# Webster's New Dictionary of Synonyms

*A Merriam-Webster*

REG. U.S. PAT. OFF.

A DICTIONARY
OF
DISCRIMINATED SYNONYMS
WITH ANTONYMS AND
ANALOGOUS AND CONTRASTED WORDS

REG. U.S. PAT. OFF.

G. & C. MERRIAM COMPANY, *Publishers*

SPRINGFIELD, MASSACHUSETTS, U.S.A.

# CONTENTS

# PREFACE

WEBSTER'S NEW DICTIONARY OF SYNONYMS is newly edited and entirely reset but based upon *Webster's Dictionary of Synonyms*, which rapidly became a favorite book among readers and writers who wish to understand, appreciate, and make nice discriminations in English words that are similar in meaning. The earlier book filled a widespread need for a work devoted to synonymy with accessory material in the form of word lists of various kinds. The editors of this new and revised edition have rewritten and sharpened the discriminations, have increased the number of articles, and have more than doubled the number of authors quoted. Particular attention has been given to updating the quotations so that they accurately reflect today's English.

The core of this book is the discriminating articles. It is not its purpose to assemble mere word-finding lists for consultants with but a vague notion of the sort of word they seek, but rather to provide them with the means of making clear comparisons between words of a common denotation and to enable them to distinguish the differences in implications, connotations, and applications among such words and to choose for their purposes the precisely suitable words. (Compare the discussion of Roget's aims beginning on page 14a following.) In addition to the central core of discriminations this book provides auxiliary information of three types, in the form of analogous words, antonyms, and contrasted words. These three types are explained on pages 26a–31a.

Every word discussed in an article of synonymy is entered in its own alphabetical place and is followed by a list of its synonyms, with a reference (by means of an asterisk or a direction introduced by "see") to the entry where the discussion of these listed words is to be found. The words listed as analogous and those listed as contrasted are always displayed in groups, each group having a clear reference (asterisk or "see") to the term under which an article of synonymy is to be found.

The writing of the articles has been done chiefly by two associate editors of the Merriam-Webster editorial staff: Dr. Philip H. Goepp and Dr. Mairé Weir Kay. Their principal assistants were Miss Ervina E. Foss, in charge of cross-referencing, and Mr. E. Ward Gilman, in charge of proofreading, both assistant editors. Mrs. Betty Meltzer was the principal editorial assistant. Some of the articles on scientific terms were written by Mr. Hubert P. Kelsey, associate editor. All of these editors took part in the editing of *Webster's Third New International Dictionary*. The historical survey and the introductory analysis of the problems and issues in the field of English synonymy are largely the work of the late Rose F. Egan, sometime assistant editor, and have been taken over from the first edition with only minor changes. To her clear analysis and understanding this book still owes much of its quality although all of her discriminations have been revised in varying degrees.

PHILIP B. GOVE
Editor in Chief

# INTRODUCTORY MATTER

## SURVEY OF THE HISTORY OF ENGLISH SYNONYMY

Consultation of a work on synonyms is made easier if the consultant has a reasonable background of the theory and of the technique that have developed since the first English synonymy was published. The following essay [first published in 1942] is, so far as we know, the first attempt to survey broadly the course of that development from its beginnings to the present. It is not intended to be exhaustive. Some good books have been published which have not been specifically discussed because they have played no essential part in this development or have advanced no new ideas which, by challenging attention or debate, have led to further clarification of the problems involved. The purpose of this article has been primarily not to praise or to denounce but to lead up to the exposition of principles which have dominated the writing of this book. These principles, we believe, are founded upon the practice of those who have seen and known clearly what could be accomplished by a book of synonyms: there are others who disagree, but we have tried to present their case fairly.

It was not until the second half of the eighteenth century that the first book on synonyms appeared in English. The Rev. John Trusler (1735–1820) was its author, *The Difference between Words Esteemed Synonymous* its title, and 1766 its date. Its source is definitely established. In 1718, the Abbé Gabriel Girard (1677–1748) had published in France *La Justesse de la langue françoise ou les Différentes significations des mots qui passent pour être synonymes*, a work which had great vogue not only in France but also abroad, especially in England. That Trusler's book was based upon it is evidenced not only by the likeness of the titles but also (in the first edition) by an English version of Girard's preface and by the admission in the author's preface that he had translated as much of the articles as was in keeping with the peculiar genius of the English language. The second edition of 1783, however, increases the divergence between the two books: the prefaces are consolidated and the result is given as the work of the author, although many passages from Girard are included without being quoted. There are, too, many new articles dealing with peculiarly British terms, such as those which concern the church and daily life in England; but these, although they represent an enrichment of vocabulary, add little to the originality of the work, which still remains an imitation. A clear-cut distinction which sharply reveals the meanings of synonymous French terms often becomes a forced distinction when applied to English. In fact, Trusler never knew whether it was his aim to point out the "delicate differences between words reputed synonymous" or to give the particular idea of each word "which constitutes its proper and particular character." He claims both aims as one, not realizing that often they are divergent.

The next significant work was the *British Synonymy* of Hester Lynch Piozzi (1741–1821), better known as Mrs. Thrale, the close friend of Dr. Johnson. It first appeared in 1794 and was succeeded by at least two editions, the best known of which was published in Paris in 1804. That it was immediately popular is evident from the testimony of its 1804 editors, who asserted its merits on the ground of "the successive editions it has passed through being the best proof of the estimation in which it is held." That it was not written without a knowledge of Girard's work we know on the authority of these same editors.[1] "So great indeed was the estimation" in which the French work was held, "that in a few years after its publication, an imitation of it appeared in England": presumably the "imitation" was Trusler's.

The editors imply, however, that Mrs. Piozzi's work is something better than had yet been given to the public. "But it was only in the year 1794," they continue, in a tone that implies contempt for the "imitation," "that Mrs. PIOZZI (formerly Mrs. THRALE) so well known in the literary world for her different publications, and her intimacy with the learned Dr. Johnson, brought out the work we have now the pleasure of presenting to our Readers, and which is totally grounded on the structure of the English language." There is no reason to suppose, however, that she depended much on the influence of Dr. Johnson, who had died in 1784.

Mrs. Piozzi's book reveals an independence of spirit and a feminine disregard of advice. It is, in fact, never profound: it is full of errors or dubious assertions, and it is often absurdly naïve. More than this, it frequently takes issue with Dr. Johnson or, in a sprightly manner, casts doubt on his judgments. There

---

[1] Mrs. Piozzi in her own preface (p. vii) mentions Girard and says, "I should be too happy, could I imitate his delicacy of discrimination, and felicity of expression."

is the story of the milliner's apprentice who saved her chicken bones to feed a horse. Johnson contended that such an action showed that she was *ignorant*, but Mrs. Piozzi maintained that it proved her *senseless*. "I thought her an ideot [sic]" was, for her, the last word on the matter.

Great as was her respect for Dr. Johnson in his own field, she believed that she also had her field and that it was incumbent on her to remain within the limits she had set for herself. Her object is very clear. Like Girard and Trusler, she was distinguishing not synonyms (that is, words identical in meaning) but words so similar in meaning as to be "apparently synonymous." The subtitle of her book announces her aim and reveals a further limitation of purpose: "An attempt at regulating the choice of words in familiar conversation." Her preface to the 1794 edition develops these ideas:

> If then to the selection of words in conversation and elegant colloquial language a book may give assistance, the Author . . . modestly offers her's; persuaded that, while men teach to write with propriety, a woman may at worst be qualified—through long practice—to direct the choice of phrases in familiar talk.

Her book, she modestly claimed, is "intended chiefly for a parlour window" and is "unworthy of a place upon a library shelf," but it may be of help to others "till a more complicated and valuable piece of workmanship be found to further their research." She wished in particular to help those who desired to converse elegantly and to save foreigners from ridiculous mistakes in speech. "If I can in the course of this little work dispel a doubt, or clear up a difficulty to foreigners . . . I shall have an honour to boast."

For this reason she could not see that her method of discrimination had much in common with that of the lexicographer and the logician. Theirs was to define: hers was to indicate propriety in the use of words. It was not her intent to establish differences in meaning but to indicate the fitness of words for use, often depending on "the place in which they should stand" but sometimes depending on their relative fineness, strength, force, or the like. She makes a distinction between the methods of the definer and the methods of the synonymist by giving, first, two definitions of the word *fondness*, one from "an eminent logician" and one from Dr. Johnson, and, secondly, by an ideal synonymy in which she reveals the same word's meaning by showing it in use along with similar words. This was not invariably her method, but it illustrates what in the main she was trying to achieve.

> . . . I have before me the definition of *fondness*, given into my hands many years ago by a most eminent logician. . . .
>
> "*Fondness*," says the Definer, "is the hasty and injudicious determination of the will towards promoting the present gratification of some particular object."
>
> "*Fondness*," said Dr. Johnson, "is rather the hasty and injudicious attribution of excellence, somewhat beyond the power of attainment, to the object of our affection."
>
> Both these definitions may possibly be included in *fondness;* my own idea of the whole may be found in the following example:
>
> Amintor and Aspasia are models of true *love:* 'tis now seven years since their mutual *passion* was sanctified by marriage; and so little is the lady's *affection* diminished, that she sate up nine nights successively last winter by her husband's bed-side, when he had on him a malignant fever that frighted relations, friends, servants, all away. Nor can any one allege that her *tenderness* is ill repaid, while we see him gaze upon her features with that *fondness* which is capable of creating charms for itself to admire, and listen to her talk with a fervour of admiration scarce due to the most brilliant genius.
>
> For the rest, 'tis my opinion that men love for the most part with warmer *passion* than women do—at least than English women, and with more transitory *fondness* mingled with that passion. . . .

It was in her simpler versions of this method that she developed a formula that has been followed by many of her successors in the discriminated synonymy—not always felicitously. We will have opportunity to return to this method later when it becomes an object of attack and will call it for the sake of convenience the Piozzi method. At present let examples of her usage suffice:

> TO ABANDON, FORSAKE, RELINQUISH, GIVE UP, DESERT, QUIT, LEAVE . . . though at first sight apparently synonymous, conversing does certainly better shew the peculiar appropriation, than books, however learned; for . . . familiar talk tells us in half an hour—That a man *forsakes* his mistress, *abandons* all hope of regaining her lost esteem, *relinquishes* his pretensions in favour of another. . . .
>
> we say a lad of an active and *diligent spirit*, or else of an *assiduous temper*, or *sedulous disposition*. . . .
>
> we say that reports are *confirmed*, treaties *ratified*, and affairs *settled*.
>
> a hard question *puzzles* a man, and a variety of choice *perplexes* him: one is *confounded* by a loud and sudden dissonance of sounds or voices in a still night; *embarrassed* by a weight of clothes or valuables, if making escape from fire, thieves, or pursuit. . . .
>
> The gentleman who discharges a gaming debt in preference to that of a tradesman, apparently prefers *honour* to another virtue, *justice*. . . .

It seems a fair statement of her aim to say that she was attempting to indicate and establish idiomatic English. However, in determining such English, she had only two tests to apply: the drawing-room usage of her time and her own instinct. To literary use in general she was indifferent. Therefore her judgments are nearly always subjective and sometimes arbitrary. Moreover, she discounted the great help that discrimination of meanings is to the synonymist. "We must not meantime retard our own progress," she wrote in her preface, "with studied definitions of every quality coming under consideration. . . .although the final cause of definition is to fix the true and adequate meaning of words or terms, without knowledge of which we stir not a step in logic; yet *here* we must not suffer ourselves to be so detained, as synonymy has more to do with elegance than truth. . . ."

Her judgments are often limited or partial, for they represent her personal feelings or the predilections of her age. Yet, within those limits, she frequently hit upon an exact meaning of a word in a particular sense and gave it life and color. What she seldom saw was that a word might have more meanings than the one which was illustrated (as *honor* in her example of the tradesman) or that a good but narrow instance of use might be taken as idiomatic by her readers (as when by implication *puzzle* suggests a question or problem needing determination and *perplex* a variety of choices). The danger of her work is not in the falsity of the example, for it is usually true or just, but in its inadequacy in suggesting other instances of good use.

Yet in her refusal to accept her age's theory of definition and in her approach to a concept of good usage we must recognize an independent spirit. The time was not ripe for a fully developed conception of the differences between logic and lexicography, yet she was somewhat nearer the present conception than some later and cleverer persons, and she had at least a feeling of rightness in the use of language that suggested, even if it did not consciously approach, the later theory of good usage as a test of such rightness. Besides, her book has an engaging quality, often lacking in books of this character, which is not necessarily a sign of the levity with which critics have charged this book, but rather of a spirited challenge to the ideals of a hidebound age.

Mrs. Piozzi's book was followed by William Perry's *Synonymous, Etymological, and Pronouncing English Dictionary*, published in 1805. On its title page and in its preface the editor explicitly offers his work as derived from *The Dictionary* of Samuel Johnson. Perry was the compiler of the better known *Royal Standard English Dictionary* brought out in England in 1775 and in America in 1788.

The *Synonymous Dictionary*, as we will call the 1805 book, evidently did not achieve the fame or popularity of the *Royal Standard*. Chauncey Goodrich, Noah Webster's son-in-law, referred to it in 1847 in his preface to the royal octavo volume of Webster as "entirely out of print." There is no evidence to show that it passed beyond the first edition. On its title page it is described as "an attempt to Synonymise his [Johnson's] Folio Dictionary of the English Language." In its preface Perry claims that it contains "the only synonymous vocabulary ever offered to the public" and that "To the philological, critical, and other interesting observations of the above learned author [Dr. Johnson], we have superadded two exclusive advantages to our publication; the one—as a *synonymous*, the other—as a *pronouncing* nomenclature. The *former* is new and unique. . . ."

The work, he informs us, was begun in 1797, three years, therefore, after the publication of the first edition of Mrs. Piozzi's *British Synonymy*. Yet there is no indication of knowledge of that work or of the work of Girard; in fact, Perry recognized no predecessor save Johnson. From Johnson, by explicit credit, he extracted his vocabulary and his explanations of meanings. Not so openly, however, did he extract the synonyms themselves: for example, his entry *good* is followed by Johnson's definition of sense 1, but the synonyms are taken from all of Johnson's succeeding twenty-nine senses. Nor does he provide many citations, and these are chiefly in entries at the end of the book; elsewhere, at the end of an entry or in parentheses, he cites the authors Johnson quoted but not the passages.

In addition he adopted an original method of presenting his material. There were two types of entries, one in lowercase and one in capitals. The latter, which he called "radicals," were followed by an exhaustive list; the former were succeeded by a much shorter list, but one word was printed in small capitals to indicate it was the radical. Thus "marches," a lowercase entry, has "borders, limits, confines, BOUNDARIES" as its synonyms: "BOUNDARY," an entry in capitals, has a much longer list which includes "limit, bound, bourn, term, mere, but, abuttal, border, barrier, marches, confines, precinct, line of demarcation, utmost reach or verge of a territory; a landmark, a mere-stone." If, then, one wished all the synonyms of a lowercase entry such as *marches* or *abbreviation*, one must turn to BOUNDARY or ABRIDGMENT, the word entered as the radical.

There are two things to notice here that are important. Perry was not merely greatly extending the traditional definition of *synonym* (as one of two or more words of identical meaning or of apparently identical meaning) and broadening it to include a group of words which have resemblances in meaning, but was doing so in what seems to be a misunderstanding of Dr. Johnson's purposes in adding such words to his definitions and in ignorance of what he supplied as a corrective. The fact of the matter is that Johnson was aware of the difficulties of his task, that he was conscious that the part of his work on which "malignity" would "most frequently fasten is the *Explanation* [i.e., the definition]."

> I cannot hope to satisfy those, who are perhaps not inclined to be pleased, since I have not always been able to satisfy myself. To interpret a language by itself is very difficult; many words cannot be explained by synonimes, because the idea signified by them has not more than one appellation; nor by paraphrase, because simple ideas cannot be described.

That was the difficulty. Synonyms would not perfectly satisfy the need either when the word defined had many meanings or when the word defining had more significations than the one intended, for in either case one must be too broad and the other too narrow. Then, too, "simple ideas" (really those involved in simple words such as *be*, *do*, *act*) were beyond definition, as Johnson saw it.

> The rigour of interpretative lexicography requires that *the explanation, and the word explained, should be always reciprocal;* this I have always endeavoured but could not always attain. Words are seldom exactly synonimous; a new term was not introduced, but because the former was thought inadequate: names, therefore, have often many ideas, but few ideas have many names. It was then necessary to use the proximate word, for the deficiency of single terms can very seldom be supplied by circumlocution. . . .

So Johnson wrote and so Perry quotes in his preface. But instead of continuing Johnson's statement to its end, Perry broke off with "circumlocution," thereby giving the reader some reason to infer that Johnson thought the method of definition by synonym preferable to that of definition by paraphrase. He had failed to notice or possibly had deliberately ignored that this was not in any sense Johnson's meaning, that both methods were faulty, but that there was a remedy for the imperfections of each. Johnson's addition to this last sentence, "nor is the inconvenience great of such mutilated interpretations, because the sense may easily be collected entire from the examples," makes that point clear. Perry may have been obtuse rather than disingenuous when, for the most part, he omits the examples (citations) of Johnson and enters synonyms, which are not, in Johnson's language, "exactly synonymous" but only "proximate words." But he may have known what Dr. Johnson meant, though his explanation is by no means clear:

> . . .we by no means contend, that the whole of the explanations collected under such initial words as. . .we call RADICALS, are all strictly synonymous; neither, on the other hand, can we agree with those who roundly assert, that there are not two words in the whole English language of precisely the same signification; but this we take upon us to say, that we have no less than Dr. Johnson's authority for their selection and disposition as explanatory of their meaning. . . .

Dr. Johnson's example, great as was its authority and prestige at that time, was an unstable prop when his statements were misunderstood. Perry perhaps indirectly rendered a service by raising the issue as to whether the term "synonym" needed redefinition, since it was being broadened in its extension: he may also have done a service in showing to others the values implicit in word-finding lists. But he did not see that he had raised those issues, and what purports to be a dictionary succeeds chiefly in being a word finder.

Between 1805 and 1852 (the latter the date of publication of Roget's *Thesaurus of English Words and Phrases*) several works on synonyms appeared. Some were of the word-finding list type, and among these there was nothing of particular importance. On the other hand, there were as many as five works discriminating synonyms of which at least four stand out for one reason or another: *English Synonymes Discriminated* by William Taylor (1813), *English Synonymes Explained* by George Crabb (1816), *English Synonyms Classified and Explained* by George F. Graham (1846), and *A Selection of English Synonyms* by Miss Elizabeth Jane Whately (1851). Both Crabb's and Whately's books are still influential and have been reprinted in recent years.

William Taylor (1765–1836), the author of the first of these books, is better known as the translator of Burger's *Lenore*, Lessing's *Nathan the Wise*, and Goethe's *Iphigenia in Tauris* and as one of the leading promoters of knowledge of contemporary German literature during the romantic era. His *English Synonymes Discriminated* is the result of his studies in German, French, Italian, and other languages and of his conviction that no English work the equal of certain foreign treatises on synonyms had as yet been written. The work is, as a whole, uneven, but a few articles in it are not only better than any others written up to that time but the equal of any that were to be written for over ninety years. A favorite theory of his was that if one is thoroughly grounded in the original meaning of a term, one "can never be at a loss how to employ it in metaphor." Consequently, etymologies became for him an important means of showing this original meaning. They formed not an invariable part of his discrimination but a very useful part when they were needed. Usually, also, he knew when his etymology was grounded on fact and when it was merely hypothetical. His method at its best is exemplified in the article covering *austere*, *severe*, and *rigid*, which we give here in abridged form:

Austerity (says Blair[2]) relates to the manner of living: severity, of thinking, rigour, of punishing. To austerity is opposed effeminacy; to severity, relaxation; to rigour, clemency. A hermit is austere in his life; a casuist, severe in his decision; a judge, rigorous in his sentence.

In this discrimination there is little exactness. Austerity is applied not only to habit, but to doctrine, and to infliction. Solitary confinement is a severe form of life, and a severe punishment. Rigid observances, rigid opinions, are oftener spoken of than rigid sentences.

A hermit is austere, who lives harshly; is severe who lives solitarily; is rigid who lives unswervingly. A casuist is austere who commands mortification, severe, who forbids conviviality, rigid, whose exactions are unqualified. A judge is austere, who punishes slight transgressions; severe, who punishes to the utmost; rigid, who punishes without respect of persons and circumstances.

Why this? Austerity is an idea of the palate; it means crabbedness. . . .These modes of life which are painful to the moral taste, are called austere. . . .Austerity is opposed to suavity.

Severity is not traced back to the sensible idea in which the word originates. *Se* and *vereor*, to bend down apart, are perhaps the component ideas. The *lying prostrate apart* is not only characteristic of the praying anchoret, and of public penance, but of cruel infliction: and to all these cases severity is accordingly applied . . . .To severity is opposed remissness.

Rigour is stiffness: rigid means frozen: stiff with cold. . . .To rigour is opposed pliancy.

Religious competition renders sects austere, priests severe, and establishments rigid.

With the exception of *severe* (the ultimate origin of which is still doubtful) the words, in the main, conform to their etymology. *Austere* does originally mean something like "bitter-tasting" and *rigid* means "stiff," though not necessarily "stiff with cold"; also, something that is *austere* is not sweet or suave, and something that is *rigid* is not pliant or flexible. He has caught the essential difference here, and the proper application follows. If Taylor had been able to maintain this method and the penetration it involved, he might have changed the course of synonymizing. But three years later *English Synonymes Explained*, by George Crabb (1778–1851), appeared and caught the public favor. For thirty-seven years Taylor's book remained unreprinted: then between 1850 and 1876 there were three new editions. For a few years it attracted some attention and then disappeared from favor.

Crabb's book, while still highly regarded by some, meets much adverse criticism from others. In his own day it was thought of generally as the best work available, although Crabb complicated matters somewhat by frequent revisions which changed its character. In his introduction to the first edition he complained of the lack of a work on English synonyms in which the subject is treated "in a scientifick manner adequate to its importance." Englishmen though great in literature and philology had in this field fallen short of the French and Germans, who "have had several considerable works on the subject." He did not wish "to depreciate the labours of those who have preceded" him; rather he claimed to "have profited by every thing which has been written in any language upon the subject; and although I always pursued my own train of thought, yet whenever I met with any thing deserving of notice, I adopted it, and referred it to the author in a note."

Crabb's *English Synonymes Explained* is both the most laborious and the most ambitious work of its kind. In spirit and objective it is a far remove from Mrs. Piozzi's *British Synonymy*, few as are the years which intervened between their publication. For Mrs. Piozzi represented the old temper where sprightliness, elegance, and ease were paramount and Crabb the new temper in which the world had grown solemn and serious under the influence of many currents, such as the pressure of momentous events, the influence of Continental (especially German) thinkers, and the spread of all the new ideas spoken of collectively as romanticism. When the best philosophers and philosophic poets of the age were seeking to answer the questions what is beauty, what is poetry, what is art, what is genius and were discriminating the beautiful and the sublime, the naïve and the sentimental, imagination and fancy, the ugly and the grotesque, what synonymist could in conscience say that "synonymy has more to do with elegance than truth"?

Crabb was undoubtedly concerned with truth rather than elegance. He was stimulated by the thinking of his age and, like many persons of his time, responded with joy to the new philosophy that deepened and enriched the concepts of beauty, poetry, and truth. Although he was in no sense a philosopher, he had a smattering of philosophical knowledge, a small philosophical vocabulary, and a deep love of philosophical distinctions. He was also interested in philology as it was understood in his time. In the study of synonyms he found satisfaction of all these interests, all the more so since he had come to regard synonyms not as words of the same meaning but as "closely allied" words between which there are "nice shades of distinction." Discrimination not only gave him profound intellectual satisfaction: it also afforded him great opportunities. In his introduction he wrote:

My first object certainly has been to assist the philological inquirer in ascertaining the force and comprehension of the English language; yet I should have thought my work but half completed had I made it a

---

[2] Hugh Blair, rhetorician, 1718–1800.

mere register of verbal distinctions. While others seize every opportunity unblushingly to avow and zealously to propagate opinions destructive of good order, it would ill become any individual of contrary sentiments to shrink from stating his convictions, when called upon as he seems to be by an occasion like that which has now offered itself.

His justification for "the introduction of morality in a work of science" is very ingenious. In answer to anticipated objections he wrote, "a writer, whose business it was to mark the nice shades of distinction between words closely allied, could not do justice to his subject without entering into all the relations of society, and showing, from the acknowledged sense of many moral and religious terms, what has been the general sense of mankind on many of the most important questions which have agitated the world."

It is not easy to find in Crabb proofs that he was discriminating historical meanings (the interpretation that may be given to his "acknowledged sense"), but one can readily discover evidence that often he was supporting an older conception he favored rather than a new conception he heartily disliked. A good example of this is found in his discrimination of SOUL and MIND.

> There are minute philosophers, who. . .deny that we possess any thing more than what this poor composition of flesh and blood can give us; and yet, methinks, sound philosophy would teach us that we ought to prove the truth of one position, before we assert the falsehood of its opposite; and consequently that if we deny that we have any thing but what is material in us, we ought first to prove that the material is sufficient to produce the reasoning faculty of man. . . .[He continued this line of argument through several sentences.]
>
> But not to lose sight of the distinction drawn between the words *soul* and *mind*, I simply wish to show that the vulgar and the philosophical use of these terms altogether accord, and are both founded on the true nature of things.
>
> Poets and philosophers speak of the *soul* in the same strain, as the active and living principle.[3]

Arguments of this character were mostly occasional with Crabb, but the method of discriminating things which the words named or to which they were applied was characteristically infixed. He could not, for instance, mark the distinctions between *finical* and *foppish* but between a *finical gentleman* and a *foppish gentleman*.

> A *finical* gentleman clips his words and screws his body into as small a compass as possible to give himself the air of a delicate person. . . : a *foppish* gentleman seeks by extravagance in the cut of his clothes, and by the tawdriness in their ornaments, to render himself distinguished for finery.

He could not discriminate *beautiful, fine, handsome* without determining what is *the beautiful, the fine, the handsome.*

> The *beautiful* is determined by fixed rules; it admits of no excess or defect; it comprehends regularity, proportion, and a due distribution of colour, and every particular which can engage the attention: the *fine* must be coupled with grandeur, majesty, and strength of figure; it is incompatible with that which is small; a little woman can never be *fine:* the *handsome* is a general assemblage of what is agreeable; it is marked by no particular characteristic, but the absence of all deformity. . . .

Even simple words were so discriminated; each one had an abstract reference which was the test of its right use no matter how little cultivated writers and speakers respected that test.

> The *gift* is an act of generosity or condescension; it contributes to the benefit of the receiver: the *present* is an act of kindness, courtesy, or respect; it contributes to the pleasure of the receiver.
>
> What we *abhor* is repugnant to our moral feelings; what we *detest* contradicts our moral principle; what we *abominate* does equal violence to our religious and moral sentiments. . . .Inhumanity and cruelty are objects of *abhorrence;* crimes and injustice of *detestation;* impiety and profanity of *abomination.* . . .

Crabb's habitual attitude to words as names of things, or for what he might have called "true concepts of things," vitiates his entire work. It has made it of negligible value in our time when lexicography has become an independent science with clearly defined objectives and functions, the chief of which is to respect the meanings men have agreed to give words rather than the notions individuals have concerning the things named or described by those words. His concepts, however interesting, are still subjective and have not been tested to any extent by actual written or spoken language. There are many citations in his work, but the sensitive reader often finds little relevancy between the word as used there and the sense defined. For example, in illustrating the meaning of the "soul" as "the active and living principle" he cites Thomson:

> "In bashful coyness or in maiden pride,
> The soft return conceal'd, save when it stole
> In side-long glances from her downcast eyes,
> Or from her swelling *soul* in stifled sighs"

---

[3] This paragraph did not appear in the first edition.

But here *soul* as cited means simply and narrowly the rising emotions and not "the active and living principle."

His synonymies are, on the whole, hard reading because confused and inconsistent. As a rule they attempt too much yet do not fully apprehend the greatness of the task and leave the reader without any clear or definite impression or without any remembered distinctions. Also, they excite rebellion in a reader who can give any number of citations to show that Crabb's dogmatic assertions are not justified by usage. Despite these fundamental defects which, with the passage of time and changes in the basic conceptions, have come to be more and more striking, Crabb deserves recognition for some additions to the art of synonymizing. Even these, however, may not be entirely his contributions: a bit here and a bit there may have been done by others. Taylor, for example, gave etymologies when they served his purpose. Moreover, after Crabb the work of perfecting often remained to be done and many others are responsible for deeper insight into the possibilities of the method or the extent to which each possibility is serviceable. The chief contributions are three:

1. The addition of an etymology to the article. Much more, however, needed to be known before certain words could be correctly etymologized and before they could be related to the sense to be defined. In some cases Crabb's etymologies are "learned" additions to the article, in no way reflecting the words' semantic development.

2. The addition of a statement (usually introductory) as to how far the words are equivalent in meaning. There was an approach to this in the work of Mrs. Piozzi, but it was hardly of the same character. Crabb's method was not only clearer and firmer but was much less subject to idiosyncrasies. Since this was his most enduring contribution, a few examples may be given to illustrate his method.

> INGENUITY, WIT. . . . Both these terms imply acuteness of understanding, and differ mostly in the mode of displaying themselves. . . .
>
> TO DISPARAGE, DETRACT, TRADUCE, DEPRECIATE, DEGRADE, DECRY. . . .The idea of lowering the value of an object is common to all these words, which differ in the circumstances and object of the action. . . .
>
> DISCERNMENT, PENETRATION, DISCRIMINATION, JUDGMENT. . . .The first three of these terms do not express different powers, but different modes of the same power; namely the power of seeing intellectually, or exerting the intellectual sight. . . .

In clearness of statement, in pointedness, in "hitting the nail on the head" nearly all of these introductions leave something to be desired. Nevertheless, they are historically important because they represent the first tentative formulation of what has proved to be an important and essential part of the discriminated synonymy at its best.

3. In the arrangement of his word lists Crabb claims to have moved from the most comprehensive to the less comprehensive. In such articles as those discussing **form, ceremony, rite, observance;** and **short, brief, concise, succinct, summary** the principle is clear, but in others, such as those for **apparel, attire, array;** and **belief, credit, trust, faith;** and **execute, fulfill, perform,** the procedure is not perfectly clear. In general, however, he seems to have had a plan and to have stuck to it when he could.

There are other devices used by Crabb which in later and defter hands proved valuable, but these three are the ones on which he has exerted his powers and with which he had greatest success. That the success was not complete is not entirely his fault. The English language is not a symmetrical language: it was never intended to be prodded into shape by the pen of the lexicographer or of the synonymist. No method is uniformly successful: every method must achieve a degree of fluidity before it can be turned to use. What was eminently true in Crabb's case is still eminently true, but some writers of today have learned to bow to necessity, a lesson which many early synonymists could not learn easily or gracefully.

His book continued to be held in high regard for many decades. In fact, a centennial edition in honor of the first (1816) was published in 1917 in the United States. Its editors' names are not given, but it contains an eloquent introduction by John H. Finley, then commissioner of education in New York state, which ends with the sentence: "Long life to Crabb and to that for which his name is as a synonym!"

By this time—that is, particularly between the first edition of Crabb's work and the first edition of Whately's book—keen interest was being displayed in the use of synonyms in education. Several texts suitable for use in the schools were prepared. Not necessarily the best of these but the most thoughtful and suggestive was *English Synonymes Classified and Explained with Practical Exercises Designed for School and Private Tuition* by George F. Graham. The emphasis in the book is entirely upon discrimination. Since there is no attempt to supply as many synonyms as possible and every effort to make differences clear, two words only are given in each article. Although this has the effect of making the book seem purely pedagogical, it admits employment of a method of classification which would break down if more words were to be added. It is, therefore, only by courtesy that Graham's book can be called a synonymy.

The study of synonyms ought, according to Graham, to begin in the elementary schools. In the hope of making this possible, he divides all pairs of synonyms into five classes marking the relationships of these words. He calls his classes *General and Specific, Active and Passive, Intensity, Positive and Negative,* and *Miscellaneous.* The classification is obviously not clean-cut and the classes are not necessarily mutually exclusive. As illustrations of *General and Specific* relationships he compares *answer* and *reply, bravery* and *courage;* as instances of *Active and Passive* relationships he discriminates *burden* and *load,* and *actual* and *real;* and as examples of *Intensity* in relationships he considers *agony* and *anguish,* and *intention* and *purpose.* It is needless to say that a rigid classification begets a rigid method of discrimination. Sometimes, it serves to bring out a real distinction between the words, but more often it serves to confuse them by bending them to suit a set purpose. It is the best example we have had so far of the futility of applying a rigid method to the direct study of anything so nonrigid and living as a language.

Crabb's supremacy as a synonymist seems not to have been seriously threatened by a slight book which appeared in 1851, won general praise, and has been listed in practically every bibliography since that time. This book, usually called "Whately's book on synonyms," has never, so far as we know, been properly esteemed for its own values, nor has its true author ever been adequately recognized. Credit for its author-ship is often given to the famous logician Richard Whately (1787–1863), Anglican archbishop of Dublin; rightly, it belongs to his daughter, Elizabeth Jane Whately. A modern but undated edition (before 1928) from the Boston house of Lothrop, Lee, and Shepard confuses both details of title and authorship by calling it on the title page "English Synonyms Discriminated, by Richard Whately, D.D." It has two prefaces, one the editor's preface signed, in the characteristic fashion of Anglican bishops, "Richard Dublin"; the other the preface by the author, which is unsigned.

The editor's preface is very short and abstruse but pregnant with meaning. The archbishop took occasion to say that "this little work has been carefully revised by me, throughout" and that though "far from pre-suming to call it perfect, it is, I am confident, very much the best that has appeared on the subject." Some of its readers will acknowledge its value in the "cultivation of correctness and precision in our expressions." There will be those, however [we are paraphrasing, amplifying, and interpreting his very cryptic statements], who are so blinded by their adoption of "the metaphysical theory of *ideas*" that they will regard words as of little importance in themselves, and the ideas named as of great significance. There are others, such as himself, who regard words as "an indispensable instrument of thought, in all cases, where a process of *reasoning* takes place." Words are the symbols which men use in discourse. For the most part they do not name real things, for abstractions, such as the one called "beauty," or the generalized notion, such as the one called "tree," exist nowhere except in the mind and have not reality. Only in particular things can beauty be found: only particular objects which are classed together under the name "tree" exist. Therefore, if words are to serve as convenient instruments of discourse, they must often be regarded as signs not of real things but of notions of things and must have a fixed and generally accepted content. Otherwise human minds could never come together in discourse. Moreover, actual discourse is often futile because words are loosely or incorrectly used.

The preface by the author, though it avoids all references to philosophy, is in general based on the same premises. The author, as has been said, is the archbishop's daughter, and the proper title of the book is *A Selection of Synonyms.* To her, as well as to her father, words are, for the most part, the names for human ideas or concepts of things. There may be words which name approximately the same thing but which, because of differences in human points of view, are distinguishable by slight differences in meaning. Syn-onyms, or as she preferred to call them "pseudo-synonyms," have "sufficient resemblance of meaning to make them liable to be confounded together. And it is in the number and variety of these that. . .the richness of a language consists. To have two or more words with exactly the same sense, is no proof of copiousness, but simply an inconvenience." A language, in her estimation, should have no more words than it needs, just as a house should have no more chairs or tables than required for convenience.

Differences in meaning she found even in words which denote exactly the same object, act, process, quality, emotion, and the like. Such words often have different connotations. "*Swine's flesh,*" she says, is prohibited by the Mosaic Law, for "it is plain that it presents to the mind a gross idea, which *pork* does not." Some words may denote the same thing but their different origins or their varying historical associations give them a distinct character which better fits one than the other for use in certain contexts. In polite phrases such as "May I take the liberty?" the Latin derivative *liberty* is more suitable than the Saxon *freedom.* A heathen or an atheist may be called *just* but not *righteous* because Biblical use of the latter word has narrowed its application. Much more acute is her observation that two words may name the same thing but differ because they regard that thing from opposite points of view. She instances *inference* and *proof.*

> Whoever justly infers, proves; and whoever proves, infers; but the word 'inference' leads the mind from the premises which have been assumed, to the conclusion which follows from them: while the word 'proof' follows a reverse process, and leads the mind from the conclusion to the premises.

In a footnote she refers to Aristotle's admirable parallel between *anger* and *hatred,* but after summing up his distinctions, she adds significantly:

> His [Aristotle's] example. . .has not been followed in this work. . .because, though the two *passions* may often be confounded together, and mistaken one for the other, the two *words* are not liable to be mistaken; and it is with words that we have now to do.

There, one is forced to comment, is the lexicographer speaking and not the would-be philosopher who would use definition or discrimination of words as an instrument for the expression of his own ideas.

Here and there in her preface and in her synonymies, without evident plan or intention, Miss Whately advanced ideas which when brought together indicate a conception of the synonymist's function and equipment far beyond any yet presented. Not only was she, in effect if not by design, distinguishing lexicography from philosophy but she was defining and enriching the concept of the ideal synonymy and the ideal synonymist. And she did so by flying in the face of all Crabb's admirers and imitators.

Although she realized the importance per se of the "history of the *derivation* of words," she omitted etymologies "which are generally appended to every group of synonyms as an almost essential part of it." She questioned the value of "this procedure" because it tends "to confuse the subject it was intended to clear," for "in inquiring into the *actual* and *present* meaning of a word, the consideration of what it *originally* meant may frequently tend to lead us astray." Nevertheless, she made good use of her knowledge of etymology when it helped in the discrimination of words.

> *'Contentment'* may be classed among those words in the English language which adhere strictly to their etymology. Its root was undoubtedly the verb 'to contain,' and the substantive and its adjective have not departed from this meaning. A *contented* person does not indulge in fruitless wishes for what is beyond his reach; his desires are limited by what he possesses.
>
> *'Satisfaction'* implies more: this word has likewise retained the signification of its root, and means that we have obtained all we want; not that our desires are *limited*, but that they have been *gratified*. A poor and needy man may be *'contented,'* but he cannot feel *'satisfaction'* with his condition.

Her illustrations are many and reveal wide reading, a broad linguistic background, and a deep interest in developments of meaning, in differences in meaning between words of the same origin in different languages (e.g., between the English *defend* and the French *défendre* which means not only to defend but also to forbid), and in English words which have "corresponding origins" yet are "widely different in their significations," such as *substance* (printed as *substantia* in her book), *understanding*, and *hypostasis*. She was interested also in the notions which gave names to things, as " 'Heaven'. . . .conveyed with it the idea of something *heaved* or *lifted up*. . . .'Coelum'. . .referred to something hollowed out or vaulted."

> All these variations of meaning. . .are valuable and curious; but though they may occasionally help us, they must not be allowed to influence our decisions with respect to the significations of words. Our question is, not what *ought* to be, or formerly was, the meaning of a word, but what it *now* is; nor can we be completely guided by quotations from Shakespeare or Milton, or even from Addison or Johnson. Language has undergone such changes, even within the last sixty or seventy years, that many words at that time considered pure, are now obsolete; while others. . .formerly slang, are now used by our best writers. . . .The standard we shall refer to in the present work, is the sense in which a word is used by the purest writers and most correct speakers of our own days.

Although Miss Whately cannot be said to be the first to discriminate meanings of synonyms, she was, so far as we know, the first in England to make that the avowed aim of a book of synonyms and to realize clearly the distinction between the meaning of a word and the thing or idea for which it stood.

Unfortunately, Miss Whately was not so successful in finding a method of synonymizing as she was in expounding its principles. She had, in theory, thrown off the yoke of Crabb, but in practice she occasionally submitted to it. Nor had she, any more than Crabb, been able to discard completely or to transform to her own use what has been called the Piozzi method of illustration. Some of the difficulty arises from her use of other writers and from the reviser (her father) who, though sympathetic in principle, did not always agree with the exposition in detail and made many heavy-handed changes. But these sources of difficulty are superficial: the real but unassignable reason probably has its roots in something that lies in temper and lack of experience. Yet, in spite of everything, she made several significant advances not only in the theory but in the art of synonymizing. Summed up, they are:

1. The principle that knowledge of meanings and all the background that such knowledge implies (derivations, historical development of senses, usage of purest writers and speakers, especially of one's own period, the associations that affect connotations, etc.) are indispensable elements of the synonymist's equipment, to be used or discarded as the occasion warrants.

2. The principle that the synonymist goes beyond the definer, in a difference of purpose. It is the function of the one who would define a word to estimate truly the meanings men have agreed should be given to it: it is the function of the synonymist to point out the differences between words with meanings so nearly alike

that he not only gives help in their correct use but promotes precision of expression so necessary to the thinker and writer.

3. A clearer conception of the ways in which synonyms differ:

(a) Because of differences in implications.

> "Both *obstinacy* and *stubbornness* imply an excessive and vicious perseverance in pursuing our own judgment in opposition to that of others; but to be *obstinate* implies the doing what we ourselves chose. To be *stubborn* denotes rather, not to do what others advise or desire." (Quoted from Sir James Mackintosh.)
>
> A *trifling* matter is one merely of small importance: a *trivial* matter is a small matter made too much of. The word 'trivial' implies contempt, which 'trifling' does not. By saying, 'He never neglects a *trifling* matter,' we are rather supposed to praise; but in blaming a person for frivolity, we often say, 'He is always engrossed with *trivial* concerns.'

(b) Because of differences in applications.

> "*Obstinacy* is generally applied to the superior; *stubbornness* to the inferior. . .*Obstinacy* refers more to outward acts, and *stubbornness* to disposition." (Quoted from Sir James Mackintosh.)
>
> Strictly speaking, '*expense*' should be applied to the purchaser, and '*cost*' to the thing purchased. . . .Many persons are tempted to buy articles. . .because they are not *costly*, forgetting that. . .these purchases may still be too *expensive*.
>
> '*Delightful*' is applied both to the pleasures of the mind and those of the senses: '*delicious*' only to those of the senses. An excursion, a social circle, a place of abode, may be '*delightful*'; a perfume, or a fruit, '*delicious*.'

(c) Because of differences in extension, or range of meaning.

> '*Timid*' is applied both to the state of mind. . .in which a person may happen to be at the moment, and to the habitual disposition; '*timorous*,' only to the disposition. '*Timid*' is therefore, the more extensive term, and comprehends the meanings of '*timorous*.'. . .
>
> TO UNDERSTAND, TO COMPREHEND. The former of these verbs is used in a much more extended sense than the latter. Whatever we *comprehend*, we *understand;* but '*to understand*' is used on many occasions in which *to comprehend* would be inadmissible. . . .It would be quite correct to say, 'I did not *comprehend* his exposition, or his arguments, although I *understood* the language, and the grammatical import of each sentence.'

(d) Because of differences in association or origin and, therefore, in connotations.

> FATHERLY, PATERNAL; MOTHERLY, MATERNAL. . .are formed from corresponding roots in Latin and Saxon. . . the Latin word being the more polite and cold, the Saxon the more hearty and cordial. . . .We speak of 'a *paternal* government'—'*maternal* duties'; but of 'a *fatherly* kindness of manner'—'a *motherly* tenderness.'
>
> RIGHTEOUS, JUST. . .a Saxon and a Latin term, whose roots exactly correspond in meaning; but they have even more curiously diverged than many other pairs of words. '*Righteous*' is now exclusively applied to rectitude of conduct drawn from *religious* principle, while '*just*' is simply used for moral uprightness. A heathen or atheist may be called *just*, but not *righteous*.

(e) Because of the difference in the point of view from which the same thing is regarded.

> '*Anger*' is more correctly applied to the inward feeling: '*wrath*' to the outward manifestation. . . .We should not speak of the 'anger,' but of the 'wrath' of the elements. We therefore speak of 'the *wrath* of God,' more correctly than of his *anger*. We cannot attribute to Him passions like those of men: we can only describe the external effects which in man would be produced by those passions.

In 1852, the year after Whately's *Selection of Synonyms* was published, appeared the first edition of the *Thesaurus of English Words and Phrases*, by Peter Mark Roget (1779–1869), a book that was to exert very great influence on the development of interest in synonyms and to provoke a new interest in opposite or contrasted terms. The modern consultant of the *Thesaurus*, accustomed to depend on the elaborate index (provided in 1879 by the compiler's son John L. Roget), has little knowledge of the original plan of the book, though it has in no way been disturbed by revisers of the Roget family. But this plan is obviously hard to use and few consultants of the *Thesaurus*, if any, now avail themselves of it. It depends upon a classification of all words into six main categories, those dealing with Abstract Relations, Space, Matter, Intellect, Volition, and Affections, each of which is divided into smaller and appropriate subdivisions until an appropriate heading, such as *Interpretation* or *Lending*, gives the clue for the left-hand column of nouns, verbs, adjectives, and adverbs gathered under it and an appropriate heading, such as *Misinterpretation* or *Borrowing*, gives the clue for the right-hand column of nouns, verbs, adjectives, and adverbs that are theoretically opposed or in contrast. But Roget did not call these word lists *Synonyms* and *Antonyms* (the latter word indeed had not yet been coined): his usual name was "Analogous Words" for those in the left-hand column and "Correlative Words" for those in the right-hand column. Despite this, other revisers than those of the Roget family have consistently misinterpreted this volume as a book of synonyms and antonyms and have rearranged it or alphabetized it in the hope of making this clear.

It is, therefore, merely because of its historical connections with the treatment of synonyms and antonyms that this book is of immediate significance to us. Only when it is clear that the book purports to be a supplier of words—technically, a "word finder"—and nothing else, are we able to estimate correctly the heresy that has arisen out of its misunderstanding. To reach this end we must know very clearly just what Roget tried to accomplish by this book and just what he ruled out as extraneous to his purpose.

As early as 1805 Roget realized that what he needed for his own writing was a classified list of words in which he might find not only the right words to express his ideas but words that would help him in clarifying or formulating confused or vague ideas. He found the lists he made so useful to himself that he came to believe that they would prove, if amplified, of great value to others. For nearly fifty years he had this project in mind, but only at the age of seventy, after his retirement in 1849 from his position as secretary of the Royal Society of London for the Advancement of Science, was he able to realize it.

He held from the start that what was needed was not a dictionary of synonyms. Roget had in mind a consultant who not only did not know a near word but could not even recall a word somewhat similar in meaning to the word desired or only vaguely apprehended an idea because of the want of the right word or words to help him in formulating it. For example, a geologist who has found a rock, probably hitherto undiscovered, because it fitted into no known classification might be at a loss for the exact terms to describe its peculiar texture. Such a person could hope to find in the section headed "Matter" the concrete adjective he needed (such as *fissile, friable, splintery*). No word, no phrase, was too narrow in its meaning to serve Roget's purpose, or too archaic, or too slangy, or too erudite. Whether one was writing a technical treatise or a witty essay, a historical novel or a definition for a dictionary, one might hope to discover in this *Thesaurus* the expressions "which are best suited to his purpose, and which might not have occurred to him without such assistance." For words, "like 'spirits from the vasty deep' . . . come not when we call"; "appropriate terms, notwithstanding our utmost efforts, cannot be conjured up at will."

More than this, Roget did not call the words he selected *synonyms*, when they were of the same part of speech and belonged in the same column. That he understood "synonyms" as denoting words of equivalent meaning is evident in his reference to the discrimination of "apparently synonymous" terms. There can be no question that he thought word-finding lists of synonyms and of "apparently synonymous" terms would be too meager to suit the purposes he had in mind.

As for the discrimination of synonyms, that was entirely foreign to the purpose of his book. He was very explicit about that:

> The investigation of the distinctions to be drawn between words apparently synonymous, forms a separate branch of inquiry, which I have not presumed here to enter upon; for the subject has already occupied the attention of much abler critics than myself, and its complete exhaustion would require the devotion of a whole life. The purpose of this Work, it must be borne in mind, is not to explain the signification of words, but simply to classify and arrange them according to the sense in which they are now used, and which I presume to be already known to the reader. I enter into no inquiry into the changes of meaning they may have undergone in the course of time. I am content to accept them at the value of their present currency, and have no concern with their etymologies, or with the history of their transformations; far less do I venture to thrid [thread] the mazes of the vast labyrinth into which I should be led by any attempt at a general discrimination of synonyms.

It is also important to notice that Roget believed himself without a precursor "in any language." He may have known Perry and many others who worked in the word-finding field before 1852: like other cultivated men he probably knew Crabb and others working on the discrimination of synonyms; but he always thought of himself as doing something quite distinct from both. In fact, he gave his successors many reasons for refusing to believe that his two series of word-supplying lists were synonyms or antonyms or were capable of discrimination as synonyms or of opposition as antonyms.

Despite that, his purpose was misunderstood and his book misinterpreted. In 1867 appeared a small book called *A Complete Collection of Synonyms and Antonyms*, by the Rev. Charles J. Smith, which gave evidence that here and there men were quietly substituting their judgment of Roget's work for his own. It is true that there is only one sentence in the preface of Smith's book to support this inference, and that concerns the reason why its author has chosen the dictionary method of presenting his material, "from finding that the abstract classifications of words, under certain broad ideas, according to the plan of Dr. Roget, seems invalidated by the necessity, in his well-known Thesaurus, of numberless cross-divisions, and is practically disregarded in favor of the Alphabetical Index." Yet, brief as is that statement, it reveals that he thought his work and Roget's had a common purpose—to give synonyms and their opposites or, to use the word which he now coined, their "antonyms"—and that the difference between the two books was merely a matter of method.

There is no evidence that Smith realized that he was changing the time-honored definition of *synonym*. His chief object in phrasing his definition of *synonym* was to set that term in opposition to *antonym*, which he regarded as its antithesis. Nevertheless, in so doing, he introduced a subtle and important change in the definition. His statement reads as follows:

> Words which agree in expressing one or more characteristic ideas in common [with the entry word] he [i.e., Smith himself] has regarded as Synonyms, those which negative one or more such ideas he has called Antonyms.

The inference that he changed the traditional definition of *synonym* is supported not only by this statement but also by his method of selecting synonyms. One example must suffice:

> ACCELERATE, *v.t. Ad* and *celer*, quick. To quicken the speed or process of events, objects, or transactions. SYN. Quicken. Hasten. Urge. Speed. Expedite. Promote. Despatch. Facilitate.
> ANT. Delay. Obstruct. Impede. Retard. Clog. Hinder. Drag. Shackle.

The important thing to notice about these lists is not their parallelism, nor even how good or bad the synonyms or antonyms are, but their selection according to a new principle. The synonyms are not all closely allied words differing only in minor ways or words which are essentially alike in meaning, but some, such as *urge* and *promote*, are words which come together only in some part of their meaning and that not necessarily their essential meaning. Nor are the antonyms necessarily opposed to the essential meaning of *accelerate*. It is quite possible that neither Smith nor anyone else at the time fully realized what a radical change in definition he had made. In his *Synonyms Discriminated*, the work with which four years later (1871) he followed his *Synonyms and Antonyms*, he adhered to the orthodox definition of *synonym*. The later work proved the more popular, and it is probable that the inconspicuousness of *Synonyms and Antonyms* helped to obscure its definition of *synonym*, buried as it was in the preface.

Moreover, in the same year as *Synonyms Discriminated* appeared another book of undiscriminated synonyms, Richard Soule's *A Dictionary of English Synonymes and Synonymous or Parallel Expressions* (1871), which attracted far more attention than had Smith's *Synonyms and Antonyms*. New editions appeared in rapid succession, and it was revised in 1891 by Professor George H. Howison and in 1937 by Professor Alfred D. Sheffield.

Although Soule acknowledged help from Roget's *Thesaurus* and a number of other works such as the dictionaries of Webster and Worcester and the books by Crabb, Whately, and others discriminating synonyms, he claims in no particular instance to have followed them strictly or to have been influenced by them in any way. If we judge from the words of Professor Howison, who, nearly twenty years after the first edition, undertook revision at the request of Soule's family, he "found little more to do than to carry out to a greater completeness the lines of Mr. Soule's original design." That Soule's original design was clear and definite and that he saw himself as doing something quite different from Roget, on the one hand, and from Crabb and Whately, on the other, is obvious from what Professor Howison has further to say:

> A perfect manual of that sort is impossible within the compass of a single work of convenient size and arrangement. . . .A work on Synonymes may thus have for its purpose either an alphabetic list of all the more important words in the language, with their various meanings or shades of meaning set down under them, each followed by its appropriate synonymes; or a list of general notions, duly named and properly divided and subdivided, with the words and phrases that belong to the expression of each collected under them as fully as possible; or, again, the collocation of words allied in meaning with subjoined disquisitions on the shades of difference between them. The latter conception has been the prevailing one among English makers of synonymic dictionaries, and is represented by the well-known work of Crabb, as well as by any; the second is that of Roget's Thesaurus; while the first is that of Soule.

Consequently, we are not surprised to find that Soule's definition of *synonym* approaches the orthodox one. True, he gives us no detailed definition, but he does say enough to show that he does not mistake the relation between words of the same part of speech in the left-hand or the right-hand column of Roget (he is obviously not interested in their cross relation), and he does not show any knowledge—much less any interest—in Smith's definition of a synonym as a word which agrees in expressing one or more characteristic ideas in common with a given word. A synonym, he says, has "the same meaning as" the entry word under which it is listed "or a meaning very nearly the same." Within limits his lists of synonyms are about as good as is possible when they are not submitted to the test of discrimination.

Even though Soule's *Dictionary of Synonyms* has been the model for a great many works issued in imitation of it, some claiming to have improved upon it, it still remains, in both its original and its revised forms, the best dictionary of synonyms that does not provide discriminations. Like Roget's work, within its own limits it has not yet been bettered.

But beyond those limits, both in the realm of books providing discriminating synonymies and in the realm of books providing synonyms and antonyms without discriminations, there has arisen a state of affairs which makes us believe that we are at a point where a stand must be taken if we are to avert chaos in the field.

In the forefront of this battle are the American general dictionaries and certain manuals written by men who have been at one time or another members of their staffs.

The general dictionaries have so far been omitted from this survey. Not that they were inactive—for, almost from the start, they were not. A few ventures were merely tentative, such as that in James Barclay's *Complete and Universal Dictionary* issued in England in 1774. This work Chauncey Goodrich (in his preface to Webster's *A Pronouncing and Defining Dictionary*, 1856, an abridgment of the 1828 Webster) notices with the observation that discriminations of "synonymous words" were "first introduced into a general dictionary by Barclay, though in a very imperfect manner." Goodrich also calls attention to the fact that Noah Webster had often successfully used the method of discrimination as part of his definitions. But these attempts do not merit the honor of being the first discriminating synonymies in the general dictionary. No one in fact laid serious claim to their introduction before Joseph Worcester who, in 1855, issued his *Pronouncing, Explanatory, and Synonymous Dictionary*. The slight foundation for the claim is evident from the following typical examples:

> DEFEND. . . .*Syn.*—*Defend* the innocent; *protect* the weak; *vindicate* those who are unjustly accused; *repel* aggression.
> FIGURE. . . .*Syn.*—A fine *figure;* regular *shape;* circular *form;* a carved *statue;* a graven *image.*—A *metaphor* is a *figure* of speech; a lamb is an *emblem* of innocence; the paschal lamb was a *type* of Christ.

One year later (1856) William G. Webster and Chauncey A. Goodrich, the son and son-in-law of Noah Webster, brought out abridged editions of his *American Dictionary* for school, business, and family use. Short discriminating synonymies were introduced, all of them written by Chauncey Goodrich. A few typical illustrations will indicate how much better a title he had than had Worcester to the claim of having introduced such synonymies into a dictionary:

> Things are *adjacent* when they lie near to each other without touching, as *adjacent* fields; *adjoining* when they meet or join at some point, as *adjoining* farms; *contiguous* when they are brought more continuously in contact, as *contiguous* buildings.
>
> *Liveliness* is an habitual feeling of life and interest; *gayety* refers more to a temporary excitement of the animal spirits; *animation* implies a warmth of emotion and a corresponding vividness of expressing it; *vivacity* is a feeling between liveliness and animation, having the permanency of the one, and, to some extent, the warmth of the other.

The first serious attempt in a general dictionary at discriminating synonymies on a par with those published by Piozzi, Crabb, Whately, and others, came in 1859 with the publication by G. & C. Merriam Co. of a "provisional edition"[4] of Webster as a preparation for the first complete revision (issued in 1864) of the *American Dictionary*. These also were written by Chauncey A. Goodrich (1790–1860), whose articles in the smaller dictionaries of 1856 had been, according to the publishers' preface of 1859, "so highly appreciated by distinguished scholars" that they had prevailed upon him in his capacity as editor of the 1859 edition to add a treatment of synonyms to this book. For some years Goodrich had been engaged on "a distinct work on this subject" and it was the material gathered for this project that was developed and presented in the table of synonyms as part of the "front matter" of the 1859 edition.

These synonymies, with slight changes in phrasing and many additions, served for the two ensuing complete revisions of Merriam-Webster dictionaries, *Webster's Unabridged Dictionary* of 1864 and *Webster's International Dictionary* of 1890, both under the editorship of Noah Porter. In these books the articles on synonymy, instead of being grouped in the front matter, were distributed through the main vocabulary.

In the publishers' statement in the 1859 edition of the *American Dictionary*, note was made of the great advance in Goodrich's synonymies over those of preceding writers:

> This is only an application on a broad scale of one mode adopted by Dr. Webster, for giving clearness and precision to his definitions. It is also peculiarly appropriate in a work like this, which aims at great exactness as a defining dictionary; since it affords an opportunity of giving in connection with the leading terms of our language, those nicer discriminations and shades of thought which it is impossible to reach in the way of ordinary definitions. . . .Unless the distinctive meaning of the several words is previously given, little or no aid is afforded as to their proper use and application, by adducing such passages. This will be seen by turning to such a work as *Platt's Dictionary of English Synonyms*,[5] which is framed chiefly upon this plan. On the first page, we find under the words *abandon, desert, leave* &c., such examples as these: "Men are *abandoned* by their friends; we *desert* a post or station; *leave* the country," &c. But these words may be

---

[4] As stated in the preface to *Webster's Unabridged Dictionary* (1864).

[5] A small work for use in schools, published 1825.

equally well interchanged. Men may be *deserted* by their friends; we may *abandon* a post or station, &c. Such examples, therefore, afford no light or guidance as to the proper use of these words. So, if the phrase be given "the officer abandoned his post," the question may arise whether he really *abandoned,* or *deserted,* or *surrendered,* or *left* it. He may have *abandoned* it on the approach of an enemy, or as no longer important to maintain; he may have *deserted* it unworthily or treacherously; he may have *surrendered* it to a superior force; he may have *left* it temporarily.

The criticism clearly shows that the chief defect of the current discriminating synonymy was a defect in method: it was not a defect in the definition of *synonym* or in the selection of synonyms. But in the thirty years following there were signs that Perry's vague conceptions of a synonym, and Smith's freer definition were beginning to enter the minds of synonymists. Neither Perry nor Smith was largely responsible for this change in definition. Roget, because of the enormous popularity of his work, or rather those who misinterpreted Roget's aim, must be considered as originating the trend and be blamed for it. By 1889 the first evidence of its more general acceptance had made its appearance.

In that year was published the first edition of the *Century Dictionary,* and in 1894 followed Funk and Wagnalls' *Standard Dictionary.* Both were new ventures in dictionary making and had the advantage of being in the limelight. Both followed the initiative of the Merriam-Webster dictionaries and introduced discriminating synonymies as an essential part of their contribution. But neither followed Webster in its adhesion to the traditional definition of *synonym.*

Although the *Century Dictionary* attempted many new things in the way of dictionary making, such as an encyclopedic character and a format of several volumes, it placed little stress on its treatment of synonyms. The writer of these articles, Henry Mitchell Whitney, was the brother of the editor in chief, William Dwight Whitney (1827–1894): his work was given only a four-line notice in the editorial preface:

> Discussions of synonyms treating of about 7000 words. . .will be found convenient as bringing together statements made in the definitions in various parts of the dictionary, and also as touching in a free way upon many literary aspects of words.

It was probably because of the division of the *Century Dictionary* into several volumes that its editors could entertain the idea that the function of a discriminating synonymy is to assemble definitions of comparable terms from various parts of the dictionary, but such a function, because of its accidental character, has no inherent value. As a matter of fact, the synonymist of the *Century* often depended on cross reference to definitions for support or amplification of his statements and, therefore, invalidated the description (quoted above) by William Dwight Whitney in the editorial preface. Nor do his synonymies "touch in a free way upon many literary aspects of words." In the first place, it is not quite clear what is meant by that statement, and, in the second, there is no consistent proof of anything like it in the articles themselves. As a general rule, with the possible exception of Whately, synonymists had not yet felt strongly any difference between the literary and colloquial use of words.

There is not only the lack of a clearly defined policy in the preface, but there is also the lack of one in the synonymies themselves. Yet Henry M. Whitney seems to have had in him the makings of a good synonymist but to have been suffering from conditions over which he had no control. It may be that his job was too big for one man or for the time set for its completion and that he had little leisure to think through its problems: it may be that what he considered a good synonymy was not in accord with the opinion of the editor in chief. At any rate, his synonymies vary greatly in method, aim, and accomplishment. The most that can be said is that he was experimenting with different methods and aims and that he never reached definite conclusions as to the superiority of one over the other.

The most vital problem which concerned him was the selection of synonyms. Sometimes he provides a very limited selection, as at the noun **adept,** where he gives only *expert,* leaving out such words as *master, proficient,* and *specialist,* which might well have been treated as synonyms. In other places he gives a much longer and more heterogeneous list, as at **ample:** *ample, copious, plenteous,* spacious, roomy, extensive, extended, wide, capacious, abundant, sufficient, full, enough, unrestricted, plenary, unstinted. Only the italicized words are discriminated, it is true, but the others are given as synonyms. The average reader may doubt the justification of many of these words as synonyms, though he will readily find a relationship in meaning.

There was good reason for H. M. Whitney's uncertainty, in that around the eighteen-seventies and eighties synonymists were confronted with a problem that had not particularly concerned their predecessors. The demand then was not only for discriminating synonymies but for word-finding lists more or less in the manner of Roget and Soule. Crabb's work was still influential, but was not satisfying those who wanted more words synonymized and more synonyms for each word. Roget was immensely popular but extremely difficult to use, not only because of his classificatory method but because he supplied no definitions. In 1879 a "new and elaborate Index, much more complete than that which was appended to the previous editions" had been added by Roget's son, in the belief that "almost every one who uses the book finds it more convenient to have recourse to the Index first." In this way the major difficulty, the classificatory system which the elder Roget had pertinaciously believed in, became no longer an obstacle. The other difficulty, the lack of discrimination, was not touched and, in view of Roget's primary purpose, was not likely to be.

As a result there followed an attempt to provide synonymies which would combine the virtues and value of the discriminating synonymies and yet would deal with word lists that approached in number and variety those of Roget. Henry M. Whitney more or less played with the problem, but James C. Fernald (1838–1918), the editor of synonymies for Funk and Wagnalls' *Standard Dictionary* (1894) and author of a manual, *English Synonyms and Antonyms* (1896), attacked it with vigor and offered what seemed to him a solution.

Fernald and the editors of the *Standard Dictionary* set out to increase markedly the number of synonyms and antonyms at each entry. Hitherto, from two to eight words represented the norm in each of these lists: in the *Standard Dictionary* the average number lies between ten and twenty. First of all, they believed that they were justified in extending the definition of *synonym* to include both words of identical or closely allied meaning (the time-honored definition) and words which agree in some part of their meaning. The definition of *synonym* in the 1894 edition of the *Standard Dictionary* (slightly changed in later editions) reads:

> A word having the same or almost the same meaning as some other; oftener, one of a number of words that have one or more meanings in common, but that differ either in the range of application of those meanings or in having other senses not held in common; opposed to antonym. . . . Words of this class may often be used interchangeably, but discrimination in their choice is one of the most important characteristics of a good writer.

The discriminating synonymy given at the entry of *synonymous* in the main vocabulary reads:

> **Synonyms:** alike, correspondent, corresponding, equivalent, identical, interchangeable, like, same, similar, synonymic. In the strictest sense, *synonymous* words scarcely exist; rarely, if ever, are any two words in any language *equivalent* or *identical* in meaning; where a difference in meaning can not easily be shown, a difference in usage commonly exists, so that the words are not *interchangeable*. By *synonymous* words we usually understand words that coincide or nearly coincide in some part of their meaning, and may hence within certain limits be used interchangeably, while outside of those limits they may differ very greatly in meaning and use. It is the office of a work on synonyms to point out these correspondences and differences, that language may have the flexibility that comes from freedom of selection within the common limits, with the perspicuity and precision that result from exact choice of the fittest word to express each shade of meaning outside of the common limits. To consider *synonymous* words *identical* is fatal to accuracy; to forget that they are *similar*, to some extent *equivalent*, and sometimes *interchangeable*, is destructive of freedom and variety.

It is possible that definition and synonymy were designed to avoid provoking criticism from those who adhered to the commonly accepted definition of *synonym* yet at the same time to extend the sense to accord with what was believed to be Roget's practice and to satisfy the demands of those who urged more words. It may be granted that this is a legitimate practice, provided it does not force the issue, but represents a genuine change in conception among a large or even a small class of those who use the term *synonym*. That the growing demand was for more synonyms cannot be questioned but that a change in the conception of *synonym* had occurred, from the one that had been in vogue since Crabb's time, may justly be disputed. At any rate, let us see how it affected the *Standard Dictionary's* choice of synonyms. Two lists will illustrate its practice:

> ADEQUATE    able, adapted, capable, commensurate, competent, equal, fit, fitted, fitting, qualified, satisfactory, sufficient, suitable.
>
> HARMONY    accord, accordance, agreement, amity, concord, concurrence, conformity, congruity, consent, consistency, consonance, symmetry, unanimity, uniformity, union, unison, unity.

The *Standard Dictionary's* definition justifies the selection of such lists of "synonyms." Each is a word which has one or more meanings in common with the introductory word *(adequate* or *harmony)*. But if *adequate* means exactly commensurate with the requirements, only *sufficient* and *competent* (in one of its senses) with the addition of *enough* approach it in content. A person may be *adequate* if he is *able, capable, competent* (in another sense), or *qualified;* a person or thing may be *adequate* if he or it is *adapted, fitted,* or *suitable;* a thing may be *adequate* if it is equal to the requirement by being *fit* or *satisfactory:* but in all these cases, he or it may also be more than *adequate* or less than *adequate,* in some way, or the question of adequacy may never arise. *Harmony* in its musical sense may be related to *accord, concord, consonance,* in its aesthetic sense to *symmetry* and other terms not in this list; but what relation there is between it and *amity, uniformity, unanimity, agreement, concurrence, congruity,* etc., except as a cause or result or concomitant, needs to be proved. A word-finding list may consist of terms which, by agreeing in some implications and connotations, overlap, for those lists serve their purpose in helping the user to locate his word. But when the object is discrimination, only those words serve the purpose whose basic likeness can be proved by showing that they have a common denotation as well as not readily discerned differences.

It is true that Fernald found no difficulty here. His clearest expression of the method of discrimination is found in the preface to his *English Synonyms, Antonyms, and Prepositions:*

> The great source of vagueness, error, and perplexity in many discussions of synonyms is, that the writer merely associates stray ideas loosely connected with the different words, sliding from synonym to synonym with no definite point of departure or return, so that a smooth and at first sight pleasing statement really gives the mind no definite resting-place and no sure conclusion. A true discussion of synonyms is definition by comparison, and for this there must be something definite with which to compare. When the standard is settled, approximation or differentiation can be determined with clearness and certainty.

What type of synonymy Fernald was criticizing is not clear. It was probably what may be called "the chain-formula type." When a synonymist had made so poor a selection of synonyms that there could be no common ground and his list presented an array of associated rather than synonymous terms, he often fell into the habit of giving a series of definitions with a factitious relation. A repetition of a previous word was usually enough to make a connection. This was the defect of certain synonymies into which all writers of articles, good as well as bad, fell at one time or another and is probably the type to which Fernald referred when he described the "easy sliding from synonym to synonym." Yet it is not always bad: when one word carries a general meaning which serves as a substitute for the common denotation, it is possible to use it with good effect. A short example from *The New Century Dictionary* (1927) must suffice for the good use:

> BANTER is good-humored jesting. . . .RAILLERY is often sharp, sarcastic banter; PLEASANTRY, delicate and pleasant banter; BADINAGE, diverting and purposeless banter; PERSIFLAGE, light, frivolous, or flippant banter.

With lists such as Fernald's own it would be impossible to avoid this formula, unchanged. It was necessary for him to find some way of varying "the chain formula" so that he could secure the desired qualities, "unity of the group" and "some point of departure and return." Therefore, he devised the method whereby one word would be selected as the key word and all the other words should be compared or contrasted with it. A good example is afforded by his article at *money:*

> MONEY. SYN.: bills, bullion, capital, cash, coin, currency, funds, gold, notes, property, silver, specie. *Money* is the authorized medium of exchange; coined *money* is called *coin* or *specie*. What are termed in England bank-*notes* are in the United States commonly called *bills;* as, five-dollar *bill*. The *notes* of responsible men are readily transferable in commercial circles, but they are not *money;* as, the stock was sold for $500 in *money* and the balance in merchantable paper. *Cash* is *specie* or *money* in hand, or paid in hand; as, the *cash* account; the *cash* price. In the legal sense, *property* is not *money*, and *money* is not *property;* for *property* is that which has inherent value, while *money*, as such, has but representative value, and may or may not have intrinsic value. *Bullion* is either *gold* or *silver* uncoined, or the coined metal considered without reference to its coinage, but simply as merchandise, when its value as *bullion* may be very different from its value as *money*. The word *capital* is used chiefly of accumulated *property* or *money* invested in productive enterprises or available for such investment. Compare PROPERTY; WEALTH.

Nothing could be clearer than that these words are not synonyms in the generally accepted sense. They include names of kinds of money (coin, specie, bills), names of material used for money or, in figurative language, meaning money or wealth (gold, silver), and words denoting things that have some intimate association with money (bullion, property, capital). The article keeps more or less consistently before the reader the relation of these to the key word *money*. The reader is bound to see and understand the distinctions and carry away a unified impression. There can be no quarrel with such articles on the ground of their not giving useful information. It may even be argued that a discrimination of terms that coincide in some part of their meaning may be in itself a valuable thing. But neither justification touches the issue raised by the Fernald synonymies. The ground of valid objection to them is that they offer *as synonyms* many words which even by the loosest of definitions cannot be accepted as such. The point of absurdity is reached at *spontaneous*, where the key word is so important that *voluntary* and *involuntary*, *free* and *instinctive*, *automatic* and *impulsive* are included.

By 1909, the date of publication of the next complete revision of the Merriam-Webster dictionaries (the first edition of *Webster's New International Dictionary*), there had been time for consideration of these matters and for a more sober judgment. The Goodrich synonymies clearly needed revision on account of the growth of the language and, partly, because the synonym lists could be enriched. The work was entrusted to John Livingston Lowes (1867–1945; then at Washington University, St. Louis, but later at Harvard University) under the advisory supervision of George Lyman Kittredge (1860–1941) of Harvard. They were to deal only with general senses, but a few technical articles written by specialists were to be submitted to them, so as to insure uniformity in manner and method. The articles thus prepared were included in

*Webster's New International Dictionary* and reprinted, with minor changes, in *Webster's New International Dictionary, Second Edition* (1934).

Certain points of agreement were established by Lowes and Kittredge early in the course of their partnership. Very early in the writing of these articles Lowes called Kittredge's attention to the Fernald list at *adequate* and the *Century* list, *adequate, sufficient, enough*. "Is not the *Century's* list adequate?" he wrote. "I did not notice the test my question affords, but none of the other words in the *Standard's* list can be substituted for 'adequate.' Are they not better distributed among other articles? The longer I study the material, the more strongly I feel that more articles, each discriminating fewer words, are advisable. The longer articles are, as a matter of fact, confusing, and seem to have led often to strained attempts to find a single common factor for words which fall more naturally into several groups." Kittredge agreed fully.[6] Thus, the Webster tradition of discriminating synonyms that are synonyms in the accepted sense was followed. Looser synonyms or closely related words were still given in the word-finding lists, and these also were revised by Lowes, whose interests, however, were concentrated on the articles discriminating synonyms.

By temperament and training Professor Lowes was especially fitted for the task assigned him. He excels all his predecessors in philosophic grasp and powers of analysis, yet he never confuses synonymizing with philosophizing or moralizing; he outstrips them all in the range of his knowledge of literature and of his contacts with language as the medium of expressing ideas and emotions; great scholar though he was, his work is utterly free of the pedantry, dogmatism, and heaviness that so often mar the work of lesser men. Though not a lexicographer by training or experience, he almost perfectly adapted the art of synonymizing to the methods of lexicography, so that whatever can contribute in either to the advantage of the other was brought out in his articles.

It is in the clarification of the differences between terms that are to a large extent equivalent in denotation that Lowes made the greatest advances in the art of synonymizing. Practically every synonymist before him had inklings of the kinds of differences that he saw clearly; many of them, such as Miss Whately, had used the language adopted by him, but no one so fully realized its possibilities. Rambling, persistent missing of the real differences and constant confusion of the content of the word itself with the concept for which that word stood were characteristic and prevalent faults of many earlier writers of synonymies. With Lowes, direct attack at each problem became possible and, with it, swift, sure shafts that rarely fail to make the desired cleavage.

It may be said that as a rule he was careful in his synonymies to state the ground of agreement; but sometimes he neglected to do so when the likeness was obvious. But in regard to differences he was extremely particular and rarely departed from the aim he held before him. His most frequently used method may be illustrated by an excerpt from the article at **foretell** in *Webster's New International Dictionary* (1909):

> FORETELL *(Saxon)* and PREDICT *(Latin)* are frequently interchangeable; but PREDICT is now commonly used when inference from facts (rather than occult processes) is involved; as, "Some sorcerer. . .had *foretold*, dying, that none of all our blood should know the shadow from the substance" *(Tennyson);* "Mr. Brooke's conclusions were as difficult to *predict* as the weather" *(G. Eliot);* an astronomer *predicts* the return of a comet. PROPHESY connotes inspired or mysterious knowledge, or great assurance of prediction; as, "ancestral voices *prophesying* war" *(Coleridge);* "Wrinkled benchers often talked of him approvingly, and *prophesied* his rise" *(Tennyson).* FORECAST connotes conjecture rather than inference; PRESAGE implies shrewd forecast, sometimes presentiment or warning; as, "Who shall so *forecast* the years?" *(Tennyson);* "I *presage*, unless the country make an alarm, the cause is lost"*(Scott).* . . .FOREBODE. . .implies obscure prescience or premonition (esp. of evil); PORTEND. . ., threatening or ominous foretokening; as, "His heart *forebodes* a mystery" *(Tennyson);* "My father put on the countenance which always *portends* a gathering storm" *(Richardson).*

If we supply the common denotation of all these words—"to indicate what will happen"—the difference lies in other ideas involved in their meaning. In each case this difference forms part of the word's definition, the other part of which will be the common denotation. Indeed, although the dictionary definition may be presented from another point of view, a good and fair definition may be made according to this method. The synonymist, however, should find it the best method when his job is merely to show how far words agree and then to point out their individual differences. Other methods are conceivable, indeed some are necessary in special cases, but as yet no better method has been devised for the general run of synonyms. Miss Whately is largely responsible for it, but Lowes has greatly improved it.

It was (and is), however, impossible always to be equally exact, clear, and direct. This is especially true when the differences are less a matter of meaning than of coloring, as by historical and literary associations, or a matter of idiomatic usage. The difference in coloring or, in other terms, the difference in connotations— is especially difficult, requiring not only great knowledge but fine perceptions, imagination, and taste. Few

---

[6] From manuscript notes in the editorial files of G. & C. Merriam Company.

would dare to attempt to distinguish connotations, but Lowes, whose feeling for these differences is not equaled by any synonymist, is especially successful in their handling. Many of these could not be incorporated in a dictionary definition, but they must be felt if the word is to be used with the accumulated power that has been stored in it. A particularly effective synonym of this type is to be found at **idiot.**

> IDIOT, IMBECILE, FOOL, SIMPLETON are here compared esp. in their connotations; for technical distinctions, see defs. IDIOT (a learned word become popular) implies absence, commonly congenital, of intellectual or reasoning powers; it is often less strictly used to characterize one who is felt to have acted with utter stupidity; IMBECILE (less common as a popular term) implies great mental feebleness or (in its looser derogatory sense) entire fatuity; FOOL, the more vigorous word, is wholly popular, and frequently suggests lack of sense or wisdom rather than of brains; from its Biblical use, it still connotes, in elevated style, grave, pitying, or scathing condemnation; in colloquial usage, as a term of contempt, it is strongly offensive; SIMPLETON (also wholly popular) implies silliness or (sometimes) unsophisticatedness; it is often used lightly as a term of indulgent contempt; as, "He said you were. . .a senseless, driveling *idiot*" *(Wycherley);* "What an *idiot* am I, to wait here for a fellow who probably takes a delight in mortifying me" *(Goldsmith);* "custom's *idiot* sway" *(Cowper);* cf. an *idiotic* grin; "The petty passions, the *imbecile* desires. . ., daily moving her contempt" *(G. Eliot);* "She's a *fool* to stay behind her father" *(Shak.);* "*Fools* rush in where angels fear to tread" *(Pope);* "They look upon persons employing their time in making verses. . .as *simpletons* easily to be deceived" *(V. Knox);* poor, innocent little *simpleton!* "The 'Great *simpleton!*'. . .of Mr. Newman, and the 'Thou *fool!*' of the Bible, are something alike; but 'Thou *fool!*' is very grand, and 'Great *simpleton!*' is an atrocity. So too. . .Shakespeare's 'Poor venomous *fool,* be angry and dispatch!' is in the grand style" *(M. Arnold). . . .*

Differences in idiomatic usage are oftentimes not a matter that can easily be presented by definition. Many terms in a dictionary are defined almost in the same words, though written by various editors, the only clue to difference consisting in the illustrations. The consultant is often at a loss, because he does not see that these examples may constitute the only uses of the term, or a few such uses, and are not representative of a large number of uses. It was in such cases that the method which we have called the Piozzi method was first used, but without a full understanding of its dangers and limitations. Lowes avoided this method except where he was dealing with fixed idioms. Then he safeguarded his statement with a parenthetical elimination such as "one *ascends* (not *mounts*) a mountain; one *mounts* (not *ascends*) a horse." The sparing use of this method did not, however, lead to his ignoring the problem presented by such synonyms as are definable in almost identical terms yet are incapable of discrimination in implications and connotations. To get at his method let us examine parts of certain synonymies where his effectiveness is most apparent:

> One EXCUSES (either as a superior or as an equal) small faults, minor omissions, or neglects, esp. in social or conventional obligations; one PARDONS (as a superior, or by act of mercy or generosity) serious faults, crimes, or grave offenses, esp. against laws or morals; as, to *excuse* an unintentional oversight, an absence from a required exercise; "*Excuse* my glove" *(Sheridan);* to *pardon* a thief; to *pardon* a theft; "Apollo, *pardon* my great profaneness 'gainst thine oracle" *(Shak.).*

> STOP. . .applies primarily to action, or to that which is thought of as *moving;* CEASE applies also to states and conditions, or to that which is thought of as *being;* as, a train *stops,* but does not *cease;* the noise it makes both *stops* and *ceases;* one's love may *cease,* but scarcely *stop.*

> *Fast* and *rapid* are often used without distinction; but FAST frequently applies to the moving object, whereas RAPID is apt to characterize or suggest the movement itself; as, a *fast* horse, a *fast* train, boat; a *rapid* current, a *rapid* gait, *rapid* progress.

> *Hateful* and *odious* are sometimes used with little distinction. But HATEFUL more frequently applies to that which excites actual hatred, ODIOUS, to that which is excessively disagreeable, or which awakens repugnance; as, "Why shouldn't we hate what is *hateful* in people, and scorn what is mean?" *(Thackeray). . . .*"There was something more *odious* to him in her friendship than her hatred" *(Thackeray).*

In these discriminations the original contribution of Lowes is the generalization regarding usage or application. An occasional synonymist before him had experimented with it, but no one before him succeeded. He knows how to guard the expression, never claims too much, and yet, in spite of all the difficulties involved, makes statements that are just and therefore convincing. There seems to have been no inclination on his part to overstate the case. If there must be inexactness, he preferred it on the side of understatement. "This is as much as it is safe to say" was a not infrequent comment of his.[7] Much more could be said about the interesting technique developed by Lowes. Much more could be said also about other excellences and some defects which characterize his work. But when all is said and done there still remains his superiority as a discriminator, as manifested in his selection of methods according to his material. Whether his synonyms differed in implications, in connotations, or in applications or, more probably, some in one way, some in another, he was seldom at a loss.

---

[7] In manuscript notes in the editorial files of G. & C. Merriam Company.

Just a word about antonyms. There is no evidence at hand to prove that Lowes was ever asked to enter antonyms in *Webster's New International Dictionary*. He did, however, incorporate a few (though not by that name) in his articles under the general formula of "opposed to . . ." when the difference between synonyms (usually very general ones) could be apprehended more easily by knowing the term which was the direct opposite of each. He does this several times, as at **base,** where *base* is "opposed to *high-minded*," *vile* is "opposed to *pure, noble*," and *mean* is "opposed to *generous, magnanimous*." It is possible to guess his definition of *antonym*, but no more. The antonyms in *Webster's New International Dictionary, Second Edition* (1934) were added by an office editor.

There is no need to go further in the history of synonymy. Further synonymists[8] there have been, some very good, some not quite so good, and some very bad; but they have all taken sides, either with those who support the traditional definition of *synonym* as one of two or more words having the same essential meaning or with those who favor its extension to one of two or more words which coincide in some part of their meaning. There has been no compromise: it might even be said that the break has scarcely been noticed. Nevertheless, it is apparent that, unless there be some clarification in definitions, especially of *synonym* and *antonym*, the prevailing popular misunderstanding will increase—with what results no one can estimate. This clarification we propose to undertake in the essays that follow.

It is because we firmly believe in the values implicit in the study of synonyms, antonyms, and word-finding lists (in this book divided into analogous words and contrasted words) that this dictionary has been written. We hope, therefore, that it not only carries some steps forward the admirable work accomplished by Goodrich and Lowes but also removes some sources of confusion or perplexity which have arisen outside of their work. The old defect inherent in synonymies, the overuse of illustration without a sufficient background in differences of implications (which we have called the Piozzi method), has not entirely disappeared from more recent writing, but, at least, the snake was scotched by the publishers' preface of the 1859 edition of *Webster's Dictionary*. In its place has come an uncertainty in the definitions of *synonym* and *antonym* which is even more insidious. In the three essays that follow we, therefore, make clear our own position. In the first of these essays we define *synonym* briefly, in order to show what effect that definition has had on our choice of words to be discriminated and on the technique of discrimination. In the second we define *antonym* at length, for the reason that this term has never been clearly examined and that the definitions in the major dictionaries are all at variance with Smith's tentative definition and with the selections of many of his successors. In the third we explain our aims and practices with respect to the word-finding lists.

## *SYNONYM:* ANALYSIS AND DEFINITION

The chief reason for including in this introduction an article on synonyms is not to phrase a new definition of that term. It is rather to make a protest as to the loosening of the definition within the last fifty or sixty years and to restate very clearly what we believe to be the true and generally accepted meaning. In addition we will show briefly the effect of this definition upon our method.

For approximately one hundred years in the history of English synonymy there was very little real difference of opinion as to what a synonym is or as to what words should be the material of discrimination. It is true that John Trusler discriminated "words esteemed synonymous," Mrs. Piozzi "words apparently synonymous," and Miss Whately "pseudo-synonyms." Roget, who held that discrimination was foreign to his purpose, claimed that "the investigation of the distinctions to be drawn between words apparently synonymous forms a separate branch of inquiry." Nevertheless, all four made a distinction between true or actual synonyms (that is, words identical in meaning) and the terms which they discriminated or, in the case of Roget, which were discriminable (that is, terms that are so nearly alike that they appear to be synonyms). For all practical purposes, however, the words which were discriminated were not at all different from the "words closely allied" in meaning between which, according to Crabb, it is the business of the synonymist "to mark the nice shades of distinction"; nor is there any clash with Soule's simple definition

---

[8] Some of the best of these are: Francis A. March, sr., and Francis A. March, jr., *A Thesaurus Dictionary of the English Language* (Philadelphia, 1902 [New Supplement by R. A. Goodwin, New York, 1958]); C. O. Sylvester Mawson, *The Standard Thesaurus of English Words and Phrases: a Dictionary of Synonyms and Antonyms* (New York, 1911 [and 1946; revised as *Roget's International Thesaurus*, 3d ed., New York, 1962]); F. Sturges Allen, *Allen's Synonyms and Antonyms* (New York, 1920 [revised and enlarged ed., New York, 1963]); A. C. Baugh and P. C. Kitchen, *Synonyms, Antonyms and Discriminations* (included as an appendix in *The New Century Dictionary*, New York, 1927 [and 1936]); C. O. Sylvester Mawson, *The Roget Dictionary of Synonyms and Antonyms* (New York, 1931).

of a synonym as that which has "the same meaning as" the entry word under which it is listed "or a meaning very nearly the same."

It is also true that these synonymists did not always agree in their choice of synonyms. In part this was due to some confusion as to the limits of their scope, but mostly it is the result of conditions which still, to a degree, prevail. Some advances have been made in precision, but the truth was and is that there are too many factors entering into the selection of synonyms to make for absolute certainty or perfect accuracy in their choice. But these synonymists were not so far wrong as William Perry, who accepted Johnson's "proximate words" as synonyms and made no distinction between them in reference to sense. The failure of his *Synonymous . . . Dictionary* may be ascribed to this cause.

The error Perry made has renewed itself, though with slightly more justification. This renewal, also, is initially the result of the misinterpretation of a highly popular work, Roget's *Thesaurus of English Words and Phrases*, and of a belief that Roget presented two lists of terms, those that were alike *(synonyms)* and those that were opposed. It was to give voice to this interpretation that Charles J. Smith coined the word *antonym* for the opposed terms and gave to the world in 1867 his small book *A Complete Collection of Synonyms and Antonyms*. But because he was not following Roget in the arrangement of his material, choosing the dictionary (alphabetical) method rather than the classificatory method, he defined *synonym* (and *antonym*) in such a way that it would apply to Roget's lists (so far as they were of the same part of speech) and to his own. Synonyms are, in Smith's definition, "words which agree in expressing one or more characteristic ideas in common" (with the entered word). It is possible that he believed he was more careful in his selection than Roget. In line with his definition he gives lists of synonyms, such as that at **accelerate,** which are, it is true, less diverse than Roget's but which are still susceptible of criticism as synonyms. There are, for example, some that are not questionable, such as *speed, quicken,* and *hasten,* but there are others, such as *promote, urge, expedite, facilitate,* and *dispatch,* that are open to question. *Accelerate* means to make go faster: so do *speed, hasten,* and *quicken.* But *promote,* for example, stresses aid given in attaining an end and only occasionally implies to make go faster; *urge* throws the emphasis upon the force that impels rather than upon the result, which usually, but not always, is to make go faster; *expedite* stresses the removal of impediments so that a progress or process is not delayed longer than is necessary or normal and therefore usually means to make go faster than it might. But in all these three cases a making go faster may or may not be implied; if implied, this notion is subordinate to the main implication of the word. Agreement "in one or more ideas" is a poor basis for the selection of synonyms, for these may or may not form a part of the essential meaning.

As the demand grew for a large number of synonyms, even agreement in one or more characteristic ideas tended to break down. Twenty-five and more years later certain synonymists of repute were offering groups of words as synonyms of one word rather than of one another and were not restricting those words to one sense of their key term. For instance, one synonymist of this period gave as the synonyms of **stain** *blot, color, discolor, disgrace, dishonor, dye, soil, spot, sully, tarnish, tinge, tint.* It is true that not all are discriminated, *blot, disgrace, dishonor, soil, spot, sully, tarnish,* and *tint* being omitted, but even so, they are all given in alphabetical order as synonyms and without explanation. In the list as it stands some words are synonyms of *stain* in the sense of to discolor, some in the sense of to impart color to or suffuse with color, and some in the sense of to bring reproach upon; but others have only a slight idea in common with *stain* in one of its senses. Such lists are far from rare in the very late nineteenth century or the early twentieth century: to the consultant who seeks another and closer word for the one which occurs to him, they must be hopelessly confusing. They have no value in teaching the precise use of language: their only merit is to indicate some of the words which may be used when one feels the need of a word like *stain* in any of its senses.

It is against a definition so loose as that favored by Smith or implied by others who went even further that this book makes a protest. In line with the tradition of the Merriam-Webster dictionaries we believe that such a definition is destructive of all the values that have come to be recognized in synonyms. We hold that only by a clear return to something like the time-honored definition can we conserve these values and recognize a synonym when we see it. To emphasize this aim we propose in this dictionary to restate that definition fully and unequivocally so that none of the loopholes may be left through which some synonymists have escaped and to tighten the method of discrimination so that it will be very clear at points where even the best of synonymists have, in the past, unconsciously permitted vagueness.

**A synonym, in this dictionary, will always mean one of two or more words in the English language which have the same or very nearly the same *essential* meaning.** This is not a matter of mere likeness in meaning, for words may have some implications (ideas involved in their meaning) in common and yet not be synonymous. It is rather a likeness in denotation, which may be inadequately defined as the meaning which includes all the important implications but which is more strictly defined as the meaning or signification of a term as expressed in its definition. The denotation must include more than a summary of implications: it must indicate the part of speech and the relations of the ideas involved in a term's meaning.

Synonyms, therefore, are only such words as may be defined wholly, or almost wholly, in the same terms. Usually they are distinguished from one another by an added implication or connotation, or they may differ in their idiomatic use or in their application. They may be and usually are interchangeable within limits, but interchangeability is not the final test, since idiomatic usage is often a preventive of that. The only satisfactory test of synonyms is their agreement in denotation. This agreement is seldom so perfect as to make the words absolutely identical in meaning, but it is always so clear that the two or more words which are synonyms can be defined in the same terms up to a certain point.

Consequently, the statement of this common denotation is of the greatest importance. In the discriminating articles in this dictionary it is, as a general rule, presented in the first sentence, but sometimes when there is need of a preliminary statement it is put in the second sentence. For example, at **nice**, the common denotation of the words to be discriminated *(nice, dainty, fastidious, finicky, finicking, finical, particular, fussy, squeamish, persnickety, pernickety)* is given as "exacting or displaying exacting standards (as in selection, judgment, or workmanship)"; at **object** (where *object, protest, remonstrate, expostulate, kick* are discriminated) it is "to oppose something (as a course, a procedure, a policy, or a project), especially by making known one's arguments against it"; at **delusion** (where *delusion, illusion, hallucination, mirage* are discriminated) it is "something which is believed to be or is accepted as being true or real but which is actually false or unreal." Each of these sentences is so worded that the part of speech of the words discriminated is made clear. For example, the wording is in the form of a definition of an adjective where the words discriminated are adjectives, in the form of a definition of a verb where the words discriminated are verbs. Some of these synonyms have other senses than the one here given, but in each such meaning the word has other synonyms and another common denotation. A distinct attempt, it may be said here, has been made to select synonyms according to their range of meaning. It has not always been possible to do so, since, occasionally, the more general word has no synonyms except more specific words (compare *let* in the list: *let, allow, permit, suffer, leave*). As a rule, however, a division between words of wide range and words of narrow range of meaning has been made, because it permits a more definite denotation for the narrower terms and makes for closer agreement and fewer differences. It is for this reason that we have separated the general terms for a political or legal agreement *(agreement, accord, understanding)* from those that are very explicit *(contract, bargain, compact, pact, treaty,* etc.), and have separated the general terms *large, big, great* from terms which specify unusual size *(huge, vast, immense, enormous,* etc.) and from terms which imply size and impressiveness *(grand, magnificent, imposing, stately,* etc.). But the difference between groups of synonyms is not always dependent on generality: it often implies a different emphasis or a different combination of implications. There have been many times when it was a serious question whether to add a word as a synonym to one group or to another, the arguments on both sides being of equal cogency. In such cases (for example, *hellish* and *fiendish*) the decision has usually depended on many factors, such as basic rather than derived meaning and the fact that, if certain words were treated separately, terms which are synonyms of one but not of the other could be added. Occasionally when a shared meaning makes a word a logical candidate for two synonymy groups but usage, connotation, or implication set the two aspects distinctly apart it has been included in two groups. For many reasons the problem of selecting synonyms has not been an easy one, but we have always tried to base our judgment upon evidence that was not affected by any personal prejudices or predilections.

Not all the words discriminated in this dictionary are synonyms. A few articles discuss a group of words that are sometimes wrongly taken as synonyms because they are confused or their actual meanings are misunderstood or because they once had one or more meanings which made them synonymous. In articles discussing such words the reason for their not being synonyms, whatever it may be, is stated clearly and unambiguously in the first or second sentence of the article. We have added these groups not merely because we believe them useful but because we believe that they come rightly within the province of the discriminator.

The method of discrimination is not invariable, for every set of synonyms presents its own problems. But, in general, the points of distinction are in: (1) implications—here, mostly minor ideas involved in the meaning of the word; (2) connotations—the ideas which color the word's meaning and are the product of various influences, such as etymology, language of origin, and historical and literary association; (3) applications— the restrictions in a word's use as prescribed by idiom or in accordance with the nature of the other words with which it may be associated, as when an adverb may be used to modify only certain kinds of verbs or when a verb may take only certain kinds of nouns as its subject or its object. Not all of the words discriminated in a single article differ in only one of these ways, however; some may differ in implications, some in connotations, some in applications, and some in more than one way. For no method adopted by the discriminator should be so artificial as to foster merely theoretical distinctions. The distinctions drawn should be real distinctions based on the evidence of recorded use—and it is such evidence, we cannot too strongly emphasize, that has guided the editors of this dictionary and has determined the distinctions set forth in its discriminating articles.

## *ANTONYM:* ANALYSIS AND DEFINITION

There are probably few words more generally used with less understanding of their meaning than the word *antonym*. True, all the dictionaries define it, but often in such terms that the definition may be interpreted to include radically different conceptions. Is an antonym theoretically only one word or, at the most, one of two or three words which can be opposed to another word in a definite sense or is it any one of several words which may be opposed to it or to a group of synonymous terms? Probably because the latter conception is the easier one it has gained widespread acceptance, but still the dictionary definitions incline to back up the opinion of those who think of an antonym in the abstract as something more specialized and nearer to the former conception.

No one will dispute the right of a person to coin a term that fills a definite need or to give to that term the meaning he desires, though one may question whether the meaning assigned accords with the term's etymology, as in the case of *antonym*. For C. J. Smith who, in his . . .*Synonyms and Antonyms* (1867), introduced this term (which, in his own phrasing, "he has ventured, not to coin, but to reissue") adopted it primarily because of its analogy to *synonym* and knew that only by considerable stretching could the meaning he proposed for it be made to approach the meaning of what he thought of as its Greek original. Despite his recognition of this fact, the term seemed to Smith preferable to *counterterm*, though he acknowledged that some persons might still prefer the latter. As for definition, he related *synonym* and *antonym*. "Words," he wrote, "which agree in expressing one or more characteristic ideas in common [that is, with a given term] he has regarded as Synonyms, those which negative one or more such ideas he has called Antonyms."

Therefore, no one is likely to dispute the right of a later investigator to examine anew the meaning of a coined word questionably grounded and vaguely defined that has become established in the language. In fact, there is not only the right but a duty on the part of such an investigator when, as in the case of *antonym*, he finds that there is a great difference between the theory, as manifested in the definition, and the practice, as manifested in selection. There will always be strict constructionists and loose constructionists but, in this case at least, the difference is more apparent than real, for many of the latter have been forced into this position by the practical difficulties confronting them in the selection of antonyms, rather than by indifference to the concept involved.

What we propose to do here, then, is to examine the word *antonym*, to determine the concept it involves, and to state its definition in as clear terms as possible. When we find a term like this used frequently with such qualifying words as *exact* and *true* (the "exact antonym" of this word; the "true antonym"), we must suspect an attempt on the part of men to approximate an ideal.

Modern unabridged dictionaries, without exception, define *antonym* with comparative strictness. It is "a word of opposite meaning" *(Webster's New International Dictionary, Second Edition[9]),* "a term which is the opposite or antithesis of another, a counter-term" *(Oxford English Dictionary),* "a word directly opposed to another in meaning; a counterterm: the opposite of *synonym*" *(Funk and Wagnalls New Standard Dictionary),* "a counterterm; an opposite; an antithetical word: the opposite of *synonym*" *(Century Dictionary),* and "a word that is an opposite in meaning of a particular word" *(New Century Dictionary).* In all of these definitions, the burden is on the word *opposite* or *opposed;* and, it should be added, all differences of opinion as to the criteria for determining antonyms are due to uncertainty as to what is meant by *opposite* or *opposed.* The physical connotations of these words always stand in the way of a strict definition of their abstract senses. How complex is the concept of opposition may be seen from the following analysis of its physical connotations.

Opposition is a relation involved when two things are so placed that: (1) they may be connected by a straight line (straightness as distinguished from obliquity being determined by external conditions such as the lines of a room) drawn from one to another (as, *opposite* windows); (2) they lie at either end of an axis, diameter, or the like (as, *opposite* points on the earth's surface); (3) they are contiguous but reversed in position (as, the *opposite* halves of the globe); (4) they face each other, the distance apart being of no consequence (as, partners stand *opposite*); (5) they depart or diverge from each other (as, to go their *opposite* ways); (6) they work against each other (as, *opposite* forces); (7) they cannot exist together, because they reverse or undo each other (as, the *opposite* processes of growth and decay); (8) they represent the obverse and the reverse (as, the *opposite* faces of a coin).

What this relation is both materially and immaterially and in all instances is, frankly, hard to determine. It is not invariably the confrontation of one with another, for "persons who go their *opposite* ways" and "the *opposite* processes of growth and decay," for example, do not respond to this test; it is hardly complete divergence or difference, for "the *opposite* halves of the globe" and "the *opposite* faces of a coin" represent difference only in one or more particulars, otherwise remaining fundamentally alike; it is still

---

[9] Same in *Webster's Third New International.*

less antagonism or irreconcilability, for there is no hint of either in the *opposite* position of partners in a dance or in *opposite* windows. Although some of these ideas exist as implications distinguishing meanings of the word *opposite*, they do not yield any fundamental meaning which is involved in every sense. One can go no further than to say that *opposite* represents a setting of one thing against another so as to sharpen their differences or to reveal their divergencies.

It will be necessary, therefore, to get at what is meant by "opposite meaning" in another way. First, let us take the words listed as antonyms in the dictionaries and manuals of synonyms and antonyms and see into what classifications they fall. When possible, we will offer a classification known to logic, but when not possible, we will form our own, naming it in unambiguous terms.

A large number of words listed as antonyms fall into two well-known logical categories, those of *contradictory terms* (or *contradictories*) and *contrary terms* (or *contraries*).

(1) *Contradictory terms* are so opposed to each other that they are mutually exclusive and admit no possibility between them. If either is true, the other must be false; if either is false, the other must be true. Examples:—A thing is either *perfect* or *imperfect:* no matter how slight or how extensive the imperfection, the fact remains that the thing cannot be called *perfect* if any flaw, blemish, or defect exists. If a person is asked for his opinion, he may *agree* with that of others, or he may *disagree*, or *differ:* it is unimportant whether the disagreement is radical or superficial or the difference concerns a major or a very minor point; he cannot be said to *agree*.

(2) *Contrary terms* are so opposed in meaning that the language admits no greater divergence. They are the true "diametrical opposites." But they must be of or must apply to things of the same genus or fundamental kind. Thus, *white* and *black* represent the extremes in color, the former, as popularly understood, implying the absorption of all colors and the latter implying the privation of every vestige of color. *Prodigal* and *parsimonious* represent extremes in expenditure (chiefly of money), but *prodigal* implies excessive extravagance and *parsimonious* excessive frugality. *Superiority* and *inferiority* represent extremes judged by a standard of what is good. Between these extremes represented by each of these pairs of examples, there are many words which may more truly describe or designate the person or thing in question.

Other classes are the following:

(3) Many words are listed as antonyms that normally appear in pairs. Some are what the logician calls *relative terms*, pairs of words which indicate such a relationship that one of them cannot be used without suggesting the other; as, *parent* and *child*, *husband* and *wife*, *predecessor* and *successor*, *employee* and *employer*. Others are *complementary terms* involving, usually, a reciprocal relation or the incompleteness of one unless the other follows; as, *question* and *answer*, *attack* and *defend*, *stimulus* and *response*.

(4) An important class of words sometimes listed in antonymies may be called for want of a better name *reverse terms:* these comprise adjectives or adverbs which signify a quality or verbs or nouns which signify an act or state that reverse or undo the quality, act, or state of the other. Although they are neither contradictory nor contrary terms, they present a clear opposition. Their addition is usually justified in this way: if the antonym of *admit* is *reject*, what shall we do with *eject* which implies not the negative but the reverse of *admit?:* if the antonym of *destructive* is *harmless*, must we ignore *constructive*, which goes further and implies either the reverse or the undoing of *destructive?* Many words of the reverse type are often equal in value; sometimes they are even stronger than the first.

(5) There is still a class of words listed as antonyms, which are neither contradictories nor contraries nor reverse terms, which do, however, present a sharp contrast—for example, such pairs as *rich* and *destitute*, *dry* and *moist*, and *keep* and *abandon*. This is one of the most perplexing of classes and one that appears very frequently in antonym lists. Such words may be designated *contrasted terms*. We shall return to them later.

(6) The last class of so-called antonyms is very inclusive. Words in this class might be called "loosely contrasted terms," since, when they are presented side by side with the word of which they are given as antonyms, they never fully clash but show a difference in only a small part of their meaning (as, *abstruse* and *superficial*, *frank* and *hypocritical*, *vigilant* and *careless*). For the sake of uniformity, however, we will call them *incompatibles*, for they usually cannot both at the same time be said of or applied to the same person or thing. *Frank* means open and free in one's talk and uninhibited by any restraints, such as fear, whereas *hypocritical* means presenting an appearance of being other and usually better than one is; *abstruse* means so remote from the range of ordinary human experience that there is difficulty in comprehension, while *superficial*, in this limited sense, means not penetrating below the surface or exterior so as to unveil what lies behind. So put, there is not the slightest sign of a clash in meaning, yet the difference which confuses, though slight, is there, for the person who is called *frank* gives the appearance of sincerity and the person who is called *hypocritical* is adjudged insincere. Similarly, a work that is spoken of as *abstruse* differs from a work that is spoken of as *superficial* in that the one is profound, the other shallow. It is *sincere* and *insincere* (not *frank* and *hypocritical*), and *profound* and *shallow* (not *abstruse* and *superficial*) which clash

in meaning. Since this class is based upon a mistake in analysis, it will be eliminated from the discussion.

If, then, we were to make a definition of *antonym* according to the type of word which dictionaries and manuals select as such, it would be phrased something like this: "An antonym is a word that so differs from another word that it represents its contradictory, its contrary, its relative (or counterpart), its complement, its reverse, its contrasted term, or its incompatible in some way or degree." That this is too inclusive a definition is obvious. No one, it seems fair to state, would define in terms as broad as this the word *antonym* as it is understood in concept; yet everyone who has made it his business to select antonyms is aware of the dangers involved and of the difficulty in avoiding the questionable types. An easygoing attitude is not chiefly responsible for this wide diversity. The English language was clearly not made to measure: it was not devised to show likenesses or differences. The discovery both of words which are closely alike and of words which are sharply different is, for the most part, the product of the need for expressing ideas or of understanding expressed ideas. No mechanical shaping power sets words right before men begin to use them.

It must be remembered that the task of selecting antonyms is imposed upon a living structure, in a desire to know its resources and so far as possible bend it to our needs. The selection not only of antonyms but also of synonyms is similar, at least in aim, to the scientist's classification of animals into orders, families, genera, and species. Both help us in the understanding and mastery of the material involved. When an old system breaks down in its study of the animal world, a new one must arise. None is perfect, but each is a help in bringing within the range of human understanding something that would otherwise be too vast for study and beyond the range of experience of any one man. So we proceed to study synonyms, words which closely resemble each other not in particular ways but in the very heart of their meaning, that we may know them better and use them more wisely, more precisely, and more effectively.

We should like to do the same thing with antonyms. It is good, we feel, to know the exact antonym of a word, for not only will it give us a firmer grasp of the meaning of the word to which it is opposed but inversely, of itself. Is there any test that will help us in discovering such words, that we may be enabled not only to speak and to write more expressively but to have a richer understanding of the pages of men who have known how to express themselves? There is a word in Smith's definition of *antonym* which may give us the clue, "those [words] which *negative* one or more such ideas he has called Antonyms." In fact, even today, some persons argue that an antonym is "the *exact* negative" of a word. It is not clear just what this is intended to mean. Taken quite literally and expressed in the phraseology of logic an "exact negative" is a word's *contradictory term*. But this is too narrow, as even those who vigorously support this definition must agree. By the terms of its definition, a word's contradictory must be the equivalent in meaning of its *not*-compound. Otherwise the two terms (a word and its contradictory) could not be mutually exclusive. Let us see this in tabular form.

| *word* | *not-compound* | *contradictory* |
|---|---|---|
| colored | not-colored | colorless |
| perfect | not-perfect | imperfect |
| agree | not-agree | disagree *or* differ |

So put, it is obvious that there is no disagreement between the *not*-term and contradictory: in this case the negative and the opposite agree. The trouble comes, however, with the naming of the antonym. As a matter of practical policy, if we accept the "exact negative" as the antonym, we must restrict ourselves to the very few contradictories which have an independent form, and to the very few *in-, un-, dis-* and similar compounds which are obviously contradictory terms. But if we wish completeness, we must supply antonyms for the vast majority of English words by constructing a *not*-form. That might do in logic, but it would not do when greater knowledge of the English language exists as our clear aim. Moreover, we feel the lack of the clash that gives so much savor to the antonym.

On the other hand, it is clear that the other terms listed as antonyms do not equal the "exact negative." The logical contradictory of *white (not-white)* may include any chromatic color or any other achromatic color, yet the contrary, or diametrical opposite, is only *black;* the logical contradictory of *parsimonious (not-parsimonious)* may include many terms, such as *liberal, extravagant, prodigal*, yet the contrary, or diametrical opposite, is *prodigal; not-liking* may include both *indifference* and *aversion*, but no one will question that *aversion* is the contrary of *liking*. Even more obvious is the difference between the logical contradictory and the relative or the complementary term, for in this case they neither represent nor include the same thing. *Not-attack*, for example, does not equal *defend; not-husband* is not the equivalent of *wife;* and *not-stimulus* does not in any way approach *response*.

More important than relative and complementary terms (most of which may be doubted, with good reason, to be the antonyms of each other) are the terms which take a reverse as the opposite. While the *not-*

term in these cases often equals or includes a word that is called the term's *antonym*, it is never equivalent with what may be called the "reverse antonym." For instance, *not-admit* equals *reject*, but it does not cover the reverse of *admit*, which may be either *eject* or *expel; not-abandon* may include *keep*, but it cannot be interpreted to cover the reverse of *abandon*, which is *reclaim*.

One class of words listed as antonyms remains for our consideration, contrasted terms. As has been said, this class covers a large number of words the listing of which as antonyms puzzles rather than enlightens the reader. It is easy to prove that they cannot be "exact negatives." For example, *keep*, which is often given as the antonym of *abandon*, is not its contradictory, for the logical contradictory *(not-keep)* also includes *sell, lose, give away,* and many other words; *rich* is not the contradictory of *destitute*, for the logical contradictory *not-rich* includes *needy, indigent, poor, comfortable,* and many other terms as well as *destitute*. But this does not get at the heart of the matter and display what is wrong with these terms. Obviously also, they are not contraries, for they do not represent extremes of divergence as do *parsimonious* and *prodigal* or *white* and *black*. What is the matter with them? In answering this question, we will find the clue to the solution of our problem.

Superficially viewed, these contrasted terms differ sharply in some part, but not in all parts, of their meaning. They do not clash full force. One term covers more ground than the other, or one term is more explicit in its implications than the other. The logician would say that they equal each other neither in extension nor in intension. Put more simply, they differ (1) in their range of application or applicability, one being general, the other specific, or one being more inclusive or less inclusive than the other, and (2) in their depth of meaning—that is, in the number and quality of implications contained in the terms. It is clear that *keep* is more general than *abandon* and that to equal it in generality and at the same time to negative (or, much better, to negate) its implications, *relinquish* would be a better choice: it is clear that *abandon* has more specific implications than are found in *keep*, such as surrender of possession or control and relegation to the mercy of others, and that a word which exactly equates these implications in number and quality yet, at the same time, negates them must be the true antonym. There seems to be no term that fills these demands except a "reverse term," one that undoes what has been accomplished by the act of abandoning. That term is *reclaim* in its definite sense of regaining control or possession of something and giving it full care and attention. *Rich* is too broad and general to pair with the very explicit *destitute*. There are many implications in the latter which have no clear parallel in *rich*. Only *poor* could be opposed to *rich* in breadth of extension and in vagueness of intension, because *rich* suggests more possessions than one needs, and *poor* suggests fewer possessions than one requires and so negates in full the meaning of the other. On the other hand, *opulent* could be opposed to *destitute* in narrowness of extension and in explicitness of intension, for *destitute* suggests the miserable condition where one is deprived of all that is needed for bare existence and *opulent* the felicitous condition where everything that is desired is possessed in abundance. Though *rich* and *poor* come close together (the dividing line being marked by such a word as *comfortable*) and *destitute* and *opulent* are very far apart, being in fact "diametrical opposites," each represents the negation of the other.

In this way *wet*, because it equals *dry* in range of meaning and negates *dry* in number and quality of implications, is the antonym of *dry*, whereas *damp* and *moist* are merely contrasted terms to *dry; alleviate* for the same reasons is the antonym of *aggravate*, and *mitigate, assuage,* and *allay* are nothing more than contrasted terms; *elevation* in the sense of promotion is the antonym of *degradation* in the sense of demotion, for it contains implications not found in *preferment* or *advancement*.

In selecting antonyms, therefore, one should be on guard to match in range of meaning the word from which one starts and to negate every one of its implications so that the opposition is complete. Otherwise the opposing words do not clash full force, one word covering more or less ground than the other or exhibiting differences not apparent in the other. It is for this reason that in this dictionary we have preferred to give *contrasted words* as distinct from *antonyms*, not denying or ignoring the value of the former in word study but emphasizing the unique, disciplinary value of the latter.

It is for a similar reason that we have ruled out relative and complementary terms as antonyms of each other. Pairs of words of this class are, it is true, usually matched in extension, but one of the pair seldom negates the intension of the other. Rather they suggest union, convergence, or completion when taken together. *Husband* and *wife, employer* and *employee* are different elements in a combination, which we may call opposites not in the sense of negating each other but of fulfilling each other. The same is true of *stimulus* and *response*, of *question* and *answer*. Without the former the latter could not be: without the latter the former remains incomplete. An occasional instance, however, remains, such as *attack* and *defend*. Since these come as close to reverse terms as they do to complementary terms, they may be treated as the former.

The foregoing analysis would seem to leave us with three classes as possible antonyms: contradictory, contrary, and reverse terms. It is true that, in general, all antonyms may be fitted into each of these classes. But, as the first two classes are the creation of logicians, who are dealing with symbols rather than with words, they are somewhat too rigid or too artificial for our use. Whether *good* and *bad*, *right* and *wrong*, *true* and *false* are contradictories or contraries might be disputed: it is wiser, for our purposes, not to raise this issue. They still remain antonyms according to our tests. So do a large number of more specific terms, which are equated in range of meaning and are negated in their specific implications, such as *extol* and *decry*, *aboveboard* and *underhand*, *constant* and *fitful* (as applied to things), *adulation* and *abuse*. The designation "reverse term" may also be dropped now that its purpose in exposition has been served. There are only three tests which should be applied to a word selected as the antonym of another word, and these are stated in the following definition:

> **An antonym is a word so opposed in meaning to another word, its equal in breadth or range of application, that it negates or nullifies every single one of its implications.**

It is this definition that has guided the selection of antonyms in this dictionary. Not every entry, of course, exhibits an antonym, for there are many words that have no antonym. In some few cases, moreover, we have been unable to supply any word that meets the three tests of the above definition or have been obliged to resort to an approximation. In such cases, we always welcome intelligent criticism that may enable us to supply these gaps. But, for the most part, where an antonym is listed, the editors rely upon its self-justification to the consultant who will apply these tests.


## THE TREATMENT OF ANTONYMS

A few words should be added to clarify the practice of this dictionary in regard to antonyms. They form an important part of its makeup; but, as they do not require much space, their significance may be overlooked. It must be emphasized that each antonym is directly related to its entry word in the special sense in which that word is discriminated. It bears not a loose relation but a very close one to that word, and even though it may also be the antonym of some other word (especially of a synonym of the entry word) it must be judged only by the relation it bears to the entry word with which it is associated. Sometimes, however, the antonym fits that word only when it is used in a narrowed sense or in a narrow application. This limitation is indicated in a parenthetical phrase with words in italics. Thus, at **abet,** we have as antonym "deter *(with a personal subject)*" and at **actuate,** "deter *(with a motive or fear as the subject)*." A simpler instance is the antonym at **brilliant,** in the sense of *bright*, which reads "subdued *(of light, color)*." At other times, the entry word is so inclusive that it takes more than one antonym to cover it. Then some indication is given of the differing collocations in which each antonym appears. Thus, **check,** as a synonym of *restrain*, has for its antonyms "accelerate *(of speed)***:** advance *(of movements, plans, hopes)***:** release *(of feelings, energies)*." A cross reference (introduced by "see") following an antonym is merely an indication of the sense in which it is used. Thus, **close,** as a synonym of *silent* and *reticent*, takes *open* as its antonym, but the sense in which *open* is used here is made clear by the cross reference to FRANK, where the word *open* is discriminated.


## ANALOGOUS AND CONTRASTED WORDS

The essential part of this dictionary consists of the synonyms and their discriminations and of the antonyms of the words thus discriminated. With these, judged from the point of view of one who is interested in the clarification of the differences in meaning between synonyms and in finding their direct opposites, it is a complete work. Yet for those who use this book as a word finder or as a vocabulary builder, there might be something lacking if it went no further. It is in view of the needs of such consultants that we have added lists of *analogous words* and of *contrasted words*.

Some of the analogous words or terms closely related in meaning merit the name of "near synonyms," so close are they to the vocabulary entry: some contain much the same implications as the entry word, but the implication that they emphasize is not the same as that expressed in the common denotation of the discriminated group of which the entry word forms a part. Some are more general than the entry word, some more specific; some come together in only a part of their meaning. But in some important particulars they are all like the word under which they are listed.

So, too, with contrasted words, or terms sharply differing in meaning from the entry word. Some are close synonyms of its antonym, but many are opposed to it only in part of their meaning. Through these lists the consultant who is seeking a word may find exactly the one he needs or the student may discover a useful means of extending his vocabulary.

These aims are made practical and easy of attainment by an additional aid which no work on synonyms has hitherto given the consultant. Terms listed as *analogous words* and *contrasted words* are arranged in groups, all of which are discriminated in this book. Most of the words are themselves directly discriminated, cross reference to the entry where the article is given being made by means of an asterisk or a reference introduced by "see": a few that are not themselves directly discriminated are closely dependent on words that are, as by being their derivatives or inflected forms, or by being their negatives, and are thereby covered by the article to which a clear cross reference is made. Thus, at **amenity** (in the sense of courtesy) the list of analogous words contains: (1) *civility, politeness, courteousness*, plus a cross reference to the article at CIVIL, where *civil, polite, courteous* are discriminated; (2) *graciousness, affability, cordiality, geniality, sociability* plus a cross reference to GRACIOUS, where *gracious, affable, cordial, genial, sociable* are discriminated. Similarly, among the contrasted words at **banal** are *stimulating* or *stimulative, provoking* or *provocative, exciting, piquing*, which, though not discriminated themselves, are fully covered by the article at PROVOKE, where their corresponding verbs are treated. Through the cross reference, then the consultant can find the meaning of every term in the word lists, and can sharpen his sense of their differences.

It is perhaps unnecessary to point out that the selection of words in each of these lists is not determined by the group of synonyms but by the one word at whose entry the list appears. As a result, each vocabulary entry is complete in itself: it has not only its synonyms and antonym or antonyms, but also analogous words which are closely related to it and contrasted words which are sharply opposed to it. It is thus treated as a unit, and all essential information is gathered about it.

# EXPLANATORY NOTES

The left-hand column below consists of entries or, usually, parts of entries selected from the main vocabulary to illustrate the principal devices used in this dictionary. The right-hand column provides explanations of these devices.

**accustomed** wonted, customary, habitual, *usual

**1** The vocabulary entry (usually a single word; occasionally a phrase) is printed in boldface type.

**acoustic, acoustical** *auditory
**adamant, adamantine** obdurate, inexorable, *inflexible

**2** Vocabulary entries which are alphabetically close to each other are sometimes listed together.

**adept** *n* *expert, wizard, artiste, artist, virtuoso
**adept** *adj* *proficient, skilled, skillful, expert, masterly

**3** The part of speech is indicated (by means of the commonly accepted abbreviations, printed in italic type) where it is desirable or necessary to do so.

**affection** 1 *feeling, emotion, passion, sentiment
**affection** *disease, disorder, condition, ailment, malady, complaint, distemper, syndrome

**4** Words identical in spelling and part of speech, but of different etymology are given separate entry.

**aggravate** 1 heighten, *intensify, enhance
2 exasperate, *irritate, provoke, rile, peeve, nettle

**5** Two or more meanings (or senses) of a single vocabulary entry are clearly separated and each meaning is numbered with a boldface numeral.

**alarm** *n* 1 **Alarm, tocsin, alert** agree in meaning a signal that serves as a call to action or to be on guard especially in a time of imminent danger. **Alarm** is used of any signal that arouses to activity not only troops, but emergency workers (as firemen, policemen); it suggests a sound such as a cry, a pealing of a bell, a beating of drums, or a siren ⟨sound a fire *alarm*⟩ ⟨the dog's barking gave the *alarm*⟩ **Tocsin** may be either an alarm sounded by bells usually from the belfry of a church or, more often, the bells sounding an alarm ⟨the loud *tocsin* tolled their last alarm —*Campbell*⟩ but is used figuratively for any sort of warning of danger. **Alert,** a military term for a signal to be on guard and ready for expected enemy action, is often used for any warning of danger ⟨sirens sounded an air-raid *alert*⟩ ⟨the Weather Bureau issued a tornado *alert* in early afternoon . . . . The *alert* was cancelled after 5 P.M. —*Springfield Union*⟩

**6** The words to be discriminated in an article are listed in boldface type at the beginning of the article.
Each word is repeated in boldface type at the point in the article where it is individually discussed.
The meanings or applications of the words discriminated are profusely illustrated by means of familiar examples (often idiomatic or characteristic phrases) or by quotations from named authors or sources. The word illustrated is printed in italic type.
The source of a quotation is also printed in italics. A list of sources quoted is given on pp. 887 ff.

**ardor** fervor, enthusiasm, zeal, *passion
**articulation** 1 integration, concatenation (see) under INTEGRATE *vb*)
2 *joint, suture

**7** Where there is no discriminating article, the first item under an entry is a list of its synonyms or near synonyms. These synonyms are discriminated from one another in an article in this dictionary.
The place where this article is to be found is indicated by an asterisk prefixed to one of the words in the list or by a reference introduced by the word "see."

**aspersion** reflection, *animadversion, stricture
*Ana* *libel, lampoon, pasquinade, squib, skit: *abuse, vituperation, invective, obloquy: *detraction, backbiting, calumny, slander, scandal
*Con* praise, laudation, extolling, eulogizing *or* eulogy (see corresponding verbs at PRAISE): *applause, acclaim, acclamation, plaudits: commendation, complimenting *or* compliment (see corresponding verbs at COMMEND)

**8** Each vocabulary entry is provided (where the facts require or permit) with "finding lists" of two kinds: Analogous Words introduced by the label *Ana* and Contrasted Words introduced by *Con.*
Words given in these finding lists are divided into groups. Each group consists of words discriminated (or related to those discriminated) in a single article.
The groups are separated from one another by boldface colons. Words within each group are separated by commas. The place of entry of the article discussing each group is indicated by an asterisk or a "see" reference (see §7).

**assortment** see corresponding adjective *assorted* at MISCELLANEOUS
*Ant* jumble, hodgepodge
**assuage** alleviate, *relieve, mitigate, lighten, allay
*Ant* exacerbate: intensify

**9** The label *Ant* introduces the antonym or antonyms of a vocabulary entry.
In the antonym lists commas are used between words that are synonyms of one another, and boldface colons are used to separate words that do not have such a relationship.
While many of the words listed as antonyms are themselves entered as vocabulary entries and are therefore discussed in the articles in this dictionary, the selection of antonyms has not been restricted to such words. For this reason the antonym lists do not as a rule contain references to discriminating articles.

**austere** *severe, stern, ascetic
*Ant* luscious (*of fruits*): warm, ardent (*of persons, feelings*): exuberant (*of style, quality*)

**10** In the lists of Antonyms italic notations in parentheses indicate the limited use or application in which the preceding word is to be taken.

# A DICTIONARY

# OF

# DISCRIMINATED SYNONYMS

# WITH ANTONYMS

## AND ANALOGOUS AND CONTRASTED WORDS

---

**abaft, aft, astern** are nautical terms meaning behind or to or at the rear (of). *Abaft* and *aft* are applied to objects or their positions in a ship. **Abaft** (opposed to *afore*) commonly suggests position relatively nearer the stern or rear part of the ship ⟨his station is *abaft* the foremast⟩ ⟨the wave struck her *abaft* the beam⟩ **Aft** (opposed to *forward*) suggests position actually in that part of the ship to the rear of the midship section ⟨they went *aft* to hoist the mainsail⟩ ⟨a cabin *aft* of the lounge⟩ **Astern** (opposed to *ahead*) chiefly implies position outside and to the rear of a ship ⟨the wake *astern* of a ship⟩ ⟨a brisk breeze *astern*⟩
*Ana* after, rear, back, *posterior, hind, hinder
*Ant* afore —*Con* ahead, forward, *before
**abandon** *vb* **1 Abandon, desert, forsake** mean to quit absolutely. **Abandon** implies surrender of control or possession often with the implication that the thing abandoned is left to the mercy of someone or something else ⟨the ghost of grandeur that lingers between the walls of *abandoned* haciendas in New Mexico—*Mary Austin*⟩ ⟨in the frantic rush to escape the insane had usually been forgotten and *abandoned* to horrible deaths—*Heiser*⟩ ⟨*abandoning* wife and children, home and business, and renouncing normal morality and humanity—*Shaw*⟩ **Desert** commonly implies previous occupation, companionship, or guardianship and often connotes desolation ⟨*deserted* farms growing up to brush⟩ It often, especially in **deserter, desertion,** emphasizes violation of duty as guardian or protector and extreme culpability ⟨*deserted* by those that should have stood by him⟩ ⟨any person found guilty of *desertion* . . . shall be punished, if the offense is committed in time of war, by death—*Uniform Code of Military Justice*⟩ **Forsake** often retains connotation of repudiation, frequently suggests renunciation, and stresses the breaking off of an association with someone or something ⟨*forsake* the world and all its pleasures⟩ ⟨she was *forsaken* at the altar—*Deland*⟩
*Ana* *discard, cast, scrap, junk: reject, repudiate (see DECLINE)
*Ant* reclaim —*Con* hold, possess, enjoy (see HAVE): shield, safeguard, protect (see DEFEND): redeem, *rescue, save
**2** surrender, *relinquish, yield, resign, leave
*Ant* cherish (*hopes, opinions*): restrain (*oneself*) —*Con*

*keep, retain: treasure, prize (see APPRECIATE): *maintain, assert, defend: inhibit, bridle, curb (see RESTRAIN)
**abandon** *n* *unconstraint, spontaneity
*Ana* license, *freedom, liberty: relaxation, laxity *or* laxness, looseness (see LOOSE)
*Ant* self-restraint —*Con* repression, suppression (see SUPPRESS): self-possession, aplomb (see CONFIDENCE): poise (see BALANCE, TACT)
**abandoned, reprobate, profligate, dissolute** fundamentally mean utterly depraved. *Abandoned* and *reprobate* were originally applied to sinners and to their acts. One who is **abandoned** by his complete surrender to a life of sin seems spiritually lost or morally irreclaimable ⟨I disdain . . . to paint her as she is, cruel, *abandoned,* glorying in her shame!—*Cowper*⟩ One who is **reprobate** is abandoned and therefore rejected by God or by his fellows; *reprobate* implies ostracism by or exclusion from a social group for a serious offense against its code ⟨don't count on my appearing your friend too openly . . . remember always that I'm a *reprobate* old clergyman—*Hugh Walpole*⟩ *Profligate* and *dissolute* convey little if any suggestion of divine or social condemnation but both imply complete moral breakdown and self-indulgence to such an extreme that all standards of morality and prudence are disregarded. One who is **profligate** openly and shamelessly flouts all the decencies and wastes his substance in dissipation ⟨rescue the Empire from being gambled away by incapable or *profligate* aristocrats—*Froude*⟩ One who is **dissolute** has completely thrown off all moral and prudential restraints on the indulgence of his appetites ⟨see them spending and squandering and being irresponsible and *dissolute* and not caring twopence for the way two thirds of the world live—*Rose Macaulay*⟩
*Ana* depraved, debauched, perverted, debased (see under DEBASE): degenerate, corrupt (see VICIOUS): wanton, lewd, lascivious, libidinous, lecherous (see LICENTIOUS)
*Ant* redeemed, regenerate —*Con* saved, rescued, reclaimed, delivered (see RESCUE)
**abase, demean, debase, degrade, humble, humiliate** are synonymous when they denote to lower in one's own estimation or in that of others. **Abase** suggests loss of dignity or prestige without necessarily implying permanency in that loss. When used reflexively it connotes

---

A colon (:) separates groups of words discriminated. An asterisk (*) indicates place of treatment of each group.
*Ana* analogous words     *Ant* antonyms     *Con* contrasted words     See also explanatory notes facing page 1

humility, abjectness, or a sense of one's inferiority; in this reflexive use *humble* is often used interchangeably ⟨whosoever exalteth himself shall be *abased* [DV and RV *humbled*]; and he that *humbleth* himself shall be exalted —*Lk* 14:11⟩ **Demean** implies less humility than *abase* but is stronger in its implications of loss of dignity or social standing ⟨it was . . . Mrs. Sedley's opinion that her son would *demean* himself by a marriage with an artist's daughter—*Thackeray*⟩ **Debase** emphasizes deterioration in value or quality: it is more often used of things ⟨*debase* the currency⟩ but when used of persons it commonly connotes weakening of moral standards or of the moral character ⟨officeholders *debase* themselves by accepting bribes⟩ ⟨struggle with Hannibal had *debased* the Roman temper—*Buchan*⟩ **Degrade** stresses a lowering in plane rather than in rank and often conveys a strong implication of the shamefulness of the condition to which someone or something has been reduced ⟨that she and Charlotte, two spent old women, should be . . . talking to each other of hatred, seemed unimaginably hideous and *degrading*—*Wharton*⟩ Often (especially in **degradation**) it connotes actual degeneracy or corruption ⟨it was by that unscrupulous person's liquor her husband had been *degraded*—*Hardy*⟩ **Humble** is frequently used in place of *degrade* in the sense of demote when the ignominy of the reduction in rank is emphasized ⟨we are pleased . . . to see him taken down and *humbled*—*Spectator*⟩ When it is employed without any implication of demotion, it often suggests a salutary increase of humility or the realization of one's own littleness or impotence ⟨it was one of those illnesses from which we turn away our eyes, shuddering and *humbled*—*Deland*⟩ Occasionally it implies a lowering in station ⟨in such a man . . . a race illustrious for heroic deeds, *humbled,* but not degraded, may expire—*Wordsworth*⟩ **Humiliate,** once a close synonym of *humble,* now comes closer to *mortify,* for it stresses chagrin and shame ⟨when we ask to be humbled, we must not recoil from being *humiliated*—*Rossetti*⟩
*Ana* cringe, truckle, cower, *fawn, toady: grovel (see WALLOW): abash, discomfit, disconcert, *embarrass: mortify (see corresponding adjective at ASHAMED)
*Ant* exalt: extol (*especially oneself*) —*Con* magnify, aggrandize (see EXALT): elevate, *lift, raise: laud, acclaim, *praise
**abash** discomfit, *embarrass, disconcert, faze, rattle
*Ana* fluster, flurry, *discompose, perturb, disturb, agitate: chagrin, mortify (see corresponding adjectives at ASHAMED): confound, dumbfound, nonplus (see PUZZLE)
*Ant* embolden: reassure
**abate 1** *abolish, extinguish, annihilate
*Ana* end, terminate (see CLOSE): *annul, ˇvoid, abrogate: cancel, obliterate (see ERASE): *nullify, invalidate
*Ant* perpetuate —*Con* *continue, last, persist, abide
**2** reduce, diminish, *decrease, lessen
*Ana* retard, slow, slacken, *delay: *moderate, temper: mitigate, lighten, alleviate (see RELIEVE)
*Ant* augment: accelerate (*pace, speed*): intensify (*hopes, fears, a fever*) —*Con* *increase, multiply, enlarge: aggravate, heighten, enhance (see INTENSIFY): *speed, quicken, hurry
**3 abate, subside, wane, ebb** all mean to die down in force or intensity; all imply previous approach to a high point and present movement or decline towards a vanishing point. **Abate,** however, stresses the idea of progressive diminution in intensity while **subside** suggests falling to a low level and cessation of turbulence or agitation ⟨the wind is *abating;* the waves are *subsiding*⟩ ⟨the revolutionary spirit has *abated*—*Grandgent*⟩ ⟨the child's quick temper *subsided* into listlessness under the fierce Italian heat—*Rep-*

*plier*⟩ **Wane** adds to *abate* the implications of fading or weakening; it tends, therefore, to be used of things that have value or excellence as well as force and intensity ⟨after the first flush of excitement, the interest of doctors, nurses, and patients all began to *wane*—*Heiser*⟩ **Ebb** adds to *abate* the suggestion of recession or of gradual loss; it is idiomatically associated with things subject to fluctuation ⟨*ebbing* vitality is often a warning of illness⟩ ⟨there were many, many stages in the ebbing of her love for him, but it was always *ebbing*—*D. H. Lawrence*⟩
*Ana* dwindle, diminish, *decrease
*Ant* rise: revive —*Con* *increase, augment: *expand, swell, dilate: mount, soar, tower, surge (see RISE)
**abatement** *deduction, rebate, discount
*Ant* addition —*Con* increment, accretion, accession (see ADDITION): increase, augmentation, enlargement (see corresponding verbs at INCREASE)
**abbey** *cloister, convent, nunnery, monastery, priory
**abbreviate** *shorten, abridge, curtail
*Ana* reduce, *decrease, lessen: *contract, compress, shrink, condense: attenuate, extenuate (see THIN)
*Ant* elongate, lengthen —*Con* *extend, prolong, protract: enlarge, *increase: *expand, amplify, dilate
**abdicate, renounce, resign** are synonymous when they are used in the sense of to give up formally or definitely a position of trust, honor, or glory, or its concomitant authority or prerogatives. **Abdicate** is the precise word to use when that which is relinquished involves sovereign or inherent power; it is applied specifically to the act of a monarch who gives up his throne, but in extended use it may also be applied to any act involving surrender of an inherent dignity or claim to preeminence ⟨the father image of the chancellor casts a long and overpowering shadow over a people which has in the past *abdicated* its political thinking and social sovereignty to the paternalistic leader —*Handler*⟩ **Renounce** is often used in place of *abdicate* ⟨the king *renounced* his throne⟩ especially when sacrifice for a greater end is intentionally implied. So strong is this implication and also that of finality in *renounce* (see also ABJURE) that it and its derivative **renunciation** often connote self-denial or surrender for the sake of moral or spiritual discipline. Consequently one *renounces* not only a right, a title, an inheritance, but also some desired or desirable possession ⟨she remains . . . the sort of woman who has *renounced* all happiness for herself and who lives only for a principle—*T. S. Eliot*⟩ **Resign** is used in reference chiefly to positions held on tenure and formally relinquished; ordinarily it implies asking permission to leave a position or office before the expiration of a term.
*Ana* *relinquish, surrender, abandon, leave
*Ant* assume: usurp —*Con* *arrogate, appropriate, confiscate
**abdomen, belly, stomach, paunch, gut** are synonyms when naming the front part of the human trunk below the chest ⟨crawl on his *stomach*⟩ ⟨crawl on his *belly*⟩ ⟨an appendectomy scar on his *abdomen*⟩ In technical usage **abdomen** more specifically denotes the cavity below the diaphragm (and sometimes above the brim of the pelvis) together with the structures in that cavity and the walls (often the front wall) enclosing it ⟨a pain in the *abdomen*⟩ ⟨the risks inherent in all surgery on the *abdomen*⟩ **Stomach** in nontechnical use is interchangeable with *abdomen* but technically it is restricted to the saccular abdominal organ in which the earlier processes of digestion take place ⟨a blow to the *stomach*⟩ ⟨the digesting mass or chyme in the *stomach* is continually churned . . . by muscular activity of the walls—*Potter*⟩ **Belly** and **paunch** are decidedly informal terms that, when used in place of *abdomen,* suggest roundness and protuberance ⟨fell flat on his *belly* in the

A colon (:) separates groups of words discriminated. An asterisk (*) indicates place of treatment of each group.

mud⟩ ⟨a comfortable *paunch* swelled out beneath the buttons of his dinner jacket—*Basso*⟩ Gut in technical use denotes the alimentary canal or one of its parts ⟨the embryonic *gut* arises from the third germ layer⟩ ⟨the blind *gut* or cecum⟩ In general use it is interchangeable with *belly* or *paunch* but in the plural, especially when designating the abdominal contents (viscera, intestines), it is usually considered vulgar although the corresponding verb is freely used of the evisceration of a carcass for food ⟨*gut* a herring⟩

**abduct, kidnap** are sometimes employed without distinction as denoting to carry off (a person) surreptitiously for an illegal purpose. In general use **kidnap** is the more specific term because it connotes seizure and detention for ransom. In law, however, the reverse is true, for the verbs acquire their meanings from the rigid technical definitions of *kidnaping* and *abduction*. **Kidnaping** is the legal term of wider application, implying that a person has been seized by violence or fraud and detained against his will or that of his legal guardian. **Abduction** is the carrying off of a girl (usually one below the legal age of consent), either against her will or with her consent, for marriage or seduction. Consequently in law *kidnaping* and *abduction* and *kidnap* and *abduct* can be used interchangeably only when the person carried off is a girl below a fixed age, or when seizure and detention are against her will and the motive is marriage or rape.
*Ana* seduce, entice, *lure, inveigle
*Con* *rescue, ransom, redeem, deliver

**aberrant** atypical, *abnormal
*Ana* divergent, *different, disparate: *irregular, anomalous, unnatural: *exceptional: singular, peculiar, odd, *strange, eccentric
*Ant* true (*to a type*) —*Con* *usual, wonted, customary: normal, *regular, typical, natural

**aberration** 1 *deviation, deflection
*Ana* abnormality, aberrancy (see ABNORMAL): *error, blunder, mistake, slip, lapse: *fault, failing: anomaly (see PARADOX)
*Ant* conformity: regularity —*Con* normality (see REGULAR): norm, *average, mean: agreement, correspondence, accord (see corresponding verbs at AGREE)
2 aberration, derangement, alienation, as here compared, denote mental disorder. **Aberration** while usable to designate any form of mental unsoundness typically denotes a minor or transitory disorder insufficient to constitute insanity. **Derangement** applies to any functional mental disturbance whether permanent or not. **Alienation** implies an estrangement from a normal or usual mental or emotional state ⟨I had been two or three nights without sleep, and I had fallen into the state of *alienation* that fatigue brings on—*Webber*⟩ and in forensic use specifically denotes a becoming or being insane.
*Ana* *insanity, lunacy, mania, dementia: *delusion, hallucination, illusion: *mania, delirium, hysteria, frenzy
*Ant* soundness (*of mind*)

**abet** *incite, foment, instigate
*Ana* aid, assist, *help: back, *support, uphold: cooperate, concur (see UNITE): forward, further, promote (see ADVANCE)
*Ant* deter (*with a personal subject*) —*Con* *frustrate, thwart, foil, balk, circumvent

**abettor** accessory, accomplice, *confederate, conspirator

**abeyant** dormant, quiescent, *latent, potential
*Ana* deferred, suspended, postponed, stayed, intermitted (SEE DEFER): suppressed, repressed (see SUPPRESS)
*Ant* operative: active: revived —*Con* live, dynamic (see ACTIVE): *living, alive: renewed, restored, refreshed (see RENEW)

**abhor** abominate, loathe, detest, *hate
*Ana* *despise, contemn, scorn: shun, avoid, eschew (see ESCAPE)
*Ant* admire (*persons, their qualities, acts*): enjoy (*things which are a matter of taste*) —*Con* *like, love, relish, dote: cherish, treasure, prize, value (see APPRECIATE): court, woo, solicit (see INVITE): esteem, respect, regard (see under REGARD *n*)

**abhorrence** detestation, loathing, abomination, hatred, hate (see under HATE *vb*)
*Ana* distaste, repugnance, repellency (see corresponding adjectives at REPUGNANT): horror, dismay (see FEAR)
*Ant* admiration: enjoyment —*Con* esteem, *regard, respect: liking, relish (see LIKE *vb*): love, affection, *attachment

**abhorrent** 1 abominable, *hateful, detestable, odious
*Ana* *contemptible, despicable, scurvy: *execrable, damnable
*Ant* admirable: enjoyable —*Con* grateful, agreeable, *pleasant, pleasing, gratifying, welcome: *delightful, delectable
2 *repugnant, repellent, obnoxious, distasteful, invidious
*Ana* *antipathetic: uncongenial, unsympathetic (see INCONSONANT): foreign, alien (see EXTRINSIC)
*Ant* congenial —*Con* attractive, alluring, captivating (see under ATTRACT): tempting, enticing, seductive (see corresponding verbs at LURE)

**abide** 1 *stay, wait, remain, tarry, linger
*Ana* dwell, *reside, live, sojourn, lodge: *stick, cleave, cling, adhere
*Ant* depart —*Con* *go, leave, quit: *move, remove, shift
2 endure, last, persist, *continue
*Ana* *stay, remain, linger: subsist, exist, live (see BE)
*Ant* pass *vi* —*Con* flee, fly, *escape: *flit
3 endure, *bear, suffer, tolerate, stand, brook
*Ana* submit, *yield, bow, defer: acquiesce, accede, consent (see ASSENT): accept, *receive, take
*Con* withstand, oppose, combat, *resist: *decline, refuse, spurn: shun, avoid, evade, elude (see ESCAPE)

**ability**, capacity, capability are often confused in use. Ability primarily denotes the quality or character of being able (as to do or perform) and is applied chiefly to human beings. **Capacity** in its corresponding sense means the power or more especially the potentiality of receiving, holding, absorbing, or accomplishing something expressed or understood and is said of persons or things. Thus one may speak of a child's *ability* to learn but not of the hall's *ability* to seat 2000 persons; on the other hand, a child's mental *capacity* and the hall has a seating *capacity* of 2000 are both acceptable. In general, *ability* suggests actual power, whether native or acquired, whether exercised or not ⟨once more he had shown his *ability* to handle a delicate situation to the credit of his government and himself—*W. C. Ford*⟩ *Capacity* on the other hand stresses receptiveness, or in reference to man's intellectual, moral, or spiritual nature, more explicitly, responsiveness, susceptibility, or aptitude. *Capacity* therefore suggests potential, as distinguished from actual or, especially, manifest power. Thus, *ability* to weep, the *ability* to work, the *ability* to pay, are not respectively identical in meaning with the *capacity* for tears, the *capacity* for work, the *capacity* for payment. The phrases of the first group mean that one can weep (because his tear glands are normal), one can work (because strong or trained), one can pay (because he has the money): those of the second group indicate, in the first case, a special sensitiveness to what is pathetic; in the second case, a readiness to work as hard as is necessary on any or every

*Ana* analogous words     *Ant* antonyms     *Con* contrasted words     See also explanatory notes facing page 1

occasion; in the third case, the qualities of mind and character that promise earning power and imply a recognition of one's obligations ⟨if Peter had a *capacity* for friendship, these speechless years had made it dumb—*Deland*⟩ ⟨we do not acquire the ability to do new deeds, but a new *capacity* for all deeds. My recent growth does not appear in any visible new talent—*Thoreau*⟩ ⟨the *capacity* of American idealism to survive a major disillusionment—*MacLeish*⟩ **Capability** is the character in a person (less often, a thing) arising from the possession of the qualities or qualifications necessary to the performance of a certain kind of work or the achievement of a given end ⟨testing the *capability* of the ear to distinguish pitches⟩ ⟨no applicant will be considered who does not offer proof of *capability*⟩ As applied exclusively to persons, *capability* may mean competence, often special competence. This connotation is usually supplied or enforced by the context.
*Ana* *power, strength, might, force, energy: proficiency, skill, adeptness (see corresponding adjectives at PROFICIENT): aptitude, talent, genius, faculty (see GIFT): competence, qualification (see corresponding adjectives at ABLE)
*Ant* inability, incapacity —*Con* impotence, powerlessness (see corresponding adjectives at POWERLESS): incompetence, incapability (see corresponding adjectives at INCAPABLE)

**abject** *mean, ignoble, sordid
*Ana* servile, slavish, menial (see SUBSERVIENT): *miserable, wretched: cringing, truckling, cowering (see FAWN): groveling (see WALLOW): abased, demeaned, humbled, humiliated (see ABASE)
*Ant* exalted (*in rank, state, condition, mood, behavior*): imperious (*in manner speech, attitude*) —*Con* arrogant, lordly, overbearing, supercilious (see PROUD): domineering, *masterful: aristocratic, patrician (see corresponding nouns at GENTLEMAN)

**abjure, renounce, forswear, recant, retract** are synonymous when they mean to abandon irrevocably and, usually, with solemnity or publicity. Except in the extended senses of *abjure, renounce*, and *forswear* they all imply the recall of one's word. **Abjure** and **renounce** are scarcely distinguishable when they imply solemn repudiation as of an oath or vow ⟨he shall, before he is admitted to citizenship, declare on oath in open court that he . . . absolutely and entirely *renounces* and *abjures* all allegiance and fidelity to any foreign prince, potentate, state, or sovereignty—*U. S. Code*⟩ In their extended senses, however, *abjure* distinctively suggests deliberate rejection or avoidance while *renounce* specifically connotes disclaiming or disowning ⟨*abjure* force⟩ ⟨*renounce* one's principles⟩ ⟨if a man is content to *abjure* wealth and to forego marriage, to live simply without luxuries, he may spend a very dignified gentle life here—*Benson*⟩ ⟨he was later to *renounce* impressionism and to quarrel with most of the impressionists —*Read*⟩ **Forswear** often adds to *abjure* (especially in the reflexive use of the verb or in the participial adjective **forsworn**) the suggestion of perjury or of culpable violation of a solemn engagement ⟨I have sworn to obey the laws, and I cannot *forswear* myself—*Blackie*⟩ It often means little more than to swear off ⟨Mr. Dulles grants by implication that the Peking regime is the government of China. He insists that it *forswear* the use of force in advancing its ambitions—*New Republic*⟩ **Recant** and **retract** stress the withdrawal of something professed or declared; *recant* always and *retract* often imply admission of error. One *recants*, however, something that one has openly professed or taught, as religious or scientific doctrines; one *retracts* something one has written or spoken, as a charge, a promise, an order ⟨if Christians *recanted* they were to be

spared, but . . . if they persisted in their faith they were to be executed—*Latourette*⟩ ⟨a word informs your brother I *retract* this morning's offer—*Browning*⟩
*Ana* *forgo, forbear, eschew: abstain, *refrain: reject, repudiate, spurn (see DECLINE): abandon, *relinquish
*Ant* pledge (*allegiance, a vow*): elect (*a way of life, a means to an end, an end*) —*Con* plight, engage (see PROMISE): *choose, select, opt: own, avow, *acknowledge

**able, capable, competent, qualified** are close synonyms when they denote having marked power or fitness for work and are used attributively. Placed after the noun, *able* (followed by *to* and infinitive) and *capable* (followed by *of*) suggest mere possession of ability or capacity without any clear indication of its extent or quality ⟨they must be *capable* of living the life of the spirit . . . they must be *able* to cope intelligently with weighty problems of public policy—*Grandgent*⟩ In general *competent* and *qualified* in predicative use suggest mere fitness in the one case and sufficient training in the other ⟨a servant *competent* to take full charge⟩ ⟨headmasters and education authorities want to be able to distinguish between those who are *qualified* to teach . . . and those who are not—*Huxley*⟩ On the other hand all four words are manifestly richer in implications when (especially in attributive use) they are thought of as characterizing persons or their activities. **Able** then suggests ability markedly above the average; it often connotes power of mastery; it does not exclude the connotation of promise even when the emphasis is on performance ⟨*able* boys and girls will . . . submit willingly to severe discipline in order to acquire some coveted knowledge or skill—*Russell*⟩ **Capable** stresses possession of qualities such as adaptability, resourcefulness, versatility, industry, or efficiency and seldom indicates, apart from its context, the specific ability involved ⟨pretty and charming, but stupid . . . because she believes men prefer women to be useless and extravagant; if left to herself she would be a domestic and *capable* person—*Millay*⟩ **Competent** and **qualified** are used especially to characterize a person or his activities in relation to a specific calling ⟨a *competent* housekeeper⟩ ⟨a *qualified* accountant⟩ *Competent* implies the ability to satisfy capably all the special demands or requirements of a particular situation, craft, or profession, but it does not necessarily imply, as *qualified* usually does, compliance with set standards such as special training and the testing of one's competence at the end of such training ⟨a *qualified* engineer⟩ ⟨a *competent* portraitist knows how to imply the profile in the full face—*Huxley*⟩
*Ana* skilled, skillful, *proficient, expert: efficient, *effective: clever, brilliant, *intelligent, smart
*Ant* inept (*by nature, training*): unable —*Con* *incapable, incompetent, unqualified: inefficient, *ineffective: mediocre, fair, indifferent (see MEDIUM): maladroit (see AWKWARD)

**abnegate** sacrifice, *forgo, eschew, forbear
*Ana* renounce, *abdicate: surrender, abandon, *relinquish, waive: abstain, *refrain
*Ant* indulge (in) —*Con* gratify, delight, regale, rejoice, gladden, *please: *satisfy, content

**abnegation** self-abnegation, *renunciation, self-denial
*Ana* forgoing, forbearance, eschewal (see corresponding verbs at FORGO): abstinence, abstemiousness, continence, *temperance: restraining, curbing, bridling (see RESTRAIN)
*Ant* indulgence, self-indulgence —*Con* intemperance, incontinence (see affirmative nouns at TEMPERANCE)

**abnormal, atypical, aberrant** mean deviating markedly from the rule or standard of its kind. All are used in the sciences, as in biology and psychology, to express non-

---

A colon (:) separates groups of words discriminated. An asterisk (*) indicates place of treatment of each group.

conformity to type. **Abnormal** frequently connotes strangeness or excess and sometimes, as in *abnormality*, deformity or monstrosity ⟨power when wielded by *abnormal* energy is the most serious of facts—*Henry Adams*⟩ In psychology, as applied to persons, *abnormal* often suggests poorer than normal performance or poorer than normal adjustment to the conditions of life and is equivalent to *subnormal*; in general use better than normal powers are often implied ⟨can envision the future in the light of what he remembers of the past. His powers of recollection . . . are *abnormal*—*R. L. Taylor*⟩ **Atypical** stresses divergence upward or downward from the established norm of some group, kind, or stage (as of development) ⟨*atypical* reactions⟩ ⟨stealing is to be looked upon as *atypical* behavior . . . not the customarily accepted type of response that we expect from children—*G. E. Gardner*⟩ **Aberrant** seldom loses its literal implication of wandering or straying; in the sciences, where it is applied to departures from type, it carries none of the extra connotations of *abnormal* and is less restricted in its reference than *atypical* ⟨*aberrant* forms of a botanical species⟩ In general use it often suggests moral deviation ⟨such a choice must argue *aberrant* senses, or degenerate blood—*Kingsley*⟩

*Ana* *irregular, unnatural, anomalous: unusual, unwonted, uncustomary, unaccustomed (see affirmative adjectives at USUAL): *monstrous, prodigious

*Ant* normal —*Con* *regular, typical, natural: ordinary, *common, familiar: *usual, wonted, customary

**abode** dwelling, residence, domicile, *habitation, home, house

**abolish,** annihilate, extinguish, abate share the meaning to make nonexistent. **Abolish** seldom refers to purely physical objects but rather to such things as are the outgrowth of law, custom, human conception, or the conditions of human existence ⟨attempts to *abolish* slavery⟩ ⟨a proposal to *abolish* the income tax⟩ ⟨no plan will be acceptable unless it *abolishes* poverty—*Shaw*⟩ **Annihilate** distinctively implies destruction so complete that everything involved is wiped out of existence and cannot be revived in any form ⟨the realization that for the first time the homes and cities of the United States itself can be *annihilated* by enemy attack—*Crawley*⟩ **Extinguish** or its related noun **extinction** is often interchangeable with *annihilate* (or *annihilation*) but it stresses the power of the cause to overwhelm and suppress rather than the finality of the result ⟨a religion of their own which was thoroughly and painfully *extinguished* by the Inquisition—*T. S. Eliot*⟩ **Abate** in general use is far weaker in meaning than the foregoing terms and typically denotes a gradual decrease or dwindling rather than an immediate termination ⟨the wind *abated* after sundown⟩ ⟨misfortune had *abated* the grandiosity of the Roman temper—*Buchan*⟩

In law **abolish** keeps close to its general sense of to make nonexistent; **annihilate** is sometimes used as an emphatic substitute for *abolish* ⟨the appointment cannot be *annihilated*—*John Marshall*⟩ **Extinguish** implies destruction of a right or obligation by some act or decision which nullifies it or makes it void. **Abate** implies termination especially by a legal decision ⟨*abate* a nuisance⟩ ⟨*abate* an action or writ⟩ ⟨summoning me for failing to *abate* a smoky chimney—*Wodehouse*⟩

*Ana* extirpate, eradicate, wipe, *exterminate: obliterate, efface, blot out, expunge (see ERASE): negate, *nullify, annul, abrogate

*Ant* establish —*Con* *found, institute: *bear, produce, turn out: create, discover, *invent

**abominable** detestable, *hateful, odious, abhorrent

*Ana* *execrable, damnable, accursed, cursed: scurvy, despicable, *contemptible, sorry: loathsome, repulsive, revolting, repugnant, *offensive: horrid, *horrible

*Ant* laudable (*practices, habits, customs*): enjoyable, delightful —*Con* pleasing, *pleasant, gratifying: commendable, applaudable (see corresponding verbs at COMMEND): attractive, charming, enchanting (see under ATTRACT)

**abominate** loathe, detest, abhor, *hate

*Ana* *despise, contemn, scorn, disdain: *execrate, objurgate, curse, damn

*Ant* esteem: enjoy —*Con* admire, respect, regard (see under REGARD *n*): relish, *like, love, dote

**abomination** 1 abhorrence, detestation, loathing, hatred, hate (see under HATE *vb*)

*Ana* scorn, despite, contempt, disdain (see under DESPISE): execration, objurgation (see corresponding verbs at EXECRATE)

*Ant* esteem: enjoyment —*Con* admiration, respect, *regard: relish, gusto, zest, *taste

2 **Abomination,** anathema, bugbear, bête noire agree in meaning a person or thing from which one shrinks with intense dislike. Something is an **abomination** that provokes loathing, disgust, and extreme displeasure ⟨lying lips are *abomination* to the Lord: but they that deal truly are his delight—*Prov* 12:22⟩ ⟨a wonderful wooden statue . . . now replaced by the usual metal *abomination*—*Norman Douglas*⟩ Something is **anathema** (or *an anathema*) to one when it is banned from one's presence or dismissed from one's mind as being odious or beyond the pale. The word in this sense is always reminiscent of St. Paul's use ⟨if any man love not the Lord Jesus Christ, let him be *Anathema*—*1 Cor* 16:22⟩ ⟨had a flair for new writers. They were as welcome to him as they were *anathema* to most editors of that day—*Repplier*⟩ ⟨all plays are *anathema* to him, and he even disapproves of dancing bears—*Quiller-Couch*⟩ Something is a **bugbear** to one when one anticipates encountering it with detestation and dread and therefore tries to evade or avoid it; often but not invariably the word connotes an imaginary basis for one's fears ⟨what is the dire necessity and "iron" law under which men groan? Truly, most gratuitously invented *bugbears*—*T. H. Huxley*⟩ ⟨but to the world no *bugbear* is so great, as want of figure, and a small estate—*Pope*⟩ One's **bête noire** is one's pet aversion, a person or thing one habitually or particularly avoids, often with superstitious fear ⟨truth . . . the breath of the poet, the vision of the artist and prophet, the quarry of the scientist . . . the toy of the careless, the *bête noire* of the politician—*Forum*⟩

*Ana* plague, pest, annoyance (see corresponding verbs at WORRY): aversion, *antipathy

*Ant* joy —*Con* delight, *pleasure, delectation: gratification, regalement (see corresponding verbs at PLEASE)

**aboriginal** indigenous, autochthonous, *native

*Ana* primitive, primordial, primeval, pristine (see PRIMARY): savage, barbaric, *barbarian, barbarous

*Con* sequent, successive (see CONSECUTIVE): advanced, progressive (see LIBERAL): civilized, cultured (see corresponding nouns at CIVILIZATION)

**abortion,** miscarriage denote the premature expulsion of a fetus before it is capable of living independently. **Abortion** may connote purposeful induction of the process either illicitly in order to avoid childbearing or therapeutically to protect the life of the mother. In medicine, however, *abortion* sometimes denotes the expulsion of the human fetus through any cause during the first twelve weeks of pregnancy. **Miscarriage** differs from *abortion* in suggesting a natural expulsion rather than one produced artificially. In medicine *miscarriage* is used of any expul-

---

*Ana* analogous words     *Ant* antonyms     *Con* contrasted words     See also explanatory notes facing page 1

sion of the fetus occurring between the twelfth and twenty-eighth weeks and before the fetus is capable of living independently.

**abortive** fruitless, vain, *futile, bootless

*Ana* *immature, unmatured, unripe: unformed (see FORMLESS): ineffectual, *ineffective, inefficacious: unfortunate, unlucky (see affirmative adjectives at LUCKY)

*Ant* consummated  —*Con* completed, concluded (see CLOSE *vb*): finished, accomplished, *consummate: effectual, *effective, efficacious

**abound** overflow, *teem, swarm

*Ana* predominate, preponderate (see corresponding adjectives at DOMINANT)

*Ant* fail, fall short  —*Con* want, *lack, need, require: scant, skimp, scrimp (see corresponding adjectives at MEAGER)

**about, concerning, regarding, respecting** are synonymous prepositions when they take an object that names something which is the subject of talk, thought, or interest. **About** is usually interchangeable with any of the others without marked loss of meaning, but it alone may follow its object as well as precede it ⟨talk *about* many things⟩ ⟨there is nothing to complain *about*⟩ **Concerning** is more meaningful because it often retains its verbal implications of affecting and influencing ⟨make laws *concerning* public welfare⟩ *Regarding* and *respecting* suggest little more than *about:* however **regarding** is especially appropriate when its object names the goal or center of attention or thought ⟨they avoided all discussion *regarding* the scandal⟩ **Respecting** is felicitously employed when selectiveness or specification is to be implied ⟨he had nothing to say *respecting* Spain⟩ ⟨there's no outwitting you *respecting* him—*Browning*⟩

**above, over** are synonymous prepositions when they indicate elevation in position. They seldom imply contact between that which is higher and that which is lower; as a rule they allow an interval. *Over* and *above* differ in that *over* usually implies verticality while *above* may or may not. Thus the entire second story of a building is *above* but only a small part of it is directly *over* one who stands on the ground floor. Between the extended senses analogous relations hold. *Over* and *above* agree in the idea of superiority but differ in the immediacy of reference. Thus, the rank of ambassador is *above* that of minister but the British ambassador is not *over* the Portuguese minister; he stands in that relation to his own subordinates only. Similarly *above* and *over* indicate a relationship of excess ⟨his strength is *above* the average⟩ ⟨we now have *over* half the amount required⟩ ⟨we shall not be tempted *above* our power to resist⟩ *Above* only, however, implies transcendence ⟨this *above* all, to thine own self be true—*Shak.*⟩

*Ant* below

**aboveboard** *straightforward, forthright

*Ana* open, *frank, candid: honest, *upright, scrupulous: *fair, impartial, just: ingenuous, unsophisticated, artless (see NATURAL)

*Ant* underhand, underhanded  —*Con* furtive, covert, surreptitious, *secret, clandestine: *dishonest, deceitful, mendacious: *crooked, devious

**abracadabra** *gibberish, hocus-pocus, mummery

*Ana* *magic, sorcery, thaumaturgy: amulet, charm (see FETISH)

*Con* sense, *meaning, significance, import

**abrade, excoriate, chafe, fret, gall** mean to affect a surface by rubbing, scraping, or wearing away. **Abrade** usually implies rubbing or scraping by something hard or harsh: when the surface rubbed or scraped is soft, injury results, but when it approaches the other in hardness, a smoothing or

polishing (as by grinding) may be achieved ⟨the palms of his hands *abraded* by gravel⟩ ⟨the ship's side was *abraded* in the collision⟩ ⟨loose sand grains . . . may be hurled against projecting masses of rock with such force as to *abrade* . . . their surfaces by a natural sandblast—*Scientific Monthly*⟩ ⟨an abrasive is a substance used in *abrading* steel⟩ **Excoriate** which literally implies a stripping or wearing away of the skin or hide usually suggests a peculiarly painful effect on something soft or tender made by something (as an abrasive or abrasion or a corrosive substance) that removes or destroys a protective layer such as the skin or mucous membrane ⟨the ends of his fingers were *excoriated* by acid⟩ ⟨my lips . . . were *excoriated* as with vinegar and gall—*Brontë*⟩ **Chafe** suggests a slight but persistent and painful or injurious rubbing of one thing upon another ⟨objected to wearing wool which she said *chafed* her skin⟩ ⟨the hawsers were so *chafed* by rubbing against the wharf that they required replacement⟩ **Fret** suggests an eating into or wearing away ⟨the river *frets* away the rocks along its banks—*T. H. Huxley*⟩ ⟨dripping water *fretted* a channel through the stone⟩ **Gall** is used especially with reference to animals and, less often, to persons: it implies a superficial injury such as an abrasion or blister made by friction ⟨an ill-fitting saddle *galled* the horse's back⟩

All have extended usage with an implication of irritating or wearing. **Abrade** and **chafe** usually suggest a persistent cause ⟨took refuge in a subdued blubbering, which soon *abraded* the teacher's nerves—*Perelman*⟩ ⟨a theater that is so physically uncomfortable as to *chafe* the playgoer's disposition even before the curtain rises—*N. Y. Times*⟩ **Excoriate** is used rather specifically of a censuring so severe as to cause real distress or mental anguish ⟨when his programs fail, the implementation, not the directive will be *excoriated;* the subordinates and volunteers, not the dictator will suffer—*Straight*⟩ ⟨*excoriated* the morality of the Gilded Age and yet was fascinated by some of its surface trappings—*J. D. Hart*⟩ **Fret** and **gall** typically imply a causing of emotional wear and tear ⟨the *galling* frictions are in the world today—*Benedict*⟩ ⟨that hidden bond which at other moments *galled* and *fretted* him so as to mingle irritation with the very sunshine—*George Eliot*⟩

*Ana* *scrape, scratch, grate, grind, rasp: *injure, damage, impair, mar: *irritate, exasperate

**abridge** *shorten, curtail, abbreviate, retrench

*Ana* condense, *contract, compress, shrink: *cut, slash: *limit, restrict, reduce, diminish, *decrease

*Ant* expand: extend  —*Con* amplify, swell, distend (see EXPAND): lengthen, elongate, prolong, protract (see EXTEND): enlarge, augment, *increase

**abridgment, abstract, epitome, brief, synopsis, conspectus** mean a condensation of a larger work or treatment, usually one already in circulation. **Abridgment** implies reduction in compass with the retention of relative completeness ⟨the current acting versions of many of Shakespeare's plays are *abridgments*⟩ ⟨an *abridgment* of a dictionary⟩ **Abstract** implies condensation of a lengthy treatise or of a proposed lengthy treatment and stresses concentration of substance ⟨*abstracts* of state papers⟩ ⟨an *abstract* of a lecture⟩ **Epitome** implies concentration of the essence or pith of something (as a long poem, essay, or treatise) into the briefest possible statement usually so as to acquire a value of its own ⟨the *Paternoster*, Christ's prayer, which is . . . [an] *epitome* . . . of all the psalms and prayers written in the whole scripture—*Hooper*⟩ Both *abstract* and *epitome* are used also in extended senses in reference to persons or things, the former stressing one or other (of the persons or things referred to) as a summary, the latter as a type representing a whole ⟨a man who is the *abstract*

A colon (:) separates groups of words discriminated. An asterisk (*) indicates place of treatment of each group.

of all faults that all men follow—*Shak.*⟩ ⟨a man so various that he seemed to be not one, but all mankind's *epitome*—*Dryden*⟩ **Brief** is usually narrowly applied in legal use to a concise statement of a client's case made out for the instruction of counsel in a trial (called specifically *trial brief*) or to a statement of the heads or points of a legal argument submitted to the court (*brief of argument*). **Synopsis** and **conspectus** imply the giving of the salient points of a treatise or subject so that it may be quickly comprehended. *Synopsis,* however, often suggests an outline or series of headings and *conspectus* a coherent account that gives a bird's-eye view ⟨provide in advance a *synopsis* of the lectures⟩ ⟨the book will serve as a *conspectus* of Chinese history⟩
*Ana* digest, précis, *compendium, sketch, syllabus
*Ant* expansion —*Con* paraphrase (see TRANSLATION): *development
**abrogate** 1 *annul, vacate, quash, void
*Ana* *abolish, extinguish, abate
*Ant* institute (*by enacting, decreeing*) —*Con* *ratify, confirm: establish, *found
2 *nullify, annul, negate, invalidate
*Ana* *abolish, annihilate, extinguish: *destroy, demolish: *ruin, wreck: cancel, obliterate, blot out (see ERASE)
*Ant* establish, fix (*a right, a character, a quality, a custom*) —*Con* settle (see SET): uphold, *support
**abrupt** 1 *steep, precipitous, sheer
*Ana* perpendicular, *vertical, plumb
*Ant* sloping —*Con* *level, flat, plain, plane, even, smooth: slanting, inclined (see SLANT *vb*)
2 sudden, *precipitate, headlong, impetuous, hasty
*Ana* quick, speedy (see FAST): hurried, hastened (see SPEED): unceremonious (see *ceremonious* under CEREMONIAL): curt, brusque (see BLUFF)
*Ant* deliberate, leisurely —*Con* *slow, dilatory, laggard: easy, *comfortable, restful
**abscess,** boil, furuncle, carbuncle, pimple, pustule all denote a localized swollen area of infection containing pus. **Abscess** is the most general term, applying to a collection of pus surrounded by inflammation whether in the skin or in the substance of a part or organ and whether discharging through an opening or fistula or being gradually reabsorbed ⟨an *abscess* at the root of a tooth⟩ ⟨a line of small *abscesses* where his belt had chafed him⟩ **Boil** and **furuncle** both mean a swollen painful nodule in the skin caused by bacteria that enter skin glands or hair follicles and set up a purulent infection which terminates by rupture of the skin and discharge of a core of pus and broken-down tissue cells. Though *boil* is commoner in general use, *furuncle* is often preferred in medical communication. A **carbuncle** is a large and severe boil that occurs especially on the back of the neck, is often accompanied by fever, and ultimately discharges through several openings. A **pimple** or **pustule** is a small superficial pus-containing elevation of the skin that usually subsides without rupturing; more specifically *pimple* is used of the typical lesions characterizing acne while *pustule* implies no specific syndrome.
**abscond** decamp, flee, fly, *escape
*Ana* depart, leave, quit, *go
*Ant* give (*oneself*) up —*Con* stay, wait, remain, abide: confess, *acknowledge
**absence** *lack, want, dearth, defect, privation
*Ana* *need, necessity, exigency: deficiency (see corresponding adjective at DEFICIENT): destitution (see corresponding adjective at DEVOID): void, vacuum (see HOLE)
*Ant* presence —*Con* abundance, copiousness, plenty (see corresponding adjectives at PLENTIFUL)
**absent** *adj* preoccupied, *abstracted, absentminded,

distraught
*Ana* engrossed, absorbed, *intent, rapt: heedless, inadvertent (see CARELESS): oblivious, unmindful, *forgetful
*Ant* attentive —*Con* *thoughtful, considerate: attending, listening, hearkening (see ATTEND)
**absentminded** absent, *abstracted, preoccupied, distraught
*Ana* inattentive, thoughtless, inconsiderate (see affirmative adjectives at THOUGHTFUL): heedless, inadvertent (see CARELESS): unobserving, unseeing, unperceiving, unnoticing (see affirmative verbs at SEE)
*Ant* wide-awake —*Con* *watchful, alert, vigilant: attentive (see THOUGHTFUL)
**absolute** 1 *pure, simple, sheer
*Ana* *perfect, whole, entire: *real, true: *abstract, ideal: *consummate, finished
*Ant* mixed, qualified —*Con* incomplete (see affirmative adjective at FULL): imperfect, unentire, unintact (see affirmative adjectives at PERFECT)
2 **Absolute,** autocratic, arbitrary, despotic, tyrannical, tyrannous mean exercising power or authority without external restraint. **Absolute** does not of itself add any further implication to this general denotation. It is restricted in application chiefly to words for authority or for one in authority ⟨an *absolute* monarch⟩ ⟨*absolute* control⟩ ⟨they held their subjects with an *absolute* hand as all communistic leaders do—*F. M. Brown*⟩ **Autocratic** implies assumption or exercise of absolute power or authority; though it is not necessarily opprobrious, it often connotes egotistical consciousness of power and haughty imposition of one's own will ⟨let the Emperor turn his nominal sovereignty into a real central and *autocratic* power—*Belloc*⟩ **Arbitrary** implies the exercise and usually the abuse of power in accord with one's opinion of the moment, free of such reasoned guides as constitution and laws which make for consistent and reasonably predictable action ⟨all the constitutional safeguards of English freedom were swept away. *Arbitrary* taxation, *arbitrary* legislation, *arbitrary* imprisonment were powers claimed without dispute and unsparingly used by the Crown—*J. R. Green*⟩ **Despotic** and **tyrannical** are stronger than *autocratic, despotic* implying the arbitrary and imperious exercise of absolute power or control and *tyrannical* the abuse of such power or control frequently through harshness, oppression, or severity ⟨the most *despotic* system of government that history has ever known, Bolshevism, parades as the very incarnation of the principles of equality and liberty of all men—*Von Mises*⟩ ⟨proofs . . . that the people, when they have been unchecked, have been as unjust, *tyrannical,* brutal, barbarous, and cruel as any king . . . possessed of uncontrollable power—*Adams*⟩ ⟨how could I have borne to become the slave of her *tyrannical* humors?—*Burney*⟩ **Tyrannous** is more frequently used of things than of persons ⟨a . . . skeptical smile, of all expressions the most *tyrannous* over a susceptible mind—*George Eliot*⟩
*Ana* *totalitarian, authoritarian: *dictatorial, magisterial: domineering, imperious, *masterful
*Ant* restrained: limited —*Con* circumscribed, restricted (see LIMIT *vb*): irresponsible, unanswerable, unamenable (see affirmative adjectives at RESPONSIBLE)
3 *ultimate, categorical
*Ana* ideal, transcendent, transcendental (see ABSTRACT): independent, autonomous, *free, sovereign: *infinite, eternal, boundless
*Ant* conditioned —*Con* relative, *dependent, conditional, contingent: circumscribed, limited, restricted (see LIMIT *vb*)

---

*Ana* analogous words    *Ant* antonyms    *Con* contrasted words    See also explanatory notes facing page 1

**absolution** *pardon, amnesty
*Ana* forgiveness, remission (see corresponding verbs at EXCUSE)
*Ant* condemnation —*Con* censure, reprobation, reprehension (see corresponding verbs at CRITICIZE)
**absolve** exonerate, acquit, *exculpate, vindicate
*Ana* pardon, forgive, remit (see EXCUSE): release, *free, discharge
*Ant* hold (*to a promise, an obligation*): charge (*with a sin, the blame, the responsibility*) —*Con* blame (see CRITICIZE): *sentence, condemn, doom: *punish, discipline, chasten
**absorb** 1 Absorb, imbibe, assimilate can all mean to take (something) in so as to become imbued with it or to make it a part of one's being. The original meaning of **absorb**, to swallow up (both literally and figuratively), has been retained in spite of the development of a later and more common sense, to soak up (both literally and figuratively). When the former idea is stressed, *absorb* implies the loss of identity of that taken in ⟨the trust *absorbed* three small corporations⟩ ⟨in England . . . the aristocracy are subordinate to the middle class, which is gradually *absorbing* and destroying them—*T. S. Eliot*⟩ When soaking up is implied, *absorb* often suggests enrichment of the recipient ⟨the roots of plants *absorb* moisture⟩ ⟨an adult reader with trained habits of attention and concentration will *absorb* the contents of a book with . . . speed and retentiveness—*Eliot*⟩ In its literal sense **imbibe** usually implies drinking or inhaling ⟨*imbibe* intoxicating liquors⟩ ⟨we did not *imbibe* an undiluted air—*N. E. Nelson*⟩ However *imbibe*, like *absorb*, often connotes soaking up ⟨the ground *imbibes* (or *absorbs*) moisture⟩ In its figurative sense *imbibe*, like *absorb*, implies a process of learning, but it often carries the suggestions that the process has been unconscious and that the effect has been noticeable or profound ⟨the pupils *imbibe* no respect for intellectual values at home, and find none among their schoolfellows—*Inge*⟩ ⟨twelve years he wandered, *imbibing* wisdom from every source, sitting at every shrine, tasting every creed—*Durant*⟩ **Assimilate** implies not only absorption but also the conversion of what is absorbed into the substance of the assimilating body. In its narrow sense it applies especially to physiological processes ⟨the body *assimilates* digested food into its protoplasm⟩ In its figurative use it often suggests lasting enrichment without loss of integrity or unity ⟨poets . . . who *assimilate* a number of influences and construct an original speech from them—*Day Lewis*⟩ Sometimes it stresses completeness of fusion and consequent loss of identity ⟨races incapable of *assimilation*⟩
*Ana* *soak, saturate, impregnate: *receive, take: incorporate, embody (see IDENTIFY)
*Ant* exude, give out —*Con* *eject, expel: *throw, cast
2 engross, *monopolize, consume
*Ana* fix, *fasten: rivet, *secure: immerse, submerge (see DIP)
*Ant* dissipate (*time, attention, energies*) —*Con* *scatter, disperse, dispel: *deplete, drain, exhaust
**absorbed** *intent, engrossed, rapt
*Ana* immersed (see DIP): riveted (see SECURE *vb*): fixed, fastened (see FASTEN)
*Ant* distracted —*Con* absent, absentminded, distraught, *abstracted: wandering, straying, rambling (see WANDER)
**absorbing** *interesting, engrossing, intriguing
*Ant* irksome
**abstain** *refrain, forbear
*Ana* *forgo, eschew, abnegate: *decline, refuse, spurn, reject: desist (see STOP)
*Ant* indulge —*Con* pamper (see INDULGE): *satiate, sate, surfeit, cloy, gorge, glut: gratify, regale (see PLEASE)

**abstemious** see under *abstemiousness* at TEMPERANCE
**abstemiousness** abstinence, *temperance, sobriety, continence
*Ana* self-denial, self-abnegation (see RENUNCIATION): asceticism, austerity (see corresponding adjectives at SEVERE)
*Ant* gluttony —*Con* greed, rapacity (see CUPIDITY): epicurism (compare EPICURE)
**abstinence** *temperance, continence, abstemiousness, sobriety
*Ana* forbearance, refrainment (see corresponding verbs at REFRAIN): forgoing, eschewal, abnegation (see corresponding verbs at FORGO): *renunciation, self-denial, self-abnegation
*Ant* self-indulgence —*Con* greediness, covetousness, graspingness, acquisitiveness (see corresponding adjectives at COVETOUS): satisfying, contenting (see SATISFY): gorging, sating, surfeiting (see SATIATE)
**abstract** *adj* Abstract, ideal, transcendent, transcendental are closely analogous rather than synonymous terms. The difference in meaning between *abstract* and *ideal* is not apparent when they are applied to things which are admirable in actuality as well as in idea, as a virtue or a desirable quality or attribute ⟨*abstract* (or *ideal*) justice⟩ ⟨*ideal* (or *abstract*) morality⟩ When, however, they are applied to the name of a category known through actually existing representatives, they reveal their fundamental differences in meaning; for **abstract** implies the formulation of the idea by *abstraction*, a logical process in which the mind selects the characters common to every known member of a species or every known instance of a quality and builds up a conception (technically, a *concept*) which describes no one actually existing thing or instance, but covers all things of the same kind or marked by the given quality ⟨man in the *abstract*⟩ ⟨to shed tears over *abstract* justice and generosity, beauty, etc., and never to know these qualities when you meet them—*James*⟩ ⟨poetic theory is almost invariably an *abstraction* from poetic practice—*Day Lewis*⟩ **Ideal** may or may not imply abstraction; very often it suggests the exercise of imagination or the adding and the elimination of characteristics as the mind seeks a conception of a thing in its perfection ⟨*ideal* man⟩ ⟨Plato, in the construction of his *ideal* republic, is thinking . . . of the symmetry and beauty of the whole—*Dickinson*⟩ In general, therefore, *abstract* connotes apartness from reality and often lack of specific application to actual things ⟨algebra . . . is more *abstract* than geometry—*Russell*⟩ On the other hand, *ideal* very frequently connotes superiority to reality or, less often, fancifulness, and, at times, untruth ⟨that lofty order of minds who pant after the *ideal* . . . [whose] emotions are of too exquisite a character to find fit objects among their everyday fellowmen—*George Eliot*⟩ **Transcendent** and **transcendental**, though often used as equivalents of *ideal*, actually imply existence beyond experience and lack of correspondence to reality as known through the senses. Thus in careful use *transcendent* (or *transcendental*) beauty is not the perfection of the beauty that is known, but a supersensual beauty which has no parallel in experience and which cannot be apprehended through any likeness in actuality ⟨the idea that God is *transcendent* . . . exalted above the world . . . is yielding to the idea of God as immanent in his creation—*Allen*⟩ In Kant's philosophy they are distinguished. What is *transcendent* is both beyond experience and beyond human knowledge; what is *transcendental* is beyond experience yet knowable, because the mind possesses knowledge not derived from experience but inherent in its own constitution and essential to its understanding of experience. Thus space and time, in

---

A colon (:) separates groups of words discriminated. An asterisk (*) indicates place of treatment of each group.

Kant's philosophy, are *transcendental* ideas.
*Ana* *universal, general, generic: specific (see SPECIAL): *ultimate, absolute, categorical
*Ant* concrete —*Con* practical (see PRACTICABLE): *material, physical, corporeal, objective, phenomenal
**abstract** *n* brief, synopsis, epitome, *abridgment, conspectus
*Ana* sketch, précis, aperçu, *compendium, digest
*Ant* amplification —*Con* expansion, dilation (see corresponding verbs at EXPAND): enlargement (see corresponding verb at INCREASE)
**abstract** *vb* *detach, disengage
*Ana* *separate, part, divorce, divide: purloin, filch, *steal
*Ant* insert, introduce —*Con* interpolate, insinuate, interpose (see INTRODUCE): *replace
**abstracted, preoccupied, absent, absentminded, distraught** are comparable when they mean inattentive to what presently claims or demands consideration. **Abstracted** implies absorption of the mind in something other than one's surroundings, and often suggests reflection on weighty matters ⟨then he sat and thought . . . in the concentrated, *abstracted* way he has . . . almost forgetting my presence—*Rose Macaulay*⟩ **Preoccupied** implies unreadiness for any new demands on one's attention because one is already busy with other thoughts or occupations ⟨Edna was so *preoccupied* with misgivings as to whether he wanted to marry her that she had never faced squarely the more important problem of whether she wanted to marry him—*Barnes*⟩ **Absent** stresses inability to fix the mind on present concerns; it often connotes mental wandering rather than concentration on other things ⟨Sir Joshua . . . was quite *absent* all the day, not knowing a word that was said to him—*Burney*⟩ **Absentminded** implies that the mind is fixed elsewhere; it suggests abstractedness or preoccupation more than absentness ⟨she would make some *absentminded*, irrelevant remark, as if she had not heard him—*Rölvaag*⟩ It often implies a mental habit rather than a present mood ⟨*absentminded* professor⟩ **Distraught** suggests inability to concentrate and also implies an agitated state of mind caused by worry or perplexity ⟨oh, if I wake, shall I not be *distraught,* environed with all these hideous fears?—*Shak.*⟩ ⟨*distraught* with grief for the dead queen—*Millay*⟩
*Ana* *intent, engrossed: oblivious, unmindful (see FORGETFUL): ignoring, overlooking, disregarding (see NEGLECT *vb*)
*Ant* alert —*Con* wide-awake, vigilant, *watchful: attentive, *thoughtful, considerate: observant, noting, noticing, seeing (see corresponding verbs at SEE)
**abstruse** *recondite, occult, esoteric
*Ana* *complex, complicated, intricate, knotty: *abstract, ideal: enigmatic, cryptic, dark, *obscure
*Ant* obvious, plain —*Con* *evident, manifest, clear, palpable: *easy, simple, facile: *clear, perspicuous, lucid
**absurd** silly, preposterous, *foolish
*Ana* ludicrous, ridiculous, *laughable, droll, funny, comic: *irrational, unreasonable: asinine, silly, fatuous, *simple
*Ant* rational, sensible —*Con* reasonable (see RATIONAL): *wise, sane, judicious, prudent: *logical
**abundant** copious, ample, *plentiful, plenteous
*Ana* abounding, teeming, overflowing (see TEEM): *profuse, lavish, luxuriant, lush, exuberant
*Ant* scarce —*Con* *infrequent, rare, uncommon: *meager, scant, scanty, skimpy, exiguous, sparse: *deficient
**abuse** *vb* Abuse, misuse, mistreat, maltreat, ill-treat, outrage all denote to use or treat a person or thing improperly or wrongfully. *Abuse* and *misuse* are capable of wider use than the others, for they do not invariably imply either

deliberateness or wantonness ⟨I can't *abuse* your generosity to that extent. You're doing more than enough for me already—*Mackenzie*⟩ ⟨it turns a man's stomach to hear the Scripture *misused* in that way—*George Eliot*⟩ **Abuse,** however, commonly suggests perversion of the ends for which something was intended ⟨the constitution leaves them [the states] this right in the confidence that they will not *abuse* it—*John Marshall*⟩ Sometimes it implies excess in use that injures or impairs ⟨*abuse* one's strength⟩ **Misuse,** by contrast with *abuse,* emphasizes the actual mistreatment or misapplication rather than its results ⟨the intent of this regulation is highly commendable, namely to keep the Indians from being *misused*—*Hitchcock*⟩ **Mistreat, maltreat,** and **ill-treat** usually imply a fault or an evil motive in the agent, such as meanness, culpable ignorance, or spitefulness ⟨many more patients die from being *mistreated* for consumption than from consumption itself—*Lytton*⟩ ⟨the meter, though a well-known English critic has *maltreated* it of late, is a very fine one—*Saintsbury*⟩ ⟨have small compunction in *ill-treating* animals, because they have no souls—*Repplier*⟩ **Outrage** implies abuse so violent or extreme as to exceed all bounds ⟨an act that *outraged* nature and produced the inevitable tragedy of the play—*Auchincloss*⟩
*Ana* hurt, *injure, harm, damage, impair, mar, spoil: *wrong, persecute, oppress: pervert, corrupt, *debase, debauch, vitiate
*Ant* respect, honor —*Con* esteem (see corresponding noun at REGARD): *revere, venerate, reverence: *commend, applaud, compliment: cherish, treasure, prize (see APPRECIATE)
**abuse** *n* Abuse, vituperation, invective, obloquy, scurrility, billingsgate can all denote vehemently expressed condemnation or disapproval. **Abuse,** the most general term, implies the anger of the speaker and stresses the offensiveness of the language ⟨the extended vocabulary of barrack-room *abuse*—*Kipling*⟩ ⟨those thunderous comminations, that jeering and *abuse* which make Milton's prose such lively reading—*Huxley*⟩ It may, however, imply hardly more than expression of personal disapproval or displeasure ⟨a vague term of *abuse* for any style that is bad—*T. S. Eliot*⟩ **Vituperation** suggests the overwhelming of someone or something with a torrent of abuse ⟨presidents were nagged beyond endurance, and senators, and congressmen: no one could escape the vials of her *vituperation*—*Pattee*⟩ **Invective** implies vehemence and bitterness in attack or denunciation and, often in distinction from *abuse,* connotes a command of language and skill in making one's points. It is the precise term when the attack is public and made in a good cause ⟨*John Bull* stopped at nothing in the way of insult; but its blazing audacity of *invective* never degenerated into dull abuse—*Repplier*⟩ **Obloquy** suggests defamation and consequent disgrace ⟨those who . . . stood by me in the teeth of *obloquy*, taunt and open sneer—*Wilde*⟩ **Scurrility** stresses coarseness or indecency of language and emphasizes the quality of the abuse rather than the attack in itself ⟨he was . . . interrupted in his defense by ribaldry and *scurrility* from the judgment seat—*Macaulay*⟩ **Billingsgate** stresses more strongly than any of the other words the offensiveness, often foul or obscene, of the language of an attack ⟨the more I humbled myself the more he stormed . . . provoking me with scandalous names that I could not put up with; so that I . . . returned his *billingsgate*—*Smollett*⟩
*Ana* aspersion, reflection, stricture, *animadversion: reviling, railing, rating, berating (see SCOLD *vb*): vilification, malignment (see corresponding verbs at MALIGN)

---

*Ana* analogous words　*Ant* antonyms　*Con* contrasted words　See also explanatory notes facing page 1

*Ant* adulation —*Con* praise, laudation, acclaim (see corresponding verbs at PRAISE): *encomium, panegyric, eulogy: commendation, applause, compliment (see corresponding verbs at COMMEND)

**abusive, opprobrious, vituperative, contumelious, scurrilous** apply chiefly to language or utterances and to persons as they employ such language: the words agree in meaning coarse, insulting, and contemptuous in character or utterance. Abusive means little more than this ⟨*abusive* language⟩ ⟨an *abusive* master⟩ ⟨*abusive* satire⟩ All the other terms carry specific and distinctive implications. Opprobrious suggests the imputation of disgraceful actions or of shameful conduct: it implies not only abusiveness but also severe, often unjust, condemnation ⟨they desecrate the shrine . . . in every conceivable way . . . and level the most *opprobrious* language at the goddess herself—*Frazer*⟩ Vituperative implies indulgence in a stream of insulting language especially in attacking an opponent ⟨the *vituperative* controversialists of the seventeenth century⟩ ⟨to restrain this employment of *vituperative* language—*J. S. Mill*⟩ Contumelious adds to *opprobrious* the implications of insolence and extreme disrespect and usually connotes the bitter humiliation of its victim ⟨with scoffs and scorns and *contumelious* taunts—*Shak.*⟩ ⟨I . . . expose a chain of causes and effects that Roosevelt himself, if he were alive, would denounce as grossly *contumelious* to his native purity of spirit—and perhaps in all honesty—*Mencken*⟩ Scurrilous often approaches *vituperative* in suggesting attack and abuse but it always implies gross, vulgar, often obscenely ribald language ⟨they never fail to attack the passengers with all kinds of *scurrilous*, abusive, and indecent terms—*Fielding*⟩ ⟨may plaster his clean name with *scurrilous* rhymes!— *Tennyson*⟩

*Ana* insulting, affronting, offending, outraging (see OFFEND): aspersing, maligning, vilifying (see MALIGN)

*Ant* complimentary: respectful —*Con* flattering (see corresponding noun at COMPLIMENT): panegyrical, eulogistic (see corresponding nouns at ENCOMIUM): praising, lauding, extolling, acclaiming (see PRAISE *vb*)

**abutment** pier, *buttress

**abutting** contiguous, adjoining, *adjacent, tangent, conterminous, juxtaposed

*Ana* *close, near, nigh, nearby: joining, connecting (see JOIN): *nearest, next: impinging (compare *impingement* under IMPACT)

*Con* detached, disengaged (see DETACH): disconnected, disjoined, disassociated (see affirmative verbs at JOIN)

**abysm** *gulf, chasm, abyss

**abysmal** *deep, profound

*Ana* illimitable, *infinite

*Con* *superficial, shallow

**abyss** *gulf, chasm, abysm

**abyssal** pelagic, oceanic, marine (see AQUATIC)

**academic** 1 scholastic, *pedantic, bookish

*Ana* *dry, arid: erudite, scholarly, *learned

*Con* unlettered, uneducated, untaught, unlearned, illiterate, *ignorant

2 *theoretical, speculative

**accede** acquiesce, *assent, consent, agree, subscribe

*Ana* concur, cooperate (see UNITE): *yield, submit, defer, relent: allow, permit, *let

*Ant* demur —*Con* *decline, refuse, reject, spurn: shy, stickle, stick, strain, balk (see DEMUR): *object, protest, kick: oppose, *resist, withstand

**accelerate** *speed, quicken, hurry, hasten, precipitate

*Ana* forward, further, *advance, promote: drive, impel (see MOVE)

*Ant* decelerate: retard —*Con* *delay, slow, slacken:

impede, obstruct, block, *hinder: *hamper, clog

**accent** *n* 1 stress, accentuation, *emphasis

*Ana* beat, pulse, throb, pulsation (see under PULSATE): *rhythm, cadence, meter

2 intonation, *inflection

*Ana* pronunciation, enunciation, articulation (see corresponding verbs at ARTICULATE)

**accentuation** accent, stress, *emphasis

*Ana* *rhythm, cadence, meter: pronunciation, enunciation, articulation (see corresponding verbs at ARTICULATE)

*Ant* inaccentuation —*Con* evenness, steadiness, uniformity (see corresponding adjectives at STEADY)

**accept** *receive, admit, take

*Ana* *adopt, embrace, espouse: acquiesce, *assent, agree, subscribe

*Ant* reject —*Con* *decline, refuse, repudiate, spurn: disavow, disown, disacknowledge (see affirmative verbs at ACKNOWLEDGE): *deny, contradict, negative: ignore, disregard (see NEGLECT)

**acceptance, acceptation** have both at one time or another carried the meanings: the act or fact of accepting or the state of being accepted. Present usage, however, restricts their denotations. Acceptance only is used to denote the act of accepting ⟨a blind *acceptance* of authority—*Inge*⟩ or the state of one who accepts something, especially something inevitable or inescapable ⟨all settled back into a sad sort of *acceptance* of the situation—*Deland*⟩ Both *acceptance* and *acceptation* may be used to denote the state of being accepted or especially of being approved or believed ⟨metrical forms are conventional, and therefore rest . . . on *acceptance*—*Lowes*⟩ Acceptation tends, however, to confine itself to denoting the sense in which a word or expression is generally received ⟨not . . . a cultivated man in the ordinary *acceptation* of the words— *Eliot*⟩

**acceptation** 1 *meaning, sense, signification, significance, import

2 *acceptance

**access** 1 ingress, *entrance, entrée, entry

*Ana* approaching *or* approach, nearing (see APPROACH *vb*): *admittance, admission: *way, route, passage: *door, portal, gate, gateway

*Ant* outlet —*Con* departure, withdrawal, retirement (see corresponding verbs at GO): retreat, recession (see corresponding verbs at RECEDE)

2 accession, attack, *fit, paroxysm, spasm, convulsion

*Ana* onset, onslaught, assault (see ATTACK): seizure, clutch, taking (see corresponding verbs at TAKE): twinge, *pain, stitch, pang, throe

**accession** 1 *addition, accretion, increment

*Ant* discard

2 access, attack, *fit, paroxysm, spasm, convulsion

*Ana* see those at ACCESS 2

**accessory** *n* 1 appurtenance, adjunct, *appendage

*Ana* concomitant, *accompaniment: *addition, accretion, increment

2 accomplice, abettor, *confederate, conspirator

*Ant* principal

**accessory** *adj* contributory, *auxiliary, subsidiary, adjuvant, ancillary, subservient

*Ana* secondary, collateral, tributary, *subordinate: concomitant, concurrent, coincident (see CONTEMPORARY): incidental, adventitious (see ACCIDENTAL)

*Ant* constituent, integral: principal (*in law*) —*Con* *inherent, intrinsic, constitutional, ingrained: essential, indispensable, requisite, *needful, necessary: fundamental, vital, cardinal (see ESSENTIAL)

**accident** 1 *quality, character, attribute, property

---

A colon (:) separates groups of words discriminated. An asterisk (*) indicates place of treatment of each group.

*Ana* mark, *sign, note, badge, token, symptom: characteristic, peculiarity (see corresponding adjectives at CHARACTERISTIC)
*Ant* substance (*in philosophy*)
2 *chance, hazard, luck, fortune, hap
*Ana* contingency, fortuity, adventitiousness (see corresponding adjectives at ACCIDENTAL)
*Ant* design, intent —*Con* calculation, circumspection (see under CAUTIOUS): *plan, plot, project, scheme: *intention, purpose
3 **Accident, casualty, mishap** are synonyms when they designate chance or a chance event bringing injury or loss. **Accident** is broadest in its application, being used of events that involve persons or things, or injuries or losses, serious or slight ⟨he was crippled by the *accident*⟩ ⟨a railway *accident*⟩ ⟨owing to an *accident* to the machines one department was closed down⟩ **Casualty** commonly implies destruction, especially of life, and is chiefly applied to an individual whose death, serious injury, or even desertion constitutes a loss to a military (or similar) force engaged in hazardous activities ⟨the regiment suffered heavy *casualties*⟩ As applied to insurance *accident* and *casualty* are usually distinguished: *accident insurance* is a provision against injury to oneself through accident; *casualty insurance* is a provision for indemnification for loss from accident (as fire or burglary) and especially for damages incurred through one's liability for injury or loss to others. **Mishap** as a rule is applied only to slight accidents, especially those involving disappointment or frustration ⟨a day seldom passes without one *mishap* or another⟩
*Ana* *disaster, catastrophe: mischance, *misfortune, mishap

**accidental, casual, fortuitous, contingent, incidental, adventitious.** The last five of these words are synonyms of *accidental* but not always of one another. **Accidental** denotes simply either happening by chance ⟨an *accidental* meeting⟩ or not of the real or essential nature of a thing ⟨the essential and the *accidental* values of a college education⟩ *Casual, fortuitous,* and *contingent* come into comparison with *accidental* in the first of these senses; *incidental* and *adventitious* chiefly in the second sense. **Casual** so strongly stresses absence of prearrangement or premeditation that it tends to obscure the implication of chance ⟨a *casual* discovery⟩ ⟨it was no *casual* reencounter. He had been enticed into the place . . . with some sinister and perhaps deadly purpose—*Froude*⟩ As applied to persons, their actions, their clothes, it often implies heedlessness or indifference ⟨this strange landscape, which seemed so dull to the *casual* view—*Rourke*⟩ ⟨[the rector] had been very *casual* about visiting his parishioners—*Mackenzie*⟩ Sometimes it is the appearance of carelessness or nonchalance and not the reality that is suggested ⟨this sense of an audience made him deliberately *casual* in his bearing—*H. G. Wells*⟩ **Fortuitous** so strongly implies chance that it sometimes connotes the absence, or seeming absence, of a cause ⟨the good frame of the universe was not the product of chance or *fortuitous* concourse of particles of matter—*Hale*⟩ **Contingent** implies both possibility and uncertainty, the former because that which is so described may come about, the latter because the outcome is unpredictable owing to the possible operation of chance, of unseen causes, or of the possible influence of unforeseen events. *Contingent* is therefore always applied to what may come ⟨the *contingent* advantages of a new law are to be distinguished from those that are immediate and certain⟩ ⟨men are inclined . . . to resist a truth which discloses the *contingent* character of their existence—

*Niebuhr*⟩ ⟨such arguments yield a provisional and *contingent* justification of moral beliefs—*Sat. Review*⟩ **Incidental** may or may not imply chance; it typically suggests a real and often a designed relationship, but one which is secondary and nonessential. An *incidental* advantage or gain is one that may have been foreseen or sought after but not regarded as of first importance; *incidental* expenses are those that must be provided for in a budget because they are normal contingencies though they cannot be enumerated under any of the usual headings ⟨the Irish question is only *incidental* to the larger question—*J. R. Lowell*⟩ ⟨although a great deal is heard about consumer and real estate credit controls, they are *incidental* to the control of overall bank credit—*Eccles*⟩ *Incidental* sometimes implies contingency that amounts to a strong probability ⟨ills *incidental* to old age⟩ ⟨labor problems *incidental* to rapidly expanding factories—*Amer. Guide Series: Mass.*⟩ **Adventitious** conveys no necessary suggestion of chance but it does imply a lack of essential relationship. Something *adventitious* does not belong to the original and intrinsic nature of a thing but has been added ⟨in works of imagination and sentiment . . . meter is but *adventitious* to composition—*Wordsworth*⟩
*Ana* haphazard, *random, hit-or-miss, chance: unintended, undesigned, unpurposed (see affirmative verbs at INTEND): contingent, *dependent, conditional
*Ant* planned: essential —*Con* intended, designed, purposed (see INTEND): plotted, projected, schemed (see corresponding verbs under PLAN *n*): *inherent, constitutional, intrinsic, ingrained: *innate, inborn

**acclaim** *vb* extol, laud, *praise, eulogize
*Ana* *applaud, cheer, root: *exalt, magnify: glorify, honor (see corresponding nouns at FAME)
*Ant* vituperate —*Con* revile, berate, rate (see SCOLD): *execrate, objurgate, damn: denounce, censure, reprobate (see CRITICIZE)

**acclaim** *n* acclamation, *applause, plaudits
*Ana* homage, *honor, reverence: renown, glory, éclat (see FAME): cheer (see corresponding verb at APPLAUD)
*Ant* vituperation —*Con* obloquy, *abuse, invective: condemnation, denunciation, reprobation, censure (see corresponding verbs at CRITICIZE)

**acclamation** acclaim, *applause, plaudits
*Ana, Ant, Con* see those at ACCLAIM *n*

**acclimate** acclimatize, *harden, season
*Ana* accustom, *habituate: *adapt, adjust, conform

**acclimatize** acclimate, *harden, season
*Ana* see ACCLIMATE

**accommodate** 1 adjust, *adapt, conform, reconcile
*Ana* *yield, submit, bow, defer: modify, *change, alter, vary: temper, *moderate, qualify
*Ant* constrain —*Con* *estrange, alienate
2 *oblige, favor
*Ana* *help, aid, assist: gratify, gladden, *please: *indulge, humor
*Ant* incommode —*Con* *inconvenience, discommode, trouble: annoy, harass, harry, *worry: vex, irk (see ANNOY)
3 hold, *contain
*Ana* lodge, house, board, shelter, *harbor, entertain: take (in), *receive, admit

**accompaniment, concomitant** denote in common something attendant upon or found in association with another thing. Both may imply addition, but they vary chiefly in the kind of relationship connoted between the principal and the attendant things. **Accompaniment** often suggests enhancement by the addition of something appropriate ⟨the piano *accompaniment* for a violin solo⟩ ⟨the usual *accompaniments* of a turkey dinner⟩ ⟨fame is not always the *accom-*

*paniment* of success⟩ Sometimes it stresses concurrence or coincidence rather than causal connection ⟨a Roman sedition was the all but invariable *accompaniment* of a Roman coronation—*Bryce*⟩ **Concomitant,** by contrast, conveys the idea of customary or necessary association. It does not as a rule need the qualifying words (*invariable, essential, inevitable*) which so often precede it, for it implies in itself the qualities attributed by these words ⟨disruption of routine is the *concomitant* of illnesses in a staff⟩ ⟨unemployment is the *concomitant* of a financial panic⟩ ⟨tuberculosis, hookworm, and infant mortality—the pathological *concomitants* of pauperism—*Handlin*⟩

**accompany,** **attend, conduct, escort, convoy, chaperon** mean to go or be together with; they differ chiefly in their implications as to the nature or purpose of the association. **Accompany** implies companionship and often, with a personal subject, equality of status ⟨*accompany* a friend⟩ Used of things, it stresses closeness of association ⟨rain *accompanied* by wind⟩ ⟨the lightheadedness which *accompanies* fever—*Kipling*⟩ **Attend** commonly implies the subordinate or inferior status of the accompanying person or thing ⟨the prince was *attended* (rather than *accompanied*) by an equerry, a secretary, and a courier⟩ Sometimes it suggests a service or courtesy ⟨the General *attended* her himself to the street door—*Austen*⟩ Sometimes it connotes following or coming in the wake of someone or something ⟨a train of mourning friends *attend* his pall—*Gray*⟩ ⟨the Nemesis that *attends* upon human pride—*Dickinson*⟩ **Conduct** usually retains an implication of guidance even when the subject is impersonal ⟨*conduct* a blind man across the street⟩ ⟨*conduct* sightseers through a museum⟩ ⟨the pipe *conducts* water from a trough⟩ Occasionally the emphasis is not on guidance but on conveyance or transmission ⟨metals that *conduct* heat⟩ **Escort** and **convoy** add to *accompany* the implication of protection. Both words and their corresponding nouns often suggest the use of an armed force as a guard, but there is a tendency to prefer *escort* when persons and *convoy* when things are protected. Also, *escort* is more often used for journeys on land and *convoy* for journeys by sea ⟨soldiers *escorted* the caravan through the desert⟩ ⟨a destroyer *convoyed* the freighter through the submarine zone⟩ *Escort,* however, often suggests (as *convoy* no longer suggests) attending as a courtesy or honor ⟨three battleships *escorted* the visiting potentate's ship into the harbor⟩ ⟨*escort* a lady to her home after a party⟩ **Chaperon** and its corresponding noun suggest propriety and sometimes supervision as the motive of the one who accompanies ⟨agreed to *chaperon* the school picnic⟩ ⟨as if his intellect were a sort of *chaperon* to his imagination—*Evans*⟩ In ordinary use they imply the presence of a mature woman or sometimes a married couple as the companion of young people (as at a dance or party) to ensure proper behavior ⟨a literary scavenging party arranged by their English teacher who accompanied them as *chaperon* —*Morley*⟩
**Ana** associate, link, combine, *join: *guide, lead, pilot
**Con** forsake, desert, *abandon: leave, quit, withdraw (see GO)

**accomplice** *confederate, accessory, abettor, conspirator
**accomplish** achieve, effect, fulfill, discharge, execute, *perform
**Ana** complete, finish, conclude (see CLOSE): consummate (see corresponding adjective at CONSUMMATE): implement, *enforce
**Ant** undo —**Con** thwart, *frustrate, foil, circumvent: defeat, beat, lick (see CONQUER): *nullify, annul, negate
**accomplished** finished, *consummate
**Ana** *proficient, skillful, skilled, adept, expert, masterly:

*versatile, many-sided, all-around
**accomplishment** attainment, *acquirement, acquisition
**Ana** *art, skill, craft: proficiency, adeptness, expertness (see corresponding adjectives at PROFICIENT)
**accord** *vb* 1 *agree, harmonize, correspond, tally, conform, square, jibe
**Ana** concur, coincide (see AGREE): blend, fuse, merge, coalesce (see MIX): cohere, adhere (see STICK)
**Ant** conflict —**Con** clash, collide, jar (see corresponding nouns at IMPACT): *differ, disagree: contrast, *compare
2 *grant, vouchsafe, concede, award
**Ana** deign, condescend (see STOOP): bestow, present, confer, *give
**Ant** withhold —**Con** *deny, gainsay: refuse (see DECLINE): hold, hold back, detain, reserve (see KEEP)
**accord** *n* 1 concord, consonance, *harmony
**Ana** agreement, acquiescence, consent (see corresponding verbs at ASSENT): union, solidarity, *unity: sympathy, affinity, *attraction
**Ant** dissension, strife: antagonism —**Con** *discord, conflict, difference, variance, contention: antipathy, animosity, hostility (see ENMITY)
2 *agreement, understanding
**Ana** pact, compact, treaty, entente, concordat (see CONTRACT)
**accordingly** so, consequently, *therefore, hence, then
**accost** *address, greet, hail, salute
**Ana** *speak, talk, converse: affront, *offend, insult
**Con** avoid, shun, elude, evade, *escape: ignore, slight, overlook (see NEGLECT)
**account** *n* 1 *use, service, advantage, profit, avail
**Ana** benefit (see corresponding verb at BENEFIT): usefulness, utility (see USE): *worth, value
**Con** futility, vanity, fruitlessness, bootlessness (see corresponding adjectives at FUTILE): unimportance, inconsequence, insignificance (see affirmative nouns at IMPORTANCE)
2 **Account, report, chronicle, version, story** denote a statement of actual events or conditions or of purported occurrences or conditions. An **account** is an oral or written, detailed, often firsthand statement ⟨Lord Mountfalcon asked for an *account* of her passage over to the island; receiving distressingly full particulars—*Meredith*⟩ A **report** is an account, usually of something witnessed or investigated, given to an employer or a superior ⟨spies send in their *reports* in cipher⟩ ⟨the secretary gave a verbatim *report* of the conference⟩ A **chronicle** is a detailed and extended account or report of events in their order of occurrence ⟨for 'tis a *chronicle* of day by day, not a relation for a breakfast—*Shak.*⟩ A **version** or **story** is a statement of purported facts. *Version* always and *story* often imply contrast with another statement of the same events and, usually, difference in details. But whereas *version* commonly implies difference of detail or of interpretation owing to limitations in each point of view, *story* often implies actual or suspected falsification ⟨the Democratic and the Republican *version* of the state of the nation⟩ ⟨the witness had been primed to tell a different *story*⟩ ⟨he returned after a week's absence with a *story* of having been held captive by kidnapers⟩
**account** *vb* 1 *consider, deem, regard, reckon
**Ana** regard, esteem (see under REGARD *n*): rate, appraise, evaluate, assess, *estimate
**Con** underrate, underestimate, undervalue (see base words at ESTIMATE): disregard, disesteem (see affirmative verbs under REGARD *n*)
2 *explain, justify, rationalize
**Ana** *answer: expound, elucidate, interpret (see EXPLAIN)

A colon (:) separates groups of words discriminated. An asterisk (*) indicates place of treatment of each group.

**accountable** *responsible, answerable, amenable, liable
*Ant* unaccountable   *—Con* \*absolute, autocratic, despotic, tyrannical, arbitrary: irresponsible, inamenable, unanswerable (see affirmative adjectives at RESPONSIBLE)

**accountant** auditor, \*bookkeeper

**accouter** equip, arm, outfit, \*furnish, appoint
*Ana* array, attire, \*clothe, dress: deck, \*adorn, embellish, decorate
*Con* \*strip, divest, dismantle

**accredit** 1 certify, \*approve, endorse, sanction
*Ana* recommend, \*commend: vouch, attest, \*certify
*Con* reject, repudiate (see DECLINE): \*disapprove, deprecate
2 commission, \*authorize, license
3 credit, charge, assign, \*ascribe, attribute, impute
*Ana* attach, \*fasten: connect, link, associate (see JOIN)

**accretion** \*addition, increment, accession
*Ana* adjunct, \*appendage: adhesion, cohesion (see corresponding verbs at STICK): increase, augmentation, enlargement (see corresponding verbs at INCREASE)
*Con* diminution, dwindling, decrease (see corresponding verbs at DECREASE)

**accumulate, amass, hoard** imply in both literal and figurative usage a bringing together so as to make a store or great quantity. **Accumulate** implies a piling up by a series of increases rather than by a single complete act; it is applicable to almost anything that may increase in amount ⟨unused books *accumulate* dust⟩ ⟨he will ever be gathering knowledge, *accumulating* experience, as he can— *Gerould*⟩ ⟨true poetry, however simple it may appear on the surface, *accumulates* meaning every time it is read— *Day Lewis*⟩ **Amass** refers usually but not always to things that are regarded as valuable, such as money or treasures ⟨*amass* a fortune⟩ It frequently implies more imposing results than *accumulate* ⟨scientific knowledge, painstakingly *amassed* by many devotees over an extended period of human history—*Geldard*⟩ **Hoard** always implies storing up and frequently concealment of what is stored ⟨squirrels *hoard* nuts for the winter months⟩ Frequently *hoard* implies greed and, when used of money, avarice ⟨a miser is one who *hoards* gold⟩ ⟨*hoarding* money is not a safe way of saving—*Shaw*⟩
*Ana* \*gather, collect: \*heap, pile, stack
*Ant* dissipate   *—Con* \*scatter, disperse, dispel: diminish, lessen, \*decrease: \*distribute, dispense, deal, dole

**accumulative** \*cumulative, summative, additive
*Ana* aggregative, conglomerative (see corresponding nouns at AGGREGATE): multiplicative, augmentative (see corresponding verbs at INCREASE)
*Con* dissipating, dispelling, dispersing, scattering (see SCATTER): disintegrating, crumbling, decomposing (see DECAY *vb*)

**accurate** \*correct, exact, precise, nice, right
*Ana* true, veracious (see corresponding nouns at TRUTH): \*impeccable, errorless, flawless, faultless: punctilious, meticulous, \*careful
*Ant* inaccurate   *—Con* \*careless, heedless, inadvertent: \*slipshod, slovenly: fallacious (see under FALLACY)

**accursed** damnable, cursed, \*execrable
*Ana* abominable, odious, \*hateful, abhorrent, detestable: revolting, repulsive, loathsome, \*offensive, repugnant
*Ant* blessed   *—Con* admirable, estimable (see corresponding nouns at REGARD): \*holy, sacred, divine: \*honorable, honorary

**accuse, charge, incriminate, indict, impeach, arraign** denote in common to declare a person guilty of a fault or offense. **Accuse** is typically immediate and personal and often suggests directness or sharpness of imputation or censure; **charge** frequently connotes seriousness in the offense and

formality in the declaration; one may *accuse* a bystander of trying to pick one's pocket (an *accusation* which may become a formal *charge* before a magistrate); one *accuses* a man of cheating (an offense which one personally resents); one *charges* a man with cheating (an infraction of the rules of a game). **Incriminate** may mean to charge with crime or serious offense ⟨your friend thinks he can clear Ken by *incriminating* poor Wayne—*G. V. Williams*⟩ ⟨careful study . . . has failed to show that any of the cultivable bacteria can be *incriminated* as the cause of colds —*Andrewes*⟩ but in current use it more often means to involve or inculpate in crime ⟨*incriminating* evidence⟩ ⟨the answer need not reveal a crime in order to be *incriminating*. It is enough if it . . . leads to proof of an illegal act —*Gressman*⟩ **Indict** adds to *charge* in legal context the implications of a formal consideration of the evidence by a grand jury or in general use by someone acting in the role of jury and of a decision that the accused person should be called to trial or to an accounting ⟨the jury refused to *indict* the men accused of arson⟩ ⟨I *indict* those citizens whose easy consciences condone such wrongdoings— *Roosevelt*⟩ **Impeach** implies legally a charge of malfeasance in office formally brought against a public officer by a branch of the government constitutionally authorized to bring such charges ⟨the House of Representatives *impeached* President Andrew Johnson of high crimes and misdemeanors⟩ In nontechnical language *impeach* or its noun *impeachment* implies a direct charge which demands an answer ⟨any intelligent and noble-minded American can with reason take that side . . . without having either his reason or his integrity *impeached*—*Kenneth Roberts*⟩ ⟨"You buy your loves." . . . he did not plead verbally against the *impeachment*—*Meredith*⟩ To **arraign** is to call or bring a prisoner before a court to answer to the charge of an indictment ⟨I was carried down to the Sessions house, where I was *arraigned*—*Defoe*⟩ Figuratively it means to call a person or thing to public account for something done or omitted ⟨*arraigns* the monks for teaching grammar rather than things spiritual—*H. O. Taylor*⟩ ⟨a despairing soliloquy . . . in which he *arraigns* the United States policy in relation to China—*Times Lit. Sup.*⟩
*Ana* denounce, blame, reprobate, censure, \*criticize
*Ant* exculpate   *—Con* exonerate, vindicate, acquit, absolve (see EXCULPATE)

**accustom** \*habituate, addict, inure
*Ana* \*adapt, accommodate, adjust: \*harden, season, acclimatize
*Ant* disaccustom   *—Con* alienate, wean, \*estrange

**accustomed** wonted, customary, habitual, \*usual
*Ana* natural, normal, \*regular, typical: \*common, ordinary, familiar
*Ant* unaccustomed   *—Con* \*strange, singular, peculiar, odd, queer, erratic: \*infrequent, uncommon, rare, occasional

**acerbity** \*acrimony, asperity
*Ana* sourness, acidity, tartness (see corresponding adjectives at SOUR): crabbedness, surliness, dourness, saturninity (see corresponding adjectives at SULLEN): bitterness, acridity (see corresponding adjectives at BITTER): harshness, roughness (see corresponding adjectives at ROUGH)
*Ant* mellowness   *—Con* gentleness, mildness, blandness, smoothness (see corresponding adjectives at SOFT): amiableness, good nature, complaisance (see corresponding adjectives at AMIABLE)

**ache** *n* \*pain, pang, throe, twinge, stitch
*Ana* \*distress, suffering, agony, misery: anguish, heartache, heartbreak (see SORROW): hurt, \*injury: torment, torture, rack (see corresponding verbs at AFFLICT)

---

*Ana* analogous words     *Ant* antonyms     *Con* contrasted words     See also explanatory notes facing page 1

*Con* relief, alleviation, assuagement, mitigation (see corresponding verbs at RELIEVE): ease, comfort (see REST)

**achieve** 1 accomplish, effect, *perform, fulfill, execute, discharge

*Ana* complete, finish, conclude (see CLOSE): surmount, overcome, *conquer

*Ant* fail (*to do something*), fail (in) —*Con* *begin, commence, start

2 attain, *reach, gain, compass

*Ana* win, secure, obtain, acquire, *get: *realize, actualize: *come, arrive

*Ant* miss (*getting or attaining*) —*Con* deviate, depart, *swerve: *escape, avoid, elude, shun

**achievement** *feat, exploit

*Ana* deed, act, *action: *victory, conquest, triumph: consummation, accomplishment (see corresponding adjectives at CONSUMMATE)

*Ant* failure —*Con* negligence, *neglect: omission, slighting (see corresponding verbs at NEGLECT): defeat, vanquishment, beating, licking (see corresponding verbs at CONQUER)

**achromatic** *colorless, uncolored

*Ana* *neutral, negative

*Ant* chromatic —*Con* colored, tinted, tinged (see corresponding nouns at COLOR)

**acid** *adj* acidulous, tart, *sour, dry

*Ana* acrid, *bitter: *sharp

*Ant* bland: sweet: alkaline —*Con* *suave, smooth: mild, *soft, gentle: basic (see ALKALINE)

**acidulous** acid, tart, *sour, dry

*Ana* *sharp: *pungent, piquant: biting, cutting (see INCISIVE)

*Ant* saccharine —*Con* mellow, ripe (see MATURE): bland, mild, *soft: *suave, smooth, urbane

**acknowledge** 1 Acknowledge, admit, own, avow, confess are synonymous when they mean to disclose something against one's will or inclination. All usually imply some sort of pressure as that of the law or of conscience leading to the disclosure. **Acknowledge** or its noun *acknowledgment* implies making known something which has been or might have been kept back or concealed ⟨*acknowledge* a secret marriage⟩ ⟨*acknowledged* his complete ignorance of mathematics⟩ ⟨she did at last extort from her father an *acknowledgment* that the horses were engaged—*Austen*⟩ **Admit**, with less suggestion of possible concealment, stresses reluctance to grant or concede and refers rather to facts than to their implications; to *admit* a charge may involve merely the granting of the fact alleged, not necessarily (as frequently with *acknowledge*) the acceptance of the point of view which the charge implies ⟨at last the government at Washington *admitted* its mistake—which governments seldom do—*Cather*⟩ **Own** is less formal than *acknowledge* and regards the thing acknowledged in its relation to oneself ⟨*owned* himself at a loss as to what to do next⟩ ⟨*owned* to forty years⟩ ⟨when a man *owns* himself to have been in an error, he does but tell you in other words that he is wiser than he was—*Pope*⟩ **Avow** implies an open or bold acknowledgment or declaration and often one made in the face of hostility ⟨communists, fascists, and other *avowed* enemies of parliamentarism—*Ogg & Zink*⟩ ⟨made the idea of democratic nationalism intellectually respectable and thus perhaps made it easier for the Colonel publicly to *avow* nationalism as his creed —*Forcey*⟩ **Confess** usually applies to what one feels to be wrong ⟨*confess* a crime⟩ ⟨*confess* one's sins⟩ but it is often used with no such implication, suggesting merely deference to the opinion of others ⟨I am not, I *confess*, fully convinced⟩

*Ana* disclose, divulge, *reveal: *grant, concede, allow:

publish, *declare, proclaim

*Ant* deny —*Con* conceal, *hide, secrete: disavow, disown (see affirmative verbs at ACKNOWLEDGE): gainsay, contradict, impugn, negative (see DENY)

2 Acknowledge, recognize agree in meaning to take cognizance of in some way, usually in a way dictated by custom or convention and implying acceptance or assent. **Acknowledge** is found in certain idioms where the concrete method of taking notice is not stated but connoted; one *acknowledges* a letter by sending a reply; one *acknowledges* a gift by a message indicating the receipt and acceptance of the gift and one's gratitude; one *acknowledges* a greeting by an appropriate conventional response (as a bow, smile, or friendly remark). In freer expression *acknowledge* usually implies definite or formal acceptance, as of a principle as binding or of a claim as rightful or of a person as ruler ⟨he *acknowledged* the obligation of a son to support his aged parents⟩ ⟨in Italy during the fourteenth and fifteenth centuries there were two *acknowledged* sources of political power: the Empire and the Church—*Huxley*⟩ **Recognize**, though often used interchangeably with *acknowledge*, suggests more strongly authoritative sanction or full admission concerning a given or implied status or suggests actual and manifest, as contrasted with formal or merely verbal, acceptance ⟨in 1918 England, France, and the United States *recognized* Czechoslovakia as an independent state⟩ ⟨the ladies never acted so well as when they were in the presence of a fact which they *acknowledged* but did not *recognize*— *Meredith*⟩ *Recognize* sometimes implies, as *acknowledge* never does, full realization or comprehension ⟨courts . . . have been . . . slow to *recognize* that statutes . . . may imply a policy different from that of the common law —*Justice Holmes*⟩

*Ana* accept, *receive: notice, note, remark (see SEE): respond, reply, *answer

*Ant* ignore —*Con* disregard, slight, *neglect: repudiate, spurn, reject (see DECLINE)

**acme** apex, zenith, culmination, climax, *summit, peak, apogee, pinnacle, meridian

**acoustic, acoustical** *auditory

**acquaint** *inform, apprise, advise, notify

*Ana* tell, *reveal, disclose, divulge: *teach, instruct, educate, school: accustom, *habituate

*Con* conceal, *hide: withhold, reserve, hold, hold back (*information*) (see KEEP)

**acquaintance** *friend, intimate, confidant

*Ana* *associate, companion, comrade, crony

*Con* *stranger, outsider

**acquiesce** consent, agree, *assent, accede, subscribe

*Ana* accept, *receive: conform, *adapt, adjust, accommodate, reconcile (*oneself*): *yield, submit, bow: concur, coincide (see AGREE)

*Ant* object —*Con* protest, remonstrate, kick (see OBJECT): *demur, stickle, stick, shy, balk: *differ, dissent

**acquiescence** compliance, resignation (see under COMPLIANT)

*Ana* deference, obeisance (see HONOR): submissiveness (see corresponding adjective at TAME)

*Ant* rebelliousness *or* rebellion —*Con* insubordination, contumaciousness (see corresponding adjectives at INSUBORDINATE)

**acquiescent** resigned, *compliant

*Ana* submissive (see TAME): yielding, submitting, deferring, bowing, relenting (see YIELD)

*Ant* rebellious —*Con* contumacious, *insubordinate: protesting, objecting, kicking, remonstrating (see OBJECT *vb*): resisting, opposing, combating, conflicting (see RESIST)

A colon (:) separates groups of words discriminated. An asterisk (*) indicates place of treatment of each group.

acquire obtain, *get, gain, win, secure, procure
*Ana* attain, achieve, compass, *reach: annex, *add, superadd: *buy, purchase: *take, seize, snatch, grab
*Ant* forfeit —*Con* alienate, *transfer, convey: *relinquish, surrender, abandon, yield

acquirement, acquisition, attainment, accomplishment denote in common a power or skill that is the fruit of exertion or effort; in this sense they are often used in the plural. Acquirement implies achievement as a result of continued endeavor and self-cultivation rather than of natural gifts or talent ⟨a woman of considerable information and literature; *acquirements* not common amongst . . . ladies—*Edgeworth*⟩ Acquisition may add to *acquirement* the implications that the thing acquired is an addition or gain and that the endeavor to acquire has been characterized by avidity and stress ⟨perhaps it was a mistake to force her into the rigid groove of classical learning . . . from it she got very unusual *acquisitions*, but overstimulation broke her health—*Parrington*⟩ As applied to an acquired power or skill, *acquisition* usually stresses, as *acquirement* does not, the inherent value of that power or skill ⟨absolute disinterestedness is a rare *acquisition*, even in historians⟩ ⟨no philosopher would resign his mental *acquisitions* for the purchase of any terrestrial good—*Peacock*⟩ Attainment commonly refers to distinguished achievements as in the arts, in statesmanship, in science; it suggests fully developed talent ⟨artists of high *attainments*⟩ ⟨remarkable literary *attainments*⟩ Accomplishment refers to any acquired power or grace such as may make for agreeable social intercourse ⟨my new *accomplishment* of dancing—*Charles Churchill*⟩ ⟨we found that even for Men of Science this neat clean carving of words was a very necessary *accomplishment*—*Quiller-Couch*⟩ ⟨an *accomplishment* of which he was a perfect exponent, the interchange of humorous and agreeable civilities—*Repplier*⟩
*Ana* achievement (see FEAT): *addition, accretion
*Con* *lack, want, dearth, defect, privation

acquisition *acquirement, attainment, accomplishment
*Ana* *addition, accession, accretion, increment: *possessions, belongings, means, assets: *gift, genius, talent, aptitude: *art, skill, cunning

acquisitive grasping, avaricious, greedy, *covetous
*Ana* avid, *eager, keen, athirst: possessing *or* possessive, owning, enjoying (see corresponding verbs at HAVE)
*Ant* sacrificing, abnegating —*Con* forgoing, forbearing, eschewing (see FORGO): self-denying, renunciative (see corresponding nouns at RENUNCIATION)

acquit 1 absolve, exonerate, vindicate, *exculpate
*Ana* discharge, *free, release, liberate: *excuse, pardon, forgive, remit
*Ant* convict —*Con* condemn, *sentence, doom, proscribe, damn: denounce, blame (see CRITICIZE)
2 quit, *behave, conduct, demean, deport, comport
*Ana* *act, behave, work, operate, react
*Con* misbehave, misconduct, misdemean (see base words at BEHAVE)

acrid 1 *bitter
*Ana* *pungent, piquant: biting (see INCISIVE): *offensive, repugnant, loathsome
*Ant* savory —*Con* *palatable, sapid, toothsome, tasty: fragrant, *odorous, aromatic, balmy: delicious, delectable, luscious, *delightful
2 *caustic, mordant, scathing
*Ana* *sharp, keen: surly, crabbed, morose (see SULLEN): malevolent, malign, spiteful, *malicious: virulent, venomous, *poisonous
*Ant* benign, kindly —*Con* *suave, urbane, bland, smooth, politic

acrimonious *angry, irate, indignant, wrathful, wroth, mad
*Ana* testy, splenetic, choleric, *irascible, cranky, cross: rancorous, hostile, antagonistic (see corresponding nouns at ENMITY): quarrelsome, contentious, *belligerent
*Ant* irenic, peaceable —*Con* *kind, kindly, benign, benignant

acrimony, acerbity, asperity agree in denoting temper or language marked by irritation or some degree of anger or resentment. Acrimony implies bitterness or ill will and also greater stinging or blistering power in what is said than the others ⟨the controversial writings of the seventeenth century are notorious for their *acrimony*⟩ ⟨we all know how easy it is to . . . defend a pet theory with *acrimony*—*Quiller-Couch*⟩ Acerbity implies sourness as well as bitterness, sometimes as shown in words or mood, but more often as manifested in a morose, embittered nature ⟨the judge's smile seemed to operate on her *acerbity* of heart like sunshine upon vinegar, making it ten times sourer—*Hawthorne*⟩ Often it suggests crabbedness ⟨the Milton of religious and political controversy . . . is not seldom disfigured by want of amenity, by *acerbity*—*Arnold*⟩ Asperity retains implications of harshness and roughness chiefly in reference to style ⟨the elderly ladies in his audience had been shocked by the *asperities* of the new style in music—*Copland*⟩ In general use *asperity* stresses quickness of temper or sharpness of resentment but it rarely suggests bitterness ⟨told him with some *asperity* to mind his own business⟩
*Ana* bitterness (see corresponding adjective at BITTER): ill will, malignity, malignancy, spite, spleen, *malice, malevolence: rancor, animus, animosity, antipathy (see ENMITY)
*Ant* suavity —*Con* urbanity, diplomacy (see corresponding adjectives at SUAVE): courtesy, civility, politeness (see corresponding adjectives at CIVIL)

across, crosswise, crossways, athwart are synonymous when they mean so as to intersect the length of something. Across and athwart may be used as prepositions as well as adverbs but carry the same implications in either part of speech. Across usually implies extension or passage from one side to the other ⟨this board will not go *across*⟩ ⟨he could not get *across* the river that night⟩ Crossways and crossways stress intersection at right angles and usually suggest a horizontal direction ⟨the stripes run *crosswise*⟩ ⟨the defect lies *crossways* to the grain of the wood⟩ Athwart commonly implies obliquity of direction or intersection at an acute angle ⟨the tree fell *athwart* the road⟩ ⟨on the slopes the shadows lie *athwart*⟩ ⟨in some weaves the filling threads run *athwart* those of the warp⟩
Figuratively, especially with reference to plans, purposes, hopes, *across* and *crosswise* are not always synonymous because they retain and stress their distinguishing implications. Across often implies fulfillment ⟨he was able to get his point *across* to his audience⟩ while crosswise implies contrariety and therefore frustration ⟨everything goes *crosswise* with us tonight⟩

act *n* 1 *action, deed
*Ana* performance, accomplishment, achievement (see corresponding verbs at PERFORM): *feat, exploit
2 statute, law, *bill

act *vb* 1 Act, behave, work, operate, function, react are comparable when used with reference to the way in which a person or thing does what is expected or responds to external influences or circumstances. Act is not only the most general word of this group but also the most general of all English intransitive verbs except those (as *be, exist, belong*) which assert being, a state of being, or relation. Act is therefore used largely in interrogative sentences when knowledge of the specific nature of the action is sought or in declarative sentences with a qualifying adverb, adverbial element, or adjective complement ⟨how did the child *act* when you called him?⟩ ⟨he *acted* as if he were about to cry⟩ ⟨he *acted* frightened⟩ ⟨how should this powder *act* when mixed with water?⟩ ⟨this medicine *acts* as a poison to some persons⟩ **Behave** is widely applied chiefly to persons and their conduct with reference to a standard of what is right or proper or decorous ⟨one must keep one's contracts, and *behave* as persons of honor and breeding should *behave—Rose Macaulay*⟩ However, in or parallel to technical use *behave* often approaches *act* in generality ⟨study how steel *behaves* under stress⟩ ⟨how the thyroid gland *behaves* during emotional excitement⟩ ⟨two men may *behave* like a crowd . . . when their emotions are engaged—*Conrad*⟩ **Work, operate, function** agree in meaning to act in the way that is natural or intended ⟨the Swiss clock had long since ceased to *work—Bennett*⟩ ⟨but she had not thought. Her brain would not *operate—Bennett*⟩ ⟨they have *functioned* as observers rather than participants—*J. M. Brown*⟩ In distinction from one another *work* may, especially when qualified, suggest success or effectiveness ⟨the fact that a theory has actually *worked* is a better recommendation for its soundness than any amount of ingenious dialectic—*Huxley*⟩; *operate* stresses efficient activity rather than achievement except when followed by *on* or *upon* ⟨the revolutionary spirit, ceasing to *operate* in politics—*Macaulay*⟩; *function* implies activity with reference to the accomplishment of the end or office for which a thing exists or is designed ⟨consciousness ceases altogether at death, when the brain no longer *functions—Grant Allen*⟩ ⟨rules of the game which must be observed, if society is to *function* at all—*Galsworthy*⟩ **React**, a word of rapidly shifting implications, is often used as though it were a close synonym of the preceding words, especially of *act* or *behave* ⟨at this threat the civil service *reacted* in the way which is always open to any civil service, under any regime—*C. P. Fitzgerald*⟩ In discriminating use it always suggests recoil or rebound; often more narrowly, but still consistently, it implies reciprocal or counteractive influence or a reverse effect ⟨home and the school *react* (act reciprocally) on each other⟩ ⟨whilst most people's minds succumb to inculcation and environment, a few *react* vigorously: honest and decent people coming from thievish slums, and skeptics and realists from country parsonages —*Shaw*⟩ As a result of use in chemistry and psychology, *react* now often implies a favorable or desired response ⟨children *react* (respond favorably) to kind treatment⟩ **2 Act, play, impersonate** are synonyms when they mean to assume the appearance or role of another person or character. **Act** usually and **play** frequently imply feigning for theatrical representation ⟨*act* Hamlet⟩ ⟨*play* the melancholy Dane⟩ Even the idiom "to *play* one's part" has a theatrical origin and still connotes performance and a contribution to an ensemble. Whether **impersonate** implies simulation for the sake of theatrical representation or for deception can be gathered only from the context ⟨an actor who *impersonates* women⟩ ⟨he was arrested for *impersonating* an officer⟩

**acting** *adj* *temporary, supply, ad interim, provisional

**action 1 Action, act, deed** agree in designating something done or effected. **Action** refers primarily to the process of acting; **act** and **deed** to the result, the thing done. An *action* is usually regarded as occupying some time and involving more than one step; an *act* is more frequently thought of as momentary or instantaneous and as individual ⟨the rescue of a shipwrecked crew is a heroic *action*; the launching of the lifeboat, a brave *act*⟩ ⟨a course of *action*⟩ ⟨the springs of *action*⟩ ⟨an *act* of vengeance⟩

⟨caught in the *act*⟩ In the plural *action* has frequently an ethical connotation and is loosely synonymous with *conduct* ⟨by him [the Lord] *actions* are weighed—*I Sam* 2:3⟩ ⟨only the *actions* of the just smell sweet and blossom in their dust—*Shirley*⟩ **Deed** refers to a thing as done; it invariably presupposes intelligence and responsibility in the agent and therefore often connotes, as *act* does not, illustriousness or achievement ⟨the *deed* is worthy doing —*Shak.*⟩ ⟨what, are my *deeds* forgot?—*Shak.*⟩ ⟨little, nameless, unremembered *acts* of kindness and of love— *Wordsworth*⟩ **Deed** is frequently opposed to *word*, as *act* to *thought* ⟨take the word for the *deed*⟩ ⟨I'll endeavour *deeds* to match these words—*Shak.*⟩ ⟨be great in *act*, as you have been in thought—*Shak.*⟩
*Ana* *process, proceeding, procedure: performance, execution, fulfillment (see corresponding verbs at PERFORM): activity, operation, work, behavior, reaction (see corresponding verbs at ACT)
**2** cause, case, *suit, lawsuit
**3** *battle, engagement
*Ana* combat, conflict, fight, fray, affray, *contest: *encounter, skirmish, brush

**activate 1** energize, *vitalize
*Ana* animate, vivify, *quicken, enliven: *stir, rouse, arouse, rally, awaken
*Ant* arrest
**2 Activate, actuate, motivate** are sometimes confused when used with reference to persons and the motives which govern their actions. They are not interchangeable, however, because they carry divergent denotations. Some external influence or agent, rather than a motive or desire, **activates** a person or thing when it supplies an effective stimulus to activity; the motive or, at least, a latent desire for such activity being commonly presupposed ⟨Kapteyn's work . . . was not final, but it . . . attracted and *activated* others—*G. W. Gray*⟩ A motive, a principle, or a desire **actuates** a person (not an action or undertaking) when it governs or determines his actions ⟨the desire for conquest *actuated* the explorers of the sixteenth century⟩ ⟨individuals *actuated* by economic self-interest—*Bush*⟩ A dramatist or novelist **motivates** the actions of his characters or the incidents of his plot when he supplies the motives for each ⟨the novelist failed to *motivate* adequately his hero's surrender to temptation⟩ Also an objective, a desire, a passion *motivates* or gives the underlying motive of an action or undertaking ⟨ambition *motivated* Macbeth's murder of Duncan⟩
*Ana* stimulate, *provoke, excite, galvanize: spur, goad, induce (see corresponding nouns at MOTIVE): *incite, instigate, foment, abet: drive, impel, *move
*Ant* restrain, inhibit —*Con* curb, check, bridle (see RESTRAIN): thwart, foil, baffle, balk, *frustrate

**active, operative, dynamic, live** are synonyms when they mean being at work or in effective action. **Active** in general may be employed wherever the others are applicable, but it is also usable where none of the others would be appropriate. It may qualify anything that shows its nature or its existence in acts, in action, or in work ⟨an *active* volcano⟩ ⟨an *active* brain⟩ ⟨*active* sympathy⟩ and it is applicable to anything which can be worked, operated, manipulated, or wielded ⟨an *active* pen⟩ ⟨a mine still *active* after fifty years of mining⟩ It is also applicable to an agent, an operator, an instrument, a means or to something accomplished by any such agency ⟨*active* enforcement of the law⟩ ⟨an *active* propagandist⟩ ⟨an *active* search for truth⟩ *Active* may imply little more action or movement or exertion than shown in a state that is not death, rest, or inertness ⟨his pulse is low, but his heart is still *active*⟩ or it may, and usually does, imply vigor and

---

A colon (:) separates groups of words discriminated. An asterisk (*) indicates place of treatment of each group.

energy in action or movement ⟨an *active* market⟩ ⟨an *active* writer⟩ ⟨the *active* stage of a disease⟩ Often it suggests causation or activation ⟨the *active* principle in a drug⟩ In contrast with *active* **operative** is applicable only to things (as a principle, motive, emotion) that have a capacity for acting, working, or effecting ends or to those (as laws) that can be put into operation ⟨when strict ethical principles are *operative* in society, men may expect the millennium⟩ ⟨the rule has been *operative* since January first⟩ *Operative* usually is weaker in its implication of effectiveness; one's sense of duty is *operative* when it in any degree influences one's thoughts or actions; it is *active* when it serves as a spur to action or is the determinant of one's actions. **Dynamic** stresses the realization of the potential in something: it therefore often connotes release of great energy and consequent forcefulness; a *dynamic* personality is one that exhibits great power and exerts a great influence; love is a *dynamic* emotion when it sweeps away all that would obstruct its movement. **Live** is also applicable to persons, personalities, principles, laws, emotions, and motives. It stresses vitality and modernity more than forcibleness and, when used of persons, intelligent awareness of present conditions or needs and progressiveness more than effectiveness ⟨Steve had in him the making of a *live* man of affairs—*Anderson*⟩

*Ana* *agile, nimble, brisk: alert, wide-awake (see WATCHFUL): *busy, industrious, assiduous, diligent: energetic, strenuous, *vigorous

*Ant* inactive —*Con* quiescent, *latent, dormant: inert, idle, supine, passive (see INACTIVE): *lazy, indolent, slothful

**actor,** **player, performer, mummer, mime, mimic, thespian, impersonator, trouper** denote in common one who, for the entertainment or edification of an audience, takes part in an exhibition simulating happenings in real life. An **actor** makes a profession of taking part in such exhibitions (as in the theater or on television) ⟨an ambition to be an *actor*⟩ A **player** acts in a stage play either as a professional or as an amateur ⟨all the world's a stage, and all the men and women merely *players*—*Shak.*⟩ **Performer** is a wider term than the others of this group. It emphasizes actual participation in an exhibition before an audience and may denote not only an actor or player but any public entertainer (as a dancer or musician) ⟨in theatrical speaking, if the *performer* is not exactly proper and graceful, he is utterly ridiculous—*Steele*⟩ **Mummer,** *mime,* and *mimic* may all denote a performer who projects a character by means of body movements, expression, and gesture usually without the use of speech. **Mummer** is used more particularly of comic and amateurish performers or maskers, usually at some festival or holiday celebration ⟨here and there the beat of drums . . . the antics and grimaces of *mummers* held the crowd for a moment before some fantastic festival car—*A. M. Bacon*⟩ When used of the professional actor its connotation is often derogatory ⟨dubbing, that *mummer's* trick with the mouth which has . . . been responsible for an endless succession of vaudeville acts—*Rogow*⟩ **Mime** is used of both the performer and the performance ⟨mime and mimicry are confused in the public mind . . . Chaplin is a *mime,* but those who imitate him are mimics. A *mime* does not copy . . . but invents characters who have their own life . . . quite apart from their creator—*Enters*⟩ and is especially applicable to the stylized gestural language of narrative dance (as ballet) ⟨was a great *mime* and did not follow the then traditional ballet-mime (pantomime), but . . . in ballet gave first-class dramatic performances—*Nicolaeva-Legat*⟩ **Mimic** more particularly stresses imitation and often comic exaggeration of qualities ⟨had accents so grotesque that

not even Molly, an able *mimic,* could copy them—*Stafford*⟩ ⟨*mimic* . . . Entertains by presenting exaggerated imitations—*Dict. of Occupational Titles*⟩ **Thespian** is equivalent in meaning to *actor* but in connotation is often mock-heroic ⟨the gossip columns, where a well-known Silk might yet be observed in solemn conclave with a distinguished *Thespian*—*Wills*⟩ An **impersonator** is a performer who assumes the character of another (as a public figure, a class of persons, an animal) whom he imitates by makeup and in speech and action ⟨a female *impersonator*⟩ ⟨a noted *impersonator* of Abraham Lincoln⟩ A **trouper** is a member of a group and especially a traveling group of actors staging a play or repertory of plays. The term often connotes the seasoning or the sense of obligation to audience and fellow actors that characterizes an experienced actor ⟨no real *trouper* while conscious will ever confess himself too sick to go on—*Ferber*⟩

**actual** *real, true

*Ana* *material, physical, phenomenal, objective: particular (see SPECIAL)

*Ant* ideal: imaginary —*Con* *abstract, transcendent, transcendental: spiritual, divine (see HOLY): *theoretical, speculative, academic: fabulous, *fictitious, mythical

**actuality** *existence, being

*Ana* realization, actualization, materialization, externalization, incarnation (see corresponding verbs at REALIZE): attainment, achievement (see corresponding verbs at REACH)

*Ant* potentiality, possibility —*Con* abstraction, ideality, transcendence (see corresponding adjectives at ABSTRACT)

**actualize** *realize, embody, incarnate, externalize, objectify, materialize, hypostatize, reify

**actuate** 1 *move, drive, impel

*Ana* stimulate, *provoke, excite, galvanize, quicken: *stir, rouse, arouse: energize, activate, *vitalize

2 *activate, motivate

*Ana* influence, *affect, sway: *incline, dispose, predispose: *induce, prevail

*Ant* deter (*with a motive or fear as the subject*) —*Con* *hinder, impede, bar: *restrain, inhibit, curb, check

**acumen** penetration, *discernment, insight, perception, discrimination

*Ana* shrewdness, sagacity, perspicacity, astuteness (see corresponding adjectives at SHREWD): sharpness, keenness, acuteness (see corresponding adjectives at SHARP)

*Ant* obtuseness —*Con* dullness, stupidity, slowness, denseness (see corresponding adjectives at STUPID): blindness, purblindness (see corresponding adjectives at BLIND)

**acute** 1 *sharp, keen

*Ana* *incisive, trenchant, cutting: penetrating, piercing (see ENTER)

*Ant* obtuse —*Con* *dull, blunt: *stupid, slow, dull, crass, dense

2 **Acute, critical, crucial. Acute** most commonly indicates intensification, sometimes rapid, of a situation demanding notice and showing signs of some definite resolution ⟨intimately associated with Indian affairs was the pressing question of defense . . . Pontiac's rebellion made the issue *acute*—*Morison & Commager*⟩ ⟨when the food shortage became *acute* in New Haven, the junior class of Yale College was moved to Glastonbury—*Amer. Guide Series: Conn.*⟩ **Critical** may describe an approach to a crisis or turning point and may imply an imminent outcome or resolution ⟨the war has reached a new *critical* phase . . . we have moved into active and continuing battle—*Roosevelt*⟩ ⟨the *critical* lack of rubber in the last war was finally beaten by the development of synthetic rubber plants capable of turning out ·1,000,000 tons a year—*Collier's Yr. Bk.*⟩ **Crucial** applies to an actual crisis situ-

ation, often one viewed with fear, worry, or suspense, and implies a speedily ensuing decisive or definitive outcome ⟨a continuous evolution, punctuated by the sudden flaming or flowering of a *crucial* moment now and then—*Lowes*⟩ ⟨the next few months are *crucial*. What we do now will affect our American way of life for decades to come—*Truman*⟩ **Ana** culminating, climactic (see corresponding nouns at SUMMIT): *dangerous, hazardous, precarious, perilous: menacing, threatening (see THREATEN): intensified, aggravated (see INTENSIFY)

**adage** *saying, saw, proverb, maxim, motto, epigram, aphorism, apothegm

**adamant, adamantine** obdurate, inexorable, *inflexible **Ana** unyielding, unsubmitting (see affirmative verbs at YIELD): immovable, immobile (see affirmative adjectives at MOVABLE): *grim, implacable, unrelenting **Ant** yielding —**Con** submissive, subdued (see TAME): obliging, complaisant (see AMIABLE): relenting, submitting, capitulating (see YIELD)

**adapt** 1 Adapt, adjust, accommodate, conform, reconcile agree in denoting to bring into correspondence. To **adapt** is to fit or suit to something; it distinctively implies modification to meet new conditions, frequently with the added suggestion of pliability or readiness ⟨he knew how to *adapt* himself. To one correspondent he is gay . . . . To another he is gravely reflective—*Huxley*⟩ To **adjust** is to bring into as close and exact correspondence or harmony as exists between the parts of a mechanism; in contrast with *adapt*, it suggests less of flexibility or tact in the agent and more of ingenuity or calculation ⟨he must divine what men would welcome and shun what men might resent. He must delicately mold and *adjust* the popular will to his own—*Buchan*⟩ **Accommodate** is used in preference to *adjust* when there exists a somewhat marked variance or discrepancy between the objects brought into often superficial or transitory agreement or harmony ⟨man is no lawgiver to nature, he is an absorber. She it is who stands firm; he it is who must *accommodate* himself—*James*⟩ **Accommodate** is used in preference to *adapt* when yielding or compromise is to be suggested ⟨they *accommodate* their counsels to his inclination—*Addison*⟩ To **conform** is to bring into harmony or accordance with a pattern, example, or principle ⟨the liberal . . . does not wish to have to *conform* himself to any program or policy—*Inge*⟩ In current use the reflexive *to conform oneself* is comparatively rare, its place being taken usually by the intransitive *conform* (for another intransitive sense see AGREE) ⟨this officer, as his duties were prescribed by that act, is to *conform* precisely to the will of the president. He is the mere organ by whom that will is communicated—*John Marshall*⟩ Partly because of the association of this word with compulsory legislation regarding religious observances, it often implies compliance or at times slavish acceptance ⟨Mark Twain . . . had *conformed* to a moral regime in which the profoundest of his instincts could not function—*Brooks*⟩ To **reconcile** is to demonstrate to one's own or another's satisfaction the fundamental consistency or congruity of things that are or seem to be incompatible ⟨confidence in her own capacity to *reconcile* conflicting portraits of herself—*Mary Austin*⟩ ⟨the great men among the ancients understood how to *reconcile* manual labor with affairs of state —*Locke*⟩ In reflexive use *reconcile* adds to *adapt* the implication of resignation or of submission ⟨*reconciled* himself to a lonely existence⟩ **Ana** temper, qualify (see MODERATE): acclimatize, acclimate (see HARDEN) **Ant** unfit

2 *edit, rewrite, revise, redact, compile **Ana** fit, *prepare, condition, qualify

**adaptable** pliant, ductile, *plastic, pliable, malleable **Ana** tractable, amenable (see OBEDIENT): supple, flexible, resilient, *elastic **Ant** inadaptable, unadaptable —**Con** intractable, refractory (see UNRULY), unaccommodating, nonconforming, irreconcilable (see affirmative verbs at ADAPT)

**add** 1 Add, sum, total, tot, cast, figure, foot share the meaning to find or represent the amount reached by putting together arithmetically a series of numbers or quantities, and are commonly followed by *up*. **Add** is both the common and the technical word; it commonly implies strict adherence to the traditional arithmetical operation. Even in figurative use it implies a similar operation ⟨taken as a whole the vignettes and the stories *add* up to a single effect—*Aldridge*⟩ ⟨the whole undertime trend *adds* up to a major consideration for businessmen and employees—*Lack*⟩ **Sum** stresses the result attained rather than the method followed. In figurative use *sum up* implies a gathering and consolidation into a new whole, especially for the production of a single telling effect ⟨a lawyer in *summing up* summarizes in brief and logical form the evidence favorable to his case or client that has been given⟩ ⟨I *summed up* all the systems in a phrase and all existence in an epigram—*Wilde*⟩ ⟨values they can *sum up* in a few simple formulas—*Croly*⟩ **Total** tends to replace *sum up* in literal use ⟨determined the cost by *totaling* all expenditures⟩ It may also mean to reach the sum or number of ⟨absences due to colds *totaled* 253 last week⟩ *Tot, cast, figure,* and *foot* are used especially of commercial matters (as accounts and bookkeeping devices). **Tot** and **cast** often imply facility in reckoning ⟨the waiter quickly *totted* the bill⟩ ⟨if you *tot* up all the items that we owed against all the items that foreigners owed us—*Hutton*⟩ ⟨*cast* up an account⟩ **Figure** usually suggests the task or burden involved in reckoning ⟨*figure* the costs of operating an automobile⟩ **Foot** connotes bookkeeping and totals at the bottom of each column of figures ⟨his debts will *foot* up to more than he can ever pay⟩

2 Add, append, annex, subjoin, superadd. Add, the most general of these words, means to join one thing to another thing or to a group, series, or combination of other things so as to increase the original unit in numbers, size, amount ⟨*added* ten books to the library⟩ ⟨a little gossip *adds* spice to the conversation⟩ ⟨police action would *add* nothing to the protection that victims of aggression have enjoyed under the old system—*Wolfers*⟩ One **appends** when one adds something that is supplemental and accessory and does not form an integral part of the principal thing ⟨*append* notes to a book⟩ ⟨the final summary of his views which he enjoyed *appending* to his long-winded discourses—*I. V. Morris*⟩ One **annexes** when one adds something that becomes part of the original whole yet bears usually a subordinate or subsidiary relation to it or suffers loss of identity in the merging ⟨*annex* a codicil to a will⟩ ⟨*annex* conquered territory to the kingdom⟩ One **subjoins** when one adds something under another thing or especially to what has already been said or written ⟨*subjoin* a postscript to a letter⟩ ⟨*subjoin* additional matter in an appendix⟩ One **superadds** when one adds something to what is complete in itself or already at its maximum ⟨the phrase "to paint the lily" means to *superadd* decoration to that which in itself is highly decorative⟩ ⟨the horrors of pestilence *superadded* to the horrors of war⟩ **Ana** *fasten, attach, affix: augment, enlarge, *increase **Ant** subtract, deduct —**Con** lessen, *decrease, dimin-

A colon (:) separates groups of words discriminated. An asterisk (*) indicates place of treatment of each group.

ish, reduce: abstract, *detach

**addendum** supplement, *appendix

**addict** *vb* *habituate, accustom, inure

*Ana* *incline, dispose, predispose, bias: devote, apply, address, *direct

*Ant* wean —*Con* alienate, *estrange: *detach, disengage: disincline, indispose (see affirmative verbs at INCLINE)

**addict** *n* Addict, votary, devotee, habitué designate a person who by habit and strong inclination indulges in something or the pursuit of something. **Addict** implies excessive, continuous, and often compulsive indulgence typically in harmful but sometimes in harmless things ⟨a drug *addict*⟩ ⟨a detective-story *addict*⟩ **Votary** and **devotee** retain some of the implications of their religious senses such as enthusiasm, often amounting to fanaticism, and zeal. They rarely suggest attachment to that which is degrading or debasing but they do not invariably imply attachment to that which is uplifting ⟨a *votary* of science⟩ ⟨a *devotee* of vegetarianism⟩ ⟨any worthy object of study, pursued disinterestedly . . . does not permit its *votary* to be very seriously narrowed by his zeal—*Inge*⟩ **Habitué** implies frequent attendance at a place but it commonly also connotes habitual indulgence in a pleasure ⟨a *habitué* of the theater is a devotee of the drama⟩ ⟨a *habitué* of a gambling house is a gambling addict⟩

**addition,** accretion, increment, accession agree in denoting a thing that serves to increase another in size, amount, or content. **Addition** implies union with something already existing as a whole or as a unit ⟨he built an *addition* to his house last year⟩ ⟨the office boy, a recent *addition* to the staff, was busy with the copying press—*Archibald Marshall*⟩ Sometimes improvement rather than increase is stressed ⟨the paintings were an *addition* to the room⟩ **Accretion** implies attachment from the outside; it may be used of the process as well as of the thing added ⟨a rolled snowball grows by *accretion*⟩ It often suggests additions made to an original body over a considerable period of time ⟨the professional historian, whose aim is exact truth, should brush aside the glittering *accretions* of fiction that have encrusted it—*Grandgent*⟩ Nearly always it implies the addition of unessential or alien matter ⟨all progress in literary style lies in the heroic resolve to cast aside *accretions* and exuberances—*Ellis*⟩ **Increment** usually implies addition bit by bit in consecutive or serial order ⟨the salaries are raised by annual *increments*⟩ ⟨one more wave in the endless ebb and flow of action and reaction, the infinitesimal *increments* of which we call Progress—*Lowes*⟩ Sometimes it signifies increase in value ⟨benefited from an unearned *increment* in the value of his land resulting from growth of the city⟩ **Accession** denotes something acquired that constitutes an addition to contents, holdings, or possessions ⟨recent *accessions* to a library⟩ ⟨the greatest *accession* of positive knowledge has come in our own time—*Inge*⟩

**additive** summative, *cumulative, accumulative

*Ana* aggregative, conglomerative, agglomerative (see corresponding nouns at AGGREGATE): constituent, component, elemental (see corresponding nouns at ELEMENT)

**addle** muddle, *confuse, fuddle, befuddle

*Ana* confound, dumbfound, nonplus, bewilder (see PUZZLE): amaze, flabbergast, astound (see SURPRISE): fluster, flurry, agitate, upset (see DISCOMPOSE)

*Ant* refresh (*mentally*) —*Con* *quicken, enliven, vivify, animate

**address** *vb* 1 *direct, devote, apply

*Ana* bend (see CURVE): appeal, pray, sue, plead (see under PRAYER): aim, point, level (see DIRECT)

2 Address, accost, greet, salute, hail mean to speak to

or less often to write or make a sign to a person in recognition or in order to obtain recognition. **Address** usually implies formality and definite purpose; it also frequently suggests length of speech or communication ⟨*address* a petition to Congress⟩ ⟨how does one *address* a governor?⟩ ⟨it was Franklin, the thick chief mate, who was *addressing* him—*Conrad*⟩ **Accost** adds to *address* the idea of speaking first or without being introduced; it implies absence of formality and often suggests boldness or sometimes evil intent ⟨he *accosted* a passerby and asked for money⟩ ⟨the women . . . were *accosted* by two men who wanted to walk with them—*Anderson*⟩ **Greet** usually implies friendliness, goodwill, or cordiality; it is the precise word when welcoming is to be suggested ⟨the whole town appeared at the station to *greet* them⟩ ⟨my lord, the Mayor of London comes to *greet* you—*Shak.*⟩ **Salute** commonly stresses ceremoniousness or observance of courtesies demanded by custom ⟨the wife of his brother . . . must be *saluted* every day; but his paternal and maternal kinswomen need only be greeted on his return from a journey—*William Jones*⟩ ⟨then I *salute* you with this kingly title: long live Richard, England's royal king —*Shak.*⟩ Specifically *salute* applies to formal or prescribed acts of recognition ⟨the soldier *saluted* his superior officer⟩ ⟨the president was *saluted* with 21 guns⟩ **Hail** implies heartiness, joyousness, and often noisiness ⟨he smiled and nodded and saluted to those who *hailed* him—*Masefield*⟩ It often stresses the idea of calling out especially from a distance ⟨*hail* a cab⟩

*Ana* *speak, talk, converse: court, woo (see INVITE)

**address** *n* 1 *tact, savoir faire, poise

*Ana* dexterity, facility, ease, *readiness: adroitness, cleverness (see corresponding adjectives at CLEVER): graciousness, affability (see corresponding adjectives at GRACIOUS): suavity, urbanity, diplomacy (see corresponding adjectives at SUAVE)

*Ant* maladroitness, gaucherie —*Con* awkwardness, clumsiness, ineptness (see corresponding adjectives at AWKWARD): boorishness, churlishness (see corresponding adjectives under BOOR)

2 *speech, oration, harangue, lecture, talk, sermon, homily

**adduce,** advance, allege, cite may be used interchangeably in the meaning to bring forward by way of explanation, proof, illustration, or demonstration; however, they usually are clearly distinguishable in their implications and in their idiomatic associations. One **adduces** facts, evidence, instances, passages, reasons, arguments when one presents these in support of a contention ⟨at the close of the chapter Aquinas solves an objection *adduced* as damaging evidence against his position—*Clark*⟩ ⟨in the light of the parallels which I have *adduced* the hypothesis appears legitimate—*Frazer*⟩ One **advances** something (as a theory, a proposal, a claim, an argument) that is in itself contentious when one presents it for acceptance or consideration ⟨once or twice psychoanalysts have *advanced* that idea to me as a theoretical possibility— *De Voto*⟩ ⟨if such a proposal was not seriously meant, why was it *advanced* at all?—*Hartmann*⟩ ⟨half a century later when the Bourbon claim to the Spanish succession is *advanced*—*Belloc*⟩ **Allege** may indicate a bringing forward or stating as if needing no proof ⟨younger scholars nevertheless can *allege* a very strong point on their side —*H. M. Jones*⟩ It may on the other hand stress doubt about an assertion or convey a warning about or a disclaimer of responsibility for the truth of matter under discussion ⟨those whose senses are *alleged* to be subject to supernatural impressions—*Le Fanu*⟩ Its participial adjective *alleged*, especially, often serves as a disclaimer of responsibility for the assertion ⟨an *alleged* miracle⟩ ⟨the

---

*Ana* analogous words    *Ant* antonyms    *Con* contrasted words    See also explanatory notes facing page 1

*alleged* thief⟩ ⟨the presence, real or *alleged*, of some hostile group—*Dewey*⟩ One **cites** only something concrete and specific (as a passage from a book or a definite instance) when one adduces it in support of a contention; one *cites* by quoting a passage to give an authority; one *cites* an instance that serves as a precedent or illustration; one *cites* definite facts in support of something (as a claim or proposal) advanced ⟨the very real difficulties of modern physical science originate, in large degree, in the facts just *cited*—*Jeans*⟩
**Ana** *exemplify, illustrate: *remark, comment, commentate, animadvert

**adept** *n* *expert, wizard, artiste, artist, virtuoso
**Ant** bungler  —**Con** dabbler, tyro, *amateur, dilettante: apprentice, *novice, probationer

**adept** *adj* *proficient, skilled, skillful, expert, masterly
**Ana** *conversant, versed: efficient, *effective: *dexterous, adroit, deft: competent, *able, capable, qualified
**Ant** inadept, inept: bungling  —**Con** amateurish, dabbling, dilettantist (see corresponding nouns at AMATEUR): *awkward, clumsy, maladroit

**adhere** *stick, cohere, cling, cleave
**Ana** *fasten, attach, affix: unite, link, combine, *join
**Con** *separate, part, sever, divide: *detach, disengage: disunite, disjoin (see affirmative verbs at JOIN)

**adherence, adhesion** are usually distinguished in current use. In spite of exceptions the tendency prevails to use **adherence** when mental or moral attachment and **adhesion** when physical attachment is implied ⟨they gave their *adherence* to the cause of reform⟩ ⟨the *adhesion* of lung tissues to the pleura⟩ Sometimes, however, *adhesion* is used in place of *adherence* when the writer feels that the physical connotations of the former will add emphasis ⟨the iron force of *adhesion* to the old routine—*Arnold*⟩
**Ant** inadherence, nonadherence

**adherent** *follower, disciple, partisan, satellite, henchman, sectary
**Ana** supporter, upholder, backer, champion (see corresponding verbs at SUPPORT)
**Ant** renegade  —**Con** apostate, recreant (see RENEGADE): deserter, forsaker (see corresponding verbs at ABANDON): adversary, *opponent, antagonist

**adhesion** *adherence
**Ant** nonadhesion, inadhesion

**ad interim** *temporary, provisional, acting, supply
**Ant** permanent

**adjacent, adjoining, contiguous, abutting, tangent, conterminous, juxtaposed** mean being in close proximity. **Adjacent** does not always imply actual contact but it does indicate that nothing of the same kind comes between; *adjacent* lots are in contact, but *adjacent* houses may or may not be ⟨it is not likely that pure accident caused three *adjacent* windows to take a Spanish tone—*Henry Adams*⟩ Objects are **adjoining** when they meet and touch at some line or point of junction ⟨*adjoining* estates⟩ ⟨*adjoining* rooms⟩ **Contiguous** adds to *adjoining* the implication of meeting and touching on one side or a considerable part of one side ⟨streets lined with rows of *contiguous* houses⟩ It may be used figuratively of events as well as of objects ⟨adjacent events need not be *contiguous*; just as there may be stretches of a string which are not occupied by beads, so the child may experience uneventful periods of time —*Jeans*⟩ **Abutting** is usually applied to something that borders on or is in contact with something else, often with the implication of the termination of one thing by the other ⟨land *abutting* on the road⟩ ⟨the north wall, to which *abutting* rooms were added—*Hussey*⟩ **Tangent** implies contact at a single point. Its literal use is chiefly geometrical ⟨a line *tangent* to a curve⟩ but in figurative and espe-

cially in absolute use it often stresses the general apartness rather than the single point of contact ⟨his critics . . . went off at a *tangent*—*Carson*⟩ ⟨horror of the *tangent*, the extreme, the unconventional—*Norman Douglas*⟩ ⟨that moment when a whistle's final blow shall signal the deploy and we disperse alone, and *tangent* to the universe— *Wolff*⟩ Objects are **conterminous** which border on each other or have a common boundary ⟨defending the side of Germany *conterminous* to France—*Lecky*⟩ *Conterminous* applies also to things having the same bounds, limits, or ends ⟨the civil and the ecclesiastical parishes in England are sometimes, but not always, *conterminous*⟩ Things are **juxtaposed** when they are placed side by side ⟨disputes about water rights were almost inevitable between closely *juxtaposed* communities with expanding populations—*Childe*⟩ especially so as to permit comparison or contrast ⟨*juxtaposed* ideas⟩ ⟨opulence wildly *juxtaposed* to unbelievable poverty—*Vanya Oakes*⟩
**Ana** *nearest, next: successive, *consecutive: joining, connecting (see JOIN *vb*)
**Ant** nonadjacent  —**Con** *distant, removed, remote: separated, parted (see SEPARATE *vb*)

**adjoining** *adj* *adjacent, contiguous, abutting, tangent, conterminous, juxtaposed
**Ana** joined, connected (see JOIN *vb*): attached (see FASTEN)
**Ant** detached, disjoined  —**Con** removed, *distant, remote, far

**adjudge** adjudicate, *judge, arbitrate
**Ana** rule, *decide, determine, settle: award, accord, *grant: *allot, assign

**adjudicate** adjudge, *judge, arbitrate
**Ana** determine, settle, rule (see DECIDE)

**adjunct** *n* *appendage, appurtenance, accessory
**Ana** *addition, accretion: appanage (see RIGHT): attachment, affix, fixture (see corresponding verbs at FASTEN)

**adjure** entreat, *beg, beseech, implore, importune, supplicate
**Ana** pray, plead, appeal (see under PRAYER): request, *ask: bid, enjoin, charge, *command

**adjust** 1 Adjust, regulate, fix share the meaning to set right or to rights. **Adjust** implies modification to meet a need. To *adjust* a thing one brings it by some change into its exact or proper position or condition or into its right relationship with other things. One *adjusts* a telescope when one changes the distance between its eyepiece and its object glass so as to bring it into focus; one *adjusts* the temperature of a house when one changes the setting of a thermostat. Often *adjust* implies rectification or correction ⟨*adjust* an error in an account⟩ ⟨*adjust* a loose screw in a machine⟩ ⟨*adjust* spectacles that are not properly centered⟩; frequently it suggests straightening out or settling ⟨*adjust* a difficulty with a neighbor⟩ ⟨*adjust* a claim for insurance⟩ **Regulate**, on the other hand, usually implies the maintenance of something in a desired condition. To *regulate* something (as a mechanism, a device, an organ) one uses or serves as the means of making it work or operate regularly, uniformly, or accurately; thus, one *regulates* a clock when one adjusts its mechanism so that it will keep accurate time ⟨some drugs *regulate* the beat of the heart by slowing it up, others by hastening it, until its rate of speed is normal⟩ One also *regulates* something that is produced or effected by a mechanism or a bodily organ when one uses the means to keep it at a fixed or uniform rate or degree ⟨*regulate* the temperature of the house by setting the thermostat at the desired mark and keeping it there⟩ **Fix** is an informal and imprecise equivalent to these words. It is often used where *adjust* or *regulate* would be more explicit and effective ⟨the optician will

A colon (:) separates groups of words discriminated. An asterisk (*) indicates place of treatment of each group.

*fix* her glasses⟩ ⟨please *fix* the clock⟩ ⟨he will *fix* up matters for us⟩ In distinctive use it implies restoration to good order or a state of repair ⟨these shoes are not worth *fixing*⟩ ⟨*fixed* the leak in the roof⟩
*Ana* rectify, *correct: trim, steady, *stabilize, balance: *order, arrange: align, *line, line up, range
*Ant* derange —*Con* disarrange, *disorder, disturb: upset, *discompose
**2** *adapt, accommodate, conform, reconcile
*Ana* *harmonize, attune: correspond, conform, accord, square (see AGREE)

**adjuvant** *adj* *auxiliary, contributory, ancillary, accessory, subsidiary, subservient
*Ana* aiding, helping, assisting (see HELP *vb*): supporting, upholding, backing (see SUPPORT *vb*): *effective, efficient, efficacious, effectual
*Ant* counteractive —*Con* neutralizing, negativing (see NEUTRALIZE): obstructing, hindering, impeding (see HINDER *vb*)

**administer, dispense** come into comparison because they are used in certain idiomatic phrases, similar in wording but not always equivalent in meaning, such as *administer* justice or *dispense* justice; *administer* a medicine or *dispense* medicine; *administer* a sacrament or *dispense* the Sacrament. Both words imply an acting on the behalf of another in or as if in the capacity of a steward. Distinctively **administer** denotes to manage, supervise, or conduct the affairs of another while **dispense** denotes to deal out in portions or equitably to recipients. These divergent significations are often lost and the words used interchangeably especially when the object of the verb is an abstraction such as justice or charity ⟨the citizens disliked the rule of William on account of the strict justice which he *administered—Freeman*⟩ ⟨these be the sort to *dispense* justice. They know the land and the customs of the land—*Kipling*⟩ In reference to a sacrament *administer* means to perform the rites and duties prescribed for its proper observance and may be used of any of the sacraments; *dispense,* in contrast, is used only of the Eucharist and retains its underlying implication of dealing out in portions. The two words when used in reference to medicine are precisely distinguished. One *administers* a medicine when he gives the prescribed dose directly to the patient; one *dispenses* medicines when he compounds them according to the prescription of the physician. Similarly, one *administers* a blow or a rebuke when he deals it out directly to the individual. *Dispense,* in comparable phrases, retains its implication of distribution; one *dispenses* advice when he metes it out to those who in his opinion need it; one *dispenses* alms when he manages their distribution.

**admiration 1** *wonder, wonderment, amazement
*Ana* astonishment, surprise (see corresponding verbs at SURPRISE): awe, fear, *reverence: rapture, transport, *ecstasy
*Con* indifference, unconcern, aloofness (see corresponding adjectives at INDIFFERENT): boredom, *tedium, ennui
**2** esteem, respect, *regard
*Ana* appreciation (see corresponding verb at APPRECIATE): liking, loving, enjoying (see LIKE): adoration, veneration, reverence, worship (see under REVERE)
*Ant* abhorrence —*Con* loathing, detestation, hate, hatred (see under HATE *vb*)

**admire** esteem, respect, regard (see under REGARD *n*)
*Ana* *appreciate, value, prize, cherish: *revere, reverence, venerate, adore, worship
*Ant* abhor —*Con* *hate, loathe, abominate, detest: *despise, contemn, scorn, disdain

**admission** *admittance
**admit 1** *receive, accept, take
*Ana* allow, permit, suffer (see LET): *harbor, entertain, shelter, lodge, house
*Ant* eject, expel —*Con* *exclude, debar, shut out: bar, obstruct, block, *hinder
**2** *acknowledge, own, confess, avow
*Ana* concede, *grant, allow: *assent, acquiesce, agree, subscribe: divulge, disclose, *reveal
*Ant* gainsay: disdain —*Con* *deny, contradict, negative
**3** *enter, introduce
*Ana* induct, *initiate, install: *introduce, insert, interject, interpose
*Ant* exclude —*Con* debar, shut out (see EXCLUDE): expel, *eject, oust

**admittance, admission.** Admittance is mostly confined to the literal sense of allowing one to enter a locality or building ⟨no *admittance* without a pass⟩ ⟨*admittance* to the grounds⟩ Admission has acquired the figurative sense of admitting to rights, privileges, standing, membership ⟨his *admission* to the club⟩ ⟨*admission* of new words into the language⟩ When entrance into a building or a locality carries with it certain privileges, *admission* rather than *admittance* is used ⟨*admission* to a theater⟩ ⟨the *admission* of aliens into a country⟩

**admixture 1** *mixture, composite, blend, compound, amalgam
**2** Admixture, alloy, adulterant are comparable when they denote an added ingredient that destroys the purity or genuineness of a substance. Admixture suggests the addition of the foreign or the nonessential ⟨pure Indian without any *admixture* of white blood⟩ ⟨love with an *admixture* of selfishness⟩ ⟨comic verses with an occasional *admixture* of mild bawdry—*Cowie*⟩ Alloy derives its figurative implication of an addition that detracts from the value or perfection of a thing from an old literal application to a base metal added to a precious metal to give it hardness ⟨there's no fortune so good, but it has its *alloy*—*Bacon*⟩ ⟨he had his *alloy*, like other people, of ambition and selfishness—*Rose Macaulay*⟩ Adulterant, both literally and figuratively, implies the addition of something that debases or impairs a thing without markedly affecting its appearance. Consequently it usually implies the intent to deceive ⟨interests . . . trying to upgrade consumer thinking on wool by classifying the new textile fibers as *adulterants—F. A. Adams*⟩ ⟨piety without any *adulterant* of hypocrisy⟩
*Ana* *addition, accretion: *touch, suggestion, streak, dash, spice, tinge, smack, shade: infusion, suffusion, leaven (see corresponding verbs at INFUSE)

**admonish** chide, *reprove, reproach, rebuke, reprimand
*Ana* *warn, forewarn, caution: counsel, advise (see under ADVICE *n*): *criticize, reprehend, reprobate
*Ant* commend —*Con* *approve: applaud, compliment (see COMMEND)

**ado** fuss, pother, flurry, bustle, *stir
*Ana* trouble, pains, exertion, *effort
*Con* quietness, stillness, silence (see corresponding adjectives at STILL): calm, serenity, tranquillity (see corresponding adjectives at CALM)

**adolescence** *youth, puberty, pubescence
*Ant* senescence

**adopt, embrace, espouse** mean in common to make one's own what in some fashion one owes to another. One **adopts** something of which one is not the begetter, inventor, or author or which is not one's own naturally ⟨*adopt* the style of Swinburne⟩ ⟨*adopt* the British pronunciation of a word⟩ ⟨the Ralstons gave up old customs reluctantly,

---

*Ana* analogous words    *Ant* antonyms    *Con* contrasted words    See also explanatory notes facing page 1

but once they had *adopted* a new one they found it impossible to understand why everyone else did not immediately do likewise—*Wharton*⟩ **Embrace** implies willingness to accept or it may suggest eager or joyful acceptance ⟨*embrace* an opportunity⟩ ⟨*embrace* Christianity⟩ ⟨she *embraced* with ardor the fantastic ideal of the cleaning up of England—*Rose Macaulay*⟩ One **espouses** that to which one attaches oneself as closely as to a wife, giving it support or sharing the same fortunes and participating in the same experiences ⟨*espouse* a friend's quarrel⟩ ⟨the spirit of uncompromising individualism that would eventually *espouse* the principle of democracy in church and state—*Parrington*⟩
*Ana* appropriate, *arrogate, usurp: *assume, affect
*Ant* repudiate: discard —*Con* reject, spurn (see DECLINE): renounce, forswear, *abjure

**adoration** worship, veneration, reverence (see under REVERE)
*Ana* *honor, homage, obeisance: praise, laud, extolling (see corresponding verbs at PRAISE)
*Ant* blasphemy —*Con* execration, cursing (see corresponding verbs at EXECRATE): *profanation, desecration, sacrilege

**adore** 1 worship, venerate, *revere, reverence
*Ana* laud, *praise, extol: *exalt, magnify
*Ant* blaspheme —*Con* *execrate, curse
2 **Adore, worship, idolize** in their nonreligious senses mean to love or admire excessively. **Adore** commonly implies emotional surrender to the charms or attractions of an object of love or admiration; it often connotes extreme adulation if the object of love is a person ⟨this inability . . . to project his personality is a serious weakness in a country which likes to *adore* its leaders—*Doty*⟩ With other objects it may connote no more than a hearty liking ⟨like gourmets and yellow flies, sows *adore* eating truffles —*Lauber*⟩ **Worship** usually implies more extravagant admiration or more servile attentions than *adore*; it also commonly connotes an awareness of one's own inferiority or of one's distance from the object of one's love ⟨he *worships* his wife⟩ ⟨small boys who *worship* astronauts⟩ **Idolize** often implies absurdly excessive admiration or doting love ⟨*idolizing* money in life and poetry—*New School Bulletin*⟩ Sometimes, however, it comes very close to *adore* ⟨a spoiled child is often one that has been *idolized* by his parents⟩
*Ana* love, dote (see LIKE): admire, esteem (see under REGARD *n*)
*Ant* detest —*Con* *hate, loathe, abhor, abominate: *despise, scorn, contemn, disdain

**adorn, decorate, ornament, embellish, beautify, deck, bedeck, garnish** mean to add something unessential in order to enhance the appearance. These words and especially the first five are often used interchangeably; certain distinctions, however, are apparent in precise use especially when the subject of the verb is the thing that enhances rather than the agent or enhancer. An element that **adorns** not only serves to heighten the beauty of its background or setting but also is beautiful in itself ⟨few nobler poems have *adorned* our time—*Quiller-Couch*⟩ ⟨the simplicity with which great composers *adorn* their works—*Braithwaite*⟩ One that **decorates** relieves the plainness or monotony of a background by contributing beauty of color or design to it ⟨the walls are yet to be *decorated*⟩ ⟨the use of inlaying in *decorating* furniture⟩ Something **ornaments** when it is an adjunct or an accessory which sets off a thing to advantage ⟨whose bridle was *ornamented* with silver bells—*Scott*⟩ ⟨a doorway *ornamented* with pillars⟩ **Embellish** more often suggests the act of an agent than the effect of a thing. One who *embellishes* modifies his ma-

terial, especially by adding adventitious or sometimes gaudy or fictitious ornament for the sake of effect ⟨*embellishes* his style with imagery⟩ ⟨feats of virtuosity . . . with which she *embellished* the usual routine of the role —*Sargeant*⟩ **Embellish** often suggests disregard for truth ⟨that theme is then expertly *embellished* by the Communists to prove that Wall Street is on the warpath against the Kremlin—*Fischer*⟩ One that **beautifies** either enhances the beauty of something or counterbalances its plainness or ugliness ⟨an embankment swathed and *beautified* by clambering roses⟩ ⟨the eternal orbs that *beautify* the night—*Shelley*⟩ One that **decks** or **bedecks** contributes to the gaiety, splendor, or, especially in the case of *bedeck*, showiness of appearance ⟨*bedeck* oneself with jewels⟩ ⟨*decking* with liquid pearl the bladed grass—*Shak.*⟩ ⟨he likes to *deck* out his little person in splendor and fine colors—*Thackeray*⟩ One **garnishes** something when one gives it the final touch of order or ornament in preparation for use or service ⟨the drawing room was empty, swept and *garnished*, waiting for the next bout—*Panter-Downes*⟩ The word is used especially in cookery ⟨*garnish* a broiled fish with lemon slices and chopped parsley⟩
*Ana* enhance, heighten, *intensify
*Ant* disfigure —*Con* *deface: mar, spoil, impair, *injure: *deform, distort, contort

**adroit** 1 *dexterous, deft, handy
*Ana* *agile, nimble: expert, masterly, adept, skillful, skilled, *proficient: effortless, smooth, facile, *easy
*Ant* maladroit —*Con* clumsy, *awkward, inept
2 *clever, cunning, ingenious
*Ana* *shrewd, astute, perspicacious: *intelligent, quick-witted, smart: artful, crafty (see SLY)
*Ant* stolid —*Con* *impassive, apathetic, phlegmatic: *stupid, slow, dull, dense

**adulation** flattery, *compliment
*Ana* praise, laud (see corresponding verbs at PRAISE): *applause, acclaim: fulsomeness, unctuousness (see corresponding adjectives at FULSOME)
*Ant* abuse —*Con* obloquy, vituperation (see ABUSE): censure, condemnation, reprobation, criticism (see corresponding verbs at CRITICIZE)

**adult** *adj* *mature, grown-up, matured, ripe, mellow
*Ana* developed, ripened, aged (see MATURE *vb*)
*Ant* juvenile: puerile —*Con* *youthful, boyish, virgin, virginal, maiden: adolescent, pubescent (see corresponding nouns at YOUTH)

**adulterant** *n* *admixture, alloy

**adulterate, sophisticate, load, weight, doctor** mean to alter fraudulently especially for profit. **Adulterate,** the usual and technical term, especially when used with reference to foodstuffs and drugs, implies either the admixture of ingredients of similar appearance to increase the bulk or of a harmful substance as a preservative or as a restorer or improver of appearance ⟨*adulterate* maple syrup with beet-sugar syrup⟩ ⟨lime juice *adulterated* with five percent sulfuric acid, jellies with formaldehyde, peas with copper—*Heiser*⟩ In its extended use *adulterate* implies spuriousness or loss of purity; such implications come out strongly in *unadulterated,* which is the equivalent of *pure* and *sheer* in their hyperbolic senses ⟨that book is *unadulterated* trash⟩ In meaning **sophisticate** is essentially identical with *adulterate* but its use is restricted almost entirely to raw drug and essential oil trade ⟨rose oil is *sophisticated* with geraniol—*Shreve*⟩ **Load** implies the admixture of something to add weight whether as an adulterant or in the normal course of manufacture ⟨numerous adulterants have been used to *load* tea to increase its weight— *Ukers*⟩ ⟨most kinds of paper are *loaded* in some way or other . . . . The process . . . was first practiced . . . to save pulp . . . but it was found that restricted quantities of loadings improved the paper—*Jennett*⟩ **Weight** is used interchangeably with *load* but is applied more especially to textiles ⟨silk *weighted* with salts of tin⟩ **Doctor** implies tampering sometimes by adulteration but more often by alterations or falsifications which give an illusion of genuineness, of superior quality, or of great value ⟨*doctoring* poor wine with essences and brandy⟩ ⟨*doctored* his accounts to hide his thefts⟩

*Ana* *debase, vitiate, corrupt: pollute, defile, taint (see CONTAMINATE)

*Ant* refine (*sugar, oil*) —*Con* *improve, better

**adultery, fornication, incest** designate forms of illicit sexual intercourse which are clearly distinguished in legal use, both civil and ecclesiastical. **Adultery** implies unfaithfulness to one's spouse, and therefore can be applied only to sexual intercourse on the part of a married man with a woman other than his wife, or of a married woman with a man other than her husband. **Fornication** designates sexual intercourse on the part of an unmarried person; when occurring between a married and an unmarried person, the former is involved in *adultery* and the latter in *fornication*. **Incest** designates sexual intercourse between persons so closely related that their marriage is prohibited by church or state and usually by both.

*Ana* unfaithfulness, inconstancy, untrueness (see affirmative adjectives at FAITHFUL): infidelity, disloyalty (see affirmative nouns at FIDELITY)

**adumbrate** *suggest, shadow

*Ana* symbolize, typify, emblematize (see corresponding nouns at SYMBOL): signify, denote, *mean

**adumbration** shadow, umbra, penumbra, *shade, umbrage

*Ana* *symbol, type, emblem: *sign, token, symptom, note: hint, suggestion, intimation (see corresponding verbs at SUGGEST)

*Ant* revelation —*Con* disclosure, revealing, divulging, discovering (see corresponding verbs at REVEAL)

**advance** *vb* **1 Advance, promote, forward, further** all mean to move or put ahead, but they come into comparison chiefly when they imply help in moving or putting (something) ahead. **Advance** usually implies effective assistance, as in hastening a process ⟨the warm rains greatly *advanced* the spring crops⟩ or in bringing about a desired end ⟨the pact should *advance* peace among nations⟩ or in exalting or elevating a person, especially in rank or in power ⟨Ahasuerus . . . *advanced* him . . . above all the princes —*Esth* 3:1⟩ The implication of moving ahead is dominant in **promote** when the word means to advance in grade or rank, especially in a predetermined order ⟨*promote* a pupil to the next grade in school⟩ ⟨*promote* a member of a college faculty from associate professor to full professor⟩ When the dominant implication is assistance, *promote* may suggest open backing or support ⟨the objects for which a corporation is created are universally such as the government wishes to *promote*—*John Marshall*⟩ It may, especially when the subject names a person, his influence, or his acts, imply actual advance by encouraging or fostering ⟨a sound forest economy *promotes* the prosperity of agriculture and rural life—*Gustafson*⟩ It may, when said of a thing such as a practice, a policy, a habit, imply subservience to an end that may not be intended ⟨the habit of regarding the language of poetry as something dissociated from personal emotion . . . was *promoted* by the writing of Greek and Latin verse in school —*Babbitt*⟩ In one or two collocations **forward** implies not assistance but effective carrying out ⟨*forward* a shipment by express⟩ ⟨please *forward* all letters during my absence⟩ In its more common sense *forward* is often not clearly distinguishable from *advance*, except that it

is seldom if ever used with reference to persons ⟨Marie de Médicis had advanced Marillac by marrying him to one of her maids of honor . . . yet . . . she only *forwarded* the marriage because she wanted to do the girl a favor—*Belloc*⟩ **Further,** less than any other word in this group, implies movement ahead and, perhaps more than any other, emphasizes the assistance given, especially in the removing of obstacles, either to a person in an undertaking or to the project he undertakes ⟨her sole object . . . was to *further* him, not as an artist but as a popular success—*Brooks*⟩ ⟨bodies like the French Academy have such power for promoting it [genius], that the general advance of the human spirit is perhaps, on the whole, rather *furthered* than impeded by their existence—*Arnold*⟩

*Ana* *help, aid, assist: hasten, accelerate, quicken, *speed: elevate, raise, *lift

*Ant* retard: check —*Con* *hinder, impede: *restrain, curb: *arrest: *delay, slow

**2 Advance, progress** both as intransitive verbs and as nouns share the meaning to move (or movement) forward in space, in time, or in approach to a material or ideal objective. They are often employed interchangeably; however there are instances in which one is preferable to the other. **Advance** only may be used when a concrete instance is signified; though one may say that at a given time science made no *advance* (or *progress*), one must say that there were no *advances* (not *progresses*) in science at that time. *Advance* is preferable to *progress* when the context implies movement ahead such as that of an army marching to its objective, the distance traveled, or the rate of traveling ⟨bullish sentiment regained fervor . . . and stock prices *advanced* sharply—*N. Y. Times*⟩ ⟨there are some . . . who picture to themselves religion as retreating . . . before the victorious *advance* of science—*Inge*⟩ ⟨boll weevil . . . may have existed in Mexico . . . for centuries . . . it *advanced* north and east at the rate of about 100 miles per year—*Harlow*⟩ **Progress** usually carries implications derived from earlier meanings of a process, a circuit, or a cycle, and so is preferable to *advance* when the movement forward involves these implications, as by suggesting a normal course, growth, or development ⟨the trial is *progressing*⟩ ⟨moon . . . begins . . . her rosy *progress*—*Milton*⟩ ⟨[summer] oft, delighted, stops to trace the *progress* of the spiky blade—*Burns*⟩ Sometimes the word without losing these implications carries additional connotations and often stresses development through a series of steps or stages, each marking a definite change ⟨it would be . . . a dull world that developed without break of continuity; it would surely be a mad world that *progressed* by leaps alone—*Lowes*⟩ ⟨the *progress* of an artist is a continual self-sacrifice, a continual extinction of personality—*T. S. Eliot*⟩ *Progress* is the preferable word when development with improvement is implied ⟨there was a general belief in inevitable and universal *progress*—*Berger*⟩

*Ana* develop, *mature: *intensify, heighten

*Ant* recede —*Con* retreat, retrograde (see RECEDE): retire, withdraw (see GO)

**3** *adduce, allege, cite

*Ana* *offer, present, proffer: propose (see corresponding noun at PROPOSAL): broach, *express, air

**advance** *n* **1** progress (see under ADVANCE *vb* 2)

*Ana* *development, evolution: improvement, betterment (see corresponding verbs at IMPROVE)

*Ant* recession, retrogression —*Con* retrograding, retreating (see RECEDE)

**2** *overture, approach, tender, bid

*Ana* *proposal, proposition: offer, proffer (see corresponding verbs at OFFER)

---

*Ana* analogous words    *Ant* antonyms    *Con* contrasted words    See also explanatory notes facing page 1

**advanced** 1 forward, precocious, *premature, untimely *Ant* backward —*Con* retrogressive, retrograde, regressive (see BACKWARD)

2 radical, *liberal, progressive *Ana* daring, venturesome, *adventurous *Ant* conservative

**advancement, preferment, promotion, elevation** designate the act of raising a person in grade, rank, or dignity, or the honor that comes to one who is so raised. **Advancement** is the general term of widest application ⟨lose all hope of *advancement*⟩ **Preferment** especially in older use often comes close to *advancement* ⟨'tis the curse of service, *preferment* goes by letter and affection, and not by old gradation, where each second stood heir to the first—*Shak.*⟩ It now more often implies choice, especially from a series of candidates or possibilities ⟨a military record was the surest road to military *preferment* among vigorous frontiersmen—*Coulter*⟩ ⟨obedience spelled *preferment* in the civil service—*Schumpeter*⟩ **Promotion**, usually but not invariably, implies gradation or raising according to a fixed plan, often involving the passing of tests or the meeting of qualifications. It is the specific word in education to designate the end-of-the-term advance of pupils to a higher grade or in any field where members of a force or staff are given positions of higher rank with increased remuneration. **Elevation** is applicable only when the advancement carries marked increase in honor or dignity ⟨the prime minister's *elevation* to the peerage⟩ ⟨the bishop's *elevation* to the cardinalate⟩ ⟨the many men of talent who owed their *elevation* to Wolsey —*Froude*⟩

*Ant* degradation: reduction (*in rank or status*)

**advantage** 1 Advantage, handicap, allowance, odds, edge denote a factor or set of factors in a competition or rivalry giving one person or side a position of superiority over the other. **Advantage** is the general term, and implies superiority of any kind ⟨the adult, with trained powers, has an immense *advantage* over the child in the acquisition of information—*Eliot*⟩ A **handicap** is something, typically an artificial advantage, designed to equalize competition; thus, in golf, the *handicap* assigned a player is the difference between the average of a certain number of his best scores and par for the course; for instance, if the player's best-score average is 75 and par is 72, his *handicap* is 3, and when he plays in a *handicap* match the player is allowed to deduct three strokes from his total score. An **allowance** is an advantageous handicap stated as a deduction of some sort. In horse racing an *allowance* is a deduction from the weight that the rules require a horse to carry, granted to a horse considered to be at a disadvantage. **Odds** usually implies a material advantage as in strength, numbers, or resources. It is often used of such an advantage possessed by the opposite side ⟨managed to beat the *odds* against him—*O'Leary*⟩ ⟨the peculiarly British quality . . . of sticking out against *odds* —*Contemporary Review*⟩ *Advantage* is often stated as a difference, *odds* as a ratio ⟨one boxer has an *advantage* of ten pounds in weight⟩ ⟨one army has *odds* of two to one over the other⟩ *Odds* may also denote an equalizing concession made to an inferior competitor; it then differs from *handicap* and *allowance* in that the concession is made by the superior competitor and not assigned by a third party ⟨each side feels that it cannot allow any *odds* to the other—*Bryce*⟩ **Edge** may be an equivalent of *advantage* or *odds* but usually implies a slight but decisive superiority ⟨here we have the *edge* on our rivals, not only because of our superior location, but also because we are reputedly reckless about reducing prices —*Publishers' Weekly*⟩

*Ana* preeminence, superlativeness (see corresponding adjectives at SUPREME): *supremacy, ascendancy *Ant* disadvantage: handicap (*in extended sense*) —*Con* *obstacle, obstruction, impediment, bar

2 *use, service, account, profit, avail *Ana* improvement, betterment (see corresponding verbs at IMPROVE): enhancement, heightening (see corresponding verbs at INTENSIFY): benefit (see corresponding verb at BENEFIT) *Ant* detriment —*Con* harm, hurt, damage, *injury

**advantageous** beneficial, profitable *Ana* *expedient, advisable: useful, utilitarian (see corresponding nouns at USE) *Ant* disadvantageous —*Con* detrimental, deleterious (see PERNICIOUS): harmful, hurtful, injurious (see corresponding nouns at INJURY)

**advent** *arrival *Ana* coming, arriving (see COME): approaching, nearing (see APPROACH *vb*): appearing, emerging (see APPEAR) *Ant* leaving, passing

**adventitious** *accidental, incidental, fortuitous, casual, contingent *Ana* acquired (see GET): accessory, subservient (see AUXILIARY) *Ant* inherent —*Con* constitutional, essential, intrinsic, ingrained (see INHERENT): *innate, inborn, inbred

**adventure, enterprise, quest** denote an undertaking, an exploit, or an experience involving hazards and requiring boldness. **Adventure** so stresses the excitement or thrills associated with the encountering of risks or hardships that the word is applicable either to the event or to its emotional effect ⟨seek *adventures* for *adventure's* sake⟩ *Adventure* tends to emphasize the pleasurable excitement induced by newness and strangeness as much as that induced by perils or difficulties ⟨the thirst for *adventure* . . . a war, a crusade, a gold mine, a new country, speak to the imagination and offer . . . play to the confined powers —*Emerson*⟩ ⟨why fear death? Death is only a beautiful *adventure*—*Frohman*⟩ **Enterprise** is applied to an undertaking rather than an experience or to the spirit required for such an undertaking. As distinguished from *adventure* it implies arduousness in the undertaking and initiative, resourcefulness, and sustained energy in the one who carries it through ⟨ripe for exploits and mighty *enterprises* —*Shak.*⟩ ⟨fresh news is got only by *enterprise* and expense —*Justice Holmes*⟩ ⟨the nurse of manly sentiment and heroic *enterprise* is gone—*Burke*⟩ **Quest** is used chiefly in poetry or elevated phrases to suggest days of chivalry and romantic adventure and implies a search or pursuit, always of something elusive and often unattainable ⟨the *quest* of the Holy Grail⟩ *Ana* exploit, *feat, achievement: hazard, peril, risk (see DANGER)

**adventurous, venturesome, daring, daredevil, rash, reckless, foolhardy** denote in common courting danger or exposing oneself to danger in a greater degree than is required for courage. One who is **adventurous** is inclined to adventure; the word may or may not imply indiscretion or imprudence in incurring risk or hazard ⟨a mind active, ambitious, and *adventurous* . . . always aspiring—*Johnson*⟩ ⟨*adventurous* boys . . . climbed, shouting and laughing, over the rafters—*Anderson*⟩ **Venturesome** frequently implies an excessive tendency to take chances ⟨in 1919 Alcock and Brown undertook the first and highly *venturesome* crossing of the Atlantic by air—*Manchester Guardian*⟩ **Daring** heightens the implication of fearlessness ⟨a *daring* pilot in extremity, pleased with the danger, when the waves went high—*Dryden*⟩ **Daredevil** implies ostentation in daring and is often specifically applied to

A colon (:) separates groups of words discriminated. An asterisk (*) indicates place of treatment of each group.

stunts performed for hire as a public spectacle or to their performers ⟨a *daredevil* acrobat⟩ **Rash** implies imprudent hastiness or boldness in word or action; **reckless,** utter heedlessness or carelessness of consequences ⟨we must detain him . . . . If we do not I am convinced Austin will do something *rash* that he will for ever repent—*Meredith*⟩ ⟨a *reckless* disregard of the future⟩ ⟨*reckless* audacity came to be considered courage—*Derek Patmore*⟩ **Foolhardy** implies a foolish daring or recklessness and may be used of persons or of their acts ⟨the perfectly *foolhardy* feat of swimming the flood—*Sinclair Lewis*⟩
*Ana* audacious, bold, intrepid, doughty (see BRAVE): aspiring, panting (see AIM *vb*): *ambitious, emulous
*Ant* unadventurous: cautious

**adversary** *opponent, antagonist
*Ana* assailant, attacker, assaulter (see corresponding verbs at ATTACK): *enemy, foe: competitor, rival (see corresponding verbs at RIVAL)
*Ant* ally —*Con* colleague, *partner: supporter, champion, backer, upholder (see corresponding verbs at SUPPORT)

**adverse** 1 Adverse, antagonistic, counter, counteractive mean so opposed as to cause interference, often harmful or fatal interference. All four may be applied to one thing that comes into conflict with another ⟨an *adverse* policy⟩ ⟨an *adverse* wind had so delayed him that his cargo brought but half its proper price—*Lowell*⟩ ⟨an *antagonistic* associate⟩ ⟨a *counter* proposal⟩ ⟨a *counteractive* agency⟩ Only *antagonistic, counter,* and, occasionally, *counteractive* are used to express mutual or reciprocal opposition ⟨*antagonistic* principles⟩ ⟨*counter* currents⟩ ⟨*counteractive* poisons⟩ Despite their common ground of meaning, each of these four words has distinct implications which limit its applicability and greatly increase its expressiveness. **Adverse** conveys so strongly the idea of unfavorable or unpropitious opposition that it often means harmful or fatal ⟨*adverse* criticism⟩ ⟨*adverse* fortune⟩ ⟨a spirit *adverse* to the existence of democracy⟩ **Antagonistic** usually implies hostility and also, when mutual opposition is suggested, incompatibility or even irreconcilability ⟨neighboring races are often *antagonistic*⟩ ⟨the *antagonistic* principles of aristocracy and democracy —*Parrington*⟩ ⟨some sociologists believe that the welfare of the individual and the welfare of society are *antagonistic* aims⟩ **Counter,** which usually denotes acting, moving, or proceeding from the opposite side or from opposite sides, does not necessarily connote hostility but it does imply inevitable contact, with either resulting conflict or tension ⟨whirlpools are usually caused by *counter* currents in a stream⟩ ⟨the *counter* influences of authority and freedom in shaping the character of youth⟩ **Counteractive,** on the other hand, invariably implies the destruction or nullification of the thing or things opposed ⟨prescribing physicians must know the *counteractive* effects of certain medicines on others⟩ ⟨in the training of delinquents a bad influence is dealt with by the introduction of a *counteractive* good influence⟩
*Ana* harmful, hurtful, injurious (see corresponding nouns at INJURY): hindering, impeding, obstructing (see HINDER *vb*): detrimental, deleterious, *pernicious: fatal, *deadly
*Ant* propitious —*Con* auspicious, *favorable, benign: *beneficial, advantageous
2 Adverse, averse are in origin and in common use contrasted rather than synonymous terms, though they are occasionally used as though similar in meaning. **Adverse** implies opposition that interferes and it is applied to the thing that stands in the way of one's progress or success ⟨the leader would tolerate no *adverse* opinions among his followers⟩ **Averse** implies repugnance in the person

opposed to a thing rather than a quality in the thing which is opposed ⟨the leader is *averse* to all independence of opinion among his followers⟩ However they are sometimes used as synonyms with only this distinction, that *adverse* is chiefly referred to opinion or intention and *averse* to feeling and inclination ⟨I . . . hope that our periodical judges will not be very *adverse* to me, and that perhaps they may even favor me—*Cowper*⟩ ⟨the writer of critical studies . . . has to mediate between the author whom he loves and the public, who are certainly indifferent and frequently *averse*—*Stevenson*⟩ ⟨what cat's *averse* to fish—*Gray*⟩

**adversity** *misfortune, mischance, mishap
*Ana* *trial, tribulation, affliction: *distress, misery, suffering: *poverty, privation, indigence, destitution
*Ant* prosperity —*Con* felicity, *happiness, bliss: ease, comfort (see REST): wealth, affluence, opulence, richness (see corresponding adjectives at RICH)

**advert** 1 Advert, revert are sometimes confused because of a similar basic meaning when they are used in reference to discourse or contemplation. **Advert** denotes to turn from the point, topic, or incident under consideration in order to take up another. It sometimes suggests an unconscious or an illogical break in the chain of thought, but in highly discriminating use may still retain its primary implication of heeding or taking notice ⟨we are but too apt to consider things in the state in which we find them, without sufficiently *adverting* to the causes by which they have been produced—*Burke*⟩ ⟨the distinction . . . will be rendered more apparent by *adverting* to that provision in the second section . . . of the constitution—*John Marshall*⟩ **Revert** adds to *advert* the implication of return either consciously or unconsciously to a point or topic already discussed or previously in one's mind ⟨he now drops this idea, and *reverts* to his reasoning on death—*Goldsmith*⟩
2 *refer, allude
*Ana* remark, notice, note, observe (see SEE)
*Con* ignore, disregard, overlook, *neglect

**advertise** publish, announce, proclaim, broadcast, promulgate, *declare
*Ana* report, recount, *relate: *communicate, impart
*Con* *suppress, repress: conceal, *hide, bury

**advertisement** publication, announcement, broadcasting, proclamation, promulgation, declaration (see under DECLARE)
*Ana* *publicity, ballyhoo, promotion, propaganda

**advice** 1 Advice, counsel and their corresponding verbs **advise, counsel** denote recommendation or to make a recommendation as to a decision or a course of conduct. **Advice** and **advise** imply real or pretended knowledge or experience, often professional or technical, on the part of the one who advises and may apply to any of the affairs of life ⟨*advice* regarding the choice of books⟩ ⟨the extension specialist assists and *advises* the farmers⟩ ⟨legal *advice*⟩ **Counsel** often stresses the fruit of wisdom or deliberation, and presupposes weightier occasions than *advice* or more authority or a closer personal relationship in the one who counsels ⟨I do in friendship *counsel* you to leave this place—*Shak.*⟩ ⟨seek *counsel* in affairs of state⟩ The noun sometimes suggests instruction or advice of a lofty or ideal character ⟨the Christian *counsel* of perfection⟩
*Ana* admonition (see corresponding verb at REPROVE): warning, forewarning, cautioning (see WARN): instruction, teaching (see corresponding verbs at TEACH)
2 intelligence, *news, tidings

**advisable** *expedient, politic
*Ana* prudent, *wise, sensible: *beneficial, advantageous, profitable: practical, *practicable

---

*Ana* analogous words    *Ant* antonyms    *Con* contrasted words    See also explanatory notes facing page 1

*Ant* inadvisable

**advise** 1 counsel (see under ADVICE 1)
*Ana* admonish (see REPROVE): *warn, forewarn, caution: *induce, persuade
*Con* consult, *confer, advise
2 consult, *confer, commune, parley, treat, negotiate
*Ana* *discuss, debate, argue: converse, talk (see SPEAK): deliberate (see THINK)
*Con* counsel (see under ADVICE 1)
3 notify, *inform, apprise, acquaint
*Ana* tell, disclose, *reveal: *communicate (with), impart (to)

**advised** *deliberate, considered, premeditated, designed, studied

**advocate** *n* *lawyer, counselor, barrister, counsel, attorney, solicitor

**advocate** *vb* *support, uphold, champion, back
*Ana* defend, justify, vindicate, *maintain: espouse (see ADOPT): promote, forward, *advance
*Ant* impugn  —*Con* assail, *attack: combat, oppose, fight (see RESIST)

**aeon** age, era, epoch, *period

**aerate, ventilate, oxygenate, carbonate. Aerate** is the general term and interchangeable in certain phrases with any of the others; the last three are specific terms which are not freely interchangeable with each other. *Aerate* means to supply or impregnate with air or to expose to the action of air. It frequently implies a mechanical process ⟨*aerate* soil by plowing⟩ ⟨*aerate* sewage by agitation in fresh air⟩ It sometimes, however, implies a natural process ⟨the blood is *aerated* in the lungs⟩ **Ventilate** is commonly used when exposure to air especially in large quantities with the object of purifying, freshening, or cooling is implied ⟨*ventilate* a room by opening windows⟩ ⟨*ventilate* an engine by means of holes in its covering⟩ ⟨the patient is unable adequately to *ventilate* himself with air because air cannot be easily drawn through the air passages, the caliber of which has been diminished by the disease—*Science*⟩ It may be indistinguishable from *aerate* when applied to the blood but usually suggests rather the exposure to air and *aerate* the resulting gaseous exchange. More exact than either in this relation is **oxygenate** since it is the oxygen in the air that is required by the blood. Technically *aerate* and **carbonate** are not synonyms, for the latter means to impregnate with carbon dioxide but they may overlap when *aerate* is used broadly with the meaning to impregnate with a gas; hence, *aerate* or especially *aerated* is used in certain designations (as *aerated* water or *aerated* bread) where *carbonated* would correctly describe the process.

**aerial** *adj* *airy, ethereal
*Ana* immaterial, incorporeal (see MATERIAL): impalpable, *imperceptible, imponderable

**aeronautics, aviation** have to do with the operation of aircraft. **Aeronautics** is primarily a science dealing with the operation of any kind of aircraft ⟨engineers specializing in *aeronautics*⟩ **Aviation** is an art, science, or practice concerned with the operation of heavier-than-air aircraft ⟨skill in *aviation* develops only when theoretical knowledge is supplemented by practical experience⟩ Unlike *aeronautics* it has extended use in which it may denote aircraft or their manufacture, development, and design ⟨his *aviation* had sunk or damaged 52 . . . vessels—*Newsweek*⟩ ⟨recent advances in American *aviation*⟩

**aesthete, dilettante, connoisseur** all designate a person conspicuous for his enjoyment and appreciation of the beautiful, the exquisite, or the choice. **Aesthete** implies highly developed sensibilities, with acute delight in beauty of color, line, sound, and texture, and violent distaste for the ugly, shapeless, and discordant ⟨no woman could walk down the street without risk of having her hat torn off . . . by some *aesthete* who happened to think it unbecoming—*Shaw*⟩ ⟨that mystical synthetic sense, of which the modern *aesthete* dreams,—the sense that sees, hears, tastes, smells, touches, all in one—*Babbitt*⟩ It often carries derogatory connotations of absurdity, extravagance, decadence, or effeminacy ⟨it was perhaps natural for a man who had had to fight his way . . . to a recognized position in scholarly literature to be irritated by the poses of comfortable *aesthetes*—*Renwick*⟩ **Dilettante** stresses the attitude of the lover of art as distinguished from that of the creative artist. Though its application to amateurs who were neither thoroughly familiar with the technique of their particular form of art nor seriously seeking for mastery, it acquired connotations of desultoriness, dabbling, and superficiality ⟨he is a mere *dilettante*⟩ However, it may apply to one who pursues an art or studies it merely for his own delight ⟨he would always be by nature a contemplative and a *dilettante*; but he had had high things to contemplate, great things to delight in—*Wharton*⟩ ⟨a generalization with which I find myself (with all the diffidence of an unlearned *dilettante*) disagreeing—*Huxley*⟩ **Connoisseur** like *dilettante* implies high appreciation of the beautiful in art; unlike it, it implies scholarly knowledge and trained taste. Because of the latter implication *connoisseur* is applied not only to one who knows a work of art when he sees it but also to one who recognizes superiority in other things governed by taste (as foods, wine, or gems). In this relation the word often comes close to *epicure* in its meaning. It is also applied to collectors of beautiful things ⟨supposing also that the material of his Apologia was . . . defunct . . . who but a few discerning *connoisseurs* of style would ever read that book now or a century hence?—*T.S. Eliot*⟩ ⟨he has found time to make himself a *connoisseur* of porcelains, one of the most esoteric of collectors' hobbies—*Heiser*⟩

**aesthetic** *artistic
*Ant* unaesthetic

**affable** *gracious, cordial, genial, sociable
*Ana* courteous, polite (see CIVIL): open, candid, *frank: *amiable, obliging, complaisant: *talkative, loquacious: *suave, urbane
*Ant* reserved  —*Con* uncommunicative, taciturn, reticent, *silent: curt, brusque (see BLUFF): surly, glum, crabbed (see SULLEN)

**affair** 1 **Affair, business, concern, matter, thing** come into comparison only when they are little more than vague or general terms meaning something done or dealt with. Some or rarely all are used interchangeably in certain similar collocations such as his own *affair, business, concern;* public and private *affairs, concerns, matters, business;* a sorry *affair, business, matter, thing; affairs, matters, things* are in good condition. However, a degree of precision is possible, for each word carries distinctive implications which are not always obscured. **Affair** suggests action or performance; it may imply a process, an operation, a proceeding, an undertaking, a transaction ⟨seeing a book through the press is a laborious and time-wasting *affair*—*T. H. Huxley*⟩ In the plural it often denotes transactions of great importance such as those involved in the management of finances or in the carrying on of diplomatic negotiations ⟨men of *affairs*⟩ ⟨he had married a rich woman and administered her *affairs*. He was not supposed . . . to have any *affairs* of his own—*Mary Austin*⟩ **Business** usually stresses duty or office; sometimes it suggests an imposed task ⟨because a Thing is every Body's *Business*, it is no Body's *Business*—*Steele*⟩ ⟨the flight of his imagination is very swift: the following of it often a breath-

---

A colon (:) separates groups of words discriminated. An asterisk (*) indicates place of treatment of each group.

less *business—Day Lewis*⟩ **Concern** suggests personal or direct relationship: it often implies an important bearing on one's welfare, success, or interests; thus, something is not one's *concern* because it has no bearing on one's interests, welfare, or success ⟨the simplest way out of the difficulty was to do nothing and dismiss the matter as no *concern* of theirs—*Conrad*⟩ Sometimes *concern* is preferred to *affair* when that which requires attention involves a degree of anxiety or solicitude ⟨the *concerns* of state⟩ **Matter** usually is more objective as well as more vague than the preceding words. It generally refers to something that is merely an object of consideration or that is to be dealt with ⟨he will attend to these *matters* very soon⟩ ⟨this is still one *matter* in dispute⟩ ⟨never insist without carrying the *matter* through—*Russell*⟩ **Thing** is even more indefinite than *matter* and is often intentionally used when there is a desire to be vague or inexplicit ⟨he promised that *things* would be better in the future⟩ ⟨first *things* should come first⟩ ⟨more *things* are wrought by prayer than this world dreams of—*Tennyson*⟩ ⟨these *things* are managed so well in France—*Harte*⟩
2 *amour, intrigue, liaison

**affect** simulate, *assume, pretend, feign, counterfeit, sham
**affect** 1 **Affect, influence, touch, impress, strike, sway** are more or less closely synonymous when they mean to produce or to have an effect upon a person or upon a thing capable of a reaction. **Affect** always presupposes a stimulus powerful enough to evoke a response or elicit a reaction ⟨our eardrums are *affected* by ten octaves, at most, out of the endless range of sounds—*Jeans*⟩ ⟨even changes of season *affect* the townsman very little—*Huxley*⟩ Often, in addition, *affect* implies a definite alteration or modification ⟨I am afraid . . . that this adventure has rather *affected* your admiration of her fine eyes—*Austen*⟩ When the object of the verb is a person, an intellectual or emotional effect is usually implied ⟨such poetry *affects* one as trite and meaningless⟩ ⟨the sight *affected* her to tears⟩ **Influence** always presupposes an agent that moves a person or thing in some way or to some degree from a course, or effects changes in nature, character, or behavior ⟨the judge was never *influenced* in his decisions by his sympathies or prejudices⟩ ⟨the body *influences* the mind and the mind the body⟩ ⟨the Society of Friends had been *influenced* by Quietism, and adversely affected by the paralyzing rationalism of the reigns of the first two Georges—*Inge*⟩ Sometimes the implication of inducing, or inciting, or persuading, or even bribing is strong ⟨monomaniacs, having first persuaded themselves, contrive to *influence* their neighbors—*Meredith*⟩ **Touch** frequently equals *affect*, but it often carries a more vivid suggestion of close contact or of the force of an impact, and therefore variously connotes stirring, arousing, or harming ⟨he was for the first time powerfully *touched* by the presence of a woman—*Anderson*⟩ ⟨a small object whose exquisite workmanship has *touched* me with its intimate charm—*J. S. Untermeyer*⟩ **Touch**, most often, but *impress* and *strike* always, imply a mental or emotional effect. **Impress** usually stresses the depth and the lastingness of the effect, for something that impresses is commonly what is remembered or noticed or is worth remembering or noticing ⟨only one of the speeches that evening *impressed* him⟩ ⟨the men he wanted to *impress* were only amused—*Anderson*⟩ **Strike** is often felt to be more colloquial than *impress* and less rich in its suggestions ⟨a hat that *struck* her fancy⟩ However *strike* connotes suddenness or sharpness of response rather than depth of impression; it may even carry a hint of a swift passing ⟨the remark *struck* him as extremely acute⟩ ⟨they *strike* mine eyes, but not my heart—*Ben Jonson*⟩ **Sway**, which basically means to influence,

differs from the latter word in implying both the pressure or control of some force that is either not resisted or is in itself irresistible, and resulting change or fluctuation in character, opinions, or decisions of the person concerned ⟨the notion . . . of capricious deities, *swayed* by human passions and desires, was incompatible with the idea of fixed law—*Dickinson*⟩ ⟨other conditions than those of classroom have *swayed* him for good or evil—*Suzzallo*⟩ ⟨he is *swayed* by fashion, by suggestion, by transient moods—*Mencken*⟩
*Ana* *move, actuate, drive, impel: pierce, penetrate (see ENTER): *thrill, electrify
2 *concern
3 **Affect, effect** are often a source of difficulty because both verbs imply the production of an effect and take as their corresponding noun the same word, *effect*. **Affect**, the verb (see AFFECT 1), distinctively implies the action or operation of an agency rather than of an agent; it therefore means to influence ⟨moisture *affects* steel⟩ ⟨high prices *affect* our pocketbooks⟩ ⟨the climate *affected* his health⟩ **Effect**, the verb (see PERFORM), implies the achievement of an end in view, and requires as its subject an intelligent agent or the means he uses to attain his end: it therefore means to bring about ⟨the prisoners *effected* their escape⟩ ⟨the new system of accounting will *effect* a reduction in costs⟩ Since the noun *effect* may be applied to any result whether brought about unconsciously or consciously, it serves equally well whether it names a result of the influence of one thing upon another or of directed effort.

**affectation** *pose, air, mannerism
*Ana* *pretense, pretension: pretentiousness, ostentation (see corresponding adjectives at SHOWY)
*Ant* artlessness —*Con* naturalness, simplicity, ingenuousness, naïveté, unsophistication (see corresponding adjectives at NATURAL)
**affecting** *adj* touching, *moving, pathetic, poignant, impressive
*Ana* stirring, rousing, rallying (see STIR *vb*): distressing, troubling (see TROUBLE *vb*): *pitiful, piteous, pitiable
**affection** 1 *feeling, emotion, passion, sentiment
*Ana* propensity, *leaning, penchant: *predilection, bias: inclination, disposition (see corresponding verbs at INCLINE)
*Ant* antipathy —*Con* aversion (see ANTIPATHY): *hate, hatred
2 love, *attachment
*Ana* devotion, piety, *fidelity: liking, doting, enjoying (see LIKE *vb*): tenderness, warmth, sympathy (see corresponding adjectives at TENDER)
*Ant* coldness —*Con* coolness, frigidity (see corresponding adjectives at COLD): hate, detestation, hatred, abhorrence (see under HATE *vb*)
**affection** *disease, disorder, condition, ailment, malady, complaint, distemper, syndrome
*Ana* attack, access, paroxysm (see FIT): disorder, derangement (see corresponding verbs at DISORDER)
**affectionate** *loving, devoted, fond, doting
*Ana* ardent, fervent, passionate (see IMPASSIONED): *tender, sympathetic, warm
*Ant* cold: undemonstrative —*Con* apathetic, *impassive, stolid
**affidavit** deposition, testimony, *evidence
**affiliated** allied, *related, kindred, cognate
*Ana* dependent, *subordinate
*Ant* unaffiliated —*Con* independent, *free, autonomous
**affinity** 1 *attraction, sympathy
*Con* repugnance, repellency *or* repulsion, abhorrence (see corresponding adjectives at REPUGNANT): *antipathy,

*Ana* analogous words  *Ant* antonyms  *Con* contrasted words  See also explanatory notes facing page 1

aversion

**2** resemblance, *likeness, similarity, similitude, analogy
*Ana* agreement, conformity, correspondence, accord (see corresponding verbs at AGREE)

**affirm** profess, aver, avow, protest, avouch, declare, *assert, warrant, predicate
*Ana* attest, *certify, vouch, witness: state (see RELATE)
*Ant* deny —*Con* contradict, negative, traverse, gainsay (see DENY): dispute, debate (see DISCUSS)

**affirmative, positive** cause difficulties in their extended use, since each term has *negative* for its opposite and since both words may qualify identical or similar nouns. The distinctions are not clearly fixed, but tendencies in usage may be noted. In general **affirmative** implies denial as its opposite, and **positive** implies negation, or the absence of truth, reality, or actuality as its opposite. Something that is not *affirmative* may be destructive; something that is not *positive* may be null, nonexistent, or nugatory. Hence, an *affirmative* philosophy either affirms accepted principles or establishes new ones, and so is opposed to *negative* philosophies (as skepticism and nihilism). A *positive* philosophy (this often equals *positivism*) deduces its principles from something that is evident to the senses or is from the commonsense point of view regarded as real and factual. Metaphysics is from the positivist's point of view a *negative* philosophy. An investigation has an *affirmative* result when it confirms the hypothesis of the investigator; it has a *positive* result if something definite is discovered, whether the result proves or disproves the hypothesis. A person may be said to exercise an *affirmative* influence when he strengthens or improves something that exists or develops something better to take its place; he may be said to exert a *positive* influence when he affects others in definite concrete ways. A defeatist may exert a very *positive* influence which cannot be described as *affirmative;* an optimist's attitude is *affirmative,* but it often fails to exert a *positive* influence.
*Ana* *effective, effectual, efficacious
*Ant* negative —*Con* destroying, demolishing (see DESTROY): abolishing, annihilating, extinguishing (see ABOLISH)

**affix** *vb* *fasten, attach, fix
*Ana* append, *add, subjoin, annex: *stick, adhere
*Ant* detach —*Con* disengage (see DETACH)

**afflatus** *inspiration, fury, frenzy

**afflict, try, torment, torture, rack** mean to inflict upon a person something which he finds hard to bear. Something or someone that causes pain, disability, suffering, acute annoyance, irritation, or embarrassment may be said to **afflict** a person ⟨*afflicted* with heart disease⟩ ⟨blindness *afflicts* many aged persons⟩ ⟨she is *afflicted* with shyness⟩ ⟨he who *afflicts* me knows what I can bear—*Wordsworth*⟩ An affliction or a person or thing that imposes a strain upon one's physical or spiritual powers of endurance or tests one's stamina or self-control may be said to **try** a person, his body, his soul, or his character ⟨a *trying* situation⟩ ⟨his *trying* temper⟩ ⟨the great heat of the sun and the heat of hard labor . . . *try* the body and weaken the digestion—*Jefferies*⟩ An affliction or a person or thing that persecutes and causes continued or repeated acute suffering or annoyance may be said to **torment** one ⟨recurrent stomach pains *torment* him⟩ ⟨other epochs had been *tormented* by the misery of existence and the terror of the unknown—*Glicksberg*⟩ ⟨the horses are *tormented* by flies⟩ ⟨the older boys . . . bullied and *tormented* and corrupted the younger boys— *H. G. Wells*⟩ An affliction or a person or thing that severely torments one physically or mentally and causes pain or suffering under which one writhes may be said to **torture** one ⟨*torture* prisoners of war⟩ ⟨an idea of what a pulsating sciatica can do in the way of *torturing* its victim—*Bennett*⟩ ⟨the unseen grief that swells with silence in the *tortured* soul—*Shak.*⟩ A person or, especially, a thing (often a painful emotion or disease) that pulls or seems to pull one this way and that beyond endurance and in a manner suggestive of the excruciating straining and wrenching of the body on the rack, an ancient instrument of torture, may be said to **rack** a person ⟨*racked* with pain⟩ ⟨he is *racked* by doubts of his friend's loyalty⟩ ⟨vaunting aloud, but *racked* with deep despair—*Milton*⟩ ⟨how on earth can you *rack* and harry . . . a man for his losings, when you are fond of his wife, and live in the same station with him?—*Kipling*⟩
*Ana* *worry, annoy, harass, harry, plague, pester: vex, bother, irk (see ANNOY): distress, *trouble, ail
*Ant* comfort —*Con* console, solace (see COMFORT): delight, gladden, rejoice, *please

**affliction** visitation, *trial, tribulation, cross
*Ana* adversity, *misfortune, mischance, mishap: *distress, suffering, misery, agony: anguish, *sorrow, grief, woe, heartbreak
*Ant* solace, consolation —*Con* relief, assuagement, alleviation (see corresponding verbs at RELIEVE): joy, delight, *pleasure

**affluent** wealthy, *rich, opulent
*Ana* possessing, owning, holding, having, enjoying (see HAVE): acquisitive (see COVETOUS)
*Ant* impecunious: straitened —*Con* indigent, penurious, destitute, poor (see corresponding nouns at POVERTY): impoverished, bankrupt (see DEPLETE)

**afford** *give, confer, bestow, present, donate
*Ana* *offer, proffer: *furnish: *grant, accord
*Ant* deny (*something one wants, asks, hopes for*) —*Con* withhold, hold, hold back (see KEEP): refuse, *decline

**affray** *n* fray, fight, combat, conflict, *contest
*Ana* *brawl, row, fracas, melee, rumpus: *encounter, skirmish, brush: dispute, *argument, controversy

**affray** *vb* *frighten, fright, affright, scare, alarm, terrify, terrorize, startle
*Ana, Ant, Con* (see those at AFFRIGHT)

**affright** *vb* *frighten, fright, affray, scare, alarm, terrify, terrorize, startle
*Ana* daunt, horrify, appall, *dismay: cow, *intimidate, bulldoze: confound, bewilder (see PUZZLE)
*Ant* nerve, embolden —*Con* animate, fire, inspire (see INFORM)

**affront** *vb* *offend, outrage, insult
*Ana* slight, ignore, *neglect: nettle, peeve, provoke, *irritate
*Ant* gratify (*by an attention*) —*Con* humor, *indulge, pamper: flatter, compliment (see corresponding nouns at COMPLIMENT)

**affront** *n* Affront, insult, indignity denote a speech or an action having for its intention or effect the dishonoring of something (as a person, a cause, or an institution). An **affront** is a designed and usually an open mark of disrespect ⟨an *affront* to the flag⟩ ⟨an old *affront* will stir the heart through years of rankling pain—*Ingelow*⟩ An **insult** is a personal attack, either by words or actions, meant to humiliate or degrade ⟨it is incredible the *insult* made to the liberty, to the life, to the dignity of the human beings, by other human beings—*Vanzetti*⟩ An **indignity** is an outrage upon one's personal dignity ⟨whom I beseech to give me ample satisfaction for these deep shames and great *indignities*—*Shak.*⟩ ⟨to nearly all men serfdom was . . . a degrading thing, and they found trenchant phrases to describe the *indignity* of the condition—*Southern*⟩
*Ana* slighting, ignoring, overlooking, neglecting (see NEGLECT *vb*): offending, outraging (see OFFEND *vb*): im-

---

A colon (:) separates groups of words discriminated. An asterisk (*) indicates place of treatment of each group.

pudence, brazenness (see corresponding adjectives at SHAMELESS)

*Ant* gratification —*Con* deference, *honor, homage: adulation, *compliment, flattery

**afraid** *fearful, apprehensive

*Ana* alarmed, scared (see FRIGHTEN): timorous, *timid

*Ant* unafraid: sanguine —*Con* *cool, composed, imperturbable, collected: *confident, assured, sure

**aft** *abaft, astern

*Ana* *after, behind: rear, back, *posterior, hind

*Ant* fore —*Con* *before, ahead, forward

**after** *prep, adj, adv* **After, behind** are synonymous adverbs, prepositions, and adjectives when they mean following upon, especially in place or in time. They are rarely interchangeable, however, without a loss of precision. With reference to place **after** usually implies order of movement or sequence and characteristically goes with verbs or nouns implying motion ⟨the faculty marched in pairs, one *after* another⟩ So used, *after* not only conveys no suggestion of precedence in order of following, but it may, by stressing pursuit, even obscure its common implication of succession; to run *after* a person is to attempt to overtake him. When, as often happens, *after* is used with verbs of rest, the implication of movement or sequence is rarely lost but is transferred to the object or is to be gathered from the context; one stays *after* the others (who have left); one calls *after* a person (who is walking ahead); one looks *after* the children of a friend (who is away, ill, or engaged). In the same connection **behind** characteristically implies a position at the back of something at rest ⟨the chair is *behind* the door⟩ ⟨the men seated themselves *behind* the women⟩ ⟨the garden is *behind* the house⟩ When, however, the reference is to something moving, *behind* usually adds the implications of delay, lagging, or immobility; to run *behind* another is to be outstripped; to be left *behind* is to be outstripped or to remain when others have departed.

With reference to time, **after** is in far more frequent use than *behind* and is the required choice when only subsequence is implied ⟨who ruled *after* James I?⟩ ⟨*after* one o'clock no one may leave the room⟩ When **behind** is used in this connection, it usually implies a time when someone or something is due according to a schedule, a system, or a normal order of progression. Consequently it implies variously lateness, backwardness, or falling in arrears ⟨you are two hours *behind* schedule⟩ ⟨theory often runs *behind* practice⟩

*Ana* *abaft, aft, astern

*Ant* before —*Con* forward, ahead (see BEFORE)

**after** *adj* hinder, hind, rear, *posterior, back

*Con* *preceding, antecedent, prior

**aftereffect, aftermath** *effect, result, consequence, upshot, sequel, issue, outcome, event

**age** *n* 1 **Age, senility, senescence, dotage** are comparable when they denote the period in one's life when one is old in years and declining in body or mind or both. **Age** is now usually replaced by *old age* except in literary use ⟨*age* cannot wither her—*Shak.*⟩ ⟨*age,* I make light of it, fear not the sight of it—*Higginson*⟩ **Senility** adds to *age* the implication of decay, especially of mental decay ⟨rheumy old man, crumpled together . . . his mind gone down the road to *senility*—*Roberts*⟩ **Senescence** designates the period or the process of the decline which results in senility or old age; it is in the life of the individual the antithesis of youth or adolescence. **Dotage,** even more than *senility,* implies the childishness or mental decline of age and thus indirectly heightens the suggestion of extreme old age ⟨old Daniel begins; he stops short—and his eye, through the lost look of *dotage,* is cunning and sly—*Wordsworth*⟩

*Ant* youth

2 *period, era, epoch, aeon

**age** *vb* *mature, ripen, develop

**aged, old, elderly, superannuated** when applied to persons mean far advanced in years. **Aged** implies extreme old age with signs of feebleness or, sometimes, senility ⟨the *aged* creature came, shuffling along with ivory-headed wand—*Keats*⟩ **Old** stresses the years of one's life, but in itself carries no connotations of marked decline ⟨a man, *old,* wrinkled, faded, withered—*Shak.*⟩ **Elderly** may imply no more than that the prime of life has been passed ⟨when you see me again I shall be an old man—that was a slip, I meant to say *elderly*—*J. R. Lowell*⟩ **Superannuated** indicates that one has been retired or pensioned because of having reached a certain age (varying in different callings) ⟨*superannuated* teachers⟩ ⟨*superannuated* judges⟩ Sometimes the word implies merely that one has passed the years of usefulness and with this denotation it is applied to things as well as to persons.

*Ana* infirm, feeble, decrepit (see WEAK)

*Ant* youthful —*Con* juvenile, puerile, boyish, virgin, virginal, maiden (see YOUTHFUL)

**agency** *mean, agent, instrumentality, instrument, medium, vehicle, channel, organ

*Ana* *cause, determinant, antecedent: operation, action, working (see corresponding verbs at ACT): activity (see corresponding adjective ACTIVE): machinery, apparatus, gear, *equipment

**agenda** *program, schedule, timetable

**agent** *n* 1 *mean, instrument, agency, instrumentality, medium, vehicle, organ, channel

*Ana* actor, operator, worker (see corresponding verbs at ACT): activator, energizer (see corresponding verbs at VITALIZE): performer, executor *or* executive (see corresponding verbs at PERFORM)

*Ant* patient

2 **Agent, factor, attorney, deputy, proxy** agree in meaning one who performs the duties of or transacts business for another, but differ in specific application. **Agent** is very general and may be used to express this idea in any context where a specific term is not required; distinctively, however, it often implies the activity of a go-between ⟨ambassadors, ministers, emissaries, nuncios are diplomatic *agents* of their governments or sovereigns⟩ ⟨the heads of departments are the political or confidential *agents* of the executive—*John Marshall*⟩ ⟨let every eye negotiate for itself and trust no *agent*—*Shak.*⟩ **Factor** was once a near equivalent of *agent* but is now chiefly employed as a designation for a commercial agent buying and selling goods for others on commission ⟨wool *factor*⟩ ⟨flour *factor*⟩ It is also used specifically to name the official in charge of a trading post of the Hudson's Bay Company. **Attorney,** now chiefly used as a designation for a professional legal agent (see LAWYER), once was applied to one who performed the personal offices of another who was absent, incapacitated, or unqualified for the work ⟨I will attend my husband, be his nurse . . . for it is my office, and will have no *attorney* but myself—*Shak.*⟩ This sense still survives but in a narrower application to a person legally delegated to transact certain specified business for another who is absent or otherwise disqualified. Such a person is often called (in distinction from an attorney-at-law) a "private attorney" or an "attorney-in-fact," and the power delegated him is called "power of attorney." **Deputy** always implies possession through delegation of some or all of the powers of a superior (as a sovereign or a governmental or business executive). Almost always, also,

---

*Ana* analogous words    *Ant* antonyms    *Con* contrasted words    See also explanatory notes facing page 1

it connotes responsibility to the person whose powers are deputed, rather than to the organization from which these powers ultimately derive ⟨the governor-general of Canada may appoint *deputies* to exercise his powers or functions locally or temporarily⟩ ⟨a vicar-general is a *deputy* of a bishop⟩ **Proxy** implies a substitution of persons when a promise or pledge is solemnly made or a vote, as at a stockholders' meeting, is to be cast. In a marriage service a *proxy* for the bride or groom or in the baptismal service a *proxy* for a godparent merely utters the promises in the name of the absent person, the latter assuming the obligation of fulfilling them.
*Ant* principal

**agglomerate, agglomeration** conglomerate, conglomeration, *aggregate, aggregation
*Ana* combination, association (see corresponding verbs at JOIN): accumulation (see corresponding verb ACCUMULATE): heap, pile, mass (see under HEAP *vb*)

**aggrandize** *exalt, magnify
*Ana* heighten, enhance, aggravate, *intensify: elevate, raise, *lift, boost
*Ant* belittle —*Con* minimize, depreciate, disparage, *decry, detract, derogate

**aggravate** 1 heighten, *intensify, enhance
*Ana* magnify, aggrandize (see EXALT): augment, *increase, multiply, enlarge
*Ant* alleviate —*Con* lighten, mitigate, allay (see RELIEVE): *palliate, extenuate: lessen, reduce, diminish, abate (see DECREASE)
2 exasperate, *irritate, provoke, rile, peeve, nettle
*Ana* perturb, upset, disturb (see DISCOMPOSE): vex, irk, *annoy: *anger, incense, infuriate
*Ant* appease —*Con* *pacify, placate, mollify: tranquilize, calm (see corresponding adjectives at CALM)

**aggregate** *n* 1 *sum, total, whole, number, amount, quantity
*Ant* individual: particular
2 Aggregate, aggregation, conglomerate, conglomeration, agglomerate, agglomeration denote a mass formed by parts or particles that are not merged into each other. **Aggregate** and **aggregation** imply the formation of a whole but without the blending of its constituents ⟨sandstone is a natural *aggregate* of quartz and a cementing substance (as silica or iron oxide)⟩ ⟨we have no communities. Our villages even are apt, rather, to be *aggregations* —*Brownell*⟩ **Conglomerate** and **conglomeration** emphasize the heterogeneousness of the components and often suggest their assemblage from a wide variety of sources; sometimes either is applied to a heap of things, sometimes to an aggregate in which the parts are clearly distinguishable ⟨pantheism is generally a *conglomerate* of animism, poetical fancy, and mysticism—*Inge*⟩ ⟨that *conglomeration* of men we call a nation—*Liddon*⟩ **Agglomerate** and **agglomeration** in general use seldom imply coherence of parts; they suggest either a huddling together or often a fortuitous association ⟨a mere *agglomeration* of different races, without national unity, national aims—*Page*⟩ In geology *agglomerate* designates a rock aggregate composed of irregularly shaped fragments scattered by volcanic explosions as distinguished from *conglomerate*, an aggregate composed of rounded, waterworn stones.
*Ana* union, *unity, integrity: unification, consolidation (see corresponding verbs at COMPACT): complex, *system, organism, network
*Ant* constituent

**aggregation** *aggregate, conglomerate, conglomeration, agglomerate, agglomeration
*Ana & Ant* see those at AGGREGATE 2

**aggression** *attack, offense, offensive
*Ana* *invasion, incursion, raid, inroad
*Ant* resistance

**aggressive** 1 attacking, offensive (see base words at ATTACK *n*)
*Ana* invading, encroaching, trespassing (see TRESPASS *vb*)
*Ant* resisting: repelling
2 Aggressive, militant, assertive, self-assertive, pushing, pushy are here compared as applied to persons, their dispositions, or their behavior, and as meaning conspicuously or obtrusively active or energetic. **Aggressive** implies a disposition to assume or maintain leadership or domination, sometimes by bullying, sometimes by indifference to others' rights, but more often by self-confident and forceful prosecution of one's ends ⟨as intolerant and *aggressive* as any of the traditional satirists—*Day Lewis*⟩ ⟨protect themselves against a too *aggressive* prosecution of the women's business—*Shaw*⟩ **Militant,** like *aggressive,* implies a fighting disposition but seldom conveys a suggestion of self-seeking. It usually implies extreme devotion to some cause, movement, or institution and energetic and often self-sacrificing prosecution of its ends ⟨*militant* feminists⟩ ⟨*militant* trade union⟩ ⟨the cause of reform slowly went on gaining adherents— most of them . . . of the acquiescent rather than the *militant* type—*Grandgent*⟩ **Assertive** stresses self-confidence and boldness in action or, especially, in the expression of one's opinions. It often implies a determined attempt to make oneself or one's influence felt ⟨somewhat too diffident, not *assertive* enough—*Bennett*⟩ ⟨to say, with some challenging *assertive* people, that trees are more beautiful than flowers—*Lucas*⟩ **Self-assertive** usually adds to *assertive* the implication of bumptiousness or undue forwardness ⟨*self-assertive* behavior incompatible with cooperativeness⟩ **Pushing,** when used without any intent to depreciate, comes very close to *aggressive* in the current sense of the latter; however, the word is more commonly derogatory and implies, variously, officiousness, social climbing, or offensive intrusiveness ⟨an energetic, *pushing* youth, already intent on getting on in the world—*Anderson*⟩ **Pushy** is very close in meaning to *pushing* but is more consistently derogatory in connotation ⟨his motive power derives from . . . the *pushiest* ambition since Alexander the Great —*R. L. Taylor*⟩ ⟨careful not to sound *pushy* or over-eager—*McClung*⟩
*Ana* energetic, strenuous,*vigorous: *masterful, domineering, imperious: fighting, combating *or* combative (see corresponding nouns at CONTEST)

**aggrieve** *wrong, oppress, persecute
*Ana* *afflict, try, torment: harass, harry, plague, annoy, *worry: *injure, hurt, harm
*Ant* rejoice —*Con* gladden, delight, *please: *benefit, profit

**agile,** nimble, brisk, spry mean acting or moving with quickness and alacrity. **Agile** implies dexterity and ease in the management of one's limbs or, by extension, one's wits ⟨*agile* as a monkey⟩ ⟨in a flow of racy comment, skimming from one topic to another with an *agile* irrelevance—*Rose Macaulay*⟩ **Nimble** suggests surpassing lightness and swiftness of movement or action, and often implies a darting here and there ⟨*nimble* as a squirrel⟩ ⟨Madame Defarge knitted with *nimble* fingers—*Dickens*⟩ ⟨*nimble* feet scudding over the springy turf—*Webb*⟩ **Brisk** implies liveliness, animation, or vigor of movement ⟨a *brisk* canter⟩ ⟨a *brisk* walking pace⟩ ⟨to have *brisk* and intelligent talk—*Benson*⟩ It is sometimes applied to things that do not move but are invigorating or exhilarating ⟨*brisk* day⟩ ⟨*brisk* reply⟩ ⟨she walked briskly in the

---

A colon (:) separates groups of words discriminated. An asterisk (*) indicates place of treatment of each group.

brisk air—*George Eliot*⟩ **Spry** stresses alacrity arising from vigor or health; however it is frequently applied to those from whom alacrity or briskness of movement is not to be expected ⟨the old lady is as *spry* as a cricket⟩ ⟨she is down one day, and up and *spry* the next⟩
*Ana* *dexterous, adroit, deft: quick, fleet, speedy (see FAST): limber, lithesome, *supple: *lively, sprightly
*Ant* torpid　—*Con* *lethargic, sluggish, comatose: inert, *inactive, passive, supine

**agitate** 1 *shake, rock, convulse
*Ana* *stir, rouse, arouse: *move, actuate, drive, impel
*Ant* quiet, lull, still
2 perturb, *discompose, upset, fluster, flurry, disturb, disquiet
*Ana* *irritate, provoke, rile, exasperate, peeve: *worry, harass, plague: *annoy, vex, irk, bother
*Ant* calm, tranquilize　—*Con* *pacify, placate, appease, mollify
3 argue, dispute, debate, *discuss
*Ana* controvert (see DISPROVE): assail, *attack: *consider: air, ventilate, broach (see EXPRESS)

**agitation** *commotion, tumult, turmoil, turbulence, confusion, convulsion, upheaval
*Ana* *motion, movement: *stir, bustle, ado: disturbance, perturbation, disquiet (see corresponding verbs at DISCOMPOSE)
*Ant* tranquillity

**agnostic** *n* *atheist, deist, freethinker, unbeliever, infidel
**agog** *eager, keen, anxious, avid, athirst
*Ana* excited, galvanized, stimulated (see PROVOKE): roused, aroused, stirred (see STIR *vb*): *impatient, restive
*Ant* aloof　—*Con* *indifferent, unconcerned, incurious, detached, uninterested, disinterested
**agonize** *writhe, squirm
*Ana* suffer, endure, *bear: torment, rack, torture, *afflict
**agonizing** *excruciating, racking
*Ana* torturing, tormenting, racking (see AFFLICT): *intense, vehement, fierce, exquisite, violent
*Con* *comfortable, easy, restful: comforting, solacing, consoling (see COMFORT)
**agony** suffering, passion, *distress, misery, dolor
*Ana* pang, throe, ache, *pain, twinge: *trial, tribulation, affliction, visitation
*Con* *rest, repose, ease, comfort: solace, consolation (see corresponding verbs at COMFORT): relief, assuagement, mitigation (see corresponding verbs at RELIEVE)
**agrarian, agricultural** are sometimes confused because they carry common implications and are used to qualify like terms (as an *agrarian* or an *agricultural* society, an *agrarian* or an *agricultural* crisis, an *agrarian* or an *agricultural* policy). Both terms have reference to land, the conditions under which it is held, and its profitable use. **Agrarian** usually stresses the economic or political issues involved in the ownership of land, in the conditions of tenancy, and in the right of the individual to the profits of his labor on the land ⟨*agrarian* crises were frequent in Ireland in the eighteenth and nineteenth centuries when the issue of tenant rights became acute⟩ **Agricultural** stresses rather the successful and profitable use of land for the production of crops and the breeding of animals ⟨*agricultural* crises are likely to occur when overproduction and a restriction of markets coincide⟩ When, however, agricultural interests are at stake and political action is held to be necessary, a party formed to promote these ends may be called an *agrarian* rather than an *agricultural* party, and a measure advocated as an *agrarian* rather than an *agricultural* measure.
**agree** 1 *assent, accede, consent, acquiesce, subscribe
*Ana* *grant, concede, allow: accept, *receive: admit,

*acknowledge
*Ant* protest (*against*): differ (*with*)　—*Con* *object, kick, expostulate, remonstrate: *demur, balk, jib: oppose, *resist, withstand
2 **Agree, concur, coincide** are comparable when they mean to come into or to be in harmony regarding a matter of opinion or a policy. **Agree** implies unison in thought or a complete accord: even if the context suggests previous discussion, the word usually indicates that argument is ended ⟨this is a point upon which all persons *agree*⟩ ⟨*agree* upon a price⟩ **Concur** usually implies reference to a specific or definite agreement or suggests a thinking, acting, or functioning cooperatively or harmoniously toward a given end or for a particular purpose ⟨for the creation of a masterwork of literature two powers must *concur*, the power of the man and the power of the moment—*Arnold*⟩ **Coincide** implies an agreement amounting to complete identity of opinion. Only occasionally is it used of persons; more frequently opinions, judgments, wishes, or interests *coincide* ⟨I had hoped that our sentiments *coincided*—*Austen*⟩ ⟨private groups whose interests did not *coincide* with national defense—*T. W. Arnold*⟩ Often *coincide* implies an agreement in time of occurrence (less often an agreement in place occupied) and therefore frequently stresses synchronousness of events ⟨the fall of Granada and the discovery of America *coincided*⟩ (see *coincident* under CONTEMPORARY)
*Ana* *unite, cooperate
*Ant* differ: disagree　—*Con* *contend, fight, battle: dispute, argue, debate (see DISCUSS): quarrel, wrangle, squabble, bicker (see under QUARREL *n*)
3 **Agree, square, conform, accord, harmonize, correspond, tally, jibe** mean to exist or go together without conflict or incongruity. One thing **agrees** with another when their comparison or association reveals no discrepancy, no inequality, or no untoward effects ⟨the conclusion *agrees* with the evidence⟩ ⟨the two accounts *agree* in every particular⟩ ⟨pronouns must *agree* with their antecedents in person, number, and gender⟩ One thing **squares** with another when there is exact, almost mathematically exact, agreement between the two ⟨force facts to *square* with a theory⟩ ⟨the corporation must, if it is to survive, *square* itself with the basic beliefs of the American people—*Lindeman*⟩ One thing **conforms** to or with another when there is likeness or agreement in form, in nature, or in essential character ⟨since theology was philosophy's queen, medieval philosophy *conformed* to that system which Augustine employed in his theology—*H. O. Taylor*⟩ ⟨my views of conduct . . . *conform* with what seem to me the implications of my beliefs—*T. S. Eliot*⟩ One thing **accords** with another when there is perfect fitness in the relation or association as in character, spirit, quality, or tone ⟨the speaker's remarks did not *accord* with the sentiments of those who listened to him⟩ ⟨the common doctrine of liberty *accorded* with the passions released by the Revolution—*Parrington*⟩ One thing **harmonizes** with another when, in spite of their real and often marked differences, their combination or juxtaposition produces an agreeable or aesthetic effect ⟨from the waves, sound . . . broke forth *harmonizing* with solitude—*Shelley*⟩ ⟨the need for the United States to *harmonize* its practices in foreign affairs more closely than in the past with its professed ideals—*Dean*⟩ One thing **corresponds** to or with another when, however far apart or however close the two things may be, they belong together because they match each other, complement each other, or answer to each other. Sometimes *correspond* implies agreement ⟨fulfillment seldom *corresponds* to anticipation⟩ ⟨I should never *correspond* to your pattern of a lady—*George Eliot*⟩ Sometimes it implies an analogous

relation ⟨the bird's wing *corresponds* to the human arm⟩ Sometimes it implies commensurateness ⟨incomes do not always *correspond* with the efforts or skill that appear to be involved—*Hobson*⟩ One thing **tallies** with another when the correspondence is so close that they either complement each other or agree with each other ⟨pain and pleasure no more *tally* in our sense than red and green—*Browning*⟩ **Jibe** is sometimes equivalent to *agree*, sometimes to *harmonize*, and sometimes to *accord* ⟨his actions do not *jibe* with his words⟩ ⟨his looks *jibed* with the stage driver's description of him—*Luke Short*⟩
*Ant* differ (*from*) —*Con* negative, counteract, *neutralize: negate, *nullify

**agreeable** grateful, pleasing, *pleasant, gratifying, welcome
*Ana* *comfortable, easy, restful: *delightful, delectable: attractive, charming, alluring (see under ATTRACT)
*Ant* disagreeable —*Con* *repugnant, repellent, obnoxious, distasteful: *hateful, abhorrent, abominable, odious: *offensive, loathsome, repulsive

**agreement, accord, understanding** are comparable chiefly in their political and legal uses. They agree in designating a settlement reached by parties to a dispute or negotiation. All these terms imply concurrence as to what should be done or not done; all imply reconciliation of differences. **Agreement** is the most positive word; it usually implies a final settlement of terms. An *agreement* may or may not be put into writing (as in the form of a contract or treaty); it may or may not be accompanied by a consideration. An **accord** is, in controversies between governments, an informal agreement; use of this term often implies that all details have not yet been settled or that the terms of the agreement are not yet ready for publication, but that the conditions necessary to a final agreement have been fulfilled. In law an *accord* is an agreement between the parties concerned in a case where satisfaction for an injury is demanded. The execution of such an accord bars further litigation. An **understanding** is the least binding of accepted settlements. If the term is used to denote the final stage in a negotiation or in settlement of a dispute, it implies the existence of definite engagements or the exchange of promises, and dependence on the honor of the parties to the agreement for the keeping of such engagements or promises.
*Ana* pact, entente, concordat, convention, cartel (see CONTRACT)

**agricultural** *agrarian

**agriculture, farming, husbandry** mean the science or the business of raising plants and animals useful to man. **Agriculture** is by far the most comprehensive of these terms; in common with *farming* and *husbandry* it implies the cultivation of the soil, the production and harvesting of crops, the care and breeding of livestock; it includes in addition other pursuits that may or may not be connected with farming and husbandry such as horticulture, forestry, dairying, sugar making, and beekeeping. It often stresses the technological as contrasted with the traditional aspects of such activities and may include in varying degrees the preparation of agricultural products for man's use. **Farming,** the term in common use, emphasizes land devoted to the production of crops or animals for the market; it may imply small or extensive holdings, but it usually suggests the inclusion of tilled land bearing crops, of pastureland for cattle, and of meadowland for hay. **Husbandry** usually suggests small holdings and production for the use of a household or community rather than for a distant market. It often suggests more varied employments than farming (as dairying or beekeeping) and often denotes management of a particular branch of farming ⟨animal *husbandry*⟩

**ahead** forward, *before
*Ant* behind —*Con* *after: *abaft, aft, astern

**aid** *vb* *help, assist
*Ana* *support, uphold, back: *relieve, lighten, alleviate, mitigate: abet (see INCITE)
*Ant* injure —*Con* harm, hurt, damage (see INJURE): *hinder, impede, block

**aid** *n* **1** help, assistance (see under HELP *vb*)
*Ana* relief, assuagement, alleviation, mitigation (see corresponding verbs at RELIEVE): *remedy, cure, medicine: support, backing (see SUPPORT *vb*)
*Ant* impediment —*Con* *obstacle, bar, obstruction: restraint, curb, check (see corresponding verbs at RESTRAIN)
**2** *assistant, helper, coadjutor, aide, aide-de-camp

**aide** *assistant, aide-de-camp, coadjutor, helper, aid

**aide-de-camp** aide, *assistant, aid

**ail** *vb* *trouble, distress
*Ana* *afflict, try: *annoy, vex, irk, bother
*Con* *comfort, solace, console: *relieve, assuage, alleviate, mitigate

**ailment** disorder, condition, affection, malady, *disease, complaint, distemper, syndrome

**aim** *vb* **1** point, *direct, level, train, lay
*Ana* bend, *curve, twist
**2 Aim, aspire, pant** all may mean to have as a controlling desire something beyond one's present power of attainment. **Aim** stresses a clearly defined end toward which one's efforts are directed or which one holds as a goal to be reached through endeavor or striving ⟨men *aiming* to advance in life with glory—*Hardy*⟩ ⟨Christianity *aims* at nothing less than absolute truth—*Inge*⟩ ⟨get honor, and keep honor free from flaw, *aim* at still higher honor—*Browning*⟩ **Aspire,** especially when followed by an infinitive, often adds little to *aim* except the suggestion of ambition ⟨those who do not *aspire* to be scholars—*Crothers*⟩ ⟨*aspiring* to be the leader of a nation of third-rate men—*Mencken*⟩ It may, however, imply urgency of longing for something that is high, often too high for attainment ⟨since first my thirsting soul *aspired* to know the secrets of their wondrous world—*Shelley*⟩ ⟨what I *aspired* to be, and was not, comforts me—*Browning*⟩ **Pant** comes into comparison with the other words only in its extended sense of biblical origin ⟨as the hart *panteth* after the water brooks, so *panteth* my soul after thee, O God—*Ps 27:1*⟩ Even more than *aspire* it stresses the fervor of the desire and the remoteness of that which is desired. Sometimes it connotes urgent unsatisfied thirst ⟨more happy, happy love! For ever warm and still to be enjoyed, for ever *panting*, and for ever young—*Keats*⟩ It may also suggest not the gasps of one thirsting but of one toiling upward ⟨[the] Brave, and Good, and Wise, for their high guerdon not in vain have *panted*!—*Wordsworth*⟩
*Ana* *intend, purpose, propose, design: *attempt, essay, endeavor, try

**aim** *n* end, goal, objective, purpose, *intention, object, intent, design
*Ana* aspiration, *ambition: *effort, exertion, pains, trouble

**air** *n* **1 Air, atmosphere, ether, ozone. Air** designates the invisible mixture of gases which surrounds the earth and is the impalpable respirable substance essential to life ⟨the *air* we breathe⟩ or that substance mixed with or contaminated by other substances ⟨perfumed *air*⟩ ⟨smoky *air*⟩ **Atmosphere** designates the layers of air which form the envelope of the earth or a similar gaseous envelope of any celestial body ⟨the *atmosphere* of Mars⟩ It may be applied to the portion of air which permeates a particular place or is in a particular state ⟨the stale *atmosphere* of a

---

A colon (:) separates groups of words discriminated. An asterisk (*) indicates place of treatment of each group.

room⟩ ⟨a superheated *atmosphere*⟩ **Ether** usually suggests a medium more rarefied than air or one far more delicate or subtle formerly held to fill the upper regions or interstellar space. In technical use it also denotes a hypothetical medium for the transmission of transverse waves which is characterized by continuity and extreme tenuity and which permeates all space. Strictly, **ozone** is a triatomic form of oxygen that is a faintly blue pungent irritating gas found especially in the upper levels of the air and used commercially chiefly in disinfection, in oxidation, and in bleaching. In general use it denotes air that is notably pure and refreshing ⟨the fresh crisp *ozone* of morning— *Halsey*⟩

**2** *pose, affectation, mannerism

*Ana* mien, *bearing, port, presence: ostentation, pretentiousness, show (see corresponding adjectives at SHOWY): *art, artifice, craft

**3** *melody, air, tune

**air** *vb* ventilate, vent, utter, voice, *express, broach

*Ana* *reveal, disclose, divulge, tell, discover: publish, proclaim, broadcast, *declare

*Con* *hide, conceal: *suppress, repress

**airport,** airdrome, airfield, airstrip, landing strip, flying field, landing field denote a place where airplanes may take off and land in safety. **Airport** implies a well-marked and lighted nonmilitary place, either on land or water, that is used regularly and provides facilities for sheltering passengers, handling cargo, supplying fuel, making repairs, and housing planes. **Airdrome** is practically synonymous with *airport* but is applied to both civil and military places, connotes the physical installation, and has been largely replaced by *airport*. **Airfield** is used of an open area of land with one or more runways and limited or no facilities for shelter or maintenance of planes. However, in strict usage, *airfield* is applied only to the part of an airport on land where planes land and take off. An **airstrip** is a specially prepared usually hard-surfaced strip of land with few or no facilities for sheltering or maintenance of planes and is often located in an advanced military position or in a remote area for occasional or emergency use. **Landing strip** in one of its meanings is synonymous with *airstrip* and in the other meaning with *runway*. A **flying field** is an airport or military airdrome, but the term is sometimes applied especially to a small airfield for privately owned planes or to a temporary airfield. A **landing field** is a land area clear or cleared of tall trees and other obstructions for flying operations.

**airy,** aerial, ethereal can all mean as light and insubstantial as air. **Airy** seldom suggests a transcendent quality; in its widest sense it implies little more than immateriality ⟨the poet's pen . . . gives to *airy* nothing a local habitation and a name—*Shak.*⟩ When applied to persons, their words, or their manners, it may imply an affectation of grandeur or putting on airs ⟨replied with *airy* condescension⟩ mere affectation of nonchalance ⟨*airy* refusal to take good advice⟩ When used of motion or movements, it suggests lightness and buoyancy ⟨the slight harebell raised its head, elastic from her *airy* tread—*Scott*⟩ **Aerial** in figurative use is found chiefly in poetry where it usually connotes impalpability, extraordinary delicacy, or elusiveness, and is applied to things rather than to persons ⟨mountains . . . fair of aspect, with *aerial* softness clad—*Wordsworth*⟩ ⟨the *aerial* hue of fountain-gazing roses—*Shelley*⟩ ⟨fine and *aerial* distinctions—*Milman*⟩ **Ethereal** implies not the atmosphere surrounding the earth but the rarefied air once believed to fill the heavenly regions and so imputes a celestial or supramundane character to the person or thing it qualifies. Sometimes it suggests an unearthly translucency ⟨fire . . . without heat, flickering a red gold flame . . . *ethe-*

*real* and insubstantial—*Woolf*⟩ ⟨so . . . *ethereal* in appearance with its cloud colors, that . . . even . . . the most beautiful golden shades . . . seemed heavy and dull and dead-looking by comparison—*Hudson*⟩ Sometimes, especially when referred to persons, their words, or their thoughts, it suggests disembodied spirit or apartness from material interests ⟨the *ethereal* quality of Shelley's poetry⟩ ⟨at times he tends to fall into excessive subtlety, to be too vaporous and *ethereal*—*Babbitt*⟩

*Ana* tenuous, rare, *thin: delicate, dainty, exquisite (see CHOICE): light, volatile, frivolous (see corresponding nouns at LIGHTNESS)

*Ant* substantial  —*Con* *massive, massy, bulky, monumental: *material, corporeal, physical: solid, hard, *firm

**aisle** *passage, passageway, ambulatory, corridor

**akin** *like, alike, similar, analogous, comparable, parallel, uniform, identical

*Ana* *related, kindred, cognate, allied: corresponding, agreeing, harmonizing, according, conforming (see AGREE)

*Ant* alien  —*Con* foreign, extraneous (see EXTRINSIC): divergent, disparate, *different

**alacrity** *celerity, legerity

*Ana* eagerness, avidity, anxiety (see corresponding adjectives at EAGER): quickness, promptness, readiness (see corresponding adjectives at QUICK): agility, nimbleness, briskness (see corresponding adjectives at AGILE): expedition, dispatch, *haste

*Ant* languor  —*Con* *lethargy, torpidity, stupor: impassiveness, apathy, stolidity (see under IMPASSIVE): indifference, unconcern, aloofness (see corresponding adjectives at INDIFFERENT)

**alarm** *n* **1** Alarm, tocsin, alert agree in meaning a signal that serves as a call to action or to be on guard especially in a time of imminent danger. **Alarm** is used of any signal that arouses to activity not only troops, but emergency workers (as firemen, policemen); it suggests a sound such as a cry, a pealing of a bell, a beating of drums, or a siren ⟨sound a fire *alarm*⟩ ⟨the dog's barking gave the *alarm*⟩ **Tocsin** may be either an alarm sounded by bells usually from the belfry of a church or, more often, the bells sounding an alarm ⟨the loud *tocsin* tolled their last alarm— *Campbell*⟩ but is used figuratively for any sort of warning of danger. **Alert**, a military term for a signal to be on guard and ready for expected enemy action, is often used for any warning of danger ⟨sirens sounded an air-raid *alert*⟩ ⟨the Weather Bureau issued a tornado *alert* in the early afternoon . . . . The *alert* was cancelled after 5 p.m.— *Springfield Union*⟩ It may also denote the state of readiness called for by the signal or warning or the period during which this is maintained ⟨an abandon-ship *alert* was signaled. Warning for that . . . was to be four blasts of the ships whistle—*Lowell Bennett*⟩ ⟨a peacetime round-the-clock *alert* against surprise aerial attack—*N. Y. Times*⟩ **2** fright, *fear, panic, terror, horror, dismay, dread, consternation, trepidation

*Ana* frightening, scaring, startling (see FRIGHTEN): agitation, perturbation, upset (see corresponding verbs at DISCOMPOSE)

*Ant* assurance: composure  —*Con* calmness, tranquillity, serenity (see corresponding adjectives at CALM): self-possession, self-assurance (see CONFIDENCE): *equanimity, sangfroid

**alarm** *vb* *frighten, fright, scare, startle, terrify, affright, terrorize, affray

*Ana* appall, daunt, horrify, *dismay: *surprise, astound, amaze, astonish

*Ant* assure: relieve  —*Con* *comfort, solace, console

**albeit** although, *though

**alchemy** *magic, thaumaturgy, wizardry, sorcery, witch-

---

*Ana* analogous words     *Ant* antonyms     *Con* contrasted words     See also explanatory notes facing page 1

ery, witchcraft

**alcoholic** n *drunkard, inebriate, dipsomaniac, sot, soak, toper, tosspot, tippler

**alert** adj 1 *watchful, wide-awake, vigilant
Ana *agile, nimble, brisk: wary, circumspect, *cautious
Con heedless, *careless: unconcerned, aloof, detached, *indifferent
2 clever, *intelligent, smart, bright, quick-witted, brilliant, knowing
Ana *sharp, keen, acute: *quick, ready, prompt, apt: *shrewd, perspicacious
Con *languid, lackadaisical, listless: *lethargic, sluggish: *stupid, slow, dull, dense

**alert** n *alarm, tocsin

**alias** n *pseudonym, nom de guerre, incognito, nom de plume, pen name

**alibi** n excuse, pretext, plea, *apology, apologia
Ana explanation, justification, rationalization (see corresponding verbs at EXPLAIN)

**alien** adj foreign, extraneous, *extrinsic
Ana external, exterior, outside (see corresponding adjectives at OUTER): adventitious, incidental, *accidental: *repugnant, repellent, abhorrent: incompatible, incongruous, *inconsonant
Ant akin: assimilable —Con *relevant, material, pertinent, germane: compatible, *consonant, congruous, congenial: kindred, cognate, *related

**alien** n foreigner, *stranger, outlander, outsider, immigrant, émigré
Ant citizen —Con subject, national (see CITIZEN)

**alienate** 1 *transfer, convey, deed
2 *estrange, disaffect, wean
Ana convert, proselyte or proselytize (see corresponding nouns at CONVERT): *separate, part, sever, sunder, divorce
Ant unite: reunite —Con reconcile, conform, accommodate, adjust, *adapt: associate, link, *join

**alienation** 1 derangement, *aberration
Ana *insanity, lunacy, mania, dementia: imbecility, idiocy, moronity (see base words at FOOL)
2 *solitude, isolation, seclusion

**alienist** psychiatrist, psychopathologist, *neurologist, psychotherapist, psychoanalyst

**alight** vb 1 *descend, dismount
Con mount, *ascend, scale, climb
2 Alight, light, land, perch, roost share the meaning to come to rest after or as if after a flight, a descent, or a fall. Alight suggests previous controlled or gentle movement through the air or open space (as of a flying bird or a floating snowflake) ⟨skylarks alight on the ground⟩ Light, sometimes the equivalent of alight, more often presupposes a falling or jumping than flying or floating, and sometimes merely a wandering or roving ⟨he sprang from the roof and lighted on his feet⟩ ⟨we came smack down on the animal tent; when we lit the tent began to tear— Sandburg⟩ Land applies to a boat coming to land or an airplane grounding. Though often used interchangeably with light, it may connote arrival at a destination and sometimes driving force or power ⟨the airplane landed in a swamp⟩ ⟨he fell headlong and landed on his face⟩ ⟨his blow landed in the spot he aimed at⟩ ⟨he has landed where he hoped, in an executive position⟩ Perch and roost basically imply alighting of birds, but perch suggests settling on something elevated to which the claws may cling (as to a pole, bar, or twig) and roost, the settling for rest or sleep, especially by domestic fowls, on the perches and in the shelters prepared for them. So perch often implies elevation of position and tenuousness of grasp or hold ⟨twenty or more [rooks] perched aloft, cawing and con-

versing comfortably—Jefferies⟩ ⟨a lofty perpendicular cliff . . . with a castle . . . perched on the distant top— Lucas⟩ Roost, when used of persons, often suggests a position like that of roosting fowls ⟨boys roosting on the rail of a fence⟩
Con *rise, arise, soar, ascend, rocket

**align** *line, line up, range, array
Ana *order, arrange, marshal: regulate, fix, *adjust
Con *disorder, disarrange, derange, unsettle

**alike** *like, similar, analogous, comparable, akin, parallel, uniform, identical
Ana *same, selfsame, equivalent, identical
Ant different —Con *distinct, separate: *different, divergent, diverse, disparate, various

**aliment** *food, pabulum, nutriment, nourishment, sustenance, pap
Con *poison, venom, bane

**alive** 1 *living, animated, animate, vital
Ana *active, dynamic, live, operative: *lively, vivacious, sprightly: being, existing (see BE)
Ant dead, defunct —Con lifeless, inanimate, deceased (see DEAD): inert, *inactive: torpid, comatose (see LETHARGIC)
2 *aware, awake, sensible, cognizant, conscious
Ana alert, wide-awake, vigilant, *watchful: *intelligent, knowing, quick-witted
Ant blind (to): anesthetic (to) —Con *indifferent, unconcerned, aloof: insensitive, *insensible, impassible

**alkaline, basic** are closely related and in many aspects of their use synonymous terms. Both are opposites or correlatives of the adjective acid and denote some aspect of relationship to bases (alkalies). Distinctively, alkaline suggests the properties (as neutralizing acids, turning litmus paper blue) of bases ⟨alkaline taste⟩ ⟨alkaline solution⟩ ⟨alkaline earth⟩ ⟨a strong alkaline reaction⟩ Basic relates more directly to the bases themselves, especially in implying derivation from or capacity to react as a base ⟨a basic salt⟩ ⟨basic dye⟩

**all** adj 1 *whole, entire, total, gross
Ana complete, plenary, *full
2 All, every, each, when applied to the individuals of a group, imply inclusion of the entire membership with no exceptions. All is applied to the aggregate of individuals and implies consideration of it as a unit without regard to the individuals as distinct persons or things ⟨all men are mortal⟩ ⟨all books are written to be read⟩ Every is applied to any of the individuals comprising the group, regarded not as a concrete person or thing but as the type or representative of the entire membership ⟨every man is mortal⟩ ⟨every book published should be worth reading⟩ Each is applied to any or every individual of the group, but unlike every it implies reference to him or to it as a distinct, recognizable, and therefore concrete person or thing ⟨he knows the weaknesses of each batter on the team⟩ ⟨each book on this shelf is worth reading⟩ ⟨each person in this club must pay his share of the expense⟩
Ant no

**all-around** *versatile, many-sided
Ana complete, *full: apt, ready, *quick

**allay** *relieve, alleviate, lighten, assuage, mitigate
Ana abate, lessen, *decrease, diminish: mollify, *pacify, appease: *moderate, temper
Ant intensify —Con *provoke, excite, stimulate: *stir, rouse, arouse: aggravate, enhance (see INTENSIFY)

**allege** *adduce, cite, advance
Ana affirm, *assert, declare, profess, avouch, avow: recite, recount, rehearse, state (see RELATE)
Ant contravene: (in law) traverse —Con *deny, contradict, gainsay, negative, impugn: *disprove, refute,

A colon (:) separates groups of words discriminated. An asterisk (*) indicates place of treatment of each group.

rebut, controvert

**allegiance** fealty, loyalty, *fidelity, devotion, piety
*Ana* faithfulness, steadfastness, constancy, staunchness (see corresponding adjectives at FAITHFUL): obeisance, deference, homage, *honor: obedience (see corresponding adjective OBEDIENT): *obligation, duty
*Ant* treachery: treason —*Con* traitorousness, perfidy, faithlessness, disloyalty (see corresponding adjectives at FAITHLESS): disaffection, alienation (see corresponding verbs at ESTRANGE)

**allegory 1 Allegory, symbolism** designate methods of representation in art. Both characteristically aim to represent concretely something that is abstract or for some other reason not directly representable. **Allegory** is applied to a form of representation found not only in literature but also in painting and sculpture. It evokes a dual interest, one in the story, scene, or characters presented and the other in the ideas they convey or the significance they bear; it demands not only aesthetic enjoyment but intellectual interpretation. The incidents, scenes, or characters may be historical or fictitious or fabulous, but if the artist has given to the historical an added meaning or has invented his material to convey an idea or truth, he has employed *allegory*. **Symbolism** is applied to a form of representation used not only in literature, painting, and sculpture but also in music, architecture, ceremonial, and pageantry. It implies an attempt to represent what by its very nature is incapable of direct representation because it is immaterial, ideal, or spiritual. Originally *symbolism* denoted representation by an accepted sign or symbol (see SYMBOL 1); in painting and sculpture the divinity of Jesus was represented by a nimbus enclosing a cross and sainthood by a simple nimbus usually enclosing rays. In modern use *symbolism* also implies artistic imitation and invention as a means of suggesting not only something that eludes representation because of its nature but also something of which the literal representation is taboo (as by reason of defiance of the generally accepted moral code). Thus, a poet employs *symbolism* when his images, his rhythms, or his words evoke ideas or emotions that escape analysis; a painter employs *symbolism* when he uses arrangements of colors and of lines not to represent definite objects but to suggest something that is impalpable or intangible; a novelist or dramatist employs *symbolism* when his novel or play carries more than its surface meaning or offers hints of an underlying significance. Especially in literature *symbolism* is not always clearly distinguishable from *allegory*. The latter term, however, implies organization and a pattern in which the characters, incidents, and setting serve as symbols.

**2 Allegory, parable, myth, fable** are comparable as literary forms that typically tell a story for the sake of presenting a truth or of enforcing a moral. An **allegory** veils its true meaning (its underlying or allegorical sense) by leaving it to be deduced from the story it tells (the outward or literal sense). Its characters and incidents are therefore either figurative or typical; they serve as a bait to the consideration of dull or unpleasant truths (as in Bunyan's *Pilgrim's Progress*), as a graded approach to the apprehension of ideas too difficult for the ordinary man (as in Dante's *Divine Comedy*), or as a cloak for an attack on persons (as in Dryden's *Absalom and Achitophel*) or for an exposure of vices and follies (as in Swift's *Gulliver's Travels*). When the allegory is very short and simple and narrates or describes a familiar occurrence in nature or life that by analogy conveys a spiritual truth, it is called a **parable**. The term is specifically applied to the brief allegories used by Jesus in his sermons (as the one likening the kingdom of heaven to the growth of a mustard

seed). **Myth** is applied to a type of brief allegory used especially by Plato in expounding a difficult philosophical conception. Such myths are, as a rule, invented and their characters and incidents are purely imaginary. In a **fable** the moral is usually clearly stated at the end. Its characters are animals (as in Orwell's *Animal Farm*) or inanimate things (as by talking and acting as human beings reflect the weaknesses and follies of men.

**alleviate** *relieve, lighten, assuage, mitigate, allay
*Ana* *moderate, temper: lessen, reduce, diminish, *decrease: remedy, *cure
*Ant* aggravate —*Con* *intensify, heighten: *provoke, excite, stimulate: arouse, awaken, rouse, *stir

**alliance, league, coalition, fusion, confederacy, confederation, federation** agree in the idea of combination, chiefly political, for a common object. **Alliance** applies particularly to a joining of interests on the part of families (by marriage) or of states (by compact or treaty); it is also less formally used of a connection for mutual benefit between other bodies, organized or not ⟨a defensive *alliance*⟩ ⟨an *alliance* between producers and consumers⟩ **League** though often used without distinction from *alliance* typically suggests a more formal compact or more definite object ⟨the Solemn *League* and Covenant⟩ and may frequently (unlike *alliance*) be taken in a bad sense ⟨to be in *league* with the powers of darkness⟩ **Coalition** refers to a temporary alliance of otherwise opposing interests, parties, or factions ⟨Mr. Fox, and his famous *coalition* with Lord North—*Gibbon*⟩ ⟨a *coalition* government⟩ **Fusion** is a coalition of political parties for the purpose of defeating another party in an election ⟨a *fusion* of Republicans and independent Democrats in New York City opposed the Tammany Democratic ticket⟩ **Confederacy** and **confederation** apply specifically to a union by compact or treaty of independent states under a government to which powers are delegated for dealing primarily with common external relations ⟨the Southern *Confederacy*⟩ ⟨the Articles of *Confederation*⟩ ⟨the German *Confederation*⟩ **Federation** in its broad sense includes any union under the terms of a league or covenant ⟨the *Federation* of Labor⟩ but specifically it designates a sovereign state or city formed by the union of other states or cities with a central general government and several local governments ⟨the United States of America constitutes a *federation*⟩ ⟨*federation* was the name given to the scheme for blending the Five Towns into one town—*Bennett*⟩ ⟨the *Federation* of Malaysia⟩

**allied** *related, cognate, kindred, affiliated
*Ana* akin, parallel, similar (see LIKE): linked, associated, united, connected (see JOIN): cooperating, uniting, conjoining (see UNITE)
*Ant* unallied —*Con* alien, foreign, extraneous (see EXTRINSIC): *different, divergent, diverse, various, disparate

**allocate** *allot, assign, apportion
*Ana* *distribute, dispense, divide, deal, dole: *grant, accord, award
*Con* withhold, detain, retain, hold, hold back, *keep

**allot,**  **assign, apportion, allocate** mean to give as one's share, portion, role, or place. **Allot** implies more or less arbitrary or haphazard selection and in itself conveys no suggestion of a fair or equal distribution ⟨*allotted* himself an hour a day for exercise⟩ ⟨*allot* 500 square feet to an exhibitor⟩ ⟨he had been *allotted* a small sitting room—*Mackenzie*⟩ ⟨Brutus and Cassius . . . were *allotted* the minor governments of Crete and Cyrene—*Buchan*⟩ **Assign** stresses authoritative and usually fixed allotment; it too carries no hint of an even division ⟨this original and supreme will organizes the government, and *assigns* to different departments their respective powers—*John*

*Marshall*⟩ ⟨to each month there has been *assigned* by tradition a birthstone considered appropriate to that month—*Nurnberg & Rosenblum*⟩ **Apportion**, on the other hand, implies a principle of fair division, sometimes of equivalence in sharing, but more often of a proportionate distribution ⟨after each decennial census Congress *apportions* the number of representatives to be elected by each state⟩ ⟨his guardians had *apportioned* to him an allowance . . . adequate to his position—*Disraeli*⟩ **Allocate** is used chiefly in reference to money, property, territory, or powers, and suggests definite appropriation to a particular person or group or dedication to a particular use ⟨*allocate* a sum of money for the construction of a bridge⟩ ⟨districts of Czechoslovakia *allocated* to Germany by the Munich Agreement⟩ ⟨the Marine Corps would be *allocated* primary responsibility for amphibious development and doctrine pertaining to landing forces—*Collier's Yr. Bk.*⟩

*Ana* divide, dispense, *distribute, deal, dole: *give, bestow

*Con* *keep, retain, withhold, detain, hold, hold back: confiscate, appropriate, *arrogate

**allow** 1 permit, suffer, *let, leave

*Ana* tolerate, endure, stand, brook (see BEAR): accede, acquiesce (see ASSENT): *yield, submit, defer

*Ant* inhibit —*Con* *forbid, prohibit, enjoin: *prevent, avert, ward

2 *grant, concede

*Ana* admit, *acknowledge, confess: acquiesce, accede, *assent

*Ant* disallow —*Con* reject, refuse (see DECLINE): *disapprove, deprecate: *deny, gainsay, contradict, traverse

**allowance** 1 *ration, dole, pittance

*Ana* allotment, apportionment, assignment (see corresponding verbs at ALLOT): share (see corresponding verb SHARE): grant, *appropriation, subsidy

2 **Allowance, concession** both signify a change made by way of compromise or adjustment. **Allowance** usually implies a modification or variation of a requirement or a standard made for a good reason (as probable contingencies or mitigating circumstances) ⟨make *allowance* for the current in steering toward the opposite bank⟩ ⟨make *allowance* for his inexperience⟩ ⟨make *allowance* for wear through friction in designing the parts of a machine⟩ ⟨if business imposes its restraints and its silences and impediments, Mr. Darnay as a young gentleman of generosity knows how to make *allowance* for that circumstance—*Dickens*⟩ **Concession** implies that the change has been made reluctantly and usually as a favor or indulgence ⟨they would make no *concession* to a candidate's youth and inexperience⟩ ⟨the sole *concession* to leisure allowed me out of the year was one month on a farm—*Heiser*⟩ ⟨any *concession* to fashion was, they felt, unbecoming to their age—*Sackville-West*⟩

*Ana* adjustment, accommodation, adaptation (see corresponding verbs at ADAPT): modification, variation (see under CHANGE *vb*)

3 *advantage, handicap, odds, edge

**alloy** *admixture, adulterant

**allude** *refer, advert

*Ana* *suggest, imply, hint, intimate

**allure** *vb* *attract, captivate, charm, fascinate, enchant, bewitch

*Ana* *lure, entice, seduce: *invite, solicit, woo, court: beguile, delude (see DECEIVE)

*Ant* repel —*Con* alienate, *estrange, disaffect, wean: shun, avoid, elude, eschew (see ESCAPE)

**alluring** attractive, charming, fascinating, bewitching, enchanting, captivating (see under ATTRACT *vb*)

*Ana* lovely, fair, *beautiful, pretty, bonny: seductive, enticing, tempting, luring (see corresponding verbs at LURE): beguiling, delusive (see corresponding verbs at DECEIVE)

*Ant* repulsive —*Con* *offensive, loathsome, repugnant, revolting: repellent, abhorrent, distasteful, obnoxious (see REPUGNANT)

**ally** colleague, *partner, copartner, confederate

*Ana* *associate, comrade, companion: supporter, upholder, backer (see corresponding verbs at SUPPORT): cooperator (see corresponding verb at UNITE)

*Ant* adversary —*Con* *enemy, foe: competitor, rival (see corresponding verbs at RIVAL): *opponent, antagonist

**almost** *nearly, approximately, well-nigh

**alms** benefaction, contribution, *donation

*Ana* *charity, philanthropy: dole, pittance, allowance, *ration

**alone** *adj* 1 **Alone, solitary, lonely, lonesome, lone, lorn, forlorn, desolate** may all refer to situations of being apart from others or emotions experienced while apart. **Alone** stresses the fact of physical isolation and also may connote feelings of isolation from others ⟨the captain of a ship at sea is a remote, inaccessible creature, something like a prince of a fairy tale, *alone* of his kind—*Conrad*⟩ **Solitary** may indicate a state of being apart that is desired and sought for ⟨Netta loved these *solitary* interludes . . . . She could dream things there and tell herself stories there, untroubled—*Powys*⟩ It often connotes sadness at the loss or lack of usual or close connections or consciousness of isolation or remoteness ⟨being *solitary* he could only address himself to the waiter—*Woolf*⟩ ⟨an only child, he was left *solitary* by the early death of his mother . . . whose loss he felt severely—*Fulton*⟩ **Lonely** may simply indicate the fact of being alone but more often suggests isolation accompanied by a longing for company ⟨he was *lonely*, but not in an unhappy sense . . . it was no hardship for him to be alone—*Canby*⟩ ⟨his grim look, his pride, his silence, his wild outbursts of passion, left William *lonely* even in his court—*J. R. Green*⟩ ⟨he felt more *lonely* and forsaken than at any time since his father's death—*Archibald Marshall*⟩ **Lonesome**, often more poignant, suggests sadness after a separation or bereavement ⟨you must keep up your spirits, mother, and not be *lonesome* because I'm not at home—*Dickens*⟩ ⟨her flight . . . yet smote my *lonesome* heart more than all misery—*Shelley*⟩ **Lone** especially in poetical use may replace either *lonely* or *lonesome* ⟨in his *lone* course the shepherd oft will pause—*Wordsworth*⟩ ⟨the mother's dead and I reckon it's got no father; it's a *lone* thing—*George Eliot*⟩ **Lorn** suggests recent separation or bereavement ⟨when *lorn* lovers sit and droop—*Praed*⟩ **Forlorn** indicates dejection, woe, and listlessness at separation from someone dear ⟨as *forlorn* and stupefied as I was when my husband's spirit flew away—*Hardy*⟩ ⟨as *forlorn* as King Lear at the end of his days—*G. W. Johnson*⟩ **Desolate** is most extreme in suggesting inconsolable grief at loss or bereavement ⟨fatherless, a *desolate* orphan—*Coleridge*⟩ ⟨for her false mate has fled and left her *desolate*—*Shelley*⟩

*Solitary, lonely, lonesome, desolate* are applied to places and locations more than the other words discriminated above. **Solitary** may be applied either to something that is apart from things similar or that is uninhabited or unvisited by human beings ⟨a *solitary* chamber, or rather cell, at the top of the house, and separated from all the other apartments by a gallery and staircase—*M.W. Shelley*⟩ **Lonely** may be applied to what is either far apart from things similar and seldom visited or to what is inhabited by only one person or group and conducive to loneliness ⟨heard not only in the towns but even in *lonely* farmhouses

---

A colon (:) separates groups of words discriminated. An asterisk (*) indicates place of treatment of each group.

—*Anderson*⟩ **Lonesome** has much the same suggestion ⟨like one that on a *lonesome* road doth walk in fear and dread—*Coleridge*⟩ **Desolate** indicates either that a place is abandoned by people or that it is so barren and wild as never to have attracted them ⟨as if nothing had life by day, in that lifeless *desolate* spot—*Trollope*⟩
*Ana* *single, sole, lone, unique: deserted, abandoned, forsaken (see ABANDON): isolated, secluded (see corresponding nouns at SOLITUDE)
*Ant* accompanied —*Con* attended, escorted, convoyed, chaperoned (see ACCOMPANY): aided, assisted, helped (see HELP *vb*)
**2 Alone** *adj & adv* *only
**aloof** *indifferent, detached, uninterested, disinterested, unconcerned, incurious
*Ana* disdainful, haughty, arrogant, *proud: cool, *cold: reserved, reticent, *silent
*Ant* familiar, close —*Con* friendly, neighborly (see AMICABLE): intimate, confidential, chummy (see FAMILIAR)
**alp** peak, *mountain, mount
**also, too, likewise, besides, moreover, furthermore** denote in addition and are used when joining (not necessarily in the same sentence) one proposition or consideration to another. **Also** adds to a statement something that may be affirmed equally with what precedes ⟨that where I am, there ye may be *also*—*Jn* 14:3⟩ ⟨every simile ought not only to be well adapted to the subject, but *also* to include every excellence of description—*Goldsmith*⟩ **Too** is less formal than *also*, and adds with a lighter touch ⟨like Twilight's, *too*, her dusky hair—*Wordsworth*⟩ ⟨I can like now, and admire you *too*, sir—*Thackeray*⟩ **Likewise** is more formal and slightly more explicit than *also;* it sometimes implies specific likeness or connection between the ideas which it unites ⟨have I not seen—ye *likewise* may have seen—*Wordsworth*⟩ ⟨Greek, was your ambition *likewise* doomed to failure?—*Browning*⟩ **Besides, moreover, furthermore** introduce a statement which must be taken into consideration along with the matter which precedes. **Besides** usually introduces a statement that strengthens what has been said ⟨his project is an excellent one; *besides*, it is likely to help a great many persons⟩ **Moreover** is more emphatic than *besides*, and often serves as a transitional word between sentences: it often implies that the stronger of two considerations is yet to be presented ⟨the mountain was steep and rugged; *moreover*, its sides were coated with ice⟩ **Furthermore** is sometimes the most formal of these words; its chief use, however, is in a chain of additions where *besides* or *moreover* has already been used ⟨he is well-liked; moreover, he is absolutely dependable; *furthermore*, there is no one who can take his place⟩
**alter** 1 *change, vary, modify
*Ana* adjust, accommodate, *adapt: qualify, temper (see MODERATE): *transform, metamorphose, convert
*Ant* fix —*Con* *set, settle, establish: preserve, conserve (see SAVE): *continue, last, endure, abide, persist
2 *sterilize, castrate, spay, emasculate, mutilate, geld, caponize
**alteration** change, variation, modification (see under CHANGE *vb*)
*Ana* adjustment, adaptation, accommodation (see corresponding verbs at ADAPT): transformation, metamorphosis, conversion (see under TRANSFORM)
*Ant* fixation: fixity —*Con* permanence, stability, perdurability (see corresponding adjectives at LASTING): continuance, endurance, persistence (see corresponding verbs at CONTINUE)
**altercate** *vb* quarrel, wrangle, squabble, bicker, spat, tiff (see under QUARREL *n*)

*Ana* fight, *contend, battle, war: dispute, debate, agitate (see DISCUSS)
*Ant* concur —*Con* *agree, coincide: conform, reconcile, accommodate, *adapt
**altercation** *quarrel, wrangle, squabble, bickering, spat, tiff
*Ana* fight, conflict, combat, *contest: *discord, dissension, contention, difference, variance, strife: controversy, dispute, *argument
*Ant* concurrence: accord —*Con* agreement, coincidence (see corresponding verbs at AGREE): *harmony, concord, consonance
**alternate** *adj* *intermittent, recurrent, periodic
*Ana* alternating, rotating (see ROTATE): *reciprocal, corresponding, complementary
*Ant* consecutive —*Con* successive, sequent (see CONSECUTIVE)
**alternate** *vb* *rotate
*Ana* recur, *return, revert: oscillate, fluctuate, sway, waver (see SWING)
*Con* *follow, succeed
**alternate** *n* *substitute, supply, understudy, double, stand-in, pinch hitter, locum tenens
**alternation** vicissitude, *change, mutation, permutation
*Ana* rotation (see corresponding verb ROTATE): oscillation, fluctuation, wavering (see corresponding verbs at SWING): turning, revolving, rotating, wheeling (see TURN *vb*): recurrence, return, reversion (see under RETURN *vb*)
**alternative** option, *choice, preference, selection, election
**although** *though, albeit
**altitude** *height, elevation
*Ana* highness, tallness, loftiness (see corresponding adjectives at HIGH): *summit, peak, apex
*Con* depth, profundity (see corresponding adjectives at DEEP)
**altruistic** benevolent, *charitable, humanitarian, philanthropic, eleemosynary
*Ana* self-abnegating, self-denying (see corresponding nouns at RENUNCIATION): generous, bountiful, bounteous, openhanded, *liberal
*Ant* egoistic —*Con* egotistic, self-loving, self-esteeming, conceited (see corresponding nouns at CONCEIT): self-indulging, self-pampering (see base words at INDULGE)
**amalgam** *mixture, admixture, compound, blend, composite
**amalgamate** blend, commingle, merge, coalesce, fuse, *mix, mingle
*Ana* combine, unite, link, associate, *join: consolidate, unify, *compact
*Con* disintegrate, crumble, decompose (see DECAY): disperse, dissipate, *scatter: *separate, part, divide
**amalgamation** *consolidation, merger
**amass** *accumulate, hoard
*Ana* collect, *gather, assemble: *heap, pile, mass, stack
*Ant* distribute —*Con* dissipate, *scatter, disperse: dispense, divide, deal, dole (see DISTRIBUTE)
**amateur, dilettante, dabbler, tyro** denote a person who follows a pursuit without attaining proficiency or a professional status. **Amateur** may denote one who has a taste or liking for something rather than an expert knowledge of it; in this sense it is distinguished from *connoisseur* ⟨an *amateur* of cameos⟩ ⟨affected the pose of the gentleman *amateur* of the arts—*F. H. Ellis*⟩ **Amateur** is also applied to a person whose participation in an activity requiring skill is due to a personal rather than a professional interest. It usually but not invariably implies a lack of mastery. This latter implication is not often found in sports, where a technical distinction between an *amateur*

(one who competes without remuneration) and a *professional* (one who competes for reward) prevails. In other use the word is opposed to *expert* and *adept*, as well as *professional*. Sometimes it suggests lack of experience or apprenticeship ⟨every artist was first an *amateur*— *Emerson*⟩; sometimes it connotes indulgence in a particular pursuit as a pastime or as an avocation ⟨how could an *amateur* venture out and make an exhibition of himself after such splendid rowing!—*Jefferies*⟩ Very often, especially in contrast to *expert* or *adept*, it connotes superficiality, bungling, or indifference to professional standards ⟨it is beginning to be hinted that we are a nation of *amateurs*—*Rosebery*⟩ ⟨the third earl of Shaftesbury . . . illustrated this unsystematic method of thinking. He was an *amateur*, an aristocratic *amateur*, careless of consistency —*Ellis*⟩ **Dilettante** is applied to an amateur (in the older underogatory sense of that word) in the fine arts (see AESTHETE). It stresses enjoyment rather than effort, a frittering rather than a concentration of one's energies, and, sometimes, the point of view of the aesthete ⟨the *dilettante* lives an easy, butterfly life, knowing nothing of . . . toil and labor—*Osler*⟩ ⟨we continue to respect the erudite mind, and to decry the appreciative spirit as amateurish and *dilettante*—*Benson*⟩ **Dabbler** implies a lack of serious purpose, but it suggests desultory habits of work and lack of persistence ⟨your *dabblers* in metaphysics are the most dangerous creatures breathing—*Tucker*⟩ ⟨the certainty of touch which marks the difference between an artist and the *dabbler* . . . can come only after patient study —*Wendell*⟩ **Tyro** does not necessarily imply youth but does suggest comparable inexperience or audacity with resulting incompetence or crudeness ⟨it is to be fancy on the part of a *tyro* in music to suggest that a change from poetry to prose occurs when Beethoven introduces in the last movement of the Choral Symphony . . . a subject in words—*Alexander*⟩ ⟨"a noble theme!" the *tyro* cried, and straightway scribbled off a sonnet. "A noble theme," the poet sighed, "I am not fit to write upon it"—*Wells*⟩ **Ana** *novice, apprentice, probationer
**Ant** professional: expert —**Con** adept, wizard, virtuoso (see EXPERT)

**amative** amorous, amatory, *erotic
**amatory** *erotic, aphrodisiac, amative, amorous
**amaze** *vb* astound, flabbergast, astonish, *surprise
**Ana** dumbfound, bewilder, confound, nonplus (see PUZZLE): impress, touch, strike, *affect
**amazement** *wonder, wonderment, admiration
**amazon** *virago, termagant
**ambassador, legate, nuncio, minister, envoy, internuncio, chargé d'affaires** all designate a diplomatic agent serving his sovereign or government in a foreign country and are here compared with reference to their order of precedence as fixed by international regulations and protocol. *Ambassador, legate,* and *nuncio* designate a diplomatic agent of the first rank who is accredited to the head of the state in which he serves, is considered to represent both the government and the person of the head of state whom he serves, and as the personal representative of his sovereign or chief executive enjoys certain privileges and precedences not shared by diplomats of lesser rank. An **ambassador** (in full **ambassador extraordinary and plenipotentiary**) is almost always a resident agent, though the term may also denote one who goes on a special mission as the chief executive's diplomatic agent. In this case he may be distinguished as an **ambassador-at-large.** The comparable diplomatic agents of the pope are called **legate** and **nuncio,** the difference between them being that a *legate* goes on a special mission and is clothed with authority to act in the name of the pope and a *nuncio* serves as the

accredited resident ambassador of the Holy See at a foreign court or seat of government. **Minister** designates a diplomatic agent of the second or of the third rank. He, too, is accredited to the head of the state to which he is sent but as the representative solely of the government and not of the person of the head of his own state. As an agent of the second rank, he may also be called an **envoy,** for his full title is **envoy extraordinary and minister plenipotentiary. Internuncio** is the designation of the papal diplomatic agent of the second rank equivalent to an *envoy extraordinary and minister plenipotentiary.* Agents of the third rank, called more fully **ministers resident** are now uncommon. They perform essentially the same function as the *envoy extraordinary and minister plenipotentiary* but are usually assigned to less important capitals.
A **chargé d'affaires** is an agent of the fourth rank who directs diplomatic affairs in place of an ambassador or minister in the absence or lack of such higher-ranked agent. He is accredited to the head of the department dealing with foreign affairs rather than to the head of the state and his appointment may be on a permanent footing and by his home government or on an interim basis by the head of a mission (an ambassador or minister).

**ambiguity, equivocation, tergiversation, double entendre** are comparable when they denote expression or, more often, an expression, capable of more than one interpretation. **Ambiguity** is referable to an expression that admits of two or sometimes more interpretations; commonly, however, it suggests the use of a word or phrase rather than a construction that may be taken in either of two senses ⟨where no *ambiguity* arises, the word polygon may be used to refer either to the broken line, or to the part of the plane enclosed by it—*R. R. Smith*⟩ *Ambiguity* does not in itself suggest intentional lack of explicitness; when that idea is to be conveyed or when an attempt to mislead or an indifference to accuracy in statement is to be suggested, **equivocation** is the preferable word ⟨the first cardinal sin from the logician's standpoint is *equivocation.* Thus Hobbes has declared that "in all discourses wherein one man pretends to instruct or convince another, he should use the same word constantly in the same sense" —*Philip Wheelwright*⟩ ⟨*equivocation* is halfway to lying —*Penn*⟩ But *equivocation* may imply that the writer or speaker is himself confused. **Tergiversation** stresses a shifting of senses, especially of a word or words important to an argument. It implies evasion and looseness of thought; more specifically it connotes intentional subterfuge and often a low standard of intellectual honesty ⟨humanism depends very heavily, I believe, upon the *tergiversations* of the word *human;* and in general, upon implying clear and distinct philosophic ideas which are never there—*T. S. Eliot*⟩ **Double entendre** designates an ambiguity which invites or allows a twofold meaning, one sense being a cover for a subtle implication, especially a stinging or an indelicate implication ⟨sometimes with these parliamentary comedies, the humor lay in a kind of *double entendre,* using the phrase in an innocent sense— *Manchester Guardian*⟩ ⟨bedroom farce with many of the *double entendres* . . . that go with that form of entertainment—*McCarten*⟩
**Ant** lucidity: explicitness —**Con** clearness, perspicuousness (see corresponding adjectives at CLEAR): definiteness, specificity, expressness (see corresponding adjectives at EXPLICIT)
**ambiguous** equivocal, cryptic, enigmatic, vague, *obscure, dark
**Ana** dubious, *doubtful, questionable
**Ant** explicit —**Con** lucid, perspicuous, *clear: express, definite, specific, categorical (see EXPLICIT)

---

A colon (:) separates groups of words discriminated. An asterisk (*) indicates place of treatment of each group.

**ambition, aspiration, pretension** mean strong desire for advancement. **Ambition** has personal advancement or preferment as its end; it may be praiseworthy but is sometimes inordinate ⟨*ambition* for fame⟩ ⟨*ambition* to hold office⟩ ⟨*ambition* to acquire wealth⟩ ⟨vaulting *ambition,* which o'erleaps itself—*Shak.*⟩ **Aspiration** implies as its object something felt to be above one, the striving after which is uplifting or ennobling ⟨*aspiration* after knowledge⟩ ⟨that spirit of his in *aspiration* lifts him from the earth—*Shak.*⟩ *Aspiration,* however, is sometimes used especially in the plural in a derogatory sense of ambition which is felt to be unwarranted or presumptuous ⟨his *aspirations* must be nipped in the bud⟩ **Pretension** (see also CLAIM, PRETENSE) may be preferred to *aspiration* in this latter sense, for it carries a hint of presumptuousness and, therefore, of lack of real claim to the powers which fulfillment of the ambition or aspiration requires ⟨they are always looked upon, either as neglected, or discontented because their *pretensions* have failed—*Montagu*⟩ More often *pretension* implies less driving power than *ambition* or *aspiration* and suggests the guidance of mere desire rather than the possession of the necessary gifts ⟨it was the undergraduate literary club, whose membership included all nice boys with literary *pretensions*—*Marquand*⟩
*Ana* urge, lust, *desire: eagerness, avidity, keenness, anxiety (see corresponding adjectives at EAGER): spur, ˋgoad, incentive, *motive
*Con* contentment, satisfaction (see corresponding verbs at SATISFY): resignation, *patience: indolence, faineance, sloth (see corresponding adjectives at LAZY)

**ambitious 1 Ambitious, emulous** both mean extremely desirous of something that will give one power, fame, success, or riches. **Ambitious** often implies inordinate, sometimes presumptuous, eagerness to advance oneself or to attain something beyond one's present reach; it may, in addition, connote aggressiveness in the pursuit of one's ends ⟨the noble Brutus hath told you Caesar was *ambitious:* if it were so, it was a grievous fault—*Shak.*⟩ **Emulous** stresses the desire to equal or surpass others; it can suggest covetous rivalry or merely the spirit of competition ⟨men of pedigree . . . *emulous* always of the nearest place to any throne, except the throne of grace—*Cowper*⟩
*Ana* *eager, avid, anxious, keen: aspiring, panting, aiming (see AIM *vb*): daring, venturesome, *adventurous
*Ant* unambitious —*Con* apathetic, phlegmatic, stolid (see IMPASSIVE): indolent, faineant, slothful, *lazy
**2 Ambitious, pretentious, utopian** are comparable when they are applied to such matters as plans, designs, programs, or policies and mean straining or exceeding the capacity of their authors or executants. Something is **ambitious** which is either so far beyond what can with certainty be accomplished that its realization or execution is doubtful or which, if realized, is accomplished only by excessive effort or by testing one's powers to the utmost ⟨the philosopher has the *ambitious* aim of unifying, or harmonizing, these points of view—*Inge*⟩ ⟨his last novel was his most *ambitious* and possibly his best⟩ Something is **pretentious** which so far exceeds one's powers or resources that any attempt to carry it out reveals one's inadequacy, inexperience, or lack of sufficient skill; in this sense it often but not necessarily implies ostentation ⟨the program was too *pretentious* for so young a violinist⟩ Something is **utopian** which is utterly impracticable or unattainable under present or sometimes, any conditions. *Utopian,* if it does not suggest an idealistic approach, invariably implies indifference to actualities ⟨the reformers started out with an ambitious program which its critics called *utopian;* time has shown that it was too pretentious⟩
*Ana* audacious, bold (see BRAVE): daring (see ADVENTUR-

OUS): ostentatious, *showy
*Ant* modest —*Con* lowly, *humble: *moderate, temperate
**amble** *vb* *saunter, stroll
*Ana* loiter, dawdle (see DELAY): meander, ramble, roam (see WANDER)
**ambulant** ambulatory, peripatetic, *itinerant, nomadic, vagrant
*Ant* bedridden (*of patients*)
**ambulatory** *adj* ambulant, peripatetic, *itinerant, nomadic, vagrant
**ambulatory** *n* *passage, passageway, aisle, gallery, cloister, arcade, hall, hallway
**ambuscade** *ambush
**ambush** *vb* *surprise, waylay
*Ana* *attack, assault, assail: trap, entrap, snare, ensnare, capture, *catch
**ambush** *n* Ambush, ambuscade mean a device to entrap an enemy by lying in wait under cover for an opportune moment to make a surprise attack. **Ambush,** however, is also used to designate an act of lying in wait or in concealment (as for spying, frightening, or obtaining an advantage); when used of nonmilitary activity it sometimes connotes unfairness or cowardliness ⟨*ambushes* of cutthroats—*Thackeray*⟩ ⟨when he was a boy he had . . . spied on the Pecos men . . . . He had lain in *ambush* for two nights on the mountain—*Cather*⟩ **Ambuscade** usually implies the legitimate strategic disposition of troops in concealment, but in military use is more often applied to the body of troops or to their position than to the trap ⟨the knights and gentlemen volunteered for an *ambuscade* to cut off the convoy—*Froude*⟩ ⟨feared in every wavering brake an *ambuscade*—*Tennyson*⟩
*Ana* trap, snare, *lure: *attack, onset, onslaught, assault
**ameliorate** *improve, better, help
*Ana* amend, remedy, reform, rectify, *correct: mitigate, alleviate, *relieve, lighten
*Ant* worsen: deteriorate *vt* —*Con* *injure, harm, hurt, damage, impair, mar, spoil: *intensify, aggravate
**amenable 1** answerable, liable, accountable, *responsible
*Ana* open, subject, *liable: *subordinate, dependent, subject
*Ant* independent (*of*): autonomous —*Con* autocratic, arbitrary, *absolute: *free, autarchic
**2** tractable, *obedient, docile, biddable
*Ana* pliant, adaptable, pliable (see PLASTIC): responsive (see TENDER): sensitive, open (see LIABLE): submissive, *tame, subdued
*Ant* recalcitrant, refractory —*Con* intractable, *unruly, ungovernable, headstrong: truculent, *fierce: *obstinate, stubborn, mulish
**amend** reform, *correct, rectify, revise, emend, remedy, redress
*Ana* *improve, better, ameliorate: *mend, repair: elevate, raise, *lift
*Ant* debase: impair —*Con* corrupt, vitiate, deprave, debauch, pervert (see DEBASE): *injure, mar, spoil, damage, harm, hurt
**amends** redress, *reparation, indemnity, restitution
*Ana* compensation, recompense (see corresponding verbs at PAY): atonement, expiation (see under EXPIATE)
**amenity 1 Amenity, luxury** both denote something (as an object, a feature, a quality, or an experience) that gives refined or exquisite pleasure or is exceedingly pleasing to the mind or senses. **Amenity** typically implies a delightful mildness, gentleness, or softness, especially in contrast to an uncomfortable or distressing harshness, roughness, or crudeness ⟨many English go to the Riviera in the winter because of the *amenity* of its climate⟩ It may imply no

*Ana* analogous words          *Ant* antonyms          *Con* contrasted words          See also explanatory notes facing page 1

more than a vague conducing to physical or material comfort or convenience ⟨every *amenity* . . . including . . . showers, central heating, and first-class cuisine—*H. G. Smith*⟩ **Luxury** stresses keen, often voluptuous, enjoyment and unalloyed gratification of the mind or senses, usually without a special suggestion of opulence in the thing enjoyed or sensuality in the pleasure ⟨and learn the *luxury* of doing good—*Goldsmith*⟩ ⟨Mark decided to walk back by the road . . . instead of indulging himself in the *luxury* of once more rejoicing in the solitude of the green lanes—*Mackenzie*⟩ ⟨a dressing room with a marble bath that made cleanliness a *luxury* instead of one of the sternest of the virtues—*Shaw*⟩

*Ana* \*pleasure, delight, joy, enjoyment: ease, comfort, relaxation (see REST): mildness, softness, blandness, lenity *or* leniency (see corresponding adjectives at SOFT)

*Ant* rigor  —*Con* harshness, roughness, ruggedness (see corresponding adjectives at ROUGH): disagreeableness, unpleasantness (see affirmative adjectives at PLEASANT): hardship, \*difficulty, vicissitude

**2** \*courtesy, attention, gallantry

*Ana* civility, politeness, courteousness (see corresponding adjectives at CIVIL): graciousness, affability, cordiality, geniality, sociability (see corresponding adjectives at GRACIOUS): \*form, convention, convenance: ceremony, formality (see FORM)

*Ant* acerbity, asperity: rudeness  —*Con* glumness, moroseness, crabbedness, surliness (see corresponding adjectives at SULLEN): \*acrimony: \*affront, insult, indignity: discourtesy, incivility, impoliteness (see corresponding adjectives at RUDE)

**amerce** fine, mulct, \*penalize

**amercement** fine (see under PENALIZE)

**amiable, good-natured, obliging, complaisant** mean having or manifesting the desire or disposition to please. All may refer either to moods or to temperaments. **Amiable** usually implies friendliness, affability, or kindliness, qualities that inspire liking ⟨from what he said of Miss Darcy, I was thoroughly prepared to see a proud, reserved, disagreeable girl. Yet he . . . must know that she was as *amiable* and unpretending as we have found her—*Austen*⟩ Often, however, the word suggests little more than a sweet temper ⟨preferred an *amiable* softness to a tragic intensity—*Glasgow*⟩ Occasionally it additionally connotes lack of firmness or strength ⟨she suddenly married a poor, good-for-nothing, *amiable* fellow—*Deland*⟩ **Good-natured** implies a disposition not only to please but to be pleased; consequently it often connotes undue compliance or indifference to imposition ⟨he was too *good-natured* a man to behave harshly—*Macaulay*⟩ ⟨horseplay and practical jokes . . . at weddings . . . require *good-natured* toleration—*Sumner*⟩ **Obliging** stresses a readiness to be helpful, or to accommodate to the wishes of others ⟨Keppel had a sweet and *obliging* temper—*Macaulay*⟩ ⟨he always had the courtesy to answer me, for he was a most *obliging* fellow—*Keith*⟩ **Complaisant** implies a courteous or sometimes a weakly amiable desire to please or to be agreeable ⟨her importunity prevailed with me and I am extremely glad I was so *complaisant*—*Montagu*⟩

*Ana* \*gracious, cordial, affable, genial: warmhearted, warm, responsive, \*tender: kindly, \*kind, benignant, benign

*Ant* unamiable: surly  —*Con* ungracious, \*rude, ill-mannered, discourteous, impolite: \*sullen, glum, morose, crabbed, dour

**amicable, neighborly, friendly** are applied to the attitudes and actions of persons, communities, and states that have intercourse with each other and mean marked by or exhibiting goodwill or absence of antagonism. **Amicable** frequently implies little more than that the parties concerned are not disposed to quarrel or are at peace with each other ⟨an *amicable* adjustment⟩ ⟨the sometimes *amicable* processes of bargaining between a federation of employers and a trade union—*Hobson*⟩ **Neighborly** sometimes suggests goodwill and kindliness and a disposition to live on good terms with those with whom one must associate because of their proximity ⟨the only encirclement sought is the encircling bond of good old-fashioned *neighborly* friendship—*Roosevelt*⟩ Very often, however, because of connotations acquired from scriptural uses of *neighbor*, especially in the parable of the Good Samaritan ("which now of these three . . . was *neighbor* unto him that fell among the thieves?") it implies the duty of helpfulness and the spirit of fellowship ⟨he hath a *neighborly* charity in him—*Shak.*⟩ ⟨he in a very *neighborly* manner admonished me—*Swift*⟩ **Friendly** is more positive in its implications of cordiality than either of the others and often suggests greater warmth of feeling ⟨a *friendly* nod⟩ ⟨a *friendly* call⟩ ⟨their relations are *friendly*⟩ ⟨a *friendly* correspondence as neighbors and old acquaintances—*Franklin*⟩

*Ana* peaceful, \*pacific, peaceable: harmonious, concordant, accordant (see corresponding nouns at HARMONY): \*social, gregarious, cooperative, hospitable

*Ant* antagonistic  —*Con* quarrelsome, contentious, \*belligerent, bellicose, pugnacious, combative: hostile, antipathetic (see corresponding nouns at ENMITY)

**amiss, astray** share the meaning wrong or otherwise than intended. **Amiss** implies failure (as of an arrow) to reach the mark aimed at and frequently suggests a shortcoming or defect (as by failure to reach a standard, an expectation, a definite conclusion, or the point of being useful) ⟨his shafts of wit went *amiss*⟩ ⟨she seemed unconcerned, as though nothing had happened *amiss*⟩ ⟨no information came *amiss* to him⟩ Sometimes *amiss* suggests a divergence from the normal or usual order ⟨whether his general health had been previously at all *amiss*—*Dickens*⟩ ⟨"What's *amiss* in the Square?" . . . "Just now I saw a man running along Wedgwood Street"—*Bennett*⟩ **Astray** emphasizes wandering from a predetermined path or the right way or course; it usually suggests moral or intellectual errancy ⟨lest in temptation's path ye gang *astray*—*Burns*⟩ ⟨in many an hour when judgment goes *astray*—*Wordsworth*⟩

*Ana* wrong (*or* wrongly), \*bad (*or* badly)

*Ant* aright, right

**amity** \*friendship, comity, goodwill

*Ana* \*harmony, concord, accord: amicableness, neighborliness, friendliness (see corresponding adjectives at AMICABLE)

*Ant* enmity  —*Con* hostility, animosity, antipathy, antagonism (see ENMITY): \*discord, strife, contention, dissension, conflict, difference, variance

**ammunition** artillery, matériel, munitions, \*armament, ordnance, arms

**amnesty** \*pardon, absolution

**among** \*between

**amoral** nonmoral, unmoral, \*immoral

**amorous** amative, \*erotic, amatory

*Ana* passionate, fervid, ardent, \*impassioned: \*enamored, infatuated: lustful, lascivious (see LICENTIOUS)

*Ant* frigid  —*Con* \*indifferent, aloof, detached: \*cold, cool: \*impassive, apathetic

**amount** *n* \*sum, total, quantity, number, aggregate, whole

**amour, liaison, intrigue, affair** denote an instance of illicit sexual relationship. **Amour** is particularly applied to the illicit attachment of prominent persons; it stresses passion as the motivating force and often connotes transience.

---

A colon (:) separates groups of words discriminated. An asterisk (\*) indicates place of treatment of each group.

**Liaison** implies duration but not necessarily permanence in the attachment; it is commonly used to designate the relation between a man and his mistress. **Intrigue** emphasizes the clandestine element in the relation and is often closer to *amour* than to *liaison* in its other implications. **Affair** is the least specific term and often suggests equivocal rather than definitely illicit relations or may be used without imputation of impropriety.

**amour propre** self-esteem, self-love, egoism, egotism, *conceit

*Ana* *pride, vanity, vainglory: complacency, self-complacency, smugness, self-satisfaction (see corresponding adjectives at COMPLACENT)

**ample** 1 *spacious, capacious, commodious

*Ana* expanded, distended, swelled *or* swollen, inflated (see EXPAND): *large, big, great

*Ant* meager: circumscribed —*Con* limited, restricted, confined (see LIMIT *vb*): contracted, compressed, condensed, shrunken (see CONTRACT *vb*): scant, skimpy, exiguous, spare (see MEAGER)

2 abundant, *plentiful, plenteous, copious

*Ana* *liberal, generous, handsome, bountiful, bounteous: *profuse, lavish, prodigal

*Ant* scant, meager —*Con* skimpy, scrimpy (see MEAGER): *stingy, niggardly

**amplify** *expand, swell, distend, dilate, inflate

*Ana* develop (see MATURE): enlarge, augment (see INCREASE)

*Ant* abridge, condense —*Con* *shorten, abbreviate: *contract, compress

**amplitude** *expanse, spread, stretch

*Ana* largeness, bigness, greatness (see corresponding adjectives at LARGE): spaciousness, commodiousness, capaciousness (see corresponding adjectives at SPACIOUS): magnitude, extent, *size: *bulk, mass, volume

*Ant* straitness: limitation —*Con* restriction, circumscription (see corresponding verbs at LIMIT)

**amulet** charm, talisman, *fetish

**amuse**, **divert**, **entertain**, **recreate** mean to cause or enable one to pass one's time in pleasant or agreeable occupations. Their corresponding nouns **amusement**, **diversion**, **entertainment**, **recreation** are also synonyms denoting such an occupation or its effect. Although these words are used more or less interchangeably, they have fundamentally different implications. **Amuse** and **amusement** stress the engagement of one's attention, especially during hours of leisure, in a source of interest or engrossment. They do not necessarily imply play or sport; nevertheless they often suggest light, purposeless, trivial, or laughter-provoking pastimes ⟨what he wanted was to be *amused*, to get through the twenty-four hours pleasantly, without sitting down to dry business—*Macaulay*⟩ ⟨I don't write because I've got things to say .... I write because it *amuses* me—*Rose Macaulay*⟩ ⟨may speculate, for *amusement*, whether it would not have been beneficial ... to Britain in particular, to have had a more continuous religious history—*T. S. Eliot*⟩ **Divert** and **diversion**, on the other hand, stress the distraction of the attention from something (as routine interests or worry) which is occupying it and its capture by something different, especially by something that enlivens or promotes gaiety ⟨after the novelty of their surroundings had ceased to attract and *divert* the lepers, they often became homesick—*Heiser*⟩ ⟨only men of leisure have the need for beautiful women to *divert* them—*Buck*⟩ ⟨I believe that the drama has something else to do except to *divert* us—*T. S. Eliot*⟩ ⟨there is a place for farce and *diversion* in experience—*Dewey*⟩ **Entertain** and **entertainment** imply the activities of others to provide amusement or diversion. The words therefore suggest more or less formal

expedients or more or less formal circumstances, which are usually implied in the context ⟨Mrs. Brown will *entertain* the Burtons over the weekend⟩ ⟨a church *entertainment*⟩ ⟨*entertainment* is what schoolboys are now led to expect ... ; they are disappointed if the school is not a hall of unbroken amusement—*Grandgent*⟩ **Recreate** and the far more common **recreation** usually imply a change of occupation or an indulgence in diversions for the sake of relaxation or refreshment of body or mind ⟨the Lord Chancellor was *recreating* himself, after a long stretch of arduous business, with a journey in Scotland—*Martineau*⟩ ⟨just to sit in the sun, to bask like an animal in its heat—this is one of my country *recreations*—*L. P. Smith*⟩

*Ana* engross, absorb (see MONOPOLIZE): beguile, *while, wile: enliven, *quicken, animate: *thrill, electrify

*Ant* bore —*Con* *tire, weary, fatigue: *depress, oppress: irk, vex, *annoy

**amusement** diversion, entertainment, recreation (see under AMUSE *vb*)

*Ana* engrossment, absorption (see corresponding verbs at MONOPOLIZE): play, sport, *fun, jest: disporting, frolicking, rollicking, romping (see PLAY *vb*): jollity, *mirth

*Ant* boredom —*Con* *tedium, ennui: languidness, listlessness, spiritlessness (see corresponding adjectives at LANGUID): languor, *lethargy

**anachronism**, **solecism** are occasionally used interchangeably to mean something that does not properly belong to the setting or background in which it is placed and that is incongruous with it. More specifically, **anachronism** implies a mistake in associating things which do not belong to the same time or age ⟨an automobile in a story of American Civil War times would be an *anachronism*⟩ ⟨an eighteenth-century Chippendale chair is an *anachronism* in a seventeenth-century Jacobean room⟩ When applied to something that does exist at the time under consideration, *anachronism* implies that the thing is behind the times or antiquated and useless ⟨born a thousand years ... too late and an *anachronism* in this culminating century of civilization—*London*⟩ **Solecism**, on the other hand, implies lack of concord or consonance through an association of things that does not accord with some standard (as of decency, propriety, or logic). One who in affectation introduces foreign words into English speech commits a *solecism* in language ⟨I feel certain that a *solecism* of this kind—the introduction into a particular rite of features not sanctioned by the texts—would have seemed a shocking thing to ... so accurate a scholar—*L. P. Smith*⟩ ⟨it is a *solecism* in Belize to describe people by their color ... the colony prides itself ... on absolute freedom from any taint of racial prejudice—*Norman Lewis*⟩

**anagogic** *mystical, mystic, cabalistic

*Ana* allegorical, symbolical (see corresponding nouns at ALLEGORY): occult, esoteric, *recondite

**analgesia** anesthesia, anodynia (see under ANODYNE 1)

**analgesic** *anodyne, anesthetic

*Ant* irritant

**analogous** *like, alike, similar, comparable, akin, parallel, uniform, identical

*Ana* corresponding, convertible (see RECIPROCAL): kindred, *related, allied, cognate

**analogue** counterpart, *parallel, correlate

**analogy** 1 *likeness, similitude, resemblance, similarity, affinity

2 Analogy, simile, metaphor designate a comparison between things essentially or generically different but strikingly alike in one or more pertinent aspects. **Analogy** is the general term since the simile and the metaphor are kinds of analogies: it is, however, usually restricted in its application to a comparison which brings out the analogy (for this

---

*Ana* analogous words     *Ant* antonyms     *Con* contrasted words     See also explanatory notes facing page 1

sense see LIKENESS) between two things for the sake of elucidating something hard to understand ⟨God cannot be described except by *analogy*⟩ ⟨the supreme example of *analogy* in English is *Pilgrim's Progress*. This overwhelms us with direct *analogy*, that is to say, the personification of allegory—*Stevens*⟩ A **simile** is an imaginative analogy used largely for the sake of literary effect by carrying over the emotion aroused by one image or idea to the other with which it is compared. A simile (for example, "fishing is at best almost as unpredictable as New England weather," "blue were her eyes as the fairy-flax, her cheeks like the dawn of day," "a job full of more headaches than a case of bourbon") is often brief but it characteristically indicates (as by the use of *like, as, so*) that comparison is intended ⟨of the *simile*, we say that two essentially unlike things are explicitly compared . . . and we are to understand that, though some likeness is suggested between the two, the likeness is not literally intended—*Margolis*⟩ A **metaphor** differs from a simile in not stating explicitly that it is an analogy: it therefore imaginatively identifies one object with another (as in "a heart of stone," "Thy word is a lamp unto my feet," "the moon was a ghostly galleon") and ascribes to the first one or more of the qualities of the second or invests the former with emotional or imaginative associations attached to the latter ⟨though by *metaphor* we point to objects and convey emotions, what we chiefly do is to convey knowledge by forging new symbols that are themselves patterns of meaning—*Waggoner*⟩

**analysis** resolution, dissection, breakdown (see under ANALYZE)

*Ana* separation, division (see corresponding verbs at SEPARATE): disintegration, decomposition (see corresponding verbs at DECAY)

*Ant* synthesis —*Con* uniting *or* union, combining *or* combination (see corresponding verbs at JOIN): integration, concatenation (see under INTEGRATE)

**analytical** subtle, *logical

*Ana* acute, keen, *sharp: profound, *deep: penetrating, piercing (see ENTER): organizing, ordering, marshaling (see ORDER *vb*)

*Ant* creative, inventive, constructive

**analyze,** resolve, dissect, break down mean to divide a complex whole or unit into its component parts or constituent elements. When their corresponding nouns (**analysis, resolution, dissection, breakdown**) denote such a division, they are similarly applied and are distinguishable by the same implications. **Analyze** and **analysis** presuppose a personal agent and stress division for the sake of determining a thing's true nature or the inner relationship of its parts ⟨*analyze* a sentence⟩ ⟨*analyze* the plot of a novel⟩ ⟨Liebig, by *analyzing* foodstuffs of every kind, came to the conclusion that the principal elements of food are proteins, fats, and carbohydrates⟩ ⟨he would take a place or a fork or a bell, set it to ringing by a blow, and *analyze* the combination of musical notes which it emitted—*Darrow*⟩ ⟨*analysis* of material objects into electrons and protons—*Inge*⟩ Sometimes these words specifically suggest an intent to discover or uncover qualities, causes, effects, motives, or possibilities often as a basis for action or for a judgment ⟨*analyze* the condition of a business before investing in it⟩ ⟨*analyze* the potential market for cotton⟩ ⟨I could not then so far *analyze* all that is roughly lumped together as "religion" as to disentangle the essential from the accidental—*Ellis*⟩ Often, especially in chemistry and other sciences, the words imply close examination as for detecting impurities or the quantity or quality of each of the constituent elements ⟨*analyze* a city's water supply⟩ ⟨*analyze* a hypothesis⟩ **Resolve** and **resolution** only occasionally

imply a personal agent; they therefore seldom suggest more than the actual division or separation into elements or parts ⟨star clusters . . . so distant that even in telescopes of great power they could not be *resolved*—*Lockyer*⟩ ⟨nothing but death was strong enough to shatter that inherited restraint and *resolve* it into tenderness—*Glasgow*⟩ Sometimes, especially in medicine, *resolve* or *resolution* implies a breaking up or disintegration and usually, as a consequence, a dissipation or scattering ⟨*resolution* of the exudate during recovery from pneumonia⟩ **Dissect** and **dissection** stress the actual and visible separation of parts; thus, one *dissects* or cuts into sections an animal or a plant so that its physical structure can be studied; in extended or figurative use, one *dissects* something when one takes it to pieces and offers it for examination from every angle and in every detail, pleasant or unpleasant ⟨we *dissect* the senseless body, and why not the mind?—*Wordsworth*⟩ ⟨the student who is willing . . . to discipline his mind by the patient correlation of facts and the fearless *dissection* of theories—*Baerlein*⟩ ⟨when you . . . *dissect* the Odyssey, what amazing artifice is found under that apparently straightforward tale! —*Quiller-Couch*⟩ **Break down** and **breakdown** are used chiefly with reference to topics (as financial reports, statements, or estimates) that involve numbers or quantities, or to substances separated by chemical agents. In both situations these words imply reduction to simpler parts or divisions ⟨a consolidated balance sheet is often accompanied by a *breakdown* giving a detailed statement for each of the main items involved⟩ In chemistry division into simpler substances rather than into elements is typically implied ⟨proteins are *broken down* by enzymes into amino acids⟩

*Ana* *separate, divide, part: classify, pigeonhole, *assort

*Ant* compose, compound: construct —*Con* *integrate, concatenate, articulate

**anarchic** anarchistic, anarchist (see under ANARCHY 1)

**anarchism** *anarchy

**anarchist** anarchic, anarchistic (see under ANARCHY 1)

**anarchistic** anarchic, anarchist (see under ANARCHY 1)

*Ant* authoritarian

**anarchy** 1 Anarchy, anarchism overlap in their implications but are not synonyms because of differing denotations. **Anarchy** may denote a state or condition of society where there is no law or imposed order because social evolution has rendered these unnecessary ⟨first the proletarian revolution . . . then the dictatorship of the proletariat; and lastly, the classless society: that is the Marxian order of advance towards communism and *anarchy*, towards justice, equality and perfect freedom—*Plamenatz*⟩ It may, on the other hand, denote one of complete disorder resulting from the breakdown of normal controls ⟨for our people liberty so often means only license and *anarchy*—*Sulzberger*⟩ **Anarchism** denotes a theory that government is an evil because it imposes limitations upon the freedom of the individual ⟨nihilism is a form of *anarchism*⟩ The same distinctions extend to their respective adjectives **anarchic** and **anarchistic** ⟨*anarchic* disorder⟩ ⟨*anarchic* conditions⟩ ⟨*anarchistic* influences⟩ ⟨*anarchistic* doctrines⟩ **Anarchist** when used adjectivally is often ambiguous since it is related to both *anarchism* and *anarchy* ⟨an *anarchist* plot to assassinate the prime minister⟩

2 Anarchy, chaos, lawlessness denote in common absence, suspension, breakdown, or widespread defiance of government, law, and order. **Anarchy** is the total absence or suspension of government ⟨by the adoption of the Constitution our country passed from weakness to strength, from *anarchy* to order, from death to life—*Muzzey*⟩

A colon (:) separates groups of words discriminated. An asterisk (*) indicates place of treatment of each group.

Chaos is the utter negation of order ⟨a process calculated to reduce the orderly life of our complicated societies to *chaos—Huxley*⟩ **Lawlessness** signifies a prevalent or habitual disregard of law and order rather than their absence or suspension ⟨the traditional *lawlessness* of the frontier community⟩ When *anarchy* and *lawlessness* (or their adjectives) are used of actions rather than of a state of things, there is often little distinction of meaning ⟨the hydrogen atom was not conforming to the canons of the classical music of physics, and yet it was not *anarchic* in the least, for . . . it was flawlessly obeying the laws of a different music—*Darrow*⟩ ⟨illusion is not *lawless*. It is a world apart, if you please, but within it are its own necessities, which exact inexorable adherence to their mandates—*Lowes*⟩
*Ant* order: discipline

**anathema** 1 *abomination, bête noire, bugbear
2 *curse, malediction, imprecation
*Ana* denunciation, condemnation, reprobation, censure (see corresponding verbs at CRITICIZE)
**anathematize** curse, damn, *execrate, objurgate
*Ana* denounce, condemn, censure, reprobate (see CRITICIZE): proscribe, *sentence
**anatomy** *structure, skeleton, framework
**ancestor,** progenitor, forefather, forebear mean a person from whom one is descended. **Ancestor,** especially in genealogical and in historical use, implies lineal descent through one's father or mother ⟨he had three *ancestors* who were judges⟩ but it is seldom applied to a grandparent. In more general use, *ancestor* (especially in the plural) may imply kinship through collaterals or through race ⟨the gentleman will please remember that when his half-civilized *ancestors* were hunting the wild boar in Silesia, mine were princes of the earth—*Benjamin*⟩ *Ancestor* often suggests knowledge of identities and family pride in them as persons ⟨*ancestor* worship⟩ ⟨they had plenty of money, but apparently no *ancestors*⟩ **Progenitor** differs from *ancestor* chiefly in its connotations rather than in its implications. It does not exclude parents or grandparents; it usually carries no hint of family or racial feeling, and it often suggests a reference to heredity or the transmission of characters ⟨do as your great *progenitors* have done, and, by their virtues, prove yourself their son—*Dryden*⟩ ⟨men resemble their contemporaries even more than their *progenitors*—*Emerson*⟩ Whenever an evolution is suggested, *ancestor* and *progenitor* may be used of living things or of nonliving things (as races, social castes, or literary or artistic forms) that are subject to development; they then often denote one or a kind or group from which a later or a presently existing kind or group has been derived ⟨the wild *ancestors* of our domestic animals⟩ ⟨Fielding was . . . the *progenitor* of the modern realistic novel—*New Yorker*⟩ **Progenitor,** even more than *ancestor,* names the ultimate source or root ⟨he sang of the nuptials of Janus and Comesena, *progenitors* of the Italian people—*Quiller-Couch*⟩ **Forefather** is used less often than *ancestor* in historical writing but is probably more common in poetic and in general use, especially when simplicity of life, strength of family feeling, or persistence of a family in one locality is connoted ⟨each in his narrow cell forever laid, the rude *forefathers* of the hamlet sleep—*Gray*⟩ ⟨think of your *forefathers*! Think of your posterity!—*J. Q. Adams*⟩ **Forebear** is not only less rich in its implications than *forefather,* but it is also less connotative of sentiment ⟨the land had been owned by his *forebears* for generations⟩ ⟨his *forebears* emigrated from Scotland around 1800⟩
*Ant* descendant

**ancestry,** lineage, pedigree mean either one's progenitors collectively or their quality or character as a whole. The words, however, are clearly distinguishable. **Ancestry** in its most restricted use evokes the image of a family tree with its ramification by geometrical progression of branches or roots the further it is traced forward or backward ⟨only by the fusion of two parent cells can an offspring cell enjoy the advantages of joint heredity and pass on the traits of both *ancestries—La Barre*⟩ In broader use *ancestry* often suggests one's progenitors in general, known or unknown, a cause of pride often, but sometimes of indifference or of shame ⟨no one is responsible for his *ancestry,* but his *ancestry* is to a certain extent responsible for his qualities⟩ **Lineage** stresses descent in a line; it evokes therefore the image of a list of the persons who in order of generation are descended from a single ancestor ⟨the evangelist Matthew traced the *lineage* of Jesus by each step from Abraham down⟩ ⟨*lineage* is reckoned through the mother; the Zuñi are matrilineal —*Kardiner*⟩ For this reason *lineage* is often used as the equivalent of *race* ⟨though of a *lineage* once abhorred —*Wordsworth*⟩ **Pedigree** is even more definite in its suggestions, for it implies a known and recorded ancestry that is typically distinguished or notable ⟨who proud of *pedigree,* is poor of purse—*Pope*⟩ ⟨the deference due to a man of *pedigree—Gilbert*⟩ The term is applied to the ancestry of persons, and to that of animals and plants propagated under controlled conditions.
*Ant* descendants: posterity
**anchor** *vb* moor, *secure, rivet
*Ana* *fasten, attach, fix, affix
**anchorite** hermit, eremite, *recluse, cenobite
*Ana* *ascetic, mystic: *religious, monk, friar
**ancient** *old, venerable, antediluvian, antique, antiquated, archaic, obsolete
*Ana* primeval, pristine, primal, primordial (see PRIMARY)
*Ant* modern —*Con* *new, new-fashioned, new-fangled, fresh, novel, modernistic: current, *prevailing
**ancillary** *auxiliary, contributory, subsidiary, adjuvant, subservient, accessory
*Ana* assisting, aiding, helping (see HELP *vb*): secondary, *subordinate: supplementary, complementary (see corresponding nouns at COMPLEMENT)
**androgynous** *bisexual, hermaphroditic, hermaphrodite, epicene
**anecdote** *story, tale, yarn, narrative
*Ana* incident, episode, event, *occurrence: narration, relation, recital (see corresponding verbs at RELATE)
**anemic** bloodless, *pale
*Ant* full-blooded: florid
**anesthesia** analgesia, anodynia (see under ANODYNE 1)
**anesthetic** *adj* insensitive, *insensible, impassible
*Ana* *dull, obtuse: *impassive, apathetic, stolid: impervious, impermeable, impenetrable, *impassable
*Ant* alive —*Con* *aware, awake, conscious, cognizant: responsive (see TENDER)
**anesthetic** *n* *anodyne, analgesic
*Ant* stimulant
**angel** backer, *sponsor, patron, surety, guarantor
**anger** *n* **Anger,** ire, rage, fury, indignation, wrath denote emotional excitement induced by intense displeasure. **Anger,** the generic term of this group, names merely the emotional reaction; the word in itself suggests no definite degree of intensity and carries no necessary implication of outward manifestation ⟨tried to conceal his *anger*⟩ ⟨easily aroused to *anger*⟩ ⟨self-destroying *anger*⟩ ⟨he saw the calf, and the dancing: and Moses' *anger* waxed hot—*Exod* 32:19⟩ **Ire** is literary and suggests greater intensity than *anger* unqualified and usually

a display of that feeling in looks, acts, or words ⟨Belinda burns with more than mortal *ire*—*Pope*⟩ ⟨"Then, my lad, ye've come to tell me a lie!" Farmer Blaize looked straight at the boy, undismayed by the dark flush of *ire* he had kindled—*Meredith*⟩ **Rage** adds to *anger* the implications of lost self-control and of violent boiling over of feeling; it often connotes variously a sense of frustration, a temporary derangement of the mind, or a determination to get revenge ⟨terrible and impotent *rage*—*Wilde*⟩ ⟨his first hot anger against the beast had changed into a cold *rage*: at all costs now he must get it—*Cloete*⟩ **Fury** is overmastering destructive rage verging on madness ⟨what *fury* drove us into saying the stupid, intolerant, denunciatory things we said?—*L. P. Smith*⟩ ⟨the war against physical evil, like every other war, must not be conducted with such *fury* as to render men incapable of the arts of peace—*Russell*⟩ **Indignation** implies depth and intensity of anger, often righteous or generous anger, aroused by something one considers mean, shameful, or otherwise unworthy of a man or men ⟨whose souls no honest *indignation* ever urged to elevated daring—*Shelley*⟩ ⟨the question now placed before society . . . is this: Is man an ape or an angel? I, my lord, I am on the side of the angels. I repudiate with *indignation* and abhorrence those newfangled theories—*Disraeli*⟩ **Wrath** may imply either rage or indignation as its emotional basis, but more strongly than either of these it suggests existence of a grievance and a desire or intent to avenge or punish or to get revenge ⟨the *wrath* of God⟩ ⟨let not the sun go down upon your *wrath*—*Eph* 4:26⟩ ⟨nursing her *wrath* to keep it warm—*Burns*⟩

*Ana* *acrimony, asperity: exasperation, irritation, provocation (see corresponding verbs at IRRITATE)

*Ant* pleasure, gratification: forbearance —*Con* *patience, longanimity, long-suffering: forgiveness, condonation, pardon (see corresponding verbs at EXCUSE): indulgence, clemency, leniency (see under FORBEARING)

**anger** *vb* Anger, incense, enrage, infuriate, madden. All these verbs carry in common with **anger**, their general term, the denotation to make angry or to rouse to anger ⟨laugh then at any, but at fools or foes; these you but *anger*, and you mend not those—*Pope*⟩ ⟨*angered* by his son's repeated disobedience⟩ **Incense** implies hotness of anger, especially as provoked by something excessively irritating and offensive ⟨Mr. Critchlow, aged and unaccustomed to interference, had to render accounts of his trusteeship to this young man, and was *incensed*—*Bennett*⟩ ⟨magistrates and populace were *incensed* at a refusal of customary marks of courtesy and respect for the laws—*Inge*⟩ **Enrage** suggests a violent display of wrath or fury ⟨I pray you, speak not . . . question *enrages* him—*Shak.*⟩ **Infuriate** may imply a sense of being outraged or sometimes no more than of being thoroughly irritated or exasperated ⟨how it *infuriates* a bigot, when he is forced to drag into the light his dark convictions!—*L. P. Smith*⟩ ⟨his colleagues and his subordinates had been alternately delighted and *infuriated* by his assumed reluctance to deal with any practical question—*Sackville-West*⟩ **Madden** is often not distinguishable from *infuriate* ⟨can it be fancied that Deity ever vindictively made in his image a mannikin merely to *madden* it?—*Poe*⟩ Like the former it may imply merely excessive annoyance or vexation ⟨*maddening* delays⟩

*Ana* *offend, outrage, affront: exasperate, provoke, *irritate, nettle, rile: vex, *annoy, irk

*Ant* please, gratify: pacify —*Con* placate, mollify, appease, propitiate (see PACIFY): rejoice, delight, gladden, tickle (see PLEASE)

**angle** *vb* *fish

**angle** *n* **1** *point of view, viewpoint, standpoint, slant

*Ana* attitude, *position, stand

**2** aspect, facet, side, *phase

*Ana* *item, detail, particular

**angry, irate, indignant, wrathful, wroth, acrimonious, mad** mean feeling or showing strong displeasure or bad temper. **Angry** is applied to persons or their moods, acts, looks, or words; it is also applied to animals ⟨an *angry* bull⟩ and by extension, because of some of its implications, to things ⟨an *angry* boil⟩ ⟨an *angry* sky⟩ In reference to persons it implies both emotional and physical excitement, usually exhibited as by an inflamed countenance or inflamed words or by threatening looks or speeches ⟨the king is *angry*: see, he bites the lip—*Shak.*⟩ ⟨the adulteress! What a theme for *angry* verse!—*Cowper*⟩ **Irate** is applied only to persons or their looks, acts, or words; it often suggests greater exhibition of feeling than *angry* and, as a rule, implies loss of self-control ⟨the men were getting . . . more *irate* and violent in their language —*Trollope*⟩ Often it suggests a comic aspect of anger (as from the disparity between the emotion and its exciting cause) ⟨refractory children, over whom Mr. Spratt . . . exercised an *irate* surveillance—*George Eliot*⟩ **Indignant,** in contrast with *irate,* suggests righteousness in the anger and sufficiency of provocation. Often its use imputes injustice or indignity to the cause of the anger ⟨let the sword speak what the *indignant* tongue disdains to brand thee with—*Shelley*⟩ **Wrathful** and the less common **wroth** are capable of being used where *irate* or *indignant* would be more explicit ⟨his partner retreated with a *wrathful* shake of his head—*Sassoon*⟩ However, they usually connote more justification of the anger than *irate* and more vehemence in its expression than *indignant* ⟨the blurring and the blotching of the later Chinese school . . . provoke his *wrathful* condemnation—*Binyon*⟩ ⟨I did not know how greatly they were fools, and this made me *wroth*—*Kipling*⟩ *Wrathful* like *angry* may be extended to things ⟨the *wrathful* thunder of God—*Tennyson*⟩ ⟨a vagrant shaft of sunlight struck the ocean and turned its surface to *wrathful* silver—*London*⟩ **Acrimonious,** though sometimes still applied to a person's temper or mood, is chiefly used to characterize intercourse and utterances. It invariably adds to *angry* the implication of irreconcilable difference of opinion and consequent bitterness of feeling that may be shown in accusations and recriminations ⟨the dispute dragged on, becoming progressively more *acrimonious,* for another eleven years —*Huxley*⟩ **Mad** (see INSANE) as a close equivalent of angry is used chiefly in informal speech or writing ⟨I was so *mad* the way father was talking—*O'Flaherty*⟩ ⟨she looked *mad* for a second but then she began to laugh—*Lowry*⟩

*Ana* *impassioned, passionate: angered, incensed, enraged, infuriated, maddened (see ANGER *vb*)

**anguish** woe, heartache, heartbreak, grief, *sorrow, regret

*Ana* *distress, suffering, dolor, misery, agony: worry, anxiety (see CARE): *pain, pang, throe, ache: torture, torment, affliction (see corresponding verbs at AFFLICT)

*Ant* relief —*Con* comfort, solace, consolation (see corresponding verbs at COMFORT): assuagement, alleviation, mitigation (see corresponding verbs at RELIEVE): *ecstasy, rapture, transport

**angular** gaunt, rawboned, lank, lanky, *lean, spare, scrawny, skinny

*Ana* *thin, slender, slim: *awkward, clumsy: cadaverous, *haggard

*Ant* rotund —*Con* plump, chubby, *fleshy, stout, portly

**animadversion,** stricture, aspersion, reflection denote a

---

A colon (:) separates groups of words discriminated. An asterisk (*) indicates place of treatment of each group.

remark or statement that is an adverse criticism. **Animadversion** (compare *animadvert* at REMARK) implies as its motive deep-seated prejudice or ill will or a tendency to carp or cavil ⟨given to *animadversions* on the clergy⟩ ⟨Maty's *animadversions* hurt me more. In part they appeared to me unjust, and in part ill-natured—*Cowper*⟩ **Stricture** implies censure, which may be either ill-natured or judicious ⟨foreign *strictures* on the dress, looks, and behavior of the English abroad—*Arnold*⟩ ⟨the lash of the merciless Porson . . . [whose] *strictures* are founded in argument, enriched with learning, and enlivened with wit—*Gibbon*⟩ **Aspersion** imputes a slanderous character to the criticism ⟨who by *aspersions* throw a stone at th' head of others, hit their own—*Herbert*⟩ ⟨at Cambridge (they tell me) while you speak very well, you write less expertly . . . . you will not set the *aspersion* down to me—*Quiller-Couch*⟩ **Reflection** often implies indirect aspersion or a defamatory imputation which may be inferred from what has been said ⟨he cannot restrain himself from *reflections* on kings and priests when he is most .contending for them—*Hallam*⟩ ⟨the *reflections* on certain named persons' chastity and honesty—*Geographical Jour.*⟩

*Ana* criticism, reprehension, censure (see corresponding verbs at CRITICIZE): observation, comment, *remark: captiousness, faultfinding, caviling, carping, censoriousness (see corresponding adjectives at CRITICAL)
*Ant* commendation —*Con* praise, laudation, extollation, acclaim (see corresponding verbs at PRAISE): *approbation, approval

**animadvert** comment, commentate, *remark
*Ana* *criticize, reprehend, censure, reprobate: deprecate, *disapprove: depreciate, disparage, *decry
*Con* ignore, disregard, overlook (see NEGLECT): *commend, applaud, compliment

**animal** *adj* *carnal, fleshly, sensual
*Ana* physical, corporeal, *bodily: bestial, *brutal
*Ant* rational —*Con* intellectual, *mental, psychic: spiritual (see HOLY)

**animalism** *animality
*Ana* sensualism, voluptuousness (see corresponding adjectives at SENSUOUS): lustfulness, lasciviousness, lecherousness (see corresponding adjectives at LICENTIOUS)

**animality, animalism** are not always clearly distinguished when they are used to denote animal nature, character, or springs of action in a man or in men. **Animality** is often preferred when it is desired to suggest likenesses between men and animals rather than differences, and **animalism** when one wishes to convey in addition all the derogatory implications of *sensuality* or *sensualism* ⟨he disliked union with a woman whom he had never seen; moreover, when he did see her, she disappointed him, and he begat his first child in mere *animality*—*Forster*⟩ ⟨puritanism was a natural and necessary revolt . . . against that naturalism which threatened to end in sheer *animalism*—*Kingsley*⟩
*Ana* virility, maleness, masculinity (see corresponding adjectives at MALE)

**animate** *adj* *living, alive, animated, vital
*Ana* physical, corporeal, *bodily: animal, *carnal, fleshly
*Ant* inanimate —*Con* lifeless, *dead

**animate** *vb* **1** *quicken, vivify, enliven
*Ana* *vitalize, activate, energize
**2** *inform, inspire, fire
*Ana* motivate, actuate, *activate: *move, drive, impel, actuate: *stir, rouse, arouse
*Ant* inhibit —*Con* *restrain, curb, check: *frustrate, thwart

**animated** **1** alive, *living, animate, vital

*Ana* *active, live, dynamic: vitalized, energized, activated (see VITALIZE)
*Ant* inert —*Con* *inactive, passive: lifeless, inanimate, *dead
**2** *lively, vivacious, sprightly, gay
*Ana* buoyant, volatile, effervescent (see ELASTIC): *agile, brisk, spry, nimble: *spirited, high-spirited
*Ant* depressed, dejected —*Con* *languid, listless, spiritless, enervated: *lethargic, torpid, comatose

**animosity** animus, rancor, *enmity, hostility, antipathy, antagonism
*Ana* hatred, hate, detestation, abhorrence (see under HATE *vb*): vindictiveness, revengefulness, vengefulness (see corresponding adjectives at VINDICTIVE): *malice, ill will, malevolence, spite
*Ant* goodwill —*Con* *friendship, amity, comity: friendliness, neighborliness, amicableness (see corresponding adjectives at AMICABLE)

**animus** animosity, rancor, *enmity, hostility, antipathy, antagonism
*Ana* ill will, spite, spleen, grudge (see MALICE): prejudice, bias (see PREDILECTION)
*Ant* favor —*Con* *predilection, partiality: *sympathy, empathy

**annals** chronicle, *history.

**annex** *vb* *add, append, subjoin, superadd
*Ana* *join, unite, connect, link, associate: attach, affix, *fasten
*Con* *detach, disengage, abstract: divorce, *separate, part

**annex** *n* **Annex, extension, wing, ell** designate an addition to a main (and, often, the original) building. An **annex** may be attached to the main building or it may even not be adjacent to it. When used of an addition to a hotel, an office building, or a commercial or educational establishment it usually implies a provision for expanded activity. An **extension** is attached to a main or central building; when it projects from the central building and is connected with it at only one point it is called a **wing**; when it extends at right angles from one end of the building it is called an **ell**.
*Ana* *addition, increment, accretion

**annihilate** extinguish, *abolish, abate
*Ana* obliterate, efface, expunge, blot out, cancel, *erase: extirpate, *exterminate, eradicate, wipe
*Con* create, *invent, discover: *make, form, fashion, forge, shape: *renew, restore

**annotate, gloss** and their corresponding nouns **annotation, gloss** mean, as verbs, to add or append comment, or as nouns, an added or appended comment intended to be helpful in interpreting a passage or text. One **annotates** a text (as of a literary work) when one furnishes it with critical, historical, or explanatory notes (as footnotes, marginal notes, or notes in an appendix) ⟨*annotate* the works of Milton⟩ ⟨an *annotated* edition of Shakespeare's sonnets⟩ The subject of an annotation may be any word, passage, or detail which is capable of being explained to the advantage of the reader or student. One **glosses** a word or phrase which is obscure in meaning because foreign, obsolete, rare, or technical by providing its definition (as in a marginal or interlinear note) or one *glosses* a text when one supplies definitions of its difficult words and phrases ⟨medieval scholars, when they found in a Latin text a word not familiar to them, were accustomed to *gloss* it—*Krutch*⟩ The word sometimes conveys (possibly by confusion with *gloss,* to give a luster to) a derogatory implication of perversion or sophistication of meaning or fact ⟨trying to *gloss* away the irrationalities of the universe—*Edman*⟩
*Ana* elucidate, interpret, construe, *explain, expound: comment, commentate, *remark

---

*Ana* analogous words      *Ant* antonyms      *Con* contrasted words      See also explanatory notes facing page 1

**annotation** gloss (see under ANNOTATE)
*Ana* commentary, comment, observation, note, *remark
**announce** publish, proclaim, *declare, promulgate, advertise, broadcast
*Ana* disclose, *reveal, divulge, tell: *communicate, impart
*Con* *suppress, repress: conceal, *hide, bury: withhold, hold, hold back, reserve (see KEEP)
**announcement** publication, proclamation, declaration, promulgation, advertisement, broadcasting (see under DECLARE)
**annoy** *vb* 1 **Annoy, vex, irk, bother** mean to disturb and nervously upset a person. **Annoy** stresses loss of equanimity or patience as a result of being forced to endure something that one finds obnoxious or offensive or sometimes merely displeasing or distasteful. It seldom implies more than a temporary disturbance or display of irritation ⟨Richard's absence *annoyed* him. The youth was vivacious, and his enthusiasm good fun—*Meredith*⟩ ⟨it was . . . his lack of the ghost of a notion what anyone else was feeling that *annoyed* her, had always *annoyed* her—*Woolf*⟩ **Vex** usually implies greater provocation and a stronger disturbance than *annoy*; it often connotes a degree of anger but at other times it suggests deep perplexity or some worry ⟨faulty translation that so *vexes* teachers—*Grandgent*⟩ ⟨pointlessly *vexing* their minds with insoluble problems⟩ ⟨Mr. Darcy's behavior astonished and *vexed* her. "Why, if he came only to be silent, grave, and indifferent," said she, "did he come at all?" —*Austen*⟩ ⟨such petty details as now *vexed* the brooding soul of the old gentlewoman—*Hawthorne*⟩ **Irk** emphasizes difficulty in enduring and resulting weariness of spirit; it is most often used in reference to something that persists or recurs annoyingly ⟨the speed and the clatter *irk* me—*Kipling*⟩ ⟨the overiterated becomes the monotonous, and the monotonous *irks* and bores—*Lowes*⟩ **Bother** implies a usually mild interference with one's comfort or peace of mind such as may arise on the one hand from something that calls for activity or effort or on the other from something that excites, puzzles, worries, concerns, or confuses ⟨the sight of him *bothered* her and set her heart beating faster⟩ ⟨he would be too accessible and excessively *bothered* with details and complaints—*Crozier*⟩ ⟨let dozens of little matters go, rather than *bother* myself—*Bennett*⟩ ⟨I am not really *bothered* by these questions—the hoary old puzzles of ethics and philosophy—*L. P. Smith*⟩
*Ana* *irritate, nettle, aggravate, exasperate, rile: perturb, disturb, upset, agitate (see DISCOMPOSE)
*Ant* soothe  —*Con* *comfort, solace, console: *please, gratify, tickle
2 *worry, pester, plague, tantalize, tease, harass, harry
*Ana* fret, chafe (see ABRADE): badger, hector, heckle, chivy, *bait: trouble (see INCONVENIENCE)
*Con* *neglect, ignore, overlook: mollify, appease (see PACIFY)
**annul** 1 *nullify, negate, invalidate, abrogate
*Ana* *neutralize, negative, counteract: cancel, efface, obliterate, blot out, *erase: annihilate, *abolish, extinguish
2 **Annul, abrogate, void, vacate, quash** are used chiefly in legal context and mean to deprive of validity, force, or authority. Though varying little in denotation, these words are not always interchangeable, their appropriate selection being dependent on the character or status of the invalidating agent and on the character of the thing invalidated. **Annul** is the most general term, applicable to something (as a right, marriage, charter, or statute) that may be adjudged invalid or void. It implies the exercise of competent legal authority ⟨had parliament, immediately after the emanation of this charter . . . *annulled* the instrument . . .

the perfidy of the transaction would have been universally acknowledged—*John Marshall*⟩ To **abrogate** is the act of one having force and authority, and often legal jurisdiction. A ruler or an arbiter as well as a court may *abrogate* something (as a law, a treaty, or a convention) previously effective and in effect or in intent abolish it ⟨we are not . . . called upon to *abrogate* the standards of values that are fixed, not by you and not by me, but by . . . time—*Lowes*⟩ **Void** in legal context retains much of its basic meaning, to make empty or null. It is often interchangeable with *annul* ⟨the state supreme bench . . . *voided* the referendum—*Aswell & Michelson*⟩ Unlike the latter it need not imply the action of a legally competent authority ⟨it is the insanity of the testator that *voids* his will, not the act of a court⟩ Only competent legal authority can **vacate** or make ineffectual or invalid something that previously was effectual or valid ⟨*vacate* proceedings after the discovery of fraud⟩ ⟨*vacate* a grant of crown property⟩ **Quash** is a strictly legal term applied chiefly to indictments thrown out of court as defective.

**anodyne** 1 **Anodyne, analgesic, anesthetic** all denote something used to relieve or prevent pain, all are freely used both substantively and adjectivally, and all have a related noun, **anodynia, analgesia, anesthesia,** denoting the corresponding state. **Anodyne** is the oldest and most inclusive of these terms; it may be applied to any agent used primarily to relieve pain whether by dulling perception of pain or by altering the pain-causing situation (as by local stimulation of blood flow), often has a literary or popular rather than medical connotation, and is the only one of these terms given broad figurative use (see ANODYNE 2). **Analgesic** is narrower in scope; it is applied especially to a medicinal substance or preparation used locally or systemically to dull the perception of pain (as by action on the nervous system) usually without other major disturbance of consciousness. An **anesthetic** is a medicinal agent that produces insensibility both to pain and to all other sensations either of a particular part or area (*local anesthesia*) or of the whole body (*general anesthesia*): *anesthetic* is the one term to use of an agent designed to prevent anticipated pain (as from surgery) as distinct from one designed to assuage existent pain; thus, one is administered an *anesthetic* before a tooth is pulled and given an *analgesic* to relieve pain after the *anesthesia* has worn off.
2 **Anodyne, opiate, narcotic, nepenthe** mean something used to dull or deaden one's senses or one's sensibility and are often used adjectivally. **Anodyne** is frequently used as the opposite of *stimulant* ⟨had . . . made *anodyne* translations from Homer and Sophocles in "rhymic" and sleepy prose —*Santayana*⟩ It usually suggests something that allays excitement or mitigates mental distress often by inducing forgetfulness or oblivion ⟨this kind of religion cannot be anything better than an *anodyne*; but an *anodyne* is unfortunately just what many people want from their religion—*Inge*⟩ ⟨mutiny among the crews of Columbus was too much of a menace for the comforting daily sight of drifting vegetation not to be a very real mental *anodyne*—*Beebe*⟩ **Opiate** usually is applied to something that induces a dream state and a delusion of happiness; it also commonly suggests indifference to actual evils and a false sense of security or well-being with consequent stilling of all disturbing thoughts ⟨price-fixing is a most dangerous economic *opiate*—*T. W. Arnold*⟩ ⟨no military swagger of my mind, can smother from myself the wrong I've done him, —without design, indeed,—yet it is so,—and *opiate* for the conscience have I none—*Keats*⟩ **Narcotic** implies a putting to sleep or into a stupor; in figurative use, it suggests merely a pleasant drowsiness which overcomes one and has a lulling effect on mind and body ⟨many lovers of

the arts find in music, poetry, painting, and the novel escapes, as *narcotic* as they are delightful, from the pressures and exigencies in which we are involved—*Edman*⟩ ⟨the promise that religion offers of a larger reward is less likely to serve as a moral stimulant than as a moral *narcotic—Garvin*⟩ **Nepenthe**, the designation of a legendary drug or potion of the ancient Greeks, said to allay pain and sorrow, is used in modern English with the implication of something sweet and pleasurable substituted for something painful ⟨after the fiery stimulants, compounded of brimstone and bigotry, offered by the polemic theologians, the gentle sedative of Montaigne's conversation comes like a draft of *nepenthe—Preserved Smith*⟩ It is also freely used to denote the state of placid peace resulting from the use of a *nepenthe* ⟨only . . . in idle chatter and consoling gossip and scandal, and in the more unendurable cases in drink, can they find *nepenthe—Nathan*⟩

*Ant* stimulant: irritant

**anodynia** analgesia, anesthesia (see under ANODYNE 1)

**anoint** *oil, cream, grease, lubricate

**anomalous** *irregular, unnatural

*Ana* *abnormal, aberrant, atypical: *monstrous, prodigious: singular, unique, peculiar, *strange

*Con* normal, natural, *regular, typical: *usual, wonted, accustomed, customary

**anomaly** *paradox, antinomy

**answer** *n* reply, response, rejoinder, retort (see under ANSWER *vb* 1)

*Ana* defense, vindication, justification (see corresponding verbs at MAINTAIN): refutation, rebuttal (see corresponding verbs at DISPROVE)

*Con* question, query, inquiry, interrogation (see corresponding verbs at ASK): summoning *or* summons, call (see corresponding verbs at SUMMON)

**answer** *vb* 1 Answer, respond, reply, rejoin, retort (and their corresponding nouns **answer, response, reply, rejoinder, retort**) mean to say or write or sometimes to do something (or something that is said, written, or done) in return (as to a question, a call, a request, or a charge). One **answers** or makes an **answer** to a question, call, or appeal, or to the person or thing questioning, calling, or appealing, when one gives the attention or service demanded by one's situation or office or required by courtesy ⟨*answer* a query⟩ ⟨*answer* the telephone⟩ ⟨*answer* the doorbell⟩ In specific collocations the words carry more definite implications; thus, in *answering* an accusation one gives a detailed and sometimes, by suggestion, a successful defense; in having the *answers* to all the problems one has their correct solutions ⟨he could talk; he could assert; produce opinions and information, but he couldn't meet or *answer* arguments—*Rose Macaulay*⟩ One **responds** or makes a **response** to a person who endeavors to elicit an answer or to a thing which serves as a stimulus when one reacts, often spontaneously and usually without resistance, to the influence ⟨*respond* immediately to an appeal for help⟩ ⟨an unsatisfactory *response* to a call for recruits⟩ ⟨when she smiled, even strangers *responded*⟩ ⟨is it true that antiquated legal ideas prevent government from *responding* effectively to the demands which modern society makes upon it?—*Frankfurter*⟩ ⟨a trustful affectionate disposition . . . creates the *response* which it expects—*Russell*⟩ Respond and response are used in preference to *answer* and *reply* when they refer to the set answers to supplications (as in a litany) or to questions (as in a catechism) ⟨he answered by a deep, gravely accented: "Thanks, I will," as though it were a *response* in church—*Conrad*⟩ One **replies** or makes a **reply** (as to a question, charge, argument, or salute or to a questioner or an accuser) when one answers so as to cover the same

ground as the question or charge; thus, one may *answer* a letter by merely acknowledging its receipt, but one *replies* to it only when one answers all its questions or touches on all points requiring attention; an *answer* to a salute is uncertain in its nature if no details are given; a *reply* to a salute usually indicates that the salute has been returned in the same form or in kind and spirit. Often *reply* is equivalent to *answer back* (as by echoing, protesting, or when the question is rhetorical agreeing) ⟨the nymph exulting fills with shouts the sky; the walls, the woods, and long canals *reply—Pope*⟩ ⟨theirs not to make *reply*, theirs not to reason why, theirs but to do and die—*Tennyson*⟩ ⟨who is here so vile that will not love his country? If any, speak; for him have I offended. I pause for a *reply—Shak.*⟩ One **rejoins** or makes a **rejoinder** when one answers a reply ⟨the assembly took the governor's reply . . . into consideration, and prepared a suitable *rejoinder—Franklin*⟩ The terms are often used to indicate an answer to an unspoken question or to an objection ⟨"He can't sleep comfortably on that ship," she said. "In his present state," *rejoined* Andrew, "he might not sleep comfortably anywhere"—*Douglas*⟩ ⟨to an abstract objection an abstract *rejoinder* suffices—*James*⟩ One **retorts** or makes a **retort** to an explicit or implicit charge, criticism, or attack when one responds with an answer that is in effect a retaliation, or a counter charge, criticism, or attack ⟨it amused me . . . to read the interview and learn that I had . . . uttered a number of trenchant sayings upon female novelists. But the amusement changed to dismay when the ladies began to *retort—Quiller-Couch*⟩

*Ana* *acknowledge, recognize: *disprove, refute, rebut: defend, justify, vindicate, *maintain

*Con* question, *ask, interrogate, query, inquire, quiz: *summon, call

2 meet, *satisfy, fulfill

**answerable** *responsible, accountable, amenable, liable

*Ana* obliged, constrained, compelled (see FORCE *vb*): subject, *subordinate

**antagonism** antipathy, *enmity, hostility, animosity, rancor, animus

*Ana* opposition *or* opposing, resistance, withstanding, contesting, fighting, combating, conflict *or* conflicting (see corresponding verbs at RESIST): strife, conflict, difference, variance, dissension, contention, *discord

*Ant* accord: comity —*Con* *agreement, understanding: concord, *harmony, consonance

**antagonist** *opponent, adversary

*Ana* foe, *enemy: rival, competitor (see corresponding verbs at RIVAL): assailant, attacker (see corresponding verbs at ATTACK)

*Ant* supporter —*Con* ally, *partner, colleague

**antagonistic** counteractive, counter, *adverse

*Ana* opposing, resisting, withstanding, contesting, fighting, combating, conflicting (see RESIST): incompatible, discordant, *inconsonant: hostile (see corresponding noun at ENMITY): *antipathetic, averse

*Ant* favoring, favorable —*Con* propitious, auspicious, benign (see FAVORABLE): advantageous, *beneficial

**antagonize** *resist, withstand, contest, oppose, fight, combat, conflict

*Ana* *attack, assail, assault: *offend, outrage, affront, insult: *incite, foment, instigate

*Ant* conciliate —*Con* *pacify, placate, propitiate, mollify, appease

**ante** stake, pot, *bet, wager

**antecedent** *n* *cause, determinant, reason, occasion

*Ana* precursor, *forerunner: progenitor, forebear (see ANCESTOR)

*Ant* consequence —*Con* *effect, result, issue, sequel,

aftereffect, aftermath, outcome, upshot

**antecedent** *adj* *preceding, precedent, foregoing, previous, prior, former, anterior

*Ant* subsequent: consequent

**antediluvian** ancient, antiquated, obsolete, antique, venerable, archaic, *old

*Ana* primordial, primeval, primal, pristine (see PRIMARY): *early

**anterior** *adj* *preceding, precedent, previous, prior, foregoing, antecedent, former

*Ant* posterior —*Con* rear, hind, back, hinder, after (see POSTERIOR)

**anthropoid, anthropomorphic, anthropomorphous** all mean resembling man. **Anthropoid** in its basic meaning is used primarily of certain apes (as the chimpanzee and gorilla) and certain prehuman primate fossils that approach modern man in structure ⟨the *anthropoid* apes of the Miocene⟩ In extended use the reference to manlike apes rather than man predominates; thus, an *anthropoid* pelvis is a human pelvis that in shape and proportions resembles that of an anthropoid ape ⟨the revolutionary thug who has the fine art of bursting Razumov's eardrums . . . is an *anthropoid* forerunner of thousands who have gone one better than that in the police states—*Pritchett*⟩ **Anthropomorphic** and the less common **anthropomorphous** are used interchangeably when implying a physical resemblance to man ⟨the *anthropomorphic* deities of primitive peoples⟩ ⟨an *anthropomorphous* carving⟩ and both may replace *anthropoid* in its basic meaning especially when it is desired to avoid taxonomic implications ⟨*anthropomorphous* apes—*Darwin*⟩ ⟨Darwin himself carefully described men and apes as having evolved separately from some common "ancient . . . *anthropomorphic* subgroup"—*High School Biology*⟩ *Anthropomorphic* is the preferable term to modify a noun denoting something immaterial or to attribute human personality or quality as distinct from human physique ⟨expectancy is too *anthropomorphic* a concept . . . its use leads the reader to attribute to animals what in fact only occurs at the level of human beings equipped with language—*Charles Morris*⟩ ⟨the categories of cause, force, law, are *anthropomorphic* in origin and were thus originally metaphors—*Cohen*⟩

**anthropology, ethnology, archaeology** are clearly distinguishable sciences, but they are often confused by laymen because the investigations of scholars in these fields are largely concerned with ancient or primitive races. **Anthropology** is a general term covering many sciences which deal with the physical and cultural evolution of the human species from prehistoric times to the present. One branch of anthropology is **ethnology**, which is concerned with the origin, development, geographical distribution, and distinguishing character of the human races and often includes comparative cultural studies of existent peoples. **Archaeology** forms a link between history and anthropology. Its province is the investigation of prehistoric and ancient cultures and civilizations and a study of their material remains (as artifacts, monuments, and traces of agriculture).

**anthropomorphic, anthropomorphous** *anthropoid

**antic** *n* monkeyshine, caper, *prank, dido

*Ana* *trick, wile, artifice: *caprice, freak, vagary, whim: gambol, frolic, romp (see under PLAY *vb*)

**antic** *adj* grotesque, bizarre, *fantastic

*Ana* preposterous, absurd, *foolish: ludicrous, ridiculous, comic, comical, farcical, *laughable

*Con* *serious, solemn, somber, grave, sedate: sensible, prudent, *wise: conventional, formal (see CEREMONIAL)

**anticipate** 1 forestall, *prevent

*Ana* introduce, *enter: *foretell, forecast, presage: *frustrate, thwart, balk

*Ant* consummate —*Con* finish, complete, terminate, *close

**2** apprehend, *foresee, foreknow, divine

*Ana* *foretell, forecast, prognosticate: foretaste (see corresponding noun at PROSPECT): await, *expect

**anticipation** foretaste, *prospect, outlook

*Ana* foreseeing, foreknowing (see FORESEE): presentiment, foreboding, *apprehension: forecast, prophecy, prediction, presage (see corresponding verbs at FORETELL): conceiving, envisioning, imagining (see THINK)

*Ant* retrospect —*Con* recollection, reminiscence, remembrance, *memory: realization, actualization (see corresponding verbs at REALIZE)

**antidote** *corrective, check, control

*Ana* counteractive, neutralizer (see corresponding verbs at NEUTRALIZE): nullifier, negator, annuller (see corresponding verbs at NULLIFY): *remedy, medicine, physic

**antinomy** *paradox, anomaly

*Ana* opposite, contradictory, contrary, antithesis (see under OPPOSITE *adj*): contradiction, denial (see corresponding verbs at DENY): conflict, variance, *discord

**antipathetic, unsympathetic, averse** are often used as if they were synonyms. They are, however, not interchangeable if employed in accord with careful usage. Strictly, **antipathetic** is applied to things or to persons objectively considered that are disagreeable, distasteful, uncongenial, abhorrent, or repellent ⟨the whole place and everything about it was *antipathetic* to her—*Trollope*⟩ ⟨settlers to whom this formula was *antipathetic* were asked to go elsewhere—*Repplier*⟩ ⟨ushering in the year with a series of calls on the most remote and the most personally *antipathetic* of our innumerable relations—*Huxley*⟩ In broader use the word is applied to persons or groups of persons as though it were the antonym of *sympathetic*; it may imply animosity and not merely the absence of sympathy ⟨he really disliked Sir Theodosius, who was in every way *antipathetic* to him—*Joseph Shearing*⟩ **Unsympathetic**, on the other hand, is with rare exceptions applied to persons or to things personified or thought of as expressing personal feeling and suggests an attitude of indifference or insensitiveness or the absence of a response to an appeal to one's interest or emotions ⟨an *unsympathetic* nurse⟩ ⟨an *unsympathetic* review of a new book⟩ **Averse** (for synonyms in this sense see DISINCLINED) is closer to *unsympathetic* than to *antipathetic* in that it suggests the spirit in which a person meets something objective rather than the effect of a thing upon a person. However, *averse* implies not merely a lack of response but a definite turning away and consequently either avoidance or rejection ⟨*averse* to a suggestion⟩ ⟨*averse* to exercise on a hot day⟩ Thus, a man may be *unsympathetic* by nature yet not be *averse* to helping the poor. In general, it may be said that one is *averse* to (or, chiefly British, from) anything which is *antipathetic* to one.

*Ana* repellent, *repugnant, distasteful, abhorrent, obnoxious: *offensive, loathsome, repulsive, revolting

*Ant* congenial —*Con* attractive, alluring, charming (see under ATTRACT): sympathetic, compatible, *consonant: agreeable, grateful, gratifying, pleasing, *pleasant

**antipathy** 1 antagonism, *enmity, hostility, animosity, rancor, animus

*Ana* repugnance, abhorrence, repellency, distaste (see corresponding adjectives at REPUGNANT): avoidance, evasion, eschewal, escape (see corresponding verbs at ESCAPE)

*Ant* taste (*for*): affection (*for*) —*Con* *attraction, sym-

---

A colon (:) separates groups of words discriminated. An asterisk (*) indicates place of treatment of each group.

pathy: *predilection, partiality, prepossession: *attachment, love

2 **Antipathy, aversion** are closer synonyms than their corresponding adjectives when they denote the state of mind created by what is antipathetic to one. **Antipathy** distinctly implies an emotional state, often a settled emotion, which prevents reconciliation or contact or which more often definitely implies hostility (see ENMITY). **Aversion** on the other hand suggests a predisposition or an unwillingness to meet, encounter, or entertain, which shows itself in avoidance or rejection rather than in hatred; thus, one has an *antipathy* to cats who is violently repelled by them and drives them from his presence; one has an *aversion* to cats who merely avoids contact with them.

*Ana, Ant, Con* see those at ANTIPATHY 1

**antipodal, antipodean** antithetical, contrary, *opposite, contradictory, antonymous

**antipode** antithesis, contrary, opposite, contradictory, antonym (see under OPPOSITE *adj*)

**antiquated** archaic, obsolete, antediluvian, antique, *old, ancient, venerable

*Ana* superannuated, *aged

*Ant* modernistic: modish —*Con* modern, new-fashioned, novel, newfangled, *new: *stylish, fashionable, smart

**antique** ancient, *old, venerable, antiquated, antediluvian, obsolete, archaic

*Ant* modern: current

**antiseptic** *adj* germicidal, bactericidal, disinfectant (see under ANTISEPTIC *n*)

**antiseptic** *n* **Antiseptic, germicide, bactericide, disinfectant** all denote an agent that interferes with the growth and activity of microorganisms. An **antiseptic** is an agent that prevents or arrests the growth and activity of microorganisms, especially disease germs, without necessarily killing them. The word is used especially of substances mild enough to be used on living tissue. **Germicide** is used of an agent that kills microorganisms and especially disease germs. It is commonly applied to strong chemicals which cannot safely be used on living tissues. A **bactericide** is a germicide that destroys all kinds of bacteria (but does not necessarily kill bacterial spores). A **disinfectant** is an agent that frees from infection and especially a chemical germicide used to kill disease germs and other harmful microorganisms in sources of infection (as drains, sickrooms, clothing, bedding, laboratories, and stables). *Disinfectant* may be used of substances (as chloride of lime) which destroy disagreeable odors by interfering with the activity of the bacteria causing putrefaction. The same distinctions hold for the corresponding adjectives **antiseptic, germicidal, bactericidal, disinfectant.**

**antisocial** asocial, *unsocial, nonsocial

*Ana* anarchic, anarchistic, anarchist (see under ANARCHY): misanthropic, pessimistic, *cynical

*Ant* social

**antithesis** 1 contrast, *comparison, parallel, collation
2 opposite, antipode, contradictory, contrary, antonym (see under OPPOSITE *adj*)

**antithetical** *opposite, contrary, contradictory, antonymous, antipodal, antipodean

**antonym** opposite, contradictory, contrary, antithesis, antipode (see under OPPOSITE *adj*)

**antonymous** *opposite, contradictory, contrary, antithetical, antipodal, antipodean

**anxiety** worry, *care, concern, solicitude

*Ana* *distress, suffering, misery: *fear, dread, alarm, panic: *apprehension, foreboding, misgiving: doubt, *uncertainty, mistrust

*Ant* security —*Con* *certainty, assurance, certitude:

*confidence, self-possession, aplomb: composure, *equanimity, sangfroid

**anxious** 1 worried, concerned, solicitous, careful (see under CARE *n*)

*Ana* *fearful, apprehensive, afraid: uneasy, jittery, *impatient: perturbed, agitated, upset (see DISCOMPOSE)

*Ant* composed —*Con* *cool, unruffled, imperturbable, unflappable, collected: *confident, assured, sanguine, sure

2 *eager, keen, agog, avid

*Ana* desiring *or* desirous, wishing *or* wishful, craving (see corresponding verbs at DESIRE): yearning, longing, pining (see LONG *vb*)

*Ant* loath —*Con* reluctant, hesitant, *disinclined, indisposed, averse

**apartment** *room, chamber

**apathetic** phlegmatic, stolid, *impassive, stoic

*Ana* insensitive, impassible, *insensible, anesthetic: callous, *hardened: unaffected, untouched, unimpressed (see affirmative verbs at AFFECT): listless, spiritless, *languid

*Ant* alert (sense 1): aghast —*Con* stirred, roused, aroused, awakened (see STIR *vb*): vigilant, *watchful, wide-awake

**apathy** phlegm, stolidity, impassivity, impassiveness, stoicism (see under IMPASSIVE)

*Ana* inertness, inactivity, passiveness, supineness (see corresponding adjectives at INACTIVE): indifference, unconcern, aloofness, detachment (see corresponding adjectives at INDIFFERENT): *lethargy, torpidity, torpor

*Ant* zeal: enthusiasm —*Con* ardor, fervor, *passion: anxiety, concern, solicitude (see CARE *n*)

**ape** *vb* *copy, imitate, mimic, mock

*Ana* caricature, burlesque (see under CARICATURE *n*): emulate, *rival

**aperçu** sketch, précis, survey, digest, pandect, *compendium, syllabus

*Ana* epitome, brief, abstract, *abridgment

**apéritif** *appetizer

**aperture, interstice, orifice** denote an opening allowing passage through or in and out. **Aperture** is applied especially to any opening in a thing that otherwise presents a solid or closed surface or structure; it may be applied both to an opening that is a flaw (as a crack or cleft) or to one that is structurally essential ⟨daylight filtered through small *apertures* in the dungeon's outside wall⟩ ⟨windows are *apertures* to admit light and air⟩ ⟨the *aperture* of a camera⟩ ⟨pores are minute *apertures* in the skin that are the openings of skin glands⟩ **Interstice** is applied to any unfilled space or gap or interval especially in a fabric (in its widest sense) or in a mass. It is especially applicable to any of the openings in something that is loose in texture, coarse-grained, layered, or piled up ⟨the *interstices* between the stones of the wall were not filled with mortar⟩ ⟨a mesh is one of the *interstices* in a fish net⟩ *Interstice* is also used of time in the sense of an empty interval ⟨what . . . do they do . . . in all the mysterious *interstices* of their lives?—*L. P. Smith*⟩ **Orifice** is applied to any opening that serves chiefly as a mouth or as a vent ⟨the *orifice* of the bladder⟩ ⟨the *orifice* of a chimney⟩ ⟨the *orifice* of a wound⟩ ⟨horror . . . when Mongibello belches forth from all its *orifices* its sulphureous fires—*Borrow*⟩

*Ana* perforation, puncture, bore, prick (see corresponding verbs at PERFORATE): *hole, hollow, cavity: slit, slash, cut (see corresponding verbs at CUT)

**apex** 1 **Apex, vertex** are so often used interchangeably with reference to the tip or top point of a cone, a pyramid, or a conic section that a fundamental difference in implications is often ignored. **Apex** has particular reference to the sharpness or angularity of the point or tip; it may or may not in its literal application to things imply that this is the highest point ⟨the *apex* of the heart is its lower and pointed end⟩ ⟨the *apex* of a lung is its upper cone-shaped end⟩ *Apex* may also refer to the converging point of two lines whether they extend in a vertical plane or not ⟨*apex* of a leaf⟩ ⟨*apex* of a vein in a mine⟩ **Vertex** as a rule, and apart from some technical senses in mathematics, implies a base (real or assumed) and therefore a top or highest point. This implication is retained when the word is applied to concrete things; thus, the *vertex* of the head or of the skull is the highest point or the upper end of its axis; *vertex* in astronomy is the zenith either with reference to the observer or to the particular body under observation. **2** peak, *summit, culmination, pinnacle, climax, acme, meridian, zenith, apogee

**aphorism** apothegm, epigram, *saying, saw, maxim, adage, proverb, motto

**aphrodisiac** *erotic, amatory, amorous
*Ant* anaphrodisiac

**apiece** *each, severally, individually, respectively

**aplomb** assurance, self-assurance, self-possession, *confidence, self-confidence
*Ana* coolness, collectedness, nonchalance, imperturbability (see corresponding adjectives at COOL): *equanimity, composure, sangfroid: poise, savoir faire (see TACT)
*Ant* shyness —*Con* embarrassment, discomfiture (see corresponding verbs at EMBARRASS): confusion, befuddlement (see corresponding verbs at CONFUSE): perplexity, bewilderment, distraction (see corresponding verbs at PUZZLE)

**apocalypse** vision, *revelation, prophecy

**apocalyptic** see under REVELATION
*Ana* visionary, *imaginary, chimerical, quixotic: *mysterious, arcane, inscrutable: mystic, *mystical, anagogic: grandiose, magnificent, august, *grand

**apocryphal** mythical, *fictitious, legendary, fabulous
*Ana* questionable, dubious, *doubtful
*Con* genuine, *authentic, veritable, bona fide

**apogee** climax, peak, culmination, apex, acme, meridian, zenith, *summit, pinnacle
*Ant* perigee

**apologia** *apology, excuse, plea, alibi, pretext
*Ana* defense, justification, vindication (see corresponding verbs at MAINTAIN): interpretation, elucidation, explanation (see corresponding verbs at EXPLAIN)

**apology, apologia, excuse, plea, pretext, alibi** denote the reason or reasons offered in explanation or defense of something (as an act, a policy, or a view). In general use **apology** implies that one has been, at least apparently, in the wrong; it suggests either a defense that brings forward palliating circumstances or a frank acknowledgment of error with an expression of regret, by way of reparation ⟨"Pardon us the interruption of thy devotion . . ." —"My lord, there needs no such *apology*"—*Shak.*⟩ In its older sense, still found in very discriminating use, it implies no admission of guilt or error but a desire to make clear the grounds for some course, belief, or position that appears wrong to others ⟨*apologies* for various . . . doctrines of the faith—*Newman*⟩ **Apologia** is often used in place of *apology* in this latter sense ⟨Basil de Selincourt's *apologia* for Ruskin in the *Contemporary Review*—*The Nation*⟩ ⟨Viscount Grey of Fallodon . . . the other day delivered an *apologia* for democracy—*N. Y. Times*⟩ **Excuse** implies an intent to remove or avoid blame (as for a neglect of duty, a failure to accomplish an end, or a violation of a rule, law, or custom) ⟨"Achilles will not to the field tomorrow"—"What's his *excuse*?"—*Shak.*⟩

⟨we have forty million reasons for failure, but not a single *excuse!*—*Kipling*⟩ ⟨his pride . . . does not offend me so much as pride often does, because there is an *excuse* for it—*Austen*⟩ **Plea** stresses argument or appeal to others for understanding or sympathy ⟨old Hepzibah's scowl could no longer vindicate itself entirely on the *plea* of nearsightedness—*Hawthorne*⟩ ⟨he mumbled something about not having a license [for hunting], and was putting that in for a *plea* against the expedition—*Meredith*⟩ **Pretext** invariably suggests subterfuge and the offering of one reason or motive in place of the true one ⟨he made my health a *pretext* for taking all the heavy chores, long after I was as well as he was—*Cather*⟩ **Alibi** in law designates a plea of having been in another place at the time a crime was committed. In its broader use it implies a desire to shift blame or to evade punishment. It commonly connotes plausibility rather than truth in the excuse offered ⟨federal taxes are already being used as an *alibi* for cuts in local school budgets—*Groves*⟩
*Ana* defense, justification, vindication (see corresponding verbs at MAINTAIN): extenuation, palliation, glozing, whitewashing (see corresponding verbs at PALLIATE): amends, *reparation

**apostasy** desertion, *defection

**apostate** *n* *renegade, turncoat, recreant, backslider
*Ana* deserter, forsaker, abandoner (see corresponding verbs at ABANDON): *heretic, schismatic, dissenter, nonconformist
*Con* *convert, proselyte

**apothecary** pharmacist, *druggist, chemist

**apothegm** aphorism, epigram, *saying, saw, maxim, adage, proverb, motto

**apotheosis** *paragon, nonpareil, nonesuch

**appall** horrify, *dismay, daunt
*Ana* terrify, affright, *frighten: confound, dumbfound, bewilder (see PUZZLE)
*Ant* nerve, embolden —*Con* energize, *vitalize, activate: *comfort, solace, console

**appalling** *fearful, dreadful, terrible, horrible, frightful, shocking, awful, terrific, horrific
*Ana* dismaying, horrifying, daunting (see DISMAY *vb*): bewildering, dumbfounding, confounding (see PUZZLE *vb*)
*Ant* reassuring

**appanage** prerogative, privilege, perquisite, birthright, *right

**apparatus** **1** *equipment, gear, tackle, outfit, paraphernalia, machinery, matériel
*Ana* tool, *implement, utensil, instrument: network, *system, scheme
**2** *machine, mechanism, machinery, engine, motor
*Ana* *device, contrivance, contraption, gadget

**apparel** *vb* *clothe, attire, dress, array, robe
*Ana* outfit, accouter, appoint, equip (see FURNISH)
*Ant* divest —*Con* *strip, bare, dismantle, denude

**apparel** *n* *clothes, clothing, dress, attire, raiment

**apparent** **1** *evident, manifest, patent, distinct, obvious, palpable, plain, clear
*Ana* discernible, noticeable (see corresponding verbs at SEE): *perceptible, ponderable, tangible, appreciable
*Ant* unintelligible —*Con* *obscure, dark, enigmatic, vague, ambiguous, cryptic
**2 Apparent, illusory, seeming, ostensible** mean not really or actually being what it appears to be. Something is **apparent** that, however evident it may be from the point of view of the unaided senses, is not borne out by scientific investigation or by a knowledge of all the facts or circumstances ⟨the *apparent* size of the sun⟩ ⟨the *apparent* loss of weight of a body immersed in water—*Darrow*⟩ ⟨I am anxious to leaven our *apparent*, for it is really more *apparent* than

---

A colon (:) separates groups of words discriminated. An asterisk (*) indicates place of treatment of each group.

real, our *apparent* worldliness—*Mackenzie*⟩ Something is **illusory** that is the result of a false impression and acquires a character or appearance other than that found in the real thing or that seems to exist when it is actually non-existent. The deception may be the result of one's sense limitations (as in an optical illusion), of a misleading appearance assumed by certain natural phenomena (as a mirage or will o' the wisp), of one's own state of mind which colors or alters the objective reality, or of the strong stimulation of the imagination (as by a work of art) that causes one to accept as real something purely imaginary ⟨lengthwise stripes give an *illusory* height to the figure⟩ ⟨*illusory* pools of water on a highway⟩ ⟨a lover often attributes an *illusory* beauty to his beloved⟩ ⟨the beautiful is in a certain sense *illusory,* or rather contains an element of illusion—*Alexander*⟩ Something is **seeming** that is so like the reality in appearance that it may be mistaken for it. *Seeming* usually implies a character in the thing observed rather than, as with the two preceding words, a defect of observation. Often it suggests an intent to produce or delude ⟨Miss Wilmot's reception [of him] was mixed with *seeming* neglect, and yet I could perceive she acted a studied part—*Goldsmith*⟩ ⟨the whole of Burns's song has an air of straight dealing . . . but these *seeming* simplicities are craftily charged . . . with secondary purposes, ulterior intimations—*Montague*⟩ Something (as an aim or motive) is **ostensible** that is explicitly declared, professed, or avowed or that has the outward marks of the character ascribed to it yet has in fact another hidden aim, motive, or character; thus, to say that the *ostensible* purpose of a naval review is the celebration of a national holiday may imply the presence of another, deeper, and more significant purpose not revealed (as mobilization for war) ⟨natives from independent and feudatory courts whose *ostensible* business was the repair of broken necklaces . . . but whose real end seemed to be to raise money for angry Maharanees or young Rajahs—*Kipling*⟩
*Ana* \*false, wrong: deceptive, delusory, delusive, \*misleading: specious, credible, \*plausible
*Ant* real  —*Con* actual, true (see REAL): intrinsic, \*inherent, essential

**apparition, phantasm, phantom, wraith, ghost, spirit, specter, shade, revenant** mean a visible but immaterial appearance of a person or thing, especially a likeness of a dead person or of a person or thing that is not physically present. *Apparition, phantasm,* and *phantom* all stress the illusory character of what appears to the sight. **Apparition** often connotes suddenness or unexpectedness of coming ⟨[enter the ghost of Caesar] . . . I think it is the weakness of mine eyes that shapes this monstrous *apparition—Shak.*⟩ while **phantasm** often suggests the workings of a disordered or overexcited imagination ⟨horrible forms, what and who are ye? never yet there came *phantasms* so foul through monster-teeming Hell—*Shelley*⟩ and **phantom** a dreamlike character and form without substance or shape without body or mass ⟨so live and laugh, nor be dismayed as one by one the *phantoms* go—*E. A. Robinson*⟩ **Wraith** specifically denotes an apparition of a living person that appears to a friend or relative and portends the former's death but is also used of an apparition of a dead person ⟨she was uncertain if it were the gypsy or her *wraith—Scott*⟩ In extended use it stresses the insubstantial and evanescent character of the apparition ⟨O, hollow *wraith* of dying fame, fade wholly, while the soul exults—*Tennyson*⟩ The remaining words in their literal senses all denote an apparition of a dead person. **Ghost** and **spirit** are the familiar and general terms for a disembodied soul; **specter** (not necessarily human) connotes more of the mysterious or terrifying ⟨*ghosts,* wandering here and there, troop

home to churchyards—*Shak.*⟩ ⟨I am thy father's *spirit,* doomed for a certain term to walk the night—*Shak.*⟩ ⟨grisly *specters,* which the Fiend had raised—*Milton*⟩ ⟨lo! when the service was ended, a form appeared on the threshold . . . why does the bridegroom start and stare at the strange apparition . . . ? Is it a phantom of air . . . ? Is it a *ghost* from the grave . . . ?—*Longfellow*⟩ **Shade** usually connotes impalpability but it stresses personality rather than mode of appearance ⟨mighty heroes' more majestic *shades—Dryden*⟩ ⟨followed . . . by the *shade* of their dead relative—*Frazer*⟩ **Revenant,** when it denotes a ghost, carries none of the implications of the other terms for a disembodied spirit except the return from the grave; it is therefore used often in straight prose or where a term without emotional connotations is desirable ⟨thus, our *revenant* from a hundred years ago would find us occupied yet with measuring intensities of force—*Darrow*⟩ ⟨I felt for a queer moment of hallucination more of a ghost than the ghost I had come to visit—a *revenant* out of a rowdy present into the more stately epoch—*L. P. Smith*⟩
*Ana* illusion, \*delusion, hallucination

**appeal** *n* plea, \*prayer, petition, suit
*Ana* entreating *or* entreaty, beseeching, supplicating *or* supplication, imploring (see corresponding verbs at BEG): soliciting *or* solicitation, requesting *or* request, asking (see corresponding verbs at ASK)
*Con* demanding *or* demand, exacting *or* exaction, claim (see corresponding verbs at DEMAND): protesting *or* protest, objecting *or* objection, kicking (see corresponding verbs at OBJECT)

**appeal** *vb* plead, pray, sue, petition (see under PRAYER)
*Ana* implore, \*beg, beseech, entreat, supplicate: solicit, request, \*ask
*Con* \*demand, exact, claim: protest, kick, \*object

**appear** 1 Appear, loom, emerge mean to come out into view. In use, however, they are only rarely interchangeable. **Appear** is weakest in its implication of a definite physical background or a source; consequently it sometimes means merely to become visible or to become apparent (see EVIDENT) ⟨one by one the stars *appeared* in the sky⟩ ⟨nothing *appears* in the testimony to cause doubt of the defendant's guilt⟩ Sometimes it means to present oneself in public in a particular capacity or to be presented or given out to the public ⟨Clarence Darrow *appeared* as counsel for the defendant⟩ ⟨Booth *appeared* nightly as Hamlet for the last two weeks of his run⟩ ⟨the new biography of Lincoln will *appear* next month⟩ ⟨weeklies usually *appear* on Thursday or Friday⟩ **Loom** means appearing as through a mist or haze ⟨a smear of . . . lead-colored paint had been laid on to obliterate Henchard's name, though its letters dimly *loomed* through like ships in a fog—*Hardy*⟩ ⟨between the bed and the ottoman . . . the cot *loomed* in the shadows—*Bennett*⟩ Because things seen in a fog are often magnified by their indistinct outlines, *loom,* especially when followed in figurative use by *large* or *great* or when followed by *up,* suggests apparent and sometimes appalling magnitude ⟨some mornings it [a mesa] would *loom* up above the dark river like a blazing volcanic mountain—*Cather*⟩ ⟨that which *loomed* immense to fancy low, before my reason lies—*Browning*⟩ **Emerge** definitely implies a coming out into the open from something that envelops: the word therefore presupposes a period or condition of concealment, obscurity, gestation, or insignificance ⟨the sun *emerged* from the clouds⟩ ⟨after a long hunt for him, we saw him *emerging* from the crowd⟩ ⟨that part of northern Ohio where the Bentley farms lay had begun to *emerge* from pioneer life—*Anderson*⟩ ⟨Lord Sligo *emerges* from this account as an able and conscientious administrator—*Times Lit. Sup.*⟩

---

*Ana* analogous words      *Ant* antonyms      *Con* contrasted words      See also explanatory notes facing page 1

*Ana* *come, arrive: issue, emanate, rise, arise, *spring
*Ant* disappear: vanish —*Con* depart, retire, withdraw, *go, leave

2 *seem, look

**appearance, look, aspect, semblance** denote the outward show presented by a person or thing. **Appearance** often carries no additional implications ⟨judge not according to the *appearance—Jn* 7:24⟩ ⟨in drawing, represent the *appearances* of things, never what you know the things to be —*Ruskin*⟩ The word, however, frequently implies an apparent as opposed to an actual or genuine character and therefore often connotes hypocrisy, dissembling, or pretense when used of persons or their actions ⟨to be able to tyrannize effectively they needed the title and *appearance* of constitutional authority—*Huxley*⟩ ⟨they spent their lives trying to keep up *appearances,* and to make his salary do more than it could—*Cather*⟩ **Look** is often indistinguishable from *appearance* except that it more often occurs in the plural ⟨never judge a thing merely by its *looks*⟩ They are not interchangeable, however, in all instances. When a personal impression or a judgment is implied, *appearance* is the precise word ⟨Aristotle . . . while admitting that Plato's scheme has a plausible *appearance* of philanthropy, maintains that it is inapplicable to the facts of human nature—*Dickinson*⟩ When the emphasis is upon concrete details (as of color, shape, or expression) observable to everybody, *look* is a better choice ⟨he had the *look* of a man who works indoors and takes little exercise⟩ ⟨I choose my friends for their good *looks,* my acquaintances for their good characters, and my enemies for their good intellects—*Wilde*⟩ Specifically *look* is often applied to a person's expression as manifest in his face or posture ⟨she had a *look* about her that I wish I could forget —the *look* of a scared thing sitting in a net!—*Millay*⟩ **Aspect,** like *look,* stresses the features of a person or thing but when applied to persons, it usually distinctively suggests the characteristic or habitual appearance and expression, especially facial expression ⟨not risking a landing because of the fierce *aspect* of the natives—*Heiser*⟩ ⟨he was a very handsome man, of a commanding *aspect*— *Austen*⟩ *Aspect* often specifically implies reference to a facet or to the features that give something (as a place, an age, or a situation) its peculiar or distinctive character ⟨the *aspect* of affairs was very alarming—*Dickens*⟩ ⟨fifty years from now, it may be, the olive tree will almost have disappeared from southern France, and Provence will wear another *aspect—Huxley*⟩ ⟨democracy' . . . has different *aspects* in different lands—*Sulzberger*⟩ **Semblance** basically implies outward seeming without necessarily suggesting a false appearance ⟨it is the *semblance* which interests the painter, not' the actual object—*Times Lit. Sup.*⟩ Nevertheless it is rarely used in this sense without an expressed or implied contrast between the outward appearance and the inner reality ⟨thou, whose exterior *semblance* doth belie thy soul's immensity—*Wordsworth*⟩ Sometimes, however, the word stresses the likeness of the thing to something else without suggesting deceptiveness in the appearance ⟨a piked road that even then had begun to take on the *semblance* of a street—*Anderson*⟩

**appease** *pacify, placate, mollify, propitiate, conciliate
*Ana* assuage, alleviate, mitigate, lighten, *relieve: *palliate, extenuate: *satisfy, content
*Ant* exasperate, aggravate —*Con* perturb, upset, disturb, *discompose: vex, irk, *annoy, bother: *anger, incense, enrage, infuriate

**appellation** *name, title, designation, denomination, style
**append** *add, subjoin, annex, superadd
*Ana* affix, attach, *fasten
*Con* *detach, disengage: curtail (see SHORTEN)

**appendage, appurtenance, accessory, adjunct** designate something regarded as additional and at the same time as subsidiary to another object. **Appendage** implies a certain closeness of attachment or connection yet often stresses the idea of subordination or even uselessness ⟨the caudal *appendage*⟩ ⟨the smaller borough is a mere *appendage* of the larger⟩ ⟨those graceful and useless *appendages,* called Directors—*Scott*⟩ **Appurtenance** is applied to something that belongs to the principal object or goes with it customarily yet is not an integral part of it (as the barns, worksheds, garages, gardens on a piece of land or the permanent fixtures in a building) ⟨the bed itself, with all *appurtenances* of palliasse, mattresses, etc.—*Barham*⟩ **Accessory** is applied usually to something that is dispensable yet contributes to the appearance, usefulness, comfort, or convenience of the principal thing ⟨automobile *accessories*⟩ ⟨wore a beige suit with brown purse, gloves, and other *accessories*⟩ **Adjunct** is applied to something that is or may be added or joined to the principal thing without becoming an essential part of it ⟨in the great age of Louis XIV, it [the ballet] became an established institution, still an *adjunct* of opera—*Ellis*⟩ ⟨meter and rhyme are not mere *adjuncts* of poetry—*Alexander*⟩

**appendix, addendum, supplement** designate additional matter subjoined to a book. **Appendix** is used of appended material which contributes (as by way of illustration, amplification, or citation of documents) to the effectiveness of a treatment that is still relatively complete in itself. **Addendum** and **supplement,** however, agree in implying that the additional matter is essential to completeness of treatment but differ in that *addendum* suggests greater brevity and is frequently used of material added to supply omissions while *supplement* implies larger compass and is often applied to material added after some lapse of time, frequently as a separate publication, to embody later information. When the additional matter of an addendum is a list (as of words or items), the plural *addenda* is often used instead of *addendum.*

**apperception** assimilation, identification, *recognition
**appertain** pertain, belong, relate, *bear, apply
**appetite** *desire, lust, passion, urge
*Ana* hungering *or* hunger, thirsting *or* thirst, yearning, longing (see LONG *vb*): craving, wishing, coveting (see DESIRE *vb*): impulse, spring, *motive: *cupidity, greed
*Con* abnegation, self-abnegation, self-denial, *renunciation: asceticism (see under ASCETIC *n*): repugnance, distaste (see corresponding adjectives at REPUGNANT)

**appetizer, hors d'oeuvre, aperitif. Appetizer** is the comprehensive term denoting food or drink served in advance of a meal as a whet to the appetite; it may include cocktails and a savory tidbit served before going to the table or a first course (as of oysters, clams, fruit cocktail, or canapé) served at the table. **Hors d'oeuvre** may be used of a savory, salt, smoked, tart, or uncooked food served with cocktails or as a first course at table. Its more common plural form, *hors d'oeuvres,* generally suggests a tray of such foods from which one selects what pleases one's taste. An *aperitif* is a small drink of liquor and especially of a fortified and usually specially flavored wine taken shortly before lunch or dinner for the purpose of or under the pretext of stimulating the appetite.

**appetizing** *palatable, relishing, tasty, toothsome, flavorsome, savory, sapid
*Ant* nauseating

**applaud 1 Applaud, cheer, root** mean to demonstrate one's feeling, especially one's approbation or joy, audibly and enthusiastically. **Applaud** specifically and usually implies hand clapping ⟨it is not the custom to *applaud* preachers⟩ ⟨the audiences at grand opera are asked to *applaud* only at

---

A colon (:) separates groups of words discriminated. An asterisk (*) indicates place of treatment of each group.

the end of an act or scene⟩ ⟨each graduate was *applauded* as he came up to receive his diploma⟩ **Cheer** suggests shouting, usually of meaningless words (as *rah-rah-rah* or *hip-hip-hooray*) or of a set form of words adopted by a school, college, or organization as its own; in one use it implies organized rather than spontaneous effort and includes singing as well as shouting. *Cheer* differs from *applaud* also in its purpose, which is chiefly that of encouraging individuals or a team taking part in a competition or contest; often, however, it suggests jubilation aroused by a successful play or a brilliant feat. **Root** may imply cheering or applauding, but it stresses encouragement as the motive. Consequently it implies strong partisanship and vocal public championship of what one favors ⟨*root* for a candidate⟩ ⟨*root* for the home team⟩

*Ana* acclaim, extol (see PRAISE)

*Ant* hiss: boo —*Con* deride, taunt, *ridicule, mock

2 *commend, compliment, recommend

*Ana* *praise, eulogize, laud: *approve, endorse, sanction

*Ant* disparage: criticize —*Con* *decry, depreciate, belittle: censure, reprobate (see CRITICIZE): *disapprove, deprecate

**applause,** acclamation, acclaim, plaudits denote public expression of approbation. **Applause** usually suggests loudness or liveliness of demonstration and often carries its literal implication of clapping hands ⟨she waited until the *applause* died down⟩ ⟨round after round of *applause* greeted him⟩ However, it may be used to designate any other noisy or emphatic expression of approval (as stamping of feet, cheering, or waving of flags) ⟨*applause* rang out from a hundred thousand throats—*Froude*⟩ **Acclamation** adds to *applause* the implications of eagerness, enthusiasm, and often unanimity of assent: it often retains its basic implication of crying out ⟨he was nominated to the office by *acclamation* without a ballot, and with emphatically voiced approval⟩ ⟨his speech was received with *acclamation*⟩ **Acclaim** is more poetic than *acclamation* though often interchanged with the latter; it sometimes carries implications of loftier deeds and more enduring esteem than *acclamation* ⟨the heroes were hailed with *acclaim*⟩ ⟨his poetry met with universal *acclaim*⟩ **Plaudits,** though literally equal to *applause,* may suggest polite or gracious rather than demonstrative expressions of approval ⟨the colonel bowed and smiled with very pleasant good nature at our *plaudits*—*Thackeray*⟩

*Ana* cheering *or* cheers, rooting (see corresponding verbs at APPLAUD)

*Ant* hisses: boos —*Con* deriding *or* derision, taunting *or* taunts, ridiculing *or* ridicule, twitting, mocking (see corresponding verbs at RIDICULE)

**appliance** tool, *implement, instrument, utensil

*Ana* accessory, adjunct (see APPENDAGE): *device, contrivance, gadget

**applicable** *relevant, pertinent, apposite, apropos, germane, material

*Ana* *fit, suitable, appropriate, apt, felicitous, happy, meet, fitting, proper

*Ant* inapplicable —*Con* *impertinent: inept, *awkward

**applicant** aspirant, *candidate

**application** concentration, *attention, study

*Ana* intentness, engrossment, absorption (see corresponding adjectives at INTENT): toil, grind, drudgery (see WORK): sedulousness, assiduousness, industriousness *or* industry, diligence (see corresponding adjectives at BUSY)

*Ant* indolence —*Con* abstractedness *or* abstraction, absentmindedness (see corresponding adjectives at ABSTRACTED): laziness, slothfulness, faineance (see corresponding adjectives at LAZY)

**appliqué** *vb* *overlay, superpose, superimpose

*Ana* ornament, *adorn, decorate: affix, attach, *fasten

**apply** 1 *use, employ, utilize, avail

2 devote, *direct, address

*Ana* attend, mind, *tend: addict, accustom, *habituate: toil, labor, work, grind (see corresponding nouns at WORK)

*Con* *neglect, slight: divert (see AMUSE)

3 go, turn, *resort, refer

*Ana* appeal, petition (see under PRAYER): *beg, beseech, implore, supplicate

4 *bear, relate, pertain, appertain

**appoint** 1 name, *designate, nominate, elect

*Ana* *choose, select, pick, single: commission, *authorize, accredit

*Con* *dismiss, discharge, cashier

2 *furnish, equip, accouter, outfit, arm

*Ana* garnish, beautify, embellish, bedeck, deck (see ADORN): array (see CLOTHE)

*Con* dismantle, divest, denude, *strip

**appointment** *engagement, rendezvous, tryst, assignation, date

**apportion** 1 allocate, *allot, assign

*Ana* *distribute, divide, dispense, deal, dole: *share, participate, partake

*Con* *gather, collect, assemble: consolidate, concentrate, *compact

2 Apportion, portion, parcel, ration, prorate mean to divide something carefully and distribute it among a number. **Apportion** suggests division on a just, fair, or equitable basis; it does not, however, imply equality in the divisions or in the persons or things affected by the distribution ⟨*apportioned* his time among various employments⟩ ⟨*apportion* the residue of an estate according to the terms of a will⟩ ⟨to *apportion* the judicial power between the supreme and inferior courts—*John Marshall*⟩ **Portion** (often with *out*) commonly suggests division into more or less equal shares ⟨in the *portioning* out of war resources China had been left at the end of the table—*Feis*⟩ ⟨the country was *portioned* out among the petty chiefs⟩ **Parcel** (usually with *out*) does not always imply immediate distribution, but it does imply division for the sake of ultimate distribution (as among purchasers or heirs); it is the preferred word when what is divided is cut into pieces, separated into lots, or distributed in small amounts ⟨it could be *parceled* out into lots fifty by one hundred feet at five hundred dollars per lot—*Dreiser*⟩ ⟨colonies were estates to be exploited for the benefit of the home merchants, and the world was *parceled* out among privileged companies—*Randall*⟩ **Ration** usually implies authoritative allowance and an equal division of necessities (as fuel, food, or clothing) according to some principle (as of adequacy, sufficiency, or dietary variety or, when the available supply is limited or scanty, of fairness to all) ⟨*ration* the food for the horses⟩ ⟨where capital is short, it must be *rationed* intelligently, in the same way as gasoline and sugar were *rationed* in wartime—*Lans*⟩ ⟨the drinking water was *rationed* during the prolonged voyage⟩ **Prorate** implies proportional division (sometimes proportional assessment) for the sake of fairness to those concerned: it may imply an authoritative decision as by a legislature, or an agreement among those concerned ⟨*prorate* employment among the workers during slack seasons⟩ ⟨*prorate* overhead expenses among the various departments of a company⟩ ⟨the entire field was to be put in truck crops, and the yield *prorated* to the workers—*Lord*⟩

*Ana* *grant, accord, award: *give, bestow: *separate, divide, part

**apposite** pertinent, germane, *relevant, apropos, applicable, material

---

*Ana* felicitous, happy, apt, appropriate, suitable, *fit, fitting: pat, timely, opportune, *seasonable
*Ant* inapposite, inapt —*Con* *impertinent: *awkward, inept: casual, hit-or-miss, haphazard, *random

**appraise** value, *estimate, evaluate, assay, rate, assess
*Ana* *judge, adjudge: determine, ascertain, *discover: inspect, examine, *scrutinize, audit

**appraising** (see under ESTIMATE *vb*)

**appreciable** *perceptible, sensible, ponderable, palpable, tangible
*Ana* apparent, *evident: discernible, noticeable (see corresponding verbs at SEE)
*Ant* inappreciable —*Con* impalpable, imponderable, *imperceptible, intangible, insensible

**appreciate** 1 comprehend, *understand
*Ana* appraise, value, rate, *estimate, evaluate: *judge, adjudge: *apprehend, comprehend
*Ant* depreciate —*Con* disparage, derogate, detract, belittle, *decry

**2 Appreciate, value, prize, treasure, cherish** mean to hold in high estimation. One **appreciates** what one understands sufficiently to admire critically or to enjoy with discrimination of its values, especially its aesthetic values ⟨relatively few persons are able to *appreciate* the fugues of Johann Sebastian Bach⟩ ⟨he liked to be near people and have his talent as a whittler *appreciated*—*Anderson*⟩ *Appreciate* may not always carry this strong implication of intelligent admiration but may stress rather a response of warm approval, keen enjoyment, or gratitude ⟨those who are just beginning to *appreciate* the idea—*Mackenzie*⟩ ⟨nature actually made him ache, he *appreciated* it so—*Galsworthy*⟩ ⟨children easily *appreciate* justice—*Russell*⟩ One **values** what one rates highly or as worth more than other persons or things ⟨*value* honor more than life⟩ ⟨there is nothing he *values* so much as the respect of his children⟩ ⟨the tragedy of plain women; to be *valued*, but not loved—*Mary Austin*⟩ One **prizes** what one values highly, especially as a possession, and takes deep pride in or sets great store by ⟨the good we never miss we rarely *prize*—*Cowper*⟩ ⟨what is freedom and why is it *prized*? —*Dewey*⟩ One **treasures** what one keeps safe from danger of being lost or stolen, especially because one regards it as precious or attaches great sentimental value to it ⟨she *treasures* every memento of her youth⟩ ⟨those who value money because it makes them independent are the reverse of those who *treasure* every penny they acquire and become slaves to their avarice⟩ When used in reference to persons, *treasure* implies a clinging to more often than appreciation or love ⟨pay me no homage, Mario, —but if it be I have your friendship, I shall *treasure* it —*Millay*⟩ **Cherish** may often be used interchangeably with *prize* and *treasure* but carries a stronger implication of love or affection for what is cherished and often suggests closer, more intimate association or attentions ⟨*cherish* a few books only, and those few chosen not for their fame in the world but wholly for the pleasure that they give you —*Montague*⟩ ⟨he was a man who *cherished* his friends. He liked to call at the Bishop's house to advise him about the care of his young orchard, or to leave a bottle of home-made cherry brandy for Father Joseph—*Cather*⟩
*Ana* admire, esteem, respect, regard (see under REGARD *n*): enjoy, *like, relish
*Ant* despise —*Con* contemn, scorn, disdain (see DESPISE): depreciate, disparage, *decry

**apprehend** 1 *arrest, detain, attach
*Ana* seize, *take: capture, *catch
*Con* release, discharge, liberate, *free

**2 Apprehend, comprehend** mean to lay hold of something with the mind so as to know it but together with their derivative nouns **apprehension** and **comprehension** are clearly distinguished in psychological use. **Apprehend** and **apprehension** do not imply attainment of full knowledge or of complete understanding but only a glimpsing of the nature, meaning, or significance of the object of thought; **comprehend** (see also UNDERSTAND) and **comprehension** imply an understanding of the object of thought in its entire compass and extent. *Apprehend* may suggest a single act of the mind and *comprehend* a complex and laborious process, but this distinction is not so essential as that between imperfect and perfect understanding; thus, one *apprehends* many things (as infinity or beauty) which one can never *comprehend;* one *apprehends* many things as a child (as mother love) which one does not *comprehend* until late in life ⟨who shall say how quickly the babe *apprehends* the relation between the causative howl and its effect, the demanded ministration?—*Grandgent*⟩ ⟨the thirteenth century which cared little to *comprehend* anything except the incomprehensible—*Henry Adams*⟩
*Ana* *understand, appreciate: grasp (see TAKE 1): perceive, observe, notice, note (see SEE)
**3** divine, anticipate, *foresee, foreknow
*Ana* fear, dread (see corresponding nouns at FEAR): forecast, predict, forebode, *foretell

**apprehension** 1 arrest, detention, attachment (see under ARREST *vb*)
*Ana* seizing *or* seizure, taking (see corresponding verbs at TAKE): capturing *or* capture, catching (see corresponding verbs at CATCH)
*Con* releasing *or* release, discharging *or* discharge, liberation (see corresponding verbs at FREE)
**2** comprehension (see under APPREHEND 2)
*Ana* understanding, appreciation (see corresponding verbs at UNDERSTAND): perceiving *or* perception, observing *or* observation, noticing *or* notice, noting (see corresponding verbs at SEE)
**3 Apprehension, foreboding, misgiving, presentiment** denote fear (or an instance of it) that something is going wrong or will go wrong. **Apprehension** usually implies fear that obsesses the mind and keeps one anxious and worried ⟨be under *apprehension* concerning a child's health⟩ ⟨peasants who have survived a famine will be perpetually haunted by memory and *apprehension*—*Russell*⟩ **Foreboding** particularly designates oppressive anticipatory fear or superstitious, unreasoning, or inadequately defined fear; thus, one may relieve a person's *apprehensions* yet find it hard to dispel his *forebodings* ⟨there was a sadness and constraint about all persons that day, which filled Mr. Esmond with gloomy *forebodings* —*Thackeray*⟩ **Misgiving** suggests uneasiness and mistrust rather than anxiety or dread; it is often applied to sudden fears (as a suspicion that one is making a mistake, a doubt of one's capacity to accomplish what one has undertaken, or a disturbing loss of courage) ⟨in the midst of my anecdote a sudden *misgiving* chilled me—had I told them about this goat before?—*L. P. Smith*⟩ ⟨his self-confidence had given place to a *misgiving* that he had been making a fool of himself—*Shaw*⟩ **Presentiment** implies a vague feeling or a dim, almost mystical, perception of something (not necessarily unpleasant) that seems bound to happen; however, because it frequently suggests an element of anticipatory fear and, in many cases, of foreboding, it comes into comparison with the other words of this group ⟨the delicious repose of the soul . . . had been shaken . . . and alarmed with dim *presentiment*—*George Eliot*⟩
*Ana* *fear, dread, alarm, panic: worry, anxiety, *care
*Ant* confidence —*Con* *trust, faith: assurance, self-

A colon (:) separates groups of words discriminated. An asterisk (*) indicates place of treatment of each group.

possession (see CONFIDENCE): *equanimity, sangfroid, composure

**apprehensive** *fearful, afraid
*Ana* anxious, worried, solicitous (see under CARE *n*): nervous, uneasy, jittery (see IMPATIENT)
*Ant* confident —*Con* assured, sanguine, sure (see CONFIDENT): unruffled, imperturbable, unflappable, composed, *cool, nonchalant

**apprentice** *novice, novitiate, probationer, postulant, neophyte
*Ana* beginner, starter (see corresponding verbs at BEGIN): tyro, *amateur
*Con* *expert, adept, wizard

**apprise** *inform, advise, notify, acquaint
*Ana* tell, *reveal, disclose, divulge, discover, betray: publish, proclaim, *declare, announce

**approach** *vb* 1 Approach, near, approximate mean to come or draw close (to). Approach is by far the widest in its range of application. Very often it implies a coming close in space ⟨he left the group and *approached* us⟩ ⟨the storm was *approaching*⟩ Often also it suggests a drawing close in time ⟨it was *approaching* three o'clock⟩ ⟨the day of the wedding *approached*⟩ Sometimes a closeness in order of thought or in an intellectual relation (as likeness or identification) is implied ⟨her interest in others sometimes *approaches* intrusiveness⟩ ⟨students are expected to *approach* the standard set for them by their teachers⟩ ⟨many words of distinctly different origin gradually *approach* each other in meaning⟩ Though the word retains its implication of coming close, often it also implies actual or imminent contact; to *approach* a man with a proposal is actually to make advances to him; to *approach* a topic with reluctance is actually to enter upon a discussion of it. Hence, *approach* often stresses the manner or method of beginning, especially one calculated to evoke the response or effect desired ⟨he did not know how to *approach* the subject⟩ ⟨every problem in painting was to Leonardo a problem in science, every problem in physics he *approached* in the spirit of the artist—*Ellis*⟩ In a still more specific sense, when used in reference to persons, *approach* suggests advances made by the agent for some ulterior motive (as diplomatic negotiation, solicitation, or bribery) ⟨the committee awaited a favorable opportunity to *approach* the governor concerning his candidacy⟩ ⟨the attorney for the prosecution declared that two jurors had been *approached* during the trial⟩ Near is interchangeable with *approach* only when used in reference to persons or things that draw close in space or time. Because of its simplicity and familiarity it is sometimes preferred to *approach* in poetry but it is not as frequent in speech as might be expected, the expressions "get near" and "come near" often being used in preference ⟨the lark could scarce get out his notes for joy . . . as he *neared* his happy home, the ground—*Tennyson*⟩ ⟨the echoed hoof *nearing* the distant shore—*Wordsworth*⟩ ⟨as the time of the birth of our Lord *neared*—*Pusey*⟩ Approximate, on the other hand, is interchangeable with *approach* chiefly in reference to things which come close to each other in some intellectual relation (as the actual to the ideal, the material to the spiritual, or one idea or entity to another) ⟨results that *approximate* perfection⟩ ⟨for law, at any given moment, even under the most favorable conditions, cannot do more than *approximate* to its own ideal—*Dickinson*⟩ ⟨the candidate's memory should closely *approximate* a hypothetical norm—*Armstrong*⟩ Approximate is specifically used in reference to a sum, an amount, or a quantity that approaches but does not necessarily equal a given sum or amount ⟨a tablespoonful *approximates* three teaspoonfuls⟩ ⟨their fund now *approximates*

$5000⟩
*Ana* accost, *address: *begin, commence, initiate: consult, *confer, advise, negotiate
*Con* avoid, elude, shun, evade, *escape: *refrain, abstain, forbear: retreat, *recede: withdraw, retire, depart, leave, *go
2 touch, equal, *match, rival
*Con* diverge, deviate (see SWERVE)

**approach** *n* *overture, advance, tender, bid
*Ana* attempt, endeavor, essay, try (see under ATTEMPT *vb*)
*Ant* repulse

**approbation, approval** are closely related in meaning. Approbation stresses admiration or high favor and is applied either to actual expressions of such feeling or to the state of mind of a person whose favorable opinion is manifest ⟨his speech won general *approbation*⟩ ⟨terms of *approbation*⟩ ⟨feels pleasure in the *approbation* of his superiors⟩ Approval requires qualification by words like *warm, hearty,* or *enthusiastic* to be interchangeable with *approbation,* especially when the latter denotes expression of favor. For *approval,* in itself, implies no greater favor than that involved in giving full consent with no reservations or in sanctioning. It therefore is applied especially to the formal act of approving or to a formal statement of permission, endorsement, or confirmation ⟨no interscholastic games are to be played without the *approval* of the principal⟩ ⟨the president gave his *approval* to the proposed legislation in yesterday's conference with reporters⟩
*Ana* admiration, esteem, respect, *regard: *applause, acclaim, acclamation, plaudits
*Ant* disapprobation —*Con* odium, opprobrium, disrepute (see DISGRACE): hatred, detestation, abhorrence (see under HATE *vb*): censuring *or* censure, condemning *or* condemnation, reprehension (see corresponding verbs at CRITICIZE)

**appropriate** *vb* preempt, *arrogate, confiscate, usurp
*Ana* *take, seize, grab: annex, *add

**appropriate** *adj* fitting, proper, *fit, suitable, apt, meet, happy, felicitous
*Ana* apposite, pertinent, germane, *relevant: pat, timely, *seasonable, opportune
*Ant* inappropriate —*Con* wrong, *false: incongruous, incompatible, *inconsonant

**appropriation, grant, subvention, subsidy** mean money or property given or set apart by an authorized body for a predetermined use by others. Appropriation is the comprehensive term used in government, business, or an institution controlling large sums of money for the amount formally and officially allotted to any one of its departments, projects, services, or beneficiaries in advance of the expenditure of that money ⟨every department must keep within its *appropriation*⟩ ⟨since the bill just signed carries no *appropriation* for the new bridge, it is obvious that construction will not begin this year⟩ Grant usually applies to a gift made by a government or by a corporation (as an educational or charitable foundation) to a beneficiary on the condition that certain terms be accepted or certain engagements fulfilled. The beneficiary may be a specific institution, a corporation, or even an individual; the gift may be a sum of money, but when the government is the benefactor, it is often a tract of land or a valuable franchise ⟨*grants* of land from the federal government were made to various railroads building new lines and to various colleges and universities providing agricultural and industrial courses in the mid-nineteenth century⟩ ⟨foundations that make *grants* to institutions engaged in health and medical research⟩ Subvention is more re-

*Ana* analogous words    *Ant* antonyms    *Con* contrasted words    See also explanatory notes facing page 1

stricted than *grant* since it always implies pecuniary aid especially to a person or institution in straits; it more often applies to a grant-in-aid to an artistic, literary, or scientific undertaking than a commercial one ⟨opera in many places is possible only because of a *subvention*⟩ **Subsidy** applies to a grant made to an individual or a company to enable him (or it) to carry on some work regarded as advantageous to the public but not for one reason or another self-supporting. *Subvention* is often preferred when the grant is made by an educational or charitable foundation or similar agency; *subsidy,* when it is made by the government ⟨the Carnegie Corporation makes *subventions* to libraries and educational institutions⟩ ⟨the British government provides *subsidies* for mail-carrying vessels⟩

**approval** *approbation
*Ana* commending *or* commendation, applauding *or* applause, compliment (see corresponding verbs at COMMEND): endorsing *or* endorsement, sanction (see corresponding verbs at APPROVE)
*Ant* disapproval —*Con* criticizing *or* criticism, reprehension, censure (see corresponding verbs at CRITICIZE): disparagement, depreciation, derogation (see corresponding verbs at DECRY)

**approve, endorse, sanction, accredit, certify** mean to have or to express a favorable opinion of. **Approve** often means no more than this ⟨daring them . . . to *approve* her conduct —*Conrad*⟩ Sometimes, however, it suggests esteem or admiration ⟨Jane secretly *approved* his discernment— *Rose Macaulay*⟩ **Endorse** adds to *approve* the implication of backing or supporting (as by an explicit statement): it is therefore used chiefly in reference to things requiring promotion or publicity ⟨*endorse* a person's candidacy⟩ ⟨*endorse* the platform of a new political party⟩ ⟨*endorse* a brand of cigarette⟩ **Sanction** not only implies approval but also authorization ⟨the school dances were *sanctioned* by the board of education⟩ The one that sanctions may be not only a person or group but something that provides a standard by which something can be approved and authorized or disapproved and discountenanced ⟨proposed laws not *sanctioned* by public opinion⟩ ⟨some churches permit divorce, but do not *sanction* remarriage⟩ ⟨these statements are *sanctioned* by common sense—*Joseph Gilbert*⟩ ⟨the court has also *sanctioned* recently some federal efforts to protect Negroes in the South from violence—*Barth*⟩ **Accredit** and **certify** usually imply official endorsement and conformity with certain standards. Their selection is dependent on idiom rather than on distinctions in meaning ⟨an *accredited* herd of dairy cattle⟩ ⟨*certified* milk⟩ ⟨an *accredited* school⟩ ⟨a *certified* teacher⟩ ⟨a *certified* public accountant⟩ ⟨labels by which brain merit is advertised and *certified*—medals, honors, degrees—*Woolf*⟩ *Accredited,* however, is sometimes used generally as implying public approval or general acceptance ⟨if any . . . break away from *accredited* custom—*Inge*⟩ ⟨sages so fully *accredited* as Mr. Bertrand Russell—*Montague*⟩
*Ana* *commend, applaud, compliment: *ratify, confirm
*Ant* disapprove —*Con* reject, refuse, repudiate, spurn (see DECLINE): condemn, reprehend, *criticize

**approximate** *vb* *approach, near
**approximately** *nearly, almost, well-nigh
*Ant* precisely, exactly

**appurtenance** accessory, adjunct, *appendage
*Ana* furnishing *or* furniture, equipment, appointment (see corresponding verbs at FURNISH)

**apropos** apposite, pertinent, *relevant, germane, applicable, material
*Ana* pat, timely, opportune, *seasonable: appropriate,

fitting, *fit, suitable, apt, proper, meet, happy
*Ant* unapropos

**apt 1** happy, felicitous, appropriate, fitting, *fit, suitable, meet, proper
*Ana* apposite, pertinent, *relevant, apropos: pat, timely, opportune (see SEASONABLE): telling, convincing, compelling (see VALID): right, nice, precise, exact (see CORRECT)
*Ant* inapt, inept —*Con* *awkward, maladroit: wrong, *false
**2 Apt, likely, liable** are often interchangeable when followed by *to* and the infinitive, but clear differences may be descried. **Apt** implies an inherent or habitual tendency (as an inclination, bent, or predisposition); it refers to the past and the present as much as if not more than to the future; it applies commonly to persons, but may apply to things that show a tendency or drift ⟨you are just a little *apt* to let yourself be a slave to that house of yours— *Bennett*⟩ ⟨the upper circles . . . are *apt* to favor a pronunciation derived . . . from that which prevailed in England—*Grandgent*⟩ ⟨long poems are always *apt* to drop in places into what is only not called prose because it is metrical—*Alexander*⟩ **Likely** stresses probability; it refers in time to the future and therefore has its place in predictions ⟨he is *likely* to succeed⟩ ⟨the wedding is *likely* to cost her parents more than they can afford⟩ ⟨it is *likely* to rain today⟩ ⟨"How now! is Jack Cade slain?" "No, my lord, nor *likely* to be slain; for they have won the bridge"—*Shak.*⟩ **Liable** (see also LIABLE, RESPONSIBLE) implies exposure to a risk or danger; it suggests a chance rather than a probability and is therefore often used in warnings, in cautions, or in the expression of fears ⟨children who play in the street are *liable* to be injured by automobiles⟩ ⟨drivers must remember that cars are *liable* to skid on wet roads⟩ ⟨anyone who disobeys this rule is *liable* to be punished severely⟩ Thus, a person who is *apt* to lose his head under stress knows that he is *likely* to fail when he is put to a test and therefore forms the habit of avoiding situations in which he is *liable* to encounter difficulties.
*Ana* inclined, disposed, predisposed (see INCLINE *vb*): prone, *liable
*Con* averse, *disinclined, indisposed, loath
**3** *quick, prompt, ready
*Ana* clever, prompt, smart, bright, *intelligent, quick-witted, alert: gifted, talented (see corresponding nouns at GIFT)
*Con* *slow, laggard: *lethargic, sluggish: *stupid, slow, dull, dense, crass

**aptitude** bent, turn, talent, faculty, *gift, knack, genius
*Ana* *taste, gusto, zest: propensity, *leaning, penchant, flair
*Ant* inaptitude

**aquatic, lacustrine, fluvial, fluviatile, marine, oceanic, thalassic, neritic, pelagic, abyssal** all refer to water and especially to a body of water but all except *aquatic* are highly specific in their applications and all are more or less technical terms in the geographical and biological sciences and in geology. **Aquatic** may imply a habitat in water, but as applied to animals and plants it often means living in water (but not necessarily submersed) or on the water or around a body of water. It is specifically applicable to any plant (as the water hyacinth and the water lily) that has its roots in or below water. It is also applicable to any animal that frequents the water, especially to a swimming bird or mammal (as a gull or an otter). A frog is more often described as an amphibious animal but as compared to a toad its habits may be said to be *aquatic.* **Lacustrine** relates only to a lake; it is used in biology ⟨*lacustrine* shells⟩ ⟨*lacustrine* fauna and flora⟩, in geology ⟨*lacustrine* deposits⟩, and in archaeology

A colon (:) separates groups of words discriminated. An asterisk (*) indicates place of treatment of each group.

⟨the *lacustrine* period, a prehistoric period when dwellings were erected over lakes⟩ **Fluvial** and **fluviatile** are used interchangeably to suggest the action, operation, or influence of flowing water though geologists perhaps somewhat prefer *fluvial* and biologists distinctly prefer *fluviatile* ⟨a *fluvial* plain⟩ ⟨*fluviatile* communities generally have a smaller standing crop of phytoplankters—*Park*⟩ When denoting a specific relationship to a particular stream or a relation to streams as such as distinct from their action or effects *fluvial* is the term of choice ⟨international *fluvial* law⟩ ⟨coastal and *fluvial* shipping—*Welles*⟩ ⟨sketched a geographical interpretation of the history of civilization through three stages: the *fluvial*, the thalassic, and the oceanic—*Sat. Review* (*London*)⟩ In reference to salt water **marine** (see also MARINE) is the comprehensive term, applicable not only to things that pertain to the open ocean but to those that pertain to contiguous salt or brackish waters (as bays, harbors, salt marshes, or salt ponds) ⟨*marine* shells⟩ ⟨*marine* vegetation⟩ ⟨*marine* deposits⟩ When specific reference to the open ocean or to mid ocean is intended, **oceanic** is the preferred word ⟨*oceanic* fauna⟩ ⟨*oceanic* currents⟩ ⟨*oceanic* storms⟩ When reference is to seas or gulfs, as distinguished from the ocean, **thalassic** is often the term preferred especially by historians ⟨*thalassic* empire⟩ These terms, however, are neither so definitely restricted nor so precise as the succeeding terms, which usually name definite zones of the ocean. **Neritic** refers only to the belt of shallow water surrounding a landmass. **Pelagic,** which in general use implies definitely the open sea or the high seas ⟨*pelagic* sealing⟩, in its stricter technical application has reference in its extent only to the realm of the open ocean and in its depth only to so much of the water covering that expanse as is penetrable by light. Below the pelagic zone in the deeper parts of the ocean lies the **abyssal** zone, where no plant life exists and animals are carnivorous and are usually blind or luminescent.

**aqueduct** *channel, canal, conduit, duct

**Arab** Arabic, *Arabian

**Arabian** *adj* **Arabian, Arab, Arabic** are not freely applicable to the same things and are, consequently, often a source of confusion. **Arabian** is used chiefly with reference to a place, the large peninsula in southwestern Asia which includes the modern kingdom of Saudi Arabia. Thus, one speaks of the *Arabian* peninsula, desert, kingdoms, flora, fauna, history, intending in each case to convey a consciousness of geographic relationship. **Arab** is used chiefly with reference to a people who still dwell in Arabia or their descendants who are common in northern, eastern, and central Africa, in Madagascar, India, and the Malay Archipelago, and in some parts of Syria and Persia. The word, therefore, often implies characteristics or habits associated with Arabs (as a nomadic life, equestrian skill, or Muslim practices) ⟨*Arab* customs⟩ ⟨*Arab* descent⟩ ⟨*Arab* harems⟩ Distinctively, an *Arabian* horse is a particular horse bred in or imported from Arabia whereas the *Arab* horse is the kind of horse bred and used by Arabs; an *Arabian* caravan travels in Arabia, an *Arab* caravan is made up of Arabs. **Arabic** refers usually to a language, originally the language of the Arabs, but now used in several countries whose inhabitants are not exclusively Arab in origin (as Palestine, Syria, Iraq, Egypt, and northern Africa) ⟨the *Arabic* language⟩ *Arabic* is also applicable to a culture associated with the use of the Arabic language or to any manifestations of that culture ⟨*Arabic* architecture⟩ ⟨*Arabic* numerals⟩ Distinctively, *Arab* literature is the literature of Arabs whereas *Arabian* literature is produced specifically in Arabia and *Arabic* literature is written in Arabic.

**Arabic** Arab, *Arabian

**arbiter** *judge, arbitrator, umpire, referee

**arbitrary** autocratic, *absolute, despotic, tyrannical, tyrannous
*Ana* *dictatorial, authoritarian, magisterial, oracular: domineering, *masterful, imperious, peremptory, imperative
*Ant* legitimate —*Con* *lawful, legal, licit

**arbitrate** adjudicate, adjudge, *judge
*Ana* mediate, intervene (see INTERPOSE): *decide, determine, settle: conciliate, placate, appease (see PACIFY)

**arbitrator** *judge, referee, arbiter, umpire

**arc** *curve, arch, bow

**arcade** 1 arcature, *colonnade, portico, peristyle
2 gallery, cloister, ambulatory, *passage, passageway

**arcane** *mysterious, inscrutable
*Ana* occult, esoteric, *recondite: cabalistic, anagogic, mystic, *mystical

**arcature** arcade, *colonnade

**arch** *n* *curve, bow, arc

**arch** *adj* *saucy, pert
*Ana* roguish, waggish, impish, •mischievous, *playful: mocking, deriding *or* derisive, twitting (see corresponding verbs at RIDICULE)

**archaeology** *anthropology, ethnology

**archaic** obsolete, antiquated, antique, *old, ancient, antediluvian, venerable
*Ant* up-to-date —*Con* fresh, novel, *new, newfangled, new-fashioned, modern, modernistic: fashionable, modish (see STYLISH)

**architect** *artist, artificer, artisan

**architectonic** *adj* architectural (see under ARCHITECTURE)

**architectonics** *n* *architecture

**architectural** architectonic (see under ARCHITECTURE)

**architecture, architectonics** and their corresponding adjectives **architectural** and **architectonic** are often indistinguishable, but they tend to diverge in emphasis. The nouns mean the science of planning and building structures (as churches, houses, bridges, and ships) that involve problems of artistic design, engineering, and adaptation to the ends in view. In general use **architecture** and hence **architectural** often suggest that artistry or beauty in design is the end and goal of the architect; in technical use they stress design as the result of attention to practical as well as artistic ends and imply that the profession is both a science and an art. **Architectonics** and its corresponding adjective **architectonic** place the emphasis on constructive skill; they suggest attention to the framework, skeleton, or supporting structure, sometimes without reference to the details necessary for the completion or elaboration of the structure; when one speaks of Chartres Cathedral as a triumph of *architecture,* he calls attention to its beauty of design and ornamentation; but when one speaks of it as a triumph of *architectonics,* he calls attention to it as a great work of engineering where the supporting parts of pillars, props, and ribs are united so as to form a stone skeleton capable of carrying the enormous weight of stone roof and high towers yet permitting many windows in its enclosing walls. *Architectonics* and its adjective are far more common in extended use than *architecture* and *architectural,* for the latter seldom escape their suggestions of building with stone, wood, or steel. *Architectonics* and more especially *architectonic,* on the other hand, often are referable to a system of ideas or philosophy or to a work of art and especially to an epic or a poetic drama where there is not only perfect articulation of parts but their combination into an integral or organic whole ⟨creative energy . . . is . . . *architectonic,* and it imposes upon the lyric impulse an ordered sequence and an organic unity—

*Lowes*⟩ ⟨Dante's . . . *architectonic*[*s*] of the relationships of authority and obedience—*Knox*⟩

**archive** 1 in plural form **archives** library, *museum, treasury, gallery
2 *document, record, monument

**arctic** frigid, freezing, frosty, icy, gelid, glacial, *cold, chilly, cool
*Ant* torrid

**ardent** passionate, fervid, perfervid, fervent, *impassioned
*Ana* *intense, fierce: enthusiastic, zealous (see corresponding nouns at PASSION): *eager, avid, keen: glowing, flaming (see BLAZE *vb*)
*Ant* cool —*Con* *cold, frigid: composed, imperturbable, nonchalant (see COOL): dispassionate, impartial (see FAIR): apathetic, *impassive, phlegmatic

**ardor** fervor, enthusiasm, zeal, *passion
*Ana* excitement, stimulation, quickening, galvanizing (see corresponding verbs at PROVOKE): eagerness, avidity (see corresponding adjectives at EAGER): zest, gusto (see TASTE)
*Ant* coolness: indifference —*Con* unconcernedness *or* unconcern, aloofness, detachment, uninterestedness, disinterestedness (see corresponding adjectives at INDIFFERENT): listlessness, languidness *or* languor, lackadaisicality (see corresponding adjectives at LANGUID)

**arduous** *hard, difficult
*Ana* laborious, toilsome (see corresponding nouns at WORK): exhausting, wearying *or* wearisome, tiring, fatiguing (see corresponding verbs at TIRE): *onerous, exacting, oppressive
*Ant* light, facile —*Con* *easy, simple, effortless, smooth

**area** 1 **Area, tract, region, zone, belt** mean an extent of space especially of ground or surface that is distinguishable from its surroundings in appearance or in certain distinctive features. **Area** still carries its original implication of clearly marked bounds, but it may be used with reference to a space defined on a map or chart as well as to one the limits of which are actually visible ⟨an oasis is a green or fertile *area* in a desert⟩ ⟨there are vast uncultivated *areas* even in the most populous of the states⟩ ⟨two colors—aspen and evergreen, not intermingled but lying in solid *areas* of light and dark—*Cather*⟩ **Tract**, on the other hand, stresses extent rather than limits; it is therefore preferred to *area* in designating a space that might otherwise be described as an expanse or is thought of as widespread or far stretching and uniform in character ⟨beyond the *area* of small farms lay larger *tracts* that were immensely productive—*Anderson*⟩ ⟨a *tract* of grass, furze and rushes, stretching away to the western horizon—*Shaw*⟩ **Tract** is often used in an extended sense in reference to anything that has extent or duration ⟨wide *tracts* of life—*Day Lewis*⟩ ⟨a large *tract* of unwritten history—*T. S. Eliot*⟩ **Region** suggests reference to some definite place or locality (as on the earth's surface, in the atmosphere, or in the human body) distinguished from other localities by certain features or by being subject to a particular condition or influence ⟨the upper *region* of the air⟩ ⟨the Finger Lakes *region* of central New York State⟩ ⟨what *region* of the brain is the seat of consciousness?⟩ **Zone** denotes an area or region that suggests a girdle or an encircling band especially on a map or chart ⟨the torrid, arctic, and temperate *zones*⟩ ⟨parcel post *zones*⟩ ⟨the pelagic *zone* of the ocean⟩ In broader use it is often applied to an area that forms a band or strip and is distinctly set off from its environs by some peculiarity of feature ⟨the firing *zone* of a battlefield⟩ ⟨the business *zones* of a city⟩ ⟨that milky way which nightly as a circling *zone* thou seest powdered with stars—*Milton*⟩ Basically **belt** is a synonym of *zone;* distinctively, it implies an area

characterized by the presence of some distinguishing natural feature (as a particular flora or mineral) ⟨the corn *belt* of the U.S.⟩ ⟨a coal *belt*⟩ In strict technical usage *belt* is applied to an area less extensive than a *zone* ⟨a *belt* of conifers extending into the northern mixed forest zone⟩
*Ana* *locality, district: *expanse, stretch
2 extent, *size, dimensions, magnitude, volume

**argot** cant, jargon, slang, *dialect, lingo, vernacular, patois

**argue** 1 debate, dispute, agitate, *discuss
*Ana* *prove, demonstrate: *disprove, refute, rebut, controvert: expostulate, protest, *object, remonstrate
2 bespeak, prove, attest, betoken, *indicate
*Ana* *show, manifest, evidence, demonstrate, evince: imply, *suggest, intimate

**argument** 1 proof, *reason, ground
*Ana* proving, demonstrating *or* demonstration (see corresponding verbs at PROVE): disproving *or* disproof, refuting *or* refutation, rebutting *or* rebuttal (see corresponding verbs at DISPROVE)
2 **Argument, dispute, controversy** mean a vigorous and often heated discussion of a moot question. **Argument** usually stresses the appeal to the mind and the use of evidence and reasoning to support one's claims; it implies the hope of each side to prove its case and to convince its opponents ⟨if Winthrop had not by force of *argument* . . . obtained the lifting of duties from goods sent to England . . . the Boston colony would have been bankrupt—*Repplier*⟩ In informal use it may be indistinguishable from *dispute* ⟨obeying orders without *argument*⟩ **Dispute** fundamentally implies the contradiction of something maintained by another and therefore a challenge to argument ⟨the decrees of a dictator are not subject to *dispute*⟩ When applied to a verbal contention, *dispute* suggests not only a challenger and one challenged but an effort on the part of each to get the upper hand. Hence it often implies more or less anger or disturbance of the peace ⟨a *dispute* begun in jest . . . is continued by the desire of conquest, till vanity kindles into rage, and opposition rankles into enmity—*Johnson*⟩ ⟨"You dislike an argument, and want to silence this." "Perhaps I do. Arguments are too much like *disputes*"—*Austen*⟩ **Controversy** emphasizes a profound difference of opinion not so often between persons as between parties; the term is applied chiefly to debates over issues of importance or of widespread interest involving two or more religions, governments, schools of thought, or political parties and carried on mainly by writings addressed to the public or by speeches on public platforms ⟨the Shakespeare-Bacon *controversy*⟩ ⟨when a thing ceases to be a subject of *controversy*, it ceases to be a subject of interest—*Hazlitt*⟩
*Ana* *argumentation, disputation, debate: controverting, refuting, rebutting (see DISPROVE): contention, dissension (see DISCORD)
3 theme, *subject, matter, subject matter, topic, text, motive, motif, leitmotiv

**argumentation,** disputation, debate, forensic, dialectic mean the act or art of argument or an exercise of one's powers of argument. In contrast with *argument, dispute, controversy* (see ARGUMENT 2) they stress formality and a more or less didactic intention. **Argumentation** is the designation given to a form of discourse the aim of which is to prove or disprove propositions or to an oral or written exercise having such proof or disproof for its end ⟨a course in exposition and *argumentation*⟩ ⟨the next theme will be an *argumentation*⟩ **Disputation** and **debate** both imply the handling of a proposition with the intent to sustain one's position not only by advancing arguments in its support but by attacking the position of

---

A colon (:) separates groups of words discriminated. An asterisk (*) indicates place of treatment of each group.

one's opponent and by defending one's own from his attacks. *Disputation*, however, is more often applied to a formal exercise common in medieval universities and still found in some modern universities in which a thesis is tested by the ability of its proponent or defender to sustain it in the face of severe critical attack; *debate*, to a two-sided contest between persons or teams which is governed by strict rules of procedure and in which the victory goes to the person or team regarded by the appointed judges as manifesting the greater ability. **Forensic** in its academic use is applied to an argumentative exercise intended to convince its readers or hearers; the word suggests emphasis on the qualities of successful legal argument such as the ability to marshal evidence, to make telling points, to persuade as well as to convince. **Dialectic** is a term more common among philosophers than in general or academic use. It is usually applied to a method of reasoning especially by weighing and resolving contradictory or juxtaposed arguments, the aim of which is to reach the truth by the correct application of the rules of logic, but is sometimes applied to argument or argumentation that merely observes what its writer believes to be the laws of reasoning 〈Newman's masterly English, and his competent, if not supreme, *dialectic—Saintsbury*〉
*Ana* *argument, dispute, controversy
**arid** *dry
*Ana* barren, infertile, *sterile, unfruitful: *bare, bald, barren: desiccated, dehydrated, parched (see DRY)
*Ant* moist: verdant —*Con* *wet, damp, dank, humid: *living, alive, vital: lush, luxuriant (see PROFUSE): *fertile, fruitful, fecund
**arise 1** *rise, ascend, mount, soar, levitate, surge, tower, rocket
*Ana* *lift, raise, elevate, rear
*Ant* recline: slump
**2** rise, *spring, originate, derive, flow, issue, emanate, proceed, stem
*Ana* emerge, *appear, loom: *begin, commence, start: ensue, succeed, *follow
**aristocracy 1** plutocracy, *oligarchy
**2** Aristocracy, nobility, gentry, county, elite, society denote a body of persons who constitute a socially superior caste. **Aristocracy** often refers to an ideally superior caste and therefore does not invariably apply to a fixed or definite group of persons 〈there is a natural *aristocracy* among men. The grounds of this are virtue and talents —*Jefferson*〉 Usually the term connotes superiority in birth, breeding, and social station and is applicable to all those persons generally recognized as first in family and in personal importance 〈he comes of the Brahmin caste of New England. This is the harmless, inoffensive, untitled *aristocracy—Holmes*〉 However, in countries where there is a privileged and titled class, the **nobility**, *aristocracy* is often used to designate the same group with this difference in implication: that *nobility* stresses rank inferior to that of royalty but superior to that of all other classes, and *aristocracy* stresses the possession of power over the people through ownership of land and through long-established and generally acknowledged superiority 〈the word *cousin* in the mouth or from the pen of a royalty signified a recognition of rank superior to *nobility—Belloc*〉 〈the distinguishing characteristic of an *aristocracy* is the enjoyment of privileges which are not communicable to other citizens simply by anything they can themselves do to obtain them—*Hallam*〉 However, *nobility* in British use does not include titled commoners (as baronets and knights). These latter are thought of as members of the *aristocracy*. **Gentry** and

**county** are distinctively British terms applied to a class, essentially a leisured class, who by birth and breeding can be described as gentlemen (in the technical sense) and ladies but who are without hereditary title and are classed as commoners. In British use *gentry* refers to a class in rank just below the nobility but often having in its membership persons of equally high birth or breeding. *County*, however, carries a suggestion of an association of the family with the county or section and usually of ownership of an estate in the country 〈the *gentry* and the *nobility* were on friendliest terms〉 〈the newcomers were slow in being accepted by the *county*〉 〈the advantage claimed for this plan is that it provides us with a *gentry*: that is, with a class of rich people able to cultivate themselves by an expensive education—*Shaw*〉 **Elite** is referable not to a social rank but to those members of any group or class who stand out as its flower or the ones most frequently sought after 〈the *elite* of the nobility〉 〈few others of the mathematical *elite*— *Darrow*〉 When used without qualification *elite* usually means the group regarded as the highest, especially as judged by social or cultural standards 〈it is the business of the college to produce an *elite*—superior men—*North American Review*〉 **Society** is applied to that portion of a community which marks itself apart as a leisured class much given to formal entertainments, fashionable sports, and other pursuits characteristic of an active social life 〈*society* is now one polished horde, formed of two mighty tribes, the Bores and Bored—*Byron*〉 〈there are only about four hundred people in New York *Society* —*McAllister*〉
*Ant* people, proletariat
**aristocrat** patrician, *gentleman
*Ant* commoner
**arm** *vb* accouter, outfit, equip, *furnish, appoint
*Ant* disarm
**armament,** matériel, munitions, arms, ordnance, artillery, ammunition as used in modern warfare are not all synonyms of one another, but they are frequently confused. In general they mean material used in military, naval, and air operations. **Armament** is by far the most inclusive term, for it comprehends everything that must be considered in determining a nation's military strength, such as trained soldiers, sailors, and fliers, land fortifications, battleships and all other war vessels (as transports, submarines, destroyers), aircraft, guns, provisions, equipment, available manpower and resources. **Matériel** is less inclusive; it comprehends materials only and includes all the requirements of a military establishment other than personnel. **Munitions** is often coextensive with *matériel* but typically stresses supplies of war including military equipment of all kinds, especially all weapons of attack and defense and the missiles, projectiles, and propellants necessary for their use. **Arms** is less definite in its application than either of the preceding words, but in general, when used as an inclusive term, it covers whatever weapons soldiers or sailors need in actual fighting (as cannon, guns, rifles, pistols, swords, and bayonets). **Ordnance** is used in two senses, the more general of which is probably the less common. In that sense the term includes not only everything which is covered by *arms*, but every other weapon of attack or defense (as tanks) and everything needed for the equipment and use of these weapons (as mounts, carriages, projectiles, and missiles) or for their manufacture or repair (as tools and machinery). More narrowly and also more commonly, *ordnance* is a comprehensive term for all kinds of heavy firearms, especially those discharged from mounts (as cannon, guns, howitzers, and mortars). **Artillery** is

a close synonym of *ordnance* in this latter sense, but it suggests actual warfare and therefore implies group service in the management of mounted firearms. It sometimes, like the broader sense of *ordnance,* comprehends also the mounts, ammunition, and other items essential to the work of the branch of an army dealing with the operation of heavy guns (called also the *artillery*). **Ammunition,** though once used as a general term nearly equal to *munitions,* is now restricted in its application to the projectiles used in warfare (as bullets, shells, grenades, or bombs) and their necessary propellants, detonators, fuses, and primers.
*Ana* *fort, fortress, citadel, stronghold: *bulwark, breastwork, rampart, bastion, parapet

**armistice** *truce, cease-fire, peace

**armory, arsenal, magazine** have related but usually distinguishable technical military senses. **Armory** once carried the meanings now associated with *arsenal* and *magazine,* but in current use it has commonly two applications: one, a public building in which troops (as of the National Guard) have their headquarters and facilities (as for drill and storage); the other, an establishment under government control for the manufacture of arms (as rifles, pistols, bayonets, and swords). **Arsenal** in its narrow sense is applied to a government establishment for the manufacture, storage, and issue of arms, ammunition, and related equipment: in popular and especially in figurative use the word usually suggests a store of or a storehouse for weapons and ammunition ⟨weapons from the *arsenal* of poetic satire—*Reed*⟩ ⟨make America the *arsenal* of the democracies⟩ **Magazine** is strictly applied to a storehouse for all sorts of military and naval supplies including especially arms and ammunition. In extended use it often more narrowly suggests a storehouse for explosives ⟨a powder *magazine*⟩ ⟨as when high Jove his sharp artillery forms, and opes his cloudy *magazine* of storms—*Pope*⟩ ⟨an educated man stands, as it were, in the midst of a boundless arsenal and *magazine,* filled with all the weapons and engines which man's skill has been able to devise from the earliest time—*Carlyle*⟩ In extended use *magazine* is applied to a supply chamber (as in a gun for cartridges, in a camera for films, or in a typesetting machine for matrices).

**arms** ordnance, artillery, matériel, munitions, *armament, ammunition

**army** host, legion, *multitude
*Ana* throng, press, crush, *crowd, mob, rout, horde

**aroma** odor, scent, *smell
*Ana* *fragrance, perfume, redolence, incense, bouquet: savor (see TASTE)
*Ant* stink, stench  —*Con* stinkingness, rankness, malodorousness (see corresponding adjectives at MALODOROUS)

**aromatic** balmy, redolent, fragrant, *odorous
*Ana* spicy, *pungent, piquant: savory (see PALATABLE)
*Ant* acrid (*of odors*)  —*Con* *malodorous, fetid, musty, fusty, noisome, rank, putrid

**arouse** rouse, awaken, waken, *stir, rally
*Ana* stimulate, quicken, galvanize, excite, *provoke: electrify, *thrill: kindle, fire (see LIGHT): *move, drive, impel
*Ant* quiet, calm  —*Con* allay, assuage, alleviate, mitigate, *relieve: *pacify, mollify, placate

**arraign** charge, *accuse, impeach, indict, incriminate
*Ana* *summon, cite: try, test (see PROVE)
*Con* *answer, rejoin, reply, respond: acquit, exonerate, *exculpate, absolve, vindicate: defend, justify (see MAINTAIN)

**arrange** 1 *order, marshal, organize, systematize, methodize

*Ana* dispose (see corresponding noun DISPOSAL): *line, line up, range, array, align: *assort, classify, pigeonhole, sort
*Ant* derange, disarrange  —*Con* *disorder, disorganize, unsettle, disturb: disperse, *scatter
2 *negotiate, concert
*Ana* plan, design, scheme, project (see under PLAN *n*)

**arrant** out-and-out, *outright, unmitigated

**array** *vb* 1 *line, line up, range, align
*Ana* marshal, arrange, *order
*Ant* disarray
2 *clothe, apparel, attire, robe, dress

**array** *n* *display, parade, pomp
*Ana* showing *or* show, exhibiting *or* exhibition, exposing *or* exposition (see corresponding verbs at SHOW): arranging *or* arrangement, marshaling (see corresponding verbs at ORDER): disposition (see DISPOSAL)

**arrear** *debt, indebtedness, debit, obligation, liability

**arrest** *vb* 1 **Arrest, check, interrupt** mean to stop in mid-course. **Arrest** implies a holding fixed in the midst of movement, development, or progress and usually a prevention of further advance until someone or something effects a release ⟨*arrest* the progress of a disease⟩ ⟨discouragement sometimes *arrests* a child's development⟩ ⟨books that *arrest* attention⟩ **Check** (see also RESTRAIN) suggests suddenness and force in stopping as though bringing to a halt sharply or with a jerk ⟨the teacher *checked* the disturbance in the schoolroom⟩ ⟨he *checked* himself just as he was about to blurt out his indignation⟩ ⟨he caught her by the arm as she ran past and . . . without trying to *check* her, simply darted in with her and up the stairs—*Conrad*⟩ **Interrupt** stresses a breaking in and a consequent stopping, but it carries no clear suggestion that continuation is impossible or improbable ⟨*interrupt* a lecture with a question⟩ ⟨their talk was *interrupted* by the arrival of visitors⟩ ⟨he was discouragingly *interrupted* at the point when ideas and words were flowing freely⟩
*Ana* *interpose, intervene, interfere: *delay, detain, retard: *frustrate, thwart, balk
*Ant* activate: quicken  —*Con* *vitalize, energize: *stir, rouse, arouse, awaken: prolong (see EXTEND)
2 **Arrest, apprehend, attach, detain** mean to seize and hold under restraint or in custody by authority of the law. The same likenesses and differences in meaning are manifest in the comparable use of **arrest, apprehension, attachment, detention. Arrest** (verb or noun) is the most widely used of these words for the seizing of a person and holding him in custody. It refers both to civil cases where a person is placed under restraint, and to criminal cases, where **apprehend** and **apprehension** are also used; strictly, one *arrests* a person for debt, but one *apprehends* a thief; witnesses are under *arrest;* the *apprehension* of the rioters is demanded. Ordinarily laymen seldom use *arrest* except in the sense of *apprehend,* for it carries connotations which make its use avoided in reference to witnesses or even suspects. The words commonly used when property is seized and held (as for payment of a debt) are **attach** and **attachment** ⟨*attach* the accounts of a firm suspected of falsification of income tax reports⟩ *Attach* and *attachment* are used in reference to persons chiefly when the intent is to make them appear in court (as to answer for contempt or to serve as a witness). **Detain** and **detention** usually imply holding in custody (as for inquiry or inspection). They are not strictly legal terms but are often used when there is the desire to avoid the stigma associated with the word *arrest* ⟨the health officers *detained* the ship⟩ ⟨*detain* a suspect⟩ ⟨*detain* a witness⟩

---

A colon (:) separates groups of words discriminated. An asterisk (*) indicates place of treatment of each group.

*Ana* seize, *take: *catch, capture: *imprison, incarcerate, jail

*Con* discharge, release, liberate, *free

**arrest** *n* apprehension, detention, attachment (see under ARREST *vb*)

*Ana* seizing *or* seizure, taking (see corresponding verbs at TAKE): capturing *or* capture, catching (see corresponding verbs at CATCH)

*Con* liberation, discharging *or* discharge, releasing *or* release (see corresponding verbs at FREE)

**arresting** striking, remarkable, *noticeable, outstanding, salient, signal, prominent, conspicuous

*Ana* impressive, *moving, touching, affecting, poignant: fascinating, attractive, enchanting (see under ATTRACT)

*Con* *common, ordinary, familiar: hackneyed, stereotyped, *trite

**arrival,** advent denote in common the reaching of a destination. Arrival implies precedent travel or movement ⟨the *arrival* and departure of trains⟩ ⟨the morning of my *arrival*⟩ Advent is sometimes applied to an important or even momentous arrival ⟨look forward to the *advent* of the Messiah⟩ Except when it connotes birth, it usually stresses appearance on the scene more than the coming or reaching of the end of a journey ⟨life . . . with the *advent* of an attractive young woman took on acknowledged connotations of interest—*Mary Austin*⟩

*Ana* coming (see COME): appearing *or* appearance, emerging *or* emergence (see corresponding verbs at APPEAR)

*Ant* departure —*Con* going, leaving, withdrawing *or* withdrawal (see corresponding verbs at GO)

**arrive** *come

*Ant* depart —*Con* *go, leave, withdraw, retire

**arrogant** *proud, haughty, lordly, insolent, overbearing, supercilious, disdainful

*Ana* imperious, domineering, *masterful, peremptory, imperative: pretentious, ostentatious (see SHOWY)

*Ant* meek: unassuming —*Con* *humble, modest, lowly: yielding, submitting *or* submissive, deferring *or* deferential (see corresponding verbs at YIELD)

**arrogate** *vb* Arrogate, usurp, preempt, appropriate, **confiscate** mean to seize or assume something by more or less high-handed methods. **Arrogate** (commonly followed by *to* and a reflexive pronoun) implies an unwarranted and usually an insolent or presumptuous claim to something assumed, frequently to the exclusion of others ⟨by *arrogating* to himself too much, he was in danger of losing that degree of estimation to which he was entitled—*Johnson*⟩ ⟨he *arrogated* to himself the right of deciding dogmatically what was orthodox doctrine—*Macaulay*⟩ ⟨the exploitation of the tourists was a monopoly which the most active of the children had *arrogated* by force and cunning to themselves—*Huxley*⟩ Usurp stresses unlawful or wrongful intrusion of oneself into the place held by another (as through law, custom, or natural right) and the seizure for oneself of the territory, power, authority, prerogatives, or rights pertaining to such place ⟨*usurp* a throne⟩ ⟨the dictator *usurped* the powers not only of the king but of the parliament⟩ ⟨literature, or culture, tended with Arnold to *usurp* the place of religion—*T. S. Eliot*⟩ Preempt implies beforehandedness in taking something desired by others and keeping it in one's own possession. Historically it implies the right to purchase or acquire (as land or property) before others and often on more favorable terms: this implication is now sometimes found in discriminating figurative use ⟨prose has *preempted* a lion's share of the territory once held, either in sovereignty or on equal terms, by poetry—*Lowes*⟩ In current use it more often suggests arrogation or usurpation than lawful methods

such as purchase ⟨when the townspeople arrived they found that the visitors had *preempted* all the parking places⟩ ⟨the best of the slogans suggested had already been *preempted* by a rival manufacturer⟩ ⟨in the game of bridge, to *preempt* is to make a bid aimed at shutting out shifts by the partner or bids by the opponents⟩ **Appropriate** more often suggests conversion to one's own use than a setting apart for a particular or peculiar use. However, the latter implication is often retained ⟨congress *appropriated* three billion dollars for flood control⟩ It usually suggests an acquiring for oneself or an annexing sometimes by lawful but often by unscrupulous or even by unlawful means ⟨growing plants *appropriate* whatever elements they need from the soil and the air⟩ ⟨a plagiarist *appropriates* the ideas of others⟩ ⟨if we could by any means *appropriate* to our use some of the extraordinary digestive power that a boa constrictor has—*Meredith*⟩ **Confiscate** implies seizure (as of others' property or goods) through an exercise of authority; it does not, like *appropriate*, suggest conversion to the use of the one exercising authority; thus, one might note that the sheriff *appropriated* the liquor *confiscated* when the still was raided, if he took for his own use without authority what had been taken from another in a proper exercise of authority ⟨the teacher *confiscated* all packages of chewing gum⟩ ⟨if miners, or any other sort of workers, find that the local authorities will *confiscate* the incomes of the ratepayers to feed them when they are idle, their incentive to pay their way by their labor will be . . . perceptibly slackened—*Shaw*⟩

*Ana* seize, *take, grab

*Ant* renounce: yield —*Con* *relinquish, surrender, cede, resign

**arsenal** *armory, magazine

**art** *n* **1** Art, skill, cunning, artifice, craft can mean the faculty of performing or executing expertly what is planned or devised. Art is not actually a comprehensive term but is so variable in its implications that it is interchangeable with any one of the others and capable of carrying its specific implications; hence the last four words are synonyms of *art,* but they are not always closely synonymous with each other and may even at times be used in distinction from each other. The earliest and still common implications of *art* are those which are now associated specifically with **skill**: technical knowledge, and proficiency or expertness in its exercise or practical application ⟨true ease in writing comes from *art,* not chance, as those move easiest who have learned to dance —*Pope*⟩ ⟨'tis hard to say, if greater want of *skill* appear in writing or in judging ill—*Pope*⟩ Both words are also used concretely with these implications ⟨there's a great *art* in doing these things properly. I have often had to carry off a man of fourteen stone, resting him all the time as if he was in bed—*Shaw*⟩ ⟨able boys and girls will . . . submit willingly to severe discipline in order to acquire some coveted . . . *skill*—*Russell*⟩ Art also at times comes close to **cunning** where it adds to *skill* such implications as great or recondite knowledge, inventive or creative power, and capacity for perfection in execution. This sense prevails especially in the phrase "a work of *art.*" Sometimes either word may be substituted for the other without change of meaning ⟨high-ribbed vault . . . with perfect *cunning* framed—*Wordsworth*⟩ ⟨praised be the *art* whose subtle power could stay yon cloud, and fix it in that glorious shape—*Wordsworth*⟩ Art may be used interchangeably also with **artifice** (see also TRICK) when the later stresses skill and intelligence in contriving, devising, or constructing, and suggests lack of creative power. In this sense both *art* and *artifice* in their emphasis

on contrived skill imply a contrast with power derived from nature or inspiration ⟨gaining his ends by one *art* or another⟩ ⟨when you come to dissect the *Odyssey,* what amazing *artifice* is found under that apparently straightforward tale—*Quiller-Couch*⟩ *Art* and **craft** (see also TRADE) were once close synonyms but now tend to become contrasted terms. Both words still imply ingenuity and subtlety in workmanship ⟨a gem carved with classic *art*⟩ ⟨a bracelet wrought with all the *craft* of a Cellini⟩ ⟨naturalism in prosody . . . is after all only defensible as one element in the *craft*, the artifice of poetry—*Carruth*⟩ Both may suggest, but *art* less often suggests, trickery or guile in the attainment of one's ends ⟨Henry, out of a lifetime of political *craft*, coached Cranmer how to turn the tables on his accusers—*Hackett*⟩ Both words are also affected by their use as designations of pursuits, *craft* tending to be applied to a lower kind of skill or inventive power revealing itself in the mastery of materials or technique and in effects that can be analyzed and imitated, and *art* to a higher creative power capable of expressing a personal vision and of achieving results which defy analysis and imitation; thus, an artist may demonstrate his *craft* in painting sunlight but he manifests his *art* in painting a composition that conveys his intent to the spectator ⟨like many of the hard-boiled writers, he will allow himself *craft*, but not art—*Portz*⟩
2 craft, handicraft, profession, *trade
3 **Art, science** designate a branch of learning. **Art** as it is found in the phrases the liberal *arts,* bachelor of *arts,* master of *arts* refers to one of the fundamental branches of learning regarded as necessary to every educated person and serving as an instrument for his advancement in knowledge not only generally but specifically in his professional studies. In the Middle Ages the liberal arts were grammar, logic, rhetoric, arithmetic, geometry, music, and astronomy; with these as a foundation, a student was ready to proceed with his studies in philosophy, theology, law, or medicine. In modern times the liberal arts, as interpreted by various colleges giving arts degrees, may be the disciplinary or instrumental branches of learning as distinguished from those that are technical or professional in their character or may comprise the cultural as distinguished from the vocational studies. **Science** was also used in the late Middle Ages and the Renaissance of a branch of learning. It was not identical with *art*, however, because it was not restricted to studies giving the rudiments or providing the apparatus for further study but was applied to any branch of learning that was a recognized subject of study ⟨I do present you with a man of mine, cunning in music and the mathematics, to instruct her fully in those *sciences*—*Shak.*⟩ ⟨a gentleman of Tyre; my name, Pericles; my education been in *arts* and arms—*Shak.*⟩ Since the nineteenth century, especially in reference to departments of knowledge or courses given in schools, colleges, and universities, these words show a wider divergence in implications and applications and a tendency (especially in the plural forms) to be used as generic terms. On the one hand, **art** is applied to those courses which have for their end teaching students to make or do something that requires skill and a knowledge of technique and also, usually, special gifts such as inventiveness, taste, or ingenuity ⟨the manual *arts*⟩ ⟨the fine *art* of painting⟩ ⟨instruction in the *arts* of design⟩ On the other hand, **science** is applied only to such courses or studies as deal with the gathering and classification of facts, the drawing of correct inferences from them, and the establishment of verifiable general laws ⟨the *sciences* of physics, botany, and economics⟩ ⟨major in *science*⟩ ⟨teachers of *science*⟩ Still other distinctions are drawn

between the two, when *art* or *science* refers not so much to a branch of learning as to a pursuit for which one is prepared by the study of an art or science; thus, questions arise as to whether architecture is an *art* or a *science,* that is (1) whether its essential demands of the architect are inventiveness, taste, and technical skill, or a knowledge of the principles of physics, engineering, and related sciences; (2) whether the end to be served is to give aesthetic pleasure or to produce something useful ⟨rhetoric was for Rome both an *art* and a *science.* . . . It had obvious utilitarian value, and its materials were not only exact logical concepts, but the sonorous words and the noble rhythms which were the glory of their tongue—*Buchan*⟩
**artery** route, course, *way, passage, pass
**artful** wily, guileful, crafty, cunning, tricky, *sly, foxy, insidious
*Ana* adroit, *dexterous: politic, diplomatic, smooth, *suave
*Ant* artless —*Con* simple, *natural, ingenuous, unsophisticated, naïve: candid, open, *frank
**article** *n* 1 clause, plank, count, *paragraph, verse
2 *thing, object
*Ana* *item, detail, particular
3 *essay, paper, theme, composition
**articled** indentured, *bound, bond
**articulate** *adj* 1 *vocal, oral
*Ana* distinct, clear (see EVIDENT): uttered, voiced (see EXPRESS *vb*)
*Ant* inarticulate, dumb
2 *vocal, fluent, eloquent, voluble, glib
*Ana* expressing, voicing, uttering, venting (see EXPRESS *vb*): *expressive, meaningful, significant: voluble, glib, *talkative
*Ant* inarticulate, dumb
**articulate** *vb* 1 *integrate, concatenate
*Ana* unite, *join, connect, link, relate: organize, systematize, methodize, *order
*Con* dissect, resolve, *analyze: *separate, part, divide
2 **Articulate, pronounce, enunciate** are comparable when they mean to form speech sounds. To **articulate** is to break up, by manipulation of the vocal organs, an expiration of breath into distinct parts (as phones or words) such that a sequence of these constitutes intelligible speech ⟨his agitation was so great that he could not *articulate*—*Macaulay*⟩ In a precise phonetics use to *articulate* is to close or narrow the vocal organs in such a manner as to produce a sound, especially a consonant, of a language, more specifically by the adjustment of the tongue with relation to the palate, at the place where the tongue has, for that sound, its maximum elevation ⟨many foreigners . . . use a *t articulated* by the tip of the tongue against the upper teeth . . . . This articulation produces a very unnatural effect when used in English—*Daniel Jones*⟩ In slightly extended usage *articulate* may also mean to make the manipulations or articulations for the sounds as a whole in one's speech with such care or carelessness that one's speech is distinctly or indistinctly heard. To **pronounce** is to employ articulations, accentuation, and intonation with an acceptability whose yardstick is the usage of others ⟨*colonel* is *pronounced* the same as *kernel*⟩ ⟨*s* in his is *pronounced z*⟩ ⟨*c* at first had the value of hard *g*. During the classical Latin period it was *pronounced k*—*Goudy*⟩ To **enunciate** is to articulate with an effectiveness whose yardstick is a listener's ease of understanding ⟨*enunciating* their words with peculiar and offensive clarity—*Household*⟩
**articulated** integrated, concatenated (see under INTEGRATE)
*Ana* united, joined, connected, linked, related (see JOIN):

---

A colon (:) separates groups of words discriminated. An asterisk (*) indicates place of treatment of each group.

organized, systematized, methodized, ordered (see ORDER *vb*)

**Con** dissected, resolved, analyzed (see ANALYZE): separate, *distinct, discrete

**articulation** 1 integration, concatenation (see under INTEGRATE *vb*)

**Ana** organization, systematizing, methodizing (see corresponding verbs at ORDER): *system, organism, economy, scheme, complex

2 *joint, suture

**artifact** product, *work, production, opus

**artifice** 1 *art, cunning, craft, skill

**Ana** ingeniousness *or* ingenuity, cleverness, adroitness (see corresponding adjectives at CLEVER): adeptness, proficiency, expertness (see corresponding adjectives at PROFICIENT)

2 *trick, ruse, wile, stratagem, maneuver, gambit, ploy, feint

**Ana** *deception, chicanery, chicane, trickery: *deceit, guile, duplicity, dissimulation

**Con** *mean, instrument, instrumentality, vehicle, channel: *device, contrivance: expedient, shift, makeshift (see RESOURCE)

**artificer** artisan, *artist, architect

**Ana** craftsman, handicraftsman, mechanic, workman (see WORKER)

**artificial,** factitious, synthetic, ersatz mean not brought into being by nature but by human art or effort or by some process of manufacture. They are not often interchangeable because of differences in some of their implications and in their range of application. **Artificial** is far more extensive in scope than the others. It may be applied to anything that is not produced by natural conditions but is in some sense a human creation ⟨most of the inequalities in the existing world are *artificial—Russell*⟩ ⟨the family is a natural society, the state is an *artificial* society⟩ In law a corporation or an institution that may be the subject of rights or duties is called an *artificial* person in distinction from a human being, who is a natural person. *Artificial* is also applicable to something produced by human effort that has its counterpart in nature ⟨civilization may be said to have begun when the *artificial* heat and light of burning fuel were first used to supplement the natural heat and light of the sun⟩ *Artificial* is applied also to things which imitate and sometimes serve the same purposes as something found in nature but which are of quite different origin and constitution and usually of inferior worth ⟨*artificial* flowers of wax⟩ ⟨*artificial* jewels made from colored glass⟩ *Artificial* is also applicable to persons or to their acts, utterances, and behavior; it then implies lack of naturalness or spontaneity and often connotes affectation, conventionality, or formalism ⟨set him to write poetry, he is limited, *artificial,* and impotent; set him to write prose, he is free, natural, and effective— *Arnold*⟩ ⟨the strained *artificial* romanticism of Kotzebue's lugubrious dramas—*Krutch*⟩ **Factitious** is applied largely to such intangible things as emotions, states of mind, situations, relations, reasons, which are not naturally caused or are not the product of real circumstances but are invented or worked up for one's own ends or purposes ⟨create a *factitious* demand for shares of a stock⟩ ⟨the vogue was short-lived because *factitious*⟩ ⟨his trick of doing nothing with an air, his salon manners and society smile, were but skin-deep, *factitious—Watson*⟩ ⟨they stood for Parliament and played the game of politics upon *factitious* issues—*H. G. Wells*⟩ **Synthetic** is applicable to an end product so far removed from its ultimate natural source that it has become a wholly different thing ⟨*synthetic* perfumes originally dug from the ground as coal⟩

It is preferred to *artificial* when the noun modified denotes a class to which the thing in question actually belongs and it is free from the implication of inferiority that commonly clings to *artificial;* thus, *artificial* silk is not silk since it is woven from *synthetic* fibers which are fibers man-made from substances that are not themselves fibrous. To some degree differences in usage are purely idiomatic; thus, one ordinarily refers to *synthetic* rubber but *artificial* food coloring, *synthetic* fabrics but *artificial* flavoring. **Ersatz** is frequently used as a synonym of *artificial* or *synthetic* always, however, with the implication of use as a substitute; it is used chiefly with the name of a natural product ⟨*ersatz* coffee⟩ ⟨*ersatz* butter⟩ ⟨*ersatz* wool⟩ thereby implying imitation and inferiority and, often, suggesting a cheap or disagreeable origin ⟨the search for *ersatz* . . . materials was unceasing. Sugar from sawdust; flour from potato meal; gasoline from wood and coal—*Gunther*⟩

**Ana** fabricated, manufactured, fashioned (see MAKE *vb*): simulated, feigned, counterfeited *or* counterfeit (see corresponding verbs at ASSUME)

**Ant** natural —**Con** genuine, veritable, bona fide, *authentic: *real, true, actual

**artillery** ordnance, *armament, matériel, munitions, arms, ammunition

**artisan** 1 artificer, *artist, architect

2 mechanic, workman, workingman, *worker, operative, craftsman, handicraftsman, hand, laborer, roustabout

**artist** 1 Artist, artificer, artisan, architect mean one who makes something beautiful or useful or both. In their wider senses the words are often confused. The earliest and the continuing implication of **artist** is skill or proficiency (see *artist* under EXPERT); it was formerly applied to anyone who made or did things requiring learning and skill; thus, a teacher, a philosopher, a physician, a scientist, an alchemist, or a craftsman was called an *artist* ⟨the wise and fool, the *artist* and unread—*Shak.*⟩ ⟨I will give you more directions concerning fishing; for I would fain make you an *artist—Walton*⟩ Gradually, however, the word has come to be associated with those whose aim is to produce something which gives aesthetic pleasure, first with musicians, dancers, actors, and later with poets, painters, and sculptors. The two ideas of skill and the aim to give pleasure were combined, so that since the early nineteenth century *artist* (when it does not mean specifically a painter) is usually applied to a gifted person who works in the fine arts and especially to one who reveals his skill, taste, and power to create beautiful things ⟨of the faults of Scott as an *artist* it is not very necessary to speak —*Chesterton*⟩ ⟨the counsels of Marcus Aurelius . . . are more fit for a moralist than for an *artist—Conrad*⟩ **Artificer** still retains its earliest meaning of one who makes something by means of art and skill. Originally it was applied especially to mechanics. In current use it suggests craftsmanship and is applied especially to those who work in some plastic material which responds to the exercise of skill, taste, and ingenuity in contrivance ⟨a fine cook and *artificer* of strange English dishes—*Bennett*⟩ ⟨the teacher has been only one of the *artificers* in the making of this changing personality—*H. Suzzallo*⟩ **Artisan** was formerly and is still sometimes applied to the practitioner of any art and especially an industrial art chiefly in distinction from an *artist* ⟨the Germans . . . are better *artisans* than artists; better at handicrafts than at head craft—*Cotgrave*⟩ This difference between *artisan* and *artist* widened as *artist* came to imply the power to create or produce beautiful things and became restricted in its application to a worker in the fine arts. In current use *artisan* is a general term almost equal to *workman* and names one engaged in a craft, a handicraft, or a trade; it comprehends in its range

all the skills often subsumed as skilled labor. In extended use it is still often contrasted with *artist,* the latter now implying imaginative power and a passion for perfection, the former mere mechanical industry ⟨free verse is not yet out of the experimental stage, and the artists who practice it have still the *artisans* in their own craft to reckon with —*Lowes*⟩ **Architect** has never lost its basic implication of a master builder, though it has come to stress more the designing of something to be built than actual participation in its erection. Specifically it designates a person whose profession it is to plan buildings or structures in detail and to exercise supervision over their construction in order to see that the design is executed in every particular. In extended use the word usually implies the power to conceive a thing as a whole and in detail in advance of its coming into being as well as to control its execution. It is often applied specifically to God as the Creator. Although it comes close to *artist* in its implications of imaginative power and constructive ability, it differs from the former in its greater emphasis upon design than upon execution ⟨the poet is an artificer by profession, an *architect* experimenting with a variety of materials, concerned with . . . new designs—*Day Lewis*⟩
*Ana* craftsman, workman (see WORKER): creator, *maker: *writer, composer, author
2 artiste, virtuoso, *expert, adept, wizard
**artiste** artist, virtuoso, adept, *expert, wizard
**artistic,** aesthetic are often understood as equivalent terms, especially when used in such collocations as the *artistic* or *aesthetic* temperament; *artistic* or *aesthetic* satisfaction; *artistic* or *aesthetic* standards or values; for *artistic* or *aesthetic* reasons. But **artistic** may stress the point of view of the artist or of one who actually produces a work of art, who thinks in terms of technique, of the relationship of details to the design of the whole, or of the effects to be gained and who therefore regards beauty as a thing that results from his attention to these matters and that is his creation. By extension *artistic* may imply also the point of view of one who studies or judges art objectively from the artist's angle. On the other hand **aesthetic** stresses the point of view of one who contemplates a finished work of art or beauty that exists and who thinks in terms of the effect it has upon him and especially of the sensations it stimulates and the feelings it excites. Strictly, the *artistic* temperament shows itself in an urge to fashion or to express and to create out of materials, words, or sounds the beautiful thing that the artist designs or conceives: the *aesthetic* temperament shows itself in responsiveness to beauty wherever it is found, and by contrast, in aversion to that which is ugly. *Artistic* satisfaction is the gratification that comes to one who can look at a work of art (his own or another's) and call it good: *aesthetic* satisfaction is the content that accompanies the enjoyment of beauty for its own sake and independently of all other considerations. For *aesthetic,* largely because of its connection with *aesthetics,* the branch of philosophy dealing with beauty, usually implies a distinction between that which is beautiful and that which is moral or useful or merely pleasing. *Artistic* standards are therefore the tests of perfection in a work of art which artists and critics have accepted: *aesthetic* standards are the usually subjective criteria which have been set up by aestheticians or by the individual to enable him to distinguish the beautiful from the merely pleasing or gratifying.
**artless** *natural, simple, ingenuous, naïve, unsophisticated, unaffected
*Ana* *spontaneous, impulsive: candid, open, plain, *frank: *straightforward, aboveboard, forthright
*Ant* artful: affected —*Con* *sly, cunning, wily, insid-

ious: designing (see INTEND)
**as** since, *because, for, inasmuch as
**ascend** 1 *rise, arise, mount, soar, tower, rocket, levitate, surge
*Ana* elevate, raise, rear, *lift: *advance, progress
*Ant* descend
2 Ascend, mount, climb, scale mean to move upward to or toward a summit. Ascend is the most colorless of these terms, for it implies little more than progressive upward movement ⟨*ascend* a mountain⟩ ⟨the car rapidly *ascended* the steep grade⟩ It may be specifically used of movement along a river in the direction of its source ⟨the Amazon can be *ascended* by seagoing ships 2300 miles⟩ **Mount** usually implies getting up on something above the level of the ground and is therefore preferred to *ascend* in some collocations; thus, one *mounts* or less commonly *ascends* a platform or a scaffold but one may *ascend* or *mount* a throne while one invariably *mounts* a horse. **Climb** usually suggests effort and ascent by the use of various means (as the hands and feet or gears or extra power) ⟨*climb* a tree⟩ ⟨*climb* the social ladder⟩ ⟨to *climb* steep hills requires slow pace at first—*Shak.*⟩ **Scale** adds to *climb* not only the suggestion of progression by steps but that of great difficulty; it is referable therefore to feats of climbing ⟨*scale* a wall⟩ ⟨a ladder quaintly made of cords . . . would serve to *scale* another Hero's tower—*Shak.*⟩
*Ant* descend
**ascendancy** *supremacy
*Ana* dominance, predominance (see corresponding adjectives at DOMINANT): command, sway, dominion, control, *power, authority: sovereignty (see under FREE *adj*)
**ascension,** ascent denote the act of moving upward or the movement upward. **Ascension** may occur where there is no implication of effort or difficulty in rising, and where there is usually the suggestion of movement activated by some property in the thing which ascends ⟨a balloon *ascension*⟩ In religious use *ascension* refers specifically to the translation of the risen Jesus into heaven. **Ascent,** on the other hand, is preferred when there is any implication of effort or of a human agent or operator ⟨during their *ascent* of the mountain⟩ ⟨the scientists effected an *ascent* to the stratosphere⟩ ⟨her rapid *ascent* in the social scale⟩ ⟨make an *ascent* of three miles in an airplane⟩
**ascent** *ascension
**ascertain** determine, *discover, unearth, learn
*Ana* inquire, query, interrogate, *ask: study, contemplate, weigh, *consider: observe, survey (see SEE)
*Con* *conjecture, surmise, guess: presume, assume (see PRESUPPOSE)
**ascetic** *adj* austere, *severe, stern
*Ana* disciplined, trained, schooled (see TEACH): self-denying, self-abnegating (see corresponding nouns at RENUNCIATION): abstaining *or* abstinent, forbearing (see corresponding verbs at REFRAIN): abstemious (see corresponding noun at TEMPERANCE)
*Ant* luxurious, voluptuous (see SENSUOUS) —*Con* *sensuous, sensual, epicurean, sybaritic: dissolute, *abandoned
**ascetic** *n* Ascetic, mystic and their derivative nouns **asceticism, mysticism** though not true synonyms are not always clearly distinguished, partly because of overlapping implications but largely because the first two are often applicable to the same person. Historically many of the great mystics have been ascetics. But **ascetic** suggests an austere mode of life in which everything that does not contribute to or may interfere with the end in view (usually spiritual or sometimes intellectual perfection) is sacrificed, and certain acts (as fasting and mortification) are practiced not for their own sake but for their disciplinary effect especially in strengthening one's powers of contemplation. **Mystic,** on

A colon (:) separates groups of words discriminated. An asterisk (*) indicates place of treatment of each group.

the other hand, suggests the possession of a power (as a high capacity for contemplation) or of an inner revelation, by means of which one overpasses the limits of human reason and by spiritual insight comes to a knowledge of that which is divine or supernatural. *Ascetic* and *mystic,* therefore, when applied to the same person, regard him from different points of view; the former implies that he practices austerities believed favorable to spiritual contemplation; the latter, that he has had the mystical experiences that are the end of contemplation. But the two terms do not necessarily imply each other; *ascetic,* even when applied to those who aim at spiritual perfection, does not connote attainment of mystical knowledge; *mystic,* on the other hand, does not in itself imply a connection with an ascetic life. Although **asceticism** and **mysticism** may denote doctrines or practices, their chief differences are apparent when they denote the theory upon which such doctrines and practices are based. *Asceticism* often designates the theory that abstinence from otherwise lawful acts or pleasures and the practice of austerities are conducive to spiritual and intellectual perfection; *mysticism,* the theory that immediate knowledge of God or ultimate reality is attainable through a faculty that transcends the reason and makes no use of ordinary human perceptive or ratiocinative powers ⟨one is sometimes tempted to think that to approve *mysticism* is to preach *asceticism.* Certainly many *mystics* have been *ascetic.* But that has been the accident of their philosophy and not the essence of their religion—*Ellis*⟩
*Ana* anchorite, hermit, eremite, cenobite (see RECLUSE): monk, friar, nun, *religious
*Ant* bon vivant  —*Con* *epicure, gourmet, gourmand, glutton: sensualist, voluptuary, sybarite (see corresponding adjectives at SENSUOUS)

**asceticism** mysticism (see under ASCETIC *n*)

**ascribe, attribute, impute, assign, refer, credit, accredit, charge** mean to lay something (creditable, discreditable, or neutral) to the account of a person or thing. The first four of these words are often used interchangeably without marked loss in precision, but they have distinctions in discriminating use. One **ascribes** *to* a person or thing something which is not outwardly apparent but which may be inferred or conjectured (as a motive, a feeling, an opinion, or a value) ⟨whatever else might be in her head, it was . . . neither love, nor romance, nor any of the emotions usually *ascribed* to the young—*Sackville-West*⟩ Also, one *ascribes* something whose origin is unknown or disputed *to* its conjectured source, cause, or author ⟨a poem formerly *ascribed* to Chaucer⟩ ⟨that conceit always *ascribed* to a lack of intelligence—*Brownell*⟩ One **attributes** *to* a person or thing something (as a quality, a character, or a value) believed, usually on good grounds, to belong to it or to be appropriate to it, or something for which that person or thing is judged to be responsible or accountable ⟨if he disclaimed the virtues *attributed* to him he should only accentuate his embarrassment—*Mackenzie*⟩ ⟨a combination . . . might have *attributed* to it . . . the character of a monopoly merely by virtue of its size—*Justice Holmes*⟩ ⟨the French had then given up their conventional trick of *attributing* Eleanor's acts to her want of morals —*Henry Adams*⟩ One **imputes** when one so definitely ascribes something *to* a person or, less often, a thing that the ascription is impressed on that person or thing. For this reason *impute* commonly but not invariably implies accusation and, often, its resulting stigma ⟨how dare you, sir, *impute* such monstrous intentions to me?—*Shaw*⟩ One **assigns** something *to* a person or thing when one deliberately and often as a result of critical study places it in a class (as of values, things, or occurrences) ⟨more

than one rejoinder declared that the importance I here *assigned* to criticism was excessive—*Arnold*⟩ ⟨the temple of Baal Lebanon, which is *assigned* to the eleventh century B.C.—*Clodd*⟩ Also, one *assigns* a reason *for* something when one definitely fixes or states the ground, excuse, or motive for that thing ⟨it is impossible to *assign* any reason for his failure⟩ Sometimes *assign* suggests allegation, but this connotation is usually derived from the context ⟨whatever reason of discontent the farmers may *assign,* the true cause is this—*Coleridge*⟩ One **refers** a thing or rarely a person *to* the class to which it belongs or to its origin when, after tracing it back, one assigns it to its proper category or to its ultimate cause or source ⟨the aurora borealis is commonly *referred* to the class of electric phenomena⟩ ⟨I am convinced that at least one half of their bad manners may be *referred* to their education—*Quiller-Couch*⟩ One **credits** someone *with* something or something *to* someone when one ascribes the thing to some person or thing as its author, its agent, its source, or its explanation ⟨people *credited* Moriarty's queerness of manner and moody ways to the solitude—*Kipling*⟩ ⟨I am sure both parties *credited* them with too much idealism and too little plain horse sense—*Rose Macaulay*⟩ Sometimes *credit* suggests unwarranted belief ⟨Aunty Rosa had *credited* him in the past with petty cunning and stratagem that had never entered into his head—*Kipling*⟩ One **accredits** a person (rarely, a thing) *with* something (as a statement, an accomplishment, or a quality) or *accredits* something *to* a person when one accepts him as author, agent, or possessor ⟨when a person stimulates us . . . we *accredit* him with an attractive personality—*Weaver*⟩ ⟨savings accumulated in good times . . . must doubtless be *accredited* with some expectation of future . . . dividends—*Hobson*⟩ ⟨several Bangor houses have been *accredited* to Bulfinch—*Amer. Guide Series: Me.*⟩ Like *credit, accredit* is typically used of favorable attributions. One **charges** something *on* or *upon* a person or thing when one fixes the responsibility for a fault, crime, or evil on him or it ⟨crimes as base as any *charged* on me?—*Cowper*⟩ ⟨the tyrannies . . . *charged* upon the New England oligarchy—*Parrington*⟩
*Ana* attach, *fasten, affix: *conjecture, surmise, guess: allege, advance, *adduce, cite

**ash, cinders, clinkers, embers** mean the remains of combustible material after it has been destroyed by fire. **Ash,** especially as the plural *ashes,* implies perfect combustion and a powdery residue consisting only of incombustible and thoroughly disintegrated mineral or earthy substances ⟨devices used to trap fly *ash*⟩ ⟨wood *ashes* are used as a fertilizer⟩ ⟨the house and its furnishings were reduced to *ashes*⟩ Sometimes the singular *ash* suggests a solid mass, not yet disintegrated ⟨the *ash* of a cigar⟩ **Cinders** carries the implication of either incomplete combustion or incombustibility and is applied to a residue, usually of a coal fire, consisting of coarse particles which, if the combustion is incomplete, are capable of further burning ⟨sift the ashes from the *cinders*⟩ or which are the remains of incombustible impurities in the fuel and may also be called **clinkers.** Strictly, a *clinker* is a fused or vitrified stony mass such as is formed in burning impure coal or in smelting metals containing impurities, or is ejected from a volcano; thus, *cinders* composed mainly of small *clinkers* are often used for surfacing paths, driveways, and tracks for footraces. **Embers** is applied to the still glowing or still smoldering remains of a fire just before it is reduced to ashes or cinders.

**ashamed, mortified, chagrined** mean acutely or manifestly conscious of embarrassment and humiliation. One is **ashamed** whose embarrassment and humiliation are mixed

sometimes with a sense of guilt and always with the awareness of being discredited or disgraced by one's own or vicariously another's shameful or indecorous act, behavior, or situation ⟨he sees he has nothing to be *ashamed* of in you—rather everything to be proud of—*Meredith*⟩ ⟨suddenly Joe began to cry. He was *ashamed* and did not want his wife to see—*Anderson*⟩ One is also *ashamed* who by anticipating such feelings is reluctant or unwilling to do something that seems shameful ⟨what shall I do? for my lord taketh away from me the stewardship: I cannot dig; to beg I am *ashamed*—*Lk* 16:3⟩ One is **mortified** whose embarrassment and humiliation are mixed with a strong sense of being put in a false or disagreeable light and who suffers more because of loss of esteem or a hurt to his own pride than because of the shameful or indecorous character of the act, behavior, or situation; thus, one might say that the boy was not *ashamed* of his conduct (because he did not consider it wrong) but he was *mortified* when he was suspended from the team (because others viewed his conduct in a light that resulted in injury to his pride and position) ⟨"Don't spare him; let the university expel him! . . . Let Robert be ashamed, if you would save his soul alive!" . . . Robert was sullen and *mortified*, but, alas, not ashamed—*Deland*⟩ One is **chagrined** whose embarrassment and humiliation are accompanied by vexation or annoyance ⟨Tony, somewhat *chagrined* at his mistake, said he should like to see the other pictures—*Archibald Marshall*⟩ ⟨I was as much *chagrined* as they were flabbergasted by this involuntary outbreak—*L. P. Smith*⟩
*Ana* embarrassed, discomfited, abashed (see EMBARRASS): humiliated, humbled, abased (see ABASE): abject, *mean: contrite, penitent, repentant (see corresponding nouns at PENITENCE)
*Ant* proud —*Con* vain, vainglorious (see under PRIDE *n*): arrogant, overbearing (see PROUD)
**ashen** ashy, livid, pallid, wan, *pale
*Ana* *ghastly, grim, macabre: blanched, bleached, decolorized (see WHITEN)
**ashy** ashen, livid, pallid, wan, *pale
*Ana* (see those at ASHEN)
**asinine** *simple, fatuous, silly, foolish
*Ana* *stupid, crass, dumb, dense, dull, slow: puerile (see YOUTHFUL): *irrational, unreasonable
*Ant* sensible, judicious —*Con* *wise, sane, prudent, sapient, sage: *intelligent, clever, knowing, smart: *rational, reasonable
**ask 1** Ask, question, interrogate, query, inquire, catechize, quiz, examine mean to address a person in an attempt to elicit information. **Ask** is the general or colorless term for putting a question ⟨*ask* and you will find⟩ ⟨*ask* the price of an article⟩ ⟨*ask* your brother if he will join us⟩ ⟨none of them understood how to *ask* the question which they were trying to answer—*Ellis*⟩ **Question** usually suggests asking one question after another as in teaching or in searching out the ramifications of a topic ⟨*question* a suspect at length⟩ ⟨Socrates preferred *questioning* his disciples to lecturing them⟩ **Interrogate** stresses formal or systematic questioning ⟨they examined many witnesses . . . whom they *interrogated*, not only upon the express words of the statute, but upon all . . . collateral or presumptive circumstances—*Burnet*⟩ **Query** usually strongly implies a desire for authoritative information or the resolution of a doubt ⟨should not one *query* whether he had not those proofs in his hands antecedent to the cabinet?—*Walpole*⟩ It is specifically so used by proofreaders ⟨do not *query* a misspelled word in ordinary text . . . . Never *query* style to the author—*Manual of Style*⟩ **Inquire** has for its fundamental implication a search for the facts or the truth; only when it distinctly implies in addition to such

an intention the asking of a question or questions does it come into comparison with the other words of this group ⟨*inquire* the best route to New York City⟩ ⟨*inquire* when the public library would be open⟩ ⟨it was soon evident that this was the ruddleman who had *inquired* for her—*Hardy*⟩ **Catechize** adds to *interrogate* the suggestion of an aim to elicit a certain kind of answer. Often the answers expected are definite statements of doctrine already phrased in a catechism (a book supplying questions and answers concerning the doctrines of a church) ⟨*catechize* a candidate for the ministry⟩ In extended use, however, there is often the implication of a desire to lead the person who is questioned into making answers that are self-condemnatory or that will reveal his weaknesses ⟨it was their policy to *catechize* every candidate for a doctor's degree at the beginning of his advanced studies⟩ **Quiz** implies an informal but often thoroughgoing interrogation (as of a class) to determine how well a series of lectures has been understood or (as of a murder suspect) to determine the facts of the case. **Examine** implies interrogation or catechizing for the purpose of drawing answers that indicate how much or how little a person knows (as from students when their fitness for promotion is to be decided, from candidates for a position when it is necessary to determine the extent of their preparation and the adequacy of their training, from those giving testimony in a trial, or when the lawyers on each side try to elicit information of value to their clients) ⟨the students in this course are *examined* at the end of the year⟩ ⟨no candidate for a civil service position is considered until he has been *examined* with all other candidates and given a satisfactory rating⟩ ⟨it took the whole day to *examine* and to cross-examine the principal witness⟩
*Con* reply, *answer, respond, rejoin, retort
**2** Ask, request, solicit mean to seek to obtain by making one's wants or desires known. **Ask** implies expectation of a response, often an affirmative response ⟨I am going to *ask* a favor of you⟩ ⟨he *asked* the close attention of all his audience⟩ ⟨*ask* the citizens for their full cooperation⟩ **Request** carries a suggestion of greater courtesy and formality in the manner of asking and is preferable to *ask* when one feels that what one wants may not be granted, whether for lack of power or means or from lack of interest on the other side or when one wishes to be exceedingly polite or ingratiating ⟨*request* a loan⟩ ⟨*request* the presence of a person at a reception⟩ ⟨*requesting* an opportunity to present their opinions⟩ **Solicit** (compare BEG) seldom implies earnest entreaty or urging; its most common suggestion is that of calling attention to one's wants and desires in the hope of having them satisfied; ⟨a merchant *solicits* trade by means of letters, or handbills, or advertisements in journals⟩ ⟨a magazine *solicits* subscriptions when it sends an agent to interview possible subscribers⟩
*Ana* appeal, petition, plead, pray, sue (see under PRAYER): *address, accost
*Con* *get, obtain, acquire, secure: *decline, refuse, spurn: *deny, gainsay
**askance** askew, *awry
*Ana* mistrustfully, distrustfully (see corresponding verbs at DISTRUST): enviously, jealously (see corresponding adjectives at ENVIOUS)
*Ant* straightforwardly, directly
**askew** *awry, askance
*Ana* crookedly, obliquely (see corresponding adjectives at CROOKED)
*Ant* straight
**asocial** *unsocial, antisocial, nonsocial
*Ant* social

---

A colon (:) separates groups of words discriminated. An asterisk (*) indicates place of treatment of each group.

**aspect** 1 look, *appearance, semblance
*Ana* *face, countenance, visage: *bearing, mien, port, presence
2 *phase, side, facet, angle
*Ana* angle, slant, *point of view, viewpoint, standpoint
**asperity** *acrimony, acerbity
*Ana* sharpness, keenness (see corresponding adjectives at SHARP): causticity, mordancy (see corresponding adjectives at CAUSTIC): snappishness, waspishness, irritability (see corresponding adjectives at IRRITABLE)
*Ant* amenity —*Con* *courtesy, gallantry: suavity, urbanity, blandness (see corresponding adjectives at SUAVE)
**asperse** *vb* vilify, *malign, traduce, calumniate, slander, defame, libel
*Ana* disparage, depreciate, derogate, detract, *decry: revile, vituperate (see SCOLD): defile (see CONTAMINATE)
*Con* *praise, extol, laud, acclaim, eulogize: *commend, applaud, compliment
**aspersion** reflection, *animadversion, stricture
*Ana* *libel, lampoon, pasquinade, squib, skit: *abuse, vituperation, invective, obloquy: *detraction, backbiting, calumny, slander, scandal
*Con* praise, laudation, extolling, eulogizing *or* eulogy (see corresponding verbs at PRAISE): *applause, acclaim, acclamation, plaudits: commendation, complimenting *or* compliment (see corresponding verbs at COMMEND)
**asphyxiate** *suffocate, stifle, smother, choke, strangle, throttle
**aspirant** *candidate, applicant, nominee
**aspiration** *ambition, pretension
*Ana* aim, goal, objective (see INTENTION): *desire, passion, lust
**aspire** *aim, pant
*Ana* crave, covet, *desire: *long, yearn, hunger, thirst, pine
*Con* *stoop, condescend, deign: grovel, *wallow
**assail** bombard, *attack, assault, storm
*Ana* beset (see INFEST): belabor, pummel, buffet, pound, *beat
**assassin, cutthroat, gunman, bravo** designate a murderer or one who can be hired to murder in cold blood. **Assassin** stresses secrecy and treachery in operation ⟨like *assassins,* these destructive animals do their work in the dark⟩ It is chiefly applied to murderers of important personages ⟨tyrants always live in dread of *assassins*⟩ ⟨revolutions breed *assassins*⟩ **Cutthroat** and *gunman* usually designate professional hired murderers. **Cutthroat** is chiefly literary or merely figurative because daggers and knives are no longer the weapons usually employed by such criminals, but the word still commonly suggests brutal methods of murder ⟨I am a soldier, sir, and not a *cutthroat* —*Froude*⟩ **Gunman** is used somewhat more broadly than the foregoing terms since it may denote not only one who murders with a firearm but one (as a gangster) who goes armed and is prepared to shoot to prevent interference with his criminal activities or at the orders of a leader or employer. Basically a **bravo** is a blustering unscrupulous ruffian or desperado ⟨a few halfhearted catcalls from young *bravos* of the opposing party—*Barker*⟩ The word is especially applicable in an historical situation and commonly implies a venality sufficient to perform murder for hire ⟨unfolds all of seventeenth-century Italy and its dramas—its predatory noblemen, its murderous *bravos* —*Rolo*⟩ ⟨the hired *bravos* who defend the tyrant's throne —*Shelley*⟩
*Ana* murderer, slayer, killer (see corresponding verbs at KILL)
**assassinate** murder, *kill, slay, dispatch, execute
**assault** *n* *attack, onslaught, onset

*Ana* assailing, bombarding *or* bombardment, storming *or* storm (see corresponding verbs at ATTACK): *invasion, incursion, raid
**assault** *vb* storm, *attack, bombard, assail
*Ana* smite, slug, *strike: *beat, pound, buffet, pummel
*Con* *resist, withstand, oppose, combat: *defend, protect, shield, guard
**assay** *vb* assess, evaluate, *estimate, appraise, value, rate
*Ana* *analyze, resolve: *calculate, compute, reckon: *prove, test, try, demonstrate
**assemblage** 1 assembly, collection, congregation, gathering (see under GATHER)
*Ana* *aggregate, aggregation: *crowd, throng, horde, crush, press
2 **Assemblage, assembly** are not always interchangeable in concrete use. **Assemblage** may be used freely in reference either to persons or to things ⟨an *assemblage* of farmers from every section of the state⟩ ⟨an *assemblage* of the city's manufactured products for exhibition⟩ It may imply a unit that is a collection of individuals of the same general kind or one that is a whole formed by the union of miscellaneous things ⟨an *assemblage* of logs⟩ ⟨an automobile is an *assemblage* of various distinct parts⟩ It may be applied to something that can be seen as a unit or whole or that can be conceived as such ⟨we have just been picturing nature as an *assemblage* of particles set in a framework of space and time—*Jeans*⟩ **Assembly,** on the other hand, was until recently restricted in its application to a group of persons who gather together in a given place usually for the purpose of acting as a unit or of social enjoyment or, in a more specific sense, in order to serve as a deliberative or legislative body ⟨the mayor decided to call an *assembly* of the citizens⟩ ⟨the New York State *Assembly*⟩ There is a tendency to use *assembly* instead of *assemblage* of a structure or machine and especially of part of a machine that is formed by the union of different parts ⟨a hub *assembly*⟩
*Ana* (see those at ASSEMBLAGE 1)
**assemble** congregate, collect, *gather
*Ana* convene, convoke, muster (see SUMMON): combine, associate, unite (see JOIN)
*Ant* disperse —*Con* *scatter, dissipate, dispel: *distribute, dispense, divide, deal, dole
**assembly** 1 assemblage, congregation, gathering, collection (see under GATHER)
*Ana* *company, party, troop, band: *crowd, throng, crush, press
2 *assemblage
*Ana* (see those at ASSEMBLY 1)
**assent** *vb* **Assent, consent, accede, acquiesce, agree, subscribe** and their corresponding nouns express in common the idea of concurrence with what someone else has stated or proposed. **Assent** implies primarily an act of the understanding and applies to opinions or propositions ⟨one was convinced and believed and *assented*—*Webster*⟩ ⟨whatever is expressed with art—whether it be a lover's despair or a metaphysical theory—pierces the mind and compels *assent* and acceptance—*Huxley*⟩ **Consent** involves the will or the feelings and indicates compliance with what is requested or desired; thus, a lady may *assent* to a gentleman's opinion on the weather, but if he makes a proposal of marriage she must either *consent* to or reject his offer ⟨if a thing has been practiced for two hundred years by common *consent,* it will need a strong case for the Fourteenth Amendment to affect it—*Justice Holmes*⟩ Neither *assent* nor *consent* necessarily implies approval ⟨a parent may *assent* against his better judgment⟩ **Accede** implies a yielding either of one's adherence (as to a cause) or of one's assent (as to a statement or proposal) ⟨even if

---

*Ana* analogous words    *Ant* antonyms    *Con* contrasted words    See also explanatory notes facing page 1

Americans once worked a revolution of which they are proud, we need not feel so bound by this fact that we demurely *accede* to every other revolution, regardless of its methods, purposes, and consequences—*Yale Review*⟩ ⟨Mr. Bennet could have no hesitation in *acceding* to the proposal before him—*Austen*⟩ **Acquiesce** implies tacit acceptance or forbearance of opposition ⟨no organism *acquiesces* in its own destruction—*Mencken*⟩ **Agree** may or may not imply previous difference of opinion, but it very often carries an implication of this and also of previous discussion, negotiation, or attempts at persuasion ⟨he reluctantly *agreed* that his son be allowed to choose his own college⟩ ⟨post, my lord, to France; *agree* to any covenants—*Shak.*⟩ **Subscribe** denotes assent but it implies in addition hearty approval; it seldom implies actually signing one's name in token of assent, but it does connote a willingness to go on record ⟨no one would *subscribe* at present to the Kantian doctrine, that mathematics derive their validity from their applicability to sensible experience—*Alexander*⟩
*Ana* accept, *receive: *adopt, embrace, espouse: believe, credit (see corresponding nouns at BELIEF)
*Ant* dissent —*Con* *deny, gainsay, impugn: reject, spurn, refuse (see DECLINE): *object, protest

**assert** 1 Assert, declare, profess, affirm, aver, protest, avouch, avow, predicate, warrant agree in meaning to state positively usually either in anticipation of denial or objection or in the face of it. **Assert** implies absence of proof: it usually ascribes to the speaker or writer either assurance of the grounds for his statement or such confidence in his opinions as to make him indifferent to evidence ⟨that rigid sect which *asserts* that all real science is precise measurement—*Ellis*⟩ ⟨Hobart . . . could talk; he could *assert* . . . but he couldn't meet or answer arguments—*Rose Macaulay*⟩ **Declare** and *profess* add to *assert* the implication of open or public statement and are often interchangeable. In precise usage **declare** is somewhat more formal and impersonal than **profess** which is especially suitable for conveying a personal or emotional involvement in what is under discussion; thus, a government *declares* war while a citizen *professes* complete trust in his government; a jury *declares* a man guilty but his mother *professes* continued belief in his innocence ⟨they do not, for the most part . . . *declare* . . . that no war can ever be right—*Inge*⟩ ⟨he talked well, *professed* good opinions—*Austen*⟩ **Profess** but not *declare* may carry a suggestion of insincerity ⟨our princes of darkness . . . have become what they *profess* to scorn—angels of light—*Sullivan*⟩ **Affirm** implies conviction of truth and willingness to stand by one's statement because it is supported by evidence or one's experience or faith ⟨yet, with the evidence before us . . . we cannot *affirm* that this is the later play—*T. S. Eliot*⟩ ⟨politicians more often *affirm* their desire for retirement than show that they really mean it—*Times Lit. Sup.*⟩ **Aver** suggests complete confidence and certainty of truth ⟨for all *averred*, I had killed the bird —*Coleridge*⟩ **Protest** stresses emphasis in affirmation, especially in the face of doubt or contradiction ⟨I here *protest*, in sight of heaven . . . I am clear—*Shak.*⟩ ⟨he *protested* that, except Lady Catherine and her daughter, he had never seen a more elegant woman—*Austen*⟩ **Avouch** usually imputes authority or personal knowledge to the maker of a positive statement ⟨his own deposition, as three Cardinals *avouched* that he had made it before them—*Yonge*⟩ **Avow** implies open and emphatic declaration and personal responsibility for the statement ⟨we affirm and *avow* that the very meanest translation of the Bible in English . . . containeth the word of God—*Bible: Preface to A. V., 1611*⟩ **Predicate**, though occa-

sionally used as a close synonym of the preceding words, usually implies the affirmation of something as a quality, a property, or a concomitant of something ⟨logic works by *predicating* of the single instance what is true of all its kind—*James*⟩ ⟨to *predicate* of diabolic agencies, which are gifted with angelic intellects, the highly ridiculous activities which are so characteristic of poltergeist visitations—*J. McCarthy*⟩ **Warrant** (see also JUSTIFY 3) carries a strong implication of assurance and positiveness, sometimes suggesting little or no fear that one will be doubted or contradicted, and at other times connoting one's personal guarantee ⟨I *warrant* that's just what will happen⟩ ⟨I'll *warrant* he's as good a gentleman as any—*Buchan*⟩ ⟨as smooth as silk, I *warrant* ye—*L'Estrange*⟩ ⟨cheap-jacks who sell at dockyard gates a pill *warranted* to cure measles, toothache and rupture—*Montague*⟩
*Ana* allege, advance, cite, *adduce
*Ant* deny: controvert —*Con* gainsay, contradict, negative, traverse, contravene (see DENY): *disprove, refute, rebut, confute
2 vindicate, justify, *maintain, defend
*Ana* proclaim, *declare, publish, advertise: *express, voice, utter
**assertive** self-assertive, *aggressive, pushing, pushy, militant
*Ana* positive, *affirmative: blatant, clamorous, *vociferous: cocksure, certain, *sure, positive: *confident, assured, sanguine, presumptuous
*Ant* retiring: acquiescent —*Con* *shy, bashful, diffident, modest: docile, *obedient, amenable, biddable
**assess** assay, appraise, value, evaluate, *estimate, rate
*Ana* *calculate, compute, reckon
**asset** 1 (in plural form **assets**) resources, means, *possessions, effects, belongings
*Ant* liabilities
2 *credit
*Ant* handicap
**assiduous** sedulous, diligent, industrious, *busy
*Ana* *indefatigable, tireless, untiring, unwearied
*Ant* desultory —*Con* *random, haphazard, casual, hit-or-miss, happy-go-lucky: *lazy, slothful, indolent, faineant: remiss, lax, slack (see NEGLIGENT)
**assign** 1 *allot, allocate, apportion
*Ana* fix, *set, establish, settle: *distribute, deal, dole, dispense
2 refer, *ascribe, attribute, impute, credit, accredit, charge
*Ana* attach, *fasten, affix: relate, link, associate (see JOIN): pigeonhole, classify (see ASSORT)
3 *prescribe, define
*Ana* determine, settle, *decide: consign, relegate, *commit, entrust
**assignation** rendezvous, tryst, date, *engagement, appointment
**assignment** *task, duty, job, stint, chore
**assimilate** 1 *identify, incorporate, embody
*Ana* *change, alter, modify, vary: *transform, metamorphose, transmute: blend, fuse, merge, commingle, *mix
2 *absorb, imbibe
*Ana* engross, absorb, *monopolize: *adopt, embrace, espouse: *infuse, imbue, ingrain, suffuse, inoculate, leaven
**assimilation** apperception, identification, *recognition
**assist** *help, aid
*Ana* *support, uphold, back, champion: profit, avail, *benefit: attend, *accompany, escort: cooperate, concur (see UNITE)
*Ant* hamper: impede —*Con* *hinder, obstruct, block: trammel, clog, fetter (see HAMPER): *prevent, forestall
**assistance** help, aid (see under HELP *vb*)

A colon (:) separates groups of words discriminated. An asterisk (*) indicates place of treatment of each group.

*Ana* service, advantage, profit, avail, *use: supporting, upholding, backing (see SUPPORT *vb*): subsidy, grant, subvention, *appropriation: cooperation, concurrence (see corresponding verbs at UNITE)
*Ant* impediment: obstruction

**assistant** *n* Assistant, helper, coadjutor, aid, aide, aide-de-camp all denote persons who take over part of the duties of another, especially in a subordinate capacity. Assistant is applicable to a person who meets this description, regardless of the status of his work ⟨a baker's *assistant*⟩ ⟨a bishop's *assistant*⟩ ⟨a superintendent's *assistant*⟩ Helper often implies apprenticeship in a trade or the status of an unskilled laborer ⟨a bricklayer's *helper*⟩ ⟨a mother's *helper* often performs the duties of a nursemaid⟩ Coadjutor usually implies equivalence except in authority; it may be used either of a co-worker or a volunteer assistant ⟨in working so complex a mechanism as the government of the empire he must have willing *co-adjutors—Buchan*⟩ ⟨at St. James I met with a kind and cordial *coadjutor* in my biblical labors in the bookseller of the place—*Borrow*⟩ ⟨decided to share the government of the Roman world with a *coadjutor—R. M. French*⟩ In a specific use it names or is applied to a bishop who serves as an assistant to the bishop having jurisdiction over a diocese. Especially in Roman Catholic and Protestant Episcopal use it implies the right of succession. Aid and aide are often interchangeable synonyms of *assistant* ⟨a laboratory *aid*⟩ ⟨*aides* and orderlies . . . assist the professional nurses—*Nursing World*⟩ Aide frequently but *aid* rarely denotes a special and often highly qualified assistant able to act as an adviser to his principal ⟨questioned the use of presidential *aides* in foreign affairs⟩ ⟨with their chief *aides* they will discuss the problems of the interregnum—*N. Y. Times*⟩ Aide and aide-de-camp designate a military or naval officer who personally attends a general or a sovereign, a president or a governor, often as an escort but sometimes with definitely prescribed duties.

**associate** *vb* connect, relate, link, *join, conjoin, combine, unite
*Ana* merge, mingle, *mix, blend, amalgamate, coalese: organize (see ORDER *vb*)
*Con* alienate, *estrange: *separate, part, divorce, sever, sunder, divide

**associate** *n* Associate, companion, comrade, crony mean a person frequently found in the company of another. Associate is the general term, referable to anyone whose company one enjoys or tolerates more or less regularly and usually on terms of equality because of a business, social, fraternal, or similar connection or because of a community of interests or aims ⟨a person is known by his *associates*⟩ ⟨his *associates* included all the prominent young men of the town⟩ ⟨he became a leader of fashion. Then, to the visible embarrassment of his young *associates*, he suddenly tired of it all—*Day Lewis*⟩ Companion refers to a person who actually accompanies or attends one; a person who walks along the street with one or who sits with one at a restaurant table may be called a *companion* for the time being even if one has never seen him before and never sees him afterwards. However, the word often implies more habitual association and closer personal relationship than *associate* ⟨his wife was his lifelong *companion*⟩ ⟨he no longer stood alone; the *companions* of his youth had become in the full sense his coadjutors—*Buchan*⟩ ⟨he was her darling brother, her beloved *companion* in adventure—*Rose Macaulay*⟩ Sometimes the association is not the result of friendship or of relationship but of a business arrangement ⟨the old lady sought a competent paid *companion*⟩ Comrade implies association in a common calling or pursuit, and more or less familiarity

in companionship ⟨*comrades* in arms⟩ ⟨school *comrades*⟩ Commonly it connotes more sentiment than either *associate* or *companion*, even though that sentiment is sometimes no more than a sense of shared fortunes or experiences, or a consciousness of having worked or played together ⟨return to her . . . ? no, rather I abjure all roofs, and choose . . . to be a *comrade* with the wolf and owl—*Shak.*⟩ ⟨which weep the *comrade* of my choice . . . the human-hearted man I loved—*Tennyson*⟩ Crony is seldom used of a young person, though often applied to an older person who was an intimate friend in school days or with whom one has been on intimate terms for a very long time ⟨an old *crony* of his turned up after a long absence from England⟩ ⟨the two old ladies are great *cronies*⟩
*Ana* *partner, colleague, ally, confederate: accomplice, abettor, accessory (see CONFEDERATE): *assistant, helper, coadjutor, aide
*Con* antagonist, adversary, *opponent: *enemy, foe: rival, competitor (see corresponding verbs at RIVAL)

**association**, society, club, order denote a body of persons who unite in the pursuit of a common aim or object. Association is in general used of an organization which is inclusive in its membership, excluding only those whose personal affiliations, interests, and needs are different from those of the typical member or, if the object of the organization is service of some sort, those who do not belong to the business, the industry, or the profession served ⟨the Young Men's Christian *Association*⟩ ⟨the Modern Language *Association*⟩ ⟨the National *Association* of Manufacturers⟩ Society is often used interchangeably with *association*, but it tends to suggest a more restricted aim, a closer union of members, and their more active participation, and sometimes a narrower field of choice of membership ⟨the Christian Endeavor *Society*⟩ ⟨*Society* for the Prevention of Cruelty to Animals⟩ ⟨a missionary *society*⟩ ⟨a secret *society*⟩ ⟨the Philological *Society*⟩ ⟨*Society* for Ethical Culture⟩ Club usually suggests such privacy that admission to membership is only through election and invitation; it often also implies quarters for the meeting and entertainment of members and therefore is applied to the buildings or rooms as well as to the organization ⟨going to the country *club* to play golf⟩ ⟨a political *club*⟩ ⟨a bridge *club*⟩ ⟨most large cities have a university *club*⟩ Order is applied chiefly to a society whose members have common aims and accept common obligations (as of working together in brotherly union and of practicing certain virtues) ⟨a religious *order*⟩ ⟨a fraternal *order*⟩ Order usually suggests in addition a ritual, a uniform, and honorary distinctions ⟨the Independent *Order* of Odd Fellows⟩ ⟨the Benevolent and Protective *Order* of Elks⟩

**assort**, sort, classify, pigeonhole mean to arrange in systematic order or according to some definite method of arrangement or distribution. Assort (see also *assorted* under MISCELLANEOUS) implies division into groups of like things or of things intended for the same purpose or destination ⟨*assort* the jumbled contents of an attic⟩ ⟨*assorted* his bills and papers⟩ When used in reference to homogeneous material, *assort* usually implies grading (as according to size, condition, or value) ⟨*assort* oranges for the market⟩ ⟨*assort* the books by author and subject⟩ Often, additionally, it implies selection, either of what is to be eliminated or of what is to be chosen or preserved ⟨her mind was busily *assorting* and grouping the faces before her —*Glasgow*⟩ ⟨the company indeed was perfectly *assorted*, since all the members belonged to the little inner group of people who, during the long New York season, disported themselves together daily and nightly—*Wharton*⟩ Sort usually equals *assort* but is often preferred to it when

the latter would seem too literary or too technical ⟨*sort* mail⟩ ⟨*sort* stockings⟩ ⟨*sort* yarns⟩ Frequently, especially with *out, sort* implies culling or selection even more than arrangement ⟨he *sorted* and re-sorted his cargo, always finding a more necessary article for which a less necessary had to be discarded—*Cather*⟩ **Classify** is more often used of things that fall into intellectual categories than of those which can be physically grouped. It usually implies a division into kinds or types and an arrangement for convenience in dealing with material that cannot be assembled or that is not before one ⟨*classify* bodies of water⟩ ⟨*classify* poems as epic, lyric, and dramatic⟩ ⟨*classify* languages according to the way in which words are formed⟩ **Pigeonhole** suggests an arrangement of small compartments in a writing desk or of boxes in a post office, each compartment being a receptacle for one group of letters or papers that are sorted or classified; it implies the ability to put each of a number of things in its right class or category ⟨he *pigeonholes* the wild flowers he meets on a day's walk by assigning each to its proper classification or by being able to give it its proper specific or generic name⟩ ⟨he *pigeonholes* every bit of information that comes to him by filing it away in his memory properly labeled and in its right place with relation to the rest of his knowledge⟩
*Ana* arrange, methodize, systematize, *order
*Con* *mix, mingle, commingle: derange, disarrange, disorganize, *disorder

**assorted** *miscellaneous, heterogeneous, motley, promiscuous
*Ana* diverse, *different, various, disparate, divergent: selected, picked, chosen, preferred (see CHOOSE): mixed, mingled (see MIX)
*Ant* jumbled —*Con* *like, similar, identical, uniform

**assortment** see corresponding adjective *assorted* at MISCELLANEOUS
*Ana* *mixture, blend, compound: combining or combination, associating or association, uniting or union (see corresponding verbs at JOIN)
*Ant* jumble, hodgepodge

**assuage** alleviate, *relieve, mitigate, lighten, allay
*Ana* temper, *moderate: *comfort, solace, console: mollify, placate, appease, *pacify
*Ant* exacerbate: intensify —*Con* kindle (see LIGHT *vb*): aggravate, heighten (see INTENSIFY): *increase, augment

**assume 1** Assume, affect, pretend, simulate, feign, counterfeit, sham mean to put on a false or deceptive appearance. **Assume** often implies a pardonable motive rather than an intent to deceive ⟨it sometimes happens that by *assuming* an air of cheerfulness we become cheerful in reality—*Cowper*⟩ To **affect** is to make a show of possessing or using something, usually for effect, but sometimes because of one's liking for it ⟨*affect* plainness of speech⟩ ⟨*affect* a gesture, an opinion, a phrase, because it is the rage with a large number of persons—*Hazlitt*⟩ ⟨Jones had really that taste for humor which others *affect*—*Fielding*⟩ **Pretend** implies overt profession of what is false ⟨that *pretended* liking called politeness—*L. P. Smith*⟩ ⟨*pretend* to be insane⟩ ⟨even their clowns had to be learned or to *pretend* learning—*Highet*⟩ To **simulate** is to assume the characteristics of something else by imitating its appearance or outward signs ⟨trees hewn to *simulate* formidable artillery pieces were dragged into position all along the ramparts—*Amer. Guide Series: La.*⟩ **Feign** implies more invention than *pretend,* less specific imitation of life than *simulate* ⟨I grow angry and I curse them, and they *feign* penitence, but behind my back I know they call me a toothless old ape—*Kipling*⟩ But *feign* and *simulate* are often interchangeable. **Counterfeit** implies the highest degree

of verisimilitude of any of the words in this group ⟨are you not mad indeed? or do you but *counterfeit?—Shak.*⟩ ⟨many noblemen gave the actor-manager access to their collections of armor and weapons in order that his accouterment should exactly *counterfeit* that of a Norman baron —*Shaw*⟩ **Sham** implies feigning with an intent to deceive; it usually connotes deception so obvious that it fools only the gullible ⟨*sham* sickness⟩ ⟨*sham* sleeping⟩ ⟨when the curtain falls there are more actors *shamming* dead upon the stage than actors upright—*H. A. L. Craig*⟩
*Ana* dissemble, *disguise, cloak, mask, camouflage
**2** *presuppose, postulate, presume, premise, posit
*Ana* *conjecture, surmise: *grant, concede, allow: *assert, affirm, aver, predicate, profess

**assumption** presupposition, postulate, posit, presumption, premise (see under PRESUPPOSE)
*Ana* *hypothesis, theory: *principle, fundamental, axiom, theorem: conjecture, surmise (see under CONJECTURE *vb*)

**assurance 1** certitude, *certainty, conviction
*Ana* *belief, faith, credence, credit: *trust, confidence, reliance, dependence: positiveness, sureness, cocksureness (see corresponding adjectives at SURE)
*Ant* mistrust: dubiousness —*Con* doubt, *uncertainty, skepticism, suspicion: disbelief, *unbelief, incredulity
**2** self-assurance, *confidence, self-confidence, self-possession, aplomb
*Ana* sangfroid, composure, *equanimity: sureness, sanguineness (see corresponding adjectives at CONFIDENT): mettle, resolution, spirit, *courage, tenacity: effrontery, *temerity, nerve
*Ant* diffidence: alarm —*Con* timorousness, timidity (see corresponding adjectives at TIMID): shyness, bashfulness, modesty (see corresponding adjectives at SHY)

**assure** insure, *ensure, secure
*Ant* alarm —*Con* *frighten, scare, fright, terrify: abash, discomfit, *embarrass: *intimidate, cow

**assured** *confident, sanguine, sure, presumptuous
*Ana* fearless, unapprehensive, unafraid (see affirmative adjectives at FEARFUL): *cool, composed, unruffled, imperturbable, unflappable, collected
*Ant* abashed: timorous —*Con* discomfited, embarrassed, rattled, disconcerted (see EMBARRASS): *fearful, apprehensive, afraid: hesitant, reluctant (see DISINCLINED)

**astern** *abaft, aft
*Ana* after, hind, rear, back (see POSTERIOR)
*Ant* ahead —*Con* *before, forward

**astonish** *surprise, astound, amaze, flabbergast
*Ana* nonplus, dumbfound, bewilder, confound (see PUZZLE): impress, strike, touch, *affect

**astound** *surprise, astonish, amaze, flabbergast
*Ana* dumbfound, confound, nonplus, bewilder (see PUZZLE): startle, affright, alarm, terrify (see FRIGHTEN)

**astral** *starry, stellar, sidereal

**astray** *amiss

**astute** *shrewd, perspicacious, sagacious
*Ana* *sharp, keen, acute: discreet, prudent, foresighted (see under PRUDENCE): knowing, *intelligent, clever, smart: wily, crafty, cunning, *sly
*Ant* gullible —*Con* ingenuous, naïve, simple, unsophisticated (see NATURAL): candid, open, plain, *frank: forthright, *straightforward, aboveboard

**asylum** *shelter, refuge, retreat, sanctuary, cover

**at 1** At, in, on cause difficulty when used in phrases giving the place or locality of an action. When reference to the interior of any place is made prominent, **in** is used; when a place is regarded as a mere local point, **at** is more commonly employed; when the direction is indicated, **on** is sometimes used in place of *at* ⟨look for a book *in* the

---

A colon (:) separates groups of words discriminated. An asterisk (*) indicates place of treatment of each group.

library⟩ ⟨meet a friend *at* the library⟩ ⟨sit *on* my right⟩ ⟨the town lies *on* the east coast⟩ ⟨he appointed regular meetings of the States of England twice a year *in* London —*Hume*⟩ ⟨an English king was crowned *at* Paris— *Macaulay*⟩ *In* is commonly employed before the names of countries or districts and *at* before names of institutions, public offices, or business houses ⟨*in* America⟩ ⟨*in* the South⟩ ⟨Milton was educated *at* Christ's College⟩ ⟨*at* the customhouse⟩ ⟨*at* the jeweler's⟩ With names of towns and cities the choice between *in* or *at* usually depends upon whether the place designated is felt respectively (1) as an including area or scene, especially with an implication of destination or permanence of occupancy, or of having familiar associations for the speaker or (2) merely as a point (as along a journey or course) on a map or in space or at a remove from the speaker ⟨on our way to visit *in* Troy we lunched *at* Albany⟩ ⟨after a stopover *at* Chicago, we arrived *in* Sioux Falls on Friday⟩ ⟨a man born here *in* Zenith is consul *at* Hong Kong⟩ In giving a town address we say *at* 141 Wood Street *in* Springfield. In giving the street without the number, *in* is preferred in Great Britain, *on* in the United States.
**2 At, in, on** are clearly distinguishable when used to introduce a phrase giving the time of an action. When reference is to time by the clock or to a point of time registered by a clock, **at** is commonly used ⟨*at* two o'clock⟩ ⟨promptly *at* the hour appointed⟩ ⟨*at* three minutes to six⟩ When the reference is not to a point but to a period in the course of which an action occurs, **in** is the usual preposition ⟨at two o'clock *in* the afternoon⟩ ⟨September 1st *in* the year 1939⟩ ⟨*in* the month of May⟩ When the reference is to a particular day in the course of which something occurs, **on** is used ⟨*on* July fourth there will be a celebration⟩ ⟨it happened *on* a Sunday⟩ *On* is sometimes used also with reference to a point of time with which there is, or should be, coincidence ⟨be here *on* the hour⟩ ⟨he is always *on* the dot⟩

**atavism** *reversion, throwback

**atavistic** reversionary (see under REVERSION)

**atheist,** agnostic, deist, freethinker, unbeliever, infidel designate a person who rejects some or all of the essential doctrines of religion and particularly the existence of God. An **atheist** is one who denies the existence of God; an **agnostic** is one who withholds belief (though he may not deny the possible existence of a supreme being) because he does not know and is unwilling to accept as proof the evidence of revelation and spiritual experience; a **deist** is one who rejects the conception of a supreme being as ruler and guide of men and the universe, but still believes in a god who is the creator and the final judge of men. Since deism implies a denial of revelation and supernaturalism, *deist* has often been used as though it were the equivalent of *atheist*. **Freethinker** suggests loss of faith and the rejection of any or all of the tenets of revealed religion in favor of what seems rational or credible. **Unbeliever** is more negative than *freethinker,* because it carries no implication of a substitute for faith. **Infidel** denotes one who is not a Christian or who opposes Christianity; it is used by Christians especially to designate monotheists (as Muslim) who do not subscribe to the Judeo-Christian concept of God and in such usage is distinguishable from *heathen* and *pagan*. From the Muhammedan point of view, especially as presented in English fiction and poetry, *infidel* often means a Christian. *Ant* theist

**athirst** avid, *eager, keen, anxious, agog
*Ana* thirsting, hungering, pining, yearning, longing (see LONG *vb*): craving, coveting *or* covetous, desiring *or* desirous (see corresponding verbs at DESIRE)

*Con* *indifferent, unconcerned, incurious, aloof: *languid, lackadaisical, listless: apathetic, *impassive

**athlete,** gymnast agree in denoting a person skilled in physical performance requiring agility, powers of endurance, and, often, muscular strength. **Athlete** also usually implies the status of a contender in games or in sports involving a contest, whether outdoor or indoor; school or college *athletes* are the students who participate in school sports (as football, baseball, basketball, or track) ⟨an outstanding *athlete* who had participated in several college sports⟩ A **gymnast** is one who is skilled in bodily exercises and calisthenics performed often with the aid of apparatus for the development of nimbleness, strength, and control in the use of the body ⟨leaping back a yard . . . with the speed and security of a trained *gymnast* —*Stevenson*⟩

**athletic** *muscular, husky, sinewy, brawny, burly
*Ana* *strong, stalwart, sturdy: lusty, *vigorous, strenuous, energetic
*Con* frail, fragile, *weak

**athletics,** sports, games denote physical activities engaged in for exercise or play. **Athletics** is a collective term (not used in the singular) for exercises for the performance of which one acquires and maintains agility, skill, stamina by regular and systematic training and practice usually with the aim of competing, singly or as a member of a team, with others similarly trained, whether for pleasure, to keep the body in trim, to win honor for oneself, one's team, school, or club, or to earn a livelihood ⟨college *athletics* include football, basketball, hockey, baseball, rowing, and tennis⟩ ⟨baseball, hockey, football, and tennis are among the better-known professional *athletics*⟩ **Sports** are forms of physical activity, usually outdoor, that afford pleasure or diversion. The term may be used in the singular for any of the various forms of athletics, since whatever the main purpose of athletic activity may be, a certain amount of pleasure is usually derived ⟨football, basketball, hockey, baseball, rowing, and tennis are among the popular *sports* with those who go out for athletics in college⟩ ⟨major-league baseball is a professional *sport*⟩ The idea of training to develop agility, skill, or stamina, prominent in *athletics,* is frequently wanting in *sports,* which may involve so little exertion or be engaged in for so short a period or so infrequently as not to require it; thus, an impromptu baseball game between two pickup teams falls under the head of *sport,* but hardly of *athletics*. So also the idea of competition, usually present in *athletics,* is frequently wanting in *sports* ⟨noncompetitive skating, skiing, canoeing, and swimming are *sports*⟩ The term is wider than *athletics,* including such activities as hunting and fishing (in which the pleasure derives from pursuit of quarry). Since sports contests are often an object of interest to others, the term *sports* is applied also to contests which provide amusement or diversion for spectators as well as or often rather than contestants; horse racing, dog racing, bullfighting, and cockfighting are *sports* ⟨we . . . have every source of amusement open to us, and yet follow these cruel *sports*—*Windham*⟩ **Games** (for singular see FUN) are athletic or sports contests, usually those which are of a somewhat artificial nature and therefore require more extensive rules than such contests as rowing, boxing, wrestling, and skiing. Thus, practically all forms of competition that make use of a ball or similar object are called *games* (as baseball, football, hockey, golf, tennis, and polo). Although the plural *games* may be used interchangeably with *meet* of a competition consisting chiefly or only of track-and-field events ⟨Olympic *games*⟩ the singular *game* is applied to few of the individual events of such a competition.

---

*Ana* analogous words     *Ant* antonyms     *Con* contrasted words     See also explanatory notes facing page 1

**athwart** crosswise, crossways, *across

**atmosphere** 1 *air, ether, ozone

2 Atmosphere, **feeling, feel, aura** denote an intangible and usually unanalyzable quality or aggregate of qualities which gives something an individual and distinctly recognizable character. **Atmosphere** is used chiefly in reference to places, to groups of persons, or to periods of time that have a definite identity. It frequently denotes a character that accrues to something or that pervades it as a whole and determines the impression it produces on those who come within the range of its influence; thus, a place that has no *atmosphere* is by implication a place that leaves no clear impression of its difference from other places of the same type or kind; a poet who re-creates the *atmosphere* of the Middle Ages is one who by implication gives a true and vivid impression of the life of that time. *Atmosphere* may also denote an environment (regarded as a sum total of physical, social, intellectual, and spiritual conditions) that not only produces a distinct impression but exerts a definite influence (as on the state of mind, habits of work, or views) of those who are encompassed by it ⟨genius can only breathe freely in an *atmosphere* of freedom— *J. S. Mill*⟩ ⟨any judge who has sat with juries knows that . . . they are extremely likely to be impregnated by the environing *atmosphere—Justice Holmes*⟩ **Feeling** (see also FEELING, SENSATION) may refer either to the character one ascribes to something when one has a clear and unified impression of its distinctive qualities or atmosphere, or to the aesthetic effect of a work of art which not only represents a thing but re-creates its atmosphere or conveys the impression the artist seeks to produce ⟨a collection of scenic wallpapers that . . . have a slight Japanese *feeling* —*New Yorker*⟩ ⟨they bring the notion of the things described to the mind, they do not bring the *feeling* of it to the imagination—*Arnold*⟩ **Feel** may be used interchangeably with *feeling* and also with *atmosphere*, especially when the quality of a thing is known through frequent experience or intimate knowledge ⟨the factory had a homely *feel—D. H. Lawrence*⟩ ⟨the sensitive reader may discover in them, also, something of the quality and *feel* of Shakespeare's own poetry—*Day Lewis*⟩ **Aura** is used chiefly in reference to persons who seem to be enveloped by an ethereal spirit which is an emanation of their inner life or of their secret thoughts; it is also used of things that are invested with a mysterious quality or character ⟨in their company, he was always conscious of an *aura* of disapproval⟩ ⟨there was about her the *aura*, the glow, the roseate exhalation that surrounds the woman in love— *Ferber*⟩ ⟨throughout the Middle Ages the Taunus and the Harz had about them an *aura* of the uncanny as the last haunt of the primeval gods—*Buchan*⟩

*Ana* *quality, character, property: peculiarity, individuality, characteristic (see corresponding adjectives at CHARACTERISTIC): *impression, impress

**atom** 1 *particle, molecule, corpuscle

2 *particle, bit, mite, smidgen, jot, tittle, iota, whit

*Ana* smack, spice, dash, suspicion, soupçon, *touch, suggestion, tincture, tinge, shade

**atone** *expiate

*Ana* compensate, *pay: propitiate, conciliate, appease (see PACIFY)

**atonement** expiation (see under EXPIATE)

*Ana* compensating *or* compensation, offsetting (see corresponding verbs at COMPENSATE): conciliation, propitiation, appeasement (see corresponding verbs at PACIFY): *reparation, amends

**atrabilious** hypochondriac, *melancholic, melancholy

*Ana* morose, glum, saturnine, crabbed, *sullen: *despondent, hopeless, forlorn: depressed, dejected, gloomy

(see corresponding nouns at SADNESS)

*Ant* blithe —*Con* *merry, jocund, jovial, jolly: *glad, happy, cheerful, lighthearted, joyful, joyous

**atrocious** heinous, monstrous, *outrageous

*Ana* *flagrant, gross, rank, glaring: nefarious, flagitious, infamous, iniquitous, *vicious: barbaric, savage, barbarous, *barbarian

*Ant* humane: noble (see MORAL) —*Con* righteous, virtuous (see MORAL)

**attach** 1 *arrest, apprehend, detain

*Ana* seize, *take, grab: capture, *catch

*Con* release, discharge, deliver, *free

2 *fasten, affix, fix

*Ana* *join, link, unite, connect: annex, *add, append: *tie, bind

*Ant* detach —*Con* disengage (see DETACH): disencumber, disentangle, disembarrass (see EXTRICATE): sever, sunder, divorce, part, *separate

**attachment** 1 arrest, apprehension, detention (see under ARREST *vb*)

2 Attachment, **affection, love** denote the feeling which animates a person who is genuinely fond of someone or something. **Attachment** and **affection** differ in that *affection* usually has for its object a sentient being, whereas that of *attachment* may be even an inanimate thing ⟨an *attachment* to his profession⟩ ⟨feels a strong *attachment* to the house in which he lived⟩ *Attachment* implies strong liking, devotion, or loyalty; *affection*, rather warmth and tenderness of sentiment ⟨a profound *attachment* to the King as king—*Belloc*⟩ ⟨it cannot show lack of *attachment* to the principles of the Constitution that she thinks it can be improved—*Justice Holmes*⟩ ⟨widespread American *affection* for France—*George*⟩ *Affection* and *love* differ in that *affection* implies a feeling more settled and regulated, less intense or ardent, than *love*, which alone of the three may connote passion. Thus to one's friends any one of the three terms may be applicable; to the members of one's own family, *love* or *affection*, but usually not *attachment;* to God, *love* (in the sense of reverent devotion), but not *affection* or *attachment;* to one's country, *love*, especially if ardent patriotism is implied, *affection*, if the emphasis is upon genuine but not blind devotion, *attachment*, if allegiance and loyalty are definitely connoted.

*Ana* fondness, devotedness (see corresponding adjectives at LOVING): devotion, piety, fealty, *fidelity, allegiance

*Ant* aversion —*Con* *antipathy: estrangement, alienation, disaffection (see corresponding verbs at ESTRANGE)

**attack** *vb* Attack, **assail, assault, bombard, storm** are comparable not only in their military but also in their extended senses. All carry as their basic meaning to make a more or less violent onset upon. **Attack** originally connoted a fastening upon something as a beast of prey fastens upon its victim. It now implies aggression or aggressiveness in all its senses and usually the initiative in entering into an engagement or struggle (as with a person or thing that is opposed or that one intends to conquer) ⟨plan to *attack* the enemy at dawn⟩ ⟨*attacked* the position of his opponents in a debate⟩ ⟨*attack* a problem in engineering⟩ ⟨they lack the courage to *attack* their other studies with the vigor requisite to success—*Grandgent*⟩ ⟨it had become increasingly apparent that the logical method of eradicating disease was to *attack* it at its source—*Heiser*⟩ **Assail** suggests the action of one who would conquer by force of repeated blows rather than by brute strength. Its chief distinction from *attack* is in this suggestion of repetition of means (as blows, strokes, shots, or thrusts) of breaking down resistance ⟨*assail* an enemy with shells⟩ ⟨*assail* with reproaches⟩ ⟨*assailed* by temptations⟩ ⟨property interests . . . *assailed* by attempts to put industry upon a

---

A colon (:) separates groups of words discriminated. An asterisk (*) indicates place of treatment of each group.

more reasonable and more equitable footing—*Hobson*⟩ ⟨old pains keep on gnawing at your heart, old desires . . . old dreams, *assailing* you—*Conrad*⟩ **Assault** implies close contact or a direct confrontation; in contrast with *assail,* it suggests the use of brute strength and an attempt to overpower by suddenness and violence of onslaught ⟨*assault* a person with a club⟩ ⟨*assault* a stronghold on all sides⟩ ⟨while other aircraft *assaulted* supply buildings —*N. Y. Times*⟩ ⟨a universal hubbub wild of stunning sounds . . . *assaults* his ear—*Milton*⟩ **Bombard** literally means to assail continuously and devastatingly with bombs or shells ⟨the advancing German army in 1914 expected to *bombard* Paris and bring a quick end to the war⟩ It is, in its stronger implication of importunity or of continuous pestering, distinguishable from *assail* ⟨he *bombarded* Cicero with letters asking for advice—*Buchan*⟩ ⟨the reporters *bombarded* the district attorney with questions⟩ **Storm** means to assault with the violence, rush, and effectiveness of a sudden and devastating storm or wind; it connotes an attempt to sweep from its path every obstacle to a victory ⟨several of their bravest officers were shot down in the act of *storming* the fortress—*Irving*⟩ ⟨who think to *storm* the world by dint of merit—*Burns*⟩ *Ana* fight, *contend, battle, war: beset, overrun (see INFEST): *surprise, waylay, ambush *Con* *defend, shield, guard, protect: *resist, withstand, oppose, combat

**attack** *n* **1** **Attack, assault, onslaught, onset** denote an attempt made on another or on others to injure, destroy, or defame. An **attack** may be upon the physical person or it may be upon the character, the reputation, or the writings of a person or persons; it often suggests animosity or definite enmity as its cause, but it may imply motives as various as wanton cruelty, partisan feeling, or a critical intention ⟨the victim of a cowardly *attack* by hoodlums⟩ ⟨the speech was a severe *attack* upon the policies of the administration⟩ ⟨the book was the object of *attacks* from all sides⟩ ⟨an unprovoked *attack* upon the fairness of the court⟩ **Assault** implies more violence, more malice or viciousness, and often the infliction of greater damage or less reparable damage than *attack.* However, an *assault* upon the person is legally an apparently violent attempt or a willful offer with force or violence to injure or hurt that person physically. When the hurt has been inflicted, the precise legal term for the act is *assault and battery.* Rape is sometimes specifically called an *assault.* In military language an *assault* is sometimes distinguished from an *attack* upon the enemy, the former term being applied only to the last phase of an *attack* or offensive movement, when the aggressors close upon their opponents and the issue is determined. Usually *assault* and *attack* are not clearly distinguishable except in emphasis; thus, an *assault* upon a person's character suggests violent emotion (as hatred or vindictiveness); an *attack* upon a person's character need not imply strong feeling as its motive ⟨the passage . . . shows how alarmed a Hegelian may be by an *assault* upon the authority of science—*Inge*⟩ **Onslaught** suggests a vigorous and destructive method of attack; it usually implies an attempt to overwhelm by force of momentum or of numbers or by the fury of the assault ⟨the defenders, taken by surprise, were unable to repel the *onslaught*⟩ ⟨no play can withstand such an *onslaught* from the critics⟩ ⟨he sees I am no man to take rebuff. . . . quick to the *onslaught,* out sword, cut and thrust!—*Browning*⟩ **Onset** is applicable not only to the first furious rush that initiates an attack (as an offensive movement, an act of aggression, or a fit of illness) but to any such succeeding rush that marks a renewal of vigor in the attack ⟨at the *onset,* the twelfth regiment bore the brunt of the attack⟩

⟨a pause in the fighting gave the officers time to rally their scattered troops and to prepare for a fresh *onset* from the enemy⟩ ⟨at every *onset* of the gale convulsive sounds came from the branches—*Hardy*⟩ *Ana* action, *battle: striking, hitting, smiting, slugging (see STRIKE): criticism, condemnation, denouncing *or* denunciation (see corresponding verbs at CRITICIZE) *Con* defending *or* defense, vindication, justification (see corresponding verbs at MAINTAIN): resistance, opposition (see corresponding verbs at RESIST)

**2** **Attack, aggression, offense, offensive** and their corresponding adjectives **attacking, aggressive, offensive** denote or describe action in a struggle for supremacy which must be met with defense or by means of defenses. The terms are used not only of military operations but of competitive games or exhibitions of skill (as in boxing and fencing). **Attack** implies the initiation of action; commonly, also, it suggests an attempt to catch the enemy or opposition off guard and therefore connotes suddenness, and often violence, of onset ⟨the first raiding *attack* was . . . repulsed with heavy losses—*H. G. Wells*⟩ **Aggression,** which also implies initiation of hostile action, stresses rather a lack of provocation and a desire for conquest or domination. *Attack* is applicable to any movement or action in a series of operations; *aggression* is applied chiefly to a war or to a type of fighting that involves invasion or encroachment on another's territory and usually further connotes a determination to maintain the advantage of the attacking side ⟨pledged never to fight in a war of *aggression*⟩ ⟨the business of government is to check *aggression* only—*Smith*⟩ ⟨an *aggressive* war, as distinguished from mere plundering inroads—*Freeman*⟩ **Offense** and **offensive** characterize the position or the methods of the attacking side. The noun is interchangeable with *attack* only when the latter word does not refer to a concrete action; thus, one may speak of methods of *attack* (or of *offense*) as contrasted with methods of defense but one would use "a war of *offense*" (rather than of *attack*) and "readiness for an *attack*" (rather than for an *offense*). Both words are distinguishable from *aggression* and *aggressive,* which in many ways they closely resemble, by their absence of suggestion of any motive or aim other than that of a desire for supremacy. **Offensive** implies vigorously aggressive action especially in war; thus, when taking the *offensive* one carries on *offensive* operations. *Offensive* may also denote a particular campaign or episode marked by such action ⟨an economic *offensive* can often prevent the necessity for a more costly military defense—*Draper*⟩ ⟨to be *offensive* means to carry the war to the enemy. And this as well is the most effective sort of defense—*Ageton*⟩ **3** *fit, access, accession, paroxysm, spasm, convulsion

**attacking** *adj* aggressive, offensive (see under ATTACK *n*) **attain** *reach, compass, gain, achieve *Ana* *come, arrive: win, acquire, secure, obtain, *get: accomplish, effect (see PERFORM) **attainment** accomplishment, *acquirement, acquisition **attaint** *vb* taint, pollute, defile, *contaminate **attempt** *vb* **Attempt, try, endeavor, essay, strive, struggle** as verbs mean to make an effort to do something that may or may not be successful and as nouns (the single exception in form being **striving**) mean the effort made to accomplish such an end. **Attempt** implies an actual beginning of or venturing upon something that one hopes to accomplish or carry through and often suggests failure ⟨formed a plan and yet made no *attempt* to execute it⟩ ⟨the troops were driven back when they *attempted* to break through the enemy's line⟩ ⟨after many *attempts* to construct a flying machine the Wright brothers succeeded⟩ ⟨nothing

---

*Ana* analogous words     *Ant* antonyms     *Con* contrasted words     See also explanatory notes facing page 1

*attempted,* nothing gained⟩ ⟨here Shakespeare tackled a problem which proved too much for him. Why he *attempted* it at all is an insoluble puzzle—*T. S. Eliot*⟩ **Try** is often thought of as a simpler equivalent of *attempt;* in discriminating use, however, the two terms are distinguishable by subtle differences in meaning. *Try* seldom loses the implication of effort or experiment directed toward the end of ascertaining a fact or of testing or proving a thing. This implication is especially apparent in some idiomatic phrases; thus, one *tries* a window by attempting to open it so as to find out if it is fastened; one *tries* one's hand at something by attempting to do something new to test one's ability or aptitude; one *tries* one's luck with the horses by betting on horse races in the hope of proving one's luck. *Try* is the word of choice when effort or experiment or testing are stressed rather then a venturing upon or undertaking ⟨*try* to find which of two methods is the better⟩ ⟨make a *try* at solving the problem⟩ ⟨succeed at the first *try*⟩ ⟨freedom in thought, the liberty to *try* and err, the right to be his own man— *Mencken*⟩ **Endeavor** heightens the implication of exertion and should be avoided as too strong when likelihood of success is implied. It often connotes a striving to fulfill a duty or obey a sense of fitness ⟨she walked up and down the room *endeavoring* to compose herself—*Austen*⟩ ⟨the Good, which is the goal of all moral *endeavor*—*Inge*⟩ ⟨in Arnold's phrases the first step for every aspirant to culture is to *endeavor* to see things as they are, or "to learn, in short, the will of God"—*Eliot*⟩ ⟨we all *endeavor,* as Spinoza says, to persist in our own being; and that *endeavor* is, he adds, the very essence of our existence— *L. P. Smith*⟩ **Essay** implies that the thing to be accomplished is especially difficult; otherwise it combines the foremost implications of *attempt* (that is, making a beginning) by suggesting a tentative effort and of *try* (that is, experiment) by suggesting the testing of a thing's feasibility ⟨sculpture which attempted to unite repose and action, the "far off" and the familiar, in a way which Phidias and Donatello were too prudent to *essay*— *Brownell*⟩ ⟨conventions frequently take their rise . . . from the faulty *essays* of an early and as yet undeveloped technique—*Lowes*⟩ The last terms of this group, **strive** and **struggle,** not only carry heightened implications of difficulty and of correspondingly greater exertion, but also connote greater opposition to be overcome. *Strive* and *striving* suggest persistent endeavor to surmount obstacles created by one's weaknesses, one's lack of experience, the height of one's ambitions, or the power of resisting forces ⟨*strive* to overcome a bad habit⟩ ⟨a *striving* to reach the top of his class⟩ ⟨*striving* to come out of the filth, the flies, the poverty—*Anderson*⟩ ⟨sick of self and tired of vainly *striving*—*James*⟩ ⟨the bitter, desperate *striving* unto death of the oppressed race—*Rose Macaulay*⟩ **Struggle** literally and figuratively implies straining or stretching that suggests a tussle, a wrestling, or an effort to extricate oneself from what impedes or fetters ⟨*struggled* to free himself from his attackers⟩ ⟨a *struggle* to reach the shore⟩ So strong at times is this implication that the word loses or nearly loses its implication of endeavor ⟨he clambered over half-visible rocks, fell over prostrate trees, sank into deep holes and *struggled* out— *Cather*⟩ ⟨the *struggle* between two strong-willed women to control one weak-willed man is the usual motive of the French drama in the nineteenth century—*Henry Adams*⟩

*Ana* *begin, commence, start, initiate, inaugurate

*Ant* succeed —*Con* accomplish, achieve, effect, fulfill, execute, *perform: attain, compass, *reach, gain

**attempt** *n* endeavor, essay, try, striving, struggle (see

under ATTEMPT *vb*)

*Ana* trial, test (see under PROVE): beginning, commencement, starting *or* start, initiation (see corresponding verbs at BEGIN)

**attend** 1 *tend, mind, watch

*Ana* *nurse, foster, nurture, cherish: supervise, oversee (see corresponding nouns at OVERSIGHT)

2 escort, *accompany, chaperon, convoy

**attention** 1 **Attention, study, concentration, application** can mean the direct focusing of the mind on something, especially on something to be learned, worked out, or dealt with. **Attention** is applicable to the faculty or power as well as to the act ⟨noises that distract one's *attention*⟩ ⟨if we had to think about breathing or digesting . . . we should have no *attention* to spare for anything else— *Shaw*⟩ ⟨every awareness is the simple form of *attention* —*Alexander*⟩ Since the word carries no inherent implications about the power or the act or of the length of the latter's duration, it usually requires qualifying words or phrases ⟨close *attention*⟩ ⟨trained habits of *attention*⟩ ⟨a few moments' *attention*⟩ **Study** stresses continuity and closeness of attention; it usually also implies an aim such as the acquisition of knowledge, or the analysis of something that is complex or confusing, or the working out of a plan (as for action) or of a design (as for a book) ⟨the president said that he would not comment upon the proposal until he had given it further *study*⟩ ⟨of making many books there is no end; and much *study* is a weariness of the flesh—*Eccles* 12:12⟩ **Concentration** emphasizes the centering of the attention on one thing to the exclusion of everything else ⟨amazing powers of *concentration*⟩ ⟨the learning to read poetry takes as much patience and *concentration* as the learning to write it—*Day Lewis*⟩ **Application** usually implies persistence in fixing one's attention, and diligence and assiduity in the performance of all that is required; it suggests therefore a virtue won by effort and sheer force of will rather than (as with *concentration*) a power that has its origin in one's temperament or is the result of profound interest ⟨*application* for ever so short a time kills me —*Lamb*⟩ ⟨her *application* to her studies in school— *Anderson*⟩

*Ana* diligence, assiduity, sedulousness, industriousness (see corresponding adjectives at BUSY)

*Ant* inattention —*Con* preoccupation, abstraction, absentmindedness (see corresponding adjectives at ABSTRACTED)

2 *courtesy, gallantry, amenity

*Ana* courting *or* court, wooing (see corresponding verbs at INVITE): deference, homage, *honor, reverence: solicitude (see CARE)

*Con* neglect, *negligence: indifference, aloofness, unconcernedness *or* unconcern (see corresponding adjectives at INDIFFERENT): rudeness, discourteousness *or* discourtesy, impoliteness (see corresponding adjectives at RUDE)

**attentive** *thoughtful, considerate

*Ana* courteous, polite, gallant, chivalrous, *civil: solicitous, concerned (see under CARE *n*)

*Ant* inattentive: neglectful —*Con* *indifferent, unconcerned, aloof: *negligent, remiss: heedless, thoughtless, *careless

**attenuate** *vb* *thin, rarefy, dilute, extenuate

*Ana* *weaken, sap: reduce, lessen (see DECREASE): dissipate (see SCATTER): *contract, shrink, constrict, deflate

*Ant* enlarge: dilate: enrich —*Con* *expand, amplify, swell, distend, inflate: *increase, augment

**attest** 1 witness, *certify, vouch

*Ana* *confirm, corroborate, substantiate, verify

*Con* *disprove, controvert, refute, confute: *deny, con-

---

A colon (:) separates groups of words discriminated. An asterisk (*) indicates place of treatment of each group.

tradict, gainsay
**2** argue, prove, bespeak, *indicate, betoken
*Ana* demonstrate, test (see PROVE): *confirm, authenticate, substantiate
*Ant* belie —*Con* *misrepresent, falsify
**attire** *vb* *clothe, apparel, array, dress, robe
*Ana* accouter, appoint, equip, outfit, arm (see FURNISH)
*Ant* divest —*Con* *strip, bare, denude, dismantle
**attire** *n* *clothes, clothing, apparel, raiment, dress
**attitude 1** *posture, pose
*Ana* mien, *bearing, port, presence, demeanor
**2** *position, stand
*Ana* *point of view, angle, slant, viewpoint, standpoint: bias, prepossession, prejudice, *predilection
**attorney 1** *agent, deputy, proxy, factor
*Ana* *substitute, supply, alternate
**2** *lawyer, solicitor, counselor, barrister, counsel, advocate
**attract** *vb* **Attract, allure, charm, fascinate, bewitch, enchant, captivate** mean to draw another by exerting an irresistible or compelling influence over him. The same distinctions in implications and connotations are observable in the adjectival forms of these words, **attractive, alluring, charming, fascinating, bewitching, enchanting, captivating. Attract** always implies a drawing of one thing to another either because of qualities or properties in the agent or because of an affinity in the one attracted for that which draws it or a susceptibility to its influence ⟨a magnet *attracts* iron⟩ ⟨positive electricity *attracts* negative⟩ ⟨a store of honey *attracts* a bear⟩ ⟨a stimulating new book *attracts* attention⟩ When used in reference to persons of different sexes, it suggests the arousing of strong admiration or the awakening of love or desire in the person attracted ⟨talking, in that beautiful voice which made everything she said sound like a caress, to Papa, who had begun to be *attracted* rather against his will—*Woolf*⟩ **Allure** implies not only attraction but enticement by something that is fair, pleasing, or seductive. It may, like *lure*, suggest enticement into evil or danger ⟨ancient fables of men *allured* by beautiful forms and melodious voices to destruction—*Hudson*⟩ More often the stress is on the overcoming of resistance or indifference by the use of winning methods (as delicate flattery or the enhancement of feminine appeal) or by the bait of a pleasant prospect ⟨an *alluring* advertisement of a summer resort⟩ ⟨she did not naturally attract men, but she became accomplished in *alluring* them⟩ ⟨the prospect of an interesting, vivid life *allures* many young women to the big cities⟩ ⟨young children should rather be *allured* to learning by gentleness and love, than compelled to learning by beating and fear—*Ascham*⟩ **Charm** implies a power in the agent to cast a spell over and so dominate the person or thing affected ⟨only his daughter had the power of *charming* this black brooding from his mind—*Dickens*⟩ In its commonest use *charm* implies a power to evoke or attract admiration, but it usually heightens that implication by retaining the suggestion of casting a spell over the senses or over the mind ⟨there was a grace about him which *charmed*, and a hint of latent power which impressed—*Buchan*⟩ ⟨Cyril, having taken a fancy to his brilliant aunt, had tried to *charm* her as he seldom or never tried to *charm* his mother—*Bennett*⟩ **Fascinate,** like *charm,* implies the casting of a spell, but it usually suggests the ineffectiveness of resistance or helplessness to escape from the one that fascinates ⟨the younger and weaker man was *fascinated* and helpless before the creeping approach of so monstrous a wrath—*G. D. Brown*⟩ ⟨personality . . . so *fascinating* that . . . it would absorb my whole nature, my whole soul, my very art itself—

*Wilde*⟩ **Bewitch** and **enchant** likewise imply the exertion of a magical influence; the former, in its literal sense, suggesting witchcraft, and the latter, sorcery but these implications are often either exceedingly weak or actually lost. *Bewitch,* in its commonest sense, implies the exertion of a power of fascination that causes another to succumb to one's charms or allurements and to be under one's domination. *Enchant,* on the other hand, usually suggests a power to evoke joy or rapture or ecstatic admiration in the person fascinated ⟨*enchanted* by the girl's beauty⟩ ⟨*bewitched* by her charms⟩ ⟨heavens grant that Warwick's words *bewitch* him not!—*Shak.*⟩ ⟨Sophia enjoyed the intimacy with Constance. As for Constance, she was *enchanted*—*Bennett*⟩ **Captivate** is the weakest of these words in its suggestion of an irresistible influence or attraction. It implies a capturing of the fancy or feelings and a holding them in thrall for the time being, but it carries no suggestion of prolonged influence or of enslavement ⟨the child *captivates* everyone with his sunny smile⟩ ⟨just the hero to *captivate* a romantic girl —*Irving*⟩
*Ana* *invite, solicit, court: entice, *lure, tempt, seduce: *catch, capture
*Ant* repel —*Con* *offend, affront, outrage, insult
**attraction,** **affinity,** **sympathy** are comparable when they denote the relationship between persons or things that are involuntarily or naturally drawn together and exert, to some degree, an influence over each other. **Attraction** implies the possession by one person or thing of qualities with the power to draw another person or thing so that the latter moves toward the former or, in the case of things, is brought into contact with it or clings to it. *Attraction* also implies the existence in the thing attracted of susceptibility to the influence of what attracts; in the case of persons it may be a natural inclination for, a predisposition to, or an innate liking of what attracts or, in the case of things, a tendency to unite or combine with the attractant. This natural or constitutional susceptibility is called **affinity.** Therefore *affinity* is the complement of *attraction* and not its synonym; thus, *attraction* is a force whereby a magnet draws iron to it, but iron is one of the few metals that have an *affinity* for the magnet; chemistry has a powerful *attraction* for minds that have an *affinity* for it ⟨he too yearns as they do for something unattained by him. What an *affinity* for Christianity had this persecutor of the Christians!—*Arnold*⟩ The words are interchangeable only when used of persons and things that are mutually attracted or have a reciprocal affinity for each other; even in these cases, however, the fundamental distinction in meaning prevails; thus, two persons may have an *attraction* (or an *affinity*) for each other; atoms remain in combination in a substance because of their *affinity* or *attraction* for each other. It is not by chance that in physics, the science concerned with energy, *attraction* is the word used in reference to atomic cohesion and that in chemistry, the science concerned with the composition of substances, *affinity* is the technical term. **Sympathy** stresses not so much the drawing together of persons or things as their reciprocal influence or their susceptibility to the same influences. When used in reference to things, it commonly implies interaction ⟨the tides rise and fall in *sympathy* with the moon⟩ ⟨there is close *sympathy* between the heart and the lungs⟩ When used in reference to persons, *sympathy* usually connotes spiritual affinity, or compatibility in tastes, interests, or aims ⟨union of hearts, not hands, does marriage make, and *sympathy* of mind keeps love awake—*Hill*⟩
**attractive** alluring, charming, fascinating, bewitching, enchanting, captivating (see under ATTRACT)

*Ana* lovely, fair, *beautiful, bonny, pretty, comely: luring, enticing, tempting, seductive (see corresponding verbs at LURE)
*Ant* repellent: forbidding —*Con* *repugnant, abhorrent, distasteful, obnoxious: *offensive, repulsive, revolting, loathsome
**attribute** *n* 1 *quality, property, character, accident
2 emblem, *symbol, type
*Ana* *sign, mark, token, badge, note: *character, symbol, sign
**attribute** *vb* *ascribe, impute, assign, credit, accredit, refer, charge
*Ana* *fasten, attach, fix: predicate (see ASSERT): blame (see CRITICIZE): *accuse, charge
**attrition** contrition, repentance, *penitence, remorse, compunction
*Ana* regret, *sorrow, grief, anguish
**attune** tune, *harmonize
*Ana* *adapt, adjust, accommodate, reconcile, conform: accord, *agree, harmonize: temper (see MODERATE): balance, counterbalance, *compensate
*Con* alienate, *estrange, wean
**atypical** *abnormal, aberrant
*Ana* *irregular, anomalous, unnatural: divergent, *different: deviating, departing (see SWERVE *vb*): *exceptional
*Ant* typical: representative —*Con* ordinary, *common, familiar: *usual, customary
**audacious** *brave, courageous, unafraid, fearless, intrepid, valiant, valorous, dauntless, undaunted, doughty, bold
*Ana* daring, daredevil, reckless, venturesome, *adventurous, rash, foolhardy: brazen, brash, *shameless
*Ant* circumspect —*Con* *cautious, wary, chary, calculating: prudent, sane, judicious, *wise
**audacity** *temerity, hardihood, effrontery, nerve, cheek, gall
*Ana* intrepidity, boldness, courageousness (see corresponding adjectives at BRAVE): daring, daredeviltry, recklessness, rashness, foolhardiness (see corresponding adjectives at ADVENTUROUS): *courage, mettle, spirit: brazenness *or* brass (see corresponding adjective at SHAMELESS)
*Ant* circumspection —*Con* caution, wariness, calculation (see under CAUTIOUS): timidity, timorousness (see corresponding adjectives at TIMID): fearfulness, apprehensiveness (see corresponding adjectives at FEARFUL)
**audible** *aural, auricular
*Ant* inaudible
**audience** 1 *hearing, audition
2 public, *following, clientele
*Ana* devotees, votaries (see singular nouns at ADDICT)
**audit** *n* examination, inspection, scrutiny, scanning (see under SCRUTINIZE)
*Ana* check, *corrective, control: investigation, probe, *inquiry
**audit** *vb* examine, inspect, *scrutinize, scan
**audition** *hearing, audience
**auditor** *bookkeeper, accountant
*Ana* examiner, inspector, scrutinizer (see corresponding verbs at SCRUTINIZE): verifier, authenticator (see corresponding verbs at CONFIRM)
**auditory, acoustic, acoustical** mean of or relating to the hearing of sounds. **Auditory** often stresses hearing more than sound ⟨the *auditory* powers of a dog⟩ ⟨the *auditory* sensitivity of an individual's organs of hearing⟩ **Acoustic** emphasizes sound with reference to its capacity for being heard or the conditions under which it is heard ⟨the *acoustic* quality of a person's voice⟩ ⟨*acoustic* properties of a hall⟩ Both words are used in anatomy with little distinction, except that some human anatomists prefer

*acoustic* ⟨the *auditory* nerve⟩ ⟨the *acoustic* area of the brain⟩ **Acoustical** is often interchangeable with *acoustic* but when direct reference to the science of acoustics is intended, the former is preferred ⟨*acoustical* engineering⟩
**augment** *increase, enlarge, multiply
*Ana* *intensify, aggravate, enhance, heighten: swell, *expand, amplify, dilate
*Ant* abate (sense 2) —*Con* reduce, diminish, *decrease, lessen, dwindle: curtail, abridge, *shorten
**augur** prognosticate, presage, portend, forebode, prophesy, forecast, *foretell, predict
*Ana* betoken, *indicate, bespeak, argue: apprehend, anticipate, divine, foreknow, *foresee
**augury** omen, portent, presage, prognostic, *foretoken
*Ana* *sign, symptom, token, note, badge, mark: precursor, *forerunner, harbinger, herald
*Con* fulfillment, accomplishment, effecting *or* effect (see corresponding verbs at PERFORM): realization, actualization, materialization (see corresponding verbs at REALIZE)
**august** majestic, imposing, stately, noble, grandiose, *grand, magnificent
*Ana* impressive, *moving: *splendid, sublime, superb: awful, *fearful
*Ant* unimpressive: unimposing
**aura** *atmosphere, feeling, feel
**aural, auricular, audible** mean heard or perceived by the ear but they are not often interchangeable. **Aural** is applicable to any sensation or impression which affects the auditory sense rather than other senses ⟨insensitiveness to *aural* stimuli⟩ ⟨prefer the *aural* to the visual method in learning a language⟩ **Auricular** is applicable not only to what is heard as distinguished from what is read but also especially to something communicated privately and addressed to the ear of a particular person; thus, *auricular confession* is used of the private confession of sins to a priest as distinguished from open confession before a congregation ⟨you shall . . . by an *auricular* assurance have your satisfaction—*Shak.*⟩ **Audible** is applicable only to sounds, voices, or conversations which are heard as distinguished from those which are not heard because too faint, too low, or uttered in a whisper ⟨his voice being distinctly *audible* in the street—*Hardy*⟩
**aureate** *adj* euphuistic, flowery, *rhetorical, grandiloquent, magniloquent, bombastic
*Ana* *ornate, florid, flamboyant, rococo, baroque
*Ant* austere (*in style*)
**auricular** *aural, audible
**auspicious** *favorable, propitious, benign
*Ana* *lucky, fortunate, happy, providential: *hopeful, roseate: indicating *or* indicative, betokening (see corresponding verbs at INDICATE)
*Ant* inauspicious: ill-omened —*Con* *sinister, baleful, malign, malefic, maleficent: *adverse, antagonistic, counter: *ominous, portentous, unpropitious, fateful
**austere** *severe, stern, ascetic
*Ana* bald, *bare: unembellished, unadorned, unornamented, undecorated (see affirmative verbs at ADORN): dispassionate (see FAIR): rigorous, strict (see RIGID): grave, somber, *serious, sober, earnest
*Ant* luscious (*of fruits*): warm, ardent (*of persons, feelings*): exuberant (*of style, quality*) —*Con* lush, prodigal, *profuse: clement, lenient, indulgent (see FORBEARING): grandiloquent, magniloquent, aureate, flowery, *rhetorical: *impassioned, passionate, fervid, fervent
**autarchic** autarkic, autonomous, independent, *free, sovereign
**autarchy** autarky, autonomy, independence, freedom, sovereignty (see under FREE *adj*)
**autarkic** autarchic, autonomous, independent, *free,

---

A colon (:) separates groups of words discriminated. An asterisk (*) indicates place of treatment of each group.

sovereign

**autarky** autarchy, autonomy, independence, freedom, sovereignty (see under FREE *adj*)

**authentic,** genuine, veritable, bona fide denote being exactly what the thing in question is said to be or professes to be. The prevailing sense of **authentic** is authoritative or trustworthy with the implication of actuality or accordance with fact ⟨confirmed both by legend and *authentic* record—*Froude*⟩ ⟨an *authentic* description of the Great Fire of London⟩ The prevailing sense of **genuine** is real or true (see REAL) often with the implication of descent without admixture from an original stock or of correspondence without adulteration to the natural or original product called by that name ⟨*genuine* maple syrup⟩ ⟨a *genuine* Russian wolfhound⟩ ⟨this is real merino, the *genuine* article⟩ Often the stress is on sincerity or lack of factitiousness ⟨*genuine* piety⟩ ⟨true simplicity and *genuine* pathos—*Wordsworth*⟩ Both terms are used— genuine more frequently than *authentic*—as opposed to *spurious, counterfeit, apocryphal* ⟨let them contrast their own fantastical personages . . . with the *authentic* rustics of Burns—*Jeffrey*⟩ ⟨what is *genuine* knowledge, and what is its counterfeit—*Newman*⟩ It is idiomatic to say of a work (as a portrait) "this is an *authentic* portrait of George Washington" (that is, it was painted from life) and "this is a *genuine* Gilbert Stuart portrait of Washington" (that is, it is properly ascribed to Gilbert Stuart, the painter). **Veritable** implies a correspondence with truth; it is seldom used without a suggestion of asseveration or of affirmation of belief ⟨I who am now talking . . . am the *veritable* Socrates—*Blackie*⟩ ⟨though Christ be the *veritable* Son of God—*Quiller-Couch*⟩ It also is applied to words or phrases used figuratively or hyperbolically to assert the justice of the designation or of its truth in essentials ⟨his fits of passion are *veritable* hurricanes⟩ ⟨he is a *veritable* fool⟩ **Bona fide,** though often used as though it were the equivalent of *genuine* or *authentic*, is properly applied when good faith or sincerity is in question ⟨a *bona fide* sale of securities⟩ ⟨a *bona fide* bid for a piece of property⟩

**Ana** authoritarian, oracular (see DICTATORIAL): *reliable, trustworthy, dependable: *correct, right, exact: true, *real, actual

**Ant** spurious —**Con** *fictitious, apocryphal, fabulous, mythical, legendary: *false, wrong: deceptive, *misleading, delusive, delusory: *supposed, supposititious, putative, purported, hypothetical

**authenticate** validate, verify, *confirm, substantiate, corroborate

**Ana** certify, accredit, endorse, *approve: *prove, try, test, demonstrate: avouch, warrant (see ASSERT)

**Ant** impugn: —**Con** *deny, gainsay, contradict, traverse, negative, contravene: reject, repudiate, spurn (see DECLINE)

**author** 1 *maker, creator
2 *writer, composer

**authoritarian** 1 dogmatic, *dictatorial, magisterial, doctrinaire, oracular

**Ana** despotic, autocratic, arbitrary, tyrannical, tyrannous, *absolute: domineering, imperious, *masterful

**Ant** liberal, libertarian: anarchistic, anarchic
2 *totalitarian

**authority** 1 *power, jurisdiction, command, control, dominion, sway

**Ana** ascendancy, *supremacy: government, ruling *or* rule (see corresponding verbs at GOVERN)
2 *influence, weight, credit, prestige

**Ana** exemplar, ideal, standard, pattern, *model, example: *expert, adept, artist: connoisseur, *aesthete

**authorize,** commission, accredit, license denote in common to invest with power or the right to act. One **authorizes** a person to act for oneself when he is given the necessary legal right or power with or without instructions of a specific character. Often discretionary powers are implied ⟨*authorize* a friend to make an answer to an attack on one's character⟩ ⟨our clerks are *authorized* to receive contributions for the Red Cross⟩ One **commissions** a person when one not only authorizes but instructs him to perform a definite duty or office ⟨I am *commissioned* to make you an offer which I have told him . . . you would not accept—*Gray*⟩ **Commission** may imply appointment as one's business agent (as in buying, selling, or supplying goods) or it may suggest an order to do a certain kind of work, especially work of a professional or artistic nature ⟨*commissioned* an artist to paint his children's portraits⟩ One **accredits** a person when one sends him, invested with authority and possessed of the proper credentials, as a representative, delegate, or ambassador ⟨John Hay was *accredited* to the Court of St. James's⟩ ⟨the sovereign to whom I am *accredited*—*Motley*⟩ One **licenses** a person or a business, a trade, or a craft when one grants formal legal permission to act in a certain capacity or to carry on a particular business, trade, or craft ⟨*license* a teacher⟩ ⟨*license* medical school graduates to practice medicine⟩ ⟨a *licensed* dental laboratory⟩ **License** sometimes stresses permission so strongly that the implication of authorization is obscured and that of regulation substituted ⟨*license* beggars⟩ ⟨*license* a restaurant to sell liquor⟩

**Ana** empower, *enable: permit, allow, *let
**Con** enjoin, *forbid, prohibit, interdict

**autobiography** memoir, life, *biography, confessions

**autochthonous** indigenous, *native, aboriginal, endemic
**Ant** naturalized
**Con** foreign, alien, extraneous, *extrinsic

**autocratic** arbitrary, *absolute, despotic, tyrannical, tyrannous
**Ana** *dictatorial, magisterial: authoritarian, *totalitarian: *masterful, domineering, imperious: overbearing, arrogant (see PROUD)
**Con** yielding, deferring, submitting, capitulating (see YIELD *vb*): tolerant, lenient, *forbearing, indulgent

**automatic** *adj* 1 Automatic, spontaneous are not close synonyms but they agree in meaning brought into being or action by an internal as opposed to an external agency. **Automatic** was originally used to describe a thing that was self-acting or self-activated because it contained the principle of motion within itself ⟨in the universe, nothing can be said to be *automatic*—*Davy*⟩ Now it is applied more often to machines and mechanical contrivances which, after certain conditions have been fulfilled, continue to operate indefinitely without human supervision or until the conditions have materially changed; thus, an *automatic* firearm is so constructed that after the first round is exploded the force of the recoil or gas pressure loads and fires round after round until the ammunition is exhausted or the trigger is released; a thermostat is an *automatic* device which maintains the temperature of artificially heated rooms by operating the appropriate parts of a furnace when the temperature exceeds or falls below the point at which it is set. **Spontaneous** (see also SPONTANEOUS) applies not so much to objective things as to processes, particularly natural processes, thought of as originating without external agency or without human agency; thus, *spontaneous* generation implies origin of living directly from nonliving matter; *spontaneous* combustion implies a generation of heat through chemical changes in matter causing it to burn; a *spontaneous* growth

---

*Ana* analogous words　　*Ant* antonyms　　*Con* contrasted words　　See also explanatory notes facing page 1

refers to vegetation produced neither from humanly sown seed nor from plantings.

**2** mechanical, instinctive, *spontaneous, impulsive
*Ana* trained, disciplined, schooled, instructed (see TEACH): prompt, *quick, ready
*Con* deliberate, *voluntary, intentional

**autonomous** independent, sovereign, *free, autarchic, autarkic

**autonomy** independence, freedom, sovereignty, autarky, autarchy (see under FREE *adj*)

**auxiliary, subsidiary, accessory, contributory, subservient, ancillary, adjuvant** mean supplying aid or support. **Auxiliary** may imply subordinate rank or position ⟨an *auxiliary* organization⟩ ⟨an *auxiliary* bishop⟩ ⟨the conclusion that the humanistic point of view is *auxiliary* to and dependent upon the religious point of view—*T. S. Eliot*⟩ It often suggests something kept in reserve ⟨an *auxiliary* motor in a sailboat⟩ **Subsidiary** stresses subordinate or inferior status or capacity, often to the obscuring or loss of the notion of supplying aid ⟨*subsidiary* streams⟩ ⟨a *subsidiary* company controlled by another company that holds a majority of the shares of its stock⟩ **Accessory** so strongly stresses association or accompaniment that the notion of assistance or support is often obscured or lost; thus, an *accessory* mineral is one present in a rock but not an essential constituent; a person *accessory* to a crime (as the hirer of an assassin or a receiver of stolen goods) need not actively participate in its commission (see also *accessory n* under CONFEDERATE). **Contributory** stresses the assistance rather than the subordinate status of the assistant and usually implies the effecting of an end or result ⟨resentment against the unjust tax was one of the *contributory* causes of the revolt⟩ ⟨*contributory* negligence on the part of a person suffering an injury may impair his right to recover damages⟩ **Subservient** usually stresses the subordinate nature of the assistance ⟨a catastrophe to which every incident should be *subservient*—*Crabbe*⟩ It may stress the importance or usefulness of the end it serves and the nature of its motive (as commendable self-subordination or a sense of order and due relation) ⟨he has uniformly made his talents *subservient* to the best interests of humanity—*Coleridge*⟩ ⟨those features of a work of art which by themselves would be unattractive or repulsive, like an "ugly" face, but in the work are *subservient* to the total effect and may even heighten its beauty—*Alexander*⟩ **Ancillary** more than the other terms stresses the intimacy of the assistance ⟨some practice in the deft use of words, with its correspondent defining of thought, may well be *ancillary* even to the study of natural science—*Quiller-Couch*⟩ **Adjuvant** differs from *auxiliary*, its closest synonym, in attributing greater importance, more noticeable effectiveness, or a more definite influence to the thing so qualified; an *adjuvant* ingredient in a prescription often modifies the action of the major ingredient so as to make it effective ⟨asceticism is merely an *adjuvant* discipline to ... pathological forms of mysticism—*Ellis*⟩
*Ana* *subordinate, secondary, tributary: supporting, upholding, backing (see SUPPORT *vb*): helping, aiding, assisting (see HELP *vb*): supplementary, complementary (see corresponding nouns at COMPLEMENT)

**avail** *vb* **1** *benefit, profit
*Ana* meet, answer, *satisfy, fulfill: *help, aid
*Con* harm, hurt, *injure, damage
**2** utilize, employ, *use, apply
*Con* *abuse, misuse: *neglect, ignore, slight, overlook: reject, refuse, spurn (see DECLINE)

**avail** *n* *use, service, account, advantage, profit

**avarice** greed, *cupidity, rapacity

*Ana* avariciousness, covetousness, acquisitiveness (see corresponding adjectives at COVETOUS): stinginess, niggardliness, miserliness, parsimoniousness (see corresponding adjectives at STINGY)
*Ant* prodigality —*Con* extravagance (see corresponding adjective at EXCESSIVE): liberality, generosity, munificence, bountifulness, bounteousness, openhandedness (see corresponding adjectives at LIBERAL)

**avaricious** *covetous, acquisitive, grasping, greedy
*Ana* miserly, close, closefisted, parsimonious, *stingy
*Ant* generous —*Con* *liberal, bountiful, bounteous, openhanded, munificent: lavish, prodigal (see PROFUSE)

**avenge, revenge** mean to inflict punishment on a person who has wronged oneself or another. Once close synonyms, these verbs are now increasingly divergent in implications. One may *avenge* or *revenge* (oneself or another who is wronged), but **avenge** is to be preferred when the motive is a desire to vindicate or to serve the ends of justice or when one visits just or merited punishment on the wrongdoer ⟨*avenge*, O Lord, thy slaughtered saints—*Milton*⟩ ⟨I swear on my knees, on these stones, to *avenge* you on Foulon—*Dickens*⟩ ⟨he had *avenged* himself on them by havoc such as England had never before seen—*Macaulay*⟩ On the other hand, one **revenges** oneself or, rarely, another when one inflicts injury *on* or *upon* an offender in a desire to exact satisfaction for his offense. *Revenge* may imply a desire for vindication or an aim to serve the ends of justice, but more often it suggests a desire to get even, to pay back in kind or degree, and therefore variously connotes malice, spite, or an unwillingness to forgive ⟨the hope of *revenging* himself on me was a strong inducement—*Austen*⟩ ⟨the novelist obsessed with the errors of his past ... is irresistibly drawn to *revenge* himself on his past by rewriting it—*Rolo*⟩ ⟨he saw that his true policy was not to *revenge* himself by executions and confiscations—*Stubbs*⟩ Also, one may either *avenge* or *revenge* a wrong or injury but *avenge* usually implies that the end is just retribution whether the activity is in one's own or another's behalf, whereas *revenge* implies that the end is retaliation and the compelling spirit of the act hatred or bitterness; thus, Orestes *revenged* his father's murder by killing the murderess, his mother, but the gods *avenged* his matricide by driving him mad.
*Ana* requite, recompense, compensate, *pay: vindicate, defend, justify (see MAINTAIN): *punish, chasten, chastise
*Con* forbear, *refrain, abstain: remit, pardon, forgive (see EXCUSE)

**aver** declare, avouch, avow, profess, affirm, *assert, protest
*Ana* *maintain, defend, justify
*Ant* deny —*Con* gainsay, negative, contradict, traverse (see DENY)

**average** *n* Average, mean, median, norm, par denote something and usually a number, a quantity, or a condition that represents a middle point between extremes. Of these words **average, mean, median,** and **par** are also used as adjectives. **Average** is an arithmetical term applied to a quotient obtained by dividing a total by the number of items entering into this total so that the quotient represents the value each item would have if all were alike; thus, the *average* of 10, 12, 14, 16, 18, 20 is 15 (that is, 90 ÷ 6). Such averages are computed to give one a fair estimate of a group or a series in which there are inequalities ⟨his *average* for his high school course was 82⟩ ⟨the daily *average* of the apple pickers was 25 bushels⟩ When (as in sports) the total represents the number of chances taken or of opportunities offered or provided, the *average* is obtained by dividing the number of successes or successful

---

A colon (:) separates groups of words discriminated. An asterisk (*) indicates place of treatment of each group.

performances by this total. Such an average may be expressed as a percentage or a permillage and gives a fair estimate of a player's performance and a basis for comparison with others; thus, a baseball first baseman who handles a total of 1114 chances and makes 6 errors has a fielding *average* of .9946 (that is, 1108 ÷ 1114); a baseball batter who is credited with 605 appearances at bat and has made 201 hits has a batting *average* of .332 (that is, 201 ÷ 605). A similar method is used in estimating probabilities (as the chances of death for a person between given ages and the length of the period between recurrences of an unpredictable phenomenon); thus, the *average* of mortality for persons of a given age is computed from statistics of deaths at that age and of the population group consisting of persons of that age. *Average* also may be applied to a concept of what is the typical or ordinary person or thing of its kind (see also *average*, under MEDIUM) ⟨the boy is above the *average* for his age and background⟩ ⟨the play is below the season's *average* in dramatic interest⟩ **Mean** originally and still in certain idioms named a condition, quality, intensity, or rate that is midway between two extremes ⟨observe a happy *mean* between abjectness and arrogance or between effusiveness and reserve⟩ ⟨he that holds fast the golden *mean*, and lives contentedly between the little and the great—*Cowper*⟩ In its mathematical use *mean* is more general than *average* (for which another name is *arithmetical mean*): it covers also the *geometric mean*, that is, the square root of the product of two numbers or quantities (or the *n*th root of the product of *n* quantities); thus, 10 is the *arithmetical mean* or *average* of 4, 16; while 8 is the *geometric mean* of 4, 16. **Median** refers to a midway point in position; in statistics it names the figure or quantity which represents the point at which there are as many instances below as there are above it; thus, the *average* of a group of 5 workers earning respectively 6, 8, 10, 16, and 20 dollars a day is 12 dollars a day, whereas the *median* for the same group is 10 dollars, because one half of them earn less than 10 dollars a day and one half more. **Norm** suggests a rule for guidance or a definite pattern to be followed; it also denotes especially in such fields as psychology and sociology, an average, whether mathematically computed or estimated, of performance or achievement of a group, class, or category that can be set up as a standard for or a minimum of accomplishment by a similar larger group, class, or category; thus, a course of study for a particular school grade is based upon a *norm* determined by the performance of children of the age, experience, and background commonly found in that grade ⟨crime is merely a name for the most obvious, extreme, and directly dangerous forms of . . . departure from the *norm* in manners and customs—*Ellis*⟩ ⟨it is everything to have acquired and to possess such a *norm* of Poetry within us that we know whether or not what he wrote was Poetry—*Quiller-Couch*⟩ **Par** usually refers to an average for an individual that is like the *norm* for a group. It often refers to an individual person's average in health, accomplishment, or performance ⟨I feel below *par* (that is, below my average in health) today⟩ ⟨this theme is above *par* for that student⟩ In British use *par* may be employed in reference to an average in amount ⟨the *par* of crop production for this farm⟩

*Ant* maximum: minimum

**average** *adj* **1** mean, median, par (see under AVERAGE *n*)
**2** middling, *medium, indifferent, fair, moderate, mediocre, second-rate

*Ana* *common, ordinary, familiar: *usual, customary
*Ant* exceptional: extraordinary —*Con* outstanding, prominent, conspicuous, *noticeable: superlative, *su-

preme, surpassing, preeminent

**averse** **1** *disinclined, indisposed, loath, reluctant, hesitant
*Ana* recoiling, shrinking, flinching, quailing (see RECOIL *vb*): uncongenial, unsympathetic (see INCONSONANT): balky, *contrary, perverse
*Ant* avid (*of* or *for*): athirst (*for*)
**2** unsympathetic, *antipathetic
**3** *adverse

**aversion** **1** *dislike, distaste, disfavor
*Ana* antipathy, hostility, antagonism (see ENMITY): horror, dread, *fear
*Ant* predilection —*Con* partiality, bias (see PREDILECTION): *leaning, propensity
**2** *antipathy
*Ana* repugnance, repellency, abhorrence, distaste *or* distastefulness (see corresponding adjectives at REPUGNANT): horror, dread, *fear
*Ant* attachment, predilection —*Con* partiality, bias, prejudice (see PREDILECTION): *leaning, penchant, propensity, flair

**avert** **1** *turn, deflect, sheer, divert
*Ana* bend, twist, *curve: shift, remove, transfer, *move
**2** ward, *prevent, obviate, preclude
*Ana* *escape, avoid, shun, eschew, evade, elude: forestall, anticipate (see PREVENT): *frustrate, balk, thwart, foil

**aviation** *aeronautics

**avid** *eager, keen, anxious, agog, athirst
*Ana* desiring *or* desirous, craving, coveting *or* covetous (see corresponding verbs at DESIRE): longing, yearning, pining, hankering, hungering, thirsting (see LONG *vb*)
*Ant* indifferent: averse —*Con* indisposed, *disinclined, loath: aloof, disinterested (see INDIFFERENT): listless, *languid: apathetic, *impassive

**avoid** *escape, shun, eschew, evade, elude
*Ana* avert, ward, *prevent, obviate: forestall, anticipate (see PREVENT): flee, fly (see ESCAPE)
*Ant* face: meet —*Con* *incur, contract, catch: court, solicit, *invite

**avouch** aver, affirm, avow, profess, declare, *assert, protest, warrant, predicate
*Ana* *confirm, corroborate
*Con* gainsay, contradict, *deny, negative, traverse, impugn

**avow** **1** affirm, profess, declare, aver, avouch, warrant, *assert, protest, predicate
*Ana* *maintain, defend, vindicate
**2** own, *acknowledge, confess, admit
*Ana* proclaim, *declare, publish, announce: *reveal, discover, disclose, divulge, tell
*Ant* disavow —*Con* repudiate, reject, refuse (see DECLINE *vb*): *deny, gainsay, negative, contradict

**await** *expect, hope, look
*Ana* wait, abide, *stay
*Ant* despair

**awake** *adj* *aware, alive, cognizant, conscious, sensible
*Ana* alert, vigilant, *watchful: roused, aroused, stirred up, awakened (see STIR)
*Con* *sleepy, drowsy, somnolent, slumberous: *inactive, inert, supine

**awaken** waken, rouse, arouse, *stir, rally
*Ana* excite, galvanize, quicken, stimulate, *provoke: kindle, fire (see LIGHT): elicit, evoke (see EDUCE)
*Ant* subdue —*Con* *arrest, check: *frustrate, thwart, baffle, balk, foil

**award** *vb* *grant, accord, vouchsafe, concede
*Ana* bestow, confer, present, *give: assign, *allot, apportion, allocate: adjudicate, adjudge, *judge, arbitrate
**award** *n* prize, *premium, reward, guerdon, meed, bonus,

bounty

**aware, cognizant, conscious, sensible, alive, awake** mean having knowledge of something, especially of something that for some reason is not obvious or apparent to all. One is **aware** of something through information or through one's own vigilance in observing or in drawing inferences from what one sees, hears, or feels ⟨few, so far as I am *aware*, now claim the free speech to call a knave a knave—*T. S. Eliot*⟩ ⟨would not . . . have been worthy of his reputation had he not been *aware* . . . of the existence of this League. Journalists have to be *aware* of such things—*Rose Macaulay*⟩ ⟨Americans were becoming *aware* that American destiny can be pursued only in a world framework—*Lerner*⟩ One who is **cognizant** of something has had it called to his attention or has become aware of it through his own powers of observation; in careful use the word commonly implies firsthand or certain knowledge ⟨he is not, as yet, fully *cognizant* of the facts⟩ ⟨through the servants, or from other means, he had made himself *cognizant* of the projected elopement—*Trollope*⟩ One is **conscious** of something that he sees, hears, feels, or apprehends when he allows it to enter his mind so that he recognizes its existence or fixes his attention on it; thus, one may or may not be *conscious* of his heartbeat or of someone passing through the room ⟨he stood there motionless and in wonder, dimly *conscious* that Hallward was speaking to him—*Wilde*⟩ ⟨to be happy or miserable without being *conscious* of it seems to me utterly inconsistent and impossible—*Locke*⟩ ⟨lifelong short-sightedness . . . of which he has never ceased to be *conscious*—*Ellis*⟩ One is **sensible** of something who through intuitive feeling or a rational perception realizes its existence ⟨she was disturbing him extremely . . . but he was much too *sensible* of her goodwill to wound her feelings by telling her so—*Mackenzie*⟩ ⟨even he was *sensible* of the decorous atmosphere—*Joyce*⟩ One who is **alive** to something is acutely susceptible to its influence or sensible of its existence ⟨the Spring finds thee not less *alive* to her sweet force than yonder upstarts—*Cowper*⟩ ⟨they were fully *alive* to the danger of thwarting Barbara—*Galsworthy*⟩ One who is **awake** to something is aroused to it or on the alert for developments ⟨the country is not *awake* to the potential evils of a strict censorship⟩

*Ana* *sure, certain, positive: informed, acquainted, apprised (see INFORM)

*Ant* unaware —*Con* *insensible, insensitive, impassible, anesthetic: *ignorant

**awe** *n* fear, *reverence

*Ana* respect, esteem, *regard: *wonder, wonderment, admiration, amazement

*Con* contempt, scorn, disdain, despite (see under DESPISE): insolence, superciliousness, arrogance (see corresponding adjectives at PROUD)

**awful** *fearful, dreadful, frightful, terrible, horrible, shocking, appalling, terrific, horrific

*Ana* impressive, *moving: solemn, *serious, grave: imposing, august, majestic (see GRAND): sublime, superb, *splendid: *ominous, portentous

**awkward, clumsy, maladroit, inept, gauche** mean not adapted by constitution or character to act, operate, or achieve the intended or desired ends with ease, fitness, or grace. *Awkward* and *clumsy* are by far the widest of these terms in their range of application. **Awkward** often involves the idea of unfitness for easy handling or dexterous management. It may suggest unhandiness or inconvenience ⟨an *awkward* tool⟩ ⟨*awkward* arrangement of controls⟩ It may suggest embarrassment or discomfiture ⟨an *awkward* situation⟩ ⟨an *awkward* silence⟩ ⟨an *awkward* meeting⟩ ⟨how earnestly did she then wish that her former opinions had been more reasonable, her expressions more moderate! It would have spared her from explanations . . . which it was exceedingly *awkward* to give—*Austen*⟩ When applied to persons, their build, their movements, or their manners, *awkward* usually implies a lack of ease or grace and often suggests inadequate muscular coordination or deficiency in poise; thus, an *awkward* gait implies lack of muscular control; an *awkward* greeting implies want of tact or address ⟨an *awkward* dancer⟩ ⟨I, sitting in silence, felt *awkward;* but I was too shy to break into any of the groups that seemed absorbed in their own affairs—*Maugham*⟩ ⟨his manners were *awkward* and unconciliatory—*Buchan*⟩ **Clumsy** stresses stiffness or heaviness with consequent want of flexibility or dexterity and is often applied to something so constructed or contrived as to be lumbering or ponderous ⟨a boy of *clumsy* build⟩ ⟨a bear is the most *clumsy* of animals⟩ ⟨a *clumsy* narrative style⟩ ⟨*clumsy* boots⟩ ⟨when a great writer . . . creates a speech of his own which is too *clumsy* to be flexible and too heavy to be intimate—*Ellis*⟩ ⟨a great play in spite of . . . the *clumsy* machinery of the plot—*T. S. Eliot*⟩ Often, and especially when applied to persons and their acts, it implies a lack of expertness or adroitness in manipulation often with a suggestion of bungling ⟨the *clumsy* attempts of governments or other social bodies to interfere . . . will only make matters worse—*Hobson*⟩ ⟨he was a *clumsy* dissector because of his injury—*H. G. Wells*⟩ **Maladroit** and *inept* imply awkwardness or clumsiness in managing whatever requires mental or social dexterity and are applicable only to persons and their acts or utterances. **Maladroit** implies a lack of tact or of skill in avoiding difficult situations in human intercourse and is often opposed to *politic* or *diplomatic* in their extended senses ⟨a *maladroit* reply to a letter⟩ ⟨a *maladroit* remark⟩ ⟨it was more correct to "break" a piece of bad news to a person by means of a (possibly *maladroit* and unfeeling) messenger—*Thackeray*⟩ **Inept** stresses inappropriateness or lack of aptness especially in a person's acts or utterances; often, in addition, it carries a suggestion of futility or absurdity; thus, a remark may be *inept* because it is so out of keeping with the topic under discussion as to seem pointless and also *maladroit* if it gives an awkward turn to the conversation ⟨the conviction that the British were everywhere so *inept* that they deserved to lose—*Abend*⟩ ⟨one of the most often encountered weaknesses in the trial of criminal cases is the *inept* and unconvincing testimony of the law enforcement officer —*Paul Wilson*⟩ ⟨the sharp-eyed and penetrating critic for whom . . . this extraordinary and extraordinarily *inept* society has in fancied security unwittingly been waiting—*Brownell*⟩ **Gauche** suggests a lack of social graces that makes for clumsiness or ineptness: it may imply also shyness, inexperience, or ill breeding ⟨this journey . . . tended to reduce my shy, taciturn, and somewhat *gauche* manner—*G. G. Scott*⟩

*Ana* *stiff, wooden, rigid: embarrassing, discomfiting, disconcerting (see EMBARRASS)

*Ant* handy, deft: graceful —*Con* adroit, *dexterous: skillful, adept, *proficient: *easy, simple, facile, effortless

**awry, askew, askance** mean deviating from a straight line or direction. They may all imply divergence from what is straight or straightforward, direct, symmetrical, or orderly, but they are seldom applicable to the same things. **Awry** carries a strong implication of disorderliness, of disarrangement, or of confusion ⟨the blinds all hang *awry*⟩ ⟨everything in the kitchen was *awry*⟩ ⟨their plans went *awry*⟩ **Askew** stresses crookedness or distortion. It implies that the thing so described is set at a wrong angle, is twisted out of its proper position, or goes off in the wrong direction ⟨every chair in this room is *askew*⟩ ⟨since the hurricane many of the trees are *askew*⟩ ⟨the seam in the front of your skirt runs *askew*⟩ **Askance** is used chiefly in the set phrases "to look, or eye, or view *askance*" which all mean to observe or examine with mistrust, suspicion, disfavor, jealousy, or disapproval ⟨aside the Devil turned for envy; yet with jealous leer malign eyed them *askance* —*Milton*⟩ ⟨both . . . were viewed *askance* by authority —*Gladstone*⟩

**axiom** *principle, fundamental, law, theorem

# B

**babble** *vb* gabble, jabber, prattle, chatter, patter, prate, gibber, gab, *chat
*Ana* *gossip, blab, tattle: converse, talk, *speak
**babel** hubbub, clamor, racket, *din, uproar, hullabaloo, pandemonium
*Ana* clamorousness *or* clamor, vociferousness (see corresponding adjectives at VOCIFEROUS): *confusion, disorder
*Con* stillness, quietness *or* quiet, silentness *or* silence, noiselessness (see corresponding adjectives at STILL)
**baby** *vb* mollycoddle, humor, pamper, *indulge, spoil
**bacillus** bacterium, virus, *germ, microbe
**back** *n* *spine, backbone, vertebrae, chine
**back** *adj* *posterior, rear, hind, hinder, after
*Ant* front
**back** *vb* 1 *support, uphold, champion, advocate
*Ana* assist, aid, *help: favor, accommodate, *oblige: abet (see INCITE)
*Con* *weaken, undermine, disable, cripple: subvert, upset (see OVERTURN): oppose, *resist, combat, fight
2 retrograde, *recede, retreat, retract
*Con* *advance, progress
**backbiting** *n* *detraction, slander, scandal, calumny
*Ana* aspersion, *animadversion, reflection, stricture: *abuse, invective, obloquy, vituperation: vilifying *or* vilification, defaming *or* defamation (see corresponding verbs at MALIGN)
*Ant* vindication (see corresponding verb at MAINTAIN)
—*Con* *compliment, flattery, adulation: praising *or* praise, eulogizing *or* eulogy, extolling (see corresponding verbs at PRAISE)
**backbone** 1 back, *spine, vertebrae, chine
2 grit, guts, sand, *fortitude, pluck
*Ana* *courage, resolution, tenacity, mettle, spirit: courageousness, intrepidity, dauntlessness, valiancy (see corresponding adjectives at BRAVE): nerve, *temerity, hardihood
*Ant* spinelessness
**backdrop** *background, setting, milieu, mise-en-scène, environment
**backer** *sponsor, surety, guarantor, patron, angel
**background, setting, environment, milieu, mise-en-scène, backdrop** are comparable when they refer to persons and their actions as found in real life or as represented in art and denote the place, time, circumstances, and conditions in which those persons live or carry on their activities. However they vary widely in their derivations and are not always interchangeable. **Background** refers primarily to a dramatic performance and to the back and usually dimly lighted part of the stage as distinguished from the better-lighted foreground where the main action usually takes place; it may be used similarly of pictorial art to denote that part of a picture which seems most remote from the spectator and against which the figures or principal objects represented seem to be projected ⟨many of the Renaissance painters preferred a natural *background*, such as mountain peaks and blue sky, others preferred an architectural *background*, such as a group of buildings or an interior⟩ In its common extended use the term is often widened in scope to include the whole aspect of the environment of something (as an historical event, a movement, a career, or a phase of a person's or a people's development) that is capable of being seen in perspective and that may be viewed as antecedent, causal, or intimately related to the fundamental quality of what it environs ⟨to know a person well one needs to know his *background*⟩ ⟨students of English literature must have as *background* a knowledge of English history⟩ ⟨landscape is treated as an accessory to human life and a *background* to human events—*Binyon*⟩ **Setting** also derives its basic implications from the arts, originally from the jewelers' art, where the term is used of the framework of precious metal in which a gem is mounted, and later from the dramaturgists' art, where it is used of the framework (as scenic paintings and furniture) which indicates to the spectator the surroundings in which the action of a play takes place. Hence *setting* is preferred to *background* as a designation of the element in a novel, a play, or other literary representation of human life which is distinguished from the plot and the characters and which is the author's imaginative reconstruction of the time, place, and conditions in which his characters live and act. When used in reference to real life, *setting* commonly connotes the standpoint of one who looks at human beings and their activities as though they were dramatic or literary representations ⟨what a social *setting* it was, that little world into which Mark Twain was born! It was drab, it was tragic—*Brooks*⟩ **Environment** basically denotes the surroundings and especially the natural surroundings (as of a town, a body of water, or an individual) ⟨relaxed . . . in a cozy *environment* of apple-green furniture and art linoleum—*Punch*⟩ When relating to a person or a living being *environment* commonly suggests not only natural surroundings but any or all external factors (as social or economic conditions, nutrient supply, or crowding) that are important in the physical, mental, and moral development of the species or the individual or as formative influences ⟨the *environment* which produced Jonathan Edwards and Cotton Mather—*Brownell*⟩ When the formative influences in a person's development are the result of heredity or nature, *background* is the preferred term; when they are the product of his surroundings or his nurture, *environment* is the more likely choice; thus, one may say that, although it is impossible to change a child's *background*, he may turn out well if brought up in a different *environment*. **Milieu** carries none of the scientific implications of *environment*, yet it also means surroundings and is used chiefly in reference to the physical and social surroundings of a person or group of persons. It is preferred to *environment* when there is the intent to evoke a clear picture or to suggest the specific character or atmosphere of such surroundings; it may be used in reference to imagined as well as to actual

persons and therefore is often interchangeable with *setting* ⟨his chief object . . . is not to make an isolated study of this or that *milieu*, or to describe a particular social sphere —*Athenaeum*⟩ **Mise-en-scène** is the equivalent of *setting*, especially as referred to a theatrical performance. However its stronger suggestion of the use of properties to achieve a given atmosphere or theatrical effect is the reason for its preference by some writers when the reference is not specifically to a dramatic performance or even to invented scenes ⟨in *The Scarlet Letter* how truly in the spirit of art is the *mise-en-scène* presented . . . . The material investiture of the story is presented . . . by the reserved, fastidious hand of an artist, not by the gaudy fingers of a showman or the mechanical industry of a department-store window dresser—*Cather*⟩ **Backdrop** denotes a drop curtain at the rear of the stage which provides the decorative or realistic background for the action of a play and brings players and their movements into relief; it is increasingly common in an extended sense as a substitute for *background* or *setting* or *milieu* when there is the intent to stress pictorial effect rather than social influence or spiritual significance ⟨against the multitowered *backdrop* of New York he has pictured . . . the passions and hopes, the dreams and desolations, the greeds and corruptions, of the seven million souls that are its lifeblood —*Atlantic*⟩

**backslide** *vb* relapse, *lapse
*Ana* revert, *return: deteriorate, degenerate, decline (see corresponding nouns at DETERIORATION): *recede, retreat, retrograde

**backslider** *renegade, apostate, recreant, turncoat

**backsliding** *n* relapse, lapse (see under LAPSE *vb*)
*Ana* retrogressiveness *or* retrogression, retrogradation (see corresponding adjectives at BACKWARD): abandoning, deserting, forsaking (see ABANDON)

**backward, retrograde, retrogressive, regressive** all involve the idea of not moving or going ahead, or forward, or in advance. Only when applied to motion or a movement does **backward** imply the reverse of forward motion ⟨a *backward* thrust of a hand⟩ ⟨the *backward* swimming of a crayfish⟩ Its commonest implication is failure to move ahead; in this sense it is chiefly applied to human beings who do not or cannot progress or develop with others of their age, kind, or class or to persons or things that hold back or are held back from doing what is normal or to be expected; thus, a child who is unable to keep up with others of his age in school because of some degree of mental deficiency is described as *backward;* a person who holds back from expressing his appreciation, or in urging his candidacy for a position, because of shyness or self-distrust is also describable as *backward;* when cold weather and frosts delay the development of vegetation beyond the normal or usual time, the season may be called *backward* ⟨England, throughout the middle ages, was one of the *backward* countries of Europe: it was on the outskirts of the great continental civilization—*Mumford*⟩ **Retrograde** is not only applicable to backward motion and backward movement but also to any moving or seemingly moving thing that proceeds in a direction which is contrary to the direction usually followed by things of its kind ⟨*retrograde* motion of a wheel⟩ ⟨a *retrograde* planet seemingly moving from east to west⟩ It is also applicable to a process (as of natural development) in which the events occur in an order contrary to the usual or progressive; thus, an animal that passes from a more complex to a simpler and often degenerate state during development is said to manifest *retrograde* development. *Retrograde* when applied to races, cultures, institutions, or movements differs from *backward* in implying decline or degeneration; thus, a *backward* society is one that does not progress, while a *retrograde* society is one that is relapsing into barbarism or sinking into an inferior state. **Retrogressive** implies opposition to *progressive*. Like *retrograde*, and unlike *backward*, it implies movement in the direction that is the reverse of forward; unlike *retrograde*, however, it is seldom applied to physical movement; thus, one speaks of a *retrograde* (but not a *retrogressive*) movement or rotation, but one might speak of *retrogressive* (or *retrograde*) cruelties or behavior when stressing decline from some higher or more progressive level. *Retrogressive* is sometimes preferred as a milder term when the reverse of improvement or betterment rather than positive decline from an improved or better state is implied ⟨a *retrogressive* policy⟩ ⟨objections were made to the proposed legislation on the ground of its probable *retrogressive* effect⟩ **Regressive** carries a stronger implication of going backward by steps or degrees and often, also, a weaker implication of failure to progress or move ahead than any of the others. Consequently it is often the preferred term when a colorless or uncolored statement of fact is intended; thus, when one infers a cause from an effect or a principle from a number of facts he follows a *regressive* process of reasoning; the process of growing old may be described as a *retrograde* development when the emphasis is on its backward direction, as a *retrogressive* development when the stress is on the absence of progress, and a *regressive* development when the intent is to indicate that it is marked by an inversion of order in its stages; a *regressive* loss of memory implies that the most recent memories disappear first and the earliest linger longest.
*Ana* laggard, dilatory, *slow: *stupid, slow, dull, dense: *lethargic, sluggish: *abnormal, atypical
*Ant* advanced —*Con* civilized, cultured (see corresponding nouns at CIVILIZATION): cultivated, cultured, refined (see corresponding nouns at CULTURE): educated, instructed (see TEACH)

**bactericidal** *adj* germicidal, antiseptic, disinfectant (see under ANTISEPTIC *n*)

**bactericide** germicide, *antiseptic, disinfectant

**bacterium** *germ, microbe, bacillus, virus

**bad** 1 Bad, evil, ill, wicked, naughty are comparable when they mean not meeting with the approval of the ethical consciousness. **Bad** is a very general term and applies to anyone or anything reprehensible, for whatever reason and to whatever degree ⟨almost as *bad*, good mother, as kill a king, and marry with his brother—*Shak.*⟩ ⟨Johnnie's been a *bad* boy today: he's emptied the cookie jar⟩ ⟨*bad* dog! you've torn up my scarf⟩ **Evil** is a stronger term than *bad* and usually suggests the sinister or baleful as well as the reprehensible ⟨*evil* deeds⟩ ⟨the *evil* eye⟩ ⟨he knew nothing bad about him, but he felt something *evil*—*Cather*⟩ ⟨an *evil* and treacherous folk, and they lied and murdered for gold—*Morris*⟩ ⟨the *evil* counselors who . . . abused his youth—*J. R. Green*⟩ **Ill** is close to *evil* in basic meaning and may suggest an active malevolence or vicious intent ⟨an *ill* deed⟩ ⟨it was *ill* counsel had misled the wife—*Tennyson*⟩ Often *ill* may be used in a weaker sense to suggest the imputing or implying of evil or sometimes of mere objectionableness or inferiority to someone or something ⟨held in *ill* repute by his fellows⟩ ⟨attached an *ill* significance to the statement⟩ ⟨had an *ill* opinion of their abilities⟩ **Wicked** implies the actual often conscious or deliberate contravention or violation of moral law ⟨God is angry with the *wicked* every day—*Ps 7:11*⟩ ⟨*wicked* designs⟩ It is sometimes used with weakened, even playful, force ⟨you are the *wickedest* witty person I know— *Lytton*⟩ **Naughty** was once serious ⟨a most vile flagitious man, a sorry and *naughty* governor as could be—*Barrow*⟩

---

A colon (:) separates groups of words discriminated. An asterisk (*) indicates place of treatment of each group.

but is now trivial in its application. Mostly it implies mischievousness on the part of a child too young to have a lively sense of right and wrong ⟨Charles never was a *naughty* boy. He never robbed birds' nests, or smoked behind the barn, or played marbles on Sunday—*Deland*⟩ Sometimes it expresses charitable censure of a person of responsible age who has done wrong ⟨it was only one *naughty* woman out of the world. The clergyman of the parish didn't refuse to give her decent burial—*Meredith*⟩ Often it is applied to what is impolite, impudent, or amusingly risqué ⟨the still popular, and still *naughty,* and perpetually profane *Decameron*—*Highet*⟩
*Ana* iniquitous, *vicious, villainous: *base, low, vile: *immoral, unmoral, amoral
*Ant* good —*Con* righteous, virtuous, *moral, ethical, noble
**2 Bad, poor, wrong** are comparable when they mean not measuring up to a standard of what is satisfactory. **Bad** implies a failure to meet one's approval; it need not imply positive condemnation, but it always suggests that the thing so described falls below the mark or is not up to what one would call good ⟨he is a *bad* correspondent⟩ ⟨her handwriting is very *bad*⟩ ⟨it's a *bad* day for a long walk⟩ It often also implies positive harmfulness ⟨a *bad* light for the eyes⟩ ⟨*bad* food for the young⟩ ⟨a *bad* book for a depressed person⟩ ⟨a *bad* environment⟩ ⟨it is *bad* for her to live alone⟩ Sometimes it suggests corruption or pollution ⟨this meat is *bad*⟩ ⟨*bad* air⟩ ⟨*bad* water⟩ Often also it may suggest unpleasantness in any degree, in this sense ranging from the merely displeasing to the strongly offensive or painful or distressing ⟨it leaves a *bad* taste in the mouth⟩ ⟨have *bad* news⟩ ⟨he always comforted himself when things were *bad* by thinking how much worse they might have been⟩ **Poor** also implies a failure to reach a satisfactory point or level, but it usually imputes to the thing so described a deficiency in amount or in returns or a lack of a quality or qualities essential to excellence; thus, a *poor* crop is one that is relatively scanty; *poor* land is wanting in fertility, while *bad* land lacks the potentiality for agricultural development; a *poor* book may be devoid of interest or artistic quality, but a *bad* book is commonly offensive to one's sense of propriety; a *poor* carpenter is one lacking in skill ⟨business was *poor* this year⟩ ⟨a *poor* dancer⟩ ⟨*poor* bread⟩ ⟨a *poor* return for one's effort⟩ **Wrong** (see also FALSE) implies a failure to conform to a strict standard; it suggests deviation from a standard of what is satisfactory or, more specifically, fit, appropriate, proper, or orderly ⟨I know that something is *wrong* with this suit⟩ ⟨do not make a *wrong* choice in selecting your profession⟩ ⟨hang a picture in the *wrong* light⟩ ⟨there is nothing *wrong* in this arrangement of the furniture⟩
*Ant* good —*Con* excellent, perfect, meritorious (see corresponding nouns at EXCELLENCE): right (see GOOD)
**badge** *sign, token, mark, note, symptom
**badger** *vb* *bait, hound, chivy, hector, ride, heckle
*Ana* *annoy, vex, bother, irk: harass, harry, *worry, pester, plague, tease
**badinage, persiflage, raillery** denote a kind of banter. **Badinage** is applied to banter that is playful and delicate, **persiflage** to banter that is derisive but not cutting, and **raillery** to banter that is keen and often sarcastic in its ridicule ⟨love . . . permits itself even gentle mocking and friendly *badinage*—*Ward*⟩ ⟨I have the fresh and charming letter she wrote to her husband on the occasion . . . with a trace of gay *persiflage* of all the old people at Sudbury and their meetinghouse—*Ellis*⟩ ⟨a company in which you have been galled by the *raillery* of some wag by profession—*Beresford*⟩
*Ana* bantering *or* banter, chaffing, kidding, joshing, jolly-

ing (see corresponding verbs at BANTER): *fun, game, jest, sport
**badlands** *waste, desert, wilderness
**baffle** balk, circumvent, outwit, foil, thwart, *frustrate
*Ana* *puzzle, mystify, confound, dumbfound: discomfit, rattle, faze, *embarrass, disconcert: *confuse, addle, muddle: *hamper, fetter, hog-tie: *hinder, impede, obstruct, block
**bag** *n* **Bag, sack, pouch** denote a container made of a flexible material (as paper, cloth, or leather) and open or opening at the top. **Bag** is the widest in its range of application and is referable to anything that comes under this general description and is used to hold something ⟨money *bag*⟩ ⟨traveling *bag*⟩ ⟨paper *bag*⟩ ⟨saddle*bag*⟩ ⟨mail-*bag*⟩ **Sack** is usually more restricted in its application than *bag;* within these limits, however, the terms are interchangeable. *Sack* commonly suggests oblong shape, a coarse material and, often, crude workmanship ⟨gunny-*sack*⟩ ⟨paper *sack*⟩ ⟨flour *sack*⟩ It is probably more often used than *bag* when it refers to containers and their contents ⟨deliver 1000 *sacks* of grain⟩ ⟨*sacks* of potatoes⟩ ⟨sell coal by the *sack*⟩ **Pouch** is applied chiefly to a small bag carried on the person or in the hand and used as a substitute for a pocket; it often specifically designates a bag that is opened or closed by means of a gathering string, zipper, or flap ⟨tobacco *pouch*⟩ ⟨*pouch* for bullets⟩ ⟨*pouch*-shaped handbag⟩ ⟨mail *pouch*⟩
**bag** *vb* capture, trap, snare, entrap, ensnare, *catch
**bail** *n* bond, surety, security, *guarantee, guaranty
**bail** *vb* *dip, ladle, scoop, spoon, dish
**bailiwick** province, domain, territory, *field, sphere
**bait** *vb* **Bait, badger, heckle, hector, chivy, hound, ride** mean to persist in tormenting or harassing another. **Bait** derives its implications from its basic reference to the action of dogs set on to bite and worry an animal (as a chained bear, boar, or bull). Both in this and in extended use it suggests wanton cruelty or malicious delight in persecution ⟨the diversion of *baiting* an author has the sanction of all ages—*Johnson*⟩ **Badger** is more specific than *bait.* Basically it suggests the baiting of a badger that has been trapped in a hole or barrel and can neither escape nor adequately defend itself from attack; in reference to persons it implies pestering or persecuting that drives the victim into a hopelessly confused or frenzied state of mind ⟨*badger* a witness being cross-examined⟩ ⟨the mill foreman so taunted the workers, so *badgered* them and told them that they dared not quit—*Sinclair Lewis*⟩ **Heckle** implies persistent questioning of a speaker (as a candidate for election, a legislator discussing a bill before the house, or a person advocating or condemning a movement or cause) and an attempt to bring out his weaknesses or to destroy the effect of his argument. It suggests an intent to harass and confuse a speaker by frequent interruptions and by inconvenient or embarrassing questions ⟨the advocates of any unpopular cause must learn to endure *heckling*⟩ ⟨infuriates some of his fellow Justices by *heckling* lawyers who appear before the Court—*Sat. Review*⟩ **Hector** always carries a suggestion of bullying and implies a spirit-breaking scolding or maddeningly domineering treatment ⟨we are . . . not to be *hectored,* and bullied, and beat into compliance—*Fielding*⟩ ⟨they had hard times when they were little . . . and were *hectored* and worried when they ought to have been taking some comfort—*Stowe*⟩ **Chivy** *and* **hound** both stress relentless chasing and pursuing. **Chivy,** however, often also suggests teasing or annoying past the endurance of the victim ⟨having seen two successive wives of the delicate poet *chivied* and worried into their graves—*Conrad*⟩ **Hound** implies persistent and long-continued persecution till the tormentor's

*Ana* analogous words  *Ant* antonyms  *Con* contrasted words  See also explanatory notes facing page 1

end is achieved or the victim acknowledges himself defeated ⟨he was *hounded* by reporters until he made his stand known⟩ ⟨grandfather had been *hounded* out of his congregation because he couldn't hold her to their standards of behavior for a minister's wife—*Mary Austin*⟩ **Ride** implies persistent goading or spurring (as by unfair criticism, ridicule, or onerous impositions) ⟨a hard taskmaster *rides* those who serve him⟩ ⟨he was *ridden* so hard by the coach that he was no longer fit to remain on the team⟩
*Ana* *worry, annoy, harass, harry: torment, rack, torture, try, *afflict

**bait** *n* *lure, snare, trap, decoy
*Ana* allurement, attraction (see corresponding verbs at ATTRACT): enticement, temptation (see corresponding verbs at LURE)

**bake** parch, *dry, desiccate, dehydrate

**balance** *n* 1 Balance, equilibrium, equipoise, poise, tension are comparable when denoting the stability or efficiency resulting from the equalization or exact adjustment of opposing forces. **Balance** suggests a steadiness that results when all parts are properly adjusted to each other, when no one part or constituting force outweighs or is out of proportion to another ⟨kept her *balance* on the icy street⟩ ⟨keeping his emotional *balance* under stress⟩ ⟨the *balance* between civilian and military needs—*Collier's Yr. Bk.*⟩ ⟨establish an acceptable *balance* between satisfactions and frustrations—*Kardiner*⟩ ⟨I doubt that Thoreau would be thrown off *balance* by the fantastic sights and sounds of the 20th century—*E. B. White*⟩ **Equilibrium** may be interchangeable with *balance* ⟨retain physical and emotional *equilibrium* under stress⟩ but is more often restricted to a mechanically produced or producible property deriving from a thing's construction, support, or relation to external forces and then often suggests a tendency to return to an original position after disturbance ⟨a ship's *equilibrium*⟩ ⟨an *equilibrium* of opposing human impulses —*Sinclair Lewis*⟩ ⟨establishing an *equilibrium* between the Western forces and a possible aggressor—*Current History*⟩ ⟨a fundamental lack of *equilibrium* between different aspects of the constitutional distribution of power—*R. M. Dawson*⟩ **Equipoise** suggests perfection of balance or stability of equilibrium ⟨to maintain . . . *equipoise* among contending interests—*Butterfield*⟩ ⟨the structure remains upright, a marvel of *equipoise*—*Norman Douglas*⟩ ⟨the *equipoise* of intellectual and pietistic interests in him—*H. O. Taylor*⟩ **Poise** denotes an equality of opposing or different things or forces and often implies a state or an appearance of perfect balance or serenity especially of mind ⟨the condition of a *poise* between widely divergent impulses and emotions that produces a strange serenity—*Leavis*⟩ ⟨the main characteristic of their blond gray-eyed colleague is quiet *poise* that stands her in good stead in the exciting, high-pressure work—*Newsweek*⟩ **Tension** in this relation implies strain, either a pull from both ends or an outward pressure in every direction, of such equality that there results a tautness without undue strain at any point; applied to a mental condition it implies an inner balanced vital opposition of moral or intellectual forces, powers, or qualities ⟨indolent as he was on all occasions which required *tension* of the mind, he was active and persevering in bodily exercise—*Macaulay*⟩ ⟨the whole *tension* of Gide's work is characterized in those sentences: the incessant dialectic of a man who knows no peace but the precarious equilibrium of opposites—*Times Lit. Sup.*⟩ ⟨in letting the whole physical system lose tone, for lack of the *tension* which gaiety imparts—*Brownell*⟩
2 *symmetry, proportion, harmony

3 *remainder, rest, residue, residuum, leavings, remnant, remains

**balance** *vb* 1 counterpoise, counterbalance, *compensate, countervail, offset
*Ana* attune, *harmonize, tune: correspond, accord, square, *agree
2 poise, ballast, trim, *stabilize, steady
*Ana* settle, *set: waver, sway, oscillate, fluctuate (see SWING): rock, *shake
*Con* *overturn, upset, capsize

**bald** *bare, barren, naked, nude
*Ana* austere, *severe: unembellished, unadorned, unornamented (see affirmative verbs at ADORN): *colorless, uncolored
*Con* *ornate, florid

**balderdash** *nonsense, twaddle, drivel, bunk, poppycock, gobbledygook, trash, rot, bull

**bale** *n* *bundle, package, pack, parcel, bunch, packet

**baleful** maleficent, malefic, malign, *sinister
*Ana* threatening, menacing (see THREATEN): *ominous, portentous, fateful: hellish, *infernal: diabolical, *fiendish, devilish
*Ant* beneficent —*Con* *beneficial, advantageous: salutary, wholesome, *healthful: benign, *favorable, propitious, auspicious

**balk** *vb* 1 *frustrate, thwart, foil, baffle, circumvent, outwit
*Ana* defeat, beat, lick, *conquer, overcome: block, obstruct, impede, *hinder: *prevent, forestall
*Ant* forward —*Con* further, promote, *advance: abet (see INCITE): assist, aid, *help: *support, uphold, back
2 jib, shy, boggle, stickle, scruple, *demur, strain, stick
*Ana* *hesitate, falter, waver: refuse, *decline: shrink, flinch, quail, *recoil
*Con* *yield, submit, capitulate, succumb, relent

**balky** *contrary, restive, perverse, froward, wayward
*Ana* hesitant, reluctant, averse, loath, *disinclined, indisposed: *obstinate, stubborn, mulish: refractory, recalcitrant, *unruly
*Con* amenable, docile, tractable, *obedient, biddable: submissive, subdued, *tame

**ballast** *vb* *stabilize, steady, balance, trim, poise

**ballot** *n* vote, *suffrage, franchise

**ballyhoo** *n* *publicity, promotion, propaganda
*Ana* advertisement, broadcasting (see under DECLARE)

**balmy** 1 aromatic, fragrant, *odorous, redolent
*Ana* refreshing, restoring, rejuvenating (see RENEW): pleasing, grateful, welcome, *pleasant
*Ant* rank, noisome —*Con* *malodorous, fetid, stinking, fusty, musty, putrid
2 *soft, gentle, smooth, bland, mild, lenient
*Ana* agreeable, *pleasant, gratifying, grateful: gladdening, delighting, rejoicing, regaling (see PLEASE): assuaging, allaying, lightening, relieving (see RELIEVE): salubrious, salutary (see HEALTHFUL)
*Con* *intense, vehement, fierce, exquisite, violent: vexing, bothering *or* bothersome, irking *or* irksome, annoying (see corresponding verbs at ANNOY)

**bamboozle** trick, hoodwink, *dupe, gull, hoax, befool
*Ana* delude, *deceive, beguile, mislead: outwit, circumvent (see FRUSTRATE): defraud, cozen, overreach, *cheat, swindle

**ban** *vb* prohibit, *forbid, interdict, inhibit, enjoin
*Ana* bar, block, *hinder: *prevent, preclude: *exclude, debar, rule out
*Con* allow, permit, suffer, *let: tolerate, abide, suffer (see BEAR)

**banal** flat, jejune, inane, vapid, wishy-washy, *insipid
*Ana* *trite, hackneyed: *simple, fatuous, silly, asinine: commonplace, platitudinous, bromidic (see corresponding

A colon (:) separates groups of words discriminated. An asterisk (*) indicates place of treatment of each group.

nouns at COMMONPLACE)
*Ant* original: recherché —*Con* fresh, *new, novel: pithy, terse, succinct (see CONCISE): stimulating *or* stimulative, provoking *or* provocative, exciting, piquing (see corresponding verbs at PROVOKE)

**band** *n* 1 *bond, tie
*Ana* connection, link, joining (see corresponding verbs at JOIN): *joint, articulation, suture
2 *strip, stripe, ribbon, fillet
3 troop, troupe, *company, party
*Ana* coterie, clique, *set, circle: horde, mob, *crowd: society, club, *association, order

**bandy** *vb* *exchange, interchange

**bane** *poison, venom, virus, toxin

**baneful** *pernicious, noxious, deleterious, detrimental
*Ana* harmful, injurious, mischievous, hurtful (see corresponding nouns at INJURY): malign, *sinister, baleful: *poisonous, venomous, toxic
*Ant* beneficial —*Con* advantageous, profitable (see BENEFICIAL): salutary, wholesome, *healthful

**banish,** exile, expatriate, ostracize, deport, transport, extradite are comparable when denoting to remove by authority or force from a country, state, or sovereignty. To **banish** is to compel one, usually by public edict or sentence, to leave a country or section, although not necessarily one's own, either permanently or for a fixed time and with or without restriction to a given place ⟨*banish* an enemy of the King⟩ ⟨the Newtonian scheme of the universe does not *banish* God from the universe—*Times Lit. Sup.*⟩ To **exile** is to banish or cause to depart under constraint from one's own country; it may connote either expulsion by formal sentence or decree or the compulsion of circumstances and an enforced absence or sometimes a prolonged voluntary absence; thus, Russians and foreigners alike may be *banished* from Russia, but only Russians can be *exiled* to Siberia; Dante was *banished* from his native Florence because of political troubles, but he *exiled* himself for the rest of his life as a protest against conditions there. **Expatriate** differs from *exile* sometimes in its implication of loss of citizenship in one's own country ⟨*expatriate* Jews from Germany⟩ but oftener in its implication of voluntary exile or naturalization in another country ⟨Henry James *expatriated* himself from the United States⟩ *Exile* often suggests a possibility of return with full rights to one's own country; *expatriate*, however, may imply the exclusion of that possibility. In historical context **ostracize** denotes a temporary banishment by popular vote from one of the cities of ancient Greece; the term is used more commonly in an extended sense which implies not expatriation, but a forced exclusion by common consent, from recognition or acceptance by society ⟨the dangers inherent in *ostracizing* from public service men of eminence—*Kimmis Hendrick*⟩ ⟨exposed as a cheat and *ostracized* by his fellow officers⟩ To **deport** is to send a person out of a country of which he is not a citizen either because his presence is considered inimical to the public welfare or because he has not lawfully entered that country. It often implies return to the country of which the deported person is a citizen or subject or from which he has emigrated, especially if he is without funds to go where he chooses. To **transport** is to banish to a penal colony a person convicted of a crime ⟨convicts were *transported* to Australia⟩ To **extradite** is to deliver over an alleged criminal at the request of the sovereignty or state having jurisdiction to try the charge ⟨since no treaties existed between the Allied Control Commission and neutral states, it follows that no duty to *extradite* existed among the latter—*Neumann*⟩ ⟨the escaped prisoner was *extradited* by the State of Illinois at the request of the State

of Georgia⟩
*Ana* *eject, expel, oust: *exclude, debar, eliminate, shut out
*Con* admit, *receive, accept: *harbor, shelter, entertain: protect, shield (see DEFEND)

**bank** *n* 1 *shoal, bar, reef
2 *shore, strand, coast, beach, foreshore, littoral
3 mass, heap, pile, stack, shock, cock (see under HEAP *vb*)
*Ana* *aggregate, aggregation, conglomerate, conglomeration: assemblage, assembly, collection, gathering (see under GATHER)

**bank** *vb* mass, *heap, pile, stack, shock, cock
*Ana* collect, assemble, *gather
*Con* *scatter, disperse

**bank** *vb* *rely, count, reckon, trust, depend

**bankrupt** *vb* impoverish, exhaust, *deplete, drain
*Ana* denude, *strip, bare: sap, cripple, disable, undermine (see WEAKEN)

**banner** *n* *flag, standard, ensign, color, streamer, pennant, pendant, pennon, jack

**banquet** *dinner, feast

**banter** *vb* Banter, chaff, kid, rag, rib, josh, jolly are comparable when denoting to make fun of good-naturedly (as by reminding one of an actual fault, foible, failure, or shortcoming, by exaggerated praise obviously remote from the truth, or by playful imputation of undeserved success). The same distinctions in implications and connotations are found in their corresponding nouns. **Banter** is the generic term and may usually be substituted for any of the others, though not without loss of specificness ⟨"Why didn't you get tipsy, Sir? Don't you ever intoxicate yourself but at lawful marriages? . . ." Ripton endured his *bantering* that he might hang about Richard—*Meredith*⟩ To **chaff** is to nettle with rough banter ⟨they *chaffed* me for leaving so early—*Price*⟩ **Kid** is frequently as general in meaning as *banter* ⟨he is very fond of placing his hand on his heart and declaiming about his warm virtues. He gets a lot of *kidding* for it—*Gunther*⟩ More often than perhaps any other word in this group, however, it specifically implies an attempt at good-natured imposition on one's gullibility; thus, "No *kidding?*" is a common way of asking "Are you serious?" of one who has made a statement that sounds incredible ⟨she says he's going to do a portrait of her. I think he's *kidding* her—*Harper's*⟩ Used with a reflexive pronoun, *kid* implies a shutting one's eyes to the truth ⟨if you think you can avoid hard work and long hours and yet write something memorable, you are just *kidding* yourself⟩ To **rag** is to banter repeatedly or persistently and often annoyingly to the victim ⟨there were, even, no unpleasantnesses (aside from a bit of *ragging* about his galoshes . . .)—*Bergen Evans*⟩ **Rib** implies bantering under conditions which make it impossible or inadvisable for the butt to retort or defend himself and also may imply specifically the enactment of a role on the part of the ribber ⟨high government officials are *ribbed* in the skits presented yearly before the Gridiron Club in Washington⟩ ⟨*ribs* her fellow Russians as the temperamental ballerina who introduces her equals as her "supporting cast"—*Time*⟩ *Josh* and especially *jolly* imply transparent good humor in the funmaker. **Josh** usually suggests homeliness and unsophistication ⟨for children he has jokes and candy. He cheers the men . . . and *joshes* the women—*Time*⟩ ⟨running the chatty, homespun, *joshing* sort of thing that actually goes on in a town—*S.R.L.*⟩ **Jolly** often implies an ulterior aim such as putting the person bantered into good humor so that he will grant a favor ⟨he was a good salesman who *jollied* his customers, but not too obviously⟩ ⟨*jollied* and joked with sailors in the street—*Wecter*⟩

---

*Ana* twit, rally, deride, *ridicule

**baptize, christen** mean to make one a Christian or to admit one to a Christian communion by a ceremony in which water is poured or sprinkled on the head or in which the body is immersed in water. **Baptize** is at once the precise and the general term for this ceremony because it implies both the rite and its ends, and it may be used in reference to both infants and adults. **Christen** is the popular word, but for several centuries it has so emphasized the giving of a name, which is in some churches a part of the ceremony of baptism, that it now is used at times without any reference to the religious ceremony and even with reference to inanimate objects which are formally named, often with a ceremony analogous to that of baptism; thus, "the baby has not yet been *christened*" may mean either "not yet baptized" or "not yet named," though both are commonly implied; a ship is *christened* by performing the ceremony of breaking a bottle of liquid (as champagne) against its sides while pronouncing its name.

**bar** *n* **1 Bar, barrier, barricade** mean something which hinders or obstructs. Both *bar* and *barrier* apply to something that prevents free communication or passage; more specifically, **bar** frequently suggests a restriction of ingress or egress, while **barrier** suggests an obstacle to advance, progress, or attack; *bar* also may suggest a simple structure and *barrier* a more extensive or elaborate one ⟨the *bars* of a prison⟩ ⟨a harbor *bar*⟩ ⟨a mountain *barrier*⟩ ⟨erect dikes as a *barrier* against the sea⟩ ⟨a *barrier* reef⟩ ⟨religious myths may come to be a *bar* to progress in science —*Inge*⟩ ⟨a perpetual and impassable *barrier* . . . between the white race and the one which they had reduced to slavery—*Taney*⟩ **Barricade** is chiefly used in the sense of an obstruction thrown across a street or way to check a hostile advance ⟨the fighting at the *barricades* in Paris during the Commune⟩
**2** *obstacle, obstruction, impediment, snag
*Ana* hindrance, block, dam (see corresponding verbs at HINDER): *difficulty, hardship, vicissitude
*Ant* advantage —*Con* odds, edge (see ADVANTAGE): help, aid, assistance (see under HELP *vb*)
**3** *shoal, bank, reef
**bar** *vb* obstruct, block, dam, impede (see HINDER)
*Ana* shut out, debar, *exclude: *prevent, preclude, obviate: *forbid, prohibit, interdict: *close, shut
*Ant* admit: open —*Con* accept, *receive, take
**barbarian** *adj* **Barbarian, barbaric, barbarous, savage** are comparable when applying to people or characteristics of people that are not fully civilized. **Barbarian** frequently applies to a state about midway between full civilization and tribal savagery ⟨some *barbarian* peoples have brought their mores into true adjustment to their life conditions and have gone on for centuries without change—*Sumner*⟩ **Barbaric** and **barbarous** may also be used to express this notion ⟨they had passed the *barbaric* stage when they invaded Chaldea. They knew the use of metals; they were skillful architects and . . . good engineers—*Clodd*⟩ ⟨Caesar's short sketch of the Germans gives the impression of *barbarous* peoples . . . they had not yet reached the agricultural stage, but were devoted to war and hunting—*H. O. Taylor*⟩ **Savage** implies an even less advanced and more primitive state ⟨for *savage* or semicivilized men . . . authority is needed to restrain them from injuring themselves—*Eliot*⟩ **Barbarous** and *savage* are somewhat more commonly used than *barbaric* and *barbarian* to indicate uncivilized cruelty, but all may be so used ⟨he required as a condition of peace that they should sacrifice their children to Baal no longer. But the *barbarous* custom was too inveterate—*Frazer*⟩ ⟨the King's greed passed into *savage* menace. He would hang all, he swore—man,

woman, the very child at the breast—*J. R. Green*⟩ ⟨they had further traits and customs which are *barbaric* rather than specifically Teutonic: cruelty and faithlessness toward enemies, feuds, wergeld—*H. O. Taylor*⟩ ⟨for him those chambers held *barbarian* hordes, hyena foeman, and hot-blooded lords—*Keats*⟩
*Barbaric* and *barbarous* are more common in relation to taste and refinement. **Barbaric** suggests a wild, profuse lack of restraint ⟨this audacious and *barbaric* profusion of words—chosen always for their color and their vividly expressive quality—*Symons*⟩ ⟨the march became rather splendid and *barbaric*. First rode Feisal in white, then Sharraf at his right in red headcloth and henna-dyed tunic and cloak, myself on his left in white and scarlet, behind us three banners of faded crimson silk with gilt spikes—*T. E. Lawrence*⟩ **Barbarous** implies an utter lack of cultivated taste and refinement ⟨a race of unconscious spiritual helots. We shall become utterly *barbarous* and desolate—*Lewisohn*⟩ ⟨but this deeply *barbarous* book may, in its very vulgarity of expression, be in advance of its time—*Dorothy Thompson*⟩
*Ant* civilized
**barbarian** *n* *obscurantist, philistine
**barbaric** *barbarian, savage, barbarous
*Ana* *showy, ostentatious: florid, *ornate, flamboyant: *gaudy, garish, flashy, meretricious
*Ant* restrained: refined: subdued
**barbarism, barbarity** are frequently confused. **Barbarism** is used chiefly of a state of society or of a culture that may be described as *barbarian*, or as neither savage and crude nor civilized and highly refined ⟨the savage mystic is also the savage man of science, the priest and the doctor are one. It is so also for the most part in *barbarism*—*Ellis*⟩ ⟨the human race . . . is as yet only a little bit civilized and . . . in time of serious trouble . . . has a very strong tendency to stampede back into *barbarism*—*Lippmann*⟩ **Barbarity** is used chiefly in reference to a temper or to practices that may be described as barbarous, or uncivilized, brutal, and inhumane ⟨*barbarity* seldom equaled by the fiercest of savages⟩ ⟨his dream of eating pâtés de foie gras to the sound of trumpets ignored the calculated *barbarity* which produced the food he loved—*Repplier*⟩ Sometimes, however, *barbarity* denotes a taste that is barbaric ⟨the supposed influence of Seneca on the *barbarity* of Elizabethan tragedy—*T. S. Eliot*⟩
*Ant* civilization —*Con* *culture, cultivation, refinement
**barbarity** *barbarism
*Ana* barbarousness, savagery, ferociousness *or* ferocity, cruelty, inhumanity (see corresponding adjectives at FIERCE)
*Ant* humaneness —*Con* gentleness, mildness, smoothness, lenity *or* leniency (see corresponding adjectives at SOFT)
**barbarous 1** savage, barbaric, *barbarian
*Ana* *rough, harsh: untutored, untaught, uneducated, illiterate, *ignorant: *rude, rough, crude
*Ant* civilized: humane
**2** savage, inhuman, ferocious, *fierce, cruel, fell, truculent
*Ana* pitiless, ruthless, uncompassionate (see corresponding nouns at SYMPATHY): atrocious, monstrous, *outrageous
*Ant* clement —*Con* merciful, *forbearing, tolerant, lenient: *tender, compassionate, sympathetic: humane, humanitarian, benevolent (see CHARITABLE)
**bard** *n* *poet, minstrel, troubadour, rhymer, rhymester, versifier, poetaster
**bare** *adj* **1 Bare, naked, nude, bald, barren** are comparable when they mean destitute or divested of the naturally or conventionally appropriate covering or clothing. **Bare**

---

A colon (:) separates groups of words discriminated. An asterisk (*) indicates place of treatment of each group.

strongly suggests the removal or, often, the rejection of something additional, superfluous, dispensable, or acquired; thus, a *bare* head is one without a hat; *bare* legs suggest lack of socks or stockings; *bare* trees have lost all their leaves; one takes another's *bare* word for a thing when one demands no confirmation or documentary proof; a *bare* room may be empty of furniture or may have only such furniture as is indispensable ⟨the *bare* statement that "art is useless" is so vague as to be really meaningless, if not inaccurate and misleading—*Ellis*⟩ **Naked** suggests absence of all covering, especially in the way of protective or ornamental covering. When used with regard to persons and implying absence of clothing, the word is not uniform in its pictorial and emotional evocations; it may suggest many conditions, such as a state of nature and of physical beauty, a state of destitution and of pitiful suffering, a state of privacy and of admirable modesty or purity, a state of shameful publicity or of wanton exhibitionism ⟨Eve . . . in *naked* beauty more adorned, more lovely, than Pandora, whom the gods endowed with all their gifts—*Milton*⟩ ⟨poor *naked* wretches, wheresoe'er you are, that bide the pelting of this pitiless storm—*Shak.*⟩ In extended use, therefore, *naked* is preferred to *bare* when the emphasis is on revelation or exposure, or on the power of revealing or exposing something as it is in its severe outlines or structure, in its plain truth or without disguise, or in its hidden weakness or strength ⟨craft must have clothes, but truth loves to go *naked*—*Fuller* d. 1734⟩ ⟨it is not asked that poetry should offer *naked* argument—*Day Lewis*⟩ ⟨the power of striking out, in a few *naked,* simple words, a picture which is ineffaceable—*Lowes*⟩ **Nude** and *naked* are very close synonyms when they are used in reference to persons, but *nude,* because of its association with the representation of undraped figures in art, tends to suggest little more than the absence of covering and to be comparatively a colorless word with little extended use and with few, if any, significant and distinctive implications. Because of its unequivocal meaning, *nude* is preferred to *naked* when the mere fact of being without clothing is indicated and there is no intent to convey an aesthetic or ethical implication ⟨three *nude* statues in the exhibition⟩ ⟨residents of the houses along the river objected to *nude* swimmers⟩ **Bald** implies absence of the hair of the head or, sometimes, actual or apparent absence of another covering (as of foliage, feathers, or vegetation); thus, the *bald* eagle is the common eagle after it has reached an age when its head and neck feathers are white and inapparent at a distance; a *bald* tree is one that no longer bears leaves at its top; a *bald* mountain is one whose peak is bare of vegetation. In extended use *bald* implies austere or colorless bareness and a conspicuous absence of qualities that might add charm, vividness, or interest; thus, a *bare* style is one that employs economy of means or a meagerness of ornament; a *naked* style is one that disguises nothing and shows not the slightest obscurity or hesitancy in presenting the thought; a *bald* style is bare and plain to the point of severity ⟨his expression may often be called *bald* . . . but it is *bald* as the bare mountaintops are *bald,* with a baldness which is full of grandeur—*Arnold*⟩ **Barren** (see also STERILE) implies a lack of fertility or productive power and therewith also implies absence of natural or appropriate covering as an outward sign of impoverishment, impotence, or aridity; thus, *barren* lands are not only bare but they are waste, desolate lands incapable of producing crops; a *barren* style is the style of a person who has not the mind, heart, or imagination to give his style any signs of life or vitality or any coloring of fancy ⟨without social history,

economic history is *barren* and political history is unintelligible—*Trevelyan*⟩
**Ana** stripped, divested, denuded (see STRIP *vb*): unclothed, undressed, unrobed (see affirmative verbs at CLOTHE)
**Ant** covered
**2** *mere
**bare** *vb* denude, divest, *strip, dismantle
**Ant** cover —**Con** *clothe, dress, apparel, robe, attire: *disguise, cloak, mask, dissemble, camouflage
**barefaced** brazen, *shameless, brash, impudent
**Ana** open, plain, *frank, candid: indecent, unseemly, *indecorous
**Ant** furtive —**Con** covert, surreptitious, stealthy, *secret
**bargain** *n* *contract, compact, pact
**bark** *vb* Bark, bay, howl, growl, snarl, yelp, yap mean to make the sound of or a sound suggestive of a dog. **Bark** implies the sharp, explosive utterance characteristic of dogs; it may be used not only of them and of another animal (as a seal) that produces a similar noise but also of a person or a sonorous thing that gives the same effect ⟨heard the *barking* of wolves in the distance⟩ ⟨the guns *barked* all night long⟩ ⟨they [critics] had . . . *barked* at you, foamed at you day after day, now you were ended. They praised you . . . and laid you away—*Lindsay*⟩ ⟨thunder . . . *barked* in the distance—*McFee*⟩ **Bay** implies a repeated or almost continuous barking in deep prolonged tones that is characteristic of hounds in pursuit of quarry ⟨I had rather be a dog, and *bay* the moon, than such a Roman—*Shak.*⟩ ⟨dogs *baying* and driving him up a tree—*Darwin*⟩ **Bay** is seldom used of any animals other than members of the dog family (including mythical ones such as Cerberus) and is infrequently used in reference to men. When it is so used, it generally implies the action not of an individual but of a group (as a mob) that acts like a pack of dogs baying ⟨I dare avouch you'd stand up for yourself, though all the world should *bay* like winter wolves—*Tennyson*⟩ **Howl** implies a long, loud, mournful cry made by dogs seemingly in distress and often interpreted as evidence of hunger or loneliness. The term implies also similar sounds made by other animals, but its strongest association has been with dogs and wolves ⟨a dog *howled* each night⟩ ⟨pursued by *howling* wolves⟩ *Howl* (see also ROAR) may be used in reference to human beings to imply loud crying, laughing, or derisive calling, and to other sounds that suggest the howling of animals (as in loudness and prolongation). **Growl** applies to the long, low rumbling sound suggesting a threat that is made by an angry dog; less often it is used in reference to other animals (as the bear or cat). Like *howl,* it is applied to persons and to inanimate things (as thunder and winds). When used of persons, it suggests utterance in a surly or grumbling mood ⟨he *growled,* "What are you doing there?"⟩ ⟨he's no business to *growl* . . . about money—*Holland*⟩ **Snarl** implies not only a growling but a snapping and baring of fangs; it, too, is used typically of dogs and suggests an aggressive or infuriated state ⟨the dog never *snarled* until he was mistreated⟩ ⟨children run from a *snarling* dog⟩ *Snarl* when used of a person's manner or speech implies a highly disagreeable quality and usually suggests spite or malignity and a menacing attitude ⟨the midwife wondered and the women cried "O, Jesus bless us, he is born with teeth!" And so I was; which plainly signified that I should *snarl* and bite and play the dog—*Shak.*⟩ **Yelp** has as its basic implication the utterance of short, shrill barks by a dog (as in eagerness, in pain, or in fear); when used in reference to men, the word often implies a number of short, shrill utterances, especially indicating surprise, fear, or excitement ⟨a . . . huntsman

clad for the field, with his fresh pack *yelping* . . . about him—*Dickens*⟩ ⟨the nominations have accordingly furnished something to *yelp* on—*Jefferson*⟩ ⟨"Look out," *yelps* the crowd and the high walls fall—*Lindsay*⟩ **Yap** comes close to *yelp,* but it chiefly implies the short, shrill barking of a small dog or excited, staccato sounds that are comparable ⟨half a dozen little *yapping* dogs . . . assailed me—*Braddon*⟩ It may suggest excessive talking that conveys little but is usually uttered in an insistent or offensive and often high-pitched voice.
*Ana* bellow, vociferate, bawl, *roar: yell, *shout, scream, shriek

**bark** *n* *skin, rind, peel, hide, pelt

**baroque** *adj* *ornate, florid, rococo, flamboyant

**barren 1** *sterile, unfruitful, infertile, impotent
*Ant* fecund —*Con* *fertile, prolific, fruitful
**2** bald, *bare, naked, nude
*Ana* arid, *dry: desolate, forlorn (see ALONE): impoverished, exhausted, depleted (see DEPLETE): austere, *severe, stern
*Con* luxuriant, lush, *profuse: opulent, *luxurious, sumptuous

**barricade** *n* barrier, *bar

**barrier** *n* barricade, *bar

**barrister** *lawyer, counselor, counsel, advocate, attorney, solicitor

**basal** basic, underlying, *fundamental, radical

**base** *n* Base, basis, foundation, ground, groundwork are comparable when meaning something on which another thing is reared or built or by which it is supported or fixed in place. **Base** may be applied to the lowest part or bottom of something without strong implication of purpose as a support or prop ⟨the *base* of a tree⟩ ⟨*base* of a mountain⟩ but more often it implies specific reference to a broad bottom or to a substructure on which a thing rests or seems to rest for support or by which it is kept upright or stable ⟨the *base* of a pyramid⟩ ⟨the *base* of a lamp⟩ ⟨the *base* of a triangle⟩ ⟨the first of four cabinets the liberal leader was to form . . . in attempts to achieve a combination of ministers with a wide enough *base* to ensure effective support—*Current Biog.*⟩ The word may fail to stress an underlying and then applies to something which serves either as a starting point of a development, an operation, or a process ⟨a *base* of operations⟩ ⟨a submarine *base*⟩ ⟨coal tar is the *base* from which whole families of useful compounds are derived⟩ or as a necessary ingredient that carries or contains the active ingredient of a mixture ⟨lanolin is the *base* of many cosmetics⟩ ⟨dynamite often has an absorbent *base* such as sawdust⟩ **Basis** like *base* may be used in reference to something that underlies and supports or to something that serves as a starting point, but the term is rarely applied to a physical or material thing; thus, one may speak of the *base* (but not the *basis*) of a monument, or of the *basis* (not the *base*) for a certain belief ⟨implicit trust is the *basis* of a lasting friendship⟩ ⟨phrase a question as a *basis* for discussion⟩ ⟨tradition forms a *basis* for the acquiring of literary taste —*Day Lewis*⟩ **Foundation** usually implies solidity in what underlies and supports and fixity or stability in whatever is erected on that support; thus, a house has a *base* even if it rests directly on the ground but it may properly be said to have a *foundation* only when it rests on a substructure (as a wall of stones or bricks lining an excavation and usually rising above the surface of the ground); a report may be said to have its *basis* (not *foundation*) in speculation, but a report that is said to be without *foundation* has no *basis* in fact ⟨let me pry loose old walls; let me lift and loosen old *foundations*— *Sandburg*⟩ ⟨as the happiness of the people is the sole end of government, so the consent of the people is the only *foundation* of it—*Adams*⟩ ⟨how firm a *foundation,* ye saints of the Lord, is laid for your faith in His excellent Word!—*Old Hymn*⟩ **Ground** implies something solid or firm beneath, or a substratum comparable to the earth or ground in its firmness and capacity for support; the term is therefore applied to a material, a substance, or a surface upon which another thing is built or against which it is displayed; thus, a piece of net may serve as a *ground* upon which a pattern is worked in lacemaking; before a decorative design is applied to a wall, the *ground,* or wall surface, must be treated and colored so that it will take the pattern and display it properly. **Groundwork** is applied not to a substratum but to a substructure; like *foundation,* the term suggests something built up before the superstructure is erected, but, unlike *foundation,* it is used chiefly in a figurative sense ⟨early training is the *groundwork* of good habits⟩ ⟨lay a *groundwork* in college for one's professional studies⟩ ⟨the *groundwork* of all happiness is health—*Hunt*⟩
*Ant* top —*Con* *summit, peak, apex

**base** *vb* Base, found, ground, bottom, stay, rest are comparable when they mean to supply or to serve as a basis. **Base** now rarely suggests a material support upon which a material superstructure is built ⟨the pile . . . I reared up to the cloud . . . *based* on the living rock—*Browning*⟩ but rather something material or immaterial that underlies a nonmaterial superstructure (as a belief, a system, a judgment, a hope or an action) ⟨is it not the conviction that action should be *based* . . . on solid fact?—*Eliot*⟩ ⟨shares, or bonds, or other pieces of paper, the value of which is *based* upon the estimated future earnings or profits—*Hobson*⟩ **Found** comes so close to *base* as often to be indistinguishable from it and, therefore, to be interchangeable with it ⟨and the rain descended, and the floods came, and the wind blew . . . and it fell not: for it was *founded* upon a rock—*Mt* 7:25⟩ Often, however, it suggests not what merely underlies but what is consciously advanced as support (as for an opinion, a principle, a judgment, a belief, or an affection) ⟨a man that all his time hath *founded* his good fortunes on your love—*Shak.*⟩ ⟨certain fixed laws and principles which he proceeds to *found* upon Aristotle—*Babbitt*⟩ ⟨this criticism is *founded* in misconception—*Cardozo*⟩ **Ground** denotes an implanting (as into the earth) that gives solidity and firmness; it may apply to something (as personal virtue, education, or an institution) which can grow and thrive only when it is firmly based (as if by deep roots) ⟨that ye, being rooted and *grounded* in love, may be able to comprehend with all saints . . . and to know the love of Christ, which passeth knowledge—*Eph* 3:17-19⟩ ⟨ofttimes nothing profits more than self-esteem, *grounded* on just and right— *Milton*⟩ But *ground* may be used, less strictly, in a sense approaching that of *base* and *found* ⟨he *grounds* his theory on evidence gathered over a long period of time⟩ ⟨their quarrel was *grounded* on a dispute over petty matters⟩ **Bottom** implies a broad or strong base ⟨*bottomed* upon solid principles of law and policy—*Burke*⟩ **Stay** implies a support that keeps upright or prevents from falling and may suggest adding a supplementary support to correct an observed or anticipated tendency ⟨*stay* a weakened wall with props⟩ ⟨his nature looked coldly upon its early faith and sought to *stay* itself with rational knowledge— *H. O. Taylor*⟩ **Rest** stresses reliance or dependence on something as a base or fundamental support ⟨their academic reputations *rest,* quite largely, upon their academic power—*Mills*⟩ ⟨metrical forms are conventional, and therefore *rest,* like all matters of usage, on acceptance— *Lowes*⟩ ⟨if the Germans are to justify the high claims

---

A colon (:) separates groups of words discriminated. An asterisk (*) indicates place of treatment of each group.

they make for Lessing as a critic, they must *rest* them on other grounds than his intellectual originality or the fineness of his taste—*Babbitt*⟩
*Ana* *support, sustain: *set, establish, fix, settle

**base** *adj* Base, low, vile mean contemptible because beneath what is expected of the average man. What is **base** excites indignation because devoid of all nobility or even of humanity; the term usually implies the setting (as through cowardice or avarice) of self-interest ahead of duty to others ⟨peace had brought only the shabby, dispiriting spectacle of Versailles, with its *base* greeds and timidities—*Montague*⟩ What is **low** outrages one's sense of decency or propriety. The term, when implying moral contemptibility, often suggests a taking advantage (as by cunning, deceit, or other devious practice) of a person who is helpless or not in a position to defend himself ⟨no one thought he could be *low* enough to steal a nickel from a blind beggar's cup⟩ ⟨whenever a dramatist wished to introduce intrigue, chicanery, or other dirty work, his dramatis personae included a *low* attorney—*Law Times*⟩ Low also is often used of persons, thoughts, language, or actions that strongly offend one's sense of propriety ⟨*low* humor⟩ ⟨they were *low,* those sensual feelings; they were ignoble—*Huxley*⟩ What is **vile** is inexpressibly base or low; the word often implies disgusting foulness or depravity ⟨it was *vile* indeed to unaccustomed and unhardened senses. Every little habitation . . . left its own heap of refuse on its own landing, besides flinging other refuse from its own windows—*Dickens*⟩ ⟨the *vilest* epithet in the English language—*Freeman*⟩
*Ana* *mean, ignoble, abject, sordid: *bad, evil, ill, wicked: ignominious, infamous, disgraceful (see corresponding nouns at DISGRACE)
*Ant* noble —*Con* *moral, ethical, virtuous, righteous: honorable, *upright, honest, just

**baseless, groundless, unfounded, unwarranted** mean not justified or justifiable in any way. **Baseless** implies an entire lack of foundation; it imputes to a thing lack of actuality in itself or in the events or facts upon which it is supposedly based ⟨the *baseless* fabric of this vision —*Shak.*⟩ ⟨he proved the rumors *baseless*⟩ ⟨no claim could have been more utterly *baseless*—*J. R. Green*⟩ **Groundless** stresses the absence of a cause or reason; it is applied especially to thoughts, emotions, or feelings that arise seemingly from nothing and have no perceptible or justifying cause ⟨*groundless* fears⟩ ⟨*groundless* suspicions⟩ **Unfounded** sometimes implies baselessness but more often suggests lack of support or want of evidence, authority, or proof ⟨his theory is not entirely *unfounded*⟩ ⟨an *unfounded* belief⟩ **Unwarranted** emphasizes the fact of exceeding the bounds of what is authorized, sanctioned, believable, or reasonable ⟨the *unwarranted* proceedings of a lower court⟩ ⟨take *unwarranted* liberties⟩ ⟨an *unwarranted* assumption⟩
*Ana* *false, wrong: unsupported, unsustained (see corresponding affirmative verbs at SUPPORT)
*Con* true, actual, *real: *authentic, veritable, bona fide, genuine

**bashful** *shy, diffident, modest, coy
*Ana* shrinking, recoiling (see RECOIL *vb*): timorous, *timid: embarrassed, abashed (see EMBARRASS)
*Ant* forward: brazen —*Con* brash, barefaced, impudent, *shameless: bold, intrepid (see BRAVE)

**basic** 1 basal, *fundamental, underlying, radical
*Ana* principal, capital, *chief, main: primordial, *primary
*Ant* top: peak
2 *alkaline

**basis** *base, foundation, ground, groundwork
*Ana* *principle, fundamental, axiom, law, theorem:

premise, postulate, presupposition, presumption, assumption (see under PRESUPPOSE)

**baste** *vb* *beat, pummel, thrash, buffet, pound, belabor
*Ana* chastise, castigate, *punish, discipline

**bastion** breastwork, parapet, *bulwark, rampart

**bathos** *pathos, poignancy
*Ana* mawkishness, maudlinism, soppiness, mushiness (see corresponding adjectives at SENTIMENTAL)

**batter** *vb* mangle, *maim, mutilate, cripple
*Ana* *beat, pound, pummel, thrash, buffet, belabor, baste

**batter** *n* *dough, paste

**battle** *n* Battle, engagement, action denote a hostile meeting between opposing military forces. **Battle** is commonly used of a general and prolonged combat and is distinguished, therefore, from such terms as *skirmish* or *brush* (see ENCOUNTER). **Engagement** stresses the actual encountering of forces and may be applied to either a general encounter (as between entire armies) or a minor encounter (as between subdivisions or outposts). **Action** is often employed in place of *battle* or *engagement* when the stress is on the idea of active, frequently sharp offensive and defensive operations ⟨clear the warship's decks for *action*⟩ ⟨Gustavus Adolphus, King of Sweden, was killed in *action* at Lutzen, 1632⟩ ⟨a brisk *action* between scouting patrols⟩
*Ana* *encounter, skirmish, brush: *attack, assault, onslaught, onset: combat, conflict, fight, *contest

**battle** *vb* war, fight, *contend
*Ana* combat, oppose, *resist, withstand, fight: *attack, assail, assault, bombard: kick, protest, *object

**bawl** *vb* 1 *roar, bellow, bluster, vociferate, clamor, howl, ululate
*Ana* yell, *shout, scream, shriek: bay, *bark, growl, yelp: *cry, wail
2 rate, berate, tongue-lash, upbraid, *scold, chew out, wig, rail, revile, vituperate
*Ana* reprimand, rebuke, reproach, *reprove, chide: censure, denounce, condemn, reprehend, reprobate (see CRITICIZE)

**bay** *vb* *bark, howl, growl, snarl, yelp, yap
*Ana* bellow, vociferate, clamor, *roar: yell, holler (see SHOUT)

**be** *vb* Be, exist, live, subsist are comparable when they mean to have actuality or reality. **Be** applies to whatever has a place in the realm of things describable as real in a material or immaterial sense; only its context makes clear whether it asserts physical or spiritual reality ⟨to *be,* or not to *be:* that is the question—*Shak.*⟩ ⟨I think, therefore I *am*—*translation*⟩ ⟨whatever *is,* is right—*Pope*⟩ **Exist** adds to *be* the implication of continuance in time; it also commonly implies a place in the realm of things which are describable as entities or as having independent, objective being ⟨a fact which has *existed* cannot be made never to have *existed*—*John Marshall*⟩ ⟨everybody saw the drawings of the temples, strange walls and columns, but nobody believed these things *existed*—*Stark Young*⟩ **Live** basically implies existence in the realm of things possessing the character called *life,* which distinctively characterizes plants and animals and is manifest especially in metabolism, growth, and reproduction ⟨many men *live* to be threescore and ten⟩ ⟨plants cannot *live* without moisture⟩ ⟨whatever *lives* must have sustenance⟩ Live, however, is often applied in an extended sense to immaterial entities (as ideas or beliefs); in this use it may carry a suggestion of qualities associated with life (as persistent existence, vigor, activity, and development) ⟨his name will *live* as long as his country *lives*⟩ ⟨poems that *live*⟩ **Subsist** may be used in place of *be,* or *exist,* or *live* because it may imply the kind of reality or actuality connoted by

---

*Ana* analogous words    *Ant* antonyms    *Con* contrasted words    See also explanatory notes facing page 1

one of those terms, but it (or more particularly its related adjective, *subsistent*) often additionally suggests a relation to or dependence on something; thus, a thing that *subsists* by itself (a self-*subsistent* thing) is independent and self-contained; an idea *subsists* or maintains its existence only so long as it appeals to the mind of thinking men ⟨those secret distributions without which the body cannot *subsist* in its vigor—*Addison*⟩ In philosophical use *subsist* is used often in reference to purely mental conceptions and implies logical validity or the character of being true or logically conceivable ⟨the round square . . . is an object, which neither exists, nor *subsists,* nor has any kind of being at all—*Chisholm*⟩

**beach** *n* strand, coast, foreshore, *shore, bank, littoral

**beak** *bill, neb, nib

**beam** *n* *ray

*Ana* flash, gleam, glint, scintillation, coruscation (see corresponding verbs at FLASH)

**beaming** *adj* radiant, refulgent, effulgent, *bright, brilliant, luminous, lustrous, lambent, lucent, incandescent

*Ana* flashing, gleaming, glittering, glistening, glinting, sparkling, coruscating, scintillating (see FLASH *vb*): glowing, flaming (see BLAZE *vb*)

**bear** *vb* 1 *carry, convey, transport, transmit

*Ana* *move, remove, shift, transfer: hold, *contain

**2 Bear, produce, yield, turn out** are comparable when they mean to bring forth as products. *Bear* usually implies a giving birth to offspring or a bringing of fruit to maturity, though it may be extended to something which tends to reproduce itself or to aid reproduction ⟨she *bore* three children⟩ ⟨the apple trees *bear* every year⟩ ⟨the soil is not rich enough to *bear* crops⟩ ⟨the seed he sowed *bore* fruit⟩ ⟨the bank deposit *bears* a low interest⟩ **Produce** is far wider in its range of application, for it, unlike *bear,* carries no clear implication of a carrying during a period of development prior to the bringing forth; it may be used of almost any bringing forth or into view whether by human or natural agency ⟨he *produced* the book for his friends' inspection⟩ ⟨nobody could *produce* the desired witness⟩ It may apply more specifically to the bringing forth of something as issue of one's body, one's mind, or one's imagination or as an output of labor or effort ⟨it is necessary for the colleges to *produce* straight thinkers⟩ ⟨the plantation *produces* a vast amount of cotton⟩ ⟨the factory *produces* more shoes than ever⟩ ⟨Raphael *produced* an unusual number of widely known paintings⟩ ⟨he feels he can never *produce* another book as good as the one he has just written⟩ ⟨the glands *produce* secretions⟩ **Yield** (see also RELINQUISH, YIELD) fundamentally implies a giving out (as of something within the confines of a thing or within one's power of production); it therefore stresses the outcome, result, return, or reward and not the previous effort or endurance ⟨land that could be counted on to *yield* good crops year after year⟩ ⟨two kinds of classics . . . those that *yield* their meaning at the first encounter and those that we have to discover by effort and insight —*Brooks*⟩ ⟨the discovery of . . . its [calcium carbide's] reaction with ordinary water to *yield* a highly flammable gas, acetylene—*Morrison*⟩ **Turn out,** like *yield,* stresses the outcome or result, but it implies previous and especially mechanical labor or effort ⟨the company promises to *turn out* 300 airplanes a month⟩ ⟨the main object is to *turn out* good Englishmen—*Inge*⟩

*Ana* reproduce, propagate, breed, *generate

**3 Bear, suffer, endure, abide, tolerate, stand, brook** denote to sustain something trying or painful. *Bear* and *suffer* are also synonyms in their more comprehensive denotation, to sustain whatever is imposed ⟨this theory will *bear* examination⟩ ⟨the stone *suffers* no alteration in a colder climate⟩ Both verbs, however, are more often used in their specific senses because of their customary reference, with *bear,* to things that are heavy or difficult or, with *suffer,* to things that are painful or injurious. **Bear** suggests more the power to sustain than the manner in which something is sustained ⟨water as hot as one can *bear* it⟩ ⟨his decency which has made him *bear* prolonged and intolerable humiliation with control and courtesy— *Mannes*⟩ ⟨*bear* affliction⟩ **Suffer** more often implies acceptance of infliction than patience or courage in bearing ⟨I am waylaid by Beauty . . . Oh, savage Beauty, *suffer* me to pass—*Millay*⟩ ⟨being a man of uncommon spirit, he never *suffered* the least insult or affront to pass unchastised—*Smollett*⟩ **Endure** and *abide* usually refer to long-continued trials or sufferings borne without giving in. **Endure** usually connotes stamina or firmness of mind, while **abide** suggests patience and submission ⟨I am able now, methinks . . . to *endure* more miseries and greater far—*Shak.*⟩ ⟨what fates impose, that men must needs *abide*—*Shak.*⟩ *Tolerate* and *stand* imply overcoming one's own resistance to what is distasteful or antagonistic. **Tolerate** often connotes failure to resist through indifference or, sometimes, through a desire for peace or harmony ⟨*tolerate* differences in opinion⟩ ⟨Archer's New York *tolerated* hypocrisy in private relations; but in business matters it exacted . . . impeccable honesty—*Wharton*⟩ **Stand** is often used in place of *bear,* but distinctively it implies the ability to keep from flinching ⟨he can *stand* teasing⟩ ⟨he *stood* the attack well⟩ **Brook** occurs chiefly in negative constructions and implies self-assertion and defiance ⟨restraint she will not *brook*—*Milton*⟩ ⟨he is not well-born enough to succeed there, and his sense of intellectual superiority did not *brook* subordination— *Laski*⟩ The other verbs are also used commonly in negative clauses but with weakened emphasis. In such constructions *bear* (with the negative) commonly implies dislike, *suffer* rejection, *endure* intolerance, *abide* impatience, *tolerate* contempt, and *stand* repugnance.

*Ana* accept, *receive: *afflict, try, torment, torture

**4** *press, bear down, squeeze, crowd, jam

*Ana* weigh, oppress, *depress: *burden, encumber, load, saddle

**5 Bear, relate, pertain, appertain, belong, apply** are comparable when used intransitively with the meaning to have a connection, especially a logical connection. One thing **bears** *on* or *upon* another thing when the first touches so directly upon the second (usually something in question) as to carry appreciable weight in its solution or in the understanding of issues it involves ⟨ignore all facts except those that *bear* upon this particular case⟩ ⟨this situation *bears* directly upon the question under discussion⟩ One thing **relates** *to* another thing when there is some connection between them which permits or, more often, requires them to be considered together with reference to their effect upon each other. The connection implied is usually closer in the intransitive than in the transitive verb (see JOIN), being commonly one of dependence or interdependence ⟨in an organism each part *relates* to every other part⟩ ⟨show how the demand *relates* to the supply⟩ ⟨each incident *relates* to the plot⟩ ⟨a detail in a painting *relates* to the design of the whole⟩ ⟨the duties of the citizen, as he understood them, *related* not only to acts, but also to thoughts—*Mencken*⟩ One thing **pertains** or **appertains** to another when there is a connection that permits their association in practice or thought. Both of these words are more widely applicable than *bear* and *relate,* for they cover not only the connections specifically implied in those words but also those close connections implied by *belong* and those remote connections

A colon (:) separates groups of words discriminated. An asterisk (*) indicates place of treatment of each group.

implied by *have to do with;* thus, the things that *pertain* to happiness are all the things that can be thought of as causing, contributing to, preventing, or affecting the quality of happiness ⟨moral philosophy is the branch of philosophy that deals with all problems *pertaining* to morals or ethics⟩ *Pertain* more often implies a necessary connection or a very close relation than the more formal *appertain,* which commonly suggests an incidental or acquired connection ⟨a . . . faithful high priest in things *pertaining* to God—*Heb* 2:17⟩ ⟨the crown and all wide-stretched honors that *pertain* by custom and the ordinance of times unto the crown of France—*Shak.*⟩ ⟨to that simple object *appertains* a story—*Wordsworth*⟩ **Belong,** usually with *to,* implies a relation in which one thing is a part or element without which another cannot exist, function, have its true character or being, or be complete. In this sense a thing that *belongs* is a property, an attribute, a duty, or a proper concern ⟨the Government of the United States . . . does not possess all the powers which usually *belong* to the sovereignty of a nation—*Taney*⟩ ⟨nor does value *belong* to what concerns man only—*Alexander*⟩ But *belong* also may be used of things as they pertain to persons, then implying possession ⟨the watch *belongs* to James⟩ ⟨this land *belongs* to the government⟩ or informally of persons with reference to their qualifications for fitting into a group, especially a social group ⟨she's smart and jolly and everything, but she just doesn't *belong*—*Ferber*⟩ **Apply,** also with *to,* implies a relation in which a more inclusive category (as a law, a principle, a rule, a theory, a general term) covers a less inclusive specific instance, usually also explaining, interpreting, or describing the latter or having some clear bearing upon it ⟨the rules of addition *apply* to our debts as rigorously as to our assets—*James*⟩ ⟨he really was the one child to whom the "spare-the-rod" precept did not *apply*—he was naturally good—*Deland*⟩
*Ana* *concern, affect: touch, influence, *affect: weigh (see DEPRESS)

**beard** *vb* *face, brave, challenge, dare, defy
*Ana* confront, *meet, encounter

**bear down** *press, bear, squeeze, crowd, jam

**bearing** *n* **Bearing, deportment, demeanor, mien, port, presence** are comparable when they denote the way in which or the quality by which a person outwardly manifests his personality and breeding. **Bearing** is the most general of these words; it may imply reference to a person's mental attitude to others, his conduct in society, or his characteristic posture or way of holding himself ⟨if 'twere so, she could not sway her house, command her followers . . . with such a smooth, discreet and stable *bearing*—*Shak.*⟩ ⟨"You should have seen him as a young man," she cried . . . drawing herself up to imitate her husband's once handsome *bearing*—*D. H. Lawrence*⟩ **Deportment** applies especially to a person's actions in their relations to the external, often conventional amenities of life; it so strongly suggests the influence of breeding or training that in current use it often means little more than *behavior* ⟨lessons in *deportment*⟩ ⟨naturalism is limited to neurasthenics; while Style means a British *deportment*—stiff upper lip, stiff limbs, and stiffer backbone—and an elocutionary Oxonian delivery—*Bentley*⟩ **Demeanor** applies rather to one's attitude as shown in one's behavior in the presence of others ⟨his *demeanor* in public was still, silent, almost sepulchral. He looked habitually upon the ground when he conversed, was chary of speech, embarrassed—*Motley*⟩ ⟨the child who has been treated wisely and kindly has a frank look in the eyes, and a fearless *demeanor* even with strangers—*Russell*⟩ **Mien** implies reference both to bearing and demeanor,

often as suggestive of mood ⟨for truth has such a face and such a *mien,* as to be loved needs only to be seen—*Dryden*⟩ ⟨his *mien* of settled woe—*Robertson Davies*⟩ **Port** implies reference to physique and, especially through long association with such adjectives as *majestic, regal,* and *proud,* to a stately or dignified physique ⟨pride in their *port,* defiance in their eye, I see the lords of humankind pass by—*Goldsmith*⟩ ⟨people with a dignity of *port,* an amplitude of back, an emphasis of vocabulary—*L. P. Smith*⟩ **Presence** is more explicit than *bearing;* it denotes a person's bearing with reference to its power to impress his personality on others or to attract their attention, interest, or admiration ⟨in mature life he became "a bulky person," with strong health and a commanding *presence*—*Inge*⟩ ⟨a small, birdlike person, of no *presence*—*Rose Macaulay*⟩ ⟨by a *Port,* one may understand them to indicate something unsympathetically impressive; whereas a *Presence* would seem to be a thing that directs the most affable appeal to our poor human weaknesses—*Meredith*⟩
*Ana* *posture, attitude, pose: *behavior, conduct: attitude, stand, *position: poise, address (see TACT)

**beastly** bestial, *brutal, brute, brutish, feral
*Ana* abominable, detestable, *hateful: loathsome, repulsive, revolting, *offensive: disgusting, sickening, nauseating (see DISGUST)
*Con* agreeable, gratifying, grateful, *pleasant, pleasing: delicious, *delightful, delectable

**beat** *vb* **1 Beat, pound, pummel, thrash, buffet, baste, belabor** are comparable when they mean to strike repeatedly. **Beat,** the usual and general word of this group, may imply no more than the simple action of repeated striking (as with one's hands or an implement). The purpose is usually suggested by the object beaten, even when the manner of beating or the kind of implement used is not specifically stated ⟨clean a rug by *beating* it⟩ ⟨*beat* his breast in anguish⟩ ⟨the shocking increase in the battered child syndrome, the physical result of viciously *beating* a young child⟩ ⟨the horse restlessly *beat* the ground with his hooves⟩ **Pound** suggests beating with a weight or pestle to crush or reduce to a pulp or powder (as in grinding meal). More often the term implies heavier, more damaging blows than *beat;* it may suggest repeated striking (as by a heavy hammer, strong doubled fists, the hooves of horses, bombs, or shells), and it often also suggests rhythmical, loud, and heavy sounds ⟨the big boys who sit at the tables *pound* them and cheer—*Hughes*⟩ ⟨the hooves of the horses *pounding* on the bridge—*Anderson*⟩ ⟨he could hear his own heart *pounding*⟩ ⟨he *pounded* on the door in an effort to rouse the sleeping family⟩ ⟨night after night the port was *pounded* by bombs⟩ **Pummel** implies the beating of a person with one's fists: although it does not suggest as heavy blows as *pound,* it carries a stronger suggestion of continuous raining of blows and, often, of the infliction of injury than *beat* ⟨a desire to *pummel* and wring the nose of the aforesaid Stiggins—*Dickens*⟩ ⟨he *pummeled* and slapped and scrubbed the somewhat obese nudity of his companion—*Buchan*⟩ **Thrash** in its basic sense means to separate the grain (as of wheat) from the husks and straw, originally by beating or striking again and again (as with a flail). Consequently *thrash* usually means to strike repeatedly in a manner suggestive of strokes with a flail and usually with an implement (as a stick or whip) ⟨*thrash* a hedge with a cane in order to drive out the rabbits⟩ ⟨propelled himself through the water with wildly *thrashing* arms⟩ ⟨everyone fought fire. Everyone went to the woods and *thrashed* out some new blaze—*Vorse*⟩ **Buffet** implies a repeated striking with or as if with an open hand: it therefore suggests a slapping rather than a pounding and in extended use is employed chiefly with reference to something which dashes against the face or the body in the manner of a slap or which one fights as if by slapping ⟨the two hands of Madame Defarge *buffeted* and tore her face—*Dickens*⟩ ⟨*buffeted* by high waves⟩ **Baste** implies a sound vigorous thrashing with any weapon (including the tongue) ⟨I took a broom, and *basted* her, till she cried extremely—*Pepys*⟩ ⟨if you will give me the loan of a horsewhip, I'll *baste* the backs of these lazy fellows of yours—*Wheelwright*⟩ **Belabor** implies a prolonged and mighty basting or buffeting ⟨he saw Virago Nell *belabor,* with Dick's own staff his peaceful neighbor—*Swift*⟩ ⟨a group of demonstrating Egyptians being *belabored* by police—*Doty*⟩

*Ana* slug, clout, swat, punch, *strike, hit, smite, slap, box, cuff

**2** defeat, lick, *conquer, vanquish, subdue, subjugate, reduce, overcome, surmount, overthrow, rout

*Ana* surpass, excel, outstrip (see EXCEED): confound, nonplus (see PUZZLE)

**3** *pulsate, throb, pulse, palpitate

*Ana* quiver, quaver, quake (see SHAKE): vibrate, oscillate, fluctuate, pendulate (see SWING)

**beat** *n* pulsation, pulse, throb, palpitation (see under PULSATE)

*Ana* accent, accentuation, stress (see EMPHASIS): *rhythm, cadence

**beatitude** blessedness, bliss, felicity, *happiness

*Ana* rapture, *ecstasy, transport: joy, fruition, enjoyment, *pleasure

*Ant* despair: dolor —*Con* tribulation, affliction, *trial, cross: anguish, woe, *sorrow, grief: suffering, agony, misery, *distress

**beau** *n* *fop, exquisite, dandy, coxcomb, dude, buck

**beau ideal** ideal, exemplar, pattern, *model, example, mirror, standard

**beauteous** pulchritudinous, fair, good-looking, handsome, pretty, comely, bonny, lovely, *beautiful

*Ana* alluring, attractive, fascinating, charming (see under ATTRACT)

**beautiful** *adj* Beautiful, lovely, handsome, pretty, bonny, comely, fair, beauteous, pulchritudinous, good-looking are comparable when they express judgment of a person or a thing perceived or contemplated with sensuous or aesthetic pleasure. Although they differ widely not only in their implications and connotations but also in their range of reference, they carry in common the meaning very pleasing or delightful to look at. Of all these adjectives **beautiful** is usually the richest in significance; since the abstraction it represents (*the beautiful*) has been for many centuries the subject of discussion by philosophers, artists, and aestheticians, its content in a particular context often depends upon the speaker's or writer's cultural background, his chosen philosophy, or his own peculiar definition. In general, however, both in learned and in ordinary use *beautiful* is applied to what excites the keenest pleasure not only of the senses but also through the medium of the senses of mind and soul. It also suggests an approach to or a realization of perfection, often specifically the imagined perfection associated with one's conception of an ideal. That is why *beautiful* is applicable not only to things that are directly perceived by the senses ⟨a *beautiful* woman⟩ ⟨a *beautiful* scene⟩ ⟨the *beautiful* "Winged Victory"⟩ ⟨an exquisitely *beautiful* painting⟩ but to things that are actually mental constructions formed in the mind through the instrumentality of language or as a result of inferences from certain outward manifestations ⟨a *beautiful* poem⟩ ⟨a *beautiful* plan⟩ ⟨a

*beautiful* character⟩ **Lovely,** like *beautiful,* usually suggests a more than sensuous pleasure, but it implies keen emotional delight rather than profound intellectual or spiritual pleasure. It is applied therefore to what is so pleasant to look upon, to hear, to smell, or to touch that the person affected dwells delightedly, sensuously, or amorously upon it or the sensations it produces ⟨why ever wast thou *lovely* in my eyes?—*Shak.*⟩ ⟨in after years . . . thy mind shall be a mansion for all *lovely* forms —*Wordsworth*⟩ ⟨a sailing ship—that *loveliest* of human creations—*Ellis*⟩ **Handsome,** on the other hand, carries little connotation of emotional or spiritual pleasure; it implies rather a judgment of approval occasioned by something that is pleasant to look upon because it conforms to one's conception of what is perfect in form and detail or in perfect taste, and pleasing because of its due proportions, symmetry, or elegance. It is applied chiefly to what can be regarded unemotionally and with detachment; thus, a woman who is described as *handsome* rather than as *beautiful* or *lovely* is by implication one whose appearance aesthetically satisfies the observer but does not markedly stir his deeper feelings ⟨a *handsome* dress⟩ ⟨a *handsome* house⟩ ⟨a *handsome* table⟩ ⟨"They say I'm *handsome.*" "You're lovely, Bella!" She drank in his homage—*Meredith*⟩ **Pretty,** in contrast to *handsome,* is applied largely to what pleases by its delicacy, grace, or charm rather than by its perfection or elegance of form or style. It is seldom used to describe something large or impressive; consequently it often connotes diminutiveness, daintiness, or exquisiteness ⟨a group of *pretty* girls⟩ ⟨a very *pretty* child⟩ ⟨a *pretty* cottage⟩ *Pretty* is often used depreciatively to suggest mere pleasingness of appearance and the absence of qualities that make for beauty, grandeur, or strength ⟨a *pretty* poem⟩ ⟨a *pretty* view⟩ **Bonny,** which is more common in British and especially Scottish use, implies approbation of a person's or thing's looks but it may also imply various pleasing qualities (as sweetness, simplicity, healthiness, plumpness) ⟨a *bonny* day⟩ ⟨a great actress and a *bonny* girl—*Donn Byrne*⟩ ⟨a *bonny* baby⟩ ⟨what the sentimental women of the neighborhood called a "*bonny* man." His features were remarkably regular, and his complexion was remarkably fair—*G. D. Brown*⟩ **Comely** implies an opposition to what is homely and plain and suggests pleasant wholesomeness with a measure of good looks or physical attractiveness ⟨a *comely* barmaid⟩ ⟨the *comeliest* woman in the club⟩ ⟨Jack was so *comely,* so pleasant, so jolly—*Dibdin*⟩ ⟨once a moorland Helen, and still *comely* as a blood horse and healthy as the hill wind—*Stevenson*⟩ **Fair** applies especially to something which gives delight because of the purity, the flawlessness, or the freshness of its beauty ⟨*fair* as a star, when only one is shining in the sky—*Wordsworth*⟩ ⟨forever wilt thou love, and she be *fair*—*Keats*⟩ **Beauteous** and **pulchritudinous** are used especially in ironic or journalistic prose where they often carry a suggestion of derogation or imply an emphasis on mere physical attractiveness ⟨*beauteous* candidates for the title of "Miss America"⟩ ⟨a *beauteous* platinum blonde⟩ ⟨*pulchritudinous* chorus girls⟩ *Beauteous* in poetical and dignified use often carries a stronger implication of opulence of charms than *beautiful* ⟨how *beauteous* mankind is! O brave new world, that has such people in't!—*Shak.*⟩ **Good-looking** is a less expressive word than *handsome* or *pretty* but is often used as a close synonym ⟨the children of that family are all *good-looking*⟩

*Ana* *splendid, resplendent, glorious, sublime, superb: exquisite, elegant, *choice

*Ant* ugly —*Con* repulsive, repugnant, revolting, *offensive

---

A colon (:) separates groups of words discriminated. An asterisk (*) indicates place of treatment of each group.

**beautify** embellish, deck, bedeck, \*adorn, ornament, decorate, garnish

*Ana* enhance, heighten (see INTENSIFY)

*Ant* uglify —*Con* \*deface, disfigure: \*deform, distort, contort: mar, spoil, \*injure, damage

**because,** for, since, as, inasmuch as are the chief causal conjunctions in English. **Because** assigns a cause or reason immediately and explicitly; as, I hid myself, *because* [=for the express reason that, or as caused to do so by the fact that] I was afraid; he must have passed this way, *because* [=owing to the specific fact that] there is no other road or *because* [=as is directly proved by the fact that] his footprints are here. **For** is a particle of less immediate reference than *because;* it regards the statement to which it is subjoined as relatively independent and proceeds to adduce for it some ground, reason, evidence, proof, explanation, or justification; as, I hid myself, *for* [=as I may add by way of explanation] I was afraid; he must have passed this way, *for* [=as you may readily see] here are his footprints; I like him, *for* [=I ask, in justification of the fact] who can help it? **Since** is less formal and more incidental than *because;* **as** assigns a reason even more casually than *since;* each of them frequently begins its sentence; as, *Since* (or *As*) I was afraid, I hid myself ⟨I will come, *since* you asked me⟩ ⟨*as* I knew him to be out of town, I did not call⟩ **Inasmuch as** assigns a reason in a somewhat concessive or qualified fashion; as, *Inasmuch as* [=in view of, or considering, the fact that] I was afraid, I hid myself; I am ready to accept your proposal, *inasmuch as* [=seeing that] I believe it is the best you can offer.

**becloud** cloud, eclipse, fog, befog, dim, bedim, \*obscure, darken, obfuscate

*Ana* \*confuse, muddle, addle, befuddle: \*puzzle, perplex, distract

**bedeck** deck, garnish, embellish, beautify, decorate, ornament, \*adorn

**bedim** dim, eclipse, cloud, becloud, fog, befog, obfuscate, \*obscure, darken

*Ana* cloak, mask, \*disguise: conceal, \*hide, screen

**beetle** *vb* overhang, jut, project, \*bulge, protuberate, protrude, stick out

*Ana* menace, \*threaten

**befall** betide, occur, \*happen, chance, transpire

**befog** fog, cloud, becloud, eclipse, \*obscure, darken, dim, bedim, obfuscate

*Ana* \*puzzle, perplex, distract, bewilder, dumbfound: \*confuse, muddle, addle

**befool** trick, hoax, hoodwink, \*dupe, gull, bamboozle

*Ana* \*cheat, cozen, overreach: \*deceive, delude, beguile, mislead: blandish, cajole, wheedle, \*coax

**before,** ahead, forward are comparable when they mean in advance, especially in place or in time. **Before** is more commonly used in reference to time than to place. Its most frequent implication is previousness or priority ⟨I have heard that *before*⟩ ⟨not dead, but gone *before*—*Rogers*⟩ ⟨dreams no mortal ever dared to dream *before*—*Poe*⟩ Sometimes, however, it implies futurity ⟨we look *before* and after, and pine for what is not—*Shelley*⟩ This use is not a contradiction of the temporal sense, but an extension of the adverb in its less frequent meaning of in front or in the van ⟨thou art so far *before* that swiftest wing of recompense is slow to overtake thee—*Shak.*⟩ *Ahead* and *forward* are the commonest adverbs indicating position in advance or in front of something and have practically supplanted *before;* **ahead,** however, usually implies a position outside of a thing, often a moving thing, and **forward** frequently implies a front position in the thing itself. Thus, to send a group of scouts *ahead* im-

plies their detachment from an advancing body of troops; to send a company *forward* usually means to send them to a position nearer the front or in the van of a regiment. In nautical context *ahead* (opposed to *astern*) indicates a position or direction in front of and outside of the ship ⟨breakers *ahead*⟩ ⟨a sail *ahead*⟩ ⟨full speed *ahead*⟩ while *forward* (opposed to *aft*) indicates one in front of the midships section of the vessel ⟨the guns were placed *forward*⟩ The same distinction is often found in extended use; thus, one who looks *ahead* can foresee the remote consequences of a decision and ignore the immediate results, while one who looks *forward* anticipates something likely or bound to occur ⟨no longer *forward* nor behind I look in hope or fear—*Whittier*⟩ There is no difference between *ahead* and *forward* in reference to mechanisms which can be reversed or the opposite, except as determined by idiom ⟨set a clock *ahead*⟩ ⟨drive an engine *forward*⟩ *Forward,* unlike *ahead,* is rarely used in reference to time except in its sense of onward (see ONWARD) ⟨from that time *forward* I believed what he told me⟩ *Ahead,* on the other hand, comes close to *before* in its implication of previousness or priority. Thus, a person finds himself *forward* of an appointment when he arrives *ahead* of time; idiomatically, one puts the clock *forward* (or sets it *ahead*) when he changes the position of the hands so that they record a later time.

*Ant* after —*Con* behind (see AFTER): \*abaft, aft, astern

**beforehand** \*early, betimes, soon

*Ant* behindhand

**befoul** foul, dirty, sully, \*soil, smirch, besmirch, grime, begrime, tarnish

*Ana* \*spot, spatter, sprinkle

**befuddle** fuddle, addle, muddle, \*confuse

*Ana* bewilder, distract, confound, perplex (see PUZZLE): intoxicate, inebriate (see corresponding adjectives at DRUNK)

*Ant* clarify, clear

**beg,** entreat, beseech, implore, supplicate, adjure, importune mean to ask or request urgently. **Beg** suggests earnestness or insistence especially in asking a favor ⟨why, boy, before I left, you were constantly *begging* to see Town—*Meredith*⟩ **Entreat** implies an attempt to persuade or to overcome resistance in another especially by ingratiating oneself ⟨he was accustomed to command, not to *entreat*—*Cather*⟩ **Beseech** implies great eagerness and often anxiety or solicitude ⟨she *besought* him, for his soul's sake, to speak the truth—*Kipling*⟩ **Implore,** often used interchangeably with *beseech,* at times suggests even greater urgency in the plea or more manifest anguish ⟨the last look of my dear mother's eyes, which *implored* me to have mercy—*Dickens*⟩ **Supplicate** adds to *entreat* the suggestion of fervent prayer or of a prayerful attitude ⟨invite, entreat, *supplicate* them to accompany you—*Chesterfield*⟩ ⟨fall on his knees and *supplicate* the God of his fathers—*Terrien*⟩ **Adjure** implies an injunction as well as a plea and is strengthened by the expressed or implied invocation of a sense of responsibility or duty or of something sacred ⟨I *adjure* thee by the living God, that thou tell us whether thou be the Christ—*Mt* 26:63⟩ It may sometimes suggest little more than urgency or peremptoriness ⟨so E company . . . doubled for the dear life, and in the rear toiled the perspiring sergeant, *adjuring* it to double yet faster—*Kipling*⟩ **Importune** commonly suggests repeated attempts to break down resistance and often connotes annoying pertinacity ⟨a valued adviser who was wont to *importune* me with the dear old doctrines of the church—*Emerson*⟩

*Ana* solicit, request, \*ask: plead, pray, petition, sue (see under PRAYER): \*demand, exact

---

*Ana* analogous words   *Ant* antonyms   *Con* contrasted words   See also explanatory notes facing page 1

**beget** get, *generate, sire, procreate, engender, breed, propagate, reproduce
*Ana* *bear, produce, yield

**beggarly** cheap, scurvy, shabby, sorry, *contemptible, despicable, pitiable
*Ana* paltry, measly, *petty, trifling: *mean, abject, sordid

**begin, commence, start, initiate, inaugurate** are comparable when they mean to set something going or in progress or to take the first step in a course, process, or operation. *Begin, commence,* and *start* are also used intransitively with the activity, work, or instrument as the subject in the sense of to get going or in progress ⟨he *began* the letter⟩ ⟨play *begins* when the whistle blows⟩ ⟨*start* a race⟩ ⟨the race *starts* at ten⟩ **Begin** (implying opposition to *end*) and **commence** (implying opposition to *conclude*) are identical in meaning; the former is often preferred because less formal than the latter ⟨*begin* work⟩ ⟨the lecture *began* with an apology⟩ ⟨well *begun* is half done⟩ ⟨things never *began* with Mr. Borthrop Trumbull; they always *commenced*—*George Eliot*⟩ Traditional usage often supports the choice of *commence* in reference to court proceedings, religious or other ceremonies, or military operations ⟨*commence* a lawsuit⟩ ⟨divine service *commences* promptly at eleven⟩ ⟨directs the commission to *commence* its work not later than thirty days from the adoption of this resolution—*Current History*⟩ **Start** is often used as though it also were identical in meaning with *begin* and *commence;* the term, however, carries implications which distinguish it sharply from the other words. *Start* implies opposition to *stop;* it therefore suggests a setting out from a particular point (as on a journey, a race, or a course) often after inaction or waiting ⟨the horses are ready to *start* (that is, to begin the race)⟩ ⟨the children like to see the train *start* (that is, set out from the station at which it has stopped)⟩ ⟨conversation *started* and stopped and after an embarrassing pause *started* again⟩ *Start* also frequently takes as its subject not the person or agency that begins a process or course but the one that causes, enables, or permits him or it to begin ⟨his father *started* him in business⟩ ⟨he quickly *started* the engine working by pressing a button⟩ **Initiate** (see also INITIATE) suggests reference to the first step in a process and carries no implication of an end or ending; it often suggests a contrast with *carry on, continue,* or *maintain;* thus, a person *initiates* (more precise than *begins* or *starts* except in informal speech) a custom or practice when he is its originator; a diplomat *initiates* negotiations between the government he represents and another when he takes the first step leading to future discussions in which he may or may not take part, but he *begins* negotiations on behalf of his government when he enters into actual discussions which in the natural course of events will end only when there is agreement or hopeless disagreement ⟨Taft had to make himself popular as a necessary incident to *initiating* a civil government—*Heiser*⟩ **Inaugurate** retains, from its more frequent sense of to induct into office (see INITIATE), a hint of a ceremonial beginning. Often it is an inflated term for *begin* or *commence* ⟨the Curies *inaugurated* a new era in science by their discovery of radium⟩ ⟨*inaugurate* proceedings on behalf of the heirs⟩ The word sometimes takes as its subject the act, action, or incident that serves as the first step in a course or procedure ⟨the discovery of radium *inaugurated* a new era in science⟩ ⟨prayers and scripture *inaugurated* the official day—*H. G. Wells*⟩
*Ana* *found, institute, establish, organize: introduce, admit, *enter: originate, derive, *spring, arise, rise
*Ant* end —*Con* *close, terminate, conclude, finish, complete: *stop, cease, quit, discontinue, desist: achieve,

accomplish, effect, fulfill (see PERFORM)

**beginning, genesis, rise, initiation** are comparable when they mean the first part or stage of a process or development. Although **beginning,** often in the plural form **beginnings,** may mean the point at which a person or thing commences its existence (compare BEGIN) it is more often used as denoting the period when something takes form or shape ⟨the *beginning* of justice is the capacity to generalize and make objective one's private sense of wrong, thus turning it to public account—*Earl Warren*⟩ Often, especially when applied to something whose entire course can be viewed, *beginning* or *beginnings* is contrasted with middle and end or with end alone ⟨a drama, according to Aristotle, is composed of three parts, a *beginning,* a middle, and an end⟩ ⟨he eschews speculation on first *beginnings* and ultimate ends, on the ground that no theory about them will assist him to produce . . . an end to suffering—*Humphreys*⟩ ⟨Canada has had a dramatic and colorful history, particularly in her *beginnings*—*J. D. Adams*⟩ ⟨in the *beginning* God created the heaven and the earth—*Gen 1:1*⟩ **Genesis** is usually distinguished from *origin* (see ORIGIN) in that the latter applies to the point at which or from which a thing started, and the former to the stage in which a thing came into its distinctive form or shape or was brought into being; usually, therefore, *genesis* suggests the gradual formulation, formation, or unfolding, but not the full development or evolution of the thing in question; thus, one speaking of the *origin* of the phrase "art for art's sake" gives the first use discoverable of the phrase, whereas one speaking of the *genesis* of the theory of "art for art's sake" dwells upon what happens between the origin of the phrase and its attachment to definite ideas, or upon the period when the theory is receiving its first formulation ⟨the *genesis* and growth of his ideas and attitudes—*G. L. Kline*⟩ ⟨the *genesis* of personality is in all probability determined largely by the anatomical and physiological makeup of the individual—*Sapir*⟩ ⟨the little theater movement . . . had its *genesis* in small groups of idealists eager to experiment with new methods and new media—*Amer. Guide Series: Va.*⟩ **Rise,** although sometimes used in place of *genesis,* usually denotes the upward course of a new thing as opposed to its downward course or decline. It differs, therefore, from *genesis,* which represents a period comparable to gestation, in commonly representing a period comparable to that between a man's birth and his full maturity or prime of life ⟨the *rise* and fall of a great state⟩ ⟨this use of an old word in a slightly new sense took its *rise* out of the same milieu that led . . . to the addition of *lynch law*—*Mathews*⟩ ⟨the *rise* of large newspapers brought special problems, for their power of inflicting injury was enormous—*Plucknett*⟩ *Rise,* however, is sometimes more limited in its significance, often being referred to that part of a growth or development which precedes its full flowering ⟨the greater French novelists . . . chronicle the *rise,* the regime, and the decay of the upper bourgeoisie in France—*T. S. Eliot*⟩ **Initiation** may refer to the period of indoctrination (as in the mysteries, rites, and ordeals of a religion or state of life or in the performance of one's duties or functions); usually this indoctrination is by instructions which follow a system or it may be the unconscious result of many influences, but in any event it is felt as the beginning of a new period or state characterized by maturity fully attained ⟨that universal preoccupation among men everywhere with *initiation,* that mysterious male rebirth of the youth into full membership in the society of men—*La Barre*⟩ ⟨such a love is the *initiation* into the higher life, the spring at once of virtue, of philosophy, and of religion—*Dickin-*

---

A colon (:) separates groups of words discriminated. An asterisk (*) indicates place of treatment of each group.

*son*⟩ But often *initiation* loses this clear suggestion of attained maturity and is then essentially interchangeable with *beginning* ⟨resolutely opposed the *initiation* and development of the researches that lead to the thermonuclear bomb—*Times Lit. Sup.*⟩ ⟨the platform . . . called for civic reform . . . and for the *initiation* of the city-manager form of government—*Current Biog.*⟩
*Ana* *origin, source, inception, root: rise, derivation, emanation (see corresponding verbs at SPRING): emergence, appearance (see corresponding verbs at APPEAR)
*Con* termination, ending, *end: conclusion, completion, closing (see corresponding verbs at CLOSE)
**begrime** grime, smirch, besmirch, dirty, sully, *soil, foul, befoul, tarnish
*Ana* *spot, spatter, sprinkle
**begrudge** *covet, envy, grudge
**beguile** 1 delude, *deceive, mislead, betray, double-cross
*Ana* *dupe, gull, befool, trick, hoax, hoodwink, bamboozle: cajole, wheedle, blandish, *coax: *cheat, cozen: *lure, entice, seduce
2 *while, wile, beguile, fleet
*Ana* divert, *amuse, entertain: *comfort, solace: *speed, hasten, hurry
**behave** 1 Behave, conduct, comport, demean, deport, acquit, quit are comparable when they mean to act or to cause or allow (oneself) to act in a specified way or in a way that evokes comment. **Behave** denotes the performing of various actions or the saying of various things in the manner indicated by modifiers ⟨one must keep one's contracts, and *behave* as persons of honor and breeding should behave—*Rose Macaulay*⟩ ⟨you will bitterly reproach him in your own heart, and seriously think that he has *behaved* very badly to you—*Wilde*⟩ Used without modifiers, it indicates action and conduct adjudged proper and seemly; in this use it is common in relation to children and adolescents ⟨the average parent is likely to say that the child *behaves* if the child conforms to what the parent thinks is right—*Fishbein*⟩ **Conduct** often applies to actions showing direction or control of one's actions or bearing with command, will, knowledge, and resolution ⟨he *conducted* himself with patience and tact, endeavoring to enforce the laws and to check any revolutionary moves—*W. E. Stevens*⟩ **Comport**, in this sense always reflexive, is somewhat more formal than *behave* and *conduct* but usually lacks any other special suggestion though it sometimes may convey the notion of conformance to the expected (as of one's class) or suitable (as to one's position) ⟨the missionaries . . . *comported* themselves in a way that did not rouse general antagonism or they could have been easily ousted—*Spicer*⟩ ⟨a man is judged now by how well he *comports* himself in the face of danger—*Aldridge*⟩ ⟨after having seen him thus publicly *comport* himself, but one course was open to me—to cut his acquaintance—*Thackeray*⟩ In this sense **demean** and **deport** are close synonyms for *comport;* the former is becoming rare ⟨it shall be my earnest endeavor to *demean* myself with grateful respect towards her—*Austen*⟩ The latter may suggest deportment according to a code ⟨Dido and Aeneas, in the *Roman d'Eneas, deport* themselves in accordance with the strictest canons of courtly love—*Lowes*⟩ **Acquit** and **quit,** the latter archaic, are always used reflexively in this sense; they are likely to apply to action deserving praise or meeting expectations ⟨I trust we *acquit* ourselves worthily as custodians of this sacred mystery—*Wylie*⟩ ⟨he then *acquitted* himself well as a hardworking and level-headed chairman of the judiciary committee of the House—*Pearson*⟩ ⟨the endless heroes of life and death who still bravely meet their separate

hours . . . and *quit* themselves like men—*Yale Review*⟩ ⟨a border action in which the Dogra companies of the Loodhiana Sikhs had *acquitted* themselves well—*Kipling*⟩
*Ana* bear, *carry: manage, control, direct (see CONDUCT)
*Ant* misbehave
2 *act, react, operate, work, function
**behavior, conduct, deportment** are comparable when denoting a person's actions in general or on a particular occasion, so far as they serve as a basis of another's judgment of one's qualities (as character, temperament, mood, manners, or morals). **Behavior** may be used in reference to a human being regardless of status (as in age, development, or social standing), for it need not imply consciousness of what one is doing. *Behavior* may be thought of as instinctive or as voluntary and, hence, as either a spontaneous expression of personality or character or as the result of training or breeding ⟨the captain's *behavior* to his wife and to his wife's father . . . was as if they had been a pair of not very congenial passengers—*Conrad*⟩ ⟨courageous *behavior* is easier for a man who fails to apprehend dangers—*Russell*⟩ ⟨grandfather had been hounded out of his congregation because he couldn't hold her to their standards of *behavior* for a minister's wife—*Mary Austin*⟩ Since *behavior* is increasingly used in the various sciences in reference to animals and even substances, the term as referred to human beings tends in present usage to become more sharply differentiated from **conduct** than in the past. The latter term consistently carries a hint of moral responsibility and is less likely to confuse or mislead than *behavior* when this thought is prominent; thus, one dismisses a servant because of his *conduct* (better than *behavior* because it implies violation of principles) ⟨no animal's *behavior* is controlled by moral principles. Generally speaking, they do not rise from *behavior* to *conduct*—*Clarke*⟩ **Deportment** (see also BEARING) is often used of behavior as taught or as the result of discipline; its strongest implication is that of degree of conformity to the accepted code of good manners or the conventions governing one's relations to one's fellows, one's superiors, or one's inferiors ⟨children held up as models of *deportment*⟩ ⟨his old-fashioned *deportment* marked him out from others⟩
*Ana* demeanor, mien, deportment, *bearing: *action, act, deed
**behest** *n* bidding, dictate, injunction, *command, order, mandate
*Ana* precept, rule, *law: request, solicitation (see corresponding verbs at ASK)
**behind** *after
*Ant* ahead
**behindhand** *tardy, late, overdue
*Ana* dilatory, laggard, *slow: delayed, retarded, detained (see DELAY *vb*)
*Ant* beforehand —*Con* *early, soon, betimes: punctual (see CAREFUL): *quick, prompt
**behold** *see, view, survey, observe, descry, espy, notice, perceive, discern, remark, note, contemplate
*Ana* watch, look, *see: regard, *consider
**beholder** onlooker, looker-on, observer, witness, eyewitness, *spectator, bystander, kibitzer
**being** 1 *existence, actuality
*Ana* personality, individuality, character (see DISPOSITION)
*Ant* becoming: nonbeing
2 *entity, creature, individual, person
*Ana* *thing, object, article: *idea, concept, thought
**belabor** *beat, pound, pummel, thrash, buffet, baste
*Ana* *strike, hit, smite, slug, clout, swat, punch, box, cuff, slap

*Ana* analogous words    *Ant* antonyms    *Con* contrasted words    See also explanatory notes facing page 1

**belch** *vb* Belch, burp, vomit, disgorge, regurgitate, spew, throw up are comparable when they mean to eject matter (as food or gas) from the stomach by way of the mouth or, in extended use, from a containing cavity by way of an opening. Belch denotes the noisy voiding of gas from the stomach and may be extended to something ejected in volume and often with noise (as smoke and fire from a cannon or a volcano) ⟨there stood a hill not far, whose grisly top *belched* fire and rolling smoke—*Milton*⟩ ⟨the war-fiend shrieks and *belches* out his fury—*Capern*⟩ **Burp** in its basic sense in interchangeable with *belch* ⟨mopping his face solemnly with his cologne-scented handkerchief, and *burping* surreptitiously under it—*Mencken*⟩ but in extended use is much less forceful and usually refers to something sounding like a human belch ⟨the engine *burped* and ran out of gas—*Road and Track*⟩ **Vomit** is the usual word for the ejection through the mouth of what has been eaten or swallowed; ordinarily it implies nausea, but it may suggest a previous gorging or surfeiting or the use of an emetic ⟨and the Lord spake unto the fish, and it *vomited* out Jonah upon the dry land—*Jonah* 2:10⟩ It is often used to suggest a forcible rejection or an emission or a discharge of contents ⟨that huge black-mouthed sewer, *vomiting* its pestilential riches across the mud—*Kingsley*⟩ **Disgorge**, though close to *vomit*, more specifically implies an ejection of something swallowed, in essentially its original state ⟨Jonah was *disgorged* by the whale after three days and three nights⟩ Especially in extended use it may suggest an ejection or yielding up (as of something held or secreted) that is induced by force or pressure from without ⟨make the French generals *disgorge* the church plate which they have stolen—*Wellington*⟩ Basically **regurgitate** implies a flowing or gushing back, typically of food from the stomach to the esophagus or mouth ⟨cattle *regurgitate* small cuds of herbage for further chewing⟩ In extended use *regurgitate* may reflect quite neutrally its basic meaning ⟨"Mind you," he said *regurgitating* his article slowly phrase by phrase, "the subject doesn't make the work of art"—*Huxley*⟩ but more often it carries some suggestion of the unpleasantness of the physiological phenomenon ⟨Henry was incapable of reversing himself or of *regurgitating* Cromwell's wealth—*Hackett*⟩ ⟨read greedily and without abatement, and *regurgitated* his formal culture in the same feverish spasms—*Gurko*⟩ **Spew** is rare in modern usage as a synonym for *vomit* but has extended use as connoting a pouring forth in a stream that cannot be restrained or, sometimes, a spurting or spitting forth ⟨the steer . . . dying *spews* a flood of foamy madness, mixed with clotted blood—*Dryden*⟩ It also may imply specifically a pouring forth of something offensive (as abusive or foul language) ⟨Thersites *spews* over everything that we had deemed high and sacred, his foul . . . insults—*Dowden*⟩ Basically **throw up** is closely equivalent to *vomit,* though it may stress the matter ejected rather than the physiological process. In extended use it is distinctly less vigorous than *vomit* and usually implies no more than a producing or bringing forth of something ⟨all the voluminous information *thrown up* by successive . . . investigations—*Bemis*⟩
*Ana* *eject, expel

**beleaguer** *besiege, invest, blockade
*Ana* *surround, environ, encircle, encompass, hem, gird: *enclose, envelop: harass, pester, *worry, annoy

**belie** *misrepresent, falsify, garble
*Ana* contradict, contravene, negative (see DENY): controvert, *disprove
*Ant* attest —*Con* *reveal, discover, disclose: *indicate, bespeak, betoken

**belief** 1 Belief, faith, credence, credit are comparable when they mean the act of one who assents intellectually to something proposed or offered for acceptance as true or the state of mind of one who so assents. Belief is less restricted in its application than the other terms, for it may or may not imply certitude or certainty in the one who assents; it may even suggest nothing more than his mere mental acceptance ⟨his conclusions are beyond *belief*⟩ ⟨the theory merits *belief*⟩ ⟨nothing could shake his *belief* in the Bible as the word of God⟩ ⟨hope is the *belief*, more or less strong, that joy will come—*Sydney Smith*⟩ ⟨*belief* consists in accepting the affirmations of the soul; unbelief, in denying them—*Emerson*⟩ Faith implies full assent of the mind and therefore certitude, but it adds to this a strong implication of complete trust or confidence in the source (as the divinity, the institution, or the person) that proposes something or offers itself for belief and confidence. Consequently, although *belief* may represent the mind's act or state when something is assented to, regardless of whether it is or is not fully supported by evidence, *faith* characteristically represents the mind's act or state only when something is assented to on grounds other than merely those of the evidence of one's senses or of conclusions entirely supported by reason ⟨*faith* is the substance of things hoped for, the evidence of things not seen—*Heb* 11:1⟩ ⟨to believe only possibilities is not *faith,* but mere philosophy —*Browne*⟩ ⟨such tales, whether false or true, were heard by our ancestors with eagerness and *faith—Macaulay*⟩ *Faith* often carries a strong suggestion of credulity or overreadiness to accept authority ⟨he takes everything on *faith*⟩ **Credence** stresses mere intellectual assent without implying weak or strong grounds for belief and without suggesting credulity or its absence. Consequently it is seldom used in reference to religious or philosophical doctrines and is commonly employed in reference to reports, rumors, and opinions ⟨there is no superstition too absurd to find *credence* in modern England—*Inge*⟩ ⟨we are not now concerned with the finality or extent of truth in this judgment. The point is that it gained a widespread *credence* among the cultured class in Europe—*Day Lewis*⟩ **Credit** (see also INFLUENCE) carries a weaker implication than any of the preceding words of certitude or of acceptance as a result of conviction; often it specifically suggests as its ground a reputation for truth in the person who offers something for acceptance ⟨anything he will tell you about the circumstances is entitled to *credit*⟩ ⟨full faith and *credit* shall be given in each State to the public acts, records, and judicial proceedings of every other State—*U.S. Constitution*⟩
*Ana* certitude, assurance, *certainty, conviction: assenting *or* assent, acquiescing *or* acquiescence (see corresponding verbs at ASSENT)
*Ant* unbelief, disbelief —*Con* incredulity (see UNBELIEF): *uncertainty, doubt, mistrust
2 conviction, persuasion, view, *opinion, sentiment
*Ana* *doctrine, dogma, tenet: *principle, fundamental: conclusion, judgment (see under INFER)

**believable** credible, *plausible, colorable, specious
*Ana* *probable, possible, likely
*Ant* unbelievable —*Con* fabulous, mythical (see FICTITIOUS): *doubtful, dubious, questionable

**belittle** depreciate, disparage, derogate, detract, minimize, *decry
*Ana* underestimate, undervalue, underrate (see base words at ESTIMATE): diminish, reduce, lessen, *decrease
*Ant* aggrandize, magnify —*Con* *exalt: heighten, *intensify, enhance, aggravate: vaunt, gasconade, brag, *boast, crow

A colon (:) separates groups of words discriminated. An asterisk (*) indicates place of treatment of each group.

**bellicose** *belligerent, pugnacious, combative, contentious, quarrelsome
*Ana* militant, *aggressive, assertive: antagonizing *or* antagonistic, combating *or* combative (see corresponding verbs at RESIST): fighting, warring, battling, contending (see CONTEND): rebellious, factious, seditious, mutinous (see INSUBORDINATE)
*Ant* pacific: amicable —*Con* peaceful, pacifist, peaceable (see PACIFIC)
**belligerent** *adj* Belligerent, bellicose, pugnacious, combative, quarrelsome, contentious mean having or taking an aggressive or fighting attitude. **Belligerent** usually implies actual engagement in hostilities 〈the *belligerent* powers in the World War〉 〈define a nation's status as not neutral yet not *belligerent*〉 When applied to such things as tones, speeches, or gestures, the term implies an actively hostile mood or warlike temper 〈a *belligerent* reply to a diplomatic note〉 **Bellicose** applies usually to a state of mind or temper; it suggests a desire or readiness to fight or sometimes a disposition to stir up a fight 〈a *bellicose* tribe〉 〈an intoxicated man in a *bellicose* mood〉 〈an editorial in a *bellicose* vein〉 **Pugnacious** and **combative** differ from *bellicose* (which is sometimes given an ironic or mock-heroic turn) in applying more commonly to disposition or character; they need not, however, convey the impression of pettiness or ill nature or of readiness to fight without genuine cause, so frequently implied in **quarrelsome** 〈the Scotch are certainly a most *pugnacious* people; their whole history proves it—*Borrow*〉 〈combat in the field of sports . . . [is] generally approved. The *combative* impulses in human nature may find an expression—*Cohen*〉 〈soon every father bird and mother grew *quarrelsome,* and pecked each other—*Cowper*〉 〈on the days they worked they were good-natured and cheerful . . . on our idle days they were mutinous and *quarrelsome*—*Franklin*〉 **Contentious** frequently suggests perversity of temper and wearisome persistence in dispute 〈a very kind woman, though saying what she liked about her neighbors, and *contentious* toward all antireformers—*Canby*〉
*Ana* hostile, antagonistic (see corresponding nouns at ENMITY): fighting, warring, battling, contending (see CONTEND): warlike, *martial
*Ant* friendly —*Con* neighborly, *amicable: *neutral, indifferent
**bellow** *vb* *roar, bluster, bawl, vociferate, clamor, howl, ululate
*Ana* yell, *shout, scream, shriek: bay, *bark, yelp: *cry, wail, keen
**belly** *abdomen, stomach, paunch, gut
**belong** pertain, appertain, relate, apply, *bear
**belongings** *possessions, effects, means, resources, assets
**below, under, beneath, underneath** mean in a lower position relatively to some other object or place. **Below** (opposed to *above*) applies to something which is anywhere in a lower plane than the object of reference; **under** (opposed to *over*) to something which is below in a relatively vertical line, and it may imply actual covering 〈*below* sea level〉 〈the valley far *below* us〉 〈*under* a tree〉 〈*under* the bed〉 〈hide one's light *under* a bushel〉 〈the Whirlpool Rapids are *below,* and the Cave of the Winds is *under* Niagara Falls〉 〈the whole visible landscape is *below,* but only a small portion of it *under,* an observer in a balloon〉 **Beneath** is an equivalent of both *below* and *under* 〈heaven above, or . . . the earth *beneath*—*Exod* 20:4〉 〈*beneath* the spreading tree—*Goldsmith*〉 **Underneath** is often employed in place of *under* or *beneath*. It is, however, the preferred term when there is the intent to imply complete or nearly complete concealment 〈mines

underneath the city〉 〈garments worn *underneath* a dress〉
In their extended senses *below* and *under* agree in expressing inferiority but differ (like *above* and *over*) in the immediacy of the relation expressed; thus, one officer may be *below* another in rank without being *under* him in immediate subordination. Similarly, with reference to deficiency, *below* is commonly used in general, *under* in more specific, relations 〈*below* the accepted standard〉 〈*below* normal temperatures〉 〈*under* six years of age〉 *Beneath* frequently suggests social, moral, or general inferiority 〈married *beneath* herself〉 〈criticism *beneath* his notice〉 〈*beneath* contempt〉 *Underneath* suggests, not inferiority, but something underlying and not indicated clearly by what is outwardly manifest 〈*underneath* his ingratiating manner one felt a sinister intention〉 〈there is something *underneath* this announcement, I am sure〉
*Ant* above —*Con* over (see ABOVE)
**belt** zone, *area, tract, region
**bemoan** bewail, lament, *deplore
*Ana* *grieve, mourn, sorrow
*Ant* exult
**bemuse** *daze, stun, stupefy, benumb, paralyze, petrify
*Ana* *confuse, muddle, addle, fuddle, befuddle
*Con* *illuminate, enlighten: arouse, rouse, *stir, awaken: excite, stimulate, *provoke
**bend** *vb* *curve, twist
*Ana* contort, *deform: deflect, divert (see TURN)
*Ant* straighten
**beneath** underneath, under, *below
*Ant* above, over
**benefaction** *donation, contribution, alms
*Ana* *gift, present, largess, boon: endowment (see corresponding verb at DOWER): grant, subvention (see APPROPRIATION): *charity, philanthropy
**beneficent** *benevolent
*Ana* *charitable, humanitarian, philanthropic, eleemosynary, altruistic: munificent, bountiful, bounteous, openhanded, generous (see LIBERAL)
*Ant* maleficent
**beneficial, advantageous, profitable** are applied to what brings good or gain. **Beneficial** refers to what promotes health or well-being; **advantageous,** to what more directly conduces to relative superiority or subserves a desirable end; **profitable,** to what yields useful or lucrative returns 〈a climate *beneficial* to rheumatism〉 〈measures . . . *beneficial* to the kingdom—*J. R. Green*〉 〈the enemy were in an *advantageous* position on the hill〉 〈you see . . . how swift and *advantageous* a harbinger it [a good reputation] is, wherever one goes—*Chesterfield*〉 〈a *profitable* study〉 〈*profitable* investments〉
*Ana* salutary, *healthful, wholesome: *favorable, benign, propitious
*Ant* harmful: detrimental —*Con* *pernicious, deleterious, baneful, noxious
**benefit** *vb* Benefit, profit, avail mean to do good or to be of advantage to someone. **Benefit** usually implies personal betterment or improvement (as of one's physical, intellectual, moral, or spiritual condition), but it may suggest enrichment or a furtherance of one's ends 〈a summer at the seashore *benefits* the entire family〉 〈we all *benefit* greatly by lighthouses, even those of us who have never seen the sea and never expect to—*Shaw*〉 〈the expansion of the city's industries *benefits* everyone indirectly〉 **Profit** carries a strong implication of gain, especially material gain. It is therefore preferred to *benefit* when an increase or yield, as opposed to a decrease or loss, in one's store (as of wealth, power, or knowledge) is to be suggested; thus, he always *profits* (not *benefits*, unless one wishes to imply a salutary effect) by the misfortunes of

*Ana* analogous words    *Ant* antonyms    *Con* contrasted words    See also explanatory notes facing page 1

others; no one *benefits* from a war except those who seek to *profit* by it ⟨it will *profit* you as a congressman to pay more attention to your constituency's wishes⟩ ⟨what is a man *profited,* if he shall gain the whole world, and lose his own soul?—*Mt* 16:26⟩ ⟨do we not lose something . . . when we hurry by and disregard what does not seem to *profit* our own existence?—*Binyon*⟩ **Avail,** which has an archaic and literary flavor that makes it rare in speech except in historical novels or in sermons or orations, stresses efficacy ⟨ah wretched shepherd, what *avails* thy art, to cure thy lambs, but not to heal thy heart!—*Pope*⟩ ⟨say not the struggle nought *availeth,* the labor and the wounds are vain—*Clough*⟩
*Ana* better, *improve, ameliorate: *help, assist, aid
*Ant* harm —*Con* *injure, hurt, damage, impair
**benevolent** 1 *charitable, philanthropic, eleemosynary, humanitarian, humane, altruistic
*Ana* benign, benignant, kindly, *kind: generous, *liberal, bountiful, bounteous, openhanded: obliging, complaisant, *amiable
*Ant* malevolent —*Con* *malicious, malignant, malign, spiteful: *stingy, close, miserly
2 **Benevolent, beneficent** are closely related rather than strictly synonymous terms. **Benevolent,** which applies primarily to persons, means kindly in feelings and disposed to be generous or charitable, thereby emphasizing the will to do good, while **beneficent,** which applies to persons and things, means doing or effecting good, thereby emphasizing the fact of doing good. Consequently *benevolent* is not only applied to a person, a group, or an institution, but to matters (as looks, attitudes, intentions, manners, and tones) that suggest a kindly disposition or a wish to help ⟨beloved old man! *benevolent* as wise—*Pope*⟩ ⟨the mild precepts of a *benevolent* religion—*John Moore*⟩ ⟨the heart *benevolent* and kind the most resembles God—*Burns*⟩ *Benevolent* may sometimes take on a new connotation either seriously or ironically and suggest the attitude of a person on the outside who is little more than a well-wisher ⟨the mission of the United States is one of *benevolent* assimilation, substituting the mild sway of justice and right for arbitrary rule—*McKinley*⟩ ⟨few persistent novelists, I suppose, have ever received in one lifetime so generous a measure of *benevolent* neglect—*Glasgow*⟩ *Beneficent* heightens the implication of doing good. It is therefore preferred when the emphasis is upon accomplishment rather than upon intention ⟨a *beneficent* economic policy⟩ ⟨a *beneficent* sovereign⟩ ⟨the stars were no longer regarded as malignant or *beneficent* powers —*L. P. Smith*⟩ ⟨certain influences appear, specifically that of Lipchitz, but these are *beneficent,* and they suggest no feeling of constraint in the artist—*Coates*⟩ Unlike *benevolent, beneficent* may be used without any hint of volition and is then applicable to the benefits produced by things ⟨overflows its banks and leaves *beneficent* layers of fertile soil—*Mumford*⟩ ⟨the *beneficent* Gulf stream prevents things from really getting cold—*Joseph*⟩
*Ana, Ant, Con* see those at BENEVOLENT 1
**benign** 1 benignant, kindly, *kind
*Ana* *gracious, genial, cordial, affable: sympathetic, *tender, compassionate: *suave, urbane, bland
*Ant* malign —*Con* malignant, malevolent, *malicious, spiteful: *caustic, acrid, mordant
2 auspicious, *favorable, propitious
*Ana* fortunate, happy, providential, *lucky: gentle, mild (see SOFT): benevolent, humane, *charitable: merciful, clement, *forbearing
*Ant* malign —*Con* *sinister, baleful, malefic, maleficent: threatening, menacing (see THREATEN)
**benignant** benign, *kind, kindly

*Ana* benevolent, humane, *charitable, humanitarian, philanthropic, eleemosynary: *gracious, affable: compassionate, *tender, sympathetic
*Ant* malignant —*Con* malevolent, spiteful, *malicious: merciless, unrelenting, implacable, relentless, *grim
**bent** *n* turn, talent, aptitude, knack, *gift, faculty, genius
*Ana* propensity, penchant, *leaning, proclivity, flair: *predilection, bias, prepossession, prejudice, partiality: capacity, *ability, capability
*Con* disinclination, indisposition, reluctance (see corresponding adjectives at DISINCLINED): aversion, *antipathy
**benumb** *daze, stun, bemuse, stupefy, paralyze, petrify
*Ana* chill, freeze (see corresponding adjectives at COLD): congeal (see COAGULATE): dumbfound, confound, nonplus, bewilder (see PUZZLE)
*Con* rouse, arouse, *stir, rally: kindle, fire (see LIGHT)
**bequeath** *will, devise, leave, legate
*Ana* *give, present, bestow: *distribute, dispense
**berate** rate, tongue-lash, upbraid, jaw, bawl, chew out, *scold, wig, rail, revile, vituperate
*Ana* censure, denounce, condemn, reprehend, reprobate, *criticize: rebuke, reprimand, reproach, *reprove, chide
**berth** 1 *room, play, elbowroom, leeway, margin, clearance
2 *wharf, dock, pier, quay, slip, jetty, levee
**beseech** entreat, implore, supplicate, *beg, importune, adjure
*Ana* pray, petition, sue, plead, appeal (see under PRAYER)
**beset** overrun, *infest
*Ana* *worry, annoy, harass, harry, pester, plague: assail, *attack, assault
**beside, besides** are occasionally interchangeable. More often **beside** is employed as a preposition in a local sense, meaning by the side of ⟨he stood *beside* her⟩ ⟨the house *beside* the river⟩ On the other hand, **besides** has almost entirely replaced *beside* as a preposition in the sense of other than ⟨a man knowing little *besides* the basic skills of his trade⟩ and as a preposition in the sense of in addition to ⟨he received other gifts *besides* the watch⟩ and as an adverb in the senses of otherwise and moreover (see ALSO).
**besides** *adv* moreover, furthermore, *also, too, likewise
**besides** *adv & prep* *beside
**besiege, beleaguer, invest, blockade** mean to surround an enemy in a fortified or strong position so as to prevent ingress or egress. **Besiege** implies a sitting down before the entrances to a fortified place (as a castle or a walled town), and it may be used to denote the operation of attackers of a strongly fortified or naturally protected position of the enemy and usually implies the surrounding of it and frequent assaults upon it in order to break down the resistance of the enemy ⟨Troy was *besieged* by Greek armies for ten years⟩ **Beleaguer** does not materially differ from *besiege* in meaning, although it springs from a different type of warfare, one where fortifications are less the objects of attack than open cities or occupied positions. *Beleaguer* suggests the presence of camps and therefore of great numbers of troops; often it carries the connotations of besetting or harassing rather than of confining or imprisoning ⟨a *beleaguered* garrison⟩ ⟨but Richelieu's general, Harcourt, besieged the town from the outside, himself surrounded and *beleaguered* by the Spanish governor of Milan—*Belloc*⟩ ⟨as in a *beleaguered* city there spread circumstantial rumors of happenings in the world outside—*Eddington*⟩ In extended use *besiege* stresses a blocking up ⟨they will *besiege* your doors⟩ or an assailing with importunities ⟨I was *besieged* by four small Bedouin children who had been whimpering for money as I read the papers—*Liebling*⟩ and *beleaguer* emphasizes a pestering or annoying ⟨the girl

---

A colon (:) separates groups of words discriminated. An asterisk (*) indicates place of treatment of each group.

is ... *beleaguering* ... a worthy gentleman—*Richardson*⟩ ⟨the family is *beleaguered* by peddlers⟩ **Invest** comes very close to *besiege,* but it does not, by comparison, carry as strong an implication of strength or of persistence in attack. In many cases it implies the use of men and weapons to prevent ingress or egress, but it carries little suggestion of frequent assaults upon the position ⟨Astorga is *invested,* but has not been vigorously attacked—*Wellington*⟩ ⟨Charleston was never besieged nor was any serious effort made ... to *invest* it on the land side—*Spaulding*⟩ **Blockade** usually stresses a closing of all sea-lanes to those who wish to enter or leave hostile territory. The term usually implies the use of ships or mines to attain this end, but if the attacking country is sufficiently strong, it may imply prohibition of neutral or enemy vessels entering or leaving and efforts to seize or detain those that disobey. The object of blockading is usually to starve the enemy or to prevent the entrance of essential supplies ⟨in any showdown the West's ultimate power to *blockade* might make the Russians think twice—*Time*⟩
*Ana* *enclose, envelop, pen: *surround, environ, encircle, encompass, hem: beset (see INFEST): assail, *attack, assault

**besmirch** smirch, dirty, sully, *soil, foul, befoul, grime, begrime, tarnish
*Ana* *spot, spatter, sprinkle
*Ant* cleanse

**besotted** infatuated, *fond, insensate
*Ana* fatuous, asinine, foolish, silly, *simple: *drunk, drunken, intoxicated, inebriated: *stupid, slow, dull, dense, crass
*Con* sensible, sane, *wise, judicious, prudent: *rational, reasonable: sober, *serious, earnest

**bespangle** spangle, *spot, spatter, sprinkle, mottle, fleck, stipple, marble, speckle
*Ana* *illuminate, illumine, lighten, light: glow, *blaze, flame: *flash, gleam, sparkle, scintillate, twinkle

**bespangled** spangled, spotted, spattered, sprinkled, mottled, flecked, stippled, marbled, speckled (see under SPOT *vb*)
*Ana* *bright, brilliant, radiant, luminous: illuminated, illumined, lighted (see ILLUMINATE)

**bespeak** betoken, attest, *indicate, argue, prove
*Ana* manifest, evidence, *show, evince, demonstrate: imply, hint, *suggest

**bestial** brutish, brute, *brutal, feral, beastly
*Ana* debased, depraved, corrupted *or* corrupt (see under DEBASE): degenerate, *vicious: degraded (see ABASE): sensual, fleshly, *carnal

**bestow** confer, present, donate, *give, afford
*Ana* *distribute, dispense, divide: *grant, award

**bet** *n* Bet, wager, stake, pot, ante denote in common something of value, usually money, risked in the confidence or hope that something is true or will turn out in a certain way, something else of value being risked by at least one other party in support of an opposing confidence or hope. **Bet** and **wager** are used with little distinction of meaning either of what is risked or of the act of risking it. **Stake** implies money or valuables bet and actually produced and entrusted to a neutral party (stakeholder) or placed in the pot in a card game. By extension a stake is anything material or nonmaterial that one stands in jeopardy of losing ⟨and will probably always have the largest commercial *stake* in the African continent—*Livingstone*⟩ ⟨with my most affectionate wishes for Dr. Johnson's recovery, in which his friends ... have so deep a *stake*—*Dick*⟩ A **pot** is an aggregate of the bets made by all the bettors or players especially in poker ⟨won several big *pots* in successive deals⟩ An **ante** typically is a stake which each player in a poker game who

wishes to continue a particular hand puts up after he has seen his original five cards but before he draws other cards, but in some games of stud or draw poker and in blackjack the ante is a compulsory stake put up by each player before the cards are seen. By extension an ante is a share or amount which must be put up, usually as a price or as a prelude to a joint venture ⟨considerations that tend to raise the *ante* so as to discourage all but the most efficient producers—*Amer. Fabrics*⟩ ⟨the *ante* of these shareholders and other private sources of financing the steel expansion will come to about 1.7 billion dollars—*Atlantic*⟩

**bête noire** *abomination, bugbear, anathema

**bethink** recollect, remind, *remember, recall, reminisce, mind

**betide** befall, *happen, chance, occur, transpire

**betimes** *early, soon, beforehand
*Ant* unseasonably, inopportunely

**betoken** bespeak, attest, *indicate, argue, prove
*Ana* presage, augur, portend, forebode (see FORETELL): import, signify, denote, *mean: evidence, manifest, *show, evince, demonstrate

**betray** 1 mislead, delude, *deceive, beguile, double-cross
*Ana* trap, entrap, snare, ensnare (see CATCH): *dupe, trick, befool, hoodwink, gull
2 discover, *reveal, disclose, divulge, tell
*Ana* manifest, evidence, evince, *show, demonstrate: attest, betoken, bespeak, argue, *indicate
*Con* shield, guard, safeguard, protect, *defend

**better** *adj* Better, superior, preferable mean more worthy or more pleasing than another or others. **Better,** which often serves as the comparative of *good,* in this sense implies a quality or character in a person or thing that surpasses or exceeds that in the one or ones called good ⟨the theme is good, but I think you can write a *better* one⟩ ⟨he proposed a *better* scheme than any that had been discussed⟩ Often, however, *better* is used in comparison or contrast with something that can be described as bad ⟨give him time to show his *better* nature⟩ ⟨looking upon myself as no *better* than a dead man—*Steele*⟩ or with something that may be good, bad, or indifferent yet from the point of view of the speaker or writer is to be rejected as totally undesirable in comparison ⟨it is *better* for him that a millstone were hanged about his neck, and he were cast into the sea—*Mk 9:42*⟩ ⟨*better* to reign in Hell than serve in Heaven—*Milton*⟩ **Superior** in all its uses retains some feeling of its basic meaning, higher in physical position, which is now largely restricted to technical contexts in which it implies opposition to what is below (*inferior*); thus, the upper jaw or maxilla is sometimes distinguished as the *superior* maxilla from the lower jaw or mandible which is then designated the *inferior* maxilla. *Superior* often implies a scale (as of values or ranks) and emphasizes height (as of status, quality, or worth); thus, if a student is doing good work one might suggest that he could do *better* (as compared with his previous accomplishment) if he tried, and might hope that his added efforts would produce a truly *superior* result (as compared either with any relevant accomplishment or with a scale of possible accomplishments); one might like an author's new book *better* than his last but rate it *superior* to anything he had previously written ⟨a sergeant is *superior* to a corporal⟩ ⟨certain rights are *superior* to constitutions and to statute laws—*Lippincott*⟩ ⟨the *superior* durability of parchment—*Coulton*⟩ ⟨*superior* wisdom derived from experience—*Trewartha*⟩ **Preferable** implies a choice between two things or one thing and all others usually on the ground that the thing chosen is better by comparison or is superior in quality, status, or kind. But its chief emphasis is upon relative desirability, and the other implications may be greatly

obscured or lost upon occasion ⟨he finds a walk in the country *preferable* to reading a book⟩
*Ana* *choice, delicate, dainty: selected, culled, picked, preferred (see CHOOSE)
**better** *vb* *improve, ameliorate, help
*Ana* *correct, amend, reform, rectify, remedy, redress: enhance (see INTENSIFY)
*Ant* worsen —*Con* impair, mar, harm, damage, *injure: *debase, vitiate, corrupt
**between, among** are comparable when they take as object two or more persons or things and indicate their relation (as in position, in a distribution, or in participation). **Between** in its basic sense applies to only two objects ⟨*between* Scylla and Charybdis⟩ ⟨*between* two fires⟩ When this word is used of more than two objects, it brings them severally and individually into the relation expressed ⟨a treaty *between* three powers⟩ ⟨the three survivors had but one pair of shoes *between* them⟩ ⟨I hope that *between* public business, improving studies, and domestic pleasures, neither melancholy nor caprice will find any place for entrance—*Johnson*⟩ **Among** always implies more than two objects which it brings less definitely into the relation expressed ⟨*among* so many candidates one must find a good one⟩ ⟨*among* the survivors were two boys⟩ ⟨five barley loaves, and two small fishes: but what are they *among* so many?—*Jn 6:9*⟩
**bewail** lament, *deplore, bemoan
*Ana* sorrow, *grieve, mourn: wail, weep, *cry
*Ant* rejoice
**bewilder** mystify, perplex, distract, *puzzle, confound, nonplus, dumbfound
*Ana* *confuse, addle, fuddle, muddle: fluster, flurry, perturb, agitate, upset (see DISCOMPOSE): baffle, foil (see FRUSTRATE)
**bewitch** enchant, captivate, fascinate, charm, allure, *attract
*Ana* *thrill, electrify: delight, *please: infatuate, enamor (see corresponding adjectives at ENAMORED)
**bewitching** enchanting, captivating, fascinating, charming, alluring, attractive (see under ATTRACT)
**biannual, biennial, semiannual,** though not synonymous, are frequently confused. The chief source of confusion is **biannual,** which is used to mean either twice a year or every two years. If no clue to its meaning is given by the text, the reader will often be at a loss to determine the time represented. Because of this ambiguity there is a tendency to avoid *biannual* and use the other two terms to express the two meanings. **Biennial** unequivocally means existing for two years or happening every two years ⟨*biennial* plants⟩ ⟨a *biennial* convention⟩ ⟨a *biennial* reunion⟩. **Semiannual** is also unequivocal, since it means half-yearly, that is, twice a year ⟨a *semiannual* publication⟩ ⟨*semiannual* payments⟩
**bias** *n* prejudice, prepossession, partiality, *predilection
*Ana* slant, standpoint, *point of view, viewpoint, angle: *leaning, propensity: inclining *or* inclination, predisposition, disposition (see corresponding verbs at INCLINE)
*Con* fairness, justness, impartiality, dispassionateness (see corresponding adjectives at FAIR)
**bias** *vb* *incline, dispose, predispose
*Ana* sway, influence, *affect, impress
**bicker** squabble, spat, tiff, quarrel, wrangle, altercate (see under QUARREL *n*)
*Ana* *contend, fight, battle, war
**bickering** spat, tiff, squabble, *quarrel, wrangle, altercation
*Ana* *discord, contention, dissension, strife, conflict
**bid** *vb* 1 *command, order, enjoin, direct, instruct, charge
*Ana* *summon, summons, call, cite

*Ant* forbid —*Con* prohibit, enjoin, interdict, inhibit (see FORBID)
2 *invite, solicit, court, woo
*Ana* *ask, request
**bid** *n* tender, *overture, advance, approach
*Ana* offering *or* offer, proffering *or* proffer (see corresponding verbs at OFFER): *proposal, proposition: inviting *or* invitation, soliciting *or* solicitation (see corresponding verbs at INVITE)
**biddable** docile, amenable, tractable, *obedient
*Ana* *compliant, acquiescent: obliging, complaisant, good-natured, *amiable: submissive, *tame
*Ant* willful —*Con* intractable, refractory, recalcitrant, headstrong, ungovernable, *unruly: *obstinate, stubborn, stiff-necked, mulish
**bidding** behest, *command, order, injunction, mandate, dictate
*Ana* direction, instruction (see corresponding verbs at COMMAND): summoning *or* summons, calling *or* call, citing *or* citation (see corresponding verbs at SUMMON)
**biennial** *biannual, semiannual
**big** *large, great
*Ana* *grand, magnificent, imposing, grandiose, majestic, august: *huge, immense, enormous, gigantic, colossal
*Ant* little —*Con* *small, diminutive, wee, tiny, petite, minute, microscopic, miniature
**bigot** fanatic, *enthusiast, zealot
**bigoted** *illiberal, narrow-minded, narrow, intolerant, hidebound
*Con* tolerant, *forbearing, lenient: *liberal, progressive, advanced, radical
**bill** *n* Bill, beak, neb, nib denote the jaws of a bird together with their projecting horny covering. **Bill** is the general term and is used inclusively by ornithologists for such a structure; in popular usage, however, *bill* suggests a structure that is straight and often flattened or long and slender (as in the duck, swan, hummingbird, crane, heron, sandpiper, or snipe) or one that is short, stout, and conical (as in the cardinal bird or hawfinch). **Beak** is associated with striking or tearing and is the usual term for a structure, characteristic especially of birds of prey, in which the tip of the upper mandible has a sharp downward curvature and overhangs the lower mandible (as in the eagle, vulture, or hawk) ⟨although the kite soar with unbloodied *beak*—*Shak.*⟩ **Neb** and **nib** are equivalent to *bill* or *beak* chiefly in dialect or poetry but derive from this use their commoner extended sense of a jutting or pointed thing or part ⟨the *nib* of a pen⟩
**bill** *n* Bill, act, statute, law are frequently confused when used to designate a legislative measure. **Bill** is properly applied only to the draft of a measure submitted to a legislature for its acceptance or rejection. The other terms are properly applied only to bills which have been passed. In actual use they are practically identical. Strictly, however, a bill becomes an **act** when it is passed and duly signed by an executive officer; an act becomes a **statute** when it is legally effective and a part of the written law of the state; a statute is one kind of **law** (see LAW).
**billingsgate** scurrility, vituperation, *abuse, invective, obloquy
**bind** *tie
*Ana* *fasten, attach: *join, link, unite, connect
*Ant* unbind
**biography, life, memoir, autobiography, confessions** are comparable when they mean a more or less detailed account of the events and circumstances of a person's life. **Biography** is the technical, neutral term for this kind of writing or for an example of it; the term suggests neither length nor brevity of treatment, neither factuality nor in-

A colon (:) separates groups of words discriminated. An asterisk (*) indicates place of treatment of each group.

terpretation of facts, neither partisanship nor detachment, for it may be characterized by any of these qualities, but it does imply that the course of a career is covered at least in its main events ⟨the official *biography* . . . written by his son is still in print and easily available—*Nock*⟩ ⟨Lytton Strachey's *biography* of Queen Victoria restricts itself to the facts which develop his conception of her⟩ **Life** usually suggests a fuller and more intimate treatment than *biography;* a work so designated may, however, be written on a brief scale or be drawn out so that very little is escaped. *Life* is often used in place of *biography* when the author especially wishes to suggest a vivid or graphic or interpretive account or to imply the addition of firsthand material (as letters or a journal); the term is also often used in the combination "life and times" as the title for a biography placing the subject in the background of his period ⟨Boswell's *Life of Dr. Johnson*⟩ ⟨Ray Stannard Baker's *Life and Letters of Woodrow Wilson*⟩ ⟨*Life and Times of Jesus* by J. F. Clarke⟩ **Memoir** (or often the plural **memoirs**) refers to a biography written by one who has intimate knowledge of its details; although it does not necessarily imply that the subject of the biography is the writer, it very frequently does so. Also, *memoir* may suggest reminiscences of a whole or of part of a life; the term therefore carries no promise of completeness, or fullness, but it does connote a more personal approach than *biography* or, usually, than *life* ⟨Hallam Tennyson's biography of his father is called *Alfred, Lord Tennyson: A Memoir*⟩ ⟨its spirit is so devout as to make it almost more a *memoir* than a biography—*Nock*⟩ **Autobiography** refers to a biography of oneself typically written toward the end of one's life or at the completion of one's active career. *Autobiography* usually implies some distinction in the writer and a demand for or the desire to give information about the personalities and events of his time or about the background of the events in which he has played a part. The term is seldom used in the titles of books and is preferred as a designation of a type ⟨*My Life* is Havelock Ellis's *autobiography*⟩ ⟨what would we give for such an *autobiography* of Shakespeare—*Carlyle*⟩ **Confessions** as a type belong to the genre of autobiography. *Confessions* are usually written by a person who desires to avow fully the experiences of his life, both shameful and creditable. The motive of such a book is as varied as the books themselves; thus, to give extremes, the *Confessions* of St. Augustine were written for the glorification of God, who has brought him out of a life of sin; the *Confessions* of Rousseau were written to reveal truly and sincerely all his experiences without reference to the opinions of men ⟨De Quincey's *Confessions of an English Opium-Eater*⟩

**biologic** *n* *drug, simple, medicinal, pharmaceutical
**biotype** *habitat, range, station
**birthright** 1 *right, appanage, prerogative, privilege, perquisite
2 patrimony, *heritage, inheritance
**bisexual** *adj* Bisexual, hermaphroditic, hermaphrodite, **androgynous, epicene** are comparable when meaning combining male and female qualities. The first four of these terms may be used interchangeably to mean being structurally or functionally both male and female; they may apply to all kinds of living beings and may designate a normal or an abnormal state. **Bisexual** also is applied to human mental or behavioral qualities ⟨careers catastrophically broken by the vagaries of *bisexual* personality —*New Republic*⟩ and, more precisely, designates the individual who responds sexually to members of both sexes ⟨the ancient Greeks who were notoriously *bisexual* (women for breeding and boys for pleasure)—*Gerber*⟩ Such use need not imply abnormality ⟨the author accepts

the notion of the *bisexual* character of man—*Mullahy*⟩ **Hermaphroditic** and **hermaphrodite** when applied to human beings usually indicate primarily the presence of physical characteristics and especially of actual gonads of both sexes in the same individual and imply an abnormal state ⟨*hermaphroditic* children, where both ovaries and testes are present—*Newsweek*⟩ *Hermaphrodite* frequently or *hermaphroditic* occasionally has extended use in which it suggests the combination of two readily distinguishable and often more or less incongruous elements; thus, a *hermaphrodite* wagon is one made up of a two-wheeled cart with an extra pair of wheels and a rack added; *hermaphrodite* calipers have one caliper and one divider leg ⟨a young Königsberg architect, a Balt (that is to say a kind of *hermaphrodite* Russian and Prussian too)— *Clare Sheridan*⟩ ⟨everybody in every war, barring the *hermaphrodite* soldier who wears a uniform but doesn't fight, lives in a sort of hell—*Kenneth Roberts*⟩ **Androgynous** in reference to human beings or to qualities or characteristics rarely connotes abnormality but rather suggests a congruous and pleasing blending ⟨has the *androgynous* Greek beauty which suits a youth or a goddess equally well, combining the vigor of one sex with the grace of the other—*The Critic*⟩ ⟨if one is a man, still the woman part of the brain must have effect; and a woman must also have intercourse with the man in her. Coleridge perhaps meant this when he said that a great mind is *androgynous*—*Woolf*⟩ *Androgynous* is also the preferred term for use in respect to deities, their attributes or appearances ⟨a somewhat *androgynous* Apollo—*Grigson*⟩ ⟨the *androgynous* character of the Bodhisattva: masculine Avalokiteshvara, feminine Kwan Yin—*Joseph Campbell*⟩ Unlike the preceding terms, **epicene** has no technical application to physical or functional status; however, in its often allusive reference to sex in characterizing human beings, their attributes, or the products of their being it may approach the other terms in meaning ⟨decapitated by a hero disguised as a woman . . . his brothers suspect the *epicene* wife because of her masculine arms—*Lowie*⟩ More often *epicene* suggests deficient sexuality and may imply intersexuality, effeminacy, or sexlessness ⟨the hearty sportsman who is really *epicene* beneath his tweeds—*Gibbs*⟩ ⟨if only all this messy business of sex could be done away with and we could all remain . . . happy, *epicene* Peter Pans—*Dwight Macdonald*⟩ In some contexts *epicene* loses all direct reference to sex and suggests rather the weakness inherent in deficiency which may be expressed on the one hand in extreme delicacy ⟨something dreamy, ambiguous, almost *epicene*—*Norman Douglas*⟩ or on the other in utter decadence ⟨the glass of fashion and the mold of form, so dainty a figure, indeed, that he turned Mark Twain's stomach and appears as an *epicene* clown in the American's robust story—*G. W. Johnson*⟩

**bit** *particle, mite, smidgen, whit, atom, iota, jot, tittle
*Ana* piece, fragment, detail, fraction, *part, portion
**bite, gnaw, champ, gnash** are comparable when they mean to attack with or as if with the teeth. **Bite** fundamentally implies a getting of the teeth, especially the front teeth, into something so as to grip, pierce, or tear off ⟨*bite* an apple deeply⟩ ⟨*bite* into a cookie⟩ ⟨*bite* off a piece of molasses candy⟩ Sometimes *bite* denotes to wound by biting ⟨the dog has *bitten* a boy⟩ ⟨unable to fight with hands or feet, he savagely *bit* his antagonist⟩ In extended use *bite* implies unusual power of penetration or power of cutting into something so that it stings or pricks, or gives support to a good grip or hold ⟨scissors that snip sheet steel and *bite* off heavy bars—*Shaw*⟩ ⟨*bite* an etching plate with acid⟩ ⟨saws . . . as they . . . *bite* the

*Ana* analogous words     *Ant* antonyms     *Con* contrasted words     See also explanatory notes facing page 1

wood—*Frost*⟩ ⟨heel nails *bit* on the frozen ruts—*Hemingway*⟩ ⟨a summer *bitten* into Joan's memory—*H. G. Wells*⟩ **Gnaw,** on the other hand, implies an effort to bite something hard or tough; it implies repeated action and a slow wearing away, sometimes stressing one in preference to the other ⟨the dog *gnaws* a bone⟩ ⟨rats have *gnawed* the rope into shreds⟩ ⟨*gnaw* at a crust of bread⟩ ⟨life goes on forever like the *gnawing* of a mouse—*Millay*⟩ Therefore *gnaw* is used of what eats, frets, or corrodes something that is strong, resistant, or not easily affected ⟨old pains keep on *gnawing* at your heart—*Conrad*⟩ ⟨they were both . . . *gnawed* with anxiety—*D. H. Lawrence*⟩ **Champ** implies vigorous and noisy action of the teeth and jaws as they attempt to penetrate something hard or, sometimes, inedible. The word usually is associated with animals (as horses) and connotes impatience or extreme hunger, but it is also used of men who avidly apply themselves to the task of biting with their teeth and crushing with their jaws: often it suggests the flow and foaming of saliva ⟨the horse *champed* at its bit until its mouth was covered with foam⟩ ⟨he ate in a ruthless manner, *champing* his food—*Waugh*⟩ ⟨others, devoted themselves to the sodden and lee-dyed pieces of the cask, licking, and even *champing* the moister wine-rotted fragments with eager relish—*Dickens*⟩ **Gnash** usually implies the striking of the teeth against each other or a grinding of them (as in anguish, despair, or extreme rage); it often emphasizes this action as the visible sign of an overpowering emotion or distress ⟨but the children of the kingdom shall be cast out into outer darkness: there shall be weeping and *gnashing* of teeth—*Mt* 8:12⟩ Sometimes, however, it implies a savage biting that rends a thing in two or tears it apart ⟨I strove . . . to rend and *gnash* my bonds in twain—*Byron*⟩ ⟨the tiger *gnashed* the fox, the ermine and the sloth—*Landor*⟩
*Ana* *eat, consume, devour

**biting** cutting, crisp, trenchant, *incisive, clear-cut
*Ana* *caustic, mordant, acrid: *pungent, poignant, piquant, racy

**bitter,** acrid are applied to things with an unpleasant taste (also smell, in the case of *acrid*) that is neither sweet nor bland yet seldom distinctly sour or really sickening. **Bitter** is traditionally associated with the repellent taste of wormwood, quinine, and aloes, but it is also used to describe the taste of beer, unsweetened chocolate, and the rind of citrus fruits. Something *bitter* usually lacks the pleasant tang and freshness of an acid flavor (as of lemon juice) and has a penetrating and persistent quality difficult to mask. **Acrid** implies a bitterness in taste that has an astringent or irritating effect (as the taste of chokecherries, various unripe fruits, or alum). It is also applied to something both bitter and salty (as sweat). An *acrid* smell is a penetrating, suffocating, repugnant odor. It is especially associated with certain fumes (as from burning sulphur) or with certain noxious vapors (as of a heavy city fog).
*Ana* *sour, acid, acidulous, tart: *pungent, piquant
*Ant* delicious  —*Con* delectable, luscious, *delightful

**bizarre** grotesque, *fantastic, antic
*Ana* outlandish, erratic, eccentric, *strange, singular, odd, queer, curious: extravagant, extreme (see EXCESSIVE)
*Ant* chaste: subdued

**blab** tattle, *gossip
*Ana* babble, gabble, chatter, prate, *chat: divulge, disclose, betray (see REVEAL)

**blackball** *vb* debar, shut out, *exclude, eliminate, rule out, disbar, suspend
*Con* admit, accept, *receive

**blackguard** *villain, scoundrel, knave, rascal, rogue,

scamp, rapscallion, miscreant

**blame** *vb* reprehend, reprobate, condemn, denounce, censure, *criticize
*Ana* *accuse, charge, indict, impeach: impute, attribute, *ascribe: implicate, *involve
*Con* exonerate, vindicate, *exculpate, absolve, acquit: *excuse, remit, forgive

**blame** *n* **Blame, culpability, guilt, fault** are comparable when they mean responsibility for misdeed or delinquency. **Blame** is a term of shifting denotations, sometimes meaning the reprehension, criticism, or censure of those who find fault or judge one's work or acts ⟨I have never desired praise . . . I have been indifferent to, if not indeed contemptuous of, *blame*—*Ellis*⟩ or sometimes a charge or accusation of some fault, misdeed, or delinquency ⟨fear of incurring *blame* in Wiltstoken for wantonly opposing her daughter's obvious interests—*Shaw*⟩ When the term denotes responsibility for wrongdoing or delinquency, it also implies the meriting of reproof, censure, or the appropriate penalty ⟨he took on himself all the *blame* for the project's failure⟩ ⟨they tried to shift the *blame* for their defeat⟩ Often the term means ultimate rather than immediate responsibility ⟨the *blame* [for backwardness in American education] has sometimes been put, and with some justice, upon our migratory habits and upon the heterogeneous character of our population—*Grandgent*⟩ **Culpability** usually means little more or no more than the fact or the state of being responsible for an act or condition that may be described as wrong, harmful, or injurious ⟨they could not prove his *culpability* for the accident⟩ ⟨as if the estrangement between them had come of any *culpability* of hers—*Dickens*⟩ ⟨an inescapable responsibility rests upon this country to conduct an inquiry . . . into the *culpability* of those whom there is probable cause to accuse of atrocities and other crimes—*R. H. Jackson*⟩ **Guilt** usually carries an implication of a connection with misdeeds of a grave or serious character from the moral and social points of view. Also it usually implies a deserving of severe punishment (as condemnation, loss of freedom, or, in the case of sin, loss of salvation) or of a definite legal penalty (as a fine, imprisonment, or death). Therefore, when the term denotes responsibility for a crime or sin, it also carries implications of need of proof before punishment can be determined or forgiveness granted ⟨though she was strongly suspected of murder, her *guilt* was not established until after her death⟩ ⟨since he admitted his *guilt*, he saved the state the cost of a trial⟩ ⟨to confess one's sins is to acknowledge one's *guilt* for those sins⟩ **Fault** (see also FAULT 2) is often used in place of *culpability* as a simpler word ⟨the *fault* is her parents', not the child's⟩ ⟨the *fault*, dear Brutus, is not in our stars, but in ourselves, that we are underlings—*Shak.*⟩
*Ana* responsibility, accountability, answerability (see corresponding adjectives at RESPONSIBLE): censure, condemnation, denunciation, reprehension (see corresponding verbs at CRITICIZE)
*Con* commendation, compliment (see corresponding verbs at COMMEND): *applause, acclaim, plaudits, acclamation

**blameworthy,** guilty, culpable are comparable when they mean deserving reproach and punishment for a wrong, sinful, or criminal act, practice, or condition. One (as a person or his act or work) is **blameworthy** that deserves blame or criticism and must suffer or receive reproach, censure, or even more severe punishment ⟨thee therefore still, *blameworthy* as thou art . . . thee I account still happy, and the chief among the nations, seeing thou art free—*Cowper*⟩ A person is **guilty** who is justly chargeable with responsibility for a delinquency, crime, or sin,

---

A colon (:) separates groups of words discriminated. An asterisk (*) indicates place of treatment of each group.

either in his own knowledge or in that of others, by his confession or by proof (often legal proof) of his responsibility; the term may stress either the fact that guilt has been proved or the fact or the fear of resulting punishment ⟨the defendant was found *guilty*⟩ ⟨suspicion always haunts the *guilty* mind; the thief doth fear each bush an officer—*Shak.*⟩ ⟨let no *guilty* man escape, if it can be avoided—*Grant*⟩ Often the term suggests merely a state of mind (as a consciousness that one has committed a sin or a crime or a fear that one is justly suspected of wrongdoing or of a misdeed) ⟨a *guilty* conscience⟩ ⟨there is no use in making the refractory child feel *guilty*— *Russell*⟩ A person is **culpable** who has been shown to be blameworthy and open to severe censure or condemnation ⟨the judge . . . remarked that those whom Smith had gulled were almost as *culpable* as he—*Altick*⟩ The term is also applicable to a blameworthy act, condition, or practice for which one is responsible or which leads to wrong or harm ⟨*culpable* ignorance⟩ ⟨*culpable* neglect⟩ ⟨is it not . . . *culpable* and unworthy, thus beforehand to slur her honor?—*Shelley*⟩
*Ant* blameless —*Con* faultless, *impeccable, flawless

**blanch** *vb* *whiten, bleach, decolorize, etiolate

**bland** *adj* **1** smooth, *suave, urbane, diplomatic, politic
*Ana* benign, benignant, *kind, kindly: *amiable, complaisant, obliging, good-natured: slick, unctuous (see FULSOME)
*Ant* brusque —*Con* *bluff, blunt, gruff, curt, crusty
**2** mild, gentle, smooth, *soft, balmy, lenient
*Ana* *neutral, indifferent: temperate, *moderate: *insipid, flat, vapid, wishy-washy
*Ant* *pungent, piquant: savory, tasty (see PALATABLE) —*Con* stimulating, exciting, quickening (see PROVOKE): thrilling, electrifying (see THRILL *vb*)

**blandish** wheedle, cajole, *coax
*Ana* allure, charm, bewitch, captivate (see ATTRACT): *lure, entice, seduce: beguile, delude (see DECEIVE)
*Con* constrain, oblige, coerce, compel, *force: drive, impel (see MOVE): *intimidate, cow, bulldoze, browbeat, bully

**blank** *adj* void, *empty, vacant, vacuous
*Ana* *bare, barren: *clean
*Con* *expressive, meaningful, significant, pregnant

**blasé** *sophisticated, worldly-wise, worldly, disillusioned
*Ana* *indifferent, unconcerned, incurious: nonchalant, imperturbable, unruffled (see COOL)

**blasphemous** *impious, profane, sacrilegious
*Ana* cursing, damning, execrating, anathematizing, objurgating (see EXECRATE): *irreligious, ungodly, godless
*Ant* reverent

**blasphemy** **1** Blasphemy, profanity, swearing, cursing are comparable when meaning impious or irreverent speech. **Blasphemy,** the strongest term (see also PROFANATION), applies strictly to an intentional or malicious utterance in which the Supreme Being is defied or offered indignity; as such it is regarded as a serious sin in theology and as a crime at the common law ⟨genuine *blasphemy,* genuine in spirit and not purely verbal, is the product of partial belief and is as impossible to the complete atheist as to the perfect Christian—*T. S. Eliot*⟩ **Profanity** has a wider range and includes all irreverent reference to holy things; it is particularly applied to speech in which the names of God, Jesus, and the Virgin Mary are used lightly and irreverently, especially in expressing rage or passion in oaths, curses, and imprecations ⟨he had what one might call a preliminary recourse in his *profanity,* those "scorching, singeing blasts" he was always directing at his companions—*Brooks*⟩ **Swearing** and **cursing** are forms of profanity, the former stressing indulgence in profane and

often meaningless oaths; the latter, indulgence in profane curses or imprecations (as by calling on God to damn or punish the object of one's wrath or hatred) ⟨among laborers and others, that ungodly custom of *swearing* is too frequently heard, to the dishonor of God and contempt of authority—*Wren*⟩ ⟨why, what an ass am I! . . . that I . . . must . . . unpack my heart with words, and fall a-*cursing*—*Shak.*⟩
*Ana* insult, *affront, indignity: scurrility, vituperation (see ABUSE *n*)
*Ant* adoration —*Con* worship, reverence, veneration (see under REVERE)
**2** *profanation, desecration, sacrilege
*Ana* debasement, corruption, perversion (see corresponding verbs at DEBASE): misrepresentation, falsehood, untruth, *lie

**blast** *n* blight, nip (see under BLAST *vb*)
*Ana* destruction (see corresponding verb at DESTROY): extermination, extirpation, wiping out (see corresponding verbs at EXTERMINATE): ruin, wreck (see RUIN *vb*)

**blast** *vb* Blast, blight, nip mean as verbs, to ruin or to injure severely, suddenly, or surprisingly and as nouns, the effect of such ruin or injury. **Blast** which basically implies a violent onrush (as of wind) carries the implication of something pernicious that comes with sweeping force to destroy or demolish or to bring with it complete frustration ⟨I'll cross it, though it *blast* me—*Shak.*⟩ ⟨O fairest flower, no sooner blown but *blasted*—*Milton*⟩ ⟨the thunder crackled again. It is terrifying in the tropics, that sound. . . . You expect to be annihilated, *blasted,* burned to a crisp—*McFee*⟩ ⟨our shelter from the stormy *blast*—*Watts*⟩ ⟨the East bowed low before the *blast*— *Arnold*⟩ **Blight** primarily implies a withering and killing of plant tissue by some natural agency (as disease, pests, or adverse weather) ⟨dahlias *blighted* by an unseasonable frost⟩ ⟨late *blight* of potatoes⟩ Similarly in extended use the term implies a destructive altering (as of a plan, a hope, or a life) by some external but relevant agency ⟨a secret marriage . . . was a *blight* on his life—*George Eliot*⟩ ⟨when the true scholar gets thoroughly to work, his logic is remorseless, his art is implacable, and his sense of humor is *blighted*—*Henry Adams*⟩ ⟨a Peloponnesian or a European war lays its *blight* on whole peoples—*Montague*⟩ ⟨*The Moonstone* is very near to *Bleak House.* The theft of a diamond has some of the same *blighting* effect on the lives about it as the suit in Chancery—*T. S. Eliot*⟩ **Nip** may imply a squeezing, a pinching, or more specifically, a cutting off between two edges, surfaces, or points; in extended use, it implies the acting of something comparable (as a killing frost or a bitter wind) that has power to damage, to check, or to distress ⟨so have I seen some tender slip saved with care from winter's *nip*—*Milton*⟩ ⟨the wind that blows between the worlds, it *nipped* him to the bone—*Kipling*⟩ ⟨most of the flowers had been *nipped* by a heavy frost⟩ In the idiomatic phrase "to nip in the bud" *nip* harks back to the implication of cutting off and suggests a terminating or destroying of something before it has fully developed or matured ⟨the plans for an uprising were *nipped* in the bud⟩ ⟨*nip* a scandal in the bud⟩
*Ana* *destroy: *ruin, wreck: *exterminate, extirpate, wipe: *injure, damage, spoil

**blatant** clamorous, *vociferous, strident, boisterous, obstreperous
*Ana* assertive, self-assertive, pushing, *aggressive, militant: *vocal, articulate, voluble, glib: vulgar, *coarse, gross
*Ant* decorous: reserved —*Con* *silent, uncommunicative, reticent, taciturn: subdued, *tame: discreet, prudent (see under PRUDENCE)

---

*Ana* analogous words    *Ant* antonyms    *Con* contrasted words    See also explanatory notes facing page 1

**blaze** *n* flare, flame, glare, glow (see under BLAZE *vb*)
**Ana** firing *or* fire, kindling, igniting *or* ignition (see corresponding verbs at LIGHT): effulgence, refulgence, radiance, brilliance *or* brilliancy (see corresponding adjectives at BRIGHT)

**blaze** *vb* Blaze, flame, flare, glare, glow are comparable both as verbs meaning to burn or appear to burn brightly and as nouns denoting a brightly burning light or fire. **Blaze** implies great activity in burning, the thorough kindling of the burning substance or material, and the radiation of intense light and often heat ⟨the sun *blazed* down upon them with a crushing violence—*Forester*⟩ ⟨everyone fought fire. Everyone went to the woods and thrashed out some new *blaze—Vorse*⟩ ⟨her eyes *blazing* in her white face—*Stevenson*⟩ **Flame** suggests a darting tongue or tongues of fire formed by rapidly burning gas or vapor; it therefore often connotes less steadiness than *blaze* and sometimes less intense heat and light ⟨the burning house was soon a mass of *flames*⟩ ⟨the torches *flamed* in the wind⟩ ⟨the dry fuel soon burst into *flame*⟩ ⟨dimmed hope's newly kindled *flame—Shelley*⟩ **Flare** implies flame, especially a flame darting up suddenly against a dark background or from a dying fire ⟨torches that guttered and *flared* —*Hewlett*⟩ ⟨he . . . lighted a cigarette and then remembered that the *flare* of the match could probably be seen from the station—*Anderson*⟩ **Glare** (see also GAZE) emphasizes the steady emission or reflection of bright light; it sometimes connotes an almost unendurable brilliancy ⟨dazed by the lantern *glare—Kipling*⟩ ⟨the snow *glares* in the sunlight⟩ ⟨the *glare* of a forest fire in the sky⟩ ⟨he . . . lets the fire *glare* on the sullen face for a moment, and it sears itself into the memory forever—*J. R. Lowell*⟩ ⟨his days were passed in the *glare* of publicity—*Buchan*⟩ **Glow** also stresses the emission of light, but it suggests an absence of flame and therefore connotes steadiness, intensity, radiance without brilliance, and often warmth and duration ⟨the *glow* of coals⟩ ⟨her fine effect of *glowing* from within as a lamp glows—*Mary Austin*⟩ ⟨the fire that burned within him, that *glowed* with so strange and marvelous a radiance in almost all he wrote—*Huxley*⟩
**Ana** *illuminate, illumine, light: *burn: *flash, gleam, glance

**bleach** *vb* *whiten, etiolate, decolorize, blanch
**Ant** dye

**bleak** cheerless, dispiriting, *dismal, dreary, desolate
**Ana** *cold, chilly, frigid, freezing: barren, *bare, bald: stripped, denuded (see STRIP *vb*)

**blemish** *n* Blemish, defect, flaw all denote an imperfection. **Blemish** applies to something (as a spot or stain) that is external or superficial and mars or disfigures the appearance of an object ⟨on their sustaining garments not a *blemish—Shak.*⟩ ⟨he studiously perfected nature by correcting all the little *blemishes* of manner and little weaknesses of character in order to produce an immaculate effect—*Parrington*⟩ ⟨a reputation without a *blemish*⟩ **Defect** implies the lack or want of something which is essential to completeness or perfection but which is not necessarily superficially apparent ⟨a *defect* in a mechanism⟩ ⟨a *defect* in the organs of vision⟩ ⟨the *defects* of this poem are not obvious⟩ ⟨*defects* of understanding based on ignorance and unfamiliarity—*Oppenheimer*⟩ A **flaw** is a defect in continuity or cohesion (as a break, a crack, or a fissure), that may either mar a perfect surface or cause a weakness in structure ⟨a *flaw* in a crystal⟩ ⟨or some frail China jar receive a *flaw—Pope*⟩ ⟨my love to thee is sound, sans crack or *flaw—Shak.*⟩ ⟨style is not a sheet of glass in which the only thing that matters is the absence of *flaws—Ellis*⟩ ⟨we most enjoy, as a spectacle, the downfall of a good man, when the fall is justified by some *flaw* in his

being—*Guérard*⟩
**Ana** blot, stain, *stigma: tainting *or* taint, pollution, defilement (see corresponding verbs at CONTAMINATE): *fault, failing, frailty: *lack, want, privation
**Ant** immaculateness   **—Con** purity, simplicity (see corresponding adjectives at PURE): cleanness, cleanliness (see corresponding adjectives at CLEAN): clearness, transparency, pellucidness (see corresponding adjectives at CLEAR)

**blench** quail, shrink, *recoil, flinch, wince
**Ana** evade, elude, avoid, shun, eschew, *escape: tremble, quiver, shudder, quake, *shake
**Con** *bear, suffer, endure, abide, stand

**blend** *vb* fuse, *mix, merge, coalesce, mingle, commingle, amalgamate
**Ana** combine, unite, conjoin (see JOIN): *integrate: consolidate, unify, *compact
**Ant** resolve   **—Con** *analyze, break down: *separate, part, divorce: decompose, disintegrate (see DECAY)

**blend** *n* *mixture, admixture, compound, composite, amalgam

**blessed** *holy, sacred, divine, spiritual, religious
**Ant** accursed

**blessedness** beatitude, bliss, *happiness, felicity
**Ana** enjoyment, fruition, joy, *pleasure
**Ant** misery, dolor   **—Con** suffering, *distress, agony: woe, anguish, *sorrow, grief

**blight** *n* blast, nip (see under BLAST *vb*)
**Ana** *injury, damage, hurt, harm: frustration, thwarting (see corresponding verbs at FRUSTRATE)

**blight** *vb* *blast, nip
**Ana** *injure, damage, hurt, harm, spoil: *maim, cripple, batter: *frustrate, thwart

**blind** *adj* Blind, sightless, purblind mean lacking or deficient in the power to see or to discriminate objects. **Blind** is used to imply absence or deprivation or gross restriction of the power of vision, either by congenital defect or as a result of disease or of an injury to the organs of vision ⟨the very years when the *blind* Milton was dictating the last books of *Paradise Lost* to his amanuensis—*Altick*⟩ ⟨if the *blind* lead the *blind*, both shall fall into the ditch—*Mt* 15:14⟩ It is as often employed in an extended sense, especially as implying a lack of the mental, moral, or spiritual vision essential to the perception or discernment of what actually exists or what is really true ⟨His divine power hath given unto us all things that pertain unto life and godliness . . . . But he that lacketh these things is *blind—2 Pet* 1:3-9⟩ ⟨expound the merits to me if you think me *blind—Justice Holmes*⟩ *Blind* is also applicable to things devoid of intelligence or of ability to know whither they are moving or tending ⟨*blind*, mechanical forces of society—*Wilde*⟩ or to acts, emotions, and attitudes which are the result of or which produce mental, moral, or spiritual blindness ⟨*blind* terror⟩ ⟨*blind* acceptance of authority⟩ or to something (as a space or a structure) that is so dark or obscure or obstructed that one cannot see through, into, or around it ⟨a *blind* wall⟩ ⟨*blind* alley⟩ ⟨a *blind* corner⟩ **Sightless** is sometimes the preferred term when permanent total blindness is implied ⟨the *sightless* Homer⟩ ⟨rehabilitation of the *sightless* and partially blind—*Current Biog.*⟩ **Purblind** is disused in the sense of totally blind ⟨*purblind* Argus, all eyes and no sight—*Shak.*⟩ but it persists in the sense of nearly blind, or without sight enough to do one's work or make one's way successfully ⟨*purblind* with cataracts, he gets a living by misprinting, by hand, a four-page paper—*Gerald Kersh*⟩ More usually, *purblind* implies the imperfection or even the absence of mental, moral, or spiritual vision and usually connotes obtuseness or shortsightedness that comes from ignorance, stupidity, or indifference

---

A colon (:) separates groups of words discriminated. An asterisk (*) indicates place of treatment of each group.

〈the intolerable narrowness and the *purblind* conscience of the society—*George Eliot*〉 〈in Washington *purblind* congressmen, sensitive only to the demands of big business, fastened . . . the McKinley tariff—*Nevins & Commager*〉 *Con* seeing, perceiving, discerning, noticing, noting (see SEE): *aware, alive, conscious, sensible, cognizant, awake

**blind** *n* Blind, shade, shutter mean a device that serves as a screen for a window. **Blind** is used especially in British countries to designate a window covering, usually of fabric and operating on a roller, that shuts out the sunlight or at night prevents those outside from seeing in. In this sense **shade** is more usual in the United States. The use of the term *blind* as an element of or as a shortened form for *venetian blind* is common both in American and British countries. *Venetian blind* refers to a flexible inside curtain composed of light and narrow laths fixed on tapes which may be raised or lowered as desired and whose laths may be opened or closed according to the amount of light needed. But *blind* (or *blinds,* since a pair of the devices is usually fitted to a single window) is used chiefly for a device fitted on the outside or on the inside of a window, made of a wooden frame with slats that are movable or fixed, and typically hinged at the side so that when opened it lies flat against the outside wall or folds into an inner recess of the window frame. This device is also called a **shutter.** But *shutter* is actually a more inclusive term and implies a device that can be shut (as to exclude light, rain, or wind, to insure privacy, or to make safe against intruders). The term therefore includes such devices as those made of solid panels whether used singly or in pairs or sets to each window, and whether left permanently in place or hung when desired 〈storm *shutters*〉 〈hurricane *shutters*〉 〈each night the shopkeeper put up his *shutters*〉

**blink** *vb* *wink
*Ana* ignore, disregard, overlook, slight, *neglect: evade, elude, avoid, shun (see ESCAPE)
*Con* *see, note, notice, observe, remark

**bliss** beatitude, blessedness, felicity, *happiness
*Ana* enjoyment, joy, delectation, fruition, *pleasure: rapture, *ecstasy, transport
*Ant* anguish: bale —*Con* misery, suffering, *distress, agony, dolor: woe, *sorrow, grief: gloom, dejection, melancholy, *sadness

**blithe** jocund, *merry, jovial, jolly
*Ana* gay, *lively, animated, vivacious, sprightly: joyful, joyous, lighthearted, *glad, happy, cheerful: buoyant, effervescent, volatile (see ELASTIC)
*Ant* morose: atrabilious —*Con* sad, depressed, dejected, gloomy (see corresponding nouns at SADNESS): *sullen, glum, dour, saturnine: *melancholic, melancholy

**bloc** party, *combination, faction, ring, combine

**block** *vb* obstruct, bar, dam, impede, *hinder
*Ana* check, *arrest, interrupt: *hamper, clog, trammel: prohibit, *forbid, inhibit: *frustrate, thwart, foil: *prevent, forestall
*Con* *advance, forward, further, promote

**blockade** *n* Blockade, siege are comparable when denoting an attempt of a belligerent force to break down the resistance of the enemy by preventing egress or ingress of men or entrance of supplies over a considerable period of time. **Blockade** is used chiefly of an attempt made to close a port, harbor, or coast, especially by effectively investing it with warships or with mines so that fresh supplies (as of food, fuel, and ammunition) are cut off from the enemy 〈run a *blockade*〉 〈raise a *blockade*〉 〈the allied *blockade* of the North Sea avenues to the German coast during the war〉 **Siege** is applied chiefly to a military as opposed to a naval attempt. The term implies investment with troops on all sides of a fortified place (often a city). It also suggests, as

*blockade* does not, frequent assaults by the besieging forces as efforts to compel surrender 〈the *siege* of Troy〉 〈the *siege* of Vicksburg in the American Civil War〉

**blockade** *vb* *besiege, beleaguer, invest
*Ana* *close, shut: block, impede, obstruct (see HINDER): *enclose: *surround, environ, encircle

**bloodless** anemic, *pale
*Ana* *colorless, uncolored: wishy-washy, vapid, inane (see INSIPID)
*Ant* sanguine: plethoric —*Con* vital, alive, *living: vivid, *graphic: *vigorous, lusty, nervous

**bloody,** sanguinary, sanguine, sanguineous, gory are comparable when they mean affected by or involving the shedding of blood. **Bloody** may be used in place of any of the succeeding words, but it specifically and distinctively applies to that which is covered with blood or is actually or apparently made up of blood 〈a *bloody* knife〉 〈*bloody* hands〉 〈a *bloody* discharge from a wound〉 **Sanguinary** usually and *bloody* also when a simpler, more forcible word is desired apply to something attended by or someone bent upon bloodshed 〈a *sanguinary* conflict〉 〈*sanguinary* deeds〉 〈my thoughts be *bloody,* or be nothing worth—*Shak.*〉 〈a *bloody* battle〉 **Sanguine** and **sanguineous** are used chiefly in a literary context in place of either of the preceding words or in specifically implying an association with bleeding or bloodthirstiness or the color of blood 〈to find his way through the *sanguine* labyrinth of passion through which he was wandering—*Wilde*〉 〈his passion, cruel grown, took on a hue fierce and *sanguineous*—*Keats*〉 **Gory** sometimes suggests clotted blood, but more often it suggests a profusion of blood that testifies to slaughter 〈a *gory* fight〉 〈never shake thy *gory* locks at me—*Shak.*〉

**bloom** *n* flower, blow, blossom (see under BLOSSOM *vb*)

**bloom** *vb* flower, blow, *blossom
*Ana* flourish, thrive, prosper (see SUCCEED)

**blossom** *n* flower, bloom, blow (see under BLOSSOM *vb*)

**blossom** *vb* Blossom, bloom, flower, blow are comparable as verbs when meaning to become florescent and as nouns when meaning the period or state of florescence or (except for *blow*) meaning the florescent part itself. **Blossom** may be used of a plant that reaches the condition of florescence, but typically it applies to trees, shrubs, and herbaceous plants (and to their florescent parts) that normally proceed to bear what is ordinarily (not technically) called a fruit 〈the cherry trees are in *blossom*〉 〈the apple trees will *blossom* next month〉 〈the tomatoes have shed their *blossoms*〉 **Bloom,** though sometimes employed interchangeably with *blossom,* is typically used of such herbaceous plants, shrubs, or trees (or their florescent parts) as have reached the height of their beauty during the period of florescence 〈the roses are in *bloom*〉 〈the iris is *blooming*〉 〈the rhododendron has *blooms* in early June in this locality〉 **Flower** in technical use as a noun refers to the part of a seed plant which normally bears reproductive organs; in popular use it is usually restricted to such part when its gross structure is showy and conspicuously colored or white. Fragrance, freshness, shortness of life or of beauty are the implications in the popular use of the noun and the verb that distinguishes *flower* from *bloom* chiefly but also from *blossom;* also *flower* is often thought of as apart from the plant where it has grown 〈a bouquet of *flowers*〉 〈the rambler's period of *flowering* is short〉 〈one after another the garden plants *flowered,* but always in the meantime some had faded 〈as for man, his days are as grass: as a *flower* of the field, so he flourisheth—*Ps* 103:15〉 〈full many a *flower* is born to blush unseen, and waste its sweetness on the desert air—*Gray*〉 〈there can be no perfect *flower* without fragrance—*Symons*〉 **Blow,** in this sense, has an archaic or poetic flavor except in the combination *full-blown.* Usually it suggests a bursting into flower or bloom and often, especially in the noun, connotes a great display of blooms ⟨I know a bank where the wild thyme *blows—Shak.*⟩ ⟨the blossoms *blow;* the birds on bushes sing—*Dryden*⟩ ⟨such a *blow* of tulips, as was not to be matched—*Addison*⟩

All of these words have extended use. **Blossom** usually suggests something analogous to a natural blossom (as in freshness or rich development) ⟨after a shy girlhood she is *blossoming* out in college⟩ **Bloom** usually suggests a time or period of perfection, vigor, or beauty ⟨the *bloom* of perfect manhood—*Hamerton*⟩ ⟨the hills are full of marble before the world *blooms* with statues—*Phillips Brooks*⟩ **Flower** implies the choicest part, specimen, or product of something or its coming into being ⟨the *flower* of a nation died in that war⟩ ⟨always the *flower* of courtesy —*Cather*⟩ ⟨I think it [Greek literature] one of the brightest *flowers* of the human spirit—*Benson*⟩ ⟨art, he thought, should *flower* from an immediate impulse towards self-expression or communication—*Huxley*⟩ **Blow,** by far the least frequent of these terms in such use, implies a bursting into beauty or perfection.

**blot** *n* *stigma, brand, stain
*Ana* taint, defilement, pollution (see corresponding verbs at CONTAMINATE): *blemish, flaw, defect: shame, *disgrace, ignominy, obloquy

**blot out** *vb* delete, obliterate, expunge, *erase, cancel, efface
*Ana* *abolish, annihilate, extinguish: wipe, *exterminate, extirpate
*Con* preserve, *save, conserve: imprint, print, impress, stamp (see corresponding nouns at IMPRESSION)

**blow** *vb* *blossom, bloom, flower
*Ana* *expand, swell: enlarge, augment (see INCREASE)

**blow** *n* blossom, bloom, flower (see under BLOSSOM *vb*)

**blowsy** frowzy, *slatternly, dowdy
*Ana* flashy, tawdry, *gaudy, garish: slovenly, sloppy, disheveled, unkempt, *slipshod: florid, flamboyant (see ORNATE): vulgar, *coarse
*Ant* smart, spruce: dainty —*Con* *neat, tidy, trim, trig: fastidious, particular, *nice

**blubber** *vb* *cry, weep, wail, keen, whimper

**bluejacket** *mariner, sailor, seaman, tar, gob

**blueprint** *n* sketch, draft, tracing, plot, diagram, delineation, outline (see under SKETCH *vb*)

**blueprint** *vb* *sketch, draft, trace, plot, diagram, delineate, outline

**blues** dejection, depression, melancholy, gloom, dumps, *sadness

**bluff** *adj* **Bluff, blunt, brusque, curt, crusty, gruff** mean abrupt and unceremonious in speech or manner. **Bluff,** the only term of the group used in a complimentary sense, connotes outspokenness, rough good nature, and unconventionality which bespeak a sincerity that scorns the forms of politeness ⟨*bluff* King Hal—*Scott*⟩ ⟨*bluff* good humor⟩ ⟨a *bluff,* burly, hearty-looking man in a short blue jacket —*Kenneth Roberts*⟩ **Blunt** (see also DULL) implies such directness and plain speaking as to suggest lack of consideration for the feelings of others and some disregard for the amenities of life ⟨a *blunt* reply⟩ ⟨the petition was rejected in a *blunt,* one-sentence letter of refusal—*Blanshard*⟩ ⟨a *blunt* man. He is often brutal. He has never seemed to me to be devious—*Welles*⟩ **Brusque** suggests a certain sharpness of manner and ungraciousness of speech ⟨a *brusque* refusal⟩ ⟨I was nettled by her *brusque* manner of asserting her folly—*Conrad*⟩ ⟨Markham was forthright, *brusque,* and, on occasion, domineering, taking life with grim and serious conscience—*S. S. Van Dine*⟩ **Curt** im-

plies disconcerting shortness or rude conciseness ⟨a *curt* answer⟩ ⟨a *curt* message . . . bade her return at once to Rome—*Buchan*⟩ **Crusty** implies a forbidding exterior and a manner marked by asperity or acerbity that sometimes belies real kindness of heart ⟨he was a *crusty* old fellow, as close as a vise—*Hawthorne*⟩ **Gruff** carries a stronger implication of surliness and roughness than *crusty* and distinctively suggests curt and hoarse or guttural utterance but like the former may suggest an underlying kindliness ⟨*gruff,* disagreeable, sarcastic remarks—*Thackeray*⟩ ⟨covered his essentially warm and friendly nature with a *gruff* exterior—*Bliven* b.1889⟩
*Ana* hearty, *sincere: plain, open, *frank, candid: abrupt, *precipitate
*Ant* suave, smooth —*Con* urbane, diplomatic, bland (see SUAVE): courteous, courtly, gallant, polite, *civil

**blunder** *vb* lurch, flounder, *stumble, trip, lumber, galumph, lollop, bumble
*Ana* stagger, *reel, totter: *wallow, welter

**blunder** *n* mistake, *error, bull, howler, boner, slip, lapse, faux pas
*Ana* *fault, failing, frailty, vice: *anachronism, solecism: aberration, *deviation: transgression, violation, *breach

**blunt** 1 *dull, obtuse
*Ant* keen, sharp —*Con* acute (see SHARP): penetrating, piercing, probing (see ENTER)
2 brusque, curt, *bluff, gruff, crusty
*Ana* plain, candid, *frank: *rude, discourteous, ungracious, uncivil, impolite: *forthright, downright
*Ant* tactful: subtle —*Con* diplomatic, politic, smooth, *suave, urbane

**blurb** puff, review, critique, *criticism

**blush** *vb* **Blush, flush** are comparable as verbs primarily when meaning to turn or grow red in the face and as nouns when meaning a turning or growing red in the face. **Blush** implies a sudden heightening of color usually as the result of shame or embarrassment ⟨caused Mrs. Tolliver to *blush* as if it were herself who had sinned—*Bromfield*⟩ ⟨she *blushed* to a crisp when she found her mistake—*White*⟩ ⟨Lucy *blushed,* as one who has something very secret to tell, very sweet, very strange, but cannot quite bring herself to speak it—*Meredith*⟩ **Blush** is often extended to matters (as the dawn, the sunset, or a fresh growth of pink in the garden) that suggest a delicate glow or warmth of color ⟨a faint *blush* of color tinged the eastern sky⟩ ⟨in the hedges there were bushes of faintly *blushing* dog rose in full blossom—*David Garnett*⟩ ⟨full many a flower is born to *blush* unseen—*Gray*⟩ **Flush** basically suggests a flooding (as by a rush of water) or a sudden brilliant flashing or glowing. In reference to the face both of these ideas are involved, for *flush* may imply a reddening of the face that brightens or floods the countenance sometimes transiently like a flame or it may imply the more or less persistent redness of the face that is associated with robust health, anger, elation, fever, or hard drinking. *Flush,* therefore, connotes modesty or shame much less often than does *blush* ⟨the hard dull *flush* of the steady heavy drinker —*Wolfe*⟩ ⟨no one could look more beautiful . . . when she was *flushed* from the fire—*D. H. Lawrence*⟩ ⟨a *flush* of anger came to his cheeks—*Anderson*⟩ ⟨*flushed* with a new humane glow, he would go singing on his way—*Lucas*⟩ In extended usage *flush* refers to lights or colors that flash and dart and glow ⟨straying beams . . . in copper-colored patches *flush* the sky—*Clare*⟩
*Ana* color, tint, tinge (see corresponding nouns at COLOR)

**blush** *n* flush (see under BLUSH *vb*)
*Ana* *color, tint, tinge, hue

**bluster** *vb* *roar, bellow, bawl, vociferate, clamor, howl, ululate

---

A colon (:) separates groups of words discriminated. An asterisk (*) indicates place of treatment of each group.

*Ana* *boast, brag, vaunt, crow: *threaten, menace

**board** *vb* house, lodge, *harbor, shelter, entertain

*Ana* *feed, nourish

**boast** *vb* Boast, brag, vaunt, crow, gasconade mean to give vent in speech to one's pride in oneself or something (as family, connections, race, or accomplishments) intimately connected with oneself. *Boast* and *vaunt* are often used transitively as well as intransitively; the other words are chiefly intransitive. **Boast** is the general term; it may or may not carry a suggestion of contempt or impute exaggeration, ostentation, or vaingloriousness to the boaster ⟨what folly then to *boast* what arms can do!—*Milton*⟩ ⟨the wretch . . . abhors the craft he *boasted* of before—*Cowper*⟩ ⟨he was childishly anxious to *boast* that he had walked the whole of the six or seven miles—*Mackenzie*⟩ **Brag** is more forceful than *boast* and carries a stronger implication of exaggeration and conceit; it often also implies glorying in one's superiority or in what one can do as well as in what one is, or has, or has done ⟨nor shall death *brag* thou wander'st in his shade—*Shak.*⟩ ⟨even when they *brag*, their eyes are generally self-mocking, mildly wise—*Lord*⟩ ⟨that we may *brag* we hae a lass, there's nane again sae bonie—*Burns*⟩ **Vaunt** is more literary than either of the preceding terms; it usually connotes more pomp and bombast than *boast* and less crudeness or naïveté than *brag* ⟨charity *vaunteth* not itself, is not puffed up—*1 Cor* 13:4⟩ ⟨and ye *vaunted* your fathomless power, and ye flaunted your iron pride—*Kipling*⟩ **Crow** usually implies exultant boasting or especially blatant bragging in a manner suggestive of the triumphal crowing of a cock ⟨the barrister *crowed* with triumph but the professor was in no way put out—*Kersh*⟩ **Gasconade** is the least common of these terms and implies habitual or extravagant self-vaunting ⟨an enlightened statesman and not a *gasconading* militarist —*Bowers*⟩

*Ana* flaunt, parade (see SHOW): *pride, plume, pique, preen: *exalt, magnify, aggrandize

*Ant* depreciate (*oneself, one's accomplishments*) —*Con* *decry, disparage, belittle, minimize: deprecate (see DISAPPROVE)

**boat,** vessel, ship, craft are comparable when they denote a floating structure designed to carry persons or goods over water. **Boat** is sometimes used as a general designation of such a structure but more specifically it is applicable to a small, typically open structure operated by oars, paddles, or poles ⟨a row*boat*⟩ or by sails or a power mechanism ⟨a sail*boat*⟩ ⟨a motor*boat*⟩ **Vessel** suggests a purpose as well as a form, the term in general applying to anything hollowed out so as to serve as a receptacle. Hence, *vessel* is appropriate when the containing and transporting of goods and persons is stressed; it is applied chiefly to large boats, especially seagoing boats, in the business of carrying passengers or freight or serving as a base of operations at sea (as in fishing or in war) ⟨steam *vessels*⟩ ⟨a fleet of war *vessels* including dreadnoughts, cruisers, destroyers, and submarines⟩ ⟨fishing *vessels*⟩ **Ship** is the preferred term for the large seagoing vessel, especially when its navigation rather than its business is emphasized ⟨a sailing *ship*⟩ ⟨a steam*ship*⟩ ⟨a battle*ship*⟩ ⟨the captain stands by his *ship*⟩ **Ship** also suggests more personality, more romance, and more beauty than the other words and therefore is far more common in poetry and in figurative use ⟨sailing, like a stately *ship* . . . sails filled, and streamers waving—*Milton*⟩ ⟨O Captain! my Captain! our fearful trip is done! The *ship* has weathered every wrack, the prize we sought is won—*Whitman*⟩ **Craft** may be used as a singular or collective noun and is now applicable to any type of boat or ship that plies the water. Originally it was found only in the phrase *small craft* ànd was applied to smaller vessels, especially to those in the service of ships (as lighters, tugs, and fireboats) or to those forming part of a navy or fleet ⟨when the winds increased the Coast Guard sent out small *craft* warnings⟩ The word may still be used in the sense of *small craft* but it tends to become a comprehensive term covering all kinds of boats and vessels ⟨the harbor is filled with *craft*⟩ As a singular, *craft* unqualified is often a vague and general term ⟨for me, my *craft* is sailing on, through mists today, clear seas anon—*Bangs*⟩ However, for that very reason, *craft* is often, when it is qualified, a better choice than *boat, ship,* or *vessel* ⟨a huge, lumbering *craft*⟩ ⟨for she is such a smart little *craft* —*Gilbert*⟩

**bodily,** physical, corporeal, corporal, somatic are comparable when used narrowly to mean of or relating to the human body. **Bodily** suggests opposition to *mental* or *intellectual* ⟨so engrossed in thought as to be unaware of his *bodily* needs⟩ ⟨he has never known *bodily* pain⟩ ⟨*bodily* illness is more easy to bear than mental—*Dickens*⟩ **Physical** (see also MATERIAL), though often used interchangeably with *bodily,* does not carry so strong a suggestion of organic structure; thus, *bodily* suffering implies some disturbance within the organism or, if external, some stimulus directly affecting the organism; *physical* suffering may also mean this, but often it is vaguer and less explicit in its implications or reference ⟨bodily pains induced by *physical* exhaustion⟩ ⟨a sense of *physical* well-being is often the result of freedom from bodily ailments⟩ **Corporeal** refers more specifically to the substance or matter of which the body is composed; like *physical* it has a more inclusive sense (see MATERIAL) but when used with reference to the human body, it implies an opposition to *immaterial* or to *spiritual* as applied to substance or nature ⟨our notion of man, for instance, necessarily includes its specific parts, rational soul and *corporeal* body— *Connally*⟩ ⟨until, the breath of this *corporeal* frame . . . almost suspended, we are laid asleep in body, and become a living soul—*Wordsworth*⟩ **Corporal** applies almost exclusively to things that have for their object an often painful effect upon the body ⟨subjected to *corporal* punishment⟩ In some contexts (as in "*corporal* works of mercy") it may stand in contrast to *spiritual*. **Somatic,** because of its freedom from theological and poetic connotations, is now preferred to *bodily* and *corporeal* by physiologists, psychologists, and physicians with an implied opposition to *psychical* ⟨*somatic* reactions to a stimulus⟩ ⟨a *somatic* disturbance⟩ ⟨*somatic* behavior⟩

*Ana* *carnal, fleshly, animal, sensual

*Con* *mental, psychic, intellectual: spiritual (see HOLY)

**body,** corpse, carcass, cadaver denote the physical organism of a man or animal (especially one of the larger animals). **Body** refers to the animal organism, living or dead; but its commonest use is in reference to man, then often implying an opposition to *mind* or *soul* ⟨absent in *body,* but present in spirit—*1 Cor 5:3*⟩ ⟨women take great care of their *bodies*⟩ ⟨they removed the *body* to a morgue⟩ **Corpse** and **carcass** (of man and animal respectively) refer to the dead body ⟨make a ring about the *corpse* of Caesar— *Shak.*⟩ ⟨there was a swarm of bees and honey in the *carcass* of the lion—*Judg 14:8*⟩ *Carcass* is also used as a term of contempt for the human body, dead or alive ⟨on the bleak shore now lies th' abandoned king, a headless *carcass,* and a nameless thing—*Dryden*⟩ **Cadaver** (compare *cadaverous* at HAGGARD) applies to a corpse used for the purpose of dissection in a laboratory. The term is sometimes applied to living men and then suggests extreme emaciation or the appearance of a skeleton.

*Con* *soul, spirit: *mind, intellect, psyche, intelligence

**boggle** *vb* stickle, stick, strain, scruple, *demur, balk, jib, shy

*Ana* *object, protest, kick, remonstrate, expostulate: *recoil, shrink, flinch, wince, blench, quail

*Ant* subscribe (*to*) —*Con* acquiesce, accede, *assent, agree: accept, admit, *receive

**bogus** *adj* *counterfeit, spurious, fake, sham, pseudo, pinchbeck, phony

*Ana* fraudulent, deceitful, deceptive (see corresponding nouns at IMPOSTURE): duping, hoaxing, gulling, hoodwinking (see DUPE)

*Con* *authentic, genuine, bona fide, veritable

**boil** *n* *abscess, furuncle, carbuncle, pimple, pustule

**boil** *vb* Boil, seethe, simmer, parboil, stew mean to prepare (as food) in a liquid heated to the point where it emits considerable steam. **Boil** implies the bubbling of the liquid and the rapid escape of steam; it may be applied to the liquid alone, but usually it suggests a fast method of accomplishing an end (as cooking or cleansing) ⟨boil water⟩ ⟨the water is boiling⟩ ⟨boil eggs⟩ ⟨boil clothes⟩ **Seethe** differs only slightly from boil. It emphasizes the subjection of something to the influence of a boiling liquid in order to cook it thoroughly or to make an infusion of it ⟨tomorrow is the rest of the holy sabbath unto the Lord: bake that which ye will bake today, and seethe that ye will seethe —Exod 16:23⟩ This difference, though slight, is also apparent in extended senses of boil and of seethe, for boil suggests a sudden rise and ebullition ⟨he boiled with anger⟩ and seethe suggests the agitation and turmoil which follows a cause of excitement ⟨the crowd was seething with excitement⟩ **Simmer** suggests that the liquid is at the point of boiling; it implies less steam and less bubbling than boil and is used, therefore, to denote a gentle and slower form of cooking ⟨corned beef should be simmered, not boiled⟩ ⟨simmer milk⟩ **Parboil** usually implies boiling for a limited time to prepare some food for further cooking (as by roasting or frying) ⟨parboil potatoes prior to roasting them with beef⟩ ⟨parboil a chicken before frying it⟩ **Stew** implies long slow simmering, usually in a closed vessel; it is used especially in reference to meats or fruits cooked until they are tender or broken up ⟨stew beef and kidneys together⟩ ⟨stew fruit for dessert⟩

**boisterous** obstreperous, clamorous, blatant, *vociferous, strident

*Ana* sporting, disporting, rollicking, frolicking, gamboling (see PLAY *vb*): *unruly, ungovernable: *indecorous, unseemly

*Con* quiet, noiseless, *still: peaceful, *calm, tranquil, serene, placid: staid, sedate, *serious, sober

**bold** *brave, courageous, unafraid, fearless, intrepid, valiant, valorous, dauntless, undaunted, doughty, audacious

*Ana* daring, reckless, venturesome, *adventurous, daredevil, rash, foolhardy: mettlesome, *spirited: fearless, unapprehensive, unafraid (see affirmative adjectives at FEARFUL)

*Ant* cowardly —*Con* *timid, timorous: quailing, flinching, shrinking, recoiling (see RECOIL)

**bolster** *vb* prop, *support, sustain, buttress, brace

*Ana* *strengthen, reinforce, fortify: uphold, champion (see SUPPORT)

**bombard** assail, storm, assault, *attack

**bombast, rhapsody, rant, fustian, rodomontade** all designate a style of speech or writing characterized by high-flown pomposity or pretentiousness of language disproportionate to the thought or subject matter. All of them are derogatory in some degree; some of them are frankly contemptuous. **Bombast** does not necessarily connote emptiness of thought, but it implies inflation or a grandiosity or impressiveness in language and style which so outruns the thought that the attention is distracted from the matter and

concentrated upon the manner of expression. When used in description rather than in censure, *bombast* often additionally suggests a soaring eloquence or a kind of oratorical grandeur, such as is found in Marlowe's *Tamburlaine the Great* or is characteristic of Elizabethan drama in comparison with modern realistic drama; when used in depreciation, it suggests padding, windiness, verbosity, and exaggeration ⟨to outbrave better pens with the swelling *bombast* of a bragging blank verse—*Nash*⟩ ⟨their eloquence is all *bombast*—*Kingsley*⟩ ⟨it looks like mere "rhetoric," certainly not "deeds and language such as men do use." It appears to us, in fact, forced and flagitious *bombast*—*T. S. Eliot*⟩ **Rhapsody**, like *bombast*, may be scarcely or obviously derogatory. It designates an ecstatic or effusive utterance or writing in which the language or style is governed by the feelings rather than by logical thought. It may, at one extreme, suggest inspired utterance (as in rapture) or, at the other, a maudlin loquaciousness ⟨O then my breast should warble airs, whose *rhapsodies* should feast the ears of seraphims—*Quarles*⟩ ⟨his characters . . . are excellently drawn, but he writes as though he had uncovered a new religion and thought it deserved a *rhapsody*—*New Yorker*⟩ In scholarly and critical use it is often applied to a kind of writing that has no perceptible argument and is seemingly incoherent, yet moves by a kind of logic of its own from one expression of feeling or one image to another ⟨the traditional assumption that it [Kubla Khan] was a *rhapsody* of enchanting images which "led to nothing"—*Times Lit. Sup.*⟩ **Rant** and **fustian** are definitely terms of derogation. Both are applicable to bombast and rhapsody at their worst, but *rant* stresses its extravagance or violence of expression or utterance and *fustian* the banality of its quality or the preposterousness of its character ⟨the hoarse *rant* of that demagogue fills the air and distracts the people's minds—*Ascoli*⟩ ⟨he, whose *fustian's* so sublimely bad, it is not poetry but prose run mad—*Pope*⟩ ⟨romantic *fustian;* which may be defined as the enormous disproportion between emotion and the outer object or incident on which it expends itself. Victor Hugo abounds in *fustian* of this kind—*Babbitt*⟩ **Rodomontade** is applied especially to the rant of the braggart, of the demagogue, or of anyone given to bluster and magniloquence ⟨the brothers set about abusing each other in good round terms and with each intemperate sally their phrases became more deeply colored with the tincture of Victorian *rodomontade*—*Marsh*⟩

*Ana* grandiloquence, magniloquence, rhetoric (see corresponding adjectives at RHETORICAL): inflatedness, turgidity, tumidity, flatulence (see corresponding adjectives at INFLATED)

*Con* temperateness *or* temperance, soberness *or* sobriety, unimpassionedness (see corresponding adjectives at SOBER): dispassionateness, justness (see corresponding adjectives at FAIR)

**bombastic** grandiloquent, magniloquent, *rhetorical, aureate, flowery, euphuistic

*Ana* *inflated, turgid, tumid: verbose, diffuse, *wordy: eloquent, voluble, fluent, articulate, *vocal

*Con* temperate, unimpassioned, *sober: *sincere: unaffected, *natural, simple, artless: dispassionate, just, impartial, *fair

**bona fide** *authentic, genuine, veritable

*Ana* true, *real, actual: *reliable, dependable, trustworthy: *pure, absolute, simple, sheer

*Ant* counterfeit, bogus —*Con* simulated, feigned, pretended, affected, shammed, assumed (see ASSUME)

**bond** *adj* *bound, indentured, articled

*Ant* free —*Con* emancipated, manumitted, liberated, freed (see FREE *vb*): independent (see FREE *adj*)

---

A colon (:) separates groups of words discriminated. An asterisk (*) indicates place of treatment of each group.

**bond** *n* **1** **Bond, band, tie** all denote something which serves to bind or bring two or more things firmly together, but they differ from each other not only in implications but in their specific applications. **Bond** often retains its basic implication of restraint upon the freedom of the individual. It may be applied to a restraining device (as a rope, a chain, a fetter, or a manacle) which prevents a prisoner from escaping or, more broadly, to something that interferes with one's liberty and holds one down ⟨it has been said that only the dying man is free, for death breaks every *bond*⟩ But *bond* is equally applicable to something that connects or brings together two individuals (persons or things) or all the individuals comprising a group or mass into a stable union. In this sense the term may and often does refer to a connection that is primarily spiritual; occasionally, especially when the plural is used, there is also a hint of restraint or constraint ⟨the *bond* (or *bonds*) of marriage⟩ ⟨the *bond* of faith⟩ ⟨the *bond* of fellowship⟩ ⟨the *bonds* of a common tradition⟩ ⟨the religion of the Greeks [was] . . . the *bond* of their political life—*Dickinson*⟩ **Band** (see also STRIP) may imply, like *bond*, a restraint, a fastening, or a connection, but it more usually also implies something material in the form of a flat and narrow piece of material, often one that forms a hoop or ring; thus, a *band* around the hair is worn to confine the hair and may be a ribbon with ends tied together or a hoop or half hoop (as of metal or plastic); an endless strip of rubber or elastic material is called a rubber *band*; a hooplike piece which holds together two parts of a structure (as the barrel and stock of a gun or two sections of a pillar) is called a *band;* also, a straight member of a wall (as continuous molding, a frieze, or a strip of brickwork in a different pattern) often serves not only as an ornament but also as a union or connection between two sections of the wall or structure, and is therefore called in architecture a *band.* **Tie** basically applies to a bond or band for fastening or restraining which is of a flexible substance (as rope, cord, or string) and can be secured by knotting the loose ends together or one end to the thing fastened and the other to its support. Consequently, in extended use, *tie* tends to suggest a less integral union and often more flexibility in the connection than *bond,* which it otherwise closely resembles; thus, one breaks the *bond* of friendship but one severs the *tie* of friendship; the *ties* of blood suggest the pull exerted by blood relationship, but the *bond* of blood suggests an obligation or a duty. *Tie,* as applied to specific fastenings or connections, is used chiefly when the object of the connection is not (as in *bond*) to form into an integral unit or (as in *band*) to keep closely united or together but to bring together two things that are affected by common forces so that when they are subjected to strain or tension they will not spread or pull apart; thus, the transverse bars on which rails rest and which serve to keep the rails equidistant from each other are called *ties;* a piece (as a beam, a post, or a rod) which connects two parts or sides of a structure (as the ribs of a vessel or the two sides of a pointed arch) and serves to brace and stay the whole is called a *tie.*
**2** surety, security, bail, *guarantee, guaranty
**bondage** *servitude, slavery
**boner** blunder, mistake, *error, howler, bull, slip, lapse, faux pas
**bonny** comely, pretty, good-looking, fair, lovely, *beautiful, handsome, beauteous, pulchritudinous
*Ana* pleasing, agreeable, *pleasant: attractive, charming, captivating (see under ATTRACT)
*Ant* homely
**bonus** bounty, *premium, reward, guerdon, award, prize, meed

**bon vivant** gastronome, gourmet, gourmand, *epicure, glutton
*Ant* ascetic
**bookish** academic, scholastic, *pedantic
**bookkeeper, accountant, auditor.** A **bookkeeper** keeps a regular, concise, and accurate record of business transactions by making the proper entries in the various books of account for that purpose. An **accountant** is a person skilled in the art of bookkeeping and may be employed either to organize and set up a system of records suitable to the needs of a particular organization or to investigate and report upon the financial condition of an organization by a study and analysis of its books of record. An **auditor** is an examiner who checks and verifies the financial records of an organization to see that these records correctly represent its condition.
**boon** favor, *gift, present, gratuity, largess
*Ana* benefaction, *donation, contribution
*Ant* calamity —*Con* *misfortune, mischance, mishap: *trial, cross, tribulation, affliction
**boor, churl, lout, clown, clodhopper, bumpkin, hick, yokel, rube** are comparable when meaning an uncouth, ungainly fellow. Most of these words may be applied to rustics, but they tend increasingly to imply reference to breeding, manners, and appearance rather than to origin or social status. The same distinctions in connotations and implications are apparent in the adjectives derived from the first four of these nouns, **boorish, churlish, loutish, clownish.** **Boor** implies an opposition to *gentleman,* especially in respect to characteristics indicative of good breeding and fineness of feeling. As a rule *boor* and **boorish** imply variously rudeness of manner, insensitiveness, lack of ceremony, or unwillingness to be agreeable in the presence of others ⟨love makes gentlemen even of *boors,* whether noble or villain—*Henry Adams*⟩ ⟨to the European mind, with all its goodwill, the very things that make us more powerful make us also more *boorish*—*Lerner*⟩ **Churl** may suggest low birth or social status but more often ill-bred surly meanness of expression or attitude. The latter implication is far more common in the adjective **churlish,** which characteristically implies surliness, irresponsiveness, or ungraciousness ⟨warns all whom it concerns, from King to *churl*—*John Morley*⟩ ⟨by what magic was it that this divine sweet creature could be allied with that old *churl* —*Meredith*⟩ ⟨they object to the dairymaids and men crossing the elm vista . . . . It seems *churlish*—*Shaw*⟩ **Lout** and **loutish** apply especially to hulky youths or men without regard to origin and usually suggest stupidity, clumsiness, and sometimes, abjectness of bearing or demeanor. Both words are terms of contempt frequently applied to idlers or loafers of particularly unprepossessing appearance ⟨it was inevitable that the older boys should become mischievous *louts;* they bullied and tormented and corrupted the younger boys because there was nothing else to do—*H. G. Wells*⟩ **Clown** and **clownish** come close to *lout* and *loutish* in connotation. Instead of stupidity, however, the terms often connote ignorance or simplicity and instead of hulkiness they suggest the ungainliness of a person whose body and movements reveal hard plodding labor ⟨the *clown,* the child of nature, without guile— *Cowper*⟩ When used in reference to those who are not countrymen the terms still imply general uncouthness and awkwardness and often, by association with the other sense of *clown,* a propensity for absurd antics ⟨he was the sort of boy that becomes a *clown* and a lout as soon as he is not understood, or feels himself held cheap—*D. H. Lawrence*⟩ **Clodhopper** distinctively suggests the frame and the heavy movements generally associated with plowmen but is not restricted in application to rustics ⟨though hon-

est and active they're most unattractive and awkward as awkward can be—can be. They're clumsy *clodhoppers—Gilbert*⟩ **Bumpkin** implies a loutishness suggestive of unfamiliarity with city ways and manners ⟨bashful country *bumpkins—Irving*⟩ **Hick** comes close to *bumpkin* and suggests the unsophisticated simple rustic ⟨*hicks* of the hinterlands mistrusting city politicians⟩ **Yokel** and **rube** more particularly suggest a rustic lack of polish or an obtuse gullibility ⟨his mouth was agape in *yokel* fashion—*Crane*⟩ ⟨always a new crop of *rubes* waiting to be tricked out of their money⟩
*Ant* gentleman

**boorish** loutish, clownish (see under BOOR)
*Ana* *awkward, clumsy, maladroit, inept: *rude, discourteous, ungracious, uncivil, impolite, ill-mannered
*Ant* gentlemanly  —*Con* *suave, urbane, smooth: courteous, courtly, gallant, polite, *civil

**boost** *vb* *lift, raise, elevate, hoist, rear, heave
*Ana* *exalt, aggrandize: heighten, enhance (see INTENSIFY): mount, soar, levitate, surge, ascend, *rise

**bootleg** *smuggled, contraband

**bootless** fruitless, *futile, vain, abortive
*Ana* idle, empty, hollow, nugatory, *vain, otiose
*Con* *beneficial, advantageous, profitable

**bootlicker** sycophant, toady, lickspittle, hanger-on, *parasite, favorite, leech, sponge, sponger

**booty** *spoil, loot, plunder, prize, swag

**border** *n*  Border, margin, verge, edge, rim, brim, brink mean the line or relatively narrow space which marks the limit or outermost bound of something. A **border** is the part of a surface which is just within its boundary line ⟨the *border* of a rug⟩ or it may be the boundary line itself ⟨I had at last reached the *border* of the forest—*Hudson*⟩ **Margin** denotes a border of definite width usually distinguished in some way from the remaining surface; it also applies to the space immediately contiguous to a body of water ⟨the *margin* of a page⟩ ⟨the *margin* of a lake or river⟩ ⟨they wandered onward till they reached the nether *margin* of the heath, where it became marshy, and merged in moorland—*Hardy*⟩ **Verge** applies to the line or to a very narrow space which sharply marks the limit or termination of a thing (as a surface or an expanse) ⟨the sky was clear from *verge* to *verge*—*Hardy*⟩ **Verge** may also be applied to the extreme limit of something with an implication that it is being approached either from within or from without ⟨it is not enough that a statute goes to the *verge* of constitutional power. We must be able to see clearly that it goes beyond that power—*Justice Holmes*⟩ ⟨he is on the *verge* of ruin⟩ An **edge** is a sharply defined terminating line made by the converging of two surfaces (as of a blade, a dish, a plank, or a box). *Edge* often implies sharpness (as opposed to bluntness) and therefore power to cut ⟨a tool with a fine *edge* may do mischief—*Godwin*⟩ ⟨put an *edge* on this knife⟩ It is this implication that comes out strongest in extended use where it often suggests asperity, trenchancy, or keenness ⟨there was an *edge* in his tone⟩ ⟨his calming words took the *edge* off their fear⟩ **Rim** usually applies to the verge or edge of something circular or curving ⟨the *rim* of the moon⟩ ⟨the *rim* of a bucket⟩ ⟨the *rim* of a wheel⟩ **Brim** applies to the inner side of the rim of a hollow vessel ⟨fill the pot to the *brim*⟩ or to the topmost line of the basin of a river, lake, or other body of water ⟨the river has risen to the *brim*⟩ **Brink** denotes the edge of something steep (as a precipice); thus, one would speak of the river's *brink* when stressing the abruptness of the bank or shore but of the river's *brim* when the notion of the close approach of the water to the basin's rim is uppermost in mind. *Brink* may also be used of immaterial things with the implication

of a possibility or risk of abrupt transition (as from one state to another) ⟨a policy that brought the nation to the *brink* of war⟩ ⟨on the *brink* of a horrible danger—*Wilde*⟩
*Ana* *limit, bound, confine, end
*Con* inside, interior (see corresponding adjectives at INNER)

**bore** *vb* *perforate, drill, puncture, punch, prick
*Ana* penetrate, pierce, *enter

**boredom** *tedium, ennui, doldrums
*Ant* amusement  —*Con* diversion, entertainment, recreation (see under AMUSE)

**boring** *irksome, tiresome, wearisome, tedious
*Ana* *dull, humdrum, monotonous, dreary, stodgy, pedestrian
*Con* *interesting, absorbing, engrossing, intriguing: exciting, stimulating, provoking *or* provocative (see corresponding verbs at PROVOKE)

**botch** *vb*  Botch, bungle, fumble, muff, cobble mean to handle or treat awkwardly or unskillfully. **Botch** may imply repairing or mending, but it frequently implies a making or forming by patching or by putting together out of pieces. It consistently suggests incompetence and a spoiling or marring of the thing produced, whatever its character ⟨*botch* a job⟩ ⟨an assemblage of ill-informed gentlemen who have *botched* every business they have ever undertaken—*Shaw*⟩ ⟨the suit was vilely *botched* and skimped . . . and now it was too late to remedy the defect—*Wolfe*⟩ **Bungle** implies ignorance, ineffectualness, or clumsiness in design or execution or an inability to use materials with skill or competence ⟨the plans were badly *bungled*⟩ ⟨he has completely *bungled* the matter⟩ ⟨some singularly excellent recordings side by side with some pretty *bungled* ones—*P. H. Lang*⟩ ⟨some Occupation officials said and did stupid things, and inexperience led to *bungling*—*Sat. Review*⟩ **Fumble** stresses clumsy or unskillful use of the hands especially in uncertain attempts to reach, take, or grasp something or in groping in the dark for something ⟨a football player who seldom *fumbles*⟩ ⟨recovered himself, *fumbled* with his cap, and made a bow—*Dickens*⟩ ⟨his old fingers *fumbling* absently for the beard which wasn't there—*Mary Austin*⟩ ⟨so she *fumbled* about in the dim light, and brought her brother his bread and butter and meat—*Deland*⟩ Occasionally it suggests the awkward uncertainty not of hands or fingers but of mind or soul ⟨a hesitant speaker *fumbling* for the right words⟩ ⟨never *fumbling* with what she has to say, never . . . imperfectly presenting her thought—*Arnold*⟩ **Muff**, a word much used in sports, especially implies an unskillful performance or a bad play (as in catching a ball, firing a shot, or wielding a golf stick) ⟨*muff* a stroke⟩ ⟨he *muffed* the ball⟩ Consequently *muff* in more general use often means to fail by bungling or fumbling ⟨*muff* an opportunity⟩ ⟨he *muffed* his chances for the nomination⟩ **Cobble** is much like *botch*, though it basically implies the mending or patching of shoes; in more general use it stresses a patching or putting together of something in a crude or clumsy manner ⟨even generous critics . . . attribute to him a limit in narrative stamina . . . his wind gave out too soon, forcing him to *cobble* things up out of tone—*J. C. Furnas*⟩
*Ana* patch, *mend, repair: *treat, handle: multilate (see MAIM): wreck, *ruin

**bother** *vb* vex, *annoy, irk
*Ana* *worry, harass, harry, pester, tease, tantalize: interfere, *meddle, tamper: *puzzle, perplex, distract: trouble, *inconvenience, incommode, discommode
*Ant* comfort  —*Con* solace, console (see COMFORT): appease, placate, *pacify, mollify, propitiate

**bottom** *vb* *base, found, ground, stay, rest
*Ana* *support, sustain: *set, fix, establish

---

**bough** branch, limb, *shoot

**bounce** *vb* *dismiss, drop, sack, fire, discharge, cashier

**bound** *n* *limit, confine, end, term
  *Ana* *border, verge, edge

**bound** *adj* **Bound, bond, indentured, articled** are comparable when they mean obliged to serve a master or in a clearly defined capacity for a certain number of years by the terms of a contract or mutual agreement. **Bound** not only stresses the obligation, but it also often connotes a condition of or approaching servitude. It frequently implies the status of an apprentice, one obliged to serve a master for an agreed term in return for being taught a trade, a craft, an art, or a profession. It may, however, imply the status of an unskilled laborer (as a domestic servant) who agrees to serve (as in a distant colony) in return for transportation, keep, and, sometimes, a wage ⟨he emigrated from England to the American colonies as a *bound* servant⟩ When the condition of servitude is emphasized and service without a wage is implied, **bond** (placed before the noun) is often used in place of *bound* ⟨*bond* servant⟩ ⟨a *bond*woman⟩ **Indentured** implies apprenticeship and emphasizes the fact that the agreement is in writing, has been executed in duplicate, and has legal validity. Usually it carries the implication of fairness and equity to both parties to the agreement ⟨a tailor's *indentured* employees⟩ ⟨a solicitor's *indentured* clerk⟩ Sometimes, especially in reference to an apprentice in a law office, **articled** is preferred to *indentured,* though there seems to be no clear distinction between the two ⟨he started out as an *articled* clerk in an attorney's office⟩

**bound** *n* jump, leap, spring, vault (see under JUMP *vb*)
  *Ana* advance, progress (see under ADVANCE *vb*): *haste, hurry, speed, expedition

**bound** *vb* **1** *jump, leap, spring, vault
  *Ana* *advance, progress: *speed, precipitate, hasten, hurry
**2** *skip, ricochet, hop, curvet, lope, lollop
  *Ana* dart, skim, skud (see FLY): *rebound, recoil, resile

**bounder** *cad, rotter

**boundless** *infinite, uncircumscribed, illimitable, eternal, sempiternal
  *Ana* vast, immense, enormous (see HUGE): *monstrous, prodigious, tremendous, stupendous
  *Con* circumscribed, limited, confined, restricted (see LIMIT *vb*)

**bountiful, bounteous** generous, openhanded, munificent, *liberal, handsome
  *Ana* *charitable, philanthropic, benevolent: prodigal, lavish (see PROFUSE)
  *Ant* niggardly  —*Con* *stingy, parsimonious, penurious, close, miserly: avaricious, *covetous, greedy, grasping: frugal, *sparing, economical

**bounty** award, reward, meed, guerdon, prize, *premium, bonus
  *Ana* gratuity, largess, *gift, boon: grant, subvention, subsidy (see APPROPRIATION)

**bouquet** perfume, *fragrance, redolence, incense
  *Ana* odor, aroma, *smell, scent

**bout** *n* stint, turn, trick, tour, *spell, shift, go

**bow** *vb* defer, *yield, submit, capitulate, succumb, relent, cave

**bow** *n* arc, arch, *curve

**bow** *vb* *flex, crook, buckle
  *Ana* bend, *curve, twist

**box** *vb* *strike, hit, smite, punch, slug, slog, swat, clout, slap, cuff

**boyish** *youthful, juvenile, puerile, maiden, virgin, virginal

**brace** *n* *couple, pair, yoke

**brace** *vb* *support, sustain, buttress, prop, bolster

*Ana* *strengthen, reinforce, fortify, energize, invigorate

**brag** *vb* *boast, vaunt, crow, gasconade
  *Ana* plume, pique, *pride, preen: flaunt, parade (see SHOW)
  *Ant* apologize  —*Con* extenuate, *palliate, whitewash, gloze, gloss

**braid** *vb* plait, *weave, knit, crochet, tat

**brain** *mind, intellect, intelligence, wit, psyche, soul

**branch** *n* limb, bough, *shoot

**brand** *n* **1** mark, stamp, label, tag, ticket (see under MARK *vb*)
  *Ana* *impression, impress, imprint, print
**2** *stigma, blot, stain
  *Ana* sear, burn, scorch (see BURN): tainting *or* taint, defilement (see corresponding verbs at CONTAMINATE): *blemish, defect, flaw

**brand** *vb* *mark, stamp, label, tag, ticket

**brandish** flourish, shake, *swing, wave, thrash
  *Ana* wield, swing, *handle, manipulate, ply: flaunt, parade, display, exhibit, *show

**brash** *adj* brazen, barefaced, impudent, *shameless
  *Ana* bold, audacious (see BRAVE): rash, reckless (see ADVENTUROUS): impetuous, headlong, abrupt, *precipitate: intrusive, officious, *impertinent
  *Ant* wary  —*Con* *cautious, chary, circumspect: *timid, timorous: reserved (see SILENT): discreet (see under PRUDENCE)

**brave** *adj* **Brave, courageous, unafraid, fearless, intrepid, valiant, valorous, dauntless, undaunted, doughty, bold, audacious** are comparable when they mean having or showing no fear when faced with something dangerous, difficult, or unknown. **Brave** usually indicates lack of fear in alarming or difficult circumstances rather than a temperamental liking for danger ⟨the *brave* soldier goes to meet Death, and meets him without a shudder—*Trollope*⟩ ⟨he would send an explosion ship into the harbor . . . a *brave* crew would take her in at night, right up against the city, would light the fuses, and try to escape—*Forester*⟩ **Courageous** implies stouthearted resolution in contemplating or facing danger and may suggest a temperamental readiness to meet dangers or difficulties ⟨I am afraid . . . because I do not wish to die. But my spirit masters the trembling flesh and the qualms of the mind. I am more than brave, I am *courageous*—*London*⟩ ⟨a man is *courageous* when he does things which others might fail to do owing to fear—*Russell*⟩ **Unafraid** simply indicates lack of fright or fear whether because of a courageous nature or because no cause for fear is present ⟨enjoy their homes *unafraid* of violent intrusion—*MacArthur*⟩ ⟨a young, daring, and creative people—a people *unafraid* of change—*MacLeish*⟩ **Fearless** may indicate lack of fear, or it may be more positive and suggest undismayed resolution ⟨joyous we too launch out on trackless seas, *fearless* for unknown shores—*Whitman*⟩ ⟨he gives always the impression of *fearless* sincerity . . . one always feels that he is ready to say bluntly what every one else is afraid to say—*T. S. Eliot*⟩ **Intrepid** suggests either daring in meeting danger or fortitude in enduring it ⟨with the *intrepid* woman who was his wife, and a few natives, he landed there, and set about building a house and clearing the scrub—*Maugham*⟩ ⟨the *intrepid* guardians of the place, hourly exposed to death, with famine worn, and suffering under many a perilous wound—*Wordsworth*⟩ **Valiant** suggests resolute courage and fortitude whether in facing danger or in attaining some end ⟨this *valiant*, steadfast people [of Yugoslavia], whose history for centuries has been a struggle for life—*Sir Winston Churchill*⟩ **Valorous** suggests illustrious bravery and, more often than *valiant*, qualifies accomplishments rather than persons or their exertions; thus,

*Ana* analogous words      *Ant* antonyms      *Con* contrasted words      See also explanatory notes facing page 1

one might refer to the *valorous* deeds of a *valiant* band of knights ⟨the regiment itself is a proud one, with a *valorous* record—*Infantry Jour.*⟩ **Dauntless** emphasizes determination, resolution, and fearlessness despite danger or difficulty ⟨the *dauntless* English infantry were receiving and repelling the furious charges—*Thackeray*⟩ ⟨nothing appalled her *dauntless* soul—*Beckford*⟩ **Undaunted** indicates continued courage and resolution after danger, hardship, or defeat ⟨he watched them at the points of greatest danger falling under the shots from the scorpions, and others stepping *undaunted* into their places to fall in the same way—*Froude*⟩ **Doughty** combines the implications of *formidable, sturdy,* and *brave* but may have an archaic or humorous suggestion ⟨when Fisk reached the head of the stairs leading to the boardroom, the *doughty* president of the endangered railway knocked him down to the ground floor—*Charles & Mary Beard*⟩ ⟨so *doughty* a warrior must break a lance—*Parrington*⟩ **Bold** may indicate a forward or defiant tendency to thrust oneself into difficult or dangerous situations ⟨it was a *bold* man who dared to walk alone through hundreds of miles of lion-infested country with nothing but a spear in his hand to seek work and adventure—*Cloete*⟩ ⟨these fellows who attacked the inn tonight—*bold,* desperate blades, for sure—*Stevenson*⟩ ⟨he knew a fool and a tyrant in high places, and was *bold* to call them by their true names—*Parrington*⟩ When used of immaterial things (as plans, experiments, or deeds) *bold* suggests a disregard for danger, risk, or convention ⟨a *bold* scheme to corner the wheat market⟩ **Audacious** implies spirited and sometimes reckless daring ⟨the place where the fiery Ethan Allen first sketched his *audacious* move against Ticonderoga—*Schulberg*⟩ ⟨hitherto no liberal statesman has been so *audacious* as to . . . lay profane hands on the divine right of nations to seek their own advantage at the cost of the rest—*Veblen*⟩
*Ana* daring, venturesome, daredevil, *adventurous: heroic, gallant (see corresponding nouns at HEROISM): plucky, gritty (see corresponding nouns at FORTITUDE)
*Ant* craven —*Con* *timid, timorous: shrinking, flinching, blenching (see RECOIL *vb*)

**brave** *vb* dare, defy, beard, *face, challenge
*Ana* confront, *meet, encounter: oppose, combat, *resist, fight

**bravo** *assassin, cutthroat, gunman

**brawl** *n* Brawl, broil, fracas, melee, row, rumpus, scrap are comparable when meaning a noisy fight or quarrel. **Brawl** implies angry contentions, blows, and a noisy racket; it usually suggests participation by several persons ⟨a family *brawl* that kept the neighbors awake⟩ ⟨street *brawls*⟩ ⟨a howling *brawl* amongst vicious hoodlums—*Stafford*⟩ **Broil** stresses disorder, confusion, and turmoil among the combatants more than the disturbance they cause others. The term may be used contemptuously in place of *war, conflict,* or *controversy* ⟨plunging us in all the *broils* of the European nations—*Jefferson*⟩ but it is more often used of a violent fight or quarrel where the issues are not clear or significant or where the opposing parties are not clearly distinguished ⟨but village mirth breeds contests, *broils,* and blows—*Shelley*⟩ **Fracas** is applicable to a noisy quarrel or excited disturbance whether leading to blows or not; the term does not suggest as much vulgarity or as many participants as *brawl,* but it may imply as much noise and excitement ⟨they were hot-tempered, frequently embroiled in quarrels. John Adams, after such a *fracas,* listed his new enemies in his diary—*C. D. Bowen*⟩ **Melee** is applied to a more or less disorganized hand-to-hand conflict or to a dispute which resembles such a combat. In many instances the emphasis is so strongly on confusion and mix-up that the implication

of combat or contention is weakened or lost ⟨the calmness of the platform was transformed into a *melee.* Little Constance found herself left on the fringe of a physically agitated crowd which was apparently trying to scale a precipice surmounted by windows and doors—*Bennett*⟩ **Row** is applicable to a demonstration or fight, whether a quarrel, a squabble, or a dispute, that is so public or so noisy as to attract attention ⟨during the recent *row* over atomic-energy legislation their feuding was epic—*Friendly*⟩ **Rumpus** suggests even greater agitation and disturbance than *row,* for it usually connotes an uproar ⟨you incur my serious displeasure if you move one inch in this contemptible *rumpus*—*Scott*⟩ **Scrap** usually suggests a physical tussle but often implies little more than a noisy, sharp quarrel ⟨the boys are good friends, but they have many a *scrap*⟩
*Ana* conflict, fight, fray, affray (see CONTEST): contention, dissension, strife, *discord: wrangle, altercation, *quarrel, squabble: uproar, racket, *din, hubbub, clamor

**brawny** *muscular, burly, husky, sinewy, athletic
*Ana* stalwart, *strong, sturdy, stout, tough: *fleshy
*Ant* scrawny —*Con* lanky, lank, gaunt, rawboned, *lean, spare, skinny: *thin, slender, slight, slim

**brazen** *shameless, brash, impudent
*Ana* callous, *hardened, indurated: insolent, arrogant (see PROUD): rash, reckless (see ADVENTUROUS): bold, audacious (see BRAVE)
*Ant* bashful —*Con* *shy, diffident, modest, coy: *timid, timorous: stealthy, surreptitious, underhand, *secret

**breach** *n* 1 Breach, infraction, violation, transgression, trespass, infringement, contravention are comparable when denoting the act or the offense of one who fails to keep the law or to do what the law, one's duty, or an obligation requires. **Breach** occurs rarely by itself except in phrases such as "a law more honored in the *breach* than in the observance." The word is usually followed by *of* and a noun or pronoun which indicates the thing which is broken or not kept ⟨his action constitutes a *breach* of faith⟩ ⟨he was found guilty of *breach* of the peace by reason of his noisy, disorderly, and annoying conduct⟩ ⟨sued for *breach* of contract⟩ **Infraction** is now more often used than *breach* (except in certain time-honored idioms) for a breaking of a law or obligation ⟨an *infraction* of the school rules⟩ ⟨an *infraction* of a treaty⟩ ⟨an *infraction* of canon law⟩ ⟨we have scrutinized the case, but cannot say that it shows an *infraction* of rights under the Constitution of the United States—*Justice Holmes*⟩ **Violation** adds to *breach* and *infraction* the implication of flagrant disregard of the law or of the rights of others and often suggests the exercise of force or violence; thus, the *violation* of a treaty suggests positive, often aggressive and injurious action, while its *infraction* may imply a mere failure strictly to adhere to its terms ⟨a *violation* of military discipline⟩ ⟨the police interference was a *violation* of the right to free assembly⟩ ⟨when more of the people's sustenance is exacted through the form of taxation than is necessary to meet the just obligations of Government . . . such exaction becomes ruthless extortion and a *violation* of the fundamental principles of a free Government—*Cleveland*⟩ **Transgression** is applied to any act that goes beyond the limits prescribed by a law, rule, or order; often the term is used specifically of an infraction of the moral law or of one of the commandments ⟨for sin is the *transgression* of the law—*1 Jn 3:4*⟩ ⟨"I was forgetting," she said. "I am forbidden tea." . . . She looked at the cup, tremendously tempted. . . . An occasional *transgression* could not harm her—*Bennett*⟩ **Trespass** also implies an overstepping of prescribed bounds, but it carries in addition a strong implication of encroachment upon the rights, the comfort, or the prop-

---

A colon (:) separates groups of words discriminated. An asterisk (*) indicates place of treatment of each group.

erty of others. In Scriptural and religious use a *trespass* is particularly an offense against God or one's neighbor ⟨if ye forgive not men their *trespasses,* neither will your Father forgive your *trespasses—Mt* 6:15⟩ In law a *trespass* is an unlawful act, involving some degree of force or violence, committed against the person, the property, or the rights of another ⟨the passing through another's premises against his wish or without his invitation constitutes a *trespass*⟩ ⟨a burglar who is frightened away before he actually enters a house is liable to arrest for *trespass*⟩ **Infringement** is sometimes used as though it were identical in meaning with *infraction* ⟨an *infringement* of the law⟩ ⟨an *infringement* of a treaty⟩ More often it implies *trespass* rather than *violation* and therefore is the idiomatic term when trespass involving an encroachment upon a legally protected right or privilege is at issue; thus, the unauthorized manufacture of something which has been patented constitutes an *infringement* (rather than an *infraction* or *violation*) of a patent ⟨the unauthorized reproduction and sale of matter already copyrighted constitutes an *infringement* of the copyright⟩ ⟨an *infringement* on the liberty of the American people⟩ **Contravention** applies specifically to a going contrary to the intent of the law or to an act in defiance of what is regarded as right, lawful, or obligatory ⟨warrants in *contravention* of the acts of Parliament—*Macaulay*⟩ ⟨if there is in a work of art a *contravention* of nature—*Lowes*⟩
*Ant* observance

**2 Breach, break, split, schism, rent, rupture, rift** are comparable when they mean a pulling apart in relations or in connections. **Breach,** the most general in application of any of these terms, is capable of being referred to any such pulling apart in itself, as apart from the context, throwing light on its cause, its magnitude, or its seriousness ⟨a *breach* in unity⟩ ⟨widen the *breach* between old friends⟩ ⟨having followed the high banks of the Tom to the furthest extremity . . . they happily found a *breach* in the inclosure—*Kingston*⟩ ⟨it may be one man's privilege and duty to heal the *breach* between the Arab and the Jew—*Douglas*⟩ **Break** (see also BREAK *n*) is often substituted for *breach* when one wishes to emphasize the strain that is inducing or has induced a disruption (as between persons or groups) ⟨efforts to avoid an open *break* with the conservative faction⟩ ⟨the *break* was final, and there was no course open for the nation except war⟩ **Split** usually implies a complete breach, suggesting a division such as would be made by an ax or knife; often, also, it hints at the impossibility of bringing together again the two parts (as parties or factions) that once formed a whole. *Split* often implies a division of friends or friendly groups into opposing parties or factions ⟨a major *split* between the United States and most of the rest of the free world—*Bundy*⟩ ⟨I fear the *split* betwixt Constable and Cadell will render impossible what might otherwise be hopeful enough—*Scott*⟩ **Schism** implies a clear-cut separation between divisions of an original group and consequent discord and dissension between the two parts; typically the term is used of such a division in a religious communion, but it may be applied to any union of rational beings (as a political party or a philosophical school) ⟨he succeeded in dividing the American Quakers into two bodies; and this *schism* . . . lasted on till the present year—*Inge*⟩ ⟨a school of literalists arose with all the mad consequence of *schism* and heresy—*Blackmur*⟩ **Rent** suggests an opening made by tearing or rending and may impute characteristics (as irregularity, jaggedness, and narrowness) to a break to which it is applied ⟨thy stately mansion, and the pride of thy domain, strange contrast do present to house and home in many a craggy *rent* of the wild Peak—*Words-*

*worth*⟩ ⟨through the wide *rent* in Time's eternal veil, hope was seen beaming—*Shelley*⟩ ⟨a *rent* in the social fabric—*Millstein*⟩ **Rupture** approaches *breach* in meaning, but it carries a more clearly defined stress upon a break in relations between people or groups; in addition, it frequently is affected by its special medical use and then often suggests an actual but not always clearly apparent break ⟨mother and son avoided an open *rupture* by never referring to their differences—*Santayana*⟩ ⟨it was still the policy of the Cardinal . . . to carry on the convention that he had not provoked any direct *rupture* with Vienna—*Belloc*⟩ **Rift** implies a breach that is made usually by some natural process (as one that produces a separation of rocks in a mountain or a cracking of the earth); consequently it is often applied to a breach that is small at first and is in danger of growing larger ⟨this little *rift* it was that had widened to a now considerable breach—*H. G. Wells*⟩ ⟨it is the little *rift* within the lute, that by and by will make the music mute—*Tennyson*⟩ ⟨it was, I believe, the terrible Wars of Religion that made the fatal *rift* between religion and science which we are now trying to close—*Inge*⟩
*Ana* division, severance, separation (see corresponding verbs at SEPARATE): dissension, *discord, difference, variance, strife: estrangement, alienation (see corresponding verbs at ESTRANGE)
*Con* union, *unity, solidarity, integrity: accord, *harmony, concord

**bread, bread and butter** sustenance, *living, livelihood, subsistence, maintenance, support, keep
**break** *vb* **Break, crack, burst, bust, snap, shatter, shiver** are comparable as general terms meaning fundamentally to come apart or cause to come apart. **Break** basically implies the operation of a stress or strain that will cause a rupture, a fracture, a fissure, or a shattering either in one spot or in many ⟨*break* a dish by dropping it⟩ ⟨*break* a bone⟩ ⟨the column *broke* when subjected to too great a weight⟩ ⟨a flood resulted when the dam *broke*⟩ But *break* goes much further than this. Often, with or without the help of an adverb, it suggests the disruption of something material or immaterial, either in whole or in part. It may then imply a collapsing or causing to collapse ⟨the wagon *broke* down⟩ ⟨*broke* the enemy by the only methods possible—starvation, attrition, and a slow, deadly . . . envelopment—*Buchan*⟩ ⟨his spirit was *broken*⟩ Similarly it may imply a destruction of completeness, integrity, or wholeness; thus, one *breaks* a set of china by losing or destroying one or more pieces of the set; one *breaks* a ten-dollar bill by spending part of it and getting the remainder in smaller bills or coins ⟨*break* a solid group into factions⟩ With the same underlying notion it may imply a destruction of continuity (as by interrupting, terminating, or disintegrating) ⟨*break* a circuit⟩ ⟨*break* a journey⟩ ⟨*broke* his silence⟩ ⟨*break* up a friendship⟩ ⟨it was the only time that day he saw her pale composure *break*—*Cather*⟩ Sometimes the sense of disruption is not obvious, and the idea of piercing so as to let someone or something make entrance or exit predominates ⟨*broke* his way through the crowd⟩ ⟨*break* a new path⟩ ⟨*break* the news gently⟩ ⟨she had just *broken* into her fifty-second year—*Woolf*⟩ Most common of the senses that bear only a slight relation to the primary sense of *break* is one that implies violation or transgression ⟨*break* the law⟩ ⟨*break* the Sabbath⟩ ⟨all rules, in education, should be capable of being *broken* for special reasons—*Russell*⟩ Basically **crack** means to make the sudden, sharp sound characteristic of a breaking of something brittle (as ice, bone, or glass). It is often applied with this denotation to things which make a similar sound yet do not necessarily break ⟨*crack* a whip⟩ ⟨the

thunder *cracks*⟩ ⟨his voice *cracked*⟩ *Crack* more frequently implies a breaking of something hard or brittle or of something also hollow, often with a sudden sharp sound and usually without a separation of the parts ⟨the dish was *cracked,* not broken⟩ ⟨*cracking* nuts between two stones⟩ ⟨the mirror was *cracked* by the explosion⟩ ⟨the sound of *cracking* glass⟩ ⟨the thin ice *cracked* under the skater's weight⟩ Occasionally it implies merely the breaking of something that has grown dry or parched ⟨fever has made his lips *crack*⟩ ⟨the prolonged drought has caused the earth to *crack*⟩ **Burst** usually implies a breaking (as into pieces) with a scattering of contents by the force of internal pressure ⟨*burst* a blood vessel⟩ ⟨the boiler *burst* under too great pressure⟩ ⟨bombs *bursting* in air—*Key*⟩ ⟨the willow scarce holds the sap that tightens the bark and would *burst* it if it did not enlarge to the pressure—*Jefferies*⟩ Sometimes the implication is merely the sudden release or the likelihood of such release of something seeking utterance but hitherto suppressed or held back ⟨*burst* into laughter⟩ ⟨*bursting* with suppressed merriment⟩ ⟨*burst* into tears⟩ Sometimes a breaking under tension, under concussion, or through limitations is the only implication that the word carries ⟨*burst* the bonds which tied him⟩ or it may stress the violence of the force that opens ⟨*burst* open the doors⟩ or the suddenness with which someone or something comes out or in ⟨the lilacs *burst* into bloom⟩ ⟨she *burst* into the living room⟩ ⟨the news of the attack *burst* upon the nation⟩ **Bust** may be used informally in place of *burst* especially in the sense of to break under the strain of pressure, of tension, or of concussion ⟨this westernmost province . . . is beginning to *bust* its industrial britches —*Wall Street Jour.*⟩ **Snap** fundamentally implies a quick, sudden effort to seize (as by biting or by snatching at), but usually this action is accompanied by a short sharp sound (as a report or a click). Hence *snap* is often used to imply the action of breaking or bursting when the intent is to suggest a quick, clean-cut break and the sharp sound which accompanies it ⟨branch after branch *snapped* during the storm⟩ ⟨a string of his violin *snapped*⟩ ⟨sharp the link of life will *snap*—*Housman*⟩ **Shatter** literally implies a breaking into many pieces, but unlike *burst,* which emphasizes the cause, it stresses the effect, a scattering of the pieces far and wide, and a total destruction of the thing involved ⟨the flying debris *shattered* the window⟩ ⟨*shatter* a rock by an explosion of dynamite⟩ ⟨a bolt of lightning *shattered* the oak tree⟩ Consequently, especially as applied to intangible things, *shatter* consistently implies a far more devastating and destructive effect than *break;* thus, "his health was *broken* by the experience" means that it was seriously impaired, but "his health was *shattered* by the experience" means that it was impaired beyond the point of complete recovery ⟨the *shattering* of his illusions⟩ ⟨the pathetic gropings after the fragments of a *shattered* faith—*Day Lewis*⟩ ⟨the Great War shook civilization to its base; . . . another conflict on the same scale would *shatter* it—*Inge*⟩ ⟨the legend of Rome's invincibility had been *shattered*—*Buchan*⟩ **Shiver,** a chiefly rhetorical term, implies a shattering by dashing, smashing, or any usually external force and a wide scattering of fragments or splinters; in extended use it ordinarily preserves a context approaching the literal and so has never acquired a detached secondary sense ⟨the knight's lance *shivered* against his opponent's shield⟩ ⟨as he crossed the hall, his statue fell, and *shivered* on the stones—*Froude*⟩ ⟨the upshot of which, was, to smash this witness like a crockery vessel, and *shiver* his part of the case to useless lumber—*Dickens*⟩

*Ana* disintegrate, crumble (see DECAY): *detach, disen-

gage: demolish, *destroy
*Ant* cleave (*together*): keep (*of laws*) —*Con* cohere, cling, *stick: unite, *join, combine: observe (see KEEP)
**break** *n* 1 **Break, gap, interruption, interval, interim, hiatus, lacuna** all denote a lapse in continuity. **Break** applies not only to a lapse in continuity in something material or substantial ⟨a *break* in geological strata⟩ ⟨a *break* in the clouds⟩ ⟨he tried to find a *break* in the fence⟩ but also in things (as a course of action or something having extension in time) that may be considered in reference to their continuity ⟨he ran the long race without a *break*⟩ ⟨the book was written with no *breaks* except for eating and for sleeping⟩ ⟨a holiday makes a pleasant *break* in routine⟩ ⟨there was no *break* in the long, cold winter⟩ ⟨yet he felt that he was going away forever, and was making the final *break* with everything that had been dear to him—*Cather*⟩ **Gap** basically applies to an opening (as in a wall or fence) made either by natural decay or by deliberate effort as a means of ingress or egress; the term may also include an opening (as a gorge between mountains) that serves as a passage inward or outward ⟨the Delaware Water *Gap*⟩ or that seems like a chasm or void, in representing either a break in continuity or in leaving an unfilled or unfillable space ⟨here's our chief guest. If he had been forgotten, it had been as a *gap* in our great feast—*Shak.*⟩ ⟨so that the jest is clearly to be seen, not in the words—but in the *gap* between—*Cowper*⟩ ⟨a fatal *gap* in our security structure—*Truman*⟩ ⟨one would like to cling to the old-fashioned theory that there is a *gap* between accusation and proof—*Schlesinger* b. 1917⟩ **Interruption** implies a break that not only makes for a lapse in continuity but that disturbs the procedure (as of an action, a work, or a discourse) and causes a temporary stop or that, less often, makes a void or gap in space or order ⟨the growing infirmities of age manifest themselves in nothing more strongly, than in an inveterate dislike of *interruption*—*Lamb*⟩ ⟨those who hope to render themselves . . . oblivious to the harsh *interruptions* of reality —*Day Lewis*⟩ ⟨the mountain range continues without *interruption* until it meets the sea⟩ **Interval** refers to the distance (as in time or in space) that exists between two things that are basically alike; the term often serves simply as a basis for measuring or suggesting this distance ⟨at present, perhaps, it was as well to be asunder. She was in need of a little *interval* for recollection—*Austen*⟩ ⟨how soft the music of those village bells falling at *intervals* upon the ear in cadence sweet—*Cowper*⟩ ⟨there stretches on either side of the rivers . . . a region of hills and lakes and swamps among which the farms are only upland *intervals* —*Canby*⟩ **Interim** applies to the interval between two events (as the death or abdication of a sovereign and the accession of his successor or the discarding of one method and the instituting of another) ⟨many contended that the child born to Lucrezia in the *interim* between her divorce from Pesaro and her marriage to Bisceglie was sired by Cesare—*Beuf*⟩ ⟨in a healthy mind there is an *interim* between one duty and another—*Crothers*⟩ **Hiatus** applies mainly to an interruption or lapse in time or continuity, and so implies that something important or essential is missing ⟨Charles II had been restored to his kingdom . . . after an enforced *hiatus* of twelve years—*Abernethy*⟩ ⟨we are likely to be disconcerted by . . . *hiatuses* of thought, when certain links in the association of ideas are dropped down into the unconscious mind—*Edmund Wilson*⟩ ⟨"The war," they said, "has caused a *hiatus,* and thought has broken with tradition"—*Rose Macaulay*⟩ **Lacuna** may stress the vacuity of a gap or void ⟨fills a *lacuna* in our knowledge as to the whereabouts of many manuscripts—*Gohdes*⟩ ⟨one of the rare *lacunae* in this map—*Lebon*⟩ and is often

A colon (:) separates groups of words discriminated. An asterisk (*) indicates place of treatment of each group.

used specifically of a blank in a text (as of a manuscript or inscription) where a few words have been omitted or effaced ⟨translated the whole work anew, and succeeded in filling many *lacunae* in the text—*Mezger*⟩ In anatomical use the term more often stresses the minuteness than the vacuity of a gap (as a pit or chamber) ⟨cartilage cells are isolated in scattered *lacunae*⟩
*Ana* division, separation, severance (see corresponding verbs at SEPARATE): falling, sinking, dropping (see FALL): respite, lull, intermission, recess, *pause
2 *breach, split, schism, rent, rupture, rift
*Ana, Con* see those at BREACH 2
3 chance, *opportunity, occasion, time
**break down** *analyze, resolve, dissect
*Con* concatenate, articulate, *integrate
**breakdown** *n* analysis, resolution, dissection (see under ANALYZE)
**breastwork** *bulwark, bastion, parapet, rampart
**breed** *vb* *generate, engender, propagate, reproduce, procreate, beget, sire, get
**breed** *n* *variety, subspecies, race, cultivar, strain, clone, stock
**breeding** cultivation, *culture, refinement
*Ana* *tact, address, poise, savoir faire: *courtesy, amenity, gallantry: grace, dignity, *elegance
*Ant* vulgarity —*Con* boorishness, churlishness (see corresponding adjectives under BOOR): grossness, coarseness (see corresponding adjectives at COARSE): rudeness, discourteousness *or* discourtesy, ungraciousness (see corresponding adjectives at RUDE)
**breeze** *wind, gale, hurricane, zephyr
**bridle** *vb* 1 check, curb, *restrain, inhibit
*Ana* repress, *suppress: *govern, rule: control, direct, manage (see CONDUCT)
*Ant* vent —*Con* *express, utter, air, voice, ventilate
2 bristle, *strut, swagger
*Ana* plume, preen, pique, *pride
*Con* grovel, *wallow: cringe, cower (see FAWN): wince, flinch (see RECOIL)
**brief** *adj* Brief, short are the most comprehensive adjectives in English meaning not long. Brief refers primarily to duration; short, to either duration or linear extent ⟨a *brief* interview⟩ ⟨a *short* sermon⟩ ⟨a *short* distance⟩ ⟨*short* legs⟩ As applied to duration, *brief* and *short* are sometimes complete synonyms ⟨a *brief* struggle⟩ ⟨a *short* battle⟩ But *short* frequently suggests incompleteness, curtailment, or sudden stoppage, and *brief* sometimes implies condensation ⟨he cut his speech *short*⟩ ⟨he made his speech as *brief* as possible⟩ As applied to linear extent, *brief* is facetious and means extremely short ⟨a *brief* skirt⟩
*Ana* *transient, fleeting, passing, momentary, short-lived: *concise, terse, succinct, laconic, pithy: compacted *or* compact, concentrated (see corresponding verbs at COMPACT): shortened, abbreviated, abridged, curtailed (see SHORTEN)
*Ant* prolonged, protracted —*Con* lengthened *or* lengthy, extended *or* extensive, elongated (see corresponding verbs at EXTEND)
**brief** *n* abstract, epitome, *abridgment, synopsis, conspectus
**bright** *adj* 1 Bright, brilliant, radiant, luminous, lustrous, effulgent, refulgent, beaming, lambent, lucent, incandescent are comparable when they mean actually or seemingly shining or glowing with light. Bright implies an opposition to *dim* or *dull;* it applies chiefly to things that vary in the degree in which they shed light or are pervaded by light, according to circumstances; thus, when used in reference to a fire or burning material (as coals), it sug-

gests a good draft and flames; when used in reference to a day, it implies lack of clouds, fog, smoke, or other obstacles to the passage of sunlight ⟨a *bright* sky⟩ ⟨a *bright* star⟩ ⟨a *bright* sword⟩ ⟨*bright* eyes⟩ ⟨a *bright* color⟩ Brilliant (see also INTELLIGENT) implies conspicuous or intense brightness; it also often connotes scintillating or flashing light ⟨a well-cut diamond is the most *brilliant* of gems⟩ ⟨the sun is too *brilliant* for the human eye⟩ ⟨a *brilliant* smile⟩ ⟨Madame Olenska's face grew *brilliant* with pleasure—*Wharton*⟩ ⟨what one saw when one looked about was that *brilliant* blue world of stinging air and moving cloud—*Cather*⟩ Radiant, in contrast with *bright* and *brilliant,* stresses the emission or seeming emission of rays of light; it suggests, therefore, a property or power possessed by a thing rather than a quality ascribed to it because of its effect on the vision; thus, a celestial body is properly described as *radiant* only when it emits rays of light; a planet, no matter how bright it appears to the eye, is preferably described as *bright* or *brilliant* because it shines by reflected light ⟨Virtue could see to do what Virtue would by her own *radiant* light, though sun and moon were in the flat sea sunk—*Milton*⟩ The term, however, is sometimes used of anything that seems to give out light in the manner of the sun or a star ⟨in warlike armor drest, golden, all *radiant!*—*Shelley*⟩ Luminous, like *radiant,* suggests emission of light, but, unlike it, implies the sending forth of steady suffused glowing light; it is applicable to anything that shines by reflected light or that glows in the dark because of some special quality (as of physical state or chemical activity); thus, all celestial bodies are *luminous,* but only self-*luminous* bodies (stars in the strict astronomical sense) are also *radiant* ⟨phosphorus is a *luminous* substance⟩ As applied to color or to colored things the term implies more than *bright,* for it usually suggests a jewel-like quality ⟨the *luminous* green of the emerald⟩ or iridescence ⟨the blue off Nantucket is not the miracle of *luminous,* translucent color off Sardinia—*Lowes*⟩ As applied to ideas or their expression, the term implies crystallike clearness and the absence of all obscurity ⟨a *luminous* treatment of a subject⟩ ⟨a *luminous* statement—*Brougham*⟩ Lustrous is applied only to an object whose surface reflects light; it therefore seldom implies pervading light but, rather, a brilliant or iridescent sheen or gloss ⟨the *lustrous* brass of a burnished lamp⟩ ⟨a *lustrous* enameled surface⟩ ⟨*lustrous* satin⟩ Effulgent and refulgent indicate resplendent or gleaming brilliance, and the latter implies further that the brilliance is reflected, sometimes from an unseen source ⟨*effulgent* loveliness⟩ ⟨a chandelier of *refulgent* crystal⟩ ⟨in arms they stood of golden panoply, *refulgent* host—*Milton*⟩ Beaming literally implies emission of a beam (see *beam* under RAY) ⟨rising moon, fair *beaming,* and streaming her silver light the boughs amang—*Burns*⟩ In its commonest use (as applied to looks or expression) *beaming* suggests a display of happiness, satisfaction, or benevolence ⟨the *beaming* eyes of children greeting Santa Claus⟩ ⟨broad *beaming* smile—*George Eliot*⟩ Lambent is applied to a thing (as a flame or a luminous body) which throws a play of light over an object or surface without rendering it brilliant or lustrous ⟨the *lambent* flame of genius . . . lights up the universe—*Hazlitt*⟩ ⟨*lambent* lightning-fire—*Shelley*⟩ Often *lambent* suggests the emission of soft gleams of light ⟨kind, quiet, nearsighted eyes, which her round spectacles magnified into *lambent* moons —*Deland*⟩ Lucent is a highly poetical or literary adjective that approaches *luminous* or, less often, *lustrous* in its meaning; it is usually applied to something transfigured by light (as from the sun or a fire) ⟨the *lucent* fume of

the city's smoke rising up—*Mackenzie*⟩ ⟨till every particle glowed . . . and slowly seemed to turn to *lucent* amber—*Gibson*⟩ **Incandescent** suggests intense glowing brightness of or as if of an intensely heated body ⟨pots *incandescent* in the kiln⟩ ⟨an *incandescent* lamp⟩ ⟨set thoughts aglowing in *incandescent* language—*Iglesias*⟩ *Ana* illuminated, illumined, lighted, lightened, enlightened (see ILLUMINATE): flashing, gleaming, glistening, sparkling (see FLASH *vb*): glowing, flaming (see BLAZE *vb*)
*Ant* dull: dim —*Con* dusky, murky, gloomy, *dark, obscure: *colorless, uncolored: *pale, pallid, ashen, livid
2 smart, quick-witted, brilliant, clever, *intelligent, knowing, alert
*Ana* *sharp, keen, acute: *quick, ready, prompt, apt: precocious, advanced (see PREMATURE)
*Ant* dense, dull —*Con* *stupid, slow, crass, dumb: *lethargic, sluggish: phlegmatic, stolid, *impassive
**brilliant** 1 radiant, luminous, *bright, effulgent, lustrous, refulgent, beaming, lambent, lucent, incandescent
*Ana* flashing, scintillating, sparkling, gleaming, glittering, coruscating (see FLASH *vb*): blazing flaming, flaring, glowing (see BLAZE *vb*)
*Ant* subdued (*of light, color*) —*Con* gloomy, murky, obscure, dim, dusky (see DARK)
2 *intelligent, clever, bright, smart, alert, quick-witted, knowing
*Ana* erudite, *learned, scholarly: sage, sapient, *wise
*Ant* crass —*Con* *stupid, slow, dull, dense, dumb
**brim** rim, edge, brink, *border, verge, margin
**bring**, take, fetch are comparable but not interchangeable when used in the sense of to convey from one place to another. **Bring** implies carrying, leading, or transporting from a distance to the point where the speaker or agent is or will be; **take**, a carrying, leading, or conducting to a point away from the one where the speaker or agent is or will be; thus, a mother asks her boy setting out for school to *take* a note to the teacher and to *bring* home a reply; a farmer *takes* his cattle to the market and *brings* back a supply of sugar, flour, and fresh meat. **Fetch** implies going to a place where something is to be found, getting it, and bringing it back to the starting point ⟨please *fetch* me a chair from the next room⟩ ⟨I shall *fetch* whatever you need⟩ ⟨he called to her, and said, *Fetch* me, I pray thee, a little water in a vessel, that I may drink. And as she was going to *fetch* it, he called to her, and said, *Bring* me, I pray thee, a morsel of bread in thine hand—*I Kings* 17:10-11⟩
*Ana* bear, *carry, convey: obtain, procure, *get
*Ant* withdraw, remove
**brink** verge, edge, rim, *border, margin
*Ana* *limit, bound, end, confine: *shore, strand, coast
**brisk** nimble, *agile, spry
*Ana* *fast, quick, rapid, fleet, swift, speedy: ready, prompt, *quick: dynamic, live, *active
*Ant* sluggish —*Con* *lethargic, torpid, comatose: *lazy, indolent, slothful, faineant: *inactive, inert, idle
**bristle** *vb* bridle, *strut, swagger
*Ana* preen, plume *pride, pique: evince, manifest, *show, evidence: flaunt, parade, display, exhibit (see SHOW)
*Con* conceal, *hide, bury
**brittle** crisp, *fragile, frangible, short, friable
*Ana* *hardened, indurated
*Ant* supple —*Con* *elastic, resilient, springy, flexible: tough, tenacious, *strong, stout
**broach** *vb* voice, utter, *express, vent, air, ventilate
*Ana* *reveal, disclose, divulge: *introduce, interject, interpose
**broad** *adj* Broad, wide, deep are comparable chiefly when

they refer to horizontal extent. **Broad** and **wide** apply to surfaces or areas as measured from side to side ⟨a picture two feet *wide*⟩ and **deep** (see also DEEP) to those as measured from front to back ⟨a closet that was narrow but *deep*⟩ *Broad* and *wide* always and *deep* in some instances may be used of surfaces that spread away from one; thus, a river may be *wide* or *broad* (but not *deep*, which would here refer only to vertical distance) at a given point, but a flower border may be four feet *wide*, *broad*, or, if the far side is not ordinarily accessible, *deep*. When a plot of ground or similar area is measured, *broad* or, especially, *wide* is used of the distance from one side to the other and *deep* of that from front line to back line ⟨the lot is 70 feet *wide* and 100 feet *deep*⟩ *Broad* and *wide* are frequently interchangeable when used descriptively to mean having relatively great extent across or from side to side ⟨a *broad* or *wide* street, ribbon, margin⟩ But *broad* commonly applies only to surfaces or areas as such ⟨a *broad* leaf⟩ ⟨a *broad*-headed tack⟩ ⟨*broad*-shouldered⟩ *Wide* applies also to apertures or to something that opens or spreads. *Wide*, therefore, is the preferred term when the emphasis is upon the distance between limits rather than on the extent of the intervening surface ⟨a *wide* gash in his arm⟩ ⟨a *wide* opening⟩ ⟨a *wide* view⟩ ⟨the doorway is four feet *wide*⟩ *Deep* in similar descriptive use, when it carries an implication only of horizontal extent, is applicable only to something that has great extent backward (as from an opening or from the front) ⟨a *deep* forest⟩ ⟨a *deep* cavern⟩ ⟨a *deep* lot⟩
*Ana* extended *or* extensive (see corresponding verb at EXTEND): *spacious, capacious, commodious, ample: vast, immense (see HUGE): expanded, dilated (see EXPAND)
*Ant* narrow —*Con* confined, circumscribed, limited, restricted (see LIMIT *vb*)
**broadcast** *vb* 1 *strew, straw, scatter, sow
*Ana* *spread, circulate, disseminate, propagate
2 promulgate, publish, advertise, announce, *declare, proclaim
**broadcasting** promulgation, publication, advertisement, announcement, declaration, proclamation (see under DECLARE)
**Brobdingnagian** *huge, vast, immense, enormous, elephantine, mammoth, giant, gigantic, gigantean, colossal, gargantuan, Herculean, cyclopean, titanic
*Ant* lilliputian
**broil** *n* fracas, melee, row, *brawl, rumpus, scrap
*Ana* fray, affray, fight, conflict, combat, *contest: altercation, wrangle, *quarrel: contention, strife, dissension, conflict (see DISCORD)
**bromide** cliché, platitude, truism, *commonplace
**brook** *vb* stand, abide, *bear, tolerate, suffer, endure
**browbeat** bulldoze, bully, *intimidate, cow
*Ana* terrorize, terrify, *frighten, scare
*Con* *coax, cajole, wheedle, blandish
**bruise** *vb* *crush, mash, smash, squash, macerate
*Ana* batter, mangle, *maim: *press, squeeze
**bruise** *n* *wound, contusion, trauma, traumatism, lesion
**brush** *vb* Brush, graze, glance, shave, skim are comparable when they mean to touch lightly in passing. **Brush** implies a movement like the flick of a brush upon a surface: sometimes it suggests no more than an almost impalpable touching, but sometimes it suggests a light touching or rubbing that disperses something that it touches ⟨ye tinsel Insects! whom a court maintains . . . . The Muse's wing shall *brush* you all away—*Pope*⟩ ⟨fair dewy roses *brush* against our faces—*Keats*⟩ ⟨trees, filled with birds, *brushed* the roof—*Pollet*⟩ ⟨their eyes met and *brushed*

---

A colon (:) separates groups of words discriminated. An asterisk (*) indicates place of treatment of each group.

like birds' wings—*F. S. Fitzgerald*⟩ **Graze** implies the swift passage of a bullet or any rapidly moving object so that it touches a person or thing abrading the surface or, in the case of a person, the skin ⟨whose solid virtue the shot of accident nor dart of chance could neither *graze* nor pierce—*Shak.*⟩ ⟨the bullet *grazed* the young lady's temple—*Scott*⟩ ⟨the missile *grazed* the spot where the shrike sat, and cut the ends of his wings—*Burroughs*⟩ **Glance** (see also FLASH) basically implies a blow (as from a sword, a spear, or an ax) that owing to the hardness or resistance of what is struck turns aside or slips and so fails of its full effect; hence *glance* in its participial form *glancing* is often used to describe such a blow either in its course or effect ⟨he struck a *glancing* blow⟩ ⟨the blow *glanced* off his shoulder without even jarring him⟩ ⟨the blade *glanced,* I did but shear a feather—*Tennyson*⟩ **Shave** implies a touching as lightly and closely as a razor that passes over the face; although it comes near to *graze,* it carries no implication of abrasion but rather in some contexts suggests a dangerous approach or a narrow escape ⟨now *shaves* with level wing the deep, then soars up to the fiery concave—*Milton*⟩ ⟨three hansoms *shaved* him by an inch—*Barrie*⟩ **Skim** (see also FLY) also implies a light touch in passing ⟨kingfishers . . . darted across the water, their wings just *skimming* the surface—*Walden*⟩ but it never suggests the action of anything (as a bullet, a razor, or a weapon) that is even slightly dangerous; rather it suggests an avoidance of depths by someone or something that touches upon the surface or dips only into shallows ⟨*skim* a book in reading⟩ ⟨am pleased to *skim* along the surfaces of things—*Wordsworth*⟩
*Ana* touch, contact (see corresponding nouns at CONTACT): *scatter, disperse, dispel: *slide, slip, glide

**brush** *n* skirmish, *encounter
*Ana* *contest, conflict, combat, fight, fray: engagement, action, *battle: *attack, assault, onset, onslaught

**brusque** curt, blunt, gruff, *bluff, crusty
*Ana* ungracious, *rude, impolite, uncivil, discourteous: *rough, harsh
*Ant* unctuous: bland —*Con* *suave, urbane, smooth: *gracious, cordial, affable, genial: courteous, gallant, polite, *civil

**brutal, brute, brutish, bestial, beastly, feral** are not close synonyms, though all suggest a likeness to or the nature of a lower animal and all, especially as applied to persons, tend to express strong derogation. **Brutal** is almost exclusively applied to men or their acts, characters, or words; it implies qualities (as sensuality, lack of intelligence or feeling, or inhumanity) that relate them to the lower animals ⟨a *brutal* beating⟩ ⟨a senseless and *brutal* war⟩ ⟨the consistently *brutal* ways of the English-speaking peoples in dealing with native populations—*Mumford*⟩ **Brute** is sometimes employed in distinguishing an animal from a man ⟨a *brute* creature⟩ ⟨*brute* beings⟩ ⟨why am I shut out like a *brute* beast?—*Shaw*⟩ but more often it applies to something inanimate that can be likened to the lower animals (as in its soullessness, its irrationality, its blindness, its immobility, or its inflexibility) ⟨*brute* matter⟩ ⟨*brute* force⟩ ⟨as we proceed in an inquiry we adjust our laws to the *brute* facts—*Alexander*⟩ ⟨words are . . . the careless, unfeeling *brute* mass that will not respond—*Montague*⟩ **Brutish,** like *brutal,* is usually applied to men or their acts, their minds, and their passions; it differs from *brutal* in that it rarely suggests cruelty and inhumanity but stresses likeness to an animal in stupidity, in lack of control over appetites, or in government by instinct ⟨how *brutish* is it not to understand—*Spenser*⟩ ⟨the English mistrust of the intellectual, the *brutish* aesthetic apathy and contempt for the creative artist

must go—*Connolly*⟩ ⟨whoso loveth instruction loveth knowledge: but he that hateth reproof is *brutish*—*Prov* 12:1⟩ **Bestial** likewise applies to men and their acts, their minds, and their manners, but it usually stresses neither inhumanity nor a low-grade mind but a depravity or state of degradation unworthy of man and fit only for beasts and is therefore usually a term of severe reprobation ⟨*bestial* habits⟩ ⟨living in *bestial* filth⟩ ⟨inclined to describe any sexual indulgence of which he does not approve as *bestial*—*Krutch*⟩ **Beastly** may come close to *bestial* in its suggestion of utter depravity or abominable character ⟨*beastly* cruelty⟩ but more often it is weakened and implies no more than disapprobation of something unpleasant or distasteful to a greater or less degree ⟨a *beastly* stench pervaded the house⟩ ⟨a *beastly* day⟩ ⟨*beastly* weather⟩ **Feral,** when applied to men, suggests savagery or ferocity ⟨the *feral* instincts of men⟩ ⟨her wrath, savage and *feral,* utterly possessed her. She was like a wild animal, cornered and conscious of defeat—*S. S. Van Dine*⟩
*Ana* sensual, animal, fleshly, *carnal: *coarse, gross, vulgar: *stupid, dull, dense, crass: barbarous, savage (see BARBARIAN)
*Con* humane, humanitarian (see CHARITABLE): gentle, mild (see SOFT): chivalrous, courteous (see CIVIL)

**brute** *adj* *brutal, brutish, bestial, beastly, feral
*Ana* inanimate, lifeless, *dead: inert, supine, *inactive: impotent, *powerless

**brutish** *brutal, brute, bestial, beastly, feral
*Ana* dull, dense, crass, *stupid: sluggish, comatose, *lethargic: stolid, *impassive, apathetic
*Con* *intelligent, alert, quick-witted: responsive, sensitive, impressionable (see SENTIENT)

**buccaneer** *pirate, freebooter, privateer, corsair

**buck** *n* dude, *fop, dandy, beau, coxcomb, exquisite

**buckle** *vb* *flex, crook, bow
*Ana* *break, crack, snap, burst: bend, twist, *curve

**bucolic** pastoral, *rural, rustic
*Ana* boorish, loutish, clownish, churlish (see under BOOR): *natural, simple, naïve, ingenuous
*Ant* urbane

**buffet** *vb* baste, pummel, *beat, pound, belabor, thrash
*Ana* *strike, smite, hit, slap, slug: batter (see MAIM)

**bugbear** bête noire, *abomination, anathema

**build** *vb* Build, construct, erect, frame, raise, rear are comparable when they mean to form or fashion a structure or something comparable to a structure. **Build** strictly implies a fitting together of parts and materials to form something which may be large (as a house, a factory, a church, or a bridge) or small (as a bird's nest, a fence, or a child's toy) but of which the forming must involve some measure or degree of complication in the bringing together of parts and materials ⟨*build* a cathedral⟩ ⟨*build* a shack⟩ ⟨the robins *built* their nest in the fork of a tree⟩ ⟨*build* a battleship⟩ When used in reference to something immaterial *build* (often followed by *up*) may suggest an analogy between the immaterial thing and an edifice especially by implying an adding of part to part or bit to bit in the attainment of an end ⟨*build* up a man's ego⟩ ⟨*built* up a fortune bit by bit⟩ ⟨*build* a theory on slight evidence⟩ **Construct** comes close to *build* in its implication of the putting together the material given or at hand to form something. But it is not quite equivalent, for it stresses not the labor, especially the manual labor, involved but the problem involved in the fitting together of parts. *Construct* therefore emphasizes the discovering by the mind of how the parts or the materials should be combined in order to gain the desired end. To *build* is the work of men who use their hands or by analogy their brains to bring something into being;

to *construct* is the work of men who use their brains, though sometimes their hands in obedience to their brains, to solve the problem of how a thing should be or is built or made or brought into being; hence *construct* implies composition or design and may take as its object anything brought into material or immaterial existence by one or the other process ⟨*construct* a plot⟩ ⟨*construct* a dam⟩ ⟨the mind of the scientist *constructs* its own world—*Inge*⟩ ⟨each *constructed* and consolidated a realm—*Belloc*⟩ *Construct* is also often used as the opposite of *destroy* without a specific reference to these implications ⟨it is proverbially easier to destroy than to *construct*—*T. S. Eliot*⟩ ⟨roughly speaking, we *construct* when we increase the potential energy of the system in which we are interested, and we destroy when we diminish its potential energy—*Russell*⟩ **Erect** basically means to set upright. Although the term may carry this as its essential meaning ⟨*erect* a flagpole⟩ ⟨the cobra *erected* itself to strike⟩ it was early applied to high structures and has accordingly come to imply building in its most usual sense. The word is often used in place of *build* without any marked implication of putting together parts and materials ⟨many huge factories *erected* during the war now stand idle⟩ but it always carries some suggestion of the sense of to set up (as by building or establishing) ⟨*erect* a statue to his memory⟩ ⟨*erect* a scaffold⟩ ⟨a very much denser obstruction is in the process of being *erected* now by literary critics—*Day Lewis*⟩ **Frame** approaches *construct* but in respect to physical structures more specifically applies to the bringing together and joining of parts (as sills, plates, and joists) that define the form of the final structure ⟨a cottage *framed* of pine and sheathed with cedar⟩ In extended use it throws the stress upon a forming or fashioning to suit a design, an intention, a purpose, or the facts and may be applied to anything so constructed ⟨*frame* an answer⟩ ⟨*frame* a hypothesis⟩ ⟨picture him excuses *framing*—going from her far away—*Gilbert*⟩ ⟨all those who have *framed* written constitutions contemplate them as forming the fundamental and paramount law of the nation—*John Marshall*⟩ ⟨it is in order to overcome these obstacles that the notes and questions in this volume have been *framed*—*Notes and Queries on Anthropology*⟩ **Raise** and **rear** (see also LIFT) often replace *build*, especially when the idea of height is emphasized ⟨now after this he built a wall without the city . . . and *raised* it up a very great height—*2 Chron* 33:14⟩ ⟨those arts which were destined to *raise* our Gothic cathedrals—*Coulton*⟩ ⟨this tower; it is my own; though it was *reared* to Beauty—*Millay*⟩

*Ana* fabricate, fashion, manufacture (see MAKE): produce, turn out, yield, *bear

*Ant* unbuild, destroy —*Con* demolish, raze (see DESTROY): *ruin, wreck

**build** *n* *physique, habit, constitution

*Ana* *form, figure, shape, conformation, configuration: *structure, framework: contour, *outline: style, *fashion

**building** *n* Building, edifice, structure, pile are comparable when they mean a construction (as of wood, brick, or stone) intended to house a family, a business, or an institution. **Building** is the common and in most cases the adequate term ⟨a school *building*⟩ ⟨a new *building* going up⟩ ⟨the *buildings* of the temple—*Mt* 24:1⟩ **Edifice** usually applies to large and elegant buildings ⟨should I go to church and see the holy *edifice* of stone . . .?—*Shak.*⟩ **Structure** retains more frequently than the others the sense of something constructed, often in a particular way ⟨a tumbledown *structure*⟩ ⟨a modern steel *structure*⟩ Like *edifice, structure* is often used of buildings of some size or magnificence ⟨the civic auditorium . . . is the city's most important public *structure*—*Amer. Guide Series:*

*Mich.*⟩ **Pile** is a somewhat literary term for a very large building or sometimes a cluster of buildings especially of stone; it usually suggests a public or official structure (as a palace, a cathedral, or a government building) ⟨contrast between the vast *pile* of the cathedral and the pygmy men in the street—*Laski*⟩

**bulge** *vb* Bulge, jut, stick out, protuberate, protrude, project, overhang, beetle mean to extend outward beyond the usual and normal line. **Bulge** suggests a swelling out in an excessive or abnormal fashion; it may be used when the impression to be given is that there is an imperfection, a defect, or a cause of strain that explains the swelling ⟨the wall *bulged* in the center⟩ ⟨above her boots . . . the calves *bulged* suddenly out—*Bennett*⟩ ⟨good little Fyne's eyes *bulged* with solemn horror—*Conrad*⟩ **Jut** (often with *out*) and **stick out** do not imply abnormality as a rule but construction, formation, or position that permits a thing to extend outside or beyond the flat line of a surface ⟨rocks *jutting* from the water⟩ ⟨the nun took Father Latour to a window that *jutted* out and looked up the narrow street—*Cather*⟩ ⟨one building *stuck out* from the straight line made by the rest⟩ **Protuberate,** which is currently much less used than the corresponding adjective *protuberant* and the corresponding noun *protuberance,* implies a swelling or sticking outward (as in a rounded or angular prominence); it does not differ greatly from *bulge,* but it often carries less implication of something radically wrong ⟨the point of his elbows markedly *protuberated*⟩ **Protude** implies a thrusting forth especially in an unexpected place; it applies especially to something that does not seem to belong or that sticks out obviously ⟨whenever a small tuft of heather . . . *protruded* itself through the grass . . . and entangled her feet—*Hardy*⟩ ⟨through the leaves . . . a slender dead stem *protruded,* and from a twig at its summit depended a broken spider's web—*Hudson*⟩ ⟨the great rollers piled up on the sandy beach where great boulders *protruded* here and there—*Heiser*⟩ In literal use **project** is more often intransitive, though in extended uses it is chiefly transitive. Intransitively it may mean to jut out or to protrude ⟨the eaves usually *project* far beyond the roof in semitropical and tropical climates⟩ ⟨this great rimrock, which *projected* out over the erosions like a granite shelf—*Cather*⟩ In its transitive use, however, it carries implications of throwing or casting forward both in literal use ⟨*project* a shadow⟩ ⟨*project* the colors from a prism upon a wall⟩ and especially in extended use when it refers to thoughts, conceptions, or feelings; thus, one *projects* not only his ideas or thoughts but his powers (as of imagination or comprehension), as if by throwing them out, so that they reach their goal effectively ⟨one couldn't formulate and express one's ideas and *project* them into that spate of charming, inconsequent talk, that swept on gaily over anything one said—*Rose Macaulay*⟩ ⟨all the knowledge we possess . . . is of the past, and the further back we can *project* our vision, the more comprehensive, the more thorough, the more efficient is that knowledge—*Grandgent*⟩ Often the idea of extending beyond the usual and normal line gives way to other implications derived especially from psychology, mathematics, and magic, and the word then means simply to externalize or to free oneself from ⟨*project* one's thoughts⟩ ⟨she *projected* her own guilt into the other person—*Overstreet*⟩ Both **overhang** and **beetle** imply a jutting out over the support or base; **overhang** sometimes connotes a threatening position, while **beetle** often suggests precariousness or ominousness ⟨then lend the eye a terrible aspect . . . let the brow o'erwhelm it as fearfully as doth a galled rock *o'erhang*

---

A colon (:) separates groups of words discriminated. An asterisk (*) indicates place of treatment of each group.

and jutty his confounded base—*Shak.*⟩ ⟨an *overhanging* roof⟩ ⟨*beetling* brows⟩ ⟨the dreadful summit of the cliff that *beetles* o'er his base—*Shak.*⟩ ⟨an isolated hill that *beetled* over the western edge of the ridge—*Cather*⟩
*Ana* swell, distend, dilate, *expand

**bulge** *n* protuberance, *projection, protrusion
*Con* cavity, hollow, *hole, pocket

**bulk** *n* **Bulk, mass, volume** mean a body of usually material substance that constitutes a thing or unit. **Bulk** is applied mainly to what is or appears to be inordinately large or heavy ⟨the *bulk* of ancient minster—*Wordsworth*⟩ and often more or less shapeless or unshapely ⟨on the living sea rolls an inanimate *bulk*—*Shelley*⟩ ⟨a blue night set with stars, the *bulk* of the solitary mesas cutting into the firmament—*Cather*⟩ ⟨Dr. Lanskell sank his gouty *bulk* into the armchair behind his desk—*Wharton*⟩ **Mass** is applied mainly to something, whether material or immaterial, that is or gives the appearance of being built up by the piling or gathering together of things of the same kind so that they cohere and have a real or apparent unity ⟨the towering *mass* of the Sierras⟩ ⟨pieces of obsolete science, imprisoned . . . in the solid *mass* of a religious creed—*Inge*⟩ ⟨the *mass* [of people] never comes up to the standard of its best member, but on the contrary degrades itself to a level with the lowest —*Thoreau*⟩ **Volume** usually applies to something that flows and is therefore without outline and often continuous in extent ⟨a tremendous *volume* of water⟩ ⟨a *volume* of gas poured into the room⟩ ⟨it [the voice] rose through progressive gradations of sweetness and power, until its *volume* seemed to envelop her—*Hawthorne*⟩ These three terms also come into comparison when they designate quantity or amount. But *bulk* and *mass* mean the greater part or a large majority of something objective ⟨some must know medicine, but for the *bulk* of mankind it is sufficient to have an elementary knowledge of physiology and hygiene—*Russell*⟩ ⟨the great *mass* of the articles on which impost is paid is foreign luxuries— *Jefferson*⟩ *Volume*, however, may denote either the total amount or quantity especially of something subject to seasonal, periodic, or other fluctuations ⟨the *volume* of travel increases greatly in the vacation season⟩ ⟨enlarge the *volume* of the currency⟩ ⟨the *volume* of business has decreased recently⟩ or a considerable or relatively great amount ⟨profits are made by selling *volume* at market price—*Wall Street Jour.*⟩ ⟨crops will fail unless we soon get rain in *volume*⟩
*Ana* *form, figure, shape

**bulky** *massive, massy, monumental, substantial
*Ana* *huge, gigantic, colossal, mammoth, elephantine, enormous: corpulent, obese, portly, *fleshy: burly, husky (see MUSCULAR)
*Con* petite, diminutive, *small, little

**bull** *n* 1 blunder, howler, boner, mistake, *error, slip, lapse, faux pas
2 *nonsense, twaddle, drivel, bunk, balderdash, poppycock, gobbledygook, trash, rot

**bulldoze** bully, browbeat, *intimidate, cow
*Ana* *threaten, menace: terrorize, terrify, *frighten: *worry, harass, harry
*Con* cajole, wheedle, blandish, *coax

**bullheaded** pigheaded, stiff-necked, stubborn, mulish, *obstinate, dogged, pertinacious

**bully** *vb* bulldoze, browbeat, *intimidate, cow
*Ana* torment, rack, torture (see AFFLICT): *threaten, menace: terrorize, terrify, *frighten, scare
*Ant* coax —*Con* wheedle, cajole, blandish (see COAX): *lure, entice, inveigle, decoy

**bulwark** *n* Bulwark, breastwork, rampart, parapet, bastion

are comparable when they denote a structure above the ground that forms part of a fortification and is specifically intended for purposes of defense. **Bulwark** is the most general and the least technical of these terms. It is or has been applied to various defensive structures (as a wall intended to keep out an enemy, a structure of logs, earth, or stones from behind which defenders can safely attack besiegers or an assaulting force, and a breakwater or sea wall). The term is also extended to a person or a thing regarded as a firm, steadfast, or powerful defense or defender ⟨he stood, the *bulwark* of the Grecian band —*Pope*⟩ ⟨the support of the State governments in all their rights, as the most competent administrations for our domestic concerns, and the surest *bulwarks* against anti-republican tendencies—*Jefferson*⟩ **Breastwork** applies chiefly to a structure of earth, often hastily thrown up and usually only a few feet in height, behind which defenders may crouch or stand so as to fire their guns from a protected position ⟨the mud *breastworks* had long been leveled with the earth—*Irving*⟩ **Rampart** and *parapet* are the common technical terms especially when fortifications of the type that prevailed before World War I are under consideration. In this sense a **rampart** is an embankment round a place often, especially in old castles, built inside a moat and rising high enough to conceal forces lying behind it yet broad enough on its top level to permit the movement of men and of guns when they are needed in action. A **parapet** is a structure rising above the top level of a rampart and serving as a breastwork for those aiming and firing guns and as a bulwark against the missiles of the enemy. But in less technical use *rampart* is applied to a wall or to an elevation or level on which defenders may operate when in action or which may be thought of as suitable for such action, and *parapet* is applied to a structure (as a low wall or a balustrade) resembling a parapet of a fortification ⟨populous No, that was situate among the rivers, that had the waters round about it, whose *rampart* was the sea— *Nah* 3:8⟩ ⟨on a summer's day Wolstanbury Hill is an island in sunshine; you may lie on the grassy *rampart*, high up in the most delicate air—*Jefferies*⟩ ⟨the terrace surrounded with a stone *parapet* in front of the house— *George Eliot*⟩ **Bastion** applies to a projection extending from the main wall of a fortification; typically a bastion is a four-sided projection ending in an acute angle and providing a means whereby the enemy may be covered in several directions and the fortification protected from at least four angles. In extended use *bastion* may differ from *rampart* in carrying a stronger suggestion of attack than of defense ⟨they build each other up . . . as *bastions* set point-blank against God's will—*Cowper*⟩
*Ana* stronghold, fortress, *fort, citadel

**bum** *n* *vagabond, vagrant, tramp, hobo, truant

**bumble** *vb* *stumble, trip, blunder, lurch, flounder, lumber, galumph, lollop

**bump** *vb* **Bump, clash, collide, conflict** are comparable when they mean to come or cause to come into violent contact or close or direct opposition. **Bump** is used primarily of physical matters and then implies a forceful knocking or running against, typically with thudding impact ⟨the ferry *bumped* into the mooring post⟩ ⟨he *bumped* his foot on the stove⟩ It may also suggest encountering an obstacle or difficulty ⟨the builder *bumped* up against the problem of shoring up the wall⟩ **Clash** may suggest hitting, knocking, or dashing together or against with sharp force and jangling metallic din ⟨the swords *clashed*⟩ ⟨where ignorant armies *clash* by night —*Arnold*⟩ or sharp, although sometimes short-lived, variance, incompatibility, or opposition ⟨Cavour and

Victor Emmanuel *clashed* sharply, and on these occasions it was usually the King who won—*Times Lit. Sup.*⟩ ⟨when the new demands of our changing economic life *clash* with the old dogmas—*Cohen*⟩ **Collide** denotes a more or less direct running together or against with a definite and often destructive force or shock ⟨the tanker sank after it *collided* with the freighter⟩ or it may indicate a forceful direct disagreement or opposition ⟨an English East India Company was using the Portuguese route around Africa and *colliding* with the Portuguese in India —*Barr*⟩ **Conflict** is archaic in senses involving physical contact and is used to convey the notion of variance, incompatibility, or opposition ⟨*conflicting* testimony by two witnesses⟩ ⟨to stand up amid *conflicting* interests —*Wordsworth*⟩
*Ana* hit, *strike, smite: impinge, jolt, jar (see corresponding nouns at IMPACT)

**bumpkin** hick, yokel, rube, clodhopper, clown, lout, *boor, churl

**bunch** *n* 1 *group, cluster, parcel, lot
*Ana* see those at BUNCH 2
2 *bundle, bale, parcel, pack, package, packet
*Ana* collection, assemblage, gathering (see under GATHER): quantity, number, aggregate (see SUM)

**bundle** *n* Bundle, bunch, bale, parcel, pack, package, packet denote things done up for storage, sale, or carriage. A **bundle** is a collection of articles bound or rolled together ⟨a *bundle* of papers⟩ ⟨a *bundle* for the laundry⟩ ⟨a *bundle* of old clothes⟩ A **bunch** is a collection of things, usually of the same sort, fastened closely together in orderly fashion ⟨a *bunch* of violets⟩ ⟨a *bunch* of radishes⟩ A **bale** is a large bundle of goods bound up for storage or transportation and especially one composed of materials (as rags, hay, straw, cotton, or wool) which are closely pressed together so as to form a mass, usually rectangular, tightly bound with stout cord or wire, and often wrapped in paper or burlap. Because there is in various localities a uniform size for a bale of a certain commodity, the word often also implies an average or approximate weight ⟨a United States *bale* of cotton weighs approximately 500 pounds⟩ **Parcel** (see also PART) implies a state of being wrapped and tied and a small or moderate size, and it carries no suggestion of the number or kind of things so wrapped and tied ⟨a shopping bag for *parcels*⟩ ⟨loaded down with *parcels*⟩ ⟨send *parcels* through the mail⟩ **Pack** implies more careful and more compact arrangement than *bundle;* specifically it denotes a conveniently packed bundle of goods or supplies that is carried on the back (as by a peddler, a soldier on the march, or a mule). A **package** is specifically something packed (as in a box or receptacle of moderate size or in a compact bundle) especially for convenience in sale or transportation ⟨an express *package*⟩ ⟨a *package* of envelopes⟩ ⟨candy in the original *package*⟩ ⟨*package* goods⟩ It may also be applied to a group of intangibles (as contracted services or performances) forming, offered, or dealt with as a unit ⟨sell them a . . . complete *package* (lot, house, equipment and financing in a single transaction)—*Gutheim*⟩ ⟨a series of treaties and agreements forming a single *package*—*Fay*⟩ A **packet** is a small package or parcel ⟨a *packet* of letters or dispatches⟩
*Ana* collection, assemblage, gathering (see under GATHER): *bag, sack

**bungle** *vb* *botch, fumble, muff, cobble
*Ana* *confuse, muddle, addle, befuddle: confuse, confound, *mistake: *disorder, disarrange, disorganize, derange: *entangle, enmesh

**bunk** *n* *nonsense, twaddle, drivel, balderdash, poppycock, gobbledygook, trash, rot, bull

**buoyant** volatile, expansive, resilient, effervescent, *elastic
*Ana* *spirited, high-spirited, mettlesome, gingery: *lively, vivacious, animated, sprightly: jocund, blithe, *merry: optimistic, *hopeful
*Ant* depressed, dejected —*Con* doleful, lugubrious, *melancholy: *sullen, morose, glum, dour: *despondent, despairing, hopeless, forlorn

**burden** *n* *load, cargo, freight, lading

**burden** *vb* Burden, encumber, cumber, weigh, weight, load, lade, tax, charge, saddle are comparable when they mean to lay a heavy load upon or to lie like a heavy load upon a person or thing. **Burden** implies the imposition or the carrying of a load that makes one conscious of its weight and that is therefore regarded as grievous, trying, or oppressive. The term often suggests something that is or seems to be too much to be borne by the mind or spirit ⟨*burdened* with too many responsibilities⟩ ⟨exorbitant taxes that *burden* the workingman⟩ ⟨but this murder—was it to dog him all his life? Was he always to be *burdened* by his past?—*Wilde*⟩ ⟨when the aesthetic sense deviates from its proper ends to *burden* itself with moral intentions . . . it ceases to realize morality—*Ellis*⟩ **Encumber** specifically suggests the presence of something that impedes, obstructs, hampers, or embarrasses. Even when the term connotes too great a weight, it stresses the fact that the weight is an annoyance or a clog to one's progress ⟨he was *encumbered* by mountains of luggage⟩ Consequently it is oftener used of things than of persons ⟨the father had left his inheritance *encumbered*—*Belloc*⟩ ⟨the vast quantity of mere survivals (customs and beliefs) which *encumber* modern life—*Inge*⟩ ⟨awaiting release from the . . . *encumbering* bulk of gross matter—*Montague*⟩ **Cumber** is close to *encumber* but it is less likely to stress motion and more likely to stress what perplexes, worries, discommodes, or inconveniences ⟨he *cumbers* himself never about consequences, about interests: he gives an independent, genuine verdict—*Emerson*⟩ ⟨such an enterprise might well have seemed to him beyond the reach of Rome, *cumbered* already with so many duties—*Buchan*⟩ **Weigh** suggests a load of something (as sorrow, fears, or anxiety) that lies upon the heart, the spirit, or the mind so that it oppresses or depresses it ⟨canst thou not . . . with some sweet oblivious antidote cleanse the stuffed bosom of that perilous stuff which *weighs* upon the heart—*Shak.*⟩ ⟨mortality *weighs* heavily on me like unwilling sleep—*Keats*⟩ **Weight** differs from *weigh* in suggesting not a load that oppresses or depresses the heart, mind, or spirit but one that serves as a handicap in a struggle or a disadvantage to be met; the term may be so used that the handicap or disadvantage either may be thought of as residing in the person or thing considered or in the person or thing set against it ⟨*weighted* as he was with faults . . . he fought his battle bravely—*Froude*⟩ ⟨it wants to have a House of Commons which is not *weighted* with nominees of the landed class—*George Eliot*⟩ **Load** and **lade** carry an implication of overloading but may imply an overabundance that is agreeable as well as one that entails a burden or impresses one as a superfluity ⟨a store *loaded* with merchandise of every sort⟩ ⟨*load* human life with frustration and grief—*Cort*⟩ ⟨*load* one with reproaches⟩ ⟨the butler entered with a *laden* tea tray—*Wilde*⟩ ⟨come unto me, all ye that labor and are heavy *laden,* and I will give you rest—*Mt* 11:28⟩ **Tax** in its relevant sense means to place an exacting burden or demand upon; it suggests something that strains one to the uttermost ⟨it may *tax* the highest wisdom of the race to preserve civilization at all—*F. N. Robinson*⟩ ⟨the war severely *taxed* the resources of the country⟩ **Charge** basically means to load a thing up to its

A colon (:) separates groups of words discriminated. An asterisk (*) indicates place of treatment of each group.

capacity to receive ⟨*charge* a battery⟩ To this sense have been added new connotations especially of loading beyond a capacity to receive or to contain so that the word now often implies a burdening, an overloading, or a weighing down ⟨the youth was too *charged* with emotion to speak —*Meredith*⟩ ⟨songs . . . must not be too *charged* with meaning . . . or they will fail of their effect—*Binyon*⟩ ⟨all the . . . elemental processes of nature, all the changing, yet abiding physiognomy of earth and sky, were *charged* for psalmist and prophet with spiritual significance— *Lowes*⟩ **Saddle** usually implies the imposition of a burden or encumbrance, ordinarily by another, though sometimes as a result of one's own fault ⟨he is *saddled* with cares because of a hasty marriage⟩ ⟨by what mismanagement . . . had a project like this been *saddled* with Lord Comfrey as chairman?—*Jan Struther*⟩ ⟨*saddling* the nation with restrictive laws—*New Republic*⟩
*Ana* oppress, *depress, weigh: *crush, mash
*Con* lighten, alleviate, mitigate, *relieve: *moderate, temper

**burden** *n* *substance, purport, gist, core, pith
*Ana* *subject, matter, subject matter, theme, text, topic

**burdensome** oppressive, *onerous, exacting
*Ana* *heavy, ponderous, cumbersome, cumbrous, weighty: *irksome, wearisome: fatiguing, exhausting, fagging, tiring (see TIRE): arduous, *hard, difficult
*Ant* light —*Con* *easy, facile, simple, smooth, effortless

**burglar** thief, robber (see under THEFT)
*Ana* stealer, pilferer, filcher, purloiner (see corresponding verbs at STEAL): plunderer, looter, rifler (see corresponding verbs at ROB)

**burglarize** *rob, plunder, rifle, loot
*Ana* *steal, pilfer, filch, purloin, lift, pinch, snitch, cop, swipe: sack, pillage, *ravage, despoil

**burglary** *theft, larceny, robbery

**burlesque** *n* *caricature, parody, travesty
*Ana* mimicry, mockery, imitation (see corresponding verbs at COPY): *fun, jest, sport, game: satire, sarcasm, humor, *wit: derision, ridicule (see corresponding verbs at RIDICULE)

**burlesque** *vb* caricature, parody, travesty (see under CARICATURE *n*)
*Ana* mimic, ape, mock, imitate, *copy: *ridicule, deride

**burly** husky, *muscular, brawny, athletic, sinewy
*Ana* corpulent, *fleshy, portly: bulky, substantial, *massive: *vigorous, lusty: *powerful, forceful, potent
*Ant* lanky, lank —*Con* *lean, spare, gaunt, rawboned, angular, scrawny, skinny

**burn** *vb* **Burn, scorch, char, sear, singe** mean to injure by exposure to fire or intense heat. **Burn** is the most comprehensive of these terms, for it is applicable regardless of the extent of injury or of whether fire or heat is the destructive agency ⟨the cake was *burned* to a crisp in the oven⟩ ⟨only the lower edge of his coat was *burned* by the flames⟩ ⟨the grass was badly *burned* by the sun⟩ ⟨the child *burned* his hand by touching the hot stove⟩ **Burn** is also applicable when a similar injury or effect is produced by another agency ⟨*burn* plants by using too strong a fertilizer⟩ ⟨a sharp wind *burns* the face⟩ **Scorch** implies superficial burning that changes the color (especially to brown or black) or texture of something ⟨*scorch* a dress in ironing it⟩ ⟨the paint of the house was badly *scorched* by the flames from the grass fire⟩ **Char** usually implies total or partial reduction to carbon or charcoal by fire ⟨*charred* wood⟩ ⟨*char* coffee beans in roasting them⟩ ⟨the lower parts of the rafters were *charred* in the fire⟩ **Sear** applies basically to the burning or scorching of animal tissues by fire or intense heat (as in cauterizing a wound, branding an animal, or quickly browning the out-

side of meats so that they will retain their juices in later and slower cooking⟩ ⟨*seared* the damaged tissue with an electric needle⟩ ⟨many cooks still *sear* beef before roasting it⟩ **Singe** implies a very superficial burning ⟨the fire next door merely *singed* our house⟩ Sometimes such burning is intentional, especially when the short hairs or bristles covering a carcass being prepared for market or for cooking are quickly destroyed by a flame ⟨*singe* a chicken before broiling it⟩
*Ana* kindle, fire, ignite, *light: *blaze, flame, glow

**burp** *belch, vomit, disgorge, regurgitate, spew, throw up

**burst** *vb* *break, crack, bust, snap, shatter, shiver
*Ana* distend, swell, *expand: *push, shove, thrust, propel

**bury** secrete, cache, *hide, conceal, screen, ensconce
*Con* expose, display, parade, flaunt, exhibit, *show: unearth, *discover, ascertain, learn, determine

**business** *n* 1 *work, occupation, pursuit, calling, employment
*Ana* *trade, craft, handicraft, art, profession
2 *affair, concern, matter, thing
*Ana* *function, office, duty, province: *task, job, assignment, chore, stint
3 **Business, commerce, trade, industry, traffic** are comparable chiefly when they denote one of the forms or branches of human endeavor which have for their objective the supplying of commodities. **Business** specifically applies to the combined activities of all those who are engaged in the barter, purchase, or sale of commodities of any sort either as wholesale or retail transactions or in financial transactions connected with such activities; in this sense *business* is thought of as the combined activities of all kinds of dealers (as merchants) and financiers (as bankers) as opposed to those of all kinds of producers (as manufacturers and farmers). The term is also used more broadly to include the activities of producers and transporters of goods as well as of merchants and bankers, since all these have for their ultimate aims the supplying of commodities and the increase of private wealth ⟨there should be no conflict between government and *business*⟩ ⟨*business* is greatly depressed throughout the world⟩ **Commerce** and **trade**, on the other hand, apply to the activities of those who are engaged in the exchange of commodities, especially such exchange as involves transactions on a large scale and the transportation of goods from place to place. The words are often used interchangeably; thus, in the United States the Interstate *Commerce* Commission regulates common carriers of all kinds (rail, water, motor) engaged in interstate transportation of passengers or goods; the Federal *Trade* Commission was created to prevent use of unfair methods of competition in interstate *commerce* and to investigate *trade* conditions in and with foreign countries. But in general *commerce* is preferred when different countries or states are involved, when transportation is across seas or by sea, and when the dealings are not only in merchandise but also in media of exchange (as money, bills of exchange, and notes) and *trade*, when different business organizations in the same country are involved or when the dealings are in merchandise ⟨laws regulating interstate *commerce*⟩ ⟨ships engaged in *commerce* with the West Indies⟩ ⟨a slump in the sale of automobiles has adversely affected the *trade* between the manufacturers and the steel companies⟩ ⟨free *trade* designates a policy of permitting entry of natural and manufactured products from foreign countries without duties or tariff restrictions⟩ **Industry** applies chiefly to the activities of those who are engaged in production, especially in the processing of natural products, the manufacture of artificial products, the erection of buildings and other structures, on so large a scale that problems of capi-

tal and labor are involved. The term may be used generally to include all activities covered by this definition ⟨automation is rapidly revolutionizing *industry*⟩ It may also be used more narrowly of any branch of industry as determined by the thing produced ⟨the sugar *industry* comprises all business organizations engaged in the processing and refining of sugar⟩ ⟨the steel *industry*⟩ ⟨the automobile *industry*⟩ **Traffic** (see also INTERCOURSE) applies to the activities of those who are engaged in the operation of public carriers (as ships, railroads, bus lines, and systems of trucking) and who are therefore primarily responsible for the transportation not only of commodities and articles of manufacture but also of persons from one part of a country or of the world to another ⟨the *traffic* interests were also represented at the conference⟩

**bust** *vb* *break, crack, burst, snap, shatter, shiver
  *Ana* see those at BURST

**bustle** *n* flurry, *stir, ado, fuss, pother
  *Ana* *business, commerce, trade, industry, traffic: movement, *motion: hubbub, clamor, racket, babel, *din
  *Con* inactivity, idleness, inertness, passiveness, supineness (see corresponding adjectives at INACTIVE)

**busy,** **industrious, diligent, assiduous, sedulous** mean actively engaged or occupied in work or in accomplishing a purpose or intention. **Busy** may imply nothing more than that the person or thing referred to is not idle, that is, that he is at work or that it is in use ⟨the doctor is *busy* just now⟩ ⟨the telephone is *busy*⟩ In attributive use and some predicative use *busy* usually implies habitual or temporary engrossment in activity or the appearance of such engrossment ⟨the *busy* bee⟩ ⟨a *busy* life⟩ ⟨nowhere so *busy* a man as he there was, and yet he seemed *busier* than he was—*Chaucer*⟩ ⟨*busy* offices full of bustling clerks—*Nevins & Commager*⟩ **Industrious** applies to one who is characteristically attentive to his business, work, or avocation; it implies habitual or continual earnest application ⟨a willing, *industrious* boy ever striving to please⟩ ⟨at once the most *industrious* and the least industrial of the great nations—*Brownell*⟩ **Diligent** may stress care, constancy, attentiveness, and thoroughness, but it often implies application of these to some specific object or pursuit; thus, one may be *diligent* in seeking some favorite end without being in general *industrious* ⟨the Yankee's boots were missing, and after a *diligent* search were not to be found—*Melville*⟩ ⟨a *diligent* student of the scriptures⟩ **Assiduous** implies studied and unremitting, and **sedulous,** painstaking and persevering application to a business or enterprise ⟨acquire the power to speak French fluently by *assiduous* practice⟩ ⟨an *assiduous* nurse⟩ ⟨a *sedulous* but not brilliant student⟩ ⟨attempted to gain his end by *sedulous* flattery⟩ ⟨even the most *assiduous* critic can scarcely hope to keep abreast of the growing flood of translated books—*Times Lit. Sup.*⟩ ⟨I read with *sedulous* accuracy . . . the metrical romances—*Coleridge*⟩ ⟨she would never fail in *sedulous* attention to his wants—*M. E. Freeman*⟩
  *Ana* engrossed, absorbed, *intent: working, toiling, laboring, travailing (see corresponding nouns at WORK)
  *Ant* idle: unoccupied  —*Con* *inactive, inert, passive: indolent, slothful, *lazy: slack, relaxed (see LOOSE)

**butchery** slaughter, *massacre, carnage, pogrom
  *Ana* murdering *or* murder, slaying, killing (see corresponding verbs at KILL)

**butt in** *vb* *intrude, obtrude, interlope
  *Ana* interfere, *meddle, intermeddle: *interpose, intervene, interfere, mediate, intercede
  *Con* withdraw, retire (see GO): *refrain, abstain, forbear

**buttress** *n* **Buttress, pier, abutment** are architectural terms for auxiliary structures designed to serve as a prop, shore, or support for a wall (as of a building). A **buttress** is a structure (as of masonry) projecting from and supporting a wall and often designed especially for receiving and carrying the outward pressure or thrust exerted on the wall by the weight of an arch or vault. In a *flying buttress* the pressure or thrust is carried over an open space. A **pier** is a thickened piece of masonry designed to stiffen a wall. A pier may be built as a part of the wall or it may be a detached mass used as the vertical part of a flying buttress and carrying the thrust of a masonry bar or rod extending between it and the wall. An **abutment** is the particular section of either a buttress or a pier which actually receives the pressure or thrust exerted by the weight of an arch or vault.

In bridge building an **abutment** is the support at either extreme end of the structure or, by extension, the anchorage of the cables for a suspension bridge; a **pier** is any intermediate support between the ends of a bridge.

**buttress** *vb* *support, sustain, prop, bolster, brace
  *Ana* uphold, back, champion (see SUPPORT): *strengthen, reinforce, fortify: *defend, protect, shield, guard

**buy,** **purchase** mean to acquire something for money or an equivalent. **Buy** is at once the more general and the homelier word; consequently, while it may be freely used of any such transaction, it is distinctly the word of choice in respect to small, casual, or day-to-day exchanges of money for goods. **Purchase,** on the other hand, frequently implies a transaction of some dignity or importance and negotiations or other efforts to obtain it. Thus, one *buys* (rather than *purchases*) a dozen eggs, a glass of beer, or a new hat, but one *purchases* (or *buys*) a yacht or a country estate ⟨peace, how oft, how dearly *bought*—*Pope*⟩ ⟨thou hast thought that the gift of God may be *purchased* with money —*Acts* 8:20⟩ Whereas *buy* may almost always be substituted for *purchase* without disadvantage, the use of *purchase* instead of *buy* often weakens the effect or strikes a jarring note.
  *Ana* obtain, acquire, procure, *get: *pay, compensate, remunerate

**by,** **through, with** are comparable as prepositions followed by a word or phrase naming the agent, means, or instrument. **By** is followed commonly by the agent or causative agency ⟨a wall built *by* the Romans⟩ ⟨a novel *by* Scott⟩ ⟨destroyed *by* fire⟩ ⟨devoured *by* wolves⟩ ⟨blessed *by* a priest⟩ ⟨inflamed *by* the jibes of officers⟩ ⟨impressed *by* the evidence⟩ **Through** implies intermediacy; it is followed by the name of the person or thing that serves as the medium or the means by which an end is gained or an effect produced ⟨speak *through* an interpreter⟩ ⟨procure a rare book *through* a friend⟩ ⟨express ideas *through* words⟩ ⟨acquire a position *through* influence⟩ ⟨an opportunity lost *through* indecision⟩ **With,** on the other hand, is often followed by the name of the instrument which accompanies the action ⟨write *with* a pen⟩ ⟨eat *with* a fork⟩ ⟨defend oneself *with* a stick⟩ It may, however, take for its object something not consciously used as an instrument but serving as the instrumentality by which an effect is produced ⟨he amused the crowd *with* his anecdotes⟩ ⟨do not kill us *with* kindness⟩

**bystander** onlooker, looker-on, witness, eyewitness, *spectator, observer, beholder

**byword** *catchword, shibboleth, slogan
  *Ana* proverb, *saying, saw, motto: *abuse, invective: legend, caption (see INSCRIPTION)

---

A colon (:) separates groups of words discriminated. An asterisk (*) indicates place of treatment of each group.

# C

**cabal** intrigue, conspiracy, machination, *plot
**cabalistic** anagogic, mystic, *mystical
  *Ana* occult, esoteric, *recondite, abstruse: cryptic, enigmatic, *obscure: arcane, *mysterious
  *Con* plain, clear, obvious, manifest, *evident, palpable, apparent
**cache** *vb* secrete, bury, *hide, conceal, ensconce, screen
  *Con* expose, exhibit, display, *show: unearth, *discover
**cad, bounder, rotter** mean one who shows himself to be no gentleman. Usually they are somewhat vague terms of contempt for bad behavior or manners. **Cad** is applied especially to a man who violates in some way or another the code of morals or of manners by which he has been brought up and is supposed to be guided ⟨Napoleon III—in whom the *cad*, the coward, the idealist, and the sensualist were inextricably mixed—*Birrell*⟩ ⟨I pretended to gloat over the sight . . . . I have rarely in my life felt such a *cad*—*Buchan*⟩ **Bounder** usually applies to a man who apes the gentleman but who in some definite way (as undue stylishness of dress or faulty habits of speech) marks himself as a mere imitation; the term condemns him as ignorant, obtrusive, or vulgar in a measure that puts him beyond the pale of good society ⟨that is an antisocial proceeding, the conduct of a *bounder*—*Archer*⟩ ⟨this breezy, cocksure, self-assertive Englishman was what we today should be inclined to call a *bounder*—*Cyril Robinson*⟩ **Rotter** may be applied to a man who is extremely objectionable especially on moral grounds ⟨a regular *rotter;* that man is about as bad as they make them—*George Moore*⟩ The term is sometimes used of one who is felt as objectionable because of some failure, however great or small, to conform and then may suggest no more than mild disapproval ⟨there were a few *rotters* among the schoolboys, but fortunately not very many⟩ ⟨he's a bit of a *rotter* but a jolly good fellow for all that⟩
**cadaver** corpse, *body, carcass
**cadaverous** wasted, pinched, *haggard, worn, careworn
  *Ana* gaunt, skinny, scrawny, angular, rawboned, lank, lanky, *lean, spare
  *Ant* plump, stout —*Con* *fleshy, fat, corpulent, obese, portly, rotund
**cadence** *rhythm, meter
  *Ana* accentuation, accent, stress, *emphasis: beat, pulse, throb, pulsation (see under PULSATE)
**cage** *vb* *enclose, envelop, fence, pen, coop, corral, wall
  *Ana* confine, circumscribe (see LIMIT): *imprison, incarcerate, jail: *surround, environ, encompass, hem
**cajole** wheedle, blandish, *coax
  *Ana* entice, inveigle, seduce, decoy, *lure: beguile, delude, *deceive: tease, tantalize (see WORRY)
  *Con* browbeat, bully, bulldoze, cow, *intimidate: constrain, oblige, compel, coerce, *force
**cake** *vb* *harden, solidify, indurate, petrify
  *Ana* *compact, consolidate: *contract, compress, condense, shrink
**calamitous** *unlucky, disastrous, ill-starred, ill-fated, unfortunate, luckless, hapless
**calamity** *disaster, catastrophe, cataclysm
  *Ana* *accident, casualty, mishap: *misfortune, mischance, adversity, mishap: tribulation, visitation, affliction, *trial, cross: ruin, wreck (see RUIN)
  *Ant* boon —*Con* fortune, luck (see CHANCE): favor, *gift: benefaction (see DONATION)
**calculate, compute, estimate, reckon** mean to determine

something (as cost, speed, or quantity) by mathematical and especially arithmetical processes. **Calculate** is usually preferred when highly advanced, intricate, or elaborate processes are followed with precision and care and when the result arrived at is not readily proven by a physical confirmation (as by measuring or enumerating) ⟨*calculate* the distance between the sun and the earth⟩ ⟨*calculate* the number of atoms in a cubic centimeter of hydrogen⟩ **Compute** is preferred where the data are given or the actual figures involved are known and at hand and not arrived at indirectly; it therefore commonly implies the use of simple though often lengthy arithmetical processes ⟨*compute* the interest due⟩ ⟨*compute* the cost of running a business during a given year⟩ **Estimate** carries so strong an implication from its more common sense (see ESTIMATE) of an evaluation based on one's experience and good judgment that even when it implies careful calculation or computation it still connotes a result that is not necessarily exact but approximates the exact result; for he who *estimates* deals with data or figures that are to some extent unsatisfactory. Hence *estimate* is preferred to *calculate* and *compute* when the cost of a piece of work to be done is computed at present prices ⟨a contractor's bid on a projected building is based on its *estimated* cost to him⟩ ⟨a printer *estimates* a printing job when he names the price he will probably ask for doing it⟩ **Reckon** is used in place of *compute* and usually connotes simpler mathematical processes especially such as can be carried on in one's head or aided by the use of counters ⟨*reckon* the cost of a trip to the city⟩ ⟨*reckon* the number of eggs laid by the hens during the month⟩
  *Ana* weigh, study, *consider: *ponder, ruminate: determine, ascertain, *discover
  *Con* guess, *conjecture, surmise
**calculating** circumspect, *cautious, wary, chary
  *Ana* *deliberate, designed, considered, studied, premeditated: designing, scheming, plotting (see corresponding verbs under PLAN *n*): wily, guileful, crafty, artful, cunning, *sly
  *Ant* reckless, rash —*Con* foolhardy, daring, venturesome, *adventurous: improvident, imprudent, indiscreet (see affirmative adjectives at PRUDENT)
**calculation** circumspection, caution, wariness, chariness (see under CAUTIOUS)
  *Ana* *prudence, forethought, foresight, providence, discretion: *care, concern, solicitude: astuteness, perspicacity, sagacity, shrewdness (see corresponding adjectives at SHREWD)
  *Ant* recklessness, rashness
**caliber** *quality, stature
  *Ana* capability, capacity, *ability: force, *power
**call** *vb* *summon, summons, cite, convoke, convene, muster
  *Ana* assemble, *gather, collect: *invite, bid
**call** *n* *visit, visitation
**caller** *visitor, visitant, guest
**calling** occupation, pursuit, business, *work, employment
  *Ana* profession, *trade, craft, art, handicraft
**callous** *hardened, indurated
  *Ana* tough, tenacious, stout, *strong: *firm, solid, hard: *inflexible, adamant, obdurate, inexorable: insensitive, impassible, *insensible, anesthetic
  *Ant* tender —*Con* *soft, lenient, gentle, smooth: yielding, submitting, relenting (see YIELD): compassionate,

responsive, sympathetic (see TENDER): sensitive, susceptible, open, exposed, subject, *liable

**callow** green, crude, raw, *rude, rough, uncouth
*Ana* puerile, boyish, juvenile, *youthful: naïve, ingenuous, simple, unsophisticated, artless, *natural: adolescent, pubescent (see corresponding nouns at YOUTH)
*Ant* full-fledged, grown-up   —*Con* *mature, adult, matured

**calm** *adj* Calm, tranquil, serene, placid, peaceful, halcyon mean quiet and free from all that disturbs or excites. **Calm** is primarily applied to sea or weather, usually conveys an implicit contrast with its opposite, *stormy,* and suggests freedom, real or assumed, from agitation of whatever sort ⟨as men for ever temp'rate, *calm,* and wise—*Pope*⟩ **Tranquil** implies a more settled composure, a more inherent quiet, than *calm* with less suggestion of previous agitation overcome ⟨farewell the *tranquil* mind! farewell content!—*Shak.*⟩ ⟨the *tranquil* beauty of Greek sculpture—*FitzGerald*⟩ ⟨a *tranquil* trust in God amid tortures and death too horrible to be related—*Motley*⟩ **Serene** suggests a lofty and unclouded tranquillity ⟨regions mild of calm and *serene* air, above the smoke and stir of this dim spot which men call Earth—*Milton*⟩ ⟨the *serene* monotony that so often wears the aspect of happiness—*Glasgow*⟩ **Placid** connotes lack of excitement and suggests an unruffled and equable aspect or temper or even sometimes, in derogatory use, a hint of stupidity ⟨to confirm by *placid* silences the fact that the wine had been good—*Henry James*⟩ ⟨the *placid* common sense of Franklin—*J. R. Lowell*⟩ ⟨she is as *placid* as a cow⟩ **Peaceful** (see also PACIFIC) implies repose or the attainment of undisturbed tranquillity ⟨I am grown *peaceful* as old age tonight—*Browning*⟩ ⟨they harried his hitherto *peaceful* domains—*Irving*⟩ **Halcyon** implies an almost magic or golden calmness especially of weather or of spirit ⟨soft blue stone, the color of robins' eggs, or of the sea on *halcyon* days of summer—*Cather*⟩ ⟨the long uproar over the passage of the Reform Bill compared to which the stormiest days of the New Deal were *halcyon*—*Dwight Macdonald*⟩
*Ana* *still, quiet, stilly, noiseless: *pacific, peaceable: *impassive, stoic: unruffled, composed, collected, imperturbable, unflappable, *cool
*Ant* stormy: agitated   —*Con* shaken, rocked, convulsed (see SHAKE): disturbed, perturbed, discomposed, upset (see DISCOMPOSE)

**calm** *vb* Calm, compose, quiet, quieten, still, lull, soothe, settle, tranquilize are comparable when they relate to persons and their feelings and moods and mean essentially to bring to an end or relieve from whatever distresses, agitates, or disturbs. **Calm** implies a previous disordered state and denotes a returning to inner quietude especially as aided by judgment, fortitude, or faith ⟨Christian faith *calmed* in his soul the fear of change and death—*Wordsworth*⟩ ⟨her also I with gentle dreams have *calmed*—*Milton*⟩ **Compose,** often reflexive, retains its basic notion of arranging in order, specifically in an order that results in repose; it may heighten suggestions of conscious effort, resolution, and fortitude ⟨my child, if ever you were brave and serviceable in your life . . . you will *compose* yourself now—*Dickens*⟩ ⟨a most *composed* invincible man; in difficulty and distress, knowing no discouragement —*Carlyle*⟩ **Quiet** and **quieten** may connote a temporary external calmness in speech and demeanor rather than lasting inner calm ⟨the most unreasonable of Franklin's impulses had now been *quieted* by this most reasonable of marriages—*Van Doren*⟩ These terms are likely to be used in indicating the effect of actions of persons in authority on others ⟨threats to the physical well-being of the unborn baby can *quieten* a noisy and uncooperative

patient in labor—*Lancet*⟩ **Still** is somewhat literary or poetic and stresses the fact of cessation of agitation ⟨flattened, silenced, *stilled*—*Woolf*⟩ ⟨a voice *stilled* by death⟩ It may suggest more peremptory action than the other terms compared and often connotes a return to quietude induced by power, authority, or awe ⟨the debate was *stilled* by the crash of guns⟩ ⟨it was Mary who *stilled* the hideous bawling of Peter—*H. G. Wells*⟩ **Lull** suggests the somnolence of *lullaby,* to which it is related ⟨Aiken has *lulled* the reader with a seductive music and has transported him into the dreamworld of Freudian fantasy—*Matthiessen*⟩ It may, on the one hand, apply to the gentle easing of an infant into sleep (as by song or rocking) or, on the other hand, imply a sleepy relaxation into repose, complacence, unawareness, or apathy when one should be vigilant ⟨we must not let a year or two of prosperity *lull* us into a false feeling of security—*Truman*⟩ **Soothe** suggests bland, gentle mitigation, assuagement, or solace ⟨cooled their fevered sleep, and *soothed* them into slumbers full and deep—*Keats*⟩ ⟨when they [babies] wake screaming and find none to *soothe* them—*Lamb*⟩ **Settle** (see also DECIDE) stresses the subsiding of swirling agitation and implies a stabilizing and easing of a mind or body previously upset (as by emotional excitement, illness, or intoxication) ⟨*settled* her stomach with peppermint tea⟩ ⟨I'll read a bit before supper to *settle* my mind—*Turnbull*⟩ ⟨if I can't *settle* my brains, your next news of me will be that I am locked up—*Montagu*⟩ **Tranquilize** in general use stresses the serenity and depth of peace achieved ⟨when contemplation . . . sends deep into the soul its *tranquilizing* power—*Wordsworth*⟩ but in recent years it has acquired a more specific though closely related medical application in which it implies a relieving of mental tension and agitation by means of medication ⟨tranquilizers will calm nervous cows for milking. . . . The most hopeful prospect in *tranquilizing* the animal world lies in the possibility it may change the attitude of some dogs toward postmen—*Sacramento Bee*⟩
*Ana* allay, assuage, mitigate, alleviate, *relieve: mollify, placate, appease, *pacify
*Ant* agitate, arouse   —*Con* upset, perturb, disturb, disquiet, *discompose

**calumniate** defame, slander, asperse, traduce, *malign, vilify, libel
*Ana* revile, vituperate (see SCOLD): *decry, derogate, detract, belittle, disparage
*Ant* eulogize: vindicate   —*Con* extol, laud, *praise, acclaim: defend, justify (see MAINTAIN)

**calumny** slander, *detraction, backbiting, scandal
*Ana* aspersion, reflection, *animadversion, stricture: defaming *or* defamation, maligning, traducing, vilifying *or* vilification, libeling *or* libel (see corresponding verbs at MALIGN *vb*)
*Ant* eulogy: vindication   —*Con* *encomium, panegyric, tribute: *compliment, adulation, flattery

**camouflage** *disguise, cloak, mask, dissemble

**can** *vb* Can, may are often confused in use. In its commonest sense **can** expresses ability, whether physical or mental ⟨he *can* climb this pole⟩ ⟨he is only four, but he *can* read⟩ ⟨he will do it if he possibly *can*⟩ ⟨when Duty whispers low, thou must, the youth replies, I *can*—*Emerson*⟩ But *can* may imply ability that is granted (as by the will of the people or one in authority) ⟨the law does all that is needed when it does all that it *can*—*Justice Holmes*⟩ **May** fundamentally expresses not ability but possibility ⟨he *may* go if the day is pleasant⟩ ⟨you *may* be right⟩ When the possibility depends for its fulfillment on the permission or sanction of another, *may* is the usual term ⟨I shall call tomorrow if I *may*⟩ ⟨you *may* go, if you

---

A colon (:) separates groups of words discriminated. An asterisk (*) indicates place of treatment of each group.

wish⟩ ⟨*may* we take your coach to town?—*Thackeray*⟩ The use of *can* for *may* in asking or granting permission is widespread.

**canal** *channel, conduit, duct, aqueduct

**cancel** efface, obliterate, expunge, delete, *erase, blot out
*Ana* invalidate, annul, *nullify: void, *annul, abrogate: *deface, disfigure: *neutralize, counteract, negative
*Con* confirm, *ratify: *enforce, implement

**cancer** *tumor, neoplasm, malignancy

**candid** open, *frank, plain
*Ana* truthful, veracious (see corresponding nouns at TRUTH): *fair, dispassionate, impartial, unbiased, just: *sincere: honest, scrupulous, *upright
*Ant* evasive —*Con* *dishonest, deceitful, lying, mendacious, untruthful

**candidate, aspirant, nominee, applicant** denote one who seeks an office, honor, position, or award. **Candidate** is applied not only to a seeker but to one who is put forward by others or is considered as a possibility by those whose function it is to make a choice. It implies therefore an examination of qualifications and is applicable wherever selection is dependent upon others' judgment of one's fitness ⟨the Republican *candidate* for governor⟩ ⟨*candidates* for the degree of doctor of philosophy⟩ ⟨*candidates* for holy orders⟩ Since the word often implies previous training or grooming for a position or honor, it is sometimes used more widely of a person whose career is such that he seems headed for a certain place or end ⟨a grafter is a *candidate* for prison⟩ **Aspirant** definitely implies that one seeks an office, honor, post, or promotion because of one's own desire or decision; it therefore often connotes ambition or laudable efforts to improve one's state or condition ⟨the preliminary physical examination was so rigid that twelve *aspirants* were promptly ruled out—*Heiser*⟩ ⟨in consequence of the resignations . . . the way to greatness was left clear to a new set of *aspirants*—*Macaulay*⟩ **Nominee** is applied to a candidate for office who has been chosen to represent a party or a faction in a coming election or who has been proposed as the appropriate person to fill a particular office ⟨the president's *nominee* to the post was approved by the Senate⟩ **Applicant** is applied to one who definitely or formally submits himself as a possibility for a post or position. It is often used interchangeably with *candidate* when personal solicitation is implied in the latter, but unlike *candidate*, it conveys no suggestion of consideration by those who make the selection ⟨weed out *applicants* without experience⟩ ⟨there are plenty of unemployed seamstresses and laborers starving for a job, each of them trying to induce you to give it to her or him rather than to the next *applicant*—*Shaw*⟩

**canon** *law, precept, regulation, rule, statute, ordinance
*Ana* *principle, fundamental, axiom: criterion, *standard, yardstick, touchstone, gauge

**cant** *n* **1** jargon, argot, *dialect, lingo, vernacular, slang, patois
*Ana* phraseology, vocabulary, diction, *language: idiom, speech (see LANGUAGE)
**2** *hypocrisy, sanctimony, pharisaism

**canting** hypocritical, sanctimonious, pharisaical (see under HYPOCRISY)

**capability** *ability, capacity
*Ana* competence, qualification *or* qualifications (see corresponding adjectives at ABLE): proficiency, adeptness, expertness, skillfulness (see corresponding adjectives at PROFICIENT): *art, skill, cunning
*Ant* incapability, incompetence —*Con* *inability, disability

**capable** competent, qualified, *able

*Ana* efficient, *effective, effectual, efficacious
*Ant* incapable —*Con* incompetent, unqualified (see INCAPABLE)

**capacious** *spacious, commodious, ample
*Ana* *broad, wide: extended *or* extensive (see corresponding verb EXTEND): expanded *or* expansive (see corresponding verb EXPAND)
*Ant* exiguous (*of quarters, spaces, containers*) —*Con* circumscribed, limited, confined, restricted (see LIMIT *vb*)

**capacity** *ability, capability
*Ana* amplitude, *expanse, spread: extent, magnitude, *size, volume: aptitude, *gift, faculty, talent, bent, turn, knack
*Ant* incapacity —*Con* powerlessness, impotence (see corresponding adjectives at POWERLESS)

**caper** *n* *prank, monkeyshine, antic, dido
*Ana* gamboling *or* gambol, rollicking *or* rollick, romping *or* romp, frolicking *or* frolic (see corresponding nouns under PLAY *vb*): skipping *or* skip, hopping *or* hop, bounding *or* bound (see SKIP)

**capital** *adj* *chief, principal, main, leading, foremost
*Ana* *primary, primordial, primal: *fundamental, basic, radical, underlying: cardinal, vital, *essential

**capitulate** submit, *yield, succumb, relent, defer, bow, cave
*Ana* surrender, abandon, waive, cede (see RELINQUISH)

**capitulation** *surrender, submission
*Ana* yielding, relenting, succumbing, caving in (see YIELD): *truce, cease-fire, armistice, peace

**caponize** *sterilize, castrate, spay, emasculate, alter, mutilate, geld

**caprice,** **freak, fancy, whim, whimsy, conceit, vagary, crotchet** are comparable when denoting an arbitrary notion that usually lacks a logical basis and therefore may be unsound, impractical, or even irrational. **Caprice** emphasizes the lack of apparent motivation and implies a certain willfulness or wantonness ⟨they . . . without reason or judgment, beyond the *caprice* of their good pleasure, threw down the image from its pedestal—*Byron*⟩ ⟨my cousin's pet *caprice* is to affect a distaste for art, to which she is passionately devoted—*Shaw*⟩ **Freak** suggests an impulsive, seemingly causeless change of mind, like that of a child or a lunatic ⟨a light word flung in the air, a mere *freak* of perverse child's temper—*Thackeray*⟩ ⟨follow this way or that, as the *freak* takes you—*Stevenson*⟩ **Fancy** stresses casualness and lack of reflection in forming an idea and may sometimes suggest a kind of harmless perverseness in the idea formed ⟨coddle ourselves into the *fancy* that our own [life] is of exceptional importance—*Stevenson*⟩ ⟨consoled myself with *fancies* of doing good—curing sick friends by an occult exploration plus pure willpower—*Gold*⟩ **Whim** and **whimsy** suggest not so much a sudden as a quaint, fantastic, or humorous turn or inclination, but *whim* often stresses capriciousness, and *whimsy* fancifulness ⟨a young lady of some birth and fortune . . . who had strange *whims* of fasting—*George Eliot*⟩ ⟨Mr. Wilder is unconcerned with fads, with *whims* of the moment; he is attempting to write permanently about permanent things—*Fadiman*⟩ ⟨Augustus was as free as any man who ever lived from *whimsies* about his own divinity—*Buchan*⟩ ⟨now and again a *whimsy* seized my master and he declared that we must work and earn our daily bread by the sweat of our brows—*W. J. Locke*⟩ **Conceit** suggests more strongly than *whim* or *whimsy* the quaint, fantastic, or erratic character of the notion formed and also may suggest the firmness and persistence with which it is held ⟨it is one of Freud's quaint *conceits* that the child in its mother's womb is the happiest of living creatures—*Krutch*⟩ ⟨fortified him in the *conceit* that in

dealing perfect justice to his son he was doing all that was possible—*Meredith*⟩ **Vagary** suggests still more strongly the erratic, extravagant, or irresponsible character of the notion or fancy ⟨straight they changed their minds, flew off, and into strange *vagaries* fell—*Milton*⟩ ⟨a great force of critical opinion controlling a learned man's *vagaries*, and keeping him straight—*Arnold*⟩ **Crotchet** implies even more perversity of temper or more indifference to right reason than *vagary;* it often is applied to a capriciously heretical opinion on some frequently unimportant or trivial point ⟨the impracticable *crotchets* you are fond of airing are not recognized in England as sane political convictions—*Shaw*⟩ ⟨this political view may now seem to have been the *crotchet* of a particular set of historical scholars—*Dewey*⟩
*Ana* humor, *mood, temper, vein: notion, *idea: impulse (see MOTIVE): irrationality, unreasonableness (see corresponding adjectives at IRRATIONAL): perverseness, contrariness (see corresponding adjectives at CONTRARY)
*Con* intent, purpose, *intention, design: project, scheme, *plan: deciding *or* decision, determining *or* determination, resolving *or* resolution (see corresponding verbs at DECIDE)
**capricious** mercurial, unstable, *inconstant, fickle
*Ana* *changeable, changeful, protean, variable: moody, humorsome (see corresponding nouns at MOOD): volatile, effervescent (see ELASTIC)
*Ant* steadfast —*Con* constant, resolute, staunch, loyal, *faithful: *steady, constant
**capsize** *vb* upset, *overturn, overthrow, subvert
**caption** *inscription, legend
**captious** caviling, carping, *critical, hypercritical, fault-finding, censorious
*Ana* *contrary, perverse: exacting, demanding (see DEMAND *vb*): peevish, petulant, snappish, *irritable: testy, choleric, *irascible
*Ant* appreciative —*Con* reasonable, *rational: judicious, *wise, sensible
**captivate** fascinate, bewitch, enchant, charm, allure, *attract
*Ana* delight, *please, gratify: win, gain (see GET)
*Ant* repulse
**captivating** fascinating, bewitching, enchanting, charming, alluring, attractive (see under ATTRACT)
*Ana* pleasing, *pleasant, agreeable, grateful: *delightful, delectable: lovely, bonny, fair, *beautiful
*Ant* repulsive —*Con* repellent, *repugnant, distasteful, obnoxious: *offensive, loathsome, revolting
**captive** *n* *prisoner
**capture** *vb* *catch, trap, snare, entrap, ensnare, bag
*Ana* seize, *take, grasp, clutch, snatch: *arrest, apprehend
*Con* release, *free, liberate: surrender, yield, *relinquish
**carbonate** *vb* *aerate, ventilate, oxygenate
*Ant* decarbonate
**carbon copy** copy, duplicate, transcript, *reproduction, facsimile, replica
**carbuncle** *abscess, boil, furuncle, pimple, pustule
**carcass** corpse, cadaver, *body
**cardinal** *adj* vital, *essential, fundamental
*Ana* requisite, necessary, indispensable, *needful: radical, *fundamental, basic: capital, principal, *chief, main, leading: important, significant, momentous (see corresponding nouns at IMPORTANCE)
*Ant* negligible
**care** *n* Care, concern, solicitude, anxiety, worry are comparable when meaning either a state of mind in which one is engrossed and troubled by something pertinent to oneself or another, or the pertinent thing that engrosses and

troubles one. The same distinctions in implications and connotations are evident in their corresponding adjectives (**careful, concerned, solicitous, anxious, worried**) when they mean engrossed and troubled by a particular matter. **Care** and **careful** (which is archaic in this sense; see also CAREFUL 2) imply preoccupation and oppression of mind because of heavy responsibilities or disquieting fears or apprehensions ⟨the king . . . most sovereign slave of *care* —*Thoreau*⟩ ⟨her face was worn with *care*⟩ ⟨she was free . . . to go where she liked and do what she liked. She had no responsibilities, no *cares*—*Bennett*⟩ ⟨be *careful* for nothing; but in every thing . . . let your requests be made known unto God—*Phil* 4:6⟩ **Concern** and **concerned** stress absence of indifference, but they also imply a degree of care because of one's interest, affection, respect, or responsibility ⟨his child's future was his greatest *concern*⟩ ⟨an adult who falls on the street is the object of *concern* and commiseration—*Repplier*⟩ ⟨it was quite characteristic of the state of mind of England in the summer of 1914 that Mr. Britling should be mightily *concerned* about the conflict in Ireland, and almost deliberately negligent of the possibility of a war with Germany— *H. G. Wells*⟩ **Solicitude** and **solicitous** imply profound concern; sometimes they connote extreme apprehensiveness, but more often they suggest thoughtfulness for another's welfare, well-being, or success and sometimes an almost hovering attentiveness in another's misfortune ⟨they . . . tended the wounded man with the gentlest *solicitude*—*Dickens*⟩ ⟨with motherly *solicitude*, he insisted that Tom get to his feet—*Anderson*⟩ ⟨they . . . were as *solicitous* to see it through for me as though I had been an only child among a lot of maiden aunts—*Mary Austin*⟩ The last two pairs of words in this group imply far more agitation and depression than the first three. **Anxiety** and **anxious** stress the anguish of fear coupled with uncertainty or of the anticipation of impending failure, misfortune, or disaster ⟨poor Miss Maria! she was *anxious*, no doubt . . . over money matters. Ladies ought not to have such *anxieties*—*Deland*⟩ ⟨the child's inner life is often a turmoil of terrors and *anxieties* of which his parents know almost nothing—*Inge*⟩ **Worry** and **worried** usually suggest more mental activity, often futile, than *anxiety* and *anxious* or more fretting or stewing over problems or situations or persons that are a cause of solicitude or anxiety ⟨because the list of her *worries* is too long, it is difficult to feel as sorry for her as one ought—*Moorehead*⟩ ⟨the high command . . . had begun to wrinkle their brows. They were perplexed, vexed and *worried*—*Pyle*⟩ ⟨*worried* . . . by the need for keeping up their social positions—*Shaw*⟩
*Ana* trouble, pains, *effort, exertion: disquieting *or* disquiet, perturbing *or* perturbation, discomposing *or* discomposure (see corresponding verbs at DISCOMPOSE): vigilance, watchfulness, alertness (see corresponding adjectives at WATCHFUL)
**careful** 1 solicitous, anxious, worried, concerned (see under CARE *n*)
*Ana* disquieted, perturbed, discomposed, disturbed, upset (see DISCOMPOSE): troubled, distressed (see TROUBLE *vb*): *watchful, vigilant, alert
2 Careful, **meticulous, scrupulous, punctilious, punctual** are comparable in their basic sense of showing or revealing close attention to details or care in execution or performance. **Careful** implies great concern for the persons or things in one's charge or for the way in which one's duties or tasks are performed. With regard to the former, the term implies solicitude or watchfulness ⟨a *careful* mother⟩ ⟨a *careful* nurse⟩ ⟨a *careful* spender of money⟩ and with regard to the latter, it usually implies painstaking efforts, thoroughness, cautiousness in avoiding errors, and

A colon (:) separates groups of words discriminated. An asterisk (*) indicates place of treatment of each group.

a desire for perfection ⟨a *careful* piece of work⟩ ⟨a *careful* examination by the doctor⟩ ⟨a *careful* mapping out of the plan of battle⟩ All of the other words mean exceedingly careful, but they vary in their implications of the motives which inspire such carefulness and, to a less extent, in regard to the objects of attention. **Meticulous** usually suggests timorousness lest one make the slightest error or fall short of a high standard; in addition, it implies extreme fussiness or fastidiousness in attention to details ⟨Mr. Prufrock . . . like most converts, *meticulous* over points of ritual—*Day Lewis*⟩ ⟨the *meticulous* care with which the operation in Sicily was planned has paid dividends. For our casualties . . . have been low—*Roosevelt*⟩ ⟨there were men who ploughed clumsily . . . leaving banks of land untouched . . . but Hendrik was not one of these, his work was *meticulous*—*Cloete*⟩ **Scrupulous** (see also UPRIGHT) implies the promptings of conscience, not only of one's moral conscience but of one's sense of what is right and wrong (as in fact, in logic, or in aesthetics); it therefore also implies strict or painstaking adherence to what one knows to be true, correct, or exact ⟨*scrupulous* fairness of statement⟩ ⟨*scrupulous* observation of details⟩ ⟨Bradley, like Aristotle, is distinguished by his *scrupulous* respect for words, that their meaning should be neither vague nor exaggerated—*T. S. Eliot*⟩ **Punctilious**, on the other hand, implies knowledge of the fine points (as of law, etiquette, ceremony, or morality) and usually connotes excessive or obvious attention to the details or minutiae of these ⟨I am sorry . . . to see you so *punctilious* as to stand upon answers, and never to come near me till I have regularly left my name at your door—*Gray*⟩ ⟨the *punctilious* gods who judged them according to the principles laid down in some celestial Book of Etiquette—*Krutch*⟩ **Punctual** may occasionally come close to *punctilious* in its stress on attention to the fine points of a law or code, but in such use the term carries a much stronger implication than *punctilious* of emphasis on their observance and a weaker implication of concentration upon the minutiae ⟨we are not altogether so *punctual* as the French, in observing the laws of comedy—*Dryden*⟩ ⟨his *punctual* discharge of his duties—*Froude*⟩ More usually the term implies near perfection in one's adherence to appointed times for engagements or in following a schedule and then means punctiliously prompt ⟨I made Mr. Middleditch *punctual* before he died, though when he married me he was known far and wide as a man who could not be up to time—*Mackenzie*⟩ ⟨*punctual*, commonplace, keeping all appointments, as I go my round—*L. P. Smith*⟩
*Ana* *cautious, circumspect, wary: provident, foresighted, prudent (see under PRUDENCE): accurate, precise, nice, exact (see CORRECT): studied, *deliberate
*Ant* careless —*Con* heedless, thoughtless, inadvertent (see CARELESS): neglectful, *negligent, lax, slack, remiss

**careless** *adj* Careless, heedless, thoughtless, inadvertent mean showing lack of concern or attention. **Careless** often implies the absence of such cares as responsibilities or worries; it then usually connotes casualness, spontaneity, and lightheartedness and carries little or no suggestion of culpability ⟨her *careless* refinement of manner was so different from the studied dignity and anxious courtesy of the actor-manager—*Shaw*⟩ ⟨he presented to the world the appearance of a *careless* and hospitable millionaire strolling into his own drawing room with the detachment of an invited guest—*Wharton*⟩ Often, however, the term implies a more or less culpable indifference which at its best is the product of independence or of concentration on other and more important things ⟨raise all kinds of hope, *careless* of the disillusionment that will certainly

follow—*Hicks*⟩ and at its worst is the result of laziness or negligence and manifests itself in blameworthy lack of pains or thought ⟨a *careless* bookkeeper⟩ ⟨a *careless* piece of work⟩ ⟨*careless* errors⟩ **Heedless** also implies indifference, but it stresses inattentiveness or a failure to see, observe, take note of, or remark rather than laziness or negligence; the term often also connotes light-mindedness, frivolousness, or flightiness ⟨heaps of flies . . . fell dead. . . . Their decease made no impression on the other flies out promenading. . . . Curious to consider how *heedless* flies are!—*Dickens*⟩ ⟨discreetly *heedless*, thanks to her long association with nobleness in art, to the leaps and bounds of fashion—*Henry James*⟩ **Thoughtless** may emphasize lack of reflection or of forethought ⟨*thoughtless* of tomorrow and God—*Guthrie*⟩ More frequently it suggests lack of thoughtfulness or consideration for others ⟨now and then, however, he is horribly *thoughtless*, and seems to take a real delight in giving me pain—*Wilde*⟩ **Inadvertent** usually implies heedlessness; the term is rarely applied to persons or their minds but is used in qualifying their acts and especially such of their mistakes, errors, or blunders as ensue from heedlessness or inattention resulting from concentration on other things rather than from ignorance or intention ⟨an *inadvertent* wakening of a person who is asleep⟩ ⟨an *inadvertent* error in spelling or in pronunciation⟩ ⟨they are in a bad fix . . . and sometimes with an *inadvertent* child or two to support —*Rand*⟩
*Ana* *negligent, neglectful, lax, slack, remiss: casual, desultory, haphazard, *random, hit-or-miss, happy-go-lucky
*Ant* careful —*Con* meticulous, scrupulous, punctilious, punctual (see CAREFUL): accurate, precise, exact, nice (see CORRECT)

**caress** *vb* Caress, fondle, pet, cosset, cuddle, dandle mean to show affection or love by touching or handling. **Caress** implies an expression of tender interest (as by soft stroking or patting) or of affection ordinarily without undue familiarity ⟨soothing with a touch the wild thing's fright . . . *caressed* it into peace with light, kind palms—*Edwin Arnold*⟩ ⟨the little Isaac . . . leans . . . against his father's knee . . . while Abraham's left hand quiets him and *caresses* the boy's face—*Henry Adams*⟩ **Fondle** implies doting fondness and frequently lack of dignity; it usually suggests attentions (as hugging or kissing) more obvious and less gentle than caressing ⟨*fondle* a baby⟩ ⟨all that he was good for, she said, was to *fondle* and fumble and kiss—*Graves*⟩ ⟨dwarf trees that had to be *fondled* and humored—*Brooks*⟩ **Pet**, sometimes, and **cosset** imply special attentions and indulgences including more or less fondling ⟨the *petted* child of the family⟩ ⟨died . . . in the newest and largest of hospitals *petted* by all her nurses—*Jarrell*⟩ ⟨soothed and *cosseted* by his aunt—*Cather*⟩ In recent use *pet* more often stresses flirtatious or amorous fondling and sometimes suggests undue familiarity ⟨a *petting* party⟩ **Cuddle** chiefly suggests the action of a mother or nurse in drawing a child close to her breast to keep it warm, happy, and quiet ⟨little boys . . . who have kind mammas to *cuddle* them—*Kingsley*⟩ The term may be extended to other attentions which imply a desire to protect and keep warm and contented ⟨Temple seems . . . to have been coaxed, and warmed, and *cuddled* by the people round about him—*Thackeray*⟩ ⟨we might *cuddle* up to the world in a comfortable attitude—*Langer*⟩ **Dandle** suggests playful handling of a child (as by moving him up and down lightly on one's knee) ⟨the mother cuddles, but the father *dandles*, their little boy⟩ In its extended use *dandle* usually implies toying with especially in a playful but pampering manner ⟨editors, scholars, mer-

---

*Ana* analogous words     *Ant* antonyms     *Con* contrasted words     See also explanatory notes facing page 1

chants, even the noble lords and ladies feted and *dandled* him—*Eastman*⟩

*Ana* \*trifle, toy, dally, flirt, coquet: cherish, \*nurse

**careworn** worn, \*haggard, pinched, wasted, cadaverous

*Ana* troubled, distressed (see TROUBLE *vb*): \*lean, gaunt, scrawny, skinny: exhausted, fagged, jaded, tuckered (see TIRE *vb*)

*Ant* carefree

**cargo** burden, \*load, freight, lading

**caricature** *n* Caricature, burlesque, parody, travesty are comparable as nouns meaning a grotesque or bizarre imitation of something and as verbs meaning to make such an imitation. **Caricature** implies ludicrous exaggeration or distortion (often pictorial) of characteristic or peculiar features (as of a person, a group, or a people) for the sake of satire or ridicule ⟨cartoonists who *caricature* prominent politicians⟩ ⟨that propensity to *caricature* which tempts clever writers . . . to transform into objects of derision the venerated Great—*L. P. Smith*⟩ ⟨his portrait of Addison, for example . . . depends upon . . . the apparent determination not to exaggerate. The genius of Pope is not for *caricature*—*T. S. Eliot*⟩ **Burlesque** implies mimicry (especially of words or actions in the theater) that arouses laughter. The term usually also suggests distortion (as by treating a trifling subject in mock-heroic vein or by giving to a serious subject a frivolous or laughable turn) for the sake of the comic effect ⟨in *Don Quixote* Cervantes *burlesques* the old romances of chivalry⟩ ⟨*burlesque* is . . . of two kinds; the first represents mean persons in the accouterments of heroes; the other describes great persons acting and speaking like the basest among the people—*Spectator*⟩ **Parody** basically denotes a writing in which the language and style of an author or work are closely imitated for comic effect or in ridicule ⟨*parody* may be regarded as an unique combination of both creative and cognitive criticism. At its best, it is creative because it is genuine self-expression through imitation of another's self-expression. It debunks aesthetic illusion by means of a mock-aesthetic illusion of its own—*J. L. Davis*⟩ Parody, like *caricature*, may involve exaggeration or, like *burlesque*, distortion but ordinarily is more subtle and sustained than the first and quieter and less boisterous than the second ⟨burlesque or *parody* may be aimed at the most august object, but surely it must imply an understanding of that object—*Bentley*⟩ ⟨one of the richest sources of their humor lies in their ability to *parody* the most solemn efforts of radio and television as these media attempt the dramatic slush known as soap operas—*G. S. Perry*⟩ In extended use *parody* may apply, often with more than a hint of bitterness or disgust, to a feeble or inappropriate imitation ⟨his art had become *parody*, his body a gutted edifice—there was nothing left but to drink in the company of friends and to hope to die with dignity—*Rogow*⟩ or to a poor inadequate substitute ⟨subsidized football results in some queer *parodies* of education—*Eaton*⟩ ⟨the mechanically produced *parodies* of period designs hitherto offered by the furniture trade—*Gloag*⟩ **Travesty** is usually a harsher word than others of this group; it implies a palpably extravagant and often debased or grotesque imitation and more often and more intensely than parody suggests repulsion ⟨it should never be the object of a satirist to make a *travesty* of a genuine work of art—*Kitchell*⟩ ⟨racist explanations of the fall of Rome are a *travesty* of the facts—*Benedict*⟩ ⟨later examples of the Greek revival *travestied* the classic style rather than copied it—*Amer. Guide Series: Mass.*⟩

*Ana* satire, humor, sarcasm (see WIT): grotesqueness, fantasticality, bizarreness (see corresponding adjectives at FANTASTIC): lampoon, \*libel, skit, squib, pasquinade

**caricature** *vb* burlesque, parody, travesty (see under CARICATURE *n*)

*Ana* mimic, mock, ape, imitate, \*copy: distort, \*deform: simulate, counterfeit (see ASSUME): \*ridicule, deride

**carnage** slaughter, butchery, \*massacre, pogrom

**carnal, fleshly, sensual, animal** are comparable when they are used in reference to human beings, their acts, works, desires, and interests and mean having or showing a physical rather than an intellectual or spiritual character or origin. Both *carnal* and *fleshly* imply a connection with the body or flesh especially when thought of as distinct from the spirit. **Carnal** need not in itself imply condemnation ⟨armed against ghostly as well as *carnal* attack—*Stoker*⟩ Often it is a purely descriptive or classificatory term ⟨a . . . flier with a lyrical gift for conveying the *carnal* élan of men fighting, was the first writer ever to treat air combat in epic style—*Flanner*⟩ but through its frequent opposition to the spiritual it has come to suggest not merely man's bodily but his lower nature and appetites ⟨the superiority of the spiritual and eternal over the *carnal* and temporal had to be vindicated—*H. O. Taylor*⟩ ⟨medieval Christianity tended to restore the conviction that sex, being *carnal* and not spiritual, is low, lascivious, and wicked—*Garvin*⟩ and ultimately to be applied more or less specifically and usually derogatorily to the sexual and the lustful as the most bodily of appetites and the most antithetical to the spiritual nature ⟨to make herself a *carnal* object, the prey of another, is in contradiction to her self-worship: it seems to her that embraces blight and sully her body or degrade her soul—*Parshley*⟩ ⟨he has also three partner antagonists: his wife Lucy and his two mistresses, one a *carnal* affair, the other "idealistic"—*Bentley*⟩ ⟨who more *carnal* than a recent virgin—*Steinbeck*⟩ ⟨had an instant succès du scandale. It titillated the prurient with the frankness of its *carnal* detail—*S. H. Adams*⟩ **Fleshly**, though it implies a connection with the flesh thought of as man's lower nature, is often less suggestive of condemnation than *carnal* ⟨turn to Bernard's love of God, and rise with him from the *fleshly* to the spiritual—*H. O. Taylor*⟩ ⟨the godly dame, who *fleshly* failings damns—*Pope*⟩ **Sensual** implies a connection with sensations, but it further implies an indulgence in bodily sensation for its own sake rather than for an aesthetic end ⟨his feet and hands were always cold and there was for him an almost *sensual* satisfaction to be had from just lying perfectly still . . . and letting the hot sun beat down on him—*Anderson*⟩ Very often the word carries implications of grossness marked by concentration on bodily satisfaction and the absence of intellectual or spiritual qualities ⟨a sloping meaty jaw, and large discolored buckteeth which showed unpleasantly in a mouth . . . always half open . . . that gave his face its *sensual*, sly, and ugly look—*Wolfe*⟩ **Animal** implies a connection with man's physical nature as distinguished chiefly from his rational nature. It comparatively seldom implies an intent to depreciate ⟨he could never find his Nirvana in mere sensuousness; he could not sink into the mud of *animal* existence—*Parrington*⟩ ⟨the first mood at any war's end is sheer *animal* joy in survival—*Wecter*⟩ ⟨he taught the boy boxing, and shooting, and . . . superintended the direction of his *animal* vigor—*Meredith*⟩

*Ana* physical, \*bodily, corporeal, corporal, somatic: \*sensuous: gross, \*coarse, vulgar, obscene: \*earthly, earthy, worldly, mundane: lustful, lewd, wanton, lascivious (see LICENTIOUS)

*Ant* spiritual: intellectual —*Con* \*moral, ethical, virtuous, noble, righteous: ethereal, aerial (see AIRY): pure, \*chaste, modest, decent

**carol** *vb* \*sing, troll, descant, warble, trill, hymn, chant,

---

A colon (:) separates groups of words discriminated. An asterisk (\*) indicates place of treatment of each group.

intone

**carping** *adj* caviling, faultfinding, captious, *critical, hypercritical, censorious

*Ana* blaming, reprehending, reprobating, criticizing (see CRITICIZE): upbraiding, jawing, railing (see SCOLD): depreciating *or* depreciative, disparaging, decrying (see corresponding verbs at DECRY)

*Ant* fulsome —*Con* commending *or* commendatory, applauding, complimenting (see corresponding verbs at COMMEND): praising, lauding, extolling (see PRAISE *vb*): approving, endorsing (see APPROVE)

**carry** *vb* Carry, bear, convey, transport, transmit are comparable when they mean to be or to serve as the agent or the means whereby something or someone is moved from one place to another. **Carry** often implies the use of a cart or carriage or more recently of a train, ship, automobile, or airplane, but it may imply a personal agent or a beast of burden or some natural or artificial passage (as an artery or a pipe) ⟨the ship *carries* a heavy cargo⟩ ⟨airplanes *carry* mail⟩ ⟨a bus built to *carry* sixty passengers⟩ ⟨*carry* news⟩ ⟨please *carry* the basket to the house⟩ ⟨the arteries *carry* the blood from the heart to the various parts of the body⟩ **Bear** stresses the support of the weight of whatever is being moved; in its extended senses, even though actual weight may not be implied, *bear* is preferred to *carry* when effort is suggested or the importance or the significance of what is carried is to be connoted ⟨let four captains *bear* Hamlet, like a soldier, to the stage—*Shak.*⟩ ⟨over his head was *borne* a rich canopy—*Johnson*⟩ ⟨then came the envoys *bearing* rich gifts⟩ ⟨come *bearing* good news⟩ **Convey** is more often used than *carry* of things that move continuously or in the mass or that pass through natural or artificial channels or mediums ⟨an endless belt for *conveying* dirt from an excavation to the trucks removing it⟩ ⟨freight cars for *conveying* coal from the mines to the various cities and towns⟩ ⟨pipelines to *convey* natural gas from one section to another⟩ ⟨language *conveys* thought⟩ **Transport** is used in place of *carry* or *convey* when the stress is on the movement of persons or goods especially in numbers or bulk and typically over a considerable distance and by a professional carrier (as a railway or steamship line) ⟨fast liners were used to *transport* troops to France⟩ ⟨trucks *transporting* farm produce to market⟩ ⟨most modern well-to-do Englishmen and Americans, if they were *transported* by magic into the Age of Elizabeth, would wish themselves back in the modern world —*Russell*⟩ **Transmit** emphasizes the causative power in an agent or instrument; it implies either an actual sending by some means of conveyance or transportation ⟨the telegraph company *transmits* messages to all parts of the world⟩ ⟨the steamship company will *transmit* your baggage whenever it receives the word⟩ or the power or the property of permitting passage through or from one place to another ⟨glass *transmits* light⟩ ⟨metals *transmit* electricity⟩

*Ana* take, *bring, fetch: *move, remove, shift, transfer: drive, *ride

**cartel** 1 compact, pact, convention, *contract, bargain, concordat, treaty, entente

2 pool, syndicate, corner, *monopoly, trust

*Ana* combine, *combination: *consolidation, merger, amalgamation

**carve** 1 *cut, slit, hew, chop, slash

*Ana* shape, fashion, form (see MAKE): *separate, divide, part

2 Carve, incise, engrave, etch, chisel, sculpture, sculpt, sculp are comparable when they denote to cut an outline or a shape out of or into some substance (as stone, wood,

or metal). They are, however, not close synonyms, for few of the terms keep within the limits of this meaning. **Carve** (see also CUT) suggests working with an instrument (as a knife or a chisel) in order to adorn a surface or to fashion a solid figure; the term may connote an artistic purpose (as representation or decoration) and a method of work involving the cutting of a pattern into a surface (*intaglio carving*) or the cutting away of parts of the original surface so as to leave a raised design or raised figures upon a new ground (*relief carving*) or the fashioning of a whole or partial figure by cutting or chipping away excess material ⟨*carve* an inscription on a tombstone⟩ ⟨the legs of chairs and table were *carved* with oak leaves⟩ ⟨a figure *carved* in stone is fine carving when one feels that not the figure, but the stone . . . has come to life—*Sweeney*⟩ **Incise** implies cutting into with an instrument (as a knife) that leaves traces; more specifically it implies a cutting into some hard or resistant material so that figures, letters, or devices are marked upon its surface ⟨*incise* an epitaph upon a monument⟩ ⟨the gem had been *incised* with his coat of arms and was used as his seal⟩ **Engrave** often implies a cutting into and may be used as an equivalent of *incise;* in general use, however, it more often implies a cutting (as upon wood, stone, or metal) with a graving tool in order to form an inscription or a pictorial representation that can be printed either from the incised lines, spaces, or points (as in *copperplate engraving*) or from parts of the surface left in relief (as in *wood engraving*). The noun *engraving* denotes a picture printed from a plate or block thus made, but the verb usually emphasizes the work of the one who actually cut the plate or block ⟨was asked to *engrave* a portrait of Daniel Webster⟩ ⟨prints made from an *engraved* copper plate⟩ *Engrave* also may be used to connote an indelible impression upon the heart, mind, or memory ⟨no stone stands over where he lies. It is on our hearts that his life is *engraved*— *Galsworthy*⟩ **Etch** differs from *engrave* only in implying that the lines and dots which form a picture are incised not upon the metal but through a hard, acid-resisting surface (as of varnish) covering the metal of a plate and are then eaten into the plate by coating this surface with acid. **Chisel,** though used widely by workers in stone and wood to suggest the various processes (as of cutting or shaping) that are executed with a chisel, is in general use more often employed to suggest either literally or figuratively the process of carving an image from resistant material; the emphasis in such use is upon the skill of the maker and the artistic quality of the product ⟨it was a great artist who *chiseled* the vital figure of the Winged Victory out of stone⟩ ⟨finely *chiseled* features⟩ **Sculpture** and the related **sculpt** and **sculp** imply the formation of primarily three-dimensional figures especially in stone or metal. Basically *sculpture* suggests carving or chiseling out of some hard substance, but all three terms stress the end result over the technique and may be extended to include the making of three-dimensional art forms by such diverse methods as modeling and molding, welding, or construction as well as by the traditional carving and chiseling, and all three, but especially *sculpture,* may be further extended to processes and results suggesting the work of a sculptor ⟨a *sculptured* bronze head⟩ ⟨because it was God Who had *sculptured* the mountains . . . while it was men who had bricked the cities and that was why they were sometimes so ugly—*Bruce Marshall*⟩ ⟨does not so much sing Mozart's phrases as *sculpt* them, with the sure instincts of a master craftsman—*Gelatt*⟩ ⟨Brancusi . . . *sculps* what Plato had in mind by the idea of form—*Time*⟩

*Ana* shape, fashion, form (see MAKE): produce, turn out

---

*Ana* analogous words     *Ant* antonyms     *Con* contrasted words     See also explanatory notes facing page 1

(see BEAR)

**case** 1 *instance, illustration, example, specimen, sample
*Ana* *occurrence, event, incident, episode, circumstance: situation, condition, *state
2 cause, action, *suit, lawsuit

**casement** *window, dormer, oriel

**cash** *n* currency, *money, legal tender, specie, coin, coinage

**cashier** *vb* *dismiss, discharge, drop, fire, sack, bounce
*Ana* *eject, expel, oust: eliminate, disbar, *exclude, suspend
*Con* engage (see PROMISE): elect, appoint, *designate, name

**cast** *vb* 1 *throw, fling, hurl, pitch, toss, sling
*Ana* *direct, aim, point, level, train, lay: *scatter, disperse
2 *discard, shed, molt, slough, scrap, junk
*Ana* *relinquish, abandon, yield, surrender, leave: repudiate, reject (see DECLINE): *dismiss, drop
3 figure, foot, *add, sum, total, tot
*Ana* compute, *calculate, reckon

**castaway** *n* derelict, *outcast, reprobate, pariah, untouchable

**castigate** *vb* chastise, *punish, chasten, discipline, correct
*Ana* *beat, baste, thrash, pummel, belabor: berate, tongue-lash, rate, upbraid, wig, rail (see SCOLD): *penalize, fine, amerce, mulct

**castrate** *sterilize, spay, emasculate, alter, mutilate, geld, caponize

**casual** 1 *accidental, incidental, adventitious, contingent, fortuitous
*Ana* unpremeditated (see EXTEMPORANEOUS): *indifferent, unconcerned, incurious: *negligent, slack, lax, remiss: inadvertent, *careless, heedless
*Con* intentional, *voluntary: premeditated, *deliberate, studied, considered, advised, designed: *careful, meticulous, punctilious, scrupulous
2 desultory, *random, haphazard, chancy, hit-or-miss, happy-go-lucky
*Ana* offhand, impromptu, improvised, *extemporaneous, extempore: *spontaneous, impulsive: unmethodical, unsystematic (see affirmative adjectives at ORDERLY)
*Ant* deliberate —*Con* formal, conventional, ceremonious (see CEREMONIAL)

**casualty** *accident, mishap
*Ana* *disaster, calamity, catastrophe, cataclysm: *misfortune, mischance, mishap

**casuistical** sophistical, fallacious (see under FALLACY)
*Ana* *plausible, specious: tortuous (see WINDING): oblique, devious, *crooked: *misleading, delusive, deceptive, delusory
*Con* sound, cogent, convincing, *valid

**casuistry** sophistry, sophism, *fallacy

**cataclysm** catastrophe, *disaster, calamity
*Ana* convulsing *or* convulsion, rocking, shaking, agitation (see corresponding verbs at SHAKE): revolution (see REBELLION): *misfortune, mischance, mishap

**catalog** *n* *list, inventory, table, schedule, register, roll, roster

**catalog** *vb* *record, register, list, enroll
*Ana* enumerate, number, *count: *enter, admit

**cataract** *n* *flood, deluge, inundation, torrent, spate

**catastrophe** *disaster, calamity, cataclysm
*Ana* *trial, tribulation, visitation: defeating *or* defeat, overthrowing *or* overthrow, routing *or* rout (see corresponding verbs at CONQUER)
*Con* *victory, triumph

**catch** *vb* 1 Catch, capture, trap, snare, entrap, ensnare, bag are comparable when meaning to get into one's possession or under one's control either by taking or seizing or by means of skill, craft, or trickery. Catch, the ordinary and general term of this group, distinctively implies that the thing laid hold of has been in flight, in concealment, or in constant movement and that possession has been gained by pursuit, force, strategy, or surprise or by means of a device or accident which brings it within one's reach physically, visually, or mentally ⟨after several days' search the detectives *caught* the murderer⟩ ⟨not able to *catch* the man who snatched her purse⟩ ⟨*catch* fish⟩ ⟨*catch* a ball⟩ ⟨*catch* a pupil cheating in an examination⟩ ⟨his eyes *caught* the skirt of her dress—*Dickens*⟩ ⟨Yancey Cravat *caught* the word beneath his teeth and spat it back—*Ferber*⟩ ⟨he smiled back like a child *caught* in a lie—*Steinbeck*⟩ Sometimes the power of laying hold of is ascribed not to a person, his vision or other sense, or his mind, heart, or imagination but to the thing which draws to itself his attention, his eye, or his fancy ⟨the fact *caught* her interest, just as sometimes a point in a wide dull landscape *catches* the eye—*Deland*⟩ ⟨two recent imports . . . offer striking new surprises which may *catch* unaware even the veteran reader—*Anthony Boucher*⟩ **Capture** implies heavier odds (as greater opposition or difficulty or more competition) than does *catch* and suggests a taking possession that amounts to an overcoming or a victory ⟨*capture* a stronghold of the enemy⟩ ⟨*capture* a company of retreating soldiers⟩ ⟨he was making plans . . . to *capture* the banking of the country—*Belloc*⟩ ⟨no artist can set out to *capture* charm; he will toil all the night and take nothing —*Benson*⟩ **Trap, snare, entrap,** and **ensnare** imply catching by a device which holds the one caught in a position that is fraught with danger or difficulty or from which escape is difficult or impossible. *Trap* and *snare* imply the use of a trap or snare (see LURE *n*), but *entrap* and *ensnare* suggest trickery in capture more often than the use of an actual trap or snare: all four terms impute craft to the catcher and unwariness or lack of caution to the one that is caught. Distinctively, *trap* and *entrap* suggest a being held in a position where one is at the mercy of the captor and his designs, and *snare* and *ensnare* a being held so that the more one struggles the more desperate becomes one's situation ⟨*trap* an animal⟩ ⟨*snare* a bird⟩ ⟨*trap* a detachment of soldiers with an ambush⟩ ⟨themselves in bloody toils were *snared*—*Scott*⟩ ⟨as if he would clear away some entanglement which had *entrapped* his thoughts —*Bromfield*⟩ ⟨*entrap* a person by a sudden question into making a dangerous admission⟩ ⟨sympathetic to the regime that *ensnared* them in its monstrous net—*B. D. Wolfe*⟩ **Bag** carried a double implication of catching (as game or specimens) and of putting into a container (as a game bag) for transportation or storage ⟨he *bagged* several rare butterflies within the last month⟩ ⟨*bag* pheasants⟩ So strong is the implication of catching and killing game in this use that the word is often employed without suggestion of putting in a bag ⟨they *bagged* three bears on their last hunting expedition⟩ ⟨*bagged* the British rights to John Hersey's *Hiroshima* while other English publishers were asleep—*Cerf*⟩
*Ana* seize, *take, grasp, grab, clutch, snatch: apprehend, *arrest
*Ant* miss
2 *incur, contract

**catching** contagious, *infectious, communicable

**catchword,** byword, shibboleth, slogan mean a phrase that catches the eye or the ear and is repeated so often that it becomes a formula. Catchword usually applies to a phrase that serves as the formula or identification mark of an emotionally charged subject (as a school of thought, a political party, or a cause) and that is often used by those who have only a superficial knowledge of the subject and

---

A colon (:) separates groups of words discriminated. An asterisk (*) indicates place of treatment of each group.

its philosophy and basic tenets ⟨"the new deal" became the *catchword* of supporters and critics of Franklin Roosevelt as "the square deal" was that of the friends and the enemies of Theodore Roosevelt⟩ ⟨man is a creature who lives not upon bread alone, but principally by *catchwords* —*Stevenson*⟩ ⟨these *catchwords* which you repeat when people ask you for intelligence—*Masefield*⟩ **Byword** sometimes denotes a significant phrase that is repeated far and wide until it has become a proverb ⟨the old *byword* of necessity being the mother of invention—*Kroeber*⟩ The more usual sense is a person or thing that has become proverbial as the type of certain evil, ludicrous, or shameful characteristics and whose name, therefore, has become the object of concentrated scorn or contempt ⟨I had disgraced that name eternally. I had made it a low *byword* among low people—*Wilde*⟩ ⟨even those public departments that were *bywords* for incompetence and red tape were far more efficient than the commercial adventurers who derided them—*Shaw*⟩ ⟨*Emerson* . . . was still an impossible puzzle in the popular mind, even a national joke, a *byword* of the country paragraphers—*Brooks*⟩ **Shibboleth** was the word which, in *Judges* 12, the Ephraimites fleeing from the Gileadites could not correctly pronounce when tested, thus giving away their identity to Jephthah as his enemies; it typically applies to a fixed usage (as a word, phrase, or speech sound) whose employment identifies a person as belonging to a particular party, class, profession, ethnic group, or time. The term basically stresses help in placing a person ⟨a child who . . . has not yet learned sufficiently well the phonemic *shibboleths,* the arbitrary sound-gamuts, which his society insists upon —*La Barre*⟩ ⟨our listeners type us—stereotype us— according to the impression they gain from our verbal habits . . . every word we speak is a *shibboleth*—G. A. *Miller*⟩ but may also imply the emptiness and triteness of such usage and then approach *platitude* in meaning ⟨some truth in the *shibboleth* that crime does not pay— *Rogow*⟩ **Slogan,** originally a cry used in battle, has come to mean a phrase that is a shibboleth of the party or group using it ⟨that was in fact the position that the Dadaists took up. "Art is a private matter: the artist does it for himself" was one of their *slogans*—*Day Lewis*⟩ It may be a phrase deliberately invented for the sake of attracting attention to a party or group ⟨a *slogan* . . . is a short message designed to be repeated over and over again, word for word—*Kleppner*⟩ ⟨traditional schoolbook platitudes and campaign *slogans*—*Frankfurter*⟩ or it may be an eye-catching or ear-catching bit used as an advertising device ⟨the Heinz "57 Varieties" label . . . provided the company with both a trademark and an advertising *slogan*—*Current Biog.*⟩
*Ana* caption, legend (see INSCRIPTION): *phrase, expression, idiom: *commonplace, platitude, truism, bromide, cliché

**catechize** interrogate, quiz, examine, question, *ask, query, inquire

**categorical** 1 *ultimate, absolute
*Con* hypothetical, conjectural, supposititious (see SUPPOSED): conditional, contingent, relative, *dependent
2 express, definite, *explicit, specific
*Ana* positive, certain, *sure: *forthright, downright
*Con* ambiguous, equivocal, vague, cryptic, enigmatic, *obscure: dubious, *doubtful, questionable, problematic

**category** *class, genus, species, denomination, genre
*Ana* division, section, *part: classification (see corresponding verb at ASSORT)

**cater** *vb* Cater, purvey, pander are comparable when they mean to furnish with what satisfies the appetite or desires. **Cater** basically implies the provision of what is needed in

the way of food and drink ⟨he that doth the ravens feed, yea, providently *caters* for the sparrow—*Shak.*⟩ The term especially implies provision of food and drink ready for the table ⟨a firm that *caters* for dinners, weddings, and receptions⟩ In extended use *cater* often implies the provision of something that appeals to a specific appetite ⟨*catering* to the national taste and vanity—*Thackeray*⟩ Often, especially when followed by *to,* the term implies a certain subserviency (as to popular standards or uncultivated tastes) ⟨too many movies, novels, and comic books do *cater* to an appetite for violence—*Sisk*⟩ ⟨*cater* to the public demand for the sensational⟩ **Purvey** usually suggests the provision of food but sometimes of such other material necessities as lodgings and clothes. In contrast with *cater,* however, it suggests service as a source of supply, either as an agent through whom what is wanted may be found or as a merchant who sells the needed articles ⟨merchants who *purveyed* to the troops during the Seven Years' War⟩ In extended use, especially when followed by *for, purvey* implies the provision of whatever is needed to satisfy, delight, or indulge ⟨the function of the eye is now merely ministerial; it merely *purveys* for the ear—*Lanier*⟩ **Pander,** which basically means to act as a procurer or as a go-between in an illicit amour, in its frequent extended use may imply a purveying of something which will gratify desires and passions that are degrading or base ⟨*pander* to depraved appetites⟩ ⟨*pander* to morbid tendencies⟩ or may connote mere servile truckling ⟨denounced legislative *pandering* to special interests—*Time*⟩ ⟨institutions which *pandered* to the factory workers . . . —a movie house, a quick-lunch wagon —*F. S. Fitzgerald*⟩ or even no more than a deferring to or a reasonable indulgence of tastes ⟨choose a plan to suit your type of land and to *pander* to your own particular tastes—*Sydney Bulletin*⟩ ⟨such things, as being traditional, may *pander* to your sense of the great past. Histrionically, too, they are good—*Beerbohm*⟩
*Ana* *furnish, equip, appoint, accouter: pamper, *indulge, humor: *satisfy, content

**catholic** *adj* *universal, cosmic, ecumenical, cosmopolitan
*Ana* *whole, entire, total: all-around, many-sided, *versatile: prevalent, *prevailing, current
*Ant* parochial: provincial   —*Con* bigoted, fanatic, enthusiastic (see corresponding nouns at ENTHUSIAST)

**catnap** nap, snooze, *sleep, slumber, drowse, doze

**cause** *n* 1 Cause, determinant, antecedent, reason, occasion are comparable when denoting what in whole or in part produces an effect or result. **Cause** is applicable to an agent (as a circumstance, condition, event, or force) that contributes to the production of an effect or to any combination (as of circumstances, conditions, or events) that inevitably or necessarily brings about a result ⟨one of the *causes* of the French Revolution was the bankruptcy of the government⟩ ⟨every effect must have an adequate *cause*⟩ ⟨what was the *cause* of this outbreak?⟩ ⟨water and soil pollution are the root *causes* of mortality in the tropics—*Heiser*⟩ *Cause* is sometimes used of a personal agent whose activities are instrumental in bearing consequences ⟨he is the *cause* of all our troubles⟩ or of the motive which prompts one to action ⟨he claimed to have just *cause* for his attack⟩ A **determinant** is a circumstance, factor, element, quality, or motive that by itself or in combination with other factors conditions or fixes the nature of a result and especially of a product or outcome ⟨environment is an important *determinant* of character⟩ ⟨the ideals and the character of citizens are the final *determinants* of their form of government⟩ ⟨"imponderables," which in philosophy as in politics are the most important factors of experience and *determinants* of action—*Inge*⟩

⟨strength of organization, shelter from foreign or other distant competition, command of markets in key industries —these . . . are the main direct *determinants* of wage rates —*Hobson*⟩ **Antecedent** is applicable to a person or thing (as an object or a circumstance, condition, or event) that is responsible, usually in part, for a later existing person or thing, most often as a progenitor, precursor, or predeterminant ⟨it is certainly true that these twelfth-century windows . . . had no *antecedent,* and no fit succession— *Henry Adams*⟩ ⟨the *antecedents* of emperor-worship lay far back in history—*Buchan*⟩ ⟨phenomena like these have other social, cultural, or superorganic phenomena as their immediate causes or *antecedents*—*Kroeber*⟩ **Reason** is interchangeable with *cause* when it means specifically a traceable or explainable cause; it always implies, therefore, that the effect is known or has actually been brought about ⟨there was a *reason* for Mark Twain's pessimism, a *reason* for that chagrin . . . . That bitterness of his was the effect of a certain miscarriage in his creative life, a balked personality, an arrested development—*Brooks*⟩ **Occasion** applies to a situation or to a person, place, or event which provides such a situation that serves to set in motion causes already existing or to translate them into acts; thus, the *cause* of a war may be a deep-rooted enmity between two peoples, the *occasion* of it such a relatively unimportant incident as the murder of a citizen of one country within the confines of the other; an *occasion* of sin may be a visit to a place (as a saloon) where the real *cause,* a propensity to drink, is not resisted ⟨a formula that has been the *occasion* for a considerable amount of misunderstanding—*Richards*⟩
*Ana* \*motive, spring, incentive, inducement, spur, goad, impulse: motivation, activation, actuation (see corresponding verbs at ACTIVATE): agent, agency (see MEAN): \*origin, root, source, prime mover
*Con* \*effect, result, consequence, outcome, issue
**2** \*suit, lawsuit, action, cause, case

**caustic, mordant, acrid, scathing** are comparable when they mean stingingly incisive. **Caustic** usually implies a biting wit, a ready tongue or pen, and the power to drive disagreeable truths home ⟨"I really do not know what to do with my books," he said, and looked round for sympathy. "Why not read them?" said a . . . *caustic* Fellow opposite—*Benson*⟩ **Mordant** is not always clearly distinguishable from *caustic.* In distinctive use it suggests perhaps greater blighting power or deadlier effectiveness in the thrusts of wit ⟨the *mordant* humor of G. B. Shaw⟩ ⟨the *mordant* things you try to say to listeners, cruelties invariably regarded as merely gently whimsical—*Edman*⟩ **Acrid** adds to *caustic* the implications of bitterness and, often, malevolence ⟨most satirists are indeed a public scourge . . . . Their *acrid* temper turns . . . the milk of their good purpose all to curd—*Cowper*⟩ ⟨an *acrid* denunciation of the use of the House floor to broadcast falsehoods—*Roy*⟩ **Scathing** retains its basic implication of injuring chiefly in its suggestion of a deliberate intent to scorch or blister. It seldom implies, as the other words of this group often imply, insensitiveness or maliciousness, and it often connotes both righteous indignation and fierce and withering severity ⟨*scathing* satire⟩ ⟨a *scathing* exposure of graft⟩ ⟨young Wendell Phillips, aristocratic, handsome, ironical, *scathing,* bitter . . . with the bitterness of a man in anguish—*Sandburg*⟩
*Ana* biting, cutting, \*incisive, trenchant: \*bitter: \*sharp, keen, acute: \*sarcastic, satiric, ironic
*Ant* genial —*Con* \*suave, urbane, bland, diplomatic: \*gracious, cordial: gentle, mild (see SOFT)

**caution** *n* circumspection, wariness, chariness, calculation (see under CAUTIOUS)

*Ana* watchfulness, vigilance, alertness (see corresponding adjectives at WATCHFUL): \*prudence, providence, foresight, forethought, discretion
*Ant* temerity: adventurousness —*Con* audacity, hardihood, nerve (see TEMERITY): rashness, recklessness, foolhardiness, daring, daredeviltry (see corresponding adjectives at ADVENTUROUS)

**caution** *vb* \*warn, forewarn
*Ana* admonish (see REPROVE): counsel, advise (see under ADVICE)

**cautious, circumspect, wary, chary, calculating** are comparable when meaning prudently attentive to the dangers one may encounter or the risks one may face, or revealing such attentiveness. The same differences in implications and connotations are apparent in the nouns **caution, circumspection, wariness, chariness, calculation** when they denote the quality of the character or the mental processes of one who is so attentive. **Cautious** and **caution** usually imply both the prompting of fear, especially of fear of failure or of harm to oneself or others, and the exercise of forethought in planning or of prudence in proceeding so that the dangers of failure or the risks of disaster may be avoided or minimized ⟨the troops advanced with great *caution*⟩ ⟨a *cautious* investor⟩ ⟨for the most part, he generalizes with a sobriety and a *caution* worthy of the highest praise—*Huxley*⟩ ⟨the old man, *cautious* in all his movements, always acting as if surrounded by invisible spies, delayed setting out until an hour after dark— *Hudson*⟩ **Circumspect** and **circumspection** frequently imply less fear than *cautious* and *caution;* commonly, however, they suggest the exercise of great prudence and discretion, especially in making decisions or in acting, and the surveying of all possible consequences, lest moral, social, business, or political harm may inadvertently occur ⟨and in all things that I have said unto you be *circumspect*—*Exod* 23:13⟩ ⟨they do not live very happy lives, for they even more than the others are restricted in their movements, and they must live the most *circumspect* of lives—*Steinbeck*⟩ ⟨the . . . *circumspection* with which it approaches the consideration of such questions—*John Marshall*⟩ **Wary** and **wariness** usually carry a far stronger suggestion of suspiciousness than *cautious* and *caution* and sometimes, as a result, connote less well-grounded fear. Often, also, the terms imply alertness in watching out for difficulties or dangers or cunning in escaping them ⟨they . . . had a *wary* eye for all gregarious assemblages of people, and turned out of their road to avoid any very excited group of talkers—*Dickens*⟩ ⟨we must always be *wary* of those who with sounding brass and a tinkling cymbal preach the "ism" of appeasement—*Roosevelt*⟩ ⟨our domestic dogs are descended from wolves . . . they may not have gained in cunning, and may have lost in *wariness*—*Darwin*⟩ **Chary** and **chariness** imply the cautiousness of those who are careful of what they have or what they can give, say, or do and proceed with great reserve or discretion ⟨I am *chary* of admitting native differences between the sexes, but I think that girls are less prone than boys to punish oddity by serious physical cruelty—*Russell*⟩ ⟨my business experience has taught me to be *chary* of committing anything of a confidential nature to any more concrete medium than speech— *Faulkner*⟩ ⟨there was no fastidious overrefined *chariness* in the use of that name—*F. W. Robertson*⟩ **Calculating** and **calculation** imply the caution of one who carefully and deliberately plans the way to attain his own and often selfish end taking into account every possible danger and the way in which it can be met ⟨some day the American boy's outlook upon the future may be as clear and *calculating* as that of his European brother—*Grandgent*⟩

A colon (:) separates groups of words discriminated. An asterisk (\*) indicates place of treatment of each group.

⟨only in regard to la France do they [the French] permit themselves illusions. Only here does sentiment triumph freely and completely over *calculation—Brownell*⟩ The suggestion of selfish prudence that disregards the cruelty of the means, provided the end is attained, is often so strong in these words that the implication of cautiousness is lost and that of coldhearted scheming or of deliberate cruelty takes its place ⟨the terrible men are the men who do everything in cold blood, icily, with *calculation—Hearn*⟩
*Ana* \*watchful, vigilant, alert: prudent, provident, foresighted, forethoughtful, discreet (see under PRUDENCE): heedful, careful (see negative adjectives at CARELESS)
*Ant* adventurous, temerarious —*Con* venturesome, daring, rash, reckless, foolhardy (see ADVENTUROUS): \*precipitate, impetuous, headlong

**cavalcade** \*procession, parade, cortege, motorcade
*Ana* \*succession, progression, chain, train: array, \*display

**cave** succumb, submit, \*yield, capitulate, relent, defer, bow

**caviling** *adj* captious, faultfinding, censorious, carping, \*critical, hypercritical
*Ana* exacting, demanding (see DEMAND): \*contrary, perverse: objecting, protesting, expostulating, kicking (see OBJECT)
*Con* accommodating, obliging, favoring (see OBLIGE): complaisant, \*amiable, good-natured: conciliating, pacifying, mollifying, appeasing (see PACIFY)

**cavity** hollow, \*hole, pocket, void, vacuum
*Con* bulge, protuberance, protrusion, \*projection

**cease** \*stop, quit, discontinue, desist
*Ana* end, terminate, \*close, conclude, finish: stay, suspend, intermit (see DEFER)
*Con* \*spring, arise, rise, originate: \*begin, commence, start, initiate, inaugurate: \*extend, prolong, protract: \*continue, persist

**cease-fire** \*truce, armistice, peace

**cede** surrender, abandon, waive, resign, yield, \*relinquish, leave
*Ana* \*grant, concede, award, accord, vouchsafe
*Con* withhold, hold, hold back, keep back, retain (see KEEP)

**celebrate** commemorate, solemnize, observe, \*keep

**celebrated** renowned, \*famous, famed, eminent, illustrious
*Ana* prominent, conspicuous, outstanding, signal (see NOTICEABLE)
*Ant* obscure

**celebrity** \*fame, renown, glory, honor, éclat, reputation, repute, notoriety
*Ana* prominence, conspicuousness (see corresponding adjectives at NOTICEABLE)
*Ant* obscurity

**celerity, alacrity, legerity** are comparable when they are used in reference to human beings and denote quickness in movement or action. **Celerity** stresses speed in moving or especially in accomplishing work ⟨she could, when she chose, work with astonishing *celerity—Bennett*⟩ ⟨the human brain, we are reminded, acts at times with extraordinary *celerity—Cardozo*⟩ **Alacrity** emphasizes promptness in response more than swiftness in movement, though the latter is usually implied ⟨"You must wait till she sends for you—" and she winced a little at the *alacrity* of his acceptance—*Wharton*⟩ Very often, also, it connotes eagerness or cheerful readiness ⟨working away at his subject with the *alacrity* . . . of a man . . . fulfilling the very office . . . for which nature had designed him—*L. P. Smith*⟩ **Legerity**, a less common word than the others, refers more

to the quality than to the rate of speed and implies nimbleness and ease ⟨cover the ground with the *legerity* of a trained runner⟩ ⟨when the mind is quickened . . . the organs . . . newly move, with . . . fresh *legerity—Shak.*⟩ ⟨the *legerity* of the French mind made the Gallic visitor quick to comprehend his desire for solitude—*Wylie*⟩
*Ana* expedition, dispatch, speed, hurry, \*haste: quickness, rapidity, swiftness, fleetness (see corresponding adjectives at FAST): velocity, \*speed: agility, briskness, nimbleness (see corresponding adjectives at AGILE)
*Ant* leisureliness —*Con* slowness, deliberateness or deliberation, dilatoriness (see corresponding adjectives at SLOW): \*lethargy, languor

**celestial** *adj* Celestial, heavenly, empyrean, empyreal mean of, relating to, or fit for heaven or the heavens. **Celestial** (opposed to *terrestrial*) may refer either to the visible heavens (the region surrounding the earth and seemingly enclosed by the sky) or to the religious conception of heaven or the heavens (in Christian use, the abode of God, the angels, and the blessed dead); thus, a *celestial* globe is one on whose surface the stars, planets, comets, and nebulae are depicted; a *celestial* body is a star, planet, or other aggregation of matter that forms a unit for astronomical study; a *celestial* visitant is an angel or other spirit from the spiritual heaven; *celestial* bliss is the happiness enjoyed by the residents of heaven ⟨angels by Raphael . . . whose serene intelligence embraces both earthly and *celestial* things—*Hawthorne*⟩ **Heavenly**, although it is applicable, especially in nontechnical use, to the visible heavens ⟨*heavenly* bodies—*Bacon*⟩ or to pagan conceptions of Olympus or other abodes of the gods ⟨the immortal sun, who, borne by *heavenly* steeds his race doth run—*Shelley*⟩ is far more often applied to heaven as conceived by Jews and Christians and is apt, therefore, to suggest spiritual qualities ⟨your *heavenly* Father—*Mt 6:14*⟩ ⟨they desire a better country, that is, an *heavenly—Heb 11:16*⟩ ⟨I thought that liberty and heaven to *heavenly* souls had been all one—*Milton*⟩ **Empyrean** and **empyreal** suggest association with the empyrean, either as thought of in ancient and medieval cosmology as the highest celestial sphere, a region of light or fire ⟨from the courts of the *empyrean* dome came forth . . . a fiery car—*Praed*⟩ or, more often, as conceived by various theologians and poets as the highest of the spiritual heavens, where God is and reigns in spiritual light the fire ⟨into the Heaven of Heavens I have presumed . . . and drawn *empyreal* air—*Milton*⟩ The words are often weakened in idiomatic use to mean little more than outstanding of its kind ⟨well-meaning ineptitude, that rises to *empyreal* absurdity—*Dworkin*⟩ ⟨*empyrean* aplomb—*Basso*⟩
*Ana* ethereal, aerial, \*airy: divine, spiritual, \*holy
*Ant* terrestrial —*Con* \*earthly, mundane, earthy, worldly, sublunary: \*infernal, hellish, chthonian

**celibate** *adj* \*unmarried, single, virgin, maiden

**cenobite** \*recluse, eremite, hermit, anchorite
*Ana* monk, friar, \*religious, nun

**censorious** faultfinding, \*critical, hypercritical, captious, carping, caviling
*Ana* reproaching or reproachful, chiding (see corresponding verbs at REPROVE): condemning or condemnatory, denouncing or denunciatory, reprehending (see corresponding verbs at CRITICIZE)
*Ant* eulogistic —*Con* praising, extolling, lauding or laudatory, acclaiming (see corresponding verbs at PRAISE): complimenting or complimentary, flattering, adulatory (see corresponding nouns at COMPLIMENT)

**censure** *vb* \*criticize, reprehend, blame, condemn, denounce, reprobate

---

*Ana* analogous words     *Ant* antonyms     *Con* contrasted words     See also explanatory notes facing page 1

*Ana* reprimand, rebuke, reproach, *reprove: upbraid, berate, tongue-lash (see SCOLD)

*Ant* commend —*Con* applaud, compliment, recommend (see COMMEND): eulogize, laud, *praise

**center** *n* Center, middle, midst, core, hub, focus, nucleus, heart are comparable when meaning the point, spot, or portion of a thing which is comparable to a point around which a circle is described. **Center** approximates more or less closely its strict geometrical sense as the point within a circle or sphere that is equidistant from every other point on the circumference or is the average distance from the exterior points of a body or figure ⟨the *center* of a table⟩ ⟨the *center* of the earth⟩ *Center* may be extended to a thing or a part of a thing which suggests a geometrical center especially in being the point around which the rest rotates or revolves ⟨each airy thought revolved round a substantial *center—Wordsworth*⟩ ⟨the old school was the *center* of our lives, somehow: dances, socials, Sunday services—*McCourt*⟩ or at which all lines (as of activity) converge ⟨draw to one point, and to one *center* bring beast, man, or angel, servant, lord, or king—*Pope*⟩ or from which every line, or branch radiates ⟨a railroad *center*⟩ ⟨a power *center*⟩ or which lies midway between extremes ⟨in Europe a party of moderate views, neither conservative nor radical, is often called the *center*⟩ **Middle** is less precise than *center* and suggests a space rather than a point; it is the part of an object which includes and surrounds the center; thus, the *middle* of a room is the central portion of it ⟨they have what they call a central depot here, because it's the *middle* of England—*Bennett*⟩ *Middle,* unlike *center,* also applies to what has duration ⟨the *middle* of the night⟩ and to merely linear extension ⟨the *middle* of the road⟩ *Middle* may be applied freely to something which lies between the beginning and end (as of a process, a course, or a piece of work) ⟨in this, as in most questions of state, there is a *middle—Burke*⟩ ⟨he was stopped in the *middle* of his speech⟩ ⟨a play should have a beginning, *middle,* and end⟩ **Midst** is often used in place of *middle* for a point or spot well within a group or number of enveloping persons or objects or of things (as duties, affairs, and burdens) that surround or beset one; however it seldom occurs except in a prepositional phrase introduced by *in, into, from, out of* ⟨he stood in the *midst* of a crowd⟩ ⟨he penetrated into the *midst* of the forest⟩ ⟨why it was he should feel in the *midst* of all these people so utterly detached and so lonely—*Bromfield*⟩ ⟨sense of right, uppermost in the *midst* of fiercest strife—*Wordsworth*⟩ **Core** basically denotes the central portion of certain fruits (as the apple) which is made up of papery or leathery envelopes containing seeds and is often extended to something that similarly lies at the center of a thing and that resembles an apple core in being unconsumed or unused ⟨the *core* is the unburnt portion of a coal or of a lump of lime⟩ or in forming a firm central mass in a growth ⟨the *core* of a boil⟩ or in having a different character from that which surrounds or encloses it ⟨a corncob is the *core* of an ear of Indian corn⟩ ⟨in cabinetmaking soft wood on which veneers are glued is called a *core*⟩ or often in being the very center of a thing's life, significance, or power ⟨I will wear him in my heart's *core,* ay, in my heart of heart—*Shak.*⟩ ⟨the Romans . . . proved rebellious to the idea that living is an art; yet it may well be that they still retained that idea at the *core* of their morality—*Ellis*⟩ ⟨a hard *core* of perhaps ten percent who have been in the Party for fifteen years—*Schlesinger* b. 1917⟩ **Hub,** which primarily denotes the central and usually solid part of a wheel from which the spokes radiate and which rotates on (or with) the axle, is often extended to a place, person, or thing on which other places, persons,

or things depend for their life, activity, ideas, or progress ⟨Boston Statehouse is the *hub* of the solar system—*Holmes*⟩ **Focus** is applicable to a point of convergence or concentration or, sometimes, in nontechnical use, of emanation; thus, the point at which rays of light meet after reflection or refraction is called a *focus;* a person to whom all eyes are turned is the *focus* of attention ⟨a place of exchange for the merchandise of East and West . . . the *focus* of a network of trade routes—*Buchan*⟩ **Nucleus** applies especially to a vital and usually small and stable center about which matter is gathered or concentrated or to which accretions are made ⟨the *nucleus* of a cell⟩ ⟨the *nucleus* of an atom⟩ ⟨a small but good collection of books as a *nucleus* for his library⟩ ⟨unable to re-create a satisfactory social group from the *nucleus* of his own individuality—*Day Lewis*⟩ **Heart** applies to a place or thing that lies well within something (as a region or system) and which determines the essential character of the whole or serves as a vital, positive, or motivating part ⟨the economic *heart* of the nation has gradually shifted to the west⟩ ⟨exploits done in the *heart* of France—*Shak.*⟩ ⟨Rome was the *heart* and pulse of the empire—*Buchan*⟩ ⟨the discernment and understanding with which he penetrates to the *heart* and essence of the problem—*Cardozo*⟩

*Con* *circumference, periphery, perimeter, compass: bounds, confines, limits (see singular nouns at LIMIT)

**center** *vb* Center, focus, centralize, concentrate are comparable (though not closely synonymous) because all mean to draw to or fix upon a center. **Center** strongly implies a point upon which things turn or depend; typically the term is followed by a prepositional phrase (as with *in, on,* or *upon*) that names the thing (or sometimes the person) upon which all responsibility or all attention is placed or around which anything or everything of a specified kind (as hopes, fears, or joys) turns ⟨the authority was *centered* in one person⟩ ⟨the incident upon which the plot *centers*⟩ ⟨a common belief about art is that it *centers* about emotion—*Alexander*⟩ ⟨the man whose hopes and fears are all *centered* upon himself can hardly view death with equanimity, since it extinguishes his whole emotional universe—*Russell*⟩ **Focus** implies a point at which a number and usually the total number of things of the same sort (as rays of light, waves of sound, attentions, or interests) converge and become one ⟨the attention of the audience was *focused* upon the speaker⟩ ⟨the essential characteristic of poetry is its power of *focusing* the whole range of our sensibilities—*Binyon*⟩ ⟨how to get the sense of equity or fair play which prevails in many other spheres of action to *focus* upon these . . . disturbing economic questions is thus distinctively a moral issue—*Hobson*⟩ **Centralize** is used of things (as government, authority, or administrative procedure) that may be either gathered about a center or divided, distributed, or diffused; it especially implies the placing of power and authority under one head or in one central organization or the bringing together of similar things at one point ⟨authority is said to be *centralized* wherever a manager tends not to delegate authority to his subordinates—*Koontz & O'Donnell*⟩ ⟨the supporters of reorganization point out that the *centralized* type of administrative organization has worked well with the national government, with the better-governed cities, and with American business—*Dimond & Pflieger*⟩ ⟨by *centralizing* . . . the reserves of the member banks within a district, the Federal Reserve System builds up a large sum of money and credit upon which any member bank may call—*Goodman & Moore*⟩ **Concentrate** differs from the other words not only in being more widely applicable but also in its greater emphasis upon human

A colon (:) separates groups of words discriminated. An asterisk (*) indicates place of treatment of each group.

skill and human methods, discipline, or effort in effecting its purpose; the word may be used not only with reference to what may be centralized or focused and to much that may be centered but is applicable also to material substances that can be reduced in volume (as by dehydration or evaporation), thereby gaining in strength or intensity (see also COMPACT) ⟨here Hannibal . . . *concentrated* the forces which had been gathered from such distant countries—*R. B. Smith*⟩ ⟨but neither of the men paid much attention to these things, their eyes being *concentrated* upon the little flat stone—*Hardy*⟩ ⟨I think that it is a test which we may apply to all figure-painters . . . if we ask whether the figures are really occupied by what they are doing, if the movements of the body are *concentrated* on the particular business of the moment—*Binyon*⟩
*Ana* *depend, hinge, hang, turn: rest, *base, ground

**central,** focal, pivotal are more closely comparable when they mean dominant or most important than when they refer to a literal or material point (as a center, focus, or pivot). **Central** applies to what is regarded as the center because more important than all the rest in that everything else of the same kind depends on it or derives from it ⟨the *central* virtues . . . courage, honor, faithfulness, veracity, justice—*Lippmann*⟩ ⟨the *central* character in a story⟩ ⟨the *central* policy of a nation⟩ ⟨the *central* trouble with America is conformity, timorousness, lack of enterprise and audacity—*Mencken*⟩ **Focal** implies usually a center that is a focus (as of interest, concern, or significance) or that becomes the point on which or in which every or all attention, interest, or activity is concentrated ⟨the *focal* position of the president as formulator or expositor of the nation's opinion is obvious—*Rossiter*⟩ ⟨if we are to make some sense out of this galaxy of recorded experience we are in need of some *focal* ideas about which to organize the material—*Kardiner*⟩ The term occurs frequently in the phrase *focal point* which equals *focus* ⟨quite unaccustomed to being a *focal* point of interest on the part of such highbrows, I made the most of the situation, and was very extravagant in my replies—*Sidney Lovett*⟩ *Focal* may shift its emphasis and attribute such importance to the thing qualified as to suggest that it deserves to be the focus (as of attention or interest) ⟨Miss Grau's tendency to blur or confuse her own point of view with that of her *focal* characters—*Peden*⟩ ⟨the other *focal* elements in American policy toward Europe—*Bundy*⟩ **Pivotal** implies an importance that equals that of pivot (a fixed pin or axis upon which something turns) and suggests that the item so qualified is one on which some larger issue is wholly dependent and that it is therefore cardinal or vital ⟨so we return to the president as the *pivotal* point, the critical element in reaching decisions on foreign policy—*Acheson*⟩ ⟨something important is about to happen . . . a succession of events that will be *pivotal* in her experience—*DeVoto*⟩ ⟨the *pivotal* issue in this controversy⟩ ⟨the presidential election will be decided by the vote in a few *pivotal* states⟩
*Ana* *dominant, paramount, predominant, preponderant: outstanding, salient, signal (see NOTICEABLE): important, significant (see corresponding nouns at IMPORTANCE)

**centralize** *center, focus, concentrate
*Ana* *gather, collect, assemble: *accumulate, amass: *compact, consolidate, unify
*Con* *scatter, disperse, dispel, dissipate: *distribute, divide: apportion, *allot, allocate

**cerebral** *mental, intellectual, psychic, intelligent

**ceremonial** *adj* Ceremonial, ceremonious, formal, conventional, solemn are comparable when they mean characterized or marked by attention to the forms, procedures, and details prescribed as right, proper, or requisite. Both **ceremonial** and **ceremonious** imply strict attention to and regard for what is prescribed by the etiquette or tradition of a court or of polite society, by the ritual of a church, or by the formalities of the law for a ceremony or a proceeding. They are sometimes interchangeable ⟨Duncan dropped back, whether from reverence or ridicule his father had never discovered, into the *ceremonial* usages of the past—*Glasgow*⟩ ⟨an age in which no lady was too frail to attend a play alone . . . seemed to her, on the whole, better worth living in than the *ceremonious* era that had witnessed her fall—*Glasgow*⟩ ⟨its worship is not highly *ceremonious*—*Shepherd*⟩ but more often *ceremonial* distinctively suggests the existence of and conformance to an elaborate, prescribed, and usually ritualistic code of procedures, while *ceremonious* stresses elaborate, often punctilious and dignified procedures or, in reference to persons, a tendency to formality and ceremony; thus, a wedding is a *ceremonial* occasion but not one at which the participants need be excessively *ceremonious* ⟨grave *ceremonial* occasions, like birth and death and the assumption of manhood—*Buchan*⟩ ⟨the president is . . . the *ceremonial* head of the American government . . . . He greets distinguished visitors, lays wreaths on the tomb of the Unknown Soldier, bestows the Medal of Honor on flustered pilots—*Rossiter*⟩ ⟨the Zuñi are a *ceremonious* people, a people who value sobriety and inoffensiveness above all other virtues. Their interest is centered upon their rich and complex *ceremonial* life—*Benedict*⟩ ⟨wine is a *ceremonial* drink in Normandy, where none is grown or made. It is not expected to taste good—*Liebling*⟩ **Formal** in comparison to *ceremonial* suggests set form or procedure rather than external ceremonies ⟨a *formal* call⟩ ⟨*formal* dress⟩ and in comparison to *ceremonious, formal* suggests stiffness, restraint, decorousness rather than impressive dignity or punctiliousness ⟨rules are an integral part of German life, rules for behavior . . . for persons of every status, for every *formal* situation—*Mead*⟩ ⟨the habits of the family . . . may be termed *formal,* and old-fashioned by such visitors as claim to be the pink of the mode—*Scott*⟩ **Conventional** applies to whatever is in accord with or governed by recognized, frequently artificial conventions or standards; it connotes lack of originality or independence ⟨a *conventional* expression of regret⟩ ⟨the *conventional* white tie with men's full evening dress⟩ ⟨a highly *conventional* person⟩ ⟨a skillful . . . journalist, *conventional* and conformist except in a strong bent toward liberal humanitarianism—*Canby*⟩ **Solemn** is used in relation to religious observances or services and to certain acts the conduct of which is prescribed by law. The term implies, usually, strict attention to every detail that is prescribed or allowed by the ritual of the church or by the formalities of the law; thus, a *solemn* Mass is one in which the full liturgy is followed; a *solemn* feast is one celebrated not only by the full liturgy but by such other ceremonial observances as processions and pageants ⟨funerals . . . were as much social events as *solemn* obsequies—*Schlesinger* d. 1965⟩ ⟨having taken the *solemn* oath of office in the presence of my fellow countrymen—in the presence of our God—*Roosevelt*⟩
*Ana* liturgical, ritualistic (see corresponding nouns at FORM)

**ceremonial** *n* ceremony, ritual, rite, liturgy, *form
**ceremonious** *ceremonial, formal, solemn, conventional
*Ana* impressive, *moving: *decorous, seemly, proper: stately, imposing, majestic, grandiose (see GRAND)
*Ant* unceremonious, informal

**ceremony** ceremonial, ritual, liturgy, rite, *form, formality

**certain** *adj* **1** positive, *sure, cocksure

---

*Ana* analogous words     *Ant* antonyms     *Con* contrasted words     See also explanatory notes facing page 1

*Ana* *confident, assured, sanguine

*Ant* uncertain —*Con* *doubtful, dubious, questionable

**2 Certain, inevitable, necessary** are comparable when they mean bound to follow in obedience to the laws of nature or of thought. What is **certain** does not admit of being described as probable even in the highest conceivable degree and is beyond question or dispute ⟨death is the only future event we can regard as *certain*⟩ ⟨it is *certain* that effects must have a cause—*Bp. Butler*⟩ What is **inevitable** (see also INEVITABLE) is as it must be (sometimes should be) according to some unchangeable law (as of nature, of logic, or of beauty). *Inevitable* often carries little suggestion of unavoidability but stresses finality (as in truth or rightness) or an ultimate character (as perfection) ⟨the results obtained in an actual experiment . . . seem nonsensical . . . when we picture light as bullets, but perfectly natural and *inevitable* when we picture it as waves—*Jeans*⟩ ⟨the design is, indeed, so happy, so right, that it seems *inevitable;* the design is the story and the story is the design—*Cather*⟩ What is **necessary** is logically or naturally inevitable and cannot be denied without resulting contradiction or frustration ⟨most of the distinctions of law are distinctions of degree. If the states had any power it was assumed that they had all power and that the *necessary* alternative was to deny it altogether—*Justice Holmes*⟩ ⟨his plays are the *necessary* expression of his mind and character, not the *necessary* conditions of his existence—*Inge*⟩

*Ant* probable: supposed —*Con* possible, likely (see PROBABLE): precarious (see DANGEROUS)

**certainty, certitude, assurance, conviction** are comparable when denoting a state of mind in which one is free from doubt. **Certainty** and **certitude** both imply the absence of all doubt as to the truth of something; they are not always distinguishable in use, although philosophers and psychologists have often tried to distinguish the states of mind which they designate. The psychological differentiation of *certainty* as the state of mind induced by something of which there is objectively as well as subjectively not the slightest question, from *certitude* as the state of mind of one whose faith or belief is so strong that it resists all attack, has indubitably affected the meanings and the use of these terms in general use ⟨some philosophies tend to destroy man's *certainty* of his own existence⟩ ⟨one has *certainty* of nothing in the future, even that the sun will rise tomorrow, but that does not weaken one's *certitude* that the world will go on indefinitely⟩ ⟨*certitude* is not the test of *certainty*. We have been cocksure of many things that were not so—*Justice Holmes*⟩ *Certitude* is usually more personal and less objective than *certainty* and suggests deeper roots for one's freedom from doubt and less likelihood of a change of belief ⟨one thing, however, we feel with irresistible *certitude*, that Mark Twain's fate was once for all decided there—*Brooks*⟩ In its greater objectivity *certainty* also provides a term that may logically designate the quality of a thing believed ⟨*certitude* is a mental state: *certainty* is a quality of propositions—*Newman*⟩ ⟨the suspense which was more terrible than any *certainty*—*Glasgow*⟩ **Assurance** (see also CONFIDENCE 2) stresses sureness and confidence rather than certainty; the grounds of such sureness need not be objective proofs or the evidence of one's senses, for something of which one has assurance is typically something that is indemonstrable or is yet to happen; the word usually suggests implicit reliance on oneself or on one's powers, one's intuitions, or one's methods or complete trust in another (as a source of information, a supporter, a sovereign, or God) ⟨I'll make *assurance* double sure, and take a bond of fate—*Shak.*⟩ ⟨faith is the *assurance* of things hoped for—

*Heb* 11:1 *(RV)*⟩ ⟨rather, it might be said that he went beyond hope to the *assurance* of present happiness—*More*⟩ **Conviction** usually implies previous doubt or uncertainty. It involves the idea of *certitude* but is not its equivalent, for *certitude* may or may not imply a rational basis for one's freedom from doubt, and *conviction* (see also OPINION) usually does. It differs from *certainty* in stressing one's subjective reaction to evidence rather than the objective validity of the evidence itself. *Conviction* is therefore commonly applied to the state of mind of one who has been or is in the process of being convinced ⟨have lost the old American *conviction* that most people are good and that evil is merely an accident—*Malcolm Cowley*⟩ ⟨she does not wish me to go unless with a full *conviction* that she is right—*Conrad*⟩

*Ana* *belief, faith, credence: proof, demonstration (see under PROVE)

*Ant* uncertainty —*Con* doubt, skepticism, mistrust (see UNCERTAINTY)

**certify** **1 Certify, attest, witness, vouch** are comparable when they mean to testify to the truth or genuineness of something. **Certify** usually implies a statement in writing, especially one that carries one's signature or seal or both or one that is legally executed; thus, a *certified* check carries the guarantee of a bank that the signature is genuine and that there are sufficient funds on deposit to meet it ⟨they said their chemists . . . could *certify* on their honor that their extract contained no salicylic acid—*Heiser*⟩ **Attest** (see also INDICATE) implies oral or written testimony from a person in a position to know the facts, usually but not invariably given under oath or on one's word of honor; thus, when one says that something is well *attested,* he implies that there is sufficient documentary or oral testimony from competent persons to warrant its acceptance ⟨the pleader . . . had witness ready to *attest* . . . that every article was true—*Swift*⟩ ⟨Washington's strong natural love of children, nowhere *attested* better than in his expense accounts—*Fitzpatrick*⟩ In technical legal use *attest* is used chiefly in reference to the official authentication of a document (as a will, a deed, or a record) or to the guaranteeing of the genuineness of a signature or a statement or an oath by a qualified public agent (as a notary public or a commissioner of deeds) ⟨an *attested* copy of the marriage record—*Cather*⟩ **Witness** implies attestation, not necessarily official or notarial, of a signature (as of a statement, a will, or a bond) by one who has seen that signature actually made and who subscribes his own name to the document as evidence of its genuineness ⟨he called in two of his servants to *witness* the signature to his will⟩ **Vouch** (usually with *for*) rarely implies official or legal proof, which the other words in this group usually do imply, but it suggests that the one who testifies is a competent authority or a reliable person who will stand behind his affirmation and support it further if necessary ⟨for the exactness of this story [of a purported miracle] in all its details, Bishop James of Voragio could not have *vouched,* nor did it greatly matter. What he could *vouch* for was the relation of intimacy and confidence between his people and the Queen of Heaven—*Henry Adams*⟩

*Ana* avouch, avow, aver, *assert, profess

**2** endorse, accredit, *approve, sanction

*Ana* vouch (see CERTIFY): *authorize, commission, license

*Con* reject, repudiate, refuse (see DECLINE)

**certitude** *certainty, assurance, conviction

*Ana* *belief, faith, credence, credit: sureness, positiveness, cocksureness (see corresponding adjectives at SURE)

*Ant* doubt —*Con* *uncertainty, skepticism, mistrust

---

A colon (:) separates groups of words discriminated. An asterisk (*) indicates place of treatment of each group.

chafe *abrade, excoriate, fret, gall
 Ana *injure, hurt, damage, impair: flay, *skin, peel:
 *abuse, maltreat, outrage: *irritate, exasperate
chaff vb *banter, kid, rag, jolly, rib, josh
 Ana tease, tantalize, *worry: *ridicule, deride, twit,
 taunt
chagrined mortified, *ashamed
 Ana discomfited, abashed, embarrassed, disconcerted
 (see EMBARRASS): humiliated (see ABASE): discomposed,
 perturbed, upset (see DISCOMPOSE)
chain n series, train, string, sequence, *succession,
 progression
challenge vb *face, brave, dare, defy, beard
 Ana question (see ASK): dispute (see DISCUSS): claim,
 *demand, require: *invite, solicit
chamber *room, apartment
champ vb *bite, gnaw, gnash
 Ana· *crush, smash, mash, macerate
champion n vanquisher, *victor, winner, conqueror
champion vb back, advocate, uphold, *support
 Ana *contend, fight, battle: espouse (see ADOPT):
 defend, justify, vindicate, *maintain: aid, assist, *help
 Ant combat —Con oppose, *resist, withstand, fight:
 condemn, denounce (see CRITICIZE)
chance n 1 Chance, accident, fortune, luck, hap, hazard
 denote something that happens without an apparent or
 determinable cause or as a result of unpredictable forces.
 Chance serves often as a general term for the incalculable
 and fortuitous element in human existence and in nature
 and is usually opposed to law (see PRINCIPLE) ⟨it is
 incorrect to say that any phenomenon is produced by
 chance; but we may say that two or more phenomena
 are conjoined by chance . . . meaning that they are in no
 way related by causation—J. S. Mill⟩ Chance often
 retains implications derived from its early association
 with the casting of dice or lots and the selection of one
 out of many possibilities by this means; consequently
 it may mean determination by irrational, uncontrollable
 forces ⟨leave things to chance⟩ or it may mean degree
 of probability ⟨his chance of success is one in ten⟩ or
 it may mean one possibility of success among many possibilities of failure ⟨he is always willing to take a chance⟩
 Accident is interchangeable with chance only when a
 particular event or situation is in mind ⟨it happened by
 accident (or by chance)⟩ It differs from chance mainly
 in its emphasis on lack of intention ⟨buildings are not
 grouped like that by pure accident—Cather⟩ ⟨meeting
 by accident, we hovered by design—Emily Dickinson⟩
 Fortune, owing to its historical connection with the ancient
 Roman goddess of chance, Fortuna, often designates the
 hypothetical cause of what happens fortuitously ⟨fortune
 favored him in his first attempt⟩ It also often suggests
 qualities ascribed to the goddess (as variability, fickleness, and malignity) ⟨I may conquer fortune's spite by
 living low, where fortune cannot hurt me—Shak.⟩ ⟨vicis-
 situdes of fortune—Gibbon⟩ Fortune is also applied to
 the issue or outcome of an undertaking the success of
 which is problematical ⟨the fortunes of war⟩ ⟨the country
 virtually drops everything . . . to follow the fortunes of
 the two teams engaged in the World Series—Harold
 Rosenthal⟩ Luck differs from fortune chiefly in its connotations. It not only lacks the dignity accruing to fortune
 through the latter's mythological associations, but it is
 somewhat colored by its association with gambling. It
 is preferable in contexts where fortune would seem
 bookish ⟨bad luck followed him all his days⟩ ⟨it was just
 our luck to miss that train⟩ ⟨the fisherman had good luck
 today⟩ Luck unqualified can, however, imply success
 or a happy outcome, as fortune unqualified rarely does

⟨I wish you luck⟩ ⟨he had luck in all his adventures⟩
 ⟨with luck and the help of atomic research our children
 may be safe from this grim disease—A. E. Stevenson⟩
 Hap is rather neutral and commonly denotes what falls
 or, more often, has already fallen to one's lot ⟨lives
 that had known both good and evil hap⟩ ⟨by some bad
 tide or hap . . . the ill-made catamaran was overset—
 Melville⟩ Hazard, which basically denotes a game of
 dice in which the chances are complicated by arbitrary
 rules, is often used in place of accident, especially when
 there is the traceable but not predictable influence of existing conditions or of concomitant circumstances ⟨men and
 women danced together, women danced together, men
 danced together, as hazard had brought them together—
 Dickens⟩ ⟨the choice [of examples] has been determined
 more by the hazards of my recent reading than by anything else—Huxley⟩
 Ana contingency, emergency, pass, *juncture, exigency
 Ant law (see PRINCIPLE) —Con inevitableness or
 inevitability, necessariness or necessity, certainty (see
 corresponding adjectives at CERTAIN)
 2 *opportunity, occasion, break, time
 Ana possibility, likelihood, probability (see corresponding adjectives at PROBABLE): *prospect, outlook, foretaste, anticipation
chance vb 1 *happen, befall, betide, occur, transpire
 2 *venture, hazard, risk, jeopardize, endanger, imperil
 Ana dare, beard, *face: *meet, encounter, confront
chance adj *random, haphazard, chancy, casual, desultory,
 hit-or-miss, happy-go-lucky
chancy haphazard, chance, hit-or-miss, happy-go-lucky,
 *random, casual, desultory
change vb Change, alter, vary, modify (and their corresponding nouns change, alteration, variation, modification)
 are comparable when denoting to make or become different (or when denoting a difference effected). Change
 and alter are sometimes interchangeable; thus, conditions
 may change (or alter) for the better. Change, however,
 usually implies either an essential difference, even a loss
 of identity, or the substitution of one thing for another
 ⟨can the Ethiopian change his skin, or the leopard his
 spots?—Jer 13:23⟩ ⟨and Earth be changed to Heaven,
 and Heaven to Earth—Milton⟩ ⟨this chamber changed
 for one more holy—Poe⟩ while alter stresses difference
 in some particular respect (as in form or detail) without
 implying loss of identity ⟨one may alter a coat without
 changing its style⟩ ⟨the whole existing order must be,
 if ever so slightly, altered—T. S. Eliot⟩ ⟨external circumstances may change catastrophically, as during a war;
 or gradually, as when means of production are altered
 —Huxley⟩ Vary frequently implies a difference or a series
 of differences due to change (as by shifting, diversifi-
 cation, or growth) ⟨the temperature varies greatly during
 the day⟩ ⟨any intelligent effort to vary or improve the
 effect—Henry Adams⟩ Sometimes it implies a deviation
 from the normal, the conventional, or the usual ⟨the
 prospectus tendered by the Communists to the peasants
 varies with the type of discontent in the particular area
 —W. O. Douglas⟩ ⟨this is not a proceeding which may be
 varied . . . but is a precise course . . . to be strictly pursued
 —John Marshall⟩ Modify suggests a difference that
 limits or restricts; thus, an adjective is said to modify
 a noun because it definitely reduces the range of application of that noun (as old in "old men" and red in "a red
 rose"). Often the word implies moderation (as of severity)
 or toning down (as of excess) ⟨the proximity of the ocean
 modifies the temperature—Amer. Guide Series: R. I.⟩
 ⟨Sophia was at first set down as overbearing. But in a
 few days this view was modified—Bennett⟩ Modify may

---

**Ana** analogous words    **Ant** antonyms    **Con** contrasted words    See also explanatory notes facing page 1

sometimes suggest minor changes or absence of radical changes ⟨history shows you men whose master-touch not so much *modifies* as makes anew—*Browning*⟩ ⟨the *aeroplane*—as it was called for many years before the word was *modified* to *airplane*—*Harlow*⟩
*Ana* \*transform, metamorphose, transmute, convert, transmogrify: \*exchange, interchange: fluctuate, oscillate (see SWING *vb*)
*Con* settle, \*set, establish, fix: endure, abide, \*continue, persist
**change** *n* **1** alteration, variation, modification (see under CHANGE *vb*)
*Ana* \*variety, diversity: divergence, \*deviation, aberration
*Ant* uniformity: monotony
**2 Change, mutation, permutation, vicissitude, alternation** are comparable especially in their concrete senses. **Change,** the inclusive term, denotes not only any variation, alteration, or modification in a thing (as in its form, substance, or aspect) but also any substitution of one thing for another ⟨he could detect no *change* in her when they met again⟩ ⟨the body undergoes *changes* during puberty⟩ ⟨a *change* of season⟩ ⟨a *change* of clothes often makes a *change* in one's appearance⟩ ⟨poor faithful dogs, lovers of novelty and *change* of scene—*Repplier*⟩ *Mutation* and *permutation* are applied to a change within a thing or in a combination of things regarded or functioning as a unit. **Mutation** stresses lack of permanence or stability; it has been applied to variations or alterations that are expected only because they are inherent in the nature of things but are otherwise fortuitous or unaccountable ⟨O world! But that thy strange *mutations* make us hate thee, life would not yield to age—*Shak.*⟩ More typically the term connotes suddenness and unpredictableness but seldom implies impossibility of explanation; often also it implies orderly change ⟨so far as reality means experienceable reality, both it and the truths men gain about it are everlastingly in process of *mutation*—*mutation* towards a definite goal, it may be—*James*⟩ **Permutation** implies transposition within a group or combination of things without change in the constituent elements or parts of that group or combination. It is now used largely in reference to a change in position within a group of differentiable items (as digits, letters, colors, or sounds) ⟨the 26 letters of the alphabet are capable of endless combinations and *permutations*⟩ It may imply a rearrangement of constituent elements that effects a change in relations, emphasis, or significance and so gives a new form to what is substantially the same material ⟨conventions beget conventions, to be sure, and their ramifications and *permutations* are endless—*Lowes*⟩ ⟨by whatever *permutations* and combinations may be necessary, we may gradually move somewhat nearer to that reign of law—*Davis*⟩ **Vicissitude** (see also DIFFICULTY) implies a change so great as to seem a substitution for, or a reversal of, what has been. Sometimes it is applied to such changes as occur in natural succession or from one extreme to another ⟨Nature indeed vouchsafes for our delight the sweet *vicissitudes* of day and night—*Cowper*⟩ ⟨like walking in a wood where there is . . . a constant *vicissitude* of light and shade—*J. R. Lowell*⟩ More often it is applied to a sweeping and unpredictable change that overturns what has been and so has the character of a revolution or an upheaval ⟨the place and the object gave ample scope for moralizing on the *vicissitudes* of fortune, which spares neither man nor the proudest of his works, which buries empires and cities in a common grave—*Gibbon*⟩ This implication of reversal is now so strong that the original implication of succession in turn is disappearing. **Alternation,** though logically used

only of the succession of two things in turn, is also used, as *vicissitude* once was, of two or more things ⟨the *alternation* of the seasons⟩
*Ana* metamorphosis, transformation, conversion, transmutation, transmogrification (see under TRANSFORM): substitute, surrogate, shift (see RESOURCE)
**changeable, changeful, variable, mutable, protean** are comparable when meaning having or showing a marked capacity for changes or a marked tendency to alter itself or be altered under slight provocation. **Changeable,** the ordinary and most comprehensive term of this group, usually suggests this as a characteristic or property that is the result of such reactions as inconstancy, fickleness, an unsettled state, a ready responsiveness to certain influences, or a roving habit ⟨*changeable* weather⟩ ⟨she was a fresh, cool, dewy thing . . . fitful and *changeable* with the whim of the moment—*Hawthorne*⟩ ⟨a *changeable* silk is one that seems to change its color with each change of position or point of view⟩ **Changeful** is a more poetic term than *changeable;* it throws greater stress on the fact of changing frequently than on the underlying characteristic or property which manifests itself in such changes ⟨the *changeful* April day—*Southey*⟩ ⟨he felt that life was *changeful*, fluid, active, and that to allow it to be stereotyped into any form was death—*Wilde*⟩ ⟨all your charms more *changeful* than the tide—*Millay*⟩ **Variable** carries an implication of subjection to frequent and often deeper changes than either of the preceding words; it stresses shifting or fluctuation as a characteristic or property and therefore usually connotes uncertainty or unpredictability ⟨a region of *variable* winds⟩ ⟨man himself was a *variable*, mixed and transitory creature; he could not escape the law of his own being—*L. P. Smith*⟩ ⟨the methods of statistics are so *variable* and uncertain . . . that it is never possible to be sure that one is operating with figures of equal weight—*Ellis*⟩ **Mutable** also implies subjection to change, but it suggests an opposition to *unchanging, fixed,* or *permanent* and therefore is less often applied to something fluctuating and variable than to something living, growing, or developing that shows changes due to progression or retrogression or to external influences or conditions over which the thing affected has no control ⟨my lord, you know what Virgil sings, woman is various and most *mutable*—*Tennyson*⟩ ⟨our view of any of these concepts, say justice, is *mutable*, changing from century to century, from place to place—*G. W. Johnson*⟩ ⟨our valuation of poetry . . . depends upon several considerations, upon the permanent and upon the *mutable* and transitory—*T. S. Eliot*⟩ **Protean** suggests a capacity for assuming many different forms or shapes without loss of identity; the term therefore implies changeability with respect to outer manifestations rather than inner character or nature ⟨an amoeba is a *protean* animalcule⟩ ⟨the *protean* genius of Shakespeare⟩ ⟨for poetry is *protean* in its moods and dispositions, and its diction changes with its bents and its occasions—*Lowes*⟩ ⟨but an idea is a misty, vague object that takes on *protean* shapes, never the same for any two people—*Dwight Macdonald*⟩
*Ana* unstable, \*inconstant, mercurial, capricious, fickle: mobile, \*movable
*Ant* stable: unchangeable —*Con* set, fixed, settled, established (see SET *vb*): unceasing, \*everlasting: enduring, abiding, persisting *or* persistent (see corresponding verbs at CONTINUE)
**changeful** \*changeable, variable, protean, mutable
*Ana* fluid (see LIQUID *adj*): \*active, dynamic, live: progressing, advancing (see ADVANCE *vb*): declining, deteriorating, degenerating (see corresponding nouns

A colon (:) separates groups of words discriminated. An asterisk (\*) indicates place of treatment of each group.

at DETERIORATION)

*Ant* changeless: stereotyped —*Con* constant, uniform, *steady: stable, *lasting, durable, perdurable

**channel** 1 passage, *strait, narrows, sound

2 **Channel, canal, conduit, duct, aqueduct** all mean something through which a fluid (as water) is led or flows. **Channel** implies the natural bed of a stream of running or moving waters; the term is also applied to a deep portion of a stream or body of water either where the main current flows or where a good passage for boats exists ⟨the brook's *channel* is nowhere more than three feet deep⟩ ⟨the *channel* for ships into the harbor needs to be dredged frequently on account of the drifting sands⟩ *Channel* often applies also to a natural or an artificial passageway (as a tube, a gutter, a ditch, or a trough) through which something (as waste) flows or (as chain or wire) runs ⟨the poison *channel* in a snake's fangs⟩ ⟨the *channel* of a tackle block through which the rope runs⟩ **Canal** is used for an artificial waterway which connects two bodies of water ⟨the New York State Barge *Canal* connecting Lake Erie and the Hudson river⟩ ⟨the Panama *Canal* connecting the Atlantic and Pacific oceans⟩ It is also used in designations of various anatomical grooves or tubular channels (as for the containing of some structure or the passage of some substance) ⟨blood vessels of bone occupy the haversian *canals*⟩ ⟨the alimentary *canal* through which food passes in the course of digestion⟩ **Conduit** may be applied to an artificial or natural passageway that serves to convey or transmit a fluid ⟨volcanoes . . . made by discharge of material through a more or less cylindrical *conduit* in the earth's crust—*Howel Williams*⟩ but the term is more often used specifically for a large heavy pipe which conveys water from a reservoir to a point where it is distributed or for a pipe that carries the wires or cables of an electric system ⟨into it through underground arteries of *conduits* and pipes, are fed the electric power, gas, and water supply —*Science*⟩ **Duct** has specific application to one of the small anatomical tubes through which a secretion is conveyed to where it is needed or is excreted from the organism ⟨thoracic *duct*⟩ ⟨bile *duct*⟩ The term is also used in reference to any of the pipes of a furnace or an air-conditioning system through which air is taken in, circulated, or discharged. **Aqueduct** is applied to an artificial channel for water (as a conduit) and especially to an artificial structure, in appearance like a bridge, for carrying water over a river, or over a gorge or gap between elevations.

*Ana* passage, pass (see WAY)

3 vehicle, *mean, instrument, instrumentality, organ, agency, agent, medium

**chant** *vb* *sing, troll, carol, descant, warble, trill, hymn, intone

**chaos** 1 *confusion, disorder, disarray, jumble, clutter, snarl, muddle

*Ant* system —*Con* ordering *or* order, organization (see corresponding verbs at ORDER)

2 *anarchy, lawlessness

**chaperon** *vb* *accompany, attend, escort, convoy, conduct

*Ana* protect, shield, guard, safeguard (see DEFEND)

**char** *vb* *burn, scorch, sear, singe

**character** *n* 1 **Character, symbol, sign, mark** are comparable in the specific sense of an arbitrary or conventional device that is used in writing and in printing, but is neither a word nor a phrase nor a picture. **Character** suggests the distinctive form or shape of such a device ⟨an inscription in runic *characters*⟩ It is applicable to a letter of an alphabet, to a digit in arithmetical notation, to a note in musical notation, or to a single and simple figure or

diagram which is the conventional representation of such a directive or indicative value as a comma (,), a direction to delete (𝛝), a minute in degree ('), or an indication of G clef in music ( 𝄞 ). **Symbol** may be used interchangeably with *character* in this sense; more typically it is employed when the meaning or significance of the character rather than its shape is stressed; thus, for each letter in the English alphabet there are various *characters* (as small letter and capital or italic and boldface) for use in writing and printing but each letter, whatever the *character* used to express it, is a *symbol* for a speech sound; the *character* ? is the *symbol* used to indicate that a question has been asked. *Symbol* is sometimes extended to other devices than those strictly called *characters*, such as abbreviations ⟨O is the *symbol* for oxygen⟩, as diagrams or schematic figures ⟨☺ is the *symbol* for full moon in calendars⟩, or as more or less arbitrary arrangements of numerals, letters, or other characters ⟨12mo or 12° is the *symbol* for duodecimo⟩ **Sign**, like *symbol*, stresses the meaning rather than the form of the device; unlike *symbol*, however, it is seldom interchangeable with *character*, either because it may be a complicated device involving many characters or because it is less arbitrary and actually suggests through its shape or form the thing which it signifies. There is a tendency therefore to prefer *sign* to *symbol* when the device is complicated or in its form gives a hint of what it represents, either because it is a schematic representation of the thing ⟨ ∿ is a highway *sign* for double right curves⟩ or because it has figurative associations with the idea represented ⟨→, an arrow, or *sign* indicating direction⟩ *Sign*, however, is used idiomatically of characters indicating a mathematical operation ⟨the plus *sign* +⟩ ⟨the minus *sign* −⟩ and of those indicating one of the twelve divisions of the zodiac ⟨ ♈ is the *sign* of Aries, the Ram⟩ **Mark** comes closer to *character* than *symbol* or *sign*, because it carries little, if any, suggestion of reference to an idea. It is the ordinary designation of any of various characters that are used to make clear the meaning of a passage but that add nothing to that meaning ⟨punctuation *marks*, such as the comma , or the question *mark* ?⟩ or that indicate to the eye how words should be pronounced ⟨pronunciation *marks* such as the acute accent ′ or the cedilla ç⟩ ⟨diacritical *marks* such as ¨ over the vowel a⟩

2 *quality, property, attribute, accident

*Ana* characteristic, peculiarity, distinctiveness *or* distinction, individuality (see corresponding adjectives at CHARACTERISTIC)

3 individuality, personality, complexion, temperament, temper, *disposition

*Ana* *mind, intellect, soul, intelligence: *soul, spirit: *courage, mettle, spirit, resolution

4 nature, description, *type, kind, ilk, sort, stripe, kidney

5 reference, recommendation, testimonial, *credential

**characteristic** *adj* **Characteristic, individual, peculiar, distinctive** are comparable when they mean indicating or revealing the special quality or qualities of a particular person or thing or of a particular group of persons or things. **Characteristic** stresses the indication or revelation not only of what is essential or typical, but of what distinguishes and serves to identify the person, the thing, or the group; the word, however, fixes the attention on the thing considered more as it is in itself than as it seems in contrast or relation to other things ⟨he answered with *characteristic* courtesy⟩ ⟨it was *characteristic* of the relationship between these two that, in all the pleadings and protests of the poor deferred lover, Sally never made the offer of convention and custom to release him— *Deland*⟩ ⟨a fertile oasis possesses a *characteristic* color scheme of its own—*Huxley*⟩ **Individual** (see also

SPECIAL) not only implies a reference to a particular person or thing but also places much more stress on qualities that distinguish him or it from all other members of the same class or kind than does *characteristic;* it therefore usually applies to something that indicates or reveals a personality or a nature that is different from others ⟨that singularly *individual* voice of Tom's—mature, confident, seldom varying in pitch, but full of slight, very moving modulations—*Cather*⟩ ⟨the *individual* idiosyncrasies of each member of the great family—*Anderson*⟩ **Peculiar** (see also STRANGE) comes close to *individual;* it usually implies a reference to a person or thing as he or it is in himself or itself and as differentiated from all others of the same kind. It may, however, apply to such a class as a sex, a race, or a people. In this use, the term does not, as in its more common derived sense, necessarily carry any hint of strangeness or oddness; rather it suggests private and undisputed possession (as of a quality, a character, an emotion, or a significance) ⟨a grief that was private and *peculiar*—*Meredith*⟩ ⟨a drowsy fervor of manner and tone which was quite *peculiar* to her—*Hardy*⟩ ⟨in these aspects . . . of his work we pretend to find what is individual, what is the *peculiar* essence of the man—*T. S. Eliot*⟩ ⟨habits both universal among mankind and *peculiar* to individuals—*Allport*⟩ **Distinctive** implies the possession of an individuality or peculiarity that marks the thing so described as apart from all others of its class or type and often, therefore, as worthy of special recognition or praise ⟨it is this . . . *distinctive* vision of the world as a whole which seems to give Leonardo that marvelous flair for detecting vital mechanism in every field—*Ellis*⟩ ⟨it is . . . the exquisite craftsmanship . . . that has given to free verse, alike in England and America, its most *distinctive* qualities—*Lowes*⟩
*Ana* *special, especial, specific, particular: typical, natural, normal, *regular

**characteristic** *n* **Characteristic, trait, feature** mean something that marks or sets apart a person or thing. **Characteristic** designates a constant property or quality that stands out in such a way as to distinguish a person or thing from others or to reveal him or it as he or it is; the term is applicable not only to persons and concrete objects but to things which are immaterial, intangible, or the product of abstraction ⟨here we must note in the man one very striking *characteristic* . . . he appreciated the singularity of his talent—*Belloc*⟩ ⟨what was only an incidental and local damage . . . became a widespread *characteristic* of Western civilization—*Mumford*⟩ ⟨a constant alternation of lyricism and flatness . . . is the salient *characteristic* of postwar verse technique—*Day Lewis*⟩ **Trait** applies especially to persons, peoples, or types and to their sharply accented qualities of character or of mind; otherwise, the term differs from *characteristic* only in its suggestions of clear definition and of distinctiveness ⟨Marino Lucero had not one *trait* in common with Martinez, except the love of authority—*Cather*⟩ ⟨what they like to do . . . not at all what they are fitted to do, is the rule of their effort. And it is the unfailing *trait* of the amateur—*Brownell*⟩ **Feature,** on the other hand, suggests not a quality or property, but a part or detail of a thing (as a face, a view, an object, or a character) which attracts and holds the attention by reason of its shape or form or by reason of its importance, its conspicuousness, or its being pressed upon one's attention ⟨her eyes are her most admirable *feature*⟩ ⟨the great *feature* of the exposition is the new coliseum⟩ ⟨though the gloom had increased sufficiently to confuse the minor *features* of the heath, the white surface of the road remained almost as clear as ever—*Hardy*⟩ ⟨*features* so un-Egyptian

that they practically prove that her cult was a local one—*G. W. Murray*⟩ In the United States the term *feature* is often applied specifically to something exhibited or advertised as particularly attractive and especially to the principal attraction in a motion-picture entertainment or to a distinctive or prominent article, story, or cartoon in a periodical ⟨a *feature* writer⟩
*Ana* *quality, property, character: peculiarity, individuality (see corresponding adjectives at CHARACTERISTIC)

**characterize, distinguish, mark, qualify** are comparable when they mean to be a peculiar or significant quality or feature of something. **Characterize** stresses that quality or feature (or those qualities or features) which stands out and identifies the person or thing considered; often an obvious or striking feature rather than a fundamental or basic quality is implied ⟨metaphor *characterizes* the language of poetry—*R. M. Weaver*⟩ ⟨that mien of assured authority, of capacity tested in many a crisis, which *characterized* Mrs. Baines—*Bennett*⟩ **Distinguish** (see also DISTINGUISH), on the other hand, stresses a feature, a quality, or a characteristic that makes a person or thing different from others or that sets him or it apart from and sometimes above others ⟨a peculiar sort of sweet pudding . . . *distinguished* the days of his coming—*Lamb*⟩ ⟨was *distinguished* for ignorance; for he had only one idea, and that was wrong—*Disraeli*⟩ ⟨once writers were a class apart, *distinguished* by ink-stained fingers, unkempt hair, and a predilection for drinking cheap wine in cellars—*Uhlan*⟩ **Mark** (see also MARK *vb*) implies the presence of noteworthy qualities or features that are the outward signs of an inward character ⟨no triumph—no exaltation . . . *marks* her manner—*Cowden Clarke*⟩ ⟨are we so sure that the qualities that *mark* successful climbers—self-assertion, acquisition, emulation—are highly desirable?—*Ellis*⟩ **Qualify** (see also PREPARE, MODERATE) occasionally implies a quality, characteristic, or description that is attributed by the immediate writer or speaker to a person or thing as fitted to him or it ⟨the "Devil's drawing room," as some have *qualified* that wondrous place—*Byron*⟩ ⟨cannot *qualify* it as . . . either glad or sorry—*T. S. Eliot*⟩
*Ana* *distinguish, differentiate, demarcate: individualize, peculiarize (see corresponding adjectives at CHARACTERISTIC)

**charge** *vb* **1** *burden, encumber, cumber, weigh, weight, load, lade, tax, saddle
**2** direct, instruct, bid, enjoin, *command, order
*Ana* request, solicit, *ask: adjure (see BEG)
**3** *accuse, incriminate, indict, impeach, arraign
*Ana* denounce, blame, censure, condemn (see CRITICIZE)
*Ant* absolve —*Con* *exculpate, exonerate, vindicate, acquit: pardon, remit, forgive, *excuse
**4** *ascribe, attribute, impute, assign, refer, credit, accredit
*Ana* *fasten, attach, fix, affix: *join, connect, link
**5** *rush, dash, tear, shoot
*Ana* impel, drive (see MOVE): *fly, dart, scud
**charge** *n* *price, cost, expense
**chargé d'affaires** *ambassador, legate, nuncio, minister, envoy, internuncio
**chariness** circumspection, caution, wariness, calculation (see under CAUTIOUS)
*Ana* *prudence, providence, discretion, foresight, forethought
**charitable, benevolent, humane, humanitarian, philanthropic, eleemosynary, altruistic** are comparable when they mean having or showing interest in or being concerned with the welfare of others. **Charitable** stresses either active generosity to the poor or leniency and mercifulness in one's judgments of others, but in each case it

---

A colon (:) separates groups of words discriminated. An asterisk (*) indicates place of treatment of each group.

usually retains in some degree the implications of fraternal love or of compassion as the animating spirit behind the gift or the judgment ⟨generous and *charitable,* prompt to serve—*Wordsworth*⟩ ⟨Mrs. Hawthorne had been rude . . . to a friend of his, but that friend, so much more *charitable* and really good than she was, had made excuses for her—*Archibald Marshall*⟩ ⟨it is more *charitable* to suspend judgment—*Glasgow*⟩ **Benevolent** also stresses some inner compulsion (as native kindliness, a desire to do good, or an interest in others' happiness and well-being). In contrast with *charitable,* however, it more often suggests an innate disposition than an inculcated virtue ⟨his intentions are *benevolent*⟩ ⟨old Dimple with his *benevolent* smile—*H. G. Wells*⟩ ⟨my mother . . . always employed in *benevolent* actions while she uttered uncharitable words—*Wharton*⟩ ⟨the administrator of the future must be the servant of free citizens, not the *benevolent* ruler of admiring subjects—*Russell*⟩ **Humane** implies tenderness and compassion, sometimes as qualities of one's temperament, but sometimes as required qualifications of enlightened and sensitive human beings; it is referable chiefly, but not exclusively, to methods and policies affecting the welfare of others ⟨*humane* treatment of prisoners or of animals⟩ ⟨with reasonable men, I will reason; with *humane* men I will plead; but to tyrants I will give no quarter, nor waste arguments where they will certainly be lost—*Garrison*⟩ **Humanitarian** suggests an interest in the welfare or well-being of mankind or of a particular class or group of men more than of the individual; it is applied especially to acts, outlooks, and policies (as of institutions, rulers, or governments) ⟨as a nation we have been sharing our abundance with the world's hungry people . . . primarily from a *humanitarian* standpoint—*Hope*⟩ ⟨such *humanitarian* issues as the repeal of the brutal debtor laws—*Parrington*⟩ ⟨a part of the nation became *humanitarian,* and with a tender conscience turned . . . toward the perfectibility of man— *Canby*⟩ ⟨to use the A-bomb . . . was . . . wrong . . . on *humanitarian* grounds—*Zacharias*⟩ **Philanthropic** and **eleemosynary** also suggest interest in humanity rather than in the individual, but they commonly imply (as *humanitarian* does not) the giving of money on a large scale to organized charities, to institutions for human advancement or social service, or to humanitarian causes ⟨*philanthropic* foundations⟩ ⟨found time to devote to church, civic, and *philanthropic* affairs—*Silveus*⟩ ⟨*eleemosynary* institutions⟩ ⟨contractors, rarely known for wearing *eleemosynary* halos, cheerfully pocketed a loss . . . while they waited for the self-help workers . . . to catch up —*Olivier*⟩ ⟨an institution of higher education is not a commercial enterprise . . . . Its character is *eleemosynary,* strictly *eleemosynary*—*Himstead*⟩ **Altruistic** presupposes the guidance of an ethical principle: that the interests of others should be placed above those of self; it usually implies the absence of selfishness and often indifference to one's own welfare or interests ⟨if it is assumed that the objectives of American policy are wholly *altruistic,* it follows that non-Americans who participate . . . must be wholly virtuous—*Muggeridge*⟩ ⟨*altruistic* motives⟩ ⟨an *altruistic* physician⟩
*Ana* generous, *liberal, bountiful, bounteous, openhanded, munificent: merciful, *forbearing, lenient, clement, tolerant: *tender, compassionate, warmhearted, sympathetic
*Ant* uncharitable —*Con* merciless, relentless, implacable (see GRIM): *stingy, close, closefisted, parsimonious, niggardly, cheeseparing
**charity** 1 *mercy, clemency, grace, lenity
*Ana* love, affection, *attachment: benevolence, humane-

ness, altruism (see corresponding adjectives at CHARITABLE): benignity, benignancy, kindness, kindliness (see corresponding adjectives at KIND): generousness *or* generosity, liberalness *or* liberality, bountifulness *or* bounty, openhandedness (see corresponding adjectives at LIBERAL): goodwill, amity, *friendship
*Ant* malice, ill will —*Con* malevolence, malignity, malignancy, spite, spleen (see MALICE)
2 **Charity, philanthropy** are comparable in several of their meanings. Both words denote basically a love for one's fellowmen and a disposition to help those who are in need. But **charity** in this sense tends to suggest a Christian virtue and the will to help, as well as the deed, whenever the occasion arises ⟨alas for the rarity of Christian *charity* under the sun!—*Hood*⟩ ⟨melt not in an acid sect the Christian pearl of *charity*—*Whittier*⟩ **Philanthropy** in this sense is much vaguer because it usually implies a love of mankind and a disposition to help the community or one's fellowmen rather than the individual ⟨this *philanthropy* . . . is everywhere manifest in our author— *Dryden*⟩ Consequently there is a tendency to think of charity as benevolence manifested especially in public or private provision for the relief of the poor, and of philanthropy as benevolence manifested in efforts to promote the welfare or well-being of one's fellowmen; thus, out of *charity* one provides for the support of a destitute orphan; out of *philanthropy* one sends a large gift of money to an educational institution ⟨in benevolence, they excel in *charity,* which alleviates individual suffering, rather than in *philanthropy,* which deals with large masses and is more frequently employed in preventing than in allaying calamity—*Lecky*⟩ The terms also may be applied to what is done or given out of charity or philanthropy or to an institution or cause which is the object of such benefaction ⟨the cold *philanthropies,* the ostentatious public *charities* . . . he exposed with utter and relentless scorn—*Wilde*⟩ ⟨many *charities* and many *philanthropies* were aided by him during his lifetime⟩
**charlatan** mountebank, quack, *impostor, faker
*Ana* humbug, fraud, cheat, fake (see IMPOSTURE): pretender, feigner, counterfeiter (see corresponding verbs at ASSUME)
**charm** *n* talisman, amulet, *fetish
**charm** *vb* fascinate, allure, captivate, enchant, bewitch, *attract
*Ana* delight, rejoice, *please, gratify
*Ant* disgust
**charming** fascinating, alluring, captivating, enchanting, bewitching, attractive (see under ATTRACT *vb*)
*Ana* *delightful, delectable, delicious: pleasing, agreeable, grateful, *pleasant
*Ant* forbidding
**chart** *n* **Chart, map, graph** are comparable as nouns meaning a graphic and explanatory representation by means of lines, dots, colors, and symbols of something incapable of verbal or pictorial representation (because too large, too detailed, or too abstract) and as verbs meaning to make such a representation of something. **Chart** is the most inclusive of these terms; it implies the aim of making clear to the mind through the eye by graphic projection of data something (as solutions of an equation, points on the face of the earth, or values of a variable at specified times and places) that cannot be viewed directly ⟨a *chart* of coastal rainfall⟩ ⟨a nomographic conversion *chart* for an equation relating two variable quantities consists of two scales and a pivot point—*French & Vierck*⟩ ⟨a star *chart*⟩ ⟨*charting* the shifting channel of a river⟩ ⟨at 30,000 feet, in clear skies above the boiling cloud cap of a hurricane, an Air Force plane *charts* the size

---

*Ana* analogous words   *Ant* antonyms   *Con* contrasted words   See also explanatory notes facing page 1

chart 142 chat

of the disturbance—*N. Y. Times*⟩ *Chart* often specifically denotes a map designed as an aid to air or water navigation by stressing features and hazards of the area depicted ⟨the modern nautical *chart* is the end product of all the field operations. Into its construction enter the results of the geodetic, topographic, hydrographic, tidal, and magnetic work of the Survey—*Shalowitz*⟩ ⟨an un*charted* rock⟩ **Map** usually implies a representation of the earth's surface or of a part of it that shows directly according to some given scale or projection the relative position and size of cultural features (as streets, buildings, cities, towns, villages, counties, states, provinces, or countries) as well as the shape and proportionate extent of natural features (as bodies of water, mountain ranges, and coasts) ⟨a *map* of Europe⟩ ⟨*map* a newly explored country⟩ It may also be used in reference to a representation of the celestial sphere or of a particular heavenly body ⟨*mapping* the surface of the moon⟩ ⟨a *map* of the northern heavens⟩ **Graph** applies specifically to a chart or diagram in which two variable factors (for example, the prices of a commodity and the times at which these varying prices were asked) are so represented as to indicate their interrelationship. The usual method of preparing a graph is to locate by means of coordinates a series of points and often to join them with a curve or a series of straight lines ⟨a *graph* of a patient's fever⟩ ⟨*graph* the course of business since 1962⟩
*Ana* \*plan, plot, scheme, design, project

**chart** *vb* map, graph (see under CHART *n*)
*Ana* see those at CHART *n*

**charter** *vb* \*hire, let, lease, rent

**chary** \*cautious, circumspect, wary, calculating
*Ana* prudent, discreet, provident (see under PRUDENCE): \*sparing, economical, frugal, thrifty: reluctant, hesitant, loath, \*disinclined

**chase** *vb* \*follow, pursue, trail, tag, tail
*Con* flee, fly, \*escape: elude, evade, \*escape: \*abandon, forsake, desert

**chasm** \*gulf, abyss, abysm

**chaste** *adj* **Chaste, pure, modest, decent** are comparable when they mean free from all taint of what is lewd or salacious. **Chaste** fundamentally implies an opposition to *immoral* in the sense of that word in which it connotes lustfulness and licentiousness. The term therefore suggests a refraining from all acts or thoughts that incite desire or are not in accordance with virginity or marriage vows ⟨strew me over with maiden flowers, that all the world may know I was a *chaste* wife to my grave—*Shak.*⟩ It particularly stresses restraint and an avoidance of anything thought to defile or make unclean not only the love of man and woman but whatever should be free from cheapness, debasement, or vulgarization ⟨a *chaste* style⟩ ⟨the *chaste* beauty of a work of art⟩ ⟨one of the most striking characteristics of a man who is really in love, is that his conversation is *chaste*. He is willing to analyze sentiment, but not sensation—*Dimnet*⟩ ⟨the *chaste* and abstracted intellect of the scholar—*Wylie*⟩ **Pure** differs from *chaste* mainly in its suggestion of freedom from all taint of evil thought or immoral desires; it implies innocence and absence of temptation rather than, as *chaste* implies, control over one's impulses and actions ⟨come, pensive nun, devout and *pure*—*Milton*⟩ ⟨blessed are the *pure* in heart: for they shall see God—*Mt* 5:8⟩ ⟨it may have been that . . . he had never known any woman, that he had been *pure* as a saint—*Bromfield*⟩ **Modest** and **decent** are frequent in this sense as applied especially to behavior and to dress as outward manifestations of an inward chastity or purity. **Modest** usually also implies an absence of brazenness, boldness, or other characteristics unbefitting one who is by nature chaste or pure; *decent,* a due concern for what is regarded as seemly or proper (see also DECOROUS) ⟨fair, sweet, and *modest* maid forgive my thoughts—*Beaumont & Fletcher*⟩ ⟨dressing in so *modest* a way and behaving with such decorum—*Graves*⟩ ⟨*decent* men leading *decent* lives⟩ ⟨a paper *decent* people don't see—*Rose Macaulay*⟩
*Ana* virtuous, \*moral, righteous, ethical: \*faithful, true, constant, loyal: austere, \*severe
*Ant* lewd, wanton, immoral: bizarre (*of style, effect*) —*Con* obscene, gross, \*coarse, vulgar, ribald: \*licentious, lustful, lascivious, lecherous: \*fantastic, grotesque

**chasten** discipline, correct, \*punish, chastise, castigate
*Ana* humble, humiliate, \*abase: try, \*afflict: test, try, \*prove
*Ant* pamper, mollycoddle —*Con* \*indulge, humor, baby, spoil

**chastise** \*punish, discipline, correct, castigate, chasten
*Ana* \*beat, thrash, pummel, baste, belabor

**chat** *vb* **Chat, gab, chatter, patter, prate, prattle, babble, gabble, jabber, gibber** denote to emit a loose and ready flow of inconsequential talk or as nouns the talk so emitted. To **chat** is to talk in light, easy, and pleasant fashion ⟨in easy mirth we *chatted* o'er the trifles of the day before—*William Whitehead*⟩ ⟨passed an hour in idle *chat*⟩ To **gab** is to talk trivia glibly and long, often tiresomely ⟨came in to tea and sat there *gabbing* till ten o'clock—*J. W. Carlyle*⟩ ⟨luncheon *gab* among women—*Portz*⟩ To **chatter** is to talk aimlessly, incessantly, and (often) with great rapidity ⟨it was she who *chattered, chattered,* on their walks, while . . . he dropped a gentle word now and then—*Conrad*⟩ ⟨my *chatter* was as gay and sprightly as birdsong—*Warren*⟩ To **patter** is to speak or repeat rapidly and mechanically ⟨*pattering* prayers half inaudibly⟩ or glibly and volubly often without much regard to sense ⟨they're college-reared and can *patter* languages—*Buchan*⟩ ⟨the *patter* of an auctioneer⟩ To **prate** is to talk idly and boastfully ⟨a *prating* fool shall fall—*Prov* 10:8⟩ The word is often specifically used in reproach implying platitudinous or fulsome boasting or a readiness to talk at length about things of which the speaker is really ignorant or has only superficial knowledge ⟨we may *prate* of democracy, but actually a poor child in England has little more hope than had the son of an Athenian slave to be emancipated into that intellectual freedom of which great writings are born—*Quiller-Couch*⟩ To **prattle** is to talk like a child (as in artlessness and freedom or sometimes in lack of substance and sense) ⟨*prattled* on . . . in this vein, spewing up the squalid confusion of his thoughts—*Anthony West*⟩ ⟨we are . . . charmed with the pretty *prattle* of children—*Sidney*⟩ **Babble, gabble, jabber,** and **gibber** basically imply a making of sounds suggestive of speech but lacking the meaning content, intelligibility, and articulateness of normal adult human speech ⟨a brook *babbled* among the stones⟩ ⟨the noisy *gabble* of geese⟩ ⟨monkeys *jabbering* in the trees⟩ ⟨an idiot mewling and *gibbering*⟩ As applied to human speaking or speech all four terms are somewhat derogatory and especially suggest lack of clarity in both articulation and content ⟨the *babble* of four or more voices going on at once—*G. A. Miller*⟩ ⟨saying nothing comprehensible, just *babbling* and *gabbling,* half unconsciously—*Bennett*⟩ ⟨subjected to *gabble* about fifteenth-century politics—*McCarten*⟩ ⟨must we fall into the *jabber* and babel of discord—*Sir Winston Churchill*⟩ ⟨listened to *gibber* about . . . our present form or methods of government—*The Nation*⟩ ⟨the sheeted dead did squeak and *gibber* in the Roman streets—*Shak.*⟩
*Ana* converse, talk, \*speak: \*gossip

**chatter** *vb* *chat, gab, patter, prate, babble, gabble, jabber, gibber
*Ana* see those at CHAT

**cheap** beggarly, shabby, pitiable, sorry, *contemptible, despicable, scurvy
*Ana* *mean, ignoble, sordid, abject: paltry, *petty, measly, trifling: meretricious, tawdry (see GAUDY): low, *base, vile: poor, *bad, wrong
*Ant* noble

**cheat** *n* fraud, fake, deceit, deception, *imposture, counterfeit, sham, humbug
*Ana* hoaxing *or* hoax, bamboozling *or* bamboozlement (see corresponding verbs at DUPE): *deception, trickery, chicanery, chicane: charlatan, quack, mountebank, faker, *impostor: swindler, defrauder, cozener (see corresponding verbs at CHEAT)

**cheat** *vb* Cheat, cozen, defraud, swindle, overreach are comparable when meaning to obtain something and especially money or valuables from or an advantage over another by dishonesty and trickery. Cheat suggests deceit and, usually, tricks that escape or are intended to escape the observation of others ⟨*cheat* at cards⟩ ⟨*cheat* in a written examination⟩ ⟨she and her husband had *cheated* every one with whom they had dealings—*Anderson*⟩ ⟨he is not *cheated* who knows he is being *cheated*—*Coke*⟩ Cozen implies more artfulness or craft and often more allurements than *cheat;* it usually suggests the victim's loss of something of value to him whether of real worth or not ⟨soldiers *cozened* of their pay by clever girls⟩ ⟨cousins, indeed; and by their uncle *cozen'd* of comfort, kingdom, kindred, freedom, life—*Shak.*⟩ ⟨the Popular Front—that famous opportunity for men of goodwill to be *cozened* by the Communists—*Poore*⟩ Defraud implies depriving another of something that is his by right whether by taking it from him or by withholding it; the word, however, implies misleading statements or deliberate perversion of the truth more often than it implies craft, artfulness, or wiles ⟨*defraud* a widow of a piece of property⟩ ⟨the stockholders held that they had been *defrauded* by those who reorganized the company⟩ ⟨thou shalt not *defraud* thy neighbor, neither rob him—*Lev* 19:13⟩ ⟨freedom of speech and press does not include . . . the right to deceive or *defraud*—*Neill*⟩ Swindle implies either gross cheating or defrauding especially by imposture or by gaining the victim's confidence; it usually implies the obtaining of money or something quickly or easily convertible into money by false pretenses ⟨the forger *swindled* the merchants of the city out of large sums of money⟩ ⟨the despised Chinese, who were cuffed and maltreated and *swindled* by the Californians—*Brooks*⟩ Overreach implies getting the better of a person with whom one is dealing or negotiating or bargaining by unfair or dishonest means; often it implies cheating or defrauding or swindling ⟨he never made any bargain without *overreaching* (or, in the vulgar phrase, cheating) the person with whom he dealt—*Fielding*⟩
*Ana* *dupe, gull, hoax, hoodwink, bamboozle, trick, befool: *deceive, delude, beguile, double-cross, mislead

**check** *n* *corrective, control, antidote
*Ana* *oversight, supervision, surveillance

**check** *vb* 1 *arrest, interrupt
*Ana* stay, suspend (see DEFER): *stop, cease, discontinue, desist: repress, *suppress: *frustrate, thwart, foil, circumvent
2 bridle, curb, *restrain, inhibit
*Ana* *hinder, impede, obstruct, block: *prevent, preclude, obviate: baffle, balk (see FRUSTRATE): control, manage (see CONDUCT *vb*)
*Ant* accelerate (*of speed*): advance (*of movements, plans,*

hopes): release (*of feelings, energies*)

**checked, checkered** *variegated, parti-colored, motley, pied, piebald, skewbald, dappled, freaked

**cheek** nerve, effrontery, hardihood, gall, *temerity, audacity
*Ana* boldness, intrepidity (see corresponding adjectives at BRAVE): impudence, brazenness, shamelessness, brashness (see corresponding adjectives at SHAMELESS)
*Ant* diffidence —*Con* shyness, modesty, bashfulness (see corresponding adjectives at SHY): timorousness, timidity (see corresponding adjectives at TIMID): reservedness *or* reserve, reticence (see corresponding adjectives at SILENT)

**cheep** *vb* *chirp, chirrup, peep, tweet, twitter, chitter

**cheep** *n* chirp, chirrup, peep, tweet, twitter, chitter (see under CHIRP *vb*)

**cheer** *vb* 1 *encourage, inspirit, hearten, embolden, nerve, steel
*Ana* *comfort, console, solace: gladden, gratify (see PLEASE): stimulate, excite, quicken, *provoke
*Ant* deject: dismay —*Con* *discourage, dishearten, dispirit
2 root, *applaud
*Ana* acclaim, laud, *praise
*Con* deride, mock, *ridicule, taunt

**cheerful** lighthearted, joyful, joyous, *glad, happy
*Ana* jolly, jovial, *merry, blithe, jocund: mirthful, gleeful (see corresponding nouns at MIRTH): gay, vivacious, *lively, animated
*Ant* glum, gloomy —*Con* *sullen, saturnine, dour, morose: dejected, depressed, melancholy, sad (see corresponding nouns at SADNESS): doleful, lugubrious, rueful (see MELANCHOLY)

**cheerless** *dismal, dreary, dispiriting, bleak, desolate
*Ana* discouraging, disheartening, dejecting (see DISCOURAGE)
*Ant* cheerful

**cheeseparing** *stingy, close, closefisted, tight, tightfisted, niggardly, penny-pinching, parsimonious, penurious, miserly

**chemist** *druggist, apothecary, pharmacist

**cherish** 1 prize, treasure, value, *appreciate
*Ana* love, enjoy, *like: esteem, respect, regard (see under REGARD *n*): *revere, venerate, reverence: protect, *defend, shield, safeguard, guard
*Ant* neglect —*Con* ignore, overlook, slight, disregard, forget (see NEGLECT): desert, forsake (see ABANDON)
2 foster, *nurse, nurture, cultivate
*Ana* preserve, conserve, *save: *harbor, shelter, entertain
*Ant* abandon —*Con* repudiate, scorn, reject (see DECLINE *vb*): contemn, *despise, disdain

**chew out** *scold, upbraid, rate, berate, tongue-lash, jaw, bawl, wig, rail, revile, vituperate

**chic** *adj* smart, fashionable, modish, *stylish, dashing

**chicane, chicanery** trickery, double-dealing, *deception, fraud
*Ana* artifice, stratagem, maneuver, ruse, feint, *trick, wile, gambit, ploy: intrigue, machination, *plot: underhandedness, furtiveness, surreptitiousness (see corresponding adjectives at SECRET)
*Con* straightforwardness, forthrightness (see corresponding adjectives at STRAIGHTFORWARD): *honesty, integrity, probity, honor

**chide** reproach, *reprove, rebuke, reprimand, admonish
*Ana* *criticize, reprehend, censure, blame, condemn, denounce: *scold, upbraid, rate, berate
*Ant* commend —*Con* applaud, compliment (see COMMEND): *praise, laud, extol

---

*Ana* analogous words     *Ant* antonyms     *Con* contrasted words     See also explanatory notes facing page 1

**chief** *n* Chief, chieftain, head, headman, leader, master are comparable when they mean the person in whom resides authority or ruling power but they differ in their applications and associations. **Chief** is the most comprehensive of these terms, being applicable as a general term to anyone from an absolute monarch to one's immediate superior ⟨the *chief* of a court of inquisition was called the grand inquisitor⟩ ⟨the chargé d'affaires reports daily to his *chief*⟩ Usually, however, the term is applied specifically to one who is supreme in power or authority over a tribe or clan ⟨an Indian *chief*⟩ or to the superior officer in a civil department ⟨fire *chief*⟩ ⟨*chief* of police⟩ or to one who is vested with authority and power to act by the organization over which he presides ⟨the chairmen of the national committees of the leading political parties are virtually party *chiefs*⟩ The phrase *in chief* is often added to a title, held by two or more, to indicate the one who is the first in authority ⟨commander *in chief*⟩ ⟨editor *in chief*⟩ **Chieftain** has never obtained the generality of *chief,* and still usually carries implications derived from its early and still leading application to the chief of a tribe, a clan, or of a primitive, savage, or barbaric group ⟨the *chieftain's* plaid⟩ ⟨a robber *chieftain*⟩ **Head,** though seemingly as comprehensive as *chief,* is applied most frequently to the person of a group who serves as its chief executive or on whose shoulders the responsibility finally rests ⟨the *head* of the family⟩ ⟨the *head* of a school⟩ ⟨the British prime minister is actually the *head* of the government⟩ ⟨the *head* of a department⟩ **Headman** comes close to *chieftain* in that it usually applies to the person who serves as the chief of his tribe or village; the term, even more than *chieftain,* implies a condition of savagery or barbarism. **Leader** implies headship, sometimes of a nation or people but more often of an organized body (as a political party, a society, or a band of musicians) or of an informal assembly (as of persons or animals) ⟨a rangy red steer was the *leader* of the stampede⟩ The term usually implies a capacity for guidance, direction, or for the assumption of full control and of winning the support of those under one ⟨the *leader* of an orchestra⟩ ⟨the *leader* of the opposition in the British parliament⟩ **Master,** on the other hand, applies to a head who has another or others under him subject to his direction or control and necessarily obedient to his will: the term stresses his authority rather than his capacity for guidance ⟨a man cannot serve two *masters*⟩ In general use the term is applied as a designation to an employer of servants and to the head of a school or of a class. It is also applied generally to anyone who exerts great and controlling influence over others or who is regarded as one to be followed or obeyed. The chief specific use of *master* is as the title of the person qualified to command a merchant vessel; in this use it is commonly superseded by *captain* as a courtesy title.
*Ana* governor, ruler (see corresponding verbs at GOVERN)
*Con* *follower, disciple, henchman, adherent, satellite

**chief** *adj* Chief, principal, main, leading, foremost, capital mean first in importance or in standing. **Chief** is applicable to a person that serves as the head of his class or group or to a thing that stands out as above all the rest of its class or kind in rank, importance, dignity, or worth; the term therefore usually implies the subordination of all others ⟨*chief* justice of the supreme court⟩ ⟨president of a republic is its *chief* magistrate⟩ ⟨the cathedral is the *chief* church of a diocese⟩ ⟨the *chief* topic of conversation⟩ ⟨duty, not pleasure, is the *chief* aim of living—*Glasgow*⟩ **Principal** is applicable to whatever is the first in order of power or importance, and so is applied chiefly to a person to whom is given direction, control, or government of others or to a thing (or person thought of as a

thing) that, because of its size, its position, or its intrinsic importance precedes all others of its class or kind ⟨the *principal* dancer in a ballet⟩ ⟨the *principal* keeper in a prison⟩ ⟨the *principal* gate to the grounds of an institution⟩ ⟨the *principal* streets of a city⟩ ⟨the *principal* witness against the accused⟩ ⟨a chicken stew of which the *principal* ingredient was not chicken but sea cucumber—*Steinbeck*⟩ **Main** is applicable to something (often a part, unit, or division of a large or extensive thing) that excels all the others of its class or kind in size, potency, or importance ⟨the *main* line of a railroad⟩ ⟨the *main* street of a small city⟩ ⟨the *main*land⟩ ⟨words have been used so long as the *main* channel for communication—*Day Lewis*⟩ ⟨the literary critic . . . will yet find, like the historian, his *main* subject matter in the past—*L. P. Smith*⟩ **Leading,** like *principal,* implies precedence, but it often distinctively implies, in addition, a capacity or fitness for drawing others, for guiding them, or for giving a particular quality or character to a movement ⟨the *leading* men of the city⟩ ⟨he had been the *leading* counsel for the seven Bishops—*Macaulay*⟩ ⟨the *leading* automobile in a procession⟩ ⟨another *leading* object in education for efficiency is the cultivation of the critical discernment of beauty and excellence in things and in words and thoughts, in nature and in human nature—*Eliot*⟩ **Foremost** differs from *leading,* which it otherwise closely resembles, in its stronger implication of being first in an advance or progressive movement; it is preferable for that reason whenever there is a suggestion of the person's or thing's having forged ahead to that position ⟨one of us, that struck the *foremost* man of all this world—*Shak.*⟩ ⟨"handedness," of course, is the *foremost* primate characteristic—*La Barre*⟩ **Capital** is applicable to a thing that stands at the head of its class or kind because of its importance, its significance, its excellence, or its seriousness ⟨a *capital* plan⟩ ⟨his *capital* offense was that he had omitted to mention her at all⟩ ⟨the seven *capital* sins are the most important sins theologically not because they are the worst sins but because they lead to other sins and are fatal to spiritual progress⟩ ⟨with a little managing . . . she would have gained every point as easily as she had gained the *capital* one of taking the foundling baby under her wing —*Wharton*⟩
*Ana* *dominant, paramount, sovereign, predominant, preponderant, preponderating: *primary, prime: *supreme, preeminent
*Ant* subordinate —*Con* secondary, dependent, subject (see SUBORDINATE): subservient, ancillary, subsidiary, *auxiliary

**chiefly** *largely, greatly, mostly, mainly, principally, generally

**chieftain** *chief, head, leader, master

**childish** *childlike
*Ana* puerile, boyish, *youthful: *simple, foolish, silly, fatuous, asinine
*Ant* mature, grown-up —*Con* adult, matured (see MATURE): manly, manful, virile, manlike (see MALE): womanly, womanlike (see FEMALE)

**childlike,** childish agree in meaning having or showing the manner, spirit, or disposition of a child. Both are applicable to adolescents and to adults as well as to children. **Childlike,** however, usually suggests such qualities of childhood as innocence, simplicity, or straightforwardness which are worthy of admiration or emulation; **childish** suggests such less pleasing and less admirable characteristics as helplessness, peevishness, or undeveloped mentality ⟨her arias have the *childlike* quality Puccini wanted—*Hume*⟩ ⟨the same thought which clothed

---

A colon (:) separates groups of words discriminated. An asterisk (*) indicates place of treatment of each group.

in English seems *childish,* and even foolish, assumes a different air in Latin—*Cowper*⟩ ⟨was angry with himself for his *childish* petulance—*Hersey*⟩ ⟨to lose sight of such distinctions is to show one's self, not *childlike,* but *childish*—*Babbitt*⟩ ⟨the earnestness of the young people endows their sketches with a certain charm lacking in their imitators, whose pictures are *childish,* not *childlike*—*Argus*⟩

**Ana** naïve, unsophisticated, ingenuous, artless (see NATURAL): docile, *obedient, tractable, biddable

**chilly** cool, *cold, frigid, freezing, frosty, gelid, icy, glacial, arctic

**Ant** balmy

**chimerical** fantastic, fanciful, visionary, *imaginary, quixotic

**Ana** utopian, *ambitious, pretentious: illusory, *apparent: delusive, delusory, *misleading, deceptive: fabulous, mythical (see FICTITIOUS): preposterous, absurd (see FOOLISH)

**Ant** feasible  —**Con** *possible, practicable: reasonable, *rational: sensible, sane, *wise, prudent

**chine** backbone, back, *spine, vertebrae

**chink** *crack, cleft, fissure, crevasse, crevice, cranny

**Ana** *break, gap, interruption: split, rift, *breach

**chirp** *vb* **Chirp, chirrup, cheep, peep, tweet, twitter, chitter** can all mean as verbs to make the little sounds characteristic of small animals and as nouns the little sounds so made, and all can be extended to sounds and the making of sounds (as by human beings) that suggest such small animal sounds. **Chirp** implies the short, sharp, and thin sound that is made by practically all small birds and some insects; it regularly connotes cheerfulness but often also busyness and immaturity ⟨there was no sound save the *chirping* of birds⟩ ⟨the linnet . . . *chirps* her vernal song of love—*Southey*⟩ ⟨one of these birds . . . began to ascend, by short hops and flights, through the branches, uttering a sharp, preliminary *chirp*—*Burroughs*⟩ ⟨someone turned on the water down the hall and all the second-floor faucets *chirped* at once, like so many crickets—*Algren*⟩ ⟨wait until the boldest *chirps:* "It was tonight, dear, wasn't it?"—*MacLeish*⟩ **Chirrup** implies a more sustained effect than *chirp,* as though a bird is singing or is learning to sing; it also often heightens the connotations of cheerfulness or liveliness ⟨untucked his head from under his wing and *chirruped* drowsily—*Sinclair*⟩ ⟨the shrill persistent *chirrup* of a fledgling sparrow⟩ ⟨there is a new *chirrup* in their talk, feeling that they shall feel livelier in a livelier land—*O'Casey*⟩ ⟨made her little *chirruping* sound of welcome—*Woolf*⟩ ⟨the bullets *chirruped* by in the soft buzzing sound of insects on the wing—*Mailer*⟩ **Cheep** implies feebleness yet shrillness of sound such as that made by a very young bird or by a mouse, a bat, or a squirrel ⟨the persistent *cheep* of a crate of new-hatched chicks⟩ ⟨a brood of ducklings, which had lost their mother, filed into the barn, *cheeping* feebly—*George Orwell*⟩ ⟨fog seemed to rise from his raincoat and his shoes *cheeped*—*Dorothy Parker*⟩ **Peep** differs from *cheep* chiefly in stressing the weakness of the sound and so suggesting its faintness or the animal's helplessness ⟨the *peep* of a chick just struggling from the shell⟩ ⟨a worrisome mother . . . hovers over her child. Every time he *peeps,* she jumps to see what's the matter—*Spock*⟩ ⟨all the little boats *peeped* their klaxons, and the bells . . . suddenly burst into crashing, bashing peals—*Panter-Downes*⟩ ⟨consisted for the most part of odd little squeals from the woodwinds. These *peeps* . . . added up to a fairly meaningless and silly score—*Philip Hamburger*⟩ **Tweet** usually implies the monosyllabic note of a very small bird or the call of small game birds (as the quail or bob-

white) ⟨a redstart . . . sat on the fence near my hut till dusk, *tweeting* rather plaintively on one note—*Kingdon-Ward*⟩ ⟨the referee checked the play with sharp *tweets* of his whistle⟩ **Twitter** implies a succession of notes or sounds, uttered tremulously or excitedly; when applied to persons or their utterances or doings it can suggest feverish or disorderly excitement ⟨the trees *twittered* feverishly, and cool winds swept the ground—*Peggy Bennett*⟩ ⟨the swallow *twittering* from the straw-built shed—*Gray*⟩ ⟨these youngest girls . . . stood around *twittering,* trying to appear prim, but only succeeded in looking more and more excited—*Styron*⟩ The noun, especially, is often used to express a state of agitation ⟨in a *twitter* of excitement⟩ ⟨a nerve-racking place full of the *twitters* and colors and smells and giggles and screeches of too many unlovely shoving girls—*Wouk*⟩ **Chitter,** like *twitter,* implies a succession of sounds, but distinctively it can imply a briskness and sharpness of tone that belong also to chattering and then may carry such connotations as alarm, irritation, or fear ⟨heard a squirrel *chitter* in alarm, as if it had scurried around the trunk of a tree after something had startled it—*Frazee*⟩ ⟨the cawings of jackdaws, the *chittering* of sparrows—*Powys*⟩ ⟨from close by came the *chitter* of a screech owl—*Saxon*⟩ ⟨some teeth in angry fit may *chitter*—*Alexander Boswell*⟩

**chirp** *n* chirrup, cheep, peep, tweet, twitter, chitter (see under CHIRP *vb*)

**chirrup** *vb* *chirp, cheep, peep, tweet, twitter, chitter

**chirrup** *n* chirp, cheep, peep, tweet, twitter, chitter (see under CHIRP *vb*)

**chisel** *vb* sculpture, sculpt, sculp, *carve, incise, engrave, etch

**Ana** *cut, chop: produce, turn out (see BEAR): shape, fashion, form (see MAKE)

**chitter** *vb* *chirp, chirrup, cheep, peep, tweet, twitter

**chitter** *n* chirp, chirrup, cheep, peep, tweet, twitter (see under CHIRP *vb*)

**chivalrous** gallant, courtly, courteous, polite, *civil

**Ana** *spirited, mettlesome, high-spirited

**Ant** churlish  —**Con** *rude, ungracious, discourteous: boorish, loutish, clownish (see under BOOR)

**chivy** *vb* *bait, badger, heckle, hector, hound, ride

**Ana** *worry, annoy, harry, harass, tease: chase, pursue, trail, *follow: torment, try, *afflict

**choice** *n* **Choice, option, alternative, preference, selection, election** are comparable when they mean the act or opportunity of choosing or the thing chosen. **Choice** usually implies the right or the privilege to choose freely from a number (as of persons, things, or courses) ⟨take your *choice* of rooms⟩ ⟨he had no *choice* in the determination of his profession⟩ ⟨everyone admires his *choice,* for she is a very attractive young woman⟩ **Option** stresses a specifically given right or power to choose one from among two or more mutually exclusive actions or courses of action ⟨the state constitution gives local *option* to the cities and towns in the matter of granting or withholding licenses for the sale of intoxicants⟩ ⟨the court sentenced the convicted speeder to one month's imprisonment with the *option* of a fine⟩ ⟨the students have no *option* in the matter of vacations⟩ In business transactions, an *option* is usually purchased and enables one to demand during an agreed length of time fulfillment of a contract to sell (as a specified quantity of a commodity) or buy (as a particular parcel of real estate) at a price and on terms agreed upon when drawing the option ⟨acquire an *option* on a tract of land⟩ ⟨buying and selling *options* on the stock exchange⟩ **Alternative** typically stresses restriction of choice between two mutually exclusive things (as propositions, theories, courses, or policies). Commonly it implies that all other comparable things are ruled out by force of circumstances ⟨the *alternatives* before the country were peace with dishonor or war with honor⟩ or by unconquerable personal aversion ⟨the only *alternative* to liberty, in Patrick Henry's estimation, was death⟩ or by logical necessity ⟨if the States had any power it was assumed that they had all power and that the necessary *alternative* was to deny it altogether—*Justice Holmes*⟩ *Alternative,* however, is sometimes used of more than two possible choices. **Preference** emphasizes the guidance of one's choice by one's bias or predilections or by one's judgment of values or of desirability ⟨he was promised his *preference*⟩ ⟨he said he had no *preference* and would wait until others had declared their *preferences*⟩ **Selection** implies a wide range of choice and the need of discrimination or taste in choosing ⟨he was commended for his *selection* of books⟩ ⟨she did not have time for the careful selection of a hat⟩ **Election** adds to *selection* the implication of an end or purpose which necessitates the exercise of judgment ⟨the students will make their *election* of courses before returning to college⟩ ⟨the doctrine of predestination holds that men are destined to heaven or hell by divine *election*⟩

**choice** *adj* **Choice, exquisite, elegant, recherché, rare, dainty, delicate** are comparable when they mean having qualities that appeal to a fine or highly refined taste. **Choice** stresses preeminence in quality or kind rather than careful selection of the best, although the latter may also be connoted; consequently, the word usually suggests an appeal to a highly cultivated and discriminating taste ⟨the *choice* and master spirits of this age—*Shak.*⟩ ⟨when education in America began, it was intended for the fit and was designed to produce a *choice* type—*Grandgent*⟩ **Exquisite** implies consummate perfection in workmanship, in choice, in quality, or in impression produced—a perfection so fine and unobtrusive that it attracts only the most sensitive and fastidious ⟨he paints with *exquisite* art the charm of the deep country and the lure of the simple life—*Buchan*⟩ ⟨angels, supporting, saluting, and incensing the Virgin and Child with singular grace and *exquisite* feeling—*Henry Adams*⟩ **Elegant** differs widely from *exquisite;* it implies either an impressive richness or grandeur restrained by fine taste, or grace and dignity characterized by a noble simplicity ⟨whoever wishes to attain an English style . . . *elegant* but not ostentatious, must give his days and nights to the volumes of Addison—*Johnson*⟩ ⟨charming to look at and *elegant* to her fingertips—*John Martin*⟩ ⟨the handsomest man of the company, very *elegant* in velvet and broadcloth—*Cather*⟩ **Recherché** like the preceding terms implies care in selection; it often suggests a studied exquisiteness or elegance ⟨the sangfroid, grace, abandon, and *recherché* nonchalance with which Charles Yates ushers ladies and gentlemen to their seats in the opera house—*O. Henry*⟩ ⟨giving long and *recherché* dinners—*Saintsbury*⟩ Very frequently, however, it implies a search for the novel or fresh as well as the choice, and it may carry a connotation of artificiality or of straining for effect ⟨the word *devastating* . . . was thought to be *recherché;* the discerning reader is likely to call it affected—*Beach*⟩ **Rare** derives from its ordinary senses (see INFREQUENT, THIN) connotations of uncommonness and of a fineness associated with the rarefied air of the upper regions; nevertheless, its major implication is distinction in merit or excellence or a superlative quality ⟨the *rarest* cordials old monks ever schemed to coax from pulpy grapes—*Lowell*⟩ ⟨he [W. H. Hudson] is, of living writers that I read, the *rarest* spirit—*Galsworthy*⟩ **Dainty** (see also NICE 1) may come close to *choice,* but is then used chiefly

to describe things which give delight to the fastidious taste, especially to the eye, and often also the palate ⟨her house is elegant and her table *dainty—Johnson*⟩ More often, however, the term implies smallness and exquisiteness ⟨those *dainty* limbs, which Nature lent for gentle usage and soft delicacy—*Milton*⟩ ⟨the spirit of romance, gross and tawdry in vulgar minds, *dainty* and refined in the more cultivated—*Parrington*⟩ **Delicate,** like *dainty,* implies exquisiteness and an appeal to a fastidious taste, but it ascribes fineness, subtlety, and often fragility to the thing rather than smallness, and it implies an appeal not only to the eye or palate, but to any of the senses or to the mind or spirit ⟨the more *delicate* perfume of the pink-flowering thorn—*Wilde*⟩ ⟨not, however, an effervescing wine, although its *delicate* piquancy produced a somewhat similar effect—*Hawthorne*⟩ ⟨I have, alas! only the words we all use to paint commoner, coarser things, and no means to represent all the exquisite details, all the *delicate* lights, and shades—*Hudson*⟩ ⟨an irony so quiet, so *delicate,* that many readers never notice it is there . . . or mistake it for naïveté—*Priestley*⟩

*Ana* preeminent, surpassing, peerless, incomparable, *supreme, superlative: picked, selected, culled, chosen (see CHOOSE)

*Ant* indifferent (see MEDIUM) —*Con* mediocre, secondrate, middling, fair, average, *medium: *common, ordinary

**choke** *suffocate, asphyxiate, stifle, smother, strangle, throttle

**choleric** splenetic, testy, *irascible, touchy, cranky, cross

*Ana* *irritable, fractious, huffy, querulous, petulant, peevish: *angry, acrimonious, wrathful, wroth, indignant, mad, irate: fiery, peppery, spunky (see SPIRITED): captious, carping, faultfinding (see CRITICAL)

*Ant* placid: imperturbable —*Con* *calm, tranquil, serene: *cool, composed, nonchalant

**choose,** select, elect, opt, pick, cull, prefer, single are comparable when they mean to fix upon one of a number of things as the one to be taken, accepted, or adopted or to make such a determination. **Choose** commonly implies both an act of judgment and the actual taking or adoption of what is fixed upon ⟨that he may know to refuse the evil, and *choose* the good—*Isa* 7:15⟩ ⟨between them . . . we can see little to *choose—Henry Adams*⟩ ⟨the disinterested search for truth is certainly one of the highest and noblest careers that a man can *choose—Inge*⟩ **Select** usually implies a wide range of choice and discrimination or discernment of values in making one's choice ⟨one particular nation to *select* from all the rest—*Milton*⟩ ⟨the difficult task of *selecting* a presidential candidate—*H. D. Jordan*⟩ ⟨his temperament was *selecting* the instances he should narrate, his mind *selecting* the words to employ—*F. M. Ford*⟩ **Elect** often implies a deliberate choice, especially between alternatives, or a careful selection of some out of many possibilities; ordinarily, it carries a stronger implication of the rejection of that not chosen than either of the preceding words ⟨*elect* a president⟩ ⟨according to the doctrine of predestination, God *elects* those who are to be saved⟩ ⟨will it not look a little odd . . . when you have so many devoted children, that you should *elect* to live alone—*Sackville-West*⟩ ⟨having *elected* deliberately . . . that stern land and weather—*Faulkner*⟩ **Opt** (often with *for*) implies an election between alternatives ⟨give the people an opportunity to *opt* for statehood—*Rupert Emerson*⟩ often specifically, in the case of inhabitants of territory transferred by treaty, between retaining one's former citizenship or acquiring citizenship in the new state ⟨*opt*

A colon (:) separates groups of words discriminated. An asterisk (*) indicates place of treatment of each group.

to remain a British subject⟩ **Pick** implies a careful selection, often on personal grounds; **cull,** a nice or fastidious choice ⟨attempts to *pick* an exact synonym—*Johnson O'Connor*⟩ ⟨*pick* an all-star team from the players in the city⟩ ⟨*pick* a winner⟩ ⟨his dictionary had no vulgar word in it, no harsh one, but all *culled* from the luckiest moods of poets—*J. R. Lowell*⟩ **Prefer** implies choice that indicates what one favors or desires; it does not, however, always carry an implication of taking or adopting what one chooses or of getting one's choice ⟨*prefer* the blue dress to the brown one⟩ ⟨certain colors were *preferred* . . . for reasons of association and tradition —*Binyon*⟩ ⟨experience has taught me, when the versions of the same story . . . differ materially, to *prefer* the less exciting—*Davis*⟩ **Single** (usually with *out*) implies choice or election usually of an individual person or thing from a number ⟨*singles* out for special praise the guidebook to Wells cathedral—*Pyke Johnson*⟩
*Ana* *adopt, espouse, embrace: *desire, wish, crave
*Ant* reject: eschew —*Con* *forgo, forbear, abnegate: refuse, *decline, spurn, repudiate

**chop** *vb* hew, *cut, slit, slash, carve
*Ana* split, cleave, rive (see TEAR *vb*)

**chore** *task, duty, assignment, job, stint
*Ana* *work, occupation, employment, business

**christen** *baptize

**chronic** *inveterate, confirmed, deep-seated, deep-rooted
*Ana* established, fixed, settled (see SET): *hardened, indurated, callous
*Ant* acute (*of illness*)

**chronicle** 1 *history, annals
2 *account, story, report, version
*Ana* narration, recital, recountal (see corresponding verbs at RELATE)

**chthonian** *infernal, Hadean, stygian, hellish, Tartarean

**chubby** rotund, plump, fat, *fleshy, stout, portly, corpulent, obese
*Ana* chunky, stubby, dumpy, squat (see STOCKY)
*Ant* slim

**chummy** intimate, close, thick, confidential, *familiar

**chunky** *stocky, thickset, thick, stubby, squat, dumpy
*Ana* rotund, chubby (see FLESHY)

**church** *religion, denomination, sect, communion, creed, faith, cult, persuasion

**churl** *n* *boor, lout, clown, clodhopper, bumpkin, hick, yokel, rube
*Ant* *gentleman, aristocrat

**churlish** boorish, loutish, clownish (see under BOOR)
*Ana* ungracious, ill-mannered, discourteous, *rude, uncivil, impolite: curt, blunt, brusque, gruff, crusty (see BLUFF): surly, dour (see SULLEN)
*Ant* courtly —*Con* *civil, polite, courteous, gallant: urbane, *suave, diplomatic, bland, politic, smooth

**cinders** clinkers, embers, *ash

**circle** *n* *set, coterie, clique
*Ana* friends, acquaintances, intimates (see singular nouns at FRIEND): associates, companions, comrades (see singular nouns at ASSOCIATE)

**circle** *vb* 1 *surround, environ, encircle, encompass, compass, hem, gird, girdle, ring
*Ana* *enclose, envelop: circumscribe, restrict (see LIMIT)
2 revolve, rotate, *turn, gyrate, wheel, spin, twirl, whirl, eddy, swirl, pirouette

**circuit** compass, *circumference, perimeter, periphery
*Ana* route, course, *way: tour, *journey

**circuitous** roundabout, *indirect
*Ana* *winding, serpentine, sinuous, tortuous, flexuous: *crooked, devious

*Ant* straight

**circulate** *spread, disseminate, diffuse, propagate, radiate
*Ana* revolve, rotate (see TURN): interchange, *exchange

**circumference,** perimeter, periphery, circuit, compass are comparable because all in their basic senses denote a continuous line enclosing an area or space. They differ, however, in the extent to which they retain this meaning and in the number and character of their acquired implications and connotations. Precisely, **circumference** designates either the line that describes a circle or an ellipse or the length of such a line; in extended use it is applied to something felt as having a center (see CENTER) ⟨nature set from center to *circumference*—*Milton*⟩ ⟨that mysterious intellectual magnetism that enlarges the *circumference* of his ego—*Powys*⟩ **Perimeter** is more comprehensive than *circumference;* it includes not only the line that bounds any circular figure or area, but also the broken line that encloses any polygon; moreover it may designate the whole outer boundary of a body, especially a more or less spherical body ⟨the *perimeter* of a hexagon⟩ ⟨the *perimeter* of the globe⟩ **Periphery** is sometimes interchangeable with *perimeter* but it is more frequently used in an extended sense. More often than any other word in this group it is referred to the actual edge or border or boundaries of something concrete ⟨the sections of an orange extend from the center to the *periphery*⟩ ⟨we had just time enough to explore the *periphery* (the encircling shore) of the island⟩ ⟨the *periphery* (the wall) of a blood vessel⟩ Occasionally it suggests limits which cannot be exceeded ⟨stimuli beyond the *periphery* of consciousness⟩ ⟨the fixed stars at the *periphery* of the universe were stationary— *S. F. Mason*⟩ **Circuit** has become so tied up with the idea of a journey round the periphery of something that the two ideas are fused ⟨the hour hand of a clock covers its *circuit* every twelve hours⟩ ⟨he also completed the great *circuit* of coast highways—*Buchan*⟩ On the other hand, **compass** usually refers to the area or space within an enclosing line or the ground that figuratively might be covered by the leg of a compass describing such a line ⟨within thy crown, whose *compass* is no bigger than thy head—*Shak.*⟩ ⟨another soldier . . . followed his trail, went on to make a wide *compass*, and got as far as Zuñi—*De Voto*⟩
*Ana* *outline, contour

**circumlocution** periphrasis, pleonasm, *verbiage, redundancy, tautology
*Ana* prolixity, diffuseness, wordiness, verbosity (see corresponding adjectives at WORDY)
*Con* compactness (see corresponding adjectives at CLOSE): conciseness or concision, terseness, succinctness, pithiness (see corresponding adjectives at CONCISE)

**circumscribe** confine, *limit, restrict
*Ana* *restrain, inhibit, curb, check: *hamper, trammel, fetter
*Ant* expand, dilate —*Con* distend, amplify, inflate, swell (see EXPAND): enlarge (see INCREASE *vb*)

**circumspect** *adj* *cautious, wary, calculating, chary
*Ana* *careful, punctilious, punctual, meticulous, scrupulous: vigilant, *watchful, alert
*Ant* audacious —*Con* venturesome, rash, reckless, daring, daredevil, foolhardy, *adventurous: bold (see BRAVE): heedless, *careless

**circumspection** caution, wariness, calculation, chariness (see under CAUTIOUS)
*Ana* carefulness *or* care, punctiliousness, punctuality, meticulosity, scrupulousness (see corresponding adjectives at CAREFUL): discretion, forethought, foresight, providence, *prudence

---

*Ana* analogous words      *Ant* antonyms      *Con* contrasted words      See also explanatory notes facing page 1

*Ant* audacity —*Con* venturesomeness, rashness, reck- lessness, daring, daredeviltry, foolhardiness (see corre- sponding adjectives at ADVENTUROUS): boldness (see corresponding adjective at BRAVE): heedlessness, careless- ness (see corresponding adjectives at CARELESS)

**circumstance** *occurrence, event, incident, episode
*Ana* *item, detail, particular: factor, constituent, com- ponent, *element

**circumstantial, minute, particular, particularized, de- tailed, itemized** are comparable when they mean dealing with a matter point by point. **Circumstantial** applies especially to accounts of events or to narratives, but it is applicable also to the persons who recount or narrate or to their memories. The term implies full and precise reference to the incidents or circumstances attending an event ⟨a *circumstantial* account of the battle has not yet been written⟩ ⟨generally speaking, a historical novel . . . must be documented with the news of what once hap- pened, and full of *circumstantial* life—*Garrigue*⟩ ⟨my memory is exact and *circumstantial*—*Dickens*⟩ **Minute,** in addition, applies to investigations, researches, inspec- tions, and descriptions; it stresses interest in or inclusion of every detail, no matter how trivial or insignificant. It therefore usually connotes exhaustiveness or meticulous exactness ⟨he prolonged the flower-picking process by *minute* and critical choice—*Deland*⟩ ⟨Plato . . . in the Laws . . . provides for the state a perfect jungle of *minute* regulations—*Buchan*⟩ ⟨she was interested in the little details and writes with *minute* care about the change of fashion—*Bradford*⟩ **Particular** differs little from *circum- stantial* except in being applicable also to descriptions and lists; it may therefore imply attention to every feature or item rather than to every incident or circumstance ⟨a *particular* description of every musical instrument in the collection⟩ ⟨it is as *particular* as the four-sheet maps from which it is taken—*Jefferson*⟩ ⟨I think myself obliged to be very *particular* in this relation, lest my veracity should be suspected—*Swift*⟩ **Particularized** often replaces *particular* as applied to narratives, descriptions, and lists; it is not used of those who so narrate, describe, or list, but it may be applied to the circumstances, features, and items that they present ⟨Scott's *particularized* descriptions of his characters⟩ ⟨a most concrete, *particularized,* earthy series of small diurnal recognitions—*Powys*⟩ **Detailed** ap- plies to a circumstantial or minute account, description, study, or representation; it implies, however, abundance of rather than exhaustiveness in detail ⟨Perera in the six- teenth century . . . presents a *detailed* picture of Chinese life—*Ellis*⟩ ⟨the *detailed* study of history should be supple- mented by brilliant outlines—*Russell*⟩ **Itemized** implies complete enumeration of details, especially of those that indicate the separate purchases or separate credits in a mercantile account, or of those that indicate the articles or groups of articles in the possession of a person or business (as in an inventory) ⟨an *itemized* bill⟩ ⟨*itemized* list of his expenditures⟩ The term is also applicable to descriptions, narratives, or accounts which in addition to being particu- larized have something of the formality of an inventory ⟨an *itemized* description of a room⟩
*Ana* precise, nice, exact, accurate (see CORRECT): *full, complete, replete
*Ant* abridged: summary —*Con* succinct, terse, laconic, *concise, pithy, compendious: shortened, abbreviated, curtailed (see SHORTEN)

**circumvent** outwit, baffle, balk, *frustrate, thwart, foil
*Ana* forestall, anticipate, *prevent: evade, *escape, elude, avoid: trick, befool, hoodwink, *dupe
*Ant* conform (to *laws, orders*): cooperate (with *persons*) —*Con* promote, further, *advance, forward: abet (see INCITE)

**citadel** stronghold, fortress, *fort, fastness

**citation** *encomium, eulogy, tribute, panegyric
*Ana* commendation, recommendation, complimenting *or* compliment (see corresponding verbs at COMMEND): award, guerdon, reward (see PREMIUM)

**cite** *vb* **1** *summon, summons, call, convoke, convene, muster
*Ana* bid, *invite: *arrest, detain, apprehend: *praise, extol, eulogize, laud, acclaim: award, accord (see GRANT)
**2** *quote, repeat
**3** *adduce, advance, allege
*Ana* enumerate, tell, *count, number: recount, recite, narrate, rehearse (see RELATE)

**citizen 1** *inhabitant, resident, denizen
*Con* *stranger, outsider
**2 Citizen, subject, national** are comparable when denoting a person who is regarded as a member of a sovereign state, entitled to its protection, and subject to its laws. **Citizen** implies *alien* as its opposite. It is applicable to a native or naturalized person, regardless of sex or age, who owes allegiance to a government and is entitled to its protection of his life, liberty, and property at home or abroad. Ordi- narily (as in the United States) citizenship does not imply possession of all political rights (as the right to vote). *Citizen* often implies allegiance to a government in which the sovereign power (theoretically or absolutely) is re- tained by the people; it is usually the preferred term in designating those persons in a republic whose status is not that of aliens ⟨American *citizens* living in Mexico⟩ ⟨all persons born or naturalized in the United States, and subject to the jurisdiction thereof, are *citizens* of the United States and of the State wherein they reside—*U. S. Constitution*⟩ **Subject** is applicable to a person, no matter where he resides, who by right of birth or naturalization owes allegiance to a personal sovereign (as a king or em- peror) whether this sovereign rules directly or is a figure- head in whose name an often representative government is conducted; thus, *subject* is the preferred term in the British Commonwealth of Nations largely for historical reasons in spite of the limitations on the power of the sovereign and in spite of the representative form of gov- ernment in Great Britain and in its dominions ⟨British *subjects* living in the United States⟩ ⟨the millions of *sub- jects* of Queen Elizabeth⟩ The term is also applicable to any person residing in territory governed by another state that has gained power over it by force of arms or by con- quest, whether the sovereign power in that state is vested in a person or in the people ⟨the line of distinction between the citizen and the *subject,* the free and the subjugated races—*Taney*⟩ **National** belongs with this group of terms in spite of its shifting significance and more or less con- flicting implications. It is applicable chiefly to any of a body of persons of the same nation or people living in a country other than the one in which they have or have had the status of citizen or subject. In diplomatic use the term is often applied to one's fellow countrymen ⟨the consul in each of the large cities is responsible for protecting the rights of his own *nationals*⟩ Still other denotations, not so common, have come into use. Chief among these is the definition of a *national* as anyone who has been born in the territory of a given government, even though he now resides in another country, either as an alien or, by natural- ization, as a citizen or subject of that country ⟨some Euro- pean governments claim authority over their *nationals* in North and South America⟩ There is also a tendency to prefer *national* to *subject* or *citizen* in some countries where the sovereign power is not clearly vested in a mon- arch or ruler or in the people or where theories of racism

---

A colon (:) separates groups of words discriminated. An asterisk (*) indicates place of treatment of each group.

prevail. In some use, especially in international law, *national* is applied to anyone entitled to the protection of a government regardless of whether his status is that of citizen or not; in this sense, the Filipinos were formerly *nationals,* though never *citizens,* of the United States. *Ant* alien —*Con* foreigner (see STRANGER)

**civic,** civil, civilian are not close synonyms but rather words whose meanings lend themselves to confusion. In a sense they have a common meaning: of, relating to, or characteristic of a citizen—but in each case the word *citizen* has a specific or particular meaning. **Civic** implies some relation to a city and its citizens; *city,* however, is used loosely so as to cover any community having closely related interests (as a town, a village, or a city proper) or any municipality or corporation having powers of local self-government: in this sense *civic* is used in distinction from *state, federal,* and *national* (London took the lead in this new development of *civic* life—*J. R. Green*) (civic interests gave way to national interests) (organizations for *civic* betterment) Often the word comes close in meaning to *public* when used to modify acts, functions, obligations, or qualities, the chief distinction consisting in its closer application to the life of the community (his personal virtues were no less outstanding than his *civic* virtues) (for the theme of her life is that we are public as well as private beings and that civilization depends on the spread of *civic* virtue—*Bentley*) **Civil,** in general, has reference to a citizen as a member of the state, or to citizens as members of the state. In this sense *state* denotes usually a larger organized unit than that denoted by *city* and comes close in meaning to *country, nation,* and *people.* The term *civil* implies reference to this organization; thus, *civil* liberty is the liberty permitted to a citizen by the laws of the state or exemption from arbitrary government interference; a *civil* war (as opposed to a foreign war) is a conflict between citizens of the same state. More specifically, there is often a definitely implied contrast in the use of *civil*; the *civil* authorities are those that prevail in all affairs except where ecclesiastical authorities, or military authorities have the final say; *civil* service denotes service of the state in any capacity that does not distinctively belong to the military organization; thus, *civil* architecture applies to architecture which is neither ecclesiastical nor military; in law, *civil* actions are distinguished from criminal actions as relating to proceedings in connection with the private or individual rights of citizens; also, in law, a *civil* death implies not a natural (that is, actual) death, but the loss or renunciation of all legal rights or status (saw the Bible as . . . containing the complete, final, and absolute code for all matters spiritual and civil—*J. D. Hart*) (a program to make of the Atlantic Alliance a *civil* and not merely a military Community—*Ascoli*) **Civilian** refers to persons who are not members of the armed forces and is used chiefly in contrast to *military* (civilian personnel) (civilian duties in time of war) (rationing of gasoline among *civilian* consumers) (glad to get back to *civilian* clothes)

**civil** *adj* **1** *civic, civilian
**2** Civil,** polite, courteous, courtly, gallant, chivalrous are comparable as applied to persons or their words and acts when in intercourse with others with the meaning observant of the forms required by good breeding. **Civil** commonly suggests the bare fulfillment of the ordinary requirements of social intercourse; it frequently implies little more than forbearance from rudeness (it was an entirely *civil* greeting, but that was all you could say of it—*Christopher La Farge*) (this man . . . cut short one of our party, and addressed a silly remark to Spencer . . . . Spencer's answer was *civil,* but brief and not inviting—*Fiske*)

**Polite,** while sometimes suggesting a merely perfunctory attitude, is more positive than *civil;* it commonly implies thoughtfulness for the feelings of others, united with polish of manners and address (nothing was ever so serene as his countenance, so unembarrassed as his manner, so *polite* as his whole demeanor—*Landor*) (the Bishop seldom questioned Jacinto about his thoughts or beliefs. He didn't think it *polite*—*Cather*) **Courteous** implies more considerate and dignified, **courtly,** more stately and ceremonious, observance of due civilities (owns a fine old historical painting in Châteldon and he was *courteous* enough to permit me to view it—*Upton Sinclair*) (be *courteous* to all, but intimate with few—*Washington*) (his great-uncle, a *courtly* and stately old gentleman—*Symonds*) **Gallant** and *chivalrous* imply courteous attentiveness to women. But **gallant** suggests spirited and dashing or ornate and florid expressions of courtesy (the General attended her himself to the street door, saying everything *gallant* . . . admiring the elasticity of her walk, which corresponded exactly with the spirit of her dancing —*Austen*) (the qualities . . . of surface chivalry and *gallant* attentiveness in her brilliant American friend had for a moment seemed to reveal a lack in me—*Ellis*) (in a moment he was all *gallant* anxiety and solicitude—*Wylie*) **Chivalrous** suggests high-minded, disinterested, sometimes self-sacrificing attentions (nothing can beat a true woman for a clear vision of reality; I would say a cynical vision if I were not afraid of wounding your *chivalrous* feelings— *Conrad*) (with what *chivalrous* accents would he address . . . those witty and wise women of old worlds—*L. P. Smith*) (she had fainted from weakness and he had felt strangely *chivalrous* and paternal—*Glasgow*) *Ana* complaisant, obliging, *amiable: *gracious, affable, cordial: politic, diplomatic, bland, urbane, *suave *Ant* uncivil, rude —*Con* churlish, boorish, loutish (see under BOOR): ill-mannered, impolite, discourteous, ungracious (see RUDE)

**civilian** *adj* *civic, civil

**civilization,** culture are comparable when meaning the particular state or stage of advancement in which a race, a people, a nation, a specific class, or an integrated group of these finds itself at a given period. **Civilization** always implies a definite advance from a state of barbarism; often it suggests the absence of all signs of barbarism or a divorce from all the ways of living, all the beliefs, all the conditions that distinguish a primitive from a civilized society (the *civilization* of France has been for centuries and is still the central and dominating *civilization* of Europe— *L. P. Smith*) (this mesa had once been like a beehive; it was full of little cliff-hung villages, it had been the home of a powerful tribe, a particular *civilization*—*Cather*) **Culture** (see also CULTURE), on the other hand, suggests rather the complex of attainments, beliefs, customs, and traditions which forms the background of a particular people or group, which distinguishes them from all other peoples or groups, and which gives their particular civilization, no matter how little or how far advanced, its peculiar quality or character (Greece for our purposes means not a race, but a *culture,* a language and literature, and still more an attitude towards life, which for us begins with Homer, and persists, with many changes but no breaks, till the closing of the Athenian lecture rooms by Justinian—*Inge*) (it would no doubt have been more satisfactory to select a people like the Fijians rather than the Lifuans, for they represented a more robust and accomplished form of a rather similar *culture,* but their *culture* has receded into the past— *Ellis*) *Ana* cultivation, *culture, breeding, refinement *Ant* barbarism —*Con* barbarity (see BARBARISM):

---

*Ana* analogous words      *Ant* antonyms      *Con* contrasted words      See also explanatory notes facing page 1

barbarousness, savagery (see corresponding adjectives at BARBARIAN)

**claim** *vb* *demand, exact, require
*Ana* *maintain, assert, defend, vindicate, justify: allege, *adduce, advance
*Ant* disclaim: renounce —*Con* disavow, disown, disacknowledge (see affirmative verbs at ACKNOWLEDGE): reject, repudiate, refuse (see DECLINE *vb*): concede, allow, *grant: waive, cede, *relinquish: *forgo, abnegate

**claim** *n* Claim, title, pretension, pretense are comparable when they denote an actual or alleged right to demand something as one's possession, quality, power, or prerogative. Claim carries the strongest implication of any of these terms of a demand for recognition; only the context can indicate whether that demand is regarded as justifiable or not or whether the right is actually asserted by the person involved ⟨though the house was legally the daughter's, the father, as the one who had paid for it and had taken care of all taxes and insurance, had a moral *claim* to live there the rest of his life⟩ ⟨intelligent persons cannot accept the *claims* made for many patent medicines⟩ ⟨he advanced no *claim* to scholarly knowledge⟩ ⟨searching for truth as against all the *claims* and all the counterclaims of all the partisans—*Lippmann*⟩ ⟨liberty itself became . . . a principle of anarchy rather than a body of *claims* to be read in the context of the social process—*Laski*⟩ Claim also occurs in a more concrete sense as denoting the property or possession for which one sets up a claim ⟨stake out a *claim* in an oil field⟩ Title (see also NAME), on the other hand, distinctively imputes validity or justice to the claim, or its substantiation in law or in reason ⟨his distinguished success as the governor of a great state gives him a *title* to our support of his candidacy for president⟩ ⟨many of the people who masquerade under the name of "men of science" have no sort of *title* to that name—*Ellis*⟩ ⟨they were discussed by men each of whom, in his own way, had some *title* to speak on them—*Sat. Review*⟩ Pretension (see also PRETENSE, AMBITION) is sometimes used in place of *claim* ⟨gifts and excellences to which Wordsworth can make no *pretension*—*Arnold*⟩ and less often, in place of *title* ⟨the courtier, the trader, and the scholar, should all have an equal *pretension* to the denomination of a gentleman—*Steele*⟩ Very often, however, *pretension* connotes a lack of warrant or a weakness in the claim and may attribute to it a measure of hypocrisy or deceit ⟨this court disclaims all *pretensions* to such power—*John Marshall*⟩ ⟨his *pretension*, deftly circulated by press agents, was that he was a man of brilliant and polished mind—*Mencken*⟩ Pretense has become rare in the sense of *claim* (see PRETENSE). Usually the term applies to an asserted claim ⟨Marlborough calmly and politely showed that the *pretense* was unreasonable—*Macaulay*⟩ but it may apply to a claim that is tacitly made in that one is assumed by another to be something that one is not or to have a right that one does not actually possess ⟨she knew that she was in the house under false *pretenses*, for her host and hostess had warmly welcomed her as a daughter of old friends of the same name⟩
*Ana* assertion, affirmation, protestation, declaration (see corresponding verbs at ASSERT): *right, prerogative, birthright, privilege

**clamor** *n* *din, uproar, pandemonium, hullabaloo, babel, hubbub, racket

**clamor** *vb* *roar, bellow, bluster, bawl, vociferate, howl, ululate
*Ana* *shout, yell, scream, shriek, screech, holler: agitate, dispute, debate (see DISCUSS): *demand, claim

**clamorous** *vociferous, blatant, strident, boisterous, obstreperous

*Ana* importuning *or* importunate, begging, imploring, adjuring (see corresponding verbs at BEG): *vocal, articulate, voluble, eloquent: protesting, expostulating, remonstrating (see OBJECT *vb*)
*Ant* taciturn —*Con* *silent, reserved, uncommunicative, close-lipped: *still, noiseless, quiet

**clandestine** *secret, covert, surreptitious, furtive, underhand, underhanded, stealthy
*Ana* concealed, hidden (see HIDE): *sly, artful, foxy: illicit, illegitimate (see affirmative adjectives at LAWFUL)
*Ant* open —*Con* aboveboard, *straightforward, forthright: obvious, manifest, *evident, clear, patent

**clash** *vb* *bump, collide, conflict
*Ana* *contend, fight, battle, war: compete, vie, *rival: *resist, combat, withstand, oppose: disagree, *differ
*Ant* blend

**clash** *n* collision, *impact, impingement, shock, concussion, percussion, jar, jolt
*Ana* conflict, strife, *discord: noise, *sound: incompatibility, incongruousness, discordance (see corresponding adjectives at INCONSONANT)
*Con* concord, accord, consonance, *harmony

**class** *n* Class, category, genus, species, denomination, genre are compared here only in their general, nonspecialized use, and the following comments may be inapplicable to such technical fields as philosophy and the sciences. Class is a very general term for a group including all individuals with a common characteristic ⟨as soon as we employ a name to connote attributes, the things . . . which happen to possess those attributes are constituted ipso facto a *class*—*J. S. Mill*⟩ Class consistently implies division which may involve abstraction of a single group from a greater unclassified mass or the separation of a larger group into discrete subgroups; the basis of such a division may be strictly logical or a mere matter of convenience, and often it involves a value judgment ⟨Hickey is the first *class* of English memoirists—*Times Lit. Sup.*⟩ ⟨the *class* of nominal Christians for whom there might be a chance—*Lovett*⟩ Category may be interchangeable with *class* but is sometimes more precise in suggesting classification or grouping on the basis of a certain readily perceived criterion or on a predication, often an explicit one ⟨we cannot approach a work of art with our laws and *categories*. We have to comprehend the artist's own values—*Ellis*⟩ ⟨none of the writings of the fathers of the English Church belongs to the *category* of speculative philosophy —*T. S. Eliot*⟩ Genus and species, scientific in their suggestion, differ in that the first implies a larger less specific group, the latter a smaller more specific one ⟨English society, in other words, is . . . a *species* of a larger cultural *genus*—*Watnick*⟩ ⟨the word *infringement* is almost never used to describe acts of the *genus*, unfair competition. It is applied only to the *species*, namely trademark misuse—*Pattishall*⟩ Denomination usually indicates that the group under consideration has been or may be named explicitly and clearly; it is common in religious use ⟨Methodist, Presbyterian, and other *denominations*⟩ and use with a series of closely related units ⟨*denominations* of currency⟩ Genre refers to a specific, named type; its use is mainly restricted to literature and art ⟨some of his prose poems, a *genre* . . . which he invented—*Sat. Rev.*⟩ ⟨the larger literary types or *genres*, such as the drama or novel—*Lerner & Mims*⟩
*Ana* division, section (see PART): classification (see corresponding verb at ASSORT): grade, rank, gradation, rating (see corresponding verbs at CLASS)

**class** *vb* Class, grade, rank, rate, graduate, gradate are synonyms in that they all involve the idea of ordering a number of things according to a scale or of placing a thing in

---

A colon (:) separates groups of words discriminated. An asterisk (*) indicates place of treatment of each group.

its due order. **Class** usually presupposes a division of a number of things of the same nature into groups; it implies, therefore, an arranging based upon some such principle as age, advancement, quality, or convenience, and a placing of items within one of the resulting groups ⟨*class* Shakespeare among the greatest dramatists of all time⟩ ⟨men who are *classed* as low in the human scale⟩ ⟨"She has nothing of me that matters," rather inaccurately *classing* under the head of what did not matter, his children, his name, and the right to his bed and board—*Rose Macaulay*⟩ What *class* presupposes, **grade** definitely implies as a fact or a possibility: *grade* also carries a clearer implication of division into groups based on an ascending or descending order (as of quality, merit, advancement, or social status) ⟨*grade* the schools of the state according to certain standards for equipment and teaching⟩ ⟨*grade* oranges according to their size⟩ ⟨we must have instruction *graded* to suit the recipients—*Grandgent*⟩ **Rank** primarily means to arrange in rows or in any serial formation; it, like *class,* presupposes a division, but, more specifically than *class,* it implies a division based upon merit, proved worth, or social standing, and a placing of any one person or type or sometimes thing in its proper place or in order of precedence ⟨the artisan, for example, *ranks* . . . lower than the professional man; but no one maintains that he is . . . incapable by nature . . . of the characteristic excellence of man—*Dickinson*⟩ ⟨the coast road from Egypt to Syria has some claim to *rank* as the most famous of all the roads of history—*Buchan*⟩ ⟨he cannot *rank* Leonardo as an artist higher than Botticelli—*Ellis*⟩ **Rate** (see also ESTIMATE, DESERVE) suggests a determination of the class, or grade, or rank and is used especially of ships and of seamen or ships' officers or of motors or generators with respect to units of power ⟨the ship is *rated* a heavy cruiser⟩ ⟨on board that ship I was *rated* as surgeon—*Besant*⟩ **Graduate** like *grade* implies the existence of an ascending or descending order by which something may be classified or into which it may be fitted; the term, however, stresses rather the existence of differences than an actual division into classes ⟨the hierarchy of officialdom *graduated* like a vast family—*Owen & Eleanor Lattimore*⟩ ⟨the Alhambra possesses retreats *graduated* to the heat of the weather—*Irving*⟩ ⟨specialists whose interest in branches of the law was nicely *graduated*—*Radin*⟩ **Gradate** carries further the trend of *graduate* and implies a changing or passing usually by imperceptible degrees in the direction of either an ascending or a descending scale. The verb is used especially of colors and is less common than the related noun **gradation** which is of far wider application ⟨retiring shades, which *gradate* or go off by degrees—*Hogarth*⟩ ⟨Rembrandt used large areas of delicately *gradated* darks and Veronese large areas of delicately *gradated* lights—*Charles Johnson*⟩ ⟨endless *gradations* in the balance between the denotation of words and their connotation—*Lowes*⟩ ⟨through every *gradation* of increasing tenderness—*Austen*⟩
*Ana* divide, *separate, part: assign, *allot: *distribute

**classify** pigeonhole, *assort, sort
*Ana* *order, arrange, systematize, methodize, marshal

**clause** *paragraph, verse, article, plank, count

**clean** *adj* **Clean, cleanly** are often confused. **Clean** is applied to a person or thing that is actually free from dirt; **cleanly** to a person or animal whose habit or tendency is to be clean; thus, one who is *cleanly,* though not always able to keep *clean,* will never remain dirty by choice ⟨an ant is a very *cleanly* insect—*Addison*⟩
*Ana* cleaned, cleansed (see CLEAN *vb*): pure, decent, *chaste
*Ant* dirty  —*Con* filthy, foul, nasty, squalid (see DIRTY)

**clean** *vb* **Clean, cleanse** mean to remove whatever soils, stains, or contaminates from someone or something. **Clean** is the word in common and literal use for the removal of foreign matter (as dirt, litter, and debris) typically by washing, sweeping, dusting, or clearing away ⟨*clean* a dress⟩ ⟨*clean* a room⟩ ⟨*clean* off a table⟩ **Cleanse** in this relation seldom wholly loses some hint of its basic notion of making morally or spiritually pure; it is, therefore, the term of choice when the matter to be removed is or is felt as foul, polluting, or noxious or the action is rather one of purifying than of merely restoring to order, freshness, or neatness; thus, one would *clean* a house but, more often, *cleanse* a sickroom; one would *cleanse* a wound but *clean* one's teeth ⟨*cleanse* the bowels with a laxative⟩ Unlike *clean, cleanse* is common in essentially metaphoric extension in which it always retains the suggestion of removing what is vile, harmful, or obnoxious ⟨the brilliant campaign which *cleansed* Havana from yellow fever—*S. H. Adams*⟩ ⟨young soldiers who are now being *cleansed* of subversive ideas at Valley Forge Army Hospital—*D. H. Gillis*⟩ ⟨take part in an attempt to *cleanse* the public life of the country—*Ewer*⟩ ⟨the air was purer for the *cleansing* rain—*Macdonald*⟩
*Ant* soil

**cleanly** *adj* *clean
*Ana* spick-and-span, *neat, tidy, trim, snug: *orderly: dainty, fastidious, fussy, *nice
*Ant* uncleanly  —*Con* slovenly, unkempt, disheveled, sloppy, *slipshod

**cleanse** *clean
*Ana* *sterilize, disinfect, sanitize
*Ant* defile, besmirch

**clear** *adj* **1** **Clear, transparent, translucent, lucid, pellucid, diaphanous, limpid** are comparable when they mean having the property of being literally or figuratively seen through. Something is **clear** which is free from all such impediments to the vision as clouds, mist, or haze ⟨*clear* air⟩ ⟨a *clear* day⟩ or from muddiness, cloudiness, or turbidity ⟨*clear* glass⟩ ⟨*clear* crystals⟩ ⟨the launch moved slowly through water *clear* as air—*Nordhoff & Hall*⟩ or from obscurity, vagueness, or indistinctness of any sort ⟨*clear* thinking⟩ ⟨a *clear* mind⟩ ⟨a *clear* style⟩ ⟨a *clear* vision of reality—*Conrad*⟩ Something is **transparent** which is either so clear or so thin that objects can be easily seen or perceived through it ⟨the water . . . is as *transparent* as the air, so that the stones and sand at the bottom seem, as it were, trembling in the light of noonday—*Shelley*⟩ ⟨*transparent* gauze⟩ ⟨guavas, with the shadows of their crimson pulp flushing through a *transparent* skin—*Melville*⟩ ⟨rushing away from the discussion on the *transparent* pretense of quieting the dog—*Conrad*⟩ ⟨his writings . . . are so flat, so *transparent,* so palpably taken from the nearest authorities—*H. O. Taylor*⟩ Something is **translucent** which admits the passage of light through it but which does not permit a clear sight of what lies beyond ⟨frosted glass is *translucent*⟩ ⟨under the glassy, cool, *translucent* wave—*Milton*⟩ ⟨*translucent* amber that cages flies—*Wylie*⟩ ⟨*translucent* phrases, which mirror . . . the woodland lights and shadows—*L. P. Smith*⟩ Something is **lucid** (see CLEAR 2) which is both transparent and luminous; this use is chiefly literary ⟨gods, who haunt the *lucid* interspace of world and world where never creeps a cloud, or moves a wind—*Tennyson*⟩ ⟨the thought may be obscure, but the word is *lucid,* or rather translucent—*T. S. Eliot*⟩ Something is **pellucid** which is clear as crystal ⟨more *pellucid* streams, an ampler ether, a diviner air—*Wordsworth*⟩ ⟨[Goldsmith's] *pellucid* simplicity—*Harrison*⟩ Something is **diaphanous** which is so delicate and gossamerlike in texture that it is almost transparent or is actually translucent

⟨a *diaphanous* veil⟩ ⟨I like *diaphanous* illusions, with the shapes of things as they are showing not too faintly through them—*L. P. Smith*⟩ Something is **limpid** which has the soft clearness of or as if of pure water ⟨the whole atmosphere has a luminous serenity, a *limpid* clearness—*Ward*⟩ ⟨that . . . simple, *limpid* style which is the supreme style of all—*Arnold*⟩ ⟨Archer's New York . . . in business matters . . . exacted a *limpid* and impeccable honesty —*Wharton*⟩

*Ana* *bright, luminous: *liquid: *pure, sheer
*Ant* turbid: confused —*Con* dim, obscure, murky, dusky, gloomy (see DARK): muddy, roily (see TURBID): muddled, addled, fuddled, befuddled (see CONFUSE)

**2 Clear, perspicuous, lucid** are comparable, as used in reference to qualities of thought or style with the meaning, quickly and easily understood. **Clear** implies freedom from obscurity, ambiguity, or the danger of being misunderstood ⟨"many are called," there is a *clear* truth: "few are chosen," there is an obscure truth—*Arnold*⟩ ⟨there are more obscure poems written and printed every year than *clear* ones—*R. B. West*⟩ **Perspicuous** lays more stress than *clear* upon the medium of expression regarded for itself; it frequently connotes a certain simplicity and elegance of style ⟨extreme conciseness of expression, yet pure, *perspicuous,* and musical, is one of the grand beauties of lyric poetry—*Gray*⟩ ⟨the ode is not wholly *perspicuous.* Wordsworth himself seems to have thought it difficult—*Trilling*⟩ **Lucid** especially implies clearness of order or arrangement ⟨he thought little of recasting a chapter in order to obtain a more *lucid* arrangement— *G. O. Trevelyan*⟩ ⟨his descriptions of the most complicated organic structures are astonishingly *lucid*—*Huxley*⟩
*Ana* express, *explicit, definite: *graphic, vivid: clearcut, *incisive, trenchant
*Ant* unintelligible: abstruse —*Con* vague, *obscure, ambiguous, equivocal, cryptic, enigmatic: turgid, tumid (see INFLATED): *recondite, occult, esoteric
**3** manifest, *evident, obvious, distinct, apparent, patent, palpable, plain
*Con* *doubtful, dubious, questionable, problematic

**clear** *vb* *rid, unburden, disabuse, purge
*Ana* *free, release, liberate, deliver: *clean, cleanse: eliminate, rule out (see EXCLUDE)

**clearance** *room, berth, play, elbowroom, leeway, margin

**clear-cut** trenchant, *incisive, cutting, biting, crisp
*Ana* distinct, plain, clear, manifest, *evident: definite, *explicit, express: precise, exact, nice (see CORRECT)
*Con* confused, muddled (see CONFUSE): hazy, misty, fogged (see corresponding nouns at HAZE)

**cleave** cling, *stick, adhere, cohere
*Ana* *fasten, attach, fix, affix: unite, *join, associate, link, combine, conjoin
*Ant* part —*Con* *separate, divorce, divide, sever, sunder: *detach, disengage: *estrange, alienate

**cleave** split, rive, rend, *tear, rip
*Ana* *separate, divide, sever, sunder, part, divorce: *cut, hew, chop, slit
*Con* *join, unite, link: attach, *fasten

**cleft** *n* *crack, fissure, crevasse, crevice, cranny, chink
*Ana* split, rift, *breach: gap, *break, interruption

**clemency 1** lenity, *mercy, charity, grace
*Ana* compassion, pity, commiseration, *sympathy, ruth: gentleness, mildness (see corresponding adjectives at SOFT): fairness, equitableness, justness (see corresponding adjectives at FAIR)
*Ant* harshness —*Con* severity, sternness, austerity (see corresponding adjectives at SEVERE): rigorousness, strictness, rigidity (see corresponding adjectives at RIGID):

inflexibility, obduracy, inexorableness (see corresponding adjectives at INFLEXIBLE)
**2** mercifulness, leniency, indulgence, forbearance, tolerance (see under FORBEARING)
*Ana, Ant, & Con* see CLEMENCY 1

**clement** merciful, lenient, indulgent, *forbearing, tolerant
*Ana* compassionate, *tender, sympathetic: benign, benignant, kindly, *kind: humane, benevolent, *charitable
*Ant* harsh: barbarous —*Con* *severe, stern, austere: *rigid, rigorous, strict, stringent: implacable, merciless, relentless, unrelenting, *grim

**clemently** forbearingly, tolerantly, mercifully, leniently, indulgently (see under FORBEARING)

**clever 1** *intelligent, quick-witted, brilliant, bright, smart, alert, knowing
*Ana* *quick, apt, ready, prompt: *versatile, all-around, many-sided: capable, competent, *able: *sharp, keen, acute
*Ant* dull —*Con* *stupid, slow, dense, crass: *simple, foolish, fatuous, asinine
**2 Clever, adroit, cunning, ingenious** are comparable when they mean having or showing a high degree of practical intelligence or of skill in contrivance. **Clever** often carries an implication of physical dexterity but it usually stresses mental quickness or resourcefulness ⟨I became so *clever* with the gloves that Ned matched me against a lightweight—*Shaw*⟩ ⟨but Jane's mother had been too *clever* for him. . . . she had come to the dinner table primed to do just that thing—*Mary Austin*⟩ ⟨his judgments were wise rather than *clever,* his appreciations scholarly rather than sophisticated—*Hilton*⟩ ⟨Lowell was too *clever* to be sound—*Brooks*⟩ Sometimes it suggests a native aptitude or knack ⟨a dull fellow but very *clever* with horses⟩ **Adroit** usually suggests greater shrewdness and astuteness than *clever* and often implies the skillful (sometimes the crafty) use of expedients to attain one's ends in the face of difficulties ⟨the *adroit* William Penn . . . found means to stand well at the court of the persecuting James the Second—*Montague*⟩ ⟨one of the most *adroit* technicians ever to have employed the English language—*J. M. Brown*⟩ **Cunning** (see also SLY) may retain its older implications of learning and expert knowledge and is then chiefly applied to craftsmen or artists whose work exhibits a high degree of constructive or creative skill ⟨gnomes and brownies: the *cunning* little people who know how to use the bellows, the forge, the hammer, and the anvil—*Mumford*⟩ ⟨he knew how . . . to construct a plot, he was *cunning* in his manipulation of stage effects —*T. S. Eliot*⟩ **Ingenious** stresses inventive power or skill in discovery; sometimes it implies brilliancy of mind, sometimes little more than cleverness ⟨powerful and *ingenious* minds . . . may, by a course of . . . refined and metaphysical reasoning . . . explain away the constitution of our country—*John Marshall*⟩ ⟨this *ingenious* Yankee, quick to adapt himself everywhere, easily extricating himself from situations—*Josephson*⟩
*Ana* *dexterous, deft, handy: nimble, *agile: *proficient, skillful, skilled, adept, expert, masterly
*Con* inept, maladroit, *awkward, clumsy, gauche: *slow, laggard, dilatory

**cliché** platitude, truism, *commonplace, bromide

**clientele** *following, public, audience

**climax** *n* culmination, peak, apex, acme, zenith, apogee, *summit, pinnacle, meridian

**climb** *vb* *ascend, mount, scale
*Ant* descend

**cling** cleave, *stick, adhere, cohere
*Ana* depend, *rely, trust, count, bank, reckon: attach, affix, *fasten: *hang, dangle, suspend

---

A colon (:) separates groups of words discriminated. An asterisk (*) indicates place of treatment of each group.

*Con* desert, forsake, *abandon: *relinquish, leave, resign, yield

**clinkers** cinders, *ash, embers

**clip** *vb* *shear, poll, trim, prune, lop, snip, crop
*Ana* *cut, chop, slash, slit: curtail (see SHORTEN): sever, *separate

**clique** *set, circle, coterie
*Ana* party, faction, bloc, ring, combine, *combination

**cloak** *vb* mask, *disguise, dissemble, camouflage
*Ana* conceal, *hide, screen
*Ant* uncloak —*Con* *reveal, disclose, discover, betray

**clodhopper** bumpkin, hick, yokel, rube, *boor, lout, clown, churl

**clog** *vb* fetter, hog-tie, shackle, manacle, *hamper, trammel
*Ana* impede, obstruct, *hinder, block: balk, baffle, *frustrate: check, curb (see RESTRAIN)
*Ant* expedite, facilitate —*Con* *free, liberate, release: forward, further, *advance, promote

**cloister** *n* 1 Cloister, convent, monastery, nunnery, abbey, priory. *Cloister* and *convent* are general terms denoting a place of retirement from the world for members of a religious community; they may apply to houses for recluses of either sex. In such use **cloister** stresses the idea of seclusion from the world; **convent**, of community of living. Basically a **monastery** is a cloister for monks; in actual use it is often applied to a convent for men or occasionally for women who combine the cloistered life with teaching, preaching, or other work. **Nunnery**, which specifically denotes a cloister for nuns, is often displaced by *convent* with the same specific meaning. A monastery or nunnery governed by an abbot or an abbess is called an **abbey**; by a prior or prioress, a **priory**. A priory is subordinate in rank to, but often independent of, an abbey.
2 arcade, *passage, passageway, ambulatory, gallery, corridor, aisle, hall, hallway

**clone** *variety, subspecies, race, breed, cultivar, strain, stock

**close** *vb* 1 Close, shut are very close synonyms in the sense of to stop or fill in an opening by means of a closure (as a door, a gate, a lid, or a cover) and are often used interchangeably. However, they may have distinctive nuances of meaning and quite different implications in idiomatic use. **Close** is the more general term, usually implying both the act of stopping an opening and the result produced by such an act but stressing exclusion of those who would enter or pass through. **Shut** stresses the act or process and the means employed in this process; it not only carries a more emphatic implication or a more vivid suggestion of drawing a door, gate, lid, or window into a position which closes the opening, but it often also evokes an image of fastening securely (as by drawing a bar or a bolt or locking); hence, in *closing* a door or gate one merely draws it into a position which bars entrance or egress until it is again opened but in *shutting* a door or gate one pushes or pulls it into the position where it is closed. Idiomatically, one *closes* (not *shuts*) an opening or a gap or one *closes* (not *shuts*) a park or a church to the public, because in neither case is the use of a door, gate, or other means of exclusion clearly or definitely implied. On the other hand, in idiomatic use *shut*, especially when followed by *up, out,* or *against,* carries a stronger and often a more direct and emphatic suggestion than *close* of the interposition of a barrier or obstacle (often an immaterial one) that effectually prevents ingress or egress ⟨he found every road to the accomplishment of his desires *shut* against him⟩ ⟨he *shut* his eyes to everything he did not wish to see⟩ ⟨*closed* his

eyes in death⟩ ⟨he was warned to *shut* his mouth⟩
*Ana* *exclude, debar: block, bar, dam (see HINDER)
*Ant* open
2 Close, end, conclude, finish, complete, terminate are comparable as transitive verbs meaning to bring something to a stopping point or to its limit, or, with the exception of *complete,* as intransitive verbs meaning to come to that point. **Close** usually has latent in it the idea of action upon something which may be regarded as in some sense *open* as well as unfinished (see CLOSE *vb* 1) ⟨*close* an account, a debate, or a subscription list⟩ ⟨recall those nights that *closed* thy toilsome days— *Pope*⟩ ⟨the Peace of Westphalia . . . which *closed* the Thirty Years' War—*Barr*⟩ **End** conveys a stronger sense of finality; it frequently has implicit reference to a progress or development which is thought of as having been carried through ⟨the harvest is past, the summer is *ended,* and we are not saved—*Jer 8:20*⟩ ⟨*ended* his life⟩ ⟨*ended* his labors upon a book⟩ **Conclude** is a more formal term and applies particularly to transactions, proceedings, or writings that have a formal or special close ⟨*concluded* his speech with a peroration⟩ ⟨*conclude* a meeting with a benediction⟩ ⟨I shall *conclude* this essay upon laughter with observing that the metaphor of laughing . . . runs through all languages—*Spectator*⟩ **Finish** implies that what one set out to do is done; often, therefore, it connotes the completion of the final act in a process of elaboration (as polishing or perfecting) ⟨gave the festive table a *finishing* touch⟩ ⟨I have *finished* the work which thou gavest me to do—*Jn 17:4*⟩ ⟨it wants but seventeen lines of having an end, I don't say of being *finished*— *Gray*⟩ ⟨I shall *finish* with a Chopin nocturne—*Hellman*⟩ **Complete** implies the removal of all deficiencies or a finishing of all that has been attempted ⟨when Blondel paused about the middle, the king began the remainder, and *completed* it—*Warton*⟩ ⟨*complete* their education in Europe⟩ ⟨art partly *completes* what nature is herself sometimes unable to bring to perfection—*Ellis*⟩ ⟨he may well have thought that his days would be few on earth, and that it would be foolish to put his hand to a task which he could not *complete*—*Buchan*⟩ **Terminate** implies the setting of a limit in time or space ⟨Ben Lomond *terminates* the view —*Dorothy Wordsworth*⟩ ⟨the age at which the youth of each nation *terminates* full-time education—*Conant*⟩ ⟨he had never seen the instrument that was to *terminate* his life—*Dickens*⟩ ⟨hostilities *terminate* at sundown⟩
*Ana* *stop, cease, quit, desist
*Con* *begin, commence, start, inaugurate, initiate

**close** *adj* 1 Close, near, nigh, nearby are comparable both as adjectives and as adverbs when they mean not far (as in place, time, or relationship) from the point, position, or relation that is indicated or understood. **Close** (see also CLOSE *adj* 2) commonly implies so slight a difference that the two things (sometimes persons) under consideration may be said to be almost in contact if the difference is in distance or almost coincident if the difference is in time, to be of the immediate family if the difference is in relationship, or to be very like the original if the difference is in a copy ⟨the houses on this street are *close* together⟩ ⟨*close* relatives⟩ ⟨*close* friends⟩ ⟨hold one *close*⟩ ⟨the more accurately we use words the *closer* definition we shall give to our thoughts—*Quiller-Couch*⟩ ⟨a *close* shave⟩ ⟨give *close* attention to a problem⟩ ⟨a *close* translation of a passage⟩ **Near** may often be used in place of *close* ⟨events that come *near* to each other⟩ ⟨*near* relatives⟩ but it carries a much less explicit suggestion of contiguousness or adjacency and may be used of persons or things that, though not far off (as in place, time, or relationship) are not almost in contact, almost coincident, or of the immediate family ⟨come *near* where I can see you⟩ ⟨a *near* concern of all of us⟩ *Near* also is applied to things reproduced (as by copying, imitating, or translating) that more or less closely resemble but are far from replicas of the original; in this sense the term is often used in depreciation ⟨*near* beer⟩ ⟨a *near* translation⟩ ⟨*near* silk⟩ ⟨*near*-leather upholstery⟩ **Nigh** is somewhat outmoded or poetic in the sense of *near*. As an adverb it, even more often than *near*, is followed by *to, unto, about, on, upon* ⟨he was sick *nigh* unto death—*Phil* 2:27⟩ ⟨now the day is over, night is drawing *nigh*—*Baring-Gould*⟩ As an adjective it differs little from *near* except in sometimes being given preference in the comparative and superlative degrees to *nearer* and *nearest* ⟨friend, brother, *nighest* neighbor—*Whitman*⟩ **Nearby** indicates a position near in distance or close at hand ⟨*nearby* towns⟩ ⟨the *nearby* houses⟩ ⟨there is no hotel *nearby*⟩

*Ana* adjoining, *adjacent, contiguous, abutting: *related, kindred

*Ant* remote *or* remotely —*Con* *distant, removed, far, faraway, far-off

**2 Close, dense, compact, thick** are comparable when they mean having constituent parts (as filaments, particles, cells, or atoms) that are massed tightly together. **Close** may apply to the texture or weave of something ⟨between the *close* moss violet-inwoven—*Shelley*⟩ ⟨a paper of fine, *close* texture⟩ ⟨a cloth of *close* weave⟩ More often, however, the term applies to something that is made up of a number of single things pressed or seemingly pressed together ⟨he writes a *close* hand⟩ ⟨the troops fought in *close* formation⟩ Especially as applied to literary expression, *close* implies a compression of what is to be said into the fewest and most telling words possible ⟨it is a relief to turn back to the austere, *close* language of *Everyman*—*T. S. Eliot*⟩ **Dense** applies to something in which the arrangement of parts or units is exceedingly close ⟨*dense* clouds⟩ ⟨a *densely* populated district⟩ ⟨a *dense.* star⟩ ⟨a *dense* flower spike⟩ The term commonly implies impenetrability ⟨a *dense* thicket⟩ and in extended use may lose the basic notion of close packing of parts ⟨a *dense* mind⟩ ⟨*dense* stupidity⟩ ⟨*dense* silence⟩ ⟨Proust's book is a gigantic *dense* mesh of complicated relations—*Edmund Wilson*⟩ **Compact** suggests close and firm union or consolidation of parts, especially within a small compass; it often also implies neat or effective arrangement ⟨he was all *compact* and under his swart, tattooed skin the muscles worked like steel rods—*Melville*⟩ ⟨small, *compact,* homogeneous communities such as the Greek city state or Elizabethan England—*Day Lewis*⟩ **Thick** (see also STOCKY) usually applies to something which is condensed or is made up of abundant and concentrated parts ⟨make the gruel *thick* and slab—*Shak.*⟩ ⟨a *thick* swarm of bees⟩ ⟨a *thick* grove⟩ ⟨a *thick* head of hair⟩

*Ana* compressed, condensed, constricted (see CONTRACT *vb*): concentrated, compacted (see COMPACT *vb*)

*Ant* open —*Con* scattered, dispersed (see SCATTER): expanded (see EXPAND)

**3** close-lipped, closemouthed, tight-lipped, secretive, reserved, taciturn, reticent, uncommunicative, *silent

*Ant* open (see FRANK) —*Con* *frank, candid, plain: garrulous, loquacious, *talkative, voluble, glib

**4** intimate, confidential, chummy, thick, *familiar

*Ant* aloof

**5** closefisted, tight, tightfisted, niggardly, parsimonious, penurious, *stingy, cheeseparing, penny-pinching

*Ana* *sparing, economical, frugal, thrifty

*Ant* liberal —*Con* generous, bountiful, bounteous, openhanded (see LIBERAL): lavish, prodigal (see PROFUSE)

**closefisted** *stingy, close, tight, tightfisted, niggardly,

parsimonious, penurious, miserly, cheeseparing, penny-pinching

*Ana, Ant, & Con* see those at CLOSE *adj* 5

**close-lipped** close, closemouthed, uncommunicative, taciturn, reserved, reticent, secretive, *silent, tight-lipped

*Ant & Con* see those at CLOSE *adj* 3

**closemouthed** close, close-lipped, tight-lipped, reticent, reserved, uncommunicative, *silent, taciturn, secretive

*Ant & Con* see those at CLOSE *adj* 3

**clot** *vb* congeal, curdle, *coagulate, set, jelly, jell

**clothe, attire, dress, apparel, array, robe. Clothe,** the least specific of these terms, means to cover or to provide what will cover (one's body or whatever is bare) with or as if with garments ⟨*clothe* the child warmly⟩ ⟨*clothe* your thoughts in words⟩ ⟨rugged hills *clothed* and softened with snow⟩ The other words convey the same meaning but each one adds to it distinctive implications and connotations. **Attire** suggests a more careful process and more formality than *clothe* and therefore is avoided except when the context requires that note ⟨he said it was for the honor of the Service that he *attired* himself so elaborately; but those who knew him best said that it was just personal vanity—*Kipling*⟩ **Dress** is far less formal than *attire* and much richer in its connotations than *clothe*. It often suggests care in the choice and arrangement of clothes and sometimes, especially in *dress up,* preening and prinking or selection of one's best or choicest clothes ⟨children warmly but simply *dressed* for school⟩ ⟨every afternoon she *dresses up* and goes out⟩ ⟨*dressed up* in his Sunday clothes⟩ *Dress up* sometimes distinctively implies an assuming of the dress of or a dress suitable to another ⟨*dress up* as Cleopatra⟩ while *dress,* especially in its intransitive or reflexive forms, often implies a change of clothes to those that are appropriate for a special occasion; thus, to *dress* for dinner implies a change into dinner or evening clothes ⟨I shall not have time to *dress*⟩ The idea of decking or adorning is frequently associated with *dress* especially in its extended senses ⟨*dress* the hair with flowers⟩ ⟨*dress* the table for an elaborate dinner⟩ ⟨yet shall thy grave with rising flow'rs be *dressed*—*Pope*⟩ **Apparel** and **array** are chiefly literary words used when there is the intent to connote splendor, elegance, or gorgeousness in what a person or thing is clothed with ⟨she had a garment of divers colors upon her: for with such robes were the king's daughters . . . *appareled*—*2 Sam* 13:18⟩ ⟨a time when meadow, grove, and stream . . . to me did seem *appareled* in celestial light —*Wordsworth*⟩ ⟨consider the lilies of the field, how they grow; they toil not, neither do they spin: and yet I say unto you, that even Solomon in all his glory was not *arrayed* like one of these—*Mt* 6:28, 29⟩ ⟨I rode with him to court, and there the Queen *arrayed* me like the sun —*Tennyson*⟩ **Robe** implies a dressing with or as if with a robe and has the same wide range of use as the noun but it typically suggests the enveloping apparel worn by a king, queen, or noble on state occasions, by a judge or a professor when the conventions of his office demand it, or by a bishop or other high ecclesiastic when formally but not liturgically attired ⟨helped to *robe* him . . . in a quilted robe of scarlet silk—*Waln*⟩ ⟨love *robed* her in a blush—*Lynch*⟩

*Ant* unclothe —*Con* *strip, divest, dismantle

**clothes, clothing, dress, attire, apparel, raiment** are comparable when they denote a person's garments considered collectively. **Clothes** and **clothing** are general words which do not necessarily suggest a wearer or personal owner but sometimes a manufacturer or a merchant ⟨evening *clothes*⟩ ⟨summer *clothing* for men⟩ ⟨her *clothes* are always immaculate⟩ ⟨each child has ample *clothing*⟩

A colon (:) separates groups of words discriminated. An asterisk (*) indicates place of treatment of each group.

**Dress** is used with reference only to a wearer's outer clothes; it is not only far less inclusive than *clothes* and *clothing* but less concrete in its suggestions except when qualified ⟨both men and women are expected to wear full *dress*⟩ ⟨the actors will be costumed in the *dress* of the period⟩ ⟨a man of sense carefully avoids any particular character in his *dress*—*Chesterfield*⟩ ⟨in pilgrimage *dress* on his way to Mecca—*Doty*⟩ **Attire** usually stresses the appearance or the total impression produced by one's clothes; it is therefore rarely used with reference to one's own clothes except in affectation or humorously; when applied to another person's, it is as a rule qualified ⟨our speech, our color, and our strange *attire*—*Pope*⟩ ⟨his unfashionable *attire* and clumsy manners—*Cole*⟩ **Apparel** (often specifically *wearing apparel*) carries a weaker suggestion of the effect produced and a stronger implication of a collection or assemblage of clothes than *attire*, which otherwise it closely resembles in meaning; therefore one says an article of *apparel* (rather than *attire*) and the richness of her *attire* (rather than *apparel*) ⟨a blue serge suit, a grey shirt, a blue and red necktie, a gray homburg, and black shoes and gloves comprised his *apparel*⟩ ⟨the *apparel* oft proclaims the man—*Shak.*⟩ ⟨his daily *apparel* was rough and shabby—*Cather*⟩ **Raiment** is a more or less literary term that is nearly as comprehensive as *clothes*, for it includes everything that is worn for decency, comfort, and adornment and therefore suggests reference to undergarments as well as to outer garments ⟨brought a change of *raiment* with him⟩ When the quality or the texture of the clothing is to be indicated, *raiment* is the appropriate word ⟨fine *raiment*⟩ ⟨the coarse *raiment* of a penitent pilgrim⟩ ⟨but what went ye out for to see? A man clothed in soft *raiment*? behold, they ,that wear soft clothing are in kings' houses—*Mt* 11:8⟩ ⟨if these strangers were of important air and costly *raiment*—*O'Nolan*⟩

**clothing** *clothes, dress, attire, apparel, raiment

**cloud** *vb* *obscure, dim, bedim, darken, eclipse, becloud, fog, befog, obfuscate
*Ana* *confuse, muddle, addle, befuddle: *puzzle, perplex, distract

**clout** *vb* *strike, hit, smite, punch, slug, slog, swat, slap, cuff, box
*Ana* *beat, pummel, thrash, baste, belabor

**clown** *boor, clodhopper, lout, bumpkin, hick, yokel, rube, churl
*Ana* simpleton, natural (see FOOL)

**clownish** loutish, boorish, churlish (see under BOOR)
*Ana* *awkward, clumsy, gauche: *rude, rough, raw, green, uncouth
*Ant* urbane  —*Con* *suave, bland, smooth, polite

**cloy** *vb* *satiate, sate, surfeit, pall, glut, gorge
*Ant* whet  —*Con* stimulate, pique, excite, *provoke

**club** society, *association, order

**clumsy** *awkward, gauche, maladroit, inept
*Ana* *rude, rough, green, callow, uncouth: loutish, clownish, boorish (see under BOOR): *stiff, wooden, tense, rigid
*Ant* dexterous, adroit: facile  —*Con* deft (see DEXTEROUS): graceful, dignified, elegant (see corresponding nouns at ELEGANCE): *elastic, resilient, flexible, supple, springy: *easy, effortless, smooth

**cluster** *n* *group, bunch, parcel, lot
*Ana* collection, assemblage (see under GATHER): aggregate, number, quantity (see SUM)

**clutch** *vb* grasp, grab, *take, seize, snatch
*Ana* capture, *catch: hold, *have, possess, own

**clutch** *n* *hold, grip, grasp
*Ana* seizing, grabbing, taking (see TAKE)

**clutter** *n* *confusion, disorder, disarray, jumble, chaos, muddle, snarl

**coadjutor** *assistant, helper, aid, aide, aide-de-camp

**coagulate,** congeal, set, curdle, clot, jelly, jell are comparable when meaning to form or cause to form a stiff mass that is solid or at least cohesive. **Coagulate** implies a thickening or solidification of a liquid and usually the making insoluble (as by chemical reaction) of something that was soluble ⟨fresh blood exposed to air rapidly *coagulates*⟩ ⟨heat *coagulates* the white of egg⟩ ⟨waterborne impurities which *coagulate* when aluminum sulfate is added can be removed by filtration⟩ **Congeal** specifically implies a thickening or solidification by means of cold; the mass thus affected may dissolve or become liquid when the temperature rises again ⟨freezing temperatures have *congealed* the surface waters of the river⟩ ⟨here no hungry winter *congeals* our blood—*Longfellow*⟩ **Set** (see also SET) carries no implication of how the stiffening, or making solid or viscid, occurs but only of the nature of the effect ⟨rennet may be used in *setting* milk for cheese⟩ ⟨give the jelly time to *set* before adding a paraffin cover⟩ **Curdle** basically implies the coagulation of milk (as through souring or the addition of rennet) into a soft but solid part (the curd) from which cheese is made, and the separation of this part from the watery part (the whey); in more general use the term connotes a thickening and sometimes a souring ⟨Mark Twain was expressing his true opinions, the opinions of the cynic he had become owing to . . . the constant *curdling* as it were of the poet in him—*Brooks*⟩ ⟨envy soon *curdles* into hate—*Froude*⟩ **Clot** implies the coagulation or congealing of a liquid into lumps or masses or, less often, the gathering of something light and diffuse into hard accumulations or lumps ⟨the blood not yet had *clotted* on his wound—*Southey*⟩ ⟨*clotted* cream⟩ ⟨the bed becomes uneasy by the feathers *clotting* together into hard knobs—*Tucker*⟩ **Jelly** specifically implies the setting during cooling of a cooked liquid (as broth or juice of meats) containing gelatin from animal tissue or one (as fruit juice and sugar) containing the pectin of acid fruits ⟨the *jellied* juice of the veal roast⟩ ⟨jellies and marmalades *jelly* readily if pectin is added to the boiling juice⟩ **Jell** is basically identical with *jelly* ⟨the jelly won't *jell*—*Alcott*⟩ but unlike the latter it is often used especially in negative constructions to imply the state when nonmaterial things (as ideas or plans) attain fixity or cohesiveness ⟨public opinion has not yet *jelled* on this question⟩ ⟨his ideas for the story would not *jell*, no matter how much he kept turning them over in his mind⟩
*Ana* solidify, *harden: cohere, *stick: coalesce, fuse, blend (see MIX): concentrate, consolidate, *compact

**coalesce** merge, fuse, blend, mingle, commingle, *mix, amalgamate
*Ana* *compact, consolidate, concentrate, unify: *contract, condense, compress: cohere, adhere, *stick, cleave, cling: mass (see HEAP)
*Con* disintegrate, crumble, decompose (see DECAY): *separate, part, divide: deliquesce (see LIQUEFY): dissipate, disperse (see SCATTER)

**coalition** fusion, confederacy, confederation, federation, *alliance, league

**coarse,** vulgar, gross, obscene, ribald are comparable when applied to persons, their language, or behavior and mean offensive to a person of good taste or moral principles. **Coarse** is opposed to *fine* not only with reference to material things (as fiber, texture, or structure) but also with reference to quality of mind, spirit, manners, or words; it implies roughness, rudeness, crudeness, or insensitivity ⟨whose laughs are hearty, though his jests are coarse—*Pope*⟩ ⟨simple parables of the *coarse* business-man and the sensitive intellectual—*De Voto*⟩ ⟨some of the royal family were as *coarse* as the king was delicate in manners—*Henry Adams*⟩ **Vulgar** (see COMMON 3) suggests something that is offensive to good taste or decency, frequently with the added implication of boorishness or ill breeding ⟨Caliban is coarse enough, but surely he is not *vulgar*—*Hazlitt*⟩ ⟨Burns is often coarse, but never *vulgar*—*Byron*⟩ ⟨it was, in fact, the mouth that gave his face its sensual, sly, and ugly look, for a loose and *vulgar* smile seemed constantly to hover about its thick coarse edges—*Wolfe*⟩ **Gross** (see FLAGRANT) is opposed to *fine* in the sense of delicate, subtle, ethereal; it implies either a material, as contrasted to a spiritual, quality or a bestiality unworthy of man ⟨the *grosser* forms of pleasure—*Wharton*⟩ ⟨*gross* habits of eating⟩ ⟨Caliban . . . is all earth, all condensed and *gross* in feelings and images—*Coleridge*⟩ ⟨my anger and disgust at his *gross* earthy egoism had vanished—*Hudson*⟩ **Obscene** stresses more strongly the idea of loathsome indecency or utter obnoxiousness ⟨the war to him was a hateful thing . . . waged for the extension of the *obscene* system of Negro slavery—*Parrington*⟩ ⟨an *obscene* allusion⟩ ⟨the jest unclean of linkboys vile, and watermen *obscene*—*Pope*⟩ ⟨the rabble of Comus . . . reeling in *obscene* dances—*Macaulay*⟩ ⟨it was, of course, easy to pick out a line here and there . . . which was frank to indecency, yet certainly not *obscene*—*Canby*⟩ **Ribald** suggests vulgarity and often such impropriety or indecency as provokes the laughter of people who are not too fastidious ⟨a *ribald* folksong about fleas in straw—*Lowes*⟩ ⟨their backs . . . shaking with the loose laughter which punctuates a *ribald* description—*Mary Austin*⟩ ⟨we stare aghast, as in the presence of some great dignitary from behind whom, by a *ribald* hand, a chair is withdrawn when he is in the act of sitting down—*Beerbohm*⟩ *Ana* rough, crude, *rude, raw, green, callow, uncouth: *rank, rampant: boorish, loutish, clownish (see under BOOR) *Ant* fine: refined —*Con* delicate, dainty, exquisite, *choice: cultivated, cultured (see corresponding nouns at CULTURE)

**coast** *n* *shore, strand, beach, bank, foreshore, littoral

**coast** *vb* toboggan, *slide, glide, slip, skid, glissade, slither

**coax, cajole, wheedle, blandish** mean to use ingratiating art in persuading or attempting to persuade. **Coax** implies gentle, persistent efforts to induce another or to draw what is desired out of another ⟨in a *coaxing* voice, suited to a nurse soothing a baby—*Burney*⟩ It most often suggests artful pleading or teasing in an attempt to gain one's ends ⟨little by little, he *coaxed* some of the men whom the measure concerned most intimately to give in their views—*Kipling*⟩ ⟨one . . . who can linger over and taste a phrase, *coaxing* its flavor to the palate as if it were an old wine—*Moody*⟩ ⟨his skill in *coaxing* . . . the attention of the variable human mind to divine objects—*T. S. Eliot*⟩ but it may be extended to other situations in which persevering yet careful efforts are used to attain an end ⟨*coax* embers into a blaze⟩ **Cajole** may stress deceit (as by flattering or making specious promises) ⟨they . . . should be treated as they themselves treat fools, this is, be *cajoled* with praises—*Pope*⟩ It more often implies enticing or alluring and suggests beguilement rather than duplicity ⟨I think a vein of sentiment . . . induced me to take the journey, and to *cajole* a reluctant friend into accompanying me—*Repplier*⟩ **Wheedle** suggests more strongly than *cajole* the use of soft words, artful flattery, or seductive appeal ⟨she could *wheedle* the soul out of a saint—*Hewlett*⟩ ⟨he had *wheedled* the Abeyta woman out

of her geraniums, and left her pleased with herself for surrendering them—*Mary Austin*⟩ ⟨no hucksters to *wheedle* you into buying souvenirs—*Nebel*⟩ **Blandish** implies less artfulness than wheedle and more open flattery and a more apparent desire to win over by charming or alluring ⟨would the *blandishing* enchanter still weave his spells around me—*Dickens*⟩ ⟨found herself being *blandished* by millionaires—*Rogow*⟩ *Ana* *induce, persuade, prevail, get: tease, pester (see WORRY): inveigle, entice, tempt, *lure *Ant* bully —*Con* bulldoze, browbeat, *intimidate, cow: *threaten, menace: compel, coerce, oblige, *force, constrain

**cobble** *vb* *botch, bungle, fumble, muff *Ana* patch, *mend, repair: fabricate, forge, manufacture (see MAKE): impair, mar, spoil (see INJURE)

**cock** *vb* stack, shock, pile, *heap, mass, bank *Ana* *gather, collect, assemble *Con* *scatter, disperse

**cock** *n* stack, shock, pile, heap, mass, bank (see under HEAP *vb*)

**cocksure** positive, certain, *sure *Ana* *confident, assured, sanguine, presumptuous: pretentious (see SHOWY): *decided, decisive *Ant* dubious, doubtful —*Con* modest, diffident (see SHY)

**coerce** compel, *force, constrain, oblige *Ana* *intimidate, bulldoze, bully, browbeat, cow: *threaten, menace: drive, impel (see MOVE): terrorize (see FRIGHTEN) *Con* *induce, persuade, prevail, get: *coax, cajole, wheedle, blandish: *lure, entice, tempt, seduce, inveigle

**coercion** compulsion, *force, violence, duress, constraint, restraint *Ana* *power, might, puissance, strength: intimidation, bulldozing, bullying, browbeating (see corresponding verbs at INTIMIDATE): threatening *or* threat, menacing *or* menace (see corresponding verbs at THREATEN)

**coetaneous** coeval, contemporaneous, *contemporary, synchronous, simultaneous, coincident, concomitant, concurrent

**coeval** coetaneous, synchronous, concurrent, simultaneous, coincident, concomitant, *contemporary, contemporaneous

**cogent** convincing, compelling, telling, *valid, sound *Ana* forceful, forcible, potent, *powerful, puissant: compelling, constraining (see FORCE *vb*): inducing, persuading *or* persuasive (see corresponding verbs at INDUCE): proving, demonstrating (see PROVE): *effective, effectual

**cogitate** *think, reflect, deliberate, reason, speculate *Ana* *ponder, ruminate, meditate, muse: *consider, excogitate, weigh, contemplate, study: *think, conceive, imagine, envisage, envision

**cognate** *related, allied, kindred, affiliated *Ana* akin, alike, identical, similar (see LIKE): common, generic, general, *universal *Con* diverse, *different, divergent, disparate, various

**cognizant** *aware, conscious, sensible, alive, awake *Ana* *conversant, versed: informed, acquainted, apprised (see INFORM) *Ant* ignorant —*Con* *insensible, insensitive, impassible, anesthetic: ignoring, overlooking, slighting, neglecting (see NEGLECT): oblivious, unmindful, *forgetful

**cohere** *stick, adhere, cleave, cling *Ana* coalesce, fuse, merge, blend (see MIX): *fasten, attach, affix: *join, combine, unite, connect, associate *Con* *detach, disengage: disentangle, untangle, disembarrass (see EXTRICATE)

---

A colon (:) separates groups of words discriminated. An asterisk (*) indicates place of treatment of each group.

coherence, cohesion mean the quality or character of a whole all of whose parts cohere or stick together. Coherence usually implies a unity of such immaterial or intangible things as the points of an argument, the details of a picture, or the incidents, characters, and setting of a story, or of material or objective things that are bound into unity by a spiritual, intellectual, or aesthetic relationship (as through their clear sequence or their harmony with each other); it commonly connotes an integrity which makes the whole and the relationship of its parts clear and manifest ⟨to treat the subject with the clearness and *coherence* of which it is susceptible—*Wordsworth*⟩ ⟨is there or is there not a spiritual *coherence* in Christianity, or is it only a gathering of laws and precepts, with no inherent connected spiritual philosophy?—*Galsworthy*⟩ ⟨scientific work . . . may indeed possess the appearance of beauty, because of the inner *coherence* which it shares with fine art—*Alexander*⟩ ⟨no more *coherence* than the scattered jangle of bells in the town below—*Quiller-Couch*⟩ Cohesion more often implies a unity of material things held together by such a physical substance as cement, mortar, or glue or by some physical force (as attraction or affinity) ⟨a house stands and holds together by the natural properties, the weight and *cohesion* of the materials which compose it—*T. H. Huxley*⟩ ⟨what am I, Life? A thing of watery salt held in *cohesion* by unresting cells which work they know not why, which never halt—*Masefield*⟩ Cohesion may also be used of either material or immaterial things when the emphasis is on the process by which things cohere rather than on the resulting unity ⟨a state composed of discordant races incapable of *cohesion*⟩
*Ana* *unity, integrity, solidarity, union: clearness, perspicuousness, lucidity (see corresponding adjectives at CLEAR)
*Ant* incoherence

**cohesion** *coherence
*Ana* unification, consolidation, concentration, compacting (see corresponding verbs at COMPACT): coalescence, fusing *or* fusion, blending *or* blend, merging (see corresponding verbs at MIX)
*Con* disintegration, decomposition, crumbling (see corresponding verbs at DECAY): deliquescence (see corresponding verb at LIQUEFY)

**coil** *vb* *wind, curl, twist, twine, wreathe, entwine
*Ana* *turn, revolve, rotate, circle

**coin** *n* coinage, currency, specie, legal tender, cash, *money

**coinage** coin, currency, cash, specie, legal tender, *money

**coincide** concur, *agree
*Ana* accord, correspond, jibe, harmonize, tally (see AGREE): *match, equal
*Ant* differ —*Con* diverge (see SWERVE)

**coincident** synchronous, simultaneous, concurrent, concomitant, coeval, coetaneous, contemporaneous, *contemporary

**cold,** cool, chilly, frigid, freezing, frosty, gelid, icy, glacial, arctic mean having a temperature below that which is normal or comfortable. Cold is the general term, often implying nothing more than a lack of warmth ⟨a *cold* day⟩ ⟨a *cold* hand⟩ ⟨*cold* meat⟩ It may also connote discomfort ⟨shivering in her *cold* room⟩ ⟨battered by a *cold* wind⟩ Cool suggests moderate and often refreshing coldness ⟨a *cool* breeze⟩ ⟨a *cool* hand on a fevered brow⟩ ⟨a *cool* drink⟩ but when hotness or warmth is desirable it, too, connotes something disagreeable ⟨*cool* soup⟩ ⟨a *cool* radiator⟩ Chilly implies coldness that makes one shiver ⟨a *chilly* morning⟩ ⟨a *chilly* room⟩ Frigid, freezing, and frosty imply temperatures below 32° Fahrenheit. Frigid

stresses the intensity of the cold ⟨a *frigid* climate⟩ ⟨*frigid* weather⟩ and freezing its congealing effect (as on man, vegetation, and water) ⟨a *freezing* wind⟩ ⟨*freezing* temperature⟩ while frosty applies rather specifically to times or conditions in which fine ice crystals are deposited from atmospheric moisture onto a cold surface ⟨*frosty* nights are usually clear and cold with little wind⟩ Gelid is equivalent to *freezing,* but it somewhat more often stresses the resultant discomfort ⟨so the leaden hours passed in the *gelid* darkness—*Sitwell*⟩ ⟨while sea-born gales their *gelid* wings expand—*Goldsmith*⟩ Icy, when used to indicate a kind of coldness, implies frigidity so great as to be painful and cutting; it is applicable chiefly to winds, storms, and water ⟨an *icy* rain⟩ ⟨an *icy* northeast wind⟩ Basically glacial is very close to *icy* ⟨the air in the cave was *glacial,* penetrated to the very bones—*Cather*⟩ but its later association with *glacier* has given it an ambiguous cast in many locutions; thus, a *glacial* lake might be, according to context, either a painfully cold lake or one formed by the action of a glacier. Arctic is the strongest of these words in its suggestion of intense coldness. It connotes the frigidity of the polar regions and is usually a hyperbolic rather than an exact term ⟨a winter notable for its *arctic* temperatures⟩
When applied to persons, their temperaments, their acts and words, and their responses to stimuli, these words are also marked by differences in implications. Cold suggests absence of feeling or emotion, or less than normal human sympathy, friendliness, sensitiveness, or responsiveness ⟨his plea left us *cold*⟩ ⟨*cold* words⟩ ⟨he treated us with *cold* justice⟩ ⟨their *cold* intelligence, their stereotyped, unremitting industry repel me—*L. P. Smith*⟩ ⟨Okio, in spite of his unerring eye and his incomparable cunning of hand, was of too *cold* a temperament to infuse a powerful current of life into the old tradition—*Binyon*⟩ Cool (see also COOL 2) stresses control over one's feelings or emotions, and therefore absence of excitement or agitation ⟨this wonder, that when near her he should be *cool* and composed, and when away from her wrapped in a tempest of desires—*Meredith*⟩ ⟨both looked at life with a *cool* realism which was not allowed to become cynical—*Buchan*⟩ Chilly, frosty, and freezing usually stress the effect of another's coldness: chilly connotes a depressing or repressive influence ⟨a *chilly* greeting⟩ ⟨a *chilly* reception⟩ while frosty connotes a checking or restraining of advances ⟨a *frosty* smile⟩ and freezing connotes a blighting or repelling ⟨a *freezing* reply to a letter⟩ ⟨many . . . had been repelled by his *freezing* looks—*Macaulay*⟩ Frigid suggests such a deficiency of natural feeling as is abnormal or repellent; it is specifically applicable to persons who are sexually passionless and averse to sexual intercourse, but it is often applied to things which are not, but by their nature could be, impassioned or infused with feeling or warmth ⟨*frigid* verse⟩ ⟨a *frigid* religion⟩ ⟨*frigid* hospitality⟩ Gelid and icy suggest a discomfiting chill (as in manner or conduct), the former sometimes stressing the power to benumb, the latter the power to pierce or stab ⟨immediately, the long *gelid,* nightly silence fell between us—*Spina*⟩ ⟨sweeping her sympathizers with a *gelid* gaze—*Patton*⟩ ⟨her voice dropped into an *icy* gravity—*Yerby*⟩ ⟨a lady of the most arresting beauty and *icy* good breeding—*Max Peacock*⟩ Glacial suggests a chilling lack of vitality or animation ⟨Boston, for all its *glacial* perfection, has no intimacy at all—*Virgil Thomson*⟩ ⟨his manner more *glacial* and sepulchral than ever—*Motley*⟩ Arctic frequently adds to *frigid* a connotation of remoteness from all that is human or referable to humanity ⟨exact and *arctic* justice—*Mencken*⟩
*Ant* hot

**collate** *compare, contrast

**collateral** adj *subordinate, secondary, dependent, subject, tributary
Ana *related, allied, kindred, cognate: correlative, complementary, corresponding, *reciprocal

**collation** *comparison, parallel, contrast, antithesis
Ana corroboration, verification, confirmation, authentication (see corresponding verbs at CONFIRM): emending or emendation, revising or revision, correcting or correction (see corresponding verbs at CORRECT)

**colleague** *partner, copartner, ally, confederate
Ana *associate, companion, comrade

**collect** *gather, assemble, congregate
Ana mass, *heap, pile: *accumulate, amass, hoard: consolidate, concentrate, *compact
Ant disperse: distribute —Con *scatter, dissipate, dispel: dispense, divide, deal, dole (see DISTRIBUTE): *separate, part, sever, sunder: *assort, sort

**collected** composed, *cool, unruffled, imperturbable, unflappable, nonchalant
Ana *calm, placid, tranquil, serene: quiet, *still: assured, *confident, sure, sanguine: *complacent, smug, self-satisfied
Ant distracted, distraught —Con agitated, perturbed, upset, disturbed, flustered, flurried (see DISCOMPOSE)

**collection** assemblage, assembly, gathering, congregation (see under GATHER vb)
Ana heap, pile, mass, stack (see under HEAP vb): accumulation, hoarding or hoard (see corresponding verbs at ACCUMULATE)

**collide** *bump, clash, conflict
Ana hit, *strike: impinge, impact (see corresponding nouns at IMPACT): dash, charge, *rush

**collision** *impact, impingement, clash, shock, concussion, percussion, jar, jolt
Ana striking, hitting (see STRIKE vb): wrecking or wreck, ruining or ruin, dilapidation (see corresponding verbs at RUIN): demolishment, destruction (see corresponding verbs at DESTROY)

**colonnade, arcade, arcature, portico, peristyle** are discriminable as used in architecture. A **colonnade** is a row of columns (typically on the outside of a building) spaced at regular intervals and carrying an architrave or horizontal member lying directly across their capitals, so that the opening between each pair of columns is square-topped. *Colonnade* is usually applied not only to the columns but to the entire structure consisting of columns, roof, and pavement or to the space which they enclose. The word is used especially in reference to classical architecture. An **arcade** is a long series of arches with their supporting columns and piers together with the other members that complete the structure as an architectural feature. An arcade may be either inside or outside of a building; it may be a purely decorative feature or a means of admitting light and air. When purely decorative, the spaces between the arches and the piers may be filled in (sometimes providing niches for statues); this type of arcade is also called an **arcature**. An arcade may take the place of an outer wall (as of a gallery or cloister). *Arcade* is used especially of types of architecture (as the late Romanesque and the Gothic) in which the arch is an essential feature. *Portico* and *peristyle* are used in reference to architectural features employing the colonnade. When the colonnade extends across, or nearly across, one side of a building and serves as an entrance, it is called a **portico**; when it is continued so as to extend along three or, usually, all four sides of a building, it is called a **peristyle**.

**color** n 1 Color, hue, shade, tint, tinge, tone are comparable when they mean a property or attribute of a visible thing that is recognizable only when rays of light fall upon the thing and that is distinct from properties (as shape or size) apparent in dusk. **Color** is the ordinary term and, in precise use, the only generic term of this group. It may apply to the quality of blood which one describes as redness, of grass as greenness, of the sky as blueness, of snow as whiteness, or of ebony as blackness, or to the optical sensation which one experiences when one sees these things respectively as red, green, blue, white, and black. It may refer to any of the bands of the spectrum or to any of the variations produced by or as if by combination of one or more of these with another or with white, black, or gray ⟨Walden is blue at one time and green at another. . . . Lying between the earth and the heavens, it partakes of the *color* of both—*Thoreau*⟩ Color is also specifically applicable to the attribute of things seen as red, yellow, blue, orange, green, purple (the chromatic *colors*) as distinct from the attribute of things seen as black, white, or gray (the achromatic *colors*) ⟨give a white house touches of *color* by painting the window sashes and shutters green⟩ **Hue**, especially in poetry or elevated prose, is often synonymous with *color* ⟨as brown in *hue* as hazelnuts and sweeter than the kernels—*Shak.*⟩ ⟨all the gradational *hues* of the spectrum from red through yellow, green, blue, to violet—*Scientific Monthly*⟩ More specifically, *hue* suggests some modification of color ⟨their shining green has changed to a less vivid *hue*; they are taking bluish tones here and there—*Hearn*⟩ **Shade** is often used in the sense of one of the gradations of a color, especially as its hue is affected by its brilliance ⟨seek a darker *shade* of blue⟩ ⟨a brighter *shade* of green⟩ ⟨various *shades* of gray⟩ ⟨the dark ultramarine of the west turns a *shade* paler—*J. C. Van Dyke*⟩ **Tint** is also used as meaning a gradation of color in respect to brilliance, but it always suggests hue and is commonly used in reference to light colors that seem to be given by a light or delicate touching; thus, what are often called "pastel *colors*" or "pastel *shades*" are known also as *tints*. The term is not infrequently used in contrast to *shade*, especially when the latter word connotes comparative darkness or dullness ⟨the flags by the shore were turning brown; a *tint* of yellow was creeping up the rushes—*Jefferies*⟩ ⟨dark it appeared, but the precise *tint* was indeterminable—*Hudson*⟩ ⟨the sprays of bloom which adorn it are merely another *shade* of the red earth walls, and its fibrous trunk is full of gold and lavender *tints*—*Cather*⟩ **Tinge** implies more of interfusion or stain than *tint* ⟨autumn bold, with universal *tinge* of sober gold—*Keats*⟩ ⟨the water . . . imparts to the body of one bathing in it a yellowish *tinge*—*Thoreau*⟩ **Tone** is a rather general word, sometimes equivalent to *color* but more often suggesting *hue* or a modification of hue (as a tint or tinge) ⟨from strand to cloud-capped peak, the *tone* was purple—*Beebe*⟩ ⟨*tone*, which he plays with as has no other of the moderns, modifying color brightness to achieve his foreseen tonal harmony—*Cheney*⟩

Nearly all of these terms carry extended meanings derived from or related to the senses previously considered. **Color** usually suggests an outward character or aspect such as may be changed by circumstances ⟨your love for him has changed its *color* since you have found him not to be the saint you thought him—*Hardy*⟩ ⟨it had been an essentially aristocratic movement . . . . But . . . it took on a strongly democratic *color*—*Mencken*⟩ or may be imparted to a thing to brighten and vivify it ⟨people talk of matters which I had believed to be worn threadbare by use, and yet communicate a rich *color* . . . to them—*Benson*⟩ **Hue** is less often so used than *color*; it usually suggests a character rather than an aspect, but it does not necessarily imply an ingrained character ⟨our

mental *hue* depends . . . completely on the social atmosphere in which we move—*Horace Smith*⟩ **Tint** applies to a character that is not dominant but imparted as if by contact or influence ⟨our inborn spirits have a *tint* of thee—*Byron*⟩ **Shade** and **tinge** are used in the sense of *trace, touch, trifle* (for this sense, see TOUCH) ⟨eyes that . . . had some *tinge* of the oriental—*Edmund Wilson*⟩ ⟨a *shade* less cordial than usual⟩ ⟨a *tinge* of sadness⟩
**2** usually in plural **colors** *flag, ensign, standard, banner, streamer, pennant, pendant, pennon, jack
**colorable** *plausible, credible, believable, specious
*Ana* convincing, compelling, telling, cogent, sound, *valid
**colorless** uncolored, achromatic mean without color. However, they are not freely interchangeable. **Colorless** is applied to something that is transparent ⟨water is a *colorless* liquid⟩ or to something that is bleached, blanched, or pallid ⟨*colorless* leaves⟩ ⟨*colorless* cheeks and lips⟩ **Uncolored** is applied to something that is left in its natural state or is not dyed or stained ⟨*uncolored* oranges⟩ or to objects which have not been touched or touched up with color ⟨an *uncolored* photograph⟩ **Achromatic** is applied to something that is free from any of the hues in the spectrum or from any hues formed by combinations of these or that gives images which are free from extraneous colors produced by refraction ⟨an *achromatic* color⟩ ⟨an *achromatic* telescope⟩ A color (in its inclusive sense) may be *chromatic* or *achromatic:* if the former, it has a hue; if the latter, it has not and is, therefore, white, black, or a pure gray.
*Ana* *pale, pallid, ashen, wan: whitened, blanched, bleached, decolorized (see WHITEN)
*Ant* colorful
**colossal** *huge, vast, immense, enormous, elephantine, mammoth, giant, gigantic, gigantean, gargantuan, Herculean, cyclopean, titanic, Brobdingnagian
*Ana* monumental, stupendous, tremendous, prodigious, *monstrous
**column** *pillar, pilaster
**comatose** torpid, sluggish, *lethargic
*Ana* *languid, languorous, listless, languishing: phlegmatic, *impassive: *insensible, anesthetic, impassible: inert, passive, supine (see INACTIVE)
*Ant* awake
**comb** *vb* *seek, search, scour, hunt, ferret out, ransack, rummage
*Ana* *scrutinize, inspect, examine: investigate, probe (see corresponding nouns at INQUIRY)
**combat** *vb* *resist, withstand, contest, oppose, fight, conflict, antagonize
*Ana* fight, *contend, battle, war: *attack, assail, assault, bombard, storm
*Ant* champion: defend —*Con* protect, shield, guard (see DEFEND): *support, uphold, advocate: *maintain, justify, vindicate
**combat** *n* conflict, fight, *contest, affray, fray
*Ana* *battle, engagement, action: *encounter, skirmish, brush: controversy, dispute, *argument: contention, strife, conflict, *discord
**combative** *belligerent, bellicose, pugnacious, quarrelsome, contentious
*Ana* *aggressive, militant: strenuous, energetic, *vigorous: virile, manly, manful (see MALE)
*Ant* pacifistic
**combination,** combine, party, bloc, faction, ring denote a union, either of individuals or of organized interests, for mutual support in obtaining common political or private ends. **Combination** is the most comprehensive of these terms, being applicable to any such union whether a trust, an alliance, or simply an association for the purpose of

urging demands or resisting claims ⟨a *combination* of citizens devoted to holding down taxes⟩ ⟨a *combination* of railroads to maintain existing rates⟩ **Combine** is often interchangeable, especially in informal use, with *combination* ⟨the coal *combine*⟩ Often it may connote a combination with an improper or illegal aim in view ⟨how the Mafia operates has been duplicated . . . in Ed Reid's book of that infamous . . . *combine*—*Kogan*⟩ ⟨a *combine* that understands it must destroy . . . if it is actually to control—*The Commonweal*⟩ A **party** is a number of persons united in support of some opinion, cause, or principle; it usually implies a similar body in opposition, especially when used in reference to a political organization built up to continue the action and policies of government through election of its candidates to office ⟨in the United States there are usually only two strong *parties*⟩ ⟨the Labour *party* in England⟩ ⟨he who draws his pen for one *party* must expect to make enemies of the other—*Dryden*⟩ ⟨who, born for the universe, narrowed his mind, and to *party* gave up what was meant for mankind—*Goldsmith*⟩ **Bloc** implies a combination of persons or groups who otherwise differ in party or in interests for the sake of achieving a common and often temporary end; thus, in France and in Italy, a *bloc* is a combination of members of two or more political parties; in the United States, a *bloc* is a combination not of parties but of members of different parties who have a common end ⟨the farm *bloc* formed by members from the agricultural states wishing to secure legislation helpful to their constituents⟩ **Faction** frequently suggests a smaller body than *party* and commonly implies selfish ends and the use of unscrupulous or turbulent means ⟨so several *factions* from this first ferment work up to foam and threat the government—*Dryden*⟩ ⟨the Whigs and Tories in Rome, Athens, and Jerusalem never forgot national points with more zeal, to attend to private *faction*, than we have lately—*Walpole*⟩ **Ring** is applicable to an exclusive, often more or less secret, combination for a selfish and often corrupt or criminal purpose (as the control of a market, of political patronage, or of distribution of narcotics) ⟨the Tweed *Ring* was in control of New York City politics for six years⟩ ⟨innocent women were frequently framed by a *ring* consisting of police officers, stool pigeons, bondsmen and lawyers—*Ploscowe*⟩
*Ana* *monopoly, corner, pool, cartel, syndicate, trust
**combine** *vb* **1** unite, associate, link, conjoin, *join, connect, relate
*Ana* *mix, mingle, commingle, blend, fuse, amalgamate: consolidate, unify (see COMPACT *vb*)
*Ant* separate —*Con* part, divide, sever, sunder, divorce (see SEPARATE): *detach, disengage
**2** *unite, cooperate, concur, conjoin
*Ana* coalesce, merge (see MIX): coincide, *agree, concur
**combine** *n* *combination, party, bloc, faction, ring
*Ana* see those at COMBINATION
**combustible** *adj* Combustible, inflammable, flammable, incendiary, inflammatory, which are not close synonyms, since they apply to different types of nouns, are comparable because they mean showing a tendency to catch or be set on fire. **Combustible** applies chiefly to material which is of such a nature that it catches fire easily and usually burns quickly ⟨excelsior is very *combustible*⟩ ⟨a *combustible* roof of pine shingles⟩ **Inflammable** applies to materials ready to flame up at the slightest cause; the term, however, suggests more than the ease with which a thing burns, for it stresses a capacity for flaring up dangerously ⟨the fire soon gutted the attic, which had been full of old papers and other *inflammable* materials⟩ *Inflammable* as applied to persons, their natures, their

*Ana* analogous words　　　*Ant* antonyms　　　*Con* contrasted words　　　See also explanatory notes facing page 1

hearts, and their temperaments stresses the danger as well as the ease in arousing them (as to anger, excitement, or passion); it applies also to a subject or situation that can induce such arousal ⟨the vision of a single young woman is said to have overcome the *inflammable* monk —*Meredith*⟩ ⟨"Don't trouble about it, Clym. They may get to be friends." He shook his head. "Not two people with *inflammable* natures like theirs"—*Hardy*⟩ ⟨a very *inflammable* subject to be raised at election time⟩ **Flammable** is equivalent to *inflammable* and used chiefly in respect to materials dangerously likely to flare up or explode ⟨gasoline is a highly *flammable* substance requiring special care in storage and transportation⟩ **Incendiary** not only stresses a capacity for starting up or causing a conflagration but a malicious intent to do the same. Therefore the term applies not only to something that is designed to cause fire but to fire that is caused by intent or design ⟨an *incendiary* bomb⟩ ⟨an *incendiary* conflagration⟩ The term may be extended to something (as an act, practice, speech, or publication) that tends to arouse something (as sedition, evil passions, or violence) that acts as destructively or disastrously as fire ⟨*incendiary* ideas⟩ ⟨an *incendiary* policy⟩ While the adjective is seldom applied to persons, the noun *incendiary* chiefly, except when used as short for such phrases as *incendiary bomb,* designates a person who maliciously or willfully sets fire to a building or other property or who deliberately incites quarrels, unrests, sedition, or violence. **Inflammatory,** like *incendiary,* emphasizes the power to cause a fire, especially in the hearts or minds of people, but it carries less suggestion of a malicious intent ⟨taking to politics, he became a Chartist, and was found to be a capable *inflammatory* speaker—*Lucas*⟩ ⟨this gentleman . . . having been imprisoned fourteen months for *inflammatory* language anent the Federal Government—*Repplier*⟩

*Ana* burnable (see corresponding verb at BURN): kindling, firing, igniting (see LIGHT *vb*)

**come, arrive** are comparable because both basically mean to get to one point from another more or less distant in space, time, relation, or development. *Come* (with *to*) and *arrive* (with *at*) are synonyms of *reach* (see REACH); thus, one *comes* to or *arrives* at the end of a journey; one *comes* to or *arrives* at a decision. **Come** is one of the elementary intransitive verbs of motion, always implying movement toward, and may be used wherever such movement, actual or apparent, physical or spiritual, is implied. **Arrive,** however, stresses rather the reaching of and the end of movement toward a destination. *Come,* therefore, may be used with or without the implication that the destination is reached; *arrive* consistently carries that implication ⟨I can see them *coming*⟩ ⟨they will *arrive* at three o'clock⟩ When used in reference to things that move or progress without an agent or agency (as because of some law of nature or in obedience to some inner law or principle) *come* is usually preferable unless a definite end or termination or, often, fulfillment (as of expectation) is suggested ⟨the days *come* and go⟩ ⟨at last the day of departure *arrived*⟩ ⟨the longed-for breeze was slow in *coming,* but when it *arrived* it brought joy to all⟩ ⟨success never *comes* to those who await it idly; it usually *arrives* only after years of patient endeavor⟩ *Come* often suggests or requires statement of a source of place from which a thing has issued; *arrive,* on the other hand, often suggests or requires a statement of an end, a goal, or a climax to a progress or development ⟨the family *comes* from peasant stock⟩ ⟨the family *arrived* socially when the grandfather of the present baron was elevated to the peerage⟩ In such cases *come* and *arrive* are not inter-

changeable, for the former is loosely synonymous with *issue, emanate, originate,* or *arise* and the latter with *succeed, triumph,* or (when followed by *at*) with *acquire.*

*Ana* *approach, near: rise, arise, *spring, proceed, emanate, issue, stem

*Ant* go —*Con* leave, depart, quit, withdraw, retire (see GO)

**comely** *adj* fair, pretty, bonny, handsome, lovely, *beautiful, good-looking, beauteous, pulchritudinous

*Ant* homely

**comestibles** provisions, viands, victuals, *food, feed, provender, fodder, forage

**comfort** *n* ease, *rest, repose, relaxation, leisure

*Ana* contentedness *or* content, satisfaction (see corresponding adjectives under SATISFY *vb*): enjoyment, joy, fruition, *pleasure: relief, assuagement, alleviation (see corresponding verbs at RELIEVE)

*Ant* discomfort —*Con* *distress, suffering, misery

**comfort** *vb* **Comfort, console, solace** are comparable when meaning to give or offer a person help or assistance in relieving his suffering or sorrow. **Comfort,** the homelier, more intimate word, suggests relief afforded by imparting positive cheer, hope, or strength as well as by the lessening of pain and distress ⟨he hath sent me . . . to *comfort* all that mourn—*Isa* 61:1-2⟩ ⟨a mother *comforts* her sobbing child⟩ ⟨but there was about him a certain reserve, and she dared not *comfort* him, not even speak softly to him —*D. H. Lawrence*⟩ **Console,** the more formal term, emphasizes rather the alleviation of grief or the mitigation of the sense of loss than the communication of pleasure; it frequently implies some definite source of relief ⟨the presence of his friend *consoled* him⟩ ⟨*console* oneself by philosophic reflections⟩ ⟨if you really want to *console* me, teach me rather to forget what has happened—*Wilde*⟩ ⟨his father's letter gave him one of his many fits of melancholy over his own worthlessness, but the thought of the organ *consoled* him—*Butler* d.1902⟩ **Solace** frequently suggests relief from distressful emotions (as weariness, despondency, chagrin, loneliness, or dullness) rather than from grief or pain, and often, specifically, a lift of the spirits; the source of that relief is more often things than persons ⟨*solace* oneself with books⟩ ⟨though you rail against the bar and the imperfect medium of speech, you will be *solaced,* even in your chagrin, by a sense of injured innocence—*Cardozo*⟩

*Ana* delight, gladden, rejoice, *please: *relieve, assuage, mitigate, alleviate: refresh, restore (see RENEW)

*Ant* afflict: bother. —*Con* *distress, trouble: torment, torture, try (see AFFLICT): vex, *annoy, irk

**comfortable, cozy, snug, easy, restful** are comparable when they mean enjoying or providing conditions or circumstances which make for one's contentment and security. **Comfortable** usually implies the absence of whatever gives trouble, pain, or distress in any degree or of any kind to the body or mind ⟨a *comfortable* chair⟩ ⟨a *comfortable* room both in summer and in winter⟩ ⟨he is never *comfortable* except in his own home⟩ ⟨a makeshift arrangement not altogether agreeable or *comfortable* for either of us—*Ellis*⟩ but it often applies to persons or things that encourage in one serenity of mind, tranquillity, a sense of well-being, or complacency ⟨the family was left in *comfortable* circumstances⟩ ⟨a *comfortable,* motherly woman⟩ ⟨diverted from senseless controversy into *comfortable* monologue—*Jan Struther*⟩ **Cozy** suggests comfortableness derived from warmth, shelter, ease, and friendliness ⟨a *cozy* fire⟩ ⟨a *cozy* armchair⟩ ⟨close all the windows and doors so as to make the house *cozy*⟩ ⟨the *cozy* talk by the fireside—*J. R. Green*⟩ ⟨Wimsey gratefully took in the *cozy* sitting room, with

---

A colon (:) separates groups of words discriminated. An asterisk (*) indicates place of treatment of each group.

its . . . fire roaring behind a chaste canopy of velvet overmantel—*Sayers*⟩ **Snug** (see also NEAT) suggests the state or the frame of mind of one who has as much room, or responsibility, or freedom, or money as is essential to his well-being but no more than he actually needs to be cozy, content, or secure; the term usually connotes such comfort as is associated with small but comfortable quarters as distinguished from those that are spacious or with a quiet, restricted, but pleasant way of life as distinguished from one where there is little time for one's own interests or where one is driven by ambitions or restlessness; often, specifically, the term emphasizes protection from the elements, and warmth and dryness, as contributions to one's comfort ⟨all the gypsies and showmen . . . lay *snug* within their carts and tents—*Hardy*⟩ ⟨Arnold the heartbroken outcast from the *snug* household of faith, wearying in spiritual wastes of sand and thorns—*Montague*⟩ **Easy** (see also EASY 2) implies relief from all that makes for discomfort or hardships, with the result that one is happy or free from care, anxiety, trouble, or doubt ⟨he is in *easy* circumstances for the first time in his life⟩ ⟨she could now enjoy herself with an *easy* conscience⟩ ⟨people of the right sort are never *easy* until they get things straight—*Shaw*⟩ ⟨Mrs. Struthers's *easy* Sunday hospitality—*Wharton*⟩ **Restful** usually suggests a state of mind of one who is comfortable, cozy, or easy, as well as relaxed, or a quality in a thing that induces such a state of mind ⟨it's *restful* to arrive at a decision, and *restful* just to think about New Hampshire—*Frost*⟩ ⟨a *restful,* friendly room, fitted to the uses of gentle life—*Mary Austin*⟩
*Ana* comforting, consoling, solacing (see COMFORT *vb*): content *or* contented, satisfied (see under SATISFY): grateful, welcome, agreeable, gratifying (see PLEASANT) *Ant* uncomfortable: miserable —*Con* wretched (see MISERABLE): distressing, troubling (see TROUBLE *vb*): annoying, vexing, irking, bothering (see ANNOY)

**comic** *adj* comical, *laughable, farcical, funny, droll, risible, ludicrous, ridiculous
*Ana* diverting, amusing, entertaining (see AMUSE): *witty, humorous, facetious: grotesque, antic, *fantastic *Ant* tragic —*Con* *serious, solemn, grave, sober: pathetic, touching, poignant, *moving, affecting

**comical** comic, farcical, ludicrous, ridiculous, *laughable, risible, droll, funny
*Ana* absurd, silly, *foolish: jocular, jocose, humorous (see WITTY): waggish, impish, roguish, sportive (see PLAYFUL): deriding *or* derisive, ridiculing, mocking (see corresponding verbs at RIDICULE)
*Ant* pathetic —*Con* *melancholy, doleful, lugubrious, dolorous: *moving, poignant, touching, affecting

**comity** amity, goodwill, *friendship
*Ana* *association, society: companionship, comradeship (see base words at ASSOCIATE): concord, accord, *harmony

**command** *vb* Command, order, bid, enjoin, direct, instruct, charge mean to issue orders to someone to give, get, or do something. **Command** and **order** agree in stressing the idea of authority, *command* implying its more formal and official exercise ⟨the chairman *commands* the undertaking—*Kefauver*⟩ and *order,* its more peremptory, sometimes even arbitrary, exercise; thus, a king, a military officer, the captain of a ship, *commands*; a landowner *orders* a trespasser off his premises; one is apt to resent being *ordered,* except by those who have a right to *command.* But *order* is used by a physician with no such connotation ⟨the doctor *ordered* outdoor exercise⟩ **Bid** in this sense is usually somewhat literary or informal; it usually implies an ordering or directing (often with a

suggestion of peremptoriness) directly and by speech ⟨she *bade* him be seated⟩ ⟨he seized him by the collar and sternly *bade* him cease making a fool of himself —*Shaw*⟩ **Enjoin, direct,** and **instruct** are all less imperative than *command* or *order,* but they all connote expectation of obedience. **Enjoin** adds to the idea of authority the implication of urging or warning; **direct** and **instruct** suggest especially business, official, or diplomatic relations, *direct* being perhaps the more mandatory, *instruct* the more formal, of the two ⟨a parent *enjoins* his children to be quiet⟩ ⟨the church *enjoins* certain duties⟩ ⟨the editor *directed* his secretary to admit no callers during a conference⟩ ⟨*instruct* an assistant to gather certain information⟩ ⟨St. Peter . . . *enjoins* us to be ready always to give an answer to every man that asks us a reason for the faith that is in us—*Lowes*⟩ ⟨why otherwise does it [the Constitution of the United States] *direct* the judges to take an oath to support it?—*John Marshall*⟩ **Charge,** chiefly a literary term, implies not only enjoining but the imposition of a task as a duty ⟨Mrs. Yeobright gave him the moneybags, *charged* him to go to Mistover—*Hardy*⟩ ⟨Gustavus . . . considered himself *charged* by God with the defense of the true Lutheran faith—*Barr*⟩
*Ana* control, manage, *conduct, direct: exact, *demand, require: *force, compel, coerce, constrain, oblige
*Ant* comply, obey

**command** *n* 1 Command, order, injunction, bidding, behest, mandate, dictate mean a direction, that must or should be obeyed, to do or not do something. **Command** imputes to the person who issues the directions either unquestioned authority ⟨the *commands* of a general⟩ or complete control of a situation ⟨at the *command* of the intruder he held up his hands⟩ The term usually connotes either peremptoriness or imperativeness ⟨at the *command* of his father he returned to the house⟩ ⟨every request of hers he interpreted as a *command*⟩ ⟨encroachment to some extent there is by every *command* or prohibition—*Cardozo*⟩ **Order** is not always clearly distinguishable from *command;* is, however, the preferred word for directions to subordinates that are instructions as well as commands; in such use it commonly implies explicitness in detail ⟨the troops were awaiting *orders* from headquarters⟩ ⟨in response to the principal's *order,* the pupils maintained silence while passing through the corridors⟩ ⟨refusal to recognize the authority of the emperor amounted to a refusal to take *orders*—*Pharr*⟩ **Injunction** carries a weaker implication of imperativeness than the preceding words except in legal use, where it is applied to a court order commanding a person to do or more often to refrain from doing something on the penalty of being adjudged guilty of contempt of court. In general use the word stresses admonition without losing the implication of expected or demanded obedience ⟨the high *injunction* not to taste that fruit—*Milton*⟩ ⟨she carefully obeyed the *injunctions* laid upon her by her physician⟩ ⟨delivered stern *injunctions*⟩ **Bidding,** chiefly literary, usually implies the status of master or parent in the person who issues the orders and therefore stresses expected obedience or the fact of being obeyed ⟨thousands at his *bidding* speed—*Milton*⟩ ⟨at the ghostly *bidding* of the cloud, . . . the surly summons of the sun —*Aiken*⟩ **Behest** is also distinctly literary and equivalent to *bidding* in its implications ⟨do his master's high *behest* —*Scott*⟩ ⟨during the war, it is true, at the *behest* of government agencies, many writers worked into their serials incidents and dialogue of a worthy sociological nature —*Thurber*⟩ **Mandate** (see also MANDATE 2) carries the strongest implication of imperativeness of all of these words, for it denotes a command or order issued by a

very high, often the highest, authority. It has or has had specific applications, such as an order from a superior court or official to an inferior one or from a Roman emperor to the commander of his military forces. It is often applied to something inexorably demanded (as by the exigencies of the situation) rather than actually or verbally commanded ⟨he accepted the nomination, believing that his huge majority indicated a *mandate* from his party⟩ ⟨it was a bold step, for he had no legal military command, and no *mandate* from senate or people —*Buchan*⟩ ⟨Poe's doctrine of brevity, as a *mandate* laid upon poetry by the inflexible nature of things—*Lowes*⟩ **Dictate** basically denotes a command given orally ⟨he . . . received his suggestions, and bowed to his *dictates* —*Meredith*⟩ More often it applies to a command or authoritative judgment uttered by an inner voice (as of the conscience) or formulated in a principle or law ⟨the government which has a right to do an act, and has imposed on it the duty of performing that act, must, according to the *dictates* of reason, be allowed to select the means—*John Marshall*⟩ ⟨a suspicion that . . . the moral law speaks in equivocal tones to those who listen most scrupulously for its *dictates*—*L. P. Smith*⟩
*Ana* direction, instruction, charging *or* charge (see corresponding verbs at COMMAND): precept, ordinance, *law, statute, canon, rule
**2** control, authority, *power, jurisdiction, sway, dominion
*Ana* ascendancy, *supremacy: sovereignty (see under FREE *adj*)
**commemorate** *vb* celebrate, observe, *keep, solemnize
**commence** *begin, start, initiate, inaugurate
*Ana* institute, *found, organize, establish
*Con* finish, complete, conclude, terminate, end, *close
**commend,** **recommend, applaud, compliment** are comparable when they mean to voice or otherwise manifest to others one's warm approval. **Commend** usually implies judicious or restrained praise, but it suggests as its motive a desire to call attention to the merits of a person or a thing ⟨the police commissioner publicly *commended* the officers who made the arrest⟩ ⟨his wife seriously *commended* Mr. Collins for having spoken so sensibly— *Austen*⟩ ⟨it is always dangerous and impertinent to *commend* a poem for anything but its poetry—*Day Lewis*⟩ ⟨embodying in his work the qualities of righteousness which will *commend* it to men of other times and places—*Cohen*⟩ **Recommend** adds to *commend* the implication of offering something that is praised for acceptance, use, or employment by another ⟨the physician *recommended* the treatment of bruises with alternating cold and hot applications⟩ ⟨his present employers highly *recommended* him to his prospective employers⟩ ⟨for a spare hour, I can *recommend* no more diverting pursuit —*Skinner*⟩ **Applaud** implies an enthusiastic expression of approval; it usually suggests approval by a large number of persons or by the public ⟨the president was *applauded* for his closing of all banks in the crisis⟩ ⟨everybody *applauded* the mayor's proposed entertainment, especially when it became known that he meant to pay for it all himself—*Hardy*⟩ **Compliment** stresses either courtesy in the commendation or, sometimes, flattery in the manner or words of praise ⟨the visitors to the convention *complimented* the townspeople on the arrangements made for their comfort⟩ ⟨"Marvelous cognac this, madame!" It was the first time it had ever been so *complimented,* and Madame Defarge knew enough of its antecedents to know better—*Dickens*⟩
*Ana* *praise, laud, extol, eulogize, acclaim
*Ant* censure: admonish —*Con* *criticize, reprehend,

reprobate, blame: *reprove, reproach, rebuke, reprimand, chide
**commensurable** commensurate, proportionate, *proportional
*Ana* equivalent, equal, identical, tantamount (see SAME): *reciprocal, corresponding
*Ant* incommensurable
**commensurate** commensurable, proportionate, *proportional
*Ana* corresponding *or* correspondent, according *or* accordant, squaring, conforming (see corresponding verbs at AGREE): balancing, counterbalancing, compensating, offsetting (see COMPENSATE)
*Ant* incommensurate
**comment** *n* commentary, *remark, observation, note, obiter dictum
*Ana* interpreting *or* interpretation, elucidation, explication, expounding *or* exposition, explaining *or* explanation (see corresponding verbs at EXPLAIN): annotation, gloss (see under ANNOTATE)
**comment** *vb* commentate, *remark, animadvert
*Ana* interpret, elucidate, expound, *explain, construe, explicate: *annotate, gloss: *criticize: illustrate, *exemplify
**commentary** comment, *remark, observation, note, obiter dictum
*Ana* see those at COMMENT *n*
**commentate** *vb* comment, *remark, animadvert
*Ana* see those at COMMENT *vb*
**commentator** see under *commentate* at REMARK *vb*
**commerce** **1** trade, *business, industry, traffic
**2** traffic, *intercourse, dealings, communication, communion, conversation, converse, correspondence
**commercial** *adj* **Commercial, mercantile** are comparable when they mean of, relating to, or dealing with the supplying of commodities. **Commercial** is the more widely applicable term: it may be used in reference to anything which has to do with the buying or selling of commodities for profit, with their transportation, and sometimes, even, with their production, or with business affairs in general; thus, a *commercial* transaction is any piece of business involving a buyer and seller of goods or property that is for the financial benefit of the seller; *commercial* law deals with all matters (as contracts, negotiable papers, liens, payment of debts, and partnerships) that have reference to business; a *commercial* attaché is, in the United States, an officer of the Department of Commerce attached by the Department of State to an embassy or legation in a country where trade is important. Also, *commercial* is used to describe whatever has for its aim financial profit or is guided by the methods or practices of business ⟨the *commercial* theater⟩ ⟨*commercial* aviation⟩ ⟨*commercial* sports⟩ ⟨*commercial* radio programs are programs paid for by advertisers⟩ **Mercantile** is often used interchangeably with *commercial* with little difference in meaning; thus, a *mercantile* transaction is not ordinarily distinguishable from a *commercial* transaction, nor *mercantile* law from *commercial* law. The term, however, more often suggests actual buying and selling (the occupation of a merchant) than commerce in general including production and transportation and is therefore more restricted in its application; thus, a *commercial* house is a business or company engaged in foreign or domestic commerce; a *mercantile* house is a business, usually wholesale, engaged in merchandising ⟨*mercantile* agent⟩ ⟨*mercantile* establishment⟩
**commingle** mingle, blend, *mix, merge, coalesce, fuse, amalgamate
*Ana* combine, unite, conjoin, associate (see JOIN):

A colon (:) separates groups of words discriminated. An asterisk (*) indicates place of treatment of each group.

*integrate

**commiseration** compassion, pity, condolence, *sympathy, ruth, empathy

*Ana* compassionateness, ténderness, warmheartedness (see corresponding adjectives at TENDER): mercifulness, clemency (see under FORBEARING): lamenting *or* lamentation, bewailing, bemoaning (see corresponding verbs at DEPLORE): pitifulness, piteousness, pitiableness (see corresponding adjectives at PITIFUL)

*Ant* ruthlessness, pitilessness

**commission** *vb* *authorize, accredit, license

*Ana* appoint, *designate, name, nominate: empower, *enable: instruct, enjoin, charge, bid, order, *command

**commit** *vb* 1 Commit, entrust, confide, consign, relegate are comparable when they mean to assign to a person or place for some definite end or purpose (as custody or safekeeping). **Commit** is the widest term; it may express merely the general idea of delivering into another's charge ⟨*commit* the management of an estate to an agent⟩ ⟨on landing in Boston in 1872, my father and I were able safely to *commit* our trunk to the expressman—*Santayana*⟩ or it may have the special sense of a transfer to a superior power or to a place of custody ⟨into thine hand I·*commit* my spirit—*Ps* 31:5⟩ ⟨we therefore *commit* his body to the ground; earth to earth, ashes to ashes, dust to dust—*Book of Common Prayer*⟩ ⟨*commit* a person to prison⟩ ⟨*commit* one's thoughts to paper⟩ To **entrust** is to commit with trust and confidence; to **confide** is to entrust with entire reliance and assurance ⟨*entrusted* him with her secret⟩ ⟨a government, *entrusted* with such ample powers . . . must also be *entrusted* with ample means for their execution—*John Marshall*⟩ ⟨the right of naturalization was therefore, with one accord, surrendered by the States, and *confided* to the Federal Government—*Taney*⟩ ⟨never to those bloodstained accursed hands will the future of Europe be *confided*—*Sir Winston Churchill*⟩ **Consign** implies a more formal act and frequently suggests such transfer or delivery as removes its object from one's immediate control ⟨*consign* goods to an agent fór sale⟩ ⟨he must now . . . *consign* him to a living tomb again—*Hawthorne*⟩ ⟨the barber and the curate of La Mancha . . . felt bound to wall up Don Quixote's library, and *consigned* to the flames many of the volumes which had so unsettled the poor knight's wits—*Muggeridge*⟩ To **relegate** is to consign to some particular class, position, or sphere usually with the implication of setting aside or getting rid of ⟨[man] is *relegated* to his place in a classification—*Newman*⟩ ⟨he supposed that he had disappointed the Bishop and that he was being *relegated* into the limbo of moderately satisfactory young parsons—*Mackenzie*⟩

*Ana* transfer, shift, remove, *move: assign, *allot

2 Commit, perpetrate mean to be responsible for or to be guilty of some offense or mistake. **Commit** is the term regularly used in prohibiting (as in some of the Ten Commandments) or to describe engaging in an action that is counted a sin, crime, or offense ⟨*commit* murder⟩ ⟨*commit* adultery⟩ ⟨*commit* blasphemy⟩ In less specific use the word may mean little more than *do* or *perform*, but it retains to a greater or less degree its implication of reprehensibility ⟨*commit* a stupid blunder⟩ ⟨*commit* needless errors⟩ **Perpetrate** basically implies the committing of a crime ⟨*perpetrate* arson⟩ ⟨*perpetrate* treason⟩ and often so strongly carries the notion of crime or offense that a neutral word can be used as the object of the verb without any doubt as to its offensive character ⟨the deed was *perpetrated* at midnight⟩ However, *perpetrate* is also freely used of acts or actions which though not criminal are morally, socially, intellectually, or artistically reprehensible and which may range from the utterly outrageous to the mildly deplorable ⟨hastened to *perpetrate* the partition of your country before the Polish nation could consolidate its position—*Sir Winston Churchill*⟩ ⟨the colossal waste they *perpetrate* probably does not exceed the financial blunders and stuffed overhead in big corporations—*Paul*⟩ ⟨Peter Cornelius, who at Munich was quite successfully *perpetrating* . . . about the worst art of the century—*Mather*⟩ ⟨went away feeling I had *perpetrated* a delightful fraud—*L. P. Smith*⟩

*Ana* offend, sin, scandalize (see corresponding nouns at OFFENSE): transgress, trespass, violate, contravene (see corresponding nouns at BREACH)

**commodious** capacious, *spacious, ample

*Ana* *comfortable: *large, big, great: *broad, wide, deep

*Con* circumscribed, confined, limited, restricted (see LIMIT *vb*): inconvenient, incommodious (see corresponding verbs at INCONVENIENCE)

**common** *adj* 1 *universal, general, generic

*Ana* shared, partaken, participated (see SHARE *vb*): joined *or* joint, united, conjoined, connected, associated (see corresponding verbs at JOIN): merged, blended, amalgamated (see MIX)

*Ant* individual

2 mutual, *reciprocal

*Ana & Ant* see those at COMMON 1

3 Common, ordinary, familiar, popular, vulgar are comparable when they mean being or having the character of what is generally or usually met with and not in any way special, strange, or unusual. **Common** implies the lack of distinguishing, conspicuous, or exceptional qualities; positively, it suggests usualness, everyday character or quality, or frequency of occurrence ⟨the *common* people⟩ ⟨a *common* soldier⟩ ⟨the *common* chickweed⟩ ⟨a *common* error⟩ ⟨he lacks *common* honesty⟩ ⟨for *common* men and women two or three of the *common* loves will suffice—the love of family and home, of school and church, of mountain and sea—*Eliot*⟩ Often the term also connotes inferiority, coarseness, lack of breeding, or low station ⟨the *common* herd⟩ ⟨of *common* clay⟩ ⟨O hard is the bed . . . and *common* the blanket and cheap—*Housman*⟩ ⟨a *common* fellow with no notion of politeness or manners⟩ **Ordinary** expresses more definitely accordance with the regular order or run of things ⟨the *ordinary* intercourse of man with man—*Newman*⟩ ⟨it is not an *ordinary* war. It is a revolution . . . which threatens all men everywhere—*Roosevelt*⟩ It usually implies qualities not above, and frequently below, the average ⟨choice word and measured phrase, above the reach of *ordinary* men—*Wordsworth*⟩ ⟨let others expatiate on trivial objects, *ordinary* characters, and uninteresting events—*Landor*⟩ As a term of depreciation *ordinary* is similar to but less contemptuous than *common* ⟨a very *ordinary*-looking person⟩ ⟨his ability is no more than *ordinary*⟩ **Familiar** stresses something that is generally known and easily recognized because of its frequency of occurrence or one's constant association with it rather than because of its lack of distinguishing qualities ⟨the tyranny of *familiar* surroundings over the imagination—*Russell*⟩ ⟨to remind you of what is so *familiar* as to be frequently forgotten—*Frankfurter*⟩ ⟨the doctrine of Einstein, which sweeps away axioms so *familiar* to us that they seem obvious truths, and substitutes others which seem absurd because they are unfamiliar—*Ellis*⟩ **Popular** and **vulgar** (see also COARSE) imply commonness that arises from use or acceptance by or prevalence among the vast majority of persons, often specifically among the common people of a country or an age ⟨*popular* fallacies⟩ ⟨the *vulgar* tongue⟩ *Popular* more often stresses the implication of widespread prevalence, currency, or favor among the

people than does *vulgar,* which even in this sense nearly always carries derogatory connotations (as of inferiority or coarseness) ⟨a *popular* song⟩ ⟨dancing . . . of all the arts . . . most associated in the *popular* mind with pleasure —*Ellis*⟩ ⟨this mode of interpreting Scripture is fatal to the *vulgar* notion of its verbal inspiration—*Arnold*⟩ ⟨a *popular* instead of an accurate and legal conception of what the word *monopolize* in the statute means—*Justice Holmes*⟩ ⟨we were reluctant to expose those silent and beautiful places to *vulgar* curiosity—*Cather*⟩
**Ana** prevalent, *prevailing, rife, current: *usual, customary: *plentiful, abundant, ample
**Ant** uncommon: exceptional —**Con** rare, *infrequent, occasional: singular, unique, peculiar, odd, *strange
**commonplace** *n* **Commonplace, platitude, truism, bromide, cliché** mean an idea or expression lacking in originality or freshness. A **commonplace** is a stock idea or expression which is frequently little more than the obvious, conventional, and easy thing to think or say on a given subject ⟨the machinery as well as the characters of those novels became the *commonplaces* of later romancers—*Raleigh*⟩ ⟨the superficial *commonplaces* which pass as axioms in our popular intellectual milieu—*Cohen*⟩ **Platitude** adds to *commonplace* the suggestions of flatness or triteness and, often, utterance with an air of importance or novelty ⟨what is that sentimental *platitude* of somebody's . . . about the sun being to flowers what art is to life?— *Hewlett*⟩ ⟨traditional schoolbook *platitudes* and campaign slogans—*Frankfurter*⟩ A **truism** is a self-evident truth; it differs from an axiom (see *axiom* at PRINCIPLE) in frequently implying a somewhat superfluous insistence upon the obvious ⟨Pope's palpable *truism* "The proper study of mankind is man"⟩ ⟨it is a *truism* that a sound society makes for sound individuals—*Day Lewis*⟩ **Bromide** applies to a commonplace, platitude, or truism that strikes the listener or reader as especially dull or hackneyed and, often, as an evidence of its maker's low-grade mentality ⟨despite the silly old *bromide,* the fat man is more often than not the best loved of men— *McClure's Mag.*⟩ ⟨under the circumstances the usual, indeed the expected, Chamber of Commerce *bromides* would have been acceptable—*J. M. Brown*⟩ **Cliché** applies to an expression which when new was fresh and full of meaning but which by constant iteration has become not only dull but hackneyed and stereotyped ⟨the *cliché* is merely the sometime novel, that has been loved not wisely but too well—*Lowes*⟩ ⟨the pathetic *cliché,* "for the sake of the children," has perpetuated many unsuccessful marriages—*D. B. Lewis*⟩
**Ana** expression, *phrase, idiom, locution: banality, jejuneness, inanity, wishy-washiness (see corresponding adjectives at INSIPID): triteness, threadbareness (see corresponding adjectives at TRITE)
**common sense** see SENSE 2
**commotion, agitation, tumult, turmoil, turbulence, confusion, convulsion, upheaval** are comparable when they designate great physical, mental, or emotional excitement. All carry this general meaning yet have applications which fit them for narrower use in specific senses. **Commotion** always implies movement to and fro that may be violent and disturbing or that may be merely sharply in contrast to a usual calm. It is used physically of storms, especially as they affect the movement of the seas ⟨beneath the endless surges of the deep . . . a host of mariners perpetual sleep, too hushed to heed the wild *commotion's* roar—*Channing* d. 1901⟩ and of unusual bustle or hubbub ⟨there was *commotion* all over the house at the return of the young heir—*Meredith*⟩ Even when *commotion* represents mental or emotional excitement, it indirectly suggests

movement in heightening the ideas of unrest and perturbation ⟨eighteen years of *commotion* had made the majority of the people ready to buy repose at any price—*Macaulay*⟩ **Agitation,** on the other hand, suggests a stirring up or a shaking up comparable physically to that accompanying a fermentation or to boiling or seething ⟨the *agitation* of the earth's crust during an earthquake⟩ Usually it describes strong emotional excitement that, whether controlled or not, causes distress or pain to the person involved ⟨that sickening *agitation* of the heart which arises from hope deferred—*Scott*⟩ ⟨"Pray," said Mr. Lorry . . . bringing his left hand . . . to lay it on the supplicatory fingers that clasped him in so violent a tremble, "pray control your *agitation*"—*Dickens*⟩ It also may refer to the stirring up of men's minds and emotions on some usually emotionally charged matter or question ⟨political *agitation* by foreign agents⟩ ⟨an anti-Catholic *agitation* that was marked by the destruction of churches— *Amer. Guide Series: N. Y.*⟩ **Tumult** may mean, generally, either commotion or agitation that is characterized by uproar, din, or great disorder ⟨the *tumult* and the shouting dies, the captains and the kings depart—*Kipling*⟩ It also may apply specifically to a riot or fracas or to an insurrection or rebellious outbreak ⟨the *tumults* and disorders of the Great Rebellion had hardly been subdued—*T. S. Eliot*⟩ but it is equally applicable to other things (as a violent disturbance of the elements or an agitating conflict of passions) that suggest in combination noise, disorder, and intense excitement ⟨it thunders and lightens . . . what *tumult's* in the heavens?—*Shak.*⟩ ⟨the gods approve the depth, and not the *tumult,* of the soul— *Wordsworth*⟩ **Turmoil** implies a state where nothing is at rest and where everything seethes with excitement. It is applicable to a state of physical commotion or to a condition of mental or emotional agitation, but in all cases it carries a suggestion of harassment and of ferment from which there seems no escape. In fact, it often connotes the point of view of a person who loves peace and hates disturbance ⟨her life had been calm, regular, monotonous . . . now it was thrown into . . . indescribable *turmoil*— *Bennett*⟩ ⟨the child's inner life is often a *turmoil* of terrors and anxieties of which his parents know almost nothing— *Inge*⟩ ⟨the great peace beyond all this *turmoil* and fret compassed me around—*L. P. Smith*⟩ **Turbulence** implies an excitement that cannot be easily put down or allayed; it may suggest impetuosity, insubordination, unruliness, lack of discipline, or comparable qualities in inanimate things ⟨yon foaming flood seems motionless as ice; its dizzy *turbulence* eludes the eye, frozen by distance— *Wordsworth*⟩ ⟨it required all the personal influence of the king to check the *turbulence* of his irritated followers— *Pattison*⟩ ⟨the rest exhibited plenty of the *turbulence* of passion, but none of the gravity of thoughtful emotion— *Quiller-Couch*⟩ **Confusion** (see also CONFUSION) applies chiefly to a mental state which may affect one person or many and which is marked by such a condition that the mind is at sea and unable to function; usually it suggests perturbation and inability to think coherently often as a result of embarrassment or discomfiture ⟨the crown was thrown into *confusion* by the news⟩ ⟨overcome with *confusion,* and unable to lift up her eyes—*Austen*⟩ ⟨she was slowly emerging from the mental *confusion* which followed the fall—*Ellis*⟩ ⟨to cover his *confusion,* he half turned away—*Anderson*⟩ **Convulsion** and **upheaval** suggest large-scale violent activity, commotion, or agitation. More particularly **convulsion** implies a sudden, surging, confused, or spasmodic action (as in the earth's crust, the individual's mind, or the body politic) ⟨flourishing cities were demolished by the earth's *convulsion*—*Martin*

A colon (:) separates groups of words discriminated. An asterisk (*) indicates place of treatment of each group.

*Gardner*⟩ ⟨a *convulsion* of wild laughter⟩ ⟨the vast social *convulsions* of a continent in travail—*Niebuhr*⟩ while **upheaval** implies a violent and forceful thrusting that results in a heaving up or overthrowing ⟨an emotional *upheaval* as shattering as an earthquake—*Goudge*⟩ ⟨there had also been social *upheavals* before the Reformation— —*J. R. Lowell*⟩

*Ana* hubbub, racket, *din, uproar, pandemonium: *motion, movement: *stir, bustle, flurry, ado

*Con* calmness *or* calm, placidity, tranquillity (see corresponding adjectives at CALM): quietness *or* quiet, silentness *or* silence, stillness (see corresponding adjectives at STILL)

**commune** *vb* *confer, consult, advise, parley, treat, negotiate

*Ana* converse, talk, *speak: *discuss, debate, argue

**communicable** *infectious, contagious, catching

**communicate,** **impart** mean to convey or transfer something (as information, feelings, or qualities) neither tangible nor concrete; they differ chiefly in emphasis, *communicate* stressing the result, *impart* rather the process, of the transfer. To **communicate** (the more general term) is to make common to both parties or objects involved the knowledge or quality conveyed; to **impart** is to share with another what is regarded as primarily one's own ⟨his courage *communicated* itself to his men⟩ ⟨the smoke *imparted* its odor to his clothes⟩ ⟨teaching is essentially an *imparting* of one's knowledge or skill to others⟩ ⟨I wonder do we ever succeed really in *communicating* our thoughts to one another—*Shaw*⟩ ⟨you are worth to society the happiness you are capable of *imparting*—*Holland*⟩

*Ana* acquaint, apprise, *inform, advise, notify: tell, disclose, *reveal, divulge, discover: convey, *transfer

*Con* conceal, *hide: *suppress, repress: withhold, hold, hold back, keep back, reserve (see KEEP)

**communication** *intercourse, commerce, traffic, dealings, conversation, converse, correspondence, communion

*Ana* exchanging *or* exchange, interchanging *or* interchange (see corresponding verbs at EXCHANGE): conversing, talking (see SPEAK): *news, tidings, advice, intelligence

**communion** 1 *intercourse, commerce, traffic, converse, dealings, communication, conversation, correspondence

*Ana* empathy, *sympathy: mysticism (see under ASCETIC): contemplation (see corresponding verb at CONSIDER): *ecstasy, rapture, transport

2 *religion, denomination, faith, church, creed, sect, cult, persuasion

**compact** *adj* dense, *close, thick

*Ana* compressed, condensed, contracted (see CONTRACT *vb*): concentrated, consolidated, compacted (see COMPACT *vb*): solid, *firm, hard: *tight

*Con* *loose, slack: diffuse, prolix, verbose, *wordy: tenuous, rare, *thin

**compact** *vb* **Compact, consolidate, unify, concentrate** are comparable when meaning to bring or gather together the parts, particles, elements, or units of a thing so as to form a close mass or an integral whole. **Compact** stresses the process more than the effect. It usually suggests a packing or pressing together of many things so as to form a closely arranged mass or a dense substance and may be used in reference both to material and immaterial things; sometimes it carries so strong an implication of solid formation or construction that it fundamentally means to build firmly or to strengthen ⟨heat and lack of rain have *compacted* the soil⟩ ⟨*compact* matted fibers of wool and hair into felt by rolling and pressing⟩ ⟨sweet spring . . . a box where sweets *compacted* lie—*Herbert*⟩ ⟨it

is based on solid facts, nay, is *compacted* of solid facts from the first sentence to the last—*Times Lit. Sup.*⟩ **Consolidate** implies a merging or uniting, often in an exceedingly close union, of previously distinct but usually homogeneous or complementary things. The term may take as its object such a whole as a nation, a people, or an empire or as a substance or material and may imply a process which promotes the binding together of the parts, elements, or individuals so that solidarity or solidity is achieved ⟨war tends to *consolidate* a people⟩ ⟨organize state leagues for political action in order to *consolidate* the labor vote—*Watkins*⟩ ⟨rolling and cooling *consolidated* the newly laid asphalt into a firm smooth pavement⟩ But *consolidate* can also take as its objects the units (as parts, elements, individuals, or groups) which have been brought together in close union ⟨these organizations worked independently, and subsequently they were partially *consolidated*—*Heiser*⟩ ⟨two marriages with the Dutch Vandergraves had *consolidated* these qualities of thrift and handsome living—*Wharton*⟩ **Unify** implies a union of heterogeneous or homogeneous parts, elements, or individuals that results in the making or producing of a thing that has oneness and integrity and that stands by itself as a thing apart; the term does not, however, carry as strong an implication of solidarity as does *consolidate* but, on the other hand, it places stress on the integration of parts so that each does its appointed work or serves its own purpose to the benefit not only of itself but of the whole; thus, a dramatist *unifies* (not *consolidates*) the play he composes; after a civil war, the task of the government is to *unify* (rather than *consolidate*) a nation; the imagination of a great poet *unifies* a mass of images and impressions; the Homeric poems may have been originally a collection of narrative poems, but it seems likely that one person *unified* them ⟨would now be technically possible to *unify* the world and abolish war—*Russell*⟩ **Concentrate** usually carries the implication of bringing together a number of things that are scattered or diffused and of massing them around a point or center; ⟨*concentrate* troops at places where an attack is expected⟩ ⟨*concentrate* one's efforts on a single piece of work⟩ ⟨the science of that age was all divination, clairvoyance . . . seeking in an instant of vision to *concentrate* a thousand experiences—*Pater*⟩ **Concentrate** may be extended to imply the fixing of the mind or attention on one thing so that all distracting objects or thoughts are eliminated ⟨her excitement made her unable to *concentrate* on the task⟩ A similar implication of eliminating whatever weakens, dilutes, or adulterates is found in technical use; thus, the chemist *concentrates* a solution by evaporating the solvent; a miner *concentrates* ores (i. e., separates the base from the precious metals) by a machine or by washing.

*Ana* compress, condense, *contract: bind, *tie: unite, combine (see JOIN): knit, *weave

*Con* dissipate, disperse, *scatter: *separate, part, divide

**compact** *n* pact, entente, convention, concordat, treaty, cartel, *contract, bargain

**companion** *n* comrade, *associate, crony

*Ana* *friend, confidant, intimate, acquaintance: *partner, colleague: attendant, escort, chaperon (see corresponding verbs at ACCOMPANY)

**companionable** *social, cooperative, convivial, gregarious, hospitable

*Ana* friendly, neighborly, *amicable: *amiable, obliging, complaisant, good-natured: sociable, affable, *gracious, cordial

*Con* uncongenial, unsympathetic (see INCONSONANT): reserved, taciturn, uncommunicative (see SILENT)

---

*Ana* analogous words      *Ant* antonyms      *Con* contrasted words      See also explanatory notes facing page 1

**company,** party, band, troop, troupe are comparable when they denote a group of persons who are associated in a joint endeavor or who are assembled for a common end. **Company** is the general term for either a temporary assemblage or a permanent association of individuals who join forces ⟨the glorious *company* of the apostles —*Book of Common Prayer*⟩ ⟨the whole *company* of thinkers who have written philosophy—*Sullivan*⟩ A **party** is a company assembled temporarily for a common purpose ⟨search *party*⟩ ⟨dinner *party*⟩ ⟨a *party* of visitors from the country⟩ A **band** is a company united by a common tie or purpose; the term implies closer organization and a less casual coming together than does *company* ⟨the robbers worked in *bands*⟩ ⟨a *band* of musicians⟩ ⟨that small, transfigured *band* . . . whose one bond is, that all have been unspotted by the world—*Arnold*⟩ A **troop** is a company or band that works or acts together in close formation or in unanimity; the term frequently suggests a throng or multitude ⟨there entertain him all the saints above, in solemn *troops,* and sweet societies—*Milton*⟩ ⟨a mobile and dynamic *troop* whose major aims are the improvement of the mind —*Hauser*⟩ In specific use **troop** is applied to a band of soldiers or, in the plural *troops,* to soldiers collectively ⟨farewell the plumed *troop,* and the big wars—*Shak.*⟩ ⟨British *troops*⟩ When the reference is to a company of performers (especially on the stage) **troupe** is the preferred spelling ⟨a circus *troupe*⟩
*Ana* \*set, circle, coterie, clique: \*association, society, club, order: \*crowd, throng, mob, horde

**comparable** \*like, alike, similar, analogous, akin, parallel, uniform, identical
*Ant* disparate —*Con* \*different, divergent, diverse, various

**compare,** contrast, collate mean to set two or more things side by side in order to show likenesses and differences. **Compare** implies as an aim the showing of relative values or excellences or a bringing out of characteristic qualities, whether they are similar or divergent; **contrast** implies as the aim an attempt to emphasize their differences; thus, one may *compare* the movement of the *Odyssey* with that of the *Aeneid* to arrive at their distinctive qualities; one may thereupon *contrast* the buoyancy and rapidity of the one with the stateliness and dignity of the other. One object is *compared with* another, as above: it is *compared to* another when it is formally represented on the basis of a real or imagined similarity as being like that other; thus, Pope *compares* Homer *with* (not *to*) Vergil; he *compares* Homer *to* (not *with*) the Nile, pouring out his riches with a boundless overflow, Vergil *to* (not *with*) a river in its banks, with a gentle and constant stream. **Collate** suggests a minute or critical comparison in order to note points of agreement and divergence; it applies especially to the minute comparison of books and manuscripts containing different versions of the same work for the sake of ascertaining or establishing the correct text ⟨he has visited all Europe . . . not to collect medals, or *collate* manuscripts: but . . . to compare and *collate* the distresses of all men in all countries—*Burke*⟩
*Ana* \*match, equal, approach, touch, rival

**comparison,** contrast, antithesis, collation, parallel mean a setting of things side by side so as to discover or exhibit their likenesses and differences, especially their generic likenesses and differences. **Comparison** is often used as the comprehensive term; it is preferred when the differences are obvious, and an intent to lay bare resemblances and similarities for the sake of expounding or judging is implied ⟨despite the fact that Communism and Fascism are antagonistic ideologies, there is ground for a *comparison* between them⟩ ⟨students who make a *comparison* of Shakespeare's *Hamlet* and the play which was its source acquire intimate knowledge of the great dramatist's indebtedness to others⟩ Because measuring one thing in terms of another is usually implied by *comparison,* the word often imputes an offensive character either to the association ⟨the *comparison* of "the colonel's lady" and "Judy O'Grady"⟩ or to the judgment ⟨*comparisons* are odious⟩ ⟨a tactful person never makes *comparisons*⟩ ⟨he will lose nothing by the *comparison*⟩ ⟨make no *comparisons*; and if any of the company be commended for any brave act of virtue, commend not another for the same—*Washington*⟩ **Contrast** more specifically implies an intent to distinguish or discriminate things which are so much alike that their differences are not obvious ⟨the correct use of close synonyms can be shown only by *contrast*⟩ ⟨you cannot value him alone; you must set him, for *contrast* and comparison, among the dead—*T. S. Eliot*⟩ **Contrast** often also suggests an aesthetic rather than an expository aim or an artistic effect gained by the exhibition of startling differences ⟨in physical appearance that *contrast* is glaring . . . the square, full-blooded, blunt face of the one, the pointed chin and finely cut, pale features of the other—*Belloc*⟩ **Antithesis** also implies contrast for the sake of revealing startling differences, but it distinctively suggests such opposition in the things contrasted that they either represent balancing extremes or negate each other. The word may imply an expository intent; it then presupposes that the true nature of one thing is fully understood only when it is presented as opposed to what is unlike it in every particular ⟨the century-old *antitheses* of heavenly justice and earthly fallibility, sin and innocence, Heaven and Hell, God and the Devil dominate Melville's mind—*Weir*⟩ **Collation** and *parallel* denote a kind of comparison for the purpose of revealing both likenesses and differences. Both imply a close study and usually a specific aim. **Collation** more specifically implies a comparison of different versions, accounts, editions, texts, or manuscripts of the same thing for the purpose of verification, coordination, correction, or selection of the original ⟨make a *collation* of the Scriptural accounts of the Resurrection⟩ ⟨of these [corrupt passages in Shakespeare] the restoration is only to be attempted by *collation* of copies or sagacity of conjecture—*Johnson*⟩ and **parallel** usually a minute comparison of passages, articles, or works which are believed to have a different origin in order to detect correspondences, or of accounts, records, or stories told at different times which ought to agree, in order to detect discrepancies; thus, by what is often called "the deadly *parallel*," a comparison of two articles may reveal such correspondences in language and thought as to give ground for a charge of plagiarism, or a comparison of testimony given by the same witness on two occasions may reveal discrepancies that make him liable to arrest for perjury.
*Ana* \*likeness, similarity, resemblance, analogy, similitude, affinity: \*parallel, counterpart, analogue, correlate

**compass** *vb* 1 \*surround, environ, encircle, circle, encompass, hem, gird, girdle, ring
*Ana* \*enclose, envelop: confine, circumscribe, restrict (see LIMIT)
2 gain, attain, achieve, \*reach
*Ana* effect, fulfill, accomplish, \*perform: complete, finish (see CLOSE *vb*)

**compass** *n* 1 \*circumference, perimeter, periphery, circuit
*Ana* area, extent, magnitude, \*size: \*field, sphere, domain
2 \*range, gamut, reach, radius, sweep, scope, orbit,

A colon (:) separates groups of words discriminated. An asterisk (\*) indicates place of treatment of each group.

horizon, ken, purview
**Ana** circumscription, limitation, restriction (see corresponding verbs at LIMIT): limits, bounds, confines (see singular nouns at LIMIT)
**compassion** pity, commiseration, ruth, *sympathy, empathy, condolence
**Ana** tenderness, compassionateness, responsiveness, warmheartedness (see corresponding adjectives at TENDER): *mercy, charity, grace, lenity, clemency
**Con** indifference, aloofness, unconcern (see corresponding adjectives at INDIFFERENT): mercilessness, relentlessness, implacability (see corresponding adjectives at GRIM)
**compassionate** *tender, sympathetic, warmhearted, warm, responsive
**Ana** *pitiful, piteous: merciful, *forbearing, clement, lenient: humane, benevolent, *charitable
**Con** merciless, unrelenting, relentless, implacable, *grim: obdurate, inexorable, *inflexible, adamant
**compatible** congruous, *consonant, consistent, congenial, sympathetic
**Ana** suitable, appropriate, proper, meet, fitting, *fit: harmonizing, corresponding *or* correspondent, according *or* accordant (see corresponding verbs at AGREE): harmonious (see corresponding noun HARMONY)
**Ant** incompatible —**Con** incongruous, *inconsonant, inconsistent, uncongenial, discordant, discrepant: *adverse, antagonistic, counter
**compel** *force, coerce, constrain, oblige
**Ana** impel, drive, *move: *command, order, enjoin
**Con** prevail, *induce, persuade, get: *coax, cajole, wheedle, blandish
**compelling** telling, convincing, cogent, sound, *valid
**compendious** summary, pithy, succinct, *concise, terse, laconic
**Ana** compact, *close: condensed, contracted (see CONTRACT *vb*): abridged, abbreviated, shortened (see SHORTEN)
**Con** amplified, expanded, inflated (see EXPAND): *full, complete: diffuse, prolix (see WORDY)
**compendium,** syllabus, digest, pandect, survey, sketch, précis, aperçu are comparable when they mean a treatment of a subject or of a topic in brief compass. A **compendium** gathers in brief, orderly, and intelligible form, sometimes outlined, the facts, principles, or details essential to a general understanding of some matter; the word typically implies compilation rather than original investigation ⟨*A Treatise on Epidemic Cholera* which contained little original matter but was published as a *compendium* of the existing knowledge of this disease —*Steiner*⟩ A **syllabus,** often presented with a series of headings, points, or propositions, gives concise statements affording a view of the whole and an indication of its significance ⟨no party program, no official *syllabus* of opinions, which we all have to defend—*Inge*⟩ A **digest** presents a body of information gathered from many sources and arranged and classified for ready accessibility, often alphabetized and indexed; the word also indicates a condensed easy-to-read version ⟨the only hope of gaining such knowledge lies in a summarization and thorough *digest* of the huge body of county statistics already available—*Bogue*⟩ ⟨the *Current Digest of the Soviet Press,* now in its fifth year of uninterrupted weekly appearance, a seventy-thousand word a week *digest* of forty Russian newspapers and periodicals—*Mortimer Graves*⟩ A **pandect** is a systematic digest covering the whole of a monumental subject ⟨no printed body of modern social history, either by purpose or accident, contains a richer *pandect* of the efficient impulses of its age—*Morley*⟩ A **survey** is a brief comprehensive presen-

tation giving main outlines, often as a preliminary aid to thorough study or more detailed treatment ⟨the policy of the Board and its founder being to make first of all a . . . *survey* of the educational needs of the country —*J. D. Greene*⟩ ⟨an essay on the Renaissance, not a history of the Renaissance. It omits mention of many interesting details of that vast transformation in an effort to determine, through a broad *survey* of its more salient features, the fundamental nature of the movement— *Sellery*⟩ A **sketch** is a slight tentative preliminary presentation subject to later change, emendation, and amplification ⟨to give anything but the most fragmentary *sketch* of the winter of '94 and '95 in Berlin is impossible— *Fairchild*⟩ ⟨*The American Chancery Digest,* including state and federal equity decisions, with an introductory *sketch* of equity courts and their jurisdiction—*Wilkinson*⟩ A **précis** is a concise clear-cut statement or restatement of main matters, often in the form of a report or a summary that suggests the style or tone of an original ⟨a carefully prepared critical text of Guido, with a short critical introduction, a full critical apparatus, and English *précis* printed concurrently—*Times Lit. Sup.*⟩ An **aperçu** is a sketch giving a very brief and sometimes impressionistic compression of the whole, with all details omitted ⟨popular books which give an *aperçu* of recent research, in order to have some idea of the general scientific purpose served by particular facts and laws—*Russell*⟩
**Ana** conspectus, epitome, brief, abstract (see ABRIDGMENT)
**compensate** *vb* **1** Compensate, countervail, balance, offset, counterbalance, counterpoise are comparable when meaning to make up for or to undo the effects of. **Compensate** is by far the broadest of these terms both in mode of use and scope of application. It may be used transitively and especially passively with either the one to be made up to or the thing to be made up for as object, or it may be used intransitively. In either case it is commonly modified by a phrase governed by *for* denoting a cause, by *with* specifying an equivalent, or by *by* indicating an action. It is freely applicable to the purely physical ⟨*compensate* a pendulum for the effects of temperature change⟩ ⟨a weakened heart *compensated* by muscular hypertrophy⟩ to the economic (see also PAY) ⟨*compensate* a wounded soldier with a pension⟩ ⟨the Assembly put through this Bill, for *compensating* persons who had suffered losses through the Rebellion of 1837—*Sandwell*⟩ or to the immaterial ⟨an air of dignity and distinction *compensated* the deficiencies of beauty—*Bromfield*⟩ ⟨dreams, drives, and yearnings . . . which may be pleasant or unpleasant in themselves but which at all events console and *compensate*—*Bentley*⟩ ⟨*compensate* for his feelings of loneliness by assertions of superiority—*Auden*⟩ One thing **countervails** another, or *against* another, when the former is sufficiently strong, powerful, or efficient to counteract the influence exerted or the harm or damage done by the latter or suffered in consequence of it ⟨so shall my credit *countervail* your shame—*Browning*⟩ ⟨the absence of fuss . . . *countervailed* any tendency to self-importance—*S. T. Warner*⟩ ⟨the fact . . . shall, in the absence of strong *countervailing* testimony, be deemed conclusive evidence —*Lincoln*⟩ One thing **balances** another, or two things *balance* (or *balance* each other) when both are so adjusted that they are either equal or properly proportioned (as in numbers, quantity, size, importance, or effectiveness) and the combination is harmonious because neither one outweighs the other or can exert a harmful influence on the whole ⟨in sentencing prisoners, the judge *balanced* justice and mercy⟩ ⟨in the healthy human body the salt intake and the salt loss through excretion *balance*⟩

---

**Ana** analogous words     **Ant** antonyms     **Con** contrasted words     See also explanatory notes facing page 1

⟨the general tendency to the degradation or dissipation of energy is *balanced* . . . by a building-up process in the cell and in the organism—*Inge*⟩ ⟨that, like a ground in painting, *balances* all hues and forms, combining with one tone whatever lights or shades are on it thrown—*Bridges*⟩ ⟨the pressures of business, labor, and farmers . . . manage to check and *balance* each other—*Ascoli*⟩ One thing **offsets** another (this and the following terms have no intransitive use) when the former, as the exact opposite of the latter and its equal (as in importance, in effectiveness, in power, or in numbers), neutralizes the latter's good or evil effect, gain or loss, or benefit or harm ⟨his loss of thousands of votes from his own party was *offset* by his gain in independent votes⟩ ⟨the disadvantages of the plan are sufficient to *offset* its clear advantages⟩ ⟨the benefits of favorable climatic environment are oftentimes more than *offset* by the inconveniences of travel, loneliness, and homesickness—*Heiser*⟩ ⟨it is difficult to see any need for it that *offsets* in the slightest all the trouble it may cause—*Chafee*⟩ One thing **counterbalances** another when the former serves or is intended to serve to offset some quality (as an excess, a deficiency, or an evil) in the latter ⟨in his second book, there has to be rather more about religion to *counterbalance* the detailed, joyless descriptions of the heroine's sex life—*Punch*⟩ or when the former acts as a corrective of any tendency in the latter to loss of equilibrium or proper balance, especially when it, or one of its parts, is subjected to undue pressure, strain, or tension ⟨a heavy weight suspended on a cable which is attached to an elevator and passes over a pulley at the top of the shaft serves to *counterbalance* the increased load when the elevator carries passengers or freight⟩ ⟨mine hoists are often operated by the *counterbalancing* of an ascending and a descending car⟩ One thing **counterpoises** another when the former provides the equivalent of the latter in weight or value (physical, spiritual, artistic) and insures the balance of the whole ⟨like scales, in which the weight on one side must be *counterpoised* by a weight in the other —*Jefferies*⟩ ⟨the new tower is a little wanting in repose for a tower whose business is to *counterpoise* the very classic lines of the old one—*Henry Adams*⟩
*Ana* counteract, *neutralize, negative: *nullify, negate, annul, abrogate, invalidate: complement, supplement (see under COMPLEMENT *n*): correspond, square, tally, jibe, *agree
2 remunerate, *pay, recompense, repay, reimburse, satisfy, indemnify

**compete** 1 Compete, contend, contest are comparable especially in their intransitive senses when they mean to strive to gain the mastery or upper hand. **Compete** (see also RIVAL) implies a struggle to overcome or get the better of in an activity requiring two or more participants and involving rivalry (as an athletic match or a debate); the term may sometimes connote an additional incentive or inducement (as a prize or reward) ⟨the two classes *competed* in a spelling bee⟩ ⟨*compete* for places on the football team⟩ ⟨there were several boys anxious to *compete* for the scholarship⟩ **Contend**, which may suggest a straining or stretching (see CONTEND), usually implies opposition that has equal or better chances of succeeding and therefore a vigorous endeavor to win or to attain or to down or to frustrate; the term usually connotes competition, but it stresses the need of fighting or struggling ⟨strength of shade *contends* with strength of light—*Pope*⟩ ⟨the passions and hopes which he had excited had become too strong for him to *contend* against—*Froude*⟩ ⟨forced to *contend* with an army that outnumbered them⟩ **Contest** usually implies a competing but, since the word may

be qualified with respect to the way in which the rivalry manifests itself, it often suggests a contending. The term may be used in reference to a debate, dispute, or controversy, a race or an athletic competition, or a physical fight or struggle but it invariably involves the idea of proving one's mastery or superiority ⟨the election for the office of district attorney was hotly *contested*⟩ ⟨the rivals *contested* lukewarmly for the crown⟩
*Ana* battle, fight (see CONTEND): *rival, vie: oppose, combat, withstand (see RESIST)
2 vie, *rival, emulate
*Ana* *contend, fight: *match, rival, approach, equal, touch

**competent** capable, qualified, *able
*Ana* *proficient, skillful, skilled, adept, expert, masterly: efficient, *effective
*Ant* incompetent —*Con* *incapable, unqualified: inefficient, *ineffective

**compile** *edit, revise, redact, rewrite, adapt

**complacent, self-complacent, self-satisfied, smug, priggish** are comparable when they mean feeling or showing satisfaction especially in one's own possessions, attainments, accomplishments, or virtues. **Complacent** implies that a feeling of pleasure accompanies this satisfaction; it may suggest merely a sense of well-being that comes from having no complaint to make, or, at the other extreme, it may imply gloating over the success of something for which one is in some way or in some degree responsible ⟨Mrs. Baines laughed with the *complacent* ease of obesity—*Bennett*⟩ ⟨"nothing in my brain I bring" —he seems to hymn with a pious and *complacent* humility his freedom from intellectual baggage—*Montague*⟩ ⟨*complacent* when they should have been self-critical —*Nevins & Commager*⟩ Although *complacent* usually suggests an attitude toward oneself, it does not carry that implication so clearly that there is left no room for doubt. For this reason **self-complacent** or **self-satisfied** is often preferred when an unequivocal or an unambiguous word is desired; both carry a strong implication either of a comparison made between oneself and others to the great disadvantage of the others or of a feeling that one can rise no higher ⟨all nature may be represented as groaning and travailing to produce at last her consummate masterpiece, our noble selves. There is a certain provincialism about this last assumption, characteristic of a *self-complacent* age—*Inge*⟩ ⟨the strong, *self-complacent* Luther declares . . . that "God himself cannot do without wise men"—*Emerson*⟩ ⟨no bandit fierce, no tyrant mad with pride, no caverned hermit, rests *self-satisfied*—*Pope*⟩ **Smug** usually implies a habitual self-satisfaction that arouses in some degree dislike or contempt; the term often implies both self-satisfaction and conscious respectability, and it may additionally connote narrowness or provinciality or a degree of self-righteousness ⟨his worldwide sympathy . . . with everything but the *smug* commonplace—*Birrell*⟩ ⟨a *smug* . . . quality . . . had crept into that stern piety—*Bates*⟩ ⟨those late Georgian days which were the *smuggest* known to fame—*Replier*⟩ **Priggish**, like *smug*, is difficult to confine to any one sense or to any constant emphasis on certain implications; while it typically connotes either self-satisfaction, self-sufficiency, or self-righteousness, it usually also suggests either a more or less conscious assumption of one's own superiority or an obvious effort to live up to what one considers one's high principles or one's high ideals ⟨a serious, earnest lad who gave many the impression that he was *priggish*⟩ ⟨that unpromising young man with high collar and pince-nez whose somewhat *priggish* air of superiority infuriated most of the

Democrats—*Schlesinger* b. 1917⟩
*Ana* self-assured, self-confident, self-possessed, assured, confident (see corresponding nouns at CONFIDENCE): conceited, egotistic, egoistic (see corresponding nouns at CONCEIT): proud, vain, vainglorious (see under PRIDE *n*)
*Con* *humble, modest: diffident, *shy

**complaint** ailment, *disease, disorder, condition, affection, malady, distemper, syndrome

**complaisant** obliging, good-natured, *amiable
*Ana* affable, genial, cordial, *gracious: courteous, courtly, gallant, polite, *civil: *suave, urbane, politic, diplomatic, smooth, bland: agreeable, *pleasant, pleasing
*Ant* contrary, perverse —*Con* disagreeable, unpleasant (see affirmative adjectives at PLEASANT): uncongenial, unsympathetic (see INCONSONANT): *cold, chilly, frigid

**complement** *n* Complement, supplement are comparable both as nouns meaning one thing that makes up for a want or deficiency in another thing and as verbs meaning to supply what is needed to make up for such a want or deficiency. **Complement** implies a completing; it may suggest such a relation between two things or two groups of things that if they are put together they form a whole, or the full number, amount, or quantity necessary for a given purpose; thus, a grammatical *complement* is a word or phrase which must be added to a predicate if the latter is to make a definite assertion (as *well* in "he feels *well*," *free* in "to set him *free*," *of no use* in "it proved *of no use*") ⟨bought a farm complete with its *complement* of implements and livestock⟩ ⟨you need two more chairs to *complement* those you already have in the room⟩ However, the term even more often suggests such disparity in two things that what is supplied by either one is lacking in the other, with the result that their actual or theoretical combination gives a completeness that constitutes or approaches perfection ⟨had found someone whose . . . masculinity was the very *complement* of his own fragile graces—*Horace Gregory*⟩ ⟨no adequate conception of the pictorial art of Asia can be attained without taking account of these wonderful works [of Japanese figure painting], *complementing,* as they do, the philosophic and poetic art which culminated in the Chinese painting of the Sung era—*Binyon*⟩ ⟨the chief products of Belgium and the Netherlands appeared to *complement* more than to duplicate one another—*Valentine*⟩ **Supplement** implies an addition to something relatively complete but capable of improvement, enrichment, or enhancement by such an addition; thus, a *supplement* to a newspaper (often, a "book *supplement*" or "literary *supplement*") is an additional section which enriches the character of the issue. Usually the term means exactly this ⟨a year of foreign travel is an excellent *supplement* to a college education⟩ ⟨*supplement* a work with an index⟩ ⟨the detailed study of history should be *supplemented* by brilliant outlines—*Russell*⟩ Sometimes, however, the term carries the implication of needless addition ⟨the policy of apartheid is only a political *supplement* to an economic policy—*Ross*⟩ Sometimes, on the other hand, it comes close to *complement* in suggesting essential differences or a need of combination if perfection is to be attained ⟨physics, history, and religion have their different valuations of experience . . . . A complete philosophy would find room for all and would show how they *supplement* each other—*Inge*⟩ ⟨the settle, which is the necessary *supplement* to a fire so open that nothing less than a strong breeze will carry up the smoke—*Hardy*⟩
*Ana* counterpart, correlate, *parallel

**complement** *vb* supplement (see under COMPLEMENT *n*)
*Ana* complete, finish, *close

**complementary, complemental** *reciprocal, correlative,

corresponding, convertible
*Ana* complementing, supplementing (see corresponding verbs under COMPLEMENT *n*): completing, finishing (see CLOSE *vb*): related, associated (see JOIN)
*Con* *different, diverse, divergent, disparate: *inconsonant, incompatible, incongruous, inconsistent

**complete** *adj* *full, plenary, replete
*Ana* entire, *whole, total, all: *perfect, intact, whole, entire
*Ant* incomplete

**complete** *vb* finish, conclude, *close, end, terminate
*Ana* effect, fulfill, achieve, execute, accomplish, *perform, discharge
*Con* initiate, inaugurate, start, *begin, commence

**complex** *adj* Complex, complicated, intricate, involved, knotty are comparable when they mean having parts or elements that are more or less confusingly interrelated. Something is **complex** which is made up of so many different interrelated or interacting parts or elements that it requires deep study or expert knowledge to deal with it ⟨the *complex* mechanism of a watch⟩ ⟨our general failure to grasp the need of knowledge and thought in mastering the *complex* modern world—*Russell*⟩ ⟨the *complex* details of naval, ground, and air activities—*Roosevelt*⟩ Something is **complicated** which is so complex that it is exceedingly difficult to understand, solve, explain, or deal with ⟨a *complicated* problem in mathematics⟩ ⟨his descriptions of the most *complicated* organic structures are astonishingly lucid—*Huxley*⟩ Something is **intricate** which, because of the interwinding or interlacing of its parts, is perplexing or hard to follow out ⟨the *intricate* tracery of an arabesque⟩ ⟨nature utilizes the sunshine, the air and the earth as raw materials for creating myriad perfumes, but so *intricate* are her processes . . . that man cannot follow precisely in her footsteps—*Morrison*⟩ ⟨the economic situation is so complex, so *intricate* in the interdependence of delicately balanced factors—*Dewey*⟩ Something is **involved** in which the parts are or are thought of as so intertwined or interwoven or so turned upon themselves as to be separated or traced out only with difficulty; the term, therefore, in reference especially to financial affairs, implies extreme complication or disorder ⟨the *involved* patterns of heraldic knots⟩ ⟨an *involved* sentence or argument⟩ ⟨her husband . . . at his death . . . had left his affairs dreadfully *involved* —*Austen*⟩ ⟨public issues are so large and so *involved* that it is only a few who can hope to have any adequate comprehension of them—*Dickinson*⟩ Something is **knotty** which is not only complicated but is so full of perplexities, difficulties, or entanglements that understanding or solving seems almost impossible ⟨that brings up at last the *knotty* question, what is enough?—*Shaw*⟩ ⟨the *knotty* problems of a complex society—*Parrington*⟩ The same object may often be regarded from more than one of the above points of view; a sailor's knot may be *intricate* and *complicated,* as well as *involved;* a network of railroad trucks may be *complicated* as well as *intricate,* though not *involved.*
*Ana* mixed, mingled, blended, merged, fused, amalgamated (see MIX): composite, compound (see corresponding nouns at MIXTURE)
*Ant* simple (see PURE)

**complex** *n* *system, scheme, network, organism, economy
*Ant* component —*Con* member, *part, portion, piece: constituent, *element, factor: *item, particular, detail

**complexion** temperament, temper, *disposition, character, personality, individuality
*Ana* humor (see WIT): *mood, humor, vein, temper: nature, kind, *type, sort

**compliance** acquiescence, resignation (see under COM-

PLIANT)

*Ana* obedience, docility, amenableness, tractableness (see corresponding adjectives at OBEDIENT): submitting *or* submission, yielding, deferring *or* deference (see corresponding verbs at YIELD)

*Ant* frowardness —*Con* obstinacy, stubbornness (see corresponding adjectives at OBSTINATE)

**compliant, acquiescent, resigned,** and their corresponding nouns **compliance, acquiescence, resignation,** are comparable when used in reference to a person, a mood, or a disposition that manifests acceptance (as of another's will or of something disagreeable or hard to endure). **Compliant** suggests a flexibility or lack of firmness in mood or temperament and frequently implies readiness to accept meekly and without question ⟨educational methods that make children *compliant*⟩ ⟨a naturally *compliant* race⟩ **Acquiescent** implies acceptance without protest or rebellion; it often also connotes a temperamental lack of self-assertiveness ⟨the cause of reform slowly went on gaining adherents—most of them . . . of the *acquiescent* rather than the militant type—*Grandgent*⟩ **Resigned** usually presupposes a disposition or a temperament neither compliant nor acquiescent and implies deliberate but not necessarily happy acceptance and resolute forbearance from repining ⟨he had become *resigned* to her perpetual lamentation—*Meredith*⟩ ⟨*resignation* to inevitable evils is the duty of us all—*Austen*⟩

*Ana* *obedient, amenable, tractable, docile: submissive, *tame, subdued: accommodating, conforming, adapting *or* adaptable (see corresponding verbs at ADAPT)

*Ant* froward —*Con* *contrary, perverse, balky, restive, wayward: refractory, recalcitrant, *unruly, ungovernable, intractable, willful, headstrong

**complicated** intricate, involved, *complex, knotty

*Ana* difficult, arduous, *hard: abstruse, *recondite: perplexing, puzzling, mystifying (see PUZZLE *vb*)

*Ant* simple —*Con* *easy, facile, light

**compliment** *n* **Compliment, flattery, adulation** all denote praise addressed directly to a person. A **compliment** is a courteous expression of commendation and may be either sincere or merely formal ⟨in the noble dedication . . . to the Duchess of Ormond we have an example of Dryden's most polished and magnificent style in elaborate personal *compliment*—*Gosse*⟩ ⟨pay the craftsmen the *compliment* of making a study of their language—*Ullyett*⟩ **Flattery** implies insincerity in compliment or a play upon self-love or vanity by means of artful or obsequious praise ⟨when one is flagging, a little praise (if it can be had genuine and unadulterated by *flattery*) . . . is a cordial —*Scott*⟩ ⟨it is better to leave genuine praise unspoken than to expose yourself to the suspicion of *flattery*—*Shaw*⟩ **Adulation** adds to *flattery* the implications of servility or fulsomeness ⟨he fascinated others into believing him a superior being; feasted his self-esteem on their *adulation* until it swelled to monstrous proportions—*Huxley*⟩

*Ana* *encomium, tribute, panegyric, eulogy: praise, lauding *or* laudation, extolling *or* extollation (see corresponding verbs at PRAISE)

*Ant* taunt —*Con* *affront, insult, indignity: depreciation, disparagement (see corresponding verbs at DECRY): criticism, censure, reprehension, reprobation, denunciation (see corresponding verbs at CRITICIZE)

**compliment** *vb* *commend, applaud, recommend

*Ana* *praise, laud, extol, eulogize, acclaim

*Con* *criticize, censure, reprehend, condemn, denounce: *decry, depreciate, disparage

**comply** *obey, mind

*Ana* accede, consent, agree, acquiesce (see ASSENT):

*yield, submit, defer, bow

*Ant* command, enjoin —*Con* *resist, withstand: thwart, balk, *frustrate

**component** constituent, ingredient, *element, factor

*Ana* member, *part, detail, portion, piece: *item, particular

*Ant* composite: complex —*Con* *mixture, compound, blend, admixture, amalgam

**comport** acquit, quit, demean, *behave, conduct, deport

**compose** *calm, quiet, quieten, still, lull, soothe, settle, tranquilize

*Ana* *pacify, mollify, propitiate, conciliate: *moderate, temper

*Ant* discompose —*Con* disquiet, disturb, perturb, agitate, upset (see DISCOMPOSE)

**composed** collected, *cool, unruffled, imperturbable, unflappable, nonchalant

*Ana* quiet, *still: serene, placid, tranquil, *calm: sedate, staid, *serious: repressed, suppressed (see SUPPRESS)

*Ant* discomposed: anxious —*Con* agitated, perturbed, upset, disquieted, flustered, flurried (see DISCOMPOSE): worried, concerned (see under CARE *n*)

**composer** *writer, author

*Ana* *maker, creator, author: *artist, artificer

**composite** admixture, blend, compound, amalgam, *mixture

*Ana* combining *or* combination, uniting *or* union (see corresponding verbs at JOIN)

**composition** theme, paper, article, *essay

**composure** *equanimity, sangfroid, phlegm

*Ana* coolness, collectedness, imperturbability, nonchalance (see corresponding adjectives at COOL): self-possession, aplomb (see CONFIDENCE): placidity, serenity, calmness (see corresponding adjectives at CALM)

*Ant* discomposure, perturbation —*Con* agitation, disquieting *or* disquiet, flustering *or* fluster (see corresponding verbs at DISCOMPOSE): alarm, consternation, terror, *fear, panic: discomfiture, embarrassment (see corresponding verbs at EMBARRASS)

**compound** *n* *mixture, amalgam, composite, admixture, blend

*Ana* combining *or* combination, uniting *or* union (see corresponding verbs at JOIN): coalescence, fusing *or* fusion, merging *or* merger (see corresponding verbs at MIX)

*Ant* element

**comprehend** 1 *understand, appreciate

*Ana* seize, grasp (see TAKE): conceive, envisage, envision (see THINK)

2 *apprehend

*Ana* see those at COMPREHEND 1

3 embrace, involve, *include, imply, subsume

*Ana* *contain, hold: classify, pigeonhole (see ASSORT)

**comprehension** apprehension (see under APPREHEND)

*Ana* understanding, appreciating *or* appreciation (see corresponding verbs at UNDERSTAND): *knowledge, science, learning, erudition

**compress** *vb* constrict, deflate, *contract, condense, shrink

*Ana* *compact, concentrate, consolidate: bind, *tie

*Ant* stretch: spread —*Con* *expand, dilate, distend, swell, inflate: disperse, *scatter, dissipate

**compulsion** coercion, constraint, duress, *force, violence, restraint

*Ana* impelling *or* impulsion, driving *or* drive (see corresponding verbs at MOVE): pressure, *stress: necessity, exigency, *need

*Con* persuasion, inducement (see corresponding verbs at INDUCE): *choice, option, election, preference

**compunction** 1 remorse, *penitence, repentance, contrition, attrition

A colon (:) separates groups of words discriminated. An asterisk (*) indicates place of treatment of each group.

*Ana* regret, *sorrow: conscientiousness, scrupulousness *or* scrupulosity (see corresponding adjectives at UPRIGHT) 2 scruple, demur, *qualm
*Ana* *hesitation, hesitancy: reluctance, disinclination (see corresponding adjectives at DISINCLINED)
**compute** *calculate, reckon, estimate
*Ana* *count, enumerate, number: sum, total, tot, figure, cast, *add
**comrade** *associate, companion, crony
*Ana* *friend, intimate, confidant: colleague, *partner, confederate, ally
**conation** *will, volition
*Ana* *effort, exertion: *action, act: *choice, selection, option
**concatenate** *vb* articulate, *integrate
*Ana* link, connect, relate, unite, combine, *join, associate: fuse, blend, merge, coalesce (see MIX): organize, systematize (see ORDER *vb*)
*Con* break down, resolve, *analyze, dissect
**concatenated** articulated, integrated (see under INTEGRATE *vb*)
*Ana* *cumulative, accumulative, additive: linked, connected, united, related (see JOIN): organized, systematized (see ORDER *vb*)
**concatenation** articulation, integration (see under INTEGRATE *vb*)
*Ana* sequence, *succession, chain, train
**conceal** *hide, screen, secrete, bury, cache, ensconce
*Ana* cloak, mask, *disguise, dissemble, camouflage
*Ant* reveal —*Con* disclose, discover, divulge, betray (see REVEAL): expose, exhibit, display, *show, parade, flaunt: manifest, evidence, *show, evince
**concede** 1 *grant, allow
*Ana* admit, *acknowledge: waive, cede (see RELINQUISH)
*Ant* dispute —*Con* argue, debate, *discuss, agitate
2 *grant, vouchsafe, accord, award
*Ana* *yield, submit: surrender, resign, cede, *relinquish
*Ant* deny (*something to somebody*) —*Con* refuse (see DECLINE)
**conceit** 1 Conceit, egotism, egoism, self-esteem, self-love, amour propre mean an attitude of regarding oneself with favor. Conceit implies a conviction of superiority in one or more lines of achievement or an overweeningly favorable opinion of one's powers or accomplishments. It often connotes a failure to see oneself truly or an offensive, bumptious manner ⟨to have lost the godlike *conceit* that we may do what we will, and not to have acquired a homely zest for doing what we can, shows a . . . mind that . . . forswears compromise—*Hardy*⟩ ⟨*conceit* may puff a man up, but never prop him up—*Ruskin*⟩ ⟨it was part of the author's formidable *conceit* that he wrote only for the most learned of his professional colleagues—*Galbraith*⟩ Egotism stresses the tendency to attract attention to and center interest on oneself, one's thoughts, and one's achievements. The word sometimes implies contempt for but more often an overriding of or disregard for others' interests or opinions ⟨a man and a boy of ten are perhaps better company than a man and a boy of fifteen. There's so much less *egotism* between them—*H. G. Wells*⟩ ⟨*egotism* resides more in a kind of proud isolation, in a species of contempt for the opinions and aims of others—*Benson*⟩ Egoism emphasizes concentration on oneself, one's interests, and one's needs. It seldom suggests a tendency to display oneself or to attract attention to oneself, but it commonly implies self-interest, especially as opposed to altruism or interest in others, as the inner spring of one's acts or as the measure by which all things are judged ⟨she preferred to be herself, with the *egoism* of women—*Meredith*⟩ ⟨the essence of a self-reliant and

autonomous culture is an unshakable *egoism*. It must not only regard itself as the peer of any other culture; it must regard itself as the superior of any other—*Mencken*⟩ Self-esteem implies a proper and balanced pride in oneself ⟨ofttimes nothing profits more than *self-esteem*, grounded on just and right—*Milton*⟩ ⟨love, hope, and *self-esteem*, like clouds depart and come, for some uncertain moments lent—*Shelley*⟩ ⟨woman had the feeling of being a constructive factor in the economic process; thus she was provided with a sound basis for *self-esteem*—*Horney*⟩ Self-love usually implies an abnormal regard for oneself that excludes or overshadows all other interests or affections. On the other hand it occasionally designates that degree of love for oneself or interest in one's well-being which is the proper and necessary complement of one's love for others ⟨but 'tis not easy with a mind like ours . . . to bid the pleadings of *self-love* be still—*Cowper*⟩ ⟨*self-love* but serves the virtuous mind to wake, as the small pebble stirs the peaceful lake . . . friend, parent, neighbor, first it will embrace; his country next; and next all human race—*Pope*⟩ Amour propre comes closer to *self-esteem*, for it stresses pride, usually pardonable pride, in oneself. It is therefore used when the idea of sensitiveness to others' opinions is indicated ⟨the *amour propre* of the French people had been outraged—*Holt & Chilton*⟩ ⟨she flattered his *amour propre* by asking that from his generosity which she could have taken as a right—*Reade*⟩
*Ana* *pride, vanity, vainglory: arrogance, superciliousness, insolence (see corresponding adjectives at PROUD): complacency, smugness, priggishness (see corresponding adjectives at COMPLACENT)
*Ant* humility —*Con* humbleness, modesty, meekness, lowliness (see corresponding adjectives at HUMBLE): diffidence, shyness, bashfulness (see corresponding adjectives at SHY)
2 *caprice, freak, fancy, whim, whimsy, vagary, crotchet
**conceive** *think, imagine, fancy, realize, envisage, envision
*Ana* *consider, excogitate: speculate, cogitate, *think: *ponder, ruminate, meditate
**concentrate** *vb* 1 *center, focus, centralize
*Ana* fix, *set, settle, establish: muster, convoke, convene (see SUMMON)
2 *compact, consolidate, unify
*Ana* *gather, collect, assemble: mass, *heap, pile: fix, *fasten, attach: engross, *monopolize, absorb
*Ant* dissipate —*Con* disperse, dispel, *scatter: dilute, *thin, attenuate, extenuate, rarefy: *distribute, divide, dispense, deal
**concentration** application, *attention, study
*Ana* intentness, raptness, engrossment, absorption (see corresponding adjectives at INTENT)
*Ant* distraction
**concept** *idea, conception, notion, thought, impression
*Con* percept, sense-datum, sensum, image, *sensation
**conception** concept, *idea, thought, notion, impression
*Ana* *opinion, view, belief, conviction, persuasion, sentiment: theory, *hypothesis
**concern** *vb* Concern, affect are sometimes confused. Concern implies the bearing or influence, affect, the direct operation or action, of one thing on another; thus, a piece of legislation may *concern* (that is, have to do with, have reference or relation to) certain vested interests without *affecting* them (that is, producing an effect upon them, changing them in any way).
*Ana* *bear, pertain, appertain, apply, relate, belong: influence, sway, *affect, touch
**concern** *n* 1 *affair, business, matter, thing
2 solicitude, *care, anxiety, worry
*Ana* thoughtfulness, considerateness *or* consideration,

attentiveness *or* attention (see corresponding adjectives at THOUGHTFUL)

*Ant* unconcern —*Con* indifference, aloofness, incuriousness, uninterestedness, disinterestedness (see corresponding adjectives at INDIFFERENT)

**concerned** solicitous, careful, anxious, worried (see under CARE *n*)

*Ana* engrossed, absorbed, *intent: impressed, affected, influenced, touched (see AFFECT *vb*): troubled, distressed (see TROUBLE *vb*)

*Ant* unconcerned —*Con* *indifferent, incurious, aloof, detached, uninterested, disinterested: *negligent, neglectful, remiss

**concerning** regarding, respecting, *about

**concert** *vb* *negotiate, arrange

*Ana* *discuss, debate, argue: concur, cooperate, *unite, conjoin, combine

**concession** *allowance

*Ana* favor, boon, *gift: indulgence, leniency, tolerance, forbearance (see under FORBEARING)

**conciliate** *pacify, appease, placate, propitiate, mollify

*Ana* arbitrate, adjudicate (see JUDGE *vb*): mediate, intervene (see INTERPOSE): persuade, prevail (see INDUCE): calm, tranquilize (see corresponding adjectives at CALM): adjust, accommodate, reconcile, *adapt

*Ant* antagonize —*Con* *estrange, alienate, disaffect: *provoke, excite, stimulate, pique: *incite, foment

**concise,** terse, succinct, laconic, summary, pithy, compendious are comparable when meaning briefly stated or presented or given to or manifesting brevity in statement or expression. A person is **concise** who speaks or writes briefly; a thing is *concise* that is brief because all superfluities have been removed and all elaboration avoided ⟨a *concise* report⟩ ⟨I hadn't known Jane spoke so well. She has a clever, coherent way of making her points, and is *concise* in reply if questioned—*Rose Macaulay*⟩ A thing is **terse** that is both concise and finished; the word often implies both pointedness and elegance ⟨pure, *terse,* elegant Latin—*Edwards*⟩ ⟨*terse* headlines are another part of the *Tribune's* campaign to save newsprint—*New Yorker*⟩ A person or thing is **succinct** that compresses or is marked by compression into the smallest possible space; the term suggests great compactness and the use of no more words than are necessary ⟨*succinct* directions⟩ ⟨a strict and *succinct* style is that where you can take away nothing without loss, and that loss to be manifest—*Ben Jonson*⟩ ⟨a book must have a title, and today it must have a *succinct* title; therefore this book appears as *Richelieu*—*Belloc*⟩ A person or thing is **laconic** that is characterized by such succinctness as to seem curt, brusque, unperturbed, or mystifying ⟨this *laconic* fool makes brevity ridiculous—*Davenant*⟩ ⟨I cannot exactly say with Caesar, "Veni, vidi, vici": however, the most important part of his *laconic* account of success applies to my present situation—*Byron*⟩ ⟨*laconic,* these Indians—*La Barre*⟩ A thing is **summary** that presents only the bare outlines or the main points without details ⟨a *summary* account of the year's events under a few main headings⟩ The term often suggests almost rude curtness or extreme generality ⟨the terms I use here are exceedingly *summary.* You may interpret the word *salvation* in any way you like—*James*⟩ ⟨her diary and her letters continued to be mainly the swift and *summary* record of crowded and delightful days—*Ellis*⟩ A thing is **pithy** that is not only terse or succinct but full of substance and meaning and therefore especially forcible or telling ⟨*pithy* epigrams⟩ ⟨a brief, *pithy,* and, as it then appeared to him, unanswerable argument against the immortality of the human soul—*Hawthorne*⟩ ⟨his speech

was blacksmith-sparked and *pithy*—*Masefield*⟩ Something is **compendious** which is concise, summary, and weighted with matter; the word suggests the type of treatment that distinguishes the typical compendium ⟨a *compendious* account of the Reformation⟩ ⟨a *compendious* style⟩ ⟨the *compendious* scholarly words which save so much trouble—*T. E. Brown*⟩

*Ana* condensed, compressed (see CONTRACT *vb*): compacted, concentrated (see COMPACT *vb*): abridged, abbreviated, shortened (see SHORTEN): *brief, short

*Ant* redundant —*Con* prolix, diffuse, verbose, *wordy

**conclude** 1 *close, finish, terminate, end, complete

*Ant* open —*Con* commence, *begin, start, initiate, inaugurate

2 judge, gather, *infer, deduce

*Ana* reason, speculate (see THINK): *conjecture, surmise, guess

**concluding** *adj* *last, final, terminal, latest, ultimate

*Ana* closing, terminating, ending, finishing, completing (see CLOSE *vb*)

*Ant* opening —*Con* beginning, commencing, starting, initiating *or* initial, inaugurating *or* inaugural (see corresponding verbs at BEGIN)

**conclusion** judgment, deduction, inference (see under INFER)

**conclusive,** decisive, determinative, definitive are comparable when they mean having or manifesting qualities that bring something to a finish or end. **Conclusive** applies most frequently to an argument, evidence, or reasoning that is irrefutable or so convincing that it compels certainty or certitude and puts an end to question or debate concerning a matter ⟨there is one very convincing text which so strongly supports the tradition that it seems *conclusive*—*Belloc*⟩ ⟨a very persuasive if not a *conclusive* argument—*John Marshall*⟩ **Decisive** (see also DECIDED) applies to something (as an act, event, influence, or argument) that puts an end to controversy or competition, to vacillation, to uncertainty, or to insecurity; it often comes close in meaning to *critical* ⟨the *decisive* battle of the war had not yet been fought⟩ ⟨my words had been *decisive.* At least they put an end to the discussion—*London*⟩ **Determinative** applies especially to matters (as decisions, judgments, operative causes, or influences) which put an end to uncertainty, wavering, and fluctuation and serve to give a fixed direction, goal, or character (as to a life, a course, or a movement) ⟨the *determinative* influence in shaping his career⟩ ⟨an appeal covering similar merchandise is pending . . . which will be *determinative* of this issue—*U. S. Treasury Decisions*⟩ **Definitive,** which is often opposed to *tentative* and, sometimes, to *provisional,* applies to whatever is put forth as final and as serving to make further questioning, dispute, uncertainty, or experiment needless or as serving to put an end to an unsettled state or condition where temporary measures have been necessary ⟨the decisions of the Supreme Court of the United States are *definitive*⟩ ⟨a *definitive* treaty⟩ ⟨a *definitive* edition of an author's works is one that claims to have said the last word on all textual problems⟩ ⟨not until there is a settled and *definitive* world order can there be such a thing as a settled and *definitive* version of human history—*Huxley*⟩

*Ana* convincing, compelling, telling, cogent (see VALID): *certain, inevitable, necessary

*Ant* inconclusive —*Con* *doubtful, dubious, questionable, problematic: *theoretical, speculative, academic: *plausible, credible, specious

**concoct** *contrive, devise, invent, frame

*Ana* *make, fabricate, fashion, manufacture: create, discover (see INVENT): conceive, envisage, envision,

---

A colon (:) separates groups of words discriminated. An asterisk (*) indicates place of treatment of each group.

*think

**concomitant** *adj* coincident, concurrent, synchronous, simultaneous, contemporaneous, *contemporary, coeval, coetaneous

*Ana* attending *or* attendant, accompanying (see corresponding verbs at ACCOMPANY): associated, connected, related, linked (see JOIN)

*Con* antecedent, *preceding, foregoing, previous, precedent: following, succeeding, ensuing (see FOLLOW)

**concomitant** *n* *accompaniment

**concord** *harmony, consonance, accord

*Ana* agreement, concurrence, coincidence (see corresponding verbs at AGREE): peacefulness *or* peace, tranquillity, serenity, placidity, calmness (see corresponding adjectives at CALM): amity, comity, goodwill, *friendship

*Ant* discord —*Con* strife, conflict, dissension, contention, difference, variance (see DISCORD)

**concordat** compact, pact, treaty, entente, convention, cartel, *contract, bargain

**concourse** *junction, confluence

**concur** 1 conjoin, *unite, combine, cooperate

*Ana* accord, harmonize, *agree, jibe

2 *agree, coincide

*Ana* consent, *assent, accede, acquiesce, agree

*Ant* contend: altercate —*Con* fight, battle, war (see CONTEND): quarrel, wrangle (see under QUARREL *n*): dispute, debate, argue (see DISCUSS)

**concurrent** coincident, simultaneous, synchronous, concomitant, contemporaneous, *contemporary, coeval, coetaneous

**concussion** shock, percussion, *impact, impingement, collision, clash, jar, jolt

*Ana* beating, pounding, buffeting (see BEAT *vb*): striking, smiting, swatting, slapping (see STRIKE *vb*)

**condemn** 1 denounce, censure, blame, reprobate, reprehend, *criticize

*Ana* *judge, adjudge: *decry, belittle, depreciate, disparage: *disapprove, deprecate

*Con* *commend, applaud, compliment: *praise, laud, extol, acclaim, eulogize: condone, *excuse, pardon, forgive

2 *sentence, doom, damn, proscribe

*Con* *free, release, liberate, discharge: acquit, absolve, exonerate, *exculpate, vindicate: *rescue, redeem, save, deliver

**condense** *contract, shrink, compress, constrict, deflate

*Ana* abridge, abbreviate, *shorten, curtail: reduce, diminish, *decrease: *compact, concentrate, consolidate

*Ant* amplify (*a speech, article*) —*Con* *expand, swell, distend, dilate, inflate

**condescend** *stoop, deign

*Ana* favor, accommodate, *oblige: vouchsafe, concede, *grant

*Ant* presume

**condign** *due, rightful

*Ana* just, equitable, *fair: merited, deserved (see corresponding nouns at DUE)

**condition** *n* 1 Condition, stipulation, terms, provision, proviso, reservation, strings are comparable when meaning something that is established or is regarded as the prerequisite of a promise or agreement being fulfilled or taking effect. Condition implies the laying down of something as a prerequisite which must be observed or satisfied if the validity of the whole agreement, promise, dispensation, or gift is not to be destroyed ⟨he was to go to Oxford or Cambridge . . . if he succeeded in gaining a scholarship. . . . That was the *condition* his father had laid down—*Archibald Marshall*⟩ ⟨though they regarded the diplomatic service as a preserve for their younger sons, they attached

to it the *condition* that no youth should be eligible for it without a private income of four hundred a year—*Shaw*⟩ ⟨just had to keep writing—writing was a profession, a way of life, a *condition* of his survival—*Anderson*⟩ Stipulation differs from *condition* chiefly in implying a formal, explicit, and often written statement (as a contract) binding a party thereto to a specified course ⟨he made the *stipulation* that payments be in gold⟩ ⟨one consequence of this contract by the law that governed it and by the *stipulation* of the lessor was that if the lessee held over he held over for a year—*Justice Holmes*⟩ ⟨a *stipulation* is a statement of conditions that are agreed to in the conduct of some affair—*Kaufmann*⟩ Terms indicates conditions offered or agreed upon by one or both parties to a contract, agreement, or deal; thus, two parties may come to *terms* (i.e., may agree upon such a matter as work to be done, prices to be paid, or a division of property) ⟨only a general of repute could get recruits, and for that service he could make his own *terms*—*Buchan*⟩ ⟨the *terms* of the lease are not harsh—*Montague*⟩ ⟨a certain despair of her ever understanding . . . the *terms* of a contract—*Mary Austin*⟩ Provision applies chiefly to a documentary statement which provides measures for the treatment of certain matters legally ⟨the admission of Arkansas with a *provision* in its constitution forbidding the abolition of slavery without the consent of the slaveowners—*L. B. Evans*⟩ ⟨according to the *provisions* of the constitution the state courts have no jurisdiction in this controversy⟩ It may be specifically used of a clause or of a part of such a document or of a document that is comparable in laying down a condition or making a stipulation ⟨into his will he wrote a *provision* that all of his children should accept his decision regarding the disposal of his property on pain of being disinherited⟩ Proviso denotes a condition or a stipulation, especially one that is clearly stated and binding ⟨passionate feeling is desirable, provided it is not destructive; intellect is desirable, with the same *proviso*—*Russell*⟩ ⟨it is because the practical businessman always forgets this *proviso* that he is such a hopeless idiot politically—*Shaw*⟩ Reservation indicates a qualification or modification of the terms of an agreement or statement, often to cover contingencies. It may become a stipulation or proviso if the other party or parties concerned agree or acquiesce ⟨she [Spain] had already in the treaty of Madrid promised to leave the Valtelline, but with such *reservations* that she could still hold on—*Belloc*⟩ or it may be avowed only to oneself (*mental reservation*) in evading the generally understood sense of a promise or an oath or other statement that one is impelled to make for reasons of necessity or expediency ⟨the issues that won him most votes were issues that, at bottom, he didn't believe in; there was always a mental *reservation* in his rhetoric—*Mencken*⟩ Strings suggests strands which the maker of a promise, a proposal, or an offer keeps in his hands so that he may pull them back if what he lays down as a condition or imposes as a stipulation is not kept; the term usually denotes conditions or provisos, often unexpected or concealed, that may radically alter or even annul an agreement ⟨make me a cash offer, with no *strings*⟩

*Ana* prerequisite, requisite, *requirement

2 *state, situation, mode, posture, status

*Ana* circumstance, *occurrence, event: occasion, antecedent, *cause: *phase, aspect, side, facet, angle

3 *disease, disorder, affection, ailment, malady, complaint, distemper, syndrome

**condition** *vb* *prepare, fit, qualify, ready

**conditional** *dependent, contingent, relative

*Ana* problematic, questionable (see DOUBTFUL): *provisional, tentative: subject, prone, *liable, open: *acci-

---

*Ana* analogous words     *Ant* antonyms     *Con* contrasted words     See also explanatory notes facing page 1

dental, fortuitous, incidental
*Ant* unconditional

**condolence** *sympathy, pity, commiseration, compassion, ruth, empathy
*Ana* consoling *or* consolation, solacing *or* solace, comforting (see corresponding verbs at COMFORT)
*Con* felicitation, congratulation (see corresponding verbs at FELICITATE)

**condone** *excuse, forgive, pardon, remit
*Ana* disregard, overlook, forget, ignore (see NEGLECT *vb*): *exculpate, absolve, acquit
*Con* *punish, chastise, discipline, castigate, correct: condemn, denounce, censure, reprobate, reprehend (see CRITICIZE): *disapprove, deprecate

**conduct** *n* *behavior, deportment
*Ana* act, deed, *action: demeanor, mien, deportment, *bearing

**conduct** *vb* **1** escort, convoy, *accompany, attend, chaperon
*Ana* *guide, lead: convey, transmit, *carry
**2 Conduct, manage, control, direct** are comparable when they mean to use one's skill, authority, or other powers in order to lead, guide, command, or dominate persons or things. **Conduct** may imply the act of an agent who is both the leader and the person responsible for the acts and achievements of a group having a common end or goal ⟨*conduct* an orchestra⟩ ⟨the minister *conducts* the prayer meetings⟩ ⟨Douglas *conducted* conferences and studies which led to a reorganization of the Stock Exchange—*Current Biog.*⟩ but often the idea of leadership is lost or obscured and the stress is placed on a carrying on by all or by many of the participants ⟨debates, *conducted* seriously with a view to ascertaining the truth, could be of great value—*Russell*⟩ ⟨it was judged desirable for him to see how affairs were *conducted* in the United States—*Heiser*⟩ **Manage** usually implies the handling, manipulating, or maneuvering of a person or persons or a thing or things so as to bring about a response or submission to one's wishes or attempts to use, guide, lead, or command ⟨he *manages* the sailboat admirably⟩ ⟨he cannot *manage* himself, so how can he be expected to *manage* others⟩ ⟨*manage* a refractory child⟩ ⟨the boy . . . could not yet *manage* his "r's" and "th's" aright—*Kipling*⟩ ⟨the first condition for an artist in glass is to know how to *manage* blue—*Henry Adams*⟩ ⟨now do you leave this affair in my hands. Only tell me which woman it is and I will *manage* the affair—*Buck*⟩ But *manage* is also often used to imply the action of one who is in authority and charged with the handling of the details of a business or industry or of one of its departments or of any complex or intricate system or organization ⟨he *manages* a theater⟩ ⟨*manage* the financial affairs of a company⟩ ⟨the delight she would take in *managing* a real house, not in any sense as its drudge, but magnificently as its mistress—*Dell*⟩ ⟨*manage* a chain of restaurants⟩ **Control** stresses the idea of authoritative guidance and suggests a keeping within set or desired bounds (as of accuracy, efficiency, propriety, or discipline); it implies a regulating or a restraining often by getting or keeping the upper hand ⟨no attempt was made . . . to *control* by public authority the production and distribution of wealth —*Dickinson*⟩ ⟨in order to make its highways most useful, the business traffic upon them must be *controlled*—*Justice Holmes*⟩ ⟨he started things moving and then was caught up in the repercussions of the movement. He mounted an act as if it were a horse, found himself unable to *control* it—*Cloete*⟩ Sometimes, however, *control* implies little more than domination or the complete subjection of the dominated person or thing to one's will ⟨he has learned to *control* himself⟩ ⟨the struggle between two strong-willed women to *control* one weak-willed man is the usual motive of the French drama in the nineteenth century—*Henry Adams*⟩ ⟨pirates at one time practically *controlled* the coasts of Florida—*Amer. Guide Series: Fla.*⟩ **Direct** (see also COMMAND, DIRECT 1, DIRECT 2) implies a regulation of the activities (as of a group of persons) or of the course or courses to be followed; it carries no suggestion of a desire or aim to dominate, but of an intent or purpose to keep the persons or things involved straight, well organized, or properly administered ⟨the president and trustees *direct* the affairs of the institution⟩ ⟨the architect *directed* the building of the bank⟩ ⟨*direct* American taste and mold the genius of the young republic—*Brooks*⟩
*Ana* supervise, oversee (see corresponding nouns at OVERSIGHT): *govern, rule: engineer, pilot, steer, lead (see GUIDE *vb*): operate, work, function (see ACT *vb*)
**3** demean, deport, *behave, comport, acquit, quit

**conduit** *channel, canal, duct, aqueduct

**confederacy, confederation** federation, coalition, fusion, *alliance, league

**confederate** *n* **1** *partner, copartner, colleague, ally
*Ana, Ant, & Con* see those at ALLY
**2 Confederate, conspirator, accessory, abettor, accomplice.** As used in law these words all convey the idea of complicity or common guilt in a wrongful act. **Confederate** is the general term applied to any person who in conjunction with others intentionally contributes to the commission of an unlawful act, whether the act be a crime or a civil injury. For civil joint wrongdoers the specific term is **conspirator**. An **accessory** is neither the chief actor (*principal*) in an offense nor a person present at its performance but one who accedes to or becomes involved in its guilt by some act (as of instigating, encouraging, aiding, or concealing) either previous or subsequent to the commission of the offense. In the case of certain classes of offenses (as treason or misdemeanors) the law ordinarily recognizes no distinction between an accessory and a principal. An **abettor** is one who is actually or constructively present at the commission of the deed and contributes to it by moral or physical force. An **accomplice** is one who with criminal intent participates in the commission of an offense whether as principal, abettor, or accessory. Legal usage does not recognize the distinction made by laymen between *principal* and *accomplice*.

**confer 1** bestow, present, *give, donate, afford
*Ana* accord, award, vouchsafe, *grant
**2 Confer, commune, consult, advise, parley, treat, negotiate** are synonyms when they are used intransitively and bear the meaning to carry on a conversation or discussion especially in order to reach a decision or settlement. **Confer** implies comparison of views or opinions and, as a rule, equality in those participating in the discussion ⟨the executives *confer* weekly about important business affairs⟩ ⟨the Dauphin and his train approacheth, to *confer* about some matter—*Shak.*⟩ **Commune**, once a close synonym of *confer*, now is rare in this sense ⟨we were *communing* on important matters—*Walpole*⟩ In current use it usually implies spiritual intercourse (as in prayer or meditation or in a close union of minds and spirits) ⟨there, sitting on the ground, the two [mother and child] would *commune* with each other by the hour—*Hudson*⟩ **Consult** adds to *confer* the implication of seeking or taking counsel ⟨the president will not make his reply to the ambassador until he has *consulted* with the cabinet⟩ ⟨the three powers would *consult* on how to ameliorate the internal political conflict—*Vucinich*⟩ **Advise** often is not clearly distinguishable from *consult* except that it is more suitable for use regarding personal matters on which one seeks advice ⟨before he makes his decision, he will

---

A colon (:) separates groups of words discriminated. An asterisk (*) indicates place of treatment of each group.

*advise* with his friends⟩ *Parley, treat,* and *negotiate* all imply conference for the sake of settling differences or of coming to an agreement on terms. **Parley** stresses the talk involving the discussion of terms ⟨they are at hand, to *parley* or to fight—*Shak.*⟩ ⟨the . . . government was forced to *parley* with the rebels—*Harrington*⟩ **Treat** adds to *parley* the implication either of a common will to adjust differences or of the need of diplomacy ⟨the warring nations were ready to *treat* for peace⟩ ⟨the commander in chief . . . was to *treat* for an armistice—*Pares*⟩ **Negotiate** implies compromise or bargaining ⟨after the preliminaries were over, they proceeded to *negotiate*⟩
*Ana* converse, talk, *speak: *discuss, debate, argue
**confess** avow, *acknowledge, admit, own
*Ana* *grant, concede, allow: disclose, divulge, *reveal, discover: *declare, proclaim, publish
*Ant* renounce (*one's beliefs, principles*)
**confessions** *biography, life, memoir, autobiography
**confidant** intimate, *friend, acquaintance
*Ana* comrade, crony, companion (see ASSOCIATE *n*)
**confide** entrust, *commit, consign, relegate
*Ana* bestow, present, *give: *grant, vouchsafe, accord, award
**confidence** 1 *trust, reliance, dependence, faith
*Ana* certitude, assurance, conviction, *certainty: credence, credit, *belief, faith
*Ant* doubt: apprehension —*Con* *distrust, mistrust: despair, hopelessness (see under DESPONDENT)
2 **Confidence, self-confidence, assurance, self-assurance, self-possession, aplomb** are comparable when denoting either a state of mind free from diffidence, misgivings, or embarrassment or the easy, cool, or collected bearing or behavior resulting from this attitude. **Confidence** stresses faith in oneself and in one's powers; it does not as a rule imply conceit nor preclude the suggestions of support from external agencies or influences or of modest recognition of that assistance ⟨far better that the task should be entrusted to one who had . . . a sincere *confidence* in his power of dealing with the difficulties of the situation—*Benson*⟩ ⟨the *confidence* that springs from complete mastery of his subject—*Grandgent*⟩ When self-sufficiency is connoted, **self-confidence** commonly replaces *confidence* ⟨he has the *self-confidence* of one who has made money—*Shaw*⟩ ⟨in extreme youth one has to be secondhand . . . one lacks *self-confidence*—*Rose Macaulay*⟩ **Assurance** is distinguishable from *confidence* only by its far stronger implication of certainty and its frequent suggestion of arrogance; thus, one meets a situation with *confidence* when one's belief in one's powers is strong, but with *assurance* when one never questions the outcome or the rightness of what one is saying or doing ⟨there was indeed in the personality of that little old lady the tremendous force of accumulated decision—the inherited *assurance* of one whose prestige had never been questioned—*Galsworthy*⟩ ⟨no experience so far served to reveal the whole offensiveness of the man's *assurance*—*Mary Austin*⟩ **Self-assurance** implies an assured self-confidence ⟨the serene *self-assurance* . . . of the Abbey is unlike the baffling compound of modesty and self-assertiveness in a Nonconformist chapel—*Sperry*⟩ ⟨he wrote with that pleasing *self-assurance* which the civilized man occasionally shares with the savage—*Repplier*⟩ **Self-possession** implies an ease or coolness arising from command over one's powers; it connotes, usually, controlled but not repressed emotions and actions, or speech free from flurry and appropriate to the situation ⟨she was rather afraid of the *self-possession* of the Morels, father and all. . . . It was a cool, clear atmosphere, where everyone was himself, and in harmony

—*D. H. Lawrence*⟩ ⟨had that carefully cultivated air of quiet *self-possession*, suggesting inner repose and serenity —*Strauss*⟩ **Aplomb** describes the behavior or, less often, the bearing of one whose assurance or self-possession is conspicuously but not necessarily disagreeably evident ⟨ignoring with admirable *aplomb* the fact that we are tardy—*Lowes*⟩ ⟨it is native personality, and that alone, that endows a man to stand before presidents and generals . . . with *aplomb*—*Whitman*⟩
*Ana* *courage, resolution, mettle, spirit, tenacity
*Ant* diffidence —*Con* modesty, bashfulness, shyness (see corresponding adjectives at SHY): misgiving, *apprehension
**confident,** assured, sanguine, sure, presumptuous are comparable as applied to a person or to his temperament, looks, manner, acts, or utterances with the meaning not inhibited by doubts, fears, or a sense of inferiority. **Confident** may imply a strong belief in oneself or one's powers but it nearly always implies freedom from fear of failure, frustration, or attack and, as a corollary, certitude of success, fulfillment, or approval. As a rule, it is not a depreciative term, and often is complimentary ⟨his voice was manly and *confident*⟩ ⟨the happy and joyous temper which characterizes a fresh and *confident* faith— *Inge*⟩ ⟨do you grapple the task that comes your way with a *confident*, easy mind?—*Guest*⟩ ⟨a *confident* feeling of immense reserves in strength and endurance—*T. E. Lawrence*⟩ **Assured** suggests the absence of question in one's mind as to whether one is right or wrong, secure or insecure in one's position, or likely to fail or to succeed; it may also imply certitude of one's rightness, security, success, but this is not one of its consistent or emphatic implications ⟨talking with *assured* authority about places we have not visited, plays we have not seen—*Lucas*⟩ ⟨the *assured* gaze of one who is accustomed to homage— *Bennett*⟩ ⟨she had the casual, *assured* way of speaking —*Wolfe*⟩ **Sanguine** implies a greater measure of optimism than *confident*, sometimes suggesting this as a weakness rather than as a virtue ⟨Mr. Britling's thoughts were quick and *sanguine* and his actions even more eager than his thoughts—*H. G. Wells*⟩ ⟨*sanguine* and very susceptible to flattery, Haydon was always ready to believe that the smallest stroke of good fortune must be the herald of complete success—*Huxley*⟩ ⟨a surgeon's commission for the doctor, and a lieutenancy for myself, were certainly counted upon in our *sanguine* expectations—*Melville*⟩ **Sure** implies that one's freedom from doubts or fears is rather the consequence of certainty or of complete confidence in one's skill than of temperament or health. The word also often connotes a steady and disciplined mind, mental or emotional stability, or unfailing accuracy ⟨a *sure* scholar⟩ ⟨a *sure* craftsman⟩ ⟨as he is slow he is *sure*—*Steele*⟩ ⟨she tempted the young man into kissing her, and later lay in his arms for two hours, entirely *sure* of herself—*Anderson*⟩ **Sure** is applicable also to any part of the body equipped to do a certain kind of work under the control of the brain, or to the work itself; thus, a *sure* hand works with unfaltering skill and accuracy; *sure* feet pick their way fearlessly over slippery rocks; a *sure* eye is necessary for a *sure* aim ⟨the *sure* rhythm of their tiny moccasined feet—*Cather*⟩ **Presumptuous** implies an excess of confidence that is usually displayed boldly or insolently. The term is distinctly depreciative and suggests that the one so characterized is lacking in courtesy, judgment, and savoir faire ⟨she enforced the doctor's orders in a way which seemed . . . loud and *presumptuous*—*Wescott*⟩
*Ana* courageous, intrepid, *brave, bold, dauntless, undaunted, valiant, fearless, unafraid: positive, certain,

---

*Ana* analogous words    *Ant* antonyms    *Con* contrasted words    See also explanatory notes facing page 1

*sure

*Ant* apprehensive: diffident —*Con* *fearful, afraid: nervous, uneasy, jittery (see IMPATIENT): *shy, bashful, modest: dubious, *doubtful

**confidential** close, intimate, *familiar, chummy, thick
*Ana* *secret: trusty, tried, trustworthy (see RELIABLE)

**configuration** conformation, figure, shape, *form
*Ana* *outline, contour, silhouette, profile, skyline

**confine** *vb* circumscribe, *limit, restrict
*Ana* bind, *tie: *restrain, curb, inhibit, check: *hamper, trammel, fetter, shackle, hog-tie, manacle: *imprison, incarcerate, immure, intern, jail

**confine** *n* bound, *limit, end, term
*Ana* verge, edge, *border: *circumference, periphery, compass

**confirm** 1 *ratify
*Ana* *assent, consent, acquiesce, accede, subscribe: validate (see CONFIRM 2): sanction, *approve, endorse
*Con* reject, refuse, *decline
2 Confirm, corroborate, substantiate, verify, authenticate, validate mean to attest to the truth, genuineness, accuracy, or validity of something. *Confirm* and *corroborate* are both used in reference to something doubtful or not yet proved. **Confirm,** however, usually implies the resolving of all doubts typically by an authoritative statement or by indisputable facts ⟨his failure to pay his debts *confirmed* their suspicion that he was not to be trusted⟩ ⟨there is a rumor—which cannot of course be *confirmed*—*Gorrell*⟩ ⟨it was expectation exquisitely gratified, superabundantly *confirmed*—*Henry James*⟩ **Corroborate** suggests particularly the strengthening of one statement or piece of evidence by another ⟨the bystanders *corroborated* his story⟩ ⟨in general the material illustrates and *corroborates* what has already become known from other sources—*Kennan*⟩ **Substantiate** presupposes something needing to be demonstrated or proved and implies the offering of evidence sufficient to sustain the contention or to create a strong presumption in its favor ⟨they were able to *substantiate* their claim to the property when the long-lost deed was found⟩ ⟨Darwin spent nearly a lifetime in gathering evidence to *substantiate* his theory of the origin of species⟩ ⟨no proof had to be brought forward to *substantiate* the claims they made—*Anderson*⟩ **Verify** has for its distinctive implication the established correspondence of the actual facts or details to those that are given in an account or statement. When what is in question is a suspicion, a fear, or a probability, it can be *verified* only in the result, event, or fulfillment ⟨the prediction of a severe storm was *verified* in every detail⟩ ⟨it [faith] begins as a resolution to stand or fall by the noblest hypothesis . . . ; but it is *verified* progressively as we go on—*Inge*⟩ In more general use *verify* implies a deliberate effort to establish the accuracy or truth of something usually by comparison (as with ascertainable facts, an original, or a series of control experiments) ⟨*verify* all the citations in a book⟩ ⟨statements of accounts due are not sent out until they are *verified*⟩ ⟨the careful scientist *verifies* every step in an experiment⟩ ⟨he has explored most of Trans-Jordan, *verified* biblical accounts by his findings and excavations—*Current Biog.*⟩ ⟨a government survey party was *verifying* the neighboring landmarks—*Furphy*⟩ **Authenticate** presupposes question of a thing's genuineness or validity and therefore implies a demonstration of either of these by someone (as an expert or the proper authority) in a position to know or to determine ⟨the collector refused to purchase the manuscript until it had been *authenticated* by experts⟩ ⟨the bank *authenticated* the signatures on the note⟩ ⟨an *authenticated* copy of the Declaration—*Dumas Malone*⟩ **Validate** is more often

used than *authenticate* when applied to legal papers requiring an official signature or seal before becoming valid ⟨*validate* a passport⟩ It is, however, also used when the soundness of a judgment, of a belief, or of a policy is in question ⟨the expansion of demand which alone can *validate* the policy—*Hobson*⟩ ⟨he *validated* his conclusion when he demonstrated that his facts and his reasoning were correct in every detail⟩
*Ana* *support, uphold, back: vouch, attest, *certify
*Ant* deny: contradict —*Con* gainsay, traverse, impugn, contravene, negative (see DENY): confute, refute, controvert, *disprove

**confirmed** *inveterate, chronic, deep-seated, deep-rooted
*Ana* established, fixed, set, settled (see SET *vb*): *hardened, indurated, callous

**confiscate** appropriate, *arrogate, usurp, preempt
*Ana* seize, *take, grab: condemn, proscribe (see SENTENCE *vb*)

**conflagration** *fire, holocaust

**conflict** *n* 1 combat, fight, *contest, affray, fray
*Ana* engagement, *battle, action: *encounter, skirmish, brush: controversy, dispute, *argument
2 strife, contention, dissension, difference, variance, *discord
*Ana* clash, collision, impingement, *impact: antagonism, hostility, *enmity: incompatibility, incongruousness, inconsistency, inconsonance, discordance (see corresponding adjectives at INCONSONANT)
*Ant* harmony —*Con* consonance, concord, accord (see HARMONY): comity, amity, *friendship: compatibility, congruity (see corresponding adjectives at CONSONANT)

**conflict** *vb* 1 *resist, withstand, contest, oppose, fight, combat, antagonize
2 *bump, clash, collide
*Ana* *contend, fight: *differ, vary, disagree
*Ant* accord —*Con* harmonize, *agree: *match, equal, touch, rival

**confluence** *junction, concourse

**conform** 1 *adapt, adjust, accommodate, reconcile
*Ana* *harmonize, tune, attune: *assent, accede, acquiesce: accept, *receive
2 *agree, accord, harmonize, correspond, square, tally, jibe
*Ant* diverge —*Con* *differ, disagree

**conformation** configuration, *form, shape, figure
*Ana* *structure, anatomy, framework, skeleton

**confound** 1 dumbfound, nonplus, bewilder, mystify, *puzzle, perplex, distract
*Ana* flabbergast, amaze, astound, astonish, *surprise: discomfit, faze, rattle, abash, *embarrass, disconcert
2 confuse, *mistake
*Ana* muddle, addle, *confuse: *mix, mingle
*Ant* distinguish, discriminate

**confront** *vb* *meet, face, encounter
*Ana* defy, beard, challenge, brave, dare (see FACE): oppose, withstand, *resist
*Ant* recoil from

**confuse** 1 Confuse, muddle, addle, fuddle, befuddle mean to throw one out mentally so that one cannot think clearly or act intelligently. **Confuse** usually implies intense embarrassment or bewilderment ⟨you *confuse* me, and how can I transact business if I am *confused*? Let us be clearheaded—*Dickens*⟩ **Muddle** often suggests stupefaction (as by drink) and usually implies blundering, aimless, but not necessarily unsuccessful attempts to deal with ideas, situations, or tasks beyond one's powers of analysis or one's capacity ⟨a subject so abstruse as to *muddle* the brains of all but exceptional students⟩ ⟨we have

---

A colon (:) separates groups of words discriminated. An asterisk (*) indicates place of treatment of each group.

*muddled* through so often that we have come half to believe in a providence which watches over unintelligent virtue—*Inge*⟩ **Addle** suggests staleness or emptiness of mind and resulting mental impotence ⟨I have *addled* my head with writing all day—*Dickens*⟩ **Fuddle** and the more common **befuddle** imply confusion from or as if from tippling or indulgence in a drug that clouds the mind and makes one's thinking and speech absurdly incoherent ⟨Shakespeare's Falstaff is most amusing when he is completely *befuddled*⟩ ⟨corridors, archways, recesses . . . combined to *fuddle* any sense of direction—*Elizabeth Bowen*⟩ ⟨perhaps his best would be a little better if he didn't *befuddle* his mind with . . . slander—*Frank*⟩
*Ana* confound, bewilder, mystify, perplex, *puzzle: discomfit, disconcert, faze, rattle (see EMBARRASS): fluster, flurry (see DISCOMPOSE)
*Ant* enlighten
2 *mistake, confound
*Ant* differentiate
**confusion** 1 Confusion, disorder, chaos, disarray, jumble, clutter, snarl, muddle are comparable when they mean the state or a condition in which things are not in their right places or arranged in their right relations to each other, or an instance of such a state or condition. **Confusion** suggests such mixing or mingling as obliterates clear demarcation or distinction; **disorder** (see also DISEASE) implies lack or more frequently disturbance or breach of due order or arrangement; thus, a busy worker might leave his desk in *confusion* with objects mingled together and no arrangement apparent to an observer, but a burglar searching it for money would probably leave it in *disorder* with contents thrown about and out of their normal (though not necessarily orderly) arrangement ⟨the dark *confusion* of German history—*Guérard*⟩ ⟨mid the misery and *confusion* of an unjust war—*Shelley*⟩ ⟨cowardice has succeeded to courage, *disorder* to discipline—*Dickinson*⟩ ⟨our last chance to substitute order for *disorder,* government for anarchy—*E. B. White*⟩ **Chaos** suggests an absolute or sometimes hopeless confusion suggestive of the ancient Greek conception of Chaos as the unorganized state of primordial matter before the creation of distinct and orderly forms; the term therefore more often implies innate lack of organization rather than disturbance of an existent order ⟨the Essays of Montaigne . . . a *chaos* indeed, but a *chaos* swarming with germs of evolution—*J. R. Lowell*⟩ When *chaos* does imply a disturbing, it usually suggests a reducing to the utter confusion of primordial matter ⟨back not merely to the dark ages but from cosmos to *chaos*—*Baruch*⟩ **Disarray,** more even than *disorder,* implies disarrangement; it is therefore preferable when the breaking up of order or discipline is to be suggested ⟨the *disarray* into which society had been thrown by this deplorable affair made their presence in town more necessary than ever—*Wharton*⟩ **Jumble** implies the mixing of incongruous things with resulting confusion ⟨the house they lived in . . . was a heterogeneous architectural *jumble*—*Meredith*⟩ **Clutter** implies confusion and crowding and often suggests a disagreeable or more or less messy state ⟨Lord, what a mess this set is in! If there's one thing I hate above everything else . . . it's *clutter*—*Millay*⟩ **Snarl,** basically applied to a tangle of filaments (as hairs or threads), implies confusion and entanglement and suggests great difficulty in unraveling and ordering ⟨his affairs are in a *snarl*⟩ ⟨held up by a traffic *snarl*⟩ **Muddle** (compare *muddle* at CONFUSE 1) also implies confusion and entanglement, but in addition it suggests the influence of bungling and a more or less hopeless condition ⟨we both grub on in a *muddle*—*Dickens*⟩ ⟨the world's been confused and poor, a thorough

*muddle;* there's never been a real planned education for people—*H. G. Wells*⟩
*Ana* derangement, disarrangement, disorganization, disturbance (see corresponding verbs at DISORDER): *din, babel, pandemonium, hullabaloo: *anarchy, lawlessness
*Con* ordering *or* order, systematization, organization (see corresponding verbs at ORDER): system, *method
2 *commotion, agitation, tumult, turmoil, turbulence, convulsion, upheaval
*Ana* disorder, disorganization, disturbance (see corresponding verbs at DISORDER): perturbation, agitation, disquiet, upset (see corresponding verbs at DISCOMPOSE): discomfiture, embarrassment (see corresponding verbs at EMBARRASS)
**confute** controvert, refute, *disprove, rebut
**congeal** *vb* *coagulate, set, curdle, clot, jelly, jell
*Ana* solidify, *harden: *compact, concentrate, consolidate: cool, chill, freeze (see corresponding adjectives at COLD)
*Con* melt, *liquefy, deliquesce
**congenial** *consonant, consistent, compatible, congruous, sympathetic
*Ana* companionable, cooperative, *social: sociable, genial, cordial, *gracious, affable: pleasing, *pleasant, agreeable
*Ant* uncongenial: antipathetic (*of persons*): abhorrent (*of tasks, duties*)
**congenital** inborn, *innate, hereditary, inherited, inbred
*Ana* *inherent, constitutional, ingrained: *native
*Con* acquired (see GET): *accidental, adventitious
**conglomerate, conglomeration** agglomerate, agglomeration, *aggregate, aggregation
*Ana* mass, heap, pile, stack (see under HEAP *vb*): accumulation, amassment, hoarding *or* hoard (see corresponding verbs at ACCUMULATE)
**congratulate** *felicitate
*Con* console, solace, *comfort: commiserate, condole with, pity (see corresponding nouns at SYMPATHY)
**congregate** *gather, assemble, collect
*Ana* swarm, *teem
*Ant* disperse
**congregation** assembly, assemblage, gathering, collection (see under GATHER *vb*)
*Ana* audience, *following, public: *crowd, throng, press, crush
**congruous** compatible, congenial, *consonant, sympathetic, consistent
*Ana* harmonizing *or* harmonious, according *or* accordant, corresponding *or* correspondent, agreeing *or* agreeable (see corresponding verbs at AGREE): seemly, proper (see DECOROUS): meet, appropriate, fitting, *fit
*Ant* incongruous   —*Con* incompatible, uncongenial, *inconsonant, discordant, discrepant
**conjectural** hypothetical, suppositious, *supposed, supposititious, reputed, putative, purported
*Ana* presumed, assumed, postulated (see PRESUPPOSE): *theoretical, speculative: alleged (see ADDUCE)
*Con* proved, demonstrated (see PROVE)
**conjecture** *vb* Conjecture, surmise, guess are comparable as verbs, meaning to draw an inference from slight evidence, and as nouns, denoting an inference based upon such evidence. **Conjecture** implies formation of an opinion or judgment upon what is recognized as insufficient evidence ⟨Washington *conjectured* that at least 300 of the enemy were killed—*Amer. Guide Series: Pa.*⟩ ⟨mysteries which must explain themselves are not worth the loss of time which a *conjecture* about them takes up—*Sterne*⟩ **Surmise** implies still slighter evidence, and exer-

cise of the imagination or indulgence in suspicion ⟨what thoughts he had beseems not me to say, though some *surmise* he went to fast and pray—*Dryden*⟩ ⟨just how long the small multiplied impressions will take to break into *surmise* . . . nobody can tell—*Quiller-Couch*⟩ ⟨we are not told what their business was but we may *surmise* it was the fur trade—*G. F. Hudson*⟩ **Guess** implies a hitting upon or an attempting to hit upon either at random or from insufficient, uncertain, or ambiguous evidence ⟨you would never *guess* from meeting them that anyone would pay them for their ideas—*Rose Macaulay*⟩ ⟨my daughter Lucie is . . . such a mystery to me; I can make no *guess* at the state of her heart—*Dickens*⟩
*Ana* *infer, gather, conclude, judge, deduce: speculate, reason, *think: imagine, fancy, conceive (see THINK)
*Con* ascertain, determine, learn, *discover: *prove, demonstrate, test, try
**conjecture** *n* surmise, guess (see under CONJECTURE *vb*)
*Ana* theory, *hypothesis: *opinion, view, belief, sentiment: inference, deduction, conclusion, judgment (see under INFER)
*Ant* fact
**conjoin** 1 *join, combine, unite, connect, link, associate, relate
2 combine, *unite, concur, cooperate
**conjugal** *matrimonial, marital, connubial, nuptial, hymeneal
*Ant* single
**connect** *join, link, associate, relate, unite, conjoin, combine
*Ana* attach, *fasten, affix: articulate, concatenate, *integrate
*Ant* disconnect —*Con* sever, sunder, divorce, *separate, part, divide: *detach, disengage
**connoisseur** dilettante, *aesthete
*Ana* *epicure, gourmet, bon vivant: *expert, adept
*Con* *amateur, tyro, dabbler
**connotation** denotation (see under DENOTE)
*Ana* suggestion, implication, intimation (see corresponding verbs at SUGGEST): evoking *or* evocation (see corresponding verb at EDUCE): import, signification, *meaning, significance, sense
**connote** *denote
*Ana* *suggest, imply, intimate, hint: *express, voice, utter: import, signify, *mean, denote
**connubial** conjugal, *matrimonial, marital, nuptial, hymeneal
**conquer,** defeat, vanquish, overcome, surmount, subdue, subjugate, reduce, overthrow, rout, beat, lick all mean to get the better of or to bring into subjection whether by the exercise of force or of strategy. *Conquer* and *defeat* are perhaps the most general. **Defeat** usually signifies merely the fact of getting the better of or winning against and may imply no more than a temporary checking or frustrating ⟨the enemy were successfully *defeated*⟩ ⟨he *defeated* the older man in the tennis tournament⟩ ⟨a distortion of the news picture which *defeats* the whole purpose to which our system is committed—*Mott*⟩ **Conquer,** however, usually implies a large and significant action (as of a large force in war) or an action involving an all-inclusive effort and a more or less permanent result ⟨Caesar *conquered* most of Gaul⟩ ⟨culture *conquers* more surely than the sword—*A. M. Young*⟩ ⟨science has *conquered* yellow fever—*Amer. Guide Series: La.*⟩ ⟨the 21-year-old Englishman who *conquered* the most dangerous river in the world—*N. Y. Times Book Rev.*⟩ **Vanquish** suggests a significant action of a certain dignity usually in the defeat of a person rather than a thing and usually carrying the suggestion of complete defeat ⟨to

overthrow the enemy solely by his own strength—to *vanquish* him solely by his own effort—*Hearn*⟩ ⟨*vanquish* an opponent in a championship match at tennis⟩ **Overcome** usually implies an opposing, more or less fixed obstacle to be dealt with and a high degree of effectiveness in dealing therewith whether by direct conflict or perhaps more often by indirect means (as evasion or substitution) ⟨*overcome* the enemy's shore fortifications⟩ ⟨*overcoming* difficult legal obstacles—*Americana Annual*⟩ ⟨using the airlift to *overcome* the blockade—*Collier's Yr. Bk.*⟩ ⟨*overcome* a speech defect⟩ **Surmount,** like *overcome,* implies an opposing, more or less fixed obstacle but carries the idea of surpassing or exceeding rather than overcoming in face-to-face conflict ⟨the technical problems to be *surmounted*—*K. F. Mather*⟩ ⟨many petty faults which he is apparently unable to *surmount*—*New Republic*⟩ ⟨Simon . . . has an inner force that is capable of *surmounting* conditions—*Malcolm Cowley*⟩ **Subdue,** *subjugate,* and *reduce* all throw emphasis upon the condition of subjection resulting from defeat. **Subdue** signifies to bring under control by or as if by overpowering ⟨in 1803 Commodore Edward Preble *subdued* the Barbary Coast pirates—*Amer. Guide Series: Me.*⟩ ⟨in their last century of conquest they almost succeeded in *subduing* the whole island—*Blanshard*⟩ ⟨all violence or recklessness of feeling has been finally *subdued*—*Cather*⟩ ⟨the wilderness had been almost completely *subdued* by cutting down the forests and building roads and cities⟩ **Subjugate** signifies to bring into and keep in subjection, often as a slave is in subjection ⟨authoritarian reaction which overwhelmed Italy and *subjugated* it for two centuries—*R. A. Hall*⟩ ⟨the heart and imagination *subjugating* the senses and understanding—*Arnold*⟩ **Reduce** signifies surrender and submission but usually of a town or fortress under attack or siege ⟨the town and finally the province were *reduced* by the invaders⟩ **Overthrow** is much like *overcome* but carries the strong idea of disaster to the overthrown ⟨*overthrow* the established government by violence⟩ ⟨get swiftly through the field of fire and pierce and *overthrow* the enemy lines—*Wintringham*⟩ ⟨a huge body of evidence . . . completely *overthrows* the older view —*Comfort*⟩ **Rout** always suggests a defeat so complete as to cause flight or the complete dispersion of the opposition ⟨twelve hundred French and a large force of Indians . . . were intercepted . . . and utterly *routed,* only 200 of the French escaping capture or death—*Bingham*⟩ ⟨Weaver with the assistance of two other gunboats *routed* a large force of Texas cavalry when they attacked Fort Butler—*Bolander*⟩ **Beat** and *lick* are characteristic of a less formal style of expression or level of usage than the preceding verbs. Both come close to *defeat* in meaning but distinctively **beat** (see also BEAT 1) is rather neutral in this sense, except that occasionally it may imply the finality though not the scope of *vanquish* ⟨the local ball team won the state championship by *beating* all comers⟩ while **lick** usually implies a complete humbling or reduction to impotency and ineffectiveness of the one defeated ⟨the fighter must be confirmed in the belief that he can *lick* anybody in the world—*Liebling*⟩ ⟨with the problem growing, the railroads have redoubled their efforts to *lick* it —*Faulkner*⟩
*Ana* *frustrate, thwart, foil, circumvent, outwit, baffle, balk
*Con* surrender, submit, capitulate (see corresponding nouns at SURRENDER): *yield, succumb, bow, cave
**conqueror** vanquisher, *victor, winner, champion
**conquest** *victory, triumph
*Ana* subjugation, subdual, defeating *or* defeat, overthrowing *or* overthrow, routing *or* rout (see corresponding verbs

at CONQUER)

**conscientious** scrupulous, honorable, honest, *upright, just

*Ana* righteous, virtuous, ethical, *moral: strict, *rigid: particular, fastidious, finicky, *nice: meticulous, punctilious, *careful

*Ant* unconscientious, unscrupulous —*Con* slack, lax, remiss, *negligent, neglectful: *careless, heedless, thoughtless

**conscious** sensible, *aware, cognizant, alive, awake

*Ana* attending *or* attentive, minding *or* mindful, watching (see corresponding verbs at TEND): *watchful, alert, vigilant: perceiving, noticing, noting, remarking, observing (see SEE)

*Ant* unconscious —*Con* ignoring, overlooking, disregarding (see NEGLECT *vb*): *forgetful, unmindful, oblivious

**consecrate** hallow, dedicate, *devote

*Con* desecrate, profane (see corresponding nouns at PROFANATION): defile, pollute (see CONTAMINATE)

**consecutive,** successive, sequent, sequential, serial are comparable when meaning following one after the other in order. *Consecutive* and *successive* apply to objects which follow one another without interruption or break. But **consecutive** is somewhat more emphatic, stressing the immediacy of the succession, the regularity or fixedness of the order, and the close connection (as in time, space, or logic) of the units while **successive** is applicable to things that follow regardless of differences (as in duration, extent, or size) or of the length of the interval between the units; thus, one would speak of nine, ten, and eleven as *consecutive* numbers since they follow one another in immediate and regular order, but of flashing the *successive* numbers three, eleven, and nine on a screen since the order would then be neither immediate nor regular; one would speak of *successive* (not *consecutive*) leap years since the order though regular is not immediate and of *successive* strokes of a piston since, though immediate, it need not be regular ⟨the most important cause . . . has run throughout our post-Conquest history like a *consecutive* thread —*Coulton*⟩ ⟨the product of the *successive* labors of innumerable men—*Mumford*⟩ *Consecutive* is also applicable to a person or to thought that manifests logical sequence ⟨*consecutive* thinking absolutely requires personal initiative—*Eliot*⟩ **Sequent** and **sequential** apply to an arrangement or to things (sometimes a thing) following a sequence (as a causal, logical, or chronological sequence) or some settled order ⟨the events of the narrative do not follow in *sequent* order⟩ ⟨the galleys have sent a dozen *sequent* messengers this very night at one another's heels—*Shak.*⟩ ⟨changes which proceed with *sequential* regularity⟩ ⟨combination of two *sequential* courses into one—*Pressey*⟩ **Serial** implies that the thing or things so qualified form a series or will appear as a series; it therefore suggests likeness or uniformity in the units and, usually, a prearranged order especially in time or space ⟨the fifth of the *serial* concerts⟩ ⟨from the publisher's point of view mystery stories make good *serial* narratives⟩ ⟨wrote her a *serial* account of his adventures—*Krutch*⟩

*Ana* following, succeeding, ensuing (see FOLLOW): continuous, *continual, incessant: coherent (see corresponding noun COHERENCE): *logical

*Ant* inconsecutive —*Con* alternate, *intermittent, recurrent, periodic: desultory, *random, haphazard, hit-or-miss

**consent** *vb* *assent, accede, acquiesce, agree, subscribe

*Ana* *yield, submit, defer, relent: permit, allow, *let: *approve, sanction: concur (see AGREE)

*Ant* dissent —*Con* refuse, *decline: *disapprove, deprecate: *demur, balk, stick, stickle, strain

**consequence** 1 result, *effect, upshot, aftereffect, aftermath, sequel, issue, outcome, event

*Ant* antecedent —*Con* *cause, determinant, reason, occasion: *origin, source, root

2 *importance, moment, weight, significance, import

*Ana* necessity, *need, exigency: *worth, value: renown, honor, reputation, repute, *fame: eminence, illustriousness (see corresponding adjectives at FAMOUS)

**consequently** *therefore, hence, then, accordingly, so

**conserve** *vb* preserve, *save

*Ana* protect, shield, safeguard, guard, *defend

*Ant* waste, squander

**consider** 1 Consider, study, contemplate, weigh, excogitate are comparable chiefly as transitive verbs meaning to fix the mind for a time on something in order to increase one's knowledge or understanding of it or to solve a problem involved in it. **Consider** often suggests little more than an applying of one's mind ⟨a proposal so unreasonable that one does not need to *consider* it⟩ but sometimes it also carries such a restricting implication as that of a definite point of view ⟨in the last paragraphs we have *considered* science as a steadily advancing army of ascertained facts —*Inge*⟩ or as that of thinking over ⟨the publishers told him they would *consider* his book⟩ ⟨marriage is an action too freely practiced and too seldom adequately *considered* —*Rose Macaulay*⟩ ⟨in Florida *consider* the flamingo, its color passion but its neck a question—*Warren*⟩ or as that of casting about in order to reach a suitable conclusion, opinion, or decision ⟨when I came to *consider* his conduct, I realized that he was guilty of a confusion —*T. S. Eliot*⟩ **Study** implies greater mental concentration than *consider;* usually it also suggests more care for the details or minutiae and more of an effort to comprehend fully or to learn all the possibilities, applications, variations, or relations ⟨the president said that the bill must be *studied* before he reached a decision regarding the signing or vetoing of it⟩ ⟨a work of architecture that deserves to be *studied* closely⟩ ⟨*study* a patient's reactions to a new treatment⟩ ⟨I like very naturally to think that I am being read; but the idea that I am being *studied* fills me, after the first outburst of laughter, with a deepening gloom— *Huxley*⟩ ⟨Bryce, who had *studied* the matter so thoroughly, was wont to insist it is the smallest democracies which today stand highest in the scale—*Ellis*⟩ **Contemplate** (see also SEE) implies, like *meditate* (see under PONDER), the focusing of one's attention upon a thing and a close dwelling upon it; the term, however, does not always carry a clear implication of the purpose or result. When the object on which the mind rests is a plan, a project, or an imaginative conception, the word usually suggests its formulation in detail or its enjoyment as envisioned ⟨Henchard bent and kissed her cheek. The moment and the act he had *contemplated* for weeks with a thrill of pleasure—*Hardy*⟩ ⟨the poet "has an idea," and in the course of *contemplating* it he draws up from his subconscious a string of associated ideas and images—*Day Lewis*⟩ When the object contemplated lies outside the mind and has either material or immaterial existence, the term suggests an attempt to increase one's knowledge and comprehension of it through minute scrutiny and meditation ⟨nature is beautiful only to the mind which is prepared to apprehend her beauty, to *contemplate* her for her own sake apart from the practical delight she brings—*Alexander*⟩ ⟨the opinion . . . widely held, that while science, by a deliberate abstraction, *contemplates* a world of facts without values, religion contemplates values apart from facts—*Inge*⟩ **Weigh** (compare PONDER) implies evaluation of something and especially of one thing in respect to another and relevant thing or things; it suggests an attempt to get at

the truth by a balancing (as of counterclaims, contradictory data, or conflicting evidence) ⟨in teaching the young to think hard, any subject will answer. The problem is to get them to *weigh* evidence, draw accurate inferences . . . and form judgments—*Eliot*⟩ ⟨it is not enough to count, we must evaluate; observations are not to be numbered, they are to be *weighed*—*Ellis*⟩ **Excogitate** is often replaced by *think out* and implies the application of the mind to something so that one may find the solution of the problems involved ⟨*excogitate* a plan whereby poverty may be relieved without unduly burdening the taxpayers⟩ ⟨there may have been a time when the scientific inquirer sat still in his chair to *excogitate* science—*Dewey*⟩
*Ana* *ponder, meditate, ruminate, muse: reflect, cogitate, *think, reason, speculate: inspect, examine, *scrutinize, scan
*Con* ignore, *neglect, overlook, disregard, slight
**2 Consider, regard, account, reckon, deem** denote to hold the view or opinion that someone or something is in fact as described or designated. They are often used interchangeably, but there are shadings of meaning that allow them to be discriminated. **Consider** suggests a conclusion reached through reflection ⟨he *considers* exercise a waste of energy⟩ ⟨it seems, however, best to *consider* as literature only works in which the aesthetic function is dominant —*René Wellek & Austin Warren*⟩ **Regard** may retain its primary implication of looking upon. Sometimes it suggests a judgment based on appearances ⟨I was . . . plainly *regarded* as a possible purchaser—*L. P. Smith*⟩ Often it implies a point of view, sometimes merely personal, sometimes partisan ⟨the regulations of the state were not *regarded* by the Greeks—as they are apt to be by modern men—as so many vexatious, if necessary, restraints on individual liberty—*Dickinson*⟩ ⟨a church . . . which *regarded* all dissentients as rebels and traitors—*Inge*⟩ **Account** and **reckon** to some extent retain their basic implications of counting or calculating, and in comparison with the other terms they stress such value-related factors as evaluation and differentiation ⟨these trees were not *reckoned* of much value⟩ ⟨another field where the dominance of the method of sociology may be *reckoned* as assured—*Cardozo*⟩ ⟨I *account* the justice which is grounded on utility to be the . . . most sacred and binding part of all morality—*J. S. Mill*⟩ **Deem** is somewhat literary. It is often used as the equivalent of *consider*, but it distinctively stresses judgment rather than reflection ⟨behind the economic problem lies a psychological or ethical problem, that of getting persons to recognize truths which they *deem* it to their interest to avoid—*Hobson*⟩ ⟨the first time he made a helmet, he tested its capacity for resisting blows, and battered it out of shape; next time he did not test it, but *deemed* it to be a very good helmet—*Russell*⟩ ⟨investigation of all the facts which it *deems* relevant—*Truman*⟩
*Ana* *think, conceive, imagine, fancy: judge, gather, *infer, conclude
**considerate** *thoughtful, attentive
*Ana* kindly, *kind: *tender, sympathetic, warmhearted, compassionate: obliging, complaisant, *amiable
*Ant* inconsiderate  —*Con* *forgetful, unmindful, oblivious: *careless, heedless, thoughtless
**considered** *deliberate, premeditated, advised, designed, studied
*Ana* intentional, *voluntary, willful: planned, projected, schemed (see corresponding verbs under PLAN *n*)
*Ant* unconsidered  —*Con* *precipitate, impetuous, headlong: impulsive, *spontaneous, instinctive
**consign** *commit, entrust, confide, relegate
*Ana* transfer, *move, remove, shift: assign, allocate,

*allot: resign, surrender, yield (see RELINQUISH)
**consistent** congruous, *consonant, compatible, congenial, sympathetic
*Ana* conforming *or* conformable, tallying, jibing, squaring (see corresponding verbs at AGREE): matching, equaling (see MATCH *vb*): identical, alike, similar, *like
*Ant* inconsistent  —*Con* discrepant, discordant, incongruous, *inconsonant, incompatible: contradictory, contrary, *opposite, antithetical
**console** *vb* *comfort, solace
*Ana* assuage, alleviate, mitigate, *relieve, allay: calm, tranquilize (see corresponding adjectives at CALM): *satisfy, content
*Con* *trouble, distress: *discompose, disturb, perturb, agitate, upset, disquiet
**consolidate** *compact, unify, concentrate
*Ana* *integrate, articulate, concatenate: amalgamate, merge, fuse, blend (see MIX): condense, compress (see CONTRACT *vb*): *weave, knit
*Con* melt, *liquefy: *separate, sever, sunder, part: *distribute, dispense, divide: dissipate, *scatter, disperse
**consolidation, merger, amalgamation** are comparable when denoting a union of two or more business corporations. **Consolidation** is often used as a general term; more precisely it implies a unification of the companies or corporations with dissolution of their separate corporate identities and transference of their combined assets, franchises, and goodwill to a single new corporate unit, often under an entirely new name. **Merger** usually implies a unification in which one or more companies or corporations are absorbed by another and the assets (as property, franchises, and goodwill) of the former are transferred to or merged into the latter whose corporate status and name remain unchanged. In a merger additional shares of stock may be issued by the absorbing company or corporation to replace on an agreed basis the shares of the units absorbed or a monetary transaction may be involved. **Amalgamation** is often used interchangeably with *consolidation* in its general sense and applied to any form of consolidation or merger. It is sometimes restricted to a consolidation in which a new corporation with an entirely new name and corporate identity results or, in British use, to a union of the merger type.
*Ant* dissolution
**consonance** *harmony, concord, accord
*Ana* agreement, conformity, correspondence (see corresponding verbs at AGREE): concurrence, coincidence (see corresponding verbs at AGREE): compatibility, congruity (see corresponding adjectives at CONSONANT)
*Ant* dissonance (*in music*): discord  —*Con* inconsonance, discordance, incompatibility, incongruity, discrepancy (see corresponding adjectives at INCONSONANT)
**consonant** *adj* **Consonant, consistent, compatible, congruous, congenial, sympathetic** are comparable when they mean being in agreement one with another or agreeable one to the other. **Consonant** implies agreement with a concurrent circumstance or situation, or conformity to an accepted standard, or harmony between two things that must come into contact or comparison with each other; the term suggests absence of discord ⟨Fijians possessed a physical endurance *consonant* with their great stature—*Heiser*⟩ ⟨it is . . . more *consonant* with the Puritan temper to abolish a practice than to elevate it and clear away abuses—*Quiller-Couch*⟩ ⟨to pursue callings more *consonant* with Buddha's teaching—*Binyon*⟩ ⟨nature has no ends *consonant* with . . . the desires of man which would make it possible for him to accord himself to her—*Krutch*⟩ **Consistent** suggests such agreement or harmony between things or between the details of the same thing as implies

---

A colon (:) separates groups of words discriminated. An asterisk (*) indicates place of treatment of each group.

the absence or avoidance of contradiction ⟨that their letters should be as kind as was *consistent* with proper maidenly pride—*De Quincey*⟩ ⟨did not think it to be *consistent* with his dignity to answer this sally—*Trollope*⟩ ⟨no one has yet imagined a *consistent* picture of what the electron and proton really are—*Jeans*⟩ **Compatible** implies a capacity for existing or coming together without disagreement, discord, or disharmony; the term does not necessarily suggest positive agreement or harmony, but it does imply the absence of such conflict between two or more things as would make their association or combination impossible or incongruous ⟨with all the eagerness *compatible* with . . . elegance, Sir Walter and his two ladies stepped forward to meet her—*Austen*⟩ ⟨to combine, in the highest measure in which they are *compatible,* the two elements of refinement and manliness—*Froude*⟩ ⟨many bad qualities are of course *compatible* with vitality —for example, those of a healthy tiger. And many of the best qualities are *compatible* with its absence— *Russell*⟩ **Congruous** implies more positive agreement or harmony than *compatible* does; ordinarily it implies the fitness, suitability, or appropriateness of one thing to another so that their association or combination, no matter how much they are in contrast, produces a pleasing or at least a not disagreeable impression ⟨*congruous* furnishings of a room⟩ ⟨not *congruous* to the nature of epic poetry—*Blair*⟩ ⟨thoughts *congruous* to the nature of their subject—*Cowper*⟩ The negative form *incongruous* is currently far more common than *congruous.* **Congenial** is most often used of persons or things that are in such harmony with the taste of a person that they afford him pleasure or delight or satisfaction ⟨a *congenial* companion⟩ ⟨a pair of not very *congenial* passengers—*Conrad*⟩ ⟨the reticence and understatement of the method made it specially *congenial* [to the Chinese]—*Binyon*⟩ ⟨[Hobbes's] theory of government is *congenial* to that type of person who is conservative from prudence but revolutionary in his dreams—*T. S. Eliot*⟩ ⟨the ideal of a Greek democracy was vastly *congenial* to his aristocratic temperament—*Parrington*⟩ Occasionally *congenial* is used of things in the sense of wholly and satisfyingly congruous ⟨all such introduced ideas are *congenial* to the subject—*Alexander*⟩ ⟨statement, overstatement, and understatement in letters given a *congenial* context, every one of them is right—*Montague*⟩ **Sympathetic** (see also TENDER), like *congenial,* usually suggests qualities in the person or thing so described that make him or it in agreement with another person's likings or tastes, but, in contrast with *congenial,* it suggests a more subtle appeal and often a less hearty acceptance ⟨every author who is *sympathetic* to them—*Bradley*⟩ ⟨Arnold does still hold us. . . . To my generation . . . he was a more *sympathetic* prose writer than Carlyle or Ruskin—*T. S. Eliot*⟩ ⟨a tête-à-tête with a man of similar tastes, who is just and yet *sympathetic,* critical yet appreciative—*Benson*⟩
*Ana* conforming or conformable, harmonizing or harmonious, agreeing or agreeable, according or accordant (see corresponding verbs at AGREE): concurring or concurrent, coinciding or coincident (see corresponding verbs at AGREE)
*Ant* inconsonant: dissonant (*in music*) —*Con* discordant, discrepant, inconsistent, incompatible, incongruous (see INCONSONANT)

**conspectus** synopsis, epitome, *abridgment, abstract, brief
*Ana* *compendium, syllabus, digest, survey, sketch, précis, aperçu

**conspicuous** prominent, salient, signal, *noticeable, remarkable, striking, arresting, outstanding

*Ana* patent, manifest, *evident, distinct, obvious: eminent, celebrated, illustrious (see FAMOUS)
*Ant* inconspicuous —*Con* *common, ordinary: *obscure, vague: lowly, *humble, modest: hidden, concealed (see HIDE): *secret, covert

**conspiracy** cabal, intrigue, machination, *plot
*Ana* *sedition, treason: treacherousness or treachery, perfidiousness or perfidy, disloyalty, faithlessness, falseness or falsity (see corresponding adjectives at FAITHLESS)

**conspirator** *confederate, accessory, accomplice, abettor

**constant** adj 1 *faithful, true, loyal, staunch, steadfast, resolute
*Ana* abiding, enduring, persisting or persistent, lasting (see corresponding verbs at CONTINUE): dependable, trustworthy, *reliable, trusty, tried
*Ant* inconstant, fickle —*Con* unstable, capricious, mercurial (see INCONSTANT): disloyal, *faithless, false, perfidious
2 *steady, uniform, even, equable
*Ana* established, settled, set, fixed (see SET *vb*): invariable, immutable, unchangeable (see affirmative adjectives at CHANGEABLE): *regular, normal, typical, natural
*Ant* variable —*Con* *changeable, changeful, mutable, protean: fluctuating, wavering (see SWING)
3 *continual, incessant, unremitting, continuous, perpetual, perennial
*Ana* persisting or persistent, persevering (see corresponding verbs at PERSEVERE): pertinacious, dogged, *obstinate, stubborn: chronic, confirmed, *inveterate
*Ant* fitful —*Con* *intermittent, alternate: spasmodic (see FITFUL): occasional, sporadic, *infrequent

**consternation** panic, terror, alarm, fright, *fear, dread, dismay, horror, trepidation
*Ana* confusion, muddlement or muddle (see corresponding verbs at CONFUSE): bewilderment, distraction, perplexity (see corresponding verbs at PUZZLE): agitation, perturbation (see corresponding verbs at DISCOMPOSE)
*Con* sangfroid, composure, *equanimity, phlegm: aplomb, self-possession (see CONFIDENCE)

**constituent** n component, *element, ingredient, factor
*Ana* *part, portion, piece, detail, member: *item, particular
*Ant* whole, aggregate —*Con* *system, complex, organism, economy: composite, compound, blend, amalgam (see MIXTURE)

**constitution** *physique, build, habit
*Ana* temperament, temper, personality (see DISPOSITION): organism, *system: *structure, framework, anatomy

**constitutional** adj *inherent, intrinsic, essential, ingrained
*Ana* congenial, *innate, inborn: *native: natural, normal (see REGULAR): *characteristic, individual, peculiar
*Ant* advenient —*Con* *accidental, adventitious, fortuitous: unnatural, *irregular, anomalous: foreign, alien, extraneous, *extrinsic

**constrain** oblige, coerce, compel, *force
*Ana* impel, drive, *move, actuate: require, exact, *demand

**constraint** compulsion, coercion, duress, restraint, *force, violence
*Ana* suppression, repression (see corresponding verbs at SUPPRESS): impelling or impulsion, driving or drive (see corresponding verbs at MOVE): goad, spur, *motive, spring: *obligation, duty

**constrict** compress, *contract, shrink, condense, deflate
*Ana* *tie, bind: restrict, confine, circumscribe, *limit: *restrain, curb
*Con* *expand, dilate, distend, swell, inflate: enlarge, *increase

**construct** *build, erect, frame, raise, rear

*Ana* fabricate, manufacture, fashion, *make: produce, turn out, yield (see BEAR)
*Ant* demolish: analyze —*Con* *destroy, raze: *ruin, wreck

**constructive** *implicit, virtual
*Ana* inferential, ratiocinative (see under INFERENCE): implied, involved (see INCLUDE)
*Ant* manifest —*Con* express, *explicit, definite: *evident, patent, obvious

**construe** *vb* explicate, elucidate, interpret, expound, *explain
*Ana* *analyze, resolve, break down, dissect: *understand, comprehend, appreciate

**consult** *confer, advise, parley, commune, treat, negotiate
*Ana* *discuss, debate: deliberate, cogitate (see THINK): counsel, advise (see under ADVICE)

**consume** 1 *waste, squander, dissipate, fritter
*Ana* exhaust, *deplete, drain: dispel, disperse, *scatter
*Con* *save, preserve, conserve
2 *eat, swallow, ingest, devour
3 engross, absorb, *monopolize

**consummate** *adj* Consummate, finished, accomplished are comparable when meaning brought to completion or perfection. Their distinctions lie chiefly in the degree of perfection, in the means by which this perfection is attained, and, at times, in their application: *consummate* and *finished* apply to persons or to things; *accomplished,* as a rule, to persons only. Something is **consummate** which attains the highest possible point or degree of perfection or which possesses the highest possible qualities, whether natural or acquired ⟨*consummate* skill⟩ ⟨*consummate* happiness⟩ ⟨a *consummate* hypocrite⟩ ⟨the little band held the post with *consummate* tenacity—*Motley*⟩ ⟨a man of perfect and *consummate* virtue—*Addison*⟩ ⟨Pope . . . is . . . one of the most *consummate* craftsmen who ever dealt in words—*Lowes*⟩ Something which is **finished** (see also *finish* at CLOSE *vb* 2) manifests such care and exquisiteness in performance or workmanship that nothing additional is required to perfect it or to increase its technical excellence ⟨a *finished* gentleman is always courteous⟩ ⟨*finished* actors usually give *finished* performances⟩ ⟨he's the most *finished* blackmailer in America—*Donn Byrne*⟩ ⟨written with the *finished* workmanship which always delights us—*Edward Sackville-West*⟩ One is **accomplished** who is distinguished for his skill, his versatility, and his finesse; the word often suggests mastery in whatever is attempted ⟨an *accomplished* musician⟩ ⟨an *accomplished* villain⟩ ⟨they . . . are more *accomplished* and ingenious in this sort of rationalizing than Arnold was—*T. S. Eliot*⟩ *Accomplished* sometimes implies merely the acquirement of social arts and graces or accomplishments ⟨*accomplished* young ladies⟩
*Ana* *perfect, whole, entire, intact: complete, *full: flawless, *impeccable, faultless: *supreme, superlative, transcendent, peerless, surpassing
*Ant* crude —*Con* rough, *rude, callow, green, raw, uncouth: primitive, primeval (see PRIMARY): defective, *deficient

**contact** *n* Contact, touch mean the state or fact of coming into direct connection or close association with someone or something. **Contact** implies the mutual relation between two bodies that impinge upon each other ⟨the tangent at its point of *contact* with the circle⟩ ⟨the two boats are coming into *contact*⟩ ⟨break the *contact* in an electric circuit⟩ **Touch** primarily implies the action involved when a tactile organ, especially of a human being, comes in contact with someone or something or the sensation involved when one feels through a tactile organ the presence of another person or object ⟨one *touch* of the snake was

enough to make her scream⟩ ⟨ruffian! let go that rude uncivil *touch*—*Shak.*⟩ ⟨but O for the *touch* of a vanished hand—*Tennyson*⟩ Although these two words are often interchangeable in general use, *contact* may be preferable when the intent is to stress a connection or association whether between bodies, between persons, or between persons and things and the sensation or emotional response is not emphasized, or when an impersonal or unexplict word without clearly defined connotations is wanted ⟨the New York firm established business *contacts* in Australia⟩ ⟨an adult with whom a child is in constant *contact* may easily become . . . dominant in the child's life—*Russell*⟩ ⟨it was her first *contact* with the nether side of the smooth social surface—*Wharton*⟩ ⟨his mind turned away from the hunger for human *contact*—*Anderson*⟩ On the other hand *touch* is usually preferable when the idea of the sensation or of the emotion involved is more important than the abstract or literal idea of coming into contact or when lightness or delicacy is to be implied ⟨the whole secret . . . lay in the development of the sense of *touch* in the feet, which comes with years of night rambling in little-trodden spots—*Hardy*⟩ ⟨she felt his nearness intimately, like a *touch*—*Conrad*⟩ ⟨lost *touch* with all his old friends⟩
*Ana* impingement, *impact: connection, association, relation (see corresponding verbs at JOIN): union, *unity: closeness, nearness (see corresponding adjectives at CLOSE)
*Con* separation, division, severance (see corresponding verbs at SEPARATE): *breach, split, rupture, rift

**contagious** *infectious, communicable, catching
*Ana* toxic, pestilential, pestilent, virulent, mephitic, miasmic (see POISONOUS)

**contain,** hold, accommodate denote to have or be capable of having within. To **contain** is to have within or to have as an element, fraction, or part; to **hold** is to have the capacity to contain or to retain; thus, a bookcase that *holds* (is capable of containing) one hundred volumes may *contain* (actually have in it) only fifty; a bushel *contains* (not *holds*) four pecks but a bushel basket *holds* (not *contains*) four pecks of potatoes ⟨these boxes *contain* apples⟩ ⟨his philosophy *contains* some elements of truth⟩ ⟨of Plato himself we know nothing . . . that could not be *held* in a single sentence—*Ellis*⟩ But the distinction between *hold* and *contain* is often inconsiderable or disregarded. To **accommodate** (see also OBLIGE 2) is to hold without crowding and inconvenience ⟨thirty passengers were crowded into a bus built to *accommodate* twenty⟩ ⟨the parking lot *accommodates* fifty cars⟩ ⟨the earth can *accommodate* its present population more comfortably than it does or ever did—*Shaw*⟩ ⟨the hotel was unable to *accommodate* all who applied for rooms⟩
*Ana* *receive, admit, take: *harbor, shelter, lodge, house

**contaminate,** taint, attaint, pollute, defile mean to debase by making impure or unclean. **Contaminate** implies the presence or the influence of something external which by entering into or by coming in contact with a thing destroys or may destroy the latter's purity ⟨the city's water supply was in danger of being *contaminated* by surface drainage⟩ ⟨refused to allow her children to play with other children for fear their manners and morals might be *contaminated*⟩ ⟨air *contaminated* by noxious gases⟩ ⟨dispersing from the sky vast quantities of radioactive dust particles . . . *contaminating* entire cities—*Cousins*⟩ **Taint** differs from *contaminate* in stressing the effect rather than the cause; something *contaminated* has been touched by or mixed with what will debase or corrupt; whatever is *tainted* is no longer pure, clean, unspoiled, or wholesome but is in some measure or degree sullied

---

A colon (:) separates groups of words discriminated. An asterisk (*) indicates place of treatment of each group.

or stained or in process of corruption or decay ⟨*tainted* meat⟩ ⟨his unkindness may defeat my life, but never *taint* my love—*Shak.*⟩ ⟨the Claudii, brilliant, unaccountable, *tainted* with some deep congenital madness—*Buchan*⟩ ⟨directed toward the purge from the public service rolls of those *tainted* with fascism—*Taylor Cole*⟩ The less common **attaint** may be closely synonymous with *taint* ⟨our writers have been *attainted* by the disease they must help to cure—*Frank*⟩ More often it retains a hint of its primary meaning of to sentence to outlawry or death and then suggests a sullying (as of one's name) or a degrading especially as a result of actual or reputed misconduct ⟨wherein a good name hath been wrongfully *attainted*—*Milton*⟩ ⟨no breath of calumny ever *attainted* the personal purity of Savonarola—*Milman*⟩ **Pollute** implies that the process which begins with contamination is complete and manifest and that what was pure and clean has lost its clearness or fairness and has become muddy or filthy or poisoned ⟨the nuisance set forth in the bill was one which would be of international importance—a visible change of a great river from a pure stream into a *polluted* and poisoned ditch—*Justice Holmes*⟩ **Pollute** is especially apt when the reference is to something that ideally is clean, clear, or bright ⟨*pollute* the minds of children by obscenities⟩ ⟨you . . . are *polluted* with your lusts—*Shak.*⟩ **Defile** strongly implies befouling of something which ought to be kept clean and pure or held sacred. It usually suggests violation, profanation, or desecration and is highly opprobrious in its connotations ⟨an evil bird that *defiles* his own nest—*Latimer*⟩ ⟨scenes such as these, 'tis his supreme delight to fill with riot, and *defile* with blood—*Cowper*⟩ ⟨cruelty is not only the worst accusation that can be brought against a man, *defiling* the whole character—*Belloc*⟩
*Ana* *debase, vitiate, corrupt, deprave: impair, spoil, *injure, harm

**contemn** *despise, disdain, scorn, scout
*Ana* repudiate, reject (see DECLINE): slight, *neglect, disregard: flout, *scoff, jeer
*Con* venerate, *revere, reverence: respect, esteem, admire, regard (see under REGARD *n*)

**contemplate** 1 study, *consider, weigh, excogitate
*Ana* *ponder, meditate, muse, ruminate: reflect, cogitate, speculate, *think
2 observe, survey, notice, remark, note, perceive, discern, *see, view, behold, descry, espy
*Ana* *scrutinize, inspect, examine, scan

**contemplative** meditative, reflective, *thoughtful, speculative, pensive
*Ana* *intent, rapt, engrossed, absorbed: musing, ruminating, pondering (see PONDER): reflecting, cogitating, reasoning, thinking (see THINK)

**contemporaneous** *contemporary, coeval, coetaneous, synchronous, simultaneous, coincident, concomitant, concurrent
*Con* *preceding, antecedent, previous, prior, foregoing: following, ensuing, succeeding (see FOLLOW)

**contemporary** *adj* Contemporary, contemporaneous, coeval, coetaneous, synchronous, simultaneous, coincident, concomitant, concurrent are comparable when they mean existing, living, or occurring at the same time. In **contemporary** and **contemporaneous** (of which *contemporary* is applied somewhat more frequently to persons, *contemporaneous* to events), the time regarding which agreement is implied is determined only through the context ⟨Shakespeare was *contemporary* with Cervantes, who died in the same month⟩ ⟨Shelley's last year was *contemporaneous* with Matthew Arnold's first⟩ ⟨the reign of Louis XIV was *contemporaneous* with the Commonwealth in

England and also with the Restoration and the revolution of 1688⟩ ⟨a recent history of the 15th century based on *contemporary* accounts⟩ ⟨love of school is not *contemporaneous* with residence therein; it is an after product —*Grandgent*⟩ Contemporary, but not *contemporaneous*, may imply reference to the present; it then means of the same time as that of the speaker or writer ⟨we are not without *contemporary* talent—*Wharton*⟩ ⟨most *contemporary* novels Jane found very bad—*Rose Macaulay*⟩ **Coeval** usually implies contemporaneousness for a long time or at a remote time ⟨everyone knows that the Roman Catholic religion is at least *coeval* with most of the governments where it prevails—*Burke*⟩ ⟨the theory requires that these *coeval* stars should be of nearly the same mass and brightness—*Eddington*⟩ **Coetaneous** is a close synonym of *coeval*, but it may more specifically suggest contemporaneity of origin ⟨the maturation of Veblen's thought led him to note two forces . . . whose *coetaneous* presence acted first in the promotion of reason and then in its derangement—*Rosenberg*⟩ ⟨ancient and *coetaneous* mountain ranges⟩ **Synchronous** implies an exact correspondence between the usually brief periods of time involved; **simultaneous** more frequently denotes agreement in the same point or instant of time ⟨two pendulums so adjusted that their movements are *synchronous*⟩ ⟨the two shots were *simultaneous*⟩ ⟨French speech has run a similar and almost *synchronous* course with English —*Ellis*⟩ ⟨it was proposed that there should be *simultaneous* insurrections in London . . . and at Newcastle—*Macaulay*⟩ **Coincident** applies to events that are regarded as falling or happening at the same time; it ordinarily minimizes the notion of causal relation ⟨the discovery of America was almost *coincident* with the capture of Granada⟩ ⟨the growth of the mine union movement was *coincident* with the growth of business and manufacturing —*Hay*⟩ **Concomitant** carries so strong an implication of attendance or association that it often imputes a subordinate character; however, only when it implies coincidence or synchronousness is it truly a synonym of the other words ⟨the *concomitant* circumstances of this event cannot be ignored⟩ ⟨as the beauty of the body always accompanies the health of it, so certainly is decency *concomitant* to virtue—*Spectator*⟩ **Concurrent** adds to *synchronous* the implication of parallelism or agreement (as in length of existence or in quality or character) ⟨*concurrent* terms in prison⟩ ⟨the *concurrent* operation of many machines⟩ ⟨great cultural achievements have not been inevitably, or even generally, *concurrent* with great material power—*Bryson*⟩
*Ana* living, existing, subsisting (see BE)
*Con* see those at CONTEMPORANEOUS

**contempt** despite, disdain, scorn (see under DESPISE *vb*)
*Ana* abhorrence, detestation, loathing, hatred, hate (see under HATE *vb*): aversion, *antipathy: repugnance, distaste (see corresponding adjectives at REPUGNANT)
*Ant* respect  —*Con* esteem, admiration, *regard: *reverence, awe, fear

**contemptible** *adj* Contemptible, despicable, pitiable, sorry, scurvy, cheap, beggarly, shabby are comparable when they mean arousing or deserving scorn or disdain. **Contemptible** applies to whatever inspires such scorn or disdain for any reason however great or small ⟨with that property he will never be a *contemptible* man—*Austen*⟩ ⟨the one disgraceful, unpardonable, and to all time *contemptible* action of my life was to allow myself to appeal to society for help and protection—*Wilde*⟩ **Despicable** is a stronger term and frequently implies both keen and scornful, sometimes indignant, disapprobation and a sufficient cause for such a reaction ⟨the immorality of James's Court was hardly

more *despicable* than the imbecility of his government—
*J. R. Green*⟩ ⟨even excellent science could and did often
make *despicable* morality—*Gauss*⟩ **Pitiable** (see also
PITIFUL) implies the inspiring of pity mixed with contempt ⟨a *pitiable* show of weakness⟩ ⟨a *pitiable* attempt
at reform⟩ ⟨the resorting to epithets . . . is a *pitiable*
display of intellectual impotence—*Cohen*⟩ **Sorry** is
often used interchangeably with *pitiable* without marked
loss, but it often distinctively implies contemptible or
ridiculous inadequacy, wretchedness, or sordidness
⟨*sorry* accommodations for the travelers⟩ ⟨mounted . . .
upon a lean, *sorry*, jackass of a horse—*Sterne*⟩ **Scurvy**
implies extreme despicability and meanness and the
arousing of disgust as well as scornful contempt ⟨a *scurvy*
trick⟩ ⟨a *scurvy* impostor⟩ ⟨what difference betwixt
this Rome and ours . . . between that *scurvy* dumbshow
and this pageant sheen . . . ?—*Browning*⟩ **Cheap** often
implies contemptibility that results from undue familiarity
or accessibility ⟨had I so lavish of my presence been . . .
so stale and *cheap* to vulgar company—*Shak.*⟩ More
often, however, *cheap* and *beggarly* imply contemptible
pettiness, *cheap* by falling far below the standard of what
is worthy, *beggarly* by its remoteness from what is adequate ⟨*cheap* politics⟩ ⟨a *cheap* and nasty life—*Shaw*⟩
⟨about his shelves a *beggarly* account of empty boxes—
*Shak.*⟩ ⟨the South in 1800 was a land of contrasts, of
opulence and squalor . . . fine mansions, *beggarly* taverns
—*Brooks*⟩ **Shabby** comes close to *cheap* and *beggarly*
in implying contemptible pettiness and to *scurvy* in implying meanness and the arousing of disgust; distinctively
it may stress the poverty, the paltriness, or the ungenerous
nature of what is so characterized ⟨the *shabby* way in
which this country . . . treated a poet so deeply devoted
to it—*Engle*⟩ ⟨the explorer's mistress shows up with the
*shabby* truth of the man's life—*Hewes*⟩
*Ana* detestable, abominable, abhorrent, odious, *hateful: vile, low, *base: abject, *mean, sordid, ignoble
*Ant* admirable, estimable: formidable —*Con* *splendid,
sublime, glorious, superb

**contend** 1 Contend, fight, battle, war come into comparison
when they mean to strive in opposition to someone or
something. **Contend,** the most general of these words,
always implies a desire or an effort to overcome that
which is opposed, but it may imply rivalry rather than
animosity, the use of argument rather than the exercise
of physical strength or skill or the employment of weapons,
a nonhuman rather than a human antagonist ⟨the river was
stronger than I, and my arms could not for many hours
*contend* with the Thames—*Jefferies*⟩ ⟨since they had left
the Española country behind them, they had *contended*
first with wind and sandstorms, and now with cold—
*Cather*⟩ ⟨the Manichean theory of a good and an evil
spirit *contending* on nearly equal terms in the arena—
*Inge*⟩ **Fight** in its earliest and still most common sense
implies a struggle involving physical strength or prowess,
originally between men with the fists or with weapons
and later also between animals ⟨*fight*, gentlemen of
England! *fight*, bold yeomen!—*Shak.*⟩ ⟨*fight* fiercely,
Harvard—*Lehrer*⟩ ⟨a dog that will *fight* other dogs
larger then himself⟩ In extended use (see also RESIST)
*fight* differs from *contend* not so much in its range of
application, for both may imply other than a human adversary, as in its stress on a rigorous effort to achieve one's
ends, and in its suggestion of a struggle against odds or
great difficulties ⟨*fight* for the defeat of a bill⟩ ⟨*fight* for
breath⟩ ⟨*fight* against a growing evil⟩ ⟨he had *fought*
like a demon every inch of the way against poverty and
discouragement—*Long*⟩ **Battle** and **war** are more picturesque or more poetic terms than *fight;* they are used

chiefly in an extended sense, the first to suggest a continuous assailing or attacking of the enemy or other method
characteristic of open battle, and the second to suggest
the noise, fury, or tumult of war ⟨he found he must *battle*
his way to success⟩ ⟨sometimes a patriot, active in debate,
mix with the world, and *battle* for the state—*Pope*⟩
⟨he *wars* with darkling powers (I *war* with a darkling sea)
—*Kipling*⟩
*Ana* quarrel, wrangle, altercate, squabble (see under
QUARREL *n*): *resist, combat, withstand, oppose, fight:
compete, vie, *rival
2 *compete, contest
*Ana* battle, war (see CONTEND): oppose, *resist, withstand, combat, fight
**content, contented** satisfied (see under SATISFY)
*Ana* gratified, pleased (see PLEASE): sated, satiated,
cloyed, surfeited (see SATIATE): replete (see FULL)
**content** *vb* *satisfy
*Ana* gratify, *please: sate, *satiate, surfeit, cloy
*Con* tantalize, tease (see WORRY): pique, stimulate, *provoke, excite
**contention** dissension, difference, variance, strife, *discord, conflict
*Ana* *quarrel, wrangle, altercation, squabble: controversy, dispute, *argument: contending, fighting, warring
(see CONTEND)
*Con* agreement, concurrence, coincidence (see corresponding verbs at AGREE): *harmony, accord, concord,
consonance
**contentious** quarrelsome, bellicose, *belligerent, pugnacious, combative
*Ana* *contrary, perverse, froward: captious, faultfinding,
caviling, carping (see CRITICAL): *aggressive, militant
*Ant* peaceable —*Con* *pacific, peaceful, irenic: serene,
tranquil, *calm: *amiable, good-natured, complaisant,
obliging
**conterminous** contiguous, abutting, adjoining, *adjacent,
tangent, juxtaposed
**contest** *vb* 1 *compete, contend
*Ana* struggle, strive, endeavor (see ATTEMPT): fight,
battle (see CONTEND)
2 *resist, withstand, oppose, fight, combat, conflict,
antagonize
**contest** *n* Contest, conflict, combat, fight, affray, fray
denote a battle between opposing forces for supremacy,
for power, or for possessions. **Contest** is the broadest
term; originally it referred solely to strife in argument
but it is now applicable to any struggle, whether friendly
or hostile, for a common object that involves a test of
ability, strength, endurance, or strategic skill ⟨a swimming
*contest*⟩ ⟨a *contest* of wits⟩ ⟨what mighty *contests* rise
from trivial things—*Pope*⟩ ⟨boundary controversies or
other *contests* between states—*Frankfurter*⟩ **Conflict**
implies discord and warfare; it also suggests a closer engagement than *contest* ⟨arms on armor clashing brayed
. . . dire was the noise of *conflict*—*Milton*⟩ *Conflict* may
be extended to denote a struggle (often spiritual or mental)
between opposing or contradictory principles or forces
⟨there is [in a Shakespearean tragedy] an outward *conflict* of persons and groups, there is also a *conflict* of
forces in the hero's soul—*Bradley*⟩ **Combat** is less commonly used in an extended sense ⟨a *combat* against
despair⟩ It implies an encounter, especially an armed
encounter, between two (individuals, parties, or forces),
frequently for the determination of a dispute ⟨let these
have a day appointed them for a single *combat* in convenient place—*Shak.*⟩ ⟨these progressive leaders in both
parties rose only after bitter struggle. They were the
product of more than a lively contest. Sometimes the

---

A colon (:) separates groups of words discriminated. An asterisk (*) indicates place of treatment of each group.

contests were *combats—White*⟩ **Fight** usually implies a hand-to-hand conflict and therefore emphasizes the individual participants. It ranges in dignity from a spiritual struggle ⟨fight the good *fight* of faith—*1 Tim* 6:12⟩ to actual blows with fists or weapons ⟨a prize*fight*⟩ **Affray** commonly refers to a tumultuous disturbance (as a street fight between mobs or factions) that inspires terror. Legally an affray is a fight that disturbs the public peace; in literary use the word is often applied to an unseemly or acrimonious dispute ⟨the suppressing of riots and *affrays—Burke*⟩ ⟨days of European crises, diplomatic *affrays*, hecatombic accidents—*Montague*⟩ ⟨some bloody *affray* between scholars—*Quiller-Couch*⟩ **Fray** is usually either a literary term, often with more dignified connotations than *affray* of which it is otherwise a very close synonym, or it is a poetic or hyperbolical substitute for *battle, contest,* or *game* ⟨"Where are the vile beginners of this *fray?*" "O noble prince, I can discover all the unlucky manage of this fatal brawl"—*Shak.*⟩
*Ana* *encounter, skirmish, brush: competition, emulation, rivalry (see corresponding verbs at RIVAL): *battle, engagement, action

**contiguous** adjoining, abutting, conterminous, *adjacent, tangent, juxtaposed
*Ana* *nearest, next: *close, near, nigh, nearby

**continence** *temperance, abstemiousness, sobriety, abstinence
*Ana* chasteness *or* chastity, purity (see corresponding adjectives at CHASTE): moderateness *or* moderation, temperateness (see corresponding adjectives at MODERATE)
*Ant* incontinence    —*Con* lecherousness, lustfulness, lewdness, lasciviousness, licentiousness, wantonness (see corresponding adjectives at LICENTIOUS): excessiveness, inordinateness (see corresponding adjectives at EXCESSIVE)

**continent** *adj* temperate, unimpassioned, *sober
*Ana* restrained, bridled, curbed, inhibited (see RESTRAIN): decent, *chaste, pure: self-denying, self-abnegating (see corresponding nouns under RENUNCIATION)
*Ant* incontinent

**contingency** emergency, exigency, pinch, *juncture, pass, strait, crisis
*Ana* chance, break, *opportunity, occasion, time

**contingent**   1 *accidental, fortuitous, casual, incidental, adventitious
*Ana* possible, *probable, likely: unforeseen *or* unforeseeable, unanticipated (see affirmative verbs at FORESEE)
*Con* inevitable, necessary, *certain
2 conditional, *dependent, relative
*Ana* subject, *liable, open, exposed
*Con* absolute, *ultimate, categorical

**continual,**   **continuous, constant, incessant, unremitting, perpetual, perennial** are comparable when meaning characterized by continued occurrence or recurrence over a relatively long period of time. **Continual** implies a close or unceasing succession or recurrence; **continuous,** an uninterrupted continuity or union (as of objects, events, or parts) ⟨ensure a *continual* supply of provisions at regular intervals⟩ ⟨*continual* and regular impulses of pleasurable surprise from the metrical arrangement—*Wordsworth*⟩ ⟨analytic studies are *continuous,* and not to be pursued by fits and starts, or fragmentary efforts—*De Quincey*⟩ ⟨the *continual* suggestion of the landscape ... entering ... into the texture of *continuous* intelligent narration—*Stevenson*⟩ As applied to a single object, *continual* also stresses frequently the idea of going on indefinitely, though not without interruptions, in time rather than (like *continuous*) that of unbroken connection or substance; thus, *continual* industry implies that one is always at it; *continuous* labor, that the work itself is per-

formed at a stretch ⟨he that is of a merry heart hath a *continual* feast—*Prov* 15:15⟩ ⟨that dull and *continuous* burden of the sea heard inland before or after a great storm—*J. R. Lowell*⟩ *Continuous* refers to both time and space, *continual* only to time; thus, one may speak of a *continuous* (not *continual*) expanse, but of a *continual* (or *continuous*) noise ⟨humanism has been sporadic, but Christianity *continuous—T. S. Eliot*⟩ **Constant** implies uniform, steady, or persistent occurrence or recurrence and usually connotes lack of change or variation (as in character, degree, or rate ⟨*constant* throbbing of the engine⟩ ⟨such a career meant *constant* toil—*Buchan*⟩ ⟨unfortunately, perhaps, experience does not grow at a *constant,* but at an accelerated, rate—*Krutch*⟩ **Incessant** implies ceaseless or uninterrupted activity; **unremitting,** unceasing activity without slackening or halting; and **perpetual** (see also LASTING), unfailing repetition or lasting duration ⟨an *incessant* cough⟩ ⟨a life of *unremitting* toil⟩ ⟨*perpetual* colds⟩ ⟨sporadic outbursts are converted by the rationalization into purposive and *unremitting* activity—*Huxley*⟩ ⟨the *perpetual* fuel of controversy—*Newman*⟩ ⟨sins unatoned for and uncondoned bring purgatorial or *perpetual* torment after death—*H. O. Taylor*⟩ ⟨his *incessant* talking and shouting and bellowing of orders had been too much—*London*⟩ **Perennial** carries the implication of existence over an indeterminate number of years; especially in older use this idea may be stressed and that of exhaustlessness often connoted ⟨the *perennial* beauty and heroism of the homeliest human nature—*J. R. Lowell*⟩ ⟨the *perennial* feeling of silent worship—*Carlyle*⟩ In current use, probably because of the application of the term to plants that die down to the roots and spring up again seasonally over a number of years, the implication of continual recurrence or constant renewal is perhaps more common ⟨revolt is *perennial—Lowes*⟩ ⟨the *perennial* question of the relation between *ought* and *is,* of obligation and fact—*Alexander*⟩
*Ana* unceasing, endless, interminable, *everlasting: eternal (see INFINITE): *lasting, permanent, perdurable
*Ant* intermittent   —*Con* recurrent, periodic, alternate (see INTERMITTENT): *fitful, spasmodic

**continuance** *continuation, continuity
*Ana* endurance, persistence, lasting (see corresponding verbs at CONTINUE): perseverance, persistence (see corresponding verbs at PERSEVERE): remaining, staying, tarrying (see STAY)

**continuation,**   **continuance, continuity** are often confused, especially when meaning the quality, the act, or the state of continuing or of being continued or an instance revealing such a quality, action, or state. **Continuation** suggests prolongation or resumption ⟨the *continuation* of a line⟩ ⟨it's the *continuation* of a philosophic plan—*Meredith*⟩ ⟨the boy from a good classical school finds that his college Latin, Greek, and mathematics are the natural *continuation* of what he has already acquired—*Grandgent*⟩ **Continuance** implies duration, perseverance, or stay ⟨eleven years' *continuance—Shak.*⟩ ⟨patient *continuance* in well doing—*Rom* 2:7⟩ ⟨our *continuance* in the city depends on our boy's health⟩ ⟨the idleness and vice of many years *continuance—Austen*⟩ **Continuity** stresses uninterrupted or unbroken connection, sequence, or extent ⟨the *continuity* of a series⟩ ⟨*continuity* of attention⟩ ⟨the entire breach of *continuity* in your history made by the Revolution—*Arnold*⟩ ⟨space and time are thus vehicles of *continuity* by which the world's parts hang together—*James*⟩ In the technical language of those engaged in making motion pictures or in radio and television broadcasting, *continuity* denotes material written in advance (as the scenario of a motion picture or the

---

*Ana* analogous words     *Ant* antonyms     *Con* contrasted words     See also explanatory notes facing page 1

lines to be spoken in a radio broadcast) as provision for perfection in sequence and in timing of the performance. *Ana* extending *or* extension, prolonging *or* prolongation, protracting *or* protraction (see corresponding verbs at EXTEND)
*Ant* cessation

**continue, last, endure, abide, persist** are comparable when meaning to remain indefinitely in existence or in a given condition or course. **Continue** distinctively refers to the process and stresses its lack of an end rather than the duration of or the qualities involved in that process. Often, in addition, it suggests an unbroken course ⟨what a man is as an end perishes when he dies; what he produces as a means *continues* to the end of time—*Russell*⟩ ⟨the illusion *continues* that civilization can somehow be reconciled with atomic war—*Fleming*⟩ **Last** especially in its derivative *lasting* (see LASTING) when unqualified usually stresses length of existence exceeding what is normal or expected ⟨the anger of slow, mild, loving people has a *lasting* quality—*Deland*⟩ When qualified, *last* often loses this distinctive implication ⟨the work that Michelangelo did complete has *lasted* well—*Barr*⟩ ⟨the refrigerator is guaranteed to *last* five years⟩ ⟨the tire *lasted* only three months⟩ **Endure** adds to *last* the implication of resistance, especially to destructive forces or agencies ⟨for living things, who suffer pain, may not *endure* till time can bring them ease—*Lowell*⟩ ⟨an art . . . which *endured* . . . until man changed his attitude toward the universe—*Henry Adams*⟩ **Abide** and its derivative *abiding* imply stability or constancy, especially in opposition to mutability or impermanence ⟨though much is taken, much *abides*—*Tennyson*⟩ ⟨notwithstanding the countless features of London's living which were *abiding*, the changes made themselves felt—*J. M. Brown*⟩ **Persist** adds to *continue* the implication of outlasting the appointed or normal time; it often also connotes recurrence, especially in sporadic instances ⟨an attitude towards life, which . . . *persists*, with many changes but no breaks, till the closing of the Athenian lecture rooms by Justinian—*Inge*⟩
*Ana* remain, *stay: survive, *outlive, outlast
*Con* *arrest, interrupt, check: *stop, cease, desist, quit, discontinue: suspend, stay, intermit, *defer, postpone

**continuity** *continuation, continuance
*Ana* *succession, sequence, chain, train, progression
*Con* intermittence, recurrence, alternation, periodicity (see corresponding adjectives at INTERMITTENT): fitfulness (see corresponding adjective at FITFUL)

**continuous** constant, perpetual, perennial, *continual, incessant, unremitting
*Ana* connected, related, linked (see JOIN): successive, *consecutive, sequent, serial: *steady, constant, uniform
*Ant* interrupted —*Con* *intermittent, recurrent, periodic, alternate

**contort** distort, warp, *deform
*Ana* twist, bend, *curve

**contour** *outline, silhouette, skyline, profile
*Ana* configuration, shape, *form, conformation, figure

**contraband** *adj* *smuggled, bootleg

**contract** *n* Contract, bargain, compact, pact, treaty, entente, convention, cartel, concordat designate an agreement reached after negotiation and ending in an exchange of promises between the parties concerned. **Contract** applies especially to a formal written agreement, often of a business nature, couched in such explicit terms as to be enforceable at law ⟨a regular *contract* to the above effect was drawn up by a lawyer, and signed and sealed in the presence of witnesses—*Hawthorne*⟩ **Bargain** applies especially to an agreement regarding purchase and sale ⟨this *bargain* provides for an exchange of so much Ameri-

can wheat and cotton for so much British rubber and tin⟩ A **compact** is an earnest or solemn exchange of promises, sometimes between state or political groups and often between persons. A compact may be unwritten or undocumented, the only assurance of its execution being the trust which each party places in the honor of the other. The word is used when a keen sense of the obligation which it imposes is assumed of each of the parties ⟨men and women . . . marry and promise loyalty to some one person. They can keep that *compact* and yet not shut themselves away from other men and other women—*Rose Macaulay*⟩ ⟨let us make a *compact*. I shall do everything to please you, and you must promise to do everything to please me—*Hudson*⟩ ⟨the National Assembly, inspired by Thiers's patriotism, adopted . . . the "*Compact* of Bordeaux," whereby it was agreed that political differences should be put aside in order to carry through expeditiously the work of reconstruction—*Schapiro*⟩ **Pact** as used of an agreement between persons or groups is usually interchangeable with *compact* ⟨suicide *pact*, an agreement between two persons to commit suicide⟩ ⟨an unvoiced *pact* between us to read him with . . . skepticism—*Horace Gregory*⟩ Perhaps because of its popularity with newspaper headline writers which its brevity won for it, *pact* is used with increasing frequency in the (often unofficial) title of agreements between states ⟨the *Pact* of Corfu was a constitutional *pact* wherein leaders of the southern Slavs agreed to join in a unitary kingdom—*The Nation*⟩; in this use it is frequently interchanged with **treaty**, which is the generic term for an agreement between states made by negotiation or diplomacy ⟨the Lateran *Pact* or *Treaty* establishing Vatican City⟩ ⟨a nonaggression *pact*⟩ ⟨a trade *pact*⟩ ⟨a commercial *treaty*⟩ ⟨the president . . . shall have power, by and with the advice and consent of the Senate, to make *treaties*—*U. S. Constitution*⟩ *Treaty*, and never *pact*, however, is the term for an agreement establishing peace after a period of armed hostility ⟨the *Treaty* of Versailles⟩ An **entente** is a cordial or amicable agreement between nations in regard to their foreign affairs, usually involving a promise of joint military action in case of aggression against an adherent to the entente ⟨the Triple *Entente* between France, Great Britain, and Russia⟩ An *entente* may be in writing set forth in a published document or it may be based simply on an exchange of promises between heads of government, or may be merely a state of mind of the peoples concerned ⟨it changes the *entente* into an alliance, and alliances . . . are not in accordance with our traditions—*Grey*⟩ The word is also used of an understanding between groups (as of economic competitors) ⟨a broader "peace treaty" between leaders of industry, labor, and agriculture governing both price and wage adjustments. This kind of *entente* would seem to be central to the management of an economy such as ours—*L. G. Reynolds*⟩ A **convention** is usually an agreement which is either less formal or more specific than a treaty; it may be an agreement between several states regulating matters affecting all of them (as postage, copyright, or the conduct of war) or an agreement between commanders of armies in respect to military operations ⟨the *conventions* for suspending hostilities agreed upon by me with Marshals Soult and Suchet—*Wellington*⟩ A **cartel** (see also MONOPOLY) is a written agreement or convention between opposing nations, usually for the regulation of intercourse between them in view of or during war. *Cartels* provide for such matters as the treatment and exchange of prisoners, postal and telegraphic communication, the mode of reception of bearers of flags of truce, and the treatment of the wounded. **Concordat** usually applies to

---

A colon (:) separates groups of words discriminated. An asterisk (*) indicates place of treatment of each group.

an agreement between the pope and a secular government for regulating the relations between church and state ⟨the *Concordat* of Worms was an agreement with Germany (1122) regulating investiture of bishops and abbots⟩ Less often the term is used for an agreement regulating ecclesiastical matters ⟨the prospect of a union of the Protestant Episcopal church and the Presbyterian Church . . . which a *concordat* proposed a year ago—*Springfield Republican*⟩

**contract** *vb* **1** pledge, covenant, engage, *promise, plight
**2** catch, *incur
*Con* *escape, avoid, evade, elude, shun, eschew: avert, ward, *prevent
**3 Contract, shrink, condense, compress, constrict, deflate** denote to decrease in bulk, volume, or content, but they vary widely in their suggestion as to how this decrease is effected and what consequences it has. **Contract** means to draw together the sides or the particles of, especially by a force from within, with a consequent reduction in compass or a compacting of the mass ⟨the heart, by *contracting* and dilating rhythmically, keeps up the circulation of the blood⟩ ⟨molten iron *contracts* as it cools⟩ **Shrink** means to contract so as to fall short of an original length, bulk, or volume ⟨*shrink* cloth⟩ ⟨his assets have *shrunk*⟩ ⟨apples often *shrink* before rotting⟩ **Condense** denotes reduction, usually of something more or less homogeneous, to greater compactness without material loss of content ⟨*condense* a gas to a liquid⟩ ⟨*condense* a speech into a few paragraphs⟩ **Compress,** which also means to reduce to a compact state, differs from *condense* in that it connotes a pressing or squeezing of something formless or diffused into definite shape or into a small compass ⟨*compress* air⟩ ⟨*compress* cotton into bales⟩ ⟨*compress* the events of a lifetime into a play taking three hours to present⟩ **Constrict** means to make narrow or smaller in diameter either by contraction or by squeezing ⟨the pores of certain bodies are *constricted* under the influence of cold⟩ ⟨the throat is *constricted* by too tight a collar⟩ **Deflate** means to cause to shrink by exhausting of a gas, air, or something insubstantial ⟨*deflate* a balloon⟩ ⟨*deflate* a wild rumor⟩ ⟨*deflate* an undeserved reputation⟩
*Ana* dwindle, diminish, *decrease, reduce
*Ant* expand —*Con* dilate, swell, distend, inflate (see EXPAND)

**contradict** *deny, gainsay, negative, contravene, traverse, impugn
*Ana* dispute (see DISCUSS): controvert, *disprove, refute, confute: belie, falsify, garble (see MISREPRESENT)
*Ant* corroborate —*Con* *confirm, verify, authenticate, substantiate

**contradictory** *n* contrary, antithesis, opposite, antonym, antipode (see under OPPOSITE *adj*)
*Ana* *converse, reverse

**contradictory** *adj* contrary, antithetical, *opposite, antonymous, antipodal, antipodean
*Ana* negating, nullifying (see NULLIFY): counter, counteractive, antagonistic, *adverse
*Con* agreeing, squaring, tallying, jibing (see AGREE)

**contraption** gadget, *device, contrivance
*Ana* appliance, tool, instrument, *implement, utensil: *machine, mechanism, apparatus: expedient, makeshift (see RESOURCE)

**contrary** *n* antithesis, opposite, contradictory, antonym, antipode (see under OPPOSITE *adj*)
*Ana* *converse, reverse

**contrary** *adj* **1** antithetical, *opposite, contradictory, antonymous, antipodal, antipodean
*Ana* divergent, disparate, *different: counter, antagonis-

tic, *adverse: negating, nullifying (see NULLIFY)
**2 Contrary, perverse, restive, balky, froward, wayward** are comparable when they mean given to opposing or resisting wishes, commands, conditions, or circumstances. A person is **contrary** who by nature or disposition is so self-willed that he cannot or will not accept dictation or advice ⟨she is the most *contrary* child I have ever seen⟩ or who vigorously objects to any arrangements or plans made by others ⟨they've been in your way all these years, and you've always complained of them, so don't be *contrary*, sir—*Cather*⟩ A person or sometimes one of his acts, utterances, or desires is **perverse** when he or it as a result of temperament or disposition, or sometimes of physical constitution or moral character, runs counter to what is right, true, correct, or in keeping with human nature, especially as determined by the moral law, by custom, or by the laws of nature or the state. Like *contrary*, the term may suggest obstinate willfulness, but even then it usually carries a stronger suggestion of wrongheadedness ⟨*perverse* disputings of men of corrupt minds, and destitute of the truth—*1 Tim* 6:5⟩ ⟨they will not be resolute and firm, but *perverse* and obstinate—*Burke*⟩ More often, however, the term suggests defiance of or disobedience to the law, especially the moral law or the established proprieties ⟨Rimbaud was the rebel incarnate . . . he was *perverse*, untractable, adamant—until the very last hour—*Henry Miller*⟩ ⟨the poet's sense of responsibility to nothing but his own inner voice is perhaps his only way of preserving poetic integrity against the influences of a *perverse* generation—*Day Lewis*⟩ **Perverse** sometimes suggests perversion or a sexual maladjustment that reveals itself in aberrant or abnormal desires or acts ⟨the presence of a small minority of abnormal or *perverse* persons . . . affords no excuse for restricting the liberty of the many to the standard of the few—*Ellis*⟩ ⟨the last *perverse* whim which has taken possession of the debauchee—*Krutch*⟩ A person is **restive** (see also IMPATIENT) who obstinately refuses to obey the commands or the will of another; the term may imply inaction or a turning in another direction but more often it suggests intractability or unruliness ⟨the common man . . . is increasingly *restive* under the state of "things as they are"—*Veblen*⟩ ⟨your colonies become suspicious, *restive*, and untractable—*Burke*⟩ A person or, more often, an animal (as a horse) is **balky** when he or it stops short and refuses to go further in the desired direction or in the performance of something undertaken ⟨the horse was never *balky* unless he was overloaded⟩ ⟨a child may become *balky* when he is confused by too many orders⟩ ⟨examination of witnesses, mostly reluctant if not downright *balky*—*The Nation*⟩ A person (often a child) is **froward** who is so contrary or so prone to disobedience that he will not comply with the most reasonable of requests or suggestions; the term usually suggests a characteristic rather than an occasional or a justifiable reaction ⟨all the words of my mouth are in righteousness; there is nothing *froward* or perverse in them—*Prov* 8:8⟩ ⟨I never entered on disobedience without having settled with myself that the fun of it would be worth the pains, scorned repentance, and endured correction with a philosophy which got me the reputation of being a hardened and *froward* child—*Mary Austin*⟩ A person is **wayward** who is so perverse that he is incapable of government by those in authority over him and therefore goes his own way, however wanton, capricious, or depraved it may be ⟨an institution for *wayward* girls⟩ ⟨I have been wild and *wayward*, but you'll forgive me now —*Tennyson*⟩ Things that are erratic or follow no clear law or principle are also describable as *wayward* ⟨*wayward* fancies⟩ ⟨a *wayward* breeze⟩

---

*Ana* analogous words    *Ant* antonyms    *Con* contrasted words    See also explanatory notes facing page 1

*Ana* refractory, recalcitrant, intractable, headstrong, *unruly: contumacious, rebellious, *insubordinate
*Ant* good-natured, complaisant  —*Con* *amiable, obliging: *compliant, acquiescent: amenable, tractable (see OBEDIENT)

**contrast** *n* *comparison, collation, parallel, antithesis
*Ana* distinction, difference, divergence, divergency, *dissimilarity, unlikeness: conflict, *discord

**contrast** *vb* *compare, collate

**contravene** *deny, contradict, traverse, impugn, negative
*Ana* oppose, combat, *resist, fight: controvert, *disprove: *trespass, encroach, infringe
*Ant* uphold (*law, principle*): allege (*right, claim, privilege*)

**contravention** trespass, transgression, violation, infringement, *breach, infraction
*Ana* *offense, vice, sin, crime
*Con* compliance, acquiescence (see under COMPLIANT)

**contribution** *donation, benefaction, alms
*Ana* grant, subvention, subsidy, *appropriation: *gift, present, largess, boon

**contributory** *auxiliary, ancillary, adjuvant, subservient, accessory
*Ana* concurring, cooperating (see UNITE): helping *or* helpful, aiding, assisting *or* assistant (see corresponding verbs at HELP)

**contrition** attrition, repentance, *penitence, compunction, remorse
*Ana* *sorrow, grief, regret

**contrivance** *device, gadget, contraption
*Ana* invention, creation, discovery (see corresponding verbs at INVENT): *implement, tool, instrument, appliance, utensil: *machine, mechanism, apparatus

**contrive, devise, invent, frame, concoct** mean to find a way of making or doing something or of achieving an end by the exercise of one's mind. **Contrive** implies ingenuity or cleverness in planning, designing, or in scheming; it is a matter of indifference whether the end or object is good or bad, since the word stresses the manner of making, doing, or achieving rather than the character of the end ⟨in every deed of mischief he had a heart to resolve, a head to *contrive,* and a hand to execute—*Gibbon*⟩ ⟨if we were perfectly satisfied with the present, we should cease to *contrive,* to labor, and to save with a view to the future—*Macaulay*⟩ ⟨she was forced to hurry. And she had risen that morning with plans perfectly *contrived* for the avoidance of hurry—*Bennett*⟩ ⟨*contrive* a way of helping them without their knowing it⟩ **Devise** often comes very close to *contrive,* but in general it throws more stress upon mental effort than upon ingenuity; the term often implies the serious reflection and experimentation that precedes the bringing of something into being, especially something new or quite different ⟨*devise* new and dainty dishes for a fastidious taste⟩ ⟨*devise* an engine of triple the power⟩ ⟨*devise* a plan of campaign⟩ ⟨*devise* a new method of teaching a subject⟩ ⟨grossly contriving their dear daughter's good—poor souls, and knew not what they did, but sat ignorant, *devising* their own daughter's death—*Tennyson*⟩ ⟨Leonardo was a child even . . . in *devising* fantastic toys and contriving disconcerting tricks—*Ellis*⟩ **Invent,** though often used interchangeably with *devise,* commonly retains from its primitive senses some notion of finding, but the term comes closer in its implication to originating, especially after thought and reflection, but sometimes more quickly, as the result of a happy accident ⟨the telescope was *invented* by Galileo in 1609⟩ ⟨Huxley claims to have *invented* the term *agnostic*⟩ ⟨his pains to *invent* a complete, generally unlovely terminology of his own—*Muller*⟩ ⟨she was tired of *inventing* means for making the days and nights pleasant and capriciously

variable for others—*Van Vechten*⟩ **Frame** (see also BUILD) implies the exact fitting of one thing to another (as in devising or inventing a story, a theory, or a rule); usually the term suggests an exact fitting (as of the words to the thought, or of the plot, character, and actions to the story as a whole, or of the expression to the spirit, or of the means to the end) ⟨it will take me some time to *frame* a proper reply to this letter⟩ ⟨statutes . . . which must needs have been *framed* for some purpose or other—*Kingsley*⟩ ⟨never, it may be safely asserted, was a plan of society *framed* so consistent, harmonious and beautiful in itself—*Dickinson*⟩ **Concoct** especially suggests a bringing together of ingredients in new or unexpected combinations, arrangements, or order so as to enhance their effectiveness (as in writing, in imagining, or in fashioning) ⟨from the scraps of conversation he had overheard he *concocted* a plausible and amusing yarn⟩ ⟨the most horrible monsters and tortures . . . his fervid imagination could *concoct* out of his own bitter experiences and the manners and customs of his cruel times—*Eliot*⟩
*Ana* plan, scheme, project (see under PLAN *n*): manipulate, ply, swing (see HANDLE)

**control** *vb* direct, manage, *conduct
*Ana* *govern, rule: regulate, *adjust: *guide, lead, pilot, engineer, steer: *restrain, curb, check

**control** *n* 1 command, dominion, authority, *power, jurisdiction, sway
*Ana* ascendancy, *supremacy: might, puissance, *power, force: management, direction (see corresponding verbs at CONDUCT)
*Con* mutiny, revolt, *rebellion
2 *corrective, check, antidote
*Ana* regulation, *law, ordinance, rule, precept, statute, canon

**controversy** dispute, *argument
*Ana* contention, dissension (see DISCORD): disputation, *argumentation, forensic, debate

**controvert** *vb* rebut, refute, *disprove, confute
*Ana* contravene, traverse, impugn, *deny, gainsay: oppose, combat, fight (see RESIST): dispute, debate, agitate, argue, *discuss
*Ant* assert  —*Con* defend, justify, *maintain, vindicate

**contumacious** rebellious, *insubordinate, mutinous, seditious, factious
*Ana* *contrary, perverse, froward: refractory, recalcitrant, intractable, ungovernable, *unruly, headstrong
*Ant* obedient  —*Con* *compliant, acquiescent, resigned: amenable, tractable, docile (see OBEDIENT)

**contumelious** *abusive, opprobrious, vituperative, scurrilous
*Ana* insolent, overbearing, arrogant, disdainful (see PROUD): humiliating, demeaning, debasing, abasing (see ABASE): flouting, scoffing, jeering, sneering (see SCOFF)
*Ant* obsequious  —*Con* complimenting *or* complimentary, commending *or* commendatory, applauding (see corresponding verbs at COMMEND)

**contusion** bruise, *wound, trauma, traumatism, lesion

**conundrum** puzzle, riddle, enigma, problem, *mystery

**convalesce** *improve, recover, recuperate, gain
*Ana* progress, *advance: *strengthen, invigorate: *cure, heal, remedy

**convenance** convention, usage, *form

**convene** convoke, muster, *summon, summons, call, cite
*Ana* *gather, congregate, assemble, collect
*Ant* adjourn  —*Con* disperse, *scatter: dismiss, *eject

**convent** *cloister, nunnery, monastery, abbey, priory

**convention** 1 entente, compact, pact, treaty, cartel, concordat, *contract, bargain

---

A colon (:) separates groups of words discriminated. An asterisk (*) indicates place of treatment of each group.

*Ana* *agreement, accord, understanding
2 *form, convenance, usage
*Ana* custom, practice (see HABIT): canon, precept, rule, *law: etiquette, propriety, *decorum
**conventional** formal, ceremonious, *ceremonial, solemn
*Ana* *decorous, proper, seemly, decent: *correct, right, precise
*Ant* unconventional —*Con* *negligent, slack, lax, remiss: *natural, simple, unsophisticated, ingenuous, naïve, artless
**conversant, versed** are comparable when they mean being familiar with something; they are seldom found in attributive use. **Conversant** (usually followed by *with*) implies a familiarity with a subject or a field of knowledge or with the writings on that subject or in that field that comes from long association, long experience, frequent intercourse, or many dealings with them ⟨like Walpole . . . he was thoroughly *conversant* with questions of finance—*Lecky*⟩ ⟨*The Pilgrim's Progress* is known not only to everyone who is *conversant* with the other writings of the period, but to thousands, the world around, who never heard of . . . [Bacon's] *Essays—Lowes*⟩ ⟨British officers . . . must be *conversant* with the ways of a dozen or more castes—*Rand*⟩ **Versed** (followed by *in*) may be used interchangeably with *conversant* or it may be used distinctively to convey not only an implication of familiarity with something, but of skill, adeptness, or proficiency (as in an art or a profession); thus, a person *versed* in law need not be *conversant* with the laws of all European countries; a specialist in forensic medicine though *versed* in medicine may not be *conversant* with all the new methods of treating pneumonia. Because of this added implication, *versed* is often used in combination ⟨well-*versed*⟩ ⟨ill-*versed*⟩ ⟨poorly *versed*⟩ ⟨I don't think him deeply *versed* in life—*Byron*⟩ ⟨political minutemen excited by the issues of the day, informed on these issues and at the same time fully *versed* in the problems of the community—*Humphrey*⟩ ⟨*versed* in all the arts of procrastination, indolence, and evasion—*A. R. Williams*⟩
*Ana* intimate, *familiar: informed, acquainted (see INFORM): *learned, erudite: adept, *proficient, skilled, expert, skillful, masterly
*Ant* ignorant
**conversation, converse** communion, communication, *intercourse, commerce, traffic, dealings, correspondence
*Ana* conversing, talking *or* talk, speaking *or* speech (see corresponding verbs at SPEAK)
**converse** *vb* talk, *speak
*Ana* *express, voice, broach, air, ventilate, vent, utter: *chat, chatter, gabble: *gossip, tattle: *discourse, descant, expatiate, dilate
**converse** *n* see CONVERSATION
**converse** *n* **Converse, obverse, reverse** are frequently confused when they mean something which is the opposite of another thing. **Converse** applies chiefly to statements or to propositions; typically it implies an interchange or transposition of the important terms ⟨the relation of wife to husband is called the *converse* of the relation of husband to wife—*Russell*⟩ ⟨the *converse* of "none but the brave deserves the fair" is "none but the fair deserves the brave"⟩ *Converse* is not to be confused with *contradictory* (see under OPPOSITE *adj*); so long as the important terms are transposed, one proposition is the *converse* of another whether or not it is its opposite ⟨the feeling that society needs protection against the individual rather than the *converse*—*Brownell*⟩ **Obverse** and **reverse** specifically apply to the two faces of a coin or medal, *obverse* applying to the one containing the head or principal inscription, *reverse* to the other; in more general use, *obverse* refers

to the more, *reverse* to the less, apparent or intentionally conspicuous side or face of something ⟨looking at the fair tapestry of Life, with its royal and even sacred figures, he dwells not on the *obverse* alone, but here chiefly on the *reverse;* and indeed turns out the rough seams, tatters, and manifold thrums of that unsightly wrong side—*Carlyle*⟩
*Ana* opposite, contrary, antithesis, contradictory (see under OPPOSITE *adj*)
**conversion** transformation, metamorphosis, transmutation, transmogrification, transfiguration (see under TRANSFORM)
**convert** *vb* *transform, metamorphose, transmute, transmogrify, transfigure
*Ana* manufacture, fabricate, forge, *make: apply, utilize, employ, *use
**convert** *n* **Convert, proselyte** are synonyms only in being applicable to the same person. Both denote a person who has embraced another creed, opinion, or doctrine than the one he has previously accepted or adhered to. **Convert** commonly implies a sincere and voluntary change of belief; it is, therefore, the designation preferred by the church, the party, or the school of thought of which such a person becomes a new member ⟨the first American novelist to become a . . . *convert* to naturalism—*Malcolm Cowley*⟩ *Convert* is also applied to a person who undergoes the religious experience called *conversion* or a turning from a life of sin or indifference to one guided by religious (specifically, Christian) principles and motives. **Proselyte** basically denotes a convert to another religion. It is still used in reference to a convert to Judaism who manifests his sincerity and fidelity by strict adherence to religious laws and practices. In general use, however, the term may suggest less a reverent or convicted and voluntary embracing than a yielding to the persuasions and urgings of another, be it an earnest missionary or zealot or someone with less praiseworthy motives ⟨ye compass sea and land to make one *proselyte—Mt* 23:15⟩ *Proselyte* is often the designation chosen by the members of a church for one formerly of their number who has been converted to another faith. The term is also applied to a person won over to a party, a cause, or a way of life in which he has formerly expressed disbelief or disinterest ⟨you agree with the rest of the married world in a propensity to make *proselytes—Shenstone*⟩
*Ana* neophyte, *novice
*Con* apostate, *renegade, backslider, recreant, turncoat
**convertible** *reciprocal, corresponding, correlative, complementary, complemental
*Ana* interchangeable, exchangeable (see corresponding verbs at EXCHANGE)
**convey** 1 transport, *carry, transmit, bear
*Ana* *move, remove, shift, transfer: take, fetch, *bring
2 *transfer, deed, alienate
*Ana* consign, *commit, relegate
**convict** *n* *criminal, felon, malefactor, culprit, delinquent
*Ana* miscreant, blackguard, scoundrel, *villain: offender, sinner (see corresponding nouns at OFFENSE)
**conviction** 1 assurance, certitude, *certainty
*Ana* faith, *belief, credence, credit
*Con* doubt, *uncertainty, dubiety, dubiosity, skepticism: disbelief, *unbelief, incredulity
2 belief, persuasion, *opinion, view, sentiment
*Ana* tenet, dogma, *doctrine: judgment, conclusion (see under INFER)
**convincing** compelling, telling, cogent, *valid, sound
*Ana* proving, demonstrating (see PROVE): persuading *or* persuasive, inducing (see corresponding verbs at INDUCE): forceful, forcible, potent, *powerful
**convivial** companionable, *social, gregarious, hospitable, cooperative

---

*Ana* analogous words      *Ant* antonyms      *Con* contrasted words      See also explanatory notes facing page 1

*Ana* sociable, genial, cordial, affable, \*gracious: gay, \*lively, vivacious: \*merry, jocund, jolly, jovial: hilarious, mirthful (see corresponding nouns at MIRTH)
*Ant* taciturn: staid  —*Con* reserved, reticent, \*silent: \*serious, sober, grave, sedate, solemn, somber: asocial, \*unsocial

**convoke** convene, muster, \*summon, summons, call, cite
*Ana* assemble, \*gather, congregate, collect: \*invite, bid
*Ant* prorogue, dissolve  —*Con* disperse, \*scatter

**convoy** *vb* escort, conduct, \*accompany, attend, chaperon
*Ana* protect, shield, guard, safeguard, \*defend: \*guide, lead, pilot

**convulse** rock, \*shake, agitate
*Ana* \*discompose, disturb, disquiet, perturb

**convulsion** 1 spasm, paroxysm, \*fit, attack, access, accession
2 \*commotion, agitation, tumult, turmoil, turbulence, confusion, upheaval
*Ana* shaking, rocking (see SHAKE): quaking, trembling, tottering (see SHAKE): revolution, revolt, \*rebellion: cataclysm, \*disaster

**convulsive** spasmodic, \*fitful
*Con* \*steady, uniform, even, equable, constant

**cool** 1 chilly, \*cold, frigid, freezing, frosty, gelid, icy, glacial, arctic
*Ant* warm
2 **Cool, composed, collected, unruffled, imperturbable, unflappable, nonchalant** are comparable when applied to persons, their manners, appearance, temper, or acts, in the sense of showing or seeming to show freedom from agitation or excitement. **Cool** (see also COLD) basically implies such self-control that no hint is given of any emotion or motive that might warm, inflame, excite, or impassion. Specifically, it may further imply detachment or dispassionateness ⟨modest youth, with *cool* reflection crowned—*Pope*⟩ ⟨my work, I am often told, is *cool* and serene, entirely reasonable and free of passion—*Ellis*⟩ or calm courage in assault or under attack ⟨soldiers *cool* under fire⟩ or deliberateness or determination in gaining one's ends ⟨the coquette [Queen Elizabeth I] of the presence chamber became the *coolest* and hardest of politicians at the council board—*J. R. Green*⟩ or cold assurance or effrontery ⟨the sudden change in her voice, from *cool* imperial arrogance to terrified pleading—*Graves*⟩ or actual or seeming indifference ⟨a *cool* lover⟩ **Composed** implies the freedom from signs of agitation or excitement that is characteristic of a decorous sedate temperament or is the result of self-discipline ⟨in her *composed,* schooled manner she despised and disliked both father and daughter exceedingly—*Conrad*⟩ ⟨she was *composed* without bravado, contrite without sanctimoniousness—*Repplier*⟩ ⟨she was pale, and looked as if she hadn't slept, but *composed,* as she always is—*Rose Macaulay*⟩ **Collected** stresses a concentration of the mind or spirit with resulting elimination of all distractions; otherwise it differs little from *composed* ⟨be *collected:* no more amazement—*Shak.*⟩ ⟨Mrs. Hawthorne wore her *collected* Sunday expression, and Tony knew that she did not allow them to talk of mundane affairs on these expeditions to and from church—*Archibald Marshall*⟩ ⟨the Queen . . . remained, as she herself said, "very much *collected;* civil and high, and betrayed no agitation"—*Sitwell*⟩ **Unruffled** implies coolness, placidity, and often, poise, in the midst of excitement or when there is cause for agitation ⟨while others fretted and fumed, he remained *unruffled*⟩ ⟨her mind was *unruffled* by the spiritual problems which were vexing the minds around her—*J. R. Green*⟩ ⟨an efficient organizer, smooth and *unruffled* —*Flora Lewis*⟩ **Imperturbable** implies such coolness

and assurance that one cannot be abashed, annoyed, disconcerted, alarmed, or otherwise disturbed; it usually implies a temperamental rather than an acquired frame of mind ⟨Franklin's *imperturbable* common sense—*Arnold*⟩ ⟨a very good-looking, rosy little man with . . . a soft voice and a manner of *imperturbable* urbanity—*H. G. Wells*⟩ **Unflappable** is a somewhat informal synonym of *imperturbable,* and like the latter stresses ability to resist what tends to disturb ⟨from his encounters with lions and hippos . . . Mr. Hillaby emerges *unflappable* and subtly triumphant —*Times Lit. Sup.*⟩ ⟨un *unflappable* debater, he never let a Soviet accusation go unanswered—*Newsweek*⟩ ⟨an *unflappable* management of affairs that might otherwise become bothersome—*Wicker*⟩ **Nonchalant** stresses an easy coolness of manner or casualness that suggests indifference or unconcern; it often connotes lightheartedness or offhandedness ⟨God . . . knows, if he is not as indifferent to mortals as the *nonchalant* deities of Lucretius—*Byron*⟩ ⟨at the back [of the ambulance], haughty in white uniform, *nonchalant* on a narrow seat, was The Doctor —*Sinclair Lewis*⟩ ⟨he walked in a *nonchalant* fashion— *D. H. Lawrence*⟩
*Ana* \*calm, tranquil, serene, placid: detached, aloof, \*indifferent: \*impassive, stoic, phlegmatic
*Ant* ardent: agitated  —*Con* fervid, fervent, passionate, perfervid, \*impassioned: perturbed, discomposed, disturbed, upset, flustered, flurried (see DISCOMPOSE)

**coop** *vb* \*enclose, envelop, fence, pen, corral, cage, wall
*Ana* confine, circumscribe, \*limit, restrict: \*hinder, impede, obstruct, block, bar

**cooperate** conjoin, \*unite, combine
*Ana* coincide, \*agree, concur
*Ant* counteract  —*Con* \*neutralize, negative: \*nullify, negate, annul

**cooperative** \*social, companionable, gregarious, convivial, hospitable
*Ana* sociable, cordial, genial, affable, \*gracious: helping *or* helpful, aiding, assisting (see corresponding verbs at HELP)
*Ant* uncooperative  —*Con* \*unsocial, asocial

**cop** *vb* \*steal, filch, pinch, snitch, swipe, lift, pilfer, purloin

**copartner** \*partner, colleague, ally, confederate
*Ana* \*associate, companion, comrade

**copious** \*plentiful, abundant, ample, plenteous
*Ana* \*profuse, lavish, exuberant, prodigal, luxuriant, lush
*Ant* meager  —*Con* scanty, scant, scrimpy, sparse, exiguous, spare (see MEAGER): \*thin, slight, tenuous, slim, slender

**copy** *n* \*reproduction, duplicate, carbon, carbon copy, transcript, facsimile, replica
*Ana* counterpart, \*parallel: imprint, print, \*impression, impress: \*image, effigy
*Ant* original

**copy** *vb* **Copy, imitate, mimic, ape, mock** mean to make something like an already existing thing in form, appearance, or obvious or salient characteristics. **Copy** implies duplication of an original and thereby as close a resemblance as is possible under the circumstances ⟨*copy* a letter⟩ ⟨*copy* Da Vinci's "Mona Lisa"⟩ ⟨*copy* the clothes of a fashionable designer⟩ ⟨later examples of the Greek revival travestied the classic style rather than *copied* it —*Amer. Guide Series: Mass.*⟩ **Imitate** stresses following something as a pattern or model; it does not therefore preclude variations from the original; thus, a writer who *imitates* Keats may merely reecho enough of that poet's rhythms, images, or sentiments to produce poetry reminiscent of Keats. *Imitate* may imply emulation ⟨she slept for hours in the daytime, *imitating* the cats—*Stafford*⟩ ⟨*imitated* the example of his elders⟩ or it may imply

representation in another medium ⟨art *imitates* nature⟩ ⟨the dramatist *imitates* life⟩ ⟨the music *imitates* a storm⟩ or it may imply simulation ⟨fabrics that *imitate* leather⟩ ⟨their pots seemed to *imitate* leather vessels—*Childe*⟩ **Mimic** usually implies an exact copying, especially of a person's movements, gestures, voice, mannerisms, sometimes for the sake of making sport of them, but often with the intention of giving a lifelike representation of them ⟨I am sure I repeat her words, though I cannot *mimic* either the voice or air with which they were spoken— *Fielding*⟩ The word sometimes suggests a counterfeiting clever enough to seem real; it therefore often implies the skill of an actor ⟨I might *mimic* a passion that I do not feel, but I cannot *mimic* one that burns me like fire— *Wilde*⟩ ⟨he learned to call wild turkeys with a piece of bone through which he was able to *mimic* the notes of the bird—*Brooks*⟩ **Ape** also implies close copying sometimes seriously, sometimes in the spirit of mimicry ⟨in dress and habits, *ape* the Arabs around them—*G. W. Murray*⟩ Often it suggests an attempt to emulate what one admires and then may connote such failure of the attempt as is likely to subject one to contempt ⟨clods *aping* their betters⟩ ⟨the lower classes *aped* the rigid decorum of their "betters" with laughable results—*Harrison Smith*⟩ **Mock** commonly adds to *mimic* the implication of a derisive intent. It often distinctively suggests immediate repetition of the words or actions mimicked ⟨*mocked* his teacher⟩ ⟨the babbling echo *mocks* the hounds—*Shak.*⟩ ⟨her shadow still glowered about . . . as though . . . to *mock* behind her back—*Keats*⟩ ⟨she contended every point, objected to every request, shirked her work, fought with her sisters, *mocked* her mother—*Mead*⟩
*Ant* originate

**coquet** *vb* flirt, *trifle, dally, toy

**cordial** genial, affable, *gracious, sociable
*Ana* warm, warmhearted, responsive, sympathetic, *tender: *sincere, heartfelt, hearty, wholehearted
*Con* cool, *cold, frosty, frigid: *indifferent, aloof, detached, disinterested: reserved, taciturn, *silent

**core** *n* 1 *center, middle, midst, hub, focus, nucleus, heart
2 *substance, purport, gist, burden, pith
*Ana* import, significance, *importance, consequence: *center, heart, nucleus

**corner** pool, *monopoly, syndicate, trust, cartel

**corporal** *adj* corporeal, *bodily, physical, somatic
*Ana* fleshly, *carnal, animal, sensual

**corporeal** 1 *material, physical, sensible, phenomenal, objective
*Ana* actual, *real: tangible, palpable, ponderable, *perceptible
*Ant* incorporeal  —*Con* intangible, impalpable, *imperceptible, insensible, imponderable
2 *bodily, physical, corporal, somatic
*Ana* see those at CORPORAL

**corpse** carcass, cadaver, *body
*Ana* remains (see REMAINDER)

**corpulent** *fleshy, portly, fat, stout, obese, rotund, plump, chubby
*Ana* burly, husky, brawny, *muscular: thickset, chunky, stubby, dumpy (see STOCKY)
*Ant* spare  —*Con* *lean, gaunt, rawboned, angular, lanky, lank, skinny, scrawny: slender, slim, slight, *thin

**corpuscle** *particle, atom, molecule

**corral** *vb* *enclose, envelop, fence, pen, coop, cage, wall

**correct** *vb* 1 Correct, rectify, emend, remedy, redress, amend, reform, revise mean to set or make right something which is wrong. One **corrects** something which is inaccurate, untrue, or imperfect or which contains errors, faults, or defects, when one by substitutions brings it into con-

formity with a standard or rule of accuracy, truth, or perfection ⟨*corrected* his mistakes in pronunciation⟩ ⟨*correct* printers' proofs⟩ ⟨appellate jurisdiction . . . revises and *corrects* the proceedings in a cause already instituted— *John Marshall*⟩ Also, one *corrects* a person when one points out his errors or faults for disciplinary purposes (see also PUNISH) ⟨she's been with me such a long time . . . . She takes liberties. I've *corrected* her once or twice— *Bennett*⟩ One thing *corrects* another thing when the former serves to counteract or neutralize the bad effect of the latter ⟨alkaline tablets to *correct* stomach acidity⟩ ⟨his head *corrects* his heart in the choice of friends⟩ One **rectifies** something which requires straightening out or ordering because it deviates from the rule or standard of what is right, just, equitable, or properly controlled or directed ⟨*rectify* a mistake in an account⟩ ⟨*rectify* an error of judgment⟩ ⟨reason is here no guide, but still a guard: 'tis hers to *rectify*, not overthrow, and treat this passion more as friend than foe—*Pope*⟩ ⟨an incredible, disgraceful blunder, which should be *rectified* at the earliest possible moment—*New Republic*⟩ One **emends** a thing when one frees it from error or defects; specifically an editor *emends* a corrupt text when he replaces doubtful readings with others that are judged to be closer to the original or to the intention of the author ⟨the eighteenth-century editors of Shakespeare freely *emended* the texts of his plays⟩ One **remedies** something which is a source of evil or harm when one makes such corrections as will either bring about its eradication or restore what is harmed to a normal, sound, or prosperous condition ⟨the crime can never be *remedied*, it can only be expiated—*Day Lewis*⟩ ⟨*remedy* an abuse of a privilege⟩ ⟨*remedy* the maldistribution of relief⟩ ⟨*remedy* a social evil⟩ One **redresses** something which involves unfairness, injustice, or lack of proper balance; the word usually suggests reparation or compensation ⟨there is no calamity which right words will not begin to *redress*—*Emerson*⟩ ⟨the wrongs that were to be righted, the grievances to be *redressed*, the abuses to be done away with—*Muggeridge*⟩ One **amends** something when one makes such corrections or changes in it that it is bettered or raised to a higher standard ⟨*amend* his life⟩ ⟨the work once done he could not or would not *amend* it—*Yeats*⟩ ⟨laws that are not repealed are *amended* and amended—*Shaw*⟩ One **reforms** something when one makes drastic changes in it in an attempt to eliminate imperfections; the word usually implies a new form or character ⟨*reform* the church⟩ ⟨the fact is that the world does not care to be *reformed*. . . . This makes the way of the improver hard—*Crothers*⟩ One **revises** something when one looks it over to discover where it requires correction or amendment and makes the necessary changes ⟨*revise* a book before its second printing⟩ ⟨*revise* a state constitution⟩ ⟨there can be no doubt as to the jurisdiction of this court to *revise* the judgment of a Circuit Court—*Taney*⟩
*Ana* *improve, better, ameliorate: offset, *compensate, countervail, counterbalance, balance: *neutralize, counteract: *adjust, regulate, fix: *reprove, reprimand, admonish, chide
*Con* impair, spoil, mar, *injure, damage, harm, hurt: aggravate, *intensify
2 discipline, *punish, chastise, chasten, castigate
*Con* *indulge, pamper, spoil, humor, baby: condone, *excuse

**correct** *adj* Correct, accurate, exact, precise, nice, right are comparable when meaning conforming to standard, fact, or truth. **Correct,** the most colorless term, implies scarcely more than freedom from fault or error, as judged by some (usually) conventional or acknowledged standard

⟨socially *correct* dress⟩ ⟨*correct* school deportment⟩ ⟨a supposed center of *correct* information, *correct* judgment, *correct* taste—*Arnold*⟩ ⟨it is our custom at Shangri-La to be moderately truthful, and I can assure you that my statements about the porters were almost *correct*—*Hilton*⟩ **Accurate** implies more positively fidelity to fact or truth attained by the exercise of care ⟨an *accurate* statement⟩ ⟨an *accurate* observer⟩ ⟨a reasonably *accurate* and refined use of the mother tongue —*Eliot*⟩ **Exact** emphasizes the strictness or rigor of the agreement, which neither exceeds nor falls short of the fact, a standard, or the truth ⟨an *exact* likeness⟩ ⟨the *exact* value⟩ ⟨his *exact* words⟩ ⟨the acquisition of *exact* knowledge . . . is essential to every kind of excellence— *Russell*⟩ **Precise** stresses sharpness of definition or delimitation, or scrupulous exactness ⟨*precise* statements of principles—*Benson*⟩ ⟨she did not . . . understand . . . the *precise* nature of what she was doing—*Conrad*⟩ **Nice** implies great, occasionally excessive, precision and delicacy (as in discrimination, adjustment, or statement) ⟨a *nice* calculation⟩ ⟨an over*nice* distinction⟩ ⟨overbalance the *nice* adjustment on either side of the scale, and loss is the inevitable result—*Lowes*⟩ ⟨it was a time of revolution, when *nice* legal distinctions are meaningless —*Buchan*⟩ **Right** (see also GOOD) stresses an absence of deviation from and, therefore, a strict accordance with the facts, the truth, or a standard. Often it is so close in meaning to *correct* that it is only in collocations where the latter's stress on freedom from error or fault is set up against *right's* emphasis on strict accordance with the facts, truth, or a standard that one can determine which word is preferable; thus, an answer to a problem in arithmetic may be said to be either *correct* or *right;* a gentleman of faultless manners and dress is said to be *correct* (not *right*); one seeking a friend in conformance with some socially or personally acceptable standard watches for the *right* (not *correct*) person ⟨though he gave an assumed name the police know his *right* name⟩ ⟨the *right* man for the job—*Redman*⟩
*Ana* *impeccable, faultless, flawless: punctilious, punctual, scrupulous, meticulous, *careful
*Ant* incorrect —*Con* *false, wrong: fallacious, casuistical (see under FALLACY)

**corrective** *adj* remedial, restorative, sanative, *curative
*Ana* helping, aiding, assisting (see HELP *vb*): salutary, hygienic, *healthful

**corrective** *n* Corrective, control, check, antidote are comparable in their extended senses where they denote something which serves to keep another thing in its desired place or condition. **Corrective** is applied to an agency or influence which keeps true a thing that is subject to aberration or deviation, or which rectifies or remedies a departure in it from truth, balance, soundness, or health ⟨the sight of the product [of our work] put to its full uses. . . is the best *corrective* to our blunders—*Suzzallo*⟩ ⟨a salutary *corrective* to the sometimes facile optimism and mass-hypnotized rhetoric of the revolutionary poets—*Day Lewis*⟩ **Control** is applied to a predetermined device, rule, agency, or procedure which sets a guard upon a person or thing so as to prevent his or its overpassing prescribed limits or so as to enable him or it to be discovered if in error ⟨the Constitution of the United States sets up various *controls* for the three branches of government, such as the veto power of the president⟩ ⟨a scientific investigator sets up a *control* for an experiment when he provides a means (usually a similar experiment identical in all but one factor) for testing the accuracy of his findings⟩ ⟨the only government *controls* authorized by law are marketing quotas—*New Republic*⟩ **Check** is applied

to something which affords a means of securing or insuring accuracy, uniformity in quality, or the maintenance of a standard ⟨duplicate records are kept by different clerks as a *check* upon each other⟩ ⟨by means of statewide examinations of pupils, the regents keep a *check* on the efficiency of the schools⟩ ⟨any arbitrary formula too rigidly adhered to may endanger good writing, but a good set of principles used as a *check* and an aid may be very helpful—*Mott*⟩ **Antidote,** basically a remedy that counteracts a poison, implies that harm has been done and that a corrective which will neutralize or nullify these effects is necessary ⟨there is no *antidote* against the opium of time—*Browne*⟩ ⟨the whole truth is the best *antidote* to falsehoods which are dangerous chiefly because they are half-truths—*Coleridge*⟩

**correlate** *n* *parallel, analogue, counterpart
**correlative** *adj* corresponding, complementary, complemental, *reciprocal, convertible
**correspond** *agree, square, accord, tally, jibe, harmonize, conform
*Ana* approach, touch, *match, rival, equal
**correspondence** *intercourse, communication, conversation, converse, communion, commerce, traffic, dealings
**corresponding** *adj* correlative, complementary, complemental, *reciprocal, convertible
*Ana* similar, analogous, *like, parallel, comparable
**corridor** passageway, *passage, hall, hallway, gallery, arcade, cloister, aisle, ambulatory
**corroborate** *confirm, substantiate, verify, authenticate, validate
*Ana* attest, vouch, *certify: *support, uphold, back
*Ant* contradict —*Con* invalidate, negate, *nullify
**corrupt** *vb* deprave, debauch, pervert, *debase
*Ana* degrade, debase, *abase: *ruin, wreck: pollute, defile, *contaminate
*Con* reform, amend, *correct
**corrupt** *adj* 1 also **corrupted** debased, vitiated, depraved, perverted (see under DEBASE)
*Ana* *abandoned, dissolute, profligate, reprobate
*Con* *upright, honorable, honest, just, conscientious, scrupulous: virtuous, righteous, *moral, ethical, noble
2 iniquitous, nefarious, flagitious, infamous, *vicious, villainous, degenerate
*Ana* *crooked, devious, oblique: venal, *mercenary: *base, low, vile: *pernicious, noxious, deleterious, detrimental, baneful: degraded, abased (see ABASE)
**corsair** *pirate, freebooter, buccaneer, privateer
**cortege** *procession, cavalcade, parade, motorcade
*Ana* train, string, *succession: followers, satellites, disciples, partisans, henchmen (see singular nouns at FOLLOWER)
**coruscate** *flash, gleam, scintillate, glance, glint, sparkle, glitter, glisten, twinkle
**cosmic** *universal, catholic, ecumenical, cosmopolitan
*Con* *earthly, terrestrial, mundane, worldly
**cosmopolitan** *adj* catholic, *universal, ecumenical, cosmic
*Ana* *liberal, progressive: all-around, many-sided, *versatile
*Ant* provincial: insular: parochial
**cosmos** universe, macrocosm, *earth, world
**cosset** *caress, fondle, pet, cuddle, dandle
**cost** *n* expense, *price, charge
**costly** *adj* Costly, expensive, dear, valuable, precious, invaluable, priceless mean having a high value or valuation, especially in terms of money. *Costly, expensive, dear* refer to the expenditure or sacrifice involved in obtaining or procuring a thing. **Costly** applies to something which actually costs much; it usually implies such justi-

A colon (:) separates groups of words discriminated. An asterisk (*) indicates place of treatment of each group.

fication as sumptuousness, rarity, or fine workmanship ⟨their hòme is filled with *costly* furniture⟩ ⟨I took a *costly* jewel from my neck. A heart it was, bound in with diamonds—*Shak.*⟩ ⟨they are clad in very *costly* robes of silk; they are girdled like queens—*Hearn*⟩ **Expensive** applies chiefly to something which is high-priced, especially with the implication of a cost beyond the thing's value or the buyer's means ⟨an *expensive* suit of clothes⟩ ⟨the father . . . was unable to give the child as *expensive* an education as he had desired—*Froude*⟩ Both *costly* and *expensive* may also be applied to whatever involves great losses or is a drain upon one's resources, not only in money but in such matters as time, effort, or health ⟨an *expensive* error⟩ ⟨*costly* litigation⟩ ⟨expeditions which might prove *costly* in lives as well as money— *Stefansson*⟩ ⟨the rat is *expensive* to get rid of, but even more *expensive* to maintain—*Heiser*⟩ **Dear** is opposed to *cheap* and commonly suggests a high, often an exorbitant, price or excessive cost; usually it implies a relation to other factors than the intrinsic worth of a thing ⟨butter is cheap when it is plentiful, and *dear* when it is scarce— *Shaw*⟩ ⟨relatively high wages of building labor bring *dearer* housing—*Hobson*⟩ ⟨their stout resistance was destined to cost them *dear*. . . . Many thousand citizens were ruined—*Motley*⟩ **Valuable** when applied to things which have monetary value usually suggests the price they will bring in a sale or exchange ⟨the most *valuable* dog in the kennel⟩ ⟨he stores away all his *valuable* effects when he goes on a tour⟩ ⟨a *valuable* piece of property⟩ *Valuable*, however, often suggests worth that is not measured in material goods, but in such qualities as usefulness, serviceableness, or advantageousness ⟨a *valuable* citizen⟩ ⟨the most *valuable* course in a college career⟩ ⟨a *valuable* piece of evidence⟩ ⟨food is *valuable* to the animal and moisture to the plant—*Alexander*⟩ ⟨beauty which is humanly *valuable* but biologically useless— *Krutch*⟩ **Precious** originally came closer in meaning to *costly* than to *valuable*, of which it is now a very close synonym. But it carries a heightened implication of worth and often applies to something or someone whose value can scarcely be computed in terms of money ⟨*precious* friends hid in death's dateless night—*Shak.*⟩ ⟨happy is the man who findeth wisdom . . . she is more *precious* than rubies—*Prov 3:13-15*⟩ ⟨to any one who has ever looked on the face of a dead child or parent the mere fact that matter could have taken for a time that *precious* form, ought to make matter sacred ever after—*James*⟩ ⟨and these two things, judgment and imagination, are, with knowledge itself, the most *precious* results of well directed schooling—*Grandgent*⟩ When applied to a thing of monetary value, *precious* usually means that it is one of the rarest and most costly of the class that is named ⟨*precious* stones⟩ ⟨an alabaster box of very *precious* ointment— *Mt 26:7*⟩ but it may mean that the thing so described is too scarce and therefore, often, too expensive to use freely or generally ⟨be careful of the butter; it's too *precious* to waste⟩ **Invaluable** and **priceless** imply worth that cannot be estimated. In practice they are sometimes used when *precious* is actually meant but would seem not quite in keeping for one reason or another ⟨an *invaluable* servant⟩ ⟨this *invaluable* liquor was of a pale golden hue, like other of the rarest Italian wines—*Hawthorne*⟩ ⟨a *priceless* jewel⟩ ⟨the colleges of this country have been a *priceless* element in the making of the freedom and might of this nation—*L. M. Chamberlain*⟩ Therefore their use tends to be hyperbolical and often, especially in the case of *priceless*, intensive ⟨I've just heard a *priceless* story⟩ ⟨isn't that dress *priceless?*⟩
*Ana* exorbitant, extravagant, *excessive: sumptuous,

*luxurious, opulent
*Ant* cheap —*Con* beggarly, sorry, scurvy, *contemptible: poor, *bad
**coterie** circle, *set, clique
**couchant** recumbent, dormant, supine, *prone, prostrate
**counsel** *n* **1** *advice
*Ana* admonishing *or* admonition, chiding, reproaching *or* reproach (see corresponding verbs at REPROVE): warning, forewarning, cautioning *or* caution (see corresponding verbs at WARN): precept, rule (see LAW)
**2** *lawyer, counselor, barrister, *advocate, attorney, solicitor
**counsel** *vb* advise (see under ADVICE)
*Ana* admonish, chide (see REPROVE): *warn, forewarn, caution: remonstrate, expostulate (see OBJECT *vb*): instruct, direct (see COMMAND *vb*)
**counselor** *lawyer, barrister, counsel, advocate, attorney, solicitor
**count** *vb* **1** Count, tell, enumerate, number are comparable when they mean to ascertain the total of units in a collection by noting one after another or one group after another. **Count** (see also RELY) implies computation of a total by assigning to each unit or each group of units as noted its proper numeral in succession, such as one, two, three . . . or three, six, nine . . . ⟨they were *counting* the books one by one when he told them it would be quicker to *count* them by fives⟩ ⟨as many as thirty bonfires could be *counted* within the whole bounds of the district— *Hardy*⟩ **Tell**, which is somewhat old-fashioned in general use, usually stresses a counting one by one ⟨look now toward heaven, and *tell* the stars, if thou be able to number them—*Gen 15:5*⟩ ⟨all *told* there were 27 public schools —*Jones*⟩ or it may suggest a lingering counting interspersed with meditation on each unit counted ⟨thus will he *tell* like beads the memories of his days—*Powys*⟩ *Tell* is more common in current use in the collocation *tell off* which adds to the notion of counting that of setting apart the units counted ⟨*told* off a detail and put them to opening a trench—*Dobie*⟩ **Enumerate** implies a listing or mentioning of each one in a series not only that their total may be ascertained, but that they may be individually known or specified ⟨*enumerate* the powers of the supreme court⟩ ⟨*enumerate* the species of plants found on an island⟩ ⟨*enumerate* the various dishes served at a dinner⟩ **Number** is a somewhat literary equivalent of either *count* or *enumerate;* in some uses it carries an additional suggestion of allotment or limit ⟨the days of every man are *numbered*⟩ ⟨*number* the flowers of the field⟩ ⟨but even the very hairs of your head are all *numbered*—*Lk 12:7*⟩ ⟨his hosts of blind and unresisting dupes the despot *numbers*—*Shelley*⟩
*Ana* *calculate, compute, reckon, estimate: *add, sum, figure, total, tot, cast, foot
**2** *rely, depend, bank, trust, reckon
**count** *n* *paragraph, verse, article, clause, plank
**countenance** *n* *face, visage, physiognomy, mug, puss
**countenance** *vb* *favor, encourage
*Ana* *approve, sanction, endorse: *commend, applaud: *support, uphold, champion, back
*Con* *criticize, reprehend, reprobate: *reprove, reproach: deride, *ridicule
**counter** antagonistic, counteractive, *adverse
*Ana* contrary, *opposite, antithetical, antipodal, antipodean, antonymous, contradictory: hostile, inimical (see corresponding nouns at ENMITY)
**counteract** *neutralize, negative
*Ana* *correct, rectify: offset, counterbalance, countervail, counterpoise, balance, *compensate
*Ant* cooperate —*Con* conjoin, concur, *unite, combine

**counteractive** counter, *adverse, antagonistic
*Ana* countervailing, counterbalancing, counterpoising, compensating, offsetting, balancing (see COMPENSATE): correcting (see CORRECT *vb* 1): neutralizing (see NEUTRALIZE)
**counterbalance** *vb* offset, *compensate, countervail, balance, counterpoise
*Ana* *stabilize, steady, poise: *correct (sense 1)
*Con* *overturn, upset, capsize
**counterfeit** *vb* feign, sham, simulate, pretend, *assume, affect
*Ana* *copy, imitate, mimic, ape: dissemble, *disguise
**counterfeit** *adj* **Counterfeit, spurious, bogus, fake, sham, pseudo, pinchbeck, phony** are comparable when meaning not at all what it is said to be or purports to be. **Counterfeit** implies that what is so qualified is an imitation of something else and usually of something finer, rarer, or more valuable and that the imitation is intended to deceive or defraud; thus, play money intended for the use of children at play is imitation but not *counterfeit* money; a clipped coin, though intended to defraud, is a real coin and not *counterfeit;* but a false banknote is both imitation and intended to deceive or defraud and is *counterfeit* ⟨planned to substitute a *counterfeit* gem for the historic original⟩ ⟨the austere word of genuine religion is: save your soul! The degenerate counsel of a *counterfeit* religion is: salve your soul!—*Sullivan*⟩ **Spurious** designates something as false rather than true or genuine; it carries no strong implication of being an imitation; thus, a *spurious* painting is one that is falsely attributed to a well-known painter; *spurious* writings attributed to Shakespeare are those thrown out of a canon of his work; a *spurious* condition is one which only superficially resembles the genuine condition ⟨*spurious* pregnancy⟩ The word does not necessarily connote a fraudulent purpose; it may suggest an honest mistake, confusion, or lack of scholarship ⟨it is certain that the letter, attributed to him, directing that no Christian should be punished for being a Christian, is *spurious*—*Arnold*⟩ ⟨it would have been unfair to call his enthusiasm for social reform *spurious*. It was real enough in its way—*Galsworthy*⟩ ⟨no *spurious* argument, no appeal to sentiment . . . can deceive the American people—*Roosevelt*⟩ **Bogus** carries the implications of fraudulence or deceit and applies to whatever may be passed off on one or may attempt to deceive one as to its true nature ⟨*bogus* certificates⟩ ⟨*bogus* statesmen⟩ ⟨*bogus* legal actions⟩ ⟨he had figured . . . the night before, in red cambric and *bogus* ermine, as some kind of a king—*Mark Twain*⟩ ⟨Herman Melville made a habit of breaking out, whenever he was excited, into *bogus* Shakespeare—*Huxley*⟩ **Fake** and **sham** are often equal to the past participial adjectives *faked* and *shammed,* both usually implying a more or less obvious imitation of something real. But **fake** emphasizes the idea of a false fabrication or of fraudulent manipulation ⟨give *fake* news⟩ ⟨Americans who cling to illusions about communism and its *fake* Utopia—*A. E. Stevenson*⟩ ⟨sell a *fake* medicine⟩ ⟨a *fake* diamond⟩ and **sham** stresses the thinness and obviousness of the disguise, the naïveté of the deception, or often the lack of intent to imitate exactly ⟨a *sham* battle⟩ ⟨*sham* jewelry⟩ ⟨a *sham* crown⟩ ⟨a garden adorned with *sham* ruins and statues—*L. P. Smith*⟩ **Pseudo** actually means false in any way; as an adjective modifying a noun or in the combining form joined with a separate noun it frequently implies pretense rather than fraud or spuriousness rather than counterfeiting ⟨these *pseudo* evangelists pretended to inspiration —*Jefferson*⟩ ⟨luxuries which, when long gratified, become a sort of *pseudo* necessaries—*Scott*⟩ ⟨o'er taste awhile these *pseudo*-bards prevail—*Byron*⟩ **Pinchbeck** implies

a cheap, tawdry, or worthless imitation often of something precious, costly, or grand; it rarely implies an intent to deceive and is therefore closer to *sham* than to *counterfeit* ⟨a *pinchbeck* age of poetry—*Symonds*⟩ ⟨*pinchbeck* imitations of the glory of ancient Rome—*Manchester Guardian*⟩ **Phony** stigmatizes something which does not impose but puzzles or perplexes since it has a dubious appearance of reality ⟨a *phony* message⟩ ⟨a *phony* examination⟩ ⟨journalists described as a *phony* war the period of relative inactivity near the beginning of World War II⟩
*Ana* simulated, feigned, pretended (see ASSUME): fraudulent (see corresponding noun at DECEPTION): deceptive, *misleading, delusive, delusory
*Ant* bona fide, genuine —*Con* *authentic, veritable: true, *real, actual
**counterfeit** *n* fraud, sham, fake, *imposture, cheat, humbug, deceit, deception
*Ana* *reproduction, copy, facsimile
**counterpart** correlate, *parallel, analogue
*Ana* *complement, supplement: duplicate, copy, facsimile, replica, *reproduction
*Con* antithesis, opposite, contradictory (see under OPPOSITE *adj*)
**counterpoise** *vb* balance, countervail, counterbalance, *compensate, offset
*Ana* poise, *stabilize, steady, balance, ballast, trim
*Con* upset, capsize, *overturn
**countervail** *vb* offset, balance, *compensate, counterbalance, counterpoise
*Ana* *correct (sense 1): counteract, *neutralize, negative: overcome, surmount (see CONQUER): foil, thwart, *frustrate
**county** gentry, *aristocracy, elite, nobility, society
**coup, coup d'etat** *rebellion, revolution, uprising, revolt, insurrection, mutiny, putsch
**couple** *n* **Couple, pair, brace, yoke** are comparable when meaning two things of the same kind. **Couple** applies to two things of the same sort, regarded as in some way associated, but not necessarily (except in the case of a married or mated pair) matched or belonging together; it frequently means no more than *two* ⟨a *couple* of hours⟩ ⟨a *couple* of dollars⟩ **Pair** applies to two things that belong or are used together, frequently so that one is useless or defective without the other; it also applies to a single object (as trousers, spectacles, scissors, or tongs) composed of two corresponding or complementary parts ⟨a *pair* of compasses⟩ ⟨a matched *pair* of carriage horses⟩ **Brace** applies especially to a couple of certain animals ⟨a *brace* of pheasants⟩ ⟨a *brace* of greyhounds⟩ or occasionally, to a couple of inanimate objects ⟨a *brace* of pistols⟩ or rarely and usually with contemptuous connotations to persons ⟨a *brace* of dukes—*Goldsmith*⟩ **Yoke** applies to two animals linked together ⟨a *yoke* of oxen⟩ It is used of persons only in contempt ⟨a *yoke* of his discarded men—*Shak.*⟩
**courage** *n* **Courage, mettle, spirit, resolution, tenacity** are comparable when they mean a quality of mind or temperament which makes one resist temptation to give way in the face of opposition, danger, or hardship. **Courage** stresses firmness of mind or purpose and a casting aside of fear (for *courage* meaning *courageousness,* see *courageous* under BRAVE); it implies a summoning of all one's powers in order that one's desires or ends may be achieved ⟨a reformer must have the *courage* of his convictions⟩ ⟨but screw your *courage* to the sticking place, and we'll not fail—*Shak.*⟩ ⟨the unconquerable will . . . and *courage* never to submit or yield—*Milton*⟩ ⟨*courage* to act on limited knowledge, *courage* to make the best of what is here and not whine for more—*Time*⟩ **Mettle** suggests an

ingrained or characteristic capacity for meeting strain or stress in a manner suggestive of a finely tempered sword blade ⟨the challenge put him on his *mettle*⟩ It often implies qualities (as resiliency, ardor, fearlessness, fortitude, or gallantry associated less with physical strength than with mental or spiritual vigor ⟨now I see there's *mettle* in thee, and even from this instant do build on thee a better opinion than ever before—*Shak.*⟩ ⟨doing one's bit, putting one's shoulder to the wheel, proving the *mettle* of the women of England, certainly had its agreeable side—*Rose Macaulay*⟩ **Spirit,** like *mettle,* refers to a temperamental quality but suggests something more volatile or fragile. It implies an ability to hold one's own, to assert oneself or one's principles, or to keep up one's morale when opposed, interfered with, frustrated, or tempted ⟨I do not think I can forgive you entirely, even now—it is too much for a woman of any *spirit* to quite overlook—*Hardy*⟩ ⟨to quit a comrade on the road, and return home without him: these are tricks which no boy of *spirit* would be guilty of—*Meredith*⟩ ⟨successive crop failures had broken the *spirit* of the farmers—*Cather*⟩ **Resolution,** like *courage,* implies firmness of mind and purpose, but it stresses determination to achieve one's ends in spite of opposition or interference of men or of circumstances rather than a casting aside of fear of danger or a dread of hardship ⟨good-humored-looking on the whole, but implacable-looking, too; evidently a man of a strong *resolution* and a set purpose; a man not desirable to be met rushing down a narrow pass with a gulf on either side, for nothing would turn the man—*Dickens*⟩ ⟨the General . . . had no *resolution,* no will of his own, was bullied into the favors he bestowed—*Pargellis*⟩ ⟨he saw that England was saved a hundred years ago by the high spirit and proud *resolution* of a real aristocracy—*Inge*⟩ **Tenacity** adds to *resolution* the implications of stubborn persistence and of unwillingness to acknowledge defeat ⟨the *tenacity* of the bulldog breed⟩ ⟨this is not to say that the French lack *tenacity.* . . . Having determined upon a thing, the French character tends to exceed in its pursuit, and, while fighting for it, to hold out to the death—*Belloc*⟩ ⟨maintained this conviction with a fearless *tenacity*—*Kirk*⟩
*Ana* bravery, boldness, audacity, dauntlessness, intrepidity, doughtiness, fearlessness (see corresponding adjectives at BRAVE): valor, *heroism, gallantry: *fortitude, grit, pluck, guts, backbone, sand
*Ant* cowardice —*Con* timorousness, timidity (see corresponding adjectives at TIMID)

**courageous** *brave, unafraid, fearless, intrepid, valiant, valorous, dauntless, undaunted, doughty, bold, audacious
*Ana* mettlesome, *spirited, high-spirited, fiery: resolute, staunch (see FAITHFUL): stout, tenacious, *strong
*Ant* pusillanimous —*Con* *fearful, apprehensive, afraid: *timid, timorous

**course** *n* *way, route, passage, pass, artery
*Ana* circuit (see CIRCUMFERENCE): orbit, scope (see RANGE *n*): drift, trend, *tendency: procedure, *process

**court** *vb* *invite, woo, bid, solicit
*Ana* allure, *attract, captivate, charm: toady, truckle, *fawn, cringe

**courteous** polite, *civil, courtly, gallant, chivalrous
*Ana* *gracious, affable, cordial: *suave, urbane, politic, diplomatic: considerate, *thoughtful, attentive: obliging, complaisant (see AMIABLE)
*Ant* discourteous —*Con* *rude, impolite, uncivil, ill-mannered, ungracious: curt, brusque, gruff, blunt (see BLUFF): insolent, supercilious, overbearing (see PROUD)
**courtesy,** **amenity, attention, gallantry** are comparable when they denote a manner or an act which promotes

agreeable or pleasant social relations. **Courtesy** suggests consideration for others or deference (as to their rank, sex, or age); it usually implies good breeding and acquired graces but it sometimes connotes innate gentleness or instinctive politeness rather than social training ⟨the beauty of an inherited *courtesy* . . . of a thousand little ceremonies flowering out of the most ordinary relations and observances of life—*Binyon*⟩ ⟨rising to receive him . . . with all the engaging graces and *courtesies* of life—*Dickens*⟩ **Amenity** implies a disposition to make easy the approach to or the continuance of pleasant social relations; when used concretely it may be applied not only to words or acts but to pursuits, interests, or facilities that bring men into rapport ⟨he was . . . a charming letter-writer; above all, an excellent and delightful talker. The gaiety and *amenity* of his natural disposition were inexhaustible —*Arnold*⟩ ⟨he is a man of informed tastes who happens to prize the *amenities*. A snob, however, he is not and never has had to be—*J. M. Brown*⟩ ⟨would she be interested to read it? Might he send it to her? Joan's chaperon . . . put no bar upon these *amenities*—*H. G. Wells*⟩ **Attention** implies a singling out of a particular person for special favor or consideration, or as the recipient of courtesies showing one's admiration or love (as in courting) ⟨the elder son is paying *attention* to his roommate's sister⟩ ⟨many of his visitors were busily deferential toward the young lord, and evidently flattered by his *attentions*— *Carlos Baker*⟩ ⟨she loved her children, but did not unduly spoil them or turn their heads with injudicious *attentions* —*Rose Macaulay*⟩ **Gallantry** stresses devoted attention, sometimes amorous attention, to a lady; it also often connotes ingratiating personal qualities (as ease of address, a dashing style, or a polished manner) ⟨"Now despise me if you dare." "Indeed I do not dare." Elizabeth, having rather expected to affront him, was amazed at his *gallantry—Austen*⟩ ⟨Cashel, in a businesslike manner, and without the slightest air of *gallantry,* expertly lifted her and placed her on her feet—*Shaw*⟩
*Ana* graciousness, cordiality, affability, geniality (see corresponding adjectives at GRACIOUS): politeness, courteousness, courtliness, chivalrousness *or* chivalry, civility (see corresponding adjectives at CIVIL): considerateness *or* consideration, attentiveness, thoughtfulness (see corresponding adjectives at THOUGHTFUL)
*Ant* discourtesy —*Con* churlishness, boorishness (see corresponding adjectives under BOOR): rudeness, impoliteness, ungraciousness, incivility (see corresponding adjectives at RUDE)

**courtly** courteous, gallant, chivalrous, polite, *civil
*Ana* ceremonious, formal, conventional, *ceremonial: elegant, dignified, graceful (see corresponding nouns at ELEGANCE): finished, *consummate
*Ant* churlish —*Con* ungracious, discourteous, ill-mannered, impolite, *rude, uncivil: *coarse, vulgar, gross: boorish, loutish (see under BOOR)

**covenant** *vb* pledge, engage, *promise, plight, contract
*Ana* *agree, concur, coincide: *unite, combine, conjoin, cooperate

**cover** *vb* **Cover, overspread, envelop, wrap, shroud, veil** are comparable when meaning to put or place over or to be put or placed over or around. **Cover** may imply the putting or placing by a conscious agent or unconscious agency of something on top ⟨*cover* a box⟩ ⟨*cover* a garbage pail⟩ ⟨the lid *covers* the kettle tightly⟩ or on or over a surface (as of a circumscribed area or body) ⟨snow *covered* the ground⟩ ⟨*cover* a table with a cloth⟩ ⟨clothes that *cover* the entire body⟩ ⟨*cover* the shore with wreckage⟩ In these uses *cover* often carries an additional implication of hiding, enclosing, protecting, or sheltering; indeed, in some use

---

*Ana* analogous words    *Ant* antonyms    *Con* contrasted words    See also explanatory notes facing page 1

the emphasis is upon one of these implications, the basic idea being obscured ⟨their advance was *covered* by squadrons of airplanes⟩ ⟨he *covered* his anxiety by joining in the laugh⟩ ⟨there is nothing *covered,* that shall not be revealed—*Mt* 10:26⟩ In still another sense *cover* implies an extending so far as to include, embrace, or comprise something ⟨left scarcely enough money to *cover* his debts⟩ ⟨this point has already been *covered* in the argument⟩ ⟨Chaucer's life *covered* the last sixty years of the fourteenth century⟩ ⟨I think your statement *covers* the matter completely⟩ ⟨a situation not *covered* by the rules⟩ **Overspread** usually implies a covering by something that diffuses itself or spreads over a surface; the word carries no clear implication of concealing, sheltering, or protecting, but it does suggest the activity of something that flows, expands, or scatters until the entire surface is covered ⟨clouds *overspread* the sky⟩ ⟨the ground is *overspread* with weeds⟩ ⟨a blush *overspread* his face⟩ ⟨the rising waters quickly *overspread* the valley⟩ **Envelop** suggests the presence or addition of something that surrounds and therefore covers or nearly covers a person or thing on all sides; it is often used of a gas or a liquid or of clothing ⟨*enveloped* in a fur overcoat⟩ ⟨*enveloped* in water up to his chin⟩ ⟨till the sweet . . . incense-laden atmosphere . . . *enveloped* her like a warm and healing garment—*Rose Macaulay*⟩ *Envelop* lends itself to extension and often connotes something impalpable or immaterial as the enveloping element ⟨words stir our feelings . . . through their *enveloping* atmosphere of associations—*Lowes*⟩ ⟨we are surely justified in . . . calling the spiritual presence which *envelops* us the spirit of Christ—*Inge*⟩ **Wrap** comes very close to *envelop* in meaning, but it suggests something that folds or winds about so as to enclose rather than surround; the difference, although sometimes slight, is usually important to idiomatic usage; thus, one *wraps* (better than *envelops*) oneself in blankets or one *wraps* up (not *envelops*) several bars of soap ⟨a closely *wrapped* female figure approached—*Hardy*⟩ In extended use *wrap* usually suggests something that enfolds, enshrouds, or entangles ⟨all the household were *wrapped* in slumber⟩ ⟨the place was suddenly *wrapped* in darkness when the lights gave out⟩ ⟨he found the roots of the poplar *wrapped* closely about the drainpipe⟩ ⟨the mother was *wrapped* up in the welfare of her son⟩ **Shroud** and *veil,* in their extended senses, imply a covering that protects, conceals, or disguises, but **shroud** usually emphasizes the density and **veil** the comparative tenuity of the surrounding element ⟨the queen, *shrouded* in deepest mystery—*Carlyle*⟩ ⟨its proceedings were impenetrably *shrouded* from the public eye—*Prescott*⟩ ⟨the hills, *shrouded* in grey mist—*Buchan*⟩ ⟨their [women's] beauty, softened by the lawn that thinly *veiled* it—*Radcliffe*⟩ ⟨her eyes were quick under a faint dimness that merely *veiled* their vigor—*Roberts*⟩
*Ana* *hide, conceal, screen: *close, shut: *enclose, envelop: shield, protect, *defend
*Ant* bare —*Con* expose, exhibit, display (see SHOW): evince, demonstrate, manifest, *show

**cover** *n* *shelter, retreat, refuge, asylum, sanctuary
*Ana* hiding *or* hiding place, concealment, screening *or* screen (see corresponding verbs at HIDE): safety, security (see corresponding adjectives at SAFE)
*Ant* exposure

**covert** *secret, clandestine, surreptitious, underhand, underhanded, stealthy, furtive
*Ana* hidden, concealed, screened (see HIDE): disguised, dissembled, masked, cloaked, camouflaged (see DISGUISE *vb*)
*Ant* overt —*Con* open, plain, candid, *frank: plain,

clear, manifest, patent, *evident, obvious

**covet** 1 Covet, envy, grudge, begrudge though not closely synonymous all carry the implication of a selfish desire to have something for one's own enjóyment or possession. To **covet** (for fuller treatment see DESIRE) is to long inordinately for something which belongs to another ⟨*covet* a neighbor's piece of property because of its fine view⟩ To **envy** is to regard another with more or less chagrin, repining, jealousy, or hatred because he possesses something one covets or feels should have come to oneself ⟨*envy* a person his good fortune or his promotion⟩ To **grudge** or **begrudge** implies reluctance or hesitation (often through selfishness, meanness, or stinginess) in giving another what he (or it) ought to have because it is his (or its) due or need ⟨surely you wouldn't *grudge* the poor old man some humble way to save his self-respect—*Frost*⟩ ⟨*begrudges* every penny he spends on taxis⟩ ⟨she *grudges* every moment spent on housekeeping chores⟩
2 crave, *desire, wish, want
*Ana* yearn, *long, pine, hanker, thirst, hunger: pant, aspire, *aim
*Ant* renounce (*something desirable*) —*Con* resign, *relinquish, yield, surrender: *abjure, forswear: *decline, refuse, reject

**covetous,** greedy, acquisitive, grasping, avaricious mean having or manifesting a strong desire for possessions, especially material possessions. **Covetous** implies inordinateness of desire; very often, with allusion to the Ten Commandments, it implies longing for something that is rightfully another's ⟨*covetous* of Shakespeare's beauty—*Cowper*⟩ ⟨first settlers brought fine hunting dogs . . . of which the Indians were so *covetous* that a day was set each year when settlers traded dogs—*Amer. Guide Series: Va.*⟩ It is, however, used with derogatory intent or effect only when envy is implied or wrongful means of acquiring possession are suggested ⟨is not thy kindness subtle, *covetous* . . . expecting in return twenty for one?—*Shak.*⟩ **Greedy** emphasizes absence of restraint in desire; it is a censorious term only when the object of longing is evil either in itself or in immoderation, or cannot be possessed without harm to oneself or to others ⟨*greedy* for gold⟩ ⟨exploitation [of provinces] by *greedy* proconsuls—*Buchan*⟩ ⟨he loved learning; he was *greedy* of all writings and sciences—*Coulton*⟩ **Acquisitive** implies not only eagerness to possess but the capacity for acquiring and retaining what is desired. Thus, an *acquisitive* mind is not only greedy for knowledge but is capable of absorbing it in large amounts; the *acquisitive* classes of society not only covet possessions but have the means whereby they can constantly add to their possessions ⟨one of those strenuous, *acquisitive* women—*Weeks*⟩ **Grasping** implies eagerness and capacity to acquire wealth and selfishness in its acquisition and often suggests use of wrongful or unfair means ⟨people who are hard, *grasping* . . . and always ready to take advantage of their neighbors, become very rich—*Shaw*⟩ **Avaricious** also implies eagerness and capacity to acquire wealth, but especially wealth in a form (as money) which can be hoarded. It, more than any of the others, emphasizes extreme stinginess ⟨an unremitting, *avaricious* thrift—*Wordsworth*⟩
*Ana* *envious, jealous: desirous, lustful (see corresponding nouns at DESIRE): avid, athirst, *eager: rapacious, ravening, gluttonous, ravenous, *voracious
*Con* self-denying, self-abnegating (see corresponding nouns at RENUNCIATION): renouncing, abjuring, forswearing (see ABJURE)

**cow** *vb* *intimidate, browbeat, bulldoze, bully
*Ana* *frighten, terrorize, terrify: daunt, *dismay, appall: abash, discomfit, rattle, faze, disconcert, *embarrass

---

A colon (:) separates groups of words discriminated. An asterisk (*) indicates place of treatment of each group.

*Con* animate, *quicken, vivify, enliven: cringe, cower, *fawn

**cower** cringe, truckle, *fawn, toady
*Ana* shrink, quail, flinch, blench, wince, *recoil
*Con* cow, bully, bulldoze, browbeat, *intimidate: *strut, swagger, bristle

**coxcomb** *fop, dandy, beau, exquisite, dude, buck

**coy** bashful, *shy, diffident, modest
*Ana* nice, proper, seemly, *decorous, decent: aloof, detached (see INDIFFERENT): *cautious, wary, chary
*Ant* pert —*Con* *saucy, arch: brazen, brash, impudent (see SHAMELESS)

**cozen** *cheat, defraud, swindle, overreach
*Ana* *dupe, bamboozle, gull, trick, hoax, hoodwink, befool: delude, beguile, *deceive, mislead

**cozy** *comfortable, snug, easy, restful
*Ana* sheltering, harboring, housing, lodging (see HARBOR *vb*): *safe, secure: contenting, satisfying (see SATISFY)
*Con* *miserable, wretched

**crabbed** *sullen, surly, glum, morose, gloomy, sulky, saturnine, dour
*Ana* crusty, gruff, brusque, blunt (see BLUFF): testy, choleric, cranky, cross, splenetic, *irascible: snappish, huffy, *irritable
*Con* *amiable, good-natured, obliging, complaisant: kindly, *kind, benign, benignant: *pleasant, agreeable: genial, affable, *gracious

**crack** *vb* *break, burst, bust, snap, shatter, shiver
*Ana* split, rend, cleave, rive (see TEAR)

**crack** *n* 1 Crack, cleft, fissure, crevasse, crevice, cranny, chink are comparable when meaning an opening, break, or discontinuity made by or as if by splitting or rupture. Crack basically applies to substances or structures that are subjected to drying, slow disintegration, or shrinking or are fragile or brittle ⟨a *crack* in dry earth⟩ ⟨a *crack* in the plaster⟩ ⟨a *crack* in a china plate⟩ ⟨little rifts and *cracks* are beginning to appear in the whole bland, ecclesiastical facade of Victorian England—*Day Lewis*⟩ **Cleft** implies an opening or break wider and deeper than a crack and often in a natural structure; it may suggest a defect that is constitutional or an opening that is left by nature ⟨a *cleft* in a great rock⟩ ⟨a *cleft* in a palate⟩ ⟨this belief in an irremediable *cleft* within our intelligence must destroy our confidence that either our facts or our values are anywhere near the truth—*Inge*⟩ **Fissure** does not differ materially from *cleft* except that it usually suggests a narrow and deep opening and does not carry so strong an implication of inherent defect. The term may denote a normal structural feature ⟨the *fissures* of the brain are deep dividing lines between certain of its lobes⟩ or an abnormal condition ⟨a *fissure* in the earth's crust⟩ ⟨painful *fissures* at the corners of the mouth—*JAMA*⟩ In extended use it usually suggests something abnormal or undesirable ⟨the loss of Illyria would have made a dangerous *fissure* between East and West—*Buchan*⟩ **Crevasse** is applied generally and usually in its extended use to a fissure or cleft that is broad and deep ⟨an angry clamor which rang down the *crevasse* of Wall Street—*Fortune*⟩ but is particularly applicable to a deep break in the surface of a glacier or a wide breach in a levee ⟨a glacier, riven with deep *crevasses*, yawning fifty or sixty feet wide—*King*⟩ ⟨where the current of a flood locally and violently breaks across a levee a *crevasse* is cut—*von Engeln*⟩ **Crevice** and **cranny** apply especially to a space made by a break or crack (as in a wall or a cliff) that forms a place for dirt to gather or for plants to root and grow ⟨a pile of purple rock, all broken out with red sumac and yellow aspens up in the high *crevices* of the cliffs—*Cather*⟩ ⟨the log church whose *crannies* admitted the drifting snow—*Everett*⟩ **Cranny**

often (*crevice* occasionally) conveys so strongly the notion of an obscure, remote, or hidden nook that it loses completely all suggestion of a mode of formation ⟨a first-rate guidebook for adventurous tourists. It searches into every *cranny* of an exotic world—*Lehrman*⟩ ⟨pursuing their subtleties into the last refuge and *cranny* of logic—*Parrington*⟩ ⟨makes its way into every crack and *crevice* of our being—*Cardozo*⟩ **Chink** implies a small break or hole sufficient for one to see through or for something to come through ⟨sleep on straw ticks exposed to winter snows that came through *chinks* in the logs—*Amer. Guide Series: Ind.*⟩ ⟨watch a game through *chinks* in the fence⟩ ⟨*chinks* in the wall admitted the only light there was⟩
*Ana* split, rent, rift (see BREACH)
2 wisecrack, witticism, *joke, jest, jape, quip, gag

**craft** 1 skill, cunning, *art, artifice
*Ana* adeptness, expertness, proficiency (see corresponding adjectives at PROFICIENT): ingeniousness *or* ingenuity, cleverness (see corresponding adjectives at CLEVER): competence, capability (see corresponding adjectives at ABLE): efficiency (see corresponding adjective at EFFECTIVE)
2 *trade, handicraft, art, profession
*Ana* occupation, employment, pursuit, *work
3 *boat, ship, vessel

**craftsman** handicraftsman, mechanic, artisan, *worker, workman, workingman, laborer, hand, operative, roustabout

**crafty** tricky, *sly, cunning, insidious, foxy, guileful, wily, artful
*Ana* adroit, *clever, cunning: *shrewd, astute: *sharp, keen, acute
*Con* *stupid, slow, dull, dense, crass, dumb: obtuse, *dull

**cram** *vb* *pack, crowd, stuff, ram, tamp
*Ana* *press, squeeze, jam: compress (see CONTRACT): *compact, consolidate: *force, compel

**cranky** cross, choleric, splenetic, testy, *irascible, touchy
*Ana* *irritable, fractious, peevish, petulant, snappish: *contrary, perverse, froward: *impatient, nervous, jittery
*Con* *calm, tranquil, serene, placid: good-natured, *amiable, obliging, complaisant

**cranny** *crack, cleft, fissure, crevasse, crevice, chink
*Ana* *hole, cavity, pocket, hollow: perforation, puncture, bore (see corresponding verbs at PERFORATE): interstice, *aperture

**crass** *adj* dense, *stupid, slow, dull, dumb
*Ana* obtuse, *dull: crude, raw, *rude, rough, uncouth
*Ant* brilliant —*Con* *intelligent, clever, alert, quick-witted, bright, smart

**crave** covet, *desire, wish, want
*Ana* *long, hanker, yearn, pine, hunger, thirst
*Ant* spurn —*Con* reject, repudiate, refuse, *decline: abhor, abominate, detest, loathe, *hate: *despise, contemn, scorn, disdain

**crawl** *vb* *creep

**craze** vogue, fad, rage, *fashion, style, mode, dernier cri, cry

**crazy, crazed** *insane, mad, demented, lunatic, maniac, deranged, non compos mentis
*Con* *rational, reasonable: sane, sensible, *wise, sapient

**cream** *vb* grease, *oil, lubricate, anoint

**create** *invent, discover
*Ana* *make, form, fashion, shape, forge: design, plan, scheme (see under PLAN *n*)

**creator** *maker, author
*Ana* *artist, architect, artificer: composer, *writer, author

**creature** *entity, being, individual, person

**credence** credit, *belief, faith
*Ana* conviction, assurance, certitude, *certainty: accept-

ing *or* acceptance, admitting *or* admission, receiving *or* reception (see corresponding verbs at RECEIVE): assenting *or* assent, acquiescing *or* acquiescence (see corresponding verbs at ASSENT): reliance, confidence, *trust, faith **Con** doubt, *uncertainty, skepticism: mistrust, *distrust: disbelief, *unbelief, incredulity

**credential,** testimonial, recommendation, character, reference mean something presented by one person to another in proof that he is what or who he claims to be. **Credential** (usually in the plural **credentials**) implies material evidence and especially a letter or document indicating that a person (occasionally a thing) is what he claims (or it seems) to be; the term was originally and is still used of the letter from the sovereign or head of one state to another carried by a new envoy or ambassador and formally presented to the sovereign or head of the state in which he is to serve ⟨an envoy extraordinary from Savoy . . . presented his *credentials* in the Banqueting House—*Macaulay*⟩ The term is often used of a letter presented to show competency or to attest identity, or of statements made or acts performed that serve as proof of what is to follow ⟨if we turn out to be poor managers of our own affairs, we will have inferior *credentials* to present abroad—*W. O. Douglas*⟩ ⟨the putative Professor Moriarty of the fight business, who may or may not die of old age before his *credentials* as an archfiend are established—*Lardner*⟩ ⟨these statements I put forward by way of *credentials* for a comparison which I purpose to make—*Grandgent*⟩ **Testimonial** usually implies a written statement from a person competent to judge the character, qualifications, or merits of another and to testify to his fitness to hold or to fill an office or a position ⟨six *testimonials* were received affirming his fitness for the ministry⟩ ⟨selected what seemed to me from the *testimonials* to be the two best men—*Crofts*⟩ However, the word is often used as an equivalent of **recommendation,** a term which implies that the statement comes from one (as a former employer or teacher) who commends a person to the notice of a possible employer ⟨armed with several *recommendations* he started out to seek a job⟩ **Character,** which in this sense is used chiefly in Great Britain, is the designation given to a statement furnished by a former employer about the qualities and habits of a person as manifested while in his employ ⟨then came . . . the coachman, the grooms, the sweeper. For each and all of these I had to write *characters*—*John Lang*⟩ Although **reference** may imply no more than the giving of the name of a person from whom information regarding another may be obtained (as by a possible employer or landlord) it increasingly tends to be employed as a synonym of *recommendation* or *character* ⟨Mrs. Blank told the woman she would let her know when she had examined her *references*⟩ ⟨she had lost all her *references* and was afraid to apply for a job⟩
**Ana** certification, accreditation, endorsement, sanction (see corresponding verbs at APPROVE)

**credible** believable, *plausible, colorable, specious
**Ana** *probable, likely, possible: reasonable, *rational: trustworthy, *reliable, dependable
**Ant** incredible —**Con** fabulous, mythical, apocryphal, *fictitious: dubious, *doubtful, questionable

**credit** *n* 1 *belief, faith, credence
**Ana** reliance, *trust, confidence, faith: assurance, certitude, conviction, *certainty
**Con** *unbelief, disbelief, incredulity: *distrust, mistrust: doubt, *uncertainty
2 prestige, authority, *influence, weight
**Ana** reputation, repute, *fame, renown: authority,

*power, sway
**Ant** discredit —**Con** opprobrium, obloquy, ignominy, disrepute (see DISGRACE)
3 **Credit, asset** are comparable when they mean a person or a thing that enhances another. Someone or something is a **credit** *to* another when he or it is a source of honor or of increase in good repute ⟨the boy is a *credit* to his school⟩ ⟨his integrity is a *credit* to his upbringing⟩ Someone or something is an **asset** *to* another when he or it adds to the usefulness, the worth, the advantages, or the attractiveness of another ⟨the new teacher is an *asset* to the school⟩ ⟨his knowledge of how to deal with people made him an *asset* to his employer⟩

**credit** *vb* accredit, *ascribe, assign, attribute, impute, refer, charge

**credulity** gullibility (see under CREDULOUS)
**Ana** credence, credit, *belief
**Ant** incredulity: skepticism —**Con** *uncertainty, doubt, suspicion, mistrust

**credulous,** gullible both mean unduly trusting or confiding but they differ significantly in their implications as do their corresponding nouns **credulity** and **gullibility**. **Credulous** and **credulity** stress a tendency to believe readily and uncritically whatever is proposed for belief without examination or investigation; typically they suggest inexperience, naïveté, or careless habits of thought rather than inherent incapacity ⟨far from being unconscious of heredity . . . men were insanely *credulous* about it; they not only believed in the transmission of qualities and habits from generation to generation, but expected the son to begin mentally where the father left off—*Shaw*⟩ ⟨Hess, who was as deeply interested in psychic matters as Lanny, and far more *credulous*—*Upton Sinclair*⟩ ⟨we know from the satiric comments of Lucian and from the ingenuousness of Pliny the deep *credulity* of the average Roman—*Buchan*⟩ **Gullible** and **gullibility**, on the other hand, stress the idea of being duped; they suggest more the lack of necessary intelligence than the lack of skepticism, and connote the capacity for being made a fool of ⟨it was discovered that this man who had been raised to such a height by the credulity of the public was himself more *gullible* than any of his depositors—*Conrad*⟩ ⟨that any of us may be so *gullible* and so forgetful as to be duped into making "deals" at the expense of our Allies—*Roosevelt*⟩ ⟨monstrous was the *gullibility* of the people. How could an overcoat at twelve and sixpence be "good"—*Bennett*⟩
**Ana** assenting, acquiescing *or* acquiescent, agreeing, subscribing (see corresponding verbs at ASSENT): believing, crediting (see corresponding nouns at BELIEF)
**Ant** incredulous: skeptical —**Con** uncertain, doubtful, suspicious, mistrustful (see corresponding nouns at UNCERTAINTY)

**creed** faith, persuasion, *religion, denomination, sect, cult, communion, church

**creep** *vb* **Creep, crawl** mean to move slowly along a surface in a prone or crouching position. **Creep** is more often used of quadrupeds or of human beings who move on all fours and proceed slowly, stealthily, or silently ⟨a baby *creeps* before it walks⟩ ⟨crouching down . . . in a corner . . . he made out the three fishermen *creeping* through some rank grass—*Dickens*⟩ and **crawl** of elongated animals with no legs (as snakes and some worms) or with many small legs (as centipedes) that seem to move by drawing the body along the ground or a surface, or of human beings who imitate such movement ⟨when she saw the snake *crawling* along the path, she screamed⟩ ⟨he was so badly injured that he could only *crawl* to the open door⟩ In extended use both words often imply

---

A colon (:) separates groups of words discriminated. An asterisk (*) indicates place of treatment of each group.

intolerable slowness ⟨tomorrow, and tomorrow, and to-morrow, *creeps* in this petty pace from day to day—*Shak.*⟩ ⟨that sad, disappointing, disillusioning . . . war *crawled* through that bitter winter of defeat—*Rose Macaulay*⟩ Both often imply a slow movement of a person, especially into another's favor or into a given status or position, but *creep* usually suggests stealthy and insinuating methods ⟨*creep* along the hedge-bottoms, an' thou'll be a bishop yet—*Tennyson*⟩ ⟨even in later and more enlightened times, the study of literature has *crept* its way into official Cambridge—*Quiller-Couch*⟩ and *crawl,* procedure by abjectness, servility, cringing, or groveling ⟨Cranmer . . . hath *crawled* into the favor of the king—*Shak.*⟩ ⟨pomp-fed king . . . art thou not the veriest slave that e'er *crawled* on the loathing earth? —*Shelley*⟩ Both also imply a sensation such as might be produced by lice, fleas, or other human or animal parasites, but *creep* suggests a shivering, nervous re-action, and *crawl,* an intense feeling of distress and dis-comfort ⟨something in their countenances that made my flesh *creep* with a horror I cannot express—*Swift*⟩ ⟨his flesh was *crawling* with the need of alcohol—*Doherty*⟩

**crevasse**   *crack, cleft, fissure, crevice, cranny, chink
*Ana* chasm, *gulf: *breach, split, rent, rift

**crevice**   *crack, cleft, fissure, crevasse, cranny, chink
*Ana* *breach, split, rift, rent: *break, gap

**crime**   *offense, vice, sin, scandal
*Ana* *fault, failing, frailty, foible, vice
*Con* virtue, *excellence, merit, perfection

**criminal** *n* Criminal, felon, convict, malefactor, culprit, delinquent mean, in common, one guilty of a transgression or an offense especially against the law. **Criminal** desig-nates one who commits some serious violation of the law, of public trust, or of common decency, as vicious unwar-ranted attack, embezzlement, or murder. **Felon,** the legal term for one popularly called a criminal, designates one guilty of a felony, which used with legal exactness covers all lawbreaking punishable by death or prolonged con-finement (as in a state penitentiary) and is distinguished from a misdemeanor ⟨men were transported with the worst *felons* for poaching a few hares or pheasants—*Shaw*⟩ ⟨the casual or accidental *felon* who is impelled into a misdeed by force of circumstances—*Banay*⟩ **Convict** basically denotes one convicted of a crime or felony but has come more generally to signify any person serving a long prison term ⟨the stranger turned out to be a *con-vict* who had escaped on the way to prison⟩ ⟨a riot among *convicts* in a state penitentiary⟩ **Malefactor** signifies one who has committed an evil deed or serious offense but suggests little or no relation to courts or punish-ment ⟨most of our *malefactors,* from statesmen to thieves —*T. S. Eliot*⟩ ⟨a *malefactor* robbing small stores at night and setting fire to them⟩ **Culprit** often carries the weak-ened sense of one guilty of a crime ⟨after the series of crimes, the police tried for several weeks to find the *culprit*⟩ but more generally either suggests a trivial fault or offense, especially of a child ⟨the *culprits* were two boys, one about twelve years old, the other about ten—*Green Peyton*⟩ or applies to a person or thing that causes some undesirable condition or situation ⟨another group of supposed *culprits* who are being blamed for the present inflationary situation—*Waage*⟩ ⟨the *culprit* holding up world peace and understanding—*Lydgate*⟩ **Delinquent** applies to an offender against duty or the law especially in a degree not constituting crime; in its present semilegal use, in application to juvenile offenders against civil or moral law, it usually implies a habitual tendency to commit certain offenses and contrasts with *criminal* in implying a sociological or psychological rather than

judicial attitude toward the offender ⟨whether a customer who has missed a payment is . . . a habitual *delinquent* —*Phelps*⟩ ⟨we label as *delinquents* those who do not conform to the legal and moral codes of society—*Federal Probation*⟩
*Ana* offender, sinner (see corresponding nouns at OFFENSE): transgressor, trespasser, violator (see corre-sponding nouns at BREACH)

**cringe**   cower, truckle, *fawn, toady
*Ana* *recoil, quail, flinch, blench, wince: bow, cave, *yield, submit, defer

**cripple** *vb* 1 *maim, mutilate, batter, mangle
*Ana* *injure, hurt
2 disable, *weaken, enfeeble, debilitate, undermine, sap
*Ana* damage, harm, impair, mar (see INJURE)

**crisis**   exigency, emergency, pinch, *juncture, pass, contingency, strait

**crisp** 1 brittle, short, friable, *fragile, frangible
*Con* *limp, flabby, flaccid
2 clear-cut, cutting, *incisive, trenchant, biting
*Ana* terse, pithy, laconic, succinct, *concise: piquing, stimulating, provoking *or* provocative (see corresponding verbs at PROVOKE)

**criterion**   *standard, touchstone, yardstick, gauge
*Ana* test, proof, trial, demonstration (see under PROVE): *principle, axiom, law: judging *or* judgment, adjudgment, adjudication (see corresponding verbs at JUDGE)

**critical**   1 Critical, hypercritical, faultfinding, captious, caviling, carping, censorious are comparable when they mean exhibiting the spirit of one who detects and points out faults or defects. **Critical,** when applied to persons who judge and to their judgments, is the one of these terms that may imply an effort to see a thing clearly, truly, and impartially so that not only the good in it may be dis-tinguished from the bad and the perfect from the imperfect, but also that it as a whole may be fairly judged or valued ⟨a tête-à-tête with a man of similar tastes, who is just and yet sympathetic, *critical* yet appreciative . . . is a high intellectual pleasure—*Benson*⟩ Critical may also imply a keen awareness of faults or imperfections with often the suggestion of loss of fairness in judgment ⟨the attitude of Euripides towards the popular religion is . . . clearly and frankly *critical*—*Dickinson*⟩ ⟨the vast audience . . . was wont to be exceedingly *critical.* Bungling work drew down upon the headsman the execrations of the mob, and not infrequently placed his own life in danger—*Repplier*⟩ When this loss of fairness is to be implied or when the judge's undue awareness of defects and over-emphasis of them is to be suggested, writers often prefer **hypercritical** to *critical* ⟨the audience that night was, as the actors soon knew, *hypercritical*⟩ ⟨he was . . . exceedingly difficult to please, not . . . because he was *hypercritical* and exacting, but because he was indiffer-ent—*Bennett*⟩ ⟨constant *hypercritical* belittling of the efforts of others—*Rosen & Kiene*⟩ **Faultfinding** some-times takes the place of *critical,* sometimes of *hyper-critical,* but usually suggests less background, less ex-perience, or less fastidiousness than either; it is there-fore frequently used when an unreasonably exacting or a querulous temperament is also to be suggested ⟨a continually *faultfinding* reviewer of books⟩ ⟨a *fault-finding* parent⟩ ⟨Mrs. Stebbins's book would be better throughout for a more critical (I don't mean *faultfinding*) account of her authors' works—*Bentley*⟩ **Captious** im-plies a readiness, usually a temperamental readiness, to detect trivial faults or to take exceptions on slight grounds, because one is either unduly exacting or perversely hard to please ⟨is it *captious* to say that, when Manoah's

# criticism　200　criticize

locks are called "white as down," whiteness is no characteristic of down?—*Landor*〉 〈after reading a work of such amplitude it seems *captious* to protest that the motivating forces . . . are inadequately analyzed—*Bruun*〉 Caviling usually implies a captious disposition but stresses the habit or act of raising picayune or petty objections 〈*caviling* legislators who delay the passage of a bill〉 〈the most *caviling* mind must applaud their devoted sense of duty—*Willis*〉 〈those *caviling* critics who snipe from the musty back rooms of libraries—*Ramsdell*〉 Carping, far more than *hypercritical* or *faultfinding,* implies ill-natured or perverse picking of flaws and often in addition suggests undue emphasis upon them as blameworthy 〈and to that end we wished your lordship here, to avoid the *carping* censures of the world—*Shak.*〉 〈that *carping* spirit in which she had been wont to judge of his actions —*Trollope*〉 Censorious implies a disposition or a tendency to be both severely critical and condemnatory of what one criticizes 〈such is the mode of these *censorious* days, the art is lost of knowing how to praise—*Sheffield*〉
*Ana* judicious (see WISE): *judicial: fastidious, finicky, particular, *nice, fussy, squeamish: discriminating, discerning, penetrating (see corresponding nouns at DISCERNMENT): understanding, comprehending, appreciating (see UNDERSTAND)
*Ant* uncritical —*Con* *superficial, shallow, cursory
2 crucial, *acute
*Ana* decisive, determinative, *conclusive: momentous, consequential, weighty, significant, important (see corresponding nouns at IMPORTANCE)

criticism, critique, review, blurb, puff are comparable when meaning a discourse (as an essay or report) presenting one's conclusions after examining a work of art and especially of literature. None of these terms has a clearly established and narrowly delimited meaning, but, in general, each can be distinguished from the others with reference to its leading implications and its place in usage. Criticism is of all these terms the most nearly neutral and the least capable of carrying derogatory connotations. The proper aim and the content of a criticism have never been definitely fixed and are still subjects of controversy, but the term usually implies an author who is expected to have expert knowledge in his field, a clear definition of his standards of judgment, and an intent to evaluate the work under consideration 〈read every *criticism* of a new play the day following its first performance〉 *Criticism* is more often applied to the art, craft, or collective writings of such writers or speakers than to the individual article 〈this feeling, that contemporary judgments are apt to turn out a little ludicrous . . . has converted much *criticism* of late from judgment pronounced into impression recorded—*Galsworthy*〉 〈I go on the assumption that a review is simply a short piece of *criticism,* and that it should be as good criticism as its writer can make it—*Matthiessen*〉 Because of this tendency to restrict the use of *criticism* to its general sense, critique is sometimes preferred as a designation of a critical essay, especially of one dealing with a literary work; but currently it is often avoided as an affectation 〈Jeffrey's *critiques* in the *Edinburgh Review*〉 Review is now the common designation of a more or less informal critical essay dealing particularly with new or recent books and plays. The term is frequently preferred by newspaper and magazine critics as a more modest designation of their articles than *criticism* or *critique* and as permitting less profound or exhaustive treatment or as requiring only a personal rather than a final judgment of the merits and faults of the work. *Review* gener-

ally suggests literary criticism of a less pretentious kind, giving in general a summary of a book's contents and the impressions it produces on the reviewer 〈the Sunday editions of many newspapers have a supplement devoted to book *reviews*〉 Blurb is applied chiefly to a publisher's description of a work printed usually on the jacket of a book for the purposes of advertisement 〈as a term of reprobation for fulsomeness on the "jackets," or dust-cloaks, of new books, *blurb* is a peach of the first order —*Montague*〉 Puff, a word once common for any unduly flattering account (as of a book or play), in current use applies especially to a review that seems obviously animated by a desire to promote the sale of a book or the success of a play regardless of its real merits or to one that is markedly uncritical in its flattering comments 〈*puffs* . . . with which booksellers sometimes embroider their catalogs—*John Carter*〉

criticize, reprehend, blame, censure, reprobate, condemn, denounce are comparable when they mean to find fault with someone or something openly, often publicly, and with varying degrees of severity. Criticize in its basic sense does not carry faultfinding as its invariable or even major implication; rather it suggests a discernment of the merits and faults of a person or thing 〈know well each ancient's [classic poet's] proper character; his fable, subject, scope in ev'ry page; religion, country, genius of his age: without all these at once before your eyes, cavil you may, but never *criticize*—*Pope*〉 In ordinary use, however, the word does commonly imply an unfavorable judgment or a pointing out of faults and is probably the term most frequently used to express this idea 〈*criticize* a play severely〉 〈averse to being *criticized*〉 〈avoid *criticizing* a person's errors in speech〉 〈it is foolish . . . to *criticize* an author for what he has failed to achieve —*Huxley*〉 〈we are trying to get away from the word "management" because it has been lambasted, ridiculed, *criticized,* and blasted—*Personnel Jour.*〉 Reprehend in present-day English takes a person as an object far less often than a thing, a quality, or an action. In such use it not only explicitly suggests the approach of a critic and his disapproval but implies a more or less severe rebuke 〈*reprehend* not the imperfection of others— *Washington*〉 〈the thing to be *reprehended* is the confusing misuse of the word "verse"—*Grandgent*〉 Blame fundamentally implies speaking in dispraise of a person or thing rather than in his or its favor; in general it also suggests the mental approach of a critic or detector of faults 〈some judge of authors' names, not works, and then nor praise nor *blame* the writings, but the men—*Pope*〉 〈Heine . . . cared . . . whether people praised his verses or *blamed* them—*Arnold*〉 〈Aristotle, while *blaming* the man who is unduly passionate, *blames* equally the man who is insensitive—*Dickinson*〉 Blame sometimes loses much of its opposition to *praise* and then may strongly convey an imputation or accusation of wrongdoing 〈one cannot *blame* starving children who steal food〉 or of guilt 〈there is no one to *blame* but yourself〉 Again *blame* may connote ultimate responsibility rather than actual guiltiness and then can take a thing as well as a person for its object 〈the German family, whose patriarchical authoritarianism has been *blamed* . . . for militarism and despotism—*Padover*〉 〈the drug-fiend will get drugs somewhere: if he finds his poppy and mandragora in poetry, you must *blame* his habit, not the poet—*Day Lewis*〉 Since *blame* no longer invariably implies the simple reverse of commendation, censure is usually preferred to *blame* as the antonym of *praise.* This word carries a stronger suggestion of authority or competence in the critic or judge than does

A colon (:) separates groups of words discriminated. An asterisk (*) indicates place of treatment of each group.

*blame,* as well as a clearer connotation of reprehension or, sometimes, of a reprimand ⟨the judge *censured* the jury for their failure to render a verdict on the evidence⟩ ⟨the official was not dismissed until after he had more than once been severely *censured* for his mistakes of judgment⟩ ⟨I lose my patience, and I own it too, when works are *censured,* not as bad but new—*Pope*⟩ ⟨it is not one writer's business to *censure* others. A writer should expound other writers or let them alone—*F. M. Ford*⟩ **Reprobate** is often used as though it were a close synonym of *reproach* or *rebuke* ⟨"I put it to you, miss," she continued, as if mildly *reprobating* some want of principle on Lydia's part—*Shaw*⟩ Distinctively, however, it may imply not only strong disapproval and, usually, vigorous censure but also a rejection or a refusal to countenance ⟨he *reprobated* what he termed the heresies of his nephew—*Irving*⟩ ⟨that wanton eye so *reprobated* by the founder of our faith—*L. P. Smith*⟩ **Condemn** carries even stronger judicial connotations than *censure,* for it implies a final decision or a definitive judgment; it commonly also suggests an untempered judgment which is wholly unfavorable and merciless ⟨*condemn* the fault, and not the actor of it? Why, every fault's *condemned* ere it be done—*Shak.*⟩ ⟨the freedom with which Dr. Johnson *condemns* whatever he disapproves, is astonishing—*Burney*⟩ ⟨no conceivable human action which custom has not at one time justified and at another *condemned*—*Krutch*⟩ **Denounce** adds to *condemn* the implication of public declaration or proclamation ⟨in all ages, priests and monks have *denounced* the growing vices of society—*Henry Adams*⟩ ⟨nothing . . . makes one so popular as to be the moral denouncer of what everybody else *denounces*—*Brooks*⟩
*Ana* inspect, examine, *scrutinize, scan: *judge, adjudge: appraise, evaluate, assess (see ESTIMATE)

**critique** *criticism, review, blurb, puff
**crochet** *vb* knit, *weave, plait, braid, tat
**crony** comrade, companion, *associate
*Ana* intimate, *friend, confidant
**crook** *vb* *flex, bow, buckle
*Ana* *curve, bend, twist: contort, *deform
**crooked, devious, oblique** mean not straight or straightforward. **Crooked** may imply the presence of material curves, turns, or bends ⟨a *crooked* back⟩ ⟨a *crooked* road⟩ ⟨the *crooked* trunk of a tree⟩ In its frequent extended use it applies especially to practices (as fraud, cheating, or graft) involving marked departures from rectitude ⟨*crooked* dealings⟩ ⟨a *crooked* politician⟩ ⟨*crooked* policies⟩ ⟨they are a perverse and *crooked* generation—*Deut* 32:5⟩ **Devious** implies departure from a direct, appointed, regular, or fixed course and hence suggests wandering or errancy and, often, circuitousness ⟨we sought with relief the empty roads of the fens, and, by *devious* routes, wound our way between golden buttercups and brown cattle—*Lucas*⟩ ⟨he went by *devious* ways, a little proud of himself for knowing the shortcuts, through a building used as a thoroughfare from one street to another, through what had once been the churchyard of an ancient church—*Archibald Marshall*⟩ The term as applied to persons and their acts or practices usually implies unreliability and often trickiness or shiftiness ⟨the *devious* policies of the administration⟩ ⟨he had been a *devious* rascal—*Bennett*⟩ ⟨the marks of the thoroughbred were simply not there. The man was blatant, crude, overly confidential, *devious*—*Mencken*⟩ **Oblique** implies a departure from the perpendicular or horizontal direction, or a slanting course ⟨an *oblique* tower⟩ ⟨an *oblique* sunbeam⟩ and in extended use suggests indirection or lack of perfect straightfor-

wardness ⟨an *oblique* glance⟩ ⟨all censure of a man's self is *oblique* praise—*Johnson*⟩ ⟨their rebellion was an act of *oblique* homage—*Collet*⟩ ⟨people . . . who think that . . . the Japanese people are maddeningly *oblique* —*Faubion Bowers*⟩
*Ana* *awry, askew: twisted, bended *or* bent (see corresponding verbs at CURVE): distorted, contorted, deformed, warped (see DEFORM): tortuous, *winding: corrupt, nefarious, iniquitous, *vicious: stealthy, furtive, underhand (see SECRET)
*Ant* straight —*Con* *straightforward, aboveboard, forthright: *upright, honest, scrupulous, conscientious, honorable, just
**crop** *vb* *shear, poll, clip, trim, prune, lop, snip
*Ana* *cut, chop, hew, slash: *detach, disengage
**cross** *n* *trial, tribulation, affliction, visitation
**cross** *adj* cranky, testy, touchy, choleric, splenetic, *irascible
*Ana* captious, carping, caviling, faultfinding (see CRITICAL): *irritable, fractious, peevish, petulant, snappish, waspish, querulous
**crosswise, crossways** *across, athwart
**crotchet** *caprice, freak, fancy, whim, whimsy, conceit, vagary
**crow** *vb* *boast, brag, vaunt, gasconade
**crowd** *vb* 1 *press, bear, bear down, squeeze, jam
*Ana* *push, shove, thrust, propel: *force, compel, constrain
2 *pack, cram, stuff, ram, tamp
*Ana* compress (see CONTRACT): *compact, consolidate, concentrate
**crowd** *n* **Crowd, throng, press, crush, mob, rout, horde** are comparable when they mean a more or less closely assembled multitude usually of persons. **Crowd** basically implies a close gathering and pressing together ⟨the *crowd* came pouring out with a vehemence that nearly took him off his legs—*Dickens*⟩ It often implies a merging of the individuality of the units into that of the mass ⟨study the psychology of *crowds*⟩ ⟨no one in European art has rivalled Keion in the mastery of *crowds* of men each individually alive yet swept along by a common animating impulse, whether the raging passion of the victors or the panic of the routed—*Binyon*⟩ ⟨all our ideas are *crowd* ideas—*Ferril*⟩ **Throng** varies so little in meaning from *crowd* that the two words are often used interchangeably without loss. *Throng* sometimes carries the stronger implication of movement and of pushing and the weaker implication of density ⟨*throngs* circulating through the streets⟩ ⟨so they went northward . . . past droves and droves of camels, armies of camp followers, and legions of laden mules, the *throng* thickening day by day—*Kipling*⟩ ⟨sailors hung from yards and bowsprits to shout the names of vessels to the bewildered, harried *throng*—*Kenneth Roberts*⟩ **Press** differs from *throng* in being more often applied to a concentrated mass in which movement is difficult because of the numbers, but otherwise it also suggests pushing or pressing forward ⟨perched on the folded-down top of a convertible, to roll down the boardwalk with a *press* of people following her car—*Pete Martin*⟩ **Crush** carries a stronger implication than either *crowd* or *throng* of compactness of the group, of offering difficulty to one who wishes to make his way through it, or of causing discomfort to one who is part of it ⟨the *crush* was terrific for that time of day . . . for the street was blocked—*Woolf*⟩ ⟨a *crush* of dancing couples packed the floor —*Basso*⟩ **Mob** strictly applies to a crowd or throng bent on the accomplishment of riotous or destructive acts ⟨the citizens were terrorized for weeks by *mobs*⟩

*Ana* analogous words     *Ant* antonyms     *Con* contrasted words     See also explanatory notes facing page 1

⟨a *mob* . . . which pulled down all our prisons—*Burke*⟩ Especially in the United States and in Australia *mob* may be employed as an intensive of *crowd,* sometimes implying more disorganization ⟨it is the tendency of a large crowd to become a *mob*⟩ but at other times denoting merely an extremely large crowd ⟨you could scarcely call it a crowd; it was a *mob*⟩ In theatrical use *mob* applies to any large and manifestly agitated crowd of persons that has to be directed as a unit to achieve the proper or the intended effects. **Rout** applies to an especially disorderly or tumultuous mob ⟨a hireling *rout* scraped together from the dregs of the people—*Milton*⟩ ⟨the busy *rout* of the street could be seen. He loved the changing panorama of the street—*Dreiser*⟩ **Horde** usually applies to an assemblage or to a multitude massed together. It is sometimes preferred to *crowd, throng, mob,* or *rout* when a contemptuous term is desired, especially one that suggests the rude, rough, or savage character of the individuals who constitute the multitude or mass ⟨*hordes* of small boys roving through the streets⟩ ⟨the *horde* of excursionists took possession of the beach⟩ ⟨*hordes* of sturdy rogues and vagrants—*Fussell*⟩ *Ana* *multitude, army, host, legion

**crucial** critical, *acute
*Ana* threatening, menacing (see THREATEN): trying, afflicting, torturing *or* torturous (see corresponding verbs at AFFLICT)

**crude** *rude, rough, uncouth, raw, callow, green
*Ana* primitive, primeval (see PRIMARY): *immature, unmatured: *coarse, vulgar, gross
*Ant* consummate, finished —*Con* cultivated, refined, cultured (see corresponding nouns at CULTURE): *mature, mellow, adult: matured, developed, ripened (see MATURE *vb*)

**cruel** inhuman, fell, *fierce, truculent, ferocious, barbarous, savage
*Ana* atrocious, *outrageous, monstrous, heinous: *brutal, bestial: merciless, relentless, implacable, *grim
*Ant* pitiful —*Con* compassionate, *tender, sympathetic: merciful, clement, *forbearing, lenient: humane (see CHARITABLE)

**cruise** *n* voyage, tour, trip, *journey, jaunt, excursion, expedition, pilgrimage

**crumble** disintegrate, decompose, *decay, rot, putrefy, spoil

**crush** *vb* **1** Crush, mash, smash, bruise, squash, macerate are comparable when they mean to reduce or be reduced to a pulpy or broken mass. **Crush** implies a compressing between two hard or resistant surfaces that succeeds, usually, in destroying the shape and integrity of the mass; the result depends on the texture of what is crushed, whether it is permanently deformed and destroyed, broken into fragments, or capable of springing back into shape ⟨*crushed* her fingers between the rollers of a mangle⟩ ⟨[the ostrich] leaveth her eggs in the earth . . . and forgetteth that the foot may *crush* them—*Job* 39:14-15⟩ ⟨many persons were *crushed* to death in the panic⟩ ⟨this hat *crushes* easily⟩ ⟨the *crushed* leaves of mint have a strong smell⟩ **Mash** implies the beating or pounding of something, often deliberately, to a soft pulp; in this sense *mash* may come close to *crush* in meaning ⟨this hand shall . . . *mash* all his bones—*Pope*⟩ but it is more often used in reference to the preparation of certain vegetables and fruits in the kitchen by similar means ⟨*mash* cooked potatoes⟩ ⟨*mash* strawberries for jam⟩ **Smash** carries a stronger implication of violence in implying a force that shatters or batters; it also often suggests the uselessness for all purposes of what is smashed ⟨*smash* a bottle to bits⟩ ⟨the upshot of which, was, to

smash this witness like a crockery vessel, and shiver his part of the case to useless lumber—*Dickens*⟩ ⟨his hair was black and close-cut; his skin indurated; and the bridge of his nose *smashed* level with his face—*Shaw*⟩ **Bruise,** though more commonly used in reference to an injury of the flesh, also carries a sense related to that of *crush, smash,* or *mash* in which it implies the pressing or beating of something so as to break it down with the effect of setting the juices running or of softening the fibers ⟨nor *bruise* her flowerets with the armed hooves of hostile paces—*Shak.*⟩ ⟨some scatt'ring pot-herbs . . . *bruised* with vervain—*Dryden*⟩ **Squash** differs from the preceding words chiefly in its applicability to objects that are very soft (as through overripeness or immaturity) or that require little effort to crush by pressure ⟨every pear that fell from the tree was *squashed*⟩ ⟨he *squashed* under his foot every beetle he could find⟩ **Macerate** is used chiefly in reference to a process of steeping something in a liquid so as to soften or detach its fibers or to wear away its soft parts; the softening or detachment of fibers is chiefly emphasized, and *macerate* often refers to a step in an industrial process or to a part of a digestive process ⟨*macerate* rags as the first step in papermaking⟩ ⟨corn is *macerated* in the gizzard of a fowl⟩ The term may, however, imply a wearing away of the soft part from whatever cause; it particularly suggests a wasting away of the body (as through fasting or worry) ⟨the fierce unrest, the deathless flame, that slowly *macerates* my frame—*Martin*⟩
*Ana* *press, squeeze, crowd, jam: batter, mangle, *maim: *beat, pound

**2** Crush, quell, extinguish, suppress, quench, quash are comparable when they mean to bring to an end by destroying or defeating. **Crush** in this sense retains from its basic meaning the implication of being destroyed or injured severely by pressure from without, but it differs in being more often applied to immaterial than to material things and in implying a force at work that makes for the destruction of effective opposition or operation especially by preventing resistance or by depriving of the freedom necessary for expansion or thriving ⟨truth, *crushed* to earth, shall rise again—*Bryant*⟩ ⟨the free play of passion and thought, the graces and arts of life . . . were *crushed* out of existence under this stern and rigid rule —*Dickinson*⟩ ⟨the mere volume of work was enough to *crush* the most diligent of rulers—*Buchan*⟩ **Quell** means to overwhelm completely and reduce wholly to submission, to inactivity, or to passivity; the term may be used in respect to people or animals or to (usually immaterial) things; thus, one may *quell* a riot or the rioters; *quell* a mutiny or the mutineers ⟨the nation obeyed the call, rallied round the sovereign, and enabled him to *quell* the disaffected minority—*Macaulay*⟩ ⟨had some difficulty in *quelling* the tumult that arose when the bell was answered—*Shaw*⟩ **Extinguish** (see also ABOLISH) implies an end as sudden or as complete as the blowing out of a candle or the putting out of a fire with water ⟨the sudden and soon *extinguished* genius of Marlowe —*T. S. Eliot*⟩ ⟨lives that were to be *extinguished* in Hitler's gas chambers—*Deutscher*⟩ **Suppress** differs from *crush* especially in implying conscious action, in more strongly suggesting a power or force that openly quells or extinguishes, and in more often taking as its object a definite objective person or thing ⟨*suppress* a political organization⟩ ⟨one purpose of the purchase was to *suppress* competition between the two roads —*Justice Holmes*⟩ ⟨deeply as the Cistercians disliked and distrusted Abelard, they did not violently *suppress* him—*Henry Adams*⟩ **Quench,** which is close to *extinguish*

A colon (:) separates groups of words discriminated. An asterisk (*) indicates place of treatment of each group.

in its basic meaning, differs from it in extended use in stressing a satisfying, dampening, cooling, or decreasing (as of ardor) as the cause of extinction. Although it is used specifically of thirst, it is also frequently referred to emotions, sensations, and desires ⟨many waters cannot *quench* love—*Song of Solomon* 8:7⟩ ⟨to be damned by the praise that *quenches* all desire to read the book—*T. S. Eliot*⟩ ⟨he then turns to those who do not belong to the leisure class, and *quenches* their aspirations after wisdom—*Crothers*⟩ Quash basically implies a shaking or dashing that destroys; in the present sense (see also ANNUL) it implies a sudden and summary extinction ⟨*quash* a rebellion⟩ ⟨he foresaw that the dreadful woman . . . would *quash* his last chance of life—*Dickens*⟩ ⟨the lady, together with her family, was dispatched to the safe distance of the Far East. . . . Thus was *quashed* an idyll—*S. H. Adams*⟩
*Ana* *destroy, demolish: *ruin, wreck: annihilate, *abolish: obliterate, blot out, efface (see ERASE)

**crush** *n* press, throng, *crowd, horde, mob, rout
*Ana* *multitude, army, legion, host

**crusty** brusque, gruff, blunt, curt, *bluff
*Ana* snappish, waspish, *irritable: choleric, splenetic, cranky, testy, *irascible: crabbed, surly, saturnine, dour (see SULLEN)

**cry** *vb* Cry, weep, wail, keen, whimper, blubber mean to show one's grief, pain, or distress by tears and utterances, usually inarticulate utterances. *Cry* and *weep* (the first the homelier, the second the more formal term) are frequently interchanged. Cry is more apt to stress the audible lamentation, weep, the shedding of tears ⟨if you hear a child *cry* in the night, you must call to the nurse—*Shak.*⟩ ⟨*weep* not, sweet queen; for trickling tears are vain—*Shak.*⟩ ⟨*wept* unseen, unheeded *cried*—*Millay*⟩ Wail usually implies expressing grief without restraint, in mournful and often long-drawn-out cries, moans, and lamentations ⟨"Where is my father, and my mother, nurse?" "Weeping and *wailing* over Tybalt's corpse"—*Shak.*⟩ ⟨hear him, o'erwhelmed with sorrow, yet rejoice; no womanish or *wailing* grief has part—*Cowper*⟩ ⟨soon as she . . . saw the lifeblood flow . . . *wailing* loud she clasped him—*Shelley*⟩ Keen implies the wailing lamentations or dirges of a professional mourner ⟨*keen* [means] hideous, dismal wailing or howling practiced in Ireland among the humbler classes in token of grief, at funerals, and on hearing news of a death or other calamity—*Wyld*⟩ ⟨*keened* our sorrow—*Punch*⟩ ⟨*keened* like a squaw bereft—*M. H. Moody*⟩ Whimper implies low, whining, broken cries (as made by a baby or puppy) ⟨*whimpering* in fright⟩ ⟨had seen the old woman *whimper* like a whipped dog —*F. M. Ford*⟩ Blubber implies scalding, disfiguring tears and noisy, broken utterances (as of a child who cannot have his way) ⟨he always *blubbers* until those who oppose him give in to him⟩ ⟨tears came easy to him; he could *blubber* like a child over a slight or a disappointment—*S. H. Adams*⟩
*Ana* lament, bewail, bemoan, *deplore: sob, moan, *sigh, groan

**cry** *n* vogue, rage, *fashion, style, mode, fad, craze, dernier cri

**crying** *adj* *pressing, urgent, imperative, importunate, insistent, exigent, instant
*Ana* outstanding, conspicuous (see NOTICEABLE): compelling, constraining (see FORCE *vb*)

**cryptic** enigmatic, *obscure, dark, vague, ambiguous, equivocal
*Ana* puzzling, perplexing, mystifying (see PUZZLE *vb*): occult, esoteric, *recondite: *mysterious, arcane

**cuddle** fondle, dandle, pet, cosset, *caress

**cuff** *vb* *strike, hit, smite, punch, slug, slog, swat, clout, slap, box

**cull** *vb* pick, single, *choose, select, elect, opt, prefer

**culmination** peak, climax, apex, acme, *summit, pinnacle, meridian, zenith, apogee

**culpability** *blame, guilt, fault
*Ana* responsibility, accountability (see corresponding adjectives at RESPONSIBLE)

**culpable** guilty, *blameworthy
*Ana* *responsible, accountable, answerable, amenable, liable

**culprit** *criminal, felon, convict, malefactor, delinquent
*Ana* *prisoner: offender, sinner (see corresponding nouns at OFFENSE): scoundrel, blackguard, miscreant, rogue, rascal (see VILLAIN)

**cult** sect, denomination, *religion, communion, faith, creed, persuasion, church

**cultivar** *variety, subspecies, race, breed, strain, clone, stock

**cultivate** nurture, *nurse, foster, cherish
*Ana* develop, *mature, ripen: raise, rear (see LIFT): educate, train, instruct, *teach: *improve, better, ameliorate
*Con* *neglect, ignore, disregard, slight

**cultivation** breeding, *culture, refinement

**culture** *n* 1 Culture, cultivation, breeding, refinement are comparable when they denote a quality of a person or group of persons which reflects his or their possession of excellent taste, manners, and social adjustment. Culture implies a high degree of enlightenment that has been acquired by familiarity with what is best in the civilized life of many ages and lands; in addition, it usually suggests fineness of taste, delicacy of perception, and gracious urbanity of manners ⟨a man of *culture*⟩ ⟨*culture*, the acquainting ourselves with the best that has been known and said in the world—*Arnold*⟩ Cultivation is often preferred to *culture* because it suggests the continuous pursuit of culture and the self-discipline which accompanies such pursuit, rather than its achievement, and is therefore more modest and often more appropriate ⟨he has found many persons of *cultivation* in the city to which he has recently moved⟩ ⟨gratitude is a fruit of great *cultivation*; you do not find it among gross people—*Johnson*⟩ ⟨a work of prose fiction written by one who not only possesses obvious *cultivation* but is also a distinguished practicing poet—*Steegmuller*⟩ Breeding implies such training or lifelong experience in courtesy and the amenities of gracious living that one is never at a loss how to act or what to say; moreover the word often suggests poise, tact, an ability to come forward or to retire at will or at need, and other social qualities which mark one out even among one's social equals ⟨I am a gentleman of blood and *breeding*—*Shak.*⟩ ⟨as men of *breeding*, sometimes men of wit, t'avoid great errors, must the less commit—*Pope*⟩ ⟨politely learned, and of a gentle race, good *breeding* and good sense gave all a grace—*Cowper*⟩ Refinement implies not only the absence (often the eradication) of all that is gross, vulgar, or merely common but also the presence of fineness of feeling, delicacy of perception or understanding, and fastidiousness ⟨he had true *refinement;* he couldn't help thinking of others, whatever he did—*Galsworthy*⟩
2 *civilization

**cumber** *burden, encumber, weigh, weight, load, lade, tax, charge, saddle
*Ana* see those at ENCUMBER

**cumbersome, cumbrous** ponderous, *heavy, weighty, hefty
*Ana* burdensome, *onerous: *awkward, clumsy: *irksome, wearisome, tiresome

*Ana* analogous words    *Ant* antonyms    *Con* contrasted words    See also explanatory notes facing page 1

*Con* compact, *\*close: \*easy, light, facile

**cumulative, accumulative, additive, summative** are comparable when meaning increasing or produced by the addition of like or assimilable things. Something is **cumulative** which is constantly increasing or is capable of constant increase (as in size, amount, power, or severity) by successive additions, successive accretions, or successive repetitions; thus, the *cumulative* effect of a drug may be harmful even though the immediate effect of each dose has, apparently, been beneficial; terror is *cumulative* because one fear tends to inspire another ⟨groupings of fact and argument and illustration so as to produce a *cumulative* and mass effect—*Cardozo*⟩ Something is **accumulative** which is constantly increasing in amount or bulk through successive additions or which has reached its sum total or magnitude through many such additions ⟨the art of nations is to be *accumulative* . . . the work of living men not superseding, but building itself upon the work of the past—*Ruskin*⟩ ⟨such persons cannot understand the force of *accumulative* proof—*Whately*⟩ *Cumulative* is now used more often than *accumulative* especially where increasing severity or enhancement in influence or power are to be suggested. Something is **additive** which is of such a nature that it is capable either of assimilation to or incorporation in something else or of growth by additions. An *additive* detail, element, or factor is one that has such affinity for another thing that it becomes a constituent part of that thing; thus, red, green, and blue-violet are the *additive* colors and are used in color photography because they blend to form any color ⟨this new hypothesis assigns to the atom properties which are in no way inconsistent with the inverse-square attraction of its electrons and protons; rather they are *additive* to it—*Jeans*⟩ ⟨this pluralistic view, of a world of *additive* constitution, is one that pragmatism is unable to rule out from serious consideration—*James*⟩ Something is **summative** which is capable of association or combination with other things so as to produce such a sum total as an additive whole or a cumulative effect ⟨the *summative* action of a drug and its adjuvant⟩ ⟨if the student could not add up his achievements, if there was nothing *summative* in his education—*Educational Review*⟩

*Ana* accumulated, amassed (see ACCUMULATE): multiplying, increasing, augmenting (see INCREASE)

*Con* dissipated, dispersed, scattered (see SCATTER)

**cunning** *adj* **1** ingenious, *\*clever, adroit

*Ana* skillful, skilled, adept, *\*proficient, expert, masterly

**2** crafty, tricky, artful, *\*sly, foxy, insidious, wily, guileful

*Ana* devious, oblique, *\*crooked: *\*sharp, acute, keen: *\*shrewd, astute: knowing, smart (see INTELLIGENT)

*Ant* ingenuous —*Con* artless, unsophisticated, naïve (see NATURAL)

**cunning** *n* **1** skill, *\*art, craft, artifice

*Ana* dexterousness *or* dexterity, adroitness, deftness (see corresponding adjectives at DEXTEROUS): proficiency, adeptness, expertness (see corresponding adjectives at PROFICIENT): ingeniousness *or* ingenuity, cleverness (see corresponding adjectives at CLEVER)

**2** guile, *\*deceit, duplicity, dissimulation

*Ana* craftiness, insidiousness, wiliness, guilefulness, trickiness *or* trickery, artfulness, slyness (see corresponding adjectives at SLY): stratagem, ruse, maneuver, feint, *\*trick, wile, gambit, ploy

*Ant* ingenuousness

**cupidity, greed, rapacity, avarice** are comparable when meaning intense desire for wealth or possessions. **Cupidity** stresses the intensity and compelling nature of the desire and often suggests covetousness as well ⟨the sight of so much wealth aroused his *cupidity*⟩ ⟨the vast *cupidity* of

business in preempting the virgin resources of California—*Parrington*⟩ **Greed,** more than *cupidity,* implies a controlling passion; it suggests not strong but inordinate desire, and it commonly connotes meanness as well as covetousness ⟨a low, incessant, gnawing *greed* . . . for power, for money, for destruction—*White*⟩ **Rapacity** implies both cupidity and actual seizing or snatching not only of what one especially desires but of anything that will satisfy one's greed for money or property; it often suggests extortion, plunder, or oppressive exactions ⟨the *rapacity* of the conquerors knew no bounds⟩ ⟨the woman's greed and *rapacity* . . . disgusted me—*Thackeray*⟩ ⟨the *rapacity* of the warlords—*Peffer*⟩ **Avarice,** although it involves the idea of cupidity and often carries a strong suggestion of rapacity, stresses that of miserliness and implies both an unwillingness to let go whatever wealth or property one has acquired and an insatiable greed for more ⟨such a stanchless *avarice* that, were I king, I should cut off the nobles for their lands, desire his jewels and this other's house: and my more-having would be as a sauce to make me hunger more—*Shak.*⟩ ⟨they scrimped and stinted and starved themselves . . . out of *avarice* and the will-to-power—*Mumford*⟩

*Ana* covetousness, avariciousness, greediness, acquisitiveness (see corresponding adjectives at COVETOUS): avidity, eagerness (see corresponding adjectives at EAGER): lust, *\*desire

**curative, sanative, restorative, remedial, corrective** are comparable when they mean returning or tending to return to a state of normalcy or health. **Curative** is applicable to whatever effects or, sometimes, seeks or tends to effect a complete recovery especially from disease of body or of mind ⟨a *curative* drug⟩ ⟨*curative* regimens⟩ ⟨most medicines are alleviative in their action and not definitely *curative*. Rather, they overcome the symptoms of disease and give the patient a chance to recover—*Morrison*⟩ **Sanative** is a general term applicable to whatever is conducive either to the restoration of or the maintenance of health, whether of body and mind or of spirit or morals; the term often comes close to *salutary* in meaning ⟨the *sanative* virtue of action . . . to dispel doubt and despair—*Masson*⟩ **Restorative** is occasionally applicable to what restores to health but more often to what revives someone unconscious or renews or refreshes someone or something overstrained or exhausted ⟨the *restorative* effect of rain on parched fields⟩ ⟨take a *restorative* drink before dinner⟩ ⟨that voyage proved entirely beneficial and *restorative*—*Ellis*⟩ **Remedial** is much the broadest term of this group and like the related noun (see REMEDY *n*) and verb (see CURE *vb*) is applicable not only to whatever alleviates or cures disease or injury of body or mind but to whatever tends to relieve or correct a faulty or evil condition (as of the community, the law, or the body politic) ⟨while . . . the teacher's greatest contribution lies in the prevention of maladjustment, he must also assume a major responsibility in *remedial* work with the student who has become poorly adjusted—*C. C. Dunsmoor & L. M. Miller*⟩ ⟨whatever action the court takes towards a convicted offender . . . is in fact a punishment; and it does not cease to be so because it may also be used as a form of *remedial* treatment, adapted to the personality of the offender and directed to his social rehabilitation—*Fox*⟩ ⟨with poverty and humility she overcame the world, and cast down the devil with prayer and *remedial* tears—*H. O. Taylor*⟩ ⟨the communities affected entered upon a patient course of *remedial* action and successfully labored to prevent a recurrence of these disorders—*Handlin*⟩ **Corrective** (compare CORRECTIVE *n*) in many of its uses comes close to *remedial,* but, unlike the latter, it cannot ordinarily re-

---

A colon (:) separates groups of words discriminated. An asterisk (*) indicates place of treatment of each group.

place *curative;* specifically it applies to what is designed to restore something to a norm or standard or bring it up (or down) to a desirable level from which it has deviated. In this relation the term is peculiarly applicable to material objects that supplement or compensate for a defective function or part, but it may be used interchangeably with *remedial* in most contexts, though the emphasis may be more on making good a defect or deficiency than (as in *remedial*) on relieving the distress it causes; thus, one would speak of *corrective* (rather than *remedial*) shoes for the relief of weak ankles, but one could say that among *remedial* (or *corrective*) measures for weak ankles are shoes with special lifts in the soles ⟨constantly called upon their *corrective* lenses to decipher documents—*Ace*⟩ ⟨such *corrective* declines need not, necessarily, represent the end of this greatest of all bull markets—*Van Loan*⟩ ⟨there is today special need for the balancing and *corrective* sanity of not taking ourselves and our time over-seriously—*Alain Locke*⟩
  *Ana* healing, curing, remedying (see CURE *vb*)

**curb** *vb* check, bridle, \*restrain, inhibit
  *Ana* repress, \*suppress: shackle, manacle, fetter, \*hamper, hog-tie: thwart, foil, balk, \*frustrate
  *Ant* spur  —*Con* \*indulge, pamper, humor

**curdle** *vb* \*coagulate, congeal, set, clot, jelly, jell

**cure** *n* \*remedy, medicine, medicament, medication, specific, physic

**cure** *vb* Cure, heal, remedy mean to rectify an unhealthy or undesirable condition especially by some specific treatment (as medication). **Cure** and **heal** may apply interchangeably to both wounds and diseases ⟨pierced to the soul with slander's venomed spear, the which no balm can *cure*—*Shak.*⟩ ⟨physician, *heal* thyself—*Lk* 4:23⟩ Often, however, they tend to be differentiated in such applications, *cure* more frequently implying restoration to health after disease, *heal* implying restoration to soundness of an affected part after a wound or lesion ⟨the treatment failed to *cure* his headache⟩ ⟨the salve will *heal* slight burns⟩ ⟨his fever . . . might *cure* him of his tendency to epilepsy—*Byron*⟩ ⟨I . . . must not break my back to *heal* his finger—*Shak.*⟩ In extended use a similar distinction often holds, with *cure* applicable when a condition (as a state of mind or a habit of behavior) is under discussion and *heal* when a specific incident or event is involved; thus, one would seek to *cure* (not *heal*) mistrust but to *heal* (rather than *cure*) a breach between friends ⟨if you can compass it, do *cure* the younger girls of running after the officers—*Austen*⟩ ⟨we are denied the one thing that might *heal* us . . . that might bring balm to the bruised heart, and peace to the soul in pain—*Wilde*⟩ **Remedy** (see also REMEDY *n*) applies to the using of whatever will correct or relieve an abnormal condition (as of body or mind) whether affecting physical or mental health or causing mere local or occasional discomfort ⟨who . . . may likeliest *remedy* the stricken mind—*Southey*⟩ In extended use (see also CORRECT *vb* 1) *remedy* is often used in reference to evil conditions corrected, relieved, or counteracted by any means ⟨*remedy* an abuse⟩ ⟨*remedy* the breakdown of international prestige—*Ascoli*⟩

**curious** 1 Curious, inquisitive, prying, snoopy, nosy are comparable when meaning interested in finding out or in a search for facts that are not one's personal concern. **Curious** need not imply objectionable qualities such as intrusiveness or impertinence, but it suggests an eager desire to learn, especially to learn how or why things have happened or are happening ⟨children are naturally *curious* about almost everything⟩ ⟨*curious* onlookers were held back by the police⟩ ⟨she did not wish to seem *curious* about her neighbor's affairs⟩ ⟨a Latin poet whose reputa-

tion would deter any reader but the most *curious*—*T. S. Eliot*⟩ ⟨Edgar was a rationalist, who was *curious,* and had a sort of scientific interest in life—*D. H. Lawrence*⟩ **Inquisitive** implies habitual and impertinent curiosity and usually suggests the asking of many questions regarding something secret or unrevealed ⟨they grew *inquisitive* after my name and character—*Spectator*⟩ ⟨we had no lack of visitors among such an idle, *inquisitive* set as the Tahitians—*Melville*⟩ **Prying** adds to *curious* and *inquisitive* the implications of busy meddling and of officiousness ⟨the world might guess it; and I will not bare my soul to their shallow *prying* eyes—*Wilde*⟩ **Snoopy** and **nosy** are somewhat informal terms highly expressive of contempt. *Snoopy* adds to *prying* suggestions of slyness or sneaking ⟨a *snoopy* legal investigator⟩ ⟨everyone felt that she was *snoopy* and soon refused to welcome her as a visitor⟩ *Nosy* suggests the methods of a dog pursuing a scent and implies a desire to discover the ins and outs of every situation that arouses one's curiosity ⟨a *nosy,* disagreeable child⟩ ⟨doesn't want *nosy* state officials or city slickers prying into its manners and morals—*Fortnight*⟩
  *Ana* meddling, intermeddling, interfering, tampering (see MEDDLE): scrutinizing, inspecting, examining (see SCRUTINIZE): intrusive, meddlesome, \*impertinent
  *Ant* incurious: uninterested  —*Con* \*indifferent, aloof, detached, unconcerned: apathetic, stolid, \*impassive, phlegmatic
  **2** singular, \*strange, peculiar, unique, odd, queer, quaint, outlandish, eccentric, erratic

**curl** *vb* \*wind, coil, twist, twine, wreathe, entwine
  *Ana* \*curve, bend: \*flex, crook

**currency** cash, \*money, legal tender, specie, coin, coinage

**current** *adj* \*prevailing, prevalent, rife
  *Ana* general, \*universal, common: popular, ordinary, familiar, \*common: \*usual, customary
  *Ant* antique, antiquated: obsolete

**current** *n* stream, \*flow, flood, tide, flux

**curse** *n* Curse, imprecation, malediction, anathema are comparable when they denote a denunciation that conveys a wish or threat of evil. **Curse** (opposed to *blessing*) usually implies a call upon God or a supernatural power to visit punishment or disaster upon a person; in dignified use it commonly presupposes a profound sense of injury and a plea to a divine avenger for justice. No other word in this group suggests so strongly the certainty of the threatened evil ⟨the untented woundings of a father's *curse* pierce every sense about thee!—*Shak.*⟩ ⟨an orphan's *curse* would drag to hell a spirit from on high—*Coleridge*⟩ **Imprecation** also implies an invocation of evil or calamity, but it often suggests as its provocation wrath rather than a sense of injury and a desire for revenge rather than for justice as its aim ⟨with *imprecations* thus he filled the air, and angry Neptune heard the unrighteous prayer—*Pope*⟩ Both *curse* and *imprecation* are applied to profane swearing involving blasphemy, but, again, the latter is the weaker in its implications. **Malediction** (opposed to *benediction*) is applied chiefly to bitter reproaches or denunciations publicly proclaimed and bringing disgrace or ignominy to their object ⟨my name . . . to all posterity may stand defamed, with *malediction* mentioned—*Milton*⟩ ⟨Cleopatra has long ago passed beyond the libels with which her reputation was blackened by a terrified Rome—even the *maledictions* of great poets—*Buchan*⟩ ⟨a passage in one of the recently discovered Ras Shamra poems . . . pronounces a *malediction* . . . "may Horon break thy head"—*Mercer*⟩ **Anathema** basically denotes a solemn authoritative ecclesiastical ban or curse accompanied by excommunication ⟨the third letter to Nestorias . . . con-

tained the *anathemas—R. M. French*⟩ In more general use the term applies to a strong or violent denunciation by one in authority or in a position to judge of something as grossly wrong, as productive of evil, or as accursed ⟨the Pope . . . has condemned the slave trade—but no more heed is paid to his *anathema* than to the passing wind—*Gladstone*⟩ ⟨continued openly . . . to flaunt their beauties, in spite of the *anathemas* from the pulpits—*Wellman*⟩ or it may be used in a much weakened sense to mean no more than a vigorous denunciation ⟨no *anathema* pronounced by any psychologist against such words as "purpose" will exorcise this initiative as a distinctive and observable character of certain modes of conscious doing —*C. I. Lewis*⟩ ⟨[people] of self-respect who would like to teach our children . . . are afraid to hire themselves out to communities and states . . . where they may be under the continuous censorship of politicians, petty moralists, and those businessmen for whom the mere subscription to a liberal journal is a reason for *anathema—Ulich*⟩
*Ana* execration, objurgation (see corresponding verbs at EXECRATE): profanity, *blasphemy, swearing
*Ant* blessing

**curse** *vb* damn, anathematize, *execrate, objurgate
*Ana* condemn, denounce, reprobate (see CRITICIZE): blaspheme, swear (see corresponding nouns at BLASPHEMY)
*Ant* bless

**cursed** accursed, damnable, *execrable
*Ana, Ant, & Con* see those at ACCURSED

**cursing** profanity, swearing, *blasphemy
*Ana* *curse, imprecation, malediction, anathema: execration, objurgation (see corresponding verbs at EXECRATE)

**cursory** *superficial, shallow, uncritical
*Ana* hasty, speedy, quick, rapid, swift, *fast: *brief, short: casual, desultory, *random, haphazard
*Ant* painstaking —*Con* meticulous, *careful, scrupulous, punctilious

**curt** brusque, blunt, crusty, gruff, *bluff
*Ana* laconic, terse, summary, *concise: *brief, short: snappish, waspish, *irritable: peremptory, imperious (see MASTERFUL)
*Ant* voluble

**curtail** *shorten, abbreviate, abridge, retrench
*Ana* reduce, *decrease, lessen: *cut, slash
*Ant* protract, prolong —*Con* *extend, lengthen, elongate

**curve** *vb* **Curve, bend, twist** are comparable when they mean to swerve or cause to swerve or deviate from a straight line or a normal direction or course. **Curve** is the word of widest application, and it may describe any deviation or swerving from the straight or level that suggests an arc of a circle or an ellipse ⟨his lips were *curved* in a smile—*Kenneth Roberts*⟩ ⟨over the roof a few swallows were *curving—Glasgow*⟩ **Bend** is likely to refer to an angular turning or a curving at a certain point under a degree of force or pressure ⟨*bend* the steel strips as required⟩ ⟨*bend* the glass tube at the point indicated⟩ In extended use *bend* may imply some forcing or distortion of materials or of facts or some pressure on or persuasion of people ⟨was somewhat prone to *bend* logic to meet the demands of argument—*E. S. Bates*⟩ ⟨not all prescriptive speech aims purely and typically at *bending* the hearer's attitudes to those of the speaker—*Falk*⟩ **Twist** is likely to suggest a force having a spiraling effect throughout the object involved rather than an effect at one point, and it may imply, especially in extended use, a wrenching out of shape or distorting rather than a giving of a desired or desirable shape ⟨the light steel rods *twisted* together by

the explosion⟩ ⟨hands gnarled and *twisted* with age⟩ ⟨mend a break in a fence by *twisting* two wires together⟩ ⟨an unconquerable confidence . . . which understates, or *twists* into a wry joke, the fatal moment of war—*Times Lit. Sup.*⟩
*Ana* deflect, divert, *turn: *swerve, veer, deviate

**curve** *n* **Curve, arc, bow, arch** mean a line or something which follows a line that is neither straight nor angular but rounded. **Curve** is the general term and the most widely applicable. It may be used in reference to a line, edge, outline, turn, or formation that keeps changing its direction without interruption or angle ⟨the *curve* of a ship's side⟩ ⟨the deep *curve* of the back of a wing chair⟩ ⟨a serpentine *curve*⟩ ⟨the *curve* of the greyhound is not only the line of beauty, but a line which suggests motion—*Jefferies*⟩ **Arc** is used specifically to denote a part or section of the circumference of a circle; in more general use it is applied to things that have or assume a strongly curved form ⟨with eyebrows raised in a quizzical *arc*⟩ **Bow**, unlike the preceding words, has always designated concrete things that are curved, and draws its implications especially from its reference to the archer's bow with its long, gradually curving strip of wood that may be bent almost into a **U**. Hence many things which resemble an archer's bent bow are describable or designatable as a *bow* ⟨the *bows* of spectacles⟩ ⟨an ox*bow*⟩ ⟨*bow*legs⟩ ⟨the moon, like to a silver *bow*, new-bent in heaven—*Shak.*⟩ **Arch**, though once equivalent to *arc* in denotation, is now basically applied to a supporting structure built up of wedge-shaped pieces of stone or other substance in such a way that they form a semicircular curve with a keystone at the apex or two opposite curves with a joint at the apex and provide an opening underneath (as for a window, a door, or a passageway). Hence *arch* is applied to any similarly curved structure ⟨the *arch* of the eyebrow⟩ ⟨the *arch* of the foot⟩ ⟨an *arch* formed by meeting treetops⟩
*Ana* circuit, compass, *circumference

**curvet** *vb* *skip, bound, hop, lope, lollop, ricochet

**custom** *n* usage, habitude, *habit, practice, use, wont
*Ana* convention, *form, usage, convenance: rule, precept, canon, *law

**customary** *usual, wonted, accustomed, habitual
*Ana* *regular, normal, typical, natural: *prevailing, prevalent, current: familiar, ordinary, *common: general, *universal
*Ant* occasional —*Con* *infrequent, uncommon, rare, sporadic: *exceptional

**cut** *vb* **Cut, hew, chop, carve, slit, slash** mean to penetrate and divide something with a sharp-bladed tool or instrument (as a knife, ax, or sword). **Cut** is by far the most comprehensive term, for it is not only interchangeable with any other word in the group but also with any of a large number of verbs that suggest use of a specific instrument (as *knife, shear, reap,* or *mow*) or dividing in a certain way (as *mince* or *shred*) or an operation having a definite end (as *prune, lop,* or *amputate*). Often it requires an adverb to describe the process or purpose more clearly ⟨*cut* down a tree⟩ ⟨*cut* off dead branches⟩ ⟨*cut* up a carcass of beef⟩ ⟨*cut* out a paper doll⟩ Its extended uses are many: usually it implies a result (as separation or isolation) similar to one produced by cutting ⟨*cut* off a member of the family⟩ ⟨she is *cut* off from all her friends⟩ or one (as distress or pain) suggestive of a stabbing or hurting ⟨the remark *cut* her to the heart⟩ **Hew** is not only more restricted in its application than *cut* but it carries far more explicit implications. It usually suggests the use of a heavy tool (as an ax, a sword, or chisel) which calls for the expenditure of much effort in

---

A colon (:) separates groups of words discriminated. An asterisk (*) indicates place of treatment of each group.

the cutting or shaping of large, difficult, or resistent objects or material ⟨*hew* them to pieces, hack their bones asunder—*Shak.*⟩ ⟨a wall of *hewn* stones⟩ ⟨and now also the axe is laid unto the root of the trees: every tree . . . which bringeth not forth good fruit is *hewn* down, and cast into the fire—*Lk* 3:9⟩ ⟨there's a divinity that shapes our ends, rough*hew* them how we will—*Shak.*⟩ **Chop** implies a cleaving or dividing by a quick, heavy blow (as of an ax, a cleaver, or a hatchet) or, more often, a dividing into pieces by repeated blows of this character ⟨*chop* off branches of a tree⟩ ⟨*chop* the trunk of a tree into firewood⟩ ⟨*chop* meat into small pieces⟩ **Carve** has come to be restricted to two types of cutting. The first requires the use of special tools (as chisels and gouges) and has for its end the artistic shaping, fashioning, or adornment of a material (as stone, ivory, or wood) ⟨a sculptor *carves* a statue out of marble⟩ ⟨the back and legs of the chair were elaborately *carved*⟩ ⟨an exquisite ivory box *carved* with figures⟩ The second requires a sharp knife and has for its end the cutting up and especially the slicing of meat at table in pieces suitable for serving ⟨*carve* a roast of beef⟩ ⟨the head of the family *carves* the turkey⟩ **Slit** implies the making of a lengthwise cut; except that it suggests the use of a sharp clean-cutting instrument (as scissors, a scalpel, a sword, or a knife) it carries no clear connotations as to the extent of the cut in depth or in length ⟨the surgeon *slit* the abdominal wall in front of the appendix⟩ ⟨the long skirt was *slit* to the knee⟩ ⟨*slit* a sealed envelope⟩ **Slash** also implies a lengthwise cut but usually suggests a sweeping stroke (as with a sharp sword, knife, or machete) that inflicts a deep and long cut or wound: very frequently it connotes repeated cuts and often furious or rough-and-tumble fighting ⟨*slashing* desperately at his circling enemies⟩ ⟨tires *slashed* by vandals⟩
*Ana* split, cleave, rive (see TEAR): sever, sunder (see

SEPARATE *vb*): curtail (see SHORTEN)
**cutthroat** *assassin, gunman, bravo
**cutting** *incisive, trenchant, clear-cut, biting, crisp
*Ana* *sharp, keen, acute: piercing, penetrating, probing (see ENTER)
**cyclone** *whirlwind, typhoon, hurricane, tornado, waterspout, twister
**cyclopean** *huge, vast, immense, enormous, elephantine, mammoth, giant, gigantic, gigantean, colossal, gargantuan, Herculean, titanic, Brobdingnagian
**cynical, misanthropic, pessimistic, misogynic** are comparable when meaning deeply and often contemptuously distrustful. **Cynical** implies a sneering disbelief in sincerity and integrity ⟨the ease with which she asserted or denied whatever suited her purpose was only equaled by the *cynical* indifference with which she met the exposure of her lies—*J. R. Green*⟩ ⟨but people are nowadays so *cynical*—they sneer at everything that makes life worth living—*L. P. Smith*⟩ **Misanthropic** implies a rooted dislike and distrust of one's fellowmen and aversion to their society ⟨Swift was of an unhappy, *misanthropic* state of mind⟩ ⟨he . . . viewed them not with *misanthropic* hate—*Byron*⟩ ⟨his loathing . . . hardened into a *misanthropic* mania—*Powys*⟩ **Pessimistic** suggests a distrustful and gloomy view of things in general ⟨the *pessimistic* philosophy of Schopenhauer⟩ ⟨of kindly heart, though of violent speech . . . and of *pessimistic* temperament—*Ellis*⟩ **Misogynic** implies a deep-seated aversion to, and a profound distrust of, women ⟨his *misogynic* soul—*Meredith*⟩ ⟨a *misogynic* old bachelor⟩
*Ana* sneering, girding, flouting, scoffing (see SCOFF): captious, caviling, carping, censorious, *critical: disbelieving, unbelieving (see corresponding nouns at UNBELIEF)
*Con* *hopeful, optimistic, roseate

# D

**dabbler** tyro, *amateur, dilettante
*Con* adept, *expert, wizard, artist

**daily, diurnal, quotidian, circadian** mean of each or every day. **Daily** is used with reference to the ordinary concerns and customary happenings of life ⟨*daily* wants⟩ ⟨*daily* visits⟩ ⟨the *daily* newspaper⟩ Sometimes however it implies an opposition to *nightly* ⟨the *daily* anodyne, and nightly draught—*Pope*⟩ **Diurnal** is commonly either astronomical (with special reference to the movements of the heavenly bodies) or poetic in its use ⟨the *diurnal* revolution of the earth⟩ ⟨rolled round in earth's *diurnal* course—*Wordsworth*⟩ **Diurnal** also implies opposition to *nocturnal* ⟨the *diurnal* and *nocturnal* offices of the monks⟩ ⟨hunting dogs are mainly *diurnal* animals—*Stevenson-Hamilton*⟩ **Quotidian** adds to *daily* the implication of recurrence each day ⟨a *quotidian* fever⟩ It often suggests also a commonplace, routine, or everyday character or quality ⟨that quality of strangeness which puts a new light on all *quotidian* occupations—*Bennett*⟩ ⟨he has found in *quotidian* interests and affections and appetites so complete an escape from the labors and the struggles of the creative spirit—*Brooks*⟩ ⟨as *quotidian* as catching the 8:52 from Surbiton to go to business on a Monday morning—*Huxley*⟩ **Circadian** is a chiefly technical term of recent coinage that differs from *daily* or *quotidian* in implying only approximate

equation with the twenty-four hour day ⟨*circadian* rhythms in insect behavior⟩
*Con* *nightly, nocturnal: periodic, alternate, recurrent, *intermittent: occasional, *infrequent, sporadic
**dainty** 1 delicate, exquisite, *choice, elegant, recherché, rare
*Ana* petite, diminutive, little, *small: pretty, bonny, fair, lovely, *beautiful: *delightful, delectable, delicious
*Ant* gross — *Con* *coarse, vulgar: *common, ordinary
2 fastidious, finicky, finicking, finical, *nice, particular, fussy, squeamish, persnickety, pernickety
*Ana* *careful, meticulous, punctilious, scrupulous: discriminating, discerning (see corresponding nouns at DISCERNMENT)
**dally** flirt, coquet, toy, *trifle
*Ana* *play, sport, frolic, gambol: *caress, fondle, pet
**dam** *vb* bar, block, obstruct, *hinder, impede
*Ana* clog, *hamper, trammel, shackle, fetter, hog-tie: *suppress, repress
*Con* *advance, forward: *express, vent, utter, air
**damage** *n* harm, *injury, hurt, mischief
*Ana* impairment, marring (see corresponding verbs at INJURE): ruining, dilapidation, wrecking (see corresponding verbs at RUIN): detriment, deleteriousness (see corresponding adjectives at PERNICIOUS)

*Con* improvement, betterment (see corresponding verbs at IMPROVE): benefiting *or* benefit, profiting *or* profit (see BENEFIT *vb*): advantage, service, *use

**damage** *vb* harm, *injure, impair, mar, hurt, spoil
*Ana* *ruin, dilapidate, wreck: *deface, disfigure: *abuse, misuse, mistreat, ill-treat, maltreat, outrage
*Con* *improve, better, ameliorate: *benefit, profit, avail: repair, *mend

**damn** *vb* **1** doom, condemn, *sentence, proscribe
*Ana* *judge, adjudge: *punish, castigate, discipline
*Ant* save (*from eternal punishment*) —*Con* redeem, ransom, *rescue, deliver
**2** curse, *execrate, anathematize, objurgate
*Ana* denounce, condemn (see CRITICIZE): revile, vituperate (see SCOLD)

**damnable** accursed, cursed, *execrable
*Ana* atrocious, *outrageous, monstrous, heinous: *hateful, abominable, detestable, odious, abhorrent
*Con* admirable, estimable (see corresponding verbs at REGARD *n*): laudable, praiseworthy (see corresponding verbs at PRAISE)

**damp** *adj* moist, dank, humid, *wet
*Con* *dry, arid

**dandle** cuddle, pet, cosset, fondle, *caress
*Ana* *trifle, toy, dally: *play, sport, disport: *handle, swing

**dandy** *n* *fop, beau, coxcomb, exquisite, dude, buck
*Ant* sloven

**danger** *n* Danger, peril, jeopardy, hazard, risk mean either the state or fact of being threatened with loss of life or property or with serious injury to one's health or moral integrity or the cause or source of such a threat. **Danger** is the general term and implies contingent evil in prospect but not necessarily impending or inescapable ⟨to win renown even in the jaws of *danger* and of death—*Shak.*⟩ ⟨where one *danger's* near, the more remote, tho' greater, disappear—*Cowley*⟩ ⟨troubled by the *danger* that the manuscript might be lost—*Van Doren*⟩ ⟨a frame of adamant, a soul of fire, no *dangers* fright him—*Johnson*⟩ **Peril** usually carries a stronger implication of imminence than *danger* and suggests even greater cause for fear and a much higher degree of probability of loss or injury ⟨in *perils* of waters, in *perils* of robbers . . . in *perils* in the city, in *perils* in the wilderness, in *perils* in the sea—*2 Cor* 11:26⟩ ⟨he lived in constant *peril*—*Buchan*⟩ ⟨the *perils* which threaten civilization—*Ellis*⟩ **Jeopardy** implies exposure to extreme or dangerous chances ⟨why stand we in *jeopardy* every hour?—*1 Cor* 15:30⟩ The term is much used in law in reference to persons accused of serious offenses, being tried in court, and therefore exposed to the danger of conviction and punishment ⟨nor shall any person be subject for the same offense to be twice put in *jeopardy* of life or limb—*U. S. Constitution*⟩ ⟨it seems to me that logically and rationally a man cannot be said to be more than once in *jeopardy* in the same cause, however often he may be tried—*Justice Holmes*⟩ **Hazard** implies danger from something fortuitous or beyond one's control; it is not so strong a term as *jeopardy* ⟨the amusements . . . of most of us are full of *hazard* and precariousness—*Froude*⟩ ⟨there would have been no triumph in success, had there been no *hazard* of failure—*Newman*⟩ ⟨travel on the thoroughfares of Manila was not without its *hazards*—*Heiser*⟩ **Risk**, more frequently than *hazard,* implies a voluntary taking of doubtful or adverse chances ⟨no adventure daunted her and *risks* stimulated her—*Ellis*⟩ ⟨life is a *risk* and all individual plans precarious, all human achievements transient—*Edman*⟩
*Ana* threatening *or* threat, menacing *or* menace (see corresponding verbs at THREATEN): precariousness (see

corresponding adjective at DANGEROUS): emergency, exigency, pass (see JUNCTURE)
*Ant* security —*Con* safety (see corresponding adjective SAFE): immunity, *exemption: safeguarding *or* safeguard, guarding *or* guard, protection, defending *or* defense, shielding *or* shield (see corresponding verbs at DEFEND)

**dangerous,** hazardous, precarious, perilous, risky all mean attended by or involving the possibility of loss, evil, injury, harm; however, they are frequently not freely interchangeable in usage. **Dangerous** applies to persons, things, or situations that should be avoided or treated with exceeding care because contact with them or use of them is unsafe and exposes one or causes one to expose others at least to danger ⟨a *dangerous* weapon⟩ ⟨a *dangerous* occupation⟩ ⟨a *dangerous* practice⟩ ⟨a *dangerous* doctrine⟩ ⟨conditions *dangerous* to health⟩ ⟨the child discovers that grown-ups lie to him, and that it is *dangerous* to tell them the truth—*Russell*⟩ ⟨a wide circuit must be made to avoid a fierce and *dangerous* tribe called Snake Indians—*Parkman*⟩ **Hazardous** carries a far stronger implication of dependence on chance than *dangerous* carries: it is often the preferred term when the chances of loss, death, or severe injury are comparatively great; thus, a *hazardous* occupation (especially from the point of view of insurability) is one in which the worker must run significantly greater than average risks of accident or loss of life; a *hazardous* enterprise is one which has as many (if not more) chances of failing as of succeeding ⟨no one should be deluded into believing that we can ever have completely assured lives. Living is a *hazardous* business at the best—*Furnas*⟩ ⟨the *hazardous* game of secret service in enemy country —*Alexander Forbes*⟩ **Precarious** is often used inaccurately where *dangerous* or even *hazardous* would be the better word. The basic meaning of this word is *uncertain* or *insecure:* therefore, it may be used without implication of threatened danger or of possible hazards; in strict use *precarious* health is uncertain health rather than a physical condition threatening death; a *precarious* occupation is one that may be neither dangerous nor hazardous but uncertain (as in its tenure or remunerativeness) ⟨whoever supposes that Lady Austen's fortune is *precarious* is mistaken. . . . It is . . . perfectly safe—*Cowper*⟩ ⟨a National Church in the early Caroline sense depended upon the *precarious* harmony of the king, a strong archbishop, and a strong first minister—*T. S. Eliot*⟩ The term often carries also an implication of attendance by danger or hazards especially as a factor in or source of insecurity or uncertainty; thus, a *precarious* hold or footing is one that is so insecure that it involves danger ⟨the *precarious* track through the morass—*Scott*⟩ ⟨keeping a *precarious* and vital balance, like a man walking on high on a tightrope—*Montague*⟩ **Perilous** carries a stronger implication of the immediacy of a threatened evil than *dangerous* ⟨after all their intolerable toils, the sounding tumult of battle, and *perilous* sea-paths, resting there . . . amid the epitaphs and allegorical figures of their tombs—*L. P. Smith*⟩ ⟨we all know how *perilous* it is to suggest to the modern woman that she has any "sphere"—*Babbitt*⟩ **Risky** comes close to *perilous* in suggesting high possibility of harm or loss, but it is usually applied to an action or activity which a person undertakes voluntarily and often with knowledge of the perils or risks to which it exposes him ⟨undertake a *risky* job⟩ ⟨make a *risky* investment⟩ ⟨so *risky* was travel that the Indiana legislature specifically permitted travelers to carry concealed weapons—*Sandburg*⟩
*Ana* unsafe, insecure (see affirmative adjectives at SAFE): chancy, chance, haphazard, *random, hit-or-miss

---

A colon (:) separates groups of words discriminated. An asterisk (*) indicates place of treatment of each group.

*Ant* safe, secure

**dangle** suspend, *hang, sling

*Ana* oscillate, sway, pendulate, fluctuate (see SWING): *swing, wave

**dank** damp, humid, moist, *wet

*Ana* soaked, saturated, sopped *or* soppy, drenched (see corresponding verbs at SOAK)

**dappled** *variegated, parti-colored, motley, checkered, checked, pied, piebald, skewbald, freaked

**dare** *vb* *face, brave, challenge, defy, beard

*Ana* *venture, risk, chance, hazard

**daredevil** *adj* daring, rash, reckless, foolhardy, venturesome, *adventurous

*Ana & Con* see those at DARING

**daring** rash, reckless, daredevil, foolhardy, venturesome, *adventurous

*Ana* bold, intrepid, audacious (see BRAVE)

*Con* *timid, timorous: *cautious, wary, circumspect, chary: prudent, sensible, sane, *wise, judicious

**dark** *adj* 1 Dark, dim, dusky, obscure, murky, gloomy mean partly or wholly destitute of light. **Dark,** the ordinary word and the most general of these terms, implies a lack of the illumination necessary to enable one to see or to identify what is before him. It may imply lack of natural illumination (as by the sun or moon) ⟨a *dark* forest⟩ ⟨a *dark* night⟩ or of artificial illumination (as by gas or electricity) ⟨ a *dark* room⟩ or a lack of immaterial light (as cheerfulness) ⟨a *dark* mood⟩ ⟨a *dark* countenance⟩ or of moral or spiritual light ⟨a *dark* deed⟩ or of brilliance—that is, the quality of lightness in color ⟨a *dark* blue⟩ **Dim** suggests just so much darkness that the things before one cannot be seen clearly or in their distinct or characteristic outlines: it may be applied equally to things viewed or to a source of illumination ⟨the light has grown *dim*⟩ ⟨*dim* stars⟩ ⟨he could just make out *dim* figures in the distance⟩ It may designate a usually bright thing that is dulled or softened ⟨a . . . *dim* and tender red—*Hudson*⟩ ⟨a *dim* image of their glorious vitality—*Krutch*⟩ or a place or time that is nearly dark ⟨scrambled over to join the other ghosts out on the *dim* common—*Galsworthy*⟩ ⟨the hazy light . . . reminded him of the *dim* distances of his own . . . country—*Anderson*⟩ **Dim** as applied to eyes, sight, or insight suggests a loss of functional keenness ⟨eyes *dim* with tears⟩ ⟨*dim* eyesight⟩ **Dusky** suggests the halfway state between light and dark characteristic of twilight: like *dim* it implies faintness of light but unlike that word definitely connotes grayness and an approach to darkness ⟨*dusky* winter evenings⟩ ⟨the *dusky* windowless loft⟩ ⟨*dusky* clouds⟩ ⟨but comes at last the dull and *dusky* eve—*Cowper*⟩ **Obscure** is more often used in its extended senses (see OBSCURE) than in its literal sense, but it is employed literally when there is a suggestion of darkening by covering, concealment, or overshadowing that deprives a thing of its lightness, brightness, or luster ⟨*obscurest* night involved the sky—*Cowper*⟩ ⟨*obscure* stars⟩ ⟨an *obscure* corner of the attic⟩ **Murky** originally implied and still sometimes implies intense darkness or a darkness in which things are not even faintly visible ⟨Hell is *murky!*—*Shak.*⟩ In current use, the term more often suggests a thick, heavy darkness suggestive of smoke-laden fogs or of air filled with mist and dust ⟨an atmosphere *murky* with sand—*Cather*⟩ ⟨as if its [London's] low sky were the roof of a cave, and its *murky* day a light such as one reads of in countries beneath the earth—*L. P. Smith*⟩ **Gloomy** (see also SULLEN) implies imperfect illumination owing to causes that interfere seriously with the radiation of light (as dense clouds or the heavy shade of many closely set trees): in addition, it often connotes pervading

cheerlessness ⟨the day was especially *gloomy* for June⟩ ⟨the *gloomiest* part of the forest⟩ ⟨the room was *gloomy* and depressing with only a dim light from a small candle⟩ ⟨their *gloomy* pathway tended upward, so that, through a crevice, a little daylight glimmered down upon them—*Hawthorne*⟩

*Ant* light —*Con* *bright, brilliant, radiant, luminous: illumined, illuminated, enlightened, lighted (see ILLUMINATE)

2 *obscure, vague, enigmatic, cryptic, ambiguous, equivocal

*Ana* abstruse, occult, *recondite, esoteric: *mystical, mystic, anagogic, cabalistic: intricate, complicated, knotty, *complex

*Ant* lucid —*Con* *clear, perspicuous: simple, *easy, light, facile

**darken** *obscure, dim, bedim, eclipse, cloud, becloud, fog, befog, obfuscate

*Ant* illuminate —*Con* enlighten, illumine (see ILLUMINATE): elucidate, *explain

**dart** *vb* *fly, scud, skim, float, shoot, sail

*Ana* *speed, precipitate, hasten, hurry

**dash** *vb* *rush, tear, shoot, charge

*Ana* dart, *fly, scud

**dash** *n* 1 *vigor, vim, spirit, esprit, verve, punch, élan, drive

*Ana* force, energy, might, *power: vehemence, intensity (see corresponding adjectives at INTENSE): impressiveness (see corresponding adjective at MOVING)

2 *touch, suggestion, suspicion, soupçon, tincture, tinge, shade, smack, spice, vein, strain, streak

**dashing** smart, *stylish, fashionable, modish, chic

**date** *n* *engagement, rendezvous, tryst, appointment, assignation

**daunt** appall, *dismay, horrify

*Ana* cow, *intimidate, browbeat: discomfit, disconcert, faze (see EMBARRASS): foil, thwart, baffle (see FRUSTRATE): *frighten, alarm, scare, terrify

*Con* rally, rouse, arouse, *stir, waken, awaken: impel, drive, *move, actuate: activate, *vitalize, energize

**dauntless** *brave, courageous, unafraid, fearless, intrepid, valiant, valorous, undaunted, doughty, bold, audacious

*Ana* indomitable, unconquerable, *invincible: heroic, gallant (see corresponding nouns at HEROISM)

*Ant* poltroon —*Con* *fearful, afraid, apprehensive

**dawdle** *delay, procrastinate, loiter, lag

*Ana* linger, tarry, wait, *stay: *trifle, toy, dally: *play, sport, disport

*Con* *stir, rally, rouse, arouse: hurry, hasten, *speed

**daydream** *n* dream, *fancy, fantasy, phantasy, phantasm, vision, nightmare

*Ana* imagining *or* imagination, conceiving *or* conception, fancying (see corresponding verbs at FANCY): illusion, *delusion, hallucination

**daze** *vb* Daze, stun, bemuse, stupefy, benumb, paralyze, petrify all mean to dull or deaden the powers of the mind through some disturbing experience or influence. **Daze** may imply any of numerous causes (as a blow on the head, an excess of light, or a physical or mental shock) which prostrates one's powers and leaves one confused or bewildered or dazzled ⟨till I felt I could end myself too with the dagger—so deafened and *dazed*— . . . with the grief that gnawed at my heart—*Tennyson*⟩ ⟨the cattle gather and blare, roused by the feet of running men, *dazed* by the lantern glare—*Kipling*⟩ **Stun** usually suggests a sudden deprivation of one's powers of thought or a loss of consciousness as a result of a heavy blow or a violent fall, but it is also used in an extended and often hyperbolic sense to describe the devastating effect of noise, surprise, or astonishment ⟨*stunned* his assailant with the butt of his rifle⟩ ⟨*stunned* by the news of his son's drowning⟩ ⟨where wild Oswego spreads her swamps around, and Niagara *stuns* with thundering sound—*Goldsmith*⟩ ⟨ye little children, *stun* your grandame's ears with pleasure of your noise!—*Wordsworth*⟩ ⟨or has the shock . . . confused . . . and *stunned* me from my power to think—*Tennyson*⟩ **Bemuse** implies an addling or muddling of the mind whether through intoxication or through employment, preoccupation, or engrossment that dulls or abstracts the mind ⟨a Prussian was regarded in England as a dull beer-*bemused* creature—*M'Carthy*⟩ ⟨his senses so *bemused* in the intensity of calculation —*Scott*⟩ ⟨people with brains and intelligence . . . play cards until they are *bemused* and stupid—*McClure's Mag.*⟩ **Stupefy** heightens the implication of stupor or stupidity by weakening not only the implication of shock or surprise but that of overwork or fatigue; it therefore usually implies something (as an injury, an illness, a grief or anxiety long-continued, or intoxication) that dulls both the senses and the mind ⟨sun elated them; quiet rain sobered them, weeks of watery tempest *stupefied* them—*Hardy*⟩ **Benumb** is used chiefly of the effect of cold in deadening or immobilizing the muscles, but it is used also of anything that becomes so inert that it seems as if frozen ⟨it is so cold, so dark, my senses are so *benumbed* —*Dickens*⟩ ⟨Mrs. Ralston drew back a step or two. Charlotte's cold resolution *benumbed* her courage, and she could find no immediate reply—*Wharton*⟩ **Paralyze** is often used figuratively to imply an inability to act or to function, on the part of a thing as well as of a person, that comes as the result of a dire event, a burden too heavy to be borne, or an astounding disclosure ⟨in these wild places . . . a snowstorm . . . does not . . . paralyze traffic as London permits itself to be *paralyzed* under similar circumstances—*Jefferies*⟩ ⟨a certain helplessness in the presence of what is unfamiliar that fairly *paralyzes* even Gallic curiosity—*Brownell*⟩ **Petrify** (see also HARDEN) emphasizes the immediate effect of fear, amazement, shock, or awe and suggests complete inability to move, to think, or to act, as though one were turned to stone ⟨the spectators were *petrified* with horror⟩ ⟨she was too *petrified* to answer the question⟩ More than any other word in this group, *petrify* is often used hyperbolically ⟨I was too *petrified* to pay any attention to him⟩

**Ana** confound, bewilder, mystify (see PUZZLE): *confuse, muddle, befuddle: dazzle, dizzy (see corresponding adjectives at GIDDY)

**dazzled** *giddy, dizzy, vertiginous, swimming
**Ana** confused, addled, befuddled, muddled (see CONFUSE): confounded, bewildered, puzzled, perplexed (see PUZZLE)

**dead** *adj* **Dead, defunct, deceased, departed, late, lifeless, inanimate** all mean devoid of life. **Dead** applies strictly to anyone or to anything that has been deprived of life and has therefore ceased to grow or to function ⟨a *dead* person⟩ ⟨a *dead* animal⟩ ⟨a *dead* tree⟩ ⟨every plant in the garden is *dead* as a result of the intensely severe winter⟩ *Dead* is also applicable to things which have not had life (in its literal sense) but have existed for a time and have been used or accepted or have proved effective or influential; thus, a *dead* language is no longer in spoken use by any people; a *dead* belief no longer has any acceptance; a *dead* journal no longer is printed and circulated; a *dead* issue or question no longer arouses interest or debate. Figuratively the term implies lack or loss of sensation, consciousness, feeling, activity, energy, or any of the qualities associated with life ⟨*dead*

fingers⟩ ⟨a *dead* engine⟩ ⟨a *dead* cigar⟩ ⟨the *dead* season in a business⟩ **Defunct** differs little in its literal sense from *dead,* except that it is somewhat bookish ⟨Charlotte had entered society in her mother's turned garments, and shod with satin sandals handed down from a *defunct* aunt—*Wharton*⟩ The term is more often applied to a thing that by failure or dissolution has ceased to function or to operate ⟨a *defunct* newspaper⟩ ⟨a *defunct* corporation⟩ **Deceased** applies only to a person and especially to one who has died comparatively recently or who, though dead, is at the moment under consideration especially in some legal context ⟨laws prohibiting the marriage of a man with his *deceased* wife's sister⟩ ⟨the legal heirs of the *deceased* millionaire were never found⟩ **Departed** is distinctly euphemistic (especially in religious use) ⟨pray for the souls of *departed* relatives and friends⟩ **Late** is used in place of *deceased* or *departed* especially when stressing a relationship to a surviving person or an existent institution ⟨under the terms of his *late* father's will⟩ ⟨the *late* chairman of the board of directors⟩ ⟨the *late* master of the house⟩ **Lifeless,** unlike the preceding words, does not necessarily imply deprivation of life, for it is applicable not only to something literally dead but also to something which never had life or is incapable of life. In comparison with *dead,* however, *lifeless* stresses the absence (sometimes, when loss of consciousness is implied, the apparent absence) of the phenomena characteristic of being alive; thus, one speaks of a *dead* man, but a *lifeless* body (that is, a body that shows no signs of life) ⟨there in the twilight cold and grey, *lifeless,* but beautiful, he lay—*Longfellow*⟩ In its extended use *lifeless* is especially applicable to things (far less often to persons) that have not or never have had vitality, power, or spirit ⟨a *lifeless* color⟩ ⟨a *lifeless* poem⟩ ⟨she has been *lifeless* since her recovery from a prolonged illness⟩ ⟨dull *lifeless* mechanical systems that treat people as if they were things—*Wilde*⟩ ⟨monochrome is a starved and *lifeless* term to express the marvellous range and subtlety of tones of which . . . Chinese ink is capable —*Binyon*⟩ **Inanimate** is more consistently used than *lifeless* in describing something which never had life; it is the preferred term when a contrast between that which is devoid of life and that which possesses life is expressed or implied ⟨objects which consist of *inanimate* matter —*Jeans*⟩ ⟨a transition . . . from the inorganic to the organic, from the *inanimate* to the living—*Inge*⟩ ⟨harnessing *inanimate* power to carry us and our burdens—*Furnas*⟩ But *inanimate* is also applicable in extended use to that which is spiritless, inactive, or not lively, and therefore dull ⟨an *inanimate* style⟩ ⟨her *inanimate* movement when on the stage—*Yeats*⟩
**Ant** alive —**Con** *living

**deadlock** *n* *draw, tie, stalemate, standoff
**Ana** situation, condition, *state, posture: *predicament, plight, dilemma, quandary

**deadly** *adj* 1 **Deadly, mortal, fatal, lethal** mean causing or causative of death. **Deadly** may imply an extremely high degree of probability rather than a certainty of death; the term therefore applies to something with the capacity of or a marked potentiality for causing death; a *deadly* disease is one usually ending fatally; a *deadly* weapon is one capable of inflicting death; the seven *deadly* sins in theology are those sins which must be avoided because they are the source of other sins and are destructive of spiritual life and progress ⟨two brave vessels matched in *deadly* fight, and fighting to the death —*Wordsworth*⟩ ⟨poisons more *deadly* than a mad dog's tooth—*Shak.*⟩ ⟨the neglect of form . . . was even deadlier to poetry—*Viereck*⟩ **Mortal** implies that death has

---

A colon (:) separates groups of words discriminated. An asterisk (*) indicates place of treatment of each group.

occurred or is certain to occur; the term therefore is applicable only to that which actually has caused or is about to cause death; a *mortal* disease is one that ends fatally; a *mortal* wound is one that caused or will inevitably cause death; a *mortal* sin (in contrast with a *deadly* sin) is a grievous sin deliberately committed and actually inflicting spiritual death. *Deadly* applies to the instrument that deals the wound or blow that proves mortal ⟨a *deadly* lance⟩ ⟨a *mortal* stab⟩ ⟨Gigi took off his mask and hid it under a rock; it would be no help to him now, but on the contrary a *mortal* danger —*Upton Sinclair*⟩ **Fatal** stresses inevitability and applies to a potential or actual result of death, destruction, or disaster. The term is often used in place of *mortal* as applied to wounds, blows, or illnesses especially when some time has intervened between the wounding or sickening and the dying. *Fatal* rather than *mortal* is used in predictions ⟨to remove him to the hospital would be *fatal*⟩ ⟨at her age . . . it [diabetes] was not speedily or necessarily *fatal*—*Ellis*⟩ ⟨I will not repeat your words . . . because the consequences to you would certainly be *fatal*—*Henry Adams*⟩ **Lethal** applies only to something which by its very nature is bound to cause death or which exists for the purpose of destroying life ⟨the morphia he gave was a full *lethal* dose, and presently the body on the deck found peace—*Nevil Shute*⟩ ⟨a *lethal* gas⟩ ⟨a *lethal* chamber for the execution of those condemned to death⟩ ⟨a *lethal* weapon⟩ All of these terms except *lethal* may be used in a lighter sense not implying physical or spiritual death, but something dreaded or greatly feared; a *deadly* shaft of irony causes complete discomfiture; *mortal* terror always suggests extreme terror, but only occasionally the terror of losing one's life; a *fatal* error or a *fatal* slip may imply the destruction of one's plans or hopes rather than of one's life.
*Ana* destroying *or* destructive (see DESTROY): killing, slaying (see KILL *vb*): malignant, malign (see MALICIOUS): baneful, *pernicious: toxic, virulent, *poisonous, pestilential, pestilent: ruinous (see corresponding verb at RUIN)
**2 Deadly, deathly** are frequently confused although in precise use they are not synonyms. **Deadly** applies to an agent which is bound or extremely likely to cause death (see DEADLY 1); in one of its extended senses, it applies to something which is so implacable or virulent or so relentless that it can result only in death, destruction, or ruin ⟨a *deadly* enmity existed between them⟩ ⟨the two railroads are engaged in a *deadly* conflict over rates⟩ *Deadly* may imply no more than an extreme of something ⟨*deadly* monotony⟩ ⟨why are you in such *deadly* haste?⟩ or it may suggest a disgusting extreme of some depressing or spirit-destroying quality ⟨the city is *deadly* in summer⟩ **Deathly** applies only to that which suggests the appearance or the presence of death ⟨his *deathly* pallor⟩ ⟨the *deathly* stillness of the place⟩
**deal** *vb* **1** *distribute, divide, dispense, dole
*Ana* apportion, *allot, assign, allocate: *share, participate, partake
*Con* collect, *gather, assemble: *receive, take: *keep, retain, withhold, hold, hold back, detain, reserve
**2** *treat, handle
*Ana* manage, control, *conduct, direct: *rid, clear, unburden
**dealings** *intercourse, commerce, traffic, communication, communion, conversation, converse, correspondence
**dear** expensive, *costly, precious, valuable, invaluable, priceless
*Ana* exorbitant, *excessive, extravagant, inordinate
*Ant* cheap

**dearth** *lack, want, absence, defect, privation
*Ana* scarcity, infrequency, rareness, uncommonness (see corresponding adjectives at INFREQUENT): scantiness, meagerness, scantness (see corresponding adjectives at MEAGER)
*Ant* excess
**death,** decease, demise, passing denote the end or the ending of life. **Death** is the general word and is used for the termination of plants and animals as well as of men and also of inanimate things marked by continuity or development ⟨the *death* of an enterprise⟩ **Decease** and **demise** apply only to human beings except in figurative use. *Decease* is preferred in legal context but in ordinary use conveys a slightly euphemistic or rhetorical quality. *Demise* in literal use has become somewhat pompous or affected ⟨the lady's *demise* had been ascribed to apoplexy—*Hynd*⟩ In figurative use it frequently lacks such connotation ⟨organized labor, which promised his political *demise* if he signed the bill against jurisdictional strikes—*Beverly Smith*⟩ **Passing** is a euphemism for the death of a person.
*Ant* life
**deathless** *immortal, undying, unfading
*Ana* *everlasting, endless: eternal (see INFINITE): enduring, abiding, persisting (see CONTINUE)
*Con* ephemeral, *transient, transitory, evanescent, passing
**deathly** *deadly
*Ana* *ghastly, macabre, gruesome, grisly
*Ant* lifelike
**debar** *exclude, blackball, disbar, suspend, shut out, eliminate, rule out
*Ana* preclude, obviate, *prevent: *forbid, prohibit, ban, interdict
*Con* *invite, court, woo, solicit, bid: permit, allow, *let
**debase** **1** Debase, vitiate, deprave, corrupt, debauch, pervert mean to cause a person or thing to become impaired and lowered in quality or character and share certain distinctions in implications and connotations with the adjectives (usually participial adjectives) corresponding to the verbs, **debased, vitiated, depraved, corrupted** (but more often, **corrupt**), **debauched, perverted**. **Debase** (see also ABASE) and **debased** imply a loss of worth, value, or dignity and are widely applicable ⟨plays that *debase* the taste of the people⟩ ⟨a *debased* coinage⟩ ⟨the life-and-death struggle with Hannibal . . . had permanently *debased* the Roman temper and left in it a core of hard inhumanity—*Buchan*⟩ ⟨success permits him to see how those he has converted distort and *debase* . . . his teaching—*Huxley*⟩ ⟨the fine old language which has been slowly perfected for centuries, and which is now being . . . *debased* by the rubbishy newspapers which form almost the sole reading of the majority—*Inge*⟩ ⟨human values cruelly and systematically *debased* by the Nazis —*Dean*⟩ **Vitiate** and **vitiated** imply impairment through the introduction of a fault, a defect, or anything that destroys the purity, validity, or effectiveness of a thing ⟨a style *vitiated* by exaggeration⟩ ⟨inappropriate and badly chosen words *vitiate* thought—*Huxley*⟩ ⟨the fox . . . *vitiates* his line of scent with the gas fumes on the macadam highways—*Heinold*⟩ ⟨the *vitiated* air of a crowded hall⟩ ⟨party jealousies *vitiated* the whole military organization —*Times Lit. Sup.*⟩ ⟨a final decree . . . *vitiated* by the judge's assumption that he was bound by the master's findings of fact—*Justice Holmes*⟩ **Deprave** and **depraved** usually imply pronounced moral deterioration; thus, a person who has a *debased* taste cannot enjoy what is really good or beautiful if it lacks showy surface qualities which catch his attention, but a person with a *de-*

*praved* taste finds satisfaction only in what is wholly or partly obscene or prurient ⟨the belief that a witch was a person who leagued herself with the Devil to defy God and *deprave* man—*The Spectator*⟩ ⟨the servants, wicked and *depraved,* corrupt and *deprave* the children—*Henry James*⟩ **Corrupt** (both verb and adjective: for the latter see also VICIOUS) and **corrupted** imply a loss of soundness, purity, integrity through forces or influences that break down, pollute, or destroy: the terms are applicable to things which are subject to decay, disintegration, or irreparable contamination of any sort ⟨lay not up for yourselves treasures upon earth, where moth and rust doth *corrupt*—*Mt* 6:19⟩ ⟨we must not so stain our judgment, or *corrupt* our hope—*Shak.*⟩ ⟨the idea of beauty has been *corrupted* by those who would make it purely impressionistic or expressive—*Babbitt*⟩ ⟨our schools teach the morality of feudalism *corrupted* by commercialism—*Shaw*⟩ Often also, the terms imply seduction, bribery, or influence as leading to a moral breakdown or to an immoral act ⟨they were not able to *corrupt* the new legislators⟩ ⟨*corrupted* courts⟩ ⟨at sixteen the girl was further *corrupted* by a "perverse and wicked" young man—*Edmund Wilson*⟩ **Debauch** and **debauched** imply a demoralizing and depraving through such corrupting influences as a life of pleasure, ease, or sensual indulgence: they suggest the weakening, more often than the loss, of such qualities as loyalty to one's allegiance or duties, fitness for responsibility or high endeavor, and moral purity or integrity, and they often also connote dissoluteness or profligacy ⟨to betray their master and *debauch* his army—*Mill*⟩ ⟨she takes them to an enchanted isle, where she *debauches* them with enervating delights and renders them oblivious to their duty—*R. A. Hall*⟩ ⟨the gay, *debauched,* quite inconsequent lad was managed like a puppet—*Belloc*⟩ **Pervert** and **perverted** imply a twisting or distorting of something (sometimes someone) from what it is in fact or in its true nature, so as to debase it completely or make it incapable of proper or correct application; to *pervert* the meaning of a text is to twist that meaning in interpreting it so that it will serve one's own ends or seem to prove one's thesis; to *pervert* the facts in a case is to give a distorted and, usually, personally advantageous view of them; to *pervert* the ends of nature· is to use one's appetites or natural desires for other ends than those which are normal and in accordance with nature ⟨subjugation of the eternal to the temporal in a *perverted* set of values—*Times Lit. Sup.*⟩ ⟨these nothings which . . . people are so prone to start a row about, and nurse into hatred from an idle sense of wrong, from *perverted* ambition—*Conrad*⟩ ⟨the truth to him . . . is not only not to be spoken at all times, but it is now and then to be *perverted*—*Brownell*⟩
*Ana* defile, pollute, taint, *contaminate: *adulterate, sophisticate, load, weight, doctor: impair, spoil, mar, damage, harm, *injure
*Ant* elevate (*taste, character*): amend (*morals, way of life*) —*Con* enhance, heighten (see INTENSIFY): raise, *lift: *improve, better, ameliorate
2 degrade, demean, *abase, humble, humiliate
*Ana* *weaken, undermine, sap, enfeeble, debilitate, cripple, disable
*Con* *vitalize, energize, activate: vivify, enliven, *quicken: *renew, restore, refresh, rejuvenate
**debased** vitiated, depraved, corrupted, debauched, perverted (see under DEBASE 1)
*Ana* deteriorated, degenerated *or* degenerate, decadent (see corresponding nouns at DETERIORATION)
*Con* improved, bettered, ameliorated (see IMPROVE): raised, elevated, lifted (see LIFT *vb*)

**debate** *n* disputation, forensic, *argumentation, dialectic
*Ana* controversy, *argument, dispute: contention, dissension (see DISCORD)
**debate** *vb* dispute, argue, *discuss, agitate
*Ana* *contend, fight, battle, war: wrangle, altercate, quarrel (see under QUARREL *n*): controvert, refute, confute, rebut, *disprove: *prove, demonstrate
**debauch** corrupt, deprave, pervert, *debase, vitiate
*Ana* *injure, harm, damage, spoil, mar: seduce, inveigle, decoy, tempt, *lure: pollute, defile, taint (see CONTAMINATE)
**debauched** corrupted, depraved, perverted, debased, vitiated (see under DEBASE)
*Ana* dissolute, reprobate, *abandoned, profligate: *licentious, libertine, lascivious, libidinous, lecherous, lewd, wanton
**debilitate** enfeeble, *weaken, undermine, sap, cripple, disable
*Ana* impair, *injure, damage, harm, hurt, mar, spoil
*Ant* invigorate —*Con* energize, *vitalize: *renew, restore, rejuvenate, refresh
**debit** indebtedness, liability, *debt, obligation, arrear
*Ant* credit
**debris** *refuse, waste, rubbish, trash, garbage, offal
**debt, indebtedness, obligation, liability, debit, arrear** mean something, and especially a sum of money, that is owed another. **Debt** usually implies that the amount is owed in return for goods, property, or services and can be definitely computed or, if something other than money is owed, that it equals in value if not in kind the thing sold or the service given ⟨incur a heavy *debt* for repairs to his house⟩ ⟨pay one's social *debts*⟩ ⟨this *debt* is now due⟩ ⟨the firm has no *debts* at present⟩ **Indebtedness** is applied either to the total amount owed one's creditors or a single creditor ⟨the *indebtedness* of the city exceeds the legal limit⟩ ⟨his *indebtedness* to his father fell just short of a thousand dollars⟩ **Obligation,** which is chiefly a legal term in this sense, implies a formal agreement to pay a certain amount or to do something or an acknowledgment of such an agreement (as by a contract or a bond) ⟨a contract is said to be "performed" . . . when all the *obligations* have been fulfilled on both sides—*Rubinstein*⟩ **Liability** is an accountant's term used chiefly in reference to general balance sheets of a company or corporation and is the opposite of *asset.* It is also used of the affairs of individuals especially in bankruptcy actions. It applies to any amount which constitutes an item of indebtedness. Liabilities include accounts payable, accrued interest, taxes, such obligations as notes, bonds, and debentures, and even capital stock. **Debit** is also a term in accounting for any item shown on the left side of an account; it usually designates a purchase and its price and is opposed to *credit,* or any entry on the right side (that is, for an article returned or an amount paid on account). **Arrear** especially in its plural *arrears* usually implies that some of a debt, but not all, has been paid, but it always implies that the amount owed is overdue ⟨pay off the *arrears* of one's rent⟩ ⟨the servants found it difficult to obtain the *arrears* of their wages⟩
**decadence** decline, declension, *deterioration, degeneration, devolution
*Ana* retrogressiveness *or* retrogression, regressiveness *or* regression *or* regress, retrograding *or* retrogradation (see corresponding adjectives at BACKWARD)
*Ant* rise: flourishing —*Con* advance, progress (see under ADVANCE *vb*): *progress, progression
**decamp** *escape, flee, fly, abscond
*Ana* depart, quit, leave, *go: elude, evade, *escape, shun, avoid

---

A colon (:) separates groups of words discriminated. An asterisk (*) indicates place of treatment of each group.

**decay** *vb* Decay, decompose, rot, putrefy, spoil, disintegrate, crumble mean to undergo or, in some cases, to cause something to undergo destructive dissolution. **Decay** implies change, commonly a natural and gradual change, from a state of soundness or perfection; it may or may not suggest the certainty of complete destruction ⟨teeth *decaying* from lack of care⟩ ⟨infirmity, that *decays* the wise—*Shak.*⟩ ⟨as winter fruits grow mild ere they *decay*—*Pope*⟩ ⟨nor shall I discuss the causes why science *decayed* and died under the Roman Empire—*Inge*⟩ **Decompose** stresses the idea of breaking down by separation into constituent parts or elements (as by chemical action in the laboratory or, in respect to animal and vegetable matter in nature, by the action of living microorganisms) ⟨whenever molecules combine or *decompose* or atoms change partners, it is chemistry—*Furnas*⟩ ⟨the action of bacteria in *decomposing* the organic products contained and forming gases useful for power and heat—*Morrison*⟩ ⟨the odor of *decomposing* meats⟩ ⟨after slaying his colleague, he chemically *decomposed* the body—*Guild*⟩ **Rot** implies decay and decomposition, usually of or as if of animal or vegetable matter; the term may or may not imply offensiveness or foulness; figuratively it differs from *decay* in stressing stagnation or corruption rather than decline ⟨blossoms . . . which fall before they wither rather than cling *rotting* to the stalk—*Binyon*⟩ ⟨there shall they *rot*, ambition's honored fools!—*Byron*⟩ ⟨it was this garrison life. Half civilian, half military, with all the drawbacks of both. It *rotted* the soul, robbed a man of ambition, faith—*Irwin Shaw*⟩ **Putrefy** not only suggests the rotting of or as if of animal matter but also stresses its extreme offensiveness to sight and smell ⟨corpses *putrefying* on the sun-drenched battlefields⟩ ⟨flesh in that long sleep is not *putrefied*—*Donne*⟩ **Spoil** (see also INJURE) is often used in place of *decay*, *rot*, or *putrefy* when foodstuffs, especially in the home or the market, are referred to ⟨roasted pork *spoils* quickly if not kept in a refrigerator⟩ **Disintegrate** implies either a breaking down or a breaking apart so that the wholeness or integrity of the thing or the cohesiveness of its particles is destroyed or is in process of destruction ⟨the London atmosphere tends to *disintegrate* bricks⟩ ⟨Rutherford and Soddy found that radioactive substances *disintegrate* in a way they described as "spontaneous"—the rate of decay cannot be expedited or retarded by any known physical process—*Jeans*⟩ ⟨the other great civilizations with which it was once contemporary have passed away or been *disintegrated* and transformed—*Ellis*⟩ **Crumble** implies disintegration of or as if of a substance that breaks into fine particles; neither it nor *disintegrate* need imply, as the remaining terms almost inevitably do, an alteration at the chemical level ⟨*crumbled* a piece of bread in his fingers⟩ ⟨winter rains had washed and washed against its . . . old bricks until the plaster between them had *crumbled*—*Deland*⟩ ⟨great periods of human culture which flourished at their height just as the substructure *crumbled*—*Krutch*⟩
*Ana* *weaken, undermine, sap, debilitate, enfeeble: taint, *contaminate, defile, pollute: dilapidate, *ruin, wreck: deliquesce (see LIQUEFY)

**decease** *death, demise, passing

**deceased** departed, late, *dead, defunct, lifeless, inanimate

**deceit** 1 Deceit, duplicity, dissimulation, cunning, guile mean the quality, the habit, the act, or the practice of imposing upon the credulity of others by dishonesty, fraud, or trickery. **Deceit** usually implies the intent to mislead or delude; otherwise, it is the most comprehensive of these terms, for it may imply deliberate mis-

representation or falsification, the assumption of a false appearance, the use of fraud or trickery or craft ⟨the fox barks not when he would steal the lamb. No, no, my sovereign! Gloucester is a man unsounded yet and full of deep *deceit*—*Shak.*⟩ ⟨no! there my husband never used *deceit*—*Browning*⟩ ⟨there is an element of sham and *deceit* in every imitation—*Dewey*⟩ **Duplicity** commonly implies double-dealing or bad faith; usually it suggests a pretense of feeling one way and an acting under the influence of another and opposite feeling ⟨I should disdain myself as much as I do him, were I capable of such *duplicity* as to flatter a man whom I scorn and despise—*Burney*⟩ The word may sometimes imply no more than the appearance of deceit arising out of a complexity of motives or a lack of singlemindedness ⟨it was chiefly that the simplicity and openness of their lives brought out for him the *duplicity* that lay at the bottom of ours—*Mary Austin*⟩ **Dissimulation** implies deceit by concealing what one truly is or what one actually feels and therefore often suggests duplicity ⟨Archer looked at her perplexedly, wondering if it were lightness or *dissimulation* that enabled her to touch so easily on the past at the very moment when she was risking her reputation in order to break with it—*Wharton*⟩ ⟨the levity of Hamlet, his repetition of phrase, his puns, are not part of a deliberate plan of *dissimulation*, but a form of emotional relief—*T. S. Eliot*⟩ **Cunning** implies deceit by the use of trickery, wiles, or stratagems; it often connotes a perverted intelligence and almost vicious shrewdness in attaining one's end ⟨surely the continual habit of dissimulation is but a weak and sluggish *cunning*, and not greatly politic—*Bacon*⟩ ⟨he . . . had come to the belief that I was incapable of the *cunning* and duplicity they practiced . . . to deceive with lies and false seeming was their faculty and not mine—*Hudson*⟩ **Guile** carries an even stronger implication of lack of obviousness in the arts practiced or tricks used than does *cunning;* in strict use it carries a strong implication of insidiousness or treacherousness ⟨we now return to claim our just inheritance of old . . . by what best way, whether of open war or covert *guile*, we now debate—*Milton*⟩ ⟨but Father Vaillant had been plunged into the midst of a great industrial expansion, where *guile* and trickery and honorable ambition all struggled together—*Cather*⟩ The word has, however, so long been used in such phrases as "without *guile*" and "devoid of *guile*" that it often is used in a very much weaker sense than *cunning*, sometimes implying little more than artfulness or the use of wiles ⟨her heart innocent of the most pardonable *guile*—*Conrad*⟩ ⟨there is a note of unconscious *guile*, the *guile* of the peasant, of the sophisticated small boy, in the letter he wrote—*Brooks*⟩
*Ana* *deception, fraud, trickery, double-dealing, chicane, chicanery: craft, artifice (see ART): cheating, cozening, defrauding, overreaching (see CHEAT *vb*)
*Con* honesty, uprightness, scrupulousness (see corresponding adjectives at UPRIGHT): openness, candidness or candor, frankness (see corresponding adjectives at FRANK): straightforwardness, forthrightness (see corresponding adjectives at STRAIGHTFORWARD)
2 *imposture, cheat, fraud, sham, fake, deception, counterfeit, humbug
*Ana* ruse, wile, *trick, feint, stratagem, maneuver, artifice, gambit, ploy

**deceitful** *dishonest, mendacious, lying, untruthful
*Ana* crafty, tricky, wily, guileful, foxy, insidious, cunning, *sly, artful: underhand, underhanded, stealthy, furtive, clandestine (see SECRET): *crooked, devious, oblique: delusory, deceptive, delusive, *misleading
*Ant* trustworthy —*Con* *reliable, dependable, trusty

**deceive,** mislead, delude, beguile, betray, double-cross mean to lead astray or into evil or to frustrate by underhandedness or craft. A person or thing *deceives* one by leading one to take something false as true, something nonexistent as real, something counterfeit as genuine, something injurious as helpful: the term may imply no more than a chance or inadvertent confusing or it may suggest a deliberate ensnaring or entrapping for the agent's own and often evil ends ⟨*deceived* by a chance resemblance into the belief that he had seen his dead sister's spirit⟩ ⟨"No woman's safe with him." "Ah, but he hasn't *deceived* me, Mrs. Berry. He has not pretended he was good"—*Meredith*⟩ ⟨a person who first subconsciously *deceives* himself and then imagines that he is being virtuous and truthful—*Russell*⟩ A person or thing **misleads** one by causing one to follow a wrong path, way, or course or to fall into error ⟨*misled* by a confusing traffic signal⟩ ⟨we never find them *misled* into the conception that such gifts are an end in themselves—*Dickinson*⟩ ⟨nor is there any safeguard against the nations being *misled* and deceived by their governments into sanctioning another great war—*Inge*⟩ ⟨Thrasyllus never told lies but he loved *misleading* people—*Graves*⟩ A person or thing **deludes** one by deceiving or misleading one so completely as to make one a fool, a dupe, or so befuddled as to be incapable of distinguishing the false from the true ⟨I began to wonder whether I, like the spider that chased the shadow, had been *deluded,* and had seemed to hear a sound that was not a sound—*Hudson*⟩ ⟨did he, did all the people who said they didn't mind things, know that they really did? Or were they indeed *deluded?*—*Rose Macaulay*⟩ A person or, less often, a thing, **beguiles** one by using such subtle and usually agreeable or alluring devices as to mislead, deceive, or delude one ⟨the male propensity to be *beguiled*—*Mary Austin*⟩ ⟨I recalled some of the Indian beliefs, especially that of the . . . man-devouring monster who is said to *beguile* his victims into the dark forest by mimicking the human voice—*Hudson*⟩ ⟨marshlights to *beguile* mankind from tangible goods and immediate fruitions—*Mumford*⟩ A person or thing **betrays** one by using deception or treachery to deliver one into the hands of an enemy or put one in a dangerous or false position ⟨verily I say unto you, that one of you shall *betray* me—*Mt 26:21*⟩ ⟨knowing that nature never did *betray* the heart that loved her—*Wordsworth*⟩ ⟨so, times past all number deceived by false shows, deceiving we cumber the road of our foes, for this is our virtue: to track and *betray*—*Kipling*⟩ A person **double-crosses** another and usually a friend, partner, or accomplice by deceiving or betraying him, especially by double-dealing or duplicity ⟨said he had been *double-crossed* by his partner⟩ ⟨De Valera charged that his own trusted negotiators had *double-crossed* him by signing an agreement to take the detested oath of loyalty to the British king—*Blanshard*⟩ **Ana** *cheat, cozen, defraud, overreach: outwit, circumvent (see FRUSTRATE): *dupe, gull, befool, trick, hoax, hoodwink, bamboozle **Ant** undeceive: enlighten

**decency** *decorum, propriety, dignity, etiquette **Ana** seemliness, decorousness (see corresponding adjectives at DECOROUS): fitness, suitability, fittingness, appropriateness (see corresponding adjectives at FIT)

**decent** 1 *decorous, seemly, proper, nice **Ana** fitting, *fit, appropriate, suitable, meet: conventional, formal, ceremonious (see CEREMONIAL) **Con** *awkward, gauche, inept, maladroit, clumsy: crude, rough, *rude, uncouth
2 modest, pure, *chaste **Ana** virtuous, *moral, ethical, noble: pleasing, grateful,

welcome, agreeable, *pleasant **Ant** indecent: obscene —*Con* lewd, lascivious, wanton, libertine, *licentious: ribald, gross, *coarse, vulgar: dissolute, profligate, reprobate, *abandoned

**deception** 1 Deception, fraud, double-dealing, trickery, chicane, chicanery mean the act or practice of, or the means used by, one who deliberately deceives in order to accomplish his ends. **Deception** may or may not imply blameworthiness, for it may be used not only of cheating, swindling, and tricking but also of many arts or games in which the object is illusion or mystification ⟨he is incapable of *deception*⟩ ⟨there is, as the conjurers say, no *deception* about this tale—*Kipling*⟩ ⟨magicians are adepts in *deception*⟩ *Deception* also may be used for the state of being deceived ⟨fall into *deception*⟩ ⟨he is surely greedy of delusion, and will hardly avoid *deception*—*Browne*⟩ **Fraud,** on the other hand, except in casual use, always implies guilt, often criminality, in act or practice. Distinctively, it usually suggests the perversion of the truth for the sake of persuading someone to surrender some valuable possession or a legal right ⟨the elder brother gained control of the property by *fraud*⟩ ⟨he will never stoop to *fraud,* no matter how much he desires to get rich⟩ The term may suggest an act or practice involving concealment of truth, violation of trust and confidence, or nonperformance of contracted acts by which one (as an agent, an attorney, an executor, an employer, or an employee) gains an advantage over another to the injury of the latter ⟨according to one legal decision "silence where necessity requires speech may sometimes constitute *fraud*"⟩ ⟨I think that obtaining money by *fraud* may be made a crime as well as murder or theft; that a false representation, expressed or implied at the time of making a contract of labor, that one intends to perform it and thereby obtaining an advance, may be declared a case of fraudulently obtaining money—*Justice Holmes*⟩ **Double-dealing** usually implies duplicity in character and in actions, for it frequently suggests an act that in its essence is contrary to one's professed attitude ⟨one does not always believe them . . . they often say one thing and mean another, so that we may fairly accuse them of *double-dealing*—*Jernigan*⟩ The term may imply secret treating with each of two opposed persons or groups as though one were friendly to that person or group and inimical to the other ⟨Saville . . . by his *double-dealing* with the King and the Scots, proved himself a political traitor—*D'Israeli*⟩ **Trickery** implies acts or practices that are intended to dupe or befool others; it often implies sharp practice or actual dishonesty ⟨we rely not upon management or *trickery,* but upon our own hearts and hands—*Jowett*⟩ ⟨they held that the basest *trickery* or deceit was not dishonorable if directed against a foe—*Amer. Guide Series: R. I.*⟩ **Chicane** and **chicanery** imply petty or paltry trickery and often subterfuge especially in legal proceedings ⟨to wrest from them by force, or shuffle from them by *chicane* —*Burke*⟩ ⟨many scenes of London intrigues and complex *chicanery*—*De Quincey*⟩ ⟨making a tremendous fight, chiefly by *chicane*—whooping for peace while preparing for war, playing mob fear against mob fear—*Mencken*⟩ **Ana** *deceit, duplicity, dissimulation, cunning, guile: cheating, cozening, defrauding, overreaching (see CHEAT): duping, gulling, hoaxing, hoodwinking, bamboozling, befooling (see DUPE)
2 *imposture, cheat, fraud, sham, fake, humbug, counterfeit, deceit **Ana** illusion, *delusion, hallucination, mirage

**deceptive** *misleading, delusory, delusive **Ana** specious, *plausible, colorable: *false, wrong **Con** genuine, *authentic, veritable, bona fide: true, *real,

---

A colon (:) separates groups of words discriminated. An asterisk (*) indicates place of treatment of each group.

actual

**decide,** determine, settle, rule, resolve mean to come or to cause to come to a conclusion. **Decide** presupposes previous consideration of a matter causing doubt, wavering, debate, or controversy and implies the arriving at a more or less logical conclusion that brings doubt or debate to an end: the word may take as its subject the person or persons arriving at such a conclusion or the thing or things that bring them to the conclusion ⟨the time for deliberation has then passed. He has *decided*—*John Marshall*⟩ ⟨this exordium, and Miss Pross's two hands in quite agonized entreaty clasping his, *decided* Mr. Cruncher—*Dickens*⟩ ⟨the . . . mistress of the household referred to her whether we should have another round or go in to supper. Of course, she always *decided* as she supposed the hostess wished—*Jefferies*⟩ ⟨it should disturb the complacency of those network officials who *decided* . . . that not enough people were watching to justify the expense—*Seldes*⟩ **Determine** (see also DIS-COVER 2) may mean to set limits or bounds to: when it means basically to decide, this implication of definitely fixing something so that its identity, its character, its scope, its direction is clear and beyond doubt distinguishes it from *decide;* one *decides* to give a dinner party but *determines* the guests to be invited; a legislature *decides* that the state constitution should be revised and appoints a committee with power to *determine* what changes shall be made. In a slightly different sense *determine* implies the arrival at a conclusion that either is a fixed and unalterable purpose or intention ⟨can you weep [i.e., move by weeping] fate from its *determined* purpose?—*Middleton*⟩ ⟨she was . . . obviously tormented by shyness, but as obviously *determined* to conquer it—*Mackenzie*⟩ or is the inevitable result, outcome, or end of what precedes ⟨what we notice *determines* what we do; what we do again *determines* what we experience—*James*⟩ ⟨their civilization was one of "city-states," not of kingdoms and empires; and their whole political outlook was necessarily *determined* by this condition—*Dickinson*⟩ **Settle** implies the arrival at a conclusion, often a mental or logical conclusion but sometimes a termination for which no individual is responsible, that brings to an end all doubt, all wavering, all dispute ⟨the Supreme Court of the United States has power to *settle* all questions of law⟩ ⟨time has *settled* few or none of the essential points of dispute—*Henry Adams*⟩ ⟨death *settled* all their problems⟩ **Rule** (see also GOVERN) implies a decision or determination by authority, especially by the authority of the court ⟨the judge *ruled* that the question was inadmissible⟩ **Resolve** implies an expressed or clear decision or determination to do or refrain from doing something ⟨*resolve* to get up earlier in the mornings⟩ ⟨*resolve* to give up smoking⟩ ⟨he was *resolved* to win through to fortune, but he must first discover his tools—*Buchan*⟩
*Ana* conclude, judge, gather (see INFER): *judge, adjudge, adjudicate
*Con* vacillate, waver, *hesitate, falter

**decided,** decisive are often confused, especially when they mean positive and leaving no room for doubt, uncertainty, or further discussion. In this sense the words are applied chiefly to persons, their natures, their utterances or manner of utterance, their opinions, or their choices. **Decided** implies a contrast with what is undetermined, indefinite, and neither this nor that; thus, a *decided* blue raises no question of its greenness or blackness; a *decided* success so far overpasses the line between success and failure that no one can question its favorable termination; a *decided* answer leaves no doubt of a person's meaning, wishes, or intentions. When applied to a person's char-

acter, expression, or movements *decided* suggests such qualities or outward signs of qualities as determination, resolution, and lack of all hesitation or vacillation ⟨the mother was a *decided* person to whose will everyone in the family submitted⟩ ⟨he has very *decided* opinions⟩ ⟨I see too many ways of saying things; a more *decided* mind hits on the right way at once—*Ward*⟩ ⟨then with a *decided* step she turned toward home—*Wharton*⟩ **Decisive,** on the other hand, implies an opposition to what is unsettled, uncertain, or wavering between this and that (for this sense as applied to things see CONCLUSIVE). When used in reference to persons it implies ability or intent to settle or success in settling a controverted matter once and for all ⟨this was enough to determine Sir Thomas, and a *decisive* "Then so it shall be" closed that stage of the business—*Austen*⟩ ⟨she stood up and surveyed herself in the pier glass. The *decisive* expression of her great florid face satisfied her—*Joyce*⟩
*Ana* *definite, definitive: determined, resolved (see DE-CIDE): positive, cocksure, certain, *sure: categorical, *explicit, express
*Con* dubious, *doubtful, questionable, problematic

**decipher** *vb* *solve, resolve, unfold, unravel
*Ana* interpret, construe, elucidate (see EXPLAIN): translate, paraphrase (see corresponding nouns at TRANS-LATION)

**decisive** 1 *conclusive, determinative, definitive
*Ana* critical, crucial, *acute: momentous, significant, consequential, important (see corresponding nouns at IMPORTANCE)
*Ant* indecisive
2 *decided
*Ana* peremptory, imperative, *masterful, imperious: certain, *sure, positive, cocksure: resolute, steadfast (see FAITHFUL)
*Ant* irresolute —*Con* wavering, fluctuating (see SWING): hesitant, reluctant (see DISINCLINED)

**deck** *vb* bedeck, *adorn, decorate, ornament, garnish, embellish, beautify
*Ana* array, apparel, attire, dress, *clothe

**declaration** announcement, publication, advertisement, proclamation, promulgation, broadcasting (see under DECLARE 1)

**declare** 1 Declare, announce, publish, advertise, proclaim, promulgate, broadcast (and their corresponding nouns declaration, announcement, publication, advertisement, proclamation, promulgation, broadcasting) denote to make known (or a making known) openly or publicly. To declare is to make known explicitly or plainly and usually in a formal manner ⟨if Lord Wolseley should *declare* his preference for a republic—*Brownell*⟩ ⟨the law . . . *declares* all such marriages absolutely null and void—*Taney*⟩ ⟨here the results of research are presented, here the progress of knowledge is *declared*—*De Voto*⟩ To **announce** is to declare especially for the first time something presumed to be of interest or intended to satisfy curiosity ⟨*announce* a discovery⟩ ⟨*announced* his candidacy for the mayoralty⟩ ⟨*announce* a forthcoming book⟩ ⟨she could not live without *announcing* herself to him as his mother—*Hardy*⟩ To **publish** is to make public especially through the medium of print ⟨he was . . . exercising great self-denial, for he was longing to *publish* his prosperous love—*Austen*⟩ ⟨there were no newspapers to *publish* every mystery—*Leland*⟩ To **advertise** is to call public attention to by repeated or widely circulated statements. In its general sense it often connotes unpleasant publicity or extravagance in statement ⟨an issue which *advertised* me . . . throughout the Church as a supporter of heresy—*William Lawrence*⟩ ⟨deliberately

*advertising* his willingness to make concessions—*Time*⟩ In its specific sense, as implying publicity for the sake of gaining patronage or support for an article of merchandise, it implies the use of communication media (as the press, the radio, handbills, or billboards); so used, it is devoid of unfavorable connotation ⟨*advertise* a new model of automobile⟩ To **proclaim** is to announce orally, sometimes by means of other sound (as of a trumpet), and loudly in a public place; by extension, to give wide publicity to, often insistently, proudly, boldly, or defiantly ⟨a lie is as much a lie, when it is whispered, as when it is *proclaimed* at the market cross—*Wollaston*⟩ ⟨you *proclaim* in the face of Hellas that you are a Sophist—*Jowett*⟩ To **promulgate** is to make known to all concerned something that has binding force (as a law of the realm or a dogma of the church) or something for which adherents are sought (as a theory or doctrine) ⟨the Doctrine of the Immaculate Conception was *promulgated* in December 1854—*Robertson*⟩ ⟨that for the training of the young one subject is just as good as another . . . is surely . . . an amazing doctrine to *promulgate*—*Grandgent*⟩ To **broadcast** is to make known (as by radio or television) in all directions over a large area ⟨the doctrine of missionary zeal . . . has been *broadcast* over Christendom—*Isaac Taylor*⟩ ⟨the largest . . . wireless station that can *broadcast* to the world—*Daily Mail*⟩ ⟨the book he has written to *broadcast* this conviction—*Gordon Harrison*⟩
*Ana* *inform, apprise, acquaint, advise, notify: impart, *communicate: *reveal, disclose, discover, divulge
**2** *assert, profess, affirm, aver, avouch, avow, protest, predicate, warrant
*Ana* *express, voice, utter, vent, broach, air, ventilate
*Con* *suppress, repress: *hide, conceal

**declass** *degrade, demote, reduce, disrate

**declension** decline, decadence, *deterioration, degeneration, devolution
*Ana* decaying *or* decay, disintegration, crumbling (see corresponding verbs at DECAY): retrogressiveness *or* retrogression, regressiveness *or* regression (see corresponding adjectives at BACKWARD)
*Con* ascent, *ascension: rising *or* rise (see corresponding verb RISE): advance, progress (see under ADVANCE *vb*): *progress, progression

**decline** *vb* Decline, refuse, reject, repudiate, spurn are comparable when they mean to turn away something or someone by not consenting to accept, receive, or consider it or him. **Decline** is the most courteous of these terms and is used chiefly in respect to invitations, offers (as of help), or services ⟨*decline* an invitation to dinner⟩ ⟨she *declined* the chair the Judge pushed toward her—*Cather*⟩ ⟨I am very sensible of the honor of your proposals, but it is impossible for me to do otherwise than *decline* them—*Austen*⟩ **Refuse** is more positive, often implying decisiveness, even ungraciousness ⟨meats by the law unclean . . . young Daniel could *refuse*—*Milton*⟩ ⟨the employers *refused* to "recognize" the unions—*Shaw*⟩ Refuse, however, may imply, as *decline* does not, the denial of something expected or asked for ⟨*refuse* a child permission to go out⟩ ⟨Mark knew that Mrs. Pluepott only lived to receive visitors, and he had not the heart to *refuse* her the pleasure of a few minutes—*Mackenzie*⟩ **Reject** stresses a throwing away, a discarding, or abandoning; it implies a refusal to have anything to do with a person or thing ⟨those who accepted the offer and those who *rejected* it—*Montague*⟩ ⟨Plotinus definitely *rejects* the notion that beauty is only symmetry—*Ellis*⟩ ⟨the poor man must be forgiven a freedom of expression, tinged at rare moments with a touch of bitterness, which magnanimity as well as caution would *reject* for one triumphant—*Cardozo*⟩

⟨common sense, *rejecting* with scorn all that can be called mysticism—*Inge*⟩ **Repudiate** implies a casting off (as of a wife whom one refuses any longer to recognize or accept); it usually connotes either a disowning or a rejection with scorn as untrue, unauthorized, or unworthy of acceptance ⟨*repudiate* a son⟩ ⟨the state has *repudiated* its debts⟩ ⟨*repudiate* a religious doctrine or a scientific theory⟩ ⟨I do not see how the United States could accept the contract and *repudiate* the consequence—*Justice Holmes*⟩ ⟨it is the law of nature that the strong shall rule; a law which everyone recognizes in fact, though everyone *repudiates* it in theory—*Dickinson*⟩ **Spurn** carries an even stronger implication of disdain or contempt in rejection than *repudiate* ⟨the proposals which she had proudly *spurned* only four months ago—*Austen*⟩ ⟨he would be *spurned* out of doors with a kick—*Snaith*⟩ ⟨must *spurn* all ease, all hindering love, all which could hold or bind—*Lowell*⟩
*Ana* *demur, balk, shy, boggle, jib, stick, stickle, scruple
*Ant* accept —*Con* take, *receive: consent, *assent, acquiesce, accede

**decline** *n* declension, decadence, *deterioration, degeneration, devolution
*Ana & Con* see those at DECLENSION

**decolorize** blanch, bleach, etiolate, *whiten

**decompose** *decay, rot, putrefy, spoil, disintegrate, crumble
*Ana* deliquesce, *liquefy, melt

**decorate** ornament, embellish, beautify, *adorn, deck, bedeck, garnish
*Ana* enhance, heighten, *intensify

**decorous,** decent, seemly, proper, nice apply to persons, their utterances, and their behavior, and mean conforming to an accepted standard of what is right or fitting or is regarded as good form. Something is **decorous** when it is marked by observance of the proprieties; the term usually implies a dignified, sometimes ceremonious, sometimes prim, formality ⟨the *decorous* platitudes of the last century—*J. R. Lowell*⟩ ⟨done something strange and extravagant and broken the monotony of a *decorous* age—*Emerson*⟩ ⟨on Sunday mornings the whole school went to church; in the afternoon it had a *decorous* walk —*H. G. Wells*⟩ Something is **decent** (for other sense, see CHASTE) when it keeps within the bounds of what is appropriate or fitting to its kind or class, not only from the points of view of morality or social propriety but also from those of good taste or the exigencies of a situation ⟨to praise a man's self, cannot be *decent,* except it be in rare cases—*Bacon*⟩ ⟨he cast only one glance at the dead face on the pillow, which Dolly had smoothed with *decent* care—*George Eliot*⟩ ⟨his *decent* reticence is branded as hypocrisy—*Maugham*⟩ Something is **seemly** when it is not only decorous or decent, but also pleasing to the eye, ear, or mind of the observer ⟨to make a *seemly* answer —*Shak.*⟩ ⟨a *seemly* display of enthusiasm⟩ ⟨it was not *seemly* that one so old should go out of his way to see beauty, especially in a woman—*Galsworthy*⟩ ⟨the safety of human society lies in the assumption that every individual composing it, in a given situation, will act in a manner hitherto approved as *seemly*—*Mencken*⟩ Something is **proper** when it is exactly what it should be according to accepted ethical or social standards or conventions ⟨Henchard's creed was that *proper* young girls wrote ladies'-hand—nay, he believed that bristling characters were as innate and inseparable a part of refined womanhood as sex itself—*Hardy*⟩ ⟨a few pages back I was expressing a *proper* diffidence about any conclusions in view, and here I am, almost shouting in favor of one—*Montague*⟩ Something is **nice** (see also NICE 1; CORRECT)

---

A colon (:) separates groups of words discriminated. An asterisk (*) indicates place of treatment of each group.

when it satisfies a somewhat fastidious taste in behavior, manners, or speech ⟨his conduct is not always so *nice*⟩ ⟨it is not enough for the knight of romance that you agree that his lady is a very *nice* girl—*Justice Holmes*⟩ ⟨the undergraduate literary club, whose membership included all *nice* boys with literary pretensions—*Marquand*⟩ *Ana* formal, conventional, ceremonious, *ceremonial: dignified, elegant (see corresponding nouns at ELEGANCE) *Ant* indecorous: blatant

**decorticate** *skin, peel, pare, flay

**decorum,** decency, propriety, dignity, etiquette are comparable either when they mean a code of rules respecting what is right, fitting, or honorable in behavior or, more often, when they mean the quality or character of rightness, fitness, or honorableness in behavior resulting from the observance of such a code. The first three words are somewhat literary; the last two are the most common in speech. Both *decorum* and *decency* imply that the code is based upon the nature of things or the circumstances which attend them, and therefore the rules which it embodies have their basis in nature or sound reason. **Decorum** especially suggests a code of rigid rules or laws governing the behavior of civilized men under given or understood conditions ⟨if gentlemen of that profession [the army] were at least obliged to some external *decorum* in their conduct—*Swift*⟩ ⟨that continual breach of . . . *decorum* which, in exposing his wife to the contempt of her own children, was so highly reprehensible—*Austen*⟩ ⟨he enjoyed a distinguished reputation for the excellence of his sermons, for the conduct of his diocese . . . and for the *decorum* and devotion of his private life—*T. S. Eliot*⟩ The term may suggest also order, moderation, and a high degree of intelligibility as a basis of literary or artistic beauty ⟨that *decorum* and orderliness without which all written speech must be ineffective and obscure—*Ellis*⟩ **Decency** often stresses a freedom from immodesty or obscenity ⟨*decency* in dress⟩ ⟨*decency* in conduct⟩ It may imply a seemliness or appropriateness that is based upon the right relation of one thing to another (as of a person to his profession, rank, or condition in life or of a thing to its use or end) ⟨for himself, Father Joseph was scarcely acquisitive to the point of *decency*. He owned nothing in the world but his mule—*Cather*⟩ ⟨there are those . . . for whom St. Paul's [in London], in comparison with St. Peter's [in Rome], is not lacking in *decency*—*T. S. Eliot*⟩ ⟨there were May [his wife], and habit, and honor, and all the old *decencies* that he and his people had always believed in—*Wharton*⟩ **Propriety** stresses conformity to a standard of what is proper or correct. When used in reference to language, it implies a regard for the established meanings of words and a refusal to accept what is not countenanced by good usage ⟨the severe *propriety* of his diction⟩ More often the word refers to social matters and implies adherence or conformity to a code respecting conduct or manners accepted as correct, proper, and essential by either the generality or a particular class of society ⟨my whole life has been at variance with *propriety*, not to say decency—*Byron*⟩ ⟨in the reign of James I the conduct of ladies and gentlemen was not marked by the same prim *propriety* as in the reign of the highly respectable Victoria—*Ellis*⟩ ⟨with characteristic independence she had made her reception rooms upstairs and established herself (in flagrant violation of all the New York *proprieties*) on the ground floor of her house—*Wharton*⟩ *Propriety* is sometimes preferred to *decency* when merely seemly or fitting correctness (and not conformity to convention) is implied ⟨the *propriety* and necessity of preventing interference with the course of justice—*Justice Holmes*⟩ **Dignity** (see also

ELEGANCE) seldom applies directly to a code or a rule but it does often denote a state of being that arises from obedience to what one, one's class, or one's profession regards as elevated, noble, or in full accordance with his rank, status, or position, and thereby it implies governance by a code or by forces which often correspond to the decencies or proprieties ⟨lost his *dignity*⟩ ⟨not in accord with the *dignity* of man as a son of God⟩ ⟨I had half a mind to save my *dignity* by telling him that—*Conrad*⟩ ⟨it is of the essence of real *dignity* to be self-sustained, and no man's *dignity* can be asserted without being impaired —*Henry Taylor*⟩ **Etiquette** is the usual term for the code of manners and behavior governing one's conduct in society or in particular circumstances (as in a court or legislature). It may replace *propriety,* for the conventional observance of these rules ⟨trained in the complex *etiquette* and protocol of the Diplomatic Corps⟩ ⟨unaware of the *etiquette* governing the setting of a table for a formal dinner⟩ ⟨the pompous *etiquette* of the court—*Prescott*⟩ ⟨Augustus had kept to the strict constitutional *etiquette*, indicating his preference but leaving the choice of his successor to the Senate—*Buchan*⟩ *Ana* formality, conventionality, ceremoniousness, solemnity (see corresponding adjectives at CEREMONIAL): *form, convention, convenance, usage *Ant* indecorum: license

**decoy** *n* *lure, bait, snare, trap

**decoy** *vb* *lure, entice, inveigle, tempt, seduce *Ana* snare, ensnare, trap, entrap, capture, *catch, bag: beguile, delude, *deceive, mislead

**decrease** *vb* **Decrease, lessen, diminish, reduce, abate, dwindle** denote to make or grow less, but they are not freely interchangeable. *Decrease* and *lessen* are often employed in place of any of the others. **Decrease** normally retains, even in the transitive, an implication of the process of growing less, and suggests progressive decline ⟨forces that *decrease* the population⟩ ⟨his temperature *decreases*⟩ ⟨his fears *decreased* as dawn approached⟩ ⟨the rise of the public high school . . . *decreased* the number and lessened the importance of the academies —*Amer. Guide Series: Vt.*⟩ **Lessen** is a close synonym of *decrease* but the latter is to be preferred in contexts employing specific numbers; thus, it is idiomatic to say that a fever has *lessened* or that it has *decreased* from 101° to 99° ⟨I hoped to obtain your forgiveness, to *lessen* your ill opinion—*Austen*⟩ **Diminish** is a more precise word when the ideas of taking away or subtraction by an agent and of resultant perceptible loss are to be emphasized ⟨their funds were greatly *diminished* by their extravagance⟩ ⟨his sense of personal initiative is cultivated instead of being *diminished*—*Russell*⟩ **Reduce** adds to *diminish* the implication of bringing down, or lowering; it suggests more than any of the others the operation of a personal agent ⟨*reduce* the time needed for an operation⟩ ⟨prices were *reduced* to below cost⟩ ⟨*reduce* budget estimates drastically⟩ *Reduce* also is applicable to lowering in rank, status, or condition ⟨*reduce* a sergeant to the ranks⟩ ⟨suddenly *reduced* from riches to absolute penury—*Conrad*⟩ **Abate** differs from *diminish* and *reduce* in its presupposition of something excessive in force, intensity, or amount and in its strong implication of moderation or, especially when referred to taxes or imposts, of deduction ⟨physically weakened by a stomach disorder that will not *abate*—*Alpert*⟩ **Dwindle,** like *decrease,* implies progressive lessening, but is more often applied to things capable of growing visibly smaller. It specifically connotes approach to a vanishing point ⟨hull down—hull down and under—she *dwindles* to a speck —*Kipling*⟩

---

*Ana* analogous words      *Ant* antonyms      *Con* contrasted words      See also explanatory notes facing page 1

*Ana* curtail, *shorten, retrench, abridge, abbreviate: *contract, shrink

*Ant* increase —*Con* augment, multiply, enlarge (see INCREASE): *extend, protract, prolong, lengthen, elongate: *expand, amplify, swell, dilate, distend

**decree** *vb* *dictate, prescribe, ordain, impose

*Ana* *command, order, enjoin, charge, direct: constrain, oblige, compel, *force

**decrepit** infirm, feeble, *weak, frail, fragile

*Ana* worn, wasted, *haggard: *aged, superannuated, old: tottering, quavering, shaking (see SHAKE)

*Ant* sturdy —*Con* *strong, stalwart, stout, tough, tenacious: *vigorous, lusty, energetic

**decry, depreciate, disparage, derogate, detract, belittle, minimize** mean to write, speak, or otherwise indicate one's feeling in regard to something in such a way as to reveal one's low opinion of it. **Decry** implies open or public condemnation or censure with the intent to discredit or run down someone or something ⟨there seems almost a general wish of *decrying* the capacity and undervaluing the labor of the novelist—*Austen*⟩ ⟨you've had a Western education . . . but you're *decrying* everything Western science has contributed to the world—*Heiser*⟩ **Depreciate** implies a representation of a person or thing as of smaller worth than that usually ascribed to it ⟨to prove that the Americans ought not to be free, we are obliged to *depreciate* the value of freedom itself—*Burke*⟩ ⟨he seems to me to *depreciate* Shakespeare for the wrong reasons—*T. S. Eliot*⟩ ⟨shocked to learn that professional art critics today *depreciate* his works—*Mary McCarthy*⟩ **Disparage** implies depreciation by more subtle or indirect methods (as slighting, invidious reference, or faint praise) ⟨the critic . . . is generally *disparaged* as an artist who has failed— *L. P. Smith*⟩ ⟨cities . . . which they sometimes pretended to *disparage,* but of which they were secretly and inordinately proud—*Repplier*⟩ **Derogate** and **detract** (both with *from*) stress the idea of taking away, positively and injuriously, especially from reputation or merit; *derogate from* may be used with an impersonal subject only, *detract from* with either a personal or an impersonal subject ⟨a few instances of inaccuracy or mediocrity can never *derogate from* the superlative merit of Homer and Vergil—*Goldsmith*⟩ ⟨far am I from *detracting from* the merit of some gentlemen . . . on that occasion—*Burke*⟩ ⟨the advocates of pure poetry are apt to take the line that any admixture of logical, of "prose" meaning *detracts from* the value of a poem—*Day Lewis*⟩ **Belittle** and **minimize** both imply depreciation, but *belittle* suggests an effort to make a thing contemptibly small, and *minimize* to reduce it to a minimum or to make it seem either disparagingly or defensively as small as possible ⟨he was inclined to *belittle* the assistance he had received from others⟩ ⟨he *minimized* the dangers of the task⟩ ⟨let there be no *belittling* of such qualities as Archer's—his coherent thinking, his sense of the worth of order and workmanship—*Montague*⟩ ⟨always delighted at a pretext for *belittling* a distinguished contemporary—*Edmund Wilson*⟩ ⟨"Don't think that I am trying to *minimize* your excellent work among the hop pickers this year," he told his curate—*Mackenzie*⟩

*Ana* *disapprove, deprecate: *criticize, denounce, reprehend, censure, reprobate, condemn

*Ant* extol —*Con* acclaim, laud, eulogize, *praise: *exalt, magnify

**dedicate** consecrate, hallow, *devote

*Ana* devote, *direct, address, apply

**deduce** *infer, gather, conclude, judge

*Ana* reason, cogitate, *think, speculate

**deduct, subtract** mean to take away one quantity from another. **Deduct** usually is used in reference to amounts (as of costs, payments, or credits) while **subtract** is used in reference to numbers or to figures obtained by a computation or calculation ⟨*deduct* the cost of transportation from the profits⟩ ⟨*deduct* the price of the returned article from his bill⟩ ⟨*subtract* five from nine⟩ ⟨*deduct* five percent of the receipts for his commission⟩ ⟨*subtract* the area of the triangular northeast section from the area of the whole plot of ground⟩

*Ant* add

**deduction** 1 Deduction, abatement, rebate, discount are comparable when they mean an amount subtracted from a gross sum. **Deduction** is interchangeable with any of the others but not without some loss in precision. An **abatement** is a deduction from a levied tax or impost ⟨an *abatement* of the duties levied at the customhouse⟩ A **rebate** is an amount deducted and returned after payment either in adjustment of an overcharge or to gain a competitive advantage ⟨a *rebate* on an income tax⟩ ⟨a *rebate* on an insurance premium⟩ A **discount** is a deduction from an amount owed or a price asked in consideration of a cash or prompt payment ⟨this bill is subject to 2 percent *discount* if paid within thirty days⟩ It also may denote an advance deduction of the amount of interest payable on a loan or note from the time the loan is made or the note purchased until the due date ⟨the bank credited his account with the proceeds of the note less the *discount*⟩ 2 inference, conclusion, judgment (see under INFER) 3 Deduction, induction and their corresponding adjectives **deductive, inductive** are comparable as used in logic to designate forms of reasoning. **Deduction** and **deductive** imply reasoning from premises or propositions antecedently proved or assumed as true or certain and procedure from the general or universal to a particular conclusion; thus, the conclusion that one must die someday is based on the premises that all men are mortal and that one is a man; therefore one infers by *deduction* or *deductive* reasoning that one must necessarily be mortal. **Induction** and **inductive** imply reasoning from particular facts to a conclusion that is general or universal in its nature. In its simplest form *induction* implies a knowledge of every particular and a generalization from these; thus, the conclusion that all of a certain man's books have red bindings is reached by *induction* or *inductive* reasoning when one has surveyed his library and has found no exception to this rule. In its more complicated forms, since knowledge of every particular is usually impossible, *induction* often implies the use of postulates or assumptions which are generally accepted (as the uniformity of nature), more or less tentative conclusions, and constant observation and experiment and reexamination of the evidence. In this sense many of the laws of nature stated in the various sciences are derived by *induction,* but when these laws are used as premises and become the bases for further inferences, the reasoning becomes *deductive.*

**deductive** inductive (see under DEDUCTION 3)

*Ana* inferential, ratiocinative (see under INFERENCE)

**deed** *n* *action, act

*Ana* exploit, *feat, achievement

**deed** *vb* *transfer, convey, alienate

**deem** *consider, regard, account, reckon

*Ana* conclude, gather, *infer

**deep** 1 Deep, profound, abysmal. *Deep* and *profound* denote extended either downward from a surface or, less often, backward or inward from a front or outer part. **Deep** is the most general term ⟨a *deep* pond⟩ ⟨a slope cut by *deep* gullies⟩ As applied to persons or to mental states or processes, *deep* implies the presence or a necessity for the exercise of penetration or subtlety, some-

A colon (:) separates groups of words discriminated. An asterisk (*) indicates place of treatment of each group.

times of craft ⟨a *deep* politician⟩ ⟨*deep* plots⟩ ⟨a little knowledge often estranges men from religion, a *deeper* knowledge brings them back to it—*Inge*⟩ ⟨a *deep* study of the inner meaning of the work—*Braithwaite*⟩ **Profound** connotes exceedingly great depth ⟨a gulf *profound* as that Serbonian bog . . . where armies whole have sunk—*Milton*⟩ ⟨canyons more *profound* than our deepest mountain gorges—*Cather*⟩ It may imply the presence or need of thoroughness ⟨a *profound* thinker⟩ ⟨a *profound* treatise⟩ ⟨are, in their meditative depths, among the few *profound* poems of our day—*Untermeyer*⟩ As expressing intensity, *profound* is commonly stronger than *deep* ⟨motherhood, this queer, sensuous, cherishing love . . . an emotion more *profound* than most—*Rose Macaulay*⟩ **Abysmal** carries the idea of *abyss*, infinite depth, and implies fathomless distance downward, backward, or inward from a surface ⟨mountain roads . . . within a few inches of *abysmal* precipices —*W. R. Arnold*⟩ It may imply measureless degree and is then used with words denoting a lack of something ⟨*abysmal* ignorance⟩ ⟨*abysmal* darkness⟩ ⟨plays of an *abysmal* foolishness—*Brooks*⟩
**Con** shallow, *superficial: flat, plane, plain, *level
2 *broad, wide

**deep-rooted** deep-seated, chronic, confirmed, *inveterate
*Ana* established, fixed, set, settled (see SET *vb*)
**Con** eradicated, extirpated, uprooted, wiped out (see EXTERMINATE)

**deep-seated** chronic, deep-rooted, confirmed, *inveterate
*Ana* ingrained, constitutional, *inherent: profound, *deep

**deface, disfigure** mean to mar the appearance of a thing. **Deface** usually suggests a marring of the face or external appearance of something; it frequently implies the effacement, obliteration, or removal of some part or detail ⟨earth has yet a little gilding left, not quite rubbed off, dishonored, and *defaced*—*Hazlitt*⟩ ⟨a door *defaced* by innumerable incised inscriptions—*Shaw*⟩ ⟨bad poets *deface* what they take [from others], and good poets make it into something better—*T. S. Eliot*⟩ **Disfigure**, as applied to a surface, implies deeper or more permanent injury than *deface;* as applied to figure or conformation, it frequently suggests such impairing of beauty or attractiveness as results from other than structural injury ⟨a book *disfigured* by many serious faults⟩ ⟨the smallpox . . . fell foul of poor little Oliver's face . . . and left him scarred and *disfigured* for his life—*Thackeray*⟩ ⟨where trees, *disfigured* by no gaudy lanterns, offered the refreshment of their darkness and serenity—*Galsworthy*⟩ ⟨in the midst of the political investigations which *disfigure* our time—*Sat. Review*⟩
*Ana* *injure, damage, mar: *deform, distort, contort: mutilate, batter, mangle (see MAIM)

**defame** vilify, calumniate, *malign, traduce, asperse, slander, libel
*Ana* vituperate, revile (see SCOLD): *decry, disparage, detract, derogate
**Con** *praise, laud, eulogize, extol, acclaim

**default** *n* *failure, neglect, miscarriage, dereliction
*Ana* absence, *lack, want, privation: *imperfection, deficiency, shortcoming, fault

**defeat** *vb* beat, *conquer, vanquish, lick, subdue, subjugate, reduce, overcome, surmount, overthrow, rout
*Ana* *frustrate, thwart, foil, baffle, balk, circumvent, outwit
**Con** *yield, submit, capitulate, succumb, cave, bow, defer

**defect** 1 *lack, want, dearth, absence, privation
*Ana* deficiency, defectiveness (see corresponding adjectives at DEFICIENT): *need, necessity, exigency
2 flaw, *blemish
*Ana* *fault, failing, frailty, foible
**Con** *excellence, perfection, virtue, merit

**defection, desertion, apostasy** mean an abandonment that involves the breaking of a moral or legal bond or tie and that is highly culpable from the point of view of the person, cause, or party abandoned. **Defection** emphasizes both the fact of one's falling away and the loss that is sustained by his failure to adhere to his allegiance; in itself as apart from the context it commonly gives no certain indication of motive, though at times disaffection or loss of confidence is connoted ⟨the conversions are probably balanced by the *defections* and in some countries the Church seems even to be losing ground—*Times Lit. Sup.*⟩ ⟨the news of the *defection* of Lepidus caused the Senate to declare him a public enemy—*Buchan*⟩ ⟨a single *defection* would throw the Senate into a deadlock of 48 to 48—*Neuberger*⟩ **Desertion** (see also under ABANDON) presupposes an oath of allegiance or a duty or an obligation to guard, protect, or support, the violation of which constitutes a crime or a distinctly blameworthy act. It also suggests a base motive (as cowardly fear or a desire to shirk) ⟨the penalty for *desertion* from an army in time of war is usually death⟩ ⟨many persons considered Wordsworth's defection from the liberal cause a *desertion*⟩ ⟨the crisis of our times is not such as to justify *desertion* of basic traditions—*Chapman*⟩ **Apostasy** implies a repudiation of something one has formerly and voluntarily professed; it connotes therefore a retreat (as in weakness) from a position or stand one has taken. The term is used chiefly with reference to a repudiation of religious beliefs, but it is employed also when moral, philosophical, or other principles are involved ⟨when Raphael . . . had forewarned Adam, by dire example, to beware *apostasy*—*Milton*⟩ ⟨marriage is to me *apostasy* . . . sale of my birthright, shameful surrender—*Shaw*⟩ ⟨my political *apostasy* . . . was attended with no diminution of reverence for that great citizen army that defended and saved the Union—*Nicholson*⟩
*Ana* disaffection, alienation, estrangement (see corresponding verbs at ESTRANGE): abandonment, forsaking (see corresponding verbs at ABANDON)
**Con** faithfulness, loyalty, constancy (see corresponding adjectives at FAITHFUL): allegiance, *fidelity, fealty

**defective** *deficient
*Ana* impaired, damaged, injured, marred (see INJURE): vitiated, corrupted, debased (see under DEBASE): deranged, disordered (see DISORDER)
*Ant* intact —**Con** *perfect, entire, whole: complete, *full, plenary: sound, *healthy

**defend** 1 Defend, protect, shield, guard, safeguard mean to keep secure from danger or against attack. **Defend** implies the use of means to ward off something that actually threatens or to repel something that actually attacks ⟨raise a large army to *defend* the country from aggression⟩ ⟨guns used in *defending* the explorers against hostile incursions of the natives⟩ ⟨the independence of the Supreme Court of the United States should be *defended* at all costs—*Lippmann*⟩ **Protect** implies the use of a covering as a bar to the admission or impact of what may injure or destroy ⟨*protect* one's estate from intruders by a high wall⟩ ⟨*protect* one's eyes from the sun by dark glasses⟩ ⟨*protect* one's family by ample insurance⟩ ⟨*protect* tobacco plants by a cheesecloth screen⟩ ⟨the ring of old forts which so far had *protected* the city successfully—*P. W. Thompson*⟩ **Shield** differs from *protect*

---

*Ana* analogous words      *Ant* antonyms      **Con** contrasted words      See also explanatory notes facing page 1

especially in its suggestion of a protective intervention comparable to a medieval warrior's shield before one exposed to imminent danger or actual attack ⟨Heavens *shield* Lysander, if they mean a fray!—*Shak.*⟩ ⟨I could scarcely believe that she would wish to *shield* her husband's murderer, if he were that—*Rose Macaulay*⟩ **Guard** implies a standing watch at or over for the sake of defense; it usually connotes vigilance ⟨the entrances to the palace are well *guarded*⟩ ⟨the president is always *guarded* by secret service men⟩ ⟨the accumulation of private wealth in Boston, thriftily *guarded* by the canny Whigs—*Brooks*⟩ ⟨inmates of a fortress are defended by its guns, protected by its walls, and *guarded* by sentries against surprise⟩ **Safeguard,** much more strongly than any of the preceding words, implies use of protective measures where merely potential danger exists ⟨*safeguard* children who play on the streets⟩ ⟨*safeguard* our shores from attack⟩ ⟨in all this he was more than worldlywise. He was *safeguarding* his own self-respect—*Repplier*⟩
*Ana* ward, avert, *prevent: oppose, *resist, withstand: fight, battle, war, *contend
*Ant* combat: attack —*Con* assault, assail, bombard, storm (see ATTACK): submit, cave, *yield, capitulate
2 assert, *maintain, justify, vindicate
*Ana* voice, vent, utter, *express, air: *explain, account, justify, rationalize: *support, champion, uphold, back

**defer, postpone, intermit, suspend, stay** mean to cause a delay in an action, activity, or proceeding. **Defer** suggests little more than a putting off till a later time; ordinarily it implies an intentional delaying ⟨*defer* a discussion of a proposal until more members are present⟩ ⟨*defer* payment on a note⟩ ⟨he *deferred* giving his son needed advice until he found the boy in a less refractory mood⟩ It may imply a delay in fulfillment, attainment, or fruition that is occasioned by conditions beyond one's control ⟨hope *deferred* maketh the heart sick—*Prov* 13:12⟩ ⟨reluctantly, he made up his mind to *defer* the more exacting examinations until another time—*Cronin*⟩ **Postpone** implies an intentional deferring, commonly until a definite time ⟨*postpone* a meeting for a week⟩ ⟨her dentist was willing to *postpone* her appointment until Saturday⟩ ⟨I think that we had better *postpone* our look round the church until after lunch—*Mackenzie*⟩ **Intermit** implies a stopping for a time, usually as a measure of relief, and typically with an expectation of starting again after an interval ⟨pray to the gods to *intermit* the plague—*Shak.*⟩ ⟨when seriously urged to *intermit* his application [to study], and allow himself a holiday—*Pattison*⟩ **Suspend** denotes a stopping or making inoperative for a time and usually for a reason (as personal desire or a legal restriction) that is implicit or explicit in the context ⟨Eleanor's work was *suspended* while she gazed with increasing astonishment —*Austen*⟩ ⟨*suspend* trolley service during the parade⟩ ⟨Henchard gave orders that the proceedings were to be *suspended*—*Hardy*⟩ ⟨Congress has authorized the president to *suspend* the operation of a statute—*Justice Holmes*⟩ ⟨*suspend* one's judgment of a person charged with a crime⟩ **Stay** implies the interposition of an obstacle to something that is in progress; it may suggest bringing it to a complete stop, but more often it suggests an intermitting or suspending or a slackening of pace ⟨two spectators started forward, but she *stayed* them with a motion of her hand—*Dickens*⟩ ⟨they couldn't *stay* the flow of her ideas by reminding her how much the alteration would cost—*Mary Austin*⟩ ⟨when his mind fails to *stay* the pace set by its inventions, madness must ensue—*Day Lewis*⟩
*Ana* *delay, retard, slow

*Con* hasten, hurry, *speed, accelerate
**defer** bow, *yield, submit, cave, capitulate, succumb, relent
*Ana* accede, acquiesce, *assent, agree: conform, accommodate, *adapt, adjust: truckle, *fawn, cringe
**deference** reverence, homage, *honor, obeisance
*Ana* veneration, worship, adoration (see under REVERE): respect, esteem, admiration, *regard
*Ant* disrespect —*Con* disdain, scorn, contempt, despite (see under DESPISE)
**deficiency** *imperfection, shortcoming, fault
*Ana* *lack, want, dearth, defect: flaw, *blemish: *failure, neglect, default, miscarriage, dereliction
*Ant* excess
**deficient** *adj* Deficient, defective mean showing lack of something necessary. The words are sometimes used interchangeably though they tend to diverge in their meanings. **Deficient** typically implies a falling short in the amount, quantity, or force considered essential to adequacy or sufficiency; **defective** on the other hand typically implies existence of some definite fault, injury, or flaw that impairs the completeness or efficiency of something; thus, a person is *deficient* in courage when he has not sufficient courage to meet his difficulties; he is mentally *deficient* when he has not sufficient intelligence to enable him to take care of himself; he is mentally *defective* (or a mental *defective*) when some fault or defect in his nervous system impairs his ability to think coherently; he suffers from *defective* hearing when by disease or injury the organ of hearing has become defective ⟨*deficient* sympathies⟩ ⟨a *deficient* supply of food⟩ ⟨a *defective* crystal⟩ ⟨a *defective* mechanism⟩
*Ana* *meager, scanty, scant, sparse, exiguous: scarce, rare, *infrequent, uncommon
*Ant* sufficient, adequate: excessive —*Con* *plentiful, plenteous, ample, abundant: *excessive, inordinate, immoderate, extravagant
**defile** pollute, taint, *contaminate, attaint
*Ana* *debase, vitiate, deprave, corrupt, pervert, debauch: profane, desecrate (see corresponding nouns at PROFANATION)
*Ant* cleanse: purify —*Con* hallow, consecrate (see DEVOTE)
**define** *vb* *prescribe, assign
*Ana* *limit, circumscribe: fix, *set, establish
*Con* *mix, merge, mingle: *mistake, confuse, confound
**definite** 1 Definite, definitive are sometimes confused. What is **definite** (see also EXPLICIT) has limits so clearly fixed or defined or so unambiguously stated that there can be no doubt concerning the scope or the meaning of something so qualified ⟨he has very *definite* opinions on the matter⟩ ⟨*definite* accomplishments⟩ ⟨appointments are made for *definite* periods of time⟩ What is **definitive** (for fuller treatment see CONCLUSIVE) fixes or settles something else and therefore is final or decisive ⟨a *definitive* statement of a doctrine⟩ ⟨a *definitive* judicial decision by the highest court of the land⟩ ⟨a *definitive* biography⟩
*Ana* defined, prescribed, assigned (see PRESCRIBE): limited, restricted, circumscribed (see LIMIT *vb*): determined, settled, decided (see DECIDE)
*Ant* vague: loose —*Con* *obscure, ambiguous, equivocal
2 *explicit, express, specific, categorical
*Ana* clear, plain, distinct (see EVIDENT): *full, complete, downright, *forthright: precise, exact (see CORRECT *adj*) clear-cut, *incisive
*Ant* indefinite: equivocal —*Con* *doubtful, dubious, questionable

A colon (:) separates groups of words discriminated. An asterisk (*) indicates place of treatment of each group

**definitive** 1 determinative, decisive, *conclusive
*Ana* settling, deciding, determining (see DECIDE): final, concluding, *last, terminal, ultimate
*Ant* tentative, provisional
2 *definite
*Ana, Ant* see those at DEFINITIVE 1

**deflate** compress, shrink, *contract, condense, constrict
*Ana* reduce, *decrease, lessen: exhaust, *deplete, drain: puncture, prick (see PERFORATE): attenuate, extenuate (see THIN)
*Ant* inflate  —*Con* distend, *expand, dilate, swell

**deflect** *turn, divert, avert, sheer
*Ana* deviate, depart, diverge, *swerve, veer, digress: bend, *curve, twist

**deflection** *deviation, aberration, divergence
*Ana* bending, curving, twisting (see CURVE): swerving *or* swerve, veering *or* veer, departing *or* departure (see corresponding verbs at SWERVE)

**deform,** distort, contort, warp mean to mar or spoil a person's or thing's appearance, character, true nature, or development by or as if by twisting. **Deform** is the least specific of these terms in its implications; sometimes, it carries no significance other than that expressed above; sometimes, however, it suggests a loss of some particular excellence or essential (as comeliness, perfection of line, or attractiveness) ⟨soul-killing witches that *deform* the body—*Shak.*⟩ ⟨to *deform* thy gentle brow with frowns—*Rowe*⟩ ⟨I suspect Mr. Babbitt at times of an instinctive dread of organized religion, a dread that it should cramp and *deform* the free operations of his own mind—*T. S. Eliot*⟩ ⟨with the best intentions in the world, Mr. Imam is incessantly at work to *deform* and degrade the content of poetry—*Times Lit. Sup.*⟩ **Distort** usually carries a clear implication of twisting or wresting away from or out of the natural, regular, or true shape, posture, or direction; the term, however, is used not only in reference to physical or material things, but also in reference to minds, judgments, facts, or statements that may be twisted by conditions, circumstances, or, when a personal agent is involved, a dominating purpose or intent ⟨*distorted* as a living thing by pain—*Wilde*⟩ ⟨the upward slant of the candlelight *distorted* Mary Adeline's mild features, twisting them into a frightened grin—*Wharton*⟩ ⟨there is an element of truth in what you say, grossly as you may *distort* it to gratify your malicious humor—*Shaw*⟩ ⟨some accident of immediate overwhelming interest which appeals to the feelings and *distorts* the judgment—*Justice Holmes*⟩ **Contort** implies a more involved or continuous twisting together or upon itself; it therefore differs from *distort* in suggesting a grotesque or a painful effect rather than a departure from the natural, the true, or the normal ⟨that most perverse of scowls *contorting* her brow—*Hawthorne*⟩ ⟨the baby's face muscles *contorted* in a manner that only Mammy Clo could have interpreted as an expression of merriment—*Roark Bradford*⟩ ⟨one generation of fearless women could transform the world, by bringing into it a generation of fearless children, not *contorted* into unnatural shapes, but straight and candid, generous, affectionate, and free—*Russell*⟩ **Warp** denotes a twisting or bending or drawing out of a flat plane by some force (as drying and shrinking) ⟨the covers of the book are *warped*⟩ ⟨the back of the chair is *warped*⟩ It often may imply the operation of a force that twists or wrests a thing so as to give it a bias, a wrong slant, an abnormal direction, or a distorted significance ⟨cares have *warped* her mind⟩ ⟨*warped* opinions⟩ ⟨so they [trees] slowly come to full growth, until *warped*, stunted, or risen to fair and gracious height, they stand open to all the winds—*Galsworthy*⟩ ⟨to cut me off from all natural

and unconstrained relations with the rest of my fellow creatures would narrow and *warp* me if I submitted to it—*Shaw*⟩ ⟨I'm sure you are disinterested … but, frankly, I think your judgment has been *warped* by events—*Cather*⟩ ⟨their lives and minds have been *warped,* twisted, and soured—*Lardner*⟩
*Ana* *maim, cripple, mutilate, mangle, batter: disfigure, *deface: *injure, mar, damage, impair

**defraud** swindle, overreach, *cheat, cozen
*Ana* trick, bamboozle, hoax, gull, *dupe, befool: outwit, circumvent, foil (see FRUSTRATE)

**deft** *dexterous, adroit, handy
*Ana* nimble, *agile, brisk: *quick, ready, apt, prompt: skillful, skilled, adept, *proficient: sure, assured, *confident
*Ant* awkward  —*Con* clumsy, maladroit, inept, gauche (see AWKWARD)

**defunct** deceased, departed, late, *dead, lifeless, inanimate
*Ant* alive: live

**defy** *face, brave, challenge, dare, beard
*Ana* mock, deride, *ridicule: flout (see SCOFF): withstand, *resist, oppose, fight: confront, encounter, *meet
*Ant* recoil from

**degenerate** *adj* corrupt, infamous, *vicious, villainous, iniquitous, nefarious, flagitious
*Ana* degraded, demeaned (see ABASE): debased, depraved, debauched, perverted (see under DEBASE): dissolute, *abandoned, reprobate, profligate

**degeneration** devolution, decadence, *deterioration, decline, declension
*Ana* retrogressiveness *or* retrogression, regressiveness *or* regression (see corresponding adjectives at BACKWARD): debasement, degradation (see corresponding verbs at ABASE)

**degradation** see under *degrade* at ABASE

**degrade** 1 Degrade, demote, reduce, declass, disrate mean to lower in station, rank, or grade. **Degrade** may be used of any such lowering ⟨babies … *degrade* one to the state of anxious, fawning suppliants for a smile—*Wallace*⟩ ⟨turkeys not in prime condition are *degraded* on the market⟩ ⟨that the Duke of York should have concurred in the design of *degrading* that crown which it was probable that he would himself … wear—*Macaulay*⟩ It usually implies a real or presumed fault in what is acted on and often adds to the basic meaning a suggestion of humiliation (see *degrade* under ABASE) ⟨ridiculed and *degraded* for his ideas, he maintained his integrity in the prison cell —*D. M. Wolfe & E. M. Geyer*⟩ ⟨the world is weary of statesmen whom democracy has *degraded* into politicians—*Disraeli*⟩ It sometimes denotes a formal or ceremonial stripping (as of a priest or a military officer) of outward evidences of station or rank ⟨Dreyfus is *degraded* before the Army, January 5, 1895—*Guérard*⟩ **Demote** in itself and as distinct from its context does not imply fault to or humiliation of the one *demoted* ⟨he returns a captain (temporary), is promoted and *demoted* in the same order, made first lieutenant (permanent)—*Mailer*⟩ ⟨the secretaryship was *demoted* to a subordinate bureau in the Department of the Interior—*Neill*⟩ **Reduce** (see also DECREASE and CONQUER) never wholly loses its basic sense of to make less or smaller; it denotes a lessening in status or dignity whether involving an actual lowering in rank or not ⟨a sergeant *reduced* to the ranks⟩ ⟨people in *reduced* circumstances⟩ ⟨an old crusader … *reduced* to menial work—*Costain*⟩ **Declass** is typically used with respect to social classes; it may imply a loss of social position especially as a result of one's own actions ⟨even today a woman may *declass* herself by acts tolerated of her brothers⟩ Perhaps more frequently it may imply an altering of or a freeing from the restrictions of social status ⟨the growing masses of modern society that stand outside all class-strata. These *declassed* groups, composed . . . of individuals from all strata of society—*Arendt*⟩ ⟨a younger generation which feels that the writer ought to be at least a spiritual vagabond, a *declassed* mind —*The Dial*⟩ ⟨members of the *declassed* intelligentsia —*Ridgely Cummings*⟩ **Disrate** implies a reduction in military and more especially in naval or nautical rank and is used chiefly with reference to petty or noncommissioned officers ⟨the witness had been chief mate . . . but had been *disrated* . . . for drunkenness—*Mercantile Marine Mag.*⟩

*Ana* humble, humiliate, *abase, debase: disbar, rule out (see EXCLUDE)

*Ant* elevate

2 debase, demean, humble, *abase, humiliate

*Ana* *debase, deprave, debauch, pervert, corrupt, vitiate

*Ant* uplift —*Con* *exalt, magnify, aggrandize

**dehydrate** *vb* desiccate, *dry, parch, bake

**deign** condescend, *stoop

*Ana* vouchsafe, accord, concede, *grant, award

**deist** freethinker, *atheist, agnostic, unbeliever, infidel

**deject** *vb* *discourage, dishearten, dispirit

*Ana* *depress, weigh, oppress: distress, *trouble

*Ant* exhilarate: cheer

**dejected** depressed, dispirited, *downcast, disconsolate, woebegone

*Ana* weighed down, oppressed (see DEPRESS): *despondent, forlorn, hopeless: morose, glum, gloomy (see SULLEN)

**dejection** depression, melancholy, melancholia, gloom, *sadness, blues, dumps

*Ana* despondency, hopelessness, forlornness, despair, desperation (see under DESPONDENT)

*Ant* exhilaration

**delay** *vb* 1 Delay, retard, slow, slacken, detain are not always close synonyms, but they carry the same basic meaning: to cause someone or something to be behind in his or its schedule or usual rate of movement or progress. **Delay** implies the operation, usually the interference, of something that keeps back or impedes, especially from completion or arrival at a set or given time ⟨a plague upon that villain Somerset, that thus *delays* my promised supply—*Shak.*⟩ ⟨a criminal court jury . . . *delayed* a verdict all afternoon—*C. G. Jameson*⟩ **Retard** applies especially to motion, movement, or progress and implies something which causes it to reduce its speed ⟨*retard* the revolution of a wheel⟩ ⟨the snow *retards* our progress⟩ ⟨children *retarded* in development⟩ ⟨mental evolution has perhaps *retarded* the progress of physical changes—*Inge*⟩ ⟨the rate of decay [of radioactive substances] cannot be expedited or *retarded* by any known physical process—*Jeans*⟩ **Slow** (often followed by *up* or *down*) and **slacken** also imply a reduction in speed or rate of progress, but *slow* usually implies deliberation or intention and *slacken,* an easing or letting up or a relaxation of some sort ⟨the engineer *slowed* down the train as he approached the city⟩ ⟨the doctor administered digitalis to *slow* up his pulse⟩ ⟨as we turned into Compton Street together he *slowed* his step—*Brace*⟩ ⟨he *slackened* his pace to a walk⟩ ⟨having never *slackened* her . . . search for your father—*Dickens*⟩ **Detain** (see also ARREST 2) implies a being held back beyond an appointed time, often with resulting delay in arrival or departure or in accomplishment of what one has in mind ⟨I had been *detained* by unexpected business in the neighborhood—*Conrad*⟩ ⟨tell him that as I have a headache I

won't *detain* him today—*Hardy*⟩ ⟨you will not thank me for *detaining* you from the bewitching converse of that young lady—*Austen*⟩ ⟨I slipped my arm around her slender body to *detain* her—*Hudson*⟩

*Ana* impede, obstruct, *hinder, block: *defer, postpone, stay, suspend, intermit

*Ant* expedite: hasten —*Con* *speed, hasten, hurry, accelerate, quicken, precipitate

2 Delay, procrastinate, lag, loiter, dawdle mean to move or act slowly so that progress is hindered or work remains undone or unfinished. **Delay** (for transitive sense see DELAY 1) usually carries an implication of putting off something (as departure, initiation of an action or activity, or accomplishment of necessary work) ⟨when he had his instructions, he did not *delay* an instant⟩ ⟨time and again were we warned of the dykes, time and again we *delayed*—*Kipling*⟩ **Procrastinate** implies blameworthy or inexcusable delay usually resulting from laziness, indifference, hesitation, or the habit of putting off until tomorrow what should be done today ⟨the less one has to do, the less time one finds to do it in. One yawns, one *procrastinates,* one can do it when one will, and therefore one seldom does it at all—*Chesterfield*⟩ ⟨a timid, unsystematic, *procrastinating* ministry—*Burke*⟩ ⟨to fumble, to vacillate, to *procrastinate* and so let war come creeping upon us almost unawares—*White*⟩ **Lag** implies a failure to maintain a speed or pace, either one set by and therefore in comparison with that of another or one requisite to some end or goal ⟨after an hour's brisk walk, two of the hikers *lagged* behind the rest⟩ ⟨it was a time of great men, but our learning and scholarship *lagged* far behind those of Germany—*Inge*⟩ ⟨military preparation does *lag* at a shameful rate—*Carlyle*⟩ ⟨the production of certain parts necessary for airplanes is *lagging*⟩ **Loiter** implies delay while in progress, commonly while one is walking but sometimes while one is trying to accomplish a piece of work; it also suggests lingering or aimless sauntering or lagging behind ⟨very little remained to be done. Catherine had not *loitered;* she was almost dressed, and her packing almost finished—*Austen*⟩ ⟨the caravan has to go on; to *loiter* at any distance behind is to court extinction—*Montague*⟩ ⟨the children sauntered down Sloane Street, *loitering* at the closed shop windows, clinking their shillings in their pockets—*Rose Macaulay*⟩ **Dawdle** carries a slighter implication of delay in progress (especially in walking) than *loiter* but an even stronger connotation of idleness, aimlessness, or of a wandering mind; consequently it usually implies a wasting of time or a taking of more time than is warranted ⟨*dawdle* through four years of college⟩ ⟨the new maid *dawdles* over her work⟩ ⟨I did not hurry the rest of the way home; but neither did I *dawdle*—*Heiser*⟩ ⟨the sun *dawdles* intolerably on the threshold like a tedious guest—*Jan Struther*⟩

*Ana* linger, tarry, wait (see STAY): *hesitate, falter, vacillate, waver

*Ant* hasten, hurry

**delectable** *delightful, delicious, luscious

*Ana* gratifying, grateful, agreeable, pleasing, welcome, *pleasant: exquisite, rare, delicate, dainty, *choice: *palatable, savory, sapid, toothsome

*Con* *offensive, repulsive, revolting, loathsome: repellent, *repugnant, distasteful, abhorrent, obnoxious

**delectation** enjoyment, delight, *pleasure, joy, fruition

*Ana* amusement, diversion, entertainment (see under AMUSE): gratifying *or* gratification, regaling *or* regalement (see corresponding verbs at PLEASE)

**delegate** *n* Delegate, deputy, representative designate a person who stands in place of another or others. It is not always possible to distinguish these words, for they are all used in different places or at different times to designate persons whose offices and functions are much the same. Nevertheless there are broad or general differences in meaning which may be observed, although they will not always afford a clue as to why this person or that is called a *delegate*, a *deputy*, or a *representative*. **Delegate** applies to a person who is sent or is thought of as being sent with a commission to transact business for another or for others; it often specifically designates a person who is sent by an organized or unorganized body (as a branch of a larger organization or a group of employees) to a meeting where questions pertaining to the welfare of the entire organization or industry will be discussed and voted upon. *Delegate* usually implies powers that are not plenary but are somewhat modified (as by the delegate's own power to influence or convince others and by the need of his bowing to the will of the majority) ⟨a lay *delegate* to a Protestant Episcopal synod⟩ ⟨each branch of the American Legion sends two *delegates* to the national convention⟩ ⟨the workers and the employers each sent three *delegates* to the conference⟩ **Deputy** applies to a person who is given authority to act for another or for others as a substitute or as an agent; it is particularly applicable to a person who has been chosen to perform a part or the whole of an official's duties ⟨the sheriff of each county appoints one or more *deputies*⟩ ⟨since he could not be present at the conference, he sent a *deputy*⟩ **Representative** applies fundamentally to a person who takes the place of one or more persons in a situation where for some reason the latter cannot be. It may be used of a person engaged to do or to transact business for another or others ⟨the firm's legal *representative*⟩ ⟨the king's *representative* at the peace conference⟩ However it is more often employed in reference to one who takes the place of a larger group (as the electorate of a particular region) and thereby belongs to a body of men who as a whole are charged with making the laws for the state or nation ⟨even in a democracy the people as a whole cannot make the laws but assign that work to their *representatives* in Congress or in Parliament⟩ ⟨the elected became true *representatives* of the electors—*Steele*⟩ The terms are often used to imply the same or very similar functions in different places; thus, approximately the same body is called the House of *Representatives* in the United States and the Chamber of *Deputies* in the Republic of France; there is little difference except in voting powers between a *representative* from a state in the United States Congress and a *delegate* from a territory.

**delete** cancel, efface, obliterate, blot out, expunge, *erase
*Ana* eliminate, *exclude, rule out: omit (see NEGLECT *vb*)
**deleterious** detrimental, *pernicious, baneful, noxious
*Ana* injuring *or* injurious, harming *or* harmful, hurting *or* hurtful (see corresponding verbs at INJURE): destroying *or* destructive (see corresponding verb DESTROY): ruining *or* ruinous (see corresponding verb RUIN)
*Ant* salutary —*Con* *beneficial, advantageous, profitable: wholesome, *healthful, healthy
**deliberate** *adj* **1** willful, intentional, *voluntary, willing
*Ana* purposed, intended (see INTEND): conscious, cognizant, *aware: mortal, *deadly
*Ant* impulsive —*Con* inadvertent, *careless, heedless, thoughtless
**2 Deliberate, considered, advised, premeditated, designed, studied** are comparable when applied to a person's acts, words, or accomplishments with the meaning thought out in advance. **Deliberate** implies full awareness of the nature of what one says or does and often a careful and unhurried calculation of the intended effect or of the

probable consequences ⟨a *deliberate* lie⟩ ⟨a *deliberate* snub⟩ ⟨Poe's consummate and *deliberate* technique—*Lowes*⟩ ⟨the *deliberate* insertion into a lyrical context of pieces of slang and "prosaic" words—*Day Lewis*⟩ ⟨the tone of most comment, whether casual or *deliberate*, implies that ineptitude and inadequacy are the chief characteristics of government—*Frankfurter*⟩ **Considered,** unlike *deliberate*, which it closely resembles in meaning, is seldom applied to questionable acts or practices; it suggests careful study from all angles rather than calculation and often, therefore, connotes soundness or maturity of judgment ⟨there was no time for a *considered* reply⟩ ⟨the committee had before it many half-baked and a few *considered* proposals⟩ ⟨it [the press] is against Democrats, so far as I can see, not after a sober and *considered* review of the alternatives, but automatically, as dogs are against cats—*A. E. Stevenson*⟩ ⟨he saw no reason to parade his *considered* and decided loyalty—*Wylie*⟩ **Advised** mostly is used with deprecatory or intensifying adverbial modifiers and denotes so well thought out and considered that possible criticisms and objections have been reviewed and answers to them prepared ⟨she felt well *advised* to visit him before deciding to be his wife—*Forster*⟩ ⟨the public is well-*advised* to leave methodological decisions to members of the medical profession—*Woodring*⟩ Its related adverb *advisedly* is often used to carry the implications of *considered* (which has no adverb) ⟨he told them he used the offending word *advisedly*⟩ ⟨everything in this difficult situation has been done *advisedly*⟩ ⟨I often say that one must permit oneself, and that quite *advisedly* and deliberately, a certain margin of misstatement—*Cardozo*⟩ **Premeditated** emphasizes forethought and planning but often falls far short of *deliberate* in implying careful calculation and awareness of consequences ⟨certain self-conscious preciosities in his *premeditated* style—*Powys*⟩ It is applied especially to things (as crimes or insults) which are morally or socially unacceptable and for which only overwhelming impulse or overmastering passion (as of fear or rage) could reasonably be offered as extenuating circumstances; in such relation, then, *premeditated* implies wrongdoing unmitigated by circumstances ⟨a *premeditated* murder⟩ ⟨plain that Thady's presence on the scene at the moment was accidental and that the attack could not have been *premeditated*—*Trollope*⟩ **Designed** and its adverb *designedly* are often applied to what has the appearance of being accidental, spontaneous, or natural but which is actually the result of intention ⟨the *designed* failure of a project⟩ ⟨useless to seek to know whether he has been for years overlooked, or always *designedly* held prisoner—*Dickens*⟩ **Studied** is applied chiefly to effects gained or qualities achieved as a result of painstaking effort or careful attention to detail; it connotes absence of spontaneity ⟨a rather *studied* performance of a Beethoven symphony⟩ ⟨the *studied* dignity and anxious courtesy of the actor-manager—*Shaw*⟩ It is also applied to offensive acts committed with cool deliberation and with attention to their probable effect ⟨treat the opposition with *studied* discourtesy⟩
*Ana* planned, schemed, projected (see corresponding verbs under PLAN *n*): calculated (see CALCULATE): *careful, meticulous, scrupulous
*Ant* casual —*Con* haphazard, *random, hit-or-miss, desultory, happy-go-lucky, chance, chancy
**3** leisurely, *slow, dilatory, laggard
*Ana* *cautious, circumspect, wary, chary, calculating: *cool, collected, composed, imperturbable
*Ant* precipitate, abrupt —*Con* impetuous, headlong, sudden, hasty (see PRECIPITATE)

**deliberate** *vb* reflect, cogitate, *think, reason, speculate
*Ana* *ponder, meditate, ruminate, muse

**delicate** exquisite, dainty, rare, *choice, recherché, elegant
*Ana* delectable, *delightful, delicious: *soft, gentle, mild, lenient, balmy: ethereal, *airy, aerial
*Ant* gross —*Con* *coarse, vulgar: rank, rancid, *malodorous

**delicious** delectable, luscious, *delightful
*Ana* *palatable, sapid, savory, toothsome, appetizing: delicate, dainty, exquisite, *choice, rare
*Con* distasteful, obnoxious, *repugnant, repellent: *insipid, vapid, flat, wishy-washy, inane, jejune, banal

**delight** *n* *pleasure, delectation, enjoyment, joy, fruition
*Ana* glee, *mirth, jollity, hilarity: rapture, transport, *ecstasy: satisfaction, contentment (see corresponding verbs at SATISFY)
*Ant* disappointment: discontent

**delight** *vb* gratify, *please, rejoice, gladden, tickle, regale
*Ana* *satisfy, content: divert, *amuse, entertain: charm, enchant, fascinate, allure, *attract
*Ant* distress: bore —*Con* *trouble: *afflict, try: *grieve: *annoy, vex, irk, bother

**delightful, delicious, delectable, luscious** mean extremely pleasing or gratifying to the senses or to aesthetic taste. **Delightful,** the least restricted in its application of these words, may refer to anything that affords keen, lively pleasure and stirs the emotions agreeably, whether the direct appeal is to the mind, the heart, or the senses ⟨a *delightful* view⟩ ⟨a *delightful* talk⟩ ⟨a *delightful* companion⟩ ⟨my ears were never better fed with such *delightful* pleasing harmony—*Shak.*⟩ ⟨the experience of overcoming fear is extraordinarily *delightful*—*Russell*⟩ ⟨the most charming and *delightful* book I have read in many a day—*Canby*⟩ **Delicious** commonly refers to sensuous pleasures, especially those of taste and smell ⟨*delicious* food⟩ ⟨a *delicious* sense of warmth⟩ but may be applied to anything which is so delightful that one dwells upon it with sensuous gratification ⟨her gestures *delicious* in their modest and sensitive grace—*Bennett*⟩ ⟨I am not staying here, but with the Blenkers, in their *delicious* solitude at Portsmouth—*Wharton*⟩ ⟨there are people whose society I find *delicious*—*L. P. Smith*⟩ **Delectable** in its implications is often indistinguishable from *delightful* and especially from *delicious,* though it often suggests more refined or discriminating enjoyment ⟨the trees of God, *delectable* both to behold and taste—*Milton*⟩ ⟨a *delectable* tale⟩ ⟨the *delectable* fragrance of freesia⟩ ⟨its scoring is *delectable,* with the subtlest of balances, mixed colors and shifting sonorities —*Musical America*⟩ The term is more often used than either *delightful* or *delicious* with a humorous or ironical connotation ⟨the spoken word of some *delectable* Sarah Gamp—*Montague*⟩ **Luscious** adds to *delicious* an implication of richness (as of flavor, fragrance, coloring, or sound) ⟨*luscious* music⟩ As applied to fruits, it suggests fullness of flavor and rich ripe juiciness ⟨*luscious* sun-warmed peaches⟩ Like *delectable* it may be used humorously or ironically, but it then commonly adds the implication of extravagance, exaggeration, or, more specifically, voluptuousness ⟨*luscious* passages of description⟩ ⟨those Don Juans, those melting beauties . . . those *luscious* adventuresses—*Huxley*⟩
*Ana* enchanting, charming, fascinating, alluring, attractive (see under ATTRACT): lovely, fair, *beautiful: ineffable (see UNUTTERABLE)
*Ant* distressing: boring: horrid —*Con* *miserable, wretched: distasteful, obnoxious, repellent, *repugnant

**delineate** 1 trace, outline, *sketch, diagram, draft, plot, blueprint

*Ana* describe, *relate: design, plan (see under PLAN *n*)
2 *represent, depict, portray, picture, limn
*Ana* see those at DELINEATE 1

**delineation** tracing, outline, sketch, diagram, plot, blueprint (see under SKETCH *vb*)
*Ana* map, *chart, graph: design, *plan

**delinquent** *n* *criminal, felon, convict, malefactor, culprit

**deliquesce** *liquefy, melt, fuse, thaw
*Ana* *decay, decompose, disintegrate

**delirious** *furious, frantic, frenzied, wild, frenetic, rabid
*Ana* excited, stimulated (see PROVOKE): enthusiastic, fanatic (see corresponding nouns at ENTHUSIAST): ecstatic, rapturous, transported (see corresponding nouns at ECSTASY)

**delirium** frenzy, hysteria, *mania

**deliver** 1 *free, release, liberate, discharge, emancipate, manumit, enfranchise
*Ana* *escape, elude, evade: *extricate, disencumber, disentangle: voice, utter, vent, *express
*Con* confine, circumscribe, restrict, *limit
2 *rescue, redeem, save, ransom, reclaim
*Con* *imprison, incarcerate, jail, immure, intern: *catch, capture, trap, snare, entrap, ensnare

**delude** beguile, *deceive, mislead, betray, double-cross
*Ana* *dupe, gull, hoodwink, befool, bamboozle, hoax, trick: *cheat, cozen, overreach
*Ant* enlighten

**deluge** *n* *flood, inundation, torrent, spate, cataract
*Ana* *flow, stream, current, flux, tide

**delusion, illusion, hallucination, mirage** denote something which is believed to be or is accepted as being true or real but which is actually false or unreal. **Delusion** in general implies self-deception or deception by others; it may connote a disordered state of mind, extreme gullibility, or merely an inability to distinguish between what only seems to be and what actually is true or real ⟨suffer from *delusions* of persecution⟩ ⟨he recovered consciousness slowly, unwilling to let go of a pleasing *delusion* that he was in Rome—*Cather*⟩ ⟨old Nuflo, lately so miserable, now happy in his *delusions*—*Hudson*⟩ ⟨she labored under the *delusion* that the constitution and social condition of her country were . . . on the upward plane—*Rose Macaulay*⟩ ⟨wild oats were to be sown early under the common *delusion* that they would not have to be sown again—*Simmons*⟩ **Illusion** seldom implies mental derangement or even the inability to distinguish between the true and the false; rather it implies an ascription of truth or reality to what only seems to be true or real, especially to the eyes ⟨an optical *illusion*⟩ or to the imagination ⟨artistic *illusion*⟩ or to one's mind as influenced by one's feelings or sentiments ⟨a lover's *illusions*⟩ ⟨during a quake, when I used to . . . observe the houses swaying toward one another, I would have the *illusion* that they were actually bumping heads—*Heiser*⟩ ⟨nature, we know, first taught the architect to produce by long colonnades the *illusion* of distance—*Hudson*⟩ ⟨if you have built up an immunity against the *illusion* that you know the whole truth—*Lippmann*⟩ ⟨most modern great men are mere *illusions* sprung out of a national hunger for greatness—*Anderson*⟩ **Hallucination** implies the perception of visual images or, less often, of other sensory impressions (as sounds or odors) that have no reality but are the product of disordered sensory organs, nerves, or mind or are associated with particular disorders (as delirium tremens or intense fever) ⟨the burglar in her room was only a *hallucination*⟩ ⟨the flying-saucer *hallucination* may be attributed, in part, to the public's conviction that all sorts of strange objects are flying through the sky—*Leonard*⟩ ⟨suffers from the *hallucination*

---

A colon (:) separates groups of words discriminated. An asterisk (*) indicates place of treatment of each group.

that he is being pursued⟩ ⟨he had *hallucinations* as a child. Mediaeval figures from the *Faerie Queene* had walked beside him on his way to school—*Brooks*⟩ **Mirage** is comparable with the preceding terms only in its extended sense in which it usually applies to a vision, dream, hope, or aim which one takes as a guide, not realizing that it is merely an illusion ⟨this hope to find your people . . . is a *mirage,* a delusion, which will lead to destruction if you will not abandon it—*Hudson*⟩
*Ana* *deception, trickery, chicane, chicanery: *imposture, counterfeit, cheat, fraud, sham, fake, humbug, deceit: fantasy, vision, dream, daydream, *fancy
**delusive, delusory** deceptive, *misleading
*Ana* fantastic, chimerical, visionary, *imaginary, fanciful, quixotic: fallacious, sophistical, casuistical (see under FALLACY): illusory, seeming, ostensible, *apparent
**delve** *dig, spade, grub, excavate
**demand** *vb* **Demand, claim, require, exact** are comparable not as close synonyms but as sharing the basic meaning to ask or call for something as due or as necessary or as strongly desired. **Demand** strongly implies peremptoriness or insistency; if the subject is a person or sometimes an expression of his will (as a law), it usually implies that he possesses or believes he possesses the right or the authority not only to issue a peremptory request but also to expect its being regarded as a command ⟨the physician *demanded* payment of his bill⟩ ⟨the court *demands* fair treatment of the accused by the prosecutor⟩ ⟨the father *demanded* knowledge of what had occurred during his absence from home⟩ ⟨can he [the keeper of a public record] refuse a copy thereof to a person *demanding* it on the terms prescribed by law?—*John Marshall*⟩ ⟨instincts which the conventions of good manners and the imperatives of morality *demand* that they should repress —*Huxley*⟩ If the subject of the verb is a thing, the verb implies the call of necessity or of imperative need ⟨the fire that the cool evenings of early spring *demanded*— *Mary Austin*⟩ ⟨the mind and body of a child *demand* a great deal of play—*Russell*⟩ ⟨he is best in his plays when dealing with situations which·do not *demand* great emotional concentration—*T. S. Eliot*⟩ **Claim** implies a demanding either of the delivery or concession of something due one as one's own, one's right, or one's prerogative or of the admission or recognition of something which one asserts or affirms; thus, one who *claims* a piece of property *demands* its delivery tó him as his own; one who *claims* that he has solved a problem *demands* recognition of the truth of his assertion ⟨there is no right to freedom or life. But each man does *claim* such freedom—*Alexander*⟩ ⟨a genius, say his detractors, can be perverse, and they *claim* the right to tell this genius when and where and why he is perverse—*Read*⟩ **Require** is often used interchangeably with *demand,* but it usually distinctively implies imperativeness such as arises from inner necessity ⟨consecutive thinking absolutely *requires* personal initiative —*Eliot*⟩ or the compulsion of law or regulation ⟨*require* that every member of the bank's staff be bonded⟩ or the exigencies of the situation ⟨I shall not go away till you have given me the assurance I *require*—*Austen*⟩ **Exact** implies not only demanding something but getting what one demands ⟨*exact* payment of overdue rent⟩ ⟨*exact* a promise from a friend⟩ ⟨she . . . kept a keen eye on her Court, and *exacted* prompt and willing obedience from king and archbishops—*Henry Adams*⟩ ⟨the mistake of *exacting* reparations in money and then lending Germany the money with which to pay—*Truman*⟩
*Ana* request, *ask, solicit: order, *command, charge, enjoin, direct, bid: call, *summon, summons, cite
*Con* waive, resign, *relinquish: concede, allow, *grant

**demarcate** *distinguish, differentiate, discriminate
*Ana* *limit, restrict, circumscribe, confine: define, assign, *prescribe
**demean** deport, comport, *behave, conduct, acquit, quit
*Ana* *carry, bear (*as reflexive verbs*)
**demean** *abase, degrade, debase, humble, humiliate
*Con* heighten, enhance (see INTENSIFY): *exalt, magnify, aggrandize
**demeanor** deportment, *bearing, mien, port, presence
*Ana* *behavior, conduct, deportment: *posture, attitude, pose: air, mannerism, *pose, affectation
**demented** *insane, mad, crazy, crazed, deranged, lunatic, maniac, non compos mentis
*Ana* *irrational, unreasonable: delirious, hysterical, frenzied (see corresponding nouns at MANIA)
*Ant* rational
**dementia** *insanity, lunacy, mania, psychosis
*Ana* *mania, delirium, hysteria, frenzy
**demise** *death, decease, passing
**demolish** *destroy, raze
*Ana* wreck, *ruin, dilapidate: devastate, *ravage, waste, sack
*Ant* construct
**demoniac, demonic** diabolic, diabolical, *fiendish, devilish
*Ana* hellish, *infernal: crazed, crazy, maniac, *insane: inspired, fired (see INFORM)
*Con* *celestial, heavenly
**demonstrate 1** manifest, evince, *show, evidence
*Ana* *reveal, disclose, discover, betray: display, exhibit, parade, flaunt, expose, *show
*Con* *hide, conceal, secrete: dissemble, cloak, mask, *disguise, camouflage
**2** *prove, try, test
*Ana* argue, debate (see DISCUSS): substantiate, verify, authenticate, *confirm, corroborate, validate
**demonstration** proof, trial, test (see under PROVE)
*Ana* substantiation, confirming *or* confirmation, corroboration, verification (see corresponding verbs at CONFIRM)
**demote** *degrade, reduce, declass, disrate
*Ant* promote (*in rank, grade*)
**demur** *vb* **Demur, scruple, balk, jib, shy, boggle, stick, stickle, strain** are comparable when they mean to hesitate or show reluctance because of difficulties in the way. One **demurs** *to* or *at* something when one raises objections to it, casts doubt upon it, or takes exception to it, thereby interposing obstacles which delay action, procedure, or decision ⟨our colleagues in the university who *demur* on academic grounds to the inclusion of theology— *Moberly*⟩ In older use the stress was on delay ⟨notwithstanding he hoped that matters would have been long since brought to an issue, the fair one still *demurs*— *Spectator*⟩ In modern use the emphasis is commonly on objection ⟨Jerry . . . proposed that . . . we stretch a point by going to supper at Reeves's. Sarah and I *demurred* as women will at such a proposal from a man whose family exigencies are known to them—*Mary Austin*⟩ ⟨it would seem hazardous to *demur* to a proposition which is so widely accepted—*Alexander*⟩ One **scruples** *to do* or *at doing* something when he is reluctant because his conscience bothers or because he is doubtful of the propriety, expediency, or morality of the action; the word is increasingly common in a negative construction ⟨*scruple* to accept any gift that might seem a bribe⟩ ⟨he does not *scruple* to ask the most abominable things of you—*Meredith*⟩ ⟨Greece and in particular Athens was overrun by philosophers, who . . . did not *scruple* to question the foundations of social and moral obligation—*Dickinson*⟩ One **balks** (often *at* something) when he stops short and obstinately refuses to go further in his course because he has reached

the limit of strength, courage, credulity, or tolerance ⟨the horse *balked* at the leap⟩ ⟨he never *balks* at any task no matter how difficult it is⟩ ⟨there is the opposite case of the man who yields his poetic faith too readily, who does not *balk* at any improbability—*Babbitt*⟩ ⟨one rather *balks* at the idea of synthetic roughage—excelsior, wood chips, or whatever may be at hand—*Furnas*⟩ One *jibs* (often *at* something) when he balks like a horse and backs away or out ⟨I had settled to finish the review, when, behold . . . I *jibbed*—*Scott*⟩ ⟨he *jibbed* at alliance with the Catholic League—*Belloc*⟩ ⟨his soldiers, many of whom had served with Antony, *jibbed* at the attack on their old leader—*Buchan*⟩ One *shies at, away from,* or *off from* something when like a suddenly frightened horse he recoils or swerves aside in alarm or distaste or suspicion and is unable to proceed or act ⟨*shy* at the sight of blood⟩ ⟨these turns of speech . . . have the old virtue in them; you see the old temperament of the race still evincing itself; still *shying* away from the long abstract word—*Montague*⟩ One *boggles at, over,* or *about* something from which he by temperament, instinct, or training shies away. In addition, *boggle* often implies scrupling or fussing ⟨when a native begins perjury he perjures himself thoroughly. He does not *boggle* over details—*Kipling*⟩ ⟨we [lovers of poetry] do not *balk* at the sea-wave washing the rim of the sun, which we know it does not do, any more than we *boggle* at blackberries that are red when they are green—*Lowes*⟩ ⟨it was in the essence a snobbish pleasure; why should I *boggle* at the word?—*L. P. Smith*⟩ One *sticks at* something to which he demurs because of scruples, especially scruples of conscience; the term is used frequently in the idiom "*stick* at nothing," which is another way of saying be absolutely unscrupulous ⟨was in a hole and would *stick* at little to get out of it—*Buchan*⟩ One *stickles at, about,* or *over* something to which he demurs or raises objections because it is offensive, distasteful, or contrary to his principles ⟨the purist *stickles* at using clipped words such as *gas* for *gasoline, phone* for *telephone, exam* for *examination*⟩ ⟨there is no time in a serious emergency to *stickle* over means if they achieve the desired ends⟩ ⟨presumably that is his method—so the reader, eager to get good things where he can, will not *stickle* at it—*K. D. Burke*⟩ One *strains at* something when he demurs to it as beyond his power to believe, accept, understand, or do. This usage is chiefly dependent on the scriptural passage "ye blind guides, which *strain* at a gnat, and swallow a camel." The object of *at* is commonly something which might without real difficulty be believed, accepted, understood, or done ⟨persons who *strain* at the truth yet accept every wild rumor without question⟩ ⟨I do not *strain* at the position,—it is familiar,—but at the author's drift—*Shak.*⟩
*Ana* *hesitate, falter, vacillate, waver: oppose, *resist, combat, fight: *object, remonstrate: *disapprove, deprecate
*Ant* accede —*Con* accept, admit, *receive, take: acquiesce, agree, *assent, consent, subscribe
**demur** *n* *qualm, compunction, scruple
*Ana* *hesitation, hesitancy: reluctance, loathness, aversion, disinclination (see corresponding adjectives at DISINCLINED): objection, remonstrance (see corresponding verbs at OBJECT)
*Con* readiness, promptness, quickness (see corresponding adjectives at QUICK)
**denizen** *inhabitant, resident, citizen
**denomination** 1 *name, designation, appellation, title, style
2 *class, category, genus, species, genre
3 sect, communion, *religion, faith, creed, cult, persuasion,

church
**denotation** connotation (see under DENOTE)
*Ana* *meaning, signification, significance, sense, acceptation, import
**denote** 1 signify, *mean, import
*Ana* betoken, bespeak, *indicate, attest, argue, prove: *intend, mean: *suggest, imply, hint, intimate, insinuate
2 Denote, connote and their corresponding nouns **denotation, connotation** are complementary rather than synonymous. Taken together, the verbs as used in reference to terms equal *mean* (see MEAN *vb* 2). Taken singly, a term **denotes** or has as its **denotation** whatever is expressed in its definition: in a noun the thing or the definable class of things or ideas which it names, in a verb the act or state which is affirmed. A term **connotes** or has as its **connotation** the ideas or emotions that are added to it and cling to it, often as a result of experience but sometimes as a result of something extraneous (as a poet's effective use of the term, or its constant association with another term or idea, or a connection between it and some historical event); thus, "home" *denotes* the place where one lives with one's family, but it *connotes* comforts, intimacy, and privacy. What a term *denotes* (or the *denotation* of a term) can be definitely fixed; what a term *connotes* (or its *connotation*) often depends upon the experience or background of the person using it ⟨I have used the term "post-war poets" to *denote* those who did not begin to write verse till after the war—*Day Lewis*⟩ ⟨there is no word that has more sinister and terrible *connotations* in our snobbish society than the word *promiscuity*—*Shaw*⟩
In logic *denote* and *connote,* though still complementary and still predicated of terms, carry very different implications. They are dependent on two highly technical terms, both collective nouns, *denotation* and *connotation.* A term **denotes** (or bears as **denotation**) the entire number of things or instances covered by it; thus, "plant" *denotes* the aggregate of all things that come under the definition of that word; the *denotation* of "plant" is far more inclusive than the *denotation* of "shrub." A term **connotes** (or bears as **connotation**) the sum total of the qualities or characteristics that are implied by it and are necessarily or commonly associated with it; thus, "plant" *connotes* (or bears as *connotation*) life, growth and decay, lack of power of locomotion, and, commonly, roots and cellular structure invested with a cellulose wall.
**denounce** condemn, censure, reprobate, reprehend, blame, *criticize
*Ana* *accuse, charge, arraign, impeach, incriminate, indict: *decry, disparage, depreciate: revile, vituperate (see SCOLD)
*Ant* eulogize —*Con* *commend, applaud, compliment, recommend: *praise, extol, laud, acclaim
**dense** 1 compact, *close, thick
*Ana* consolidated, concentrated, compacted (see COMPACT *vb*): compressed, condensed (see CONTRACT *vb*): massed, heaped, piled, stacked (see HEAP *vb*)
*Ant* sparse (*of population, forests*): tenuous (*of clouds, air, masses*) —*Con* scattered, dispersed, dissipated (see SCATTER): *thin, rare: *meager, scanty, scant, exiguous
2 crass, *stupid, slow, dull, dumb
*Ana* obtuse, *dull: stolid, phlegmatic, *impassive
*Ant* subtle: bright —*Con* *intelligent, brilliant, clever, alert, quick-witted
**denude** bare, *strip, divest, dismantle
*Ant* clothe
**deny, gainsay, contradict, negative, traverse, impugn, contravene** are comparable as meaning, when they refer to an act, to declare something untrue, untenable, or unworthy of consideration or, when they refer to a condition, to go

A colon (:) separates groups of words discriminated. An asterisk (*) indicates place of treatment of each group.

counter to what is true or to the facts as they are. **Deny** commonly implies a refusal and usually a firm or outspoken refusal to accept as true, to grant or concede, or to acknowledge the existence or claims of ⟨*deny* the report that the British ambassador has resigned⟩ ⟨he is no vulgar and stupid cynic who *denies* the existence . . . of any feelings higher than the merely physical—*Huxley*⟩ ⟨*deny* citizenship to certain applicants⟩ ⟨*deny* a request for more books⟩ ⟨for he's a jolly good fellow, which nobody can *deny!*⟩ ⟨the necessities of his own life . . . not any longer to be *denied*—*Mary Austin*⟩ ⟨it would seem that I was *denying* God—*Meredith*⟩ In the reflexive form *deny* usually implies abstinence or renunciation often, but not necessarily, for religious or moral reasons ⟨she *denied* herself all luxuries⟩ ⟨he resolved to *deny* himself the pleasure of smoking⟩ (compare *self-denial* at RENUNCIATION). **Gainsay** is somewhat formal or literary; it implies opposition, usually by way of disputing the truth of what another has said ⟨facts which cannot be *gainsaid*⟩ ⟨but she's a fine woman—that nobody can *gainsay*—*Meredith*⟩ ⟨his mother, whom he could not *gainsay*, was unconsciously but inflexibly set against his genius—*Brooks*⟩ ⟨no one would *gainsay* the right of anyone, the royal American right, to protest—*White*⟩ **Contradict** differs from *gainsay* not only in usually implying a more open or a flatter denial of the truth of an assertion but also in commonly suggesting that the contrary of the assertion is true or that the statement is utterly devoid of truth; thus, " to *contradict* a rumor " is a stronger expression than "to *deny* a rumor"; one may *contradict* (never in this sense *deny*) a person, whereas one may *deny* or *contradict* (the stronger term) an assertion of his ⟨a report which highly incensed Mrs. Bennet, and which she never failed to *contradict* as a most scandalous falsehood—*Austen*⟩ ⟨"Nobody *contradicts* me now," wrote Queen Victoria after her husband's death, "and the salt has gone out of my life"—*Ellis*⟩ *Contradict* is also used without implication of a spoken or written denial: it then suggests that an assertion, a doctrine, or a teaching runs counter to something else, and therefore either it cannot be true or the other must be false ⟨all the protestations of the employers that they would be ruined by the Factory Acts were *contradicted* by experience—*Shaw*⟩ ⟨they insisted on teaching and enforcing an ideal that *contradicted* the realities—*Henry Adams*⟩ **Negative** is usually a much milder term than those which precede; often it implies merely a refusal to assent to something (as a suggestion, a proposition, a nomination, or a bill) ⟨the senate *negatived* the proposed taxation⟩ ⟨after a polite request that Elizabeth would lead the way, which the other as politely . . . *negatived*—*Austen*⟩ ⟨Beaufort stood, hat in hand, saying something which his companion seemed to *negative*—*Wharton*⟩ When the idea of going counter to is uppermost, *negative* usually implies disproof ⟨the omission or infrequency of such recitals does not *negative* the existence of miracles—*Paley*⟩ **Traverse** occurs chiefly in legal use and implies a formal denial (as of the truth of an allegation or the justice of an indictment) ⟨it *traverses* the theory of the Court—*Corwin*⟩ **Impugn** usually retains much of its basic implication of attacking and carries the strongest suggestion of any of these terms of directly disputing or questioning or of forcefully contradicting a statement, proposition, or less often a person; it sometimes connotes prolonged argument in an attempt to refute or confute ⟨the idealists . . . took up the challenge, but their reply was to disparage the significance, and even to *impugn* the reality, of the world as known to science—*Inge*⟩ ⟨the morality of our Restoration drama cannot be *impugned*. It assumes orthodox Christian morality, and laughs (in its

comedy) at human nature for not living up to it—*T. S. Eliot*⟩ ⟨no one cares to *impugn* a fool; no one dares to *impugn* a captain of industry—*Brooks*⟩ **Contravene** implies strongly a coming into conflict but less strongly than the other terms an intentional opposition, suggesting rather some inherent incompatibility ⟨no state law may *contravene* the United States Constitution or federal laws enacted under its authority—*Fitzsimmons*⟩ ⟨steps toward the mitigation of racial segregation and discrimination are often forestalled, since . . . these *contravene* the dicta of Southern customs and tradition—*R. E. Jackson*⟩
**Ana** *decline, refuse, reject, repudiate: controvert, refute, rebut, confute, *disprove
**Ant** confirm: concede　—**Con** aver, affirm, *assert: *acknowledge
**depart** 1 leave, withdraw, retire, *go, quit
**Ant** arrive: remain, abide　—**Con** *stay, tarry, linger, wait: *come
2 digress, deviate, *swerve, diverge, veer
**Ana** forsake, *abandon, desert: reject, repudiate (see DECLINE *vb*): *discard, cast
**departed** deceased, late, *dead, defunct, lifeless, inanimate
**depend** 1 *rely, trust, count, reckon, bank
**Ana** lean, incline (see SLANT *vb*)
2 **Depend, hinge, hang, turn** are comparable when they mean to rest or, especially, to be contingent upon something uncertain or variable or indeterminable. All are normally followed by *on* or *upon*. **Depend**, which literally means to hang or be suspended, suggests an element of mental suspense which makes forecasting impossible. It often suggests uncertainty of a thing with reference to circumstances yet to take place, facts not yet known, or a decision yet to be made ⟨our trip *depends* upon the weather⟩ ⟨his going to college will *depend* on his ability to earn enough money to cover his living expenses⟩ ⟨another motive is the conviction that winning the best satisfaction of later life will *depend* on possessing this power to think—*Eliot*⟩ It may suggest also a variability that rests upon a difference in attitude or point of view ⟨the sterling morale of strikers. This may mean either a staunch fidelity to law and order, or willingness to overturn a motor bus in the street. . . . It *depends* on who is speaking—*Montague*⟩ **Hinge** is sometimes used interchangeably with *depend;* it may retain much of its literal suggestion of a movable part (as a door or a gate) that opens or closes upon hinges and then usually implies the cardinal (see under ESSENTIAL 2) point upon which a decision, a controversy, or an outcome ultimately rests. In such use it suggests not so much mental suspense as uncertainty tempered by the certainty that the matter will go one way or the other ⟨the outcome of the war *hinges* on the ability of our forces to outmove every strategic move of the enemy⟩ ⟨the point on which the decision must finally *hinge*—*Thirlwall*⟩ ⟨the whole case being built up by Mr. Kennon was going to *hinge* in large part upon a single issue—was Clifford under the influence of liquor—*Basso*⟩ **Hang** likewise may interchange with *depend,* but more precisely it suggests a point of support such as is characteristic of the literal action of hanging; the term therefore stresses not so much the uncertainty of the event as the weakness or the strength of what gives validity, authority, or credibility to something (as a doctrine, a belief, or a course of action) or of what points the way to fulfillment or successful performance ⟨the truth of the testimony *hangs* on his word only⟩ ⟨the election *hangs* on a single vote⟩ ⟨a good deal . . . *hangs* on the meaning, if any, of this short word *full*—*T. S. Eliot*⟩ **Turn** often comes close to *hinge* in its meaning ⟨great

---

**Ana** analogous words　　　**Ant** antonyms　　　**Con** contrasted words　　　See also explanatory notes facing page 1

events often *turn* upon very small circumstances—*Swift*⟩ It as often differs from *hinge* in suggesting a rotation or pivoting rather than a going one way or the other and, therefore, in implying a dependence upon something that may be variable or casual ⟨the action of the play *turns* upon a secret marriage⟩ ⟨his plots *turn* on the vicissitudes of climbing the success-ladder—*Fadiman*⟩ ⟨the great anxiety of each disputant seemed to *turn* upon striking the first blow—*Thorp*⟩

**dependable** *reliable, trustworthy, trusty, tried
*Ana* sure, assured, *confident: *responsible: staunch, steadfast, constant, *faithful
*Con* *doubtful, questionable, dubious: capricious, fickle, unstable, *inconstant, mercurial

**dependence** reliance, *trust, confidence, faith

**dependent** *adj* **1 Dependent, contingent, conditional, relative** mean having its existence or nature determined by something else. Something is **dependent** which cannot exist or come into existence by itself quite without aid or support ⟨we are all *dependent* on one another, every soul of us on earth—*Shaw*⟩ ⟨the color of the skin is *dependent* on an adequate supply of blood—*Fishbein*⟩ What is **contingent** takes its character from something that already exists or may exist and therefore is limited or qualified by something extraneous or is incapable of ·existence apart from it ⟨a person's conception of love is *contingent* both on his past experience and on the nature of that experience⟩ ⟨if propriety should die, there could be no impropriety, inasmuch as the continuance of the latter is wholly *contingent* on the presence of the former—*Grandgent*⟩ ⟨war is *contingent;* even dictatorship is *contingent.* Both depend on . . . ignorance—*Pound*⟩ Something is **conditional** which depends for its realization, fulfillment, execution, or expression on what may or may not occur or on the performance or observance of certain terms or conditions. *Conditional* and *contingent* are often interchangeable, but the former is preferred when eventualities are in the power of the human will ⟨the pardon is *conditional* on his behavior during probation⟩ ⟨while the validity of *conditional* recognition is a matter of debate, it would be entirely novel . . . if the conditions for recognition were set forth by a new government—*I-Kua Chou*⟩ Something is **relative** which cannot be known, considered, or determined apart from its reference to something else and which therefore is affected by the limitations, the instability, or the imperfections of the other thing ⟨market values are always *relative* to the demand⟩ ⟨the idea of civilization is *relative* . . . any community and any age has its own civilization and its own ideals of civilization—*Ellis*⟩
*Ana* subject, *liable, open, exposed, susceptible
*Ant* absolute: infinite: original —*Con* *ultimate, categorical: uncircumscribed, boundless, eternal, illimitable (see INFINITE): underived (see affirmative verb at SPRING)
**2** subject, tributary, *subordinate, secondary, collateral
*Ana* relying, depending, trusting, reckoning, counting (see RELY): subsidiary, subservient, *auxiliary: abased, humbled, debased (see ABASE)
*Ant* independent

**depict** *represent, portray, delineate, picture, limn
*Ana* describe, narrate, *relate: *sketch, draft, outline, trace

**deplete** *vb* **Deplete, drain, exhaust, impoverish, bankrupt** are comparable when they mean to deprive a thing in whole or in part of what is essential or necessary to its existence or potency. **Deplete** is often used as though it implied merely a reduction in numbers, in quantity, or in mass or volume; it may be used specifically to suggest the potential harm of such a reduction or the impossibility of restoring what has been lost before such consequences

are evident; thus, bloodletting *depletes* the system, not only by reducing the quantity of blood but by depriving the system of elements essential to its vitality and vigor; an epidemic *depletes* an army when it reduces the army not only in size but in effective strength, especially at a time when that strength is needed ⟨he would have us fill up our *depleted* curriculum with subjects whose worth has not even been tried—*Grandgent*⟩ ⟨cattle herds *depleted* by the heavy slaughter last year—*Time*⟩ **Drain** when precisely employed retains its basic implications of slow withdrawal of liquid (as by straining, seepage, or suction) until the substance which is drained becomes dry or the container which holds the liquid is emptied; hence it connotes a gradual depletion and ultimate deprivation of the figurative lifeblood of a thing or the essential element of its existence or well-being ⟨the Thirty Years' War nearly *drained* Germany of men and materials⟩ ⟨their country's wealth our mightier misers *drain*—*Pope*⟩ ⟨a burden of arms *draining* the wealth and labor of all peoples— *Eisenhower*⟩ **Exhaust** (see also TIRE) is very close to *drain*, but it stresses emptying or evacuation rather than gradual depletion. Unlike *drain*, which usually implies loss without compensating gain, *exhaust* need not suggest ultimate loss of what is removed; thus, a mine is *exhausted* when all its ore has been removed for refining; a soil is *exhausted*, or *drained* of nutrients, by growing crops on it without adequate fertilizing; but, a person is *drained* of vitality when overwork or illness reduces him to a weak or ineffective state ⟨*exhaust* a subject by treating it so fully that nothing more can be said about it⟩ ⟨molasses is *exhausted* when no further sugar can be extracted from it⟩ ⟨the theme of mother and child has proved a theme which no age has ever *exhausted* or ever will *exhaust*— *Binyon*⟩ ⟨evidently the old ideas had been *exhausted* and the time was ripe for new ideologies—*R. W. Murray*⟩ ⟨seven hundred years of glorious and incessant creation seem to have *exhausted* the constructive genius of Europe —*Clive Bell*⟩ **Impoverish** implies a depletion or a draining of something as essential to a thing as money or its equivalent is to a human being; it stresses the deprivation of qualities essential to a thing's strength, richness, or productiveness ⟨*impoverish* the body by too meager a diet⟩ ⟨a brilliant sun scorched the *impoverished* trees and sucked energy from the frail breezes—*Farrell*⟩ **Bankrupt** stresses such impoverishment of a thing that it is destitute of qualities essential to its continued existence or productiveness; it connotes a complete or imminent collapse or breaking down ⟨argued that science by inattention to immaterial phenomena is *bankrupting* itself⟩ ⟨dainty bits make rich the ribs, but *bankrupt* quite the wits— *Shak.*⟩
*Ana* undermine, sap, debilitate, *weaken, enfeeble, cripple, disable: reduce, diminish, *decrease, lessen
*Con* augment, *increase, enlarge

**deplore, lament, bewail, bemoan** mean to· manifest grief or sorrow for something. All carry an implication of weeping or crying which is commonly purely figurative. **Deplore** implies keen and profound regret especially for what is regarded as irreparable, calamitous, or destructive of something good or worth keeping ⟨ev'n rival wits did Voiture's death *deplore*—*Pope*⟩ ⟨*deplore* a quarrel between friends⟩ ⟨they *deplore* the divorce between the language as spoken and the language as written—*T. S. Eliot*⟩ **Lament** commonly implies a strong or demonstrative expression of sorrow or mourning. In contrast to *deplore*, it usually does imply utterance, sometimes passionate, sometimes fulsome ⟨yet I *lament* what long has ceased to be—*Shelley*⟩ ⟨he made the newly returned actress a tempting offer, instigating some journalist friends

---

A colon (:) separates groups of words discriminated. An asterisk (*) indicates place of treatment of each group.

of his at the same time to *lament* over the decay of the grand school of acting—*Shaw*⟩ **Bewail** and **bemoan** imply poignant sorrow finding an outlet in words or cries, *bewail* commonly suggesting the louder, *bemoan,* the more lugubrious expression of grief or, often, of a mere grievance or a complaint ⟨the valet *bewailing* the loss of his wages—*Alexander*⟩ ⟨even at the time when our prose speech was as near to perfection as it is ever likely to be, its critics were *bemoaning* its corruption—*Ellis*⟩ ⟨and all wept, and *bewailed* her—*Lk* 8:52⟩ ⟨the silver swans her hapless fate *bemoan,* in notes more sad than when they sing their own—*Pope*⟩

*Ana* deprecate, *disapprove: *grieve, mourn, sorrow: weep, wail, *cry

*Con* vaunt, crow, *boast, brag

**deport** 1 demean, comport, *behave, conduct, acquit, quit

*Ana* see those at DEMEAN

2 transport, *banish, exile, expatriate, ostracize, extradite

**deportment** 1 *behavior, conduct

*Ana* see those at BEHAVIOR

2 demeanor, *bearing, mien, port, presence

*Ana* *form, formality, ceremony, ceremonial, ritual: *culture, cultivation, breeding, refinement: dignity, grace, *elegance

**deposit** *n* Deposit, precipitate, sediment, dregs, lees, grounds mean matter which settles to the bottom of or is let fall from suspension in a fluid (as air or water). **Deposit,** the most comprehensive term, refers to matter let fall by a natural or mechanical process to remain where it settles until there is a visible layer or accumulation ⟨a *deposit* of soot in a chimney⟩ ⟨a *deposit* of gravel on the bed of a river⟩ ⟨rich *deposits* of coal⟩ ⟨the walls of the houses are clean and less discolored by the *deposit* of carbon than usual in most towns—*Jefferies*⟩ **Precipitate** denotes a usually solid substance separated from a solution or suspension by some chemical interaction or by some physical force (as heat, cold, or centrifugal force) ⟨camphor may be obtained as a *precipitate* from an alcoholic solution by addition of water⟩ ⟨some finely divided *precipitates* (as silver chloride and zinc sulfide) coalesce into amorphous, curdy, or flocculent masses that remain suspended near the surface of the liquid⟩ **Sediment** applies to matter that settles to the bottom of a liquid ⟨sharp rocks hidden by *sediment* spoiled the cove for diving⟩ The word may be used of other matters with emphasis on a foreign element that disturbs the clarity or purity of something ⟨the poetry of all these men contained a deep *sediment* of prose meaning—*Day Lewis*⟩ **Dregs** and **lees** typically apply to the sediment found at the bottom of a cask or a bottle of some alcoholic or fermenting liquor, but the terms may be used of other things that, like a sediment, suggest that something now fair has been formerly turbid, foul, or offensive, or that imply the worthlessness of what lies at the bottom or is left over ⟨destined to drain the cup of bitterness, even to its *dregs*—*Southey*⟩ ⟨the very *dregs* of the population—*C. M. Davies*⟩ ⟨I will drink life to the *lees*—*Tennyson*⟩ ⟨the angler . . . has left for his day's work only the *lees* of his nervous energy—*Kingsley*⟩ ⟨the sonnet became . . . a thing of frigid conceits worn bare by iteration; of servile borrowings; of artificial sentiment, flat as the *lees* and *dregs* of wine—*Lowes*⟩ **Grounds** is used of the small particles left after serving or drinking a beverage (as coffee); usually the term carries no implication of a disagreeable sediment but simply of one from which all the flavor has been exhausted.

*Ana* falling, dropping, sinking, subsiding (see FALL)

**deposition** affidavit, testimony, *evidence

*Ana* *account, report, version

**deprave** *debase, vitiate, corrupt, debauch, pervert

*Ana* defile, pollute, taint, *contaminate: *injure, impair, damage, spoil

*Con* *improve, better, ameliorate: *exalt, magnify

**depraved** debased, vitiated, corrupted, corrupt, debauched, perverted (see under DEBASE)

*Ana* dissolute, *abandoned, reprobate, profligate: degenerate, infamous, villainous, *vicious: degraded, debased (see ABASE)

**deprecate** *disapprove

*Ana* *deplore, lament, bewail, bemoan: reprobate, reprehend, condemn (see CRITICIZE)

*Ant* endorse —*Con* *approve, sanction: *commend, applaud

**depreciate** *decry, disparage, derogate, detract, belittle, minimize

*Ana* underestimate, undervalue, underrate (see base words at ESTIMATE): asperse, *malign

*Ant* appreciate —*Con* prize, cherish, treasure, value (see APPRECIATE): *understand, comprehend

**depreciative, depreciatory** *derogatory, disparaging, slighting, pejorative

*Ana* decrying, belittling, minimizing (see DECRY): aspersing, maligning (see MALIGN *vb*): underrating, underestimating, undervaluing (see base words at ESTIMATE)

**depress, weigh, oppress** mean to put such pressure or such a load upon a thing or person as to cause it or him to sink under the weight. **Depress** implies a lowering of something by the exertion of pressure or by an overburdening; it most commonly implies a lowering of spirits by physical or mental causes ⟨the long dull evenings in these dull lodgings when one is weary with work *depress* one sadly— *J. R. Green*⟩ ⟨the mere volume of work was enough to crush the most diligent of rulers and *depress* the most vital—*Buchan*⟩ ⟨he was *depressed* by his failure— *Anderson*⟩ It may suggest lowering of bodily vigor or the power of certain organs to function (as by a drug, a disease, or an external condition) ⟨the drug aconite *depresses* heart action⟩ In reference to other things (as market prices or social or cultural states) *depress* often suggests a lowering in activity, intensity, or vigor ⟨the first effect of the World War was greatly to *depress* the prices of stocks⟩ ⟨a grain market *depressed* by the existence of a large surplus⟩ ⟨to *depress* the culture of the minority below the point at which a full understanding of poetry becomes possible— *Day Lewis*⟩ **Weigh** in this relation is used with *down, on,* or *upon* and carries a weaker implication of the result or lowering than *depress* but a stronger implication of the difficulty or burdens imposed upon a person or thing ⟨he is *weighed down* with cares⟩ ⟨the responsibility *weighs* heavily *upon* him⟩ ⟨Walter's mind had cleared itself of the depression which had *weighed on* him so heavily— *Costain*⟩ ⟨a melancholy damp . . . to *weigh* thy spirits *down*—*Milton*⟩ Like *weigh,* **oppress** stresses the burden which is borne or is imposed and, like *depress,* the consequent ill effects (as the lowering of spirits or of power to function) or in its more common sense (see WRONG), a trampling down, a harassing, or a subjection to heavy penalties ⟨the weary world of waters between us *oppresses* the imagination—*Lamb*⟩ ⟨the butler, *oppressed* by the heat . . . was in a state of abstraction bordering on slumber —*Shaw*⟩ ⟨she is so *oppressed* by fear that she may lose her mind⟩

*Ana* distress, *trouble, ail: *afflict, try, torment: weary, fatigue, exhaust, fag, jade, tucker

*Ant* elate: cheer —*Con* gladden, rejoice, delight, gratify, *please

**depressed** dejected, dispirited, *downcast, disconsolate, woebegone

---

*Ana* analogous words     *Ant* antonyms     *Con* contrasted words     See also explanatory notes facing page 1

*Ana* gloomy, glum, morose (see SULLEN): discouraged, disheartened (see DISCOURAGE): *melancholy, lugubrious

**depression** dejection, gloom, blues, dumps, *sadness, melancholy, melancholia
*Ana* despondency, forlornness, hopelessness, despair, desperation (see under DESPONDENT): doldrums, boredom, ennui, *tedium
*Ant* buoyancy —*Con* cheerfulness, lightheartedness, gladness, joyousness (see corresponding adjectives at GLAD): *mirth, hilarity, glee

**deputy** 1 attorney, *agent, factor, proxy
*Ana* substitute, surrogate (see RESOURCE)
2 *delegate, representative

**deracinate** uproot, eradicate, extirpate, *exterminate, wipe
*Ana* *abolish, extinguish, annihilate, abate: *destroy, demolish

**derange** disarrange, unsettle, *disorder, disturb, disorganize
*Ana* upset, *discompose, perturb: discommode, incommode, *inconvenience
*Ant* arrange (*a scheme, plan, system*): adjust

**deranged** demented, non compos mentis, crazed, crazy, *insane, mad, lunatic, maniac

**derangement** *aberration, alienation

**derelict** *n* *outcast, castaway, reprobate, pariah, untouchable
*Ana* *vagabond, vagrant, tramp, hobo

**dereliction** *failure, neglect, default, miscarriage
*Ana* abuse, misuse, outrage (see ABUSE *vb*)

**deride** *ridicule, mock, taunt, twit, rally
*Ana* *scoff, jeer, gibe, flout, sneer, gird, fleer: chaff, *banter, kid, rag, jolly, rib

**derive** originate, arise, rise, *spring, emanate, issue, stem, flow, proceed

**dernier cri** *fashion, style, mode, vogue, fad, rage, craze, cry

**derogate** disparage, detract, belittle, minimize, depreciate, *decry
*Ana* reduce, lessen, *decrease, diminish
*Con* enhance, heighten, *intensify

**derogatory, depreciatory, depreciative, disparaging, slighting, pejorative** mean designed or tending to belittle. **Derogatory** may be used of one's own action or activity that tends to detract from his reputation or to lower him in the estimation of others ⟨though it was supposed to be proper for them to have an occupation, the crude fact of moneymaking was still regarded as *derogatory*—*Wharton*⟩ ⟨will grub in a garden all day, or wash dogs or rid them of vermin . . . without considering the dirt involved in these jobs in the least *derogatory* to their dignity—*Shaw*⟩ More often the term is applied to expressions or modes of expression (as choice of words or tone of voice) and then implies an intent to detract or belittle by suggesting something that is discreditable ⟨the *derogatory* use of the term *politician*⟩ ⟨he makes remarks about miracles, quite *derogatory* remarks—*H. G. Wells*⟩ ⟨there is no one so situated that he cannot refrain from telling race jokes and using *derogatory* names—*Lillian Smith*⟩ **Depreciatory** and **depreciative** are used chiefly of something written or spoken that tends to lower a thing in value or in status ⟨a *depreciatory* comparison of man's mortal nature with the persistence of cosmic phenomena—*Lowie*⟩ They often also describe words or modes of using words that bear connotations tending to discredit or to bring into discredit the person or thing referred to ⟨what people might refer to, slightingly, as being mere subjective feelings . . . have more significance than that *depreciatory* way of speaking about them—*Hendel*⟩ ⟨in the classic world of antiquity they called outsiders . . . "barbarians"—a

denomination which took on an increasingly *depreciative* sense—*Ellis*⟩ **Disparaging** definitely implies an intent to depreciate usually by the use of oblique and indirect methods. The term suggests an attempt to make little of or to discourage by belittling and often carries a clearer implication of intentional detraction than *derogatory* and of resulting undervaluing than *depreciatory* or *depreciative* ⟨a *disparaging* review of a book⟩ ⟨criticism is in many cases just a calling of laudatory or *disparaging* names—*Huxley*⟩ ⟨nothing can be further from the truth than to call the Greeks "intellectualists" in the *disparaging* sense in which the word is now often used—*Inge*⟩ **Slighting** applies to anything that may convey or imply a slight or indicate the little respect in which one is held by the speaker; it sometimes implies disparagement but, more often, indifference or disdain ⟨to hear yourself . . . glanced at in a few *slighting* terms—*Ben Jonson*⟩ ⟨a *slighting* allusion to his book⟩ ⟨the constable felt the full effect of this *slighting* reception—*Scott*⟩ ⟨her chief complaint is my *slighting* reference to Henry James—*J. D. Adams*⟩ **Pejorative** is nearly equal to *depreciatory* or *depreciative* in meaning ⟨it might be argued, without any *pejorative* implication, whether Gide's is essentially a religious temperament or whether . . . he has found in the traditions and doctrines of Christianity . . . an adequate and sympathetic psychology—*Farrelly*⟩ ⟨the Grand Jury . . . is here put in a *pejorative* light—*Stein*⟩ It is used especially in reference to words which have acquired a later and baser meaning or to derogatory words formed from another word or root by the addition of a suffix or prefix that gives them a derogatory twist ⟨the earlier meaning of "imp"—a child—has now given way to its *pejorative* meaning of a mischievous child, or rogue⟩ ⟨it was drifting, all right, but not drifting in any nasty *pejorative* sense, like . . . a cake of soap in the gray water before you pull the plug in the bathtub—*Warren*⟩ ⟨euphemism . . . is the motive force behind many *pejorative* developments. If a euphemistic substitute ceases to be felt as such . . . this will result in a permanent depreciation of its meaning—*Ullmann*⟩ ⟨resort to *pejorative* epithets as their argument—*Cohen*⟩ ⟨*poetaster* is the *pejorative* word for poet⟩ ⟨*pseudo-* is often used in English with *pejorative* force⟩
*Ana* belittling, minimizing, decrying (see DECRY): aspersing, maligning (see MALIGN)

**descant** *vb* 1 *sing, troll, carol, warble, trill, hymn, chant, intone
2 *discourse, expatiate, dilate

**descend, dismount, alight** mean to get or come down from a height. One **descends** when one climbs down a slope (as of a hill or mountain), a ladder, a step, a stair, a wall, or a tree; one **dismounts** when one gets down from a horse or from a bicycle or motorcycle; one **alights** when one comes down from a perch or out of a vehicle (as a carriage, a car, or an airplane) with a spring or especially with lightness and grace.
*Ant* ascend, climb

**descendant** *offspring, young, progeny, issue, posterity

**describe** *relate, narrate, state, report, rehearse, recite, recount
*Ana* delineate, *sketch, outline

**description** kind, sort, *type, character, nature, stripe, kidney, ilk

**descry** espy, *see, behold, observe, notice, remark, note, perceive, discern, view, survey, contemplate

**desecration** *profanation, sacrilege, blasphemy
*Ana* defilement, pollution (see corresponding verbs at CONTAMINATE)

**desert** *n* *waste, badlands, wilderness

**desert** *n* *due, merit

A colon (:) separates groups of words discriminated. An asterisk (*) indicates place of treatment of each group.

*Ana* meed, guerdon, reward (see PREMIUM): punishment, chastisement, chastening, disciplining *or* discipline (see corresponding verbs at PUNISH)

**desert** *vb* forsake, *abandon
*Ana* leave, quit, depart (see GO)
*Ant* stick to, cleave to

**deserter** see under *desert* at ABANDON *vb*

**desertion** 1 *defection, apostasy
*Ana* perfidiousness *or* perfidy, treacherousness *or* treachery, disloyalty, faithlessness (see corresponding adjectives at FAITHLESS)
2 see under *desert* at ABANDON *vb*

**deserve, merit, earn, rate** mean to be or become worthy of something as recompense whether by way of reward or punishment. **Deserve** implies a just claim which entitles one to something good or evil, usually on the ground of actions done or qualities shown; it does not necessarily imply that the claim has been won or recognized 〈when at your hands did I *deserve* this scorn?—*Shak.*〉 〈that he should be supported at the public expense as one who had *deserved* well of his country—*Dickinson*〉 〈it is largely owing to his insight and enthusiasm, as well as to his editorial toil, that the Tudor translators have become recognized as they *deserve*—*T. S. Eliot*〉 **Merit** is so close a synonym of *deserve* that it is often used interchangeably with it without loss. Even so, slight differences in meaning may be detected. *Merit*, although it implies a just claim, seldom suggests that the claim has been urged by oneself or another, a connotation that is not essential to but may often be found in *deserve; merit* also more often implies qualities of character, of life, or of action that entitle one to reward or punishment 〈give him the words of praise that he *merits*〉 〈he *merited* a reproof, but he did not deserve dismissal〉 〈a compliment . . . to the grandeur of the family, *merited* by the manner in which the family has sustained its grandeur—*Dickens*〉 **Earn** may suggest a due correspondence between the efforts exerted or the time or energy spent and the recompense that ensues; it fundamentally implies a deserving or meriting as well as a getting and therefore may suggest a return in evil as well as in good 〈"Indeed, he hath an excellent good name." "His excellence did *earn* it, ere he had it"—*Shak.*〉 〈an active, ardent mind . . . a generous spirit, and a body strong . . . had *earned* for him sure welcome—*Wordsworth*〉 〈his devotion to self-interest has *earned* for him nothing but contempt〉 **Rate** implies recognition of deserts or merits usually upon a carefully calculated basis, but it does not carry any suggestion of whether what is deserved or merited has been given 〈he *rates* a promotion〉 〈the magazine *rates* our support〉
*Ana* gain, win, *get: evaluate, value, *estimate: claim, *demand

**desiccate** *vb* *dry, dehydrate, parch, bake

**design** *vb* 1 mean, *intend, propose, purpose
*Ana* *aim, aspire
2 plan, plot, scheme, project (see under PLAN *n*)
*Ana* *sketch, outline, diagram, delineate, blueprint, draft: *invent, create
*Con* execute, fulfill, effect, accomplish, achieve, *perform

**design** *n* 1 *plan, plot, scheme, project
*Ana* delineation, sketch, draft, outline, tracing, diagram (see under SKETCH *vb*): conception, *idea
*Con* execution, fulfillment, accomplishment, achievement, performance (see corresponding verbs at PERFORM)
2 *intention, intent, purpose, aim, end, object, objective, goal
*Ana* *will, volition, conation: deliberation, reflection, thinking *or* thought (see corresponding verbs at THINK): intrigue, machination, *plot

*Ant* accident —*Con* impulse (see MOTIVE)
3 *figure, pattern, motif, device

**designate, name, nominate, elect, appoint** are comparable in the sense to declare a person one's choice for incumbency of an office, position, post, or benefice. **Designate** implies selection by the person or body having the power to choose an incumbent or to detail a person to a certain post; it often connotes selection well in advance of incumbency 〈Harold contended that he had been *designated* by Edward the Confessor as the latter's successor to the English throne〉 〈a clergyman who has been *designated* by the proper ecclesiastical authority as the incumbent of an episcopacy is usually called bishop-designate until he has been consecrated or has been installed〉 **Name** varies little in meaning from *designate* except that it stresses announcement rather than selection; it is more informal, however, and is usually preferred when the reference is to a political or government office within the gift of an executive or of an executive body 〈the mayor has not yet *named* the commissioner of public safety〉 〈only one member of the incoming president's cabinet remains to be *named*〉 **Nominate**, though etymologically the equivalent of *name*, is rarely used as its equivalent in meaning 〈the House of Commons was crowded with members *nominated* by the Royal Council—*J. R. Green*〉 Usually it implies merely the presentation of the name of one's choice for an office for approval or rejection by others who have the final say; thus, a person from the floor at a convention may *nominate* his choice for a particular office; a state convention of a political party meets to *nominate* the party's candidates for governor and other state officers. Either *nominate* or *name* may be used when the executive's choice must be confirmed by a body having that power. **Elect**, as distinguished from *nominate*, implies a final selection (as by the electorate) from the candidates who have been previously nominated 〈all the liberal candidates were *elected*〉 〈not one person on the nominating committee's slate was *elected* at today's meeting〉 **Appoint** always implies that the selection is determined without a general vote (as of an electorate) and represents the choice of the person or the body in whom such power is legally vested. *Appoint* may be used even when confirmation (as by the U. S. Senate) has been necessary to make the designation valid 〈three justices of the Supreme Court have been *appointed* by the president within twelve months〉 〈he [the president] shall nominate, and by and with the advice and consent of the Senate, shall *appoint* ambassadors, other public ministers and consuls, judges of the Supreme Court—*U. S. Constitution*〉
*Ana* *choose, select, single, opt, pick

**designation** *name, denomination, appellation, title, style
*Ana* identification, *recognition: classification, pigeonholing *or* pigeonhole (see corresponding verbs at ASSORT)

**designed** ³ premeditated, *deliberate, considered, advised, studied
*Ana* intentional, *voluntary, willful, deliberate, willing: purposed, intended (see INTEND): resolved, determined, decided (see DECIDE)
*Ant* accidental —*Con* fortuitous, casual (see ACCIDENTAL): *spontaneous, impulsive: natural, normal, *regular, typical

**desire** *vb* Desire, wish, want, crave, covet mean having a longing for something. *Desire, wish,* and *want* are often used with identical intent though in such situations (usually everyday ones) that the degree of intensity of longing or need is not at issue 〈we can order whichever model you *wish*〉 In such use **desire** is often felt as more formal and dignified, and it may even be decidedly pompous in effect ⟨cleaning lady *desires* situation⟩ *Desire* in more general use, however, emphasizes the strength or ardor of feeling and often implies strong intention or aim ⟨more than any other thing on earth *desired* to fight for his country—*White*⟩ ⟨unions which *desired* to avail themselves of the benefits of the law—*Collier's Yr. Bk.*⟩ **Wish** is less strong, often suggesting a not usually intense longing for an object unattained, unattainable, or questionably attainable ⟨Newton's law of gravitation could not be *wished* into existence —*Overstreet*⟩ ⟨not to have property, if one *wished* it, was almost a certain sign of shiftlessness—*Brooks*⟩ **Want** (see also LACK) is a less formal term than *wish* and so is often interchangeable with it in situations where dignity of the subject or respectfulness is not at issue, though generally *want* implies that the longing is for something the attainment of which would fill a real need and which is actively hoped for ⟨those who *wanted* to live long—*Fishbein*⟩ ⟨the French *wanted* European unity—*N. Y. Times*⟩ **Crave** implies strongly the force of physical or mental appetite or need (as of hunger, thirst, love, or ambition) ⟨crave peace and security after war⟩ ⟨that eternal *craving* for amusement —*Donn Byrne*⟩ ⟨what he *craved* was books of poetry and chivalry—*Weeks*⟩ **Covet** implies a strong, eager desire, often inordinate and envious and often for what belongs to another ⟨where water is the most *coveted* and essential resource because its supply is limited —*Amer. Guide Series: Texas*⟩ ⟨we hate no people, and *covet* no people's land—*Willkie*⟩

*Ana* *long, yearn, hanker, pine, hunger, thirst: aspire, pant, *aim

*Con* abhor, abominate, loathe, detest, *hate: spurn, repudiate, reject, refuse, *decline

**desire** *n* Desire, appetite, lust, passion, urge are comparable as meaning a longing for something regarded as essential to one's well-being or happiness or as meaning an impulse originating in a man's nature and driving him toward the object or the experience which promises him enjoyment or satisfaction in its attainment. **Desire** may be used of every conceivable longing that stirs one emotionally, whether that longing originates in man's physical or in his spiritual nature, whether it is natural and normal or unnatural and perverted, whether it is generally regarded as low or high in the scale of moral or spiritual values ⟨the *desire* for food⟩ ⟨the *desire* for an education⟩ ⟨a *desire* for change⟩ ⟨the *desire* for peace⟩ ⟨his physical *desire* to sit in the sun and do nothing—*Anderson*⟩ ⟨the keen *desire* . . . to pay their debts—*Repplier*⟩ ⟨nothing dies harder than the *desire* to think well of oneself —*T. S. Eliot*⟩ ⟨Congreve's characters have inclinations, not *desires;* habits, not ecstasies—*J. M. Brown*⟩ It may be used specifically to denote sexual longing, but it does not always convey derogatory connotations when so restricted in meaning ⟨like the flesh of animals distended by fear or *desire*—*Cather*⟩ *Desire* is often used in implicit contrast to *will* or *volition,* for in itself it carries no implication of a determination or effort to possess or attain ⟨she had the *desire* to do something which she objected to doing—*Bennett*⟩ ⟨guiltless even of a *desire* for any private possession or advantage of their own —*Dickinson*⟩ **Appetite** is almost as extensive in its range of application as *desire,* and it invariably implies an imperative demand for satisfaction. It is specifically applied to the longings (as hunger, thirst, and sexual desire) which arise out of man's physical nature and which may be thwarted only by circumstances beyond one's control or by deliberate self-control ⟨a slave to his *appetite* for drink⟩ ⟨the child is losing his *appetite* and

only picks at his food⟩ ⟨impose restraints upon one's physical *appetites*⟩ ⟨he collected guns and women and his sexual *appetite* was awesome—*E. D. Radin*⟩ The word may be applied also to equally exacting longings which drive one to their satisfaction, whether they originate in his nature or are acquired ⟨man's distinguishing characteristic is the *appetite* for happiness⟩ ⟨an insatiable *appetite* for news⟩ ⟨almost pathological in his *appetite* for activity—*Mencken*⟩ **Lust** combines the specific denotation of *desire* as a longing that stirs emotion and that of *appetite* as a longing that exacts satisfaction; often it implies domination by the emotion or insatiability of the appetite ⟨Jansen . . . utterly condemned, as abominable concupiscence, not only sensuality (the *lust* of the flesh) but scientific curiosity (the *lust* of knowing) and ambition (the *lust* of power)—*Preserved Smith*⟩ ⟨whose ruling passion was the *lust* of praise—*Pope*⟩ When used specifically to denote sexual longing, *lust* unlike *desire* automatically carries derogatory connotations ⟨in his morning litany he could pray to be kept from lasciviousness, but when night came *lust* might come with it—*Van Doren*⟩ **Passion** is applied to any intense and preoccupying emotion which gives one's mind its particular bent or which serves as an outlet for and gives direction to one's energies. Though it comes close to *lust* in suggesting the energizing of desire by the vehemence of the emotions, *passion* is the better choice when personal predilection is implied; thus, he, too, knew the *lust* (better than *passion*) for power; but, his work reveals a *passion* (better than *lust*) for perfection ⟨avarice, he assured them, was the one *passion* that grew stronger and sweeter in old age. He had the lust for money as Martinez had for women—*Cather*⟩ ⟨the dream, the ambition, the *passion* of Mr. Raycie's life was (as his son knew) to found a Family—*Wharton*⟩ **Urge**, which basically means a force or motive which drives one to action, often more specifically denotes a strong, persistent, and compelling desire that has its origin in one's physical nature or one's peculiar temperament. The word is sometimes applied to the physical appetites (the sexual appetite is often called "the biological urge"), but it is more often used of a desire so strong and insistent that it must be satisfied or a sense of frustration ensues ⟨an *urge* to travel⟩ ⟨an *urge* to marry⟩ ⟨that almost mystic *urge* to climb can dominate your whole life— *Vaughan-Thomas*⟩

*Ana* longing, yearning, hankering, pining, hungering *or* hunger, thirsting *or* thirst (see LONG *vb*): *cupidity, greed, avarice, rapacity

*Ant* distaste —*Con* repugnance, repellency *or* repulsion, abhorrence (see corresponding adjectives at REPUGNANT)

**desist** discontinue, cease, *stop, quit

*Ana* *refrain, abstain, forbear: *relinquish, yield, abandon, resign

*Ant* persist —*Con* *continue: *persevere

**desolate** 1 forlorn, lorn, lonesome, lone, solitary, lonely, *alone

*Ana* deserted, forsaken, abandoned (see ABANDON): *miserable, wretched

*Con* cheerful, lighthearted, joyful, joyous, happy, *glad

2 *dismal, dreary, cheerless, dispiriting, bleak

*Ana* *bare, barren, bald: destitute, poverty-stricken, *poor

**despair** *n* hopelessness, desperation, despondency, forlornness (see under DESPONDENT *adj*)

*Ana* dejection, melancholy, *sadness, gloom, depression

*Ant* hope: optimism: beatitude —*Con* rapture, trans-

---

A colon (:) separates groups of words discriminated. An asterisk (*) indicates place of treatment of each group.

port, *ecstasy

**despairing** adj hopeless, desperate, *despondent, forlorn
**Ana** melancholy, *melancholic, atrabilious: pessimistic, misanthropic, *cynical: depressed, weighed down (see DEPRESS)
**Ant** hopeful —**Con** optimistic, roseate, rose-colored (see HOPEFUL): sanguine, *confident, assured, sure

**desperate** hopeless, despairing, *despondent, forlorn
**Ana** reckless, rash, foolhardy, venturesome (see ADVENTUROUS): *precipitate, headlong: thwarted, foiled, frustrated, outwitted, circumvented, baffled, balked (see FRUSTRATE)
**Con** *cool, collected, composed, nonchalant: sanguine, assured, *confident, sure

**desperation** hopelessness, despair, despondency, forlornness (see under DESPONDENT adj)
**Ana** fury, frenzy (see INSPIRATION): grit, pluck, guts, sand, *fortitude: recklessness, rashness, foolhardiness (see corresponding adjectives at ADVENTUROUS): *temerity, audacity
**Con** *confidence, assurance, aplomb: *equanimity, composure, sangfroid, phlegm

**despicable** *contemptible, pitiable, sorry, scurvy, cheap, beggarly, shabby
**Ana** *base, low, vile: ignominious, infamous, disgraceful (see corresponding nouns at DISGRACE): ignoble, *mean, abject, sordid
**Ant** praiseworthy, laudable

**despise,** contemn, scorn, disdain, scout mean to regard a person or thing as beneath one's notice or as unworthy of one's attention or interest. The same differences in implications and connotations are observable in the corresponding nouns **despite, contempt, scorn, disdain** when they denote such an attitude toward or such treatment of a person or thing. **Despise** and **despite** may imply an emotional reaction from strong disfavor to loathing, but in precise use it stresses a looking down upon a thing and its evaluation as mean, petty, weak, or worthless ⟨he must learn, however, to *despise* petty adversaries. No good sportsman ought to shoot at crows—*Scott*⟩ ⟨bird and beast *despised* my snares, which took me so many waking hours at night to invent—*Hudson*⟩ ⟨receive thy friend, who, scorning flight, goes to meet danger with *despite*—*Longfellow*⟩ ⟨the *despite* in which cunners are held is a convention—*Yale Review*⟩ **Contemn** and **contempt** imply even a harsher judgment than *despise* or *despite*, for *despise* and *despite* may connote mere derision, whereas *contemn* and especially *contempt* usually suggest vehement, though not necessarily vocal, condemnation of the person or thing as low, vile, feeble, or ignominious ⟨I *contemn* their low images of love—*Steele*⟩ ⟨his own early drawings of moss roses and picturesque castles—things that he now mercilessly *contemned*—*Bennett*⟩ ⟨and in *contempt* of hell and heaven, dies rather than bear some yoke of priests or kings—*Masefield*⟩ ⟨it was to proclaim their utter *contempt* for the public and popular conceptions of art, that the Dadaists launched into a series of outrageous practical jokes—*Day Lewis*⟩ **Scorn** implies quick, indignant, or profound contempt ⟨instructed from her early years to *scorn* the art of female tears—*Swift*⟩ ⟨I knew he'd *scorn* me. He hates frumps—*Meredith*⟩ ⟨Voltaire, with his quick intellectual *scorn* and eager malice of the brain—*Dowden*⟩ ⟨common sense, rejecting with *scorn* all that can be called mysticism—*Inge*⟩ **Disdain** suggests a visible manifestation of pride and arrogance or of aversion to what is base ⟨a great mind *disdains* to hold anything by courtesy—*Johnson*⟩ ⟨the psychiatric patient is *disdained* and ridiculed by his fellow inmates—*Banay*⟩ ⟨his *disdain*

of affectation and prudery was magnificent—*Mencken*⟩ **Scout** stresses not only derision but a refusal to consider the person or thing concerned as of any value, efficacy, or truth. It therefore suggests rejection or dismissal ⟨many great philosophers have not only been *scouted* while they were living, but forgotten as soon as they were dead—*Hazlitt*⟩ ⟨Alice would have *scouted* . . . any suggestion that her parent was more selfish than saintly —*Shaw*⟩
**Ana** abominate, loathe, abhor, detest, *hate: spurn, repudiate (see DECLINE)
**Ant** appreciate —**Con** admire, esteem, respect (see under REGARD n): value, prize, cherish, treasure (see APPRECIATE)

**despite** n 1 spite, ill will, malevolence, spleen, grudge, *malice, malignity, malignancy
**Ana** contempt, scorn, disdain (see under DESPISE): abhorrence, loathing, detestation, abomination, hatred, hate (see under HATE vb)
**Ant** appreciation: regard —**Con** admiration, esteem, respect (see REGARD n): *reverence, awe, fear
2 contempt, scorn, disdain (see under DESPISE)

**despite** prep in spite of, *notwithstanding

**despoil** *ravage, devastate, waste, sack, pillage, spoliate
**Ana** plunder, *rob, rifle, loot: *strip, bare, denude

**despondency** despair, desperation, hopelessness, forlornness (see under DESPONDENT adj)
**Ana** dejection, depression, melancholy, melancholia, *sadness, blues, dumps
**Ant** lightheartedness —**Con** cheerfulness, gladness, happiness, joyfulness, joyousness (see corresponding adjectives at GLAD)

**despondent** adj Despondent, despairing, desperate, hopeless, forlorn mean having lost all or practically all hope. The same distinctions in implications and connotations are to be found in their corresponding nouns **despondency, despair, desperation, hopelessness, forlornness** when they denote the state or feeling of a person who has lost hope. **Despondent** and **despondency** imply disheartenment or deep dejection arising out of a conviction that there is no longer any justification of hope or that further efforts are useless ⟨a *despondent* lover⟩ ⟨whenever . . . the repressed spirit of the artist . . . perceived . . . the full extent of its debacle, Mark Twain was filled with a *despondent* desire, a momentary purpose even, to stop writing altogether—*Brooks*⟩ ⟨we poets in our youth begin in gladness; but thereof come in the end *despondency* and madness—*Wordsworth*⟩ ⟨England, they said, was wont to take her defeats without *despondency,* and her victories without elation—*Repplier*⟩ **Despairing** and **despair** imply sometimes the passing of hope, sometimes the utter loss of hope, and often accompanying despondency ⟨the author . . . ended with a *despairing* appeal to the democracy when his jeremiads evoked no response from the upper class . . . or from the middle class—*Inge*⟩ ⟨to fortify ourselves against the ultimate disaster—which is *despair*—*Times Lit. Sup.*⟩ ⟨*despair* of her ever understanding either the terms of a contract or the nature of working conditions—*Mary Austin*⟩ ⟨the bitter weariness of a fathomless resignation and *despair*—*Wolfe*⟩ **Desperate** and **desperation** imply despair but not the cessation of effort; rather, they often suggest violence and recklessness as a last resource especially in the face of anticipated defeat or frustration ⟨the bitter, *desperate* striving unto death of the oppressed race, the damned *desperation* of the rebel—*Rose Macaulay*⟩ ⟨a *desperate* determination that nothing should interfere with her marriage with Hugh had taken possession of her—*Anderson*⟩ ⟨he was fighting a fight of *desperation,* and knew it—*Meredith*⟩ ⟨not knowing . . . how near my

pursuer might be, I turned in *desperation* to meet him—*Hudson*⟩ Hopeless and hopelessness imply both the complete loss of hope and the cessation of effort ⟨the *hopeless* look in the faces of the doomed men⟩ The words do not necessarily suggest despondency, dejection, or gloom, for sometimes they imply acceptance or resignation ⟨"Why should you say such desperate things?" "No, they are not desperate. They are only *hopeless*"—*Hardy*⟩ ⟨not that Dr. Lavendar was *hopeless;* he was never *hopeless* of anybody . . . but he was wise; so he was deeply discouraged—*Deland*⟩ ⟨the little *hopeless* community of beaten men and yellow defeated women—*Anderson*⟩ Forlorn (see also ALONE 1) and forlornness stress utter hopelessness, but they differ from *hopeless* and *hopelessness* in implying hopelessness even in the act of undertaking something because its failure is all but certain ⟨[we] sit down in a *forlorn* skepticism—*Berkeley*⟩ ⟨poor prince, *forlorn* he steps . . . and proud in his despair—*Keats*⟩ Desperate, hopeless, and forlorn and their corresponding nouns are applicable not only to men, their moods, words, and acts, but to the things which make men despairing or hopeless ⟨*desperate* straits⟩ ⟨the *hopeless* situation of a beleaguered garrison⟩ ⟨*desperate* grime and greasiness—*McFee*⟩ ⟨all the high ardor and imaginative force which the Celt has ever thrown into a *forlorn* and failing cause—*Cyril Robinson*⟩
*Ana* grieving, mourning, sorrowing (see GRIEVE): depressed, dejected, melancholy, sad (see corresponding nouns at SADNESS)
*Ant* lighthearted —*Con* cheerful, joyful, joyous, happy, *glad: buoyant, volatile, resilient, *elastic

despotic tyrannical, tyrannous, arbitrary, autocratic, *absolute
*Ana* domineering, imperious, *masterful, imperative: *dictatorial, authoritarian, magisterial

destiny *fate, lot, doom, portion
*Ana* *end, termination, terminus, ending: goal, objective (see INTENTION)

destitute 1 *devoid, void
*Ana* lacking, wanting (see LACK *vb*): *deficient: *empty: barren, *bare: depleted, drained, exhausted, bankrupted *or* bankrupt (see corresponding verbs at DEPLETE)
*Con* *full, replete, complete
2 *poor, indigent, needy, penniless, impecunious, poverty-stricken, necessitous
*Ant* opulent

destitution want, indigence, *poverty, penury, privation
*Ana* *need, necessity, exigency: *lack, absence, want, privation, dearth: adversity, *misfortune: strait (see JUNCTURE)
*Ant* opulence

destroy, demolish, raze mean to pull or tear down. Destroy is so general in its application that it may imply the operation of any force that wrecks, kills, crushes, or annihilates ⟨*destroy* a nest of caterpillars⟩ ⟨*destroy* affection⟩ ⟨a building *destroyed* by fire⟩ ⟨grinding poverty that *destroys* vitality⟩ Its opposition to *construct* is often apparent ⟨it is proverbially easier to *destroy* than to construct—*T. S. Eliot*⟩ ⟨very few established institutions, governments and constitutions . . . are ever *destroyed* by their enemies until they have been corrupted and weakened by their friends—*Lippmann*⟩ Demolish implies a pulling or smashing to pieces; when used in reference to buildings or other complex structures (as of wood, stone, or steel), it implies complete wreckage and often a heap of ruins ⟨houses *demolished* by a hurricane⟩ ⟨the automobile was *demolished* in a collision with the train⟩ The term implies the destruction of all coherency or integrity in a nonmaterial thing and, consequently, of all its usefulness

⟨*demolish* an opponent's argument⟩ ⟨people are inclined to believe that what Bradley did was to *demolish* the logic of Mill and the psychology of Bain—*T. S. Eliot*⟩ ⟨his research has been painstaking, and he *demolishes* a good many legends—*Pratt*⟩ Raze implies a bringing to the level of the ground; it may or may not imply an orderly process with no destruction of usable parts ⟨several buildings were *razed* to make room for the new city hall⟩ ⟨in 1865 a Gulf hurricane *razed* the town—*Amer. Guide Series: Texas*⟩ The term may imply obliteration or effacement, more, however, with reference to the implication of scraping than to the sense of pulling or tearing down ⟨canst thou not minister to a mind diseased . . . *raze* out the written troubles of the brain . . .?—*Shak.*⟩
*Ana* *ruin, wreck, dilapidate: *abolish, extinguish, annihilate: *ravage, devastate, sack
*Con* *found, establish, institute, organize: *make, form, shape, fashion, fabricate, forge, manufacture: preserve, conserve, *save

destruction *ruin, havoc, devastation
*Ana* demolishing *or* demolition, razing (see corresponding verbs at DESTROY): annihilation, extinction (see corresponding verbs at ABOLISH)

desultory casual, hit-or-miss, haphazard, *random, happy-go-lucky, chance, chancy
*Ana* *fitful, spasmodic: unsystematic, unmethodical, disorderly (see affirmative adjectives at ORDERLY): capricious, mercurial, *inconstant, fickle
*Ant* assiduous (*study, search, or other activity*): methodical (*something designed, planned, constructed*)

detach, disengage, abstract mean to remove one thing from another with which it is in union or association. One detaches something when one breaks a literal or figurative connection, tie, or bond and thereby isolates it or makes it independent ⟨*detach* sheets from a loose-leaf book⟩ ⟨*detach* a ship from a fleet⟩ ⟨*detach* oneself from one's prejudices⟩ ⟨the mature critic whose loyalties quietly *detached* themselves from the gods of his generation—*Parrington*⟩ One disengages something that is held by or involved with something else and thereby sets it free ⟨she *disengaged* her hand⟩ ⟨it is hard for the mind to *disengage* itself from depressing thoughts⟩ ⟨I could not rest satisfied until I . . . had *disengaged* . . . his good work from the inferior work joined with it—*Arnold*⟩ One abstracts something by withdrawing it from the place where it belongs or by separating it from a mass of like things so as to put it in another place or another relation ⟨a vast cigar-shaped body of gas was raised and eventually *abstracted* from the surface of the sun—*Swinton*⟩ ⟨*abstract* papers from a file⟩ Abstract may imply furtiveness and theft ⟨*abstract* eggs from a nest⟩ ⟨*abstract* money from a till⟩ It may imply an intention of shortening ⟨*abstract* the essential points from an argument⟩ or of concentrating elsewhere ⟨*abstract* one's attention from one's surroundings⟩ (see also ABSTRACT *adj*)
*Ana* *separate, part, sever, sunder, divorce: disjoin, disconnect, disunite (see affirmative verbs at JOIN)
*Ant* attach, affix —*Con* *fasten, fix: *tie, bind: *unite, combine, conjoin

detached aloof, uninterested, disinterested, *indifferent, unconcerned, incurious
*Ana* impartial, dispassionate, objective, unbiased, *fair: altruistic (see CHARITABLE)
*Ant* interested: selfish —*Con* *mercenary: concerned (see under CARE)

detail *n* 1 *item, particular
*Con* *structure, framework, anatomy, skeleton: whole, aggregate, total, *sum: mass, *bulk: design, scheme, *plan, plot

---

A colon (:) separates groups of words discriminated. An asterisk (*) indicates place of treatment of each group.

**2** *part, portion, piece, parcel, member, division, segment, sector, fraction, fragment

**detailed** itemized, particularized, *circumstantial, minute, particular
*Ana* *full, complete, replete: copious, abundant (see PLENTIFUL): exhausting *or* exhaustive (see corresponding verb at DEPLETE)

**detain 1** *arrest, apprehend, attach
*Ana* *catch, capture: seize, *take: *imprison, incarcerate, intern, jail
**2** withhold, hold, hold back, keep back, keep out, retain, reserve, *keep
**3** *delay, retard, slow, slacken
*Ana* curb, check, *restrain, inhibit: *arrest, interrupt: *defer, suspend, stay
*Con* *advance, promote, forward, further: *speed, hasten, hurry

**detention** arrest, apprehension, attachment (see under ARREST *vb*)
*Ana* imprisonment, internment, incarceration (see corresponding verbs at IMPRISON)

**deter** *dissuade, discourage, divert
*Ana* *prevent (sense 2): *hinder, impede, obstruct, block: debar, shut out (see EXCLUDE): *frighten, scare: *restrain, inhibit
*Ant* abet: actuate, motivate —*Con* *incite, instigate: stimulate, excite, *provoke

**deterioration,** degeneration, devolution, decadence, decline, declension are comparable as meaning either the process of falling from a higher to a lower level or the state of a thing when such a falling has occurred. **Deterioration** is the least specific of these terms and applies to any process or condition in which there are signs of impairment in quality, in character, or in value ⟨chemicals that reduce the *deterioration* of rubber in aging⟩ ⟨the *deterioration* of his memory is marked in recent years⟩ ⟨man the toolmaker has made "inanimate instruments". . . do his manual work for him; he is now trying to make them do his mental work . . . . The price may be the progressive *deterioration* of our faculties—*Inge*⟩ ⟨to promise that warfare will be nuclear . . . is to assure the further *deterioration* of our position throughout Asia—*Straight*⟩ **Degeneration** usually implies retrogression and a return to a simpler or more primitive state or condition; when used in reference to plants, animals, or their parts, it usually suggests changes in physical structure, but it may imply a progressive deterioration in structure and function resulting from disease ⟨the sea squirt in its adult stage evidences *degeneration* through the loss of the vertebrate characters apparent in its larval stage⟩ ⟨fatty *degeneration* of the heart⟩ When applied to persons in groups or as individuals or to states or empires, it suggests physical, intellectual, and often moral degradation and a reversion toward barbarism or, in the case of individuals, bestiality ⟨the *degeneration* of the American Indians confined to reservations⟩ ⟨the *degeneration* of the ancient Roman Empire⟩ ⟨of all the dangers that confront a nation at war, this *degeneration* of national purpose . . . is the greatest—*New Republic*⟩ **Devolution** in technical use may take the place of *degeneration* ⟨the *devolution* of the sea squirt⟩ but in general use it carries even a stronger implication of opposition to *evolution* ⟨the process of human evolution is nothing more than a process of sifting, and where that sifting ceases evolution ceases, becomes, indeed, *devolution*—*Ellis*⟩ **Decadence** presupposes a previous maturing and usually a high degree of excellence; it implies that the falling takes place after a thing (as a people, a literature or other form of art, or

a branch of knowledge) has reached the peak of its development ⟨there seems to be no more pronounced mark of the *decadence* of a people and its literature than a servile and rigid subserviency to rule—*Ellis*⟩ ⟨a sharply falling rate of population growth, an abnormally high death rate, extensive illness and the like, are an indication of social *decadence* and ample cause for alarm on the part of political leaders—*Roucek*⟩ In reference to matters of art *decadence* may imply no more than excessive refinement and studied attention to esthetic detail ⟨at the turn of the century we all thought we knew what *decadence* meant—overripeness, overcivilization, a preoccupation with refined sensations . . . the essence of *decadence* is an excessive subjectivism—*Times Lit. Sup.*⟩ ⟨Van Vechten produced a kind of mock *decadence* unique in American literature. His novels are hyperaesthetic, perverse, and often devoted to esoteric or archaic lore—*Lueders*⟩ **Decline** is often interchangeable with *decadence* because it, too, suggests a falling after the peak has been reached in power, prosperity, excellence, or achievement, but it usually suggests more momentum, more obvious evidences of deterioration, and less hope of a return to the earlier state ⟨the rise and *decline* of the imperial power⟩ ⟨he is in the *decline* of life⟩ ⟨the association so often noted between the flowering of the intellect and the *decline* of national vigor—*Krutch*⟩ **Declension** differs from *decline* only in connoting less precipitancy or a slower or more gradual falling toward extinction or destruction ⟨seems to mark a *declension* in his career as an illustrator—*Mather*⟩ ⟨the moral change, the sad *declension* from the ancient proud spirit . . . was painfully depressing —*Bennett*⟩
*Ana* impairment, spoiling (see corresponding verbs at INJURE): decaying *or* decay, decomposition, disintegration, rotting, crumbling (see corresponding verbs at DECAY): debasement, degradation (see corresponding verbs at ABASE)
*Ant* improvement, amelioration

**determinant** antecedent, *cause, reason, occasion
*Ana* factor (see ELEMENT): *influence, weight, authority

**determinative** *conclusive, decisive, definitive
*Ana* determining, deciding, settling (see DECIDE): influencing, affecting (see AFFECT): shaping, fashioning, forming *or* formative (see corresponding verbs at MAKE)
*Con* *ineffective, ineffectual, inefficacious, inefficient

**determine 1** settle, rule, *decide, resolve
*Ana* fix, *set, establish: dispose, predispose, *incline, bias: drive, impel, *move, actuate: *induce, persuade
**2** ascertain, *discover, unearth, learn

**detest** *hate, abhor, abominate, loathe
*Ana* *despise, contemn, scorn, disdain: spurn, repudiate, reject (see DECLINE *vb*)
*Ant* adore (sense 2) —*Con* love, *like, dote, fancy, relish: cherish, prize, treasure, value, *appreciate

**detestable** odious, *hateful, abominable, abhorrent
*Ana* *contemptible, despicable, sorry, scurvy: atrocious, *outrageous, monstrous, heinous: *execrable, damnable, accursed

**detestation** hate, hatred, abomination, abhorrence, loathing (see under HATE *vb*)
*Ana* *antipathy, aversion: despite, contempt, scorn, disdain (see under DESPISE)
*Con* admiration, esteem, respect, *regard: love, affection, *attachment: tolerance, indulgence, forbearance (see under FORBEARING)

**detract** belittle, minimize, disparage, derogate, *decry, depreciate
*Ana* asperse, *malign, traduce, defame, vilify, calumni-

ate, slander, libel: reduce, lessen, diminish, *decrease
*Con* enhance, heighten, *intensify: magnify, aggrandize, *exalt

**detraction,** **backbiting, calumny, slander, scandal** are comparable when they denote either the offense of one who defames another or casts aspersions upon him or what is uttered by way of defamation or aspersion. **Detraction** stresses the injurious effect of what is said and the loss through it of something (as the esteem of others or his credit, his deserts, or even his good name) precious to the person affected ⟨bring candid eyes unto the perusal of men's works, and let not . . . *detraction* blast well-intended labors—*Browne*⟩ ⟨to listen to *detraction* is as much an act of *detraction* as to speak it—*Manning*⟩ **Backbiting** imputes both furtiveness and spitefulness to the one who asperses or defames; it suggests an unfair, mean, and cowardly attack when the victim is absent and unable to defend himself ⟨refrain your tongue from *backbiting:* for there is no word so secret, that shall go for nought—*Wisdom of Solomon* 1:11⟩ ⟨jealousy and intrigue and *backbiting,* producing a poisonous atmosphere—*Russell*⟩ **Calumny** stresses malicious misrepresentation; it therefore implies that the detractor is a liar and that his intent is to blacken another's name ⟨be thou as chaste as ice, as pure as snow, thou shalt not escape *calumny*—*Shak.*⟩ ⟨*calumny* differs from most other injuries in this dreadful circumstance: he who commits it can never repair it—*Johnson*⟩ ⟨to persevere in one's duty and be silent is the best answer to *calumny*—*Washington*⟩ **Slander** (for legal use, see MALIGN) stresses the dissemination of calumnies, especially those of a highly defamatory character; thus, a person who is given to *calumny* is prone to malicious misrepresentation of the acts, the motives, or the character of others; a person who is given to *slander* is prone to repeat calumnies or defamatory reports without ascertaining or with complete indifference to their truth or falsehood ⟨who spake no *slander,* no, nor listened to it —*Tennyson*⟩ ⟨this charge cannot be excused as a reckless *slander*. It was a deliberate falsehood, a lie—*New Republic*⟩ **Scandal** (see also OFFENSE, DISGRACE) usually suggests the activity of a gossip, especially of an idle, irresponsible gossip (a scandalmonger), who spreads abroad shocking details, whether true or untrue, that reflect discredit on another or that tend to tarnish or blacken his reputation ⟨it is difficult for a man to remain long in public life untouched by *scandal*⟩ ⟨her tea she sweetens, as she sips, with *scandal*—*Rogers*⟩ ⟨the reappearance of the priest upon the scene cut short further *scandal*—*Cather*⟩
*Ana* *injury, damage, harm, hurt: *injustice, injury, wrong: defaming *or* defamation, aspersion, maligning, traducing, slandering *or* slander, calumniation, vilification, libeling *or* libel (see corresponding verbs at MALIGN)

**detriment** *disadvantage, handicap, drawback
*Ana* damage, *injury, harm, hurt: impairment, spoiling, marring (see corresponding verbs at INJURE)
*Ant* advantage, benefit

**detrimental** deleterious, noxious, *pernicious, baneful
*Ana* harming *or* harmful, hurting *or* hurtful, injuring *or* injurious, damaging, impairing (see corresponding verbs at INJURE)
*Ant* beneficial —*Con* advantageous, profitable (see BENEFICIAL): helping *or* helpful, aiding (see corresponding verbs at HELP)

**devastate** waste, *ravage, sack, pillage, despoil, spoliate
*Ana* *destroy, demolish, raze: *ruin, wreck: plunder, loot, *rob, rifle

**devastation** *ruin, havoc, destruction
*Ana* demolishment, razing (see corresponding verbs at DESTROY): ravaging, sacking, pillaging, despoliation (see corresponding verbs at RAVAGE)

**develop 1** *unfold, evolve, elaborate, perfect
*Ana* actualize, *realize, materialize: attain, achieve, compass, *reach
**2** *mature, ripen, age
*Ana* *advance, progress: *expand, dilate
*Con* *wither, shrivel, wizen

**development,** **evolution** are comparable when they mean growth from a lower to a higher state. **Development** stresses the bringing out of the hidden or latent possibilities in a thing whether through growth and differentiation and therefore through a series of natural stages ⟨*development* of a seed into a plant⟩ ⟨*development* of a human being from the embryo⟩ or through the exercise of human energy, ingenuity, or art ⟨the *development* of an industry⟩ ⟨*development* of a tract of land⟩ ⟨*development* of an argument⟩ **Evolution,** on the other hand, stresses an orderly succession of events or of living things, each growing out of the preceding yet marked by changes which transform it and give it a particular identity and usually a more elaborate or more advanced character ⟨the *evolution* of species⟩ ⟨the *evolution* of the drama⟩ *Development* is appropriately used when the emphasis is on the realization of the full possibilities of a particular thing through natural or artificial means, and *evolution* when the stress is on transformations which occur in a type, class, or order of things, the individual instances of which retain a likeness to the parent but manifest differences especially in the direction of complexity and progress ⟨the Aristotelian canon that the "nature" of a thing must be sought in its completed *development,* its final form—*Inge*⟩ ⟨no, "revolution" is not the proper word! What is happening in modern physics is a tremendously rapid *evolution*—*Darrow*⟩
*Con* decline, declension, decadence, devolution, *deterioration, degeneration

**deviate** digress, diverge, *swerve, veer, depart
*Ana* deflect, *turn, divert, avert, sheer: stray, *wander, rove

**deviation,** **aberration, divergence, deflection** denote departure or an instance of departure from a straight course or procedure or from a norm or standard. **Deviation,** the term of widest application, usually requires qualification or a context to complete its meaning ⟨no *deviation* from traditional methods was permitted⟩ ⟨there were many *deviations* from fact in his account⟩ ⟨the road proceeds without any *deviation* for two miles⟩ **Aberration** adds to *deviation* definite implications of error, fault, or abnormality and therefore has highly technical significations in some of the sciences. In general use it commonly implies transgression of the moral law or the social code and is often used euphemistically for a reprehensible act or reprehensible behavior ⟨the *aberrations* of his youth had long been forgotten⟩ **Divergence** is sometimes used interchangeably with *deviation,* but ordinarily it denotes deviation of two or more things which from a common starting point proceed in different directions ⟨an angle is formed by the *divergence* of two lines⟩ ⟨at no point in the discussion was there *divergence* of opinion on this question⟩ **Deflection** adds to *deviation* the implication of bending or curving ⟨*deflection* of rays of light passing through a prism⟩

**device 1 Device, contrivance, gadget, contraption** mean something usually of a mechanical character which is invented as a means of doing a particular piece of work or of effecting a given end. **Device** is the most widely

A colon (:) separates groups of words discriminated. An asterisk (*) indicates place of treatment of each group.

applicable of these terms; it may be used of a thing that serves as a tool or instrument or as an effective part of a machine, especially one which shows some ingenuity in invention ⟨a *device* for controlling the speed of a car⟩ ⟨he invented several handy household *devices* including one for whipping cream and one for hulling strawberries⟩ It may be used also of an artifice or stratagem concocted as a means of accomplishing an end ⟨her *device* for keeping the children quiet⟩ ⟨he will . . . entrap thee by some treacherous *device—Shak.*⟩ or of a pattern or design that shows the play of fancy, especially of one that proves useful to the less inventive ⟨first-person narrative is a common literary *device*⟩ ⟨that old stale and dull *device* [in painting] of a rustic bridge spanning a shallow stream—*Jefferies*⟩ **Contrivance** stresses skill and dexterity in the adaptation of means and especially of the means at hand to an end; it sometimes carries a suggestion of crudity of or of contempt for the resulting device or system ⟨a *contrivance* for frightening birds that were eating his corn⟩ ⟨all sorts of *contrivances* for saving more time and labor—*Shaw*⟩ ⟨he would look at none of the *contrivances* for his comfort—*Conrad*⟩ **Gadget** is sometimes used of a device for which one does not know the name; more often it applies to a small and novel device and especially to an accessory or an appliance intended to add to a person's comfort, convenience, or pleasure ⟨the garden tools and *gadgets* which make gardening so much more fun—*Van der Spuy*⟩ ⟨their new car has all the latest *gadgets*⟩ **Contraption** is usually more depreciative than *contrivance* or *gadget* and often suggests a clumsy substitute rather than an ingenious invention ⟨he has rigged up a *contraption* which he calls a radio⟩ ⟨her husband's little perch-in-the-sun . . . is a simple enough *contraption*—a wooden stump with the seat of an old kitchen chair nailed across the top of it —*Glover*⟩ It also may denote something viewed with skepticism or mistrust primarily because new, unfamiliar, or untried ⟨the *contraption* ran so well that the Detroit Common Council was forced to pass the city's first motor traffic regulation—*Amer. Guide Series: Mich.*⟩ ⟨a seventy-two-foot-long, eleven-ton finless rocket . . . . In the nose of this *contraption—Daniel Lang*⟩
*Ana* instrument, tool, *implement, appliance, utensil: apparatus, *machine, mechanism: expedient, *resource, shift, makeshift, resort: invention, creation (see corresponding verbs at INVENT): artifice, ruse, *trick, gambit, ploy
**2** *figure, design, motif, pattern
*Ana* *symbol, emblem, attribute, type

**devilish** diabolical, diabolic, *fiendish, demoniac, demonic
*Ana* *infernal, hellish: nefarious, iniquitous, villainous, *vicious
*Ant* angelic

**devious** *crooked, oblique
*Ana* deviating, diverging, digressing (see SWERVE): aberrant, *abnormal: tricky, crafty, artful, cunning, foxy, insidious, *sly
*Ant* straightforward   —*Con* downright, *forthright

**devise 1** *contrive, invent, frame, concoct
*Ana* create, discover (see INVENT): fashion, forge, fabricate, shape, form, *make: design, plan, scheme, plot (see under PLAN *n*)
**2** *will, bequeath, leave, legate

**devoid,** **void, destitute** are comparable when they are followed by *of* and mean showing entire want or lack. **Devoid** stresses the absence or the nonpossession of a particular quality, character, or tendency ⟨I was not *devoid* of capacity or application—*Gibbon*⟩ ⟨they will steal from you before your very face, so *devoid* are they

of all shame—*Hudson*⟩ ⟨a human being *devoid* of hope is the most terrible object in the world—*Heiser*⟩ **Void** (see also EMPTY 1) usually implies freedom from the slightest trace, vestige, tinge, or taint of something ⟨a man *void* of honor⟩ ⟨a conscience *void* of offence—*Acts* 24:16⟩ ⟨a drama which, with all its preoccupation with sex, is really *void* of sexual interest—*Shaw*⟩ **Destitute** stresses deprivation or privation; it therefore is seldom used with reference to what is evil or undesirable ⟨a domestic life *destitute* of any hallowing charm—*George Eliot*⟩ ⟨men of genius . . . wholly *destitute* of any proper sense of form—*J. R. Lowell*⟩ ⟨no woman . . . so totally *destitute* of the sentiment of religion—*J. R. Green*⟩
*Ana* barren, *bare: lacking, wanting (see LACK *vb*): *empty

**devolution** decadence, decline, declension, *deterioration, degeneration
*Ana* retrogressiveness *or* retrogression, regressiveness *or* regression (see corresponding adjectives at BACKWARD): receding *or* recession, retrograding *or* retrogradation (see corresponding verbs at RECEDE)
*Ant* evolution   —*Con* *development: *progress, progression

**devote 1 Devote, dedicate, consecrate, hallow** mean to set apart something or less often someone for a particular use or end. **Devote** often implies a giving up or setting apart because of motives almost as impelling as those that demand a vow ⟨*devotes* her full time to the care of the unfortunate⟩ ⟨the administrative work . . . deprived him of the time and energy which he longed to *devote* to historical research—*Callender*⟩ ⟨eloquence, erudition, and philosophy . . . were humbly *devoted* to the service of religion—*Gibbon*⟩ ⟨he cared too little for diplomacy to *devote* himself to it—*Commins*⟩ **Dedicate** implies solemn and exclusive devotion and often a ceremonial setting apart for a serious and often a sacred use ⟨*dedicate* a memorial⟩ ⟨I will *dedicate* all the actions of my life to that one end—*Belloc*⟩ ⟨I had devoted the labor of my whole life, and had *dedicated* my intellect . . . to the slow and elaborate toil of constructing one single work—*De Quincey*⟩ **Consecrate** implies the giving of a sacred or exalted character ⟨his effect was to *consecrate* the Prussian State and to enshrine bureaucratic absolutism—*Dewey*⟩ especially by rites (as those by which a building is set apart for the service or worship of God or by which a bishop or king is elevated to his throne or by which ground is set apart as a burial place of the dead) ⟨kings of England are *consecrated* in Westminster Abbey⟩ ⟨the right of burial in *consecrated* ground⟩ In more general applications *consecrate* while not implying such rites does carry a stronger connotation of almost religious devotion than *dedicate* ⟨a night of memories and of sighs I *consecrate* to thee—*Landor*⟩ **Hallow** is a still stronger term, partly because of its use in the Lord's Prayer ⟨"Our Father which art in heaven, *hallowed* be thy name"⟩ and partly because it often implies an ascription of intrinsic sanctity. Unlike the foregoing terms *hallow* is not normally used of oneself; thus, one may *devote* or *dedicate* or occasionally *consecrate* oneself to something (as a duty, a responsibility, or an interest), but one *hallows* something or more rarely someone ⟨his marriage was *hallowed* and made permanent by the Church—*Barr*⟩ ⟨but in a larger sense we cannot dedicate, we cannot consecrate, we cannot *hallow* this ground —*Lincoln*⟩ *Hallow* may also be used to imply a mere respecting or making respectable (as by reason of age or custom) without suggesting a sacred character ⟨you justify everything, *hallow* everything—*Elizabeth Taylor*⟩

*Ana* analogous words     *Ant* antonyms     *Con* contrasted words     See also explanatory notes facing page 1

⟨dirty yellow varnish no longer interposes here its *hallowing* influence between the spectator and the artist's original creation—*Fry*⟩
*Ana* *commit, consign, confide, entrust: assign, *allot: *sentence, doom
2 apply, *direct, address
*Ana* endeavor, strive, struggle, try, *attempt
**devoted** *loving, affectionate, fond, doting
*Ana* *faithful, loyal, true, constant: attentive, considerate, *thoughtful
**devotee** votary, *addict, habitué
*Ana* *enthusiast, zealot, fanatic
**devotion** loyalty, fealty, *fidelity, piety, allegiance
*Ana* fervor, ardor, zeal, enthusiasm, *passion: love, affection, *attachment: dedication, consecration (see corresponding verbs at DEVOTE)
**devour** *eat, swallow, ingest, consume
*Ana* *waste, squander, dissipate: *destroy, demolish: wreck, *ruin
**devout,** **pious, religious, pietistic, sanctimonious** apply mainly to persons, their acts, and their words and mean showing fervor and reverence in the practice of religion. **Devout** stresses an attitude of mind or a feeling that leads one to such fervor and reverence ⟨a *devout* man, and one that feared God—*Acts* 10:2⟩ ⟨all those various "offices" which, in Pontifical, Missal, and Breviary, *devout* imagination had elaborated from age to age—*Pater*⟩ **Pious** emphasizes rather the faithful and dutiful performance of one's religious obligations; although often used interchangeably with *devout* it tends to suggest outward acts which imply faithfulness and fervor rather than, as does *devout,* an attitude or feeling which can only be inferred ⟨*pious* churchmen⟩ ⟨happy, as a *pious* man is happy when after a long illness, he goes once more to church—*Hichens*⟩ ⟨were *pious* Christians, taking their Faith devoutly. But such religious emotion as was theirs, was reflected rather than spontaneous—*H. O. Taylor*⟩ The term often, however, carries a hint of depreciation, sometimes of hypocrisy ⟨the saying that we are members one of another is not a mere *pious* formula to be repeated in church without any meaning—*Shaw*⟩ ⟨a hypocrite—a thing all *pious* words and uncharitable deeds—*Reade*⟩ **Religious** may and usually does imply both devoutness and piety, but it stresses faith in a God or gods and adherence to a way of life believed in consonance with that faith ⟨a man may be moral without being *religious,* but he cannot be *religious* without being moral—*Myers*⟩ ⟨they are not *religious:* they are only pew renters—*Shaw*⟩ In its basic meaning **pietistic** stresses the emotional rather than the intellectual aspects of religion ⟨in the Catholic Church it [use of the Bible] is threefold, doctrinal, liturgical, and *pietistic*—*New Catholic Dict.*⟩ ⟨while probably a very late psalm, it brings to a kind of spiritual climax the *pietistic* utterances found in earlier parts of the Bible—*Baab*⟩ ⟨an emotional person with *pietistic* inclinations that nearly carried him over at different times to the Plymouth Brethren—*H. G. Wells*⟩ Often this opposition of the emotional to the intellectual is overlooked and *pietistic* is used derogatorily of someone or something felt to display overly sentimental or unduly emotional piety ⟨Gibbon's analysis of the causes of the growth of Christianity was very valuable, because he redressed the balance against a heavy weight of *pietistic* flapdoodle that passed for ecclesiastical history—*Trevelyan*⟩ **Sanctimonious** has entirely lost its original implication of a holy or sacred character and implies a mere pretension to or appearance of holiness or piety ⟨a *sanctimonious* hypocrite⟩ ⟨*sanctimonious* phrases⟩ Often it connotes a hypocritical aloofness or superiority of manner ⟨if it only takes some of the *sanctimonious*

conceit out of one of those pious scalawags—*Frost*⟩
*Ana* fervent, fervid, ardent (see IMPASSIONED): worshiping, adoring, venerating (see REVERE)
**dexterity** facility, ease, *readiness
*Ana* dexterousness, adroitness, deftness (see corresponding adjectives at DEXTEROUS): expertness, adeptness, skillfulness, proficiency (see corresponding adjectives at PROFICIENT)
*Ant* clumsiness —*Con* awkwardness, ineptness *or* ineptitude, maladroitness (see corresponding adjectives at AWKWARD)
**dexterous,** **adroit, deft, handy** mean having or showing readiness and skill in the use of one's hands, limbs, or body and may also imply physical or mental readiness or skill. **Dexterous** implies expertness with consequent facility and agility in manipulation or movement ⟨seized one corner of the blanket, and with a *dexterous* twist and throw unrolled it—*C. G. D. Roberts*⟩ ⟨one of the most *dexterous* novelists now writing, with an enviable command of styles —*Bellow*⟩ **Adroit** is only occasionally used with reference to physical skill. It more commonly implies resourcefulness or artfulness and ability to cope effectively or cleverly with situations; thus, an *adroit* fencer or an *adroit* magician is, by implication, not only *dexterous* in his manipulations but able to cope quickly and without bungling with every situation that arises ⟨a daring but consummately *adroit* transference of conventions—*Lowes*⟩ **Deft** stresses lightness, neatness, and sureness of touch or handling ⟨a *deft* watch repairer⟩ ⟨*deft* in every cunning, save the dealings of the sword—*Morris*⟩ ⟨waltzed off with the prettiest girl, sliding, swinging, *deft*—*Sinclair Lewis*⟩ **Handy** usually implies lack of formal or professional training but a degree of skill in doing small jobs (as of carpentry, plumbing, or repairing) ⟨some men are what is known as "*handy* around the house." They can, if need be, fix a dripping faucet, plane off a door that sticks, put up a hook in the back hall—*Rorick*⟩ It is sometimes applied to a jack-of-all-trades.
*Ana* nimble, *agile: skilled, skillful, expert, masterly, adept, *proficient: *easy, effortless, smooth, facile
*Ant* clumsy —*Con* *awkward, maladroit, inept, gauche
**diabolical, diabolic** devilish, *fiendish, demoniac, demonic
*Ana & Ant* see those at DEVILISH

**diagnosis,** **prognosis** should perhaps be called near synonyms; but they can be confused because both are employed in a specific medical sense with clear, sharp implications that are often carried over into their general and extended use. **Diagnosis** applies to the act or art of recognizing or of identifying a disease or diseased condition by analysis of such factors as the history of the case, its subjective symptoms, and its objective signs as revealed by observation or by special laboratory tests (as a count of the blood cells or an X-ray examination) ⟨if a physician is not confident of his own *diagnosis,* he should call in another who has had much experience in similar cases⟩ ⟨operates an experimental auto *diagnosis* and repair center—*Wall Street Jour.*⟩ ⟨heat-flow measurements in the earth can aid in our *diagnosis* of the earth's condition—*Benfield*⟩ ⟨if he cannot find the cure at least he can help in the *diagnosis* of our social ills—*Firth*⟩ **Prognosis** applies to the act or art of foretelling the course and the termination of a disease; the term usually implies a correct diagnosis and knowledge of how the disease will affect the patient as it runs its course and of how it will end ⟨the physician was so confident of his patient's powers of resistance that he could give a favorable *prognosis* in the case⟩ ⟨a *prognosis* is based on observation and analysis, and consists of the application to particular in-

A colon (:) separates groups of words discriminated. An asterisk (*) indicates place of treatment of each group.

**diagram** 239 **dictate**

stances of generalizations about the actual and hypothetical connections between facts and events—*Streeten*⟩ ⟨in my opinion the book *Brave New World* is no longer a *prognosis,* but a *diagnosis*—*Peerman*⟩

**diagram** *n* outline, draft, tracing, sketch, delineation, plot, blueprint (see under SKETCH *vb*)
*Ana* design, *plan, plot, scheme

**diagram** *vb* outline, plot, blueprint, draft, trace, *sketch, delineate
*Ana* design, plan, plot, scheme (see under PLAN *n*)

**dialect** *n* **1** Dialect, vernacular, patois, lingo, jargon, cant, argot, slang denote a form of language or a style of speech which varies from that accepted as the literary standard. **Dialect** (see also LANGUAGE 1) is applied ordinarily to a form of a language that is confined to a locality or to a group, that differs from the standard form of the same language in peculiarities of vocabulary, pronunciation, usage, and morphology, and that persists for generations or even centuries. It may represent an independent development from the same origin as the standard form (as the Sussex *dialect*) or a survival (as the *dialect* of the Kentucky mountaineers). It is sometimes applied to any form of language differing from the standard ⟨a Babylonish *dialect* which learned pedants much affect—*Butler* d. 1680⟩ **Vernacular** (usually *the vernacular*) has several applications, though it always denotes the form of language spoken by the people in contrast with that employed by learned or literary men. In the Middle Ages when the language of the church, of the universities, and of learned writings was Latin, the *vernacular* was the native language of the people whatever it might be in the locality in question ⟨translate the Bible into the *vernacular*⟩ ⟨the first Christian missionaries from Rome did not teach their converts to pray and give praise in the *vernacular*—*Quiller-Couch*⟩ When a contrast with the literary language rather than with Latin is implied, *the vernacular* is an underogatory designation for the spoken language, the language that represents the speech of the people as a whole, that is colloquial but not inherently vulgar, and that is marked chiefly by the spontaneous choice of familiar, often native as opposed to exotic words and phrases ⟨Pope . . . is absolute master of the raciest, most familiar, most cogent and telling elements of the *vernacular*—*Lowes*⟩ Vernacular often implies a contrast with scientific nomenclature ⟨taxonomic and *vernacular* names for flowers⟩ **Patois** is often used as if it were the equivalent of *dialect*. It tends, however, to be restricted especially in North America to designating a form of speech used by the uneducated people in a bilingual section or country; the word often specifically refers to the hybrid language (of mingled English and Canadian French) spoken in some parts of Canada. **Lingo** is a term of comtempt applied to any language that is not easily or readily understood. It is applicable to a strange foreign language, a dialect, or a patois or to the peculiar speech of a class, cult, or group ⟨I have often warned you not to talk the court gibberish to me. I tell you, I don't understand the *lingo*—*Fielding*⟩ **Jargon,** which may be applied to an unintelligible or meaningless speech (as in a foreign tongue or a patois), is used chiefly in reference to the technical or esoteric language of a subject, a class, a profession, or a cult and usually expresses the point of view of one unfamiliar with it and confused or baffled by it ⟨cockets, and dockets, and drawbacks, and other *jargon* words of the customhouse—*Swift*⟩ ⟨Whitman . . . has a somewhat vulgar inclination for technical talk and the *jargon* of philosophy—*Stevenson*⟩ **Cant,** related to *chant,* seems to have been applied first to the whining speech of beggars. It has been applied more or less specifically to several different forms of language (as the secret language of gypsies

and thieves, the technical language of a trade or profession, and the peculiar phraseology of a religious sect or of its preachers). From the last of these applications a new sense has been developed (see HYPOCRISY). When referring to the peculiar language of a subject or profession *cant* usually suggests the hackneyed use of set words or phrases, often in a specialized sense, and, unlike *jargon,* does not usually imply unintelligibility; thus, the language of sportswriters is a *cant* rather than a *jargon*; the scientific nomenclature used by physicians in official reports may be called medical *jargon* rather than *cant* by those who do not understand it; a person who repeatedly calls an investigation a "probe," a large book a "tome," a preacher a "parson," or his wife "my better half" may be said to be given to *cant*. **Argot** is applicable chiefly to the cant of the underworld; it is now sometimes used of any form of peculiar language adopted by a clique, a set, or other closely knit group. **Slang** does not as often denote a form of language or a type of speech as it does a class of recently coined words or phrases or the type of word which belongs to that class ⟨in the *slang* of college students a drudge is a "grind"⟩ ⟨the characteristic differences between American *slang* and British *slang*⟩ Slang implies comparatively recent invention, the appeal of the words or phrases to popular fancy because of their aptness, picturesqueness, grotesqueness, or humorousness, and usually an ephemeral character.
**2** *language, tongue, speech, idiom

**dialectic** *argumentation, disputation, debate, forensic
**diaphanous** limpid, pellucid, transparent, translucent, *clear, lucid

**diatribe** *n* *tirade, jeremiad, philippic
*Ana* invective, vituperation, obloquy, *abuse

**dictate** *vb* Dictate, prescribe, ordain, decree, impose mean to lay down expressly something to be followed, observed, obeyed, or accepted. **Dictate** implies an authoritative direction by or as if by the spoken word which serves in governing or guiding one's course of action ⟨they *dictated* the conditions of peace—*Gibbon*⟩ ⟨a man and woman who love each other and their children ought to be able to act spontaneously as the heart *dictates*—*Russell*⟩ ⟨all the other papers had traditions; their past principles *dictated* their future policy—*Rose Macaulay*⟩ **Prescribe** (see also PRESCRIBE) implies a formulated rule, law, or order; it suggests an authoritative pronouncement which is clear, definite, and cannot be gainsaid ⟨my teachers should have *prescribed* to me, 1st, sincerity; 2d, sincerity; 3d, sincerity—*Thoreau*⟩ ⟨establishments maintained by general taxation and filled with children whose presence is *prescribed* by law—*Grandgent*⟩ **Ordain** implies institution, establishment, or enactment by a supreme or unquestioned authority or power; usually it suggests an inalterable settlement of a problem or question ⟨we still accept, in theory at all events, the Mosaic conception of morality as a code of rigid and inflexible rules, arbitrarily *ordained,* and to be blindly obeyed—*Ellis*⟩ ⟨a blessed custom of my infancy *ordained* that every living room should be dominated by a good-sized center table—*Repplier*⟩ ⟨nature inexorably *ordains* that the human race shall perish of famine if it stops working—*Shaw*⟩ **Decree** implies a decision made and formally pronounced by absolute authority or by a power whose edicts are received with the same attention. It is used particularly of ecclesiastical, civil, or judicial power, whether absolute or limited in its scope, or more broadly of anything whose authoritative pronouncements are blindly obeyed ⟨the king *decreed* that all foreigners should be excluded from the state⟩ ⟨fashion *decrees* that skirts be shorter and jackets somewhat longer than last year⟩ ⟨if statues were *decreed* in Britain, as in ancient Greece and Rome, to public benefactors—*Dickens*⟩ ⟨the

---

*Ana* analogous words    *Ant* antonyms    *Con* contrasted words    See also explanatory notes facing page 1

old man was used to the order of his monastery, and though he slept on the ground, as the Rule *decrees,* preferred a decency in these things—*Kipling*⟩ **Impose** implies a subjecting to what must be borne, endured, or submitted to. It may suggest infliction by a paramount authority ⟨each time I attempted to speak he *imposed* silence—*Hudson*⟩ ⟨the ever more stringent regulations we found it necessary to *impose*—*Heiser*⟩ More often it suggests limitations intended to make for order, beauty, or efficiency ⟨patience and industry . . . could only be secured . . . by the enforcement of good habits *imposed* by external authority—*Russell*⟩ ⟨when the language, the stresses, the very structure of the sentences are *imposed* upon the writer by the special mood of the piece—*Cather*⟩
*Ana* direct, control, manage (see CONDUCT): *guide, lead: *govern, rule: tell, utter, *say

**dictate** *n* behest, bidding, injunction, *command, order, mandate
*Ana* *law, rule, precept, canon, ordinance, statute, regulation

**dictatorial,** magisterial, authoritarian, dogmatic, doctrinaire, oracular are comparable in the sense of imposing or having the manner or disposition of one who imposes his will or his opinions upon others. **Dictatorial** implies the powers of a dictator, but it has acquired so strong an implication of the assumption of such power that it often stresses autocratic or high-handed methods and a domineering, overbearing temper ⟨a captain who has been entrusted with *dictatorial* power—*Macaulay*⟩ ⟨he is . . . very learned, very *dictatorial,* very knock-me-down—*Mitford*⟩ **Magisterial** derives its chief implications from its reference to a magistrate or, more often, to a schoolmaster. It seldom implies an assumption of power, high-handedness, or a bad temper but does suggest excessive use or display of the powers or prerogatives associated with the offices of a magistrate or schoolmaster (as in controlling and disciplining or in enforcing the acceptance of one's opinions) ⟨we are not *magisterial* in opinions, nor . . . obtrude our notions on any man—*Browne*⟩ *Magisterial* is applied also to opinions or ideas which are so deeply impressed on the mind, especially the popular mind, that they cannot easily be eradicated ⟨the "possible," as something less than the actual and more than the wholly unreal, is another of these *magisterial* notions of common sense—*James*⟩ **Authoritarian** is used chiefly in reference to states or governments (for this use see TOTALITARIAN), to churches, to bodies, persons, or their policies or attitudes. It implies assumption of one's own (or another's) power to exact obedience or of the right to determine what others should believe or do; often it suggests an opposition to *liberal* or *libertarian* and sometimes to *anarchic* or *anarchistic* ⟨*authoritarian* system of education⟩ ⟨the *authoritarian* type of mind⟩ ⟨the decline of *authoritarian* control and the rapid changes in our ways of living have made changes in our education imperative—*Christian Century*⟩ ⟨in an *authoritarian* regime, on the other hand, it is usual to impose stringent tests of partisanship—*Robson*⟩ **Dogmatic** implies the attitude of an authoritative or authoritarian teacher or preacher and the laying down of principles or dogmas as true and beyond dispute ⟨art is never *dogmatic*; holds no brief for itself—you may take it or you may leave it—*Galsworthy*⟩ ⟨now physics is, or should be, un*dogmatic*; mathematics is, and must be, *dogmatic.* No mathematician is infallible; he may make mistakes; but he must not hedge. Even in this age which dislikes dogma, there is no demand for an un*dogmatic* edition of Euclid—*Eddington*⟩ *Dogmatic* may imply depreciatively an assertive and sometimes an arrogant attitude that discourages if it does not inhibit debate ⟨Mr. Raycie made no pretence to book-

learning. . . . But on matters of art he was *dogmatic* and explicit, prepared to justify his opinions—*Wharton*⟩ **Doctrinaire** usually implies a dogmatic disposition; it typically suggests an opposition to *practical,* for it emphasizes a disposition to be guided by one's theories or the doctrines of one's school of thought in teaching, in framing laws, or in policies or decisions, especially those affecting others ⟨the rationalist mind . . . is of a *doctrinaire* and authoritative complexion: the phrase "must be" is ever on its lips—*James*⟩ ⟨the most profound contribution to political thought in America, namely, the *Federalist,* was not the work of *doctrinaire* thinkers but of men of affairs —*Frankfurter*⟩ **Oracular,** with its implied reference to an ancient oracle, suggests the possession of hidden knowledge and the manner of one who delivers his opinions or views in cryptic phrases or with pompous dogmatism ⟨his habit of *oracular* utterance when and possibly whenever he had a conviction—*Pound*⟩
*Ana* *masterful, domineering, imperative, imperious, peremptory: despotic, tyrannical, arbitrary, autocratic, *absolute

**diction** *language, vocabulary, phraseology, phrasing, style
*Ana* speech, tongue, idiom, *language: enunciation, pronunciation, articulation (see corresponding verbs at ARTICULATE)

**dido** *prank, caper, antic, monkeyshine

**differ,** vary, disagree, dissent mean to be unlike or out of harmony. **Differ** stresses the fact of unlikeness in kind or nature or in opinion but does not indicate except through the context the extent or degree of divergence ⟨the houses in the row *differ* only in small details⟩ ⟨minds *differ,* as rivers *differ*—*Macaulay*⟩ ⟨they *differed* sharply about the college to which their son should be sent⟩ **Vary** (see also CHANGE) though often interchangeable with *differ* may call attention to readily apparent differences and sometimes suggests a range of differences. The term commonly introduces a statement of the points, the ways, or the degree in which the things or the persons under discussion differ ⟨the two editions *vary* only in small particulars⟩ ⟨the northern and southern races *vary* chiefly in size⟩ ⟨the strength and direction of sea currents *vary* considerably at different times of the year—*Dowdeswell*⟩ **Disagree** emphasizes lack of agreement and not only may imply differences between things or variance between persons or opinions, but often may suggest incompatibility, unfitness, or disharmony ⟨the two accounts *disagree* in important details⟩ ⟨the verb should not *disagree* with the subject noun either in person or number⟩ ⟨who shall decide when Doctors *disagree?*—*Pope*⟩ ⟨one can *disagree* with his views, but one can't refute them—*Henry Miller*⟩ Of the words here compared only *disagree* is used in reference to lack of harmony between a thing and a person that results in mental or physical disorder of the latter ⟨the climate *disagreed* with him⟩ ⟨fried foods *disagree* with many people⟩ **Dissent** denotes a difference in opinion between persons or groups; it may imply refusal to assent to or the withholding of consent from something that is proposed or offered ⟨*dissenting* to the most outrageous invasion of private right ever set forth as a decision of the court—*Boyd*⟩ ⟨it has . . . taken on the worst intolerance of ignorance and stupidity . . . . All who *dissent* from its orthodox doctrines are scoundrels—*Mencken*⟩ or it may imply the expression of a difference in opinion from a person or persons holding an opposite view ⟨a great number of people in England would *dissent* from that judgment—*C. L. R. James*⟩
*Ana* diverge, deviate, depart (see SWERVE)
*Ant* agree

A colon (:) separates groups of words discriminated. An asterisk (*) indicates place of treatment of each group.

**difference** 1 unlikeness, *dissimilarity, divergence, divergency, distinction
*Ana* discrepancy, inconsistency, inconsonance, discordance (see corresponding adjectives at INCONSONANT): variation, modification (see under CHANGE *vb*): disparity, diversity (see corresponding adjectives at DIFFERENT)
*Ant* resemblance —*Con* similarity, *likeness, similitude, analogy, affinity
2 *discord, strife, conflict, contention, dissension, variance

**different,** diverse, divergent, disparate, various are comparable when they are used to qualify plural nouns and mean not identical or alike in kind or character. **Different** often implies little more than distinctness or separateness ⟨four *different* persons told me the same story⟩ Sometimes, however, it implies contrast or contrariness ⟨they approached the subject from *different* points of view⟩ ⟨vastly *different* in size than it was twenty-five years ago—N. M. Pusey⟩ **Diverse** is stronger and implies marked difference and decided contrast ⟨I obtained from three cultivated Englishmen at different times three *diverse* pronunciations of a single word—J. R. Lowell⟩ ⟨a curious fusion of *diverse* elements—Van Vechten⟩ **Divergent** implies movement apart or along different courses and usually connotes the impossibility of an ultimate meeting, combination, or reconciliation ⟨they took *divergent* paths⟩ ⟨he was bothered very much by *divergent* strands in his own intellectual composition—H. G. Wells⟩ ⟨he recognized that labor and capital have *divergent* interests—Cohen⟩ **Disparate** implies absolute or essential difference, often as between incongruous or incompatible elements ⟨two divergent, yet not wholly *disparate* emotions—Myers⟩ ⟨for if men are so diverse, not less *disparate* are the many men who keep discordant company within each one of us—Pater⟩ **Various** (see also MANY) commonly lays stress on the number of sorts or kinds ⟨in *various* shapes of parsons, critics, beaus—Pope⟩ ⟨an exuberant energy which displayed itself in *various* fields—Ellis⟩
*Ana* *distinct, separate, several: *single, particular: various, sundry, divers (see MANY)
*Ant* identical, alike, same —*Con* similar, *like, uniform, akin, analogous, comparable

**differentiate** *distinguish, discriminate, demarcate
*Ana* *separate, divide, part: *detach, disengage
*Ant* confuse —*Con* confound, *mistake

**difficult** *hard, arduous
*Ana* perplexing, puzzling, mystifying (see PUZZLE): intricate, involved, complicated, *complex, knotty: *obscure, enigmatic, cryptic: exacting, *onerous, burdensome
*Ant* simple —*Con* *easy, facile, light, effortless, smooth: *clear, perspicuous, lucid

**difficulty,** hardship, rigor, vicissitude are synonyms only when they mean something which demands effort and endurance if it is to be overcome or one's end achieved. **Difficulty,** the most widely applicable of these terms, applies to any condition, situation, experience, or task which presents a problem extremely hard to solve or which is seemingly beyond one's ability to suffer or surmount; it does not imply insolubility or insurmountability or even intolerableness, but it does suggest the need of skill and perseverance or patience ⟨the wise gods have put *difficulty* between man and everything that is worth having —J. R. Lowell⟩ ⟨ten thousand *difficulties* do not make one doubt, as I understand the subject; *difficulty* and doubt are incommensurate—Newman⟩ ⟨the simplest way out of the *difficulty* was to do nothing and dismiss the matter as no concern of theirs—Conrad⟩ **Hardship** stresses suffering, toil, or privation that is almost beyond endurance or is extremely hard to bear; it does not necessarily imply any effort to overcome or any patience in enduring ⟨men to

much misery and *hardship* born—Milton⟩ ⟨the *hardships* of life in a slum area⟩ However, it is so frequently applied to the suffering, toil, and privation encountered in an attempt to accomplish an end that it often comes very close to *difficulty* in its implications ⟨the search for truth . . . makes men and women content to undergo *hardships* and to brave perils—Eliot⟩ ⟨they had practically overcome the worst *hardships* that primitive man had to fear—Cather⟩ **Rigor** usually applies to a hardship that is imposed upon one, sometimes by oneself (as through asceticism or ambition) but more often by an austere religion, a tyrannical government or other power, a trying climate, or an extremely exacting enterprise or undertaking ⟨to undergo much pain, many hardships, and other *rigors*—Burnet⟩ ⟨the *rigors* of an explorer's life⟩ ⟨a vast deal of sympathy has been lavished upon the Puritan settlers because of the *rigors* of their religion—Repplier⟩ ⟨a European custom which nowhere survived the *rigors* of the frontier—W. P. Webb⟩ ⟨the *rigors* of an arctic winter⟩ **Vicissitude** (see also CHANGE *n* 2) applies to a difficulty or hardship incident to a way of life especially as it is subjected to extraneous influences, to a career, or to a course of action; it usually suggests reference to something that demands effort and endurance if it is to be overcome ⟨the fierce *vicissitudes* of deadly combat—Lecky⟩ ⟨it is the work he performed during these years, often in illness, danger, and *vicissitudes,* that should earn him particular gratitude from his Church—T. S. Eliot⟩ ⟨the dwarfing *vicissitudes* of poverty —Hackett⟩
*Ana* *obstacle, impediment, snag, obstruction: *predicament, dilemma, quandary, plight, scrape, fix, jam, pickle: pinch, strait, emergency, exigency, pass (see JUNCTURE)

**diffident** modest, bashful, *shy, coy
*Ana* shrinking, flinching, blenching (see RECOIL): hesitant, reluctant (see DISINCLINED): timorous, *timid
*Ant* confident —*Con* assured, sure, sanguine, presumptuous (see CONFIDENT): self-confident, self-assured, self-possessed (see corresponding nouns at CONFIDENCE): brash, brazen, impudent, *shameless

**diffuse** *adj* prolix, redundant, verbose, *wordy
*Ana* *profuse, lavish, exuberant: desultory, casual, *random: copious (see PLENTIFUL): *loose, relaxed, slack, lax
*Ant* succinct —*Con* *concise, terse, laconic, pithy, summary: compact, *close

**diffuse** *vb* *spread, circulate, disseminate, propagate, radiate
*Ana* disperse, dissipate (see SCATTER): *extend: *expand
*Ant* concentrate —*Con* *compact, consolidate: focus, *center, centralize

**dig** *vb* Dig, delve, spade, grub, excavate mean to use a spade or similar utensil in breaking up the ground to a point below the surface and in turning or removing the earth or bringing to the surface of something below it. **Dig,** the commonest word, implies a loosening of the earth around or under something so as to bring it to the surface, or a disturbing of the earth by such loosening ⟨dig in the ruins of Pompeii⟩ ⟨dig for gold⟩ ⟨dig potatoes⟩ Dig may imply also a result comparable to that obtained by spading ⟨the woodchuck *dug* a burrow in the field⟩ or a bringing to the surface or out of concealment ⟨dig up a man's past⟩ or prolonged laborious effort as in study or research ⟨ Laurie *dug* to some purpose that year, for he graduated with honor—Alcott⟩ **Delve** implies the use of a spade or more often of efforts comparable to the use of a spade and carries a stronger connotation of laboriousness and depth of penetration (as in the work of a gardener or of one who cultivates an interest) ⟨eleven, twelve, dig and *delve*— Old Nursery Rhyme⟩ ⟨a smug and spectacled best scholar, spending . . . time *delving* among the chronicles . . . in

the reading room of the British Museum—*Rose Ma-caulay*⟩ **Spade** is often interchangeable with *dig* but even more frequently than the latter is applied to a turning of the earth in manual (as opposed to mechanical) preparation of soil for planting ⟨*spade* up a garden⟩ ⟨she had *spaded* a pit in the backyard for barbecues—*Joseph Mitchell*⟩ ⟨has spent her writing career (28 years, eleven books) *spading* up the New England past—*Time*⟩ **Grub** may denote a digging and turning of soil but more often implies a clearing of soil by digging out something (as roots, stumps, and stones); often it suggests the hard, dirty, exhausting nature of such work and with this feeling may be used of various tasks, labors, or duties ⟨women and children helped to *grub* the land—*Collis*⟩ ⟨surviving on roots he *grubbed* from the soil⟩ ⟨shuffled among the ruins of their cities, and *grubbed* in the countryside for food and fuel—*The Lamp*⟩ ⟨fortunes were made in a day of *grubbing* and lost in a night of faro or red dog—*Billington*⟩ In some cases *grub* reflects the disorder of the land-clearing process and denotes a haphazard and laborious rummaging ⟨I *grubbed* in the dark alone, groping among shoes and boots . . . painfully garnering the scattered pictures—*Phelan*⟩ ⟨rag-pickers . . . *grubbing* about among a pile of human refuse—*Times Lit. Sup.*⟩ ⟨*grubbing* around cemeteries⟩ **Excavate** suggests making a hollow in or through something (as the ground, a mass of rock, or a mountainside) by or as if by means of a spade or shovel or a machine which performs the operations of spading and shoveling ⟨*excavate* the ground for a cellar⟩ ⟨*excavate* a tomb⟩ ⟨*excavate* a tunnel⟩ ⟨archaeologists engaged in *excavating* the site of an ancient city⟩
*Ana* pierce, penetrate, probe, *enter

**digest** *n* *compendium, syllabus, pandect, survey, sketch, précis, aperçu
*Ana* collection, assemblage, gathering (see under GATH-ER): *abridgment, conspectus, abstract, brief, synopsis, epitome

**digit** *n* *number, numeral, figure, integer

**dignify, ennoble, honor, glorify** mean to invest a person or thing with something that elevates or uplifts his or its character or raises him or it in human estimation. **Dignify** distinctively implies the addition of something that adds to the worth of a person or thing or, more often, to the estimation in which he or it is held or should be held ⟨from lowest place when virtuous things proceed, the place is *dignified* by the doer's deed—*Shak.*⟩ ⟨'tis true, no turbots *dignify* my boards, but gudgeons, flounders, what my Thames affords—*Pope*⟩ ⟨*dignify* crude verses by calling them poetry⟩ ⟨this "tea-party" diplomacy, if it may be *dignified* with that name—*Salisbury*⟩ **Ennoble,** though closely akin to *dignify,* does not so much suggest an added grace or dignity as a grace or dignity that comes as a natural result; literally it denotes a raising to the nobility ⟨the activities of the merely rich or the merely *ennobled* —*Huxley*⟩ but typically it implies a raising in moral character or in moral esteem or in qualities that rid the person or thing of all suspicion of pettiness, meanness, or selfishness and exalt him or it above ordinary status ⟨the Christian religion *ennobleth* and enlargeth the mind—*Berkeley*⟩ ⟨a confirmed realist who *ennobled* his prose by his breadth of style and dignity—*Mereness*⟩ **Honor** may imply the giving of reverence or of deep respect to that to which it is due ⟨*honor* thy father and thy mother—*Exod* 20:12⟩ ⟨*honor* a man for his steadfastness of principle⟩ It may imply also the giving of something to a person or sometimes a thing that increases the distinction or the esteem in which he or it is held; in neither sense, however, is there any suggestion of an effect that touches the one honored except in externals

⟨our feast shall be much *honored* in your marriage—*Shak.*⟩ ⟨several soldiers were *honored* by the president when he presented them with medals for bravery⟩ ⟨we that had loved him so, followed him, *honored* him —*Browning*⟩ **Glorify** rarely except in religious use carries its basic implication of exalting a man to heavenly beatitude or of advancing the glory of God through prayer or good works ⟨Jesus was not yet *glorified*— *Jn* 7:39⟩ but it retains the suggestions of casting a transfiguring light upon or of honoring in such a way as to increase a person's or thing's glory. In general, it implies investing with a splendor or with a glory that lifts above the ugly, the commonplace, the ordinary, or, often, the true ⟨in old days it was possible to *glorify* it [war] as a school of chivalry, courage, and self-sacrifice—*Inge*⟩ ⟨poetical truth becoming here . . . the servant of common honesty . . . so far from being cramped and degraded, is enlarged and *glorified*—*Day Lewis*⟩ ⟨knowing that the talent that had made them rich is but a secondary talent . . . they employ men to *glorify* it—*Anderson*⟩
*Ana* elevate, raise, *lift: *exalt, magnify, aggrandize: heighten, enhance, *intensify
*Con* disparage, depreciate, belittle, minimize, detract, *decry, derogate: demean, *abase, debase

**dignity** **1** *decorum, decency, propriety, etiquette
*Ana* *excellence, virtue, merit, perfection: nobleness *or* nobility, morality, ethicalness *or* ethics (see corresponding adjectives at MORAL)
**2** *elegance, grace
*Ana* *worth, value: beautifulness *or* beauty, loveliness, comeliness (see corresponding adjectives at BEAUTIFUL): grandness *or* grandeur, magnificence, stateliness, nobleness *or* nobility, majesty, augustness (see corresponding adjectives at GRAND)

**digress** deviate, diverge, depart, *swerve, veer
*Ana* *wander, stray

**digression, episode, excursus, divagation** are comparable when they denote a departure from the main course of development, especially of a narrative, a drama, or an exposition. **Digression** applies to a deviation, especially if at the expense of unity of effect, from the main subject of a discourse; it may or may not suggest intention or design ⟨in this long *digression* which I was accidentally led into—*Sterne*⟩ ⟨a word of *digression* may be pardoned, however, for the two subjects are allied—*Cardozo*⟩ **Episode** (see also OCCURRENCE) usually applies to an incidental narrative which, though separable from the main subject, arises naturally from it; sometimes an episode is definitely a purposeful digression (as for giving variety to the narration, heightening the illusion of reality, or elucidating a motive); thus, in *Paradise Lost* Raphael's account of the war in heaven is in this sense an *episode* because it breaks the chronological order of the poem and reverts to events which occurred prior to those told in the first book ⟨descriptive poetry . . . may be interspersed with dramatic *episodes*—*Alexander*⟩ **Episode** is used not only of a literary work but of other art forms or of life in reference to something that seems apart from the main subject or course of a thing ⟨delight in the virginal beauty of fresh blossoms, in the dewy green of water-meadows . . . is evident in numberless pictures of the earlier schools of Europe; but there these amenities of nature are but an *episode*—*Binyon*⟩ ⟨Miss Dix's biographer . . . considers her war work an *episode,* not equal in quality to her lifework—*Baker*⟩ **Excursus** applies to an avowed and usually formal digression elucidating at some length an incidental point ⟨this started an ethnological *excursus* on swineherds, and drew from Pinecoffin long tables showing the proportion per thousand of the caste in the Derajat

---

A colon (:) separates groups of words discriminated. An asterisk (*) indicates place of treatment of each group.

—*Kipling*⟩ **Divagation** is often used in preference to *digression* when aimless wandering from the main course or inattentiveness to logic is implied ⟨Froissart's style of poetry invites the widest . . . liberty of *divagation*, of dragging in anything that really interested him— *Saintsbury*⟩ ⟨the author of it would need to keep an extremely clear head, reject stuffing and *divagation* —*Swinnerton*⟩

**dilapidate** *ruin, wreck
*Ana* *decay, disintegrate, crumble, decompose: *neglect, ignore, disregard, forget, slight, overlook
*Con* repair, rebuild, *mend: *renew, restore, renovate, rejuvenate

**dilapidated** *shabby, dingy, faded, seedy, threadbare
*Ana* damaged, injured, impaired, marred (see INJURE): ruined, wrecked (see RUIN *vb*)

**dilate 1** *discourse, expatiate, descant
*Ana* *relate, recount, rehearse, recite, narrate, describe: expound, *explain: *discuss, argue
**2** *expand, distend, swell, amplify, inflate
*Ana* enlarge, *increase, augment: *extend, protract, prolong, lengthen: widen, broaden (see corresponding adjectives at BROAD)
*Ant* constrict: circumscribe: attenuate —*Con* *contract, shrink, compress, condense

**dilatory** *slow, laggard, deliberate, leisurely
*Ana* procrastinating, delaying, dawdling (see DELAY): *negligent, neglectful, lax, slack, remiss
*Ant* diligent —*Con* *busy, assiduous, sedulous, industrious: *quick, prompt, ready

**dilemma** *predicament, quandary, plight, scrape, fix, jam, pickle
*Ana* perplexity, bewilderment, mystification (see corresponding verbs at PUZZLE): *difficulty, vicissitude

**dilettante 1** *amateur, dabbler, tyro
*Con* artist, *expert, adept
**2** *aesthete, connoisseur
*Con* *artist, artificer, architect: *writer, composer, author: craftsman, workman (see WORKER)

**diligent** assiduous, sedulous, industrious, *busy
*Ana* persevering, persisting *or* persistent (see corresponding verbs at PERSEVERE): *indefatigable, tireless, untiring, unwearied, unflagging
*Ant* dilatory —*Con* *slow, laggard, deliberate, leisurely: desultory, casual, happy-go-lucky (see RANDOM)

**dilute** *vb* attenuate, *thin, rarefy
*Ana* temper, *moderate, qualify: *weaken, enfeeble: *liquefy, deliquesce: *adulterate, sophisticate
*Ant* condense: concentrate (*in chemistry, especially in past participial form*)

**dim** *adj* dusky, *dark, obscure, murky, gloomy
*Ant* bright: distinct —*Con* brilliant, radiant, luminous, effulgent (see BRIGHT): manifest, patent, *evident, plain, clear

**dim** *vb* *obscure, bedim, darken, eclipse, cloud, becloud, fog, befog, obfuscate
*Ana* screen, conceal, *hide: cloak, mask, camouflage, *disguise
*Ant* illustrate

**dimensions** extent, *size, area, magnitude, volume

**diminish** reduce, *decrease, lessen, abate, dwindle
*Ana* wane, ebb, *abate, subside: *moderate, temper: lighten, alleviate, mitigate (see RELIEVE): attenuate, extenuate (see THIN)
*Con* enlarge, augment: *increase: *extend: *intensify, enhance, heighten, aggravate

**diminutive** *adj* little, *small, wee, tiny, minute, miniature
*Con* *large, big, great: enormous, immense, *huge, vast, colossal, mammoth

**din** *n* **Din, uproar, pandemonium, hullabaloo, babel, hubbub, clamor, racket** mean a disturbing or confusing welter of sounds or a scene or situation marked by such a welter of sounds. **Din** emphasizes the distress suffered by the ears and the completely distracting effect of the noise as a whole; it often suggests prolonged and deafening clangor or insistent ear-splitting metallic sounds ⟨the *din* of a machine shop⟩ ⟨escape the *din* of heavy traffic⟩ ⟨the *din* of a New Year's Eve party⟩ ⟨think you a little *din* can daunt mine ears? . . . Have I not heard great ordnance in the field, and heaven's artillery thunder in the skies?—*Shak.*⟩ ⟨the general had forbidden the tolling of funeral bells so that the incessant mournful *din* might not pound perpetually at our ears—*Kenneth Roberts*⟩ **Uproar** and **pandemonium** both imply tumult or wild disorder, typically of a crowd of persons but often among wild animals or in the elements; when the reference is to men, *uproar* usually suggests the sound of a multitude vociferously, sometimes riotously, protesting, arguing, or defying and *pandemonium,* the din produced when a group or crowd usually under discipline breaks bounds and runs riot or becomes uncontrollably boisterous ⟨often throw the parliamentary debates into an *uproar* —*Blanshard*⟩ ⟨*pandemonium* followed the announcement of the armistice⟩ ⟨draw not the sword; 'twould make an *uproar,* Duke, you would not hear the end of —*Keats*⟩ ⟨the modern parent . . . does not want a fictitious Sabbath calm while he is watching, succeeded by *pandemonium* as soon as he turns his back—*Russell*⟩ **Hullabaloo** is often interchangeable with *din* or *uproar* especially in a construction following *make,* but it seldom carries the suggestions of piercing, earsplitting noise or of vociferation and turmoil which are respectively so strong in *din* and *uproar.* When it refers to a welter of sounds, it suggests great excitement and an interruption of peace or quiet ⟨the *hullabaloo* made by hunters and hounds in the chase⟩ ⟨the children are making a great *hullabaloo* at their party⟩ When it refers to a situation, it suggests a storm of protest, an outburst of passion or wrath, or a torrent of comment or sensational gossip ⟨the current political *hullabaloo*—*New Republic*⟩ ⟨the project was not again brought before the public until the *hullabaloo* about it had died down⟩ ⟨the music stopped and the familiar *hullabaloo* was reestablished in the room—*Stafford*⟩ **Babel** stresses the confusion of sounds that results from a mingling of languages and vocal qualities and the seeming meaningless or purposeless quality of the sound ⟨young and old, fat and thin, all laughed and shouted in a *babel* of tongues—*Bambrick*⟩ ⟨must we fall into the jabber and *babel* of discord—*Sir Winston Churchill*⟩ **Hubbub** denotes the confusing mixture of sounds characteristic of activities and business; it implies incessant movement or bustle rather than turmoil ⟨a sound heard above the *hubbub* of the city streets⟩ ⟨strollers on the common could hear, at certain hours, a *hubbub* of voices and racing footsteps from within the boundary wall— *Shaw*⟩ **Clamor** and **racket,** like *din,* stress the psychological effect of noises more than their character or origin. They usually imply annoyance or disturbance rather than distress and distraction and are applicable to any combination of sounds or any scene that strikes one as excessively or inordinately noisy ⟨the *clamor* was such that votes could not be taken until at last the shouting subsided— *W. P. Webb*⟩ ⟨the crow began to shriek . . . . In a few seconds the *clamor* had attracted the attention of a bevy of wild crows—*Kipling*⟩ ⟨we wanted quiet, not *racket*— *Steele*⟩ ⟨something like forty feet of chain and wire rope, mixed up with a few heavy iron blocks, had crashed down

---

*Ana* analogous words  *Ant* antonyms  *Con* contrasted words  See also explanatory notes facing page 1

from aloft on the poop with a terrifying *racket—Conrad*⟩
*Ana* clamorousness, stridency, boisterousness, blatancy
(see corresponding adjectives at VOCIFEROUS): clash,
percussion (see IMPACT)
*Ant* quiet

**dingy** *shabby, dilapidated, faded, seedy, threadbare
*Ana* soiled, grimed, sullied, smirched, tarnished (see
SOIL): *dull (sense 2): dusky, murky, gloomy (see DARK)
*Con* *bright, luminous, brilliant: fresh, *new: *clean,
cleanly

**dinner,** banquet, feast are comparable when denoting
an elaborate meal that is served to guests or to a group
(as of members of a club or association) and that often
marks some special occasion (as an anniversary) or honors
a particular person. **Dinner** which basically means the
chief meal of the day is the most general of these terms;
it is appropriately used of any elaborate and formal meal
served to guests or to a group and is the preferred term
for use in invitations and in colorless reference to such
an affair ⟨popular as a speaker at public *dinners*⟩ ⟨planned
a birthday *dinner* for her cousin⟩ ⟨worn out by state *dinners* and receptions⟩ Typically, **banquet** suggests the
sumptuousness of the meal, the magnificence of its setting, and often the ceremonial character of the occasion
and entertainment ⟨a certain rigid decorum between guest
and geisha is invariably preserved at a Japanese *banquet—Hearn*⟩ ⟨entreating him, his captains, and brave
knights, to grace a *banquet—Keats*⟩ It may stress the
excellence and elaborateness of food and service ⟨the
widows and other women prepare a special dinner, which
may be so elaborate as to become a *banquet—Amer.
Guide Series: Ariz.*⟩ or especially in popular use it may
imply no more than a formal dinner held elsewhere
than in a private home ⟨not so long ago the word "banquet" evoked pictures of barons of beef, turtle soup,
boar's heads and ten courses served on solid gold plate
. . . "banquet" today has become the generic word for
any meal served in a private room in a hotel—*Britannia & Eve*⟩ ⟨father's club gave a *banquet* at the hotel
—*L. E. Billington*⟩ **Feast** is often interchangeable with
*banquet* but it may carry over a feeling of its other meaning of a festival of rejoicing and then stresses the shared
enjoyment and pleasure in the occasion that gives rise
to the meal ⟨a white cat purring its way gracefully among
the wine cups at a *feast* given in honor of Apuleius
—*Repplier*⟩ ⟨to share our marriage *feast* and nuptial
mirth?—*Keats*⟩ ⟨it is not the quantity of the meat,
but the cheerfulness of the guests, which makes the
*feast—Clarendon*⟩ Unlike the other terms of this group
*feast* has frequent extended use with the notion of a
source of, often shared, enjoyment ⟨treasures his memories of that . . . visit, with vegetarian meals and a *feast*
of conversation—*Fogg*⟩ ⟨human beings have always
loved these perceptual *feasts* of sensuous satisfaction
—*Hunter Mead*⟩

**dip** *vb* 1 Dip, immerse, submerge, duck, souse, dunk
are·comparable when meaning to plunge a person or thing
into or as if into liquid. **Dip** implies a momentary or
partial plunging into a liquid or a slight or cursory entrance into a subject ⟨the priest shall *dip* his finger in
the blood—*Lev* 4:6⟩ ⟨*dip* a dress in cleansing fluid⟩
⟨*dip* into a book⟩ ⟨she had *dipped* in the wells of blissful oblivion—*Meredith*⟩ **Immerse** implies that the person
or thing is covered by the liquid or buried or engrossed
in something ⟨*immerse* the persons being baptized⟩
⟨*immerse* a dress in boiling dye for several minutes⟩
⟨*immerse* oneself in thought⟩ ⟨I am at present wholly
*immersed* in country business—*Addison*⟩ **Submerge**
implies complete and often prolonged immersion (as

in an inundation) or a being overwhelmed or, sometimes,
overpowered and made helpless ⟨the submarine *submerged*⟩ ⟨several houses were completely *submerged*
by the flood⟩ ⟨the last and most violent religious rebellion
. . . seemed likely to *submerge* that monarchy—*Belloc*⟩
It may suggest a sinking to the lowest state, grade, or
status ⟨personality had been *submerged* by organization
—*W. P. Webb*⟩ ⟨almost unheard of for such a girl to
enter into relations with a man of that *submerged* class
—*Mencken*⟩ **Duck** implies a sudden plunging and an
almost immediate withdrawal ⟨I say, *duck* her in the
loch, and then we will see whether she is witch or not
—*Scott*⟩ ⟨*ducked* into a doorway to avoid a bore⟩
**Souse** adds to *duck* the suggestion of more prolonged
immersion and often of a thorough soaking ⟨the boy was
*soused* before he was freed from his captors⟩ ⟨a blazing
caldron in which Beelzebub is *sousing* the damned
—*Arnold*⟩ ⟨after being *soused* in the Atlantic ocean
—*Aldrich*⟩ **Souse** sometimes implies steeping of meat,
fish, or other food in a pickle or tart liquid for the sake
of preserving and flavoring it ⟨*soused* mackerel⟩ It
may often imply not only immersion but a being saturated
and, hence, after liquor drinking a becoming intoxicated
⟨came home night after night thoroughly *soused*⟩ **Dunk**
in its basic use means to dip and soak something (as bread
or a doughnut) in coffee, tea, or milk before eating it,
but in many contexts it is equivalent to *duck* or *immerse*
⟨men dangling from lines, being *dunked* in the cold sea
as the ship rolled—*Cronk*⟩

2 Dip, bail, scoop, ladle, spoon, dish mean to remove a liquid or a loose or soft substance from a container by means
of an implement (as a pail, spoon, or scoop). They are
often followed by *up* or *out*. **Dip** suggests the process
of plunging the utensil (usually called a *dipper*) into the
substance and lifting it out full; it is the preferred word
when the labor involved is to be implied or the action
is described ⟨*dip* drinking water from a spring⟩ ⟨*dip*
into one's memory for facts one has nearly forgotten⟩
**Bail** is used chiefly in reference to something (as a boat)
in which water has accumulated or is accumulating;
it implies emptying or an attempt to empty by means of
repeated dipping ⟨*bail* the water out of a rowboat⟩
⟨by the help of a small bucket and our hats we *bailed*
her [a boat] out—*Dana*⟩ **Scoop, ladle, spoon** throw
the emphasis on the kind of implement employed in an
operation consisting usually of dipping, conveying, and
pouring. **Scoop** suggests a shovellike implement, either
a small kitchen utensil for dipping out loose dry material
(as flour, sugar, or coffee beans) or for gouging out pieces
of a soft substance (as cheese) or a much larger and
heavier implement used in digging or excavating operations or in the removal of a heap of things from one
place to another ⟨*scoop* out three cups of sugar⟩ ⟨*scoop*
up the catch of fish into barrels⟩ ⟨*scooping* gravel from
the pit into waiting trucks⟩ **Ladle** implies the use of a
ladle, or long-handled implement with a bowl-shaped
end and often a pouring lip; it is especially used of substances which are liable to be spilled ⟨*ladle* soup into
bowls⟩ ⟨*ladle* out the punch⟩ The term sometimes implies
the use of a mechanical device for removing and conveying
liquid (as molten metal) from one container to another.
**Spoon** implies the use of a spoon in lifting and depositing
something (as food or medicine) ⟨the girl who *spoons*
out vegetables in the cafeteria⟩ ⟨slowly *spooning* up
the hot soup⟩ **Dish** implies transference to the individual
plate or dish of a portion of food (as by ladling or spooning) ⟨*dish* out the vegetables⟩ ⟨*dish* up the ice cream⟩

**diplomatic** politic, smooth, bland, *suave, urbane
*Ana* astute, *shrewd: courteous, courtly, polite (see

---

A colon (:) separates groups of words discriminated. An asterisk (*) indicates place of treatment of each group.

CIVIL): artful, wily, guileful, crafty (see SLY): tactful, poised (see corresponding nouns at TACT)

**dipsomaniac** alcoholic, inebriate, *drunkard, sot, soak, toper, tosspot, tippler

**direct** *vb* **1** Direct, address, devote, apply are comparable when used reflexively with the meaning to turn or bend one's attention, energies, or abilities to something or when meaning to turn, bend, or point (as one's attention, thoughts, or efforts) to a certain object or objective. Between **direct** and **address** there is often no perceptible difference; thus, one *directs* or *addresses* oneself to a task, or to his work, or to the study of a problem; one *directs* or *addresses* one's attention to a certain thing, his remarks to a given person, his book to a special type of reader; also, one *directs* or *addresses* a letter when he writes on the envelope the name of the recipient and the place of delivery. There is, however, a tendency to prefer *direct* when an intent or aim is implied or indicated and *address* when an appeal to the mind or feelings is expressed or understood ⟨the Democratic members *directed* their energies to the defeat of the measure⟩ ⟨a demagogue *addresses* his arguments to the least intelligent in his audience⟩ ⟨sat by the breakfast table . . . her eyes listlessly *directed* towards the open door—*Hardy*⟩ ⟨a story *addressed* . . . to his sense of honor and humanity—*Lee*⟩ ⟨asked myself to what purpose I should *direct* my energies—*Cohen*⟩ **Devote** often adds to *direct* and *address* the implication of persistence; thus, one *devotes* himself to a task, a work, or the study of a problem when he resolutely continues towards its completion; one *directs* his attention to a problem but *devotes* his energies to its solution. Quite as often, and in distinction from the other words, *devote* implies dedication or setting apart for a certain end or use ⟨*devote* himself to the public good⟩ ⟨*devote* his leisure to charity⟩ ⟨small farms *devoted* to fruit and berry raising—*Anderson*⟩ **Apply** distinctively suggests concentration. One *applies* himself to a task or to his work when he gives his entire attention to what he has *directed* or addressed himself. In idiomatic use *apply oneself* and *apply one's mind* often equal "concentrate" or "give one's entire attention" ⟨he learned early to *apply himself*⟩ ⟨an anxious person cannot *apply his mind* to the task in hand⟩ ⟨he cannot *apply himself* to study—*Garnett*⟩ Sometimes *apply* comes very close to *direct* and *address* with, however, the additional implication of employment ⟨that they may sample several kinds of knowledge . . . and have a chance to determine wisely in what direction their own individual mental powers can be best *applied*—*Eliot*⟩

*Ana* bend (see CURVE): *set, fix, settle: endeavor, strive, try, *attempt

*Con* divert, deflect, *turn: digress, diverge, deviate, *swerve

**2** Direct, aim, point, level, train, lay are comparable when they mean to turn something toward its appointed or intended mark or goal. One **directs** something or someone *to* its or his destination or objective when he heads it or him toward the proper course or guides it or him along that course ⟨*directed* his eyes to the door⟩ ⟨*direct* a stranger to the railroad station⟩ ⟨*direct* a searchlight to the opposite shore⟩ ⟨'tis heav'n each passion sends, and diff'rent men *directs* to diff'rent ends—*Pope*⟩ One **aims** a weapon or something used as a weapon when he by careful calculation or estimation of counterinfluences turns it toward the exact spot or the object he designs to hit ⟨*aim* a pistol at a burglar⟩ ⟨*aim* a blow at a man's stomach⟩ ⟨a law *aimed* at tax evaders⟩ One **points** something *at* or less often *to* or *toward* a person

or thing when he turns its point or tip toward a particular spot (as in indicating or directing) ⟨*point* your finger at your choice⟩ ⟨*point* a sword at an opponent's breast⟩ ⟨*point* a boat to shore⟩ One **levels** a weapon (as a spear, a lance, or a rifle) or something which serves as a weapon *at* or *against* something when he brings it to the position or line (often a horizontal position or line) where it will do its most deadly or most effective work ⟨*level* a spear at a foe⟩ ⟨*level* a rifle at a deer⟩ ⟨*level* a charge against the mine owners⟩ ⟨like an arrow shot from a well-experienced archer hits the mark his eye doth *level* at—*Shak.*⟩ One **trains** or **lays** a firearm (as a cannon) when he sets it in a position pointed directly at its mark ⟨kept their guns *trained* on the enemy cruiser⟩ One *trains* something (as a telescope or a camera) but rarely if ever *lays* other things than firearms ⟨the distinguished visitors could go nowhere without finding a battery of cameras *trained* upon them⟩ ⟨*lay* a gun for a shot⟩

*Ana* steer, pilot, *guide, lead, engineer

*Ant* misdirect

**3** manage, control, *conduct

*Ana* *govern, rule: lead, *guide

**4** *command, order, bid, enjoin, instruct, charge

*Ana* *prescribe, assign, define

**direct** *adj* Direct, immediate, as applied to relations and as meaning marked by the absence of interruption (as between the cause and the effect, the source and the issue, or the beginning and the end), are frequently used with little distinction, although their connotations may be quite dissimilar. **Direct** suggests unbroken connection between one and the other or a straight bearing of one upon the other, while **immediate** suggests the absence of any intervening medium or influence; thus, *direct* knowledge is knowledge gained firsthand, but *immediate* knowledge is that attained by intuition or insight rather than through inference from facts or premises; *direct* contact stresses the bearing of one thing upon the other, but *immediate* contact implies the coherence or cohesion of one and the other; *direct* descent implies descent in a straight line from an ancestor; one's *immediate* family is composed only of those who are the nearest in relation, or one's father, mother, brothers, and sisters; a *direct* cause leads straight to its effect, but an *immediate* cause (which may or may not be the *direct* cause) is the one which serves as the last link in a chain of causes and brings about a result.

**directly** *presently, shortly, soon

**dirty** *adj* Dirty, filthy, foul, nasty, squalid mean conspicuously unclean or impure. **Dirty** is the general term for what is sullied or defiled with dirt of any kind ⟨*dirty* hands⟩ ⟨*dirty* linen⟩ ⟨*dirty* streets⟩ ⟨he was *dirty* and bloodstained and his clothes were bedaubed with mud and weeds—*Sayers*⟩ **Filthy** is a much stronger term than *dirty* in its suggestion of offensiveness; it often suggests gradually accumulated dirt which besmears or begrimes rather than merely soils ⟨he was constantly drunk, *filthy* beyond all powers of decent expression—*Stephen*⟩ ⟨a *filthy* hovel⟩ **Foul** carries a still stronger implication of revolting offensiveness; it often implies an unwholesome or malodorous state resulting from the decay of putrescible matter ⟨a *foul* sewer⟩ ⟨a *foul* dungeon⟩ ⟨a *foul* pond⟩ ⟨the Arabs explained that the Turks had thrown dead camels into the pool to make the water *foul*—*T. E. Lawrence*⟩ It may come near to loathsome or disgusting ⟨a *foul* sight⟩ **Nasty** applies chiefly to what is repugnant to a person who is fastidious about cleanliness ⟨a *nasty* ship⟩ ⟨a *nasty* odor⟩ ⟨the care of pigs is *nasty* work⟩ Sometimes *nasty* is softened to a mere synonym for "objectionable, disagreeable" ⟨a *nasty* fall⟩ ⟨a *nasty* temper⟩ ⟨be *nasty* to someone⟩ **Squalid** adds to the idea of dirtiness or filth that of extreme slovenliness or neglect ⟨*squalid* poverty⟩ ⟨the East, so *squalid* and splendid, so pestilent and so poetic—*Wharton*⟩

All of these terms may imply moral uncleanness or baseness or obscenity. **Dirty,** however, stresses meanness or despicability ⟨the creature's at his *dirty* work again —*Pope*⟩ **Filthy** and **foul** imply disgusting obscenity, *filthy* stressing the presence of obscenity and *foul,* its ugliness ⟨*filthy* talk⟩ ⟨a *foul* jest⟩ **Nasty** implies a peculiarly offensive unpleasantness ⟨a *nasty* mind⟩ ⟨he hated it as a gentleman hates to hear a *nasty* story— *E. E. Hale*⟩ ⟨squandered all their virile energy on greasy slave girls and *nasty* Asiatic-Greek prostitutes—*Graves*⟩ **Squalid** implies sordidness as well as baseness ⟨the *squalid* scenes and situations through which Thackeray portrays the malign motives and unclean soul of Becky Sharp —*Eliot*⟩ The first four terms are used also of weather, meaning the opposite of clear and thereby implying rainy, snowy, stormy, or foggy weather.
*Ant* clean

**dirty** *vb* *soil, sully, tarnish, foul, befoul, smirch, besmirch, grime, begrime
*Ana* pollute, defile, *contaminate: *spot, spatter

**disability** *inability

**disable** cripple, undermine, *weaken, enfeeble, debilitate, sap
*Ana* *injure, damage, harm, hurt, impair, mar, spoil: *maim, mutilate, mangle, batter: *ruin, wreck
*Ant* rehabilitate (*a disabled person*)

**disabuse** *rid, clear, unburden, purge
*Ana* *free, liberate, release: enlighten, *illuminate
*Con* mislead, delude, *deceive: *dupe, gull

**disadvantage** *n* Disadvantage, detriment, handicap, drawback mean something which interferes with the success or well-being of a person or thing. **Disadvantage** often implies an act, circumstance, or condition which threatens to affect or does actually affect a person or thing unfavorably or injuriously ⟨the best-known area of *disadvantage* is the transitional zone, or deteriorated area, adjacent to the main business district of growing American cities—*Carr*⟩ It may therefore suggest a mere deprivation of advantage ⟨working at a *disadvantage* because the narrow space prevented complete freedom of movement⟩ ⟨I was brought here under the *disadvantage* of being unknown by sight to any of you—*Burke*⟩ or, more positively, an appreciable loss or injury ⟨his attempts to reach his enemy's face were greatly to the *disadvantage* of his own—*Shaw*⟩ ⟨spread rumors to a candidate's *disadvantage*⟩ **Detriment** usually implies a suffering of harm or a sustaining of damage or a cause of harm or damage but carries no direct indication of the extent of actual or probable harm or damage; it is therefore often used in the negative phrase "without detriment" assuring safety with regard either to the past or to the future ⟨the physiological machinery of the body is so adjusted that great variations of atmospheric temperature can be supported without *detriment*—*Heiser*⟩ ⟨rotation of farm crops . . . may very well be a benefit rather than a *detriment*—*Furnas*⟩ ⟨it is not unfashionable to pit one form . . . against another—holding up the naturalistic to the disadvantage of the epic . . . the fantastic to the *detriment* of the naturalistic—*Galsworthy*⟩ **Handicap** retains a suggestion of its application to a competitive struggle (see ADVANTAGE) but greatly extends that application to include various struggles into which an ordinary individual may be pushed by inclination or circumstances; it also refers to a disadvantage under which the person so placed must live or work ⟨his lame-

ness was a lifelong *handicap*⟩ ⟨his inability to master mathematics proved to be a serious *handicap* to him after his school years⟩ ⟨the *handicap* under which the student and lawyer labored at that time . . . the lack of a dictionary containing legal information—*Rose*⟩ ⟨truthfulness is . . . a *handicap* in a hypocritical society, but the *handicap* is more than outweighed by the advantages of fearlessness—*Russell*⟩ **Drawback** applies especially to a disadvantage that serves to retard a person's or thing's progress or advance in any way ⟨one of the *drawbacks* of French agriculture is the scarcity of farm labor—*Van Valkenburg & Huntington*⟩ Often, however, it means no more than an objectionable feature of a person or thing that constitutes a disadvantage from some point of view usually implicit in the context ⟨there is always some alloying ingredient in the cup, some *drawback* upon the triumphs, of grown people —*Bagehot*⟩ ⟨all the *drawbacks* of town life—*Jefferies*⟩
*Ana* *obstacle, impediment, bar: barrier (see BAR): hindrance, blocking (see corresponding verbs at HINDER):
*Ant* advantage —*Con* help, aid, assistance (see under HELP *vb*): service (see USE)

**disaffect** alienate, *estrange, wean
*Ana* upset, agitate, *discompose, disquiet, disturb: sever, sunder, divorce (see SEPARATE)
*Ant* win (*men to a cause, allegiance*)

**disagree** *differ, vary, dissent
*Ana* *object, protest: *demur, balk, jib: *disapprove, deprecate: conflict, clash (see BUMP)
*Ant* agree —*Con* accord, harmonize (see AGREE): concur, coincide (see AGREE): *assent, acquiesce

**disallow** *vb* *disclaim, disavow, repudiate, disown
*Ana* reject, refuse, spurn (see DECLINE): *deny, gainsay, traverse: debar, shut out, *exclude
*Ant* allow —*Con* *grant, concede: acquiesce, accede, *assent

**disappear** *vanish, evanesce, evaporate, fade
*Ana* depart, leave (see GO)
*Ant* appear —*Con* emerge, loom (see APPEAR): *come, arrive: issue, emanate (see SPRING)

**disapprove, deprecate** mean to feel or to express an objection to or condemnation of a person or thing. **Disapprove** implies an attitude of dislike or distaste on any good grounds (as social, ethical, or intellectual) and an unwillingness to accept or to praise; the word may sometimes connote rejection or the expression of condemnation ⟨Gard loved his sister, but there were times when he wished for a way of making her understand how thoroughly he *disapproved* of her—*Mary Austin*⟩ ⟨*disapproved* of too much knowledge, on the score that it diminished men's sense of wonder—*Huxley*⟩ **Deprecate** stresses the implication of regret, frequently profound, occasionally diffident or apologetic ⟨shaping the plays to modern taste by the very excisions which scholars will most *deprecate*—*FitzGerald*⟩ ⟨Wallace earnestly *deprecates* the modern tendency to disparage reason—*Inge*⟩ ⟨there is nothing I more *deprecate* than the use of the Fourteenth Amendment . . . to prevent the making of social experiments—*Justice Holmes*⟩
*Ana* reprehend, reprobate, censure, *criticize: *decry, disparage
*Ant* approve —*Con* *commend, recommend, applaud, compliment: endorse, sanction (see APPROVE)

**disarrange** derange, disorganize, *disorder, unsettle, disturb
*Ana* *misplace, mislay: displace, *replace: upset, *overturn
*Ant* arrange —*Con* *order, systematize, methodize

**disarray** disorder, chaos, *confusion, jumble, clutter,

snarl, muddle

**Con** *method, system: ordering *or* order, arrangement, marshaling, organization (see corresponding verbs at ORDER)

**disaster,** **calamity, catastrophe, cataclysm** are comparable when they denote an event or situation that is regarded as a terrible misfortune. A **disaster** is an unforeseen mischance or misadventure (as a shipwreck, a serious railroad accident, or the failure of a great enterprise) which happens either through culpable lack of foresight or through adverse external agency and brings with it destruction (as of life and property) or ruin (as of projects, careers, or great hopes) ⟨such a war would be the final and supreme *disaster* to the world—*MacLeish*⟩ **Calamity** is a grievous misfortune, particularly one which involves a great or far-reaching personal or public loss or which produces profound, often widespread distress; thus, the rout at Bull Run was a *disaster* for the North but the assassination of President Lincoln was a *calamity;* the wreck of the *Don Juan* was a *disaster* and, as involving the loss of Shelley, it was a *calamity* ⟨we have heard of his decision . . . . It is a disaster—for me a *calamity* —*Galsworthy*⟩ ⟨Hamlet's bloody stage is now our world, and we are beginning to trace our own *calamity* back to its sources—*Battenhouse*⟩ **Catastrophe** is used of a disastrous conclusion; it often emphasizes the idea of finality ⟨the captain's folly hastened the *catastrophe*⟩ ⟨what had become of them [the inhabitants of a deserted village]? What *catastrophe* had overwhelmed them? —*Cather*⟩ **Cataclysm** is often used of an event or situation that brings with it an overwhelming of the old order or a violent social or political upheaval ⟨in the general upheaval of doctrine . . . during the Reformation *cataclysm*—*Blunt*⟩ ⟨a thought so imperishably phrased that it sums up not only the *cataclysm* of a world, but also the stoic and indomitable temper that endures it —*Lowes*⟩

**Ana** mishap, *accident, casualty: adversity, *misfortune, mischance

**disastrous** *unlucky, ill-starred, ill-fated, unfortunate, calamitous, luckless, hapless

**Ana** malign, *sinister, baleful: unpropitious, inauspicious, *ominous, portentous, fateful

**disavow** *disclaim, repudiate, disown, disallow

**Ana** *deny, gainsay, traverse: *disapprove, deprecate: reject, refuse (see DECLINE)

**Ant** avow —**Con** *maintain, assert, justify: *express, voice: *declare, proclaim

**disbar** shut out, eliminate, rule out, suspend, debar, *exclude, blackball

**disbelief** *unbelief, incredulity

**Ana** atheism, deism (compare nouns at ATHEIST): rejection, repudiation, spurning (see corresponding verbs at DECLINE)

**Ant** belief —**Con** faith, credence, credit (see BELIEF)

**disburse** *spend, expend

**Ana** *distribute, dispense: apportion, *allot, allocate: *pay

**discard** *vb* **Discard, cast, shed, molt, slough, scrap, junk** mean to get rid of as of no further use, value, or service. **Discard** literally denotes the getting rid of a card from one's hand in a card game, usually because they are worthless or can be replaced by better cards; in its more common general sense, it implies a getting rid of something which one can no longer use to advantage or which has become a burden, an annoyance, or an interference ⟨he sorted and re-sorted his cargo, always finding a more necessary article for which a less necessary had to be *discarded*—*Cather*⟩ ⟨modern research, which *discards*

obsolete hypotheses without scruple or sentiment—*Inge*⟩ ⟨in portrait painting, where a painter *discards* many trivial points of exactness, in order to heighten the truth of a few fundamentals—*Montague*⟩ **Cast** (see also THROW) may imply a seasonal process of discarding (as the throwing off of skin by a reptile) ⟨creatures that *cast* their skin are the snake, the viper—*Bacon*⟩ Especially when followed by *off, away,* or *out,* it more frequently implies a discarding, a rejection, a discharging, or a repudiation ⟨his wife was *casting* him off, half regretfully, but relentlessly— *D. H. Lawrence*⟩ ⟨an Englishman like an Ethiopian cannot change his skin any more than a leopard can *cast* off his spots—*Cloete*⟩ **Shed** is the ordinary, general term for the seasonal or periodic casting of skin, hair, antlers, or leaves ⟨deciduous trees *shed* their leaves every autumn⟩ ⟨male deer *shed* their antlers annually⟩ The term is used also to imply a throwing off or discarding of anything that is a burden to carry, that represents a past stage in one's development, or that is no longer useful or comfortable ⟨found it warm enough to *shed* his overcoat⟩ ⟨statesmen may try to *shed* their responsibility by treating the situation as a natural phenomenon—*Hobson*⟩ ⟨Jane . . . was acquiring new subtleties, complexities, and comprehensions, and *shedding* crudities—*Rose Macaulay*⟩ **Molt** is the specific term for the periodic shedding of feathers, skin, shells, hair, or horns by various animals and the growth of new corresponding parts. It often suggests a process of a change in plumage including the shedding of feathers and their renewal ⟨the eagle when he *molts* is sickly—*Carlyle*⟩ ⟨while hens are *molting* they do not lay eggs⟩ In general use *molt* even more often than *shed* implies change, flux, or transition ⟨England is *molting*. Opinions . . . are . . . in a state of flux—*Goldwin Smith*⟩ ⟨belief . . . that society can *molt* its outer covering and become new in shape and spirit—*J. D. Hart*⟩ **Slough** implies the shedding of tissue (as the skin by a reptile or, especially in intransitive use, of necrotic or cicatricial tissue from the surface of a sore or wound) ⟨the snake often *sloughs* its skin in mid-September⟩ ⟨the scab is *sloughing* off from the sore⟩ The term is also common in the sense of to discard or throw off what has become objectionable, burdensome, or useless ⟨*slough* a bad habit⟩ ⟨this talented author has *sloughed* off most of her more irritating sentimentalities—*Times Lit. Sup.*⟩ ⟨as though her gaunt and worldly air had been only a mockery she began to *slough* it off—*Bromfield*⟩ The last two words, *scrap* and *junk,* have literal reference to the throwing away of fragments, parts, or pieces that are useless to the owner or can no longer be used by him. **Scrap** suggests a discarding as rubbish or refuse, but it may carry an implication of some use to another (as a processor or a dealer in parts or accessories) ⟨*scrap* out-of-date machinery⟩ ⟨*scrap* a plan as impractical⟩ ⟨all the old ideas of combat had to be *scrapped*⟩ ⟨the English language that Shakespeare was born to had used up and *scrapped* a good deal of the English of Chaucer—*Montague*⟩ **Junk** differs little from *scrap* except in stressing a throwing away and in carrying little implication of value to a second-hand dealer or to a processor of waste ⟨*junk* all their old furniture before moving into their new home⟩ ⟨in its astonishing quest for perfection, can *junk* an entire system of ideas almost overnight—*Davidson*⟩

**Ana** *abandon, forsake, desert: reject, repudiate, spurn (see DECLINE *vb*): dismiss, *eject, oust

**Con** *adopt, embrace, espouse: utilize, employ, *use: retain, *keep, hold, hold back

**discern** perceive, descry, observe, notice, remark, note, espy, behold, *see, view, survey, contemplate

**Ana** *discover, ascertain: divine, apprehend, anticipate, *foresee: pierce, penetrate, probe (see ENTER)

---

**Ana** analogous words     **Ant** antonyms     **Con** contrasted words     See also explanatory notes facing page 1

**discernment,** discrimination, perception, penetration, insight, acumen are comparable when they denote keen intellectual vision. All imply power to see below the surface and to understand what is not evident to the average mind. **Discernment** stresses accuracy (as in reading character or motives or in appreciation of art) ⟨she had not had the *discernment* to discover the caliber of this young favorite—*Belloc*⟩ **Discrimination** emphasizes the power to distinguish and select the excellent, the appropriate, or the true ⟨there was a time when schools attempted . . . to cultivate *discrimination* and to furnish the material on which selection can be founded—*Grandgent*⟩ ⟨nobody should reproach them for reading indiscriminately. Only by so doing can they learn *discrimination*—*Times Lit. Sup.*⟩ **Perception** implies quick discernment and delicate feeling ⟨of a temperament to feel keenly the presence of subtleties; a man of clumsier *perceptions* would not have felt as he did—*George Eliot*⟩ ⟨persecutors were ordinary, reasonably well-intentioned people lacking in keen *perception*—*Sykes*⟩ **Penetration** implies a searching mind and power to enter deeply into something beyond the reach of the senses ⟨it did not require any great *penetration* to discover that what they wished was that their letters should be as kind as was consistent with proper maidenly pride—*De Quincey*⟩ ⟨good little novels, full of Gallic irony and *penetration*—*Time*⟩ **Insight** emphasizes depth of discernment or of sympathetic understanding ⟨throughout the years he has used . . . techniques or *insights* provided by abstract art, to express better his statements about men and the world—*Current Biog.*⟩ **Acumen** suggests characteristic penetration and keenness and soundness of judgment ⟨a paradox which your natural *acumen,* sharpened by habits of logical attention, will enable you to reconcile in a moment—*Cowper*⟩
*Ana* intuition, understanding, *reason: perspicaciousness *or* perspicacity, sagaciousness *or* sagacity, shrewdness, astuteness (see corresponding adjectives at SHREWD)
*Con* stupidity, slowness, dullness, density, crassness (see corresponding adjectives at STUPID): blindness (see corresponding adjective BLIND)
**discharge** *vb* **1** *free, release, liberate, deliver, emancipate, manumit, enfranchise
*Ana* *eject, expel, oust, dismiss: eliminate, *exclude
**2** *dismiss, cashier, drop, sack, fire, bounce
*Ana* displace, supplant, supersede, *replace
**3** *perform, execute, accomplish, achieve, effect, fulfill
*Ana* finish, complete, *close, end, terminate
**disciple** adherent, *follower, henchman, satellite, sectary, partisan
*Ana* votary, devotee (see ADDICT *n*): *enthusiast, zealot, fanatic
**discipline** *n* *morale, esprit de corps
*Ana* self-control, self-command (see base words at POWER): self-confidence, self-possession (see CONFIDENCE): nerving, steeling (see ENCOURAGE)
*Ant* anarchy, lawlessness —*Con* enervation (see corresponding verb at UNNERVE): disorganization, disorder (see corresponding verbs at DISORDER)
**discipline** *vb* **1** train, educate, *teach, instruct, school
*Ana* lead, *guide: control, manage, direct, *conduct: drill, exercise, *practice
**2** *punish, chastise, castigate, chasten, correct
*Ana* subdue, overcome, reduce, subjugate (see CONQUER): *restrain, curb, bridle, check, inhibit
**disclaim,** disavow, repudiate, disown, disallow mean to refuse to admit, accept, or approve. **Disclaim** implies refusal to admit or accept a claim, but it may apply specifically to a legal claim one has upon property or to a title ⟨the son *disclaimed* all right to his father's small estate⟩

or to the claim or imputation of something evil made by another to one's chagrin or dismay ⟨this court *disclaims* all pretensions to such a power—*John Marshall*⟩ ⟨I entirely *disclaim* the hatred and hostility to Turks . . . which you ascribe to me—*Gladstone*⟩ or, even more frequently, to the implied or expressed praise of oneself by another ⟨Mark was embarrassed by the Rector's talking like this; but if he *disclaimed* the virtues attributed to him he should . . . give an impression of false modesty—*Mackenzie*⟩ **Disavow** often comes close to *disclaim* in meaning, but it much less often implies reference to a legal claim and fastens the attention upon a vigorous denial either of personal responsibility for something or personal acceptance or approval of something ⟨Melfort never *disavowed* these papers—*Macaulay*⟩ ⟨the boys *disavowed* any intention to set the stable on fire⟩ ⟨this Court always had *disavowed* the right to intrude its judgment upon questions of policy or morals—*Justice Holmes*⟩ **Repudiate** originally applied to a casting away of one's wife (see also *repudiate* under DECLINE); it may also imply a casting off or a denial of responsibility for something that has been previously acknowledged, recognized, or accepted ⟨they *repudiated* their heresies⟩ ⟨the state has *repudiated* its debts⟩ ⟨a law which everyone recognizes in fact, though everyone *repudiates* it in theory—*Dickinson*⟩ ⟨the liberal mind . . . had *repudiated* the doctrine of original sin—*Straight*⟩ **Disown** usually stresses a repudiation or renunciation and often applies to something that has stood in close relationship to the person disowning; it may specifically imply disinheritance or abjuration ⟨*disowned* his son⟩ ⟨*disowned* his allegiance to the country of his birth⟩ ⟨the prince . . . was . . . required to *disown* . . . the obligations contracted in his name—*Froude*⟩ **Disallow** implies the withholding of sanction or approval and sometimes suggests complete rejection or condemnation ⟨*disallowed* the jockey's claim of a foul⟩ ⟨*disallow* a bill for the entertainment of the officers⟩ ⟨it was known that the most eminent of those who professed his own principles, publicly *disallowed* his proceedings—*Swift*⟩ ⟨your claim upon her hand is already *disallowed*—*G. P. R. James*⟩
*Ana* *deny, gainsay, traverse, contradict: reject, refuse, spurn (see DECLINE): deprecate (see DISAPPROVE): belittle, minimize, disparage (see DECRY)
*Ant* claim
**disclose** *reveal, divulge, tell, discover, betray
*Ana* confess, admit, own, *acknowledge, avow: *declare, proclaim, announce, publish, broadcast, advertise
*Con* conceal, *hide: cloak, mask, dissemble, *disguise, camouflage
**discomfit** disconcert, *embarrass, faze, abash, rattle
*Ana* *annoy, vex, irk, bother: perturb, *discompose, agitate, upset, disturb: check, *arrest, interrupt
**discommode** incommode, *inconvenience, trouble
*Ana* disturb, perturb, upset, fluster, flurry, *discompose: vex, irk, bother (see ANNOY)
**discompose,** disquiet, disturb, perturb, agitate, upset, fluster, flurry are comparable when they mean to excite one so as to destroy one's capacity for clear or collected thought or prompt action. **Discompose** is sometimes only slightly more suggestive of mental confusion than *disconcert* or *discomfit*; usually, however, it implies greater emotional stress and an actual loss of self-control or self-confidence ⟨he was still *discomposed* by the girl's bitter and sudden retort. It had cast a gloom over him—*Joyce*⟩ **Disquiet** stresses the loss, not of composure, but of something deeper (as one's sense of security or of well-being or one's peace of mind) ⟨why art thou cast down, O my soul? and why art thou *disquieted* within me?—*Ps 42:11*⟩ ⟨he was indubitably not happy at bottom, restless and

---

A colon (:) separates groups of words discriminated. An asterisk (*) indicates place of treatment of each group.

*disquieted,* his disquietude sometimes amounting to agony —*Arnold*⟩ ⟨why should we *disquiet* ourselves in vain in the attempt to direct our destiny—*Crothers*⟩ **Disturb,** unlike the preceding words, carries no implication of a loss of one's balance or of an excess of emotion; usually it implies marked interference with one's mental processes (as by worry, perplexity, disappointment, or interruption) ⟨profoundly *disturbed* by the prospective dissolution of a bond which dated from the seventies—*Bennett*⟩ ⟨nothing is more *disturbing* than the upsetting of a preconceived idea—*Conrad*⟩ **Perturb** implies deep disturbance and unsettlement of mind; it usually connotes a cause for disquietude or alarm ⟨in this *perturbed* state of mind, with thoughts that could rest on nothing, she walked on— *Austen*⟩ ⟨*perturbed* by excursions into verbal coquetry, and later into political arguments—*Hillyer*⟩ **Agitate** emphasizes the loss of calmness and self-control and implies obvious signs of nervous or emotional excitement. It does not, however, always suggest distress of mind or a cause of worry ⟨so *agitated* that she was incoherent—*Deland*⟩ ⟨growing more and more irritated, more and more *agitated*—*Woolf*⟩ ⟨it was a happiness that *agitated* rather than soothed her—*Crothers*⟩ **Upset,** like *agitate,* implies a nervous reaction, but it usually presupposes a cause that brings disappointment or distress or sorrow ⟨they wouldn't have believed they could be so *upset* by a hurt woodpecker—*Cather*⟩ ⟨what *upset* me in the . . . trial was not the conviction, but the methods of the defense—*Laski*⟩ **Fluster** may carry a suggestion of the excitement and confusion induced by drinking intoxicants ⟨*flustered* with new wine—*Tennyson*⟩ but it usually suggests the agitation, bewilderment, and sometimes fright induced by sudden and often unexpected demands, commands, needs, or crises ⟨the aged housekeeper was no less *flustered* and hurried in obeying the numerous . . . commands of her mistress—*Scott*⟩ **Flurry** suggests the excitement, commotion, and confusion induced by great haste or alarm ⟨they reached the station, hot and *flurried,* just as the train pulled out⟩ ⟨thoughts, with their attendant visions, which . . . *flurried* her too much to leave her any power of observation—*Austen*⟩ ⟨he recognized her and sat down immediately, *flurried* and confused by his display of excitement—*O'Flaherty*⟩

*Ana* discomfit, disconcert, rattle, faze, \*embarrass: vex, irk, bother, \*annoy: \*worry, harass, plague, pester

*Con* appease, \*pacify, conciliate, mollify, placate, propitiate

**disconcert** rattle, faze, discomfit, \*embarrass, abash

*Ana* bewilder, nonplus, perplex, \*puzzle: \*discompose, fluster, flurry, disturb, perturb

**disconsolate** woebegone, \*downcast, dejected, depressed, dispirited

*Ana* inconsolable, comfortless (see affirmative verbs at COMFORT): sorrowful, woeful (see corresponding nouns at SORROW): \*melancholy, doleful

**discontinue** desist, cease, \*stop, quit

*Ana* suspend, intermit, stay (see DEFER): \*arrest, check, interrupt

*Ant* continue

**discord** *n* Discord, strife, conflict, contention, dissension, difference, variance mean a state or condition marked by disagreement and lack of harmony or the acts or circumstances which manifest such a state or condition. **Discord** implies not only a want of harmony or of concord between persons or between things but also, usually, a positive clashing which manifests itself in personal relations by quarreling, factiousness, or antagonism, in relations between· sounds by a resulting dissonance or unpleasant noise, and in relations between other things that are incon-

gruous or incompatible by creating unpleasant impressions or mental disturbance ⟨they were firm and understanding friends. I know of but one approach to *discord* in their relations—*Repplier*⟩ ⟨in this state of enlightenment there is no more *discord* between the will, the intellect, and the feelings, and the objects of our reverence—*Inge*⟩ ⟨the seeker after truth . . . must disclaim responsibility for the way in which his discoveries fit into the general scheme of things. For the moment they may seem to produce *discord* rather than harmony—*Crothers*⟩ **Strife** throws the emphasis on a struggle for superiority rather than on the incongruity or incompatibility of the persons or things that disagree. It applies chiefly to relations between persons, and when used in reference to things it is nearly always figurative. Also, the term may imply any of widely different motives for the struggle (as rivalry, emulation, difference in opinion, disagreement, deep antagonism, or violent hostility) ⟨domestic fury and fierce civil *strife*—*Shak.*⟩ ⟨yet live in hatred, enmity, and *strife* among themselves— *Milton*⟩ ⟨I strove with none, for none was worth my *strife* —*Landor*⟩ ⟨a face in which a strange *strife* of wishes, for and against, was apparent—*Hardy*⟩ ⟨the crowd swells, laughing and pushing toward the quays in friendly *strife* —*Lowell*⟩ **Conflict** (see also CONTEST) implies a clashing and a struggle, but it stresses not the aim or end but the process, the uncertainty of the outcome, or the trials, difficulties, or torments it involves. In this sense the term may apply to actual battles or wars, but usually it applies to a mental, moral, or spiritual state of a person or group of persons or to its outward manifestations ⟨pale with *conflict* of contending hopes and fears—*Cowper*⟩ ⟨no more for him life's stormy *conflicts*—*Whitman*⟩ ⟨the *conflict* of passion, temper, or appetite with the external duties— *T. S. Eliot*⟩ The term is also used in a milder sense to imply an incompatibility between or the impossibility of reconciling two things which come together at the same time or upon the one person ⟨a *conflict* of engagements⟩ ⟨a *conflict* of duties⟩ **Contention** may be used in place of *strife* in any of ,the senses of the latter word; more often it applies to strife that manifests itself in quarreling, disputing, or controversy; it may even be applied to a condition of affairs marked by altercations or brawls ⟨cast out the scorner, and *contention* shall go out; yea, strife and reproach shall cease—*Prov* 22:10⟩ ⟨let the long *contention* cease! Geese are swans, and swans are geese, let them have it how they will—*Arnold*⟩ ⟨we were never friends. There was always a certain *contention* between us—*Max Peacock*⟩ **Dissension** may imply discord or strife between persons or parties, but it lays greater stress on a breach between them than do any of the preceding words; thus, to say that there is *dissension* in a church or political party is to imply that it is broken up into contentious or discordant factions ⟨France, torn by religious *dissensions,* was never a formidable opponent—*Macaulay*⟩ ⟨left the seeds of philosophic *dissension* vigorous in French soil—*Belloc*⟩ **Difference** (often in the plural) and **variance** usually imply a clash between persons or things owing to dissimilarity in opinion, character, or nature that makes for discord or strife. The terms may also suggest apparent or actual incompatibility or impossibility of reconciliation ⟨nationalists have always used force to settle their *differences*—*Fowler*⟩ ⟨I might very possibly have quarreled and skirmished with anyone of less unvarying kindness and good temper. As it is, we have never had a word or thought of *difference*—*Henning*⟩ ⟨to remain at *variance* with his wife seemed to him . . . almost a disaster —*Conrad*⟩ ⟨I never saw a child with such an instinct for preventing *variance,* or so full of tact—*Yonge*⟩ ⟨sectarian *variances* in the town had delayed the erection of a house

of worship—*Amer. Guide Series: Vt.*⟩
*Ana* incompatibility, incongruity, inconsonance, inconsistency, uncongeniality, discrepancy (see corresponding adjectives at INCONSONANT): antagonism, hostility, *enmity, rancor, animosity, antipathy
*Con* *harmony, consonance, accord
**discordant** *inconsonant, incongruous, uncongenial, unsympathetic, incompatible, inconsistent, discrepant
*Con* *consonant, congruous, congenial, sympathetic, compatible: harmonizing *or* harmonious, according *or* accordant, agreeing (see corresponding verbs at AGREE)
**discount** *deduction, rebate, abatement
**discourage** *vb* **1** Discourage, dishearten, dispirit, deject mean to weaken in qualities that maintain interest, zeal, activity, or power to continue or to resist. **Discourage** implies not only the loss of courage and confidence but the entrance of fear and the marked diminution of all power to summon up one's forces ⟨the long winter and the lack of fuel *discouraged* the settlers⟩ ⟨his failure had completely *discouraged* his wife⟩ **Dishearten** differs little from *discourage*, but it stresses not so much a mood or a state of mind as a loss of heart or will to accomplish a purpose or to achieve an end ⟨the slight response to ·their appeal *disheartened* the promoters of the fund⟩ ⟨his answers were at the same time so vague and equivocal, that her mother, though often *disheartened*, had never yet despaired of succeeding at last—*Austen*⟩ **Dispirit** distinctively implies the loss of cheerfulness or hopefulness; it often suggests a prevailing gloom that casts a blight upon a gathering, a project, or whatever depends for its success upon the spirits of those who enter into it. It may also, more strongly than *discourage*, suggest the way an individual or group affects others ⟨in quelling a local Armenian revolt he was badly wounded. Sick and *dispirited*, he gave up his Arabian plan—*Buchan*⟩ ⟨*dispirited* by their futile efforts—*Grandgent*⟩ ⟨the shabby, *dispiriting* spectacle of Versailles, with its base greeds and timidities —*Montague*⟩ **Deject**, even more strongly than *dispirit*, implies a casting down, with resulting loss of cheerfulness or hopefulness, but, unlike *dispirit*, it refers usually to the individual alone ⟨she has been much *dejected* lately⟩ ⟨nothing *dejects* a trader like the interruption of his profits —*Johnson*⟩
*Ana* *depress, weigh: try, *afflict: vex, bother, irk (see ANNOY)
*Ant* encourage —*Con* inspirit, hearten, embolden, nerve, steel (see ENCOURAGE)
**2** deter, *dissuade, divert
*Ana* *restrain, inhibit: *prevent (sense 2): *frighten, scare
**discourse** *n* Discourse, treatise, disquisition, dissertation, thesis, monograph designate in common a systematic, serious, and often learned consideration of a subject or topic. **Discourse,** the widest of these terms, may refer to something written or spoken but, since it fundamentally implies a passing from one link in a chain of reasoning to another, always suggests a careful formulation and usually a plan made in advance of expression ⟨read a *discourse* on the fundamental causes of war before the Foreign Policy Association⟩ ⟨his *discourses* from the pulpit were always long remembered⟩ **Treatise** implies a written work and suggests a formal, methodical, and more or less extended treatment, usually expository but sometimes argumentative or narrative; it often differs from *discourse* in not emphasizing reasoning and in referring to a lengthy work ⟨Turretin's history . . . (a dry, heavy, barren *treatise*) —*John Wesley*⟩ ⟨a *treatise* on insects⟩ ⟨a philosophical *treatise*⟩ **Disquisition** stresses limitation of a subject and its investigation and discussion in writing; it carries no

suggestion of failure or of success but throws its emphasis upon the exploratory nature of the discussion ⟨for . . . grave *disquisition* he was not well qualified—*Macaulay*⟩ ⟨in his initial *disquisition*, he tells how he has searched many books—*S. R. L.*⟩ **Dissertation** presupposes examination and often independent examination of a subject and its discussion at length, usually in writing; it often denotes a treatise dependent on individual research by a candidate for a higher academic degree ⟨the sermon is a *dissertation*, and does violence to nature in the effort to be like a speech—*Gladstone*⟩ ⟨Lamb's playful "*Dissertation* upon Roast Pig"⟩ ⟨present a *dissertation* upon "The Pedant as a stock character in the Elizabethan Drama" for the doctor of philosophy degree⟩ **Thesis** basically denotes a proposition which a person (as a candidate for an academic degree) advances and offers to maintain but is also often used interchangeably with *dissertation* ⟨it is my *thesis* that people are growing not worse but better⟩ ⟨write a doctoral *thesis* on Chaucer's minor poems⟩ although some restrict it to a dissertation or other work (as one incorporating the results of a series of experiments) intended to maintain or prove a proposition laid down or clearly stated. In practice, however, it may be difficult to tell whether the proposition or its treatment is in the user's mind, so inextricably are the two notions intertwined ⟨a *thesis* maintaining that man's economic condition can be closely correlated with weather records⟩ ⟨Miss Lynch's extremely suggestive *thesis* is that the transition from Elizabethan-Jacobean to later Caroline comedy is primarily economic—*T. S. Eliot*⟩ **Monograph** implies a learned treatise on a single topic (as a particular biological species, a clearly restricted literary genre, or an author). It typically refers to a work of this character published in a learned journal or as a pamphlet or small book ⟨a *monograph* on "The Ballade in England"⟩ ⟨a *monograph* on the catfishes of the Great Lakes region⟩
*Ant* paper, article, *essay: *speech, lecture, talk, sermon
**discourse** *vb* Discourse, expatiate, dilate, descant are comparable when meaning to talk or sometimes write more or less formally and at length upon a subject. **Discourse** frequently implies the manner or attitude of the lecturer, the monologist, or the preacher; it may suggest detailed or logical and sometimes profound, witty, or brilliant discussion ⟨Jonson is a real figure—our imagination plays about him *discoursing* at the Mermaid, or laying down the law to Drummond of Hawthornden—*T. S. Eliot*⟩ ⟨we talk in the bosom of our family in a way different from that in which we *discourse* on state occasions—*Lowes*⟩ **Expatiate** implies ranging without restraint or wandering at will over a subject; it connotes more copiousness than *discourse* and often carries a hint of long-windedness ⟨we will *expatiate* freely over the wide and varied field before us—*Landor*⟩ ⟨the promoter of the raffle . . . was *expatiating* upon the value of the fabric as material for a summer dress—*Hardy*⟩ ⟨in another lecture I shall *expatiate* on the idea—*James*⟩ **Dilate** implies a discoursing that enlarges the possibilities of a subject (as by dwelling on each small detail) ⟨she proceeded to *dilate* upon the perfections of Miss Nickleby—*Dickens*⟩ ⟨those joys on which Stevenson *dilates* in that famous little essay in *Virginibus Puerisque*—*Quiller-Couch*⟩ ⟨he reverted to his conversation of the night before, and *dilated* upon the same subject with an easy mastery of his theme—*Wylie*⟩ **Descant** stresses free comment, but it often also connotes delight or pleasure in this free expression of one's opinions or observations ⟨to praise his stable, and *descant* upon his claret and cookery—*Goldsmith*⟩ ⟨he *descanted* to his heart's content on his favorite topic of the [prize] ring—*Shaw*⟩

A colon (:) separates groups of words discriminated. An asterisk (*) indicates place of treatment of each group.

*Ana* *discuss, argue, dispute: converse, talk, *speak: lecture, harangue, orate, sermonize (see corresponding nouns at SPEECH)

**discourteous** impolite, uncivil, ungracious, *rude, ill-mannered
*Ana* brusque, curt, crusty, gruff, blunt (see BLUFF): boorish, churlish (see under BOOR)
*Ant* courteous —*Con* *civil, polite, courtly, gallant, chivalrous

**discover** 1 *reveal, disclose, divulge, betray
*Ana* impart, *communicate: *declare, announce, publish, advertise, proclaim
2 Discover, ascertain, determine, unearth, learn mean to find out something not previously known to one. Discover may presuppose investigation or exploration, or it may presuppose accident, but it always implies that the thing existed, either actually or potentially, in fact or in principle but had not been hitherto seen or known or brought into view, action, use, or actual existence ⟨*discover* an island⟩ ⟨*discover* a new writer⟩ ⟨*discover* uses for a weed⟩ ⟨*discover* the laws of heredity⟩ ⟨those rules of old *discovered*, not devised—*Pope*⟩ ⟨the historian of our times . . . will surely *discover* that the word *reality* is of central importance in his understanding of us—*Trilling*⟩ ⟨he was fifteen and beginning to become solid. This fall he'd *discovered* football—*La Farge*⟩ **Ascertain** seldom if ever implies accidental discovery; it usually presupposes an awareness of one's ignorance or uncertainty and conscious efforts (as by study, investigation, observation, and experiment) to find the truth or discover the facts ⟨old paintings were compared to *ascertain* the dresses of the period —*Shaw*⟩ ⟨it has been *ascertained* by test borings that salt extends for 2200 feet below the surface—*Amer. Guide Series: La.*⟩ **Determine** (see also DECIDE) differs from *ascertain* only in its greater emphasis upon the intent to establish the facts or the truth or to decide a dispute or controversy. Its use is largely legal and scientific ⟨experts were called to *determine* the presence or absence of poison in the vital organs⟩ ⟨if the site of his birthplace can be *determined*, the memorial will be erected there⟩ ⟨*determine* the degree of reaction when ragweed pollen is injected beneath the skin⟩ ⟨the executor must assemble all available records to *determine* the decedent's assets and liabilities—*Gehman*⟩ **Unearth** is freely used in the sense of to bring to light or out into the open something that has been hidden, forgotten, or lost or that is exceedingly difficult to trace. Frequently it also suggests intensive or prolonged investigation preceding discovery ⟨*unearth* old records⟩ ⟨*unearth* the evidence necessary for a conviction⟩ ⟨accurate scholarship can *unearth* the whole offense from Luther until now that has driven a culture mad—*Auden*⟩ ⟨an early-nineteenth-century globe that Dinah had *unearthed* in one of the basement rooms—*Basso*⟩ **Learn** implies acquirement of knowledge; it commonly suggests little or no effort on the part of the one who discovers ⟨it was only today that I *learned* his name⟩ ⟨Judy *learned* that the ayah must be left behind—*Kipling*⟩ ⟨they have not yet even *learnt* that "science" is not the accumulation of knowledge . . . but the active organization of knowledge —*Ellis*⟩
*Ana* discern, observe, perceive, espy (see SEE)
3 *invent, create

**discreet** prudent, forethoughtful, foresighted, provident (see under PRUDENCE)
*Ana* *cautious, circumspect, wary: politic, diplomatic (see SUAVE)
*Ant* indiscreet —*Con* rash, reckless, foolhardy (see

ADVENTUROUS): foolish, fatuous, asinine, *simple

**discrepant** inconsistent, *inconsonant, discordant, incompatible, incongruous, uncongenial, unsympathetic
*Ana* divergent, disparate, *different, diverse
*Ant* identical (*as accounts, explanations*) —*Con* agreeing, squaring, conforming, corresponding, jibing, tallying (see AGREE): uniform, parallel, alike, *like, similar

**discrete** separate, *distinct, several
*Ana* individual, distinctive, peculiar (see CHARACTERISTIC)
*Con* blended, merged, fused, mingled (see MIX)

**discretion** *prudence, forethought, foresight, providence
*Ana* caution, circumspection, wariness (see under CAUTIOUS): judgment, *sense, wisdom, gumption
*Ant* indiscretion —*Con* foolishness, fatuousness, asininity, simplicity (see corresponding adjectives at SIMPLE): rashness, recklessness, foolhardiness (see corresponding adjectives at ADVENTUROUS)

**discriminate** *vb* *distinguish, differentiate, demarcate
*Ana* *compare, contrast, collate: *separate, divide, part: *detach, disengage
*Ant* confound —*Con* confuse, *mistake

**discrimination** penetration, insight, *discernment, perception, acumen
*Ana* wisdom, judgment, *sense: subtlety, logicalness *or* logic (see corresponding adjectives at LOGICAL)
*Con* crassness, density, dullness, slowness, stupidity (see corresponding adjectives at STUPID)

**discuss,** argue, debate, dispute, agitate mean to discourse about something in order to arrive at the truth or to convince others. **Discuss** implies an attempt to sift or examine especially by presenting considerations pro and con; it often suggests an interchange of opinion for the sake of clarifying issues and testing the strength of each side ⟨Hobart couldn't *discuss*. He could talk; he could assert . . . but he couldn't meet or answer arguments—*Rose Macaulay*⟩ ⟨not even the loon, in whose voice there is a human note, means to *discuss* the weather. You are living in a world almost devoid of communication —*Laird*⟩ **Argue** usually implies conviction and the adducing of evidence or reasons in support of one's cause or position ⟨Agrippa advised a republican restoration and Maecenas *argued* for a principate—*Buchan*⟩ ⟨deep-seated preferences cannot be *argued* about—you cannot *argue* a man into liking a glass of beer—*Justice Holmes*⟩ **Debate** stresses formal or public argument between opposing parties ⟨they had gathered a wise council to them of every realm, that did *debate* this business—*Shak.*⟩ **Dispute,** in the sense of *discuss* or *debate,* is somewhat uncommon ⟨[Paul] spake boldly for the space of three months, *disputing* and persuading the things concerning the kingdom of God—*Acts* 19:8⟩ It more usually implies contentious or heated argument (compare *dispute n* at ARGUMENT). **Agitate** stresses both vigorous argument and a practical objective; it usually implies active propaganda and a determination to bring about a change ⟨when workers working ten hours a day *agitate* for an eight-hour day, what they really want is . . . sixteen hours off duty instead of fourteen—*Shaw*⟩ ⟨if you really expect success, *agitate, agitate, agitate*—*Paget*⟩
*Ana* *explain, expound, interpret, elucidate, explicate: *discourse, expatiate, dilate, descant

**disdain** *n* scorn, despite, contempt (see under DESPISE)
*Ana* aversion, *antipathy: insolence, superciliousness, arrogance (see corresponding adjectives at PROUD)
*Con* *regard, admiration, respect, esteem: *reverence, awe, fear

**disdain** *vb* scorn, scout, *despise, contemn

*Ana* spurn, repudiate, reject (see DECLINE *vb*)

*Ant* favor: admit —*Con* accept, *receive, take: *acknowledge, own

**disdainful** supercilious, overbearing, insolent, arrogant, lordly, *proud, haughty

*Ana* spurning, repudiating, rejecting (see DECLINE *vb*): scorning, despising, contemning, scouting (see DESPISE): averse, *antipathetic, unsympathetic

*Con* obliging, complaisant, *amiable: considerate, attentive, *thoughtful

**disease** *n* Disease, disorder, condition, affection, ailment, malady, complaint, distemper, syndrome denote a deranged bodily state usually associated with or amounting to a loss of health. Disease in its usual and broadest use implies an impairment of the normal state of the living body or of one or more of its parts marked by disturbance of vital functions and usually traceable to a specific cause (as a parasite, a toxin, or a dietary deficiency) ⟨his suffering is caused by *disease*⟩ As used in names of specific abnormal states, *disease* implies the existence of a regularly occurring identifying group of symptoms and, often, of a known cause ⟨such dreaded *diseases* as smallpox and plague⟩ ⟨possibly celiac *disease* is a symptom complex with a multiple etiology rather than a single *disease* entity—*Yr. Bk. of Endocrinology*⟩ Disorder is commonly interchangeable with *disease* ⟨a nutritional *disorder* caused by a lack of calcium and phosphorus —*Time*⟩ but typically it stresses the disordered state without regard to cause ⟨a specialist in *disorders* of the liver⟩ *Disease* may sometimes be used more narrowly to distinguish an abnormal state resulting from an infective process ⟨*disease* is conceived as being limited to malfunctioning of the organism initiated and maintained by an infectious process—*Ashley Montagu*⟩ and is then distinguished from or subordinated to *disorder* ⟨his distinction between *disease* (morbid change in tissue due to specific microorganisms) and *disorder* (disturbance in structure or function from any cause) is an artificial one—*Roney*⟩ ⟨*diseases* and other *disorders* of turf—*Lukens & Stoddard*⟩ Condition and the less common **affection** both imply a particular and usually an abnormal state of the body or more often of one of its parts; neither suggests anything about the cause or severity of such state ⟨pulmonary *affections*⟩ ⟨a severe heart *condition*⟩ Ailment, malady, and *complaint* are used chiefly of human disorders, and all imply a degree of indefiniteness ⟨the pattern of *ailments* is changing and the "degenerative diseases," like heart, circulation, and nerve diseases and cancer, are increasing—*New Statesman*⟩ ⟨had suffered from an obscure *malady*, an injury to the spine—*Glasgow*⟩ ⟨a digestive *complaint* of long standing⟩ Ailment often suggests a trivial or chronic disorder ⟨the pesthouses of the period of our Civil War, in which patients suffering from minor *ailments* were infected with all manner of diseases—*Morrison*⟩ ⟨constantly complaining of her *ailments*⟩ Malady, on the other hand, usually stresses the mysterious or serious character of a disorder ⟨suspicion in the Oriental is a sort of malignant tumor, a mental *malady*—*Forster*⟩ ⟨told by his physician that he had a fatal *malady*—*Cather*⟩ Complaint carries no inherent implication about the seriousness of the disorder but in stressing the invalid's point of view may suggest the distress that accompanies ill health ⟨taking all sorts of medicine for vague *complaints*—*Fishbein*⟩ Distemper, which formerly applied to human disorders, is now used almost entirely of diseases of lower animals and more particularly to denote specifically certain severe infectious diseases (as a destructive virus disease of the dog and related

animals, strangles of the horse, or panleucopenia of the cat). Syndrome is often used interchangeably with *disease* to denote a particular disorder, but in precise professional thinking such interchangeability does not imply strict synonymy, since *syndrome* denotes the group or pattern of signs and symptoms that constitute the evidence of disease and carries no implication about causation; thus, one might use either Ménière's *disease* or Ménière's *syndrome* to denote a particular disorder centered in the inner ear; however, one would say that the *syndrome* (not *disease*) of recurrent dizziness, ringing in the ears, and deafness suggests the presence of Ménière's *disease* ⟨a condition characterized by splenomegaly, hypochromic anemia, leukopenia, and icterus . . . this symptom complex may be produced by a variety of pathological states. It is therefore more properly classified as a *syndrome* than as a disease entity—*W. M. Fowler*⟩

Certain of these terms also are comparable in other uses and especially as applied to mental, spiritual, or emotional abnormal states. Disease usually connotes evident derangement requiring remedies or a cure ⟨*diseases* of the body politic⟩ ⟨this strange *disease* of modern life, with its sick hurry, its divided aims—*Arnold*⟩ Ailment implies something wrong that makes for unsoundness, weakness, or loss of well-being ⟨a bodily disease . . . may, after all, be but a symptom of some *ailment* in the spiritual part—*Hawthorne*⟩ Malady, especially as contrasted with *disease*, implies a deep-seated morbid condition or unwholesome abnormality ⟨how would they be troubled by this beauty, into which the soul with all its *maladies* had passed—*Pater*⟩ Distemper usually harks back to its earlier reference to human ailments and stresses a lack of balance or of a sense of proportion ⟨to seek of God more than we well can find, argues a strong *distemper* of the mind—*Herrick*⟩ Syndrome retains its implication of a group of contributory signs and symptoms ⟨lying is one of a *syndrome* or constellation of character traits that tend to be found in one another's company—*Garvin*⟩ ⟨partition . . . is no more decisive in the Irish *syndrome* than emigration or the decline of rural marriage or the fallen state of Irish literature—*Kelleher*⟩

**diseased** *unwholesome, morbid, sickly, pathological

**disembarrass** disencumber, disentangle, untangle, *extricate

*Ana* release, *free, liberate: *relieve: disengage, *detach

*Con* *hamper, trammel, clog, fetter, shackle

**disencumber** disembarrass, disentangle, untangle, *extricate

*Ana* *relieve, alleviate, lighten: disengage, *detach: liberate, release, *free

*Con* *depress, weigh, oppress: *hamper, fetter, shackle, manacle, trammel, clog

**disengage** *detach, abstract

*Ana* disembarrass, disencumber, disentangle, untangle, *extricate: release, liberate, *free: disconnect, disjoin, dissociate, disunite (see affirmative verbs at JOIN)

*Ant* engage (*one part, one thing with another*) —*Con* involve, *include, embrace, comprehend, imply: link, associate, connect, unite, *join

**disentangle** untangle, *extricate, disembarrass, disencumber

*Ana* disengage, *detach: *separate, part, sever, sunder: *free, release, liberate

*Ant* entangle

**disfavor** *n* *dislike, distaste, aversion

*Ana* disapproval, deprecation (see corresponding verbs at DISAPPROVE): distrust, mistrust (see under DISTRUST *vb*)

---

A colon (:) separates groups of words discriminated. An asterisk (*) indicates place of treatment of each group.

**disfigure** *deface
*Ana* mangle, batter, *maim, mutilate: *deform, distort, contort, warp: *injure, damage, mar, impair
*Ant* adorn —*Con* embellish, beautify (see ADORN)
**disgorge** *belch, burp, vomit, regurgitate, spew, throw up
**disgrace** *n* Disgrace, dishonor, disrepute, shame, infamy, ignominy, opprobrium, obloquy, odium mean the state, condition, character, or less often the cause of suffering disesteem and of enduring reproach or severe censure. **Disgrace** may imply no more than a loss of the favor or esteem one has enjoyed ⟨Queen Elizabeth's favorites were constantly in danger of *disgrace* if they offended her in the slightest degree⟩ ⟨he was shut up in an attic . . . and forbidden to speak to his sisters, who were told that he was in *disgrace*—*Russell*⟩ The term, however, often implies complete humiliation and, sometimes, ostracism ⟨you may find yourself at any moment summoned to serve on a jury and make decisions involving the *disgrace* or vindication . . . of your fellow creatures—*Shaw*⟩ **Dishonor** may often be employed in place of *disgrace*, but typically it suggests a previous condition of being honored or of having a high sense of honor; it therefore may imply the loss of the honor that one has enjoyed or the loss of one's self-respect or self-esteem ⟨prefer death to *dishonor*⟩ ⟨but now mischance hath trod my title down, and with *dishonor* laid me on the ground—*Shak.*⟩ ⟨wouldst thou . . . harp on the deep *dishonor* of our house—*Byron*⟩ **Disrepute** stresses either the loss of one's good name or the attribution of a bad name or reputation ⟨the actions of certain of its guests have brought the hotel into *disrepute*⟩ ⟨the *disrepute* into which this once famous name has now fallen⟩ ⟨the habit of pub-crawling—so much the fashion when I was their age—seems to have happily fallen into *disrepute*—*O'Connor*⟩ **Shame** implies particularly humiliating disgrace or disrepute such as is caused by an illicit union, illegitimate birth, inferior blood, relationship to a traitor or criminal, or commission of a crime ⟨live in *shame*⟩ ⟨a child of *shame*⟩ ⟨"Is it not . . . a pity to live no better life?" "God knows it is a *shame*!"—*Dickens*⟩ ⟨*shame* is a reaction to other people's criticism. A man is shamed either by being openly ridiculed and rejected or by fantasying to himself that he has been made ridiculous —*Benedict*⟩ **Infamy** usually implies notoriety as well as exceeding shame ⟨men who prefer any load of *infamy*, however great, to any pressure of taxation, however light —*Sydney Smith*⟩ ⟨I have come, not from obscurity into the momentary notoriety of crime, but from a sort of eternity of fame to a sort of eternity of *infamy*—*Wilde*⟩ **Ignominy**, more than *infamy*—which in some ways it closely resembles—stresses the almost unendurable contemptibility or despicability of the disgrace or its cause ⟨the *ignominy* he had been compelled to submit to— *Meredith*⟩ ⟨was she now to endure the *ignominy* of his abandoning her?—*D. H. Lawrence*⟩ ⟨the *ignominy* of returning to Spain, having accomplished nothing, became more obvious the more it was considered—*Froude*⟩ **Opprobrium** adds to *disgrace* the implication of being severely reproached or condemned ⟨the *opprobrium* which often attaches itself to the term *politician*⟩ ⟨Spain . . . has been plundered and oppressed, and the *opprobrium* lights on the robbers, not on the robbed—*Buckle*⟩ ⟨the name "educator," for many intelligent people, has become a term of *opprobrium*—*Grandgent*⟩ **Obloquy** (see also ABUSE *n*) adds to *disgrace* the implication of being abused or vilified ⟨and undergo the perpetual *obloquy* of having lost a kingdom—*Clarendon*⟩ ⟨that unmerited *obloquy* had been brought on him by the violence of his minister —*Macaulay*⟩ **Odium** applies to the disgrace or the opprobrium that is attached to the fact or state of being an object

of widespread or universal hatred or intense dislike ⟨whatever *odium* or loss her maneuvers incurred she flung upon her counselors—*J. R. Green*⟩ ⟨as a preliminary Augustus . . . revised the senatorial roll. This was always an invidious task . . . . in the end he was compelled to make the nominations himself and face the *odium*— *Buchan*⟩ ⟨many materialists . . . seek to eliminate the *odium* attaching to the word *materialism,* and even to eliminate the word itself—*James*⟩
*Ana* degradation, debasement, abasement, humbling, humiliation (see corresponding verbs at ABASE): *stigma, brand, blot, stain
*Ant* respect, esteem —*Con* admiration, *regard: *reverence, awe, fear: honor, repute, glory, renown, *fame
**disguise** *vb* Disguise, cloak, mask, dissemble, camouflage are comparable when meaning to assume a dress, an appearance, or an expression that conceals one's identity, intention, or true feeling. **Disguise**, which basically implies an alteration in one's dress and appearance, frequently retains this implication with the added suggestion either of concealment of identity or of the assumption (as on the stage) of another identity ⟨escape captivity *disguised* as a woman⟩ ⟨they *disguise* themselves as Turks for a joke⟩ The term, however, may apply to a feeling, an intention, or a motive when one's words, expression, or acts imply a contrary reaction ⟨I *disguised* my impatience and suspicion of him and waited—*Hudson*⟩ ⟨however we may *disguise* it by veiling words we do not and cannot carry out the distinction between legislative and executive action with mathematical precision—*Justice Holmes*⟩ ⟨our author, *disguised* as Jonathan Oldstyle, contributed a series of letters . . . protesting with admirable chivalry against jesting at maiden ladies—*Commins*⟩ **Cloak** implies the assumption of something which covers and conceals identity or nature ⟨the appearance of goodwill *cloaked* a sinister intention⟩ ⟨intolerance and public irresponsibility cannot be *cloaked* in the shining armor of rectitude and righteousness—*A. E. Stevenson*⟩ **Mask** implies a disguise, comparable to a covering for the face or head, which prevents recognition of a thing's true character, quality, or presence ⟨icy spots *masked* by newly fallen snow⟩ ⟨*masking* with a smile the vain regrets that in their hearts arose—*Morris*⟩ ⟨his pessimism . . . became an obvious pose, an attempt to *mask* his porky complacence—*Hicks*⟩ **Dissemble** stresses simulation for the purpose of deceiving as well as disguising; it, therefore, is the preferred term when actual deception is achieved ⟨Ross bears, or *dissembles,* his disappointment better than I expected of him—*Gray*⟩ ⟨the Scripture moveth us . . . to acknowledge and confess our manifold sins and wickedness; and that we should not *dissemble* nor cloak them before the face of Almighty God—*Book of Common Prayer*⟩ **Camouflage** in its basic military use implies a disguising (as with paint, garnished nets, or foliage) that reduces the visibility or conceals the nature or location of a potential target (as a ship, a factory, or an airfield), and in its common extended use tends to imply a comparable disguising quality or element, often specifically one that tends to minimize some undesirable aspect (as of a person or his acts or attributes) ⟨Soulé is five feet five inches tall and . . . inclines to stoutness, but his erect bearing and quick movements tend to *camouflage* this—*Wechsberg*⟩ ⟨the absolute character of these dictatorships was *camouflaged* somewhat by an elaborate parliamentary system—*C. E. Black & E. C. Helmreich*⟩
*Ana* conceal, *hide: *misrepresent, belie, falsify, garble: *assume, pretend, feign, counterfeit, sham, simulate, affect
*Con* expose, exhibit, display, parade, flaunt (see SHOW

*vb*): *reveal, disclose, discover, betray

**disgust** *vb* Disgust, sicken, nauseate are comparable when meaning to arouse an extreme distaste for. **Disgust** implies a stomach that is revolted by food offered or taken; in its extended use it implies sensibilities which are revolted by something seen, heard, or otherwise known that creates strong repugnance or aversion ⟨a *disgusting* medicine⟩ ⟨a *disgusting* smell⟩ ⟨*disgusted* by the vulgarity of men who ate noisily and greedily⟩ ⟨the very thought of such an occupation *disgusted* his fastidious nature⟩ ⟨the majority of women that he meets offend him, repel him, *disgust* him —*Mencken*⟩ **Sicken** usually implies not only the exciting of distaste but of actual physical distress (as faintness or a turning of the stomach); often, however, it is used merely as a more emphatic word for *disgust*, or it may suggest a disgust born of weariness or exhaustion ⟨the smell of certain flowers is *sickening* in its sweetness⟩ ⟨mine eyes did *sicken* at the sight, and could not endure a further view—*Shak.*⟩ ⟨she was *sickened* by the girl's affectations⟩ ⟨for a few evenings it had interested the sisters . . . but they had soon *sickened* of it and loathed it —*Bennett*⟩ ⟨his unctuous morality, which *sickens* later ages—*Lewis & Maude*⟩ **Nauseate** carries a stronger implication than *disgust* or *sicken* of loathsomeness (as to the taste, sight, or mind), and often suggests retching or vomiting ⟨he always finds castor oil *nauseating*⟩ ⟨just now, even the thought of food *nauseates* the patient⟩ ⟨they were all *nauseated* by the foul odor⟩ ⟨*nauseating* behavior⟩ ⟨we also cannot bring ourselves to deny him that famous, if dangerous, charm of his, *nauseated* as we may be by the excesses into which it so often misled him—*J. M. Brown*⟩
*Ana* revolt, repulse, offend (see corresponding adjectives at OFFENSIVE)
*Ant* charm —*Con* tempt, entice (see LURE): gratify, delight, rejoice, *please

**dish** *vb* ladle, spoon, *dip, bail, scoop

**dishearten** *discourage, dispirit, deject
*Ana* *depress, weigh: despair, despond (see corresponding adjectives at DESPONDENT)
*Ant* hearten —*Con* *encourage, inspirit, embolden, cheer, nerve, steel

**disheveled** unkempt, sloppy, *slipshod, slovenly
*Ana* *negligent, neglectful, lax, slack, remiss: *slatternly, blowsy, frowzy, dowdy

**dishonest,** deceitful, mendacious, lying, untruthful are comparable especially when applying to persons, their utterances, and their acts and meaning deficient in honesty and unworthy of trust or belief. **Dishonest** may apply to any breach of honesty or trust (as by lying, deceiving, stealing, cheating, or defrauding) ⟨a *dishonest* statement⟩ ⟨a *dishonest* employee⟩ ⟨while it would be *dishonest* to gloss over this weakness, one must understand it in terms of the circumstances that conspired to produce it—*Mumford*⟩ ⟨years ago a few *dishonest* men traveled about the country, saying that they could make rain—*Craig & Urban*⟩ **Deceitful** usually implies the intent to mislead or to impose upon another in order to obscure one's real nature or actual purpose or intention, or the true character of something offered, given, or sold; it therefore usually suggests a false or specious appearance, indulgence in falsehoods, cheating, defrauding, or double-dealing ⟨*deceitful* propaganda⟩ ⟨*deceitful* testimony⟩ ⟨she was a *deceitful*, scheming little thing—*Zangwill*⟩ **Mendacious** is typically more formal than, often less derogatory than, but otherwise closely equivalent to **lying,** the ordinary, direct, unequivocal word ⟨silly newspapers and magazines for the circulation of *lying* advertisements—*Shaw*⟩ ⟨a *lying* account of the accident⟩ ⟨go aboard the ships

that caught his interest where the masters . . . set out wine and told him *mendacious* tales of their trade—*Wheelwright*⟩ ⟨while the communication was deceptive and so intended, it was not technically *mendacious*—*S. H. Adams*⟩ As applied to persons *mendacious* more often suggests the habitude of deceit while *lying* suggests guilt in respect to a particular instance; thus, one might describe a person as *mendacious* with primary reference to his character or habit but would ordinarily prefer *lying* when a particular instance is in view ⟨a *mendacious* child is doubted even when telling the truth⟩ ⟨only a *lying* scoundrel would tell such a tale⟩ **Untruthful** is often used in place of *mendacious* or *lying* as a slightly less brutal word; however, the term distinctively implies lack of correspondence between what is said or represented and the facts of the case or the reality, and is often applied to statements, accounts, reports, or descriptions with little stress on dishonesty or intent to deceive ⟨an *untruthful* account of an incident⟩ ⟨the artist's representation of the scene at Versailles was *untruthful* in many of its details⟩
*Ana* *crooked, devious, oblique: false, *faithless, perfidious: cheating, cozening, defrauding, swindling (see CHEAT *vb*)
*Ant* honest —*Con* *upright, honorable, scrupulous, conscientious, just: *straightforward, forthright, aboveboard: candid, open, *frank, plain

**dishonor** *n* *disgrace, disrepute, shame, infamy, ignominy, opprobrium, obloquy, odium
*Ana* humiliation, humbling, debasement, degradation, abasement (see corresponding verbs at ABASE): *stigma, brand, blot, stain
*Ant* honor —*Con* glory, renown, repute, *fame: reverence, veneration (see under REVERE): prestige, *influence, credit, authority, weight: esteem, respect, *regard, admiration

**disillusioned** *sophisticated, worldly-wise, worldly, blasé
*Ana* undeceived (see corresponding affirmative verb at DECEIVE): disenchanted (see corresponding affirmative verb at ATTRACT)

**disinclined** *adj* Disinclined, indisposed, hesitant, reluctant, loath, averse mean manifesting neither the will nor the desire to do or to have anything to do with something indicated or understood. **Disinclined** implies a lack of taste or inclination for something for which one has no natural bent or which meets one's disapproval ⟨I should not be *disinclined* to go to London, did I know anybody there—*Richardson*⟩ ⟨*disinclined* to come to real grips with the vexed question of public control in industry—*Cohen*⟩ ⟨he was preoccupied and *disinclined* for sociability⟩ **Indisposed** implies an unfavorable or often a hostile or unsympathetic attitude ⟨unfit to rule and *indisposed* to please—*Crabbe*⟩ ⟨*indisposed* to take part in the feasting and dancing—*Hardy*⟩ **Hesitant** suggests a holding back through fear, distaste, uncertainty, or irresolution ⟨she was *hesitant* to accept the invitation⟩ ⟨*hesitant* in seeking advice⟩ ⟨a *hesitant* suitor⟩ ⟨*hesitant* about spending the money required to build an experimental plant— *Griffin*⟩ **Reluctant** adds to *hesitant* a definite resistance or sense of unwillingness ⟨I was simply persuading a frightened and *reluctant* girl to do the straight and decent and difficult thing—*Rose Macaulay*⟩ ⟨people were *reluctant* to charge a dead man with an offense from which he could not clear himself—*Wharton*⟩⟨*reluctant* to expose those silent and beautiful places to vulgar curiosity—*Cather*⟩ *Reluctant* is also applied directly to the thing which is done reluctantly or to a thing which seems reluctant ⟨the constant strain of bringing back a *reluctant* and bored attention —*Russell*⟩ ⟨they wring from *reluctant* soil food enough to keep . . . alive—*Repplier*⟩ **Loath** stresses the lack of

A colon (:) separates groups of words discriminated. An asterisk (*) indicates place of treatment of each group.

harmony between something one anticipates doing and his likes or dislikes, tastes or distastes; or sympathies or antipathies; thus, a tender person may be *loath* to punish a refractory child but a strict disciplinarian would be *loath* to allow that child to go unpunished; one may be *loath* to believe a well-founded report that discredits a friend and equally *loath* to disbelieve a rumor that confirms his bad opinion of a person ⟨*loath* to publish translations of anything except our surefire sex-and-mayhem fiction—*Whyte*⟩ **Averse** suggests a turning away from something distasteful or repugnant ⟨*averse* to all advice⟩ ⟨his impulses were generous, trustful, *averse* from cruelty—*J. R. Green*⟩
*Ana* *antipathetic, unsympathetic: opposing, resisting (see RESIST): balking, shying, boggling, sticking, stickling (see DEMUR): objecting, protesting (see OBJECT *vb*)
*Con* *eager, avid, keen, anxious: inclined, disposed, predisposed (see INCLINE *vb*)

**disinfect** *sterilize, sanitize, fumigate
*Ant* infect
**disinfectant** *n* *antiseptic, germicide, bactericide
**disinfectant** *adj* antiseptic, germicidal, bactericidal (see under ANTISEPTIC *n*)
**disintegrate** crumble, decompose, *decay, rot, putrefy, spoil
*Ana* deliquesce (see LIQUEFY): *scatter, disperse, dissipate: break down, resolve, *analyze, dissect
*Ant* integrate —*Con* articulate, concatenate (see INTEGRATE): fuse, blend, merge, coalesce (see MIX): unite, conjoin, combine, link, associate, *join, connect
**disinterested** uninterested, detached, aloof, unconcerned, *indifferent, incurious
*Ana* dispassionate, unbiased, impartial, *fair, just: *neutral, negative
*Ant* interested: prejudiced, biased
**dislike** *n* Dislike, distaste, aversion, disfavor mean the state of mind of one who is not drawn to or turns from or avoids a person or thing; often these terms imply the manifestation of the state of mind. **Dislike** normally suggests the finding of something unpleasant or repugnant or of a kind one is unwilling to meet or to face ⟨an aristocratic disdain and *dislike* of the bourgeoisie—*Inge*⟩ ⟨differentiating between mere aversion and *dislike* and morbid unreasonable fear or dread—*Armstrong*⟩ In itself *dislike* is rather neutral but it is readily intensified by context to the point of suggesting complete detestation ⟨I was on fire with the same anger, *dislike*, and contempt that burned in Hobart towards me—*Rose Macaulay*⟩ **Distaste**, which implies a lack of taste for, usually stresses a squeamishness or a repugnance but allows a good deal of range in intensity to this squeamishness or repugnance; it may imply such other feelings as fear occasioned by the difficulties involved ⟨a pronounced *distaste* for mathematics⟩ or rebellion at constraint or confinement ⟨for sheer pity of the repressed . . . *distaste* on Nettie's face, you . . . drove her down to the movies—*Mary Austin*⟩ or simply an unexplained reluctance ⟨great as was his need of shelter, the Bishop . . . was struck by a reluctance, an extreme *distaste* for the place—*Cather*⟩ **Aversion** suggests a disinclination for someone or something which manifests itself especially in attempts to avoid, evade, or escape. An *aversion* may be temperamental or it may be the result of training; it may or may not suggest an accompanying feeling, but it consistently implies a definite reaction on the part of one manifesting it ⟨he tried to take hold of her feet with his hands, but she shrank from him with *aversion*—*Hudson*⟩ ⟨unless we can give them an *aversion* from cruelty, they will not abstain from it—*Russell*⟩ ⟨the natural human *aversion* to cold, noise, vibration, . . . and

the unfriendly and lonesome environment at high altitude —*Armstrong*⟩ **Disfavor**, the weakest of these words, usually suggests no more than a lack of liking or approval but it may imply contempt, lack of confidence, or disdain as motives ⟨the proposal met with general *disfavor*⟩ ⟨the young prince had fallen into open *disfavor* at court⟩ ⟨*Punch* . . . eyed the house with *disfavor*—*Kipling*⟩
*Ana* hate, hatred, detestation (see under HATE *vb*): disapproval, deprecation (see corresponding verbs at DISAPPROVE)
*Ant* liking —*Con* affection, *attachment, love: *predilection, partiality
**disloyal** *faithless, false, perfidious, traitorous, treacherous
*Ana* disaffected, estranged, alienated (see ESTRANGE): *inconstant, fickle, unstable
*Ant* loyal —*Con* *faithful, constant, true, staunch, steadfast, resolute
**dismal,** dreary, cheerless, dispiriting, bleak, desolate are comparable when they mean devoid of all that makes for cheer or comfort. *Dismal* and *dreary* are often interchangeable. **Dismal** may indicate extreme gloominess or somberness utterly depressing and dejecting ⟨*dismal* acres of weed-filled cellars and gaping foundations—*Felix Morley*⟩ ⟨rain dripped . . . with a *dismal* insistence—*Costain*⟩ ⟨the most *dismal* prophets of calamity—*Krutch*⟩ **Dreary** may differ in indicating what discourages or enervates through sustained gloom, dullness, tiresomeness, or futility, and wants any cheering or enlivening characteristic ⟨the most *dreary* solitary desert waste I had ever beheld—*Bartram*⟩ ⟨it was a hard *dreary* winter, and the old minister's heart was often heavy—*Deland*⟩ ⟨had the strength been there, the equipment was lacking. Harding's *dreary* appreciation of this was part of his tragedy—*S. H. Adams*⟩ **Cheerless** stresses absence of anything cheering and is less explicit than but as forceful as the others in suggesting a pervasive disheartening joylessness or hopelessness ⟨he would like to have done with life and its vanity altogether . . . so *cheerless* and dreary the prospect seemed to him—*Thackeray*⟩ **Dispiriting** refers to anything that disheartens or takes away morale or resolution of spirit ⟨it was such *dispiriting* effort. To throw one's whole strength and weight on the oars, and to feel the boat checked in its forward lunge—*London*⟩ **Bleak** is likely to suggest chill, dull, barren characteristics that dishearten and militate against any notions of cheer, shelter, warmth, comfort, brightness, or ease ⟨the *bleak* upland, still famous as a sheepwalk, though a scant herbage scarce veils the whinstone rock—*J. R. Green*⟩ ⟨the sawmill workers of the *bleak* mountain shack towns—*Amer. Guide Series: Calif.*⟩ ⟨the *bleak* years of the depression—*J. D. Hicks*⟩ **Desolate** applies to what disheartens by being utterly barren, lifeless, uninhabitable or abandoned, and remote from anything cheering, comforting, or pleasant ⟨a semibarren, rather *desolate* region, whose long dry seasons stunted its vegetation—*Marvel*⟩ ⟨some *desolate* polar region of the mind, where woman, even as an ideal, could not hope to survive—*Glasgow*⟩
*Ana* murky, gloomy, *dark: forlorn, hopeless (see DESPONDENT): barren, *bare
*Con* gay, *lively, animated: cheerful, joyous (see GLAD)
**dismantle** divest, *strip, denude, bare
*Con* *furnish, equip, outfit, appoint
**dismay** *vb* Dismay, appall, horrify, daunt mean to unnerve and check or deter by arousing fear, apprehension, or aversion. **Dismay** suggests a loss of power to proceed either because a prospect is terrifying or disheartening, or, more often, because one is balked and perplexed or at a loss concerning how to deal with a situation ⟨be not afraid nor *dismayed* by reason of this great multitude; for

the battle is not yours, but God's. Tomorrow go ye down against them—*2 Chron* 20:15-16⟩ ⟨here was an opponent that more than once puzzled Roosevelt, and in the end flatly *dismayed* him—*Mencken*⟩ ⟨who in one lifetime sees all causes lost, herself *dismayed* and helpless—*Rukeyser*⟩ **Appall,** in its most forceful use, implies an overwhelming and paralyzing dread or terror ⟨the sight *appalled* the stoutest hearts⟩ ⟨"Are you a man?" "Ay, and a bold one, that dare look on that which might *appall* the devil"—*Shak.*⟩ The word more often implies the sense of impotence aroused when one is confronted by something that perturbs, confounds, or shocks, yet is beyond one's power to alter ⟨an *appalling* waste of human life⟩ ⟨*appalling* statistics⟩ ⟨the unpunctuality of the Orient . . . is *appalling* to those who come freshly from a land of fixed mealtimes and regular train services—*Huxley*⟩ ⟨*appalled* by the magnitude of the tragedy—*Bowers*⟩ **Horrify** may emphasize a reaction of horror or of shuddering revulsion from what is ghastly or hideously offensive ⟨to developed sensibilities the facts of war are revolting and *horrifying*—*Huxley*⟩ ⟨this theme—a man ready to prostitute his sister as payment for a debt of honor—is too grotesque even to *horrify* us—*T. S. Eliot*⟩ Often *horrify* comes close to *shock* in meaning and implies momentary agitation occasioned by a surprising breach of the proprieties or decencies ⟨they were *horrified* by his playing golf on Sunday⟩ ⟨she *horrified* London society by pouring hot tea on a gentleman who displeased her—*Amer. Guide Series: Va.*⟩ **Daunt** presupposes an attempt to do something that requires courage and implies therefore a checking or scaring off by someone or something that cows or subdues ⟨he had been completely *daunted* by what he had found . . .; the Revolution . . . had been something against which self-assertion had been of no avail—*Mary Austin*⟩ *Daunt* perhaps most often occurs in negative constructions ⟨nothing can *daunt* the man whose last concern is for his own safety⟩ ⟨no adventure *daunted* her and risks stimulated her—*Ellis*⟩ *Ana* perplex, confound, bewilder, nonplus, dumbfound, mystify, *puzzle: disconcert, rattle, faze, abash, discomfit, *embarrass: alarm, *frighten, terrify *Ant* cheer  —*Con* assure, secure, *ensure: pique, quicken, stimulate, galvanize, excite, *provoke

**dismay** *n* alarm, consternation, panic, *fear, dread, fright, terror, horror, trepidation
*Ana* perturbing *or* perturbation, agitation, disquieting *or* disquietude, discomposing *or* discomposure, upsetting *or* upset (see corresponding verbs at DISCOMPOSE): *apprehension, foreboding
*Con* *confidence, assurance, aplomb, self-possession: *courage, mettle, spirit, resolution

**dismiss** 1 Dismiss, discharge, cashier, drop, sack, fire, bounce are comparable when they mean to let go from one's employ or service. **Dismiss** basically denotes a giving permission to go ⟨he *dismissed* the assembly—*Acts* 19:41⟩ ⟨*dismissed* the night-watchers from the room, and remained with her alone—*Meredith*⟩ When used in respect to employment it carries apart from the context no suggestion of the reason for the act and is, therefore, often preferred as the softer or as the more comprehensive term ⟨with the letup in business, thousands of employees were *dismissed*⟩ ⟨the new governor *dismissed* the staff that served his predecessor and appointed members of his own party in their places⟩ **Discharge** is usually a harsher term, implying dismissal for cause and little or no likelihood of being called back ⟨*discharge* an employee for insubordination⟩ ⟨she has the habit of *discharging* her servants without notice⟩ ⟨a rich man can *discharge* anyone in his employment who displeases him—*Shaw*⟩ Only

in military and court use does it, when unqualified, carry no implication of dissatisfaction on the part of the employer ⟨the enlisted man will be *discharged* after three years' service⟩ ⟨the three convicted soldiers were dishonorably *discharged*⟩ ⟨the judge *discharged* the jury with thanks⟩ **Cashier** implies a summary or ignominious discharge from a position of trust or from a position that is high in the scale ⟨*cashier* a suspected official⟩ ⟨many a duteous and knee-crooking knave . . . wears out his time, much like his master's ass, for nought but provender, and when he's old, *cashiered*—*Shak.*⟩ ⟨the few sentimental fanatics who . . . proceeded upon the assumption that academic freedom was yet inviolable, and so got themselves *cashiered*—*Mencken*⟩ *Drop, sack, fire,* and *bounce* are all rather informal. **Drop** is a common and colorless synonym of *dismiss* ⟨many employees were *dropped* when business slackened⟩ **Sack** stresses a being discarded or thrown out of employ ⟨he was *sacked* after long years of service⟩ ⟨Blum had *sacked* him because he wore blue undershirts—*Bennett*⟩ while **fire** stresses a dismissal as sudden and peremptory as the action of firing a gun ⟨he *fired* his clerk one day in a fit of anger, but the next day he called him back⟩ and **bounce,** a kicking out ⟨he *bounced* the boy after one day of unsatisfactory service⟩
2 *eject, oust, expel, evict
*Ana* *discard, cast, shed, slough: spurn, repudiate, reject, refuse (see DECLINE *vb*): scorn, scout (see DESPISE)
*Con* accept, *receive, admit: entertain, *harbor

**dismount** alight, *descend
*Ant* mount

**disorder** *vb* Disorder, derange, disarrange, disorganize, unsettle, disturb are comparable when they mean to undo the fixed or proper order of something. **Disorder** is commonly used in reference to something that depends for its proper functioning or effectiveness upon being properly ordered (see ORDER *vb* 1) or in good order or array ⟨tresses all *disordered*—*Milton*⟩ ⟨too rich a diet will *disorder* his digestive system⟩ **Derange** implies a throwing out of proper arrangement of the parts, or of an important part, of something in which all the parts or elements are ordered with reference to each other or are so carefully adjusted or so closely related to each other that they work together as a unit. The term usually carries a strong implication of resulting confusion or a destruction of normal or healthy conditions ⟨war *deranges* the life of a nation⟩ ⟨fear has *deranged* his mind⟩ ⟨within the power of man irreparably to *derange* the combinations of inorganic matter and organic life—*Lord*⟩ **Disarrange** often implies little more than the changing of a fixed, neat, or perfect order of arrangement and may carry no suggestion of confusion ⟨she . . . would not let his chamber be *disarranged* just at present—*Martineau*⟩ ⟨someone had *disarranged* the papers on his desk⟩ ⟨the wind *disarranged* her hair⟩ **Disorganize** implies usually the destruction of order and functioning in a body or whole all the parts of which have an organic connection with each other or have been so ordered with reference to each other that what affects one part affects every other part; the term therefore usually suggests a disordering that impedes the functioning or impairs the effectiveness of the affected system ⟨subversive methods intended to *disorganize* the internal communications of the enemy's country⟩ ⟨the Whigs . . . though defeated, disheartened, and *disorganized*, did not yield without an effort—*Macaulay*⟩ ⟨an expenditure which would *disorganize* his whole scheme of finance—*Buchan*⟩ **Unsettle** implies a disordering or disarrangement that causes instability, unrest, inability to concentrate, or turbulence ⟨the cold war has

A colon (:) separates groups of words discriminated. An asterisk (*) indicates place of treatment of each group.

*unsettled* the minds of men—*Travis*⟩ ⟨constant rumors that keep one *unsettled*⟩ **Disturb** (see also DISCOMPOSE) usually implies a force or combination of forces that *unsettles* or *disarranges*; frequently it also suggests an interruption or interference that affects a settled or orderly course, plan, growth, or progress ⟨the attraction of planets *disturbs* the course of comets⟩ ⟨regulation . . . produces a uniform whole, which is as much *disturbed* and deranged by changing what the regulating power designs to leave untouched, as that on which it has operated—*John Marshall*⟩ ⟨the warps and strains of civilized life . . . seem to *disturb* the wholesome balance of even the humblest elements of the possessive and aesthetic instincts—*Ellis*⟩ **Ant** order  —**Con** arrange, marshal, organize, methodize, systematize (see ORDER *vb*): array, align, range, *line, line up: regulate, *adjust, fix

**disorder** *n* **1** *confusion, disarray, clutter, jumble, chaos, snarl, muddle
**Ana** derangement, disarrangement, disorganization, disturbance, unsettlement (see corresponding verbs at DISORDER): *anarchy, chaos, lawlessness
**Ant** order  —**Con** arrangement, organization, methodization, systematization (see corresponding verbs at ORDER): system, *method
**2** *disease, condition, affection, ailment, malady, complaint, distemper, syndrome

**disorganize** disturb, unsettle, *disorder, derange, disarrange
**Ant** organize  —**Con** systematize, methodize, arrange, marshal, *order

**disown** *disclaim, disavow, repudiate, disallow
**Ana** reject, spurn, refuse (see DECLINE)
**Ant** own  —**Con** *acknowledge, avow

**disparage** *decry, depreciate, derogate, detract, belittle, minimize
**Ana** asperse, *malign, traduce, defame, slander, libel: deprecate, *disapprove
**Ant** applaud  —**Con** *praise, laud, extol, eulogize, acclaim: *commend, compliment: *exalt, magnify, aggrandize

**disparaging** *derogatory, depreciatory, depreciative, slighting, pejorative
**Ana** belittling, decrying, minimizing (see DECRY): underestimating, undervaluing, underrating (see base words at ESTIMATE)
**Con** extolling, acclaiming, praising (see PRAISE): magnifying, exalting (see EXALT)

**disparate** diverse, divergent, *different, various
**Ana** *inconsonant, incompatible, incongruous, discrepant, discordant, inconsistent: *distinct, separate
**Ant** comparable, analogous  —**Con** similar, *like, parallel

**dispassionate** unbiased, impartial, objective, uncolored, *fair, just, equitable
**Ana** disinterested, detached, aloof, *indifferent: *cool, collected, composed: candid, open, *frank
**Ant** passionate: intemperate

**dispatch** *vb* **1** *send, forward, transmit, remit, route, ship
**Ana** hasten, quicken, *speed
**2** *kill, slay, murder, assassinate, execute

**dispatch** *n* **1** speed, expedition, *haste, hurry
**Ana** *celerity, alacrity, legerity: quickness, fleetness, swiftness, rapidity (see corresponding adjectives at FAST): diligence (see corresponding adjective at BUSY)
**Ant** delay
**2** message, note, *letter, epistle, report, memorandum, missive

**dispel** dissipate, disperse, *scatter
**Ana** expel, *eject, oust, dismiss: disintegrate, crumble

(see DECAY)
**Con** *accumulate, amass: *gather, collect, assemble
**dispense** **1** *distribute, divide, deal, dole
**Ana** *allot, assign, apportion, allocate: portion, parcel, ration, prorate, *apportion
**2** *administer

**disperse** *scatter, dissipate, dispel
**Ana** *separate, part, divide: *dismiss, discharge
**Ant** assemble, congregate (*persons*): collect (*things*)  —**Con** *summon, convoke, convene, muster, cite, call

**dispirit** *discourage, dishearten, deject
**Ana** *depress, weigh
**Ant** inspirit  —**Con** *encourage, hearten, embolden, cheer, nerve, steel

**dispirited** depressed, dejected, *downcast, disconsolate, woebegone
**Ana** sad, melancholy (see corresponding nouns at SADNESS): gloomy, glum, morose (see SULLEN): discouraged, disheartened (see DISCOURAGE)
**Ant** high-spirited  —**Con** encouraged, inspirited, heartened (see ENCOURAGE)

**dispiriting** *dismal, dreary, cheerless, bleak, desolate
**Ana** disheartening, discouraging, dejecting (see DISCOURAGE): depressing, oppressing *or* oppressive (see corresponding verbs at DEPRESS)
**Ant** inspiriting  —**Con** heartening, cheering, encouraging, emboldening (see ENCOURAGE)

**displace** supplant, *replace, supersede
**Ana** transpose, *reverse, invert: shift, remove, transfer, *move: derange, disarrange, *disorder: *eject, oust, expel, dismiss

**display** *vb* exhibit, *show, expose, parade, flaunt
**Ana** manifest, evidence, evince, demonstrate, *show: *reveal, disclose, discover
**Con** *disguise, cloak, mask, dissemble, camouflage: *hide, conceal, secrete

**display** *n* **Display, parade, array, pomp** are comparable when denoting a striking or spectacular show or exhibition for the sake of effect. **Display** commonly suggests a spreading out or an unfolding of something that is usually concealed or visible only in the mass or in individual instances, so that the observer is impressed by the extent, the detail, the beauty, or the lavishness of what is revealed to him ⟨a *display* of meteors⟩ ⟨a parvenu's *display* of wealth⟩ ⟨a nation's *display* of military power⟩ ⟨fine editions that make an impressive *display* in an oilman's library —*Green Peyton*⟩ **Parade** implies ostentatious or flaunting exhibition; *display* may or may not suggest a conscious endeavor to impress, but *parade* definitely does carry such an implication ⟨Mr. Cruncher could not be restrained from making rather an ostentatious *parade* of his liberality—*Dickens*⟩ ⟨he does not make the least *parade* of his wealth or his gentility—*Snaith*⟩ **Array** stresses order and brilliancy in display of or as if of marshaled ranks of armed soldiers and therefore may be used of displays that strike one as beautiful, as terrible, or as merely astonishing ⟨an *array* of tulips⟩ ⟨an *array* of silver on a sideboard⟩ ⟨the terrible *array* of evils around us and dangers in front of us—*Shaw*⟩ ⟨clouds . . . each lost in each, that marvelous *array* of temple, palace, citadel—*Wordsworth*⟩ **Pomp** stresses ceremonial grandeur or splendor. Once often but now rarely used of a pageant or solemn procession it still suggests an outward spectacular show of magnificence or glory ⟨it [Independence Day] ought to be solemnized with *pomp* and parade, with . . . bonfires, and illuminations—*Adams*⟩ ⟨pride, *pomp* and circumstance of glorious war—*Shak.*⟩ ⟨lo, all our *pomp* of yesterday is one with Nineveh and Tyre—*Kipling*⟩

---

**Ana** analogous words     **Ant** antonyms     **Con** contrasted words     See also explanatory notes facing page 1

**Ana** ostentatiousness *or* ostentation, pretentiousness *or* pretension, showiness *or* show (see corresponding adjectives at SHOWY)

**disport** *n* sport, play, frolic, rollick, romp, gambol (see under PLAY *vb*)

**Ana** recreation, diversion, amusement, entertainment (see under AMUSE): merriment, jollity (see corresponding adjectives at MERRY)

**disport** *vb* sport, *play, frolic, rollick, romp, gambol

**Ana** divert, *amuse, recreate, entertain

**disposal, disposition** are frequently used without clear distinction when they mean the act or the power of disposing of something. However, when the emphasis is upon what shall be done with money, property, or possessions, **disposal** tends to imply a getting rid of (as by selling, giving away, assigning to others, or destroying) and **disposition,** a proper or orderly distribution or utilization ⟨the *disposal* of her jewels seemed necessary to pay her debts⟩ ⟨the *disposition* of the intestate's property has been agreed upon by the heirs⟩ ⟨incinerators used for the *disposal* of garbage⟩ ⟨I am happy that the speedy *disposal* of the pictures will enable you . . . to settle this unpleasant affair—*Mitford*⟩ ⟨the donors have stipulated for the future *disposition* . . . of those funds—*John Marshall*⟩ When the idea of arrangement or ordering or of making arrangements is stressed, *disposition,* rather than *disposal,* is the more accurate term ⟨while the *disposition* of the branches is unsymmetrical, balance is maintained—*Binyon*⟩ ⟨a deserter had informed Octavian of the general plan . . . and he made his *dispositions* accordingly—*Buchan*⟩ The idiomatic phrases *at one's disposal* and *at* (or *in*) *one's disposition* differ in that, though both imply a placing under one's control, the former suggests use as one sees fit and the latter, subjection to one's direction, arrangement, or command ⟨they put their summer home at the *disposal* of the bridal couple⟩ ⟨had at his *disposition* no inconsiderable sums of money—*Trench*⟩

**Ana** destroying *or* destruction, demolishing *or* demolition (see corresponding verbs at DESTROY)

**dispose** predispose, bias, *incline

**Ana** influence, *affect, sway

**disposition** 1 *disposal

**Ana** administering *or* administration, dispensing *or* dispensation (see corresponding verbs at ADMINISTER): management, direction, controlling *or* control, conducting *or* conduct (see corresponding verbs at CONDUCT): arrangement, ordering (see corresponding verbs at ORDER)

**2 Disposition, temperament, temper, complexion, character, personality, individuality** are comparable when they mean the prevailing and dominant quality or qualities which distinguish or identify a person or group. **Disposition** applies to the predominating bent or constitutional habit of one's mind or spirit ⟨ages of fierceness have overlaid what is naturally kindly in the *dispositions* of ordinary men and women—*Russell*⟩ ⟨the taint of his father's insanity perhaps appeared in his unbalanced *disposition*—*E. S. Bates*⟩ **Temperament** applies to the sum total of characteristics that are innate or inherent and the result of one's physical, emotional, and mental organization ⟨a nervous, bilious *temperament*⟩ ⟨I verily believe that nor you, nor any man of poetical *temperament,* can avoid a strong passion of some kind—*Byron*⟩ ⟨shall I ever be cheerful again, happy again? Yes. And soon. For I know my *temperament*—*Mark Twain*⟩ **Temper** (compare *temper* under MODERATE *vb*) implies a combination of the qualities and especially those acquired through experience which determine the way one (as a person, a people, an age) meets the situations, difficulties, or problems that

confront him ⟨there was a general confidence in her instinctive knowledge of the national *temper*—*J. R. Green*⟩ ⟨the leaders of forlorn hopes are never found among men with dismal minds. There must be a natural resiliency of *temper* which makes them enjoy desperate ventures—*Crothers*⟩ Unlike the foregoing terms *temper* may suggest an acquired or transient state of mind controlling one's acts and decisions ⟨after four years of fighting, the *temper* of the victors was such that they were quite incapable of making a just settlement—*Huxley*⟩ **Complexion** implies some fundamentally distinctive quality based on mood, attitude, and ways of thinking that determines the impression one produces on others ⟨the rationalist mind . . . is of a doctrinaire and authoritative *complexion:* the phrase "must be" is ever on its lips—*James*⟩ ⟨great thinkers of various *complexion,* who, differing in many fundamental points, all alike assert the relativity of truth—*Ellis*⟩ **Character** applies to the aggregate of qualities, especially moral qualities, which distinguish an individual at any one time in his development, which constantly tend to become more or less fixed, and which must be taken as a whole into consideration in any ethical judgment of him ⟨he is a man of *character*⟩ ⟨in his youth his *character* was weak and unstable⟩ ⟨that inexorable law of human souls that we prepare ourselves, for sudden deeds by the reiterated choice of good or evil that determines *character*—*George Eliot*⟩ Often *character* means such an aggregate of qualities brought to a high state of moral excellence by right principles and right choices and by the rejection of anything that weakens or debases ⟨when we say of such and such a man that he has . . . *character,* we generally mean that he has disciplined his temperament, his disposition, into strict obedience to the behests of duty—*Brownell*⟩ **Personality** also applies to the aggregate of qualities which distinguish an individual, but the term differs from *character* in that it implies his being distinguished as a person rather than as a moral being. In general personality may be said to be revealed in unconscious as well as in conscious acts or movements, in physical and emotional as well as in mental and moral behavior, and especially in a person's relations to others; thus, one may know very little about the *character* of an acquaintance, yet have a very definite idea of his *personality.* Therefore *personality* is qualified not as good or bad but by an adjective implying the extent to which it pleases, displeases, or otherwise impresses the observer ⟨there was a pious and good man, but an utterly negligible *personality*—*Mackenzie*⟩ ⟨the mere presence of *personality* in a work of art is not sufficient, because the *personality* revealed may be lacking in charm—*Benson*⟩ Hence *personality* often distinctively means personal magnetism or charm ⟨*personality* is not something that can be sought; it is a radiance that is diffused spontaneously—*Ellis*⟩ **Individuality** implies a personality that distinguishes one from all others; often it connotes the power of impressing one's personality on others ⟨a man of marked *individuality*⟩ ⟨she is a pleasant person but has no *individuality*⟩ ⟨Sophia quietened her by sheer force of *individuality*—*Bennett*⟩ ⟨an *individuality,* a style of its own—*Cather*⟩

**disprove, refute, confute, rebut, controvert** mean to show or attempt to show by argument that a statement, a claim, a proposition, or a charge is not true. **Disprove** stresses the success of an argument in showing the falsity, erroneousness, or invalidity of what is attacked ⟨he could not *disprove* the major contention of his opponents⟩ ⟨I speak not to *disprove* what Brutus spoke, but here I am to speak what I do know—*Shak.*⟩ ⟨the final values of life, the ultimate meanings of experience, are just those that no man

---

A colon (:) separates groups of words discriminated. An asterisk (*) indicates place of treatment of each group.

can prove, and that no man can *disprove* either—*Hedley*⟩
**Refute** stresses the method more than the effect of argument in disproof; it therefore is preferred to *disprove* when one wishes to convey implications of the adducing of evidence, of a bringing forward of witnesses, experts, or authorities, and of close reasoning. It connotes a gathering of forces and an elaboration of arguments not present in *disprove* ⟨with respect to that other, more weighty accusation, of having injured Mr. Wickham, I can only *refute* it by laying before you the whole of his connection with my family—*Austen*⟩ ⟨there is great force in this argument, and the Court is not satisfied that it has been *refuted*—*John Marshall*⟩ ⟨one can disagree with his views but one can't *refute* them. . . . Every particle of him asseverates the truth which is in him—*Henry Miller*⟩
**Confute** emphasizes a destruction of arguments or a reducing to silence of opponents by clearly revealing the falsity or the untenability of the points which have been made; the term usually implies refutation, but it may also suggest such methods as raillery, denunciation, and sarcasm ⟨Satan stood . . . *confuted* and convinced of his weak arguing and fallacious drift—*Milton*⟩ ⟨Elijah . . . *confuted* the prophets of Baal in precisely that way, with . . . bitter mockery of their god when he failed to send down fire from heaven—*Shaw*⟩ ⟨hypotheses which may be *confuted* by experience—*Ayer*⟩ **Rebut** differs from *refute*, its closest synonym, in suggesting greater formality of method (as that used in organized debate or in courts of law). Although its aim is disproof of an opponent's contentions, the term does not necessarily imply the achievement of one's end, but it does suggest the offering of argument, evidence, or testimony that contradicts argument, evidence, or testimony given in support of the other side ⟨at the end of the formal arguments, each member of the debating team was allowed three minutes for *rebutting* the arguments of his opponents⟩ ⟨the Tractarians were driven to formulate a theory of the Church . . . which should justify the exclusive claim of Anglicanism to be the Church of Christ in these islands, while *rebutting* the arguments of Rome—*Inge*⟩ ⟨the author carefully examined and *rebutted*, point by point, many of the arguments—*Ashley Montagu*⟩ **Controvert** usually carries a dual implication of denying or contradicting a statement, proposition, or doctrine, or a set of these, and of refuting or attempting to refute it. It does not necessarily suggest disproof but it does connote a valiant effort to achieve that end ⟨this doctrine has been *controverted*; it is, however, very ably defended by Mr. Hargrave—*Cruise*⟩ ⟨I am glad that this year we are assembled not to *controvert* the opinions of others, nor even to defend ourselves—*Inge*⟩
*Ana* negative, traverse, impugn, contravene (see DENY)
*Ant* prove, demonstrate
**disputation** debate, forensic, *argumentation, dialectic
*Ana* *argument, dispute, controversy
**dispute** *vb* argue, debate, *discuss, agitate
*Ana* see those at DEBATE
*Ant* concede —*Con* *grant, allow
**dispute** *n* *argument, controversy
*Ana* *argumentation, disputation, debate, forensic, dialectic: contention, dissension, strife, *discord, conflict
**disquiet** *discompose, disturb, agitate, perturb, upset, fluster, flurry
*Ana* *annoy, vex, irk, bother: *worry, harass, harry: *trouble, distress
*Ant* tranquilize, soothe
**disquisition** dissertation, thesis, *discourse, treatise, monograph
*Ana* paper, *essay, article: *inquiry, investigation

**disrate** *degrade, demote, reduce, declass
**disregard** *vb* ignore, overlook, slight, forget, *neglect
*Con* attend, mind, watch, *tend: observe, notice, note, remark (see SEE)
**disrepute** *n* *disgrace, dishonor, shame, infamy, ignominy, opprobrium, obloquy, odium
*Ant* repute —*Con* *fame, reputation, renown, honor, glory
**dissect** *analyze, break down, resolve
*Ana* *scrutinize, examine, inspect: pierce, penetrate, probe (see ENTER)
**dissection** breakdown, analysis, resolution (see under ANALYZE)
**dissemble** mask, cloak, *disguise, camouflage
*Ana* simulate, feign, counterfeit, sham, pretend, *assume, affect
*Ant* betray —*Con* *reveal, disclose, discover: *show, manifest, evidence, evince, demonstrate
**disseminate** *spread, circulate, diffuse, propagate, radiate
*Ana* *scatter, disperse: *distribute, dispense, divide: *share, participate
**dissension** difference, variance, strife, conflict, contention, *discord
*Ana* altercation, wrangle, *quarrel, bickering: *argument, dispute, controversy
*Ant* accord (sense 1): comity —*Con* *harmony, concord, consonance: *friendship, goodwill, amity
**dissent** *vb* *differ, vary, disagree
*Ana* *object, protest: *demur, balk, boggle, shy, stickle
*Ant* concur: assent: consent —*Con* acquiesce, subscribe, agree, accede (see ASSENT)
**dissenter** nonconformist, sectarian, sectary, schismatic, *heretic
**dissertation** disquisition, thesis, treatise, monograph, *discourse
*Ana* *exposition: *argumentation, disputation: article, paper, *essay
**dissimilarity,** unlikeness, difference, divergence, divergency, distinction are comparable when they mean lack of agreement or correspondence (or an instance of such lack) in appearance, in qualities, or in nature brought out by a comparison of two or more things. **Dissimilarity** and **unlikeness**, the most general terms in this group, are often used interchangeably without loss, but when there is little basis for comparison and the contrast is obvious, *dissimilarity* is usually preferred ⟨the effectiveness of a metaphor depends, in part, on the *dissimilarity* of the things which are compared⟩ ⟨the injunction that the most recent comers slough off all the traits of their *dissimilarity* also implied that homogeneity was itself socially desirable —*Handlin*⟩ **Unlikeness** is commonly the preferred term, however, when the things contrasted belong to a common category, and there are fundamental likenesses between them ⟨but he was rich where I was poor, and he supplied my want the more as his *unlikeness* fitted mine —*Tennyson*⟩ ⟨the likenesses among human beings as well as the *unlikenesses*—*Wiggam*⟩ **Difference** suggests notice of a quality or feature which marks one thing as apart from another. The term may imply want of resemblance in one or more particulars ⟨note the *differences* between the first poems of Keats and those written after he had achieved mastery of his art⟩ ⟨there are both resemblances and *differences* in the designs of these two cathedrals⟩ or want of identity ⟨*difference* of opinion is the one crime which kings never forgive—*Emerson*⟩ ⟨*difference* of religion breeds more quarrels than *difference* of politics—*Phillips*⟩ or a disagreement or cause of disagreement which separates individuals or makes them hostile to each other ⟨there have been *differences*

---

between them for some time⟩ **Divergence** or **divergency** applies to a difference between things or less often persons having the same origin, the same ends, or the same background or belonging to the same type or class; there is usually an implication of a difference that makes for cleavage or increasing unlikeness ⟨an illustration of the *divergences* between countries both highly democratic—*Bryce*⟩ ⟨the greatest *divergence* in the educational value of studies is due to the varying degree to which they require concentration, judgment, observation, and imagination—*Grandgent*⟩ ⟨increasing *divergencies* between British and French policies—*Welles*⟩ **Distinction** usually implies want of resemblance in detail, especially in some minute or not obvious detail; it therefore commonly applies to a difference that is brought out by close observation, study, or analysis or that marks the line of division between two like things ⟨point out the *distinction* in meaning between two close synonyms⟩ ⟨a hairsplitting *distinction* between "original" and "creative" writing⟩ ⟨apprehend the vital *distinction* between religion and criticism—*Arnold*⟩ ⟨so intoxicated with dreams of fortune that he had lost all sense of the *distinction* between reality and illusion—*Brooks*⟩ ⟨this is not a *distinction* without a difference. It is not like the affair of "an old hat cocked" and "a cocked old hat" . . . but there is a difference here in the nature of things—*Sterne*⟩
*Ana* difference, diversity, disparity (see corresponding adjectives at DIFFERENT): discrepancy, discordance, inconsonance (see corresponding adjectives at INCONSONANT)
*Ant* similarity —*Con* \*likeness, resemblance, similitude: correspondence, agreement, conformity (see corresponding verbs at AGREE)
**dissimulation** duplicity, \*deceit, cunning, guile
*Ana* dissembling, cloaking, masking, disguising, camouflaging (see DISGUISE): hiding, concealing, secreting (see HIDE): pretending *or* pretense, feigning, shamming (see corresponding verbs at ASSUME): \*hypocrisy, pharisaism, sanctimony
*Con* candidness *or* candor, openness (see corresponding adjectives at FRANK): sincerity (see corresponding adjective SINCERE)
**dissipate 1** dispel, disperse, \*scatter
*Ana* disintegrate, crumble (see DECAY): \*separate, part, divide: deliquesce, melt (see LIQUEFY)
*Ant* accumulate (*possessions, wealth, a mass of things*): absorb (*one's energies, one's attention*): concentrate (*one's thoughts, powers, efforts*)
**2** \*waste, squander, fritter, consume
*Ana* \*spend, expend, disburse: \*scatter, disperse: \*vanish, evanesce, disappear, evaporate
**dissolute** profligate, reprobate, \*abandoned
*Ana* \*licentious, libertine, wanton, lewd: inebriated, intoxicated, drunken, \*drunk: debauched, depraved, corrupt, debased, perverted (see under DEBASE)
**dissuade,** deter, discourage, divert mean to turn one aside from a purpose, a project, or a plan. **Dissuade** carries the strongest implication of advice, argument, or exhortation; like the affirmative form *persuade*, it usually suggests gentle or effective methods and carries no suggestion of bullying or browbeating, though it equally carries little or no suggestion of coaxing or wheedling ⟨Sir Walter had at first thought more of London; but Mr. Shepherd . . . had been skillful enough to *dissuade* him from it, and make Bath preferred—*Austen*⟩ ⟨wrote a book to *dissuade* people from the use of tobacco—*Scudder*⟩ ⟨Galton was eagerly interested and wanted to experiment on himself, though ultimately *dissuaded* on account of his advanced age—*Ellis*⟩ While **deter** often implies the operation of fear as

the cause of turning aside from the fulfillment of a project, it may suggest no more than a changing of purpose for cause rather than from mere caprice ⟨the fear of reprisals *deterred* them from using poison gas⟩ ⟨he vowed that nothing should *deter* him from his purpose⟩ ⟨the Judge's remark about hanging around the stable did not *deter* Theophilus from playing there all that winter—*Deland*⟩ ⟨Peter for a time abandoned both smoking and alcohol, and was only *deterred* from further abstinences by their impracticability—*H. G. Wells*⟩ ⟨he then hazards the conjecture that Aristotle wrote so obscurely in order that he might *deter* slow-witted and indolent men from reading him—*Babbitt*⟩ In *deterrent* the implication that it is fear which is the cause of holding back is stronger than in the verb. **Discourage** (see also DISCOURAGE) implies a deterring by undermining spirit or enthusiasm or by weakening intent or sense of purpose ⟨*discouraged* him from prosecuting the inquiry⟩ ⟨the incessant hurry and trivial activity of daily life . . . seem to prevent, or at least *discourage*, quiet and intense thinking—*Eliot*⟩ ⟨I definitely wished to *discourage* his intimacy with my family—*Rose Macaulay*⟩ **Divert** (see also TURN and AMUSE) implies a turning aside, but here the mind or some of its functions is usually the thing diverted or turned aside, and another object of interest or attention is generally expressed or understood as the alternative; in this sense *divert* is often used of the very young, or of the preoccupied or the worried ⟨the children's attention was *diverted* to a more interesting game⟩ ⟨thank God for colonels, thought Mrs. Miniver; sweet creatures, so easily entertained, so biddably *diverted* from senseless controversy into comfortable monologue—*Jan Struther*⟩
*Ana* advise, counsel (see under ADVICE *n*): \*urge, exhort, prick
*Ant* persuade —*Con* \*induce, prevail, get: influence, touch, \*affect
**distant,** far, faraway, far-off, remote, removed mean not near or close but separated by an obvious interval especially in space or in time. **Distant** carries a stronger reference to the length of the interval (whether long or short) than the other terms; only when it directly qualifies a noun does it necessarily imply that the interval is markedly long ⟨a book held six inches *distant* from the eyes⟩ ⟨the sun is about 93,000,000 miles *distant* from the earth⟩ ⟨a *distant* city⟩ ⟨the other item, on a *distant* page, was cheerfully headed "Food from Sewage"—*Krutch*⟩ ⟨at a *distant* date⟩ ⟨I do not ask to see the *distant* scene,—one step enough for me—*Newman*⟩ **Far,** except for the possible reference to a short distance involved in the question "How *far*?", applies (as adverb as well as adjective) only to what is a long way off ⟨[he] took his journey into a *far* country—*Lk 15:13*⟩ ⟨take a *far* view in planning for future needs of the city⟩ ⟨go back in the *far* past to a common origin—*Kroeber*⟩ ⟨across the hills, and *far* away beyond their utmost purple rim—*Tennyson*⟩ **Faraway** and **far-off** not only mean extremely far but are preferred when distance in time is specifically implied ⟨old, unhappy, *far-off* things, and battles long ago—*Wordsworth*⟩ However, both may suggest distance in space ⟨a cheer that started the echo in a *faraway* hill—*Stevenson*⟩ ⟨the *far-off* places in which he had been wandering—*Dickens*⟩ **Remote** suggests a far removal, especially from something (as one's present location, one's point of view, or one's time) regarded as a center or vantage ground ⟨some forlorn and naked hermitage, *remote* from all the pleasures of the world—*Shak.*⟩ ⟨the sands of a *remote* and lonely shore—*Shelley*⟩ ⟨whose nature it was to care more for immediate annoyances than for *remote* consequences—*George Eliot*⟩ **Removed,** which is usually a predicate adjective,

---

A colon (:) separates groups of words discriminated. An asterisk (\*) indicates place of treatment of each group.

carries a stronger implication of separateness and distinction than *remote*; it therefore usually implies a contrast between two things apart not only in space or in time but in character or quality ⟨an age far *removed* from the present age in its accomplishments and ideals⟩ ⟨he sought a retreat *removed* from all centers of population⟩ ⟨with peace as far *removed* as it had been at the time of his election—*Paxson*⟩

Figuratively, **distant** implies slightness of connection or aloofness of manner ⟨a *distant* resemblance⟩ ⟨a *distant* nod⟩ **Remote** imputes to the thing so described a foreign or alien character or an inaccessible nature ⟨I told Oliver about your modern monastery; but the thing is too *remote* from his experience to have any interest for him—*Santayana*⟩ ⟨the captain of a ship at sea is a *remote*, inaccessible creature . . . alone of his kind, depending on nobody—*Conrad*⟩ **Removed** stresses difference, often a diametrical or antithetical difference ⟨to Queen Scheherazade the dream might have seemed not far *removed* from commonplace—*Hardy*⟩ ⟨he was not an oracle *removed* from the people, but a real human being—*Bok*⟩ ⟨he accepted the nomination for considerations entirely *removed* from those influencing the average candidate⟩
*Con* near, *close, nigh, nearby

**distaste** *dislike, aversion, disfavor
*Ana* repugnance, repulsion, abhorrence (see corresponding adjectives at REPUGNANT): antipathy, hostility (see ENMITY)
*Ant* taste —*Con* relish, zest (see TASTE): *predilection, partiality

**distasteful** obnoxious, *repugnant, repellent, abhorrent, invidious
*Ana* *hateful, odious, detestable, abominable: *offensive, loathsome, repulsive, repugnant, revolting
*Ant* agreeable: palatable —*Con* *pleasant, pleasing, gratifying, grateful, welcome: delectable, *delightful, delicious

**distemper** complaint, syndrome, *disease, malady, ailment, disorder, condition, affection

**distend** swell, dilate, *expand, inflate, amplify
*Ana* enlarge, *increase, augment: *extend, lengthen
*Ant* constrict —*Con* *contract, shrink, compress, condense, deflate

**distinct** 1 Distinct, separate, several, discrete are comparable when used in reference to two or more things (sometimes persons) and in the sense of not being individually the same. **Distinct** always implies a capacity for being distinguished by the eye or by the mind as apart from the other or others, sometimes in space or in time but more often in character, nature, or identity ⟨I see three *distinct* objects in the distance, but I cannot identify them⟩ ⟨the novel has two related, but nevertheless *distinct*, plots⟩ ⟨there has been endless discussion whether we have a *distinct* faculty for the knowledge of God—*Inge*⟩ ⟨for him the work of literature is not *distinct* or separable from its author—*L. P. Smith*⟩ **Separate** (see also SINGLE) is often used interchangeably with *distinct* and often in combination with it, as if one strengthened the other ⟨the power . . . is given in two *separate* and *distinct* sections of the constitution—*John Marshall*⟩ ⟨these two characteristics were not *separate* and *distinct* . . . they were held together in vital tension—*Ellis*⟩ But *separate* stresses, as *distinct* does not, the lack of a connection between the things considered, usually by reason of the distance in space or time or the difference in identity of the things in question; thus, a drama with two *separate* plots is not the same as one with two *distinct* plots, for *separate* implies no connection (or, often, only a factitious connection) between the plots, while *distinct* suggests only that they

can be distinguished ⟨a nicety and force of touch, which is an endowment *separate* from pictorial genius, though indispensable to its exercise—*Hawthorne*⟩ ⟨the reestablishment of ethics and esthetics as *separate* and autonomous realms—*Krutch*⟩ **Separate** is also often used in preference to *distinct* when an opposition to *common* or *shared* is implied ⟨please give us *separate* rooms⟩ ⟨the children had *separate* toys and *separate* books⟩ **Several** (see also MANY) is somewhat formal or old-fashioned in this sense; it implies an existence, a character, a status, or a location separate or distinct from that of similar items. It may modify a singular noun, especially when "each" precedes, as well as a plural noun ⟨conduct these knights unto their *several* lodgings—*Shak.*⟩ ⟨each individual seeks a *sev'ral* goal—*Pope*⟩ ⟨will call the members . . . for their *several* opinions—*New Republic*⟩ ⟨a network of concrete highways upon the *several* states—*W. H. Hamilton*⟩ **Discrete**, even more than *separate*, implies that the individuals are not the same and are not connected; it is often more precise than *separate* because it stresses numerical distinctness (that is, distinctness as individuals) rather than difference in kind, nature, or goal; thus, *discrete* things may be exactly the same in appearance, nature, or value, but they are not selfsame and are physically disconnected ⟨the dumb creation lives a life made up of *discrete* and mutually irrelevant episodes—*Huxley*⟩ ⟨[the phage] has been identified as existing in *discrete* units, that is, it is a particle like granulated sugar and not a continuum like molasses—*Furnas*⟩ ⟨the conclusion that gases are made up of *discrete* units (molecules)—*Hogben*⟩
*Ana* individual, distinctive, peculiar (see CHARACTERISTIC): *single, sole, separate, particular: particular, individual, *special, especial: *different, diverse, disparate, divergent
*Con* *same, selfsame, identical
2 *evident, manifest, patent, obvious, apparent, palpable, plain, clear
*Ana* defined, prescribed (see PRESCRIBE): *explicit, definite, express, specific, categorical: perspicuous, *clear, lucid: clear-cut, *incisive, trenchant
*Ant* indistinct: nebulous —*Con* vague, *obscure, dark, enigmatic, cryptic

**distinction** difference, divergence, divergency, *dissimilarity, unlikeness
*Ant* resemblance —*Con* *likeness, similarity, analogy, similitude, affinity

**distinctive** peculiar, individual, *characteristic
*Ana* *special, particular, specific, especial: unique, particular, separate, *single: *distinct, separate, several, discrete
*Ant* typical —*Con* *common, ordinary, familiar, popular, vulgar: similar, *like, alike, identical, comparable, parallel, analogous: *same, equivalent, equal: generic, general, *universal

**distinguish** 1 Distinguish, differentiate, discriminate, demarcate are synonymous when they mean to point out or mark the differences between things that are or seem to be much alike or closely related. **Distinguish** presupposes sources of confusion; the things considered may or may not be alike, but if not alike, they are so closely connected, so indissolubly related, so open to misunderstanding that the differences must be noted or marked out if confusion is to be eradicated; hence, maturity of intellect or of judgment is implicit in the power to distinguish ⟨a child under four will hardly *distinguish* between yesterday and a week ago, or between yesterday and six hours ago—*Russell*⟩ ⟨the aesthetic and ethical spheres, in fact, were never sharply *distinguished* by the Greeks—*Dickinson*⟩ **Differ-**

**entiate** implies either the possession of a distinguishing character or characters, or more commonly capacity to ascertain differences between things susceptible of confusion ⟨we find in Chinese art a strong synthetic power, which *differentiates* it and lifts it beyond the art of Persia and the art of India—*Binyon*⟩ ⟨if poetry is art, it must produce its effects through a medium which *differentiates* it, without divorcing it, from reality—*Lowes*⟩ ⟨we must have classes small enough to enable the teacher to *differentiate* the strong and the willing from the sluggards—*Grandgent*⟩ **Discriminate** involves the idea of perception; it implies the power to perceive or discern differences, often slight differences, between things that are very much alike ⟨*discriminate* synonyms⟩ ⟨irritated by the wasp's inability to *discriminate* a house from a tree—*E. K. Brown*⟩ ⟨whenever you have learned to *discriminate* the birds, or the plants, or the geological features of a country, it is as if new and keener eyes were added—*Burroughs*⟩ ⟨to *discriminate* between true and false Aristotelianism —*Babbitt*⟩ **Demarcate** implies the setting of literal limits or the marking of literal boundaries, but it can be freely used to suggest a distinguishing between things as clear as if there were lines between them ⟨how shall we *demarcate* Reproduction from Growth?—*Lewes*⟩ ⟨only in periods when a common idea of style pervades the whole production of a people does . . . the work of the craftsman merge, with no *demarcating* difference, in the art which expresses thought and emotion—*Binyon*⟩
*Ana* *separate, part, divide: *detach, disengage
*Ant* confound —*Con* confuse, *mistake
2 *characterize, mark, qualify
*Ana* individualize, peculiarize (see corresponding adjectives at CHARACTERISTIC)
**distort** contort, warp, *deform
*Ana* twist, bend, *curve: disfigure, *deface: *injure, damage, mar, impair: misinterpret, misconstrue (see affirmative verbs at EXPLAIN)
**distract** bewilder, nonplus, confound, dumbfound, mystify, perplex, *puzzle
*Ana* *confuse, muddle, addle, fuddle, befuddle: baffle, balk (see FRUSTRATE): agitate, upset, fluster, flurry, perturb, *discompose
*Ant* collect (*one's thoughts, one's powers*)
**distraught** absentminded, absent, *abstracted, preoccupied
*Ana* distracted, bewildered, nonplused (see PUZZLE *vb*): muddled, addled, confused (see CONFUSE): agitated, perturbed, discomposed, flustered (see DISCOMPOSE)
*Ant* collected —*Con* *cool, composed, unruffled, imperturbable, unflappable, nonchalant
**distress** *n* Distress, suffering, misery, agony, dolor, passion are comparable when denoting the state of one that is in great trouble or in pain of mind or body. **Distress** commonly implies conditions or circumstances that cause physical or mental stress or strain; usually also it connotes the possibility of relief or the need of assistance ⟨to pity *distress* is human; to relieve it is Godlike—*Mann*⟩ The word is applicable to things as well as to persons; thus, a ship in *distress* is helpless and in peril because of some untoward circumstance (as a breakdown in machinery); a community's *distress* may be the result of a disaster or of an event imposing extreme hardships on the people; When used to designate a mental state, *distress* usually implies the stress or strain of fear, anxiety, or shame ⟨the original shock and *distress* that were caused by the first serious work of scholars on the Bible—*Montague*⟩ ⟨it had evidently been a great *distress* to him, to have the days of his imprisonment recalled—*Dickens*⟩ ⟨she therefore dressed exclusively in black, to her husband's vast amusement and her

mother's rumored *distress*—*Wylie*⟩ **Suffering** is used especially in reference to human beings; often it implies conscious awareness of pain or distress and conscious endurance ⟨extreme sensibility to physical *suffering* . . . characterizes modern civilization—*Inge*⟩ ⟨the losses and hardships and *sufferings* entailed by war—*Russell*⟩ **Misery** stresses the unhappy or wretched conditions attending distress or suffering; it often connotes sordidness, or dolefulness, or abjectness ⟨for bleak, unadulterated *misery* that dak bungalow was the worst . . . I had ever set foot in—*Kipling*⟩ ⟨she had . . . cheated and shamed herself . . . exchanged content for *misery* and pride for humiliation—*Bennett*⟩ **Agony** suggests suffering so intense that both body and mind are involved in a struggle to endure the unbearable ⟨fell with a scream of mortal *agony*—*Mason*⟩ ⟨the *agony* of being found wanting and exposed to the disapproval of others—*Mead*⟩ **Dolor** is a somewhat literary word applied chiefly to mental suffering that involves sorrow, somber depression, or grinding anxiety ⟨heaviness is upon them, and *dolor* thickens the air they walk through—*Frank*⟩ **Passion** is now rare in this sense except in reference to the sufferings of Jesus in the garden at Gethsemane and culminating in his crucifixion.
*Ana* affliction, *trial, tribulation: *sorrow, grief, anguish, woe, heartbreak: strait, pass, pinch, exigency (see JUNCTURE): hardship, *difficulty, rigor, vicissitude: *pain, pang, ache
*Con* comforting *or* comfort, solacing *or* solace, consolation (see corresponding verbs at COMFORT): alleviation, assuagement, mitigation, allaying, relieving *or* relief (see corresponding verbs at RELIEVE)
**distress** *vb* *trouble, ail
*Ana* *afflict, try, torment, torture, rack: *worry, annoy, harass, harry, plague, pester: *depress, oppress, weigh
*Con* *comfort, console, solace: *help, aid, assist: *relieve, alleviate, lighten, mitigate, assuage, allay
**distribute,** dispense, divide, deal, dole are comparable when they mean to give out, usually in shares, to each member of a group. **Distribute** implies either an apportioning among many by separation of something into parts, units, or amounts, and by assigning each part, unit, or amount to the proper person or place, or a scattering or spreading more or less evenly over an area ⟨distributed his possessions among his heirs⟩ ⟨*distribute* fertilizer by spreading or scattering it over a garden⟩ ⟨*distribute* profits among shareholders in the form of dividends⟩ ⟨*distribute* type by returning each piece of used type to its proper compartment in a case⟩ ⟨the old habit of centralizing a strain at one point, and then dividing and subdividing it, and *distributing* it on visible lines of support to a visible foundation—*Henry Adams*⟩ ⟨all modern societies aim . . . to *distribute* impartially to all the burdens and advantages of the state—*Dickinson*⟩ **Dispense** (see also ADMINISTER 1) differs from *distribute* in not usually implying a spreading out that affects a large number or a separation that reduces the size or amount of each part or portion; rather, it suggests the giving of a carefully weighed or measured portion to each of a group as a right or as due, or as accordant to need ⟨*dispense* alms to the needy⟩ ⟨if every just man that now pines with want had but a moderate and beseeming share . . . nature's full blessings would be well-*dispensed*—*Milton*⟩ ⟨let us . . . receive whatever good 'tis given thee to *dispense*—*Wordsworth*⟩ ⟨a pulsating, metallic, fluorescent sound, in which Olympian judgments are *dispensed* by worried word fanciers from their thirty-ninth floor cubicles—*Hilton*⟩ **Divide** (see also SEPARATE) stresses the separation of a whole into parts but it implies as the purpose of that

---

A colon (:) separates groups of words discriminated. An asterisk (*) indicates place of treatment of each group.

separation a dispensing of those parts to, or a sharing of them by, each of a group; the term usually implies, if the context gives no further information, that the parts are equal ⟨the three partners *divide* the profits of the business, the size of each share depending on the size of the partner's investment⟩ ⟨claimed that his confederates would not *divide* the booty fairly⟩ ⟨of the rent, a large proportion was *divided* among the country gentlemen— *Macaulay*⟩ ⟨if, for example, he is an evildoer, it is a great comfort to him to know that others likewise are evildoers. *Dividing* the blame lightens the load—*Over-street*⟩ **Deal** (usually followed by *out*) emphasizes the delivery of something piece by piece, or in suitable portions, especially to those who have a right to expect it ⟨*deal* the cards for a game of bridge⟩ ⟨*deal* out equipment and supplies to each soldier⟩ ⟨our fellows were very methodical about the death they were *dealing* out. They dispensed it in the firm, tranquil-seeming way of clerks— *Wolfert*⟩ Often, the term carries no suggestion of distribution, and means little more than to give or deliver ⟨*dealt* his opponent a blow⟩ ⟨should employ one special man whose sole job is to keep inventing fresh phrases of delight to be *dealt* out in regular doses to authors at work—*Dawson & Wilson*⟩ **Dole** (also frequently followed by *out*) may imply a dispensing of alms to the needy ⟨*dole* out daily one thousand loaves of bread⟩ ⟨a prince *doling* out favors to a servile group of petitioners —*Dreiser*⟩ but since in this sense it usually suggests a carefully measured portion, it often suggests scantiness or niggardliness in the amount dispensed and does not necessarily suggest a charitable intent ⟨this comfort . . . she *doled* out to him in daily portions—*Fielding*⟩ ⟨I can accept what is given in love and affection to me, but I could not accept what is *doled* out grudgingly or with conditions—*Wilde*⟩
*Ana* apportion, *allot, allocate, assign: ration, portion, parcel, prorate, *apportion: *administer, dispense
*Ant* collect (*supplies*): amass (*wealth, a fortune*) —*Con* *gather, assemble: *accumulate, hoard
**district** *locality, vicinity, neighborhood
*Ana* *area, tract, region, zone, belt: section, sector, division, parcel (see PART *n*): *field, province, territory, sphere
**distrust** *vb* **Distrust, mistrust** are comparable both as verbs meaning to lack trust or confidence in someone or something and as nouns denoting such a lack of trust or confidence. **Distrust,** however, implies far more certitude that something is wrong than *mistrust;* often it suggests conviction of another's guilt, treachery, or weakness ⟨Octavius had imbibed sufficient philosophy to *distrust* the sword as a cure for all ills—*Buchan*⟩ ⟨the same *distrust* and horror of the unnatural forms into which life for the majority of people is being forced— *Day Lewis*⟩ **Mistrust** suggests domination by suspicion and, usually, fear ⟨he took me into a place so wild that a man less accustomed to these things might have *mistrusted* and feared for his life—*Cather*⟩ ⟨something . . . roused in him a suspicion that in the near future he was not going to have matters quite so much his own way. However, he concealed his *mistrust* as well as he could —*Mackenzie*⟩
*Con* *rely, trust, depend, count, bank, reckon: confide, entrust, *commit, consign
**distrust** *n* mistrust (see under DISTRUST *vb*)
*Ana* doubt, *uncertainty, dubiety, dubiosity, suspicion: *apprehension, foreboding, misgiving, presentiment
*Con* confidence, *trust, reliance, dependence, faith
**disturb** 1 unsettle, derange, *disorder, disarrange, disorganize

*Ana* displace, *replace: shift, remove, *move: *arrest, interrupt, check: *meddle, intermeddle, interfere, tamper
*Con* settle, *set, fix, establish: regulate, *adjust: *order, arrange, organize, systematize
2 *discompose, perturb, upset, disquiet, agitate, fluster, flurry
*Ana* *frighten, alarm, terrify, scare: perplex, *puzzle, bewilder, distract: discomfit, rattle, faze, disconcert (see EMBARRASS): discommode, incommode, trouble, *inconvenience
**dither** *vb* *shake, tremble, quake, quiver, shiver, quaver, wobble, teeter, shimmy, shudder, totter
**diurnal** *daily, quotidian, circadian
*Con* see those at DAILY
**divagation** *digression, episode, excursus
**dive** *vb* *plunge, pitch
*Ana* leap, *jump, spring, bound: *move, drive, impel: *push, propel
**diverge** *swerve, veer, deviate, depart, digress
*Ana* *differ, disagree, vary: divide, part, *separate
*Ant* converge (*as paths, roads, times*): conform (*as customs, habits, practices*)
**divergence** 1 *deviation, deflection, aberration
*Ana* division, separation, parting (see corresponding verbs at SEPARATE): differing, disagreeing, varying (see DIFFER)
*Ant* convergence —*Con* agreement, concurrence, coincidence (see corresponding verbs at AGREE)
2 divergency, difference, *dissimilarity, unlikeness, distinction
*Ana* diversity, *variety
*Ant* conformity, correspondence —*Con* consonance, accord, *harmony, concord
**divergency** divergence, difference, *dissimilarity, unlikeness, distinction
*Ana, Ant, & Con* see those at DIVERGENCE 2
**divergent** *different, diverse, disparate, various
*Ana* *opposite, contradictory, contrary, antithetical
*Ant* convergent —*Con* similar, *like, parallel, identical, uniform
**divers** *many, several, sundry, various, numerous, multifarious
**diverse** *different, divergent, disparate, various
*Ana* contrasted *or* contrasting (see corresponding verb at COMPARE): contrary, *opposite, contradictory: *distinct, separate
*Ant* identical, selfsame —*Con* *same, equivalent, equal
**diversion** amusement, recreation, entertainment (see under AMUSE *vb*)
*Ana* play, sport, disport (see under PLAY *vb*): levity, frivolity (see LIGHTNESS)
**diversity** *variety
*Ana* divergence, divergency, difference, *dissimilarity, unlikeness, distinction: multifariousness (see corresponding adjective at MANY)
*Ant* uniformity: identity
**divert** 1 *turn, deflect, avert, sheer
*Ana* bend, *curve, twist: deviate, digress, diverge, *swerve, veer: *change, alter, modify
*Con* fix, *set, settle: absorb, engross, *monopolize
2 *amuse, entertain, recreate
*Ana* beguile, *while, wile, fleet: regale, delight, gladden, tickle, *please
*Con* *tire, weary, fatigue, exhaust, jade, fag
3 *dissuade, deter, discourage
*Ana* *detach, disengage, abstract
**divest** *strip, denude, bare, dismantle
*Ant* invest, vest (*in robes of office, with power or author-*

*ity*): apparel, clothe

**divide** *vb* 1 *separate, part, sever, sunder, divorce
*Ana* cleave, split, rend, rive (see TEAR): *cut, carve, chop
*Ant* unite

2 *distribute, dispense, deal, dole
*Ana* *apportion, portion, prorate, ration, parcel: *share, participate, partake: *allot, assign, allocate

**divine** *adj* *holy, sacred, spiritual, religious, blessed

**divine** *vb* *foresee, foreknow, apprehend, anticipate
*Ana* discern, perceive, descry (see SEE): predict, prophesy, prognosticate, presage (see FORETELL)

**division** section, segment, sector, *part, portion, piece, detail, member, fraction, fragment, parcel

**divorce** *vb* *separate, sever, sunder, part, divide
*Ana* alienate, *estrange, wean, disaffect

**divulge** tell, disclose, *reveal, betray, discover
*Ana* impart, *communicate: announce, *declare, publish, advertise, proclaim: blab, tattle, *gossip

**dizzy** *giddy, vertiginous, swimming, dazzled
*Ana* reeling, whirling (see REEL): confounded, bewildered, puzzled (see PUZZLE)

**docile** *obedient, biddable, tractable, amenable
*Ana* *compliant, acquiescent: pliant, pliable, adaptable (see PLASTIC): yielding, submitting *or* submissive (see corresponding verbs at YIELD)
*Ant* indocile: unruly, ungovernable —*Con* intractable, refractory, recalcitrant, willful, headstrong (see UNRULY): stubborn, *obstinate

**dock** *wharf, pier, quay, slip, berth, jetty, levee

**doctor** *vb* *adulterate, sophisticate, load, weight

**doctrinaire** dogmatic, magisterial, oracular, *dictatorial, authoritarian

**doctrine, dogma, tenet** are synonymous only when they mean a principle (usually one of a series or of a body of principles) accepted as authoritative (as by members of a church, a school of philosophers, or a branch of science). Doctrine is often used in a much broader sense to denote a formulated theory that is supported by evidence, backed by authority, and proposed for acceptance ⟨the *doctrine* of evolution⟩ ⟨Einstein's *doctrine* of relativity⟩ In the narrower sense *doctrine* retains its basic implication of authoritative teaching, but it presupposes acceptance by a body of believers or adherents ⟨a catechism of Christian *doctrines*⟩ ⟨a . . . mathematical *doctrine* of waves which nowadays has almost come to dominate . . . physics—*Darrow*⟩ Dogma also stresses authoritative teaching but unlike *doctrine* it seldom implies proposal for acceptance. A dogma is not advanced as reasonable and worthy of acceptance but laid down as true and beyond dispute ⟨the *dogmas* of a church are usually stated in a creed or confession⟩ ⟨in 1870 Pope Pius IX defined the *dogma* of papal infallibility⟩ Dogma (or especially its derivative *dogmatic*) often connotes insistence, sometimes arrogant insistence, on authority or imposition by authority ⟨the *dogma* that the king can do no wrong⟩ Tenet emphasizes acceptance and belief rather than teaching. It is therefore thought of as a principle held or adhered to and implies a body of adherents ⟨the *tenets* of modern Socialism are not in every instance identical with the doctrines of Karl Marx⟩
*Ana* teaching, instruction (see corresponding verbs at TEACH): *principle, fundamental

**document** 1 Document, monument, record, archive denote something preserved and serving as evidence (as of an event, a situation, or the thought of its time). Document commonly designates something written or printed (as a letter, a charter, a deed, a will, or a book) or something carrying an inscription (as a coin, a tombstone, or a medal) that has value as evidence because of its contemporaneousness ⟨while the poor little affairs of obscure, industrious men of letters are made the subject of intensive research, the far more romantic, thrilling, and illuminating *documents* about the seekers and makers of great fortunes, are neither gathered nor cherished—*H. G. Wells*⟩ ⟨*The Waste Land* seems to me chiefly important as a social *document*. It gives an authentic impression of the mentality of educated people in the psychological slump that took place immediately after the war—*Day Lewis*⟩ Monument is applicable to whatever serves as a memorial of the past; it is usually applied to a building, work of art, or other relic of the past, especially one that serves as a reminder (as of a country's greatness, a nation's triumphs in war, or a period's accomplishments in art) ⟨the French government has taken over many of the ancient cathedrals in order to preserve them as public *monuments*⟩ ⟨the English Church has no literary *monument* equal to that of Dante, no intellectual *monument* equal to that of St. Thomas, no devotional *monument* equal to that of St. John of the Cross—*T. S. Eliot*⟩ Record implies the intent to preserve evidence of something; it denotes matter recorded (as by writing or taping) so that exact knowledge of what has occurred will be perpetuated ⟨keep a *record* of a conversation⟩ ⟨the *records* of the trial were destroyed in a fire⟩ ⟨made six motion-picture *records* of his undersea expeditions —*Current Biog.*⟩ ⟨it is not only the right, but it is the judicial duty of the court, to examine the whole case as presented by the *record*—*Taney*⟩ Archive (see also MUSEUM) is applicable to a document or record preserved especially throughout a long period ⟨some rotten *archive*, rummaged out of some seldom-explored press—*Lamb*⟩ Its more common plural form archives suggests a miscellaneous accumulation, rather than a carefully selected collection, of records and documents ⟨the *archives* of the Vatican are now accessible to scholars⟩ ⟨the *archives* of every city—*Dryden*⟩
*Ana* *evidence, testimony

2 instrument, *paper

**dodge** *vb* Dodge, parry, sidestep, duck, shirk, fence, malinger are comparable when meaning to avoid or evade by some maneuver or shift. Dodge implies quickness of movement or a sudden evasive shift of position (as in avoiding a blow or pursuit) ⟨they ran to the Abbey, *dodged* the Baronet, armed themselves—*Meredith*⟩ ⟨he was able to *dodge* so that the man's knife went through his sleeve, wounding him only slightly—*Heiser*⟩ It may imply artfulness, or craft, or clever deceit in evading not only the attack of an enemy but similarly the thrusts of a debater, or an examiner, or the demands of an authoritative power ⟨some *dodging* casuist with more craft than sincerity—*Milton*⟩ ⟨the trouble . . . is always being *dodged* or minimized by the moralist—*Forster*⟩ ⟨dodged the issue again and again⟩ Parry does not imply dodging so much as warding off a blow and turning aside the weapon; it suggests skill and adroitness in defending oneself not only from blows with a weapon but from whatever threatens or proves awkward (as a question or demand) ⟨*parry* an argument by shifting the ground⟩ ⟨*parry* a demand for the payment of a claim by making a counterclaim⟩ ⟨I *parried* her questions by the best excuses I could offer—*Wilkie Collins*⟩ Sidestep comes very close to *dodge* in its suggestion of a quick maneuver to evade a blow or the facing of an issue; it usually suggests dexterous action in avoiding something imminent but often, on the other hand, suggests not ultimate avoidance but temporary delay or postponement ⟨the boxer neatly *sidestepped* the blow⟩ ⟨sidestep the decision

---

A colon (:) separates groups of words discriminated. An asterisk (*) indicates place of treatment of each group.

of a matter⟩ ⟨he can no longer *sidestep* the issue⟩ **Duck** implies evasion or avoidance by or as if by a sudden bending or stooping ⟨he never once *ducked* at the whiz of a cannonball—*Pope*⟩ ⟨some ministers and teachers have *ducked* the facts of life—*Bundy*⟩ ⟨the way for a reviewer to *duck* such a question—*Newsweek*⟩ **Shirk** implies evasion or avoidance by means that suggest meanness, cowardice, laziness, or sneakiness ⟨*shirked* his duty to his family⟩ ⟨*shirk* a difficult or dangerous task⟩ ⟨that is my duty and I shall not *shirk* it—*Truman*⟩ ⟨a war which must be fought out and not *shirked*—*Moberly*⟩ ⟨he had . . . *shirked* telling her that no marriage would occur that day—*Bennett*⟩ **Fence** suggests a maneuver comparable to one used in fencing; it may connote parrying, or thrusting, or guarding, but it typically implies more dexterity or more boldness in baffling inquiry than skill in warding off what is awkward ⟨*fence* skillfully on the witness stand⟩ ⟨the president showed a new capability for *fencing* with the press—*Time*⟩ **Malinger** implies, usually, a shirking (as of one's duties or a hard task) through feigning illness or weakness ⟨some were half inclined to suspect that he was, to use a military phrase, *malingering*—*Macaulay*⟩ ⟨the question whether hysteria is an unintentional device or whether it represents a process of *malingering*—*Bagby*⟩
*Ana* evade, avoid, elude, *escape: *slide, slip
*Ant* face —*Con* brave, dare, defy, beard, challenge (see FACE)

**dogged** *obstinate, pertinacious, mulish, stubborn, stiff-necked, pigheaded, bullheaded
*Ana* determined, resolved, decided (see DECIDE): tenacious (see STRONG): persevering, persistent (see corresponding verbs at PERSEVERE): resolute, steadfast (see FAITHFUL)
*Ant* faltering

**dogma** *doctrine, tenet
*Ana* belief, conviction, persuasion, view (see OPINION): *principle, fundamental

**dogmatic** magisterial, doctrinaire, oracular, *dictatorial, authoritarian
*Ana* peremptory, *masterful, imperative, imperious, domineering

**doldrums** boredom, ennui, *tedium
*Ana* dejection, depression, gloom, blues, dumps (see SADNESS)
*Ant* spirits, high spirits

**dole** *n* allowance, pittance, *ration
*Ana* apportioning *or* apportionment, parceling *or* parcel, portioning *or* portion (see corresponding verbs at APPORTION): sharing *or* share (see corresponding verb SHARE)

**dole** *vb* dispense, deal, *distribute, divide
*Ana* *apportion, ration, portion, parcel, prorate: bestow, confer, present, *give

**doleful** lugubrious, dolorous, *melancholy, plaintive, rueful
*Ana* mourning *or* mournful, sorrowing *or* sorrowful, grieving (see corresponding verbs at GRIEVE): piteous, *pitiful
*Ant* cheerful, cheery

**dolor** agony, suffering, passion, *distress, misery
*Ana* anguish, woe, *sorrow, grief: tribulation, *trial, affliction, cross, visitation
*Ant* beatitude, blessedness

**dolorous** doleful, *melancholy, plaintive, lugubrious, rueful
*Ana & Ant* see those at DOLEFUL

**domain** sphere, province, *field, territory, bailiwick
*Ana* *area, region, zone: district, *locality: jurisdiction, dominion (see POWER)

**domicile** dwelling, abode, residence, house, home, *habitation

**dominant,** predominant, paramount, preponderant, preponderating, sovereign mean superior to all others in power, influence, position, or rank. Something is **dominant** which is thought of as ruling, as commanding, or as uppermost ⟨a *dominant* race⟩ ⟨the idea of beauty and of a human nature perfect on all its sides, which is the *dominant* idea of poetry—*Arnold*⟩ ⟨I will not say that money has ceased to be the *dominant* force in American life—*Lerner*⟩ Something is **predominant** which is for the time being in the ascendant or exerts the most marked influence ⟨the power of . . . modifying a series of thoughts by some one *predominant* thought or feeling —*Coleridge*⟩ ⟨a variety of subjects . . . in which no particular one is *predominant*—*Cowper*⟩ ⟨the painter whose *predominant* aim is moral instruction—*Binyon*⟩ Something is **paramount** which has preeminence or supremacy in importance, order, rank, or jurisdiction ⟨time is of *paramount* importance—*Roosevelt*⟩ ⟨for most American newsmen the ideal of accurate and objective news reports is fundamental and *paramount*—*Mott*⟩ Something is **preponderant** or **preponderating** which outweighs or overbalances every other thing of its kind in power, influence, force, or number; these terms are commonly used without clear distinction in meaning, but *preponderating* sometimes suggests active operation ⟨the *preponderating* tendency⟩ and *preponderant* the actual effect ⟨for several years this political party has been the *preponderant* party in the affairs of the nation⟩ ⟨the *preponderant* influence of a group of banks⟩ ⟨if the net result was beneficial to the university—and this seems to be the *preponderant* opinion around Madison—it was detrimental to La Follette—*Davis*⟩ Something is **sovereign** (see also FREE) when every other comparable thing is subordinate, inferior, or of lower value; the term therefore imputes unquestioned supremacy to the thing so described ⟨the *Sovereign* Ruler of the universe⟩ ⟨the *sovereign* power in the United States of America is vested in the people⟩ ⟨a *sovereign* remedy⟩ ⟨wearing . . . an amulet *sovereign* against all passion—*Browning*⟩ ⟨promote . . . the *sovereign* good of the community—*Grote*⟩
*Ana* *prevailing, prevalent: preeminent, *supreme, transcendent, surpassing: outstanding, salient, signal (see NOTICEABLE): governing, ruling (see GOVERN)
*Ant* subordinate

**domineering** *masterful, imperious, imperative, peremptory
*Ana* arrogant, overbearing, lordly, insolent (see PROUD): magisterial, *dictatorial
*Ant* subservient —*Con* obsequious, servile (see SUBSERVIENT)

**dominion** control, command, sway, authority, jurisdiction, *power
*Ana* ascendancy, *supremacy: sovereignty (see under FREE *adj*)

**donate** present, bestow, *give, confer, afford
*Ana* *grant, accord, award

**donation,** benefaction, contribution, alms are comparable when they denote a gift of money or its equivalent for a charitable, philanthropic, or humanitarian object. **Donation** is freely used for such a gift ⟨blood *donations*⟩ ⟨seeking small *donations* for myriad worthy causes⟩ It may, however, retain in this sense some feeling of its earlier meaning of the act or right (as of a state, a ruler, or a patron) of granting or giving to a subordinate (as a subject or a client) and is, therefore, the normal term to apply to a gift of substantial value, presented more

or less publicly, and usually without reference to other givers or gifts ⟨the endowment funds of the great universities are increased mainly by *donations* and bequests⟩ ⟨a list of the Rockefeller *donations*⟩ **Benefaction** is often used in place of *donation*, especially when there is the intent to compliment the donor and to imply his benevolence or the beneficence of his gift. The latter, however, is the basic implication and the word may be appropriately used of any benefit conferred or received whether it has money value or not ⟨her *benefactions* are remembered by many philanthropic agencies⟩ ⟨the *benefactions* of the American GIs to the . . . children of Korea—*Hartford Times*⟩ ⟨this *benefaction* totals almost $5 million—*Americana Annual*⟩ **Contribution** implies participation in giving; it is applicable to small as well as large amounts of money; it is the modest term which one may apply to his own gift, though others may rightly call it a *donation* or *benefaction* ⟨please accept my *contribution* to the endowment fund of your institution⟩ ⟨a community chest *contribution*⟩ ⟨but the Government quickly came to the rescue, and, aided by private *contribution*, built a cutoff wall—*Amer. Guide Series: Minn.*⟩ **Alms** implies the aim of relieving poverty either in former times as the fulfillment of a religious obligation or as a practical manifestation of the virtue of charity ⟨the gift without the giver is bare; who gives himself with his *alms* feeds three,—himself, his hungering neighbor, and me [Christ]—*J. R. Lowell*⟩ or in more recent times as an indication of casual benevolence displayed chiefly in the giving of petty sums to beggars or paupers ⟨though poor and forced to live on *alms*—*Wordsworth*⟩ ⟨a few filthy . . . children, waiting for stray tourists, cried for an *alms*—*Harper's*⟩
*Ana* grant, subvention, *appropriation, subsidy
**doom** *n* *fate, destiny, lot, portion
**doom** *vb* damn, condemn, *sentence, proscribe
**door, gate, portal, postern, doorway, gateway** are comparable chiefly as meaning an entrance to a place. **Door** applies chiefly to the movable and usually swinging barrier which is set in the opening which serves as an entrance to a building or to a room or apartment in a building ⟨an oak *door*⟩ ⟨the front *door* of a house⟩ Sometimes *door* is used also of the opening ⟨children came running through the *door*⟩ **Gate** may apply to an opening in a wall, fence, or enclosure but it more commonly denotes a movable and often swinging barrier (especially one made of a grating or open frame or a heavy or rough structure) set in such an opening and closed or opened at will ⟨the north *gate* to the campus⟩ ⟨opening the garden *gate*⟩ **Portal** applies usually to an elaborate and stately door or gate, with its surrounding framework ⟨the *portal* to the temple⟩ ⟨the knights were admitted through the *portal* to the palace⟩ **Postern** denotes a private or retired door or gate (as at the back of a castle or fortress). **Doorway** and **gateway** apply not to the structure but to the passage when a door (in a *doorway*) or a gate (in a *gateway*) is opened for ingress or egress ⟨stand in the *doorway* awaiting the postman⟩ ⟨automobiles passed through the *gateway* in constant succession⟩
In their extended use these words are still more sharply distinguished. **Door** usually applies to what provides opportunity to enter or withdraw or makes possible an entrance or exit ⟨the love of books, the golden key that opens the enchanted *door*—*Lang*⟩ ⟨I know death hath ten thousand several *doors* for men to take their exit—*John Webster*⟩ **Gate** differs from *door* chiefly in its connotations of facility in admission or of entrance into something large, impressive, wide, or even infinite ⟨what sweet contentments doth the soul enjoy by the senses! They are the

*gates* and windows of its knowledge—*William Drummond*⟩ ⟨to wade through slaughter to a throne and shut the *gates* of mercy on mankind—*Gray*⟩ **Portal** often carries similar connotations, but it usually applies to a definite place or thing which is itself splendid or magnificent and through which something (as the sun at rising and at setting) is admitted or allowed exit ⟨Heaven, that opened wide her blazing *portals*—*Milton*⟩ ⟨since your name will grow with time . . . have I made the name a golden *portal* to my rhyme—*Tennyson*⟩ **Postern,** on the other hand, implies an inconspicuous or even a hidden means of entrance or escape ⟨it finds a readier way to our sympathy through a *postern* which we cannot help leaving sometimes on the latch, than through the ceremonious portal of classical prescription—*J. R. Lowell*⟩ **Gateway** is usually preferred to **doorway** in figurative use because it more strongly suggests a passage through which entrance is gained to something desirable or difficult ⟨the city was once more the *gateway* to half a continent—*Harold Sinclair*⟩ ⟨the senses were regarded as *gateways* or avenues of knowledge—*Dewey*⟩
*Ana* *entrance, entry, entrée, ingress, access
**doorway** *door, portal, postern, gate, gateway
**dormant** 1 quiescent, *latent, abeyant, potential
*Ana* *inactive, inert, passive, idle
*Ant* active, live
2 couchant, *prone, recumbent, supine, prostrate
**dormer** *n* *window, casement, oriel
**dotage** senility, *age, senescence
*Ant* infancy
**dote** love, relish, enjoy, fancy, *like
*Ant* loathe —*Con* abhor, abominate, detest, *hate: *despise, contemn, scorn
**doting** fond, devoted, *loving, affectionate
*Ana* infatuated, *enamored: fatuous, foolish, silly, asinine, *simple
**double** *n* understudy, stand-in, *substitute, supply, locum tenens, alternate, pinch hitter
**double-cross** delude, betray, beguile, *deceive, mislead
**double-dealing** *n* chicanery, chicane, trickery, *deception, fraud
*Ana* duplicity, dissimulation, *deceit, guile, cunning
**double entendre** equivocation, *ambiguity, tergiversation
**doubt** *n* *uncertainty, skepticism, suspicion, mistrust, dubiety, dubiosity
*Ana* dubiousness, doubtfulness, questionableness (see corresponding adjectives at DOUBTFUL): incredulity, *unbelief, disbelief
*Ant* certitude: confidence —*Con* *certainty, conviction, assurance: *trust, reliance, dependence, faith
**doubtful, dubious, problematic, questionable** are comparable when they mean not affording assurance of the worth, soundness, success, or certainty of something or someone. *Doubtful* and *dubious* are sometimes used with little distinction. **Doubtful,** however, is commonly so positive in its implication as almost to impute worthlessness, unsoundness, failure, or uncertainty to the thing in question ⟨it is *doubtful* whether the captain had ever had so much fun—*Steinbeck*⟩ **Dubious** stresses suspicion, mistrust, or hesitation (as in accepting, believing, following, or choosing); thus, a man of *doubtful* repute is by implication more distrusted than one of *dubious* repute; one who is *doubtful* of the outcome of a project has by implication better grounds for fearing its failure than one *dubious* about it, for the latter may imply mere vague suspicions and fears and little evidence ⟨a *doubtful* prospect⟩ ⟨a *dubious* transaction⟩ ⟨a *doubtful* title to an estate⟩ ⟨*dubious* friends⟩ ⟨whispers and glances were interchanged, accompanied by shrugs and *dubious*

---

A colon (:) separates groups of words discriminated. An asterisk (*) indicates place of treatment of each group.

shakes of the head—*Irving*⟩ ⟨she takes me in, telling me there's nobody there. I'm *doubtful,* but she swears she's alone—*Hammett*⟩ **Problematic** is the only one of the terms here considered that is free from a suggestion of a moral judgment or suspicion; it is especially applicable to things whose existence, meaning, fulfillment, or realization is very uncertain, sometimes so uncertain that the probabilities of truth and of falsehood or of success and of failure are nearly equal ⟨the very existence of any such individual [Homer] . . . is more than *problematic—Coleridge*⟩ ⟨excellent acoustics, always so *problematic* a quality in halls built for the hearing of music—*Wharton*⟩ ⟨publishing is now in a very *problematic* state—*Farrell*⟩ **Questionable** may imply little more than the existence of doubt respecting the thing so qualified ⟨the legality of this action is *questionable*⟩ ⟨a *questionable* theory⟩ It more commonly suggests doubt about propriety and may imply well-grounded suspicions (as of immorality, crudity, or dishonesty) that for one reason or another need to be expressed in guarded terms; thus, to say that a man is a *questionable* character is to cast a reflection on his honesty or morality; *questionable* dealings suggest underhandedness and dishonesty ⟨women of *questionable* virtue⟩ ⟨the propriety of Lydia's manners was at least *questionable—Shaw*⟩ ⟨the illustration is *questionable,* but the notion implied may be sound—*Alexander*⟩
*Ana* distrusting *or* distrustful, mistrusting *or* mistrustful (see corresponding verbs at DISTRUST): *fearful, apprehensive, afraid
*Ant* cocksure, positive

**dough,** **batter, paste** are quasi-synonyms often confused in their modern cookery senses. All denote a mixture of flour, liquid, salt, and supplementary ingredients, but each suggests a difference both in consistency as a result of the variety and proportion of ingredients and in use. **Dough** applies to a mixture with only enough liquid in relation to the flour to bind the ingredients while leaving the mixture sufficiently stiff to knead or to shape before baking. Ordinarily other ingredients (as a leavening agent, fat, and sugar) are included to improve the texture, flavor, and nutritive qualities of the ultimate product which includes such items as bread, biscuit, rolls, and some kinds of cake and cookies. **Batter** applies to a thinner mass in which the proportion of liquid is much greater than in dough; characteristically, also, it contains eggs, and often baking powder, sugar, and fat. It may be used for cakes that are shaped by the pan in which they are baked or for those that are poured in small amounts on a hot griddle or pan and quickly cooked. *Batter* also designates a similar mixture of flour, liquid, and eggs into which raw food (as fish or oysters) are dipped before frying in hot fat. **Paste** applies to a mixture like *dough* in its stiffness and in its admitting of being rolled and shaped but differs in implying the use of a large proportion of fat and a very small proportion of liquid; it names, therefore, the mixture out of which pastries (as pies and tarts) are made.

**doughty** *brave, courageous, unafraid, fearless, intrepid, valiant, valorous, dauntless, undaunted, bold, audacious
*Ana* venturesome, *adventurous, daring

**dour** saturnine, glum, gloomy, *sullen, morose, surly, sulky, crabbed
*Ana* *severe, stern, austere: rigorous, strict, *rigid: *grim, implacable

**dowdy** *slatternly, frowzy, blowsy
*Ana* slovenly, *slipshod, unkempt, disheveled, sloppy
*Ant* smart (*in dress, appearance*) —*Con* fashionable, *stylish, modish, chic: flashy, *gaudy, garish

**dower** *vb* **Dower, endow, endue** are comparable when meaning to furnish or provide with a gift. **Dower** specifically denotes the provision of the dowry which a woman brings to a husband in marriage ⟨a well-*dowered* bride⟩ It may also imply the bestowal of a gift, talent, or good quality ⟨poets *dowered* with genius⟩ ⟨nature had so richly *dowered* him—*Symonds*⟩ **Endow** in its basic sense implies the bestowing of money or property on a person or institution for its support or maintenance ⟨with all my worldly goods I thee *endow—Book of Common Prayer*⟩ ⟨erect and *endow* a hospital⟩ ⟨a large bequest sufficient to *endow* the new college⟩ Like *dower* it may be extended to the giving of any good thing, often with a suggestion of enhancing or enriching the recipient ⟨Shakespeare took these words . . . and *endowed* them with new significance—*Kilby*⟩ ⟨a fascinating woman *endowed* with every grace⟩ **Endue** may mean to clothe or invest with something (as a garment, a dignity, a right, or a possession) ⟨a loose gown . . . such as elderly gentlemen loved to *endue* themselves with—*Hawthorne*⟩ ⟨to make him a citizen of the United States, and *endue* him with the full rights of citizenship—*Taney*⟩ ⟨a new and penetrating light descends on the spectacle, *enduing* men and things with a seeming transparency—*Hardy*⟩ *Endue* has become so confused with *endow* in its extended sense of to bestow upon one a faculty, power, or other spiritual or mental gift that it is difficult to trace any differences in meaning between the two words. But *endow* in precise use usually implies a permanent enriching, and *endue* an investing or clothing (either temporarily or permanently) with a specific quality or character ⟨those who are the most richly *endowed* by nature, and accomplished by their own industry—*Spectator*⟩ ⟨finer faculties with which the continued process of evolution may yet *endow* the race—*Montague*⟩ ⟨the Revolution awakened it [French democracy] into consciousness . . . and *endued* it with efficient force—*Brownell*⟩
*Ana* *furnish, equip, outfit, appoint, accouter

**downcast,** **dispirited, dejected, depressed, disconsolate, woebegone** mean affected by or showing very low spirits. **Downcast** implies a being overcome by shame, mortification, or loss of hope or confidence; it usually suggests an inability to face others or an utter lack of cheerfulness ⟨his abstraction, and *downcast,* but not melancholy, air—*Meredith*⟩ ⟨she comes into the room very determinedly: the two men, perplexed and *downcast,* following her—*Shaw*⟩ **Dispirited** implies extreme low-spiritedness occasioned by failure to accomplish or to get what one wants or to achieve what one wishes to attain; it usually implies discouragement or a being disheartened ⟨he, *dispirited,* left the talking all to her—*Meredith*⟩ ⟨*dispirited* by their futile efforts—*Grandgent*⟩ ⟨sick and *dispirited,* he gave up his Arabian plan and started on the return voyage to Italy—*Buchan*⟩ **Dejected** implies greater prostration of the spirits than either *downcast* or *dispirited* with sudden but often temporary loss of hope, courage, or vigor ⟨Catherine took up her work directly, saying, in a *dejected* voice, that her head did not run upon Bath—much—*Austen*⟩ ⟨I may, as I lie on the sand, be happy, *dejected,* in vacant or in pensive mood —*Lowes*⟩ **Depressed** suggests a sinking under a heavy weight or a burden too great to be borne; it may express a temporary or a chronic mood or reaction and may, unlike the other terms of this group, indicate a serious inability to be normally active and happy ⟨*depressed* by his failures to the point of suicide⟩ ⟨my spirits have been more *depressed* than is common, even with me —*Cowper*⟩ ⟨when nothing happens they become sad and *depressed—Anderson*⟩ **Disconsolate** fundamentally implies comfortlessness and carries a strong suggestion

of being inconsolable or exceptionally uncomfortable; it may sometimes suggest no more than a frame of mind in which depression and disappointment are associated with discomfort or grief ⟨the Jews sat *disconsolate* on the poop; they complained much of the cold they had suffered in their exposed situation—*Borrow*⟩ ⟨Adrian hurried after Richard in an extremely *disconsolate* state of mind. Not to be at the breakfast and see the best of the fun, disgusted him—*Meredith*⟩ **Woebegone** usually suggests a frame of mind but it emphasizes the impression of dejection and defeat produced on an observer not only by the facial expression and posture of the one observed but also by his surroundings or quarters: it may imply dejection, depression, or merely discouragement in the persons affected or desolation or dilapidation in their surroundings, but the overall impression is that of a defeated, spiritless condition ⟨it was the most *woebegone* farm I had ever seen⟩ ⟨the *woebegone* expression on the countenances of the little children⟩ ⟨a poor mendicant approached, old and *woebegone*—*Lockhart*⟩
*Ana* weighed down, oppressed (see DEPRESS): distressed, troubled (see TROUBLE *vb*): *despondent, forlorn
*Ant* elated —*Con* cheerful, happy, joyous (see GLAD)
**downright** *adj* also *adv* *forthright
*Ana* blunt, *bluff, brusque, curt: candid, plain, open, *frank: *straightforward, aboveboard
*Con* devious, oblique, *crooked
**doze** *vb* drowse, snooze, slumber, nap, catnap
**draft** *n* outline, diagram, sketch, delineation, tracing, plot, blueprint (see under SKETCH *vb*)
**draft** *vb* outline, diagram, *sketch, delineate, trace, plot, blueprint
**drag** *vb* draw, *pull, haul, hale, tug, tow
*Con* *push, shove, thrust, propel: drive, impel, *move
**drain** *vb* *deplete, exhaust, impoverish, bankrupt
*Ana* sap, undermine, debilitate, *weaken
**dramatic,** theatrical, dramaturgic, melodramatic, histrionic are not close synonyms although all imply special reference to plays as performed by actors or to the effects which are produced by acted plays. **Dramatic** basically denotes relationship to the drama as written or as produced ⟨a *dramatic* critic⟩ ⟨a *dramatic* performance⟩ It may imply an effect or a combination of effects appropriate to the drama (as a stirring of the imagination and emotions by vivid and expressive action, speech, and gesture, or by the exciting complications of a plot) ⟨the *dramatic* appeal of a great orator⟩ ⟨the *dramatic* storytelling . . . of incidents which have a sympathetic hero—*Russell*⟩ ⟨an idyll of Theocritus . . . is today as much alive as the most *dramatic* passages of the *Iliad*—stirs the reader's feeling quite as much—*Cather*⟩ **Theatrical** denotes relationship to the theater ⟨a *theatrical* office⟩ ⟨a *theatrical* agent⟩ It may imply effects appropriate to the theater as the place where plays are produced, and to the demands which its limitations, its convention, and, often, its need of financial success make both upon a play and its performance; the term therefore usually implies a marked degree of artificiality or conventionality, a direct and sometimes a blatant appeal to the senses and emotions, and often an overdoing or exaggeration in gesture, in speech, or in action ⟨the situations are in the most effective sense *theatrical,* without being in the profounder sense dramatic—*T. S. Eliot*⟩ ⟨he had already learned that with this people religion was necessarily *theatrical*—*Cather*⟩ **Dramaturgic,** which stresses the technical aspects of the drama and its presentation, may be used in place of *theatrical* when the more or less derogatory connotations of that word are to be avoided and the emphasis is upon those elements in a play which fit it for repre-

sentation in a theater ⟨poetic plays are often lacking in *dramaturgic* quality⟩ ⟨a play that is said to be "good theater" is both dramatic and *dramaturgic* in its character⟩ ⟨every *dramaturgic* practice that subordinates the words to any other medium has trivialized the drama —*Bentley*⟩ **Melodramatic** implies a manner characteristic of melodrama; it, therefore, usually connotes exaggerated emotionalism or inappropriate theatricalism ⟨make a *melodramatic* speech⟩ ⟨employ *melodramatic* gestures⟩ ⟨for the first time in his centuries of debate with the Tozers, he was *melodramatic*. He shook his fist under Bert's nose—*Sinclair Lewis*⟩ ⟨but suppose . . . the most lurid or *melodramatic* solution you like. Suppose the servant really killed the master—*Chesterton*⟩ **Histrionic** is more limited than *theatrical* for it implies reference to the tones of voice, gestures, movements, and appearance characteristic of actors, especially in times before realism was attempted in dramatic performances ⟨good looks are more desired than *histrionic* skill—*Shaw*⟩ ⟨a tall, *histrionic,* dark man with a tossing mane—*S. E. White*⟩
**dramaturgic** theatrical, *dramatic, histrionic, melodramatic
**draw** *vb* drag, *pull, tug, tow, haul, hale
*Ana* *bring, fetch: *attract, allure: *lure, entice: extract, elicit, evoke, *educe
*Con* see those at DRAG
**draw** *n* Draw, tie, stalemate, deadlock, standoff mean an indecisive ending to a contest or competition or a contest or competition ending indecisively. **Draw** usually implies equally matched contestants who compete (as in fighting, performing, or playing) with equal skill and between whom there can be no clear decision as to the superiority of one or the other ⟨the prizefight ended in a *draw*⟩ ⟨the chess match was a *draw*⟩ **Tie** implies a numerical equality (as in the scores attained by competitors or contestants, or in the votes obtained by candidates for office); usually a tie does not remain indecisive, since provisions are often made (as by law or by the rules of a game) for reaching a decision when a tie occurs ⟨there was a *tie* between the two candidates for governor, which was decided by a vote of the legislature⟩ ⟨when a contest ends in a *tie,* a further match is often played to determine the winner⟩ **Stalemate** is fundamentally a term of chess which designates the position of a player when his king, although not in check, cannot be moved without being placed in check and the game is thereby drawn; in extended use, *stalemate* represents a condition from which neither contestant can derive an advantage ⟨was advised to cut his losses by withdrawing . . . but refused, and expended much precious material there in a costly *stalemate*—*D. N. Rowe*⟩ ⟨they believed that they could hold the triumvirs to a *stalemate* till hunger or sedition broke down their armies—*Buchan*⟩ **Deadlock** implies a counteraction or neutralization of the efforts of contending elements (as parties, forces, or factions) that leads to a stoppage of action; it connotes an immobilization because of the equal power of the opposing elements usually in a situation other than a formal competition or contest ⟨it often happens that one party has a majority in the Senate, another party in the House, and then . . . a *deadlock* results—*Bryce*⟩ ⟨so the *deadlock* continues, and neither side is prepared to yield—*Blanshard*⟩ **Standoff** is an informal term usually for a draw or tie but sometimes for a situation where two opponents counteract or neutralize each other, so evenly are they matched ⟨they fought several hours to a *standoff*⟩ ⟨the availability of the bomb to the two greatest powers may mean a *standoff* as far as atomic war is concerned—*Atlantic*⟩

A colon (:) separates groups of words discriminated. An asterisk (*) indicates place of treatment of each group.

⟨a *standoff* between the Communist party and the Army, a sort of uneasy truce with each watching the other carefully—*W. L. Ryan*⟩

**drawback** *disadvantage, detriment, handicap
*Ana* *evil, ill: inconvenience, trouble (see INCONVENIENCE): obstruction, hindrance (see corresponding verbs at HINDER)

**dread** *n* *fear, horror, terror, fright, alarm, trepidation, panic, consternation, dismay
*Ana* *apprehension, foreboding, misgiving, presentiment: timidity, timorousness (see corresponding adjectives at TIMID)

**dreadful** horrible, horrific, appalling, *fearful, awful, frightful, terrible, terrific, shocking

**dream** *n* *fancy, fantasy, phantasy, phantasm, vision, daydream, nightmare
*Ana* *delusion, illusion, hallucination

**dreary** 1 *dismal, cheerless, dispiriting, bleak, desolate
*Ana* discouraging, disheartening (see DISCOURAGE): barren, *bare: forlorn, hopeless (see DESPONDENT)
2 *dull, humdrum, monotonous, pedestrian, stodgy
*Ana* *irksome, tiresome, wearisome, tedious, boring: fatiguing, exhausting, fagging, tiring (see TIRE *vb*)

**dregs** sediment, *deposit, precipitate, lees, grounds

**drench** *soak, saturate, sop, steep, impregnate, waterlog
*Ana* *permeate, pervade, penetrate, impenetrate

**dress** *vb* *clothe, attire, apparel, array, robe
*Ant* undress

**dress** *n* *clothes, clothing, attire, apparel, raiment

**drift** *n* trend, *tendency, tenor
*Ana* *flow, stream, current: movement, *motion, progression, *progress: *intention, purpose, end, objective, goal, intent, aim

**drill** *vb* 1 bore, *perforate, punch, puncture, prick
*Ana* pierce, penetrate, *enter, probe
2 *practice, exercise
*Ana* train, discipline, *teach, instruct, school: *habituate, accustom

**drill** *n* practice, exercise (see under PRACTICE *vb*)

**drive** *vb* 1 impel, *move, actuate
*Ana* *push, shove, propel: compel, *force, coerce: *incite, instigate
*Con* *restrain, curb, check, inhibit: lead, *guide, pilot, steer
2 *ride

**drive** *n* 1 ride (see under RIDE *vb*)
2 *vigor, vim, spirit, dash, esprit, verve, punch, élan
*Ana* *power, force, energy, strength, might: impetus, momentum, *speed, velocity

**drivel** *nonsense, twaddle, bunk, balderdash, poppycock, gobbledygook, trash, rot, bull
*Ana* *gibberish, mummery, abracadabra

**droll** *laughable, risible, comic, comical, funny, ludicrous, ridiculous, farcical
*Ana* amusing, diverting, entertaining (see AMUSE): absurd, preposterous (see FOOLISH): humorous, *witty, facetious

**droop** *vb* Droop, wilt, flag, sag are comparable when they mean to sink or to lose in vigor, firmness, or freshness. Droop stresses a hanging or bending downward (as through exhaustion, discouragement, or lack of nourishment) ⟨some of the watchers were *drooping* from weariness—*Cather*⟩ ⟨he sat down heavily, his shoulders *drooping,* his arms falling between his outspread legs —*Caldwell*⟩ In extended use it implies a languishing or a subsiding of something previously thriving or flourishing ⟨oh, ye so fiercely tended, ye little seeds of hate! I bent above your growing early and noon and late, yet are ye *drooped* and pitiful,—I cannot rear ye straight!—*Millay*⟩

Wilt applies especially to plants and suggests a loss of freshness or firmness in flower, leaves, or stems through lack of water or through excessive heat ⟨most cut flowers *wilt* quickly unless given plenty of fresh water⟩ The term often may be extended to various things that grow flaccid or weak in response to some stress (as fear, exhaustion, boredom, or a physical agent) ⟨collars *wilted* in the damp heat⟩ ⟨the witness *wilted* under the cross-examiner's sarcasm⟩ ⟨nor did I ever see the nation droop and *wilt* as we saw it wither under the panic of 1907—*White*⟩ ⟨the romance . . . blossomed for six or seven months and then *wilted*—*Commins*⟩ Flag may be used of flexible things that hang loosely and limply and, with reference to plants, may be interchangeable with *droop* ⟨leaves *flagging* in the heat⟩; more often it is used of something that loses in vigor or in force so that it suggests dullness, weariness, or languor ⟨the conversation *flagged*⟩ ⟨*Tristan and Isolde;* it's wonderful beyond words—a sustained ecstasy of love that never *flags* or grows monotonous—*Ellis*⟩ This effect of wearying or boring may be attributed not to the thing which drops in interest or stimulating power but to the energy, spirits, interest, or attention that are concentrated on that thing ⟨for a couple of hours he wrote with energy, and then his energy *flagged*—*H. G. Wells*⟩ ⟨these devices succeed . . . in stimulating our interest afresh just at the moment when it was about to *flag*—*T. S. Eliot*⟩ Sag implies a sinking or subsiding, especially at one point, through undue weight, pressure, or improper distribution of stresses ⟨the ceiling shows signs of *sagging*⟩ ⟨the bridge *sagged* under the weight of the truck⟩ In extended uses it implies a loss of firmness, resiliency, or power to stand up against pressure, and a consequent drooping or decline ⟨though it *sags* in the middle, the novel is readable throughout—*Havighurst*⟩ ⟨his heart *sagged* with disappointment—*Mason*⟩ ⟨prices on the market *sagged*⟩
*Ana* sink, slump, subside, *fall, drop: languish (see languishing under LANGUID): *wither, shrivel, wizen

**drop** *vb* 1 *fall, sink, slump, subside
*Ana* *descend, dismount: *lapse, relapse, backslide: slip, *slide: expire, elapse (see PASS)
*Ant* mount
2 *dismiss, discharge, cashier, sack, fire, bounce

**drowse** doze, snooze, *sleep, slumber, nap, catnap

**drowsy** *sleepy, somnolent, slumberous
*Ana* comatose, *lethargic, sluggish, torpid
*Con* alert, vigilant, *watchful: *active, live, dynamic: animated, *lively, vivacious

**drudgery** toil, travail, labor, *work, grind
*Ana* exertion, *effort, pains, trouble

**drug** *n* Drug, medicinal, pharmaceutical, biologic, simple are comparable when they denote a substance used by itself or in a mixture with other substances for the treatment of or in the diagnosis of disease. Drug is the ordinary comprehensive term in both general and professional use for such a substance, whether of plant, animal, or mineral origin, or produced synthetically, and in its broadest use denotes any substance used as a medicine or in making medicines. Especially in technical use the term also has certain more specific uses; sometimes it may denote a medicinal substance recognized in an official pharmacopoeia or formulary as distinguished from one used in folk medicine or proprietary remedies; even more specifically it may denote a narcotic and especially an addictive narcotic substance. Medicinal is interchangeable with *drug* in the latter's comprehensive sense and is often preferred, especially in commerce, in manufacture, and in law where indication of the ultimate use of the substance is for one reason or another desirable

⟨exports of *medicinals* to China⟩ ⟨*medicinals* are not contraband⟩ **Pharmaceutical** is also often preferred to *drug* by pharmacists and manufacturers, especially as a designation of drugs (as quinine, cod-liver oil, and aspirin) which are commercially refined or prepared or synthetically manufactured. The term is also used to distinguish strictly therapeutic substances from other substances of similar origin or composition ⟨the company produces *pharmaceuticals,* dyes, and cosmetics⟩ **Biologic** is the increasingly frequent designation for a therapeutic product (as a globulin, serum, vaccine, or antibody) that is ultimately a product of living organisms. **Simple** usually denotes a plant product used for its real or fancied medicinal value especially in primitive or folk medicine ⟨boneset, tansy, and other homely *simples*⟩ It may also be used of a plant drug or medicinal preparation containing only one active ingredient.
*Ana* medicine, medicament, medication, *remedy, physic, specific, cure

**druggist,** pharmacist, apothecary, chemist denote one who deals in medicinal drugs. **Druggist** is the broadest of these terms and may designate a seller of drugs or medicinal preparations at wholesale or retail and as owner, manager, or employee of the sales establishment; it may often replace the more precise **pharmacist** to denote one who is skilled in compounding drugs and dispensing medicines prescribed by a physician especially when he is thought of primarily as selling these. *Pharmacist,* however, specifically implies, as *druggist* does not, special training in pharmacy, professional standing, and usually licensing following a test of qualifications. **Apothecary** in early use was distinguished from *druggist,* which then designated one who sold crude drugs (as herbs, roots, and other ingredients of medicines) while *apothecary* designated one who compounded these ingredients or made them up into medicines and was, therefore, equivalent to *pharmacist.* The distinction has tended to disappear and *apothecary* may be interchangeable with either *druggist* or *pharmacist* although it is increasingly rare except in historical situations. In England **chemist** is the popular or commercial equivalent of *druggist.*

**drunk,** drunken, intoxicated, inebriated, tipsy, tight are comparable when they mean being conspicuously under the influence of intoxicating liquor. **Drunk** and **drunken** are the plainspoken, direct, and inclusive terms ⟨*drunk* as a fiddler⟩ ⟨*drunk* as a lord⟩ ⟨dead *drunk*⟩ ⟨I have seen Sheridan *drunk,* too, with all the world; but his intoxication was that of Bacchus, and Porson's that of Silenus—*Byron*⟩ **Drunk** and *drunken* differ in that *drunk* is commonly used predicatively, while *drunken* is chiefly attributive ⟨front yards littered with empty bottles, and three *drunken* boys sprawling on the grass —*Glasgow*⟩ **Drunken** frequently suggests habitual drinking to excess; it also applies to whatever pertains to or proceeds from intoxication ⟨Stephano, my *drunken* butler —*Shak.*⟩ ⟨a *drunken* brawl⟩ **Intoxicated** may be exactly synonymous with *drunk,* though it is generally felt to be a less offensive term and has thus come to be applied often to a person but slightly under the influence of liquor ⟨my friend requested me to add, that he was firmly persuaded you were *intoxicated* during a portion of the evening, and possibly unconscious of the extent of the insult you were guilty of—*Dickens*⟩ **Inebriated** implies such a state of intoxication that exhilaration or undue excitement results ⟨*inebriated* revelers⟩ All these words are used in a figurative sense as implying excess of emotion ⟨*drunk* with joy⟩ ⟨*drunk* with divine enthusiasm—*Shelley*⟩ ⟨Spinoza saw no recalcitrancy in the face of

the universe and this led Novalis to characterize him as the God-*intoxicated*—*Ginnetti*⟩ ⟨*intoxicated* poetry, difficult and dense but flashing sparks of overwhelming insight—*Time*⟩ ⟨a sweet *inebriated* ecstasy—*Crashaw*⟩ **Tipsy** implies a degree of intoxication that deprives one of muscular or sometimes of mental control ⟨drinking steadily, until just manageably *tipsy,* he contrived to continue so—*Melville*⟩ **Tight** usually implies obvious intoxication, but does not suggest loss of power over one's muscles ⟨he was *tight,* and, as was characteristic of him, he soon dropped any professional discretion that he might have been supposed to exercise—*Edmund Wilson*⟩
*Ana* fuddled, befuddled, confused (see CONFUSE): maudlin, soppy (see SENTIMENTAL)
*Ant* sober

**drunkard,** inebriate, alcoholic, dipsomaniac, sot, soak, toper, tosspot, tippler designate one who drinks to excess. **Drunkard** and **inebriate** suggest the habitude of intoxication but in themselves imply nothing about the causes or effects of such intoxication. **Alcoholic** and *dipsomaniac* both denote a person with defective ability to control his use of intoxicants. In technical usage **alcoholic** is the usual term and often specifically distinguishes the person physically and mentally impaired by compulsive drinking; in more general and often distinctly derogatory use it may approach *drunkard* and *inebriate* but normally carries at least some suggestion of loss of control. **Dipsomaniac,** once nearly coextensive with *alcoholic,* is now little used except to denote a person subject to periodic bouts of compulsive drinking. **Sot** and **soak** are closely comparable in implying excessive and habitual drinking. **Sot** in addition suggests the dulling of faculties and degradation of habits that accompany such drinking. **Soak,** on the other hand, may stress a spongelike capacity for intoxicants and even carry a hint of wry admiration; like the next two terms but unlike *sot* it may be used as a casual or even friendly epithet without connoting any strong disparagement. *Toper, tosspot,* and *tippler* all imply habitual drinking but carry no inherent implication of intoxication. **Toper** and **tosspot** commonly stress the conviviality and jovialness of group drinking (as in taverns and bars) and may suggest a capacity for heavy drinking without obvious intoxication. **Tippler** carries the idea of light but constant and often secret drinking.
*Ant* teetotaler

**drunken** *drunk, intoxicated, inebriated, tipsy, tight
*Ana & Ant* see those at DRUNK

**dry** adj 1 Dry, arid mean devoid of moisture. **Dry** may suggest freedom from noticeable moisture either as a characteristic or as a desirable state ⟨a *dry* climate⟩ ⟨*dry* clothing⟩ ⟨*dry* land⟩ ⟨*dry* provisions⟩ ⟨*dry* floors⟩ or it may suggest deficiency of moisture or the lack of normal or necessary moisture ⟨*dry* soil⟩ ⟨a *dry* summer⟩ ⟨*dry* seedy berries⟩ or, again, it may suggest exhaustion or dissipation of water or other liquid ⟨a *dry* fountain pen⟩ ⟨*dry* pond⟩ ⟨*dry* well⟩ ⟨*dry* bones⟩ **Arid** implies destitution or deprivation of moisture and therefore extreme rather than relative dryness. In its chief applications to regions or territory, it suggests waste or desert land ⟨*arid* sections of the southwestern United States⟩ ⟨*arid* plains⟩ ⟨an *arid* condition of soil⟩ In extended use, as applied to such matters as subjects, books, or sermons, *dry* suggests the lack of qualities which compel interest or attention ⟨the course is *dry* but useful⟩ ⟨in the *driest* passages of her historical summaries these delightful descriptions come running to the rescue—*Payne*⟩ **Arid,** on the other hand, connotes absence of all qualities which mark the thing so

---

A colon (:) separates groups of words discriminated. An asterisk (*) indicates place of treatment of each group.

qualified as worthwhile, fruitful, or significant ⟨an *arid* treatise on poetry⟩ ⟨the frank elucidation of such a principle . . . might imply only bleak and *arid* results—*Holbrook Jackson*⟩ As applied to persons, their manner, or their words and expressions, *dry* implies a loss of normal or often of youthful human warmth, freshness, responsiveness, or enthusiasm; *arid*, an absence of these qualities or an incapacity for them ⟨his *dry* schoolmaster temperament, the hurdy-gurdy monotony of him—*James*⟩ ⟨some *arid* matron made her rounds at dawn sniffing, peering, causing blue-nosed maids to scour—*Woolf*⟩ Specifically, *dry* often suggests the repression of feeling for the sake of outwardly appearing aloof or imperturbed ⟨a *dry* comic style⟩ ⟨comments which did not seem to be censures because uttered in a *dry* tone of voice⟩ *Arid*, on the other hand, often connotes a deadening of feeling, especially as shown by a loss of fervor or hope ⟨if Shakespeare himself ever had that "dark period" . . . it was at least no darkness like that bleak and *arid* despair which sometimes settles over modern spirits —*Krutch*⟩
*Ana* barren, *bare, bald: dehydrated, desiccated, dried, parched, baked (see DRY *vb*): drained, depleted, exhausted, impoverished (see DEPLETE): sapped (see WEAKEN)
*Ant* wet —*Con* damp, moist, humid, dank (see WET): *tender, sympathetic, warm, responsive: exuberant, lush, luxuriant, prodigal, *profuse
2 *sour, acid, acidulous, tart
*Ant* sweet (*wine*)
**dry** *vb* Dry, desiccate, dehydrate, bake, parch are comparable when meaning to treat or to affect so as to deprive of moisture. Dry is the comprehensive word and may be used whatever the process (as evaporation, absorption, or solidification) or method (as heating, draining, or aerating) by which the result is attained ⟨clothes *dried* in the wind⟩ ⟨*dry* up a ditch⟩ ⟨*dry* dishes with a towel⟩ ⟨*dry* bricks in a kiln⟩ Desiccate is narrower in its range of reference and implies a complete deprivation of moisture, especially of vital juices, and often therefore, in its common extended use, a withering or shriveling. It is applicable to animal and vegetable products preserved by thorough drying ⟨*desiccated* fish⟩ or it may be applied to persons or to their attitudes, activities, or expression which have lost all their spiritual or emotional freshness or vitality ⟨analysis is *desiccating* and takes the bloom off things—*Babbitt*⟩ ⟨they were all . . . living on the edge of their nerves, a harsh, angular, *desiccated* existence— *Brooks*⟩ Dehydrate implies extraction or elimination of water; it is often preferred to *desiccate*, of which it is a close synonym, when the reference is to foods ⟨*dehydrate* vegetables⟩ It is the usual word when the removal of water (or hydrogen and oxygen in the proportion to form water) is by chemical rather than physical means ⟨*dehydrated* alums⟩ and in extended use suggests a removal of what strengthens, inspires, or makes meaningful or pleasing ⟨touches nothing that he does not *dehydrate*— *Economist*⟩ Bake implies not only dehydrating by means of heat, but a hardening or caking of what is dried ⟨sun-*baked* earth⟩ ⟨*bake* bricks⟩ Parch stresses the damaging effect of drying by intense heat or drought; it is preferred to *bake*, therefore, when the restoration of the proper amount of water is necessary or highly desirable ⟨a *parched* throat⟩ ⟨record heat waves which have *parched* mid-America's usually productive plains—*N. Y. Times Mag.*⟩
*Ana* drain, *deplete, exhaust: *wither, shrivel, wizen
*Ant* moisten, wet
**dubiety** *uncertainty, dubiosity, doubt, skepticism, suspicion, mistrust

*Ana* *hesitation, hesitancy: wavering, vacillation, faltering (see corresponding verbs at HESITATE)
*Ant* decision —*Con* *certainty, certitude, assurance, conviction: decisiveness, decidedness (see corresponding adjectives at DECIDED)
**dubiosity** dubiety, *uncertainty, doubt, skepticism, suspicion, mistrust
*Ana* confusion, muddlement, addlement (see corresponding verbs at CONFUSE): wavering, vacillation, faltering, hesitation (see corresponding verbs at HESITATE)
*Ant* decidedness —*Con* assurance, certitude, *certainty: cocksureness, positiveness (see corresponding adjectives at SURE)
**dubious** *doubtful, questionable, problematic
*Ana* suspicious, skeptical, mistrustful, uncertain (see corresponding nouns at UNCERTAINTY): hesitant, reluctant, *disinclined
*Ant* cocksure (*state of mind, opinion*): reliable (*of things in general*): trustworthy (*of persons*) —*Con* dependable, trusty, tried (see RELIABLE): *sure, certain, positive
**duck** *vb* 1 *dip, immerse, submerge, souse, dunk
2 *dodge, parry, shirk, sidestep, fence, malinger
*Ana* avoid, elude, shun, evade (see ESCAPE): avert, ward, *prevent
*Con* *face, brave, challenge, dare, defy, beard
**duct** *channel, canal, conduit, aqueduct
**ductile** *plastic, pliable, pliant, malleable, adaptable
*Ana* tractable, amenable (see OBEDIENT): responsive (see TENDER): yielding, submitting (see YIELD): fluid, *liquid: flexible, *elastic, resilient
*Con* refractory, intractable (see UNRULY): rigid, *stiff, inflexible: obdurate, *inflexible, adamant
**dude** *fop, dandy, beau, coxcomb, exquisite, buck
**dudgeon** umbrage, huff, pique, resentment, *offense
*Ana* *anger, indignation, wrath, rage, fury, ire: temper, humor, *mood
**due** *adj* Due, rightful, condign are comparable when they mean being in accordance with what is just and appropriate. Due, which basically means owed or owing as a debt, carries over in the sense here considered a strong implication that the thing so described is grounded upon an obligation, duty, or debt which should not or cannot be ignored; thus, one who takes *due* precautions uses the care that is required by his obligation to look out for his own or for others' safety or well-being; one who has a *due* sense of another person's rights accords to that person all that belongs to him by natural or moral right; one who has *due* respect for the law observes the individual laws as the duty of a responsible citizen. Often the term implies little more than an accordance with what is right, reasonable, or necessary ⟨the *due* relation of one thing with another—*Galsworthy*⟩ ⟨your *due* and proper portion— *Meredith*⟩ ⟨many noncommissioned officers have a firm belief that without a *due* admixture of curses, an order is inaudible to a private—*Montague*⟩ Rightful carries a much stronger and more consistent implication than *due* of a ground in right and justice, and usually suggests a moral or legal claim ⟨the *rightful* heir to the estate⟩ ⟨possess the *rightful* authority⟩ ⟨looked askance, jealous of an encroacher on his *rightful* domain—*Hawthorne*⟩ ⟨the disloyal subject who had fought against his *rightful* sovereign—*Macaulay*⟩ Condign applies to something that is distinctly deserved or merited and usually something that neither exceeds nor falls below one's deserts or merits; the term is used chiefly of punishment, often with the implication of severity ⟨he had been brought to *condign* punishment as a traitor—*Macaulay*⟩ ⟨the particular troubles which involved Messrs. Buecheler and Vahlen in such *condign* castigation—*Housman*⟩ ⟨con-

*dign* punishments set up for violations of the rules of control—*Baruch*⟩
*Ana* appropriate, meet, suitable, *fit, fitting, proper: right, *good: just, *fair, equitable
*Con* *excessive, inordinate, immoderate, extravagant, exorbitant: *deficient
**due** *n* **Due, desert, merit** are comparable when they mean what is justly owed to a person (sometimes a thing), especially as a recompense or compensation. **Due** usually implies a legal or moral right on the part of the person or thing that makes the claim or is in a position to make the claim and suggests a determination of what is owed by strict justice ⟨more is thy *due* than more than all can pay —*Shak.*⟩ ⟨carve to all but just enough, let them neither starve nor stuff, and that you may have your *due,* let your neighbor carve for you—*Swift*⟩ ⟨giving each man his *due* . . . impartial as the rain from Heaven's face—*Lindsay*⟩ **Desert** (often in plural **deserts**) suggests not a legal right but a moral right based upon what one actually deserves, whether it be a reward or a penalty ⟨"My lord, I will use them according to their *desert.*" "God's bodykins, man, much better: use every man after his *desert,* and who should 'scape whipping?"—*Shak.*⟩ ⟨you have deprived the best years of his life of that independence which was no less his due than his *desert*—*Austen*⟩ ⟨any Federal officer, regardless of his *deserts,* has much prestige— *Heiser*⟩ **Merit** is a somewhat complex term, often shifting in its major implication but (see also EXCELLENCE) commonly implying a deserving either of reward or punishment on the ground of what has been accomplished or of commendation, esteem, or acceptance on the ground of intrinsic and usually excellent qualities ⟨no tribute can be paid to them which exceeds their *merit*—*John Marshall*⟩ ⟨deal with every case on its *merits*⟩ ⟨as a pilgrim to the Holy Places I acquire *merit*—*Kipling*⟩
*Ana* compensation, recompensing *or* recompense, repayment, satisfaction, payment (see corresponding verbs at PAY): retribution, *retaliation, reprisal, vengeance, revenge: reward, meed, guerdon (see PREMIUM)
**dulcet** *sweet, engaging, winning, winsome
*Ana* *soft, gentle, mild, balmy, lenient: serene, *calm, tranquil: harmonious, consonant, accordant, concordant (see corresponding nouns at HARMONY)
*Ant* grating
**dull** *adj* **1** *stupid, slow, dumb, dense, crass
*Ana* *lethargic, sluggish, comatose: phlegmatic, stolid, *impassive, apathetic: *backward: retarded (see DELAY *vb*)
*Ant* clever, bright —*Con* *intelligent, alert, quick-witted, smart, brilliant, knowing
**2 Dull, blunt, obtuse** are comparable when they mean the reverse of *sharp, keen,* and *acute.* As used of things, especially of tools, weapons, and instruments, **dull** refers to either an edge or a point that has lost its sharpness by use ⟨a *dull* knife⟩ ⟨a *dull* razor⟩ ⟨a *dull* pencil⟩ **Blunt** refers to an edge or point that through use, nature, or intention, is not sharp or keen ⟨use the *blunt* side of the knife in prying⟩ ⟨an ax is a *blunt* instrument as compared with a razor, but its edge should not be allowed to become dull through use⟩ **Obtuse** applies to the shape of something whose sides converge at an angle that is broader than a right angle or to a thing terminating in a broad blunt point ⟨the *obtuse* apex of a wing⟩ ⟨an *obtuse* leaf⟩
In the extended senses of these words, **dull** (see also STUPID) is the most widely applicable and the richest as well as the most variable in its connotations. It implies, in general, a lack or the loss of what gives keenness, intensity, or activity ⟨a *dull* pain⟩ ⟨*dull* red⟩ ⟨a *dull* market⟩ ⟨*dull* anger⟩ **Blunt** (see BLUFF for application to manners

and utterances) usually implies a lack of edge or point in the figurative senses of these words. Often, it refers to a person's powers of perception or to his sensibilities, which normally should be sharp or keen ⟨she . . . is *blunt* in perception and feeling, and quite destitute of imagination— *Bradley*⟩ ⟨to the age of twelve . . . all my emotions were wholesomely undeveloped and *blunt,* never at any point exasperated into acute sensibility—*Ellis*⟩ It may also apply to matters (as contrasts, critical judgments, and analyses) normally requiring sharp distinction or differentiation and then imply exceptional conciseness and corresponding loss of fine detail ⟨the function of diplomacy, in the *bluntest* analysis, is to get what you want— *Newsweek*⟩ **Obtuse** suggests such bluntness of perception or sensibilities as makes one insensitive to emotions or ideas ⟨there was, one vaguely feels, something a little *obtuse* about Dr. Burney. The eager, kind, busy man, with his head full of music and his desk stuffed with notes, lacked discrimination—*Woolf*⟩ ⟨an *obtuse* insensibility to the rich and subtle variety of human relations—*Cohen*⟩
*Ant* sharp (*edge, point*): poignant (*sensation, feeling, reaction*): lively (*action or activity*)
**3 Dull, humdrum, dreary, monotonous, pedestrian, stodgy** mean so unvaried and uninteresting as to provoke boredom or tedium. **Dull** (see also STUPID) implies the lack of all that gives brightness, edge, or point to the person or thing; it need not imply inferiority, but it does suggest, from the point of view of one who judges, a want of interesting character ⟨compared with her, other women were . . . *dull;* even the pretty ones seemed lifeless—*Cather*⟩ ⟨for instance, you draw no inference from your facts. It's *dull.* Why not round the thing off into a good article?— *Rose Macaulay*⟩ **Humdrum** implies a commonplace and routine character; it suggests a lack of variation that persists and colors the life or the people who lead that life ⟨a plain, *humdrum* domestic life, with eight hundred a year, and a small house, full of babies—*Trollope*⟩ ⟨they regarded their adversaries as *humdrum* people, slaves to routine, enemies to light—*Arnold*⟩ **Dreary** (see also DISMAL) applies to something that from the writer's or speaker's point of view seems uninteresting and dull; the word may imply an absence of enlivening character in the thing itself but more often it reveals an attitude of mind ⟨I see that many people find the world *dreary*—and, indeed, there must be spaces of dreariness in it for us all —some find it interesting—*Benson*⟩ **Monotonous** implies an irksome sameness (as of what never changes in quality, character, or appearance); it may be widely applied (as to work, to play, to persons, to scenes, or to noises) ⟨incessant recurrence without variety breeds tedium; the overiterated becomes the *monotonous*—*Lowes*⟩ ⟨we may thus bring a little poetry and romance into the *monotonous* lives of our handworkers—*Inge*⟩ ⟨the sky was as full of motion and change as the desert beneath it was *monotonous* and still—*Cather*⟩ **Pedestrian,** which basically means walking on foot, is applied chiefly to something written, especially in verse, that lacks any quality (as originality in thought or freshness in expression or in imagery) which raises the spirits and that, therefore, is monotonous and uninspired; the term may connote a dull prosaic quality and implies the impossibility of lifting the reader's thoughts, emotions, or imagination ⟨who wandering with *pedestrian* muses, contend not with you on the winged steed—*Byron*⟩ ⟨Crane's verse is of a very *pedestrian* order—*Sidney Lee*⟩ **Stodgy,** which also implies the lack of a quality which inspirits or inspires, is wider in its application, for it emphasizes the heaviness, the solidity, or the lumpishness of something (as a person, a book, or an affair) that should be lighter, brighter, or gayer ⟨a

---

A colon (:) separates groups of words discriminated. An asterisk (*) indicates place of treatment of each group.

*stodgy* discussion⟩ ⟨the reception was a *stodgy* affair⟩ ⟨in England, art must be obvious and *stodgy* before people think it's respectable—*Guy Thorne*⟩ *Ana* \*irksome, tiresome, wearisome, tedious, boring: prosy, \*prosaic, matter-of-fact *Ant* lively —*Con* gay, animated, sprightly (see LIVELY): exciting, stimulating (see PROVOKE)

**dumb** *adj* **1 Dumb, mute, speechless, inarticulate** mean lacking the power to speak. **Dumb** and **mute** are often used interchangeably, but when used in distinction from each other, *dumb* implies an incapacity for speech (as in the case of animals and inanimate objects or of human beings whose organs of speech are defective); *mute* implies an inability to speak, owing to one's never having heard speech sounds (as in the case of one who is deaf congenitally or has lost his hearing before being old enough to reproduce heard sounds); thus, persons once called deaf and dumb are usually deaf-mutes who have healthy speech organs and can be trained to speak through the senses of sight and touch ⟨*dumb* stones whereon to vent their rage —*Arnold*⟩ ⟨a *mute* child⟩ When used of persons who are normally able to speak, *dumb* (see also STUPID) usually suggests deprivation of the power to speak; *mute* stresses a compelling cause for keeping or maintaining silence ⟨deep shame had struck me *dumb*—*Shak.*⟩ ⟨how terrible is that *dumb* grief which has never learned to moan— *Galsworthy*⟩ ⟨all sat *mute,* pondering the danger with deep thoughts—*Milton*⟩ ⟨some *mute* inglorious Milton —*Gray*⟩ **Speechless** commonly implies momentary deprivation of the power of speech ⟨struck *speechless* with terror⟩ ⟨I can remember, across the years, standing there with that paper in my hand; dumb, *speechless,* and probably tearful—*White*⟩ **Inarticulate** implies either lack of the power to speak at all ⟨the *inarticulate* people of the dead—*Shelley*⟩ ⟨the *inarticulate* hungers of the heart— *Sherman*⟩ or, especially, inability to speak intelligibly or clearly, usually on account of some powerful emotion but sometimes because of lack of power to express one's thoughts or feelings ⟨*inarticulate* with rage⟩ ⟨stood looking down on her in *inarticulate* despair—*Wharton*⟩ **2** dull, \*stupid, slow, dense, crass *Ana & Con* see those at DULL 1 *Ant* articulate (sense 2)

**dumbfound** confound, nonplus, bewilder, distract, mystify, perplex, \*puzzle *Ana* astound, flabbergast, amaze, astonish, \*surprise: \*confuse, muddle, addle, fuddle: disconcert, rattle, faze, discomfit (see EMBARRASS)

**dumps** dejection, gloom, blues, depression, melancholy, melancholia, \*sadness *Ana* despondency, forlornness, hopelessness, despair (see under DESPONDENT): doldrums, ennui, boredom, \*tedium

**dumpy** \*stocky, thickset, thick, chunky, stubby, squat

**dunk** *vb* \*dip, immerse, souse, submerge, duck *Ana* \*soak, saturate, sop

**dupe** *vb* **Dupe, gull, befool, trick, hoax, hoodwink, bamboozle** mean to delude a person by underhand means or for one's own ends. **Dupe** suggests unwariness or unsuspiciousness on the part of the person or persons deluded and the acceptance of what is false as true, what is counterfeit as genuine, or what is worthless as valuable ⟨the public is easily *duped* by extravagant claims in advertising⟩ ⟨he was so softhearted that he was constantly being *duped* into helping impostors⟩ ⟨William had too much sense to be *duped*—*Macaulay*⟩ **Gull** implies great credulousness or a disposition that lends itself to one's being easily imposed upon or made a laughingstock of ⟨if I do not *gull* him into a nayword, and make him a common recreation, do not think I have wit enough to lie straight in my bed—*Shak.*⟩

⟨if the world will be *gulled,* let it be *gulled*—*Burton*⟩ ⟨*gull* who may, they will be *gulled!* They will not look nor think —*Browning*⟩ **Befool** stresses the effect on the victim, that of being made a fool of in his own eyes or in those of others; it does not so strongly suggest a temperamental weakness in the victim as the preceding words, nor so clearly imply an intent to delude on the part of the agent, as most of the words that follow ⟨confess themselves *befooled* by the candidate, his personable appearance, and his promises⟩ ⟨innocent philosophic critics, too easily *befooled* by words—*Ellis*⟩ ⟨pictures supplant one another so swiftly as to *befool* the eye with the illusion of continuity—*S. H. Adams*⟩ **Trick** implies the intent to delude on the part of the agent by means of a stratagem or ruse, by wiles, or by fraud; it suggests the deliberate intent to deceive, but it need not imply a base end. It may, for example, imply illusion as the end ⟨a skillful dramatist *tricks* the spectators into accepting the impossible as probable⟩ ⟨a magician's success depends partly upon his ability to *trick* his audience⟩ It more often suggests deliberate misleading and the use of cunning or craft ⟨pills are coated with sugar or chocolate in order to *trick* children into taking them⟩ ⟨he was *tricked* out of his savings by the promises of large returns on an investment⟩ ⟨the people felt that they had been *tricked* into approval of the project⟩ ⟨it enables some lawyers to *trick* us into bringing in the wrong verdict—*Reilly*⟩ **Hoax** may imply indulgence in tricking as a sport or for the purpose of proving how gullible a person or persons can be when a skillful imposture or fabrication is presented to them; it more often suggests a fraud intended to deceive even the most skeptical and often, also, to work for one's own profit or personal advantage ⟨after having been *hoaxed* for the past 40 years, British scientists have discovered that the jaw and teeth of the world-famous "Piltdown man" belong to a modern ape—*Farmer's Weekly*⟩ ⟨a get-rich-quick scheme intended to *hoax* the public⟩ ⟨did Mark Twain intend to *hoax* people by his *Personal Recollections of Joan of Arc,* published without his name and as the work of one of her contemporaries?⟩ **Hoodwink** connotes either a deliberate confusing intended to blind the mind of another to the truth, or, less often, self-delusion arising from one's inability to distinguish the false from the true ⟨he will not be *hoodwinked* by sentimental platitudes into doing things that are against reason⟩ ⟨to *hoodwink* everybody by pretending to conform—*Cabell*⟩ ⟨since she'd *hoodwinked* your uncle, she thought she could pull the wool over my eyes, too—*Kenneth Roberts*⟩ **Bamboozle** usually implies the use of such methods as cajolery, humbug, or illusion to dupe or confuse; the word is often used interchangeably with *trick, hoax,* or *hoodwink,* but it is less definite or fixed in its implications ⟨*bamboozled* into a belief that he was a great man⟩ ⟨what Oriental tomfoolery is *bamboozling* you?—*Newman*⟩ *Ana* \*deceive, beguile, delude, mislead, double-cross, betray: \*cheat, cozen, defraud, overreach: outwit, baffle, circumvent (see FRUSTRATE)

**duplicate** *n* \*reproduction, facsimile, copy, carbon copy, transcript, replica *Ana* counterpart, \*parallel, analogue

**duplicity** \*deceit, dissimulation, cunning, guile *Ana* double-dealing, chicanery, chicane, trickery, \*deception, fraud: treacherousness *or* treachery, perfidiousness *or* perfidy, faithlessness (see corresponding adjectives at FAITHLESS) *Con* straightforwardness, forthrightness (see corresponding adjectives at STRAIGHTFORWARD)

**durable** \*lasting, perdurable, permanent, stable, perpetual *Ana* enduring, abiding, persisting (see CONTINUE):

*strong, stout, tenacious
*Con* fragile, frail, feeble, *weak: *transient, transitory, fleeting, ephemeral, fugitive
**duress** constraint, coercion, compulsion, violence, *force, restraint
**dusky** dim, *dark, obscure, murky, gloomy
**duty** 1 *obligation
*Ana* responsibility, accountability, amenability, answerability, liability (see corresponding adjectives at RESPONSIBLE)
2 office, *function, province
*Ana* concern, business, *affair
3 *task, assignment, job, stint, chore
*Ana* *work, business, employment, occupation, calling: *trade, craft, art, profession
**dwarf** *n* Dwarf, pygmy, midget, manikin, homunculus, runt are comparable when they mean an individual and usually a person of diminutive size. **Dwarf** is the general term not only for a human being but for any animal or plant that is definitely below the normal size of its kind; often the term suggests stunted development ⟨his [the fool's] value was trebled in the eyes of the king by the fact of his being also a *dwarf* and a cripple—*Poe*⟩ **Pygmy** originally was applied to one of a race of fabled dwarfs mentioned by Homer and others; now it is used especially of one of a people of small stature found in central Africa. In general application the term carries a stronger connotation of diminutiveness and a weaker suggestion of arrested development than *dwarf*; when used in reference to a person, it often implies relative tininess, sometimes in body but more often in intellect ⟨to him all the men I ever knew were *pygmies*. He was an intellectual giant—*Byron*⟩ **Midget** stresses abnormal diminutiveness but, unlike *dwarf*, carries little suggestion

of malformation or deformity; the term is applied usually to a tiny but otherwise more or less normally shaped person exhibited in a circus or employed in place of a child in theatrical performances ⟨P. T. Barnum's famous *midget, Tom Thumb*⟩ **Manikin** is often applied not only to a dwarf but to any human being who for one reason or another seems despicably small or weak ⟨can it be fancied that Deity ever vindictively made in his image a *manikin* merely to madden it?—*Poe*⟩ Often it suggests an animated doll ⟨a bright-eyed little *manikin,* naked like all his people—*Forester*⟩ **Homunculus** usually suggests even greater diminutiveness and often greater perfection in form than *midget*; it is the specific term for an exceedingly small artificial human being such as was supposedly developed by Paracelsus, a famous Renaissance alchemist. **Runt,** usually a contemptuous designation, applies to a dwarf or undersized person, especially to one who is conspicuously puny or undeveloped ⟨I always did admire a good, sizable, stout man. I hate a *runt*—*McClure's Mag.*⟩ The term is also applied to an animal, especially a domestic animal, small of its kind; and it is used specifically of the undersized one of a litter (as of pigs).
**dwell** *reside, live, lodge, sojourn, stay, put up, stop
**dwelling** abode, residence, domicile, home, house, *habitation
**dwindle** diminish, lessen, *decrease, reduce, abate
*Ana* wane, ebb, *abate, subside: attenuate, extenuate, *thin: *moderate: disappear (see affirmative verb at APPEAR 1)
**dynamic** live, *active, operative
*Ana* potent, forceful, forcible, *powerful: *intense, vehement, fierce, exquisite, violent: vitalizing, energizing, activating (see VITALIZE)

# E

**each** *adj* every, *all
**each** *adv* Each, apiece, severally, individually, respectively are comparable when they refer to every one of the many or several persons or things comprising a group. All imply distribution. **Each** and **apiece** usually connote equality in the amount or value of what is distributed unless the context indicates otherwise ⟨he gave the five children a dollar *apiece*⟩ ⟨the students have a bedroom and study *each*⟩ **Severally** stresses the apartness of each of the persons and things involved but at the same time often, especially in legal use, implies that each of them is favored, bound, guilty, or responsible in the same degree as the group as a whole; thus, to try a group of conspirators *severally* is to try them not jointly, or together, but one at a time and usually on the identical charge; to be bound jointly and *severally* is to be under obligation as a group and singly as individuals, damages being recoverable from all or from any member of the group. **Individually,** like *severally,* implies a distinction between each member of the group, but it goes further in not suggesting equality (as in responsibility, favor, or disfavor); thus, to try a group of conspirators *individually* is to try each one on a specific charge, usually on the assumption that they are not equally guilty; to greet each member of a visiting delegation *individually* is to greet him separately and personally. **Respectively** is used only when the persons or things involved in the distribution follow a given order and what is distributed goes to each in the same order ⟨he gave John, James, and Edward

ten dollars, five dollars, and three dollars *respectively*⟩ ⟨the suites of offices 101, 102, 103 are assigned *respectively* to the president, the treasurer, and the secretary of the company⟩
**eager,** avid, keen, anxious, agog, athirst mean actuated by a strong and urgent desire or interest. **Eager** implies ardor and, often, enthusiasm; it frequently also connotes impatience ⟨it is not a life for fiery and dominant natures, *eager* to conquer—*Benson*⟩ **Avid** adds to *eager* the implication of greed or of unbounded desire ⟨a too *avid* thirst for pleasure—*Æ*⟩ ⟨cultivated, excitable, *avid* of new things —*Buchan*⟩ ⟨he was convivial, bawdy, robustly *avid* for pleasure—*F. S. Fitzgerald*⟩ **Keen** suggests intensity of interest and quick responsiveness in action ⟨boys in white flannels—all *keen* as mustard, and each occupied with his own game, and playing it to the best of his powers—*Quiller-Couch*⟩ ⟨Tories who are as *keen* on State interference with everything and everybody as the Socialists —*Shaw*⟩ **Anxious** emphasizes fear lest one's desires be frustrated or one's hopes not realized; it often additionally connotes insistence or perseverance in making one's desires known ⟨visibly *anxious* that his wife should be on easy terms with us all—*Repplier*⟩ ⟨schoolmasters may be pathetically *anxious* to guide boys right, and to guard them from evil—*Benson*⟩ **Agog** suggests being caught up in the excitement and bustle attending something interesting about to be begun or an event eagerly awaited ⟨six precious souls, and all *agog* to dash through thick and thin—

A colon (:) separates groups of words discriminated. An asterisk (*) indicates place of treatment of each group

*Cowper*⟩ ⟨the abrupt announcement . . . left everybody . . . *agog*—*Cerf*⟩ **Athirst** implies yearning or longing more vividly than the others; it seldom connotes readiness for action ⟨I that forever feel *athirst* for glory—*Keats*⟩ ⟨one or two great souls *athirst* for pure aesthetic rapture—*Clive Bell*⟩

**Ana** desiring, coveting, craving (see DESIRE *vb*): longing, yearning, hungering, thirsting (see LONG *vb*): *impatient, restless, restive

**Ant** listless —*Con* *indifferent, unconcerned, incurious, aloof, uninterested: apathetic, *impassive, stolid

**early** *adv* **Early, soon, beforehand, betimes** share the meaning of at or nearly at a given point of time or around the beginning of a specified or implied period of time. **Early** is used chiefly in reference to a period of time (as a day, a lifetime, an age, or a term) and in dating a happening with reference to the beginning of that period. In such use it implies occurrence shortly after the time at which the period is set to begin or is regarded as beginning ⟨crocuses blossomed *early* this spring⟩ ⟨migrations took place *early* in the Middle Ages⟩ ⟨*early* to bed and *early* to rise, makes a man healthy, wealthy, and wise—*Franklin*⟩ ⟨Voltaire perceived very *early* in life that to be needy was to be dependent—*John Morley*⟩ Sometimes, especially when the reference is to a point of time, *early* may mean in advance of the time set or expected or of the usual time; thus, a person who arrives *early* at a meeting and leaves *early* comes slightly before (sometimes just at) the time set or noticeably ahead of the others and leaves before the gathering breaks up; winter came *early* (that is, ahead of the expected or normal time) this year. **Soon** usually refers to a definite point of time (as the present or the beginning of a period, a process, or a course), but it commonly implies occurrence after the moment in mind; thus, when a physician tells a patient to come *early*, he by implication asks that patient to come in advance of the time set for the beginning of his office hours so that the patient may be attended to *soon*, or shortly after the office hours begin; on the other hand, when he asks a patient to come *soon*, he by implication requests another visit shortly after the present one. But *soon* carries not only the implication of subsequence to a specified or implied point of time but also, even more strongly, that of quickness or promptness or lack of delay ⟨I called, and he *soon* appeared⟩ ⟨the absconder was apprehended *soon* after his disappearance⟩ ⟨I hope you will find your ring very *soon*⟩ *Soon*, however, is sometimes used in place of *early*, though with greater emphasis on promptness, in poetry, in some idiomatic expressions, and in the comparative and superlative degrees ⟨late and *soon*, getting and spending, we lay waste our powers—*Wordsworth*⟩ ⟨must you go so *soon*?⟩ ⟨excuse my not writing *sooner*⟩ ⟨the spirit . . . may know how *soonest* to accomplish the great end—*Shelley*⟩ **Beforehand** sometimes implies a time in advance of that set or expected or customary ⟨he promised to be here *beforehand*⟩ More often it refers to a time in advance of a possible, probable, or certain occurrence, and it then usually implies anticipation or anticipatory measures ⟨if one knows a thing *beforehand* one can be prepared⟩ ⟨try to be *beforehand* in dealing with an enemy⟩ ⟨had . . . taken unusual pains to inform himself *beforehand* concerning the subject matter—*Dean*⟩ **Betimes** is a somewhat old-fashioned or literary word that may replace either *early* or *soon* ⟨not to be abed after midnight is to be up *betimes*—*Shak.*⟩ ⟨he tires *betimes* that spurs too fast—*Shak.*⟩ More often it implies occurrence at the proper or due time and therefore stresses seasonableness. Something which happens *betimes* is neither too early nor too late ⟨know the art of giving advice *betimes*⟩ ⟨because he had learned his lesson

*betimes*, he was able to give perfect satisfaction afterwards⟩ ⟨if we had taken steps *betimes* to create an air force half as strong again . . . we should have kept control of the future—*Sir Winston Churchill*⟩

**Ant** late

**earn** *deserve, merit, rate

**Ana** gain, win (see GET)

**earnest** *adj* *serious, solemn, grave, somber, sober, sedate, staid

**Ana** zealous, enthusiastic, passionate (see corresponding nouns at PASSION): diligent, *busy, industrious, assiduous, sedulous: *sincere, wholehearted, whole-souled

**Ant** frivolous —*Con* volatile, effervescent, buoyant, *elastic: flippant, flighty, light (see corresponding nouns at LIGHTNESS)

**earnest** *n* token, *pledge, pawn, hostage

**earsplitting** *loud, stentorian, hoarse, raucous, strident, stertorous

**earth** *n* **Earth, world, universe, cosmos, macrocosm** are comparable when they mean the entire area or extent of space in which man thinks of himself and of his fellow men as living and acting. **Earth** applies, however, only to part of what he knows by sight or by faith to exist; the term usually suggests a distinction between the sphere or globe called astronomically the earth, which he knows to be composed of land and water, and the bodies which he sees in the heavens ⟨this goodly frame, the *earth*—*Shak.*⟩ ⟨land is part of *Earth's* surface which stands at a given time above sea level—*Lord*⟩ It may imply a distinction from heaven and hell ⟨Thy will be done in *earth*, as it is in heaven—*Mt* 6:10⟩ ⟨the infinite loftiness of Mary's nature, among the things of *earth*, and above the clamor of kings—*Henry Adams*⟩ **World** is a far less definite term than *earth*. When applied to a physical entity, it may denote all that illimitable area which to man's senses, at least, includes not only the earth and other planets but all the space surrounding the earth and all the bodies contained within it ⟨it is not accident that wherever we point the telescope . . . wherever we look with the microscope there we find beauty. It beats in through every nook and cranny of the mighty *world*—*R. M. Jones*⟩ To persons who accept the account of creation in Genesis the term denotes the entire system that was brought into being by the word of God ⟨God made the *world*⟩ ⟨expect the destruction of the *world*⟩ The term, nevertheless, is usually used as equivalent to *earth*, the globe ⟨a trip around the *world*⟩ ⟨he wanted to visit every corner of the *world*⟩ As applied to an immaterial entity, world may imply the sum total of all the inhabitants of earth and of their interests and concerns ⟨all the *world* loves a lover⟩ ⟨the *world* was one in desiring peace⟩ ⟨the doctrine of imperialism which condemns the *world* to endless war—*Willkie*⟩ or that section or part of this larger world which comes within the knowledge of the individual ⟨man's relation to the *world* about him⟩ ⟨his family and his business comprised his *world*⟩ ⟨among the friends of his three *worlds*, the intellectuals, the Concord family circle, and the farmers, he was always a little on edge with the first—*Canby*⟩ or the section or part of the larger world which is devoted to secular, as distinct from religious or spiritual, concerns ⟨retire from the *world*⟩ ⟨the *world*, the flesh, and the devil⟩ ⟨the *world* is too much with us—*Wordsworth*⟩ ⟨I too love the earth and hate the *world*. God made the first, and man . . . has made the second—*Santayana*⟩ **Universe**, in its most precise sense, denotes the entire system of created things or of physical phenomena, regarded as a unit both in its organization and in its operation ⟨ancient and medieval astronomers regarded the earth as the fixed center of the *universe*⟩ ⟨the astronomers of today teach that the *uni-*

verse is finite but that it is constantly expanding⟩ ⟨what was true for the development of man, the microcosm, must have been true for the genesis of the *universe* as a whole, the macrocosm—*S. F. Mason*⟩ *Universe,* however, is also used in reference to an entire system of phenomenal things as that system appears to the limited vision of the typical man or of the individual ⟨from the *universe* as we see it both the Glory of God and the Glory of Man have departed—*Krutch*⟩ ⟨he inhabited a different *universe* from that of common men—*Huxley*⟩ **Cosmos,** because of its opposition to *chaos,* carries a stronger implication of order and harmony in operation than *universe,* which it otherwise closely resembles in meaning ⟨were it not for the indwelling reason the world would be a chaos and not a *cosmos*—*Blackie*⟩ **Macrocosm** applies to the universe thought of as a great whole characterized by perfect organic unity exhibited elsewhere only in the small whole, the individual man or *microcosm* ⟨the microcosm repeats the *macrocosm*—*T. H. Huxley*⟩ ⟨should these ephemera [flying disks] exist in the *macrocosm,* it is likely . . . that they would be known to . . . observers of the atmosphere—*Mauer*⟩

**earthly,** **terrestrial, earthy, mundane, worldly, sublunary** are comparable when they mean of, belonging to, or characteristic of the earth. **Earthly** is used chiefly in opposition to *heavenly* ⟨*earthly* love⟩ ⟨the *earthly* paradise⟩ ⟨if I have told you *earthly* things, and ye believe not, how shall ye believe, if I tell you of heavenly things?—*Jn 3:12*⟩ ⟨a peace above all *earthly* dignities, a still and quiet conscience—*Shak.*⟩ ⟨there could be a new order, based on vital harmony, and the *earthly* millennium might approach—*Forster*⟩ **Terrestrial** is sometimes used in place of *earthly* as a more sonorous term; frequently, however, it implies an opposition to *celestial* rather than to *heavenly* (see CELESTIAL) ⟨a *terrestrial* globe⟩ ⟨a *terrestrial* telescope⟩ or it may imply a distinction of earth from the other planets ⟨*terrestrial* magnetism⟩ ⟨whose vision is cosmic, not *terrestrial*—*Lowes*⟩ ⟨carbon dioxide is, of course, of great importance in long-wave *terrestrial* radiation, but plays a minor role in solar radiation absorption—*Compendium of Meteorology*⟩ or more specifically in astronomy, a distinction of certain planets assumed to be like the earth from others assumed to be unlike the earth ⟨the *terrestrial* planets are Earth, Mars, Venus, and Mercury⟩ ⟨there are also celestial bodies, and bodies *terrestrial:* but the glory of the celestial is one, and the glory of the *terrestrial* is another—*1 Cor 15:40*⟩ ⟨when from under this *terrestrial* ball he fires the proud tops of the eastern pines—*Shak.*⟩ *Terrestrial* in some use suggests land as a habitat, rather than water or trees ⟨*terrestrial* reptiles⟩ ⟨*terrestrial* plants⟩ ⟨they will still obey natural laws and, if manned, they will still be manned by normal, *terrestrial* airmen—*Time*⟩ **Earthy,** in the historical development of its senses, has stressed a connection with the earth as soil rather than the earth as the abode of men ⟨an *earthy* smell⟩ Even when it comes close to *earthly* in its meaning, it carries a stronger implication of grossness of substance or of material interests than *earthly* and is opposed more to *spiritual* than to *heavenly* ⟨the first man is of the earth, *earthy:* the second man is the Lord from heaven—*1 Cor 15:47*⟩ ⟨my anger and disgust at his gross *earthy* egoism had vanished—*Hudson*⟩ ⟨with much *earthy* dross in her, she was yet preeminently a creature of "fire and air"—*Buchan*⟩ **Mundane** and **worldly** both imply a relationship to the world thought of as the affairs, concerns, and activities of human beings especially as they are concentrated on practical ends or on immediate pleasures. *Mundane* specifically suggests an opposition to what is eternal and stresses transitoriness or impermanence ⟨mundane

glory⟩ ⟨there I quaff the elixir and sweet essence of *mundane* triumph—*L. P. Smith*⟩ ⟨Tony knew that she did not allow them to talk of *mundane* affairs on these expeditions to and from church—*Archibald Marshall*⟩ ⟨the occupations and distractions of *mundane* life—*Harold Nicolson*⟩ *Worldly,* which is applied chiefly to persons and their interests, specifically implies indifference to things of the spirit and concentration on whatever satisfies one's love of success, one's desire for pleasure, or one's self-esteem ⟨the obvious thing to say of her was that she was *worldly; cared* too much for rank and society and getting on in the world—*Woolf*⟩ ⟨the most *worldly* of the eighteenth-century ecclesiastics—*Belloc*⟩ **Sublunary** is a distinctly literary or poetic term variously interchangeable with *earthly, mundane,* and *terrestrial* ⟨all things *sublunary* are subject to change—*Dryden*⟩ ⟨what then would matter the quakes and *sublunary* conflicts of this negligible earth? —*L. P. Smith*⟩

*Ana* temporal, *profane, secular: *material, physical, corporeal

*Con* *celestial, heavenly, empyrean, empyreal: spiritual, divine (see HOLY)

**earthy** mundane, worldly, *earthly, terrestrial, sublunary

*Ana* *material, physical, corporeal: fleshly, *carnal, sensual: gross, *coarse

**ease** *n* **1** comfort, relaxation, *rest, repose, leisure

*Ana* inactivity, idleness, inertness, passiveness, supineness (see corresponding adjectives at INACTIVE): tranquillity, serenity, placidity, calmness, peacefulness (see corresponding adjectives at CALM)

*Con* toil, travail, *work, labor: *distress, suffering, misery

**2** facility, dexterity, *readiness

*Ana* effortlessness, smoothness, easiness (see corresponding adjectives at EASY): grace (see ELEGANCE): expertness, adeptness, skillfulness, proficiency (see corresponding adjectives at PROFICIENT): deftness, adroitness (see corresponding adjectives at DEXTEROUS)

*Ant* effort —*Con* exertion, pains, trouble (see EFFORT): awkwardness, clumsiness, ineptness, maladroitness (see corresponding adjectives at AWKWARD)

**easy** *adj* **1** *comfortable, restful, cozy, snug

*Ana* *soft, lenient, gentle: commodious, *spacious: *calm, tranquil, serene, placid: unconstrained, spontaneous (see corresponding nouns at UNCONSTRAINT)

*Ant* disquieting *or* disquieted —*Con* disturbed, perturbed, agitated, upset, discomposed (see DISCOMPOSE): anxious, worried, concerned (see under CARE *n*)

**2** **Easy, facile, simple, light, effortless, smooth** are comparable when meaning not involving undue effort or difficulty (as in doing, making, giving, or understanding). **Easy** is applicable both to persons and things that make demands for physical or mental effort or that impose a task upon a person and to the acts or activities involved in satisfying such demands or in accomplishing such a task ⟨the book was *easy* to read⟩ ⟨I would like some more *easy* reading⟩ ⟨our teacher was *easy* today; her assignment for tomorrow is short and *easy*⟩ ⟨an *easy* riddle⟩ ⟨the place is *easy* to reach⟩ ⟨the place is within *easy* reach of the city⟩ ⟨it will not be *easy* for him to understand your breaking of your promise⟩ ⟨take my yoke upon you, and learn of me . . . for my yoke is *easy,* and my burden is light—*Mt 11:29-30*⟩ ⟨I have been a dreamer and an artist, a great dreamer, for that is *easy,* not a great artist, for that is hard—*Ellis*⟩ ⟨it was *easy* to sit on a camel's back without falling off, but very difficult to . . . get the best out of her—*T. E. Lawrence*⟩ **Facile** was once and to some extent is still used as a very close synonym of *easy* ⟨having won . . . his *facile* victory—*Froude*⟩ ⟨the *facile* modes of measurement which we now employ—*Tyndall*⟩ But it now chiefly applies to something which comes, or moves, or works, or gains its ends seemingly without effort or at call; it therefore is often used in derogation implying lack of constraint or restraint, undue haste, dexterity rather than meticulousness, or fluency with shallowness ⟨a writer's *facile* pen⟩ ⟨a woman's *facile* tears⟩ ⟨I am not concerned with . . . offering any *facile* solution for so complex a problem—*T. S. Eliot*⟩ ⟨she was a prey to shoddy, *facile* emotions and moods, none of which had power to impel her to any action—*Rose Macaulay*⟩ ⟨Chrétien was a *facile* narrator, with little sense of the significance that might be given to the stories—*H. O. Taylor*⟩ **Simple** stresses ease in apprehending or understanding; it implies freedom from complication, intricacy, elaboration, or other involvements which render a thing difficult to see through ⟨problems in arithmetic too *simple* to hold the interest of pupils of that age⟩ ⟨true poetry, however *simple* it may appear on the surface, accumulates meaning every time it is read—*Day Lewis*⟩ ⟨the English mother or the English nurse has a *simpler* job. She must teach her charge to start as few fights as possible and that there are rules—*Mead*⟩ **Light** implies an opposition to *heavy* in nearly all of its senses, but in the one here considered it suggests freedom from burdensomeness or from exactions that make undue or difficult demands on one ⟨a *light* task⟩ ⟨his work is very *light*⟩ ⟨one generation's *light* reading often becomes another's heavy text—*J. D. Hart*⟩ ⟨*light* punishment⟩ **Effortless**, though it carries many of the connotations characteristic of *facile*, suggests more the appearance of ease than actual absence of effort; often it implies mastery, skill, or artistry, and the attainment of such perfection that the movements or technique seem to involve no strain ⟨the *effortless* dancing of a Pavlova⟩ ⟨that *effortless* grace with which only a true poet can endow his work—*M. O. Smith*⟩ ⟨a natural, *effortless* style⟩ ⟨the swallows . . . glided in an *effortless* way through the busy air—*Jefferies*⟩ **Smooth** suggests an absence of, or the removal of, all difficulties or obstacles that makes a course or a career easy to follow or to pursue ⟨the car sped along over the *smooth* road⟩ ⟨floated over the expanse within, which was *smooth* as a young girl's brow—*Melville*⟩ ⟨making the lives of the needy a little more *smooth*—*Shields*⟩

*Ant* hard  —*Con* difficult, arduous (see HARD): exacting, *onerous, burdensome, oppressive

**eat, swallow, ingest, devour, consume** mean to take food into the stomach through the mouth and throat. **Eat**, the common and ordinary term, implies the process of chewing as well as of taking into the stomach and therefore distinguishes itself from **swallow**, which implies merely the passing from the mouth through the throat to the stomach. *Eat* is often used, however, without any clear reference to chewing or swallowing ⟨cattle do not *eat* meat⟩ ⟨the worms have *eaten* into the timber⟩ and, especially in extended use, without implying anything but a slow, gradual process that is comparable to the biting or gnawing that precedes eating in that it wastes or wears away the substance ⟨the waves have *eaten* a channel through the rocks⟩ ⟨a knife *eaten* by rust⟩ ⟨the acid *eats* into the metal⟩ In many idiomatic expressions the literal phrasing recalls the implications of the original meaning but nothing more ⟨*eat* one's heart out (grieve in silence)⟩ ⟨*eat* one's words (take back what one has said)⟩ *Swallow* basically implies the second part of the eating process ⟨he has difficulty in *swallowing*⟩ ⟨the tablets are to be *swallowed* without chewing⟩ More often it is used of hurried eating without proper mastication of food ⟨he *swallowed* his breakfast and rushed for the train⟩ In extended use it implies a seizing and taking in or a being seized and taken in (as by engulfment, engrossment, or suppression) ⟨the ship was *swallowed* up by the sea⟩ ⟨*swallow* one's resentment⟩ **Ingest** is a physiological term that implies a taking in through the mouth and throat into the stomach and is commonly opposed to *egest* ⟨does a man dine well because he *ingests* the requisite number of calories?—*Lippmann*⟩ **Devour** throws the emphasis on greediness; it suggests intense hunger or gluttony in man and voracity in a wild animal ⟨the tramp rapidly *devoured* the food that was set before him⟩ ⟨they saw the tiger rushing on them as if it would *devour* them⟩ In extended use *devour* applies to something (as fire or disease) which destroys or wastes completely ⟨the flames *devoured* the houses one by one⟩ ⟨he that is in the city, famine and pestilence shall *devour* him—*Ezek* 7:15⟩ or to something which preys upon one as insistently as a beast or bird of prey ⟨*devoured* by fear⟩ Sometimes, however, it approaches *swallow* in its reference to something which engrosses the mind, but it heightens the implications of avidity and zest in taking in ⟨*devoured* all the books on aviation that he could get⟩ ⟨*devoured* the scene before him⟩ **Consume** (see also WASTE, MONOPOLIZE) usually means little more than *eat* and *drink,* for which it serves as a term including both or either ⟨whoever came late had to start with the course which the captain was then . . . *consuming*—*Heiser*⟩ ⟨after taking a piece of asparagus in her hand, she was deeply mortified at seeing her hostess *consume* the vegetable with the aid of a knife and fork—*Shaw*⟩ Very often, however, it adds to *eat* the implications of using up ⟨my stock of provisions had been so long *consumed* that I had forgotten the flavor of pulse and maize and pumpkins and purple and sweet potatoes—*Hudson*⟩

*Ana* *bite, champ, gnaw

**ebb** *vb* subside, *abate, wane

*Ana* dwindle, diminish, *decrease, lessen: *recede, retrograde, retreat

*Ant* flow (*as the tide*)  —*Con* *advance, progress: *rise, mount, ascend

**eccentric** erratic, odd, queer, peculiar, *strange, singular, unique, quaint, outlandish, curious

*Ana* *abnormal, atypical, aberrant: *irregular, anomalous, unnatural: *exceptional, exceptionable: *fantastic, bizarre, grotesque

*Con* *common, ordinary, familiar: *usual, customary, habitual: normal, natural, typical, *regular

**eccentricity,** **idiosyncrasy** are not always clearly distinguished when they denote an act, a practice, or a characteristic that impresses the observer as strange or singular. **Eccentricity** (compare STRANGE) emphasizes the idea of divergence from the usual or customary; **idiosyncrasy** implies a following of one's peculiar temperament or bent especially in trait, trick, or habit; the former often suggests mental aberration, the latter, strong individuality and independence of action ⟨as the country became more thickly settled and its economy more tightly knit, *eccentricity* declined and conformity became a virtue—*Commager*⟩ ⟨[his] house . . . had an outer and visible aspect of proud reserve, and appeared to have developed some of the *eccentricities* which come of isolation—*Bierce*⟩ ⟨letters to native princes, telling them . . . to refrain from kidnapping women, or filling offenders with pounded red pepper, and *eccentricities* of that kind—*Kipling*⟩ ⟨this decided love of the slope, or bank above the wall, rather than below it, is one of Turner's most marked *idiosyncrasies*—*Ruskin*⟩ ⟨what I learned of mathematics and science has been . . . of great intrinsic value, as affording subjects of contemplation and reflection, and touchstones of truth in a deceitful world. This is, of course, in part a personal *idiosyncrasy*—*Russell*⟩

---

*Ana* analogous words    *Ant* antonyms    *Con* contrasted words    See also explanatory notes facing page 1

**Ana** *deviation, aberration, divergence: peculiarity, oddity, queerness, singularity (see corresponding adjectives at STRANGE): freak, conceit, vagary, crotchet, *caprice, fancy, whim, whimsy

**echelon** *line, row, rank, file, tier

**éclat** renown, glory, celebrity, notoriety, repute, reputation, *fame, honor
**Ana** prominence, conspicuousness, remarkableness, noticeableness (see corresponding adjectives at NOTICEABLE): illustriousness *or* luster, eminence (see corresponding adjectives at FAMOUS)

**eclipse** *vb* *obscure, dim, bedim, darken, cloud, becloud, fog, befog, obfuscate
**Ana** *hide, conceal, screen: cloak, mask, camouflage (see DISGUISE)
**Con** expose, exhibit, *show, display: emerge, *appear, loom

**economical** frugal, thrifty, *sparing
**Ana** prudent, provident (see under PRUDENCE): close, cheeseparing, parsimonious, penurious (see STINGY)
**Ant** extravagant —**Con** lavish, prodigal, exuberant, *profuse

**economy** *system, scheme, network, complex, organism
**Ana** organization, institution, establishment, foundation (see corresponding verbs at FOUND)

**ecstasy** *n* **Ecstasy, rapture, transport** denote a feeling or a state of intense, sometimes excessive or extreme, mental and emotional exaltation. **Ecstasy** in its earlier sense, which is now found chiefly in religious and poetical writings, implies a trancelike state in which consciousness of one's surroundings is lost and the mind is intent either on what it contemplates (as does the mystic) or on what it conceives and creates (as does the inspired poet or artist) ⟨like a mad prophet in an *ecstasy*—*Dryden*⟩ ⟨anthems clear, as may with sweetness, through mine ear, dissolve me into *ecstasies,* and bring all Heaven before mine eyes—*Milton*⟩ In later and now general use the term implies overmastering, entrancing joy, or other emotion that exalts the mind and overcomes the senses ⟨men in whom the manual exercise of combat seems to light a wonderful fire in the blood. To them battle brings *ecstasy.* They are ravished above pain and fear—*Montague*⟩ ⟨she loved him with an acute, painful *ecstasy* that made her dizzy and blinded her to all the world besides—*Rose Macaulay*⟩ ⟨their faces were fixed in a calm *ecstasy* of malevolence—*Wylie*⟩ **Rapture** in its early religious use and still occasionally in theology, mysticism, and poetry differs from *ecstasy* in implying a lifting of the mind or soul out of itself by divine power, so that it may see things beyond the reach of human vision; the experiences narrated by the Apostle Paul of being caught up to the third heaven are in this sense *raptures.* In its chief current sense *rapture* merely implies intense bliss or beatitude with or without the connotation of accompanying ecstasy or loss of perception of everything else ⟨I drank it in, in a speechless *rapture*—*Mark Twain*⟩ ⟨as a child I first read Pope's Homer with a *rapture* which no subsequent work could ever afford—*Byron*⟩ ⟨she burned again with the same *ecstasy,* the same exaltation. How fine it had been, to live in that state of *rapture!*—*Sackville-West*⟩ ⟨continual ups and downs of *rapture* and depression—*Wharton*⟩ **Transport** applies to any violent or powerful emotion that lifts one out of oneself and, usually, provokes enthusiastic or vehement expression ⟨I mean to . . . support with an even temper, and without any violent *transports* . . . a sudden gust of prosperity—*Fielding*⟩ ⟨*transports* of rage—*Austen*⟩ ⟨what a *transport* of enthusiasm!—*Landor*⟩ ⟨in art, as in poetry, there are the *transports* which lift the artist out of . . . himself—*Pater*⟩ ⟨a periodical that is weekly moved to *transports* of delight

about contemporary America—*Bliven* b. 1889⟩
**Ana** bliss, beatitude, blessedness, felicity, *happiness: joy, delectation, delight, *pleasure: *inspiration, fury, frenzy, afflatus

**ecumenical** *universal, cosmic, catholic, cosmopolitan
**Ant** provincial: diocesan

**eddy** *n* **Eddy, whirlpool, maelstrom, vortex** mean a swirling mass especially of water. **Eddy** implies swift circular movement (as in water, wind, dust, or mist) caused by a countercurrent or, more often, by something that obstructs; it is usually thought of less as dangerous than as annoying or confusing ⟨it is blunt tails [of ships] rather than blunt noses that cause *eddies*—*W. H. White*⟩ ⟨a thick brown fog, whirled into *eddies* by the wind . . . abolished the landscape from before our smarting eyes—*Huxley*⟩ **Whirlpool** suggests a more extensive and more violent eddy in water; usually it implies a force of swirling water (as at a meeting of countercurrents) so great as to send whatever enters whirling toward a center where it is sucked down ⟨pass safely through the *whirlpool* of the Niagara River in a barrel⟩ but it may also be extended to other things that draw or suck one in like a swirl of raging water ⟨live in a *whirlpool* of excitement⟩ ⟨Europeans . . . have assumed . . . that public life will draw . . . enough of the highest ability into its *whirlpool*—*Bryce*⟩ **Maelstrom** is basically the name of a very powerful whirlpool off the west coast of Norway which was supposed to suck in all vessels that passed within a wide radius; the term is extended to any great turmoil that resistlessly drags men into it ⟨in one wild *maelstrom* of affrighted men —*J. S. C. Abbott*⟩ ⟨in the *maelstrom* of wild controversy⟩ ⟨the ancient taboos were gone, lost in the *maelstrom* of war—*Coulton Waugh*⟩ **Vortex** usually suggests a mass of liquid (as water) or gas (as air) rapidly circulating around a hollow center; it is visualized principally as something which draws all that become involved in the swirling into its center ⟨the cleansing power of the *vortex* of water in a washing machine⟩ ⟨the noise of the *vortex* of soapy water draining from the bathtub⟩ ⟨conventions are shifting, and undergoing metamorphosis. . . . But it is hard to estimate justly the significance of their contemporary behavior, because we are caught in the *vortex*—*Lowes*⟩ ⟨it is Koestler and Silone, who went deepest into the *vortex* of revolutionary activity, who emerge with the profoundest insights—*Time*⟩ ⟨drawn back into the emotional *vortex* of a youthful love affair—*Geismar*⟩

**eddy** *vb* rotate, gyrate, circle, spin, whirl, revolve, *turn, twirl, wheel, swirl, pirouette

**edge** *n* **1** verge, rim, brink, margin, *border, brim
**Ana** *limit, end, bound, confine: *circumference, periphery, compass
**2** odds, *advantage, handicap, allowance

**edifice** *n* structure, pile, *building

**edit** *vb* **Edit, compile, revise, redact, rewrite, adapt,** though not strict synonyms, are sometimes confused when used of the preparation of material for publication. **Edit** covers a wide range of meaning, sometimes stressing one implication, sometimes another. It fundamentally implies preparation for publication of a work, often the work of another or of others; thus, to *edit* a text (as a play of Shakespeare) usually means to present the text as nearly as possible in the form intended by the author, but it often suggests the modernization of spelling, the giving of variant readings, or the addition of comments or glosses; to *edit* a newspaper or magazine means, in general, to become responsible for the contents and policy of the periodical as a whole, sometimes by doing all or most of the work involved but far oftener by supervising the work of a staff, by exercising surveillance of all outside writers or of the articles they write, and sometimes by writing editorials or leaders; to *edit* a work of reference (as a dictionary or encyclopedia) means to plan and execute a new work or one of its later editions, or, more often, to supervise the work of subordinates charged with the execution of those plans. Because the details of editing vary according to the nature of the work edited, the verb is often used narrowly with a stress on one of these implications; thus, to *edit* often currently implies the cutting out of material for the sake of improvement or to meet limitations of space but often for other reasons that concern the person or the institution involved ⟨*edit* a classic for high school use⟩ **Compile** in reference to literary material stresses a gathering together of material, whether written by oneself or obtained from varied sources, to form a collection, an anthology, or a work of reference; often, in addition, it implies the performance of the tasks of an editor, for it suggests need of skill in arrangement, in interpretation, and in dealing with textual problems ⟨Palgrave *compiled* in the first volume of the Golden Treasury one of the best anthologies of English poetry⟩ ⟨the French Academy . . . took forty years to *compile* their Dictionary—*William Adams*⟩ **Revise** (see also CORRECT) implies a review of an earlier draft or edition to see where it can be improved and the actual work of improving ⟨twenty years after Dr. Smith's death his standard work on this subject was *revised* and brought up-to-date by Dr. Jones⟩ ⟨the society finally decided to *revise* its bylaws⟩ **Redact** is used mostly by literary and historical scholars, especially in its derivative forms *redaction* and *redactor,* to imply the presentation of something in form for use or for publication. It may imply careful framing of or giving expression to some material ⟨council of ministers . . . engaged in *redacting* the two proclamations—*W. G. Clark*⟩ but it more often suggests editing of materials ⟨the *redaction* of this great work . . . was ultimately confided to Diderot—*Jefferies*⟩ or even, especially in the form *redactor,* the giving of a new form to an old work (as by revision, rearrangement, or addition) ⟨the visit of Julius Caesar to Egypt in the *Pharsalia* is seized upon by its [medieval] *redactor* to introduce . . . the liaison between Caesar and Cleopatra —*Lowes*⟩ ⟨whatever delicacy and poignancy the tale has in Ovid's version eludes the Elizabethan *redactor*— *PMLA*⟩ **Rewrite** implies a putting into a form suitable for publication of a set of facts or of material gathered by another (as a reporter). The verb often occurs in this sense but is not so common as the noun *rewrite* designating such an article ⟨made a complete *rewrite* of his earlier draft⟩ ⟨it is this journalist's function to *rewrite* stories sent in by local representatives in nearby towns⟩ ⟨an old song which Burns has simply *rewritten*—*Kilby*⟩ ⟨the reporter at the scene of the catastrophe telephoned his story to a *rewrite* man in his editorial office⟩ **Adapt** (for fuller treatment see ADAPT) implies a free alteration of the work of someone else to make it suitable for other readers or for another medium ⟨the play was *adapted* from a French farce⟩ ⟨the book was *adapted* with success for the stage—*J. D. Hart*⟩ ⟨the tunes he *adapted* freely from French vaudeville—*Edward Sackville-West & Desmond Shawe-Taylor*⟩

*Ana* \*make, fabricate, fashion, form

**edition,** impression, reprinting, printing, reissue are capable of being distinguished when used to designate the total number of copies of the same work printed during a stretch of time. **Edition,** as now used by publishers and to some extent by printers, applies to all the books and also to all the newspapers printed from the same type or plates made from it. Terms such as *special edition,*

*limited edition,* and *anniversary edition* are sometimes used to indicate the particular form or format in which a fixed text is presented; but in United States copyright law a different edition must incorporate some material addition to or revision of the original matter. Hence, when the first edition gives way to the second edition, the second edition to the third edition, and so on, a definite change in content is implied. The work may have been revised in whole or in part, whether by bringing it up-to-date or by varying it (this is especially true of newspapers) to suit a particular clientele, but in all cases there must have been changes involving an entire or partial resetting of type before a work can be said to go into a new edition ⟨the 14th *edition* of the Encyclopaedia Britannica⟩ ⟨you will find it in the city *edition* of the *New York Times* for January 17th⟩ **Impression** applies to all of the books (also prints or engravings) run off by the press at one time. The standing type or plates are then stored until a later impression (often called a **reprinting**) is needed. It is now the general practice among publishers to speak of the aggregate number of copies of a new book run off from the press in a large number and at one time (or, in technical language, printed in a continuous run from a single makeready) as an *impression* rather than an *edition,* thereby respecting the latter word's implication of substantial changes in content ⟨a work which went through several *impressions*⟩ **Printing** is often used as practically equivalent to *impression* or *reprinting* but it is sometimes preferred as implying some minor corrections ⟨the book is already in its tenth *printing*⟩ **Reissue** is used to denote a republication, usually after some time, of a work which is out of print. The reissue may differ in price from the original edition or impression owing to changes in paper or in binding, and it may differ in further ways requiring a resetting of type in whole or in part.

**educate** train, discipline, school, \*teach, instruct

**educe,** evoke, elicit, extract, extort mean to bring or draw out what is hidden, latent, or reserved. **Educe** usually implies the development and outward manifestation of something potential or latent ⟨Gray, with the qualities of mind and soul of a genuine poet . . . could not fully *educe* and enjoy them—*Arnold*⟩ ⟨seem to be able to *educe* from common sense a more or less clear reply to the questions raised—*Sidgwick*⟩ **Evoke** basically suggests the voice or the words of a magician compelling spirits to leave the other world or the dead to arise from their graves ⟨*evoke* a demon⟩ ⟨*evoked* the ghost of his father⟩ In current use the term ordinarily implies the operation of a powerful agency that produces an effect instantly or that serves as a stimulus in arousing an emotion, a passion, or an interest ⟨the delight which growing flowers and blossoming trees *evoke*—*Binyon*⟩ ⟨it is useless to obtrude moral ideas [upon children] at an age at which they can *evoke* no response—*Russell*⟩ ⟨all harmonies . . . are latent in the complex mechanism of an organ, but a master's hand is necessary to *evoke* them—*Lowes*⟩ **Elicit** usually implies pains, trouble, or skill in drawing something forth or out; it often implies resistance either in the person or thing that is the object of effort ⟨*elicit* important information from a witness by cross-examination⟩ ⟨it is the trouble we take over our children that *elicits* the stronger forms of parental affection—*Russell*⟩ **Extract** implies the action of a force (as pressure or suction) ⟨*extract* the juice of an orange⟩ ⟨*extract* a tooth⟩ ⟨to *extract* all the dramatic value possible from the situation—*T. S. Eliot*⟩ ⟨he had not that faculty of *extracting* the essence from a heap of statements—*Dickens*⟩ ⟨to make the comparison at all was . . . to return to it

often, to brood upon it, to *extract* from it the last dregs of its interest—*Henry James*⟩ **Extort** implies a wringing or wresting especially from one who is reluctant or resisting ⟨*extort* money from one's relatives⟩ ⟨*extort* a promise⟩ ⟨she did at last *extort* from her father an acknowledgment that the horses were engaged—*Austen*⟩ ⟨whose income is ample enough to *extort* obsequiousness from the vulgar of all ranks—*Bennett*⟩
*Ana* draw, drag (see PULL): produce, *bear, yield, turn out: *summon, call

**eerie** *weird, uncanny
*Ana* *fantastic, bizarre, grotesque: *mysterious, inscrutable, arcane: *fearful, awful, dreadful, horrific: *strange, odd, queer, curious, peculiar

**efface** obliterate, *erase, expunge, blot out, delete, cancel
*Ana* remove, *move, shift: eradicate, extirpate, wipe (see EXTERMINATE): eliminate, *exclude, rule out

**effect** *n* **1** Effect, result, consequence, upshot, aftereffect, aftermath, sequel, issue, outcome, event are comparable in signifying something, usually a condition, situation, or occurrence, ascribable to a cause or combination of causes. **Effect** is the correlative of the word *cause* and in general use implies something (as a bodily or social condition or a state of mind) necessarily and directly following upon or occurring by reason of a cause ⟨the *effect* of the medicine was an intermittent dizziness⟩ ⟨tanning is the *effect* of exposure to sunlight⟩ ⟨low mortality, the *effect* of excellent social services available in every village—*Petersen*⟩ **Result,** close to *effect* in meaning, implies a direct relationship with an antecedent action or condition, usually suggests an effect that terminates the operation of a cause, and applies more commonly than *effect* to tangible objects ⟨his limp was the *result* of an automobile accident⟩ ⟨the subsiding flood or surface waters cause mineral deposits and the *result* is a mound—*Duncan-Kemp*⟩ **Consequence** may suggest a direct but looser or more remote connection with a cause than either *effect* or *result,* sometimes implying an adverse or calamitous effect and often suggesting a chain of intermediate causes or a complexity of effect ⟨one of the *consequences* of his ill-advised conduct was a loss of prestige⟩ ⟨this refined taste is the *consequence* of education and habit—*Reynolds*⟩ **Upshot** often implies a climax or conclusion in a series of consequent occurrences or the most conclusive point of a single complex gradual consequence ⟨we spent the time swimming at Glenelg and dancing at the Palais Royal in the city. The *upshot* was that, before we left . . . we were engaged—*Ingamells*⟩ ⟨they won the battle, and the *upshot* was a short-lived bourgeois republic—*Lewis & Maude*⟩ ⟨the *upshot* of the whole matter was that there was no wedding—*Colum*⟩ **Aftereffect** and *aftermath* both usually designate secondary rather than direct or immediate effects. **Aftereffect** besides designating a secondary effect sometimes suggests a side effect but more generally implies an effect ascribable to a previous effect that has become a cause ⟨the *aftereffects* of an atomic-bomb explosion—*Current Biog.*⟩ ⟨although the pioneer effort had reached a dead end, its *aftereffects* were all too apparent—*Kohler*⟩ ⟨to the left of the highway the blackened appearance is the *aftereffect* of a fire that has recently swept across the flat—*G. R. Stewart*⟩ **Aftermath** often suggests a more complex effect or generalized condition than *aftereffect* and usually carries the notion of belated consequences that appear after the effects, especially disastrous effects, seem to have passed ⟨the serious dislocations in the world as an *aftermath* of war—*U. S. Code*⟩ ⟨the *aftermath* of the epidemic in Memphis was worse than the dismal days of Recon-

struction—*Amer. Guide Series: Tenn.*⟩ **Sequel** usually signifies a result that follows after an interval ⟨spinal curvature . . . may be a symptom or a *sequel* to many different diseases—*Fishbein*⟩ ⟨she lay rigid experiencing the *sequel* to the pain, an ideal terror—*Stafford*⟩ **Issue** adds to *result* the implication of exit or escape (as from difficulties); it therefore usually designates a result that is a solution or a resolution ⟨a contest in which the *issue* is still the greatest and gravest of all, life or death—*A. C. Ward*⟩ ⟨the war was by then obviously proceeding towards a successful *issue*—*F. M. Ford*⟩ **Outcome,** though often interchangeable with *result* or *issue,* may put less stress on the notion of finality than does *issue* ⟨the *outcome* of the presidential election⟩ ⟨the enduring organisms are now the *outcome* of evolution—*Whitehead*⟩ ⟨one *outcome* of this report was the formation of the Southern Conference for Human Welfare—*Current Biog.*⟩ **Event,** which is both uncommon and somewhat archaic in this relation, usually carries the notion of an unpredictable or unforeseeable outcome and comes very close to the related *eventuality* in its implication of a possible or contingent effect or result ⟨the happiness of Rome appeared to hang on the *event* of a race—*Gibbon*⟩ ⟨he employed himself at Edinburgh till the *event* of the conflict between the court and the Whigs was no longer doubtful—*Macaulay*⟩ ⟨the calm assumption that I should live long enough to carry out my extensive plan at leisure . . . has in the *event* been justified—*Ellis*⟩
*Ant* cause —*Con* determinant, antecedent, reason, occasion (see CAUSE): basis, ground, *base, foundation, groundwork
**2** in plural form **effects** *possessions, belongings, means, resources, assets

**effect** *vb* **1** accomplish, achieve, *perform, execute, discharge, fulfill
*Ana* *reach, attain, achieve, compass, gain: finish, complete, conclude, end, terminate, *close: implement, *enforce: *realize, actualize
**2** *affect

**effective,** effectual, efficient, efficacious all mean producing or capable of producing a result or results, but they are not freely interchangeable in idiomatic use. **Effective** emphasizes the actual production of an effect or the power to produce a given effect ⟨*effective* thinking⟩ ⟨an *effective* speaker⟩ ⟨an *effective* rebuke⟩ ⟨the law becomes *effective* on the 1st of next month⟩ ⟨research chemists . . . are actively investigating to learn why particular materials are *effective* and to make them more so—*Morrison*⟩ ⟨persons who will do nothing unless they get something out of it for themselves are often highly *effective* persons of action—*Shaw*⟩ **Effectual** suggests the accomplishment of a desired result or the fulfillment of a purpose or intention, so that the term frequently becomes synonymous with *decisive* or *final* and looks backward after the event ⟨an *effectual* measure⟩ ⟨an *effectual* refutation⟩ ⟨his recommendation was *effectual,* and I was . . . chosen—*Gibbon*⟩ ⟨an appeal to the emotions is little likely to be *effectual* before lunch—*Maugham*⟩ **Efficient** may apply to what is actively operative and producing a result and then comes close to *operant* in meaning ⟨it should be obvious that it is the conditions producing the end effects which must be regarded as the *efficient* causes of them—*Ashley Montagu*⟩ More often it suggests an acting or a capacity or potential for action or use in such a manner as to minimize the loss or waste of energy in effecting, producing, or functioning ⟨an *efficient* apparatus⟩ ⟨a setup designed for the *efficient* production of small parts⟩ ⟨a strong tendency to break up cumbersome estates into small, *efficient* farms—*Nevins*

A colon (:) separates groups of words discriminated. An asterisk (*) indicates place of treatment of each group.

& *Commager*⟩ As used of human beings with this denotation *efficient* suggests the exercise of such qualities as skill, pains, and vigilance and often becomes synonymous with *capable* and *competent* ⟨an *efficient* housewife takes care of her equipment⟩ ⟨because pasturage is the best and cheapest feed for dairy cows, the *efficient* dairyman takes the best possible care of his pastures—*R. E. Hodgson & W. J. Sweetman*⟩ ⟨a small seedy village grocer is more *efficient* for the limited task he must perform than a supermarket—*Wiles*⟩ **Efficacious** implies the possession of the quality or virtue that gives a thing the potency or power that makes it effective ⟨quinine is *efficacious* in cases of malaria⟩ ⟨good wishes being so cheap, though possibly not very *efficacious*—*Hawthorne*⟩ ⟨certain formulae of blessing especially *efficacious* against devils—*Wylie*⟩
*Ana* forceful, forcible, potent, *powerful: producing *or* productive, bearing, turning out (see corresponding verbs at BEAR): telling, cogent, convincing, compelling (see VALID): operative, *active, dynamic
*Ant* ineffective: futile —*Con* vain, fruitless, bootless, abortive (see FUTILE): nugatory, idle, otiose, *vain, empty, hollow
**effectual** *effective, efficacious, efficient
*Ana* effecting, accomplishing, achieving, fulfilling (see PERFORM): operative, dynamic, *active: decisive, determinative, *conclusive
*Ant* ineffectual: fruitless —*Con* *futile, vain, bootless, abortive
**effeminate** *adj* womanish, womanlike, womanly, feminine, *female, ladylike
*Ana* emasculated, enervated, unmanned (see UNNERVE): epicene (see BISEXUAL): *soft, mild, gentle, lenient, bland: pampered, indulged, humored, mollycoddled (see INDULGE)
*Ant* virile —*Con* mannish (see MALE)
**effervescent** volatile, buoyant, expansive, resilient, *elastic
*Ana* *lively, vivacious, sprightly, gay, animated: hilarious, jolly, gleeful, mirthful (see corresponding nouns at MIRTH)
*Ant* subdued
**efficacious** effectual, *effective, efficient
*Ana* potent, *powerful, puissant: cogent, telling, sound, convincing, compelling (see VALID)
*Ant* inefficacious: powerless
**efficient** *effective, effectual, efficacious
*Ana* competent, qualified, *able, capable: expert, skillful, skilled, *proficient, adept, masterly
*Ant* inefficient
**effigy** *image, statue, icon, portrait, photograph, mask
**effort,** exertion, pains, trouble mean the active use or expenditure of physical or mental power in producing or attempting to produce a desired result. **Effort** may suggest either a single action or continued activity, but it usually implies consciousness that one is making an attempt or sometimes, even, is laboring or straining to achieve an end ⟨make a final supreme *effort*⟩ ⟨the constant *effort* of the dreamer to attain his ideal—*Henry Adams*⟩ ⟨utterly absorbed in the writing of a private letter—how you lose count of time and have no sense of disagreeable *effort*—*Montague*⟩ **Exertion** in general stresses the active, often vigorous, exercise of a power or faculty ⟨the continued *exertion* of vigilance⟩ ⟨wearied by over*exertion*⟩ ⟨a . . . man, capable of close application of mind, and great *exertion* of body—*Dickens*⟩ Often, however, especially when not followed by *of*, *exertion* means a laborious effort ⟨his work was done with remarkable grace, but with *exertions* which it was painful to witness; for he had but one leg, and had to use a crutch—*Deland*⟩ **Pains** implies toilsome or solicitous effort; **trouble** implies exertion that inconveniences or wastes time and patience ⟨was at *pains* to emphasize the nonpolitical character of the visit—*Morgenthau*⟩ ⟨the Indians had exhaustless patience; upon their blankets and belts and ceremonial robes they lavished their skill and *pains*—*Cather*⟩ ⟨is twenty hundred kisses such a *trouble?*—*Shak.*⟩ ⟨"I feel that I am beginning to get a grip of the people . . . ." "I should hope so, after the amount of time and *trouble* you've taken"—*Mackenzie*⟩
*Ana* *work, labor, toil, travail: energy, force, *power, might, puissance: endeavor, essay (see under ATTEMPT *vb*)
*Ant* ease
**effortless** *easy, smooth, facile, simple, light
*Ana* *proficient, skilled, skillful, expert, adept, masterly
*Ant* painstaking
**effrontery** *temerity, audacity, hardihood, nerve, cheek, gall
*Ana* impudence, brazenness, brashness (see corresponding adjectives at SHAMELESS): impertinence, intrusiveness, officiousness (see corresponding adjectives at IMPERTINENT)
**effulgent** radiant, luminous, brilliant, *bright, lustrous, refulgent, beaming, lambent, lucent, incandescent
*Ana* flaming, blazing, glowing, flaring (see BLAZE *vb*): flashing, gleaming (see FLASH *vb*): resplendent, *splendid, glorious
*Con* murky, gloomy, *dark, dim, obscure, dusky
**egg** *vb* *urge, exhort, goad, spur, prod, prick, sic
*Ana* stimulate, excite, *provoke, pique: *incite, instigate: rally, arouse, rouse, *stir
**egoism** egotism, *conceit, amour propre, self-love, self-esteem
*Ana* self-confidence, self-assurance, self-possession (see CONFIDENCE): self-satisfaction, self-complacency, complacency, smugness, priggishness (see corresponding adjectives at COMPLACENT)
*Ant* altruism —*Con* humility, meekness, modesty, lowliness (see corresponding adjectives at HUMBLE)
**egotism** egoism, *conceit, self-love, amour propre, self-esteem
*Ana* vanity, vainglory, *pride: boasting *or* boastfulness, vaunting *or* vauntfulness, gasconading (see corresponding verbs at BOAST): pluming, piquing, priding, preening (see PRIDE *vb*)
*Ant* modesty —*Con* humility, meekness, lowliness (see corresponding adjectives at HUMBLE): diffidence, bashfulness, shyness (see corresponding adjectives at SHY)
**eject** *vb* Eject, expel, oust, evict, dismiss mean to force or thrust something or someone out. **Eject,** although it is the comprehensive term of this group and is often interchangeable with any of the others, carries the strongest implication of throwing out from within. So emphatic is this suggestion that the term covers actions so far apart as those implied by *dislodge, disgorge, vomit, emit, discharge,* and many other terms ⟨the volcano *ejected* lava for three days in succession⟩ ⟨*eject* an intruder from one's house⟩ ⟨the chimney *ejected* flames rather than smoke⟩ ⟨he was being *ejected* for taunting the pianist—*Atkinson*⟩ **Expel** stresses a thrusting out or a driving away; it therefore more regularly implies the use of voluntary force or compulsion than does *eject* and indicates more clearly than *eject* an intent to get rid of for all time; thus, the stomach *ejects* (rather than *expels*) material in vomiting since the emphasis is on casting out from within; one *expels* (rather than *ejects*) air from the lungs since in this case a degree of voluntary force and permanent ridding are both implicit ⟨*expel*

---

*Ana* analogous words       *Ant* antonyms       *Con* contrasted words       See also explanatory notes facing page 1

a student from college〉 〈a curse . . . in his blood . . .
which no life of purity could *expel*—*Meredith*〉 〈Octavian
. . . forbade the practice of certain eastern cults, and
*expelled* from Rome Greek and Asiatic magicians—
*Buchan*〉 **Oust** implies a removal or dispossession by the
power of the law or, in more general use, by the exercise
of force or by the compulsion of necessity 〈in America
. . . a new set of officials *oust* the old ones whenever the
Opposition *ousts* the Government—*Shaw*〉 〈insidious
attempts to disparage the findings of Reason, or to *oust*
it from its proper province—*Inge*〉 **Evict** means to turn
out (as from house or home or one's place of business)
by legal or equally effective process, commonly for nonpayment of rent 〈after not paying their rent for six months,
they were *evicted* by the sheriff〉 〈the revolutionary artists
. . . in the first flush of victory . . . literally *evicted* the
members and officers of the Imperial Academy—*Read*〉
〈he volunteered to become foster father to a 400-pot
family [of orchids] temporarily *evicted* from a nearby
greenhouse—*JAMA*〉 **Dismiss** (see also DISMISS) stresses
a getting rid of something such as a legal case by rejecting
a claim or prayer and refusing it further consideration
〈this court reversed the judgement given in favor of the
defendant, and remanded the case with directions to
*dismiss* it—*Taney*〉 or a fear, a grudge, or a hatred by
ejecting it from the mind or thoughts 〈I declare to you
. . . that I have long *dismissed* it from my mind—*Dickens*〉
or an unwelcome subject, duty, or prospect by taking adequate measures to ensure its no longer annoying or confronting one 〈the Judge was sharply angry . . . because he
found himself unable to *dismiss* the whole thing by
packing the child off—*Deland*〉
**Ana** *exclude, eliminate, shut out, rule out, debar, disbar:
*dismiss, discharge, cashier, fire, sack: *discard, cast,
shed: reject, repudiate, spurn (see DECLINE)
**Ant** admit (sense 1)

**elaborate** *vb* *unfold, evolve, develop, perfect
**Ana** *expand, amplify, dilate: enlarge, augment (see
INCREASE): heighten, enhance (see INTENSIFY)

**élan** *vigor, vim, spirit, dash, esprit, verve, punch, drive

**elapse** *pass, pass away, expire
**Ana** slip, *slide, glide: end, terminate (see CLOSE)

**elastic** *adj* **1** Elastic, resilient, springy, flexible, supple
are comparable when they mean able to endure strain
(as extension, compression, twisting, or bending) without
being permanently affected or injured. *Elastic* and *resilient* are both general and scientific terms; the scientific
senses are later and are in part derived from the earlier
meanings. **Elastic** in nontechnical use is applied chiefly
to substances or materials that are easy to stretch or
expand and that quickly recover their shape or size when
the pressure is removed 〈a rubber band is *elastic*〉
〈*elastic* cord for hats〉 〈a toy balloon is an *elastic* bag
which can be blown up greatly beyond its original size〉
In scientific use *elastic* is applicable to a solid that may
be changed in volume or shape, or to a fluid (gas or liquid)
that may be changed in volume, when in the course of the
deformation of such a solid or fluid forces come into play
which tend to make it recover its original volume or shape
once the deforming force or forces are removed. The term
in such use describes a property (*elasticity*) which a
substance possesses up to the point (the *elastic limit*)
beyond which it cannot be deformed without permanent
injury 〈a body . . . is *elastic* when, and only when, it tends
to recover its initial condition when the distorting force
is removed . . . . Steel, rubber, air . . . are more or less
*elastic*—*Foley*〉 **Resilient** in nontechnical use is applicable
to whatever springs back into place or into shape especially after compression; thus, rising bread dough is said
to be *resilient* because it quickly recovers from a deforming
pressure by the hand; a tree's branch may be described as
*resilient* when it snaps back into its former position
once a pull is released. Scientifically, *resilient* is not
the equivalent of *elastic*, but it may be used as its counterpart; *elastic* stresses the capacity for deformation without permanent injury, *resilient* the capacity for recovering
shape or position after strain or pressure has been removed; thus, when an *elastic* substance is stretched or
compressed, it shows itself *resilient*; as arteries gradually
become less *elastic* with age, to the same extent they
become less *resilient*. **Springy** is a nontechnical term
that carries the meanings and suggestions of both *elastic*
and *resilient* and stresses at once the ease with which
a thing yields to pressure or strain and the quickness of
its return 〈walk on *springy* turf〉 〈firm, *springy* muscles〉
〈a laughing schoolboy . . . riding the *springy* branches
of an elm—*Keats*〉 **Flexible** is applicable to whatever can
be bent or turned without breaking; the term may or may
not imply resiliency, or quick recovery of shape 〈lead
pipe is *flexible* and may be bent into shape〉 〈a *flexible*
young tree often endures a heavy windstorm better than
a rigid, fully developed one〉 〈*flexible* and gracious
as the willow—*Binyon*〉 **Supple** applies to things which
are, in general, not as solid or firm in structure as some
which may be described as *flexible;* it also implies ease
in bending, twisting, or folding or flexing, together with
resistance to accompanying injury (as from breaking,
cracking, or splitting) 〈*supple* joints and muscles〉 〈a
*supple* leather〉 〈mere manual labor stiffens the limbs,
gymnastic exercises render them *supple*—*Jefferies*〉
In extended use these words often carry the implications
of their literal senses. **Elastic** stresses ease in stretching
or expanding beyond the normal or appointed limits
〈an *elastic* conscience〉 〈some principles there must
be, however *elastic*—*Buchan*〉 〈an *elastic* term〉 **Resilient** implies a tendency to rebound or recover quickly
(as in health or spirits) especially after subjection to stress
or strain (see ELASTIC 2) 〈a *resilient* constitution〉 **Springy,**
which is less common in extended use, may suggest youth,
freshness, or buoyancy 〈a *springy* step〉 **Flexible** implies
an adaptable or accommodating quality or, when applied
to persons, pliancy or tractability 〈a *flexible* scheme〉
〈a *flexible* arrangement〉 〈his mind became more *flexible*
with age—*Crothers*〉 **Supple,** in its extended use, is applied chiefly to persons or their utterances. Sometimes
it suggests little more than flexibility; at other times it
implies obsequiousness or complaisance or a show
of these with what is actually astute mastery of a situation 〈in . . . Bismarck, the *supple* spirit is hidden under
an external directness and rough assertion—*Belloc*〉
**Ana** pliable, pliant, ductile, *plastic, malleable: limber,
lithe, *supple
**Ant** rigid —**Con** *stiff, inflexible, tense
**2** Elastic, expansive, resilient, buoyant, volatile, effervescent are comparable when describing persons, their
temperaments, moods, acts, or words and meaning indicative of or characterized by ease or readiness in the
stimulation of spirit and especially of high spirits. **Elastic**
implies an incapacity for being kept down in spirits;
specifically it may suggest an ability to recover quickly
from a state of depression 〈those *elastic* spirits . . . had
borne up against defeat—*Macaulay*〉 or a tendency to
moods of exaltation, elation, or optimism 〈there are times
when one's vitality is too high to be clouded, too *elastic*
to stay down—*Cather*〉 〈not an *elastic* or optimistic nature
—on the contrary, rigid and circumscribed, depressed
by a melancholy temperament—*Symonds*〉 〈to him whose
*elastic* and vigorous thought keeps pace with the sun,

A colon (:) separates groups of words discriminated. An asterisk (*) indicates place of treatment of each group.

the day is a perpetual morning—*Thoreau*⟩ **Expansive** implies exaltation of spirit that tends to make a person unusually genial, communicative, or sociable ⟨she had an *expansive* temperament, a brilliant personality, a widely sympathetic disposition, troops of friends—*Ellis*⟩ ⟨in an *expansive* and not very sober moment, she had told Tod about her adventure—*Sayers*⟩ ⟨while not *expansive* toward visitors, she received them with courtesy—*Raymond Weeks*⟩ **Resilient** usually implies a return to normal good spirits, which may or may not be high spirits ⟨he was as *resilient* as ever, one day utterly exhausted, and the next day ready for fresh labors⟩ ⟨evidently her *resilient* strength was going; she could no longer react normally to the refreshment of food—*Ellis*⟩ ⟨already the shock and horror of it was fading from her *resilient* mind—*Ruth Park*⟩ **Buoyant** implies such lightness or vivacity of heart or spirits as is either incapable of depression or that readily shakes it off ⟨no such immaterial burden could depress that *buoyant*-hearted young gentleman for many hours together—*George Eliot*⟩ ⟨his *buoyant* spirits were continually breaking out in troublesome frolics—*Prescott*⟩ **Volatile** implies diametrical opposition to all that is serious, sedate, or settled; it therefore suggests lightness, levity, or excessive buoyancy of spirits and often flightiness or instability ⟨as giddy and *volatile* as ever —*Swift*⟩ ⟨he seemed to them so *volatile* and unstable. He was an enigma to which they never secured the key —*Ellis*⟩ **Effervescent** implies liveliness, often boisterousness of spirits; it often suggests the effect of release after restraint and even more than *buoyant* implies the impossibility of suppression so long as the mood or temper lasts ⟨an *effervescent* sort of chap with an enthusiasm that takes off like a rocket—*Joseph*⟩
*Ana* *spirited, high-spirited, mettlesome: *lively, vivacious, sprightly, animated, gay
*Ant* depressed —*Con* dejected, gloomy, melancholy, sad, blue (see corresponding nouns at SADNESS): flaccid, *limp
**elbowroom** *room, berth, play, leeway, margin, clearance
**elderly** old, *aged, superannuated
*Ant* youthful
**elect** *adj* picked, *select, exclusive
*Ana* *choice, exquisite, rare: selected, preferred, chosen, singled out (see CHOOSE): redeemed, saved, delivered (see RESCUE *vb*)
*Ant* reprobate (*in theology*) —*Con* rejected, repudiated, spurned, refused (see DECLINE *vb*): scorned, disdained (see DESPISE): doomed, damned (see SENTENCE *vb*)
**elect** *vb* 1 select, pick, prefer, single, opt, *choose, cull
*Ana* *decide, determine, settle, resolve: conclude, judge (see INFER): *receive, accept, admit, take
*Ant* abjure —*Con* reject, spurn, repudiate, refuse, *decline: dismiss, *eject, oust, expel
2 *designate, name, nominate, appoint
**election** selection, option, *choice, preference, alternative
*Ana* deciding *or* decision, determining *or* determination, settling *or* settlement (see corresponding verbs at DECIDE)
**electrify** *thrill, enthuse
*Ana* galvanize, excite, stimulate, quicken, *provoke: *stir, rouse, arouse, rally
**eleemosynary** *charitable, benevolent, humane, humanitarian, philanthropic, altruistic
**elegance,** grace, dignity are comparable only when they denote an impressive beauty of form, appearance, or behavior. **Elegance** is used in reference to persons chiefly when their grooming, their clothes, and the way they wear them are specifically considered; it then often implies fashionableness and good taste, but it stresses perfection

of detail and exquisiteness or, sometimes, overexquisiteness (as in materials, lines, and ornamentation) ⟨the *elegance* in dress of a Beau Brummell⟩ When used in reference to such things as the furnishings of a home, the details of a dinner, or a literary style, the term also implies the perfection and propriety in detail that indicate excellence of taste, a nice selective instinct, and often a restrained luxuriousness ⟨a very pretty sitting room, lately fitted up with greater *elegance* and lightness than the apartments below—*Austen*⟩ ⟨a cultivated man should express himself by tongue or pen with some accuracy and *elegance*—*Eliot*⟩ **Grace** is more commonly applied to what is inward and native than to what is outward and acquired, especially when used in reference to persons; it always suggests a quality or a harmonious combination of qualities that gives aesthetic pleasure through a natural or simple beauty such as is shown in suppleness or rhythm of movement, in clean-flowing lines or contours, or in spontaneity and felicitousness of manner, mood, expression, or style ⟨a behavior so full of *grace* and sweetness, such easy motions, with an air so majestic, yet free from stiffness or affectation—*Montagu*⟩ ⟨the effect upon the observer of this exquisite little edifice ... was of an unparagoned lightness and *grace*—*Mackenzie*⟩ ⟨she took the congratulations of her rivals and of the rest of the company with the simplicity that was her crowning *grace*—*Wharton*⟩ **Dignity** applies to what compels respect and honor. The term often suggests stateliness, majesty, and elevation of character or style as the compelling cause ⟨the qualifications which frequently invest the facade of a prison with far more *dignity* than is found in the facade of a palace double its size—*Hardy*⟩ ⟨there was a *dignity* in his Client, an impressiveness in his speech, that silenced remonstrating Reason—*Meredith*⟩ ⟨those who are just beginning to appreciate the idea of lending greater *dignity* to the worship of Almighty God—*Mackenzie*⟩ Very frequently in modern use the term suggests the compulsion of intrinsic worth or merit apart from any superficial characteristics that give it external beauty ⟨the *dignity* of work⟩ ⟨the *dignity* of motherhood⟩ ⟨it matters not how trivial the occupation, if the man or woman be wholly given to it, there will be a natural compelling *dignity* in the figure—*Binyon*⟩
*Ana* beautifulness *or* beauty, handsomeness, comeliness (see corresponding adjectives at BEAUTIFUL): fastidiousness, niceness *or* nicety, daintiness (see corresponding adjectives at NICE): perfection, *excellence: *taste (sense 2)
**elegant** *adj* exquisite, *choice, recherché, rare, dainty, delicate
*Ana* majestic, stately, noble, august, *grand: *beautiful, handsome: fastidious, *nice: *consummate, finished: sumptuous, *luxurious, opulent
*Con* crude, *rude, rough, uncouth: ostentatious, *showy, pretentious: bizarre, grotesque, *fantastic
**element,** component, constituent, ingredient, factor are comparable when they mean one of the parts, substances, or principles which make up a compound or complex thing. **Element** is, except in its specific sense in science, the most widely applicable of these terms, being referable both to material and immaterial and to tangible and intangible things ⟨the native and foreign *elements* in English⟩ ⟨words are the *elements* of a sentence⟩ ⟨the basic *element* of his character⟩ ⟨his life was gentle, and the *elements* so mixed in him that Nature might stand up and say to all the world "This was a man!"—*Shak.*⟩ Always in its scientific sense, often in its general sense, the term implies irreducible simplicity or, if applied to a substance, incapacity for separation into simpler substances ⟨gold, silver, carbon, lead are among the chemical *elements*, or

ultimate building units of matter⟩ ⟨analyze the *elements* of a situation⟩ ⟨another *element* common to all novels is characterization—*Jacobs*⟩ *Component* and *constituent* are often used interchangeably for any of the substances (whether elements or compounds) which enter into the makeup of a mixed thing or for any of the principles or qualities which comprise an intangible composite. **Component**, however, stresses the separate identity or distinguishable character of the substance; **constituent** stresses its essential and formative character ⟨springs, gears, levers, pivots, and other *components* of a watch mechanism⟩ ⟨hydrogen and oxygen are the *constituents* of water⟩ ⟨the *components* of the typical novel are its plot, its characters, and its setting⟩ ⟨the *components* of knowledge can never be harmonized until all the relevant facts are in—*De Voto*⟩ ⟨break a ray of light into the colors which are its *constituents*⟩ ⟨the *constituents* of a perfume⟩ **Ingredient** applies basically to any of the substances or materials which when combined form a particular mixture (as a drink, a medicine, a food, an alloy, or an amalgam) ⟨the *ingredients* of a cocktail⟩ ⟨iron and carbon are the *ingredients* of steel⟩ The term, however, may be extended to any component or constituent that can be thought of as added or as left out ⟨in this transaction every *ingredient* of a complete and legitimate contract is to be found—*John Marshall*⟩ ⟨two very necessary *ingredients* of the scientific process are curiosity and lack of haste—*Sears*⟩ **Factor** is somewhat remotely synonymous with the foregoing words. The term is applicable to a constituent, element, or component only when the latter exerts an effectuating force enabling the whole of which it is a part to perform a certain kind of work, to produce a specific and definite result, or to move or trend in a particular direction ⟨God . . . is not one of the *factors* for which science has to account—*Inge*⟩ ⟨various *factors* entered the inception of the American enterprise—*Ellis*⟩ ⟨the word *vitamins* was coined to designate these essential food *factors*—*Morrison*⟩
*Ana* *principle, fundamental: *part, portion, member: *item, detail, particular
*Ant* compound (*in science*): composite —*Con* mass, *bulk, volume: aggregate, whole, total, *sum

**elemental** *elementary
*Ana* *ultimate, categorical, absolute: *primary, prime, primordial

**elementary**, **elemental** are often confused. Something is **elementary** which pertains to rudiments or beginnings; something is **elemental** which pertains to the elements, especially to the ultimate and basic constituents or forces ⟨an *elementary* treatise⟩ ⟨an *elementary* knowledge of physics⟩ ⟨an *elementary* virtue⟩ ⟨an *elementary* school⟩ ⟨the *elemental* sounds of language⟩ ⟨an *elemental* substance⟩ ⟨they . . . busied themselves with the *elemental*, enduring things: sex, fatherhood, work—*Rose Macaulay*⟩
*Ana* basic, *fundamental: primal, *primary
*Ant* advanced

**elephantine** *huge, vast, immense, enormous, mammoth, giant, gigantic, gigantean, colossal, gargantuan, Herculean, cyclopean, titanic, Brobdingnagian

**elevate** *lift, raise, rear, hoist, heave, boost
*Ana* *exalt, aggrandize, magnify: heighten, enhance (see INTENSIFY): *rise, mount, ascend, tower, soar, rocket
*Ant* lower —*Con* *abase, debase, degrade, demean, humble

**elevation** 1 altitude, *height
*Ana* *ascension, ascent
2 promotion, *advancement, preferment
*Ana* exaltation, aggrandizement (see corresponding verbs at EXALT)

*Ant* degradation

**elicit** *vb* evoke, *educe, extract, extort
*Ana* draw, drag, *pull: *bring, fetch

**eliminate** rule out, *exclude, debar, blackball, disbar, suspend, shut out
*Ana* *eject, oust, dismiss, expel, evict: eradicate, extirpate, *exterminate, uproot, wipe: expunge, *erase, delete, efface

**elite** society, *aristocracy, nobility, gentry, county
*Ant* rabble

**ell** wing, extension, *annex

**elongate** lengthen, *extend, prolong, protract
*Ant* abbreviate, shorten —*Con* abridge, curtail, retrench (see SHORTEN): shrink, compress, *contract

**eloquent** 1 articulate, voluble, *vocal, fluent, glib
*Ana* *impassioned, passionate, fervid, perfervid, ardent, fervent: expressing, voicing, venting, uttering (see EXPRESS *vb*): forceful, forcible, potent, *powerful
2 *expressive, significant, meaningful, pregnant, sententious
*Ana* revealing, disclosing, telling, betraying (see REVEAL): impressive, *moving, poignant, touching, affecting

**elucidate** interpret, construe, expound, *explain, explicate
*Ana* illustrate, *exemplify: demonstrate, *prove

**elude** *escape, evade, avoid, shun, eschew
*Ana* thwart, foil, outwit, circumvent, baffle (see FRUSTRATE): flee, fly, *escape
*Con* *follow, pursue, chase, trail, tag, tail

**emanate** issue, proceed, *spring, rise, arise, originate, derive, flow, stem
*Ana* emerge, loom, *appear: *begin, commence, start, initiate

**emancipate** manumit, enfranchise, *free, liberate, release, deliver, discharge

**emasculate** 1 *sterilize, castrate, spay, alter, mutilate, geld, caponize
2 enervate, unman, *unnerve
*Ana* *weaken, enfeeble, debilitate, sap, undermine
*Con* energize, *vitalize

**embarrass, discomfit, abash, disconcert, rattle, faze** mean to balk by confusing or confounding, but each word is capable of expressing precise and distinctive shades of meaning. **Embarrass** characteristically implies some influence which impedes freedom of thought, speech, or action and may be used with reference not only to persons but also to the things they plan or desire to do ⟨a course of legislation . . . which . . . *embarrassed* all transactions between individuals, by dispensing with a faithful performance of engagements—*John Marshall*⟩ When said of persons it commonly implies and often stresses resulting uneasiness or constraint ⟨he had, he knew, a sort of charm—it *embarrassed* him even to admit it—*Mary Austin*⟩ ⟨I was upset . . . and *embarrassed* by the crude and childish manner in which the townspeople were reduced to caricatures—*J. M. Brown*⟩ **Discomfit** in this sense typically retains some of its basic denotation of to put to rout; in such use it implies opposition and the competence with which one opponent routs the other and crushes his self-esteem or self-complacency ⟨an answer that completely *discomfited* the brash young man⟩ or throws him into confusion ⟨Bradley's polemical irony and his obvious zest in using it, his habit of *discomfiting* an opponent with a sudden profession of ignorance, of inability to understand, or of incapacity for abstruse thought—*T. S. Eliot*⟩ ⟨the Prime Minister began badly. *Discomfited* by Labor heckling from the front bench opposite, Eden lost his usual urbanity—*Time*⟩ or, sometimes, thwarts his wishes, his hopes, or his plans ⟨thieves *discomfited* by a wakeful dog⟩ ⟨he practiced the Socratic method . . . and earned among generations of

A colon (:) separates groups of words discriminated. An asterisk (*) indicates place of treatment of each group.

*discomfited* students the designation Stinker Taussig—*Lovett*⟩ At times *discomfit* is used with much weakened force and then loses its suggestion of active opponency and implies no more than to make uncomfortable or embarrass ⟨it is *discomfiting* to recall the high hopes with which the states that had joined hands to defeat Fascism founded the United Nations—*Sat. Review*⟩ ⟨he drew *discomfited* chuckles from them in response to his garish laughter—*Straight*⟩ ⟨she may heckle the dealer, add a running commentary to the demonstrations, or just assume a *discomfiting* smugness—*Fortune*⟩ **Abash** presupposes self-confidence or self-possession and implies a usually sudden check to that mood by some influence that awakens shyness or a conviction of error or inferiority or, sometimes, of shame ⟨a man whom no denial, no scorn could *abash*—*Fielding*⟩ ⟨*abashed* by the base motives she found herself attributing to Charlotte—*Wharton*⟩ **Disconcert**, like *embarrass*, may be used in reference to actions and plans, but it is more frequently referred to persons. In either case it implies an upsetting or derangement; in the latter it suggests temporary loss of equanimity or of assurance ⟨when she saw him there came that flicker of fun into her eyes that was so *disconcerting* to Mr. Ezra-Deland⟩ **Rattle** more than *disconcert* stresses the emotional agitation accompanying the upset and implies a more complete disorganization of one's mental processes ⟨the jeering *rattled* the team and caused them to play badly⟩ ⟨*rattled* by hypothetical eyes spying on her—*Stafford*⟩ **Faze** is found chiefly in negative expressions, where it comes close to *disconcert* but sometimes carries the implications of *abash* and *rattle* ⟨neither rebuffs nor threats *faze* him in the least⟩ ⟨it hit Marciano flush on the right side of the jaw, but it didn't seem to *faze* him a bit—*Liebling*⟩
*Ana* *discompose, disturb, perturb, fluster, flurry: bewilder, nonplus, perplex (see PUZZLE): *trouble, distress: vex, *annoy, bother, irk: impede, obstruct, block, *hinder: *hamper, fetter, shackle, hog-tie
*Ant* relieve: facilitate

**embellish** beautify, deck, bedeck, garnish, *adorn, decorate, ornament
*Ana* enhance, heighten, *intensify: apparel, array (see CLOTHE)
*Con* denude, *strip, bare, divest

**embers** *ash, cinders, clinkers

**emblem** attribute, *symbol, type
*Ana* device, motif, design, *figure, pattern: *sign, mark, token, badge

**embody** 1 incarnate, materialize, externalize, objectify, *realize, actualize, hypostatize, reify
*Ana* invest, *clothe: illustrate, *exemplify: manifest, demonstrate, evidence, evince, *show
*Ant* disembody
2 incorporate, assimilate, *identify
*Ana* *add, annex, superadd, append: *introduce, insert, interpolate, interject: comprehend, *include, embrace, involve, imply

**embolden** *encourage, inspirit, hearten, cheer, nerve, steel
*Ana* *strengthen, fortify: *venture, chance, hazard
*Ant* abash —*Con* discourage, deter (see DISSUADE): dishearten, dispirit, deject (see DISCOURAGE)

**embrace** *vb* 1 *adopt, espouse
*Ana* accept, *receive: seize, grasp, *take
*Ant* spurn —*Con* reject, refuse, repudiate, *decline: scorn, disdain (see DESPISE)
2 comprehend, *include, involve, imply, subsume
*Ana* *contain, hold, accommodate: embody, incorporate (see IDENTIFY)

*Con* *exclude, rule out, shut out, debar, eliminate
**emend** *correct, rectify, revise, amend, remedy, redress, reform
*Ana* *mend, repair: *improve, better, ameliorate
*Ant* corrupt (*a text, passage*)

**emerge** *appear, loom
*Ana* issue, emanate, *spring, flow, arise, rise, proceed, stem, derive, originate

**emergency** exigency, contingency, crisis, pass, *juncture, pinch, strait
*Ana* situation, condition, posture, *state: *difficulty, vicissitude

**emigrant, immigrant** are comparable but not interchangeable when denoting a person who leaves one country in order to settle in another. **Emigrant** (so also **emigrate** and **emigration**) is used with reference to the country from which, **immigrant** (so also **immigrate** and **immigration**) with reference to the country into which, migration is made. The former marks the going out from a country; the latter, the entrance into a country ⟨a large crowd of Italian *emigrants* boarded the ship at Naples⟩ ⟨Ireland lost heavily through *emigration* in the middle of the nineteenth century⟩ ⟨our surplus cottage children *emigrate* to Australia and Canada—*H. G. Wells*⟩ ⟨Scandinavian *immigrants* settled large parts of the Middle Western United States⟩ ⟨*immigration* from Europe into the United States has gradually decreased⟩

**emigrate** immigrate (see under EMIGRANT)
**emigration** immigration (see under EMIGRANT)
**émigré** immigrant, alien, foreigner, outlander, outsider, *stranger

**eminent** illustrious, renowned, celebrated, *famous, famed
*Ana* signal, outstanding, prominent, remarkable, conspicuous, *noticeable

**emolument** stipend, salary, fee, *wage *or* wages, pay, hire
*Ana* compensation, remuneration, recompensing *or* recompense (see corresponding verbs at PAY): reward, meed, guerdon (see PREMIUM)

**emotion** *feeling, affection, passion, sentiment
**empathy** *sympathy, pity, compassion, commiseration, ruth, condolence
*Ana* *imagination, fancy, fantasy: appreciation, understanding, comprehension (see corresponding verbs at UNDERSTAND)

**emphasis, stress, accent, accentuation** denote exerted force by which one thing stands out conspicuously among other things; they also often designate the effect produced or the means used in gaining this effect. **Emphasis** implies effort to bring out what is significant or important ⟨he puts the *emphasis* on discipline in his teaching⟩ ⟨an effective orator knows how to be sparing in his use of *emphasis*⟩ Sometimes it also suggests vigor or intensity of feeling ⟨anyone, however ignorant, can feel the sustained dignity of the sculptor's work, which is asserted with all the *emphasis* he could put into it—*Henry Adams*⟩ **Stress**, though often used interchangeably with *emphasis*, is distinguishable from it both in some of its implications and in its association with particular arts, where it has acquired specific meanings. It rarely loses entirely its original implication of weight that causes pressure or strain, though this is often merely suggested ⟨"I wouldn't lay too much *stress* on what you have been telling me," I observed quietly—*Conrad*⟩ At times *stress* strongly implies urgency or insistency ⟨Jane secretly approved his discernment. But all she said was, with her cool lack of *stress*, "It's not so bad" —*Rose Macaulay*⟩ In phonetics and prosody *stress* is the general term referring to the prominence given to certain syllables by force of utterance. It may also be used of the natural emphasis on certain words in a sentence. It

---

*Ana* analogous words     *Ant* antonyms     *Con* contrasted words     See also explanatory notes facing page 1

may even suggest degree of emphasis ⟨there were volumes of innuendo in the way the "eventually" was spaced, and each syllable given its due *stress—Wharton*⟩ **Accent** implies contrast for the sake of effect, very frequently an aesthetic effect. *Accent* carries no connotation of weight, but it strongly suggests relief in both senses, that of relieving monotony and that of bringing out sharply or into relief ⟨the room was quiet and neutral in coloring, but it was given *accent* by bowls of bright flowers⟩ ⟨sun and sea, the heady fragrance of the plane trees, the tropical *accent* of palms—*Cassidy*⟩ In prosody accent is the form of stress characteristic of English verse, akin to the beat in music and involving force in utterance. In English phonetics *accent* and *stress* are commonly used interchangeably. Since force of utterance (*stress*) is the principal means by which a syllable, a word, or a group of words is accented or brought into sharp contrast with the others, one may speak of syllabic *accent* or *stress,* or word *accent* or *stress.* **Accentuation,** though close to *accent* (except in technical senses), often goes beyond it in its emphasis on increased conspicuousness; it also often suggests disagreeableness in the contrast ⟨the essential defect of their polity . . . its excessive *accentuation* of the corporate aspect of life —*Dickinson*⟩

**employ** *vb* *use, utilize, apply, avail
*Ana* *practice, exercise, drill: engross, absorb, *monopolize: *choose, select, pick

**employment** *work, occupation, business, calling, pursuit
*Ana* *trade, craft, handicraft, art, profession

**empower** *enable
*Ana* *authorize, commission, accredit, license: train, instruct, discipline, *teach: endow, endue (see DOWER)
*Con* debar, disbar, shut out, rule out, *exclude

**empty** *adj* **1** Empty, vacant, blank, void, vacuous mean lacking the contents that could or should be present. Something is **empty** which has nothing in it; something is **vacant** which is without an occupant, incumbent, tenant, inmate, or the person or thing it appropriately contains ⟨an *empty* bucket⟩ ⟨his purse was *empty*⟩ ⟨*empty*-handed⟩ ⟨a *vacant* professorship⟩ ⟨a *vacant* apartment⟩ When qualifying the same nouns the words usually suggest distinctly different ideas; thus, an *empty* house has neither furniture nor occupants; a *vacant* house is without inmates and presumably for rent or for sale; an *empty* chair has no one sitting in it at the time; a *vacant* chair is one that has lost its usual occupant by death or other cause; an *empty* space has nothing in it; a *vacant* space is one left to be filled with what is appropriate ⟨[it] enabled him to fill a place which would else have been *vacant*— *Hawthorne*⟩ Something, especially a surface, is **blank** which is free from writing or marks or which has vacant spaces that are left to be filled in ⟨a *blank* page⟩ ⟨a *blank* application⟩ Something is **void** which is absolutely empty so far as the senses can discover ⟨a conscience *void* of offense⟩ ⟨sandy wilderness, all black and *void*—*Wordsworth*⟩ ⟨the *void*, hollow, universal air—*Shelley*⟩ Something is **vacuous** which exhibits the absolute emptiness of a vacuum ⟨the *vacuous* globe of an incandescent lamp⟩
  In extended use the same distinctions hold: an **empty** mind is destitute of worthwhile ideas or knowledge; a **vacant** mind lacks its usual occupant, the soul or intellect; a **blank** look is without expression; a person is said to be **void** of learning or of common sense when not the slightest evidence of either one can be detected; a **vacuous** mind, look, or expression is so deficient in alertness or spirit as to suggest a vacuum in its inanity ⟨the unthinking mind is not necessarily dull, rude, or impervious; it is probably simply *empty*—*Eliot*⟩ ⟨the loud laugh that spoke the *vacant* mind—*Goldsmith*⟩ ⟨his eyes had that *blank*

fixed gaze . . . that babies' eyes have—*M. E. Freeman*⟩ ⟨it is dull and *void* as a work of art—*Montague*⟩ ⟨there was nothing to be read in the *vacuous* face, blank as a school notice board out of term—*Greene*⟩
*Ana* *devoid, destitute, void: *bare, barren: exhausted, drained, depleted (see DEPLETE)
*Ant* full —*Con* replete, complete (see FULL)
**2** idle, hollow, *vain, nugatory, otiose
*Ana* inane, *insipid, vapid, flat, jejune, banal: trifling, trivial, paltry, *petty: fruitless, *futile, vain, bootless
*Con* significant, meaningful, pregnant (see EXPRESSIVE): genuine, *authentic, veritable, bona fide

**empyrean, empyreal** *celestial, heavenly

**emulate** *rival, compete, vie
*Ana* imitate, *copy, ape: *match, equal, approach, touch

**emulous** *ambitious
*Ana* aspiring, aiming, panting (see AIM *vb*): *eager, avid, keen, anxious, athirst, agog

**enable, empower** are comparable when meaning to make one able to do something. In ordinary usage **enable** implies provision of the means or opportunity, **empower,** the granting of the power or the delegation of the authority, to do something ⟨an income that *enables* him to live with dignity⟩ ⟨a letter *empowering* him to act in his father's behalf⟩ ⟨to give to the Cathedral fund a sum sufficient to *enable* Father Latour to carry out his purpose—*Cather*⟩ ⟨these courts of appeal are also *empowered* to review and enforce orders of federal administrative bodies— *Sayre*⟩
*Ana* permit, allow, *let
*Con* *forbid, prohibit, inhibit: *prevent, preclude

**enamored, infatuated** are very frequently used interchangeably, though with a loss in precision, in the sense of being passionately in love. **Enamored** usually connotes complete absorption in the passion ⟨Elizabeth-Jane . . . did not fail to perceive that her father . . . and Donald Farfrae became more desperately *enamored* of her friend every day—*Hardy*⟩ **Infatuated,** when applied to lovers and their acts, carries much the same implications as *enamored* but may add the implications of its primary sense (see FOND 1) of blind folly and unreasoning ardor ⟨you, Scythrop Glowry, of Nightmare Abbey . . . *infatuated* with such a dancing . . . thoughtless, careless . . . thing as Marionetta—*Peacock*⟩
*Ana* bewitched, captivated, fascinated (see ATTRACT): fond, devoted, doting, *loving

**enchant** charm, captivate, allure, fascinate, bewitch, *attract
*Ana* delight, rejoice, gladden, gratify, *please
*Ant* disenchant

**enchanting** charming, captivating, alluring, fascinating, bewitching, attractive (see under ATTRACT)
*Ana* *delightful, delectable: *pleasant, pleasing, grateful, gratifying
*Con* repulsive, repugnant, revolting, loathsome, *offensive: distasteful, obnoxious, repellent, abhorrent, *repugnant

**encircle** *surround, environ, circle, encompass, compass, hem, gird, girdle, ring
*Ana* *enclose, envelop: circumscribe, confine, *limit

**enclose** *vb* Enclose, envelop, fence, pen, coop, corral, cage, wall mean to surround so as to shut in or confine actually or apparently. **Enclose** implies a shutting in by barriers (as walls) or in an enveloping cover (as a case); the term may be used without connotations, or it may suggest protection, defense, privacy, or monastic seclusion ⟨a high hedge *encloses* the garden⟩ ⟨the larger fir copses, when they are *enclosed,* are the resort of all

---

A colon (:) separates groups of words discriminated. An asterisk (*) indicates place of treatment of each group

kinds of birds of prey yet left in the south—*Jefferies*⟩ ⟨you will find *enclosed* our price list⟩ ⟨walked across the *enclosed* porch, knocked, and opened the inside door—*Bradbury*⟩ **Envelop** (see also COVER) implies enclosure in or by something usually yielding or penetrable that surrounds it on all sides and serves to screen it, to protect it, or to separate it from others ⟨each specimen was *enveloped* in cotton and packed in a box⟩ ⟨the heart is *enveloped* by a serous sac, called the pericardium⟩ ⟨clouds *envelop* the mountaintops⟩ ⟨drew off his coat and *enveloped* him in a white robe—*Krey*⟩ **Fence** in this sense is usually followed by *in* or *about* and means only to enclose with or as if with a fence (as by a row of palings, a wall, or a hedge); the term usually connotes a means of barring trespassers, of keeping animals from wandering about or intruding, or of securing privacy ⟨the farm was *fenced* about with a stone wall⟩ ⟨we will have to *fence* in the garden with wire netting to keep out the rabbits⟩ ⟨the chickens were not *fenced in*⟩ ⟨a tall hedge of hemlocks *fenced in* the estate⟩ In extended use the term is a synonym of *enclose* only when that by which a thing is shut in is a man-made limitation ⟨the men themselves were . . . *fenced* by etiquette—*Emerson*⟩ ⟨*fenced* by your careful fathers, ringed by your leaden seas, long did ye wake in quiet and long lie down at ease —*Kipling*⟩ **Pen,** usually followed by *up* or *in,* implies confinement in or as if in an enclosure with narrow limits and suggests irksome restraint ⟨the troops were *penned* up for days in inadequate barracks⟩ ⟨where shepherds *pen* their flocks at eve, in hurdled cotes—*Milton*⟩ ⟨practically the whole of the population is *penned* in on a narrow coastal strip—*W. A. Lewis*⟩ **Coop,** usually followed by *up,* also implies confinement in a limited enclosure but it carries even a stronger implication of cramping limitations ⟨*coop* up the chickens only at night⟩ ⟨they are at present *cooped* up in a very small apartment⟩ ⟨her illness has kept her *cooped* in for a week⟩ **Corral** implies a shutting up in or as if in a strongly fenced enclosure and is used primarily of animals or persons who would scatter, escape, or flee if not securely confined ⟨at night they *corralled* their horses⟩ ⟨here they *corralled* us [prisoners] to the number of seven or eight thousand—*Century*⟩ In extended use *corral* may largely lose its basic notion of shutting up and stress, rather, the difficulty of catching or bringing under control ⟨the vitamins are being *corralled* one by one and the proteins are being brought under control—*Furnas*⟩ **Cage** is often used, especially with *in* or *up,* to imply confinement with severe or humiliating restrictions ⟨I don't stay *caged* in my shop all day—*George Eliot*⟩ ⟨the feeling of *caged* muscular tightness has provoked a fairly widespread desire to emigrate from Britain—*Chamberlain*⟩ **Wall** means enclosed by a wall which may be material or may be made up of harsh or rigid and impenetrable restraints ⟨*walled* round with rocks as an inland island, the ghost of a garden fronts the sea—*Swinburne*⟩ ⟨*walled* in by conventions⟩
*Ana* confine, circumscribe, *limit, restrict: environ, *surround, encircle, circle, encompass, compass, hem

**encomium,** eulogy, panegyric, tribute, citation denote a more or less formal and public expression of praise. **Encomium** implies enthusiasm or warmth in praising a thing or more often a person ⟨*encomium* in old time was poet's work—*Cowper*⟩ ⟨the *encomiums* by my friend pronounced on humble life—*Wordsworth*⟩ ⟨every worthy quality which he had in mind when he rolled out his unctuous *encomiums* of Americanism—*S. H. Adams*⟩ **Eulogy** implies a more studied form than *encomium;* as a rule it applies to a speech (or writing) extolling the virtues and the services of a person; the term is especially and specifically applied to a funeral oration or sermon of this character ⟨great minds should only criticize the great who have passed beyond the reach of *eulogy* or faultfinding—*Lang*⟩ ⟨I would rather have a plain coffin without a flower, a funeral without a *eulogy,* than a life without . . . love and sympathy—*Childs*⟩ **Panegyric** carries a far stronger implication of elaborate, high-flown, often poetical or rhetorical compliment than either of the preceding terms but it does not now emphasize publicity as much as it once did ⟨but verse, alas! your Majesty disdains; and I'm not used to *panegyric* strains—*Pope*⟩ ⟨all *panegyrics* are mingled with an infusion of poppy—*Swift*⟩ **Tribute** applies not only to spoken or written praise but to any act or situation which can be construed as taking its place ⟨no *tribute* can be paid to them which exceeds their merit—*John Marshall*⟩ ⟨I am appointed sole executor, a confidence I appreciate as a *tribute* to my lifelong friendship—*H. G. Wells*⟩ **Citation** is used in designating either the formal eulogy accompanying the awarding of an honor (as an honorary degree) or the specific mention of a person in military service in an order or dispatch ⟨Columbia's *citation* praised Mr. Rhee as an "indomitable leader, implacable enemy of Communist totalitarianism" and "a scholar and statesman"—*Christian Science Monitor*⟩ ⟨he had received the Croix de Guerre, with a divisional *citation,* for his service in Belgium—*Malcolm Cowley*⟩
*Ana* lauding *or* laudation, extolling *or* extollation, praising *or* praise (see corresponding verbs at PRAISE): plaudits, *applause, acclaim, acclamation: commending *or* commendation, complimenting *or* compliment (see corresponding verbs at COMMEND)
*Con* invective, *abuse, vituperation, obloquy

**encompass** *surround, environ, encircle, circle, compass, hem, gird, girdle, ring
*Ana* envelop, *enclose, wall: circumscribe, confine (see LIMIT)

**encounter** *vb* *meet, face, confront
*Ana* collide, conflict, clash, *bump: brave, beard, defy, challenge (see FACE)

**encounter** *n* Encounter, skirmish, brush. In their military senses (compare BATTLE), an **encounter** is a sudden hostile meeting that is typically both violent and unexpected; a **skirmish,** a slight and desultory, often preliminary, encounter, commonly between light detachments of troops; a **brush,** a short but brisk skirmish. All three words are used of other than military contests ⟨a sharp *encounter* of wits⟩ ⟨a *skirmish* preliminary to a political campaign⟩ ⟨a *brush* between opposing legal counsel⟩
*Ana* *battle, engagement: *contest, combat, conflict, fight, fray: clash, collision, *impact, impingement

**encourage** 1 Encourage, inspirit, hearten, embolden, cheer, nerve, steel mean to fill with courage or strength of purpose especially in preparation for a hard task or purpose. **Encourage** in its basic and still common sense implies the raising of confidence to such a height that one dares to do or to bear what is difficult; it then usually suggests an external agent or agency stimulating one to action or endurance ⟨the teacher's praise *encouraged* the pupil to try even harder⟩ ⟨whatever appeals to the imagination . . . wonderfully *encourages* and liberates us—*Emerson*⟩ ⟨the treatment should begin by *encouraging* him to utter freely even his most shocking thoughts —*Russell*⟩ Sometimes it may suggest merely an increase in strength of purpose or in responsiveness to advice or inducement fostered by a person or an influence or event ⟨there they listened, and retained what they could remember, for they were not *encouraged* to take notes —*Henry Adams*⟩ *Encourage* is often used with an impersonal object, sometimes as if the object were a person ⟨we wish to *encourage* no vice⟩ but often as if it were the object not of *encourage* but of an ellipsis meaning to encourage a person or persons to act (as by doing, making, forming, or using) ⟨they are donations to education; donations, which any government must be disposed . . . to *encourage—John Marshall*⟩ ⟨if a state sees fit to *encourage* steam laundries and discourage hand laundries, that is its own affair—*Justice Holmes*⟩ **Inspirit** is chiefly literary; it retains its implication of putting spirit into, especially in the sense of life, energy, courage, or vigor, and therefore often comes close to *enliven* or to *animate* in meaning ⟨those great men, who, by their writings, *inspirited* the people to resistance—*Buckle*⟩ ⟨the early tea which was to *inspirit* them for the dance—*George Eliot*⟩ ⟨how *inspiriting* to escape from here and now and wander wildly in a world of lutes and roses—*Woolf*⟩ ⟨the book is an astonishing and *inspiriting* record of what human ingenuity can accomplish—*Basil Davenport*⟩ **Hearten** implies a putting heart into and carries suggestions that are stronger than those carried by either *encourage* or *inspirit*. It presupposes a state of low courage, depression, despondency, or indifference and therefore implies a lifting of mind or spirit that rouses one with fresh courage or zeal ⟨gifts . . . which both strengthen our resources and *hearten* our endeavors—*Conant*⟩ ⟨people . . . who were merry or wise or comforting or revealing, whose presence either *heartened* the spirit or kindled the mind —*Jan Struther*⟩ **Embolden** implies a giving of boldness to or, more especially, a giving of just enough courage or bravery to do what one wants to do or is expected to do and suggests not brazenness but the overcoming of timidity or reluctance ⟨she was *emboldened* to descend and meet him under the protection of visitors—*Austen*⟩ ⟨*emboldened* by the utter stillness pervading the room he addressed himself to Mrs. Fyne—*Conrad*⟩ **Cheer** in its basic sense is very close to *hearten* and implies a renewing of flagging strength of mind, body, or spirit ⟨drink the cup that *cheers*⟩ ⟨my royal father, *cheer* these noble lords and hearten those that fight in your defense—*Shak.*⟩ But *cheer* (usually with *on*) may also imply a more vigorous encouraging (as by applause, commendation, or aid) intended not merely to strengthen and refresh but to stimulate to the utmost or sometimes to an ultimate attempt to do, succeed, or conquer ⟨*cheering* on the home team⟩ ⟨as to some great advent'rous fight this bravo *cheers* these dastards all he can—*Daniel*⟩ **Nerve** comes close to *embolden* in meaning, but it implies a harder task to be performed and the need of summoning all one's powers to accomplish it; the term therefore connotes greater effort or greater impulsion from within than the other words ⟨the open resistance of the northern barons *nerved* the rest of their order to action—*J. R. Green*⟩ ⟨*nerving* myself with the thought that if I got crushed by the fall I should probably escape a lingering and far more painful death, I dropped into the cloud of foliage beneath me—*Hudson*⟩ **Steel**, like *nerve*, may imply a great effort or impulsion from within, but it often also suggests an imparting from without, either of which gives a man the power to endure or to accomplish something by making him insensible to pain, suffering, or insults, and by filling him with resolution or determination ⟨O God of battles, *steel* my soldiers' hearts, possess them not with fear—*Shak.*⟩

*Ana* stimulate, excite, *provoke, quicken, pique, galvanize: *strengthen, fortify, energize, invigorate: rally, *stir

*Ant* discourage —*Con* dishearten, dispirit, deject (see DISCOURAGE)

2 *favor, countenance

*Ana* sanction, endorse, *approve: *incite, instigate, abet: *induce, prevail

*Ant* discourage —*Con* deter, *dissuade, divert: *restrain, inhibit

**encroach** *trespass, entrench, infringe, invade

*Ana* *enter, penetrate, pierce, probe: *intrude, butt in, obtrude, interlope: interfere, intervene, *interpose

**encumber** *burden, cumber, weigh, weight, load, lade, tax, charge, saddle

*Ana* discommode, incommode, *inconvenience: clog, fetter, *hamper: impede, obstruct, block (see HINDER)

**end** *n* 1 *limit, bound, term, confine

*Ana* *extreme, extremity

2 End, termination, ending, terminus are comparable when opposed to *beginning* or *starting point* and meaning the point or line beyond which a thing does not or cannot go (as in time or space or magnitude). **End** is not only the ordinary but also the most inclusive of these terms, and it may be used of almost any final limit and in such varied applications as time ⟨the *end* of a period⟩ ⟨at the *end* of his life⟩ or space ⟨the *end* of the road⟩ or movement or action ⟨the *end* of his journey⟩ or magnitude ⟨there is no *end* to his energy⟩ or range of possibility ⟨his statement put an *end* to speculation⟩ **Termination** and **ending** apply especially to the end in time or, less often, in space of something that is brought to a close typically as having a set term or bounds or predetermined limits or as being complete, finished, or futile ⟨the *termination* of a lease⟩ ⟨the *termination* of the period agreed upon⟩ ⟨the *termination* of a search⟩ ⟨a fair beginning but a bad *ending*⟩ ⟨the maiden sang as if her song could have no *ending—Wordsworth*⟩ **Terminus** applies to the end (often in clear opposition to *starting point*) to which a person or a thing moves or progresses. The term usually suggests spatial relations and often indicates a definite point or place ⟨the *terminus* of his tour⟩ ⟨New York is the *terminus* of several important railroads⟩ ⟨an airway *terminus*⟩ ⟨the object is the starting point, not the *terminus,* of an act of perception—*Jeans*⟩

*Ana* closing *or* close, concluding *or* conclusion, finishing *or* finish, completion (see corresponding verbs at CLOSE): culmination, climax (see SUMMIT): term, bound, *limit

*Ant* beginning —*Con* inception, *origin, source, root

3 objective, goal, aim, object, *intention, intent, purpose, design

*Ana* destiny, *fate, lot, doom, portion: *function, office, duty

**end** *vb* *close, conclude, terminate, finish, complete

*Ant* begin —*Con* commence, start, initiate, inaugurate (see BEGIN): originate, derive, arise, rise, *spring

**endanger** *venture, hazard, risk, chance, jeopardize, imperil

*Ana* encounter, confront, *meet, face: dare, brave (see FACE): *incur, contract, catch

**endeavor** *vb* *attempt, try, essay, strive, struggle

*Ana* apply, devote, *direct, address: determine, resolve, *decide

**endeavor** *n* essay, striving, struggle, attempt, try (see under ATTEMPT *vb*)

*Ana* toil, labor, travail, *work: *effort, exertion, pains, trouble

**endemic** *adj* indigenous, *native, autochthonous, aboriginal

*Ant* exotic: pandemic —*Con* foreign, alien, extraneous, *extrinsic

**ending** *n* *end, termination, terminus

---

A colon (:) separates groups of words discriminated. An asterisk (*) indicates place of treatment of each group.

*Ana, Ant, & Con* see those at END *n* 2

**endless** interminable, *everlasting, unceasing
*Ana* *lasting, perdurable, perpetual, permanent: eternal, illimitable, boundless, *infinite: *immortal, deathless, undying
*Con* transitory, *transient, fugitive, passing, short-lived, ephemeral, evanescent

**endorse** *approve, sanction, accredit, certify
*Ana* vouch, attest, *certify, witness: *commend, recommend: *support, uphold, champion, back, advocate
*Con* *disapprove, deprecate: condemn, denounce, reprobate, reprehend, censure, *criticize: reject, repudiate, spurn (see DECLINE)

**endow** *dower, endue
*Ana* bestow, confer (see GIVE): *grant, award, accord: empower, *enable: *furnish, equip
*Con* denude, *strip, divest, bare: despoil, spoliate, *ravage: exhaust, drain, *deplete, impoverish

**endue** endow, *dower
*Ana* *clothe, invest, vest: *furnish, equip, outfit, accouter: bestow, confer (see GIVE)
*Con* see those at ENDOW

**endure** 1 *continue, last, abide, persist
*Ana* survive, outlast, *outlive: *stay, remain, wait, linger, tarry, abide
*Ant* perish —*Con* disintegrate, crumble, *decay
2 abide, tolerate, suffer, *bear, stand, brook
*Ana* accept, *receive, take: submit, *yield
*Con* reject, refuse, *decline, spurn, repudiate

**enemy, foe** denote an individual or body of individuals that is hostile or that manifests hostility to another. **Enemy** usually stresses antagonism that arises from a cherished hatred or a desire to harm or destroy, but it may suggest nothing much more than active or evident dislike or a habit of preying upon ⟨a man with many friends and no *enemies*⟩ ⟨the anarchist is the *enemy* of government⟩ ⟨the woodpecker is a natural *enemy* of insects that infest the bark of trees⟩ ⟨let the teacher appear always the ally of the pupil, not his natural *enemy*—*Russell*⟩ ⟨time is at once the *enemy* and the ally of life and of love—*Millett*⟩ **Foe,** on the other hand, implies active warfare ⟨he is the *foe* of all reform measures⟩ ⟨give me the avowed, the erect, the manly *foe,* bold I can meet,—perhaps may turn his blow!—*Canning*⟩ When the reference is to a nation or group of nations with whom a country is at war, *enemy* is preferred in general use, *foe* being used in this sense chiefly in poetry or rhetorical prose ⟨we have met the *enemy,* and they are ours—*O. H. Perry*⟩ ⟨whispering with white lips—"The *foe!* They come!"—*Byron*⟩
*Ana* *opponent, adversary, antagonist: rival, competitor (see corresponding verbs at RIVAL)
*Con* *friend, ally, *partner, confederate, colleague: adherent, *follower, partisan

**energetic** *vigorous, strenuous, lusty, nervous
*Ana* forceful, forcible, *powerful, potent: *active, dynamic, live: *busy, industrious, diligent: *strong, stout, sturdy, stalwart, tough, tenacious
*Ant* lethargic —*Con* *languid, enervated, spiritless, listless: phlegmatic, apathetic, stolid, *impassive: sluggish (see LETHARGIC): indolent, slothful, *lazy

**energize** 1 *vitalize, activate
*Ana* stimulate, quicken, galvanize, excite (see PROVOKE): *stir, arouse, rouse, rally
*Con* enervate, emasculate (see UNNERVE): *weaken, enfeeble, debilitate
2 *strengthen, invigorate, fortify, reinforce
*Ana* empower, *enable: *stir, rally, rouse, arouse

**energy** force, *power, strength, might, puissance

*Ana* dynamism, activity, operativeness *or* operation (see corresponding adjectives at ACTIVE): momentum, impetus, *speed, velocity, headway
*Ant* inertia —*Con* weakness, feebleness, decrepitude (see corresponding adjectives at WEAK): powerlessness, impotence (see corresponding adjectives at POWERLESS)

**enervate** *unnerve, emasculate, unman
*Ana* *weaken, enfeeble, debilitate, undermine, sap, disable: *abase, demean, debase, degrade: exhaust, jade, fatigue, *tire, weary
*Ant* harden, inure —*Con* energize, *vitalize, activate: galvanize, stimulate, quicken (see PROVOKE)

**enervated** languishing, *languid, languorous, lackadaisical, spiritless, listless
*Ana* decadent, degenerated, deteriorated (see corresponding nouns at DETERIORATION): enfeebled, debilitated, weakened (see WEAKEN)
*Con* hardened, seasoned (see HARDEN): stout, sturdy, tough, tenacious, *strong, stalwart: *vigorous, lusty, energetic, strenuous

**enfeeble** *weaken, debilitate, sap, undermine, cripple, disable
*Ana* impair, mar, harm, *injure: enervate, emasculate, *unnerve, unman
*Ant* fortify

**enforce, implement** are comparable when they mean to put something into effect or operation. **Enforce** is used chiefly in reference to laws or statutes. The term suggests the exercise of executive rather than legislative power or the use of the authority and the means given to the magistrates and police to maintain order and security in the community ⟨blue laws more often ignored than *enforced*⟩ ⟨*enforce* traffic laws and regulations strictly⟩ But *enforce* is also used in reference to agreements, contracts, rights, and ends which have legal sanction or a legal character and require the compulsory powers of the government or of the courts to ensure their fulfillment or their protection in case of violation ⟨Congress, as incident to its power to authorize and *enforce* contracts for public works—*Justice Holmes*⟩ ⟨there was no legal process by which a citizen could *enforce* his rights against the state—*Buchan*⟩ **Implement** usually suggests reference to bills or acts which have been passed, proposals or projects which have been accepted, or policies which have been adopted and implies the performance of such acts as are necessary to carry them into effect or ensure their being put into operation ⟨proposed that any further medical aid to the aged be *implemented* by increased Social Security taxation⟩ ⟨he also urged that military equipment be given to the nations of western Europe to *implement* the Brussels pact—*Current Biog.*⟩
*Ana* execute, fulfill, discharge, *perform: compel, constrain, oblige, *force
*Ant* relax *(discipline, rules, demands)* —*Con* ignore, forget, disregard, *neglect

**enfranchise** emancipate, manumit, *free, release, liberate, deliver, discharge

**engage** pledge, plight, *promise, covenant, contract
*Ana* bind, *tie: agree, accede, acquiesce, *assent, consent, subscribe

**engagement** 1 Engagement, appointment, rendezvous, tryst, assignation, date mean a promise or an agreement to be in an agreed place at a specified time, usually for a particular purpose. **Engagement** is the general term usable in place of any of the others ⟨he has no business *engagements* for the rest of the week⟩ ⟨an *engagement* to play golf at four o'clock⟩ ⟨the lecturer can make no more *engagements* for the season⟩ **Appointment** is applied chiefly to an engagement with a person who

because of the exigencies of his office, his profession, or his position in life must keep a calendar and apportion his time carefully among those who wish to consult him professionally or confer with him ⟨the governor sees visitors only by *appointment*⟩ ⟨the doctor's secretary said it was impossible to make an *appointment* before Thursday⟩ **Rendezvous** may designate a place agreed upon for the meeting of persons, often a group of persons ⟨the old soldiers made the town hall their *rendezvous*⟩ but it usually connotes a pledge or covenant (often an implicit one) to meet something or someone that cannot be escaped without violation of one's honor ⟨this generation of Americans has a *rendezvous* with destiny— *Roosevelt*⟩ **Tryst** is chiefly poetic; like *rendezvous*, it may designate the place of meeting (which, however, is more often termed *trysting place*) as well as the agreement to meet at a certain place, but the latter is the commoner denotation of *tryst* ⟨a lovers' *tryst*⟩ ⟨hurrying to keep their *tryst* in the wood⟩ **Assignation** usually denotes a lovers' tryst, but it commonly conveys a suggestion of an illicit love or of a clandestine meeting ⟨make *assignations* for them with ladies of the street —*Shaw*⟩ **Date** is used especially of casual engagements between friends or of an agreed meeting between a young man and young woman ⟨remembering suddenly he had a riding *date* with Major Thompson's wife at 12:30— *James Jones*⟩
2 *battle, action
*Ana* *encounter, skirmish, brush: *contest, conflict, combat, fight

**engaging** *sweet, winning, winsome, dulcet
*Ana* alluring, attractive, enchanting, charming, captivating (see under ATTRACT *vb*): *interesting, intriguing
*Ant* loathsome

**engender** *generate, breed, beget, get, sire, procreate, propagate, reproduce
*Ana* produce, *bear, yield: *provoke, excite, stimulate, quicken: rouse, arouse (see STIR)

**engine** *machine, mechanism, machinery, apparatus, motor

**engineer** *vb* *guide, pilot, lead, steer
*Ana* manage, direct, *conduct, control

**engrave** incise, *carve, etch, sculpture, sculpt, sculp, chisel
*Ana* delineate, depict, limn, portray (see REPRESENT): imprint, impress, print (see corresponding nouns at IMPRESSION)

**engross** *monopolize, absorb, consume
*Ana* utilize, employ, *use, apply: control, manage (see CONDUCT)
*Con* distract, bewilder (see PUZZLE): dissipate, *scatter, disperse

**engrossed** absorbed, *intent, rapt
*Ana* monopolized, consumed (see MONOPOLIZE): fixed, set, settled (see SET *vb*): *busy, industrious, diligent, sedulous, assiduous
*Con* distracted, bewildered (see PUZZLE *vb*): distraught (see ABSTRACTED): *indifferent, unconcerned, detached, uninterested, disinterested

**engrossing** *interesting, absorbing, intriguing
*Ana* monopolizing, consuming (see MONOPOLIZE): controlling, managing, directing (see CONDUCT *vb*): transporting, ravishing, enrapturing, entrancing (see TRANSPORT)
*Ant* irksome

**enhance** heighten, *intensify, aggravate
*Ana* *lift, elevate, raise: *exalt, magnify, aggrandize: augment, *increase: *adorn, embellish, beautify
*Con* diminish, reduce, lessen, *decrease: attenuate,

extenuate, *thin: belittle, minimize, depreciate, detract (see DECRY)

**enigma** riddle, puzzle, conundrum, *mystery, problem

**enigmatic** cryptic, *obscure, dark, vague, ambiguous, equivocal
*Ana* puzzling, perplexing, mystifying, bewildering (see PUZZLE *vb*): abstruse, occult, esoteric, *recondite: dubious, problematic, *doubtful
*Ant* explicit —*Con* express, specific, definite (see EXPLICIT): *clear, perspicuous, lucid: plain, candid, open, *frank

**enjoin** 1 direct, order, *command, bid, instruct, charge
*Ana* advise, counsel (see under ADVICE): admonish (see REPROVE): *warn, forewarn, caution
2 interdict, prohibit, *forbid, inhibit, ban
*Ana* debar, shut out, rule out (see EXCLUDE): bar, *hinder, impede
*Con* permit, allow, *let, suffer

**enjoy** 1 *like, love, relish, fancy, dote
*Ana* delight, rejoice, gratify, gladden, regale, tickle, *please
*Ant* loathe, abhor, abominate —*Con* *hate, detest: *despise, contemn, scorn
2 possess, own, *have, hold

**enjoyment** delight, *pleasure, joy, delectation, fruition
*Ana* delighting, rejoicing, gratifying, regaling, gladdening, pleasing (see PLEASE): *happiness, felicity, bliss, beatitude: zest, relish, gusto, *taste
*Ant* abhorrence —*Con* aversion, *antipathy: distastefulness *or* distaste, repugnance, repellency *or* repulsion (see corresponding adjectives at REPUGNANT)

**enlarge** *increase, augment, multiply
*Ana* *extend, lengthen, elongate, prolong, protract: amplify, *expand, distend, dilate, inflate: magnify, aggrandize (see EXALT)
*Con* *thin, attenuate, extenuate: abridge, abbreviate, *shorten, curtail, retrench: compress, shrink, *contract, condense: *compact, concentrate

**enlighten** illustrate, *illuminate, illume, light, lighten
*Ana* educate, instruct, train, *teach, school: *inform, apprise, acquaint, advise
*Ant* confuse, muddle —*Con* mystify, perplex, *puzzle, bewilder: addle, fuddle (see CONFUSE)

**enliven** animate, *quicken, vivify
*Ana* refresh, *renew, restore, rejuvenate: stimulate, excite, quicken, galvanize, *provoke: entertain, recreate, divert, *amuse: inspire, fire, *inform, animate
*Ant* deaden: subdue —*Con* *depress, oppress, weigh

**enmesh** *entangle, involve
*Ana* ensnare, entrap, snare, trap, capture, *catch: *hamper, clog, hog-tie, fetter
*Con* *extricate, disentangle, untangle, disembarrass: disengage, *detach

**enmity, hostility, antipathy, antagonism, animosity, rancor, animus** mean intense deep-seated dislike or ill will or a manifestation of such a feeling. **Enmity** implies more than the absence of amity or a friendly spirit; it suggests positive hatred which may or may not be dormant or concealed ⟨I will put *enmity* between thee and the woman —*Gen* 3:15⟩ ⟨angry friendship is sometimes as bad as calm *enmity*—*Burke*⟩ **Hostility** suggests strong and usually open enmity manifesting itself actively (as in warfare, in violent attacks, or in ostracism) ⟨the unremitting *hostility* with which . . . [these poems] have each and all been opposed—*Wordsworth*⟩ ⟨if we could read the secret history of our enemies, we should find in each man's life sorrow and suffering enough to disarm all *hostility* —*Longfellow*⟩ **Antipathy** and *antagonism* usually imply a temperamental or constitutional basis for one's hatred

---

A colon (:) separates groups of words discriminated. An asterisk (*) indicates place of treatment of each group.

or dislike. **Antipathy** suggests aversion or repugnance and often, in consequence, avoidance or repulsion of the person or thing hated ⟨inveterate *antipathies* against particular nations and passionate attachments for others should be excluded—*Washington*⟩ ⟨found it so hard to conceal his *antipathy* that he could not understand the way in which Dayrell went out of his way to cultivate his society—*Mackenzie*⟩ **Antagonism** stresses the clash of temperaments and the quickness with which hostilities are provoked or the spirit of resistance is aroused ⟨Karl Marx believed that the hostility of one nation to another will come to an end when the *antagonism* between classes within these nations vanishes⟩ ⟨some note of viceregal authority must have lingered in her voice for the caretaker's *antagonism* changed to a sort of bedraggled obsequiousness—*Sackville-West*⟩ *Animosity* and *rancor* denote emotions of such intensity or violence that they may, if not given release, provide the ground for active hostility. **Animosity** usually suggests anger, vindictiveness, and sometimes a desire to destroy or injure what one hates ⟨the Bishop had let the parish alone, giving their *animosity* plenty of time to cool—*Cather*⟩ ⟨her hatred of the idea of it was intensified into a violent *animosity*—*Bennett*⟩ **Rancor** stresses bitterness and ill will amounting to malevolence; it often implies the nursing of a grudge or grievance ⟨'tis not my speeches that you do mislike, but 'tis my presence that doth trouble ye. *Rancor* will out: proud prelate, in thy face, I see thy fury—*Shak.*⟩ ⟨small wonder at her feeling an unchristian *rancor* against the nation which had caused his death—*Forester*⟩ **Animus** suggests less emotional violence than *animosity*, but it implies more definitely a prejudice or ill will that seeks to find expression ⟨there was no mistaking his intentions; he had transferred his *animus* to me, convinced I was to blame for his rejection —*Heiser*⟩
*Ana* hate, hatred, detestation, abhorrence, loathing (see under HATE *vb*): aversion (see ANTIPATHY): malignity, malignancy, ill will, malevolence, *malice
*Ant* amity —*Con* friendliness, amicability (see corresponding adjectives at AMICABLE): *friendship, comity, goodwill

**ennoble** *dignify, honor, glorify
*Ana* *exalt, magnify: elevate, raise, *lift: heighten, enhance, *intensify

**ennui** doldrums, boredom, *tedium
*Ana* depression, dejection, dumps, blues, melancholy, *sadness: listlessness, languidness, languorousness *or* languor, spiritlessness (see corresponding adjectives at LANGUID): satiation *or* satiety, surfeiting *or* surfeit, cloying (see corresponding verbs at SATIATE)

**enormity, enormousness** both mean the state or the quality of being enormous but are rarely interchangeable in modern usage. **Enormity** imputes an abnormal quality; it applies especially to the state of exceeding all bounds in wickedness or evil, and therefore of being abnormally, monstrously, or outrageously evil ⟨Newson . . . failed to perceive the *enormity* of Henchard's crime—*Hardy*⟩ ⟨the sensation of standing there . . . and wishing her dead, was so strange, so fascinating and overmastering, that its *enormity* did not immediately strike him—*Wharton*⟩ **Enormousness** applies to the state or quality of grossly exceeding comparable things in size or amount ⟨the *enormousness* of a whale⟩ ⟨the *enormousness* of the cost of war⟩ ⟨covers 885 close-printed pages of thin paper. Readers who brave its *enormousness* are likely to emerge both crushed and impressed—*Time*⟩ **Enormity**, but not *enormousness*, may also be used of an instance of what is characterized by enormity or monstrous wickedness

⟨the *enormities* of which Caligula was guilty⟩
*Ana* outrageousness, atrociousness *or* atrocity, heinousness, monstrousness (see corresponding adjectives at OUTRAGEOUS): flagrancy, grossness, rankness (see corresponding adjectives at FLAGRANT)

**enormous** *huge, vast, immense, elephantine, mammoth, giant, gigantic, gigantean, colossal, gargantuan, Herculean, cyclopean, titanic, Brobdingnagian
*Ana* prodigious, stupendous, tremendous, *monstrous, monumental: inordinate, exorbitant, *excessive, extravagant

**enormousness** *enormity
*Ana* immenseness *or* immensity, hugeness, vastness (see corresponding adjectives at HUGE): tremendousness, prodigiousness, stupendousness, monstrousness (see corresponding adjectives at MONSTROUS)

**enrage** infuriate, madden, incense, *anger
*Ana* exasperate, provoke, aggravate, rile (see IRRITATE)
*Ant* placate  —*Con* *pacify, appease, mollify, propitiate, conciliate

**enrapture** *transport, ravish, entrance
*Ana* rejoice, delight, gladden, *please, gratify: charm, enchant, captivate, fascinate, *attract

**enroll** *record, register, list, catalog
*Ana* *enter (sense 2): insert (see INTRODUCE)

**ensconce** screen, secrete, *hide, conceal, cache, bury
*Ana* shield, guard, safeguard, protect, *defend: shelter, lodge (see HARBOR)
*Con* expose, exhibit, display, *show

**ensign** *flag, standard, banner, color, streamer, pennant, pendant, pennon, jack

**ensnare** snare, entrap, trap, bag, *catch, capture
*Ana* *lure, entice, inveigle, decoy

**ensue** *follow, succeed, supervene
*Ana* issue, emanate, proceed, stem, *spring, derive, originate, rise, arise: pursue, *follow, chase

**ensure, insure, assure, secure** are comparable because they all carry the underlying meaning to make a person or thing sure. *Ensure, insure,* and *assure* all indicate a making of an outcome or event sure, certain, or inevitable as a consequence or concomitant. **Ensure** in such use may come very close to *guarantee* ⟨good farming practices that go far toward *ensuring* good harvests⟩ ⟨certain rules of conduct for the purpose of *ensuring* the safety and victory of the absent warriors—*Frazer*⟩ ⟨for the remainder of his life he so constrained the expression of his thoughts as to *ensure* his safety—*H. O. Taylor*⟩ **Insure** is often interchangeable with *ensure* ⟨shipbuilders, who wished to *insure* a profitable career for their vessels —*Amer. Guide Series: Mich.*⟩ ⟨the structural division of the buildings, with no more than four apartments opening on any hallway, *insures* privacy and quiet— *Amer. Guide Series: N. Y. City*⟩ but it is also the general word for reference to making certain arrangements for indemnification for loss by contingent events ⟨to *insure* the car against theft and fire damage⟩ **Assure** may in its more general use be indistinguishable from *ensure* and *insure* ⟨protected by game laws and reared in state hatcheries, this bird is now *assured* a permanent place among the game birds of the state—*Amer. Guide Series: Tenn.*⟩ ⟨policies and plans for *assuring* the necessary labor force for defense and essential civilian production —*Current Biog.*⟩ but distinctively it more definitely expresses the notion of removal of doubt, uncertainty, or worry from a person's mind ⟨I *assured* him that I was far from advising him to do anything so cruel— *Conrad*⟩ ⟨*assured* the inhabitants that France intended to grant autonomy—*Current Biog.*⟩ **Secure** implies purposive action to ensure safety, protection, or certainty against adverse contingencies ⟨lock the door to *secure* us from interruption—*Dickens*⟩ ⟨one other battalion moved up to *secure* the first battalion's flank—*Bernstein*⟩ **entangle, involve, enmesh** are comparable when meaning to catch or to hold as if in a net from which it is difficult to escape. **Entangle** usually carries the implications of impeding and of the difficulty or impossibility of escape; although basically the word implies being caught in a net, a snare, or a maze, it may suggest only a condition that is similar in forming a complication of difficulties ⟨the fly became *entangled* in the spider's web and could not escape⟩ ⟨like a bird *entangled* in a snare⟩ ⟨*entangle* themselves in the mazes of sophistry⟩ ⟨the firm is *entangled* in financial difficulties⟩ ⟨peace, commerce, and honest friendship with all nations, *entangling* alliances with none—*Jefferson*⟩ ⟨had *entangled* the king in a false marriage with her—*Sitwell*⟩ **Involve** (see also INVOLVE 3; compare *involved* under COMPLEX) implies the addition, often the conscious addition, of ideas, words, or projects which tend to make difficulties (as by confusing or perplexing) for oneself or another ⟨his sentences are *involved* because he tries to express too many ideas⟩ ⟨the controversies . . . moved on in all their ugliness to *involve* others—*J. M. Brown*⟩ ⟨I plead frankly for the theistic hypothesis as *involving* fewer difficulties than any other—*Inge*⟩ **Enmesh** comes very close to *entangle* in meaning but may be preferred when an involvement in or as if in the meshes of a net is strongly felt ⟨declining to haul up the net when the fish were already *enmeshed*—*Grote*⟩ ⟨his eye was *enmeshed* in no tangle of foreground, but was led across great tracts of country to the distant mountains—*Binyon*⟩ **Ana** *hamper, trammel, fetter, clog, hog-tie: *embarrass, discomfit: ensnare, snare, entrap, trap, capture, *catch **Ant** disentangle —**Con** untangle, *extricate: disengage, *detach

**entente**    treaty, pact, compact, concordat, convention, cartel, *contract, bargain

**enter** 1 **Enter, penetrate, pierce, probe** are comparable when meaning to make way into something so as to reach or pass through the interior. **Enter** (see also ENTER 2) is the most comprehensive of these words and the least explicit in its implications. When the word takes a person for its subject, it often means little more than to go in or to go into ⟨he *entered* the house⟩ ⟨came riding out of Asia on the very first horses to *enter* Africa—*G. W. Murray*⟩ but sometimes it also suggests the beginning of a course of study, a career, or a proceeding ⟨*enter* college⟩ ⟨*enter* Parliament⟩ ⟨there are many who are aghast at the type of world which we are now *entering*, in which a war could cause obliteration—*Vannevar Bush*⟩ When *enter* takes a thing for its subject, it implies a making way through some medium and especially a dense or resisting medium ⟨the rain could not *enter* the frozen earth⟩ ⟨the bullet *entered* the body near the heart⟩ ⟨such an idea never *entered* his mind⟩ **Penetrate** (see also PERMEATE) carries a far stronger implication than *enter* of an impelling force or of a compelling power that makes for entrance ⟨the salt rain . . . *penetrates* the thickest coat—*Jefferies*⟩ and it also more often suggests resistance in the medium ⟨Frémont had tried to *penetrate* the Colorado Rockies—*Cather*⟩ ⟨his sight could not *penetrate* the darkness⟩ It may imply either a reaching the center or a passing through and an issuing on the further side ⟨*penetrate* the depths of a forest⟩ ⟨armor plate so thick that no cannonball can *penetrate* it⟩ *Penetrate*, especially as an intransitive verb, often specifically takes as its subject something that is intangible or at least not objective but that has (in affirmative expressions)

the power of making its way through ⟨the influence of Christianity has *penetrated* to the ends of the earth⟩ ⟨a *penetrating* odor⟩ ⟨a *penetrating* voice⟩ Often also, as distinguished from the other terms, *penetrate* suggests the use of a keen mind or the exercise of powers of intuition or discernment in the understanding of the abstruse or mysterious ⟨we cannot *penetrate* the mind of the Absolute—*Inge*⟩ ⟨in seeking to *penetrate* the essential character of European art—*Binyon*⟩ ⟨Aunty Rosa could *penetrate* certain kinds of hypocrisy, but not all—*Kipling*⟩ **Pierce** in the earliest of its English senses implies a running through with a sharp-pointed instrument (as a sword, a spear, or a knife) ⟨they *pierced* both plate and mail—*Spenser*⟩ In all of its extended senses it carries a far stronger implication than *penetrate* of something that stabs or runs through or of something that cuts into the very center or through to the further side ⟨feel the *piercing* cold in every nerve⟩ ⟨a passion like a sword blade that *pierced* me through and through—*Lindsay*⟩ ⟨how was one to *pierce* such hidebound complacency?—*Mackenzie*⟩ Often the term imputes great poignancy or aesthetic effectiveness beyond what is usual to the thing that pierces ⟨the remembrance of all that made life dear *pierced* me to the core—*Hudson*⟩ ⟨whatever is expressed with art— whether it be a lover's despair or a metaphysical theory —*pierces* the mind and compels assent and acceptance —*Huxley*⟩ **Probe** derives its implications from the earliest of its senses, to explore (as a wound, a cavity, or the earth) with a long slender instrument especially in order to determine depth, condition, or contents. In its extended senses it implies penetration so far as circumstances allow or so far as one's powers or skills permit, and it usually suggests an exploratory or investigatory aim ⟨the bog or peat was ascertained, on *probing* it with an instrument, to be at least fifteen feet thick—*Lyell*⟩ ⟨the only one . . . with whom he cared to *probe* into things a little deeper than the average level of club and chophouse banter—*Wharton*⟩ In some cases *probe* means little more than to investigate thoroughly (as by questioning those in a position to know facts) ⟨a rascally calumny, which I was determined to *probe* to the bottom—*Scott*⟩ **Ana** invade, entrench, *trespass, encroach: *intrude, butt in: *begin, commence, start **Ant** issue from

2 **Enter, introduce, admit** are comparable when they mean to cause or permit to go in or get in. **Enter,** in its causative sense, is used chiefly in idiomatic phrases, though occasionally it is employed in the sense to drive or force in ⟨he could not *enter* the wedge between the layers of rock⟩ In idiomatic use it commonly implies writing down (as in a list, a roll, a catalogue, or a record), but in some of these phrases it also connotes the observance of other formalities; thus, to *enter* a word in a dictionary is to list it in alphabetical order and define its meaning; to *enter* one's son at a private school is to send in his name as a candidate for admission; to *enter* a judgment is to put it upon record in the proper legal form and order ⟨the judge could *enter* a judgment of conviction and send Woodfall to prison—*Chafee*⟩ **Introduce** is often preferred to *enter* when it implies insertion ⟨the painter who was *introducing* a tree into his landscape —*Ellis*⟩ ⟨when a bit of finely filiated platinum is *introduced* into a chamber containing oxygen and sulphur dioxide—*T. S. Eliot*⟩ ⟨Aunt Harriet . . . *introduced* herself through the doorway . . . into the interior of the vehicle—*Bennett*⟩ It is the precise word when used of things not native and brought into a country or locality for the first time ⟨plants *introduced* into America by the

A colon (:) separates groups of words discriminated. An àsterisk (*) indicates place of treatment of each group.

colonists⟩ Sometimes its use connotes an alien character in that whose entrance is effected ⟨*introduce* one's own ideas into the interpretation of a poem⟩ **Admit** in this relation usually means let in; it may imply a human agent ⟨the maid *admitted* the callers to the drawing room⟩ ⟨I wanted to put in more poems by young poets than he was willing to *admit*—*Spender*⟩ but often a means of getting or passing in ⟨small windows *admit* light to the cell⟩
*Ana* insert, interpolate, intercalate, insinuate, *introduce

**enterprise** *n* *adventure, quest
*Ana* exploit, *feat, achievement: struggle, striving, endeavor, essay, attempt (see under ATTEMPT *vb*)

**entertain** 1 *harbor, shelter, lodge, house, board
*Ana* *receive, admit: cultivate, cherish, foster (see NURSE): *feed, nourish
2 divert, *amuse, recreate
*Ana* *please, delight, gratify, rejoice, gladden, regale: beguile, *while, wile

**entertainment** diversion, amusement, recreation (see under AMUSE)
*Ana* *dinner, banquet, feast: play, sport, disport (see under PLAY *vb*)

**enthuse** *thrill, electrify

**enthusiasm** fervor, ardor, *passion, zeal
*Ant* apathy —*Con* impassivity, phlegm, stolidity (see under IMPASSIVE): unconcern, detachment, aloofness, indifference (see corresponding adjectives at INDIFFERENT)

**enthusiast** *n* Enthusiast, fanatic, zealot, bigot denote a person who manifests excessive ardor, fervor, or devotion in his attachment to some cause, idea, party, or church. **Enthusiast** commonly denotes a person of keen and ardent interests and may carry either favorable or unfavorable connotations (as of mental or spiritual vitality or of a subordination of judgment to enthusiasm) ⟨increasing number of chess *enthusiasts*⟩ ⟨folk-singing *enthusiasts*⟩ ⟨we are a nation of *enthusiasts*—*Meeker*⟩ In earlier use and still in historical works the term applies particularly to a preacher, a member of a religious sect, or, sometimes, a poet who claims to be immediately inspired or who outwardly manifests signs (as rapture, madness, or intense emotionalism) associated with divine inspiration or possession by a god. In such context the term has been applied more or less contemptuously to a member of one of the strongly evangelical sects that arose in the seventeenth and eighteenth centuries ⟨the visions, voices, revelations of the *enthusiast*—*Glanvill*⟩ ⟨harmonic twang! . . . such as from lab'ring lungs th' *enthusiast* blows —*Pope*⟩ **Fanatic,** even more than *enthusiast*, carries a hint of madness or irrationality. In contrast to *enthusiast*, however, the term suggests extreme monomaniac devotion and a concentration of attention, sometimes on the end to be gained but, possibly more often, on the chosen means to one's end regardless of the real value of that end. *Fanatic*, therefore, in distinction from *enthusiast*, connotes determination, often silent determination, and an uncompromising temper ⟨a virtuous *fanatic*, narrow, passionate . . . regarding all ways as wrong but his own —*Froude*⟩ ⟨a *fanatic*, in Santayana's famous definition, is a man who redoubles his efforts after he has forgotten his aims—*Waters*⟩ ⟨this creature Man, who in his own selfish affairs is a coward to the backbone, will fight for an idea like a hero. He may be abject as a citizen; but he is dangerous as a *fanatic*—*Shaw*⟩ **Zealot** often implies fanaticism; it suggests ardent devotion, but it distinctively emphasizes vehement activity in the service of one's cause, party, or church. It may or may not connote blinding partisanship, but it usually suggests jealous vigilance in pro-

tecting one's beliefs or institutions ⟨for modes of faith let graceless *zealots* fight—*Pope*⟩ ⟨a furious *zealot* may think he does God service by persecuting one of a different sect—*Gilpin*⟩ **Bigot** implies obstinate, often blind, devotion to one's own (especially religious) beliefs or opinions; as compared with *fanatic* and *zealot*, the term implies dogged intolerance and contempt for those who do not agree, rather than enthusiasm or zeal ⟨the hell that *bigots* frame to punish those who err—*Shelley*⟩ ⟨one of the marks of a *bigot* is that he thinks he does a service to God when he persecutes his fellowmen—*Gillis*⟩
*Ana* devotee, votary, *addict

**entice** *lure, inveigle, decoy, tempt, seduce
*Ana* snare, ensnare, trap, entrap (see CATCH): cajole, blandish, *coax, wheedle
*Ant* scare —*Con* *frighten, alarm, terrify, fright

**entire** 1 *whole, total, all, gross
*Ana* complete, *full, plenary
*Ant* partial
2 *perfect, whole, intact
*Ana* integrated, concatenated (see under INTEGRATE *vb*): unified, consolidated, compacted (see COMPACT *vb*)
*Ant* impaired

**entity,** being, creature, individual, person are comparable when meaning something which has real and independent existence. **Entity,** the most consistently abstract of these terms, implies such existence not only in the actual world but also in the realm of thought. An *entity* may be seen or heard or it may be invisible, intangible, or imaginary, but it may be thought of as really existing ⟨that *entity* which we call an automobile⟩ ⟨is democracy an *entity?*⟩ ⟨his country is to him an *entity*, a concrete and organic force, with whose work in the world he is extremely proud to be natively associated—*Brownell*⟩ ⟨I introduce the *entity* called *light* to the readers of this book: as an *entity* consisting of particles—*Darrow*⟩ ⟨for the good of that mystical *entity*, different from and superior to the mere individuals composing it, the Nation—*Huxley*⟩ **Being** is for practical purposes definable in much the same terms as *entity*; however, it seldom retains the abstract meaning given to it by philosophers but easily slides into another and related sense, that of something or someone having material or immaterial existence, possessing qualities, properties, and attributes, and exciting thought or feelings ⟨the Supreme *Being*⟩ ⟨a human *being*⟩ ⟨a corporation is an artificial *being*, invisible, intangible, and existing only in contemplation of law—*John Marshall*⟩ ⟨a period during which there exist in the universe *beings* capable of speculating about the universe and its fluctuations—*Eddington*⟩ ⟨doing her best to do the extraordinary things required of her, but essentially a *being* of passive dignities, living chiefly for them—*H. G. Wells*⟩ **Creature,** in its most general sense, is the correlative of *creator*: it refers to any created thing, whether viewed as the creation of God or of natural influences ⟨we are all God's *creatures*⟩ ⟨as a child, I was inordinately fond of grasshoppers. For one of these *creatures*—*Grandgent*⟩ In this, its usual sense, *creature* is a general term including all living beings, but especially all animals and men. Often, as a modification of this sense, *creature* refers to a human being regarded as an object of pity, scorn, congratulation, or reprobation ⟨Mrs. Long is as good a *creature* as ever lived—*Austen*⟩ ⟨it was against a *creature* like this that we plotted—*Meredith*⟩ In a narrower sense *creature* often refers to someone or something that is the creation of some power or influence and that, usually, is subject to it or obedient to its will ⟨he . . . was the Queen Mother's *creature*—*Belloc*⟩ ⟨the evil in the moral order of the

---

*Ana* analogous words    *Ant* antonyms    *Con* contrasted words    See also explanatory notes facing page 1

world is part of that world—and its own *creature—
Alexander*⟩ ⟨imagination is always the *creature* of desire—*Krutch*⟩ **Individual,** in its fundamental sense, refers to whatever may be regarded as an entity or being, but the term stresses rather its incapacity for being divided and its existence as a unit ⟨an *individual* is that which cannot be divided without ceasing to be what it is—*Archbishop Thomson*⟩ *Individual,* therefore, in ordinary language applies to a single member of a conceivable group, especially of human beings, and is often used in contrast with such general or comprehensive terms as *society, race,* or *family* ⟨the *individual* rebelled against restraint; society wanted to do what it pleased—*Henry Adams*⟩ ⟨art . . . tends to reconcile the *individual* with the universal, by exciting in him impersonal emotion—*Galsworthy*⟩ ⟨the equipment of the higher animals . . . is needed less for the good of the *individual* than for the good of the race—*Ellis*⟩ Concretely, *individual* is often used of a person who strikes one as rich in nature and as standing strongly alone or independently ⟨Donne would have been an *individual* at any time and place—*T. S. Eliot*⟩ but occasionally it is used contemptuously to describe one who makes himself unpleasantly conspicuous (as by undue familiarity, blatancy, or general obnoxiousness) ⟨the *individual* who had sat himself down by me produced a little box and offered me a lozenge—*Jefferies*⟩ **Person** in its most common modern use denotes an individual human being without reference to sex, age, or identity ⟨there were five thousand *persons* at the meeting⟩ ⟨he knew but one *person* in the throng⟩ ⟨a commission of inquiry empowered to examine *persons* and papers⟩ *Person* is often found in other and richer senses, most of which involve the idea of the manifestation or the sustaining of a clearly defined character; sometimes it implies an entity distinguished from one's body yet somehow associated with it ⟨we observe . . . to begin with, that our bodies are not we,—not our proper *persons*—*Mozley*⟩ ⟨never needing to assert the dignity of his *person*⟩ and sometimes it implies this character as manifest to others ⟨the boy is becoming a real *person*⟩ ⟨everybody recognized him as a *person*⟩ Sometimes (as in law) *person* may refer not only to a man ⟨a natural *person*⟩ but to a corporate body ⟨an artificial, or juristic, *person*⟩ either of which has rights and duties that are recognized ⟨a state, a church, and a corporation are in the eyes of the law *persons*⟩ Again (as in Christian theology), *person* denotes one of the distinct modes of being in which the Supreme Being manifests Himself to men ⟨one God in three divine *Persons,* the Father, the Son, and the Holy Ghost⟩ Sometimes, also, *person* may refer to the body of a human being or to his appearance, but even in these uses it usually suggests a body informed by a spirit or personality ⟨he suffered injury to his *person* and damage to his property⟩ ⟨Mr. Wickham was . . . far beyond them all in *person,* countenance, air, and walk—*Austen*⟩ ⟨appear in *person*⟩ ⟨England . . . had stolen a kingdom . . . in Africa, and seized the *person* of its king—*Shaw*⟩

**entrance** *n* **Entrance, entry, entrée, ingress, access** are comparable when meaning the act, fact, or privilege of going in or coming in. All but *entrée* also carry the denotation of a way or means of entering. Their differences are largely in their applications and in their connotations. **Entrance** is the widest in its range of application and the thinnest in its specific implications; it fits in with nearly every context ⟨await the *entrance* of the king⟩ ⟨a season ticket gives you *entrance* to all the events⟩ ⟨the *entrance* is through a gate south of the stadium⟩ ⟨gained their *entrance* to the game through a hole in the fence⟩ **Entry,**

by comparison, typically imputes a formal or ceremonial character to the act of entering ⟨the trumpet will announce the Nuncio's *entry—Browning*⟩ When used with reference to a place where one enters, it usually signifies a door, a gate, a portico, or more commonly a vestibule or entrance hall ⟨the postman throws the letters in the *entry*⟩ ⟨I hear a knocking at the south *entry—Shak.*⟩ It has largely yielded its meaning of the privilege or right of entrance to **entrée.** The latter word, however, is usually restricted in its application and suggests exclusiveness in those admitting or distinction or social gifts in those admitted ⟨my mother's introductions had procured me the *entrée* of the best French houses—*Lytton*⟩ ⟨commented on the *entrée* which his son had with the president—*New Republic*⟩ **Ingress,** because of legal use, carries more than any of the others the implication either of permission to enter or of encroachment ⟨his deed gives him use of the path with free *ingress* and egress⟩ ⟨we pardon it; and for your *ingress* here upon the skirt and fringe of our fair land—*Tennyson*⟩ ⟨it puts a great strain on an armadillo to open his mouth wide enough to permit the *ingress* of a copper cent edgewise—*G. S. Perry*⟩ When used concretely it more often suggests a natural passageway than an architectural structure ⟨a narrow gap is the only *ingress* to the valley⟩ **Access,** like *ingress,* implies admission where barriers are imposed, but they may be of many kinds: social, legal, or personal, as well as natural ⟨he is here at the door and importunes *access* to you—*Shak.*⟩ *Access* is distinguished from the other words of this group by its emphasis on approach rather than on entrance ⟨explorers still find the North Pole difficult of *access,* in spite of their use of airplanes⟩ ⟨the *access* to the harbor was through a long narrow channel⟩
*Ant* exit

**entrance** *vb* *transport, ravish, enrapture
*Ana* delight, gladden, rejoice, *please: enchant, captivate, bewitch, charm (see ATTRACT)

**entrap** trap, snare, ensnare, bag, *catch, capture
*Ana* seize, *take, clutch: *lure, inveigle, decoy, entice

**entreat** *beg, beseech, implore, supplicate, importune, adjure
*Ana* *ask, request, solicit: pray, appeal, plead, petition, sue (see under PRAYER)
*Con* withstand, *resist, oppose: dare, *face, brave, challenge

**entrée** *entrance, entry, ingress, access
*Ana* admission, *admittance

**entrench** encroach, *trespass, infringe, invade
*Ana* *monopolize, engross, consume, absorb: *interpose, interfere, intervene

**entrust** confide, *commit, consign, relegate
*Ana* *allot, assign, allocate: *rely, trust, depend, count, bank, reckon
*Con* suspect, doubt (see corresponding nouns at UNCERTAINTY): mistrust, *distrust

**entry** *entrance, entrée, ingress, access
*Ana* *door, doorway, gate, gateway, portal, postern

**entwine** *wind, coil, curl, twist, twine, wreathe
*Ana* *curve, bend: interweave, interplait (see base words at WEAVE): *entangle, enmesh

**enumerate** *count, tell, number
*Ana* compute, *calculate, reckon: *add, sum, total, figure: rehearse, recount, recite (see RELATE)

**enunciate** pronounce, *articulate

**envelop** *vb* **1** *cover, overspread, wrap, shroud, veil
*Ana* *surround, environ, encompass: cloak, mask (see DISGUISE)
**2** *enclose, fence, pen, coop, corral, cage, wall

---

A colon (:) separates groups of words discriminated. An asterisk (*) indicates place of treatment of each group.

*Ana* confine, circumscribe (see LIMIT): protect, shield, guard (see DEFEND)

**envious,** **jealous,** though not close synonyms, are comparable because both carry as their basic meaning that of grudging another's possession of something desirable. Envious stresses a coveting of something (as riches, possessions, or attainments) which belongs to another or of something (as success or good fortune) which has come to another. It may imply either a gnawing, often a malicious, desire to deprive one of what gives him gratification, or a spiteful delight in his dispossession or loss of it ⟨still in thy right hand carry gentle peace, to silence *envious* tongues—*Shak.*⟩ ⟨some *envious* hand has sprinkled ashes just to spoil our slide—*Field*⟩ Frequently, however, the stress is on coveting rather than on a desire to injure ⟨we are all *envious* of your good fortune⟩ ⟨tried to look disappointed and angry but . . . only succeeded in looking *envious*—*Hervey Allen*⟩ **Jealous** often stresses intolerance of a rival for the possession of a thing which one regards as peculiarly one's own or on the winning of which one has set one's heart, but sometimes it merely implies intensely zealous efforts to keep or maintain what one possesses. The term often is used without derogation ⟨thou shalt have no other gods before me . . . for I the Lord thy God am a *jealous* God—*Exod* 20:3-5⟩ ⟨proud of their calling, conscious of their duty, and *jealous* of their honor—*Galsworthy*⟩ However the term usually carries a strong implication of distrust, suspicion, enviousness, or sometimes anger ⟨a *jealous* wife⟩ ⟨he was *jealous* of Carson's fame as an Indian fighter—*Cather*⟩ ⟨stabbed by a *jealous* lover⟩
*Ana* *covetous, grasping, greedy: grudging, coveting, envying (see COVET): malign, malignant, spiteful, *malicious, malevolent
*Con* generous, *liberal, bountiful, openhanded: kindly, *kind, benign, benignant

**environ** *vb* *surround, encircle, circle, encompass, compass, hem, gird, girdle, ring
*Ana* *enclose, envelop, fence: circumscribe, confine (see LIMIT)

**environment** *background, setting, milieu, backdrop, mise-en-scène

**envisage, envision** conceive, imagine, *think, realize, fancy
*Ana* view, behold, survey, contemplate (see SEE): objectify, externalize, materialize, *realize

**envoy** *ambassador, legate, minister, nuncio, internuncio, chargé d'affaires

**envy** *vb* *covet, grudge, begrudge
*Ana* *long, pine, hanker, yearn

**ephemeral** *transient, transitory, passing, fugitive, fleeting, evanescent, momentary, short-lived
*Ana* *brief, short

**epicene** hermaphroditic, hermaphrodite, *bisexual, androgynous
*Ana* effeminate, womanish (see FEMALE *adj*)

**epicure, gourmet, gourmand, glutton, bon vivant, gastronome** mean one who takes pleasure in eating and drinking. An **epicure** is one who is choice and fastidious while at the same time voluptuous in enjoyment of food and drink; the term is also applied to a connoisseur in an art involving both feasting and delicacy of taste ⟨I am become a perfect *epicure* in reading; plain beef or solid mutton will never do—*Goldsmith*⟩ ⟨an *epicure* in many of the delights of the senses—*Canby*⟩ A **gourmet** is a connoisseur in delicate or exotic dishes, liquors, and wines; the term carries as its distinctive connotation the savoring as of each morsel of food or sip of wine, and the power to distinguish delicate differences in flavor or

quality ⟨the most finished *gourmet* of my acquaintance —*Thackeray*⟩ ⟨eating habits . . . of a determined *gourmet*, verging at times on those of a gourmand—*Kahn*⟩ **Gourmand** implies less fastidiousness and less discernment than *gourmet*, but it suggests a hearty interest in and enjoyment of good food and drink rather than, as **glutton** does, greedy and voracious eating and drinking ⟨I dare say, their table is always good, for the Landgrave is a *gourmand*—*Chesterfield*⟩ ⟨youth is a *gourmand* when it cannot be a gourmet—*McClure's Mag.*⟩ ⟨it would be difficult to determine whether they were most to be distinguished as *gluttons* or epicures; for they were, at once, dainty and. voracious, understood the right and the wrong of every dish, and alike emptied the one and the other—*Burney*⟩ **Bon vivant** differs little from *gourmand* except in its stronger connotation of a lively or spirited enjoyment of the pleasures of the table, especially in the company of others ⟨the Major was somewhat of a *bon vivant*, and his wine was excellent—*Scott*⟩ ⟨he was also a *bon vivant*, a diner-out, and a storyteller —*Fraser's Mag.*⟩ **Gastronome** is equivalent to *epicure*, with perhaps greater stress on expert knowledge and appreciation of fine food and wine and of the ritual of preparation and serving of them ⟨a conversation on the mysteries of the table, which . . . a modern *gastronome* might have listened to with pleasure—*Scott*⟩
*Ana* connoisseur, *aesthete, dilettante

**epicurean** sybaritic, luxurious, *sensuous, sensual, voluptuous
*Ana* fastidious, dainty, *nice, particular
*Ant* gross

**epigram** aphorism, apothegm, *saying, saw, maxim, adage, proverb, motto

**episode** 1 *digression, divagation, excursus
*Ana* *deviation, divergence, deflection: departing *or* departure (see corresponding verb at SWERVE)
2 incident, event, *occurrence, circumstance

**epistle** *letter, missive, note, message, dispatch, report, memorandum

**epitome** conspectus, synopsis, *abridgment, abstract, brief
*Ana* précis, aperçu, sketch, digest, *compendium

**epoch** era, age, *period, aeon

**equable** even, constant, *steady, uniform
*Ana* regular, *orderly, methodical, systematic: invariable, immutable, unchangeable (see affirmative adjectives at CHANGEABLE): *same, equal, equivalent
*Ant* variable, changeable   —*Con* fluctuating, wavering (see SWING): *fitful, spasmodic

**equal** *adj* equivalent, *same, very, identical, identic, tantamount
*Ana* equable, even, uniform (see STEADY): *like, alike: proportionate, commensurate (see PROPORTIONAL)
*Ant* unequal   —*Con* *different, diverse, disparate, various, divergent

**equal** *vb* *match, rival, approach, touch
*Ana* *compare: square, accord, tally, correspond, *agree

**equanimity,** **composure, sangfroid, phlegm** mean the mental temper of one who is self-possessed or not easily disturbed or perturbed. **Equanimity** suggests either a proper mental balance or a constitutionally equable temper; it therefore may imply either a delicate adjustment of one's emotional and mental powers that is liable to disturbance only under great strain or a settled attitude of mind which repels all that disturbs ⟨his placidity of demeanor . . . arose from . . . the *equanimity* of a cold disposition rather than of one well ordered by discipline —*Trollope*⟩ ⟨it was some time before Wildeve recovered his *equanimity*—*Hardy*⟩ ⟨stoicism teaches men . . . to accept with proud *equanimity* the misfortunes of life—*Inge*⟩ **Composure** commonly implies the conquest of mental agitation or disturbance by an effort of will, though it may imply a temperamental freedom from agitation ⟨his passions tamed and all at his control, how perfect the *composure* of his soul!—*Cowper*⟩ ⟨we have to call upon our whole people—men, women, and children alike—to stand up with *composure* and fortitude to the fire of the enemy—*Sir Winston Churchill*⟩ **Sangfroid** implies great coolness and steadiness especially under strain ⟨no being ever stood in a pedagogue's presence with more perfect *sangfroid*—*Disraeli*⟩ ⟨at all these [gambling games] she won and lost, with the same equable *sangfroid*—*Rose Macaulay*⟩ **Phlegm** suggests an apathy of mind or sluggishness of temperament that results from a physical condition rather than from discipline or self-control; it therefore suggests even greater imperturbability and insensitiveness than any of the preceding terms ⟨he chose the eldest daughter whose numb composure he mistook for *phlegm*—*Patton*⟩ ⟨there was a busy, bustling, disputatious tone about it, instead of the accustomed *phlegm* and drowsy tranquillity—*Irving*⟩ **Ana** poise, equipoise, *balance, equilibrium: self-possession, self-assurance, aplomb (see CONFIDENCE): tranquillity, serenity, placidity, calmness (see corresponding adjectives at CALM)

**Con** discomposure, agitation, disquieting *or* disquiet, perturbing *or* perturbation, disturbance (see corresponding verbs at DISCOMPOSE)

**equilibrium** equipoise, poise, *balance, tension
**Ana** stableness *or* stability (see corresponding adjective at LASTING): stabilization, steadying (see corresponding verbs at STABILIZE): counterbalancing *or* counterbalance, counterpoising *or* counterpoise (see corresponding verbs at COMPENSATE)

**equip** *furnish, outfit, appoint, accouter, arm
**Con** divest, dismantle, denude, *strip: despoil, spoliate, *ravage

**equipment, apparatus, machinery, paraphernalia, outfit, tackle, gear, matériel** are comparable when they mean all the things that are used in a given work or are useful in effecting a given end. **Equipment** usually covers everything needed for efficient operation or efficient service except the personnel; thus, the *equipment* for a polar expedition would include not only the vessels, instruments, and implements required but also the sleds, dogs, and supplies (as clothing, food, and medicines) ⟨the *equipment* of furnishings, utensils, and supplies required for setting up housekeeping⟩ Sometimes *equipment* is more limited in its application; thus, in railroading it covers only the rolling stock and not the roadbed and stations. In extended use *equipment* is also employed in reference to persons and covers the qualities and skills necessary to their efficiency or competency in a given kind of work ⟨knowledge, penetration, seriousness, sentiment, humor, Gray had them all; he had the *equipment* and endowment for the office of poet—*Arnold*⟩ ⟨a health officer needed more than technical training . . . . It appeared that diplomacy should constitute a major part of his *equipment*—*Heiser*⟩ **Apparatus** usually covers the instruments, tools, machines, and appliances used in a given craft or profession or in a specific operation or the equipment used in a recreation or sport; thus, the *apparatus* of a dentist includes all the mechanical and electrical devices he uses in his professional work; the *apparatus* of a laboratory, as distinguished from its equipment, consists of all the mechanical requisites for carrying on operations or experiments. When used in reference to persons or employments not requiring mechanical devices, *apparatus* denotes all

the external aids useful in prosecuting a particular kind of work; thus, the *apparatus* of a scholar in Old English includes the reference books (as texts, glossaries, and bibliographies) that he finds essential to or helpful in his investigations ⟨formal lectures, with an appalling *apparatus* of specimens, charts, and wall pictures—*Grandgent*⟩ **Machinery** covers all the devices, means, or agencies which permit a thing (as an organism, a government, an institution, or a law) to function or which enable it to accomplish its ends (as a movement, a political party, or propaganda) ⟨the physiological *machinery* of the body is so adjusted that great variations of atmospheric temperature can be supported without detriment—*Heiser*⟩ ⟨public meetings, harangues, resolutions, and the rest of the modern *machinery* of agitation had not yet come into fashion—*Macaulay*⟩ ⟨if the peoples wanted war, no *machinery* could prevent them from having it—*Inge*⟩ **Paraphernalia** usually suggests a collection of the miscellaneous articles or belongings that constitute the usual accompaniments (often the necessary equipment) of a person or group of persons in a particular employment or activity ⟨the *paraphernalia* of a circus⟩ ⟨the *paraphernalia* of a tourist⟩ ⟨little piles of wheels, strips of unworked iron and steel, blocks of wood, the *paraphernalia* of the inventor's trade—*Anderson*⟩ The word may be slightly contemptuous and imply a trivial or worthless character to the items included ⟨clear a boy's room of all its *paraphernalia*⟩ **Outfit** is sometimes interchangeable with *equipment*, but it has a slightly less formal flavor and is preferred when the latter term might seem pretentious ⟨a camper's *outfit*⟩ ⟨a beginner's beekeeping *outfit*, consisting of a bee veil, a pair of bee gloves, and the makings of a first-rate beehive—*New Yorker*⟩ It often specifically suggests wearing apparel and other necessities for a journey, a school year, or a new employment ⟨a bride's *outfit*⟩ ⟨a college girl's *outfit*⟩ ⟨beside this neat, black figure the American business man's *outfit* is as garish as a clown's—*Barbara Beecher*⟩ **Tackle** is also less formal than *apparatus*, which otherwise it closely resembles ⟨fishing *tackle*⟩ ⟨the girl sprucely habited, with her pretty *tackle* on the shining blood [horse] was a glad sight—*Miles Franklin*⟩ **Gear** is variously used, sometimes approaching *equipment* ⟨you've got a good six hours to get your *gear* together—*Conrad*⟩ or sometimes *apparatus* ⟨sportsman's *gear*⟩ or again *outfit*, or *wearing apparel* ⟨servants . . . ready in waiting at Pathankote with a change of *gear*—*Kipling*⟩ It is also occasionally the most general of these terms and equivalent to one's belongings collectively ⟨they are all, as far as worldly *gear* is concerned, much poorer than I—*Shaw*⟩ **Matériel** is used in industry and in military affairs as a comprehensive and unambiguous term that covers everything but the personnel ⟨a heavy drain on both the manpower and *matériel* resources—*N. Y. Times*⟩

**equipoise** equilibrium, poise, *balance, tension
**equitable** *fair, just, impartial, unbiased, dispassionate, uncolored, objective
**Ana** *proportional, proportionate, commensurate, commensurable: equal, equivalent, *same, identical
**Ant** inequitable, unfair —**Con** unreasonable, *irrational
**equity** *justice
**equivalent** *adj* equal, *same, identical, identic, selfsame, very, tantamount
**Ana** like, alike, comparable, parallel, uniform (see SIMILAR): proportionate, commensurate (see PROPORTIONAL): *reciprocal, corresponding, convertible
**Ant** different —**Con** disparate, diverse, divergent, various (see DIFFERENT): discrepant, discordant, *inconsonant, incompatible

A colon (:) separates groups of words discriminated. An asterisk (*) indicates place of treatment of each group.

**equivocal** ambiguous, *obscure, dark, vague, enigmatic, cryptic
*Ana* dubious, questionable, *doubtful
*Ant* unequivocal —*Con* *explicit, express, definite, specific, categorical: perspicuous, lucid, *clear
**equivocate** prevaricate, *lie, palter, fib
*Ana* *deceive, mislead, delude: evade, elude, *escape
**equivocation** *ambiguity, tergiversation, double entendre
*Ana* prevarication, lying *or* lie, paltering, fibbing *or* fib (see corresponding verbs at LIE): duplicity, dissimulation, *deceit
**era** age, epoch, *period, aeon
**eradicate** uproot, deracinate, extirpate, *exterminate, wipe
*Ana* *abolish, annihilate, extinguish, abate: *destroy, demolish, raze: obliterate, efface, *erase, blot out
*Con* *set, fix, establish, settle: *implant, inculcate, instill: propagate, engender, breed, *generate

**erase, expunge, cancel, efface, obliterate, blot out, delete** mean to strike out something so that it no longer has effect or existence. **Erase** basically implies a scraping or rubbing out of something that is written, engraved, or painted ⟨*erase* a word⟩ ⟨*erase* a line of an inscription⟩ In extended use *erase* often refers to something that has been eradicated as if by scraping or rubbing out after it has impressed or imprinted itself on the memory or has become part of an unwritten record ⟨have a few years totally *erased* me from your memory?—*Gray*⟩ ⟨the old boyhood notion . . . that a town and a people could remake him and *erase* from his body the marks of what he thought of as his inferior birth—*Anderson*⟩ **Expunge** implies, possibly through confusion with *sponge,* so thoroughgoing an erasure that the thing affected is wiped out completely ⟨a woman's history, you know: certain chapters *expunged*—*Meredith*⟩ ⟨the most primitive ways of thinking may not yet be wholly *expunged*—*James*⟩ Basically **cancel** means to strike out written material (originally with lines crossed latticewise), but it also may apply to an invalidating or nullifying by other means; thus, a postage stamp is *canceled* to prevent reuse, usually with a hand device or a machine that stamps an indelible mark or device on its face; a transportation ticket is similarly *canceled* with a punch that removes a part of it; a will is *canceled* by physically destroying it ⟨the worn or soiled currency declared unfit for further circulation is transferred to our custodians of unfit currency for cancellation on a *canceling* machine which is designed to punch the symbol "L" in each corner of each package of 100 bills, and to simultaneously cut each package in half lengthwise—*George Parker*⟩ In extended use *cancel* implies an action that completely negatives something, whether by a legal annulling ⟨cancellation consists of any act, such as the surrender or intentional destruction of the instrument, that indicates the intention to *cancel* or renounce the obligation—*Fisk & Snapp*⟩ or by a revoking or rescinding ⟨*cancel* a meeting⟩ ⟨the laboratory door does not lock behind him and bar his return any more than it swung shut to imprison Darwin and forever *cancel* his status as a naturalist—*Amer. Naturalist*⟩ or often by a neutralization of one thing by its opposite ⟨the qualities that in the end nullified his great strength of character and remarkable gifts, just as his irritability *cancelled* out his natural kindness—*Osbert Sitwell*⟩ ⟨ironies breed before our eyes, *cancel* each other out—*Kristol*⟩ **Efface,** more strongly than *erase,* implies the complete removal of something impressed or imprinted on a surface ⟨constant use gradually *effaces* the figures and letters on a coin⟩ ⟨*efface* the offensive murals in a public building⟩ As a result,

in its extended use, *efface* often implies destruction of every visible or sensible sign of a thing's existence ⟨while nations have *effaced* nations, and death has gathered to his fold long lines of mighty kings—*Wordsworth*⟩ ⟨the attempt to *efface* the boundaries between prose and verse—*Lowes*⟩ Often, especially in reflexive use, it implies an attempt to make inconspicuous or vague ⟨*efface* oneself in the company of others⟩ **Obliterate** and **blot out** both imply rendering a thing undecipherable by smearing it with something which hides its existence ⟨a smear of decisive lead-colored paint had been laid on to *obliterate* Henchard's name—*Hardy*⟩ ⟨*blot out* with ink a passage in a manuscript⟩ Both terms are more often used, however, with the implication of the removal of every trace of a thing's existence ⟨the falling snow rapidly *obliterated* all signs of approaching spring⟩ ⟨a successful love . . . *obliterated* all other failures—*Krutch*⟩ ⟨then rose the seed of chaos, and of night, to *blot out* order, and extinguish light—*Pope*⟩ **Delete** implies marking something in a manuscript or proof for omission from a text that is to be published or distributed ⟨whenever you feel an impulse to perpetrate a piece of exceptionally fine writing, obey it—wholeheartedly—and *delete* it before sending your manuscript to press—*Quiller-Couch*⟩ But *delete* also often suggests eradication or elimination by the exercise of arbitrary power ⟨the censor *deleted* all the interesting parts of the letter⟩ ⟨a compulsion to make plays out of books, musicals out of plays . . . to insert scenes, *delete* characters, include commentators—*Kronenberger*⟩
*Ana* annul, *nullify, negate: *abolish, extinguish
*Con* imprint, impress, print, stamp (see corresponding nouns at IMPRESSION)
**erect** *vb* *build, construct, frame, raise, rear
*Ana* fabricate, fashion, form (see MAKE): *lift, raise, elevate
*Ant* raze
**eremite** hermit, anchorite, *recluse, cenobite
**erotic, amatory, amorous, amative, aphrodisiac** all involve the idea of love for the opposite sex, but they are not freely interchangeable because of differences in denotation as well as in implications. **Erotic,** though the strongest in its suggestions of love as a violent passion or as a physical appetite, is rarely applied to persons as distinct from their behavior, reactions, or emotions, and it is especially used in characterizing or classifying emotions, motives, or themes in art ⟨*erotic* tendencies⟩ ⟨*erotic* music⟩ ⟨an *erotic* poet⟩ ⟨*erotic* poetry⟩ ⟨it was the persuasion that the deprivation was final that obsessed him with *erotic* imaginations . . . almost to the verge of madness—*H. G. Wells*⟩ ⟨describes his *erotic* adventures with prostitutes—*Sat. Review*⟩ **Amatory** is a synonym of *erotic* but weaker in its suggestion of sexual desire; it sometimes connotes little more than ardent admiration; thus, one might more correctly describe the youthful love poems of Tennyson as *amatory* than as *erotic* poetry ⟨Sir Lucius . . . has been deluded into thinking that some *amatory* letters received by him from Mrs. Malaprop are from Lydia—*Harvey*⟩ **Amorous** is applied chiefly to persons, their words, or their acts especially when they are falling in love or making love ⟨came many a tiptoe, *amorous* cavalier, and back retired . . . her heart was otherwhere—*Keats*⟩ ⟨yielded, with coy submission, modest pride, and sweet, reluctant, *amorous* delay—*Milton*⟩ ⟨the shady lawns and thickets along the river give nightly sanctuary to *amorous* couples—*Green Peyton*⟩ The word often suggests ripeness or eagerness for love ⟨the English . . . are not an *amorous* race. Love with them is more sentimental than passionate—*Maugham*⟩ In this

sense it is also applied, chiefly in poetry, to animals ⟨the *amorous* dove—*Gilbert*⟩ **Amative** implies merely a disposition to fall in love or a propensity for loving; it is chiefly used in describing temperaments or in analyzing character ⟨that crudely *amative* public to which our modern best sellers appeal—*N. Y. Times*⟩ ⟨he is not normally *amative*⟩ **Aphrodisiac** is applied to things (as drugs or writings) that arouse or tend to arouse sexual desire ⟨the labored unreserve of *aphrodisiac* novels and plays—*Montague*⟩
*Ana* passionate, *impassioned, fervid, perfervid, ardent, fervent: *carnal, fleshly, sensual

**erratic** eccentric, odd, queer, *strange, singular, peculiar, unique, quaint, outlandish, curious
*Ana* aberrant, *abnormal, atypical: *irregular, unnatural, anomalous: capricious, fickle, mercurial, *inconstant
*Con* normal, *regular, typical, natural: *usual, customary, wonted, habitual: *common, ordinary, familiar: conventional, formal (see CEREMONIAL): *decorous, decent, seemly, proper

**error,** mistake, blunder, slip, lapse, faux pas, bull, howler, boner are comparable when they denote something (as an act, statement, or belief) that involves a departure from what is, or what is generally held to be, true, right, or proper. **Error** implies a straying from a proper course and suggests such guilt as may lie in failure to take proper advantage of a guide (as a record or manuscript, a rule or set of rules, or a principle, law, or code); thus, a typographical *error* results when a compositor misreads a manuscript; an *error* in addition involves some failure to follow the rules for addition; an *error* in conduct is an infraction of an accepted code of manners or morals ⟨those who, with sincerity and generosity, fight and fall in an evil cause, posterity can only compassionate as victims of a generous but fatal *error*—*Scott*⟩ ⟨without understanding grievous and irreparable *errors* can be made—*Donald Harrington*⟩ **Mistake** implies misconception, misunderstanding, a wrong but not always blameworthy judgment, or inadvertence; it expresses less severe criticism than *error* ⟨he made a serious *mistake* when he chose the law as his profession⟩ ⟨a child makes many *mistakes* in spelling⟩ ⟨there is a medium between truth and falsehood, and (I believe) the word *mistake* expresses it exactly. I will therefore say that you were mistaken—*Cowper*⟩ **Blunder** is harsher than *mistake* or *error*; it commonly implies ignorance or stupidity, sometimes blameworthiness ⟨we usually call our *blunders* mistakes, and our friends style our mistakes *blunders*—*Wheatley*⟩ ⟨one's translation is sure to be full of gross *blunders*, but the supreme *blunder* is that of translating at all when one is trying to catch not a fact but a feeling—*Henry Adams*⟩ **Slip** carries a stronger implication of inadvertence or accident than *mistake* and often, in addition, connotes triviality ⟨the wrong date on the check was a *slip* of the pen⟩ ⟨a social *slip* which makes us feel hot all over—*L. P. Smith*⟩ Often, especially when it implies a transgression against morality, the word is used euphemistically or ironically ⟨let Christian's *slips* before he came hither . . . be a warning to those that come after—*Bunyan*⟩ ⟨the minister . . . comes when people are in extremis, but they don't send for him every time they make a slight moral *slip*—tell a lie, for instance, or smuggle a silk dress through the customhouse—*Holmes*⟩ **Lapse,** though sometimes used interchangeably with *slip,* stresses forgetfulness, weakness, or inattention more than accident; thus, one says a *lapse* of memory or a *slip* of the pen, but not vice versa ⟨writes well, despite occasional *lapses* into polysyllabic humor—*Geographical Jour.*⟩ When used in reference to a moral transgression,

it carries a weaker implication of triviality than *slip* and a stronger one of a fall from grace or from one's own standards ⟨for all his . . . *lapses,* there was in him a real nobility, an even ascetic firmness and purity of character —*Ellis*⟩ **Faux pas** is most frequently applied to a mistake in etiquette ⟨she was carefully instructed so that there was no danger of her making a *faux pas* when she was presented at the Court of St. James's⟩ ⟨John and I, horrified, hustled him out before he could commit any further *faux pas*—*S. H. Adams*⟩ **Bull,** *howler,* and *boner* all three are rather informal terms applicable to blunders (and especially to blunders in speech or writing) that typically have an amusing aspect. A **bull** may be a grotesque blunder in language typically characterized by some risible incongruity ⟨the well-known *bull* stating that "one man is just as good as another—and sometimes more so"⟩ or it may be a mere stupid or gauche blunder ⟨he really committed a *bull* when he solemnly introduced his new friend to the latter's ex-wife⟩ A **howler** is a gross or ludicrous error based on ignorance or confusion of ideas; the term is used especially of laughable errors in scholastic recitations or examinations ⟨a collection of schoolboy *howlers*⟩ ⟨a *howler* that turns the title "Intimations of Immortality" into "Imitations of Immorality"⟩ A **boner** may be a grammatical, logical, or factual blunder in a piece of writing that is usually so extreme as to be funny ⟨a few historical *boners* . . . such as dinosaurs surviving until medieval times—*Coulton Waugh*⟩ or it may be a ridiculous or embarrassing slip of the kind that results from a sudden lapse (as of attention or from tact or decorum) ⟨is the proprietor of a large and varied selection of diplomatic *boners*—*Rosenthal*⟩

**errorless** flawless, faultless, *impeccable
*Ana* *correct, accurate, exact, precise, right, nice

**ersatz** *adj* *artificial, synthetic, factitious

**erudite** *learned, scholarly

**erudition** learning, scholarship, *knowledge, science, information, lore

**escape** *vb* **1 Escape,** flee, fly, decamp, abscond mean to run away especially from something which limits one's freedom or threatens one's well-being. **Escape** so stresses the idea of flight from confinement or restraint that it very often conveys no suggestion of wrongdoing or of danger ⟨one of the most powerful motives that attract people to science and art is the longing to *escape* from everyday life—*Ellis*⟩ ⟨eager to *escape* from the army and go back to his hometown—*Wecter*⟩ **Flee** implies haste and often abruptness in departure ⟨there was evidence that the burglars had been frightened and had *fled*⟩ It often connotes disappearance, especially when extended to things ⟨the mists *fled* before the rising sun⟩ **Fly** is interchangeable with *flee* but its use is restricted in idiomatic English to the present tense ⟨*fly,* father, *fly!* for all your friends are fled—*Shak.*⟩ **Decamp** usually suggests a sudden departure to elude discovery or arrest; it commonly carries a disparaging or belittling connotation ⟨having imparted my situation to my companion, she found it high time for us to *decamp*—*Smollett*⟩ ⟨came to town, took orders, received advances of goods or money, and then *decamped*—*Jones*⟩ **Abscond** adds to *decamp* the distinctive implications of clandestine withdrawal and concealment usually to avoid the consequences of fraudulent action ⟨he had the appearance of a bankrupt tradesman *absconding*—*Meredith*⟩ ⟨determined to be a poet at any price, he *absconded* from college with his clothes and took refuge in a lonely farmhouse—*Brooks*⟩
*Con* *follow, chase, pursue, trail, tag

**2 Escape,** avoid, evade, elude, shun, eschew are comparable

---

A colon (:) separates groups of words discriminated. An asterisk (*) indicates place of treatment of each group.

when meaning to get away or to keep away from something which one does not wish to incur, endure, or encounter. **Escape** when referred to persons (sometimes to animals) usually implies a threat to their liberty or well-being; in this sense it may not imply running away from or even an effort to miss what threatens, but it does suggest the latter's imminence or likelihood ⟨*escape* suspicion⟩ ⟨*escape* discovery⟩ ⟨*escape* the family tendency to tuberculosis⟩ ⟨*escape* annoyance⟩ ⟨*escape* a blow by dodging it⟩ ⟨few fish can *escape* this net⟩ When extended to things and especially to inanimate or intangible things *escape* connotes something comparable to a net which holds and confines yet permits passage through it ⟨details which *escape* the mind⟩ ⟨nothing *escaped* the kind eyes —*Deland*⟩ ⟨the exquisite beauty of this passage, even in translation, will *escape* no lover of poetry—*Dickinson*⟩ **Avoid,** in contrast with *escape,* suggests a keeping clear of what one does not wish to risk or knows to be a source of danger, rather than a getting away from what actually threatens; thus, one may *escape* suspicion by *avoiding* persons or places that are being watched; one may *avoid* all known sources of contagion yet not *escape* infection ⟨he kept himself somewhat aloof, seeming to *avoid* notice rather than to court it—*Arnold*⟩ *Avoid,* however, is often used interchangeably with *escape*; it may be preferred when a danger is averted by forethought, prudence, or caution ⟨mother and son *avoided* an open rupture by never referring to their differences—*Santayana*⟩ ⟨by pooling our difficulties, we may at least *avoid* the failures which come from conceiving the problems of government to be simpler than they are—*Frankfurter*⟩ **Evade** implies escape or the intent to escape, but it also commonly suggests avoidance by the use of adroit, ingenious, or, sometimes, underhand means; thus, one *evades* suspicion who escapes it by spreading rumors that throw others off the scent; one *evades* a question one does not wish to answer by seeming not to hear it ⟨the exacting life of the sea has this advantage over the life of the earth, that its claims are simple and cannot be *evaded*—*Conrad*⟩ ⟨wisdom consists not in premature surrender but in learning when to *evade,* when to stave off and when to oppose head on—*Howe*⟩ **Elude** comes closer to *escape* than to *avoid* but stresses a slippery or baffling quality in the thing which gets away or cannot be captured ⟨whose secret presence, through creation's veins running quicksilverlike, *eludes* your pains—*FitzGerald*⟩ ⟨for are we not all fated to pursue ideals which seem eternally to *elude* us—*L. P. Smith*⟩ *Elude,* however, is sometimes used in place of *evade* when there is a strong suggestion of shiftiness or unreliability or of the use of stratagems ⟨she is adept in *eluding* her obligations⟩ ⟨in the game of hide-and-seek the players try to *elude* discovery by the one seeking their hiding places⟩ **Shun** differs from *avoid* chiefly in its added implication of an abhorrence or aversion that is sometimes temperamental in its origin but oftentimes rational and dictated by conscience, experience, or sense of prudence ⟨[lepers] *shunned* and rebuffed by the world—*Heiser*⟩ ⟨to *shun* for his health the pleasures of the table—*Quiller-Couch*⟩ ⟨thus have I *shunned* the fire for fear of burning—*Shak.*⟩ ⟨I used to live entirely for pleasure. I *shunned* suffering and sorrow of every kind—*Wilde*⟩ **Eschew** comes very close to *shun* in meaning but tends to stress practical, moral, or prudential rather than temperamental reasons for the avoidance ⟨trained to *eschew* private passions and pursuits —*Mowrer*⟩ ⟨what cannot be *eschewed* must be embraced —*Shak.*⟩ ⟨observers . . . thought that capitalists would *eschew* all connection with what must necessarily be a losing concern—*Macaulay*⟩

**Con** *incur, contract, catch: *bear, endure, suffer, tolerate, abide

**eschew** *vb* 1 shun, elude, avoid, evade, *escape
**Ant** choose —**Con** *adopt, embrace, espouse: *incur, contract, catch
2 forbear, *forgo, abnegate, sacrifice
**Ana** abstain, *refrain, forbear

**escort** *vb* conduct, convoy, chaperon, *accompany, attend
**Ana** protect, shield, guard, safeguard, *defend: lead, *guide, pilot, steer

**esoteric** occult, *recondite, abstruse
**Ana** mystic, *mystical, anagogic, cabalistic: arcane, *mysterious

**especial** *special, specific, particular, individual
**Ana** preeminent, surpassing, *supreme: paramount, *dominant, predominant, preponderant, sovereign: *exceptional

**espousal** *marriage, matrimony, nuptial, wedding, wedlock

**espouse** embrace, *adopt
**Ana** *support, uphold, advocate, champion, back
**Con** renounce, *abjure, forswear: forsake, *abandon, desert

**esprit** *vigor, vim, spirit, dash, verve, punch, élan, drive
**Ana** wit, brain, intelligence, *mind: *courage, mettle, tenacity: ardor, fervor, *passion, enthusiasm

**esprit de corps** *morale, discipline

**espy** descry, behold, *see, perceive, discern, notice, remark, note, observe, survey, view, contemplate

**essay** *vb* endeavor, strive, struggle, *attempt, try
**Ana** work, labor, toil, travail (see corresponding nouns at WORK)

**essay** *n* 1 endeavor, striving, struggle, attempt, try (see under ATTEMPT *vb*)
**Ana** *effort, exertion, trouble, pains: toil, labor, *work, travail
2 **Essay, article, paper, theme, composition** are comparable when denoting a relatively brief discourse written for others' reading or consideration. **Essay** is the only one of these terms which suggests a literary character or is included in classifications of literary types. It may designate any writing that attempts to cover a subject briefly, competently, and interestingly, whether the attempt is successful or not and whether it is intended for publication or for submission to a teacher or others for criticism. In such usage an essay is often distinguished from a short story or an argument, and though use of the word does not debar the introduction of a narrative or argumentative method, it typically has an expository or descriptive aim. **Article** carries the implication found in all senses of this word: that of membership in a whole without sacrifice of distinctness and individuality. Therefore *article* is appropriately applied only to one of the separate and in itself complete writings which make up a single issue of a journal or a magazine or such a book as a history written by different persons ⟨have you read the *article* on the prospects of war in today's newspaper?⟩ ⟨a writer of *articles* for magazines⟩ ⟨the encyclopedia's *article* at "carpet" will furnish you information concerning Oriental rugs⟩ **Paper** is applied to a writing, chiefly an informative writing, that is intended for reading (as at a meeting of a club or a learned society) or for publication (as in a scientific or learned journal) or as a college exercise especially in a nonliterary course ⟨the most interesting *paper* on the program of the Woman's Club was one on the history of dolls⟩ **Theme** and **composition** are applied to writings that are school exercises and submitted for criticism. Although they are seldom distinguished

---

**Ana** analogous words      **Ant** antonyms      **Con** contrasted words      See also explanatory notes facing page 1

in their use, except that *theme* is more often employed in colleges and high schools and *composition* in the lower schools, there can be a real difference in the implications of the words. *Theme* may imply the development and elaboration of a definite subject; its tests are chiefly adequacy, as evinced by its completeness of treatment within limitations, and readability, as evinced by its power to interest those who read it and impress its points on their minds. *Composition,* on the other hand, implies organization of details, facts, and ideas or sometimes of sentences and paragraphs so that the result is a unified and clear piece of writing.

**essential** *adj*   1 *inherent, intrinsic, constitutional, ingrained
*Ana* *innate, inborn, inbred, congenital: *inner, inward: elemental (see ELEMENTARY): *characteristic, individual, peculiar, distinctive
*Ant* accidental  —*Con* adventitious, fortuitous, incidental (see ACCIDENTAL): contingent, *dependent, conditional
2 **Essential, fundamental, vital, cardinal** mean so important as to be indispensable. Something is **essential** which belongs to the very nature or essence of a thing and which therefore cannot be removed without destroying the thing itself or its distinguishing character ⟨the *essential* doctrines of Christianity⟩ ⟨the *essential* ingredient in a medicine⟩ ⟨the most *essential* characteristic of mind is memory—*Russell*⟩ Something is **fundamental** upon which everything else in a system, institution, or construction is built up, by which the whole is supported, or from which each addition is derived and without which, therefore, the whole construction would topple down ⟨certainly all those who have framed written constitutions contemplate them as forming the *fundamental* and paramount law of the nation—*John Marshall*⟩ ⟨the power of concentrated attention as the *fundamental* source of the prodigious productiveness of great workers —*Eliot*⟩ Something is **vital** which is as necessary to a thing's existence, continued vigor, or efficiency as food, drink, and health are to living things ⟨a question the solution of which is *vital* to human happiness⟩ ⟨the *vital* interests of a people⟩ ⟨the capture of the fortified town was *vital* to the invaders⟩ ⟨Germany is extremely important to Russia, but Poland, the gateway of invasion, is *vital*—*Hartmann*⟩ Something is **cardinal** upon which something else turns or hinges or actively depends; thus, the *cardinal* virtues (prudence, fortitude, temperance, justice, and sometimes, patience and humility) are not, in Christian theology, the highest virtues (which are the Christian virtues faith, hope, and charity), but they are fundamental and without them moral progress would be impossible ⟨*cardinal* arguments in a brief⟩ ⟨the *cardinal* defects in a character⟩ ⟨*cardinal* events are not to be forgotten—*De Quincey*⟩ ⟨I repeat this sentence, with emphasis on its *cardinal* words—*Darrow*⟩
*Ana* basic, basal, underlying, *fundamental: principal, foremost, capital, *chief, main, leading: prime, *primary, primal
*Con* *subordinate, secondary, dependent: *auxiliary, subsidiary, accessory, contributory, subservient
3 indispensable, requisite, necessary, *needful
*Ana* required, needed, wanted (see LACK *vb*)
*Ant* nonessential

**establish**   1 *set, settle, fix
*Ana* *implant, inculcate, instill: *secure, rivet, anchor, moor
*Ant* uproot (*a tree, a habit, a practice*): abrogate (*a right, a privilege, a quality*)  —*Con* eradicate, extirpate, wipe, *exterminate

2 *found, institute, organize
*Ana* start, inaugurate, *begin, commence, initiate
*Ant* abolish (*a society, an institution*)

**esteem** *n*   respect, admiration, *regard
*Ana* *honor, homage, reverence, deference, obeisance: veneration, reverence, worship, adoration (see under REVERE)
*Ant* abomination: contempt  —*Con* despite, scorn, disdain (see under DESPISE): abhorrence, loathing, hatred, hate, detestation (see under HATE *vb*)

**esteem** *vb*   respect, admire, regard (see under REGARD *n*)
*Ana* prize, value, *appreciate, treasure, cherish: *revere, reverence, venerate
*Ant* abominate  —*Con* abhor, loathe, *hate, detest: contemn, *despise, scorn, disdain

**estimate** *vb*   1 **Estimate, appraise, evaluate, value, rate, assess, assay** are comparable when meaning to judge a thing with respect to its worth. **Estimate** usually implies a personal and sometimes a reasoned judgment which, whether considered or casual, is by the nature of the case neither thoroughly objective nor definitive ⟨we have first to *estimate* their effects upon complicated social conditions (largely a matter of guesswork)—*Dewey*⟩ ⟨small and manageable numbers of birds must be counted precisely; huge flocks can only be *estimated* —*Time*⟩ ⟨to *estimate* the Frenchwoman's moral nature with any approach to adequacy it is necessary . . . to avoid viewing her from an Anglo-Saxon standpoint—*Brownell*⟩ **Appraise** implies the intent to fix definitely and in the capacity of an expert the monetary worth of the thing in question usually in terms of the price it ought to bring in the market if sold, or in case of its loss (as by fire or theft) the monetary compensation due its owner from an insuring company ⟨*appraise* the decedent's real estate⟩ ⟨*appraise* a fire loss⟩ In extended use *appraise,* in contrast to *estimate,* implies an intent to give a final, an accurate, or an expert judgment of a thing's worth; *estimate,* therefore, is often preferred by persons speaking of their own judgments because *appraise* seems presumptuous or pretentious ⟨it is not my business to *appraise.* Appraisements imply censures and it is not one writer's business to censure others—*F. M. Ford*⟩ ⟨this difficulty of *appraising* literature absolutely inheres in your study of it from the beginning—*Quiller-Couch*⟩ The participial adjective **appraising** is often used to qualify *eye, glance, look;* it then suggests close, critical inspection or scrutiny ⟨addressing him with a watchful *appraising* stare of his prominent black eyes —*Conrad*⟩ ⟨the monumental and encyclopedic critic is to be regarded with a carefully *appraising* eye—*T. S. Eliot*⟩ **Evaluate,** like *appraise,* suggests an intent to arrive at a mathematically correct judgment; it seldom suggests, however, an attempt to determine a thing's monetary worth, but rather to find its equivalent in other and more familiar terms ⟨a teacher *evaluates* a student's work by marks in numbers or in letters⟩ ⟨many persons find it impossible to *evaluate* a work of art except in terms of morals⟩ ⟨conventional ethical codes are assumed to be invalid or at least impractical for *evaluating* life as it is—*Walcutt*⟩ **Value** (see also APPRECIATE 2) comes very close to *appraise* in that it also implies an intent to determine or fix the market price but differs from *appraise* in that it carries no implication of an authoritative or expert judgment and must depend on the context to make that point if it is essential ⟨the appraiser *valued* at $10,000 condemned property which had already been *valued* by the owner at $15,000 and by the city at $8000⟩ ⟨experts were called in to appraise the gems which the alleged smuggler had *valued* at $1000⟩ In extended use and in

---

A colon (:) separates groups of words discriminated. An asterisk (*) indicates place of treatment of each group.

reference to things not marketable, *value* is often found with a negative or with a restrictive word such as *only* ⟨he *values* success only as a stepping-stone⟩ ⟨who *values* his own honor not a straw—*Browning*⟩ ⟨*valued* himself on his tolerance of heresy in great thinkers—*Frost*⟩ **Rate** often adds to *estimate* the implication of fixing in a scale of values ⟨*rate* one profession above another in usefulness⟩ ⟨*rate* one person's qualifications as superior to another's⟩ ⟨we English are capable of *rating* him far more correctly if we knew him better—*Arnold*⟩ **Assess** implies valuing for the sake of determining the tax to be levied; in extended use it implies a determining of the exact value or extent of a thing prior to judging it or to using it as the ground for a decision ⟨the task of defining that influence or of exactly *assessing* its amount is one of extraordinary difficulty—*Huxley*⟩ ⟨striving to *assess* the many elements upon which Rome's future depended—*Buchan*⟩ **Assay** basically implies chemical analysis for the sake of determining a substance's (usually a metal's) quality, quantity, or value; in extended use it implies a critical analysis for the sake of measuring, weighing, and appraising ⟨to *assay* . . . changes which the great reformers within and without the Catholic Church accomplished—*Randall*⟩
*Ana* *judge, adjudge, adjudicate: determine, *discover, ascertain: settle, *decide, determine
**2** reckon, *calculate, compute
*Ana* *figure, cast, sum (see ADD): *count, enumerate: *conjecture, surmise, guess
**estimate** *n* *estimation
*Ana* valuation, evaluation, appraisal, assessment (see corresponding verbs at ESTIMATE): cost, expense, *price
**estimation,** **estimate** both mean the act of valuing or appraising, but they are rarely interchangeable. In general, **estimation** implies the manner or measure in which a person or thing is valued or esteemed ⟨the degree in which he is held in *estimation* by scholars cannot be appreciated by the average man⟩ ⟨men's *estimation* follows us according to the company we keep—*Steele*⟩ Often the term comes close to *personal opinion* or *point of view*, especially in respect to a thing's value ⟨in my *estimation* the article, though interesting, is not in keeping with the policies and purposes of this periodical⟩ ⟨the crown . . . in the . . . *estimation* of law . . . had ever been perfectly irresponsible—*Burke*⟩ In general, **estimate** applies to the result of an appraisal or an evaluation (as of a thing's worth, its cost, its size, or its prospects). It may connote an approximation to the truth that has been reached either by guessing or conjecture or as the outcome of careful consideration, expert knowledge, or profound study ⟨his *estimate* of the value of the stolen jewels was $50,000⟩ ⟨the young man has justified the high *estimate* of his promise expressed some years ago by his teachers⟩ ⟨a scientific *estimate* of the distance between the earth and Saturn⟩ ⟨economic forecasts are at best mere *estimates*⟩ In a technical sense *estimate* implies the sum for which a piece of work (as the erection or repair of a building) can or will be undertaken.
*Ana* esteem, *regard, respect: *opinion, view: conjecture, guess, surmise (see under CONJECTURE *vb*)
**estrange,** **alienate, disaffect, wean** are comparable when meaning to cause one to break a bond or tie of affection or loyalty. **Estrange** implies separation with consequent indifference or hostility; **alienate** may or may not suggest actual separation, but it does imply loss of affection or interest or withdrawal of support and often connotes a diversion of that affection or interest to another object ⟨a little knowledge often *estranges* men from religion, a deeper knowledge brings them back to it—*Inge*⟩ ⟨the

colossal impudence of his comment on his former and now *alienated* associate—*Lucas*⟩ **Estrange** is preferable when the indifference or hostility is mutual, *alienate* when the blame can be fixed on one person or on a third person ⟨Mr. and Mrs. Brown have been *estranged* for a year⟩ ⟨she *alienated* him by her extravagance⟩ ⟨his affections were *alienated* by another woman⟩ **Disaffect** is more often used with reference to groups from whom loyalty is expected or demanded; it stresses such effects of alienation without separation as unrest, discontent, or rebellion ⟨the workers were *disaffected* by paid agitators⟩ ⟨the disloyalists tried to *disaffect* the militia, preaching treason—*Bowers*⟩ **Wean** implies separation from something which has a strong hold on one or on which one depends in the manner of a nursling on its mother. Unlike the other words, it often suggests merit rather than fault in the person who breaks the bond ⟨*wean* a person from a bad habit⟩ ⟨to *wean* your minds from hankering after false Germanic standards—*Quiller-Couch*⟩ ⟨low prices of movies may have *weaned* large sections of the public away from the legitimate theater—*Messenger*⟩
*Ana* *separate, part, divide, sunder, sever, divorce
*Ant* reconcile —*Con* conciliate, propitiate, appease, *pacify: unite, *join, link
**etch** *vb* incise, engrave, *carve, chisel, sculpture, sculpt, sculp
**eternal** sempiternal, *infinite, boundless, illimitable, uncircumscribed
*Ana* *everlasting, endless, unceasing, interminable: *lasting, perdurable, perpetual, permanent: *immortal, deathless, undying
*Ant* mortal
**ether** atmosphere, *air, ozone
**ethereal** *airy, aerial
*Ana* *celestial, heavenly, empyrean, empyreal: tenuous, rare, *thin
*Ant* substantial
**ethical** *moral, righteous, virtuous, noble
*Ant* unethical —*Con* iniquitous, nefarious, flagitious (see VICIOUS): unbecoming, improper, unseemly, *indecorous, indecent
**ethnology** *anthropology, archaeology
**etiolate** *vb* decolorize, blanch, bleach, *whiten
**etiquette** propriety, *decorum, decency, dignity
*Ana* deportment, demeanor, mien, *bearing
**eulogize** extol, acclaim, laud, *praise
*Ana* *exalt, magnify, aggrandize: *commend, applaud, compliment
*Ant* calumniate, vilify —*Con* *malign, traduce, asperse, defame, slander, libel
**eulogy** *encomium, panegyric, tribute, citation
*Ana* *compliment, flattery, adulation: lauding *or* laudation, extolling *or* extollation, praising *or* praise (see corresponding verbs at PRAISE)
*Ant* calumny: tirade —*Con* *abuse, invective, obloquy
**euphuistic** flowery, aureate, grandiloquent, *rhetorical, magniloquent, bombastic
**evade** elude, avoid, *escape, shun, eschew
*Ana* flee, fly, *escape: thwart, foil, circumvent, outwit (see FRUSTRATE)
**evaluate** appraise, value, rate, assess, assay, *estimate
*Ana* *judge, adjudge: *criticize
**evanesce** *vanish, evaporate, disappear, fade
*Ana* *escape, flee, fly: *scatter, dissipate, dispel, disperse: squander, dissipate, consume, *waste
**evanescent** ephemeral, passing, fugitive, fleeting, *transient, transitory, momentary, short-lived
**evaporate** *vanish, evanesce, disappear, fade

---

*Ana* analogous words     *Ant* antonyms     *Con* contrasted words     See also explanatory notes facing page 1

*Ana* *escape, decamp, flee, fly: dissipate, dispel (see SCATTER)

**even** *adj* **1** smooth, *level, flat, plane, plain, flush
*Ant* uneven —*Con* curving, bending, twisting (see CURVE *vb*): *crooked, devious: rugged, *rough, scabrous, harsh
**2** uniform, equable, *steady, constant
*Ana* *same, equal, identical: continuous, constant, incessant, *continual
*Con* *irregular: varying, changing (see CHANGE *vb*): fluctuating, wavering, undulating (see SWING *vb*)
**event** **1** incident, *occurrence, episode, circumstance
*Ana* *action, act, deed: exploit, *feat, achievement: *chance, accident, fortune: happening, befalling, transpiring (see HAPPEN)
**2** *effect, result, consequence, upshot, aftereffect, aftermath, sequel, issue, outcome
**eventual** ultimate, concluding, terminal, final, *last, latest
*Ana* ensuing, succeeding (see FOLLOW): terminating, closing, ending (see CLOSE *vb*)
**everlasting** *adj* **Everlasting, endless, interminable, unceasing** are comparable when they mean continuing on and on without end. Unlike *infinite, eternal,* and similar words (see INFINITE), these terms do not presuppose the absence of a beginning and therefore usually have reference only to continued extent or duration. However, **everlasting** is often used interchangeably with *eternal,* differing from it only in placing more stress on the fact of enduring throughout time than on the quality of being independent of time or of all similar human limitations ⟨the eternal God is thy refuge, and underneath are the *everlasting* arms—*Deut* 33:27⟩ ⟨and these shall go away into *everlasting* punishment: but the righteous into life eternal—*Mt* 25:46⟩ Therefore, in serious use, *everlasting,* rather than *eternal,* is applied to material things or earthly conditions which endure, or seem to endure, forever ⟨see Cromwell damned to *everlasting* fame—*Pope*⟩ ⟨these mighty gates of *everlasting* rock—*De Quincey*⟩ ⟨each man dreamed of a square meal, new boots, a full powder horn, an end to the *everlasting* shortages—*Mason*⟩ In lighter use the word is little more than a hyperbolic term expressing loss of patience or extreme boredom and more often applying to recurrence than to duration or extent ⟨these *everlasting* headaches⟩ ⟨his *everlasting* stupidity⟩ **Endless** is applicable not only to things which continue in time but also in extent; the word is used especially when a circular form or construction is implied ⟨*endless* belt⟩ or it may imply no known or apparent or determinable end ⟨an *endless* chain of letters⟩ ⟨an *endless* road through the mountains⟩ ⟨there has been *endless* discussion whether we have a distinct faculty for the knowledge of God—*Inge*⟩ ⟨*endless* masses of hills on three sides, *endless* weald or valley on the fourth—*Jefferies*⟩ **Interminable** is somewhat uncommon in its sense of having no end or incapable of being brought to an end or termination ⟨the forest trees above were wild with the wind, but the *interminable* thickets below were never stirred—*Trollope*⟩ More often it applies to something so extended or prolonged or protracted that it is exceedingly wearisome or exhausts one's patience ⟨the weeks were *interminable,* and papa and mamma were clean forgotten—*Kipling*⟩ ⟨spleen, chagrin, . . . discontent, misanthropy, and all their *interminable* train of fretfulness, querulousness, suspicions, jealousies—*Peacock*⟩ **Unceasing,** like *interminable,* suggests undue prolonging or protracting, but it emphasizes the extraordinary capacity for going on and on rather than the psychological effect produced (usually on others) by long-continuing activity or continual recurrence ⟨*unceasing* effort⟩ ⟨Jules de Goncourt . . . died from the mental exhaustion of his *unceasing* struggle

to attain an objective style adequate to express the subtle texture of the world as he saw it—*Ellis*⟩
*Ana* eternal, boundless, *infinite: *lasting, perdurable, perpetual: *immortal, deathless, undying
*Ant* transitory —*Con* *transient, passing, fleeting, fugitive, ephemeral, evanescent, momentary, short-lived
**every** each, *all
**evict** *eject, oust, expel, dismiss
*Ana* *exclude, eliminate, shut out: reject, repudiate, spurn (see DECLINE): *dismiss, fire, cashier, discharge
**evidence** *n* **Evidence, testimony, deposition, affidavit** are, in their legal senses, closely related but not synonymous terms. The last three designate forms of **evidence,** or material submitted to a competent legal tribunal as a means of ascertaining where the truth lies in a question of fact. *Evidence* also implies the intention of the side offering the material to use it as a basis for inference and argument and as a medium of proof. **Testimony** is evidence offered by persons (as eyewitnesses or experts) who are in a position to provide pertinent information. It implies declaration under oath or affirmation, usually on the stand in open court. Testimony does not necessarily constitute favorable evidence for the side that calls the witness, for its effect may vary with such matters as inferences that may be drawn from it favorable to the opposition or new aspects and emphases elicited by cross-examination. **Deposition,** though occasionally used interchangeably with *testimony,* is more usually used to designate a form of testimony that replaces testimony in open court or, more often, provides information for pretrial procedures and is given orally in response to questioning by competent officers, taken down in writing, and sworn to or properly affirmed. **Affidavit** designates a written declaration made upon solemn oath before a recognized magistrate or officer. An affidavit may sometimes be used as testimony, but when so used it is as a rule because a witness cannot take the stand. An affidavit submitted as testimony may be distinguished from a deposition; when used specifically and in contrast with *deposition, affidavit* always implies that the declaration has been obtained by one side to the dispute and that there has been no cross-examination.
**evidence** *vb* evince, manifest, demonstrate, *show
*Ana* *reveal, disclose, betray, divulge: display, exhibit, expose, *show: prove, *indicate, betoken, attest, bespeak
**evident, manifest, patent, distinct, obvious, apparent, palpable, plain, clear** are comparable when they mean readily perceived or apprehended. **Evident** implies the existence of visible signs, all of which point to the one conclusion; it may be applied to something (as another person's state of mind, a hidden condition, or an imminent event) which is beyond the range of the senses but can be inferred from the outward indications ⟨her *evident* delight in the gift⟩ ⟨even in his vices the contradiction was *evident.* His conscience was severe—*Carlos Baker*⟩ ⟨the sustained impartiality and *evident* learning of his work—*Cheyney*⟩ **Manifest** implies an outward revelation or expression or an open exhibition; it is applied as a rule to something which is displayed so clearly that its recognition seemingly involves no inference ⟨his joy in the prospect of departure from the Five Towns, from her . . . was more *manifest* than she could bear—*Bennett*⟩ ⟨where the work of such a master [as Milton] is at its best, the greatness of his spirit is most greatly *manifest*—*L. P. Smith*⟩ **Patent** implies an opposition to what is imperceptible or obscure but existent; it therefore is applied to things (as a cause, an effect, a mistake, or an imperfection) which are not invariably or as a class evident or manifest ⟨the seller is required by law to disclose to the buyer latent as well as *patent* defects in the article sold⟩ ⟨a man is . . . in jeopardy even when the

A colon (:) separates groups of words discriminated. An asterisk (*) indicates place of treatment of each group.

error is *patent* on the face of the record, as when he is tried on a defective indictment—*Justice Holmes*⟩ ⟨three very *patent* reasons for the comparatively slow advance of our children—*Grandgent*⟩ **Distinct** (see also DISTINCT) implies such sharpness of outline or of definition that the thing requires no effort of the eyes to see or discern ⟨*distinct* features⟩ ⟨his handwriting is unusually *distinct*⟩ or of the ears to hear or interpret ⟨*distinct* utterance⟩ ⟨*distinct* enunciation⟩ or of the mind to apprehend or comprehend without confusion ⟨the course of his reasoning is not only evident, it is *distinct*⟩ ⟨he gave a *distinct* account of everything that occurred⟩ **Obvious** stresses ease in discovery or, sometimes, in accounting for and often connotes conspicuousness in what is discovered or little need of perspicacity in the discoverer; it is therefore often applied to something not successfully concealed or something crudely manifest ⟨*obvious* heirs he had none, any more than he had *obvious* progenitors—*Sackville-West*⟩⟨the avidity with which he surrendered himself to her perfectly *obvious* methods—*Mary Austin*⟩ ⟨acting on the conviction of Mr. Justice Holmes that "at this time we need education in the *obvious* more than investigation of the obscure"—*Frankfurter*⟩ **Apparent** (see also APPARENT 2) is often so close to *evident* in meaning that the two words are difficult to distinguish. But *evident* usually implies inference directly from visible signs or effects, and *apparent* from evidence plus more or less elaborate reasoning; therefore *apparent* is especially applicable to something which is apprehended through an induction, a deduction, or a similar course of reasoning ⟨the absurdity of their contention is *apparent* to one who knows the effects produced by the same causes in the past⟩ ⟨as experience accumulated it gradually became *apparent* that the oils of any of the trees . . . were equally efficacious—*Heiser*⟩ ⟨deposits of transported material . . . are perhaps the most widely *apparent* results of the glaciation—*Amer. Guide Series: N. H.*⟩ **Palpable** (see also PERCEPTIBLE) basically implies perceptibility through the sense of touch; it is often extended to perception by the other senses, excluding sight, or by the mind and typically suggests ease of perception or readiness of interpretation ⟨'tis probable that thou hast never lived, and *palpable* that thou hast never loved—*Garnett*⟩ ⟨yet, despite these precautions, a *palpable* uneasiness persists—*Moorehead*⟩ ⟨beneath it all was a hush, almost *palpable*—*Mailer*⟩ **Plain** and **clear** are less formal and literary than the preceding terms. Both are applied to something that is immediately apprehended or unmistakably understood, but **plain** implies familiarity or distinctness or a lack of intricacy or complexity, while **clear** suggests an absence of whatever confuses or muddles the mind or obscures the issues ⟨a *plain* answer to a direct question—*Crothers*⟩ ⟨yes, that makes much which was dark quite *clear* to me—*Galsworthy*⟩ ⟨proof as sharp and *clear* as anything which is known—*Darrow*⟩
*Ana* \*perceptible, sensible, palpable, tangible, appreciable, ponderable: conspicuous, prominent, \*noticeable

**evil** *adj* \*bad, ill, wicked, naughty
*Ana* \*base, low, vile: iniquitous, nefarious, flagitious, \*vicious, villainous, infamous: \*pernicious, baneful: \*execrable, damnable
*Ant* exemplary: salutary

**evil** *n* **Evil, ill** are comparable when they mean whatever is harmful or disastrous to morals or well-being. **Evil** is the ordinary term capable of use in all contexts and referable not only to deeds and practices actually indulged in or to conditions actually suffered ⟨lead a life of *evil*⟩ ⟨the *evils* of war⟩ ⟨correct the *evils* in a system of government⟩ but also to motivating desires or actuating causes of such deeds, practices, or conditions ⟨think no *evil*⟩ ⟨shun

*evil*⟩ and to their harmful effects or consequences ⟨the *evil* that men do lives after them—*Shak.*⟩ ⟨*evils* which our own misdeeds have wrought—*Milton*⟩ *Evil* is also the term in general use for the abstract conception of whatever is the reverse of good, especially of the morally good, or as a designation of whatever is thought of as the reverse of a blessing ⟨able to distinguish good from *evil*⟩ ⟨the origin of *evil*⟩ ⟨St. Francis of Assisi accounted poverty a blessing rather than an *evil*⟩ ⟨*evil* no nature hath; the loss of good is that which gives to sin a livelihood—*Herrick*⟩ ⟨*evil* is not a quality of things as such. It is a quality of our relation to them—*Lippmann*⟩ Although **ill**, like *evil,* may imply an antithesis to *good,* it is seldom used to designate the abstraction except in a poetic context and in direct contrast to *good* ⟨O, yet we trust that somehow good will be the final goal of *ill*—*Tennyson*⟩ Also, it is now rare in the sense of moral evil. In present use, as in the past, *ill* is applied chiefly to whatever is distressing, painful, or injurious and is more often used in reference to what is actually suffered or endured than to what may be inflicted or imposed on one ⟨and makes us rather bear those *ills* we have than fly to others that we know not of—*Shak.*⟩ ⟨they could never in such a Utopian State feel any other *ills* than those which arise from bodily sickness—*Hume*⟩ ⟨there mark what *ills* the scholar's life assail—toil, envy, want, the patron, and the jail—*Johnson*⟩ ⟨servitude, the worst of *ills*—*Cowper*⟩
*Ant* good

**evince** manifest, evidence, demonstrate, \*show
*Ana* betoken, \*indicate, attest, prove, argue, bespeak: display, exhibit, expose, \*show: disclose, \*reveal, discover, betray
*Con* \*suppress, repress: \*hide, conceal

**evoke** elicit, \*educe, extract, extort
*Ana* \*provoke, excite, stimulate: arouse, rouse, rally, awaken, waken, \*stir

**evolution** \*development

**evolve** \*unfold, develop, elaborate, perfect
*Ana* progress, \*advance: \*mature, develop, ripen

**exact** *vb* require, \*demand, claim
*Ana* \*ask, request, solicit: compel, \*force, constrain, coerce, oblige

**exact** *adj* accurate, \*correct, right, precise, nice
*Ana* \*careful, meticulous, scrupulous, punctilious: agreeing, squaring, tallying, jibing, conforming (see AGREE)

**exacting** *adj* \*onerous, burdensome, oppressive
*Ana* \*severe, stern: \*rigid, rigorous, strict, stringent: arduous, difficult, \*hard
*Ant* easy: lenient

**exaggeration, overstatement, hyperbole** all mean an overstepping of the bounds of truth, especially in describing the goodness or the greatness or the smallness of something. **Exaggeration** does not always or even often imply dishonesty or an intent to deceive on the part of one making a statement, a representation, or a claim; it may merely imply an often temperamental unwillingness to be held down by the facts or a bias, whether favorable or unfavorable, so great that one cannot clearly see or accurately estimate the exact state of affairs depicted ⟨men of great conversational powers almost universally practise a sort of lively sophistry and *exaggeration* which deceives for the moment both themselves and their auditors—*Macaulay*⟩ ⟨to say that Mrs. Ralston's son and daughter were pleased with the idea of Tina's adoption would be an *exaggeration*—*Wharton*⟩ Unlike *exaggeration,* **overstatement** rarely carries any hint of depreciation; it is therefore often the term chosen by one desiring to stress the fact of exceeding the truth without any additional implications ⟨this . . . is one of those *overstatements* of a true principle,

---

*Ana* analogous words   *Ant* antonyms   *Con* contrasted words   See also explanatory notes facing page 1

often met with in Adam Smith—*J. S. Mill*⟩ ⟨if all costs applicable to revenue are charged thereto, *overstatement* of net income . . . is avoided—*Paton & Littleton*⟩ ⟨he invariably avoids *overstatement;* not for him is the heavy underlining of a musical phrase—*N. Y. Times*⟩ **Hyperbole** implies the use of exaggeration as a literary device. Though such use may arise from overpowering emotion, it more often suggests a desire to create a planned impression or particular effect; in either case *hyperbole* implies obvious extravagance in statement often producing a rhetorical effect that could not be gained otherwise ⟨the speaking in a perpetual *hyperbole* is comely in nothing but in love—*Bacon*⟩ ⟨an Arabic interpreter expatiated, in florid *hyperbole,* on the magnanimity and princely qualities of the Spanish king—*Prescott*⟩ ⟨that rather startling "terrible" is not *hyperbole;* it is precisely what Mr. Blackmur means —*Mizener*⟩ *Hyperbole* is often used as the name of a figure of speech that produces its effect by overstatement as its opposite, *litotes,* does by understatement.
*Ana* misrepresentation, untruth (see LIE): *fallacy, sophistry

**exalt, magnify, aggrandize** are comparable when meaning to increase in importance or in prestige. *Exalt* and *magnify* also come into comparison in their older sense of to extol or to glorify ⟨O *magnify* the Lord with me, and let us *exalt* his name together—*Ps* 34:3⟩ In modern general use **exalt** retains its implication of lifting up but emphasizes a raising in a scale of values without necessarily affecting the quality of the thing raised. Therefore one *exalts* something above another or at the expense of another ⟨Rousseau's readiness to *exalt* spontaneity even at the expense of rationality—*Babbitt*⟩ ⟨there is a valid reason for not preventing games, but . . . not . . . for *exalting* them into a leading position in the school curriculum—*Russell*⟩ **Magnify** stresses increase in size; it commonly suggests an agency (as an optical device) which affects the vision and causes enlargement of apparent size or one (as a vivid imagination) which affects the judgment and leads to exaggeration ⟨kind, quiet, nearsighted eyes, which his round spectacles *magnified* into lambent moons—*Deland*⟩ ⟨the public opinion which . . . *magnifies* patriotism into a religion—*Brownell*⟩ **Aggrandize** emphasizes increase in greatness or mightiness; it implies efforts, usually selfish efforts, directed to the attainment of power, authority, or worldly eminence ⟨if we *aggrandize* ourselves at the expense of the Mahrattas—*Wellington*⟩ ⟨have we a satisfaction in *aggrandizing* our families . . . ?—*Fielding*⟩ ⟨to those of us who are engaged in constructive research and in invention, there is serious moral risk of *aggrandizing* what we have accomplished—*Wiener*⟩
*Ana* elevate, raise, *lift: heighten, enhance, *intensify: extol, laud, *praise
*Ant* abase —*Con* demean, debase, degrade, humble, humiliate (see ABASE): disparage, depreciate, detract, derogate, *decry, belittle, minimize

**examination** inspection, scrutiny, scanning, audit (see under SCRUTINIZE *vb*)
*Ana* questioning, interrogation, inquiry, catechism, quizzing *or* quiz (see corresponding verbs at ASK)
**examine** 1 inspect, *scrutinize, scan, audit
*Ana* *analyze, dissect, resolve: contemplate, observe, survey, view, notice, note (see SEE)
2 question, interrogate, quiz, catechize, *ask, query, inquire
*Ana* penetrate, probe (see ENTER): test, try (see PROVE)
**example** 1 sample, specimen, *instance, case, illustration
*Con* anomaly, *paradox
2 *model, exemplar, pattern, ideal, standard, beau ideal, mirror

*Ana* *paragon, apotheosis
*Con* precept, rule, *law
**exasperate** provoke, nettle, *irritate, aggravate, rile, peeve
*Ana* vex, *annoy, irk, bother: *anger, incense, enrage, madden, infuriate
*Ant* mollify —*Con* *pacify, placate, appease, propitiate, conciliate
**excavate** *dig, delve, spade, grub
**exceed, surpass, transcend, excel, outdo, outstrip** mean to go or to be beyond a stated or implied limit, measure, or degree. **Exceed** may imply an overpassing of a limit set by one's right, power, authority, or jurisdiction ⟨this task *exceeds* his ability⟩ ⟨he has *exceeded* his authority in allowing such use of our land⟩ or by prescription (as in time or space) ⟨they were penalized if they *exceeded* the allotted time by even one day⟩ The term may also imply superiority in size, amount, degree, or number according to a given standard or measure ⟨my wrath shall far *exceed* the love I ever bore—*Shak.*⟩ ⟨an Inferno which *exceeds* anything that Dante imagined—*Henry Miller*⟩ **Surpass** often replaces *exceed,* especially when superiority to a standard or measure is implied ⟨the reality *surpassed* our expectations⟩ When the intent is to imply superiority in quality (as in virtue, in merit, or in skill) rather than in quantity or extent, *surpass* is usually preferred to *exceed* ⟨it is safe to say that in this play Middleton is *surpassed* by one Elizabethan alone, and that is Shakespeare—*T. S. Eliot*⟩ ⟨he *surpasses* all others in keenness of mind⟩ **Transcend** carries so strong an implication of rising across or above a limit or measure that, although it is sometimes used in place of *exceed* ⟨the powers of government are limited and . . . its limits are not to be *transcended*— *John Marshall*⟩ and often in place of *surpass* ⟨this sorrow *transcending* all sorrows—*Hudson*⟩ It is the precise term to use when a higher than human or earthly limit, standard, or measure is implied ⟨a point of view *transcending* the purely human outlook on the universe— *Binyon*⟩ ⟨in the rather sloppy Socialism which pervades this document there is nothing which seems to *transcend* the limits of unaided human intelligence—*Inge*⟩ In intransitive use **excel** implies reaching a preeminence in accomplishment or achievement ⟨he *excelled* in the painting of miniatures⟩ but in transitive use it differs little from *surpass* ⟨love divine, all love *excelling*— *Wesley*⟩ ⟨he *excelled* his friends in archery⟩ ⟨during their seminary years he had easily surpassed his friend in scholarship, but he always realized that Joseph *excelled* him in the fervor of his faith—*Cather*⟩ **Outdo** is less formal than *excel* or *surpass,* but it is often preferred when there is the intent to connote the breaking of a previously established record ⟨he hath in this action *outdone* his former deeds doubly—*Shak.*⟩ ⟨a competition in deceit in which, I admit, he *outdid* them—*Wister*⟩ **Outstrip** is often preferred to *excel* or *surpass* when one wishes to suggest a race, a competition, or a strenuous effort to get ahead ⟨he would not allow anyone to *outstrip* him in zeal⟩ ⟨instead of allowing his reader the easy victory, he takes pride in *outstripping* him completely —*Edmund Wilson*⟩

**excel** surpass, transcend, *exceed, outdo, outstrip
**excellence, merit, virtue, perfection** are comparable when meaning a quality or feature of a person or thing that gives him or it especial worth or value. **Excellence** applies to a quality or feature in which the person or thing excels or surpasses others; since the term carries no implication of absence of fault, defect, or blemish, it is often qualified (as by *particular, specific,* or *distinctive*) ⟨the particular *excellence* of this cake is its lightness⟩ ⟨the great *excellence* of the eastern tableland was . . . in

---

A colon (:) separates groups of words discriminated. An asterisk (*) indicates place of treatment of each group.

pasture and in forest—*Stanley*⟩ ⟨spoke of the rude health of their children as if it were a result of moral *excellence* —*Conrad*⟩ **Merit** (see also DUE) may be used interchangeably with *excellence*, but it typically carries no suggestion of a surpassing quality; rather, it applies to a quality or feature that has evident worth or value or is highly commendable. It is used especially in critical estimates in which good points (*merits*) are displayed against bad points (*defects* or *faults*) ⟨Mr. Wright's version of the Iliad, repeating in the main the *merits* and defects of Cowper's version—*Arnold*⟩ ⟨the faculty of discerning and using conspicuous *merit* in other people distinguishes the most successful administrators, rulers, and men of business—*Eliot*⟩ **Virtue**, because of the long association of the term with moral goodness (for this sense see GOODNESS) is chiefly applied to a moral excellence or a conspicuous merit of character ⟨one is inclined to ask whether, when the right path is so easy to them, they really have any *virtues*—*Ellis*⟩ ⟨reverence for age and authority, even for law, has disappeared; and in the train of these have gone the *virtues* they engendered and nurtured—*Dickinson*⟩ But the term may also apply to the quality or feature that is the source of a person's or thing's peculiar or distinctive strength, power, or efficacy ⟨the special *virtue* of a newly discovered remedy for pneumonia⟩ ⟨that unsparing impartiality which is his most distinguishing *virtue*—*Macaulay*⟩ **Perfection** suggests an attainment of the ideal and is usually found in less restrained writing or speech than the other terms when it applies to an excellence in the highest degree ⟨but eyes, and ears, and ev'ry thought, were with his sweet *perfections* caught—*Spenser*⟩ ⟨what tongue can her *perfections* tell?—*Sidney*⟩ ⟨Fitzgerald's *perfection* of style and form, as in The Great Gatsby, has a way of making something that lies between your stomach and your heart quiver a little—*Thurber*⟩
*Ana* value, *worth: property, *quality, character
*Ant* fault —*Con* *blemish, defect, flaw: failing, frailty, foible, vice (see FAULT)

**exceptionable** *exceptional
*Ana* *offensive, repugnant, loathsome, repulsive, revolting: repellent, distasteful, obnoxious, invidious, *repugnant
*Ant* unexceptionable: exemplary —*Con* pleasing, agreeable, gratifying, *pleasant, grateful, welcome

**exceptional, exceptionable,** although not synonyms, are liable to confusion. Something is **exceptional** which is itself an exception, and so is out of the ordinary, being either extraordinary or unusual ⟨this is an *exceptional* opportunity⟩ ⟨the bath was habitual in the twelfth century and *exceptional* at the Renaissance—*Henry Adams*⟩ Something is **exceptionable** to which exception may be taken (that is, to which an objection may be made) and which is therefore displeasing or offensive to others ⟨there was nothing *exceptionable* in his comment⟩ ⟨this is something of a tour de force, in which the only *exceptionable* thing is a schoolboy brand of mild vulgarity —*Times Lit. Sup.*⟩
*Ana* outstanding, remarkable, *noticeable, conspicuous, prominent, salient, signal: rare, *infrequent, uncommon, scarce: singular, unique, *strange: anomalous, *irregular
*Ant* common (sense 3): average —*Con* ordinary, familiar, popular, vulgar (see COMMON)

**excerpt** *n* *extract

**excess** *n* **Excess, superfluity, surplus, surplusage, overplus** denote something which goes beyond a limit or bound. **Excess** applies to whatever exceeds a limit, measure, bound, or accustomed degree ⟨in measure rein thy joy; scant this *excess*—*Shak.*⟩ ⟨the proper point between sufficiency and *excess*—*Henry James*⟩ ⟨I think poetry should surprise by a fine *excess*—*Keats*⟩ Often it specifically implies intemperance or immoderation ⟨early *excesses* the frame will recover from—*Meredith*⟩ ⟨restrain the *excesses* of the possessive instinct—*Ellis*⟩ **Superfluity** applies to an excess (as of money, clothes, or possessions) that is above or beyond what is needed or desired ⟨the inventory of thy shirts, as, one for *superfluity*, and another for use!—*Shak.*⟩ ⟨I succumb easily to anyone who asks me to buy *superfluities* and luxuries —*Huxley*⟩ **Surplus** applies to the amount or quantity of something that remains when all that has been needed has been disposed of (as by using, spending, or selling) ⟨his salary was so small that there was no *surplus* for investment⟩ ⟨the problem is how to dispose of the large *surplus* in this year's cotton crop⟩ ⟨huge unused *surpluses* pile up beyond the reach of consumers—*La Barre*⟩ **Surplusage** may be used in place of *surplus* but may especially imply wasteful or useless excess ⟨the subsequent part of the section is mere *surplusage*, is entirely without meaning, if such is to be the construction—*John Marshall*⟩ ⟨say what you have to say . . . with no *surplusage*—*Pater*⟩ **Overplus** is often used in place of *surplus*, but it less often implies a remainder than an addition to what is needed ⟨the *overplus* of a great fortune—*Addison*⟩ ⟨there was no *overplus* in the proceeds this year⟩ ⟨the wild *overplus* of vegetation which was certainly not that of a normal garden—*Wyndham Lewis*⟩
*Ana* lavishness, prodigality, profuseness *or* profusion, luxuriance, exuberance (see corresponding adjectives at PROFUSE): inordinateness, immoderation, extravagance (see corresponding adjectives at EXCESSIVE)
*Ant* deficiency: dearth, paucity —*Con* meagerness, scantiness, scantness, exiguousness (see corresponding adjectives at MEAGER)

**excessive, immoderate, inordinate, extravagant, exorbitant, extreme** are comparable when meaning characterized by going beyond or above its proper, just, or right limit. **Excessive** implies an amount, quantity, or extent too great to be just, reasonable, or endurable ⟨the *excessive* heat of a midsummer afternoon⟩ ⟨*excessive* lenity and indulgence are ultimately *excessive* rigor—*John Knox*⟩ ⟨an *excessive* penchant for intellectual and verbal hairsplitting —*Beach*⟩ **Immoderate** is often used interchangeably with *excessive* ⟨*immoderate* heat⟩ but, distinctively, it may imply lack of restraint especially in the feelings or their expression ⟨*immoderate* zeal⟩ ⟨*immoderate* laughter⟩ ⟨Mass gave him extreme, I may even say *immoderate*, satisfaction. It was almost orgiastic—*T. S. Eliot*⟩ **Inordinate** implies an exceeding of the bounds or limits prescribed by authority or dictated by good judgment ⟨the great difficulty of living content is the cherishing of *inordinate* and unreasonable expectations—*T. E. Brown*⟩ ⟨I am always staggered . . . by the *inordinate* snobbery of the English press—*Huxley*⟩ **Extravagant** often adds to *excessive* or *immoderate* the implications of a wild, lawless, prodigal, or foolish wandering from proper restraints and accustomed bounds ⟨make *extravagant* claims for an invention⟩ ⟨abandoned herself to all the violences of *extravagant* emotion—*Stoker*⟩ ⟨went off in a second *extravagant* roar of laughter—*Hudson*⟩ The term often specifically implies prodigality in expenditure ⟨she was rapacious of money, *extravagant* to excess —*Fielding*⟩ **Exorbitant** implies excessiveness marked by a departure from what is the customary or established amount or degree; it typically connotes extortion or excessive demands on the part of the agent or the infliction of hardships on the person affected ⟨a resolution to con-

tract none of the *exorbitant* desires by which others are enslaved—*Spectator*⟩ ⟨the men who worked in the brick-kilns lived in this settlement, and paid an *exorbitant* rent to the Judge—*Deland*⟩ ⟨the law for the renegotiation of war contracts—which will prevent *exorbitant* profits and assure fair prices to the government—*Roosevelt*⟩ **Extreme** implies an excessiveness or extravagance that seems to reach the end of what is possible; it is often hyperbolic in actual use ⟨the result gave him *extreme* satisfaction⟩ ⟨the *extreme* oddness of existence is what reconciles me to it—*L. P. Smith*⟩ ⟨the most *extreme* . . . statement of such an attitude would be: nothing is poetry which can be formulated in prose—*Day Lewis*⟩ ⟨the fascination of crime is perpetual, especially in its *extreme* form as murder—*A. C. Ward*⟩ **Ana** *superfluous, surplus, supernumerary, extra, spare: *intense, vehement, fierce, exquisite, violent: redundant (see WORDY)
**Ant** deficient —**Con** *meager, scanty, scant, skimpy, exiguous, sparse

**exchange** *vb* **Exchange, interchange, bandy** mean to give a thing to another in return for another thing from him. **Exchange** may imply a disposing of one thing for another by or as if by the methods of bartering or trading ⟨*exchange* horses⟩ ⟨the hostile forces *exchanged* prisoners of war⟩ ⟨*exchange* farm products for manufactured goods⟩ Sometimes the term specifically implies a substitution of one thing for another without any definite suggestion of bartering or trading ⟨wedding presents are often *exchanged* by the bride for things of which she has greater need⟩ ⟨well satisfied to *exchange* the stratified suburb of Hyde Park for the amorphous neighborhood of Halsted Street—*Lovett*⟩ or an alternation of things by two, sometimes more, persons ⟨*exchange* letters⟩ ⟨*exchange* a few words with each other⟩ **Interchange** is rarely used in place of *exchange* except when alternation (as in reciprocal giving and receiving) is implied, often with the connotation of a continuous succession ⟨the townspeople and the summer residents *interchanged* courtesies with each other⟩ ⟨there were repeated cheerings and salutations *interchanged* between the shore and the ship—*Irving*⟩ **Bandy** may imply a careless or casual tossing back and forth or from one to another ⟨a firearm is no toy to be *bandied* about⟩ and it is often used in place of *interchange* when vigorous, rapid, and more or less prolonged action is implied ⟨*bandy* hasty words⟩ ⟨*bandy* compliments⟩ The term also may imply heated or active discussion or a passing of information from one to another ⟨your name is . . . frequently *bandied* at table among us —*Irving*⟩ ⟨the stories they invent . . . and *bandy* from mouth to mouth!—*Dickens*⟩

**excitant** *stimulus, stimulant, incitement, impetus

**excite** *provoke, stimulate, pique, quicken, galvanize
**Ana** *stir, rouse, arouse, rally, waken, awaken: agitate, disturb, perturb, *discompose, disquiet: animate, inspire, fire (see INFORM)
**Ant** soothe, quiet (*persons*): allay (*fears, anxiety*)

**exclude, debar, blackball, eliminate, rule out, shut out, disbar, suspend** are comparable when meaning to prevent someone or something from forming part of something else as a member, a constituent, or a factor. **Exclude** implies a keeping out of what is already outside; it therefore suggests a prevention of entrance or admission ⟨*exclude* light from a room by closing the shutters⟩ ⟨*exclude* a subject from consideration⟩ ⟨*exclude* a class from certain privileges⟩ **Debar** implies the existence of a barrier which is effectual in excluding someone or something on the outside from entering into a group, body, or system, from enjoying certain privileges, powers, or

prerogatives, or from doing what those not so restrained do naturally or easily ⟨a high wall *debarred* boys from entering⟩ ⟨the qualifications demanded . . . would be likely to *debar* 99 percent of the secondary school instructors in America—*Grandgent*⟩ ⟨the Japanese designer was *debarred* by instinct and tradition from using the resources of texture and of light and shade—*Binyon*⟩ **Blackball** basically implies exclusion from a club or society by vote of its members (originally by putting a black ball into a ballot box) ⟨he was very nearly *blackballed* at a West End club of which his birth and social position fully entitled him to become a member—*Wilde*⟩ The term has some extended use, but it usually implies a deliberate decision or effort to exclude a person from social, professional, or economic intercourse. **Eliminate** differs from the preceding words in implying a getting rid of, or a removal of what is already in, especially as a constituent element or part ⟨*eliminate* a quantity from an equation⟩ ⟨*eliminate* a subject from a curriculum⟩ ⟨*eliminate* a poison from the system⟩ ⟨it is always wise to *eliminate* the personal equation from our judgments of literature —*J. R. Lowell*⟩ ⟨in most poets there is an intermittent conflict between the poetic self and the rest of the man; and it is by reconciling the two, not by *eliminating* the one, that they can reach their full stature—*Day Lewis*⟩ **Rule out** may imply either exclusion or elimination, but it usually suggests a formal or authoritative decision ⟨*rule* a horse *out* of a race⟩ ⟨*rule out* certain candidates for a position⟩ ⟨*rule* such subjective and moral judgments *out* of our biology—*Kroeber*⟩ **Shut out** may imply exclusion of something by preventing its entrance or admission ⟨close the windows to *shut out* the rain⟩ or, in sports use, to prevent from scoring ⟨the home team was *shut out* in the second game⟩ **Disbar** (often confused with *debar*) implies the elimination by a legal process of a lawyer from the group of those already admitted to practice, thereby depriving him for cause of his status and privileges. **Suspend** implies the elimination of a person who is a member of an organization or a student at a school or college, often for a definite period of time and, usually, because of some offense or serious infraction of the rules; the term seldom if ever implies that the case is closed or that readmission is impossible ⟨*suspend* ten members of a club for nonpayment of dues⟩ ⟨there was but one course: to *suspend* the man from the exercise of all priestly functions—*Cather*⟩
**Ana** *hinder, bar, block: preclude, obviate, ward, *prevent: *banish, exile, ostracize, deport
**Ant** admit (*persons*): include (*things*) —**Con** comprehend, embrace, involve (see INCLUDE)

**exclusive** *select, elect, picked
**Ana** excluding, eliminating, debarring, shutting out, ruling out (see EXCLUDE): aristocratic, patrician (see corresponding nouns at GENTLEMAN)
**Ant** inclusive —**Con** catholic, cosmopolitan, *universal: *common, ordinary, familiar, popular, vulgar

**excogitate** weigh, *consider, study, contemplate
**Ana** *ponder, meditate, ruminate, muse: cogitate, reflect, deliberate, speculate, *think

**excoriate** *abrade, chafe, fret, gall
**Ana** *strip, divest, denude, bare: flay, *skin: torture, torment, rack (see AFFLICT): tongue-lash, revile, berate (see SCOLD)

**excruciating, agonizing, racking** mean intensely and, usually, unbearably painful. All are commonly used as strong intensives and applied to pain, suffering, and torture. When used to qualify other things, they mean causing intense pain or suffering. **Excruciating** carries strong suggestions of acute physical torture or of exquisitely

---

A colon (:) separates groups of words discriminated. An asterisk (*) indicates place of treatment of each group.

painful sensation ⟨suffered *excruciating* pain from an abscessed tooth⟩ ⟨*excruciating* noises⟩ ⟨the hearty merrymakings of the population at large were an *excruciating* torment to narrow-minded folk—*Amer. Guide Series: Md.*⟩ **Agonizing** stresses anguish of mind even when it strongly implies physical suffering ⟨an *agonizing* spasm of pain—a memento mori—shot through me and passed away—*W. J. Locke*⟩ ⟨lives there a man so firm, who, while his heart feels all the bitter horror of his crime, can reason down its *agonizing* throbs—*Burns*⟩ **Racking** suggests sensations of pulling and straining and tearing comparable to those suffered by a person on the rack ⟨*racking* pains in the chest⟩ ⟨a *racking* headache⟩ ⟨*racking* doubts⟩
*Ana* torturing, tormenting, racking (see AFFLICT): *intense, vehement, fierce, exquisite, violent

**exculpate,** absolve, exonerate, acquit, vindicate mean to free from a charge or burden. **Exculpate** implies simply a clearing from blame, often in a matter of small importance ⟨*exculpate* oneself from a charge of inconsistency⟩ ⟨directly Harding was blameless for what was going on. Indirectly he cannot be wholly *exculpated*—*S. H. Adams*⟩ **Absolve** implies a release, often a formal release, either from obligations or responsibilities that bind the conscience or from the consequences or penalties of their violation ⟨*absolve* a person from a promise⟩ ⟨society cannot be *absolved* of responsibility for its slums⟩ **Exonerate** implies relief, often in a moral sense, from what is regarded as a load or burden ⟨no reason for *exonerating* him [a judge] from the ordinary duties of a citizen—*Justice Holmes*⟩ In general *exonerate* more frequently suggests such relief from a definite charge that not even the suspicion of wrongdoing remains ⟨*exonerate* a person charged with theft⟩ **Acquit** implies a decision in one's favor with reference to a specific charge ⟨*acquit* a suspect of all participation in a crime⟩ ⟨you do *acquit* me then of anything wrong? You are convinced that I never meant to deceive your brother . . . ?—*Austen*⟩ **Vindicate,** unlike the preceding words, may have reference to things as well as to persons that have been subjected to attack, suspicion, censure, or ridicule. As here compared (see also MAINTAIN) it implies a clearing through proof of the injustice or the unfairness of such criticism or blame and the exoneration of the person or the justification of the thing ⟨both his knowledge and his honesty were *vindicated* when the river was discovered—*G. R. Stewart*⟩ ⟨the . . . politicians were *vindicated* on all counts—*Rovere*⟩
*Ana* justify, *explain, rationalize: *excuse, condone, pardon, forgive, remit
*Ant* inculpate: accuse —*Con* blame, denounce, reprehend, reprobate, censure (see CRITICIZE): charge, arraign, indict, incriminate, impeach (see ACCUSE)

**excursion** trip, jaunt, tour, cruise, *journey, voyage, expedition, pilgrimage
*Ana* ride, drive (see under RIDE *vb*)

**excursus** divagation, *digression, episode

**excuse** *vb* Excuse, condone, pardon, forgive, remit are comparable when meaning not to exact punishment or redress for (an offense) or from (an offender). In polite use *excuse, pardon,* and *forgive* usually suggest a hope that one is not annoyed. Both *excuse* and *condone* imply an overlooking or passing over either without censure or without adequate punishment; distinctively, one may **excuse** specific acts (as faults, omissions, or neglects) especially in social or conventional obligations or the person committing them ⟨please *excuse* my interruption⟩ ⟨the injustice with which he had been treated would have *excused* him if he had resorted to violent methods of

redress—*Macaulay*⟩ but one more often **condones** either a kind of behavior (as dishonesty, folly, or violence) or a course of conduct or an institution especially when constituting a grave breach of the moral code or a violation of law ⟨we *condone* everything in this country—private treason, falsehood, flattery, cruelty at home, roguery, and double-dealing—*Thackeray*⟩ ⟨slavery struck no deep roots in New England soil, perhaps because the nobler half of the New England conscience never *condoned* it—*Repplier*⟩ **Pardon** (opposed to *punish*) and *forgive* (opposed to *condemn*) are often employed interchangeably, but their implications may be distinct. One **pardons** when one frees from the penalty due for an offense or refrains from exacting punishment for it ⟨*pardon* ten prisoners at Christmas⟩ ⟨will you *pardon* my intrusion?⟩ ⟨it became necessary . . . to fly for our lives . . . . We could not look to be *pardoned*—*Hudson*⟩ and one **forgives** when one gives up not only all claim to requital or retribution but also all resentment or desire for revenge ⟨to err is human, to *forgive,* divine—*Pope*⟩ ⟨the wrath . . . is past . . . and I, lo, I *forgive* thee, as Eternal God *forgives!*—*Tennyson*⟩ **Remit** is a synonym only in the idiomatic phrase *to remit sins,* in which it means to free from the punishment due for one's sins.
*Ana* justify, *explain, account, rationalize: acquit, vindicate, *exculpate, absolve, exonerate: *palliate, extenuate, gloze, gloss, whitewash
*Ant* punish —*Con* censure, reprobate, reprehend, blame, *criticize: chastise, castigate, discipline, chasten, correct (see PUNISH)

**excuse** *n* plea, pretext, *apology, apologia, alibi
*Ana* explanation, justification, rationalization (see corresponding verbs at EXPLAIN): palliation, extenuation, whitewashing, glossing (see corresponding verbs at PALLIATE)

**execrable,** damnable, accursed, cursed mean so odious as to deserve cursing or condemning. In actual use they vary little if any in force and only slightly in implications, although usage to a certain extent limits their applications. **Execrable** is applied chiefly to what is bad beyond description ⟨*execrable* poetry⟩ ⟨an *execrable* performance of Hamlet⟩ ⟨the concurrent possession of great wealth and *execrable* taste—*Wylie*⟩ **Damnable** and **accursed** are applied most often either to persons, their acts, and their vices or to things that excite righteous indignation and strong condemnation ⟨unless that man in there is to be given a chance of expiation in another life, then capital punishment is a *damnable* horror—*Mackenzie*⟩ ⟨*accursed* tower! *accursed* fatal hand that hath contrived this woeful tragedy!—*Shak.*⟩ **Cursed** varies in dignity, sometimes being applied to what merely excites profanity and sometimes to what is intrinsically worthy of imprecation ⟨merciful powers, restrain in me the *cursed* thoughts that nature gives way to in repose! —*Shak.*⟩
*Ana* *outrageous, atrocious, heinous, monstrous: *base, low, vile: loathsome, revolting, repulsive, *offensive, repugnant

**execrate,** curse, damn, anathematize, objurgate are comparable when meaning to denounce violently and indignantly. **Execrate** implies intense loathing or hatred and, usually, a fury of passion ⟨they *execrate* . . . their lot —*Cowper*⟩ ⟨*execrated* the men who were responsible for their misery⟩ It often suggests acts as well as words which give an outlet to these emotions ⟨for a little while he was *execrated* in Rome; his statues were overthrown, and his name was blotted from the records—*Buchan*⟩ **Curse** in reference to earlier custom may imply an invocation to the Supreme Being to visit deserved punish-

---

*Ana* analogous words    *Ant* antonyms    *Con* contrasted words    See also explanatory notes facing page 1

ment upon a person or to afflict him for his sins ⟨he that withholdeth corn, the people shall *curse* him: but blessing shall be upon the head of him that selleth it—*Prov* 11:26⟩ In more general use *curse* and **damn** (see also SENTENCE) do not markedly differ in meaning. Both usually imply angry denunciation by blasphemous oaths or profane imprecations ⟨I heard my brother *damn* the coachman, and *curse* the maids—*Defoe*⟩ **Anathematize** implies solemn denunciation (as of an evil, a heresy, or an injustice). It is used chiefly in reference to the impassioned denunciations of preachers or moralists ⟨*anathematize* the violation of a treaty⟩ ⟨*anathematize* graft in politics⟩ ⟨a quasi idealism which has been *anathematized* by the empirical foundations and purposes of realistic philosophy —*Nemetz*⟩ **Objurgate** implies a vehement decrial or criticism ⟨*objurgated* the custom of garnishing poems with archaisms—*T. R. Weiss*⟩ and often suggests the use of harsh or violent language in the expression of one's views so that it may approach *curse* or *damn* in some of its uses ⟨command all to do their duty. Command, but not *objurgate*—*Taylor*⟩ ⟨violently had he *objurgated* that wretch of a groom—*Vaughan*⟩

*Ana* denounce, condemn, reprobate, censure, reprehend (see CRITICIZE): revile, berate, rate (see SCOLD)

*Con* *commend, applaud, compliment, recommend: *praise, laud, extol, acclaim, eulogize

**execute** 1 effect, fulfill, discharge, *perform, accomplish, achieve

*Ana* complete, finish, conclude, *close: *realize, actualize, externalize, objectify

2 *kill, dispatch, slay, murder, assassinate

**exemplar** pattern, ideal, beau ideal, example, *model, mirror, standard

*Ana* apotheosis, *paragon, nonpareil, nonesuch: type, *symbol

**exemplify,** **illustrate** are comparable when they mean to use in speaking or writing concrete instances or cases to make clear something which is difficult, abstract, general, or remote from experience or to serve as an instance, case, or demonstration of a point or matter under examination. **Exemplify** implies the use of examples for clarification of a general or abstract statement or as aid in revealing the truth of a proposition or assertion ⟨a good preacher usually *exemplifies* each point that he seeks to impress upon his congregation⟩ ⟨the notes of Coleridge *exemplify* Coleridge's fragmentary and fine perceptions—*T. S. Eliot*⟩ ⟨each, in his way, *exemplifies* the peril that besets a highly gifted poetic nature—*Lowes*⟩ **Illustrate** implies the use not only of concrete examples but also sometimes of pictures or sketches and the intent not only to clarify but to make vivid or real what is being explained or to drive home most effectively a point that is being made ⟨the textbook is adequately *illustrated* with photographs and diagrams⟩ ⟨I will *illustrate* the word a little further—*J. R. Lowell*⟩ ⟨the assertion . . . leans for support . . . upon the truth conveyed in those words of Cicero, and wonderfully *illustrates* and confirms them—*Arnold*⟩ ⟨the world was no more made to serve us by *illustrating* our philosophy than we were made to serve the world by licking its boots—*Santayana*⟩

**exemption,** **immunity** are comparable when meaning the act or fact of freeing or the state of being free or freed from something burdensome, disagreeable, or painful. **Exemption** is more restricted in its meaning, for it applies usually to a release from some legal or similarly imposed obligation or burden to which others in the same circumstances and not similarly freed are liable ⟨married men with families may apply for *exemption* from military service⟩ ⟨[they] have no vices, but they buy that *exemption*

at a price, for one is inclined to ask whether . . . they really have any virtues—*Ellis*⟩ **Immunity** covers all cases for which an exemption may be given or obtained, but the term carries so strong an implication of privilege and of freedom from certain common restrictions that it is often used in reference to persons or classes of persons especially favored by the law or by nature ⟨entitled to the rights of a citizen, and clothed with all the rights and *immunities* which the Constitution and laws of the State attached to that character—*Taney*⟩ ⟨the question of the *immunities* of the clergy had been publicly raised—*Froude*⟩ ⟨the man of creative imagination pays a ghastly price for all his superiorities and *immunities*—*Mencken*⟩

**exercise** *n* practice, drill (see under PRACTICE *vb*)

*Ana* *action, act, deed: using *or* use, employment, utilization, application (see corresponding verbs at USE): operation, functioning, behavior (see corresponding verbs at ACT)

**exercise** *vb* *practice, drill

*Ana* *use, employ, utilize: display, exhibit, *show: wield, ply, manipulate, *handle

**exertion** *effort, pains, trouble

*Ana* labor, toil, travail, *work, grind, drudgery: struggle, striving, endeavor (see under ATTEMPT *vb*)

*Con* relaxation, *rest, repose, leisure, ease: inactivity, inertness *or* inertia, idleness (see corresponding adjectives at INACTIVE)

**exhaust** *vb* 1 drain, *deplete, impoverish, bankrupt

*Ana* sap, undermine, *weaken: consume, absorb, engross, *monopolize: dissipate, disperse, dispel, *scatter

*Con* conserve, preserve, *save: restore (see RENEW)

2 fatigue, jade, weary, *tire, fag, tucker

*Ana* *unnerve, enervate, emasculate: disable, cripple, debilitate, enfeeble, *weaken

*Con* refresh, restore, rejuvenate, *renew: vivify, *quicken, animate, enliven

**exhibit** *vb* display, expose, *show, parade, flaunt

*Ana* *reveal, disclose, discover, divulge: *show, manifest, evidence, evince, demonstrate

*Con* *suppress, repress: *hide, conceal, secrete, bury

**exhibit** *n* *exhibition, show, exposition, fair

**exhibition,** **show, exhibit, exposition, fair** are comparable when meaning a public display of objects of interest. **Exhibition** and, less often in strictly formal use except in art circles, **show** are applicable to any such display of objects of art, manufacture, commerce, or agriculture or to a display (as by pupils, members, or associates) of prowess or skill (as in gymnastics, oratory, or music) ⟨the annual *exhibition* of the Academy of Fine Arts⟩ ⟨an *exhibition* of Navaho blankets⟩ ⟨a one-man *show* of paintings⟩ ⟨a gymnastic *exhibition*⟩ ⟨a cattle *show*⟩ ⟨an industrial *exhibition*⟩ **Exhibit** typically denotes an object or collection displayed by a single person, group, or organization in an *exhibition* ⟨our club had a fine *exhibit* in the school fair⟩ but in some uses it is not clearly distinct from *exhibition* or *show,* since the scope of an *exhibit* may vary from a single object to a collection coextensive with an exhibition; thus, an artist might present a one-man *show* which would be at once an *exhibition* and an *exhibit* of his work. **Exposition** is the usual term for a very large exhibition, especially one involving the participation of many states and countries ⟨the World's Columbian *Exposition* at Chicago in 1893⟩ ⟨the annual Eastern States *Exposition* at West Springfield, Massachusetts⟩ **Fair** may be equivalent to *exposition* ⟨a world's *fair*⟩ or it may apply to a small exhibition of wares, produce, or stock sometimes for the promotion of sales, sometimes in competition for prizes for excellence; it suggests a variety of kinds of display and entertainment

A colon (:) separates groups of words discriminated. An asterisk (*) indicates place of treatment of each group.

and usually an outdoor setting ⟨a county *fair*⟩

**exhort** *urge, egg, goad, spur, prod, prick, sic
*Ana* plead, appeal (see under PRAYER): entreat, implore, beseech (see BEG): stimulate, excite, *provoke: advise, counsel (see under ADVICE *n*)

**exigency** 1 pass, emergency, pinch, strait, crisis, contingency, *juncture
*Ana* *difficulty, vicissitude, rigor, hardship: *predicament, plight, fix, quandary, dilemma, jam, pickle, scrape
2 necessity, *need
*Ana* demanding *or* demand, requirement, exacting *or* exaction, claiming *or* claim (see corresponding verbs at DEMAND): compulsion, coercion, constraint, duress (see FORCE *n*)

**exigent** *adj* 1 *pressing, urgent, imperative, crying, importunate, insistent, instant
*Ana* critical, crucial, *acute: threatening, menacing (see THREATEN): compelling, constraining (see FORCE *vb*)

**exiguous** *meager, scant, scanty, skimpy, scrimpy, spare, sparse
*Ana* diminutive, tiny, *small, little: tenuous, slender, slight, *thin: limited, restricted, confined (see LIMIT *vb*)
*Ant* capacious, ample

**exile** *vb* *banish, expatriate, ostracize, deport, transport, extradite
*Ana* proscribe, condemn (see SENTENCE): expel, *eject, oust

**exist** *be, live, subsist

**existence, being, actuality** are closely related in meaning but not always interchangeable. **Existence** is the inclusive term which designates the state or condition of anything regarded as occurring in space or time, as distinct and apart from all other things, and as having a nature or substance of its own ⟨customs that have recently come into *existence*⟩ ⟨a mathematical point has no real *existence*⟩ ⟨wars that threaten the *existence* of civilization⟩ ⟨his misfortunes have *existence* only in his imagination⟩ ⟨concepts . . . are tyrants rather than servants when treated as real *existences*—*Cardozo*⟩ The opposite of *existence* is its complete negation *nonexistence*. **Being**, when it denotes existence, adds varying implications. Sometimes it implies life, consciousness, or personality ⟨in him we live, and move, and have our *being*—*Acts* 17:28⟩ Sometimes it implies fullness or completeness of existence and absence of imperfection ⟨everything else is in a state of becoming, God is in a state of *being* —*F. W. Robertson*⟩ Sometimes it suggests the complex of qualities or characteristics that constitute the nature of a person or a personified thing ⟨all the forces of his *being* were massed behind one imperious resolve— *Buchan*⟩ **Actuality** as a synonym of *existence* stresses realization or attainment; it usually implies opposition to *possibility* or *potentiality* ⟨ambition is the spur that makes dreams come into *actuality*⟩ ⟨risks which have been seized upon as *actualities* when they have been merely potentialities—*T. S. Eliot*⟩
*Ana* *state, condition, situation, status: subsisting *or* subsistence, living *or* life (see corresponding verbs at BE)
*Ant* nonexistence

**exonerate** acquit, vindicate, absolve, *exculpate
*Ana* *relieve, lighten, alleviate: *excuse, remit
*Ant* charge (*a person with a task, a duty, a crime*)

**exorbitant** inordinate, extravagant, *excessive, immoderate, extreme
*Ana* *onerous, burdensome, oppressive, exacting: greedy, grasping, *covetous: extorting *or* extortionate (see corresponding verb at EDUCE)
*Ant* just (*price, charge*) —*Con* *fair, equitable: reason-

able, *rational

**exordium** preamble, preface, *introduction, foreword, prologue, prelude

**expand, amplify, swell, distend, inflate, dilate** mean to increase or to cause to increase in size, bulk, or volume. **Expand** is the most inclusive term in this group and may often be used interchangeably with any of the others. It distinctively implies enlargement by opening out, unfolding, or spreading and may be used when the enlarging force is either internal or external ⟨tulips *expand* in the sun⟩ ⟨the flag *expanded* in the breeze⟩ ⟨*expand* a sponge by soaking it in water⟩ ⟨*expand* one's chest by breathing deeply⟩ ⟨their business is *expanding*⟩ **Amplify** implies extension of something which is inadequate or obscure (as by filling out with details or by magnifying the volume) ⟨*amplify* a statement by adding details⟩ ⟨devices for *amplifying* sounds⟩ ⟨the author follows the Vulgate narrative closely . . . but *amplifies* and embroiders— *Saintsbury*⟩ **Swell** implies expansion beyond a thing's original circumference or normal limits ⟨warm spring rains cause the leaf buds to *swell*⟩ ⟨the river is *swelling*⟩ ⟨his hand is *swollen*⟩ ⟨gifts to *swell* the endowment fund⟩ Often it implies increase in intensity, force, or volume ⟨the laughter *swelled* to hooting—*Galsworthy*⟩ ⟨Caesar's ambition, which *swelled* so much that it did almost stretch the sides of the world—*Shak.*⟩ or it may imply puffing up or puffing out to the point of bursting ⟨*swollen* veins⟩ ⟨his heart *swelled* with pride⟩ **Distend** implies swelling caused by pressure from within forcing extension outward in all directions. It may presuppose a previous void or flaccid state ⟨a rubber bag *distends* when filled with water⟩ ⟨sails *distended* by the wind⟩ or it may imply an exceeding of normal bounds ⟨a stomach *distended* by gas⟩ ⟨like the flesh of animals *distended* by fear— *Cather*⟩ ⟨the bat's body was so *distended* that it appeared spherical—*Ditmars & Greenhall*⟩ **Inflate** usually implies distention by artificial means (as by the introduction of gas or by puffing up with something as insubstantial or as easily dissipated as gas) ⟨*inflate* a balloon⟩ ⟨*inflate* values⟩ ⟨an *inflated* idea of one's own importance⟩ ⟨poems . . . so *inflated* with metaphor, that they may be compared to the gaudy bubbles blown up from a solution of soap—*Goldsmith*⟩ ⟨the psychological problems of *inflated* national ego, heroic delusions of grandeur, and theories of historical inevitability—*Newhall*⟩ **Dilate** implies expansion in diameter; it therefore suggests a widening out of something circular rather than a puffing up of something globular or spherical ⟨as round a pebble into water thrown *dilates* a ring of light—*Longfellow*⟩ ⟨half-frighted, with *dilated* eyes—*Tennyson*⟩ ⟨some stirring experience . . . may swiftly *dilate* your field of consciousness—*Montague*⟩
*Ana* enlarge, *increase, augment: *extend, protract, prolong
*Ant* contract: abridge (*a book, article*): circumscribe (*a range, a scope, a power*)

**expanse, amplitude, spread, stretch** are comparable when they denote an area or range of considerable or conspicuous extent. **Expanse** is applied chiefly to vast areas open to view and usually uniform in character ⟨pure as the *expanse* of Heaven—*Milton*⟩ ⟨thy mariners explore the wide *expanse*—*Cowper*⟩ ⟨great *expanse* of country spread around and below—*D. H. Lawrence*⟩ **Amplitude** implies in general use an ampleness in what it describes and suggests relative largeness (as in size or range) ⟨with a face dark and proud as a Borgia's, though not cruel; with a figure of noble *amplitude*—*Donn Byrne*⟩ ⟨the *amplitude* of his vision found supreme expression in a style that is meticulous, colorful, and luminous—*Millett*⟩ or great-

---

*Ana* analogous words     *Ant* antonyms     *Con* contrasted words     See also explanatory notes facing page 1

ness (as in character or quality) ⟨he displayed a Miltonic *amplitude* of ambition and style—*Bush*⟩ ⟨a red-curtained English inn . . . stood sideways in the road, as if standing aside in the *amplitude* of hospitality—*Chesterton*⟩ but in technical contexts in which the word is specifically applied to the range of a variable (as wavelength or a statistical array) the notion of ampleness has given way to that of magnitude, and *amplitude* means no more than size or extent ⟨the size or extent of the swing is known as the *amplitude* of the pendulum—*Taffel*⟩ ⟨the maximum distance the curve rises above or falls below the horizontal axis . . . is known as its *amplitude*—*F. E. Seymour & P. J. Smith*⟩ **Spread** is applied to an expanse drawn out in all directions ⟨the water . . . a ripply *spread* of sun and sea—*Browning*⟩ ⟨a trackless *spread* of moor—*Blackmore*⟩ ⟨under the immense *spread* of the starry heavens—*Stevenson*⟩ **Stretch** is applied to an expanse in one of its two dimensions ⟨the beach was a narrow *stretch* of sand⟩ ⟨a *stretch* of farmland extending as far as the distant mountains⟩ ⟨the great *stretches* of fields that lay beside the road—*Anderson*⟩
*Ana* \*range, reach, scope, compass, sweep, orbit: domain, territory, sphere, \*field

**expansive** \*elastic, resilient, buoyant, volatile, effervescent
*Ana* exuberant, luxuriant, lavish, prodigal (see PROFUSE): generous, \*liberal, bountiful, bounteous, open-handed: exalted, magnified, aggrandized (see EXALT)
*Ant* tense: reserved —*Con* \*stiff, inflexible, rigid: stern, austere, \*severe: taciturn, \*silent, reticent

**expatiate** \*discourse, descant, dilate
*Ana* \*speak, talk, converse: \*expand, amplify: \*discuss, argue, dispute: expound, \*explain: \*relate, narrate, recount, recite, rehearse

**expatriate** *vb* exile, \*banish, ostracize, deport, transport, extradite
*Ant* repatriate

**expect,** hope, look, await are comparable when they mean to have something in mind as more or less certain to happen or come about. They vary, however, so greatly in their implications and in their constructions that they are seldom interchangeable. **Expect** usually implies a high degree of certainty, but it also involves the idea of anticipation (as by making preparations or by envisioning what will happen, what one will find, or what emotions one will feel) ⟨he told his mother not to *expect* him for dinner⟩ ⟨she had reason to *expect* that the trip would be exciting⟩ ⟨he seems to require and *expect* goodness in his species as we do a sweet taste in grapes and China oranges—*Mandeville*⟩ ⟨what can you *expect* of a girl who was allowed to wear black satin at her coming out ball?—*Wharton*⟩ **Hope** (often with *for*) implies some degree of belief in the idea that one may expect what one desires or longs for; although it seldom implies certitude, it usually connotes confidence and often especially in religious use implies profound assurance ⟨he dared not *hope* that he would succeed in his venture, for he feared disappointment⟩ ⟨what I *hope* for and work for today is for a mess more favorable to artists than is the present one—*Forster*⟩ ⟨encouraged to *hope* for a college education—*Scudder*⟩ **Look** (usually followed by *to* with an infinitive and sometimes also by *to* with a personal object) is less literary than *expect;* it often also suggests more strongly than *expect* a counting upon or a freedom from doubt ⟨they *look* to profit by their investment⟩ ⟨they *looked* to their son to help them in their old age⟩ ⟨I never *look* to have a mistress that I shall love half as well—*Brooke*⟩ With *for,* on the other hand, *look* does not imply as much assurance; it suggests rather an attitude of expectancy and watchfulness ⟨they are *looking* for news in the next post⟩ ⟨there is no use *looking* for their return tonight⟩ ⟨finality is not to be *looked* for in . . . translation—*Swaim*⟩ **Await** often adds to *look for* the implication of being ready mentally or, sometimes, physically for the event; it also suggests waiting, often patient waiting ⟨we *await* your reply with interest⟩ ⟨the two armies are eager for action, each *awaiting* an attack by the other⟩ ⟨I . . . had known it would happen to me, and now it was there with all the strangeness and dark mystery of an *awaited* thing—*Wolfe*⟩ *Await* also differs from the other words in this group in its capacity for taking as subject the thing expected and as object the person who is expecting ⟨good fortune *awaits* you⟩ ⟨death *awaits* all men⟩
*Ana* \*foresee, foreknow, anticipate, apprehend, divine
*Ant* despair of

**expedient** *adj* **Expedient, politic, advisable** are comparable when they are used to imply a choice (as of course, action, or method) and to mean dictated by practical wisdom or by motives of prudence. Something is **expedient** from which definite and usually immediate advantages accrue. Originally and still occasionally the word carries no derogatory implication ⟨it is *expedient* for you that I go away: for if I go not away, the Comforter will not come unto you; but if I depart, I will send him unto you—*Jn* 16:7⟩ In its sense development *expedient* came to imply determination by immediate conditions and to mean necessary or suitable under present circumstances ⟨there shall be appointed . . . such number of . . . justices of the peace as the president of the United States shall, from time to time, think *expedient*—*John Marshall*⟩ As a result *expedient* now commonly implies opportuneness (sometimes with a strong hint of timeserving) as well as advantageousness ⟨they decided that it was not *expedient* (that is, neither opportune nor of advantage) to interfere now⟩ Very frequently also it connotes such an ulterior motive as self-interest ⟨purely for *expedient* reasons he let the Iroquois alone—*Hervey Allen*⟩ Consequently *expedient* is often opposed to *right*, the former suggesting a choice determined by temporal ends, the latter one determined by ethical principles ⟨too fond of the right to pursue the *expedient*—*Goldsmith*⟩ Something is **politic** which is the judicious course, action, or method from the practical point of view. Though often used interchangeably with *expedient*, *politic* may be applied discriminatively to choices involving tactics or the effective handling of persons, and *expedient* to choices involving strategy, or the gaining of objectives ⟨the move was a *politic* one, for it served to win friends to the cause and to placate its enemies⟩ ⟨community of race . . . is mainly a *politic* fiction, at least in countries of European civilization, in which the races are inextricably mixed up—*Encyc. Brit.*⟩ Like *expedient*, however, *politic* often implies material motives ⟨whether it is not your interest to make them happy . . . . Is a *politic* act the worse for being a generous one?—*Burke*⟩ Something is **advisable** which is expedient in the original, underogatory sense of that word. *Advisable* has now nearly lost its original derivative sense and is preferred by writers or speakers who wish to avoid any of the unpleasant implications of *expedient* or of *politic* ⟨I don't think that it's altogether *advisable* to mention Dickens in a sermon . . . . Some people might be offended at mentioning a novelist in church—*Mackenzie*⟩ ⟨he was told it was not *advisable* to drive on through the mountains because of the night fogs—*Sylvester*⟩
*Ana* advantageous, \*beneficial, profitable: useful, utilitarian (see corresponding nouns at USE): \*seasonable, opportune, timely, well-timed: feasible, practicable,

---

A colon (:) separates groups of words discriminated. An asterisk (\*) indicates place of treatment of each group.

*possible

**Ant** inexpedient —**Con** detrimental, deleterious (see PERNICIOUS): harming *or* harmful, hurting *or* hurtful, injuring *or* injurious (see corresponding verbs at INJURE): *futile, vain, fruitless

**expedient** *n* *resource, resort, shift, makeshift, stopgap, substitute, surrogate
**Ana** *device, contrivance, contraption: *mean, agency, instrument, instrumentality, medium

**expedition 1** dispatch, speed, *haste, hurry
**Ana** *celerity, legerity, alacrity: agility, nimbleness, briskness (see corresponding adjectives at AGILE)
**Ant** procrastination —**Con** delaying *or* delay, retarding *or* retardation, slowing, slackening (see corresponding verbs at DELAY)
**2** *journey, voyage, tour, trip, jaunt, excursion, cruise, pilgrimage

**expeditious** speedy, swift, *fast, rapid, fleet, quick, hasty
**Ana** efficient, *effective, efficacious, effectual: brisk, *agile, nimble: *quick, ready, prompt
**Ant** sluggish —**Con** inefficient, *ineffective, inefficacious, ineffectual: *slow, dilatory, leisurely, laggard, deliberate

**expel** *eject, oust, dismiss, evict
**Ana** *banish, exile, ostracize: *dismiss, discharge, cashier, fire: *discard, cast: *exclude, shut out, eliminate
**Ant** admit (sense 1)

**expend** *spend, disburse
**Ana** *pay, repay, compensate, reimburse, remunerate: *distribute, dispense

**expense** cost, *price, charge

**expensive** *costly, dear, valuable, precious, invaluable, priceless
**Ana** exorbitant, extravagant, *excessive, immoderate
**Ant** inexpensive

**experience** *vb* Experience, undergo, sustain, suffer are comparable when they mean to pass through the process of actually coming to know or to feel. **Experience** means little more than this. It implies that something (as a sensation, an emotion, or an occasion) is known not from hearsay but from an actual living through it or going through it ⟨the disgust he had inspired in me before . . . was a weak and transient feeling to what I now *experienced*— *Hudson*⟩ ⟨we cannot *experience* the sweetness of a single molecule of sugar, nor the smell of a single molecule of musk—*Jeans*⟩ **Undergo** carries a strong implication of bearing or enduring or of being subjected to that is almost lacking in *experience;* it frequently takes as an object a distressing experience (as pain, suffering, or hardships) when the subject names a person ⟨*undergo* great disappointment⟩ ⟨*undergo* a serious operation⟩ ⟨his fine spirit was broken by the anxieties he had *undergone*— *Martineau*⟩ ⟨the search for truth . . . makes men and women content to *undergo* hardships—*Eliot*⟩ But when it is used with objects which represent a process which covers years or ages of time, it comes closer to *experience* in meaning, though it seldom takes an individual as its subject ⟨a man *experiences* a change of heart, but a race *undergoes* changes which are not apparent for many generations⟩ Very occasionally, when the idea of submission to or imposition upon is stressed, the subject of *undergo* in the active voice may be impersonal ⟨the bridge must *undergo* inspection before it is accepted by the government⟩ **Sustain** suggests undergoing infliction or imposition without implying as a necessary concomitant courage in resisting or enduring ⟨*sustain* a great loss through fire⟩ ⟨*sustain* an injury⟩ ⟨the two dropped supine into chairs at opposite corners of the ring as if they had *sustained* excessive fatigue—*Shaw*⟩ ⟨must be prepared to *sustain*

heavy losses—*Bliven* b. 1889⟩ **Suffer,** which is frequently used interchangeably with *sustain* in this sense, carries a more marked implication of the harm done or injury wrought and is preferable when what is affected is a thing; moreover, *suffer* may also be used intransitively ⟨all *suffered* the same fate⟩ ⟨the very language of France has *suffered* considerable alterations since you were conversant in French books—*Burke*⟩ ⟨a great author necessarily *suffers* by translation—*Inge*⟩ Sometimes *suffer* loses its distinctive quality and is then nearly equal to *experience* ⟨Gard *suffered* an odd impulse to get up and kick his chair over—*Mary Austin*⟩ ⟨most or all genes *suffer* mutational changes from time to time—*Dobzhansky*⟩
**Ana** *see, perceive, behold, view, survey

**expert** *adj* *proficient, adept, skilled, skillful, masterly
**Ana** practiced, drilled (see PRACTICE *vb*): trained, schooled (see TEACH): *dexterous, deft, adroit
**Ant** amateurish —**Con** inept, maladroit, *awkward, clumsy

**expert** *n* Expert, adept, artist, artiste, virtuoso, wizard are comparable when they designate a person who shows mastery in a subject, an art, or a profession or who reveals extraordinary skill in execution, performance, or technique. **Expert** implies successful experience, broad knowledge of one's subject, and distinguished achievements; it is applied specifically to one who is recognized as an authority in his field ⟨an *expert* in city planning⟩ ⟨a handwriting *expert*⟩ ⟨this problem in triangulation was extremely difficult, and an *expert* in geodesy was brought from the United States—*Heiser*⟩ ⟨in philosophy he naturally looks for guidance to the *experts* and professionals —*James*⟩ **Adept** connotes understanding of the mysteries of some art or craft or penetration into secrets beyond the reach of exact science ⟨thou art an *adept* in the difficult lore of Greek and Frank philosophy—*Shelley*⟩ It tends to imply sublety or ingenuity ⟨he is an *adept* in intrigue⟩ ⟨he is an *adept* at evasion⟩ ⟨an *adept* at understatement— *Buchan*⟩ **Artist** stresses creative imagination and extraordinary skill in execution or in giving outward form to what the mind conceives. More than any other word in this group it stresses skill in performance and the factors (as perfection in workmanship, loving attention to detail, and a feeling for material) that are pertinent thereto ⟨the good craftsman . . . becomes an *artist* in so far as he treats his materials also for themselves . . . and is perpetually besieged by dreams of beauty in his work—*Alexander*⟩ ⟨it came to pass that after a time the *artist* was forgotten, but the work lived—*Schreiner*⟩ **Artiste** applies especially to public performers (as actors, singers, and dancers) but may occasionally be applied to workers in crafts where adeptness and taste are indispensable to distinguished achievement ⟨that milliner is an *artiste*⟩ ⟨groups of *artistes* rehearsing every kind of act—*Bambrick*⟩ **Virtuoso,** though often close to *artist* in meaning, stresses the outward display of great technical skill or brilliance in execution rather than the inner passion for perfection or beauty. It is applied chiefly to performers on musical instruments and especially to pianists, violinists, and cellists ⟨the compositions of Liszt are the delight of *virtuosos*⟩ ⟨this precise evocation of forms and colors by the great *virtuosos* ˙of description—*Babbitt*⟩ **Wizard** implies such skill and knowledge or such excellence in performance as seems to border on the magical ⟨a *wizard* with a billiard cue⟩ ⟨that Sauerbruch, as thoracic surgeon, was a genius and something of a *wizard* seems to have been generally accepted—*Brit. Book News*⟩
**Ant** amateur —**Con** tyro, dabbler, dilettante (see AMATEUR): *novice, apprentice, probationer

---

**Ana** analogous words      **Ant** antonyms      **Con** contrasted words      See also explanatory notes facing page 1

**expiate** *vb* Expiate, atone mean to make amends or give satisfaction for an offense, a sin, a crime, or a wrong. The same distinctions in implications and connotations are observable in their derivative nouns **expiation** and **atonement**. Expiate and expiation imply an attempt to undo the wrong one has done by suffering a penalty, by doing penance, or by making reparation or redress ⟨let me here, as I deserve, pay on my punishment, and *expiate,* if possible, my crime—*Milton*⟩ ⟨unless that man in there is to be given a chance of *expiation* in another life, then capital punishment is a damnable horror—*Mackenzie*⟩ Atone and **atonement** have been greatly colored in their meanings by theological controversies. The basic implication of reconciliation became mixed with and sometimes subordinated to other implications (as appeasement, propitiation, or reparation). In general use *atone* (usually with *for*) and *atonement* emphasize a restoration through some compensation of a balance that has been lost. When the reference is to an offense, sin, or crime the words usually imply expiation, but they stress the rendering of satisfaction for the evil that has been done by acts that are good or meritorious; thus, one *expiates* a sin by doing penance for it, but one *atones* for it by leading a good life afterwards ⟨she hated herself for this movement of envy . . . and tried to *atone* for it by a softened manner and a more anxious regard for Charlotte's feelings—*Wharton*⟩ Sometimes a deficiency or a default rather than an offense may be *atoned* for (as by an excess of something else that is equally desirable) ⟨for those who kneel beside us at altars not Thine own, who lack the lights that guide us, Lord, let their faith *atone!*—*Kipling*⟩
*Ana* redress, remedy, rectify, *correct, amend: redeem, deliver, save (see RESCUE)

**expiation** atonement (see under EXPIATE *vb*)
*Ana* *penitence, repentance, contrition: *trial, tribulation, cross, visitation

**expire** *pass, pass away, elapse
*Ana* end, terminate, *close: cease, discontinue (see STOP)
*Con* *begin, commence, start

**explain** 1 Explain, expound, explicate, elucidate, interpret, construe are comparable when they mean to make oneself or another understand the meaning of something. Explain, the most general term, implies a making of something plain or intelligible to someone by whom it was previously not known or clearly understood ⟨*explain* to a boy the mechanism of an engine⟩ ⟨the teacher *explained* the meanings of the new words in the poem⟩ ⟨a poet whose words intimate rather than define, suggest rather than . . . *explain*—*Edman*⟩ Expound implies careful, elaborate, often learned setting forth of a subject in order to explain it (as in a lecture, a book, or a treatise) ⟨a clergyman *expounding* a biblical text⟩ ⟨*expound* a point of law⟩ ⟨Sir A. Eddington in two masterly chapters . . . *expounds* the law of gravitation—*Alexander*⟩ ⟨*expound* the duties of the citizen⟩ Explicate, a somewhat learned term, adds to *expound* the idea of development or detailed analysis ⟨the mind of a doctor of the Church who could . . . *explicate* the meaning of a dogma—*T. S. Eliot*⟩ Elucidate implies a throwing light upon something obscure (as a subject, a work, or a passage) especially by clear or luminous exposition or illustration ⟨*elucidate* an obscure passage in the text⟩ ⟨the simplicity of the case can be addled . . . when the object is to addle and not to *elucidate*—*Shaw*⟩ ⟨the author's linguistic erudition has allowed him to consult the original sources and to *elucidate* and interpret them authentically—*Reinhardt*⟩ Interpret implies the making clear to oneself or to another the meaning of something (as a poem, a dream, an abstraction, or a work in a foreign language) which presents more than intellectual

difficulties and requires special knowledge, imagination, or sympathy in the person who would understand it or make it understood ⟨I have tried in this all too hasty sketch to *interpret* . . . the indwelling spirit and ideal of the art of the Far East—*Binyon*⟩ ⟨it is a sophistry to *interpret* experience in terms of illusion—*Sullivan*⟩ ⟨an inscription which no one could understand or rightly *interpret*—*Hudson*⟩ Construe is preferred to *interpret* when the difficulties are textual either because of the strangeness of the language (as by being foreign, ancient, dialectal, or technical) or because of ambiguities or equivocations in it. It therefore may suggest either translation involving careful analysis of grammatical structure ⟨*construe* ten lines of Vergil⟩ or a highly individual or particular interpretation ⟨the phrase "every common carrier engaged in trade or commerce" may be *construed* to mean "while engaged in trade or commerce" without violence to the habits of English speech—*Justice Holmes*⟩ ⟨had *construed* the ordinarily polite terms of his letter of engagement into a belief that the Directors had chosen him on account of his special and brilliant talents—*Kipling*⟩
*Ana* *analyze, resolve, dissect, break down: *discuss, argue, dispute: *exemplify, illustrate

2 Explain, account, justify, rationalize are comparable when they mean to give or tell the cause, reason, nature, or significance of something obscure or questionable. One **explains** what is hard to understand because it is mysterious in its origin or nature or lacks an apparent or sufficient cause or is full of inconsistencies ⟨these sciences have not succeeded in *explaining* the phenomena of life —*Inge*⟩ ⟨this . . . study of Napoleon, which, while free from all desire to defend or admire, yet seems to *explain* Napoleon—*Ellis*⟩ Explain often implies an attempt to excuse or to set oneself right with others ⟨one can do almost anything . . . if one does not attempt to *explain* it—*Wharton*⟩ One **accounts** for something, rather than *explains* it, when one shows how it fits into a natural order or a logically consistent pattern ⟨we fail, we are told, to *account* for the world. Well, the world is a solid fact, which we have to accept, not to *account* for— *Inge*⟩ ⟨going about her business as if nothing had happened that needed to be *accounted* for—*Wharton*⟩ ⟨their presence could not be *accounted* for by some temporary catastrophe, such as the Mosaic Flood—*S. F. Mason*⟩ One **justifies** himself or another when he explains certain acts or behavior in an attempt to free himself or another from blame. It may or may not imply consciousness of guilt or a definite accusation ⟨Powell . . . began to *justify* himself. "I couldn't stop him," he whispered shakily. "He was too quick for me"—*Conrad*⟩ ⟨so far is he from feeling the pangs of conscience that he constantly *justifies* his act—*Dickinson*⟩ ⟨in her heart she did not at all *justify* or excuse Cyril—*Bennett*⟩ One **rationalizes** something that is or seems to be contrary to reason when he attempts an explanation that is in accord with scientific principles or with reality as known to the senses ⟨*rationalize* the Greek myths⟩ ⟨*rationalize* the Genesis story of creation⟩ Rationalize may come close to *justify* without, however, so strong an implication of blame and with the added implication of self-deception and, at times, of hypocrisy ⟨in other countries the plutocracy has often produced men of reflective and analytical habit, eager to *rationalize* its instincts—*Mencken*⟩ ⟨easy for men of principle to *rationalize* lapses from high standards where the cause seems to them good—*Pimlott*⟩
*Ana* *excuse, condone: *exculpate, exonerate, acquit, absolve

**explicate** *vb* *explain, expound, elucidate, interpret,

construe

**explicit,** express, specific, definite, categorical are comparable when applied to statements, utterances, and language and when meaning perfectly clear in significance or reference. Something is **explicit** which is stated so plainly and distinctly that nothing is left to be inferred or to cause difficulty by being vague, equivocal, or ambiguous ⟨*explicit* directions or promises⟩ ⟨to give an *explicit* and determinate account of what is meant—*Bentham*⟩ Something is **express** which is both explicit and is uttered or expressed with directness, pointedness, or force ⟨an *express* prohibition⟩ ⟨*express* testimony⟩ ⟨the defendant should be enjoined from publishing news obtained from the Associated Press for — hours after publication by the plaintiff unless it gives *express* credit to the Associated Press; the number of hours . . . to be settled by the District Court—*Justice Holmes*⟩ ⟨she sent me the now famous drawings, with the *express* injunction that I was to show them to no one—*Pollitzer*⟩ Something is **specific** which is perfectly precise in its reference to a particular thing or in its statement of the details covered or comprehended ⟨he made two *specific* criticisms of the school, one dealing with its lack of a playground, the other with the defective ventilation of certain rooms⟩ ⟨government workers, by *specific* law, must be fired if they resort to the Fifth Amendment—*Time*⟩ Something is **definite** which leaves no doubt as to its reference or to its details or as to what is excluded; *definite,* far more than *specific,* suggests precise and determinate limitations ⟨he was asked to make a *definite* statement concerning the young man's prospects with the company⟩ ⟨it was a simple, clear, *definite* question—*Sinclair Lewis*⟩ In practice *specific* and *definite* are often used interchangeably without loss; but *specific* may be preferred when the intent is to stress particularization of reference or specification of details, and *definite* when it is to emphasize clear limitations; thus, a worker may be given *specific* instructions about the sequence in which his tasks are to be performed but a *definite* order not to smoke on the job. **Categorical** (see also ULTIMATE 2) implies explicitness without the least suggestion of a qualification or condition; thus, a *categorical* answer is demanded of a person testifying in court when he is compelled to answer yes or no; a *categorical* denial is a denial that is complete and contains not the slightest reservations ⟨it is perilous to make *categorical* assertions—*Lowes*⟩
**Ana** precise, exact, accurate (see CORRECT): *clear, lucid, perspicuous
**Ant** ambiguous —**Con** equivocal, vague, enigmatic, cryptic, dark, *obscure: *implicit, virtual, constructive
**exploit** *n* *feat, achievement
**Ana** act, deed, *action: *adventure, enterprise, quest
**expose** display, exhibit, *show, parade, flaunt
**Ana** *reveal, disclose, discover, divulge: demonstrate, evince, manifest, evidence, *show: air, ventilate, vent, voice, utter, *express: publish, advertise, proclaim, broadcast, *declare
**exposé** *n* exposure, *exposition
**exposed** open, *liable, subject, prone, susceptible, sensitive
**Ana** threatened, menaced (see THREATEN)
**Con** protected, shielded, guarded, safeguarded, defended (see DEFEND)
**exposition 1** fair, *exhibition, exhibit, show
**2 Exposition,** exposure, exposé are comparable when they mean a setting forth or laying open of a thing or things hitherto not known or fully understood. **Exposition** (see also EXHIBITION) often implies a display of something (as wares, manufactures, or a collection of rarities or

antiquities); more often it implies a setting forth of something which is necessary for the elucidation or explanation of something else such as a theory, a dogma, or the law ⟨you know the law, your *exposition* hath been most sound —*Shak.*⟩ or the events or situations preceding a story or play ⟨the first quarter of the first act is devoted to the *exposition*⟩ In a more general sense, especially in academic use, *exposition* applies to the type of writing which has explanation for its end or aim and is thereby distinguished from other types in which the aim is to describe, to narrate, or to prove a contention. **Exposure** is now preferred to *exposition* as a term implying a laying bare or open especially to detrimental or injurious influences or to reprobation, contempt, or severe censure ⟨fabrics faded by *exposure* to the sun⟩ ⟨*exposure* to a contagious disease⟩ ⟨the *exposure* of a candidate's unsavory past⟩ ⟨the *exposure* of a person's motives⟩ *Exposure* is the term for the time during which the sensitive surface of a photographic film is laid open to the influence of light ⟨an *exposure* of two seconds⟩ **Exposé** is often used in place of *exposure* for a revealing and especially a formal or deliberate revealing of something that is discreditable to a person or group ⟨an *exposé* of an allegedly charitable association⟩ ⟨an *exposé* of the judge's graft⟩
**expostulate** remonstrate, protest, *object, kick
**Ana** oppose, *resist, combat, fight: argue, debate, dispute, *discuss
**exposure** exposé, *exposition
**Ant** cover: covering —**Con** *shelter, refuge, asylum, retreat
**expound** *explain, explicate, elucidate, interpret, construe
**Ana** dissect, break down, *analyze, resolve: illustrate, *exemplify
**express** *adj* *explicit, definite, specific, categorical
**Ana** expressed, voiced, uttered (see EXPRESS *vb*): lucid, *clear, perspicuous: distinct, plain (see EVIDENT): precise, exact, accurate (see CORRECT)
**Con** *implicit, constructive, virtual: vague, *obscure, cryptic, enigmatic, ambiguous, equivocal
**express** *vb* **Express,** vent, utter, voice, broach, air, ventilate are comparable when they mean to let out what one feels or thinks. **Express,** the most comprehensive of these words, implies an impulse to reveal not only thoughts or feelings but also experiences, imaginative conceptions, and personality; it implies revelation not only in words but also in gestures, in action, in dress, or in what one makes or produces, especially as works of art ⟨once again I have to *express* surprise and satisfaction—*Lucas*⟩ ⟨in speaking or writing we have an obligation to put ourselves into the hearer's or reader's place . . . . To *express* ourselves is a very small part of the business— *Quiller-Couch*⟩ ⟨there were so many different moods and impressions that he wished to *express* in verse—*Joyce*⟩ **Vent** stresses such an inner compulsion to expression as a pent-up emotion that seeks an outlet or a powerful passion that cannot be controlled ⟨he *vented* his spleen in libelous caricatures⟩ ⟨his heart's his mouth: what his breast forges, that his tongue must *vent*—*Shak.*⟩ ⟨by means of ferocious jokes . . . he could *vent* his hatred of pioneer life and all its conditions—*Brooks*⟩ **Utter** stresses the use of voice; it does not, however, always imply speech ⟨*utter* a yell⟩ ⟨*utter* one's relief by sobbing⟩ When speech is implied, it is typically both short and significant ⟨*utter* a command⟩ ⟨his tongue and pen *uttered* heavenly mysteries—*Walton*⟩ and the context may suggest a reason for secrecy as well as for revelation ⟨he was caught up into paradise, and heard unspeakable words, which it is not lawful for a man to *utter*—*2 Cor* 12:4⟩ ⟨begin by encouraging him to *utter*

---

**Ana** analogous words     **Ant** antonyms     **Con** contrasted words     See also explanatory notes facing page 1

freely even his most shocking thoughts—*Russell*⟩ **Voice** does not necessarily imply vocal utterance, but it invariably suggests expression in words ⟨I revelled in being able to *voice* my opinions without being regarded as a dangerous lunatic—*Mackenzie*⟩ Very often *voice* suggests that the writer or speaker serves as a spokesman expressing a shared view ⟨the editorial *voices* the universal longing for peace⟩ ⟨one, bolder than the rest, *voiced* their disapproval of the proposal⟩ ⟨Webster contributed a pamphlet . . . which effectively *voiced* the Federalist opposition—*Cole*⟩ **Broach** stresses mention for the first time, especially of something long thought over and awaiting an opportune moment for disclosure ⟨the mayor did not *broach* the project until he felt that public opinion was in its favor⟩ ⟨the idea of religious radio broadcasts was first *broached* in 1923—*Current Biog.*⟩ **Air** implies exposure, often in the desire to parade one's views, sometimes in the hope of attracting attention or sympathy ⟨*air* one's opinions of the government⟩ ⟨*air* a grievance⟩ ⟨he did not *air* his politics in the pulpit—*Murdock*⟩ **Ventilate** implies exposure also but usually suggests a desire to get at the truth by discovering the real issues or by weighing the evidence pro and con; it often means to investigate freely, openly, and thoroughly ⟨the question [the future of literature] has thus been *ventilated* from every point of view—*Times Lit. Sup.*⟩
*Ana* *speak, talk: pronounce, *articulate, enunciate: *reveal, disclose, divulge, tell: *declare, proclaim, announce
*Ant* imply —*Con* hint, intimate, *suggest, insinuate
**expression** *phrase, locution, idiom

**expressive, eloquent, significant, meaningful, pregnant, sententious** mean clearly conveying or manifesting a thought, idea, or feeling or a combination of these. Something is **expressive** which vividly or strikingly represents the thoughts, feelings, or ideas which it intends to convey or which inform or animate it; the term is applicable not only to language but to works of art, to performances (as of music or drama), and to looks, features, or inarticulate sounds ⟨a forcible and *expressive* word⟩ ⟨an *expressive* face⟩ ⟨he laid great stress on the painting of the eyes, as the most *expressive* and dominating feature—*Binyon*⟩ ⟨a growing emphasis on the element [in beauty] that is described by such epithets as vital, characteristic, picturesque, individual—in short, on the element that may be summed up by the epithet *expressive*—*Babbitt*⟩ Something is **eloquent** (see also VOCAL 2) which reveals with great or impressive force one's thoughts, ideas, or feelings ⟨there was a burst of applause, and a deep silence which was even more *eloquent* than the applause—*Hardy*⟩ ⟨I could scarcely remove my eyes from her *eloquent* countenance: I seemed to read in it relief and gladness mingled with surprise and something like vexation—*Hudson*⟩ or which gives a definite and clear suggestion of a condition, situation, or character ⟨a tremulous little man, in greenish-black broadcloth, *eloquent* of continued depression in some village retail trade—*Quiller-Couch*⟩ ⟨a sidewalk *eloquent* of official neglect—*Brownell*⟩ **Eloquent** is also applicable to words, style, and speech when a power to arouse deep feeling or to evoke images or ideas charged with emotion is implied ⟨words *eloquent* of feeling⟩ ⟨a simple but deeply *eloquent* style⟩ Something is **significant** which is not empty of ideas, thoughts, or purpose but conveys a meaning to the auditor, observer, or reader. The term sometimes is applied to words that express a clearly ascertainable idea as distinguished from those words (as prepositions and conjunctions) that merely express a relation or a connection ⟨his honored client had a meaning and so deep it was, so subtle, that no wonder he experienced a difficulty in giving it fitly *significant* words—

*Meredith*⟩ ⟨those who lay down that every sentence must end on a *significant* word, never on a preposition—*Ellis*⟩ or to works of art or literature that similarly express a clearly ascertainable idea (as a moral, a lesson, or a thesis) as distinguished from works that exist purely for their beauty or perfection of form and have no obvious purpose or import ⟨art-for-art's-sake men deny that any work of art is necessarily *significant*⟩ More often, *significant* applies to something (as a look, gesture, or act) that suggests a covert or hidden meaning or intention ⟨by many *significant* looks and silent entreaties, did she endeavor to prevent such a proof of complaisance—*Austen*⟩ ⟨she could not feel that there was anything *significant* in his attentions—*Deland*⟩ Something is **meaningful** which is significant in the sense just defined; the term is often preferred when nothing more than the presence of meaning or intention is implied and any hint of the importance or momentousness sometimes associated with *significant* would be confusing ⟨of two close synonyms one word may be more *meaningful* because of its greater richness in connotations than the other⟩ ⟨it was a . . . *meaningful* smile—*Macdonald*⟩ ⟨I suppose the most *meaningful* thing that can be said of her is that she has restored delight (repeat, delight) to poetry—*Charles Jackson*⟩ Something is **pregnant** which conveys its meaning with richness or with weightiness and often with extreme conciseness or power ⟨it is pretty and graceful, but how different from the grave and *pregnant* strokes of Maurice's pencil—*Arnold*⟩ ⟨the *pregnant* maxim of Bacon that the right question is the half of knowledge—*Ellis*⟩ ⟨he had no talent for revealing a character or resuming the significance of an episode in a single *pregnant* phrase—*Maugham*⟩ Something is **sententious** which is full of significance; when applied, as is usual, to expressions, the word basically connotes the force and the pithiness of an aphorism ⟨*sententious* and oracular brevity—*Gibbon*⟩ ⟨*sententious* maxims⟩ But even as an aphorism may become hackneyed, so has *sententious* come to often connote platitudinousness or triteness ⟨"Contentment breeds happiness" . . . a proposition . . . *sententious,* sedate, obviously true—*Quiller-Couch*⟩
*Ana* revealing *or* revelatory, disclosing, divulging (see corresponding verbs at REVEAL): *graphic, vivid, picturesque, pictorial: suggesting *or* suggestive, adumbrating, shadowing (see corresponding verbs at SUGGEST)
*Con* *stiff, wooden, rigid, tense, stark: stern, austere, *severe: inane, jejune, flat, banal, vapid, *insipid: vacuous, *empty

**expunge** *erase, cancel, efface, obliterate, blot out, delete
*Ana* wipe, eradicate, extirpate (see EXTERMINATE)
**exquisite** *adj* 1 *choice, recherché, rare, dainty, delicate, elegant
*Ana* precious, valuable, priceless, *costly: *consummate, finished: flawless, *impeccable, faultless: *perfect, intact, whole, entire
2 *intense, vehement, fierce, violent
*Ana* *consummate: *perfect: *supreme, superlative: heightened, aggravated, intensified, enhanced (see INTENSIFY): exalted, magnified (see EXALT)
**exquisite** *n* *fop, coxcomb, beau, dandy, dude, buck
**extemporaneous, extempore, extemporary, improvised, impromptu, offhand, unpremeditated** mean composed, concocted, devised, or done at the moment rather than beforehand. **Extemporaneous, extempore,** and **extemporary** in their more general applications stress something made necessary by the occasion or situation and may suggest sketchiness or crudity in the thing modified ⟨*extemporaneous* cover during the snowstorm⟩ ⟨the old woman had erected a clothesline as a sort of *extempore* tent—*Powys*⟩

A colon (:) separates groups of words discriminated. An asterisk (*) indicates place of treatment of each group.

⟨there was enthusiasm over the *extemporary* throwing together and dispatching of the United Nations Emergency Force—*Panter-Downes*⟩ The terms may retain this value when applied to modes of expression or to persons as sources of expression ⟨a detective who has had to resort to *extemporaneous* prevarications on numerous occasions to crash police lines—*Gardner*⟩ ⟨the aesthetic horror of *extempore* prayer—*Laski*⟩ but more usually, and in technical context routinely, they imply a well thought-out plan or outline that is given spontaneity in presentation by fresh, unstudied choice of words ⟨*extempore* speaking is a form of prepared speaking on a selected topic in which everything is ready for delivery except the exact words to be used . . . . *Extempore* speaking is neither impromptu speech, manuscript reading, nor memorized speech—it is different from all other types and in many ways superior to them—*Holley*⟩ ⟨guided by notes rather than by a regular script, her own comment is largely *extemporaneous* in style—*Current Biog.*⟩ **Improvised** stresses the absence of foreknowledge of what is to be accomplished and therefore the composing, concocting, devising, or constructing of something without advance thought or preparation and often without the necessary tools, instruments, or other equipment ⟨an *improvised* musical accompaniment⟩ ⟨an *improvised* pantomime⟩ ⟨an *improvised* bed for the night in the open⟩ ⟨when an emergency came an army had to be *improvised*—*Buchan*⟩ **Impromptu** stresses the immediate response to a need or suggestion and the spontaneous character of what is composed or concocted on the spur of the moment; thus, an *impromptu* speech is one prepared at a moment's notice and delivered without notes or a preconceived plan; an *impromptu* meal is one prepared from what is available usually at an unusual time or for an unexpected number of people ⟨postponements or changes of plan were always *impromptu*—*Davenport*⟩ **Offhand**, both as adjective and adverb, carries so much stronger an implication of casualness, carelessness, or indifference than any of the preceding terms that at times it loses its suggestion of an impromptu character and means little more than *curt* or *brusque* ⟨an *offhand* comment⟩ ⟨an *offhand* salute⟩ ⟨a father can't make *offhand* remarks to a 4-year-old and have them gently slip into oblivion—*McNulty*⟩ ⟨an *offhand* manner of dealing with strangers⟩ **Unpremeditated** emphasizes less strongly than *extemporaneous* and *impromptu* the immediate stimulus of an occasion, but it usually suggests some strong, often suddenly provoked emotion which drives one to action ⟨[skylark] that from heaven, or near it, pourest thy full heart in profuse strains of *unpremeditated* art—*Shelley*⟩ ⟨*unpremeditated* murder⟩
*Ana* *spontaneous, impulsive: ready, prompt, apt, *quick
*Con* planned, designed, projected, schemed (see corresponding verbs under PLAN *n*): *deliberate, considered, studied, advised, premeditated: formal, ceremonious, *ceremonial, conventional

**extemporary, extempore** *extemporaneous, improvised, impromptu, offhand, unpremeditated
*Ana & Con* see those at EXTEMPORANEOUS

**extend,** lengthen, elongate, prolong, protract all mean to draw out or add to so as to increase in length. Both **extend** and **lengthen** (opposed to *shorten*) connote an increase of length either in space or in time, but *extend* is also used to connote increase in range (as of kinds, of influence, or of applicability); thus, a road may be *extended* or *lengthened*; one may *extend* or *lengthen* his stay; the power of a monarch, however, may be *extended* but not *lengthened* ⟨words with *extended* meanings⟩ ⟨delays *lengthened* their trip⟩ **Elongate** (usually opposed to *abbreviate*) denotes to increase in spatial length and has

wider technical than general use ⟨fibers *elongated* by stretching⟩ **Prolong** (opposed to *cut short, arrest*) means to extend in duration beyond usual or normal limits ⟨*prolong* one's childhood⟩ ⟨*prolong* the process of digestion⟩ ⟨exercise *prolongs* life⟩ **Protract** (opposed to *curtail*) adds to the denotation of *prolong* the connotations of indefiniteness, needlessness, or boredom ⟨*protracted* debate⟩ ⟨an unduly *protracted* visit⟩
*Ana* *increase, enlarge, augment: *expand, amplify, distend, dilate
*Ant* abridge, shorten —*Con* abbreviate, curtail, retrench (see SHORTEN): *contract, shrink, condense

**extension** wing, ell, *annex
**extent** *size, dimensions, area, magnitude, volume
*Ana* *range, scope, compass, sweep, reach, radius: stretch, spread, amplitude, *expanse

**extenuate** *vb* 1 attenuate, *thin, dilute, rarefy
*Ana* diminish, lessen, reduce, *decrease: *weaken, enfeeble, debilitate: *moderate, temper, qualify
*Ant* intensify —*Con* aggravate, heighten, enhance (see INTENSIFY)
2 *palliate, gloze, gloss, whitewash, whiten
*Ana* condone, *excuse: rationalize, *explain, justify

**exterior** *adj* *outer, external, outward, outside
*Ana* *extrinsic, extraneous, foreign, alien
*Ant* interior —*Con* *inner, inward, internal, inside, intestine: intrinsic, *inherent, ingrained

**exterminate,** extirpate, eradicate, uproot, deracinate, wipe are comparable when they mean to effect the destruction or abolition of something. **Exterminate** implies utter extinction; it therefore usually implies a killing off ⟨efforts to *exterminate* such pests as mosquitoes, rats, and ragweed have been only partly successful⟩ ⟨the tribe had been *exterminated*, not here in their stronghold, but in their summer camp . . . across thé river—*Cather*⟩ **Extirpate** implies extinction of a group, kind, or growth, but it may carry less an implication of killing off, as *exterminate* carries, than one of the destruction or removal of the things essential to survival and reproduction; thus, wolves might be *exterminated* by hunting in a particular area, but large carnivores in general are *extirpated* by changed conditions in thickly settled regions; a heresy is often *extirpated*, rather than *exterminated*, by the removal of the leaders from a position of influence; a vice cannot easily be *extirpated* so long as the conditions which promote it remain in existence ⟨the ancient Athenians had been *extirpated* by repeated wars and massacres—*Graves*⟩ **Eradicate** stresses the driving out or elimination of something that has taken root or has established itself ⟨diphtheria has been nearly *eradicated* from the United States⟩ ⟨it is difficult to *eradicate* popular superstitions⟩ ⟨he must gradually *eradicate* his settled conviction that the Italians and the French are wrong—*Grandgent*⟩ **Uproot** differs from *eradicate* chiefly in being more definitely figurative and in suggesting forcible and violent methods similar to those of a tempest that tears trees out by their roots ⟨hands . . . red with guiltless blood . . . *uprooting* every germ of truth —*Shelley*⟩ ⟨end forthwith the ruin of a life *uprooted* thus —*Browning*⟩ ⟨refugees from the peoples *uprooted* by war⟩ **Deracinate** basically is very close to *uproot* ⟨disemboweling mountains and *deracinating* pines—*Stevenson*⟩ ⟨he fascinated the young Anderson's intellect and *deracinated* certain convictions—*Benét*⟩ but in much recent use it denotes specifically to separate (as oneself or one's work) from a natural or traditional racial, social, or intellectual group ⟨although the author is himself a Negro, his book is . . . *deracinated*, without any of the lively qualities of the imagination peculiar to his people —*Commentary*⟩ **Wipe** (in this sense used with *out*)

often implies extermination ⟨the entire battery was *wiped out* by shellfire⟩ but it equally often suggests a canceling or obliterating (as by payment, retaliation, or exhaustion of supply) ⟨*wipe* out a debt⟩ ⟨*wipe* out an old score⟩ ⟨*wipe* out a disgrace⟩ ⟨the fall in share prices *wiped* out his margin⟩
*Ana* \*abolish, extinguish, annihilate, abate: obliterate, efface, expunge, blot out, \*erase: \*destroy, demolish, raze

**external** *adj* \*outer, exterior, outward, outside
*Ana* \*extrinsic, extraneous, foreign, alien
*Ant* internal —*Con* interior, intestine, \*inner, inward, inside: intrinsic, ingrained, \*inherent

**externalize** materialize, actualize, \*realize, embody, incarnate, objectify, hypostatize, reify

**extinction** see under *extinguish* at ABOLISH

**extinguish** 1 \*crush, quell, suppress, quench, quash
*Ana* obliterate, expunge, efface, delete (see ERASE): \*destroy: \*ruin, wreck
*Ant* inflame
2 \*abolish, annihilate, abate
*Ana* extirpate, \*exterminate, eradicate, uproot, wipe: obliterate, efface, blot out, expunge, \*erase: \*suppress, repress

**extirpate** \*exterminate, eradicate, uproot, deracinate, wipe
*Ana* extinguish, \*abolish, annihilate: obliterate, efface, expunge, \*erase, blot out: \*destroy, demolish, raze
*Con* propagate, \*generate, engender, breed

**extol** laud, \*praise, eulogize, acclaim
*Ana* applaud, \*commend, compliment: \*exalt, magnify, aggrandize
*Ant* decry: abase (*oneself*) —*Con* depreciate, disparage, detract, derogate, belittle, minimize (see DECRY): denounce, condemn, censure, reprobate, reprehend, \*criticize

**extort** extract, \*educe, elicit, evoke
*Ana* draw, drag, \*pull: compel, \*force, constrain, oblige, coerce: exact, \*demand, require

**extra** *adj* supernumerary, spare, surplus, \*superfluous

**extract** *vb* extort, elicit, \*educe, evoke
*Ana* draw, \*pull, drag: \*demand, require, exact: obtain, procure, gain, win, acquire, \*get

**extract** *n* Extract, excerpt denote a passage transcribed or quoted from a book or document. Extract is the general term referring to any such passage regardless of the principle of its selection or its further use ⟨*extracts* for citation are copied by the typists as indicated to them by the readers⟩ ⟨he makes many *extracts* from every book he reads⟩ Excerpt differs from *extract* in implying careful selection for a definite purpose that is commonly indicated in the context ⟨back up his points by *excerpts* from the authoritative writers on the subject⟩ ⟨*excerpts* from his letters were entered as evidence⟩

**extradite** deport, transport, expatriate, \*banish, exile, ostracize
*Ana* surrender, \*relinquish, yield, resign

**extraneous** \*extrinsic, foreign, alien
*Ana* external, exterior, outside, \*outer, outward: adventitious, \*accidental, incidental
*Ant* relevant —*Con* intrinsic, \*inherent, ingrained, constitutional: intestine, internal, \*inner, inside, interior, inward: pertinent, germane, material (see RELEVANT)

**extravagant** inordinate, immoderate, \*excessive, exorbitant, extreme
*Ana* preposterous, absurd, \*foolish, silly: \*profuse, prodigal, lavish, exuberant
*Ant* restrained —*Con* frugal, \*sparing, economical

**extreme** *adj* exorbitant, inordinate, \*excessive, immod-

erate, extravagant

**extreme** *n* Extreme, extremity are comparable when they mean the utmost limit or degree of something. Extreme usually applies to either of two limits which are diametrically opposed or are as far removed from each other as possible ⟨a climate where *extremes* of heat and cold are unknown⟩ ⟨twixt two *extremes* of passion, joy and grief —*Shak.*⟩ ⟨my tendency is to unite *extremes* rather than to go between them—*Ellis*⟩ ⟨he aroused *extremes* of admiration and hostility—*Robert Lawrence*⟩ The term may, however, when used with a verb of motion or one suggesting movement, imply a definite direction and therefore denote the utmost limit or degree in that direction ⟨he is always dressed in the *extreme* of fashion⟩ ⟨carried their enthusiasm to *extremes*⟩ Extremity, on the other hand, usually implies the utmost removal from what is reasonable, sane, safe, tolerable, or endurable ⟨the *extremity* of their opinions⟩ ⟨an *extremity* of caution—*H. G. Wells*⟩ ⟨an *extremity* of suffering⟩ Often the term applies concretely to the state or condition of one in extreme pain, grief, anxiety, suffering, or poverty ⟨the queen's in labor, they say, in great *extremity*—*Shak.*⟩ ⟨those ... who succor heroic minds in their worst *extremities*—*L. P. Smith*⟩
*Ana* antithesis, antipode, contrary (see under OPPOSITE *adj*)

**extremity** \*extreme
*Ana* \*limit, bound, end, confine, term

**extricate** *vb* Extricate, disentangle, untangle, disencumber, disembarrass are comparable when meaning to free or release from what binds or holds back. Extricate, the most widely useful of these words, implies a situation in which someone or something is so entangled (as in difficulties or perplexities) or so restrained (as from freedom of action or movement) that great force or ingenuity is required to bring about a release ⟨the fly was not able to *extricate* itself from the spider's web⟩ ⟨*extricate* himself from financial difficulties⟩ ⟨*extricate* his car from the mud into which its wheels had sunk⟩ ⟨my success in having *extricated* myself from an awkward predicament—*Heiser*⟩ Disentangle adheres far more closely than *extricate* to its basic sense of to free from what entangles; also, it is used typically of things rather than of persons and therefore seldom involves the ideas of difficulty or perplexity except for the person who seeks to free the thing entangled or to unravel what is intricately complicated ⟨*disentangle* a strand from a twisted skein⟩ ⟨[Seneca] is a dramatist . . . whom the whole of Europe in the Renaissance delighted to honor. It is obviously a task of some difficulty to *disentangle* him from his reputation—*T. S. Eliot*⟩ ⟨I could not then so far analyze all that is roughly lumped together as "religion" as to *disentangle* the essential from the accidental—*Ellis*⟩ Untangle is sometimes used in place of *disentangle* with much the same implications ⟨leaned down to *untangle* his foot from a vine in which it was caught⟩ ⟨drank, set down his glass, and *untangled* his legs—*Basso*⟩ Disencumber implies a freeing from what weighs down, clogs, or imposes a very heavy burden ⟨he can call a spade a spade, and knows how to *disencumber* ideas of their wordy frippery—*George Eliot*⟩ ⟨the trees, laden heavily with their new and humid leaves, were now suffering more damage than during the highest winds of winter, when the boughs are specially *disencumbered* to do battle with the storm—*Hardy*⟩ Disembarrass implies a release from what embarrasses by or as if by impeding, hampering, or hindering ⟨*disembarrass* himself of his companion—*Scott*⟩ ⟨*disembarrass* ourselves of the curse of ignorance and learn to work together—*Alvin Johnson*⟩ ⟨Chamberlain, at several critical junctures, preferred to *disembarrass* himself of trained, expert advisers—*Na-*

---

A colon (:) separates groups of words discriminated. An asterisk (\*) indicates place of treatment of each group.

*mier*⟩

**Ana** disengage, *detach, abstract: liberate, release, *free: *rescue, deliver

**Con** *hamper, fetter, trammel, shackle, clog, hog-tie, manacle: impede, obstruct, *hinder, block

**extrinsic, extraneous, foreign, alien** are comparable when they mean external to something or someone or to the true nature or original character of such thing or person. **Extrinsic** applies to something which is distinctly outside the thing in question or is derived from something apart from it; thus, a ring may have *extrinsic* value because of sentimental or historical associations; such *extrinsic* influences as chance or the assistance of friends may help a man to succeed ⟨[those] who would persuade us . . . that style is something *extrinsic* to the subject, a kind of ornamentation laid on—*Quiller-Couch*⟩ ⟨even life itself might arise from lifeless matter through the influence of favorable *extrinsic* conditions—*Conklin*⟩ **Extraneous,** though often used interchangeably with *extrinsic,* applies more specifically to something which is introduced from outside and may or may not be capable of becoming an integral part of the thing ⟨advance arguments *extraneous* to the real issue⟩ ⟨water is rarely pure and free from *extraneous* matter⟩ ⟨style . . . is not—can never be—*extraneous* ornament—*Quiller-Couch*⟩ ⟨whatever we gain comprehension of, we seize upon and assimilate into our own being . . .; that which had been *extraneous* is become a part of ourselves—*H. B. Alexander*⟩ **Foreign** applies to something which is so different from the thing under consideration that it is either inadmissible because repellent or, if admitted, incapable of becoming identified with it, assimilated by it, or related to it ⟨much coal contains *foreign* matter⟩ ⟨inflammation caused by a *foreign* body in the eye⟩ ⟨the mysticism so *foreign* to the French mind and temper—*Brownell*⟩ ⟨look round our world . . . . Nothing is *foreign*: parts relate to whole . . . ; all served, all serving: nothing stands alone—*Pope*⟩ **Alien** applies to something which is so foreign that it can never be made an inherent or an integral part of a thing. The word often suggests repugnance or at least incompatibility or irreconcilableness ⟨a voluptuous devotionality . . . totally *alien* to the austerity and penetrating sincerity of the Gospel!—*Inge*⟩ ⟨he would often adopt certain modes of thought that he knew to be really *alien* to his nature—*Wilde*⟩

**Ana** external, *outer, outside, exterior, outward: acquired, gained (see GET)

**Ant** intrinsic —**Con** internal, *inner, inside, inward, interior, intestine

**exuberant** lavish, *profuse, prodigal, luxuriant, lush

**Ana** prolific, *fertile, fruitful, fecund: *vigorous, lusty, energetic, nervous: rampant, *rank: copious (see PLENTIFUL)

**Ant** austere: sterile

**eyewitness** witness, onlooker, looker-on, *spectator, observer, beholder, bystander, kibitzer

# F

**fable** 1 *fiction, fabrication, figment

2 myth, parable, *allegory

**fabricate** *make, fashion, forge, form, shape, manufacture

**Ana** *invent, create: produce, turn out (see BEAR): devise, contrive (see corresponding nouns at DEVICE)

**fabrication** *fiction, figment, fable

**Ana** invention, creation (see corresponding verbs at INVENT): art, craft, handicraft (see TRADE): *work, product, production, opus, artifact

**fabulous** *fictitious, mythical, legendary, apocryphal

**Ana** astonishing, amazing, astounding (see SURPRISE *vb*): extravagant, inordinate (see EXCESSIVE): *monstrous, prodigious, stupendous

**Con** credible, believable, colorable (see PLAUSIBLE): veritable, genuine, *authentic

**face** *n* Face, countenance, visage, physiognomy, mug, puss denote the front part of a human or, sometimes, animal head including the mouth, nose, eyes, forehead, and cheeks. **Face** is the simple and direct word ⟨your *face* is dirty⟩ ⟨she struck him in the *face*⟩ ⟨to feel the fog in my throat, the mist in my *face*—*Browning*⟩ ⟨was this the *face* that launched a thousand ships and burnt the topless towers of Ilium?—*Marlowe*⟩ **Countenance** applies especially to the face as it reveals mood, character, or changing emotions ⟨a benign *countenance*⟩ ⟨his face was not the cheerful *countenance* of yesterday—*Cather*⟩ ⟨his *countenance* changed when he heard the news⟩ ⟨something feminine—not effeminate, mind—is discoverable in the *countenances* of all men of genius—*Coleridge*⟩ Especially in the phrases "to keep in *countenance*" (maintain one's composure) and "to put out of *countenance*" (cause one to lose one's composure) the term denotes the normal, composed facial expression of one free from mental distress. Sometimes the word is used in place of *face* when a formal term is desired ⟨that vile representation of the royal *countenance*—*Swift*⟩ Both *face* and *countenance* may be used in personifications when the outward aspect or appearance of anything is denoted ⟨startling transformations in the outward *face* of society are taking place under our very eyes—*Frankfurter*⟩ ⟨beholding the bright *countenance* of truth in the quiet and still air of delightful studies—*Milton*⟩ **Visage** is a more literary term than the preceding words; it often suggests attention to the shape and proportions of the face, but sometimes to the impression it gives or the changes in mood which it reflects ⟨black hair; complexion dark; generally, rather handsome *visage*—*Dickens*⟩ ⟨his *visage* all agrin—*Tennyson*⟩ ⟨the very *visage* of a man in love—*Millay*⟩ **Physiognomy** may be preferred when the reference is to the contours of the face, the shape of the features, and the characteristic expression as indicative of race, character, temperament, or disease ⟨he has the *physiognomy* of an ascetic⟩ ⟨nor is there in the *physiognomy* of the people the slightest indication of the Gaul—*Landor*⟩ The term may be extended to the significant or sharply defined aspect of things ⟨not exactly one of those styles which have a *physiognomy* . . . which stamp an indelible impression of him on the reader's mind—*Arnold*⟩ ⟨the changing yet abiding *physiognomy* of earth and sky —*Lowes*⟩ **Mug,** used in informal context, usually carries a suggestion of an ugly but not necessarily displeasing physiognomy ⟨getting your *mug* in the papers is one of the shameful ways of making a living—*Mailer*⟩ ⟨among all the ugly *mugs* of the world we see now and then a face made after the divine pattern—*L. P. Smith*⟩ **Puss** sometimes denotes a facial expression (as of anger or pouting) ⟨she put on a very sour *puss* when she saw the priest along with me—*Frank O'Connor*⟩ but it more often denotes the physiognomy ⟨it had the head of a bear, the very head and *puss* of a bear—*Gregory*⟩

**face** *vb* **1** *meet, encounter, confront
*Ana* look, watch (see SEE): *gaze, stare, glare: await, look, *expect
**2 Face, brave, challenge, dare, defy, beard** are comparable because all carry the meaning to confront with courage or boldness. **Face** carries no more than this general sense; basically it suggests the confrontation of an enemy or adversary ⟨here we are together *facing* a group of mighty foes—*Sir Winston Churchill*⟩ but in its extended use it implies a recognition of the power of a force, a fact, or a situation which cannot be escaped to harm as well as to help and a willingness to accept the consequences ⟨must *face* the consequences of your own wrongdoing⟩ ⟨strict justice, either on earth or in heaven, was the last thing that society cared to *face*—*Henry Adams*⟩ ⟨like . . . a tailor's bill, something that has to be *faced* as it stands and got rid of—*Montague*⟩ **Brave** may imply a show of courage or bravado in facing or encountering ⟨I must hence to *brave* the Pope, King Louis, and this turbulent priest—*Tennyson*⟩ More often, however, it implies fortitude in facing and in enduring forces which ordinarily would strike the spirit with terror ⟨firemen *braving* danger and death to rescue persons trapped in the blazing hotel⟩ ⟨women . . . for his sake had *braved* all social censure—*Wilde*⟩ ⟨the search for truth . . . makes men and women content to undergo hardships and to *brave* perils—*Eliot*⟩ ⟨if you find yourself in trouble before then, call on your courage and resolution: *brave* out every difficulty—*Kenneth Roberts*⟩ **Challenge** generally implies a confrontation of a person or thing opposed in such a way that one seems an accuser imputing weakness or fault in the one confronted. Often it may lose the feeling of accusation and then may mean no more than to dispute or question ⟨our thoughts and beliefs "pass," so long as nothing *challenges* them—*James*⟩ ⟨that "Testament" the authenticity of which, foolishly *challenged* by Voltaire, is sufficiently established—*Belloc*⟩ or, on the other hand, it may go farther and suggest a bold invitation to a contest (as a duel or other test of rightness or skill) which the one challenged cannot refuse ⟨the degree of courage displayed by Malakai, the best medical practitioner turned out by the School, who once dared to *challenge* the power of the chief of the witch doctors—*Heiser*⟩ or it may suggest bold measures inviting a response or retaliation ⟨*challenge* criticism⟩ ⟨*challenge* attention⟩ **Dare** also usually emphasizes boldness rather than fortitude, but it rarely suggests the critical or censorious attitude so frequently evident in *challenge.* Rather, it implies venturesomeness, love of danger, or moral courage and may connote great or especial merit or mere rashness in the action ⟨*dare* the perils of mountain climbing⟩ ⟨*dare* to be true: nothing can need a lie —*Herbert*⟩ ⟨and what they *dare* to dream of, *dare* to do —*J. R. Lowell*⟩ ⟨to wrest it from barbarism, to *dare* its solitudes—*Century*⟩ ⟨among the newspapers only the *Irish Times dared* to discuss the issue frankly— *Blanshard*⟩ ⟨no American *dared* to be seen reaching for a sandwich by the side of a known Communist— *Sulzberger*⟩ **Defy,** like the others, usually implies a personal agent, but it may be said of things as well. When the idea of challenging is uppermost, the connotation of daring one to test a power which the challenger believes undefeatable or to do what the challenger be-

lieves impossible is usually its accompaniment. In either case there is a stronger implication of certainty in one's belief than there is in *challenge,* and often a clearer suggestion of mockery ⟨from my walls I *defy* the pow'rs of Spain—*Dryden*⟩ ⟨fiend, I *defy* thee! . . . foul tyrant both of gods and humankind, one only being shalt thou not subdue—*Shelley*⟩ ⟨I *defy* the enemies of our constitution to show the contrary—*Burke*⟩ ⟨I *defy* him to find the gate, however well he may think he knows the city— *Kipling*⟩ When the idea of resistance is uppermost, there is a suggestion in *defy* of a power to withstand efforts, opposition, or rules. It is in this sense that a personal agent is most often not implied, for resistance does not always suggest an exercise of will ⟨scenes that *defy* description⟩ ⟨words that *defy* definition⟩ ⟨a wooden seat put together with nails—a flimsy contrivance, which *defies* all rules of gravity and adhesion—*Jefferies*⟩ ⟨the tall erect figure, *defying* age, and the perfectly bald scalp *defying* the weather—*Upton Sinclair*⟩ **Beard,** although it implies defiance, often differs from *defy* in suggesting resolution rather than daring or mockery as its motive; in that way it comes somewhat closer to *face* and to *brave* ⟨what! am I dared and *bearded* to my face?—*Shak.*⟩ ⟨a bold heart yours to *beard* that raging mob!—*Tennyson*⟩ ⟨for years she led the life of a religious tramp, *bearding* bishops and allowing herself many eccentricities—*Coulton*⟩
*Ana* confront, encounter, *meet: oppose, withstand, *resist: *contend, fight
*Ant* avoid —*Con* evade, elude, shun, *escape
**facet** aspect, side, angle, *phase
**facetious** humorous, jocose, jocular, *witty
*Ana* joking, jesting, quipping, wisecracking (see corresponding nouns at JOKE): jolly, jovial, jocund, *merry, blithe: comical, comic, droll, funny, ludicrous, *laughable
*Ant* lugubrious —*Con* grave, solemn, somber, *serious, sober, sedate, staid
**facile** *easy, smooth, light, simple, effortless
*Ana* adroit, deft, *dexterous: fluent, voluble, glib (see VOCAL): *superficial, shallow, uncritical, cursory
*Ant* arduous *(with reference to the thing accomplished)*: constrained, clumsy *(with reference to the agent or his method)*
**facility** ease, dexterity, *readiness
*Ana* spontaneity, *unconstraint, abandon: address, poise, *tact: lightness, effortlessness, smoothness (see corresponding adjectives at EASY)
*Con* ineptness, clumsiness, awkwardness, maladroitness (see corresponding adjectives at AWKWARD): stiffness, rigidity, woodenness (see corresponding adjectives at STIFF): *effort, exertion, pains: *difficulty, hardship
**facsimile** copy, carbon copy, *reproduction, duplicate, replica, transcript
**faction** bloc, party, *combination, combine, ring
*Ana* clique, *set, coterie, circle
**factious** contumacious, seditious, mutinous, rebellious, *insubordinate
*Ana* contending, fighting, warring (see CONTEND): contentious, quarrelsome (see BELLIGERENT): disaffected, estranged, alienated (see ESTRANGE)
*Ant* cooperative —*Con* companionable, gregarious, *social: *compliant, acquiescent: loyal, true, *faithful
**factitious** *artificial, synthetic, ersatz
*Ana* manufactured, fabricated (see MAKE *vb*): forced, compelled, constrained (see FORCE *vb*): simulated, feigned, counterfeited, shammed, pretended, affected, assumed (see ASSUME)
*Ant* bona fide, veritable —*Con* *authentic, genuine: *natural, simple, artless, naïve, unsophisticated

---

A colon (:) separates groups of words discriminated. An asterisk (*) indicates place of treatment of each group.

**factor** 1 *agent, attorney, deputy, proxy
2 constituent, *element, component, ingredient
*Ana* determinant, *cause, antecedent: *influence:
agency, agent, instrument, instrumentality, *mean

**faculty** 1 *power, function
2 *gift, aptitude, knack, bent, turn, genius, talent
*Ana* *ability, capacity, capability: property, *quality:
penchant, flair, propensity, proclivity, *leaning: *predilection

**fad** vogue, *fashion, style, rage, craze, mode, dernier
cri, cry
*Ana* fancy, whim, whimsy, *caprice, conceit, vagary

**fade** *vanish, evanesce, evaporate, disappear
*Ana* deliquesce, melt (see LIQUEFY): *thin, rarefy,
attenuate: reduce, lessen (see DECREASE)

**faded** *shabby, dilapidated, dingy, seedy, threadbare
*Ana* worn, wasted, *haggard: dim, murky, gloomy (see
DARK): *colorless, achromatic: *pale, pallid, ashen, wan

**fag** vb exhaust, jade, fatigue, *tire, weary, tucker

**failing** n frailty, foible, *fault, vice
*Ana* *blemish, flaw, defect: weakness, infirmity (see
corresponding adjectives at WEAK)
*Ant* perfection (in concrete sense) —*Con* *excellence,
merit, virtue

**failure,** neglect, default, miscarriage, dereliction are
comparable when they mean an omission on the part of
someone or something of what is expected or required
of him or of it. **Failure** basically implies a being found
wanting; it implies a lack or absence of something that
might have been expected to occur or to be accomplished,
performed, or effected ⟨there was a general *failure* of
crops that year⟩ ⟨a distressing confusion in discussions
of the human-interest story has been caused by a common
*failure* to define the term—*Mott*⟩ ⟨you will hear a great
deal of talk about the *failure* of Christianity; but where
in the Holy Gospels . . . do you find any suggestion that
Christianity is to be an easy triumph?—*Mackenzie*⟩
**Neglect** (see also NEGLIGENCE) implies carelessness and
inattentiveness on the part of a person, so that what is expected or required of him is either left unattended to or
is not adequately performed ⟨in wartime a charge of
*neglect* of duty is a very serious one⟩ ⟨his *neglect* of
his health is a source of much worry to his friends⟩
⟨the property has become dilapidated through the owner's
*neglect*⟩ ⟨we made a nice tidy cleanup . . . . If I hadn't
done it I ought . . . to have been shot for *neglect*—*H. G.
Wells*⟩ **Default** is now chiefly found in legal use, where
it implies a failure to perform something required by
law (as a failure of a plaintiff or of a defendant to appear
at the appointed time to prosecute or defend an action
or a proceeding) ⟨in case of *default* on the part of the
plaintiff, he may be nonsuited⟩ ⟨in case of *default* on
the part of the defendant, he may have a judgment rendered
against him, this being called a *judgment by default*⟩
*Default* may also imply a failure to pay one's debts at
the appointed time ⟨convicted of *default* in the payment of a fine⟩ or in extended use a failure to perform
something required, usually by total omission of pertinent action ⟨betraying by *default* the privileges of citizenship in a democratic society—*Dean*⟩ ⟨lose a tennis match
by *default*⟩ **Miscarriage** does not so definitely point the
blame for a failure of someone or something to live up
to expectations or to accomplish certain ends as do the
preceding words; it is often used when there are no
definite persons or things to which culpability can be
assigned or when for some reason or other there is a
desire to avoid casting of blame ⟨there was a serious
*miscarriage* of justice in that trial⟩ ⟨the causes of the
*miscarriage* of the project were not clear⟩ ⟨we fear . . .

some *miscarriage* in the details of our plan—*Krutch*⟩
⟨these various *miscarriages* cannot all be ascribed to
ill fortune—*Grenfell*⟩ **Dereliction,** of all these terms,
carries the strongest implication of a neglect that amounts
to an abandonment of, or a departure from, the thing and
especially the duty, the principle, or the law that should
have been uppermost in a person's mind; ordinarily it
implies a morally reprehensible failure rather than one
resulting from carelessness and inattention or from mishap ⟨they would be answerable with their lives for any
further *dereliction* of duty—*Ainsworth*⟩ ⟨it revealed in
him . . . the indisputable signs of a certain *dereliction*
from some path of development his nature had commanded
him to follow—*Brooks*⟩
*Ana* *fault, failing: shortcoming, deficiency, *imperfection: *lack, want, absence, privation, dearth: negligence, laxness, slackness, remissness (see corresponding
adjectives at NEGLIGENT): indifference, unconcernedness or unconcern (see corresponding adjectives at
INDIFFERENT)

**faineant** adj indolent, slothful, *lazy
*Ana* supine, passive, *inactive, inert, idle: apathetic,
*impassive, phlegmatic: *lethargic, sluggish: languorous,
lackadaisical, *languid

**fair** adj 1 comely, lovely, *beautiful, pretty, bonny,
handsome, beauteous, pulchritudinous, good-looking
*Ana* delicate, dainty, exquisite (see CHOICE): charming,
attractive, enchanting (see under ATTRACT): pure, *chaste
*Ant* foul: ill-favored
2 **Fair, just, equitable, impartial, unbiased, dispassionate,
uncolored, objective** are comparable when they are applied
to judgments or to judges or to acts resulting from or
involving a judgment and mean free from undue or
improper influence. **Fair,** the most general term, implies
the disposition or the intention to regard other persons
or things without reference to one's own interests, feelings,
or prejudices, often even to the point of conceding every
reasonable claim of the weaker side or of giving oneself
or the stronger side no undue advantage ⟨a *fair* distribution of one's estate⟩ ⟨a *fair* decision by a judge⟩
⟨*fair* play⟩ ⟨when we consider how helpless a partridge
is . . . it does seem *fairer* that the gunner should have
but one chance at the bird—*Jefferies*⟩ ⟨I believe you
will find them a *fair* solution of this complicated and
difficult problem—*Roosevelt*⟩ **Just** implies no divergence from the standard or measure of what has been
determined or is accepted as right, true, or lawful and
dealings that are exactly in accordance with those de-
terminations, no matter what one's personal inclinations
or interests may be or what considerations in favor of
the person or thing judged may be adduced ⟨a *just* judge⟩
⟨some *juster* prince perhaps had . . . safe restored me to
my native land—*Pope*⟩ ⟨how much easier it is to be generous than *just*—*Junius*⟩ ⟨to divert interest from the poet
to the poetry . . . would conduce to a *juster* estimation
of actual poetry, good and bad—*T. S. Eliot*⟩ **Equitable** implies a freer and less rigid standard than *just*,
often the one which guides a court of equity as distinguished from a court of law and which provides relief
where rigid adherence to the law would make for unfairness ⟨he has an *equitable* claim to the property⟩ More
often the word implies fair and equal treatment of all
concerned ⟨a form of society which will provide for an
*equitable* distribution of . . . riches—*Krutch*⟩ ⟨it depended wholly on their individual characters whether
their terms of office were *equitable* or oppressive—
*Buchan*⟩ **Impartial** implies absence of favor for or
absence of prejudice against one person, party, or side
more than the other ⟨an *impartial* tribunal⟩ ⟨*impartial*

summing up of evidence⟩ ⟨the law provides for the examination by neutral, *impartial* psychiatric experts of all persons indicted for a capital offense—*Current Biog.*⟩ **Unbiased** expresses even more strongly the absence of all prejudice or prepossession and a disposition to be fair to all ⟨an *unbiased* history⟩ ⟨give an *unbiased* opinion⟩ ⟨presents an able, fair, and singularly *unbiased* picture of the Russian scene—*Marquand*⟩ **Dispassionate** implies freedom from the influence of passion or strong feeling, often also implying great temperateness or even coldness in judgment ⟨a *dispassionate* judgment of the young actor's abilities⟩ ⟨*dispassionate* men, precise in laboratories, with nothing to consider but the facts—*Ciardi*⟩ **Uncolored** (see also COLORLESS) implies freedom from influences (as personal feeling or a desire to embellish) that would affect the truth or accuracy of an account, a statement, or a judgment ⟨an *uncolored* story of a battle⟩ ⟨an *uncolored* record of one's experiences⟩ ⟨a statement of facts, *uncolored* by personal prejudice⟩ **Objective** implies a tendency to view events or phenomena as apart from oneself and therefore to be judged on purely factual bases and without reference to one's personal feelings, prejudices, opinions, or interests ⟨nor must we be content with a lazy skepticism, which regards *objective* truth as unattainable—*Russell*⟩ ⟨we shall be like ice when relating passions and adventures . . . we shall be . . . *objective* and impersonal—*Troy*⟩

*Ana* disinterested, detached (see INDIFFERENT): reasonable, *rational

*Ant* unfair —*Con* partial, prepossessed, biased, prejudiced (see corresponding nouns at PREDILECTION)

**3** average, *medium, middling, mediocre, second-rate, moderate, indifferent

*Ana* ordinary, *common

*Con* *good, right: *bad, poor, wrong

**fair** *n* exposition, *exhibition, show, exhibit

**faith 1** *belief, credence, credit

*Ana* assurance, conviction, *certainty, certitude: assenting *or* assent, acquiescence, agreement (see corresponding verbs at ASSENT)

*Ant* doubt —*Con* *uncertainty, skepticism, dubiety, dubiosity: *unbelief, disbelief, incredulity

**2** dependence, reliance, confidence, *trust

*Ana* assurance, certitude (see CERTAINTY)

*Con* incredulity, *unbelief, disbelief: mistrust, suspicion, *uncertainty, doubt: misgiving, *apprehension

**3** creed, *religion, persuasion, church, denomination, sect, cult, communion

*Ana* tenets, dogmas, doctrines (see singular nouns at DOCTRINE)

**faithful** *adj* Faithful, loyal, true, constant, staunch, steadfast, resolute are comparable when meaning firm in adherence to the person, the country, or the cause to whom or to which one is bound by duty or promise. **Faithful** in its most common sense implies firm and unswerving adherence to a person or thing to whom or to which one is united by some tie (as marriage, friendship, political allegiance, gratitude, or honor) or to the oath, pledge, or promise made when one has accepted a position, an office, or an obligation ⟨a *faithful* husband is *faithful* to his marriage vows⟩ ⟨a *faithful* public servant is *faithful* to his oath of office⟩ ⟨[Cleopatra] was *faithful* to the main policy of her life, the restoration of Egypt to the position which it had held under the first Ptolemies—*Buchan*⟩ The term is also used when only firm adherence to actuality or reality (as in representation or portrayal) is implied; it then comes close to *accurate* or *exact* in meaning ⟨the photograph is a *faithful* likeness⟩ ⟨the *faithful* rendering of the observed facts—*Encounter*⟩ ⟨a *faithful* description

of village life⟩ **Loyal** implies faithfulness to one's pledged word or continued allegiance to the leader, the country, the institution, or the principles to which one feels oneself morally bound; the term suggests not only adherence but resistance to being lured or persuaded away from that adherence ⟨most of the subjects remained *loyal* to their sovereign⟩ ⟨your wife, my lord; your true and *loyal* wife—*Shak.*⟩ ⟨"I've been *loyal* to Arch Gunnard for a long time now," Lonnie said, "I'd hate to haul off and leave him like that"—*Caldwell*⟩ **True** (see also REAL) is somewhat stronger than *loyal* and *faithful* in stressing a personal or emotional quality as well as steadiness in one's allegiance, devotion, or fidelity ⟨a *true* friend⟩ ⟨he is a New England poet, perhaps the New England poet, and reaps all the advantage there is in being *true* to a particular piece of earth—*Mark Van Doren*⟩ **Constant** also stresses firmness or steadiness in attachment, devotion, or allegiance, but it carries a weaker implication of strict adherence to one's vows, pledges, or obligations. Consequently it often implies a state of mind that is the opposite of fickleness rather than a course of action that is the opposite of unfaithfulness and disloyalty ⟨even Rochester, utterly bad and ignoble, was not only a poet and a wit but a loyal husband (*constant* if not faithful)—*Repplier*⟩ ⟨I never knew a pair of lovers more *constant* than those two—*Millay*⟩ **Staunch** carries far more strongly than *loyal* an implication of one's unwillingness to be turned aside from those to whom one owes allegiance or to whom one has pledged one's troth or from an institution (as a church or political party) to which by conviction one belongs. From its earliest and still current nautical sense of being watertight and sound it retains a suggestion of an inherent imperviousness to all influences that would weaken one's loyalty or steadiness in faith ⟨a *staunch* believer⟩ ⟨a *staunch* Republican⟩ ⟨*staunch* fidelity to law and order—*Montague*⟩ ⟨you, who from a girl have had a strong mind and a *staunch* heart—*Dickens*⟩ **Steadfast** so stresses unwavering or unswerving adherence that the term is applicable not only to persons but to things that maintain a steady course or an unchanging quality or character ⟨which hope we have as an anchor of the soul, both sure and *steadfast*—*Heb* 6:19⟩ ⟨the blue, the *steadfast*, the blazing summer sky—*Woolf*⟩ However its most usual application is to persons or their attachments ⟨therefore, my beloved brethren, be ye *steadfast*, unmoveable—*I Cor* 15:58⟩ ⟨if love . . . survives through all sorrow, and remains *steadfast* with us through all changes—*Thackeray*⟩ ⟨narrow of vision but *steadfast* to principles—*Repplier*⟩ **Resolute** implies steadfastness and, often, staunchness, but it throws the emphasis upon a determination which cannot be broken down as a quality of character and may suggest firm adherence to one's own purposes or ends rather than to those of others ⟨not . . . *resolute* and firm, but perverse and obstinate—*Burke*⟩ ⟨she sat there *resolute* and ready for responsibility—*Conrad*⟩ ⟨an earthquake in the midst of the proceedings terrified every prelate but the *resolute* Primate—*J. R. Green*⟩

*Ana* devoted, *loving, affectionate: tried, trustworthy, *reliable, dependable

*Ant* faithless —*Con* disloyal, false, perfidious, traitorous, treacherous (see FAITHLESS): fickle, *inconstant, unstable

**faithless,** false, disloyal, traitorous, treacherous, perfidious mean untrue to a person, an institution, or a cause that has a right to expect one's fidelity or allegiance. **Faithless** applies to a person, utterance, or act that implies a breach of a vow, a pledge, a sworn obligation, or allegiance. Although often used interchangeably with the

---

A colon (:) separates groups of words discriminated. An asterisk (*) indicates place of treatment of each group

strongest of the terms here discriminated, then implying a betrayal of a person or cause, it is also capable of implying untrustworthiness, unreliability, or loss or neglect of an opportunity to prove one's devotion or faith ⟨and hopeless, comfortless, I'll mourn a *faithless* woman's broken vow—*Burns*⟩ ⟨the remnant . . . have been abandoned by their *faithless* allies—*Shelley*⟩ ⟨he abandoned one wife and was *faithless* to another—*J. R. Green*⟩ **False** differs from *faithless* in its greater emphasis upon a failure to be true or constant in one's devotion or adherence than upon an actual breach of a vow, pledge, sworn promise, or obligation; however it may, like *faithless,* carry varying connotations with respect to the gravity or heinousness of that failure ⟨betrayed by a *false* friend⟩ ⟨never was Plantagenet *false* of his word —*Marlowe*⟩ ⟨we hope that we can give a reason for the faith that is in us without being *false* to the strictest obligations of intellectual honesty—*Inge*⟩ ⟨the conception of a lordly splendid destiny for the human race, to which we are *false* when we revert to wars and other atavistic follies—*Russell*⟩ **Disloyal** implies lack of faithfulness in thought, in words, or in actions to one (as a friend, superior, sovereign, party, or country) to whom loyalty is owed ⟨a *disloyal* subject⟩ ⟨good party people think such open-mindedness *disloyal;* but in politics there should be no loyalty except to the public good—*Shaw*⟩ ⟨assumed a tone in their correspondence which must have seemed often *disloyal,* and sometimes positively insulting, to the governor—*Motley*⟩ **Traitorous** implies either actual treason or a serious betrayal of trust or confidence ⟨a *traitorous* general⟩ ⟨a *traitorous* act⟩ ⟨*traitorous* breach of confidence⟩ ⟨by the *traitorous* connivance of the Bulgarian King and Government, advance parties of the German Air Force . . . were gradually admitted to Bulgaria—*Sir Winston Churchill*⟩ **Treacherous** is of wider application than *traitorous;* as used of persons it implies readiness, or a disposition, to betray trust or confidence ⟨a *treacherous* ally⟩ and as used of things it suggests aptness to lead on to peril or disaster by false or delusive appearances ⟨*treacherous* sands⟩ ⟨the *treacherous* ocean—*Shelley*⟩ ⟨up steep crags, and over *treacherous* morasses, he moved . . . easily—*Macaulay*⟩ **Perfidious** is a more contemptuous term than *treacherous;* it implies baseness or vileness as well as an incapacity for faithfulness in the person concerned ⟨*perfidious* violation of a treaty⟩ ⟨*perfidious* dealings⟩ ⟨Spain . . . to lavish her resources and her blood in furtherance of the designs of a *perfidious* ally—*Southey*⟩
*Ana* *inconstant, unstable, fickle, capricious: wavering, fluctuating (see SWING *vb*): *changeable, changeful
*Ant* faithful —*Con* loyal, true, staunch, steadfast, resolute, constant (see FAITHFUL)

**fake** *n* sham, humbug, counterfeit, *imposture, cheat, fraud, deceit, deception

**fake** *adj* *counterfeit, spurious, bogus, sham, pseudo, pinchbeck, phony
*Ana* fabricated, forged (see MAKE): framed, invented, concocted (see CONTRIVE)
*Con* *authentic, bona fide, genuine, veritable: true, *real, actual

**faker** *impostor, mountebank, charlatan, quack
*Ana* defrauder, cheater *or* cheat, swindler, cozener (see corresponding verbs at CHEAT)

**fall, drop, sink, slump, subside** are comparable when they mean to go or to let go downward freely. They are seldom close synonyms, however, because of various specific and essential implications that tend to separate and distinguish them. **Fall,** which in the relevant sense is intransitive, suggests a descent by the force of gravity

and implies a loss of support opposing gravity; in extended use *fall* may apply to whatever extends downward or gives an effect of going in a downward direction ⟨let a glass *fall* to the ground and shatter⟩ ⟨the supports gone, the structure *fell* in a heap⟩ ⟨the roof had *fallen* in on another speaker—*Cerf*⟩ ⟨hair *falling* over a woman's shoulders⟩ ⟨the birthrate *fell* over a 6-month period, then rose⟩ ⟨let *fall* a remark about the weather⟩ **Drop** may suggest a falling drop by drop or bit by bit, but usually it stresses a speed, directness, unexpectedness, or casualness in falling or allowing to fall ⟨*dropped* a coin into a pond⟩ ⟨*dropped* seeds into holes⟩ ⟨*dropping* to the ground at the sound of an air-raid warning⟩ ⟨*dropping* a hint of coming trouble⟩ ⟨income *dropped* during the slow winter season⟩ **Sink** fundamentally implies a gradual descending motion, especially into something, often to the point of total submersion ⟨the ship *sank* gradually into the placid sea⟩ ⟨the float on the fish line *sank* a moment, then bobbed furiously⟩ ⟨the thermometer *sank* to far below zero—*Carruthers*⟩ but in frequent somewhat extended use the stress is so strongly on a slow or gradual falling or descent that the notion of submergence is largely or wholly lost ⟨*sinking* to her knees from exhaustion⟩ ⟨the sun is *sinking* in the west⟩ ⟨his voice *sank* to a whisper⟩ **Slump** usually implies a sudden falling or collapsing (as of someone suddenly powerless or suddenly totally enervated) ⟨*slumping* to the ground unconscious⟩ ⟨*slumped* in his seat⟩ ⟨prices *slumped* badly in the winter⟩ ⟨when a bird falls asleep, it relaxes and *slumps* down until its body rests against the perch —*J. H. Baker*⟩ **Subside** suggests a gradual descent or return to a normal or usual position, action, or condition after an undue rising, expanding, or boiling up; often it can suggest a sinking below a normal or usual level ⟨a wind rising, then *subsiding*⟩ ⟨he lost a quarter of an hour waiting for the flood to *subside*—*Mary Austin*⟩ ⟨the bustle *subsides* and relative calm is resumed—*Amer. Guide Series: N. C.*⟩ ⟨the child's quick temper *subsided* into listlessness—*Repplier*⟩ ⟨after the boom prices *subsided* to a level far below normal⟩ ⟨their voices *subsided* to a whisper⟩
*Ana* *descend, dismount, alight: *droop, sag, flag, wilt: ebb, *abate, wane: *recede
*Ant* rise —*Con* *lift, raise, elevate, hoist: ascend, arise, mount, soar, tower (see RISE)

**fallacious** sophistical, casuistical (see under FALLACY)
*Ana* *irrational, unreasonable: *misleading, deceptive, delusive, delusory: equivocal, ambiguous (see OBSCURE)
*Ant* sound, valid

**fallacy,** sophism, sophistry, casuistry are comparable when meaning unsound and misleading reasoning or line of argument. The same distinctions in implications and connotations are distinguishable in the corresponding adjectives **fallacious, sophistical, casuistical. Fallacy** and **fallacious** in specific logical use imply an error or flaw in reasoning that vitiates an entire argument; thus, a syllogism in which one argues from some accidental character as though it were essential and necessary (as, The food you buy, you eat; you buy raw meat; therefore you eat raw meat) contains a *fallacy* or is *fallacious* ⟨the many *fallacies* that lurk in the generality and equivocal nature of the terms "inadequate representation"—*Burke*⟩ In more general use *fallacy* and *fallacious* apply to a conception, belief, or theory that is erroneous and logically untenable, whether it has been arrived at by reasoning or by conjecture or has been taken over from others ⟨the arguments of the *Federalist* are intended to prove the *fallacy* of these apprehensions— *John Marshall*⟩ ⟨the separatist *fallacy,* the belief that

---

*Ana* analogous words    *Ant* antonyms    *Con* contrasted words    See also explanatory notes facing page 1

what may be good for any must be good for all—*Hobson*⟩ ⟨parents . . . console themselves by the American *fallacy* that one can only be young once—*Elizabeth Bowen*⟩ ⟨the contention of some that the debt is not serious because we owe it to ourselves is *fallacious*—*Ogg & Ray*⟩ **Sophism** and **sophistry** and **sophistical** imply, as *fallacy* and *fallacious* do not necessarily imply, either the intent to mislead or deceive by fallacious arguments or indifference to the correctness of one's reasoning provided one's words carry conviction; the terms, therefore, often connote confusingly subtle, equivocal, or specious reasoning. *Sophism*, however, applies usually to a specific argument of this character, *sophistry* often to the type of reasoning employing sophisms ⟨skilled to plead, with a superficial but plausible set of *sophisms*, in favor of . . . contempt of virtue—*Shelley*⟩ ⟨the juggle of *sophistry*—*Coleridge*⟩ ⟨this evil is . . . inexcusable by any *sophistry* that the cleverest landlord can devise—*Shaw*⟩ ⟨Rousseau does not often indulge in such an unblushing *sophism*—*Babbitt*⟩ ⟨the *sophistical* plea that matter is more important than manner—*Montague*⟩ **Casuistry** and **casuistical** imply sophistry only in their extended senses. In their basic senses both have reference to the science that deals with cases of conscience, or the determination of what is right and wrong in particular cases where there is justifiable uncertainty ⟨we now have to lay the foundation of a new *casuistry,* no longer theological and Christian, but naturalistic and scientific—*Ellis*⟩ In their extended use both terms usually imply sophistical and often tortuous reasoning in reference to moral, theological, and legal problems ⟨those who hold that a lie is always wrong have to supplement this view by a great deal of *casuistry*—*Russell*⟩ ⟨*casuistical* hairsplitting⟩

**false** *adj* **1** **False, wrong** mean not in conformity with what is true or right. **False** in all of its senses is colored by its original implication of deceit; the implication of deceiving or of being deceived is strong when the term implies a contrariety between what is said, thought, or concluded and the facts or reality ⟨*false* statements⟩ ⟨thou shalt not bear *false* witness against thy neighbor —*Exod 20:16*⟩ ⟨whether it is a genuine insight into the workings of his own mind or only a *false* explanation of them—*Day Lewis*⟩ ⟨you can take a chessboard as black squares on a white ground, or as white squares on a black ground, and neither conception is a *false* one—*James*⟩ An intent to deceive or a deceptive appearance is implied when the term connotes an opposition to what is real or genuine or authentic ⟨*false* tears⟩ ⟨*false* pearls⟩ ⟨a box with a *false* bottom⟩ ⟨a *false* arch is an architectural member which simulates an arch in appearance but does not have the structure or serve the function of a true arch⟩ The term is applied in vernacular names of plants to a kind related to, resembling, or having properties similar to another kind that commonly bears the unqualified vernacular ⟨the pinkster flower is sometimes called *false* honeysuckle⟩ Even when the word stresses faithlessness (see FAITHLESS) there is usually a hint of a deceptive appearance of faithfulness or loyalty or of self-deception in one's failure to be true ⟨so far as outward appearances went, one could not believe him to be a *false* friend⟩ Only in the sense of incorrect or erroneous ⟨a *false* note⟩ ⟨a *false* policy⟩ is this implication obscured, though there is often a suggestion of being deceived into believing that the thing so described is true or right. **Wrong,** on the other hand, is colored in all of its senses by its original implication of wryness or crookedness; in general it implies a turning from the standard of what is true, right (especially morally right), or correct to its

reverse. In comparison with *false, wrong* is simple and forthright in its meaning; thus, a *wrong* conception is one that is the reverse of the truth, but a *false* conception is not only *wrong* but the result of one's being deceived or of one's intent to deceive; a *wrong* answer to a question is merely an erroneous answer, but a *false* answer to a question is one that is both erroneous and lying; *wrong* principles of conduct are the reverse of ethically right principles, but *false* principles of conduct are not only wrong but are bound to lead astray those who accept them ⟨give a person *wrong* advice through bad judgment⟩ ⟨believed that a lie is always *wrong*⟩ ⟨there is something *wrong* about his appearance⟩ ⟨there is something *false* in his courtesy⟩ ⟨he may be *wrong* in his opinions, but he is not *false* to his country in trying to impress them upon others⟩ ⟨the book is a chic little piece . . . often amusing, always arch and clever, and usually *wrong*—*Farrelly*⟩ ⟨the man who, having out of sheer ignorance eaten the *wrong* end of his asparagus, was thenceforce compelled to declare that he preferred that end—*Ellis*⟩
*Ana* *misleading, deceptive, delusive, delusory: fallacious, sophistical (see under FALLACY): mendacious, deceitful, *dishonest, untruthful: factitious (see ARTIFICIAL)
*Ant* true  —*Con* *real, actual: veritable, *authentic, genuine, bona fide: veracious, truthful (see corresponding nouns at TRUTH)
**2** perfidious, disloyal, traitorous, treacherous, *faithless
*Ana* recreant, apostate, renegade, backsliding (see corresponding nouns at RENEGADE): *inconstant, unstable: *crooked, devious
*Ant* true  —*Con* staunch, steadfast, loyal, *faithful, constant, resolute
**falsehood** untruth, *lie, fib, misrepresentation, story
*Ant* truth (*in concrete sense*)
**falsify** *misrepresent, belie, garble
*Ana* *change, alter, modify, vary: distort, contort, warp (see DEFORM): pervert, corrupt (see DEBASE): contradict, contravene, traverse, *deny
**falter** *vb* waver, vacillate, *hesitate
*Ana* flinch, blench, *recoil, quail, shrink: fluctuate, oscillate, *swing: *shake, tremble, quake, shudder
*Con* *persevere, persist: resolve, determine, *decide
**fame** *n* **Fame, renown, honor, glory, celebrity, reputation, repute, notoriety, éclat** are comparable when they mean the character or state of being widely known by name for one's deeds and, often, one's achievements. **Fame** is the most inclusive and in some ways the least explicit of these terms, for it may be used in place of any of the others, but it gives no clear suggestion of how far the knowledge of one's name extends, of the reasons for it, or of the creditableness of those reasons; although the term often implies longevity and usually implies a cause or causes to one's credit, it does not invariably carry these favorable implications ⟨acquired some *fame* for his inventions⟩ ⟨his *fame* was short-lived⟩ ⟨*fame* is the spur that the clear spirit doth raise . . . to scorn delights and live laborious days—*Milton*⟩ ⟨*fame* : . . that second life in others' breath—*Pope*⟩ ⟨popularity is neither *fame* nor greatness—*Hazlitt*⟩ ⟨*fame* is the thirst of youth—*Byron*⟩ ⟨I had won a great notoriety and perhaps even a passing *fame*—*Maugham*⟩ **Renown** implies widespread fame and widespread acclamation for great achievements (as in war, in government, in science, or in art) ⟨those other two equalled with me in fate, so were I equalled with them in *renown*—*Milton*⟩ ⟨Niten's paintings are prized, but it is as a swordsman that he won supreme *renown*—*Binyon*⟩ ⟨the *renown* of *Walden* has grown; schools and colleges have made it required reading—*Frank*⟩ ⟨he once achieved a singular

---

A colon (:) separates groups of words discriminated. An asterisk (*) indicates place of treatment of each group.

mechanical triumph that won him wide *renown—Anderson*⟩ **Honor** (see also HONOR 2, HONESTY) implies a measure of fame (as in a section, a country, a continent, or the civilized world), but it also implies that the knowledge of one's achievements has earned for one esteem or reverence ⟨length of days is in her right hand; and in her left hand riches and *honor—Prov* 3:16⟩ ⟨one must learn to give *honor* where *honor* is due, to bow down . . . before all spirits that are noble—*Benson*⟩ **Glory** usually suggests renown, but more especially it implies a position where attention is fixed on one's brilliancy of achievement and the accompaniment of enthusiastic praise or of high honor ⟨the paths of *glory* lead but to the grave—*Gray*⟩ ⟨to be recognized . . . as a master . . . in one's own line of intellectual or spiritual activity, is indeed *glory—Arnold*⟩ ⟨no keener hunter after *glory* breathes. He loves it in his knights more than himself; they prove to him his work—*Tennyson*⟩ **Celebrity** is often used in place of *fame* when the widespread laudation of one's name and accomplishments in one's own time is implied; the term usually carries a stronger implication of famousness and of popularity than it does of deep-seated or long-lived admiration and esteem ⟨the lonely precursor of German philosophy, he still shines when the light of his successors is fading away; they had *celebrity*, Spinoza has *fame—Arnold*⟩ ⟨made a sensational debut as a pianist at the age of six . . . but by adolescence her *celebrity* was finished—*Tunley*⟩ **Reputation** often denotes nothing more than the character of a person or place, not necessarily as it really is but as it is conceived to be by those who know of him or of it ⟨he has a good *reputation* in the community⟩ ⟨it is a shame to injure a man's *reputation*⟩ but in the sense in which it is here particularly considered, the term implies a measure of fame, typically for creditable reasons ⟨his *reputation* for wit was countrywide⟩ ⟨a man of doubtful *reputation*⟩ ⟨a painter of growing *reputation*⟩ ⟨the purest treasure mortal times afford is spotless *reputation—Shak.*⟩ ⟨the fame (*reputation* is too chilly a word) of Arnold J. Toynbee is a phenomenon in itself worth noting—*Brogan*⟩ **Repute** is sometimes used interchangeably with *reputation* in either sense ⟨only a general of *repute* could get recruits—*Buchan*⟩ More often, however, *repute* suggests a relation that is closer to *honor* than to *fame*, and denotes rather the degree of esteem accorded to a person or thing than the measure of fame it acquires ⟨the book has no little *repute* among the best critics⟩ ⟨his work is held in high *repute*⟩ ⟨he won a great deal of *repute* for his bravery⟩ **Notoriety** implies public knowledge of a person or deed; it usually suggests a meretricious fame and imputes sensationalism to the person or thing that wins such repute ⟨he achieved *notoriety* as the author of a most salacious novel⟩ ⟨that brilliant, extravagant, careless Reverend Doctor Dodd who acquired some fame and much *notoriety* as an eloquent preacher—*Ellis*⟩ **Éclat** may be used in place of *renown* or of *notoriety*. To either idea is added the connotation of great brilliancy or display, but when the basic meaning is renown, illustriousness is especially suggested ⟨consider what luster and *éclat* it will give you . . . to be the best scholar, of a gentleman, in England—*Chesterfield*⟩ and when it is notoriety, flashiness or ostentation is usually implied ⟨his success in such a pursuit would give a ridiculous *éclat* to the whole affair—*Scott*⟩

*Ana* acclaim, acclamation, *applause: recognizing *or* recognition, acknowledgment (see corresponding verbs at ACKNOWLEDGE): eminence, illustriousness (see corresponding adjectives at FAMOUS)

*Ant* infamy: obscurity —*Con* ignominy, obloquy, *disgrace, dishonor, odium, opprobrium, disrepute, shame

**famed** *famous, renowned, celebrated, eminent, illustrious
*Ant* obscure

**familiar** 1 Familiar, intimate, close, confidential, chummy, thick are comparable when meaning near to one another because of constant or frequent association, shared interests and activities, or common sympathies, or, when applied to words or acts, indicative of such nearness. **Familiar** suggests relations or manifestations characteristic of or similar to those of a family, where long-continued intercourse makes for freedom, informality, ease of address, and the taking of liberties; consequently *familiar* may apply to the relations, words, and acts of persons actually in such a situation and to the attitude or the style of speaking or writing of persons who assume the freedom and ease of address of those who are ⟨*familiar* essays⟩ ⟨time and intercourse have made us *familiar—Johnson*⟩ ⟨a simpler and more *familiar* speech, able to express subtleties or audacities that before seemed inexpressible—*Ellis*⟩ ⟨the *familiar*, if not rude, tone in which people addressed her—*Hawthorne*⟩ ⟨she was a fearless and *familiar* little thing, who asked disconcerting questions—*Wharton*⟩ **Intimate** suggests relations characteristic of those who are in close contact with one another (as through ties of blood, of friendship, or of common interests or aspirations) and who have opened their hearts or their minds to such a degree that they deeply know and understand one another ⟨the *intimate* political relation subsisting between the president of the United States and the heads of departments, necessarily renders any legal investigation of the acts of one of those high officers peculiarly . . . delicate—*John Marshall*⟩ ⟨they establish and maintain . . . more *intimate* and confiding relations with us—*J. R. Lowell*⟩ ⟨though Farfrae must have so far forgiven him as to have no objection to . . . him as a father-in-law, *intimate* they could never be—*Hardy*⟩ **Intimate** may also apply to a connection between a person and a thing, especially something he says, does, wears, or uses; it then implies a very close relation between that thing and his inmost thoughts or feelings or his life in the privacy of his home ⟨official receptions were few, but small, *intimate* teas were frequent in the governor's home⟩ ⟨the indecency of publishing *intimate* letters which were never written to be published—*Ellis*⟩ ⟨her eyes, lively, laughing, *intimate*, nearly always a little mocking—*Cather*⟩ ⟨a shirt-sleeved populace moved . . . with the *intimate* abandon of boarders going down the passage to the bathroom—*Wharton*⟩ As applied directly or indirectly to knowledge, *intimate* differs from *familiar* not only in idiom but also in implying not merely acquaintance but close or deep study ⟨he has an *intimate* knowledge of the situation⟩ ⟨he is *familiar* with the facts pertaining to the situation⟩ ⟨he is *familiar* with the poem in question⟩ ⟨he has gained, through long study, an *intimate* knowledge of the poem⟩ **Close** is often used in place of *intimate* when one wishes to imply an attachment drawing persons together in such a way as to suggest the exclusion of others or a very strong bond of affection between them ⟨*close* friends⟩ ⟨a *close* friendship⟩ ⟨seeing them so tender and so *close—Tennyson*⟩ ⟨too *close* to Theodore Roosevelt ever to receive the confidence of Woodrow Wilson—*Paxson*⟩ **Confidential** implies a relationship based upon mutual trust or confidence or upon a willingness to confide intimate matters (as one's hopes, thoughts, or feelings) ⟨the growing harmony and *confidential* friendship which daily manifest themselves between their Majesties—*Chatham*⟩ ⟨he slipped his arm through his father's with a *confidential* pressure—*Wharton*⟩ **Chummy** and *thick* are less formal terms and usually convey some degree of contempt, derision, or envy of a close association. **Chummy** suggests an easy informal intimacy ⟨it is an unprecedented thing, I take it, for a captain to be *chummy* with the cook—*London*⟩ **Thick** stresses constant association more than the strength of the attachment ⟨the two former enemies are now as *thick* as thieves⟩ but often it carries a sinister suggestion ⟨a friend of gangsters and rumrunners, very *thick* with people like Jake the Barber—*Bellow*⟩

*Ana* friendly, neighborly, *amicable: sociable, cordial, genial, affable, *gracious: easy, *comfortable, cozy, snug: intrusive, obtrusive, officious, *impertinent

*Ant* aloof —*Con* *indifferent, detached, unconcerned, incurious: formal, conventional, ceremonious, *ceremonial 2 ordinary, *common, popular, vulgar

*Ana* *usual, wonted, accustomed, customary, habitual

*Ant* unfamiliar: strange —*Con* novel, newfangled, new-fashioned, *new: rare, uncommon, *infrequent: fantastic, chimerical (see IMAGINARY)

**famous, famed, renowned, celebrated, eminent, illustrious** are comparable when meaning known far and wide among men. **Famous** and **famed** apply chiefly to men, events, and things that are much talked of or are widely or popularly known throughout a section, a country, a continent, or a cultural tradition; they also imply good repute or a favorable reputation. Normally these terms are applied without qualification only to those persons or things that are still so known or that were so known in the time under consideration ⟨the once *famous* poems of Owen Meredith⟩ ⟨a *famous* American aviator⟩ ⟨some of our most *famous* physicians have had to struggle pitiably against insufficient means until they were forty or fifty—*Shaw*⟩ ⟨time has spiraled them from rebellion to eminence. They are respectably *famous,* and the poet Edith even fashionable—*W. T. Scott*⟩ ⟨a corpulent, jolly fellow, *famed* for humor—*Hawthorne*⟩ **Renowned** implies more glory or honor and more widespread acclamation than either *famous* or *famed*; it is, however, often employed as a stronger or more emphatic term than *famous* with little actual difference in meaning except for a suggestion of greater longevity of fame ⟨royal kings . . . *renowned* for their deeds . . . for Christian service and true chivalry—*Shak.*⟩ ⟨those far-*renowned* brides of ancient song—*Tennyson*⟩ **Celebrated** stresses reception of popular or public notice or attention and frequent mention, especially in print; it may also suggest public admiration or popular honor ⟨the *celebrated* kidnapping of Charley Ross⟩ ⟨the most *celebrated* of the cases pending before the Supreme Court⟩ ⟨Benjamin Franklin's *celebrated* kite⟩ ⟨the greatest, but the least *celebrated*, general in the war⟩ ⟨it is characteristic that in this whole "Notebook" Maugham seldom mentions any of his *celebrated* friends—*Behrman*⟩ **Eminent** implies conspicuousness for outstanding qualities; it is applicable chiefly to persons or things that are recognized as topping others of their kind ⟨the age produced no *eminent* writers⟩ ⟨many *eminent* men of science have been bad mathematicians—*Russell*⟩ ⟨*eminent* manifestations of this magical power of poetry are very rare and very precious—*Arnold*⟩ **Illustrious** carries a stronger implication of renown than *eminent;* it also imputes to the thing so described a gloriousness or splendor that increases its prestige or influence ⟨*illustrious* deeds of great heroes⟩ ⟨his right noble mind, *illustrious* virtue—*Shak.*⟩ ⟨boast the pure blood of an *illustrious* race—*Pope*⟩

*Ant* obscure

**fanatic** *n* bigot, *enthusiast, zealot

**fanciful** *imaginary, visionary, fantastic, chimerical, quixotic

*Ana* *fictitious, fabulous, mythical, apocryphal, legendary: bizarre, grotesque, *fantastic: preposterous, absurd (see FOOLISH): *false, wrong

*Ant* realistic —*Con* matter-of-fact, *prosaic: truthful, veracious (see corresponding nouns at TRUTH)

**fancy** *n* 1 *caprice, freak, whim, whimsy, conceit, vagary, crotchet

2 *imagination, fantasy

*Ant* experience

3 **Fancy, fantasy, phantasy, phantasm, vision, dream, daydream, nightmare** are comparable when they denote a vivid idea or image, or a series of such ideas or images, present in the mind but having no concrete or objective reality. **Fancy** (see also IMAGINATION) is applicable to anything which is conceived by the imagination, whether it recombines the elements of reality or is pure invention ⟨surely this great chamber . . . did not exist at all but as a gigantic *fancy* of his own—*Galsworthy*⟩ ⟨the status of archaeological fact and *fancy* in the world today—*W. W. Taylor*⟩ **Fantasy** applies to a fancy and especially to an organized series of fancies (as one presented in art) that is the product of an unrestrained imagination freed from the bonds of actuality ⟨Shakespeare's *Midsummer Night's Dream* is a pure *fantasy*⟩ ⟨a thousand *fantasies* begin to throng into my memory, of calling shapes, and beckoning shadows dire, and airy tongues that syllable men's names —*Milton*⟩ **Phantasy,** though sometimes used in place of *fantasy,* both as the power of free inventive imagination and as a product of that power, may apply particularly to the image-making power of the mind, whether the image is the result of sense perception or of the imagination, or to a product of that power and then may be strongly antonymous to *truth* and *reality* ⟨probably in his life, certainly in his poetry, there is no sharp boundary between *phantasy* and reality—*Canby*⟩ ⟨*phantasies* created by the reading of *Kubla Khan*⟩ **Phantasm** may be applied either to a phantasy, the mental image ⟨figures . . . of which the description had produced in you no *phantasm*—*Taylor*⟩ or to a fantasy, especially to one that is hallucinatory ⟨the *phantasms* of a disordered mind⟩ **Vision** often implies an imagining, but it as frequently implies a seeing or a revelation. Specifically, however, the term is applied to something which the mind perceives as clearly or concretely as if revealed to it by a supernatural or mysterious power (see REVELATION), or as if viewed by a kind of spiritual sight or intuition, or as if seen in a dream; *vision* therefore often suggests a sight of something that is actually spiritual in essence or is beyond the range or power of the eyes or mind to grasp as a whole ⟨a whole life . . . devoted to the patient pursuit of a single *vision* seen in youth—*Eliot*⟩ ⟨each word's . . . power of touching springs in the mind and of initiating *visions*—*Montague*⟩ ⟨our *vision* of world law and some sort of worldwide law-enforcement agency—*Sat. Review*⟩ **Dream** is the general term for the ideas or images present to the mind in sleep ⟨thus have I had thee, as a *dream* doth flatter, in sleep a king, but waking no such matter—*Shak.*⟩ ⟨your old men shall dream *dreams,* your young men shall see visions—*Joel* 2:28⟩ In extended use *dream,* like **daydream,** suggests vague or idle, commonly happy, imaginings of future events or of nonexistent things ⟨childhood's sunny *dream*—*Shelley*⟩ ⟨a busy person has no time for *daydreams*⟩ **Nightmare** applies to a frightful and oppressive dream which occurs in sleep or, by extension, to a vision or, sometimes, an actual experience which inspires terror or which cannot easily be shaken off ⟨how many of our daydreams would darken into *nightmares,* were there a danger of their coming true! —*L. P. Smith*⟩

*Ana* figment, fabrication, fable, *fiction: notion, conception, *idea, concept

*Ant* reality (*in concrete sense*)

**fancy** *vb* 1 dote, *like, love, enjoy, relish

---

A colon (:) separates groups of words discriminated. An asterisk (*) indicates place of treatment of each group.

*Ana* *approve, endorse, sanction
*Con* *disapprove, deprecate
2 imagine, conceive, envisage, envision, realize, *think
*Ana* *conjecture, surmise, guess
**fantastic** 1 chimerical, visionary, fanciful, *imaginary, quixotic
*Ana* extravagant, extreme (see EXCESSIVE): incredible, unbelievable, implausible (see affirmative adjectives at PLAUSIBLE): preposterous, absurd (see FOOLISH): *irrational, unreasonable: delusory, delusive, deceptive, *misleading
*Con* familiar, ordinary, *common: *usual, customary
2 Fantastic, bizarre, grotesque, antic are comparable when they describe works of art, effects produced by nature or art, ideas, or behavior and mean conceived or made, or seemingly conceived or made, without reference to reality, truth, or common sense. Fantastic stresses the exercise of unrestrained imagination or unlicensed fancy. It therefore variously connotes absurd extravagance in conception, remoteness from reality, or merely ingenuity in devising ⟨*fantastic* figures, with bulbous heads, the circumference of a bushel, grinned enormously in his face—*Hawthorne*⟩ ⟨one need not have a very *fantastic* imagination to see spirits there—*Gray*⟩ ⟨he wove *fantastic* stories of the hunting bridle—*Kipling*⟩ Bizarre is applied to what is unduly, often sensationally, strange or queer; it suggests the use of violent contrasts (as in color, in sound, or in emotional effects) or of strikingly incongruous combinations (as of the tragic and the comic or of the horrible and the tender) ⟨it was *bizarre* in the extreme. It was as if a judge, wearing the black cap, had suddenly put out his tongue at the condemned—*Powys*⟩ ⟨temple sculpture became *bizarre*—rearing monsters, fiery horses, great pillared halls teeming with sculptures—*Atlantic*⟩ Grotesque emphasizes distortion of the natural to the point either of comic absurdity or of aesthetically effective ugliness. Technically the word is applied to a type of painting or sculpture of ancient Roman origin which serves a decorative rather than a pictorial purpose and which employs natural details (as animals, men, flowers, and foliage) and conventional designs and figures (as scrolls, garlands, and satyrs) in unnatural combinations or to the comic exaggerations or distortions of human and animal figures in the sculptured decorations and especially the gargoyles of Gothic architecture. It is from the latter association that the adjective in general use derives its leading implications of ridiculous ugliness or ludicrous caricature ⟨the camel was crouching . . . with his *grotesque* head waving about in dumb protest to the blows—*Hoffman*⟩ ⟨she differed from other comedians. There was nothing about her of the *grotesque;* none of her comic appeal was due to exaggeration—*T. S. Eliot*⟩ Sometimes the word suggests an absurdly irrational combination of incompatibles ⟨the attempts . . . to dress up the Labour movement as a return to the Palestinian Gospel, are little short of *grotesque*—*Inge*⟩ Antic, chiefly in literary use, though once indistinguishable from *grotesque*, has come to stress ludicrousness or buffoonery more than unnaturalness or irrationality ⟨he came running to me . . . making a many *antic* gesture—*Defoe*⟩ ⟨an outrageously funny novel . . . basically the product of an *antic* imagination—*Gibbs*⟩ ⟨irrepressibly *antic* and unabashedly outspoken, he affects a brassy impudence that many of his staid associates appear to find refreshing—*Kahn*⟩
*Ana* imagined, fancied, conceived (see THINK): externalized, objectified (see REALIZE): ingenious, adroit, *clever: eccentric, erratic, singular, *strange, odd, queer
**fantasy** 1 fancy, *imagination
*Ana* imagining, fancying, conceiving, envisioning (see

THINK): externalizing, objectifying (see REALIZE)
2 *fancy, phantasy, phantasm, vision, dream, daydream, nightmare
*Ana* *delusion, illusion, hallucination: vagary, *caprice, whimsy, whim, freak, fancy: grotesquerie, bizarrerie (see corresponding adjectives at FANTASTIC)
**far, faraway, far-off** *distant, remote, removed
*Ant* near, nigh, nearly
**farcical** comical, comic, ludicrous, *laughable, ridiculous, risible, droll, funny
**farfetched** *forced, labored, strained
*Ana* *fantastic, grotesque, bizarre: eccentric, erratic, *strange, queer
*Con* natural, normal (see REGULAR): *spontaneous, impulsive: *usual, wonted, accustomed
**farming** *agriculture, husbandry
**farther, further** are often used without distinction though originally different words, **farther** being the comparative of *far* and **further**, in its adverbial form (as an adjective, it is without a positive), being the comparative of *fore* or *forth*. At any rate *farther* basically implies a greater distance from a given point in space or sometimes in time; *further* implies onwardness or an advance or an addition (as in movement or progression) not only in space but in time, quantity, or degree ⟨the *farther* tree is blocking my view⟩ ⟨Germany is *farther* from the United States than England⟩ ⟨move *farther* away from the city⟩ ⟨no *further* steps are necessary⟩ ⟨the incident happened *farther* back than I can remember⟩ ⟨circumstances such as the present . . . render *further* reserve unnecessary—*Shaw*⟩ In spite of this fundamental distinction in meaning, there are many occasions where it is difficult to make a choice, since the ideas of distance from a given point and of advance in movement may both be implied. In such cases either word may be used ⟨to go *further* and fare worse—*Old Proverb*⟩ ⟨my ponies are tired, and I have *further* to go—*Hardy*⟩ ⟨as we climb higher, we can see *further*—*Inge*⟩ ⟨"What! . . . was Pat ever in France?" "Indeed he was," cries mine host; and Pat adds, "Ay, and *farther*—*Lover*⟩
**fascinate** charm, bewitch, enchant, captivate, allure, *attract
*Ana* influence, impress, *affect, sway, strike, touch: delight, rejoice, gladden, *please
**fascinating** charming, bewitching, enchanting, captivating, alluring, attractive (see under ATTRACT)
*Ana* *delightful, delectable: luring, enticing, seducing *or* seductive, tempting (see corresponding verbs at LURE)
*Con* *repugnant, repellent, distasteful, obnoxious, abhorrent
**fashion** *n* 1 manner, way, *method, mode, system
*Ana* practice, *habit, custom, usage, wont
2 Fashion, style, mode, vogue, fad, rage, craze, dernier cri, cry are comparable when denoting a way of dressing, of furnishing and decorating rooms, of dancing, or of behaving that is generally accepted at a given time by those who wish to follow the trend or to be regarded as up-to-date. Fashion is thought of in general as the current conventional usage or custom which is determined by polite society or by those who are regarded as leaders especially in the social, the intellectual, the literary, or the artistic world ⟨the dictates of *fashion*⟩ ⟨follow the *fashion*⟩ ⟨nowhere . . . is *fashion* so exacting, not only in dress and demeanor, but in plastic art itself—*Brownell*⟩ ⟨took the view . . . that externals count for much, since they sway opinion, and opinion sways *fashion*, and *fashion* is reflected in conduct—*Buchan*⟩ Fashion is also applicable to the particular thing (as costume, furniture, behavior, or subject in literature or art) which is dictated by fashion ⟨this poem . . . provided . . . the fake-progressive

with a new *fashion—Day Lewis*⟩ ⟨it is the latest *fashion* in hats⟩ **Style,** in this as in its other senses (see LANGUAGE 2, NAME) implies a manner or way that is distinctive; though often interchangeable with *fashion* ⟨a dress in the latest *style*⟩ it particularly suggests the elegant or distinguished way of dressing, furnishing, and living characteristic of those who have wealth and taste ⟨live in *style*⟩ ⟨judging from the *style* they keep, they are both wealthy and cultivated⟩ ⟨their clothes, their homes, their tables, their cars have that somewhat elusive quality called *style*⟩ ⟨an authentic opera queen, temperamental, colorful, obstreperous, who considered traveling in *style* as important as singing in tune—*Kupferberg*⟩ **Mode,** especially in the phrase "*the mode*," suggests the peak of fashion or the fashion of the moment among those who cultivate elegance in dress, behavior, and interests ⟨the easy, apathetic graces of the man of the *mode—Macaulay*⟩ ⟨that summer Russian refugees were greatly the *mode—Rose Macaulay*⟩ ⟨sleeping on top of television sets is the *mode* of the day for cats—*New Yorker*⟩ **Vogue** stresses the prevalence or wide acceptance of the fashion and its obvious popularity ⟨the slender, undeveloped figure then very much in *vogue—Cather*⟩ ⟨the word *morale*, in italics, had a great *vogue* at the time of the War—*Montague*⟩ ⟨yet I am told that the *vogue* of the sermon is passing—*Quiller-Couch*⟩ *Fad, rage, craze, dernier cri* all apply to an extremely short-lived fashion. **Fad** stresses caprice in taking up and in dropping ⟨many people are inclined to see in the popularity of this new subject a mere university *fad—Babbitt*⟩ ⟨a fashion is not in France the mere "*fad*" it is in England and with us—*Brownell*⟩ **Rage** and **craze** imply short-lived and often markedly senseless enthusiasm ⟨Mr. Prufrock fitted in very well with his wife's social circle, and was quite the *rage—Day Lewis*⟩ ⟨dog racing had begun as an enthusiasm, worked through to being a *craze*, and ended as being a habit—*Westerby*⟩ **Dernier cri** or its equivalent **cry** (especially in "*all the cry*") applies to whatever is the very latest thing in fashion ⟨a woman whose clothes are always the *denier cri*⟩ ⟨open-toed shoes were all the *cry* that summer⟩

*Ana* trend, drift, *tendency: convention, *form, usage

**fashion** *vb* form, shape, *make, fabricate, manufacture, forge

*Ana* devise, contrive (see corresponding nouns at DEVICE): design, plan, plot (see under PLAN *n*): produce, turn out (see BEAR)

**fashionable** *stylish, modish, smart, chic, dashing

*Ant* unfashionable: old-fashioned

**fast, rapid, swift, fleet, quick, speedy, hasty, expeditious** mean moving, proceeding, or acting with great celerity. *Fast* and *rapid* are often used without distinction; but **fast** frequently applies to the moving object and emphasizes the way in which it covers ground, whereas **rapid** is apt to characterize the movement itself and often to suggest its astonishing rate of speed ⟨a *fast* horse⟩ ⟨a *fast* train⟩ ⟨a *fast* boat⟩ ⟨a *rapid* current⟩ ⟨a *rapid* gait⟩ ⟨*rapid* progress⟩ ⟨a *fast* worker⟩ ⟨*rapid* work⟩ **Swift** suggests great rapidity, frequently coupled with ease or facility of movement ⟨fleeter than arrows, bullets, wind, thought, *swifter* things—*Shak.*⟩ ⟨more *swift* than swallow shears the liquid sky—*Spenser*⟩ ⟨the flight of his imagination is very *swift;* the following of it often a breathless business—*Day Lewis*⟩ **Fleet,** which is chiefly in poetic or nimble use, connotes lightness or nimbleness as well as extreme fastness or rapidity ⟨antelope as *fleet* of foot⟩ ⟨how the *fleet* creature would fly before the wind—*Melville*⟩ **Quick** (see also QUICK 2) applies especially to something that happens promptly or occupies

but little time; it suggests alacrity or celerity, especially in action, rather than velocity of movement ⟨*quick* thinking saved him from the trap⟩ ⟨thy drugs are *quick*. Thus with a kiss I die—*Shak.*⟩ ⟨slow to resolve, but in performance *quick—Dryden*⟩ **Speedy,** when applied to persons or their motions or activities, implies extreme quickness and often hurry or haste; when applied to things and their motion or movement, it also often suggests great velocity; in general, it is opposed to *dilatory* ⟨no mode sufficiently *speedy* of obtaining money had ever occurred to me—*De Quincey*⟩ ⟨hope for their *speedy* return⟩ ⟨be *speedy*, darkness—*Keats*⟩ ⟨make *speediest* preparation for the journey!—*Shelley*⟩ **Hasty** suggests hurry or precipitousness rather than speed and often connotes the resulting confusion, disorder, or inattention ⟨gobbled down a *hasty* meal⟩ ⟨we must, this time, have plans ready—instead of waiting to do a *hasty*, inefficient, and ill-considered job at the last moment—*Roosevelt*⟩ **Expeditious** adds to *quick* or *speedy* the implication of efficiency; it therefore implies the absence of waste, bungling, and undue haste ⟨an *expeditious* movement of troops⟩ ⟨there is no *expeditious* road to pack and label men for God, and save them by the barrel load—*Thompson*⟩

*Ant* slow

**fasten, fix, attach, affix** mean to make something stay firmly in place or in an assigned place. All but *fix* (and that sometimes) imply a uniting or joining of one thing to another or of two things together. **Fasten** implies an attempt to keep a thing from moving by uniting it (as by tying, binding, nailing, or cementing) to something else or by restraining it by means of some mechanical device (as a lock, a screw, or a hook and eye) ⟨*fasten* a horse to a post⟩ ⟨*fasten* down the lid of a box⟩ ⟨*fasten* a calendar to a wall⟩ ⟨*fasten* a door⟩ ⟨*fasten* a dress in the back⟩ **Fix** implies an attempt to keep something from falling down or from losing hold; it suggests such operations as driving in or implanting deeply, usually with care and accuracy ⟨*fix* a stake in the ground⟩ ⟨unless their roots are deeply *fixed*, plants will not be strong⟩ It is more common in its extended than in its basic sense, but the implications remain the same ⟨*fix* a face in one's memory⟩ ⟨*fix* facts in one's mind⟩ ⟨*fix* a color in a fabric by use of a mordant⟩ In some phrases where *fasten* and *fix* are used interchangeably there may be a distinction in meaning which is subtle but justified; thus, to *fix* one's affections on someone connotes concentration and fidelity while to *fasten* one's affections on someone may, and often does, suggest covetousness or an attempt to hold or control; to *fix* the blame upon a person implies solid grounds for the accusation, but to *fasten* the blame upon someone often suggests factitious grounds or selfish motives ⟨his heart is *fixed*, trusting in the Lord—*Ps* 112:7⟩ ⟨society wanted to do what it pleased; all disliked the laws which Church and State were trying to *fasten* on them—*Henry Adams*⟩ **Attach** stresses connection or union in order to keep things together or to prevent their separation; it usually implies a bond, link, or tie ⟨the lid is *attached* to the box by hinges⟩ ⟨*attach* loose sheets by means of a staple⟩ ⟨the collarbone is *attached* to the shoulder blade at one end and to the breastbone at the other⟩ ⟨he *attached* himself to the cause in his youth⟩ ⟨in some countries little odium is *attached* to drunkenness⟩ ⟨*attach* a condition to a promise⟩ ⟨she undertakes to *attach* him to her by strong ties: a child, or marriage—*Parshley*⟩ **Affix** usually implies imposition of one thing upon another; it may convey no further information ⟨*affix* a seal to a document⟩ ⟨Felton *affixed* this bull to the gates of the bishop of London's palace—*Hallam*⟩ but it more often than not suggests

---

A colon (:) separates groups of words discriminated. An asterisk (*) indicates place of treatment of each group.

either attachment by an adhesive (as paste, gum, or mucilage) ⟨*affix* a stamp to an envelope⟩ or subscription (as of a name to a document) ⟨he's old enough to *affix* his signature to an instrument—*Meredith*⟩
*Ana* *secure, rivet, moor, anchor: *join, connect, link, unite: adhere, cleave, cling, *stick, cohere: bind, *tie
*Ant* unfasten: loosen, loose —*Con* *separate, part, sever, sunder, divorce, divide
**fastidious** finicky, finicking, finical, particular, fussy, *nice, dainty, squeamish, persnickety, pernickety
*Ana* exacting, demanding (see DEMAND *vb*): *critical, hypercritical, captious: *careful, meticulous, punctilious, scrupulous
*Con* *negligent, remiss, neglectful, slack, lax: uncritical, cursory (see SUPERFICIAL)
**fastness** stronghold, *fort, fortress, citadel
**fat** *adj* *fleshy, stout, portly, plump, corpulent, obese, rotund, chubby
*Ant* lean —*Con* spare, lank, lanky, skinny, gaunt, scrawny, rawboned, angular (see LEAN): *thin, slender, slim, slight
**fatal** mortal, *deadly, lethal
*Ana* killing, slaying (see KILL *vb*): destroying *or* destructive (see corresponding verb DESTROY): baneful, *pernicious
**fate,** destiny, lot, portion, doom are comparable when they denote the state, condition, or end which is decreed for one by a higher power. **Fate** presupposes such a determining agent or agency as one of the ancient goddesses called Fates, the Supreme Being, or the law of necessity; the term usually suggests inevitability and, sometimes, immutability ⟨he either fears his *fate* too much, or his deserts are small, that dares not put it to the touch to gain or lose it all—*Montrose*⟩ ⟨let us, then, be up and doing, with a heart for any *fate*—*Longfellow*⟩ ⟨he maintained that the *fate* of the Southern Negro depended on his right to protect himself by voting—*C. L. Thompson*⟩ **Destiny** may imply an irrevocable determination or appointment (as by the will of the gods or of God); even in this sense, however, it carries little or no suggestion of something to be feared; on the contrary, it may even imply a great or noble state or end ⟨the conception of a lordly splendid *destiny* for the human race—*Russell*⟩ ⟨Lawrence was . . . unescapably an artist . . . . There were moments when he wanted to escape from his *destiny*—*Huxley*⟩ **Destiny** may also be applied to whatever one envisions as his end or goal, sometimes retaining a slight implication that it is, or has the inevitability of, the will of God ⟨the intoxication of victory swept Hitler's fears away; they were never voiced again, drowned with cries of defiant belief in his *destiny*—*Times Lit. Sup.*⟩ **Lot** and *portion* carry a strong implication of distribution in the decreeing of one's fate. **Lot** stresses the action of blind chance or as if by determination through the casting of lots, and **portion,** the more or less fair apportioning of good and evil ⟨it was her unhappy *lot* to be made more wretched by the only affection which she could not suspect—*Conrad*⟩ ⟨with whom would she be willing to exchange *lots?*—*Bennett*⟩ ⟨so has my *portion* been meted out to me; and . . . I have . . . been able to comprehend some of the lessons hidden in the heart of pain—*Wilde*⟩ ⟨poverty was his *portion* all his days—*Malone*⟩ **Doom,** more than any of these words, implies a final and usually an unhappy or calamitous award or fate ⟨with the sea approaches lost, her [La Rochelle's] *doom* was certain—*Belloc*⟩ ⟨involution is as much a law of nature as evolution. There is no escape from this *doom*—*Inge*⟩
*Ana* issue, outcome, upshot, consequence, result, *effect: *end, ending, termination

**fateful** *ominous, portentous, inauspicious, unpropitious
*Ana* momentous, significant, important (see corresponding nouns at IMPORTANCE): decisive, determinative, *conclusive: crucial, critical, *acute
**fathom** *vb* Fathom, sound, plumb all mean to measure the depth (as of a body of water) typically with a weighted line. **Fathom** implies a measuring in fathoms (units of six feet). **Sound** typically suggests the use of a sounding line in measuring, but it may come close to *probe* (see under ENTER 1) when it deals with the investigation of a body of water to ascertain not only its depth but the character of its bottom or floor ⟨men went overboard with poles in their hands, *sounding* . . . for deeper water—*Defoe*⟩ **Plumb** implies the use of a plumb line, a wire or cord to which is attached a plummet that keeps the line in a vertical position as it falls. These differences are seldom apparent, because such measurements are usually taken by similar means, but in extended usage they take on importance and usually determine the specific implications of the words. **Fathom** implies an attempt to get through or beneath the obscuring layers of something mysterious or incomprehensible so as to reveal or comprehend its true nature ⟨the aims of the artist must first be *fathomed*—*Charles Johnson*⟩ ⟨if we can *fathom* the mystery of the structure of the Milky Way, we shall have learned much about the arrangement of the universe —*B. J. Bok*⟩ ⟨it involved a speculative *fathoming* of the uncertainties of the human mind—*Davis*⟩ **Sound** implies particularly the use of such indirect methods as cautious questioning or examination to elicit information as to someone's views or feelings, as to the real state of affairs in a particular case, or as to the worth, status, or possibility of something ⟨*sound* out the attitude of the candidate towards Medicare⟩ ⟨sent commissioners . . . to *sound* for peace—*Jefferson*⟩ ⟨when Delia *sounded* her cousin, the girl's evasive answer and burning brow seemed to imply that her suitor had changed his mind —*Wharton*⟩ ⟨told Tiberius that Castor was *sounding* various senators as to their willingness to support him —*Graves*⟩ **Plumb** suggests the ascertaining of something hidden usually by minute and critical examination ⟨she succeeded in *plumbing* his motives⟩ ⟨there were depths . . . beneath the story that he had never *plumbed* —*Brooks*⟩ Sometimes, however it comes pretty close to *fathom* ⟨who can *plumb* what the future holds in store?⟩
**fatigue** *vb* exhaust, jade, *tire, weary, fag, tucker
*Ana* *deplete, drain: debilitate, disable, *weaken
*Ant* rest —*Con* refresh, restore, rejuvenate, *renew: *relieve, assuage
**fatuous** asinine, silly, foolish, *simple
*Ana* idiotic, imbecile, moronic (see corresponding nouns at FOOL): *fond, infatuated, besotted, insensate
*Ant* sensible —*Con* sane, prudent, judicious, *wise, sage, sapient
**fault** *n* 1 *imperfection, deficiency, shortcoming
*Ana* flaw, defect, *blemish: weakness, infirmity (see corresponding adjectives at WEAK)
*Ant* excellence
2 Fault, failing, frailty, foible, vice are comparable when they mean an imperfection in character or an ingrained moral weakness. **Fault** implies failure, but not necessarily serious or even culpable failure, to attain a standard of moral perfection in disposition, deed, or habit ⟨have many virtues and few *faults*⟩ ⟨he is all *fault* who hath no *fault* at all—*Tennyson*⟩ ⟨our modern appreciativeness is often only the amiable aspect of a *fault*—an undue tolerance for indeterminate enthusiasms and vapid emotionalism—*Babbitt*⟩ **Failing** is even less censorious than *fault,* for it usually implies a shortcoming, often a

weakness of character for which one is not entirely responsible or of which one may not be aware ⟨pride . . . is a very common *failing,* I believe—*Austen*⟩ ⟨a knowledge of his family *failings* will help one man in economizing his estate—*Quiller-Couch*⟩ ⟨while in other statesmen these *failings* are usually thought of as sorrowful necessities, in Lloyd George they are commonly held to show his essential nastiness—*Sykes*⟩ **Frailty** often implies a weakness in character which makes one prone to fall when tempted ⟨God knows our *frailty,* pities our weakness—*Locke*⟩ The term therefore often denotes a pardonable or a petty fault ⟨a purely human *frailty,* like a fondness for detective stories—*Lowes*⟩ **Foible** denotes a harmless, sometimes an amiable, sometimes a temperamental, weakness or failing ⟨I can bear very well to hear my *foibles* exposed, though not my *faults*—*Shenstone*⟩ ⟨he had all the *foibles* of the aesthete—*Buchan*⟩ **Vice** (see also OFFENSE 3) is stronger than *fault* and *failing* in its suggestion of violation of the moral law or of giving offense to the moral senses of others, but it does not necessarily imply corruptness or deliberate defiance of the law and may be rather a general term attributable to an imperfection or flaw that impairs the soundness of a character or an ability ⟨knowledge . . . of all the virtues and *vices,* tastes and dislikes of all the people—*Galsworthy*⟩ ⟨she had been proud. She was criminally proud. That was her *vice*—*Bennett*⟩ ⟨as Professor Whitehead has lately said, the intolerant use of abstractions is the major *vice* of the intellect—*Inge*⟩ *Ana* weakness, infirmity (see corresponding adjectives at WEAK): flaw, defect, *blemish
*Ant* merit  —*Con* *excellence, virtue, perfection
**3** *blame, culpability, guilt
*Ana* responsibility, answerability, accountability (see corresponding adjectives at RESPONSIBLE): sin, *offense, crime

**faultfinding** *adj* captious, caviling, carping, censorious, hypercritical, *critical
*Ana* exacting, demanding, requiring (see DEMAND *vb*): fussy, particular, finicky, pernickety (see NICE)
*Con* appreciating *or* appreciative, valuing, prizing, cherishing (see corresponding verbs at APPRECIATE): approving, endorsing (see APPROVE)

**faultless** *impeccable, flawless, errorless
*Ana* *correct, right, nice, accurate, exact, precise: *perfect, intact, entire, whole
*Ant* faulty

**faux pas** blunder, slip, *error, mistake, lapse, bull, howler, boner

**favor** *n* boon, largess, *gift, present, gratuity
*Ana* token, *pledge, earnest: concession, *allowance: *honor, homage, deference: benefaction, *donation, contribution

**favor** *vb* **1** Favor, countenance, encourage are comparable when they mean to give the support of one's approval to. **Favor** may be used in reference to a well-disposed inclination, an expressed preference, or active support or sometimes to a circumstance or agency conducive to a result ⟨a number of wealthy and influential Newport folk *favored* dramatic performances, although a majority of their fellow citizens continued to condemn them—*Amer. Guide Series: R. I.*⟩ ⟨in general the marshmen *favor* a broad, roomy canoe—*Thesiger*⟩ ⟨we had been *favored* by tail winds and would put down at Idlewild —*Cerf*⟩ ⟨the summer weather at Maudheim *favored* the formation of this type of snow—*Schytt*⟩ **Countenance** may indicate mere toleration; more often it implies a positive favoring ⟨really fail to see why you should *countenance* immorality just to please your father—

*Kaye-Smith*⟩ ⟨her popularity had been retrieved, grievances against her silenced, her past *countenanced,* and her present irradiated by the family approval—*Wharton*⟩ ⟨several of them appeared at the bar to *countenance* him when he was tried at the Horsham assizes—*Macaulay*⟩ **Encourage** carries the notion of heartening stimulation, inciting or inducing especially by expressions of approval, confidence, liking, or comfort ⟨openly *encouraged* from Germany and Italy, fascist organizations, although from time to time banned, carried on insidious and demoralizing propaganda—*Ogg & Zink*⟩ ⟨*encouraged* her in her ambition to be an actress—*Current Biog.*⟩
*Ana* *approve, endorse: *support, uphold, back
*Ant* disapprove  —*Con* *decry, depreciate, disparage
**2** accommodate, *oblige
*Ana* *help, aid, assist: *indulge, pamper, humor: *benefit, profit
*Con* foil, thwart, baffle, circumvent, *frustrate: *inconvenience, incommode, discommode

**favorable,** benign, auspicious, propitious mean being of good omen or presaging a happy or successful outcome. **Favorable** implies that the persons or circumstances involved tend to assist in attaining one's ends—persons by being kindly disposed or actually helpful and circumstances by being distinctly advantageous or encouraging ⟨lend a *favorable* ear to a request⟩ ⟨it was feared that many of the small countries were *favorable* to the enemy⟩ ⟨a *favorable* breeze⟩ ⟨a hot dry summer, *favorable* to contemplative life out of doors—*Conrad*⟩ ⟨they won't take a chance of battle unless they can feel sure of most *favorable* conditions—*Alexander Forbes*⟩ **Benign** (see also KIND) is applicable chiefly to someone or to something that has power to make or mar one's fortunes by his or its aspect and is thought of as looking down with favor on one or of presenting a favorable countenance to one ⟨so shall the World go on, to good malignant, to bad men *benign*—*Milton*⟩ ⟨on whose birth *benign* planets have certainly smiled—*Brontë*⟩ ⟨a *benign* rather than a malevolent phenomenon—*Margaret Halsey*⟩ **Auspicious,** like the related *augur* (see under FORETELL), suggests the presence of signs or omens and is applicable to something that is marked by favorable signs or is in itself regarded as a good omen ⟨an *auspicious* beginning of what proved to be a great career⟩ ⟨for sure the milder planets did combine on thy *auspicious* horoscope to shine—*Dryden*⟩ ⟨pay the boy . . . he brought *auspicious* news—*Kipling*⟩ **Propitious** suggests an allusion to favoring gods or powers more strongly than *favorable* but not quite so explicitly as *auspicious*; it may therefore be preferred to *favorable* when such a connotation is desired ⟨if the fates are *propitious,* there is no doubt of his success⟩ ⟨they looked upon the present moment as *propitious* for starting their project⟩ ⟨after so *propitious* an opening it seemed that acerbities might be quelled, rivalries mitigated—*S. H. Adams*⟩
*Ana* advantageous, *beneficial, profitable: salutary, wholesome, *healthful: benignant, kindly, *kind
*Ant* unfavorable: antagonistic

**favorite** *n* sycophant, toady, lickspittle, *parasite, bootlicker, hanger-on, leech, sponge, sponger

**fawn** *vb* Fawn, toady, truckle, cringe, cower are comparable when they mean to act or behave with abjectness in the presence of a superior. **Fawn** implies a courting of favor by such acts of a sycophant as servile flattery and exaggerated deference ⟨they *fawn* on the proud feet that spurn them lying low—*Shelley*⟩ ⟨courtiers who *fawn* on a master while they betray him—*Macaulay*⟩ ⟨they *fawn* and slaver over us—*Jeffers*⟩ ⟨died, still *fawning* like the coward that he had always been—*Pares*⟩ **Toady** carries a strong

---

A colon (:) separates groups of words discriminated. An asterisk (*) indicates place of treatment of each group.

implication of a menial as well as of a fawning attitude in an attempt to ingratiate oneself; often also it suggests the close following of a hanger-on or parasite or the vulgarly imitative behavior of a social climber ⟨*toadying* to the rich boys in his school⟩ ⟨her generosity encouraged *toadying* among her neighbors⟩ ⟨he *toadied* and worshipped and worried: he became timid and obsequious, feeling himself to be a flaw, a little scratching cinder among immensities—*Enright*⟩ ⟨in proportion as he submits and *toadies,* he also will dominate and bully—*Mead*⟩ **Truckle** implies subordination of self or submission of one's desires, judgments, or opinions to those of a superior ⟨everybody must defer. A nation must wait upon her decision, a dean and chapter *truckle* to her wishes—*Sackville-West*⟩ ⟨there are people who will always *truckle* to those who have money—*Archibald Marshall*⟩ **Cringe** implies obsequious bowing or crouching as if in awe or fear; it usually connotes abject abasement ⟨we are sneaking and bowing and *cringing* on the one hand, or bullying and scorning on the other—*Thackeray*⟩ ⟨she is very humble and careless of self. "My poor, humble self" . . . is often on her lips; but she never *cringes* or loses dignity —*Symonds*⟩ **Cower** always implies abject fear, often cowardly fear, especially in the presence of those who tyrannize or domineer ⟨the whole family *cowered* under Lady Kew's eyes and nose, and she ruled by force of them—*Thackeray*⟩ ⟨having found . . . every incentive to *cower* and cringe and hedge, and no incentive . . . to stand upright as a man—*Brooks*⟩
*Ana* blandish, cajole, wheedle, *coax: defer, bow, cave, *yield, submit: court, woo, *invite
*Ant* domineer

**faze** disconcert, discomfit, rattle, *embarrass, abash
*Ana* nonplus, confound, dumbfound, perplex, mystify, *puzzle: *confuse, muddle: fluster, flurry, perturb, *discompose

**fealty** *fidelity, loyalty, devotion, allegiance, piety
*Ana* faithfulness *or* faith, trueness *or* truth, constancy, staunchness, steadfastness (see corresponding adjectives at FAITHFUL): *obligation, duty
*Ant* perfidy —*Con* perfidiousness, treacherousness *or* treachery, traitorousness, faithlessness, disloyalty, falseness (see corresponding adjectives at FAITHLESS)

**fear** *n* 1 Fear, dread, fright, alarm, dismay, consternation, panic, terror, horror, trepidation denote the distressing or disordering agitation which overcomes one in the anticipation or in the presence of danger. **Fear** is the most general term; like **dread,** it implies apprehension and anxiety, but it also frequently suggests a loss of courage amounting to cowardice ⟨*fear* came upon me, and trembling—*Job* 4:14⟩ ⟨he had, indeed, an awful *dread* of death, or rather "of something after death"—*Boswell*⟩ ⟨do you know what *fear* is? Not ordinary *fear* of insult, injury or death, but abject, quivering *dread* of something that you cannot see—*Kipling*⟩ ⟨the only thing we have to fear is *fear* itself—*Roosevelt*⟩ **Fright** implies the shock of sudden, startling, and usually short-lived fear; **alarm** suggests the fright which is awakened by sudden awareness of imminent danger ⟨she had taken *fright* at our behavior and turned to the captain pitifully—*Conrad*⟩ ⟨she stared at her husband in *alarm*; her golden-hazel eyes were black with apprehension—*Wylie*⟩ ⟨thou wast born amid the din of arms, and sucked a breast that panted with *alarms*—*Cowper*⟩ **Dismay** implies deprivation of spirit, courage, or initiative, especially by an alarming or disconcerting prospect ⟨the storm prevails, the rampart yields a way, bursts the wild cry of horror and *dismay!*—*Campbell*⟩ **Consternation** heightens the implication of prostration or confusion of the faculties ⟨'tis easy to believe, though not to describe, the *consternation* they were all in—*Defoe*⟩ **Panic** is overmastering and unreasoning, often groundless, fear or fright ⟨a blockhead, who was in a perpetual *panic* lest I should expose his ignorance—*De Quincey*⟩ **Terror** suggests the extremity of consternation or dread ⟨the *terror* by night—*Ps* 91:5⟩ ⟨frozen with *terror*—*Beckford*⟩ ⟨soul-chilling *terror*—*Shelley*⟩ **Horror** adds the implication of shuddering abhorrence or aversion, for it usually connotes a sight, activity, or demand rather than a premonition as a cause of fear ⟨the *horror* of supernatural darkness—*Pater*⟩ ⟨shrank from the task with all the *horror* of a well-bred English gentleman—*Woolf*⟩ **Trepidation** adds to *dread* the implication of timidity, especially as manifested by trembling or by marked hesitation ⟨the Stubland aunts were not the ladies to receive a solicitor's letter calmly. They were thrown into a state of extreme *trepidation*—*H. G. Wells*⟩ It is often used for a polite pretense of fear or timidity ⟨I take up with some *trepidation* the subject of program music—*Babbitt*⟩
*Ana* *apprehension, foreboding, misgiving, presentiment: anxiety, worry, concern (see CARE)
*Ant* fearlessness —*Con* boldness, bravery, intrepidity, valiancy (see corresponding adjectives at BRAVE): *courage, mettle, spirit, resolution: *confidence, assurance, aplomb
2 awe, *reverence
*Ana* veneration, worship, adoration (see under REVERE): admiration, *wonder, amazement: respect, esteem (see REGARD *n*)
*Ant* contempt

**fearful** 1 Fearful, apprehensive, afraid are comparable when they mean inspired or moved by fear. In such use they are normally followed by *of, that,* or *lest, afraid* being never and *fearful* and *apprehensive* infrequently used attributively in this sense. **Fearful** carries no suggestion of a formidable cause of fear; it often connotes timorousness, a predisposition to worry, or an active imagination ⟨the child is *fearful* of loud noises⟩ ⟨they were *fearful* that a storm would prevent their excursion⟩ ⟨*fearful* lest his prize should escape him—*J. R. Green*⟩ **Apprehensive** suggests a state of mind rather than a temperament and grounds for fear that at least seem reasonable. It always implies a presentiment or anticipation of evil or danger ⟨in July 1914 all civilized peoples were *apprehensive* of war⟩ ⟨had driven before them into Italy whole troops of . . . provincials, less *apprehensive* of servitude than of famine—*Gibbon*⟩ **Afraid** may or may not imply sufficient motivation of fears, but it typically connotes weakness or cowardice and regularly implies inhibition of action or utterance ⟨the trained reason is disinterested and fearless. It is not *afraid* of public opinion—*Inge*⟩ ⟨I was too *afraid* of her to shudder, too *afraid* of her to put my fingers to my ears—*Conrad*⟩
*Ana* *timid, timorous: anxious, worried, concerned (see under CARE *n*): hesitant, reluctant, *disinclined
*Ant* fearless: intrepid —*Con* bold, audacious, *brave, courageous, dauntless, valiant, unafraid
2 Fearful, awful, dreadful, frightful, terrible, terrific, horrible, horrific, shocking, appalling are comparable in that all and especially their adverbs are used informally as intensives meaning little more than *extreme* (or *extremely*), but each term has a definite and distinct value when applied to a thing that stimulates an emotion in which fear or horror is in some degree an element. Something is **fearful** which makes one afraid or alarmed. In literary or formal use the word usually implies a deep and painful emotion and a loss of courage in the face of possible or imminent danger ⟨all torment, trouble, wonder and amazement inhabits here: some heavenly power guide us out of this

*fearful* country!—*Shak.*⟩ ⟨a sight too *fearful* for the feel of fear—*Keats*⟩ ⟨our *fearful* trip is done, the ship has weathered every rack—*Whitman*⟩ In less formal English *fearful* may not imply apprehension of danger, but it may at least imply that the thing so qualified is a cause of disquiet ⟨the *fearful* tenacity of a memory⟩ ⟨a *fearfully* distressing situation⟩ Something is **awful** which impresses one so profoundly that one acts or feels as if under a spell or in the grip of its influence; the word often implies an emotion such as reverential fear or an overpowering awareness of might, majesty, or sublimity ⟨and wring the *awful* scepter from his fist—*Shak.*⟩ ⟨God of our fathers . . . beneath whose *awful* Hand we hold dominion over palm and pine—*Kipling*⟩ ⟨men living among the glooms and broken lights of the primeval forest, hearing strange noises in the treetops when the thunder crashed, and *awful* voices in the wind—*Buchan*⟩ With somewhat weakened force *awful* may be applied to qualities or conditions which are unduly weighted with significance or which strike one forcibly as far above or beyond the normal ⟨no tribunal can approach such a question without a deep sense . . . of the *awful* responsibility involved in its decision—*John Marshall*⟩ ⟨a moment of *awful* silence before the questions began—*Deland*⟩ ⟨suddenly, with the *awful* clarity and singleness of purpose of the innocent and intelligent, she believed in Captain Remson—*McFee*⟩ Something is **dreadful** from which one shrinks in shuddering fear or in loathing ⟨the *dreadful* prospect of another world war⟩ ⟨cancer is a *dreadful* disease⟩ ⟨she felt her two hands taken, and heard a kind voice. Could it be possible it belonged to the *dreadful* father of her husband?—*Meredith*⟩ ⟨*dreadful* things should not be known to young people until they are old enough to face them with a certain poise—*Russell*⟩ In weakened use *dreadful* is applicable to something from which one shrinks as disagreeable or as unpleasant to contemplate or endure ⟨a *dreadful* necessity⟩ ⟨wouldn't it be *dreadful* to produce that effect on people—*L. P. Smith*⟩ Something is **frightful** which, for the moment at least, paralyzes one with fear or throws one into great alarm or consternation ⟨a *frightful* sound broke the quiet of the night⟩ ⟨a *frightful* tornado⟩ ⟨the Ghost of a Lady . . . a scar on her forehead, and a bloody handkerchief at her breast, *frightful* to behold—*Meredith*⟩ *Frightful* is also often employed without direct implication of fright, but in such use it imputes to the thing so qualified a capacity for startling the observer (as by its enormity, outrageousness, or its shocking quality) ⟨a *frightful* disregard of decency⟩ ⟨a *frightful* scandal⟩ ⟨this *frightful* condition of internal strain and instability—*Shaw*⟩ ⟨the labor of sifting, combining, constructing, expunging, correcting, testing: this *frightful* toil is as much critical as creative—*T. S. Eliot*⟩ Something is **terrible** which causes or is capable of causing extreme and agitating fear or which both induces fright or alarm and prolongs and intensifies it ⟨millions of voices arose. The clamor became *terrible*, and confused the minds of all men—*Anderson*⟩ ⟨one of those *terrible* women produced now and then by the Roman stock, unsexed, implacable, filled with an insane lust of power—*Buchan*⟩ ⟨I have never read a more *terrible* exposure of human weakness—of universal human weakness—than the last great speech of Othello—*T. S. Eliot*⟩ ⟨a human being devoid of hope is the most *terrible* object in the world—*Heiser*⟩ When the word carries no implication of terrifying or of capacity for terrifying, it usually suggests that the thing so described is almost unendurable in its excess (as of force or power) or too painful to be borne without alleviation or mitigation ⟨knowledge . . . is no longer thought to be a secret, precious, rather *terrible* possession—*Benson*⟩ ⟨an evil passion may give great

physical and intellectual powers a *terrible* efficiency—*Eliot*⟩ ⟨Saint-Beuve believed that the truth is always *terrible*—*L. P. Smith*⟩ Something is **terrific** which is fitted or intended to inspire terror (as by its size, appearance, or potency) ⟨eyes and hairy mane *terrific*—*Milton*⟩ ⟨assume a *terrific* expression⟩ ⟨one little tool . . . transforms the spark [of electricity] from a form too brief and bright and *terrific* to be intelligible into one of the most tractable and lucid of the phenomena . . . of Nature—*Darrow*⟩ *Terrific* may be preferred to *terrible* when there is an implication of release of stored-up energy, physical, emotional, or intellectual, and of its stunning effect ⟨a *terrific* explosion⟩ ⟨a *terrific* outburst of rage⟩ ⟨the most admired single phrase that Shakespeare ever wrote—Ripeness is all . . . derives a *terrific* and pure dramatic impact from its context—*Day Lewis*⟩ Something is **horrible** the sight of which induces not only fear or terror but also loathing and aversion; thus, a *fearful* precipice may not be *horrible*; in the practice of the ancient Greek dramatists, murder on the stage was avoided as *horrible* ⟨now that wars are between nations, no longer between governments or armies, they have become far more *horrible*—*Inge*⟩ Horrible, like the other words, may be used in a weaker sense; in such cases it seldom suggests horror, but it does suggests hatefulness or hideousness ⟨a *horrible* suspicion arose in his mind⟩ ⟨a *horribly* shrill voice⟩ ⟨a *horrible* taste⟩ *Horrible* emphasizes the effect produced on a person, **horrific** the possession of qualities or properties fitted or intended to produce that effect ⟨that *horrific* yarn [Stevenson's] "The Body-Snatcher"—*Montague*⟩ ⟨his yearning for the *horrific*, the revolting, the transcendent mystery of whatever is not "nice"—*Times Lit. Sup.*⟩ Something is **shocking** which startles or is capable of startling because it is contrary to one's expectations, one's standards of good taste, or one's moral sense ⟨likes to tell *shocking* stories⟩ ⟨find a *shocking* change in a friend's appearance⟩ ⟨the treatment should begin by encouraging him to utter freely even his most *shocking* thoughts—*Russell*⟩ Often in extended use *shocking* does not imply a capacity for startling so much as a blamable or reprehensible character ⟨it is *shocking* of me, but I have to laugh when people are pompous and absurd—*Rose Macaulay*⟩ ⟨a solecism of this kind . . . would have seemed a *shocking* thing to . . . so accurate a scholar—*L. P. Smith*⟩ Something is **appalling** which strikes one with dismay as well as with terror or horror ⟨her overthrow would have been the most *appalling* disaster the Western world had ever known—*Henry Adams*⟩ ⟨the defectives are *appallingly* prolific—*Shaw*⟩ Sometimes *appalling* comes close to *amazing* but then retains the notion of dismaying and carries a stronger suggestion of dumbfounding than of surprising ⟨his *appalling* quickness of mind⟩ ⟨he was squatting in some septic Indian village talking to unwashed old men, and eating the most *appalling* food—*La Farge*⟩

*Ana* frightening, terrifying, alarming (see FRIGHTEN): *ghastly, gruesome, grisly, grim, macabre, lurid: *sinister, baleful, malign: sublime (see SPLENDID)

**fearless** unafraid, dauntless, undaunted, bold, intrepid, audacious, *brave, courageous, valiant, valorous, doughty
*Ana* daring, venturesome, *adventurous: heroic, gallant (see corresponding nouns at HEROISM): plucky, gritty (see corresponding nouns at FORTITUDE)
*Ant* fearful —*Con* *timid, timorous

**feasible** *possible, practicable
*Ana* practical, *practicable: advisable, *expedient, politic: advantageous, *beneficial, profitable: suitable, appropriate, fitting, *fit
*Ant* unfeasible, infeasible: chimerical (*schemes, projects, suggestions*) —*Con* fantastic, visionary, quixotic (see

A colon (:) separates groups of words discriminated. An asterisk (*) indicates place of treatment of each group.

IMAGINARY): utopian, *ambitious, pretentious

**feast** *dinner, banquet

**feat** *n* Feat, exploit, achievement denote a remarkable deed or performance. Feat applies particularly to an act involving physical strength, dexterity, and often courage; an **exploit** is an adventurous, heroic, or brilliant deed; **achievement** emphasizes the idea of distinguished endeavor especially in the face of difficulty or opposition; all are used frequently with some degree of irony ⟨sleights of art and *feats* of strength went round—*Goldsmith*⟩ ⟨*feats* of daring⟩ ⟨I must retreat into the invalided corps and tell them of my former *exploits,* which may very likely pass for lies—*Scott*⟩ ⟨great is the rumor of this dreadful knight, and his *achievements* of no less account—*Shak.*⟩ ⟨*achievements* of science⟩

*Ana* deed, act, *action: triumph, conquest, *victory: enterprise, *adventure, quest

**feature** *n* *characteristic, trait

*Ana* detail, particular, *item: speciality, particularity (see corresponding adjectives at SPECIAL): *quality, character, property

**fecund** fruitful, prolific, *fertile

*Ana* bearing, producing, yielding (see BEAR): breeding, propagating, reproducing, generating (see GENERATE)

*Ant* barren —*Con* *sterile, unfruitful, infertile, impotent

**fecundity** fruitfulness, prolificacy, fertility (see under FERTILE)

*Ana* producing *or* productiveness (see corresponding verb at BEAR): profuseness *or* profusion, luxuriance, lavishness, prodigality, lushness, exuberance (see corresponding adjectives at PROFUSE)

*Ant* barrenness

**federation** confederacy, confederation, coalition, fusion, *alliance

**fee** stipend, emolument, salary, *wage *or* wages, pay, hire

*Ana* remuneration, compensation (see corresponding verbs at PAY): charge, *price, cost, expense

**feeble** *weak, infirm, decrepit, frail, fragile

*Ana* unnerved, enervated, emasculated, unmanned (see UNNERVE): debilitated, weakened, enfeebled, disabled, crippled (see WEAKEN): *powerless, impotent

*Ant* robust —*Con* *strong, sturdy, stout, stalwart: *vigorous, lusty, energetic: hale, *healthy

**feed** *vb* Feed, nourish, pasture, graze are comparable when they mean to provide the food that one needs or desires. **Feed** is the comprehensive term applicable not only to persons and animals but also to plants and, by extension, to whatever consumes something or requires something external for its sustenance ⟨*feed* the baby⟩ ⟨*feed* a family of ten on fifty dollars a week⟩ ⟨use bone meal to *feed* the chrysanthemums⟩ ⟨*feed* a furnace with coal⟩ ⟨Hugh's growing vanity was *fed* by the thought that Clara was interested in him—*Anderson*⟩ ⟨the press exploits for its benefit human silliness and ignorance and vulgarity and sensationalism, and, in exploiting it, *feeds* it—*Rose Macaulay*⟩ In American but not in British use *feed* sometimes takes for its object the thing that is fed ⟨*feed* oats to the horses⟩ ⟨*feed* coal to the furnace⟩ ⟨he has been *feeding* bread and butter to the dog—*Wiggin*⟩ **Nourish** implies feeding with food that is essential to growth, health, well-being, or continuing existence. *Nourish* more often takes as its subject the thing that serves as a sustaining or a building-up food than the person who provides such food ⟨milk, eggs, and meat *nourish* the bodies of growing boys and girls⟩ ⟨the humid prairie heat, so *nourishing* to wheat and corn, so exhausting to human beings—*Cather*⟩ ⟨freedom *nourishes* self-respect—*Channing* d. 1842⟩ ⟨his zeal seemed *nourished* by failure and by fall—*Whit-*

*tier*⟩ **Pasture** is applied chiefly to animals and especially to domestic animals (as cattle, sheep, or horses) fed on grass ⟨cattle are *pastured* on the ridges and mounds that rise . . . above the swamps—*Amer. Guide Series: La.*⟩ **Graze** is often preferred specifically to *pasture* when the emphasis is on the use of growing herbage for food ⟨a field or two to *graze* his cows—*Swift*⟩ ⟨*graze* sheep on the common⟩

*Ana* *nurse, nurture, foster, cherish: support, sustain, maintain (see corresponding nouns at LIVING)

*Ant* starve

**feed** *n* fodder, forage, provender, *food, victuals, viands, provisions, comestibles

**feel** *vb* *touch, palpate, handle, paw

*Ana* *apprehend, comprehend: perceive, observe, notice (see SEE)

**feel** *n* feeling, *atmosphere, aura

*Ana* see those at FEELING 3

**feeling** *n* 1 sensibility, *sensation, sense

*Ana* reacting *or* reaction, behaving *or* behavior (see corresponding verbs at ACT): responsiveness (see corresponding adjective at TENDER): sensitiveness, susceptibility (see corresponding adjectives at LIABLE)

2 Feeling, affection, emotion, sentiment, passion. **Feeling,** the general term, denotes a partly mental and partly physical, but not primarily sensory, reaction or state that is characterized by an emotional response (as pleasure, pain, attraction, or repulsion). Unless it is qualified or a clue is given in the context, *feeling* gives no indication of the nature, the quality, or the intensity of the response ⟨whatever *feelings* were in Sophia's heart, tenderness was not among them—*Bennett*⟩ ⟨a *feeling* of sadness and longing—*Longfellow*⟩ Often *feeling* implies a contrast with *judgment* and connotes lack of thought ⟨her humanity was a *feeling,* not a principle—*Henry Mackenzie*⟩ ⟨she had a *feeling* that all would be well—*Parker*⟩ **Affection** is applied mainly to such feelings as are also inclinations or likings; the word therefore suggests desire or striving ⟨the heart . . . we are, by foolish custom . . . impelled to call the seat of the *affections*—*Rose Macaulay*⟩ ⟨that serene and blessed mood, in which the *affections* gently lead us on—*Wordsworth*⟩ ⟨music played with *affection* and understanding—*Kolodin*⟩ **Emotion** usually suggests a condition that involves more of the total mental and physical response than does *feeling* or implies feelings marked by excitement or agitation ⟨eagerness for *emotion* and adventure—*Sydney Smith*⟩ ⟨means of exciting religious *emotion*—*Ruskin*⟩ ⟨a sensation of strength, inspired by mighty *emotion*—*George Eliot*⟩ **Sentiment** connotes a larger intellectual element in the feeling than any of the others; it often is applied specifically to an emotion inspired by an idea ⟨his own antislavery *sentiments* were sincere—*Boatfield*⟩ Commonly the word suggests refined, sometimes romantic, occasionally affected or artificial, feeling ⟨that moral *sentiment* which exists in every human breast—*Bancroft*⟩ ⟨his opinions are more the result of conviction than of *sentiment*—*J. R. Lowell*⟩ ⟨Sterne has been called a man overflowing with *sentiment* on paper but devoid of real feeling⟩ **Passion** suggests powerful or controlling emotion; more than *affection,* it implies urgency of desire (as for possession or revenge) ⟨hark! how the sacred calm, that breathes about, bids every fierce tumultuous *passion* cease—*Gray*⟩ ⟨the ruling *passion,* be it what it will, the ruling *passion* conquers reason still—*Pope*⟩ ⟨give me that man that is not *passion's* slave—*Shak.*⟩

*Ana* impressing *or* impression, touching, affecting *or* affection (see corresponding verbs at AFFECT *vb* 1): *mood, humor, temper, vein

---

*Ana* analogous words    *Ant* antonyms    *Con* contrasted words    See also explanatory notes facing page 1

3 feel, *atmosphere, aura

*Ana* *impression, impress, imprint: peculiarity, individuality, characteristic (see corresponding adjectives at CHARACTERISTIC): *quality, property, character, attribute

**feign** simulate, counterfeit, sham, pretend, affect, *assume

*Ana* fabricate, manufacture, forge (see MAKE): dissemble, *disguise, cloak, mask, camouflage

**feint** *n* artifice, wile, ruse, gambit, ploy, stratagem, maneuver, *trick

*Ana* *pretense, pretension, make-believe: hoaxing *or* hoax, hoodwinking, befooling (see corresponding verbs at DUPE): resort, expedient, shift (see RESOURCE)

**felicitate, congratulate** mean to express one's pleasure in the joy, success, elevation, or prospects of another. Felicitate is the more formal term and carries perhaps a stronger implication that the person who felicitates regards the other as very happy or wishes him happiness ⟨*felicitate* parents upon the birth of a child⟩ ⟨*felicitated* His Majesty upon his coronation⟩ ⟨a young pianist came backstage to *felicitate* Milstein—*Current Biog.*⟩ Congratulate is the more common and often more intimate term; it usually implies that the congratulator regards the other as a person to whom good fortune has come or on whom fortune smiles ⟨it is good manners to *congratulate* a bridegroom and to *felicitate* a bride⟩ ⟨*congratulate* a friend on his promotion⟩ ⟨*congratulated* himself that he had escaped a trying situation⟩

**felicitous** happy, apt, fitting, appropriate, *fit, suitable, meet, proper

*Ana* telling, convincing (see VALID): pat, timely, opportune, *seasonable, well-timed: apposite, pertinent, *relevant

*Ant* infelicitous: inept, maladroit —*Con* *awkward, clumsy, gauche: unfortunate, unhappy, unlucky (see affirmative adjectives at LUCKY)

**felicity** *happiness, bliss, beatitude, blessedness

*Ana* rapture, transport, *ecstasy: joy, delight, delectation, *pleasure, fruition

*Ant* misery

**fell** *adj* cruel, inhuman, savage, barbarous, ferocious, *fierce, truculent

*Ana* baleful, malign, malefic, maleficent, *sinister: pitiless, ruthless (see corresponding nouns at SYMPATHY): relentless, unrelenting, merciless, *grim, implacable

**felon** *criminal, convict, malefactor, culprit, delinquent

**female** *n* Female, woman, lady are comparable when meaning a person and especially an adult who belongs to the sex that is the counterpart of the male sex. Female (the correlative of *male*) emphasizes the idea of sex; it applies not only to human beings but also to animals and plants. Its ordinary use as a synonym for *woman* was once frequent ⟨three smart-looking *females*—*Austen*⟩ ⟨to please the *females* of our modest age—*Byron*⟩ but this use is now felt as derogatory or contemptuous except in strictly scientific or statistical application, where the term may be employed to designate a person of the female sex whether infant, child, adolescent, or adult ⟨the city's population included 12,115 males and 15,386 *females*⟩ As compared with **woman** (the correlative of *man*), which emphasizes the essential qualities of the adult female, **lady** (the correlative of *gentleman*) connotes basically the added qualities implicit in gentle breeding, gracious nature, and cultivated background. *Woman* is preferred by many whenever the reference is to the person merely as a person ⟨the country expects the help of its *women*⟩ ⟨the following *women* assisted in receiving the guests⟩ ⟨a *woman* of culture⟩ ⟨a sales*woman*⟩ ⟨working*women*⟩ ⟨society *women*⟩ *Lady*, on the other hand, is preferred when exalted social position or refinement and delicacy

are definitely implied ⟨Alfonso XI at his death left one legitimate son . . . and five bastards by a *lady* of Seville, Doña Leonor de Guzmán—*Altamira y Crevea*⟩ ⟨Miss Nancy . . . had the essential attributes of a *lady*—high veracity, delicate honor in her dealings, deference to others, and refined personal habits—*George Eliot*⟩ but *lady* may also be used informally as a mere courteous synonym for *woman* ⟨please allow these *ladies* to pass⟩ ⟨the *ladies* were the decisive factor in rolling up the Republican landslide—*Priest*⟩ ⟨may I speak to the *lady* of the house?⟩ though its indiscriminate substitution for *woman* (as in wash *lady*, sales*lady*) carries courtesy into travesty ⟨from that hour to this, the *Gazette* has referred to all females as *women* except that police-court characters were always to be designated as *ladies*—*White*⟩

**female** *adj* Female, feminine, womanly, womanlike, womanish, effeminate, ladylike are comparable when meaning of, characteristic of, or like a female especially of the human species. Female (opposed to *male*) applies to animals and plants as well as to human beings and stresses the fact of sex ⟨the *female* bee—*Milton*⟩ ⟨*female* children were excluded from inheritance⟩ Feminine (opposed to *masculine*) alone of these words may imply grammatical gender ⟨*feminine* nouns and pronouns⟩ but it characteristically applies to features, attributes, or qualities which belong to women rather than to men; it has practically displaced all except the more strictly physiological senses of *female* ⟨her heavenly form angelic, but more soft and *feminine*—*Milton*⟩ ⟨the domestic virtues, which are especially *feminine*—*Lecky*⟩ ⟨the strangely *feminine* jealousies and religiousness—*Steinbeck*⟩ **Womanly** (often opposed to *girlish* or, from another point of view, to *manly*) is used to qualify whatever evidences the qualities of a fully developed woman ⟨*womanly* virtues⟩ It often specifically suggests qualities (as tenderness, sympathy, moral strength, and fortitude) which especially befit a woman and make her attractive especially in her functions as a wife and mother, or it may merely suggest the absence of such mannish qualities as aggressiveness ⟨'twas just a *womanly* presence, an influence unexpressed —*J. R. Lowell*⟩ ⟨all will spy in thy face a blushing, *womanly*, discovering grace—*Donne*⟩ **Womanlike** (opposed to *manlike*) is more apt to suggest characteristically feminine faults or foibles ⟨*womanlike*, taking revenge too deep for a transient wrong done but in thought to your beauty—*Tennyson*⟩ **Womanish** (compare *mannish, childish*) is a term of contempt, especially when applied to what should be virile or masculine ⟨art thou a man? Thy form cries out thou art; thy tears are *womanish* —*Shak.*⟩ ⟨*womanish* or wailing grief—*Cowper*⟩ **Effeminate** emphasizes the idea of unmanly delicacy, luxuriousness, or enervation ⟨a woman impudent and mannish grown is not more loathed than an *effeminate* man in time of action—*Shak.*⟩ ⟨an *effeminate* and unmanly foppery—*Hurd*⟩ ⟨something feminine—not *effeminate*, mind—is discoverable in the countenances of all men of genius—*Coleridge*⟩ **Ladylike** is sometimes used sarcastically, especially of men, to imply a dainty and finical affectation of the proprieties ⟨fops at all corners, *ladylike* in mien—*Cowper*⟩ ⟨that *ladylike* quality which is the curse of Southern literature—*Leech*⟩ As applied to girls and women or to their conduct, habits, or manners, *ladylike* implies conformity to a standard appropriate to a lady ⟨your daughter may be better paid, better dressed, more gently spoken, more *ladylike* than you were in the old mill—*Shaw*⟩

*Ant* male —*Con* masculine, manly, manlike, manful, mannish, virile (see MALE)

**feminine** *female, womanly, womanish, ladylike, woman-

---

A colon (:) separates groups of words discriminated. An asterisk (*) indicates place of treatment of each group.

like, effeminate

*Ant* masculine —*Con* *male, manly, mannish, virile, manlike, manful

**fence** *vb* **1** *enclose, envelop, pen, coop, corral, cage, wall

*Ana* confine, circumscribe, *limit: *surround, gird, environ

**2** *dodge, parry, sidestep, duck, shirk, malinger

*Ana* evade, avoid, shun, elude (see ESCAPE): maneuver, feint (see corresponding nouns at TRICK): baffle, foil, outwit (see FRUSTRATE)

**feral** *brutal, brute, brutish, bestial, beastly

*Ana* *fierce, ferocious

**ferocious** *fierce, truculent, barbarous, savage, inhuman, cruel, fell

*Ana* infuriated, maddened, enraged (see ANGER *vb*): rapacious, *voracious, ravening, ravenous: relentless, implacable, merciless, *grim

*Con* *tame, subdued, submissive

**ferret out** *vb* *seek, search, scour, hunt, comb, ransack, rummage

*Ana* extract, elicit (see EDUCE): penetrate, pierce, probe (see ENTER)

**fertile,** fecund, fruitful, prolific mean having or manifesting the power to produce fruit or offspring. The same distinctions in implications and connotations are observable in their corresponding nouns **fertility, fecundity, fruitfulness, prolificacy.** Fertile (opposed to *sterile, infertile*) applies particularly to something in which seeds take root and grow or may take root and grow because it contains the elements essential to their life and development ⟨*fertile* soil⟩ ⟨*fertility* of alluvial land⟩ ⟨past fields where the wheat was high . . .; it was a *fertile* country—*S. V. Benét*⟩ Consequently the term often applies to something in which ideas take root and thrive ⟨a *fertile* mind⟩ ⟨in the heath's barrenness to the farmer lay its *fertility* to the historian—*Hardy*⟩ ⟨in him were united a most logical head with a most *fertile* imagination —*Boswell*⟩ Fertile is also applicable to something which has in itself the elements essential to its growth and development ⟨a *fertile* egg⟩ ⟨*fertile* seed⟩ ⟨a *fertile* idea⟩ or to a person or animal or pair that is able to produce normal living young ⟨a *fertile* husband⟩ ⟨a *fertile* couple⟩ **Fecund** (opposed to *barren*) applies especially to something which actually yields in abundance or with rapidity fruits, offspring, or, by extension, projects, inventions, or works of art; thus, one speaks of the *fecundity* of a mother if one wishes to imply that she has a large family, but of her *fertility* if the intent is to indicate that she is not sterile; so, by extension, a *fecund* rather than a *fertile* inventive genius ⟨a good part of these inventions came to birth—or were further nourished—in the *fecund* mind of Leonardo da Vinci—*Mumford*⟩ ⟨if you had been born a Dumas—I am speaking of *fecundity* . . . and of nothing else . . . and could rattle off a romance in a fortnight—*Quiller-Couch*⟩ **Fruitful** may be preferred to *fecund* when the reference is to plants and may replace *fertile* in reference to soil or land, but it is especially applicable to something that promotes fertility or fecundity ⟨a *fruitful* rain⟩ In its extended sense it is applicable to whatever bears results, especially useful or profitable results ⟨the time has always come, and the season is never unripe, for the announcement of the *fruitful* idea—*John Morley*⟩ ⟨the enormously *fruitful* discovery that pitch of sound depends upon the length of the vibrating chord—*Ellis*⟩ ⟨Darwinism . . . is a *fruitful* theory of the means by which nature works—*Inge*⟩ ⟨the poet . . . is apt to lack the detachment which alone makes *fruitful* criticism possible—*Lowes*⟩ **Prolific** is often interchangeable with *fecund*, but it often suggests

even greater rapidity in reproduction and is therefore more frequently used than the latter term in disparagement or derogation especially when applied to types or kinds of things or beings ⟨the starling is so *prolific* that the flocks become immense—*Jefferies*⟩ ⟨uncultivated, defective people . . . are appallingly *prolific*—*Shaw*⟩ ⟨the flabby pseudoreligions in which the modern world is so *prolific*—*Krutch*⟩

*Ana* producing, bearing, yielding (see BEAR): inventing *or* inventive, creating *or* creative (see corresponding verbs at INVENT): quickening, stimulating, provoking, exciting, galvanizing (see PROVOKE)

*Ant* infertile, sterile —*Con* barren, impotent, unfruitful (see STERILE)

**fertility** fruitfulness, fecundity, prolificacy (see under FERTILE)

*Ant* infertility, sterility —*Con* impotence *or* impotency, barrenness, unfruitfulness (see corresponding adjectives at STERILE)

**fervent** ardent, fervid, perfervid, *impassioned, passionate

*Ana* *devout, pious, religious: warm, warmhearted, *tender, responsive: *sincere, wholehearted, heartfelt, hearty, whole-souled, unfeigned: *intense, vehement, fierce, exquisite, violent

*Con* cool, *cold, chilly, frigid: apathetic, *impassive, phlegmatic

**fervid** fervent, ardent, perfervid, *impassioned, passionate

*Ana* *intense, vehement, fierce, exquisite, violent: earnest, *serious, solemn: *sincere, heartfelt, hearty, wholehearted, whole-souled

*Con* collected, composed, *cool, imperturbable, nonchalant: *indifferent, aloof, detached, unconcerned

**fervor** ardor, enthusiasm, *passion, zeal

*Ana* devoutness, piousness *or* piety (see corresponding adjectives at DEVOUT): earnestness, seriousness, solemnity (see corresponding adjectives at SERIOUS): sincerity, heartiness, wholeheartedness (see corresponding adjectives at SINCERE)

**fetch** *vb* *bring, take

*Ana* *get, obtain, procure: transfer, shift, *move, remove: convey, transport, transmit, *carry, bear

**fetid** noisome, *malodorous, stinking, putrid, rank, rancid, fusty, musty

*Ana* foul, nasty (see DIRTY): *offensive, loathsome, repulsive, repugnant, revolting

*Ant* fragrant —*Con* *odorous, aromatic, redolent, balmy

**fetish,** talisman, charm, amulet are comparable when they designate an object believed to be endowed with the virtue of averting evil or of bringing good fortune. **Fetish** is applied to an object, either natural (as a snake or an animal's tooth or claw) or artificial (as a piece of carved wood or bone), which is held sacred in the belief that a supernatural spirit has entered into it and invested it with the power to bring success, luck, and freedom from evil to its owner or worshiper. In its basic sense the word is always connected with the religion of primitive or barbarous peoples ⟨the Ashanti fertility *fetish,* carried on the backs of pregnant women to help make their children beautiful—*Time*⟩ In extended use it may be applied to whatever is unreasonably or irrationally regarded as sacred or sacrosanct ⟨make a *fetish* of the Constitution⟩ ⟨the mediocre was repellent to them; they made a *fetish* of hard truth—*Rose Macaulay*⟩ **Talisman,** unlike *fetish,* presupposes a degree of enlightenment, a knowledge of astrology and other occult sciences, and a belief in magical powers. Primarily it is applied to a cut, incised, or engraved figure or image of a heavenly constellation or planet or to its sign, or to a gem or a piece of metal so cut, incised, or engraved. By virtue of this representation it is supposed to be endowed with the same occult influence as what it represents ⟨he had stolen from Henry . . . a *talisman,* which rendered its wearer invulnerable—*Stubbs*⟩ In extended use it may be applied to an object felt to exert a magical, extraordinary, and usually happy influence ⟨the little circle of the schoolboy's copper coin . . . had proven a *talisman,* fragrant with good, and deserving to be set in gold and worn next her heart—*Hawthorne*⟩ ⟨the mere touch of a leaf was a *talisman* to bring me under the enchantment—*Jefferies*⟩ ⟨there is no *talisman* in the word *parent* which can generate miracles of affection—*Butler* d. 1902⟩ ⟨if their hearts had been opened, there would have been found, engraved within, the *talisman* Education—*Brooks*⟩ **Charm** basically applies to something believed to work a spell repelling evil spirits or malign influences or attracting favorable ones. It may be used in reference to an incantation, a word, or a form of words as well as to an object; thus, fetishes and talismans were often carried as *charms* ⟨the gallant little Abruzzi cob was decorated with . . . a panoply of *charms* against the evil eye—*Mackenzie*⟩ In its extended application to a quality in persons or in things it connotes a power to attract or allure that is suggestive of spell working ⟨she has great *charm*⟩ ⟨did you feel the *charm* of the painting?⟩ ⟨one of the great *charms* of Lawrence . . . was that he could never be bored—*Huxley*⟩ **Amulet** is usually applied to something worn or carried on the person because of its supposed magical power to preserve one in danger or to protect one from evil and especially from disease ⟨the French traveler Coudreau . . . expressly states that collars made of jaguars' or bush hogs' teeth, worn round the neck by small children, are *amulets* intended to protect them, when they grow bigger, against the attack of ferocious beasts—*Karsten*⟩ In its rare extended use the word still implies protection ⟨righteousness will give you love . . . but it will not give you an invincible *amulet* against misfortune—*Farrar*⟩

**fetter** *vb*    shackle, *hamper, trammel, clog, manacle, hog-tie

*Ana* *hinder, impede, obstruct, block, bar, dam: *restrain, curb, check: baffle, balk, thwart, foil, *frustrate: bind, *tie

*Con* *free, liberate, release: *extricate, disencumber, disembarrass, disentangle, untangle: disengage, *detach

**fewer** *less, lesser, smaller

**fib** *n*   untruth, falsehood, *lie, misrepresentation, story

**fib** *vb*   equivocate, palter, *lie, prevaricate

**fickle** *inconstant, unstable, capricious, mercurial

*Ana* *changeable, changeful, variable, protean: *fitful, spasmodic: light, light-minded, frivolous, flighty, volatile (see corresponding nouns at LIGHTNESS)

*Ant* constant, true  —*Con* *faithful, loyal, staunch, steadfast

**fiction,** **figment, fabrication, fable** are comparable when meaning a story, an account, an explanation, or a conception which is an invention of the human mind. **Fiction** so strongly implies the use of the imagination that it serves as the class name for all prose or poetic writings which deal with imagined characters and situations or with actual characters or situations with less concern for the historicity of the details than for the telling of an interesting, coherent story. In the sense here particularly considered, a *fiction* is something that is made up without reference to and often in defiance of fact or reality or truth, typically for some such reason as to avoid telling an unpleasant or inconvenient truth ⟨Adrian . . . was at a loss what to invent to detain him, beyond the stale *fiction* that his father was

coming tomorrow—*Meredith*⟩ or to describe or explain someone or something about whom or which practically nothing is known ⟨Karl Joël . . . spent fifteen of the best years of his life over the Xenophontic Socrates, to discover that the figure was just as much a *fiction* as the Platonic Socrates—*Ellis*⟩ or to impose upon others an interpretation or an assumption that serves one's own ends or that satisfies the unthinking because of its accord with outward appearances ⟨the notion that a business is clothed with a public interest and has been devoted to the public use is little more than a *fiction* intended to beautify what is disagreeable to the sufferers—*Justice Holmes*⟩ ⟨few of the usual *fictions* on which society rested had ever required such defiance of facts—*Henry Adams*⟩ or, especially in legal or scientific use, to provide a convenient assumption or method whereby one can deal with what is beyond the range of rational or objective proof ⟨the Linnaean and similar classificatory systems are *fictions* . . . having their value simply as pictures, as forms of representation—*Ellis*⟩ **Fiction** may apply to something which appears to be or is believed to be true or which accords with some higher form of truth (as "poetic truth," "philosophical truth," or "spiritual truth") or with the demands of reason when these come into conflict with fact or with the world as apprehended by the senses; *figment* and *fabrication,* on the other hand, carry no implication of justification and typically suggest a defiance of truth of whatever kind or degree. **Figment** usually suggests the operation of fancy or of unlicensed imagination and neglect of fact ⟨the rude, unvarnished gibes with which he demolished every *figment* of defense—*Stevenson*⟩ ⟨a sense of unreality was creeping over him. Surely this great Chamber . . . did not exist at all but as a gigantic fancy of his own! And all these figures were *figments* of his brain!—*Galsworthy*⟩ **Fabrication** applies to something that is made up with artifice and usually with the intent to deceive; consequently it is often used of a fiction that is a deliberate and complete falsehood ⟨the common account of his disappearance is a *fabrication*⟩ ⟨the legend, though some of its details are obviously fictitious, cannot be dismissed as a pure *fabrication*⟩ ⟨it is evidence—fact, not *fabrication*—*Partridge*⟩ ⟨the Government story was not a complete *fabrication* but a careful distortion—*Devlin*⟩ **Fable** (see also ALLEGORY 2) applies to a fictitious narrative that is obviously unconcerned with fact, usually because it deals with events or situations that are marvelous, impossible, preposterous, or incredible ⟨if we may take the story of Job for a history, not a *fable*—*Defoe*⟩ ⟨nothing but whispered suspicions, old wives' tales, *fables* invented by men who had nothing to do but loaf in the drugstore and make up stories—*Anderson*⟩

*Ana* narrative, *story, tale, anecdote, yarn

**fictitious,** **fabulous, legendary, mythical, apocryphal** mean having the character of something invented or imagined as opposed to something true or genuine. **Fictitious** commonly implies fabrication and, therefore, more often suggests artificiality or contrivance than intent to deceive or deliberate falsification ⟨many authors prefer to assume a *fictitious* name⟩ ⟨he was a novelist: his amours and his characters were *fictitious*—*Gogarty*⟩ In an extended sense *fictitious* definitely connotes falseness when applied to value, worth, or significance and suggests its determination by other than the right standards ⟨the furore created by this incident gives it a *fictitious* importance⟩ ⟨in booms and in panics the market value of a security is often *fictitious*⟩ **Fabulous** stresses the marvelousness or incredibility of what is so described; only at times, however, does the adjective imply a thing's impossibility or nonexistence ⟨the *fabulous* mill which

---

A colon (:) separates groups of words discriminated. An asterisk (*) indicates place of treatment of each group.

ground old people young—*Dickens*⟩ ⟨the company paid *fabulous* dividends⟩ ⟨[Lincoln] grows vaguer and more *fabulous* as year follows year—*Mencken*⟩ Often it is little more than a vague intensive ⟨a house with a *fabulous* view of the mountains⟩ ⟨we had a *fabulous* vacation trip⟩ **Legendary** usually suggests popular tradition and popular susceptibility to elaboration of details or distortion of historical facts as the basis for a thing's fictitious or fabulous character ⟨the *legendary* deeds of William Tell⟩ ⟨the Tarquins, *legendary* kings of ancient Rome⟩ ⟨Bradford's *John Henry* . . . took a famous *legendary* Negro for its hero—*Van Doren*⟩ **Mythical**, like *legendary*, usually presupposes the working of the popular imagination, but it distinctively implies a purely fanciful explanation of facts or the creation of purely imaginary beings and events especially in accounting for natural phenomena. Therefore, *mythical* in its wider use is nearly equivalent to *imaginary* and implies nonexistence ⟨the *mythical* beings called nymphs⟩ ⟨these ancestors are not creations of the *mythical* fancy but were once men of flesh and blood—*Frazer*⟩ **Apocryphal** typically attributes dubiety to the source of something (as a story or account) and especially suggests that the source is other than it is believed or claimed to be ⟨this . . . epigram, has a certain fame in its own right. It too has been attributed to Ariosto, though it is evidently *apocryphal—Morby*⟩ ⟨the *apocryphal* work attributed to Chaucer in the 16th century—*Philip Williams*⟩ In such use it does not necessarily imply that the matter is in itself untrue, but it stresses the lack of a known responsible source. Sometimes, however, *apocryphal* loses its stress on source and then may imply dubiety or inaccuracy of the thing itself ⟨taking to themselves the upper rooms formerly belonging to the *apocryphal* invisible lodger—*Dickens*⟩ ⟨tales, possibly *apocryphal* and certainly embroidered, of his feats of intelligence work in the eastern Mediterranean—*Firth*⟩
**Ana** invented, created (see INVENT): *imaginary, fanciful, fantastic: fabricated, fashioned (see MAKE)
**Ant** historical —**Con** *real, true, actual: *authentic, veritable: veracious, truthful, verisimilar (see corresponding nouns at TRUTH)

**fidelity,** allegiance, fealty, loyalty, devotion, piety denote faithfulness to something to which one is bound by a pledge or duty. **Fidelity** implies strict adherence to what is a matter of faith or of keeping faith; it presupposes an obligation, sometimes natural, sometimes imposed as a trust, and sometimes voluntarily accepted or chosen ⟨*fidelity* to one's word⟩ ⟨*fidelity* in the performance of one's duties⟩ ⟨*fidelity* to one's friends⟩ Sometimes, even when unqualified, it implies marital faithfulness ⟨with close *fidelity* and love unfeigned to keep the matrimonial bond unstained—*Cowper*⟩ Sometimes it implies faithfulness to the original (as in representation, portrayal, or quotation) ⟨the Russian . . . finds relief to his sensitiveness in letting his perceptions have perfectly free play, and in recording their reports with perfect *fidelity—Arnold*⟩ **Allegiance** implies adherence to something objective which one serves or follows as a vassal follows his lord and which demands unswerving fidelity when conflicting obligations dispute its preeminence ⟨secret societies that exact the *allegiance* of every member⟩ ⟨but he [the critic] owes no *allegiance* to anything but to Truth; all other fidelities he must disregard when that is in question—*L. P. Smith*⟩ **Fealty,** like *allegiance*, implies a supreme obligation to be faithful, but unlike the latter it stresses the compelling power of one's sense of duty or of consciousness of one's pledged word ⟨when I do forget the least of these unspeakable deserts, Romans, forget your *fealty* to me—*Shak.*⟩ ⟨the extent to which we are accurate in our thoughts, words,

and deeds is a rough measure of our *fealty* to truth—*Ballard*⟩ **Loyalty** may imply more emotion and closer personal attachment than either *fidelity* or *fealty*; it usually connotes steadfastness, sometimes in the face of attempts to alienate one's affections or of a temptation to ignore or renounce one's obligation ⟨I will follow thee, to the last gasp, with truth and *loyalty—Shak.*⟩ but in some contexts it may be taken to imply no more than absence of anything treasonable or subversive ⟨there are the *loyalty* programs . . . which undertake to exclude Communists and other disloyal persons from the government payrolls—*Cushman*⟩ Unlike *fidelity, loyalty* sometimes suggests a personal and emotional attachment often without rational basis ⟨her chief offering, however, was a blind *loyalty* which stood every test, including the party's purge of her husband—*Time*⟩ ⟨we can draw a portrait of Jesus that does not offend our rationalism, but it is done at the expense of our *loyalty* to the textual authority—*Jung*⟩ ⟨indeed, in public life it is generally considered a kind of treachery to change, because people value what they call *loyalty* above truth—*Benson*⟩ **Devotion** stresses zeal in service often amounting to self-dedication; it usually also implies ardent attachment ⟨he set out to prove the loyalty of his nature by *devotion* to the Queen who had advanced him—*Belloc*⟩ ⟨there is . . . something outside of the artist to which he owes allegiance, a *devotion* to which he must surrender and sacrifice himself—*T. S. Eliot*⟩ **Piety** emphasizes fidelity to obligations regarded as natural or fundamental (as reverence for one's parents, one's race, one's traditions, one's country, or one's God) and observance of all the duties which such fidelity requires ⟨filial *piety* inspires respect for the wishes of parents⟩ ⟨religious *piety* is manifest in faithful and reverent worship⟩ ⟨having matured in the surroundings and under the special conditions of sea life, I have a special *piety* toward that form of my past . . . . I have tried with an almost filial regard to render the vibration of life in the great world of waters —*Conrad*⟩
**Ana** faithfulness, constancy, staunchness, steadfastness (see corresponding adjectives at FAITHFUL)
**Ant** faithlessness: perfidy —**Con** falseness *or* falsity, disloyalty, treacherousness *or* treachery, traitorousness, perfidiousness (see corresponding adjectives at FAITHLESS)

**fidgety** restless, restive, uneasy, jumpy, jittery, *impatient, nervous, unquiet

**field,** domain, province, sphere, territory, bailiwick are comparable when they denote the limits in which a person, an institution, or a department of knowledge, of art, or of human endeavor appropriately or necessarily confines his or its activity or influence and outside of which by implication he or it may not or should not go. **Field** implies restriction by choice or by necessity, but it seldom suggests permanent limitation ⟨a European war narrows the *field* of commerce for neutral American nations⟩ ⟨he chose the development of industries in the South as his *field* of investigation⟩ ⟨the philosopher and the practical man . . . each is in his own *field*, supreme—*Buckle*⟩ ⟨a writer whose reputation . . . has been pretty much confined to the whodunit *field—Kelly*⟩ **Domain** is used chiefly in reference to departments of knowledge, of art, and of human endeavor viewed abstractly; it implies exclusive possession and control of a clearly defined field and a title to regard all outside interference or all intrusion into that field as trespass or invasion ⟨the *domain* of science⟩ ⟨the *domain* of the spiritual⟩ ⟨what is the difference between the legitimate music of verse and the music it attains by trespassing on the *domain* of a sister art?—*Babbitt*⟩ ⟨those who believe in the reality of a world of the spirit —the poet, the artist, the mystic—are at one in believing

that there are other *domains* than that of physics—*Jeans*⟩ **Province** is used in reference not only to the arts and sciences, each of which may be said to have its own domain, but also to a person or institution that because of his or its office, aims, or special character can be said to have jurisdiction, competence, power, or influence within clearly defined limits ⟨it is within the *province* of a parent rather than of a teacher to discipline a pupil for misconduct out of school⟩ ⟨it is often stated that art goes beyond its *province* when it attempts to teach morals⟩ ⟨the almost impertinently realistic explorations into behavior which are the *province* of the psychiatrist—*Sapir*⟩ **Province** is also used in the sense of function (see also FUNCTION *n* 1) and in the sense of a part of a larger domain ⟨I should like the reader to accept engineering as a *province* of physics: so that the feats of the one may serve as credentials for the discoveries of the other—*Darrow*⟩ **Sphere,** even more than *domain,* throws emphasis on clear circumscription of limits; it therefore suggests apartness rather than fundamental differences and carries no hint of danger of trespass or interference ⟨the aesthetic and ethical *spheres* . . . were never sharply distinguished by the Greeks—*Dickinson*⟩ ⟨in the *sphere* of morals we must often be content to wait until our activity is completed to appreciate its beauty or its ugliness—*Ellis*⟩ ⟨in the life of a man whose circumstances and talents are not very exceptional there should be a large *sphere* where what is vaguely termed "herd instinct" dominates, and a small *sphere* into which it does not penetrate—*Russell*⟩ ⟨a long and profound process of social change . . . but this time in the economic *sphere*—*Strachey*⟩ **Territory** comes very close to *domain* in implying a field possessed and controlled and regarded as one's own; it does not, however, carry the implications so strong in *domain* of rightful ownership, of sovereignty, and of the title to inviolability; it may even suggest that the field has been usurped or taken over by the science, art, or activity in question ⟨prose has preempted a lion's share of the *territory* once held, either in sovereignty or on equal terms, by poetry—*Lowes*⟩ ⟨if passageways connect the domain of physics with the domains of life or of spirit, physics ought in time to discover these passageways, for they start from her own *territory*—*Jeans*⟩ **Bailiwick,** basically the jurisdiction of a bailiff, is increasingly used in an extended and playful sense in reference to an individual and the special and limited province or domain in which he may or does exercise authority. It often also carries a connotation of petty yet despotic display of power ⟨a politician whose influence does not extend beyond his own *bailiwick*⟩ ⟨he will not get along with others until he learns to keep within his own *bailiwick*⟩ ⟨we may neither be angry nor gay in the presence of the moon, nor may we dare to think in her *bailiwick*—*Stephens*⟩ ⟨the largest problems are in the *bailiwick* of the social scientist—*Street*⟩
*Ana* limits, bounds, confines (see singular nouns at LIMIT): extent, area, *size, magnitude

**fiendish,** devilish, diabolical, diabolic, demoniac, demonic are comparable when they mean having or manifesting the qualities associated with infernal or hellish beings called devils, demons, and fiends. **Fiendish** usually implies excessive cruelty or malignity ⟨*fiendish* tortures⟩ ⟨the *fiendish* joy that illumined his usually stolid countenance sent a sudden disgust and horror through me—*Hudson*⟩ **Devilish** frequently suggests abnormal wickedness ⟨*devilish* orgies⟩ ⟨*devilish* treachery⟩ but it often also suggests superhuman or satanic ingenuity or craft or capacity for destruction ⟨showed no compunction in planning *devilish* engines of military destruction—*Ellis*⟩ The term is often used as an intensive that substitutes for profanity ⟨*devilish*

good dinner—*Dickens*⟩ **Diabolical** often and *devilish* sometimes connote colder and more calculating malevolence than *fiendish* ⟨*diabolical* cruelty⟩ ⟨*diabolical* ingenuity⟩ ⟨a *diabolical* sneer⟩ ⟨people suffering from the paranoia of persecution often imagine that they are the victims of a *diabolical* secret society—*Huxley*⟩ **Diabolic** is often used interchangeably with *diabolical,* but the former term may be preferred when the reference is to devils as individuals of a given character or origin rather than to their malign qualities ⟨the difference between the angelic and the *diabolic* temperament—*Shaw*⟩ ⟨[the heroic age's] heroes were doughty men to whom *diabolic* visitors were no more unusual than angelic ones—*Krutch*⟩ **Demoniac** and **demonic** often suggest frenzy or excesses (as of one possessed) ⟨*demoniac* strength⟩ ⟨*demonic* laughter⟩ More frequently they suggest the inexplicable or superhuman element in life or, especially, in genius ⟨in the solidest kingdom of routine and the senses, he [Goethe] showed the lurking *demonic* power—*Emerson*⟩ ⟨the rapt, *demonic* features of the Magic Muse—*Hewlett*⟩ ⟨he rode swift horses; he fought duels; he had burning love affairs; he traveled with *demoniac* restlessness throughout Europe—*Highet*⟩
*Ana* hellish, *infernal: malign, malefic, maleficent, baleful, *sinister: malignant, malevolent, *malicious

**fierce 1** Fierce, truculent, ferocious, barbarous, savage, inhuman, cruel, fell are comparable when they mean displaying fury or malignity in looks or in actions. **Fierce** is applied to men or to animals that inspire terror because of their menacing aspect or their unrestrained fury in attack ⟨the other Shape . . . black it stood as night, *fierce* as ten Furies, terrible as Hell, and shook a dreadful dart —*Milton*⟩ ⟨no bandit *fierce,* no tyrant mad with pride —*Pope*⟩ **Truculent,** though it implies fierceness, especially of aspect, suggests the intent to inspire terror or to threaten rather than the achievement of that intention. Consequently it often implies a bullying attitude or pose. It is applied chiefly to persons, groups of persons, and nations ⟨a group of *truculent* schoolboys⟩ ⟨he must . . . worry them toward the fold like a *truculent* sheep dog —*J. R. Lowell*⟩ ⟨the America that [Theodore] Roosevelt dreamed of was always a sort of swollen Prussia, *truculent* without and regimented within—*Mencken*⟩ **Ferocious** not only connotes extreme fierceness but it implies actions suggestive of a wild beast on a rampage or in an attack on its prey; it therefore usually implies unrestrained violence, extreme fury, and wanton brutality ⟨a *ferocious* bayonet charge⟩ ⟨take a *ferocious* revenge⟩ ⟨a particularly *ferocious* dog⟩ ⟨two bloodthirsty men, more cruel than the most *ferocious* brutes—*Frazer*⟩ **Barbarous** (see also BARBARIAN) in its extended sense applies only to civilized persons or their actions; it implies a harshness, a brutality, and, often, a ferocity thought of as unworthy of human beings in an advanced state of culture ⟨the *barbarous* pleasures of the chase—*John Morley*⟩ ⟨*barbarous* treatment of prisoners⟩ ⟨*barbarous* methods of warfare⟩ ⟨you have been wantonly attacked by a ruthless and *barbarous* aggressor. Your capital has been bombed, your women and children brutally murdered —*Sir Winston Churchill*⟩ **Savage** (see also BARBARIAN) implies an absence of the restraints imposed by civilization or of the inhibitions characteristic of civilized man when dealing with those whom he hates or fears or when filled with rage, lust, or other violent passion ⟨a *savage* desire for revenge⟩ ⟨*savage* punishment of a disobedient child⟩ ⟨a *savage* criticism of a book⟩ ⟨lashed out with all the oratorical fury and *savage* invective at his command—*Sidney Warren*⟩ ⟨the *savage* wars of religion

—*Inge*⟩ **Inhuman** is even stronger than *savage,* for it suggests not so much undue violence or lack of restraint as absence of all feeling that normally characterizes a human being: on the one hand it may suggest wanton brutality, or on the other hand it may imply absence of all capacity for love, kindness, or pity ⟨an *inhuman* mother⟩ ⟨thy *deed, inhuman* and unnatural—*Shak.*⟩ **Cruel** implies indifference to the suffering of others and even a positive pleasure in witnessing it or in inflicting it ⟨her mouth *crueler* than a tiger's, colder than a snake's, and beautiful beyond a woman's—*Swinburne*⟩ ⟨as *cruel* as a schoolboy ere he grows to pity—*Tennyson*⟩ **Fell,** which is chiefly rhetorical or poetic, connotes dire or baleful cruelty ⟨unsex me here, and fill me from the crown to the toe topful of direst cruelty! . . . stop up the access and passage to remorse, that no compunctious visitings of nature shake my *fell* purpose—*Shak.*⟩ ⟨sinister men with . . . their own *fell* ends—*T. I. Cook*⟩

*Ana* menacing, threatening (see THREATEN): infuriated, maddened, enraged (see ANGER *vb*): ravening, ravenous, rapacious, *voracious: *fearful, terrible, horrible, horrific
*Ant* tame: mild

**2** *intense, vehement, exquisite, violent
*Ana* extreme, *excessive, inordinate: penetrating, piercing (see ENTER): *supreme, superlative, transcendent
**fiery** *spirited, high-spirited, peppery, gingery, mettlesome, spunky
*Ana* impetuous, *precipitate, headlong: passionate, perfervid, ardent, *impassioned, fervid: vehement, *intense, fierce, violent
**fight** *vb* **1** battle, war, *contend
*Ana* struggle, strive (see ATTEMPT): dispute, debate (see DISCUSS): wrangle, squabble, quarrel, altercate (see under QUARREL *n*)
**2** *resist, withstand, contest, oppose, combat, conflict, antagonize
**fight** *n* combat, fray, affray, conflict, *contest
*Ana* struggle, striving (see under ATTEMPT *vb*): strife, contention, conflict, dissension, *discord, difference, variance
**figment** fabrication, fable, *fiction
*Ana* *fancy, fantasy, dream, daydream, nightmare: invention, creation (see corresponding verbs at INVENT)
**figure** *n* **1** *number, numeral, digit, integer
*Ana* symbol, *character
**2** *form, shape, configuration, conformation
*Ana* *outline, contour, profile, silhouette: *character, symbol, sign, mark
**3** Figure, pattern, design, motif, device are comparable when they mean a unit in a decorative composition (as in an ornamented textile or fabric) consisting of a representation of a natural, conventionalized, or geometrical shape or a combination of such representations. **Figure** commonly refers to a small, simple unit which is repeated or is one of those repeated over an entire surface. A figure may be one of the outlines associated with geometry (as a triangle, diamond, pentagon, or circle) or such an outline filled in with color, lines, or a representation of another kind; it may, however, be a natural or conventionalized representation of a natural form (as a leaf, flower, or animal) ⟨an Oriental rug with geometrical *figures* in blue and red⟩ ⟨a silk print with a small *figure*⟩ ⟨the wallpaper has a well-spaced *figure* of a spray of rosebuds⟩ ⟨carved with *figures* strange and sweet, all made out of the carver's brain—*Coleridge*⟩ **Pattern** may be used in place of *figure* ⟨arranged in a series of simple and pleasing *patterns*—diamonds, quincunxes, hexagons—*Huxley*⟩ but *figure* is not interchangeable with the more inclusive senses of *pattern.* The latter term is applicable not only

to the simplest repeated unit, or figure, or to a larger repeated unit involving several related figures but also to the whole plan of decoration or adornment ⟨the *pattern* of a lace tablecloth⟩ ⟨the *pattern* of a rug⟩ Also, *pattern* may be used of other things than those which are visible, objective works of art and craftsmanship but which nevertheless can be viewed or studied as having diverse parts or elements brought together so as to present an intelligible and distinctive whole ⟨the true *pattern* of the campaign revealed itself after the first week⟩ ⟨when he said *pattern,* he did not mean the *pattern* on a wallpaper; he meant the *pattern* of life—*Sackville-West*⟩ ⟨as skepticism grows, the *pattern* of human conduct inevitably changes—*Krutch*⟩ ⟨the nearness of friends in those days, the familiar, unchanging streets, the convivial clubs, the constant companionship helped to knit the strands of life into a close and well-defined *pattern* —*Repplier*⟩ **Design** (see also PLAN, INTENTION) emphasizes drawing and arrangement and attention to line and the handling of figures and colors; it often specifically denotes a single unit (figure or pattern) which reveals these qualities ⟨branches and leaves were disposed, not as combinations of color in mass, but as *designs* in line —*Binyon*⟩ ⟨your golden filaments in fair *design* across my duller fiber—*Millay*⟩ **Motif** (see also SUBJECT 2) is frequently used in the decorative arts for a figure or a design which stands out not necessarily as the only one but as the leading one which gives the distinctive character of the whole ⟨in lace for ecclesiastical use a sheaf of wheat is often the *motif* of the pattern⟩ **Device** applies usually to a figure that bears no likeness to anything in nature but is the result of imagination or fancy. Unlike the other terms, it does not exclusively apply to a decorative unit, though it occurs frequently in that application ⟨set in the close-grained wood were quaint *devices; patterns* in ambers, and in the clouded green of jades —*Lowell*⟩

**figure** *vb* cast, *add, sum, total, tot, foot
*Ana* compute, *calculate, reckon, estimate: *count, enumerate, number
**filch** *vb* purloin, lift, pilfer, *steal, pinch, snitch, swipe, cop
*Ana* snatch, grab, *take, seize, grasp: *rob, plunder, loot, rifle
**file** *n* *line, row, rank, echelon, tier
**fillet** *n* *strip, band, ribbon, stripe
**filthy** *dirty, foul, squalid, nasty
*Ana* slovenly, unkempt, disheveled, sloppy, *slipshod: *offensive, loathsome, repulsive, revolting
*Ant* neat, spick-and-span —*Con* cleaned, cleansed (see CLEAN *vb*): *clean, cleanly: tidy, trim, trig, shipshape (see NEAT)
**final** terminal, concluding, *last, latest, ultimate, eventual
*Ana* closing, ending, terminating (see CLOSE *vb*): decisive, determinative, *conclusive, definitive
**financial,** monetary, pecuniary, fiscal are comparable when meaning of or relating to the possession, the making, the borrowing and lending, or the expenditure of money. **Financial** implies a relation to money matters in general, especially as conducted on a large scale ⟨the *financial* concerns of the company are attended to by the treasurer⟩ ⟨the *financial* position of the bank is sound⟩ ⟨the *financial* interests of the country⟩ ⟨the city is in *financial* difficulties⟩ **Monetary** implies a much more direct reference to money as such and therefore often connotes the coinage, distribution, and circulation of money ⟨the *monetary* unit⟩ ⟨the *monetary* systems of Europe⟩ ⟨the *monetary* standard⟩ ⟨*monetary* gifts⟩ **Pecuniary** suggests a reference to the practical uses of money; it is

often employed in preference to *financial* when money matters that are personal or on a small scale are being considered 〈to ask for *pecuniary* aid〉 〈he is always in *pecuniary* difficulties〉 〈he works only for *pecuniary* motives〉 **Fiscal** implies reference to the financial affairs of a state, a sovereign, a corporation, or an institution whose concerns with revenue and expenditures are managed by a treasurer or treasury department 〈the *fiscal* year in the United States ends on June 30〉 〈a *fiscal* officer of the crown〉

**fine** *n* amercement (see under PENALIZE)

**fine** *vb* *penalize, amerce, mulct

**finicky, finicking, finical** particular, fussy, fastidious, *nice, dainty, squeamish, persnickety, pernickety
*Ana* exacting, demanding (see DEMAND *vb*): captious, carping, hypercritical, *critical: meticulous, punctilious, *careful: conscientious, scrupulous (see UPRIGHT)
*Con* *slipshod, sloppy, slovenly: *slatternly, dowdy, blowsy, frowzy

**finish** *vb* complete, conclude, *close, end, terminate
*Ana* achieve, accomplish, effect, fulfill (see PERFORM)

**finished** *consummate, accomplished
*Ana* *perfect, entire, intact, whole: refined, cultivated, cultured (see corresponding nouns at CULTURE): *suave, urbane, smooth: elegant, exquisite (see CHOICE)
*Ant* crude —*Con* *rude, rough, raw, callow, green, uncouth

**fire** *n* Fire, conflagration, holocaust are comparable when meaning a blaze that reduces or threatens to reduce one or more buildings to ashes. **Fire** is the general term referable to such an event, whether it involves one or many buildings and whether it is checked or not 〈Chicago was nearly half destroyed by a *fire* that occurred in 1871〉 〈there was a small *fire* on our street last night〉 **Conflagration** implies a devastating fire that must be contended with by all the available forces; it usually takes a length of time to check it or to prevent its further advance 〈a disastrous *conflagration* made 2000 persons homeless〉 〈by quick work the firemen prevented the fire from developing into a *conflagration*〉 **Holocaust** basically denotes a burnt sacrifice, but in more general use it refers usually to a conflagration in which there has been a great loss of life and especially of human life 〈the burning of the Iroquois Theater at Chicago in 1903, in which nearly 600 persons lost their lives, was one of the worst *holocausts* ever known in the United States〉 In extended use *holocaust* usually stresses destruction of life, but it may blend in the notion of sacrifice 〈the Eire that had its birth in the *holocaust* of Easter Week —*Richard Watts*〉 〈an assemblage of men whose maturity has been forged in the *holocaust* of battle—*Loveman*〉
*Ana* blaze, glare, flame, flare (see under BLAZE *vb*): burning, charring, scorching (see BURN *vb*)

**fire** *vb* 1 kindle, ignite, *light
*Ana* *burn, scorch, char: *blaze, flame, flare, glare, glow: *illuminate, lighten
2 animate, inspire, *inform
*Ana* excite, *provoke, stimulate, galvanize: *thrill, electrify: *stir, rouse, arouse: enliven, *quicken, vivify
*Ant* daunt —*Con* *dismay, appall
3 discharge, *dismiss, cashier, drop, sack, bounce
*Ana* *eject, oust, expel: *discard

**firm** *adj* Firm, hard, solid are comparable chiefly as meaning having a texture or consistency that markedly resists deformation by external force. **Firm** (opposed to *loose, flabby*) suggests such closeness or compactness of texture or a consistency so heavy or substantial that the substance or material quickly returns to shape or is difficult to pull, distort, cut, or displace 〈*firm* cloth〉

〈*firm* flesh〉 〈*firm* jellies〉 〈*firm* ground〉 **Hard** (opposed to *soft*; see also HARD 2) implies impenetrability or relatively complete resistance to pressure or tension but, unlike *firm*, *hard* rarely implies elasticity 〈*hard* as adamant〉 〈*hard* as steel〉 〈diamond is one of the *hardest* substances known〉 **Solid** (opposed to *fluid*) implies such density and coherence in the mass as enable a thing to maintain a fixed form in spite of external deforming forces 〈*solid* mineral matter〉 As opposed to *flimsy*, the term implies a structure or construction that makes a thing sound, strong, or stable 〈*solid* furniture〉 〈a *solid* foundation〉 〈the bungalow was a very *solid* one—*Kipling*〉 As opposed to *hollow*, it implies the absence of empty spaces within the structure or mass and, usually, the same or similar density and hardness of material throughout 〈a *solid* rubber tire〉 〈a *solid* wall〉

In extended use **firm** implies stability, fixedness, or resolution 〈a *firm* purpose〉 〈a *firm* belief〉 〈guide with a *firm* hand〉 〈a *firm* and even tough diplomacy—*Gaitskell*〉 **Hard** implies obduracy or lack of feeling 〈a *hard* master〉 〈she was firm, but she was not *hard*—*Archibald Marshall*〉 〈a sort of scoutmaster to a *hard* gang of boys —*Lovett*〉 **Solid** usually implies substantiality or genuineness 〈a *solid* meal〉 〈*solid* facts〉 〈*solid* virtues〉 〈*solid* attainments〉 〈money, the great solvent of the *solid* fabric of the old society, the great generator of illusion—*Trilling*〉 but it may imply absolute reliability or seriousness of purpose 〈*solid* banks〉 〈a *solid* character〉 〈his scholarship was *solid* and sound—*McGiffert*〉 or unbroken continuity (as in time, group feeling, or opinion) 〈put in a *solid* week on a piece of work〉 〈the *solid* vote of the members〉
*Ana* compact, *close, dense, thick: tough, tenacious, *strong: *stiff, rigid, inflexible
*Ant* loose, flabby —*Con* flaccid, *limp, floppy, flimsy, sleazy

**fiscal** *financial, monetary, pecuniary

**fish** *vb* Fish, angle mean to attempt to catch fish. **Fish** implies the use of some apparatus and suggests nothing about the reason; **angle,** which is chiefly literary except in the derivative *angler*, implies the use of hook, bait, line, and rod and sport as the reason for the activity. Both words are used, without perceptible distinction, in the extended sense to seek to obtain or win by artifice 〈*fish* for a compliment〉 〈modesty is the only sure bait, when you *angle* for praise—*Chesterfield*〉 〈the first woman who *fishes* for him, hooks him—*Thackeray*〉 〈she knew her distance and did *angle* for me, madding my eagerness with her restraint—*Shak.*〉

**fissure** *crack, cleft, crevasse, crevice, cranny, chink
*Ana* *break, gap: *breach, split, rent, rupture, rift

**fit** *n* Fit, attack, access, accession, paroxysm, spasm, convulsion are comparable when they denote a sudden seizure or spell resulting from an abnormal condition of body or mind. The last three are too specific in their technical medical senses to be synonyms of the others (except of *fit* in its narrower significations), but in their extended senses they are frequently closely parallel. **Fit** is often used narrowly: sometimes to designate a sudden seizure of a disorder (as epilepsy or apoplexy) characterized by such symptoms as violent muscular contractions or unconsciousness 〈fall in a *fit*〉 or sometimes to designate a period in which there is a marked increase of a physical disturbance characteristic of a disease 〈hysteria often reveals itself in *fits* of alternate laughing and weeping〉 In its wider application, *fit* still may imply suddenness and violence, but it emphasizes temporariness 〈a *fit* of the blues〉 〈he works only by *fits* and starts〉 Occasionally it suggests nothing more than the un-

---

A colon (:) separates groups of words discriminated. An asterisk (*) indicates place of treatment of each group.

usual and passing character of the condition and is applied to things as well as to persons ⟨enjoy a *fit* of laziness⟩ ⟨a *fit* of bad weather⟩ **Attack** always implies a sudden and often violent onslaught but carries no suggestion of length of duration ⟨frequent *attacks* of pain⟩ ⟨an *attack* of melancholy⟩ ⟨a prolonged *attack* of bronchitis⟩ ⟨we have a second *attack* of hot weather—*Whitman*⟩ **Access** and **accession,** though often interchangeable with *attack,* distinctively imply the initiation of an attack or fit and often come close in meaning to *outbreak* or *outburst* ⟨now and then an *access* of . . . sudden fury . . . would lay hold on a man—*Kipling*⟩ ⟨one of his sudden sharp *accessions* of impatience at the leisurely motions of the Trujillo boy—*Mary Austin*⟩ Occasionally they also connote intensification (as of a mood or state of mind) to the point where control is lost or nearly lost ⟨her evident, but inexplicable, *access* of misery—*Meredith*⟩ In their technical medical senses *paroxysm, spasm,* and *convulsion* are sudden and usually short attacks especially characteristic of certain diseases. The distinguishing marks of a **paroxysm** are sudden occurrence or intensification of a symptom (as coughing) and recurrence of attacks; those of **spasm** are sudden involuntary muscular contraction, in some cases producing rigidity of the body or constriction of a passage and in others producing alternate contractions and relaxations of the muscles; those of **convulsion** are of repeated spasms of the latter kind affecting the whole or a large part of the body and producing violent contortions of the muscles and distortion of features. The implications of these technical senses are usually carried over into the extended senses. *Paroxysm* commonly occurs in the plural and suggests recurrent, violent attacks ⟨the girls went into *paroxysms* of laughter⟩ ⟨throughout the night he suffered *paroxysms* of fear⟩ *Spasm,* especially when used of emotional disturbances, often implies possession by something that for a moment grips and paralyzes ⟨she could scarcely even look at the wall without a *spasm* of fear—*Bennett*⟩ When used in the plural, it usually suggests the more or less rapid alternation of contrasting moods or states of mind ⟨he worked only by *spasms*⟩ *Convulsion* implies definite physical effects accompanying the mood or state of mind and closely resembling those symptomatic of disease ⟨the ragged crew actually laughed at me . . . some of them literally throwing themselves down on the ground in *convulsions* of unholy mirth—*Kipling*⟩

**fit** *adj* **Fit, suitable, meet, proper, appropriate, fitting, apt, happy, felicitous** are comparable when they mean right with respect to the nature, condition, circumstances, or use of the thing qualified. Something is **fit** which is adapted or adaptable to the end in view, the use proposed, or the work to be done ⟨food *fit* for a king⟩ ⟨but when to mischief mortals bend their will, how soon they find *fit* instruments of ill!—*Pope*⟩ ⟨never even in the most perfect days of my development as an artist could I have found words *fit* to bear so august a burden—*Wilde*⟩ ⟨a wooden image, movable and *fit* to be carried in procession—*Santayana*⟩ Sometimes, in addition, *fit* connotes competence or the possession of the required qualifications ⟨men *fit* to command⟩ ⟨he is not a *fit* father for his children⟩ ⟨they do not know what the boy is *fit* for⟩ Other times it suggests readiness (as in condition, state of health, mood, or inclination) ⟨the vessel is now *fit* for service⟩ ⟨he played tennis to keep *fit*⟩ Something is **suitable** which answers the requirements or demands of the occasion, the circumstances, or the conditions or suggests no incongruity with them ⟨behavior *suitable* to his age and station in life⟩ ⟨will begin instinctively to arrange these institutions into *suitable* conventional categories—*Marquand*⟩ ⟨clothes *suitable* for the occasion . . . tennis outfits, hiking outfits,

cycling outfits—*Laver*⟩ Something is **meet** which is not only suitable but nicely adapted to the particular situation, need, or circumstances; the word usually suggests rightness or justness rather than an absence of incongruity; thus, a punishment of a childish offense may be *suitable* if it is in accord with the years and mentality of the child, but it is not *meet* unless it suggests due proportion between the offense and its penalty ⟨it is very *meet,* right, and our bounden duty, that we should at all times and in all places, give thanks unto thee, O Lord—*Book of Common Prayer*⟩ ⟨Sabbath was made a solemn day, *meet* only for preaching, praying, and Bible reading—*Charles & Mary Beard*⟩ Something is **proper** (see also DECOROUS) which belongs to a thing on some justifiable grounds (as by nature, by custom, or by right reason) ⟨water is the *proper* element for fish⟩ ⟨the *proper* observance of Memorial Day⟩ ⟨the article brought only half its *proper* price⟩ When, as often happens, fitness or suitability is stressed rather than natural or rightful association, proper then implies determination of fitness or suitability by logic, reasonableness, or good judgment ⟨the *proper* study of mankind is man—*Pope*⟩ ⟨[according to Aristotle] the thing to aim at is to be angry "on the *proper* occasions and with the *proper* people in the *proper* manner and for the *proper* length of time"—*Dickinson*⟩ Something is **appropriate** which is so eminently fit or suitable that it seems to belong peculiarly or distinctively to the person or thing with which it is associated, sometimes giving him or it a distinguishing grace or charm through its very congruity ⟨an excitement in which we can discriminate two sorts of elements, the passions *appropriate* to the subject and the passion proper to the artist—*Alexander*⟩ ⟨the eighteenth-century gentleman spoke with a refined accent, quoted the classics on *appropriate* occasions—*Russell*⟩ ⟨we have agreed that our writing should be *appropriate* . . . that it should rise and fall with the subject, be grave where that is serious, where it is light not afraid of what Stevenson . . . calls "a little judicious levity"—*Quiller-Couch*⟩ Something is **fitting** which is in harmony with the spirit, the tone, the mood, or the purpose ⟨news *fitting* to the night, black, fearful, comfortless and horrible—*Shak.*⟩ ⟨it is a *fitting* paradox that he should live today . . . chiefly by those writings which contradict everything he believed—*Stewart*⟩ Something is **apt** (see also APT 2; QUICK 2) which is nicely fitted by its nature or construction to attain the end desired, to accomplish the purpose in view, or to achieve the results contemplated ⟨it was recognized that while one style was suited to one set of themes, another was *apter* for another set—*Binyon*⟩ ⟨Fourier . . . invented a mathematical process which was not only suitable for handling his problem, but proved to be so universally *apt* that there is hardly a field of science or of engineering which it has not penetrated—*Darrow*⟩ Something is **happy** (see also GLAD, LUCKY) which is singularly appropriate and apt and therefore brilliantly successful or effective considered in its relation to the situation, the conditions, or other important factors ⟨a *happy* choice of words, nicely expressing the subtlety of his thought⟩ ⟨whether a composite language like the English is not a *happier* instrument of expression than a homogeneous one like the German—*Coleridge*⟩ ⟨of all writers he perhaps best combines in his style a felicitous elegance with a *happy* vernacular—*Van Doren*⟩ Something is **felicitous** which is most opportunely, tellingly, or gracefully happy ⟨I do not like mottoes but where they are singularly *felicitous*—*Lamb*⟩ ⟨some of the most *felicitous* turns of thought and phrase in poetry are the result of a flash of inspiration under the happy guidance of a rhyme—*Lowes*⟩ ⟨let us inquire . . . whether the relation of the figures to

---

*Ana* analogous words     *Ant* antonyms     *Con* contrasted words     See also explanatory notes facing page 1

each other and of groups to the space they occupy is a *felicitous* one—*Binyon*⟩
*Ana* adapted *or* adaptable, adjusted *or* adjustable, conformed *or* conformable (see corresponding verbs at ADAPT): qualified, capable, *able, competent
*Ant* unfit

**fit** *vb* *prepare, qualify, condition, ready
*Ana* endow, endue (see DOWER): furnish, *provide, supply

**fitful,** **spasmodic, convulsive** are comparable when they mean lacking steadiness or regularity in course, movement, or succession (as of acts or efforts). **Fitful** stresses variability and intermittency; it implies an irregular succession characterized by fits and starts ⟨after life's *fitful* fever he sleeps well—*Shak.*⟩ ⟨the *fitful* gloom and sudden lambencies of the room by firelight—*De Quincey*⟩ ⟨a *fitful,* undecided rain—*Kipling*⟩ ⟨a *fitful* wind swept the cheerless waste—*Conrad*⟩ ⟨hitherto I've been gloomy, moody, *fitful*—*Gilbert*⟩ **Spasmodic** implies fitfulness, but it further suggests marked alternations (as of violent activity and inactivity or of great effort and of negligible effort or of zeal or enthusiasm and lack of interest); it therefore implies, even more than *fitful,* an opposition to what is sustained at a high pitch ⟨*spasmodic* efforts to reform municipal government⟩ ⟨*spasmodic* energy⟩ ⟨a continuous discussion of international affairs, not *spasmodic* action at times of crisis—*Attlee*⟩ ⟨a *spasmodic* movement of despair—*S. S. Van Dine*⟩ ⟨*spasmodic* industry⟩ **Convulsive** differs from the preceding terms in not implying intermittency and in stressing unsteadiness, strain or overstrain, and the lack of such regular rhythm as is the sign of control and especially of muscular, mental, or spiritual control ⟨*convulsive* rise and fall of the breast⟩ ⟨the *convulsive* movement of the earth characteristic of an earthquake⟩ ⟨he had a *convulsive* drive, a boundless and explosive fervor—*Behrman*⟩ ⟨a *convulsive* little hug—*Turnbull*⟩
*Ana* *intermittent, periodic, recurrent: desultory, hit-or-miss, *random, haphazard
*Ant* constant (sense 3) —*Con* *steady, uniform, even, equable: regular, methodical, systematic, *orderly

**fitting** *adj* appropriate, proper, meet, suitable, *fit, apt, happy, felicitous
*Ana* *relevant, pertinent, germane, apposite, apropos: seemly, *decorous, decent, proper: congruous, *consonant: harmonious, concordant, accordant (see corresponding nouns at HARMONY)
*Ant* unfitting

**fix** *vb* **1** *set, settle, establish
*Ana* *stabilize, steady: determine, *decide, rule, settle: *prescribe, define
*Ant* alter: abrogate (*a custom, rule, law*) —*Con* modify, *change, vary: supplant, supersede, displace, *replace
**2** *fasten, attach, affix
*Ana* *implant, instill, inculcate: *secure, rivet, anchor, moor
*Con* eradicate, uproot, extirpate (see EXTERMINATE): upset, *overturn, overthrow, subvert
**3** *adjust, regulate
*Ana* repair, *mend, patch, rebuild: *correct, rectify, revise, amend, emend
*Con* derange, disarrange, disorganize, unsettle, *disorder

**fix** *n* *predicament, plight, dilemma, quandary, scrape, jam, pickle

**flabbergast** amaze, astound, astonish, *surprise
*Ana* dumbfound, confound, bewilder, nonplus, perplex (see PUZZLE): disconcert, rattle, faze, discomfit (see EMBARRASS)

**flabby** flaccid, floppy, *limp, flimsy, sleazy

*Ana* *loose, relaxed, slack, lax: *soft: yielding, caving in (see YIELD *vb*): *powerless, impotent: spiritless, listless, enervated, *languid
*Ant* firm —*Con* hard, solid (see FIRM): *tight, taut, tense: tough, tenacious, sturdy, *strong: plucky, gritty (see corresponding nouns at FORTITUDE)

**flaccid** flabby, floppy, *limp, flimsy, sleazy
*Ana* slack, relaxed, lax, *loose: unnerved, enervated, emasculated (see UNNERVE): weakened, debilitated, enfeebled, sapped (see WEAKEN)
*Ant* resilient —*Con* *elastic, springy, flexible, supple: limber, lithe (see SUPPLE): *vigorous, energetic, lusty, nervous

**flag** *n* **Flag, ensign, standard, banner, color, streamer, pennant, pendant, pennon, jack** are not always clearly distinguished. **Flag,** the comprehensive term, is applied to a piece of cloth that typically is rectangular, is attached to a staff, mast, halyard, or line, and carries an arrangement of colors, an emblematic figure, or a motto. The purpose of a flag is primarily to serve as a sign or symbol of a nation, a branch of the service, an organization, or an office, but it may also serve as a signal (as in military or naval operations) or in giving information (as of a weather change or the approach of a train) ⟨the *flag* of England⟩ ⟨the admiral's *flag*⟩ ⟨a *flag* of truce⟩ ⟨a trainman's *flag*⟩ **Ensign** is applied chiefly to a flag that indicates nationality and specifically to one flown by ships at sea ⟨the Stars and Stripes is the national *ensign* of the United States⟩ ⟨of the three *ensigns* of Great Britain, the white *ensign* is flown by ships of the Royal Navy and by naval barracks, the red *ensign* by British merchant vessels, and the blue *ensign* by some vessels commanded by officers of the Royal Naval Reserve and by some classes of government vessels not part of the navy⟩ *Standard* and *banner* are more or less literary terms for the flag (as of a country, a party, or a religious, civic, or patriotic organization) thought of as a rallying point or as something to be followed. **Standard** especially suggests the former because the term originally designated and still often designates a flag or a sculptured figure raised on a pole so as to be a gathering point for all who belong under it ⟨as armies at the call of trumpet . . . troop to the *standard*—*Milton*⟩ **Banner** basically applies to a flag (often hung downward from a crosspiece instead of flying from a staff) of an individual (as an emperor, king, lord, or military leader) which was formerly flown from windows or doors or carried aloft at the head of a procession (as of troops marching to war) ⟨hang out our *banners* on the outward walls; the cry is still "They come" —*Shak.*⟩ ⟨terrible as an army with *banners*—*Song of Solomon* 6:4⟩ **Color** (most frequently found in the plural **colors**) may apply to a national flag, to a flag emblematic of affiliation or partisanship, or to a flag of most military units; the term is particularly likely to suggest military activity or display ⟨call to the *colors*⟩ ⟨hoist the *colors*⟩ ⟨troop the *colors*⟩ ⟨the British *colors* were planted on the summit of the breach—*Wellington*⟩ The remaining terms are highly specific and definite in implications. **Streamer** applies to a long narrow flag (as on the masthead of a government ship) that floats in the wind; **pennant** and **pendant,** the latter more English than American, apply to a streamer that is long, narrow, and tapering. *Pennant* even more often applies to a narrow flag, typically triangular, which is flown by ships, which is used in signaling and in decorating, or which is exhibited (as by a baseball club) as a sign of championship. **Pennon** may apply to a narrower flag or a small streamer suitable for attaching to a lance. **Jack** denotes a small oblong flag indicating nationality which is hoisted on a staff at the bow or bowsprit cap of a ship or

---

A colon (:) separates groups of words discriminated. An asterisk (*) indicates place of treatment of each group.

one used in signaling.

**flag** *vb* *droop, wilt, sag
*Ana* *fall, subside, slump, sink, drop: ebb, wane, *abate
**flagitious** nefarious, infamous, iniquitous, villainous, *vicious, corrupt, degenerate
*Ana* scandalous, criminal, sinful (see corresponding nouns at OFFENSE): shameful, disgraceful (see corresponding nouns at DISGRACE): *flagrant, gross, glaring
**flagrant, glaring, gross, rank** are comparable as derogatory intensives meaning conspicuously or outstandingly bad or unpleasant. **Flagrant** usually applies to offenses, transgressions, or errors which are so bad that they cannot escape notice or be condoned ⟨his treatise is marked by several *flagrant* errors⟩ ⟨a *flagrant* abuse of the executive power⟩ ⟨*flagrant* injustice⟩ ⟨open and *flagrant* mutiny—*Kipling*⟩ ⟨in *flagrant* violation of all the New York proprieties—*Wharton*⟩ **Glaring** carries an even stronger implication of obtrusiveness than *flagrant*; the term is often applied to something which is so evidently or so conspicuously wrong, improper, or faulty as to inflict such distress or pain upon the observer as might too vivid a color or too harsh a light ⟨a *glaring* fault in a design⟩ ⟨a *glaring* inconsistency in his argument⟩ ⟨his second novel is in *glaring* contrast to his first novel⟩ ⟨this evil is so *glaring, so inexcusable—Shaw*⟩ ⟨*glaring* imperfections which go far beyond a mere lack of verbal felicity—*Krutch*⟩ **Gross** (see also COARSE; WHOLE 2) is even more derogatory than *flagrant* or *glaring* because it suggests a magnitude or degree of badness that is beyond all bounds and wholly inexcusable or unpardonable. However, the term is not so often referred to evil acts or serious offenses as it is to human attitudes, qualities, or faults that merit severe condemnation ⟨*gross* carelessness⟩ ⟨*gross* stupidity⟩ ⟨*gross* superstition⟩ ⟨Elizabethan and Jacobean poetry . . . had serious defects, even *gross* faults—*T. S. Eliot*⟩ ⟨the hero is as *gross* an imposture as the heroine—*Shaw*⟩ ⟨they must read as the *grossest* impropriety and rankest treason—*Sperry*⟩ ⟨even illness cannot excuse such unfilial behavior and such *gross* folly—*Graves*⟩ **Rank** (see also RANK 1) applies chiefly to nouns that are terms of reproach; it implies that the person or thing described by such a term is extremely, utterly, or violently whatever he or it is declared to be ⟨O, my offense is *rank*, it smells to heaven—*Shak.*⟩ ⟨till she looked less of a *rank* lunatic—*Meredith*⟩ ⟨it was hatred, simple hatred, that *rank* poison fatal to Mr. Hazard's health, which now plagued his veins —*Wylie*⟩ ⟨*rank* heresy⟩ ⟨*rank* nonsense⟩ ⟨it would be *rank* madness to attempt such a journey in this weather⟩
*Ana* heinous, *outrageous, atrocious, monstrous: nefarious, flagitious, infamous (see VICIOUS)
**flair** proclivity, propensity, *leaning, penchant
**flamboyant** *ornate, florid, rococo, baroque
*Ana* luxuriant, exuberant (see PROFUSE): resplendent, gorgeous, glorious, *splendid: dashing (see STYLISH): ostentatious, *showy, pretentious: flashy, *gaudy
**flame** *n* blaze, flare, glare, glow (see under BLAZE *vb*)
*Ana* effulgence, radiance, brilliance *or* brilliancy, refulgence, luminosity, brightness (see corresponding adjectives at BRIGHT): ardor, fervor, *passion: flashing, coruscation, gleaming, scintillation (see corresponding verbs at FLASH)
**flame** *vb* *blaze, flare, glare, glow
*Ana* *flash, gleam, glance, glint, coruscate: *burn: fire, ignite, kindle, *light
**flammable** inflammable, incendiary, inflammatory, *combustible
**flare** *vb* glare, flame, *blaze, glow
*Ana* dart, shoot (see FLY): flutter, flicker (see FLIT): rise, arise, *spring: *flash, glance, glint, coruscate, scin-

tillate: kindle, *light, fire
*Ant* gutter out
**flare** *n* glare, flame, blaze, glow (see under BLAZE *vb*)
*Ana* rising *or* rise, surging *or* surge, towering (see corresponding verbs at RISE): darting *or* dart, shooting (see corresponding verbs at FLY): flashing *or* flash, coruscation, scintillation (see corresponding verbs at FLASH)
**flash** *vb* Flash, gleam, glance, glint, sparkle, glitter, glisten, scintillate, coruscate, twinkle mean to shoot forth light (as in rays or sparks). **Flash** implies a sudden and transient outburst of light or a sudden display of something that brilliantly reflects light or seems lighted up ⟨the headlights . . . *flashed* into barnyards where fowls slept—*Anderson*⟩ ⟨*flashed* all their sabers bare—*Tennyson*⟩ ⟨his *flashing* eyes, his floating hair—*Coleridge*⟩ **Gleam** implies a ray which shines through an intervening medium or against a background of relative darkness ⟨I see the lights of the village *gleam* through the rain and mist—*Longfellow*⟩ ⟨a light *gleamed* through the chinks in the wall—*Dickens*⟩ ⟨his dislike of me *gleamed* in his blue eyes and in his supercilious cold smile—*Rose Macaulay*⟩ **Glance** implies darting or obliquely reflected light; **glint** implies quickly glancing or gleaming light ⟨besides the *glancing* tears . . . some diamonds . . . *glanced* on the bride's hand—*Dickens*⟩ ⟨an insane light *glanced* in her heavy black eyes—*Stowe*⟩ ⟨specks of sail that *glinted* in the sunlight far at sea—*Dickens*⟩ ⟨when the first sunshine through their dewdrops *glints*—*J. R. Lowell*⟩ ⟨the large brass scales near the flour bins *glinted*—*Bennett*⟩ **Sparkle** suggests quick, bright, brief, and innumerable small flashes of light; **glitter** connotes greater brilliancy or showiness than *sparkle*, sometimes with the implication of something sinister ⟨the fireflies . . . *sparkled* most vividly in the darkest places—*Irving*⟩ ⟨the *sparkling* waves—*Wordsworth*⟩ ⟨everything *sparkled* like a garden after a shower—*Cather*⟩ ⟨eyes *sparkling* with amusement⟩ ⟨eyes *glittering* with greed⟩ ⟨*glittering* rings⟩ ⟨the sunshine sifted down . . . and the yellow flower . . . caught it, and *glittered* like a topaz—*Deland*⟩ **Glisten** implies a more or less subdued sparkle, glitter, or gleaming that suggests the lustrous shining quality of a moist surface ⟨dew *glistening* in the soft morning light⟩ ⟨snowy mountains *glistening* through a summer atmosphere—*Irving*⟩ ⟨eyes *glistening* with heavenly tears—*Carlyle*⟩ **Scintillate** implies the emission of sparks in a steady stream or a sparkling suggestive of such an emission; **coruscate** the emission of a brilliant flash or succession of flashes; both words have extended as well as literal use ⟨a night so clear that the stars seem to *scintillate*⟩ ⟨an ornate style that *coruscated* with verbal epigrams—*Huxley*⟩ ⟨*coruscating* wit⟩ **Twinkle** suggests a soft and intermittent sparkling, often wavering and lustrous ⟨*twinkle, twinkle*, little star . . . like a diamond in the sky—*Jane & Ann Taylor*⟩ ⟨sunbeams . . . *twinkled* on the glass and silver of the sideboard—*Cather*⟩ ⟨he looked at her and his eyes *twinkled*—*Anderson*⟩
*Ana* shoot, dart (see FLY): *rise, surge, tower, rocket: *blaze, flame, flare, glare, glow
**flash** *n* second, *instant, moment, minute, jiffy, twinkling, split second
**flashy** garish, *gaudy, tawdry, meretricious
*Ana* *showy, pretentious, ostentatious: flamboyant, *ornate, florid: glittering, flashing, sparkling (see FLASH *vb*)
*Con* dowdy, *slatternly: smart, chic, modish (see STYLISH): simple, *natural, unaffected
**flat** *adj* 1 *level, plane, plain, even, smooth, flush
*Con* *rough, rugged, uneven, scabrous
2 vapid, *insipid, jejune, banal, wishy-washy, inane
*Con* piquant, *pungent, poignant, racy, spicy: flavor-

---

*Ana* analogous words    *Ant* antonyms    *Con* contrasted words    See also explanatory notes facing page 1

some, savory, sapid, tasty, *palatable: zestful (see corresponding noun at TASTE)

**flattery** adulation, *compliment
**Ana** blandishment, cajolery (see corresponding verbs at COAX): fawning, toadying, truckling (see FAWN *vb*): eulogy, panegyric, *encomium: homage, obeisance, deference (see HONOR)

**flatulent** *inflated, tumid, turgid
**Ana** empty, hollow, *vain: *superficial, shallow: bombastic, grandiloquent, magniloquent, *rhetorical
**Con** weighty (see HEAVY): pithy, compendious, summary (see CONCISE): cogent, telling, convincing, compelling (see VALID): forcible, forceful, potent (see POWERFUL)

**flaunt** parade, expose, display, exhibit, *show
**Ana** *boast, brag, vaunt, gasconade: *reveal, disclose, discover, divulge: advertise, publish, broadcast, proclaim, *declare
**Con** cloak, mask, *disguise, dissemble, camouflage: conceal, *hide, screen, secrete, bury

**flavor** *n* *taste, savor, tang, relish, smack

**flavorsome** toothsome, tasty, savory, sapid, relishing, *palatable, appetizing
**Con** *insipid, vapid, flat, wishy-washy: bland, mild (see SOFT)

**flaw** *n* defect, *blemish
**Ana** cleaving *or* cleavage, riving, splitting *or* split, rending *or* rent, ripping *or* rip, tearing *or* tear (see corresponding verbs at TEAR)

**flawless** faultless, *impeccable, errorless
**Ana** intact, entire, whole, *perfect: *correct, accurate, precise, right, nice, exact
**Con** defective, *deficient: marred, impaired, damaged, injured (see INJURE): fallacious (see under FALLACY)

**flay** *vb* *skin, decorticate, peel, pare
**Ana** *abrade, excoriate, chafe: rack, torture, torment, *afflict: chastise, castigate, *punish

**fleck** *vb* *spot, spatter, sprinkle, mottle, stipple, marble, speckle, spangle, bespangle

**flecked** spotted, spattered, sprinkled, mottled, stippled, marbled, speckled, spangled, bespangled (see under SPOT *vb*)
**Ana** dappled, freaked, *variegated

**flee** fly, *escape, decamp, abscond
**Ana** evade, elude, avoid, *escape

**fleer** *vb* *scoff, jeer, gibe, gird, sneer, flout
**Ana** deride, mock, *ridicule: grin, *smile, smirk

**fleet** *vb* *while, wile, beguile
**Ana** *speed, hasten, hurry, quicken, accelerate

**fleet** *adj* swift, rapid, *fast, quick, speedy, hasty, expeditious
**Ana** *agile, brisk, nimble, spry: darting, skimming, scudding, flying (see FLY *vb*)
**Con** deliberate, leisurely, laggard, dilatory, *slow

**fleeting** evanescent, fugitive, passing, transitory, *transient, ephemeral, momentary, short-lived
**Ant** lasting

**fleshly** *carnal, sensual, animal
**Ana** physical, *bodily, corporeal, corporal, somatic: *sensuous, sensual, voluptuous, luxurious, sybaritic, epicurean
**Con** *moral, ethical, noble, virtuous: spiritual, divine, religious (see HOLY): intellectual, psychic, *mental

**fleshy, fat, stout, portly, plump, rotund, chubby, corpulent, obese** mean thick and heavy in body because of superfluous fat. **Fleshy** and **fat** are not clearly discriminated in use, although *fleshy* may imply overabundance of muscular tissue and *fat*, of adipose tissue; when a derogatory connotation is intended *fat* is usually preferred ⟨the unreasonably *fat* woman with legs like tree trunks—*K. A. Porter*⟩

⟨my appetite is plenty good enough, and I am about as *fleshy* as I was in Brooklyn—*Whitman*⟩ ⟨a *fleshy*, jolly man⟩ ⟨a dowdy *fat* woman⟩ **Stout** implies a thickset, bulky figure or build, but it is often merely a euphemistic substitute for *fat*; **portly** adds to *stout* the implication of a more or less dignified and imposing appearance ⟨a very *stout*, puffy man, in buckskins and Hessian boots—*Thackeray*⟩ ⟨one very *stout* gentleman, whose body and legs looked like half a gigantic roll of flannel, elevated on a couple of inflated pillowcases—*Dickens*⟩ ⟨a large *portly* figure . . . the very beau ideal of an old abbot—*J. W. Carlyle*⟩ ⟨an elderly gentleman, large and *portly*, and of remarkably dignified demeanor—*Hawthorne*⟩ **Plump** implies a pleasing fullness of figure and well-rounded curves ⟨the *plump* goddesses of Renaissance paintings⟩ ⟨she became *plump* at forty⟩ ⟨his wife was . . . *plump* where he was spare—*Sayers*⟩ **Rotund** suggests the shape of a sphere; it often, in addition, connotes shortness or squatness ⟨this pink-faced *rotund* specimen of prosperity—*George Eliot*⟩ **Chubby** applies chiefly to children or to very short persons who are otherwise describable as *rotund* ⟨a *chubby* cherub of a baby⟩ **Corpulent** and **obese** imply a disfiguring excess of flesh or of fat ⟨Mrs. Byron . . . was a short and *corpulent* person and rolled considerably in her gait—*Thomas Moore*⟩ ⟨a woman of robust frame, square-shouldered . . . and though stout, not *obese* —*Brontë*⟩
**Ana** *muscular, brawny, burly, husky
**Ant** skinny, scrawny —**Con** *lean, lank, lanky, gaunt, rawboned, angular, spare: *thin, slim, slender, slight

**flex** *vb* **Flex, crook, bow, buckle** mean to bend, but because of special implications and applications they are not freely interchangeable. **Flex** is used chiefly of the bending of a bodily joint especially between bones of a limb by which the angle between the bones is diminished, or it may apply to the contraction of muscles by which the bending is accomplished; in either case the word is usually opposed to *extend* ⟨*flex* the arm at the elbow⟩ ⟨*flex* the leg at the hip joint⟩ ⟨he has grown so old and stiff that he cannot easily *flex* his knees⟩ ⟨the world . . . would jeer at any eccentric who should *flex* his mental muscles in public—*Barzun*⟩ **Crook** may replace *flex* ⟨the air was so full of rheumatism that no man could *crook* his arm to write a sermon—*Blackmore*⟩ ⟨John, snickering, *crooked* his wicked thumb—*Browning*⟩ but it is also used to convey an implication of circuitousness and hence of contortion or distortion ⟨God knows, my son, by what bypaths and indirect *crook'd* ways I met this crown—*Shak.*⟩ ⟨forward then, but still remember how the course of time will swerve, *crook* and turn upon itself in many a backward streaming curve—*Tennyson*⟩ **Bow** (see also YIELD) may denote to bend as in reverence or submission ⟨at the name of Jesus every knee should *bow*—*Phil* 2:10⟩ but it often means explicitly to incline downward the head and usually the part of the body above the waist, especially as a gesture of greeting, of recognition, or of reverence ⟨*bow* pleasantly to acquaintances⟩ ⟨*bow* reverently before a shrine⟩ ⟨grasses that now were swaying and *bowing* like living things in happy dance—*Idriess*⟩ In a related use *bow* retains some suggestion of submission and implies a bending under something (as a heavy weight) that wears or oppresses ⟨trees *bowed* down with ice⟩ ⟨an old man *bowed* with years⟩ **Buckle** implies a bending under stress (as from undue pressure, weight, heat, or fright) that loosens or weakens what supports and that brings on collapse, often to the point of permanent distortion ⟨noticed the *buckling* of the girder of the bridge⟩ ⟨the freight train *buckled* as it left the track and fell over the embankment⟩ ⟨the wall *buckled* under the heat of the fire⟩ ⟨his knees *buckled*

---

A colon (:) separates groups of words discriminated. An asterisk (*) indicates place of treatment of each group.

and he fell down on the floor—*Chandler*⟩ ⟨the bulkhead had *buckled*; he had actually seen it coming forward—*Crofts*⟩

*Ana* bend, *curve, twist

*Ant* extend

**flexible** *elastic, supple, resilient, springy

*Ana* pliable, pliant, malleable, ductile, *plastic: tractable (see OBEDIENT): limber, lithe, *supple

*Ant* inflexible —*Con* *stiff, rigid, wooden: tough, tenacious (see STRONG): brittle, crisp, frangible, *fragile: *hardened, indurated, callous

**flexuous** *winding, sinuous, serpentine, tortuous

**flicker** *vb* flutter, *flit, flitter, hover

*Ana* waver, vibrate, oscillate, fluctuate, *swing: flare, flame, glare, *blaze: *flash, gleam, glance, glint, coruscate: quiver, quaver, tremble (see SHAKE)

**flightiness** light-mindedness, volatility, levity, *lightness, frivolity, flippancy

*Ana* capriciousness, unstableness *or* instability, fickleness, mercurialness *or* mercuriality, inconstancy (see corresponding adjectives at INCONSTANT): effervescence, buoyancy, elasticity (see corresponding adjectives at ELASTIC): liveliness, gaiety, sprightliness (see corresponding adjectives at LIVELY)

*Ant* steadiness: steadfastness —*Con* constancy, equableness (see corresponding adjectives at STEADY): seriousness, staidness, sedateness, earnestness (see corresponding adjectives at SERIOUS)

**flimsy** *adj* sleazy, *limp, floppy, flaccid, flabby

*Ana* *thin, slight, tenuous: *loose, slack: *weak, feeble

*Con* stout, sturdy, *strong: *heavy, weighty

**flinch** *recoil, shrink, wince, blench, quail

*Ana* falter, *hesitate, vacillate: evade, elude, shun, eschew, avoid, *escape: withdraw, retire (see GO): retreat, *recede

**fling** *vb* hurl, *throw, sling, toss, cast, pitch

*Ana* thrust, shove, propel, *push: impel, drive, *move

**flippancy** levity, *lightness, light-mindedness, frivolity, volatility, flightiness

*Ana* sauciness, pertness, archness (see corresponding adjectives at SAUCY): impishness, waggishness, roguishness, mischievousness, playfulness (see corresponding adjectives at PLAYFUL)

*Ant* seriousness —*Con* earnestness, gravity, solemnity, soberness (see corresponding adjectives at SERIOUS)

**flirt** *vb* coquet, dally, *trifle, toy

*Ana* *play, sport, disport: *caress, fondle, pet

**flit** *vb* Flit, flutter, flitter, flicker, hover suggest the movements of a bird or other flying or floating thing and mean to move in a manner like or reminiscent of such movements

Flit implies a light and swift passing from place to place or point to point ⟨birds *flitted* from tree to tree⟩ ⟨the talk *flitting* from one subject to another and never dropping so long as the meal lasts—*Arnold*⟩ ⟨seemed to pass the whole of his life *flitting* in and out of bedrooms—*Bennett*⟩ ⟨Clare Potter, flushed and gallantly gay, *flitting* about from person to person—*Rose Macaulay*⟩ Flutter implies the movement of a bird rapidly beating its wings or the restless flitting of a moth about a light; it especially implies unsteadiness and agitation ⟨till she felt the heart within her fall and *flutter* tremulously—*Tennyson*⟩ ⟨gay moods and mysterious, moth-like meditations hover in my imagination . . . but always the rarest, those freaked with azure and the deepest crimson, *flutter* away beyond my reach—*L. P. Smith*⟩ ⟨a little dark shadow *fluttered* from the wall across the floor—*Cather*⟩ ⟨her eyes . . . timidly *fluttering* over the depths of his—*Meredith*⟩ Flitter implies the lightness and quickness of movement suggested by *flit* but usually also suggests the uneasiness or uncer-

tainty connoted by *flutter* ⟨the poor silly *flittering* woman⟩ ⟨children *flittering* here and there⟩ ⟨when he was pressed and irritated to condemn the Cardinal, his eyes *flittered* uncomfortably—*Hackett*⟩ ⟨flared and *flittered* around them like light gone mad—*Rölvaag*⟩ Flicker implies a light fluttering or a fitfully wavering movement ⟨translucent *flickering* wings between the sun and me—*Stevenson*⟩ ⟨thou small flame, which, as a dying pulse rises and falls, still *flickerest* up and down—*Shelley*⟩ ⟨fireflies *flicker* in the tops of trees—*Lowell*⟩ Hover implies a hanging suspended over something like a bird maintaining its position in the air by an even usually slow movement of the wings; the word frequently connotes irresolution, sometimes menace, sometimes solicitude ⟨vultures *hovering* over a battlefield⟩ ⟨behold him perched in ecstasies, yet seeming still to *hover*—*Wordsworth*⟩ ⟨your servant . . . has been *hovering* about us and looking at you anxiously for some minutes—*Shaw*⟩ ⟨the shark was still *hovering* about—*Birtles*⟩

*Ana* *fly, dart, skim, float, scud

**flitter** *vb* *flit, flutter, flicker, hover

*Ana* *fly, dart, skim: quiver, quaver, teeter (see SHAKE)

**float** *vb* *fly, skim, sail, dart, scud, shoot

*Ana* glide, *slide, slip: *flit, hover, flitter

**flood** *n* 1 *flow, stream, current, tide, flux

*Ana* *excess, superfluity, surplus: incursion, *invasion

2 Flood, deluge, inundation, torrent, spate, cataract are comparable when they mean a great or overwhelming flow of or as if of water. Flood basically implies the flowing of water, often in great abundance, over land not usually submerged; it therefore suggests usually something (as a stream) that exceeds or breaks its normal bounds, but it carries in itself no clear implication of the ultimate cause ⟨the disastrous Mississippi river *floods* of 1936⟩ ⟨his home was washed away by the *flood*⟩ ⟨a *flood* of advertising was sent through the mail⟩ ⟨messages of sympathy came in a *flood*⟩ ⟨the rising *flood* of students is very much like the barbarian invasions—*Bush*⟩ Deluge may apply to a flood that destroys or drowns but especially to a tremendous and continuous downpour of rain; the term seldom suggests a flood which results from a melting of snows, a rising river, or a tidal wave. In its extended uses it implies, sometimes hyperbolically, a power that, through force of numbers, of volume, or of quantity cannot be resisted or that sweeps one away ⟨the rain descended in a *deluge*⟩ ⟨the waters have not yet abated from the *deluge*⟩ ⟨the memorable *deluge* of the thirteenth century out of which the Zuyder Zee was born—*Motley*⟩ ⟨a *deluge* of criticisms fell on him from all sides⟩ ⟨the frightful *deluge* of spoken and printed palaver—*Sat. Review*⟩ ⟨she becomes lost in the overflow—a formless, unending *deluge* of realistic detail—*Robert Humphrey*⟩ Inundation implies a flood caused by a stream, lake, or exceptionally high tide overflowing adjacent land; it therefore stresses something that overspreads and extends far and wide ⟨the annual *inundation* of Egypt by the Nile⟩ ⟨the threat of *inundation* by the sea—*Mumford*⟩ ⟨his tears were not drops but a little *inundation* down his cheeks—*Wescott*⟩ ⟨an *inundation* of Italy by barbarians⟩ Torrent implies an impetuous rushing or surging of waters (as of a river in flood or of a stream that follows a steep course). It stresses the violence and rapid movement of the stream rather than its destructiveness or its capacity for spreading far and wide, and in extended use may be applied to something that comes forth with the same suddenness, the same violence, and the same clear direction ⟨a *torrent* of water swept down the hillside⟩ ⟨he used to say that the mountain *torrents* were the first road builders, and that wherever they found a way, he could find one—*Cather*⟩ ⟨pouring

forth that *torrent* of stinging invective—*Hudson*⟩ ⟨philosophy . . . provided a foothold for man above the *torrent* of circumstance—*Buchan*⟩ **Spate** refers literally to a stream that has suddenly become full, agitated, and turbulent under the influence of a spring freshet or violent rains; hence in its extended applications it suggests a sudden swelling or outpouring of what usually flows in a quiet stream ⟨when you are a big man, and fish such a stream as that, you will hardly care . . . whether she be roaring down in full *spate*—*Kingsley*⟩ ⟨he had hardly sat down when he began to talk full *spate*—about the war, the war of 1914—*Henry Miller*⟩ ⟨the *spate* of books on conservatism and liberalism in America—*Niebuhr*⟩ ⟨a *spate* of inventions in the early years of the century⟩ **Cataract** denotes a waterfall or a steep rapids characterized by a great volume of water descending precipitously or headlong; it is sometimes applied to something (as a deluge of rain or of words) that suggests such a waterfall or rapids in its overwhelming downpour or rush ⟨blow, winds, and crack your cheeks! rage! blow! You *cataracts* and hurricanoes, spout —*Shak.*⟩ ⟨the *cataract* of nastiness which he poured alike on Piso and Clodius and Gabinius—*Froude*⟩ ⟨no doubt flaming *cataracts* of lava rushed down the sides of Vesuvius on that terrible day—*Lucas*⟩
*Ana* *flow, stream, tide, current

**floppy** *limp, flabby, flaccid, flimsy, sleazy
*Ana* *loose, relaxed, lax, slack
*Con* *firm, hard: *stiff, inflexible, rigid, tense, stark: taut, *tight, tense

**florid** *ornate, flamboyant, rococo, baroque
*Ana* aureate, flowery, euphuistic, grandiloquent, magniloquent, *rhetorical, bombastic: sumptuous, *luxurious, opulent: *showy, ostentatious, pretentious
*Ant* chaste (*in style, decoration*) —*Con* bald, barren, *bare: matter-of-fact, *prosaic

**flounder** *vb* *stumble, trip, blunder, lurch, lumber, galumph, lollop, bumble
*Ana* struggle, strive (see ATTEMPT): toil, travail, labor (see corresponding nouns at WORK): *wallow, welter

**flourish** *vb* 1 *succeed, prosper, thrive
*Ana* bloom, flower, *blossom, blow: *increase, augment, multiply: *expand, amplify
*Ant* languish —*Con* *wither, shrivel: shrink, *contract: ebb, *abate, wane, subside
2 brandish, shake, *swing, wave, thrash
*Ana* wield, manipulate, ply, *handle: flaunt, display, exhibit, *show

**flout** *vb* *scoff, jeer, gibe, fleer, gird, sneer
*Ana* scout, scorn, *despise, contemn, disdain: spurn, repudiate (see DECLINE): deride, *ridicule, mock
*Ant* revere —*Con* regard, respect, esteem, admire (see under REGARD *n*)

**flow** *vb* issue, emanate, proceed, stem, derive, *spring, arise, rise, originate
*Ana* emerge, *appear, loom: start, *begin, commence

**flow** *n* Flow, stream, current, flood, tide, flux are comparable when meaning something issuing or moving in a manner like or suggestive of running water. **Flow** may apply to the issuing or moving mass or to the kind of motion which characterizes it, but in either case it implies the type of motion characteristic of the movement of a fluid; the term may suggest either a gentle or a rapid pace and either a copious or a meager supply, but it consistently implies an unbroken continuity of the particles or parts ⟨the *flow* of his ideas exceeded his capacity for setting them down in writing⟩ ⟨she expressed herself in a *flow* of words⟩ ⟨the hardly perceptible *flow* of a mountain glacier⟩ ⟨the thought of never ceasing life as it expresses itself in the *flow* of the seasons—*Anderson*⟩ ⟨she would tell you what

she thought about the world and its ways in a *flow* of racy comment—*Rose Macaulay*⟩ **Stream** implies a flow characteristic of a body of running water (as a river) or of water pouring forth from a source or outlet (as a fountain or a faucet). The term places emphasis more upon the volume, the duration, and the constant succession and change of particles than upon the type of motion ⟨for weeks after the surrender a *stream* of refugees crossed the country's border⟩ ⟨music, acting, poetry proceed in the one mighty *stream;* sculpture, painting, all the arts of design, in the other—*Ellis*⟩ ⟨novelists who present their characters not in action, but through the *stream* of consciousness of each⟩ ⟨let loose a *stream* of commentary and discussion—*Southern*⟩ **Current** differs from *stream* in laying greater stress on the direction or course of the movement implied and in carrying stronger suggestions of its force or velocity ⟨*streams* of people passed him in either direction, but he was finally caught by the *current* of those moving south⟩ ⟨he could not maintain his position against the *current* of opposition⟩ ⟨*currents* of cold air swept in from the north⟩ ⟨he might drift some distance with the democratic *current* of the age, and then, with Gladstone, grow affrighted—*Kirk*⟩ ⟨Olds might have won Ford's success had his mind been more sealed against the *currents* to which it was exposed—*Burlingame*⟩ **Flood** is often used in place of *flow* or *stream* to imply extreme copiousness in the supply or to attribute to it an overwhelming or torrential power ⟨it is not, he then feels with a sudden *flood* of emotion, that America is home, but that home is America—*Brownell*⟩ ⟨this poem called forth *floods* of abuse—*Day Lewis*⟩ **Tide** applies to something that flows or courses like an ocean tide and suggests either an alternation of directions ⟨swayed by the sweeping of the *tides* of air—*Bryant*⟩ or a power to suck one into its course by the force of its outward or inward pull ⟨Stanley was caught in the *tide* of war fervor—*Rose Macaulay*⟩ **Flux,** more specifically than *stream,* stresses the unceasing change in the parts, particles, or elements and, sometimes, in the direction of what flows ⟨for this and that way swings the *flux* of mortal things though moving inly to one far-set goal—*Arnold*⟩ ⟨how idle is it to commiserate them for their instability, when not stability but *flux* is their ideal!—*Brownell*⟩ *Flux* often specifically applies to the outward aspect or appearance which is constantly changing in contrast to its real and abiding nature ⟨to distinguish between the transient, unsatisfying *flux* of things, and the permanent, satisfying reality which lies behind it—*Inge*⟩
*Ana* *succession, progression, series, sequence: continuity, *continuation, continuance

**flower** *n* blossom, bloom, blow (see under BLOSSOM *vb*)
**flower** *vb* *blossom, bloom, blow
*Ana* flourish, prosper (see SUCCEED)

**flowery** aureate, grandiloquent, magniloquent, *rhetorical, euphuistic, bombastic
*Ana* florid, *ornate, flamboyant: *inflated, tumid, turgid: *wordy, verbose, redundant, prolix, diffuse

**fluctuate** oscillate, *swing, sway, vibrate, pendulate, waver, undulate
*Ana* alternate, *rotate: waver, vacillate (see HESITATE)
*Con* fix, *set, establish, settle: resolve, determine, *decide

**fluent** eloquent, voluble, glib, articulate, *vocal
*Ana* facile, effortless, smooth, *easy: *quick, prompt, ready, apt
*Con* stuttering, stammering (see STAMMER *vb*): fettered, hampered, trammeled (see HAMPER *vb*)

**fluid** *adj* *liquid
*Ana* liquefied, melted, fused, deliquesced *or* deliquescent

A colon (:) separates groups of words discriminated. An asterisk (*) indicates place of treatment of each group.

(see corresponding verbs at LIQUEFY)

**fluid** *n* liquid (see under LIQUID *adj*)
*Ant* solid

**flurry** *n* bustle, fuss, ado, *stir, pother
*Ana* perturbation, agitation, disturbance, discomposure (see corresponding verbs at DISCOMPOSE): *haste, hurry,

**flurry** *vb* fluster, agitate, perturb, disturb, *discompose, disquiet
*Ana* bewilder, distract, perplex (see PUZZLE): quicken, excite, galvanize, stimulate, *provoke

**flush** *n* blush (see under BLUSH *vb*)
*Ana* *color, tinge, tint

**flush** *vb* *blush
*Ana* color, tinge, tint (see corresponding nouns at COLOR): surge, *rise: betray, divulge, disclose, *reveal

**flush** *adj* even, *level, flat, plane, plain, smooth

**fluster** *vb* upset, agitate, perturb, flurry, disturb, *discompose, disquiet
*Ana* bewilder, distract, confound, nonplus, mystify, perplex, *puzzle: rattle, faze, disconcert, discomfit (see EMBARRASS): *confuse, muddle, addle, fuddle

**flutter** *vb* flitter, flicker, *flit, hover
*Ana* *shake, tremble, quiver, quaver, wobble: beat, throb, *pulsate, palpitate: fluctuate, vibrate, oscillate, *swing

**fluvial, fluviatile** *aquatic, lacustrine, marine, oceanic, thalassic, neritic, pelagic, abyssal

**flux** *flow, current, tide, stream, flood
*Ana* swinging *or* swing, fluctuation, oscillation, wavering, swaying *or* sway (see corresponding verbs at SWING): shifting, moving (see MOVE *vb*): *motion, movement, stir

**fly** *vb* **1** Fly, dart, float, skim, scud, shoot, sail are comparable in their extended senses when they mean to pass, or less often to cause to pass, lightly or quickly over a surface or above a surface. **Fly** (see also ESCAPE 1) may be used to imply movement through or as if through the air that suggests swift passage, buoyancy, or lack of impediments like that of a bird or airplane ⟨swift *fly* the years—*Pope*⟩ ⟨saw the snowy whirlwind *fly*—*Gray*⟩ ⟨thy loose hair in the light wind *flying*—*Shelley*⟩ ⟨their Oriental robes flapping and their Oriental beards *flying* in the wind—*Forester*⟩ ⟨pushed one's way through the reeds, which *flew* back into place and revealed nothing—*Beebe*⟩ **Dart** in its extended intransitive sense implies movement that is as suddenly initiated and as straight and as swift in its course as that of an arrow or javelin ⟨hawks regularly beat along the furze, *darting* on a finch now and then—*Jefferies*⟩ ⟨he caught her by the arm as she ran past and . . . without trying to check her, simply *darted* in with her and up the stairs, causing no end of consternation—*Conrad*⟩ ⟨[stars] *darting* about our galaxy with speeds that range up to 200 miles per second—*Merrill*⟩ **Float** in its extended use implies a buoyant and seemingly effortless gliding through the air or along a smooth or liquid surface ⟨I wandered lonely as a cloud that *floats* on high o'er vales and hills—*Wordsworth*⟩ ⟨a bright bird which sings divinely as it *floats* about from one place to another—*L. P. Smith*⟩ **Skim** in its extended use implies a passing lightly and swiftly over the surface of something, sometimes darting into it, sometimes floating above it; often it suggests a light touching of the surface without real physical or mental penetration ⟨*skim* through an assignment⟩ ⟨some lightly o'er the current *skim*—*Gray*⟩ ⟨down the road *skims* an eave swallow, swift as an arrow—*Jefferies*⟩ ⟨she had *skimmed* gracefully over life's surface like a swallow, dipping her pretty wings in the shallows—*Rose Macaulay*⟩ ⟨the habit of *skimming* volumes in bookshops—*Times Lit. Sup.*⟩ **Scud** implies light, rapid movement (as of a hare pursued by hounds, of a sailboat driven over the surface of the water by a high wind, or of clouds driven by

an approaching hurricane); often, also, it connotes swiftness so great that the surface is barely touched by the speeding object ⟨the yacht *scuds* before the wind⟩ ⟨the *scudding* rain which drives in gusts over the . . . great shining river—*Thackeray*⟩ ⟨crisp foam-flakes *scud* along the level sand—*Tennyson*⟩ ⟨freezing weather that sent the delegates and their briefcases *scudding*—*Panter-Downes*⟩ **Shoot** differs from *dart,* its nearest synonym, in throwing less emphasis upon the suddenness of start and, often, in more definitely suggesting continuous or extended movement ⟨the lambent lightnings *shoot* across the sky—*Thomson*⟩ ⟨the automobile *shot* around the corner⟩ ⟨a wild idea *shot* into her mind—*Glasgow*⟩ **Sail** differs from its nearest synonym *float* in more frequently implying power, ostentation as if of spread sails, or steadiness and directness of course ⟨hope . . . set free from earth . . . on steady wing *sails* through the immense abyss—*Cowper*⟩ ⟨but who is this? . . . female of sex it seems—that, so bedecked, ornate, and gay, comes this way *sailing*—*Milton*⟩ ⟨held the door for us and we *sailed* through—*Deutschman*⟩
*Ana* *flit, flutter, flitter, flicker, hover: soar, mount, *rise, arise, ascend: glide, *slide, slip
**2** flee, *escape, decamp, abscond

**flying field** *airport, airdrome, airfield, airstrip, landing strip, landing field

**foam** *n* Foam, froth, spume, scum, lather, suds, yeast are comparable when they denote either a mass of bubbles gathering in or on the surface of a liquid or something as insubstantial as such a mass. **Foam** is the most comprehensive of these terms but is not interchangeable with all; it implies an aggregation of small bubbles such as rises to the top of a fermenting liquor or an effervescing or boiling liquid, or appears on the surface of the sea when agitated by high winds or covered with breaking waves; the term is also applicable to a bubbly slaver dribbling from the mouth of one in a rage or in great excitement or to the clotted sweat of an animal driven to exhaustion or suffering from intense heat ⟨the rider from the château, and the horse in a *foam,* clattered away through the village—*Dickens*⟩ Of all these words *foam* commonly has the most pleasant associations, usually connoting in poetry whiteness, delicacy, and grace ⟨Idalian Aphrodite beautiful, fresh as the foam—*Tennyson*⟩ ⟨the *foam* that looks so sunbright when the wind is kicking up the breakers—*Warren*⟩ **Froth** is applicable to any foam, but it carries a stronger implication of insubstantiality, worthlessness, or, when there is direct or indirect reference to persons or animals, of mad excitement than *foam* carries ⟨your glass of beer is half *froth*⟩ ⟨*froth* forming at the mouth of a mad dog⟩ ⟨his speech had no logical substance, being mostly *froth*⟩ ⟨in all the *froth* and ferment between capital and labor—*Furnas*⟩ **Spume** is applicable where *foam* or *froth* might also be employed ⟨they dart forth polypus-antennae, to blister with their poison *spume* the wanderer—*Shelley*⟩ but the term is chiefly used to denote the foam arising on an agitated body of water ⟨all the billows green tossed up the silver *spume* against the clouds—*Keats*⟩ ⟨as when a sandbar breaks in clotted *spume* and spray—*Kipling*⟩ ⟨shore encumbered by rain-washed boulders and ruffed with sea spume—*Han Suyin*⟩ **Scum** distinctively applies to the bubbly film that rises on boiling liquids, especially those containing organic matter ⟨*scum* on boiling currant juice⟩ or to a similar film which forms on molten metals ⟨the *scum* or scoria of iron⟩ or on the surface of a body of stagnant water ⟨the ditch is covered with a green *scum*⟩ Such scums ordinarily constitute impurities that are removed (as from broth or molten metal) or that constitute a contamination impairing the usability (as of stagnant water); this notion of worthlessness or obnoxiousness is carried over into extended use especially as applied to a class or body of persons ⟨the social *scum,* the passively rotting mass of people who lie at the bottom of the social scale—*Geismar*⟩ *Lather* and *suds* both apply to the foam produced by agitating water impregnated with soap or detergent. **Lather,** however, usually suggests a less frothy condition than *suds* and a heavier aggregation of small soapy bubbles ⟨hard water does not produce a good *lather* for shaving⟩ **Suds,** on the other hand, often denotes water so covered with a soapy foam that it is usable for laundering clothes ⟨the laundress likes the soap because it gives her plenty of *suds*⟩ ⟨soak the cloth in hot *suds*⟩ *Lather,* rather than *suds,* may be preferred when the foam induced by intense sweating or emotional excitement is denoted ⟨a hard-ridden horse working up a *lather*⟩ ⟨he was in a *lather* of rage⟩ but *suds* is more usual when the reference is to something that suggests the appearance of suds in a laundry tub or washing machine ⟨another [medicine man] whips up a mixture of water and meal into frothy *suds* symbolic of clouds—*Frazer*⟩ **Yeast** basically applies to a froth or sediment composed of an aggregate of small fungal cells and found in saccharine liquids (as fruit juices and malt worts) in which it induces fermentation. The same substance is used as a leavening agent in bread; from this stems one line of its extended use in which it suggests a sign of activity, vitality, or agitation ⟨seething with the *yeast* of revolt—*Dobie*⟩ ,But because yeast often appears as a froth on liquids and is accompanied by fermentation, the term has another line of extended use in which it is applied to a similar froth, foam, or spume, especially one appearing on the surface of an agitated sea ⟨the ship . . . swallowed with *yeast* and froth—*Shak.*⟩ ⟨they melt into thy *yeast* of waves—*Byron*⟩

**focal** *central, pivotal
*Ana* significant, important, momentous (see corresponding nouns at IMPORTANCE): salient, signal, striking, arresting, outstanding (see NOTICEABLE)

**focus** *n* heart, nucleus, core, *center, middle, midst, hub

**focus** *vb* *center, centralize, concentrate
*Ana* fix, *set, settle, establish
*Con* diffuse, disseminate, radiate, *spread

**fodder** forage, *food, feed, provender, provisions, comestibles, victuals, viands

**foe** *enemy
*Ana* antagonist, *opponent, adversary: assailant, attacker (see corresponding verbs at ATTACK): rival, competitor (see corresponding verbs at RIVAL)
*Ant* friend —*Con* ally, colleague, confederate, *partner: *associate, comrade, companion

**fog** *n* *haze, smog, mist

**fog** *vb* *obscure, dim, bedim, darken, eclipse, cloud, becloud, befog, obfuscate
*Ana* *puzzle, perplex, mystify, bewilder, distract: *confuse, muddle, addle

**foible** failing, *fault, frailty, vice
*Ana* weakness, infirmity (see corresponding adjectives at WEAK): defect, flaw, *blemish: aberration, *deviation

**foil** *vb* thwart, *frustrate, circumvent, balk, baffle, outwit
*Ana* discomfit, *embarrass, disconcert, faze, rattle: curb, check, *restrain, inhibit
*Con* *advance, further, forward, promote: abet, foment, *incite, instigate

**follow** *vb* **1 Follow, succeed, ensue, supervene** mean to come after someone or, more often, something. Although all of these verbs occur as transitives and intransitives, *ensue* and *supervene* are more commonly intransitive verbs. **Follow** is the general term and may imply a coming after in time, in sequence, in pursuit (see FOLLOW 2), in logic,

or in understanding ⟨the singing of "America" by the audience will *follow* the introductory prayer⟩ ⟨Queen Victoria *followed* William IV as British sovereign⟩ ⟨the driving force in education should be the pupil's wish to learn, not the master's authority; but it does not *follow* that education should be soft and easy and pleasant at every stage—*Russell*⟩ **Succeed** commonly implies an order (as one determined by descent, inheritance, election, or rank) by which one person or thing comes after another ⟨son *succeeded* father as head of the business for many generations⟩ ⟨the eldest son *succeeds* to the title⟩ ⟨the person who will *succeed* the late congressman will be appointed by the governor of the state⟩ *Succeed* is often used when the idea of a fixed order is lost, but it still usually retains the idea of taking the place of someone or something ⟨the link dissolves, each seeks a fresh embrace, another love *succeeds,* another race—*Pope*⟩ ⟨the anxieties of common life began soon to *succeed* to the alarms of romance—*Austen*⟩ ⟨simplicity of concept *succeeds* complexity of calculation—*Bell*⟩ **Ensue** usually implies some logical connection or the operation of some such principle of sequence as that of necessity ⟨that such a consequence . . . should *ensue* . . . was far enough from my thoughts—*Austen*⟩ ⟨each knowing the other, a conversation *ensues* under the hypothesis that each to the other is unknown . . . a very silly source of equivoque—*Poe*⟩ **Supervene** suggests a following by something added or conjoined and often unforeseen or unpredictable ⟨two worlds, two antagonistic ideals, here in evidence before him. Could a third condition *supervene,* to mend their discord?—*Pater*⟩ ⟨it was not acute rheumatism, but a *supervening* pericarditis that . . . killed her—*Bennett*⟩ ⟨it is in the philosophy that *supervened* upon the popular creed . . . that we shall find the highest . . . reaches of their thought—*Dickinson*⟩

**2 Follow, pursue, chase, trail, tag, tail** are comparable when meaning to go immediately or shortly after someone or something. **Follow** is the comprehensive term; it usually implies the lead or, sometimes, guidance of someone or something ⟨the detective *followed* the boys to their hiding place⟩ ⟨hangers-on who *follow* the circus⟩ ⟨the vengeance that *follows* crime—*Dickinson*⟩ ⟨*follow* up a clue⟩ ⟨*follow* a trade⟩ ⟨he should not desire to steer his own course, but *follow* the line that the talk happens to take—*Benson*⟩ ⟨not one of the many people I know who *followed* the hearings thought that the television reporting was slanted or unfair—*Seldes*⟩ **Pursue** in its earliest sense implies a following as an enemy or hunter ⟨*pursue* a fox⟩ ⟨*pursuing* rebels in flight⟩ ⟨*pursue* happiness⟩ The term therefore usually suggests an attempt to overtake, to reach, or to attain, and commonly in its extended senses, even when the implications of hostility or of a desire to capture are absent, it connotes eagerness, persistence, or inflexibility of purpose in following one's thoughts, ends, or desires ⟨ye who . . . *pursue* with eagerness the phantoms of hope—*Johnson*⟩ ⟨thrice happy man! enabled to *pursue* what all so wish, but want the pow'r to do!—*Pope*⟩ ⟨*pursuing* the game of high ambition with a masterly coolness—*Buchan*⟩ ⟨*pursue* the career of a diplomat⟩ **Chase** implies fast pursuit in order to or as if to catch a fleeing object or to drive away or turn to flight an oncoming thing ⟨*chase* the fleeing thieves⟩ ⟨the boys *chased* the intruder out of the school yard⟩ ⟨we were *chased* by two pirates, who soon overtook us—*Swift*⟩ ⟨if to dance all night, and dress all day . . . *chased* old age away . . . who would learn one earthly thing of use?—*Pope*⟩ **Trail** implies a following in someone's tracks ⟨*trail* a fugitive to his hiding place⟩ ⟨*trail* a lost child to the edge of a creek⟩ ⟨not daring to accost him . . . she had *trailed* him to the railroad station—*Chidsey*⟩ **Tag** implies a persistent,

---

A colon (:) separates groups of words discriminated. An asterisk (*) indicates place of treatment of each group.

annoying following or accompanying ⟨complained that his little sister was always *tagging* after him⟩ ⟨two un-armed launches *tagged* behind—*Millard*⟩ **Tail** specifically implies close following and surveillance ⟨he employed detectives to *tail* the suspect⟩

*Ana* attend, *accompany, convoy: *copy, imitate, ape: *practice, exercise

*Ant* precede (*in order*): forsake (*a teacher or his teach-ings*) —*Con* lead, *guide, pilot, steer: elude, evade, *escape: desert, *abandon

**follower,** adherent, disciple, sectary, partisan, henchman, satellite are comparable when denoting one who attaches himself to another. **Follower** is the inclusive term, de-noting a person who attaches himself to the person or opinions of another ⟨the *followers* of Jesus⟩ ⟨*followers* of Karl Marx⟩ ⟨they are creatures of the Devil, vowed to idolatry, and *followers* of Mithras—*Nevil Shute*⟩ Its synonyms divide themselves into two groups, the first three designating a follower through choice or conviction and the last three a follower in whom personal devotion overshadows or eclipses the critical faculty. **Adherent** connotes closer and more persistent attachment than *follower;* it may be used without any implication of the personality of the teacher or leader ⟨a doctrine that gained many *adherents*⟩ ⟨the candidate lost many *ad-herents* when he announced his views on reform⟩ ⟨*ad-herents* to the Communist party—*Conant*⟩ **Disciple** typically presupposes a master or teacher and implies personal, often devoted, adherence to his views or doc-trines ⟨though . . . an enthusiastic student of Fourier . . . he was never a mere *disciple*—the individualistic stamp was too strong—*Rosenzweig*⟩ but it may also imply similar adherence to a school of thought or govern-ing principle ⟨there is no angler, not even the most aes-thetic *disciple* of the dry fly—*Alexander MacDonald*⟩ ⟨during the war years the *disciples* of the extreme Left sounded very much like the worst of the Negro-hating Southerners—*Current Biog.*⟩ **Sectary** (see also HERETIC) usually implies the acceptance of the doctrines of a teacher or body ⟨*sectaries* of Mohammed⟩ ⟨there dwelt, un-changed, the spirit of the Puritans and the Friends, the stiff-necked *sectaries* of Cromwell's army—*Brooks*⟩ ⟨Aristotle . . . has suffered from the adherence of persons who must be regarded less as his disciples than as his *sec-taries—T. S. Eliot*⟩ **Partisan** suggests such devotion to the person or opinions of another or to a party, a creed, or a school of thought that there is incapacity for seeing from any other point of view. It often, therefore, connotes bigot-ry or prejudice ⟨Laura was always a passionate *partisan* of her young brother—*Mary Austin*⟩ ⟨a few *partisans* argued for him—*Mencken*⟩ **Henchman** is commonly ap-plied to a subservient follower of a political leader or boss; in extended use it connotes abject submission to the will of a dominating and, usually, unscrupulous leader or group ⟨the cat's-paw of corrupt functionaries and the *henchman* of ambitious humbugs—*Shaw*⟩ **Satellite,** more than any of the others, suggests devotion to the person of the leader and constant obsequious attendance on him ⟨Boswell was . . . made happy by an introduction to Johnson, of whom he became the obsequious *satellite* —*Irving*⟩

*Ana* devotee, votary, *addict, habitué: *parasite, syco-phant, toady

*Ant* leader

**following** *n* Following, clientele, public, audience are comparable when they denote the body of persons who attach themselves to another especially as disciples, patrons, or admirers. **Following** is the most compre-hensive term, applicable to a group that follows either

as a physical train or retinue or as the adherents of a leader, the disciples of a philosopher, the customers of a salesman, the admirers of a young woman, or the fans of an actor ⟨such a man, with a great name in the country and a strong *following* in Parliament—*Macaulay*⟩ ⟨he unconsciously enrolls a *following* of like-minded persons —*Montague*⟩ **Clientele** is chiefly used of the persons, collectively, who go habitually for services to a profes-sional man (as a lawyer or physician) or who give their patronage to a business establishment (as a hotel, a restaurant, or a shop) ⟨Dr. Doe has among his *clientele* all the leading families in the town⟩ ⟨summer hotels usu-ally send out circulars to their *clientele* in the spring⟩ **Public** basically denotes a group of people with a common interest and may come close to *following* in many of its applications (as to adherents, disciples, customers, and admirers); often, however, it distinctively conveys the notion of a group making active demands rather than one passively or admiringly following ⟨a novelist's *public,* in fact, is people who read everything he writes even when they hate it—*Cary*⟩ ⟨a public relations program must be concerned with the policies of the institution, their interpretation and announcement to the college's various *publics—Brecht*⟩ ⟨protecting movie stars from their *publics—New Yorker*⟩ ⟨these two books on Spain are different in purpose, different in scope, and aimed at different *publics—Bergin*⟩ **Audience** is applicable to a following that listens with attention to what a person has to say whenever he addresses them (as in a speech or a book) ⟨still govern thou my song, Urania, and fit *audi-ence* find, though few—*Milton*⟩ ⟨the stricken poet [Leopardi] . . . had no country, for an Italy in his day did not exist, he had no *audience,* no celebrity—*Arnold*⟩ **Audience,** rather than *spectators* (see SPECTATOR), is also the usual term for designating the body of persons attending a lecture, a play, or a concert on the assumption that they are there primarily to hear, only secondarily to see ⟨the *audience* at the opera packed the house⟩

**foment** abet, *incite, instigate

*Ana* goad, spur (see corresponding nouns at MOTIVE): stimulate, quicken, excite, galvanize, *provoke: nurture, *nurse, foster, cultivate

*Ant* quell —*Con* *suppress, repress: check, curb, *restrain

**fond** *adj* **1** Fond, infatuated, besotted, insensate are compa-rable when they mean made blindly or stupidly foolish (as by passion or drink). **Fond** implies a judgment mis-led by credulity, undue optimism, or excessive affec-tion ⟨Cowper's characterization of the *Biographia Britannica:* "Oh, *fond* attempt to give a deathless lot to names ignoble, born to be forgot!"⟩ ⟨grant I may never prove so *fond,* to trust man on his oath or bond—*Shak.*⟩ ⟨how are we to rid ourselves of our *fond* prejudices and open our minds?—*James Ford*⟩ **Infatuated** implies a weakening rather than the absence of judgment, especially under the influence of violent passion or unreasoning emotion; it is therefore correctly applied to the acts or qualities of men from whom sagacity or self-control might have been expected ⟨what the *infatuated* ministry may do, I know not; but our *infatuated* House of Com-mons . . . have begun a new war in America—*Burke*⟩ ⟨your people are so shortsighted, so jealous and selfish, and so curiously *infatuated* with things that are not . . . good—*Jefferies*⟩ **Besotted** adds to *infatuated* the impli-cations of a stupefying or intoxicating influence that de-stroys the capacity to think clearly and sometimes makes its victim disgusting or repulsive ⟨men *besotted* by drink⟩ ⟨are these so far *besotted* that they fail to see this fair wife-worship cloaks a secret shame?—*Tennyson*⟩ ⟨seemed

*Ana* analogous words     *Ant* antonyms     *Con* contrasted words     See also explanatory notes facing page 1

absolutely *besotted* about the damned woman—*Christie*⟩ **Insensate** conveys the idea of feeling and judgment lost under the influence of such passions as hatred, desire for revenge, rage, or greed; the term is also applicable to the passion ⟨the *insensate* rage⟩ ⟨the *insensate* mob uttered a cry of triumph—*Shelley*⟩ ⟨his *insensate* wrath seemed to pass all ordinary bounds—*S. S. Van Dine*⟩ ⟨*insensate* hatred for the broken man in the White House —*S. H. Adams*⟩
*Ana* foolish, silly, fatuous, asinine, *simple: *stupid, dumb
**2** devoted, affectionate, *loving, doting
*Ana* *enamored, infatuated: *tender, sympathetic, warm, responsive: ardent, passionate, *impassioned
*Con* *indifferent, unconcerned, aloof
**fondle** pet, cosset, *caress, cuddle, dandle

**food** **1** Food, feed, victuals, viands, provisions, comestibles, provender, fodder, forage are comparable when meaning things that are edible for human beings or animals. **Food** is the most general of these terms and is typically applicable to all substances which satisfy hunger and build up or repair waste in the body of men or animals ⟨conserve a nation's supply of *food*⟩ ⟨refrigerators that keep *food* fresh⟩ It is sometimes distinguished from *drink* ⟨there was no lack of *food* or drink during their sojourn on the island⟩ or applied specifically to human needs and then distinguished from **feed,** which normally denotes food for domestic animals ⟨he needed *food* for his family and *feed* for his livestock—*Gustafson*⟩ *Victuals* and *viands* basically denote food for human beings, especially food that is prepared and ready for eating. **Victuals** is a racy or pungent word used for special effect ⟨I worked hard enough to earn my passage and my *victuals*—*Shaw*⟩ ⟨when I bear in mind how elegantly we eat our *victuals* —*L. P. Smith*⟩ **Viands** is bookish or affected and occurs chiefly where daintiness, rarity, or an especially fine quality is to be suggested ⟨all the dainties and *viands* that could be wanted for a feast—*Wilde*⟩ ⟨he dashed the wine on the earth and scattered about the other *viands* —*Milman*⟩ **Provisions** applies to food in general as offered for sale in a market or kept in store as supplies ⟨a country store stocked with all sorts of staples and *provisions*⟩ ⟨there were not enough *provisions* in the hotel to care for the weekend influx of guests⟩ ⟨a basket of *provisions*⟩ **Comestibles,** which stresses edibility, is now found chiefly in playful use for *victuals* or *provisions* ⟨he resolved upon having a strong reinforcement of *comestibles*— *Hook*⟩ ⟨bills are also discussed, and butchers and groceries, and the price of *comestibles*—*Rose Macaulay*⟩ The remaining three terms, *provender, fodder,* and *forage,* basically denote feed for animals, but all may occasionally be used, typically derogatorily, of human food. **Provender** in its basic use applies to food (as hay, oats, or corn) for horses, mules, or asses ⟨they must be dieted like mules and have their *provender* tied to their mouths—*Shak.*⟩ **Fodder** applies to food for domestic cattle and especially to coarse food (as hay, silage, and straw) that is harvested and fed out, as distinguished from **forage,** food consumed by grazing or browsing.
**2** Food, aliment, pabulum, nutriment, nourishment, sustenance, pap are comparable especially when they denote material which feeds and supports the mind or the spirit. **Food** is applicable to whatever is taken in and assimilated to enlarge the mind or spirit or to contribute to its vitality and growth ⟨praise was her favorite *food*—*Phillpotts*⟩ ⟨those books that provide *food* for the imagination⟩ *Aliment* and *pabulum* are not always distinguishable from each other, but **aliment** is more often applied to what nourishes or builds one's mind and nature ⟨mischief,

love, and contradiction, are the natural *aliments* of a woman—*Richardson*⟩ ⟨the *aliments* nurturing our nobler part, the mind, thought, dreams, passions, and aims . . . at length are made our mind itself—*Lytton*⟩ and **pabulum** to something, and often something overrefined, bland, or worthless, which serves as an article or sometimes as the substance of one's mental diet ⟨many motion pictures provide poor *pabulum* for the adolescent mind⟩ ⟨where every man's hand is out for *pabulum,* and virile creativeness has given place to the patronizing favor of swollen bureaucracy—*Vannevar Bush*⟩ **Nutriment** and **nourishment** are both applied to what is needed for healthy growth (as of the body, the mind, or an institution) ⟨the central sources of the ideology, the abundant larder from which the *nutriment* of ideology is being drawn—*A. A. Cohen*⟩ ⟨self-esteem, one of the properties of the ego, is first regulated by the supply of *nourishment* from the outside—*Blum*⟩ but **nourishment** in addition suggests, as *nutriment* does not, the nourishing effect produced ⟨Professor Perry's conclusion: "The chief source of spiritual *nourishment* for any nation, must be its own past, perpetually rediscovered and renewed"—*Time*⟩ ⟨lacking the *nourishment* which enthusiasm or imagination can give, their writing is unlikely to be either robust or vivid—*Gloag*⟩ **Sustenance** stresses the supporting and maintaining rather than the upbuilding aspect of nutriment ⟨the blossoms of Beaumont and Fletcher's imagination draw no *sustenance* from the soil, but are cut and slightly withered flowers stuck into sand—*T. S. Eliot*⟩ **Pap** is found chiefly in contemptuous or ironical use and applies in its extended sense to nourishment that is as slight, as diluted, and as innocuous as soft bland food for an infant or invalid ⟨college courses that are mere intellectual *pap*⟩ ⟨a preacher whose sermons are nothing more than *pap*⟩

**fool,** idiot, imbecile, moron, simpleton, natural are often used popularly and interchangeably of one regarded as lacking sense or good judgment but each can be more precisely applied to someone mentally deficient in a given degree. **Fool,** the most general, can apply to anyone mentally deranged as well as mentally deficient, implying lack or loss of reason or intelligence; it may be used as an extremely offensive term of contempt ⟨*fools* rush in where angels fear to tread—*Pope*⟩ ⟨he was a *fool* and liable, as such, under the stress of bodily or mental disturbance, to spasmodic fits of abject fright which he mistook for religion—*Norman Douglas*⟩ ⟨I was a *fool,* if you like, and certainly I was going to do a foolish, overbold act—*Stevenson*⟩ ⟨act like a *fool*⟩ *Idiot, imbecile,* and *moron* are technical designations for one mentally deficient. An **idiot** is incapable of connected speech or of avoiding the common dangers of life and needs constant attendance. An **imbecile** is incapable of earning a living but can be educated to attend to simple wants or avoid most ordinary dangers. A **moron** can learn a simple trade but requires constant supervision in his work or recreation. In more general and nontechnical use *idiot* implies utter feeblemindedness, *imbecile* implies half-wittedness, and *moron* implies general stupidity ⟨comes like an *idiot,* babbling and strewing flowers— *Millay*⟩ ⟨actually there never is a status quo, except in the minds of political *imbeciles*—*Henry Miller*⟩ ⟨even *morons* get college degrees—*Warfel*⟩ All three, however, may imply no more than often mild derogation or disapprobation of a person or his conduct ⟨got a little high at the reunion and made a complete *idiot* of himself⟩ ⟨how could he have been such a careless *imbecile* as to mislay his manuscript?—*Mackenzie*⟩ ⟨the telephone call was a fake . . . and Peeps climbed up into the guard

---

A colon (:) separates groups of words discriminated. An asterisk (*) indicates place of treatment of each group.

chair, mumbling about the brains of certain *morons—Boys' Life*⟩ **Simpleton,** a term of indulgent contempt, implies silliness or lack of sophistication ⟨a sweet-natured *simpleton* who wrote lovely songs for children—*Damon*⟩ ⟨in spite of her experience of his lying, she had never suspected that that particular statement was a lie. What a *simpleton* she was!—*Bennett*⟩ **Natural,** which persists chiefly in historical context, may designate any congenitally feebleminded person ⟨the man is not a *natural;* he has a very quick sense, though very slow understanding —*Steele*⟩ ⟨with the vacant grin of a *natural—Charles Gibbon*⟩

**foolhardy** daring, daredevil, rash, reckless, *adventurous, venturesome
*Ana* bold, audacious (see BRAVE): headlong, *precipitate, impetuous
*Ant* wary —*Con* *cautious, circumspect, calculating

**foolish** 1 *simple, silly, fatuous, asinine
*Ana* idiotic, imbecilic, moronic (see corresponding nouns at FOOL)
*Con* *intelligent, clever, quick-witted, bright, smart
**2 Foolish, silly, absurd, preposterous,** as applied to a person, his acts, behavior, and utterances, mean ridiculous because not exhibiting good sense. Something is **foolish** which does not commend itself to the judgment of others as wise or sensible or judicious ⟨a *foolish* investment⟩ ⟨courageous behavior is easier for a man who fails to apprehend dangers, but such courage may often be *foolish—Russell*⟩ ⟨only a *foolish* optimist can deny the dark realities of the moment—*Roosevelt*⟩ Something is **silly** which seems witless, pointless, or futile ⟨a *silly* dispute⟩ ⟨a *silly* sacrifice⟩ ⟨how *silly* an ardent and unsuccessful wooer can be, especially if he's getting on in years—*Hammett*⟩ Something is **absurd** which is inconsistent with accepted ideas, common sense, or sound reason; the word is applied, therefore, to ideas and projects considered impersonally as well as to persons and their acts ⟨the *absurd* . . . dogma that the king can do no wrong—*Shaw*⟩ ⟨the *absurd* predicament of seeming to argue that virtue is highly desirable but intensely unpleasant—*Lippmann*⟩ Something is **preposterous** which is glaringly absurd ⟨if a man cannot see a church, it is *preposterous* to take his opinion about its altarpiece or painted window—*T. H. Huxley*⟩ or sometimes merely highly unsuitable or ridiculously out of keeping (as with a particular character or situation) ⟨he put on his *preposterous* old flowered cashmere dressing gown—*Deland*⟩
*Ana* ridiculous, ludicrous, *laughable
*Ant* sensible —*Con* *wise, sane, judicious, prudent, sage, sapient

**foot** *vb* figure, cast, *add, sum, total, tot

**fop** *n* Fop, dandy, beau, coxcomb, exquisite, dude, buck are comparable when denoting a man who is conspicuously fashionable or elegant in dress or manners. **Fop** is applied to a man who is preposterously concerned with fashionableness, elegance, and refinement not only in respect to dress and manners but in respect to such matters as literary or artistic taste ⟨his tightened waist, his stiff stock . . . denoted the military *fop—Disraeli*⟩ ⟨I might have taken him for a *fop,* for he wore white lace at throat and wrists—*Kenneth Roberts*⟩ ⟨his love of good clothes and good living gave Bennett a reputation as a *fop—Time*⟩ **Dandy** carries a weaker implication of affectation and overrefinement than *fop* and a stronger suggestion of concern for stylish or striking apparel and a spruce or dapper appearance ⟨that he had the tastes of a *dandy,* we learn from a letter of the time describing his "smart white hat, kid gloves, brown frock coat, yellow cassimere waistcoat, gray duck trousers, and blue silk handkerchief carelessly secured in front by a silver pin" —*Walsh*⟩ ⟨this character, one of the most comical in Stendhal, should . . . figure very high, in the list of his *dandies.* He never smiles, never thinks, and belongs to the Jockey Club—*Girard*⟩ **Beau** suggests as much attention to details of personal appearance as does *fop* ⟨a *beau* is one who, with the nicest care, in parted locks divides his curling hair; one who with balm and cinnamon smells sweet—*Elton*⟩ **Coxcomb,** like *fop,* is applicable to a beau as a term of contempt; it often stresses fatuousness and pretentiousness as much as or more than foppishness ⟨of all the fools that pride can boast, a *coxcomb* claims distinction most—*Gay*⟩ ⟨the young *coxcombs* of the Life Guards—*Emerson*⟩ **Exquisite** is a somewhat old-fashioned designation of a dandy who manifests the extreme delicacy and refinement of taste characteristic of a fop ⟨the particular styles. . . he affected had their marked influence on the young *exquisites* of the Mayfair balls and Pall Mall club windows—*Wilde*⟩ **Dude** applies chiefly to a man who makes himself conspicuously different in dress or manners from the ordinary man; it is therefore the rough man's term for the carefully dressed and groomed man, the quiet gentleman's term for the obvious dandy, or a Western American's term for an Easterner or a city-bred man ⟨her father told her he would not allow her to marry a *dude*⟩ ⟨the boys jeer at every young man wearing a high hat and call him a *dude*⟩ ⟨they were all mountain-wise, range-broken men, picked . . . for diplomacy in handling *dudes—Scribner's Mag.*⟩ ⟨the *dudes* ogled the ladies, stroking their mustaches, adjusting their ties and scooting their shoe toes up their calves to restore the shine—*Berrigan*⟩ **Buck** applies usually to a dashing fellow, a dandy in dress, but not conspicuously, or necessarily, a gentleman in manners ⟨the dashing young *buck,* driving his own equipage—*Irving*⟩ ⟨I remember you a *buck* of *bucks* when that coat first came out to Calcutta—*Thackeray*⟩

**for** *conj* *because, since, as, inasmuch as

**forage** *n* fodder, provender, *food, feed, provisions, comestibles, victuals, viands

**forbear** 1 *forgo, abnegate, eschew, sacrifice
*Ana* *restrain, curb, bridle, inhibit: avoid, *escape, evade, shun: desist, cease (see STOP)
2 *refrain, abstain
*Ana* suffer, tolerate, endure, *bear

**forbearance** 1 long-suffering, *patience, longanimity, resignation
*Ana & Ant* see those at FORBEARANCE 2
2 tolerance, clemency, mercifulness, leniency, indulgence (see under FORBEARING)
*Ana* patience, long-suffering, longanimity: *mercy, lenity, grace, charity
*Ant* vindictiveness: anger

**forbearing,** tolerant, clement, merciful, lenient, indulgent mean disinclined by nature, disposition, or circumstances to be severe or rigorous. The same differences in implications and connotations are observable in their corresponding nouns **forbearance, tolerance, clemency, mercifulness, leniency, indulgence** and adverbs **forbearingly, tolerantly, clemently, mercifully, leniently, indulgently. Forbearing, forbearance,** and **forbearingly** imply patience under provocation and deliberate abstention from judging harshly, exacting punishment, or seeking vengeance or revenge ⟨Madame Beck was . . . *forbearing* with all the world—*Brontë*⟩ ⟨the thought of old days: of his father's *forbearance,* his own wilfulness—*Meredith*⟩ ⟨spoke *forbearingly* of the lack of facilities that handicapped his work⟩ **Tolerant, tolerance,** and **tolerantly** imply both a freedom from bias or bigotry and a liberal attitude to opinions, especially to religious, philosophical, and political doctrines, other than one's own that keep one from severity or rigor in judging others who hold such opinions or doctrines or from wanting to impose restrictions upon their freedom to think as they will ⟨[Anatole] France, as usual, professed a very *tolerant* attitude. One must gratify whatever tastes one has and seek whatever happiness one may be able to find—*Krutch*⟩ ⟨of all kinds of human energy, art is surely the most free, the least parochial; and demands of us an essential *tolerance* of all its forms—*Galsworthy*⟩ **Clement, clemency** (see also MERCY), and **clemently** suggest a temperament or nature that is mild and gentle, especially in judging offenders, and is slow to exact their punishment if a pardon or forgiveness will satisfy the purpose ⟨a *clement* ruler⟩ ⟨a judge known far and wide for his *clemency*⟩ ⟨he was *clement* whenever he could be *clement* with safety, and he began to pardon the proscribed—*Buchan*⟩ **Merciful, mercifulness,** and **mercifully** imply both compassionate and forbearing treatment, especially of those who have offended or of those who merit severity or are defenseless against it ⟨good my lord, be good to me; your honor is accounted a *merciful* man—*Shak.*⟩ ⟨like a perfect nightmare, it was *mercifully* short—*W. J. Locke*⟩ **Lenient** (see also SOFT), **leniency,** and **leniently** differ from *clement* in suggesting usually softness rather than gentleness of temper, and a relaxation of discipline or rigor ⟨a too *lenient* parent⟩ ⟨I would ask you, dearest, to be . . . very *lenient* on his faults when he is not by—*Dickens*⟩ ⟨she could not show the slightest *leniency* towards the romantic impulses of her elder daughter—*Bennett*⟩ ⟨no matter how *leniently* you may try to put it, in the end we have . . . a struggle between men—*Wister*⟩ **Indulgent, indulgence,** and **indulgently** usually imply compliancy as well as leniency; they imply, even more strongly than *lenient, leniency,* and *leniently,* concessions made out of charity or the exercise of clemency in the treatment of those who offend or who are under one's government or control ⟨that one congenial friend . . . more *indulgent* of his shortcomings, and, in all respects, closer and kinder than a brother—*Hawthorne*⟩ ⟨*indulgently* dismisses them as basically nice boys—*P. D. Whitney*⟩ ⟨before her children reached school age. . . her treatment alternated spasmodically between excessive *indulgence* and petulant severity—*Gorer*⟩

**Ana** gentle, mild (see SOFT): patient, long-suffering, longanimous (see corresponding nouns at PATIENCE)

**Ant** unrelenting —**Con** implacable, merciless, relentless, *grim: *impatient, nervous, restive

**forbearingly** tolerantly, clemently, mercifully, leniently, indulgently (see under FORBEARING)

**forbid, prohibit, enjoin, interdict, inhibit, ban** are comparable when meaning to debar a person from using, doing, or entering or to order something not be used, done, or entered. **Forbid** is the more direct and familiar, **prohibit,** the more formal or official; they do not widely differ in their essential implications, for they both imply the exercise of authority or the existence of conditions which prevent with similar imperativeness. However, *forbid* carries so strong a connotation of expected obedience that it is preferred when the order is that of one in authority (as a parent, a master, an employer, or a physician) ⟨*forbid* a child to leave the house⟩ ⟨smoking is *forbidden* on these premises⟩ ⟨suffer the little children to come unto me, and *forbid* them not—*Mk* 10:14⟩ ⟨the whole attraction of such knowledge consists in the fact that it is *forbidden* —*Russell*⟩ When circumstances absolutely debar, *forbid* is also preferred ⟨his health *forbade* the use of tobacco⟩

*Prohibit* has been used for so long in reference to laws, statutes, and regulations that it tends to connote a less despotic exercise of authority and to suggest restraints imposed for the good of all or for the sake of orderly procedure ⟨*prohibit* the manufacture and sale of intoxicating liquors⟩ ⟨the powers not delegated to the United States by the Constitution, nor *prohibited* by it to the States—*U. S. Constitution*⟩ ⟨the act was wrong in the sense that it was *prohibited* by law—*Cardozo*⟩ **Enjoin** (see also COMMAND) is a legal term implying a judicial order forbidding a particular action ⟨by the decision of the Court the defendant should be *enjoined* from publishing news obtained from the Associated Press for — [a certain number of] hours after publication by the plaintiff—*Justice Holmes*⟩ **Interdict** implies prohibition by authority, usually civil or ecclesiastical authority, typically for a given time and for a salutary purpose (as the maintenance of neutrality or the prevention of the spread of disease) or as an exemplary punishment ⟨*interdict* trade with belligerents⟩ ⟨*interdict* the administration of the sacraments in a rebellious diocese⟩ ⟨Sunday . . . until two o'clock, was a solemn interval, during which all the usual books and plays were *interdicted*—*Mary Austin*⟩ **Inhibit** implies the imposition of restraints or restrictions that amount to prohibitions, not only by authority but also by the exigencies of the time or situation ⟨a clause was . . . inserted which *inhibited* the Bank from advancing money to the Crown without authority from Parliament—*Macaulay*⟩ ⟨the peril that besets a highly gifted poetic nature, when at bad moments thought *inhibits* imagination —*Lowes*⟩ In psychological use *inhibit* suggests the restraints imposed by inner psychological impediments and conflicts or by the interaction of human will with cultural and social factors of the environment which cause one to suppress certain thoughts or desires before they can find full expression ⟨*inhibited* from bold speculation by his personal loyalties and interests—*Parrington*⟩ ⟨he is *inhibited,* he *inhibits* himself, even from seeking on his own account that vital experience which is the stuff of the creative life—*Brooks*⟩ **Ban** carries an implication of legal or social pressure as the source of prohibition and with it a strong connotation of condemnation or disapproval ⟨*ban* all obscene magazines⟩ ⟨*ban* profane language⟩ ⟨categories of persons *banned* from Federal employment—*Ginzburg*⟩ ⟨more and more landlords were *banning* tenants with children—*Wecter*⟩

**Ana** debar, rule out, *exclude: preclude, obviate, *prevent: *prevent, forestall

**Ant** permit: bid —**Con** *let, allow, suffer: *authorize, license: *approve, sanction, endorse: order, *command, enjoin

**force** *n* **1** *power, energy, strength, might, puissance
**Ana** *stress, strain, pressure, tension: *speed, velocity, momentum, impetus, headway
**2 Force, violence, compulsion, coercion, duress, constraint, restraint** denote the exercise or the exertion of power in order to impose one's will on a person or to have one's will with a thing. *Force* and *violence* ordinarily apply to physical powers used upon either persons or things; *compulsion, coercion, duress, constraint, restraint* apply to either physical or moral power used upon personal agents except in certain figurative uses—*compulsion, coercion,* and *duress* usually implying exercise of such power upon others than oneself, *constraint* or *restraint* upon oneself or others. **Force** (see also POWER 1) applies to an exercise of physical strength or of power comparable to physical strength by means of which an agent imposes his will upon another against that person's will or causes a thing to move as desired in spite of its resistance ⟨rude fishermen . . .

A colon (:) separates groups of words discriminated. An asterisk (*) indicates place of treatment of each group.

by *force* took Dromio—*Shak.*⟩ ⟨to work in close design, by fraud or guile, what *force* effected not—*Milton*⟩ ⟨move a huge boulder by main *force*⟩ ⟨the skeptical criticism that "justice" is merely another name for *force*—*Dickinson*⟩ ⟨*force* used by attendants in an asylum . . . *force* used by the police when they control a crowd . . . *force* used in war—*Huxley*⟩ **Violence** is often used in place of *force,* then commonly implying a greater display of power or fury and often connoting the infliction of injury or cruelty ⟨they will by *violence* tear him from your palace —*Shak.*⟩ ⟨the rest of the party kept off the crowd by mingled persuasion and *violence*—*Shaw*⟩ *Violence* often implies a violation of another's legal rights or property, or it may imply a corruption or abuse of someone or something entitled to respect, observance, or security ⟨a burglar in entering a house by forcing a door enters it by *violence*⟩ ⟨do *violence* to no man—*Lk* 3:14⟩ ⟨all these many and varied powers had been acquired without doing *violence* to republican sentiment—*Buchan*⟩ ⟨the phrase "every common carrier engaged in trade or commerce" may be construed to mean "while engaged in trade or commerce" without *violence* to the habits of English speech—*Justice Holmes*⟩ **Compulsion** and, still more, **coercion** imply the application of physical force or of moral pressure or the exercise of one's authority in order to control the action of a voluntary agent and to make him obedient to one's will ⟨I would give no man a reason upon *compulsion*—*Shak.*⟩ ⟨*coerçion* by threat or intimidation⟩ ⟨masterpieces I read under *compulsion* without the faintest interest—*Russell*⟩ ⟨solutions forced upon a most practical mind by the stern *compulsion* of facts—*Buchan*⟩ ⟨in the submissive way of one long accustomed to obey under *coercion*—*Dickens*⟩ ⟨some form of *coercion,* overt or covert, which encroaches upon the natural freedom of individuals—*Dewey*⟩ **Duress** implies compulsion to do or forbear some act by means that are illegal (as by imprisonment or threats to imprison or by violence) ⟨a person is not guilty of *duress* when he does or threatens to do something he has a legal right to do —*Fisk & Snapp*⟩ It may also imply compulsion or coercion through fear of a penalty that will or may be exacted ⟨a false declaration of love by the heroine under *duress*— *Dyneley Hussey*⟩ ⟨we must eliminate the condition of economic *duress* under which so many human beings are unjustly forced to live—*Ashley Montagu*⟩ **Constraint** and **restraint** may imply the exercise of physical or moral power either by an active agent or by the force of circumstances; **constraint** sometimes implies an urging or driving to action but more frequently implies its forcible restriction or confinement, whereas **restraint** suggests its actual hindrance or curbing ⟨the . . . lion . . . roared with sharp *constraint* of hunger—*Shak.*⟩ ⟨prose is memorable speech set down without the *constraint* of meter— *Quiller-Couch*⟩ ⟨absolute liberty is absence of *restraint;* responsibility is *restraint;* therefore, the ideally free individual is responsible only to himself—*Henry Adams*⟩ ⟨the emotion . . . was the deeper and the sweeter for the *restraint* that he had put upon himself—*Archibald Marshall*⟩

*Ana* intensity, vehemence, fierceness (see corresponding adjectives at INTENSE): *effort, exertion, pains, trouble

**force** *vb* **Force, compel, coerce, constrain, oblige** are comparable when meaning to make a person or thing yield to the will of a person or to the strength or power of a thing. **Force,** the ordinary and most general word in this group, implies the exertion of strength, typically physical strength, or the working of something (as circumstances or logical necessity) analogous in moving power or effectiveness to such strength ⟨*force* slaves to labor⟩ ⟨*force* food upon

a child⟩ ⟨he said hunger *forced* him to steal the food⟩ ⟨his conscience *forced* him into repaying what he had stolen⟩ ⟨*force* himself to smile⟩ ⟨the man could not be *forced* from the position he had taken⟩ Sometimes the term takes a simple object, naming the person forced or the thing brought about by force; in such cases the verb often carries additional implications acquired from its idiomatic use in a particular phrase; thus, to *force* a woman is to rape her; to *force* a door is to break it open; to *force* laughter or a smile or tears is to make oneself laugh or smile or cry against one's will; to *force* bulbs is to hasten their development by artificial means ⟨*forced* language⟩ ⟨a *forced* style⟩ **Compel** differs from *force* chiefly in typically requiring a personal object; any other type of object such as a reaction or response is possible only in extended or poetic language when the specific connotations of *compel* (as the exertion of irresistible power or force or a victory over resistance) are to be carried by the verb ⟨she always *compels* admiration⟩ ⟨an argument that *compels* assent⟩ or a concrete thing ⟨such a breeze *compelled* thy canvas—*Tennyson*⟩ *Compel* commonly implies the exercise of authority, the exertion of great effort or driving force, or the impossibility for one reason or another of doing anything else ⟨[they] submit because they are *compelled;* but they would resist, and finally resist effectively, if they were not cowards—*Shaw*⟩ ⟨we see nothing in the Constitution that *compels* the Government to sit by while a food supply is cut off and the protectors of our forest and our crops are destroyed—*Justice Holmes*⟩ ⟨there is no possible method of *compelling* a child to feel sympathy or affection—*Russell*⟩ ⟨the westering sun at length *compelled* me to quit the wood—*Hudson*⟩ **Coerce** suggests more severity in the methods employed than *compel* does; commonly it connotes the exertion of violence or duress or the use of threats or intimidation ⟨there are more ways of *coercing* a man than by pointing a gun at his head—*Inge*⟩ ⟨Charles the First signed his own death warrant when he undertook to *coerce* that stubborn will [of Londoners]—*Repplier*⟩ **Constrain** stresses more than does *compel,* its closest synonym, the force exerted by what presses or binds; it usually suggests the influence of restrictions, self-imposed or placed upon one by force, by nature, by necessity, or by circumstances, that compel one to do a stated or implied thing, live a stated or implied way, or think certain thoughts ⟨I describe everything exactly as it took place, *constraining* my mind not to wander from the task—*Dickens*⟩ ⟨causes which he loathed in his heart but which he was *constrained* to consider just—*Brooks*⟩ ⟨tied him to the wall, where he was *constrained* to stay till a kind passerby released him— *Galsworthy*⟩ **Oblige** usually implies the constraint of necessity, sometimes physical necessity ⟨a sharp pain *obliged* him to close his eyelids quickly—*Hardy*⟩ but equally often moral or intellectual necessity ⟨he is *obliged,* in conscience, to undo the harm he has done to a man's good name⟩ ⟨even the so-called laws of nature are only instruments to be used . . . we are not *obliged* to believe them—*Inge*⟩ The term also is used with reference to a person or thing which is regarded as authoritative or as having the right to determine one's course or acts ⟨the discipline of their great School . . . *obliges* them to bring up a weekly essay to their tutor—*Quiller-Couch*⟩ ⟨the convention which *obliged* a satirist to be scathing—*Inge*⟩ ⟨she is *obliged* to learn by heart a multitude of songs— *Hearn*⟩

*Ana* impel, drive, *move: *command, order, enjoin: exact, *demand, require

**forced,** **labored, strained, farfetched** are comparable when they mean produced or kept up through effort and, therefore, neither natural nor easy nor spontaneous. **Forced** is the widest in range of application of any of these terms, being referred not only to what is brought about by compulsion ⟨works of a kind which had normally been performed in antiquity by the *forced* labor of slaves—*Farrington*⟩ or to what is accomplished by exerting force beyond the usual limit ⟨a *forced* march⟩ ⟨many women talk excitedly at a *forced* pitch for long periods and finish a conversation almost exhausted—*Hewitt*⟩ but also to what seems artificial because not natural, logical, or spontaneous or because constrained or affected ⟨his . . . resolute rejection of *forced* and fantastic interpretation of Holy Scripture—*Fosbroke*⟩ ⟨the old man was grinning. It was a little *forced* and a little painful, but it was a grin—*Irwin Shaw*⟩ **Labored** carries a stronger connotation of heaviness or of ponderousness or, sometimes, of tediousness as a result of great effort ⟨a *labored* style⟩ ⟨suggests that the woman loves the man because he alone can give her the baby that fulfills her femininity . . . . These explanations are ingenious, if *labored*—*La Barre*⟩ ⟨uncomfortably aware of his men behind him; of their cushioned footsteps and *labored* breathing—*Hervey*⟩ **Strained** adds to these an implication of tenseness or of a result that is unnaturally or distortedly labored ⟨*strained* attention⟩ ⟨a *strained* comparison⟩ ⟨in the style of each there is at times evidence of *strained* composition, a lack of verbal ease or elegance—*Arnold Chapman*⟩ ⟨a *strained* air of reasonableness prevails, with a good deal of nervous anxiety showing through on both sides—*Bendiner*⟩ ⟨three patients were sitting, with *strained* expectant eyes—*Glasgow*⟩ **Farfetched** applies especially to an expression, an idea, an argument, or an explanation which has been carefully sought out so that it seems unduly strained and not quite naturally used ⟨his ideas were always *farfetched*⟩ ⟨a *farfetched* comparison⟩ ⟨these methods of interpretation . . . seem gratuitously *farfetched*, fantastic—*Edmund Wilson*⟩

**Ana** compelled, coerced, constrained (see FORCE): factitious, *artificial: fatiguing, exhausting (see TIRE)

**Con** *easy, effortless, smooth: *spontaneous, instinctive, impulsive: *natural, unsophisticated, unaffected, artless

**forceful** *powerful, potent, forcible, puissant

**Ana** compelling, constraining (see FORCE *vb*): virile, manful (see MALE): cogent, telling, convincing, compelling (see VALID): *effective, efficient

**Ant** feeble  —**Con** *weak, infirm, decrepit, frail

**forcible** forceful, *powerful, potent, puissant

**Ana** vehement, *intense, violent: energetic, strenuous, *vigorous: *aggressive, militant, assertive, self-assertive: coercing *or* coercive (see corresponding verb at FORCE)

**forebear** forefather, progenitor, *ancestor

**forebode** portend, presage, augur, prognosticate, *foretell, predict, forecast, prophesy

**Ana** betoken, bespeak, *indicate: import, signify (see MEAN): fear, dread (see corresponding nouns at FEAR)

**foreboding** *n* misgiving, presentiment, *apprehension

**Ana** *foretoken, presage, omen, portent, augury, prognostic: forewarning, warning (see WARN)

**forecast** *vb* predict, *foretell, prophesy, prognosticate, augur, presage, portend, forebode

**Ana** *foresee, foreknow, anticipate, apprehend, divine: surmise, *conjecture, guess: *infer, gather, conclude

**forefather** forebear, progenitor, *ancestor

**foregoing** *adj.* antecedent, *preceding, precedent, previous, prior, former, anterior

**Ant** following

**foreign** alien, extraneous, *extrinsic

**Ana** external, outside, *outer: *inconsonant, inconsistent, incongruous, incompatible: *repugnant, repellent, obnoxious, distasteful: adventitious, *accidental

**Ant** germane  —**Con** *relevant, pertinent, material, apposite, apropos, applicable: akin, alike, uniform (see LIKE)

**foreigner** alien, *stranger, outlander, outsider, immigrant, émigré

**foreknow** divine, *foresee, anticipate, apprehend

**Ana** *foretell, predict, forecast, prophesy, prognosticate: *infer, gather, conclude

**foremost** leading, *chief, principal, main, capital

**forensic** *n* debate, disputation, *argumentation, dialectic

**forerunner, precursor, harbinger, herald** are comparable when they denote someone or something that comes before another person or thing and in some way indicates his or its future appearance. **Forerunner** may denote a messenger that goes before a personage (as a king, prince, or lord) to warn others of his approach ⟨there is a *forerunner* come from . . . the Prince of Morocco, who brings word the prince his master will be here tonight—*Shak.*⟩ ⟨there should also be one or more *forerunners* to visit each town before the company arrives, to speak . . . upon the plays—*Masefield*⟩ but more often the term is applicable to something that serves as a sign, presage, or warning of something to follow ⟨a coma is often the *forerunner* of death⟩ ⟨a black sky and a sudden squall are the usual *forerunners* of a thunderstorm⟩ ⟨the increase is a *forerunner* to a general rise in interest rates—*New Republic*⟩ **Precursor** commonly carries an implication of making ready or of paving the way for the success or accomplishments of another person or thing rather than, as *forerunner*, one of serving as an announcement or prediction of what is to come ⟨the medieval sects which Dr. Rufus Jones describes as *precursors* of Quakerism—*Inge*⟩ ⟨Kepler, more than any man, was the *precursor* of Newton—*Ellis*⟩ ⟨a long period of [chemical analysis] . . . was an essential *precursor* of the present period of synthesis which has been so fruitful of good to mankind—*Morrison*⟩ **Harbinger** occurs chiefly in an extended sense, sometimes applying to a person or thing that announces something which is coming and for which one must be prepared ⟨make all our trumpets speak; give them all breath, those clamorous *harbingers* of blood and death—*Shak.*⟩ ⟨the sinister white owl . . . the *harbinger* of destruction—*Moorehead*⟩ and sometimes applying to one which goes before as a pioneer or initiator ⟨the great legal *harbinger* of the New Deal revolution—*Time*⟩ ⟨the *harbingers* of peace to a hitherto distracted . . . people—*Livingstone*⟩ **Herald** basically denotes an official who makes a solemn and stately proclamation or announcement (as of war or peace or the birth of an heir to the throne); in extended use it is applied to something which similarly announces or proclaims ⟨it was the lark, the *herald* of the morn—*Shak.*⟩ ⟨revolutions . . . were the *heralds* of social changes—*R. W. Livingstone*⟩

**Ana** anticipator (see corresponding verb at PREVENT): announcer *or* announcement, advertiser *or* advertisement (see corresponding verbs at DECLARE): portent, prognostic, omen, *foretoken, presage, augury: forewarning, warning (see WARN)

**foresee, foreknow, divine, apprehend, anticipate** can mean to know or expect that something will happen or come into existence in advance of its occurrence or advent or to have knowledge that something exists before it is manifested or expressed. **Foresee** apart from its context gives no hint of how this knowledge is derived, whether through presentiment, inspiration, imagination, or one's ability to draw inferences ⟨it's certainly unwise to admit any

---

A colon (:) separates groups of words discriminated. An asterisk (*) indicates place of treatment of each group.

sort of responsibility for our actions, whose consequences we are never able to *foresee—Conrad*⟩ ⟨nobody can *foresee* how the necessary restriction of the population will be effected—*Shaw*⟩ ⟨the kindly-earnest, brave, *foreseeing* man—*J. R. Lowell*⟩ **Foreknow** usually implies supernatural powers or the assistance of supernatural powers (as through revelation) ⟨if thou art privy to thy country's fate, which, happily, *foreknowing* may avoid, O, speak—*Shak.*⟩ ⟨they themselves decreed their own revolt, not I [God]. If I *foreknew*, foreknowledge had no influence on their fault—*Milton*⟩ ⟨he cannot, however, *foreknow* how his opponent . . . will behave in action—*Toynbee*⟩ **Divine** is not always clearly distinguishable from *foresee*, but it often suggests a gift or a special power or sometimes unusual sagacity or discernment ⟨to Rima has been given this quickness of mind and power to *divine* distant things—*Hudson*⟩ ⟨in all the years of his traveling to and fro through Europe he *divined* hardly one of the social tendencies that had so spectacular a denouement within four years of his death—*Brooks*⟩ **Apprehend** conveys less of a sense of the certainty of what is foreseen than any of the preceding words, but it carries a far stronger implication of the emotional effects of advance knowledge. In general, where one *apprehends* an evil, one is filled with fear, anxiety, or dread ⟨they agree with me in *apprehending* that this false step in one daughter will be injurious to the fortunes of all the others —*Austen*⟩ ⟨almost every evening he saw Lucy. The inexperienced little wife *apprehended* no harm in his· visits —*Meredith*⟩ ⟨his lips quivered, and she *apprehended* rather than heard what he said—*Glasgow*⟩ **Anticipate** is a more complex term than any of its synonyms. Thus a critic may foresee the verdict of posterity on a literary work, but he *anticipates* it only when he formulates a judgment which is either accepted by posterity or is pronounced by it as though the verdict were new. One may *foreknow* one's destiny or *apprehend* a danger, but one *anticipates* one's destiny or a danger only when, through the appropriate advance enjoyment or suffering, one also has a foretaste of that destiny or that danger. One may *divine* a friend's wish in advance of its expression, but one *anticipates* it only when one also gratifies it in advance of its expression ⟨colleges and universities are expected to pay close attention to, and even *anticipate*, the many voices heard from outside the campus—*Hacker*⟩ **Anticipate** is also used as an alternative to *expect* and, more distinctively, in the sense of to look forward to (something expected) with a foretaste of the pleasure or pain it promises ⟨I must know what is in the minds of these people. I must *anticipate* revolt—*Steinbeck*⟩ ⟨pleasure not known beforehand is half wasted; to *anticipate* it is to double it—*Hardy*⟩
*Ana* forecast, predict, *foretell, prophesy, prognosticate: perceive, discern, descry, espy (see SEE)

**foreshore** beach, strand, *shore, coast, littoral

**foresight** forethought, providence, discretion, *prudence
*Ana* sagacity, perspicacity, shrewdness, astuteness (see corresponding adjectives at SHREWD): acumen, clairvoyance, *discernment, perception
*Ant* hindsight

**foresighted** forethoughtful, provident, discreet, prudent (see under PRUDENCE)
*Ana* sagacious, perspicacious, *shrewd, astute: *intelligent, alert, quick-witted, brilliant, knowing: *wise, judicious, sage, sapient
*Ant* hindsighted

**forestall** *prevent, anticipate
*Ana* ward, avert, *prevent, preclude, obviate: *frustrate,

thwart, foil, circumvent
*Con* court, woo, *invite: further, forward, *advance, promote

**foretaste** *n* anticipation, *prospect, outlook
*Ana* realization, actualization (see corresponding verbs at REALIZE): token, earnest, *pledge: presentiment, foreboding (see APPREHENSION)
*Con* fruition, enjoyment (see PLEASURE): attainment, achievement (see corresponding verbs at REACH)

**foretell, predict, forecast, prophesy, prognosticate, augur, presage, portend, forebode** are comparable when meaning to tell something before it happens through special knowledge or occult power. *Foretell* and *predict* are frequently interchangeable, but **foretell** stresses the announcement of coming events and does not, apart from a context, indicate the nature of the agent's power or the source of his information ⟨some sorcerer . . . had *foretold*, dying, that none of all our blood should know the shadow from the substance—*Tennyson*⟩ ⟨the marvelous exactness with which eclipses are *foretold—Darrow*⟩ **Predict** commonly implies inference from facts or accepted laws of nature; it often connotes scientific accuracy in foretelling ⟨ Mr. Brooke's conclusions were as difficult to *predict* as the weather—*George Eliot*⟩ ⟨an astronomer *predicts* the return of a comet⟩ ⟨Gamow *predicted* that the explanation of the sun's heat, light, and energy would be found to lie in thermonuclear reactions—*Current Biog.*⟩ **Forecast** may occasionally imply taking forethought of the future (as by anticipation, conjecture of possible eventualities, and provision for one's needs) ⟨a prudent builder should *forecast* how long the stuff is like to last—*Swift*⟩ More often it implies prediction, but it still retains the implication of anticipated eventualities ⟨*forecast* the weather⟩ ⟨since hurricanes have been *forecast,* losses in life and property have dwindled⟩ ⟨when the votes began to be counted . . . the return of the Republicans was *forecast—Paxson*⟩ **Prophesy** either connotes inspired or mystic knowledge or implies great assurance in prediction ⟨ancestral voices *prophesying* war—*Coleridge*⟩ ⟨wrinkled benchers often talked of him approvingly, and *prophesied* his rise—*Tennyson*⟩ **Prognosticate** implies prediction based upon signs or symptoms ⟨a skillful physician can *prognosticate* the course of most diseases⟩ ⟨for the last three hundred years the relation of Church to State has been constantly undergoing change . . . . I am not concerned with *prognosticating* their future relations—*T. S. Eliot*⟩ Prognosticate and the following words also are comparable in the related sense of to betoken or foreshow future events or conditions ⟨everything seems to *prognosticate* a hard winter—*Cobbett*⟩ **Augur** implies a divining or a foreshadowing of something pleasant or unpleasant often through interpretation of omens or signs ⟨the morrow brought a very sober-looking morning . . . Catherine *augured* from it everything most favorable to her wishes—*Austen*⟩ *Presage* and *portend* more often imply foreshowing than foretelling, though both senses are found. Both also typically suggest occult power or an ability to interpret signs and omens as a basis for prediction, but **presage** may be used of neutral or of favorable as well as unfavorable prognostications, whereas **portend** regularly suggests a threat of evil or disaster ⟨lands he could measure, terms and tides *presage* —*Goldsmith*⟩ ⟨the yellow and vapory sunset . . . had *presaged* change—*Hardy*⟩ ⟨some great misfortune to *portend*, no enemy can match a friend—*Swift*⟩ ⟨his sign in the high heavens *portended* war—*Kipling*⟩ **Forebode** implies unfavorable prognostication based especially upon premonitions, presentiments, or dreams ⟨oppressed by a *foreboding* of evil⟩
*Ana* divine, foreknow, *foresee, anticipate, apprehend:

---

*Ana* analogous words    *Ant* antonyms    *Con* contrasted words    See also explanatory notes facing page 1

announce, *declare, proclaim: *reveal, divulge, disclose, discover: forewarn, *warn

**forethought** foresight, providence, discretion, *prudence
*Ana* premeditatedness *or* premeditation, deliberateness *or* deliberation (see corresponding verbs at DELIBERATE): wisdom, judgment, *sense, gumption

**forethoughtful** foresighted, provident, discreet, prudent (see under PRUDENCE)
*Ana* *cautious, circumspect, wary, calculating: *deliberate, premeditated, considered, advised, studied

**foretoken** *n* Foretoken, presage, prognostic, omen, augury, portent are comparable when meaning something (as an event, a phenomenon, or a condition) that serves as a sign of future happenings. **Foretoken,** the general term, is applicable to anything observable which may be the basis of a prediction or forecast ⟨the usual *foretokens* of a thunderstorm, intense sultriness, a heavily overcast sky, and suddenly arising winds⟩ **Presage** is applied chiefly to indications which inspire such emotions as fear or hope, dread or longing, and confidence or despair and therefore give rise to presentiments rather than serve as a basis for prediction ⟨three times, while crossing the ocean, he sees a lunar rainbow and each time he takes it as a *presage* of good fortune—*Brooks*⟩ **Prognostic** applies to an advance indication or symptom from which a skilled person can infer what is coming; it is used in medicine of a symptom or sign useful to a physician in predicting the course or the termination of an illness ⟨*prognostics* do not always prove prophecies, at least the wisest prophets make sure of the event first—*Walpole*⟩ ⟨*prognostics* are those circumstances on which a prognosis is based—*Flint*⟩ **Omen** is applicable chiefly to an extraordinary event or circumstance which one feels, especially under the influence of superstition, to be a promise of something to come ⟨nay I have had some *omens:* I got out of bed backwards too this morning, without premeditation; pretty good that too; but then I stumbled coming downstairs, and met a weasel; bad *omens* those: some bad, some good, our lives are checkered —*Congreve*⟩ Consequently, an event of ill *omen* or of good *omen* is one that is felt to be a presage of ill or of good. **Augury** and *omen* are often interchangeable, but *augury* is applicable to ordinary as well as to phenomenal circumstances, and it usually suggests discernment rather than superstition in determining whether it presages good or evil ⟨achievements that he regarded as *auguries* of a successful career for his son⟩ ⟨I had felt there was a mysterious meaning in that moment, and in that flight of dim-seen birds an *augury* of ill-omen for my life—*L. P. Smith*⟩ **Portent** is applicable chiefly to prodigies or marvels (as an eclipse, a comet, or an earthquake) which are interpreted as forewarnings or supernatural intimations of evil to come ⟨what plagues and what *portents,* what mutiny, what raging of the sea, shaking of earth, commotion in the winds—*Shak.*⟩ ⟨the interest in eclipses began in seeing them as *portents* that might be avoided—*Kroeber*⟩
*Ana* *sign, symptom, token, mark, badge, note: *forerunner, harbinger, precursor, herald

**forewarn** *warn, caution
*Ana* notify, advise, apprise, *inform: admonish (see REPROVE): advise, counsel (see under ADVICE)

**foreword** preface, exordium, *introduction, prologue, prelude, preamble

**forge** *vb* fabricate, fashion, manufacture, form, shape, *make
*Ana* *beat, pound: produce, turn out (see BEAR): counterfeit, simulate (see ASSUME): *copy, imitate

**forget** overlook, ignore, disregard, *neglect, omit, slight

*Ant* remember —*Con* recollect, recall, bethink, mind (see REMEMBER)

**forgetful,** oblivious, unmindful are comparable when they mean losing or letting go from one's mind something once known or learned. **Forgetful** usually implies a propensity not to remember or a defective memory ⟨bear with me, good boy, I am much *forgetful—Shak.*⟩ ⟨she is growing *forgetful*⟩ Sometimes it implies a not keeping in mind something which should be remembered; it then connotes negligence or heedlessness rather than a poor memory ⟨he should not be *forgetful* of his social obligations⟩ ⟨be not *forgetful* to entertain strangers—*Heb* 13:2⟩ **Oblivious** stresses forgetfulness, but it rarely suggests a poor memory. Rather, it suggests a failure to remember, either because one has been robbed of remembrance by conditions beyond one's control ⟨the accident made him for a few hours *oblivious* of all that weighed upon his mind⟩ or because one has deliberately put something out of one's mind ⟨a government *oblivious* of the rights of the governed⟩ or because one has considered something too slight or trivial to note and remember it ⟨a people so long unused to aggression as to be *oblivious* of its dangers⟩ In some instances *oblivious* is employed without a clear connotation of forgetfulness, and in a sense close to *unconscious, unaware,* and *insensible* ⟨walking along whistling, *oblivious* of the passing crowds⟩ ⟨those who hope to render themselves, through absorption in the mere habit and technique of writing poetry, *oblivious* to the harsh interruptions of reality—*Day Lewis*⟩ ⟨*oblivious* of the laws and conditions of trespass—*Meredith*⟩ *Oblivious* also is sometimes used attributively and without a succeeding *of* or *to* in the sense of causing oblivion ⟨she lay in deep, *oblivious* slumber—*Longfellow*⟩ **Unmindful** is a close synonym of *forgetful* in the sense of not keeping in mind, but it may imply a deliberate consignment to oblivion as well as inattention, heedlessness, or negligence ⟨a mother, solicitous of the health of every member of her family but *unmindful* of her own⟩ ⟨every person was willing to save himself, *unmindful* of others—*Goldsmith*⟩ ⟨for at her silver voice came death and life, *unmindful* each of their accustomed strife—*Shelley*⟩ ⟨totally *unmindful* of their mutual dependence—*Amer. Guide Series: Minn.*⟩
*Ana* remiss, *negligent, neglectful, lax, slack: heedless, thoughtless, *careless
*Con* conscious, *aware, cognizant, sensible, alive, awake: *thoughtful, considerate, attentive

**forgive** pardon, remit, *excuse, condone
*Ana* absolve, *exculpate, acquit, exonerate, vindicate

**forgo,** forbear, abnegate, eschew, sacrifice are comparable when they denote to deny oneself something for the sake of an end. One **forgoes** for the sake of policy, expediency, or the welfare of others something already enjoyed or indulged in, or within reach ⟨he agreed . . . to *forgo* all remuneration until his apprenticeship was completed —*Brooks*⟩ Often the word implies surrender or abandonment ⟨in electing this peculiar freedom of its own, vers libre . . . has *forgone* the great harmonic, orchestral effects of the older verse—*Lowes*⟩ One **forbears,** through motives of prudence, kindness, or charity, doing or saying something one wishes or is tempted to do or say. *Forbear* usually implies self-restraint ⟨although . . . I do not get much help from general propositions in a case of this sort, I cannot *forbear* quoting what seems to me applicable here—*Justice Holmes*⟩ One **abnegates** what is intrinsically good but not consistent with one's aims, principles, or limitations ⟨to treat English poetry as though it had died with Tennyson . . . is to *abnegate* high hope for the sake of a barren convenience—*Quiller-Couch*⟩ Often

---

A colon (:) separates groups of words discriminated. An asterisk (*) indicates place of treatment of each group.

*abnegate* implies renunciation or self-effacement, but this distinction is not as commonly maintained in the verb as in the derivative noun *abnegation* ⟨communities dedicated to the living of a humble and self-*abnegating* life —*Mumford*⟩ One **eschews** (see also ESCAPE 2) something tempting, sometimes on moral or aesthetic grounds but more often because abstention or self-restraint is necessary for the achievement of a more significant desire or end ⟨to work within these strict limits, *eschewing* all the helps to illusion that modeling and shadow give, was doubtless an exercise of incomparable service to the artist— *Binyon*⟩ ⟨some of the millionaires *eschewed* palatial magnificence—*F. L. Allen*⟩ One **sacrifices** something highly desirable or in itself of great value for the sake of a person, ideal, or end dearer to one than the thing or person involved; the term typically connotes renunciation and self-denial and a religious or ethical motive comparable to that of self-immolation ⟨*sacrificed* a college education for the sake of supporting his mother⟩ ⟨*sacrificed* his life in defense of his country⟩ ⟨I do not mean that the well-to-do should . . . forgo educational opportunities which . . . are not open to all. To do that would be to *sacrifice* civilization to justice—*Russell*⟩ ⟨*sacrificed* their fortune in the world for theology's sake —*H. O. Taylor*⟩
*Ana* waive, *relinquish, surrender, abandon: renounce, resign, *abdicate

**forlorn** 1 lorn, lone, desolate, lonesome, lonely, *alone, solitary
*Ana* separated, parted, divorced, severed, sundered (see SEPARATE *vb*): forsaken, deserted, abandoned (see ABANDON *vb*): wretched, *miserable: depressed, weighed down, oppressed (see DEPRESS)
2 hopeless, *despondent, despairing, desperate
*Ana* pessimistic, *cynical: *futile, vain, fruitless
*Con* *elastic, resilient, buoyant, expansive, volatile: optimistic, *hopeful, roseate, rose-colored

**forlornness** hopelessness, despondency, despair, desperation (see under DESPONDENT)
*Ana* dejection, depression, gloom, melancholy, blues, dumps, *sadness

**form** *n* 1 Form, figure, shape, conformation, configuration are comparable when they denote the disposition or arrangement of content that gives a particular aspect or appearance to a thing as distinguished from the substance of which that thing is made. **Form** is not only the most widely applicable of these terms, but it is also the least definitely fixed in its meaning, largely because of its being assigned various denotations in philosophy and aesthetics and because of its frequent use in reference to literature, music, and thought, where more is involved than the disposition or arrangement of content as immediately perceived by the senses. In general, *form* more than any of the other words implies reference to internal structure and disposition of details as well as to boundary lines and suggests unity in the whole ⟨the earth was without *form*, and void—*Gen* 1:2⟩ ⟨a sense of interdependence and interrelated unity that gave *form* to intellectual stirrings that had been previously inchoate—*Dewey*⟩ ⟨you might go in for building . . . you've got a feeling for *form* —*Mary Austin*⟩ **Figure** applies usually to the form as determined by the lines which bound or enclose a thing ⟨flowers have all exquisite *figures*—*Bacon*⟩ The term also may often suggest the lines or sometimes the visible form characteristic of a kind or type ⟨Christ painted under the *figure* of a lamb⟩ ⟨because of the darkness it was hard to say whether the person had the *figure* of a man or of a woman⟩ or the lines which follow a more or less conventional pattern rather than represent something

actual ⟨cut *figures* on the ice in skating⟩ ⟨decorate the border with *figures* of scrolls, circles, and crescents⟩ ⟨a rug design in geometrical *figures*⟩ **Shape**, like *figure*, suggests reference to the boundary lines, but it carries a stronger implication of a mass or of a body than does *figure* and is therefore precisely applicable to something that is shown in its bulk rather than in its lines; thus, one draws the *figure* rather than the *shape* of a circle or a triangle, but one forms a mass of clay in the *shape* in preference to the *figure* of a ball or of a man ⟨the color of his beard, the *shape* of his leg—*Shak.*⟩ Often, *shape* applies to outlines that have been given to a mass (as by molding, carving, or pressure) ⟨Brooke is a very good fellow, but pulpy; he will run into any mold, but he won't keep *shape*—*George Eliot*⟩ ⟨it is the business of the sensitive artist in life to accept his own nature as it is, not to try to force it into another *shape*—*Huxley*⟩ **Form**, *figure*, and *shape* are also used in reference to the bodies of living creatures, especially of men and women. *Form* is perhaps the most shadowy of these terms; it is applied chiefly to persons or animals identified but not clearly seen or noted in detail ⟨the reddleman watched his *form* as it diminished to a speck on the road—*Hardy*⟩ ⟨busy *forms* bent over intolerable tasks, whizzing wheels, dark gleaming machinery—*Benson*⟩ *Figure* usually suggests closer vision than *form* and some perception of details but stresses lines, carriage, and posture ⟨here and there a *figure* . . . leaned on the rail—*Conrad*⟩ ⟨they watched her white *figure* drifting along the edge of the grove—*Cather*⟩ *Shape* differs little from *figure* except in its clearer suggestion of flesh and body ⟨some human *shapes* appearing mysteriously, as if they had sprung up from the dark ground—*Conrad*⟩ ⟨and the shade under the ash trees became deserted, save by the tall dark figure of a man, and a woman's white *shape*—*Galsworthy*⟩ **Conformation** stresses the structure of something as composed or fashioned of related or carefully adjusted parts or as constituting a harmonious whole; it carries only a slight suggestion of reference to the outer lines or shape ⟨beef steers of excellent *conformation*⟩ ⟨the *conformation* of the vocal organs⟩ **Configuration** emphasizes the disposition or arrangement of parts and the pattern that they form especially over an extent of space or territory ⟨the *configuration* of the county is represented in this relief map⟩ ⟨the remarkable *configuration* of the Atlantic seabed—*T. H. Huxley*⟩ ⟨in every province there was a network of roads following the *configuration* of the country—*Buchan*⟩
*Ana* contour, *outline, profile, silhouette: *structure, anatomy, framework, skeleton: organism, *system, economy, scheme

2 Form, formality, ceremony, ceremonial, rite, ritual, liturgy mean an established or fixed method of procedure especially as enjoined by law, the customs of social intercourse, or the church. **Form** is the comprehensive term applicable to a recognized way of doing things in accordance with rule or prescription ⟨observing the *forms* of polite society⟩ ⟨nothing could be worse *form* . . . than any display of temper in a public place—*Wharton*⟩ ⟨a transfer of property made in due *form*⟩ ⟨the occasional exercise of a beautiful *form* of worship—*Irving*⟩ *Form* often implies show without substance or suggests an outward shell devoid of its life or spirit ⟨for who would keep an ancient *form* through which the spirit breathes no more?—*Tennyson*⟩ **Formality** applies to some more or less perfunctory or conventional procedure required by law, custom, or etiquette ⟨there was now and then the *formality* of saying a lesson—*Lamb*⟩ ⟨Mr. Critchlow entered without any *formalities*, as usual—*Bennett*⟩ The

term often implies endless detail or red tape ⟨Outland was delayed by the *formalities* of securing his patent—*Cather*⟩ **Ceremony** is more specific than *form* and implies certain outward acts, usually of an impressive or dignified character, associated with some religious, public, or state occasion or, collectively, with a church or a court ⟨the marriage *ceremony*⟩ ⟨the *ceremonies* attending the coronation of a king⟩ *Ceremony* also applies to the conventional usages of civility ⟨the appurtenance of welcome is . . . *ceremony—Shak.*⟩ ⟨you need not stand on *ceremony*⟩ ⟨the beauty of an inherited courtesy of manners, of a thousand little *ceremonies* flowering out of the most ordinary relations and observances of life—*Binyon*⟩ ⟨after the death of a king, a solemn *ceremony* of purification was performed by a princess—*Frazer*⟩ **Ceremonial** (compare CEREMONIAL *adj*) is occasionally used in place of *ceremony* in its concrete applications; more often it is a collective noun applied to an entire system of ceremonies prescribed by a court or a church ⟨the gorgeous *ceremonial* of the Burgundian court—*Prescott*⟩ The last three terms of this group refer primarily to religious ceremonies and only secondarily to the ceremonies or forms of civil life. A **rite** is the form prescribed by a church or other organization for conducting one of its ceremonies or, in the case of a church, for administering one of its sacraments, giving not only the words to be uttered but the acts to be performed ⟨the marriage *rite* of the Church of England⟩ ⟨the *rite* for the ordination of priests⟩ **Ritual** is, in effect, a collective noun applied either to all the rites that make up an elaborate religious service or to all the rites or all the ceremonies of a particular church, religion, or organization; it is, however, applicable to a rite when that represents the one form in use in the specific religion or body ⟨the *ritual* of the Roman Catholic Church is traditionally in Latin⟩ ⟨sacrifices, dances, mimetic games, processions, plays, ordeals, and feasting may enter into the *ritual* of primitive religions⟩ ⟨the *ritual* of a lodge⟩ Consequently, in extended use, *rite* and *ritual* both refer to the customary or established order of procedure for conducting not only a ceremony or a series of ceremonial acts, but all kinds of formalities or forms ⟨Archer . . . went conscientiously through all the *rites* appertaining to a weekend at Highbank—*Wharton*⟩ ⟨he knew well enough how it would be at the Hondo; the black-shawled women sitting against the wall, the *ritual* of bereavement, impressive in its poverty—*Mary Austin*⟩ **Liturgy** applies primarily to the Eucharistic service, especially that of the Orthodox and the Uniate churches (specifically called "Divine *Liturgy*" in many of these) and of the Roman Catholic Church (specifically called the "Mass" in the Latin Church). In the Anglican Communion *liturgy* applies to the Book of Common Prayer, the service book of that church. It is applied also to a strictly religious rite or ritual, but this is confusing because *rite* and *ritual* stress the form to be followed and *liturgy* the complete service as followed in a particular church; thus, the Roman *rite* is now generally followed in the *liturgy* of that branch of the Roman Catholic Church called the Latin Church ⟨he insisted on . . . the maintenance of full ritual in the *liturgy—Belloc*⟩
*Ana* proceeding, procedure, *process: practice, usage, custom, *habit: rule, regulation, precept, *law, canon: *method, mode: *decorum, propriety, etiquette
**3 Form, usage, convention, convenance** are comparable when they mean a fixed or accepted way of doing or sometimes of expressing something. **Form** can apply to a prescribed or approved way of behaving, method of procedure, or technique in any sphere of activity where correctness or uniformity of method or manner is thought

essential ⟨the *forms* of good conduct⟩ ⟨the *forms* of worship⟩ ⟨good *form* in swimming⟩ ⟨a *form* of address⟩ **Usage** implies the sanction of precedent or tradition and often designates a form preserved out of respect for a class, profession, or religion ⟨descriptions of *usages* presuppose descriptions of uses, that is, ways or techniques of doing the thing, the more or less widely prevailing practice of doing which constitutes the *usage*—*Ryle*⟩ ⟨to bury in the first furrow certain fruits of a particular structure, such as figs, pomegranates, and locust beans, is a *usage* frequently observed—*Frazer*⟩ **Convention** often replaces *form* especially in application to social behavior, where it stresses general agreement and therefore applies to some set way of doing or saying something that is sanctioned or believed to be sanctioned by general unquestioning acceptance ⟨this music followed *conventions* perfectly understood by the contemporaries —*P. H. Lang*⟩ ⟨certain parliamentary *conventions* which exist to supplement the rules of procedure—*May*⟩ ⟨this genius who was too wild and elemental ever to conform to any aesthetic *convention—Ledig-Rowohlt*⟩ **Convenance** is a somewhat literary word applied to social conventions especially regarded as essential to propriety or decorum ⟨disregarding the social *convenances,* continued to chatter on—*Richard Hull*⟩ ⟨the *convenances* of life—*Benson*⟩
**form** *vb* *make, shape, fashion, fabricate, manufacture, forge
*Ana* devise, contrive (see corresponding nouns at DEVICE): *invent, create: produce, turn out (see BEAR): design, project, scheme, plan, plot (see under PLAN *n* ): organize, *found, establish
**formal** conventional, ceremonious, *ceremonial, solemn
*Ana* systematic, methodical, *orderly, regular: *decorous, proper, seemly
*Ant* informal
**formality** *form, ceremony, ceremonial, rite, liturgy, ritual
*Ana* convention, convenance, usage, *form: practice, custom, *habit, use, wont
**former** prior, previous, *preceding, antecedent, precedent, foregoing, anterior
*Ant* latter —*Con* following, succeeding, ensuing, supervening (see FOLLOW)
**formless,** **unformed, shapeless** are comparable when they mean having no definite or recognizable form. Something is **formless** which is so fluid or so shifting in its outlines, structure, or character that it does not assume, or is incapable of assuming, a fixed or determinate form ⟨the rising world of waters . . . won from the void and *formless* infinite—*Milton*⟩ ⟨sprang from the billows of the *formless* flood—*Shelley*⟩ ⟨a *formless* fear⟩ ⟨the *formless* welter of his prose works—*Saintsbury*⟩ Something is **unformed** which has existence but has not yet attained the form or character proper to it when it has reached the height of its possible growth or development ⟨an *unformed* girl of twelve⟩ ⟨an *unformed* mind⟩ ⟨*unformed* genius⟩ Often it suggests crudeness or callousness ⟨very clever in some ways—and very *unformed*—childish almost—in others—*Ward*⟩ ⟨this *unformed* government is the "legitimate" one—*Gorrell*⟩ Something is **shapeless** which lacks or has lost the clear-cut outline or contour that is regarded as proper to a thing or essential to its beauty ⟨a *shapeless* old woman⟩ ⟨beat a silver dish into a *shapeless* mass⟩ ⟨conversation, which before had a beginning and an end, now grew *shapeless* and interminable—*Richard Hughes*⟩
*Ana* fluid, *liquid: rough, raw, crude, *rude
**fornication** *adultery, incest

---

A colon (:) separates groups of words discriminated. An asterisk (*) indicates place of treatment of each group.

**forsake** desert, *abandon
*Ana* repudiate, spurn, reject (see DECLINE): *abdicate, renounce, resign: quit, leave (see GO)
*Ant* return to: revert to
**forswear** 1 *abjure, renounce, recant, retract
*Ana* *abandon, desert, forsake: repudiate, spurn, reject (see DECLINE): *deny, contravene, traverse, gainsay
2 *perjure
**fort, fortress, citadel, stronghold, fastness** denote in common a structure or place offering resistance to a hostile force. A **fort** is an enclosed, fortified structure occupied by troops. A **fortress** is a large fort of strong construction intended for long-term occupancy (as on the border of a hostile country). A **citadel** is a fortification, usually on an eminence, that protects a city or keeps it in subjection. A **stronghold** is a strongly fortified place whose resistance to attack or siege affords protection to its occupants ⟨here . . . a famous robber had his *stronghold—Ritchie*⟩ A **fastness** is a place whose inaccessibility or remoteness makes for security. It may or may not be fortified ⟨a strong and almost inaccessible *fastness—H. H. Wilson*⟩
These terms often have extended use. In such use a **fort** is something that by its very nature resists attack ⟨oft breaking down the pales and *forts* of reason—*Shak.*⟩ and a **fortress** is something that gives a feeling of security ⟨my rock and *fortress* is the Lord—*John Wesley*⟩ **Citadel** and **stronghold** are very similar in their extended uses, both being applied to a place where or, sometimes, to a class or group in which something prevails or persists in spite of attacks or encroachment ⟨the very headquarters, the very *citadel* of smuggling, the Isle of Man—*Burke*⟩ ⟨the scientific world has been the very *citadel* of stupidity and cruelty—*Shaw*⟩ ⟨the South of Somersetshire, one of the *strongholds* . . . of the Anglo-Saxon dialect—*Jennings*⟩ **Fastness** characteristically suggests impenetrability or inaccessibility ⟨in the impregnable *fastness* of his great rich nature he [the Roman] defies us—*J. R. Lowell*⟩

**forth** forward, *onward
**forthright** *adj* 1 also *adv* **Forthright, downright** are comparable because they agree in their basic sense of moving or in the habit of moving straight to the mark. **Forthright** (see also STRAIGHTFORWARD) applies to whatever gets its effect by a straight thrust as if of a sword driven by the arm of one person into the breast of another; it therefore usually connotes dexterity, directness, straightforwardness, or a deadly effectiveness ⟨reach the good man your hand, my girl: *forthright* from the shoulder, like a brave boxer—*Meredith*⟩ ⟨the home thrust of a *forthright* word—*J. R. Lowell*⟩ ⟨the practical, *forthright*, nonargumentative turn of his mind—*Farrar*⟩ **Downright,** on the other hand, suggests a falling down or descending with the straightness and swiftness of one who leaps from a cliff or of a weapon that delivers a crushing blow. The word, therefore, usually implies crude force rather than dexterity, and concern for the effect produced rather than the point reached; often, in addition, when applied to persons or things it connotes plainness, bluntness, flat-footedness, or an out-and-out quality ⟨he . . . shot to the black abyss, and plunged *downright—Pope*⟩ ⟨sculling against a swift current is work—*downright* work—*Jefferies*⟩ ⟨you seem a pretty . . . *downright* sort of a young woman—*Shaw*⟩ ⟨a baby. What a coarse, *downright* word for the little creature—*Rose Macaulay*⟩ ⟨this admirably *downright*, if not highly sophisticated, ukase has been cited in almost every trade-secrets case . . . since—*John Brooks*⟩
*Ana* *bluff, blunt, brusque: candid, open, plain, *frank
2 *straightforward, aboveboard

*Ana* honest, *upright, conscientious, just, honorable
*Ant* furtive —*Con* *secret, covert, stealthy, surreptitious, underhand: mendacious, *dishonest, untruthful, deceitful
**fortify** *strengthen, invigorate, energize, reinforce
*Ana* rally, *stir, arouse, rouse: stimulate, quicken (see PROVOKE): *renew, restore, refresh
*Ant* enfeeble —*Con* *weaken, debilitate: enervate, emasculate (see UNNERVE): dilute, *thin
**fortitude, grit, backbone, pluck, guts, sand** denote a quality of character combining courage and staying power. **Fortitude** stresses strength of mind and firmness of purpose; it implies endurance, often prolonged endurance, of physical or mental hardships or suffering without giving way under the strain ⟨the man's courage is loved by the woman, whose *fortitude* again is coveted by the man—*Coleridge*⟩ ⟨for years he led a life of unremitting physical toil and mental anxiety combined with miserable health—no small test of *fortitude—Buchan*⟩ **Grit** also implies strength and firmness of mind, but it stresses an incapacity for being downed by difficulties or hardships and usually also suggests both a willingness to suffer the privation and pain necessary to the attainment of one's ends and the fortitude to bear them ⟨it is *grit* that tells in the long run⟩ ⟨instances of men rising from the lower ranks of society into the most highly remunerated positions in the business world are sufficiently numerous to support the belief that brains and *grit* can always "make good"—*Hobson*⟩ **Backbone** emphasizes resoluteness of character; it implies either the ability to stand up in the face of opposition for one's principles or one's chosen objectives, or determination and independence that require no support from without ⟨in spite of all his gifts, he did not have the *backbone* necessary to a good statesman⟩ ⟨when mob hysteria prevails, then, if ever, *backbone* is needed in our legislators⟩ ⟨like conscience-stricken dogs they lost *backbone,* and visibly were in a condition to submit to anything—*Kenneth Roberts*⟩ **Pluck** implies a willingness to fight or continue fighting against odds; thus, it is *pluck* that keeps a sick person at work; it is *pluck* that keeps soldiers from retreating in the face of disaster ⟨the energy, fortitude, and dogged perseverance that we technically style *pluck—Lytton*⟩ ⟨decay of English spirit, decay of manly *pluck—Thackeray*⟩ **Guts,** which is often considered expressive but not entirely polite and is therefore sometimes facetiously replaced by *intestinal fortitude,* stresses possession of the physical and mental vigor essential both to facing something which repels or frightens one and to putting up with the hardships it imposes ⟨he hasn't the *guts* to be a successful surgeon⟩ ⟨they used men with *guts* for the East African missions⟩ ⟨what bothered him was not the superzealot attackers so much as the lack of plain old-fashioned *guts* on the part of the people who give in to them—*Davis*⟩ **Sand** comes close to *grit* in its meaning, but since it often carries a suggestion of pluck or of the ability to fight against odds, it does not so strongly as *grit* connote triumph over difficulties ⟨no more pride than a tramp, no more *sand* than a rabbit—*Mark Twain*⟩
*Ana* *courage, mettle, spirit, resolution, tenacity: bravery, courageousness, intrepidity, dauntlessness, valorousness (see corresponding adjectives at BRAVE)
*Ant* pusillanimity —*Con* timidity, timorousness (see corresponding adjectives at TIMID)
**fortress** *fort, citadel, stronghold, fastness
**fortuitous** *accidental, contingent, casual, incidental, adventitious
*Ana* *random, haphazard, chance, chancy, hit-or-miss
*Con* activated, actuated, motivated (see ACTIVATE):

planned, projected, designed, schemed, plotted (see corresponding verbs under PLAN n)

**fortunate** *lucky, providential, happy
*Ana* auspicious, propitious, *favorable, benign: advantageous, *beneficial, profitable: felicitous, happy (see FIT adj)
*Ant* unfortunate: disastrous —*Con* *sinister, baleful, malign, malefic, maleficent

**fortune** *chance, accident, luck, hap, hazard
*Ana* *fate, destiny, lot, portion, doom: *opportunity, occasion, break, time
*Con* *misfortune, mischance, adversity, mishap: design, intent, *intention

**forward** adj advanced, *premature, untimely, precocious
*Ant* backward —*Con* retrograde, retrogressive, regressive (see BACKWARD)

**forward** adv 1 ahead, *before
*Ant* backward
2 forth, *onward
*Ant* backward

**forward** vb 1 *advance, promote, further
*Ana* *speed, accelerate, quicken, hasten: *help, aid, assist: *support, uphold, back, champion
*Ant* hinder: balk —*Con* impede, obstruct, bar, block (see HINDER): *frustrate, thwart, baffle, outwit, foil, circumvent
2 *send, dispatch, transmit, remit, route, ship

**foster** vb *nurse, nurture, cherish, cultivate
*Ana* *support, uphold, back, champion: *harbor, shelter, entertain, lodge, house: promote, further, forward, *advance: favor, accommodate, *oblige
*Con* oppose, combat, *resist, withstand, fight: curb, inhibit, *restrain: *forbid, prohibit, interdict, ban

**foul** adj filthy, *dirty, nasty, squalid
*Ana* putrid, stinking, fetid, noisome, *malodorous: *offensive, revolting, repulsive, loathsome: obscene, gross, vulgar, *coarse
*Ant* fair: undefiled

**foul** vb *soil, dirty, sully, tarnish, befoul, smirch, besmirch, grime, begrime
*Ana* pollute, defile, *contaminate: profane, desecrate (see corresponding nouns at PROFANATION)

**found** vb 1 *base, ground, bottom, stay, rest
*Ana* *set, fix, settle, establish: sustain, *support: *build, erect, raise, rear
2 Found, establish, institute, organize are comparable when meaning to set going or to bring into existence something (as a business, a colony, or an institution). Found implies nothing more than a taking of the first steps or measures to bring into existence something that requires building up. Just what these steps and measures are vary in usage; thus, a person who provides the funds for a new educational institution may be said to have *founded* it, and those who first devised the project and won his support may also be said to have *founded* it, as may also those who took the next steps (such as the choice of a site, the erection of buildings on that site, and the selection of the staff) ⟨*found* a parish in a new section of a city⟩ ⟨the Pilgrims in 1620 *founded* Plymouth Colony in what is now the state of Massachusetts⟩ ⟨a school of philosophy *founded* by Plato⟩ Establish (see also SET) is often employed in the sense of *found*; however, it may imply not only the laying of the foundations but also a bringing into enduring existence; thus, Brook Farm was *founded* (not *established*, because its existence was short) by George Ripley and others as an experiment in communistic living; Vassar College was not *established* until some years after the date of its *founding* ⟨the . . . Sisters of Loretto, who came to found the Academy of

Our Lady of Light. The school was now well *established* —*Cather*⟩ Institute stresses an origination or an introduction; like *found*, it implies the taking of the first steps and like *establish*, the actual bringing into existence, but it differs from both words in its far wider range of application and in being referable to things (as a method, a study, or an investigation) which do not have a continuous life or a permanent existence ⟨*institute* a new society⟩ ⟨*institute* a new method of accountancy⟩ ⟨*institute* an inquiry into an official's conduct of his office⟩ Organize (see also ORDER vb 1) may imply founding, but it usually implies the taking of the steps whereby an organization (as a business, an institution, or a government) is set up so that it functions properly, with its departments clearly distinguished and governed by a responsible head and with a supervisory staff responsible for the working of the whole ⟨Smith College was founded by Sophia Smith but was *organized* by its first president and board of trustees⟩ ⟨the company sent him to Germany to *organize* its new branch there⟩
*Ana* *begin, commence, start, initiate, inaugurate: form, fashion (see MAKE)
*Con* uproot, eradicate, deracinate, extirpate, *exterminate, wipe

**foundation** basis, *base, ground, groundwork
*Ant* superstructure

**foxy** insidious, wily, guileful, tricky, crafty, cunning, *sly, artful
*Ana* devious, *crooked, oblique: deceitful, *dishonest
*Con* *straightforward, aboveboard, forthright: candid, open, plain, *frank

**fracas** *brawl, broil, melee, row, rumpus, scrap
*Ana* fray, affray, fight, conflict, combat, *contest: altercation, wrangle, *quarrel, squabble: contention, dissension, strife, *discord

**fraction** fragment, piece, *part, portion, section, segment, sector, detail, member, division, parcel

**fractious** *irritable, peevish, snappish, waspish, petulant, pettish, huffy, fretful, querulous
*Ana* *unruly, refractory, recalcitrant, ungovernable, intractable, willful: perverse, *contrary, froward, restive, wayward
*Con* complaisant, *amiable, good-natured: docile, tractable, *obedient, amenable, biddable

**fragile** 1 Fragile, frangible, brittle, crisp, short, friable mean easily broken. They are, however, not often interchangeable. Fragile (see also WEAK) is applicable to whatever must be handled or treated carefully lest it be broken ⟨a *fragile* antique chair⟩ ⟨a *fragile* dish⟩ ⟨a *fragile* flower⟩ ⟨I found the skeleton, or, at all events, the larger bones, rendered so *fragile* by the fierce heat they had been subjected to, that they fell to pieces when handled —*Hudson*⟩ ⟨this nation, molded in the heat of battle against tyranny . . . is not a *fragile* thing—*W. O. Douglas*⟩ Frangible stresses susceptibility to being broken rather than positive weakness or delicacy of material or construction ⟨*frangible* stone⟩ ⟨avoid using *frangible* materials in ship construction⟩ ⟨using the buttresses of intellect and imagination to shore up the trembling pillars of our *frangible* era—*Fadiman*⟩ Brittle implies hardness plus frangibility because of the inflexibility of, or lack of elasticity in, the substance of which a thing is made; it also suggests susceptibility to quick snapping or fracture when subjected to pressure or strain ⟨glass is especially *brittle*⟩ ⟨as a person ages, his bones grow more *brittle*⟩ ⟨*brittle* sticks of candy⟩ The term is often extended to things that are dangerously lacking in elasticity or flexibility ⟨he would take no risks with a thing so *brittle* as the Roman polity, on which depended the fate of forty-four

---

A colon (:) separates groups of words discriminated. An asterisk (*) indicates place of treatment of each group.

millions of men—*Buchan*⟩ **Crisp** usually suggests a good quality which makes a thing firm and brittle yet delicate and easily broken or crushed, especially between the teeth ⟨*crisp* toast⟩ ⟨*crisp* lettuce⟩ In extended use it implies freshness, briskness, cleanness of cut, incisiveness, or other qualities that suggest the opposite of limpness, languor, or slackness ⟨a *crisp* morning⟩ ⟨a *crisp* style⟩ ⟨a *crisp* answer⟩ ⟨a languorous work . . . with occasional interludes of *crisp* brilliance—*Anthony West*⟩ **Short** implies a tendency to crumble or break readily and is applicable to several kinds of substance ⟨a *short* biscuit is rich in butter or other fat and is crisp and crumbly when eaten⟩ ⟨*short* mortar is difficult to spread because of oversanding⟩ ⟨*short* timber is desiccated wood⟩ ⟨*short* (or hot-*short*) steel is brittle when heated beyond a certain point because of an excess of sulfur⟩ **Friable** is applicable to substances that are easily crumbled or pulverized ⟨*friable* soil⟩ ⟨*friable* sandstone⟩ ⟨*friable* blackboard chalk⟩ ⟨particles of shale, mica, or other *friable* and unsound minerals—*Bateman*⟩
*Ant* tough —*Con* *elastic, resilient, flexible: *strong, stout, sturdy, tenacious
2 frail, *weak, feeble, decrepit, infirm
*Ana* impotent, *powerless: delicate, dainty (see CHOICE): evanescent, ephemeral, *transient, transitory
*Ant* durable

**fragment** fraction, piece, *part, portion, section, segment, sector, division, detail, member, parcel
*Ana* remnant, *remainder

**fragrance, perfume, incense, redolence, bouquet** are comparable when denoting a sweet or pleasant odor. **Fragrance** usually suggests the odor diffused by flowers or other growing things, though it is applicable to odors that merely suggest the presence of flowers ⟨*fragrance* after showers —*Milton*⟩ ⟨flowers laugh before thee on their beds and *fragrance* in thy footing treads—*Wordsworth*⟩ ⟨through the open doors . . . the soft wind . . . brought in the garden *fragrance* —*Stark Young*⟩ ⟨a *fragrance* such as never clings to aught save happy living things—*Millay*⟩ **Perfume** originally applied either to the pleasantly odorous smoke emitted by some burning things (as various spices, gums, or leaves) ⟨three April *perfumes* in three hot Junes burned since first I saw you—*Shak.*⟩ or to some natural or prepared substance which emits a pleasant odor. The latter sense predominates in current use, especially in reference to a preparation in liquid form, also called a *scent* (for full treatment of this term see SMELL), that contains the essence of fragrant flowers or is a synthetic concoction ⟨rose like a steam of rich distilled *perfumes*—*Milton*⟩ ⟨a *perfume* redolent of the odor of violets⟩ When applied to an odor rather than to a preparation, *perfume* differs little from *fragrance* except that it usually, when unqualified, suggests a heavier and more redolent odor, or at least a less delicate one ⟨the *perfume* of lilies had overcome the scent of books—*Galsworthy*⟩ ⟨a gigantic rose tree which clambered over the house . . . filling the air with the *perfume* of its sweetness—*L. P. Smith*⟩ **Incense** is usually used in place of *perfume* for the agreeably odorous smoke emitted by burning spices and gums ⟨the church was filled with the odor of *incense*⟩ The term, from association with the use of incense in religious ceremonial, tends to apply to odors or things comparable to odors that are not only pleasant but grateful to the senses or that for some cause uplift or are mentally or spiritually exalting ⟨the breezy call of *incense*-breathing Morn—*Gray*⟩ ⟨grateful the *incense* from the lime-tree flower—*Keats*⟩ ⟨love wraps his wings on either side the heart . . . absorbing all the *incense* of sweet thoughts so that they pass not to the shrine of sound —*Tennyson*⟩ ⟨this is that *incense* of the heart, whose

fragrance smells to heaven—*Cotton*⟩ **Redolence** usually implies a mixture of fragrant, often pungently agreeable, odors ⟨*redolence* of a forest after a rain⟩ ⟨the fascinating *redolence* and toughness of New Orleans' red-lighted Storyville, where jazz was born—*Time*⟩ ⟨the *redolence* of a garden in spring⟩ **Bouquet** applies especially to the distinctive fragrance of a good wine, which is perceptible when one inhales the delicate and agreeable odor ⟨lifting his glass to his lips, [he] voluptuously inhaled its *bouquet*—*Lytton*⟩ but it may be extended to other delicate and distinctive odors (as of cooking food) that suggest the excellent savory character of the source of the odor ⟨the grateful smell of cooking pork grew every moment more perfect in *bouquet*—*Ethel Anderson*⟩
*Ana* *smell, scent, odor, aroma
*Ant* stench, stink

**fragrant** *odorous, aromatic, redolent, balmy
*Ana* delicious, delectable, *delightful
*Ant* fetid —*Con* *malodorous, stinking, noisome, putrid, rank

**frail** fragile, *weak, feeble, infirm, decrepit
*Ana* slight, slender, tenuous, *thin, slim: puny, *petty: flimsy, sleazy (see LIMP): *powerless, impotent
*Ant* robust —*Con* *strong, stout, sturdy, stalwart, tough, tenacious: *healthy, sound, hale: *vigorous, lusty

**frailty** *fault, failing, foible, vice
*Ana* defect, flaw, *blemish: infirmity, fragility, feebleness, weakness (see corresponding adjectives at WEAK)

**frame** *vb* 1 *build, construct, erect, raise, rear
*Ana* fabricate, manufacture, fashion, *make
2 *contrive, devise, invent, concoct
*Ana* plan, scheme, project (see under PLAN *n*): conceive, envisage, *think

**framework** *structure, skeleton, anatomy
**franchise** *suffrage, vote, ballot
**frangible** *fragile, brittle, crisp, short, friable
**frank** *adj* **Frank, candid, open, plain** are comparable when they mean showing in speech, looks, and manners the willingness to tell what one feels or thinks. **Frank** stresses lack of reserve or of reticence in the expression of one's thoughts or feelings; it therefore usually connotes freedom from such restraints as fear, shyness, inarticulateness, secretiveness, or tact ⟨this, to Anne, was a decided imperfection . . . she prized the *frank,* the openhearted, the eager character beyond all others—*Austen*⟩ ⟨things were as she had suspected: she had been *frank* in her questions and Polly had been *frank* in her answers—*Joyce*⟩ ⟨the child who has been treated wisely and kindly has a *frank* look in the eyes, and a fearless demeanor even with strangers—*Russell*⟩ **Candid** is often used interchangeably with *frank;* it may distinctively imply a fundamental honesty and fairness that make evasion impossible and suggest a refusal to dodge an issue or to be governed by bias or fear ⟨I have tried to be as *candid* as possible, to follow out every thought as far as I could without caring where it would lead and without tempering any conclusions out of consideration to either my own sensibilities or those of any one else—*Krutch*⟩ ⟨I am sure that he was *candid* with me. I am certain that he had no guile—*White*⟩ **Open** implies both frankness and candor, but it often suggests more naturalness or artlessness than *frank* and less conscientiousness than *candid* ⟨Mr. Elliot was rational, discreet, polished, but he was not *open*. There was never any burst of feeling, any warmth of indignation or delight, at the evil or good of others—*Austen*⟩ ⟨for the white man to put himself mentally on their level is not more impossible than for these aborigines to be perfectly *open*, as children are, towards the white—*Hudson*⟩ **Plain** comes closer to *candid* than to *frank,* but it suggests outspokenness, downright-

ness, and freedom from affectation more than fairness of mind ⟨I am no orator, as Brutus is; but, as you know me all, a *plain* blunt man—*Shak.*⟩ ⟨the difference between ordinary phraseology that makes its meaning *plain* and legal phraseology that makes its meaning certain—*Gowers*⟩

*Ana* ingenuous, naïve, unsophisticated, simple, *natural: *forthright, downright: *straightforward, aboveboard

*Ant* reticent —*Con* *silent, taciturn, reserved, uncommunicative: furtive, *secret, covert, underhand

**frantic** *adj* *furious, frenzied, wild, frenetic, delirious, rabid

*Ana* crazy, crazed, mad, *insane: hysterical (see corresponding noun at MANIA): *irrational, unreasonable

**fraud** *n* **1** *deception, trickery, chicanery, chicane, double-dealing

*Ana* duplicity, *deceit, guile, dissimulation: defrauding, swindling, cheating, cozening, overreaching (see CHEAT *vb*)

**2** *imposture, cheat, sham, fake, humbug, deceit, deception, counterfeit

*Ana* hoaxing *or* hoax, bamboozling *or* bamboozlement, hoodwinking, duping *or* dupery (see corresponding verbs at DUPE): *trick, ruse, stratagem, maneuver, gambit, ploy, wile, artifice

**fray** *n* affray, fight, conflict, combat, *contest

*Ana* fracas, broil, *brawl, melee: altercation, wrangle, *quarrel: contention, strife, dissension, *discord

**freak** *n* *caprice, fancy, whim, whimsy, conceit, vagary, crotchet

*Ana* notion, *idea: *fancy, fantasy, dream, daydream

**freaked** *variegated, parti-colored, motley, checkered, checked, pied, piebald, skewbald, dappled

*Ana* spotted, flecked, speckled, spattered, sprinkled (see under SPOT *vb*)

**free** *adj* Free, independent, sovereign, autonomous, autarchic, autarkic are comparable when they mean not subject to the rule or control of another. The same differences in implications and connotations are found in their corresponding nouns freedom, independence, sovereignty, autonomy, autarchy, autarky when they denote the state or condition of not being subject to external rule or control. Free and freedom (see also FREEDOM 2) stress the absence of external compulsion or determination and not the absence of restraint. For *free* as applied to a state, a people, a person, or the will implies self-government and therefore the right to determine one's own acts, one's own laws, and one's own restraints or to accept or reject those that are proposed from without ⟨for liberty is to be *free* from restraint and violence from others, which cannot be where there is no law—*Locke*⟩ ⟨*freedom* makes man to choose what he likes; that is, makes him *free*—*Quiller-Couch*⟩ Independent and independence have for their fundamental implication lack of relatedness to anyone or anything else; therefore *independent* implies that the person or thing so described stands alone ⟨words have a meaning *independent* of the pattern in which they are arranged—*Huxley*⟩ When applied to a state or government, it implies not complete detachment from other states or governments and a refusal to have allies or dominions, but a lack of connection with a state or government that has the power to interfere with one's liberty of action ⟨the Thirteen Colonies sacrificed their *independence,* but not their freedom, when they joined the federation that became the United States of America⟩ When applied to a person or his acts and opinions, it implies either a disposition to stand alone and apart from others, or refusal to accept another's judgments, or self-reliance amounting almost to a fault; thus, a person who is *independent* in politics is attached to no political party; one might wish that a person he is trying vainly to help were less *independent* ⟨an economist should form an *independent* judgment on currency questions, but an ordinary mortal had better follow authority—*Russell*⟩ Sovereign (see also DOMINANT) and sovereignty stress the absence of a superior power and imply the supremacy within its own domain or sphere of what is so described or so designated. As applied to a state or government, these words usually involve the ideas both of political independence and of the possession of original and underived power ⟨for many years before the Civil War it was debated whether the federal government was *sovereign*⟩ ⟨the powers of the general government, it has been said, are delegated by the States, who alone are truly *sovereign* .... It would be difficult to sustain this proposition—*John Marshall*⟩ ⟨although it [the government of the United States] is *sovereign* and supreme in its appropriate sphere of action, yet it does not possess all the powers which usually belong to the *sovereignty* of a nation—*Taney*⟩ When used in reference to a thing, both words impute to that thing unquestioned supremacy and imply that everything within its sphere of influence is subject to it ⟨noble and most *sovereign* reason—*Shak.*⟩ ⟨the *sovereignty* of man lieth hid in knowledge; wherein many things are reserved that kings with their treasure cannot buy, nor with their force command—*Bacon*⟩ Autonomous and autonomy may imply independence combined with freedom. The terms are much used in philosophy to describe or designate a theoretical or ideal freedom in which the individual is absolutely self-governing and acknowledges no claim of another to interference or control ⟨the question is often asked whether an *autonomous* state and an *autonomous* church can exist side by side⟩ ⟨if this preeminence and *autonomy* of the spiritual be not granted, it is misleading to use the word God at all—*Inge*⟩ In political use the words seldom imply such absolute independence and freedom, for they are employed largely in reference to states which belong to an empire, a federation, or a commonwealth of nations. In reference to such states *autonomy* and *autonomous* commonly imply independence from the central power only in matters pertaining to self-government but recognition of the central governmental sovereignty in matters (as foreign policy) affecting the empire, federation, or commonwealth of nations as a whole. When a state is granted autonomy or become autonomous, the terms of such a grant are usually precisely stated ⟨the Imperial Conference of 1926 defined the Dominions as "*autonomous* communities within the British Empire, equal in status, in no way subordinate one to another in any aspect of their domestic or foreign affairs, though united by a common allegiance to the Crown, and freely associated as members of the British Commonwealth of Nations"—*Statesman's Year-Book*⟩ Autarchic and autarchy historically implied absolute sovereignty or absolute or autocratic rule, but they have become interchangeable with autarkic and autarky, and both pairs of words imply economic and especially national economic self-sufficiency; the words are used in reference to states or governments that favor isolation through a policy of rigidly and arbitrarily planned economic self-sufficiency as a means of maintaining their independence ⟨the totalitarian countries . . . have created a self-encirclement by their abnormal economic policy, their costly and unnatural *autarky*—*Manchester Guardian*⟩ ⟨each community in Old China was cell-like, largely autonomous and *autarkic* —*Linebarger*⟩ ⟨the issue today is, therefore, whether a policy aimed at economic nationalism—self-sufficiency—*autarchy*—creates an environment favorable to the recon-

---

A colon (:) separates groups of words discriminated. An asterisk (*) indicates place of treatment of each group.

struction of a peaceful, tranquil, confident world—*Lewis Douglas*⟩ ⟨a network of more or less closed, *autarchic* economies, each trying to the best of its ability to exist on a self-sufficient basis—*Dean*⟩
**Ana** liberated, emancipated, delivered, freed, released, enfranchised (see FREE *vb*)
**Ant** bond —**Con** compelled, coerced, forced, constrained, obliged (see FORCE *vb*)

**free** *vb* **Free, release, liberate, emancipate, manumit, deliver, discharge, enfranchise** are comparable when meaning to set loose from whatever ties or binds or to make clear of whatever encumbers or holds back. **Free** is the ordinary general term interchangeable with many of the succeeding terms; it may be used not only in reference to persons that are in bondage or in a state of dependence or oppression or under restraint or constraint ⟨*free* one's slaves⟩ ⟨*free* an oppressed people⟩ ⟨*free* a person from prison or from a charge⟩ ⟨*free* one from the necessity of speaking against a proposal⟩ but also in reference to things that are confined, entangled, or encumbered and may therefore be unfastened, unloosed, disentangled, or disengaged ⟨*free* a squirrel from a trap⟩ ⟨*free* her hair from a net⟩ ⟨flower scents, that only nighttime *frees*—*Lowell*⟩ **Release** carries a stronger implication of loosing or of setting loose from confinement, restraint, or obligation ⟨*release* a prisoner⟩ ⟨*release* a person from a promise⟩ ⟨*release* me from my bands with the help of your good hands—*Shak.*⟩ ⟨activities that *released* his stored-up energy⟩ ⟨death has *released* him from his sufferings⟩ ⟨only by indulging a deep impulse towards sermonizing could he *release* those other impulses which made him the great writer he was—*Sykes*⟩ **Liberate,** a very close synonym of the preceding words, differs from them chiefly in carrying a stronger suggestion of resulting liberty. The term may therefore connote, as do the others, emergence from some more or less disagreeable bondage or restraint ⟨*liberate* all slaves by a proclamation⟩ or it may merely suggest a cutting of a tie, relationship, or connection without regard to the power of another thing or things to restrain or restrict, thereby approaching *separate, disengage,* or *detach* in meaning ⟨oxygen is *liberated* when potassium chlorate is heated⟩ ⟨an electric current will decompose water, *liberating* hydrogen⟩ ⟨the poet draws life . . . from the community . . .: to cut himself off from this source of life is much more likely to cripple than to *liberate* him—*Day Lewis*⟩ ⟨*liberate* a certain group of individuals . . . from shackles inherited from feudalism—*Dewey*⟩ **Emancipate** basically means to free one person from subjection to another (as a child from subjection to his parent or a slave from subjection to his master) ⟨little more hope than had the son of an Athenian slave to be *emancipated*—*Quiller-Couch*⟩ but the term is more frequently found in an extended sense, implying a liberation of someone or something from what controls or dominates; it usually also suggests a freedom by which one's own judgment or conscience or intelligence decrees the course to be taken or the principles to be followed ⟨if we can imagine the various County Councils of England *emancipated* from the control of Parliament and set free to make their own laws—*Dickinson*⟩ ⟨all the philanthropic and humanitarian movements to which the Quakers, now *emancipated* from the notion that all initiative in such matters is an attempt to force the hand of the Almighty, devoted themselves in the nineteenth century—*Inge*⟩ **Manumit** differs from *emancipate* in its historical sense in always implying liberation from slavery or servitude; it is therefore sometimes preferred as the more definite term ⟨Darnall . . . was the son of a white man by one of his slaves, and his father executed certain instruments to

manumit him—*Taney*⟩ **Deliver** is comparatively rare as a close synonym of *free.* But in all of its many extended senses the idea of freeing is the basic, though not the strongest, implication. It is specifically a synonym of *rescue* (see RESCUE) when it implies release from peril, danger, or other evil ⟨and lead us not into temptation, but *deliver* us from evil—*Mt* 6:13⟩ It comes close to *transfer* or *convey* when it implies a disburdening of oneself of something which belongs to another or is intended for him ⟨*deliver* a letter to the addressee⟩ ⟨*deliver* a package to the purchaser⟩ or to *utter* or *pronounce* when it implies a relieving oneself of something one must say or is charged by oneself or another with saying ⟨*deliver* a message over the telephone⟩ ⟨*deliver* a speech⟩ The term may denote the disburdening of a woman of offspring at the time of its birth ⟨the queen was safely *delivered* of a son and heir⟩ or the freeing of all prisoners confined in a prison ⟨*deliver* a jail⟩ **Discharge** (see also DISMISS 1; PERFORM) implies the release of someone or something that is held in confinement or under restraint or within the bounds of a thing; it may suggest liberation ⟨*discharge* a prisoner⟩ ⟨*discharge* a hospital patient⟩ but often it implies an ejection ⟨*discharge* a shot⟩ ⟨*discharge* an arrow⟩ or an emission ⟨*discharge* passengers from a train⟩ ⟨*discharge* a cargo⟩ or a pouring forth through an outlet or vent ⟨the smoke is *discharged* through a very large chimney⟩ ⟨the stream *discharges* its waters into the Hudson river⟩ or a payment or settlement (as of an obligation) ⟨*discharged* his debts⟩ Often *discharge* differs from *release* in carrying a stronger connotation of force or violence ⟨many creative writers have a critical activity which is not all *discharged* into their work—*T. S. Eliot*⟩ ⟨all his accumulated nervous agitation was *discharged* on Maud like a thunderbolt—*Bennett*⟩ **Enfranchise** basically implies a freeing from subjection ⟨the nobles desired . . . to *enfranchise* themselves . . . from the power of the king—*Belloc*⟩ but in its commonest sense it specifically implies the removal of political disabilities and admission to full political rights as a freeman or as a citizen ⟨slaves were emancipated by the proclamation of President Lincoln on January 1, 1863, but were not *enfranchised* until the fifteenth amendment went into effect in 1870⟩
**Con** *hamper, fetter, manacle, shackle, trammel, hog-tie: *imprison, incarcerate, jail, immure, intern: confine, circumscribe, restrict, *limit: *restrain, curb, inhibit

**freebooter** *pirate, buccaneer, privateer, corsair

**freedom** 1 independence, autonomy, sovereignty, autarchy, autarky (see under FREE *adj*)
**Ana** liberation, emancipation, release, delivery, enfranchisement, manumission (see corresponding verbs at FREE): liberty, license (see FREEDOM)
**Ant** bondage —**Con** *servitude, slavery
2 **Freedom, liberty, license** are comparable when meaning the state or condition of one who can think, believe, or act as he wishes. **Freedom** (see also under FREE *adj*) is the term of widest application; in philosophy, for example, it often implies a state or condition in which there is not only total absence of restraint but release even from the compulsion of necessity; at the other extreme, in ordinary casual use, *freedom* merely implies the absence of any awareness of being restrained, repressed, or hampered; between these two extremes the term may imply the absence of a definite restraint or of compulsion from a particular power or agency ⟨me this unchartered *freedom* tires—*Wordsworth*⟩ ⟨the *freedom* of the press⟩ ⟨he was not affected by her reserve, and talked to her with the same *freedom* as to anybody else—*Archibald Marshall*⟩ ⟨who would not say, with Huxley, "Let me be wound up every day like a watch, to go right fatally, and I ask no

better *freedom"—James*⟩ **Liberty** is often used interchangeably with *freedom,* but it often carries one of two implications which are not so marked in the use of *freedom.* The first of these implications is the power to choose what one wishes to do, say, believe, or support as distinguished from the state of being uninhibited in doing or thinking ⟨had the *liberty* to come and go as he pleased⟩ ⟨in totalitarian states there is no *liberty* of expression for writers and no *liberty* of choice for their readers—*Huxley*⟩ ⟨*freedom* in thought, the *liberty* to try and err, the right to be his own man—*Mencken*⟩ The second of these implications is deliverance or release from restraint or compulsion ⟨set a slave at *liberty*⟩ ⟨the prisoners were willing to fight for their *liberty*⟩ ⟨from bondage freed, at *liberty* to serve as you loved best—*Baring*⟩ **License** often implies the liberty to disobey the rules or regulations imposed on the many, but not necessarily governing all, when a great advantage is to be gained by disobedience ⟨poetic *license*⟩ ⟨sometimes, with truly medieval *license,* singing to the sacred music . . ∴ songs from the street—*Pater*⟩ ⟨a general must be allowed considerable *license* in the field⟩ ⟨has little truck with those who have taken literary *license*— *Horner*⟩ More often, however, the term implies an abuse of liberty in the sense of the power to do exactly what one pleases ⟨*license* they mean when they cry Liberty—*Milton*⟩ ⟨many persons think that freedom of the press and liberty of free speech often degenerate into *license*⟩ ⟨Caesar's legions . . . were enjoying their victory in the *license* which is miscalled liberty—*Froude*⟩
*Ana* *exemption, immunity: scope, *range, compass, sweep
*Ant* necessity —*Con* compulsion, constraint, coercion (see corresponding verbs at FORCE)
**freethinker** unbeliever, *atheist, agnostic, deist, infidel
**freezing** adj *cold, frigid, frosty, gelid, icy, glacial, arctic, chilly, cool
**freight** *n* cargo, *load, burden, lading
**frenetic** adj *furious, frantic, frenzied, wild, delirious, rabid
*Ana* demented, *insane, mad: *irrational, unreasonable: provoked, excited, stimulated (see PROVOKE)
**frenzied** *furious, frantic, wild, frenetic, delirious, rabid
*Ana* demented, deranged, *insane, crazed, mad: distracted, bewildered (see PUZZLE)
**frenzy** 1 delirium, *mania, hysteria
2 fury, *inspiration, afflatus
*Ana* *ecstasy, rapture, transport
**frequently** *often, oft, oftentimes
*Ant* rarely, seldom
**fresh** novel, *new, new-fashioned, newfangled, modern, modernistic, original
*Ana* gleaming, glistening, sparkling (see FLASH *vb*): virginal, *youthful: raw, green, crude, uncouth (see RUDE): naïve, unsophisticated, artless, *natural
*Ant* stale —*Con* *trite, hackneyed, shopworn, stereotyped, threadbare
**fret** *vb* *abrade, excoriate, chafe, gall
*Ana* *eat, devour, consume: *worry, harass
**fretful** peevish, *irritable, petulant, querulous, fractious, snappish, waspish, pettish, huffy
*Ana* cross, cranky, touchy, choleric, *irascible: captious, carping, caviling, faultfinding, *critical: *contrary, perverse
*Con* patient, long-suffering, forbearing, resigned (see corresponding nouns at PATIENCE): *tame, submissive, subdued
**friable** short, frangible, crisp, brittle, *fragile
*Ana* crumbling *or* crumbly, disintegrating (see corresponding verbs at DECAY)

**friar** *religious, monk, nun
**friend,** acquaintance, intimate, confidant are comparable when they designate a person, especially not related by blood, with whom one is on good and, usually, familiar terms. **Friend,** in its application, ranges from a person who is not hostile or is a well-wisher to a person whose society one seeks or accepts with pleasure because of liking, respect, or affection. **Acquaintance** is applied to a person with whom one is on speaking terms. However, when these words are used in contrast, both imply a degree of familiarity, *friend* distinctively connoting close bonds of love and affection and *acquaintance,* comparative infrequency of contact and less close personal interest ⟨you understand that I am not their *friend.* I am only a holiday *acquaintance* —*Conrad*⟩ ⟨a companion loves some agreeable qualities which a man may possess, but a *friend* loves the man himself—*Boswell*⟩ This distinction is not invariably observed, especially when *acquaintance* is used as a collective plural ⟨he has a wide circle of *friends*; he has a large *acquaintance*⟩ ⟨he never speaks much, unless among his intimate *acquaintance*—*Austen*⟩ **Intimate** adds to *friend* the implications of a depth of affection and a closeness of association that tend to preclude reserve ⟨only his *intimates* were aware of his plans⟩ **Confidant** usually designates that intimate who actually is entrusted with one's secrets or is admitted to confidential discussions.
*Ana* comrade, companion, crony, *associate: ally, colleague, *partner
*Ant* foe —*Con* *enemy: antagonist, *opponent, adversary: rival, competitor (see corresponding verbs at RIVAL)

**friendly** *amicable, neighborly
*Ana* *familiar, intimate, close: *loving, affectionate, devoted: loyal, true, steadfast, *faithful
*Ant* unfriendly: belligerent —*Con* hostile, antagonistic, antipathetic (see corresponding nouns at ENMITY)
**friendship,** amity, comity, goodwill are comparable when they denote the relation (or, in the first three instances, the alliance) existing between persons, communities, states, or peoples that are in accord and in sympathy with each other. **Friendship** is the strongest of these terms in its implications of sentiment in the relation and of closeness of attachment ⟨the *friendship* between me and you I will not compare to a chain; for that the rains might rust, or the falling tree might break—*Penn*⟩ Sometimes it suggests an alliance; at other times it excludes that suggestion ⟨peace, commerce, and honest *friendship* with all nations—*Jefferson*⟩ ⟨*friendship,* that exquisite sense of a mutual sympathy of heart and mind which occasionally arises between independent individuals —*Cecil*⟩ **Amity** implies the absence of enmity or discord. Positively, it may imply nothing more than amicable relations ⟨the colonists and the Indians seldom lived together in *amity*⟩ or it may suggest reciprocal friendliness ⟨on his arrival he found *amity* instead of enmity awaiting him. Father Vaillant had already endeared himself to the people —*Cather*⟩ Often the term suggests benevolent understanding and mutual tolerance of potentially antagonistic aims or views ⟨the *amity* that wisdom knits not, folly may easily untie—*Shak.*⟩ ⟨the less we have to do with the *amities* or enmities of Europe, the better—*Jefferson*⟩ **Comity** has come to imply comradeship based either upon an interchange of courtesies or upon a similarity of interests and aims. The word often denotes a group bound together by friendship or by common interests but without implying loss of independence by members of the group or transference of sovereignty from the members to the group ⟨outside the *comity* of the empire, beyond the border provinces and client-kingdoms, lay the unknown lands and the

A colon (:) separates groups of words discriminated. An asterisk (*) indicates place of treatment of each group.

strange peoples—*Buchan*⟩ ⟨a Europe which pretends to have founded its *comity* upon brotherhood—*La Barre*⟩ **Goodwill** derives its chief implication of a benevolent attitude or of reciprocal good feeling largely from the Authorized Version's translation of the Angelic Hymn ⟨glory to God in the highest, and on earth peace, *goodwill* toward men—*Lk* 2:14⟩ The term is often used in international diplomacy to designate a reciprocal friendliness which constitutes an informal bond between nations and works to the advantage of all concerned ⟨*goodwill* is the mightiest practical force in the universe—*Dole*⟩ ⟨to promote the exchange of intellectual ideas and *goodwill* between Belgium and America—*School and Society*⟩ ⟨be assured that none of us have anything but *goodwill* toward you personally—*Ellison*⟩
*Ana* sympathy, affinity, \*attraction: \*sympathy, empathy: accord, concord, consonance, \*harmony: \*alliance, league, coalition, fusion, federation
*Ant* animosity　—*Con* \*enmity, hostility, antagonism, antipathy, rancor: \*hate, hatred

**fright** *n* alarm, consternation, panic, \*fear, dread, dismay, terror, horror, trepidation
*Ana* scaring *or* scare, startling, affrighting, frightening (see corresponding verbs at FRIGHTEN): appalling, horrifying, daunting (see DISMAY *vb*)

**fright** *vb* \*frighten, scare, alarm, terrify, terrorize, startle, affray, affright
*Ana* see those at FRIGHTEN

**frighten, fright, scare, alarm, terrify, terrorize, startle, affray, affright** mean to strike or to fill with fear or dread. **Frighten** is perhaps the most frequent in use; it is the most inclusive, for it may range in implicaton from a momentary reaction to a stimulus to a state of mind in which fear or dread prevails. Typically, however, it implies a more or less paralyzing fear affecting either the body or the will ⟨the silence of the house . . . *frightened* Clara—*Anderson*⟩ ⟨in the world too *frightened* to be honest—*T. S. Eliot*⟩ **Fright** is an older and chiefly literary or dialect form of *frighten* ⟨you have death perpetually before your eyes, only so far removed as to compose the mind without *frighting* it—*Gray*⟩ In informal and conversational use **scare** is often equivalent to *frighten;* in more formal use it usually implies fear that causes one to run, shy, or tremble ⟨sour visages, enough to *scare* ye—*Gray*⟩ ⟨a noise did *scare* me from the tomb—*Shak.*⟩ ⟨earth shakes beneath them, and heaven roars above; but nothing *scares* them from the course they love—*Cowper*⟩ **Alarm** in the relevant sense (compare ALARM *n* 1) nearly always stresses apprehension or anxiety ⟨they are *alarmed* for his safety⟩ ⟨the girl was . . . *alarmed* by the altogether unknown expression in the woman's face—*Conrad*⟩ **Terrify** emphasizes intensity of fear and agitation; it usually suggests a state of mind in which self-control or self-direction is impossible ⟨they were *terrified* out of their wits⟩ ⟨the dread of failure *terrified* them⟩ ⟨something in his face and in his voice *terrified* her heart—*Hichens*⟩ **Terrorize,** in distinction from *terrify,* implies the effect of an intention and therefore is used in reference to voluntary agents; thus, one may say that gangs *terrorized* the neighborhood by their constant depredations and that the depredations of the gangs *terrified* the neighborhood. *Terrorize* often implies coercion or intimidation ⟨*terrorize* a people into submission⟩ ⟨he delighted in *terrorizing* the guests by his bullying—*Burkholder*⟩ **Startle** implies surprise and a sudden shock that causes one to jump or flinch; occasionally its suggestion of fright is very weak ⟨one learns in parish work not to start, however much one may be *startled*—*Rose Macaulay*⟩ ⟨investigations of scientists . . . sprung on a public shocked and *startled* by the revelation that

facts which they were accustomed to revere were conspicuously at fault—*Galsworthy*⟩ **Affray** and **affright** are uncommon in modern use, the former, as a rule, coming close to *terrify* and the latter, to *frighten.*
*Ana* appall, horrify, \*dismay, daunt: \*intimidate, cow, browbeat, bulldoze: agitate, perturb, upset, disquiet, \*discompose

**frightful** dreadful, \*fearful, awful, terrible, terrific, horrible, horrific, shocking, appalling
*Ana* \*ghastly, grisly, gruesome, macabre, grim, lurid: \*sinister, baleful, malign

**frigid** freezing, gelid, icy, glacial, arctic, \*cold, cool, chilly, frosty
*Ant* torrid (*temperature*): amorous (*persons*)

**fritter** *vb* \*waste, squander, dissipate, consume
*Ana* disperse, \*scatter: dispense, \*distribute: disburse, \*spend, expend

**frivolity** levity, flippancy, light-mindedness, volatility, flightiness, \*lightness
*Ana* trifling, flirting, dallying, coquetting, toying (see TRIFLE *vb*): play, sport, \*fun, jest, game: gaiety, liveliness, vivaciousness, sprightliness (see corresponding adjectives at LIVELY)
*Ant* seriousness, staidness —*Con* sedateness, gravity, solemnity, somberness, soberness, earnestness (see corresponding adjectives at SERIOUS)

**frolic** *vb* \*play, sport, disport, rollick, romp, gambol
**frolic** *n* play, sport, disport, rollick, romp, gambol (see under PLAY *vb*)
*Ana* \*fun, jest, game, play, sport: caper, \*prank, antic, monkeyshine, dido: levity, \*lightness, frivolity

**frolicsome** \*playful, sportive, roguish, waggish, impish, mischievous
*Ana* \*merry, blithe, jocund, jovial, jolly: mirthful, gleeful, hilarious (see corresponding nouns at MIRTH): \*lively, vivacious, sprightly, gay

**frosty** chilly, \*cold, cool, frigid, freezing, gelid, icy, glacial, arctic

**froth** *n* \*foam, spume, scum, lather, suds, yeast
*Ana* \*lightness, levity, frivolity, flippancy

**froward** \*contrary, perverse, balky, restive, wayward
*Ana* \*obstinate, stubborn, mulish, pigheaded, stiff-necked: willful, headstrong, refractory, \*unruly, ungovernable, intractable, recalcitrant: contumacious, \*insubordinate, rebellious
*Ant* compliant —*Con* docile, tractable, amenable, \*obedient, biddable: acquiescent, resigned (see COMPLIANT)

**frown** *vb* **Frown, scowl, glower, lower, gloom** are comparable when they mean to put on a dark or malignant countenance or aspect. **Frown** commonly implies a stern face and contracted brows that express displeasure, disapprobation, anger, or contempt ⟨that Stonehenge circle of elderly disapproving faces—faces of the uncles, and schoolmasters and the tutors who *frowned* on my youth—*L. P. Smith*⟩ **Scowl** carries an implication of wrinkled drawn-down brows that express ill humor, sullenness, or discontent ⟨a spinner that would not rebel, nor mutter, nor *scowl,* nor strike for wages—*Emerson*⟩ **Glower** implies a more direct stare or gaze than *frown* or *scowl* and carries a stronger connotation of anger, contempt, or defiance ⟨the steward . . . *glowered* at Powell, that newcomer, that ignoramus, that stranger without right or privileges—*Conrad*⟩ ⟨he . . . stood *glowering* from a distance at her, as she sat bowed over the child—*D. H. Lawrence*⟩ **Lower** implies a menacing darkness and sullenness of face or aspect; the term is used in reference not only to persons but to skies that give promise of a storm ⟨wandering from chamber to chamber . . . all distinguishable by the same *lowering* gloom—*Beckford*⟩ ⟨up behind the Sangre de Cristo, gathered great thunderheads, *lowering* as they came, fringed threateningly with light—*Mary Austin*⟩ **Gloom** ordinarily carries a much stronger implication of gloominess or dejection and a much weaker (often nonexistent) suggestion of threatening than does *lower* ⟨they may be wise in not *glooming* over what is inevitable—*Cabell*⟩ ⟨Skiddaw [a mountain] *gloomed* solemnly overhead —*Dowden*⟩

*Ant* smile  —*Con* *disapprove, deprecate

**frowzy** blowsy, *slatternly, dowdy

*Ana* slovenly, unkempt, disheveled, sloppy, *slipshod: squalid, *dirty, filthy: *negligent, neglectful, lax, slack, remiss

*Ant* trim: smart  —*Con* *neat, tidy, trig, spick-and-span: *clean, cleanly

**frugal** thrifty, economical, *sparing

*Ana* *careful, meticulous: provident, prudent, discreet (see under PRUDENCE): saving, preserving, conserving (see SAVE): parsimonious, cheeseparing, penny-pinching (see STINGY)

*Ant* wasteful  —*Con* extravagant (see EXCESSIVE): prodigal, lavish, *profuse

**fruitful** fecund, prolific, *fertile

*Ana* reproducing *or* reproductive, propagating, breeding (see corresponding verbs at GENERATE): bearing, producing *or* productive, yielding (see corresponding verbs at BEAR): teeming, abounding (see TEEM): luxuriant, lush, exuberant (see PROFUSE)

*Ant* unfruitful: fruitless  —*Con* *sterile, barren, impotent, infertile: *futile, vain, bootless, abortive

**fruitfulness** prolificacy, fecundity, fertility (see under FERTILE)

**fruition** enjoyment, delectation *pleasure, delight, joy

*Ana* realization, actualization, materialization (see corresponding verbs at REALIZE): fulfillment, accomplishment (see corresponding verbs at PERFORM): attainment, achievement (see corresponding verbs at REACH): possession, enjoyment (see corresponding verbs at HAVE)

**fruitless** *futile, vain, bootless, abortive

*Ana* unfruitful, barren, infertile, *sterile: *vain, idle, otiose, nugatory, empty, hollow: frustrated, thwarted, foiled (see FRUSTRATE)

*Ant* fruitful  —*Con* *effective, effectual, efficacious, efficient: *fertile, fecund, prolific

**frustrate, thwart, foil, baffle, balk, circumvent, outwit** mean either to defeat a person attempting or hoping to achieve an end or satisfy a desire or, in some cases, to defeat another's desire. To **frustrate** is to make vain or ineffectual all efforts, however feeble or however vigorous, to fulfill one's intention or desire ⟨whatever nature . . . purposes to herself, she never suffers any reason, design, or accident to *frustrate*—*Fielding*⟩ ⟨my good intentions towards you . . . are continually *frustrated*—*Cowper*⟩ ⟨nature . . . supports as well as *frustrates* our lofty aspirations—*Muller*⟩ To **thwart** is to frustrate especially by crossing or running counter to someone or something making headway ⟨others had thrust themselves into his life and *thwarted* his purposes—*George Eliot*⟩ ⟨public enforcement of hygienic practices is *thwarted* by a really obstructive neglect of the rules of health by her peasantry—*Hobson*⟩ **Foil** commonly implies a blocking or turning aside that makes further effort difficult or destroys one's inclination to proceed further ⟨his attempts to replace ambition by love had been as fully *foiled* as his ambition itself—*Hardy*⟩ ⟨intelligence as a means to *foil* brute force—*Hearn*⟩ To **baffle** is to frustrate especially by confusing or puzzling; to **balk**, by interposing obstacles or hindrances ⟨such knotty problems of

alleys, such enigmatical entries, and such sphinx's riddles of streets without thoroughfares as must, I conceive, *baffle* the audacity of porters and confound the intellects of hackney coachmen—*De Quincey*⟩ ⟨I like reading my Bible without being *baffled* by unmeaningnesses—*Arnold*⟩ ⟨when an affection as intense as that is *balked* in its direct path and repressed it usually, as we know, finds an indirect outlet—*Brooks*⟩ ⟨his inclination to dreams, *balked* by the persistent holding of his mind to definite things—*Anderson*⟩ **Circumvent** implies frustration by stratagem; **outwit**, by craft or cunning ⟨immigration laws had been growing more and more effective .... But . . . the rejected aliens soon learned a method of *circumventing* them—*Heiser*⟩ ⟨the skill with which she [Elizabeth I] had hoodwinked and *outwitted* every statesman in Europe—*J. R. Green*⟩

*Ana* negative, counteract, *neutralize: defeat, beat, overcome, *conquer: *forbid, prohibit, inhibit: *prevent, preclude, obviate: *hinder, impede, obstruct, block, bar

*Ant* fulfill  —*Con* effect, accomplish, achieve, *perform: further, forward, promote, *advance: *incite, instigate, abet, foment

**fuddle** muddle, addle, *confuse

*Ana & Ant* see those at BEFUDDLE

**fugitive** *adj* evanescent, transitory, *transient, fleeting, passing, ephemeral, momentary, short-lived

**fulfill** 1 effect, achieve, accomplish, execute, *perform, discharge

·*Ana* *enforce, implement: compass, attain, *reach, gain: *realize, actualize: finish, complete (see CLOSE)

*Ant* frustrate: fail (in)

2 *satisfy, meet, answer

*Ana* equal, approach, *match, touch, rival

*Ant* fall short (of)

**full, complete, plenary, replete** are not interchangeable with each other, but the last three are interchangeable with the most comprehensive term, *full,* in at least one of its senses. **Full** implies the presence or inclusion of everything that is wanted or required by something or that can be held, contained, or attained by it; thus, a *full* year numbers 365 days or, in leap years, 366 days; a *full* basket is one that can hold nothing more; a *full* mind is stocked to the point of overflowing with knowledge or ideas; a *full* moon has reached the height of its illumination by the sun; a *full* stomach is one that can contain no more food with comfort or is completely satisfied; a *full* meal is one lacking in none of the courses or sometimes in none of the elements to make a satisfying or balanced meal; a sponge *full* of water has absorbed all the water it can hold. **Complete** comes into comparison and close synonymity with *full* when the latter implies the entirety that is needed to the perfection, consummation, integrity, or realization of a thing; thus, a fire in which the fuel is quite consumed may be described as involving either *full* or *complete* combustion; a *complete* meal is the same as a *full* meal; a teacher should have *complete,* or *full,* control of his class ⟨if you consider the ritual of the Church during the cycle of the year, you have the *complete* drama represented. The Mass is a small drama, having all the unities; but in the Church year you have represented the full drama of creation—*T. S. Eliot*⟩ ⟨the panorama of today's events is not an accurate or *complete* picture, for history will supply posterity with much evidence which is hidden from the eyes of contemporaries—*Eliot*⟩ **Plenary** comes into comparison with *full* when *full* implies the absence of every qualification or even suggestion of qualification as to a thing's completeness. *Plenary,* however, heightens the force of *full* in this sense and carries a stronger sug-

---

A colon (:) separates groups of words discriminated. An asterisk (*) indicates place of treatment of each group.

gestion of absoluteness; thus, to give *plenary* powers is to give full power without the slightest qualification; a *plenary* indulgence implies the remission of the entire temporal punishment due for one's sins ⟨by this word "miracle" I meant to suggest to you a something like *plenary* inspiration in these . . . men; an inspiration at once supernatural and so authoritative that it were sacrilege now to alter their text by one jot or tittle—*Quiller-Couch*⟩ **Replete** (*with*), the more bookish term, as compared with *full* (*of*), heightens the implication of abundant supply or of being filled to the brim with something ⟨he is quick, unaffected, *replete* with anecdote—*Hazlitt*⟩ ⟨an anxious captain, who has suddenly got news, *replete* with importance for him—*Henry James*⟩ Often, however, the term implies fullness to satiety or to the point of being surfeited ⟨right reading makes a full man in a sense even better than Bacon's; not *replete*, but complete rather, to the pattern for which Heaven designed him—*Quiller-Couch*⟩ ⟨*replete* with hard and book-learned words, impressively sonorous—*Southern*⟩ **Ana** including *or* inclusive, comprehending *or* comprehensive (see corresponding verbs at INCLUDE): teeming, abounding (see TEEM): glutted, cloyed, gorged, surfeited, sated (see SATIATE)

**Ant** empty —**Con** void, vacant, blank (see EMPTY): *bare, barren: stripped, dismantled, divested, denuded (see STRIP)

**fulsome,** oily, unctuous, oleaginous, slick, soapy are comparable when they mean too obviously extravagant or ingratiating to be accepted as genuine or sincere. **Fulsome** stresses a surfeit of something which in proper measure is not displeasing but which in abundance is cloyingly extravagant and offensive. Typically the term is applied to praise, flattery, and compliments, with the intent to suggest that they exceed the bounds of good taste and are lacking in truth and sincerity ⟨*fulsome* flattery⟩ ⟨he was bedaubing one of those worthies with the most *fulsome* praise—*Smollett*⟩ ⟨the *fulsome* strains of courtly adulation—*Edgeworth*⟩ ⟨he could never be made ridiculous, for he was always ready to laugh at himself and to prick the bladder of *fulsome* praise—*Buchan*⟩ **Oily** and *unctuous* both suggest the smoothness and blandness of oil. **Oily,** as applied to persons and their utterances and acts, carries a strong implication of an offensively ingratiating quality and sometimes suggests· a suavity, a benevolence, or a kindliness that is assumed as a mask for evil or dubious ends ⟨an *oily* scoundrel⟩· ⟨*oily* manners⟩ ⟨*oily* smugness⟩ ⟨only *oily* and commonplace evasion—*Stevenson*⟩ ⟨an *oily*, sycophantic press agent—*Rogow*⟩ **Unctuous,** on the other hand, suggests the assumption, often in hypocrisy, of the tone or manner of one who is grave, devout, or spiritual ⟨the *unctuous* grandiloquence of Dickens's Chadband⟩ ⟨the look was, perhaps, *unctuous,* rather than spiritual, and had, so to speak, a kind of fleshy effulgence . . . . He . . . smiled with more *unctuous* benignity than ever—*Hawthorne*⟩ ⟨Mark Twain writes those words with an almost *unctuous* gravity of conviction—*Brooks*⟩ ⟨the devastating portrait of the *unctuous* literary opportunist—*Cordell*⟩ **Oleaginous** is sometimes used in place of *oily* or *unctuous* when pomposity is connoted or a mocking note is desired ⟨the lank party who snuffles the responses with such *oleaginous* sanctimony—*Farrar*⟩ **Slick** may suggest the assumption of a smooth, ingratiating manner, but it usually stresses the speciousness of that appearance and often imputes sly wily trickiness to the person who assumes it ⟨this *slick* type of youngster anticipates exactly how adults will react to him and plays on their sensibilities—*Meyer*⟩ ⟨a pair of *slick* operators

had given the district a bad name by salting a barren claim—*Oscar Lewis*⟩ **Soapy** comes close to *unctuous* in its extended sense, but it carries almost no suggestion of hypocrisy: rather it connotes an unduly soft, bland, or ingratiating manner ⟨*soapy* supplications for unity—*New Republic*⟩ **Ana** lavish, *profuse, exuberant: *excessive, extravagant: cloying, satiating, sating (see SATIATE): bombastic, grandiloquent, magniloquent (see RHETORICAL)

**fumble** *vb* *botch, bungle, muff, cobble **Ana** blunder, flounder, *stumble

**fumigate** disinfect, sanitize, *sterilize

**fun,** jest, sport, game, play are comparable when they denote something (as an activity, an utterance, or a form of expression) that provides diversion or amusement or is intended to arouse laughter. **Fun** implies amusement or an engagement in what interests as an end in itself, or it may apply to what provides this amusement or interest and then often additionally implies a propensity for laughing or for finding a usually genial cause for laughter or amusement ⟨had such a zest for everything and thought it all such *fun—Rölvaag*⟩ ⟨make living more *fun,* life more complete—*Printers' Ink*⟩ ⟨a man full of *fun*⟩ **Jest** (see also JOKE) is comparable to *fun* chiefly in fixed phrases (as *in jest*) or when applied to activity or utterance not to be taken seriously. In such uses, however, *jest* commonly carries a stronger implication of ridicule or hoaxing ⟨a man given to making his most significant remarks in *jest*⟩ ⟨make *jest* of very serious problems⟩ **Sport** (see also under PLAY vb 1) is often interchangeable with *fun* ⟨there is a good deal of *sport* in many serious activities⟩ or *jest* ⟨play a trick on a friend for the *sport* of it⟩ But its most common use is in certain idiomatic phrases (as *make sport* and *in sport*) in which it suggests an intent to induce amusement or provoke laughter by putting someone or something up to gentle or malicious ridicule ⟨make *sport* of a suggestion⟩ ⟨make a good deal of *sport* out of his friend's misfortune⟩ ⟨teasing begun in *sport* ended in an ugly brawl⟩ **Game** as a close synonym of *fun* survives chiefly in the phrase *to make game of* where, like *sport* in the corresponding idiom, it usually carries a suggestion of mischief or malice and implies a certain ridicule ⟨make *game* of an unfortunate rival⟩ In more general related use *game* (see also *games* under ATHLETICS) may apply to an activity carried on in a spirit of fun ⟨there have been few poets more successful . . . in having fun with poetry. To Mr. Frost it is a pleasant *game—Leary*⟩ **Play,** which stresses in all senses an opposition to *earnest,* may replace *fun* or *sport* or *jest* when a thoroughly innocuous implication of lack of earnestness or seriousness is desired ⟨pretend to spank a child in *play*⟩ **Ana** amusement, diversion, recreation, entertainment (see under AMUSE): merriment, jocundity, blitheness, joviality (see corresponding adjectives at MERRY): *mirth, glee, hilarity, jollity

**function** *n* 1 Function, office, duty, province are comparable when they mean the act, acts, activities, or operations expected of a person or thing by virtue of his or its nature, structure, status, or position. **Function** is the most comprehensive of these terms, capable of referring not only to a living thing or to a part or member of a living thing but to anything in nature (as the sun, the stars, or the earth) or in art (as poetry, painting, music, or an example of one of these) or to anything constructed that serves a definite end or purpose or is intended to perform a particular kind of work ⟨fulfill one's *function* as a mother⟩ ⟨the *function* of the stomach is to digest food sufficiently to enable it to pass into the intestine⟩ ⟨the

**Ana** analogous words    **Ant** antonyms    **Con** contrasted words    See also explanatory notes facing page 1

*function* of language is twofold: to communicate emotion and to give information—*Huxley*⟩ ⟨the *function* of the leaves of a plant⟩ ⟨the *function* of criticism⟩ ⟨what after all . . . is the true *function* of religion?—*Dickinson*⟩ **Office** applies usually to the function of or the work to be performed by a person as a result of his trade, profession, employment, or position with relation to others; in this sense it refers to a service that is expected of one or to a charge that is laid upon one ⟨O, pardon me for bringing these ill news, since you did leave it for my *office*, sir —*Shak.*⟩ ⟨to suppose she would shrink . . . from the *office* of a friend—*Austen*⟩ ⟨they exercise the *offices* of the judge, the priest, the counsellor—*Gladstone*⟩ **Duty** (see also TASK) applies not only to the tasks expected or required to be performed in the course of occupation or employment ⟨the *duties* of a cook⟩ ⟨the *duties* of a hotel porter⟩ but to the offices associated with status, rank, or calling and generally regarded as inherent in that status, rank, or calling and as imposing an obligation upon the person so stationed ⟨a man and wife fulfill their biological function when they produce children, but they must still perform their *duties* as parents in rearing, protecting, and educating these children⟩ ⟨the governor regarded it as his *duty* to warn the citizens of the dangers ahead⟩ ⟨it is not only the right, but it is the judicial *duty* of the court, to examine the whole case as presented by the record—*Taney*⟩ ⟨it is in large part because of our failure to discharge our peacetime responsibilities as citizens that we must do our grim *duty* in war or perish—*Lodge*⟩ **Province** (see also FIELD) denotes a function, office, or duty which comes within one's range of jurisdiction, powers, competence, or customary practice ⟨nursing does not belong to a man; it is not his *province*—*Austen*⟩ ⟨it is emphatically the *province* and duty of the judicial department to say what the law is—*John Marshall*⟩
*Ana* end, goal, object, objective, purpose (see INTENTION): business, concern, *affair: *task, job
**2** *power, faculty
*Ana* *ability, capacity, capability: action, behavior, operation (see corresponding verbs at ACT)
**function** *vb* operate, work, *act, behave, react
**fundamental** *adj* **1** Fundamental, basic, basal, underlying, radical are comparable when they mean forming or affecting the groundwork, roots, or lowest part of something. **Fundamental** is used chiefly in reference to immaterial things or to abstractions, whether they are thought of as built up on a foundation or as having their origins in roots ⟨the *fundamental* rules of poetry⟩ ⟨a *fundamental* change in his attitude to life⟩ ⟨the *fundamental* rock in a geological formation⟩ ⟨the *fundamental* absurdity of the plot . . . remains—*FitzGerald*⟩ ⟨fatigue nor worry nor professordom could extinguish his *fundamental* gaiety—*J. M. Brown*⟩ **Basic** is often used interchangeably with *fundamental* when the latter implies reference to a substructure ⟨the fundamental or *basic* argument⟩ But *basic* is preferred to *fundamental* when the reference is to a definite or concrete groundwork, bottom, or starting point ⟨the *basic* stone of a pillar⟩ ⟨a *basic* wage in the electrical industry⟩ ⟨the distinction between *basic* scientific research and applied research— *News Front*⟩ **Basal** differs from *basic* chiefly in not being used as often in reference to immaterial things and in more often implying reference to the bottom or to the lowest point or regions of a thing ⟨geologizing the *basal* parts of the Andes—*Darwin*⟩ ⟨the *basal* plane of a crystal⟩ ⟨*basal* leaves on a stem⟩ **Underlying** may be used to suggest nothing more than extension beneath something else ⟨*underlying* rock strata⟩ ⟨the *underlying* layer of

tissue⟩ However, especially when the reference is to something immaterial, the term frequently comes close to *fundamental,* differing from it chiefly in suggesting a depth that removes the thing from one's range of vision or a remoteness that demands study or research on the part of one who would detect it ⟨the *underlying* motive for his act⟩ ⟨the *underlying* causes of World War I⟩ ⟨*underlying* differences between Communism and socialism⟩ ⟨the social transformation now demanded of us by our *underlying* technical, economic and social development—*Strachey*⟩ **Radical** (see also LIBERAL 2) implies reference to the root or origin or ultimate source of a thing; thus, a *radical* change is one that is so thoroughgoing that it affects the fundamental character of the thing involved; a *radical* error touches the very center and source of a thing's life ⟨actual differences distinguishing the different races of mankind—differences that may be ascribed to *radical* peculiarities of mind—*Bridges*⟩
*Ana* *primary, primal, primordial, prime: *elementary, elemental
**2** *essential, vital, cardinal
*Ana* requisite, *needful, necessary, indispensable: paramount, *dominant: principal, capital, foremost, *chief
*Con* *superficial: *subordinate, secondary
**fundamental** *n* *principle, axiom, law, theorem
*Ana* *element, constituent, component, factor: ground, basis, foundation, *base, groundwork
**funny** *laughable, risible, ludicrous, ridiculous, comic, comical, farcical, droll
*Ana* humorous, *witty, jocose, jocular, facetious: amusing, diverting, entertaining (see AMUSE): grotesque, bizarre, *fantastic, antic
*Con* *serious, solemn, grave, sober: *melancholy, plaintive, doleful, dolorous, lugubrious
**furious,** frantic, frenzied, wild, frenetic, delirious, rabid are comparable when they mean possessed with uncontrollable excitement especially under the stress of a powerful emotion. **Furious** implies strong excitement or violence that characterizes the movements or activities of one aroused by a powerful emotion; it may be applied to the activities or to the emotion ⟨he was in a *furious* rage⟩ ⟨she worked with *furious* zeal while the mood lasted⟩ ⟨she was now entering into that stage of *furious* activity which represented the exalted phase of the mental circular state—*Ellis*⟩ **Furious** may also mean nothing more than intensely angry with or without an outward display of excitement ⟨beneath her calm she was *furious* against her favorite—*Bennett*⟩ **Frantic** implies actions or words that indicate temporary mental disturbance under the stress of a powerful emotion (as grief, worry, anxiety, fear, or rage); it usually suggests, especially when applied to actions or behavior, a situation from which it is almost impossible to escape ⟨his *frantic* efforts to free himself resulted only in his becoming worse entangled⟩ ⟨there was a full moon at the time, and . . . every dog near my tent was baying it. The brutes . . . drove me *frantic*—*Kipling*⟩ ⟨a *frantic* beating of wings —*Cather*⟩ ⟨my father, *frantic* with anxiety over my safety—*Heiser*⟩ **Frenzied** suggests uncontrollable excitement under the sway of an emotion, often one not explicitly designated, but it differs from *frantic* in carrying no clear suggestion of a desperate situation ⟨a *frenzied* welcome by the populace⟩ ⟨why do we let these abstractions and implacable dogmatisms take possession of us . . . and fight their futile, *frenzied* conflicts in our persons?—*L. P. Smith*⟩ ⟨could hear the prosecutor's *frenzied* denunciations of the accused—*H. W. Carter*⟩ ⟨ignoring the *frenzied* nervous attempts of an unprepared city to make some semblance of defense—*Gardner*⟩

A colon (:) separates groups of words discriminated. An asterisk (*) indicates place of treatment of each group.

**Wild** comes close to *frantic* in its meaning but stresses a distracted rather than a nearly deranged state of mind; it therefore may be used with reference not only to the effect of a violent emotion but to the effect produced by any undue strain on the nerves or the mind ⟨she is *wild* with grief⟩ ⟨*wild* screams of anguish⟩ ⟨the news drove the people *wild* with joy⟩ ⟨these are but *wild* and whirling words, my lord—*Shak.*⟩ ⟨*wild* with hatred and insane with baffled desire—*Thackeray*⟩ **Frenetic** suggests a loss of balance, especially a tendency to be affected by extreme excitement under the stress of religious or partisan emotions ⟨some of the more *frenetic* of the franc-tireurs of liberalism—*Pall Mall Gazette*⟩ ⟨when inspired, their [the sacred writers'] individuality was intact. They were never . . . *frenetic*—*J. P. Newman*⟩ **Delirious,** like *frenzied,* implies uncontrollable excitement, but it more specifically suggests symptoms (as lightheadedness, incoherence, and wandering) typically associated with delirium ⟨the children were *delirious* with joy over their Christmas presents⟩ ⟨the end of the war was hailed with *delirious* excitement⟩ ⟨the *delirious* applause of the audience—*Edmund Wilson*⟩ **Rabid** applies to persons or to the actions, opinions, or utterances of persons who are possessed by fixed ideas and express them with violence often to the exclusion of all others ⟨he is very *rabid* on this subject⟩ ⟨a *rabid* partisan⟩ ⟨a *rabid* Communist⟩ ⟨burning with a *rabid* ambition to be ranked the equal of her elders in vice—*Poe*⟩
*Ana* excited, stimulated, provoked (see PROVOKE): infuriated, enraged, maddened (see ANGER *vb*): violent, fierce, vehement, *intense

**furnish 1** *provide, supply
*Ana* *get, obtain, procure, acquire, secure: *prepare, fit, ready, qualify, condition
*Ant* strip

**2 Furnish, equip, outfit, appoint, accouter, arm** are comparable when they mean to supply a person or something used by him with the adjuncts necessary or appropriate to his daily living or his occupation. **Furnish** stresses the provision of all essentials; thus, a house is *furnished* when it is supplied with all the necessary conveniences that make it ready for use as a home. **Equip** stresses the provision of things or occasionally of a single thing making for efficiency in action or in use; thus, a poorly *furnished* kitchen may be short in tables or chairs, but a poorly *equipped* kitchen is not adequately provided with the utensils or appliances needed for cooking and other work carried on there; one *equips,* rather than *furnishes,* an automobile with a four-wheel drive. **Outfit** stresses provision for a journey, an expedition, or a special kind of activity (as work); it is used chiefly with reference to necessary clothes, tools, utensils, and accessories and so is narrower in its range of applications than *furnish* and broader than *equip* ⟨it took several days to *outfit* me for my journey to Washington—*Cather*⟩ **Appoint,** which is somewhat bookish in this sense, suggests complete and often elegant furnishings or equipment ⟨well-*appointed* drawing rooms⟩ ⟨the Bristol mail is the best *appointed* in the kingdom—*De Quincey*⟩ **Accouter** stresses provision of dress, array, or personal equipment, usually for a particular activity (as military service) ⟨soldiers *accoutered* for the conflict⟩ ⟨he . . . was *accoutered* in a riding dress—*Dickens*⟩ ⟨the fully *accoutered* members of a Wild West show—*Sat. Review*⟩ **Arm** stresses provision for effective action or operation; it is used chiefly with reference to equipment necessary for offense or defense ⟨*arm* a battleship⟩ ⟨*armed* to the teeth⟩ but it may imply no more than provision of a means of preparation for added strength or security ⟨*arm* the

hilt of a sword with a plate⟩ ⟨*armed* with rubbers and umbrella⟩
In their extended senses the words in this group retain their respective implications but refer to mental, moral, or physical qualifications rather than to things ⟨such education as the local schools could *furnish*—*Smythe*⟩ ⟨thus *equipped* with a philosophy Emerson was prepared to begin his work as a critic—*Parrington*⟩ ⟨required . . . the judge to *outfit* him legally—*Hackett*⟩ ⟨one weeps to see Fowler [*Modern English Usage*] stripped and re*accoutered* by an unskilled hand for ends which he would repudiate—*Barzun*⟩ ⟨he *armed* himself with patience, as was needful, having so much to endure —*Norton*⟩
*Ana* endue, endow, *dower: array, apparel, *clothe
*Con* *strip, dismantle, denude, divest: despoil, spoliate (see RAVAGE)

**further** *adv & adj* *farther
**further** *vb* forward, *advance, promote
*Ana* *help, aid, assist: back, champion, *support, uphold: propagate, *generate, engender: accelerate, *speed, hasten, quicken
*Ant* hinder: retard —*Con* *frustrate, thwart, foil, balk, baffle, circumvent, outwit: impede, obstruct, bar, block (see HINDER): *prevent, forestall

**furthermore** moreover, besides, likewise, *also, too
**furtive** stealthy, clandestine, surreptitious, underhand, underhanded, *secret, covert
*Ana* *sly, cunning, crafty, wily, guileful, artful: *cautious, calculating, wary, circumspect: disguised, cloaked, masked (see DISGUISE *vb*)
*Ant* forthright: brazen —*Con* *straightforward, aboveboard: barefaced, brash, *shameless, impudent

**furuncle** *abscess, boil, carbuncle, pimple, pustule
**fury 1** rage, ire, *anger, wrath, indignation
*Ana* *passion: exasperation, irritation, aggravation (see IRRITATE): *acrimony, asperity, acerbity
**2** frenzy, *inspiration, afflatus
**fuse** *vb* **1** *liquefy, melt, deliquesce, thaw
**2** amalgamate, merge, coalesce, blend, mingle, commingle, *mix
*Ana* consolidate, unify, *compact: *unite, combine, conjoin

**fusion** coalition, *alliance, league, federation, confederation, confederacy
**fuss** *n* pother, ado, flurry, *stir, bustle
*Ana* agitation, perturbation, disturbance, flustering *or* fluster (see corresponding verbs at DISCOMPOSE): *haste, hurry, speed

**fussy** finicky, finicking, finical, particular, persnickety, pernickety, dainty, fastidious, squeamish, *nice
*Ana* exacting, demanding, requiring (see DEMAND *vb*): querulous, fretful, *irritable

**fustian** *n* rant, rodomontade, *bombast, rhapsody
**fusty** musty, rancid, *malodorous, putrid, fetid, stinking, noisome, rank
*Ana* *dirty, squalid, nasty, filthy, foul: slovenly, unkempt, disheveled, sloppy, *slipshod

**futile, vain, fruitless, bootless, abortive** all denote barren of result. *Futile* and *vain* parallel each other only when they imply failure to realize an immediate aim ⟨it was equally in *vain,* and he soon wearied of his *futile* vigilance—*Stevenson*⟩ **Vain** (see also VAIN 1) usually implies little more than simple failure; *futile* may connote the completeness of the failure or the unwisdom of the undertaking ⟨all literature, art, and science are *vain* . . . if they do not enable you to be glad—*Ruskin*⟩ ⟨opposition . . . had been so *futile* that surrender seemed the only course open—*Jones*⟩ Though both *vain* and *futile* may be applied to something contemplated but not yet tried, *vain* more often suggests a judgment based on previous experience and *futile,* one based on reasoning from self-evident principles ⟨but it is *vain* to talk of form and symmetry to the pure expansionist—*Babbitt*⟩ ⟨it is *futile* to ask which [Shakespeare or Dante] undertook the more difficult job—*T. S. Eliot*⟩ **Fruitless** is often interchangeable with *vain.* But its basic meaning makes it especially applicable to undertakings that entail long, patient, arduous effort and severe disappointment ⟨whom he had long time sought with *fruitless* suit—*Spenser*⟩ ⟨he nursed a grievance and, with Scotch persistence, kept up for years his *fruitless* efforts at reinstatement —*Ashley*⟩ **Bootless,** chiefly poetic, is especially applied to petitions or efforts to obtain relief ⟨they would not

pity me, yet plead I must; and *bootless* unto them—*Shak.*⟩ ⟨no guides were to be found, and in the next summer the young man returned from his *bootless* errand—*Parkman*⟩ **Abortive** implies failure before plans are matured or activities begun ⟨an *abortive* conspiracy⟩ ⟨an *abortive* attempt to break jail⟩ ⟨he had stirred up the Maronites to attack us . . . had I not brought up unexpectedly so many Arabs as rendered the scheme *abortive—Scott*⟩ ⟨some of them would play a considerable part in the *abortive* renaissance of the 1890's—*Malcolm Cowley*⟩ *Ana* *vain, idle, otiose, nugatory: *ineffective, ineffectual, inefficacious *Con* effectual, *effective, efficacious: fruitful (see FERTILE)

# G

**gab** *vb* *chat, chatter, patter, prate, prattle, babble, gabble, jabber, gibber
**gabble** *vb* babble, gab, chatter, *chat, patter, prate, prattle, jabber, gibber
**gad** *vb* *wander, stray, roam, ramble, rove, range, prowl, gallivant, traipse, meander
**gadget** contraption, *device, contrivance
**gag** *n* *joke, jest, jape, quip, witticism, wisecrack, crack
**gain** *vb* **1** win, obtain, procure, secure, acquire, *get
*Ana* achieve, accomplish, effect (see PERFORM): endeavor, strive, struggle, *attempt, try
*Ant* forfeit: lose
**2** compass, *reach, achieve, attain
*Ana & Ant* see those at GAIN 1
**3** *improve, recover, recuperate, convalesce
*Ana* progress, *advance: *cure, heal, remedy: *strengthen, invigorate
**gainful** *paying, remunerative, lucrative, profitable
*Ana* productive, yielding, bearing (see corresponding verbs at BEAR)
**gainsay** *deny, contradict, impugn, contravene, negative, traverse
*Ana* controvert, refute, confute, *disprove: oppose, combat, *resist, withstand, fight
*Ant* admit (sense 2) —*Con* *grant, concede, allow
**gale** *wind, breeze, hurricane, zephyr
**gall** *n* effrontery, nerve, cheek, *temerity, hardihood, audacity
**gall** *vb* chafe, excoriate, fret, *abrade
*Ana* *injure, hurt, harm, damage: *worry, harass
**gallant** *adj* courtly, chivalrous, courteous, polite, *civil
*Ana* attentive, considerate, *thoughtful: *spirited, mettlesome, high-spirited: urbane, *suave
**gallantry** **1** *heroism, valor, prowess
*Ana* bravery, intrepidity, valorousness, dauntlessness (see corresponding adjectives at BRAVE): *courage, mettle, spirit, resolution
*Ant* dastardliness
**2** *courtesy, attention, amenity
*Ana* chivalrousness *or* chivalry, courtliness (see corresponding adjectives at CIVIL): deference, homage (see HONOR): suavity, urbanity (see corresponding adjectives at SUAVE): address, poise, *tact, savoir faire
*Con* boorishness, churlishness, loutishness, clownishness (see corresponding adjectives under BOOR): discourteousness *or* discourtesy, ungraciousness, rudeness (see

corresponding adjectives at RUDE)
**gallery** **1** *passage, passageway, corridor, arcade, cloister, ambulatory, aisle, hall, hallway
**2** *museum, treasury, archives, library
**gallivant** *wander, stray, roam, ramble, rove, range, prowl, gad, traipse, meander
**galumph** *stumble, trip, blunder, lurch, flounder, lumber, lollop, bumble
**galvanize** excite, stimulate, *provoke, quicken, pique
*Ana* rouse, arouse, rally, *stir, awaken, waken: electrify, *thrill, enthuse: kindle, fire (see LIGHT *vb*)
**gambit** *trick, ruse, stratagem, maneuver, ploy, artifice, wile, feint
**gambol** *n* frolic, disport, play, sport, rollick, romp (see under PLAY *vb*)
**gambol** *vb* frolic, disport, *play, sport, rollick, romp
**game** *n* **1** sport, play, *fun, jest
*Ana* diversion, amusement, recreation, entertainment (see under AMUSE)
**2** in plural form **games** *athletics, sports
*Ana* *contest, conflict
**gamut** *range, reach, radius, compass, sweep, scope, orbit, horizon, ken, purview
**gap** *n* *break, interruption, interval, interim, hiatus, lacuna
*Ana* *breach, split, rent, rift: *hole, hollow, cavity: division, separation (see corresponding verbs at SEPARATE): pass, passage (see WAY)
**gape** *vb* *gaze, stare, glare, gloat, peer
*Ana* regard, admire (see under REGARD *n*): look, watch, *see
**garbage** *n* *refuse, waste, offal, rubbish, trash, debris
**garble** *misrepresent, falsify, belie
*Ana* distort, contort, warp (see DEFORM): misinterpret, misconstrue (see affirmative verbs at EXPLAIN)
**gargantuan** *huge, vast, immense, enormous, elephantine, mammoth, giant, gigantic, gigantean, colossal, Herculean, cyclopean, titanic, Brobdingnagian
**garish** *gaudy, tawdry, flashy, meretricious
*Ana* resplendent, gorgeous, *splendid: *showy, ostentatious, pretentious
*Ant* somber
**garner** *reap, glean, gather, harvest
*Ana* amass, *accumulate
**garnish** *vb* embellish, beautify, deck, bedeck, *adorn, decorate, ornament
*Ana* enhance, heighten, *intensify

A colon (:) separates groups of words discriminated. An asterisk (*) indicates place of treatment of each group.

**garrulity, garrulousness** talkativeness, loquacity, volubility, glibness (see under TALKATIVE)
*Ana* *verbiage: prolixity, verboseness, diffuseness, wordiness (see corresponding adjectives at WORDY): chattering, prating, babbling, jabbering (see CHAT *vb*)
**garrulous** *talkative, loquacious, voluble, glib
*Ana* glib, voluble, fluent, *vocal, articulate, eloquent
*Ant* taciturn —*Con* reserved, reticent, *silent, uncommunicative, close: laconic, terse, *concise: curt, brusque, blunt (see BLUFF)
**gasconade** *vb* vaunt, *boast, brag, crow
**gastronome** *epicure, gourmet, gourmand, bon vivant, glutton
**gate** *door, portal, gateway, postern, doorway
**gateway** gate, portal, *door, postern, doorway
**gather** *vb* **1** Gather, collect, assemble, congregate mean to come or to bring together so as to form a group, a mass, or a unit. The same distinctions in applications and in implications characterize their derivative nouns **gathering, collection, assemblage** (which see) or **assembly, congregation**. **Gather** is the most widely applicable of these words; it may be used in reference not only to persons and objects but to intangible things ⟨a crowd *gathers* wherever there is excitement⟩ ⟨*gather* the boys and girls of the neighborhood for a picnic⟩ ⟨leaves *gather* in heaps on windy days⟩ ⟨*gather* the leaves for burning⟩ ⟨beads of moisture *gathered* on his brow⟩ ⟨*gathering* his ideas together before planning his speech⟩ In certain phrases *gather* acquires additional specific connotations; thus, *gathering* flowers or crops implies plucking and culling as well as bringing together; *gathering* a ruffle implies a drawing together or into folds on a thread; *gathering* one's wits connotes an effort at concentration or at mustering or rallying mental forces. **Collect** is often used in place of *gather* with no intended difference in meaning ⟨*collect* leaves⟩ ⟨leaves *collect*⟩ ⟨beads of moisture *collected* on his brow⟩ But *collect* may convey, as *gather* does not, the ideas of careful selection or a principle of selection, of orderly arrangement, or of a definitely understood though not always expressed end in view; thus, to *collect* butterflies implies a selection of specimens and, usually, their cataloguing; to *collect* books (as in book *collector*) implies a choice of books with regard to some such principle as rarity, beauty of binding, or authorship. There is a subtle difference between to *gather* one's thoughts, which often merely implies previous scattering, and to *collect* one's thoughts, which implies their organization; there is also a difference between to *gather* money, which may mean merely to accumulate it, and to *collect* money, which usually suggests either raising a fund by gifts, subscriptions, and contributions or taking action to obtain possession of money due. *Collect* and *collection* are often preferred to *gather* and *gathering* when various things are brought together; thus, a jumble or an omnium-gatherum is a miscellaneous *collection* rather than a *gathering*; *collect* rather than *gather* enough chairs for all the guests to sit down. **Assemble** stresses more emphatically than either *gather* or *collect* a close union of individuals and a conscious or a definite end in their coming or in their being brought together. It is used chiefly in reference to persons who gather together, either of their own will or at the call of another, so as to form a group or body that will unite in action or join in counsel or discussion ⟨the democratic rights of free speech and free *assembly*⟩ ⟨the most renowned experts on the history, geography, economics, and politics of all the nations of the world . . . *assembled* under one roof—*Alsop & Braden*⟩ ⟨even after a new crew had . . . been *assembled*, I had qualms about setting forth over the treacherous waters of

the China Sea—*Heiser*⟩ In reference to things *assemble* implies an agent who collects them in order to unite them into a single body or structure or into a distinct and isolated group; thus, the *assembly* department of an automobile plant is the department in which the workmen build the cars by *assembling* the component parts made in other departments or in other factories ⟨it took twenty years to *assemble* this collection of musical instruments⟩ **Congregate** implies a flocking together into a crowd, a huddle, or a mass ⟨cattle *congregate* during a storm⟩ ⟨pass laws forbidding persons to *congregate* on the streets⟩ ⟨*congregations* of atoms excited and lucent, mingled with free electricity—*Darrow*⟩ **Congregation** is specifically applied to an assembly meeting for religious worship, but it usually retains the suggestion of a crowd that has flocked together.
*Ana* *accumulate, amass, hoard: *heap, pile, stack, mass
**2** *reap, glean, garner, harvest
*Ana* see those at GATHER 1
**3** *infer, deduce, conclude, judge
**gathering** collection, assemblage, assembly, congregation (see under GATHER *vb*)
*Ana* *crowd, throng, press, horde, mob, rout, crush: accumulation (see corresponding verb ACCUMULATE)
**gauche** maladroit, *awkward, clumsy, inept
**gaudy, tawdry, garish, flashy, meretricious** are comparable when meaning vulgar or cheap in its showiness. Something is **gaudy** which uses gay colors and conspicuous ornaments or ornamentation lavishly, ostentatiously, and tastelessly ⟨*gaudy* floral prints⟩ ⟨false eloquence, like the prismatic glass, its *gaudy* colors spreads on ev'ry place —*Pope*⟩ ⟨another attendant, *gaudy* with jingling chains and brass buttons, led us along a corridor—*Kenneth Roberts*⟩ Something is **tawdry** which is not only gaudy but cheap and sleazy ⟨beneath the lamp her *tawdry* ribbons glare—*Gay*⟩ ⟨a fancy . . . fruitful, yet not wanton, and gay without being *tawdry*—*Cowper*⟩ ⟨he saw nothing else; the *tawdry* scenery, the soiled cotton velvet and flimsy crumpled satin, the reek of vulgarity, never touched his innocent mind—*Deland*⟩ Something is **garish** which is distressingly or offensively bright ⟨hide me from day's *garish* eye—*Milton*⟩ ⟨for this week he would produce a bunch [of flowers] as *garish* as a gypsy, all blue and purple and orange, but next week a bunch discreet as a pastel, all rose and gray with a dash of yellow—*Sackville-West*⟩ Something is **flashy** which dazzles for a moment but then reveals itself as shallow or vulgar display ⟨Tom Paine was considered for the time as a Tom Fool to him, Paley an old woman, Edmund Burke a *flashy* sophist—*Hazlitt*⟩ ⟨the *flashy* rich boy in public school, buying toadyism —*La Farge*⟩ ⟨"what the public wants" is being translated into the *flashy*, the gadgety, the spectacular—*Loewy*⟩ Something is **meretricious** which allures by false or deceitful show (as of worth, value, or brilliancy) ⟨the jewels in the crisped hair, the diadem on the polished brow, are thought *meretricious*, theatrical, vulgar— *Hazlitt*⟩ ⟨the false taste, the showy and *meretricious* element . . . invading the social life of the period and supplanting the severe elegance, the instinctive grace of the eighteenth century—*Binyon*⟩ ⟨if a writer's attitude toward his characters and his scene is as vulgar as a showman's, as mercenary as an auctioneer's, vulgar and *meretricious* will his product for ever remain—*Cather*⟩
*Ana* *showy, pretentious, ostentatious: vulgar, *coarse, gross: resplendent, gorgeous (see SPLENDID)
*Ant* quiet (*in taste or style*) —*Con* modest, *chaste, decent, pure
**gauge** *n* *standard, criterion, yardstick, touchstone

**gaunt** rawboned, angular, lank, lanky, *lean, spare, scrawny, skinny
*Ana* cadaverous, wasted, *haggard, worn: *thin, slim, slender, slight
*Con* portly, plump, *fleshy, fat, stout, corpulent, obese, rotund, chubby

**gay** vivacious, *lively, sprightly, animated
*Ana* *merry, blithe, jocund, jovial, jolly: *playful, frolicsome, sportive
*Ant* grave, sober —*Con* *serious, sedate, staid, solemn, somber, earnest: quiet, *still, silent

**gaze** *vb* Gaze, gape, stare, glare, peer, gloat are comparable when meaning to look at long and attentively, but they vary greatly in their implications of attitude and motive. Gaze implies fixed and prolonged attention (as in admiration, curiosity, or wonder) ⟨and still they *gazed*, and still the wonder grew, that one small head could carry all he knew—*Goldsmith*⟩ ⟨the black-marble Egyptian *gazing* with unwavering eyes into the sky—*Shaw*⟩ Gape adds to *gaze* the implication of stupid and openmouthed wonder or indecision ⟨a yokel *gaping* at the sights on his first visit to the city⟩ ⟨the Gurkhas . . . hitched their kukris well to hand, and *gaped* expectantly at their officers—*Kipling*⟩ ⟨depicts man lost and blindly *gaping* amidst the chaos—*Gwyn*⟩ Stare implies a fixed and direct gazing at a person or object; it may connote curiosity, astonishment, insolence, or vacant fixedness ⟨or like stout Cortez when with eagle eyes he *stared* at the Pacific—and all his men looked at each other with a wild surmise—silent, upon a peak in Darien—*Keats*⟩ ⟨*staring* at each other as if a bet were depending on the first man who winked—*George Eliot*⟩ ⟨she tried not to *stare* at Mr. Scales, but her gaze would not leave him—*Bennett*⟩ Glare adds to *stare* the implication of fierceness or anger ⟨all . . . with countenance grim *glared* on him passing—*Milton*⟩ ⟨neither Clem nor Lonnie replied. Arch *glared* at them for not answering—*Caldwell*⟩ Peer suggests a looking narrowly, especially with or as if with partly closed eyes, or curiously, especially through or from behind something ⟨Mrs. Cary kept *peering* uneasily out of the window at her husband—*M. E. Freeman*⟩ ⟨his pale, nearsighted eyes had always the look of *peering* into distance—*Cather*⟩ Gloat usually implies prolonged or frequent gazing upon something, especially in secret, often with profound, usually malignant or unhallowed, satisfaction ⟨a miser *gloating* over his hoard⟩ ⟨to gaze and *gloat* with his hungry eye on jewels that gleamed like a glowworm's spark—*Longfellow*⟩ Sometimes the implication of malignant satisfaction is so emphasized that the implication of gazing is obscured or lost ⟨in vengeance *gloating* on another's pain—*Byron*⟩
*Ana* watch, look, *see: observe, survey, contemplate (see SEE): regard, admire (see under REGARD *n*)

**gear** tackle, *equipment, paraphernalia, outfit, apparatus, machinery
*Ana* appurtenances, accessories, adjuncts, appendages (see singular nouns at APPENDAGE): *possessions, belongings, effects, means

**geld** castrate, *sterilize, spay, emasculate, alter, caponize, mutilate

**gelid** icy, frigid, freezing, frosty, *cold, glacial, arctic, cool, chilly

**general** *adj* generic, *universal, common
*Ana* *regular, typical, normal, natural
*Con* specific, *special, particular, individual: peculiar, distinctive, *characteristic, individual

**generally** mostly, chiefly, mainly, principally, *largely, greatly

**generate** *vb* Generate, engender, breed, beget, get, sire,

**procreate, propagate, reproduce** are comparable when they mean to give life or origin to or to bring into existence by or as if by natural processes. Generate, which means no more than this, is used rarely in reference to human beings, seldom in reference to animals or plants ⟨mushrooms are not *generated* from seeds⟩ but is the technical term in reference to electricity ⟨*generate* an electric current⟩ and is used commonly in reference to ideas, emotions, passions, moods, or conditions that have a traceable cause or source ⟨a habit of thought . . . only to be *generated* by intimate knowledge of good literature—*Russell*⟩ ⟨I do not think religious feeling is ever aroused, except by ideas of objective truth and value; but these ideas are certainly not *generated* by feeling—*Inge*⟩ ⟨the mood *generated* in me by the intellectual convictions current in my time—*Krutch*⟩ Engender, like generate, is chiefly found in extended use, where it more often suggests an originating or a sudden or immediate birth than a gradual bringing into fullness of life or being ⟨to hunger for the hope and happiness which . . . the dance seemed to *engender* within them—*Hardy*⟩ ⟨a sudden spontaneous illumination . . . *engendered* in the course of writing a poem—*Day Lewis*⟩ ⟨the strike, during which three men had been killed and ill-feeling *engendered* in hundreds of silent workers—*Anderson*⟩ Breed basically means to produce offspring by hatching or gestation ⟨yet every mother *breeds* not sons alike—*Shak.*⟩ Often the term carries a less specific meaning and suggests merely the production of offspring ⟨mankind will in every country *breed* up to a certain point—*Paley*⟩ sometimes by parental action but more often by the activity of those who determine the parentage, the time of mating, and the number of offspring ⟨specialists who *breed* horses for racing⟩ ⟨cattle *bred* for milk production⟩ ⟨the notion of a Government department trying to make out how many different types were necessary, and how many persons of each type, and proceeding to *breed* them by appropriate marriages, is amusing but not practicable—*Shaw*⟩ Sometimes *breed* adds the implication of nurturing or rearing to that of producing offspring and may so stress this that there is no reference to the life processes involved in generation ⟨he was *bred* in a manner befitting the son of a king⟩ ⟨he was born and *bred* in your house—*Jowett*⟩ In its extended sense *breed* usually implies a gradual or continuous process of coming into being; it may specifically suggest a period of latency or quiescence before breaking out ⟨an iniquitous government *breeds* despair in men's souls—*John Morley*⟩ ⟨the yoke a man creates for himself by wrongdoing will *breed* hate in the kindliest nature —*George Eliot*⟩ ⟨incessant recurrence without variety *breeds* tedium—*Lowes*⟩ Beget, get, and sire imply the procreating act of the male parent; usually *beget* is preferred in reference to men and *get* and *sire* in reference to animals ⟨he that *begetteth* a fool doeth it to his sorrow —*Prov* 17:21⟩ ⟨a bull may be unable to *get* calves— *Diseases of Cattle*⟩ ⟨a Thoroughbred *sired* by a famous stallion⟩ Only *beget* and *sire* have extended use derived from their basic meaning. In such use there is very little difference between *beget*, *sire*, and *engender*, the terms often being employed interchangeably without loss ⟨motion picture industry, *sired* and nourished by private enterprise—*Hays*⟩ though *beget* sometimes stresses a calling into being on the spur of the moment or without any previous preparation or expectation ⟨beauty that *begets* wonder and admiration⟩ ⟨stories . . . spring from the fillip of some suggestion, and one *begets* another— *Lowes*⟩ Procreate, a somewhat formal word, comes close in meaning to *breed* in the sense of to produce offspring. Though sometimes used as a synonym of *beget*, it more

often refers to sexual acts involved in a mating and their results in the production of children ⟨the time-honored presumption that a child born to a married woman during coverture was *procreated* by her husband—*JAMA*⟩ Unlike the foregoing terms, **propagate** carries no inherent implication of sexual activity but rather stresses the preserving and increasing of a kind of living being, be it plant, animal, or human, whether by generating, by breeding, or by growing (as from seeds, grafts, cuttings, or bulbs) ⟨the rabbit *propagates* itself with great rapidity⟩ ⟨from cuttings . . . he *propagated* what he first named the Tokay but later the Catawba grape—*Jenkins*⟩ In its extended use *propagate* implies not only giving rise to something or bringing it into existence but often also a continuation of that existence or the widespread dissemination of the thing that is brought into existence ⟨"Oh! does patience beget patience?" said Adrian. "I was not aware it was a *propagating* virtue"—*Meredith*⟩ ⟨the Rights of Man, rights which the French Revolution had *propagated*—*Barr*⟩ **Reproduce**, like *propagate*, may be used in reference to any living thing capable of bringing into existence one or more of its kind and is applicable whether the means is sexual or asexual ⟨the tribe was dying out; infant mortality was heavy, and the young couples did not *reproduce* freely —the life-force seemed low—*Cather*⟩ ⟨the residents of the urban places probably did not *reproduce* themselves —*Oscar Handlin*⟩
*Ana* \*bear, produce, yield: \*teem, abound

**generic** general, \*universal, common
*Ana* typical, \*regular, normal: specific (see SPECIAL)
*Con* individual, peculiar, distinctive, \*characteristic: particular, individual, \*special

**generous** bountiful, bounteous, openhanded, munificent, \*liberal, handsome
*Ana* lavish, prodigal, \*profuse, exuberant: benevolent, philanthropic, eleemosynary, \*charitable, altruistic
*Ant* stingy —*Con* close, closefisted, niggardly, parsimonious, penurious, miserly (see STINGY): \*mean, ignoble

**genesis** \*beginning, rise, initiation
*Ana* \*origin, source, root, inception, provenance, provenience: derivation, origination (see corresponding verbs at SPRING): commencement, start (see corresponding verbs at BEGIN)

**genial** sociable, affable, \*gracious, cordial
*Ana* \*kind, kindly, benign, benignant: friendly, neighborly, \*amicable: jocund, jovial, jolly, blithe, \*merry: cheerful, happy, \*glad
*Ant* saturnine (*manner, disposition, aspect*): caustic (*remarks, comments*) —*Con* ungracious, discourteous, uncivil, \*rude: morose, crabbed, \*sullen: ironic, sardonic, \*sarcastic, satiric

**genius** talent, \*gift, faculty, aptitude, knack, bent, turn
*Ana* \*ability, capacity, capability: originality (see corresponding adjective at NEW): \*inspiration, afflatus

**genre** \*class, category, genus, denomination, species

**gentle** \*soft, mild, smooth, lenient, bland, balmy
*Ana* \*moderate, temperate: \*pleasant, agreeable, grateful, pleasing, welcome: \*calm, tranquil, serene, placid, peaceful, halcyon
*Ant* rough, harsh —*Con* vehement, \*intense, fierce, violent: \*powerful, forcible, forceful: stimulating, exciting, provoking *or* provocative (see corresponding verbs at PROVOKE)

**gentleman** patrician, aristocrat are comparable when they denote a person of good or noble birth. **Gentleman** basically implies descent from good family, the right to bear a coat of arms, and social rank just below that of the noble and above that of the yeoman. The term has been widely extended in its application and has acquired connotations which have little or nothing to do directly with lineage or heraldic rights but suggest only such outward marks of good birth as elegance of person and of manners and a life of leisure ⟨a *gentleman* . . . I'll be sworn thou art; thy tongue, thy face, thy limbs, actions and spirit, do give thee five-fold blazon—*Shak.*⟩ ⟨somebody has said that a king may make a nobleman, but he cannot make a *gentleman*—*Burke*⟩ ⟨the *gentleman* may be a drunkard, a gambler, a debauchee . . .; he may be a man of spotless life, able and honest; but he must on no account be a man with broad palms, a workman amongst workmen— *Tom Collins*⟩ **Patrician** derives its implications from its historical applications but chiefly from its earliest reference to a Roman citizen who belonged to one of the original families of ancient Rome which, after the growth of the plebeian order, kept power and authority in their own hands. In reference to present-day persons the word suggests a distinguished ancestry, superior culture, and aloofness from what is common or vulgar; it is applied chiefly to descendants of established and influential families when they constitute a social caste, especially one marked by exclusiveness and pride in birth ⟨the merchant-*patricians* [of Boston], like those of Holland and Flanders, in times gone by, wished to perpetuate their names and glorify their capital not only in the elegance of their mansions but also in churches, parks and public buildings— *Brooks*⟩ **Aristocrat** carries fewer suggestions of inbred physical characteristics than *gentleman* or *patrician*, but it suggests a sympathy with the point of view common to them. In historical use it commonly implies an opposition to *democrat* and is applicable to a person who believes in government by superior persons or by the class which includes such persons; in more general use it is commonly applied to a person who by reason of birth, breeding, title, wealth, or outlook is accorded recognition as a member of the highest caste and especially to one who holds himself somewhat aloof from the ordinary forms and observances of social life ⟨two kinds of *aristocrats*: one that assumes the right to govern without the consent of the people; the other that assumes the privilege of an exclusive private life—*Charles Beard*⟩ ⟨a genuine *aristocrat*, he was at home in all walks of life—*Smelser & Kirwin*⟩
*Ant* boor —*Con* lout, clown, churl (see BOOR)

**gentry** \*aristocracy, county, nobility, elite, society

**genuine** \*authentic, bona fide, veritable
*Ana* true, \*real, actual: unadulterated, unsophisticated (see affirmative verbs at ADULTERATE): \*pure, sheer, absolute: \*sincere, unfeigned
*Ant* counterfeit: fraudulent —*Con* simulated, feigned, shammed *or* sham, counterfeited (see corresponding verbs at ASSUME): \*false: \*fictitious, apocryphal, mythical: factitious, \*artificial, ersatz

**genus** \*class, category, species, denomination, genre
*Ana* \*type, kind, sort, nature, description

**germ, microbe, bacterium, bacillus, virus**, though not strict synonyms, are comparable because all denote organisms invisible to the naked eye, including organisms that are the causative agents of various diseases. **Germ** and **microbe** are the ordinary nonscientific names for such an organism and especially for one that causes disease. *Bacteria,* the plural of **bacterium** and the form commonly in general use, is often employed as the equivalent of *germs* and *microbes.* Technically, it is the scientific designation of a very large group of minute fungi which are found widely distributed in water, air, soil, living things, and dead organic matter, which have structural and biological characteristics distinguishing them from other unicellular microorganisms (as protozoans), and only some of which are instrumental in producing disease in man, animals, and plants. In addition to the pathogenic or disease-causing bacteria there are the saprophytic bacteria which live upon dead or decaying organic matter and which, for the most part, are beneficial in their effects which include many natural chemical processes (as fermentation, oxidation, and nitrification). **Bacillus** is often employed as though it designated any of the pathogenic bacteria. In technical scientific usage it denotes any of a genus of bacteria which originally included all or most rod-shaped forms and is now restricted to a group of mostly soil-inhabiting, aerobic, and saprophytic forms that produce endospores. However, it is often used of rod-shaped bacteria in general, especially as distinguished from those which are globe-shaped (the coccus form, of which the streptococcus is an example) and those which are spiral (the spirillum form, of which the vibrio which causes Asiatic cholera is an example, and the spirochete form, exemplified by the treponema of syphilis). It is common, especially in medical usage, to speak of the *bacilli* of such diseases as typhoid, diphtheria, and tetanus, though none of these are true bacilli in the restricted taxonomic sense. **Virus**, in earlier use, was an imperceptible infectious principle of unknown nature occurring in the body of a diseased individual and held to be involved in the transfer of infectious diseases. In this sense it has been applied to most germs or microbes while their specific nature remained unknown, as well as to bodily fluids and discharges containing such infective agents ⟨by [virus] is understood a principle, unknown in its nature and inappreciable by the senses, which is the agent for the transmission of infectious diseases. Thus we speak of the *variolic*, *vaccine*, and *syphilitic viruses—Dunglison*⟩ A vestige of this meaning persists in immunologic usage with respect to materials (as vaccine lymph) that are antigenic but not usually infective ⟨when the doctors inoculate you . . . they give you an infinitesimally attenuated dose. If they gave you the *virus* at full strength it would overcome your resistance and produce its direct effect—*Shaw*⟩ In general modern usage *virus* is equivalent to filterable virus and is restricted to a variety of parasitic and infective agents which are able in nature to multiply only in living tissues, are so small that they pass through the pores of bacteriological filters, and are generally invisible with the ordinary light microscope. They include highly organized microbes (as the rickettsias) and bodies (as the tobacco mosaic virus) that lie on the border between the living and nonliving, may consist of a single macromolecule of DNA or RNA in a protein case, and are capable on the one hand of existing in the crystalline state and on the other, when introduced into suitable cells, of multiplying like a true organism ⟨it appears that energy for *virus* synthesis is provided by enzyme systems already present in the normal host cell. . . . Investigations carried out thus far have not detected any biochemical activity by the virus. However, if the assumption is made that the *virus* simply stimulates its own production by the host cell, it would appear that it is a very inefficient parasite—*Weiss*⟩

**germane** *relevant, pertinent, material, apposite, applicable, apropos

*Ana* appropriate, fitting, apt, happy, felicitous (see FIT): akin, analogous, comparable, parallel (see LIKE): *related, allied, cognate, kindred

*Ant* foreign  —*Con* alien, extraneous, *extrinsic: incongruous, *inconsonant, incompatible

**germicidal** antiseptic, bactericidal, disinfectant (see under ANTISEPTIC *n*)

**germicide** bacteride, *antiseptic, disinfectant

**gesticulation** *gesture

**gesture** *n*  Gesture, gesticulation are comparable when meaning an expressive movement or motion of the body or limbs or the use of such a movement or motion. **Gesture** is the more inclusive term; it may imply any such movement or motion intended to express what words cannot, or to increase the effectiveness or poignancy of words that are being uttered, or to take the place of words when for some reason or other they are unnecessary or impossible ⟨the right [hand of Niobe] is drawing up her daughter to her; and with that instinctive *gesture* . . . is encouraging the child to believe that it can give security—*Shelley*⟩ ⟨he had permitted himself his very first and last *gesture* in all these days, raising a hard-clenched fist above his head—*Conrad*⟩ ⟨the *gesture* with which he threw away the cigar-end struck her as very distinguished—*Bennett*⟩ **Gesticulation**, on the other hand, is applicable only when there is implication of unrestrained excitement, or the loss or absence of grace or dignity, or a determined effort to attract attention ⟨his human figures are sometimes "o'erinformed" with . . . feeling. Their actions have too much *gesticulation—Hazlitt*⟩ ⟨making various savage *gesticulations—Livingstone*⟩ ⟨the nineteenth-century reaction against post-Raphaelite painting . . . the twentieth-century exclusive zeal for purely formal elements in pictures, both reflect our lack of sympathy with *gesticulation*—the word itself is pejorative—*Chandler*⟩

**get**  1 Get, obtain, procure, secure, acquire, gain, win are comparable and often interchangeable when they mean to come into possession of. **Get** is very general in its meaning and simple and familiar in its use. Thus, one may *get* something by fetching ⟨*get* a book from the table⟩, by extracting ⟨*get* gold from ore⟩, by receiving ⟨*get* a present⟩, or as a return ⟨*get* interest on a loan⟩ **Obtain** is likewise rather general. It may suggest that the thing sought has been long desired or that it has come into possession only after the expenditure of considerable effort or the lapse of considerable time ⟨the satisfaction *obtained* by the sentiment of communion with others, of the breaking down of barriers—*Dewey*⟩ ⟨in western New York, where her early education was *obtained*—*Knott*⟩ **Procure** is likely to suggest planning and contriving over a period of time and the use of unspecified or sometimes questionable means ⟨the Duma laid claim to full power . . . and on March 15 *procured* the abdication of the frightened and despondent Nicholas II—*Ogg & Zink*⟩ ⟨some gifted spirit on our side *procured* (probably by larceny) a length of mine fuse—*H. G. Wells*⟩ **Secure** may suggest safe lasting possession or control ⟨the large income and fortune which a prospering business *secures* for him is of his own making—*Hobson*⟩ or it may suggest the gaining of what is hard to come by (as by reason of rarity or competition for possession); thus, one *secures*, rather than *gets* or *acquires*, a rare stamp by offering a higher price than other interested persons will pay ⟨almost absolute safety against infection could be *secured* by the simple precaution of using safe, potable water—*Heiser*⟩ **Acquire** may suggest devious acquisition ⟨the destruction of that ship by a Confederate cruiser, although it had *acquired* a British registry in order to avoid capture —*Knott*⟩ It may also indicate continued, sustained, or cumulative acquisition ⟨the habit of any virtue, moral or intellectual, cannot be assumed at once, but must be *acquired* by practice—*Grandgent*⟩ **Gain** often implies competition in acquiring something of value ⟨if a London merchant, however, can buy at Canton for half an ounce of silver, a commodity which he can afterwards sell at London for an ounce, he *gains* a hundred percent—*Smith*⟩ ⟨few men are placed in such fortunate circumstances as

A colon (:) separates groups of words discriminated. An asterisk (*) indicates place of treatment of each group.

to be able to *gain* office—*Oliver*⟩ **Win,** though often interchangeable with *gain,* may suggest, as *gain* does not, favorable qualities leading naturally to the acquisition of something desired despite competition or obstacles ⟨the errors of his time were connected with his labors to remedy them, and *win* a firmer knowledge than dialectic could supply—*H. O. Taylor*⟩ ⟨Mrs. Woolf's fiction is too negligent of the requirements of the common reader to *win* a wide following—*Millett*⟩
*Ana* fetch, *bring: extract, elicit, extort, *educe, evoke: *receive, accept: seize, *take, grasp, grab, clutch: effect, accomplish, achieve (see PERFORM): *incur, contract, catch
*Con* *forgo, eschew, abnegate, sacrifice, forbear
**2** beget, procreate, sire, *generate, engender, breed, propagate, reproduce
*Ana* see those at BEGET
**3** *induce, persuade, prevail
*Ana* *move, actuate, drive, impel: *incite, instigate, abet

**ghastly, grisly, gruesome, macabre, grim, lurid** are comparable when they mean horrifying and repellent in appearance or aspect. **Ghastly** suggests the terrifying aspects of death or bloodshed ⟨the dying man's *ghastly* pallor⟩ ⟨death grinned horrible a *ghastly* smile—*Milton*⟩ ⟨the image of a hideous—of a *ghastly* thing—of the gallows!—*Poe*⟩ The term also is used as a strong intensive equivalent to *hideous* or *horrifying* ⟨the growing conviction that the defeat was the result of a *ghastly* and unnecessary blunder⟩ ⟨detail is heaped upon *ghastly* detail with a kind of stolid objectivity until the cumulative picture is one of madness and chaos—*Edmund Fuller*⟩ **Grisly** and **gruesome** imply an appearance that inspires shuddering or uncanny horror ⟨so spake the *grisly* Terror—*Milton*⟩ ⟨look down, and see a *grisly* sight; a vault where the bodies are buried upright!—*Wordsworth*⟩ ⟨the thick 566-page text is literally horrible. It is filled with *gruesome* details of murder and torture—*Bliven b. 1916*⟩ ⟨many readers find Keats's *Isabella* too *gruesome* for enjoyment⟩ **Macabre** may imply marked or excessive preoccupation with the horrors especially of death ⟨a *macabre* tale⟩ ⟨weirdly masked, *macabre* figures that in time became . . . the hallmark of his painting—*Coates*⟩ or it may come close to *ghastly* in its implication of a hideous or horrifying quality ⟨in a *macabre* climax, a substantial portion of Berlin was blown up by the Germans themselves—*Wechsberg*⟩ **Grim** suggests a fierce and forbidding aspect ⟨so should a murderer look, so dead, so *grim*—*Shak.*⟩ ⟨with countenance *grim* glared on him passing—*Milton*⟩ ⟨an unused, airless attic, a place the reader soon begins to think of as no less *grim* than a chamber of horrors—*Stern*⟩ ⟨the *grim* hows and not the difficult whys of battle—*McCarten*⟩ **Lurid** comes into comparison with *ghastly* as referring to light or color; it suggests either a ghastly pallor or coloring reminiscent of death ⟨death . . . pale as yonder wan and horned moon, with lips of *lurid* blue—*Shelley*⟩ or more frequently a sinister and murky glow ⟨he caught the color of what was passing about him but mixed with the *lurid* and portentous hue—*Hawthorne*⟩ ⟨no *lurid* fire of hell or human passion illumines their scenes—*Eliot*⟩ Sometimes *lurid* differs little from *gruesome* except, possibly, in its stronger suggestion of sensationalism ⟨reporters who like to give all the *lurid* details of a catastrophe⟩ ⟨the detective story may be described as *lurid* rather than as mysterious⟩
*Ana* deathly, *deadly: frightful, horrible, horrific, dreadful, *fearful, appalling: repellent, *repugnant: repulsive, revolting, loathsome, *offensive

**ghost** spirit, specter, shade, *apparition, phantasm, phantom, wraith, revenant

**giant** *adj* *huge, vast, immense, enormous, elephantine, mammoth, gigantic, gigantean, colossal, gargantuan, Herculean, cyclopean, titanic, Brobdingnagian

**gibber** *vb* prate, chatter, *chat, gab, patter, prattle, babble, gabble, jabber

**gibberish, mummery, hocus-pocus, abracadabra** are comparable as terms of contempt applied to something which is in itself unintelligible or meaningless to the person concerned. They are often used interchangeably but are not true synonyms. **Gibberish** suggests language; it is applied especially to inarticulate but expressive sounds or attempts at speech ⟨a baby's *gibberish*⟩ When applied to articulate but unintelligible utterance it may imply a low-grade or disordered intelligence in the speaker, or it may suggest *jargon.* One or more of these implications is carried over when the word is used to express contempt ⟨I have often warned you not to talk the court *gibberish* to me—*Fielding*⟩ ⟨I've endured just about enough *gibberish* about the modern woman, how she complicates her life, has sacrificed her femininity and competes in a man's world —*McAuliffe*⟩ **Mummery** suggests not language but actions uninterpreted by words (as in the old dumb shows). As a term of derogation, however, it is applied chiefly to rites, proceedings, and performances which, whether or not accompanied by words, appear theatrical and ridiculous as well as meaningless to the observer ⟨it was hardly worthwhile for a Protestant to have stripped off the *mummeries* of Rome in order to fall a victim to an agile young man in a ten-foot mask—*Graves*⟩ ⟨the *mummery* and ceremonial of modern life—*W. P. Webb*⟩ **Hocuspocus** suggests jugglery and incantations. Sometimes, in its extended use, the stress is placed upon tricks intended to mystify or confuse, sometimes upon empty but impressive-sounding words ⟨the potency of movies depends upon the quality of their dramatic articulation, not upon the working of *hocus-pocus* on the eyes—*Crowther*⟩ ⟨denounced dialectics—that curious heritage from Hegelian philosophy which Marx adopted and adapted for his own thought—as meaningless *hocus-pocus*—*A. G. Meyer*⟩ **Abracadabra** basically applies to a magical formula or a mystical figure and in extended use is applied chiefly to discourse and implies not only its unintelligibility and formulism but its complete unfitness for the ends it proposes to achieve ⟨psychology is either true knowledge concerning the spiritual nature of man' or it is moonshine and *abracadabra*—*Murry*⟩

**gibe** *vb* *scoff, jeer, sneer, flout, gird, fleer
*Ana* *ridicule, deride, mock, taunt, twit, rally

**giddy, dizzy, vertiginous, swimming, dazzled** are comparable when meaning affected by or producing a sensation of being whirled about or around and consequently confused. *Giddy* and *dizzy* are often used interchangeably with one another but **giddy** is sometimes preferred for stressing the mental confusion which results and **dizzy** for emphasizing the physical quality of the sensation ⟨I am *giddy*; expectation whirls me round. The imaginary relish is so sweet that it enchants my sense—*Shak.*⟩ ⟨this universe of astronomical whirligigs makes me a little *giddy*—*L. P. Smith*⟩ ⟨how fearful and *dizzy* 'tis to cast one's eyes so low! The crows and choughs that wing the midway air show scarce so gross as beetles—*Shak.*⟩ ⟨with my heart beating and my head quite *dizzy*—*J. W. Carlyle*⟩ Both *giddy* and *dizzy* are also used in an extended sense implying a lack of balance in persons or in things and, usually, an undue lack of steadiness or seriousness ⟨*giddy* girls⟩ ⟨I got a bifocal slant on this world which was now making me *giddy* with names, dates, legends—*Henry Miller*⟩ ⟨prices rising at a *dizzy* rate⟩ ⟨the *dizzy* multitude—*Milton*⟩ **Vertiginous** retains in its extended uses much of the connotation implicit in its basic relation to *vertigo*; it may come close to *dizzy* in its suggestion of lack of steadfastness and constancy 〈inconstant they are in all their actions, *vertiginous*, restless, unapt to resolve of any business—*Burton*〉 〈his *vertiginous,* and apparently unconscious, changes of subject make heavy going after a few pages—*Corke*〉 or may attribute a dizzying effect to the thing qualified 〈events occur at *vertiginous* speed, whole civilizations are summed up in a few words, and long processes are reduced to a paragraph if not to a sentence—*Krutch*〉 〈the delicious *vertiginous* sense of human destinies hanging by slender threads—*R. W. Brown*〉 or it may stress a confusing effect like that of vertigo 〈that *vertiginous* bewilderment which comes to creatures of mere routine when they face the unfamiliar—*Cohen*〉 〈the reader . . . is inspired with the conviction that of these writers only Austin Dobson, James Russell Lowell, and Miss Godden were really sane, that the rest of them were either actually mendacious or possibly *vertiginous*— *Yale Review*〉 **Swimming** is applied especially to the head, brain, or eyes of a person suffering from dizziness; when so used, it suggests the physical sensations of swift, unimpeded, yet uncontrollable movement 〈my head is *swimming*〉 〈and slowly by his *swimming* eyes was seen a lovely female face—*Byron*〉 〈she yielded, and was borne with *swimming* brain and airy joy, along the mountainside —*Bridges*〉 **Dazzled** applies to the physical, mental, or spiritual vision when overpowered and confused by or as if by a blinding light; it connotes, therefore, an effect suggestive of dizziness but without the sensation of being about to fall 〈the sun's rays tapered into a luminous cone . . . a hypnotizing focal point for *dazzled* eyes—*Beebe*〉 〈one knew that the sun-*dazzled* summer world would soon open about one again—*Edmund Wilson*〉 〈the solicitations of the *dazzled* swains of Cambria for the honor of the two first dances—*Peacock*〉 〈*dazzled* by the prospect of a brilliant future〉

*Ana* whirling, reeling (see REEL): confusing, addling, fuddling, muddling (see CONFUSE): bewildering, distracting, mystifying (see PUZZLE *vb*): frivolous, flighty (see corresponding nouns at LIGHTNESS)

**gift** *n* **1** **Gift, present, gratuity, favor, boon, largess** are comparable when they denote something, often of value but not necessarily material, given freely to another for his benefit or pleasure. **Gift** is the most inclusive term, but it is not interchangeable with some of the others, for apart from the context the term carries no hint of remuneration for something done or received and excludes all suggestion of return〈a birthday *gift*〉 〈a *gift* to a museum〉 〈*gifts* to the poor〉 〈fear the Greeks bearing *gifts*〉 〈every good *gift* and every perfect *gift* is from above—*Jas* 1:17〉 **Present** is ordinarily applied to something tangible which is offered as a compliment or expression of goodwill 〈she used to define a *present,* "That it was a gift to a friend of something he wanted or was fond of, and which could not be easily gotten for money"—*Swift*〉 〈flowers and fruits are always fit *presents*—*Emerson*〉 〈little odd *presents* of game, fruits, perhaps wine—*Lamb*〉 **Gratuity** implies voluntary compensation, usually in money, for some service for which there is no fixed charge or for special attention or service over and beyond what is normally included in a charge 〈he distributed *gratuities* so generously that he received more attention than any other guest of the hotel〉 〈pays five or six dollars for his dinner in a smart Mayfair club and then distributes another dollar or so in *gratuities*—*Joseph*〉 **Favor** applies to something given or granted to another as a token of one's affection, regard, or partiality or as an indulgence or concession. The term is often intentionally vague, especially when

what is given is not a concrete thing 〈he said he did not deserve so many *favors* from his party〉 〈queen's *favors* might be fatal gifts, but they were much more fatal to reject than to accept—*Henry Adams*〉 Concretely the term applies to various small things (as a ribbon, a cockade, or a lady's glove) given to a lover or admirer as a token or to some knickknack or other trifle given to guests (as at a wedding, a dance, or a party). *Favor,* rather than *gift,* is used in requests for something that can be had only from the person addressed 〈ask the *favor* of a prompt reply〉 〈begging the *favor* of a copy of his beautiful book—*Meredith*〉 **Boon** applies to any gift or favor either·as petitioned for or prayed for as something much desired or needed yet not necessarily regarded as a right 〈high emperor, upon my feeble knee I beg this *boon,* with tears not lightly shed —*Shak.*〉 〈if you mean to please any people, you must give them the *boon* which they ask—*Burke*〉 〈I ask justice from you, and no *boon*—*Sheridan*〉 or as given gratuitously and bringing with it such benefits or advantages that it is regarded as a blessing or cause for gratitude 〈our forefathers have given us the *boon* of freedom〉 〈the *boon* of free and unbought justice was a *boon* for all—*J. R. Green*〉 〈Corinth was given certain *boons,* since it was a Julian colony, but Athens . . . was left to academic decay— *Buchan*〉 **Largess** is a somewhat pompous term for a bountiful gift (as of money or of food and drink) or a liberal gratuity; it usually suggests an ostentatious bestowal 〈the newly consecrated king bestowed *largesses* on all the heralds and minstrels〉 〈contrasting his [Anthony's] meager bounty with the *largess* of Octavius—*Buchan*〉 〈dependent for her livelihood on the *largess* of a moody Danish lover—*Jean Stafford*〉

*Ana* *donation, benefaction, contribution, alms

**2** **Gift, faculty, aptitude, genius, talent, knack, bent, turn** are comparable when they mean a special ability or a capacity for a definite kind of activity or achievement. **Gift** applies not only to an ability but also to a quality; it suggests an origin not easily explainable by natural laws and often implies that the recipient is favored by God, by nature, or by fortune. It is, therefore, precisely applied to an innate ability, capacity, or quality, especially to one not commonly found and not possible of acquirement 〈a *gift* of humor〉 〈she has a real *gift* for arranging flowers— *Wharton*〉 〈men have always reverenced prodigious inborn *gifts,* and always will—*Eliot*〉 〈an artist is the sort of artist he is, because he happens to possess certain *gifts*— *Huxley*〉 **Faculty** (see also POWER 2) applies to either an innate or acquired ability or capacity; it does not apart from the context impute an extraordinary value or rarity to that power, but it does usually imply distinction or distinctiveness in its quality and skill or facility in its exercise 〈he had not that *faculty* of extracting the essence from a heap of statements—*Dickens*〉 〈she seemed to have lost her *faculty* of discrimination; her power of easily and graciously keeping everyone in his proper place—*Cather*〉 **Aptitude** usually implies a natural liking and taste for a particular activity or pursuit as well as a native capacity for it and the ability to master its details or technique 〈there are all sorts of people today who write from all sorts of motives other than a genuine *aptitude* for writing —*Ellis*〉 〈at fourteen education should begin to be more or less specialized, according to the tastes and *aptitudes* of the pupil—*Russell*〉 **Genius,** when it applies to ability or capacity rather than to a person who possesses that ability or capacity, suggests an inborn gift of impressive character or a combination of such gifts. Further than this the implications of the term are various and shifting, for the word is tied up in use with psychological, aesthetic, and critical explanations of the nature of genius; however, the

A colon (:) separates groups of words discriminated. An asterisk (*) indicates place of treatment of each group.

word often retains its original implication of a controlling spirit and may denote an inner driving energy which compels utterance or performance, often of a lofty or transcendent quality ⟨the claim to possess a style must be conceded to many writers—Carlyle is one—who take no care to put listeners at their ease, but rely rather on native force of *genius* to shock and astound—*Quiller-Couch*⟩ ⟨in the contemporary novel *genius* is hard to find, talent is abundant—*Brit. Book News*⟩ The word is often employed in current English in the sense of *gift,* usually with a connotation of transcendence or of uniqueness ⟨she made her drawing room a sort of meeting place; she had a *genius* for it—*Woolf*⟩ ⟨Mr. G. K. Chesterton has a *genius* for saying new and surprising things about old subjects—*Huxley*⟩ In ironic use the connotation of transcendence is especially strong, but that of supreme unawareness is also usually evident ⟨he has a *genius* for ineptness of remark⟩ ⟨the *genius* for illogicality of the English people—*Inge*⟩ **Talent** comes very close in its meaning to *gift* when the latter term denotes a native capacity or an innate ability. *Talent,* however, often carries the implication, derived from the Scriptural parable of the servants' use of the talents (pieces of money) entrusted them by their master, that the gift is a trust and that its possessor has an obligation to develop it and put it to profitable use ⟨it is quite probable that many . . . who would make the best doctors are too poor to take the course. This involves a deplorable waste of *talent*—*Russell*⟩ ⟨was he to leave such *talents* lying idle (and that after chafing for eight years to employ them)?—*Belloc*⟩ This basic implication in *talent* has led inevitably to another implication: that the gift is under the control of its possessor because its proper exercise depends on industry and the acquirement of necessary knowledge and skill. *Talent* is sometimes opposed to *genius* in the most exalted sense of that word as a lesser kind of power, capable of development through study and industry, completely under the control of the will, and tending to facile, agreeable, and effective, rather than exalted, performance or utterance ⟨while *talent* gives the notion of power in a man's performance, *genius* gives rather the notion of felicity and perfection in it—*Arnold*⟩ ⟨to achieve conspicuous mundane success in literature, a certain degree of good fortune is almost more important than *genius,* or even than *talent*—*Benson*⟩ **Knack** stresses ease and dexterity in performance, though it usually implies an aptitude ⟨she has, certainly, something of a *knack* at characters—*Burney*⟩ ⟨an uncommon *knack* in Latin verse—*Eliot*⟩ ⟨improvisation was his *knack* and forte; he wrote rapidly and much—sometimes an entire novel in a month—*Van Doren*⟩ **Bent** usually implies a natural inclination or taste; it often carries the same implications as *aptitude* and is sometimes preferred in general use because of technical use of *aptitude* in educational psychology ⟨it doesn't seem to me that you've shown any great *bent* towards a scholastic life—*Archibald Marshall*⟩ ⟨the *bent* thus revealed for precise observation and classification—*Babbitt*⟩ **Turn** not only implies a bent but its actual proof in performance and often suggests skill or proficiency ⟨he had a *turn* for mechanics; had invented a plow in his district, had ordered wheelbarrows from England—*Woolf*⟩ ⟨must possess . . . artistic sensibility and a *turn* for clear thinking—*Clive Bell*⟩

*Ana* endowment, dowry (see corresponding verbs at DOWER): *power, faculty, function: *acquirement, attainment, accomplishment, acquisition

**gigantic, gigantean** *huge, vast, immense, enormous, elephantine, mammoth, giant, colossal, gargantuan, Herculean, cyclopean, titanic, Brobdingnagian

*Ana* prodigious, stupendous, tremendous, *monstrous, monumental

**gingery** fiery, peppery, *spirited, high-spirited, mettlesome, spunky

**gird** *vb* *surround, environ, encircle, circle, encompass, compass, hem, girdle, ring

*Ana* *enclose, envelop, wall: confine, circumscribe, *limit

**gird** *vb* sneer, flout, *scoff, jeer, gibe, fleer

*Ana* deride, mock, taunt, twit, rally, *ridicule

**girdle** *vb* *surround, environ, encircle, circle, encompass, compass, hem, gird, ring

*Ana* see those at GIRD (to surround)

**gist** *substance, purport, burden, core, pith

*Ana* *center, heart, nucleus: import, significance (see IMPORTANCE): theme, topic, *subject

**give, present, donate, bestow, confer, afford** are comparable when meaning to convey something or make something over or available to another as his possession. **Give** is the general term meaning to pass over, deliver, or transmit something which becomes the receiver's to own, to use, to enjoy, or to dispose of ⟨it is more blessed to *give* than to receive—*Acts 20:35*⟩ ⟨*give* my love to your mother and sisters—*Keats*⟩ **Present** is more formal or ceremonious ⟨on Saturday Colonel Bellingham is going to address the lads of the Brigade and *present* them with six drums—*Mackenzie*⟩ ⟨pray, *present* my respects to Lady Scott—*Byron*⟩ **Donate** usually implies publicity attending the giving or a public cause or charity as the recipient of the gift ⟨*donate* a piano to an orphanage⟩ **Bestow** implies the settling of something on one as a gift ⟨large gifts have I *bestowed* on learned clerks—*Shak.*⟩ ⟨what nature wants commodious gold *bestows*—*Pope*⟩ To **confer** is to give graciously or as a favor or honor ⟨the Queen *confers* her titles and degrees—*Pope*⟩ To **afford** is to give or bestow especially as a natural or legitimate consequence of the character of what gives ⟨this fine day *affords* us some hope—*Cowper*⟩ ⟨do the laws of his country *afford* him a remedy?—*John Marshall*⟩

*Ana* award, accord, vouchsafe, *grant, concede: assign, *allot, apportion, allocate: *distribute, dispense, deal, dole

**glacial** arctic, icy, gelid, frigid, freezing, frosty, *cold, cool, chilly

**glad, happy, cheerful, lighthearted, joyful, joyous** are comparable when meaning characterized by or expressing the mood, temper, or state of mind of a person who is pleased or delighted with something or with things in general. **Glad** may be used in opposition to *sorry* to convey polite conventional expressions of pleasure or gratification ⟨I am *glad* to hear of your recovery⟩ ⟨I shall be *glad* to have the opportunity to meet you⟩ It may also be used in opposition to *sad,* and then connotes actual delight and a lift of spirits and sometimes elation ⟨wine that maketh *glad* the heart of man—*Ps 104:15*⟩ ⟨*glad* did I live and gladly die—*Stevenson*⟩ ⟨a child's kiss set on thy sighing lips shall make thee *glad*—*E. B. Browning*⟩ ⟨his entire saintly life was *glad* with an invincible gaiety of spirit—*H. O. Taylor*⟩ **Happy** may also be used in polite conventional phrases in which its content can hardly be distinguished from that of *glad.* In more meaningful use, however, it distinctively implies a sense of contentment and well-being or a realization either of one's good fortune or of the fulfillment of one's desires ⟨he will never be *happy* until he finds work which utilizes all his talents⟩ ⟨with the tension of an unachieved task no longer felt . . . I can say with truth that the last phase of my life has been the *happiest*—*Ellis*⟩ ⟨is my girl *happy,* that I thought hard to leave, and has she tired of weeping as she lies down at eve? —*Housman*⟩ **Cheerful** suggests a strong and, often, a

spontaneous flow of good spirits either as a result of feeling glad or happy or as a result of an equable disposition or of a naturally sanguine temperament ⟨suicidal thoughts . . . could not enter the *cheerful,* sanguine, courageous scheme of life, which was in part natural to her and in part slowly built up—*Ellis*⟩ ⟨time went by as we drank and talked in a world that was rosy, *cheerful,* and full of fellowship and peace on earth—*Hammett*⟩ **Lighthearted** stresses freedom from care, worry, and discontent. Since it also implies high spirits, vivacity, or gaiety, it commonly suggests in addition youth or an easygoing and somewhat volatile temperament ⟨he whistles as he goes, *lighthearted* wretch, cold and yet cheerful—*Cowper*⟩ ⟨why, man, I was *lighthearted* in my prime, I am *lighthearted* now; what would you have?—*Browning*⟩ *Joyful* and *joyous* imply keen gladness or happiness with resulting elation; they are often used as though they were equivalent terms. However, **joyful** usually suggests a mood or an emotional reaction to an event or situation, and it implies rejoicing ⟨in the day of prosperity be *joyful*—*Eccles* 7:14⟩ ⟨and *joyful* nations join in leagues of peace—*Pope*⟩ ⟨a *joyful* countenance⟩ ⟨a bright and happy Christian, a romping optimist who laughed away sin and doubt, a *joyful* puritan—*Sinclair Lewis*⟩ **Joyous,** on the other hand, applies more to something which by its nature or character is filled with joy or is a cause of joy ⟨all that ever was *joyous,* and clear, and fresh, thy music doth surpass—*Shelley*⟩ ⟨the happy and *joyous* temper, which characterizes a fresh and confident faith—*Inge*⟩ ⟨that *joyous* serenity we think belongs to a better world than this—*Sir Winston Churchill*⟩
*Ana* pleased, delighted, gratified, tickled, rejoiced (see PLEASE): blithe, jocund, *merry, jolly, jovial: gleeful, mirthful, hilarious (see corresponding nouns at MIRTH)
*Ant* sad —*Con* depressed, dejected, melancholy (see corresponding nouns at SADNESS)
**gladden** delight, rejoice, *please, gratify, tickle, regale
*Ana* *comfort, console, solace: enliven, animate, *quicken, vivify
*Ant* sadden —*Con* *depress, weigh, oppress: vex, irk, *annoy, bother
**glance** *vb* 1 *brush, graze, shave, skim
*Ana* *slide, slip, glide: touch, contact (see corresponding nouns at CONTACT): dart, *fly
2 glint, *flash, gleam, sparkle, glitter, glisten, scintillate, coruscate, twinkle
**glance** *n* glimpse, peep, peek, *look, sight, view
*Con* scrutiny, examination, inspection (see under SCRUTINIZE): contemplation, studying *or* study, consideration (see corresponding verbs at CONSIDER)
**glare** *vb* 1 glow, flare, *blaze, flame
*Ana* *flash, gleam, glitter, glisten, scintillate, coruscate, sparkle
2 stare, peer, gloat, gape, *gaze
*Ana* glower, lower, scowl, *frown
**glare** *n* flare, glow, blaze, flame (see under BLAZE *vb*)
*Ana* effulgence, refulgence, radiance, brilliance (see corresponding adjectives at BRIGHT): glittering *or* glitter, sparkling *or* sparkle, flashing *or* flash (see FLASH *vb*)
**glaring** *adj* *flagrant, gross, rank
*Ana* *noticeable, conspicuous, outstanding: obtrusive (see IMPERTINENT): extreme, *excessive, inordinate
**glaze** *n* gloss, sheen, *luster
**gleam** *vb* *flash, glance, glint, sparkle, glitter, glisten, scintillate, coruscate, twinkle
**glean** *reap, gather, garner, harvest
*Ana* pick (see CHOOSE): *strip, divest
**glee** *mirth, jollity, hilarity
*Ana* delight, joy, *pleasure, enjoyment, delectation: merriment, jocundity, blitheness, joviality (see corre-

sponding adjectives at MERRY): gladness, happiness, cheerfulness, joyfulness, joyousness (see corresponding adjectives at GLAD)
*Ant* gloom —*Con* *sadness, dejection, depression, melancholy, blues, dumps
**glib** 1 fluent, voluble, *vocal, articulate, eloquent
*Ana* garrulous, loquacious, voluble, *talkative: facile, smooth, effortless, *easy
*Con* hesitant, hesitating (see corresponding nouns at HESITATION): stammering, stuttering (see STAMMER *vb*): deliberate, leisurely (see SLOW)
2 *talkative, loquacious, garrulous, voluble
**glibness** talkativeness, loquacity, garrulity, volubility (see under TALKATIVE)
**glide** *vb* *slide, slip, skid, glissade, slither, coast, toboggan
*Ana* float, *fly, skim, scud, sail, shoot
**glimpse** *n* glance, peep, peek, *look, sight, view
*Con* surveying *or* survey, observing *or* observation, contemplating *or* contemplation (see corresponding verbs at SEE): scrutiny, examination, inspection (see under SCRUTINIZE)
**glint** *vb* glance, gleam, *flash, sparkle, glitter, glisten, scintillate, coruscate, twinkle
**glissade** *vb* glide, *slide, slip, skid, slither, coast, toboggan
**glisten** sparkle, glitter, *flash, gleam, glance, glint, scintillate, coruscate, twinkle
**glitter** *vb* glisten, sparkle, *flash, gleam, glance, glint, scintillate, coruscate, twinkle
**gloat** *gaze, gape, stare, glare, peer
*Con* envy, *covet, grudge, begrudge
**gloom** *vb* lower, glower, *frown, scowl
*Con* *threaten, menace
**gloom** *n* dejection, depression, melancholy, melancholia, *sadness, blues, dumps
*Ana* despondency, forlornness, hopelessness, despair, desperation (see under DESPONDENT)
*Ant* glee —*Con* *mirth, jollity, hilarity: cheerfulness, gladness, happiness, joyousness, joyfulness (see corresponding adjectives at GLAD)
**gloomy** 1 murky, obscure, *dark, dim, dusky
*Ant* brilliant (*with reference to illumination*) —*Con* *bright, effulgent, radiant, luminous: illuminated, illumined, lighted, lightened (see ILLUMINATE)
2 glum, *sullen, morose, saturnine, dour, surly, sulky, crabbed
*Ana* depressed, weighed down, oppressed (see DEPRESS)
*Ant* cheerful —*Con* joyful, joyous, happy, *glad, lighthearted: *merry, blithe, jocund, jovial
**glorify** *dignify, ennoble, honor
*Ana* extol, laud, acclaim (see PRAISE): *exalt, magnify
**glorious** *splendid, resplendent, sublime, superb, gorgeous
*Ana* radiant, brilliant, effulgent, lustrous (see BRIGHT): transcendent, superlative, surpassing, peerless, *supreme: illustrious, renowned, eminent (see FAMOUS)
*Ant* inglorious
**glory** *n* renown, honor, celebrity, *fame, éclat, reputation, repute, notoriety
*Ant* ignominy, shame —*Con* *disgrace, infamy, dishonor, disrepute, opprobrium, obloquy, odium
**gloss** *n* sheen, *luster, glaze
*Ana* sleekness, slickness, glossiness (see corresponding adjectives at SLEEK)
**gloss** *vb* gloze, *palliate, extenuate, whitewash, whiten
*Ana* *disguise, cloak, mask, dissemble, camouflage: rationalize, account, justify, *explain
**gloss** *n* annotation (see under ANNOTATE)
*Ana* commentary, comment, note, *remark, observation
**gloss** *vb* *annotate

---

A colon (:) separates groups of words discriminated. An asterisk (*) indicates place of treatment of each group.

*Ana* interpret, construe, *explain, elucidate, expound, explicate

**glossy** *sleek, slick, velvety, silken, silky, satiny
*Ana* lustrous, *bright, brilliant, lucent, lambent

**glow** *vb* *blaze, flame, flare, glare
*Ana* *burn: kindle, ignite, *light: *illuminate, lighten, illumine

**glow** *n* blaze, flame, flare, glare (see under BLAZE *vb*)
*Ana* brightness, brilliance, radiance, effulgence, luminosity, incandescence (see corresponding adjectives at BRIGHT): fervor, ardor (see PASSION)

**glower** *vb* lower, *frown, scowl, gloom
*Ana* glare, stare (see GAZE): watch, look (see SEE)
*Con* grin, *smile, smirk

**gloze** gloss, whitewash, *palliate, extenuate, whiten
*Ana* condone, *excuse: justify, rationalize, *explain, account: dissemble, cloak, mask, *disguise, camouflage

**glum** gloomy, morose, *sullen, saturnine, dour, surly, sulky, crabbed
*Ana* *silent, taciturn, close-lipped, tight-lipped: depressed, weighed down, oppressed (see DEPRESS): scowling, frowning, lowering, glowering, glooming (see FROWN *vb*)
*Ant* cheerful —*Con* happy, *glad, lighthearted, joyful, joyous

**glut** *vb* gorge, surfeit, sate, cloy, pall, *satiate

**glutton** gourmand, gastronome, bon vivant, gourmet, *epicure

**gluttonous** *voracious, ravenous, ravening, rapacious
*Ana* greedy, *covetous, grasping
*Ant* abstemious —*Con* temperate, *sober: dainty, finicky, fussy, fastidious, *nice

**gnash** *bite, gnaw, champ
*Ana* grind, grate, rasp (see SCRAPE): *strike, smite

**gnaw** *vb* *bite, champ, gnash
*Ana* fret, *abrade: *worry, annoy

**go** *vb* 1 Go, leave, depart, quit, withdraw, retire are comparable when they mean to move out of or away from the place where one is. Of these terms, **go** is the most general and the least explicit in its implications; it often is used merely as the opposite of *come* ⟨he came here yesterday and *went* this morning before I was up⟩ ⟨*go*, baffled coward, lest I run upon thee—*Milton*⟩ ⟨he would not let her *go* before he had obtained her promise to sell him the property⟩ ⟨the men *go* and cut bamboos in the jungle and bring them to the beach—*Frazer*⟩ **Leave** (see also RELINQUISH, LET 2) so strongly implies a separation from someone or something that the verb in this sense is more often used transitively than intransitively; in its intransitive use the term commonly implies a more formal or a more conspicuous act than *go* implies and often requires a statement of the means of going ⟨he plans to *leave* by the noon train⟩ ⟨we shall be sorry to have him *leave*⟩ ⟨Archipenko *left* Russia to enroll at the École des Beaux Arts in Paris —*Current Biog.*⟩ ⟨do not *leave* the place until I return⟩ ⟨her servants always *leave* her after a few days in her employ⟩ **Depart** (see also SWERVE) is rarely transitive except in a few idiomatic phrases ⟨*depart* this life⟩ As an intransitive verb it not only carries a stronger implication of separation from a person, place, or status than *leave* carries, but it is somewhat more formal, especially when it is used as the opposite of *arrive* ⟨*depart* on a trip to Europe⟩ ⟨"You will not leave me yet, Richard?" .... He had no thought of *departing*—*Meredith*⟩ ⟨a goddess of gone days, *departed* long ago—*Millay*⟩ **Quit** (see also STOP 1, BEHAVE 1), like *leave*, is more often transitive than intransitive and carries a strong implication of separation from a person or thing. Unlike *leave*, it stresses a getting free or being rid of what holds, entangles, or burdens, ⟨the distinction [knighthood] . . . had given him a disgust to his business, and to his residence in a small market town; and, *quitting* them both, he had removed with his family—*Austen*⟩ ⟨he *quitted* London to take refuge among the mountains—*Meredith*⟩ ⟨he *quitted* Cambridge in January 1643, before being formally ejected by the Puritans—*Bush*⟩ **Withdraw** stresses more than *quit* a deliberate removal for reasons that seem justifiable to the person concerned or acceptable to the reader; the term therefore seldom carries (as *quit* often carries) a suggestion of cowardice, weakness, or instability; thus, one *quits* a trying job, but one *withdraws* from an insecure position. Frequently *withdraw* implies such a motive as courtesy, a sense of propriety, or a grievance ⟨the women *withdrew* from the room when the men were ready to discuss business⟩ ⟨the visitors *withdrew* when the doctor entered⟩ ⟨the perfect lyric is a poem from which the author has *withdrawn* once he has set it in motion—*Day Lewis*⟩ ⟨a hermit *withdrawn* from a wicked world—*Conrad*⟩ **Retire** is often used interchangeably with *withdraw*, but it is especially appropriate when the removal also implies a renunciation, a permanent relinquishing (as of a position), a retreat, or a recession ⟨*retire* from the world into a monastery⟩ ⟨when he dies or *retires*, a new manager must be found—*Shaw*⟩ ⟨after the Captain's terrible fall . . . which broke him so that he could no longer build railroads, he and his wife *retired* to the house on the hill—*Cather*⟩ Often *retire* carries the specific sense of to withdraw to one's bedroom and to one's bed for the night ⟨*retire* early⟩
*Ana* *escape, decamp, abscond, flee, fly
*Ant* come —*Con* arrive (see COME): *stay, remain, abide
2 *resort, refer, apply, turn
*Con* avoid, shun, elude, evade, *escape

**go** *n* *spell, shift, tour, trick, turn, stint, bout

**goad** *n* spur, incentive, inducement, *motive, spring, impulse
*Ana* impelling *or* impulsion, driving *or* drive (see corresponding verbs at MOVE): urge, lust, passion, *desire
*Ant* curb

**goad** *vb* *urge, egg, exhort, spur, prod, prick, sic
*Ana* drive, impel, *move: coerce, compel, constrain, *force: *incite, instigate: *worry, harass

**goal** objective, object, end, aim, *intention, intent, purpose, design
*Ana* *limit, bound, confine, end, term: aspiration, *ambition

**gob** sailor, seaman, tar, bluejacket, *mariner

**gobbledygook** *nonsense, twaddle, drivel, bunk, balderdash, poppycock, trash, rot, bull

**godless** ungodly, *irreligious, unreligious, nonreligious
*Ana* atheistic, agnostic, infidel (see corresponding nouns at ATHEIST)

**good** *adj* Good, right are comparable when they mean in accordance with one's standard of what is satisfactory. **Good** (as opposed to *bad*) implies full approval or commendation of someone or something in the respect under consideration (as excellence of workmanship, excellence of condition, beneficial properties, competence, agreeableness, purity, or freshness) ⟨and God saw every thing that he had made, and, behold, it was very *good* —*Gen* 1:31⟩ ⟨*good* food⟩ ⟨a *good* light⟩ ⟨a *good* book for children⟩ ⟨*good* news⟩ ⟨a *good* neighbor⟩ ⟨they are very *good* men, the monks, very pious men—*Joyce*⟩ **Good** (as opposed to *poor*) does not imply hearty approval, but it does not suggest dissatisfaction; it implies that the person or thing so described measures up to a point which is regarded as satisfactory or possesses the qualities neces-

sary to a thing of its kind ⟨a *good* crop⟩ ⟨*good* soil⟩ ⟨*good,* but not excellent, work⟩ ⟨the business for the past year was *good*⟩ ⟨a *good* return on an investment⟩ ⟨a *good* play⟩ ⟨the more general history . . . is less *good.* Partly, that is because the sources . . . are too narrow for the weight of the conclusions—*Laski*⟩ ⟨between *good* workmanship and design and that touch of rareness which makes not merely *good* but fine and lovely—*Alexander*⟩ Often the difference in meaning between these two senses of *good* is apparent only in the inflection or through the medium of a context. **Right** (see also CORRECT) often implies that the thing so described is fitting, proper, or appropriate with respect to the circumstances; thus, a book one knows to be *good* may not be the *right* book to give to a person who is unable to understand it; the *right* light for a picture may be quite different from a *good* light for reading ⟨she always does the *right* thing at the *right* time⟩ ⟨the scene in Julius Caesar is *right* because the object of our attention is not the speech of Antony . . . but the effect of his speech upon the mob—*T. S. Eliot*⟩ *Right* may also imply the absence of anything wrong in the person or thing so described ⟨God's in his heaven— all's *right* with the world!—*Browning*⟩ ⟨marry when she has found the *right* chap—*Reid*⟩
*Ant* bad: poor

**good-looking** comely, pretty, bonny, fair, beauteous, pulchritudinous, handsome, *beautiful, lovely
*Ana* attractive, alluring, charming (see under ATTRACT): pleasing, *pleasant, agreeable

**good-natured** *amiable, obliging, complaisant
*Ana* compliant, acquiescent: kindly, *kind: altruistic, benevolent, *charitable
*Ant* contrary —*Con* cross, cranky, touchy, *irascible, choleric, splenetic: glum, morose, gloomy, *sullen, surly, crabbed

**goodness,** virtue, rectitude, morality are comparable and very general terms denoting moral excellence. **Goodness** is the broadest of these terms; it suggests an excellence so deeply established that it is often felt as inherent in or innate rather than acquired or instilled. Of all these terms it is the only one applied to God ⟨the Lord God, merciful and gracious, long-suffering, and abundant in *goodness* and truth—*Exod* 34:6⟩ When applied to persons it usually suggests such appealing qualities as kindness, generosity, helpfulness, and deep sympathy ⟨the need I have of thee thine own *goodness* hath made—*Shak.*⟩ ⟨she has more *goodness* in her little finger than he has in his whole body —*Swift*⟩ ⟨he taught that evil was a transient thing, *goodness* eternal—*Samuel*⟩ **Virtue** (see also EXCELLENCE), though often coupled with *goodness* as its close synonym, is distinguishable as suggesting acquired rather than native moral excellence and, often, a greater consciousness of it as a possession; usually the term implies either close conformity to the moral law or persistent choice of good and persistent rejection of evil ⟨*virtue* is its own reward⟩ ⟨*virtue* may be assailed, but never hurt, surprised by unjust force, but not enthralled—*Milton*⟩ ⟨the highest proof of *virtue* is to possess boundless power without abusing it—*Macaulay*⟩ ⟨*virtue* is not to be considered in the light of mere innocence, or abstaining from harm, but as the exertion of our faculties in doing good—*Bp. Butler*⟩ Since *virtue* often specifically implies chastity or fidelity in marriage, **rectitude** is frequently employed in its place when moral excellence acquired through obedience to the moral law and self-discipline is implied. But *rectitude* differs from *virtue* in often having reference to motives, intentions, and habits and not merely to character, and sometimes also in placing greater stress on such stern qualities as

uprightness, integrity, and probity ⟨no one can question the *rectitude* of his purpose⟩ ⟨for various reasons all having to do with the delicate *rectitude* of his nature, Roderick Anthony . . . was frightened—*Conrad*⟩ ⟨society is, after all, a recreation and a delight, and ought to be sought for with pleasurable motives, not with a consciousness of *rectitude* and justice—*Benson*⟩ All of the preceding words refer directly or indirectly to the moral excellence involved in character. **Morality** may come close to *virtue* and *rectitude* in denoting a quality of character ⟨the will to be good and to do good—that is the simplest definition of what the world has always meant by *morality*—*Read*⟩ In this sense the term often specifically suggests a moral excellence that arises from fidelity to ethical principles as distinguished from one that arises from obedience to the divine law or the moral laws enforced by religious teachings ⟨evil must come upon us headlong, if *morality* tries to get on without religion— *Tennyson*⟩ But *morality,* unlike the other terms, commonly denotes a code of conduct ⟨ethical problems involved in the new *morality*⟩ ⟨a highly erotic people with a strict *morality,* which was always violated, a pious people who sinned with passion—*Fergusson*⟩ ⟨what do we mean by *morality?* Generally we mean those rules of conduct that appeal to people as generally conducive to a decent human life—*Cohen*⟩ From this sense derive applications, on the one hand, to behavior, whether morally excellent in terms of ordinary ethical standards or quite the reverse, that accords with such a code ⟨his behavior constituted a new low in political *morality*⟩ ⟨in Christian love and forgiveness lay some reversal of Saxon *morality,* for instance of the duty of revenge— *H. O. Taylor*⟩ and, on the other hand, to the propriety of behavior as weighed by such a code ⟨the point at issue was the *morality* of Wise's studiedly ambiguous use of the term "a few copies" in connection with the issue of . . . a facsimile edition—*Altick*⟩ ⟨our chief failure in dealing with the Communist revolution in China has been to underestimate the vigor of Chinese moral sentiment . . . and to pay too little attention to the *morality* of our own position in the eyes of the Chinese—*Atlantic Monthly*⟩
*Ana* righteousness, nobility, virtuousness (see corresponding adjectives at MORAL): *honesty, integrity, probity, honor
*Ant* badness, evil

**good sense** see SENSE n 2
**goodwill** *friendship, amity, comity
*Ant* animosity
**gorge** vb surfeit, *satiate, sate, glut, cloy, pall
**gorgeous** resplendent, *splendid, glorious, sublime, superb
*Ana* *luxurious, sumptuous, opulent: *showy, ostentatious, pretentious
**gory** *bloody, sanguinary, sanguine, sanguineous
**gossip** n *report, rumor, hearsay
*Ana* talk, conversation (see corresponding verbs at SPEAK): tattling, blabbing (see GOSSIP vb)
**gossip** vb **Gossip, blab, tattle** mean to disclose something that one would have done better to keep to oneself. To **gossip** is to communicate or exchange in conversation remarks, often uncomplimentary or damaging and of questionable veracity, about the private affairs of others, especially acquaintances or neighbors ⟨*gossip* about the squabbles of the family next door⟩ ⟨Tat always got furious when people *gossiped* about her—*Pinckney*⟩ ⟨must see that none of these reporters get into the Castle, and that nobody from the Castle *gossips* with them— *Buchan*⟩ To **blab** is to disclose something private or secret that has been confided to one or that has come to one's knowledge ⟨if he sees cards and actual money

A colon (:) separates groups of words discriminated. An asterisk (*) indicates place of treatment of each group.

passing, he will be sure to *blab,* and it will be all over the town in no time—*Conrad*⟩ ⟨confessions made to him are . . . rarely *blabbed*—*Morley*⟩ **Tattle** sometimes is more closely akin to *gossip,* sometimes to *blab,* or it may combine the implications of the two. It suggests loose and loquacious gossip, or unsolicited revelation to one having power of discipline or punishment of some trivial misdeed on the part of another, or blabbing gossip that is usually a betrayal of confidence ⟨Mary always *tattled* to the teacher when a classmate threw a spitball⟩ ⟨so that no discovery . . . might be made by any *tattling* amongst the servants—*Hook*⟩

**gourmand**    glutton, gastronome, bon vivant, *epicure, gourmet

**gourmet**    *epicure, bon vivant, gastronome, gourmand, glutton

**govern, rule** are comparable when they mean to exercise power or authority in controlling or directing another or others, often specifically those persons who comprise a state or nation. **Govern** may imply power, whether despotic or constitutional, or authority, whether assumed by force, acquired by inheritance or through election, or granted by due processes of law, but it usually connotes as its end the keeping of the one or ones directed or controlled in a straight course or in smooth operation, where perils are avoided and the good of the individual or of the whole is achieved ⟨parents who cannot *govern* their children⟩ ⟨*govern* one's emotions⟩ ⟨every prince should *govern* as he would desire to be *governed* if he were a subject—*Temple*⟩ ⟨the [Roman] Senate was more than a modern constitutional monarch, reigning and not *governing;* it had a substantial amount of *governing* to its share—*Buchan*⟩ ⟨formulating the principles which should *govern* the creation of proletarian literature—*Glicksberg*⟩ ⟨as Matthew Arnold pointed out . . . educated mankind is *governed* by two passions—one the passion for pure knowledge, the other the passion for being of service or doing good—*Eliot*⟩ **Rule** is not always clearly distinguished from *govern* ⟨the territory is *ruled* by a high commissioner—*Americana Annual*⟩ Often it implies the power to lay down laws which shall determine the action of others or to issue commands which must be obeyed; it therefore commonly suggests the exercise of arbitrary power and is not ordinarily used of one that exercises authority over the people as an elected official ⟨resolved to ruin or to *rule* the state—*Dryden*⟩ ⟨the country is *ruled* but not governed; there is little administration and much lawlessness—*Puckle*⟩ ⟨it's damnable to have to hurt the people we love—but, after all, we can't let our parents *rule* our lives—*Rose Macaulay*⟩
*Ana* *conduct, direct, control, manage: *restrain, curb, inhibit

**grab** *vb*    grasp, clutch, *take, seize, snatch
*Ana* *catch, capture

**grace** *n* **1** *mercy, clemency, lenity, charity
*Ana* kindliness, kindness, benignity, benignancy (see corresponding adjectives at KIND): tenderness, compassionateness, responsiveness (see corresponding adjectives at TENDER): indulgence, forbearance, leniency (see under FORBEARING)
**2** *elegance, dignity
*Ana* loveliness, beautifulness *or* beauty, fairness, comeliness (see corresponding adjectives at BEAUTIFUL): suppleness, litheness, lithesomeness, lissomeness (see corresponding adjectives at SUPPLE): attractiveness, alluringness *or* allurement, charmingness *or* charm (see corresponding adjectives under ATTRACT)

**gracious, cordial, affable, genial, sociable** are used to describe persons or their words or acts who or which are markedly pleasant and easy in social intercourse. **Gracious** implies kindliness and courtesy especially to inferiors. When it carries the latter implication, it more often suggests kindly consideration than condescension ⟨*gracious* to everyone, but known to a very few—*Cather*⟩ ⟨heartened by her *gracious* reception of a nervous bow—*Shaw*⟩ **Cordial** stresses warmth and heartiness ⟨a *cordial* welcome⟩ ⟨a *cordial* handclasp⟩ ⟨be on *cordial* terms⟩ ⟨they gave us a *cordial* reception, and a hearty supper —*Melville*⟩ **Affable** implies approachability and readiness to talk in the person conversed with or addressed; when applied to a social superior, it sometimes connotes condescending familiarity but more often a gracious willingness to be friendly ⟨I don't find . . . that his wealth has made him arrogant and inaccessible; on the contrary, he takes great pains to appear *affable* and gracious—*Smollett*⟩ ⟨his father was an excellent man . . . his son will be just like him—just as *affable* to the poor—*Austen*⟩ ⟨easy of approach and *affable* in conversation. They seldom put on airs—*Maugham*⟩ **Genial** sometimes emphasizes cheerfulness and even joviality. Often, however, it stresses qualities that make for good cheer among companions (as warm human sympathy and a fine sense of humor) ⟨a *genial* host⟩ ⟨he was no fanatic and no ascetic. He was *genial,* social, even convivial—*Goldwin Smith*⟩ **Sociable** implies a genuine liking for the companionship of others and readiness to engage in social intercourse even with strangers or inferiors ⟨was genial and *sociable,* approachable at all times and fond of social intercourse—*Reeves*⟩
*Ana* obliging, complaisant, *amiable: benignant, benign, kindly, *kind: courteous, courtly, chivalrous (see CIVIL)
*Ant* ungracious —*Con* churlish, boorish (see under BOOR): brusque, curt, crusty, blunt, gruff (see BLUFF): surly, crabbed, *sullen

**gradate**    *class, grade, rank, rate, graduate
*Ana* *order, arrange: divide, *separate: classify, *assort, sort: differentiate, discriminate, demarcate, *distinguish

**gradation, shade, nuance** are comparable when they mean the difference or variation between two things that are nearly alike. **Gradation** in the singular implies a small difference or variation of this kind, but the term is used more frequently in the plural, so that it usually implies the successive steps by which a thing passes from one type or kind into something else of a different type or kind; thus, if we take the primary colors of the spectrum as blue, yellow, and red, the *gradations* between these are not the colors green, orange, purple, which are clearly seen, but all of the intermediate colors by which blue gradually passes into green, and green into yellow, and yellow into orange, and so on; therefore the word is often modified by some adjective (as *sensible, apparent, perceptible,* or *imperceptible*) ⟨the *gradations* between prose and verse are fine but perceptible⟩ ⟨by insensible *gradations* shale becomes slate⟩ ⟨by imperceptible *gradations* her love was transformed into pity⟩ **Shade** implies a minute or barely perceptible degree of difference (as in thought, belief, meaning, or position) ⟨every *shade* of religious and political opinion—*Macaulay*⟩ ⟨discover fine *shades* of meaning in synonyms⟩ *Shade* is also often used adverbially in this sense with comparatives of adjectives or adverbs to imply a degree of difference that is barely noticeable ⟨he drew his chair a *shade* nearer⟩ ⟨his second attempt was a *shade* better than his first⟩ **Nuance,** though often interchangeable with *shade,* tends to stress even more the slightness or delicacy of the difference (as between musical tones, tints of color, or feelings) ⟨I . . . think that there is a shade, a *nuance* of expression . . . which does imply this; but, I confess, the only person who can really settle such a question is M.

Renan himself—*Arnold*⟩ ⟨a faint . . . *nuance* of assent in Cousin Lydia's voice seemed to admit the . . . comment —*Mary Austin*⟩ ⟨*nuances* that might have passed unperceived break startlingly upon one's consciousness —*Millan*⟩
*Ana* difference, divergence, distinction (see DISSIMILARITY): variation, modification, change (see under CHANGE *vb*)

**grade** *vb* *class, rank, rate, graduate, gradate
*Ana* *order, arrange: divide, *separate: *assort, sort, classify

**graduate** *vb* *class, grade, rank, rate, gradate
*Ana* *order, arrange: divide, *separate: *distinguish, differentiate, demarcate, discriminate

**grand** *adj* Grand, magnificent, imposing, stately, majestic, august, noble, grandiose are comparable when they mean large, handsome, dignified, and impressive. They vary somewhat in the emphasis which they respectively place on these qualities, and they differ somewhat also in their additional implications and connotations. **Grand** emphasizes magnitude or greatness of dimensions; often, however, it is not physical largeness that is implied, but a spiritual, intellectual, or aesthetic greatness that makes the thing so described preeminent among its kind. It is distinguishable, however, from other words meaning very large (as *big, huge,* and *colossal*) by its implications of handsomeness, dignity, and impressiveness ⟨the *grand* view from the summit⟩ ⟨the *grandest* of Gothic cathedrals⟩ ⟨a *grand* production of Parsifal⟩ ⟨the *grand* style arises in poetry, when a noble nature, poetically gifted, treats with simplicity or with severity a serious subject— *Arnold*⟩ ⟨the castle was considered *grand* by the illiterate; but architects . . . condemned it as a nondescript mixture of styles in the worst possible taste—*Shaw*⟩ **Magnificent** also may or may not imply actual physical largeness, but it always suggests an impressive largeness proportionate to the thing's scale, without sacrifice of dignity or violation of the canons of good taste. The term was originally and is still in historical use applied to certain rulers, notable for their great deeds, the sumptuousness of their way of living, and the munificence of their gifts ⟨Lorenzo de' Medici was known as Lorenzo the *Magnificent*⟩ In current general use it is often applied to ways of living or to the things (as houses, furnishings, clothes, and jewels) that contribute to a sumptuous and handsome way of living ⟨the drawing room, which was a truly *magnificent* apartment—*Bennett*⟩ It is also applicable to many other things which are felt to be superior (as in beauty, elegance, or worth) often as contrasted with what may be described as *plain* or *insignificant* ⟨*magnificent* clothes⟩ ⟨a *magnificent* theme⟩ ⟨so ostentatiously *magnificent* a name as Gabriele d'Annunzio—*Ellis*⟩ ⟨a *magnificent* performance of *Hamlet*⟩ ⟨much of Dryden's unique merit consists in his ability to make . . . the prosaic into the poetic, the trivial into the *magnificent*—*T. S. Eliot*⟩ **Imposing** stresses impressiveness because of size and dignity or sometimes because of magnificence ⟨though tall and heavily built, he was not *imposing*—*Mackenzie*⟩ ⟨it is between the town and the suburb, that midway habitation which fringes every American city, and which is *imposing* òr squalid according to the incomes of suburbanites— *Repplier*⟩ **Stately** usually emphasizes dignity, but there is an almost equal stress placed on handsomeness and impressiveness, and there is often an implication of larger than usual size ⟨*stately* ships under full sail⟩ ⟨solid and *stately* furniture—*Bennett*⟩ ⟨I like to think of the obscure and yet dignified lives that have been lived in these quaint and *stately* chambers—*Benson*⟩ **Majestic** combines the implications of *imposing* and *stately,* but it

adds a strong connotation of solemn grandeur; it is applicable not only to tangible things (as persons, buildings, interiors, and furniture) but also to intangible things or to things that produce an aesthetic effect ⟨his *majestic* personality and striking physical appearance—*Jack*⟩ ⟨twilight combined with the scenery of Egdon Heath to evolve a thing *majestic* without severity, impressive without showiness—*Hardy*⟩ ⟨the clash and fall of empires is a *majestic* theme when it is handled by an imaginative historian—*Bruun*⟩ ⟨the full moon shone high in the blue vault, *majestic,* lonely, benign—*Cather*⟩ **August** implies impressiveness so strongly as to impute to the thing so described a power to inspire awe, veneration, or, in ironic use, abashment and dread. But it also ascribes a lofty or exalted character to whatever it qualifies ⟨so glorious is our nature, so *august*—*Browning*⟩ ⟨how can you look round at these *august* hills, look up at this divine sky . . . and then talk like a literary hack . . .?—*Shaw*⟩ ⟨no assemblage of academic duennas, however *august*—*Montague*⟩ ⟨for in the eternal city . . . a Power *august,* benignant and supreme shall then absolve thee of all farther duties—*Poe*⟩ **Noble** in this relation (see also MORAL) carries no suggestion of a moral quality or of a social status; rather it implies a commanding grandeur or the power to impress the imagination, emotions, or the intellect as incomparably great or excellent ⟨now see that *noble* and most sovereign reason, like sweet bells jangled, out of tune and harsh—*Shak.*⟩ ⟨the Vandals of our isle . . . have burnt to dust a *nobler* pile than ever Roman saw!—*Cowper*⟩ **Grandiose** often implies an almost preposterous pretentiousness or pomposity ⟨the *grandiose* manner of the stage—*Irving*⟩ ⟨the *grandiose* aggressive schizophrenic patient is typically a disorganized self-assertive person whose dominant delusions are those of grandeur—*Cameron*⟩ but it may also be used without derogation to imply a more than usual largeness of plan or scope or a grandeur or majesty exceeding that of life or experience ⟨things painted by a Rubens . . . all better, all more *grandiose* than the life—*Browning*⟩ ⟨tend to make us forget what more *grandiose,* noble, or beautiful character properly belongs to religious constructions—*Arnold*⟩ ⟨contemplating the *grandiose* complexities of the Universe— *Krutch*⟩
*Ana* sumptuous, *luxurious, opulent: sublime, superb, *splendid, gorgeous: monumental, tremendous, stupendous, prodigious (see MONSTROUS)
*Con* *petty, puny, paltry, trivial, trifling, measly

**grandiloquent** magniloquent, *rhetorical, aureate, flowery, euphuistic, bombastic
*Ana* grandiose, imposing (see GRAND): *inflated, turgid, tumid

**grandiose** imposing, stately, *grand, august, magnificent, majestic, noble
*Ana* ostentatious, pretentious, *showy: grandiloquent, magniloquent, *rhetorical

**grant** *vb* **1** Grant, concede, vouchsafe, accord, award denote to give as a favor or as a right. One **grants,** usually to a claimant or a petitioner and often a subordinate, as an act of justice or indulgence, something that is requested or demanded and that could be withheld ⟨the governor *granted* the condemned man a week's respite⟩ ⟨he begged the Lord to *grant* him his prayer⟩ ⟨any political rights which the dominant race might . . . withhold or *grant* at their pleasure—*Taney*⟩ ⟨save . . . every drop of rain the heavens *grant*—*Lord*⟩ One **concedes** something claimed or expected as a right, prerogative, or possession when one yields it with reluctance and, usually, in response to some compelling force in the claim or the claimant ⟨if we mean to conciliate and *concede,* let us see of what nature the

---

A colon (:) separates groups of words discriminated. An asterisk (*) indicates place of treatment of each group.

concession ought to be—*Burke*⟩ ⟨as an instrument of mind-training, and even of liberal education, it [science] seems to me to have a far higher value than is usually *conceded* to it by humanists—*Inge*⟩ ⟨even his harshest critics *concede* him a rocklike integrity—*Time*⟩ One **vouchsafes** something prayed for, begged for, or expected as a courtesy, when one grants it to a person inferior in dignity or station. The word is often found in supplications where it implies humility in the suppliant ⟨*vouchsafe*, O Lord: to keep us this day without sin—*Book of Common Prayer*⟩ Often it is ironical and then usually suggests absurd condescension ⟨he *vouchsafed* no reply to our question⟩ ⟨the occasional answers that Stalin used to *vouchsafe* to inquiries from American correspondents —*Davis*⟩ One **accords** to another something admittedly his due or in keeping with his character or status ⟨he treated bishops with the superficial deference that a sergeant major *accords* to a junior subaltern—*Mackenzie*⟩ ⟨children . . . will readily *accord* to others what others *accord* to them—*Russell*⟩ One **awards** something that is deserved or merited; the word usually implies determination by legal adjudication or by judges in a contest or competition ⟨the plaintiff was *awarded* heavy damages⟩ ⟨*award* a prize for the best story⟩ ⟨his victory was duly acclaimed by Senate and People; he was given the title of Imperator and *awarded* a triumph—*Buchan*⟩ **Ana** bestow, confer, *give, present, donate: *allot, assign, apportion, allocate: cede, yield, surrender, *relinquish
**2 Grant, concede, allow** are comparable when they mean to admit something in question, especially a point or contention of one's opponent in an argument. **Grant** usually implies voluntary acceptance in advance of proof in order to clarify the issues or to center attention on what are regarded as the main issues ⟨I *grant* there is no obvious motive⟩ ⟨let us take his goodwill for *granted*⟩ ⟨the consistency of arithmetic being *granted*, that of projective geometry follows—*Sawyer*⟩ **Concede** implies reluctant acceptance either before or after proofs have been advanced; it usually suggests the strength of the opponent's contention ⟨he was unwilling to *concede* the supremacy of any group⟩ ⟨still less does he *concede* that the British have any claim to the gratitude of the inhabitants—*Michael Clark*⟩ **Allow** implies acceptance, but usually a somewhat qualified acceptance; it often suggests admission on the ground of apparent truth, logical validity, or reasonableness ⟨even Wickham had *allowed* him merit as a brother —*Austen*⟩ ⟨if one *allows* that it is impossible to define God in intelligible terms, then one is *allowing* that it is impossible for a sentence both to be significant and to be about God—*Ayer*⟩ ⟨*allowing* that Harding was her first lover—*S. H. Adams*⟩
**Ana** admit, *acknowledge: *agree, concur, coincide
**grant** *n* *appropriation, subvention, subsidy
**Ana** *donation, benefaction, contribution
**graph** *n* *chart, map
**Ana** plot, scheme, design, *plan: diagram, outline, sketch (see under SKETCH *vb*)
**graph** *vb* chart, map (see under CHART *n*)
**Ana** see those at GRAPH *n*
**graphic, vivid, picturesque, pictorial** are comparable when they mean having or manifesting a quality or character that produces a strong, clear impression, especially a visual impression. All of these words apply particularly but not exclusively to works of art and especially of literature. Something **graphic** has the power to evoke a strikingly clear-cut, lifelike picture; the term categorizes such arts as painting, drawing, engraving, and etching (the *graphic* arts), the object of each of which is to present a picture, but it is also meaningfully applied to a representation of

things in words ⟨a *graphic* description of the face of a young Hindu at the sight of castor oil—*Darwin*⟩ ⟨it is also one of the best-written works on the subject, enlivened by a keen sense of humor and a witty and *graphic* style —*Ullmann*⟩ Something **vivid** is so vigorously alive that it is felt, seen, heard, or otherwise apprehended with a sense of its intense reality. The term may apply to what actually exists and impresses itself with such sharp force on the imagination that the memory retains the sight, sound, or other impression ⟨a *vivid* sensation of fear⟩ ⟨figures so *vivid* that they seem to breathe and speak before us—*L. P. Smith*⟩ ⟨how sights fix themselves upon the mind! For example, the *vivid* green moss—*Woolf*⟩ The term may also apply to a mental state or process of which one is oneself intensely aware ⟨Ripton awoke . . . to the *vivid* consciousness of hunger—*Meredith*⟩ ⟨my sense of right or wrong—of individual responsibility—was more *vivid* than at any other period of my life—*Hudson*⟩ ⟨those for whom the belief in immortality is most *vivid*—*Krutch*⟩ or which defines its content clearly and sharply ⟨a man of wide and *vivid* interests—*Russell*⟩ ⟨a *vivid* realization of approaching danger⟩ ⟨all three had kept a *vivid* . . . recollection . . . of what they had seen—*Wharton*⟩ Frequently the term applies to whatever represents life or one's imaginative conceptions (as a picture, or a play, or a story) or to matters (as style, colors, language, or situations) which are involved in such a representation; then the implication is of a power, either in the representation itself or in the means of representation, to evoke clearly defined pictures and to give a strong sense of their distinct quality and of their living force ⟨moving pictures are only less *vivid* than reflections from a mirror—*Justice Holmes*⟩ ⟨in his odes, with their thunder of place-names, he [Horace] makes *vivid* the territorial immensity of the empire—*Buchan*⟩ Something **picturesque** has, in general, the qualities or the character which one believes essential to a striking or effective picture. The term is applicable to a place, a person, or a building or other construction ⟨a *picturesque* costume⟩ ⟨Scott's Meg Merrilies is a *picturesque* character⟩ ⟨a *picturesque* ruin⟩ as well as to a work of graphic, literary, or plastic art ⟨a *picturesque* landscape⟩ ⟨*picturesque* details⟩ and to a style or manner (as in writing or painting) ⟨the *picturesque* force of his style—*Hawthorne*⟩ and it carries in every use an implication that the thing has been observed and judged with regard for its form, color, atmosphere, striking or unfamiliar detail, or sharp contrasts rather than for qualities which are not perceptible to the eye or that do not draw the eye because they are lacking in distinctness and charm. Sometimes *picturesque* specifically implies a kind of wild, rugged beauty associated with untouched or undisciplined nature or with things being reclaimed by nature ⟨wide prospects of startling beauty, rugged mountains, steep gorges, great falls of water—all the things that are supposed to be *picturesque*—*Benson*⟩ ⟨a venerable family mansion, in a highly *picturesque* state of semidilapidation —*Peacock*⟩ In still other contexts the term implies a charm arising rather from remoteness, strangeness, quaintness, informality, or diversity ⟨though the upper part of Durnover was mainly composed of a curious congeries of barns and farmsteads, there was a less *picturesque* side to the parish—*Hardy*⟩ ⟨the Square is rather *picturesque*, but it's such a poor, poor little thing!—*Bennett*⟩ ⟨the most *picturesque* Mediterranean craft, with colored sails and lazy evolutions—*Brownell*⟩ Something **pictorial** presents or aims to present a vivid picture; thus, the *pictorial* arts are the same as the *graphic* arts, but the emphasis is upon the objective rather than upon the medium; a *pictorial* style of poetry uses words as though they were

colors or pigments by which a vivid representation is produced ⟨she has evidently been very anxious to maintain the tradition of picturesqueness in biography that Strachey founded, and in many places is more than picturesque, is in fact *pictorial—Times Lit. Sup.*⟩ ⟨he made *pictorial* drama out of the most commonplace intimacies of French bourgeois home life—*Soby*⟩
*Ana* lucid, perspicuous, *clear: clear-cut, *incisive: telling, convincing, compelling, cogent (see VALID)

**grapple** *vb* *wrestle, tussle, scuffle
*Ana* battle, fight, *contend: vie, compete (see RIVAL): oppose, combat, *resist

**grasp** *vb* clutch, grab, seize, *take, snatch
*Ana* *catch, capture: apprehend, *arrest: *apprehend, comprehend

**grasp** *n* *hold, grip, clutch
*Ana* control, *power, sway: comprehension, understanding, appreciation (see corresponding verbs at UNDERSTAND)

**grasping** greedy, avaricious, acquisitive, *covetous
*Ana* rapacious, ravening, ravenous (see VORACIOUS): extorting *or* extortionate (see corresponding verb at EDUCE)

**grate** *vb* *scrape, scratch, rasp, grind
*Ana* *abrade, chafe, gall: harass, annoy, harry (see WORRY): *offend, outrage: exasperate, *irritate

**grateful 1 Grateful, thankful** both mean feeling or expressing one's gratitude. **Grateful** is more commonly employed to express a proper sense of favors received from another person or other persons ⟨a *grateful* child⟩ ⟨a *grateful* recipient of charity⟩ ⟨the Queen herself, *grateful* to Prince Geraint for service done—*Tennyson*⟩ **Thankful** is often employed by preference to express one's acknowledgment of divine favor or of what is vaguely felt to be providential ⟨for what we are about to receive make us truly *thankful*⟩ ⟨it was really the Lord's Day, for he made his creatures happy in it, and their hearts were *thankful—Landor*⟩ ⟨I am endlessly *thankful* that I was among the last persons to see the original Rheims intact—*Ellis*⟩
*Ana* appreciating *or* appreciative, valuing, prizing, cherishing (see corresponding verbs at APPRECIATE): gratified, pleased, delighted (see PLEASE): satisfied, contented (see under SATISFY)
*Ant* ungrateful
**2** agreeable, gratifying, *pleasant, pleasing, welcome
*Ana* comforting, consoling, solacing (see COMFORT *vb*): refreshing, restoring *or* restorative, renewing, rejuvenating (see corresponding verbs at RENEW): delicious, *delightful, delectable
*Ant* obnoxious —*Con* distasteful, abhorrent, *repugnant, repellent

**gratify** *please, delight, rejoice, gladden, tickle, regale
*Ana* content, *satisfy: *indulge, humor, pamper
*Ant* anger: offend, affront (*by inattention*): disappoint (*desires, hopes*)

**gratifying** grateful, agreeable, pleasing, welcome, *pleasant
*Ana* satisfying, contenting (see SATISFY): delighting, rejoicing, gladdening, regaling (see PLEASE)
*Con* distasteful, obnoxious, invidious, repellent, *repugnant: *offensive, revolting

**gratuitous** *supererogatory, uncalled-for, wanton
*Ana* *voluntary, willing: unrecompensed, unremunerated (see corresponding affirmative verbs at PAY): unprovoked, unexcited (see affirmative verbs at PROVOKE): unjustified, unwarranted (see affirmative verbs at JUSTIFY)

**gratuity** *gift, largess, boon, favor, present

**grave** *adj* solemn, somber, sedate, sober, *serious, earnest, staid

*Ana* austere, stern, ascetic, *severe: saturnine, dour (see SULLEN)
*Ant* gay —*Con* light, light-minded, frivolous, flighty, flippant, volatile (see corresponding nouns at LIGHTNESS): *vain, idle, otiose, nugatory, empty, hollow

**graze** *vb* pasture, *feed, nourish

**graze** *vb* *brush, glance, shave, skim
*Ana* touch, contact (see corresponding nouns at CONTACT): *injure, hurt, harm: *deface, disfigure: wound, bruise, contuse (see corresponding nouns at WOUND)

**grease,** *vb* lubricate, anoint, *oil, cream

**great** *large, big
*Ana* enormous, immense, *huge, mammoth: tremendous, prodigious, stupendous, monumental, *monstrous: eminent, illustrious, renowned (see FAMOUS): *supreme, superlative, surpassing, transcendent
*Ant* little —*Con* *small, diminutive: *petty, paltry, puny, trivial, trifling, measly

**greatly** *largely, mostly, chiefly, mainly, principally, generally

**greed** *cupidity, rapacity, avarice
*Ana* greediness, covetousness, avariciousness, acquisitiveness (see corresponding adjectives at COVETOUS): voraciousness, ravenousness, rapaciousness, gluttonousness *or* gluttony (see corresponding adjectives at VORACIOUS)
*Con* prodigality, lavishness, exuberance (see corresponding adjectives at PROFUSE): bountifulness, bounteousness, openhandedness, munificence, generousness *or* generosity, liberality (see corresponding adjectives at LIBERAL)

**greedy** *covetous, acquisitive, grasping, avaricious
*Ana* rapacious, ravening, ravenous, *voracious, gluttonous: *stingy, parsimonious, miserly, close, closefisted
*Con* bountiful, bounteous, openhanded, generous, *liberal, munificent: prodigal, lavish, exuberant, *profuse

**green** *adj* callow, raw, crude, *rude, rough, uncouth
*Ant* experienced: seasoned —*Con* grown-up, ripe, matured, *mature: trained, instructed, educated (see TEACH): *proficient, skilled, skillful

**greet** salute, hail, *address, accost

**greeting, salutation, salute** denote the ceremonial words or acts of one who meets, welcomes, or formally addresses another. **Greeting** is the ordinary term which carries no suggestion of formality and no implication of inferiority in the one who greets or of superiority in the one who is greeted. On the contrary, the term usually suggests friendliness or goodwill or lack of concern for social or official inequalities ⟨O, to what purpose dost thou hoard thy words, that thou return'st no *greeting* to thy friends?— *Shak.*⟩ ⟨why meet we on the bridge of Time to 'change one *greeting* and to part?—*R. F. Burton*⟩ **Salutation** applies to a more or less formal phrase, gesture, or ceremonial act whereby one greets another; specifically it applies to such phrases as the conventional "How do you do" or the familiar "Hello," or to the words of a letter with which the writer first directly addresses his correspondent, or to such acts as a kiss, an embrace, or a bow. **Salute** is the only one of these words that applies only to gestures determined by convention or to ceremonial acts; though it seldom applies to a speech, it may be used when to the gesture or act a word or two is added ⟨waved a *salute* to the friends awaiting his arrival⟩ ⟨the presidential *salute* of twenty-one guns⟩ ⟨the officer returned his subordinate's *salute*⟩ ⟨Sir Austin bent forward, and put his lips to her forehead Carola received the *salute* with the stolidity of a naughty doll—*Meredith*⟩

**gregarious** *social, cooperative, convivial, companionable hospitable

**grief** *sorrow, anguish, woe, heartache, heartbreak

A colon (:) separates groups of words discriminated. An asterisk (*) indicates place of treatment of each group

regret
*Ana* mourning, grieving, sorrowing (see GRIEVE): lamenting *or* lamentation, bewailing, bemoaning, deploring (see corresponding verbs at DEPLORE)
*Con* comforting *or* comfort, solacing *or* solace, consolation (see corresponding verbs at COMFORT)
**grievance** wrong, *injustice, injury
*Ana* hardship, rigor (see DIFFICULTY): *trial, tribulation, affliction, cross
**grieve, mourn, sorrow** mean to feel or express one's sorrow or grief. **Grieve** implies actual mental suffering, whether it is shown outwardly or not; the term often also connotes the concentration of one's mind on one's loss, trouble, or cause of distress ⟨after so many years, she still *grieves* for her dead child⟩ ⟨he *grieved*, like an honest lad, to see his comrade left to face calamity alone—*Meredith*⟩ ⟨my days are passed in work, lest I should *grieve* for her, and undo habits used to earn her praise—*Lowell*⟩ **Mourn** may or may not imply as much sincerity as *grieve* usually implies, but it does suggest a specific cause (as the death of a relative, friend, sovereign, or national hero) and carries a much stronger implication of the outward expression of grief (as in weeping, lamenting, or the wearing of black garments) ⟨we wept after her hearse, and yet we *mourn*—*Shak.*⟩ ⟨fix a period of national *mourning* for a dead sovereign⟩ ⟨grieve for an hour, perhaps, then *mourn* a year and bear about the mockery of woe to midnight dances, and the public show—*Pope*⟩ ⟨*mourn* not for Adonais.—Thou young Dawn turn all thy dew to splendor, for from thee the spirit thou lamentest is not gone—*Shelley*⟩ **Sorrow** may imply grieving or mourning and be used in place of either term when sincere mental distress is implied; in distinctive use, however, it carries a stronger implication of regret or of deep sadness than either of its close synonyms ⟨so send them [Adam and Eve from Eden] forth, though *sorrowing*, yet in peace—*Milton*⟩ ⟨I desire no man to *sorrow* for me—*Hayward*⟩ ⟨heed not the tear that dims this aged eye! . . . . Though I *sorrow*, 'tis for myself, Aline, and not for thee—*Gilbert*⟩
*Ana* suffer, *bear, endure: lament, bemoan, bewail, *deplore: *cry, weep, wail, keen
*Ant* rejoice
**grim** 1 Grim, implacable, relentless, unrelenting, merciless are comparable when they mean so inexorable or obdurate as to repel or bar any effort to move one from one's purpose or course. **Grim** (see also GHASTLY) usually implies tenacity of purpose and stern determination which show themselves outwardly in a forbidding aspect or in a formidable appearance; the term is applicable not only to persons or their words, acts, and looks but to things which reflect or reveal the grimness of persons ⟨*grim* Death⟩ ⟨*grim* necessity⟩ ⟨the Florentines . . . prepared to do *grim* battle for their liberties—*Oliphant*⟩ **Implacable** implies the impossibility of placating, pacifying, or appeasing and is used in reference to men or to higher beings ⟨in friendship false, *implacable* in hate—*Dryden*⟩ ⟨he [an African god] is utterly and absolutely *implacable*; no prayers, no human sacrifices can ever for one moment appease his cold, malignant rage—*L. P. Smith*⟩ However, the term is increasingly used to imply an inflexibly uncompromising character or an incapacity for yielding or making concessions, and, in this sense, it is applicable not only to persons but to things ⟨when the true scholar gets thoroughly to work, his logic is remorseless, his art is *implacable*—*Henry Adams*⟩ ⟨I wanted truth presented to me as it is, arduous and honest and *implacable*—*Ellis*⟩ **Relentless** and **unrelenting** differ mainly in that the former suggests a character and the latter a mood governing action; both imply an absence of pity or of any feeling that would cause

one to relent and to restrain through compassion the fury or violence of one's rage, hatred, hostility, or vengeance ⟨*relentless* critics⟩ ⟨woe to thee, rash and *unrelenting* chief!—*Byron*⟩ Both terms often carry so strong an implication of indefinite duration or of unremitting activity that they are frequently used to describe something which promises not the slightest abatement in severity, violence, or intensity as long as life or strength lasts ⟨*relentless* pursuit⟩ ⟨the *relentless* vigilance of the secret service men⟩ ⟨the *unrelenting* fury of a storm⟩ ⟨with unwearied, unscrupulous and *unrelenting* ambition—*Macaulay*⟩ ⟨everywhere I went in town, the people knew about them, and said nothing . . . . I found this final, closed, *relentless* silence everywhere—*Wolfe*⟩ **Merciless** differs from *relentless* and *unrelenting* mainly in stressing an innate capacity for inflicting cruelty without qualms or an unparalleled fierceness or savagery; otherwise it carries much the same implications ⟨a *merciless* whipping⟩ ⟨harder than any man could be—quite *merciless*—*Cloete*⟩
*Ana* inexorable, obdurate, adamant, *inflexible: inevitable, *certain: *fierce, ferocious, cruel, fell: malignant, malevolent (see MALICIOUS)
*Ant* lenient
2 *ghastly, grisly, gruesome, macabre, lurid
*Ana* *fierce, truculent, savage: repellent, *repugnant: repulsive, revolting, loathsome, *offensive
*Con* benign, benignant, kindly, *kind
**grime** *vb* *soil, dirty, sully, tarnish, foul, befoul, smirch, besmirch, begrime
*Ana* pollute, defile (see CONTAMINATE)
**grin** *vb* *smile, smirk, simper
*Con* scowl, *frown, glower, lower, gloom
**grin** *n* smile, smirk, simper (see under SMILE *vb*)
**grind** *vb* *scrape, scratch, grate, rasp
*Ana* *abrade: sharpen (see corresponding adjective at SHARP): *press, bear, squeeze: gnash, gnaw (see BITE)
**grind** *n* drudgery, toil, travail, labor, *work
*Ana* pains, trouble, exertion, *effort
**grip** *n* *hold, grasp, clutch
*Ana* tenaciousness, toughness, stoutness (see corresponding adjectives at STRONG): *power, force: duress, coercion, restraint, constraint (see FORCE)
**grisly** *ghastly, gruesome, macabre, grim, lurid
*Ana* horrific, *horrible, horrendous, horrid: uncanny, eerie, *weird
**grit** *n* *fortitude, pluck, backbone, guts, sand
*Ana* *courage, resolution, tenacity, mettle, spirit
*Ant* faintheartedness —*Con* timorousness, timidity (see corresponding adjectives at TIMID): vacillation, faltering, wavering, hesitation (see corresponding verbs at HESITATE)
**groan** *vb* moan, *sigh, sob
*Ana* wail, weep, *cry: lament, bemoan, bewail, *deplore
**groan** *n* moan, sigh, sob (see under SIGH *vb*)
**gross** *adj* 1 total, *whole, entire, all
*Ant* net
2 vulgar, *coarse, obscene, ribald
*Ana* fleshly, *carnal, sensual, animal: *material, physical, corporeal: loathsome, *offensive, revolting, repulsive
*Ant* delicate, dainty: ethereal —*Con* spiritual, divine, *holy
3 *flagrant, glaring, rank
*Ana* extreme, *excessive, inordinate, immoderate, exorbitant: *outrageous, atrocious, monstrous, heinous
*Ant* petty —*Con* trivial, trifling, paltry (see PETTY)
**grotesque** bizarre, *fantastic, antic
*Ana* baroque, rococo, flamboyant (see ORNATE): *weird, eerie, uncanny: extravagant, extreme (see EXCESSIVE): preposterous, absurd (see FOOLISH): ludicrous, ridiculous,

comical, comic, droll (see LAUGHABLE)

**ground** *n* **1** *base, basis, foundation, groundwork
*Ana* *background, backdrop
**2** *reason, argument, proof
*Ana* *evidence, testimony: determinant, *cause, antecedent: demonstration, proof, trial, test (see under PROVE)
**3** In plural form **grounds** *deposit, precipitate, sediment, dregs, lees

**ground** *vb* *base, found, bottom, stay, rest
*Ana* establish, fix, settle, *set: *implant: sustain, *support, buttress

**groundless** *baseless, unfounded, unwarranted
*Ana* unsupported, unsustained (see corresponding affirmative verbs at SUPPORT)

**groundwork** foundation, basis, ground, *base
*Ant* superstructure

**group** *n* Group, cluster, bunch, parcel, lot mean a collection or assemblage of persons or of things. **Group** implies some unifying relationship, however tenuous (as a similarity of activity, of purpose, or of nature), and ordinarily a degree of physical closeness ⟨a *group* waiting for the bus⟩ ⟨the *group* of workers unloading the cargo⟩ ⟨a *group* of partisans⟩ ⟨a *group* of soldiers in the picture⟩ ⟨man can only make progress in cooperative *groups*—*Bagehot*⟩ ⟨a *group* of statues in the museum⟩ ⟨a *group* of islands⟩ ⟨an ethnic *group*⟩ **Cluster** basically refers to a group of things (as fruits or flowers) growing closely together ⟨a *cluster* of grapes⟩ ⟨climbing roses producing *clusters* of flowers⟩ In extended use the term may be applied to persons or things that form distinguishable groups and especially smaller groups within larger masses ⟨the people at the reception gathered in *clusters*⟩ ⟨*clusters* of small yachts in the harbor⟩ ⟨cataloging the *clusters* of stars⟩ ⟨Clem Henry's house was in a *cluster* of Negro cabins below Arch's big house—*Caldwell*⟩ **Bunch** (see also BUNDLE) often replaces *cluster* in referring to natural groups of certain edible fruits (as grapes or bananas). In its extended uses it implies a natural or homogeneous association of like persons or things and carries a weaker implication of a common origin or point of growth than *cluster* usually does ⟨Clara is by far the best swimmer of the *bunch*⟩ ⟨a *bunch* of keys⟩ ⟨girls with *bunches* of streamers which they flicked in your face as you passed—*Bennett*⟩ ⟨a piece about a *bunch* of hillbillies in the South, each one almost precisely as crazy and lovable as the next—*Gibbs*⟩ *Parcel* and *lot* refer to a separate or detached collection of persons or things. **Parcel** in this sense (see also PART, BUNDLE) usually carries some implication of disapproval of the thing so grouped ⟨a *parcel* of lies⟩ ⟨became merely a . . . *parcel* of tricks—*Binyon*⟩ ⟨lessons to a *parcel* of young girls thumping out scales with their thick fingers—*Galsworthy*⟩ ⟨a *parcel* of giddy young kids—*Mark Twain*⟩ **Lot** applies to persons or things that are associated or should for one reason or another be thought of or treated as a whole ⟨the auctioneer sold the books in *lots*⟩ ⟨the men in this battalion are an interesting *lot*⟩ ⟨the future generation of scientists will be a sorry *lot* if the best teachers leave the academic circles—*Rabi*⟩ ⟨till you have read a good *lot* of the Fathers—*Keble*⟩ ⟨I could ignore the fuzzy doings on the screen, knowing that if you have slept through one you've slept through the *lot*—*Malcolm*⟩ When the plural is used, the idea of grouping is lost or obscured and the implication of numbers or quantity increases ⟨I have *lots* of time for that⟩ ⟨there were *lots* and *lots* of children there⟩
*Ana* *company, party, band, troop, troupe: *set, circle, coterie, clique: *crowd, mob, horde

**grovel** *wallow, welter
*Ana* *fawn, cringe, cower, toady, truckle: crawl, *creep:

*abase, demean, humble
*Con* soar, mount, ascend, *rise: aspire (see AIM)

**growl** *vb* *bark, bay, howl, snarl, yelp, yap
*Ana* *threaten, menace: *irritate

**grown-up** adult, *mature, matured, ripe, mellow
*Ant* childish: callow

**grub** *vb* *dig, delve, spade, excavate

**grudge** *vb* begrudge, envy, *covet
*Ana* *deny: refuse (see DECLINE)

**grudge** *n* *malice, ill will, malevolence, spite, despite, malignity, malignancy, spleen
*Ana* animus, antipathy, animosity, rancor (see ENMITY): *hate, hatred: grievance, *injustice, injury

**gruesome** macabre, *ghastly, grisly, grim, lurid
*Ana* daunting, appalling, horrifying (see DISMAY *vb*): horrendous, horrific, *horrible: baleful, *sinister

**gruff** crusty, brusque, blunt, curt, *bluff
*Ana* surly, morose, *sullen, saturnine, crabbed, dour: churlish, boorish (see under BOOR): truculent, *fierce
*Con* *suave, urbane, bland, smooth: unctuous, oily, slick, soapy, *fulsome

**guarantee** *n* Guarantee, guaranty, surety, security, bond, bail are comparable when they mean either something that is given or pledged as assurance of one's responsibility (as for the payment of a debt, the fulfillment of a promise or obligation, or the performance of a duty) or the person who accepts such responsibility and gives or pledges something by way of assurance. *Guarantee* and *guaranty* generally imply acceptance and especially contractual acceptance of this responsibility for another in case of his default; they may, however, imply an agreement to ensure for another the possession or enjoyment of a right, privilege, or prerogative. The words may be used interchangeably not only of something given as a pledge or of the person making the pledge but also of the contract or promise accepting the responsibility or obligation. In idiomatic use, however, they are often distinguished, **guarantee** being more often applied to the person and **guaranty** the preferred term for the contract or promise; either word is acceptable as a designation for what is given or pledged ⟨stand *guarantee*⟩ ⟨the small nations begged for *guaranties* against invasion⟩ ⟨his parents gave a *guaranty* for his good behavior⟩ ⟨he even threatened the King of England with interdict, if, as *guarantee* of the treaty, he should enforce its forfeitures—*Milman*⟩ ⟨many laws which it would be vain to ask the Court to overthrow could be shown, easily enough, to transgress a scholastic interpretation of one or another of the great *guaranties* in the Bill of Rights—*Justice Holmes*⟩ *Surety* and *security* stress provision for the protection of a person who is in a position to lose by the default of another. Both words are employable as designating either the person who accepts the responsibility or the money or property turned over to be forfeited in case of default. However, **surety** is the usual term for the person or corporation that serves as guarantee or guarantor for another, and **security** for the money, property, or certificates of ownership turned over to a creditor, beneficiary, or obligee or hypothecated for a loan and forfeitable in the case of one's own or another's default ⟨every employee handling money is obliged to find a *surety*⟩ ⟨a contractor provides a *surety* (as an insurance corporation) for his performance of a job according to the terms of the contract, but he gives *security* to the bank that loans him money to begin the job⟩ ⟨unsecured debts are those for which no *security* has been given to the creditors⟩ Though *guarantee* and *surety* usually imply a legal status and documentary proof of that status, they are also subject to more general use in which no such proof is implied, and they come close to *certainty* or *assurance* in

---

A colon (:) separates groups of words discriminated. An asterisk (*) indicates place of treatment of each group.

meaning ⟨devoted exclusively to clocks, watches, and the telling of time . . . a museum has a virtual *guarantee* of popularity—*Kirby*⟩ ⟨modern men have the additional *surety* of Christ the mediator—*Bush*⟩ **Bond** implies documentary proof of one's acceptance of an obligation and a legally binding promise to repay the holder of that document a sum of money due him on one's own account or in case of the default of another for whom one serves as surety. *Bond,* therefore, is used either of the document which is given as a pledge ⟨government *bonds*⟩ ⟨give a *bond* as proof of one's suretyship⟩ ⟨his word is as good as his *bond*⟩ or for the person or corporation that serves as a legally bound surety ⟨go *bond* for another⟩ ⟨the King of England shall be *bond* for him—*Pepys*⟩ **Bail** implies responsibility for the sure reappearance, at the time prescribed by the court, of a prisoner who has been released from jail pending his trial. The term is applicable to the security given and forfeitable if the prisoner does not return ⟨the court asked $5000 as *bail*⟩ ⟨the prisoner was not released because the *bail* was not forthcoming⟩ or to the person serving as surety and providing the security ⟨sirrah, call in my sons to be my *bail*—*Shak.*⟩ ⟨his *bail* produced him in court at the appointed time⟩ or to the state of being out of prison and in the custody of a surety ⟨admit to *bail*⟩ ⟨be out on *bail*⟩
*Ana* \*pledge, earnest, token: guarantor, surety (see SPONSOR)

**guarantor** surety, \*sponsor, patron, backer, angel
*Ana* \*guarantee

**guaranty** \*guarantee, surety, security, bond, bail
*Ana* \*pledge, earnest, token: \*contract, bargain

**guard** *vb* shield, protect, safeguard, \*defend
*Ana* watch, attend, \*tend, mind: convoy, escort, chaperon, conduct, \*accompany

**guerdon** reward, meed, bounty, award, prize, \*premium, bonus

**guess** *vb* \*conjecture, surmise
*Ana* speculate, \*think, reason: imagine, fancy (see THINK): gather, \*infer, deduce: estimate, reckon (see CALCULATE)

**guess** *n* conjecture, surmise (see under CONJECTURE *vb*)
*Ana* \*hypothesis, theory: belief, \*opinion, view
*Ant* certainty

**guest** \*visitor, caller, visitant

**guide** *vb* Guide, lead, steer, pilot, engineer are comparable when meaning to direct a person or thing in his or its course or to show the way which he or it should follow. Guide usually implies assistance either by means of a person with intimate knowledge of the course or way and of all its difficulties and dangers ⟨some heavenly power *guide* us out of this fearful country—*Shak.*⟩ ⟨how shall I tread . . . the dark descent, and who shall *guide* the way?—*Pope*⟩ ⟨men who *guide* the plough—*Crabbe*⟩ ⟨the teacher, the parent, or the friend can often do much . . . to *guide* the pupil into an enjoyment of thinking—*Eliot*⟩ or by means of something (as a light, the stars, a principle, or a device on a machine) which prevents a person or thing from getting off course or going astray ⟨the fine taste which has *guided* the vast expenditure—*Disraeli*⟩ ⟨a vehement gloomy being, who had quitted the ways of vulgar men, without light to *guide* him on a better way—*Hardy*⟩ **Lead** stresses the idea of going in advance to show the way and, often, to keep those that follow in order or under control ⟨a band *led* each division of the procession⟩ ⟨the flagship *led* the fleet⟩ ⟨he longed . . . to *lead* his men on to victory—*Marryat*⟩ ⟨this influence should rather *lead* than drive—*Eliot*⟩ Often, especially in idiomatic phrases, *lead* implies the taking of the initiative, the giving of example, or the assumption of the role of leader,

director, or guide ⟨he . . . allured to brighter worlds, and *led* the way—*Goldsmith*⟩ ⟨*lead* people astray by giving them a bad example⟩ ⟨*led* the van in solving problems "susceptible of certain knowledge"—*Sellery*⟩ **Steer** stresses the guidance by one able to control the mechanism which determines the course or direction (as of a boat, an automobile, an airplane); it carries a stronger implication of governing or maneuvering than any of the preceding terms ⟨*steer* a ship safely through a narrow channel⟩ ⟨fortune brings in some boats that are not *steered*—*Shak.*⟩ ⟨I eagerly desire to *steer* clear of metaphysics—*Lowes*⟩ ⟨secure in the faith that his reasoned intelligence will *steer* him correctly at all times—*H. N. Maclean*⟩ **Pilot** implies the assistance of a person competent to steer a vessel safely through unknown or difficult waters (as into or out of a port) ⟨*pilot* a vessel through Ambrose Channel into New York harbor⟩ In its extended use it implies guidance over a course where one may easily lose one's way because of its intricacy or may run afoul of various obstacles or dangers ⟨their room steward *piloted* them to the ship's dining room⟩ ⟨we know not where we go, or what sweet dream may *pilot* us through caverns strange and fair of far and pathless passion—*Shelley*⟩ ⟨*piloting* important bills through the Senate—*Current Biog.*⟩ **Engineer** means to lay out and manage the construction of some project (as a tunnel under a river, a highway, or a bridge ⟨a firm of experts was called upon to *engineer* the irrigation project⟩ but in its more common extended sense it means to serve as a manager in carrying through something which requires contrivance and maneuvering ⟨*engineer* a resolution through the House of Representatives⟩ ⟨*engineer* an elaborate fraud⟩ ⟨the corner in grain *engineered* by parties in Chicago—*Gould*⟩ ⟨the coup d'état was *engineered* by high-ranking army officers⟩
*Ana* conduct, convoy, escort, chaperon, \*accompany: direct, manage, control, \*conduct
*Ant* misguide  —*Con* distract, bewilder, perplex, mystify, \*puzzle: mislead, delude, beguile, \*deceive

**guile** *n* duplicity, dissimulation, cunning, \*deceit
*Ana* trickery, double-dealing, chicanery, chicane, \*deception: craft, artifice (see ART)
*Ant* ingenuousness: candor

**guileful** \*sly, cunning, crafty, tricky, foxy, insidious, wily, artful

**guilt** \*blame, culpability, fault
*Ana* sin, crime, \*offense: responsibility, answerability, liability (see corresponding adjectives at RESPONSIBLE)
*Ant* innocence: guiltlessness

**guilty** \*blameworthy, culpable
*Ana* \*responsible, answerable, accountable: indicted, impeached, incriminated (see ACCUSE)
*Ant* innocent

**gulf,** chasm, abysm, abyss basically denote a hollow place of vast width and depth in the earth. *Gulf* and *chasm* suggest a depth which, though vast, is still measurable; *abysm* and *abyss* suggest immeasurable depth. **Gulf** is the most general term and may properly be used of any wide and deep hollow place ⟨slippery cliffs arise close to deep *gulfs*—*Bryant*⟩ In its extended use *gulf* suggests separation by a great, often unbridgeable distance ⟨the broad and deep *gulf* which . . . divides the living from the dead—*Inge*⟩ ⟨a mere physical *gulf* they could bridge . . . but the *gulf* of dislike is impassable and eternal—*Shaw*⟩ **Chasm** adds the implication of a deep and sometimes wide breach in a formerly solid surface ⟨the *chasm* of the Grand Canyon, worn by the Colorado river⟩ ⟨the brink of a precipice, of a *chasm* in the earth over two hundred feet deep, the sides sheer cliffs—*Cather*⟩ In extended use *chasm* still stresses a sharp break in continuity ⟨those *chasms* of momentary indifference and boredom which gape from time to time between even the most ardent lovers— *Huxley*⟩ Abysm and *abyss* may designate the bottomless gulf or cavity of ancient cosmogonies and both have been applied to hell when thought of as a bottomless pit; in other applications they usually connote not only fathomlessness but also darkness and horror. **Abysm** is somewhat old-fashioned ⟨when my good stars . . . have empty left their orbs, and shot their fires into the *abysm* of hell— *Shak.*⟩ ⟨what seest thou else in the dark backward and *abysm* of time?—*Shak.*⟩ Abyss is commoner in general modern use ⟨the *abyss* of Tartarus, fast secured with iron gates—*Thirlwall*⟩ and, like *abysm*, it carries over into its extended uses the notion of vast, immeasurable void ⟨the respectability and prosperity of the propertied and middle classes who grew rich on sweated labor covered an *abyss* of horror—*Shaw*⟩

**gull** *vb* *dupe, befool, trick, hoax, hoodwink, bamboozle
**Ana**. delude, beguile, *deceive, mislead, double-cross, betray

**gullibility** credulity (see under CREDULOUS)
*Ant* astuteness
**gullible** *credulous

*Ana* duped, befooled, hoaxed, hoodwinked (see DUPE): deluded, beguiled, deceived, misled (see DECEIVE): impressionable, susceptible (see SENTIENT)
*Ant* astute

**gumption** *sense, common sense, good sense, judgment, wisdom
*Ana* sagaciousness *or* sagacity, shrewdness, perspicaciousness *or* perspicacity, astuteness (see corresponding adjectives at SHREWD)

**gunman** *assassin, cutthroat, bravo

**gush** *vb* *pour, stream, sluice
*Ana* flow, stream, flood (see corresponding nouns at FLOW): *spring, issue, emanate

**gusto** relish, zest, *taste, palate
*Ana* enjoyment, delight, delectation, *pleasure: enthusiasm, fervor, ardor, *passion, zeal

**gut** 1 *abdomen, belly, stomach, paunch
2 In plural form **guts** grit, pluck, *fortitude, backbone, sand
*Ana* tenacity, resolution, mettle, spirit, *courage

**gymnast** *athlete

**gyrate** rotate, revolve, *turn, spin, whirl, wheel, circle, twirl, eddy, swirl, pirouette

# H

**habit** *n* 1 Habit, habitude, practice, usage, custom, use, wont are comparable when they mean a way of behaving, doing, or proceeding that has become fixed by constant repetition. These words may be used also as collective or abstract nouns denoting habits, usages, or customs, considered as a directing or impelling force. **Habit** refers more often to the way of an individual than to the way of a community or other group; the term applies to a way of behaving (as in acting or thinking) which has become so natural to one through repetition that it is done unconsciously or without premeditation ⟨he has formed the *habit* of fingering a coat button when he speaks in public⟩ ⟨break a bad *habit*⟩ ⟨*habits* acquired very early feel, in later life, just like instincts; they have the same profound grip—*Russell*⟩ ⟨it was her *habit* to write chatty letters to a number of politicians . . . discussing with them the maneuvers of politics—*R. P. Randall*⟩ ⟨we have two opinions: one private . . . and another one—the one we use—which we force ourselves to wear to please Mrs. Grundy, until *habit* makes us comfortable in it—*Mark Twain*⟩ **Habitude** more often suggests an habitual or usual state of mind or attitude than an habitual response to a given stimulus ⟨I think, Pericles, you who are so sincere with me are never quite sincere with others. You have contracted this bad *habitude* from your custom of addressing the people—*Landor*⟩ ⟨the sense of fitness and proportion that comes with years of *habitude* in the practice of an art—*Cardozo*⟩ **Practice** (see also *practice n* under PRACTICE *vb*) applies to a habit which is by its nature an act or a method which is followed regularly and often by choice ⟨it is his *practice* to rise early each morning and take a walk before breakfast⟩ ⟨it is the *practice* of this surgeon to give local anesthetics wherever possible⟩ ⟨the team made a *practice* of leaving their scenarios unfinished until actual production—*Current Biog.*⟩ **Usage** (see also FORM 3) applies mainly to a practice that has been so long continued and has been adopted so generally that it serves to guide or determine the action or choice of others ⟨it is the

*usage* in certain European countries to breakfast on a roll and a cup of coffee⟩ ⟨the . . . inveterate *usages* of our country, growing out of the prejudice of ages—*Burke*⟩ ⟨makes it difficult . . . to earn a living in a business community without yielding to its *usages*—*W. H. Hamilton*⟩ Specifically, in reference to the meanings of words, grammatical constructions, and idiomatic forms where there is a difference of opinion, *usage* implies the long-continued and established practice of the best writers and speakers as the determining factor ⟨all senses of all words are founded upon *usage*, and nothing else—*Paley*⟩ **Custom** applies to a habit, practice, or usage that has come to be associated with an individual or a group by reason of its long continuance, its uniformity of character, and, sometimes, its compulsory nature ⟨it is his *custom* to smoke each evening after dinner⟩ ⟨in contemporary society it is not a fashion that men wear trousers; it is the *custom*—*Sapir*⟩ ⟨is it the *custom* in your church for the minister to greet each member of his congregation?⟩ ⟨it is not the *custom* to speak from the floor before being recognized by the presiding officer⟩ Often *custom* denotes an established practice or usage or the body of established practices and usages of a community or of a people that has the force of unwritten law; thus, the English common law is based upon *custom* rather than upon legislation ⟨the answer, "It is the *custom*," is final for the savage, as for the lady of fashion. There is no other reason why they behave in a certain way—*Inge*⟩ Consequently, *custom* when used as a collective or abstract noun commonly implies a force as strong, as binding, and as difficult to escape as that exerted by those who enforce the law of the land ⟨and *custom* lie upon thee with a weight, heavy as frost, and deep almost as life—*Wordsworth*⟩ **Use** (see also USE *n* 1) commonly denotes an action, manner, rite, or practice that is customary to an individual or a particular group and distinguishes him or it from others ⟨more haste than is his *use*—*Shak.*⟩ ⟨it had been a family *use* . . . to make a point of saving for him anything which he might possibly eat—*Mary*

---

A colon (:) separates groups of words discriminated. An asterisk (*) indicates place of treatment of each group.

*Austin*⟩ ⟨change and turmoil . . . are surface phenomena, while, underneath, life is an affair of *use* and wont and persists substantially unchanged—*Moberly*⟩ **Wont** usually applies to a habitual manner, method, or practice distinguishing an individual or group; it not only differs little from *use* except in its narrower range of application but is often coupled with *use* as a term of equivalent content ⟨the painter followed the religious *use* and *wont* of his time—*Oliphant*⟩ ⟨sad beyond his *wont*—*Tennyson*⟩ ⟨*Renan* . . . begins after the romantic *wont* by an outburst of sympathy and comprehension for the Parthenon and the Athenians and Pallas Athene—*Babbitt*⟩
*Ana* instinct (see under INSTINCTIVE): convention, convenance, usage, *form
2 *physique, build, constitution
*Ana* *body, carcass: *structure, anatomy, framework: figure, *form, shape: *outline, contour

**habitat,** **biotype, range, station** are comparable in their technical biological senses in which they agree in denoting the place in which a particular kind of organism lives or grows. **Habitat** refers especially to the kind of environment (as desert, seacoast, grassland, marsh, or forest) in which a kind of plant or animal is normally found. **Biotype** stresses the uniformity of an environment or habitat type and the consequent uniformity of its living population. **Range** distinctively applies to the geographical extent of a habitat or biotype or to the region in which a plant or animal naturally grows or lives and throughout which it is distributed. **Station** may be used in place of *habitat* or *range,* but it is often restricted to the most typical part or to the one at which a given specimen has been collected.

**habitation,** **dwelling, abode, residence, domicile, home, house** are comparable when they mean the place where one lives. All may apply to an actual structure or part of a structure in which one lives, and all but the last also may apply to the place (as a farm, a village, or a nation) where such a structure is situated. **Habitation** suggests permanency of occupancy and may apply to a building or to an inhabited place ⟨the properties are much smaller than they are in the pastoral region, and the *habitations* are scattered —*P. E. James*⟩ ⟨Shakespeare . . . chose Verona for her *habitation* because of its agreeably sounding name—*Bennett*⟩ ⟨what did it matter where the body found itself so long as the soul had its serene *habitations*—*W. J. Locke*⟩ **Dwelling** typically refers to a building or shelter for a single family or individual, often as opposed to a building used in business ⟨laboriously dug a cave for his *dwelling* and built a floating garden of logs upon which he raised vegetables—*Amer. Guide Series: Me.*⟩ ⟨joy of heav'n, to earth come down; fix in us Thy humble *dwelling,* all Thy faithful mercies crown—*Wesley*⟩ **Abode** may apply to a building, but more often it designates a place as a seat or center of occupancy ⟨the view that other planets may be the *abode* of life⟩ ⟨Tara, the *abode* of the high king of Ireland—*H. O. Taylor*⟩ ⟨her home ever to a certain extent had been an *abode* of the arts—*Osbert Sitwell*⟩ Distinctively, *abode* may stress transience ⟨the traveler reached his night *abode* and was ascending the stairs—*Upton Sinclair*⟩ **Residence** in reference to a building may be somewhat formal and convey a suggestion of dignity and substance ⟨the architects . . . devoting their talents to designing homes for the people as well as *residences* for the rich—*Canadian Jour. of Economics & Political Science*⟩ ⟨the houses are too superior to be called villas; the house agents call them *residences*—*Susan Gillespie*⟩ But *residence* also may refer to an area or place (as a town or state) where one lives and in such use carries specific legal implications (as of actual occupancy or intention to remain) ⟨no one may vote in a given election in more

than one place; and this place must be the voter's legal *residence,* however little of his time he may actually spend there—*Ogg & Ray*⟩ ⟨the term "*residence*" means the place of general abode; the place of general abode of a person means his principal, actual dwelling place in fact, without regard to intent—*U. S. Code*⟩ **Domicile** in reference to a building carries no special connotations ⟨grandfather's *domicile* was considered an architectural curiosity; it was an oversized log cabin with a second story reached by an outside staircase—*Barkley*⟩ In wider reference to a place it may be quite neutral ⟨with the advance of astronomy, the *domicile* of the Deity had been transposed to the unknown center of the universe—*S. F. Mason*⟩ or it may have very definite legal implications (as of being the seat of one's principal and permanent home and therefore the place where one has a settled connection for such important legal purposes as determination of civil status and jurisdiction to impose personal judgments and taxes) in which it is often specifically contrasted with *residence* ⟨the term "*domicile*" has been defined by the courts of one state as follows: "The *domicile* of a person is where he has his permanent home and principal establishment, to which, whenever he is absent, he intends to return—*Ackerman*⟩ ⟨*domicile* is not to be confused with *residence.* It is of a far more permanent nature, as where a man establishes a home in a jurisdiction with the intention of remaining there more or less permanently. The six weeks' *residence* in Reno, with which we are all familiar, does not establish legal *domicile* if the *residence* is solely for the purpose of obtaining a divorce—*Payton*⟩ **Home,** like the foregoing terms, is used either of a structure or a place of residence or sometimes of origin ⟨had lived in New York for years but still thought of Georgia as his *home*⟩ ⟨built a *home* in the new section of town⟩ but of all these terms *home* distinctively conveys the notion of one's dwelling as the seat and center of family life and the focus of domestic affections ⟨without hearts there is no *home*—*Byron*⟩ ⟨some women can make a truer *home* of a shanty than others can of a mansion⟩ Unlike the other terms **house** is not used of a place as distinct from a structure; basically it applies to a building used or intended for use as a dwelling place and, especially as compared with *home,* is a very general and neutral term; thus, a landlord's *house* may become the *home* of a tenant ⟨a speculative builder of *houses*⟩

**habitual** *usual, customary, wonted, accustomed
*Ana* habituated, addicted (see HABITUATE): practiced, drilled (see PRACTICE *vb*): confirmed, *inveterate, chronic, deep-seated, deep-rooted
*Ant* occasional —*Con* *infrequent, sporadic, rare, uncommon

**habituate,** **accustom, addict, inure** mean to make used to something. **Habituate** distinctively implies the formation of habit through repetition ⟨by constant practice she *habituated* herself to accurate observation⟩ ⟨to *habituate* ourselves, therefore, to approve . . . things that are really excellent, is of the highest importance—*Arnold*⟩ ⟨language blunter than the protected executive ears were *habituated* to—*S. H. Adams*⟩ ⟨a generation *habituated* to regard properly inscribed paper as the principal, if not the only, symbol of wealth—*G. W. Johnson*⟩ **Accustom** implies adjustment to something by frequent or prolonged experience or by constant exposure ⟨*accustom* oneself to cold⟩ ⟨*accustom* students to severe criticism⟩ ⟨this opportunity to *accustom* the girl to sea life by a comparatively short trip—*Conrad*⟩ To *accustom* oneself to nagging is to become inured to nagging by another person; to *habituate* oneself to nagging is to form the habit of nagging others. Sometimes *accustom* also connotes reconciliation by

overcoming one's resistance or distaste ⟨gradually *accustomed* his ears to the din of the factory⟩ **Addict,** which is used chiefly in a reflexive construction or in the passive, adds to *habituate* the implication of overindulgence or surrender to inclination ⟨the Japanese as a nation are *addicted* to sight-seeing—*Faubion Bowers*⟩ ⟨*addicted* to study⟩ ⟨he has always . . . been *addicted* to prefacing his poems with quotations and echoing passages from other poets—*Edmund Wilson*⟩ and frequently refers to bad habits ⟨*addicted* to gambling⟩ ⟨a man gross . . . and *addicted* to low company—*Macaulay*⟩ ⟨Hugh tried to protest and to explain that he was not *addicted* to the habit of drinking—*Anderson*⟩ and specifically to compulsive use of habit-forming drugs. **Inure** is a somewhat formal word that is a close synonym of *accustom* ⟨a man *inured* to hard physical labor—*G. W. Johnson*⟩ but distinctively it may suggest a becoming callous or indifferent as a result of repeated exposure ⟨for men's minds have been *inured* to situations of measurable and surmountable danger—*Romulo*⟩ ⟨afraid that reality could not be endured unless the mind had been gradually *inured* to it—*Krutch*⟩
*Ana* train, discipline, school (see TEACH): *harden, season, acclimatize, acclimate: *practice, exercise, drill
**habitude** *habit, practice, usage, custom, use, wont
*Ana* attitude, stand, *position: *state, condition, situation
*Con* *mood, humor, temper: *caprice, whim, freak, vagary
**habitué** *addict, votary, devotee
**hack** *adj* hireling, *mercenary, venal
*Ana* toiling, drudging, grinding, laboring (see corresponding nouns at WORK): hired, employed (see HIRE *vb*): *mean, abject, sordid
**hackneyed** *trite, stereotyped, threadbare, shopworn
*Ana* antiquated, archaic, obsolete, antediluvian, *old: worn, wasted (see HAGGARD): attenuated, diluted (see THIN *vb*)
*Con* fresh, novel, original, *new
**Hadean** chthonian, *infernal, Tartarean, stygian, hellish
**haggard, worn, careworn, pinched, wasted, cadaverous** are comparable when they mean thin and drawn by or as if by worry, fatigue, hunger, or illness. **Haggard** may imply a wild frightening appearance (as of a person driven distraught by fear, anxiety, privation, or suffering) ⟨whose *haggard* eyes flash desperation—*Cowper*⟩ ⟨the strong face to which that *haggard* expression was returning—*Conrad*⟩ ⟨she stood at the door, *haggard* with rage—*Joyce*⟩ but it usually also implies an extreme thinness or gauntness that is normally associated with age but that comes to younger persons who never know physical or mental ease ⟨they grow thin and *haggard* with the constant toil of getting food and warmth—*Anderson*⟩ **Worn** is the more accurate word for the latter sense of *haggard,* for it definitely implies the attrition of flesh characteristic of senility and induced in younger persons by overwork, worry, exhaustion, or prolonged ill health ⟨the President . . . looked somewhat *worn* and anxious, and well he might—*Dickens*⟩ ⟨it was easy to see from their *worn* and anxious faces that it was business of the most pressing importance which had brought them—*Doyle*⟩ **Careworn** differs from *worn* chiefly in its implication of a being overburdened with cares and responsibilities that cause anxiety ⟨the young mother's *careworn* face⟩ ⟨years of heavy responsibility have changed him to an old *careworn* man⟩ ⟨that lean and *careworn* look which misery so soon produces—*Trollope*⟩ **Pinched** and **wasted** suggest the effects of privation or of a wasting disease ⟨*pinched* faces of poorly nourished children⟩ ⟨the *wasted* body of a consumptive⟩ ⟨thought he looked *pinched* and cold—*Carter*⟩ **Cadaverous** is often used in place of *pinched* or *wasted*

when there is the intent to suggest the appearance of a corpse; it usually implies a deathly paleness and an extreme emaciation so that the skeleton is apparent though not visible ⟨he has a *cadaverous* countenance, full of cavities and projections—*Irving*⟩ ⟨for a queer second I did see us all in that . . . mirror . . . *cadaverous,* palsied—*L. P. Smith*⟩
*Ana* gaunt, scrawny, skinny, *lean: fatigued, exhausted, wearied, fagged, jaded (see TIRE *vb*): wan, pallid, ashen, *pale
*Con* *vigorous, lusty, energetic, strenuous
**hail** *vb* salute, greet, *address, accost
**halcyon** *calm, serene, placid, tranquil, peaceful
**hale** *adj* robust, *healthy, sound, wholesome, well
*Ana* lusty, *vigorous: sturdy, stalwart, *strong, stout: spry, *agile
*Ant* infirm —*Con* feeble, frail, fragile, decrepit, *weak
**hale** *vb* haul, *pull, draw, drag, tug, tow
**hall, hallway** *passage, passageway, corridor, gallery, arcade, cloister, aisle, ambulatory
**hallow** *vb* consecrate, dedicate, *devote
*Con* see those at CONSECRATE
**hallucination** *delusion, mirage, illusion
*Ana* *apparition, phantasm, phantom, wraith: fantasy, *fancy, vision, dream, nightmare
**hamper** *vb* **Hamper, trammel, clog, fetter, shackle, manacle, hog-tie** are comparable when meaning to hinder or impede one so that one cannot move, progress, or act freely. To **hamper** is to encumber or embarrass by or as if by an impediment or restraining influence ⟨the long dress *hampered* her freedom of movement⟩ ⟨the view is vigorously urged today that rhyme and meter *hamper* the poet's free expression—*Lowes*⟩ ⟨never . . . had she so desired to be spontaneous and unrestrained; never . . . had she so felt herself *hampered* by her timidity, her self-criticism, her deeply ingrained habit of never letting herself go—*H. G. Wells*⟩ To **trammel** is more specifically to entangle or confine as if enmeshed in a net ⟨people whose speech and behavior were *trammeled* . . . by the usages of polite society—*Gibbs*⟩ ⟨their life was at once dangerously *trammeled* and dangerously free—*Buchan*⟩ To **clog** is to hamper the movement, often the ascent, of someone or something by something extraneous, encumbering, or useless ⟨the wings of birds were *clogged* with ice and snow—*Dryden*⟩ ⟨man is ever *clogged* with his mortality—*Brontë*⟩ ⟨the Cynic preached abstinence from all common ambitions, rank, possessions, power, the things which *clog* man's feet—*Buchan*⟩ To **fetter** is to confine or restrain so that one's freedom or power to progress is lost ⟨I refused to visit Shelley that I might have my own un*fettered* scope —*Keats*⟩ ⟨we reverence tradition, but we will not be *fettered* by it—*Inge*⟩ ⟨watched a world prepare for war while he was *fettered* by the nation's propensity for isolationism—*Kefauver*⟩ To **shackle** and to **manacle** differ little in their extended use, both implying such interference with one's freedom that one feels that movement, progress, or action is impossible if the bonds are not broken ⟨he would not be *shackled* in his reasoning by the rules of logic⟩ ⟨grief too can *manacle* the mind—*Lovelace*⟩ **Hog-tie** usually implies such restraint as effectively interferes with one's ability to move, act, or function ⟨industries *hog-tied* by restrictions on imports of raw materials⟩ ⟨as soon as the senator can get us *hog-tied* to that extent, he will . . . ram these unconstitutional measures down our throats—*Congressional Record*⟩
*Ana* *hinder, impede, obstruct, block, bar: *embarrass, discomfit: baffle, balk, thwart, foil, *frustrate
*Ant* assist (*persons*): expedite (*work, projects*)
**hand** *n* operative, workman, workingman, laborer, crafts-

---

A colon (:) separates groups of words discriminated. An asterisk (*) indicates place of treatment of each group.

man, handicraftsman, mechanic, artisan, roustabout, *worker

**handicap** 1 allowance, *advantage, odds, edge
*Ant* (*for common extended sense*) advantage: asset
2 *disadvantage, detriment, drawback
*Ana* burden, encumbrance, load (see corresponding verbs at BURDEN): disability (see INABILITY): impediment, *obstacle
*Ant* asset

**handicraft** craft, art, *trade, profession

**handicraftsman** craftsman, workman, artisan, mechanic, workingman, laborer, operative, hand, roustabout, *worker

**handle** *vb* 1 Handle, manipulate, wield, swing, ply are comparable when they mean to deal with or manage with or as if with the hands typically in an easy, skillful, or dexterous manner. Handle implies the acquirement of skill sufficient to accomplish one's ends ⟨a child can be taught early to *handle* a spoon, but it takes longer to teach him to *handle* a knife and fork⟩ ⟨tools to be *handled* with care—*T. S. Eliot*⟩ ⟨he knows how to *handle* men so as to get what he wants out of them⟩ ⟨Richelieu sent Charnacé out to *handle* that situation—*Belloc*⟩ Manipulate implies dexterity and adroitness in handling. Especially in its basic use the term suggests mechanical or technical skill ⟨able to *manipulate* the most delicate scientific apparatus⟩ ⟨the kind of courage required for mountaineering, for *manipulating* an airplane, or for managing a small ship in a gale—*Russell*⟩ In its extended sense the term often specifically implies crafty or artful and sometimes fraudulent handling for the attainment of one's own ends ⟨a small group of men by *manipulating* the convention were able to procure the nomination of their candidate⟩ ⟨agencies by which some human beings *manipulate* other human beings for their own advantage—*Dewey*⟩ Wield in its most common sense implies mastery and vigor in the handling of an implement (as a tool or weapon) ⟨he knows how to *wield* an axe⟩ ⟨*wield* a sword⟩ ⟨navvies *wielding* their hammers in the streets—*Ellis*⟩ Wield also may be employed with reference to such an instrument as a writer's pen, an artist's brush, or a king's scepter to imply not the vigorous movement of the implement itself but its effectiveness as a tool in producing a desired result or as a symbol of power; thus, to *wield* a scepter means to exercise sovereign power or to hold sway ⟨of Wu Tao-tzŭ it is said that it seemed as if a god possessed him and *wielded* the brush in his hand—*Binyon*⟩ The term may also take for its object such words as authority, influence, or power when their masterful exercise is implied ⟨a great editorial writer *wields* a tremendous influence over the minds of men⟩ ⟨her newborn power was *wielded* . . . by unprincipled and ambitious men—*De Quincey*⟩ Swing may be used in place of *wield* when a flourishing with a sweep is also suggested ⟨he *swings* his golf club with great effectiveness⟩ In extended and often informal use it may mean to handle successfully, often in spite of great difficulties ⟨can *swing* 20,000 workers behind the Party line—*Arke*⟩ ⟨the corporation was able to *swing* its bond issue⟩ ⟨he could not *swing* the deal⟩ Ply may be used in place of *handle* or *wield* when great diligence or industry are also suggested ⟨go *ply* thy needle; meddle not—*Shak.*⟩ ⟨*plying* patiently the chisel and mallet—*Montague*⟩ ⟨*plied* his oars⟩ The term may also be used when constant and diligent employment (as of a power or faculty or at a trade) is also suggested ⟨the housewife *plied* her own peculiar work—*Wordsworth*⟩ ⟨*plying* his trade as a bookseller⟩
*Ana* *swing, flourish, brandish, shake, wave: *direct, aim, point, level, train, lay
2 *treat, deal

*Ana* manage, control, *conduct, direct
3 *touch, feel, palpate, paw
*Ana* inspect, examine, *scrutinize: try, test (see PROVE)

**handsome** 1 generous, *liberal, bountiful, bounteous, openhanded, munificent
*Ana* lavish, prodigal, *profuse
*Con* niggardly, penurious, *stingy, parsimonious: frugal, economical, *sparing, thrifty: *meager, skimpy, scrimpy
2 *beautiful, pulchritudinous, beauteous, comely, good-looking, lovely, pretty, bonny, fair
*Ana* majestic, stately, august, noble (see GRAND): elegant, exquisite (see CHOICE): smart, modish, fashionable, *stylish

**handy** deft, *dexterous, adroit
*Ana* adept, skillful, skilled, *proficient: *able, capable, competent

**hang** *vb* 1 Hang, suspend, sling, dangle mean to place or be placed so as to be supported at one point or on one side, usually a point or side at the top. Hang typically implies a fastening to an elevated point or line so as to allow motion to what falls from such a point or line ⟨*hang* the washing on a line⟩ ⟨hundreds of plums *hang* from the tree's branches⟩ ⟨*hang* curtains⟩ ⟨carcasses of lamb were *hung* in the butcher's window⟩ ⟨*hang* out a flag from a window⟩ In extended use *hang* often implies a position or a relation suggestive of hanging, such as that of something poised or seemingly poised in the air ⟨a dim, oblong patch of light *hanging* slantwise in the darkness—*O'Flaherty*⟩ ⟨just above its [the poplar's] pointed tip, *hung* the hollow, silver winter moon—*Cather*⟩ or of one thing dependent upon another ⟨a good deal . . . *hangs* on the meaning . . . of this short word—*T. S. Eliot*⟩ or of something clinging or adhering to something else ⟨she *hangs* on his arm⟩ ⟨thereby *hangs* a tale—*Shak.*⟩ ⟨most heavily remorse *hangs* at my heart!—*Shelley*⟩ Suspend is preferred to *hang* (or *hung*) when support from a point above suggests flexibility, free motion or movement, or a display of skill ⟨hams, tongues, and flitches of bacon were *suspended* from the ceiling—*Irving*⟩ ⟨others [of the rebels] were *suspended* from the boughs of the oak—*Keightley*⟩ Suspend is also employed more often than *hang* when a floating in a fluid (as air or water) is suggested (see SUSPENDED) ⟨wasplike flies barred with yellow *suspended* themselves in the air—*Jefferies*⟩ Sling basically implies the use of a sling for hoisting or lowering heavy or bulky articles with ease. Sometimes the term implies a hanging over the shoulder, or arm, or similar support (as for ease in carrying) ⟨*slung* a basket on her arm⟩ ⟨*sling* a scaffold from a roof⟩ Dangle implies a hanging loosely in such a manner as to swing or sway or twist to and fro ⟨*dangled* his cane from a finger⟩ ⟨the children sat on the high wall, their legs *dangling*⟩ ⟨for all might see the bottlenecks still *dangling* at his waist—*Cowper*⟩ In extended use *dangle* usually implies dependence on someone, often a loose dependence or connection, in hope of a reward for attentions or services ⟨she keeps several suitors *dangling*⟩ ⟨*dangling* to them the lures of levity and life—*Beerbohm*⟩
*Ana* *stick, adhere, cling: hover (see FLIT)
2 *depend, hinge, turn

**hanger-on** *parasite, sycophant, leech, sponge, sponger, favorite, toady, lickspittle, bootlicker

**hanker** yearn, pine, *long, hunger, thirst
*Ana* crave, *desire, covet, wish, want: aspire, pant, *aim

**hap** *n* *chance, fortune, luck, accident, hazard
*Ana* *fate, destiny, lot, portion

**haphazard** *random, chance, chancy, casual, desultory, hit-or-miss, happy-go-lucky
*Ana* *accidental, fortuitous, casual
*Con* designed, planned, schemed, plotted (see corre-

sponding verbs under PLAN n): intentional, deliberate, willful, *voluntary

**hapless** *unlucky, disastrous, ill-starred, ill-fated, unfortunate, calamitous, luckless
*Ana* unhappy, infelicitous (see UNFIT): *miserable, wretched

**happen** vb Happen, chance, occur, befall, betide, transpire are comparable when they mean to come to pass or to come about. **Happen** is the ordinary and general term and may imply either obvious causation or seeming accident, either design or an absence of design; in its simplest use the term takes the event, situation, or circumstance as its subject ⟨the incident *happened* two weeks ago⟩ but it may take the impersonal *it* or the anticipatory *there* as its subject ⟨it *happened* that at Dante's time thought was orderly and strong and beautiful—*T. S. Eliot*⟩ ⟨there *happened* to be no visitors that day⟩ In still other phrases *happen* may take a person as the subject, especially when the verb implies a coming upon someone or something, or a coming into a place more or less casually or accidentally, rather than a coming to pass ⟨the miners *happened* upon a vein of gold⟩ ⟨I go nowhere on purpose: I *happen* by—*Frost*⟩ ⟨*happened* on a cottage almost hidden in elm tree boughs—*Times Lit. Sup.*⟩ ⟨*happened* upon a remarkable and neglected volume—*Laird*⟩ ⟨hoping that no wayfarer would *happen* along the lane for the next hour or so—*Conrad*⟩ **Chance** is closer to *happen* in its idiomatic uses than any of the other words, and it too is found occasionally with the event as subject; however, it differs from *happen* in uniformly implying absence of design or apparent lack of causation ⟨if a bird's nest *chance* to be before thee—*Deut 22:6*⟩ ⟨whenever it *chanced* that the feelings of people were roused—*Kinglake*⟩ ⟨things they themselves *chance* to know—*Repplier*⟩ **Occur** in distinctive use carries an implication of presenting itself (as to sight, to consciousness, or to one's thoughts); it is, in general, interchangeable with *happen* only when a definite event or incident or something that actually takes place is the subject ⟨the accident *happened* yesterday⟩ ⟨the bombing raids on the city *occurred* early in the war⟩ ⟨it is necessary for the physicist to arrange the situation so that phenomena shall *occur* in which . . . the underlying simplicity will come to light—*Darrow*⟩ Consequently *occur* is preferable to *happen* in negative expressions when the idea of presentation in the realm of fact is uppermost ⟨a naturalistic optimism which regarded an actual event as . . . of superior value to an event which did not *occur*—*Inge*⟩ ⟨this is possible in theory, but, actually, never seemed to *occur*—*Heiser*⟩ This fundamental implication of presentation to sight or mind allows *occur*, unlike *happen*, to be used to suggest a coming to one's mind ⟨that characters deteriorate in time of need possibly did not *occur* to Henchard—*Hardy*⟩ or a meeting one's eyes or ears (as in print or speech) ⟨the word seldom *occurs* except in poetry⟩ or a turning up or appearing ⟨another instance of this disease may not *occur* for several years⟩ ⟨corundum *occurs* in crystals, masses, and grains⟩ **Befall** and the less common **betide** are used in preference to any of the preceding words, especially in poetry or in literary prose, when there is an implication of a superior power determining events or of the lack of human power to foreknow or forestall them ⟨anxiety lest mischief should *befall* her—*Wordsworth*⟩ ⟨a conscienceless opening of one's hands for all that may *betide* under benign sun or watchful arrowy moon—*Times Lit. Sup.*⟩ ⟨the fate which Beria meted out to so many should now have *befallen* him—*Muggeridge*⟩ **Transpire**, which basically means to give off or escape in the form of a vapor, retains this notion in much of its extended use, in which it implies a leaking out so as to become known or

apparent ⟨it soon *transpired* that there were two . . . conceptions of this problem—*Malik*⟩ ⟨it had just *transpired* that he had left gaming debts behind him—*Austen*⟩ but through a semantic shift the term has developed a value, disapproved by some rigorous purists, in which it is interchangeable with *happen* or *occur* ⟨I gave an honest account of what *transpired*—*Michener*⟩ ⟨all memorable events . . . *transpire* in morning time and in a morning atmosphere—*Thoreau*⟩

**happiness**, felicity, beatitude, blessedness, bliss all denote the enjoyment or pleasurable satisfaction that goes with well-being. **Happiness** is the generic term applicable to almost any state of enjoyment or pleasurable satisfaction especially as based on one's well-being, security, effective accomplishments, or satisfied wishes. **Felicity**, denoting intense happiness is suited chiefly to formal expressions (as of congratulation) or dignified description. **Beatitude** is supreme felicity ⟨to understand by honorable love romance and beauty and *happiness* in the possession of beautiful, refined, delicate, affectionate women—*Shaw*⟩ ⟨I know no one more entitled by unpretending merit, or better prepared by habitual suffering, to receive and enjoy *felicity*—*Austen*⟩ ⟨we may fancy in the happy mother's breast a feeling somewhat akin to that angelic *felicity*, that joy which angels feel in heaven for a sinner repentant—*Thackeray*⟩ ⟨about him all the Sanctities of Heaven stood thick as stars, and from his sight received *beatitude* past utterance—*Milton*⟩ ⟨a sense of deep *beatitude*—a strange sweet foretaste of Nirvana—*Beerbohm*⟩ **Blessedness** implies a feeling of being highly favored, especially by the Supreme Being, and often, a deep joy arising from the purest domestic, benevolent, or religious affections; **bliss** adds to *blessedness* a suggestion of exalted or ecstatic felicity; both *blessedness* and *bliss*, like *beatitude*, often refer to the joys of heaven ⟨thrice blest whose lives are faithful prayers, whose loves in higher love endure; what souls possess themselves so pure, or is there *blessedness* like theirs?—*Tennyson*⟩ ⟨*bliss* was it in that dawn to be alive, but to be young was very Heaven!—*Wordsworth*⟩
*Ana* contentedness *or* content, satisfiedness *or* satisfaction (see participial adjectives at SATISFY): *pleasure, enjoyment, delight, delectation, joy, fruition
*Ant* unhappiness —*Con* despondency, despair, desperation, hopelessness, forlornness (see under DESPONDENT): *distress, misery

**happy** 1 fortunate, *lucky, providential
*Ana* *accidental, incidental, fortuitous, casual: *favorable, auspicious, propitious, benign: opportune, timely (see SEASONABLE)
*Ant* unhappy
2 felicitous, apt, appropriate, fitting, *fit, suitable, meet, proper
*Ana* *effective, efficacious, efficient, effectual: telling, cogent, convincing (see VALID): pat, *seasonable, well-timed: right, *correct, nice
*Ant* unhappy
3 cheerful, *glad, lighthearted, joyful, joyous
*Ana* contented, satisfied (see under SATISFY): gratified, delighted, pleased, gladdened, rejoiced (see PLEASE)
*Ant* unhappy: disconsolate —*Con* depressed, weighed down, oppressed (see DEPRESS): *despondent, despairing, desperate, forlorn, hopeless

**happy-go-lucky** *random, haphazard, hit-or-miss, chance, chancy, casual, desultory

**harangue** n oration, *speech, address, lecture, talk, sermon, homily
*Ana* rant, rodomontade, *bombast

**harass** harry, *worry, annoy, plague, pester, tease, tantalize

---

A colon (:) separates groups of words discriminated. An asterisk (*) indicates place of treatment of each group.

*Ana* \*bait, badger, hound, ride, hector, chivy, heckle: vex, irk, bother (see ANNOY)

*Con* \*comfort, solace, console: \*relieve, assuage, alleviate

**harbinger** \*forerunner, precursor, herald

**harbor** *n* Harbor, haven, port are comparable because they have at one time or another meant a place where ships may ride secure from storms. **Harbor** applies to a portion of a large body of water (as the sea) that is partially or almost wholly enclosed so that ships or boats may enter it for safety from storms or may be anchored or moored there in security ⟨two promontories whose points come near together enclose the *harbor*⟩ ⟨the great natural *harbor* at Sydney, Australia⟩ In extended uses *harbor* carries over the notion of quiet and safety inherent in its basic use ⟨the beauty and the *harbor* of a snug house—*Le Sueur*⟩ **Haven** is chiefly literary or occurs in names of towns and cities where a natural harbor (as a bay, an inlet, or a river mouth) exists and where boats may go for safety during a storm ⟨Milford *Haven* in south Wales⟩ ⟨a blessed *haven* into which convoys could slip from the submarine-infested Atlantic—*Stewart Beach*⟩ More than the other words here considered, it connotes a refuge or place of quiet in the midst of storms ⟨my . . . only *haven* . . . is in the arms of death—*Carlyle*⟩ ⟨the Colony acquired an unsavory reputation for providing a friendly *haven* for pirates—*Amer. Guide Series: R.I.*⟩ **Port** denotes both a place of security for ships and one suitable for landing men or goods ⟨to set me safe ashore in the first *port* where we arrived—*Swift*⟩ Consequently, in extended use, it suggests a destination or goal ⟨me . . . always from *port* withheld, always distressed—*Cowper*⟩ In commercial use *port* applies to a place, sometimes a harbor, sometimes, especially in place-names, a city or town and its harbor, but still more often in the case of the great ports of transatlantic and transpacific shipping all the approaches, all the inlets, all the facilities (as docks, wharves, and offices) involved in the business of loading and unloading ships or of embarking and disembarking passengers ⟨the *ports* of New York, Cherbourg, and Southampton⟩

**harbor** *vb* Harbor, shelter, entertain, lodge, house, board are comparable when they mean to provide a place (as in one's home, quarters, or confines) where someone or something may stay or be kept for a time. **Harbor** usually implies provision of a place of refuge especially for a person or an animal that is evil or hunted or noxious ⟨*harbor* thieves⟩ ⟨cellars that *harbor* rats and cockroaches⟩ ⟨deportation . . . is simply a refusal by the Government to *harbor* persons whom it does not want—*Justice Holmes*⟩ ⟨what good is he? Who else will *harbor* him at his age for the little he can do?—*Frost*⟩ In its extended sense the term suggests the receiving into and cherishing in one's mind of thoughts, wishes, or designs and especially of those that are evil or harmful ⟨nothing is more astonishing to me than that people . . . should be capable of *harboring* such weak superstition—*Pope*⟩ ⟨I did not wish him to know that I had suspected him of *harboring* any sinister designs—*Hudson*⟩ **Shelter**, more often than *harbor*, takes for its subject the place or the thing that affords (as distinguished from the person that supplies) protection or a place of retreat; it also distinctively suggests a threat to one's comfort or safety (as by the elements, by pursuers or attackers, or by a bombardment); the term further suggests, as *harbor* does not, a covering or screening ⟨in such a season born, when scarce a shed could be obtained to *shelter* him or me from the bleak air—*Milton*⟩ ⟨in Craven's Wilds is many a den, to *shelter* persecuted men—*Wordsworth*⟩ ⟨sycamore trees *sheltered* the old place from the north and west—*Gogarty*⟩ ⟨wouldn't you like to *shelter* somebody in danger, or attempt a rescue, or do something

heroic?—*Black*⟩ **Entertain** basically implies the giving of hospitality to a person as a guest at one's table or in one's home. The term often suggests special efforts to provide for his pleasure and comfort ⟨be not forgetful to *entertain* strangers: for thereby some have *entertained* angels unawares—*Heb* 13:2⟩ In its extended sense *entertain*, like *harbor*, implies admission into the mind, and consequent consideration, of ideas, notions, and fears, but unlike *harbor*, apart from the context it carries no connotations of their good or evil, benign or noxious, character, or of any prolonged dwelling upon them, or even of deep and serious consideration ⟨it had been Eudora's idea that jealousy had gone out. It wasn't *entertained* by smart people; it was bourgeois—*Mary Austin*⟩ ⟨no proposal having for its object the readmission of Master Byron to the academy could be *entertained*—*Shaw*⟩ ⟨her brothers and sister privately *entertained* a theory that their mother was rather a simpleton—*Sackville-West*⟩ **Lodge** (see also RESIDE) implies the supplying or affording a habitation, often a temporary habitation; often it suggests provision merely of a place to sleep and carries no implications of feeding or entertaining ⟨Mrs. Brown will *lodge* three of the party for the weekend⟩ ⟨every house was proud to *lodge* a knight—*Dryden*⟩ In the extended use of this sense *lodge* may imply reception as if of a guest or denizen, not only, like *harbor*, into the mind but into anything thought of as a receptacle or as a place where a thing may be deposited or imbedded ⟨the isolated, small family unit of the patriarchal type, with formal authority *lodged* in the father—*Dollard*⟩ ⟨so fair a form *lodged* not a mind so ill—*Shak.*⟩ ⟨a song . . . had *lodged* in his memory like a cork stuck fast from the tide in the cleft of shore rock—*Victor Canning*⟩ **House** usually implies the shelter of a building with a roof and side walls that affords protection from the weather ⟨he could find no place in the village to *house* his family suitably⟩ ⟨the rich man has fed himself, and dressed himself, and *housed* himself as sumptuously as possible—*Shaw*⟩ ⟨*house* gardening implements in a shed⟩ ⟨*house* an art collection in the new library building⟩ House is somewhat rare in extended use, but it usually implies enclosing or confining in a particular place ⟨the universal does not attract us until *housed* in an individual—*Emerson*⟩ ⟨so timorous a soul *housed* in so impressive a body—*Long*⟩ **Board** may mean to provide a person with meals at one's table ⟨we cannot lodge and *board* a dozen or fourteen gentlewomen —*Shak.*⟩ ⟨the question is, will she *board* as well as lodge her guest?—*Clara Morris*⟩ but often it implies provision of both room and meals for compensation ⟨Mrs. Jones *boards* four teachers at her home⟩ ⟨four teachers *board* at Mrs. Jones's⟩

*Ana* foster, cherish, nurture, \*nurse: \*hide, conceal, secrete: protect, shield (see DEFEND)

*Con* \*eject, expel, oust, evict: \*banish, exile, deport: \*exclude, eliminate, shut out

**hard** 1 solid, \*firm

*Ana* compact, dense, \*close: consolidated, compacted, concentrated (see COMPACT *vb*): \*hardened, indurated, callous

*Ant* soft —*Con* fluid, \*liquid: flabby, flaccid, \*limp: pliant, pliable, \*plastic: flexible, \*elastic, supple, resilient, springy

2 Hard, difficult, arduous are comparable when applied to tasks for mind or body to mean demanding great toil or effort in reaching the appointed or the desired end. **Hard** is the simpler, blunter, and more general term; it implies the opposite of all that is implied by *easy*, but usually suggests nothing more specific ⟨a *hard* lesson⟩ ⟨a *hard* job⟩ ⟨a *hard* book to understand⟩ ⟨your easy reading,

Sheridan said, is "damned *hard* writing"—*Montague*⟩ ⟨the American habit of tipping . . . is a *hard* one to break —*Joseph*⟩ **Difficult** commonly implies the presence of obstacles to be surmounted or of complications to be removed; it therefore suggests the necessity for skill, ingenuity, sagacity, or courage ⟨[the tutor] armed for a work too *difficult* for thee; prepared by taste, by learning, and true worth, to form thy son, to strike his genius forth— *Cowper*⟩ ⟨men like fly-fishing, because it is *difficult*; they will not shoot a bird sitting, because it is easy—*Russell*⟩ *Difficult* is more widely applicable than *hard,* because it often means specifically hard to understand because abstruse, intricate, or abstract, or hard to deal with because thorny, knotty, cumbersome, delicate, or exacting ⟨he is a very *difficult* writer—*Inge*⟩ ⟨the *difficult* beauty of many passages . . . of *Winter's Tale* or *Coriolanus*—*Alexander*⟩ ⟨I do not propose . . . to enter upon the *difficult* question of Disestablishment—*T. S. Eliot*⟩ ⟨it was a *difficult* design and had to be executed exactly right—*Roark Bradford*⟩ **Arduous** stresses the need of laborious effort, of persever- ance, and persistent exertion; thus, one may find a task *difficult,* but not *arduous,* because one has no sense of being kept at it against one's inclination; an ascent of a mountain may be *arduous,* but not especially *difficult* ⟨the *arduous* task of formulating legislation necessary to the country's welfare—*Roosevelt*⟩ ⟨determined to save him from a life of *arduous* toil—*Cole*⟩

*Ana* *onerous, burdensome, oppressive, exacting: intri- cate, knotty, complicated, involved, *complex: exhausting, fatiguing, wearying, tiring (see TIRE *vb*)

*Ant* easy  —*Con* facile, light, simple, effortless (see EASY)

**harden** **1 Harden, solidify, indurate, petrify, cake** are comparable when they mean to make or to become physi- cally hard or solid. **Harden** usually expresses an opposi- tion to *soften* and therefore may be as often used of the process as of the effect. The term suggests a change in degree with an approach toward a state of firm consistency or texture, though it need not imply impenetrability or resistance to efforts to break, cut, pierce, or bend ⟨lava as it cools *hardens* into rock⟩ ⟨*harden* candy by chilling it⟩ **Solidify,** although differing little from *harden,* usually expresses an opposition to *liquefy* and places more stress upon the effect produced than upon the process involved; the term, therefore, suggests a change in quality rather than in degree and is more often applied to a mass subject to compacting or consolidation ⟨lava becomes rock when it is *solidified*⟩ ⟨water *solidifies* into ice⟩ **Indurate,** which means to make very hard or very compact, implies usually the making of something that is firm in texture still harder ⟨heat *indurates* clay⟩ ⟨surgeons . . . spend raptures upon perfect specimens of *indurated* veins, distorted joints—*E. B. Browning*⟩ **Petrify** implies a making or becoming stone or stonelike in hardness; the word is used of organic bodies that by a process (called *petrifaction*) of infiltration by water containing mineral deposits (as silica, calcium car- bonate) and the replacement, particle by particle, of the or- ganic matter by the introduced mineral become replaced by stony mineral while the original form is more or less per- fectly retained. **Cake** implies the formation into a firm, hard, or solid mass (as by baking, fusing, or congealing) ⟨[a barrel of gunpowder] had taken water, and the powder was *caked* as hard as a stone—*Defoe*⟩ ⟨the salt had *caked* in the shakers and did not flow⟩

*Ana* *compact, consolidate, concentrate: compress, condense, *contract

*Ant* soften  —*Con* *liquefy, melt

**2 Harden, season, acclimatize, acclimate** denote to make (as a person) proof against hardship, strain, or exposure.

All imply a becoming accustomed or adapted by time or experience. **Harden** implies habituation that toughens one and makes one insensible of one's own pain or discomfort or callous and insensitive to others' misery ⟨*hardened* to the rigors of arctic exploration⟩ ⟨I could . . . hear faint echoes of their grief. It was an experience to which I never became *hardened*—*Heiser*⟩ ⟨its influence did not *harden* him; he has always risen above cynicism—*Triebel*⟩ **Season** implies a gradual bringing into mature, sound, ef- ficient condition; it does not, when referred to persons, necessarily imply that what is to be undergone is uncon- genial ⟨a *seasoned* marathon runner⟩ ⟨a *seasoned* actor⟩ ⟨with much less compass of muscle than his foe, that which he had was more *seasoned*—iron and compact— *Lytton*⟩ **Acclimatize** and **acclimate** imply adaptation to a new and adverse climate or, by extension, to new and strange surroundings in general. Some writers have distinguished *acclimatize* from *acclimate* by restricting the first to adaptation by human agency, but this distinction is not commonly observed ⟨a race . . . well seated in a region, fixed to the soil by agriculture, *acclimatized* by natural selection—*Ripley*⟩ ⟨I have not been long enough at this table to get well *acclimated*—*Holmes*⟩

*Ana* *habituate, accustom, inure: *adapt, adjust, accom- modate

*Ant* soften  —*Con* enervate, emasculate (see UNNERVE): *weaken, debilitate, enfeeble, sap, undermine

**hardened, indurated, callous** mean grown or become hard. These terms are comparable in both literal (compare HARDEN 1) and extended use. **Hardened** is the most inclu- sive because it is applicable to any substance, whether originally fluid or solid, or loose or firm in texture, or elastic or inelastic, that has become solider and firmer and increasingly resistant to efforts to cut, pierce, or bend ⟨*hardened* soap⟩ ⟨*hardened* lava⟩ ⟨*hardened* steel⟩ Consequently, in extended use *hardened* usually implies a fixing or setting with loss of qualities (as flexibility, elasticity, pliancy, susceptibility, and impressionableness) indicative of a capacity for change ⟨*hardened* beliefs⟩ ⟨*hardened* distrust⟩ ⟨a *hardened* criminal⟩ ⟨a *hardened* heart⟩ ⟨a *hardened* little reprobate—*Thackeray*⟩ **In- durated** is common in geological and in medical use with the implication of an increase of hardness or compactness usually in something already firm or hard and sometimes to the point of abnormality ⟨*indurated* clay⟩ ⟨*indurated* sandstone⟩ ⟨an *indurated* abscess⟩ In its extended use it usually stresses abnormal or excessive hardness or stoni- ness that repels all efforts to penetrate or to soften ⟨*indu- rated* stoic as I am—*Adams*⟩ ⟨her husband's *indurated* conscience—*Henry James*⟩ **Callous,** in its earliest and still common sense, implies a hardening and thickening of the skin by constant pressure or friction and a conse- quent loss of sensibility in the part affected ⟨a *callous* spot on the sole of his foot⟩ ⟨a *callous* fingertip⟩ In extended use it usually also implies a loss of sensibility or an insensi- tiveness that results from constant experience ⟨he has grown *callous* to such appeals⟩ ⟨now *callous* to criticism⟩ ⟨the tiresome and *callous* repetition of old motives which marked the decadence of the classic tradition—*Binyon*⟩ ⟨piety . . . is made *callous* and inactive by kneeling too much—*Landor*⟩ but sometimes *callous* means simply unfeeling and carries little implication of the process of hardening ⟨a *callous* answer⟩

*Ana* consolidated, compacted, concentrated (see COM- PACT *vb*)

*Ant* softened  —*Con* liquefied, melted, thawed, fused (see LIQUEFY): weakened, enfeebled, debilitated (see WEAKEN)

**hardihood** *temerity, audacity, effrontery, nerve, cheek,

A colon (:) separates groups of words discriminated. An asterisk (*) indicates place of treatment of each group.

gall

*Ana* boldness, intrepidity (see corresponding adjectives at BRAVE): brazenness, impudence, brashness (see corresponding adjectives at SHAMELESS): guts, sand, grit, pluck, *fortitude

**hardship** rigor, vicissitude, *difficulty

*Ana* adversity, *misfortune, mischance: peril, *danger, jeopardy, hazard: *trial, tribulation, affliction: toil, travail, drudgery (see WORK)

*Con* ease, comfort (see REST)

**harm** *n* damage, *injury, hurt, mischief

*Ana* detrimentalness *or* detriment, deleteriousness, perniciousness, noxiousness (see corresponding adjectives at PERNICIOUS): *misfortune, mischance, mishap: impairing *or* impairment, marring (see corresponding verbs at INJURE)

*Ant* benefit

**harm** *vb* *injure, impair, hurt, damage, mar, spoil

*Ana* *abuse, maltreat, mistreat, misuse: *ruin, dilapidate: discommode, incommode (see INCONVENIENCE): sap, undermine (see WEAKEN)

*Ant* benefit —*Con* *improve, better, ameliorate: profit, avail (see BENEFIT): *help, aid, assist

**harmless, innocuous, innocent, inoffensive, unoffending** are comparable when meaning not having hurtful or injurious qualities. **Harmless** may be applied to whatever seems incapable of doing harm ⟨poor *harmless* fly—*Shak.*⟩ ⟨be ye therefore wise as serpents, and *harmless* as doves—*Mt* 10:16⟩ or to what in comparison with others of its kind or with members of other kinds is free from all power to hurt or injure ⟨his death eclipsed the gaiety of nations, and impoverished the public stock of *harmless* pleasure—*Johnson*⟩ ⟨content with *harmless* sport and simple food—*Lowe*⟩ ⟨he comes of the Brahmin caste of New England. This is the *harmless* . . . untitled aristocracy—*Holmes*⟩ **Innocuous** differs almost imperceptibly from *harmless* in meaning ⟨*innocuous* pleasures⟩ ⟨*innocuous* occupations⟩ It is, however, the term preferred in technical use to specify the absence of the properties or substances in some members of a group that render other members of the same group harmful or dangerous ⟨*innocuous* snakes⟩ ⟨*innocuous* chemicals⟩ ⟨replacing these by *innocuous* sodium compounds—*Morrison*⟩ In extended use, therefore, it is often applied to something that seems harmless only by comparison ⟨dynamite was milky and *innocuous* beside that report of C.25—*Kipling*⟩ ⟨an apple orchard infested with snipers, who, a colonel informed me, were *innocuous* if you kept moving—*Liebling*⟩ or that is harmless to such a degree as to merit contempt ⟨seconded him as often as not in these *innocuous,* infantile ventures—*Brooks*⟩ ⟨where the *innocuous* virtues of respectability receive unquestioning homage—*Cohen*⟩ **Innocent** fundamentally implies guiltlessness and suggests an accusation which can be or has been disproved, but the term has become applicable to actions and qualities and, in this sense, carries the implication of absence of all potential evil especially in intention or in capacity to do harm ⟨I think no pleasure *innocent,* that is to man hurtful—*Franklin*⟩ ⟨much of the religiosity which unwise parents delight to observe in their children is pure imitation or *innocent* hypocrisy—*Inge*⟩ ⟨[Cicero's] *innocent* vanity, his lack of realism—*Buchan*⟩ ⟨competitiveness is natural to man and must find some outlet, which can hardly be more *innocent* than games and athletic contests—*Russell*⟩ **Inoffensive** implies harmlessness in a degree that is almost excessive or pitiful; it is usually applied to persons and animals ⟨I could not have tormented a being as *inoffensive* as a shadow—*Brontë*⟩ ⟨a poor simple *inoffensive* old man⟩ Sometimes it suggests an incapacity for offending and in this

sense equals **unoffending,** particularly when it is applied to inanimate things ⟨he lost his temper when he stubbed his toe, and kicked the *unoffending* object⟩ ⟨an *inoffensive* odor⟩ ⟨a refreshing, *inoffensive* . . . stimulant—*Americas*⟩ *Ant* harmful —*Con* injuring *or* injurious, hurtful, damaging (see corresponding verbs at INJURE)

**harmonize** 1 accord, *agree, correspond, square, conform, tally, jibe

*Ana* reconcile, adjust, *adapt, accommodate: *match, equal, approach, touch, rival

*Ant* clash: conflict

2 **Harmonize, tune, attune** mean to bring things into accord with each other. **Harmonize** stresses as its end the combination of two or more things so that they go together without loss of individual identities yet constitute a frictionless or pleasing whole ⟨*harmonize* the conflicting colors in a room by an emphasis on blue⟩ ⟨their religion is a mixture of Greek, Latin, and Hebrew elements which refuse to be *harmonized*—*Inge*⟩ ⟨*harmonize* its practices . . . with its professed ideals—*Dean*⟩ **Tune** implies the adjustment of one thing to another or of several things to each other so that they will conform to each other or work in harmony with each other; thus, to *tune* a piano is to adjust its strings so that the tones produced will conform to a standard pitch or to a predetermined temperament; to *tune* up the instruments of an orchestra is to adjust the instruments so that they will produce harmonious tones; to *tune* up an engine is to make all the finer adjustments of its parts necessary to smooth operation. In literary use *tune* still implies adjustment (as of expression to a mood or of mood to a situation or need) ⟨for now to sorrow must I *tune* my song—*Milton*⟩ ⟨a mind well strung and *tuned* to contemplation—*Cowper*⟩ ⟨she was not *tuned* to a mood of self-reproach—*Wouk*⟩ **Attune** stresses the attainment of aesthetic harmony more than *harmonize* does, and it seldom suggests the idea of mechanical operation or effect often so strong in *tune* ⟨riding, walking, gardening, driving about the level Essex lands, she, *attuned* to the soil on which she lived, was happy and serene—*Rose Macaulay*⟩ ⟨how by mastering rhythm, our prose . . . *attuned* itself to rival its twin instrument, verse—*Quiller-Couch*⟩ *Ana* adjust, reconcile (see ADAPT)

**harmony** 1 **Harmony, consonance, accord, concord** all designate the result attained or the effect produced when different things come together without clashing or disagreement. **Harmony** basically denotes the unity, order, and absence of friction produced by the perfect articulation and interrelation of distinct parts in a complex whole ⟨to heavenliest *harmony* reduce the seeming chaos—*Southey*⟩ ⟨the scientific view of the world . . . seeks to find law, *harmony,* uniformity in nature—*Inge*⟩ Largely because of its associations with music the term often suggests beauty of effect, whether achieved by order in a whole or by agreeable blending or arrangement (as of tones, colors, and features) ⟨a *harmony* of life, a fine balance of all the forces of the human spirit—*Binyon*⟩ ⟨like hues and *harmonies* of evening—*Shelley*⟩ **Consonance** may denote the blending of two or more simultaneous sounds so as to produce an agreeable effect and is then opposed to *dissonance.* More often it names the fact or the means whereas *harmony* names the result ⟨notes in *consonance* constitute *harmony,* as notes in succession constitute melody—*Chambers*⟩ In extended application *consonance* commonly retains these implications of coincidence and concurrence. Sometimes the pleasurable effect is still suggested ⟨in good poetry there always is this *consonance* of thought and song —*Alexander*⟩ Very often there is no hint of a pleasurable effect but a strong implication of consistency or congruity ⟨this was an unprecedented act, but it was in *consonance*

with Roman tradition—*Buchan*⟩ **Accord** is often interchangeable with *consonance* without loss ⟨it was in *accord* with Roman tradition⟩ However, it can imply, as *consonance* cannot, personal agreement or goodwill or, often, absence of ill will or friction ⟨for your father's remembrance, be at *accord*—*Shak.*⟩ ⟨engineers have reached a certain *accord* in regard to ethical principles—*Wagner*⟩ Hence the phrase "with one *accord*" suggests unanimity ⟨with one *accord* they gave a cheer⟩ **Concord,** like *accord,* often stresses agreement between persons but is more positive in its implications, for it suggests peace with amity rather than absence or suppression of ill will ⟨how comes this gentle *concord* in the world?—*Shak.*⟩ ⟨till heart with heart in *concord* beats—*Wordsworth*⟩ Concord also, when applied to sounds, comes close to *harmony* in its implications. However it seldom except in a technical sense in music connotes consonance of tones, but usually the pleasant succession of tones that is the quality of melody ⟨the man that hath no music in himself, nor is not moved with *concord* of sweet sounds—*Shak.*⟩ ⟨the casual poetry of her gestures and the musical *concord* of her voice—*Wylie*⟩
*Ana* integration, articulation, concatenation (see under INTEGRATE): congruousness *or* congruity, consonance, compatibility (see corresponding adjectives at CONSONANT): concurrence, agreement (see corresponding verbs at AGREE)
*Ant* conflict  —*Con* *discord, strife, contention, difference, variance, dissension
2 *symmetry, proportion, balance
*Ana* grace, *elegance, dignity: *unity, integrity
**harry** harass, *worry, annoy, plague, pester, tease, tantalize
*Ana* torment, torture, rack, *afflict, try: *trouble, distress: *bait, badger, hound, ride, hector: fret, gall, chafe (see ABRADE)
*Con* *comfort, solace, console: *relieve, assuage, alleviate, allay
**harsh** *rough, rugged, scabrous, uneven
*Ana* repellent, *repugnant, distasteful, abhorrent, obnoxious: *coarse, gross: strident, *vociferous, blatant: rigorous, strict, stringent, *rigid
*Ant* pleasant: mild  —*Con* pleasing, agreeable, grateful, gratifying (see PLEASANT): *soft, gentle, bland, smooth, lenient, balmy
**harvest** *vb* *reap, glean, gather, garner
*Ana* collect, assemble (see GATHER): *accumulate, amass, hoard
**haste** *n* Haste, hurry, speed, expedition, dispatch are comparable when meaning quickness or swiftness in movement or in action. **Haste** implies quickness or swiftness in persons rather than in machines, vehicles, or methods of transportation; thus, a business that requires *haste* demands that the persons concerned move or act swiftly ⟨she came in straightway with *haste* unto the king—*Mk* 6:25⟩ ⟨"Why this mad *haste,* Eusoff?" I asked. "Bandits," he shouted—*W. O. Douglas*⟩ But *haste* may imply other goads than urgency or pressure for time; it may imply intense eagerness ⟨his tongue, all impatient to speak . . . did stumble with *haste*—*Shak.*⟩ ⟨I feel no *haste* and no reluctance to depart—*Millay*⟩ or lack of due reflection and precipitancy in decision ⟨marry in *haste* and repent at leisure—*Old Proverb*⟩ or the impulsion of anger ⟨I said in my *haste,* all men are liars—*Ps* 116:11⟩ **Hurry,** though often used in place of *haste* as the simpler term, distinctively carries a stronger implication of confusion, agitation, and bustle ⟨whoever is in a *hurry,* shows that the thing he is about is too big for him. Haste and *hurry* are very different things—*Chesterfield*⟩ ⟨the incessant *hurry* . . . of daily

life—*Eliot*⟩ and more frequntly refers to the things which are operated or the actions which are performed with haste than to the persons concerned; thus, one makes *haste* in the preparation of a report needed immediately, but the *hurry* of its preparation may result in several errors being overlooked. Also, *hurry* may imply the state of mind or the need of one who demands haste as well as of the one who makes haste ⟨I am in a great *hurry* for the articles ordered⟩ ⟨you need not be in a *hurry* to fill my order⟩ **Speed** (see also SPEED *n* 2) usually implies mere swiftness or rapidity, primarily in motion or movement but secondarily in action, performance, or accomplishment. Unlike *haste* and *hurry,* the term, which may be used in reference to things as well as to persons, carries no connotations of precipitancy, urgency, or agitation, although it may carry a suggestion of success ⟨the more haste the less *speed*— *Old Proverb*⟩ ⟨five dark albatrosses . . . clearly took pride as well as pleasure in a performance which had the beauty of *speed* uncontaminated by haste—*Harper's*⟩ ⟨many an adult reader with trained habits of attention and concentration will absorb the contents of a book with a *speed* . . . no child can approach—*Eliot*⟩ **Expedition** and *dispatch* imply both speed and efficiency especially in business or affairs, but **dispatch** carries a stronger suggestion of promptness in bringing matters to a conclusion, and **expedition** more often carries a hint of ease or efficiency of performance ⟨they made their plans with *expedition*⟩ ⟨Sophia put her things on with remarkable *expedition*—*Bennett*⟩ ⟨serious business, craving quick *dispatch*—*Shak.*⟩ ⟨there is nothing more requisite in business than *dispatch*—*Addison*⟩ ⟨to do everything when it ought to be done is the soul of *expedition*—*Scott*⟩ ⟨the soul of *dispatch* is decision— *Hazlitt*⟩ ⟨to move with reasonable *expedition* along the narrow pavements of Rotting Hill is impossible—*Wyndham Lewis*⟩
*Ana* *celerity, alacrity, legerity: rapidity, swiftness, quickness, expeditiousness (see corresponding adjectives at FAST): readiness, promptness (see corresponding adjectives at QUICK): agility, briskness (see corresponding adjectives at AGILE)
*Ant* deliberation  —*Con* slowness, leisureliness, deliberateness, dilatoriness (see corresponding adjectives at SLOW): procrastination, delaying *or* delay, dawdling (see corresponding verbs at DELAY)
**hasten** *speed, accelerate, quicken, hurry, precipitate
*Ant* delay  —*Con* retard, slow, slacken, detain (see DELAY): lag, procrastinate, dawdle (see DELAY)
**hasty** 1 speedy, quick, expeditious, rapid, *fast, swift, fleet
*Ana* *agile, brisk, nimble: hurried, quickened (see SPEED *vb*)
*Con* *slow, deliberate, dilatory, leisurely, laggard
2 *precipitate, headlong, abrupt, impetuous, sudden
*Con* considered, advised, *deliberate, premeditated, designed, studied
**hate** *n* 1 hatred, abhorrence, detestation, abomination, loathing (see under HATE *vb*)
*Ana* *antipathy, aversion: animosity, rancor, hostility, *enmity: despite, contempt, scorn, disdain (see under DESPISE)
*Ant* love  —*Con* affection, *attachment: admiration, respect, esteem, *regard: reverence, veneration (see under REVERE)
2 **Hate, hatred** are not always interchangeable although they both denote intense, settled dislike for a person or thing that causes one either to avoid him or it scrupulously or to be his or its bitter enemy. **Hate** is the preferable term when the emotion is thought of in the abstract as the diametrical opposite of *love* or when the term is

A colon (:) separates groups of words discriminated. An asterisk (*) indicates place of treatment of each group.

used without reference to particular individuals ⟨love you cannot help, and *hate* you cannot help; but contempt is—for you—the sovereign idiocy—*Galsworthy*⟩ ⟨it takes a very remarkable poet, like Pope . . . to elevate malice into *hate*—*Day Lewis*⟩ In concrete use *hate* is seldom found outside of poetry except when contrasted with *love*, also in concrete use; it then denotes the object of one's *hate* ⟨the scum of men, the *hate* and scourge of God—*Marlowe*⟩ ⟨a generation whose finest *hate* had been big business—*Paxson*⟩ **Hatred** is the preferable term when the emotion referred to is actually experienced and is therefore personal and individual in character; *hate* is definable because men are in agreement concerning its distinguishing marks, but *hatred* escapes exact definition because its implications, other than that of intense dislike, can be gathered only from the context or with reference to its object. Usually it implies in addition one or more such emotions as antipathy, aversion, rancor, vindictiveness, resentment, or fear ⟨he had a deep-seated *hatred* of aristocrats⟩ ⟨a violent *hatred* of restrictions on his freedom⟩ ⟨a healthy *hatred* of scoundrels—*Carlyle*⟩ ⟨his special type of satire had its roots not in *hatred* but in sympathy. His wrath was an inverted love—*Perry*⟩ ⟨*hatred* is the coward's revenge for being intimidated—*Shaw*⟩ *Hatred* also is often used in reference to its effect on the one who is hated; in such cases the nature of the emotion is not stressed, but its power to harm ⟨he sowed doubtful speeches, and reaped plain, unequivocal *hatred*—*Lamb*⟩ ⟨battered by *hatred*, seared by ridicule—*Flecker*⟩ In concrete use *hatred* usually denotes a particular instance (as of obsession by the emotion of hatred or of suffering as a result of another's hatred) ⟨given to violent *hatreds*⟩ ⟨the victim of human *hatreds*⟩ ⟨a family famous for its *hatreds*—*Disraeli*⟩ ⟨the human race lives in a welter of organized *hatreds* and threats of mutual extermination—*Russell*⟩

**hate** *vb* **Hate, detest, abhor, abominate, loathe.** **Hate,** the general term, implies extreme aversion especially as coupled with enmity or malice ⟨she did not *hate* him; she rather despised him, and just suffered him—*Thackeray*⟩ ⟨whom we fear more than love, we are not far from *hating*—*Richardson*⟩ ⟨he *hates* Lucy Wales. I don't mean dislike, or find distasteful, or have an aversion for; I mean *hate*—*Basso*⟩ **Detest** connotes violent or intense antipathy or dislike but usually lacks the active hostility and malevolence associated with *hate* ⟨the mob is a monster I never could abide . . . . I *detest* the whole of it, as a mass of ignorance, presumption, malice, and brutality—*Smollett*⟩ ⟨I mortally *detest* cards—*Fielding*⟩ **Abhor** suggests profound, shuddering repugnance ⟨swelling from tears and supplications to a scene, of all things *abhorred* by him the most—*Meredith*⟩ ⟨Rome had made herself *abhorred* throughout the world by the violence and avarice of her generals—*Froude*⟩ **Abominate** suggests strong detestation (as of something ill-omened or shameful) ⟨the Egyptians . . . lived only on the fruits of the earth, and *abominated* flesh eaters—*Newton*⟩ **Loathe** implies utter disgust or intolerance ⟨except when I am listening to their music I *loathe* the whole race; great stupid, brutal, immoral, sentimental savages—*Rose Macaulay*⟩ The same distinctions in implications and connotations are evident in the derivative nouns **hate, hatred** (for a distinction between these terms see HATE *n* 2), **detestation, abhorrence, abomination, loathing.**
*Ana* *despise, contemn, scorn, disdain: *disapprove, deprecate
*Ant* love —*Con* *like, enjoy, relish, fancy, dote: respect, esteem, admire (see under REGARD *n*)

**hateful,** **odious, abhorrent, detestable, abominable** are sometimes used with little distinction. But **hateful** more frequently applies to something which excites actual hatred; **odious,** to something which is excessively disagreeable or which gives offense or arouses repugnance ⟨why shouldn't we hate what is *hateful* in people, and scorn what is mean?—*Thackeray*⟩ ⟨between these two natures, so antipathetic, so *hateful* to each other, there was depending an unpardonable affront—*Stevenson*⟩ ⟨our blind poet, who in his later day stood almost single, uttering *odious* truth—*Wordsworth*⟩ ⟨it was an *odious* face—crafty, vicious, malignant, with shifty, light gray eyes —*Doyle*⟩ Something is **abhorrent** which outrages one's sense of what is just, right, honorable, or decent ⟨she [his wife] was his property . . . . To me it is a view that has always been *abhorrent*—*Galsworthy*⟩ Something is **detestable** which deserves scorn or contempt ⟨hypocrisy is more *detestable* than shamelessness⟩ ⟨I think you're *detestable*. You're the most loathsome beast that it's ever been my misfortune to meet—*Maugham*⟩ Something is **abominable** which is so abhorrent as to deserve execration ⟨on board ship ready to sail away from this *abominable* world of treacheries, and scorns and envies and lies—*Conrad*⟩ ⟨all the living conditions were *abominable*—*Cather*⟩
*Ana* *antipathetic, unsympathetic, averse: repellent, *repugnant, obnoxious, distasteful
*Ant* lovable: sympathetic —*Con* congenial, compatible, *consonant: attractive, alluring, charming (see under ATTRACT)

**hatred** 1 *hate
*Ana* animosity, *enmity, hostility, rancor: aversion, *antipathy: malevolence, malignity, malignancy, ill will, despite, *malice: envy, jealousy (see corresponding adjectives at ENVIOUS)
*Con* love, affection, *attachment: sympathy, affinity, *attraction: charity, *mercy, lenity
2 hate, abhorrence, detestation, abomination, loathing (see under HATE *vb*)

**haughty** *proud, arrogant, insolent, lordly, overbearing, supercilious, disdainful
*Ana* aloof, detached, *indifferent: vain, vainglorious, proud (see under PRIDE *n*): contemptuous, scornful (see corresponding nouns at DESPISE)
*Ant* lowly —*Con* *humble, modest, meek: obsequious, servile, *subservient

**haul** *vb* hale, *pull, draw, drag, tug, tow
*Ana* *move, remove, shift: *lift, raise, hoist, heave, boost, elevate: convey, transport, *carry

**have, hold, own, possess, enjoy** are comparable when they mean to keep, control, retain, or experience as one's own. **Have** is the most general term and in itself carries no implication of a cause or reason for regarding the thing had as one's own ⟨he *has* considerable property⟩ ⟨they *have* five children⟩ ⟨we *have* no cow at present⟩ ⟨*have* opinions on a subject⟩ ⟨she *has* many friends⟩ ⟨they are going to *have* a baby⟩ ⟨he *has* no French⟩ ⟨we shall *have* some trouble with it⟩ **Hold** implies stronger control over than *have* and usually suggests a grasp upon, an occupancy of, or a bond between; thus, "to *have* friends" implies a mere amicable relationship, but "to *hold* one's friends" implies either the reducing of them to subjection or the retaining of their affection; "to *have* an opinion" implies merely the existence of that opinion, whereas "to *hold* an opinion" usually suggests its assertion ⟨*hold* extensive properties in New York State⟩ ⟨once did she *hold* the gorgeous East in fee—*Wordsworth*⟩ ⟨the Breton seized more than he could *hold*; the Norman took less than he would have liked—*Henry Adams*⟩ ⟨the receptive imagination . . . *holds* fast the visions genius creates—*Eliot*⟩ **Own** implies a natural

or legal right to hold as one's property and under one's full control ⟨*own* a house⟩ ⟨*own* several horses⟩ ⟨when a child is old enough, he should . . . be allowed to *own* books —*Russell*⟩ ⟨some parents treat their children as if they *owned* them⟩ **Possess** is preferred in law to *own* as implying one's having full title and right to a particular property to the exclusion of everyone else; thus, a husband and wife might say that they *own* a piece of land when legally only the husband *possesses* it. In general use *possess* differs from *own* in being referable to other things than property (as a characteristic, a quality, a power, or a faculty) ⟨*possess* contentment⟩ ⟨the States *possessed* the power to exclude or admit them [slaves]—*John Marshall*⟩ ⟨that astonishingly retentive memory which we *possessed* as little boys—*Inge*⟩ ⟨the great medicinal value *possessed* by this water—*Heiser*⟩ **Enjoy** (see also LIKE) implies the having of something as one's own or for one's use with all its benefits and advantages; in this sense there is no necessary connotation of pleasure or delight in having or using, but, except in law, the word often does carry a hint if not a definite suggestion of it ⟨during his lifetime he *enjoyed* a distinguished reputation for the excellence of his sermons —*T. S. Eliot*⟩ ⟨while man *enjoyed* . . . an unlimited freedom to be wicked—*Henry Adams*⟩ ⟨classes that *enjoy* certain rights and privileges⟩
*Con* want, *lack, need

**haven** *harbor, port
*Ana* asylum, refuge, retreat, *shelter, cover

**havoc** *ruin, devastation, destruction
*Ana* calamity, cataclysm, catastrophe (see DISASTER): ravaging, pillaging, despoiling (see RAVAGE)

**hazard** *n* 1 accident, *chance, fortune, luck, hap
2 jeopardy, peril, *danger, risk
*Ana* possibility, probability, likelihood (see corresponding adjectives at PROBABLE): contingency, exigency, emergency (see JUNCTURE)

**hazard** *vb* *venture, risk, chance, jeopardize, endanger, imperil
*Ana* dare, beard, *face: confront, encounter, *meet: expose, open, subject (see corresponding adjectives at LIABLE)

**hazardous** precarious, risky, *dangerous, perilous
*Ana* venturesome, *adventurous: chancy, chance, haphazard, happy-go-lucky, *random
*Con* secure, *safe

**haze** *n* Haze, mist, fog, smog denote an atmospheric condition which deprives the air near the earth of its transparency. **Haze** applies to such a condition as is caused by the diffusion of smoke, dust, or a light vapor through the air in such a way as to impede but not obstruct the vision and to convey little or no impression of dampness ⟨the early morning *haze* on a warm day in autumn⟩ ⟨there is *haze* today because the wind carries the smoke from the railroad yards⟩ **Mist** applies to a condition where water is held in suspension in fine particles in the air, floating or slowly falling in minute drops. A **fog** differs from a mist only in its greater density and its greater power to cut off the vision and differs from a cloud in being near to the ground ⟨not the thin glassy *mist* of twenty minutes ago, but a thick, dense, blinding *fog* that hemmed in like walls of wadding on every side—*Hugh Walpole*⟩ **Smog** applies to a fog made heavier and darker by the smoke of an industrial area ⟨a Los Angeles *smog*⟩

In extended use **haze** suggests vagueness or lack of clear definition of thought or feeling ⟨looking back through the *haze* of years—*Allen Johnson*⟩ **Mist** applies to what can be only dimly apprehended because of its remoteness ⟨its origins are lost in the *mists* of antiquity—*Coulton*⟩ or to something which prevents exact knowledge or clear

understanding ⟨times . . . half shrouded in the *mist* of legend—*Freeman*⟩ **Fog** implies an obscuring of the mental or spiritual vision or of whatever can be detected only by such vision ⟨the *fog* of ignorance in which so many live⟩ ⟨life and its few years—a wisp of *fog* betwixt us and the sun—*Reese*⟩ ⟨the subject is wrapped in *fogs* of vague thinking—*Overstreet*⟩

**head, headman** *chief, leader, chieftain, master

**headlong** *precipitate, impetuous, abrupt, hasty, sudden
*Ana* rash, reckless, daring, daredevil, foolhardy (see ADVENTUROUS)

**headstrong** ungovernable, *unruly, intractable, refractory, recalcitrant, willful
*Ana* perverse, *contrary, froward, wayward: stubborn, *obstinate, pigheaded, stiff-necked
*Con* submissive, *tame, subdued: docile, tractable, amenable, biddable, *obedient

**headway** pace, *speed, velocity, momentum, impetus
*Ana* advance, progress (see under ADVANCE *vb*): *motion, movement

**heal** *cure, remedy

**healthful,** healthy, wholesome, salubrious, salutary, hygienic, sanitary are comparable when they mean conducive or beneficial to the health or soundness of body or mind. **Healthful** is more common than **healthy** as the term carrying this sense (see also HEALTHY 2), but the two are often interchangeable ⟨a *healthful* climate⟩ ⟨one of the *healthiest* climates in England—*Bennett*⟩ ⟨*healthful* recreation⟩ ⟨the French boy gets *healthy* recreation—*Grandgent*⟩ ⟨sound sleep is *healthful*⟩ ⟨all mothers wish their children to sleep, because it is . . . *healthy*—*Russell*⟩ ⟨the second fruit of friendship is *healthful* and sovereign for the understanding—*Bacon*⟩ **Wholesome** (see also HEALTHY 2) is a more homely word than *healthful* that is typically perfectly interchangeable with the latter ⟨provide *wholesome*, well-balanced meals⟩ ⟨books that are *wholesome* reading⟩ ⟨mathematics . . . is a *wholesome* discipline because it requires a high degree of concentration and because it shows so inexorably the difference between right and wrong—*Grandgent*⟩ but *wholesome* is the one of these words that may also be used in a much weakened sense to mean not detrimental to health or well-being ⟨some sausages may contain *wholesome* filler as well as meat and seasonings⟩ ⟨reexamining our idea of a *wholesome* food, particularly from the point of view of its freedom from chemical additives which may be harmful to the consumer —*JAMA*⟩ **Salubrious** applies chiefly to climate or to air that is pleasantly invigorating yet devoid of harshness or extremes ⟨the *salubrious* mountain air and water—*C. B. Davis*⟩ **Salutary** implies a tonic, corrective, or similarly beneficial effectiveness; often it is applied to something that is in itself unpleasant ⟨*salutary* advice⟩ ⟨idle ladies and gentlemen are treated with *salutary* contempt—*Shaw*⟩ ⟨the use of force in education should be very rare. But for the conquest of fear it is, I think, sometimes *salutary*— *Russell*⟩ **Hygienic** suggests reference to the means and the rules of promoting physical or mental health, especially of the public. The term therefore commonly implies use of approved means or obedience to approved rules because they are conducive to health ⟨instruct children in the *hygienic* care of mouth and teeth⟩ ⟨stuffy schoolrooms are not *hygienic*⟩ ⟨provision is made . . . for safe and *hygienic* working conditions—*Amer. Guide Series: Mich.*⟩ **Sanitary** implies reference to measures taken or that can be taken to guard against infections or conditions that promote disease. The term therefore usually implies the promotion of health, especially public health, through interference with causes that bring about disease or epidemics ⟨*sanitary* plumbing⟩ ⟨*sanitary* regulations⟩ ⟨the

A colon (:) separates groups of words discriminated. An asterisk (*) indicates place of treatment of each group.

_sanitary_ care of foods⟩ ⟨drainage of swamps and similar _sanitary_ measures⟩ _Sanitary_ is sometimes used in place of _healthful_ but with a stronger emphasis upon effectiveness ⟨solitary communion with nature does not seem to have been _sanitary_ or sweetening in its influence on Thoreau's character—_J. R. Lowell_⟩
**Ana** *beneficial, advantageous, profitable: remedying _or_ remedial, correcting _or_ corrective (see corresponding verbs at CORRECT): helping _or_ helpful, aiding (see corresponding verbs at HELP)
**Con** deleterious, detrimental, noxious, *pernicious
**healthy** 1 *healthful, wholesome, salubrious, salutary, hygienic, sanitary
**Ana & Con** see those at HEALTHFUL
**2 Healthy, sound, wholesome, robust, hale, well** are comparable when meaning having or manifesting health of mind or body or indicative of such health. **Healthy** may imply the possession of full vigor and strength of body or mind or it may merely imply freedom from signs of disease or abnormality ⟨a _healthy_ body⟩ ⟨a _healthy_ boy⟩ ⟨during a _healthy_ and active life—_Eliot_⟩ Often the term applies not to one having health but to what manifests one's health or vigor or serves as a sign of it ⟨he had a _healthy_ color in his cheeks—_Dickens_⟩ ⟨she has a _healthy_ appetite⟩ ⟨a _healthy_ craving for the sap and savor of a more personal, national art—_Binyon_⟩ ⟨in _healthy_ reaction to the romantic fustian of the . . . nineteenth century—_Christopher Fry_⟩
**Sound** even more strongly implies the possession of perfect health or the absence of all defects and therefore suggests not even the slightest sign of disease or of physical weakness or defect ⟨a _sound_ mind in a _sound_ body⟩ ⟨that child is . . . much too emotional to be ever really _sound_—_Conrad_⟩ ⟨his tastes were healthy, his wits _sound_—_Rose Macaulay_⟩ **Wholesome** (see also HEALTHFUL) implies a healthiness that impresses others favorably, especially as indicative of a person's physical, mental, and moral soundness or often more specifically of a person's balance or equilibrium ⟨thankful . . . that he had his mother, so sane and _wholesome_—_D. H. Lawrence_⟩ ⟨such studies . . . promote . . . a _wholesome_ dislike of sophistry and rhetoric—_Inge_⟩ ⟨her eyes shining, her face aglow, looking oddly _wholesome_ in a smeared white painter's smock—_Wouk_⟩ **Robust** implies the antithesis of all that is delicate; it usually connotes manifest vigor of health as shown in muscularity, fresh color, a strong voice, and an ability to work long and hard ⟨exercise tends to develop _robust_ boys and girls⟩ ⟨a hearty, _robust_ man in his middle sixties—_Mannix_⟩ ⟨he is in _robust_ health⟩ ⟨speak in a _robust_ voice⟩ **Hale,** which is a close synonym of _sound,_ is applied chiefly to elderly or aged persons who not only show no signs of infirmity or senility but manifest qualities of men in their prime ⟨he is _hale_ and hearty at 85⟩ ⟨Pete Gurney was a lusty cock turned sixty-three, but bright and _hale_—_Masefield_⟩ **Well,** which is commoner as a predicative than as an attributive adjective, is a rather noncommittal term; it implies freedom from disease or illness but does not necessarily suggest soundness or robustness ⟨is your father _well_?⟩ ⟨he is always _well_⟩ ⟨she has never been a _well_ person⟩ ⟨however ill one has been, he can (usually) get better, and keep getting better—he can get _well_—_Menninger_⟩
**Ana** *vigorous, lusty, energetic: *strong, sturdy, stalwart, tough, tenacious
**Ant** unhealthy —**Con** infirm, frail, feeble, *weak
**heap** _n_ pile, stack, shock, cock, mass, bank (see under HEAP _vb_)
**Ana** *aggregate, aggregation, conglomerate, conglomeration: collection, assemblage (see under GATHER)
**heap** _vb_ **Heap, pile, stack, shock, cock, mass, bank** are comparable as verbs when they mean to bring together into a more or less compact group or collection a number of things and as nouns when they denote the group or collection so assembled. **Heap** is the least definite in its implications; it usually implies a moundlike shape and more or less careless or fortuitous arrangement; it may or may not imply a personal agent, an assemblage of like things, close packing, or a large quantity ⟨throw all the discarded clothes into a _heap_⟩ ⟨_heap_ the sand in this corner of the lot⟩ ⟨the miser gloated over his _heaps_ of coins⟩ ⟨the wind _heaps_ the leaves under the garden wall⟩ ⟨stacks of firewood were _heaped_ all about the stove—_Mason_⟩ **Pile** distinctively implies the laying of one thing or one layer on top of another in a more or less orderly formation; it usually implies a personal agent and an assembling of like things or things of approximately the same size or shape ⟨_pile_ magazines according to their sizes⟩ ⟨a _pile_ of letters on a desk⟩ ⟨_pile_ logs⟩ ⟨a _pile_ of bricks⟩ **Stack** more strongly implies orderly and compact arrangement and the assembling of like things; it almost invariably suggests personal agency and a particular shape or form, and it has a distinctly restricted range of idiomatic reference. Thus, one _stacks_ hay, straw, or grain in the sheaf into conical or a four-sided, round-cornered formation designed to shed rain; one _stacks_ firewood by arranging the pieces neatly into a rectangular pile; one _stacks_ arms when one sets up rifles so that they form a pyramid; one _stacks_ lumber by so arranging it in a pile that air may circulate and warping be minimized ⟨hay curing in the _stack_⟩ ⟨a _stack_ of lumber⟩ So strongly does _stack_ suggest care in arrangement that it carries specific connotations in some of its applications; thus, to _stack_ cards is to arrange them secretly for cheating; a _stack_ is in Great Britain a measure of stacked coal or firewood equal to four cubic yards. _Shock_ and _cock_ are the narrowest of these terms. **Shock** is used primarily of sheaves of grain (as wheat, rye, or oats) or of stalks of Indian corn which are stacked upright with butt ends resting on the ground ⟨when the frost is on the punkin and the fodder's in the _shock_—_Riley_⟩ Occasionally it, like **cock,** is used with reference to hay stacked in a conical pile ⟨_cock_ up the hay from the windrow⟩ **Mass** (see also _mass_ _n_ under BULK) usually suggests amorphousness; it also implies either a capacity in the things which are brought together for cohering with or adhering to each other so as to form a blended or fused whole or a highly compact or dense agglomerate, or an external process which forces them to cohere or adhere; thus, a pasty substance used in making up pills and troches is called a _mass_ by pharmacists; some flowers (as violets) tend to grow in _masses_ or to _mass_ themselves in growing; to _mass_ colors in a painting or in stained-glass windows is to combine the various colors used in any one significant portion of the whole so that they seem to flow into each other and give a unitary effect when the painting or window is viewed in perspective. _Mass,_ therefore, usually implies integration, but it may be a physical, a spiritual, an emotional, an intellectual, or a purely aesthetic integration ⟨_massed_ his arguments⟩ ⟨compounding the American people into one common _mass_—_John Marshall_⟩ ⟨dense _masses_ of smoke hung amid the darting snakes of fire—_Meredith_⟩ ⟨a vine, remarkable for its tendency, not to spread and ramble, but to _mass_ and mount—_Cather_⟩ **Bank** (the verb is often followed by _up_) is used chiefly in reference to substances which when affected by moisture, freezing, or pressure form, or seem to form, into compact masses ⟨_bank_ up the snow on each side of the path⟩ ⟨_bank_ up a sandpile⟩ ⟨build a snow_bank_⟩ ⟨cloud _banks_⟩ ⟨the wiser heads in Rome, seeing the clouds _banking_ in the North, had clamored for the employment of the ablest of Roman com-

manders—*Buchan*⟩
*Ana* *accumulate, amass, hoard: collect, assemble, *gather
*Con* *scatter, disperse, dissipate, dispel
**hearing, audience, audition** all mean a formal opportunity to be heard by persons having authority to question or the power of decision. **Hearing** is not only the general word applicable to such an opportunity not only to be literally heard but to demonstrate worth or qualities in any rational manner ⟨a new trend which is struggling for a *hearing*— *Sapir*⟩ but is also a technical term. In legal use it designates a formal listening by a judge or tribunal to the arguments and proofs offered either in interlocutory proceedings or in a preliminary examination in a criminal case; however, only in equity practice is it applicable to a trial. It is also used in government and politics for a formal opportunity offered to citizens to state their views on proposed legislation or administrative action, or to present their objections to assessments on property, or to give evidence in a legislative or other investigation. **Audience** is more often used of a hearing that is granted as a favor or mark of esteem than of one that can be demanded as a right; therefore it is used particularly in reference to interviews by appointment granted by a sovereign, a high-ranking ecclesiastic (as a pope), or a diplomatic representative of high standing ⟨the French ambassador upon that instant craved *audience;* and the hour, I think, is come to give him hearing—*Shak.*⟩ ⟨I had an *audience* . . . with the Spanish Minister—*Disraeli*⟩ **Audition** is applicable to a hearing by expert judges of a performer (as a singer, a musician, a public speaker, an actor, or a dancer) in order to test the merits of his performance with, usually, a view to his possible engagement ⟨operatic *auditions*⟩
**hearsay** *n* *report, rumor, gossip
**heart** *center, middle, core, hub, nucleus, midst, focus
**heartache, heartbreak** *sorrow, grief, anguish, woe, regret
**hearten** *encourage, inspirit, embolden, cheer, nerve, steel
*Ana* *strengthen, fortify, invigorate, energize: rally, arouse, rouse, *stir
*Ant* dishearten —*Con* *discourage, dispirit, deject: *depress, weigh
**heartfelt** *sincere, hearty, unfeigned, wholehearted, whole-souled
*Ana* genuine, veritable, *authentic, bona fide: profound, *deep
**hearty** heartfelt, *sincere, unfeigned, wholehearted, whole-souled
*Ana* warm, warmhearted, responsive (see TENDER): *deep, profound: exuberant, *profuse
*Ant* hollow
**heave** *vb* raise, *lift, hoist, elevate, boost, rear
**heavenly** *celestial, empyrean, empyreal
*Con* hellish, *infernal: *earthly, earthy, terrestrial, mundane, worldly, sublunary
**heavy, weighty, ponderous, cumbrous, cumbersome, hefty.** Something is **heavy** which is denser and more compact in substance or larger in size or amount than the average of its kind or class and so weighs more in proportion ⟨lead is a *heavy* metal⟩ ⟨a *heavy* stone⟩ ⟨a *heavy* child for his age⟩ ⟨a *heavy* silk⟩ ⟨*heavy* bread⟩ In extended use what is *heavy* weighs down the senses or the spirits or is of such nature that the mind or the body finds difficult to bear or endure ⟨there came through the open door the *heavy* scent of the lilac—*Wilde*⟩ ⟨there was the crushing sense . . . of having been put down as a tiresome and *heavy* young man—*Benson*⟩ ⟨when a great writer . . . creates a speech of his own which is too clumsy to be flexible and too *heavy*

to be intimate—*Ellis*⟩ Often, also, *heavy* is applied to the heart, the mind, or the body to imply a being weighed down (as with grief, worry, weariness, or overwork) ⟨the old minister's heart was often *heavy* in his breast—*Deland*⟩ ⟨when he was not too *heavy* with fatigue—*Mary Austin*⟩ At other times the term merely implies a lack of some quality (as lightness, vivacity, or grace) which enlivens and stimulates ⟨compared with her, other women were *heavy* and dull . . . they had not that something in their glance that made one's blood tingle—*Cather*⟩ Something is **weighty** which is actually and not merely relatively heavy ⟨the larger trucks will carry the *weighty* packages⟩ ⟨as *weighty* bodies to the center tend—*Pope*⟩ In extended use what is *weighty* is highly important or momentous ⟨*weighty* matters of state⟩ ⟨*weighty* questions for consideration⟩ ⟨a work whose *weighty* theme should give it unity enough—*Times Lit. Sup.*⟩ or produces a powerful effect or exerts an impressive influence ⟨*weighty* arguments⟩ ⟨a *weighty* speech⟩ ⟨there were also *weighty* reasons of statecraft to influence him—*Buchan*⟩ Something is **ponderous** which is exceedingly heavy because of its size or its massiveness and cannot move or be moved quickly ⟨a *ponderous* shield⟩ ⟨a *ponderous* machine⟩ ⟨the sepulcher . . . hath oped his *ponderous* and marble jaws—*Shak.*⟩ In extended use what is *ponderous* is unduly intricate, involved, complicated, or labored ⟨his *ponderous* work on the fairy mythology of Europe—*Meredith*⟩ ⟨*ponderous* jests⟩ ⟨I have heard mathematicians groaning over the demonstrations of Kelvin. *Ponderous* and clumsy, they bludgeon the mind into a reluctant assent—*Huxley*⟩ Something is **cumbrous** or **cumbersome** which is so heavy and so bulky that it is difficult to deal with (as in moving or carrying) ⟨the only currency in circulation was of iron, so *cumbrous* that it was impossible to accumulate or conceal it—*Dickinson*⟩ ⟨its space was pretty well occupied with the two beds, and the *cumbrous* furniture that had been bought for a larger house—*Archibald Marshall*⟩ ⟨the *cumbersome* old table with twisted legs—*Dickens*⟩ In extended use both words are applicable to what is both ponderous and unwieldy ⟨he is the Philistine who upholds and aids the heavy, *cumbrous,* blind, mechanical forces of society—*Wilde*⟩ ⟨he also uses a *cumbersome* and high-sounding terminology which has a mystifying effect— *Weldon*⟩ Something is **hefty** which one estimates as heavy or weighty (as by holding in one's hands or by measuring with one's eyes) ⟨a *hefty* fellow, in the habit of standing no nonsense—*Maugham*⟩ ⟨a *hefty* chair⟩ ⟨she has grown *hefty* since I saw her last⟩ In extended use the word may imply a generous amount or portion ⟨a *hefty* boost in wages⟩ ⟨a good, *hefty* slice of pie⟩
*Ana* solid, hard, *firm: oppressing *or* oppressive, weighing down *or* upon, depressing (see corresponding verbs at DEPRESS)
*Ant* light
**heckle** *vb* *bait, badger, hector, chivy, hound, ride
*Ana* plague, pester, harass, harry, *worry, annoy: disconcert, rattle, faze, discomfit, *embarrass: rack, torment (see AFFLICT)
**hector** *vb* *bait, badger, chivy, heckle, hound, ride
*Ana* tease, tantalize, plague, pester, *worry: bother, vex, irk, *annoy: fret, chafe, gall (see ABRADE)
**heedless** thoughtless, *careless, inadvertent
*Ana* *forgetful, oblivious, unmindful: *abstracted, absent, absentminded, distraught: frivolous, light-minded, flippant, volatile (see corresponding nouns at LIGHTNESS): remiss, lax, slack, *negligent, neglectful
*Ant* heedful —*Con* attentive, *thoughtful, considerate: *watchful, vigilant, alert
**hefty** *heavy, weighty, ponderous, cumbrous, cumbersome

---

A colon (:) separates groups of words discriminated. An asterisk (*) indicates place of treatment of each group.

*Ana & Ant* see those at HEAVY

**height, altitude, elevation** mean the distance a thing rises above the level on which it stands, or the vertical distance between a given level taken as a base and a thing that is above it. **Height** may be used with reference to whatever can be so measured, whether high or low by a standard of comparison ⟨letters not more than one-twentieth of an inch in *height*⟩ ⟨the tree rises to a *height* of one hundred feet⟩ It may be used interchangeably with any of the other words, but it is not so explicit. While *altitude* and *elevation* are often interchangeable, **altitude** may be preferred in referring to vertical distance above the surface of the earth or above sea level or to the vertical distance above the horizon in angular measurement ⟨an airplane flying at an *altitude* of 12,000 feet⟩ ⟨the *altitude* of a cloud⟩ ⟨the *altitude* of a star⟩ **Elevation** is used especially in reference to vertical height above sea level on the surface of the earth; thus, one would speak of the *altitude* rather than the *elevation* of a balloon; a village situated at an *elevation*, preferable to *altitude,* of 2000 feet ⟨atmospheric pressure depends on *elevation*⟩ ⟨Pike's Peak has an *elevation* of 14,110 feet⟩

**heighten** enhance, *intensify, aggravate
*Ana* *exalt, magnify, aggrandize: elevate, *lift, raise: *improve, better
*Con* diminish, reduce, lessen, *decrease: *abase, debase, degrade, humble, humiliate

**heinous** *outrageous, atrocious, monstrous
*Ana* *flagrant, glaring, gross, rank: nefarious, flagitious, infamous (see VICIOUS)
*Ant* venial —*Con* trivial, trifling, *petty, paltry

**hellish** *infernal, chthonian, Hadean, Tartarean, stygian
*Ana* devilish, diabolical, *fiendish, demoniac

**help** *vb* 1 **Help, aid, assist** and their corresponding nouns **help, aid, assistance** are often used with little distinction as meaning (for the verbs) to furnish another person or thing with what is needed (as for the accomplishment of work or the attainment of an end) or (for the nouns) the support so furnished. All usually imply cooperation or a combination of effort. **Help,** however, carries a stronger implication of advance toward the end or objective than do the others ⟨every little bit *helps*⟩ ⟨you are hindering rather than *helping*⟩ ⟨a drug that *helps* one to sleep⟩ ⟨please *help* me over the fence⟩ **Aid** strongly suggests the need of help or relief and therefore sometimes imputes weakness to the one aided and strength to the one aiding ⟨but this she knows . . . that saints will *aid* if men will call—*Coleridge*⟩ ⟨cannonballs may *aid* the truth but thought's a weapon stronger; we'll win our battles by its *aid*—*Mackay*⟩ ⟨his undergraduate work . . . was *aided* by tuition grants—*Current Biog.*⟩ **Assist,** which seldom loses its original implication of standing by, distinctively suggests a secondary role in the assistant or a subordinate character in the assistance; thus, a deputy *assists* rather than *aids* his superior; a good light *assists* the eyes in reading ⟨every additional proof that the world is a closely interwoven system . . . *assists* religious belief—*Inge*⟩ ⟨moves through the streets at a clip that suggests they have been called to *assist* at a rather serious fire—*Panter-Downes*⟩
*Ana* .*support, uphold, back, champion: *benefit, profit, avail: forward, further, promote, *advance
*Ant* hinder —*Con* impede, obstruct, block, bar (see HINDER): *frustrate, thwart, foil, baffle, balk: *embarrass, discomfit: harm, hurt, *injure
2 *improve, better, ameliorate
*Ana* *palliate, gloss, extenuate, whitewash, whiten: alleviate, *relieve, mitigate

**help** *n* aid, assistance (see under HELP *vb* 1)
*Ana* cooperation, uniting *or* union (see corresponding verbs at UNITE): supporting *or* support, backing (see SUPPORT *vb*)

**helper** *assistant, coadjutor, aid, aide, aide-de-camp

**hem** *vb* *surround, environ, encircle, circle, encompass, compass, gird, girdle, ring
*Ana* *enclose, envelop, wall, cage, fence: confine, circumscribe, restrict (see LIMIT)

**hence** consequently, *therefore, then, accordingly, so

**henchman** *follower, adherent, disciple, partisan, satellite, sectary

**herald** *n* *forerunner, harbinger, precursor

**Herculean** *huge, vast, immense, enormous, elephantine, mammoth, giant, gigantic, gigantean, colossal, gargantuan, cyclopean, titanic, Brobdingnagian

**hereditary** congenital, inborn, inherited, *innate, inbred
*Ana* transmitted, conveyed (see CARRY): *inherent, constitutional, intrinsic, ingrained

**heretic** *n* **Heretic, schismatic, sectarian, sectary, dissenter, nonconformist** are comparable when denoting a person who from the point of view of a particular church or religious faith is not orthodox in his beliefs. **Heretic** applies to one who teaches and maintains doctrines that are contrary to those which are actually taught by the church or faith to which he belongs or has belonged ⟨the precursors of Luther were for the most part regarded as *heretics*⟩ ⟨he drew a circle that shut me out—*heretic*, rebel, a thing to flout—*Markham*⟩ ⟨to delete from history its *heretics* and its radicals would be to deprive it of that rare quality known as independence of mind—*Neff*⟩ **Schismatic** applies to one who separates from or provokes division in a church or communion usually by differing on a minor point or points of doctrine; thus, from the point of view of the Roman Catholic Church, those Eastern Christians who seceded to form the Orthodox Church are *schismatics,* whereas Luther, Calvin, Cranmer, and other leaders of the Reformation are *heretics:* to the Church of England, the early Puritans and Quakers were *schismatics* ⟨it was difficult to get any bishop to run the risk of ordaining men whom Rome regarded as *schismatics*—*Moss*⟩ **Sectarian** may be applied to a member of a religious denomination or sect, often neutrally but sometimes with the implication of a rigorous and bigoted adherence. **Sectary,** which is chiefly historical, more than *sectarian,* implies membership in a sect that is relatively small and composed of ardent and often by connotation narrow-minded and bigoted partisans ⟨the passing of the bill by Parliament was advocated both by churchmen and by *sectarians*⟩ ⟨collectivist movements within Christianity have proceeded almost entirely from the Anabaptists and other *sectaries*—*Inge*⟩ **Dissenter,** which basically means one who dissents, in the present connection, applies to a person who separates himself from and worships in a communion other than an established church (as the Church of England); **nonconformist** is ordinarily synonymous with *dissenter,* but the term has been specifically applied in England to persons who refused to accept certain religious doctrines or to follow certain religious practices imposed by the established church; thus, many of the 2000 clergymen who refused to subscribe to the Act of Uniformity in 1662 were regarded as *nonconformists;* Roman Catholics in England (as a class) have been held to be *nonconformists* rather than *dissenters,* since they did not accept the Church of England at any time. Nevertheless the terms are often used interchangeably ⟨Wesley was not a schismatic, or even, in the doctrinal sense, a *dissenter*. He desired, not to secede from the Established Church, but to fill it with new life—*Atlantic*⟩ ⟨the English and Scotch *Nonconformists* have a great horror of establishments

and endowments for religion—*Arnold*⟩
*Ana* freethinker, deist, unbeliever (see ATHEIST): *renegade, apostate
**heretical** *heterodox
**heritage,** **inheritance, patrimony, birthright** denote something which one receives or is entitled to receive by succession (as from a parent or predecessor). **Heritage** is the most widely applicable of these words, for it may apply to anything (as a tradition, a right, a trade, or the effect of a cause) that is passed on not only to one's heir or heirs but to the generation or generations that succeed ⟨[Livy] made the average Roman realize the grandeur of the past and the magnitude of his *heritage*—*Buchan*⟩ ⟨our neglect of the magnificent spiritual *heritage* which we possess in our own history and literature—*Inge*⟩ ⟨but the war had left its *heritage* of poverty . . . of disease, of misery, of discontent—*Rose Macaulay*⟩ ⟨a . . . party whose *heritage* is vision and boldness—*Straight*⟩ **Inheritance** applies to what passes from parent to children, whether it be money, property, or traits of character ⟨my father's blessing, and this little coin is my *inheritance*—*Beaumont & Fletcher*⟩ but the term may be used in place of *heritage* when such descent is implied ⟨a good man leaveth an *inheritance* to his children's children—*Prov* 13:22⟩ *Inheritance,* but not *heritage,* may also apply to the fact of inheriting or to the means by which something passes into one's possession ⟨come into possession of a property by *inheritance*⟩ ⟨the power of regulating the devolution of property by *inheritance* or will upon the death of the owner—*Justice Holmes*⟩ **Patrimony** applies basically to the money or property inherited from one's father, but is also used in the more general sense of ancestral inheritance ⟨to reave the orphan of his *patrimony*—*Shak.*⟩ ⟨content . . . to leave his *patrimony* not worse but something better than he found it—*Quiller-Couch*⟩ ⟨a most important part of the intellectual *patrimony* of Italy—*R. A. Hall*⟩ **Birthright** is now more often used in its extended sense (see RIGHT) than in its original sense of the property, goods, privileges, or rank which belong to one by reason of one's birth. But in this sense *birthright* is often more specific than *inheritance,* because it usually applies only to what belongs to the firstborn son by the law of primogeniture ⟨and Jacob said, Sell me this day thy *birthright.* And Esau said, Behold, I am at the point to die: and what profit shall this *birthright* do to me? . . . and he sold his *birthright* unto Jacob—*Gen* 25:31-33⟩ ⟨a race which . . . has taught its children to struggle on though despair be their *birthright*—*Gerald Beaumont*⟩
**hermaphroditic, hermaphrodite** *bisexual, androgynous, epicene
**hermit** eremite, anchorite, *recluse, cenobite
*Con* *religious, monk, friar, nun: *ascetic, mystic
**heroism,** **valor, prowess, gallantry** are comparable when they mean conspicuous courage or bravery in conduct or behavior especially during conflict. **Heroism,** the strongest term, distinctively implies superlative, often transcendent, courage or bravery not only as exhibited by daring deeds in the presence of danger (as in a battle, a fire, or a wreck at sea) but in carrying through without submitting or yielding an eminently arduous but exalted enterprise (as an exploration) or in the same spirit fulfilling a superhumanly high purpose (as the conquest of self or the institution of a great moral reform) where the odds are against one ⟨acts of *heroism* are in the very essence of them but rare: for if they were common they would not be acts of *heroism*—*Bentham*⟩ ⟨the characteristic of genuine *heroism* is its persistency. All men have wandering impulses, fits and starts of generosity . . . . The

heroic cannot be the common, nor the common the heroic —*Emerson*⟩ **Valor** has been applied to the quality of mind of one ready to meet dangers or hazards with courage and gallantry ⟨my *valor* is certainly going . . . I feel it oozing out—*Sheridan*⟩ but far more often it implies both the possession of a high degree of sometimes moral, sometimes physical courage and the exhibition of that quality under stress (as in battle) ⟨awarded a medal for *valor* in action⟩ In contrast with *heroism, valor* implies illustrious rather than superlative courage or bravery; it carries a far weaker implication of a persistent struggle against odds but a stronger one of fearlessness and audacity in conflict with a powerful enemy ⟨real *valor* consists not in being insensible to danger, but in being prompt to confront and disarm it—*Scott*⟩ ⟨the stupid *valor* of the Englishman never knows when it is beaten; and, sometimes, . . . succeeds in not being beaten after all—*Kingsley*⟩ ⟨must men conscientiously risk their careers only for principles which hindsight declares to be correct, in order for posterity to honor them for their *valor?*—*Kennedy*⟩ **Prowess** has become essentially a literary term in its original sense, in which it differs from *valor* chiefly in its greater emphasis upon brilliant achievements or exploits in arms ⟨how insignificant a thing . . . does personal *prowess* appear compared with the fortitude of patience and heroic martyrdom—*Wordsworth*⟩ ⟨warfare was a means of demonstrating tribal *prowess* and superiority to other tribes—*Fathauer*⟩ Often *prowess* loses its basic implication of distinguished skill and bravery in arms and means little more than success in competition typically as based on the possession of manly skills (as in athletics or hunting) ⟨among male animals, the human male is . . . (at least for constancy if not for *prowess*) without doubt the best mammal in the business—*La Barre*⟩ ⟨power derived from . . . technical *prowess*—*Aron*⟩ **Gallantry** more than *valor,* its close synonym, stresses mettle and spirit as well as courage and an almost gay indifference to danger or hardship ⟨few augured the possibility that the encounter could terminate well for . . . the Disinherited Knight, yet his courage and *gallantry* secured the general good wishes of the spectators—*Scott*⟩ ⟨the desperate *gallantry* of our naval task forces—*Marshall*⟩
*Ana* bravery, intrepidity, dauntlessness, doughtiness (see corresponding adjectives at BRAVE): *courage, tenacity, resolution, mettle, spirit: *fortitude, pluck, grit, guts, sand
**hesitancy** *hesitation
*Ana* reluctance, averseness, indisposedness *or* indisposition (see corresponding adjectives at DISINCLINED): faltering, wavering, vacillation (see corresponding verbs at HESITATE)
*Con* resolution, tenacity, spirit, *courage: backbone, pluck, grit, guts, sand, *fortitude
**hesitant** reluctant, loath, averse, indisposed, *disinclined
*Ana* *fearful, afraid, apprehensive: diffident, *shy, bashful: recoiling, flinching, blenching, shrinking (see RECOIL)
*Con* *eager, avid, keen: resolute, steadfast, staunch (see FAITHFUL)
**hesitate,** **waver, vacillate, falter** all mean to show irresolution or uncertainty. **Hesitate,** the general term, usually implies a pause or other sign of indecision before one makes up one's mind what to do, say, or choose ⟨I have for many months *hesitated* about the propriety of allowing . . . any part of my narrative to come before the public eye—*De Quincey*⟩ ⟨when delivering a speech to pour it out in a copious stream, without pausing to take breath or *hesitating* over a word—*Hudson*⟩ **Waver** (see also SWING 2) implies hesitation after a decision has been

reached and so usually connotes weakness or retreat ⟨let us hold fast . . . without *wavering*—*Heb* 10:23⟩ ⟨the front line which had been advancing rapidly *wavered* under the heavy fire⟩ ⟨you *waver* in your convictions —*Jefferies*⟩ **Vacillate** implies prolonged hesitation resulting from one's inability to reach a fixed or final decision; the term connotes alternate decision and indecision or a shifting (as in opinions, choices, or loyalties) ⟨he may pause, but he must not hesitate—and tremble, but he must not *vacillate*—*Ruskin*⟩ ⟨he had *vacillated* between various substitutes for Oswald up to the very moment when he named the four upon whom he decided finally—*H. G. Wells*⟩ ⟨I have *vacillated* when I should have insisted; temporized when I should have taken definite action—*Marsh*⟩ **Falter** suggests a wavering in purpose or action that is evident or is made evident in such signs of fear or nervousness as trembling or the breaking of the voice ⟨with voice that did not *falter* though the heart was moved—*Wordsworth*⟩ ⟨neither to change, nor *falter*, nor repent—*Shelley*⟩ ⟨his eyes did not flinch and his tongue did not *falter*—*Conrad*⟩
*Ana* balk, boggle, stick, stickle, scruple, *demur, shy: fluctuate, oscillate (see SWING)

**hesitation,** **hesitancy** are often used interchangeably as meaning a hesitating. But **hesitation** more often applies to the act or fact or to a sign of hesitating ⟨without *hesitation* Flora seized her father round the body and pulled back—*Conrad*⟩ ⟨the unmistakable *hesitation* of business —*Moley*⟩ ⟨reckless audacity came to be considered courage . . . prudent *hesitation*, specious cowardice—*Derek Patmore*⟩ **Hesitancy,** on the other hand, applies primarily to the feeling or the mood of one who hesitates ⟨a displeasing quality in most modern novels is a certain *hesitancy*, a timidity—*Philip Toynbee*⟩ ⟨the *hesitancy* with which a man older than forty is considered for employment—*Bejarano*⟩ ⟨had lost that nervous *hesitancy* that had so troubled her—*Goudge*⟩
*Ana* *uncertainty, doubt, dubiety, dubiosity, mistrust: procrastination, delaying *or* delay, dawdling (see corresponding verbs at DELAY)
*Con* resolution, spirit, mettle, *courage, tenacity: *confidence, assurance, self-possession, aplomb

**heterodox,** **heretical** are comparable when they mean not in conformity with orthodox beliefs or teachings. What is **heterodox** is at variance with accepted doctrines, especially of religion or science, or interpretations (as of the Bible or the Constitution), or with views regarded as authorized by reason, revelation, tradition, or convention ⟨Milton's *heterodox* opinions on divorce and the episcopacy⟩ ⟨Darwin's contemporaries were slow in accepting his *heterodox* theory of the origin of species⟩ What is **heretical** is not only heterodox but is regarded as not merely erroneous but destructive of truth ⟨a great Christian society defending itself against *heretical* anarchy from within—*Belloc*⟩ ⟨*heretical* books⟩ ⟨the propagation of *heretical* doctrines⟩ ⟨Galileo's writings championing the heterodox Copernican theory of the solar system were condemned by the Inquisition as *heretical*⟩
*Ant* orthodox
**heterogeneous** *miscellaneous, motley, promiscuous, assorted
*Ana* diverse, disparate, various, divergent, *different: mixed, mingled, commingled (see MIX): multifarious, divers (see MANY)
*Ant* homogeneous —*Con* uniform, identical, alike, akin, analogous, comparable, parallel (see LIKE)

**hew** chop, *cut, carve, slit, slash
*Ana* cleave, rive, split (see TEAR)

**hiatus** *break, gap, interruption, interval, interim, lacuna
**hick** bumpkin, yokel, rube, clodhopper, clown, lout, *boor, churl
**hide** *vb* **Hide, conceal, screen, secrete, cache, bury, ensconce** are comparable when meaning to withdraw or to withhold from sight or observation. *Hide,* the general term, and *conceal* are often interchangeable. But **hide** may or may not suggest intent ⟨let me go, that I may *hide* myself in the field—*l Sam* 20:5⟩ ⟨the snow *hides* all the ground⟩ or a putting into a place out of the range of others' sight ⟨*hide* the money under a mattress⟩ ⟨he *hid* somewhere in his grimy little soul a genuine love for music—*Kipling*⟩ **Conceal,** on the other hand, more often implies intention ⟨hidden things that had never been *concealed,* that had merely been dropped into forgotten corners and out-of-the-way places, to be found a long while afterward—*Roberts*⟩ or effective hiding ⟨Sophia had held that telegram *concealed* in her hand and its information *concealed* in her heart—*Bennett*⟩ or a refusal to divulge ⟨I am glad to be constrained to utter that which torments me to *conceal*—*Shak.*⟩ ⟨Elizabeth was forced to *conceal* her lover from her father—*Woolf*⟩ **Screen** implies a hiding or concealment of someone or something in danger of being seen or known by interposing between him or it and others something (as a screen or curtain) which shelters and prevents discovery ⟨Wildeve *screened* himself under a bush and waited—*Hardy*⟩ ⟨the mere idea of a woman's appealing to her family to *screen* her husband's business dishonor—*Wharton*⟩ **Secrete** implies a depositing, often by stealth, in a place screened from view or unknown to others ⟨*secrete* smuggled goods in a cave⟩ ⟨squirrels *secrete* their winter supply of nuts⟩ ⟨and in mere sound *secretes* his inmost sense—*de la Mare*⟩ **Cache** implies an even more carefully chosen hiding place than *secrete,* for it usually implies protection from thieves or from the elements; sometimes the notion of secure storage more or less completely obscures that of concealment ⟨the explorers took only enough food and ammunition for the three days' trip, the rest they *cached* in pits dug for that purpose⟩ **Bury** implies a covering with or a submerging in something that hides or conceals or serves as a hiding place ⟨*buried* his face in his hands⟩ ⟨his intention had been to *bury* the incident in his bosom—*Wharton*⟩ **Ensconce** in the relevant sense implies concealment especially in a raised or enclosed place ⟨bounded into the vehicle and sat on the stool, *ensconced* from view—*Hardy*⟩ ⟨*ensconced* the boy in a cubbyhole—*Peggy Bacon*⟩
*Ana* cloak, mask, *disguise, dissemble, camouflage: *suppress, repress
*Con* expose, parade, flaunt, display, exhibit, *show: emerge, loom, *appear
**hide** *n* *skin, pelt, rind, bark, peel
**hidebound** *illiberal, narrow-minded, narrow, intolerant, bigoted
*Ana* restricted, circumscribed, limited (see LIMIT *vb*)
**hideous** *ugly, ill-favored, unsightly
*Ana* revolting, repulsive, *offensive, loathsome: repellent, obnoxious, abhorrent, distasteful (see REPUGNANT): homely, *plain
*Ant* fair —*Con* *beautiful, lovely, comely, pretty, beauteous, handsome
**high,** **tall, lofty** mean above the average in height. **High,** the general term (opposed to *low*), implies marked extension upward and is applied chiefly to things which rise from a base or foundation ⟨a *high* hill⟩ ⟨a *high* building⟩ or are placed at a conspicuous height above a lower level (as a floor or the ground) ⟨a *high* ceiling⟩ ⟨a *high*-arched bridge⟩ **Tall** (often opposed to *short*) applies to what rises

or grows high as compared with others of its kind, especially when its breadth or diameter is small in proportion to its height; thus, in idiomatic use one would ordinarily refer to a *high* hill but a *tall* man ⟨a *tall* tree⟩ **Lofty** is often poetical for *high*, but it usually implies even greater and more imposing altitude ⟨*lofty* mountain peaks⟩ ⟨a *lofty* perch⟩ ⟨the *loftiest* star of unascended heaven—*Shelley*⟩ **High** alone of these words is used to express degree or intensity ⟨*high* speed⟩ ⟨*high* power⟩ ⟨*high* color⟩ ⟨*high* seasoning⟩ ⟨a *high* wind⟩ ⟨a *high* fever⟩

In extended use **high** connotes distinction, elevation, and sometimes pride or arrogance ⟨heaven's *high* king—*Milton*⟩ ⟨she . . . thought him cold, *high*, self-contained, and passionless—*Tennyson*⟩ ⟨nobody else could utter those two words as he did, with such gravity and *high* courtesy—*Cather*⟩ **Lofty** suggests moral grandeur or dignity ⟨exultation . . . solemn, serene and *lofty*—*Shelley*⟩ ⟨that *lofty* musing on the ultimate nature of things which constitutes, for Pascal, "the whole dignity and business of man"—*Huxley*⟩ The term may also imply haughtiness or superciliousness ⟨she is greatly disliked because of her *lofty* airs⟩ ⟨looked down upon him with the *loftiest* contempt—*Dickens*⟩ **Tall** in extended use is usually slangy or informal and often implies exaggeration or departure from the strict truth ⟨indulging in *tall* talk about the vast mysteries of life—*White*⟩ ⟨he is given to *tall* stories⟩
*Ana* elevated, lifted, raised, reared (see LIFT *vb*): *deep, profound, abysmal: heightened, enhanced, intensified (see INTENSIFY): increased, augmented (see INCREASE *vb*)
*Ant* low
**high-spirited** *spirited, mettlesome, spunky, fiery, peppery, gingery
*Ana* gallant, chivalrous, courtly, courteous (see CIVIL): audacious, bold, *brave, intrepid
**hilarity** jollity, *mirth, glee
*Ana* merriment, blitheness, jocundity (see corresponding adjectives at MERRY): cheerfulness, gladness, joyfulness, joyousness, lightheartedness (see corresponding adjectives at GLAD): *fun, play, sport, jest, game
**hind** *adj* hinder, rear, *posterior, after, back
*Ant* fore, front
**hinder** *vb* Hinder, impede, obstruct, block, bar, dam all mean to put obstacles in the way of a person or thing or of his or its action. To **hinder** is to check or hold back someone or something in action or about to act, move, or start; the term usually stresses harmful or annoying delay or interference with progress ⟨from your affairs I *hinder* you too long—*Shak.*⟩ ⟨[the artist's] education is . . . *hindered* rather than helped by the ordinary processes of society which constitute education for the ordinary man—*T. S. Eliot*⟩ Sometimes, however, *hinder* definitely implies prevention ⟨the rain *hindered* their going⟩ ⟨machines are sometimes *hindered* by speed from delivering their best performance—*Diehl*⟩ To **impede** is to impose upon a person or thing that is moving or in action or in progress something that slows him or it up (as by clogging, hampering, or fettering); the term seldom suggests the stopping of movement or progress, but it commonly implies difficulties so great that movement or action are painfully slow or seriously impaired ⟨around their tattooed limbs they often wore coiled brass rings or bands, which in time became so tight that they *impeded* the circulation—*Heiser*⟩ ⟨the teaching of mathematics is . . . *impeded* by the use of Roman symbols—*Grandgent*⟩ ⟨he . . . placed his hand on hers, *impeding* the rapidity of her embroidery needle—*Rose Macaulay*⟩ To **obstruct** is to hinder free or easy passage; the word implies interference with something in motion or in progress or obstacles in the path or channel ⟨highways *obstructed* by fallen trees after a storm⟩ ⟨the

tall building *obstructed* the light from the west⟩ ⟨the view was *obstructed* by billboards⟩ ⟨the restriction of the power of the House of Lords to *obstruct* legislation—*Plummer*⟩ To **block** (often with *up*) is to obstruct so effectively as to close all means of egress or ingress and to prevent all passage ⟨shifting sand *blocked* the entrance to the channel⟩ ⟨his nose was *blocked* up by a cold⟩ ⟨in these wild places . . . a snowstorm . . . does not *block* the King's highways and paralyze traffic as [in] London—*Jefferies*⟩ To **bar** is to block or to prohibit passage, ingress, or egress ⟨a long freight train . . . *barred* the passage along the road —*Anderson*⟩ ⟨that route is *barred* to steamers—*Kipling*⟩ Sometimes the implication of prohibition is so strong that there is no hint of blocking ⟨the law of arms doth *bar* the use of venomed shot in war—*Butler* d. 1680⟩ To **dam** (often with *up*) is to obstruct with obstacles that prevent a continued flow (as of water, speech, or emotion) and so provide no outlet or exit ⟨fallen trees *dammed* up the brook⟩ ⟨the strait pass was *dammed* with dead men—*Shak.*⟩ ⟨trembling with *dammed*-up emotion⟩
*Ana* *arrest, check, interrupt: *hamper, fetter, clog, trammel, shackle, manacle, hog-tie: *restrain, inhibit, curb, check: baffle, balk, *frustrate
*Ant* further —*Con* *advance, forward, promote: *speed, accelerate, quicken
**hinder** *adj* hind, rear, *posterior, after, back
*Ant* front, fore
**hinge** *vb* *depend, hang, turn
*Ana* *swing, fluctuate, undulate
**hint** *vb* intimate, insinuate, imply, *suggest
*Ana* allude, advert, *refer
*Con* voice, utter, *express, vent: declare, *assert, affirm, aver, profess
**hire** *n* *wage *or* wages, pay, salary, stipend, fee, emolument
**hire** *vb* Hire, let, lease, rent, charter are comparable when they mean to take or engage something or grant the use of something for a stipulated price or rate. Because some of these words are referable only to the act of the owner and some only to the act of the one who engages, and because they vary in their applications, they are not always true synonyms. In their narrowest use *hire* and *let* are complementary terms, **hire** meaning to engage the use or occupancy of something at a price or rate, and **let** meaning to grant its use or occupancy for a stipulated return ⟨we *hired* a house for the summer after having some difficulty in persuading the owner to *let* it⟩ Nevertheless *hire*, especially when used of persons or, by implication, their services, may be employed in either sense ⟨*hire* a servant⟩ ⟨*hire* oneself (often with *out*) as a servant⟩ ⟨*hire* workers by the day⟩ ⟨men willing to *hire* themselves out at any wage⟩ In distinctive use **lease** means to let on a contract by which the owner conveys to another for a set term, and usually at a fixed rate, land, buildings, or similar property ⟨the lands in America [in Colonial days] . . . are in general not tenanted nor *leased* out to farmers—*Smith*⟩ But *lease* may also be employed in the sense of to hire on a lease ⟨they have *leased* the house where they live for three years⟩ **Rent** implies payment in money (or in kind) for the use of land and the buildings thereon. As long as this idea is stressed, the verb may denote either to hire or to let a property ⟨*rent* their house from the college⟩ ⟨the college *rents* these houses only to professors⟩ *Rent* (in the sense of either *hire* or *let*) is also employed in reference to various commodities other than real property ⟨*rent* books from a circulating library⟩ ⟨*rent* an automobile for the summer⟩ **Charter** means to hire by a contract (*charter party*) similar to a lease whereby the use of a ship is given for a certain time and the safe delivery of its cargo

---

A colon (:) separates groups of words discriminated. An asterisk (*) indicates place of treatment of each group.

is promised ⟨it was impossible to *charter* a ship for the purpose—*Irving*⟩ The word is often extended to other means of transportation (as buses or airplanes) and then usually implies to reserve by hiring or leasing the exclusive use of a vehicle that is normally available to the general public ⟨*charter* a bus for a club picnic⟩
*Ana* secure, obtain, *get, procure: engage, contract, *promise

**hireling** *adj* *mercenary, venal, hack
*Ana* servile, menial, *subservient: *mean, abject, sordid

**historic, historical** are sometimes distinguished in meaning. **Historic** is used when the idea of association with history in the sense of being celebrated, well-known, or deserving to be well-known is stressed ⟨we shall visit many *historic* spots on our trip⟩ ⟨this is *historic* ground on which we are standing⟩ ⟨the incident became *historic* in the Square—*Bennett*⟩ ⟨the *historic* conference in 1948, when Lysenko announced his formal endorsement by the Communist Government—*Martin Gardner*⟩ **Historical**, on the other hand, implies use of or dependence on or relation to history, especially of facts or events; thus, an *historic* event is one that is important or famous, while an *historical* event is one that is supported by the evidence of history ⟨he is conducting an *historical* investigation of the Pelagian heresy⟩ ⟨an *historical* novel⟩ ⟨we doubt the *historical* truth of his conclusions⟩ ⟨a *historical* phenomenon as deeply rooted as English snobbery is not to be swept away in a night—*Brogan*⟩ ⟨the author examines his own background and the *historical* accident which caused him to reverse the emigration of his ancestors from England to America—*R. B. West*⟩
*Ana* famed, *famous, celebrated, renowned

**history, chronicle, annals** mean a written record of events important in the life or career of a race, a nation, an institution, or a region. A **history** is more than a mere recital of what has occurred; in the modern conception, at least, it requires order and purpose in narration, but not necessarily a strictly chronological order nor a common definitely defined purpose. Usually, also, it is thought of as an interpretation of events especially in their causal relationships. It may exhibit fullness and completeness or, on the other hand, selection of details, especially when a single aspect is considered or a thesis is to be proved. A **chronicle** is a recital of events in chronological order without interpretation ⟨the Anglo-Saxon *Chronicle*⟩ ⟨Holinshed's *Chronicles* of England, Scotland, and Ireland⟩ **Annals** is not always clearly distinguishable from *chronicle* except in its emphasis upon the progress or succession of events from year to year. The term need not imply a discursive treatment or a continued narrative, for some of the ancient annals are merely records of important events in each year of the time covered. However, in the selection of titles for modern historical works these distinctions are not always observed, for *chronicle* and *annals* are sometimes chosen as less formal or pretentious than *history* or because *chronicle* stresses narrative quality and *annals* the selection of noteworthy events ⟨in the earlier Middle Ages, history was written chiefly in the form of *annals*, that is, the enumeration of the notable events of each year, or of *chronicles*, in which happenings were recorded in somewhat more continuous, but still strictly chronological and unanalytical form—*R. A. Hall*⟩

In their extended senses only *history* and *annals* are closely comparable. Both of these words designate more or less shifting abstractions. **History** usually signifies the known past, or the sum total of events that are remembered because recorded by historians or evidenced by documents, monuments, and remains ⟨nothing like this has happened hitherto in the *history* of man⟩ ⟨a land without

ruins is a land without memories—a land without memories is a land without *history*—*Ryan*⟩ **Annals** most often signifies the sum total of events, with their dates, that have become fixed in the mind because of the momentousness, often tragic momentousness, of those events ⟨the short and simple *annals* of the poor—*Gray*⟩ ⟨happy the people whose *annals* are blank—*Carlyle*⟩ **Chronicle**, on the other hand, is often applied to something concrete (as a person or thing) that records, relates, or manifests events as they happen ⟨pitch upon the veriest camp follower of the New Poetry as the abstract and brief *chronicle* of its procedure —*Lowes*⟩ ⟨the neighborhood . . . was one of those highly favored places which abound with *chronicle* and great men —*Irving*⟩

**histrionic** *adj* *dramatic, theatrical, dramaturgic, melodramatic
*Ana* acting, playing, inpersonating (see ACT *vb*)

**hit** *vb* *strike, smite, punch, slug, slog, swat, clout, slap, cuff, box
*Ana* *beat, buffet, pound, pummel, thrash

**hit-or-miss** *random, haphazard, happy-go-lucky, desultory, casual, chance, chancy

**hoard** *vb* amass, *accumulate
*Ana* collect, assemble, *gather: pile, *heap, stack, mass
*Con* dissipate, disperse, *scatter: *distribute, divide, dispense

**hoarse** raucous, strident, *loud, stentorian, earsplitting, stertorous
*Ana* harsh, *rough: gruff, crusty (see BLUFF)

**hoax** *vb* hoodwink, bamboozle, *dupe, gull, befool, trick
*Ana* delude, mislead, *deceive: *cheat, cozen, overreach, defraud

**hobo** *n* tramp, vagrant, *vagabond, truant, bum

**hocus-pocus** mummery, *gibberish, abracadabra

**hog-tie** *hamper, trammel, clog, fetter, shackle, manacle
*Ana* impede, *hinder, obstruct, block, bar, dam: curb, check, *restrain: *tie, bind

**hoist** *vb* *lift, raise, elevate, boost, heave, rear
*Ana* *rise, arise, ascend, mount, levitate

**hold** *vb* 1 hold back, withhold, reserve, detain, retain, *keep, keep back, keep out
*Ana* *restrain, inhibit, curb, check: preserve, conserve, *save
*Con* *relinquish, surrender, abandon, resign, yield
2 *contain, accommodate
*Ana* *carry, bear, convey: *receive, admit, take: house, lodge, *harbor, shelter: *include, comprehend
3 *have, own, possess, enjoy
*Ana* control, direct, manage, *conduct

**hold** *n* Hold, grip, grasp, clutch are comparable when they denote the power of getting or of keeping something in possession or under control. **Hold** is the most comprehensive of these terms, for it may apply to material, immaterial, or intangible matters and may imply mere possession or control or possession and control securely maintained ⟨lay *hold* on the deserters⟩ ⟨lost his *hold* on the side of the boat⟩ ⟨keep his *hold* on the property in dispute⟩ ⟨kept a *hold* on himself⟩ ⟨afraid they may lose their *hold* on the domestic market—*Sydney Bulletin*⟩ ⟨the *hold* of the public school upon the middle-class mind has not weakened—*Lewis & Maude*⟩ **Grip** primarily implies the power of taking hold of by the hand, but in its secondary senses it definitely suggests a firm and tenacious hold (as on a country by an oppressor, on a person's system by a disease, or on a body of facts or principles by an eager mind) ⟨he clutched Father Joseph's hand with a *grip* surprisingly strong—*Cather*⟩ ⟨the country was on the verge of bankruptcy and in the *grip* of a series of . . . insurrections—*London Calling*⟩ ⟨his interest . . . has been to strengthen the voters' *grip* on governmental machinery—*A. D. H. Smith*⟩ ⟨moreover habits acquired very early feel, in later life, just like instincts; they have the same profound *grip*—*Russell*⟩ **Grasp** implies the power to reach out and get possession or control of something; in its basic applications it may be distinguished with difficulty from *grip* ⟨did not expect to feel his hand snatched away from her *grasp* as if from a burn—*Conrad*⟩ but in its now more common extended applications especially to what can be possessed by the mind it frequently distinctively connotes remarkable powers of comprehension on the one hand or outstanding range of mastery on the other ⟨ah, but a man's reach should exceed his *grasp,* or what's a heaven for?—*Browning*⟩ ⟨his *grasp* of the singular entirety of medieval civilization—*Cram*⟩ ⟨what competent person supposes that he understands a grain of sand? That is as much beyond our *grasp* as man—*Justice Holmes*⟩ ⟨Gray and Collins were masters, but they had lost that hold on human values, that firm *grasp* of human experience, which is a formidable achievement of the Elizabethan and Jacobean poets—*T. S. Eliot*⟩ **Clutch** basically implies a seizing and holding with the avidity or rapacity of or as if of a bird of prey ⟨a rabbit in the *clutch* of an owl⟩ In its extended use it stresses, far more than any of the preceding nouns, the notion of control as distinguished from possession ⟨fell into a usurer's *clutches*⟩ ⟨in the *clutch* of a great fear⟩ ⟨in the fell *clutch* of circumstance I have not winced nor cried aloud—*Henley*⟩ or that of the act or fact of grasping with violence, with effort, or with frantic determination (as under the impulsion of terror) ⟨in the *clutches* of a desperate infatuation—*Schwartz*⟩ ⟨the *clutch* of a drowning man at a straw⟩ ⟨I can't hold on ten seconds more . . . my *clutch* is going now —*Marryat*⟩ ⟨in the dry, womanless *clutch* of the army—*Irwin Shaw*⟩

*Ana* possession, ownership (see corresponding verbs at HAVE): control, command, *power, authority

**hold back** hold, withhold, reserve, detain, retain, *keep, keep back, keep out

**hole** *n* Hole, hollow, cavity, pocket, void, vacuum are comparable when they mean an open or unfilled space in a thing. **Hole** may apply to an opening in a solid body that is or that suggests a depression or an excavation ⟨those *holes* where eyes did once inhabit—*Shak.*⟩ ⟨a gopher lives in a *hole* in the ground⟩ or to one that passes through the material from surface to surface ⟨look through a *hole* in the wall⟩ ⟨a *hole* in a garment⟩ **Hollow,** which specifically implies opposition to *solid,* basically suggests an unfilled space within a solid object, usually one that has a surface opening ⟨a cave is a *hollow* in a rock⟩ ⟨a nest in the *hollow* of a tree trunk⟩ The term, however, is often applied to a depression in a surface ⟨the ground was not quite smooth, but had many little heights and *hollows*⟩ or to a deep and narrow valley (as a gully or ravine) ⟨I hate the dreadful *hollow* behind the little wood—*Tennyson*⟩ **Cavity** is a somewhat more learned word than *hollow* with much the same implications as the latter in its basic sense ⟨an old *cavity* excavated by a woodpecker—*Burroughs*⟩ The words are often used interchangeably, but *cavity* is preferred in technical use ⟨a *cavity* in a tooth⟩ ⟨the abdominal *cavity*⟩ **Pocket** is often employed in place of *cavity* for an abnormal or irregular space (as a bubble-like one in a substance or a sacklike one in a body). It is particularly referred to one that is a source of danger, especially in possessing the tendency to hold or to collect a foreign substance (as dirt, air, or pus) ⟨a pus *pocket* in the lungs⟩ ⟨a *pocket* in an iron casting⟩ ⟨an air *pocket* in a pipe carrying a liquid interferes with the flow⟩ ⟨we found many persons at work . . . searching for veins and *pockets* of gold—*Bayard Taylor*⟩ **Void** applies to an apparently

empty space, especially one of marked extent or of conspicuous duration, whether in a thing that is normally continuous ⟨the air-filled *voids* of the soil—*A. M. Bateman*⟩ or between things that are normally separate ⟨the American planner will have . . . to give up his opaque passion for the transparent wall and go back to the alternation of solid and *void* that is characteristic of the Japanese house—*Mumford*⟩ ⟨the immense *void* between the earth and the nearest of the planets⟩ ⟨we suffer when we have time to spare and no printed matter with which to plug the *void*—*Huxley*⟩ **Vacuum** basically and especially in technical use applies to space entirely devoid of matter; more often, however, it is applied to the space within an enclosed vessel in which by mechanical means the air has been practically, though seldom completely, exhausted. In its extended use the term applies to a condition or situation which resembles a true vacuum in its emptiness of all that normally should fill it or exert influence on anyone or anything that remains in it ⟨you are not asked, as you are by so many novelists, to concern yourself with the fortunes of two or three people who live in a *vacuum* . . . but with the fortunes of all the sorts and conditions of men who make up the world in which we all live—*Maugham*⟩ ⟨he felt a sort of emptiness, almost like a *vacuum* in his soul—*D. H. Lawrence*⟩

*Ana* *aperture, orifice, interstice: perforation, puncture, bore, prick (see corresponding verbs at PERFORATE): slit, slash, cut (see CUT *vb*)

**holiness, sanctity** are often used without distinction to mean either the state or the character of one who is spiritually perfect or of something which is sacred or hallowed. **Holiness** more often implies spiritual perfection, whether intrinsic and essential ⟨the *holiness* of the Lord⟩ or acquired by effort ⟨the *holiness* of a saint⟩ than it does sacredness, although the latter implication is not uncommon ⟨and an highway shall be there, and a way, and it shall be called the way of *holiness;* the unclean shall not pass over it—*Isa* 35:8⟩ **Sanctity** may be used either as denoting saintliness or the holiness attained by a saint ⟨die in the odor of *sanctity*⟩ ⟨men of eminent *sanctity*—*Burke*⟩ or the quality of being sacred or by law and especially by natural or divine law immune from violation ⟨the sense of the dignity of human nature is an even more civilized feeling than the sense of the *sanctity* of human life—*Brownell*⟩ ⟨there is no greater *sanctity* in the right to combine than in the right to make other contracts—*Justice Holmes*⟩

*Ana* sacredness, divineness *or* divinity, spirituality, blessedness, religiousness (see corresponding adjectives at HOLY): devoutness *or* devotion, piousness *or* piety (see corresponding adjectives at DEVOUT): *goodness, virtue, rectitude

**holler** *vb* *shout, yell, shriek, scream, screech, squeal, whoop

*Ana* vociferate, clamor, bellow, *roar

**holler** *n* shout, yell, shriek, scream, screech, squeal, whoop (see under SHOUT *vb*)

*Ana* bellow, roar, vociferation, bawl (see under ROAR *vb*)

**hollow** *adj* empty, *vain, nugatory, otiose, idle

*Ana & Con* see those at EMPTY *adj* 2

**hollow** *n* cavity, *hole, pocket, void, vacuum

*Ana* excavation, digging (see corresponding verbs at DIG): *gulf, chasm, abyss: orifice, *aperture

**holocaust** *fire, conflagration

**holy, sacred, divine, spiritual, religious, blessed** are comparable chiefly as epithets applied to persons or things associated with religion or worship and therefore either regarded with special reverence or veneration or thought of as having a character apart from what is material or

A colon (:) separates groups of words discriminated. An asterisk (*) indicates place of treatment of each group.

secular. Their choice is often a matter of idiom rather than of meaning inherent in the term. **Holy** (compare HOLI-NESS) usually implies some quality or some attribute in the thing itself which makes it either suitable for use in worship or an object of veneration. As the strongest of these terms in its suggestion of a claim upon one's reverence, it is the only one directly applied to the Supreme Being in praise or laudation ⟨*holy, holy, holy,* Lord God Almighty—*Rev* 4:8⟩ It also forms a part of some titles of the godhead or of a person of the Trinity ⟨the *Holy* Spirit⟩ It is also applied to some persons or group of persons as a mark of highest reverence or esteem; thus, the *Holy* Family consists of Mary, Joseph, and Jesus; the *Holy* Father is a frequent designation of the Pope; the *Holy* Synod is the governing body in some Orthodox churches. The term is comparably applied to particular things with a similar implication of reverence and esteem; thus, the central Eucharistic service of Christian churches is often called *Holy* Communion; Palestine is known as the *Holy* Land; water blessed for use in religious services is *holy* water; *Holy* Week is a week set apart for especially pious observances. In more general use *holy* is often the word chosen when one wishes to impute to what is so described some inherent character that dissociates it from what is mundane, material, or transitory ⟨so *holy* and so perfect is my love—*Shak.*⟩ ⟨all is *holy* where devotion kneels—*Holmes*⟩ ⟨some words are considered so *holy* they must never be spoken aloud, such as the ancient Hebrew word for God—*Chase*⟩ **Sacred** (see also SACRED 2) differs from *holy* chiefly in implying a character given to a thing by blessing, dedication, consecration to religion or worship or to the uses of religion or worship, or by its being devoted wholly to such ends or uses; the term therefore usually suggests an opposition to what is profane or exists for profane uses; thus, the vessels used in a Eucharistic service are preferably called *sacred* vessels; *sacred* as opposed to *profane* history is biblical history or history dealing with biblical characters or biblical events; *sacred* as opposed to *profane* literature may denote any or all of the books of the Bible or sometimes any or all writings (as the Bible, the Talmud, and the Koran) which are regarded by various religions as sources of revealed truth ⟨*Sacred* Writ⟩ ⟨*sacred* music⟩ ⟨in its appointed compartment in the synagogue rested the *sacred* Torah—*Time*⟩ In more general use *sacred* applies chiefly to what one treasures as a thing apart, not to be violated or contaminated by being put to vulgar or low uses or associated with vulgar or low ends ⟨when they saw all that was *sacred* to them laid waste, the Navajos lost heart. They did not surrender; they simply ceased to fight—*Cather*⟩ ⟨nothing is at last *sacred* but the integrity of our own mind—*Emerson*⟩ **Divine** in its oldest and most definite sense implies either the character of deity or an origin from or an association with deity; thus, "*divine* being" implies both a difference from "human being" and from "angelic being" and the possession of the nature or essence of deity ⟨the belief that Christ is both human and *divine*⟩ ⟨a *divine* right is one that comes from God⟩ ⟨*divine* service is a service having for its end the worship of God⟩ In its weaker senses *divine* may suggest a supernatural or a superhuman character or origin or, in hyperbolical use, a perfection that is above that which is found on earth ⟨the great mystics declare that their experiences have some kind of cosmic and *divine* significance—*Jour. of Religion*⟩ ⟨that mighty orb of song, the *divine* Milton—*Wordsworth*⟩ ⟨the strains . . . of *divinest* music—*Farrar*⟩ ⟨by what magic was it that this *divine* sweet creature could be allied with that old churl!—*Meredith*⟩ **Spiritual** implies an opposition in character or in quality to what

is bodily, material, earthy, or mundane; it may suggest incorporeal existence ⟨angels are conceived of as *spiritual* beings⟩ ⟨the *spiritual* part of man⟩ or independence from the merely physical or sensible ⟨a *spiritual* marriage⟩ ⟨the leaders of Islam saw its *spiritual* foundations endangered by the subtle infidelities of pure rationalism—*Gibb*⟩ or a definite relation to the soul or spirit in its aspiration toward or dependence on a higher power or in its perception of eternal values ⟨the responsibility of human nature, not merely on the moral side, but equally on the *spiritual* side—*Mackenzie*⟩ ⟨the *spiritual* richness, the subtle emotional qualities, which illumined the great styles of the past—*Belluschi*⟩ ⟨our Declaration of Independence was written by men whose minds reached the *spiritual* level of eternal principles—*McGranery*⟩ *Spiritual* in some chiefly technical legal and theological uses is more or less equivalent to *ecclesiastical* and then usually implies an opposition to *temporal* or *civil* ⟨a *spiritual* lord, or lord *spiritual*, is a bishop or archbishop of the Church of England who has a right to sit in the House of Lords⟩ ⟨the boundary between lay and *spiritual* authority was never defined in pre-Conquest England—*Stenton*⟩ **Religious** (for the application of this term to persons, see DEVOUT) implies an opposition to *secular* and a relation of some kind to religion; thus, *religious* history is the history of a religion or religions; *religious* literature is not the same as sacred literature but has a character that is determined by religion or by religious belief or feeling; *religious* music, unlike sacred music, is not necessarily suitable for use in services or prayer, for, although it includes sacred music, the term may also apply to music not composed for church use but animated by feeling or prompted by themes associated with religion ⟨he stated that his discourses to people were to be sometimes secular, and sometimes *religious*, but never dogmatic —*Hardy*⟩ ⟨except for the nominal subjects of the legends, one sees nothing *religious* about them; the medallions, when studied . . . turn out to be less *religious* than decorative—*Henry Adams*⟩ **Blessed** basically means consecrated ⟨the *Blessed* Sacrament⟩ and usually also suggests a supremely sacred character ⟨our *Blessed* Lord⟩ ⟨the *Blessed* Virgin⟩ In its derived senses *blessed* means beatified and supremely happy because enjoying the sight of God in heaven ⟨the *blessed* spirits in heaven⟩ In general use *blessed* may mean no more than enjoyable, pleasant, or satisfying ⟨that extra *blessed* quarter hour in bed—*Spectorsky*⟩ ⟨we have no green vegetables here in winter, and no one seems ever to have heard of that *blessed* plant, the lettuce—*Cather*⟩

*Ana* hallowed, consecrated, dedicated (see DEVOTE): adored, worshiped, venerated, reverenced, revered (see REVERE): *devout, pious, religious

*Ant* unholy  —*Con* *profane, secular: *impious, blasphemous, sacrilegious, profane

**homage** reverence, deference, obeisance, *honor

*Ana* worship, adoration, veneration, reverence (see under REVERE): fealty, *fidelity, devotion, loyalty, allegiance: tribute, panegyric, eulogy, *encomium

**home** house, *habitation, dwelling, abode, residence, domicile

**homely** *plain, simple, unpretentious

*Ana* *familiar, intimate, close: *usual, wonted, customary, habitual: ill-favored, *ugly

*Ant* comely, bonny

**homily** sermon, talk, *speech, address, oration, harangue, lecture

**homunculus** manikin, midget, *dwarf, pygmy, runt

**honest** *upright, just, conscientious, scrupulous, honorable

*Ana* truthful, veracious (see corresponding nouns at

TRUTH): candid, open, plain, *frank: *straightforward, aboveboard, forthright: *fair, equitable, dispassionate, objective

*Ant* dishonest —*Con* mendacious, lying, untruthful, deceitful (see DISHONEST)

**honesty, honor, integrity, probity** are comparable when meaning uprightness as evidenced in character and actions. **Honesty** implies refusal to lie, steal, defraud, or deceive ⟨you can rely on his *honesty*⟩ ⟨he is a man of scrupulous *honesty*⟩ ⟨this crisis will be surmounted if the Church has the faith and courage, and, above all, the common *honesty*, to face it candidly—*Inge*⟩ ⟨was not greatly pleased with Lincoln, though admitting his *honesty* and fair capability—*W. C. Ford*⟩ **Honor** (see also FAME) adds to *honesty* the implication of high-mindedness or a nice sense of allegiance to the standards of one's profession, calling, or position ⟨business *honor* is the foundation of trade⟩ ⟨I could not love thee, dear, so much, loved I not *honor* more—*Lovelace*⟩ ⟨the fourth generation of Ralstons had nothing left in the way of convictions save an acute sense of *honor* in private and business matters —*Wharton*⟩ ⟨a national administration of such integrity . . . that its *honor* at home will ensure respect abroad— *Eisenhower*⟩ **Integrity** implies such rectitude that one is incorruptible or incapable of being false to a trust or a responsibility or to one's own standards ⟨his unimpeachable *integrity* as treasurer of a widows' and orphans' fund —*Hawthorne*⟩ ⟨the poet's sense of responsibility to nothing but his own inner voice, is perhaps his only way of preserving poetic *integrity* against the influences of a perverse generation—*Day Lewis*⟩ **Probity** stresses tried or proved honesty or integrity ⟨that sort of *probity* which such men as Bailey possess—*Keats*⟩ ⟨*probity* in domestic policy and wise judgment in foreign policy—*A. E. Stevenson*⟩

*Ana* veracity, *truth, verity: uprightness, justness, conscientiousness, scrupulousness (see corresponding adjectives at UPRIGHT): candidness *or* candor, openness, plainness, frankness (see corresponding adjectives at FRANK): reliability, trustworthiness, dependability (see corresponding adjectives at RELIABLE): rectitude, virtue, *goodness

*Ant* dishonesty —*Con* untruthfulness, deceitfulness, mendaciousness *or* mendacity (see corresponding adjectives at DISHONEST): guile, duplicity, *deceit

**honor** *n* **1** glory, renown, *fame, celebrity, éclat, reputation, repute, notoriety

*Ana* esteem, respect, *regard, admiration: reverence, veneration, worship, adoration (see under REVERE): prestige, credit, authority, *influence, weight

*Ant* dishonor —*Con* *disgrace, disrepute, shame, ignominy, infamy

**2 Honor, homage, reverence, deference, obeisance** all mean respect or esteem shown another as his due or claimed by him as a right. **Honor** may apply to the recognition of one's title to great respect or esteem or to an expression or manifestation of such respect and esteem ⟨hold every good and conscientious man in high *honor*⟩ ⟨he declined the *honor* that was offered him⟩ ⟨they feel deeply the *honor* of belonging to the Senate, and the necessity of protecting the Senate against dishonorable men—*New Republic*⟩ **Homage** adds to *honor* implications of accompanying praise or tributes of esteem especially from those who owe allegiance or service ⟨all these are . . . thy gentle ministers, who come to pay thee *homage*, and acknowledge thee their Lord—*Milton*⟩ In its extended use the term carries a stronger implication of a worshipful attitude than *honor* carries ⟨to the poetry of Byron the world has ardently paid *homage*—*Arnold*⟩ ⟨"They say I'm hand-

some." "You're lovely, Bella!" She drank in his *homage* —*Meredith*⟩ **Reverence** (see also REVERENCE) implies profound respect mingled with love or devotion ⟨in general those parents have the most *reverence* who deserve it— *Johnson*⟩ ⟨it behooves those of us who cherish the past to study Alfred's life and works with a special *reverence* —*Malone*⟩ **Deference** implies such respect for the person or his position or such reverence for his personality or such honor for his years or achievements that one courteously yields or submits one's own judgment, opinion, or preference to his ⟨the arrangements for the flower show were altered out of *deference* to the wishes of the duchess⟩ ⟨a certain *deference*, not to say servility, to the heads of colleges is perhaps necessary to a physician that means to establish himself here—*Gray*⟩ ⟨looked like a great man . . . deriving dignity from a carriage which, while it indicated *deference* to the court, indicated also habitual self-possession and self-respect—*Macaulay*⟩ ⟨an attitude of hostility to aristocracy because it was aristocracy, was as incomprehensible to him as an attitude of *deference*—*Galsworthy*⟩ **Obeisance** implies a show of honor or reverence by some act or gesture (as bowing or kneeling) that indicates submission, humility, or acknowledgment of defeat ⟨the Spanish prince was welcomed . . . by a goodly company of English lords, assembled to pay him their *obeisance*—*Prescott*⟩ Sometimes the term is used in place of one of the other words in this group to suggest abject humiliation on the part of the one who pays honor or reverence ⟨a throne to which conquered nations yielded *obeisance*—*Steele*⟩ ⟨continually making humble *obeisance* to supercilious superiors—*Wier*⟩

*Ana* recognition, acknowledgment (see corresponding verbs at ACKNOWLEDGE): adulation, *compliment: tribute, panegyric, eulogy, *encomium

*Con* contempt, disdain, scorn, despite (see under DESPISE)

**3** *honesty, integrity, probity

*Ana* uprightness, justness, honorableness, scrupulousness, conscientiousness (see corresponding adjectives at UPRIGHT): *truth, veracity: straightforwardness, forthrightness (see corresponding adjectives at STRAIGHTFORWARD): rectitude, virtue (see GOODNESS)

**honor** *vb* *dignify, ennoble, glorify

*Ana* *exalt, magnify, aggrandize: extol, laud, acclaim (see PRAISE): reverence, *revere, venerate

**honorable** **1 Honorable, honorary** are sometimes not clearly distinguished. **Honorable** commonly applies to something which is worthy of honor (as in being noble, high-minded, or highly commendable) ⟨an *honorable* calling⟩ ⟨*honorable* service⟩ It is also used as a prefix to the names of some persons of distinction (as members of Congress or of Parliament, mayors, and certain scions of the nobility) and as a merely courteous appellation in speaking of an opponent in a debate or controversy ⟨my *honorable* colleague says . . . ⟩ **Honorary** regularly and *honorable* occasionally apply to what is conferred, awarded, or given as an honor ⟨an *honorary* degree⟩ ⟨*honorable* mention⟩ ⟨an *honorary* title⟩ *Honorary*, but not *honorable*, is also used before a title of an office which is held without emolument or without responsibility for services ⟨the *honorary* president of a society⟩ ⟨an *honorary* pallbearer⟩

*Ana* respected, esteemed, admired (see corresponding verbs under REGARD *n*): illustrious, eminent (see FAMOUS)

**2** *upright, just, scrupulous, conscientious, honest

*Ana* trustworthy, *reliable, dependable: noble, virtuous, righteous, *moral, ethical

*Ant* dishonorable

**honorary** *honorable

**hoodwink** *vb* hoax, trick, *dupe, gull, befool, bamboozle

---

A colon (:) separates groups of words discriminated. An asterisk (*) indicates place of treatment of each group.

*Ana* delude, *deceive, mislead: cozen, *cheat, overreach: *confuse, muddle, fuddle, befuddle: baffle, outwit, circumvent (see FRUSTRATE)

**hop** *vb* *skip, bound, curvet, lope, lollop, ricochet

**hope** *vb* *expect, look, await
*Ana* aspire, *aim, pant: yearn, *long, hunger, thirst, pine: *rely, trust, depend, count, bank, reckon: anticipate, *foresee, foreknow, divine
*Ant* despair (*of*): despond

**hopeful,** optimistic, roseate, rose-colored are comparable when they mean having or showing confidence that the end or outcome will be favorable or for the best. **Hopeful,** which is often used in distinction from *sanguine* (see CONFIDENT), usually implies some ground, and often reasonably good grounds, for one's having hope; it therefore typically suggests confidence in which there is little or no self-deception or which may be the result of a realistic consideration of the possibilities ⟨the air of youth, *hopeful* and cheerful—*Milton*⟩ ⟨I am *hopeful* of purification [in politics], but not sanguine—*J. R. Lowell*⟩ ⟨the vitamins of idealistic romance have been important in the expansive, the *hopeful* view of life—*Canby*⟩ **Optimistic** usually implies a temperamental confidence that all will turn out for the best; unlike *hopeful,* it often suggests a failure to consider things closely and realistically or, even, a willingness to be guided by illusions rather than by facts ⟨the *optimistic* or sentimental hypothesis that wickedness always fares ill in the world—*John Morley*⟩ ⟨the barren *optimistic* sophistries of comfortable moles—*Arnold*⟩ Sometimes, however, the term carries a suggestion not of weakness but of a fundamental faith in the triumph of good or right ⟨there is a species of discontent which is more fervently *optimistic* than all the cheerfulness the world can boast—*Repplier*⟩ **Roseate** and **rose-colored** in their relevant extended senses imply the optimism of an aboundingly cheerful temperament which enables one to see persons, events, or situations in their most attractive and alluring aspects. The terms definitely imply illusion or delusion and therefore connote an element of falsity, though not necessarily intentional falsity ⟨a persuasive person who could depict the merits of his scheme with *roseate* but delusive eloquence—*Goldwin Smith*⟩ ⟨a *rose-colored* view of the world's future⟩ ⟨delivers a final . . . talk, capping the *rose-colored* impression of life in this particular branch of the services—*Christian Science Monitor*⟩
*Ana* expecting, hoping, awaiting (see EXPECT): anticipating, foreseeing, divining (see FORESEE): sanguine, sure, *confident, assured
*Ant* hopeless, despairing —*Con* *despondent, desperate, forlorn: pessimistic, *cynical

**hopeless** despairing, *despondent, desperate, forlorn
*Ana* dejected, depressed, melancholy, sad (see corresponding nouns at SADNESS): gloomy, glum, morose (see SULLEN): acquiescent (see COMPLIANT)
*Ant* hopeful —*Con* optimistic, roseate, rose-colored (see HOPEFUL): *confident, assured, sanguine, sure

**hopelessness** despair, despondency, desperation, forlornness (see under DESPONDENT)
*Ana* dejection, depression, melancholy, gloom (see SADNESS)
*Ant* hopefulness —*Con* optimism (see corresponding adjective at HOPEFUL): *confidence, assurance, aplomb: *courage, spirit, tenacity, resolution

**horde** *n* mob, throng, *crowd, crush, press, rout

**horizon** *range, gamut, reach, radius, compass, sweep, scope, orbit, ken, purview
*Ana* *limit, bound, confine, term, end: spread, stretch, amplitude, *expanse

**horrendous** horrific, *horrible, horrid

**horrible** 1 Horrible, horrid, horrific, horrendous mean inspiring horror or abhorrence. **Horrible** (see also FEARFUL 2) is the general term for what inspires horror ⟨some . . . *horrible* form, which might deprive your sovereignty of reason—*Shak.*⟩ ⟨wrongs and shames, *horrible,* hateful, monstrous, not to be told—*Tennyson*⟩ ⟨coconuts in the *horrible* likeness of a head shrunken by headhunters—*Sinclair Lewis*⟩ **Horrid,** often practically synonymous with *horrible,* sometimes carries a stronger implication of inherent or innate offensiveness or repulsiveness ⟨this emperor . . . from Rome retired to Capreae . . . with purpose there his *horrid* lusts in private to enjoy—*Milton*⟩ ⟨some *horrid* beliefs from which . . . human nature revolts —*Bagehot*⟩ In modern colloquial usage the word is often weakened to a general term of aversion ⟨*horrid* weather⟩ ⟨*horrid* little boys⟩ ⟨gave her a loud . . . smack on the back, with *horrid* familiarity—*O'Flaherty*⟩ **Horrific** (see also FEARFUL 2), a somewhat bookish term, stresses the power to horrify ⟨she was a brave narrator . . . her voice sinking into a whisper over the supernatural or the *horrific*—*Stevenson*⟩ ⟨*horrific* black headlines in our daily papers—*Charles Jackson*⟩ **Horrendous** is used chiefly in producing a literary effect (as the suggestion of extreme frightfulness, an apt rhyme for *tremendous* or *stupendous,* or an onomatopoeic rhythm) ⟨damnings most dreadful . . . execrations *horrendous,* blasphemies stupendous—*Edward Hooker*⟩
*Ana* abhorrent, abominable, detestable, *hateful: *repugnant, repellent, obnoxious: *offensive, repulsive, revolting, loathsome
*Ant* fascinating —*Con* *pleasant, pleasing, grateful, gratifying: attractive, alluring, charming, enchanting (see under ATTRACT)
2 horrific, shocking, appalling, *fearful, awful, dreadful, frightful, terrible, terrific
*Ana, Ant, & Con* see those at HORRIBLE 1

**horrid** *horrible, horrific, horrendous
*Ana* distasteful, repellent, *repugnant, obnoxious: loathsome, *offensive, revolting, repulsive
*Ant* delightful —*Con* attractive, alluring, fascinating, charming (see under ATTRACT): *pleasant, pleasing, gratifying, grateful

**horrific** 1 *horrible, horrid, horrendous
*Ana* horrifying, appalling, dismaying, daunting (see DISMAY *vb*): terrorizing, terrifying, frightening, alarming (see FRIGHTEN)
2 horrible, terrible, terrific, shocking, appalling, *fearful, awful, dreadful, frightful
*Ana* see those at HORRIFIC 1

**horrify** daunt, appall, *dismay
*Ana* agitate, upset, perturb, *discompose: *offend, outrage
*Con* delight, rejoice, gladden, gratify, *please

**horror** terror, *fear, dread, fright, alarm, dismay, consternation, panic, trepidation
*Ana* aversion, *antipathy: repugnance, abhorrence, repellency *or* repulsion, distastefulness *or* distaste (see corresponding adjectives at REPUGNANT): recoiling *or* recoil, flinching, shrinking, blenching (see corresponding verbs at RECOIL)
*Ant* fascination

**hors d'oeuvre** *appetizer, aperitif

**horse sense** see SENSE *n* 2

**hospitable** *social, gregarious, convivial, cooperative, companionable
*Ana* sociable, *gracious, cordial, genial, affable: generous, *liberal, bountiful, bounteous, openhanded: friendly, neighborly, *amicable

---

*Ana* analogous words    *Ant* antonyms    *Con* contrasted words    See also explanatory notes facing page 1

*Ant* inhospitable —*Con* churlish, boorish (see under BOOR): *indifferent, aloof, detached: reserved, taciturn, uncommunicative (see SILENT)

**host** *multitude, army, legion

**hostage** pawn, *pledge, earnest, token
*Ana* surety, security, *guarantee, guaranty

**hostility** *enmity, animosity, antagonism, antipathy, rancor, animus
*Ana* hatred, *hate: ill will, malevolence, malignity, malignancy, *malice: aggression, *attack: opposing *or* opposition, combating, resisting *or* resistance (see corresponding verbs at RESIST)
*Con* *friendship, amity, comity, goodwill: forbearance, tolerance, clemency, leniency, indulgence (see under FORBEARING)

**hound** *vb* ride, hector, *bait, badger, heckle, chivy
*Ana* harry, harass, *worry, annoy: torment, torture, try, *afflict: persecute, oppress, *wrong

**house** *n* home, *habitation, dwelling, abode, residence, domicile

**house** *vb* lodge, board, shelter, *harbor, entertain
*Ana* accommodate, hold, *contain
*Con* evict, *eject, oust, expel, dismiss

**hover** *flit, flutter, flitter, flicker
*Ana* *hang, suspend: poise, balance (see STABILIZE): float, *fly, skim, sail

**howl** *vb* 1 *bark, bay, growl, snarl, yelp, yap
2 *roar, bellow, bluster, bawl, vociferate, clamor, ululate
*Ana* wail, blubber, *cry: lament, bewail, *deplore

**howler** boner, *error, mistake, blunder, slip, lapse, faux pas, bull

**hub** *n* core, *center, middle, nucleus, heart, focus, midst

**hubbub** *din, uproar, pandemonium, hullabaloo, babel, clamor, racket

**hue** *color, shade, tint, tinge, tone

**huff** *n* dudgeon, pique, resentment, *offense, umbrage
*Ana* petulance, huffiness, irritability, fractiousness (see corresponding adjectives at IRRITABLE): *anger, indignation, rage, wrath

**huffy** petulant, pettish, *irritable, fractious, peevish, snappish, waspish, fretful, querulous
*Ana* *angry, mad, indignant, irate

**huge**, vast, immense, enormous, elephantine, mammoth, giant, gigantic, gigantean, colossal, gargantuan, Herculean, cyclopean, titanic, Brobdingnagian are comparable when meaning exceedingly or excessively large. **Huge** is a rather general term indicating extreme largeness, usually in size, bulk, or capacity ⟨an enormous volume of heavy, inky vapor, coiling and pouring upward in a *huge* and ebony cumulus cloud—*H. G. Wells*⟩ ⟨the Texan question and Mexican War made *huge* annexations of Southwestern territory certain—*Nevins & Commager*⟩ **Vast** denotes extreme largeness or broadness, especially of extent or range ⟨the Great Valley of California, a *vast* elliptical bowl averaging 50 miles in width and more than 400 miles long—*Amer. Guide Series: Calif.*⟩ ⟨consider the *vast* varieties of religions ancient and modern—*Cohen*⟩ **Immense** suggests size far in excess of ordinary measurements or accustomed concepts ⟨an *immense* quill, plucked from a distended albatross' wing—*Melville*⟩ ⟨found the balloon at an *immense* height indeed, and the earth's convexity had now become strikingly manifest—*Poe*⟩ ⟨the *immense* waste of war—*Brogan*⟩ **Enormous** also indicates a size or degree exceeding accustomed bounds or norms ⟨heavy wagons, *enormous* loads, scarcely any less than three tons —*Amer. Guide Series: Calif.*⟩ ⟨the princes of the Renascence lavished upon private luxury and display *enormous* amounts of money—*Mumford*⟩ **Elephantine** suggests the cumbersome or ponderous largeness of the elephant

⟨similar *elephantine* bones were being displayed . . . as relics of the "giants" mentioned in the Bible—*R. W. Murray*⟩ ⟨*elephantine* grain elevators—*Amer. Guide Series: N. Y.*⟩ **Mammoth** is similar to *elephantine* ⟨her parties were . . . *mammoth*—she rarely invited fewer than 100 people—*Time*⟩ ⟨a *mammoth* cyclotron—*Whicher*⟩ **Giant** indicates unusual size or scope ⟨loaded with a typical unit of *giant* industrial equipment, the new car weighs more than a million pounds—*Pa. Railroad Annual Report (1952)*⟩ ⟨his *giant* intellect⟩ **Gigantic** and the uncommon **gigantean** are close synonyms of *giant* perhaps more likely to be used in metaphorical extensions ⟨*gigantic* jewels that a hundred Negroes could not carry—*Chesterton*⟩ ⟨a justice of the Supreme Court . . . however *gigantic* his learning and his juridic rectitude—*Mencken*⟩ **Colossal** may suggest vast proportion ⟨three sets of *colossal* figures of men and animals . . . the largest man is 167 feet long— *Amer. Guide Series: Calif.*⟩ ⟨the sun blazed down . . . the heat was *colossal*—*Forester*⟩ **Gargantuan** suggests the hugeness of Rabelais's Gargantua and is often used in reference to appetites and similar physical matters ⟨*gargantuan* breakfasts . . . pigs' knuckles and sauerkraut, liver and bacon, ham and eggs, beef stew—*Ferber*⟩ **Herculean** suggests the superhuman power of the Greek hero Hercules or the superhuman difficulties of his famous labors ⟨a *Herculean* task confronted them. Some 1700 miles of track had to be laid through a wilderness—*Nevins & Commager*⟩ **Cyclopean** suggests the superhuman size and strength of the Cyclops of Greek mythology ⟨of *cyclopean* masonry, consisting of very large blocks of stone—*Scientific American*⟩ **Titanic** suggests colossal size and, often, primitive earth-shaking strength ⟨*titanic* water fronds speedily choked both those rivers—*H. G. Wells*⟩ ⟨it was his *titanic* energy that broke the fetters of medievalism—*Cohen*⟩ **Brobdingnagian** suggests the hugeness of the inhabitants of the Brobdingnag of *Gulliver's Travels* ⟨a brand-new *Brobdingnagian* hotel—*Disraeli*⟩
*Ana* stupendous, tremendous, prodigious, monumental, *monstrous: big, great, *large

**hullabaloo** *din, uproar, pandemonium, babel, hubbub, clamor, racket

**humane** humanitarian, *charitable, benevolent, philanthropic, eleemosynary, altruistic
*Ana* compassionate, *tender, warmhearted: gentle, lenient, mild (see SOFT): clement, merciful, tolerant, *forbearing: kindly, *kind, benign, benignant
*Ant* barbarous, inhuman: atrocious —*Con* savage, cruel, fell (see FIERCE): merciless, relentless, implacable (see GRIM)

**humanitarian** humane, benevolent, philanthropic, eleemosynary, *charitable, altruistic

**humble** *adj* **Humble, meek, modest, lowly** are comparable when they mean lacking all signs of pride, aggressiveness, or self-assertiveness either in spirit or in outward show. All are applicable to persons and their attitudes and manners, and all but *meek* may also be applied to homes, occupations, interests, and ways of life. **Humble** may suggest a virtue that consists in the absence of pride in oneself or in one's achievements and, in religious use, a consciousness of one's weakness and a disposition to ascribe to the Supreme Being all credit for whatever one is or does that is meritorious ⟨God resisteth the proud, but giveth grace unto the *humble*—*Jas 4:6*⟩ ⟨Knowledge is proud that he has learned so much; Wisdom is *humble* that he knows no more—*Cowper*⟩ Often *humble* connotes undue self-depreciation or humiliation sometimes verging on abjectness ⟨she is *humble* to abjectness—*De Quincey*⟩ As applied to a person's circumstances, *humble* suggests low social rank, poverty, or insignificance ⟨a man of *humble*

---

A colon (:) separates groups of words discriminated. An asterisk (*) indicates place of treatment of each group.

extraction⟩ ⟨a *humble* Mexican family—*Cather*⟩ ⟨he regarded no task as too *humble* for him to undertake—*Huxley*⟩ **Meek** also, especially in Christian use, may imply a virtue evident not only in the absence of passion or wrath but in a consistent mildness or gentleness of temper ⟨a *meek* and quiet spirit, which is in the sight of God of great price—*1 Pet* 3:4⟩ In more general use, however, the term so often additionally suggests spiritlessness or undue submissiveness that even when it is employed without derogation these ideas are often connoted ⟨Stephen's face grew serious . . . . "I'm sorry I upset you." Oh, so he was going to be *meek* and Christian! Tony wasn't going to stand that either—*Archibald Marshall*⟩ ⟨*meek*, humble, timid persons, who accept things as they are—*Benson*⟩ **Modest** is often preferred to *humble* in describing a person who takes no credit to himself for what he is or for what he does; the term usually connotes a lack of boastfulness or show of conceit, but it does not necessarily imply, as *humble* often does imply, a deep conviction of one's unworthiness or inferiority ⟨the model of an eighteenth-century parish priest . . . just, *modest* . . . loved and esteemed by all—*Ellis*⟩ ⟨Taft was so certain he was right he could be rather charmingly simple and *modest*—*New Republic*⟩ As applied to such things as a home, a position, or a price, *modest* suggests neither extreme lowness nor the opposite, but a reasonable and often unobtrusive medium between extremes ⟨live in *modest* circumstances⟩ ⟨my own hotel was *modest* enough, but it was magnificent in comparison with this—*Maugham*⟩ **Lowly** is often indistinguishable from *humble* except in its lack of derogatory connotations such as abjectness or sense of inferiority ⟨surely he scorneth the scorners: but he giveth grace unto the *lowly*—*Prov* 3:34⟩ ⟨thy heart the *lowliest* duties on herself did lay—*Wordsworth*⟩ ⟨men . . . of *lowly* station—hatters, curriers, tanners, dyers, and the like—*Motley*⟩
*Ana* submissive, subdued (see TAME): resigned, acquiescent, *compliant
*Con* *proud, arrogant, insolent, haughty, lordly, overbearing, disdainful: vain, vainglorious, proud (see under PRIDE *n*): ostentatious, pretentious, *showy
**humble** *vb* humiliate, *abase, demean, debase, degrade
*Ana* abash, discomfit, *embarrass: chagrin, mortify (see corresponding adjectives at ASHAMED)
*Con* *exalt, magnify, aggrandize
**humbug** *n* fake, sham, *imposture, cheat, fraud, deceit, deception, counterfeit
*Ana* *pretense, pretension, make-believe: *impostor, faker, charlatan, mountebank: hocus-pocus, mummery, *gibberish, abracadabra
**humdrum** *adj* *dull, dreary, monotonous, pedestrian, stodgy
*Ana* *irksome, tiresome, wearisome, tedious, boring
**humid** moist, damp, *wet, dank
*Con* *dry, arid
**humiliate** humble, degrade, debase, demean, *abase
*Ana* mortify, chagrin (see corresponding adjectives at ASHAMED): confound, bewilder, nonplus (see PUZZLE): *embarrass, discomfit, abash, disconcert, faze, rattle
**humor** *n* 1 *mood, temper, vein
*Ana* *caprice, freak, fancy, whim, whimsy, conceit, vagary, crotchet: attitude, *position, stand
2 *wit, irony, satire, sarcasm, repartee
**humor** *vb* *indulge, pamper, spoil, baby, mollycoddle
*Ana* gratify, delight, *please, rejoice, gladden, tickle: content, *satisfy
**humorous** *witty, facetious, jocular, jocose
*Ana* droll, comic, comical, farcical, funny, *laughable: amusing, diverting, entertaining (see AMUSE)

*Con* grave, *serious, earnest, solemn, sober
**hunger** *vb* yearn, hanker, pine, thirst, *long
*Ana* crave, *desire, covet, wish, want
**hunt** *vb* search, ransack, rummage, *seek, scour, comb, ferret out
*Ana* pursue, chase, *follow, trail
**hurl** fling, cast, *throw, pitch, toss, sling
*Con* *catch, capture: grasp, clutch, seize, grab, *take
**hurricane** 1 *wind, breeze, gale, zephyr
2 *whirlwind, cyclone, typhoon, tornado, waterspout, twister
**hurry** *vb* *speed, quicken, precipitate, hasten
*Ana* impel, drive, *move
*Ant* delay —*Con* retard, slow, slacken, detain (see DELAY): procrastinate, lag, loiter, dawdle (see DELAY)
**hurry** *n* *haste, speed, dispatch, expedition
*Ana* swiftness, rapidity, expeditiousness, quickness, speediness (see corresponding adjectives at FAST): *celerity, alacrity, legerity: flurry, *stir, bustle, pother, ado
**hurt** *vb* *injure, harm, damage, impair, mar, spoil
*Ana* *afflict, torture, torment: *trouble, distress: *wrong, oppress, persecute, aggrieve
**hurt** *n* *injury, harm, damage, mischief
*Ana* *pain, ache, pang, throe, twinge, stitch: *injustice, wrong, grievance
**husbandry** farming, *agriculture
**husky** *muscular, brawny, sinewy, athletic, burly
*Ana* stalwart, stout, *strong, sturdy, tough: *powerful, puissant, potent, forceful
**hygienic** sanitary, *healthful, healthy, wholesome, salubrious, salutary
**hymeneal** nuptial, marital, connubial, conjugal, *matrimonial
**hymn** *vb* *sing, troll, carol, descant, warble, trill, chant, intone
*Ana* extol, laud, acclaim, *praise
**hyperbole** *exaggeration, overstatement
**hypercritical** captious, caviling, carping, censorious, faultfinding, *critical
*Ana* finicky, fastidious, fussy, pernickety, squeamish, particular (see NICE)
**hypochondriac** *melancholic, melancholy, atrabilious
**hypocrisy,** sanctimony, pharisaism, cant mean the pretense or affectation of being more virtuous or more religious than one actually is. The same differences in implications and connotations are found in their corresponding adjectives, **hypocritical, sanctimonious, pharisaical, canting. Hypocrisy** and **hypocritical,** the most inclusive of these terms, imply an assumption of goodness, sincerity, or piety by one who is either not good, sincere, or pious or is actually corrupt, dishonest, or irreligious ⟨I thought where all thy circling wiles would end—in feigned religion, smooth *hypocrisy*—*Milton*⟩ ⟨be *hypocritical*, be cautious, be not what you seem but always what you see—*Byron*⟩ ⟨Archer's New York tolerated *hypocrisy* in private relations; but in business matters it exacted a limpid and impeccable honesty—*Wharton*⟩ ⟨much of the religiosity which unwise parents delight to observe in their children is . . . innocent *hypocrisy*—*Inge*⟩ ⟨the passing stranger who took such a vitriolic joy in exposing their pretensions and their *hypocrisy*—*Brooks*⟩ **Sanctimony** and **sanctimonious** are terms of opprobrium implying an affectation or merely outward pretense of holiness or of piety ⟨he took pleasure in comparing the sanctity of the early Christians with the *sanctimony* of many modern churchgoers⟩ ⟨the preacher urged his flock to seek holiness but to take care lest they fall into *sanctimony*⟩ ⟨*sanctimonious* professions of faith⟩ ⟨a woman who was religious without being

*sanctimonious—Stokes⟩* **Pharisaism** and **pharisaical** imply a stern and censorious attitude to the manners and morals of others or a conviction of one's own moral superiority, or both; the terms frequently suggest sanctimony or, less often, out-and-out hypocrisy ⟨*pharisaism,* stupidity, and despotism reign not in merchants' houses and prisons alone—*Farrell*⟩ ⟨the assured, the positive, the *pharisaical* temper, that believes itself to be impregnably in the right and its opponents indubitably in the wrong—*Benson*⟩ **Cant** (see also DIALECT) and **canting** imply the use of religious or pietistic language or phraseology in such a way as to suggest sanctimony or hypocrisy rather than genuine holiness or deep religiousness; often, however, the terms suggest reference not only to such outward indications of sanctimony and hypocrisy but to the state of mind or the attitude of one who is so pharisaical, or so deeply convinced of his righteousness or holiness, that he is unaware that he is displaying his religion in a mechanical or perfunctory rather than in a sincere manner and in a spirit of arrogance rather than of humility ⟨a *canting* moralist⟩ ⟨a *canting* assumption of his righteousness⟩ ⟨the whole spiritual atmosphere was saturated with *cant* . . . an affectation of high principle which had ceased to touch the conduct, and flowed on in . . . insincere and unreal speech —*Froude*⟩ ⟨one of those rare artists . . . who, by virtue of some inward grace, constantly flowing through the intellect, purge the mind of *cant—Brooks*⟩

*Ana* dissimulation, duplicity, guile, *deceit: *pretense, pretension, make-believe

**hypocritical** sanctimonious, pharisaical, canting (see under HYPOCRISY)

*Ana* unctuous, oily, slick, *fulsome: feigned, affected, assumed, simulated, shammed, counterfeited, pretended (see ASSUME)

*Con* genuine, veritable, bona fide, *authentic: *sincere, heartfelt, wholehearted, whole-souled, unfeigned

**hypostatize** reify, externalize, materialize, incarnate, *realize, actualize, embody, objectify

**hypothesis, theory, law** are often interchangeable in general use. In their technical senses they are usually discriminated by the scientists and philosophers who employ them. In general the terms denote an inference from data that is offered as a formula to explain the abstract and general principle that lies behind the data and determines their cause, their method of operation, or their relation to other phenomena. In such usage **hypothesis** implies tentativeness because of insufficient evidence and applies to a well-founded conjecture that serves as a point of departure for scientific discussion or as a tentative guide for further investigation or as the most reasonable explanation of an imperfectly comprehended phenomenon ⟨a scientist says in effect—"Observation shows that the following facts are true; I find that a certain *hypothesis* as to their origin is consistent with them all"—*Jeans*⟩ ⟨the resemblance to electric polarization is very close; it is in fact so close that it would not be foolish at all to make the *hypothesis* that the iron contains not only electrons but also tiny corpuscles of some subtle magnetic fluid—*Darrow*⟩ ⟨in the last chapter I proposed the *hypothesis* that a pure poetry exists, employing the term "lyric" to describe poems which "consist of poetry and nothing else"—*Day Lewis*⟩ **Theory,** in general use, often means little more than *hypothesis* or *conjecture* ⟨"Let us sit quiet, and hear the echoes about which you have your *theory.*" "Not a *theory*; it was a fancy"—*Dickens*⟩ ⟨in the course of my work in Egypt, I had formulated certain *theories* of my own about plague, and could not reconcile them to the findings of the Commission—*Heiser*⟩ but in precise technical use it presupposes more supporting evidence than *hypothesis* does, a wider range of application, and greater likelihood of truth. It is not always obvious when *hypothesis* and when *theory* should be used; in comparable applications *hypothesis* is preferred by some scientists as the more modest in its claims, *theory* being preferred by others as suggesting such confidence in the reliability of the inference and its supporting evidence as to imply that it deserves acceptance ⟨the Darwinian explanation of the origin of species is regarded by some as a *hypothesis,* but is more often designated as the *theory* of evolution⟩ ⟨that exact verbal expression of as much as we know of the facts, and no more, which constitutes a perfect scientific *theory—T. H. Huxley*⟩ ⟨in 1905 Einstein crystallized these concepts and hypotheses in his *theory* of light quanta, according to which all radiation consisted of discrete bullet-like units—*Jeans*⟩ ⟨there was also a nascent *theory* of sound waves; and out of it there grew . . . a tremendous mathematical doctrine of waves which nowadays has almost come to dominate the physics of these times—*Darrow*⟩ **Law** (for fuller treatment see PRINCIPLE) emphasizes certainty and proof and therefore applies to a statement of an order or relation in phenomena that has been found to be invariable under the same conditions ⟨in philology, Grimm's *law* is a statement of the regular changes which the stops, or mute consonants, of the primitive Indo-European consonant system have undergone in the Germanic languages⟩ However, since such laws are subject to correction or alteration by the discovery of contradictory or additional evidence, the term is often changed in the course of time to *theory*; thus, what has long been known as Newton's *law* of gravitation is currently being revised as a result of Einstein's discoveries and is sometimes designated as Newton's mathematical *theory* of universal gravitation.

*Ana* conjecture, surmise, guess (see under CONJECTURE *vb*): inference, deduction, conclusion (see under INFER)

**hypothetical** conjectural, *supposed, supposititious, reputed, putative, purported

*Ana* *theoretical, speculative, academic: *doubtful, dubious, problematic, questionable

*Con* *certain, inevitable, necessary: proved, tested, tried, demonstrated (see PROVE)

**hysteria** delirium, frenzy, *mania

---

A colon (:) separates groups of words discriminated. An asterisk (*) indicates place of treatment of each group.

# I

**icon** *image, portrait, effigy, statue, photograph, mask

**iconoclast** *rebel, insurgent

**icy** glacial, arctic, gelid, *cold, frigid, freezing, frosty, cool, chilly
*Ant* fiery

**idea,** concept, conception, thought, notion, impression mean what exists in the mind as a representation of something that it apprehends or comprehends or as a formulation of an opinion, a plan, or a design. **Idea** is the most comprehensive and widely applicable of these terms; it may be used of an image of something at one time or another actually perceived through the senses, or of something never perceived but visualized from bits of information ⟨described his *idea* of a penthouse⟩ ⟨his *idea* of heaven does not correspond to that of most persons⟩ ⟨our *ideas* of a good time aren't the same, and never will be—*Rose Macaulay*⟩ or of something that is the clearly or vaguely defined product of fancy, imagination, or inventive power ⟨he . . . invented a new kind of buoy which was found by the authorities to be excellent in *idea,* but impracticable—*Ellis*⟩ ⟨the *idea* of holiness has its history, like other religious *ideas,* and the history is not edifying—*Inge*⟩ ⟨one of those accepted *ideas,* which are always wrong, that China is and was a country of immovable and unchanging traditions—*Binyon*⟩ It may denote a mere supposition ⟨I had no *idea* that the law had been so great a slavery—*Austen*⟩ or a good or practical solution or suggestion ⟨a very clever point that . . . . You are really full of *ideas*—*Shaw*⟩ or a ridiculous or preposterous suggestion ⟨Mr. Elton in love with me! What an *idea!*—*Austen*⟩ **Concept** applies in logic to the idea of a thing which the mind conceives after knowing many instances of the category to which it belongs and which is devoid of all details except those that are typical or generic ⟨the *concept* of "horse," "table," "mountain"⟩ ⟨the author of *Mein Kampf* has abolished the whole *concept* of the citizen as we have known it from the days of Pericles—*Dorothy Thompson*⟩ In more general use the term applies to a formulated and widely accepted idea of what a thing should be ⟨we find among the Greeks germinal *concepts* which are a vital part of modern thought—*Buchan*⟩ ⟨thus the popular *concept* of what news was came more and more to be formed upon what news was printed—*Mott*⟩ **Conception** is often used in place of *concept* in this latter sense; in fact it is sometimes preferred by those who wish to keep *concept* as a technical term of logic. However *conception* so strongly suggests the activity of the mental power of bringing into existence an idea of something not yet realized or not yet given outward form that it often implies not only the exercise of the reflective powers but of the imagination as colored by feeling; the term therefore more often applies to a peculiar or an individual idea than to one held by men as a whole or by an entire class, profession, or group ⟨compare Poe's *conception* of poetry as "the rhythmical creation of beauty" with the Aristotelian *conception* of it as the imitation of human actions "according to probability and necessity"⟩ ⟨what I needed was . . . some clear *conception* of the meaning of existence—*L. P. Smith*⟩ **Conception** is also, especially in literary and art criticism, the usual term for the idea or design conceived by the writer or artist in advance of or in company with his giving it expression or form ⟨Dante's boldness of *conception*⟩ ⟨the dramatist's power to express his *conception* with frankness and daring⟩ ⟨the *conception* comes

through the actual execution—*Alexander*⟩ **Thought** applies either to an expressed or to an unexpressed idea, especially one that comes into the mind as a result of meditation, reasoning, or contemplation ⟨a child's *thoughts* about God⟩ ⟨he had not a *thought* of disaster⟩ ⟨have to wait for the occasional genius, or the occasional lucky *thought*—*Whitehead*⟩ ⟨his mind ran over the great cities . . . . Of them all, only New York was as it had always been, and he was angered at the *thought*—*Buck*⟩ **Notion** often adds to *idea*'s implication of vagueness the suggestion of caprice or whim or of half-formed or tentative purpose or intention ⟨her *notion* of a delta was a lot of channels and islands—*Forester*⟩ ⟨one never does form a just idea of anybody beforehand. One takes up a *notion,* and runs away with it—*Austen*⟩ ⟨modest, sober, cured of all her *notions* hyperbolical—*Cowper*⟩ but *notion* may also come close to *concept* in suggesting a general or universal concept ⟨arriving at the *notion* of law—*Babbitt*⟩ or to *conception* in denoting the meaning content assigned by the mind to a term ⟨have no adequate *notion* of what we mean by causation—*Sapir*⟩ **Impression** (see also IMPRESSION 1) usually suggests an idea which comes into the mind as the result of an external stimulus ⟨I should like to know your first *impressions* of this book⟩ ⟨poetry . . . aims at the transmission . . . of *impressions,* not facts—*Lowes*⟩ ⟨looking out over the steep hills, the first *impression* is of an immense void like the sea—*Jefferies*⟩
*Ana* *opinion, view, belief, conviction, sentiment: theory, hypothesis, *law

**ideal** *adj* *abstract, transcendent, transcendental
*Ana* utopian (see AMBITIOUS): surpassing, peerless, *supreme
*Ant* actual

**ideal** *n* pattern, examplar, *model, example, standard, beau ideal, mirror
*Ana* *truth, verity: perfection, *excellence

**identical** 1 *also* identic selfsame, *same, very, equivalent, equal, tantamount
*Ana* corresponding, correlative, convertible (see RECIPROCAL)
*Ant* diverse —*Con* *different, disparate, divergent: *distinct, separate, several
**2** *like, alike, similar, analogous, comparable, akin, parallel, uniform
*Ana* matching, equaling (see MATCH): agreeing, squaring, tallying, jibing, corresponding (see AGREE)
*Ant* different

**identification** *recognition, apperception, assimilation
*Ana* perception, *discernment, discrimination: image, percept, sense-datum, sensum, *sensation

**identify,** incorporate, embody, assimilate are comparable when they mean to bring (one or more things) into union with another thing. **Identify** involves the idea of a union of things that are or are thought of as identical, or the same; it may imply the actual making of a thing or things the same as another ⟨every precaution is taken to *identify* the interests of the people and of the rulers—*Ramsay*⟩ ⟨it is the writer's business to *identify* words with things, emotion with thought—*Muller*⟩ or it may refer to the mental apprehension of a real or imagined identity between things ⟨Min was *identified* with Horus the son of Isis—*Mercer*⟩ ⟨should make us wary toward those who . . . have *identified* Americanism with a partisan policy in behalf of concealed economic aims—*Dewey*⟩ This latter use may

---

*Ana* analogous words     *Ant* antonyms     *Con* contrasted words     See also explanatory notes facing page 1

connote confusion in thought or self-deception ⟨it is easy to *identify* cynicism with honesty and hence with truthfulness—*Hamburger*⟩ **Incorporate** implies a union of one or more things with another, or of different things, so that when blended, fused, or otherwise united they constitute a uniform substance, a single body, or an integral whole ⟨fertilizers should, in general, be *incorporated* with the soil⟩ ⟨what is learned is of no value until it is *incorporated* into one's stock of knowledge⟩ ⟨what he does is to *incorporate* verbatim a good many of Leonardo's notes into a narrative that is entirely his own—*William Murray*⟩ **Embody** (see also REALIZE 1) is more restricted in its range of application than *incorporate* because it can be used only when one or more things are made part of another thing that is an ordered whole (as an organized structure, a group, or a system) ⟨yet so much of these treaties has been *embodied* into the general law of Europe—*Mackintosh*⟩ ⟨a recognized scholar, whose discussion . . . *embodies* the finest fruits of contemporary opinion and research—*E. H. Swift*⟩ **Assimilate** (see also ABSORB 1) falls short of *identify* because it does not always imply the actual fusion or blending or, when self-deception is connoted, the actual confusion, of two things. Like *identify*, however, *assimilate* implies the making of two or more things exactly alike, either actually or in thought; thus, to *assimilate* one's beliefs to those of another is to change them so that they become the same as his; to *identify* one's beliefs with those of another is to make them one and indistinguishable as well as the same; the *d* of the Latin prefix *ad-* is often *assimilated* to a following consonant as in *affectus* for *adfectus* ⟨our manufacturing class was *assimilated* in no time to the conservative classes—*H. G. Wells*⟩
*Ana* fuse, blend, merge (see MIX): *mistake, confuse, confound

**idiom** 1 dialect, *language, speech, tongue
*Ana* jargon, patois, cant, argot (see DIALECT)
2 expression, locution, *phrase

**idiosyncrasy** *eccentricity
*Ana* peculiarity, individuality, distinctiveness *or* distinction, characteristicness *or* characteristic (see corresponding adjectives at CHARACTERISTIC): manner, way, *method, mode: mannerism, affectation, *pose

**idiot** imbecile, moron, *fool, simpleton, natural

**idle** *adj* 1 *vain, nugatory, otiose, empty, hollow
*Ana* fruitless, bootless, *futile, vain: *ineffective, ineffectual, inefficacious: trivial, paltry, *petty, trifling
*Con* significant, pregnant, meaningful (see EXPRESSIVE): profitable, *beneficial, advantageous
2 *inactive, inert, passive, supine
*Ana* indolent, faineant, *lazy, slothful: dawdling, lagging, procrastinating (see DELAY)
*Ant* busy —*Con* industrious, diligent, assiduous, sedulous (see BUSY)

**idle** *vb* **Idle, loaf, lounge, loll, laze** mean to spend time not in work but in idleness. **Idle** may be used with reference to persons or to things that move lazily or without purpose; it may also be employed to connote either strong censure or a pleasant or justifiable action ⟨why do you *idle* away all your days?⟩ ⟨it is impossible to enjoy *idling* thoroughly unless one has plenty of work to do—*Jerome*⟩ ⟨the brook *idles* through the pasture⟩ ⟨her fingers *idled* over the keys⟩ ⟨it is pleasant to saunter out in the morning sun and *idle* along the summer streets with no purpose—*L. P. Smith*⟩ **Loaf** suggests either a resting or a wandering about as though there were nothing to do; it does not necessarily imply contempt, although its agent noun *loafer* when used seriously nearly always carries that implication and has often affected the meaning of the verb ⟨Tennyson does

the greater part of his literary work . . . between breakfast and lunch, and *loafs* the rest of the day—*Boston Journal*⟩ ⟨I *loaf* and invite my soul, I lean and *loaf* at my ease observing a spear of summer grass—*Whitman*⟩ ⟨the idea of the university as a place of leisure where rich young men *loaf* for three or four years is dying—*Russell*⟩ ⟨men who came into the shop to *loaf* during winter afternoons—*Anderson*⟩ **Lounge,** though occasionally used as equal to *idle* or to *loaf,* typically conveys an additional implication of lazily resting or reclining against a support or of physical comfort and ease in relaxation ⟨he stood . . . *lounging* with his elbow against the bar—*Dickens*⟩ ⟨against the sunny sides of the houses, men *lounged,* or played at duck on a rock—*Mary Austin*⟩ The agent noun *lounger* is, however, usually derogatory, though slightly less so than *loafer* ⟨he is not a *loafer,* but he is a *lounger* on street corners during his free hours⟩ ⟨the *loungers* at the bar were beginning to show signs of leaving—*MacFall*⟩ **Loll** also carries an implication of a posture similar to that of *lounge,* but it places greater stress upon an indolent or relaxed attitude ⟨there were not yet any jaded people *lolling* supine in carriages—*Shaw*⟩ ⟨on Sunday afternoons . . . when a crowd was there to *loll* on the front porch and swap stories—*Caldwell*⟩ **Laze** usually implies the relaxation of a busy person enjoying a vacation or his moments of leisure ⟨I had a very pleasant time, sailing, fishing, and *lazing* about—*J. R. Lowell*⟩ ⟨it was nice *lazing* this way. About time she had a holiday!—*Christie*⟩
*Ana* rest, relax, repose (see corresponding nouns at REST): *saunter, stroll, amble

**idolize** *adore, worship
*Ana* dote, love, *like: venerate, *revere, reverence
*Con* *despise, contemn, scorn, disdain: *hate, abhor, detest, loathe, abominate

**if,** **provided** are both used to introduce conditional clauses. When merely a possibility which may or may not be true is expressed, **if** is the usual conjunction ⟨*if* this counsel . . . be of men, it will come to naught—*Acts 6:38*⟩ When the clause which follows names a stipulation or proviso, **provided** (or sometimes **providing**) is the usual form ⟨it is not hard to know God, *provided* one will not force oneself to define him—*Arnold*⟩ ⟨*providing* they pay you the fixed rent—*Ruskin*⟩

**ignite** kindle, *light, fire
*Ant* stifle: extinguish

**ignoble** *mean, sordid, abject
*Ana* *base, low, vile: churlish, boorish, loutish (see under BOOR): *petty, puny, paltry, measly, trivial: abased, debased, degraded (see ABASE)
*Ant* noble: magnanimous —*Con* lofty, *high: sublime, glorious, *splendid: illustrious, eminent (see FAMOUS)

**ignominy** infamy, shame, *disgrace, opprobrium, dishonor, disrepute, obloquy, odium
*Ana* humiliation, degradation, abasement (see corresponding verbs at ABASE): contempt, scorn, disdain, despite (see under DESPISE): mortification, chagrin (see corresponding adjectives at ASHAMED)
*Con* honor, glory (see FAME): respect, esteem, admiration, *regard

**ignorant, illiterate, unlettered, uneducated, untaught, untutored, unlearned** mean not having knowledge. One is **ignorant** who is without knowledge, whether in general or of some particular thing ⟨a very superficial, *ignorant,* unweighing fellow—*Shak.*⟩ ⟨the disputants on both sides were *ignorant* of the matter they were disputing about—*Ellis*⟩ One is **illiterate** who is without the necessary rudiments of education; the term may imply a failure to attain a standard set for the educated or cultivated man ⟨you might read all the books in the British Museum (if you

*A colon (:) separates groups of words discriminated. An asterisk (\*) indicates place of treatment of each group.*

could live long enough) and remain an utterly *illiterate, uneducated* person—*Ruskin*⟩ but when directly applied to a person it usually implies inability to read or write ⟨*illiterate* in the sense that they could not read or write, or . . . functionally *illiterate* in the sense that they were unable to understand what they read—*Kandel*⟩ ⟨*illiterate* voters⟩ When applied to words or alterations of words or grammatical constructions, it implies violation of the usage of educated men or a status below that of the standard English of the day; thus, most teachers would stigmatize the expression "I seen it" as *illiterate*. The word, however, is often used merely as a contemptuous description of one (as a person, an utterance, or a letter) that shows little evidence of education or cultivation ⟨his speech is positively *illiterate*⟩ or shows inability to read and understand ⟨it is common knowledge that our professional students and candidates for the Ph.D. are *illiterate*. One thing you learn very quickly in teaching students at the loftiest levels of education is that they cannot read—*Hutchins*⟩ One is **unlettered** who is without the learning that is to be gained through the knowledge of books. Often it implies being able to read and write, but with no facility in either reading or writing ⟨*unlettered* peasants⟩ but sometimes it implies general ignorance or illiteracy ⟨his addiction was to courses vain, his companies [companions] *unlettered*, rude and shallow—*Shak.*⟩ One is **uneducated, untaught, untutored,** or **unlearned** who either has had no training in the schools or under teachers or whose ignorance, or crudeness, or general lack of intelligence suggests such a lack; none of the words, however, is used with great precision or in a strict sense ⟨beliefs common among *uneducated* men⟩ ⟨lo, the poor Indian! whose *untutored* mind sees God in clouds, or hears him in the wind—*Pope*⟩ ⟨experiences of an *unlearned* man in the search for truth and understanding—*Brit. Book News*⟩ ⟨taught so many flat lies that their false knowledge is more dangerous than the *untutored* natural wit of savages—*Shaw*⟩
*Ana* \*rude, crude, raw, callow, green, uncouth: simple, ingenuous, unsophisticated, naïve (see NATURAL)
*Ant* cognizant (*of something*): conversant: informed —
*Con* \*learned, erudite, scholarly: conscious, \*aware
**ignore** disregard, overlook, slight, \*neglect, omit, forget
*Ana* blink, \*wink: evade, elude, \*escape, avoid, shun, eschew
*Ant* heed (*a warning, a sign, a symptom*): acknowledge (sense 2)
**ilk** kind, sort, \*type, nature, description, character, stripe, kidney
**ill** *adj* \*bad, evil, wicked, naughty
*Ana* see those at EVIL
*Ant* good
**ill** *n* \*evil
*Ant* good
**illegal** \*unlawful, illegitimate, illicit
*Ant* legal —*Con* \*lawful, legitimate, licit
**illegitimate** \*unlawful, illegal, illicit
*Ant* legitimate —*Con* \*lawful, legal, licit
**ill-fated** ill-starred, disastrous, \*unlucky, unfortunate, calamitous, luckless, hapless
*Ana* \*ominous, portentous, fateful: malefic, malign, baleful, \*sinister
**ill-favored** \*ugly, hideous, unsightly
*Ana* \*plain, homely
*Ant* well-favored: fair —*Con* handsome, comely, \*beautiful, lovely, beauteous, pretty
**illiberal** *adj* **Illiberal, narrow-minded, narrow, intolerant, bigoted, hidebound** mean so lacking in breadth of mind or experience as to be unwilling or unable to understand the point of view of others. **Illiberal** implies a lack of freedom

of spirit, mind, or thought that prevents one from entering into sympathy with the aims, beliefs, policies, or attitudes of others; it usually suggests an ungenerous or grudging mind ⟨the *illiberal* or fanatically intolerant spirit which war psychology always engenders—*Cohen*⟩ **Narrow-minded** and **narrow** stress an ingrained temperament that is incompatible with breadth of mind; they usually suggest an inability to see and understand others' beliefs or aims owing to such determining circumstances as birth, breeding, or environment ⟨the American Puritans are frequently described as *narrow-minded*⟩ ⟨there was nothing *narrow* or illiberal in his early training—*J. R. Green*⟩ ⟨he shows to the full their *narrow-minded* hatred of the preceding century—*Stephen*⟩ **Intolerant** may imply illiberality or narrow-mindedness or it may imply an avoidance of weak permissiveness, but it emphasizes unwillingness to tolerate ideas contrary to one's own or to those accepted either generally or in accord with some standard ⟨*intolerant* refusal to listen to an opponent . . . has no business in such a representative nineteenth-century drawing room—*Shaw*⟩ ⟨what force, what fury drove us into saying the stupid, *intolerant*, denunciatory things we said—*L. P. Smith*⟩ ⟨always *intolerant* of loose thinking and of verbosity, he compressed into the masterly introductory essays . . . his entire theory—*Bidwell*⟩ **Bigoted** implies complete satisfaction with one's religious or social creed and unwillingness to admit truth in others; it usually suggests unreasonableness, obstinacy, and narrow-mindedness ⟨"The heart has its reasons which the intellect knows not of." How often have these words of Pascal been abused to justify a temper too indolent to inquire, too *bigoted* to doubt—*Inge*⟩ ⟨in spite of his wide outlook and interests, he could be narrow and *bigoted* in theoretical views and general prejudices—*Malinowski*⟩ **Hidebound** implies the strong restraint of custom, tradition, or habit and aversion to change. There is less suggestion in this word of antagonism to those who hold other opinions, but a strong suggestion of unwillingness to be moved ⟨small-town persons, *hidebound* in their beliefs and conventions⟩ ⟨a nature sometimes *hidebound* and selfish and narrow to the last degree—*Coulton*⟩
*Ant* liberal —*Con* progressive, advanced, radical (see LIBERAL)
**illicit** \*unlawful, illegal, illegitimate
*Ant* licit —*Con* \*lawful, legal, legitimate: sanctioned, endorsed, approved (see APPROVE): permitted, allowed (see LET)
**illimitable** boundless, \*infinite, uncircumscribed, eternal, sempiternal
*Ana* endless, \*everlasting, interminable
**illiterate** *adj* unlettered, uneducated, untaught, \*ignorant, untutored, unlearned
*Ant* literate —*Con* taught, instructed, educated, schooled (see TEACH)
**ill-mannered** \*rude, uncivil, ungracious, impolite, discourteous
*Ana* boorish, loutish, churlish (see under BOOR)
*Ant* well-bred
**ill-starred** ill-fated, disastrous, \*unlucky, unfortunate, calamitous, luckless, hapless
*Ana* malefic, malign, baleful, \*sinister: \*ominous, portentous, fateful
**ill-treat** maltreat, mistreat, \*abuse, misuse, outrage
*Ana* \*wrong, oppress, persecute, aggrieve: \*injure, harm, hurt
**illuminate,** **illumine, light, lighten, enlighten, illustrate** are comparable when meaning to fill with light or to throw light upon. **Illuminate** implies the use of a bright light or of something comparable to it in such a way that what

is dark is made bright or what is complicated, obscure, or vague is made clear ⟨the oblique band of sunlight . . . *illuminated* her as her presence *illuminated* the heath—*Hardy*⟩ ⟨the greatest truths are perhaps those which being simple in themselves *illuminate* a large and complex body of knowledge—*Alexander*⟩ ⟨he longed . . . to hear more about the life of which her careless words had given him so *illuminating* a glimpse—*Wharton*⟩ **Illumine** is chiefly literary or poetical for *illuminate* ⟨what in me is dark *illumine*—*Milton*⟩ ⟨no lurid fire of hell or human passion *illumines* their scenes—*Eliot*⟩ **Light, lighten,** and *enlighten* carry a stronger implication of providing with light for clear seeing than of throwing a light upon. **Light** is the most consistently literal of these terms, though it often carries a suggestion of brightening the way of one who otherwise might stumble or go astray ⟨the room was brilliantly *lighted*⟩ ⟨all our yesterdays have *lighted* fools the way to dusty death—*Shak.*⟩ ⟨seas roll to waft me, suns to *light* me rise—*Pope*⟩ ⟨the old man scratched a match, the spark *lit* up the keyhole of a door—*Lowell*⟩ **Lighten,** like *light,* basically implies a making brighter or a lessening of darkness, but it has more extended and poetic use ⟨*lighten* our darkness, we beseech thee, O Lord—*Book of Common Prayer*⟩ ⟨I would not convey the thought that an opinion is the worse for being *lightened* by a smile—*Cardozo*⟩ **Enlighten,** which has almost wholly lost its basic meaning of to make physically light or bright, is common when filling with intellectual or spiritual light is implied ⟨the Chinese philosopher . . . needed no discovery of science to *enlighten* him; that enlightenment was part of his philosophy, his religion—*Binyon*⟩ Sometimes the term implies that one has been supplied with information necessary to the understanding of something ⟨in her simplicity she did not know what it [her mistake] was, till a hint from a nodding acquaintance *enlightened* her—*Hardy*⟩ and sometimes it implies sufficient education and experience to enable one to meet all needs and, especially in the adjective *enlightened,* to remove or overcome superstition, prejudice, or intolerance ⟨the civilized and *enlightened* portions of the world at the time of the Declaration of Independence—*Taney*⟩ **Illustrate** (see also EXEMPLIFY) is somewhat rare in a sense which approaches that of *illuminate* and in which it suggests the shedding of luster rather than of light, embellishment rather than elucidation, and distinct exhibition rather than a bringing into view ⟨the poet or philosopher *illustrates* his age and country by the efforts of a single mind—*Gibbon*⟩ ⟨narrow of vision but steadfast to principles, they fronted life resolutely, honoring and *illustrating* the supreme worth of freedom—*Repplier*⟩
*Ana* *light, fire, kindle: elucidate, *explain: illustrate, *exemplify
*Ant* darken, obscure —*Con* complicate, involve (see corresponding adjectives at COMPLEX)

**illusion** *delusion, mirage, hallucination
*Ana* *imagination, fancy, fantasy: *sensation, percept, sense-datum, sensum, image

**illusory** *apparent, seeming, ostensible
*Ana* chimerical, fanciful, visionary, *imaginary, fantastic: delusory, delusive, *misleading, deceptive
*Ant* factual: matter-of-fact

**illustrate** 1 enlighten, *illuminate, illumine, light, lighten
*Ana* *adorn, embellish: expose, exhibit, display, *show: *reveal, disclose, discover
*Ant* dim
2 *exemplify
*Ana* elucidate, interpret, *explain, expound: vivify, enliven (see QUICKEN): demonstrate, manifest, *show

**illustration** example, *instance, case, sample, specimen
**illustrious** eminent, renowned, celebrated, *famous, famed
*Ana* glorious, *splendid, resplendent, sublime: outstanding, signal, striking, conspicuous (see NOTICEABLE)
*Ant* infamous —*Con* ignoble, *mean, abject: ignominious, disgraceful, shameful, infamous, dishonorable (see corresponding nouns at DISGRACE)

**ill will** *malice, malevolence, malignity, malignancy, spite, despite, spleen, grudge
*Ana* animosity, antipathy, rancor, animus, hostility, *enmity: *hate, hatred
*Ant* goodwill: charity

**image** 1 Image, effigy, statue, icon, portrait, photograph, mask all mean a lifelike representation especially of a living being. **Image** (see also SENSATION 1) in its earliest English sense denotes a sculptured, cast, or modeled representation (as of a god or a sacred or saintly person) especially when intended for the veneration of the people. The term is also applicable to a representation of a person made in wax, clay, or other plastic substance (as for use in a museum or exhibit or by a sorcerer who wishes to injure or destroy the person through attack on his image). **Effigy** is commonly limited to images sculptured, especially on sepulchral monuments (as in medieval cathedrals), or engraved, especially on coins, except in the idiomatic phrase "to burn (or hang) in *effigy.*" In the latter use *effigy* often implies a crude simulacrum in clothes similar to those worn by the original which serves merely as an object on which is inflicted the sort of punishment which he is supposed to deserve ⟨in some parts of England Guy Fawkes is burned in *effigy* each fifth of November⟩ **Statue** applies not only to an image for use in a church but to a sculptured, cast, or modeled representation of the entire figure, especially as distinguished from a *bust* or *head,* of a living or dead person ⟨a colossal *statue* of Christ on the peak of a high mountain overlooking the harbor⟩ ⟨an equestrian *statue* of Washington⟩ **Icon** specifically designates the type of representation of Christ, the Virgin Mary, or a saint used in Orthodox churches and homes. Because of a literal interpretation of the Second Commandment forbidding the making of graven images an icon is never a statue but is a painting, a mosaic, or a bas-relief ⟨the walls were studded with little *icons* of saints, each one with its guttering lamp before it—*Buchan*⟩ **Portrait** implies pictorial representation, especially of the figure or of the face of a person; it may be used of such a representation as is executed by drawing, photographing, engraving, or, in its now common specific sense, by painting ⟨the Gilbert Stuart *portraits* of Washington⟩ ⟨the latest *portrait* of the chief justice of the Supreme Court⟩ **Photograph** applies only to a portrait that is made by means of a camera and sensitive plates or films. **Mask** applies primarily to a molded copy of a face made in wax or plaster; thus, a death *mask* is a copy made very soon after a person has died, especially a cast or impression taken directly from the face of the dead person.
*Ana* *reproduction, copy, duplicate, facsimile, replica: *form, figure, shape
2 percept, sense-datum, sensum, *sensation
*Ana* *idea, concept, impression, conception, notion: fabrication, figment (see FICTION): phantasy, *fancy, fantasy

**imaginable** *imaginative, imaginal, imaginary
*Ana* realized *or* realizable, conceived *or* conceivable, imagined, envisaged, envisioned (see corresponding verbs at THINK)
*Ant* unimaginable, inconceivable

A colon (:) separates groups of words discriminated. An asterisk (*) indicates place of treatment of each group.

**imaginal** *imaginative, imaginable, imaginary

**imaginary** *adj* **1** Imaginary, fanciful, visionary, fantastic, chimerical, quixotic are comparable when they are applied to conceptions or to the persons who form the conceptions and mean unreal or unbelievable and out of keeping with things as they are or conceiving such unreal or unbelievable things. Something is **imaginary** which is fictitious and purely the product of an active or an excited imagination ⟨*imaginary* ills and fancied tortures —*Addison*⟩ ⟨those nervous persons who may be terrified by *imaginary* dangers are often courageous in the face of real danger—*Ellis*⟩ Something is or, less often, one is **fanciful** which or who indicates a giving rein to the power of conceiving or producing things that have no real counterpart in nature or in fact ⟨in Wales he found a cottage perfectly roofed with fern . . . . Had a painter put this in a picture, many would have exclaimed: "How *fanciful!*"—*Jefferies*⟩ ⟨Rousseau's *fanciful* image of primitive man, uncontaminated by science or art, undepraved by thought—*Grandgent*⟩ Something is **visionary** which, although it seems real and practical to the one who conceives it, is usually the product of a dream or vision or of an unrestrained imagination and is incapable of realization ⟨*visionary* schemes for world conquest⟩ ⟨Goldsmith had long a *visionary* project, that . . . he would go to Aleppo, in order to acquire a knowledge . . . of any arts peculiar to the East, and introduce them into Britain —*Boswell*⟩ ⟨this was a *visionary* scheme . . . a project far above his skill—*Swift*⟩ One is *visionary* who is given to such dreams, visions, and fancies and inspired by the hopes they arouse ⟨if a man happens not to succeed in such an enquiry, he will be thought weak and *visionary* —*Burke*⟩ ⟨planning, as his *visionary* father might have done, to go to Brazil to pick up a fortune—*Van Doren*⟩ Something is **fantastic** (see also FANTASTIC 2) which is or, more often, seems extravagantly fanciful or queer and hence incapable of belief or, sometimes, approval ⟨in words, as fashions, the same rule will hold; alike *fantastic,* if too new, or old—*Pope*⟩ ⟨his strange coming, his strange story, his devotion, his early death and posthumous fame—it was all *fantastic*—*Cather*⟩ ⟨a *fantastic* world inhabited by monsters of iron and steel—*Bromfield*⟩ Something is **chimerical** which is wildly or fantastically visionary or unreal ⟨an universal institutional church is as *chimerical* an idea as an universal empire—*Inge*⟩ ⟨the defeat was more complete, more humiliating . . . the hopes of revival more *chimerical*—*Times Lit. Sup.*⟩ Something is or one is **quixotic** which or who is motivated by extravagantly chivalrous devotion to visionary ideals ⟨*quixotic* as a restoration of medieval knighthood— *Cohen*⟩ ⟨to insist upon clemency in the circumstances would . . . have required *quixotic* courage—*Buchan*⟩ ⟨the economic notion that our present population . . . can live on this island and produce by their work a real income that will give them a rising standard of comfort and leisure, is utterly *quixotic*—*Hobson*⟩

*Ana* *fictitious, fabulous, mythical, legendary, apocryphal: ideal, transcendent, transcendental, *abstract: utopian (see AMBITIOUS): delusory, delusive (see MISLEADING): illusory, seeming, *apparent

*Ant* real, actual

**2** *imaginative, imaginal, imaginable

**imagination,** fancy, fantasy are comparable when denoting either the power or the function of the mind by which mental images of things are formed or the exercise of that power especially as manifested in poetry or other works of art. The meanings of all of these terms have been greatly influenced by changing psychological and aesthetic theories, with the result that in the past they have often carried implications or connotations and sometimes denotations not observable in modern use. **Imagination** is not only the most inclusive of these terms but the freest from derogatory connotations. As an inclusive term it may apply either to the power of forming images of things once known but now absent ⟨our simple apprehension of corporeal objects, if present, is sense; if absent, is *imagination*—*Glanvill*⟩ or to the power of forming images of things not seen, or actually nonexistent, or incapable of actual existence ⟨one feels that a livelier melodic *imagination* would serve the needs of classical opera better—*Evett*⟩ In the first instance the term suggests the use of memory as well as of the image-making power ⟨recall the past in one's *imagination*⟩ ⟨her face haunted his *imagination*⟩ In the second it usually suggests either a new combination of elements found in one's experience or an ability to conceive of something, seen only fragmentarily or superficially, as a complete, perfected, and integral whole ⟨a man of no *imagination* is less likely to feel physical fear⟩ ⟨with *imagination* enough to see the possible consequences⟩ ⟨and as *imagination* bodies forth the forms of things unknown, the poet's pen turns them to shapes and gives to airy nothing a local habitation and a name—*Shak.*⟩ ⟨it is only through *imagination* that men become aware of what the world might be—*Russell*⟩ ⟨facts . . . give us wherewithal to think straight and they stimulate the *imagination;* for *imagination,* like reason, cannot run without the gasoline of knowledge—*Grandgent*⟩ **Fancy** (see also FANCY 3) usually means the power to conceive and give expression to images that are far removed from reality or that represent purely imaginary things ⟨she saw, with the creative eye of *fancy,* the streets of that gay bathing place covered with officers—*Austen*⟩ ⟨the world which any consciousness inhabits is a world made up in part of experience and in part of *fancy*—*Krutch*⟩ In aesthetic use there is a tendency to make *imagination* and *fancy* antithetical. *Imagination* is often used to designate the power of representing the real or what gives an illusion of reality in its entirety and organic unity and, usually, in its ideal or universal character; *fancy,* the power of inventing the novel and unreal by recombining the elements found in reality. So interpreted, *imagination* represents men not only in their outward but in their inward life, and produces a Hamlet; *fancy* presents them in alien surroundings, or essentially changed in their natural physical and mental constitution, and produces centaurs and Brobdingnagians ⟨the *imagination,* or shaping or modifying power; the *fancy,* or the aggregative and associative power—*Coleridge*⟩ ⟨Martians, the little green men of popular *fancy*⟩ ⟨Mendelssohn's *fancy* gives additional soaring power to the poet's—*Kolodin*⟩ **Fantasy** often takes the place of *fancy* in naming the power of unrestrained and often extravagant or delusive fancy or its exhibition in art ⟨[readers] . . . live a compensatory life of *fantasy* between the lines of print—*Huxley*⟩ ⟨this mechanical man or robot idea has been decidedly overdone in the writings of *fantasy*—*Furnas*⟩

*Ana* invention, creation (see corresponding verbs at INVENT): conceiving *or* conception, realizing *or* realization (see corresponding verbs at THINK):

**imaginative,** imaginal, imaginable, imaginary, though not synonymous, are sometimes confused because of their verbal likeness. **Imaginative** applies to something which is the product of the imagination or has a character indicating the exercise of the power of the imagination; thus, *imaginative* writings are often distinguished from such factual writings as historical, expository, and argumentative; an *imaginative* poet is one whose imagination

heightens his perception of people and things ⟨it is a common fallacy that a writer . . . can achieve this poignant quality by improving upon his subject matter, by using his "imagination" upon it and twisting it to suit his purpose. The truth is that by such a process (which is not *imaginative* at all!) he can at best produce only a brilliant sham —*Cather*⟩ ⟨[workaday scientists] . . . are prone to identify the poetical with the impractical, the *imaginative* with the imaginary, the fictional with the false—*Muller*⟩ **Imaginal,** meaning of the imagination or within the conceptive powers of the imagination, has been used, especially by psychologists, to fill the need for an adjective which refers to the imagination only as a function of the mind rather than as a creative power or to images as the mental representations which follow a sensation; thus, a person belongs to one *imaginal* type rather than to another because of his tendency to have sensory images of a particular kind (as visual, tactile, or auditory) ⟨perhaps they owe their *imaginal* coloration to some childhood experience—*Cutsforth*⟩ **Imaginable** often means little more than *conceivable,* but more precisely it may imply that the thing so qualified can be seen or apprehended in a clear mental image ⟨St. Thomas was perhaps of all the apostles the one most easily *imaginable* in the present —*Mackenzie*⟩ **Imaginary** (for fuller treatment see IMAGINARY 1) implies existence only in the imagination ⟨*imaginary* woes⟩ ⟨*Imaginary Conversations,* a book by Walter Savage Landor giving *imaginary* dialogues and *imaginary* letters between famous persons of long ago⟩ ⟨the vague unrest of a husband whose infidelities are *imaginary*—*Glasgow*⟩
*Ana* imagining, fancying, realizing, conceiving (see THINK): creative, inventive (see corresponding verbs at INVENT)
*Con* *prosaic, prosy, matter-of-fact
**imagine** conceive, fancy, realize, envisage, envision, *think
*Ana* *invent, create: fabricate, form, fashion, shape, *make: *conjecture, surmise, guess
**imbecile** idiot, moron, *fool, simpleton, natural
**imbibe** *absorb, assimilate
*Ana* *receive, take, admit, accept: *soak, saturate, steep, impregnate: *permeate, pervade, penetrate, impenetrate: acquire, obtain, *get
*Ant* ooze, exude
**imbue** inoculate, leaven, ingrain, *infuse, suffuse
*Ana* *inform, inspire, fire, animate: impregnate, saturate, *permeate, pervade
**imitate** *copy, mimic, ape, mock
*Ana* impersonate (see ACT *vb*): simulate, feign, counterfeit (see ASSUME): caricature, burlesque, parody, travesty (see under CARICATURE *n*)
**immaterial, spiritual, incorporeal** are comparable when meaning not composed of matter. **Immaterial** is the most comprehensive of these terms because it makes the line of cleavage between itself and its opposite, *material,* not only clear and sharp but not open to confusion. If, therefore, one wishes a word to carry no other possible implication *immaterial* is the appropriate term; it may then apply to things believed to have real but not actual (compare REAL) or phenomenal existence or to things that are purely mental or intellectual constructions ⟨*immaterial* beings⟩ ⟨you feel like a disembodied spirit, *immaterial* —*Maugham*⟩ ⟨*immaterial* forces⟩ ⟨*immaterial* objects of thought⟩ ⟨in making mind purely *immaterial* . . . the body ceases to be living—*Dewey*⟩ **Spiritual** (see also HOLY) may imply the absence of the material or tangible ⟨millions of *spiritual* creatures walk the earth unseen —*Milton*⟩ The term, however, so often applies to some-

thing which has another side or nature variously spoken of as *material, animal, physical,* or *bodily* that the word is frequently used, not to describe the character of a whole (a man, all creatures, a belief, or the world), but to distinguish the part which has the nature of a spirit or soul from the part which has not. In distinction from *immaterial* it frequently, therefore, connotes a supernatural, an intellectual, or a moral character ⟨it is the *spiritual* always which determines the material—*Carlyle*⟩ ⟨great men are they who see that *spiritual* is stronger than any material force, that thoughts rule the world—*Emerson*⟩ **Incorporeal** basically denies the possession or presence of a body or material form; in general use it usually suggests invisibility ⟨*incorporeal* intelligences⟩ ⟨the supposed activities and transactions of putative *incorporeal* beings—*Flew*⟩ but, especially in legal use, it may imply intangibility or impalpability ⟨the second group of intangibles . . . are *incorporeal* rights which do not diminish the rights of others in material things. Such rights as patents, royalties, trademarks, goodwill, and franchises fall into this category—*W. H. Anderson*⟩
*Ant* material —*Con* physical, corporeal, sensible, objective (see MATERIAL)
**immature, unmatured, unripe, unmellow** mean not fully developed. Except for this denial of full development, the terms agree in implications and connotations with the affirmative adjectives *mature, matured, ripe, mellow* discriminated at MATURE.
*Ana* crude, callow, green, *rude: *premature, precocious, untimely: childish, *childlike
*Ant* mature —*Con* matured, ripe, mellow, adult, grown-up (see MATURE *adj*)
**immediate** *direct
*Ana* *nearest, next: intuitive, *instinctive
*Ant* mediate (*knowledge, relation, operation*): distant (*relatives*)
**immense** *huge, vast, enormous, elephantine, mammoth, giant, gigantic, gigantean, colossal, gargantuan, Herculean, cyclopean, titanic, Brobdingnagian
*Ana* tremendous, prodigious, stupendous, *monstrous: *large, big, great
**immerse** *dip, submerge, duck, souse, dunk
*Ana* drench, *soak, saturate, sop, impregnate: *infuse, imbue, ingrain: engross, absorb (see MONOPOLIZE)
**immigrant** *n* 1 *stranger, alien, foreigner, outlander, outsider, émigré
2 *emigrant
**immigrate** emigrate (see under EMIGRANT)
**immigration** emigration (see under EMIGRANT)
**imminent** *impending
*Ana* threatening, menacing (see THREATEN): likely, *probable, possible: *inevitable, ineluctable, inescapable, unescapable, unavoidable: expected, awaited (see EXPECT)
*Con* *distant, remote, far-off: *doubtful, dubious, questionable, problematic
**immobile** *immovable, immotive
*Ant* mobile
**immoderate** inordinate, *excessive, exorbitant, extreme, extravagant
*Ana* *profuse, lavish, prodigal, exuberant: teeming, overflowing (see TEEM)
*Ant* moderate —*Con* temperate (see MODERATE *adj*): restrained, curbed, checked, inhibited (see RESTRAIN): reasonable, *rational
**immoral, unmoral, nonmoral, amoral** are all briefly definable as not moral, yet they are not often interchangeable and are frequently confused, largely because the implications and connotations of the second element are not the

---

A colon (:) separates groups of words discriminated. An asterisk (*) indicates place of treatment of each group.

same in each compound. **Immoral,** which implies an active opposition to what is *moral,* may designate whatever is discordant with accepted ethical principles or the dictates of conscience ⟨morality cannot be legislated but . . . legislation can be *immoral—Gallagher*⟩ ⟨in the way in which he conceded the smaller points in order to win the important objectives and mastered the political game without yielding his own integrity, Roosevelt symbolized the moral man confronted by the dilemmas that an *immoral* society creates—*Link*⟩ and then indicates that what is so designated is fundamentally wrong, unjustifiable, or sinful. But, like *moral, immoral* may often base its values not on principle but on custom and then may imply no more than discordance with accepted social custom or the general practice ⟨refusal to acknowledge the boundaries set by convention is the source of frequent denunciations of objects of art as *immoral—Dewey*⟩ ⟨for a farm settler to start out with a decent home, efficiently produced, still seems *immoral* in many quarters—*New Republic*⟩ In its frequent specific application to sexual and, especially, irregular sexual matters *immoral* tends to fluctuate between the two extremes of its usage range according to the concurrent rigidity of the social outlook. It may in the former case come close to *licentious* or *lewd* in pejorative quality and in the second lose most of its pejorative force and mean little more than *improper* or *immodest* ⟨lead an *immoral* life⟩ ⟨*immoral* people⟩ *Unmoral, nonmoral,* and *amoral* all, in contrast to *immoral,* imply in one way or another a passive negation of what is moral especially as indicated by absence of or freedom from a code that ought to prevail and the evasion of which constitutes wrongdoing. In its most typical use **unmoral** implies a lack of moral perception and ethical awareness and is appropriately applied to persons or to their behavior when these exhibit such a lack; thus, an infant or an idiot may be described as *unmoral* because in neither case is there a capacity to distinguish right from wrong ⟨a man so purely primitive that he was of the type that came into the world before the development of the moral nature. He was not immoral, but merely *unmoral—London*⟩ ⟨Gertrude Stein's discussions reflect primitiveness also in the attitude taken towards sex, for the characters are depicted as being like savages, innocently *unmoral—Braddy*⟩ But *unmoral* may sometimes imply a mere disregard of or failure to be guided by moral principles and is then close to *conscienceless* ⟨the great *unmoral* power of the modern industrial revolution—*F. L. Wright*⟩ and occasionally it may, along with *nonmoral* and *amoral,* imply that what is so qualified cannot be appraised in terms of morality since it is not a fit subject for ethical judgment ⟨it [*moral*] is used as the opposite of *unmoral* (or *amoral*) to refer to acts that come within the sphere of moral (or ethical?) consideration as opposed to those to which moral distinctions do not appropriately apply—*Garvin*⟩ While *nonmoral* and *amoral* are frequently interchangeable ⟨make religion *nonmoral,* a matter of inner experience and personal attitude—*Randall*⟩ ⟨science as such is completely *amoral—W. S. Thompson*⟩ *nonmoral* may be preferred when the thing so described is patently outside the sphere in which moral distinctions or judgments are applicable, while **amoral** may be applied discriminatively to something not customarily or universally exempted from moral judgment; thus, life in the abstract is a *nonmoral* concept although a particular personal life may well be *amoral;* perspective is a *nonmoral* aspect of painting ⟨even those who assign art a moral function must recognize that nonrepresentational painting is best judged by *amoral* standards⟩ ⟨for the most part there are no special benefits for doing good, nor any great penalties for being bad. The supernatural power of

Melanesian religion is simply *amoral—Nida*⟩
*Ana* *licentious, lewd, lascivious, libertine, libidinous, lecherous, wanton, lustful: *abandoned, profligate, dissolute, reprobate: obscene, gross, ribald (see COARSE)
*Ant* moral: chaste, pure
**immortal, deathless, undying, unfading** mean not subject to death or decay and, hence, everlasting. With the exception of *immortal,* all of these words are chiefly in poetic use and are distinguishable especially in their connotations and applications. Basically **immortal** implies little more than exemption from liability to death and is usually applied to the soul or spirit of man ⟨such harmony is in *immortal* souls; but whilst this muddy vesture of decay doth grossly close it in, we cannot hear it—*Shak.*⟩ Sometimes *immortal* equals *eternal* ⟨the first to express the belief that the soul was divine and *immortal* in duration—*Helsel*⟩ but more frequently it keeps close to the basic sense in being applied to something comparable to the soul in that it lives on in fullness of vigor after its maker or possessor has died ⟨the *immortal* epics of Homer⟩ ⟨'tis verse that gives *immortal* youth to mortal maids—*Landor*⟩ ⟨Oh may I join the choir invisible of those *immortal* dead who live again in minds made better by their presence—*George Eliot*⟩ ⟨the single *immortal* act of John Wilkes Booth in snuffing out the life of a beloved president—*Miers*⟩ **Deathless** also implies incapacity for death; it is seldom applied to the soul but rather to immaterial things that transcend the limitations of mortal existence ⟨art's *deathless* dreams—*Shelley*⟩ ⟨virtue crowned with glory's *deathless* meed—*Wordsworth*⟩ **Undying** is applied chiefly to emotions or passions marked by such intensity or vitality as to be or to seem incapable of extinction while life lasts ⟨*undying* love⟩ ⟨*undying* hatred⟩ ⟨a patriot's heart, warm with *undying* fire—*Wordsworth*⟩ ⟨Lawrence's *undying* conviction of the necessity for . . . harmonization—*Millett*⟩ **Unfading** often comes close to *undying* in meaning but connotes persistence of brightness or bloom rather than of intensity ⟨*unfading* recollections⟩ ⟨true charity . . . thrives against hope, and in the rudest scene, storms but enliven its *unfading* green—*Cowper*⟩
*Ana* *everlasting, endless
*Ant* mortal —*Con* transitory, fleeting, fugitive, ephemeral, evanescent, *transient
**immotive** *immovable, immobile
**immovable, immobile, immotive** mean incapable of moving or being moved. Except for this denial of power, the terms otherwise carry the implications and connotations of the affirmative words as discriminated at MOVABLE.
*Ant* movable
**immunity** *exemption
*Ant* susceptibility
**immure** *imprison, incarcerate, jail, intern
*Ana* confine, circumscribe, *limit, restrict
*Con* liberate, *free, release
**impact** *n* Impact, impingement, collision, clash, shock, concussion, percussion, jar, jolt mean a forcible or enforced contact between two or more things, especially a contact so violent as to affect seriously one or the other or all of the persons or things involved. **Impact,** though it often means this and no more, may be used more generally to imply contact between two things, one of which at least is driven or impelled in the direction of the other and produces a definite effect on it, though not necessarily a physical effect or one that results in injury ⟨the *impact* of a hammer upon a nail⟩ ⟨a target constructed to resist the *impact* of a bullet⟩ ⟨live in an age where every mind feels the *impact* of new ideas⟩ ⟨it is not electricity which we see, it is the air rendered incandescent by the vehemence of the *impacts* of the electrons against its molecules—

---

*Ana* analogous words    *Ant* antonyms    *Con* contrasted words    See also explanatory notes facing page 1

*Darrow*⟩ ⟨the *impact* of world war on the lives of countless millions—*R. H. Jackson*⟩ **Impingement** often means little more than *impact,* but distinctively it may imply a sharper or more forcible contact than *impact* ⟨each little *impingement* of sound struck on her consciousness—*Langley*⟩ or may carry, as *impact* does not, a suggestion of encroachment ⟨the *impingement* of scientific theories upon religious beliefs⟩ **Collision** implies the coming together of two or sometimes more things with such force that both or all are more or less damaged or their progress is seriously impeded ⟨a *collision* has occurred when any part of the automobile comes in contact with another object, whether moving or stationary—*Gee*⟩ ⟨his uneasiness grew by the recollection of the forty tons of dynamite in the body of the *Ferndale;* not the sort of cargo one thinks of with equanimity in connection with a threatened *collision*—*Conrad*⟩ Collision may be used when the things which come together so as to seriously affect one another are immaterial rather than physical entities ⟨discrepancies between ideas and *collisions* between beliefs had to be reconciled and mediated—*De Kiewiet*⟩ ⟨the *collision* of contrary false principles—*Warburton*⟩ **Clash** primarily applies to the sharp discordant sounds produced by an impact or series of impacts between two or more bodies, especially metallic bodies; it is often used in preference to *collision* when two or more things come into contact with one another in such a manner that noises of crashing and jangling are more apparent than the destruction or ruin wrought ⟨the *clash* of swords in battle⟩ ⟨the *clash* of cymbals, and the rolling of drums—*Macaulay*⟩ Clash, also, is used more often of immaterial things (as beliefs, theories, and ideas) which are irreconcilable or incompatible and lead to violent conflict or controversy ⟨a *clash* of creeds⟩ ⟨in *Le Misanthrope* . . . there is . . . a *clash* . . . between the high-strung demands of Alceste and the unbending reasonableness of the social standard—*Alexander*⟩ ⟨an appeal to the workers and employers to be good boys and not paralyze the industry of the nation by the *clash* of their quite irreconcilable interests—*Shaw*⟩ **Shock** denotes the effect (as shaking, rocking, agitating, or stunning) produced by an impact or collision. It may imply a physical, mental, or emotional effect, but in every case it carries a strong suggestion of something that strikes or hits with force and often with violence ⟨he stood the *shock* of a whole host of foes—*Addison*⟩ ⟨the *shock* of cataract seas that snap the three-decker's oaken spine—*Tennyson*⟩ ⟨the soft *shock* of wizened apples falling . . . upon the hilly rock—*Millay*⟩ ⟨for strong emotion, however, the *shock* of sudden external stimulus is necessary —*Ellis*⟩ **Concussion,** found more often than *shock* in learned and technical use, may mean a blow or collision but more often suggests the shattering or disrupting effects of a collision or explosion or the stunning weakening effects of a heavy blow ⟨the air seemed rent apart by a *concussion* like the firing of a great cannon—*Chippendale*⟩ ⟨was so careful lest his descent should shake the earth and awake the doctor, that his feet shrank from the *concussion* —*Shaw*⟩ ⟨*concussion* of the brain is actually a paralysis of the functions of the brain—*Fishbein*⟩ **Percussion** implies a deliberate or intentional striking, knocking, or tapping for the sake of something (as a sound, an explosion, or a vibration) produced by the impact of such a stroke, knock, or tap; thus, *percussion* instruments in an orchestra are those played by striking (as a drum, a gong, cymbals, bells, or a tambourine); a *percussion* bullet contains a substance that is exploded by *percussion;* a doctor by *percussion* (that is, by tapping or striking the chest or abdomen) discovers by the sounds produced the condition of a patient's lungs or abdominal organs. **Jar** applies to the

painful and disturbing but not necessarily injurious shaking suffered as a result of a collision, clash, shock, or concussion ⟨the fall gave him a *jar,* but nothing worse⟩ ⟨we felt only the *jar* of the earthquake⟩ ⟨the howl of the wind and the crash and *jar* of seas striking the ship's hull—*Crofts*⟩ ⟨must have suffered some rude *jars* during the long years in which she had observed her husband coarsen—*Ingamells*⟩ **Jolt** carries a stronger implication of jerking out of place than of shaking and therefore carries a clearer suggestion of loss or near-loss of balance ⟨received a *jolt* when the car ran over a hole in the road⟩ ⟨the stern criticism gave him the first *jolt* he had ever had⟩ ⟨lenses should also be protected from jars and *jolts—Kodak Reference Handbook*⟩
**Ana** hitting *or* hit, striking *or* stroke, smiting, slapping *or* slap (see corresponding verbs at STRIKE): beating, pounding, buffeting (see BEAT *vb*)

**impair** damage, mar, *injure, harm, hurt, spoil
**Ana** *weaken, enfeeble, debilitate, sap, undermine, disable, cripple: *deface, disfigure: *deform, distort, contort, warp
**Ant** improve, amend: repair —*Con* better, ameliorate (see IMPROVE)

**impalpable** *imperceptible, insensible, intangible, inappreciable, imponderable
**Ana** tenuous, rare, slight (see THIN *adj*): attenuated, extenuated, rarefied (see THIN *vb*)
**Ant** palpable —*Con* *perceptible, sensible, tangible, appreciable, imponderable

**impart** *communicate
**Ana** *share, participate, partake: *distribute, dispense, divide: convey, *transfer: instill, inculcate, *implant: imbue, inoculate, leaven, *infuse

**impartial** *fair, equitable, unbiased, objective, just, dispassionate, uncolored
**Ana** disinterested, detached, aloof, *indifferent
**Ant** partial —*Con* influenced, swayed, affected (see AFFECT)

**impassable,** impenetrable, impervious, impermeable are comparable when they mean not allowing passage through. **Impassable** applies chiefly to stretches of land or water which cannot be passed over or crossed because of some insuperable difficulty or obstruction ⟨the river is *impassable* in the rainy season⟩ ⟨the road between here and the city is *impassable* since the storm blew down the trees⟩ ⟨this ocean of snow, which after October is *impassable—Evelyn*⟩ ⟨the gulf is the difference between the angelic and the diabolic temperament. What more *impassable* gulf could you have?—*Shaw*⟩ **Impenetrable** applies chiefly to something which is so dense or so thick that not even the thinnest shaft (as of light or air) can find its way through ⟨*impenetrable* fog⟩ ⟨*impenetrable* darkness⟩ ⟨this gentleman was *impenetrable* to ideas—*Colum*⟩ ⟨Professor Murray has . . . interposed between Euripides and ourselves a barrier more *impenetrable* than the Greek language—*T. S. Eliot*⟩ Often, however, *impenetrable* is preferred to *impassable* when implying an exceedingly dense growth that prevents passage ⟨an *impenetrable* thicket⟩ ⟨an *impenetrable* forest⟩ **Impervious,** which implies impenetrability, applies basically to substances or materials which have been so finished or treated as to make them impenetrable (as to air, water, or sound waves) ⟨no surface coating has ever been found which is *impervious* to sun, wind and rain—*Furnas*⟩ When applied to persons or their minds or hearts, *impervious* usually implies complete resistance to anything that would affect them for better or worse ⟨*impervious* to threats or prayers or tears—*Hewlett*⟩ ⟨we become *impervious* to new truth both from habit and from desire—*Russell*⟩ ⟨so soaked

A colon (:) separates groups of words discriminated. An asterisk (*) indicates place of treatment of each group.

with the preserve "good form" that we are *impervious* to the claims and clamor of that ill-bred creature—life!—*Galsworthy*⟩ **Impermeable** implies impenetrability, whether natural or artificially acquired, by a liquid or a gas and incapacity for becoming soaked or permeated; the term applies chiefly to substances (as some clays) which do not absorb water, to cloths treated so as to be rainproof, or to materials which do not admit the passage of air, light, gas, or water ⟨osmo-regulation in the eel is achieved by an *impermeable* outer covering of slime—*Dowdeswell*⟩ ⟨*impermeable* rocks⟩ ⟨gas pipes should be made of an *impermeable* metal⟩ ⟨*impermeable* roofing⟩ ⟨he was not drunk, since the resilient composition of which his nerves were made was almost *impermeable* to alcohol—*West*⟩ *Ant* passable

**impassible** insensitive, *insensible, anesthetic

**impassioned, passionate, ardent, fervent, fervid, perfervid** mean actuated by or showing intense feeling. **Impassioned,** though applicable to persons, is more often found in reference to utterance or artistic expression or to the mood or mental state which evokes such utterance or expression. The word usually implies intensity without violence and feeling of such depth, sincerity, and potency that it passes naturally and inevitably from the person into his expression ⟨poetry is the breath and finer spirit of all knowledge; it is the *impassioned* expression which is in the countenance of all science—*Wordsworth*⟩ ⟨the letters... are written by this master of *impassioned* recollection in a style so musical, so magical and moving, that the experiences he recounts become our own—*L. P. Smith*⟩ ⟨as his *impassioned* language did its work the multitude rose into fury —*Froude*⟩ **Passionate,** on the other hand, implies vehemence and, often, violence of emotion; when the latter idea is suggested, the word also may connote loss of rational guidance or wasteful diffusion or misdirection of emotional power ⟨a *passionate* denunciation⟩ ⟨a *passionate* reformer⟩ ⟨*passionate* partisanship⟩ ⟨*passionate* feeling is desirable, provided it is not destructive—*Russell*⟩ ⟨to match mere good, sound reasons, against the *passionate* conclusions of love is a waste of intellect bordering on the absurd—*Conrad*⟩ ⟨the *passionate* and uncompromisingly ruthless war spirit, common to Communists and Fascists—*Cohen*⟩ **Ardent** differs from *passionate* largely in its freedom from derogatory implications and in its connotations of qualities suggestive of flame or fire. It is especially appropriate when vehemence is implied and the intense feeling expresses itself in eagerness, zeal, enthusiasm, or acts of devotion ⟨an *ardent* desire for the truth⟩ ⟨an *ardent* supporter of liberal ideas⟩ ⟨an *ardent* lover⟩ ⟨heredity in man is hardly the simple thing that many of the *ardent* eugenists would have us believe—*Furnas*⟩ ⟨gave constant proofs of his *ardent* longing for an education—*Merriman*⟩ **Fervent** also implies a quality of fire, but it suggests a fire that glows rather than one that bursts into flame. Hence, though it implies strength and depth of feeling, it more often suggests steadiness than vehemence and inward quiet rather than outward activity. It is applicable especially to wishes, prayers, or hopes that are heartfelt or devout, but it is also applied to an emotion, or to a person feeling such an emotion, that is free from turbulence ⟨*fervent* thanks⟩ ⟨*fervent* good wishes⟩ ⟨a *fervent* Christian⟩ ⟨*fervent* prayers⟩ ⟨Jane's feelings, though *fervent*, were little displayed—*Austen*⟩ ⟨the gods approve the depth, and not the tumult, of the soul; a *fervent*, not ungovernable, love—*Wordsworth*⟩ **Fervid,** like *impassioned,* is applied more to moods and expressions than to persons; in contrast to *impassioned,* however, it sometimes suggests more obvious, more warmly expressed, and, often, more spontaneous emotion ⟨who could help

liking her? her generous nature, her gift for appreciation, her wholehearted, *fervid* enthusiasm?—*L. P. Smith*⟩ Frequently it carries a strong suggestion of feverishness which distinguishes it sharply from *fervent;* thus, *fervent* thanks suggest the depth and sincerity of the emotion which prompts them; *fervid* thanks suggest profuseness or an overwrought state of mind ⟨his *fervid* manner of love-making offended her—*Bennett*⟩ **Perfervid** carries an implication of too great emotional excitement or of overwrought feelings; more than *fervid,* it casts doubt upon the sincerity of the emotion that is displayed with vehemence ⟨to court their own discomfiture by love is a common instinct with certain *perfervid* women—*Hardy*⟩ ⟨in his *perfervid* flag-waving moments—*S. H. Adams*⟩
*Ana* vehement, *intense, fierce, violent: *deep, profound: *sentimental, romantic, maudlin
*Ant* unimpassioned —*Con* dispassionate, uncolored, objective (see FAIR *adj*)

**impassive, stoic, phlegmatic, apathetic, stolid** are comparable when they mean slightly if at all responsive to something that might be expected to excite emotion or interest or to produce a sensation. The distinctions to be drawn between these adjectives hold true also of their corresponding nouns, **impassivity** *or* **impassiveness, stoicism, phlegm, apathy, stolidity.** One is **impassive** who feels or shows no emotion or sensation, without necessary implication of insusceptibility ⟨his majestic *impassivity* contrasting with the overt astonishment with which a row of savagely ugly attendant chiefs grinned and gaped—*Shaw*⟩ ⟨under their *impassive* exterior they preserve ... emotions of burning intensity—*Lathrop*⟩ One is **stoic** who is indifferent to pleasure or pain; the word frequently suggests unflinching fortitude ⟨not only the cataclysm of a world, but also the *stoic* and indomitable temper that endures it —*Lowes*⟩ ⟨a *stoic* atmosphere of fortitude in adversity—*Orville Prescott*⟩ **Phlegmatic** implies a temperament or constitution in which emotion is hard to arouse or, when aroused, is moderate or restrained ⟨cold and *phlegmatic* must he be who is not warmed into admiration by the surrounding scenery—*Waterton*⟩ ⟨a lofty *phlegm,* a detachment in the midst of action, a capacity for watching in silence—*Edmund Wilson*⟩ **Apathetic** usually implies either a remiss and culpable indifference or such a preoccupation with a particular depressing emotion (as care, grief, or despair) or bodily pain as makes one insensible to other emotion or pain and deficient in or devoid of the usual human interests ⟨there is only one alarming aspect of our national debt ... the *apathy* and ignorance of the American public with regard to it. The common attitude is ...: why should an ordinary citizen add the national debt to his other workaday worries—*Scherman*⟩ ⟨the row of *stolid,* dull, vacant plowboys, ungainly in build, uncomely in face, lifeless, *apathetic*—*Butler* d. 1902⟩ ⟨an uncomplaining *apathy* displaced this anguish; and, indifferent to delight, to aim and purpose, he consumed his days, to private interest dead, and public care—*Wordsworth*⟩ **Stolid** implies heavy, dull, obtuse impassivity or apathy or utter blankness of countenance mirroring or suggesting such quality; often, specifically, it suggests impassive, mechanical, plodding, unquestioning, unresourceful adherence to routine ⟨*stolid* Saxon rustics, in whom the temperature of religious zeal was little ... above absolute zero—*Huxley*⟩ ⟨the *stolidest* mask ever given to man—*Meredith*⟩
*Ana* *cool, composed, collected, imperturbable: reserved, taciturn, *silent, reticent: callous, *hardened, indurated: *insensible, insensitive
*Ant* responsive —*Con* *tender, compassionate, sympathetic, warm, warmhearted

**impassivity, impassiveness** apathy, stolidity, phlegm,

stoicism (see under IMPASSIVE)

**impatient,** nervous, unquiet, restless, restive, uneasy, fidgety, jumpy, jittery are comparable when they mean manifesting signs of unrest or an inability to keep still or quiet. Impatient implies an inability to bear some trial (as delay, opposition, discomfort, or stupidity) with composure; it therefore connotes, as a rule, not physical but mental or emotional unrest and may suggest unrestrained reactions (as of eagerness, irritableness, brusqueness, testiness, or intolerance) ⟨so tedious is this day as is the night before some festival to an *impatient* child that hath new robes— *Shak.*⟩ ⟨cease your contention, which has been too long; I grow *impatient—Pope*⟩ ⟨when we pursue the ulterior significance of the colors into yet wider regions . . . I fear the august common sense of the Occident becomes affronted and *impatient—Binyon*⟩ ⟨the temper of the youth of his country is violent, *impatient,* and revolutionary— *Fischer*⟩ Nervous implies unsteadiness of nerves and a proneness to excitability ⟨a *nervous,* fretful woman⟩ ⟨you and I, whose ordinary daily talk maintains its slow or hurried, *nervous* or phlegmatic . . . but always pedestrian gait—*Lowes*⟩ ⟨becoming more *nervous* as the gloom increased—*Hudson*⟩ Unquiet, though basically meaning no more than not quiet, is usually used with a strong implication of prolonged or conspicuous agitation or of troubling or disturbing distractions that hinder one's peace of mind or spirit or prevent concentration; the word is applicable both to the person and to the thing which troubles him ⟨these *unquiet* times⟩ ⟨*unquiet* meals make ill digestions—*Shak.*⟩ ⟨they have not the restless *unquiet* temperament associated with the Anglo-Saxon race—*Alfred Buchanan*⟩ Restless usually implies constant and more or less aimless motion or activity; often, specifically, it connotes mental agitation ⟨our heart is *restless,* until it repose in Thee—*Pusey*⟩ ⟨indubitably not happy . . . *restless* and disquieted, his disquietude sometimes amounting to agony —*Arnold*⟩ or eagerness to change ⟨he was *restless* and dissatisfied with his life—*Anderson*⟩ or continuous or unceasing movements to and fro or back and forth ⟨the *restless* sea⟩ ⟨a *restless* crowd⟩ ⟨he was as *restless* as a hyena—*De Quincey*⟩ Restive (see also CONTRARY 2), which once meant unwilling to move, has gradually become a synonym of *restless.* In this sense it implies impatience under attempts to restrain, to control, or, especially, to keep attentive and suggests either inability to keep still or to persist in what one is doing ⟨they were all becoming *restive* under the monotonous persistence of the missionary—*Cather*⟩ ⟨as *restive* and dissatisfied as a party of 7 bridge players—*Eddington*⟩ Uneasy usually implies restlessness born of anxiety, doubt, uncertainty, or insecurity ⟨he is *uneasy* over business conditions⟩ ⟨an *uneasy* conscience⟩ ⟨an *uneasy* sense that all was not well with his family⟩ ⟨*uneasy* lies the head that wears a crown —*Shak.*⟩ ⟨so we come down, *uneasy,* to look, uneasily pacing the beach. These are the dikes our fathers made: we have never known a breach—*Kipling*⟩ ⟨the first *uneasy* stir of the sleeper—*Mumford*⟩ Fidgety implies restless movements resulting from nervousness, boredom, or uneasiness of mind; it usually suggests an inability to keep one's hands, feet, or body still or to settle down to a task or occupation ⟨toward the end of the day the pupils become *fidgety*⟩ ⟨he declared if I was *fidgety* he should have no comfort—*Burney*⟩ ⟨he perhaps did not realize . . . that the persons who felt *fidgety* or disquieted about the matter were not likely to write in about it, lest they appear irreverent—*E. B. White*⟩ Jumpy and *jittery* imply extreme nervousness that exhibits itself in tremulous, uncertain movements. Jumpy, however, usually suggests a fearful or apprehensive mood and lack of control over one's temper

as well as over one's muscles ⟨if you didn't drink so much, you wouldn't be so *jumpy—Barnaby Conrad*⟩ Jittery suggests domination not only by fears but by recollections that destroy one's nervous control and impair one's mental stability ⟨soldiers still *jittery* from their experiences under heavy fire⟩ ⟨the chief factor in making children *jittery* is *jittery* parents—*Time*⟩
*Ana* fretful, querulous, *irritable, snappish, waspish: *eager, anxious, avid, keen: impetuous, *precipitate, headlong, hasty, sudden, abrupt
*Ant* patient —*Con* composed, imperturbable, unflappable, unruffled, *cool: *calm, serene, tranquil, placid
**impeach** indict, incriminate, *accuse, charge, arraign
*Ana* condemn, denounce, blame, censure (see CRITICIZE): try, test, *prove
*Con* *exculpate, vindicate, exonerate, acquit, absolve
**impeccable,** faultless, flawless, errorless are comparable when they mean absolutely correct and beyond criticism. Impeccable usually applies to something with which no fault can be found or which is irreproachably correct ⟨the only *impeccable* writers are those that never wrote—*Hazlitt*⟩ ⟨her logical process is *impeccable—Grandgent*⟩ ⟨an *impeccable* figure in trim dinner jacket and starched shirt—*Capote*⟩ Faultless is often used in place of *impeccable* without loss, but it is sometimes preferred when the emphasis is upon the absence of defect or blemish rather than upon technical correctness ⟨whoever thinks a *faultless* piece to see, thinks what ne'er was, nor is, nor e'er shall be—*Pope*⟩ ⟨in *faultless* English and with merciless logic, lashed all the miners' socialistic theories—*Collis*⟩ Its distinctive implication, however, is often that of insipidity or tediousness ⟨faultily *faultless,* icily regular, splendidly null, dead perfection, no more—*Tennyson*⟩ Flawless applies especially to natural products in which no cracks, blemishes, or imperfections can be detected ⟨a *flawless* diamond⟩ or to character or reputation which is admirably excellent ⟨destroyed his *flawless* reputation by a single act⟩ or to a work of art or its execution when comparably fine ⟨a *flawless* lyric⟩ ⟨the *flawless* technique of the pianist⟩ ⟨a *flawless* story published in 1895 . . . somewhat forecasts James's final type—*Van Doren*⟩ Errorless usually implies absence of all mistakes, especially of such mistakes as are technically regarded as errors; thus, an *errorless* baseball game may not involve *flawless* playing.
*Ana* inerrant, unerring, *infallible: *correct, accurate, precise, right, nice: *perfect, entire, whole, intact
*Con* *deficient, defective: *superficial, shallow, uncritical, cursory: culpable, *blameworthy
**impecunious** *poor, indigent, needy, destitute, penniless, poverty-stricken, necessitous
*Ant* flush —*Con* *rich, wealthy, affluent, opulent
**impede** *hinder, obstruct, block, bar, dam
*Ana* clog, *hamper, fetter, trammel, shackle, manacle, hog-tie: *embarrass, discomfit, disconcert, rattle, faze: thwart, baffle, balk, *frustrate
*Ant* assist: promote —*Con* *advance, further, forward: *help, aid
**impediment** *obstacle, obstruction, bar, snag
*Ana* *difficulty, hardship, rigor, vicissitude: barrier, *bar: handicap (see ADVANTAGE 1)
*Ant* aid, assistance: advantage (sense 1)
**impel** drive, *move, actuate
*Ana* compel, constrain, *force: *provoke, excite, stimulate: *incite, instigate, foment: goad, spur (see corresponding nouns at MOTIVE)
*Ant* restrain —*Con* curb, check, inhibit (see RESTRAIN)
**impending,** imminent are comparable when they mean very likely to occur soon or without further warning. Both retain in this sense some feeling of now rare or disused

---

A colon (:) separates groups of words discriminated. An asterisk (*) indicates place of treatment of each group.

senses in which they essentially denote being physically elevated and hanging over or projecting as if about to fall and, as a result, tend to convey an ominous or portentous note ⟨*impending* doom⟩ ⟨*imminent* disaster⟩ Occasionally this feeling may be lacking and the words imply no more than the near futurity of the thing qualified ⟨the look of anticipation, of sweet, *impending* triumph—*Weston*⟩ ⟨the mounting heat of June warned us . . . that our departure was *imminent—Repplier*⟩ Distinctively **impending** suggests that the thing likely to occur is foreshadowed far enough ahead to allow one time for worry and suspense or for aversive action ⟨at the sound of thunder we hurried in to avoid the *impending* storm⟩ ⟨worrying over his position in the *impending* reorganization of the company⟩ ⟨the country must swiftly prepare to defend itself against this *impending* economic rape—*Walinsky*⟩ **Imminent** usually implies greater immediacy and may suggest that the thing is on the point of happening ⟨thrown into sweats of suspicion that discovery was *imminent—Meredith*⟩ ⟨we were in *imminent* danger of being swamped by the whitecaps—*London*⟩ but *imminent*, unlike *impending*, may lose much or all of its suggestion of futurity and then attributes nearness in some other than temporal relation to the thing qualified ⟨they could hear the city, evocative and strange, *imminent* and remote; threat and promise both—*Faulkner*⟩ ⟨in matters where the national importance is *imminent* and direct even where Congress has been silent, the States may not act at all—*Justice Holmes*⟩ ⟨all that we had ever thought or felt for home was real again, made *imminent* and present by the arrival of the Fortresses—*Skidmore*⟩ *Ana* *close, near, nigh: approaching, nearing (see APPROACH *vb*): likely, *probable: threatening, menacing (see THREATEN)

**impenetrable** impervious, impermeable, *impassable
*Ana* *close, dense, compact, thick: solid, hard, *firm: compacted, concentrated, consolidated (see COMPACT *vb*): callous, *hardened, indurated: obdurate, adamant, *inflexible
*Ant* penetrable　—*Con* *soft, mild, gentle, lenient: indulgent, merciful, clement, *forbearing, tolerant

**impenetrate** interpenetrate, penetrate, *permeate, pervade, impregnate, saturate
*Ana* *enter, pierce, probe, penetrate: invade, entrench (see TRESPASS): drench, *soak

**imperative** **1** peremptory, imperious, *masterful, domineering
*Ana* commanding, ordering, bidding (see COMMAND *vb*): magisterial, *dictatorial, dogmatic, oracular: arbitrary, autocratic, despotic (see ABSOLUTE)
*Con* supplicating *or* supplicatory, entreating, imploring, beseeching, begging (see corresponding verbs at BEG): mild, gentle, lenient, *soft
**2** *pressing, urgent, crying, importunate, insistent, exigent, instant
*Ana* compelling, constraining (see FORCE *vb*): critical, crucial, *acute

**imperceptible,** insensible, impalpable, intangible, inappreciable, imponderable all mean incapable of being apprehended by the senses or intellect (as in form, nature, extent, or degree) even though known to be real or existent. Except for this denial of apprehensibility, these terms carry the same implications and connotations as the affirmative adjectives discriminated at PERCEPTIBLE ⟨the *imperceptible* movement of the hour hand⟩ ⟨he grew into the scheme of things by *insensible* gradations—*H. G. Wells*⟩ ⟨the almost *impalpable* beauties of style and expression—*Prescott*⟩ ⟨we shall consider that more subtle and *intangible* thing, the soul which he sought to build up in his people—*Buchan*⟩ ⟨that *inappreciable* particle of an ele-

ment called an atom⟩ ⟨the *imponderable* factors, such as temperament and mental stability, which make or mar a promising career⟩
*Ant* perceptible

**imperfection,** deficiency, shortcoming, fault mean a failure in persons or in things to reach a standard of excellence or perfection. **Imperfection** is the most general of these words; it usually does not imply a great departure from perfection and is usually replaceable by a more specific term (as *flaw, blemish, defect, failing, frailty,* or *foible*) which emphasizes its slightness rather than its enormity ⟨the statue has one *imperfection*⟩ ⟨the early Christians followed the Stoics: property was a result of man's *imperfection*. It should be accepted regretfully, and society should take care that too much did not collect in too few hands—*Agar*⟩ ⟨coffee is graded by the number of *imperfections* in the sample—*Ukers*⟩ **Deficiency** carries a clear implication of lack or of inadequacy, whether moral or mental, physical or spiritual; it applies particularly to persons, but it may refer also to an inadequacy in things which affects the persons involved. Unlike *imperfection*, it often implies a great departure from a standard of perfection or sufficiency ⟨Mr. Collins was not a sensible man, and the *deficiency* of nature had been but little assisted by education or society—*Austen*⟩ ⟨the disastrous want and weakness of Shelley . . .—his utter *deficiency* in humor—*Arnold*⟩ ⟨another food *deficiency* was responsible for one of the most debilitating and crippling diseases of the Orient—*Heiser*⟩ **Shortcoming** implies deficiency but is seldom used in quite the same sense. Often it implies a standard of perfection or of excellence which is hard to reach and then suggests not so much the degree of imperfection or deficiency as (the doer's) sense of failure to reach the standard or (the critic's or judge's) unwillingness to use a harsher or more direct term ⟨the *shortcomings* of representative government⟩ ⟨my book has many *shortcomings*, I fear⟩ ⟨do not let them, as poor people, make everyone else suffer for their *shortcomings—Shaw*⟩ ⟨let him only preach well, and all his *shortcomings* as a curate would be forgiven—*Mackenzie*⟩ ⟨management *shortcomings* in one form or another cause most business failures—*Nation's Business*⟩ **Fault** (see also FAULT) is more direct and clear-cut in statement than any of the others; it usually implies personal culpability for the failing in a person or direct blameworthiness for the shortcoming or defect in a thing; often, also, it permits description of the failing or defect ⟨he has . . . the *fault* of defective mantelpiece clocks, of suddenly stopping in the very fullness of the tick—*Conrad*⟩ ⟨Sophia observed a *fault* in the daily conduct of the house—*Bennett*⟩
*Ana* *failure, neglect, dereliction: *fault, failing, frailty, foible: *blemish, flaw, defect: weakness, infirmity (see corresponding adjectives at WEAK)
*Ant* perfection

**imperial** *kingly, regal, royal, queenly, princely
*Ana* majestic, august, stately, noble, *grand: sovereign, *dominant

**imperil** *venture, hazard, risk, chance, jeopardize, endanger
*Ana* dare, brave (see FACE): encounter, confront, *meet, face: *threaten, menace

**imperious** domineering, *masterful, peremptory, imperative
*Ana* *dictatorial, authoritarian, magisterial: despotic, tyrannical, arbitrary, autocratic (see ABSOLUTE): lordly, overbearing (see PROUD)
*Ant* abject　—*Con* obsequious, servile, menial, *subservient, slavish: *compliant, acquiescent

**impermeable** impervious, impenetrable, *impassable
*Ana* solid, hard, *firm: *tight

*Con* absorbing *or* absorbent, imbibing, assimilating *or* assimilative (see corresponding verbs at ABSORB)

**impersonate** play, *act
*Ana* imitate, mimic, ape, *copy: simulate, counterfeit, feign (see ASSUME): caricature, burlesque (see under CARICATURE *n*)

**impersonator** *actor, player, mummer, mime, mimic, performer, thespian, trouper

**impertinent, officious, meddlesome, intrusive, obtrusive** are applied to persons and their acts and utterances and mean exceeding or tending to exceed the bounds of propriety regarding the interposition of oneself in another person's affairs. **Impertinent** (see also RELEVANT) implies a concerning oneself more or less offensively with things which are another's business or, at least, not in any sense one's own business ⟨I should have liked to ask the girl for a word which would give my imagination its line. But how was one to venture so far? I can be rough sometimes but I am not naturally *impertinent*—*Conrad*⟩ ⟨approach complete strangers, ask them a battery of *impertinent* questions —*S. L. Payne*⟩ ⟨when he became hot and vulgar, she turned grande dame, so that he felt like an *impertinent* servant—*Sinclair Lewis*⟩ **Officious** implies the offering, often well-meant, of services, attentions, or assistance that are not needed or that are unwelcome or offensive ⟨'twas but the *officious* zeal of a well-meaning creature for my honor—*Sterne*⟩ ⟨I cannot walk home from office, but some *officious* friend offers his unwelcome courtesies to accompany me—*Lamb*⟩ ⟨the foremen grew more *officious* in manner and shouted their orders—*Bromfield*⟩ **Meddlesome** carries a stronger implication of annoying interference in other people's affairs than the preceding terms; it may imply the qualities of character suggested by any of the other words, but it usually also connotes a prying or inquisitive nature ⟨a *meddlesome* old man⟩ ⟨the people found the government unduly *meddlesome*⟩ ⟨it was in no way from any desire to interfere in other people's affairs . . . he had none of my own *meddlesome* quality—*Hugh Walpole*⟩ **Intrusive** applies largely to persons, actions, or words that reveal a disposition to thrust oneself into other people's affairs or society or to be unduly curious about what is not one's concern ⟨Navajo hospitality is not *intrusive*. Eusabio made the Bishop understand that he was glad to have him there, and let him alone—*Cather*⟩ **Obtrusive** is applicable like *intrusive* and often carries very similar implications. Distinctively, however, it connotes objectionable actions more than an objectionable disposition and so stresses a thrusting forward of oneself, as into a position where one can harm more often than help or where one is unduly or improperly conspicuous ⟨rebels against a social order that has no genuine need of them and is disposed to tolerate them only when they are not *obtrusive*—*Mencken*⟩
*Ana* interfering, meddling (see MEDDLE): arrogant, insolent (see PROUD): brazen, impudent, brash, barefaced, *shameless: *offensive, repugnant
*Con* decent, *decorous, seemly, proper: reserved, reticent, *silent

**imperturbable** composed, collected, *cool, unruffled, unflappable, nonchalant
*Ana* immobile, *immovable: serene, *calm, tranquil, placid: *complacent, self-satisfied, smug
*Ant* choleric, touchy —*Con* discomfited, disconcerted, rattled, fazed (see EMBARRASS): *irascible, splenetic, testy

**impervious** impenetrable, impermeable, *impassable
*Ana* resisting *or* resistant, withstanding, opposing, combating, fighting (see corresponding verbs at RESIST): *hardened, indurated, callous: obdurate, adamant,

adamantine, *inflexible
*Con* open, exposed, susceptible, sensitive, *liable, prone

**impetuous** headlong, *precipitate, abrupt, hasty, sudden
*Ana* impulsive, *spontaneous: vehement, *intense, violent: forceful, forcible, *powerful: violent (see corresponding noun at FORCE): *impatient, restive: *impassioned, passionate, fervid, ardent
*Con* *steady, even, equable: *deliberate, premeditated, considered, advised

**impetus 1** momentum, *speed, velocity, pace
*Ana* energy, force, *power: impelling *or* impulsion, driving, moving (see corresponding verbs at MOVE)
**2** *stimulus, excitant, incitement, stimulant
*Ana* incentive, impulse, spur, goad, *motive, spring

**impingement** *impact, collision, clash, shock, concussion, percussion, jar, jolt
*Ana* hitting *or* hit, striking *or* stroke, smiting (see corresponding verbs at STRIKE): encroachment, entrenchment (see corresponding verbs at TRESPASS): *impression, impress, imprint, stamp, print

**impious, profane, blasphemous, sacrilegious** mean showing marked irreverence for what is sacred or divine. **Impious** usually implies extreme disrespect for God or the laws of God or for those endowed with God-given authority particularly as shown positively in thought or in actions ⟨against the throne and monarchy of God, raised *impious* war in Heaven—*Milton*⟩ ⟨when vice prevails, and *impious* men bear sway, the post of honor is a private station— *Addison*⟩ ⟨who is there more *impious* than a backsliding priest—*Steinbeck*⟩ **Profane** (see PROFANE 1) applies to men and to words and acts that manifest not only impiety but defilement or desecration, sometimes thoughtless and sometimes intentional, of what is worthy of highest reverence or respect ⟨shall I . . . add a greater sin by prostituting holy things to idols . . . what act more execrably unclean, *profane?*—*Milton*⟩ ⟨then speech *profane,* and manners profligate, were rarely found—*Cowper*⟩ **Blasphemous** (compare BLASPHEMY) adds to *profane* the implication of indignity, either deliberate or inadvertent, offered directly or indirectly to the Supreme Being ⟨it is *blasphemous* because it attributes to God purposes which we would not respect even in an earthly parent—*Pike*⟩ ⟨we have heard him speak *blasphemous* words against Moses, and against God—*Acts* 6:11⟩ **Sacrilegious** basically implies the commission of a sacrilege (see PROFANATION), but in its more usual extended sense it implies the defilement of what is holy or sacred (as by acts of depredation, disrespect, or contempt ⟨*sacrilegious* despoilers of ancient churches⟩ ⟨a most *sacrilegious* breach of trust—*Bolingbroke*⟩ ⟨she saw that it was a terrible, a *sacrilegious* thing to interfere with another's destiny, to lay the tenderest touch upon any human being's right to love and suffer after his own fashion —*Wharton*⟩
*Ana* nefarious, iniquitous, flagitious (see VICIOUS): *irreligious, ungodly, godless
*Ant* pious: reverent —*Con* *holy, sacred, blessed, religious, spiritual, divine

**impish** roguish, waggish, mischievous, *playful, frolicsome, sportive
*Ana* *saucy, pert, arch: naughty, *bad: *sly, cunning, tricky

**implacable** relentless, unrelenting, merciless, *grim
*Ana* *inflexible, inexorable, obdurate, adamant: pitiless, ruthless, compassionless (see corresponding nouns at SYMPATHY)
*Con* yielding, submitting, capitulating (see YIELD): merciful, lenient, clement, *forbearing, indulgent, tolerant

**implant, inculcate, instill** are comparable when they mean to introduce into the mind. **Implant** usually implies teach-

A colon (:) separates groups of words discriminated. An asterisk (*) indicates place of treatment of each group.

ing, and it stresses the fixedness or permanency of what has been taught ⟨the teacher, the parent, or the friend can often do much to *implant* this conviction—*Eliot*⟩ ⟨*implanting* in their minds doubts of the political realism of their American friends—*Brogan*⟩ **Inculcate** implies persistent or repeated endeavor with the intent to impress firmly on the mind ⟨had sedulously *inculcated* into the mind of her son . . . maxims of worldly wisdom—*Edgeworth*⟩ ⟨skillful, conscientious schoolmistresses whose lives were spent in trying to *inculcate* real knowledge—*Grandgent*⟩ ⟨whatever happened, Newland would continue to *inculcate* in Dallas the same principles and prejudices which had shaped his parents' lives—*Wharton*⟩ **Instill** carries the implication of a gradual and gentle method of imparting knowledge; it usually suggests either a teaching that extends over a long period of time (as from infancy to adolescence) or a pupil that cannot, because of age, lack of background, or the like, take in at once what is taught ⟨those principles my parents *instilled* into my unwary understanding—*Browne*⟩ ⟨the Viceroy plumed himself on the way in which he had *instilled* notions of reticence into his staff—*Kipling*⟩ ⟨it would be useless, in early years, to attempt to *instill* a stoic contempt for death—*Russell*⟩

*Ana* *infuse, imbue, inoculate, ingrain, leaven: impregnate, saturate, impenetrate, penetrate, *permeate, pervade

**implement** *n* Implement, tool, instrument, appliance, utensil mean a relatively simple device for performing a mechanical or manual operation. Nearly all of these words (the distinct exception is *appliance*) are interchangeable in their general senses, but custom and usage have greatly restricted them in their specific and most common applications. An **implement**, in general, is anything that is requisite to effecting the end one has in view or to performing the work one undertakes ⟨the *implements* of modern warfare consist of all the weapons necessary to a well-equipped army, navy, and air force⟩ ⟨mathematics is still the necessary *implement* for the manipulation of nature—*Russell*⟩ In specific use *implement* is the usual term when the reference is to a contrivance for tilling the soil (as a spade, a plow, a harrow, or a cultivator) ⟨farming *implements*⟩ ⟨gardening *implements*⟩ Historically it is the preferred term for any of the articles which are essential to the performance of a religious service ⟨the *implements* of the Mass include vestments as well as chalice, paten, and altar stone⟩ It is also the usual term for the devices made especially from stone or wood by primitive peoples as weapons or for use in digging, carrying, or lifting or in making clothing and equipment. A **tool**, in general, is anything that facilitates the accomplishment of the end one has in view; it is therefore something particularly adapted in its nature or by its construction to make possible or relatively easy the work one is doing ⟨it's difficult to be a good cook without the proper *tools*⟩ ⟨a scholar needs foreign languages as *tools*⟩ ⟨comparison and analysis . . . are the chief *tools* of the critic—*T. S. Eliot*⟩ In specific use *tool* is the preferred term when reference is made to the implements used by artisans (as carpenters and mechanics) or craftsmen in accomplishing a particular kind of work (as sawing, boring, piercing, or chipping) ⟨a saw, a gimlet, an awl, a chisel are *tools*⟩ Ordinarily *tool* suggests manipulation by the hand, but some machines for doing work that may be accomplished more slowly by manual labor and tools are called *machine tools* (as the lathe). An **instrument** (see also MEAN *n* 2, PAPER 1) is in general a delicately constructed device by means of which work (not exclusively a mechanical operation) may be accomplished with precision. Many *instruments* are by definition *tools*, but *instrument* is the preferred term among

persons (as surgeons, dentists, draftsmen, surveyors, and artists) whose technique requires delicate tools and expertness and finesse in their manipulation. Some instruments, however, are not tools, but implements in the larger sense, for they are requisite to the achieving of definite purposes but do not necessarily facilitate any manual operations ⟨a thermometer and a barometer are recording *instruments* essential to the meteorologist⟩ ⟨a telescope is an astronomical *instrument*⟩ ⟨a piano, a violin, a cello are musical *instruments* by means of which a performer evokes musical sounds⟩ ⟨language is the essential *instrument* for the acquirement and communication of ideas—*Shehan*⟩ An **appliance** may be a device that adapts a tool or machine to a special purpose usually under the guidance of a hand; thus, a dentist's drill may be called an *appliance* when it is attached to a dental engine; in industry an *appliance* is often distinguished from a *tool*, though they may both do the same kind of work, in that a *tool* is manipulated by hand and an *appliance* is moved and regulated by machinery. Additionally, an *appliance* may be a device or apparatus designed for a particular use and especially one (as a mechanical refrigerator or a vacuum cleaner) that utilizes an external power supply, especially an electric current. A **utensil** is in general anything that is useful in accomplishing work (as cooking and cleaning) associated with the household; it may be applied to tools (as egg-beaters, graters, rolling pins, brooms, and mops) used in cookery and other household work, but it is most commonly applied to containers (as pots, pans, pails, and jars), especially those which form part of the kitchen, dairy, or bedroom equipment. Consequently *utensil,* in other than household use, often means a vessel ⟨sacred *utensils* of a church⟩

*Ana* *machine, mechanism, apparatus: contrivance, *device, contraption, gadget

**implement** *vb* *enforce
*Ana* effect, fulfill, execute, achieve, accomplish, *perform: *realize, actualize, materialize

**implicate** *involve
*Ana* *concern, affect: incriminate (see ACCUSE)
*Con* *exculpate, absolve, acquit, exonerate

**implication,** inference are often interchangeable, but they may be distinguished when they specifically refer to something that is hinted at but not explicitly stated. **Implication** applies to what is hinted, whether the writer or speaker is aware of it or not or whether the reader or hearer recognizes it or not ⟨speak of their own language with at least an *implication* of disparagement—*Sampson*⟩ When, however, the reader or hearer recognizes what is implied and gathers from it its full significance or makes an explicit statement of it, he has drawn or made an **inference** ⟨he said no more, waiting for someone to draw the desired *inference* from this utterance—*Wister*⟩ ⟨you misunderstood the implications of his speech, so that your *inferences* misrepresent his point of view⟩ ⟨by *implication* you are arguing that this is the only possible solution⟩ ⟨by *inference* from what you leave unsaid, I know you believe this the only possible solution⟩ ⟨he did not perceive the *implications* of his remark⟩ ⟨the *inferences* to be drawn from his remark are inescapable⟩

*Ana* hinting *or* hint, suggestion, intimation (see corresponding verbs at SUGGEST): *insinuation, innuendo

**implicit,** virtual, constructive mean being such by correct or justifiable inference rather than by direct statement or proof. Something is **implicit** (as opposed to *explicit*) which is implied (as by the words, acts, appearance, character, or methods of the person or thing concerned) but is not definitely stated or expressed ⟨a good present behavior is an *implicit* repentance for any miscarriage in what is past—

*Spectator*⟩ ⟨the distinction between poetry and drama, which Mr. Archer makes explicit, is *implicit* in the view of Swinburne—*T. S. Eliot*⟩ Something is **virtual** (as opposed to *actual*) which exists in essence or effect but is not actually designated or recognized or put forward or regarded as such ⟨his statement is a *virtual* confession⟩ ⟨the *virtual* abdication of parents from their role as educators —*Barclay*⟩ ⟨the dictator's constant associate and his *virtual* chief of staff—*Buchan*⟩ Something is **constructive** (as opposed to *manifest*) which is inferred from a text, from known acts, or known conditions and which rests therefore on an interpretation of this text, these acts, or these conditions rather than upon direct statement or direct evidence ⟨if the law explicitly gives a governor the right of removal of certain officials, he may claim the right to control and direct their official acts as a *constructive* power⟩ ⟨a mere failure to obey the orders of the court may be interpreted by the judge as *constructive* contempt⟩ ⟨an employer who confronts a foreman with an option of demotion or withdrawal from a foreman's union is guilty of a *constructive* discharge—*B. F. Tucker*⟩ **Ana** implied, suggested, intimated, hinted (see SUGGEST): inferred, deduced, gathered (see INFER)
**Ant** explicit —**Con** express, definite, specific (see EXPLICIT): expressed, voiced, uttered (see EXPRESS *vb*): stated, recited, recounted, described (see RELATE)
**implore** entreat, beseech, supplicate, *beg, importune, adjure
**Ana** pray, plead, sue, appeal, petition (see under PRAYER): *ask, request, solicit
**imply 1** involve, comprehend, *include, embrace, subsume
**Ana** import, *mean, signify, denote: *contain, hold: convey, *carry, bear
**2** *suggest, hint, intimate, insinuate
**Ana** connote, *denote: *presuppose, presume, assume, postulate: betoken, bespeak, *indicate, attest, argue, prove
**Ant** express —**Con** state, *relate: utter, voice, broach (see EXPRESS *vb*): declare, predicate, affirm, *assert, aver, profess
**impolite** uncivil, discourteous, *rude, ill-mannered, ungracious
**Ana** churlish, boorish, loutish (see under BOOR): curt, gruff, brusque, blunt (see BLUFF)
**Ant** polite —**Con** *civil, courteous, chivalrous, gallant: *suave, urbane, diplomatic, politic: *thoughtful, considerate, attentive
**imponderable** impalpable, *imperceptible, inappreciable, insensible, intangible
**Ant** ponderable, appreciable —**Con** weighty, consequential, important, significant, momentous (see corresponding nouns at IMPORTANCE)
**import** *vb* *mean, denote, signify
**Ana** *denote, connote: involve, imply, *include, comprehend: *suggest, imply, intimate, hint: mean, *intend
**import** *n* **1** significance, *meaning, sense, acceptation, signification
**Ana** denotation, connotation (see under DENOTE 2): interpreting *or* interpretation, construing *or* construction (see corresponding verbs at EXPLAIN): drift, tenor (see TENDENCY): *implication
**2** significance, *importance, consequence, moment, weight
**Ana** *worth, value: purpose, intent, design, object, objective (see INTENTION): *emphasis, stress
**importance,** consequence, moment, weight, significance, import are comparable when they denote the quality or the character or the state of someone or something that impresses others as of great or sometimes eminent worth, value, or influence. **Importance,** probably the most inclusive of these terms, implies a judgment of the mind

by which superior value or influence is ascribed to a person or thing ⟨there are no cities of *importance* in this state⟩ ⟨he always attaches *importance* to what seem to others trivial events⟩ ⟨tradition gives *importance* to the study of the classics⟩ ⟨hence flowers come to assume [in Oriental art] ... an *importance* equal to that of figure painting with us—*Binyon*⟩ ⟨issues which, whilst not of major significance, have some *importance*—*Current History*⟩ **Consequence** (see also EFFECT) is often used interchangeably with *importance* especially in implying superior social rank or distinction ⟨men of *consequence*⟩ but it usually implies importance because of the thing's possible or probable outcome, effects, or results ⟨he ... was eager to have the Cathedral begun; but whether it was Midi Romanesque or Ohio German in style, seemed to him of little *consequence*—*Cather*⟩ ⟨to marry one of the right people ... is of the greatest *consequence* for a happy life—*Rose Macaulay*⟩ ⟨to cultivate the love of truth, it is of the utmost *consequence* that children should study things as well as words, external nature as well as books—*Eliot*⟩ ⟨I cannot think of a single poet of *consequence* whose work does not ... condemn modern civilization—*Auden*⟩ **Moment** implies conspicuous or self-evident consequence ⟨enterprises of great pith and *moment*—*Shak.*⟩ ⟨a mistake of no very great *moment* —in fine, a mere slip—*Barham*⟩ **Weight** implies a judgment of the relatively great importance or of the particular moment of the thing under consideration ⟨the judge gave great *weight* to the testimony of the accused man⟩ ⟨in such a point of *weight,* so near mine honor— *Shak.*⟩ ⟨I looked for you at dinner time; I forget now what for; but then 'twas a matter of more *weight* than laying siege to a city—*Millay*⟩ **Significance** and import are often used as though they were indistinguishable in meaning from *importance* or *consequence,* but they typically imply a quality or character in a person or thing which ought to mark it as of importance or consequence but which may or may not be recognized; thus, one may miss the *significance* of an occurrence; one may recognize the *import* of a piece of testimony ⟨a widespread recognition of the *significance* of that achievement—*Ellis*⟩ ⟨the book was invested with a *significance* ... which its intrinsic literary and philosophical merits could not justify— *Huxley*⟩ ⟨a fear that the spectator might lose, in the shock of crude sensation, the spiritual *import* of the catastrophe—*Binyon*⟩
**Ana** prominence, conspicuousness, saliency (see corresponding adjectives at NOTICEABLE): eminence, illustriousness (see corresponding adjectives at FAMOUS): seriousness, gravity (see corresponding adjectives at SERIOUS): magnitude, *size, extent
**Ant** unimportance —**Con** pettiness, triviality, paltriness (see corresponding adjectives at PETTY)
**importunate** *pressing, urgent, imperative, crying, insistent, exigent, instant
**Ana** demanding, claiming, requiring (see DEMAND): persistent, persevering (see corresponding verbs at PERSEVERE): pertinacious, dogged (see OBSTINATE)
**importune** *beg, entreat, beseech, implore, supplicate, adjure
**Ana** tease, pester, plague, harry, *worry: hound, hector, badger (see BAIT): plead, appeal, sue (see under PRAYER)
**impose** *dictate, prescribe, ordain, decree
**Ana** order, enjoin, *command, charge: exact, *demand, require: constrain, oblige, compel (see FORCE)
**imposing** stately, majestic, august, noble, magnificent, *grand, grandiose
**Ana** *showy, pretentious, ostentatious: impressive, *moving: regal, imperial (see KINGLY): monumental,

A colon (:) separates groups of words discriminated. An asterisk (*) indicates place of treatment of each group.

stupendous, prodigious (see MONSTROUS)
*Ant* unimposing  —*Con* \*contemptible, despicable, sorry, cheap, scurvy, pitiable, beggarly, shabby

**impostor,** **faker, quack, mountebank, charlatan** denote a person who makes pretensions to being someone or something that he is not or of being able to do something he cannot really do. **Impostor** applies especially to one who passes himself off for someone else ⟨there is an *impostor* abroad, who takes upon him the name of this young gentleman, and would willingly pass for him—*Addison*⟩ However the word often serves as a general term for anyone who assumes a title, character, or profession that is not his own ⟨charged that Kim Il Sung was an *impostor* trading on the name of a legendary Korean resistance leader—*Time*⟩ **Faker** applies to one who gives himself the appearance of being what, in character or in profession, he is not ⟨the accused man is not insane, he is merely a clever *faker*⟩ ⟨a hypocrite is a moral or religious *faker*⟩ ⟨he is essentially a *faker* with a large contempt for the ignorance and gullibility of the American voter—*Current History*⟩ **Quack** is the popular and contemptuous term for an ignorant, untrained, or unscrupulous practitioner of medicine or law or seller of remedies or treatments, and usually carries a strong implication of fraud or self-delusion ⟨dishonesty is the raw material not of *quacks* only, but also, in great part, of dupes—*Carlyle*⟩ ⟨one of the most notorious cancer-cure *quacks* of the day—*JAMA*⟩ **Mountebank** sometimes suggests quackery, but it regularly suggests cheap and undignified efforts to win attention ⟨political *mountebanks*⟩ ⟨our Sabbaths, closed with mummery and buffoon; preaching and pranks will share the motley scene . . . God's worship and the *mountebank* between—*Cowper*⟩ **Charlatan** applies to a writer, speaker, preacher, professor, or expert who covers his ignorance or lack of skill by pretentious, flashy, or magniloquent display ⟨insolent, pretentious, and given to that reckless innovation for the sake of noise and show which was the essence of the *charlatan*—*George Eliot*⟩ ⟨replaced by the *charlatans* and the rogues—by those without learning, without scruples, or both—*Asher Moore*⟩
*Ana* cheat, fraud, fake, humbug (see IMPOSTURE): deceiver, beguiler, misleader (see corresponding verbs at DECEIVE)

**imposture,** **cheat, fraud, sham, fake, humbug, deceit, deception, counterfeit** all mean something which pretends to be one thing in its nature, character, or quality but is really another. **Imposture** applies not only to an object but to an act or practice which is passed off to another as genuine, authentic, or bona fide ⟨several of the gallery's paintings reputed to be the work of Rubens and Rembrandt were *impostures*⟩ ⟨the hero is as gross an *imposture* as the heroine—*Shaw*⟩ ⟨its values . . . are an *imposture:* pretending to honor and distinction, it accepts all that is vulgar and base—*Edmund Wilson*⟩ **Cheat** applies chiefly to something or sometimes to someone that wins one's belief in its or his genuineness, either because one is deliberately misled or imposed upon by another or is the victim of illusion or delusion ⟨when I consider life,'tis all a *cheat.* Yet fooled with hope, men favor the deceit—*Dryden*⟩ ⟨what . . . man . . . shall prove (what argument could never yet) the Bible an imposture and a *cheat?*—*Cowper*⟩ ⟨hence, pageant history! hence, gilded *cheat!*—*Keats*⟩ ⟨if I passed myself off on Miss Carew as a gentleman, I should deserve to be exposed as a *cheat*—*Shaw*⟩ **Fraud** applies to a deliberate, often criminal, perversion of the truth ⟨many persons persisted in believing that his supposed suicide was but another *fraud*—*M'Carthy*⟩ ⟨we may take it as undisputed that Swinburne . . . did something

that had not been done before, and that what he did will not turn out to be a *fraud*—*T. S. Eliot*⟩ Applied to a person it may be less condemnatory and suggest pretense and hypocrisy ⟨the pious *fraud* who freely indulges in the sins against which he eloquently preaches—*La Farge*⟩ **Sham** applies to a close copy of a thing, especially to one that is more or less obviously a fraudulent imitation ⟨a strong living soul in him, and sincerity there; a reality, not an artificiality, not a *sham!*—*Carlyle*⟩ ⟨he smiled, in his worldliest manner. But the smile was a *sham*—*Bennett*⟩ **Fake** applies either to a person that represents himself as someone he is not or, more often, to a worthless thing that is represented as being something that it is not; *fake* differs from *fraud* in not necessarily implying dishonesty in these representations, for a *fake* may be a joke or a theatrical device, or it may be a clear fraud ⟨this testimonial is clearly a *fake*⟩ ⟨one of the great *fakes* of all time was the Cardiff Giant⟩ ⟨actors using *fakes* instead of real swords on the stage⟩ ⟨he pretends everything is what it is not, he is a *fake*—*K. A. Porter*⟩ **Humbug** applies to a person or sometimes a thing that pretends or is pretended to be other and usually more important than he or it is, not necessarily because of a desire on the part of the person involved to deceive others but often because he is self-deceived ⟨you will take to politics, where you will become . . . the henchman of ambitious *humbugs*—*Shaw*⟩ ⟨what *humbugs* we are, who pretend to live for beauty, and never see the dawn!—*L. P. Smith*⟩ **Deceit** and *deception* both apply to something that misleads one or deludes one into taking it for what it is not. **Deceit,** however, usually suggests the work of a deceiver or of one that misleads or leads astray ⟨the *deceits* of the world, the flesh, and the devil—*Book of Common Prayer*⟩ ⟨they [Indians] held that the basest trickery or *deceit* was not dishonorable if directed against a foe—*Amer. Guide Series: R.I.*⟩ **Deception,** on the other hand, often suggests a quality or character in the thing which causes one to mistake it or frankly to take it as other than it really is ⟨the rising and the setting of the sun are pure *deceptions*⟩ **Counterfeit** applies to a close imitation or copy of a thing (as a coin, a banknote, or a bond) that depends upon pictorial devices or engraved designs for assurance of its genuineness; the term usually also implies the passing or circulation of such an imitation as if it were genuine ⟨the city is being flooded with *counterfeits* of five-dollar bills⟩ The term is also applicable to a thing or, less often, to a person that passes for something other than it actually or truly is ⟨his newly purchased painting by Raphael was proved to be a clever *counterfeit*⟩ ⟨she had the illusion that she was not really a married woman and a housemistress, but only a kind of *counterfeit*—*Bennett*⟩
*Ana* \*trick, ruse, feint, artifice, wile, stratagem, maneuver, gambit, ploy

**impotent** 1 \*powerless
*Ana* \*ineffective, ineffectual, inefficacious, inefficient: \*incapable, incompetent: disabled, crippled, debilitated, enfeebled (see WEAKEN)
*Ant* potent  —*Con* \*powerful, puissant, forceful, forcible: \*vigorous, energetic, strenuous: \*effective, effectual, efficacious, efficient: \*able, capable
2 \*sterile, barren, unfruitful, infertile
*Ant* virile

**impoverish** bankrupt, exhaust, \*deplete, drain
*Ant* enrich  —*Con* enhance, heighten, \*intensify: augment, \*increase

**imprecation** \*curse, malediction, anathema
*Ana* execration, damning, objurgation (see corresponding verbs at EXECRATE): \*blasphemy, profanity, swearing

---

*Ana* analogous words     *Ant* antonyms     *Con* contrasted words     See also explanatory notes facing page 1

*Ant* prayer
**impregnable** inexpugnable, unassailable, invulnerable, *invincible, unconquerable, indomitable
*Ana* secure, *safe: protected, shielded, guarded, safeguarded, defended (see DEFEND)
*Con* exposed, open, *liable, susceptible, subject
**impregnate** 1 saturate, *permeate, pervade, penetrate, impenetrate, interpenetrate
*Ana* imbue, inoculate, ingrain, *infuse, suffuse, leaven: *enter, pierce, probe, penetrate
2 *soak, saturate, drench, steep, sop, waterlog
*Ana* immerse, submerge, *dip, souse
**impress** *vb* touch, strike, *affect, influence, sway
*Ana* *move, actuate: *thrill, electrify, enthuse: *provoke, excite, stimulate, galvanize, pique
**impress** *n* *impression, imprint, print, stamp
*Ana* see those at IMPRESSION 1
**impressible** *sentient, sensitive, impressionable, responsive, susceptible
*Ana* subject, exposed, open, *liable, prone: predisposed, disposed, inclined (see INCLINE)
**impression** 1 Impression, impress, imprint, print, stamp are comparable when denoting the perceptible trace or traces left by pressure. **Impression** is the most widely applicable of these terms. It may be used with reference to a mark or trace or a series or combination of marks or traces which are produced by the physical pressure of one thing on another (as of a seal upon wax, of a foot upon mud, or of inked type or an etched plate upon paper) ⟨in general, the first *impressions* made from an etcher's plate are the most valuable⟩ ⟨the detectives found a clear *impression* of fingertips on the handle of the door⟩ ⟨the dentist must get a plaster of paris *impression* of the jaw before he can make a denture⟩ But *impression* may also be used of a definite or distinct trace or traces left on the mind, spirit, character, or memory by the impact of sensation or experience ⟨the shock has left its *impression* on her nerves⟩ ⟨his first *impression* of Paris still remains clear in his memory⟩ ⟨the incident made no *impression* on his mind⟩ **Impress** is often used in place of *impression* especially when the reference is to a clear trace left on the character or the personality by some influence ⟨his father's uprightness has left a lasting *impress* on his character⟩ ⟨he reveals the *impress* of Keats's influence in every poem he writes⟩ ⟨the dusting of the white paper . . . is a symbol of the sweeping clear from the mind of all accumulated prejudice that it may receive the *impress* of beauty in all its freshness and power—*Binyon*⟩ **Imprint** carries a strong implication of sharpness, clearness, or permanence in outline. It may be used in reference to an impression left on a plastic substance ⟨the *imprint* of a heel in the soil⟩ ⟨the children left *imprints* of their feet on the fresh cement of the walk⟩ The term specifically applies to the printed name of the publisher or, sometimes, of the printer and place and date of publication at the foot of a book's title page ⟨this book bears the *imprint* of the G. & C. Merriam Company⟩ **Print** is often interchangeable with *imprint* in the general sense of that word but is more likely to be used when the trace is considered with reference to its retention of every line or characteristic detail of the original ⟨the clear *print* of a fingertip⟩ It is the preferred term in combinations ⟨foot*prints* in the sand⟩ ⟨hoof*prints*⟩ **Stamp** applies to an impression produced by or as if by a tool or machine which strikes so hard that it leaves a distinct imprint, often one that serves to authenticate or to approve what is so imprinted, to indicate its origin, or to authorize its passage through the mails. Hence, in extended use, *stamp* designates a marked or conspicuous impress which wins almost immediate recognition ⟨we do wish as many sons of this

university as may be to carry forth that lifelong *stamp* from her precincts—*Quiller-Couch*⟩ ⟨these works have the "classic" *stamp* upon them, and have been to the artists of the Far East what Greek marbles have been to us—*Binyon*⟩
*Ana* *trace, vestige, track: mark, token, *sign: *stigma, brand, blot, stain
2 notion, thought, *idea, concept, conception
*Ana* image, percept, sense-datum, sensum, *sensation: sentiment, *opinion, view
*Con* explanation, interpretation, elucidation (see corresponding verbs at EXPLAIN)
3 *edition, reprinting, printing, reissue
**impressionable** *sentient, sensitive, impressible, responsive, susceptible
*Ana* affectable, influenceable (see corresponding verbs at AFFECT): open, *liable, subject, exposed, prone: predisposed, disposed, inclined (see INCLINE)
**impressive** *moving, affecting, poignant, touching, pathetic
*Ana* imposing, majestic, august, noble, magnificent, grandiose, *grand: sublime, superb, glorious, *splendid: striking, arresting, remarkable, *noticeable
*Ant* unimpressive —*Con* *ineffective, ineffectual, inefficacious: *vain, nugatory, empty, hollow, idle, otiose
**imprint** *n* print, *impression, impress, stamp
**imprison, incarcerate, jail, immure, intern** mean to confine closely so that escape is impossible or unlikely. The first three words *imprison, incarcerate, jail* imply a shutting up in or as if in a prison, *imprison* being the general term, *incarcerate* the bookish or journalistic term, and *jail* the common word. Distinctively, **imprison** implies seizure and detention in custody and is applicable even when the one confined is not in a prison or jail or suffering a penalty ⟨deftly and with one arm only, he *imprisoned* her—*Ertz*⟩ ⟨the tremendous forces *imprisoned* in minute particles of matter—*Inge*⟩ **Incarcerate** implies a shutting up in or as if in a prison cell ⟨he easily obtained bail and will, in all probability, not be *incarcerated* before his trial⟩ ⟨we got the bride and bridegroom quietly away . . . having *incarcerated* all the newspaper reporters in the little drawing room—*Sayers*⟩ **Jail** may be preferred to *incarcerate* as a simpler and more generally intelligible term ⟨risked being *jailed* for life⟩ Often, however, *jail,* the verb, following *jail,* the noun, in its accepted sense connotes imprisonment in a building in which persons are held for short periods, either paying the penalty for minor offenses or for the purpose of awaiting legal proceedings. **Immure** is a literary rather than technical term. When it implies punishment for a crime, it may connote burial alive within a wall; usually, however, the term suggests restriction to closely confined quarters typically as a captive or a devotee to duty or to religion ⟨Constance was now *immured* with her father, it being her "turn" to nurse—*Bennett*⟩ ⟨a convent of nuns vowed to contemplation, who were *immured* there for life, and never went outside the convent walls—*L. P. Smith*⟩ **Intern** is used chiefly of military or wartime conditions; it seldom implies incarceration and usually suggests a keeping within prescribed limits (as in a guarded camp) and under severe restraints ⟨*intern* all enemy aliens for the duration of a war⟩ ⟨*intern* all the war refugees entering a neutral country⟩ ⟨the plane was landed safely and the crew was *interned*—*Lawson*⟩
*Ana* confine, circumscribe, restrict, *limit: *restrain, curb, check
**impromptu** unpremeditated, offhand, improvised, *extemporaneous, extempore, extemporary
*Ana* *spontaneous, impulsive: ready, prompt, *quick, apt

A colon (:) separates groups of words discriminated. An asterisk (*) indicates place of treatment of each group.

*Con* considered, premeditated, \*deliberate, studied, designed, advised: finished, \*consummate

**improper** 1 inappropriate, unfitting, unsuitable, \*unfit, inapt, unhappy, infelicitous

*Ana* wrong, \*bad, poor: \*amiss, astray: incongruous, \*inconsonant

*Ant* proper —*Con* right, \*good: \*regular, natural, normal, typical: \*due, rightful, condign: legitimate, licit, \*lawful, legal

2 \*indecorous, indecent, unseemly, unbecoming, indelicate

*Ana* unconventional, unceremonious, informal (see affirmative adjectives at CEREMONIAL): \*shameless, brazen, impudent, brash, barefaced: obscene, ribald, \*coarse, vulgar, gross

*Ant* proper —*Con* right, \*correct: \*decorous, decent, seemly, nice

**improve** 1 Improve, better, help, ameliorate are comparable when denoting to mend or correct in part or in some degree. **Improve,** the general term, and **better,** more vigorous and homely, apply both to objects and to states or conditions that are not of necessity bad ⟨the faculties of the mind are *improved* by exercise—*Locke*⟩ ⟨striving to *better,* oft we mar what's well—*Shak.*⟩ With a reflexive pronoun *improve* implies a change for the better within oneself, *better* a change for the better in one's social or financial status ⟨had from her youth *improved* herself by reading—*Fordyce*⟩ ⟨girls marry merely to "*better* themselves," to borrow a significant vulgar phrase—*Wollstonecraft*⟩ To **help** is to improve while still leaving something to be desired ⟨a coat of paint would *help* that house⟩ **Ameliorate** is used chiefly in reference to conditions that are hard to bear or that cause suffering and implies partial relief or changes that make them tolerable ⟨there is no hope whatever of *ameliorating* his condition—*Peacock*⟩ ⟨abolish feudalism or *ameliorate* its vices—*W. O. Douglas*⟩

*Ana* \*benefit, profit: amend, \*correct, rectify, reform, revise: enhance, heighten (see INTENSIFY)

*Ant* impair: worsen —*Con* corrupt, pervert, vitiate, \*debase, deprave: \*injure, harm, damage, mar

2 Improve, recover, recuperate, convalesce, gain are comparable as intransitive verbs with the meaning to grow or become better (as in health or well-being). **Improve,** although often employed in respect to health, is also applicable to situations or conditions and indirectly to persons ⟨business is *improving*⟩ ⟨the prospects for peace *improved* that year⟩ ⟨he *improves* on acquaintance⟩ ⟨the general principle that as the mental equipment of the human race *improves,* its physical qualities . . . deteriorate—*Rose Macaulay*⟩ In reference to health *improve* implies nothing more than a getting better; it connotes hope but no certainty of continued progress or of final achievement of full health ⟨her health *improves* slowly⟩ ⟨he will not *improve* until the crisis is past⟩ ⟨this acute condition usually persists for from 5 to 15 minutes and then gradually *improves*—*Armstrong*⟩ **Recover** usually implies a return to or the regaining of some former or normal state (as of health); the word may, especially with reference to health, imply certainty and not merely hope ⟨will he *recover*?⟩ ⟨when she *recovered* from her faint⟩ ⟨the market quickly *recovered* from the sell-off⟩ ⟨King Paul was stricken with typhoid fever . . . but *recovered* shortly afterward—*Current Biog.*⟩ ⟨many of the older partisans had been Bryanites, and had not *recovered* from it—*Paxson*⟩ **Recuperate** comes very close to *recover* in its implication of getting back what has been lost and is perhaps more common in reference to losses of money or energy ⟨sleep gives us an opportunity to *recuperate* from the fatigues of the

day⟩ ⟨give the business a chance and it will *recuperate*⟩ In respect to health it especially implies restoration through such influences as climate and rest ⟨she will *recuperate* in a warm climate⟩ ⟨one may *recuperate* quickly from a mild attack of influenza⟩ ⟨the animals . . . would not *recuperate* until they got water—*Cather*⟩ **Convalesce** fundamentally implies a growing stronger; the term usually applies to the period between the subsidence of a confining illness and full recovery, when the patient, more or less gradually, gathers strength and regains the use of powers lost or depleted through serious illness, a serious operation, or a serious wound ⟨convalesce after a long illness⟩ ⟨he is so busy that he will not take the time he needs to *convalesce* after his operation⟩ ⟨a man *convalescing* from a great grief—*Thoreau*⟩ ⟨was advised by his doctor to remain in the West where he had gone to *convalesce*—*Martin Gardner*⟩ **Gain** simply means to make progress especially, but not always, in health. The term is used typically in periodic reports of condition and like *improve* carries no implication of whether or not progress will continue or result in permanent recovery ⟨the doctor thinks he is *gaining*⟩ ⟨he *gains* very slowly⟩

**improvised** unpremeditated, impromptu, offhand, \*extemporaneous, extempore, extemporary

*Ana & Con* see those at IMPROMPTU

**impudent** \*shameless, brazen, barefaced, brash

*Ana* \*impertinent, intrusive, obtrusive, officious, meddlesome: \*rude, impolite, discourteous, uncivil, ungracious

*Ant* respectful —*Con* \*shy, modest, diffident, bashful

**impugn** gainsay, contradict, negative, traverse, \*deny, contravene

*Ana* \*attack, assail: refute, rebut, confute, controvert, \*disprove

*Ant* authenticate: advocate —*Con* \*confirm, corroborate, substantiate: \*support, uphold, back

**impulse** *n* \*motive, spring, incentive, inducement, spur, goad

*Ana* impetus, \*stimulus, incitement, stimulant, excitant: urge, passion, lust, \*desire, appetite: moving *or* movement, driving *or* drive, impelling *or* impulsion, actuation (see corresponding verbs at MOVE)

**impulsive** \*spontaneous, instinctive, automatic, mechanical

*Ana* impetuous, \*precipitate, headlong, abrupt, sudden, hasty

*Ant* deliberate (sense 1) —*Con* \*voluntary, intentional: premeditated, considered, \*deliberate, designed: \*cautious, circumspect, calculating

**impute** attribute, \*ascribe, assign, refer, credit, accredit, charge

*Ana* attach, \*fasten, affix: \*accuse, charge, indict: allege, advance, \*adduce: intimate, insinuate, hint (see SUGGEST)

**in** *prep* 1 \*at, on

2 \*at, on

**inability,** disability are sometimes confused because of their verbal likeness. Although both denote a lack of ability to perform a given act or to follow a given trade or profession, they are otherwise clearly distinguished. **Inability** implies lack of power to perform; it may suggest mental deficiency or tempermental unfitness, but more often it suggests a limiting factor (as lack of means, lack of health, or lack of training) ⟨an *inability* to laugh—*Lucas*⟩ ⟨an *inability* to see—*Huxley*⟩ ⟨the *inability* of the economic system to effect a cure—*Hobson*⟩ **Disability** implies the loss or the deprivation of such power (as by accident, illness, or disqualification); the term is applicable not only to the resulting inability but to whatever it is that makes one unable to do a certain thing or hold a certain office or position

⟨because of *disabilities* many of the soldiers could not return to their former occupations when the war ended⟩ ⟨if these people [American Indians] were not to be counted colored, with all the *disabilities* that designation involved —*Handlin*⟩ ⟨one may be ineligible to office on account of some legal *disability* such as foreign birth⟩
*Ana* incapability, incompetence, unqualifiedness (see corresponding adjectives at INCAPABLE): unfitness, unsuitability (see corresponding adjectives at UNFIT)
*Ant* ability —*Con* capacity, capability (see ABILITY)
**inactive, idle, inert, passive, supine** mean not engaged in work or activity. **Inactive** is applicable to anyone or to anything that for any reason is not currently in action, in operation, in use, or at work ⟨*inactive* machines⟩ ⟨delicate children are usually *inactive*⟩ ⟨an *inactive* charge account⟩ ⟨in winter, when . . . mosquitoes, exceptionally large, numerous, and aggressive in this section, are *inactive*— *Amer. Guide Series: La.*⟩ **Idle** (see also VAIN 1) applies chiefly to persons who are without occupation or not busy at the moment, but it is also applicable to their powers or to the implements they use ⟨why stand ye here all the day *idle*? They say unto him, Because no man hath hired us —*Mt 20:6−7*⟩ ⟨though his pen was now *idle,* his tongue was active—*Macaulay*⟩ ⟨is a field *idle* when it is fallow?— *Shaw*⟩ ⟨every *idle* miner directly and individually is obstructing our war effort—*Roosevelt*⟩ **Inert** as applied to a thing (as matter, a substance, or a drug) implies inherent lack of power to set itself in motion or by itself to produce a given or understood effect ⟨[comets] were now shown to be mere chunks of *inert* matter, driven to describe paths round the sun by exactly the same forces as prescribed the orderly motions of the planets—*Jeans*⟩ ⟨commercial fertilizers consist of three to five hundred pounds of available plant food . . . extended with harmless *inert* materials to make a ton of product—*Morrison*⟩ As applied to persons or their activities, *inert* suggests inherent or habitual indisposition to activity or extreme difficulty in stimulating or setting in motion ⟨*inert* citizens are not easily aroused to action by evidence of graft or waste⟩ ⟨many students are too *inert* to derive much stimulation from the books they read⟩ ⟨the *inert* were roused, and lively natures rapt away!—*Wordsworth*⟩ **Passive** implies immobility or a lack of a positive reaction when subjected to external driving or impelling forces or to provocation ⟨the mind is wholly *passive* in the reception of all its simple ideas—*Locke*⟩ ⟨to sit as a *passive* bucket and be pumped into . . . can in the long run be exhilarating to no creature—*Carlyle*⟩ ⟨deprecated . . . the *passive* reception of everything that comes from a foreign press—*Warfel*⟩ In an extended sense *passive* often implies submissiveness without such positive responsiveness as would help the person or side that attacks or seeks to impose its will ⟨*passive* obedience⟩ but it still more often implies a failure to be provoked to action or resistance ⟨to be *passive* in calamity is the province of no woman—*Meredith*⟩ **Supine** implies abject or cowardly inertia or passivity usually as a result of apathy or indolence ⟨it is impossible to remain *supine* when war threatens⟩ ⟨condition of static lethargy and *supine* incuriousness—*Huxley*⟩
*Ana* *latent, quiescent, dormant, abeyant, potential: torpid, comatose, sluggish, *lethargic
*Ant* active, live —*Con* operative, dynamic (see ACTIVE): *busy, industrious, diligent: employed, used, utilized, applied (see USE *vb*)
**inadvertent** heedless, *careless, thoughtless
*Con* conscious, *aware, cognizant, alive, awake: *deliberate, advised, designed, studied: *voluntary, intentional
**inane** banal, wishy-washy, jejune, *insipid, vapid, flat
*Ana* foolish, silly, fatuous, asinine (see SIMPLE): *vain,

idle, empty, hollow, nugatory: vacuous, blank (see EMPTY)
*Con* *expressive, significant, meaningful, pregnant
**inanimate** lifeless, *dead, defunct, deceased, departed, late
*Ana* inert, *inactive
*Ant* animate —*Con* *living, alive
**inappreciable** imponderable, impalpable, *imperceptible, insensible, intangible
*Ant* appreciable, ponderable
**inappropriate** unfitting, inapt, improper, unsuitable, *unfit, unhappy, infelicitous
*Ana* unbecoming, unseemly, *indecorous: incongruous, discordant, *inconsonant
*Ant* appropriate —*Con* fitting, proper, happy, felicitous, suitable, meet, *fit
**inapt** unhappy, infelicitous, inappropriate, unfitting, unsuitable, improper, *unfit
*Ana* inept, maladroit, gauche, *awkward, clumsy: banal, flat, jejune, *insipid
*Ant* apt —*Con* happy, felicitous, appropriate (see FIT): apposite, germane, pertinent, *relevant
**inarticulate** *dumb, speechless, mute
*Ana* *silent, taciturn, reserved
*Ant* articulate —*Con* *vocal, fluent, eloquent, voluble, glib
**inasmuch as** since, *because, for, as
**inaugurate 1** install, induct, invest, *initiate
*Ana* introduce, admit, *enter
**2** initiate, start, *begin, commence
*Ana* *found, establish, institute, organize
*Con* terminate, end, conclude, *close
**inauspicious** unpropitious, *ominous, portentous, fateful
*Ana* threatening, menacing (see THREATEN): *sinister, malign, malefic, maleficent, baleful
*Ant* auspicious —*Con* *favorable, propitious, benign: fortunate, *lucky, happy, providential
**inborn** *innate, congenital, hereditary, inherited, inbred
*Ana* *inherent, intrinsic, constitutional, essential: natural, normal, *regular, typical: *native, indigenous
*Ant* acquired
**inbred** *innate, inborn, congenital, hereditary, inherited
*Ana* ingrained, *inherent, constitutional, intrinsic: deeprooted, deep-seated, *inveterate, confirmed, chronic
*Con* infused, imbued, inoculated (see INFUSE)
**incapable** *adj* **Incapable, incompetent, unqualified** mean mentally or physically unfit, or unfitted by nature, character, or training, to do a given kind of work. Except for this denial of fitness the terms otherwise correspond to the affirmative adjectives in their attributive use as discriminated at ABLE, especially when their limitations in application and their distinguishing implications are considered.
*Ana* inefficient, *ineffective: disabled, crippled, debilitated (see WEAKEN)
*Ant* capable —*Con* competent, *able, qualified: efficient, *effective
**incarcerate** *imprison, jail, immure, intern
*Ana* confine, circumscribe, restrict, *limit
**incarnate** *vb* embody, hypostatize, materialize, externalize, objectify, *realize, actualize, reify
**incendiary** *adj* *combustible, inflammable, flammable, inflammatory
**incense** *n* redolence, *fragrance, perfume, bouquet
*Ana* odor, aroma, *smell
**incense** *vb* enrage, infuriate, *anger, madden
*Ana* exasperate, *irritate, rile, provoke, nettle, aggravate: *offend, outrage, affront, insult
*Ant* placate —*Con* appease, mollify, *pacify, propitiate, conciliate

A colon (:) separates groups of words discriminated. An asterisk (*) indicates place of treatment of each group.

**incentive** inducement, *motive, spring, spur, goad, impulse
*Ana* *stimulus, incitement, stimulant, excitant, impetus: provoking *or* provocation, excitement, stimulation (see corresponding verbs at PROVOKE): reason, *cause, determinant

**inception** *origin, source, root, provenance, provenience
*Ana* beginning, commencement, starting *or* start, initiation, inauguration (see corresponding verbs at BEGIN): rising *or* rise, origination, derivation (see corresponding verbs at SPRING)
*Ant* termination —*Con* *end, ending, terminus: completion, finishing, concluding *or* conclusion, closing (see corresponding verbs at CLOSE)

**incessant** continuous, constant, unremitting, perpetual, *continual, perennial
*Ana* unceasing, interminable, endless, *everlasting: *steady, constant: vexing, irking, annoying, bothering (see ANNOY)
*Ant* intermittent —*Con* periodic, recurrent (see INTERMITTENT)

**incest** *adultery, fornication

**incident** *n* episode, event, *occurrence, circumstance

**incidental** *accidental, casual, fortuitous, contingent, adventitious
*Ana* *subordinate, secondary, collateral: associated, related, linked, connected (see JOIN)
*Ant* essential (sense 2) —*Con* fundamental, cardinal, vital (see ESSENTIAL)

**incise** engrave, etch, chisel, *carve, sculpture, sculpt, sculp
*Ana* imprint, print, stamp, impress (see corresponding nouns at IMPRESSION): depict, delineate, limn (see REPRESENT)

**incisive, trenchant, clear-cut, cutting, biting, crisp** are applied to utterances, thoughts, style, or mentalities and mean having or manifesting the qualities associated with sharpness, keenness, and acuteness, especially of mind. **Incisive** usually implies not only qualities in the thing so described which give it the power to penetrate, pierce, or cut through but also the production of such an effect upon the person impressed; thus, an *incisive* voice or tone of voice is one that is not only sharply clear and edged but one that affects the nerves of the ear as though it were cutting into them; an *incisive* command is so sharply imperative and direct that it can neither be misunderstood nor disobeyed ⟨Bismarck's will had not that *incisive,* rapier quality, that quality of highly tempered steel— flexible, unbreakable, of mortal effect, decisive . . . which had Richelieu's—*Belloc*⟩ ⟨when finally pushed into a corner, he would be more *incisive,* more deadly, than any man seated foursquare and full of importance at a governmental desk—*Sackville-West*⟩ ⟨the clear, *incisive* genius which could state in a flash the exact point at issue— *Whitehead*⟩ **Trenchant** carries a stronger implication than does *incisive* of cutting so as to define differences, categories, or classes with sharpness and perfect clearness or of probing deeply into the inmost nature of a thing so as to reveal what is hidden or concealed ⟨a *trenchant* analysis⟩ ⟨when roused by indignation or moral enthusiasm, how *trenchant* are our reflections!—*James*⟩ ⟨the *trenchant* divisions between right and wrong, honest and dishonest, respectable and the reverse, had left so little scope for the unforeseen—*Wharton*⟩ ⟨no one . . . was more *trenchant* than he in his criticism of the popular faith—*Dickinson*⟩ ⟨a most *trenchant* defender of civil rights—*Chafee*⟩ **Clear-cut** is applied chiefly to the effect of the qualities which make for penetration, incisiveness, trenchancy, or accuracy; it suggests sharp chiseling, clear definition, or distinct outlines, and the absence of all soft edges, hazi-

ness, or confusion in the thing or things so described ⟨*clear-cut* features⟩ ⟨*clear-cut* utterance⟩ ⟨*clear-cut* distinctions⟩ ⟨the demands of Communism are too imperative, too *clear-cut* for the writer who wants only the cessation of mental pain and a private peace in his own time—*Day Lewis*⟩ ⟨his description of this condition was so *clear-cut* that others readily recognized it— *Blumer*⟩ **Cutting** is often used in place of *incisive* when a less pleasant or less agreeable quality or effect is to be connoted; the term frequently suggests sarcasm, acrimony, asperity, or harshness that wounds or hurts, but it sometimes carries a hint, at least, of such mental qualities as penetrating truthfulness and acute discernment ⟨eloquence, smooth and *cutting,* is like a razor whetted with oil—*Swift*⟩ ⟨he can say the driest, most *cutting* things in the quietest of tones—*Brontë*⟩ ⟨"I suppose you'd leave me here without money or anything?" she said in a cold, *cutting* voice—*Bennett*⟩ **Biting,** when it is applied to utterances, expressed ideas, or style, suggests a power to grip and deeply impress itself on the mind or memory; it therefore often suggests a caustic or mordant quality ⟨*biting* epigrams⟩ ⟨her *biting* words⟩ ⟨domineering and censorious of any that stood in his way, with a *biting* wit—*T. D. Bacon*⟩ **Crisp** (see also FRAGILE 1) suggests not only incisiveness but either vigorous terseness of expression or a bracing, invigorating quality ⟨the blithe, *crisp* sentence, decisive as a child's expression of its needs—*Pater*⟩ ⟨it is a relief to come to a diction that is frequently *crisp,* and incisive, and terse—*Lowes*⟩ ⟨a languorous work . . . with occasional interludes of *crisp* brilliance—*Anthony West*⟩
*Ana* terse, succinct, laconic, *concise: poignant, *pungent, piquant
*Con* prolix, diffuse, verbose, *wordy: *loose, lax, slack: unctuous, *fulsome

**incite, instigate, abet, foment** are comparable when they mean to spur on to action or to excite into activity. **Incite** stresses stirring up and urging on; frequently it implies active prompting ⟨the riot was *incited* by paid agitators⟩ ⟨it was just like Lady Pinkerton . . . to have gone round to Hobart *inciting* him to drag Jane from my office—*Rose Macaulay*⟩ **Instigate,** in contrast with *incite,* unequivocally implies prompting and responsibility for the initiation of the action; it also commonly connotes underhandedness and evil intention; thus, one may be *incited* but not *instigated* to the performance of a good act; one may be *incited* or *instigated* to the commission of a crime ⟨the early persecutions were . . . *instigated* . . . by the government as a safety valve for popular discontent—*Inge*⟩ ⟨his peculiar tastes had *instigated* him to boldness in some directions—*Edmund Wilson*⟩ **Abet** tends to lose its original implication of baiting or hounding on and to emphasize its acquired implications of seconding, supporting, and encouraging ⟨unthinkingly, I have laid myself open to the charge of aiding and *abetting* the seal cutter in obtaining money under false pretenses—*Kipling*⟩ ⟨Mr. Howells . . . seconded him as often as not in these innocuous, infantile ventures, *abetting* him in the production of . . . plays of an abysmal foolishness—*Brooks*⟩ **Foment** stresses persistence in goading; thus, one who *incites* rebellion may provide only the initial stimulus; one who *foments* rebellion keeps the rebellious spirit alive by supplying fresh incitements ⟨the apparent moral certainties of the mid-thirties—such as the notion that wars are *fomented* by munitions makers—*F. L. Allen*⟩
*Ana* stimulate, excite, *provoke, pique, galvanize: arouse, rouse, *stir
*Ant* restrain —*Con* curb, check, inhibit (see RESTRAIN): *frustrate, thwart, foil, circumvent, baffle, balk, outwit

**incitement** *stimulus, stimulant, excitant, impetus
*Ana* spur, goad, incentive, inducement, impulse, *motive, spring: provoking *or* provocation, excitement, stimulation, piquing (see corresponding verbs at PROVOKE): motivation, activation, actuation (see corresponding verbs at ACTIVATE)
*Ant* restraint: inhibition
**incline** *vb* 1 lean, *slant, slope
*Ana* bend, *curve: *swerve, veer, deviate: deflect, *turn
2 Incline, bias, dispose, predispose mean to influence one to take a stated or implied attitude to something or to someone or to have such an attitude as a result of prior influences. **Incline** (see also SLANT) implies that the mind or the feelings have been so affected that one is already leaning toward one of two or more possible conclusions, projects, decisions, or objects (as of affection). The word suggests no more than the tipping of the balance toward one and therefore connotes merely a tendency to favor one more than the other or others ⟨such considerations are not supposed to be entertained by judges, except as *inclining* them to one of two interpretations—*Justice Holmes*⟩ ⟨the vast majority of people do not *incline* to be drunkards—*Fishbein*⟩ ⟨Mr. Owen *inclines* to cover up Lloyd George's odious treatment of King George V—*Sykes*⟩ ⟨on this visit I found Australia generally *inclined* to be inimical—*Heiser*⟩ **Bias** implies a stronger and more settled leaning than *incline*; it usually connotes a prejudice for or against ⟨it would be mortifying to . . . many ladies could they . . . understand how little the heart of man is affected by what is costly or new in their attire; how little it is *biased* by the texture of their muslin—*Austen*⟩ ⟨she was unfairly *biased* towards the Liberal party in the state, and too apt to approve of the measures they passed—*Rose Macaulay*⟩ **Dispose** differs from *incline* in stressing the implication of putting one into a frame of mind that is proper or necessary for the end in view or that makes one ready or willing to do something or to take some stand; therefore it often connotes the sway of one's disposition, mood, temper, or attitude ⟨his open face *disposes* one to believe him innocent⟩ ⟨the depression *disposed* many persons to become more thrifty⟩ ⟨a thinker so little *disposed* to treat the names of these religious philosophers with respect—*Inge*⟩ ⟨those *disposed* to violate or evade the decrees of the sovereign—*Cohen*⟩ **Predispose** differs from *dispose* in implying the existence of the frame of mind or of the proper disposition in advance of the opportunity to manifest itself in action ⟨circumstances are *predisposing* men to accept principles which they attacked a few years ago⟩ ⟨if she is flattered and indulged, she will be *predisposed* to be favorable to him⟩ ⟨we are much influenced in youth by sleepless nights; they disarm, they *predispose* us to submit to soft occasion—*Meredith*⟩ **Predispose** is also used of a physical tendency or condition which makes one susceptible to a given infection or disease ⟨*predisposed* to tuberculosis⟩ ⟨the coldness and dampness . . . *predispose* the miner to rheumatism—*Mumford*⟩
*Ana* influence, *affect, sway: *move, drive, impel
*Ant* disincline, indispose
**include, comprehend, embrace, involve, imply, subsume** are comparable when meaning basically to contain something within as a part or portion of a whole. **Include** suggests that the thing included forms a constituent, component, or subordinate part ⟨the genus *Viola includes* the pansy as well as various violets⟩ ⟨the collection will not *include* any examples of the artist's earlier paintings⟩ ⟨an edition of the Bible which *includes* the Apocrypha⟩ ⟨it would not be argued today that the power to regulate does not *include* the power to prohibit—*Justice Holmes*⟩ ⟨few of the great men of our

early national history extended their humanitarianism to *include* the Indian tribes—*Hyman*⟩ **Comprehend** suggests that within the scope or range of the whole under consideration (as the content of a term, a concept, a conception, or a view) the thing comprehended is held or enclosed even though it may or may not be clearly distinguished or actually distinguishable ⟨it was not tolerance; it was something greater that *comprehended* tolerance but went far beyond it—*G. W. Johnson*⟩ ⟨for philosophy's scope *comprehends* the truth of everything which man may understand—*H. O. Taylor*⟩ **Embrace** (see also ADOPT) suggests a reaching out to gather the thing embraced within the whole (as the content of a mind or of a course of study or a construction or interpretation of a law) ⟨the scene before the reddleman's eyes . . . *embraced* hillocks, pits, ridges, acclivities, one behind the other—*Hardy*⟩ ⟨by Baudelaire's time it was no longer necessary for a man to *embrace* such varied interests in order to have the sense of the age—*T. S. Eliot*⟩ ⟨whatever disagreement there may be as to the scope of the phrase "due process of law," there can be no doubt that it *embraces* the fundamental conception of a fair trial—*Justice Holmes*⟩ **Involve** suggests inclusion by virtue of the nature of the whole, whether by being its natural or inevitable consequence ⟨surrender *involves* submission⟩ ⟨it is quite probable that many of those who would make the best doctors are too poor to take the course. This *involves* a deplorable waste of talent—*Russell*⟩ or one of its antecedent conditions ⟨clerkship did not necessarily *involve* even minor orders—*Quiller-Couch*⟩ ⟨I should . . . supply the humanistic elements of education in ways not *involving* a great apparatus of learning—*Russell*⟩ or one of the parts or elements which comprise it by necessity or definition ⟨that fusion of public and private life which was *involved* in the ideal of the Greek citizen—*Dickinson*⟩ **Imply** is very close to *involve* in meaning but stresses a thing's inclusion not, as *involve* does, by the nature or constitution of the whole but as something which can be inferred because hinted at (see also SUGGEST 1) ⟨the tone of the book was *implied* by shrewd advertisements featuring the author's open, smiling face—*J. D. Hart*⟩ or because normally or customarily part of its content especially by definition ⟨embrace *implies* a reaching out to gather to oneself or within one's grasp⟩ ⟨emergency and crisis *imply* conflict—*Langfeld*⟩ or because invariably associated with the thing under consideration as its cause or its effect or as its maker or its product ⟨a watch *implies* a watchmaker⟩ For this reason *imply* may, in comparison with *involve*, suggest a degree of uncertainty; thus, silence is often said to *imply* consent, but it would be rash to say that it *involves* consent. **Subsume,** a technical term in logic, philosophy, and the classificatory sciences, implies inclusion within a class or category (as an individual in a species or a species in a genus) or a being comprehended by a general principle or proposition ⟨absolute generic unity would obtain if there were one summum genus under which all things without exception could be eventually *subsumed*—*James*⟩
*Ana* *contain, hold, accommodate
*Ant* exclude —*Con* eliminate, rule out, debar, disbar, shut out (see EXCLUDE): omit, forget (see NEGLECT *vb*)
**incognito** *pseudonym, alias, nom de guerre, pen name, nom de plume
**incommode** discommode, *inconvenience, trouble
*Ana* *hinder, impede, obstruct, block: disturb, *discompose: bother, irk, vex, *annoy
*Ant* accommodate (sense 2) —*Con* *oblige, favor: *indulge, humor: *please, gratify
**incomparable** peerless, *supreme, superlative, transcendent, surpassing, preeminent

---

A colon (:) separates groups of words discriminated. An asterisk (*) indicates place of treatment of each group.

Ana unrivaled, unmatched, unapproached, unequaled (see affirmative verbs at MATCH)
Con ordinary, *common: fair, mediocre, *medium, second-rate, average

**incompatible** incongruous, *inconsonant, inconsistent, discordant, discrepant, uncongenial, unsympathetic
Ana antagonistic, counter, *adverse: *antipathetic, averse: contrary, contradictory, antithetical, antipodal, antipodean, *opposite: irreconcilable, unconformable, un-adaptable (see corresponding affirmative verbs at ADAPT)
Ant compatible —Con congruous, *consonant, consistent, congenial: harmonizing or harmonious, corresponding or correspondent, agreeing (see corresponding verbs at AGREE)

**incompetent** unqualified, *incapable
Ana inefficient, *ineffective
Ant competent —Con *able, capable, qualified: skilled, *proficient, expert, masterly

**incongruous** *inconsonant, uncongenial, incompatible, inconsistent, discordant, discrepant, unsympathetic
Ana alien, foreign, extraneous (see EXTRINSIC): grotesque, bizarre, *fantastic
Ant congruous —Con fitting, suitable, appropriate, meet, *fit: *consonant, compatible, congenial, consistent

**inconsistent** *inconsonant, incompatible, incongruous, uncongenial, unsympathetic, discordant, discrepant
Ana divergent, disparate, diverse, *different: irreconcilable (see corresponding affirmative verb at ADAPT)
Ant consistent —Con *consonant, compatible, congruous: according or accordant, agreeing, tallying, jibing, corresponding or correspondent (see corresponding verbs at AGREE)

**inconsonant,** inconsistent, incompatible, incongruous, uncongenial, unsympathetic, discordant, discrepant mean not in agreement with one another or not agreeable one to the other. Except for this denial of reciprocal agreement or agreeableness, the first six words correspond to the affirmative adjectives as discriminated at CONSONANT especially in regard to their specific implications. **Discordant** is more common than inconsonant when applied, in the sense of devoid of harmony, to things coming into contact or comparison with each other ⟨discordant voices⟩ ⟨the discordant views of cabinet officers⟩ **Discrepant** is often preferred to inconsistent in attributive use especially when a wide variance between details of two things that should be alike or consistent is to be suggested; thus, "two discrepant accounts of an accident" suggests more obvious differences in details than "their accounts are inconsistent." Inconsistent is more frequent in predicative use.
Ant consonant —Con congruous, compatible, consistent, congenial (see CONSONANT): harmonized or harmonious, attuned (see corresponding verbs at HARMONIZE)

**inconstant,** fickle, capricious, mercurial, unstable mean lacking or showing lack of firmness or steadiness in purpose, attachment, or devotion. **Inconstant,** usually applied to persons though sometimes to things, suggests an inherent or constitutional tendency to change frequently; it commonly implies an incapacity for fixity or steadiness (as in one's affections, aspirations, or course) ⟨swear not by the moon, the inconstant moon, that monthly changes in her circled orb—Shak.⟩ ⟨people seldom know what they would be at, young men especially, they are so amazingly changeable and inconstant—Austen⟩ ⟨Spanish assistance from the sea was inconstant, almost accidental—Jones⟩ **Fickle** retains only a hint of its basic implication of deceitfulness or treacherousness, but its basic implications of instability and unreliability are colored by the suggestion of an incapacity for being true, steadfast, or

certain ⟨Fortune, Fortune! all men call thee fickle—Shak.⟩ ⟨bitter experience soon taught him that lordly patrons are fickle and their favor not to be relied on—Huxley⟩ ⟨she is fickle! How she turns from one face to another face—and smiles into them all!—Millay⟩ **Capricious** suggests qualities which manifest or seem to manifest a lack of guidance by a power (as law, authority, or reason) that tends to regularize movements or acts. When used in reference to persons, it suggests guidance by whim, mood, freak, or sudden impulse ⟨Louis XIII . . . a boy of eight at his accession . . . grows up capricious, restricted and cold, hardly normal—Belloc⟩ ⟨he judged her to be capricious, and easily wearied of the pleasure of the moment—Wharton⟩ When used in reference to things, it implies an irregularity, an uncertainty, or a variableness that seems incompatible with the operation of law ⟨a capricious climate⟩ ⟨the capricious hues of the sea—Lamb⟩ ⟨the capricious uncertain lease on which you and I hold life—Quiller-Couch⟩ ⟨the olive is slow-growing, capricious in its yield —Huxley⟩ **Mercurial** is a synonym of the other words here discriminated only when it carries a strong implication of resemblance to the metal mercury and its fluctuations when subjected to an external influence. The word, however, also carries implications (as of swiftness, eloquence, cleverness, and volatility) derived from its earlier association with the god Mercury. Consequently when it applies to persons, their temperaments, or their natures, it usually suggests a pleasing even if baffling variability, an amazing succession of gifts capable of being displayed at will or at need, and such other qualities as sprightliness, restlessness, flashing wit, and elusive charm ⟨the gay, gallant, mercurial Frenchman—Disraeli⟩ ⟨I was ardent in my temperament; quick, mercurial, impetuous—Irving⟩ ⟨it seems impossible that her bright and mercurial figure is no longer among us, that she will delight us no more with the keen precision and stabbing brilliance of that jewelled brain—New Republic⟩ **Unstable,** which is applicable to persons as well as to things, implies a constitutional incapacity for remaining in a fixed position mentally or emotionally as well as physically; it suggests, therefore, such fluctuations in behavior as frequent and often unjustified changes in occupation or in residence or sudden and startling changes of faith or of interests ⟨unstable as water, thou shalt not excel—Gen 49:4⟩ ⟨his nature, lamentably unstable, was not ignoble—Macaulay⟩ ⟨woman's love . . . is volatile, insoluble, unstable—M. L. Anderson⟩ ⟨an unstable world economy . . . subjected to periods of wars, inflation, and depression—Farmer's Weekly⟩
Ana *changeable, changeful, variable, protean, mutable: *faithless, disloyal, false, treacherous, traitorous, perfidious: volatile, frivolous, light, light-minded (see corresponding nouns at LIGHTNESS)
Ant constant —Con *reliable, dependable, trustworthy, trusty: true, loyal, staunch, steadfast, *faithful

**inconvenience** vb Inconvenience, incommode, discommode, trouble are comparable when they mean to subject to disturbance or annoyance. **Inconvenience** usually suggests little more than interference with one's plans, one's comfort, or one's freedom of action; it seldom carries suggestions of more than a temporary or slight disturbance or annoyance ⟨I hope the new arrangement will not inconvenience you⟩ ⟨do not inconvenience him by intruding upon him while he is writing⟩ ⟨she was frequently inconvenienced by the strong scent of tobacco which the fresh breeze conveyed through the porthole—Wylie⟩ **Incommode** and, even more, **discommode** carry a somewhat heightened suggestion of disturbance or annoyance, but not enough to imply actual suffering or injury; rather, they connote some mental agitation (as embarrassment or

Ana analogous words　　　Ant antonyms　　　Con contrasted words　　　See also explanatory notes facing page 1

vexation) or more or less disagreeable interference with one's comfort or plans ⟨Lucian was soon *incommoded* by the attention his cousin attracted—*Shaw*⟩ ⟨"passenger disservice"—all the things which go to delay flights or otherwise to *incommode* the passenger—*R. P. Cooke*⟩ ⟨it could not *discommode* you to receive any of his Grace's visitors or mine—*Scott*⟩ ⟨finding herself and the younger children *discommoded* in the boat—*Galt*⟩ **Trouble** is often used in polite intercourse in a sense close to that of *inconvenience,* when it suggests even less effort or disturbance ⟨may I *trouble* you to pass the salt⟩ ⟨will it *trouble* you to drop this letter in the box when you are passing?⟩ It is, however, also used to imply serious disturbance or annoyance (as worry, deep concern, or great pains); in this sense and sometimes in the lighter sense, it is frequently reflexive ⟨men *troubled* themselves about pain and death much as healthy bears did—*Henry Adams*⟩ ⟨an artist who does not *trouble* about the philosophy of things, but just obeys the dim promptings of instinct—*Montague*⟩
**Ana** disturb, *discompose: interfere, intermeddle, *meddle
**incorporate** *vb* embody, assimilate, *identify
**Ana** merge, blend, fuse, coalesce (see MIX): *unite, combine, conjoin: consolidate, unify, *compact
**incorporeal** *immaterial, spiritual
**Ant** corporeal —**Con** *material, physical, sensible, objective
**increase** *vb* Increase, enlarge, augment, multiply mean to become or cause to become greater or more numerous. **Increase** distinctively carries the idea of progressive growth; sometimes it means nothing more than this ⟨Jesus *increased* in wisdom and stature, and in favor with God and man—*Lk* 2:52⟩ ⟨Miss Anderson's reputation as an artist *increased*—*Current Biog.*⟩ Sometimes it implies growth in numbers by natural propagation ⟨Abou Ben Adhem (may his tribe *increase!*)—*Hunt*⟩ or growth in size, amount, or quantity (as by increments or accretions) ⟨their salaries *increase* annually by one hundred dollars⟩ ⟨his strength will *increase* when his health improves⟩ or growth in intensity, especially by degrees or in proportion to something else ⟨the darkness *increases* the further we advance into the forest⟩ ⟨your misery *increase* with your age!—*Shak.*⟩ ⟨a series of several situations which progressively *increase* in humorous possibilities—*Kilby*⟩ In transitive use *increase* may or may not imply progressive growth; often it so stresses the operation or the effectiveness of a cause that it loses the connotation of natural or regular progression ⟨the trustees *increased* all salaries⟩ ⟨a rich diet *increased* her weight⟩ ⟨the depression *increased* his misery⟩ ⟨the girl's actions *increased* his suspicions⟩ ⟨good teaching *increases* one's desire for knowledge⟩ ⟨many facts unearthed by psychical research and abnormal psychology *increase* the credibility of some of the more miraculous parts of the gospel narratives—*Flew*⟩ **Enlarge** stresses expansion or extension so that whatever is affected is greater in some or all of its dimensions or in its size or capacity ⟨he *enlarged* his farm by the purchase of one hundred adjoining acres⟩ ⟨*enlarge* a hotel by building a new wing⟩ In extended use *enlarge* is applicable primarily to what may be thought of as capable of being made larger or smaller in extent or size; thus, one does not *enlarge* one's interests or one's activities but the field of one's interests, or the scope of one's activities ⟨*enlarge* the circle of one's acquaintances⟩ ⟨*enlarge* one's capacity for enjoyment⟩ Nevertheless field, scope, or capacity may be merely implied ⟨its [a constitutional clause's] terms purport to enlarge . . . the powers vested in the government—*John*

*Marshall*⟩ ⟨*enlarging* our personality by establishing new affinities and sympathies with our fellowmen, with nature, and with God—*Inge*⟩ ⟨the abundant opportunities which the aesthetic realm provides to *enlarge* our experience—*Hunter Mead*⟩ **Augment**, like *increase*, basically implies growth; it rarely, however, carries the implication of progressive growth or growth by degrees, which is often so strong in *increase*. It differs from *increase* chiefly in being used in reference to things already well grown or well developed; thus, when one says "the team's confidence *increases* with every victory" one implies that its confidence was originally not strong; on the other hand, when one says "the team's confidence *augments* with every victory" one implies that its confidence was never weak. Consequently the distinctive implication of *augment* is a growing greater, more numerous, larger, or more intense ⟨even an increase of fame served only to *augment* their industry—*Reynolds*⟩ ⟨to fret over unavoidable evils, or *augment* them by anxiety—*Austen*⟩ **Multiply** implies an increase in number especially by natural generation ⟨every species of animals naturally *multiplies* in proportion to the means of their subsistence, and no species can ever *multiply* beyond it—*Smith*⟩ Sometimes, however, the word implies increase in numbers by indefinite repetition of things of the same kind ⟨if there were space, we might *multiply* illustrative citations⟩ ⟨philosophers who propose to solve certain intellectual problems by *multiplying* abstractions—*Holmer*⟩ ⟨commerce *multiplied* wealth and comfort—*Barr*⟩
**Ana** *intensify, aggravate, heighten, enhance: *expand, swell, amplify, dilate, distend, inflate: *extend, lengthen, elongate, prolong, protract
**Ant** decrease —**Con** diminish, lessen, reduce, abate, dwindle (see DECREASE): *shorten, abridge, abbreviate, curtail, retrench: *contract, condense, shrink, deflate
**incredulity** disbelief, *unbelief
**Ana** doubt, dubiety, dubiosity, skepticism, *uncertainty
**Ant** credulity —**Con** certitude, *certainty, assurance, conviction: positiveness, cocksureness, sureness (see corresponding adjectives at SURE)
**increment** accretion, *addition, accession
**incriminate** impeach, indict, *accuse, charge, arraign
**Ana** *involve, implicate
**Con** *exculpate, exonerate, absolve, acquit, vindicate
**inculcate** *implant, instill
**Ana** *infuse, inoculate, imbue, leaven: *teach, instruct, educate: impart, *communicate
**incur**, contract, catch are comparable when they mean to bring upon oneself something unpleasant, onerous, or injurious. **Incur** may or may not imply foreknowledge of what is to happen ⟨*incur* a debt⟩ ⟨*incur* criticism⟩ but it usually implies responsibility for the acts which bring about what is incurred ⟨he simply couldn't bring himself to *incur* the loss of face involved in admitting that he didn't know enough English—*Durdin*⟩ ⟨an environment containing all the classic elements for *incurring* mental fatigue—*Armstrong*⟩ **Contract** carries a stronger implication than *incur* of acquirement, but it is equally inexplicit in its lack of clear suggestion as to whether the acquisition derives from intention or accident ⟨had *contracted* considerable debts in granting loans to the king—*Cruickshanks*⟩ ⟨*contract* a disease⟩ ⟨*contract* bad habits⟩ But *contract* often distinctively implies a meeting between two things that permits either an interchange of qualities ⟨each from each *contract* new strength and light—*Pope*⟩ or a transmission of something from one to the other ⟨they say that sherry ought to live for a while in an old brandy cask, so as to *contract* a certain convincing quality from the cask's genial timbers—*Montague*⟩ **Catch**, the least

---

A colon (:) separates groups of words discriminated. An asterisk (*) indicates place of treatment of each group.

literary and most ordinary of these terms, usually implies infection or something analogous to it ⟨*catch* a heavy cold⟩ ⟨religion, in point of fact, is seldom taught at all; it is *caught,* by contact with someone who has it—*Inge*⟩
*Ana* *get, obtain, acquire
*Con* *escape, elude, evade, avoid, shun, eschew: avert, ward, *prevent

**incurious** unconcerned, *indifferent, aloof, detached, uninterested, disinterested
*Ana* *abstracted, preoccupied, absent, absentminded, distraught
*Ant* curious, inquisitive —*Con* prying, snoopy, nosy (see CURIOUS): intrusive, meddlesome, *impertinent: observing *or* observant, remarking, noticing, noting (see corresponding verbs at SEE)

**incursion** *invasion, raid, inroad

**indebtedness** *debt, debit, obligation, liability, arrear

**indecent** unseemly, indelicate, improper, *indecorous, unbecoming
*Ana* obscene, ribald, *coarse, gross, vulgar: lewd, lascivious, *licentious: *immoral: *offensive, revolting, repulsive, repugnant, loathsome
*Ant* decent —*Con* *chaste, pure, modest: virtuous, *moral, ethical

**indecorous,** improper, unseemly, indecent, unbecoming, indelicate are comparable when meaning not in conformity with the accepted standard of what is right or fitting or is regarded as good form. The first four words are in general the diametrical opposites of *decorous, proper, seemly, decent* (see DECOROUS), but the negative terms are often more sharply distinguished from each other than the affirmative terms. Something is **indecorous** which transgresses the conventions of polite society or its notions of what constitutes good form or good manners ⟨*indecorous* behavior at a funeral⟩ ⟨they regarded argument in public as *indecorous*⟩ ⟨a generation of critical circles has maintained an *indecorous* silence, not so much discreet as unbecoming, concerning John Masefield—*Salomon*⟩ Something is **improper** which violates an accepted standard of what is right, correct, or fitting, especially in etiquette, in language, in aesthetics, or in morals ⟨I am sure if I had known it to be *improper* I would not have gone with Mr. Thorpe at all—*Austen*⟩ ⟨he was telling her a funny story, probably an *improper* one, for it brought out her naughtiest laugh—*Cather*⟩ Something is **unseemly** which is not only indecorous or improper but also offensive to persons of good taste or to strict followers of the conventions ⟨I consider it very *unseemly* to talk in this loose fashion before young men —*Cather*⟩ ⟨Maurice disgraced Amy and himself by joining in an *unseemly* fracas with the police—*Rose Macaulay*⟩ ⟨we were in no danger of being betrayed into any *unseemly* manifestations of religious fervor—*L. P. Smith*⟩ Something is **indecent** which is grossly offensive to those who observe the proprieties or, in a frequent stronger sense of the word, which violates or outrages accepted standards or morals, modesty, or propriety ⟨*indecent* plays⟩ ⟨*indecent* behavior⟩ ⟨why do we regard it as *indecent* to tuck the napkin between the waistcoat buttons—*Mencken*⟩ ⟨buried him with *indecent* haste and without the proper rites—*A. M. Young*⟩ ⟨these dances, though to the eyes of Johnston . . . "grossly *indecent*" . . . are "danced reverently"—*Ellis*⟩ Something is **unbecoming** which does not befit one's character or standing or is not in accordance with one's own standards ⟨had a . . . look in her eye that was *unbecoming* in a menial position—*H. G. Wells*⟩ ⟨charged with conduct *unbecoming* to a soldier —*James Jones*⟩ Something is **indelicate** which verges upon immodesty or which betrays lack of tact or of sensi-

tive perceptions ⟨she had visions, so startling that she half repudiated them as *indelicate,* of coarse masculine belongings strewn about in endless litter—*M. E. Freeman*⟩ ⟨think no more of the matter. It is very *indelicate* for a young lady to dwell on such subjects—*Deland*⟩
*Ana* unfitting, inappropriate, unsuitable, *unfit: incongruous, *inconsonant: *rude, ill-mannered, uncivil, discourteous, impolite: *coarse, vulgar, gross
*Ant* decorous —*Con* decent, nice (see DECOROUS): ceremonious, formal, conventional (see CEREMONIAL)

**indefatigable,** tireless, weariless, untiring, unwearying, unwearied, unflagging are comparable in their basic meaning of not feeling or manifesting fatigue, but they are closer synonyms in their extended sense of capable of prolonged and arduous effort. **Indefatigable** implies being incapable of being fatigued, but in its actual use it usually suggests persistent and unremitting activity or effort ⟨the *indefatigable* pursuit of an unattainable perfection—*L. P. Smith*⟩ ⟨the strenuous, persevering, and absolutely *indefatigable* champion of every victim of oppression—*John Morley*⟩ **Tireless** and **weariless** are sometimes employed with little distinction from *indefatigable;* frequently, however, they connote less busyness and even greater or more remarkable power of continuance ⟨the *tireless* sweep of the eagle's flight⟩ ⟨a man of distinguished presence and *tireless* industry—*H. U. Faulkner*⟩ ⟨was not Arnold the *tireless* critic of his country and his age, the lifelong arraigner of British limitedness and complacency?—*Montague*⟩ ⟨a sturdy Dissenter, a *weariless* promoter of godliness—*Times Lit. Sup.*⟩ **Untiring** and **unwearying** differ from *tireless* in carrying a stronger implication of uninterrupted activity; often they specifically suggest an extraordinary ability to go on continuously and without a break while *tireless* and *weariless,* by contrast, often imply repeated returns over a very long course of time ⟨an *untiring* search for a lost child⟩ ⟨*tireless* efforts to attract attention⟩ ⟨*untiring* devotion to a cause⟩ ⟨the *tireless* reiteration of a call⟩ ⟨the *unwearying* pursuit of an ideal⟩ ⟨to the end of his life he was an *untiring* worker—*McGiffert*⟩ **Unwearied** differs little from *untiring* in its meaning, but it is more often applied directly to the person or thing concerned than to the activity engaged in ⟨I, so long a worshipper of nature, hither came *unwearied* in that service—*Wordsworth*⟩ ⟨the *unwearied* and disinterested seeker after truth—*Jowett*⟩ ⟨men who recalled the days of the Armada did not feel proud over James's *unwearied* appeasement of Spain—*Bush*⟩ **Unflagging** differs little from *tireless,* for it too stresses a display of power to continue without signs of weariness; but it also stresses no diminution of activity, and it applies to a person's powers rather than to the person himself ⟨*unflagging* attention⟩ ⟨a purpose . . . which he pursued with *unflagging* energy—*Froude*⟩ ⟨such a hold on the imaginations of scholars . . . that they pursued it with *unflagging* zeal—*Southern*⟩
*Ana* diligent, assiduous, sedulous, industrious, *busy: dogged, pertinacious (see OBSTINATE): energetic, strenuous, *vigorous
*Con* wearying, tiring (see TIRE *vb*): lagging, dawdling, procrastinating (see DELAY): indolent, faineant, slothful, *lazy

**indefinable** *unutterable, inexpressible, unspeakable, ineffable, indescribable

**indelicate** indecent, unseemly, improper, *indecorous, unbecoming
*Ana* *coarse, gross, vulgar, obscene: *rude, rough, crude, callow, uncouth: lewd, wanton (see LICENTIOUS)
*Ant* delicate, refined —*Con* pure, modest, *chaste, decent

**indemnify** reimburse, recompense, compensate, remunerate, *pay, repay, satisfy

**indemnity** *reparation, redress, amends, restitution

**indentured** articled, *bound, bond

**independence** autonomy, freedom, sovereignty, autarchy, autarky (see under FREE *adj*)
*Ana* liberty, *freedom, license
*Ant* dependence —*Con* subordination, subjection (see corresponding adjectives at SUBORDINATE): *servitude, slavery, bondage

**independent** autonomous, *free, sovereign, autarchic, autarkic
*Ana* *alone, solitary: self-governed, self-ruled (see base words at GOVERN)
*Ant* dependent —*Con* *subordinate, subject, tributary: *subservient, servile, slavish: relative (see DEPENDENT)

**indescribable** *unutterable, inexpressible, ineffable, unspeakable, indefinable

**indicate,** betoken, attest, bespeak, argue, prove can all mean to give evidence of or to serve as ground for a valid or reasonable inference. One thing **indicates** another when the former serves as a symptom or a sign pointing to the latter as a justifiable or necessary conclusion, treatment, or remedy ⟨the facts revealed by the auditor's investigation *indicate* that the peculations were not confined to one person⟩ ⟨conflicting findings *indicate* further neurological research—*Collier's Yr. Bk.*⟩ ⟨such symptoms *indicate* an operation⟩ ⟨the results . . . are believed to be the first to *indicate* a possible magnetic effect directly attributable to a solar eclipse—*Harradon*⟩ One thing **betokens** another when the former serves as visible or sensible evidence or, more narrowly, as a presage or portent of the latter ⟨his appearance *betokened* complete security—*Meredith*⟩ ⟨the black clouds *betoken* a storm⟩ ⟨like a red morn, that ever yet *betokened* wreck to the seaman, tempest to the field—*Shak.*⟩ ⟨towering business buildings, great warehouses, and numerous factories *betoken* its importance—*Amer. Guide Series: N. C.*⟩ One thing **attests** another when the former serves as indisputable evidence of the latter and has the force though not necessarily the character of legal testimony or documentary proof ⟨the great seal . . . *attests* . . .the verity of the presidential signature—*John Marshall*⟩ ⟨their success is *attested* by the marvelous exactness with which eclipses are foretold—*Darrow*⟩ One thing **bespeaks** another when the former leads to the inference that it is the outward manifestation of the latter ⟨to Him whose works *bespeak* his nature—*Cowper*⟩ ⟨the large abstention from voting in our elections must certainly *bespeak* an indifference not without meaning—*Frankfurter*⟩ ⟨a glint of pride in her eyes that *bespoke* her new dignity —*Lasswell*⟩ One thing **argues** another when the former gives good reason for belief in the existence, the reality, or the presence of the latter ⟨his evasion, of course, was the height of insolence, but it *argued* unlimited resource and verve—*Kipling*⟩ ⟨to the grub under the bark the exquisite fitness of the woodpecker's organism to extract him would certainly *argue* a diabolical designer—*James*⟩ ⟨a becoming deference *argues* deficiency in self-respect —*Whitehead*⟩ One thing **proves** another when the former serves to demonstrate or manifest the truth of the latter ⟨your language *proves* you still the child—*Tennyson*⟩ ⟨to become a writer was, however, in Thoreau's mind; his verses *prove* it, his journal *proves* it—*Canby*⟩
*Ana* intimate, hint, *suggest: evince, evidence, demonstrate, manifest, *show: import, signify, denote, *mean

**indict** incriminate, impeach, charge, arraign, *accuse
*Ana* blame, denounce, condemn (see CRITICIZE)

*Con* *exculpate, absolve, exonerate, acquit, vindicate

**indifferent** 1 Indifferent, unconcerned, incurious, aloof, detached, uninterested, disinterested mean not feeling or showing interest, especially natural or normal interest. **Indifferent** is often used in place of the other and more specific terms. It may imply neutrality of attitude arising either from a lack of bias, prejudice, or predilection when two or more persons or things are considered or from a lack of feeling for or against a particular person or thing ⟨it is impossible to remain *indifferent* to political parties when great issues are at stake⟩ ⟨he was . . . exceedingly difficult to please, not . . . because he was hypercritical and exacting, but because he was *indifferent*—*Bennett*⟩ ⟨nature had no sympathy with our hopes and fears, and was completely *indifferent* to our fate—*L. P. Smith*⟩ **Unconcerned** implies indifference such as arises from unconsciousness, insensitiveness, or selfishness which prevents one from being moved, worried, or made solicitous ⟨convincing the *unconcerned,* the apathetic, and the downright hostile—*Fine*⟩ ⟨readers *unconcerned* with style and philosophical illumination—*Cordell*⟩ **Incurious** implies indifference arising from a lack of intellectual interest or normal curiosity; it often suggests incapacity because of temperament or state of mind ⟨why . . . are we, as a race, so *incurious,* irresponsive and insensitive—*Woolf*⟩ ⟨the *incurious* ignorance of the poor about the diseases among which they live—*Edmund Wilson*⟩ **Aloof** and especially its derivative *aloofness* stress indifference that is the natural result of feeling apart or at a distance from someone or something (as from temperamental reserve, a sense of superiority, or an aversion to the inferior) ⟨young people . . . tend to become arrogant and hard, ignorant of the problems of adult life, and quite *aloof* from their parents—*Russell*⟩ ⟨it nerved him to break through the awe-inspiring *aloofness* of his captain—*Conrad*⟩ **Detached** often implies a commendable aloofness which is the result of freedom from prejudices or of selfish concern for one's personal interests ⟨the . . . frigid and *detached* spirit which leads to success in the study of astronomy or botany—*Chesterton*⟩ Sometimes it distinctively suggests a point of view or way of looking at persons or things as though they bear no relation to one's own life ⟨Rome contemplated the spectacle with the *detached,* intelligent amusement of the . . . theatergoer—*Rose Macaulay*⟩ ⟨he had been *detached* and impersonal about the great facts of life—*Webb*⟩ **Uninterested** is the most neutral of these terms and in itself suggests nothing beyond the fact of a lack of interest ⟨aware of nature as *uninterested* in him, yet able to feed or crush him—*Kelman*⟩ **Disinterested** though increasingly interchangeable with *uninterested,* in its more discriminative use suggests a freedom from thought of personal advantage or interest that permits one to detect the truth, to tell the truth, or to judge truly ⟨a *disinterested* observer⟩ ⟨will teach that one *disinterested* deed of hope and faith may crown a brief and broken life with deathless fame—*Eliot*⟩ ⟨although there are many things in which I am uninterested, I cannot be *disinterested* about the things in which I am interested—*Lowrie*⟩ ⟨a *disinterested* historian⟩
*Ana* impartial, unbiased, dispassionate, *fair: apathetic, *impassive, phlegmatic: *cool, nonchalant
*Ant* avid —*Con* *eager, keen, agog: sympathetic, responsive, compassionate (see TENDER): *antipathetic, unsympathetic, averse

2 average, moderate, *medium, middling, fair, mediocre, second-rate
*Ana* ordinary, *common
*Ant* choice —*Con* exquisite, rare, recherché (see CHOICE): superlative, surpassing, peerless, *supreme

---

A colon (:) separates groups of words discriminated. An asterisk (*) indicates place of treatment of each group.

3 *neutral, negative

**indigence** penury, want, *poverty, destitution, privation
*Ana* strait, exigency, emergency, pass (see JUNCTURE)
*Ant* affluence, opulence

**indigenous** *native, autochthonous, endemic, aboriginal
*Ant* naturalized: exotic —*Con* foreign, alien, extraneous (see EXTRINSIC)

**indigent** *adj* *poor, needy, destitute, penniless, impecunious, poverty-stricken, necessitous
*Ant* opulent —*Con* *rich, wealthy, affluent

**indignant** *angry, irate, wrathful, wroth, acrimonious, mad
*Ana* incensed, infuriated, enraged, angered, maddened (see ANGER *vb*): exasperated, riled, provoked, nettled (see IRRITATE): roused, aroused, stirred (see STIR)
*Con* *complacent, smug, self-satisfied: *indifferent, unconcerned, aloof

**indignation** wrath, *anger, ire, rage, fury
*Ana* resentment, dudgeon, *offense: *passion

**indignity** *affront, insult
*Ana* injury, wrong, *injustice, grievance: offending *or* offense, outraging *or* outrage (see corresponding verbs at OFFEND)

**indirect, circuitous, roundabout** are comparable when applied to ways, routes, or means with the meaning not leading by a straight path to a destination or goal. **Indirect** basically implies departure from the straight and short line between two points ⟨by what bypaths and *indirect* crooked ways I met this crown—*Shak.*⟩ In its extended uses *indirect* implies following a course that is not plain, obvious, explicit, or straightforward ⟨Jane's mother was making *indirect* but perfectly legitimate inquiries into his prospects—*Mary Austin*⟩ ⟨*indirect* taxation⟩ ⟨we have seen grow up . . . a whole new family of subtle, *indirect* influences—*Kefauver*⟩ ⟨man's possible development from non-Homo stock, must be based upon *indirect* evidence—*R. W. Murray*⟩ **Circuitous** implies not only indirection but usually a winding and, because of its length, slow way or course ⟨they were forced to take a *circuitous* route on account of the floods⟩ ⟨two lines possible—the one direct by sea, the other *circuitous* through Gaul—*Mahan*⟩ ⟨paths . . . more *circuitous*, but not less sure duly to reach the point marked out by Heaven—*Wordsworth*⟩ ⟨in speech and in action most Japanese are indirect and *circuitous*—*Buchanan*⟩ **Roundabout** may be used interchangeably with *circuitous*, but specifically it implies a following of a more or less circular or semicircular course from one point to another; the term more often than *indirect* or *circuitous*, especially in its extended use, implies deliberate, often blameworthy evasion or avoidance of the direct course or way ⟨take a *roundabout* course to one's destination⟩ ⟨a *roundabout* explanation⟩ ⟨the *roundabout*, diffident appeal for pity—*Day Lewis*⟩ ⟨she declared that she would have nothing to do with any *roundabout* ways, but go openly and instantly to law—*Burney*⟩
*Ana* devious, oblique, *crooked: *winding, sinuous, tortuous
*Ant* direct: forthright, straightforward

**indiscriminate, wholesale, sweeping** are comparable when they mean including all or nearly all within the range of choice, operation, or effectiveness. Something is **indiscriminate** which does not distinguish the deserving from the undeserving but acts (as in giving, treating, selecting, or including) regardless of individual deserts or merits ⟨*indiscriminate* charity⟩ ⟨*indiscriminate* praise⟩ ⟨the critic does a wrong who brings them under his *indiscriminate* censure—*Quiller-Couch*⟩ ⟨an *indiscriminate* lavish Irish meal, sausages, eggs, bacon, all together on one plate—*O'Flaherty*⟩ **Wholesale** often implies indiscriminateness, but sometimes it carries almost no such suggestion; however, it regularly stresses extensiveness, usually suggesting that no person or thing within the range of choice, operation, or effectiveness has escaped ⟨the *wholesale* vaccination of a community⟩ ⟨communism can spread only . . . as a development of existing economic civilization and not by a sudden *wholesale* overthrow of it—*Shaw*⟩ ⟨the continuous battle of this generation against *wholesale* character assassination through the application of indiscriminate labels—*Roy*⟩ **Sweeping** implies a reaching out in or as if in a wide circle to draw in everyone or everything within range; it usually carries a stronger suggestion of indiscriminateness than *wholesale* and often specifically implies exceeding the bounds of right, justice, or jurisdiction or suggests generality rather than a concrete, specific character ⟨*sweeping* reforms⟩ ⟨*sweeping* accusations⟩ ⟨a *sweeping* and consummate vengeance for the indignity alone should satisfy him—*Meredith*⟩ ⟨the statute is of a very *sweeping* and general character —*Justice Holmes*⟩
*Ana* promiscuous, motley, heterogeneous, assorted, *miscellaneous: uncritical, *superficial, shallow
*Ant* selective: discriminating

**indispensable** essential, necessary, requisite, *needful
*Ana* vital, cardinal, fundamental, *essential
*Ant* dispensable

**indisposed** *disinclined, loath, averse, hesitant, reluctant
*Ana* inimical, hostile, antagonistic, antipathetic (see corresponding nouns at ENMITY)
*Ant* disposed —*Con* *eager, avid, keen, anxious: friendly, *amicable, neighborly: sympathetic, responsive (see TENDER)

**individual** *adj* 1 particular, specific, *special, especial
*Ana* *single, sole, separate, particular
*Ant* general —*Con* generic, *universal, common
2 peculiar, distinctive, *characteristic
*Ana* unique, singular (see STRANGE): *distinct, separate, several
*Ant* common —*Con* ordinary, familiar, popular (see COMMON)

**individual** *n* *entity, being, creature, person
*Ana* aggregate

**individuality** personality, *disposition, temperament, temper, complexion, character

**individually** *each, apiece, severally, respectively

**indolent** faineant, slothful, *lazy
*Ana* *lethargic, sluggish, comatose: *inactive, inert, idle, passive, supine: *languid, languorous, lackadaisical, listless
*Ant* industrious —*Con* *busy, diligent, assiduous, sedulous: energetic, strenuous, *vigorous

**indomitable** *invincible, unconquerable, impregnable, inexpugnable, unassailable, invulnerable
*Ana* stubborn, dogged, pertinacious (see OBSTINATE): resolute, staunch, steadfast (see FAITHFUL): undaunted, dauntless, intrepid, doughty (see BRAVE)

**induce, persuade, prevail, get** are comparable when meaning to move another by arguments, entreaties, or promises to do or agree to something or to follow a recommended course. **Induce** usually implies overcoming indifference, hesitation, or opposition especially by offering for consideration persuasive advantages or gains that depend upon the desired decision being made; the term usually suggests that the decision is outwardly at least made by the one induced rather than forced upon him by the one that induces ⟨only those . . . doctors who were possessed of superior courage and capable of supreme self-sacrifice could be *induced* to continue at the work—*Heiser*⟩ ⟨the

object is to *induce* the child to lend of his own free will; so long as authority is required, the end aimed at has not been achieved—*Russell*⟩ ⟨conditions which had *induced* many persons to emigrate from the old country—*Dewey*⟩ **Persuade** implies a winning over by an appeal, entreaty, or expostulation addressed as much to feelings as to reason; it usually implies that the one persuaded is more or less won over by the one that persuades ⟨it is not very difficult to *persuade* people to do what they are all longing to do—*Huxley*⟩ ⟨deputed by the firm of lawyers . . . to *persuade* her to resume her married life—*Powell*⟩ **Prevail**, usually with *on* or *upon*, may be employed in place of either *induce* or *persuade*, but it usually carries a stronger implication of opposition to be faced or of good arguments to be overcome ⟨he had never before supposed that, could Wickham be *prevailed* on to marry his daughter, it would be done with so little inconvenience to himself as by the present arrangement—*Austen*⟩ ⟨I will go now and try to *prevail* on my mother to let me stay with you—*Shaw*⟩ ⟨*prevailed* upon the men in the sloop to sail up the river again, to rescue any survivors—*M. S. Douglas*⟩ **Get** in this relation (see also GET 1) is a much more neutral term than the others discriminated and it may replace any of them when the method by which a favorable decision is brought about is irrelevant or, sometimes, is deliberately not stressed ⟨finally *got* the boy to do his homework⟩ ⟨tried to *get* the union to accept arbitration⟩ ⟨succeeded in *getting* the Russians to relinquish certain claims for war damages—*Americana Annual*⟩
*Ana* *incite, instigate, abet: *move, actuate, drive, impel: motivate, *activate, actuate
*Con* *command, order, enjoin, direct, bid, charge: *prescribe, assign, define

**inducement** incentive, spur, *motive, goad, spring, impulse
*Ana* temptation, enticement, seduction, luring *or* lure (see corresponding verbs at LURE): *stimulus, incitement, impetus, stimulant, excitant

**induct** inaugurate, install, *initiate, invest

**induction** *deduction
*Ana* *inference, ratiocination

**inductive** deductive (see under DEDUCTION)
*Ana* ratiocinative, inferential (see under INFERENCE)

**indulge, pamper, humor, spoil, baby, mollycoddle** mean to show undue favor or attention to a person or his desires. **Indulge** implies weakness or compliance in gratifying another's wishes or desires, especially those which have no claim to fulfillment or which ought to be kept under control ⟨I would *indulge* her every whim—*Hardy*⟩ ⟨pasty-faced languid creatures . . . *indulged* in food and disciplined in play—*Russell*⟩ ⟨when schoolboys were less *indulged* with pocket money—*Archibald Marshall*⟩ **Pamper** carries an implication of inordinate gratification of an appetite or taste especially for what is luxurious or dainty and, therefore, softening in its physical, mental, or moral effects ⟨rich though they were, they refused to *pamper* their children⟩ ⟨he preserved without an effort the supremacy of character and mind over the flesh he neither starved nor *pampered*—*Dickinson*⟩ ⟨no country can afford to *pamper* snobbery—*Shaw*⟩ **Humor** stresses either attention to or an easy yielding to whim, caprice, or changing desires; it therefore often suggests accommodation to the moods of another ⟨*humoring* a pet fawn which had a predilection for soap and cigarette butts—*Corsini*⟩ ⟨the tone of your voice . . . is too gentle, as if you were *humoring* the vagaries of a blind man's mind—*Hecht*⟩ **Spoil** stresses the injurious effect on the character or disposition of one who is indulged, pampered, humored, or otherwise made the recipient of special attention; however the word

is often used to imply attentions that are likely to have this effect ⟨"She talks a great deal, sir," Elizabeth apologized. "She's our only little girl, and I'm afraid we *spoil* her"—*Deland*⟩ **Baby** implies excessive attentions, especially of the kind given to those who are unable to care for themselves and need the constant assistance of a mother or nurse; it also carries a strong implication of humoring or pampering ⟨*babying* Americans, telling them what they should read and should not read—*Sokolsky*⟩ ⟨Lydia had two methods of taking men down: *babying* them and harping on their faults—*Edmund Wilson*⟩ **Mollycoddle** usually implies babying; it distinctively suggests inordinate attention to another's health or physical comfort or undue efforts to relieve another of strain or hardship. It often also connotes, as the effect or danger of such treatment, effeminateness or infantilism ⟨schools where grown boys and girls are *mollycoddled*⟩ ⟨look here, mother dear: I'm as well as ever I was, and I'm not going to be *mollycoddled* any more—*Braddon*⟩
*Ana* favor, accommodate, *oblige: gratify, *please, regale, delight
*Ant* discipline (*others*): abstain (*with reference to oneself, one's appetite*)

**indulgence** forbearance, tolerance, clemency, mercifulness, leniency (see under FORBEARING)
*Ana* *mercy, charity, lenity, grace: kindness, benignancy *or* benignity, benignness, kindliness (see corresponding adjectives at KIND): mildness, gentleness (see corresponding adjectives at SOFT)
*Ant* strictness —*Con* severity, sternness (see corresponding adjectives at SEVERE): rigorousness, rigidity (see corresponding adjectives at RIGID): harshness (see corresponding adjective at ROUGH)

**indulgent** lenient, *forbearing, tolerant, clement, merciful
*Ana* humoring, pampering (see INDULGE): forgiving, pardoning, condoning, excusing (see EXCUSE *vb*): benignant, benign, *kind, kindly: mild, gentle (see SOFT)
*Ant* strict —*Con* stern, *severe: rigorous, stringent (see RIGID): harsh (see ROUGH)

**indulgently** forbearingly, tolerantly, clemently, mercifully, leniently (see under FORBEARING)

**indurate** *vb* *harden, solidify, petrify, cake
*Ana* season (see HARDEN): fix, establish, *set

**indurated** *hardened, callous
*Ana* rigid, *stiff, inflexible: obdurate, adamant, adamantine, inexorable, *inflexible
*Ant* pliable —*Con* *plastic, pliant, ductile, malleable: flexible, *elastic, supple, resilient

**industrious** diligent, *busy, assiduous, sedulous
*Ana* *active, operative, live, dynamic: persevering, persisting *or* persistent (see corresponding verbs at PERSEVERE): *indefatigable, tireless, untiring, unflagging, unwearied
*Ant* slothful, indolent —*Con* idle, *inactive, inert, supine: *lazy, faineant: *lethargic, sluggish, torpid

**industry** *business, trade, commerce, traffic

**inebriate** *n* *drunkard, alcoholic, dipsomaniac, sot, soak, toper, tosspot, tippler
*Ant* teetotaler

**inebriated** *adj* *drunk, drunken, intoxicated, tipsy, tight

**ineffable** *unutterable, inexpressible, unspeakable, indescribable, indefinable
*Ana* *celestial, heavenly, empyrean, empyreal: ethereal (see AIRY): spiritual, divine, *holy, sacred: transcendent, transcendental, ideal, *abstract
*Con* expressible, utterable (see corresponding verbs at EXPRESS)

**ineffective, ineffectual, inefficient, inefficacious** mean not producing or incapable of producing results. Except for

A colon (:) separates groups of words discriminated. An asterisk (*) indicates place of treatment of each group.

this denial of production or capacity for production, these adjectives correspond in their applications and implications to the affirmative adjectives as discriminated at EFFECTIVE.
*Ana* *futile, vain, fruitless, bootless, abortive: *vain, nugatory, otiose, idle, empty, hollow: *sterile, barren, unfruitful, infertile
*Ant* effective —*Con* effectual, efficacious, efficient (see EFFECTIVE): fruitful, *fertile, fecund: forceful, forcible, *powerful, potent
**ineffectual** *ineffective, inefficacious, inefficient
*Ana* see those at INEFFECTIVE
*Ant* effectual —*Con* *effective, efficacious, efficient: useful, profitable (see corresponding nouns at USE)
**inefficacious** *ineffective, ineffectual, inefficient
*Ana* *inactive, inert, idle: *futile, vain, fruitless, bootless, abortive: *powerless, impotent
*Ant* efficacious —*Con* *powerful, potent, forcible, forceful: cogent, telling, compelling (see VALID): *effective, effectual, efficient
**inefficient** *ineffective, ineffectual, inefficacious
*Ana* incompetent, unqualified, *incapable: infirm, decrepit, feeble, *weak: indolent, slothful, faineant, *lazy: remiss, lax, slack, *negligent, neglectful
*Ant* efficient —*Con* competent, *able, capable, qualified: skillful, skilled, *proficient, expert, adept, masterly
**ineluctable** *inevitable, inescapable, unescapable, unavoidable
*Ana* *certain, inevitable, necessary
*Con* escapable, avoidable, evadable *or* evasible, eludible (see corresponding verbs at ESCAPE): *doubtful, dubious, questionable: possible, *probable
**inept** *awkward, clumsy, maladroit, gauche
*Ana* inapt, *unfit, unsuitable, inappropriate: *impertinent, intrusive, obtrusive: *vain, nugatory, idle, empty, hollow, otiose: fatuous, asinine, foolish, silly (see SIMPLE)
*Ant* apt: adept: able (*as a result of nature, training*)
**inerrable** *infallible, inerrant, unerring
**inerrant** unerring, *infallible
*Ana* *impeccable, flawless, faultless: accurate, exact, *correct, precise: *reliable, dependable, trustworthy: inevitable, *certain
**inert** *inactive, passive, idle, supine
*Ana* lifeless, inanimate, *dead: impotent, *powerless: apathetic, *impassive, phlegmatic, stolid
*Ant* dynamic: animated —*Con* *active, operative, live: alert, vigilant, *watchful
**inescapable** *inevitable, ineluctable, unescapable, unavoidable
*Ana* *certain, necessary: inexorable, *inflexible
*Ant* escapable
**inevitable** 1 Inevitable, ineluctable, inescapable, unescapable, unavoidable are comparable when meaning incapable of being shunned or evaded. Inevitable (see also CERTAIN) implies that causes are already in operation or that the conditions (as of one's existence, one's work, or one's temperament) are such that the thing so described is bound to occur ⟨life is full of perils, but the wise man ignores those that are *inevitable—Russell*⟩ ⟨as soon as one lays down a rule . . . one has to face the *inevitable* exception—*Montague*⟩ ⟨she was winding up all sorts of affairs, with the *inevitable* result that she was encountering all sorts of urgent expenses which she was unable to meet—*Ellis*⟩ Ineluctable adds to *inevitable* the suggestions that struggle or defiance is futile and that no way out is possible ⟨the dangers that beset the world as the result of . . . the *ineluctable* increase in the human population—*Hutchinson*⟩ ⟨by chance or *ineluctable* destiny—*Dwight Macdonald*⟩ ⟨the pain was deep,

deep and *ineluctable—A. S. Paton*⟩ Inescapable and unescapable carry a stronger suggestion than either *inevitable* or *ineluctable* that the person concerned would, if he could, avoid what must be but is convinced of its inexorable character ⟨his *inescapable* fate⟩ ⟨continuity in design appears to be *inescapable—Gloag*⟩ ⟨the *unescapable* expansion of the nation's foreign policy—*D. S. Freeman*⟩ Unavoidable carries a weaker implication of necessary occurrence than the other terms, but it does imply that the exercise of foresight or care has not enabled one to escape what has occurred ⟨*unavoidable* delays⟩ ⟨an *unavoidable* accident⟩
*Ana* *certain, necessary: determined, settled, decided (see DECIDE): inexorable, *inflexible
*Ant* evitable —*Con* escapable, avoidable, eludible, evadable (see corresponding verbs at ESCAPE): preventable (see corresponding verb at PREVENT)
2 *certain, necessary
*Ana* *infallible, inerrant, unerring: *perfect, entire, whole: definitive, determinative, decisive, *conclusive
**inexorable** obdurate, adamant, adamantine, *inflexible
*Ana* *rigid, rigorous, strict: resolute, steadfast (see FAITHFUL): *immovable, immobile: implacable, unrelenting, relentless, merciless, *grim
*Ant* exorable —*Con* compassionate, responsive, sympathetic, *tender: merciful, clement, lenient, indulgent, *forbearing
**inexpressible** *unutterable, ineffable, unspeakable, indescribable, indefinable
*Ana* tenuous, rare (see THIN): *infinite, boundless, illimitable
*Ant* expressible
**inexpugnable** unassailable, impregnable, *invincible, unconquerable, invulnerable, indomitable
*Ana* uncombatable, irresistible, unopposable (see corresponding affirmative verbs at RESIST)
*Ant* expugnable —*Con* assailable, attackable, stormable (see corresponding verbs at ATTACK)
**infallible**, inerrable, inerrant, unerring are comparable when they mean incapable, or manifesting incapability, of making mistakes or errors. Infallible occurs in this narrow sense chiefly in reference to something (as a person, institution, or book) that is accepted as the divinely inspired medium for the revelation of moral or spiritual truth ⟨the pope is held by Roman Catholics to be *infallible* only when he speaks ex cathedra and defines a doctrine or a rule of morals held by the church⟩ ⟨believed in an *infallible* Bible—*Sweet*⟩ ⟨no mathematician is *infallible*; he may make mistakes; but he must not hedge—*Eddington*⟩ Inerrable and inerrant are erudite synonyms of *infallible* and may be preferable to the latter when it is desired to avoid connotations associated with the notion of papal infallibility ⟨decision from the *inerrable* and requisite conditions of sense—*Browne*⟩ ⟨not an *inerrable* text—*Gladstone*⟩ but *inerrant* may imply not so much the incapacity for making mistakes or errors as the fact of their absence ⟨an *inerrant* account of the battle⟩ ⟨the Church was ubiquitous, omniscient, theoretically *inerrant* and omnicompetent—*Coulton*⟩ ⟨the *inerrant* literary sense which gave us the Prayer Book Collects—*Sperry*⟩ Unerring implies inerrancy, but it stresses reliability, sureness, exactness, or accuracy (as of aim or observation) ⟨a marksman of *unerring* aim⟩ ⟨an *unerring* eye for fleeting expression of the moral features of character—*J. R. Lowell*⟩ ⟨a man is infallible, whose words are always true; a rule is infallible, if it is *unerring* in all its possible applications—*Newman*⟩ ⟨a man's language is an *unerring* index of his nature—*Binyon*⟩
*Ana* *certain, inevitable, necessary: *impeccable, flaw-

less, faultless

*Ant* fallible  —*Con* questionable, dubious, *doubtful

**infamous** nefarious, flagitious, iniquitous, *vicious, villainous, corrupt, degenerate

*Ana* ignominious, disgraceful, disreputable, shameful (see corresponding nouns at DISGRACE)

*Ant* illustrious  —*Con* glorious, *splendid, sublime

**infamy** ignominy, shame, *disgrace, dishonor, disrepute, opprobrium, obloquy, odium

*Ana* notoriety (see FAME): degradation, humiliation, debasement, abasement (see corresponding verbs at ABASE)

*Con* honor, glory, renown, celebrity, *fame, repute: prestige, authority, *influence, credit, weight

**infancy, minority, nonage** denote the state or period of being under the age established by law for the attainment of one's full civil rights and independence of guardianship. Infancy is seldom used in this denotation outside of legal documents and court reports; in these it is especially likely to be chosen when reference is made to the condition or status of the person who is not of age ⟨the defendant pleaded *infancy* at the time the lease was made⟩ **Minority** is widely used in general as well as in legal writing and is the word most often chosen when reference is made to the period or term of being under age ⟨he inherited the title during his *minority*⟩ **Nonage** is the equivalent of *infancy* and *minority* in their legal senses, but it is often distinguishable from them in its acquired connotations and by its greater susceptibility to literary and extended use. *Nonage* may suggest mere immaturity ⟨an adolescent Parisienne . . . bored with the *nonage* of her contemporaries—*Newsweek*⟩ Not infrequently it suggests adolescence and its weaknesses and strengths and may be thought of as the opposite of *dotage*, or *senility* ⟨the brook we leaped so nimbly in our *nonage* is a mere ditch or too wide for our tonnage—*Hillyer*⟩ ⟨a world which is still after all young and has plenty of time to make good the mistakes of its *nonage*—*Times Lit. Sup.*⟩

**infatuated 1** *fond, besotted, insensate

*Ana* deluded, deceived, beguiled, misled (see DECEIVE): duped, gulled, befooled (see DUPE): foolish, silly, fatuous, asinine (see SIMPLE)

*Con* sensible, prudent, sane, judicious, *wise: *rational, reasonable

**2** *enamored

**infectious 1** Infectious, contagious, communicable, catching in their basic use as applied to diseases are distinguishable though closely similar in meaning. **Infectious** designates a disease resulting from the invasion of and multiplication in the body by germs (as bacteria, protozoans, or viruses) that produce toxins or destroy or injure tissues. **Contagious** more precisely designates an infectious disease caused by receiving living germs directly from a person afflicted with it or by contact with a secretion of his or some object he has touched. **Communicable** in this relation is nearly equivalent to *infectious*, but it emphasizes the transmissibility of the disease rather than the method by which it is acquired. **Catching**, a less formal term, is close in meaning to *contagious*, but it implies even more the dangers of contact.

**Infectious, contagious**, and **catching** all have extended use but in such use the fine distinctions exhibited in their technical senses are not carried over with the result that they are nearly exact synonyms meaning rapidly imparted to others; thus, one may speak of *contagious*, or *infectious*, enthusiasm or of enthusiasm that is *catching* ⟨what a bad temper! I hope it's not *catching*⟩ ⟨fear is exceedingly *infectious*: children catch it from their elders even when their elders are not aware of having shown it—*Russell*⟩

*Ana* toxic, mephitic, pestilent, pestilential, virulent,

*poisonous

**2 Infectious, infective** as applied to agents related to the causing of disease may be interchangeable and then mean capable of infecting or tending to infect. **Infectious**, however, is more often restricted to the technical and figurative senses expounded in the preceding article. **Infective** may be distinctively applied to matter and means potentially infectious ⟨an *infective* secretion⟩ ⟨an *infective* wart⟩ In extended use it preserves the implication of corruption, strong in *infect* but often absent in *infectious* ⟨*infective* doctrines⟩

**infective** *infectious

*Ana* contaminating, tainting, polluting, defiling (see CONTAMINATE): corrupting, vitiating (see DEBASE): *poisonous, virulent, toxic, mephitic

*Con* salutary, hygienic, *healthful, wholesome

**infelicitous** unhappy, inapt, inappropriate, unfitting, *unfit, unsuitable, improper

*Ana* unbecoming, unseemly, *indecorous, improper, indelicate, indecent: inept, maladroit, gauche, *awkward

*Ant* felicitous  —*Con* happy, apt, appropriate, fitting (see FIT *adj*): apposite, apropos, germane, pertinent, *relevant

**infer, deduce, conclude, judge, gather** are comparable when they mean to arrive at by reasoning from evidence or from premises. All except *gather* are so clearly differentiated in logical use that these distinctions tend to be retained in general use. The derivative nouns **inference, deduction, conclusion, judgment**, especially as applied to the propositions or mental formulations derived by reasoning, are even more precisely fixed in usage. **Infer** basically implies a formulating (as of an opinion, a principle, a fact, or a probability) from evidence presented or premises accepted. In general use the term often connotes slightness in the evidence and so comes close to *surmise;* in logic, however, it and **inference** convey no suggestion of weakness or strength ⟨"I see motion," said Thomas: "I *infer* a motor!" This reasoning . . . is . . . stronger than some more modern *inferences* of science—*Henry Adams*⟩ ⟨"Oh, well, don't worry. Jane hasn't got any complexes." From which Gard . . . *inferred* she thought he [Gard] had—*Mary Austin*⟩ **Deduce**, in nontechnical language, usually means to infer, with added implications of very definite grounds for the inference; in strict logical use, it means to derive an inference from a general principle; that is, to make a **deduction** as opposed to an *induction* (see DEDUCTION 3). This distinction, an important one to logicians and philosophers, is nearly lost in general use ⟨what a man is as an end perishes when he dies; what he produces as a means continues to the end of time. We cannot deny this, but we can deny the consequences *deduced* from it—*Russell*⟩ ⟨the last entry was in pencil, three weeks previous as to date, and had been written by someone with a very unsteady hand. I *deduced* from this that the management was not overparticular—*Chandler*⟩ **Conclude** is often employed as an equivalent of *deduce* in its general sense. More precisely used, it means to draw the inference that is the necessary consequence of preceding propositions whether these propositions are the premises of a syllogism or the members of a series of previously drawn inferences constituting an unbroken chain of reasoning. A **conclusion** is therefore either the third proposition of a syllogism or the final, summarizing proposition in a rational process. In general use **conclude** and **conclusion** frequently preserve the implication of logical necessity in the inference ⟨do not *conclude* that all State activities will be State monopolies—*Shaw*⟩ ⟨the more one scans the later pages of Mark Twain's history the more one is forced to the *conclusion* that there was something gravely amiss with

A colon (:) separates groups of words discriminated. An asterisk (*) indicates place of treatment of each group.

his inner life—*Brooks*⟩ ⟨on the basis of years of intensive work . . . [he] *concludes* that comic books are a profound "anti-educational" influence—*Mills*⟩ **Judge** and **judgment** are nearly equivalent to *conclude* and *conclusion* but usually connote careful examination of evidence or critical testing of premises and the fitness of the conclusion for affirmation ⟨an economist should form an independent *judgment* on currency questions, but an ordinary mortal had better follow authority—*Russell*⟩ ⟨his career will inevitably be *judged* by the achievements or failures of his Government as a whole—*Wills*⟩ ⟨most of the tribes of Southern Iraq, *judged* by their physical characteristics, are of very mixed origin—*Thesiger*⟩ To **gather** is to conclude, but it connotes reflection rather than careful reasoning, and the putting of two and two together ⟨thereby he may *gather* the ground of your ill will—*Shak.*⟩ ⟨from Thomasin's words and manner he had plainly *gathered* that Wildeve neglected her—*Hardy*⟩
*Ana* reason, speculate, *think: surmise, *conjecture, guess

**inference** 1 deduction, conclusion, judgment (see under INFER)
2 **Inference, ratiocination** denote the process of arriving at conclusions from data or premises. **Inference** often connotes guesswork based on trivial or inadequate data or premises; in technical logical use it names the process of inferring (see INFER) but does not in itself suggest care in reasoning or in deduction. **Ratiocination** adds the implication of exactitude and of an extended process or the passing by steps from one inference to another. It often carries the connotation of tediousness or of hairsplitting. The same distinctions in implications are observable in the corresponding adjectives **inferential** and **ratiocinative**.
*Ana* deduction, conclusion, judgment (see under INFER): reasoning, thinking, speculation, cogitation (see corresponding verbs at THINK): surmise, conjecture (see under CONJECTURE *vb*)
*Con* intuition, understanding (see REASON): assumption, presumption, presupposition (see under PRESUPPOSE)
3 *implication

**inferential** ratiocinative (see under INFERENCE 2)
*Ana* hypothetical, putative, purported, conjectural, supposititious, *supposed: *theoretical, speculative, academic: *implicit, constructive, virtual
*Con* *explicit, express, definite, categorical: intuitive, *instinctive: proved, demonstrated, tried, tested (see PROVE)

**inferior** *n* **Inferior, underling, subordinate** mean one, usually a person, who is lower than another. **Inferior,** the most inclusive of these terms, may be applied to anyone that is lower in some significant matter as rank, station, quality, or value) than another; the term suggests, explicitly or by implication, a comparison, sometimes with those obviously and individually higher or superior but sometimes with those merely belonging to a level felt as higher ⟨that an *inferior* should punish a superior, is against nature—*Locke*⟩ ⟨he would be judged by his peers, and safeguarded against the obtuse hostility of his *inferiors* —*Mencken*⟩ ⟨Napoleon was his equal or superior in the first, gravely his *inferior* in the second—*Belloc*⟩ ⟨they are gracious to equals, abrupt to *inferiors*—*Temple Fielding*⟩ **Underling** routinely implies subjection to the will or wishes of another; it may apply to a condition from that of a slave or servant to that of one who is just below the master but ordinarily it implies some degree of contempt ⟨the fault, dear Brutus, is not in our stars, but in ourselves, that we are *underlings*—*Shak.*⟩ ⟨the disconsidered *underling* was in danger of becoming his master —*Buchan*⟩ ⟨scientists need to be used not as lackeys

or *underlings*—*Vannevar Bush*⟩ **Subordinate** likewise suggests subjection but has an entirely different flavor from *underling.* The term implies a being in subjection to the will or wishes of another but seldom carries a suggestion of disdain and usually expresses no more than relative position in a hierarchy ⟨his tendency to meddle and give orders to Welles and his *subordinates* annoyed Welles—*Beale*⟩ ⟨marked in the eyes of his young *subordinate* a subtle light—*Guy Fowler*⟩ ⟨matters . . . talked over endlessly by . . . Captain Anthony's faithful *subordinates—Conrad*⟩
*Ana* dependent, subject (see corresponding adjectives at SUBORDINATE)
*Ant* superior —*Con* *chief, head, master, leader

**infernal, chthonian, hellish, Hadean, Tartarean, stygian** mean of or characteristic of the abode of the dead. **Infernal** basically denotes of or characteristic of the underworld regions once held to be inhabited by the earth gods and spirits of the dead. Through confusion of pagan conceptions of the underworld with Jewish and Christian conceptions of hell as the abode of devils and a place of torment for the souls of the damned *infernal* has acquired connotations of horror, torturing fiends, and unendurable suffering through fire, which nearly always blur and sometimes blot out its original subterranean implications ⟨from the *infernal* Gods, 'mid shades forlorn—*Wordsworth*⟩ ⟨the most abhorred fiend in the *infernal* regions is sent to torment me—*Scott*⟩ When the classical conception of the underworld must be suggested without an admixture of alien connotations, **chthonian** is sometimes used ⟨but the worship of the dead . . . and of the *chthonian* gods, was marked off by broad lines from that of the Olympian gods—*Hastings'*⟩ **Hellish** comes close to the current meaning of *infernal* but carries so strong an implication of devilishness that it more nearly approaches *fiendish* in its meaning ⟨heavenly love shall outdo *hellish* hate— *Milton*⟩ ⟨burned them both with *hellish* mockery— *Shelley*⟩ **Hadean, Tartarean,** and **stygian** are used in poetry in place of *infernal,* sometimes without any reference to the conception of Hades, Tartarus, and the Styx in classic mythology. Very frequently **Hadean** is a loose equivalent for *chthonian,* **Tartarean** suggests darkness and remoteness, **stygian** connotes bounds with no outlet for escape, but all three are without fixed content.
*Ana* *fiendish, devilish, diabolical, demoniac: damnable, accursed, cursed, *execrable: nefarious, flagitious, iniquitous, villainous, *vicious
*Ant* supernal

**infertile** *sterile, barren, impotent, unfruitful
*Ana* *dry, arid: impoverished, exhausted, drained, depleted (see DEPLETE)
*Ant* fertile —*Con* fecund, fruitful, prolific (see FERTILE): producing *or* productive, bearing, yielding (see corresponding verbs at BEAR): reproducing, propagating, breeding, generating (see GENERATE)

**infest, overrun, beset** are comparable when they refer to disagreeable or noxious things and mean to make trouble because of their presence in swarms. Although **infest** carries only by suggestion the idea of annoyance or repugnance, since idiom does not require reference to the person so affected, the term is always derogatory ⟨wild pigs invade the airfields; Crocodiles *infest* the rivers— *Michener*⟩ ⟨to poison vermin that *infest* his plants— *Cowper*⟩ ⟨the idle rich who at present *infest* the older universities—*Russell*⟩ ⟨police agents and provocateurs who *infested* the revolutionary movement—*Rolo*⟩ **Overrun** is often interchangeable with *infest,* especially in the passive, but because it usually retains the implications of its basic sense it is the precise word when the idea of

running or spreading is to be conveyed ⟨the cellar is *overrun* with mice⟩ ⟨the garden is *overrun* with weeds⟩ ⟨heavily wooded and *overrun* with flowers—*Amer. Guide Series: Mich.*⟩ ⟨conformity of belief has . . . *overrun* whole populations like a plague—*MacLeish*⟩ ⟨he found the East already *overrun* with refugee conductors—*Green Peyton*⟩ **Beset** has usually the meaning to trouble through frequency and persistence, and often connotes assailing or attacking ⟨he was *beset* by enemies on every side⟩ ⟨she hurried at his words, *beset* with fears—*Keats*⟩ ⟨the road is *beset* with dragons and evil magicians—*Costain*⟩ ⟨subject to none of the pressures that *beset* American and English papers—*Mott*⟩
*Ana* \*teem, swarm, abound: harass, harry, pester, plague, \*worry, annoy
*Ant* disinfest —*Con* \*exterminate, extirpate, eradicate, wipe: \*abolish, annihilate, extinguish, abate

**infidel** unbeliever, \*atheist, freethinker, agnostic, deist

**infinite,** eternal, sempiternal, boundless, illimitable, uncircumscribed mean having neither beginning nor end or being without known limits. **Infinite** especially as applied to God or his attributes implies immeasurability or an incapacity for being estimated in any conceivable respect (as duration or extent) ⟨great is our Lord, and of great power: his understanding is *infinite*—*Ps* 147:5⟩ ⟨great are thy works, Jehovah! *infinite* thy power! what thought can measure thee, or tongue relate thee—*Milton*⟩ In mathematical and scientific use the term usually stresses indeterminableness; often it implies that no limits can be set to which a thing does or may extend, or that no point at which it ends can be discerned; thus, the number of positive integers is *infinite* since no one can set a limit to the number that can be indicated; an *infinite* decimal is one (as a repeating decimal) that cannot be brought to a termination ⟨the total number of stars is supposed, even by those who reject the idea of *infinite* extension, to run into thousands of millions—*Inge*⟩ In more general use, *infinite* usually implies not only exceeding greatness or vastness but indefiniteness or seeming endlessness of extent ⟨Chinese landscape [painting] is certainly preeminent . . . in suggesting *infinite* horizons, the look of mountains . . . melting away into remote sky—*Binyon*⟩ ⟨the Truth . . . is of necessity *infinite* and so is not for any poor finite creature like man—*Babbitt*⟩ ⟨the *infinite* ingenuity of man—*Webb*⟩ **Eternal,** in its earliest and still prevailing sense, implies having neither beginning nor end in time; it is therefore applied chiefly to God, in the sense of being uncaused or uncreated and unending ⟨the *eternal* God is thy refuge—*Deut* 33:27⟩ But it may be applied with essentially the same meaning to things and especially to abstractions and concepts for which no beginning is known or under present conditions is discoverable, and for which no end can be foreseen or predicted ⟨argue that matter is *eternal*⟩ ⟨the idea that the world is *eternal* is now seldom advanced⟩ ⟨the consideration of the general flux of events leads to this analysis into an underlying *eternal* energy—*Whitehead*⟩ ⟨the tradition that nature is ruled by hard, *eternal*, immutable laws—*Cohen*⟩ In more general use *eternal* may be indistinguishable in meaning from *endless* and is then applied to things with a known or evident beginning but no ending or an ending infinitely remote or completely indeterminable ⟨the Christian's hope of *eternal* life⟩ ⟨no *eternal* historical trend toward economic equality can be discovered—*Sorokin*⟩ This sense is frequent in hyperbolic use in which it may imply either endless duration or constant recurrence often to the point of weariness or disgust ⟨the *eternal* effort to discover cheap and agreeable substitutes for hard work—*Justice Holmes*⟩ ⟨the staircase door opened with

its *eternal* creak—*Bennett*⟩ but it also applies to something which, though it changes in appearance, form, or method, never dies out ⟨Macaulay, who has a special affinity for the *eternal* schoolboy—*Inge*⟩ ⟨princes were mortal, but the commonwealth *eternal*—*Graves*⟩ **Sempiternal,** a bookish word, is an intensive of *eternal* with somewhat greater emphasis upon the continuity of the thing so described ⟨all truth is from the *sempiternal* source of Light Divine—*Cowper*⟩ ⟨he did not really believe that infinity was infinite or that the eternal was also *sempiternal*—*Shaw*⟩ but it is chiefly a hyperbolic term ⟨dull dinners . . . with the *sempiternal* saddle of mutton—*Jekyll*⟩ ⟨the oldest, deepest (and seemingly *sempiternal*) controversy involves the definition of itself—*Hentoff*⟩ **Boundless** implies little more than an apparent lack of restrictions or bounds, or a capacity for extending, expanding, or increasing indefinitely; it often applies to something which so far exceeds in range, measure, or amount what is usual for a thing of its kind that it staggers the mind ⟨*boundless* wealth⟩ ⟨*boundless* impudence⟩ ⟨my bounty is as *boundless* as the sea—*Shak.*⟩ ⟨a *boundless* command of the rhetoric in which the vulgar express hatred and contempt—*Macaulay*⟩ ⟨this long and sure-set liking, this *boundless* will to please—*Housman*⟩ In mathematical and scientific usage, *boundless* applies specifically to a surface or a space (as a closed curved line or a spherical surface) which has the property of permitting an object starting from any point in the space and proceeding by one mathematical law to return to the same point without being interrupted ⟨the surface of a sphere is *boundless* but not infinite⟩ **Illimitable** also stresses a lack of bounds or limits, and may be used in place of *boundless* ⟨an *illimitable* appetite—*Stephen*⟩ but it is often applied specifically to something (as a distance) that can theoretically be measured in extent but in actuality exceeds the capacity of human ingenuity or of human instruments for measurement or determination of extent ⟨the heavens' *illimitable* height—*Spenser*⟩ ⟨the *illimitable* distances between the earth and the stars⟩ **Uncircumscribed** implies the lack of a determinable limit in any conceivable direction; it applies to something that extends or expands or seems to extend or expand in all directions in the manner of radii from the center of a circle ⟨*uncircumscribed* freedom⟩ ⟨so arbitrary and *uncircumscribed* a Power—*Charles I*⟩ ⟨the lighthouse symbol penetrates the novel with *uncircumscribed* power—*Robert Humphrey*⟩
*Ant* finite —*Con* circumscribed, limited, restricted (see LIMIT *vb*): \*dependent, conditional, contingent, relative

**infirm** feeble, decrepit, \*weak, frail, fragile
*Ana* debilitated, disabled, crippled (see WEAKEN)
*Ant* hale —*Con* \*strong, sturdy, stalwart, stout: \*healthy, robust, sound

**inflammable** \*combustible, flammable, incendiary, inflammatory
*Ana* igniting, kindling, firing, lighting (see LIGHT *vb*): flaring, blazing (see BLAZE *vb*): infuriating, enraging, incensing (see ANGER *vb*)
*Ant* extinguishable

**inflammatory** \*combustible, inflammable, flammable, incendiary
*Ana* inciting, instigating (see INCITE): stimulating, exciting (see PROVOKE): sensitive, susceptible (see LIABLE)

**inflate** distend, swell, \*expand, amplify, dilate
*Ana* enlarge, \*increase, augment: magnify, aggrandize, \*exalt
*Ant* deflate —*Con* \*contract, compress, shrink, condense, constrict

**inflated,** flatulent, tumid, turgid mean filled with some-

A colon (:) separates groups of words discriminated. An asterisk (\*) indicates place of treatment of each group.

thing insubstantial (as air or vapor). **Inflated** implies expansion by the introduction of something (as a gas) lacking in substance to the point where the walls are stretched taut or tension is evident ⟨an *inflated* tire⟩ ⟨an *inflated* balloon⟩ In its extended use *inflated* implies a stretching or expanding, often by artificial or questionable means, to a point not justified by reality or truth; thus, currency is said to be *inflated* when the amount in circulation far exceeds the amount normally necessary to meet the demands of trade and commerce; one's ego is said to be *inflated* when one is puffed up with self-confidence and pride not warranted by one's ability or achievements; a style may be described as *inflated* when it is far more pretentious or imposing than its subject matter warrants ⟨a pretentious and *inflated* tract on feminism—*Menninger*⟩ ⟨caricaturing the *inflated* elegance of Eastern culture as represented in its refined fiction—*J. D. Hart*⟩ **Flatulent** applies basically to persons or their organs when gases generating in the alimentary canal cause distention of stomach or bowels. In its extended use *flatulent* usually implies emptiness with the appearance of fullness or a lack of pith or substance ⟨*flatulent* with fumes of self-applause—*Young*⟩ ⟨a score or two of poems, each more feeble and more *flatulent* than the last—*Swinburne*⟩ ⟨enthusiasts who read into him all sorts of *flatulent* bombast—*Mencken*⟩ **Tumid** implies noticeable enlargement by swelling or bloating, especially as a result of an abnormal condition ⟨my thighs grow very *tumid*—*Johnson*⟩ ⟨his face looked damp, pale under the tan, and slightly *tumid*—*Cozzens*⟩ In its extended use *tumid* implies an abnormal or conspicuous increase in volume without a proportionate increase in substance and often suggests pretentiousness or bombast ⟨to compare, in thy *tumid* pride, with me?—*Shelley*⟩ ⟨while Shakespeare, using great words on the lowlier subject, contrives to make them appropriate, with Burke, writing on the loftier subject, the same or similar words have become *tumid*—*Quiller-Couch*⟩ **Turgid** is not always distinguishable from *tumid*; however, it is more often used when normal distention as distinct from morbid bloating is implied ⟨healthy living cells are *turgid*⟩ ⟨woody tissue *turgid* with sap⟩ Consequently, in extended use, especially as applied to literary expression or style, *turgid* often adds to *tumid* the connotation of unrestrained vitality or of undisciplined emotion, especially as manifest in bombast, rant, or rhapsody (see BOMBAST) ⟨the effects . . . already . . . show in French architecture—which is growing repulsive—and in French prose—which is growing *turgid*—*Belloc*⟩ In general, however, *turgid* may be used to describe anything that is not measured or restrained and perfectly in keeping with orderly thought ⟨the *turgid* intricacies the modern foundation gets itself into in its efforts to spend its millions—*Dwight Macdonald*⟩ ⟨football . . . a *turgid* struggle of monolithic masses—*Thurber*⟩
*Ana* bombastic, grandiloquent, magniloquent, aureate, flowery, \*rhetorical: pretentious, ostentatious, \*showy: rhapsodical, ranting, fustian (see corresponding nouns at BOMBAST): \*wordy, verbose, prolix, diffuse
*Ant* pithy　—*Con* compendious, \*concise, summary, terse, succinct, laconic

**inflection,** intonation, accent are comparable when they designate a particular manner of employing the tones of the voice in speech. **Inflection** implies change in pitch or tone; it often suggests a variation expressive of emotion or sentiment, and, usually, a momentary mood ⟨it was not her words, but her *inflection,* that hurt⟩ ⟨a slight *inflection* made one feel that one had received a great compliment—*Cather*⟩ **Intonation** is often individual but it is seldom

thought of as the result of a mood; it is applied to the rise and fall in pitch that constitutes what is called "speech melody" and that distinguishes the utterance of one individual or group from another ⟨a ministerial *intonation*⟩ ⟨we still write . . . for the actors, reckon upon their *intonations,* their gestures—*Quiller-Couch*⟩ ⟨that peculiar and pleasant *intonation* that marks the speech of the Hebridean—*Black*⟩ In some languages (as Chinese), called "tone languages," fixed pitch, or *intonation,* distinguishes the various meanings of single words. In a more specific sense, *intonation* often (as **intone** always) implies reciting or speaking religious matter (as a psalm or a prayer) in a singing voice, usually in monotone ⟨*intonation* of that majestic iambic verse whose measure would have been obscured by a rapid and conversational delivery—*Dickinson*⟩ **Accent** denotes such manner or quality of utterance or tone as may distinguish a particular variety of speech (as one peculiar to a person, race, district, or class) ⟨a Southern *accent*⟩ ⟨a Parisian *accent*⟩ ⟨speak with a refined *accent*⟩ Like the other terms in this group, it often suggests, and sometimes indicates, the speaker's feelings ⟨a different *accent* was notable in Joseph's voice when he spoke of Azariah—*George Moore*⟩
*Ana* enunciation, pronunciation, articulation (see corresponding verbs at ARTICULATE)

**inflexible 1** rigid, \*stiff, tense, stark, wooden
*Ana* hard, solid, \*firm: \*rigid, rigorous, strict, stringent: tough, tenacious, stout, \*strong: immobile, \*immovable
*Ant* flexible　—*Con* \*elastic, resilient, supple, springy: pliable, pliant, \*plastic, malleable, ductile: fluid, \*liquid
**2 Inflexible, inexorable, obdurate, adamant, adamantine** mean not to be moved from or changed in a predetermined course or purpose. All are applicable to persons, decisions, laws, and principles; otherwise, they vary in their applications. **Inflexible** usually implies firmly established principles rigidly adhered to; sometimes it connotes resolute steadfastness, sometimes slavish conformity, sometimes mere pigheadedness ⟨society's attitude toward drink and dishonesty was still *inflexible*—*Wharton*⟩ ⟨a morality that is rigid and *inflexible* and dead—*Ellis*⟩ ⟨arbitrary and *inflexible* rulings of bureaucracy—*Shils*⟩ **Inexorable,** when applied to persons, stresses deafness to entreaty ⟨more fierce and more *inexorable* far than empty tigers or the roaring sea—*Shak.*⟩ ⟨our guide was *inexorable,* saying he never spared the life of a rattlesnake, and killed him—*Mark Van Doren*⟩ When applied to decisions, rules, laws, and their enforcement, it often connotes relentlessness, ruthlessness, and finality beyond question ⟨nature *inexorably* ordains that the human race shall perish of famine if it stops working—*Shaw*⟩ It is also often applied to what exists or happens of necessity or cannot be avoided or evaded ⟨*inexorable* limitations of human nature⟩ ⟨*inexorable* destiny⟩ ⟨you and I must see the cold *inexorable* necessity of saying to these inhuman, unrestrained seekers of world conquest . . . "You shall go no further"—*Roosevelt*⟩ **Obdurate** is applicable chiefly to persons and almost invariably implies hardness of heart or insensitiveness to such external influences as divine grace or to appeals for mercy, forgiveness, or assistance ⟨if when you make your prayers, God should be so *obdurate* as yourselves, how would it fare with your departed souls?—*Shak.*⟩ ⟨the *obdurate* philistine materialism of bourgeois society—*Connolly*⟩ **Adamant** and **adamantine** usually imply extraordinary strength of will or impenetrability to temptation or entreaty ⟨Cromwell's *adamantine* courage was shown on many a field of battle—*Goldwin Smith*⟩ ⟨when Eve upon the first of men the apple pressed with specious cant, O, what a thousand

pities then that Adam was not *Adam-ant—Thomas Moore*⟩

*Ana* *rigid, strict, rigorous, stringent: intractable, refractory, headstrong, *unruly, ungovernable: implacable, relentless, unrelenting, *grim: stubborn, *obstinate, dogged, stiff-necked, mulish

*Ant* flexible —*Con* *elastic, resilient, expansive, volatile, buoyant: amenable, tractable, docile, biddable (see OBEDIENT)

**influence** *n* Influence, authority, prestige, weight, credit are comparable when they mean power exerted over the minds or acts of others either without apparent effort or as the result of the qualities, the position, or the reputation of the person or thing that exerts this power. **Influence** suggests a flowing from one thing into another of something imperceptible or impalpable; this connotation is retained when the word implies the effect or effects which one person or thing insensibly has on another or the ascendancy which one person or thing similarly acquires over another ⟨he was not strong enough to resist the *influence* of bad companions⟩ ⟨we find primitive men thinking that almost everything . . . can exert *influence* of some sort —*James*⟩ ⟨as provost of the Swedish clergymen he exercised a quickening *influence* over all the Swedish congregations—*Genzmer*⟩ However *influence* often loses this implication of insensible or unconscious operation and suggests instead the conscious use of personal power or, sometimes, of underhanded means to determine the acts of another; in this sense it often follows the verb *use* or one of its synonyms ⟨use undue *influence* over a person making a will⟩ ⟨used his *influence* in getting a bill through a legislature⟩ **Authority** originally was applied to one (as a preacher, teacher, or writer) or to writings or utterances having the power to compel belief or to win acceptance. In such cases the word usually imputed great learning, great wisdom, or divine inspiration to the person or his work ⟨by turning o'er *authorities,* I have . . . made familiar to me . . . the blest infusions that dwell in vegetives, in metals, stones—*Shak.*⟩ This sense persists and *authority* is still applicable to a person or publication that is able or qualified to gain credence or to inspire belief in its authoritativeness ⟨do not cite this historian; he is not an *authority*⟩ ⟨an economist should form an independent judgment on currency questions but an ordinary mortal had better follow *authority*—*Russell*⟩ ⟨scholars who held that Cicero was an unchallengeable "*authority*"—*Highet*⟩ From this use mainly, but also from its other sense (see POWER 3), *authority* has come to be applied also to the power resident in a person or thing that is able because of his or its inherent qualities to win the devotion or allegiance of men and to gain rather than exact their obedience and belief ⟨a book of manifest *authority*⟩ ⟨that personal *authority,* which, far more than any legal or constitutional device, was the true secret of his later power—*Buchan*⟩ ⟨a doctrine that has acquired *authority* in our own time—*Alexander*⟩ ⟨some of the new philosophies undermine the *authority* of science, as some of the older systems undermined the *authority* of religion—*Inge*⟩ ⟨to face a good orchestra with inward and outward *authority* and assurance—*Burk*⟩ **Prestige,** in contrast with *authority,* implies the power to gain ascendancy over the minds of men and to command their admiration for distinguished and superior performance, or for conspicuous excellence in its kind ⟨nothing more affects the *prestige* of a power than its dramatic and rapid defeat in the field—*Belloc*⟩ ⟨the almost magical *prestige* that had belonged to the original humanists—*Huxley*⟩ ⟨such lustre—or *prestige* or mana—as individual writers possess—*Times Lit. Sup.*⟩ **Weight** denotes measurable influence, especially in deter-

mining the acts of others ⟨Mrs. Hawthorne's authoritative air was beginning to have some *weight* with him—*Archibald Marshall*⟩ ⟨men who take the lead, and whose opinions and wishes have great *weight* with the others—*Frazer*⟩ **Credit** (see also BELIEF 1) denotes influence that arises from one's reputation for inspiring confidence or admiration ⟨Buckingham . . . resolved to employ all his *credit* in order to prevent the marriage—*Hume*⟩ ⟨as it [the ballet] declined as an art, so also it declined in *credit* and in popularity; it became scarcely respectable even to admire dancing—*Ellis*⟩

*Ana* driving *or* drive, impelling *or* impulsion, actuation (see corresponding verbs at MOVE): *power, control, dominion, sway, authority: ascendancy, *supremacy: dominance (see corresponding adjective at DOMINANT)

**influence** *vb* *affect, sway, impress, touch, strike

*Ana* *move, actuate, drive, impel: stimulate, *provoke, excite: *stir, arouse, rouse: *incline, dispose, predispose, bias

**inform** *vb* 1 Inform, animate, inspire, fire are comparable when they mean to infuse (a person or thing) with something (as a spirit, a principle, an idea, or a passion) that gives him or it effective power or an urge to action or activity. Sometimes, especially in the last three words, the idea of driving or actuating is so strong that it becomes their common denotation and the idea of infusion is merely a common connotation. To **inform** is to give character or essence to or to so permeate as to become the characteristic, peculiar, essential, and often abiding, quality of ⟨the inspiration of religion passed on to *inform* and subtly to perfume an art nominally concerned with the aspects of earth and sky, wild creatures and wild flowers—*Binyon*⟩ ⟨everything that is made from without and by dead rules, and does not spring from within through some spirit *informing* it—*Wilde*⟩ ⟨sentimental, Protestant ethos that has always *informed* his writing—*Fiedler*⟩ To **animate** is to endow with life, a vital principle, or an impulse to action. Although *animate* is often used where *inform* is also possible, it suggests, far more than *inform*, vitality and living energy ⟨religion . . . which is *animated* . . . by faith and hope—*Johnson*⟩ When what is affected is a person or when motivation of action or transiency of impulse is to be implied, *animate* is the more precise word ⟨he was *animated* with love for all men⟩ ⟨when the community is *animated* with anger against some heinous offence—*Alexander*⟩ ⟨his hatred of restraint *animated* his resistance to authority⟩ To **inspire** is to communicate to a person, as if by breathing into him, power or energy in excess of what he believes to be his own. The word usually implies both the operation of a supernatural power or of some inexplicable agency and such an effect as a spiritual illumination, or a quickening of intellectual or imaginative activity, or an exaltation of feeling ⟨great artists know or believe that they are *inspired* from something outside themselves—*Alexander*⟩ ⟨that sublimated language used by the finest minds in their *inspired* moments—*Hudson*⟩ ⟨we climb the mountains for their views and the sense of grandeur they *inspire*—*Jefferies*⟩ *Inspire* may also imply indirect rather than inexplicable influence, methods, or source (as in imparting knowledge or arousing a feeling ⟨teachers should *inspire* their pupils to work hard⟩ ⟨today's editorial on the mayor's policy was certainly *inspired;* it does not represent the editor's views but those of someone in power⟩ To **fire** is to animate or inspire so powerfully that one is inflamed with passion, ardor, or enthusiasm ⟨one step beyond the boundary of the laws *fires* him at once in Freedom's glorious cause—*Cowper*⟩ ⟨O how they *fire* the heart devout—*Burns*⟩

*Ana* *infuse, inoculate, imbue, leaven: instill, *implant,

A colon (:) separates groups of words discriminated. An asterisk (*) indicates place of treatment of each group.

inculcate: enlighten, *illuminate: fire, kindle· (see LIGHT *vb*): endue, endow (see DOWER)

2 **Inform, acquaint, apprise, advise, notify** are comparable when meaning to make (one) aware or cognizant of something. One **informs** a person of something when one imparts knowledge, particularly of occurrences or of facts necessary to the understanding of a situation ⟨*inform* a person of his success in a competition⟩ ⟨the radio announcer *informed* his audience of the accident⟩ ⟨kept the staff *informed* of Chinese public opinion concerning the American military action there—*Current Biog.*⟩ Also, one *informs* oneself when by study or investigation one gathers the pertinent facts ⟨his obligation as a citizen is to *inform* himself . . . regarding the controversial issues—*Houston*⟩ *Inform* in one specific use also carries the implication of talebearing or accusation ⟨I shall not *inform* upon you. It is not my business—*Wilde*⟩ One **acquaints** a person with something when by introducing him to the experience of it or by imparting information concerning it one makes him familiar with it ⟨in the first meeting of the class, the teacher *acquainted* his pupils with the program of study⟩ ⟨to *acquaint* people with information instead of just telling it to them—*Gowers*⟩ Familiarity is even more strongly implied in the participial adjective *acquainted* ⟨the explanation . . . is clear enough to anyone *acquainted* with the history of Puritan thought—*Parrington*⟩ ⟨a man of sorrows, and *acquainted* with grief—*Isa 53:3*⟩ One **apprises** a person of something when by a message or sign one communicates it to him ⟨he has *apprised* his employer of his intention to resign⟩ ⟨I made up my mind to send the waiter to . . . *apprise* him that I was there—*Mary Austin*⟩ One **advises** a person of something when one gives him information about it, especially of a kind that is important to him (as in making a decision, determining a policy, or arranging plans) ⟨the president asked to be kept *advised* of changes in public sentiment⟩ ⟨consulted the wine card and *advised* me that the wine I had chosen had no special merit—*Lovett*⟩ Often there is a suggestion of forewarning or counsel (see also *advise* under ADVICE 1) ⟨the passengers were *advised* of the risk before the vessel left New York⟩ ⟨against which a solemn trespass board *advised* us—*Mary Austin*⟩ One **notifies** a person of something when one sends a notice or formal communication concerning it, usually as a matter requiring his attention ⟨*notify* students of a change in the date of opening college⟩ ⟨the court clerk promised to *notify* the witnesses when to appear⟩ In commercial use, *advise* is used in preference to *notify* when information is given by letter, telegram, or cable ⟨please *advise* us when the shipment is made⟩

*Ana* *communicate, impart: *teach, instruct, school, discipline, educate, train: *warn, forewarn, caution

**information** lore, learning, *knowledge, science, erudition, scholarship

*Ana* *news, tidings, intelligence, advice

**infraction** *breach, violation, transgression, infringement, trespass, contravention

*Ana* *offense, sin, crime, vice, scandal: slip, lapse, faux pas, *error

*Ant* observance

**infrequent, uncommon, scarce, rare, occasional, sporadic** are comparable when they mean appearing, happening, or met with so seldom as to attract attention. Something is **infrequent** which does not occur often, especially within a given period of time, or which does not recur except at very wide intervals of time or of space ⟨tornadoes are *infrequent* in New England⟩ ⟨far from being *infrequent*, the crystalline state is almost universal among solids—*Darrow*⟩ ⟨*infrequent* pines dot the forest⟩ ⟨though it was

only a few hundred miles north of Santa Fe, communication with that region was so *infrequent* that news traveled to Santa Fe from Europe more quickly than from Pikes Peak—*Cather*⟩ Something is **uncommon** which does not occur or is not found ordinarily and which therefore is singular, exceptional, or extraordinary ⟨smallpox is now *uncommon* in most parts of the United States⟩ ⟨in certain country districts in Europe families of fifteen are not *uncommon* enough to be regarded as extraordinary—*Shaw*⟩ ⟨such muscular strength is *uncommon* among girls⟩ ⟨a writer possessing *uncommon* inventive ability—*A. C. Ward*⟩ ⟨Mr. Coates's life has not been especially eventful, but he has enjoyed it with *uncommon* relish—*Richard Findlater*⟩ Something is **scarce** which at the moment in mind is not easily found or which does not exist or is not produced in sufficient quantities ⟨a bad harvest makes wheat *scarce*⟩ ⟨highly skilled mechanics are now *scarce*⟩ ⟨the Boones wanted land where deer and buffalo were numerous and men and cabins *scarce*—*J. M. Brown*⟩ Something is **rare** (see also CHOICE, THIN) of which but few examples, specimens, or instances are found; also, the term often carries such implications of *uncommon* as being exceptional or of extraordinary character ⟨*rare* postage stamps⟩ ⟨*rare* books and first editions⟩ ⟨a perfect union of wit and judgment is one of the *rarest* things in the world—*Burke*⟩ ⟨great men are scarce . . . but great biographers are positively *rare* —*Seccombe*⟩ ⟨I may say again, if only *rare*, how this butterfly would be prized!—*Jefferies*⟩ ⟨reported to give very indifferent wines to the *rare* guests he received in his grim old house—*Wharton*⟩ Something is **occasional** which happens or is met with merely now and then. *Occasional* more than any of the preceding terms implies irregularity or nonconformity to a rule or law that might govern occurrences or appearances ⟨this was not an *occasional* outburst of activity; it was Wesley's routine— *Crothers*⟩ ⟨Artemus Ward was all fun and sweet reasonableness . . ., with an *occasional* barb that by its unexpectedness did the more damage—*Lucas*⟩ Something is **sporadic** which has no continuous existence or continuity in its manifestations and which comes into existence or occurs only in rare and, usually, isolated instances ⟨*sporadic* cases of an infectious disease⟩ ⟨*sporadic* outbursts of opposition to high taxes⟩ ⟨humanism and religion are thus, as historical facts, by no means parallel; humanism has been *sporadic*, but Christianity continuous—*T. S. Eliot*⟩

*Ana* *exceptional: singular, unique, *strange: *irregular, anomalous, unnatural

*Ant* frequent —*Con* *usual, customary, accustomed: ordinary, *common, familiar

**infringe** encroach, entrench, *trespass, invade

*Ana* *intrude, obtrude, butt in, interlope: violate, break, transgress (see corresponding nouns at BREACH)

**infringement** *breach, infraction, violation, trespass, transgression, contravention

*Ana* encroachment, invading *or* invasion, entrenchment (see corresponding verbs at TRESPASS): intruding *or* intrusion, obtruding *or* obtrusion (see corresponding verbs at INTRUDE)

**infuriate** enrage, incense, *anger, madden

*Ana* provoke, rile, exasperate, aggravate (see IRRITATE): outrage, insult, affront, *offend

**infuse, suffuse, imbue, ingrain, inoculate, leaven** mean to introduce one thing into another so as to affect it throughout. **Infuse** implies a permeating like that of infiltering fluid, usually of something which imbues the recipient with new spirit, life, or vigor or gives it or him a new cast or new significance ⟨thou

didst smile, *infused* with a fortitude from heaven, when I
. . . under my burden groaned—*Shak.*⟩ ⟨he *infused* his
own intrepid spirit into the troops—*Gibbon*⟩ ⟨whose
work is for the most part *infused* with the spirit of scientific materialism—*L. A. White*⟩ **Suffuse** implies an over-
spreading of a surface by or a spreading through an extent
of something that gives the thing affected a distinctive or
unusual color, aspect, texture, or quality ⟨a blush *suffused*
her cheek⟩ ⟨eyes *suffused* with tears⟩ ⟨when purple
light shall next *suffuse* the skies—*Pope*⟩ ⟨she . . . pulled
the chain of the incandescent mantle . . . . the room was
*suffused* with the sickly illumination—*Mackenzie*⟩ ⟨the
poetic faculty will, in fact, have to deal—not with an abstract idea—but with an idea *suffused* and molded by
emotion—*Day Lewis*⟩ **Imbue** implies the introduction
of something that enters so deeply and so extensively into
the thing's substance or nature that no part is left untouched or unaffected; unlike *infuse*, which it otherwise
closely resembles, *imbue* takes as its object the person or
thing affected, not the thing that is introduced ⟨*infuse*
courage into his soldiers⟩ ⟨*imbue* his soldiers with cour-
age⟩ ⟨*infuse* grace into the soul⟩ ⟨*imbue* the soul with
grace⟩ ⟨thy words, with grace divine *imbued*, bring to
their sweetness no satiety—*Milton*⟩ ⟨[Virgil] has *imbued*
every object that he touches, with the light and warmth
and color absorbed from its contact with life—*Lowes*⟩
⟨individuals or societies whose life is *imbued* with a
cheerful certitude, whose aims are clear—*Krutch*⟩
**Ingrain** is found in the past participle or passive forms
only; like *imbue*, it implies an incorporation of something
comparable to a pervading dye with the body, substance,
or nature of whatever is affected, but unlike *imbue*, it
takes for its object or, when the verb is passive, as its
subject the thing introduced rather than the person or
thing affected ⟨cruelty and jealousy seemed to be *ingrained* in a man who has these vices at all—*Helps*⟩ ⟨the
idea of absolute financial probity as the first law of a gentleman's code was . . . deeply *ingrained* in him—*Wharton*⟩
⟨the feeling . . . is so deeply *ingrained* in human nature—
*F. M. Müller*⟩ **Inoculate** implies imbuing a person with
something that alters him in a manner suggestive of a
disease germ or an antigen. Often, the term implies an
introduction of an idea, a doctrine, an emotion, or a taste
by highly surreptitious or artificial means, in order to
achieve a desired end; less often, it additionally implies
an evil and destructive quality in what is introduced
⟨students *inoculated* with dangerous ideas⟩ ⟨the theory
. . . that if the great masses of the plain people could be
*inoculated* with it [a taste for music] they would cease
to herd into the moving-picture theaters—*Mencken*⟩
**Leaven** implies a transforming or tempering of a body or
mass by the introduction of something which enlivens,
elevates, exalts, or, occasionally, causes disturbance,
agitation, or corruption ⟨knowledge . . . must be *leavened*
with magnanimity before it becomes wisdom—*A. E.
Stevenson*⟩ ⟨there was need of idealism to *leaven* the
materialistic realism of the times—*Parrington*⟩
*Ana* impregnate, saturate, impenetrate, *permeate,
pervade: *inform, inspire, animate, fire: instill, inculcate,
*implant

**ingeminate** *repeat, iterate, reiterate

**ingenious** cunning, *clever, adroit
*Ana* inventing *or* inventive, creating *or* creative, discovering (see corresponding verbs at INVENT): *dexterous,
handy, deft: skillful, adept, skilled, expert, *proficient,
masterly

**ingenuous** *natural, simple, naïve, unsophisticated,
artless
*Ana* open, *frank, candid, plain: transparent, *clear:

*childlike, childish: *straightforward, aboveboard:
*sincere, unfeigned
*Ant* disingenuous: cunning —*Con* stealthy, covert,
furtive, surreptitious, underhand (see SECRET): wily, guileful, artful, crafty, tricky, foxy, insidious, *sly

**ingest** *eat, swallow, devour, consume
*Ana* *introduce, insert: *receive, take, accept

**ingrain** *infuse, suffuse, imbue, inoculate, leaven
*Ana* impregnate, saturate, *permeate, pervade, impenetrate, interpenetrate: instill, inculcate, *implant: incorporate, embody (see IDENTIFY)

**ingrained** *inherent, constitutional, essential, intrinsic
*Ana* confirmed, *inveterate, deep-seated, deep-rooted,
chronic: implanted (see IMPLANT): imbued, inoculated
(see INFUSE)
*Con* shallow, *superficial: external, outward, *outer,
exterior, outside: extraneous, *extrinsic, alien, foreign

**ingredient** *n* constituent, component, *element, factor
*Ana* *item, detail, particular
*Con* compound, composite, amalgam, *mixture, admix-
ture, blend

**ingress** *entrance, entry, entrée, access
*Ant* egress

**inhabitant, denizen, resident, citizen** are comparable when
meaning one whose home or dwelling place is in a definite
location. **Inhabitant,** the least specific word, implies
nothing more than an abode in a given place ⟨in 1940 the
city had 243,718 *inhabitants*⟩ ⟨certain disagreeable *inhabitants* of open impounded water supplies, known as
algae—*Morrison*⟩ **Denizen** denotes one that belongs by
birth or naturalization to a given locality ⟨*denizens* of
the deep⟩ ⟨winged *denizens* of the crag—*Scott*⟩ ⟨as if the
old *denizens* of the forest had been felled with an axe—
*Maury*⟩ Even when substituted in literary use for *inhabitant,* denizen retains something of its own flavor of
belonging to the locality by birth or naturalization ⟨jaded
and oversophisticated *denizens* of towns—*Lowes*⟩ **Resident** is not always clearly distinguished from *inhabitant,*
especially when a town or city, as distinguished from a
state or country, is in question. Often the term implies
nothing more than tenancy of a room, an apartment, a
house, or a locality for a considerable length of time ⟨the
summer *residents* of Bar Harbor⟩ Often, in the case of a
person who has several residences or who lives mainly in
a place other than the one regarded as his home, the term
suggests not permanent inhabitancy but legal recognition
of one of these places as his domicile, and as the seat of
his fundamental legal rights (as of voting) and responsibilities (as of paying income tax) ⟨proof that the multi-
millionaire was a *resident* of Massachusetts brought
several million dollars in inheritance taxes to that state⟩
⟨are the students at this college considered *residents* of
the town and entitled to vote in town matters?⟩ In reference to a country, *resident* is more usual than *inhabitant*
as a designation of an alien living in that country for a
time and regarded as subject to certain taxes ⟨an alien
actually present in the United States who is not a mere
transient or sojourner is a *resident* of the United States
for purposes of the income tax—*Income Tax Regulations,
U. S.*⟩ **Citizen** when denoting a person that is an inhabitant is rarely wholly free from its political sense (see
CITIZEN 2); hence, it usually carries some suggestion of
membership in, as distinct from mere presence in, a community and of possession of the privileges and obligations
inherent in such membership. It is particularly applicable
to an adult and substantial resident of a city or town ⟨no
mere pedant, but a leading *citizen* of the town, serving as
justice of the peace and as its first postmaster—*Starr*⟩
⟨the body of *citizens* or those who were members of the

A colon (:) separates groups of words discriminated. An asterisk (*) indicates place of treatment of each group.

city and entitled to take part in its political life—*Sabine*⟩
**inherent, ingrained, intrinsic, essential, constitutional** mean being a part, element, or quality of a thing's internal character or inmost being. Something is **inherent** which is so deeply infixed in a thing that it is apparently part of its very nature or essence ⟨certain *inherent* and indestructible qualities of the human mind—*Wordsworth*⟩ ⟨is the inferiority of the modern to the ancient languages, as a means of mental discipline, *inherent* in these tongues, or does it arise from causes that can be overcome?—*Grandgent*⟩ Something is **ingrained** which seems to be wrought into the fiber or texture of a person's being ⟨*ingrained* prejudice⟩ ⟨attributable rather to the *ingrained* law-abidingness of the people than to the perfection of the Paris police system—*Brownell*⟩ ⟨her deeply *ingrained* habit of never letting herself go—*H. G. Wells*⟩ Something is **intrinsic** which belongs to or is a property of a thing itself, as considered apart from all the external relations, connections, or conditions that affect its usefulness, value, or significance ⟨when the subject has no *intrinsic* dignity, it must necessarily owe its attractions to artificial embellishments—*Johnson*⟩ ⟨the knowledge of geographical facts is useful, but without *intrinsic* intellectual value—*Russell*⟩ Something is **essential** (see also ESSENTIAL 2, NEEDFUL) which is an element of a thing's essence and therefore indissolubly involved in its very nature or being ⟨certain *essential* differences between verse and prose—*Quiller-Couch*⟩ ⟨that *essential* sweetness of the moor, born of the heather roots and the southwest wind—*Galsworthy*⟩ ⟨has not shown that the merits of puritan thought are *essential* and the defects accidental—*M. G. White*⟩ Something is **constitutional** which is inherent in the fundamental makeup of the body or mind ⟨a *constitutional* infirmity⟩ ⟨his vigor is *constitutional*⟩ ⟨thoughtful ones will assure you that happiness and unhappiness are *constitutional,* and have nothing to do with money—*Shaw*⟩ ⟨a *constitutional* optimist, emotionally addicted to the view that any adventure into the unknown is worth the risk—*Garvin*⟩
*Ana* *innate, inborn, inbred, congenital: *inner, inward, internal: natural, typical, normal, *regular: integrated *or* integral (see corresponding verb at INTEGRATE)
*Ant* adventitious —*Con* *accidental, fortuitous, incidental: extraneous, foreign, alien, *extrinsic
**inheritance** *heritage, patrimony, birthright
**inherited** hereditary, inborn, inbred, *innate, congenital
*Ana* transmitted, conveyed (see CARRY): generated, engendered, bred (see GENERATE)
*Con* acquired, gained, obtained, gotten (see GET)
**inhibit** 1 *forbid, prohibit, interdict, ban, enjoin
*Ana* *prevent, preclude, obviate, avert, ward: debar, rule out, *exclude: *hinder, impede, obstruct, block, bar
*Ant* allow —*Con* *let, permit, suffer, leave
2 *restrain, curb, check, bridle
*Ana* *suppress, repress: *prevent, forestall: *arrest, check
*Ant* animate (sense 2): activate (sense 2)
**inhuman** savage, barbarous, *fierce, truculent, ferocious, cruel, fell
*Ana* pitiless, ruthless (see corresponding nouns at SYMPATHY): malign, malignant, *malicious: merciless, relentless, unrelenting, implacable, *grim: *fiendish, diabolical, devilish
*Ant* humane —*Con* benevolent, humanitarian, *charitable, altruistic, philanthropic, eleemosynary: compassionate, *tender
**iniquitous** nefarious, flagitious, *vicious, villainous, infamous, corrupt, degenerate
*Ana* wicked, evil, ill, *bad: atrocious, heinous, *out-

rageous, monstrous: ungodly, godless, *irreligious
*Ant* righteous —*Con* virtuous, *moral, ethical, noble: just, *upright, honorable, honest
**initial** *adj* Initial, original, primordial can all mean existing at or constituting the beginning or start of a thing, especially of a thing that gradually assumes shape or form or that manifests itself in many ways. Nevertheless, in spite of this agreement in meaning, the words are rarely interchangeable, usually because of additional and differing implications, but often also because of the determination of their use by idiom. **Initial,** in general, is used in reference to things seen as a whole, often in fact but sometimes in thought; the term, therefore, usually implies an end or completion ⟨the *initial* letter of a word⟩ ⟨the *initial* stage of a disease⟩ ⟨an aggressor nation would always have the *initial* advantage—*Dean*⟩ ⟨the great incentive to effort, all through life, is experience of success after *initial* difficulties—*Russell*⟩ **Original** (see also NEW) is used especially with reference to what is the very first in order or constitutes the ultimate beginning or source; in this sense it usually connotes the idea of being underived or unimitated and implies that there is nothing from which the *original* thing has sprung. A court that has *original* jurisdiction has the right to try a cause to determine both the facts and the application of the law to them, as distinguished from a court with appellate jurisdiction. "*Original sin*" was committed by Adam and Eve as the first human beings but, in theological use, the phrase also means that sin as its leaves its traces upon every human being ⟨great books are *original* communications. Their authors are communicating what they themselves have discovered —*Adler*⟩ Sometimes, however, *original* means something more specific; thus, the *original* owner of a piece of land would strictly be the one who first held it by a natural or legal right, but in legal interpretation the phrase may be used of an earlier owner when successive owners are mentioned; an author's *original* work may be the work first produced by him, but more often it means (without regard to order of writing) a work independently conceived and executed by him ⟨an *original* print is not, of course, *original* in the same sense as a painting. With a painting there is only one true original, whereas there may be as many as 50 or 75 originals of a given print—*Cain*⟩ **Primordial** (see also PRIMARY) is comparable with *initial* and *original* through its implied reference to what forms the actual beginning or starting point or the earliest form taken by something that follows a course, an evolution, a progression, or an unfolding ⟨speculate on the nature of the *primordial* universe⟩ ⟨the *primordial* mind⟩ ⟨the new discoveries . . . strongly support the theory that the universe has been expanding ever since a *primordial* explosion in which it was born—*Walter Sullivan*⟩
*Ana* starting, beginning, commencing (see BEGIN): *primary, primal, primeval, pristine: *elementary
*Ant* final —*Con* *last, latest, terminal, concluding
**initiate** *vb* 1 *begin, commence, start, inaugurate
*Ana* *found, establish, organize, institute
*Ant* consummate —*Con* effect, fulfill, execute, accomplish, achieve, *perform: *enforce, implement
2 Initiate, induct, inaugurate, install, invest are comparable when meaning to put one through the processes, ceremonies, or other formalities regarded as essential to one's being admitted to one's duties as a member or an official. **Initiate** (see also BEGIN) usually implies admission to some organization, cult, or craft and especially to one requiring indoctrination in its mysteries or mysterious rites or ceremonies in the introduction of new members ⟨*initiate* the newly elected members of a college fraternity⟩ ⟨*initiate* young people in the elements of physical science

—*T. H. Huxley*⟩ ⟨*initiate* a new reporter into the secrets of successful news gathering⟩ **Induct** may often be used in place of *initiate,* especially when introduction under guidance is also implied ⟨*induct* a person into the duties of a new position⟩ ⟨*induct* a draftee into the army⟩ But *induct,* as well as *inaugurate, install,* and *invest,* may imply a formal or ceremonious endowing of a person with the powers and prerogatives of an office or post ⟨*induct* the new governor of a colony⟩ *Induct* is used technically of clergymen who are put in possession of a benefice or living, or of officials who are established in their office with appropriate rites or ceremonies ⟨*induct* the new rector of a parish⟩ ⟨the new superintendent of schools was *inducted* into office at last night's meeting of the board of education⟩ **Inaugurate** (see also BEGIN) usually implies more formal and dignified ceremonies and much more publicity than *induct* ⟨*inaugurate* the president of the United States⟩ ⟨*inaugurate* the new president of the university⟩ **Install** implies induction into an office associated with a seat ⟨*install* the officers of a society⟩ ⟨*install* a bishop as the archbishop of his new diocese⟩ The term also may be used in reference to persons who are formally or comfortably seated ⟨*install* the guest of honor in the most comfortable chair⟩ ⟨*install* the tottering old lady in a chair by the fireside⟩ It is also the only one of these terms which may be used in reference to things as well as to persons ⟨*install* new machinery in a factory⟩ ⟨*install* electric light fixtures⟩ **Invest** usually suggests a clothing with the robes or other insignia of an office and, by extension, with the powers of that office. It often also implies a ceremony but it may suggest only the addition of powers that come to one on one's induction into a position or office ⟨by the constitution of the United States the president is *invested* with certain important political powers—*John Marshall*⟩

*Ana* introduce, admit, *enter

*Con* *eject, oust, expel, dismiss: *exclude, eliminate, disbar, blackball, shut out: divest, *strip

**initiation** *beginning, genesis, rise

*Ana* starting *or* start, commencing *or* commencement (see corresponding verbs at BEGIN): introducing *or* introduction, entering *or* entrance (see corresponding verbs at ENTER)

*Con* finishing *or* finish, completion, conclusion, ending *or* end, termination, closing *or* close (see corresponding verbs at CLOSE)

**initiative** referendum, *mandate, plebiscite

**injunction** *command, order, bidding, behest, mandate, dictate

*Ana* instruction, direction, charging *or* charge (see corresponding verbs at COMMAND): warning (see WARN): precept, rule, regulation, *law, statute, ordinance, canon

**injure, harm, hurt, damage, impair, mar, spoil** all mean to affect someone or something so as to rob it of soundness, strength, or perfection or to reduce its value, usefulness, or effectiveness. **Injure** in its earliest and still frequent sense means to do an injustice to or to wrong another (as by robbing him of his good name or of a rightful possession); in this sense it often suggests intent or knowledge on the part of one that injures ⟨when have I *injured* thee? when done thee wrong?—*Shak.*⟩ ⟨another *injured* burgher speaking of their forfeited rights—*Cloete*⟩ The verb may also imply the infliction not of injustice but of something detrimental to one's appearance, health, success, or comfort ⟨a bullet *injured* his eye⟩ ⟨industrialism has been very injurious to art; may it not have *injured* religion also?—*Inge*⟩ ⟨has to withhold information the release of which might *injure* the national security—*Mott*⟩ **Harm** is more specific than *injure* in stressing the infliction

of pain, suffering, or loss ⟨the boy is so gentle that he would not *harm* a fly⟩ ⟨the circulation of the rumor greatly *harmed* his business⟩ ⟨for none of woman born shall *harm* Macbeth—*Shak.*⟩ ⟨bitterness among the elders must not be permitted to *harm* or wound the innocent children of either race—*Beverly Smith*⟩ ⟨every time any one of us . . . fails to make the fullest possible contribution to . . . justice, he *harms* himself spiritually—*Atlantic*⟩ **Hurt** usually implies the infliction of a wound whether to the body or feelings or to a thing capable of sustaining an injury; often, it is used where *injure* is also possible ⟨he was severely *hurt* by a falling brick⟩ ⟨*hurt* a friend's feelings⟩ ⟨it's damnable to have to *hurt* the people we love—*Rose Macaulay*⟩ ⟨a limitless desire to *hurt* and humiliate—*H. G. Wells*⟩ **Damage** implies an injury that results in lowered value or involves loss in effectiveness, attractiveness, or efficiency ⟨his automobile was *damaged* in a collision⟩ ⟨the frost *damaged* the late crops⟩ ⟨whatever psychoanalysts may say, the parental instinct is essentially different from the sex instinct, and is *damaged* by the intrusion of emotions appropriate to sex—*Russell*⟩ ⟨like Hemingway, he was permanently *damaged* and therefore permanently inspired by war—*Morton*⟩ **Impair,** though coming close to *damage* in its meaning and often interchangeable with it, more frequently suggests deterioration or diminution (as in value, strength, or validity) ⟨a weak piece of evidence often *impairs* the strength of a good argument⟩ ⟨his value as a candidate has been *impaired* by his hysterical attacks on his opponent⟩ or a weakening (as of a function or power of functioning) ⟨his eye was injured and his vision *impaired*⟩ ⟨kindness that left an impression on my heart not yet *impaired*—*De Quincey*⟩ ⟨his physical prowess of all sorts is in no way *impaired* by heavy drinking and smoking, of course—*Christopher La Farge*⟩ **Mar** implies the infliction of an injury that disfigures or maims or involves the loss of a thing's perfection or well-being ⟨striving to better, oft we *mar* what's well—*Shak.*⟩ ⟨Plato asserts that a life of drudgery disfigures the body and *mars* and enervates the soul—*Dickinson*⟩ ⟨too good a book to be *marred* by small defects—*R. A. Smith*⟩ ⟨all these gifts and qualities . . . were *marred* by prodigious faults—*Woolf*⟩ **Spoil** (see also DECAY, INDULGE) carries a stronger implication of ruin than *mar* and suggests the operation of something that not only induces the impairment of strength, vigor, or value but also brings about their inevitable destruction ⟨bitter shame hath *spoiled* the sweet world's taste—*Shak.*⟩ ⟨a man who had *spoiled* his constitution with bad living—*Shaw*⟩ ⟨when a child persistently interferes with other children or *spoils* their pleasures, the obvious punishment is banishment—*Russell*⟩ ⟨a great novel *spoiled* by hasty (and lazy) composition—*Laski*⟩

*Ana* *deface, disfigure: *deform, distort, contort: *afflict, torture, torment: *maim, cripple, mutilate, mangle, batter: *abuse, ill-treat, maltreat, outrage, mistreat, misuse

*Ant* aid —*Con* *help, assist: *benefit, profit, avail: preserve, conserve, *save

**injury** 1 Injury, hurt, damage, harm, mischief mean the act or the result of inflicting on a person or thing something that causes loss or pain. **Injury** is the comprehensive term referable to an act or to a result of that act which involves a violation of a right or of health, freedom, and soundness of body or mind, or causes a partial or entire loss of something of value ⟨an *injury* to his eyes⟩ ⟨an *injury* to his reputation⟩ ⟨forgive an *injury*⟩ ⟨the very essence of civil liberty . . . consists in the right of every individual to claim the protection of laws, whenever he receives an *injury*—*John Marshall*⟩ ⟨mental or emotional

A colon (:) separates groups of words discriminated. An asterisk (*) indicates place of treatment of each group.

upset is just as truly an *injury* to the body as a bone fracture, a burn or a bacterial infection—*G. W. Gray*⟩ ⟨a great *injury* could be done to our nation . . . if this political campaign were to descend to the level of competitive threats and veiled hints—*A. E. Stevenson*⟩ **Hurt,** applies basically to a physical injury (as a wound, lesion, or contusion) that results from a hit, a stab, or a blow ⟨get him to bed, and let his *hurt* be looked to—*Shak.*⟩ ⟨rattleweed, made into a tincture, is better than arnica for *hurts* of every sort—*Emily Holt*⟩ In extended use *hurt* applies chiefly to an act or result that involves pain, suffering, or loss; thus, a person whose rights as an heir have been violated may be said to suffer an *injury* but not a *hurt*; a person whose reputation has been damaged by a false rumor has suffered both an *injury* to his business and a *hurt* to his feelings; a dentist in drilling a tooth may cause a *hurt*, but not commonly an *injury* ⟨leaving forever to the aggressor the choice of time and place and means to cause greatest *hurt* to us—*Eisenhower*⟩ **Damage** applies to an injury that involves loss (as in property, in value, or in usefulness) ⟨the fire caused great *damage* to the house⟩ ⟨repair the *damage* done to the cathedral by the bombs⟩ ⟨deliver Helen, and all *damage* else—as honor, loss of time, travail, expense . . . shall be struck off—*Shak.*⟩ **Harm** (usually without an article) is referable to an evil that injures or may injure; often it suggests a consequent suffering (as grief or shame) ⟨I meant no *harm*⟩ ⟨almost every evening he saw Lucy. The inexperienced little wife apprehended no *harm* in his visits—*Meredith*⟩ ⟨the men were terrified of Yusuf's cruelty, and wanted to retreat out of *harm's* way—*Forester*⟩ **Mischief** carries a stronger reference to the person or thing that works harm or is capable of inflicting injury; it applies either to the harm or injury that results from an agent or agency ⟨one failure led to another, suspicion became general, and the *mischief* was done—*Todd*⟩ ⟨that's the *mischief* of the Modernists . . . . They don't claim that the Divine revelation has been supplanted or even added to, but that it has been amplified—*Mackenzie*⟩ or occasionally to the aspect of a situation that causes harm or vexation ⟨the *mischief* is that people—especially the young—do not confine themselves to one cocktail—*Bennett*⟩ ⟨and faith, 'tis pleasant till 'tis past: the *mischief* is that 'twill not last—*Housman*⟩ **Ana** *distress, suffering, agony, misery: *pain, pang: violation, transgression, trespass, infringement (see BREACH): detriment (see corresponding adjective at PERNICIOUS): *evil, ill

**2 wrong, *injustice, grievance**
**Ana** see those at INJURY 1

**injustice, injury, wrong, grievance** are comparable when they denote an act that inflicts undeserved damage, loss, or hardship on a person. **Injustice** is the general term applicable not only to an act which involves unfairness to another or a violation of his rights ⟨class privileges which make *injustices* easy—*Spencer*⟩ ⟨the *injustices* that angered him were never quite genuine—*Mailer*⟩ but, as a collective noun, to all acts which come under this description ⟨he flamed out against *injustice* because he was a lover of justice—*Perry*⟩ ⟨the appropriate attitude toward prejudice and *injustice* and cruelty is indignation—*Hicks*⟩ **Injury** applies to an injustice to a person for which the law allows an action to recover compensation or specific property, or both ⟨every person who suffers damage to his person, his property, or his reputation as a result of an infringement of the law suffers a legal *injury*—*Rubinstein*⟩ **Wrong** is, in law, a more general term than *injury* for it applies not only to all injuries as just defined (*private wrongs*) but to all misdemeanors or crimes which affect the community (*public wrongs*) and which are punishable

according to the criminal code. But in general use *wrong* differs little from *injustice,* except in carrying a stronger connotation of flagrancy or of seriousness ⟨we are . . . steel to the very back, yet wrung with *wrongs* more than our backs can bear—*Shak.*⟩ ⟨so many were the *wrongs* that were to be righted, the grievances to be redressed—*Muggeridge*⟩ **Grievance** applies to a circumstance or condition that, in the opinion of those affected, constitutes a wrong or that gives one just grounds for complaint ⟨they sent to the king a statement of their *grievances*—*Keightley*⟩ ⟨in an early state of society any kind of taxation is apt to be looked on as a *grievance*—*Freeman*⟩
**Ana** damage, hurt, harm, mischief, *injury: infringement, trespass, transgression, violation, infraction, *breach: unfairness, inequitableness (see affirmative adjectives at FAIR)
**Con** *justice, equity

**innate, inborn, inbred, congenital, hereditary, inherited** are comparable but not wholly synonymous terms that refer to qualities which either are or seem to be derived from one's inheritance or from conditions attending one's birth or origin. *Innate* and *inborn* are often used without distinction. But **innate** (opposed to *acquired*) is frequently synonymous with *inherent, essential,* or *constitutional,* and then tends to apply to qualities, characters, or elements that are not inherited but belong as part of the nature or essence to something imbued with life ⟨*innate* ideas exist in the mind as a result of its constitution and are therefore found wherever a mind exists⟩ ⟨I do not believe that a sense of justice is *innate,* but I have been astonished to see how quickly it can be created—*Russell*⟩ ⟨this stubbornness has been explained as being *innate* in the Germans, as a natural racial cussedness. But some of the stubbornness is not *innate* but acquired—*Wood*⟩ *Innate* also may apply to elements or qualities (as virtues or defects) which arise out of the very nature or character of a thing that has no life and therefore literally no birth ⟨the *innate* defect of this plan⟩ ⟨the *innate* magnetism of the proton—*Davis*⟩ ⟨the *innate* tendency of a dictatorship to overreach itself⟩ On the other hand, **inborn,** which is frequently synonymous with *natural* or *native,* retains more specific reference to what is actually born in one or is so deep-seated as to seem to have been born in one; the term is therefore usually applied to qualities or characters that are peculiar or distinctive, sometimes to the type, often to the individual ⟨*inborn* aptitudes⟩ ⟨the tendency towards schizophrenia was *inborn*—*N. Y. Times*⟩ ⟨his *inborn* ability to sing⟩ ⟨an *inborn* love of country life⟩ **Inbred** implies reference to breeding, or to the processes concerned with the generation, nourishment, and rearing of offspring; the term therefore is more readily applied to what is deeply rooted or ingrained as a result of one's immediate parentage or the circumstances attending one's earliest education or training than to what is constitutional or merely natural ⟨an *inbred* love of freedom⟩ ⟨an *inbred* feeling of superiority⟩ ⟨those *inbred* sentiments which are . . . the true supporters of all liberal and manly morals—*Burke*⟩ ⟨a methodical man, an *inbred* Yankee—*White*⟩ **Congenital** applies chiefly to something which dates from the birth or inception of the individual concerned ⟨*congenital* hip disease⟩ ⟨*congenital* blindness⟩ ⟨the theory that what was acquired habit in the ancestor may become *congenital* tendency in the offspring—*James*⟩ ⟨yet art for art's sake suffers from a *congenital* disease; it professes to create substance out of form, which is physically impossible—*Santayana*⟩ Both **hereditary** and **inherited** apply to a result of natural heredity ⟨an *inherited* hearing defect⟩ ⟨unless he had the *hereditary* dispositions which he has, he would not behave the way he does—*Pap*⟩ or sometimes of social heredity ⟨the reciter who might graft on to an *inherited* body of literature a few embellishments of his own—*Lerner & Mims*⟩ ⟨several *hereditary* enemies of the Olivares brothers—*Cather*⟩ In technical biological use *congenital* and *hereditary* are clearly distinguishable, for *congenital* implies presence at birth (as of a disease or an organic defect) from whatever cause and *hereditary* implies transmission (as of a tendency, a weakness, or a quality) from an ancestor through the chromosomal mechanism and DNA ⟨a birthmark is a *congenital* blemish of the skin⟩ ⟨the color of the eyes is *hereditary*⟩ *Ana* constitutional, *inherent, intrinsic, essential, ingrained: *instinctive, intuitive: natural, typical, *regular, normal: *native, indigenous

*Ant* acquired —*Con* *accidental, adventitious, incidental, fortuitous: assumed, affected, feigned, simulated (see ASSUME): cultivated, fostered, nurtured (see NURSE)

**inner,** inward, inside, interior, internal, intestine are comparable when they mean being or placed within something. Although in many cases interchangeable, they are more or less restricted in their applications and therefore clearly distinguished in their implications. **Inner** typically applies to something far within or near the center ⟨thrust them into the *inner* prison—*Acts* 16:24⟩ ⟨an *inner* room⟩ ⟨the *inner* bark of a tree⟩ while **inward** typically applies to something directed within or toward the center ⟨the *inward* curve of a scroll⟩ Both words apply also to the mental or spiritual, frequently with the added implication of something intimate, secret, or inaccessible ⟨the sense by which thy *inner* nature was apprised of outward shows —*Shelley*⟩ ⟨outer events only interest me here insofar as they affected my *inner* life—*Ellis*⟩ ⟨with an *inward* smile she remembered Spandrell's summary—*Huxley*⟩ ⟨the *inward* struggle of the heroes to find their own truth—*Rees*⟩ **Inside** is used chiefly of spatial relations ⟨an *inside* seat⟩ ⟨the *inside* track⟩ but it may be used with reference to persons who are so placed in their work or who have such contacts that they may be said to be figuratively *inside* a place or group; thus, *inside* work implies a contrast with field or road work; *inside* knowledge of a negotiation implies participation to some extent in that negotiation ⟨have *inside* information of what is going on in a club⟩ **Interior** and **internal** usually suggest more abstract or technical and less intimate relations than *inner* and *inward.* **Interior** frequently implies contrast with the outer limits of the thing itself; thus, the *interior* features of a country are by implication opposed to those of the coast or boundaries; *interior* decoration deals with the decoration and furnishing of the inside of a house or other building rather than with its outside; one's *interior* life is one's life as expressed in thoughts and aspirations rather than in outward activities. **Internal** implies contrast with something beyond or outside of the outer limits of a thing; thus, *internal* evidence of a poem's authorship is gained from a study of the poem itself rather than from outside sources; the *internal* affairs of a country are its domestic, as opposed to its foreign, affairs; *internal* medicine is that branch of medicine dealing with the diagnosis and treatment of diseases affecting the internal organs (as the heart, lungs, stomach, and liver). **Intestine** is a close synonym of *internal* used specifically of what may otherwise be described as *domestic* or *civil* (as opposed to *foreign*) with, however, the connotation of an evil or mischievous origin or nature ⟨misgovernment and foreign and *intestine* war occasioned the neglect . . . of these works—*Lord*⟩ ⟨a coalition . . . was paralyzed from the start by *intestine* quarrels—*Current History*⟩

*Ana* central, middle, focal, nuclear (see corresponding nouns at CENTER): intimate, close, *familiar: intrinsic,

constitutional, essential, *inherent: *instinctive, intuitive: deep-seated, deep-rooted (see INVETERATE)

*Ant* outer —*Con* outward, outside, exterior, external (see OUTER)

**innocent** *harmless, innocuous, inoffensive, unoffending *Con* harmful, hurtful, injurious, mischievous (see corresponding nouns at INJURY)

**innocuous** *harmless, innocent, inoffensive, unoffending *Ant* pernicious —*Con* *poisonous, venomous, virulent, toxic: injurious, harmful, hurtful (see corresponding nouns at INJURY)

**innuendo** *insinuation *Ana* hinting *or* hint, intimation, suggestion (see corresponding verbs at SUGGEST): *implication, inference: allusion (see corresponding verb at REFER)

**inoculate** *infuse, imbue, ingrain, leaven, suffuse *Ana* impregnate, saturate, impenetrate, interpenetrate, *permeate, pervade: introduce, admit, *enter: instill, inculcate, *implant

**inoffensive** *harmless, innocuous, innocent, unoffending *Ant* offensive —*Con* loathsome, repulsive, revolting (see OFFENSIVE): distasteful, obnoxious, repellent, *repugnant

**inordinate** *excessive, immoderate, exorbitant, extreme, extravagant *Ana* *irrational, unreasonable: *supererogatory, wanton, uncalled-for, gratuitous: *superfluous, surplus, extra *Ant* ordinate (*rare*): temperate —*Con* *moderate: restrained, curbed, checked, inhibited (see RESTRAIN): *due, rightful, condign: *fair, just, equitable

**inquest** investigation, probe, *inquiry, inquisition, research *Ana* examination, inspection, scrutiny, audit (see under SCRUTINIZE): questioning, interrogation, catechizing, examining (see corresponding verbs at ASK)

**inquire** query, *ask, interrogate, catechize, quiz, examine *Con* reply, *answer, respond, rejoin, retort

**inquiry,** inquisition, investigation, inquest, probe, research all mean a search for truth, knowledge, or information. **Inquiry** is the most general of these terms, applicable to such search regardless of the means (as questioning, observation, or experimentation) used or of the end in view ⟨make *inquiries* about a sick friend⟩ ⟨the passion for pure knowledge is to be gratified only through the scientific method of *inquiry*—*Eliot*⟩ ⟨witnesses convicted of contempt of Congressional *inquiries*—*Current Biog.*⟩ ⟨legislative *inquiry* into the acts of a man or group of men —*Thomas*⟩ ⟨a primitive but effective police *inquiry*—*T. S. Eliot*⟩ **Inquisition** ordinarily carries heightened implications of searchingness and of penetration far below the surface to uncover what is concealed or withheld ⟨strenuously protested against being subjected to an *inquisition* into his motives⟩ The term, however, is chiefly applied to a judicial inquiry aiming to unearth facts or conditions to support suspicions or charges; probably from its historical application to the ruthless ferreting out of heretics or heresy especially in the late Middle Ages and in the Reformation period, the term generally connotes relentless pursuit of a clue or of a suspect, and sometimes merciless and rigorous persecution ⟨when, as becomes a man who would prepare for such an arduous work, I through myself make rigorous *inquisition,* the report is often cheering—*Wordsworth*⟩ ⟨the whole notion of loyalty *inquisitions* is a natural characteristic of the police state—*New Republic*⟩ **Investigation** applies to an inquiry which has for its aim the uncovering of the facts and the establishment of the truth ⟨by their bullying tactics, by their having turned needed *investigations* into regrettable *inquisitions*—*J. M. Brown*⟩ In distinctive use it implies a systematic tracking

---

A colon (:) separates groups of words discriminated. An asterisk (*) indicates place of treatment of each group.

down of something that one hopes to discover or needs to know ⟨a strong movement to make American universities centers of scholarly work and scientific *investigation—Conant*⟩ ⟨an *investigation* of the causes of the prolonged depression⟩ ⟨the bank never employs a clerk or teller without an *investigation* of his habits and record⟩ **Inquest** applies chiefly to a judicial or official inquiry or examination especially before a jury, and specifically to one conducted by a coroner and jury in order to determine the cause of a death ⟨when the rumors of murder became rife, the body was exhumed and an *inquest* held⟩ In more general use, the term usually applies to an investigation that has some of the characteristics of a coroner's inquest (as the exploration of the grounds for an accusation or suspicion in relation to some disastrous or troubling event) ⟨an *inquest* on the fall of Singapore and the sinking of H. M. S. *Repulse* and H. M. S. *Prince of Wales—New Yorker*⟩ **Probe** applies to an investigation that searches deeply and extensively with the intent to determine the presence or absence of wrongdoing; it suggests methods of exploration comparable to a surgeon's probing for a bullet ⟨a legislative *probe* of banking activities⟩ ⟨another *probe* would result merely in a reshuffle in police and political circles—*Newsweek*⟩ **Research** applies chiefly to an inquiry or investigation which requires prolonged and careful study, especially of actual conditions or of primary sources of information. It is especially applicable to scholarly and creative inquiries or investigations (as by scientists, historians, or linguists) especially for the sake of uncovering new knowledge, of getting at the facts when these are not known, or of discovering laws of nature ⟨basic *research* in science is concerned with understanding the laws of nature—*Grainger*⟩ ⟨*research* is a creative activity engaged in by talented human beings—*Leedy*⟩ but it may sometimes be used for a study leading to the writing of a résumé of facts or laws already known ⟨*research* has shown and practice has established the futility of the charge that it was a usurpation when this Court undertook to declare an Act of Congress unconstitutional—*Justice Holmes*⟩ or even for quite casual or trivial investigations ⟨I . . . managed to get involved in a highway accident. All in the interest of *research,* you understand—*Joseph*⟩
*Ana* questioning, interrogation, catechizing (see corresponding verbs at ASK): examination, inspection, scrutiny, audit (see under SCRUTINIZE)
**inquisition** inquest, *inquiry, probe, investigation, research
*Ana* see those at INQUIRY
**inquisitive** *curious, prying, snoopy, nosy
*Ana* *impertinent, intrusive, meddlesome: interfering, meddling, intermeddling (see MEDDLE)
*Ant* incurious —*Con* *indifferent, unconcerned, aloof, detached, uninterested, disinterested
**inroad** *invasion, incursion, raid
*Ana* intrusion, butting in (see corresponding verbs at INTRUDE): encroachment, entrenchment, infringement, trespassing *or* trespass (see corresponding verbs at TRESPASS): *entrance, entry, ingress
**insane, mad, crazy, crazed, demented, deranged, lunatic, maniac, non compos mentis** are comparable in their general or nontechnical senses (for senses of corresponding nouns used technically see INSANITY) and as meaning afflicted by or manifesting unsoundness of mind or an inability to control one's rational processes. **Insane** as applied to persons usually implies such unsoundness of mind that one is unable to function safely and competently in ordinary human relations, usually does not recognize one's own condition, and is not responsible for one's

actions ⟨adjudged *insane* after a period of observation⟩ ⟨an extreme antisocial, perverted personality whose reactions differ widely from the normal, but are not necessarily to be classified as *insane—Foulkes*⟩ In more general use *insane* implies utter folly or irrationality; the person or the act or utterance so described is, by implication, governed by blind passion or senselessness ⟨the *insane* ambition and insatiable appetite which have caused this vast . . . war—*Sir Winston Churchill*⟩ ⟨dumbfounded by the *insane* assault—*Al Newman*⟩ ⟨now that wars . . . have become far more horrible and . . . *insane—Inge*⟩ **Mad** usually implies more frenzy than *insane* and therefore carries a stronger suggestion of wildness, rabidness, raving, or complete loss of self-control ⟨O, let me not be *mad,* not *mad,* sweet heaven! Keep me in temper: I would not be *mad!—Shak.*⟩ ⟨he's *mad.* He always was. But he's worse than *mad* now. He's possessed—*Graves*⟩ ⟨he has fallen in love . . . with a stupid cocotte who has begun by driving him *mad* with jealousy—*Edmund Wilson*⟩ **Crazy** often suggests such mental breakdown as may result from illness or old age ⟨he has gone *crazy*⟩ ⟨we will bestow you in some better place, fitter for sickness and for *crazy* age—*Shak.*⟩ ⟨"Stuff!" exploded the Doctor. "You're not *crazy* and you never were and you're not going to be, unless you keep on making such a commotion about nothing"—*Nancy Hale*⟩ or it may suggest a distraught or wild state of mind induced by some intense emotion (as anxiety, grief, joy, desire, or excitement) ⟨works fine, but goes *crazy* if she hears Murdoch's voice—just sweats and trembles all over—*Gerald Beaumont*⟩ ⟨she was *crazy* with desire for sleep—*Ruth Park*⟩ ⟨somebody had shot a squirrel and he took on about it as though he had lost a child. I said then he was *crazy—Anderson*⟩ As applied to such things as schemes, projects, or notions *crazy* usually suggests that they are the product of a disordered or ill-balanced mind ⟨no educated Socialist believes such *crazy* nonsense—*Shaw*⟩ ⟨who would pay such a *crazy* price for a book⟩ **Crazed** is often used in place of *crazy* when a temporary disorder, usually with a specific cause, is implied ⟨*crazed* with grief⟩ ⟨they were *crazed* by the famine and pestilence of that last bitter winter—*Amer. Guide Series: Wash.*⟩ **Demented** and **deranged** are more formal than the preceding words and less rich in connotations; both terms, moreover, imply a change from mental soundness to unsoundness, *demented* usually suggesting clear signs (as profound apathy or incoherence in thought, speech, or action) which indicate deterioration of the mental powers ⟨there was now no doubt that the sick man was *demented*⟩ ⟨the great part of the German army in the early stage of the war was really an army of *demented* civilians—*H. G. Wells*⟩ ⟨apparently not clearly *demented* until after 1818, he was for years dangerously near the border of insanity—*Amer. Guide Series: Va.*⟩ and *deranged* (compare *derangement* under ABERRATION 2) suggesting a loss of mental balance or a state of mental disorder resulting from a functional disturbance of the brain or nervous system ⟨he was temporarily *deranged* by the shock⟩ ⟨in our culture a person who falls sick, hears voices, communicates with shadows, and acquires special abilities from them is inevitably classed as *deranged—Kroeber*⟩ **Lunatic** is approximately the equivalent of *insane* but is less frequently applied to persons and may imply no more than extreme folly ⟨consuming with *lunatic* speed the assets of the earth—*Agar*⟩ **Maniac** comes closer to *mad,* for it commonly connotes violence, fury, or raving ⟨the *maniac* rage of the multitude⟩ ⟨the *maniac* dreamer; cruel . . . is he with fear—*Shelley*⟩ **Non compos mentis** (Latin for "not sound of mind") is a legal term which specifies a state, but does not

define the particular condition or kind, of mental unsoundness. It is often used, especially in its shortened form *non compos,* more generally with similar indefiniteness ⟨Barron's *non compos.* Lear controls him completely—*Kenneth Roberts*⟩
*Ana* *irrational, unreasonable: distracted, bewildered (see PUZZLE *vb*)
*Ant* sane —*Con* sensible, judicious, *wise, sapient, prudent

**insanity,** **lunacy, psychosis, mania, dementia** are the leading general terms denoting serious mental disorder. **Insanity** as a technical term belongs to law rather than to medicine. It is used to cover a wide variety of mental disorders, all of which have in common one characteristic—an unfitting of the afflicted individual to manage his own affairs or perform his social duties. Mental deficiency and delirious conditions are usually excluded, the former as inborn and not acquired, the latter as temporary and not long-lasting. Since in law a person's sanity or insanity becomes an issue when he is charged with a crime or when his legal capacity to make a will or contract or to transfer property is questioned, proof of insanity is tantamount to proof of his inability to act rationally and to understand the nature of his act and its natural consequences in affecting his rights, obligations, and liabilities. In general use *insanity* is commonly distinguished from *mental deficiency* and from *neuroses* and is applied to disorders involving unsoundness or derangement of mind. **Lunacy** in general use often applies to insanity manifested in spells of madness and fury or interrupted by intervals of lucidity ⟨Cervantes's hero was led into amiable but disastrous *lunacy* by a belated obsession with the literature of chivalry—*Muggeridge*⟩ ⟨it's the tangle of good and badness; it's the *lunacy* linked with sanity makes up, and mocks, humanity!—*Stringer*⟩ *Lunacy* sometimes is used interchangeably with *insanity* in law ⟨a *lunacy* commission⟩ ⟨filed a *lunacy* petition against the attorney general so that a court could pass on his mental condition—*Time*⟩ **Psychosis** is the psychiatric term for a profound disorganization of mind, personality, or behavior resulting from an individual's inability to cope with his environment. Though in content often coextensive with *insanity* or *lunacy* it carries none of the special implications of these two terms. **Mania** (for fuller treatment see MANIA 2) denotes a phase marked by sustained and exaggerated elation, excessive activity (as in emotional expression or physical action), or delusions of greatness that characterizes certain psychoses. **Dementia** implies a marked decline from a former level of intellectual capacity often accompanied by emotional apathy and is applicable to most psychoses that involve organic deterioration, not only those manifesting themselves in spells of excitement but those manifesting themselves in apathy, depression, flightiness, or personality disintegration.
*Ana* alienation, derangement, *aberration: frenzy, delirium, *mania, hysteria
*Ant* sanity

**inscription,** **legend, caption** are comparable when they mean something written, printed, or engraved (as on a coin or a medal or under or over a picture) to indicate or describe the purpose or the nature of the thing. **Inscription** may apply to something written or printed, but it more often applies to something engraved, incised, or impressed on some hard surface (as stone, bronze, or silver); the word often carries an implication of durability or of permanence that is lacking, usually, in the others, and therefore often suggests a statement that has been framed or selected with care ⟨the *inscription* on a monument⟩ ⟨the bronze tablet has the following *inscription*⟩ ⟨some god direct my judg-

ment! Let me see; I will survey the *inscriptions* back again. What says this leaden casket? "Who chooseth me must give and hazard all he hath"—*Shak.*⟩ A **legend** (see also MYTH) is basically a very short inscription (as on a coin, a medal, or a heraldic shield) that is a motto or a statement of an aim, an ideal, or a guiding principle ⟨the *legend* "In God we trust" is found on all coins of the United States of America⟩ ⟨the *legend* on the Victoria Cross is "For Valour"⟩ The term is also used for the printed statement giving the title or a brief description or explanation of an illustration or diagram (as in a textbook or a work of reference) ⟨according to the *legend,* this illustration is that of "A Roman legionary"⟩ **Caption** basically applies to a heading or title (as of a document, an article, a chapter, or a section) ⟨an editorial under the *caption* "Where are we headed?"⟩ ⟨the stories have appeared in a running series under the *caption* of "The Adventures of Brigadier Gerard"—*N. Y. Evening Post*⟩ But the implication of a catching or arresting quality in the title is often evident, and *caption* may refer to a title or name given a story, an article, or an illustration that is designed to seize the attention of the reader ⟨delighting the readers of the Athenaeum with the treasures of his . . . reading, under the *caption,* "A Budget of Paradoxes"—*Grosart*⟩ The term *caption* is also used interchangeably with *legend* for the printed statement describing or explaining a picture or illustration ⟨a diagram of a motor with all the working parts explained in the *caption*⟩ ⟨under each [picture] was an appropriate *caption,* such as Surprise, Grief—*S. E. White*⟩ *Caption* is also used in motion pictures for any of the brief statements or bits of dialogue thrown on the screen to explain the scenes of a silent motion picture or of a sound motion picture in which the actors speak in a foreign language.

**inscrutable** *mysterious, arcane
*Ana* profound, abysmal, *deep: baffling, balking, thwarting, frustrating, foiling (see FRUSTRATE): hidden, concealed, secreted (see HIDE): enigmatic, cryptic, dark, *obscure, vague: mystifying, perplexing, puzzling (see PUZZLE *vb*)
*Con* obvious, plain, clear, manifest, *evident, patent

**insensate** besotted, *fond, infatuated
*Ana* fatuous, asinine, foolish, silly (see SIMPLE): *stupid, slow, dense, crass, dull, dumb: *irrational, unreasonable
*Con* sensible, sane, judicious, *wise, prudent, sapient, sage: *rational, reasonable: *intelligent, quick-witted, knowing, alert

**insensible** 1 **Insensible, insensitive, impassible, anesthetic** mean unresponsive to stimuli or to external influences. **Insensible** usually implies total unresponsiveness, and therefore unawareness or unconsciousness such as may result from blunted powers of sensation, obtuseness of mind, apathy, or complete absorption in something else ⟨he also warned me against X, a local professor of history, as a man full of prejudice and quite *insensible* to evidence —*Laski*⟩ ⟨so engrossed in his work that he was *insensible* of the flight of time⟩ ⟨men have a keener relish for privileges and honors than for equality, and are not *insensible* to rewards—*Sédillot*⟩ **Insensitive** implies sluggishness in response or less than normal susceptibility; more specifically, it suggests dullness rather than acuteness of sensation or perception, thickness rather than thinness of skin, callousness rather than sympathy or compassion ⟨an ear *insensitive* to changes of pitch⟩ ⟨he was *insensitive* to all kinds of discourtesy—*Joyce*⟩ ⟨*insensitive* to the misery of others⟩ ⟨many . . . Europeans still think Americans are soulless and *insensitive* machines, a raw society of mass-produced healthy extroverts—*Viereck*⟩ **Impassible** basically and historically implies absence of response because of incapacity for feeling or suffering,

A colon (:) separates groups of words discriminated. An asterisk (*) indicates place of treatment of each group.

but is often used synonymously with *impassive* or in reference to persons who by discipline have conquered the normal human susceptibility to pain or suffering ⟨the Hindu striving for Nirvana renders himself *impassible*⟩ or in reference to things in contrast with persons or creatures thought of as beings who through necessity of nature suffer pain or are susceptible to injury ⟨the language of strategy and politics is designed . . . to make it appear as though wars were not fought by individuals . . . but either by impersonal and therefore wholly nonmoral and *impassible* forces, or else by personified abstractions—*Huxley*⟩ ⟨Svengali was sitting, quite *impassible,* gazing at Monsieur J---, and smiling a ghastly, sardonic smile—*du Maurier*⟩ **Anesthetic** implies a deadening of the mind or senses by or as if by such a drug as ether and therefore an induced rather than a natural insensitiveness ⟨the intelligentsia . . . neither as *anesthetic* to ideas as the plutocracy on the one hand nor as much the slaves of emotion as the proletariat on the other—*Mencken*⟩ ⟨all except the young girls are in a state of possession, blind, deaf and *anesthetic*—*Cary*⟩
*Ana* obtuse, *dull, blunt: *impassive, apathetic, phlegmatic, stolid, stoic: *hardened, indurated, callous: engrossed, absorbed, *intent, rapt
*Ant* sensible (*to* or *of something*) —*Con* conscious, *aware, cognizant, alive, awake: impressed, affected, influenced, touched (see AFFECT)
2 *imperceptible, impalpable, intangible, inappreciable, imponderable
*Ana* tenuous, rare, slight, slender (see THIN *adj*): attenuated, extenuated, diluted, rarefied (see THIN *vb*)
*Ant* sensible, palpable —*Con* *perceptible, tangible, appreciable, ponderable
**insensitive** *insensible, impassible, anesthetic
*Ana* *hardened, indurated, callous: *indifferent, unconcerned, aloof, incurious: *impassive, stoic, apathetic, phlegmatic, stolid
*Ant* sensitive —*Con* susceptible, subject, prone, open, exposed, *liable: responsive, *tender, compassionate
**insert** *vb* *introduce, interpolate, intercalate, insinuate, interpose, interject
*Ana* *intrude, obtrude, interlope: instill, inculcate, *implant: *enter, admit
*Ant* abstract: extract —*Con* disengage, *detach
**inside** *adj* interior, internal, intestine, *inner, inward
*Ant* outside —*Con* exterior, external, *outer, outward
**insidious** *sly, cunning, crafty, tricky, foxy, wily, guileful, artful
*Ana* treacherous, perfidious (see FAITHLESS): *dangerous, perilous: furtive, stealthy, covert, underhand, underhanded (see SECRET)
**insight** penetration, acumen, *discernment, discrimination, perception
*Ana* intuition, understanding, *reason: comprehension, apprehension (see under APPREHEND): appreciation, understanding (see corresponding verbs at UNDERSTAND): perspicaciousness, sagacity, shrewdness (see corresponding adjectives at SHREWD)
*Ant* obtuseness
**insinuate** 1 *introduce, insert, interject, interpolate, intercalate, interpose
*Ana* *infuse, inoculate, imbue, leaven: instill, inculcate, *implant
2 intimate, hint, *suggest, imply
*Ana* allude, advert, *refer: impute, *ascribe
*Con* voice, utter, *express, vent, air, broach: declare, *assert, affirm, aver, avouch, avow, profess
**insinuation,** **innuendo** mean covert suggestion or a covert allusion to something. **Insinuation** applies chiefly to a

remark, comment, or question which conveys or seems to convey a hint or implication, often one that is discreditable to the person at whom it is aimed ⟨by tacit agreement they ignored the remarks and *insinuations* of their acquaintances—*D. H. Lawrence*⟩ ⟨we reject any *insinuation* that one race or another, one people or another is in any sense inferior or expendable—*Eisenhower*⟩ **Innuendo** more often applies to the method of covert suggestion than does *insinuation,* and when it applies to a definite instance, it is referable to meaningful smiles, glances, inflections, as well as to remarks; in both cases the term definitely implies a suggestion of something that is injurious to the reputation of the person concerned ⟨I prefer the most disagreeable certainties to hints and *innuendos*—*Byron*⟩ ⟨in this play Middleton shows his interest . . . in *innuendo* and double meanings—*T. S. Eliot*⟩ ⟨"He—eventually—married her." There were volumes of *innuendo* in the way the *eventually* was spaced, and each syllable given its due stress—*Wharton*⟩ ⟨he learned by chance remarks overheard, from *innuendo,* a dropped word here and there, a sly, meaningful snicker—*Harold Sinclair*⟩
*Ana* hinting *or* hint, implying *or* implication, suggestion, intimation (see corresponding verbs at SUGGEST): *animadversion, aspersion, reflection: imputation, ascription (see corresponding verbs as ASCRIBE): allusion (see corresponding verb at REFER)
**insipid,** vapid, flat, jejune, banal, wishy-washy, inane mean devoid of qualities which give spirit, character, or substance to a thing. Something **insipid** is without taste, or savor, or pungency; the term is applied not only to food and drink which are so tasteless as to give no pleasure or stimulation to the palate ⟨*insipid* substitutes for coffee⟩ but also to persons and their utterances and ideas which strike one as thin, weak, and characterless and leave one completely indifferent ⟨the tepid quality of the expatriate American novel, which has escaped vulgarity to become *insipid* instead—*Connolly*⟩ ⟨happiness is a wine of the rarest vintage, and seems *insipid* to a vulgar taste—*L. P. Smith*⟩ ⟨the *insipid* veracity with which Crabbe used to report some of the most trite doings of Nature and of man—*Montague*⟩ Something **vapid** is stale, uninteresting, or pointless because it has lost its characteristic taste, freshness, spirit, sparkle, or tang ⟨the table beer was sour . . . the wine *vapid*—*Smollett*⟩ ⟨had a genius for making the most interesting things seem utterly *vapid* and dead—*Graves*⟩ ⟨we could spare a lot of the more frivolous and even *vapid* content of our papers—*Mott*⟩ Something **flat** is so vapid that it seems dead or lifeless. The word is applied chiefly to what has lost all savor, sparkle, zest, or capacity for stimulating interest or pleasure ⟨how weary, stale, *flat* and unprofitable, seem to me all the uses of this world—*Shak.*⟩ ⟨the sonnet became, in the hands of innumerable practitioners, a thing . . . of artificial sentiment, *flat* as the lees and dregs of wine—*Lowes*⟩ ⟨the action follows the standard interpretation of Russian history in a *flat* and mechanical way—*Newsweek*⟩ Something **jejune** is so devoid of substance or nutritive quality that it cannot satisfy the appetite; the word is only occasionally used with reference to physical hunger and is usually employed with reference to hunger of the mind or the emotions. It often connotes barrenness, aridity, or meagerness in addition to its basic implications ⟨read through the sermon once more. It seemed more *jejune* than ever—*Mackenzie*⟩ ⟨literary history without evaluative criteria becomes *jejune* and sterile—*Glicksberg*⟩ Something **banal** is so commonplace or so trite that it lacks all freshness or power to stimulate or appeal. The term often also

carries one or more of such various connotations as tastelessness, pedestrianism, triviality, or platitudinousness ⟨a simple person marvelously protected from vulgarity and the *banal—T. E. Brown*⟩ ⟨the "poor working girl" of the *banal* songs of the period—*Farrell*⟩ ⟨the average man, doomed to some *banal* and sordid drudgery all his life long—*Mencken*⟩ Something **wishy-washy** has the essential or characteristic qualities so weak or diluted that it strikes one as extremely insipid or vapid ⟨she is too *wishy-washy* to attract interesting friends⟩ ⟨his courage in expressing opinions that are always judicious but never *wishy-washy—W. R. Crawford*⟩ ⟨they accepted the *wishy-washy,* almost meaningless, resolution—*Spectator*⟩ ⟨Baudelaire's notion of beatitude certainly tended to the *wishy-washy—T. S. Eliot*⟩ Something **inane** is devoid of sense, significance, or point ⟨to us the book seems a very *inane,* tiresome, and purposeless affair—*Manchester Examiner*⟩ ⟨in order to cover his embarrassment, he made some *inane* remark on the weather —*Conrad*⟩
*Ana* *thin, slight, tenuous, rare: *weak, feeble: *tame, subdued: bland, mild, *soft
*Ant* sapid: zestful —*Con* *pungent, piquant, poignant, racy, spicy: *spirited, high-spirited, mettlesome, spunky, fiery, peppery, gingery: savory, tasty, *palatable, appetizing: stimulating, exciting, piquing, provoking *or* provocative (see corresponding verbs at PROVOKE)
**insistent** *pressing, urgent, imperative, crying, importunate, exigent, instant
*Ana* persistent, persevering (see corresponding verbs at PERSEVERE): pertinacious, dogged (see OBSTINATE): obtrusive, *impertinent
**insolent** arrogant, overbearing, supercilious, disdainful, haughty, lordly (see PROUD)
*Ana* domineering, *masterful, imperious, peremptory, imperative: pretentious, ostentatious (see SHOWY): *dictatorial, magisterial: scornful, contemptuous (see corresponding nouns under DESPISE *vb*)
*Ant* deferential —*Con* submissive (see TAME): courteous, polite, *civil
**inspect** *scrutinize, examine, scan, audit
*Ana* survey, view, observe, notice (see SEE): probe, penetrate (see ENTER): inquire, interrogate, question, catechize (see ASK)
**inspection** examination, scrutiny, scanning, audit (see under SCRUTINIZE *vb*)
*Ana* investigation, probe, inquest, *inquiry, inquisition, research: surveillance, *oversight, supervision
**inspiration, afflatus, fury, frenzy,** especially when qualified by *divine* or *poetic,* all designate the seemingly involuntary element in the arts of expression for which the artist often holds a power outside himself responsible. **Inspiration** may distinctively imply a preternatural enlightening and quickening of the mind and connote, especially when used by religious persons, the intervention of or as if of such a supernatural influence as the Holy Spirit ⟨among such men there remains a . . . belief in what is vaguely called *inspiration.* They know by hard experience that there are days when their ideas flow freely and clearly, and days when they are dammed up damnably—*Mencken*⟩ Often, from its use in connection with the authorship of the Scriptures, *inspiration* implies supernatural or supranatural communication of knowledge ⟨has the highest aspect of Greek religion ever been better expressed than by Wordsworth himself, to whom . . . it came by *inspiration* and not from books?—*Inge*⟩ **Afflatus** distinctively applies to the inspiring influence rather than to the process or its effects ⟨the artists and poets who but once in their lives had known the divine

*afflatus,* and touched the high level of the best—*Henry James*⟩ ⟨we imagine that a great speech is caused by some mysterious *afflatus* that descends into a man from on high—*Eastman*⟩ but it also may name a quality rather than an influence or an operation ⟨he never again achieved that delicate balance of cold, scientific investigation and imaginative *afflatus—Scalia*⟩ **Fury** and *frenzy* emphasize the emotional excitement that attends artistic creation and the tendency of the artist to be carried out of himself. **Fury** found most often in the phrases "poetic fury" and "divine fury," does not in ordinary use imply extreme agitation; it characteristically connotes profound ecstasy induced by the poet's vision or conception ⟨they are so beloved of the Gods, that whatsoever they write, proceeds of a divine *fury—Sidney*⟩ ⟨in an age of formalism, poetic *fury* itself became a formal requirement—*Babbitt*⟩ **Frenzy** usually implies agitation rather than rapture, and stresses the imaginative or inventive element in creation, sometimes to the exclusion of any extraneous influence ⟨does he compose in a *frenzy* of mystical exaltation or does he work out his lines slowly and even laboriously?—*Kilby*⟩ ⟨caught the first fire of the writer's *frenzy* in the classroom when a long dead poet was being discussed—*Dock Leaves*⟩ ⟨Mencken and his *Mercury* were anything but cold. They were always in a state of *frenzy—Angoff*⟩
*Ana* enlightenment, illumination (see corresponding verbs at ILLUMINATE): *ecstasy, rapture, transport: *revelation, vision, apocalypse, prophecy
**inspire** animate, *inform, fire
*Ana* enlighten, *illuminate: quicken, stimulate, excite, galvanize, *provoke: activate, energize, *vitalize: endue, endow (see DOWER)
**inspirit** *encourage, hearten, embolden, cheer, nerve, steel
*Ana* enliven, animate, *quicken, vivify: stimulate, excite, galvanize (see PROVOKE)
*Ant* dispirit —*Con* *discourage, dishearten, deject: *depress, weigh
**in spite of** *notwithstanding, despite
**install** induct, inaugurate, invest, *initiate
**instance** *n* **Instance, case, illustration, example, sample, specimen** mean a concrete thing which has or manifests the qualities, characters, or nature of a type, a class, or a group. **Instance** applies to an individual person or thing brought forth in support or disproof of a general statement ⟨the *instance* may be rejected, but the principle abides —*Cardozo*⟩ ⟨Herodotus is a shining *instance* of the strong Greek bent to examine and prove or disprove—*Edith Hamilton*⟩ or as a means of indicating the character of a class ⟨this novel is a good *instance* of his best work⟩ ⟨the patterns on the breasts are an *instance* of the formalism of the period—*Saunders*⟩ **Case** applies to an act, situation, condition, or event demonstrating the occurrence or the existence of something which is being considered, studied, investigated, or dealt with or exhibiting it in actual operation ⟨cite *cases* of bribes given as payments for services never performed⟩ ⟨students of the effects of poverty now base their conclusions on *cases* actually investigated⟩ ⟨there has been no *case* of malaria in this section for three years⟩ **Illustration** applies to an instance adduced or cited as a means of throwing light upon what has been explained or discussed in general terms ⟨give several *illustrations* of the use of a word in a particular sense⟩ ⟨cites indiscriminately . . . materials of such different value that they provide *illustration* rather than documentation of his points—*Dinkler*⟩ **Example** (see also MODEL) applies to a typical, representative, or illustrative instance or case ⟨if I were asked to define what this gentlemanliness is, I should say that

A colon (:) separates groups of words discriminated. An asterisk (*) indicates place of treatment of each group.

it is only to be defined by *examples—Byron*⟩ ⟨it is impossible to study a writer without *examples* of his work⟩ ⟨a most outstanding *example* of a war fought with a purpose was our own American Revolution—*Willkie*⟩ A **sample** is a usually randomly selected part or unit of a whole presumed to be typical or representative of the whole from which it is taken ⟨knowledge of the deep ocean floor comes from . . . bottom *samples—Shepard*⟩ ⟨passed out *samples* of a new candy⟩ ⟨when I deal in wine, cloth, or cheese, I will give *samples,* but of verse never—*Cowper*⟩ **Specimen** and *sample* are often used without distinction, but *specimen* is more often the choice when the whole is composed of discrete units that are independent entities ⟨a dwarf planet, revolving round a dwarf sun, which is an average undistinguished *specimen* of a large class of elderly stars which have seen better days —*Inge*⟩ ⟨there were a few boomtowns in the Middle West, but the finest *specimens* began to be seen only with the discoveries of gold and silver in the Far West—*Harlow*⟩ *Ana* proof, *reason, ground: *evidence: particular, *item, detail

**instance** *vb* *mention, name, specify
*Ana* *exemplify, illustrate: cite, *quote

**instant** *n* Instant, moment, minute, second, flash, jiffy, twinkling, split second are comparable when they mean a particular point of time or a stretch of time of almost imperceptible duration. *Instant* and *moment* are often used interchangeably ⟨to us . . . the *moment* 8.17 A.M. means something . . . very important, if it happens to be the starting time of our daily train. To our ancestors, such an odd eccentric *instant* was without significance—did not even exist—*Huxley*⟩ but **instant** carries so much stronger a suggestion of infinitely small duration that it is better fitted than *moment* for contexts that imply urgency, extreme transiency, or inconceivable swiftness ⟨to trace the visionary company of love, its voice an *instant* in the wind (I know not whither hurled)—*Hart Crane*⟩ ⟨come this *instant*⟩ ⟨he was not an *instant* too soon⟩ ⟨it passed in an *instant*⟩ **Moment,** on the other hand, is particularly serviceable when the word or the context carries the implication of a definitely apprehended, even though extremely brief, point of time ⟨wait a *moment*⟩ ⟨a *moment* of dreadful suspense—*Greene*⟩ ⟨it was the finest *moment* of her life⟩ ⟨I haven't had a *moment* to attend to it⟩ *Minute* and *second* technically apply to measured fractions of an hour, but in the present relation **minute,** even more than *moment,* suggests an appreciable though short duration of time, and **second,** quite as much as *instant,* suggests its imperceptible duration ⟨who buys a *minute's* mirth to wail a week?—*Shak.*⟩ ⟨the train will start in a *minute*⟩ ⟨I was gone only a *minute*⟩ ⟨standing in the middle of the street he would blow, and in a *minute* boys would come swarming to him —*John Reed*⟩ ⟨they showed a *second* or two of hesitation, and then plunged off the road—*Ingamells*⟩ ⟨I'll get it this *second*⟩ **Flash** suggests duration comparable to that of a flash of lightning; the term is therefore often used when incredible speed in movement, action, or thought is implied ⟨the secret of the poor wretch's death was plain to me in a *flash—Kipling*⟩ ⟨eyes that in a *flash* could pick out a friend . . . from a throng—*Cather*⟩ **Jiffy** is found chiefly in the phrase *in a jiffy,* equivalent to very quickly or directly ⟨she could have tossed off an article for *The Times* in a *jiffy—Nicolson*⟩ ⟨the fisherman raises the submerged net in a *jiffy—Nat'l Geog. Mag.*⟩ ⟨I'll be there in a *jiffy*⟩ **Twinkling,** often with an added "of the eye," suggests the quickness of a wink or blink ⟨his patient would be carried off by meningitis in the *twinkling* of an eye—*Stafford*⟩ ⟨the kettle will boil in a *twinkling*

—*Punch*⟩ **Split second,** basically denoting a fractional part of a second, heightens the implication of brevity as expressed by *second* ⟨Mr. Moon stood for one *split second* astonished—*Chesterton*⟩ ⟨one *split second* of surprise —*Sharp*⟩

**instant** *adj* *pressing, urgent, imperative, crying, importunate, insistent, exigent
*Ana* immediate, *direct: compelling, constraining, obliging (see FORCE *vb*)

**instigate** *incite, abet, foment
*Ana* *activate, actuate, motivate: *suggest, hint, insinuate: plan, plot, scheme (see under PLAN *n*)

**instill** inculcate, *implant
*Ana* *infuse, inoculate, imbue, ingrain, leaven: impregnate, *permeate, saturate, pervade, impenetrate, interpenetrate

**instinct** intuition (see under INSTINCTIVE)
*Ana* incitement, impetus, *stimulus: impulse, spring, *motive: bent, turn, faculty, aptitude, knack, *gift

**instinctive** 1 Instinctive, intuitive both mean not involving, based on, or determined by the ordinary processes of reasoning, but as applied to human mentation they are not normally interchangeable because of consistent differences in connotation. **Instinctive** in this connection (see also SPONTANEOUS) implies a relation to **instinct,** the more or less automatic and unreasoned reactive behavior characteristic of a natural group (as a species) rather than of the individual; as applied to human mental activity and behavior *instinctive* stresses sometimes the automatic quality of the reaction, sometimes the fact that it takes place below the level of conscious reasoning and volition whether as a true expression of instinct or as being through habitude as deeply ingrained as instinct ⟨a baby may be born with a fear of a loud, sudden noise and a fear of falling. Those things we call *instinctive—Fishbein*⟩ ⟨while yet a boy he was a thorough little man of the world, and did well rather upon principles which he had tested . . . and recognized as principles, than from those profounder convictions which in his father were so *instinctive* that he could give no account concerning them—*Butler* d. 1902⟩ ⟨some of our most inevitable and *instinctive* sentiments . . . cannot be brought directly under logical laws—*Coulton*⟩ **Intuitive,** correspondingly, indicates relationship to **intuition,** the highly personal intellectual capacity for passing directly from stimulus to response (as from problem to solution or from observation to comprehension) without the intervention of reasoning or inferring; as applied to the human mind and to products of its activities *intuitive* suggests activity above and beyond the level of conscious reasoning ⟨God's thought obviously differs in its character from that of man. The latter . . . proceeds in step-by-step fashion from premise to conclusion; God's thought is entirely *intuitive* . . . it grasps its object by a single flash of insight—*Thilly*⟩ ⟨every scientific generalization is *intuitive,* for while the scientist may see a phenomenon just by looking, as at Newton's apple, he must use creative imagination and intuition to relate this apple to the moon and so discover the universal law—*G. R. Harrison*⟩ ⟨an *intuitive* mind, passionate in its attempt to capture a great truth in a few words, but impatient of logical sequences—*Canby*⟩
*Ana* *innate, inborn, congenital: constitutional, *inherent, ingrained
*Ant* reasoned

2 impulsive, *spontaneous, automatic, mechanical
*Ana* natural, normal, typical, *regular: habitual, customary, wonted, accustomed: *usual
*Ant* intentional  —*Con* *voluntary, deliberate, willful, willing

---

*Ana* analogous words          *Ant* antonyms          *Con* contrasted words          See also explanatory notes facing page 1

**institute** *vb* *found, establish, organize
*Ana* *begin, commence, start, initiate, inaugurate: introduce (see ENTER)
*Ant* abrogate —*Con* end, terminate, conclude, *close, finish, complete
**instruct** 1 *teach, train, educate, discipline, school
*Ana* impart, *communicate: *inform, acquaint, apprise: lead, *guide, steer, pilot, engineer: *practice, drill, exercise
2 direct, enjoin, bid, *command, order, charge
*Ana* *prescribe, assign, define
**instrument** 1 *mean, instrumentality, agency, medium, agent, organ, vehicle, channel
*Ana* *method, system, mode, way, manner, fashion: machinery, apparatus, tackle, gear, *equipment, paraphernalia: *device, contrivance, contraption
2 tool, *implement, appliance, utensil
3 *paper, document
**instrumentality** *mean, agent, agency, instrument, medium, organ, vehicle, channel
*Ana* *work, labor, toil: *effort, exertion, trouble, pains: *power, energy, force, might: *action, deed, act
**insubordinate,** rebellious, mutinous, seditious, factious, contumacious mean having or showing defiance or indifference to constituted authority. **Insubordinate** is used primarily in reference to a person whose status is that of a subordinate and especially of a member of an organized group (as a force, a crew, or a staff) under the control of a head (as a military or naval officer, a chief, or a master) who is responsible for their service as individuals and their discipline as a group; the term implies disobedience to orders or infraction of rules either as a particular instance or as a habit ⟨*insubordinate* sailors are confined in the warship's brig⟩ ⟨insubordination . . . may consist simply in a persistent and concerted refusal or omission to obey orders, or to do duty, with an *insubordinate* intent—*Manual for Courts-Martial*⟩ **Rebellious** implies disaffection and insubordination; it may refer to a state of mind or to a temperamental tendency ⟨temperamentally *rebellious,* instinctively disliking externally imposed authority—*Biddle*⟩ but more often it suggests active or organized resistance ⟨*rebellious* troops⟩ ⟨an outlaw'd desperate man, the chief of a *rebellious* clan—*Scott*⟩ ⟨the sword his grandsire bore in the *rebellious* days of yore—*Longfellow*⟩ **Mutinous** is a stronger and more derogatory term than *rebellious* which may imply justifiable resistance, for it suggests the refusal to obey the lawful demands or commands of an officer in charge, especially a military, naval, or ship's officer, with the result that there is no longer discipline and efficiency in the group or, if the mutiny is successful, that a new and usually unlawful control is set up ⟨the master ordered the *mutinous* sailors put into irons⟩ ⟨the *mutinous* members of the crew finally gained the upper hand⟩ ⟨each one . . . gave him to understand, roughly and roundly, that to go to sea in her they would not. In the midst of this *mutinous* uproar, the alarmed consul stood fast—*Melville*⟩ *Mutinous* is also frequently applied to active forces (as passions, winds, or waters) that are exceedingly turbulent or uncontrollable ⟨I have . . . called forth the *mutinous* winds—*Shak.*⟩ ⟨*mutinous* passions, and conflicting fears—*Shelley*⟩ **Seditious** implies treasonable activities and often specifically a stirring up of discontent or of opposition to or rebellion against the government ⟨*seditious* societies⟩ ⟨*seditious* writings⟩ ⟨*seditious* factionalism went on a rampage and began to wreck our foreign policy—*Ascoli*⟩ ⟨revolutions that were not made in Boston, by Boston gentlemen, were quite certain to be wicked and *seditious*—*Parrington*⟩ **Factious** stresses the contentious, perverse, or turbulent provocation of party spirit or a tendency to break up into embittered and irreconcilable factions. Only when it implies as a result the destruction of peace in the group as a whole does it suggest indifference to or defiance of constituted authority; very frequently it suggests the opposition of legislative groups or blocs to the government ⟨a quarrelsome, *factious* race⟩ ⟨the government's plan to entertain the proposals for peace aroused the *factious* spirit of the parliament⟩ ⟨Florence . . . sowing the wind and reaping the whirlwind, wearing her soul out by *factious* struggles—*Oliphant*⟩ ⟨the Opposition will be vigilant but not *factious.* We shall not oppose merely for the sake of opposition—*Attlee*⟩ **Contumacious** is found chiefly in legal and ecclesiastical use. It implies persistent, willful, or open disobedience of the orders of a court or of one's superiors; often, it specifically suggests contempt of court by a bold refusal to obey a summons or subpoena, or open and stubborn defiance of laws or orders that are seldom disobeyed ⟨on her refusal to appear in person or by her attorney, she was pronounced *contumacious*—*Lingard*⟩ ⟨magistrates and populace were incensed at a refusal of customary marks of courtesy and respect for the laws, which in their eyes was purely *contumacious*—*Inge*⟩
*Ana* recalcitrant, refractory, *unruly, ungovernable, intractable
*Con* *obedient, amenable, docile, tractable, biddable: submissive, subdued, *tame
**insular,** provincial, parochial, local, small-town are comparable when they mean having or indicating the limited or restricted point of view considered characteristic of the geographically isolated. **Insular** is usually applied to people or the ideas of people who are in one way or another isolated, so that they become or are regarded as self-contained or self-sufficient and disinterested in matters remote from their own concerns. The term implies an aloofness that proceeds from this isolation, but it usually also connotes narrowness of attitude, circumscription of interests, or prejudices in favor of one's own people or one's own kind (as of customs, literature, and art) ⟨much of the impetus for international thinking and planning has come from our schools and our colleges, and the pressures for *insular* chauvinism have come from self-seeking groups of adults—*Brown*⟩ ⟨Bradley was fighting for a European and ripened and wise philosophy, against an *insular* and immature and cranky one—*T. S. Eliot*⟩ **Provincial** sometimes applies to what is characteristic of outlying districts as in opposition to what is characteristic of such metropolitan centers as London or New York ⟨a *provincial* accent⟩ ⟨*provincial* theaters⟩ ⟨*provincial* fashions⟩ but the word tends to connote narrowness of view or of interest as opposed to what is cosmopolitan or catholic ⟨he replaced a philosophy which was crude and raw and *provincial* by one which was, in comparison, catholic, civilized, and universal—*T. S. Eliot*⟩ ⟨firm commitment to a given ideal is not equivalent to *provincial* intolerance towards other forms of excellence—*Nagel*⟩ ⟨Stalin, a *provincial,* Victorian philistine, fancied himself as an infallible connoisseur—*Willets*⟩ **Parochial,** with its reference to a parish, a local unit of administration in the church or, in some regions, in the state, implies confinement to views and interests of a particular place and connotes extreme narrowness and, often, intolerance ⟨of all kinds of human energy, Art is surely the most free, the least *parochial*; and demands of us an essential tolerance of all its forms—*Galsworthy*⟩ ⟨even so great a historian as Pirenne is *parochial* compared with Mr. Toynbee, who has literally taken the world . . . as his province—*Brogan*⟩ ⟨small wonder that the news is often out-of-date, and that it is mostly political polemics or *parochial* gossip—*Kim-*

A colon (:) separates groups of words discriminated. An asterisk (*) indicates place of treatment of each group.

*ble*⟩ **Local** comes very close to *parochial* in meaning, but it carries a less distinct suggestion of narrowness or of intolerance; it rather implies the strong impress produced by the place in which one lives on one's speech, one's customs, or one's interests and is distinguished from *broad* or *general* ⟨the *local* and even parochial Concord mind . . . proved to be . . . national—*Brooks*⟩ ⟨the affair was only of *local* interest⟩ **Small-town** implies a relation to smaller towns as opposed to larger, or metropolitan, centers and thus comes close to *provincial* and *local;* distinctively, it often stresses the dullness or gaucheness or philistinism felt to characterize such an environment ⟨*small-town* gossip⟩ ⟨*small-town* society⟩ ⟨it needn't be much to look big to a *small-town* girl—*S. R. L.*⟩ ⟨the *small-town* mind is as formidable a factor in Irish as in American life—*New Statesman*⟩ ⟨people get married beneath them every day, and I don't see any sign of the world coming to an end. Don't be so *small-town*—*Welty*⟩ *Ana* isolated, insulated, secluded (see ISOLATE): circumscribed, limited, restricted, confined (see LIMIT *vb*): narrow, narrow-minded, *illiberal: aloof, unconcerned, *indifferent

**insulate** *vb* *isolate, segregate, seclude, sequester
*Ana* *separate, part, sever, sunder: *detach, disengage

**insult** *vb* affront, outrage, *offend
*Ana* humiliate, humble, debase, degrade, *abase: flout, *scoff, jeer, gird, gibe, fleer, sneer: mock, taunt, deride, *ridicule
*Ant* honor —*Con* gratify, *please: respect, esteem, admire (see under REGARD *n*)

**insult** *n* *affront, indignity
*Ana* *abuse, vituperation, invective, obloquy: dishonor, shame, ignominy, opprobrium, *disgrace: insolence, superciliousness, disdainfulness (see corresponding adjectives at PROUD): contempt, despite, scorn, disdain (see under DESPISE)
*Con* *compliment, flattery, adulation: *honor, homage, obeisance, deference, reverence

**insure** *ensure, assure, secure
*Ana* protect, shield, guard, safeguard (see DEFEND): indemnify, compensate (see PAY *vb*)

**insurgent** *n* *rebel, iconoclast

**insurrection** uprising, revolt, mutiny, *rebellion, revolution, putsch, coup

**intact** whole, entire, *perfect
*Ana* flawless, faultless, *impeccable: complete, replete, *full: *consummate, finished
*Ant* defective —*Con* impaired, damaged, injured, marred (see INJURE): vitiated, corrupted *or* corrupt (see DEBASE)

**intangible** impalpable, *imperceptible, insensible, inappreciable, imponderable
*Ana* tenuous, rare, slight, slender, *thin: ethereal, *airy, aerial: eluding *or* elusive, evading *or* evasive (see corresponding verbs at ESCAPE)
*Ant* tangible —*Con* palpable, *perceptible, sensible, appreciable, ponderable: *material, physical, corporeal

**integer** *n* *number, numeral, figure, digit

**integrate,** articulate, concatenate are comparable when they mean to bring or join together a number of distinct things so that they move, operate, or function as a unit. The implications of these senses are probably more often found in the participial adjectives **integrated, articulated, concatenated** and in the derived nouns **integration, articulation, concatenation** than in the finite verbs. **Integrate** implies that the things (as parts, elements, factors, or details) combined are brought into such intimate connection with each other that a perfect whole results. Usually it suggests a complete fusion or coalescence of particulars

with loss therefore of their separate identities ⟨a customs union that . . . would *integrate* the economies of the two countries—*Current Biog.*⟩ ⟨cartels or other forms of highly *integrated* organization—*J. S. Martin*⟩ ⟨he relies heavily upon the researches of others, and his condensation and *integration* of their findings perhaps form his main contribution—*Angoff*⟩ **Articulate** also implies as its result a perfect whole, but it differs from *integrate* in implying no loss of identity or of distinctness of the things (as parts, branches, and departments) combined and in suggesting a connection between them that is found in its perfection in the skeletons of vertebrate animals. For *articulate* implies organization in which each part fits into another in a manner comparable to the fitting into each other of two bones at a movable joint and a structure is built up that functions as a whole yet without loss of flexibility or distinctness in any of its component units or without any conflict between them ⟨hard put to it to devise ways of participation for children, and means of *articulating* their school life with the rest of life—*Mead*⟩ ⟨few people have definitely *articulated* philosophies of their own—*James*⟩ ⟨the two ideas have been transferred from a conglomerate to an *articulated* unity—*Weaver*⟩ ⟨in four years the principate had scarcely begun that process of *articulation* which was to make it one of the most complex and yet smooth-running systems of government known to history—*Buchan*⟩ **Concatenate** suggests neither fusion nor organization but a linking together of smaller units until figuratively a powerful chain is forged. It implies addition of one thing to another with cumulative effect ⟨not one cause brings about war, but a *concatenation* of causes⟩ ⟨the present work comprises five essays nicely *concatenated*—*Hocking*⟩ ⟨the theory of the state is developed in a closely *concatenated* line of thought—*Sabine*⟩ ⟨could not help thinking that the *concatenation* of events this evening had produced was the scheme of some sinister intelligence bent on punishing him—*Hardy*⟩ *Ana* *unite, combine, conjoin: unify, consolidate, concentrate, *compact: fuse, blend, merge, coalesce (see MIX): organize, systematize (see ORDER)
*Ant* disintegrate —*Con* crumble, decompose (see DECAY): dissipate, disperse, *scatter: *analyze, resolve, break down

**integrated** articulated, concatenated (see under INTEGRATE *vb*)
*Ana* unified, consolidated, concentrated (see COMPACT *vb*): fused, blended, coalesced, merged (see MIX): whole, entire, intact, *perfect: organized, systematized (see ORDER *vb*)
*Ant* disintegrated

**integration** articulation, concatenation (see under INTEGRATE *vb*)
*Ana* unification, consolidation, concentration (see corresponding verbs at COMPACT): integrity, union, *unity, solidarity

**integrity** 1 *unity, solidarity, union
*Ana* wholeness, entirety, perfection, intactness (see corresponding adjectives at PERFECT): consummateness (see corresponding adjective at CONSUMMATE): purity, simplicity, absoluteness (see corresponding adjectives at PURE)
2 probity, *honesty, honor
*Ana* uprightness, justness, conscientiousness, scrupulousness *or* scrupulosity (see corresponding adjectives at UPRIGHT): rectitude, virtue, *goodness, morality: *truth, veracity, verity
*Ant* duplicity —*Con* *deceit, dissimulation, guile: dishonesty, deceitfulness, mendaciousness *or* mendacity (see corresponding adjectives at DISHONEST)

---

**intellect** *mind, soul, psyche, brain, intelligence, wit
*Ana* *reason, understanding, intuition
**intellectual** *mental, psychic, cerebral, intelligent
*Ant* carnal —*Con* *bodily, physical, corporeal, corporal, somatic: fleshly, animal, sensual (see CARNAL)
**intelligence** 1 brain, *mind, intellect, soul, psyche, wit
*Ana* *sense, judgment, wisdom, gumption: *discernment, penetration, insight, acumen: sagaciousness *or* sagacity, perspicaciousness *or* perspicacity, astuteness, shrewdness (see corresponding adjectives at SHREWD)
2 *news, tidings, advice
**intelligent** 1 Intellectual, *mental, cerebral, psychic
2 Intelligent, clever, alert, quick-witted, bright, smart, knowing, brilliant are comparable when they mean mentally quick or keen. **Intelligent** implies greater than average power to use one's mind successfully when demands are made upon it (as in understanding the new or abstruse or in meeting and solving problems) ⟨Puritanism presupposed an *intelligent* clergy capable of interpreting Scripture—*Amer. Guide Series: Mass.*⟩ ⟨the vigor of his quick and lucid mind, keenly *intelligent* rather than deeply intellectual—*Lustgarten*⟩ **Clever** implies resourcefulness or aptness more strongly than *intelligent,* and it emphasizes quickness in apprehension rather than fullness of comprehension, and dexterity or adroitness, rather than soundness, in the mental processes ⟨the poor girl liked to be thought *clever,* but she hated to be thought bookish—*Henry James*⟩ ⟨he could deal competently with effects, but he was not *clever* at assigning causes—*Sinclair*⟩ Often the word suggests a contrast with higher or more substantial qualities ⟨be good, sweet maid, and let who will be *clever*—*Kingsley*⟩ ⟨a *clever* boy trains for an examination as he trains for a race; and goes out of training as fast as possible when it is over—*Inge*⟩ **Alert** stresses quickness in the mental processes, especially in comprehending a situation ⟨she seemed more feeble in body . . . but her mind was still *alert*—*L. P. Smith*⟩ ⟨after Munich *alert* observers urged more forcefully that our country must hurry to develop its military power—*Feis*⟩ **Quick-witted** also implies quickness in thinking but in addition it suggests promptness in action in an emergency, in response to a challenge, in conversation, or in debate ⟨we are not a *quick-witted* race; and we have succeeded . . . by dint of a kind of instinct for improvising the right course of action—*Inge*⟩ **Bright** and *smart* are more often applied to young or promising persons than to those who are proficient or of proved intelligence. **Bright** suggests cleverness that is manifested especially in liveness of mind or in liveliness of talk or manner ⟨how they could, who had once been so eager and *bright,* be so stodgy now—*Edman*⟩ ⟨*bright* young fellows with a charming literary swagger, they aspired to be wits—*Parrington*⟩ **Smart,** too, implies cleverness but it also suggests alertness or quick-wittedness that enables one to get ahead ⟨I wish I was *smart* enough to invent something and maybe get rich—*Anderson*⟩ ⟨the master said he was the *smartest* lad in the school—*D. H. Lawrence*⟩ ⟨the race is no longer to the strong, but to the *smart*—*Drake*⟩ Both words are used ironically, *bright* then implying dullness or stupidity and *smart,* pertness, facetiousness, or sometimes trickery or duplicity ⟨a *smart* aleck⟩ ⟨given to making *smart* retorts⟩ ⟨other *bright* ideas—some showing a superb neglect of practical feasibility, as well as of the welfare of any unfortunates who might happen to be in the experiment area—include the scattering of concentrated sulphuric acid—*The Countryman*⟩ ⟨I do not want . . . to be converted by a *smart* syllogism—*Birrell*⟩ ⟨the *smart* work is hidden in the wording of the Monroe doctrine—*Emporia Gazette*⟩ **Knowing** carries a stronger implication

than any of the preceding terms of the possession of information or knowledge that is necessary or useful under given circumstances ⟨the *knowing* collectors of records—*Sat. Review*⟩ ⟨bipartisanship, as a *knowing* Republican politician once remarked, is a fine thing—between elections—*Collins*⟩ Occasionally the term further suggests a less agreeable quality such as sophistication, secretiveness, or the possession of knowledge of others' secrets ⟨a *knowing* wink⟩ ⟨a face so mean, so *knowing*—*Thackeray*⟩ ⟨his work has a distasteful air of pretentious smartness, of being altogether too *knowing*—*Read*⟩ **Brilliant** adds to *intelligent* the implication of unusual and outstanding keenness of intellect that manifests itself so openly or effectively as to excite admiration; the term usually suggests an opposition to qualities that characterize one whose mind works more slowly or cautiously ⟨a *brilliant* mathematician⟩ ⟨John Todhunter was esteemed a shrewd sensible man—only not *brilliant*—*Meredith*⟩ ⟨Einstein's *brilliant* solution of the . . . puzzle—*Zinsser*⟩ ⟨the *brilliant* anthropologist whom de Gaulle wished to place in charge of a combined intelligence service—*Funk*⟩
*Ana* *sharp, keen, acute: *shrewd, sagacious, perspicacious, astute: cunning, ingenious, adroit, *clever
*Ant* unintelligent —*Con* foolish, idiotic, imbecilic, moronic (see corresponding nouns at FOOL): *stupid, slow, dull, dense, crass, dumb: *irrational, unreasonable
**intend, mean, design, propose, purpose** signify to have in mind as an aim, end, or function. **Intend** implies that the mind is directed to some definite accomplishment or to the achievement of a definite end ⟨if one earnestly *intends* a conspiracy, one does not commence with a series of public readings—*Kristol*⟩ ⟨*intended* twenty-four books, sketched fourteen, but left only four—*Highet*⟩ or is bent upon some person or thing (as an invention or a writing) serving a certain purpose or use, or fulfilling a certain destiny ⟨a play, *intended* for great Theseus' nuptial day —*Shak.*⟩ ⟨a strong suspicion that the new instrument with which Einstein has presented the mathematicians is being put to uses for which it was never *intended*—*Inge*⟩ ⟨a man set aside and *intended* by nature to lead a blameless life—*Anderson*⟩ *Intend* often implies an aim to express a definite idea by a given word or phrase ⟨just what the framers of the constitution *intended* by the phrase "to be twice put in jeopardy" is still a matter of some doubt⟩ ⟨he caught the phrase as it dropped from his lips with a feeling that it said more than he *intended*—*H. G. Wells*⟩ **Mean** often carries a denotation close to that of *intend* ⟨those organ tones of his were *meant* to fill cathedrals or the most exalted of tribunals—*Cardozo*⟩ but it does not convey so clear an implication of determination to effect one's end as does *intend* and, sometimes, it implies little more than volition or decision ⟨he always *means* to work harder⟩ ⟨a book that I *mean* to get when I reach Beverly—*Justice Holmes*⟩ ⟨I don't *mean* to defend Charles' errors, but before I form my judgment of either of them I intend to make a trial of their hearts—*Sheridan*⟩ ⟨he shouldn't have done it, of course; but he was thoughtless. And he *meant* to pay the money back—*Deland*⟩ **Design** (see also under PLAN *n*) usually stresses forethought and deliberation in arriving at an intention ⟨the American people . . . . did not *design* to make their government dependent on the States—*John Marshall*⟩ ⟨we wanted absolute surrender and we wanted it within a matter of hours, and the bomb of Nagasaki was *designed* to achieve just that, which it did—*Cousins*⟩ Often, the term also implies scheming or contriving, especially by underhand means, in an attempt to effect what is designed ⟨your father and sister, in their civilities and invitations, were

A colon (:) separates groups of words discriminated. An asterisk (*) indicates place of treatment of each group.

*designing* a match between the heir and the young lady —*Austen*⟩ ⟨ah! Friend! to dazzle let the vain *design;* to raise the thought, and touch the heart be thine!—*Pope*⟩ **Propose** implies a declaration of one's intention or a setting it clearly before oneself or others. It therefore usually connotes clear definition or open avowal ⟨what do you *propose* to do when your funds run out?⟩ ⟨I *propose* to describe the circumstances under which Richelieu worked when he produced and realized the centralized nation of today—*Belloc*⟩ ⟨to China, where she *proposed* to spend some time with her friends—*Salisbury*⟩ ⟨what is reached in the end may be better or worse than what was *proposed* —*James*⟩ ⟨I, for one, do not *propose* to adjust my ethics to the values of a bloodstained despotism—*A. E. Stevenson*⟩ **Purpose** differs little from *propose* except in carrying a somewhat stronger implication of determination to effect or achieve one's intention ⟨I *purpose* to write the history of England from the accession of King James the Second—*Macaulay*⟩ ⟨a promise to send her picture postcards from the Cathedral cities which he *purposed* visiting—*Hewlett*⟩ and in occasionally connoting clearer definition in one's own mind ⟨thy brother Esau, as touching thee, doth comfort himself, *purposing* to kill thee—*Gen* 27:42⟩

*Ana* *aim, aspire: *attempt, try, endeavor, strive, essay: plan, design, scheme, plot (see under PLAN *n*)

**intense,** vehement, fierce, exquisite, violent are comparable when meaning extreme in degree, power, or effect. Although several of them often are used interchangeably without clear distinction, they can be employed in ways that reveal many differences in implications and applications. **Intense** is especially appropriate when the idea of great depth (as in quality, reach, or effect) is to be implied. In such use *intense* may apply to thoughts or thinking, to feeling or emotion, to such an outstanding quality or character as color, brilliancy, or tone, or to something that suggests a straining or a being strained (as in the attainment of an end or effect) ⟨*intense* concentration⟩ ⟨*intense* hatred⟩ ⟨*intense* silence⟩ ⟨work so *intense* that it takes the last inch out of the workers—*Shaw*⟩ ⟨he was in such an *intense* mood that humor was entirely barred out— *M. E. Freeman*⟩ ⟨one of the inspired moments that come to *intense* natures, working intensely, had come to him —*Anderson*⟩ **Vehement** and **fierce** (see also FIERCE) suggest a manifestation of abundant energy or force, and connote, *fierce* to a greater degree than *vehement,* ardency, impetuosity, or urgency ⟨jealousy is cruel as the grave: the coals thereof are coals of fire, which hath a most *vehement* flame—*Song of Sol* 8:6⟩ ⟨the temper of monists has been so *vehement,* as almost at times to be convulsive —*James*⟩ ⟨if *vehement* assertions on the one side have driven me into too *vehement* dissent on the other, I crave pardon—*Quiller-Couch*⟩ ⟨she burns with a *fierce* pietistic suspiciousness of all the arts—*Trilling*⟩ ⟨so *fierce* were the passions that had been aroused, that again he was in danger of violence—*Froude*⟩ **Exquisite** (see also CHOICE) raises the implications of *intense* to a point suggesting an extreme near to consummateness or completeness. In this sense it has been applied indifferently to things good or bad but often with the result that, when applied to such things as cleanliness, some feelings, judgment, or color which may be called good, its meaning is taken as equal to that of *exquisite* at CHOICE; thus, although *exquisite* cleanliness may mean cleanliness so extreme that it suggests immoderateness, it is usually thought of as cleanliness so perfect that it gives joy to the fastidious. Consequently, *exquisite* in this sense is more often applied to what is felt or apprehended keenly or acutely ⟨with a brilliant mind, nervous temperament, intense susceptibil-

ity to artistic and spiritual impressions . . . [she] was attuned to *exquisite* pleasure and *exquisite* pain—*Hanscom*⟩ ⟨subject a person to *exquisite* torture⟩ **Violent** (for senses of acting with or caused by violence compare *violence* under FORCE) implies immoderate strength or force and, usually, the exceeding of normal bounds even in something that is strong or forcible; the term need not impute a disagreeable quality to that to which it is applied, but the possibility of this implication is more frequent than in the other terms ⟨*violent* heat⟩ ⟨his intense faith and his *violent* spiritual agonies are experiences which few of us today are able to share—*Day Lewis*⟩ ⟨an unreasoning passion of despair descended upon them both, *violent* yet essentially slight—*Wylie*⟩

*Ana* intensified, enhanced, heightened, aggravated (see INTENSIFY): accentuated, emphasized, stressed (see corresponding nouns at EMPHASIS)

*Ant* subdued (*colors, lights, emotions*)

**intensify,** aggravate, heighten, enhance mean to increase markedly in degree or measure. **Intensify** implies a deepening or strengthening of a thing or especially of its characteristic quality ⟨a clear atmosphere *intensifies* the blue of the sky⟩ ⟨an unfortunate atmosphere . . . that *intensifies* the suspicions with which the hardheaded and skeptical naturally approach such revolutionary claims— *Flew*⟩ ⟨historical circumstances of recent years have conspired to *intensify* nationalism—*Huxley*⟩ **Aggravate** implies a manifest increase in the seriousness of a situation or condition that is already unpleasant or difficult ⟨false rumors that *aggravate* racial animosities⟩ ⟨truth and frankness dispel difficulties, but the attempt at repressive moral discipline only *aggravates* them—*Russell*⟩ ⟨these considerable defects in a parish priest were *aggravated* rather than offset by his talents as an orator— *Anthony West*⟩ **Heighten** and *enhance* both imply a lifting or raising; **heighten,** however, tends to imply a lifting above the ordinary, the trite, or the commonplace, and a consequent increase in sharpness and poignancy, and **enhance** a lifting above the norm or the average in desirability or attractiveness by the addition of something that increases the value, charm, or prestige of the thing enhanced ⟨a dramatist *heightens* the effect of his scenes by rapidity of the action and he *enhances* his dialogue by the addition of witty repartee⟩ ⟨had *heightened* his appreciation of the more austere pleasures of the afternoon—*Archibald Marshall*⟩ ⟨a painter discards many trivial points of exactness, in order to *heighten* the truthfulness of a few fundamentals—*Montague*⟩ ⟨Augustus sought . . . in every way to *enhance* its [the Roman Senate's] prestige and dignity—*Buchan*⟩

*Ana* accentuate, emphasize, stress, accent (see corresponding nouns at EMPHASIS): magnify, aggrandize, *exalt

*Ant* temper: mitigate, allay: abate (sense 2) —*Con* *moderate, qualify: alleviate, lighten, *relieve: reduce, lessen, diminish, * decrease

**intent** *n* *intention, purpose, design, aim, end, object, objective, goal

*Ana* *will, volition, conation

*Ant* accident —*Con* *chance, hap, luck, fortune, hazard

**intent** *adj* Intent, engrossed, absorbed, rapt mean having one's mind or attention deeply fixed on something. **Intent** implies that one's mind, one's desires, or one's energies are eagerly bent on something; it therefore suggests a directing of the entire attention toward a particular end or thing ⟨persons whose hearts are wholly bent toward pleasure, or *intent* upon gain—*Spectator*⟩ ⟨the wise author *intent* on getting at truth—*Quiller-Couch*⟩ ⟨for all its hideous scars is no dead city, but one grimly *intent* on survival—*Cassidy*⟩ **Engrossed** implies monopolization of one's attention either by a driving purpose or emotion or an eager interest or by the force or urgency of circumstances beyond one's control ⟨he appears to have been so *engrossed* by domestic issues as to have given little attention to foreign problems—*W. L. Langer*⟩ ⟨Sieveking was naturally *engrossed* in the musical problem, which was perplexing enough—*Hilton*⟩ ⟨these constitutional changes . . . were pushed through during and after the war by a group of busybodies who were not too much *engrossed* by the agony of their country to conduct a raging agitation in all parts of England—*Inge*⟩ **Absorbed** often differs little from *engrossed* in this sense ⟨the point is that Broch is never engrossed in, and never permits the reader to become *absorbed* by, the story itself—*Arendt*⟩ but it may carry a stronger suggestion of the power of the thing on which the attention is fixed to capture one's attention and to hold it firmly so that there is difficulty in distracting it ⟨wholly *absorbed* in his preparations for saving souls in the gold camps—blind to everything else—*Cather*⟩ ⟨human beings are prone to become *absorbed* in themselves, unable to be interested in what they see and hear or in anything outside their own skins—*Russell*⟩ ⟨already they had read *Farthest North*. Imogen, at eight years old, had read it, *absorbed*, breathless, intent, tongue clenched between teeth—*Rose Macaulay*⟩ **Rapt** implies both extreme intentness and complete absorption, as though one were taken out of oneself or were in an ecstatic trance ⟨*rapt* in adoring contemplation—*Farrar*⟩ ⟨expounded the ultimate meaning of existence to the white, *rapt* faces of Humanity—*L. P. Smith*⟩ ⟨in openmouthed wonder the lama turned to this and that, and finally checked in *rapt* attention before a large alto-relief representing a coronation or apotheosis of the Lord Buddha—*Kipling*⟩

*Ana* attending *or* attentive, minding, watching (see corresponding verbs at TEND): *abstracted, preoccupied: concentrated (see COMPACT *vb*): riveted (see SECURE *vb*)
*Ant* distracted

**intention, intent, purpose, design, aim, end, object, objective, goal** are comparable when meaning what one proposes to accomplish or to attain by doing or making something, in distinction from what prompts one (the *motive*), or from the activity itself (the *means*), or from the actual or envisioned outcome (the *effect*). The first four of these words stress the clearly defined will to do or make something. **Intention**, however, often denotes little more than what one has in mind to do or to bring about ⟨she had not had an *intention* or a thought of going home—*Dickens*⟩ ⟨she had divined the *intention* behind her mother's tolerance—*Joyce*⟩ ⟨announced its *intention* to divide its Indian Empire into two dominions—*Current Biog.*⟩ **Intent** suggests clearer formulation and greater deliberateness than *intention* ⟨they become enamored of official declarations of *intent*, though not much is said about the machinery to translate *intent* into action—*Cousins*⟩ ⟨behind my look you saw such unmistakable *intent*—*Millay*⟩ **Purpose** implies more settled determination or more resolution than *intention* ⟨have a *purpose* in life⟩ ⟨the missionary was here for a *purpose*, and he pressed his point—*Cather*⟩ ⟨there lie youth and irresolution: here manhood and *purpose*—*Meredith*⟩ **Design** carries further the notion of deliberateness and purposiveness in formulating an intention; in this sense it is not always clearly distinguishable from *design* denoting plan (see under PLAN *n*), for it retains the implications of careful ordering of details, of calculation, and sometimes of scheming ⟨a great man by accident rather than *design*—*Laski*⟩ ⟨I had suspected him of harboring . . . sinister *designs*—*Hudson*⟩ ⟨the United States has no ulterior *designs* against any of its neighbors—*Vandenberg*⟩ **Aim** implies a clear definition of something

that one hopes to effect and a direction of one's efforts or energies to its attainment; thus, one who proposes to make the best of his powers and of his opportunities may be said to have a *purpose* in life: one who has clearly defined the mark he hopes to reach and determines his actions by it may be said to have an *aim* in life ⟨her steadiness and courage in the pursuit of her *aims*—*J. R. Green*⟩ ⟨the *aim* of the Elizabethans was to attain complete realism—*T. S. Eliot*⟩ The remaining words of this group, like *aim*, imply that what one does is affected by what one hopes to accomplish or attain. **End** in this relation retains some of the suggestion of remoteness and finality inherent in some of its other senses (see LIMIT, END 2) and therefore is appropriately applied to an aim or purpose which takes its nature from principle or logical necessity and of which the attainment requires a definite and planned course of action leading to the modification of existent reality ⟨holding that the good of the *end* justified all the evil of the means⟩ ⟨the relation between means and *ends* is clearly bound up with a temporal view. *Ends* are in the future, means in the present. We do control means, we do not control *ends*. Hence the foolishness of conceiving *ends* apart from means. On the contrary, *ends* must be judged, and evaluated, in the light of the means available for their attainment—*Visalberghi*⟩ ⟨provide the safeguard we need against the abuse of mankind's scientific genius for destructive *ends*—*Dean*⟩ ⟨the *end* of law was to bring about the widest possible abstract individual liberty—*Roscoe Pound*⟩ ⟨it is commonly said and commonly believed that science is completely neutral and indifferent as to the *ends* and values which move men to act: that at most it only provides more efficient means for realization of *ends* that are and must be due to wants and desires completely independent of science—*Dewey*⟩ **Object** and **objective** apply to an end as being that toward which effort or action or emotion (as hope) is directed ⟨the *object* is to gather data that can be taken only during a total solar blackout—*Cowen*⟩ ⟨one of the important *objectives* of public education has been and will always be to inspire in youth a deep appreciation of the basic spiritual and religious values which give meaning to existence—*Current Biog.*⟩ Distinctively, **object** may suggest an end based on more individually determined desires, needs, or intentions ⟨Colonel Belgrave, who is bent on abducting Amanda . . . pursues his *object* with a pertinacity and ingenuity that does credit to his understanding—*Crothers*⟩ ⟨the *object* of a legislator, he declares, is to make not a great but a happy city—*Dickinson*⟩ ⟨we call a man cruel who takes pleasure in the suffering of others and inflicts it with that *object*—*Belloc*⟩ while **objective** may suggest one which is concrete and immediately attainable or at least one which involves no obviously insurmountable problems ⟨the *objectives* of the Guild are to promote and advance the spiritual, social, educational and recreational welfare of the blind persons in the Diocese—*Hamrah*⟩ ⟨Columbia included among its earliest stated *objectives* the instruction of youth in surveying, navigation, husbandry, commerce, government, and manufacture—*Eurich*⟩ **Goal** often evokes the image of one running a race; usually it implies struggle and endurance of hardships and cessation of effort at attainment ⟨the Good, which is the *goal* of all moral endeavor—*Inge*⟩ ⟨in the average man's mind leisure is . . . a *goal* to strive for—*Furnas*⟩ ⟨equality is, of course, a *goal* or ideal rather than an immediately attainable objective—*Gallagher*⟩

*Ana* *plan, design, scheme, project: desiring *or* desire, wishing *or* wish (see corresponding verbs at DESIRE)

**intentional** *voluntary, deliberate, willful, willing

A colon (:) separates groups of words discriminated. An asterisk (*) indicates place of treatment of each group.

*Ana* intended, meant, purposed, proposed (see INTEND): considered, premeditated, advised, studied, designed, *deliberate

*Ant* instinctive —*Con* *accidental, casual, fortuitous: inadvertent, thoughtless, *careless, heedless

**intercalate** interpolate, insert, *introduce, interpose, interject, insinuate

**intercede** mediate, intervene, *interpose, interfere

*Ana* plead, petition, sue, pray (see under PRAYER)

**interchange** *vb* *exchange, bandy

*Ana* transpose, *reverse

**intercourse, commerce, traffic, dealings, communication, communion, conversation, converse, correspondence** are comparable when meaning the connection established between persons or peoples through a medium that permits interchange (as of information, of opinions, of ideas, or of goods). **Intercourse** usually means little more than this and requires a qualifying adjective to indicate the things interchanged or the medium permitting interchange ⟨business *intercourse*⟩ ⟨trade *intercourse*⟩ ⟨sexual *intercourse*⟩ ⟨social *intercourse*⟩ In ordinary use, when employed without qualification, *intercourse* means *social intercourse* or the normal interchange of such things as ideas, opinions, news, and civilities between one person or group and another with whom there are more or less intimate relations ⟨the truth was, he could not be happy for long without human *intercourse*—*Cather*⟩ ⟨the keen and animated *intercourse* with its exchange of disputable convictions—*Repplier*⟩ ⟨he welcomes extra-class *intercourse* with students and encourages them to think critically—*G. H. White*⟩ ⟨if nations are to cooperate, the first condition must be that they have social and political *intercourse*—*E. B. White*⟩ **Commerce,** which applies primarily to the interchange of goods by buying and selling (for this sense, see BUSINESS 3) also is used in the more general sense of *intercourse* ⟨*commerce* with the world has made him wiser—*Macaulay*⟩ ⟨I was less and less disposed to *commerce* with my kind, I who never was given to social functioning—*Weygandt*⟩ The word tends to be restricted in its application to intercourse, through the spirit or mind, that involves an interchange of ideas or influences without a necessary interchange of words ⟨reestablish intellectual *commerce* among them in such a way as to enable them to get on with the attack against the common enemy—*P. B. Rice*⟩ ⟨how is poetry born in us? There is, I think, some *commerce* between the outer and an inner being—*Æ*⟩ though it is occasionally used of sexual intercourse. **Traffic** (see also BUSINESS 3) is used chiefly when such connotations derived from its commercial senses are to be suggested as the interchange of goods, especially of tangible or material goods, or a rapid passing to and from the persons or things concerned ⟨years and the *traffic* of the mind with men and books did not affect you in the least—*Woolf*⟩ ⟨the State can have no *traffic* or relationship with the Church considered as a purely spiritual society—*Times Lit. Sup.*⟩ **Dealings** usually implies a closer connection and one with more familiarity or less formality or one having for its object mutual or personal gain ⟨they suspected that he was having *dealings* with the enemy⟩ ⟨being a woman is a terribly difficult trade since it consists principally of *dealings* with men—*Conrad*⟩ ⟨if a kid gets her way, she has to take some advice. That is part of the unwritten code which governs the *dealings* between generations—*Robertson Davies*⟩ Traditionally **communication** is less general than any of the preceding terms because it implies intercourse based on an exchange of symbols and especially words ⟨there had been no *communication* with the island since the storm⟩ ⟨I can try to get to know Negroes here to establish *communication*

—*Collie*⟩ ⟨*communication* is a process by which a person refers to something, either by pointing to it or using a symbol for it, in such a way as to lead another person to have a more or less similar experience of it. *Communication*, in this sense, presupposes frames of reference which are shared by the communicating persons, so that similar meanings are shared by them—*Newcomb*⟩ but *communication* suggests, as the preceding terms do not, mutuality and the shared background of experience that has given rise to a comprehensible set of symbols; it therefore is appropriately used of nonhuman interactions ⟨*communication* is a type of behavior between living creatures characterized by mutuality, rooted in biological heredity, and constituting one of the general manifestations of life—*Révész*⟩ or of the process or art of effectively interchanging symbols ⟨in order to develop and maintain that basic consensus of values, beliefs, and institutional behavior upon which its existence must rest . . . a society must maintain effective *communication* among its parts . . . . Indeed, the effectiveness of the *communication* process is a measure of the social integration of a society—*Cottrell*⟩ ⟨Lilly was not expert in *communication*, and did not try to draw Mr. Sprockett out although it would have been easy—*Ethel Wilson*⟩ or, in the plural, of the means by which spatially or temporally separated individuals or groups engage in such exchanges ⟨*communications* were disrupted by the storm⟩ ⟨there is . . . no conclusive evidence that the organized life of any Romano-British town survived the severance of its *communications* in the troubles of the fifth century—*Stenton*⟩ ⟨the poor *communications* that exist in many factories between the front office and the men at the workbenches—*Purtell*⟩ **Communion** usually implies intercourse between those who are close in love or sympathy or in mutual understanding; it often suggests rather than implies spiritual intercourse or the absence of words ⟨the consummation of *communion* with God coincides with the final resolution of the sense of estrangement from Him—*Inge*⟩ ⟨Delia sat down beside her, and their clasped hands lay upon the coverlet. They did not say much . . . their *communion* had no need of words—*Wharton*⟩ ⟨most of the time my father was buried in his religious books, and my mother recognized it as her function to keep this *communion* undisturbed—*Behrman*⟩ **Conversation** has a use, chiefly in the phrase *criminal conversation*, in which it is equivalent to *sexual intercourse*, and **converse** has a poetic sense in which it approaches *communion* ⟨to hold fit *converse* with the spiritual world—*Wordsworth*⟩ ⟨spend in pure *converse* our eternal day—*Rupert Brooke*⟩ In general use, however, both terms usually imply free and often lively oral interchange of opinions, comments, or news between two or more persons; *conversation* often applies specifically to the act of interchanging opinions, ideas, and information in talk, and *converse*, to the ideas, gossip, and opinions involved in such conversation ⟨an important general . . . deep in *converse* with the wealthiest of all the astrologers of those war years—*Han Suyin*⟩ ⟨give a freedom to resolve difference by *converse*—*Oppenheimer*⟩ ⟨we had talk enough, but no *conversation;* there was nothing discussed—*Johnson*⟩ ⟨genuine *conversation*—by which I mean something distinguishable from disputation, lamentation, and joke telling—*Krutch*⟩ **Correspondence** implies intercourse through an interchange of letters ⟨there has been no letup in their *correspondence* for fifty years⟩ ⟨the business was conducted by *correspondence*⟩

**interdict** *vb* ban, inhibit, enjoin, *forbid, prohibit

*Ana* proscribe (see SENTENCE): debar, rule out, *exclude: *restrain, curb, check

---

*Ant* sanction —*Con* *let, allow, permit

**interesting, engrossing, absorbing, intriguing** mean having a quality or qualities that secure attention and hold it for a length of time. **Interesting** implies a power in a person or thing to awaken such a mental or emotional reaction involving attention as curiosity, sympathy, a desire to know or understand, or enthusiasm, but unless the adjective is qualified or there is a fuller explanation in the context, the degree or the cause of interest is not clear ⟨after a month of visiting Mark decided that there was not one *interesting* human creature in the whole parish—*Mackenzie*⟩ ⟨Jane seemed to me to be increasingly *interesting;* she was acquiring new subtleties, complexities, and comprehensions—*Rose Macaulay*⟩ ⟨I see that many people find the world dreary . . . some find it *interesting*—*Benson*⟩ As applied to a book, a play, or a narrative the word usually means entertaining, diverting (compare verbs at AMUSE), exciting, stimulating, or provocative (compare verbs at PROVOKE), but if the context provides no real clue as to the precise implication, the word may fail to hit the mark. **Engrossing** (see also MONOPOLIZE) suggests the power to grip the attention so as to exclude everything else, but it may or may not imply a power to please, divert, or entertain, and it refers almost always to things rather than persons; thus, an *engrossing* book may seize the whole attention from such dissimilar causes as that it requires deep study or serious reflection or that it is challenging or provocative ⟨the *engrossing* nature of his task made the time pass quickly⟩ ⟨the conditions were ideal—not too much money, *engrossing* work to be done, and a sense of purpose and progress in the world—*Whitehead*⟩ ⟨synonymy books in which differences are analyzed, *engrossing* as they may have been to the active party, the analyst, offer to the passive party, the reader, nothing but boredom—*Fowler*⟩ **Absorbing** does not differ materially from *engrossing*, but its underlying notion is not the same, for it suggests in the thing that holds one's attention a power to draw one in, as if by suction; thus, a pursuit may be *engrossing*, but not *absorbing*, when it occupies one's attention to the exclusion of everything else; a book may be *absorbing*, rather than *engrossing*, when its attraction is strong enough to draw one away from attention to one's surroundings ⟨he loved the woman with a love as *absorbing* as the hatred he later felt for all women—*Anderson*⟩ ⟨the difficult and *absorbing* question of how poetry and the other arts at their best, though human creations, put us into relation with the universe of reality—*Alexander*⟩ **Intriguing**, sometimes used in the sense of *interesting*, more specifically applies to something that attracts attention by arousing one's curiosity, by baffling one's understanding, or by leading one on ⟨an *intriguing* smile⟩ ⟨one facet of one of the most *intriguing* and baffling mysteries of the Cold War—*Drew Middleton*⟩ ⟨there is an *intriguing* unknowingness about The Age of Reason—*Hardwick*⟩ *Ana* stimulating, exciting, provoking, quickening (see PROVOKE): stirring, rousing, awakening (see STIR *vb*): thrilling, electrifying (see THRILL *vb*): amusing, diverting, entertaining (see AMUSE): inspiring, animating (see INFORM *vb*)

*Ant* boring —*Con* *dull, humdrum, dreary, monotonous, stodgy, pedestrian: *irksome, tedious, tiresome, wearisome

**interfere** 1 *interpose, intervene, mediate, intercede

*Ana* impede, obstruct, block, *hinder, bar

2 *meddle, intermeddle, tamper

*Ana* *intrude, interlope, butt in, obtrude: incommode, discommode, *inconvenience, trouble: thwart, foil, balk, baffle, *frustrate

**interim** *break, gap, interruption, interval, hiatus, lacuna

**interior** *adj* inside, internal, *inner, inward, intestine

*Ana* intimate, *familiar: spiritual (see HOLY): intrinsic, constitutional, *inherent

*Ant* exterior —*Con* *outer, outward, outside, external: extraneous, foreign, *extrinsic

**interject** *introduce, interpolate, interpose, insert, intercalate, insinuate

*Ana* *throw, cast, toss: obtrude, *intrude, interlope, butt in: comment, *remark, animadvert

**interlope** *intrude, butt in, obtrude

*Ana* *trespass, encroach, invade, entrench, infringe: interfere, *interpose, intervene

**intermeddle** *meddle, interfere, tamper

*Ana* *intrude, obtrude, butt in, interlope: entrench, encroach, *trespass, invade

**interminable** unceasing, *everlasting, endless

*Ana* perpetual, *lasting, perdurable, permanent: incessant, *continual, continuous, constant: eternal, *infinite

*Con* *intermittent, periodic: stopped, discontinued (see STOP): ended, terminated, closed, finished, completed (see CLOSE *vb*)

**intermission** *pause, recess, respite, lull

*Ana* interruption, interval, gap, *break: ceasing *or* cessation, stopping *or* stop (see corresponding verbs at STOP)

**intermit** suspend, stay, *defer, postpone

*Ana* interrupt, *arrest, check: *stop, discontinue: abate, reduce, lessen, *decrease

*Con* *continue, persist: *repeat, iterate, reiterate

**intermittent, recurrent, periodic, alternate** mean recurring or reappearing more or less regularly but in interrupted sequence. Something is **intermittent** which from time to time is omitted or disappears but always returns ⟨an *intermittent* fever⟩ ⟨an *intermittent* correspondence⟩ ⟨in most poets there is an *intermittent* conflict between the poetic self and the rest of the man—*Day Lewis*⟩ Something is **recurrent** which returns or has the habit of returning after omission or disappearance. In contrast, *intermittent* stresses breaks in continuity and *recurrent* stresses repetition ⟨*intermittent* attacks of appendicitis⟩ ⟨*recurrent* shortages⟩ ⟨an *intermittent* buzzing⟩ ⟨a *recurrent* knocking⟩ ⟨an endlessly *recurrent* set of problems—*Richards*⟩ Something is **periodic** which is known to be recurrent at more or less fixed intervals over a long period of time and which, therefore, can be fairly accurately forecast ⟨*periodic* epidemics⟩ ⟨*periodic* appearances of a comet⟩ ⟨brought about *periodic* inspection of the markets, hotels, and restaurants—*G. M. Lewis*⟩ Something is **alternate** which is both intermittent and recurrent, each in turn with something else. When applied to two contrasted or different things, *alternate* implies a succession of one after the other ⟨*alternate* smiles and tears⟩ ⟨*alternate* work and play⟩ ⟨*alternate* stripes of orange and green⟩ ⟨a dismal day of *alternate* calms and black squalls—*Nordhoff & Hall*⟩ When applied to things of the same kind or description that follow each other in serial order, *alternate* means every other one ⟨the class meets on *alternate* days of the week, beginning Tuesday⟩ ⟨the *alternate* stripes are narrow and white⟩ ⟨each of the others are active on *alternate* weeks, leaving half their time available for their customary private work—*Wagley*⟩

*Ana* interrupted, checked, arrested (see ARREST *vb*): *fitful, spasmodic: sporadic, occasional, *infrequent: discontinuing *or* discontinuous, stopping, quitting (see corresponding verbs at STOP)

*Ant* incessant, continual —*Con* continuous, constant, perpetual (see CONTINUAL): *everlasting, unceasing, interminable

**intern** *vb* *imprison, immure, incarcerate, jail

A colon (:) separates groups of words discriminated. An asterisk (*) indicates place of treatment of each group.

*Ana* confine, circumscribe, restrict, *limit: *restrain, curb, check: fetter, manacle, shackle, *hamper
*Con* release, liberate, *free
**internal** interior, intestine, *inner, inward, inside
*Ana* intrinsic, constitutional, *inherent, essential
*Ant* external —*Con* exterior, *outer, outward, outside: extraneous, *extrinsic, foreign, alien
**internuncio** nuncio, legate, *ambassador, minister, envoy, chargé d'affaires
**interpenetrate** impenetrate, penetrate, *permeate, pervade, impregnate, saturate
*Ana* see those at IMPENETRATE
**interpolate** insert, intercalate, *introduce, insinuate, interpose, interject
*Ana* *enter, introduce, admit: *intrude, interlope: *add, superadd, annex, append
*Con* delete, expunge, *erase, cancel
**interpose 1** interject, *introduce, insert, insinuate, interpolate, intercalate
*Ana* *throw, toss, cast: *intrude, obtrude: *push, shove, thrust
**2** Interpose, interfere, intervene, mediate, intercede all basically mean to come or to go between two persons, two things, or a person and thing. **Interpose** (see also INTRODUCE 2) may be used in place of any of the succeeding words largely because it carries no further implications, except as these are derived from the context ⟨the tops of the trees behind him *interposed* between him and the sun— *Forester*⟩ ⟨he should not *interpose* between other engineers and their clients when unsolicited—*Wagner*⟩ ⟨our host . . . *interposed* and forbade the experiment, pleading at the same time for a change of subject—*Shaw*⟩ **Interfere** (see also MEDDLE) implies a getting in the way of a person or thing whether by crossing his or its path or, more often, by creating a condition that hinders his movement, activity, or vision or its free operation or full effectiveness ⟨parliament *interfered* to protect employers against their laborers—*Froude*⟩ ⟨the atmospheric disturbance *interfered* with radio reception⟩ ⟨wooden palings that did not *interfere* with a wide view—*Mackenzie*⟩ **Intervene** may be used with reference to something that interposes itself or is interposed between things in space or time ⟨a huge and at that time apparently barren waste . . . *intervenes* between the St. Lawrence basin and the fertile prairie—*Sandwell*⟩ ⟨the events of the *intervening* years— *Dewey*⟩ or between persons ⟨the interjection of a third party who has a valid interest, or who *intervenes* between the physician and the patient—*W. T. & Barbara Fitts*⟩ or between a person and his interests, work, or goal ⟨the trained self-consciousness, which . . . *intervenes* between the poet's moods and his poetry—*Day Lewis*⟩ ⟨fortunately, mercy and diplomacy *intervened* and the vengeful sentence was never carried out—*Thruelsen*⟩ **Mediate** often specifically implies intervention between those who are hostile, antagonistic, or otherwise opposed to each other, for the sake of reconciling them or settling their difficulties; *mediate* usually implies, as *intervene* need not imply, an interest in both sides or freedom from bias toward either side ⟨Bacon attempted to *mediate* between his friend and the Queen—*Macaulay*⟩ ⟨I want to *mediate* between the two of you now, because if this breach continues it will be the ruin of us all—*Graves*⟩ But *mediate* may also be used abstractly in reference to something that lies between extremes or contradictories and effects either their union or a transition between them ⟨critics . . . who *mediated* between extreme points of view—*Glicksberg*⟩ **Intercede** implies intervention on another's behalf and usually an offender's behalf and the use of one's good offices in imploring mercy or forgiveness for him from the one who

has been injured or offended ⟨for each at utter need— true comrade and true foeman—Madonna, *intercede*!— *Kipling*⟩ ⟨the Duchess of Aiguillon *interceded* for Marie de Médicis with Richelieu⟩ ⟨the conviction that the Western powers would not *intercede* in favor of the peoples of the satellites—*Timasheff*⟩
*Ana* *intrude, butt in, interlope: *meddle, intermeddle: interrupt (see ARREST)
**interpret** elucidate, construe, *explain, expound, explicate
*Ana* illustrate, *exemplify: gloss, *annotate: comment, commentate (see REMARK *vb*)
*Con* distort, contort, *deform: *misrepresent, garble: *mistake, confuse, confound
**interrogate** question, catechize, quiz, examine, *ask, query, inquire
*Con* *answer, reply, respond, rejoin, retort
**interrupt** *arrest, check
*Ana* suspend, stay, intermit, *defer, postpone: *intrude, obtrude, interlope, butt in: interfere, *interpose, intervene
**interruption** *break, gap, interval, interim, hiatus, lacuna
*Ana* *pause, recess, respite, lull, intermission: *breach, rupture, rent, split, rift
**interstice** *aperture, orifice
**interval** *break, gap, interruption, interim, hiatus, lacuna
*Ana* *period, epoch, age, era: *pause, respite, lull, intermission, recess: distance, remoteness, removedness (see corresponding adjectives at DISTANT): *aperture, interstice, orifice
**intervene** *interpose, mediate, intercede, interfere
*Ana* *separate, part, divide, sever: *intrude, interlope, butt in, obtrude
**intestine** internal, *inner, interior, inside
*Ant* foreign —*Con* external, *outer, exterior, outside, outward: extraneous, alien, *extrinsic
**intimate** *vb* *suggest, imply, hint, insinuate
*Ana* *indicate, betoken, attest, bespeak: allude, advert, *refer
*Con* *express, voice, utter, vent, air: declare, *assert, affirm, aver, avouch, profess: *suppress, repress: conceal, *hide
**intimate** *adj* *familiar, close, confidential, chummy, thick
*Ana* *nearest, next: devoted, fond, affectionate, *loving: *secret, privy: friendly, neighborly (see AMICABLE): companionable, convivial, *social, hospitable, cooperative
*Con* formal, conventional, ceremonious, *ceremonial: *distant, remote
**intimate** *n* *friend, confidant, acquaintance
*Ana* comrade, companion, crony, *associate
*Ant* stranger, outsider

**intimidate,** cow, bulldoze, bully, browbeat are comparable when meaning to frighten or coerce by frightening means into submission or obedience. **Intimidate** primarily implies a making timid or fearful, but it often suggests a display or application (as of force or learning) so as to cause fear or a sense of inferiority and a consequent submission ⟨a musket was, therefore, fired over them, but . . . they seemed rather to be provoked than *intimidated*—*Cook*⟩ ⟨he wasn't lazy, he wasn't a fool, and he meant to be honest; but he was *intimidated* by that miserable sort of departmental life—*Cather*⟩ ⟨the Democrats were attempting to impeach President Grant for alleged misuse of the military to *intimidate* voters—*Woodward*⟩ **Cow** implies reduction to a state where the spirit is broken or all courage is lost ⟨he flung them back, commanded them, *cowed* them with his hard, intelligent eyes, like a tamer among beasts—*Arthur Morrison*⟩ ⟨youthful hearers who might be disillusioned or *cowed* by recent history—*J. M. Brown*⟩ **Bulldoze** implies an intimidating or an overcoming of resistance usually by forceful demanding or urging or

by implied threats ⟨a mean, stingy, *bulldozing* poseur with woodchuck whiskers—*Pegler*⟩ ⟨through the sheer strength of his reputation and the force of his will *bulldozing* them into making loans—*F. L. Allen*⟩ ⟨some irate customer who had come in to *bulldoze* me . . . and had tried to bully me with mere words—*White*⟩ **Bully** implies intimidation through overbearing, swaggering threats or insults, and in schoolboy use it usually suggests bulldozing of small boys by those who are larger or more aggressive ⟨suppose the cabman *bullies* you for double fare—*Shaw*⟩ ⟨I know what you're going to call me . . . but I am not to be *bullied* by words—*L.P. Smith*⟩ **Browbeat** implies a cowing through arrogant, scornful, contemptuous, or insolent treatment ⟨he *browbeat* the informers against us, and treated their evidence with . . . little favor—*Fielding*⟩ ⟨who saw my old kind parents . . . too much trustful . . . cheated, *browbeaten*, stripped and starved, cast out into the kennel—*Browning*⟩
*Ana* terrorize, terrify, *frighten: hector, hound, ride, chivy, *bait, badger: coerce, *force, compel, constrain, oblige
*Con* *coax, wheedle, cajole, blandish: persuade, prevail, *induce

**intolerant** *illiberal, narrow-minded, narrow, bigoted, hidebound
*Ana* obdurate, *inflexible: *antipathetic, unsympathetic, averse
*Ant* tolerant —*Con* *forbearing, indulgent, lenient
**intonation** *inflection, accent
**intone** *sing, troll, carol, descant, warble, trill, hymn, chant
**intoxicated** *drunk, drunken, inebriated, tipsy, tight
*Ana* fuddled, befuddled, confused, muddled (see CONFUSE): maudlin, *sentimental
*Con* *sober, temperate
**intractable** *unruly, ungovernable, refractory, recalcitrant, willful, headstrong
*Ana* obstreperous, boisterous (see VOCIFEROUS): contumacious, rebellious, factious, *insubordinate: froward, perverse, *contrary, wayward, balky
*Ant* tractable —*Con* *obedient, docile, biddable, amenable: *tame, submissive, subdued: *compliant, acquiescent
**intrepid** *brave, courageous, unafraid, fearless, valiant, valorous, dauntless, undaunted, doughty, bold, audacious
*Ana* daring, venturesome, *adventurous, daredevil: mettlesome, high-spirited, *spirited, fiery: plucky, gritty (see corresponding nouns at FORTITUDE)
*Con* timorous, *timid: *fearful, apprehensive, afraid
**intricate** complicated, involved, *complex, knotty
*Ana* perplexing, puzzling, mystifying, bewildering (see PUZZLE *vb*): tortuous (see WINDING): difficult, *hard, arduous
*Con* *easy, simple, light, smooth, facile, effortless: obvious, plain, clear, patent, *evident, manifest
**intrigue** *n* 1 conspiracy, machination, *plot, cabal
*Ana* scheme, design, *plan: stratagem, maneuver, ruse, artifice, *trick, feint, gambit, ploy
2 liaison, affair, *amour
**intriguing** *interesting, engrossing, absorbing
*Ana* provoking *or* provocative, piquing, exciting (see corresponding verbs at PROVOKE): mystifying, puzzling (see PUZZLE): luring, tempting, enticing, inveigling (see LURE)
**intrinsic** *inherent, ingrained, constitutional, essential
*Ana* *inner, inward, internal, interior, inside, intestine: *innate, inborn, inbred, congenital: natural, normal, typical, *regular
*Ant* extrinsic —*Con* *outer, outward, external, outside, exterior: adventitious, *accidental, incidental: added, annexed, appended, superadded (see ADD): extraneous,

alien, foreign (see EXTRINSIC)
**introduce** 1 *enter, admit
*Ana* induct, install, inaugurate (see INITIATE): instill, inculcate, *implant: *infuse, inoculate, imbue
**2 Introduce, insert, insinuate, interpolate, intercalate, interpose, interject** mean to put something or someone in a place among or between other things or persons. **Introduce** (see also ENTER 2) implies a bringing forward of someone or something not already in company with the other persons or things, but it also suggests as the aim of such an act the placing of the person or thing in the midst of that group or collection so as to form a part of it ⟨*introduce* a new subject into the conversation⟩ ⟨*introduce* several amendments into a bill before the legislature⟩ ⟨domestic science was *introduced* into the high school curriculum—*Current Biog.*⟩ **Insert** implies a setting of a thing in a fixed place between or among other things; thus, to *insert* lace in a garment is to put it between two pieces of the material which forms the garment; to *insert* leaves in a book is to put leaves into their proper places (as by the use of glue) ⟨*insert* additional words in a statement⟩ ⟨nowhere else, surely, can there be such a compulsion to make plays out of books, musicals out of plays . . . to *insert* scenes, delete characters—*Kronenberger*⟩ **Insinuate** (see also SUGGEST) implies a slow, careful, often gentle or artful introduction (as into or through a narrow or winding passage) by pushing or worming its or one's way ⟨the dog liked to *insinuate* his nose into his master's closed hand⟩ ⟨slang . . . has to *insinuate* itself into the language; it cannot pressure or push its way in—*Sat. Review*⟩ ⟨trees which *insinuate* their roots into the fissures of nearby rocks⟩ ⟨slowly but surely they *insinuated* themselves through the crowd to the edge of the pavement⟩ ⟨he couldn't quite *insinuate* the Huntingtons into American society, but he did pretty well for them in England—*Behrman*⟩ **Interpolate** implies the insertion of something that does not belong to and requires to be distinguished from the original, whether because it is extraneous to the subject under discussion or because it is spurious or simply because it is in fact not part of the original ⟨although here and there, I omit some passages, and shorten others and disguise names, I have *interpolated* nothing—*Le Fanu*⟩ ⟨he has *interpolated* editorial and critical comments of his own—*Redman*⟩ **Intercalate** primarily implies an insertion in the calendar (as of a day or month) ⟨since the calendar year contained only 355 days, an extra month was occasionally *intercalated*—*R. H. Baker*⟩ but in its extended sense it implies insertion into a sequence or series, then often also connoting intrusion ⟨lava beds *intercalated* between sedimentary layers of rock⟩ ⟨some of these discrepancies . . . are obviously due to the fact that Chaucer is *intercalating* stories previously written—*H. S. Bennett*⟩ **Interpose** (see also INTERPOSE 2) differs from *interpolate* mainly in its implication that what is inserted serves as an obstacle, obstruction, or cause of delay or postponement ⟨she actually *interposed* her body between him and the street door then, as though physically to prevent him from going—*Ferber*⟩ ⟨the early Church fought against the tendency to *interpose* objects of worship between God and man—*Inge*⟩ ⟨Professor Murray has simply *interposed* between Euripides and ourselves a barrier more impenetrable than the Greek language—*T.S. Eliot*⟩ Of all of these words, **interject** carries the strongest implication of abrupt or forced introduction ⟨he remained silent for the most part but occasionally *interjected* a question⟩ ⟨as they chewed on bones and roots, they paused to *interject* grunts of encouragement for the narrator—*Mott*⟩ The word is often employed in place of *said* in introducing a remark, statement, or ques-

---

A colon (:) separates groups of words discriminated. An asterisk (*) indicates place of treatment of each group.

tion that comes more or less as an interruption or addition ⟨when he was talking about philosophers, I *interjected* what I feel confident was a tactful remark—*Henderson*⟩ *Ant* withdraw: abstract —*Con* \*eject, oust, evict: eliminate, \*exclude

**introduction,** prologue, prelude, preface, foreword, exordium, preamble are comparable when denoting something that serves as a preliminary or as an antecedent to an extended treatment, development, discussion, or presentation (as in an exposition, a dramatic or musical work, or a poem). In their extended senses many of these terms are interchangeable, but in the special or technical senses in which they are here chiefly considered they tend to be mutually exclusive. **Introduction,** the ordinary term of this group, and the comprehensive one, specifically applies to that part of a work (as a discourse, treatise, play, or musical composition) which prepares the reader or auditor for the body of the work, especially by giving him material necessary for his understanding of what follows ⟨he always writes the body of his treatise first and then adds the *introduction* and conclusion⟩ **Prologue** applies specifically to the initial and distinct part of a poetic or dramatic work which may serve the purposes of an introduction (as by describing the characters or expounding the situations in which they find themselves) ⟨Chaucer's *Prologue* to the *Canterbury Tales*⟩ or which may be a discourse preceding the opening of a play, by a character of the play or by an actor who serves as a mouthpiece for the author, and giving a hint of the author's purposes or methods or attempting to attract the auditors' attention to or interest in the play to come ⟨the *Prologue* to Shakespeare's *Troilus and Cressida* and to each act of his *King Henry V*⟩ ⟨in his *prologue*, which contains some of the finest poetry-in-prose writing of our day, Dr. MacIver explores the meaning of time —*Donald Harrington*⟩ In its extended use, therefore, *prologue* often suggests an action or an event that sets the stage or paves the way for a series of exploits, achievements, or significant events ⟨this as a *prologue* to her own later dazzling history—*Hugh Walpole*⟩ **Prelude** applies in its general sense to something (as a series of events, actions, or natural phenomena) which constitute figuratively a short play or performance and serve as a sign or indication of or a preparation for what is to follow ⟨functional changes in glands often serve as a *prelude* to structural changes⟩ ⟨that was the *prelude* to a stormy afternoon—*H. G. Wells*⟩ As a technical term in music *prelude* applies sometimes to an opening voluntary in a religious service but more often, and more specifically, to an introductory piece forming a section or a movement, especially of a fugue or a suite but sometimes of an oratorio or of an opera, and serving usually to introduce the theme or chief subject of the work. In this sense *prelude* applies sometimes to musical, or occasionally other, works which have something of the character of an introductory section or movement but are so constructed that they have intrinsic and independent value ⟨Wordsworth's poem "The *Prelude*"⟩ In ecclesiastical use **preface** applies to the prayer of exhortation to thanksgiving and of divine praise which opens the important part of a solemn Eucharistic service where the consecration of the bread and wine occurs. In its more common general sense *preface* applies specifically to a short discourse which is distinct from the literary work (as a treatise, a novel, a poem or collection of poems) which follows, is written usually by the author but sometimes by an editor or a friend, and has for its main purpose either to put the reader into the right frame of mind for the understanding or appreciation of the work he is about to read or to supply him with information that

may be necessary to his proper understanding or use of it. When, however, a work is preceded by both a preface and an introduction, *preface* is usually applied to the introductory discourse written, and often also signed, by the author or editor, and *introduction* to the one which is definitely informative rather than personal in its character and usually carries no signature. In extended use *preface* may apply to something which serves as an introduction or prelude (as an introductory work on or a more or less tentative treatment of a subject) ⟨Walter Lippmann's book entitled *A Preface to Morals*⟩ or to an act or speech, or series of acts or speeches, which has no other purpose than to prepare the way for what is to follow ⟨they walked in the rose garden. "Do you read Utopias?" said Mr. Direck, cutting any *preface*, in the English manner—*H. G. Wells*⟩ ⟨we fight for lost causes because we know that our defeat and dismay may be the *preface* to our successor's victory—*T. S. Eliot*⟩ **Foreword** when used in place of *preface* in reference to front matter of a book may suggest simplicity and brevity of treatment and more often than not applies to material prepared by someone other than the author. **Exordium,** a technical term of rhetoric, applies to a formal beginning, especially of an oration but sometimes of a written exposition or argument, in which the speaker or writer makes an approach to his subject by remarks intended to awaken the interest of his auditors or readers and to pave the way for their understanding of what he is to say or for their acceptance of his conclusions. **Preamble** applies to a formal introduction, often only an introductory paragraph (as in a statute, a constitution, a treaty, a deed, or a set of resolutions) which states the grounds, purposes, or guiding principles of what follows. It is sometimes used as a designation of a long monotonous preface.

**introductory** *adj* \*preliminary, preparatory, prefatory *Ant* closing, concluding

**intrude,** obtrude, interlope, butt in are comparable when meaning to thrust oneself or something in without invitation or authorization. **Intrude** both transitively and intransitively carries a strong implication of forcing someone or something in without leave, without right, or against the will of others; it often connotes rudeness, officiousness, or invasion of another's property, time, or personal privacy ⟨this court always had disavowed the right to *intrude* its judgment upon questions of policy or morals—*Justice Holmes*⟩ ⟨Sergeant Lumley, unfairly *intruding* his official superiority into this theological discussion —*Sayers*⟩ ⟨I stood there, feeling very abashed at *intruding* on all these busy people—*Mannix*⟩ **Obtrude** in this relation retains much of its basic notion of pushing or extending something into view; it may imply nothing beyond this fact ⟨I intended plain prose, but a rhyme *obtruded* itself and I became poetical—*Cowper*⟩ or it may suggest the impropriety and objectionableness of the act or the disagreeableness of the offense ⟨the first sin against style as against good manners is to *obtrude* or exploit personality—*Quiller-Couch*⟩ **Interlope** implies an interposition of oneself in a place or position which has an injurious effect on one or both of the persons or things concerned ⟨he regarded her new acquaintance as an *interloping* rival for her hand⟩ ⟨he dealt with the Communists as a Groton football coach with a bunch of *interloping* ruffians who don't know the rules of the game—*Time*⟩ **Butt in** implies an abrupt or offensive intrusion suggestive of the manner in which a horned animal attacks its enemy; in this sense the term usually suggests absence of ceremony, a sense of propriety, or decent restraint ⟨it's a thankless job to *butt in* and tell a man that in your important opinion his wife is a vampire bat—*Sinclair Lewis*⟩

---

*Ana* analogous words    *Ant* antonyms    *Con* contrasted words    See also explanatory notes facing page 1

⟨he left behind a big, white turkey gobbler. It would *butt in* when we fed the horses and was a general nuisance— *Siberts*⟩
*Ana* *trespass, invade, encroach, entrench, infringe: interject, interpose, insinuate, interpolate, intercalate, *introduce: interfere, intervene, *interpose: *meddle, intermeddle, interfere, tamper
*Ant* stand off —*Con* withdraw, retire (see GO): retreat, *recede

**intrusive** *impertinent, officious, meddlesome, obtrusive
*Ana* intruding, butting in, interloping, obtruding (see INTRUDE): inquisitive, prying, snoopy, nosy, *curious: interfering, meddling, intermeddling (see MEDDLE)
*Ant* retiring: unintrusive —*Con* diffident, bashful, modest, coy, *shy

**intuition** 1 understanding, *reason
*Ana* intellect, soul, *mind: insight, acumen, *discernment
*Ant* ratiocination —*Con* *inference
2 instinct (see under INSTINCTIVE)

**intuitive** *instinctive
*Ana* immediate, *direct
*Ant* ratiocinative —*Con* inferential (see under INFERENCE)

**inundation** *flood, deluge, torrent, spate, cataract

**inure** *habituate, accustom, addict
*Ana* *adapt, adjust, accommodate

**invade** encroach, *trespass, entrench, infringe
*Ana* *intrude, obtrude, butt in, interlope: *enter, penetrate, pierce, probe: *permeate, pervade, impenetrate, interpenetrate

**invalidate** *nullify, negate, annul, abrogate
*Ana* negative, counteract, *neutralize: void, vacate, quash, *annul
*Ant* validate —*Con* *enforce, implement

**invaluable** priceless, precious, valuable, dear, *costly, expensive
*Ant* worthless

**invasion, incursion, raid, inroad** are comparable when meaning an entrance effected by force or strategy. **Invasion** basically implies entrance upon another's territory with such hostile intentions as conquest, plunder, or use as a basis of operations ⟨the Roman *invasion* of Britain⟩ ⟨in a well-planned Hitlerian *invasion* there is at first no shooting save by those who are taking their own lives—*New Republic*⟩ In nonmilitary use it may imply encroachment, trespass, or an intrusion that involves an aggressive or hostile purpose ⟨I was forced by my duty to the Constitution to refuse to answer on the grounds that it was an *invasion* of a citizen's basic rights—*Driscoll*⟩ ⟨the alarmist takes every sound as an *invasion* by burglars —*Fishbein*⟩ Sometimes it implies no more than entrance with or as if with a rush by a horde or crowd ⟨the annual *invasion* of the Connecticut suburbs by what its victims call "the summer people" is complete—*Weidman*⟩ **Incursion,** especially in military use, carries a stronger connotation of suddenness, unexpectedness, or haste than *invasion;* it often also suggests an immediate end and a quick withdrawal when the end is achieved ⟨the American colonists were in constant fear of *incursions* by the Indians⟩ ⟨English intruders landed at Golfo Dulce in 1684, made an *incursion* inland, and retired—*Jones*⟩ In its extended sense *incursion* applies chiefly to an invasion in large numbers of something dreaded or harmful, undesirable, but not necessarily inimical ⟨the peace of the neighborhood was frequently broken by *incursions* of gangs of small boys⟩ ⟨the barrier should have been sufficient to protect the adjoining owner against the *incursions,* not of all pigs, but of pigs of "average vigor and obstinacy"— *Cardozo*⟩ **Raid,** frequent in military use for a swift, sudden invasion (as of cavalry or of air forces) may or may not suggest more preparation, more strategy, and more fury in attack than *incursion,* its close synonym ⟨the *raids* in the Shenandoah Valley by Forrest's Confederate cavalry during 1863⟩ ⟨nightly bombing *raids* on London⟩ In international law, however, *raid* is applicable specifically to an incursion of armed forces that are unauthorized or unrecognized by any state into a country that is at peace; thus, an *incursion* of armed persons on one side of a border or boundary line into the adjoining country for a predatory or hostile purpose is technically a *raid.* In its extended use *raid* applies to a sudden descent or a flurry of activity intended usually to obtain the use, control, or possession of something; thus, officers of the law conduct a *raid* upon a gambling resort or a place where liquor is illicitly made or sold to obtain evidence and arrest offenders ⟨the *raids* of government and industry on college personnel, especially in the fields of science —*J. R. Butler*⟩ ⟨before the last *raid* on the railroads by the various unions—*Arden*⟩ **Inroad** may apply to a sudden hostile incursion or a forcible entering ⟨aggressive war, as distinguished from mere plundering *inroads* —*Freeman*⟩ ⟨protecting their crops of barley from the *inroads* of sparrows—*Frazer*⟩ but the term is also applied to an invasion that involves encroachment or advance especially at the expense of someone or something ⟨foil and plastic are making *inroads* where glass once held undisputed sway—*Ericson*⟩ ⟨activities that make *inroads* upon his time and his health⟩
*Ana* aggression, *attack, offense, offensive: trespass, violation, transgression, infringement, infraction, *breach: intruding *or* intrusion, interloping, butting in, obtruding *or* obtrusion (see corresponding verbs at INTRUDE): encroachment, entrenchment (see corresponding verbs at TRESPASS)

**invective** *abuse, vituperation, obloquy, scurrility, billingsgate
*Ana* vilifying *or* vilification, maligning, calumniation, traducing (see corresponding verbs at MALIGN): *animadversion, stricture, aspersion, reflection

**inveigle** decoy, entice, *lure, tempt, seduce
*Ana* snare, ensnare, trap, entrap (see CATCH): beguile, mislead, delude, *deceive, betray: cajole, wheedle, blandish, *coax

**invent** 1 *contrive, devise, frame, concoct
*Ana* initiate, inaugurate (see BEGIN): institute, *found, establish
2 **Invent, create, discover** are comparable terms frequently confused in the sense of to bring into being something new. **Invent** (see also CONTRIVE) may stress fabrication of something new through the exercise of the imagination ⟨a poet is a maker, as the word signifies: and he who cannot make, that is, *invent*, hath his name for nothing— *Dryden*⟩ ⟨his fund of knowledge seemed inexhaustible, for what he didn't know he *invented*—*Alvin Redman*⟩ ⟨the little stories she had *invented* for her two small daughters—*Current Biog.*⟩ or it may stress the fabrication of something new and often useful as a result of study and thought; the word therefore often presupposes labor and ingenuity rather than inspiration ⟨if the Semitic letters were not derived from Egypt they must have been *invented* by the Phoenicians—*Clodd*⟩ However, *invent* often stresses the finding, as well as the bringing into being, of something new or hitherto unknown as the result of mental effort ⟨physicists had to save the laws of conservation of energy and conservation of angular momentum . . . a new particle had to be *invented*—*Marshak*⟩ ⟨she was tired of *inventing* means for making the days and nights pleasant and capriciously variable for

others—*Van Vechten*⟩ **Create** stresses a causing of something to exist; it not only implies previous nonexistence but it often suggests an evoking of something into being out of, or as if out of, nothing (as by fiat, by an act of the will, or by inspiration) ⟨God *created* the heaven and the earth—*Gen* 1:1⟩ ⟨the law *creates* rights⟩ ⟨the king *created* an earldom for his favorite⟩ ⟨to this strange force within him, to this power that *created* his works of art, there was nothing to do but submit—*Huxley*⟩ ⟨I do not believe that a sense of justice is innate, but I have been astonished to see how quickly it can be *created*— *Russell*⟩ ⟨modern science, which *created* this dilemma, is also capable of solving it—*Bliven* b. 1889⟩ **Discover** (see also DISCOVER 2; REVEAL) presupposes both the existence of and a lack of knowledge about something; the term therefore implies the finding of such a thing, often as the result of mental or physical effort (as by exploration, investigation, or experiment) ⟨remains of this Belgic culture have often been *discovered*—*Jacquetta & Christopher Hawkes*⟩ ⟨men who were fighting Communism long before McCarthy ever *discovered* it—*Davis*⟩ ⟨William Harvey *discovered* the circulation of the blood⟩ Thus, in discriminative use one *invents* processes or ways of doing something, as well as instruments, tools, implements, or machines, but one *discovers* things which exist but have not yet been known (as lands, stars, or natural laws) ⟨Newton *invented* the differential and the integral calculus . . . and *discovered* the laws of motion— *Darrow*⟩
*Ana* fabricate, fashion, form, shape, forge, *make: imagine, conceive, envision (see THINK): design, project, plan, plot, scheme (see under PLAN *n*): produce, turn out (see BEAR)
**inventory** *n* *list, register, schedule, catalog, table, roll, roster
**invert** *vb* transpose, *reverse
*Ana* upset, *overturn, capsize: interchange, *exchange: derange, disarrange (see DISORDER *vb*)
**invest** 1 induct, install, inaugurate, *initiate
*Ana* endue, endow (see DOWER): consecrate (see DEVOTE)
*Ant* divest, strip (*of robes, insignia, power*): unfrock
2 *besiege, beleaguer, blockade
**investigation** probe, inquest, inquisition, *inquiry, research
*Ana* inspection, examination, scrutiny, audit (see under SCRUTINIZE): surveying *or* survey, observing *or* observation (see corresponding verbs at SEE)
**inveterate, confirmed, chronic, deep-seated, deep-rooted** are comparable when meaning so firmly established or settled that change is almost impossible. **Inveterate** applies especially to something which has persisted so long and so obstinately that it has become a fixed habit or an almost inalterable custom or tradition ⟨the growing infirmities of age manifest themselves in nothing more strongly than in an *inveterate* dislike of interruption—*Lamb*⟩ ⟨supported by precedent so *inveterate* that the chance of abandonment is small—*Cardozo*⟩ When applied to a person, the term implies the formation of a seemingly ineradicable habit, attitude, or way of acting or behaving ⟨an *inveterate* smoker⟩ ⟨an *inveterate* and formidable foe—*Peacock*⟩ **Confirmed** applies chiefly to something which has grown stronger or firmer with time until it resists all attack or assault or attempts to uproot it ⟨a *confirmed* belief in God⟩ ⟨a *confirmed* hatred of a person⟩ ⟨not so easy to say that a *confirmed* anti-American mood has settled on the British people—*Barbara Ward*⟩ Like *inveterate,* it may also apply to a person who is such as he is described in the noun by the strengthening or crystallization of a taste, a vice or virtue, or an attitude ⟨a *confirmed* bache-

lor⟩ ⟨a *confirmed* invalid⟩ ⟨*confirmed* do-gooders always end by doing good by coercion—*Mortimer Smith*⟩ **Chronic** also implies long duration, but it applies either to diseases, habits, or conditions which persist without marked interruption in spite of attempts to alleviate or to cure them or to the persons who are afflicted or affected by such diseases, habits, or conditions ⟨his *chronic* state of mental restlessness—*George Eliot*⟩ ⟨*chronic* bronchitis⟩ ⟨hysterical with failure and repeated disappointment and *chronic* proverty—*Huxley*⟩ ⟨the working scientist . . . must steer a middle course between *chronic* indecision and precipitant judgment—*Eddington*⟩ ⟨a *chronic* faultfinder⟩ **Deep-seated** and **deep-rooted** in their extended senses emphasize rather the extent to which something has entered into the structure or texture of the thing (as a person's body or mind or a people's nature) in which it becomes fixed or embedded ⟨the old, dependent, chaotic, haphazard pioneer instinct of his childhood [was] so *deep-seated*, that . . . he slipped back into the boy he had been before—*Brooks*⟩ ⟨a *deep-rooted* reverence for truth—*John Morley*⟩ ⟨Wagner's bond with this woman was much stronger, more *deep-rooted* and lasting than one had thought—*Heller*⟩
*Ana* habituated, accustomed, addicted (see HABITUATE): habitual, customary, *usual: *hardened, indurated: settled, set, fixed, established (see SET): inbred, *innate: persisting *or* persistent, enduring, abiding (see corresponding verbs at CONTINUE)
**invidious** distasteful, obnoxious, *repugnant, repellent, abhorrent
*Ana* *hateful, odious, abominable, detestable: *offensive, loathsome, revolting, repulsive
*Con* agreeable, gratifying, grateful, pleasing, *pleasant: attractive, alluring, fascinating (see under ATTRACT): enticing, tempting, seducing *or* seductive (see corresponding verbs at LURE)
**invigorate** *strengthen, fortify, energize, reinforce
*Ana* *renew, restore, refresh, rejuvenate: *stir, rally, rouse: *vitalize, activate
*Ant* debilitate —*Con* *weaken, enfeeble, disable
**invincible, unconquerable, indomitable, impregnable, inexpugnable, unassailable, invulnerable** mean proof against attack or defeat. A person or thing is *invincible* or *unconquerable* that presents insuperable difficulties to his or its being overcome or displaced; **invincible**, however, usually implies a quality or character in the person or thing which makes him or it actually or seemingly incapable of being vanquished; **unconquerable** implies rather the fact of having successfully resisted all attempts at subdual or mastery ⟨a resolute, yet not *invincible*, skepticism—*Flew*⟩ ⟨is He still mythologically *invincible*? If He is bound to take up the Devil's challenge, is He equally bound to win the ensuing battle?—*Toynbee*⟩ ⟨he made plan after plan; but each one was discarded because he saw it would encounter *invincible* selfishness, or *invincible* self-sacrifice—*Deland*⟩ ⟨seems to create *unconquerable* difficulties in man's life—*Salisbury*⟩ ⟨the iron face of those men of empire and *unconquerable* will, those Caesars and Napoleons—*L. P. Smith*⟩ A person or a human quality (as mind, will, or energy) is **indomitable** that stubbornly and determinedly resists all attempts to gain mastery over or discourage him or it or endures seemingly insuperable difficulties with fortitude until they are overcome ⟨*indomitable* courage⟩ ⟨an *indomitable* will⟩ ⟨*indomitable* energy⟩ ⟨founding colonies . . . or exploring in crazy pinnaces the fierce latitudes of the polar seas—they are the same *indomitable* God-fearing men—*Froude*⟩ ⟨two centuries of Roman persistence were required to subdue the *indomitable* Iberians

---

*Ana* analogous words  *Ant* antonyms  *Con* contrasted words  See also explanatory notes facing page 1

*—H. O. Taylor⟩* Something material (as a fortress) or intangible (as virtue) is **impregnable** when it is strong enough or sufficiently guarded to repel all attacks or assaults ⟨there is no such thing as *impregnable* defense against powerful aggressors who sneak up in the dark and strike without warning—*Roosevelt*⟩ ⟨Cato . . . was a fanatic, *impregnable* to argument, and not to be influenced by temptation—*Froude*⟩ ⟨there was always a traitor in the citadel; and after he (or generally she) had surrendered the keys, what was the use of pretending that it was *impregnable?*—*Wharton*⟩ A thing is **inexpugnable** or **unassailable** either because it is impregnable or because it offers no point at which it can be attacked or no occasion or reason (as a weakness or a defect) for attacking or impugning ⟨castles were often built at the tops of craggy mountains in the hope that they might be *inexpugnable*⟩ ⟨that we are conscious, sentient, evaluating and thinking creatures . . . is an *inexpugnable* fact of existence —*Nagel*⟩ ⟨nothing but an *unassailable* alibi would save them—*Stong*⟩ ⟨an argument so logical and convincing that it is *unassailable*⟩ A person or thing is **invulnerable** that cannot be wounded or penetrated by a destructive weapon or piercing instrument ⟨they had lived through the Nazi plague and, having survived, were henceforth *invulnerable* to its poison—*Dean*⟩ ⟨ironclad warships were once believed to be *invulnerable*⟩ ⟨how was one to pierce such hidebound complacency? It was *invulnerable* except to the Grace of God—*Mackenzie*⟩
**Ana** dauntless, undaunted, intrepid (see BRAVE)
**Con** conquerable, vanquishable, surmountable, subduable (see corresponding verbs at CONQUER)
**inviolable** inviolate, *sacred, sacrosanct
**Ana** hallowed, consecrated, dedicated (see DEVOTE): *holy, sacred, blessed, divine, religious: pure, *chaste
**inviolate** sacrosanct, *sacred, inviolable
**Ant** violated —**Con** profaned, desecrated (see corresponding nouns at PROFANATION): polluted, defiled (see CONTAMINATE)
**invite, bid, solicit, court, woo** are comparable when they mean to request or encourage a person or a thing to come to one or to fall in with one's plans or desires. **Invite** in its ordinary and usual sense implies a courteous request to go somewhere, do something, or give some assistance which it is assumed will be agreeable or at least not disagreeable to the person invited ⟨*invite* a few friends to dinner⟩ ⟨*invite* an acquaintance to spend the night⟩ ⟨*invite* an audience to express their opinions⟩ ⟨he had *invited* all the girls, including Miss Tolman, to go out with him on various occasions, but . . . everyone declined his offer—*Woodfin*⟩ In this sense the word usually implies providing an opening for those who otherwise might hesitate to go, or do, or give without such a request. Consequently, in its extended sense *invite* implies providing an opening by such means as a seductive manner or a challenging statement or policy that serves as an encouragement or temptation to another ⟨dress so conspicuously as to *invite* unwelcome attentions⟩ ⟨fairly imminent collisions *invited* by the Captain's inept conning —*Heggen*⟩ ⟨the writer who brings a new revelation is not necessarily called upon to *invite* the execration of the herd—*Ellis*⟩ **Bid** (see also COMMAND *vb*) is increasingly uncommon in the sense of to request the presence of (as at a feast or great occasion) ⟨as many as ye shall find, *bid* to the marriage—*Mt* 22:9⟩ but *bid* (usually with *for*), from its sense to offer a price for something up for sale, has developed an extended use in which it means to make an effort to win or attract or an appeal (as for sympathy) and in this use sometimes comes close to *invite* in conveying the notion of offering a tempting opening

for something ⟨in his difficult position he could not *bid* for their affection; he wanted only their obedience—*Douglas*⟩ ⟨stood for Congress in this virgin district, *bidding* for the support of labor—*Green Peyton*⟩ **Solicit** (see also ASK 2) differs from *invite* in stressing urgency or need rather than courtesy in requesting or encouraging ⟨we may come to feel a little impatient at having our pity so continually *solicited*—*Edmund Wilson*⟩ ⟨moral utterances which *solicit* the obedience of children—*Melden*⟩ **Court** basically implies an endeavor to win the favor of a person (as by flattery, attentions, or making love). Only in its extended sense does it imply a providing of a favorable opportunity by tempting or encouraging something to come to one or to happen to one ⟨he kept himself somewhat aloof, seeming to avoid notice rather than to *court* it—*Arnold*⟩ ⟨so long as a scientific textbook is obsolete in a decade or less, to poetize science is to *court* mortality—*Lowes*⟩ **Woo** basically implies amorous courting; consequently, in its extended sense it frequently stresses a drawing to or upon one by allurements, blandishments, and extravagant promises ⟨Herodotus in search of a public . . . found a favorable "pitch," as we should say, and *wooed* an audience to him—*Quiller-Couch*⟩ ⟨the young author trying to *woo* his reader, via lively humor—*Keene*⟩ Occasionally the word is very close to *court* and scarcely distinguishable from it ⟨you . . . *woo* your own destruction—*Shak.*⟩
**Ana** *ask, request, solicit: *lure, tempt, entice, inveigle: excite, *provoke, stimulate
**involve 1** *entangle, enmesh
**Ana** complicate (see *complicated* under COMPLEX): confuse, confound, *mistake: perplex, mystify, nonplus, *puzzle
**2** comprehend, embrace, *include, imply, subsume
**Ana** import, *mean, signify, denote: bespeak, attest, betoken, *indicate, argue, prove
**Con** eliminate, *exclude, rule out, debar
**3 Involve, implicate** mean to bring a person or thing into circumstances or a situation from which he or it is not easily freed. **Involve** (see also INCLUDE) need not impute disgrace to the circumstances or situation but it usually implies complication or entangling and often suggests extreme embarrassment ⟨the war may not end until every nation in Europe is *involved* in it⟩ ⟨the case of a judge *involved* by the exigencies of his office in a strong conflict between public duty and private interest or affection —*Colvin*⟩ ⟨had been *involved* in some affair that made it uncomfortable for him to return to live in that city—*Anderson*⟩ ⟨the controversies . . . moved on in all their ugliness to *involve* others—*J. M. Brown*⟩ **Implicate** usually implies a disgraceful connection or one that casts a reflection on a person's reputation; it may even imply definite proof of association with a crime ⟨the detectives discovered that an uncle of the child was *implicated* in its kidnapping⟩ ⟨they were unable to *implicate* any of the suspected political leaders in the conspiracy to defraud the city⟩ ⟨all men, even the most virtuous and wise, are *implicated* in historic evil—*Niebuhr*⟩
**Ana** ensnare, entrap, snare, trap (see CATCH): connect, link, associate, relate (see JOIN): *embarrass: fetter, shackle, *hamper
**Con** *extricate, disentangle, untangle, disembarrass: disengage, *detach: *free, liberate, release
**involved** intricate, complicated, knotty, *complex
**Ana** confused, muddled (see CONFUSE): perplexing, puzzling, bewildering, mystifying (see PUZZLE): difficult, *hard, arduous
**Con** simple, *easy, facile
**invulnerable** impregnable, inexpugnable, unassailable,

*invincible, unconquerable, indomitable
*Ant* vulnerable
**inward** *inner, interior, internal, inside, intestine
*Ana* inbred, *innate, inborn: ingrained, *inherent, intrinsic, constitutional: intimate, *familiar: objective, sensible, *material: heartfelt, unfeigned, *sincere: impalpable, *imperceptible
*Ant* outward —*Con* *outer, exterior, external, outside: extraneous, *extrinsic, foreign, alien: spiritual (see corresponding noun at SOUL)
**iota** jot, tittle, whit, *particle, bit, mite, smidgen, atom
**irascible, choleric, splenetic, testy, touchy, cranky, cross** mean easily angered or enraged. Irascible implies the possession of a fiery or inflammable temper or a tendency to flare up at the slightest provocation ⟨the *irascible* but kindhearted deity who indulges in copious curses to ease his feelings—*Cohen*⟩ ⟨a peppery and *irascible* old gentleman⟩ Choleric implies excitability of temper, unreasonableness in anger, and usually an impatient and uniformly irritable frame of mind ⟨that in the captain's but a *choleric* word, which in the soldier is flat blasphemy—*Shak.*⟩ ⟨a testy and *choleric* gentleman easily wrought into passion—*Cooper*⟩ Splenetic implies a similar temperament, but one especially given to moroseness and fits of bad temper which exhibit themselves in angry, sullen, or intensely peevish moods, words, or acts ⟨that *splenetic* temper, which seems to grudge brightness to the flames of hell—*Landor*⟩ ⟨he was not *splenetic:* nay, he proved in the offending volume he could be civil, courteous, chivalrous—*Meredith*⟩ Testy implies irascibility occasioned by small annoyances ⟨the *testy* major was in fume to find no hunter standing waiting—*Masefield*⟩ ⟨he raged . . . he was ever more autocratic, more *testy*—*Sinclair Lewis*⟩ Touchy suggests readiness to take offense; it often connotes undue irritability or oversensitiveness ⟨I am not *touchy* under criticism—*Stevenson*⟩ ⟨*touchy* about their own sacred symbols and alert to interpret any slight as an insult—*Blanshard*⟩ Cranky and cross often mean little more than irritable and difficult to please. But cranky may carry an implication of the possession of set notions, fixed ideas, or unvarying standards which predispose one to anger or a show of temper when others (as in their speech, conduct, requests, or work) do not conform to these standards ⟨a *cranky* critic⟩ ⟨a *cranky* employer⟩ ⟨a *cranky* teacher⟩ ⟨old age seemed to settle on me; I grew nervous, *cranky* and thin, I quarreled with the travelers—*Rosenfeld*⟩ Cross, on the other hand, may imply a being out of sorts that results in irascibility or irritability but only for the duration of one's mood ⟨sometimes, when I am *cross* and cannot sleep, I engage in angry contests with the opinions I object to—*L. P. Smith*⟩ ⟨the attempts to persuade the Intelligent Woman that she is having a glorious treat when she is in fact being . . . bored and tired out and sent home *cross* and miserable—*Shaw*⟩
*Ana* *irritable, fractious, snappish, waspish, huffy, querulous, petulant, peevish: *impatient, restive, jumpy, jittery, nervous: crabbed, surly (see SULLEN)
*Con* good-natured, *amiable, complaisant, obliging: *calm, placid, serene, tranquil
**irate** *angry, wrathful, wroth, mad, indignant, acrimonious
*Ana* provoked, exasperated, nettled, irritated (see IRRITATE): incensed, infuriated, enraged (see ANGER *vb*)
*Con* *forbearing, tolerant, clement, lenient, indulgent, merciful
**ire** rage, fury, *anger, indignation, wrath
*Ana* *passion: temper, humor, *mood
**irenic** *pacific, peaceable, peaceful, pacifist, pacifistic
*Ana* conciliating *or* conciliatory, placating *or* placatory, propitiating *or* propitiatory (see corresponding verbs at

PACIFY)
*Ant* acrimonious
**iridescent** opalescent, opaline, *prismatic
**irk** vex, *annoy, bother
*Ana* perturb, disturb, upset, *discompose: discommode, incommode, trouble, *inconvenience: fret, chafe (see ABRADE)
**irksome, tiresome, wearisome, tedious, boring** mean burdensome because tiring or boring or both. A person or thing is **irksome** that inspires distaste, reluctance, or impatience because of its demand for effort not made easy by interest ⟨the difficulty of grasping abstract statements made learning very *irksome* to me—*Symonds*⟩ ⟨I did not feel any longer . . . the restless and *irksome* desire to contrive skimpy rendezvous—*Edmund Wilson*⟩ ⟨he laid down his *irksome* editorial duties and spent the next fifteen years in farming—*F. H. Chase*⟩ A person or thing is **tiresome** that is dull and unenlivening and therefore is either intensely boring or soon productive of fatigue ⟨it is *tiresome* to be funny for a whole evening—*Scott*⟩ ⟨the second curate was Chator, who was so good as sometimes to be nearly *tiresome*—*Mackenzie*⟩ ⟨we think of rain as *tiresome* and uncomfortable—*Binyon*⟩ ⟨the importunity of the little boys was *tiresome* when one wanted to be alone—*Huxley*⟩ A person or, especially, a thing is **wearisome** that exhausts one's strength or patience through long-continued or constant call for effort, exertion, or attention, or through tiresome uniformity of character ⟨these high wild hills and rough uneven ways draws out our miles, and makes them *wearisome*—*Shak.*⟩ ⟨the same *wearisome* round of stereotyped habits—*Wilde*⟩ ⟨the acquisition of exact knowledge is apt to be *wearisome*, but it is essential to every kind of excellence —*Russell*⟩ A person or thing is **tedious** that is tiresomely monotonous, slow, or prolix ⟨life is as *tedious* as a twice-told tale vexing the dull ear of a drowsy man—*Shak.*⟩ ⟨they had no longer any surprises for me . . . I knew pretty well what they would say; even their love affairs had a *tedious* banality—*Maugham*⟩ A person or thing is **boring** that causes boredom; the term is perhaps the most positive of the group since it implies an active depressing, wearying, or annoying ⟨the story is badly cluttered by unnecessary and *boring* wordiness—*New Yorker*⟩ ⟨he's so *boring* . . . . I hate *boring* people. I'm out for a good time—*Lowry*⟩
*Ana* dull, *stupid, slow: fatiguing, exhausting, fagging, tiring (see TIRE *vb*)
*Ant* absorbing, engrossing
**ironic** satiric, *sarcastic, sardonic
*Ana* biting, cutting, *incisive, trenchant: *caustic, mordant, scathing
**irony** *wit, satire, sarcasm, humor, repartee
**irrational, unreasonable** are comparable when meaning not governed or guided by reason. Both terms have been used occasionally in the sense of not having the power to reason ⟨nothing has a greater effect on all plants and *irrational* animals—*Hume*⟩ ⟨whilst his fellowman . . . must as the *unreasonable* beast drag on a life of labor—*Southey*⟩ Except in technical senses (as in mathematics) both words apply usually to men, their acts, utterances, feelings, policies, and demands. **Irrational** may imply a lack of usual or normal mental control and powers ⟨the patient was *irrational* during the course of his fever⟩ but more often it suggests a lack of control or guidance by the reason, or direct conflict with reason's dictates; it therefore comes close to *absurd, illogical, foolish, preposterous, senseless,* or *fantastic* ⟨governed by an *irrational* fear⟩ ⟨*irrational* beliefs⟩ ⟨an *irrational* policy⟩ ⟨his temperamental impulse to energetic practical action

. . . and the reserve, passivity, and isolation which myopia enforced, seemed to him absolutely *irrational—Ellis⟩* ⟨though normal and very intelligent in most respects Mrs. Lincoln was *irrational* on one subject: she could not think straight in matters that pertained to money—*R. P. Randall⟩* **Unreasonable** implies guidance or control by some force (as self-will, passion, ambition, greed, or stubbornness) which makes one deficient in judgment or good sense. As applied to one's acts or utterances, it suggests lack of justification by reason; the term therefore comes close to *inequitable, immoderate, excessive, unfair,* or *extravagant* ⟨you will not be so *unreasonable* as to send your child out in this storm⟩ ⟨his demands are *unreasonable*⟩ ⟨obstinate and *unreasonable* pertinacity⟩ ⟨an *unreasonable* price for beef⟩ ⟨the earnings . . . were found materially in excess of a fair return, and the general level of their rates was found unjust and *unreasonable—J. C. Nelson⟩* ⟨it is a little *unreasonable* to find fault with his maxims because they do not apply to all times and places—*A. M. Young⟩*
*Ana* absurd, preposterous, *foolish, silly: fatuous, asinine, *simple: crazy, demented, mad, *insane
*Ant* rational —*Con* reasonable (see RATIONAL): *wise, judicious, sage, sapient, prudent, sane, sensible: *logical

**irregular, anomalous, unnatural** mean outside the sphere of what conforms to or is explainable by law, rule, custom, or principle. **Irregular** implies failure to conform to a rule, a law, or a pattern, especially to one imposed for the sake of uniformity in method, practice, or conduct; thus, an *irregular* marriage is one that does not conform to the regulations of church or state; an *irregular* verse does not correspond to an accepted metrical pattern for its type; guerrilla warfare is called *irregular* because it does not accord with the practice of civilized nations or conventional military theory; *irregular* conduct may or may not be morally reprehensible, but it defies the code or standard of the community or class ⟨there are always *irregular* fluctuations of the seasonal weather—*Ellis⟩* ⟨made a strong appeal for the highest standards of medical education in an effort to combat *irregular* practitioners—*Viets⟩* ⟨the chicanery was gross, the forgery patent, the procedure *irregular* and illegal—*Woodward⟩* **Anomalous** stresses lack of conformity to what might be expected of a thing because of the class or type to which it belongs, the laws which govern its existence, or the environment in which it is found ⟨all seven of us . . . appeared on the show under pseudonyms. Which may sound highly *anomalous,* considering that we're the children of vaudevillians, a sect not usually antipathetic to publicity—*Salinger⟩* Sometimes it specifically implies inconsistency or a conflict of principles ⟨acts so *anomalous,* in such startling contradiction to all our usual ways and accepted notions of life and its value—*L. P. Smith⟩* and sometimes it specifically means unclassifiable or indefinable ⟨*anomalous* literary works such as Holmes's *Autocrat of the Breakfast Table⟩* ⟨*anomalous* emotions⟩ Again, it suggests the absence of the character or of the characteristics essential to a thing of its kind ⟨a few judges find in her last book new support for the *anomalous* opinion that its author was a great artist, but insignificant—*Beck⟩* or it suggests a contradiction between the professed aims or intentions of a person or institution and the conditions in which that person or institution exists or finds himself or itself at a given time ⟨the *anomalous* position of the free Negro in the slave states—*E. T. Price⟩* ⟨President Wilson found himself in an *anomalous* position when Congress rejected his proposal that the United States enter the League of Nations⟩ **Unnatural** is the strongest of these words in its implication of censure, especially

when it implies a violation of natural law or of principles accepted by all civilized men as based on reason and essential to the well-being of society. In such cases it often specifically connotes moral perversion ⟨an *unnatural* practice⟩ ⟨she had been vicious and *unnatural;* she had thriven on hatred—*S. S. Van Dine⟩* or abnormal indifference or cruelty ⟨an *unnatural* parent⟩ Sometimes the word merely means contrary to what is received as *natural,* either because it is not in accordance with the normal course of nature ⟨snow in May is *unnatural* in this region⟩ or because it is not in keeping with what one regards as normal, balanced, proper, or fitting under the circumstances ⟨an *unnatural* appetite for acid foods⟩ ⟨a poetic language which appears natural to one age will appear *unnatural* or artificial to another—*Day Lewis⟩* ⟨thy deed, inhuman and *unnatural* provokes this deluge most *unnatural—Shak.⟩* ⟨a daughter who left her father was an *unnatural* daughter; her womanhood was suspect—*Woolf⟩*
*Ana* aberrant, *abnormal, atypical: *exceptional: singular, unique, *strange, peculiar, odd, queer
*Ant* regular —*Con* natural, normal, typical (see REGULAR): *usual, customary, wonted, accustomed, habitual: licit, legitimate, legal, *lawful

**irreligious, unreligious, nonreligious, ungodly, godless** mean not religious or not devoted to the ends of religion. **Irreligious** is not only the most common of the negative forms of *religious* but the most clearly defined in meaning, for it implies not merely lack of religion but hostility to religion or courses in opposition to it or in violation of its precepts ⟨that non-churchgoers are not necessarily *irreligious—Streit⟩* It may even suggest impiety, immorality, or blasphemy ⟨it is unworthy a religious man to view an *irreligious* one either with alarm or aversion—*Carlyle⟩* ⟨they are so *irreligious* that they exploit popular religion for professional purposes without delicacy or scruple—*Shaw⟩* **Unreligious,** a somewhat uncommon term, implies nothing more than lack of religion; it therefore applies aptly to men, their utterances, or their works and suggests merely the absence of religion or of religious training or religious ideas ⟨the popular poetry . . . became . . . *unreligious* . . . in some parts irreligious—*Milman⟩* **Nonreligious** applies not so much to persons as to institutions, activities, projects, and themes for art that are outside the sphere or province of religion or not under the control of a religious body; it therefore comes close in meaning to *secular* (see under PROFANE 1) ⟨*nonreligious* education⟩ ⟨*nonreligious* charitable societies⟩ ⟨made it hard for them to trust a *nonreligious* institution, such as the State University—*Amer. Guide Series: Ind.⟩* **Ungodly** often comes close to *irreligious,* but it carries a stronger suggestion of disobedience to or defiance of divine law ⟨blessed is the man that walketh not in the counsel of the *ungodly—Ps* 1:1⟩ ⟨they decided to leave so *ungodly* a land—*Usher⟩* **Godless** commonly implies atheism or agnosticism and often definitely implies rejection of religion ⟨*godless* philosophers⟩ ⟨*godless* teachings⟩ ⟨here were decent *godless* people: their only monument the asphalt road—*T. S. Eliot⟩* ⟨fiercely predicting the end of Lorenzo and all his *godless* court—*Moorehead⟩*
*Ana* *impious, profane, blasphemous, sacrilegious: *immoral, amoral, unmoral
*Ant* religious —*Con* pious, *devout

**irritable, fractious, peevish, snappish, waspish, petulant, pettish, huffy, fretful, querulous** apply to persons or to their moods or dispositions in the sense of showing impatience or anger without due or sufficient cause. **Irritable** implies extreme excitability of temperament, often associated with or arising from fatigue or physical or mental

---

A colon (:) separates groups of words discriminated. An asterisk (*) indicates place of treatment of each group.

distress, that makes one exceedingly easy to annoy or difficult to please ⟨mental work brings on . . . an *irritable* and nervous disgust—*Arnold*⟩ ⟨a hot day and the clerk in the store was *irritable* . . . had not slept much the night before and he had a headache—*Saxon*⟩ **Fractious** carries a stronger implication of willfulness or of unruliness than *irritable*, and although it also implies extreme excitability, it suggests even greater loss of self-control; the term is often applied to animals as well as to persons ⟨those who are spoilt and *fractious*, who must have everything their own way—*Swinnerton*⟩ ⟨he was *fractious* in the saddling paddock and slow leaving the starting gate—*Audax Minor*⟩ **Peevish** implies childish irritability and a tendency to give expression to petty complaints or ill-humored trivial criticisms ⟨*peevish* because he called her and she did not come, and he threw his bowl of tea on the ground like a willful child—*Buck*⟩ ⟨I have heard some London wits, rather *peevish* at Macaulay's superiority, complain that he occupied too much of the talk—*Thackeray*⟩ **Snappish** implies irritability or sometimes peevishness that manifests itself in sharp, cutting questions, comments, or objections that discourage conversation or sociability ⟨an extremely unlikable, *snappish* old fellow⟩ ⟨an obbligato of bickering and *snappish* comment—*Bester*⟩ **Waspish** stresses testiness rather than irritability, but it implies a readiness to sting or hurt others without warrant or without sufficient warrant ⟨beware of his *waspish* temper⟩ ⟨her comments may be amusing but they are always *waspish*⟩ ⟨a little *waspish* woman who . . . snapped out at a man who seemed to be with her—*C. S. Lewis*⟩ **Petulant** usually suggests the sulkiness of a spoiled child as well as peevishness and capricious impatience ⟨as he had no means of confuting his nephew, all he could do . . . was to utter *petulant* remarks on his powerlessness to appear at the dinner table that day—*Meredith*⟩ ⟨in his youth the spoiled child of Boston, in middle life he was *petulant* and irritable, inclined to sulk when his will was crossed—*Parrington*⟩ **Pettish** implies sulky or childish ill humor (as of one who is slighted or offended) ⟨said many careless, many foolish, many merely *pettish* things—*Fadiman*⟩ ⟨Stephen's resistance was but the *pettish* outbreak of a ruined man—*J. R. Green*⟩ **Huffy** also implies a tendency to take offense without due cause, but it suggests more of a display of injured pride than *pettish* ⟨when he is reproved, he is *huffy* for the rest of the day⟩ ⟨I bear no grudge at all against you. I am not *huffy* and crabbed—*Gregory*⟩ **Fretful** implies irritability and restlessness that may manifest itself in complaints or in a complaining tone of voice ⟨a *fretful* child⟩ but often is merely suggested by a lack of ease and repose ⟨all the *fretful* doubts and perturbations of the conscience most men know—*Wolfe*⟩ ⟨the air, breathed many times and spent, was *fretful* with a whispering discontent—*Millay*⟩ ⟨weary days of *fretful* argument—*Charles & Mary Beard*⟩ **Querulous** implies an often habitual discontent that manifests itself in whining complaints or in fretfulness of temper; it often also suggests petulance ⟨her *querulous* and never-ending complaints—*Gaskell*⟩ ⟨the man himself grew old and *querulous* and hysterical with failure and repeated disappointment and chronic poverty—*Huxley*⟩
**Ana** cranky, cross, testy, touchy, choleric, splenetic, *irascible
**Ant** easygoing —**Con** *amiable, good-natured, complaisant, obliging: genial, sociable, affable, cordial, *gracious

**irritate, exasperate, nettle, provoke, aggravate, rile, peeve** are comparable when meaning to excite a feeling of angry annoyance in a person. Something which **irritates** greatly displeases or offends and evokes a display of feeling rang-

ing from momentary impatience to an outburst of rage ⟨the chattering crowd, with their rude jokes . . . *irritated* him sharply—*Anderson*⟩ ⟨her intensity, which would leave no emotion on a normal plane, *irritated* the youth into a frenzy—*D. H. Lawrence*⟩ Something which **exasperates** arouses bitter or intense irritation. The word, however, sometimes expresses nothing more than keen vexation or annoyance ⟨an opportunity to . . . aggravate his poor patient wife, and *exasperate* his children, and make himself generally obnoxious—*Simeon Ford*⟩ ⟨though she could *exasperate* she could never offend—*H. G. Wells*⟩ Something which **nettles** irritates sharply but momentarily and stings or piques more than angers ⟨a touch of light scorn in her voice *nettled* me—*W. J. Locke*⟩ Something which **provokes** awakens strong annoyance or vexation and often incites to action ⟨a Tory resident who *provoked* local animosities and was charged with high treason—*Amer. Guide Series: Conn.*⟩ ⟨they were definitely *provoked* to extremity before they did this deed—*Ingamells*⟩ ⟨he is *provoked* with me for not talking more—*Burney*⟩ Something which **aggravates** (see also INTENSIFY) arouses displeasure, impatience, or anger often through prolonged or repeated action ⟨nothing so *aggravates* an earnest person as a passive resistance—*Melville*⟩ ⟨it is *aggravating* to have you talking about so small a business—*Shaw*⟩ Something which **riles** disturbs one's serenity or peace and agitates as well as angers ⟨with raucous taunting and ribald remarks to *rile* up the proprietor—*White*⟩ Something which **peeves** excites often petty or querulous fretfulness or a tendency to be easily irritated ⟨he is easily *peeved* after a restless night⟩ ⟨when she ventured to criticize it, even mildly, he was *peeved*—*Auchincloss*⟩
**Ana** *annoy, vex, irk, bother: incense, *anger, madden, enrage, infuriate: *offend, affront: fret, chafe (see ABRADE)
**Con** appease, mollify, conciliate, propitiate, placate, *pacify: gratify, *please, gladden, delight

**isolate, segregate, seclude, insulate, sequester** are comparable when they mean to separate from the usual or natural environment, but they are rarely interchangeable because their other and differentiating implications are often stressed. **Isolate** implies a detachment of someone or something from his or its usual environment so that he or it will not affect or be affected by others. The word is sufficiently general that it may be employed in reference either to an actual separation or to a separation that is merely virtual, arbitrary, or speculative ⟨several villages were *isolated* by the storm⟩ ⟨find an *isolated* spot in which to live⟩ ⟨*isolate* scarlet fever patients⟩ ⟨under present conditions no country can remain *isolated*⟩ ⟨he was singularly *isolated*, untouched by the interest or the gossip or the knowledge of the life about him—*Deland*⟩ ⟨we must remember that religion, like some chemical substance, is never found pure, and it is not at all easy to *isolate* it in order to learn its properties—*Inge*⟩ **Segregate** also applies to both persons and things and usually refers to them as a group separated from the mass or main body; its secondary implication is often, therefore, a collection in one place, one class, or one mass and it may in addition imply a holding incommunicado ⟨*segregate* lepers from the rest of the population⟩ ⟨*segregate* hardened criminals from first offenders in prisons⟩ ⟨that innate instinct which ever aimed at uniting, not *segregating* groups of Christians—*D. P. Hughes*⟩ **Seclude** implies a removal or withdrawal from external influences; it is therefore often used reflexively or at least in such a way as to imply acceptance of the protection afforded by such removal or withdrawal ⟨*secluded* in their childhood from all evil influences⟩ ⟨so she sat hard and close at her writing table from half past nine to twelve every morning, *secluded* and defended from all the world—*H. G. Wells*⟩ ⟨if we are to get the most and the best out of life, we must not *seclude* ourselves from these things—*Benson*⟩ **Insulate** means to isolate, especially by something which serves as a barrier to the escape of what is within or the entrance of what is without. Consequently it implies retention of some power in a condition approaching fullness or purity ⟨none of us can touch his later work . . ., it is . . . too *insulated* to allow an easy communication of its powers —*Day Lewis*⟩ ⟨one touch of Comedy would destroy any tragedy (unless . . ., as is the case with Shakespeare, the comic scenes were kept *insulated* from instead of integrated with the others)—*Krutch*⟩ *Insulate* is employed technically to imply the use of something to cut off free passage (as of electricity or heat or sound) ⟨electric wires should be *insulated* with a nonconducting substance⟩ ⟨the house was *insulated* by interlining the walls with rock wool⟩ Basically **sequester** implies a setting apart (as from others or for a particular purpose) and in itself, as apart from context, ordinarily conveys no more than this ⟨the period when all copper was *sequestered* for war use—*Science*⟩ ⟨a confederate who had boarded the train at a previous stop to hold down the seats we were to occupy. When the train pulled in we rushed it in valiant formation and dropped panting in our nobly *sequestered* seats—*Cassidy*⟩ Colored by context it may take the place of *isolate* ⟨no crusading idealist in history ever thought it right to *sequester* himself in an estate comprising more than 300,000 acres with exclusive possession of fifty miles of California shore—*Thomas*⟩ or of *segregate* ⟨most schools . . . have *sequestered* the slow, average and quick students of both races and let each group progress at its own pace—*J. B. Martin*⟩ or of *seclude* ⟨this typical Connecticut hill town, *sequestered* from the rush of modern traffic, retains much of its old-time charm—*Amer. Guide Series: Conn.*⟩ Sometimes, however, it may imply a setting apart by taking into one's possession ⟨the divorced wife of painter André Derain, . . . had *sequestered* Derain's studio—*Time*⟩ or by confiscating ⟨the police continued to uncover and *sequester* large amounts of arms and ammunition—*Woolbert*⟩ In legal use *sequester* implies a separation, usually for the time being, of property or income from the owner until some claim or obligation has been satisfied ⟨the bishop *sequestered* the profits of the vacant benefice for use by the next incumbent⟩ ⟨*sequester* a debtor's estate⟩ *Ana* \*detach, disengage, abstract: \*separate, part, sever, sunder

*Con* associate, relate, unite, connect, link, \*join

**isolation** \*solitude, alienation, seclusion
*Ana* loneliness, solitariness, loneness, desolateness *or* desolation (see corresponding adjectives at ALONE)

**issue** *n* 1 outcome, \*effect, result, consequence, upshot, aftereffect, aftermath, sequel, event
*Ana* ending *or* end, termination, concluding *or* conclusion, closing (see corresponding verbs at CLOSE)
*Con* \*cause, antecedent, determinant: inception, \*origin, source, root
2 \*offspring, young, progeny, descendant, posterity
**issue** *vb* emanate, proceed, flow, derive, originate, \*spring, arise, rise, stem
*Ana* emerge, \*appear, loom

**item, detail, particular** are comparable when meaning one of the things, either separate and distinct or considered so, which constitute a whole. **Item** applies mainly to each thing that is put down in a list (as of things needed, things to be done, or things to be seen) or in an account, a record, or an inventory; sometimes the term applies to the actual

thing as apart from the list ⟨the bill has ten *items*⟩ ⟨each separate *item* of income—*Hobson*⟩ ⟨the dog too went: the most noble-looking *item* in the beggarly assets—*Conrad*⟩ ⟨a mere *item* in the year's publishing list—*Brogan*⟩ **Detail** (see also PART) applies to each separate thing which enters into the building or construction of some such thing as a house, a painting, or a narrative or enters into such an activity as the performance of a task or job, the pursuit of a career, or the living of a life; often, in this sense, *detail* is contrasted with *structure, outline, design,* or *plan* ⟨while . . . laboring indefatigably in the *details* of domestic life on a farm, her outlook was large —*Ellis*⟩ ⟨alike in its large outlines and its small *details*, Chinese life is always the art of balancing an aesthetic temperament and guarding against its excesses—*Ellis*⟩ Often the singular form in this sense is used as a collective noun ⟨the poet's chief aim . . . is to communicate not the exact *detail* of an experience, but its tone and rhythm— *Day Lewis*⟩ ⟨report an incident in *detail*⟩ **Particular** may imply a relation to something general or universal ⟨it foolishly derides the universal, saying that it chooses to consider the *particular* as more important—*Quiller-Couch*⟩ but more often it implies a relation to a whole and stresses that relationship more than *item* or *detail*; in this sense *particular* emphasizes the smallness and the singleness and concreteness of each item or detail; thus, in law, a bill of *particulars* is a statement of the items of a plaintiff's claim or a defendant's counterclaim ⟨I do not care to go into the *particulars* of the agreement⟩ ⟨the real question is what is the world . . . and that can be revealed only by the study of all nature's *particulars*— *James*⟩ ⟨praised the party accomplishment, and came to *particulars* in an attack upon the . . . opposition— *Paxson*⟩ ⟨we know nothing of their language and only . . . minor *particulars* of their social customs and religion— *R. W. Murray*⟩
*Ana* \*thing, object, article: constituent, component, \*element, factor

**itemized** detailed, particularized, \*circumstantial, minute, particular
*Ant* summarized

**iterate** \*repeat, reiterate, ingeminate

**itinerant** *adj* **Itinerant, peripatetic, ambulatory, ambulant, nomadic, vagrant** mean having no fixed or settled station but moving from place to place. **Itinerant** is applicable chiefly to individuals or to groups whose calling or office requires travel along a circuit or route ⟨an *itinerant* player⟩ ⟨an *itinerant* merchant⟩ ⟨an advantage *itinerant* preachers have over those who are stationary, the latter cannot well improve their delivery of a sermon by so many rehearsals—*Franklin*⟩ ⟨a parcel of shabby, *itinerant* tattooers, who . . . stroll unmolested from one hostile bay to another—*Melville*⟩ ⟨a lazy, vagabondish, *itinerant* farmer, moving from one failure to another—*Hendrick*⟩ **Peripatetic** may be applied to activities carried on while walking or moving about ⟨*peripatetic* teaching⟩ ⟨*peripatetic* habits, favorable to meditation—*Carlyle*⟩ or to persons moving about on foot ⟨they demand a *peripatetic* spectator; one must see this group from all angles to realize the purpose of the sculptor—*Upjohn*⟩ or more often traveling from place to place ⟨that *peripatetic* digester of continents, John Gunther, has at last come home— *Fadiman*⟩ ⟨he was a *peripatetic* firebrand. He had to be. Any area in which Mann was active was soon, for various reasons, too hot to hold him—*Mallon*⟩ Sometimes, and often with a light or whimsical note, the word suggests restlessness or an unsettled state or being constantly on the go ⟨his camera is never aimlessly *peripatetic*: either there is some important action that must be observed or

Brook invents fresh and interesting groupings—*Knight*⟩ ⟨Winchester rather than London was regarded as the official capital of the *peripatetic* monarchy—*Trevelyan*⟩ ⟨our *peripatetic* Scot has apparently ended his fictional travels and is now shorebound—*Barkham*⟩ **Ambulatory** and **ambulant** both basically imply a relation to walking and may be close synonyms of *pedestrian* ⟨*ambulatory* exercise⟩ ⟨an *ambulant* traveler⟩ but more often they stress, as *pedestrian* does not, ability to walk or capability of walking as distinguished from the fact or practice of walking ⟨*ambulatory* patients treated at the clinic⟩ ⟨he seemed an *ambulant* variety of cactus standing strangely in our way—*Sampley*⟩ When applied to things, *ambulatory* and *ambulant* imply lack of fixity especially in physical station ⟨an *ambulant* radio station⟩ ⟨small *ambulatory* businesses⟩ or occasionally (as in legal usage) in immaterial qualities; thus, the provisions of a will are *ambulatory* so long as the testator is alive and legally competent to alter them. **Nomadic** is applicable to individuals ⟨he merely walked off and set out upon a *nomadic* career, finding work where he could—*Lindner*⟩ but is more often used to designate groups or tribes of men who have no fixed place of residence but wander, according to season or food supply or the needs of their means of livelihood, from one place or region to another ⟨the

Bedouins are a *nomadic* tribe found in the deserts of Arabia, Syria, and North Africa⟩ ⟨a system that compels a large segment of labor to be *nomadic*, trailing endlessly from end to end of the country—*G. W. Johnson*⟩ **Vagrant** (see also *vagrant n* under VAGABOND) as applied to human beings stresses lack of a fixed place of residence but unlike *nomadic* is applicable typically to individuals rather than to groups; in this use it commonly lacks the pejorative quality of the corresponding noun ⟨the humility with which this *vagrant* and utterly original genius turned to them for wisdom—*Sinclair Lewis*⟩ ⟨I must go down to the seas again, to the *vagrant* gypsy life—*Masefield*⟩ But in its more common application to things *vagrant* usually stresses the slight, fleeting, ephemeral quality of what is vaguely wandering rather than either firmly fixed or following a fixed course ⟨to catch *vagrant* currents of air, door and window flaps were propped open—*Heiser*⟩ ⟨nature itself in its *vagrant* moods and infinite variety—*Schlesinger* d. 1965⟩ ⟨her mind, called *vagrant*, is like a butterfly, seemingly fragile and even awkward in erratic flight—*Beck*⟩ ⟨tasks too *vagrant* or too taxing ever to have been accomplished—*Hilton*⟩ ⟨the great increase in numbers of *vagrant* boys during the depression⟩ *Ana* wandering, roving, rambling, straying, roaming, ranging (see WANDER): moving, shifting (see MOVE *vb*)

# J

**jabber** chatter, *chat, gab, patter, prate, prattle, babble, gabble, gibber

**jack** *n* *flag, ensign, standard, banner, color, streamer, pennant, pendant, pennon

**jade** *vb* exhaust, fatigue, *tire, weary, fag, tucker
*Ana* oppress, *depress, weigh: enervate, *unnerve, unman, emasculate: sate, *satiate, surfeit, pall, cloy
*Ant* refresh —*Con* *renew, restore, rejuvenate

**jail** *vb* incarcerate, *imprison, immure, intern
*Ana* confine, circumscribe, restrict, *limit: shackle, manacle, fetter (see HAMPER)
*Con* release, liberate, *free

**jam** *vb* crowd, squeeze, *press, bear, bear down
*Ana* *crush, squash: *pack, cram, stuff, ram, tamp

**jam** *n* *predicament, plight, fix, dilemma, quandary, scrape, pickle
*Ana* *difficulty, vicissitude: pinch, strait, exigency (see JUNCTURE)

**jape** *n* *joke, jest, quip, witticism, wisecrack, crack, gag

**jar** *n* jolt, *impact, impingement, collision, clash, shock, concussion, percussion
*Ana* shaking *or* shake, quaking *or* quake (see SHAKE *vb*): vibration, fluctuation, swaying *or* sway (see corresponding verbs at SWING): agitation, disturbance, upsetting *or* upset (see corresponding verbs at DISCOMPOSE)

**jargon** *dialect, vernacular, patois, lingo, cant, argot, slang
*Ana* idiom, speech (see LANGUAGE): abracadabra, *gibberish

**jaunt** *n* excursion, *journey, trip, tour, voyage, cruise, expedition, pilgrimage

**jaw** *vb* upbraid, *scold, rate, berate, tongue-lash, bawl, chew out, wig, rail, revile, vituperate
*Ana* censure, denounce, reprobate, reprehend, *criticize, blame, condemn: *reprove, reproach, chide, reprimand, rebuke

**jealous** *envious

*Ana* suspicious, mistrustful (see corresponding nouns at UNCERTAINTY): *doubtful, dubious: vigilant, *watchful, alert: distrusting, mistrusting (see DISTRUST)

**jeer** *vb* *scoff, gibe, fleer, gird, sneer, flout
*Ana* deride, *ridicule, mock, taunt, twit, rally
*Con* *fawn, truckle, toady, cringe, cower

**jejune** *insipid, vapid, flat, wishy-washy, inane, banal
*Ana* *thin, slight, slim, tenuous: arid, *dry: attenuated, extenuated, diluted, thinned (see THIN *vb*): *meager, skimpy, exiguous
*Con* lavish, *profuse, lush, luxuriant, prodigal, exuberant: nutritious, nourishing, sustaining (see corresponding nouns at FOOD)

**jell, jelly** *vb* *coagulate, congeal, set, curdle, clot
*Ana* solidify, *harden: cohere, *stick: *compact, consolidate

**jeopardize** *venture, hazard, risk, chance, endanger, imperil
*Ana* brave, dare (see FACE): *meet, encounter, confront, face

**jeopardy** peril, hazard, risk, *danger
*Ana* threatening *or* threat, menacing *or* menace (see THREATEN): exposure (see EXPOSITION): liability, susceptibility, sensitiveness, openness (see corresponding adjectives at LIABLE): *chance, accident, hap
*Con* security, safety (see corresponding adjectives at SAFE): immunity, *exemption

**jeremiad** *tirade, diatribe, philippic

**jerk, snap, twitch, yank** mean to make a sudden sharp quick movement. **Jerk** implies especially such a movement that is graceless, forceful, and abrupt ⟨thought the train would never start, but at last the whistle blew and the carriages *jerked* forward—*Carter*⟩ ⟨*jerked* her head back as if she'd been struck in the face—*Dorothy Baker*⟩ **Snap** may imply a quite quick action abruptly terminated (as a biting or trying to bite sharply or a seizing, clutching, snatching, locking, or breaking suddenly) ⟨the hounds were fine beasts . . . lank and swift as they bent over the food to *snap* it into their jaws and swallow it quickly— *Roberts*⟩ or a taking of possession with avidity ⟨the syndicate *snapping* up land as soon as it is for sale⟩ or sometimes specifically an uttering with the brisk sharpness of a bite ⟨*snapped* at her because Theophilus did not eat enough—*Deland*⟩ **Twitch** may imply quick, sometimes spasmodic, and often light action combining tugging and jerking ⟨shrunken body continued to jerk and quiver, fingers *twitching* at his gray beard—*Gerald Beaumont*⟩ ⟨one Pan ready to *twitch* the nymph's last garment off— *Browning*⟩ ⟨put out his hand to *twitch* off a twig as he passed—*Cather*⟩ **Yank** implies a quick and heavy tugging and pulling ⟨watches her two-year-old stand passive while another child *yanks* his toy out of his hand—*Mead*⟩ ⟨she *yanked* the corset strings viciously—*Chidsey*⟩ ⟨by means of long blocks and tackle they set to *yanking* out logs—*S. E. White*⟩

*Ana* *pull, drag: toss, sling, fling, *throw: *wrench, wrest, wring

**jest** *n* **1** *joke, jape, quip, witticism, wisecrack, crack, gag

*Ana* *badinage, persiflage, raillery: bantering *or* banter, chaffing *or* chaff, jollying *or* jolly (see BANTER *vb*): twitting *or* twit, ridiculing *or* ridicule, deriding *or* derision (see corresponding verbs at RIDICULE)

**2** *fun, sport, game, play

*Ana* diversion, entertainment, amusement (see under AMUSE): joviality, merriment (see corresponding adjectives at MERRY)

*Con* seriousness, earnestness, soberness, gravity (see corresponding adjectives at SERIOUS)

**jetty** *wharf, dock, pier, quay, slip, berth, levee

**jib** *vb* balk, shy, boggle, stickle, stick, strain, *demur, scruple

**jibe** *agree, harmonize, accord, conform, square, tally, correspond

**jiffy** *instant, moment, minute, second, flash, twinkling, split second

**jittery** jumpy, nervous, *impatient, unquiet, restless, restive, uneasy, fidgety

*Ana* unnerved, unmanned (see UNNERVE): perturbed, agitated, disquieted, upset, discomposed (see DISCOMPOSE)

*Con* collected, composed, *cool, imperturbable, nonchalant: serene, placid, *calm, tranquil

**job** *task, duty, assignment, stint, chore

*Ana* office, *function, duty, province: business, concern, *affair, matter, thing

**jocose** jocular, facetious, humorous, *witty

*Ana* waggish, sportive, *playful, roguish: comic, comical, *laughable, ludicrous, droll, funny: *merry, jolly, jovial, jocund, blithe

*Con* *serious, earnest, grave, sober, solemn, sedate, staid

**jocular** jocose, humorous, facetious, *witty

*Ana* jovial, jolly, *merry: *playful, sportive: funny, droll, comic, comical, *laughable, ludicrous, ridiculous

*Con* grave, earnest, solemn, somber, *serious

**jocund** blithe, *merry, jolly, jovial

*Ana* joyful, joyous, cheerful, lighthearted, happy, *glad: mirthful, hilarious, gleeful (see corresponding nouns at MIRTH): sportive, *playful, mischievous

*Con* gloomy, morose, glum, *sullen, saturnine, dour: sedate, grave, solemn, somber, staid, *serious

**jog** *vb* *poke, prod, nudge

*Ana* *shake, agitate: *push, shove

**jog** *n* poke, prod, nudge (see under POKE *vb*)

**join, conjoin, combine, unite, connect, link, associate, relate** are comparable when meaning to attach or fasten one thing to another or several things to each other or to become so attached or fastened. **Join** stresses the bringing or coming together into contact or conjunction of two or more clearly discrete things ⟨*join* two pieces of wood by dovetailing them⟩ ⟨*join* skirt lengths by seams⟩ ⟨*join* hands⟩ ⟨*join* a man and woman in matrimony⟩ ⟨where the Mohawk river *joins* the Hudson⟩ ⟨the opponents of the proposal decided to *join* forces⟩ *Join* is the specific term when one becomes a member of a group or enters into the company of others as an equal ⟨*join* a society⟩ ⟨*join* a church⟩ ⟨*join* a group at a reception⟩ ⟨*join* the army⟩ **Conjoin** usually emphasizes both the separateness and distinctness of the items to be joined and the unity that results from their being joined ⟨from inborn indolence, *conjoined* with avarice, pride, and lust of power, has sprung slavery in all its protean forms—*Henry Wilson*⟩ ⟨Death Valley probably received the discharge of both the Amargosa and Mohave rivers, whose *conjoined* waters entered from the south—*Jour. of Geology*⟩ **Combine** in this relation (see also UNITE 2) adds to *join* the implications of a mingling or blending and may stress more heavily the idea of a common purpose or end; it is therefore used of two or more, often immaterial, things that may lose or seem to lose their identities and become merged in each other ⟨*combine* the ingredients for a cake⟩ ⟨a gift for *combining,* for fusing into a single phrase, two or more diverse impressions—*T. S. Eliot*⟩ ⟨with this quality of temperance was *combined* in Socrates a rare measure of independence and moral courage—*Dickinson*⟩ ⟨*combined* literary distinction with a high degree of historical objectivity—*Van Alstyne*⟩ **Unite,** like *combine,* implies a blending that effects the loss of individual identity of the elements, but, like *conjoin, unite* stresses the singleness of the result ⟨*unite* two pieces of metal by welding⟩ ⟨our peace will, like a broken limb *united,* grow stronger for the breaking —*Shak.*⟩ ⟨particles which can *unite* to form a new compound—*T. S. Eliot*⟩ ⟨in France the whole people saw at once what was upon them; the single word *patrie* was enough to *unite* them in a common enthusiasm and stern determination—*Inge*⟩ **Connect** implies a loose or, at least, an obvious attachment of things to each other and the preservation not only of each thing's identity but also of the evidence of its physical or logical separateness; in this way it is distinguishable from *join* when physical attachment is implied; thus, a wall is built up of bricks *joined,* rather than *connected,* together by cement but a chain is made by *connecting* a succession of steel links; often *connect* implies an intervening element or medium which permits joint movement and intercommunication ⟨*connect* two railway coaches by means of a coupler⟩ ⟨*connect* two islands with a bridge⟩ ⟨ligaments serve to *connect* bones at a joint⟩ ⟨a minor road which *connects* highways⟩ When the idea of logical attachment is uppermost, *connect* usually implies that the ideas, events, or things whether material or immaterial have a bearing on each other (as of cause and effect, generic likeness, or reference to the same person or thing) ⟨the two incidents were *connected*⟩ ⟨the police have now sufficient evidence to *connect* the suspect with the bombing⟩ ⟨she could not *connect* her mother's meanness with the magnitude of what had happened—*Auchincloss*⟩ ⟨anything *connected* with Napoleon is of interest to them⟩ *Connect,* especially in the passive, is preferable to *join* when used in reference to organizations or groups and looseness of attachment, impermanence, or subordination is implied ⟨nobody *connected* with the paper ever makes a public appearance without being challenged—*Bliven* b. 1889⟩ **Link,** with its underlying reference to one of the parts of a chain, is usually more emphatic than *connect* in implying firmness

---

A colon (:) separates groups of words discriminated. An asterisk (*) indicates place of treatment of each group.

of attachment; it is therefore the more precise word when one wishes to preserve the basic implications of *connect* and yet to avoid its common connotations of a weak or severable attachment; thus, to *link* a person with a crime is, by implication, to have ample evidence of his involvement with it ⟨Augustus set himself to revive the state religion . . . as part of his policy of *linking* up past and present, and as an instrument in securing the restoration of the old morality—*Buchan*⟩ ⟨none of the subjects that *linked* us together could be talked about in a bar—*Nevil Shute*⟩ ⟨mobilize civilian science and *link* it effectively with the war effort—*Baxter*⟩ **Associate** primarily implies a joining with another usually in an amiable relationship and on terms of equality ⟨a group of men *associated* in business⟩ ⟨when bad men combine, good men must *associate*—*Burke*⟩ ⟨my father's conviction that they were too lowly to *associate* with me, when it was so clear that I was too poor to *associate* with them, may have had some sort of imaginary validity for him; but for me it was snobbish nonsense—*Shaw*⟩ In its extended use as referred to things, the implication of companionship on equal terms gives way to the implication of a connection in logic or in thought which comes naturally or involuntarily to the mind of the observer either because the things traditionally go together, or naturally or rightfully belong together, or for some reason have come to be linked together in one's thoughts ⟨for the artist life is always a discipline, and no discipline can be without pain. That is so even of dancing, which of all the arts is most *associated* in the popular mind with pleasure—*Ellis*⟩ ⟨surrealism has been *associated* with psychological and intellectual atmosphere common to periods of war—*Bernard Smith*⟩ ⟨a fir tree is not a flower, and yet it is *associated* in my mind with primroses—*Jefferies*⟩ **Relate** implies a connection, or an attempt to show a connection, between two or more persons or things. In reference to persons it implies a connection through a common ancestor or through marriage ⟨John and James are remotely *related* to each other⟩ In reference to things or to persons objectively regarded, it implies that each has some bearing on the other and often indicates the existence of a real or presumed logical connection ⟨*related* his misfortunes to events which preceded them⟩ ⟨the two circumstances are not *related*⟩ ⟨their ability to *relate* what they observe to what they know or have previously observed—*Hildreth*⟩

*Ana* conjoin, *unite, combine, cooperate, concur: articulate, concatenate, *integrate: attach, affix, *fasten: knit, *weave: *tie, bind

*Ant* disjoin: part  —*Con* *separate, sever, sunder: *detach, disengage: disentangle, untangle, disembarrass (see EXTRICATE)

**joint,** articulation, suture denote a place where two things are united or the mechanism by which they are united. **Joint** is the most inclusive of these terms and is freely usable in reference both to anatomical and mechanical structures. In anatomical reference it applies to a junction whether rigidly fixed or capable of more or less complex movements of two skeletal parts (as vertebrate bones or cartilages or molluscan shell valves) and is the one of these terms that is equally applicable to the bodily region or part at which there is such a junction ⟨the knee *joint*⟩ ⟨the *joint* at the elbow is flexible⟩ ⟨he aches in every *joint*⟩ Similarly, in mechanical reference, *joint* applies to a junction between two parts that serves as a coupling and may be rigid ⟨a dovetail *joint* at the corner of a drawer⟩ ⟨a *joint* in a gas pipe⟩ ⟨mortar *joints* between bricks carefully finished to shed water⟩ or may form a flexible union ⟨a swivel *joint*⟩ ⟨the ball *joints* . . . have a

lateral as well as up-and-down action, thus cushioning against bumps—*Ford Times*⟩ or even (as in a universal joint) one through which motion is transmitted from one part to the other. **Articulation** is chiefly an anatomical term, though it has some extended use (see under INTEGRATE). Anatomically *articulation* is applicable to the same parts of the skeleton as *joint* but distinctively it implies, as *joint* does not, the fitting together or adjustment of two parts or bones with relation not only to each other but to the entire structure and its function and is therefore not applicable, as *joint* is, to the bodily region or part where a joint occurs. It is especially appropriate when the mechanism of a joint or the elements entering into its formation are under consideration ⟨ball-and-socket structure of a movable *articulation*⟩ ⟨various *articulations* are supported by ligaments⟩ ⟨the synovial membrane reduces friction at an *articulation*⟩ The word may also denote the process of joining or the adjustment in joining ⟨in the flat bones the *articulations* usually take place at the edges—*Henry Gray*⟩ **Suture** is used of a joint or articulation that suggests a seam or that has been brought about by sewing ⟨the joints of the two parts of a pea pod are called respectively the ventral and dorsal *sutures*⟩ ⟨the form of articulation observable in the skull where two flat bones meet in a line is called a *suture*⟩ Suture is used in surgery of a seam, especially of one whereby two edges of an incision are brought together so that they may ultimately unite.

**joke,** jest, jape, quip, witticism, wisecrack, crack, gag are comparable when they mean a remark, story, or action intended to evoke laughter. **Joke,** when applied to a story or remark, suggests something designed to promote good humor and especially an anecdote with a humorous twist at the end; when applied to an action, it often signifies a practical joke, usually suggesting a fooling or deceiving of someone at his expense, generally though not necessarily good humored in intent ⟨everyone knows the old *joke,* that "black horses eat more than white horses," a puzzling condition which is finally cleared up by the statement that "there are more black horses"—*Reilly*⟩ ⟨issues had become a hopeless muddle and national politics a biennial *joke—Wecter*⟩ ⟨a child hiding mother's pocketbook as a *joke*⟩ ⟨the whole tale turns out to be a monstrous *joke,* a deception of matchless cruelty—*Redman*⟩ **Jest** may connote raillery or ridicule but more generally suggests humor that is light and sportive ⟨continually . . . making a *jest* of his ignorance—*J. D. Beresford*⟩ ⟨won fame by *jests* at the foibles of his time, but . . . his pen was more playful than caustic—*Williams & Pollard*⟩ **Jape** is identical with *jest* or *joke* ⟨the merry *japes* of fundamentally irresponsible young men—*Edmund Fuller*⟩ ⟨the *japes* about sex still strike me as being prurient rather than funny—*McCarten*⟩ **Quip** suggests a quick, neatly turned, witty remark ⟨full of wise saws and homely illustrations, the epigram, the *quip,* the jest—*Cardozo*⟩ ⟨many *quips* at the expense of individuals and their villages—*Mead*⟩ ⟨enlivened their reviews with *quips—Dunham*⟩ **Witticism, wisecrack,** and **crack** all apply to a clever or witty, especially a biting or sarcastic, remark, generally serving as a retort ⟨all the charming *witticisms* of English lecturers—*Sevareid*⟩ ⟨a vicious *witticism* at the expense of a political opponent⟩ ⟨merely strolls by, makes a goofy *wisecrack* or screwball suggestion—*Hugh Humphrey*⟩ ⟨though the gravity of the situation forbade their utterance, I was thinking of at least three priceless *cracks* I could make—*Wodehouse*⟩ **Gag,** which in this relation basically signifies an interpolated joke or laugh-provoking piece of business, more generally applies to a remark, story, or piece of business considered

funny, especially one written into a theatrical, movie, radio, or television script. Sometimes the word has extended its meaning to signify a trick whether funny or not but usually one considered foolish ⟨*gags* grown venerable in the service of the music halls—*Times Lit. Sup.*⟩ ⟨the *gag* was not meant to be entirely funny— *Newsweek*⟩ ⟨gave a party the other night and pulled a really constructive *gag* . . . had every guest in the place vaccinated against smallpox—*Hollywood Reporter*⟩ ⟨a frivolous person, given to *gags* and foolishness⟩
*Ana* *prank, caper, antic, monkeyshine, dido: *trick, ruse, wile: travesty, parody, burlesque, *caricature: raillery, *badinage, persiflage: jocoseness, jocularity, facetiousness, wittiness, humorousness (see corresponding adjectives at WITTY): *wit, humor, repartee, sarcasm

**jollity** hilarity, glee, *mirth
*Ana* merriment, joviality, jocundity, blitheness (see corresponding adjectives at MERRY): sport, disport, play, frolic, rollick, gambol, romp (see under PLAY *vb*): diversion, amusement, recreation, entertainment (see under AMUSE): *fun, jest, sport, game, play
*Con* gloom, dejection, depression, melancholy, *sadness: solemnity, gravity, seriousness, earnestness, staidness, sedateness, somberness (see corresponding adjectives at SERIOUS)

**jolly** *adj* jovial, jocund, *merry, blithe
*Ana* bantering, chaffing, jollying, joshing (see BANTER *vb*): jocular, jocose, *witty, humorous, facetious: sportive, *playful, mischievous, roguish, waggish, frolicsome: gay, *lively, vivacious, animated, sprightly
*Con* solemn, somber, grave, sedate, staid, *serious, earnest: lugubrious, doleful, dolorous, *melancholy, rueful: morose, gloomy, glum, *sullen, dour, saturnine

**jolly** *vb* *banter, chaff, kid, rag, rib, josh
*Ana* blandish, cajole (see COAX): deride, *ridicule, twit, rally, mock, taunt

**jolt** *n* jar, shock, *impact, impingement, collision, clash, concussion, percussion
*Ana* shaking *or* shake, rocking *or* rock, convulsing *or* convulsion (see corresponding verbs at SHAKE)

**josh** *vb* *banter, chaff, kid, rag, rib, jolly

**jot** *n* tittle, iota, *particle, bit, mite, smidgen, whit, atom

**journal**, periodical, newspaper, magazine, review, organ are comparable when denoting a publication which appears regularly at stated times. Basically, a **journal** is a publication which is issued daily and gives an account of matters of interest occurring during the preceding twenty-four hours. Continued use, however, has made it an acceptable designation both of a publication that appears less often (as a weekly, a monthly, or a quarterly) ⟨[the *Hibbert Journal*] appeared every three months and called itself a *journal*—*Mackenzie*⟩ and of one that is the official publication of some special group ⟨the *Journal* of the American Medical Association⟩ **Periodical** applies to a publication appearing at regular intervals and especially to weeklies, biweeklies, monthlies, and quarterlies ⟨the *periodicals* are assembled in a special room of the library⟩ **Newspaper** is the usual term for a sheet or group of sheets of which the main function is to provide the news of the day and which is usually issued daily; such a publication is called a *journal* only in formal speech or writing, although those whose profession is writing for newspapers are often termed *journalists* and although the language and style believed to be typical of the newspaper is commonly called *journalese*. **Magazine** applies chiefly to a periodical, often illustrated, that offers a miscellaneous collection of articles, fiction, poetry, descriptive sketches, and commentary. **Review** applies to a periodical that emphasizes critical writings or articles commenting on

important events and significant questions of the day. **Organ** usually applies to a publication by an organization (as a political party, church, business, or institution) that gives news of interest to its members or adherents or presents its particular principles and views authoritatively ⟨*Science* is the official *organ* of the American Association for the Advancement of Science⟩

**journey,** voyage, tour, trip, jaunt, excursion, cruise, expedition, pilgrimage mean travel or a passage from one place to another. **Journey,** the most comprehensive term in general use, carries no particular implications of the distance, duration, destination, purpose, or mode of transportation involved ⟨plans a *journey* to California⟩ ⟨wished him a happy *journey* home⟩ ⟨the *journey* to Italy will not take more than two months⟩ ⟨a *journey* of twenty-five miles in Britain will often afford . . . much variety of scenery—*Stamp*⟩ ⟨the sound film took four years to make the *journey* from Hollywood to Rome—*Jarratt*⟩ **Voyage** normally implies a journey of some length over water, especially a sea or ocean ⟨with a fair sea *voyage,* and a fair land journey, you will be soon at his dear side—*Dickens*⟩ ⟨Gordon made the *voyage* from San Francisco around the Horn on a big full-rigged Glasgow sailing ship—*Current Biog.*⟩ but sometimes it may indicate a journey through air or space ⟨through the long 109-day, 180,000,000 mile *voyage,* Mariner was precisely controlled—*Christian Science Monitor*⟩ **Tour** applies to a somewhat circular journey from place to place that ends when one reaches one's starting point ⟨set out on a walking *tour*⟩ ⟨*tour* of Western Europe⟩ ⟨penologists made a *tour* of all the prisons in the state⟩ ⟨my next design was to make a *tour* round the island—*Defoe*⟩ ⟨left in September for a seven-week goodwill *tour* of northern and western Europe—*Current Biog.*⟩ **Trip** is the preferable word when referring to a relatively short journey, especially one for business or pleasure ⟨his new position requires frequent *trips* to New York⟩ ⟨the English came over in droves on the day *trips*—*A. V. Davis*⟩ ⟨surveys revealed that 59 percent of city-driver *trips* . . . were made for purposes of making a living— *Americana Annual*⟩ The term is also used in place of *journey* to refer to more extensive travels ⟨conclusions I had reached on my *trip* around the world—*Willkie*⟩ ⟨a *trip* through western Pennsylvania, then down the Ohio —*L. M. Sears*⟩ **Jaunt** carries a stronger implication of casualness and informality than any of the others and is especially applicable to a short trip away from one's home or one's business, usually for pleasure or recreation ⟨they are off for a day's *jaunt*⟩ ⟨a *jaunt* to the shore or the hills —*F. L. Allen*⟩ ⟨lip service is paid . . . to the idea of Congressional travel but the general tone throughout runs: They're off again on their *jaunts* at public expense— *H. A. Williams*⟩ **Excursion** applies to a brief pleasure trip, usually no more than a day in length ⟨the rural neighborhood of Sneyd, where they had been making an afternoon *excursion*—*Bennett*⟩ **Excursion** is the preferred term, especially in railroad and steamship use, for a round trip at reduced rates to a point of interest (as a resort or an exposition or a metropolis) ⟨the Minneapolis, Northfield & Southern Ry. runs *excursions* to Bush Lake on tournament days—*Amer. Guide Series: Minn.*⟩ When the excursion involves a voyage of some days or weeks and, often, a sight-seeing tour with frequent stops during which the participants use the ship as their living quarters, **cruise** is the usual term ⟨a Mediterranean *cruise*⟩ ⟨the steamship lines are featuring winter *cruises* through the Caribbean Sea⟩ ⟨their yacht is off with a party on a *cruise*⟩ **Expedition** applies to a journey intended to further a definite purpose ⟨he called this trip frankly a begging *expedition—Cather⟩ ⟨he made a special *expedition* to the city to try to straighten out the difficulty⟩ ⟨had charge of the *expedition* to observe the transit of Venus in China —*Rufus*⟩ ⟨an archaeological *expedition*⟩ **Pilgrimage** applies primarily to an expedition to a place hallowed by religious associations but is sometimes applied also to a journey to a place of historical or sentimental association ⟨Arabs make *pilgrimages* to worship at his tomb— *Hichens*⟩ ⟨an excited conference at Niagara Falls in 1905 and the fervid *pilgrimage* to Harpers Ferry ... were tokens of the Negroes' obdurate consciousness of their identity —*Handlin*⟩ Often it implies an arduous journey or slow and difficult passage ⟨Chaucer's *Canterbury Tales* is a collection of stories told by men and women on a *pilgrimage* to the tomb of St. Thomas à Becket at Canterbury⟩

**jovial** jolly, jocund, *merry, blithe
*Ana* jocular, jocose, facetious, humorous, *witty: genial, sociable, affable (see GRACIOUS): good-natured, *amiable: bantering, chaffing, jollying, joshing (see BANTER *vb*)
*Con* saturnine, dour, morose, gloomy, glum, *sullen: sedate, staid, grave, solemn, *serious

**joy** delight, *pleasure, enjoyment, delectation, fruition
*Ana* bliss, beatitude, *happiness, felicity: *ecstasy, rapture, transport
*Ant* sorrow (*as emotion*): misery (*as a state of mind*): abomination (*in concrete sense*)

**joyful** joyous, cheerful, happy, *glad, lighthearted
*Ana* blithe, jocund, *merry, jolly: buoyant, effervescent, expansive (see ELASTIC)
*Ant* joyless —*Con* *despondent, despairing, desperate, forlorn, hopeless: depressed, weighed down, oppressed (see DEPRESS)

**joyous** joyful, happy, *glad, cheerful, lighthearted
*Ana* blithe, jocund, *merry: rapturous, ecstatic, transported (see corresponding nouns at ECSTASY)
*Ant* lugubrious —*Con* dolorous, doleful, *melancholy: *miserable, wretched

**judge** *vb* 1 Judge, adjudge, adjudicate, arbitrate mean to decide something in dispute or controversy upon its merits and upon evidence. All these words imply the existence of a competent legal tribunal or of its equivalent. **Judge** implies mainly the investigation of evidence on both sides, a comparison of the merits of each case, and a decision as to where the truth lies ⟨the court must *judge* between the claimants⟩ ⟨the matter is to be *judged* on the facts as they appeared then—*Justice Holmes*⟩ **Adjudge** stresses decision by a court either at the end of a trial or during a legal process ⟨the evidence was *adjudged* inadmissible⟩ ⟨the court *adjudged* the will void⟩ ⟨the district court *adjudged* the 1946 agreement void—*Harvard Law Review*⟩ **Adjudicate,** on the other hand, stresses formal deliberate determination of an issue by or as if by a court and often the pronouncing of a judgment, sentence, or decree ⟨the court proceeded to *adjudicate* the rights and interests of the parties⟩ ⟨it is useless to reargue a seemingly *adjudicated* case—*Lowes*⟩ ⟨a bitter dispute that was not *adjudicated* until 1782—*Amer. Guide Series: Conn.*⟩ ⟨all former WW II POWs whose claims were *adjudicated* by the commission—*The Naval Reservist*⟩ **Arbitrate** implies deliberate determination of a matter in dispute by one or more persons who constitute a tribunal that may or may not be legally recognized and who are usually acceptable to both sides to the controversy ⟨the strikers and the employers finally agreed on a group of three men to *arbitrate* their differences⟩ ⟨litigation has virtually ceased: it is possible, of course, that the elders are *arbitrating* these cases out of court—*Gunn*⟩
*Ana* determine, *decide, settle, rule
2 conclude, deduce, *infer, gather

*Ana* *prove, demonstrate, try, test

**judge** *n* Judge, arbiter, arbitrator, referee, umpire are comparable when they denote a person who decides or helps to decide questions or issues that are unsettled or in controversy. **Judge** implies the assumption or the possession both of superior knowledge, experience, or wisdom, and of the power to determine the truth by weighing critically and impartially the merits of a case ⟨it doth appear you are a worthy *judge; you* know the law, your exposition hath been most sound—*Shak.*⟩ ⟨the polls in each district or precinct are in charge of ... two *judges,* who help decide disputes—*Ogg & Ray*⟩ ⟨the question is whether in language the results justify the quibble. Well, the public is here the best *judge*—*Barzun*⟩ **Arbiter** stresses authoritativeness of decision and is applied to one, whether or not a professed judge, whose word or example is accepted as final and indisputable ⟨the *arbiter* of taste ... the persuasive exponent of a reasonable life, the clear, sad thinker who led no man astray—*Repplier*⟩ ⟨they were the *arbiters* of fashion, the Court of last Appeal, and they knew it—*Wharton*⟩ ⟨that "common consent of mankind" which certain moralists make the *arbiter* in ethics—*Brownell*⟩ **Arbitrator,** referee, and umpire are applied to persons to whom a dispute is referred for decision. **Arbitrator,** though sometimes interchangeable with *arbiter,* usually is applied to a person chosen by the parties to a controversy or appointed under statutory authority to resolve the differences between the parties and to formulate a fair solution ⟨the governor appointed as *arbitrators* two persons recommended by the striking miners, two recommended by the mineowners, and one person agreed upon by both sides⟩ In legal use **referee** is applied to an attorney-at-law appointed either to determine a case or to report on it to the court which he serves as an officer. It is therefore clearly distinguishable from *arbitrator.* **Umpire,** on the other hand, is applied to the person selected to make a final decision when arbitrators have disagreed or are tied. In sports and games both *umpire* and *referee* are technical terms applied to the official or officials charged with the regulation and supervision of a contest (as by enforcement of rules of a game, making decisions on plays, and determining penalties for faults). In most sports either one term or the other is used; thus, these officials in baseball, cricket, and tennis are designated *umpires,* while in boxing, basketball, football, and ice hockey they are designated *referees.* In nontechnical use *referee* usually is applied to one to whom disputants have recourse when agreement seems impossible, *umpire* to one who enters in and arbitrarily ends the struggle or dispute ⟨clear-sighted, unprejudiced, sagacious ... he was the universal *referee*—*Disraeli*⟩ ⟨just death, kind *umpire* of men's miseries—*Shak.*⟩

**judgment** 1 conclusion, deduction, inference (see under INFER)
*Ana* decision, determination, ruling (see corresponding verbs at DECIDE): *opinion, conviction, persuasion, view, belief
2 *sense, wisdom, gumption
*Ana* intelligence, wit, brain, *mind: sagaciousness *or* sagacity, perspicaciousness *or* perspicacity, shrewdness, astuteness (see corresponding adjectives at SHREWD): acumen, *discernment, insight, penetration: *prudence, discretion

**judicial,** judiciary, juridical, juristic are comparable because of verbal confusion and because all imply some connection with courts of law. **Judicial,** by far the most common of these adjectives both in legal and in general use, often implies a direct reference to the courts of justice, the judge who presides over a court of justice, or the

---

*Ana* analogous words  *Ant* antonyms  *Con* contrasted words  See also explanatory notes facing page 1

judges who form such a court ⟨a *judicial* decision⟩ ⟨a *judicial* duty⟩ ⟨a *judicial* proceeding⟩ ⟨I am told at times by friends that a *judicial* opinion has no business to be literature—*Cardozo*⟩ The term is also used in distinction from *executive, legislative* when applied to that one of the powers, departments, or functions of the government which is associated with a court (as the United States Supreme Court), which gives definitive decisions on questions of law or interprets the constitution or basic law ⟨the executive, legislative, and *judicial* branches of the government⟩ ⟨government analyzes into three main functions . . . legislative, executive, and *judicial* activities —*Ogg & Ray*⟩ In extended use *judicial* is applied especially to a type of mind, mental activity, or manner suggestive of that of a judge (as in detachment or fair-mindedness) or appropriate to a judge or court of justice (as in orderliness and seriousness of procedure) ⟨to a strictly *judicial* mind . . . the quality of age or of novelty would carry no necessary implication of value—*Grandgent*⟩ ⟨the review made an evident effort to be *judicial* . . . and so exhibiting both the good and bad points of the novel it alternated favorable and unfavorable judgments—*McCloskey*⟩ **Judiciary** is occasionally used in place of *judicial*, especially when it suggests reference to the courts in general and to the administration of justice as a whole ⟨the appointment of more women to higher *judiciary* positions —*Current Biog.*⟩ In current usage, however, *judiciary* occurs predominantly as a substantive, with *judicial* its corresponding adjective. The two words *juridical* and *juristic* imply a connection with the law, especially as it is administered in the courts, rather than with the judges or those who settle questions of law. Often these terms come close to *legal* in meaning ⟨ordered . . . to grant *juridical* recognition to the Assemblies of God churches in Italy— *Time*⟩ but in learned use they are more restricted in significance. Both terms, but especially **juridical**, imply a reference to the law as it appears to learned lawyers and judges —that is, as a highly complex and involved body of principles, statutes, decisions, and precedents requiring vast knowledge, skill in interpretation, and a keen logical mind in those who put it to use; therefore, the term often means characteristic of, determinable by, or useful to a person with such knowledge and skill ⟨Eden is clearly working for the *juridical* separation of Formosa and the Pescadores from the mainland—*Healey*⟩ ⟨high time that we act on the *juridical* principle that aggressive war-making is illegal and criminal—*R. H. Jackson*⟩ **Juristic** implies rather a reference to the science of law ⟨set forth with all the circumstance of philosophical and *juristic* scholarship—*Veblen*⟩ ⟨laws and *juristic* compilations of the Norman period—*Stenton*⟩ ⟨[Justice] Holmes had struck in 1905 in his dissent in *Lochmer v. N.Y.* the high pitch of American *juristic* thought—*New Republic*⟩

**judiciary** *judicial, juridical, juristic

**judicious** *wise, sage, sapient, prudent, sensible, sane
*Ana* *rational, reasonable: just, *fair, equitable, dispassionate, objective: sagacious, perspicacious, astute, *shrewd: discreet, prudent (see under PRUDENCE)
*Ant* injudicious: asinine —*Con* *foolish, silly, absurd, preposterous: *stupid, slow, dull, dumb, crass, dense: rash, reckless, foolhardy (see ADVENTUROUS)

**jumble** *n* *confusion, disorder, chaos, disarray, clutter, snarl, muddle

**jump** *vb* **Jump, leap, spring, bound, vault** are comparable as verbs meaning to move suddenly through space by or as if by muscular action and as nouns designating an instance of such movement through space. All of these terms apply primarily to the movements of men or lower animals, but they also may be used of similar movements of inanimate things. **Jump**, the most general term, basically implies a projection of the body that results in reaching a spot which is to some extent distant, whether below, above, or on the same plane ⟨she *jumped* from a second-story window⟩ ⟨*jump* over a fence⟩ ⟨*jump* from the ground to the top of a low wall⟩ ⟨a *jump* across a ditch⟩ Since *jump* usually implies a rise and descent in a curve and a landing away from the point of origin, it is often applicable to things as well that follow a similar curve or seem to have a similar objective ⟨[the fire] then *jumped* Essex Street and burned the house of Samuel Prince— *J. D. Phillips*⟩ *Jump* may be extended to various sudden or sharp movements whether physical or not ⟨his heart *jumped* with fright⟩ ⟨prices *jumped* when war was declared⟩ ⟨the children *jumped* with joy⟩ **Leap** usually implies greater muscular effort than *jump*, though it otherwise often agrees with it in implications; it may or may not suggest suddenness, swiftness, a forward or a backward motion, or an upward or a downward motion, but it usually includes one or more of these connotations in its meaning ⟨the chamois *leaps* from crag to crag⟩ ⟨a *leap* from a window⟩ ⟨*leapt* over a wall⟩ In extended use *leap* goes further than *jump* in suggesting suddenness or intensity (as of change, response, surprise, or exaltation of thoughts) ⟨my heart would have *leaped* at sight of him —*Kenneth Roberts*⟩ ⟨ashes am I of all that once I seemed. In me all's sunk that *leapt*, and all that dreamed is wakeful for alarm—*Millay*⟩ **Spring** implies a jumping or leaping, but both as verb and as noun it additionally suggests ideas not involved in *jump* and only occasionally involved in *leap*, such as resiliency, elasticity, grace of movement, and emergence by issuing or flowing. The emphasis is often upon the action itself rather than upon the fact of movement to or over ⟨*spring* from the bed⟩ ⟨the *spring* of a cat on a bird⟩ ⟨I *sprang* to my feet, for anger had overtaken me—*Edita Morris*⟩ ⟨*sprang* across the stream, inviting those who shared his views to follow him—*Amer. Guide Series: Me.*⟩ **Bound** (see also SKIP) comes very close to *spring* in its emphasis upon the action itself, but it carries an implication of vigor and strength not apparent in *spring*, so that it often connotes a plunging or a lunging forward ⟨he *bounded* forward in order to catch the ball⟩ ⟨with a *bound*, he was at her side⟩ ⟨there were great kangaroos that . . . would descend the hillslopes in large, slow, gracious *bounds*—*Ellis*⟩ Although **vault** is often used specifically in respect to leaping as a physical exercise with the aid of a long pole as a fulcrum, it may also apply to a leap or a leaping upward with the aid of a support or a leap over an object often with a hand laid on the object ⟨unperturbed by the tumble he *vaulted* back into the saddle⟩ ⟨an acrobat . . . was *vaulting* over chair backs —*Deland*⟩ ⟨put his hand on the counter and *vaulted* over, landing heavily on the other side—*J. W. Johnson*⟩

**jump** *n* leap, spring, bound, vault (see under JUMP *vb*)

**jumpy** jittery, nervous, restless, uneasy, fidgety, *impatient, unquiet, restive
*Ant* steady

**junction,** confluence, concourse are comparable when meaning the act, state, or place of meeting or uniting. **Junction**, the most general of these words, applies to the meeting or uniting usually of material things (as roads, rivers, lines, or railroads) ⟨at all the street *junctions* along the coronation procession route, traffic is slowed— *Panter-Downes*⟩ ⟨Brattleboro spreads along the Connecticut from its *junction* with the West river—*Amer. Guide Series: Vt.*⟩ ⟨electricity produced by the *junction* of two dissimilar metals—*S. F. Mason*⟩ or less often of immaterial things ⟨the *junction* of the Senecan influence with the native tradition—*T. S. Eliot*⟩ ⟨a fairly close

---

A colon (:) separates groups of words discriminated. An asterisk (*) indicates place of treatment of each group.

*junction* of interest between Brady and the so-called Standard Oil group—*H. P. Willis*⟩ and only occasionally of persons or groups of persons ⟨another small force of Frenchmen, reinforced by Ethiopian natives, moved westward, seeking *junction* with [Major] Marchand—*Lengyel*⟩ ⟨there he proposed to effect his *junction* with the man who should make all the difference to this new civil war—*Belloc*⟩ **Confluence** suggests a flowing movement that brings things together. It is applicable to two or more things or persons viewed as things which flow or seem to flow toward a point where they merge and mingle ⟨the *confluence* of cowboys, cattle traders, and railroad men gave Dodge City a lively homicidal character—*Life*⟩. It specifically applies to the place at which streams unite, often to form a larger stream or body of water ⟨the Ohio river is formed by the *confluence* of the Monongahela and Allegheny rivers⟩ ⟨this river, which is formed by the *confluence* of the historic Tigris and Euphrates rivers—*Boschen*⟩ **Concourse** places the emphasis on a running or flocking together of great numbers of persons or things ⟨the . . . frame of the universe was not the product of chance, or fortuitous *concourse* of particles of matter —*Hale*⟩ It is commonly used of a place, sometimes out of doors but sometimes in such a great building as a railroad terminal, in which there is an endless flow of persons or things passing through ⟨just off the waiting room is the passenger *concourse*, a 24 x 1200-foot "bon voyage deck" where passengers of the *Lurline* arrive and depart and their friends greet them or wave them on their way—*Ships and the Sea*⟩

**juncture,** pass, exigency, emergency, contingency, pinch, strait, crisis denote a critical or crucial time or state of affairs (as in the life of a person or institution or the history of a country). **Juncture** emphasizes the significant concurrence or convergence of events and usually indicates a discernible turning point ⟨we *may* now be at a vital *juncture* where the ideals of liberalism can best be achieved through separate institutions and not the omnicompetent state—*Kurtz*⟩ ⟨the Church of England is at the present *juncture* the one church upon which the duty of working towards reunion most devolves—*T. S. Eliot*⟩ **Pass** implies a concurrence or convergence of events or a condition induced by such that is evil, distressing, or sometimes utterly confusing ⟨have his daughters brought him to this *pass*?—*Shak.*⟩ ⟨Constance, after . . . reflection on the frightful *pass* to which destiny had brought her, had said that she supposed she would have to manage with a charwoman until Rose's advent—*Bennett*⟩ ⟨things have come to a pretty *pass* when a professional informer . . . is himself under investigation—*New Republic*⟩ **Exigency** (see also NEED) strongly emphasizes the pressure or restrictions of necessity or the urgency of the demands created by a juncture or pass ⟨it would have been an unwise attempt to provide, by immutable rules, for *exigencies* which, if foreseen at all, must have been seen dimly and which can be best provided for as they occur—*John Marshall*⟩ ⟨regret that the *exigencies* of party politics should deprive our government of so much talent—*Altschul*⟩ **Emergency** implies a sudden or unforeseen juncture that necessitates immediate action to avoid disaster; the term need not imply that what constitutes an emergency has also the quality of an *exigency,* for the latter term is far stronger in its suggestion of extreme difficulty ⟨it was a special provision . . . to meet a present *emergency*, and nothing more—*Taney*⟩ ⟨a presence of mind which no *emergency* can perturb—*Eliot*⟩ **Contingency** is used of a prospective event or concurrence of events that is fortuitous and is uncertain in respect to either or both the time and the fact of occurrence but that, if it should come to pass,

would constitute an exigency or emergency ⟨having thus devised a plan for use in a *contingency,* Calhoun sought in various ways to prevent the *contingency* from coming —*U. B. Phillips*⟩ ⟨every citizen must have a stake in his country adequate to justify in his eyes the sacrifices that any *contingency* may entail—*W. O. Douglas*⟩ ⟨to be dug out now and then in the winter is a *contingency* the mail driver reckons as part of his daily life—*Jefferies*⟩ **Pinch** suggests pressure and the need for action but without the same intensity as *emergency* or *exigency*; it is particularly appropriate for use of a juncture in personal affairs ⟨I could always in a *pinch* pawn my microscope for three pounds—*Maugham*⟩ ⟨ready in a *pinch* to ride roughshod over opposition—*Power*⟩ ⟨this—the great *pinch* of his life —*Hawthorne*⟩ **Strait,** often in its plural **straits**, applies to a situation from which the person involved finds it difficult to escape, so hampered or fettered is he by some given or implied set of circumstances ⟨he was in great *straits* for lack of money⟩ ⟨this disagreeable companion had, of his own free will, assisted him in the *strait* of the day—*Dickens*⟩ ⟨he was at a loss what to invent to detain him . . . . He rendered homage to the genius of woman in these *straits*. "My Aunt," he thought, "would have the lie ready"—*Meredith*⟩ ⟨the army's truly desperate *straits—Mason*⟩ **Crisis** applies to a juncture or pass whose outcome will make a decisive difference, for good or ill, in a life or a history or a disease. The term usually connotes suspense, but need not imply either evil in the situation or a particular outcome ⟨the pneumonia patient has passed the *crisis*⟩ ⟨Tiberius gave one million pounds out of his own pocket to relieve the agrarian *crisis* of A.D. 33 —*Buchan*⟩ ⟨Father finally . . . brought the matter to a *crisis*. He said, after all, the boy had a right to choose— *Mary Austin*⟩ ⟨her adolescence had passed without the trace of a religious *crisis—Huxley*⟩
*Ana* *state, posture, situation, condition, status: *predicament, plight, quandary
**junk** *vb* scrap, *discard, cast, shed, molt, slough
**juridical** juristic, *judicial, judiciary
**jurisdiction** *power, authority, control, command, sway, dominion
*Ana* limits, bounds, confines (see singular nouns at LIMIT): *range, scope, compass, reach: circuit, periphery (see CIRCUMFERENCE): province, office, *function, duty: domain, territory, province, *field, sphere, bailiwick
**juristic** juridical, *judicial, judiciary
**just** *adj* 1 *upright, honorable, conscientious, scrupulous, honest
*Ana* strict, *rigid: virtuous, righteous, *moral, ethical, noble: *reliable, dependable, tried, trustworthy
*Con* *crooked, devious, oblique: corrupt, perverted, debauched, depraved (see under DEBASE): *base, low, vile: ignoble, *mean
2 equitable, *fair, impartial, unbiased, dispassionate, uncolored, objective
*Ana* detached, disinterested, aloof (see INDIFFERENT): *due, rightful, condign: *rational, reasonable
*Ant* unjust
**justice,** equity are comparable primarily in their legal uses and when they denote the act, practice, or obligation of giving or rendering to a person or thing what is his or its due (as in conformity with right, truth, or the dictates of reason). **Justice** is by far the wider-ranging term, for it may apply to an abstraction which represents an ideal ⟨he flamed out against injustice because he was a lover of *justice—Perry*⟩ or to a quality of mind which exhibits adherence to this ideal ⟨nothing escaped the kind eyes, the far-seeing love, that punished and praised with that calm *justice* which children so keenly appreciate—*Deland*⟩

or to a quality in a thing which never departs from the truth in the slightest degree ⟨he painted a psychological portrait of himself which for its serenely impartial *justice,* its subtle gradations . . . has all the qualities of the finest Velásquez—*Ellis*⟩ or to the treatment accorded one who has transgressed a law, whether a divine law, a natural law, or the law of a state, or who seeks relief when wronged or protection when his rights are threatened ⟨at the present time . . . there is more danger that criminals will escape *justice* than that they will be subjected to tyranny—*Justice Holmes*⟩ or to the system of courts of law whereby the rights of an individual or his innocence or guilt are determined in accordance with the laws of the state ⟨in the modern state . . . . *Justice* and administration are directly connected with whatever governs—*Belloc*⟩ **Equity** differs from *justice* chiefly in being more restricted in its denotation, for it usually implies a justice that transcends the strict letter of the law and is in keeping with what is reasonable rather than with what is merely legal. It is in this sense that a court of equity is, theoretically at least, distinguished from a court of law. To the former go for adjudication and settlement the unusual cases where abstract justice might not be dealt out according to the limitations of the written law while to the latter go the vast majority of cases where the determination of facts is of first importance and where the law, once the facts are established, provides the treatment to be accorded the person or parties involved ⟨in informal terms, a law case is one where the courts have only to decide who is right; an *equity* case is one where the courts have to decide not only who is right, but go on to say what must be done—*Science*⟩ But *equity* in nonlegal use implies a justice based upon a strictly impartial meting out of what is due (as rewards and punishments or praise and blame) ⟨that noble word *liberal,* which in America has become dissociated from its essential humanism and sense of *equity* —*Ustinov*⟩ ⟨the union claimed that the lower wages paid to aliens were not in keeping with any principle of *equity*⟩
**justify** 1 vindicate, defend, *maintain, assert
*Ana* *prove, demonstrate: *support, uphold, back
*Con* *disprove, refute, confute
2 account, rationalize, *explain
*Ana* *excuse, condone: *exculpate, exonerate, absolve,

acquit, vindicate: extenuate, gloze, gloss, whitewash, *palliate
*Con* incriminate, indict, arraign, *accuse: condemn, denounce, blame (see CRITICIZE)
3 **Justify, warrant** are comparable when meaning to be the thing (as evidence, a circumstance, a situation, or a state of affairs) that constitutes sufficient grounds for doing, saying, using, or believing something. **Justify** may be preferred when the stress is on providing grounds that satisfy conscience as well as reason, and usually refers to an action that, unjustified, would be looked upon with disapproval ⟨no consideration on earth *justifies* a parent in telling lies to his child—*Russell*⟩ ⟨I remember a very tenderhearted judge being of opinion that closing a hatch to stop a fire and the destruction of a cargo was *justified* even if it was known that doing so would stifle a man below —*Justice Holmes*⟩ ⟨Locke *justified* the right of revolution —*W. S. Myers*⟩ ⟨Batista *justified* his seizure of power on the grounds of an alleged conspiracy by the government to control the elections—*Americana Annual*⟩ **Warrant** is especially appropriate (see also ASSERT 1) when the emphasis is on something that requires an explanation or reason rather than an excuse and suggests support by authority, precedent, experience, or logic ⟨the deposits contain too high a percentage of sulfur to *warrant* development—*Wythe*⟩ ⟨the history and appearance clearly *warrant* such assumption—*Armstrong*⟩ ⟨a shorter course is designed for students whose graduate study and experience *warrant* it—*Smith College: The President's Report 1952-1953*⟩
*Ana* allow, permit (see LET): sanction (see APPROVE): *authorize
**jut** *bulge, stick out, protuberate, protrude, project, overhang, beetle
*Ana* *extend, lengthen, elongate: swell, distend, dilate, *expand
**juvenile** *youthful, puerile, boyish, virgin, virginal, maiden
*Ana* *immature, unmatured: callow, green, crude (see RUDE)
*Ant* adult: senile —*Con* *mature, matured, grown-up
**juxtaposed** *adjacent, adjoining, contiguous, abutting, tangent, conterminous
*Ana* *close, near, nigh

# K

**keen** *adj* 1 *sharp, acute
*Ana* piercing, penetrating, probing (see ENTER): *pungent, poignant, piquant: cutting, biting, *incisive, trenchant
*Ant* blunt —*Con* *dull, obtuse
2 *eager, avid, agog, athirst, anxious
*Ana* ardent, fervent, fervid, perfervid (see IMPASSIONED): *intense, vehement, fierce: fired (see LIGHT *vb*)
*Con* apathetic, *impassive, stolid, phlegmatic: listless, *languid: unconcerned, incurious, *indifferent, uninterested, disinterested
**keen** *vb* wait, weep, *cry, whimper, blubber
*Ana* lament, bewail, bemoan (see DEPLORE): mourn, sorrow, *grieve
**keep** *vb* 1 Keep, observe, celebrate, solemnize, commemorate are comparable when they mean to pay proper attention or honor to something prescribed, obligatory, or demanded (as by one's nationality, religion, or rank), but they vary widely in their range of reference or applica-

tion. *Keep* and *observe* are closely synonymous terms, especially when they imply heed of what is prescribed or obligatory, but they differ fundamentally in their connotations. **Keep** implies opposition to *break,* and emphasizes the idea of not neglecting or violating; thus, one *keeps,* rather than *observes,* a promise ⟨*keep* the peace⟩ ⟨*keep* the commandments⟩ **Observe** carries such positive implications as punctiliousness in performance of required acts and rites and a spirit of respect or reverence for what one heeds or honors; when these more appropriate ideas are definitely to be suggested *observe* is the more appropriate term, even though *keep* would otherwise be possible; thus, few persons *observe,* rather than *keep,* the Sabbath in the manner of the early Puritans ⟨*observed* Passover with the utmost strictness⟩ ⟨he *observes* the letter of the law⟩ *Celebrate* and *solemnize* are also close synonyms because they may take as their objects not only a day, a season, or an occasion which for religious, political, or

A colon (:) separates groups of words discriminated. An asterisk (*) indicates place of treatment of each group.

other significant reasons is observed with pomp and ceremony but also a ceremony or rite, usually a religious ceremony or rite, that is marked with unusual dignity and splendor. **Celebrate,** however, except in certain idiomatic phrases (as *celebrate* the Eucharist, *celebrate* a marriage, *celebrate* Mass) in which the gravity and forms of religion are implicit, suggests demonstrations of joy or festivity (as by singing, shouting, speechmaking, and feasting) ⟨*celebrate* Independence Day⟩ ⟨*celebrated* their golden wedding⟩ ⟨the family decided to *celebrate* the occasion by a large dinner party⟩ **Solemnize** as applied to occasions of joy and festivity stresses their grave, ceremonious, or solemn aspects and usually suggests greater formality in observance and greater dignity and splendor of ceremony than does *celebrate* ⟨Harvard each June *solemnizes* the award of degrees to students ... of the University—*Official Register of Harvard Univ.*⟩ ⟨*solemnize* this sorrowing natal day to prove our loyal truth—*Burns*⟩ The term is often specifically used of the celebrating of marriage especially with the fullest applicable religious ceremonial; thus, in the Roman Catholic Church a marriage is *solemnized* only when administration of the sacrament of matrimony is followed by a nuptial Mass and a special blessing ⟨Catholics may marry but their marriages may not be *solemnized* during Lent⟩ **Commemorate** implies remembrance and suggests observances that tend to call to mind what the occasion (as the day, the season, or the ceremony) stands for; thus, one *celebrates* Christmas by religious ceremonies that *commemorate* the birth of Christ; the people of the United States *commemorate* the birth of their independence on the 4th of July; the French people *commemorate* the fall of the Bastille on the 14th of July.
*Ana* regard, respect (see under REGARD *n*)
*Ant* break —*Con* *neglect, ignore, forget, disregard, overlook, omit, slight: violate, transgress, contravene, infringe (see corresponding nouns at BREACH)

2 **Keep, keep back, keep out, retain, detain, withhold, reserve, hold, hold back** are comparable in meaning not to let go from one's possession, custody, or control. **Keep** is the most general of these terms, often carrying no further implications ⟨*keep* this until I ask for it⟩ When, however, it positively denotes a holding securely in one's possession, custody, or control, *keep,* or more often **keep back,** is synonymous with one or another of the remaining terms. **Keep out** specifically implies a keeping back of a portion of something ⟨*kept out* a part of his salary for emergency expenses⟩ **Retain** implies continued keeping, especially as against threatened seizure or forced loss ⟨Germany was unable to *retain* her colonies after the first World War⟩ ⟨the conception of one who ... poor, sickly, and a slave perhaps, or even in prison or on the rack, should nevertheless *retain* unimpaired the dignity of manhood—*Dickinson*⟩ **Detain** (see also ARREST 2) implies a keeping (as in a place, in conversation, or in one's possession or control) through a delay in letting go that may be based on selfishness or caprice or on entirely acceptable grounds ⟨*detain* a ship in quarantine⟩ ⟨much consideration has been given to the practice of *detaining* children away from home for the sole purpose of diagnostic study—*Service to Youth*⟩ ⟨[the cat] let the rat run about his legs, but made no effort to *detain* him there—*Grahame*⟩ **Withhold** implies restraint in letting go or a refusal to let go. Sometimes it is interchangeable with *keep,* or *keep back,* especially when hindrance is also implied ⟨timidity caused him to *withhold* the advice he longed to give⟩ Sometimes, *keep* and *withhold* are widely different in meaning; thus, to *withhold* one's promise is to refuse to give one's promise; to *keep* (see KEEP 1) one's

promise is to fulfill what has been promised. **Reserve** implies either a keeping in store for other or for future use ⟨the runner *reserved* some of his energy for the final sprint⟩ ⟨*reserve* some of the milk for breakfast⟩ or a withholding from present or from others' use or enjoyment ⟨the force of will which had enabled her to *reserve* the fund intact—*Bennett*⟩ ⟨*reserved* his judgment⟩ **Hold** and **hold back** are often used in place of *withhold* or *keep back* and sometimes in place of *detain* and *reserve* when restraint in letting go, whether self-imposed or imposed by others, is implied ⟨*hold back* a portion of each week's wages for group insurance⟩ ⟨*held back* the truth in giving his testimony⟩
*Ana* *save, preserve, conserve: hold, *have, enjoy, possess, own: control, direct, manage, *conduct
*Ant* relinquish —*Con* *discard, cast, junk: refuse, reject, repudiate, spurn (see DECLINE *vb*): surrender, abandon, resign, yield (see RELINQUISH)
**keep** *n* *living, livelihood, subsistence, sustenance, maintenance, support, bread
**keep back, keep out** *keep, retain, detain, withhold, reserve, hold, hold back
**keepsake** *remembrance, remembrancer, reminder, memorial, memento, token, souvenir
**ken** *n* *range, gamut, reach, radius, compass, sweep, scope, orbit, horizon, purview
*Ana* *field, sphere, province, domain: view, sight (see LOOK *n*)
**kibitzer** onlooker, looker-on, bystander, *spectator, observer, beholder, witness, eyewitness
**kick** *vb* *object, protest, remonstrate, expostulate
*Ana* oppose, combat, *resist, withstand, fight: *criticize, denounce, condemn: objurgate, *execrate, curse, damn, anathematize
**kid** *vb* chaff, *banter, rag, rib, josh, jolly
*Ana* tease, plague, pester, harry, *worry
**kidnap** *abduct
**kidney** kind, sort, *type, nature, description, character, stripe, ilk
**kill** *vb* Kill, slay, murder, assassinate, dispatch, execute are comparable when meaning to deprive of life or to put to death. **Kill** is so general that it merely states the fact and does not, except in special phrases (as "Thou shalt not *kill*"), suggest human agency or the means of death or the conditions attending the putting to death. Also, the object of the action may be not only a person or other living thing but also an inanimate or immaterial thing with qualities suggestive of life ⟨*kill* snails in the garden⟩ ⟨a boy *killed* by a fall⟩ ⟨vegetation *killed* by frost⟩ ⟨the president *killed* the project when he vetoed the bill making an appropriation for it⟩ ⟨*kill* a friend's love by indifference⟩ ⟨he believed at that time that the League of Nations was going to *kill* war, that the Labour Party were going to *kill* industrial inequity—*Rose Macaulay*⟩ **Slay** implies killing by force or in wantonness; it is rare in spoken English, but it often occurs in written English where it may convey a dramatic quality whether in poetic or elevated writing or in journalese ⟨though he *slay* me, yet will I trust in him—*Job* 13:15⟩ ⟨the *slain* man has not yet been identified⟩ In its extended uses *slay* usually suggests wanton or deliberate destruction or annihilation ⟨to *slay* the reverence living in the minds of men—*Shelley*⟩ ⟨never had she greatly loved before; never would she greatly love again; and the great love she now had she was *slaying*—*Rose Macaulay*⟩ **Murder** definitely implies a motive and, often, premeditation and imputes to the act a criminal character; it is the exact word to use in reference to one person killing another either in passion or in cold blood ⟨Macbeth *murdered* Duncan⟩ ⟨Thomas à

K
L

Becket, archbishop of Canterbury, was *murdered* in his own cathedral⟩ It is sometimes used in place of *kill* as more expressive or in place of *slay* as more brutally direct and condemnatory, both in literal and extended use ⟨Glamis hath *murdered* sleep, and therefore Cawdor shall sleep no more; Macbeth shall sleep no more—*Shak.*⟩ ⟨the language of strategy and politics is designed . . . to make it appear as though wars were not fought by individuals drilled to *murder* one another in cold blood—*Huxley*⟩ **Assassinate** implies murder especially of a person in governmental or political power by stealth or treachery and often by an agent or hireling of an opposition. It usually suggests an attempt to get rid of a person who is believed to be an obstacle to the safety of a tyrant, the welfare of a people, the liberty of a nation, or the success of a design ⟨Marat was *assassinated* by Charlotte Corday⟩ ⟨at least two attempts were made to *assassinate* William of Orange⟩ **Dispatch** also suggests an attempt to get rid of a person by killing him, but it is far more colorless than *assassinate* ⟨and the company shall stone them with stones, and *dispatch* them with their swords—*Ezek* 23:47⟩ Because it nearly always implies taking direct means of killing (as by shooting or stabbing) and so sometimes connotes expedition or speed in killing or in ending suffering, it is applicable, as most of the other terms are not, to killing (as of a sick or injured animal) for humane reasons ⟨the policeman *dispatched* the rabid dog with a single shot⟩ Often *dispatch* is merely a euphemism for another of the terms of this group when quick killing or a sudden end is implied ⟨reached up, caught Wright by the coat, . . . and at one stab *dispatched* him—*Amer. Guide Series: La.*⟩ **Execute** is the term for putting to death one who has been condemned to such a fate by a legal or military process, or sometimes by summary action of a group ⟨*execute* a convicted assassin⟩

**kind** *n* *type, sort, stripe, kidney, ilk, description, nature, character

**kind** *adj* **Kind, kindly, benign, benignant** mean having or exhibiting a nature that is gentle, considerate, and inclined to benevolent or beneficent actions and are comparable especially as applied to persons and to their acts and utterances. *Kind* and *kindly* both imply possession of qualities (as interest in others' welfare, sympathy, and humaneness) appropriate to man as a rational, sensitive, and social being. The two words are often used interchangeably without loss, but they may be used distinctively, **kind** then implying reference to a disposition to be sympathetic and helpful, and **kindly** to the expression of a benevolent, sympathetic, or helpful nature, mood, or impulse; thus, he has a *kind*, rather than *kindly*, heart; he takes a *kindly*, rather than *kind*, interest in ambitious boys ⟨be *kind* to animals⟩ ⟨the *kindly* ministrations of a nurse⟩ ⟨*kindly* words of advice⟩ ⟨the *kindest* man, the best-conditioned and unwearied spirit in doing courtesies —*Shak.*⟩ ⟨ring in the valiant man and free, the larger heart, the *kindlier* hand!—*Tennyson*⟩ **Benign** (see also FAVORABLE) and **benignant** stress mildness, serenity, and mercifulness more than do *kind* and *kindly;* they also often imply graciousness and therefore are more frequently applied to superiors than to equals, when they are used to describe persons or their acts, utterances, or policies ⟨a *benign* master⟩ ⟨the transformation of a *benign* personality into a belligerent one—*Mumford*⟩ ⟨a *benignant* influence⟩ ⟨strange peace and rest fell on me from the presence of a *benignant* Spirit standing near—*Sill*⟩ *Ana* benevolent, *charitable, humane, altruistic, philanthropic, eleemosynary, humanitarian: sympathetic, warm, warmhearted, responsive, *tender, compassionate: clement, lenient, indulgent, merciful, *forbearing, tolerant:

*amiable, good-natured, complaisant, obliging
*Ant* unkind  —*Con* cruel, inhuman, *fierce, savage, fell: harsh, *rough: *grim, implacable, unrelenting, merciless
**kindle** ignite, fire, *light
*Ana* *blaze, flame, flare, glow: *provoke, excite, stimulate: arouse, rouse, *stir: *incite, foment, instigate
*Ant* smother, stifle
**kindly** benign, benignant, *kind
*Ana* *gracious, cordial, genial, affable, sociable: *amiable, good-natured, complaisant, obliging: friendly, neighborly (see AMICABLE): considerate, *thoughtful, attentive
*Ant* unkindly: acrid (*of temper, attitudes, comments*)
—*Con* malevolent, malign, *malicious, spiteful
**kindred** *related, cognate, allied, affiliated
*Ant* alien
**kingly, regal, royal, queenly, imperial, princely** are comparable when meaning of, relating to, or befitting one who occupies a throne. *Kingly, regal,* and *royal* are often interchanged, especially when used in reference to a monarch who is called *king;* thus, *kingly, regal,* or *royal* power are equally appropriate and idiomatic. However, usage shows a degree of preference for **kingly** when the reference is to the personal or ideal character of a king or to his feelings, disposition, aims, or actions ⟨*kingly* courtesy⟩ ⟨*kingly* condescension⟩ ⟨leave *kingly* backs to cope with *kingly* cares—*Cowper*⟩ or for **regal** when the reference is to the king's office or the state or pomp which accompanies the exercise of his powers ⟨*regal* ceremonies⟩ ⟨*regal* splendor⟩ ⟨ascend your throne majestically . . . sit *regal* and erect—*Auden*⟩ and for **royal** when the reference is to persons or things associated with the king either as a person or as a monarch, but not necessarily involving magnificence or display ⟨the *royal* family⟩ ⟨the *royal* residences⟩ ⟨a *royal* society is one under the patronage of a king or members of his family⟩ In extended use *kingly* carries the strongest implication of dignity and nobility ⟨*kingly* pride⟩ ⟨I am far better born than is the king, more like a king, more *kingly* in my thoughts—*Shak.*⟩ while *regal* suggests magnificence or majestic character ⟨a *regal* feast⟩ ⟨her rather *regal* conception of the behavior to be expected of a whorehouse madam may have a comic value—*Gibbs*⟩ ⟨"Just tell me what you would like to eat; you can have anything you want." . . . It had a *regal* ring—*Henry Miller*⟩ and *royal,* fitness or suitability for a king especially in superlative excellence ⟨a *royal* welcome⟩ ⟨had a *royal* time⟩ ⟨was treated with the *royal* acclaim of a visiting statesman —*White*⟩ **Queenly** is used in place of *kingly* when the reference is directly to a person who is a female sovereign in her own right or is the consort of a king ⟨*queenly* courtesy⟩ ⟨*queenly* prerogatives⟩ But when the reference is to the office, the family of the queen, or anything to which *regal* and *royal* are normally applied, the latter adjectives are used without reference to the sex of the sovereign. **Imperial** suggests reference to a monarch who is called *emperor* or *empress* ⟨His *Imperial* Majesty⟩ ⟨an *imperial* court⟩ ⟨the *imperial* power⟩ In extended use *imperial* implies fitness or suitability for an emperor or empress and typically suggests a more awe-inspiring quality than *kingly* and more pomp and grandeur than *regal* or *royal* ⟨I have seen New York grow from the little old town of the nineties to the *imperial* city that stands there now—*White*⟩ ⟨she was *imperial* rather than rude— *Wylie*⟩ **Princely** implies reference to one who is called a *prince* and especially to one who is so called as the monarch of a principality, as the heir to a royal throne, or as a male member of the immediate royal family ⟨the representative of the *princely* power—*Sarah Austin*⟩ ⟨among the *princely* houses of Western Europe—*Free-*

A colon (:) separates groups of words discriminated. An asterisk (*) indicates place of treatment of each group.

man⟩ In its extended use *princely* often carries a strong implication of sumptuousness ⟨two *princely* temples, rich with painting and many-colored marble—*Macaulay*⟩ or of opulence or munificence ⟨he had been told to spend his *princely* allowance in a *princely* manner, and to return home with a gallery of masterpieces—*Wharton*⟩

**knack** bent, turn, *gift, faculty, aptitude, genius, talent
*Ana* *ability, capacity, capability: aptness, readiness, quickness (see corresponding adjectives at QUICK): facility, dexterity, ease, *readiness
*Ant* ineptitude

**knave** *villain, scoundrel, blackguard, rascal, rogue, scamp, rapscallion, miscreant

**knit** *vb* *weave, crochet, braid, plait, tat
*Ana* *join, connect, link, unite

**knock** *vb* *tap, rap, thump, thud
*Ana* *strike, hit, smite: *beat, pound, pummel

**knock** *n* tap, rap, thump, thud (see under TAP *vb*)
*Ana* pounding, beating (see BEAT *vb*)

**knotty** intricate, involved, complicated, *complex

**knowing** alert, bright, smart, *intelligent, clever, quick-witted, brilliant
*Ana* *shrewd, astute, perspicacious, sagacious: *watchful, vigilant, alert: discerning, observing *or* observant, perceiving *or* perceptive (see corresponding verbs at SEE)
*Con* obtuse, *dull, blunt: dense, crass, *stupid, slow

**knowledge, science, learning, erudition, scholarship, information, lore** are comparable when they mean what is known or can be known, usually by an individual but sometimes by human beings in general. **Knowledge** applies not only to a body of facts gathered by study, investigation, observation, or experience but also to a body of ideas acquired by inference from such facts or accepted on good grounds as truths ⟨his *knowledge* is both extensive and accurate⟩ ⟨the advantage of gaining a *knowledge* of French literature⟩ ⟨strength and bustle build up a firm. But judgment and *knowledge* are what keep it established —*Hardy*⟩ ⟨the inventor of the radio . . . had the advantage of accumulated *knowledge*—*Krutch*⟩ **Science** (see also ART 3) is occasionally employed as a close synonym of *knowledge* but ordinarily it applies only to a body of systematized knowledge dealing with facts gathered over a long period and by numerous persons as a result of observation and experiment and with the general truths or laws derived by inference from such facts. The term usually connotes more exactness and more rigorous testing of conclusions than *knowledge* does and therefore is often used to denote knowledge whose certainty cannot be questioned ⟨the art of feeding preceded the *science* of nutrition by many centuries—*Hadley*⟩ ⟨the defense of nations had become a *science* and a calling—*Macaulay*⟩ ⟨perhaps all the *science* that is not at bottom physical *science* is only pretentious nescience—*Shaw*⟩ **Learning** specifically applies to knowledge gained by long and close study not only in the schools or universities but by individual research and investigation; it may be used of those who are engaged in the study of science, but it is more often employed in reference to those who devote themselves to the study of the humanities (as languages, literature, history, and philosophy) ⟨he is a man . . . of deep *learning*—*Burney*⟩ ⟨a man of good education and *learning*, of an excellent understanding, and an exact taste—*Swift*⟩ ⟨*learning* commonly connotes organized lore outside of any scientific area. It is an end in itself, it has been so honored by the world for centuries—*H. M. Jones*⟩ **Erudition** carries a stronger implication of the possession of profound, recondite, or bookish knowledge than does *learning* ⟨all the encyclopedic *erudition* of the middle ages—*Lowes*⟩ but often the terms are employed as if they were equivalent in meaning ⟨I arrived at Oxford with a stock of *erudition*, that might have puzzled a doctor—*Gibbon*⟩ ⟨it does not seem to me fitting . . . that one layman, with no special *erudition* in that subject, should publicly express his views—*T. S. Eliot*⟩ **Scholarship** implies the possession of the learning characteristic of the trained scholar; the term usually suggests mastery in detail of a field of study or investigation, the exhibition of such qualities as accuracy and skill in carrying on research intended to extend knowledge in that field, and the display of powers of critical analysis in the interpretation of the material that is gathered ⟨never fulfilled the promise of *scholarship* given by his great and precocious intellectual power and his even greater erudition—*Economist*⟩ ⟨what *scholarship* represents is a change in the temper of the human mind, in the focus of its attention and in the quality of the things it cherishes—*Frankel*⟩ **Information** usually denotes a kind or items of knowledge gathered from various sources (as observation, other persons, or books) and accepted as truth; the term carries no specific implication regarding the extent, character, or soundness of that knowledge; often it suggests no more than a collection of data or facts either discrete or integrated into a body of knowledge ⟨seeking *information* about her ancestors⟩ ⟨his sources of *information* are not always reliable⟩ ⟨the adult, with trained powers, has an immense advantage over the child in the acquisition of *information* —*Eliot*⟩ ⟨a full, rich, human book, packed with *information* lightly dispensed and fortified with learning easily worn—*Tracy*⟩ **Lore** is occasionally used in place of *learning*, but ordinarily it applies to a body of special or out-of-the-way knowledge concerning a particular subject possessed by an individual or by a group and is primarily traditional and anecdotal rather than scientific in character ⟨sacred *lore*⟩ ⟨folk, or popular, etymology does not usually create words, but it provides *lore* about words which is as pleasant as it is unreliable—*Laird*⟩ ⟨a *lore* composed of beliefs, customs, crafts, anecdotes . . . bearing in its content and terminology the unmistakable stamp of the backwoods—*Amer. Guide Series: Ind.*⟩
*Ant* ignorance

---

# L

**label** *n* mark, brand, stamp, tag, ticket (see under MARK *vb*)
**label** *vb* *mark, brand, stamp, tag, ticket
**labor** *n* *work, toil, travail, drudgery, grind
  *Ana* *effort, exertion, pains, trouble: endeavor, striving,
struggle (see under ATTEMPT *vb*)
  *Con* *rest, repose, relaxation, leisure, ease: recreation,
diversion, amusement, entertainment (see under AMUSE):
inactivity, idleness, inertness *or* inertia, passiveness
(see corresponding adjectives at INACTIVE)
**labored** *forced, strained, farfetched
  *Ana* *heavy, ponderous, weighty: *awkward, clumsy,
maladroit, inept: *stiff, wooden, rigid
**laborer** workingman, workman, *worker, craftsman,
handicraftsman, mechanic, artisan, operative, hand,
roustabout
**lack** *vb* Lack, want, need, require are comparable when
meaning to be without something, especially something
essential or greatly to be desired. **Lack** may imply either
an absence or a shortage in the supply or amount of that
something ⟨the house *lacks* a back stairway⟩ ⟨the army
*lacked* tanks and airplanes as well as rifles⟩ ⟨they are
not *lacking* in food or comforts⟩ ⟨good counselors *lack*
no clients—*Shak.*⟩ ⟨what he *lacks* in knowledge he can
make up for by talking fast—*Chase*⟩ **Want** frequently
adds to *lack* the implication of urgent necessity and may
be difficult to distinguish from its sense connoting longing
(see under DESIRE *vb*) ⟨the oldest . . . showing incipient
moustaches and long hairs on the face that *wanted* a razor
—*Sacheverell Sitwell*⟩ ⟨everything was dingy and *wanted*
paint—*Crofts*⟩ For this reason **need** may be preferred
when a clear connotation of urgent necessity is desirable
⟨he cannot get the rest he *needs*⟩ **Need** usually throws
the emphasis on urgent necessity rather than on absence
or shortage, though both implications are often present
⟨that family *needs* food and clothing ⟩ ⟨the country *needs*
the services and support of every citizen⟩ ⟨the letter
*needs* no reply, but it would be courteous to acknowledge
it⟩ ⟨that woman *needs* a lesson, Gideon. She's a public
nuisance—*Rose Macaulay*⟩ ⟨*needs* vicarious compen-
sations and manages to find them in the gossip columns
—*Huxley*⟩ ⟨implements sorely *needed* by the British
in the construction of vessels—*Breck*⟩ **Require** (see also
DEMAND) is often interchangeable with *need* but it may
heighten the implication of urgent necessity ⟨great acts
*require* great means of enterprise—*Milton*⟩ ⟨the Doctor
. . . *required* a few days of complete rest—*Dickens*⟩
  *Con* *have, hold, possess, own, enjoy
**lack** *n* Lack, want, dearth, absence, defect, privation are
comparable when denoting the fact or state of being without something. **Lack** is somewhat ambiguous in scope
since it may imply either a total or a partial failure of something that in the circumstances might be expected to be
present and often requires qualification to make its intent
unequivocal ⟨with a complete *lack* of bloodshed, the republic was proclaimed—*William Tate*⟩ ⟨the comparative
*lack* of simian fossils—*R. W. Murray*⟩ ⟨there is a slackening, a *lack* of faith in the pioneer dream that everyone
may be rich, free, and powerful—*Lord*⟩ **Want** (see also
POVERTY) may imply either a partial or a complete lack
but its range of application is far narrower than that of
*lack* since it specifically applies to deficiencies of what
is essential or at least needed or desirable; thus, one may
exhibit either a *want* or a *lack* of tact; there may be a
complete *lack*, rather than *want*, of pain immediately

after some injuries ⟨showed a certain *want* of courtesy⟩
⟨war production occasionally suffered from *want* of hands
to tend the machines or harvest the crops—*Handlin*⟩
⟨an utter and radical *want* of the adapting or constructive
power which the drama so imperatively demands—*Poe*⟩
**Dearth** implies an often distressingly inadequate supply
rather than a complete lack ⟨her vanity, *dearth* of brains,
and excessive sentimentality were compensated by her
kindness—*Simmons*⟩ ⟨there were six seasons of *dearth*
approaching famine—*Van Valkenburg & Huntington*⟩
⟨there is no *dearth* of simple violence in San Antonio—
*Green Peyton*⟩ **Absence** is perhaps the most unequivocal
of these terms; when not qualified it denotes the complete
lack of something ⟨the prolonged *absence* of rain⟩ or that
something or occasionally someone is not present ⟨in the
*absence* of his father the boy managed the farm⟩ ⟨the general *absence* of undergrowth was understood . . . to have resulted from repeated Indian-set fires—*R. H. Brown*⟩
⟨the confusion resulting from the *absence* of a critical
discriminating attitude in the discussion of religion—
*Cohen*⟩ **Defect** (see also BLEMISH) implies the absence
or lack of something required for completeness (as in
form) or effectiveness (as in function) ⟨be mine the privilege to supplement *defect*, give dumbness voice—
*Browning*⟩ ⟨*defect* in a work [of art] is always traceable
ultimately to an excess on one side or the other, injuring
the integration of matter and form—*Dewey*⟩ ⟨there are
certain obvious and superficial defects in this poem . . . .
But merit easily outweighs *defect*—*Day Lewis*⟩ **Privation**
in the sense pertinent here (see also POVERTY) is used
primarily in certain philosophical definitions of negative
qualities or states as absences of the corresponding pos-
itives ⟨cold is the *privation* of heat⟩ ⟨St. Thomas regards
evil as *privation*. In so far as a thing acts according to
its nature, which is good, it cannot cause evil—*Thilly*⟩
⟨dialectical terms . . . are terms standing for concepts,
which are defined by their negatives or their *privations*—
*R. M. Weaver*⟩ ⟨negative facts or states of affairs . . . seem
clearly to be absences, lacks, or *privations*, and as such
devoid of any properties which could possibly render
them apprehensible in experience—*Richard Taylor*⟩
  *Ana* *need, necessity, exigency: deficiency (see corresponding adjective DEFICIENT): exhaustion, impoverishment, draining, depletion (see corresponding verbs at
DEPLETE)
  *Con* abundance, ampleness, copiousness, plentifulness,
plenteousness *or* plenty (see corresponding adjectives
at PLENTIFUL): *excess, superfluity, surplus
**lackadaisical** listless, spiritless, enervated, *languid,
languishing, languorous
  *Ana* *indifferent, unconcerned, incurious: indolent,
slothful, faineant, *lazy: inert, *inactive, passive, supine,
idle: *sentimental, romantic: enervated, emasculated
(see UNNERVE)
  *Con* energetic, strenuous, *vigorous, lusty: dynamic,
live, *active
**laconic** succinct, terse, *concise, summary, pithy, compendious
  *Ana* curt, brusque (see BLUFF): *brief, short
  *Ant* verbose —*Con* *wordy, prolix, diffuse: loquacious,
*talkative, voluble, glib, garrulous
**lacuna** gap, hiatus, *break, interruption, interval, interim
**lacustrine** *aquatic, fluvial, fluviatile, marine, oceanic,
thalassic, neritic, pelagic, abyssal

A colon (:) separates groups of words discriminated. An asterisk (*) indicates place of treatment of each group.

**lade** vb load, *burden, encumber, cumber, weigh, weight, tax, charge, saddle

**lading** freight, cargo, *load, burden

**ladle** vb scoop, spoon, dish, *dip, bail

**lady** woman, *female

**ladylike** feminine, womanly, womanlike, *female, womanish, effeminate
*Ana* dainty, fastidious, finicky, particular, *nice: fashionable, modish, smart, chic, *stylish: *decorous, proper, seemly

**lag** loiter, dawdle, *delay, procrastinate
*Ana* slow, slacken, retard, *delay: tarry, linger, wait, *stay
*Con* hurry, hasten, *speed, quicken, accelerate

**laggard** adj dilatory, *slow, leisurely, deliberate
*Ana* dawdling, loitering, delaying, procrastinating (see DELAY): *lethargic, sluggish, comatose: phlegmatic, apathetic, *impassive
*Ant* prompt, quick —*Con* alert, wide-awake, vigilant, *watchful: *fast, swift, rapid, fleet, speedy, expeditious

**lambent** beaming, luminous, *bright, brilliant, radiant, lustrous, effulgent, refulgent, lucent, incandescent
*Ana* gleaming, glistening (see FLASH vb)

**lament** vb *deplore, bewail, bemoan
*Ana* weep, keen, wail, *cry: *grieve, mourn, sorrow
*Ant* exult: rejoice

**lampoon** n *libel, skit, squib, pasquinade

**land** vb *alight, light, perch, roost
*Ana* arrive, *come: *reach, gain, achieve, attain

**landing field, landing strip** *airport, airdrome, airfield, airstrip, flying field

**lane** byway, alley, alleyway, roadway, *road, street, highway, highroad, avenue, boulevard, terrace, drive, parkway, thoroughfare

**language** 1 Language, dialect, tongue, speech, idiom are comparable when they denote a body or system of words and phrases used by a large community (as of a region) or by a people, a nation, or a group of nations. **Language** may be used as a general term for a body of communicative symbols whether it is made up of words, or of sounds, gestures, and facial expressions, or of visual signals (as a code of lights, smoke, or flags), or of electrical impulses in a computer. However, in its ordinary and specific sense the term refers to a body of words that by long use by the population of a widespread territory has become the means whereby the ideas or feelings of the individual members of that population are communicated or expressed. The term suggests some degree of stability in behavior (as in vocabulary, pronunciation, and grammaticality); it usually connotes the existence of a standard determined by the usage of educated writers and speakers ⟨English and French are *languages*, that is to say they are systems of habits of speech, exactly like Eskimo or Hottentot or any other *language*—*R. A. Hall*⟩ ⟨dead *languages* such as classical Latin and ancient Greek⟩ But *language* is also applied to a body of words and phrases that is peculiar to an art, a science, a profession, or a class and that, however well understood by others of the community, is not generally adopted by them ⟨in economic *language* the "marginal saver" determines the price—*Hobson*⟩ ⟨it took the three of us, representing economics, sociology, and political science, about six weeks to learn each other's *language*—*Kerwin*⟩. **Dialect** (see also DIALECT 1) may denote a form of language which is clearly distinguishable from other forms by marked differences and an identity of its own. More often it refers to a variant of a recognized language, restricted to a limited area and not entirely unintelligible to speakers of the language of which it is a phase ⟨Venetian and

Sicilian are equally *dialects* of Italian, although as far as mutual intelligibility is concerned these two might as well be called independent languages—*Sapir*⟩ ⟨the perennial controversy as to whether Scots is a language or a *dialect*⟩ **Tongue** and **speech** both call attention to the spoken rather than written communication. **Tongue** differs from *language* chiefly in its being applicable to a dialect, a patois, an argot (for these terms, see DIALECT 1) as well as to the standard form of a language ⟨there is no poet in any *tongue*—not even in Latin or Greek—who stands so firmly as a model for all poets—*T. S. Eliot*⟩ ⟨translated the Bible into an Indian *tongue*—*Suckow*⟩ ⟨he is a New England poet . . . true to its landscape, its climate, its history, its morality, its *tongue*—*Mark Van Doren*⟩ **Speech**, with rare exceptions, means spoken language, or (as in modern technical use) language as it is spoken ⟨people of a strange *speech*—*Ezek* 3:6⟩ ⟨there are at least two sounds in the Anglo-Saxon which are unknown in our present *speech*—*Whitney*⟩ **Idiom** suggests reference to a country or sometimes to a province or section of a country with its own peculiar and distinctive tongue ⟨part of the difficulty lies in the English *idiom* which is unfamiliar to the American reader—*Stead*⟩ ⟨on the spot I read . . . the classics of the Tuscan *idiom*—*Gibbon*⟩ **Idiom** also may apply to private or peculiar language (as of a particular writer, class, literary school, or group) ⟨the eminently personal *idiom* of Swinburne—*T. S. Eliot*⟩ ⟨the medieval poetic *idiom* came after a while to seem a jargon—*Lowes*⟩ ⟨I have read very little *Runyon*, whose *idiom* I always suspected—wrongfully, I'm sure—of being more or less synthetic—*Gibbs*⟩
*Ana* *dialect, vernacular, patois, lingo, jargon, cant, argot, slang

2 Language, vocabulary, phraseology, phrasing, diction, style are comparable rather than synonymous terms when they mean oral or written expression or a quality of such expression that is dependent on the variety, or arrangement, or expressiveness of words. **Language** applies primarily to verbal expression with reference to the words employed. It may call attention to excellence or ineptness in the use of words, to their dignity or their vulgarity, to their fitness or lack of fitness, to their sonority or their stridency, or to any of the qualities which speech or writing may derive from the choice and arrangement of words ⟨he avoided harsh *language* in dealing with his children⟩ ⟨*language*, grave and majestic, but of vague and uncertain import—*Macaulay*⟩ ⟨when I read Shakespeare I am struck with wonder that such trivial people should muse and thunder in such lovely *language*—*D. H. Lawrence*⟩ **Vocabulary** calls attention chiefly to the extent or variety of the writer's or speaker's stock of words or to the sources from which such a stock is derived ⟨the constant play and contrast in English poetry between the Latin and the Anglo-Saxon *vocabularies*—*Bottrall*⟩ ⟨German, famous for its polysyllabic *vocabulary*—*G. A. Miller*⟩ ⟨even the *vocabulary* of renunciation, and its conventional gestures, were unfamiliar to him—*Wharton*⟩ **Phraseology** or **phrasing** is sometimes used in place of *vocabulary* when the reader's attention is called especially to its idiomatic or peculiar character ⟨eccentricities of *phraseology*⟩ ⟨awkward *phrasing*⟩ ⟨the exquisite *phrasing* in which we feel that every word is in its place—*Edmund Wilson*⟩ but **phraseology** in particular stresses the grouping of words as much as their choice ⟨he can say in the *phraseology* of the sentimentalist that he "loves nature"⟩ ⟨the *phraseology*, rather than the vocabulary, of Donne offers difficulty to the inexperienced reader⟩ ⟨the gaudiness and inane *phraseology* of many modern writers—*Wordsworth*⟩ ⟨this cryptic and involved

*phraseology*, obscure to the uninitiated, permeates all communist publications—*Report of Special Committee on Communist Tactics*⟩ **Diction** calls attention to the choice and arrangement of words with reference to their expression of ideas or emotions. The term is used commonly of considered language (as of poetry, literary prose, or oratory) and it usually, therefore, implies selection or arrangement with reference to such ends as impressiveness, elegance, and beauty of sound ⟨he was in a high fever while he was writing, and the blood-and-thunder magazine *diction* he adopted did not calm him—*Kipling*⟩ ⟨his choice of forceful picturesque *diction* in speech and writing—*Lawrason Brown*⟩ ⟨a poet cannot help being of his age, the *diction* and the idiom see to that —*Gogarty*⟩ **Style** denotes a mode or manner of expressing one's thoughts or emotions or imaginative conceptions in words, as distinct from or as distinguishable from the thoughts or emotions or conceptions expressed. It is sometimes thought of as a structure and diction peculiar to an age or a literary type and found in each representative work of that time and type ⟨the Renaissance epic *style* is based upon that of Vergil⟩ ⟨a poem written in the *style* of the ode⟩ but perhaps more often it is thought of as a manner of expression which in structure and diction involves artistry but is individual and characteristic of its author ⟨*style* . . . is a peculiar recasting and heightening, under a certain condition of spiritual excitement, of what a man has to say, in such a manner as to add dignity and distinction to it—*Arnold*⟩ ⟨what he believed in was *style:* that is to say, a certain absolute and unique manner of expressing a thing, in all its intensity and color—*Pater*⟩ ⟨this then is *Style.* As technically manifested in literature is the power to touch with ease, grace, precision, any note in the gamut of human thought or emotion—*Quiller-Couch*⟩

**languid, languishing, languorous, lackadaisical, listless, spiritless, enervated** are comparable when they mean lacking in vim or energy or, when applied to things, the appearance of it. **Languid** usually implies an unwillingness or an inability to exert oneself owing to fatigue, exhaustion, or physical weakness ⟨struck by something *languid* and inelastic in her attitude, and wondered if the deadly monotony of their lives had laid its weight on her also—*Wharton*⟩ ⟨walked from the room with *languid* deliberate steps; . . . she moved as though she were intolerably weary—*Wylie*⟩ **Languishing** may suggest delicate indolence, often accompanying boredom or futilely wistful pensiveness and often connotes an affected rather than a real state ⟨a *languishing* gaze⟩ ⟨with their *languishing*, sorrowful melodies . . . with their high-flown sentimentalism, these ballads reflected . . . stale romanticism—*Mooney*⟩ **Languorous** carries a suggestion of languidness and delicacy acquired through soft living, through shrinking from exertion, or through sentimentalism or overindulgence in tender or amorous emotions ⟨sought out rich words with which to re-create the *languorous*, stilling beauty of the Old South—*Springfield Republican*⟩ ⟨a poignant perfume, soft and *languorous*, all-enveloping and heart-stirring—*Kenneth Roberts*⟩ ⟨her shaded lids . . . were *languorous* from my kisses, and gave . . . an inebriating love-bemused and longing-solemn look—*Edmund Wilson*⟩ **Lackadaisical** implies a carefree or indifferent attitude that either forbids exertion or makes for futile, piddling, or halfhearted and indolent efforts ⟨at the terrific tempo of mechanized war, *lackadaisical* men, lacking in self-confidence and slow to obey are lost—*G. S. Patton*⟩ ⟨a *lackadaisical* river town that tolerated a generous amount of vice—*T. D. Clark*⟩ **Listless** need not imply physical weakness, but it almost invariably implies either a lack of interest in what is going on around one or in what one is doing, or a languid appearance that may be the result either of boredom or ennui or of fatigue or disease ⟨the child has grown thin, white, and *listless* within the past two months⟩ ⟨suddenly relaxed into a *listless* attitude of sullen tractability—*S. S. Van Dine*⟩ ⟨they were effete, weary, burnt-out revolutionists, whose *listless* voices slid sleepily over their melodies—*Mooney*⟩ **Spiritless** implies the loss or the absence of the animation or fire that gives life or dash to a person or to his words and acts ⟨a *spiritless* performance of a play⟩ ⟨dominated the starving, *spiritless* wretches under him with savage enjoyment—*Mason*⟩ ⟨no courage can repel the dire assault; distracted, *spiritless*, benumbed, and blind, whole legions sink—*Wordsworth*⟩ **Enervated** implies a destruction of qualities or powers essential to the vigorous exercise of the will and the intellect. Often it suggests the influence of luxury or of sloth but it may imply the operation of other causes, even of those that in themselves are not evil but may have deleterious effects ⟨the *enervated* and sickly habits of the literary class—*Emerson*⟩ ⟨society in Rome, *enervated* as it was by vicious pleasures, craved continually for new excitements—*Froude*⟩ ⟨that *enervated*, run-down condition that is commonly known as Southern gentility—*Basso*⟩
*Ana* \*lethargic, sluggish, comatose, torpid: phlegmatic, apathetic, \*impassive: inert, \*inactive, supine
*Ant* vivacious: chipper

**languishing** \*languid, languorous, lackadaisical, listless, spiritless, enervated
*Ana* weakened, enfeebled, debilitated (see WEAKEN): indolent, faineant (see LAZY): inert, \*inactive, supine: \*sentimental, romantic: pining, longing, yearning (see LONG *vb*)
*Ant* thriving, flourishing: unaffected —*Con* robust, \*healthy, sound, hale: \*vigorous, energetic, lusty: \*natural, artless, unsophisticated, naïve

**languor** \*lethargy, lassitude, stupor, torpor, torpidity
*Ana* exhaustion, fatigue, weariness (see corresponding verbs at TIRE): ennui, doldrums, \*tedium: depression, blues, dumps (see SADNESS)
*Ant* alacrity —*Con* \*celerity, legerity: quickness, promptness, readiness (see corresponding adjectives at QUICK): zest, gusto (see TASTE)

**languorous** languishing, \*languid, lackadaisical, listless, spiritless, enervated
*Ana* leisurely, laggard, \*slow, dilatory: indolent, slothful, faineant (see LAZY): passive, inert, \*inactive, supine: relaxed, slack, lax, \*loose: pampered, indulged (see INDULGE)
*Ant* vigorous: strenuous (*of times, seasons*)

**lank, lanky** gaunt, rawboned, \*lean, spare, angular, scrawny, skinny
*Ana* \*thin, slim, slender, slight: attenuated, extenuated (see THIN *vb*)
*Ant* burly —*Con* husky, brawny, \*muscular, sinewy: plump, portly, rotund, chubby, \*fleshy, stout

**lapse** *n* **1** slip, \*error, mistake, blunder, faux pas, bull, howler, boner
*Ana* \*offense, sin, vice, crime: \*fault, failing, frailty, foible: transgression, \*breach, violation, trespass
**2** relapse, backsliding (see under LAPSE *vb*)
*Ana* \*deterioration, decline, declension, decadence, degeneration, devolution: retrograding *or* retrogradation, receding *or* recession (see corresponding verbs at RECEDE): retrogressiveness *or* retrogression, regressiveness *or* regression (see corresponding adjectives at BACKWARD)
*Con* advance, progress (see under ADVANCE *vb*): \*development, evolution

A colon (:) separates groups of words discriminated. An asterisk (\*) indicates place of treatment of each group.

**lapse** *vb* Lapse, relapse, backslide and their corresponding nouns, **lapse, relapse, backsliding,** are comparable when they mean to fall back into a state or condition from which one has raised oneself or has been raised, or the act or state of one who has so fallen back. As distinguished from *decline, degenerate,* and *deteriorate,* these verbs do not necessarily imply the reversion of a process or development or the gradual losing and the inevitable loss of a valuable quality (as strength, power, or influence) but they do distinctively imply a failure to continue without break a course of improvement and a return, often quickly effected but not always irreparable, to an earlier bad or lower state or condition. Both *lapse* and *relapse* basically imply a sliding or slipping but they are increasingly divergent in their applications and connotations. Lapse usually presupposes reformation in manners, morals, or habits, or the acceptance of a high standard (as of rectitude, accuracy, or accomplishment). It need not imply culpability or weakness, for it often suggests no more than a sudden failure of the memory or the influence of habit or tradition or the pressure of an overwhelming emotion ⟨it is easy for the person who has acquired good manners by effort to *lapse* into old ways when he is not on guard⟩ ⟨only when she was strongly moved did she *lapse* into the dialect she spoke in her youth⟩ ⟨the moment his attention is relaxed . . . he will *lapse* into bad Shakespearean verse—*T. S. Eliot*⟩ ⟨whatever rhythmical or technical *lapses* they may contain, the conception is throughout that of a great musician —*Edward Sackville-West*⟩ When culpability is strongly implied, the word still, in comparison to the other terms in the group, often connotes extenuating circumstances; it is therefore the fitting choice when the context indicates such circumstances ⟨he constantly fought his tendency to *lapse* into easygoing ways⟩ ⟨the natives *lapsed* back into accustomed vices—*Billington*⟩ ⟨in estimating a man's place in the scale of perfection . . . the moral judgment, not withholding condemnation of a particular *lapse,* may not condemn the man wholly for it—*Alexander*⟩ **Relapse** presupposes definite improvement or an advance (as toward health or toward a higher physical, moral, or intellectual state) and it implies a complete and often dangerous reversal of direction; thus, one whose improvement in a serious illness has been marked may be said to *relapse,* or suffer a *relapse,* when his condition becomes definitely worse; a reformed thief is said to *relapse* when he returns to his old life ⟨the Arabs were once the continuators of the Greek tradition; they produced men of science. They have *relapsed* . . . into prescientific fatalism, with its attendant incuriosity and apathy —*Huxley*⟩ ⟨man's eternal tendency to *relapse* into apathy and atavism—*Stewart*⟩ ⟨his firmness of mind soon *relapsed* into a cankerous intolerance—*Cranston*⟩ ⟨the corruptions and vices which accompany the horribly swift *relapse* of a culture into barbarism—*Edmund Fuller*⟩ **Backslide** and **backsliding** also imply a reversal in direction of one who has been going forward, but unlike *relapse,* which is in many ways their close synonym, they are restricted in their reference largely to moral and religious lapses. They therefore often suggest unfaithfulness to one's duty or allegiance or to principles once professed ⟨did not I . . . *backslide* into intemperance and folly— *Marryat*⟩ ⟨this is not to say that *backslidings* fail to occur; on the contrary *backslidings* normally follow any strenuous moral experience—*G. W. Allport*⟩
*Ana* revert, *return: slip, *slide: deteriorate, degenerate, decline (see corresponding nouns at DETERIORATION): *descend: *recede, retrograde
*Con* progress, *advance: develop, *mature
**larcener, larcenist** thief, robber, burglar (see under

THEFT)
**larceny** *theft, robbery, burglary
**large, big, great** mean above the average of its kind in magnitude, especially physical magnitude. **Large** may be preferred when the dimensions, or extent, or capacity, or quantity, or amount is being considered ⟨a *large* lot⟩ ⟨a *large* hall⟩ ⟨a *large* basket⟩ ⟨a *large* meal⟩ ⟨a *large* allowance⟩ ⟨*large* crevasses and huge tunnels in many of them [icebergs] bore witness to a long voyage—*Schytt*⟩ **Big,** on the other hand, is especially appropriate when the emphasis is on bulk, or mass, or weight, or volume ⟨a *big* book⟩ ⟨a *big* pile⟩ ⟨the box is too *big* to carry⟩ ⟨a *big* voice⟩ ⟨so *big* already—so enormous in fact—that we named him Monstro, and he padded about like a furry whale—*Atlantic*⟩ As applied to material objects, **great** has been practically displaced by *large* or *big*. Where *great* is used to denote physical magnitude, it now regularly connotes some impression (as of wonder, surprise, amusement, or annoyance) associated with the size ⟨the *great* head that seemed so weighted down with thought and study—*The Nation*⟩ ⟨the *great* size of these figures—the largest man is 167 feet long . . . prevented their character from being recognized—*Amer. Guide Series: Calif.*⟩ ⟨his eyes were *great* and hollow, as a famished man forlorn— *Morris*⟩ *Great* alone, in standard English, expresses degree ⟨he was listened to with respect and, when aroused, with nearly as *great* fear—*W. C. Ford*⟩ ⟨*great* kindness⟩ ⟨*great* heat⟩ In extended use, *great* suggests eminence, distinction, or supremacy ⟨if we win men's hearts throughout the world, it will not be because we are a big country but because we are a *great* country. Bigness is imposing. But greatness is enduring—*A. E. Stevenson*⟩ while *large* suggests breadth, comprehensiveness, or generosity ⟨in intellect and humanity he is the *largest* type I have come across. Other greater men in my time were great in some one thing, not *large* in their very texture—*Ricketts*⟩ and *big* carries over the implication of mass or bulk but often suggests impressiveness or importance rather than solidity or great worth ⟨so-called *big* names, which are still *big* and still have great readership value, command high prices—*Baldwin*⟩ ⟨he didn't expect to work here all his life . . . pretty soon he'd have a new job and would be a *big* man—*Granite*⟩
*Ana* vast, immense, enormous, *huge, mammoth, colossal, gigantic: tremendous, prodigious, monumental, stupendous, *monstrous: inordinate, *excessive, exorbitant, extreme, immoderate, extravagant
*Ant* small —*Con* little, diminutive, tiny, wee, minute (see SMALL): slight, slender, slim, *thin

**largely, greatly, mostly, chiefly, mainly, principally, generally** are often interchanged, but they are capable of being used with explicitness even though they basically agree in meaning. **Largely** stresses quantity or extent; it usually connotes copiousness or abundance and often suggests an amount exceeding that of other ingredients, components, or constituents ⟨water enters *largely* into the composition of the bodies both of plants and animals—*Geikie*⟩ ⟨good country sausage is *largely* pork⟩ **Greatly** carries a heightened suggestion of greatness in degree that differentiates it from *largely* ⟨he is *greatly* admired⟩ ⟨careless and lazy is he, *greatly* inferior to me—*Kipling*⟩ ⟨the sprouting of seed is *greatly* helped by sun and rain⟩ **Mostly** usually stresses numbers ⟨the audience was made up *mostly* of children⟩ ⟨twenty-seven millions *mostly* fools—*Carlyle*⟩ **Chiefly** emphasizes the importance of one thing among other things; it may connote an outstanding or preeminent position or it may connote merely relative importance ⟨the basket contained many fruits, but *chiefly* apples⟩ ⟨the battle was won *chiefly* by the aid of the air force⟩ **Mainly** is often used interchangeably with *chiefly*, but not where preeminence is implied; rather it connotes greatest importance among a number of things, but not exclusive value ⟨be sure to take along with you all that you will need, but *mainly* informal clothes⟩ ⟨the cause depends *mainly* on the validity of this act—*John Marshall*⟩ ⟨the Pickwickian Christmas did very little to stimulate consumption; it was *mainly* a gratuitous festivity —*Huxley*⟩ **Principally** carries an idea of primary importance rather than outstanding or relative importance; the difference is not great between it and *chiefly* or *mainly* except when the idea of being first or primary is emphasized ⟨they wholly mistake the nature of criticism, who think its business is *principally* to find fault—*Dryden*⟩ ⟨his support comes *principally* from the income of invested money⟩ ⟨the cash crops are *principally* wheat and rye⟩ **Generally** stresses reference to the majority of persons, instances, or cases involved ⟨the people, not universally, but *generally*, were animated by a true spirit of sacrifice—*Froude*⟩ ⟨the news was *generally* received with joy⟩ ⟨the land breezes here are *generally* hot and dry⟩

**largess** boon, *gift, present, gratuity, favor
*Ana* benefaction, *donation, contribution: grant, subvention (see APPROPRIATION)

**lascivious** lewd, *licentious, libertine, lustful, libidinous, lecherous, wanton
*Ana* *immoral, unmoral, amoral: sensual, *carnal, fleshly, animal: obscene, gross, *coarse
*Con* *chaste, pure, modest, decent: virtuous, *moral

**lassitude** languor, *lethargy, stupor, torpor, torpidity
*Ana* exhaustion, weariness, fatigue (see corresponding verbs at TIRE): ennui, doldrums, *tedium: dumps, blues, depression (see SADNESS): impotence, powerlessness (see corresponding adjectives at POWERLESS)
*Ant* vigor —*Con* energy, strength, might, force, *power

**last** *vb* endure, *continue, abide, persist
*Ana* survive, outlast, *outlive: remain, *stay
*Ant* fleet

**last** *adj* **Last, latest, final, terminal, concluding, eventual, ultimate** are comparable when they mean following all the others in time or order or in importance. What is **last** comes at the end of a series, especially of things of the same kind or class; the term usually implies that no more will follow or have followed ⟨the *last* page of a book⟩ ⟨their *last* child is now ten years of age⟩ ⟨fairest of stars, *last* in the train of night—*Milton*⟩ but it may imply only that the thing so qualified is or was the most recent or is the closest or nearest with respect to the present or a given time or period ⟨his *last* book is his best so far⟩ ⟨their *last* visit to us was in December⟩ In this latter sense **latest** may be preferred as less ambiguous; thus, "his *latest* book" is clearer than "his *last* book" since the latter wording might suggest the author's ensuing death ⟨the *latest* number of a current magazine⟩ ⟨the *latest* news is that all is well⟩ ⟨vetoed the *latest* version of Norris's . . . bill—*Lepawsky*⟩ What is **final** definitely closes a series or process not only because it is the last in order of individuals or details ⟨the *final* day of school⟩ ⟨the *final* float in the procession⟩ ⟨the *final* event on a program⟩ but because it is decisive or conclusive ⟨the *final* answer to this question is still to be found⟩ ⟨a *final* decree of divorce⟩ ⟨judgment that is *final*, that settles a matter—*Dewey*⟩ ⟨a genuinely popular ballad can have no fixed and *final* form, no sole authentic version—*Child*⟩ What is **terminal** comes at the end of something and marks the limit of its extension, its growth, or its completion as a series or process ⟨the *terminal* point of a railroad⟩ ⟨the Tamiami Trail, a name compounded of the syllables from the names of its *terminal* cities, Tampa and Miami—*Amer. Guide Series: Fla.*⟩

⟨little newsboys crying their wares in correct Bostonese, down to broad a's and softened *terminal* r's—*Price*⟩ What is **concluding** brings something (as a speech, a book, a program, a celebration) to an end or marks its finish ⟨the *concluding* address was delivered by the chairman⟩ ⟨provoked comparison by making their *concluding* paragraphs almost identical—*R. G. Davis*⟩ What is **eventual** is bound to follow as the final effect of causes already in operation or of causes that will be operative if a given or understood contingency occurs ⟨the silent decay and *eventual* overthrow of her natural defenses—*Gladstone*⟩ ⟨it is his object to point out the necessity . . . for a deliberate and purposive art of eugenics, if we would prevent the *eventual* shipwreck of civilization—*Ellis*⟩ What is **ultimate** (see also ULTIMATE 2) is the last, final, or terminal element in a series or process ⟨this *ultimate* book of my autobiography —*Osbert Sitwell*⟩ ⟨the *ultimate* stage in a process of descent—*Ellis*⟩ or is the final outcome or end to which a person or thing is moving or working ⟨the *ultimate* effect of a drug⟩ ⟨when I think of the earth's refrigeration, and the *ultimate* collapse of our solar system—*L. P. Smith*⟩ or is the most remote in time, either past or future, or most important in a scale of values ⟨the *ultimate* effect of a war⟩ ⟨that word comes into English from French, but its *ultimate* source is Sanskrit⟩ ⟨its utopianism interferes with an interest in proximate, rather than *ultimate*, goals— *Niebuhr*⟩
*Ant* first

**lasting, permanent, perdurable, durable, stable, perpetual** mean enduring for so long as to seem fixed or established. **Lasting** may imply long continuance with no end in sight; in this sense, it may be close in connotation to *everlasting* ⟨who . . . sings his soul and body to their *lasting* rest— *Shak.*⟩ More typically, however, it does not imply endlessness, but rather a surprising capacity to continue indefinitely ⟨the anger of slow, mild, loving people has a *lasting* quality that mere bad-tempered folk cannot understand— *Deland*⟩ ⟨an excellent mind, shrewd wit, and an amazing capacity for developing *lasting* friendships—*Douglas*⟩ **Permanent** applies chiefly to things which are not temporary, tentative, transitory, or fluctuating but which continue or are likely or expected to continue indefinitely or as long as relevant; thus, a *permanent* position may be expected to continue on the one hand until death or retirement removes the employee holding it or, on the other, until fundamental changes in or termination of the business of the employer renders it superfluous; *permanent* damage to an object is damage that will remain as long as the object persists ⟨settled down and made a *permanent* home for his family⟩ ⟨the stimulation of violent emotions may leave *permanent* traces on the mind—*Inge*⟩ ⟨much of the current literature on this subject, both ephemeral and of *permanent* value, comes out of Russia—*Sokolsky*⟩ **Perdurable** carries a stronger implication than does *lasting* in its typical use of endlessness of existence; but it suggests endless or apparently endless existence especially from the point of view of human remembrance or human history ⟨makes him one of the few *perdurable* figures of our Civil War and secures him a sainthood that slander has not been able to violate—*Cargill*⟩ ⟨our literature is going to be our most *perdurable* claim on man's remembrance— *Quiller-Couch*⟩ **Durable** implies power of resistance to destructive agencies; it usually suggests a capacity for lasting that exceeds that of other things of the same kind or sort ⟨a *durable* pavement⟩ ⟨*durable* color⟩ ⟨more *durable* than brass—*Junius*⟩ ⟨many writers have longed for *durable* renown—*L. P. Smith*⟩ **Stable** applies to what is so firmly or solidly established that it cannot be moved or changed; the term therefore is applicable to things that

---

A colon (:) separates groups of words discriminated. An asterisk (*) indicates place of treatment of each group.

are lasting or durable because they are deeply rooted, or finely balanced, or infixed and not subject or likely to be subject to fluctuations ⟨a *stable* foundation⟩ ⟨a *stable* form of government⟩ ⟨*stable* institutions⟩ ⟨the *stable* earth and the changing day—*George Eliot*⟩ ⟨men as steady as . . . wheels upon their axles, sane men, obedient men, *stable* in contentment—*Huxley*⟩ ⟨a relatively *stable* society . . . where the individual remains, both physically and socially, in the place in which he was born—*Cheek*⟩ **Perpetual** (see also CONTINUAL) is in many respects closer to *permanent* than to the remaining terms but it differs from it signally in the absence of any notion of relevance and may approach *everlasting* in its suggestion of an endless course or a going on without a prospect of something intervening to bring about an end; thus, the furnace has a *permanent,* not a *perpetual,* place in the cellar since the cellar itself will ultimately crumble away; *perpetual,* rather than *permanent,* motion is considered impossible because of the inevitable interference of friction ⟨a dark, a colorless, a tasteless, a perfumeless, as well as a shapeless world: the leaden landscape of a *perpetual* winter— *Mumford*⟩ ⟨the song of the minstrel moved through a *perpetual* Maytime—*J. R. Green*⟩ ⟨a *perpetual* embargo was the annihilation, and not the regulation of commerce —*John Marshall*⟩
*Ana* enduring, abiding, persisting *or* persistent, continuing (see corresponding verbs at CONTINUE): *everlasting, endless, unceasing: *continual, continuous, incessant, unremitting, perennial: eternal, sempiternal (see INFINITE)
*Ant* fleeting —*Con* fugitive, passing, evanescent, transitory, *transient, short-lived

**late** 1 *tardy, behindhand, overdue
*Ana* delayed, retarded, detained (see DELAY)
*Ant* early: punctual, prompt —*Con* timely, *seasonable, opportune, well-timed
2 departed, deceased, defunct, *dead, lifeless, inanimate
3 *modern, recent

**latent,** dormant, quiescent, potential, abeyant are comparable when meaning not now manifest or not evincing signs of existence or activity. **Latent** implies concealment and is applied to what is present without showing itself ⟨*latent* energy⟩ ⟨a *latent* infection⟩ ⟨his sinister qualities, formerly *latent,* quickened into life—*Hardy*⟩ ⟨it remained possible that by further development, *latent* contradictions might have been revealed—*Russell*⟩ **Dormant** usually suggests sleeping and is applied to something which has once been active but now is inactive though not incapable of future activity ⟨a *dormant* plant⟩ ⟨a *dormant* volcano⟩ ⟨which power can never be exercised by the people themselves, but must be placed in the hands of agents, or lie *dormant*—*John Marshall*⟩ ⟨she pursued him with attentions, and when his passion was *dormant* sought to excite it—*Maugham*⟩ **Quiescent** emphasizes the fact of inactivity without necessary implications either of causes or of past or future activity ⟨with the increase of their wealth . . . they sank into *quiescent* Tories—*Meredith*⟩ Sometimes it connotes immobility ⟨if only we could persuade ourselves to remain *quiescent* when we are happy!—*Jefferies*⟩ **Potential** applies to something which at a time in question does not possess such being, nature, or effect as is expressed but which is likely to have or capable of having such being, nature, or effect at some future time ⟨*potential* energy⟩ ⟨disaffected citizens who are a *potential* danger to the nation⟩ ⟨this eye for a *potential* and achievable best— *Mumford*⟩ ⟨it [an infant] must from the very first be viewed seriously, as a *potential* adult—*Russell*⟩ **Abeyant** (more often, predicatively, **in abeyance**) implies a suspension of activity or active existence ⟨in Mr. Brooke the hereditary strain of Puritan energy was clearly *in abey-*

*ance—George Eliot*⟩ It usually connotes expectancy of revival ⟨nothing seemed left . . . of . . . the former Lewis Raycie, save a lurking and *abeyant* fear of Mr. Raycie senior—*Wharton*⟩ ⟨until all danger of counterrevolution should have been removed, personal rights and liberties would have to be kept strictly *in abeyance*—*Ogg & Zink*⟩
*Ana* hidden, concealed (see HIDE *vb*): *inactive, inert, idle: unripe, unmatured, *immature
*Ant* patent —*Con* *active, operative, live, dynamic: activated, vitalized, energized (see VITALIZE)

**latest** final, *last, terminal, concluding, eventual, ultimate
*Ant* earliest

**lather** *n* suds, froth, *foam, spume, scum, yeast

**laud** *vb* extol, eulogize, *praise, acclaim
*Ana* magnify, aggrandize, *exalt: worship, adore, venerate, *revere, reverence: *commend, applaud, compliment
*Ant* revile —*Con* *decry, depreciate, disparage, belittle: censure, condemn, denounce, blame, *criticize, reprobate, reprehend: *execrate, curse, damn, anathematize, objurgate

**laughable,** risible, ludicrous, ridiculous, comic, comical, farcical, droll, funny are comparable when they mean provoking or evoking laughter or mirth. **Laughable** is the general term for whatever is fit to provoke laughter ⟨modern audiences do not find Shylock a *laughable* character⟩ ⟨a *laughable* incident⟩ ⟨the lower classes aped the rigid decorum of their "betters" with *laughable* results—*Harrison Smith*⟩ **Risible** is a close synonym of *laughable* and in this sense, like the former, carries no special connotations ⟨a *risible* account of their difficulties⟩ ⟨*risible* courtroom antics—*Hatch*⟩ **Ludicrous** applies to what induces usually scornful laughter because of its absurdity, incongruity, or preposterousness ⟨the *ludicrous* mistakes called schoolboy howlers⟩ ⟨had friendships, one after another, so violent as to be often *ludicrous*—*Belloc*⟩ ⟨some of the best public school teachers in the last century were hot-tempered men whose disciplinary performances were *ludicrous*—*Inge*⟩ ⟨buildings of different materials and styles . . . thrown together in a way at times fairly *ludicrous* —*A. O. White*⟩ **Ridiculous** applies to what excites derision because of extreme absurdity, foolishness, or contemptibility ⟨good manners at the court are as *ridiculous* in the country as the behavior of the country is most mockable at the court—*Shak.*⟩ ⟨to be always harping on nationality is to convert what should be a recognition of natural conditions into a *ridiculous* pride in one's own oddities— —*Santayana*⟩ **Comic** and **comical** are becoming distinct in implications and in applications, although they are sometimes interchangeable. **Comic** is applicable especially to something that partakes of the spirit of comedy and particularly of the literary form which aims to present life in a way that does not leave a painful impression and that does evoke smiles or laughter, especially thoughtful laughter, or amused reflection ⟨it is *comic* to see poor little nonentities like Frank Potter caught in it [Christianity], tangled up in it, and trying to get free and carry on as though it wasn't there—*Rose Macaulay*⟩ ⟨has the unerring instinct for things . . . recognized all the world over as *comic.* Green vegetables are always funny, and bad poets, and winter underwear, and feet—*Morley*⟩ **Comical** applies not so much to the character of what induces laughter as to the impression it produces upon the observer; hence, it aptly describes something which arouses spontaneous and unrestrained laughter ⟨the abrupt transition of her features from assured pride to ludicrous astonishment and alarm was *comical* enough to have sent into wild uncharitable laughter any creature less humane than Constance— *Bennett*⟩ ⟨I'm just beginning to get along with them so they don't think I'm quite so *comical,* and my wife comes

sailing in . . . and orders me out—*Faith McNulty*⟩ **Farcical** is often used interchangeably with *comical* but it is especially appropriate when what creates amusement is, like dramatic farce, dependent upon extravagance, nonsense, practical jokes, or burlesque for the effect it produces ⟨boys are like monkeys . . . the gravest actors of *farcical* nonsense that the world possesses—*Meredith*⟩ ⟨almost *farcical* to suppose that Henry, as a Norman prince, could not talk his own language to his Norman bride—*Empson*⟩ *Droll* and *funny* usually impute oddity or strangeness to what makes a thing laughable, but *droll* ordinarily carries a stronger implication of unfamiliarity, quaintness, absurdity, or intentional humorousness ⟨Thackeray's names, though often ludicrous, are always happy, and often inimitably *droll*—*Athenaeum*⟩ ⟨the habit of trying to marshal all the facts, weigh them, and think things through . . . is sometimes regarded as *droll*—*Bunche*⟩ and **funny** of queerness or curiousness ⟨the night mail set me down at Marwar Junction, where a *funny* little happy-go-lucky native-managed railway runs to Jodhpore—*Kipling*⟩ ⟨children thought he was a very *funny* old Chinaman, as children always think anything old and strange is *funny*—*Steinbeck*⟩ *Funny* is, however, the ordinary informal term interchangeable with any other word of the group ⟨a *funny* story⟩ ⟨he could rarely risk being *funny* and lightening his deadly seriousness with comedy—*Anthony West*⟩
*Ana* amusing, diverting, entertaining (see AMUSE): humorous, *witty, facetious, jocular, jocose
*Con* solemn, *serious, grave: tedious, tiresome, wearisome, boring, *irksome: pathetic, poignant, touching, affecting, *moving, impressive

**lavish** *profuse, prodigal, luxuriant, lush, exuberant
*Ana* *liberal, bountiful, bounteous, openhanded, generous, munificent, handsome: sumptuous, opulent, *luxurious: *excessive, inordinate, extravagant
*Ant* sparing —*Con* *meager, scanty, scant: economical, frugal, thrifty (see SPARING): provident, prudent, discreet (see under PRUDENCE): *stingy, niggardly, parsimonious, penurious, miserly

**law 1** Law, rule, regulation, precept, statute, ordinance, canon all designate a principle laid down or accepted as governing conduct, action, or procedure. *Law, rule,* and *precept* are also used as collective nouns to denote a body of laws, rules, or precepts ⟨obey the *law*⟩ ⟨work by *rule*⟩ ⟨teach by *precept*⟩ *Law* and *precept* are often used abstractly ⟨the world demanded peace and *law*, not liberties and privileges—*Buchan*⟩ ⟨the poet's business is not with *precept*—*Lowes*⟩ **Law** (see also HYPOTHESIS) primarily implies imposition by a sovereign authority and the obligation of obedience on the part of those governed ⟨churches are taking the lead in their own Communions as being not under the *law* of states but under the *law* of God—*Graham*⟩ In more restricted use, however, it implies a will to maintain peace and justice in the community or group governed and the expression of that will in concrete injunctions or prohibitions. Laws may be written or unwritten: when unwritten they indicate derivation from established custom; when written they commonly indicate enactment by a legislative body or power ⟨the *laws* of New York State⟩ ⟨beginning with the definition of *law* in the lawyer's sense as a statement of the circumstances in which the public force will be brought to bear upon a man through the courts—*Justice Holmes*⟩ **Rule**, in contrast with *law*, suggests closer relation to individual conduct and method, or a desire for order and discipline in the group. Sometimes it implies restriction, whether prescribed or self-imposed, for the sake of an immediate end (as unity in action, uniformity in procedure, or conformity to a standard of practice) ⟨the *rules* of a game⟩ ⟨the *rules* of a school⟩ ⟨the *rules* of good writing⟩ Sometimes *rule* does not imply ordering and prohibiting but suggests a positive way of thinking or acting in order to get desired or concrete results ⟨the *rule* of three⟩ ⟨like many old-time craftsmen he worked strictly by *rule* of thumb⟩ **Regulation** often equals *rule*, but distinctively it connotes prescription by authority for the control or management of an organization or system ⟨military *regulations*⟩ ⟨*regulations* respecting interstate commerce⟩ ⟨factory *regulations*⟩ ⟨we, the artists, are individualists . . . what right have you to circumscribe us with petty rules and *regulations*?—*Hartford*⟩ ⟨this *regulation* establishes ceiling prices for producers (brewers) of domestic malt beverages—*DiSalle*⟩ **Precept**, like *law*, usually implies generality and lack of detail in the statement and an authoritative origin; like *rule*, however, it implies closer reference to individual conduct than to government ⟨he really was the one child to whom the "spare-the-rod" *precept* did not apply—*Deland*⟩ Often *precept* is applied to what is enjoined by teaching; it commonly suggests counsel or advice, and is opposed in its abstract use to *practice* or *example* ⟨by *precept* and by practice he proclaimed the lofty solitude of the individual soul—*Ellis*⟩ ⟨observe the sixth commandment, not as a *precept* of divine law but as a counsel of profitable prudence—*Sullivan*⟩ Statute, ordinance, and canon all come under the general class of *law*. A **statute** is a written law, formally enacted by a legislative body. An **ordinance** is a local law, especially one enacted by a municipal government. A **canon**, basically, is a law of a church binding upon all of its members. In extended use *canon* is applied to such laws of ethics, of society, of criticism, and of the practice of the arts, as have the sanction of accepted authority and are enforced by one's moral, social, or artistic conscience ⟨are we witnessing a violent reaction against accepted *canons* of decency in life?—*Grandgent*⟩
*Ana* mandate, dictate, *command
**2** *principle, axiom, fundamental, theorem
*Ana* necessity, exigency (see NEED *n*)
*Ant* chance
**3** *hypothesis, theory
**4** statute, act, *bill

**lawful**, legal, legitimate, licit mean permitted, sanctioned, or recognized by law or the law. **Lawful** differs from the others in implying a reference to various sorts of law (as divine law, natural law, or the law of the land, or as civil law, common law, or canon law). Consequently, the term often comes close in meaning to *allowable* or *permissible* ⟨all things are *lawful* unto me, but all things are not expedient—*1 Cor 6:12*⟩ ⟨tell me, which knave is *lawful* game, which not? Must great offenders, once escaped the Crown, like royal harts, be never more run down?—*Pope*⟩ or sometimes to *rightful* or *proper* ⟨the *lawful* heir⟩ ⟨a *lawful* prize⟩ ⟨the *lawful* sovereign⟩ ⟨that man was not Hannah's *lawful* husband—*Ingamells*⟩ ⟨William desired to reign not as a conqueror but as a *lawful* king—*J. R. Green*⟩ **Legal** implies a reference to the law as it appears on the statute books or is administered in the courts; thus, the *lawful* heir is also the *legal* heir or the *legal* owner of a piece of property is one whose *legal* right to it is certain; a moneylender is entitled only to *legal* interest on his loans. *Legal* is used more often in the sense of sanctioned by law, or in conformity with the law, or not contrary to the law, than in the sense of allowable by the terms of the law ⟨a *legal* marriage⟩ ⟨the *legal* period for the payment of a debt⟩ ⟨the capture of the neutral ship carrying contraband was held to be *legal*⟩ ⟨she became the virtual head of our family, supplanting . . . my Uncle Tiberius (the *legal*

A colon (:) separates groups of words discriminated. An asterisk (*) indicates place of treatment of each group.

head)—*Graves*⟩ ⟨the Vichy regime he considers as illegitimate, although, at first at least, it was outwardly *legal*—*Guérard*⟩ **Legitimate,** which basically applies to a child born of legally married parents, also has been used to describe the person who has legal title (as to a throne, an inheritance, or a property) ⟨the *legitimate* monarch⟩ ⟨the *legitimate* heir of an estate⟩ The word may also imply not merely recognition by law but recognition or acceptance by custom, tradition, or the proper authorities or logical admissibility ⟨a lie may be considered *legitimate* if a patient's restoration to health depends on it⟩ ⟨Jane's mother was making indirect but perfectly *legitimate* inquiries into his prospects—*Mary Austin*⟩ ⟨*legitimate* to claim that much of our truly wonderful prodigality of talent is due to the work of gifted teachers—*Michener*⟩ ⟨in the light of the parallels which I have adduced the hypothesis appears *legitimate,* if not probable—*Frazer*⟩ **Licit** usually implies strict conformity to the provisions of the law respecting the way in which something should be performed or carried on; the term therefore is used especially of what is regulated by law; thus, a *licit* marriage, from the point of view of canon law, is one in which all prerequisites and all conditions attached to the performance of the ceremony have been attended to; *licit* liquor traffic is such traffic as obeys strictly the terms of the law; since dealings in the stock market have come under the control of the government, many deals once regarded as *lawful* are no longer *licit* ⟨the state is given its right to determine what is *licit* and illicit for property owners in the use of their possessions—*Commonweal*⟩ *Ana* rightful, *due, condign: allowed *or* allowable, permitted *or* permissible (see corresponding verbs at LET): justified *or* justifiable, warranted *or* warrantable (see corresponding verbs at JUSTIFY)
*Ant* unlawful —*Con* iniquitous, nefarious, flagitious (see VICIOUS)

**lawlessness** *anarchy, chaos
*Ana* *discord, strife, dissension, contention, conflict, difference, variance: *confusion, disorder
*Ant* discipline: order

**lawsuit** *suit, action, cause, case

**lawyer, counselor, barrister, counsel, advocate, attorney, solicitor. Lawyer** is the general term designating a person versed in the principles of law and authorized to practice law in the courts or to serve clients in the capacity of legal agent or adviser. *Counselor, barrister, counsel,* and *advocate* name a lawyer who has acquired the right to plead causes in open court or whose specialty is conducting and arguing court cases. **Counselor** is the usual designation in the United States for a lawyer who accepts court cases and gives advice on legal problems. The corresponding British term is **barrister,** with, however, special emphasis on court pleading. **Counsel** may be used as the equivalent of *counselor;* it, but not *counselor,* is also used collectively ⟨a brilliant array of *counsel*⟩ **Advocate** is in its implications the equivalent of *barrister* and *counselor,* but it is used as a designation in countries (as Scotland) in which the legal system is based on Roman law and in a few special courts. *Attorney* and *solicitor* are applied chiefly to a lawyer who serves as a legal agent for clients, transacting their business in specific courts (as probate court). Other powers vary with the law of the state or country. **Attorney** is often used in the United States as equivalent to *lawyer,* but the term may be used more precisely to denote a legal agent who acts for a client (as in conveying property, settling wills, or defending or prosecuting a case in court) ⟨the *attorney* for the executors of the will⟩ ⟨the State's *attorney*⟩ In England, the term *attorney* has been supplanted by **solicitor,** with, however, emphasis on the trans-

action of legal business for a client and the preparation of cases for trial as distinct from actual court pleading.

**lax 1** relaxed, *loose, slack
*Ana* *limp, floppy, flabby, flaccid
*Ant* rigid (sense 2) —*Con* *firm, solid, hard: tense, taut, *tight: *elastic, resilient, springy
**2** slack, remiss, *negligent, neglectful
*Ana* *careless, heedless, thoughtless: *indifferent, unconcerned: *forgetful, unmindful, oblivious
*Ant* strict, stringent —*Con* *severe, stern, austere: *rigid, rigorous: conscientious, scrupulous, honest, *upright

**lay** *vb* *direct, aim, point, level, train

**lay** *adj* secular, temporal, *profane
*Con* professional (see corresponding noun at TRADE): spiritual, religious, sacred (see HOLY)

**lay analyst** see under *psychoanalyst* at NEUROLOGIST

**laze** *idle, loaf, lounge, loll
*Ana* relax, rest, repose (see corresponding nouns at REST)
*Con* toil, travail, labor, grind, drudge (see corresponding nouns at WORK)

**lazy, indolent, slothful, faineant** are comparable primarily as applied to persons, their powers, movements, and actions, but also in some degree to things. All mean not easily aroused to action or activity. **Lazy** especially when applied to persons suggests a disinclination or aversion to effort or work and usually connotes idleness or dawdling, even when one is supposedly at work; the term is commonly derogatory ⟨rubbing their sleepy eyes with *lazy* wrists—*Keats*⟩ ⟨Una, now twenty-three, grandly beautiful, alternately *lazy* and amazingly energetic—*Rose Macaulay*⟩ ⟨we were too *lazy* .... We passed our indolent days leaving everything to somebody else—*H. G. Wells*⟩ **Indolent** implies an habitual love of ease and a settled dislike of movement or activity ⟨the stretching, *indolent* ease that the flesh and the spirit of this creature invariably seemed to move with—*Wister*⟩ ⟨he was so goodnatured, and so *indolent,* that I lost more than I got by him; for he made me as idle as himself—*Cowper*⟩ **Slothful** suggests the temper or indolence of one who is inactive when he knows he should be active or who moves or acts with excessive slowness when speed is essential ⟨be not *slothful,* but followers of them who through faith and patience inherit the promises—*Heb* 6:12⟩ ⟨not despondency, not *slothful* anguish, is what you now require, —but effort—*Hawthorne*⟩ ⟨he would . . . jog a *slothful* conscience and marshal its forces—*Parrington*⟩ **Faineant** implies both a slothful temper and a disposition to remain idly indifferent in spite of pressure or urgency ⟨he does not abandon hope in the masses . . . or see the people animated only by a *faineant* desire to be ruled—*New Republic*⟩ ⟨carpet-knight . . . is used as a term of reproach for a soldier who stays at home, and avoids active service and its hardships, with a particular reference to the carpet of a lady's chamber, in which such a *faineant* soldier lingers—*Encyc. Brit.*⟩
*Ana* inert, idle, *inactive, supine, passive: torpid, comatose, sluggish, *lethargic: *languid, languorous, lackadaisical, listless: slack, remiss, lax, *negligent, neglectful

**lead** *vb* *guide, pilot, engineer, steer
*Ana* *conduct, direct, manage, control: *set, fix, establish: *command, order, direct: *induce, persuade, prevail, get
*Ant* follow —*Con* mislead, delude, *deceive: drive, impel (see MOVE *vb*): *force, compel, coerce, constrain, oblige

**leader** head, *chief, chieftain, master
*Ant* follower —*Con* disciple, adherent, henchman,

satellite, partisan (see FOLLOWER)

**leading** *adj* *chief, principal, main, foremost, capital
*Ana* governing, ruling (see GOVERN): conducting, directing, managing, controlling (see CONDUCT *vb*): prominent, outstanding (see NOTICEABLE): eminent (see FAMOUS): preeminent, *supreme, superlative
*Ant* subordinate

**league** *alliance, coalition, fusion, confederacy, confederation, federation

**lean** *vb* *slant, slope, incline
*Ana* bend, *curve: *turn, deflect, divert, sheer

**lean** *adj* Lean, spare, lank, lanky, gaunt, rawboned, angular, scrawny, skinny mean thin because of absence of superfluous flesh. **Lean** stresses the lack of fat and therefore of rounded contours ⟨*lean* as a greyhound—*Thackeray*⟩ ⟨a small, *lean*, wiry man with sunk cheeks weathered to a tan —*Masefield*⟩ **Spare** often suggests abstemiousness or sinewy strength ⟨he had the *spare* form . . . which became a student—*George Eliot*⟩ ⟨the *spare*, alert and jaunty figure that one often finds in army men—*Wolfe*⟩ **Lank** suggests tallness or length as well as leanness; often also it implies wasting ⟨meager and *lank* with fasting grown, and nothing left but skin and bone—*Swift*⟩ ⟨a pack of *lank* hounds, sore-footed and sore-eared—*H. L. Davis*⟩ **Lanky** adds the suggestions of awkwardness and loose-jointedness ⟨a *lanky* youth, all arms and legs⟩ ⟨*lanky* men and women . . . so tall and attenuated that they seem at times to approach the one-dimensional—*Coates*⟩ **Gaunt** stresses want of sufficient flesh to conceal the bones; it often connotes overwork or undernourishment ⟨her bony visage—*gaunt* and deadly wan—*Wordsworth*⟩ ⟨this one with the passing of the years had grown lean and *gaunt* and the rocklike bones of her face stood forth and her eyes were sunken—*Buck*⟩ **Rawboned** often equals *gaunt,* but it is applied particularly to persons of large, ungainly frame and it seldom implies undernourishment ⟨a long, gawky, *rawboned* Yorkshireman—*Kipling*⟩ **Angular** implies not only absence of curves, but jerkiness or stiffness in movement ⟨sudden retirement of the *angular* female in oxydated bombazine—*Holmes*⟩ **Scrawny** and *skinny* imply extreme thinness but **scrawny** may additionally suggest slightness or a shrunken meager quality ⟨lank *scrawny* chickens⟩ ⟨a barren slope covered with *scrawny* vegetation⟩ ⟨the *scrawniest,* wretchedest horse I had ever seen—*Kalischer*⟩ while **skinny** suggests a stringy fleshless condition such as is associated with a deficiency of vitality or strength ⟨*skinny* children⟩ ⟨the *skinniest* human being I ever saw. He had not enough flesh on his bones to make a decent-sized chicken—*Lynd*⟩
*Ana* slender, slim, *thin, slight: cadaverous, wasted, pinched, *haggard
*Ant* fleshy —*Con* brawny, *muscular, sinewy, burly, husky: stout, *strong, sturdy, stalwart: plump, portly, rotund, fat, obese, corpulent (see FLESHY)

**leaning** *n* Leaning, propensity, proclivity, penchant, flair mean a strong instinct or liking for something or sometimes someone. One has a **leaning** *toward* something (as a church, a party, or a school of philosophy) when one definitely inclines to attachment to it or to follow it as a pursuit, a profession, or a course of action. *Leaning,* however, indicates only the direction in which one is being drawn by the force of attraction; it carries no implication of one's final course or destination ⟨the king was suspected by many of a *leaning* towards Rome—*Macaulay*⟩ ⟨he had a *leaning* toward the law, but his father urged him to study medicine⟩ ⟨a reformer with radical *leanings,* for years he edited a weekly paper called the *Anti-Monopolist*—*Martin Gardner*⟩ One has a **propensity** (as *toward* or *for* something or *to do* something) when one has an innate or in-

herent and often uncontrollable longing or is driven by a natural appetite ⟨study the *propensities* of a group of children⟩ ⟨the inveterate *propensity* of their husbands to linger about the village tavern—*Irving*⟩ ⟨such vehement *propensities* as drove Romeo, Antony, Coriolanus, to their doom—*Bradley*⟩ ⟨his *propensity* for sweeping authoritative statement was so supported by bravura passages of description that the gaps in his knowledge were overlooked—*Ferguson*⟩ One has a **proclivity** (as *for* or *towards* something or *to do* something) when one is prone to something not only by natural inclination but also by habitual indulgence or by the peculiarities of one's constitution or temperament ⟨the vesper sparrow, whose special *proclivity* for singing at twilight gave it its name—*W. P. Smith*⟩ ⟨curb a *proclivity* to lying⟩ ⟨the cow pony often maintained the pitching *proclivities* of a bronco—*Dobie*⟩ **Proclivity** often implies a tendency toward evil; when it is used without this implication, it still implies a stronger and less controllable urge than the other words here considered ⟨it [the American national genius] is nourished and sustained by ancient traditions and strong racial *proclivities*—*Sherman*⟩ ⟨the American *proclivity* for red tape and disoriented activity—*W. A. Noyes*⟩ One has a **penchant** usually *for* something when it has an irresistible attraction for him or when he has a decided taste for it ⟨Punjabi peasants have a *penchant* for a strong yellow that leans towards orange—*Rand*⟩ ⟨authors of medical articles exhibit on occasion an unusual *penchant* for extravagant terms, inelegant phrasing—*Holman*⟩ One has a **flair** *for* something when one has such an instinct for it as leads one to it as if by the very nature of one's being ⟨had a *flair* for finding bargains⟩ ⟨reporters with a *flair* for news⟩ ⟨that marvellous *flair* for detecting vital mechanism in every field—*Ellis*⟩ Often, especially in extended use, *flair* implies acumen and an innate power of discernment that results in an ability to distinguish the genuine from the counterfeit, the valuable from the valueless, and the significant from the insignificant ⟨a collector with a *flair* for the genuine antique⟩ ⟨as an editor he had superlative courage, and a *flair* for new writers—*Replier*⟩ Sometimes, the notion of "to do" is substituted for that of "to distinguish" and *flair* becomes a close synonym of *knack, aptitude,* or *talent* ⟨she hasn't a *flair* for writing⟩
*Ana* bias, *predilection, partiality, prepossession, prejudice: inclining *or* inclination, predisposition (see corresponding verbs at INCLINE): bent, turn, aptitude, faculty, *gift
*Ant* distaste —*Con* *antipathy, aversion: repugnance, abhorrence, repellency *or* repulsion (see corresponding adjectives at REPUGNANT)

**leap** *vb* *jump, spring, bound, vault
*Ana* *rise, arise, mount, soar, ascend
*Con* *fall, drop, sink, slump

**leap** *n* jump, spring, bound, vault (see under JUMP *vb*)

**learn** ascertain, *discover, determine, unearth

**learned,** scholarly, erudite are comparable when they mean possessing or manifesting unusually wide and deep knowledge. **Learned** implies the possession of knowledge gained by study and research; it usually implies wider and deeper knowledge than do such words as *educated, cultivated,* and *cultured,* and is usually applied to those who are conspicuous in their class or profession for learning, to associations composed of such persons, to books or articles written by them, and to periodicals edited by them or publishing articles by them ⟨the *learned* professions⟩ ⟨*learned* journals⟩ ⟨colloquialisms which I should not indulge in, were I reading a formal paper before a *learned* society—*Lowes*⟩ ⟨he is, in the true sense of the term,

A colon (:) separates groups of words discriminated. An asterisk (*) indicates place of treatment of each group.

*learned.* He reads Greek and Latin easily. He can recite poetry in seven languages—*Book-of-the-Month Club News*⟩ **Scholarly** also implies learning, but it is applied particularly to persons or to the utterances, ideas, and writings of persons who have attained mastery in a field of study or investigation, who have to a greater or lesser extent advanced knowledge in that field, and who have exhibited consistently high standards in the appraisal of their own and others' discoveries ⟨never academic—still less pedantic—but always *scholarly*; with the effect of profound learning ever so lightly worn—*Storrs*⟩ Often, more narrowly, the term implies great care for accuracy or exactness ⟨a *scholarly* study of the causes of the war⟩ ⟨*scholarly* pursuits⟩ ⟨this biography . . . is *scholarly* to the point of being unreadable, with footnotes covering half the space—*New Yorker*⟩ **Erudite**, though often employed as an equivalent of *learned* or *scholarly*, usually implies a love of learning for its own sake, a taste for what is out-of-the-way or remote from the interests of the average well-read man, and often an inordinately wide range of knowledge ⟨the point of view of a profound and *erudite* student, with a deep belief in the efficacy of useless knowledge—*Benson*⟩ ⟨that excellent critic, the late Mr. Walkley, was often spoken of as *erudite*, because his charming quotations gave so many readers a feeling of having to do with a man who had all literature at his command—*Montague*⟩
*Ana* cultivated, cultured (see corresponding nouns at CULTURE): *pedantic, academic, scholastic, bookish: *recondite, abstruse, esoteric
*Con* illiterate, unlettered, uneducated, unlearned, untutored, *ignorant
**learning** erudition, scholarship, *knowledge, science, information, lore
*Ana* *culture, cultivation, breeding, refinement: enlightenment (see corresponding verb at ILLUMINATE)
**lease** *vb* let, charter, *hire, rent
**leave** *vb* 1 *will, bequeath, devise, legate
*Ana* *commit, entrust, confide, consign: assign, *allot, apportion
2 *relinquish, resign, surrender, abandon, yield, cede, waive
*Ana* forsake, *abandon, desert: *forgo, forbear, sacrifice, abnegate, eschew: *neglect, ignore, forget, omit: *grant, concede, vouchsafe: relegate, *commit, confide, entrust
3 depart, quit, *go, withdraw, retire
*Ana* *escape, flee, fly, abscond, decamp
*Con* *come, arrive: *appear, emerge, loom
4 *let, allow, permit, suffer
**leave** *n* *permission, sufferance
*Ana* consenting *or* consent, assenting *or* assent (see ASSENT *vb*): sanctioning *or* sanction, endorsement, approval (see corresponding verbs at APPROVE): authorization (see corresponding verb at AUTHORIZE)
*Con* refusing *or* refusal, rejecting *or* rejection (see corresponding verbs at DECLINE): forbidding *or* forbiddance, prohibition, interdiction (see corresponding verbs at FORBID)
**leaven** *infuse, imbue, inoculate, ingrain, suffuse
*Ana* temper, qualify, *moderate: *inform, animate, inspire: pervade, *permeate, impregnate, saturate: vivify, enliven, *quicken
**leavings** remains, *remainder, residue, residuum, rest, balance, remnant
*Ana* fragments, pieces, portions (see singular nouns at PART): discardings *or* discards, scrappings *or* scraps, junkings *or* junk (see DISCARD *vb*)
**lecherous** libidinous, lascivious, lustful, lewd, wanton, *licentious, libertine

*Ana* dissolute, *abandoned, reprobate, profligate: degenerate, corrupt (see VICIOUS)
**lecture** address, *speech, oration, harangue, talk, sermon, homily
**leech** *parasite, sponge, sponger, sycophant, toady, lickspittle, bootlicker, hanger-on, favorite
**lees** *n* *deposit, precipitate, sediment, dregs, grounds
*Ana* *refuse, waste
**leeway** *room, berth, play, elbowroom, margin, clearance
**legal** legitimate, licit, *lawful
*Ant* illegal
**legal tender** *money, cash, currency, specie, coin, coinage
**legate** *n* *ambassador, nuncio, internuncio, chargé d'affaires, minister, envoy
**legate** *vb* *will, bequeath, devise, leave
**legend** 1 *myth, saga
2 *inscription, caption
**legendary** mythical, apocryphal, fabulous, *fictitious
**legerity** *celerity, alacrity
*Ana* nimbleness, agility, briskness, spryness (see corresponding adjectives at AGILE): swiftness, fleetness, rapidity (see corresponding adjectives at FAST): dexterity, ease, *readiness, facility: dispatch, expedition, speed (see HASTE)
*Ant* deliberateness: sluggishness
**legion** host, army, *multitude
**legitimate** legal, *lawful, licit
*Ana* justified *or* justifiable, warranted *or* warrantable (see corresponding verbs at JUSTIFY): *valid, sound, cogent: recognized, acknowledged (see ACKNOWLEDGE): customary, *usual: *regular, normal, typical, natural
*Ant* illegitimate: arbitrary (*powers, means*)
**leisure** relaxation, *rest, repose, ease, comfort
*Ant* toil —*Con* *work, labor, travail, grind, drudgery
**leisurely** deliberate, *slow, dilatory, laggard
*Ana* relaxed, slack, lax (see LOOSE): slackened, retarded, delayed (see DELAY): easy, *comfortable, restful
*Ant* hurried: abrupt —*Con* hasty, speedy, quick, *fast, rapid: *precipitate, headlong, impetuous
**leitmotiv** motive, motif, theme, *subject, matter, subject matter, argument, topic, text
**lengthen** *extend, elongate, prolong, protract
*Ana* *increase, augment: *expand, amplify, distend
*Ant* shorten —*Con* abridge, abbreviate, curtail (see SHORTEN)
**leniency** clemency, mercifulness, forbearance, tolerance, indulgence (see under FORBEARING)
*Ana* lenity, clemency, *mercy, charity, grace: kindliness, benignity, benignancy, kindness (see corresponding adjectives at KIND): compassionateness, tenderness (see corresponding adjectives at TENDER)
**lenient** 1 *soft, gentle, smooth, mild, bland, balmy
*Ana* assuaging, alleviating, relieving (see RELIEVE): grateful, agreeable, welcome, gratifying, pleasing, *pleasant
*Ant* caustic —*Con* harsh, *rough
2 indulgent, merciful, clement, *forbearing, tolerant
*Ana* forgiving, excusing, condoning, pardoning (see EXCUSE *vb*): kindly, benign, benignant (see KIND): compassionate, *tender: indulging, pampering, humoring, spoiling, mollycoddling (see INDULGE): lax (see NEGLIGENT)
*Ant* stern: exacting —*Con* *rigid, rigorous, stringent: *severe, austere
**leniently** forbearingly, tolerantly, clemently, mercifully, indulgently (see under FORBEARING)
**lenity** clemency, *mercy, charity, grace
*Ana* leniency, indulgence, clemency, mercifulness, forbearance, tolerance (see under FORBEARING): benignity,

benignancy, kindliness, kindness (see corresponding adjectives at KIND): compassionateness *or* compassion, tenderness (see corresponding adjectives at TENDER): benevolence, humaneness, charitableness (see corresponding adjectives at CHARITABLE): laxity (see corresponding adjective at NEGLIGENT)
*Ant* severity —*Con* strictness, rigorousness, rigidity, stringency (see corresponding adjectives at RIGID): sternness, austerity (see corresponding adjectives at SEVERE)

**lesion** *wound, trauma, traumatism, bruise, contusion
*Ana* *injury, hurt, damage

**less** *adj* **Less, lesser, smaller, fewer** are comparable terms that approach each other in meaning but are not synonyms and are rarely interchangeable. **Less** means not as much, especially in degree, value, or amount, and its opposite is usually *more*. It applies chiefly to collective nouns or nouns denoting a mass or abstract whole ⟨the moon yields *less* light than the sun⟩ ⟨John has *less* money than James⟩ ⟨please make *less* noise⟩ ⟨humility has *less* appeal to men of today than other virtues⟩ **Lesser** means not as great, as important, or as significant as that with which the thing so qualified is compared and implies opposition to *greater* or *major* ⟨God made . . . the *lesser* light to rule the night—*Gen* 1:16⟩ ⟨humility is not, in Christian ethics, regarded as a *lesser* virtue⟩ ⟨*lesser* breaches of the law—*Locke*⟩ In vernacular names *lesser* implies that the kind of plant or animal so designated is distinguished from a very similar one carrying the same name chiefly by its comparative smallness of size ⟨the *lesser* celandine⟩ ⟨the *lesser* snipe⟩ **Smaller** means not as large as that with which the thing so qualified is compared (as in size, dimensions, or quantity) ⟨the *smaller* of two rooms⟩ ⟨give her the *smaller* table for it will take up less room⟩ **Fewer** means not as many and implies a difference in number of individuals or units; the term therefore modifies a plural noun ⟨he has *fewer* pupils than he had last year⟩ ⟨give her *fewer* lumps of sugar⟩ ⟨no *fewer* than fifty were present⟩
*Ant* more

**lessen** *decrease, diminish, reduce, abate, dwindle
*Ana* *shorten, curtail, retrench, abridge, abbreviate: shrink, *contract: lighten, mitigate, alleviate (see RELIEVE): *thin, dilute, attenuate

**lesser** smaller, *less, fewer
*Ant* major

**let** 1 lease, rent, *hire, charter
2 **Let, allow, permit, suffer, leave** denote to refrain from preventing, or to fail to prevent, or to indicate an intention not to prevent. *Let, allow,* and *permit,* though frequently used with little distinction of meaning, are capable of discrimination. **Let** is the most informal ⟨her mother wouldn't *let* her go⟩ ⟨she didn't go because her mother wouldn't *let* her⟩ Sometimes *let* implies failure to prevent through awkwardness, inadvertence, negligence, or inaction ⟨the third baseman *let* the ball get through him⟩ ⟨this dismal sketch of the future of countries that *let* themselves become dependent on the labor of other countries—*Shaw*⟩ ⟨he is usually very particular not to *let* his beasts stray —*F. D. Smith & Barbara Wilcox*⟩ and sometimes it implies failure to prevent through lack of power or inclination ⟨he'll have to be a good deal tougher than his dad, who *lets* himself be pushed around—*Mead*⟩ **Allow** and *permit* imply power or authority to prohibit or prevent. But **allow** may imply little more than acquiescence or lack of prohibition, whereas **permit** implies express signification of willingness ⟨the freedom of conscience *allowed* dissenters, the tolerance extended to all creeds—*Billington*⟩ ⟨a business or profession which *allows* you to get away when you want to—*Joseph*⟩ ⟨I blush for the weakness that *allows* me to cherish such a passion—*Gilbert*⟩ ⟨he *permitted*

none but Quaker preachers to smoke or drink in his home —*Starr*⟩ ⟨we do not give gifts, throw parties or pay bonuses at Christmas time. We do *permit* our employes to gather in the lobby and sing carols on Christmas Eve —*Wall Street Jour.*⟩ **Suffer** (somewhat bookish in this sense) is often a mere synonym for *allow* in the narrowest implication of that word ⟨*suffer* little children to come unto me—*Lk* 18:16⟩ ⟨*suffer* me to take your hand. Death comes in a day or two—*Millay*⟩ but it may imply indifference or reluctance ⟨the eagle *suffers* little birds to sing— *Shak.*⟩ ⟨she *suffered* herself to be led to the tiny enclosure where . . . other generations had been buried—*S. E. White*⟩ ⟨perhaps the whole business . . . of the death penalty will seem . . . an anachronism too discordant to be *suffered,* mocking with grim reproach—*Cardozo*⟩ **Leave** (see also GO 1) as used with the implication of letting, allowing, or permitting is not clearly distinct from the use discriminated at *relinquish,* but it tends to stress strongly the implication of noninterference; often it also suggests the departure of the person who might interfere ⟨*leave* the choice of games to be settled by the guests⟩ ⟨the defendant's attorney *left* him free to tell his story as he wished⟩ ⟨we must *leave* the children to settle their affairs for themselves— *Rose Macaulay*⟩
*Ana* sanction, endorse, *approve, accredit, certify: *authorize, license, commission
*Con* *forbid, prohibit, interdict, enjoin, ban, inhibit: *hinder, impede, obstruct, block, bar: thwart, *frustrate, foil, circumvent

**lethal** *deadly, fatal, mortal
*Ana* destroying *or* destructive (see corresponding verb at DESTROY): killing, slaying (see KILL): *pernicious, baneful, noxious: *poisonous, virulent, venomous, toxic
*Con* salutary, wholesome, hygienic, *healthful: renewing, restoring *or* restorative (see corresponding verbs at RENEW)

**lethargic, sluggish, torpid, comatose** are comparable when they mean being by constitution or condition physically and often mentally inert or inactive. **Lethargic** usually implies either a constitutional or a temporary or pathological state of sleepiness or drowsiness that makes for slowness in reactions, responses, or movements, or for temperamental apathy ⟨bullfrogs, in a recent shipment, were quite *lethargic* . . . and reacted only when they were strongly stimulated—*Giese*⟩ ⟨gone is the *lethargic* atmosphere of an apathetic people, hopeless and helpless to direct their own destinies—*Atlantic*⟩ ⟨not all the industry of a Hercules will suffice to awaken the *lethargic* brain —*Mencken*⟩ ⟨but it was no *lethargic* calm; my brain was more active than ever—*Hudson*⟩ **Sluggish** applies not only to persons but to whatever by its nature moves, acts, or functions; the term implies conditions which create stagnation, inertia, indolence, or inability to proceed at a normal or usual pace ⟨*sluggish* attention⟩ ⟨a *sluggish* pond⟩ ⟨*sluggish* circulation⟩ ⟨a *sluggish* market for securities⟩ ⟨I want no *sluggish* languor, no bovine complacency. A phenobarbital philosophy does not appeal to me—*Warren Weaver*⟩ ⟨England has become unenterprising and *sluggish* because England has been so prosperous and comfortable—*H. G. Wells*⟩ **Torpid** suggests the loss of power of feeling and of exertion; basically it implies the numb or benumbed state of a hibernating animal, but in its more common extended sense it implies a lack of the energy, vigor, and responsiveness that one associates with healthy, vital, active beings ⟨memory was not so utterly *torpid* in Silas that it could not be wakened by these words—*George Eliot*⟩ ⟨still Richard was *torpid;* could not think or move—*Woolf*⟩ ⟨Oxford was *torpid* also, droning along in its eighteenth-century grooves—

A colon (:) separates groups of words discriminated. An asterisk (*) indicates place of treatment of each group.

*Brooks⟩* **Comatose** basically implies a being in the state of profound insensibility called coma that results from a disease (as diabetes or uremia) which spreads poisons through the system or from severe injury ⟨the almost *comatose* condition which had first supervened never developed into a fatal diabetic coma—*Ellis⟩* In extended use *comatose* implies the stultification of extreme lethargy ⟨tales . . . guaranteed to shake the most *comatose* of readers out of the deepest lethargy—*advt.⟩*
*Ana* inert, idle, *inactive, supine, passive: phlegmatic, stolid, *impassive, apathetic: *languid, languorous, lackadaisical, listless: *slow, dilatory, laggard
*Ant* energetic, vigorous —*Con* alert, quick-witted, *intelligent: *quick, ready, prompt, apt: responsive (see TENDER): *spirited, gingery, peppery

**lethargy,** **languor, lassitude, stupor, torpor, torpidity** are comparable when meaning physical and mental inertness. **Lethargy** implies a state marked by an aversion to activity which may be constitutional but is typically induced by disease, extreme fatigue or exhaustion, overeating or overdrinking, or constant frustration and which exhibits itself in drowsiness or apathy ⟨what means this heaviness that hangs upon me? This *lethargy* that creeps through all my senses? Nature, oppressed and harassed out with care, sinks down to rest—*Addison⟩* ⟨the state of apathy and *lethargy* into which they had been thrust by their stunning defeat—*Political Science Quarterly⟩* **Languor** (compare LANGUID) has nearly lost its basic application to a condition of weakness, faintness, or delicacy of constitution induced by illness and serving as a bar to exertion or effort ⟨I nearly sank to the ground through *languor* and extreme weakness—*M. W. Shelley⟩* and has come to imply an inertia such as results from soft living, from an enervating climate, or from amorous emotion ⟨intervals of repose, which though agreeable for a moment, yet if prolonged beget a *languor* and lethargy that destroy all enjoyment —*Hume⟩* ⟨she is characterized essentially by *languor*. Her most familiar posture is on a bed or divan—*Fowlie⟩* ⟨instead of the *languor* of the tropics, they seem to have acquired . . . a good deal of our energy and enthusiasm— *Eleanor Roosevelt⟩* **Lassitude** implies such a listless seedy mental or physical condition as may result from strain, overwork, poor health, or intense worry; it usually connotes an inertia of mind or body which one has not the strength to fight ⟨the results of overstrained energies are feebleness and *lassitude*—*Borrow⟩* ⟨she sat for twenty minutes or more ere she could summon resolution to go down to the door, her courage being lowered to zero by her physical *lassitude*—*Hardy⟩* ⟨an overpowering *lassitude*, an extreme desire simply to sit and dream—*Moorehead⟩* **Stupor** implies a state of heaviness when the mind is deadened (as by extreme drowsiness, intoxication, narcotic poisoning, or the coma of illness); the term may imply any state from a dreamy trancelike condition to almost complete unconsciousness ⟨there is . . . something almost narcotic in such medieval poetry; one is lulled into a pleasing *stupor*—*Lowes⟩* ⟨was in a *stupor* of mental weariness—*Anderson⟩* ⟨had collapsed for the moment in a *stupor* of pain—*Steen⟩* **Torpor** and *torpidity* basically suggest the condition of a hibernating animal which has lost all power of exertion or of feeling ⟨a poorwill found during the winter . . . which was in a state of profound *torpidity*—*F. C. Lincoln⟩* Both terms, especially when employed in reference to persons, usually imply extreme sluggishness and inertness (as in some forms of insanity); **torpidity,** however, probably more often applies to a physical condition and **torpor** to a mental state ⟨blunt the discriminating powers of the mind, and . . . reduce it to a state of almost savage *torpor*—*Wordsworth⟩* ⟨a deathlike

*torpor* has succeeded to her former intellectual activity —*Prescott⟩* ⟨in a world of *torpidities* any rapid moving thing is hailed—*Birrell⟩* ⟨the *torpidity* which the last solitary tourist, flying with the yellow leaves . . . had left them to enjoy till the returning spring—*Peacock⟩*
*Ana* sluggishness, comatoseness (see corresponding adjectives at LETHARGIC): indolence, slothfulness *or* sloth, laziness (see corresponding adjectives at LAZY): inertness *or* inertia, inactivity, idleness, passiveness, supineness (see corresponding adjectives at INACTIVE): apathy, phlegm, impassivity (see under IMPASSIVE)
*Ant* vigor —*Con* quickness, readiness, promptness, aptness (see corresponding adjectives at QUICK): alertness, quick-wittedness (see corresponding adjectives at INTELLIGENT)

**letter,** **epistle, missive, note, message, dispatch, report, memorandum** are comparable when they mean a communication sent or transmitted as distinct from one conveyed directly from source to recipient (as by oral utterance). **Letter** is the ordinary term for a written, typed, or printed communication sent by one person or group to another most often by mail; the term carries no implications about the nature of the communication and no hint as to whether it deals with personal or business matters or with affairs of public concern ⟨she received a *letter* from her husband yesterday⟩ ⟨all *letters* sent out from the belligerent countries are censored⟩ ⟨he addressed an open *letter* (i.e., one given out for publication) to his constituents⟩ **Epistle** applies especially to a letter intended to be made public (as one of the scriptural letters of advice and counsel attributed to the Apostles) ⟨the First *Epistle* to Timothy⟩ ⟨the Second *Epistle* to the Corinthians⟩ or to a composition in prose or poetry taking the form of an open letter ⟨Pope's "*Epistle* to Dr. Arbuthnot"⟩ As applied to a private letter, *epistle* is an overformal word typically used with some degree of humorous or ironic implication ⟨forced to defend his praise of James Jones's *Eternity* against a barrage of indignant *epistles*—*Geismar⟩* ⟨the amiable *epistle* of a son-in-law anxious to be a little more than correct—*Bennett⟩* **Missive,** too, is a somewhat formal term and as applied to a personal letter may be somewhat ironic or whimsical in implication ⟨many of their *missives* were illiterate, and the more violent of them were unsigned—*Merriman⟩* **Note** in general use applies to a letter that is brief and pointed, whether it is formal or informal ⟨send a *note* of condolence⟩ ⟨write a *note* of acceptance⟩ In diplomatic usage *note* is applied to a formal communication sent by one government to another ⟨the Porte . . . acknowledged the validity of the Latin claims in a formal *note*—*Kinglake⟩* **Message** differs from the preceding terms in being applicable not only to a written, typed, or printed communication but to one that is orally transmitted (as over the telephone or by a messenger or servant) or is telegraphed, cabled, or radioed ⟨sent a *message* to his mother that he had been called out of town⟩ ⟨but his citizens hated him, and sent a *message* after him, saying, We will not have this man to reign over us—*Lk 19:14⟩* In official and especially governmental use *message* applies to a formal communication from the head of a state (as one sent by the president of the United States to Congress or by a governor to the law-making body of his state) ⟨President Wilson broke tradition by delivering his *messages* to Congress personally⟩ **Dispatch** applies to a usually brief message that is sent posthaste (as by telegraph, cable, or radiotelegraph). In more technical use *dispatch* applies to such messages sent by an authorized correspondent to a newspaper or news association; it also specifically applies to an official message, often one in cipher, sent by or to a government to

or by a diplomatic, military, or naval officer in its service.
**Report** (see also ACCOUNT 2) applies particularly to a communication sent by an official (as a diplomat) to his own government. The term is also applicable to an official communication giving a detailed statement of facts, proceedings, or recommendations ⟨the committee on foreign affairs is ready to make a *report* to Congress⟩ ⟨the school sends a monthly *report* of each student's work to his parents⟩ **Memorandum** is used chiefly in business for an informal communication sent to an executive or employee, conveying instructions or directions.

**levee** *wharf, dock, pier, quay, slip, berth, jetty

**level** *vb* point, train, *direct, aim, lay

**level** *adj* Level, flat, plane, plain, even, smooth, flush are comparable chiefly as applied to surfaces and as meaning having a surface comparable to that of a perfectly calm body of water with no part higher than another. Something is **level** whose surface, from every point of view, lies on a line corresponding to or parallel with that of the horizon ⟨the top of the table is not perfectly *level*⟩ ⟨the prairies are vast stretches of nearly *level* land⟩ ⟨a plot of ground made *level* by grading⟩ But *level* is also applicable to an adjacent surface lying in exactly the same plane ⟨in the spring, the river's surface is often *level* with its banks⟩ ⟨buildings whose roofs are *level* with one another⟩ In extended use *level* implies an equality of parts, or of one thing with another, so that there are no manifest fluctuations or irregularities; thus, to speak in a *level* voice is to speak without the variations in pitch or voice volume that indicate imperfect self-control; to keep a *level* head is to keep free from distracting excitement. Something is **flat** (see also INSIPID) which is marked by absence of noticeable curvatures, prominences, or depressions, whether it lies in a horizontal plane or not ⟨there is no *flat* ground hereabouts⟩ ⟨the *flat* face of a cliff⟩ ⟨the sides of a pyramid are all *flat*⟩ But *flat* may apply to something that lies directly upon or against a flat surface ⟨*flat* feet⟩ ⟨lay the map *flat* on the table⟩ ⟨the chairs have their backs *flat* against the wall⟩ ⟨lie *flat* on the ground⟩ In extended use *flat* applies sometimes to what is so lacking in variation or variety as to be monotonous ⟨a *flat* speech delivered by the new president⟩ ⟨a *flat* entertainment⟩ or to what gives no ground for doubt or for difference in description because direct, pure, complete, or unqualified ⟨a *flat* question⟩ ⟨a belief that is *flat* heresy⟩ ⟨a *flat* failure⟩ or to what is fixed or absolutely exact ⟨ask a *flat* price⟩ ⟨he ran the race in a *flat* ten seconds⟩ Something is *plane* or *plain* which is flat and usually level. **Plane** is more usual in technical and mathematical use and more often applies to angles, curves, or figures (as triangles, rectangles, and pentagons) all points of which lie in the same real or imaginary surface so that if any two points be taken within the boundary lines of the angle, curve, or figure, the straight line joining them lies wholly within that surface; thus, *plane* geometry, which deals with *plane* angles, curves, and figures, is distinguished from *solid* geometry ⟨the *plane* sides of a crystal⟩ **Plain** is much less frequent in adjectival use and applies chiefly to the ground ⟨I recovered some strength, so as to be able to walk a little on *plain* ground—*John Wesley*⟩ Something is **even** (see also STEADY) which exhibits a uniformity of all the points either of a plane surface or of a line so that the surface's flatness or levelness or the line's straightness is observable ⟨he trimmed the top of the hedge to make it *even*⟩ ⟨the hem of your skirt is not *even*⟩ ⟨the frigate was on an *even* keel—*Marryat*⟩ Something is **smooth** that exhibits perfect evenness of surface, as though polished, rolled, or planed free from the slightest traces of roughness or unevenness ⟨the *smooth* surface of a

rubbed and polished table⟩ ⟨a *smooth* lawn⟩ ⟨the tall bamboo and the long moss threw farther shadows . . . over the *smooth* bayou—*Stark Young*⟩ A surface or a line is **flush** that is in the same horizontal or vertical plane or forms a continuous surface or line with another surface or line ⟨the front of the house is *flush* with the front boundary line⟩ ⟨the river's surface is now *flush* with that of its banks⟩ ⟨a *flush* panel⟩ ⟨in the ordinary printed page, all lines are *flush* except those in titles or headings or those that are indented for paragraphing⟩
**Ana** parallel, uniform, *like, alike, akin, identical, similar: *same, equivalent, equal
**Con** undulating, fluctuating, swaying (see SWING *vb*): varying, changing (see CHANGE *vb*)

**levitate** *rise, arise, ascend, mount, soar, tower, rocket, surge
**Ant** gravitate, sink

**levity** *lightness, light-mindedness, frivolity, flippancy, volatility, flightiness
**Ana** foolishness *or* folly, silliness, absurdity (see corresponding adjectives at FOOLISH): gaiety, liveliness, sprightliness, vivaciousness *or* vivacity (see corresponding adjectives at LIVELY)
**Ant** gravity —**Con** seriousness, soberness *or* sobriety, earnestness, solemnity, somberness (see corresponding adjectives at SERIOUS): severity, sternness, austerity, asceticism (see corresponding adjectives at SEVERE)

**lewd** lustful, lascivious, libidinous, lecherous, wanton, *licentious, libertine
**Ana** *immoral, unmoral, amoral: gross, *coarse, obscene: indecent, indelicate (see INDECOROUS)
**Ant** chaste —**Con** decent, pure, modest (see CHASTE): *moral, virtuous: continent, temperate (see SOBER)

**liability** *debt, indebtedness, obligation, debit, arrear
**Ant** asset (*or* plural assets)

**liable** 1 amenable, answerable, *responsible, accountable
**Ana** obliged, constrained, compelled (see FORCE *vb*): bound, tied (see TIE *vb*)
**Con** exempt, immune (see corresponding nouns at EXEMPTION): *free, independent
2 Liable, open, exposed, subject, prone, susceptible, sensitive are used with reference to persons or things and mean being by nature or situation in a position where something stated or implied may happen. **Liable** (see also APT 2; RESPONSIBLE) is used particularly when the thing one incurs or may incur is the result of his obligation to authority, of his state in life, or of submission to forces beyond his control ⟨one of the most horrible diseases to which mankind is *liable*—*Eliot*⟩ ⟨literature is *liable* to obsolescence, not only because language changes and gradually becomes less intelligible, but because the ideas, the interests, the conception of life it expresses, the very form of the thought, the experiences which arouse emotion, all become obsolete—*Aldington*⟩ ⟨*liable* to be burned at the stake for . . . heresy—*Repplier*⟩ **Open** suggests lack of barriers or ease of access ⟨standing thus alone . . . *open* to all the criticism which descends on the lone operator—*Catton*⟩ ⟨another modern tendency in education . . . somewhat more *open* to question—I mean the tendency to make education useful rather than ornamental —*Russell*⟩ **Exposed** presupposes the same conditions as *open*, but it is more restricted in application because it implies a position or state of peril or a lack of protection or of resistance ⟨infant mortality is high because the piglets are *exposed* to diseases the sow carries—*Farmer's Weekly*⟩ ⟨Germans never tire of explaining that their *exposed* position in Central Europe has forced them to follow a policy of expansion—*Bullock*⟩ **Subject** and *prone* (see also PRONE 2) both suggest greater likelihood

A colon (:) separates groups of words discriminated. An asterisk (*) indicates place of treatment of each group.

of incurring or suffering than *liable* and even less resistance than *exposed;* they may both connote the position of being under the sway or control of a superior power, but otherwise they differ in implications. **Subject** implies openness to something which must be suffered, borne, or undergone for a reason (as a state in life or a social, economic, or political status or a quality of temperament or nature) ⟨the French people would have stood permanently weak, open to invasion and *subject* to continual interference—*Belloc*⟩ ⟨both were *subject* to constant criticism from men and bodies of men whose minds were as acute and whose learning was as great as their own—*Henry Adams*⟩ ⟨Paul was rather a delicate boy, *subject* to bronchitis—*D. H. Lawrence*⟩ ⟨the cycles to which all civilizations are *subject*—*Ellis*⟩ ⟨the constitution was strictly an unwritten one, and was avowedly *subject* to revision in the light of new developments—*Buchan*⟩ **Prone**, on the other hand, usually implies that the person, or less often the thing, concerned is more or less governed by a propensity or predisposition to something which makes him or it almost certain to incur or to do that thing when conditions are favorable ⟨you may well warn me against such an evil. Human nature is so *prone* to fall into it!—*Austen*⟩ ⟨I think that girls are less *prone* than boys to punish oddity by serious physical cruelty—*Russell*⟩ ⟨in those industries that are most *prone* to periods of depression and unemployment—*Hobson*⟩ ⟨our painters are *prone* to acquiesce in the colors of nature as they find them, rather than to use colors expressive of the mood evoked in themselves—*Binyon*⟩ **Susceptible** carries a stronger implication than the preceding terms, with the exception of *prone*, of something in the person's or thing's nature, character, constitution, or temperament that makes him or it unresistant or liable to a thing and especially to a deleterious thing or a thing that exerts a deleterious influence ⟨wheat tends to be very *susceptible* to smut—*Furnas*⟩ ⟨a mind enormously more *susceptible* to tragic impressions than your own—*Montague*⟩ ⟨a natural-born actor, who was, in childhood, *susceptible* not only to somnambulism but to mesmeric control—*Brooks*⟩ When used attributively the word often implies a readiness to fall in love ⟨a very *susceptible* young man⟩ Sometimes, however, *susceptible* stresses openness by reason of one's nature, character, or constitution, rather than liability, and when followed by *of* is equivalent to *admitting* or *allowing* ⟨a theory *susceptible* of proof⟩ ⟨today's pedagogical theory asserts that memory cannot be cultivated: it is inborn, full-grown at the start, and not *susceptible* of increase—*Grandgent*⟩ **Sensitive** differs from *susceptible* chiefly in implying a physical or emotional condition that predisposes one to certain impressions or certain reactions ⟨she was too *sensitive* to abuse and calumny—*Macaulay*⟩ ⟨she discovered that with the clarification of her complexion and the birth of pink cheeks her skin had grown more *sensitive* to the sun's rays—*Hardy*⟩ ⟨she was extremely *sensitive* to neglect, to disagreeable impressions, to want of intelligence in her surroundings—*Henry Adams*⟩ ⟨the eye is much more *sensitive* to light than the hand or the balance to weight—*Darrow*⟩

**Ant** exempt, immune

**3** likely, *apt

**liaison** intrigue, *amour, affair

**libel** *n* **Libel, skit, squib, lampoon, pasquinade** mean a public and often satirical presentation of faults or weaknesses, especially those of an individual. **Libel** (compare *libel vb* under MALIGN) is the legal term for statement or representation (as a cartoon) published or circulated without just cause or excuse, which tends to expose a person to public contempt, hatred, or ridicule ⟨cheap senseless *libels* were scattered about the city—*Clarendon*⟩ **Skit** applies to an amusing satire typically in the form of a dramatic sketch or story that may be more humorous or ironical than satirical and is usually of no very great weight or seriousness; the term seldom connotes malice, bitterness, or abusiveness, but it often suggests the infliction of a sting ⟨he did not deserve your *skit* about his "Finsbury Circus gentility"—*FitzGerald*⟩ ⟨the first of the one-act plays was a *skit* more or less obviously dealing with the prime minister's attempt to forestall war⟩ **Squib** applies to a short and clever often malicious piece of satirical writing that makes its point with a sharp thrust and evokes laughter or amusement ⟨no one was more faithful to his early friends . . . particularly if they could write a *squib*—*Disraeli*⟩ **Lampoon** suggests more virulence and abusiveness and a coarser humor than *skit* or *squib* ⟨a lust to misapply, make satire a *lampoon*, and fiction, lie—*Pope*⟩ ⟨on his master at Twyford he had already exercised his poetry in a *lampoon*—*Johnson*⟩ **Pasquinade** is preferred to *lampoon* when such circumstances as anonymity, public posting, political character, or extreme scurrility are implied ⟨the white walls of the barracks were covered with . . . *pasquinades* leveled at Cortez—*Prescott*⟩

**Ana** scurrility, invective, vituperation, *abuse: burlesque, travesty (see CARICATURE *n*)

**libel** *vb* defame, slander, *malign, traduce, asperse, vilify, calumniate

**Ana** revile, vituperate (see SCOLD): *decry, disparage, derogate, detract: caricature, travesty, burlesque (see under CARICATURE *n*)

**liberal** *adj* **1 Liberal, generous, bountiful, bounteous, openhanded, munificent, handsome** are applied to a person or to his deeds or utterances and mean showing or revealing a spirit of giving freely and without stint. **Liberal** suggests openhandedness or lack of closeness or meanness in the giver and largeness in the thing that is given ⟨make a *liberal* provision for a son at college⟩ ⟨a *liberal* offer for a house⟩ ⟨*liberal* in praise⟩ ⟨about three thousand New Hampshire men were engaged in privateering . . . receiving *liberal* rewards for the risks they took—*Amer. Guide Series: N. H.*⟩ ⟨opium smokers included the upper crust of the underworld, as well as a *liberal* representation from the socialite class—*Maurer & Vogel*⟩ **Generous** usually emphasizes some positive quality of heart and mind (as warmhearted readiness to give, forgetfulness of self, or magnanimity) that prompts the giver or the gift more than the size or importance of the gift ⟨made a *generous* provision for his servants in his will⟩ ⟨rejected a friend's *generous* offer of assistance⟩ ⟨she was *generous* beyond the dreary bounds of common sense—*Osbert Sitwell*⟩ ⟨boys "not manly enough nor brave enough" to do a *generous* action where there was a chance that it could get them into trouble?—*Brooks*⟩ **Bountiful** suggests lavish or unremitting generosity in providing or giving ⟨he is a worthy gentleman . . . as *bountiful* as mines of India—*Shak.*⟩ ⟨even the *bountiful* Queen of Berengaria had overlooked him when she distributed honors—*Glasgow*⟩ **Bounteous** carries much the same suggestions as *bountiful* but is less often applied to a person ⟨the *bounteous* yields of [crops] . . . for which the state is noted—*Amer. Guide Series: Ariz.*⟩ ⟨caused them to . . . be very *bounteous* in their avowals of interest—*Hawthorne*⟩ **Openhanded** emphasizes generosity in giving and may further suggest freedom from all taint of self-interest and sometimes of forethought in the giving (compare *closefisted* at STINGY) ⟨he was free and *openhanded* and grudged her nothing—*McCrone*⟩ ⟨a curious mixture of

*openhanded* generosity and miserly penny-pinching—*Newsweek*⟩ **Munificent** stresses splendid or princely liberality ⟨a *munificent* endowment⟩ ⟨Caesar had been most *munificent* to his soldiers. He had doubled their ordinary pay. He had shared the spoils of his conquests with them—*Froude*⟩ **Handsome** (for application to a person see BEAUTIFUL) is often a close synonym of *liberal* and may carry a suggestion of astonishing largeness when applied to a gift, an offer, or a salary ⟨in the case of the king and other public dignitaries we have arranged that they shall have *handsome* incomes—*Shaw*⟩ ⟨assuredly the archbishop . . . leaves something *handsome* for the servants—*Borrow*⟩ or it may be a close synonym of *generous* especially when applied to an act or deed that evokes admiration for its unexpected magnanimity or graciousness ⟨I should like you to think of our house as your home, Tony." . . . This was *handsome*, if it was meant, and there seemed no reason why it shouldn't be—*Archibald Marshall*⟩
*Ana* lavish, prodigal, *profuse, exuberant: benevolent, philanthropic, eleemosynary, *charitable
*Ant* close (sense 5) —*Con* *stingy, niggardly, closefisted, tight, tightfisted, penurious, miserly, parsimonious: *meager, scanty

**2 Liberal, progressive, advanced, radical** are comparable when used of a person or thing (as an idea, a writing, or an organization) to denote being freed from or opposed to what is orthodox, established, or conservative. **Liberal** implies emancipation from what binds the mind or will and connotes either indifference to tradition, convention, dogmas, or laws or the rejection of one or more of these. It therefore may suggest tolerance and broad-mindedness on the one hand, or unorthodoxy, laxness, or even lawlessness, on the other ⟨a *liberal* Christian⟩ ⟨a *liberal* Republican⟩ ⟨some people who themselves hold *liberal* views are willing that their children shall first acquire conventional morals—*Russell*⟩ **Progressive** is commonly a relative term, because it usually implies a comparison with what is reactionary or backward and a willingness to forsake old and seek out fresh methods and beliefs in the search for betterment ⟨one *progressive* publisher is now experimenting with plastic bindings—*Third Degree*⟩ ⟨*progressive* economic and social legislation designed to benefit the masses—*A. C. Gordon*⟩ ⟨mentally so *progressive* that they were agitating for schools and the vote—*Heiser*⟩ The term seldom suggests the espousal of extreme policies ⟨a *progressive* businessman⟩ ⟨*progressive* ideas in education⟩ **Advanced** is usually applied to men or to ideas and discoveries that are, or are believed to be, ahead of their time. It can favorably suggest liberalism or progressiveness and distinctively connote mental daring or it can unfavorably suggest an extreme of foolhardiness and experimental impracticality ⟨the economic interests of the *advanced* and backward peoples—*Hobson*⟩ ⟨an interdependent and technologically highly *advanced* world—*Wirth*⟩ ⟨endeavoring . . . with the aid of the most *advanced* scientific discoveries, not only to injure but also to destroy fellow beings—*Gilroy*⟩ **Radical** often is employed in place of *advanced*, but discriminatively it may imply a willingness to root up and destroy the institutions which conserve or propagate the ideas or policies condemned; it is often therefore virtually interchangeable with *revolutionary* ⟨*radical* ideas let loose by the American Revolution, the French Revolution, the revolutionary movements of 1848, have slowly but profoundly affected men's desires and their demands upon governments—*Frankfurter*⟩ All of these words are capable of being used disparagingly especially as applied to politically active individuals or their works, often with

little thought of their meaning content in more general applications.
*Ana* tolerant, *forbearing, indulgent, lenient
*Ant* authoritarian —*Con* strict, stringent, *rigid, rigorous: dogmatic, doctrinaire, *dictatorial, oracular
**liberate** release, *free, emancipate, manumit, deliver, discharge, enfranchise
*Ana* disengage, *detach: *extricate, disentangle, untangle, disencumber, disembarrass: *rescue, redeem, ransom, deliver
*Con* *imprison, incarcerate, immure, intern: confine, circumscribe, restrict, *limit: *tie, bind: ensnare, snare, entrap, trap (see CATCH)
**libertine** *licentious, lewd, wanton, lustful, lascivious, libidinous, lecherous
*Ana* debauched, corrupted *or* corrupt (see under DEBASE): *abandoned, dissolute, profligate, reprobate: *immoral, unmoral, amoral
*Ant* straitlaced —*Con* *moral, virtuous, ethical: continent, *sober, temperate: *chaste, decent
**liberty** *freedom, license
*Ana* independence, autonomy (see under FREE *adj*): *exemption, immunity: liberation, emancipation, enfranchisement, delivery (see corresponding verbs at FREE): scope, *range, compass, sweep
*Ant* restraint —*Con* constraint, compulsion, duress, coercion (see FORCE *n*): confinement, restriction, limitation, circumscription (see corresponding verbs at LIMIT)
**libidinous** lecherous, lustful, lascivious, lewd, wanton, libertine, *licentious
*Ana* sensual, animal, *carnal: *immoral: gross, obscene, *coarse: dissolute, *abandoned, profligate, reprobate
**library** *museum, archives, treasury, gallery
**license** *n* liberty, *freedom
*Ana* *exemption, immunity: looseness, laxity, slackness, relaxedness *or* relaxation (see corresponding adjectives at LOOSE): privilege, prerogative (see RIGHT)
*Ant* decorum —*Con* *obligation, duty: decency, propriety (see DECORUM): restraint, constraint, compulsion (see FORCE): continence, *temperance, sobriety
**license** *vb* *authorize, commission, accredit
*Ana* permit, *let, allow, suffer: *approve, endorse, sanction, certify: empower, *enable
*Ant* ban —*Con* interdict, inhibit, enjoin, prohibit, *forbid: *restrain, curb, check
**licentious, libertine, lewd, wanton, lustful, lascivious, libidinous, lecherous** all suggest unchaste habits, especially in being given to or indicative of immorality in sex relations. **Licentious** basically implies disregard of the restraints imposed by law or custom for the enforcement of chastity; the term stresses looseness of life and of habits rather than the imperiousness of one's desires ⟨*licentious* living⟩ ⟨*licentious* morals⟩ ⟨the precept that enjoins him abstinence forbids him none but the *licentious* joy, whose fruit, though fair, tempts only to destroy—*Cooper*⟩ ⟨an irreligious and *licentious* age had abetted depravity—*Glasgow*⟩ **Libertine** suggests a more open and a more habitual disregard of moral laws, especially those pertaining to the sex relations of men and women ⟨the frank *libertine* wit of their old stage—*Gibbon*⟩ ⟨he castigated the *libertine* lives of many of his generation⟩ ⟨by merely living together a couple is practicing *libertine* love—and the mere repetition doesn't, in some mysterious way, make it legal—*Stone*⟩ **Lewd** often carries strong connotations of grossness, vileness, and vulgarity which color its other implications of sensuality, dissoluteness, and unconcern for chastity. As a result it is applied less often than the preceding terms to persons, or to the manners, thoughts, and acts of persons, who retain in their im-

---

A colon (:) separates groups of words discriminated. An asterisk (*) indicates place of treatment of each group.

morality evidence of breeding, refinement, or gentility ⟨seen in the company of *lewd* women⟩ ⟨*lewd* songs⟩ ⟨*lewd* actions in public⟩ ⟨where dowdy women whispered *lewd* invitations from behind wooden shutters—*Baum*⟩ ⟨the whiskey had filled his body with a rosy sense of complete well-being, and vague *lewd* sensual images stroked his mind—*Mailer*⟩ **Wanton** (see also SUPEREROGATORY) implies moral irresponsibility or a disposition or way of life marked by indifference to moral restraints; it often suggests freedom from restraint comparable to that of animals, thereby connoting lightness, incapacity for faithfulness or seriousness, or a generally unmoral attitude ⟨*wanton* little creatures without character or depth of feeling—*Nordhoff & Hall*⟩ ⟨all this was done with a gay, and, as I said, a *wanton* disregard of the ill effects—*Sir Winston Churchill*⟩ ⟨so *wanton*, light and false, my love, are you, I am most faithless when I most am true—*Millay*⟩ **Lustful** implies the influence or the frequent incitement of desires, especially of strong and often unlawful sexual desires ⟨she took the greatest care of his health and comfort, and was faithful to him, not being naturally *lustful* except of power—*Graves*⟩ **Lascivious**, like *lewd*, definitely suggests sensuality, but it carries a clearer implication of an inclination to lustfulness or of a capacity for inciting lust ⟨*lascivious* desires⟩ ⟨*lascivious* thoughts⟩ ⟨*lascivious* glances⟩ ⟨*lascivious* dress⟩ ⟨tales that . . . are Rabelaisian in their coarseness and not ... . *lascivious*—*Sellery*⟩ ⟨I have seen a nanny goat repel a *lascivious* and impatient old billy goat who was making advances—*Putnam*⟩ **Libidinous** and *lecherous* are the strongest of all these terms in their implications of deeply ingrained lustfulness and of debauchery. **Libidinous** distinctively suggests a complete surrender to one's sexual desires ⟨a lewd youth . . . advances by degrees into a *libidinous* old man—*Addison*⟩ ⟨the Gauls indulged in *libidinous* orgies, in which sodomy played a part—*Putnam*⟩ **Lecherous** clearly implies habitual indulgence of one's lust, the term often being used when any of the others would seem too weak to express one's contempt ⟨remorseless, treacherous, *lecherous*, kindless villain!—*Shak.*⟩ ⟨boasted of his pornographic publications and his pornographic "library" and his own *lecherous* fornications—*Shirer*⟩

**Ana** profligate, reprobate, dissolute, *abandoned: debauched, depraved, corrupted *or* corrupt (see under DEBASE): lax, *loose, relaxed: *immoral, unmoral, amoral

**Ant** continent —**Con** *chaste, decent, pure: *moral, virtuous: strict, *rigid: austere, ascetic, *severe

**licit** *lawful, legitimate, legal

**Ana** permitted, allowed (see LET): sanctioned, approved (see APPROVE): authorized, licensed (see AUTHORIZE): regulated (see ADJUST)

**Ant** illicit —**Con** forbidden, prohibited, interdicted, inhibited, banned (see FORBID)

**lick** *vb* beat, defeat, *conquer, vanquish, subdue, subjugate, reduce, overcome, surmount, overthrow, rout

**lickspittle** *parasite, sycophant, toady, bootlicker, hanger-on, leech, sponge, sponger, favorite

**lie** *vb* Lie, prevaricate, equivocate, palter, fib mean to tell an untruth directly or indirectly. **Lie** is the straightforward word, flatly imputing dishonesty to the speaker ⟨he *lies*, and he knows he *lies*—*Johnson*⟩ ⟨the article . . . has deliberately *lied* and distorted facts—*Nation's Business*⟩ **Prevaricate** is often used in place of *lie* as a more formal or less offensive term; distinctively, it can imply evasion of the truth (as by quibbling, dodging the real point, or confusing the issue) ⟨he could *prevaricate* no longer, and, confessing to the gambling, told her the truth—*Hardy*⟩ ⟨"Even if it wos so, which I don't say it is"—"Don't *prevaricate*," said Mr. Lorry—*Dickens*⟩ **Equivocate** implies saying one

thing and meaning another; it usually suggests the use of words that carry more than one sense in the hope that the sense which gives the incorrect impression may be the one accepted by the hearer ⟨by *equivocating*, hesitating, and giving ambiguous answers, she effected her purpose —*Martineau*⟩ ⟨he was wholly in sympathy with Congregationalism, and had no mind to conceal or *equivocate* concerning its democratic tendencies—*Parrington*⟩ **Palter** implies a playing fast and loose, not only in statements but in dealings; it often specifically implies prevarication, equivocation, or the making of promises one does not intend to keep ⟨and be these juggling fiends no more believed that *palter* with us in a double sense—*Shak.*⟩ ⟨Caroline, don't go back—don't *palter* with us—abide by your own words—*Edgeworth*⟩ **Fib** (see also LIE *n*) may be used as a euphemism for *lie*, but it more often implies the telling of an untruth that is trivial either in matter or in significance ⟨she was given to *fibbing* about her admirers⟩ ⟨the child *fibs* when he thinks he can gain something by it⟩ ⟨he didn't like Janet. She *fibbed*, he said, and was a telltale—*Glasgow*⟩

**Ana** *deceive, delude, mislead, beguile

**lie** *n* Lie, falsehood, untruth, fib, misrepresentation, story are comparable when they mean a statement or declaration that does not conform to the truth. **Lie** is usually felt to be a term of extreme opprobrium because it implies a flat and unquestioned contradiction of the truth and deliberate intent to deceive or mislead ⟨you told a *lie*; an odious, damned *lie*—*Shak.*⟩ ⟨his decent reticence is branded as hypocrisy, his circumlocutions are roundly called *lies*—*Maugham*⟩ **Falsehood** may be both less censorious than *lie* and wider in its range of application. The term need not imply sinfulness or criminality, for it applies not only to lies ⟨told two flat *falsehoods* about what had happened in secret session—*Davis*⟩ but to such fictions as literary fictions, polite fictions, and legal fictions and then contrasts most directly with *fact* ⟨a man's entire life may be a *falsehood*, while with his lips he may not once directly falsify—*F. N. Scott & J. V. Denney*⟩ Like *lie*, the term implies known nonconformity to the truth, but unlike *lie*, it does not invariably suggest a desire to pass off as true something known to be untrue ⟨*falsehoods* which we spurn today were the truths of long ago— *Whittier*⟩ **Untruth** is often euphemistic for *lie* or *falsehood* and may carry similar derogatory implications ⟨his report was riddled with inaccuracies and *untruths*⟩ or it may be selected because of mitigating circumstances ⟨told you *untruths* yesterday morning merely to cheer you up— *Bennett*⟩ Sometimes, however, *untruth* may apply to an untrue statement made as a result of ignorance or a misconception of the truth ⟨so far as he knew he had never told an *untruth*⟩ ⟨the traditions and the *untruths* our cultural fathers have sometimes told us—*La Barre*⟩ **Fib** is an informal or childish term for a trivial falsehood; it is often applied to one told to save one's own or another's face ⟨not that I couldn't tell a downright *fib* if I had to . . . but a lie is to me just as silly a performance when it is about marriage or work as about the law of gravitation— *Mary Austin*⟩ ⟨the trade in drama seems to be prosecuted in a world of perfunctory *fibs* which no one believes— *Montague*⟩ **Misrepresentation** applies to a misleading and usually an intentionally or deliberately misleading statement which gives an impression that is contrary to the truth; the term implies glossing over defects or weaknesses (as in something offered for sale) or placing the emphasis upon details that highlight a character, an occurrence, or a train of events rather than on those that in reality marked it ⟨our guides deceived us with *mis-representations*—*Addison*⟩ ⟨his duty to further the in-

---

**Ana** analogous words     **Ant** antonyms     **Con** contrasted words     See also explanatory notes facing page 1

terest of his client does not require him to employ any sort of trickery, chicane, deceit, or *misrepresentation—Drinker*⟩ **Story** (see also ACCOUNT 2) in the sense relevant to this discussion is an informal term used chiefly by or with reference to children in place of any of the preceding terms, especially *falsehood, untruth,* and *fib* ⟨boys who tell *stories* are likely to be caught⟩

*Ana* prevarication, equivocation, fibbing *or* fib (see corresponding verbs at LIE): mendaciousness *or* mendacity, untruthfulness, dishonesty, deceitfulness (see corresponding adjectives at DISHONEST)

*Ant* truth  *—Con* veracity, verity, verisimilitude (see TRUTH)

**life** *biography, memoir, autobiography, confessions

**lifeless** inanimate, *dead, defunct, deceased, departed, late

*Ana* inert, *inactive, passive: *stiff, rigid, stark, wooden, inflexible: torpid (see LETHARGIC)

*Ant* living  *—Con* alive, animate, animated, vital (see LIVING): *active, operative, dynamic, live

**lift** *vb* **1** Lift, raise, rear, elevate, hoist, heave, boost are comparable when meaning to move from a lower to a higher place or position. **Lift** often carries an implication of effort exerted to overcome the resistance of weight ⟨*lift* a large stone⟩ ⟨*lift* a pail of water from the ground⟩ ⟨*lift* a child to one's shoulders⟩ but it may be extended to whatever rises high by natural or artificial means or processes ⟨high *lifted* up were many lofty towers—*Spenser*⟩ ⟨a high conical peak . . . *lifted* some four thousand feet into the sky—*Kyne*⟩ or to something immaterial that rises or is made to rise (as in spirit, in feeling, or in aspiration) ⟨the news *lifted* a weight from his mind⟩ ⟨he was *lifted* by his simple love of all creatures . . . far above right and wrong—*Webb*⟩ **Raise** may suggest less effort than *lift,* but it carries a stronger implication of bringing something to the vertical or to a high position for which it is fitted by nature or intended function; thus, one *raises* a pole by setting it on end, but one *lifts* it by picking it up; a flag is *raised* to the top of its staff, but it is *lifted* when held high enough to be seen ⟨those arts which were destined to *raise* our Gothic cathedrals—*Coulton*⟩ In extended use *raise* may imply a lifting to a higher level (as of worth, efficiency, or accomplishment) ⟨the most wholehearted attempt ever made to *raise* the individual to his highest power—*Day Lewis*⟩ **Rear** is often used in place of *raise* ⟨the mast we *rear*—*Pope*⟩ ⟨the maypole was *reared*—*Irving*⟩ but, unlike *raise,* it can be used intransitively with the meaning to raise itself or, in the case of a horse, to raise its forelegs ⟨the . . . storm clouds *reared* on high—*Millay*⟩ ⟨horses, *rearing* and prancing—*Anderson*⟩ **Elevate** may be used in place of *lift* or *raise* in certain collocations where it does not seem unduly formal or pretentious ⟨an eagle rising with wings *elevated*—*Fox-Davies*⟩ ⟨mobile field pieces . . . were *elevated* for range in even more slow and primitive ways—*Wintringham*⟩ but, in general, the word suggests exaltation, uplifting, or enhancing ⟨*elevate* a priest to a bishopric⟩ ⟨*elevate* one's standards of literary taste⟩ ⟨his renown soared still higher. He had *elevated* the white man's name in Africa again—*James Cameron*⟩ **Hoist** implies raising something heavy aloft, often by such mechanical means as a tackle ⟨*hoist* a cargo into a ship⟩ ⟨*hoist* a sail⟩ ⟨Mrs. Malins was helped down the front steps by her son and Mr. Browne and, after many maneuvers, *hoisted* into the cab—*Joyce*⟩ ⟨it takes five power winches to *hoist* this mammoth expanse of canvas—*Monsanto Mag.*⟩ **Heave** implies a lifting upward or onward with strain or effort usually by impulsion from without ⟨a boat *heaved* high by a wave⟩ ⟨nature's way of creating a mountain peak—first the *heaving* up of some blunt monstrous bulk of

rumpled rock—*Montague*⟩ **Boost** implies lifting by or as if by means of a push or other help from below, usually without the suggestion of strain or effort found in *hoist* and *heave* ⟨*boost* prices⟩ ⟨friendly critics *boosted* the sales of his books⟩ ⟨no matter how depressed he might be, a few cocktails always *boosted* his spirits⟩ ⟨David tenderly *boosted* Elimelech up the steps and through the door—*Douglas*⟩

*Ana* *rise, arise, ascend, levitate, mount, soar, tower, rocket, surge: *exalt, magnify, aggrandize: heighten, enhance, *intensify

*Ant* lower  *—Con* reduce, lessen, diminish, *decrease: *abase, debase, degrade, demean, humble, humiliate: *depress, weigh, oppress

**2** purloin, filch, *steal, pilfer, pinch, snitch, swipe, cop

**light** *vb* **1** Light, kindle, ignite, fire basically mean to set something burning or on fire. **Light** (see also ILLUMINATE), when it takes as its subject the agent or agency, usually implies such an end of the action as illumination ⟨she *lighted* the lamps⟩ or heating ⟨he will *light* a fire in the fireplace⟩ or smoking ⟨he *lit* his cigar⟩ **Kindle** often connotes difficulty or slowness in setting combustible materials (as wood, straw, or paper) afire; it is therefore the appropriate word when what is to burn requires special preparation or does not at once burst into flame ⟨using kerosene to *kindle* the damp wood⟩ ⟨a carelessly thrown match *kindled* one of the worst forest fires in the state's history⟩ ⟨bonfires were *kindled* on the top of every hill⟩ **Ignite** is not only much more common in technical than in popular use but usually shows a difference in meaning. In technical use *ignite* sometimes implies heating of a substance until it glows or becomes incandescent ⟨when the electric current is turned on, it *ignites* the tungsten filaments in the bulb⟩ but it more often implies the placing of a small flame or spark (as an electric spark) in direct or indirect contact with a flammable substance (as gasoline, fuel oil, or gunpowder) so as to produce its combustion ⟨*ignite* the mixture in the cylinder of an internal-combustion engine⟩ In more general use, *ignite* varies little from *kindle* except in being more frequently employed in reference to explosives or highly flammable substances. **Fire** suggests blazing and rapid combustion of what is set on fire; it is typically used in respect to something that lights easily and burns fiercely ⟨a lighted match was sufficient to *fire* the haystack⟩ ⟨the turnkey *fired* the little pile, which blazed high and hot—*Dickens*⟩

All of these words have extended use. **Light** in such use is purely a figure of speech ⟨a quick animation *lit* her face—*C. F. Cushman*⟩ while **kindle** implies an exciting, arousing, or stimulating ⟨real intellectual interest . . . can be *kindled* . . . by a master who really loves and believes in his subject—*Inge*⟩ ⟨armies cannot be raised by nations or parties unless the rage of the people is first *kindled* by lies and name-calling—*Kenneth Roberts*⟩ and **ignite** implies a stirring up into activity ⟨that genius for *igniting* others essential to all great teachers—*J. M. Brown*⟩ ⟨the idea of the rising, of Irish freedom, of freedom everywhere *ignites* him and begins to consume him—*S. R. L.*⟩ **Fire** implies an inspiring with strong passion, ardent desire, or intense zeal and is usually chosen when the agent or agency enables or induces energetic activity ⟨the nations of Europe were *fired* with boundless expectation—*Johnson*⟩ ⟨the subject . . . had *fired* her imagination—*Jan Struther*⟩

**2** lighten, *illuminate, illumine, enlighten, illustrate

**light** *adj* *easy, simple, facile, effortless, smooth

*Ana* slight (see THIN): trivial, trifling, *petty, puny

*Ant* heavy: arduous: burdensome  *—Con* difficult, *hard: *onerous, oppressive, exacting: rigorous, stringent

---

A colon (:) separates groups of words discriminated. An asterisk (*) indicates place of treatment of each group.

(see RIGID)

**light** *vb* \*alight, land, perch, roost

**lighten** *vb* \*illuminate, illumine, light, enlighten, illustrate
*Ant* darken

**lighten** *vb* alleviate, mitigate, \*relieve, assuage, allay
*Ana* lessen, reduce, diminish, \*decrease, abate: \*moderate, temper, qualify: attenuate, extenuate, \*thin, dilute
*Con* \*intensify, aggravate, heighten: \*increase, augment: magnify, aggrandize (see EXALT): oppress, weigh, \*depress

**lighthearted** cheerful, happy, \*glad, joyful, joyous
*Ana* buoyant, resilient, volatile, effervescent, expansive (see ELASTIC): blithe, jocund, \*merry, jolly: high-spirited, \*spirited: gay, sprightly, vivacious, \*lively
*Ant* despondent  *—Con* sad, depressed, dejected, melancholy (see corresponding nouns at SADNESS): morose, glum, gloomy, \*sullen

**light-mindedness** \*lightness, levity, frivolity, flippancy, volatility, flightiness

**lightness, light-mindedness, levity, frivolity, flippancy, volatility, flightiness** are comparable when denoting the quality, manner, or attitude of one who is irresponsibly gay or indifferent especially when seriousness is expected. **Lightness** implies a general lack of weight or seriousness (as in character, mood, conduct, or speech) ⟨the *lightness* of tone with which I uttered such serious words—*E. J. Goodman*⟩ The term may further imply instability ⟨there is a *lightness* about the feminine mind—a touch and go—*George Eliot*⟩ or carefree heedlessness ⟨looked at her perplexedly, wondering if it were *lightness* or dissimulation that enabled her to touch so easily on the past—*Wharton*⟩ or indifference to the seriousness of a situation ⟨treating with *lightness* what is matter of life and death—*Arnold*⟩ **Light-mindedness**, even more than *lightness*, suggests a temperamental lack of seriousness or stability ⟨women are often unjustly accused of *light-mindedness*⟩ **Levity** usually suggests more specifically trifling or unseasonable gaiety ⟨her *levity*, her frivolous laughter, her unwomanly jests—*J. R. Green*⟩ ⟨Molière and his audience were accustomed to regard conjugal infidelity with *levity* when it did not touch themselves—*Alexander*⟩ **Frivolity** adds to *lightness* the implication of empty or idle speech or conduct; the term often carries a strong connotation of triviality or of pettiness ⟨the extraordinary *frivolity* of much which passes for religious interest—*Inge*⟩ ⟨tried to suggest . . . that intellectual curiosity was not necessarily a form of sin or even *frivolity*—*Time*⟩ but its most frequent implication is that of such indulgence in meaningless gaieties that serious employments are disregarded ⟨people . . . whose idleness and *frivolity* and extravagance set a most corrupting moral example—*Shaw*⟩ ⟨every form of human *frivolity* from bingo to short bathing suits on Sunday—*Coons*⟩ **Flippancy** applies especially to unbecoming levity or pertness in speaking of or in dealing with serious things ⟨modest, and without anything like *flippancy*, yet without any obsequiousness—*Arthur Young*⟩ ⟨the *flippancy* with which my requests for information are treated—*Kipling*⟩ **Volatility** implies such lightness or fickleness of disposition as precludes long or serious dwelling upon any one idea or plan ⟨*volatility* of character evinces no capabilities for great affections—*Shelley*⟩ ⟨another current characteristic . . . observed is the *volatility* of the public mind at this time—*M. W. Childs*⟩ **Flightiness** may imply extreme volatility, often with a suggestion of loss of mental balance ⟨his *flightiness* has been noticeable since his severe illness⟩ but it often suggests extreme capriciousness or a gay whimsicality characteristic of one who is not long contented with what he has or does ⟨*flightiness* was her infirmity . . . . Little things filled her thoughts—*Glasgow*⟩

*Ana* buoyancy, resiliency, elasticity, effervescence, expansiveness (see corresponding adjectives at ELASTIC): gaiety, liveliness, vivaciousness *or* vivacity (see corresponding adjectives at LIVELY): lightheartedness, cheerfulness (see corresponding adjectives at GLAD)
*Ant* seriousness  *—Con* graveness *or* gravity, earnestness, soberness, sedateness, staidness, somberness (see corresponding adjectives at SERIOUS)

**like** *vb* **Like, love, enjoy, relish, fancy, dote** are comparable when meaning to be so attracted to a person or thing as to regard him or it with favor. **Like** (opposed to *dislike*), the most general and, especially when unqualified, the most colorless of these words, means merely to regard with favor or without the slightest aversion. Therefore, it is chiefly used in reference to persons or things that are pleasing but evoke no great warmth of feeling or urgency of desire ⟨Sumner whom I admire and dislike; and Shaw of Dunfermline whom I *like* but do not admire—*Laski*⟩ ⟨Arnold, having been poor, *liked* money and knew the value of it—*Osbert Sitwell*⟩ ⟨Hawthorne *liked* to sit in barrooms; Thoreau would have enjoyed doing so, and *liked* inns, and farmers, and loafers on the river—*Canby*⟩ **Love** (opposed to *hate*) implies not only strong liking but ardent attachment and is therefore used with reference to persons or things that arouse the deeper or higher emotions; thus, one *likes* his neighbors but *loves* his family; one *likes* the open country but *loves* his native land ⟨I *like* a church; I *like* a cowl; I *love* a prophet of the soul—*Emerson*⟩ ⟨this peculiar, brooding woman, who *loved* best in life the sorrow and high seriousness of things—*Balliett*⟩ **Love** also is often used with reference to trivial objects as an informal intensive of *like* ⟨I *love* ice cream⟩ ⟨old Sarah Battle . . . *loved* a good game of whist—*Lamb*⟩ **Enjoy** implies a liking or loving that awakens deep satisfaction and keen delight which may be sensuous or intellectual or often a mingling of the two ⟨we had written our first stories together . . . and together *enjoyed* the first sweets of success—*Rose Macaulay*⟩ ⟨no one but Molny and the Bishop had ever seemed to *enjoy* the beautiful site of that building,—perhaps no one ever would. But these two had spent many an hour admiring it—*Cather*⟩ ⟨it is this specific quality, the power of *enjoying* things without being reduced to the need of possessing them, which differentiates the aesthetic instinct from other instincts—*Ellis*⟩ **Relish** implies a liking, or sometimes an enjoyment, that arises because the thing relished meets one's approval, satisfies one's taste, or gives one peculiar gratification ⟨his fine taste taught him to *relish* the beauties of Virgil and Cicero—*Hallam*⟩ ⟨a few hundred (not more) choice-loving connoisseurs *relish* him as the most perfect opportunist in prose—*Morley*⟩ **Fancy** (see also THINK 1) implies a liking for something that corresponds to one's imaginative conception or sometimes one's ideal of what it should be ⟨I never yet beheld that special face which I could *fancy* more than any other—*Shak.*⟩ ⟨he should have yachts, horses, whatever he *fancied*—*Meredith*⟩ or for something that appeals to one's taste or one's eye especially at the moment ⟨while she was ill, she *fancied* only the most delicate of foods⟩ **Dote**, with *on* or *upon*, implies an infatuation or a foolish excessive liking or fondness ⟨you *dote* on her that cares not for your love—*Shak.*⟩ ⟨he *doted* on his daughter Mary; she could do no wrong—*Havighurst*⟩ Like *love* it may be used as an informal intensive of *like* ⟨two peoples, both of whom love palaver and *dote* on uproar—*Monroe*⟩ ⟨he *dotes* on bland horrors in food—*Liebling*⟩

*Ana* prefer, \*choose, select, elect: admire, esteem, respect, regard (see under REGARD *n*): \*approve, endorse:

---

appreciate, comprehend, *understand

**Ant** dislike —**Con** *hate, abhor, detest, abominate, loathe: *despise, contemn, scorn, disdain

**like** *adj* **Like, alike, similar, analogous, comparable, akin, parallel, uniform, identical** are comparable though seldom strictly synonymous terms which describe the relation between things or persons that closely resemble each other. **Like** is a general word indicating resemblance or similarity ranging from virtual identity in all characteristics to a chance resemblance in only one ⟨the children were very *like*⟩ ⟨his finest intuitions may . . . prove convincing only to himself, or to a limited circle of *like* minds—*Times Lit. Sup.*⟩ **Alike** is similar to *like* but is less likely to be used for the chance, farfetched resemblance and is generally limited to use in a predicate or postposed situation after a compounded substantive modified ⟨their resemblance as brother and sister . . . they looked utterly *alike*—*Sinclair Lewis*⟩ ⟨they were strikingly *alike* in gifts and tastes—*Starr*⟩ **Similar** often stresses the likenesses between different things, implying that differences may be overlooked or ignored for a time ⟨Virginia creeper or the deceptively *similar* poison ivy —*Amer. Guide Series: Md.*⟩ ⟨regard the attraction which illusion has for us as *similar* to that which a flame at night has for a moth—*Cohen*⟩ ⟨this is not to say that the quarterlies are all alike. But they are as *similar* as the generation of young writers who contribute to them—*R. B. West*⟩ **Analogous** calls attention to the presence of some likeness which makes it feasible or permissible to draw from it an analogy, a sustained or appropriate comparison ⟨the two new states would have a position *analogous* to that of British Dominions—*Manchester Guardian*⟩ ⟨quite *analogous* to the emotionalizing of Christian art is the example afforded by the evolution of the Latin hymn— *H. O. Taylor*⟩ **Comparable** implies a likeness on one point or a limited number of points which permits a limited or casual comparison or matching together ⟨the Syrians . . . with Arabian coffee, served thick and strong in tiny cups, as a national drink *comparable* to the Englishman's tea—*Amer. Guide Series: R.I.*⟩ The word is especially likely to be used in connection with considerations of merit, standing, rank, or power ⟨neither in military nor industrial terms is China *comparable* to the other three great powers—*Dean*⟩ **Akin**, limited to use in postpositive situations, indicates an essential likeness, often of the sort of likeness found in kinship or suggestive of common descent from an original ancestor, prototype, or ancestral stock ⟨the Mongols of Outer Mongolia . . . are *akin* to those of the neighboring Buryat-Mongol A.S.S.R.— *Foreign Affairs*⟩ ⟨real nursery tales, *akin* to Brer Rabbit —*Times Lit. Sup.*⟩ ⟨science . . . is *akin* to democracy in its faith in human intelligence and cooperative effort— *Muller*⟩ **Parallel** stresses the fact of similarities over a course of development throughout a history or account or the fact of resemblances or likenesses permitting a setting or bracketing together as though side by side ⟨the almost *parallel* growth of the Twin Cities—*Amer. Guide Series: Minn.*⟩ ⟨*parallel* to the classic and academic Italian school was one with a more distinctive native feeling—*Manship*⟩ ⟨*parallel* to the powers of the king were the powers of the father in the individual household —*Linton*⟩ **Uniform** suggests a likeness and similarity throughout and a lack of noticeable variation wherever things in question occur or operate ⟨one of the most fundamental social interests is that law shall be *uniform* and impartial—*Cardozo*⟩ ⟨schools . . . no longer expect all children to learn to read at a *uniform* rate—*Education Digest*⟩ **Identical** indicates either the fact of being the same person or thing or, in connection with things copied,

reproduced, or repeated, an exact correspondence without detectable or significant difference ⟨George Eliot and Mary Ann Evans were *identical*⟩ ⟨the interests of workers and their employers were not altogether *identical*— *Cohen*⟩ ⟨his home life and his life as a man of letters are never *identical*—*Canby*⟩

**Ana** equivalent, equal, *same, selfsame, identical: cognate, allied, *related

**Ant** unlike —**Con** *different, diverse, divergent, disparate, various: dissimilar, distinct (see corresponding nouns at DISSIMILARITY): discrepant, discordant, *inconsonant, inconsistent

**likely** 1 *probable, possible

**Ana** credible, believable, colorable, *plausible: reasonable, *rational

**Ant** unlikely —**Con** *doubtful, dubious, questionable, problematic: *certain, inevitable, necessary

2 *apt, liable

**likeness, similarity, resemblance, similitude, analogy, affinity** are comparable when they denote agreement or correspondence or an instance of agreement or correspondence in details (as of appearance, structure, or qualities) brought out by a comparison of two or more things. **Likeness** commonly implies closer correspondence than **similarity**, which often applies to things which are merely somewhat alike ⟨thou shalt not make thee any graven image, or any *likeness* of any thing that is in heaven above —*Deut* 5:8⟩ ⟨yes, I should have known you anywhere from your *likeness* to your father—*Archibald Marshall*⟩ ⟨Zaza is an old woman, while you, princess, still have youth and beauty. Nevertheless, the *likeness* is positively amazing—*Robert Standish*⟩ ⟨certain insects escape danger by their *similarity* to plants—*Lubbock*⟩ ⟨great works of art have a decided *similarity* to great human beings— they are both three-dimensional—*Hartford*⟩ **Resemblance** suggests especially similarity in appearance or in superficial or external qualities ⟨it would be as difficult to discover any *resemblance* between the two situations as between the appearance of the persons concerned—*Wharton*⟩ **Similitude**, which is somewhat infrequent and bookish, is occasionally preferred to *likeness* or *similarity* when an abstract term is desired ⟨the law which reconciles *similitude* and dissimilitude, the harmony of contrast— *Reed*⟩ ⟨all medieval variances of thought show common *similitudes*—*H. O. Taylor*⟩ **Analogy** distinctively implies comparison of things which are unlike, not only specifically or generically, but often even in substance or essence, and it more often draws attention to likeness or parallelism in relations rather than in appearances or qualities. Philosophically, it suggests such assumptions as that similar causes will produce similar effects or that what is true in one order of existence must be true in another ⟨three principal types [of ants] offering a curious *analogy* to . . . the hunting, pastoral, and agricultural stages in the history of human development—*Lubbock*⟩ ⟨such senile efforts to penetrate . . . the mystery of religion . . . have a real *analogy* to that final effort of the emotionally starved to grasp at love which has been called "old maid's insanity"—*Ellis*⟩ **Affinity** adds to *resemblance* the implications of such a relationship as natural kinship, temperamental sympathy, similar experience, or historical influence, which is responsible for the likeness ⟨in Keats, there are . . . phrases and paradoxes that have surprising *affinities* with Taoist thought—*Binyon*⟩ ⟨his face . . . had a curious *affinity* to the faces of old sailors or fishermen who have lived a simple, practical life in the light of an overmastering tradition—*Galsworthy*⟩

**Ana** equivalence, equality, sameness, identicalness *or* identity (see corresponding adjectives at SAME): agree-

A colon (:) separates groups of words discriminated. An asterisk (*) indicates place of treatment of each group.

ment, conformity, correspondence (see corresponding verbs at AGREE): analogousness, comparableness, uniformity, parallelism (see corresponding adjectives at LIKE)

*Ant* unlikeness —*Con* *dissimilarity, difference, divergence, divergency, distinction

**likewise** *also, too, besides, moreover, furthermore

**limb** bough, branch, *shoot

**limber** *adj* *supple, lithe, lithesome, lissome

*Ana* pliant, pliable, *plastic: flexible, *elastic, resilient, springy

*Con* *stiff, inflexible, rigid, tense, stark, wooden

**limit** *n* Limit, bound, confine, end, term are comparable when they mean an actual or imaginary line beyond which a thing does not or cannot extend. **Limit** is the most inclusive of these terms because it carries no necessary implication of number, that always being suggested by the context; thus, a thing (as a man's strength, the extent of his authority, or the reach of his arm) may be said to have a *limit,* implying one only; some other thing (as a race course, a lifetime, or a period of time) may be said to have its *limits,* but since linear extent and duration are specifically implied, these limits are by implication two in number ⟨the *limits* of a room are usually its four walls⟩ ⟨nightingales will not pass their *limits;* they seem to have a marked-out range as strictly defined as the lines of a geological map—*Jefferies*⟩ Also, *limit* may be applied to a line which is fixed by nature or inner necessity, established by authority, or determined by agreement ⟨within the *limits* of human reason⟩ ⟨the *limit* of the fisherman's catch is determined by the state game laws⟩ ⟨lives within the *limits* of his income⟩ ⟨determine the *limits* for the treatment of a topic⟩ ⟨the *limits* of Santayana as a poet . . . are the restraints of an academic habit— *Edman*⟩ **Bound** and **confine,** on the other hand, are applicable to only one of the limits that comprise the real or imaginary boundaries of a thing. Both terms are used chiefly in the plural, even when the boundary line is continuous and forms a circle or only one side; the same is true of a bounding surface that forms a sphere ⟨within the *bounds* of the earth⟩ ⟨thirty bonfires could be counted within the whole *bounds* of the district—*Hardy*⟩ ⟨the western *confines* of China⟩ ⟨within the *confines* of our subject⟩ ⟨the furthest *confines* of the family property— *Menen*⟩ The distinctions between these two words are not always apparent; however, **bounds** usually indicates a point of view from within and suggests restriction, and **confines** indicates a point of view either from within or without and suggests enclosure ⟨the book passes beyond the *bounds* of decency⟩ ⟨how they behaved in their spare time, nobody cared, and few knew . . . . They had no *bounds* to respect—*Fforde*⟩ ⟨strain the *confines* of formal monogamous marriage—*La Barre*⟩ **End** (see also END 2; INTENTION) applies usually to one of the two uttermost limits or extremes of a thing; this use is chiefly found in idiomatic phrases ⟨travel to the *ends* of the earth⟩ but it occurs also in reference to either extreme in an ascending or descending scale, or in a series that progresses from one extreme to its diametrical opposite ⟨at one *end* of the social scale there is the outcast or the pariah; at the other *end*, the elite⟩ ⟨admired from one *end* of Europe to the other—*Andrews*⟩ **Term** applies usually to a limit in duration ⟨neither history nor archaeology has yet put a *term* to Roman civilization in London—*William Page*⟩

*Ana* limitation, restriction, circumscription, confinement (see corresponding verbs at LIMIT): *border, margin, verge, edge, rim, brim, brink

**limit** *vb* Limit, restrict, circumscribe, confine mean to set or prescribe the bounds for a person or thing. **Limit**

usually implies the predetermination of a point (as in time, in space, in quantity, in capacity, or in production) beyond which the person or thing concerned cannot go or is not permitted to go without suffering a penalty or incurring undesirable consequences ⟨*limit* the speed of automobiles to 45 miles an hour outside of towns and cities⟩ ⟨*limit* the time allowed for the erection of a building to one year from the date of the signing of the contract⟩ ⟨*limit* the acreage planted with potatoes⟩ ⟨*limit* a day's work to five hours⟩ ⟨the great point . . . on these sacred occasions was for each man to strictly *limit* himself to half-a-pint of liquor—*Hardy*⟩ ⟨the Constitution *limits* his functions in the law-making process to the recommending . . . and the vetoing of laws—*Current History*⟩ But *limit* may also be used with reference to a bound or bounds not predetermined but inherent in a situation or in the nature or constitution of a thing ⟨the poor soil *limited* their crops⟩ ⟨a lonely young girl *limited* . . . by the absence of companionship—*Handlin*⟩ or brought about as desirable by conscious effort or by full choice ⟨medical science knows how to *limit* these evils—*Eliot*⟩ ⟨*limited* his aspirations to the search for the attainable⟩ **Restrict**, in contrast to *limit*, suggests a boundary that encircles and encloses rather than a point that ends; the term therefore often applies to something which can be thought of in the terms of the space, territory, or field that it covers. The word often also connotes a narrowing or tightening ⟨*restrict* the powers of a court⟩ ⟨*restrict* the freedom of the press⟩ ⟨*restricted* his diet on orders from his physician⟩ ⟨the bureau was dismembered, its staff dispersed, and its appropriations for research *restricted* almost to the vanishing point—*Heiser*⟩ ⟨combinations have arisen which *restrict* the very freedom that Bentham sought to attain—*Justice Holmes*⟩ **Circumscribe** differs from *restrict* in that its implication of an encircling or enclosing boundary is always clear; consequently, it is often preferred to *restrict* when the idea of being kept within too small an extent or range is to be stressed ⟨people . . . think that the emotional range, and the realistic truth, of drama is limited and *circumscribed* by verse—*T. S. Eliot*⟩ or when there is the intent to suggest a distinct, complete, but limited whole and its apartness from all that surrounds it ⟨to undertake here to inquire into the degree of its necessity, would be to pass the line which *circumscribes* the judicial department—*John Marshall*⟩ ⟨the world to which they belonged and for which they worked was strictly *circumscribed* and complete within itself—*Binyon*⟩ **Confine** may imply limitation, restriction, or circumscription, but it usually emphasizes the bounds which must not or cannot be passed; consequently, it often suggests severe restraint or restraints and carries connotations such as those of cramping, fettering, hampering, or bottling up that are not often present in the other words ⟨now I am cabined, cribbed, *confined*, bound in to saucy doubts and fears— *Shak.*⟩ ⟨the distinction between a government with limited and unlimited powers is abolished, if those limits do not *confine* the persons on whom they are imposed—*John Marshall*⟩ ⟨it is not desirable to *confine* knowledge to whatever can be put into a useful shape for examinations, drawing rooms, or the still more pretentious modes of publicity—*T. S. Eliot*⟩ ⟨we are *confined* to our senses for perceiving the world—*Darrow*⟩

*Ana* define, *prescribe, assign: *restrain, curb, check

*Ant* widen —*Con* *expand, swell, distend: enlarge, *increase: *extend, lengthen, prolong, protract

**limn** *vb* *represent, depict, portray, delineate, picture

**limp,** floppy, flaccid, flabby, flimsy, sleazy mean deficient in firmness of texture, substance, or structure and therefore unable to keep a shape or in shape. **Limp** applies to

something that lacks or has lost the stiffness or firmness necessary to keep it from drooping or losing its original sturdiness or freshness ⟨collars *limp* with perspiration⟩ ⟨a *limp* body that seemed to have been poured into his clothes as if it were sand—*Sitwell*⟩ ⟨his body was dangling in a most uncomfortable position, all loose and *limp*, and shapeless—*Dickens*⟩ ⟨squash-flowers hanging *limp* as widow's weeds on the stringy stems—*Brittain*⟩ **Floppy** applies to something that sags or hangs limply ⟨a dog with *floppy* ears⟩ ⟨foreigners—fortunately scarce—wear *floppy* ties, long hair and beards—*Kinross*⟩ ⟨an old lady in a ... *floppy* garden hat—*Greene*⟩ **Flaccid** implies a loss or lack of elasticity or resilience and therefore an incapacity to return to an original shape or condition or to keep a desired shape; the term applies primarily to flesh and other living tissues ⟨*flaccid* muscles⟩ ⟨a *flaccid* stem⟩ ⟨now, in swift collapse, he was as *flaccid* as a sick hound and as disgusting as an aged drunkard—*Bennett*⟩ In extended use the term implies lack of force or energy or substance ⟨the style is ... worthless, slipshod, *flaccid*— *Wilde*⟩ ⟨our *flaccid* culture—*T. S. Eliot*⟩ ⟨when a writer thinks clearly his prose itself is sharp and fresh, and when his thought becomes *flaccid* his words too become limp, mechanical and fogged—*Krim*⟩ **Flabby** applies to something that is so soft that it yields readily to the touch or is easily shaken ⟨her breasts had grown *flabby* and pendulous with many children—*Buck*⟩ In extended use the term implies the loss or lack of what keeps a thing up or in good sound condition; it often carries suggestions of spinelessness, spiritlessness, or lethargy ⟨the *flabby* government which was ... incapable of defending its own interests— *Owen Lattimore*⟩ ⟨very few ... are worth converting. Their minds are intrinsically *flabby* and parasitical— *Mencken*⟩ **Flimsy** applies to something that by its looseness of structure or insubstantiality of texture cannot hold up under use or strain ⟨a wooden seat put together with nails—a *flimsy* contrivance, which defies all rules of gravity and adhesion—*Jefferies*⟩ In extended use the term applies to whatever is so frail or slight as to be without value or endurance ⟨a *flimsy* excuse⟩ ⟨the story is fashioned of such *flimsy* stuff that it almost tears apart in the telling—*Krout*⟩ **Sleazy** applies especially to flimsy textiles, but it often suggests, as *flimsy* need not, fraud or carelessness in its manufacture ⟨a *sleazy* dress⟩ ⟨thin *sleazy* woolens⟩ In extended use the term may stress lack or inferiority of standards ⟨a *sleazy* little gold digger— *New Republic*⟩ ⟨the *sleazier* forms of competition— *Fortune*⟩ or inferiority of the resultant product ⟨*sleazy* new apartment blocks, their broken, rubble-salvaged brick unfaced—*Flora Lewis*⟩ but often its suggestion is one of cheap shabby inferiority ⟨a *sleazy* piece of the old, tedious reality—*Mary McCarthy*⟩ ⟨a stammered, *sleazy* chronicle, told by fits and starts—*Time*⟩
*Ana* \*loose, slack, relaxed, lax: limber, \*supple
*Con* \*stiff, rigid, inflexible, stark, wooden, tense: \*firm, hard, solid: brittle, crisp (see FRAGILE)

**limpid** \*clear, transparent, translucent, lucid, pellucid, diaphanous
*Ana* \*pure, sheer: lucid, perspicuous, \*clear
*Ant* turbid —*Con* muddy, roily (see TURBID): \*obscure, vague, dark: murky, dusky (see DARK)

**line** *n* **Line, row, rank, file, echelon, tier** are comparable when meaning a series of things arranged in continuous or uniform order. **Line** means little more than this, except when it is attached to a specific application that increases its implications; thus, a *line* of type may equal a *line* of poetry, but there is a wealth of implication in the second that is absent from the first ⟨a *line* of trees⟩ ⟨soldiers fall in *line*⟩ ⟨the crowd formed a *line* in front of the ticket office⟩ ⟨there were three *lines* of enlisted men awaiting examination by physicians⟩ ⟨a *line* of trading posts from the Mississippi ... across the Rocky Mountains—*Irving*⟩ **Row** may suggest one line or one of several parallel lines; it is applicable to lines composed of persons or of things whether they range horizontally or vertically or abreast or away from one ⟨a *row* of trees lines the south side of the street⟩ ⟨*rows* of seats in a theater⟩ ⟨the shrubs are arranged in *rows*⟩ **Rank** and *file* are found chiefly in military use, **rank** denoting a row of men side by side, **file** a row of men one behind another ⟨march in single *file*⟩ ⟨the front *rank* was ordered to take one pace forward⟩ The conjoined use of these terms in *rank and file* is an idiomatic extension meaning the masses of men as distinguished from their leaders or rulers. **Echelon** usually implies a regular arrangement or formation in which each unit (as one of a series of parallel ranks of troops or one of a fleet of vessels headed in the same direction) is a little to the left or to the right of the unit immediately behind. **Tier** applies to one of a set of rows arranged one above another; it occasionally refers to persons but usually deals with parts of a structure or framework which are repeated ⟨the seats rise in *tiers* in the great Opera House⟩ ⟨three *tiers* of arches rose on each side of the cathedral's nave⟩ ⟨their mountain-like *San Philip* [a Spanish warship] ... with her yawning *tiers* of guns—*Tennyson*⟩
*Ana* \*succession, progression, series, sequence, chain

**line** *vb* **Line, line up, align, range, array** mean to arrange in a line or in lines. **Line,** or more often **line up,** implies setting in single file or in parallel rows ⟨*line up* prisoners for identification⟩ ⟨*line up* troops for inspection⟩ ⟨four or five men were *lined up* at the bar—*Basso*⟩ **Align** stresses the bringing of points or parts that should be in a straight line into correct adjustment or into correspondence ⟨*align* the lenses of a telescope⟩ ⟨*align* the front and rear wheels of an automobile⟩ ⟨*align* type in printing⟩ ⟨the tents were *aligned* in two rows—*Mailer*⟩ **Range** stresses orderly or correct disposition, sometimes merely in straight or parallel lines, but more often with the added implication of separation into groups or classes according to some plan or design ⟨oaken benches *ranged* in seemly rows—*Wordsworth*⟩ **Array** implies actual formation in order, especially battle order, and therefore suggests full equipment and readiness for action ⟨there is a great Field-Marshal, my friend, who *arrays* our battalions; let us to Providence trust, and abide and work in our stations— *Clough*⟩ ⟨scarcely had time to *array* his men at the townward wall before arrows, stones, and heavy javelins ... began to fall upon them—*A. C. Whitehead*⟩

These words also are comparable in extended use. **Line up** stresses organization for unity or singleness of effort ⟨*line up* the opponents of a measure to achieve its defeat⟩ ⟨*line up* public opinion in favor of a proposal⟩ ⟨*lined up* on the side of those who oppose even attempting to set up peaceful coexistence with Russia is the FBI—*Newsweek*⟩ **Align** is commonly used reflexively in this connection and implies falling into line or into a lineup ⟨at the beginning of World War I France, England, and Belgium *aligned* themselves with Serbia⟩ ⟨so long as the symptoms failed to *align* themselves with any known disorder, they were supposed to be amenable to neighborly advice— *Mary Austin*⟩ **Range** implies putting or falling precisely into a group (as a class, party, rank, or category); it may suggest alignment but more often connotes partisanship or alliance or, when used of things, susceptibility of classification ⟨'tis better to be lowly born, and *range* with humble livers in content—*Shak.*⟩ ⟨they differed violently and *ranged* themselves into distinct schools of thought—*Dinsmore*⟩ **Array** in its extended use retains its implication of

A colon (:) separates groups of words discriminated. An asterisk (\*) indicates place of treatment of each group.

orderly formation; it sometimes also suggests arrangement in logical or chronological order, or as parts of a design ⟨these doubts will be *arrayed* before their minds—*Farrar*⟩ More often, however, it stresses the impressive or imposing character of an opposition ⟨several of the best legal minds were *arrayed* against the prosecution⟩ ⟨so much prejudice of one kind or another was *arrayed* against it that it was not till nearly two hundred years after its discovery that saltpeter became the god of war—*Encore*⟩
*Ana* marshal, arrange, *order
*Con* derange, disarrange, *disorder, disturb: disperse, dissipate, *scatter
**lineage** *ancestry, pedigree
**lineal, linear** share the basic meaning of or relating to a line or lines, but they are clearly distinguished in their specific senses. **Lineal** is more often applied to a direct line of succession from or to a common ancestor either physical or spiritual, and is often distinguished from *collateral;* thus, the *lineal* descendants of a man would include all his sons and daughters, all his grandsons and granddaughters, all his great-grandsons and great-granddaughters, etc. ⟨George Washington had no *lineal* kinsmen to inherit his property, for he had no children⟩ ⟨these men, the *lineal* descendants of the mystics, found the source of certainty in inner experience, in feeling and instinct—*Thilly*⟩ **Linear** tends to lay the stress on a relation to a line other than a line of succession, either in fact or in likeness; often it suggests a relation to something having or felt as having one dimension only, usually length, especially in contrast to what has two or more dimensions ⟨*linear* measures such as the inch, foot, yard, and rod are used in measuring lengths (as of cloth, rope, poles, wire, and edges or bounds)⟩ ⟨from the *linear* dimensions of a room we can compute the square feet of floor to be covered⟩ ⟨a conductor of electricity (as a wire) which is very small or negligible in two of its dimensions, is called a *linear* conductor⟩ ⟨atoms which are so small that it takes one hundred millions of them lying side by side to extend one *linear* inch—*Darrow*⟩ ⟨the longest *linear* structural features on the earth's surface are the east-west fracture zones of the northeast Pacific Ocean—*Malahoff, Strange & Wollard*⟩
**line up** *line, align, range, array
**linger** tarry, wait, *stay, remain, abide
*Ana* *delay, procrastinate, loiter, dawdle, lag
*Con* hurry, hasten, precipitate, quicken, accelerate, *speed
**lingo** *dialect, vernacular, patois, jargon, cant, argot, slang
**link** *vb* connect, relate, associate, *join, conjoin, combine, unite
*Ana* concatenate, articulate, *integrate: *tie, bind
*Ant* sunder  *—Con* *separate, part, sever, divorce
**liquefy, melt, deliquesce, fuse, thaw** are comparable when they mean to convert or to become converted to a liquid state. **Liquefy,** the general term, is applicable not only to solids but also to gases ⟨*liquefy* oxygen and nitrogen⟩ ⟨*liquefy* a solid mass of ice⟩ ⟨jellies *liquefy* if exposed to the air in a warm room⟩ **Melt** basically implies slow liquefaction, usually through heat; the term commonly suggests a softening, a loss of shape, and a running consistency ⟨butter *melts* in a warm room⟩ ⟨*melt* wax in a candle flame⟩ In its frequent extended use *melt* is applied to masses that are gradually dispersed or grow thinner or more tenuous and finally disappear ⟨mountains beyond mountains *melting* away into remote sky—*Binyon*⟩ or to persons or their emotions or reactions that grow softer, gentler, or more tender ⟨one whose subdued eyes, albeit unused to the *melting* mood, drop tears as fast as the Arabian trees their medicinal gum—*Shak.*⟩ ⟨in

*Romeo and Juliet* the profounder dramatist shows his lovers *melting* into unconsciousness of their isolated selves—*T. S. Eliot*⟩ ⟨I cannot look up to your face. You *melt* my strength—*Lowell*⟩ or to tones, colors, and sounds that have a liquid quality and merge imperceptibly with others ⟨snow-light cadences *melting* to silence—*Keats*⟩ ⟨substance and shadow *melted* into each other and into the vastness of space—*Glasgow*⟩ **Deliquesce** implies a disappearing by or as if by melting away and applies especially to gradual liquefying through exposure to the air and the absorption of moisture from it ⟨hygroscopic salts that *deliquesce* in moist air⟩ or to plant structures (as mushrooms) that liquefy in their decay ⟨a great display of specimens [of fungi] that presently dried up or *deliquesced* and stank—*H. G. Wells*⟩ In its extended use *deliquesce* stresses loss of coherence rather than disappearance ⟨Flaubert's instincts were less epical than lyrical, and drama itself was *deliquescing* into indeterminate forms—*Levin*⟩ ⟨their lives tended to *deliquesce* into a murmuring indefiniteness of language—*Matthiessen*⟩ **Fuse** (see also MIX) may sometimes replace *liquefy* or *melt* ⟨thunderstorm had *fused* the electric mains—*Finlay*⟩ but more often it stresses union (as of two or more metals into an alloy) by or as if by the action of intense heat ⟨foundries which *fuse* zinc and copper into hard, bright brass—*Newsweek*⟩ In its extended use, too, *fuse* stresses union ⟨a ship, itself a little community in which people of various backgrounds are temporarily *fused*—*Felix Morley*⟩ ⟨the strata *fused* together by heat—*Livingstone*⟩ **Thaw** may specifically replace *melt* in reference to something (as ice or snow) that is frozen or in extended use to something (as a cold heart, a cold disposition, or extreme reserve) equally stiff or rigid ⟨the midday sun has *thawed* the ice on the roads⟩ ⟨a lady ... whose very looks would *thaw* a man more frozen than the Alps—*Shirley*⟩ ⟨a native reserve being *thawed* by this genial consciousness—*Hawthorne*⟩
**liquid** *adj* **Liquid, fluid** are comparable both as adjectives meaning composed of particles that move easily and flowingly and change their relative position without any perceptible break in their continuity and as nouns denoting a substance composed of such particles. Both terms imply an opposition to *solid*, but **liquid** is the more restricted in its application, for the term implies the flow characteristic of water and refers only to substances which, like water, have a definite volume but no independent form except such as is temporarily given by their container ⟨such potable *liquids* as water, milk, and wines⟩ ⟨blood does not remain *liquid* long after removal from the blood vessels⟩ **Fluid,** on the other hand, implies flow of any sort and is applicable not only to all liquids but also to gases, which, unlike liquids, have neither independent volume nor shape ⟨air whether in the gaseous or liquid state is a *fluid*⟩ ⟨*fluid* blood⟩ *Fluid* is especially appropriate for referring to a substance that is highly viscous ⟨molasses is a *fluid* substance⟩ or to one liquefied (as by melting, dissolving, or saturating with water) ⟨*fluid* rock⟩ ⟨*fluid* wax⟩ ⟨mud is *fluid* earth⟩
In extended use **fluid** is opposed to *rigid, fixed, unchangeable* ⟨"open societies" of which the boundaries are *fluid* or indefinite, such as humanity or even the League of Nations—*Alexander*⟩ ⟨emotion, formless, chaotic, *fluid* in itself—*Lowes*⟩ ⟨in London all values and all meanings were *fluid*—*Rose Macaulay*⟩ **Liquid,** on the other hand, often implies an opposition to *harshness* ⟨*liquid* tones⟩ ⟨thy *liquid* notes that close the eye of day—*Milton*⟩ but it sometimes implies transparency or extreme softness or both ⟨his *liquid* glance—*Wharton*⟩ ⟨with what *liquid* tenderness she turned and looked back—

*Bennett*⟩ In financial circles, where both terms are used, *fluid* may distinctively apply to money or funds that are not permanently invested or that are constantly in circulation ⟨the *fluid* gold of international trade⟩ but more often the terms are used interchangeably to imply the quality or condition of assets that are in the form of money or are easily convertible into money and are therefore readily available for another use.
*Ant* solid: vaporous

**liquid** *n* fluid (see under LIQUID *adj*)
*Ant* solid: vapor

**lissome** lithesome, lithe, *supple, limber
*Ana* & *Con* see those at LITHE

**list** *n* List, table, catalog, schedule, register, roll, roster, inventory denote a series of names or of items written down or printed as a memorandum, a record, or a source of information, but, because of wide differences in their range of application, they are not freely interchangeable. List is the most comprehensive and the most widely applicable of these terms since it may or may not imply methodical arrangement (as in alphabetical or chronological order) and it may itemize units of various kinds (as persons or objects or facts or words or figures) ⟨a grocery *list*⟩ ⟨a *list* of invited guests⟩ ⟨price *list*⟩ ⟨an engagement *list*⟩ Table is also widely applicable, but it distinctively implies arrangement in an order that will assist the person who makes use of it in quickly finding the information he desires; consequently, it usually suggests presentation of items in columns, often, when the items are related or associated with each other, in parallel columns; thus, a *table* of weights may give in the first column an alphabetical list of the weights of all countries and add in the following columns, directly on a line with each of these names, the place in which it is used, its equivalent in American or British weights, and its equivalent in metric weight ⟨a *table* of contents of a book⟩ ⟨a *table* of logarithms⟩ ⟨annuity *tables*⟩ ⟨a time*table* of trains⟩ Catalog basically applies to a complete list or enumeration of all instances of a kind ⟨a *catalog* of the Lepidoptera of Michigan⟩ ⟨a *catalog* of the popes⟩ The term is used more often of an informative itemized descriptive list (as of the books in a library, the works of art in a museum, the courses given in a university or college, or the articles for sale by a company). Because business, educational, and art catalogs often contain much other information of value, the term often loses its essential meaning of *list*, although these catalogs have usually for their main object the presentation of complete lists. Schedule (see also PROGRAM) applies especially to an itemized statement of particulars, whether it is appended to a document (as a bill or statute) to provide supplementary details ⟨*Schedule* D of the tariff bill⟩ or is separate ⟨a *schedule* of a bankrupt's debts⟩ ⟨a *schedule* of assets and liabilities⟩ Register is applicable primarily to the official book, parchments, or papers in which are entered from time to time names or items of a specific character, together with pertinent details, for the sake of maintaining a record ⟨a *register* of births⟩ ⟨a *register* of marriages⟩ ⟨a *register* of seamen⟩ Since, however, these entries constitute not only a record but also a list or catalog, the term often more strongly suggests an official listing or enumeration than a series of entries ⟨his name is not in the *register* of voters⟩ Roll is applicable to a list and especially an official list of the names of those who belong to a certain group or force; thus, a muster *roll* includes the names of all the officers and men of a military body or of a ship's company present or accounted for on the day of muster; a class *roll* is a list of all students belonging to a class. Roster, which is chiefly a military term, applies basically to a table containing a roll of officers and men

or sometimes of units and specifying such matters as the order of their rotation in duties or their special assignments. **Inventory** is a catalog of the goods and chattels, and sometimes the real estate held by a person or a corporation at a particular time (as at the person's death or at the stocktaking of the corporation) ⟨the merchant makes an *inventory* of his stock annually on January 15th⟩ In extended use the term often refers to a list similar in its details to those of a true inventory ⟨nothing short of an authentic passion for concrete detail . . . can give the saving gusto and animation which carry off safely the long *inventories* of utensils and articles of food and attire in Scott and Defoe—*Montague*⟩

**list** *vb* *record, register, enroll, catalog

**listless** spiritless, *languid, languishing, languorous, lackadaisical, enervated
*Ana* apathetic, *impassive, phlegmatic: heedless, thoughtless, *careless: inert, *inactive, passive, supine, idle
*Ant* eager —*Con* avid, keen, anxious, agog (see EAGER): alert, *watchful, vigilant: *vigorous, energetic, lusty: *quick, prompt, ready

**lithe, lithesome** lissome, *supple, limber
*Ana* slender, slim, slight, *thin: *lean, spare: pliant, pliable, *plastic: nimble, *agile, brisk, spry: graceful, elegant (see corresponding nouns at ELEGANCE)
*Con* clumsy, maladroit, *awkward, gauche, inept: *stiff, tense, wooden, inflexible

**little** *small, diminutive, wee, tiny, minute, miniature
*Ana* *petty, paltry, puny, trivial, trifling: slight, slim, slender, *thin: *meager, scanty, scrimpy, skimpy
*Ant* big —*Con* *large, great: abundant, ample, *plentiful, plenteous

**littoral** *shore, coast, beach, strand, bank, foreshore

**liturgy** ritual, rite, ceremony, ceremonial, *form, formality

**live** *vb* 1 exist, *be, subsist
*Ana* endure, abide, persist, *continue
2 *reside, dwell, sojourn, lodge, stay, put up, stop

**live** *adj* *active, operative, dynamic
*Ana* *vigorous, energetic, lusty, strenuous: *powerful, potent, forcible, forceful: *effective, efficacious, effectual, efficient
*Ant* inactive, inert: dormant (*as a volcano*): defunct (*an institution, journal*)

**livelihood** *living, subsistence, sustenance, maintenance, support, keep, bread
*Ana* *trade, craft, handicraft, art, profession: *wage *or* wages, salary, pay, stipend, fee, emolument

**lively** *adj* Lively, animated, vivacious, sprightly, gay denote in common keenly alive. Lively suggests especially briskness, alertness, or energy ⟨spent an hour in *lively* talk about their respective travels in England and France⟩ ⟨she . . . was a *lively* conversationalist, advanced, original —*Gore*⟩ ⟨the horses . . . were *lively*, and sprang about the street—*Thackeray*⟩ Animated applies especially to what is also spirited or bright ⟨was not nearly so *animated* as he had been in his pre-khaki days; there was a quiet exaltation in his manner rather than a lively excitement— *H. G. Wells*⟩ ⟨the *animated* excitement and hubbub that gives the . . . institution its friendly vitality—*Saarinen*⟩ Vivacious and sprightly suggest greater lightness of spirits or quickness of wit; they apply especially to manner or language ⟨remember her as very pretty and *vivacious* . . . I never met a girl with as much zip—*Ring Lardner*⟩ ⟨in contrast to the dour, lethargic, and solitary orang, the chimpanzee is highly active, *vivacious* . . . and uninhibitedly vocal—*La Barre*⟩ ⟨he was *sprightly*, vigorous, fiery in his belief in success—*Crane*⟩ ⟨readers prefer *sprightly* trash to dull excellence—*Canby*⟩ Gay implies utter carefreeness and exuberant or overflowing spirits ⟨wild with joyful

A colon (:) separates groups of words discriminated. An asterisk (*) indicates place of treatment of each group.

expectation . . . with an heart light, *gay*, and independent—*Austen*⟩ ⟨he was a *gay* old fellow with a large paunch, a ribald sense of humor, and an ingratiating smile—*Hervey Allen*⟩
*Ana* *agile, nimble, brisk, spry: buoyant, effervescent, volatile, expansive, resilient, *elastic: *merry, blithe, jocund, jolly: mirthful, gleeful, hilarious (see corresponding nouns at MIRTH)
*Ant* dull —*Con* *lethargic, sluggish, torpid: *languid, lackadaisical, listless, languorous: stolid, apathetic, phlegmatic, *impassive: tedious, *irksome, boring

**livid** ashen, ashy, *pale, pallid, wan
*Ana* *ghastly, grisly, lurid: murky, gloomy, dusky (see DARK)
*Con* brilliant, *bright, luminous, radiant, lustrous, effulgent, lucent

**living** *adj* Living, alive, animate, animated, vital mean endowed with or manifesting life. In their primary senses where *life* means that character or quality which is peculiar to things that are capable of growth, reproduction, and, often, motion and which is lost by death, they come very close to each other. **Living** and **alive** are opposed to *dead* and, therefore, are applied to organic bodies which have life as distinguished from those from which life has departed; they are distinguishable chiefly by the fact that *alive* follows the noun it modifies either directly or as a predicative adjective ⟨among *living* men⟩ ⟨among men still *alive*⟩ ⟨all *living* things⟩ ⟨of all it ever was my lot to read, of critics now *alive*, or long since dead—*Cowper*⟩ ⟨our appreciations of *living* or dead writers—*T. S. Eliot*⟩ **Animate** is opposed to *inanimate* and is applied to living organic bodies as contrasted with dead organic bodies or, more often, with inorganic bodies having no capacity for life ⟨those who ignore the natural world around, *animate* and inanimate—*Spencer*⟩ **Animated** (see also LIVELY; compare *animate* under QUICKEN *vb*) is opposed to *lifeless* or *inert*, and may apply to something which, once devoid of life, becomes alive ⟨viruses that may behave as *animated* bodies or as lifeless crystals⟩ or may be used to perfect a comparison of something by its nature lifeless with something living ⟨a large Australian phasmid popularly known as the *animated* stick⟩ ⟨the moral relativism engendered by the notion that man is nothing more than an *animated* machine—*Nagel*⟩ **Vital** is applied chiefly to qualities (as power, force, energy, or motion) which result naturally from or are associated with life in distinction from qualities which result from purely physical or chemical causes ⟨*vital* functions⟩ ⟨it derived its growth and movement from its internal *vital* force, not from external sources of energy—*S. F. Mason*⟩

When these words are applied to things which have not life in the sense defined, they form other groupings. All, however, stress qualities suggestive of life. **Living** usually suggests continued or continuous existence with no diminution of activity or efficacy ⟨a *living* principle⟩ ⟨a *living* force⟩ ⟨ballet as an art form was *living* and not dead—*Coleman*⟩ **Alive** and **vital** are very close in their emphasis on abundance of vigor, on capacity for development, or on powers of endurance; both are applicable to persons as well as to things ⟨we are not sufficiently *alive* to feel the tang of sense nor yet to be moved by thought—*Dewey*⟩ ⟨Queen Victoria remains . . . one of the most absorbing figures of her time. Obviously she is still *alive* enough to be condemned—*Times Lit. Sup.*⟩ ⟨the veterans insist that college be made alive, dynamic, *vital*—*Fine*⟩ **Alive** and **animated** often imply the presence of living things in great numbers ⟨the stream is *alive* with trout⟩ ⟨as *animated* as water under a microscope—*Hardy*⟩ **Animated** also may stress endowment with qualities sugges-

tive of life, especially motion ⟨*animated* pictures⟩ ⟨an *animated* doll⟩ ⟨the *animated* signs that blink, bubble, and bedazzle visitors to Times Square—*Fixx*⟩
*Ana* existing, being, subsisting (see BE): *active, live, operative, dynamic
*Ant* lifeless —*Con* *dead, defunct, deceased, departed, inanimate

**living** *n* Living, livelihood, subsistence, sustenance, maintenance, support, keep, bread, bread and butter are comparable when they denote the means, especially the amount of money or goods, required to keep one supplied with the necessities of life (as food, housing, and clothing) and sometimes also the nonessentials that with the necessities supply the needs of a full life. **Living** is perhaps the most general term since it may denote either the necessities and provisions with which one supports life or the income with which these may be obtained ⟨had undertaken to work as a manager in return for a *living* and a share of the crops—*Glasgow*⟩ ⟨many of his other customers had gone . . . so that his own poor *living* was cut in impossible half—*Malamud*⟩ ⟨an industrial community, in which *livings* are insecure, incomes are inadequate—*W. H. Hamilton*⟩ Typically it is used in a few simple idioms; thus, a man usually earns or makes or gets a or his *living;* he does something (as writing, spinning, or farming) for a or his *living;* someone or something owes or provides him a *living* ⟨I am quite pleased to make my *living* by what I write, but the attempt to write for my *living* would be hopeless, for I can write nothing that is not in itself a pleasure to me to write—*Ellis*⟩ ⟨men who start out with the notion that the world owes them a *living—Sumner*⟩ **Livelihood** may be indistinguishable in meaning from *living* ⟨the population derives its *livelihood* from farming—*Americana Annual*⟩ ⟨the *livelihood* of the people of Malaya has always been uncertain because of the narrow base of their economy—*Langdon*⟩ ⟨the profession is of necessity a means of *livelihood* or of financial reward—*MacIver*⟩ but unlike the latter it may apply specifically to the means (as a trade, profession, or craft) by which one earns a living ⟨education is a preparation for life, not merely for a *livelihood*, for living not for a living—*Sampson*⟩ ⟨it is their profession and *livelihood* to get their living by practices for which they deserve to forfeit their lives—*South*⟩ ⟨had a low opinion of politics as a *livelihood—White*⟩ **Subsistence** may be a close synonym of *living* ⟨Harbor Springs relies for its *subsistence* chiefly on the summer vacationist trade—*Amer. Guide Series: Mich.*⟩ ⟨between disappointment and expectation, is soon disgusted, and returns to pursue his more legitimate means of *subsistence—Burroughs*⟩ but often it more specifically denotes means sufficient merely to maintain life and implies an amount of money or supply of goods that provides a person or his family with no more than basic necessities (as of housing, food, and clothing) ⟨the question whether people on relief shall be provided only with *subsistence*⟩ ⟨only in the meanest and most limited sense is *subsistence* a standard of living—*Harper's*⟩ **Sustenance** is often used in place of *living* when the emphasis is upon the food that is necessary not only to one's existence but to one's well-being ⟨he was able to wring only a bare *sustenance* from his farm⟩ ⟨that thin layer of topsoil that . . . provides *sustenance* for our growing population—*K. D. White*⟩ But it is also often used to imply all the necessaries of life ⟨it was the fur trade . . . which gave early *sustenance* and vitality to the great Canadian provinces—*Irving*⟩ **Maintenance** usually denotes either a complex of necessities such as food, lodging, and laundry, and sometimes clothing or the amount needed to supply such a complex ⟨advertised . . . for a general resident doctor at $300 a month and *maintenance—Greer Williams*⟩ ⟨enough to give him books, and a moderate *maintenance—Cibber*⟩ ⟨at least half of them are living parasitically on the other half instead of producing *maintenance* for themselves—*Shaw*⟩ **Support** applies not only to the amount of money that provides maintenance but to the person who provides the means by which others are maintained ⟨he is the sole *support* of his family⟩ ⟨they look for their *support* to him⟩ ⟨each son was expected to contribute to his own *support*—*C. L. Thompson*⟩ **Keep** is a less dignified synonym of *maintenance* and is applicable not only to men but to animals ⟨the horse is scarcely worth his *keep*⟩ ⟨hired men could no longer be had for ten or fifteen dollars a month and *keep—White*⟩ **Bread** and **bread and butter** are synecdoches for *living* or *sustenance*, partly as a result of the use of the former in the Lord's Prayer "Give us this day our daily *bread*" ⟨he is a fine poet, but he makes his *bread and butter* selling insurance⟩

**load** *n* **Load, burden, freight, cargo, lading** are comparable when they mean something which is carried, conveyed, or transported from one place to another. **Load** is the most comprehensive of these terms, being applicable to whatever is carried (as by a man, animal, vehicle, ship, running water, or conducting wire) ⟨the peddler carries a heavy *load*⟩ ⟨the truckman will deliver a *load* of wood tomorrow⟩ *Load* is also applicable to the quantity or amount carried (as by a wagon, a truck, or a freight car) ⟨a ship*load* of coal⟩ **Burden** may take the place of *load* ⟨a young man ... bearing a *burden* of fruit—*Edmunds*⟩ but in both primary and extended use it ordinarily takes on some of the notions of the cognate verb (see BURDEN *vb*) and suggests a load that weighs one down (as from heaviness, unpleasantness, or unwieldiness) ⟨[the river] carried an odorous *burden* from the houses, shacks, small mills and refuse heaps along its banks—*Amer. Guide Series: N.Y.*⟩ ⟨bear ye one another's *burdens—Gal 6:2*⟩ ⟨his chief *burden* was a racking doubt of his own legitimacy—*Wyndham Lewis*⟩ ⟨a woeful *burden* of debts that plagued her —*R. P. Randall*⟩ **Freight** applies to goods or merchandise in transit, especially long-distance transit (as by ship, railway train, or motor truck) ⟨the wrecked truck spilled its *freight* over the road⟩ **Cargo** applies specifically to freight carried by a ship or aircraft ⟨a tramp ship carrying a *cargo* of grain⟩ ⟨the increasing use of airplanes for the shipping of valuable or perishable *cargoes*⟩ **Lading** is chiefly a poetic or commercial synonym for *freight* or *cargo* ⟨*ladings* are protected against shrinkage and leakage—*Dun's Review*⟩

**load** *vb* **1** *burden, encumber, cumber, weigh, weight, lade, tax, charge, saddle
*Ana* bear, convey, *carry, transport
*Ant* unload
**2** *adulterate, weight, sophisticate, doctor
**loaf** *vb* *idle, lounge, loll, laze
*Ana* rest, repose, relax (see corresponding nouns at REST): *saunter, stroll, amble
*Con* work, labor, toil, travail (see corresponding nouns at WORK)
**loath** *disinclined, indisposed, averse, hesitant, reluctant
*Ana* *adverse, averse: *antipathetic, unsympathetic, averse
*Ant* anxious —*Con* *eager, keen, avid: desiring *or* desirous, wishing, wanting (see corresponding verbs at DESIRE)
**loathe** abominate, detest, abhor, *hate
*Ana* *despise, contemn, scorn, disdain: refuse, reject, spurn, repudiate, *decline: *recoil, shrink, flinch, blench, quail
*Ant* dote on —*Con* *like, love, relish, fancy, enjoy:

*desire, crave, wish, want, covet
**loathing** abhorrence, detestation, abomination, hate, hatred (see under HATE *vb*)
*Ana* aversion, *antipathy: repugnance, repellency, distaste (see corresponding adjectives at REPUGNANT)
*Ant* tolerance
**loathsome** *offensive, repulsive, repugnant, revolting
*Ana* abominable, abhorrent, detestable, odious, *hateful: repellent, *repugnant, distasteful, obnoxious, invidious
*Ant* engaging, inviting —*Con* attractive, alluring, charming, enchanting, fascinating, bewitching (see under ATTRACT)
**local** *adj* *insular, provincial, parochial, small-town
*Ana* narrow, narrow-minded (see ILLIBERAL): circumscribed, limited, restricted, confined (see LIMIT *vb*)
*Ant* cosmopolitan
**locality, district, vicinity, neighborhood** denote a more or less definitely circumscribed place or region, especially from the point of view of those who live in it. **Locality** applies to a region of undefined boundaries, but it usually suggests an area round a center (as the place where the speaker or writer lives) ⟨he no longer resides in this *locality*⟩ or round a place remarkable for some event or landmark ⟨the deliverer is to be sought in the *locality* nearest to the chief scene of the invasion—*Stanley*⟩ **District** usually applies to a locality that has clearly defined boundaries determined (as by the nation, state, or town) for such purposes as for administrative and electoral use ⟨representative of the Fifth Congressional *District*⟩ ⟨federal judicial *districts*⟩ ⟨police *district*⟩ ⟨postal *district*⟩ In a less specific but in this instance more pertinent sense *district* is often applied to a locality with reference to some of its most obvious or clearly defined characteristics rather than to the exact area it covers ⟨the agricultural *districts* of the United States⟩ ⟨the Lake *District* of England⟩ ⟨the mining *district* of Pennsylvania⟩ ⟨the theater *district* of a city⟩ **Vicinity** never loses its basic implication of nearness but, since it suggests a distinct point of view, it applies only to the locality that is very near from that point of view ⟨there are no ponds in this *vicinity*⟩ **Neighborhood** usually carries an implied reference to one's neighbors and it may be preferred to *vicinity*, which it closely resembles in denotation, when the emphasis is on the inhabitants rather than on the locality referred to ⟨there is no one of that name in this *neighborhood*⟩ ⟨lived in a good *neighborhood*⟩ ⟨she is on good terms with the entire *neighborhood*⟩ However, it is frequently interchangeable with *vicinity* when the emphasis is on proximity; thus, a man might live in the *neighborhood* or the *vicinity* of a school ⟨the country must be on guard against the establishment of hostile bases in its *neighborhood*⟩
*Ana* region, *area, zone, belt, tract: section, sector (see PART): territory, *field, bailiwick, province, sphere, domain
**location** *place, position, situation, site, spot, station
**locomotion** *motion, movement, move, stir
**locum tenens** *substitute, supply, alternate, understudy, pinch hitter, double, stand-in
**locution** *phrase, idiom, expression
**lodge** *vb* **1** house, board, *harbor, shelter, entertain
*Ana* *receive, take, accept, admit: accommodate, *contain, hold
**2** *reside, live, dwell, sojourn, stay, put up, stop
**lofty** *high, tall
*Ana* elevated, raised, lifted (see LIFT): exalted, magnified, aggrandized (see EXALT): imposing, stately, august, majestic (see GRAND): sublime, glorious, superb (see SPLENDID)
*Con* lowly, *humble, modest

A colon (:) separates groups of words discriminated. An asterisk (*) indicates place of treatment of each group.

**logical,** analytical, subtle are comparable when they are applied to persons, their minds, their mental habits, or products of their reasoning and mean having or showing skill in thinking or reasoning. They are often used interchangeably or without clear distinction, but it is possible to employ them distinctively and with precision. **Logical** may imply the power to think according to the rules of logic and therefore in an orderly fashion; more often, however, it suggests the power to impress others that clearness of thought, soundness of reasoning, and freedom from bias underlie one's arguments, one's decisions, or one's policies ⟨he had . . . the *logical* as opposed to the intuitive temper. He distrusted emotion for which he could not find a rational basis—*Montague*⟩ ⟨Keats . . . was a perfectly *logical,* straightforward, and unprejudiced thinker. His emotions might run away with him; his ideas, never—*Lowell*⟩ **Analytical** stresses the power to simplify either what is complex or complicated (as by separating it into its constituent parts) or what is chaotic or confused (as by reorganization that shows the relation of the details to each other and the whole). In derogatory use it may imply a tendency to multiply subdivisions but in favorable or neutral use it connotes a power to systematize, clarify, and interpret, as distinguished from the power to create or invent ⟨if a man is being purely *analytical* . . . the thing is then something to be classified, related to other things by cause and effect, or broken down into elements—*Pepper*⟩ ⟨his mind was *analytical* rather than constructive—*Scudder*⟩ **Subtle** stresses the power to penetrate below the surface and to perceive fine distinctions and delicate, almost imperceptible, relations ⟨John Donne . . . one of the most *subtle* . . . intellects that ever, before or since, expressed itself through the medium of verse—*Lowes*⟩ When applied to arguments its use may imply a criticism, such as being hard to follow because of being overrefined ⟨it is a *subtle* and urbane, but none the less complacent, begging of all the serious questions in the case—*Cohen*⟩ ⟨a *subtle* and intricate book which does not readily yield its full implications—*Canad. Forum*⟩ Usually, however, it connotes extraordinary skill in reasoning or in analysis ⟨that is a point of view which . . . would hardly have escaped the *subtle* intellect of the Greeks—*Dickinson*⟩ ⟨the actual facts have required for . . . their interpretation the most *subtle* speculations of modern science—*Justice Holmes*⟩ ⟨for *subtle,* acute analysis they cannot be matched in any earlier period—*Muller*⟩
*Ana* cogent, *valid, sound, telling, convincing, compelling: *clear, lucid, perspicuous: *rational, reasonable: inferential, ratiocinative (see under INFERENCE)
*Ant* illogical —*Con* intuitive, *instinctive: *irrational, unreasonable: fallacious, sophistical, casuistical (see under FALLACY)
**logistic, logistical** strategic, tactical (see under STRATEGY)
**logistics** *strategy, tactics
**loiter** dawdle, lag, procrastinate, *delay
*Ana* tarry, linger, wait (see STAY)
*Con* hasten, hurry (see SPEED *vb*)
**loll** *idle, loaf, lounge, laze
*Ana* relax, rest, repose (see corresponding nouns at REST): lean, incline (see SLANT *vb*)
**lollop** *vb* 1 *skip, bound, hop, curvet, lope, ricochet
2 *stumble, trip, blunder, lurch, flounder, lumber, galumph, bumble
**lone** 1 lonely, lonesome, *alone, forlorn, lorn, solitary, desolate
2 *single, sole, unique, solitary, separate, particular
**lonely** lonesome, lone, *alone, solitary, forlorn, lorn, desolate

*Ana* abandoned, deserted, forsaken (see ABANDON): secluded, isolated (see corresponding nouns at SOLITUDE)
*Con* teeming, swarming (see TEEM): *social, gregarious, convivial
**lonesome** lonely, lone, *alone, solitary, forlorn, lorn, desolate
*Ana & Con* see those at LONELY
**long** *vb* Long, yearn, hanker, pine, hunger, thirst mean to have a strong and urgent desire for something. One **longs** when one wishes for something, and especially something remote or not readily attainable, with one's whole heart or with great earnestness ⟨socialists who *long* to see the world a better place—*Woodrow Wyatt*⟩ ⟨ever have I *longed* to slake my thirst for the world's praises—*Keats*⟩ ⟨wretched sensitive beings like ourselves *longing* to escape—*Powys*⟩ ⟨in the midst of the finesse, and the artistry . . . one *longs* at times, not for less refinement but for more virility—*Lowes*⟩ One **yearns** when one regards or desires something with eager, restless, often tender or passionate longing ⟨but Enoch *yearned* to see her face again—*Tennyson*⟩ ⟨she gazed into his faded blue eyes as if *yearning* to be understood—*Conrad*⟩ ⟨dreamers who *yearned* for things that are not, for things to come or things that have been—*Norman Douglas*⟩ One **hankers** when one is possessed with or made uneasy by a desire because of the urgency of a physical appetite ⟨*hanker* for fresh fruit in the wintertime⟩ or because of such a passion as greed, lust, ambition, or covetousness ⟨she . . . still *hankered,* with a natural hankering, after her money—*Trollope*⟩ ⟨*hankering* from the start after the office of tribune—*Buchan*⟩ or for something beyond one's reach or one's powers even if only for the moment ⟨to wean your minds from *hankering* after false Germanic standards—*Quiller-Couch*⟩ ⟨too long a siege of the familiar . . . sets us *hankering* after the strange—*Lowes*⟩ But often *hanker* is weakened to the point that it means little if any more than *want* ⟨although collectors still *hanker* after the period pieces, the trend is for simplicity —*Tomkinson*⟩ ⟨one *hankers* after one's own order of comfort in advancing age—*de la Mare*⟩ One **pines** when one languishes or grows weak through longing for something or gives oneself up to fruitless longing for it ⟨we look before and after, and *pine* for what is not—*Shelley*⟩ ⟨Harry Temple was wise enough to give up *pining* after what he could not get—*Besant & Rice*⟩ Basically one **hungers** for food to satisfy an urgent craving for nourishment or for a particular kind of food essential to satisfy appetite, and similarly one **thirsts** for drink to satisfy an urgent need for liquid or for a particular kind of drink essential to satisfy appetite ⟨*hunger* for fresh vegetables⟩ ⟨*thirst* for cool fresh water⟩ In their extended senses one *hungers* or *thirsts* when one longs for something with the full force of one's being ⟨blessed are they which do *hunger* and *thirst* after righteousness: for they shall be filled—*Mt 5:6*⟩ ⟨she *hungered* for a new environment in which to expand her new powers—*Ellis*⟩ ⟨East Florida was a pawn in world conflict, a strategic bait for which many nations *hungered*—*Hyman*⟩ ⟨a savage, unprincipled brute who naturally *thirsted* to overturn a society—*Plumb*⟩
*Ana* crave, *desire, wish, want, covet: pant, aspire, *aim
**longanimity** *patience, long-suffering, forbearance, resignation
*Ana* *fortitude, sand, grit, pluck, backbone: endurance, toleration *or* tolerance (see corresponding verbs at BEAR): submissiveness (see corresponding adjective at TAME)
**long-suffering** *patience, resignation, forbearance
*Ana* submissiveness, subduedness (see corresponding adjectives at TAME): meekness, humbleness *or* humility, lowliness (see corresponding adjectives at HUMBLE):

---

*Ana* analogous words    *Ant* antonyms    *Con* contrasted words    See also explanatory notes facing page 1

*fortitude, grit: endurance, toleration (see corresponding verbs at BEAR)

**Con** impatience, restiveness, uneasiness (see corresponding adjectives at IMPATIENT): irksomeness, wearisomeness, tediousness (see corresponding adjectives at IRKSOME): *tedium, boredom, ennui

**look** *vb* 1 *see, watch
**Ana** *gaze, gape, stare, glare, peer: *scrutinize, scan, inspect, examine
2 *seem, appear
**Ana** *indicate, betoken, bespeak: *show, manifest, evidence, evince, demonstrate
3 *expect, hope, await
**Ana** *foresee, foreknow, anticipate, divine

**look** *n* 1 Look, sight, view, glance, glimpse, peep, peek are comparable when meaning both the act of seeing something and the thing that is seen. **Look** implies the directing of one's eyes to a thing or the use of one's power of vision ⟨let me have a *look* at the patient⟩ ⟨one dying *look* he upward cast—*Scott*⟩ ⟨darted a quick *look* at me—*Kenneth Roberts*⟩ When applied to the thing seen (see also APPEARANCE), the impression produced tends to be stressed ⟨judging by the *look* of his rash, he has scarlet fever⟩ ⟨the *look* of his face as he spoke was by no means pleasant —*Trollope*⟩ **Sight**, on the other hand, so strongly implies reference to the object that is seen that it suggests reception of an image by the visual powers or presentation to the sense of sight rather than a conscious use of that sense. When the term denotes the act or the power of seeing, one takes a *look* at something which catches his *sight;* one has far *sight* who sees things at a great distance ⟨the litter is set down stage in full *sight* of the audience—*Millay*⟩ ⟨I was out of *sight* of the rest of them—*L. A. Viereck*⟩ When the term denotes the thing that is seen, qualifying words or phrases are usually necessary to suggest its character, appearance, or the effect it produces ⟨there is no *sight* in the world equal to it⟩ ⟨a disagreeable *sight*⟩ ⟨the blossoming of a cherry orchard . . . is a *sight* eagerly awaited—*Amer. Guide Series: Mich.*⟩ ⟨the earth, and every common *sight*—*Wordsworth*⟩ **View**, especially when it denotes the act of seeing, implies chiefly the exercise of the mental rather than the physical vision or an attempt to comprehend something beyond the range of the physical vision ⟨bring the buried ages back to *view*—*Gray*⟩ ⟨the scientific *view* of the world is not indifferent to quality or value. It seeks to find law, harmony, uniformity in nature—*Inge*⟩ ⟨Unitarianism with its more cheerful *view* of human nature—*Sperry*⟩ Often, when seeing through the eyes is suggested, *view* takes the place of *sight* in either sense, with, however, a stronger implication of a directed or fixed gaze ⟨thy dales, and hills, are fading from my *view*—*Keats*⟩ ⟨a house that affords a *view* of the ocean⟩ ⟨trees that intercept the *view*⟩ **Glance** may denote something which is seen as a sudden flash or gleam, or the presence or movement of which is recognized by a swift sudden flash ⟨with winged expedition swift as the lightning *glance*—*Milton*⟩ ⟨each sword's bright *glance*, seemed summons from their fate—*Stirling*⟩ It is in this sense that "a *glance* from the eye" is often to be interpreted, especially in older writings ⟨dart not scornful *glances* from those eyes, to wound thy lord—*Shak.*⟩, but the transition in sense from the flash that is seen to the quick look that is given is not clearly marked ⟨lift our heads to heaven, and never more abase our sight so low as to vouchsafe one *glance* unto the ground—*Shak.*⟩ ⟨a *glance* satisfied him of the hopelessness of the struggle—*J. R. Green*⟩ **Glimpse** also may apply to something seen as a flash or a gleam ⟨no dear *glimpse* of the sun's lovely face, strikes through the solid dark-

ness of the place—*Cowley*⟩ ⟨a *glimpse* of the moon showed the dark and huge tower—*Scott*⟩, but more commonly implies a brief view of a thing or, even more often, as much of it as may be taken in at a glance ⟨I did indeed for a brief evening obtain a *glimpse* of the richness and still beauty of an English harvest—*Jefferies*⟩ ⟨you remember I had a *glimpse* of him once—*Conrad*⟩ ⟨it was in one of these laboratories that I had my first and only *glimpse* of the fabulous plutonium—*Douglas Brown*⟩ **Peep** and **peek** are not clearly distinguishable in meaning, but the former is generally regarded as more dignified or less childish. When they denote the act of looking, both terms imply an attempt to see what is hidden or concealed, or what can be only furtively watched (as through a hole or a crevice or through half-shut eyes ⟨take a *peek* through a keyhole⟩ When, however, they denote something which is seen by peeping or peeking, *peep* seems to be the favored word ⟨you've only seen a *peep* through the curtain—*Stowe*⟩ ⟨none of these men has so far written a popular book of *peeps* into the fairyland of reality—*T. S. Eliot*⟩
**Ana** gazing *or* gaze, staring *or* stare (see GAZE): scrutiny, inspection, examination (see under SCRUTINIZE)
2 *appearance, aspect, semblance
**Ana** *bearing, demeanor, mien: *posture, attitude, pose: *face, countenance, visage, physiognomy

**looker-on** onlooker, beholder, *spectator, observer, witness, eyewitness, bystander, kibitzer

**loom** *vb* emerge, *appear
**Ant** vanish

**loose** *adj* Loose, relaxed, slack, lax are comparable when meaning not tightly bound, held, restrained, or stretched. **Loose** is the widest of these terms in its range of application. It is referable, for example, to persons or things that are free from a usual or a temporary restraint, whether that restraint is material (as a rope, a bond, a fetter, or a prison) or immaterial (as a rule, a principle, or a law) ⟨we found the boat *loose* after the storm⟩ ⟨the bull is *loose* in the field⟩ ⟨finally he worked his hand *loose*⟩ ⟨some sheets of this book are *loose*⟩ ⟨*loose* thinking, unrestrained by concern for logic or accuracy⟩ ⟨*loose* talk that pays scant attention to its consequences or the truth of its statements⟩ ⟨*loose* habits⟩ ⟨*loose* living⟩ *Loose* is also applicable to what is not firmly or tightly held by, attached to, connected with, or fitted to something that supports or guides, or something that it is intended to cover ⟨drive with *loose* reins⟩ ⟨a *loose* belt⟩ ⟨a *loose* coat⟩ ⟨*loose* joints⟩ ⟨a *loose* sense of a word⟩ Often the word applies to a substance or fabric having particles or filaments which are not close or compact in arrangement ⟨*loose* soil⟩ ⟨a *loose* weave⟩ **Relaxed** implies a loss of some tightness, tension, strictness, or rigidity, rather than total freedom from restraint or considerable departure from a normal state (as of discipline, fitness, or firmness); not only does it not suggest wildness, lawlessness, or immorality, but it rarely suggests anything worse than an easing up, a mitigation, an alleviation of strain, or a softening ⟨*relaxed* discipline⟩ ⟨*relaxed* nerves⟩ ⟨Augustus during these months was suffering from the *relaxed* and surfeited mood which always attends success —*Buchan*⟩ ⟨White House family life had been easy and *relaxed* . . . but it had maintained the standards of gentlefolk—*S. H. Adams*⟩ ⟨the *relaxed* attitude of the British toward the sedition expressed every day in Hyde Park— *R. K. Carr*⟩ **Slack** (see also NEGLIGENT) comes close to *relaxed* in its limitations and implications but it may stress lack of firmness or steadiness rather than a release from strain or severity; thus, a *slack* rope is one that is not taut, usually one that is not as taut as is necessary or de-

A colon (:) separates groups of words discriminated. An asterisk (*) indicates place of treatment of each group.

sirable; a *slack* hold is a weak, unsteady hold ⟨the tired arms lie with every sinew *slack—Quiller-Couch*⟩ ⟨a pair of sly, keen eyes are dancing in his *slack*, clown's face— *New Yorker*⟩ ⟨the rhythms often are indistinguishable from those of prose and the effect is often flat and *slack* —*Drew*⟩ *Slack* is applied both to business or work that is subject to periods of lessened activity and to the periods or seasons when business is dull or work is hard to find ⟨it'll be play to me after I've done my day's work, or any odd bits o' time when the work's *slack—George Eliot*⟩ ⟨the *slack* season for carpenters⟩ Like *slack*, **lax** usually stresses lack of steadiness, firmness, and tone ⟨felt the *lax* droop of her shoulder against his arm—*Wylie*⟩ ⟨sat there in one of those loose *lax* poses that came to her naturally—*Woolf*⟩ In application to nonmaterial things it is not always clearly distinguishable from other senses in which its primary stress is on lack of necessary strictness, severity, or precision (see *lax* under NEGLIGENT) ⟨his laws were in advance of general public opinion, an opinion which grew *laxer* as the years passed—*Buchan*⟩ ⟨the old unity . . . has been replaced by a new unity based on the principles of chivalry and courtly love . . . . This unity is relatively *lax* and slight—*R. A. Hall*⟩
*Ana* \*limp, flabby, flaccid, flimsy: \*free, independent, disengaged, detached (see DETACH): casual, desultory, hit-or-miss, happy-go-lucky, \*random, haphazard: \*negligent, remiss, lax, slack: \*careless, heedless, thoughtless
*Ant* tight: strict   —*Con* taut, tense (see TIGHT): \*rigid, stringent, rigorous: precise, exact, \*correct: tied, bound (see TIE *vb*): restrained, curbed, checked, inhibited (see RESTRAIN)
**loot** *n* booty, plunder, \*spoil, swag, prize
**loot** *vb* \*rob, plunder, rifle, burglarize
*Ana* sack, pillage, despoil, \*ravage, spoliate, devastate, waste: \*steal, pilfer, filch, purloin
**lop** \*shear, poll, clip, trim, prune, snip, crop
*Ana* \*cut, slash, chop, hew: \*shorten, curtail
**lope** *vb* \*skip, bound, hop, curvet, lollop, ricochet
**loquacious** garrulous, voluble, glib, \*talkative
*Ana* fluent, \*vocal, articulate, glib, eloquent, voluble: chatting *or* chatty, gabbing *or* gabby, chattering, prating, jabbering (see corresponding verbs at CHAT)
*Con* reserved, taciturn, uncommunicative, reticent, \*silent: laconic, succinct, terse, \*concise: curt, brusque (see BLUFF)
**loquacity, loquaciousness** garrulity, volubility, glibness, talkativeness (see under TALKATIVE)
*Ana* chattering *or* chatter, chatting *or* chat, gabbing *or* gab, prating *or* prate, jabbering *or* jabber (see CHAT *vb*): fluency, articulateness, glibness, volubleness (see corresponding adjectives at VOCAL): \*readiness, ease, facility
*Con* taciturnity, reservedness *or* reserve, reticence, silence (see corresponding adjectives at SILENT): curtness, brusqueness (see corresponding adjectives at BLUFF)
**lordly** haughty, arrogant, overbearing, \*proud, insolent, supercilious, disdainful
*Ana* pretentious (see SHOWY): \*dictatorial, magisterial, authoritarian: imperious, domineering, \*masterful
*Con* meek, modest, \*humble, lowly: submissive, \*tame, subdued: gentle, mild (see SOFT): abject, \*mean
**lore** \*knowledge, science, learning, erudition, scholarship, information
**lorn** forlorn, lonely, lonesome, lone, \*alone, solitary, desolate
*Ana* see those at FORLORN
**lot** 1 destiny, portion, \*fate, doom
*Ana* fortune, luck, hap, \*chance, hazard
2 \*group, cluster, bunch, parcel
*Ana* collection, assemblage (see under GATHER): \*aggre-

gate, aggregation, conglomeration, conglomerate
**loud, stentorian, earsplitting, hoarse, raucous, strident, stertorous** are comparable when they apply to sounds and mean great in volume or unpleasant in effect. **Loud** suggests a volume above normal and sometimes implies undue vehemence or obtrusiveness ⟨a *loud* cry⟩ ⟨a *loud* blast on a trumpet⟩ ⟨*loud* demands for reform⟩ ⟨a *loud* and unpleasant person⟩ **Stentorian**, chiefly applying to voices, implies exceedingly great power and range ⟨a *stentorian* voice, husky from much bawling of orders— *Jesse*⟩ ⟨a few words, rendered either completely inaudible or painfully *stentorian* according to the whim of the microphone—*Times Lit. Sup.*⟩ ⟨blowing his nose in *stentorian* tones—*Rölvaag*⟩ **Earsplitting** adds the idea of a physically oppressive loudness, especially shrillness (as of screams or shrieks) ⟨suddenly he trumpeted, an *earsplitting* sound in the close stall—*W. V. T. Clark*⟩ ⟨an *earsplitting* cry of terror⟩ **Hoarse** implies harshness, huskiness, or roughness of tone, sometimes suggesting an accompanying or causal loudness ⟨the *hoarse* growling of the mob—*Kenneth Roberts*⟩ ⟨voice came to my ears . . . tense and *hoarse* with an overmastering rage—*London*⟩ ⟨the *hoarse* bellow of the bull whistle—*Amer. Guide Series: N.C.*⟩ **Raucous** implies a loud, harsh, grating tone, especially of voice, often implying rowdiness ⟨the voices often become *raucous* or shrill and any proper dignity of the spirit suffers—*Benét*⟩ ⟨music of the city, *raucous*, jazzy, witty, dramatic—*Hanson*⟩ ⟨gathering along the platform with thin, bright, *raucous* laughter—*Faulkner*⟩ ⟨the *raucous* vitality of a mining boomtown—*Agnew*⟩ **Strident** adds to *raucous* the idea of a rasping, discordant but insistent quality, especially of voice ⟨scurrying traffic whose *strident* voice mingles whistle blasts with the hollow clang of bell buoys and the screams of softly wheeling gulls—*Amer. Guide Series: N. Y. City*⟩ ⟨a sort of a *strident*, metallic quality about her, revealed in the high pitch of her voice—*Sterling & Ascoli*⟩ ⟨her vocal attack often sounds *strident* and explosive—*Newsweek*⟩ **Stertorous**, usually not applied to sounds made by the voice, suggests the loud snoring, or sounds like snoring made in breathing, especially when it is difficult, by persons or animals in sleep, in a coma, or with marked asthmatic difficulties ⟨the *stertorous* breathing of the owl—*Osbert Sitwell*⟩ ⟨the horse is trembling . . . its breathing *stertorous* like groaning—*Faulkner*⟩
*Ant* low-pitched, low
**lounge** *vb* \*idle, loaf, loll, laze
*Ana* incline, lean (see SLANT *vb*): relax, repose, rest (see corresponding nouns at REST)
**lout** *n* \*boor, churl, clown, clodhopper, bumpkin, hick, yokel, rube
*Con* \*gentleman, patrician, aristocrat
**loutish** boorish, churlish, clownish (see under BOOR)
*Ana* clumsy, gauche, maladroit, inept, \*awkward: burly, brawny, husky, \*muscular: \*rude, rough, crude, raw, callow, green, uncouth
**love** *n* \*attachment, affection
*Ana* devotion, piety, \*fidelity, allegiance, loyalty: adoration, worship, idolatry (see corresponding verbs at ADORE): \*passion, fervor, ardor, enthusiasm, zeal
*Ant* hate   —*Con* aversion, \*antipathy: \*enmity, hostility, animosity, rancor, animus: hatred, abhorrence, detestation (see under HATE *vb*)
**love** *vb* \*like, enjoy, dote, relish, fancy
*Ana* \*adore, worship, idolize: cherish, treasure, value, prize, \*appreciate
*Ant* hate   —*Con* abhor, detest, abominate, loathe (see HATE *vb*): \*despise, contemn, scorn, disdain
**lovely** \*beautiful, fair, comely, pretty, bonny, handsome,

---

*Ana* analogous words   *Ant* antonyms   *Con* contrasted words   See also explanatory notes facing page 1

beauteous, pulchritudinous, good-looking
*Ana* alluring, enchanting, charming, attractive (see under ATTRACT): *delightful, delectable: exquisite, delicate, dainty, rare (see CHOICE)
*Ant* unlovely: plain
**loving, affectionate, devoted, fond, doting** are comparable when they mean feeling or showing love or strong liking. **Loving** stresses the inward emotion and usually implies sincerity and depth of feeling ⟨a *loving* father⟩ ⟨*loving* friends⟩ ⟨looking at it with eyes at once critical and *loving*, as if recalling the glow with which he had created it—*Galsworthy*⟩ ⟨so we'll go no more a roving so late into the night, though the heart be still as *loving*, and the moon be still as bright—*Byron*⟩ **Affectionate** often stresses demonstrativeness ⟨she is a very *affectionate* child⟩ ⟨he had an *affectionate* heart. He must love somebody—*Austen*⟩ or implies the need for or fact of outward expression of inward feeling ⟨his *affectionate* care for his people was winning him love—*Buchan*⟩ **Devoted** emphasizes attentiveness, sometimes implying little more than assiduousness, sometimes connoting self-dedication or active loyalty to the person or thing one loves or likes ⟨*devoted* lover⟩ ⟨*devoted* disciple⟩ ⟨I did everything for him that the most *devoted* mother could do—*Shaw*⟩ **Fond** implies affectionate attachment and often connotes foolish tenderness ⟨a loving husband is a very amiable character. A *fond* one I think is not so—*John Wesley*⟩ ⟨her preoccupation with petty things of no importance whatever was worthy of the finest traditions of *fond* motherhood—*Bennett*⟩ When *fond* (of) and *devoted* (to) imply a strong predilection or addiction, they are not often clearly distinguished. However, one is *fond* of the theater who welcomes every opportunity to see a play; one is *devoted* to the theater who spends much of his time in seeing plays or in efforts to further the development of the drama. One may be *fond* of the country and yet not go there often, but if one is *devoted* to it, one prefers to spend most of one's time there. **Doting** implies excessive fondness that leads to overindulgence in parents or fatuousness in lovers ⟨*doting* mothers end by ruining their children—*Hallam Tennyson*⟩
*Ana* amorous, amatory, *erotic: *enamored, infatuated: attentive, considerate, *thoughtful: *impassioned, passionate, ardent, fervent: true, constant, *faithful
*Ant* unloving —*Con* *indifferent, unconcerned, aloof, detached: *cold, chilly, frigid: *faithless, false
**low** *base, vile
*Ana* abject, ignoble, *mean, sordid: *coarse, vulgar, gross, obscene, ribald: *crooked, devious, oblique
*Con* decent, seemly, *proper, *decorous: noble, *moral, ethical: lofty, *high
**lower** *vb* glower, *frown, scowl, gloom
*Ana* glare, stare, peer (see GAZE)
**lowly** meek, *humble, modest
*Ana* submissive, subdued, *tame: retiring, withdrawing (see GO): reverential, deferential, obeisant (see corresponding nouns at HONOR)
*Ant* pompous —*Con* pretentious, ostentatious, *showy: arrogant, lordly, overbearing, haughty, *proud
**loyal** *faithful, true, constant, staunch, steadfast, resolute
*Ant* disloyal —*Con* false, *faithless, perfidious, traitorous, treacherous: disaffected, alienated, estranged (see ESTRANGE): rebellious, mutinous, seditious, *insubordinate, factious, contumacious
**loyalty** *fidelity, allegiance, fealty, devotion, piety
*Ana* trueness *or* truth, faithfulness, constancy, staunchness, steadfastness (see corresponding adjectives at FAITHFUL): *attachment, affection, love
*Ant* disloyalty —*Con* faithlessness, falseness *or* falsity,

perfidiousness *or* perfidy, treacherousness *or* treachery, traitorousness (see corresponding adjectives at FAITHLESS)
**lubricate** grease, *oil, anoint, cream
**lucent** *bright, brilliant, radiant, luminous, lustrous, effulgent, refulgent, beaming, lambent, incandescent
*Ana* glowing, blazing, flaming (see BLAZE *vb*): *splendid, resplendent, glorious
**lucid 1** pellucid, *clear, transparent, translucent, diaphanous, limpid
*Ana* luminous, *bright, brilliant, lucent
*Con* murky, gloomy, dusky, *dark: *turbid, muddy
**2** *clear, perspicuous
*Ana* distinct, plain, manifest, *evident
*Ant* obscure, vague, dark —*Con* enigmatic, cryptic, ambiguous, equivocal (see OBSCURE)
**luck** fortune, hap, accident, hazard, *chance
*Ana* break, chance, occasion, *opportunity: lot, portion, destiny, *fate
**luckless** *unlucky, disastrous, ill-starred, ill-fated, unfortunate, calamitous, hapless
*Ana* unhappy, infelicitous (see UNFIT): *miserable, wretched
**lucky, fortunate, happy, providential** all mean meeting with or producing a favorable outcome or an unforeseen or unpredictable success. **Lucky** implies that the person or persons involved have been favored by chance and that the success has not been the result of merit or merits ⟨a *lucky* gambler⟩ ⟨said he was a *lucky* fellow not to be sent to school—*Meredith*⟩ ⟨it was a *lucky* day for him when he met the girl who later became his wife⟩ **Fortunate**, although it is often indistinguishable from *lucky* in its implications, is more formal and more likely to suggest an unanticipated absence of all handicaps and mischances or presence of such favorable circumstances as might argue the intervention of a higher power (compare *fortune* under CHANCE *n* 1) that watches over one ⟨in friendships I had been most *fortunate*—*Shelley*⟩ ⟨we are aware, too, that the critical discrimination which comes so hardly to us has in more *fortunate* men flashed in the very heat of creation—*T. S. Eliot*⟩ ⟨it took a very *fortunate* conjunction of events to bring about the rapid spread and seemingly complete victory of democracy—*Dewey*⟩ **Happy** differs from the preceding words chiefly in its combining the meaning of *lucky* or *fortunate* with that of its more common sense of being blessed or made glad (see GLAD); thus, a *happy* outcome is not only one that is fortunate but one that makes the person affected feel happy; a *happy* accident is an accidental event or circumstance that brings to light something that proves a treasure ⟨giving them patience under their sufferings, and a *happy* issue out of all their afflictions—*Book of Common Prayer*⟩ ⟨*Homo sapiens* is among the safest of all animals, because he is omnivorous. His heredity is a mixture of *happy* accidents—*La Barre*⟩ **Providential** often carries an implication of good fortune resulting from the help or interference of Providence ⟨a *providential* escape⟩ ⟨I thought to myself, this can't be chance. Indeed it seemed *providential*—*de la Mare*⟩ Often, however, the word carries no trace of this implication and means little more than *lucky* or *fortunate* ⟨it was *providential*: the sisters had made no remark that the Critchlows might not hear—*Bennett*⟩ ⟨it was certainly most *providential* that I looked up at that instant, as the monster would probably, in less than a minute, have seized and dragged me into the river—*Bartram*⟩
*Ana* *favorable, benign, auspicious, propitious: advantageous, *beneficial, profitable: happy, felicitous, meet (see FIT)
*Ant* unlucky —*Con* *sinister, baleful, malefic, malef-

A colon (:) separates groups of words discriminated. An asterisk (*) indicates place of treatment of each group.

icent, malign

**lucrative** *paying, gainful, remunerative, profitable

**ludicrous** *laughable, risible, ridiculous, comic, comical, farcical, droll, funny

*Ana* absurd, preposterous, *foolish, silly: grotesque, bizarre, antic, *fantastic: amusing, diverting, entertaining (see AMUSE)

*Con* lugubrious, doleful, dolorous, *melancholy: solemn, grave, *serious

**lugubrious** doleful, dolorous, *melancholy, rueful, plaintive

*Ana* depressing, oppressing *or* oppressive (see corresponding verbs at DEPRESS): sorrowful, woeful (see corresponding nouns at SORROW): gloomy, saturnine, dour, morose, glum, *sullen

*Ant* joyous: facetious —*Con* *merry, blithe, jocund, jolly, jovial: cheerful, *glad, joyful

**lull** *vb* *calm, compose, quiet, quieten, still, soothe, settle, tranquilize

*Ana* *pacify, placate, appease, mollify: *moderate, qualify, temper: allay, assuage, alleviate, *relieve

*Ant* agitate

**lull** *n* *pause, recess, respite, intermission

*Ana* quiescence, abeyance (see corresponding adjectives at LATENT): *period, epoch, era: interval, interruption, *break

**lumber** *stumble, trip, blunder, lurch, flounder, galumph, lollop, bumble

**luminous** *bright, brilliant, radiant, lustrous, effulgent, lucent, refulgent, beaming, lambent, incandescent

*Ana* glowing, blazing, flaming (see BLAZE *vb*): gleaming, glittering, flashing, scintillating (see FLASH *vb*): resplendent, glorious, *splendid

*Con* dim, dusky, obscure, murky, gloomy, *dark

**lunacy** *insanity, psychosis, mania, dementia

*Ana* alienation, derangement, *aberration: *mania, delirium, frenzy, hysteria

**lunatic** *adj* *insane, mad, crazy, crazed, demented, deranged, maniac, non compos mentis

**lurch** *vb* *stumble, trip, blunder, flounder, lumber, galumph, lollop, bumble

*Ana* *reel, stagger, totter: *plunge, pitch, dive

**lure** *n* Lure, bait, decoy, snare, trap all denote something that leads an animal or a person into a particular place or situation from which escape is difficult. **Lure** suggests something that always attracts and often deceives ⟨threw out all the *lures* of her beauty . . . to make a prize of his heart—*Peacock*⟩ yet does not necessarily lead one into evil or into danger ⟨how many have with a smile made small account of beauty and her *lures* . . . on worthier things intent!—*Milton*⟩ Often the connotation of deception is subordinated or lost and that of drawing power or seductiveness is correspondingly heightened ⟨how can they resist . . . the *lure* of so adventurous, so enchanting an invitation?—*L. P. Smith*⟩ ⟨the *lure* of the simple life—*Buchan*⟩ **Bait** basically applies to a morsel of food by which a fish or other animal is enticed into a situation where it can be caught. In extended use it is applied to something, often in itself relatively insignificant, which is held out as a temptation or as a suggestion of an inviting prospect in the hope or with the result of inveigling someone into a desired act, position, or situation ⟨shop windows filled with *baits* to shoppers⟩ ⟨ in spite of her shyness, the girl's beauty was sufficient *bait* to attract many suitors⟩ ⟨the Festival has . . . signed a big-name movie star to act as *bait* for those who must have a pinch of glamour added to their culture—*Sat. Review*⟩ ⟨the *bait* may be reunification of East and West Germany, which all Germans are loudly demanding—*A. E. Stevenson*⟩ **Decoy** may apply

to a wildfowl or the likeness of one which is used to lure other wildfowl into shooting range or into a net. In extended use it is applied to a person or sometimes to a thing that leads one to go somewhere or to do something that exposes one to the danger of being entrapped (as in the commission of crime, in compromising or unpleasant circumstances, or into being used to further another person's ends) ⟨pretty young girls were the unconscious *decoys* by means of which she assembled numbers of men at her receptions⟩ ⟨the troops were led into ambush by a *decoy*⟩ ⟨are said to have lured ships onto the dangerous Brigantine shoals in order to plunder them. The *decoy* was a lantern hanging from a pole lashed to a jackass—*Amer. Guide Series: N. J.*⟩ ⟨wealthy department stores had the idea of using their book sections as *decoys* to draw the public into their doors by offering the latest big-selling books at heavily cut prices—*Times Lit. Sup.*⟩ **Snare** basically applies to a line with a running noose for catching a bird or animal. In extended use it is applicable to a danger one may run into accidentally or unexpectedly or through lack of caution or wariness and from which, once involved, one cannot easily extricate oneself ⟨the path to bliss abounds with many a *snare*—*Cowper*⟩ ⟨thou know'st the *snares* on ev'ry hand, guide thou their steps alway—*Burns*⟩ ⟨the wish for perfect security is one of those *snares* we are always falling into—*Russell*⟩ ⟨led years before into the *snare* of matrimony with him, in consequence of which she was encumbered with the bringing up of six children—*Stowe*⟩ ⟨she meant to weave me a *snare* . . . to entangle me when we met—*Tennyson*⟩ ⟨gin's but a *snare* of Old Nick the deluder—*Barham*⟩ **Trap** basically applies to a device that shuts with a spring for capturing animals. In extended use it is, like *snare*, applied to what is a danger to the unwary or incautious. The two words are often used interchangeably as though they were indistinguishable in meaning; however, *trap* is preferred to *snare* when disastrous effects, or deliberate setting for the purposes of capture, or trickery beyond detection are implied ⟨the army feared a *trap* but rather than retreat, they advanced into it⟩ ⟨a *trap* for speeders⟩ ⟨knowing the examiner's methods, he was certain that there would be a *trap* set for him but he could discover none⟩ ⟨they accused the Western Powers of setting a *trap* for Italy so that she would be irrevocably tied to them —*Collier's Yr. Bk.*⟩ ⟨with *traps* and obstacles and hazards confronting us on every hand, only blindness or indifference will fail to turn . . . for guidance or for warning, to the study of examples—*Cardozo*⟩

**lure** *vb* Lure, entice, inveigle, decoy, tempt, seduce are comparable when they mean to draw one from a situation or a course (as of action or behavior) typically felt as right, desirable, or usual or into one felt as wrong, undesirable, or unusual. **Lure** implies the action of a strong or irresistible influence which may be baneful ⟨sensationalism that had *lured* new readers to the yellow journals during the circulation wars of the 1890's—*H. L. Smith*⟩ or perfectly innocuous or even desirable ⟨stretches of woodland dotted with lakes where hunting and fishing *lure* sportsmen from many distant points—*American Guide Series: Me.*⟩ ⟨the essential thing is to *lure* into classroom instruction the finest type of trained men and women— *Fuess*⟩ **Entice** adds to *lure* a strong suggestion of artfulness and adroitness ⟨with her . . . high-mindedness she *enticed* him into a sphere of spirituality that was not his native realm—*Stahl*⟩ ⟨she appeared to be playing with the bird, possibly amusing herself by trying to *entice* it on to her hand—*Hudson*⟩ **Inveigle** implies the use of wiles and often of deceit and flattery ⟨with patience and diplomacy, she can eventually *inveigle* him into marrying

her—*Maher*⟩ Distinctively, it may apply to the coaxing of something from someone by such means ⟨although he used the most subtle means to *inveigle* the author into the office to read the press notices, he never succeeded—*Bok*⟩ ⟨over gin and water we *inveigled* from him a pack of well-worn cards—*Beaglehole*⟩ **Decoy** may mean to entrap or lead (as into danger) by artifice and especially by false appearances ⟨the islanders had been living in relative opulence from the wreckage of ships which they had skillfully *decoyed* to destruction on the reefs—*Barbour*⟩ ⟨the female bird . . . practiced the same arts upon us to *decoy* us away—*Burroughs*⟩ **Tempt** historically meant and still may mean to entice into evil through hope of pleasure or gain ⟨[weak] . . . nations *tempt* others to prey upon them—*Richards*⟩ In more general use it may carry a suggestion of exerting such an attraction as inclines one to act against one's better judgment or higher principles ⟨the receipt of remuneration from patents or copyrights *tempts* the owners thereof to retard or inhibit research or to restrict the benefits derivable therefrom—*W. T. & Barbara Fitts*⟩ but more often implies an attracting or inducing that is morally perfectly neutral ⟨the decision to *tempt* women away from their gray flannel suits . . . with a kaleidoscope of color—*Americana Annual*⟩ ⟨had a personality that could *tempt* a female ichthyologist's interests away from fish—*Current Biog.*⟩ **Seduce** usually means to lead astray (as from the course of rectitude, propriety, or duty) by overcoming scruples ⟨the hideous beast whose craft had *seduced* me into murder—*Poe*⟩ and even in its most favorable senses in which it implies a moving or turning into a new course it commonly suggests some degree of deluding or misleading as the method employed ⟨words when used with the gift of magic can *seduce* a reader into belief that has no roots in reality—*Feld*⟩ ⟨knew how to *seduce* the interest of his pupils; he did not drive, he led—*Anspacher*⟩
*Ana* ensnare, snare, entrap, trap, capture, *catch, bag: bewitch, fascinate, allure, captivate, *attract: blandish, wheedle, cajole (see COAX)
*Ant* revolt, repel

**lurid** *ghastly, grisly, gruesome, macabre, grim
*Ana* livid, *pale, pallid, wan, ashy, ashen: *sinister, malign, baleful, malefic, maleficent

**lurk** *vb* **Lurk, skulk, slink, sneak** do not share a common denotation, but they are comparable because the major implication of each word is furtive action intended to escape the attention of others. To **lurk** is to lie in wait (as in an ambush); the term sometimes implies only a place of concealment ⟨his faithful Tom . . . with his young master's mare . . . was *lurking* in a plantation of firs—*Meredith*⟩ ⟨around the ends cluster women and children, and outside *lurk* the boys and girls who are not participating in the dancing—*Mead*⟩ but it often also suggests an evil intention, or quiet, stealthy movements, or a readiness to spring upon a victim ⟨there . . . ugly treasons *lurk*—*Shak.*⟩ ⟨if the thought of Rufus-and-Richard-slayers *lurking* behind trees doesn't bother you—*Joseph*⟩ ⟨in the lingering shadows of the great war and the unhappy peace some unseen, alien enemy still *lurked*—*Handlin*⟩ To **skulk** is usually to move furtively but sometimes to lurk; the word carries a stronger implication than the preceding word either of a sinister intention or of cowardice or fear ⟨disdainful Anger, pallid Fear, and Shame that *skulks* behind—*Gray*⟩ ⟨Death . . . is a scavenger, *skulks* in charnels, and is the dirtiest of fighters—*Sullivan*⟩ ⟨there, *skulking* like a shadow through the trees, silent as a burglar, came the trim and handsome Cooper's hawk—*Peattie*⟩ To **slink** is to move stealthily or slyly in order not to attract atten-

tion ⟨like beasts of prey *slinking* about a campfire—*Conrad*⟩ ⟨after a while I *slunk* away out of the great circle of firelight into the thick darkness beyond—*Hudson*⟩ To **sneak** is to get out of or into a place by slinking, or out of a difficulty by methods lacking in straightforwardness or definitely underhanded ⟨he *sneaked* out of the house after his parents had gone to bed⟩ ⟨rustlers had a way of *sneaking* onto ranges and dabbing their own brand on unbranded calves—*S. E. Fletcher*⟩ ⟨meanly to *sneak* out of difficulties into which they had proudly strutted—*Burke*⟩
*Ana* *hide, conceal, secrete: ambush, waylay, *surprise
*Con* *appear, emerge, loom

**luscious** delicious, delectable, *delightful
*Ana* sapid, flavorsome, toothsome, *palatable, appetizing: grateful, gratifying, pleasing, *pleasant
*Ant* austere: tasteless

**lush** luxuriant, *profuse, lavish, prodigal, exuberant
*Ana* abounding *or* abundant, teeming, swarming (see corresponding verbs at TEEM): sumptuous, opulent, *luxurious

**lust** *desire, appetite, passion, urge
*Ana* *cupidity, greed, avarice, rapacity: yearning, longing, hankering, thirsting *or* thirst, hungering *or* hunger (see LONG *vb*): craving, coveting (see DESIRE *vb*): gusto, zest, *taste

**luster, sheen, gloss, glaze** are comparable when they denote a smooth shining surface that is the natural property of a thing or is given to it by some such process as polishing, burnishing, or coating. **Luster** basically and in technical use regularly implies a giving off of often iridescent reflected light ⟨the satiny *luster* of fine pearls⟩ ⟨the soft *luster* of polished wood⟩ ⟨cut a piece of lead or of zinc, and observe the *luster* of its fresh surface—*T. H. Huxley*⟩ ⟨the *luster* of minerals can be divided into two types, metallic and nonmetallic—*Hurlbut*⟩ In literary and extended use *luster* is often used to imply radiance or brilliance (see BRIGHT 1) ⟨the sun was shining with uncommon *luster*—*Dickens*⟩ **Sheen** applies to a lustrous surface (as of a textile) or a surface luster (as of a mineral cleavage surface or a dark feather) that may be dull or bright and may be a simple shining or marked by richly iridescent or metallic tones ⟨repeated scrubbings have given the wood a silvery *sheen*—*Amer. Guide Series: Mich.*⟩ ⟨the flashing *sheen* on the bird's plume—*Sitwell*⟩ ⟨the *sheen* of their spears was like stars on the sea—*Byron*⟩ ⟨the *sheen* of his poplin and velvet—*Cather*⟩ In extended use *sheen* may stress richness and brilliance ⟨an amazing *sheen* over the orchestral sound, a definition of textures and effects not to be heard even in the concert hall—*Robert Lawrence*⟩ or it may stress a superficiality suggestive of a surface luster ⟨daughters with a *sheen* of drawing-room accomplishments upon them—*Bell*⟩ **Gloss** stresses superficiality more than *luster* or *sheen* and is appropriately applied to something that shines because coated with a shining substance ⟨the *gloss* of a newly varnished floor⟩ or because well polished ⟨buffed the leather to a high *gloss*⟩ or specially finished ⟨the *gloss* on this chintz will wash off⟩ In extended use, *gloss* often implies superficial attractiveness or plausibility ⟨Mr. France plans to put the same *gloss* . . . on the place as he does on the fancy Collins Avenue hotels—*Friedlander*⟩ ⟨writes with his usual agreeable *gloss*, but it may be that the ingredients are wearing just a bit thin—*New Yorker*⟩ **Glaze** applies particularly to a glasslike coating which provides a smooth impervious lustrous surface on ceramic wares, but it is also applicable to such comparable coatings as one made on cooked meats by pouring over them broth thickened by boiling or by

---

A colon (:) separates groups of words discriminated. An asterisk (*) indicates place of treatment of each group

addition of gelatin, or on baked goods by beaten egg or syrup, or as one formed on terrestrial surfaces ⟨walks covered with a *glaze* of ice⟩ ⟨a porcelain bowl with a thick bubbly celadon *glaze*⟩ The term also is sometimes applied to the material from which such a glaze is made ⟨new carrots dressed with a *glaze* of brown sugar and butter⟩ *Glaze* is the least common of these terms in extended usage and in such use is typically metaphorical ⟨we whites have a color *glaze* on our imaginations that makes it hard to feel with the people we have segregated ourselves from—*Lillian Smith*⟩ ⟨her skin had the healthy *glaze* that comes from sunshine and ten hours of sleep a night—*Brodkey*⟩
*Ana* iridescence, opalescence (see corresponding adjectives at PRISMATIC): brilliancy, radiance, luminosity, effulgence, refulgence (see corresponding adjectives at BRIGHT)
**lustful** lascivious, libidinous, lecherous, wanton, lewd, *licentious, libertine
*Ana* *carnal, fleshly, sensual, animal: *immoral, unmoral, amoral
*Con* pure, modest, decent, *chaste: *moral, virtuous
**lustrous** luminous, radiant, brilliant, *bright, effulgent, refulgent, beaming, lambent, lucent, incandescent
*Ana* glorious, resplendent, *splendid: glowing, blazing, flaming (see BLAZE *vb*)
**lusty** *vigorous, energetic, strenuous, nervous
*Ana* robust, sound, *healthy, hale: stout, sturdy, *strong, stalwart: husky, brawny, *muscular, sinewy, athletic
*Ant* effete   —*Con* *weak, infirm, feeble, decrepit
**luxuriant** lush, exuberant, *profuse, lavish, prodigal
*Ana* fruitful, fecund, *fertile, prolific: *rank, rampant: abounding *or* abundant, teeming (see corresponding verbs at TEEM)
*Con* barren, *sterile, unfruitful, infertile: *meager, scanty, scrimpy, skimpy: arid, *dry
**luxurious** 1 voluptuous, sybaritic, epicurean, *sensuous, sensual
*Ana* self-indulging *or* self-indulgent, self-pampering (see base words at INDULGE): languorous, languishing (see LANGUID)

*Ant* ascetic   —*Con* austere, stern, *severe: self-denying, self-abnegating (see corresponding nouns at RENUNCIATION)
2 Luxurious, sumptuous, opulent are comparable when they are applied to things and mean ostentatiously or obviously rich and magnificent. Something **luxurious** (see also SENSUOUS) is exceedingly choice and costly ⟨*luxurious* sable coat⟩ ⟨the *luxurious* appointments of their drawing room⟩ ⟨a *luxurious* cargo of wine, olive oil, and candied tropic fruits—*Wylie*⟩ Something **sumptuous** is extravagantly rich, splendid, gorgeous, or luxurious; the word usually suggests a grandeur or magnificence that almost overwhelms the senses ⟨the *sumptuous* life of the Court provided material for some painters—*Binyon*⟩ ⟨Venice, soon to be known as the most beautiful and *sumptuous* city of Europe—*Ellis*⟩ ⟨a velvet gown, *sumptuous* and wine-purple, with a white ruff that stood up . . . high and stiff —*Edmund Wilson*⟩ ⟨for the most *sumptuous* masques in England, Italian managers, engineers and artists were brought over—*T. S. Eliot*⟩ Something **opulent** (see also RICH) flaunts or seems to flaunt its luxuriousness, or luxuriance, and, in some cases costliness ⟨offered the bribe not only of her beauty but of an *opulent* and glittering eastern throne—*Buchan*⟩ ⟨the diction of poetry became, with notable exceptions, *opulent*, sumptuous, lavish, rather than pointed, terse, concrete—*Lowes*⟩
*Ana* ostentatious, pretentious, *showy: magnificent, stately, imposing, majestic, *grand: *costly, expensive, valuable, precious
*Con* frugal, thrifty, economical, *sparing: *meager, scanty, scant, skimpy, scrimpy, spare, exiguous
**luxury** *amenity
*Ana* *pleasure, joy, delight: agreeableness, gratification, gratefulness (see corresponding adjectives at PLEASANT)
*Ant* hardship   —*Con* *difficulty, rigor, vicissitude
**lying** mendacious, untruthful, *dishonest, deceitful
*Ana* *false, wrong: deceptive, *misleading, delusive, delusory
*Ant* truthtelling   —*Con* honest, just, *upright, conscientious, scrupulous, honorable: candid, *frank, open, plain: *reliable, dependable, trustworthy

# M

**macabre** gruesome, *ghastly, grisly, grim, lurid
*Ana* horrifying, daunting, appalling, dismaying (see DISMAY): horrific, horrendous, *horrible, horrid
**macerate** *crush, mash, smash, bruise, squash
*Ana* *separate, part, divide: stew, seethe, simmer (see BOIL): soften (see corresponding adjective at SOFT)
**machination** intrigue, conspiracy, *plot, cabal
*Ana* *trick, ruse, stratagem, maneuver, gambit, ploy, artifice, feint, wile
**machine, mechanism, machinery, apparatus, engine, motor** are comparable especially when they denote a device or system by which energy can be converted into useful work. **Machine** is at once the most fundamental of these terms and the most varied in its applications. Basically it denotes an assemblage of parts that transmit forces, motion, and energy from one to another in a predetermined manner and to a desired end (as sewing a seam, hoisting a load, printing a book, or maintaining an electric current) ⟨a drilling *machine*⟩ ⟨*machines* that convert rags to paper⟩ ⟨a washing *machine*⟩ But it also may apply

specifically to any of the six *simple machines* (the lever, the wheel and axle, the pulley, the inclined plane, the wedge, and the screw) that together contain the elements of which all other machines are composed. Again, it may apply to a machine in the basic sense together with its power-generating unit and sometimes with supplementary equipment (as for moving the whole complex) ⟨road-building *machines*⟩ or it may apply specifically to a conveyance and especially an automobile ⟨the term "*machine*" as used in the patent statute includes every mechanical device or combination of mechanical powers and devices to perform some function and produce a certain effect or result—*Toulmin*⟩ ⟨only an organism has its own internal purposes which belong to it intrinsically and . . . a *machine*, so far as we know, is merely an extension of the specific purpose of organisms, men—*La Barre*⟩ ⟨gears are modified simple *machines* such as the lever, pulley, wheel-and-axle, and inclined plane. They all serve to multiply force, change speed, or direction of motion and serve as connecting devices between driving units and driven mecha-

*Ana* analogous words      *Ant* antonyms      *Con* contrasted words      See also explanatory notes facing page 1

nisms—*Heitner*⟩ ⟨man uses *machines* to transform energy, transfer energy, multiply force, multiply speed, or change the direction of a force—*C. E. Dull, H. C. Metcalfe, & J. E. Williams*⟩ and *machine* is the only term of this group that is freely used collectively of machines as a class or abstractly of the technology and technological society associated with their use ⟨when I use the word *machines* hereafter I shall refer to specific objects like the printing press or the power loom. When I use the term "the *machine*" I shall employ it as a shorthand reference to the entire technological complex—*Mumford*⟩ ⟨the domination of our cultural and collective life by the *machine*—*Glicksberg*⟩ ⟨the liberty of choice allowed to the craftsman who worked by hand has almost vanished with the general use of the *machine*—*Dewey*⟩ **Mechanism** may come close to the basic sense of *machine* when it denotes an assemblage of working parts functioning together to produce an effect, but more often than not it applies to relatively simple straightforward mechanical linkages such as make up a complex machine; thus, a sewing *machine* is made up of several *mechanisms* (as one to advance the thread, another to convey the cloth, another to determine the length of the stitch, and still another to wind the bobbins) ⟨the real mechanic understands the construction of his machine; he knows the names and uses of the parts and the principles underlying the operation of the *mechanisms*—*Burghardt & Axelrod*⟩ ⟨the economic machine that provides for our everyday needs is so intricate that it is hard to see the purpose of particular cogs in its *mechanism*—*W. T. C. King*⟩ Sometimes, however, *mechanism* suggests not merely the physical parts but the various steps that lead to the final result of the process ⟨the propeller is the source of an intense sound but the exact *mechanism* by which this sound is produced is not clearly understood—*Armstrong*⟩ **Machinery** (see also EQUIPMENT) may apply to machines collectively ⟨the mill sold its old *machinery* and bought more efficient machines⟩ ⟨*machinery* for making shoes⟩ ⟨the term *machinery* is very much more comprehensive in scope than the word *machine*. . . . Unquestionably, the term is broad enough to include a number of machines and their connecting appurtenances which are operated as a unit for a given purpose—*U.S. Treasury Decisions*⟩ but it may also replace *mechanism* to denote an assemblage of working parts performing a function ⟨a strange, quiet boy, interested much less in booklearning than in what was to be learned from rusty automobiles on the junkheap or from the thousand *machineries* all around him—*Kerouac*⟩ ⟨men who are temperamentally unsuited to fiddling with the adjustment *machinery* put in the backs of most bow ties—*New Yorker*⟩ **Apparatus** (see also EQUIPMENT) basically denotes an assemblage of parts for attaining some end or doing some thing, but in itself it implies nothing about the complexity or simplicity, the efficiency or inefficiency, or the precision or crudity of the assemblage; thus, chimpanzees have been reported to put sticks together into a crude *apparatus* for reaching fruit that is beyond the reach of their hand ⟨modern heating and refrigerating *apparatuses* raise the temperature during the winter and lower it during the summer—*Carrel*⟩ ⟨the *apparatus* which took the photographs and reproduced them . . . are more sensitive and truthful than the human eye—*Day Lewis*⟩ *Engine* and *motor* in their basic relevant sense both denote a machine for converting energy (as heat, chemical, or nuclear energy) into mechanical force or motion, but in many situations they are not at all interchangeable, choice between them being firmly fixed by idiom. **Engine** is the more general term in

this relation and is applicable to such machines whether large or small, simple or complex ⟨an internal-combustion *engine*⟩ or it may apply both to a power-generating unit and a working unit that depends upon this ⟨these *engines* were built to pump out mines—*Kettering & Orth*⟩ and sometimes specifically designates certain automotive units (as a locomotive or fire engine) ⟨sent *engines*, hose carts, and ladder trucks to the fire⟩ ⟨a long freight train drawn by two *engines*⟩ From an earlier general use *engine* is still specifically applied to a few kinds of machines ⟨rose *engine*⟩ and it is the idiomatically appropriate term to designate the power plant of an aircraft ⟨with either turbojet or rocket *engines* these research airplanes would have sufficient power to permit the maximum speed aerodynamically possible—*Bonney*⟩ **Motor** is applicable to a small or light engine ⟨an outboard *motor*⟩ ⟨a spit worked by a small clockwork *motor*⟩ or to a gasoline or other internal-combustion engine; thus, one may speak of the *motor* or *engine* of an automobile; diesel *engines* or *motors* power many modern locomotives ⟨the finest machine in the world is useless without a *motor* to drive it—*Furnas*⟩ *Motor* is the specific term for a rotating machine that transforms electrical energy into mechanical energy ⟨household appliances run by electric *motors*⟩ ⟨a *motor* is a machine for transforming electrical energy into mechanical energy or power—*Cloud*⟩ Like *machine*, *motor* also applies specifically to an automotive vehicle (as an automobile or truck) ⟨we want a truck battalion of at least four companies. . . . The vehicles for this unit would be obtained by drawing on excess *motors* in various division units—*Combat Forces Jour.*⟩ ⟨the taxpayer did not then provide Ministers with carriages and coachmen as he now provides them with *motors* and chauffeurs—*Collis*⟩
*Ana* contrivance, *device, contraption, gadget: *implement, tool, instrument, utensil, appliance
**machinery** 1 *equipment, apparatus, paraphernalia, outfit, tackle, gear, matériel
*Ana* *mean, instrument, instrumentality, agency, medium, vehicle, organ, channel, agent: *machine, mechanism, apparatus, engine, motor: *device, contrivance, contraption, gadget: *implement, tool, instrument, utensil, appliance
2 *machine, mechanism, apparatus, engine, motor
**macrocosm** cosmos, universe, world, *earth
**mad** 1 *insane, crazy, crazed, demented, deranged, lunatic, maniac, non compos mentis
*Ana* frenzied, hysterical, delirious (see corresponding nouns at MANIA): *irrational, unreasonable
2 *angry, irate, wrathful, wroth, indignant, acrimonious
*Ana* maddened, incensed, infuriated, enraged (see ANGER *vb*): offended, outraged, affronted (see OFFEND)
**madden** *anger, incense, enrage, infuriate
*Ana* vex, *annoy, irk: exasperate, provoke, rile, aggravate, *irritate
*Con* *pacify, placate, mollify, appease, propitiate, conciliate: assuage, allay, mitigate, *relieve
**maelstrom** *eddy, whirlpool, vortex
**magazine** 1 *armory, arsenal
2 *journal, periodical, review, organ, newspaper
**magic** *n* **Magic, sorcery, witchcraft, witchery, wizardry, alchemy, thaumaturgy** are comparable rather than synonymous in their basic senses. In extended use they are sometimes employed indifferently without regard to the implications of their primary senses and with little distinction from the most inclusive term, *magic*, but all are capable of being used discriminatingly and with quite distinctive implications. **Magic** primarily denotes one of the arts or the body of arts whose practitioners claim supernatural

---

A colon (:) separates groups of words discriminated. An asterisk (*) indicates place of treatment of each group.

or occult powers (as in calling spirits to their assistance, in performing miracles, in divining the future, and in fixing the destinies of men). In extended use the word denotes a power or influence that produces effects akin to or suggestive of those of magic. Usually it stresses the power to call forth an image, an emotion, or a response from or as if from a void ⟨his *magic* was not far to seek—he was so human! . . . where'er he met a stranger, there he left a friend—*J. R. Lowell*⟩ ⟨the faint significance of words . . . for a common dullard, or their evocative *magic* for a Keats—*Montague*⟩ Less often it is applied to an art or an artist transcending the natural or explainable ⟨but Shakespeare's *magic* could not copied be; within that circle none durst walk but he—*Dryden*⟩ **Sorcery** is the form of magic practiced by those who use incantations and charms and cast spells in order to work their usually harmful ends. In extended use it is especially appropriate to suggest an attempt to overpower or enthrall by glamour or artful enchantment ⟨to fence my ear against thy *sorceries*—*Milton*⟩ ⟨the old evocative themes recur . . . and they are still touched with that verbal and metrical *sorcery* whose secret his younger contemporaries seem to have lost—*New Yorker*⟩ **Witchcraft, witchery,** and *wizardry* in their primary senses suggest powers derived from evil spirits or the use of human beings as the instruments for the accomplishment of Satanic ends, the only difference being that the first two are chiefly applied to the work of women, and the last to that of men. In extended use, however, they often vary in implications. **Witchcraft** is sometimes indistinguishable from *sorcery*, but it more often suggests guile rather than enchantment and wiles rather than spells ⟨there is something more than *witchcraft* in them [women], that masters even the wisest of us all—*Rowe*⟩ **Witchery,** on the other hand, occasionally implies either sorcery or guile ⟨thus has a bit of *witchery* crept into certain methods of plague control in the past—*Hubbs*⟩ but usually stresses a winning grace or an alluring loveliness ⟨the soft blue sky did never melt into his heart; he never felt the *witchery* of the soft blue sky!—*Wordsworth*⟩ ⟨the *witchery* of legend and romance—*Riker*⟩ **Wizardry** suggests a more virile and compelling power to enchant and usually connotes exceptional skill, talent, or creative power in the person who exerts such an influence ⟨that white-winged legion through whom we had plowed our way were not, could never be, to me just gulls . . .; there was the *wizardry* of my past wonder, the enchantment of romance—*Galsworthy*⟩ ⟨his playing had a grandeur that one often misses in the work of younger and more meticulous artists, and there were moments when his *wizardry* held me spellbound—*Sargeant*⟩ **Alchemy** is properly classed with *magic* only because its practitioners claimed mastery of secret forces in nature and the power to work such miracles as the changing of base into precious metals. In discriminative extended use, therefore, it implies transmutation or sometimes transfiguration ⟨gilding pale streams with heavenly *alchemy*—*Shak.*⟩ ⟨by happy *alchemy* of mind they turn to pleasure all they find—*Green*⟩ ⟨the vast majority of those who write verse are unendowed with the assimilating *alchemy* of genius—*Lowes*⟩ **Thaumaturgy** basically is applied to performing of miracles and wonders or to the art of wonder-workers (as conjurers or those who profess the power to work miracles) ⟨a world of miracles wherein all fabled or authentic *thaumaturgy* and feats of magic were outdone—*Carlyle*⟩ In extended use it is applied to what mystifies and dazzles or is designed to mislead or confuse.

**magisterial** authoritarian, *dictatorial, dogmatic, doctrinaire, oracular

*Ana* *masterful, domineering, imperious, imperative, peremptory: directing, controlling, conducting, managing (see CONDUCT *vb*)

**magnificent** imposing, stately, majestic, august, noble, grandiose, *grand
*Ana* *splendid, resplendent, glorious, sublime, superb: opulent, sumptuous, *luxurious: ostentatious, pretentious, *showy
*Ant* modest —*Con* *mean, abject, ignoble, sordid: trifling, trivial, *petty, paltry: *humble, meek, lowly

**magnify** *exalt, aggrandize
*Ana* extol, *praise, laud, acclaim, eulogize: enlarge, *increase, augment: *expand, amplify, distend, swell, inflate, dilate
*Ant* minimize, belittle —*Con* *decry, depreciate, detract, derogate: reduce, lessen, diminish, *decrease: *contract, shrink, deflate

**magniloquent** grandiloquent, aureate, flowery, *rhetorical, euphuistic, bombastic
*Ana* turgid, tumid, *inflated, flatulent: theatrical, histrionic, melodramatic, *dramatic

**magnitude** volume, *size, extent, dimensions, area
*Ana* amplitude, *expanse, stretch, spread: *bulk, mass, volume

**maiden** *adj* 1 *unmarried, single, celibate, virgin
*Ana* *youthful, virginal, juvenile
2 *youthful, juvenile, virgin, virginal, puerile, boyish
*Ant* experienced

**maim, cripple, mutilate, batter, mangle** are comparable when they mean to injure the body or an object so severely as to leave permanent or long-lasting effects. **Maim** implies the loss of a limb or member or the destruction of its usefulness usually through violence (as by war, accident, or the deliberate act of oneself or another) ⟨automobiles *maim* large numbers of persons every year⟩ ⟨maybe I wouldn't have to kill you . . . . I could just *maim* you —so you couldn't keep me from turning back—*Edison Marshall*⟩ ⟨seems to have been *maimed* psychologically by a brutal father—*N. Y. Times Book Rev.*⟩ **Cripple** (see also WEAKEN) is more restricted than *maim* because strictly it implies the loss of or serious impairment of the use of a leg or arm or part of one ⟨he is *crippled* as a result of an amputation following blood poisoning⟩ ⟨*crippled* by a congenital hip disease⟩ **Mutilate** (for specific sense of this word, see STERILIZE 1) implies the cutting off or removal of a part essential to completeness, not only of a person but also of a thing, and to his or its perfection, beauty, entirety, or fulfillment of function ⟨could make little manikins of their enemies and by *mutilating* these, inflict pains and ills on the persons they represented—*Cobban*⟩ ⟨windows . . . darkened by time and *mutilated* by willful injury—*Henry Adams*⟩ ⟨the last twelve pages of this codex have been *mutilated* by fire—*Modern Language Notes*⟩ *Batter* and *mangle* do not suggest loss of limb, member, or part, but they do suggest injuries which excessively disfigure the person or thing. **Batter** implies a pounding (literal or figurative) that bruises deeply, deforms, or mutilates ⟨he emerged from the fight *battered* and dazed⟩ ⟨the first time he made a helmet, he tested its capacity for resisting blows, and *battered* it out of shape—*Russell*⟩ ⟨so rough were the roads that we were *battered* and pitched about like cargoes in a heavy sea—*A. R. Williams*⟩ **Mangle,** on the other hand, implies a tearing or crushing and a covering (literally or figuratively) with deep wounds or lacerations ⟨*mangled* with ghastly wounds through plate and mail—*Milton*⟩ ⟨reckless people who have disregarded the warnings and been *mangled* by sharks—*Heiser*⟩
*Ana* mar, spoil, damage, *injure: *deface, disfigure

---

*Ana* analogous words     *Ant* antonyms     *Con* contrasted words     See also explanatory notes facing page 1

**main** *adj* principal, leading, *chief, foremost, capital
*Ana* cardinal, vital, *essential, fundamental: prime, *primary, primal
*Con* *subordinate, secondary, dependent, subject, collateral
**mainly** *largely, greatly, mostly, chiefly, principally, generally
**maintain,** assert, defend, vindicate, justify are comparable when they mean to uphold as true, right, just, valid, or worthy of notice or acceptance in the face of opposition or indifference. **Maintain** implies a firmness of conviction. When this implication is the only one, *maintain* usually means to argue in the spirit of one who does not admit any weakness in his contention ⟨the artisan, for example, ranks no doubt lower than the professional man; but no one *maintains* that he is a different kind of being—*Dickinson*⟩ ⟨there is . . . a Philosophic Doctrine—. . . I know that many serious people believe it—which *maintains* that all men, in spite of appearances and pretensions . . . live alike for pleasure—*L. P. Smith*⟩ Often, however, the term additionally implies persistency or insistency in upholding in defiance of all opposition ⟨before this court ought to intervene the case should be of serious magnitude clearly and fully proved, and the principle to be applied should be one which the court is prepared deliberately to *maintain* against all considerations on the other side—*Justice Holmes*⟩ **Assert** (see also ASSERT 1) so strongly implies a determination to make others accept or recognize what one puts forward as the truth, or as a claim, or as a right, that it often suggests aggressiveness or obtrusiveness ⟨the provision of the constitution never has been understood to embrace other contracts, than those which . . . confer rights which may be *asserted* in a court of justice —*John Marshall*⟩ But *assert* does not always imply the use of argument to force conviction or recognition ⟨anyone . . . can feel the sustained dignity of the sculptor's work, which is *asserted* with all the emphasis he could put into it—*Henry Adams*⟩ ⟨on the whole New Zealand was lavish with money and attention, and used force only to *assert* her sovereignty—*Heiser*⟩ **Defend** implies a maintaining in the face of attack with the intention of demonstrating the truth, rightness, or propriety of what is questioned; thus, one *defends* a thesis who, as a candidate for a degree, submits himself to examiners who assail the weak or dubious points of his argument ⟨the independence of the Supreme Court of the United States should be *defended* at all costs—*Lippmann*⟩ *Defend*, in this sense, does not imply, as it so often implies in its more common sense (see DEFEND 1), that the defender is in a weak or dubious position; however it seldom suggests as much aggressiveness as does *assert* and often connotes the aim of an apologist ⟨I have not adopted my faith in order to *defend* my views of conduct—*T. S. Eliot*⟩ **Vindicate** (see also EXCULPATE) implies an attempt, usually a successful attempt, at defense or assertion. It presupposes that whatever is being defended or asserted has been or is capable of being challenged, questioned, denied, or contemned. When the emphasis is on defense, then argument or something which has the force of argument is usually implied, and an aim not only to make one's point but to confute and confound one's opponents is often connoted ⟨writers who *vindicated* our hereditary House of Lords against a certain Parliament Act—*Quiller-Couch*⟩ ⟨the view of the informed and disinterested men turned out to be almost completely wrong, while the relatively uninformed . . . were *vindicated* on all counts—*Rovere*⟩ When the emphasis is upon assertion, *vindicate* usually implies an effort to resist triumphantly the force of encroachment or interference or to overwhelm those who deny or doubt, not so much by argument as by appropriate action ⟨arise, and *vindicate* Thy Glory; free thy people from their yoke!—*Milton*⟩ ⟨what was it that stood in his way? His unfortunate timidity! He wished to *vindicate* himself in some way, to assert his manhood—*Joyce*⟩ **Justify** (see also EXPLAIN 2, JUSTIFY 3) implies that the thing concerned can no longer be opposed or ignored because it has been conclusively shown to be true, valid, or proper by irrefutable arguments or on inescapable grounds, such as its consequences or its successful operation ⟨if the Germans are to *justify* the high claims they make for Lessing as a critic, they must rest them on other grounds than his intellectual originality—*Babbitt*⟩ ⟨fate persists in *justifying* the harsh generalizations of Puritan morals—*Bennett*⟩ ⟨it isn't by the materials you use that your claim to originality will stand *justified* or condemned; it is solely by the thing you do with them—*Lowes*⟩
*Ana* affirm, aver, protest, avow, declare, profess, avouch (see ASSERT): *contend, fight, battle, war: persist, *persevere
*Con* oppose, combat, *resist, withstand, fight: *deny, gainsay, contradict, traverse
**maintenance** sustenance, support, *living, livelihood, subsistence, keep, bread
**majestic** stately, august, noble, magnificent, imposing, *grand, grandiose
*Ana* lofty, *high: sublime, superb, glorious, *splendid, resplendent: monumental, tremendous (see MONSTROUS): *exceptional
*Con* *mean, abject, sordid, ignoble: lowly, *humble, modest, meek: ordinary, *common
**majority,** plurality are arbitrarily defined in the United States, especially by statute, when they refer to an excess of votes as determining an election. Both imply an excess of votes over the next highest candidate. The distinction between the two words applies when there are three or more candidates; then the person who is elected by a **majority** has more votes than the other candidates combined, that is, his vote is in excess of half of the total number of votes cast, and his *majority* is the number of votes cast for him in excess of one half of the total number of votes. A person is elected by a **plurality** when he has more votes than any other candidate, whether he has a *majority* of the total or not. Thus, if a total of 290,000 votes are cast in an election contested by three candidates, with candidate A polling 200,000 votes, candidate B polling 75,000, and candidate C polling 15,000, candidate A wins the election by a *majority* of 55,000, and by a *plurality* of 125,000 over candidate B, and by a *plurality* of 185,000 over candidate C. Sometimes, where the successful candidate has a vote that exceeds the total of votes cast for all opposing candidates, the term *plurality* is applied to this excess; thus, in the example given, while candidate A's *majority* is 55,000, his *plurality* over candidates B and C together is 110,000.
**make** *vb* Make, form, shape, fashion, fabricate, manufacture, forge can all mean to cause something to come into being or existence. This is the underlying meaning of **make**, the most general and the most widely applicable of these terms. *Make* may imply the operation either of an intelligent agent or of a blind agency, and either material or immaterial existence ⟨*make* a chair⟩ ⟨*make* a poem⟩ ⟨*make* a choice⟩ ⟨this factory *makes* bicycles⟩ ⟨he is unable to *make* friends⟩ ⟨God *made* the world⟩ ⟨the spider *makes* webs⟩ ⟨the liver *makes* bile⟩ **Form** adds to *make* the implication that the thing brought into being has a definite outline, design, or structure ⟨a sculptor who *forms* hands with exquisite delicacy⟩ ⟨we are ready to *form* a plan⟩ ⟨*form* a federation of states⟩ ⟨character

A colon (:) separates groups of words discriminated. An asterisk (*) indicates place of treatment of each group.

is partly *formed* by training⟩ **Shape,** though often interchangeable with *form,* is much more restricted in its application because it characteristically connotes an external agent that physically or figuratively impresses a particular form upon something (as by molding, beating, carving, or cutting) ⟨the blacksmith *shapes* a horseshoe on his anvil⟩ ⟨*shape* a hat on a block⟩ ⟨events that *shaped* his career⟩ ⟨every life is a work of art *shaped* by the man who lives it—*Dickinson*⟩ **Fashion** means to form, but it implies an intelligent and sometimes a purposeful agency and more or less inventive power or ingenuity ⟨he *fashioned* a lamp out of an old churn⟩ ⟨legislative committees often *fashion* strange bills out of miscellaneous suggestions⟩ ⟨intelligent creatures, *fashioned* by the hand and in the image of an all-wise God—*Hambly*⟩ **Fabricate** stresses a making that unites many parts or materials into a whole ⟨Dr. Hitchings and his associates alone have *fabricated* more than 500 compounds resembling one or another of the simpler chemicals out of which D. N. A. (an enormously complex substance) is fashioned in the cell—*Engel*⟩ and it usually connotes either a making according to a standardized pattern ⟨*fabricate* doors, windows, and other parts of a house⟩ or skillfulness in construction ⟨*fabricate* a good plot for a novel⟩ ⟨*fabricated* a creed fitted to meet the sordid misery of real human life—*Woolf*⟩ Very commonly *fabricate* implies an imaginative making or inventing of something false ⟨the particulars of that genealogy, embellished with every detail that memory had handed down or fancy *fabricated*—*Stevenson*⟩ ⟨his feats of legerdemain sounded so improbable that many people considered his experiences *fabricated*—*Heiser*⟩ **Manufacture** emphasizes the making of something by labor, originally by hand but now more often by machinery. The term is applied to a making in which raw materials are used and a definite process or series of processes is followed ⟨*manufacture* cloth⟩ ⟨*manufacture* kitchen utensils⟩ ⟨*manufacture* automobiles⟩ In extended use *manufacture* often is preferred to the preceding words when laboriousness or the knowledge of the mechanics of a process, rather than skill or ingenuity, is connoted ⟨*manufacture* paintings by the dozen⟩ ⟨the strain of *manufacturing* conversation for at least ten minutes—*Fienburgh*⟩ **Forge** basically suggests the operation of a smith who heats metal and beats or hammers it into shape ⟨*forge* a horseshoe⟩ ⟨*forge* a chain⟩ In its extended sense it carries a strong implication of devising or concocting by physical or mental effort so as to give the appearance of truth or reality ⟨the proud have *forged* a lie against me: but I will keep thy precepts with my whole heart—*Ps* 119:69⟩ ⟨whate'er I *forge* to feed his brainsick fits, do you uphold and maintain in your speeches—*Shak.*⟩ ⟨however feeling may render plastic the stuff of poetry, the poem, if it be worthy of the name, is *forged* in the brain—*Lowes*⟩ In specific use, both legal and ordinary, *forge* implies the making of a counterfeit, especially by imitating the handwriting of an original or of a supposed maker; thus, one *forges* a document, such as a will, deed, or check, by making or signing it in imitation of another's handwriting or by making alterations in a genuine document by the same means.
*Ana* produce, turn out, yield, *bear: accomplish, achieve, effect, fulfill (see PERFORM)
**make-believe** *pretense, pretension
**maker** *n* Maker, creator, author denote one who brings something into being or existence. When written with an initial capital letter, all three terms designate God or the Supreme Being; without the capital they ascribe similar but not equivalent powers or effects to a person. **Maker** typically implies a close and immediate relationship

between the one who makes and the thing that is made. It implies the physical or figurative handling of material and individual or personal responsibility for what is turned out; hence, in religious use (as in hymns and prayers) God is usually called one's *Maker* ⟨every soul, insisted Luther, stands in naked confrontation before its *Maker*—*Bainton*⟩ *Maker* in such terms as king*maker,* a *maker* of men, a *maker* of phrases, a *maker* of poems, suggests the use of persons, words, or ideas as instruments by which one brings something into existence through one's own labor or effort ⟨in every creative writer there is a touch of the poet, the *maker,* even if his medium is prose—*Forster*⟩ **Creator,** on the other hand, seldom suggests either literal or figurative use or handling of materials; its leading implication is that of bringing into existence what the mind conceives and the will, as the mind's instrument, carries out. As applied to God, the term usually evokes the picture of Creation as presented in Genesis; the term is used, therefore, rather than *Maker,* when His omnipotence and the greatness of His works are stressed ⟨and touched their golden harps, and hymning praised God and his works; *Creator* him they sung—*Milton*⟩ In the same way *creator* is used of a man who brings into being something new, which has form in his mind or imagination before he gives it objective existence ⟨a conservator, call me, if you please, not a *creator* nor destroyer—*Browning*⟩ ⟨they are genuine *creators:* they do not describe nor interpret reality as much as construct it —*Howard Moss*⟩ **Author** is applied to one who originates and who, therefore, is not only the source, or ultimate source, but the one responsible for a person's or thing's existence. It is applied to God chiefly in the phrase "the *Author* of one's being" when the reference is to the gift of life or its attendant circumstances ⟨then casting up my eyes, thanked the *Author* of my being for the gift of that wild forest, those green mansions where I had found so great a happiness—*Hudson*⟩ In reference to persons it is not only applied to a writer (see WRITER) but also to one (as a founder, an inventor, or an initiator) who brings something into existence ⟨the policy of which he was principally the *author*—*Belloc*⟩ ⟨the gay and bewitching . . . coquette Célimène who is the *author* of all Alceste's woes—*Alexander*⟩
**makeshift** shift, expedient, *resource, resort, stopgap, substitute, surrogate
*Ana* *device, contrivance, contraption, gadget: *mean, instrument, agency, instrumentality
**maladroit** clumsy, gauche, inept, *awkward
*Ant* adroit —*Con* *dexterous, deft, handy: *clever, cunning, ingenious: skilled, skillful, expert, adept, masterly, *proficient: politic, diplomatic, bland, smooth (see SUAVE)
**malady** ailment, disorder, condition, affection, *disease, complaint, distemper, syndrome
**male** *adj* Male, masculine, manly, manlike, mannish, manful, virile are comparable when meaning of, characteristic of, or like a male, especially of the human species. **Male** (opposed to *female*) applies to animals and plants as well as to human beings and stresses the fact of sex ⟨a *male* tiger⟩ ⟨a *male* willow tree⟩ ⟨*male* children⟩ ⟨a *male* choir⟩ **Masculine** (opposed to *feminine*) alone of these words may imply grammatical gender ⟨*masculine* nouns and pronouns⟩ but it characteristically applies to features, attributes, or qualities which belong to men rather than to women ⟨he was a big, active, *masculine* creature—*Deland*⟩ ⟨the *masculine* character lying behind the lofty idealism of Sung painting—*Binyon*⟩ ⟨his poetry is *masculine,* plain, concentrated, and energetic—*Landor*⟩ ⟨it's a *masculine* sort of town . . . with solidity rather than

style, dignity rather than sparkle, graciousness rather than grace—*Joseph*⟩ *Masculine* is sometimes interchangeable with *male* ⟨the *masculine* part of the audience⟩ ⟨although this is largely a *masculine* disease, about 5 per cent of the patients are women—*Fishbein*⟩ **Manly** (often opposed to *boyish* or, from another point of view, to *womanly*) is used to qualify whatever evidences the qualities of a fully developed man ⟨*manly* virtues⟩ It often specifically suggests the finer qualities of a man (as courage, frankness, and independence) or the physical characters and skills which come with maturity; it is applicable not only to men but to boys ⟨his big *manly* voice, turning again toward childish treble—*Shak.*⟩ ⟨what more *manly* exercise than hunting?—*Walton*⟩ ⟨it was amusing to watch the *manly* coolness with which the announcement was taken—*Meredith*⟩ **Manlike** (often opposed to *womanlike*) is more apt to suggest characteristically masculine qualities or, especially, foibles ⟨*manlike* bluntness⟩ ⟨from long association with men she had learnt a *manlike* reticence—*H. S. Scott*⟩ Often *manlike* suggests reference to man in the more general sense of the word and therefore means little more than human or like human beings ⟨there were a dozen or more of the hairy *manlike* creatures upon the ground—*Blue Book*⟩ **Mannish** (often contrasted with *womanish* or *effeminate*) applies chiefly to women or their dress, gait, and manners, when they suggest masculinity rather than femininity ⟨a woman impudent and *mannish* grown—*Shak.*⟩ ⟨a *mannish* costume⟩ ⟨those who dislike . . . *mannish* headgear, might try his simple but feminine small hats—*Lois Long*⟩ **Manful** differs from *manly* chiefly in its greater stress on sturdiness and resoluteness ⟨a *manful* effort to gain self-control⟩ ⟨his life has been one *manful* struggle against poverty—*Trollope*⟩ **Virile** (a stronger word than *masculine* and opposed to *puerile* or, in specific sense, to *impotent*) suggests such qualities of fully developed manhood as aggressiveness, masterfulness, forcefulness, and in a specific sense, procreativeness. It differs from *manly* and *manful* in being applied only to mature men ⟨*virile* controversialists—*Inge*⟩ ⟨a *virile* style⟩ ⟨ye chiefly, *virile* both to think and feel, deep-chested Chapman and firm-footed Ben—*J. R. Lowell*⟩ ⟨the *virile* story of a little man, his big wife, and his bigger bull—*Atlantic*⟩
*Ant* female —*Con* feminine, womanly, womanlike, womanish, ladylike (see FEMALE)
**malediction** *curse, imprecation, anathema
*Ant* benediction
**malefactor** *criminal, felon, convict, culprit, delinquent
*Ana* miscreant, scoundrel, *villain, blackguard
*Ant* benefactor: well-doer
**malefic, maleficent** malign, baleful, *sinister
**malevolence** ill will, malignity, malignancy, *malice, spite, despite, spleen, grudge
*Ana* animosity, rancor, animus, antipathy, antagonism, *enmity, hostility: hate, hatred, detestation, abhorrence, abomination (see under HATE vb)
*Ant* benevolence —*Con* benignity, benignancy, kindliness, kindness (see corresponding adjectives at KIND)
**malevolent** malignant, malign, *malicious, spiteful
*Ana* *sinister, baleful, malign, malefic, maleficent
*Ant* benevolent —*Con* benign, benignant, *kind, kindly: *charitable, humane, altruistic, humanitarian, philanthropic, eleemosynary
**malice, ill will, malevolence, spite, despite, malignity, malignancy, spleen, grudge** denote a feeling or a state of mind which leads one to desire that another or others should suffer pain or injury. **Malice** usually implies a deep-seated and, often, an unjustified or unexplainable desire; it frequently carries an implication of an innate pleasure in

doing evil, in inflicting injury, in seeing others suffer, or in wanton destruction ⟨with *malice* toward none; with charity for all . . . let us . . . bind up the nation's wounds—*Lincoln*⟩ ⟨there are people in the world with that degree of . . . *malice* in them that they can't bear to allow a good man his merits—*Shaw*⟩ ⟨man, with his usual monkey-like *malice*, took pleasure in pulling down what he had built up—*Henry Adams*⟩ ⟨argues that Dreyfus' court-martial and imprisonment . . . were mostly a tragedy of honest errors, not a conspiracy of racial *malice*—*Time*⟩ Often, however, it may imply mischievousness or impishness rather than a hardened, vindictive nature ⟨she was clever, witty, brilliant, and sparkling beyond most of her kind; but possessed of many devils of *malice* and mischievousness—*Kipling*⟩ ⟨we get far too little good conversation and artistic *malice* in life or art—*Coxe*⟩ In law *malice* applies to the state of mind of one who willfully commits wrong, whether in full deliberation ⟨*malice* aforethought⟩ or out of hatred and a desire to inflict injury on another ⟨*malice* in fact⟩ or out of the depravity of his nature ⟨implied *malice*⟩ **Ill will** and **malevolence** both imply an unfriendly attitude or state of mind that is rarely without some basis, real or fancied, and that need not, as *malice* so often does, lead to overt action. **Ill will** applies to an attitude or state that is definite but measured and rarely involves any marked upheaval of mind ⟨proposal to defend Formosa for Chiang and invite the *ill will* of all the rest of Asia—*Progressive*⟩ ⟨could not believe it possible that any injury or any misfortune could provoke such *ill will* against a person not connected, or, at least, not supposed to be connected with it—*Austen*⟩ **Malevolence** applies primarily to a bitter and rancorous ill will that affects the whole outlook of one possessed by it and that is both more persistent and more likely to seek outlet in malicious conduct than is ill will ⟨their society is organized by a permanent, universal animosity and *malevolence;* sullen suspicion and resentment are their chief motives—*Muller*⟩ ⟨the frigid *malevolence* with which Wilson denied this strong man's plea, made in what Wilson, being sensitive and wise, knew was excruciating abasement—*White*⟩ **Spite** suggests petty ill will and mean envy and resentment that often manifests itself in trivial harassments ⟨a man full of the secret *spite* of dullness, who interrupted from time to time, and always to check or disorder thought—*Yeats*⟩ ⟨it is, indeed, a little shabby, a little insignificant: not really hate at all, but *spite*—*Day Lewis*⟩ **Despite** (see also under DESPISE) in this sense is a rather uncommon or literary term that may imply more pride and disdain and less pettiness than *spite* ⟨not in *despite* but softly, as men smile about the dead—*Chesterton*⟩ ⟨if you will imagine a glint of moonlight running up the blade of a rapier, you may know the chill flame of spite and *despite* that bickered in her eyes then as she spoke—*Quiller-Couch*⟩ **Malignity** and **malignancy** imply deep passion and relentless driving force ⟨he is cruel with the cruelty of petrified feeling, to his poor heroine; he pursues her without pity or pause, as with *malignity*—*Arnold*⟩ ⟨blinded by *malignancy* against the class of manual worker—*Sprigge*⟩ **Spleen** implies deep-seated rancor combined with bad temper; it usually suggests wrathful release of latent spite or persistent malice and the wish to harm ⟨his countrymen vented their *spleen* at his failure . . . by sending the unfortunate naval commander into exile—*Toynbee*⟩ ⟨his just fame was long obscured by partisan *spleen*—*Parrington*⟩ **Grudge** applies to cherished ill will against an individual which seeks satisfaction; it usually suggests deep resentment for some real or fancied slight or affront and, often, a determination to get even ⟨I will feed fat the ancient *grudge* I bear him—*Shak.*⟩

⟨this same inveterate *grudge*—*Hawthorne*⟩ ⟨buried at the root of the relations between the sisters was Sophia's *grudge* against Constance for refusing to leave the Square —*Bennett*⟩ ⟨he held no *grudge* against any of the people who had misused him—*Cather*⟩ *Ana* maliciousness, spitefulness (see corresponding adjectives at MALICIOUS): venom, bane, *poison: animosity, animus, rancor, antipathy, *enmity *Ant* charity —*Con* *mercy, grace, clemency, lenity: benignity, benignancy, kindness, kindliness (see corresponding adjectives at KIND)

**malicious,** malevolent, malignant, malign, spiteful are comparable when they mean disposed to do or to inflict evil or resulting from a disposition to do or to inflict evil. A person or thing is **malicious** that is motivated or dictated by hatred or spite and, usually, by a desire to inflict injury and suffering or to see another in disgrace or an object of ridicule or contempt ⟨episodes . . . when they create a scandal, they are hushed as much as possible, so as not to offend chaste ears and rejoice *malicious* ones —*Guérard*⟩ ⟨criticism based on guesswork and even on *malicious* falsification of fact—*Roosevelt*⟩ ⟨took a *malicious* pleasure in emphasizing this point and in watching me wince—*Kipling*⟩ A person or thing is **malevolent** that evidences ill will or an intent to do evil, or a sinister influence ⟨Captain Tilney must have heard some *malevolent* misrepresentation of her—*Austen*⟩ ⟨there is no free breath to be drawn within the sphere of so *malevolent* an influence—*Hawthorne*⟩ ⟨the medicine man . . . can be *malevolent* as well as benevolent. If he desires the death of enemies he calls his spirits and bids them to harm the object of his hatred—*Corlett*⟩ A person or thing is **malignant** that is actuated or characterized by virulent ill will or extreme malevolence ⟨tested in the crucible of a *malignant* marriage—*Hewes*⟩ ⟨a great temptation to . . . insist that the lack of relation between what happens and what is supposed to happen is due to some spell or enchantment laid by a *malignant* magician—*Muggeridge*⟩ ⟨his cold, *malignant* rage—*L. P. Smith*⟩ A person or thing is **malign** (see also SINISTER) that harbors violent enmity or ill will or threatens extreme evil or danger; the term, in contrast with *malignant*, carries a stronger implication of potentiality and therefore need not suggest certainty of effect ⟨a soul that spurns the crowd's *malign* control—*Gifford*⟩ ⟨by fiends of aspect more *malign*—*Wordsworth*⟩ **Spiteful** implies a deep-seated malice or malevolence provoked especially by a desire to get even with others for real or fancied offenses; it suggests meanness or venomousness of temper and refers more often to utterances than to acts ⟨*spiteful* gossip⟩ ⟨she has a *spiteful* tongue⟩ ⟨a *spiteful* saying gratifies so many little passions—*Addison*⟩ ⟨"Well," said Mr. Potter, who was not *spiteful* to his children, and preferred his wife unruffled, "We'll let you off this time"— *Rose Macaulay*⟩ *Ana* *poisonous, venomous, virulent, toxic: *pernicious, noxious, baneful, deleterious, detrimental: *envious, jealous: wanton, gratuitous, uncalled-for, *supererogatory

**malign** *adj* 1 malignant, *malicious, malevolent, spiteful *Ana* inimical, hostile, rancorous, antipathetic, antagonistic (see corresponding nouns at ENMITY): venomous, virulent, *poisonous, toxic *Ant* benign —*Con* benignant, kindly, *kind
2 *sinister, baleful, malefic, maleficent *Ana* threatening, menacing (see THREATEN): baneful, noxious, *pernicious, deleterious: disastrous, catastrophic, cataclysmic, calamitous (see corresponding nouns at DISASTER) *Ant* benign —*Con* *favorable, auspicious, propitious: fortunate, *lucky, providential, happy

**malign** *vb* Malign, traduce, asperse, vilify, calumniate, defame, slander, libel mean to speak evil of for the purpose of injuring and without regard for the truth. **Malign** and **traduce** usually imply persecution; they commonly suggest such a blinding passion as hatred, violent prejudice, or bigotry as the motive. **Malign**, however, although it carries the implication that the person, group, or race affected is the victim of lies, does not necessarily impute deliberate lying to the speaker or writer ⟨the most *maligned* race in history⟩ ⟨gossips had *maligned* the lady— *Meredith*⟩ ⟨whether Richard III has been *maligned* by his earlier biographers or not is still an open question⟩ ⟨other British historians have *maligned* Ward in order to build up the fame of "Chinese" Gordon—*Richard Watts*⟩ **Traduce** carries these implications also, but it stresses the resulting ignominy more than *malign* ⟨if I am *traduced* by ignorant tongues . . . 'tis but the fate of place and the rough brake that virtue must go through—*Shak.*⟩ ⟨political bias or society scandalmongers fastened on them and *traduced* them and made them notorious—*Gore*⟩ ⟨a bank-owned newspaper which . . . *traduced* the members of its adversary faction in the town—*White*⟩ **Asperse** and **vilify** both imply efforts to destroy a person's good name or reputation. **Asperse** suggests an intent to detract from one's reputation or to lower one in popular esteem by direct accusations or, more often, by such subtler methods as innuendo or spreading false reports ⟨there were foul tongues to *asperse* a Douglas—*Scott*⟩ ⟨found their characters assailed and their motives *aspersed*—*Parrington*⟩ ⟨he neither *aspersed* men's idealisms nor sniffed at their aspirations—*Kronenberger*⟩ **Vilify** implies open methods and an intent to blacken one's good name and to make it vile and shameful; it usually suggests direct accusation coupled with violent abuse and scurrilous name-calling ⟨with a malignant insanity, we oppose the measures, and ungratefully *vilify* the persons, of those whose sole object is our own peace and prosperity—*Burke*⟩ ⟨the soldier of today . . . should not be blamed for falling back. He should be shot or hanged afterward . . . but he should not be *vilified* in newspapers—*Kipling*⟩ **Calumniate** imputes malice to the speaker or writer and falsity to his aspersions or accusations ⟨*calumniating* and ridiculing the Church which he had deserted—*Macaulay*⟩ and often implies that the false and malicious statements have seriously damaged the good name of the victim ⟨the verdict of history is that Benedict Arnold was not *calumniated,* but was justly charged with treason⟩ **Defame, slander,** and **libel** are found both in general and in legal use, but their strict legal definitions are more or less affecting their literary meanings. All imply calumniation, but they differ from *calumniate* mainly in their emphasis on the positive damaging effect of the lies. **Defame,** both in legal and in literary use, suggests an actual injury to one's good name or a definite loss of repute or reputation ⟨*defaming* and defacing, till she left not even Lancelot brave nor Galahad clean— *Tennyson*⟩ ⟨Captain Basil Hall . . . was publicly accused of being an agent of the British government on a special mission to blacken and *defame* this country—*Brooks*⟩ To **slander,** in legal use, is to defame orally; in general use it covers both written and printed as well as oral calumniation. It also, more strongly than *defame* or *calumniate,* connotes positive suffering on the part of the victim ⟨*slandered* to death by villains, that dare as well answer a man indeed as I dare take a serpent by the tongue—*Shak.*⟩ ⟨he was to be imprisoned again, his friends were to betray him, his name was to be *slandered*—*Woodham-Smith*⟩ **Libel** (compare LIBEL *n*) is chiefly a legal term; in general use its implications are much the same. It implies the printing or writing of something that defames a person

or his reputation and the publication or circulation of such printed or written matter ⟨it is dangerous for a careless or malicious newspaper to *libel* individuals—*Time*⟩ ⟨the month in which William Prynne was branded for *libeling* the bishops—*Times Lit. Sup.*⟩
*Ana* detract, *decry, disparage, depreciate, derogate: vituperate, revile (see SCOLD): defile, pollute (see CONTAMINATE)
*Ant* defend —*Con* vindicate, justify, *maintain: extol, eulogize, *praise
**malignancy** 1 malignity, *malice, ill will, malevolence, spite, despite, spleen, grudge
*Ant & Con* see those at MALIGNITY
2 *tumor, neoplasm, cancer
**malignant** malign, malevolent, *malicious, spiteful
*Ana* virulent, venomous (see POISONOUS): *envious, jealous: baneful, noxious, *pernicious: diabolical, devilish, *fiendish
*Ant* benignant —*Con* benign, *kind, kindly: benevolent, *charitable, altruistic, humane
**malignity** malignancy, *malice, ill will, malevolence, spite, despite, spleen, grudge
*Ana* rancor, animus, animosity, *enmity, hostility: malignancy, maliciousness, spitefulness (see corresponding adjectives at MALICIOUS): hatred, *hate: vindictiveness, revengefulness, vengefulness (see corresponding adjectives at VINDICTIVE)
*Ant* benignity —*Con* benignancy, kindliness, kindness (see corresponding adjectives at KIND)
**malinger** *dodge, parry, sidestep, duck, shirk, fence
*Ana* evade, avoid, elude, *escape, shun
**malleable** *plastic, pliable, pliant, ductile, adaptable
*Ana* tractable, amenable (see OBEDIENT)
*Ant* refractory —*Con* intractable, recalcitrant, ungovernable, *unruly
**malodorous**, stinking, fetid, noisome, putrid, rank, rancid, fusty, musty mean having an unpleasant smell. **Malodorous** is the general term which is referable to any smell of this character, from one that is noticeably unpleasant to one that is distinctly offensive ⟨*malodorous* flowers⟩ ⟨the flavor . . . like that of many *malodorous* cheeses, is delicate—*Rawlings*⟩ **Stinking**, the familiar term, and **fetid**, the literary or technical term, describe an odor or a thing that emits an odor which is peculiarly offensive; the former more obviously suggests disgusting foulness than the latter ⟨a *stinking* dungeon⟩ ⟨a *stinking* outhouse⟩ ⟨the cave . . . was indescribably foul and *stinking*—*Barbour*⟩ ⟨exploded *stinking* flashlight powder in enclosed rooms—*Mott*⟩ ⟨a *fetid* weed⟩ ⟨he detected at once a *fetid* odor, not very strong but highly disagreeable—*Cather*⟩ **Noisome** is applicable chiefly to what emits a poisonously or unwholesomely offensive odor ⟨four sewers emptied into these twenty-five acres of swamp and morass—stagnant, *noisome*, and crawling with huge snakes—*Heiser*⟩ **Putrid** is applicable primarily to organic matter in such a state of decomposition that it is loathsomely malodorous ⟨a bloated, *putrid*, noisome carcass—*Burke*⟩ ⟨the whole was *putrid* with fish corpses—*Semon*⟩ **Rank** (see also RANK 1; FLAGRANT) applies to an odor or to a thing which emits an odor that is exceedingly strong and unpleasing yet not necessarily loathsome ⟨the *rank* smell of a sunflower⟩ ⟨O, my offence is *rank*, it smells to heaven—*Shak.*⟩ ⟨wreathed in smoke from a *rank* cigar—*Ralph Watson*⟩ **Rancid** usually suggests an offensive taste as well as an offensive smell that is indicative of a loss of freshness; it is used especially of fatty substances (as oil or butter) that have undergone a chemical change or decomposition ⟨*rancid* bacon⟩ **Fusty** and *musty* both suggest lack of ventilation and sunlight, but of the two

words **fusty** carries the stronger implication of age and prolonged uncleanliness or an accumulation of dust and dirt, and **musty**, the stronger implication of moldiness or of the effects of darkness or dampness ⟨the ill-ventilated schoolroom full of boys smelled . . . *fusty*—*Ellis*⟩ ⟨the department had moved from its *fusty* old headquarters . . . to a shiny new home—*Time*⟩ ⟨the *musty* odor of a damp cellar⟩ ⟨there was an acrid, *musty* smell; the raw air was close with breathing—*Rose Macaulay*⟩
*Ant* odorous —*Con* fragrant, aromatic, redolent (see ODOROUS)
**maltreat** mistreat, ill-treat, misuse, *abuse, outrage
*Ana* see those at ILL-TREAT
**mammoth** *huge, vast, immense, enormous, elephantine, giant, gigantic, gigantean, colossal, gargantuan, Herculean, cyclopean, titanic, Brobdingnagian
*Ana* *monstrous, monumental, stupendous, tremendous, prodigious: ponderous, weighty, cumbrous, cumbersome (see HEAVY)
**manacle** *vb* *hamper, trammel, clog, fetter, shackle, hog-tie
*Ana* *hinder, impede, obstruct, bar, block: *tie, bind: *restrain, inhibit, curb, check
**manage** *conduct, control, direct
*Ana* *govern, rule: *guide, lead, steer, pilot, engineer: *handle, manipulate, wield, swing, ply
**mandate** *n* 1 dictate, *command, order, injunction, bidding, behest
*Ana* charging *or* charge, direction, instruction (see corresponding verbs at COMMAND): sanctioning *or* sanction, endorsement, approval (see corresponding verbs at APPROVE)
2 **Mandate, initiative, referendum, plebiscite** are comparable when meaning a political action or procedure whereby a constituency instructs or gives information of its desires to its legislature or legislators. **Mandate**, the most general of these terms, applies to instruction delivered by the people (as by a general vote or by a choice in an election) that makes their wishes clear not only to their representatives in a legislature but also to those who hold the executive power, or, in an extended sense, to those who represent them in any way or who by the nature of their office or duties are necessarily responsive to the will of the people ⟨the president of the United States, reelected by an enormous majority, declared that he had a *mandate* from the people to continue his policies⟩ **Initiative** often denotes a right, but when it denotes a procedure, it implies recognition of the right of a group of voters or, more often, of a clearly defined number of voters, to propose a new measure or a constitutional amendment to a legislature ⟨the *initiative*, both as a right and as a procedure, is legally recognized in many of the states of the United States of America⟩ **Referendum** applies to the practice, adopted by some states and cities in the United States, of sending measures that have been considered by or proposed to the legislative body to the voters for approval or rejection or for an expression of their wishes. **Plebiscite** basically applies to a vote of the people usually by universal suffrage on some measure submitted to them by the group or the body having the initiative. Sometimes *plebiscite* implies a vote of the population of a territorial unit that testifies to their wishes especially as to the form of government they will accept, or their choice in a proposed merger with either of two nations.
**maneuver** *n* stratagem, *trick, ruse, gambit, ploy, artifice, wile, feint
*Ana* *device, contrivance: expedient, resort, *resource, shift, makeshift: intrigue, machination, *plot
**manful** virile, mannish, manlike, manly, masculine, *male

---

A colon (:) separates groups of words discriminated. An asterisk (*) indicates place of treatment of each group.

*Ana* sturdy, stout, tenacious, stalwart, tough, \*strong: resolute, steadfast, staunch (see FAITHFUL): intrepid, bold, \*brave

**mangle** batter, mutilate, \*maim, cripple
*Ana* \*injure, damage, mar, impair: \*deface, disfigure: \*deform, contort, distort

**mania** 1 \*insanity, lunacy, psychosis, dementia
*Ana* alienation, derangement, \*aberration
*Ant* lucidity
2 **Mania, delirium, frenzy, hysteria** are comparable when they mean a state of mind in which there is loss of control over emotional, nervous, or mental processes. **Mania** (see also INSANITY) definitely implies madness or insanity; the term may designate a type of madness in which the patient manifests extreme excitability or, more precisely, the phase of manic-depressive insanity in which the patient loses control over his powers of thought, of speech, and of movement through violent excitement or excessive emotion ⟨[George III] suffered a third attack of *mania—William Hunt*⟩ **Delirium** implies extreme mental disturbance that may be associated with or induced by toxic factors (as of disease or drugs) or occur episodically in a prolonged mental disorder and that is characterized by raving, hallucinations, delusions, and extreme restlessness ⟨a raging fever accompanied with *delirium—Dickens*⟩ ⟨by pain reduced to a state approaching *delirium*⟩ But *delirium* also, in nontechnical use, applies to a state of intense emotional excitement that manifests itself in an individual or in a group and robs him or them of self-control ⟨in a *delirium* of joy⟩ ⟨the *delirium* of popular enthusiasm—*Lecky*⟩ **Frenzy** (see also INSPIRATION) suggests wilder or more violent agitation or disorder than *delirium* but no less emotional excitement; it is applicable both to a state bordering on a mania ⟨an act done in the . . . *frenzy* of despair—*Freeman*⟩ and to one in which for the time being all self-control is lost ⟨his hands released her . . . and went up to his white hair, which they tore in a *frenzy—Dickens*⟩ ⟨her intensity, which would leave no emotion on a normal plane, irritated the youth into a *frenzy—D. H. Lawrence*⟩ **Hysteria** applies strictly to a psychoneurosis simulating organic disease and manifesting such symptoms as disturbance of sensation, motion, and visceral functions expressed typically in functional paralysis, nausea, and emotional excitability ⟨a structurally normal arm paralyzed by *hysteria*⟩ In ordinary nontechnical language *hysteria* implies extreme emotional instability that may show itself in swift transitions of mood or from laughing to crying ⟨she laughed and cried together . . . in a *hysteria* which she could not control —*Bennett*⟩ ⟨they were gradually worked up to complaisance and then to enthusiasm and then to *hysteria* and then to acute mania—*Mencken*⟩
*Ana* depression, dejection, melancholia, melancholy (see SADNESS): \*ecstasy, transport: excitement, provocation (see corresponding verbs at PROVOKE)

**maniac** \*insane, mad, crazy, crazed, demented, deranged, lunatic, non compos mentis
*Ana* \*irrational, unreasonable
*Con* \*rational, reasonable

**manifest** *adj* \*evident, patent, distinct, obvious, apparent, palpable, plain, clear
*Ana* revealed, disclosed, divulged, told (see REVEAL): shown, evidenced, evinced (see SHOW *vb*): conspicuous, \*noticeable, prominent
*Ant* latent: constructive (see IMPLICIT) —*Con* \*obscure, vague, enigmatic, cryptic, dark: \*implicit, virtual

**manifest** *vb* \*show, evidence, evince, demonstrate
*Ana* exhibit, display, expose (see SHOW *vb*): \*express, vent, utter, voice: \*reveal, discover, disclose, divulge

*Ant* suggest —*Con* adumbrate, shadow (see SUGGEST)
**manikin** midget, \*dwarf, pygmy, homunculus, runt
*Ant* giant

**manipulate** \*handle, wield, swing, ply
*Ana* flourish, brandish, shake, \*swing, wave, thrash

**manlike** mannish, manful, virile, manly, masculine, \*male
*Con* womanlike, feminine, womanish, ladylike, effeminate, womanly, \*female

**manly** manlike, manful, virile, masculine, mannish, \*male
*Ana* \*mature, matured, grown-up, adult: sturdy, \*strong, stout, stalwart
*Ant* unmanly, womanly —*Con* effeminate, womanish, ladylike (see FEMALE): boyish, puerile, juvenile, \*youthful

**manner** \*method, mode, way, fashion, system
*Ana* custom, usage, use, wont, practice, \*habit, habitude

**mannerism** \*pose, air, affectation
*Ana* \*eccentricity, idiosyncrasy: peculiarity, singularity, oddness, queerness (see corresponding adjectives at STRANGE)

**mannish** manlike, virile, masculine, \*male, manful, manly
*Ant* womanish —*Con* womanly, womanlike, unmannish, ladylike, feminine, \*female

**manufacture** fabricate, forge, \*make, form, shape, fashion
*Ana* produce, turn out, yield (see BEAR)

**manumit** emancipate, enfranchise, deliver, discharge, \*free, release, liberate
*Ant* enslave

**many**, **several, sundry, various, divers, numerous, multifarious** mean consisting of a large number or comprising a large group. **Many** implies a likeness between the individuals or units in class, category, kind, or sort; except that it vaguely implies more than a few, the term gives no explicit suggestion as to how large the number is ⟨of the eleven poets who accepted (representing, in *many* cases, a second choice on the part of the committee . . .) —*Mary McCarthy*⟩ ⟨*many* inventions which we now see to be precursors of the second industrial revolution—*Wiener*⟩ **Several** (see also DISTINCT 1) is almost as vague as *many* in its implication of number. In law the term is construed as meaning more than one; thus, the *several* counts of an indictment may be two or more counts. In more general use it is usually construed as meaning at least three ⟨the journey will take *several* days⟩ ⟨they saw *several* strangers on the road⟩ ⟨there are *several* reasons why you should not go⟩ Sometimes the term means both more than a few and different each from the other; in such use, *several* is often preceded by a possessive adjective ⟨a review of our denominational theologians . . . . There have been many of them; they have served their *several* causes well—*Sperry*⟩ ⟨her *several* thoughts . . . as signaled by the changes on her face—*Hardy*⟩ ⟨chosen every second year by the people of the *several* States— *U. S. Constitution*⟩ **Sundry** also implies an indefinite number, but it carries regularly a stronger implication of the difference of each from the others than does *several;* thus, there are *several*, rather than *sundry*, eggs left; there are *sundry*, more explicit than *several*, aspects of the problem that have not been considered ⟨she differed . . . in *sundry* important features—*Quiller-Couch*⟩ ⟨all their *sundry* emotions of a moment ago were one now in a sense of submissive, unquestioning reverence—*Tasaki*⟩ **Various** (see also DIFFERENT) is often used to mean an indefinite number, with a more or less attenuated implication of difference in identity of each from each ⟨*various* persons spoke to me about it⟩ ⟨the *various* social layers of the American population—*Packard*⟩ **Divers** (compare *diverse* under DIFFERENT) also has come to imply a vague number, often meaning little more than *many* or *several*, but often retaining some of its originally strong impli-

cation of difference among the individuals ⟨he told his story to *divers* persons⟩ ⟨*divers* styles of musical expression—*Virgil Thomson*⟩ **Numerous** may qualify plural nouns or singular nouns that designate a collection or assembly of units or individuals. In each case the term implies the existence of a noticeably large number of units or individuals; sometimes, in fact, it connotes a crowding or thronging ⟨every president has *numerous* letters from *numerous* persons⟩ ⟨I have contracted a *numerous* acquaintance among the best sort of people—*Steele*⟩ ⟨the commoners who had been summoned . . . formed a *numerous* assembly—*Macaulay*⟩ **Multifarious** adds to the implications of *many* that of great diversity and often incongruity in the units, individuals, or elements involved ⟨in many of the *multifarious* activities he undertook—*Ellis*⟩ ⟨the *multifarious* Italian dialects—*Heiser*⟩ ⟨the large desk on which *multifarious* files and papers were ranged—*Bennett*⟩ ⟨the *multifarious* sufferings of the refugees⟩
*Ant* few

**many-sided** *versatile, all-around

**map** *n & vb* *chart, graph
*Ana* *plan, plot, scheme, design: *sketch, outline, diagram

**mar** *vb* *injure, damage, hurt, harm, impair, spoil
*Ana* *deface, disfigure: *deform, contort, distort, warp: *ruin, wreck
*Con* embellish, decorate, *adorn, beautify, ornament: *mend, repair, patch: amend, revise, reform, *correct, rectify, emend

**marble** *vb* *spot, spatter, sprinkle, mottle, fleck, stipple, speckle, spangle, bespangle

**marbled** spotted, spattered, sprinkled, mottled, flecked, stippled, speckled, spangled, bespangled (see under SPOT *vb*)

**margin** 1 *border, verge, edge, rim, brim, brink
*Ana* bound, end, term, confine, *limit: penumbra (see SHADE)
2 *room, berth, play, elbowroom, leeway, clearance

**marine** *adj* 1 oceanic, thalassic, neritic, pelagic, abyssal, *aquatic, lacustrine, fluvial, fluviatile
2 **Marine, maritime, nautical, naval** are not closely synonymous terms but they are so interrelated that they are sometimes a cause of confusion. *Marine* and *maritime* both imply a connection with the sea. **Marine** is the appropriate term when what is qualified is produced by or is found in the sea or in a body of salt water (for this sense see AQUATIC) or is intended for use at sea ⟨*marine* barometer⟩ ⟨*marine* chronometer⟩ or deals with the sea or with vessels that ply the sea or other large bodies of water ⟨*marine* painting⟩ ⟨*marine* engineers⟩ *Marine* is sometimes used also when there is an actual or implied reference to seamen ⟨at that time the *Marine* Board examinations took place at the St. Katherine's Dock House on Tower Hill —*Conrad*⟩ ⟨the *marine* hospital system long maintained by the United States for the care of sick and disabled merchant seamen⟩ and the term commonly applies to soldiers who serve at sea ⟨the *Marine* Corps⟩ **Maritime** is the appropriate term when the reference is to countries, climates, or peoples on the borders of a sea ⟨the *Maritime* Provinces of Canada are on its eastern coast⟩ ⟨*maritime* races⟩ or to the navigation of or commerce on the seas ⟨*maritime* pursuits such as fishing or whaling⟩ ⟨*maritime* laws⟩ ⟨*maritime* perils⟩ ⟨in the whole of British genius . . . I have estimated the *maritime* ancestry as 1.9, less than any other class—*Ellis*⟩ But *maritime* and *marine* are sometimes used interchangeably, especially in reference to law and insurance. *Nautical* and *naval*, on the other hand, imply a connection with ships and shipping, and therefore only indirectly with the

sea. **Nautical,** however, is the usual term in applications where a relationship to sailors or seamen or the sailing of ships or boats is distinctly implied ⟨*nautical* pursuits such as yachting⟩ ⟨*nautical* skill⟩ ⟨a man of *nautical* interests is never satisfied until he owns some sort of boat⟩ ⟨*nautical* clothes⟩ ⟨no one rows, very few sail . . . ; Brighton . . . is the least *nautical* of seaside places—*Jefferies*⟩ *Nautical* is usually the preferred term when reference to the art or profession of navigation is implied ⟨*nautical* charts⟩ ⟨*nautical* tables⟩ ⟨*nautical* astronomy⟩ ⟨a *nautical* mile⟩ **Naval** usually implies reference to a navy as distinguished from a merchant marine and as composed not only of ships, but of men, supplies, and armaments; at times, only from the context can a reader be sure whether ship or naval force is referred to ⟨*naval* stores⟩ ⟨a *naval* architect⟩ ⟨a *naval* engagement⟩ ⟨he belongs to the *naval* reserve⟩

**mariner,** sailor, seaman, tar, gob, bluejacket all denote a person engaged in sailing or handling a ship. In nontechnical use **mariner** generally refers to those directly involved in the navigation and operation of the ship but in legal use it is applicable to a person employed aboard a ship in any capacity and then includes not only the navigators and operators but such persons as those concerned with the ship's business and housekeeping; thus, a ship's master, officers, engineers, and stewardesses all are in this sense *mariners. Mariner* is not so common as the other terms, but it is very common in literary use ⟨ye *mariners* of England that guard our native seas—*Campbell*⟩ **Sailor** still so strongly retains its original implication of concern with the management of boats or ships that are propelled by sails that it is the appropriate term whenever this idea is specifically suggested. However the term is also applicable to a person engaged in the actual navigation or operation of a vessel regardless of the power which drives it. In ordinary use it applies especially to one more technically called a **seaman,** one of the working force sometimes including or sometimes excluding officers employed on a ship. The term *seaman* alone is not ordinarily applied to apprentices, for it suggests skill and craft in operation and guidance of a vessel. **Tar** is a familiar, often poetic, designation of a sailor; **gob** designates informally a sailor belonging to the navy and is not applied to an officer, whether commissioned or noncommissioned. **Bluejacket** is commonly applied to an enlisted man in the British or American navy; the term originally referred to the distinguishing uniform of such a seaman; it is often employed in distinguishing a sailor in the navy from a marine or a sailor in the merchant marine.

**marital** *matrimonial, conjugal, connubial, nuptial, hymeneal

**maritime** *marine, nautical, naval

**mark** *n* 1 *sign, symptom, note, token, badge
*Ana* *stigma, brand, blot, stain: criterion, touchstone, gauge, yardstick, *standard: *trace, vestige, track: stamp, print, imprint, impress, *impression
2 *character, symbol, sign
*Ana* *device, contrivance
3 brand, stamp, label, tag, ticket (see under MARK *vb*)

**mark** *vb* 1 **Mark, brand, stamp, label, tag, ticket** are comparable both as verbs meaning to affix, attach, or impress something which serves for identification and as nouns meaning the thing affixed, attached, or impressed for such a purpose. **Mark,** the comprehensive term of this group, in itself as distinct from context implies nothing about the way of affixing, attaching, or impressing and therefore may take the place of any of the remaining terms to suggest a means by which something may be identified, or

such matters as its ownership, origin, and quality may be established ⟨all her linen was *marked* by embroidered initials⟩ ⟨English gold and silver articles are *marked*, to attest their purity, with the official *mark* of the Goldsmiths' Company⟩ ⟨the *marks* of old age are appearing in his face⟩ ⟨bringing with him the *marks* of his rank and privilege, the silver and china, the linen and damask, the portraits in peeling gold frames—*Warren*⟩ **Brand** basically implies a burning or searing with a hot iron to make a permanent mark that serves to identify (as in respect to status, ownership, quality, or make) ⟨cattle on the open range were *branded* to show their owner⟩ But *brand* has been extended to other methods of marking and then commonly stresses the indelibility of the mark and this implication affects its various extended uses much as does the more basic one (see *brand n* under STIGMA) ⟨history has once again *branded* this lesson on the minds of those who choose to see—*Beachcroft*⟩ In particular the noun often implies a being the identified product of a specified maker ⟨accustomed to ask for goods by *brand*⟩ ⟨a store that carries only well-known *brands*⟩ **Stamp** (see also IMPRESSION) basically implies an impressing of a mark of identification, authentication, or authorization upon some softer material by means of a machine or instrument that hammers it in; it may imply also any comparable method of affixing a mark, usually with some suggestion of permanence or indelibility ⟨every coin is *stamped* with a particular design that certifies it as belonging to a certain country and as having such and such a value⟩ ⟨the meat was dark red with uneven white edges of fat. Blue inspection *stamps* were on the white fat—*Wirt Williams*⟩ ⟨*stamp* a bill "Paid"⟩ ⟨*stamp* a letter with the date of arrival at the post office⟩ ⟨put a ten-cent postage *stamp* on that letter⟩ ⟨this passport now bears all the necessary *stamps*⟩ ⟨his paternity was *stamped* so indelibly on his outer shell—*Costain*⟩ ⟨a poet who has left her *stamp* on her generation—*S. H. Hay*⟩ **Label** implies the affixing of a piece of material (as paper, metal, or cloth) upon something to show its name, description, origin, or the person and address to which it is being sent ⟨*label* all the minerals in the collection⟩ ⟨she affixed a small paper *label* to each jar of preserves⟩ ⟨the contents of every bottle should be carefully *labeled*⟩ In its extended use *label* usually applies to the applying of an epithet, often rather arbitrarily, to something or someone ⟨when I was at Harvard all the types of narrative were *labeled* and classified like beetles in a case—*Marquand*⟩ ⟨hanging the subversive *label* on their own liberal clergy —*Winnett*⟩ **Tag** is applied to a label loosely attached (as to a package or a piece of baggage) giving directions or information; it often implies less permanent attachment than *label* ⟨a *tag* pinned to his lapel, bearing his name and destination—*Current Biog.*⟩ ⟨*tag* a parcel for shipment⟩ ⟨*price tags*⟩ ⟨write out *tags* for all the pieces of baggage⟩ **Ticket** in the relevant sense is more common as noun than verb and basically denotes a slip (as of paper, cardboard, or metal) usually conveying information or evidencing a right. Often the word is interchangeable with *label* or *tag* without loss of meaning ⟨many retailers who attach their own store tags to the merchandise look at the manufacturers' *tags* and labels as auxiliary *tickets* supplementing their own—*Women's Wear Daily*⟩
*Ana* imprint, impress, print (see corresponding nouns at IMPRESSION): recognize, identify (see corresponding nouns at RECOGNITION)
2 *characterize, distinguish, qualify
*Ana* *indicate, betoken, attest, bespeak, prove, argue: intimate, hint, *suggest
**marriage,** matrimony, wedlock, wedding, nuptial, espousal

are comparable though not always synonymous because they all refer directly or indirectly to acts by which a man and woman become husband and wife or to the state of being husband and wife. **Marriage** is the common term; it may apply to the rite or ceremony ⟨many were present at their *marriage*⟩ ⟨a civil *marriage*⟩ but it more often applies to the legal or spiritual relation which is entered upon ⟨joined in *marriage*⟩ ⟨annul a *marriage*⟩ or to the state of being married ⟨theirs was a long and happy *marriage*⟩ or to the institution as an abstraction ⟨nor does he dishonor *marriage* that praises virginity—*Donne*⟩ In extended use the term is applicable to any similarly close and intimate union ⟨let me not to the *marriage* of true minds admit impediments—*Shak.*⟩ ⟨the same sort of poetic effect as the Romantics obtained by the *marriage* of fertile words—*Day Lewis*⟩ **Matrimony** is in most contexts interchangeable with *marriage*, but it is the more appropriate term in religious and sometimes in legal use; in many Christian churches it designates one of the seven sacraments ⟨*matrimony* is the sacrament which unites in holy wedlock a man and a woman, between whom there is no impediment that would render marriage null and void—*Currier*⟩ The term therefore may be chosen in place of *marriage* when a religious ceremony or sanction is implied ⟨joined in bonds of holy *matrimony*⟩ In general the term is more often applied to the relationship which exists between husband and wife than to the ceremony or the state of marriage ⟨so prays the Church, to consecrate a vow "The which would endless *matrimony* make"—*Wordsworth*⟩ **Wedlock,** chiefly legal or archaic, applies especially to marriage as a legally or ecclesiastically sanctioned relationship or state; thus, children born out of *wedlock* are children of parents who are not legally married ⟨grave authors say, and witty poets sing, that honest *wedlock* is a glorious thing—*Pope*⟩ **Wedding** is the common term for the ceremony that marks a marriage and the festivities that accompany it ⟨a thousand invitations to the *wedding* were sent out⟩ **Nuptial,** usually as the plural **nuptials,** is a more rhetorical term than *wedding;* it also carries a stronger implication of an elaborate ceremony ⟨I don't object to married priests, but I do strongly object to their *nuptials.* . . . When a priest . . . indulges in an immense artistic wedding, I feel there is something undignified and almost unpleasant about it—*Mackenzie*⟩ **Espousal,** often as the plural **espousals,** differs little from *nuptial* except in its extended application. In the latter use it implies a spiritual union, especially one that is dependent upon a vow or pledge ⟨let every act of worship be like our *espousals*, Lord, to thee—*John Wesley*⟩
**marshal** *vb* *order, arrange, organize, systematize, methodize
*Ana* array, range, align, *line, line up
*Con* derange, disarrange, *disorder, disorganize, unsettle, disturb: *scatter, disperse, dissipate
**martial,** warlike, military carry as their basic meaning belonging to, suitable to, or characteristic of war. **Martial** distinctively implies reference to war in general and to its essential and fundamental characteristics; it often specifically suggests the pomp and circumstance of war ⟨standing in *martial* array⟩ ⟨the army set out to the *martial* strains of a fife and drum corps—*Amer. Guide Series: Calif.*⟩ **Warlike,** as a rule, implies reference to war as a reality, its actual causes, its actual methods, its actual effects; it therefore applies more often to feelings, acts, or activities that lead to or accompany real war than to those which suggest its thrilling or stirring qualities; thus, a *warlike* temper suggests bellicosity or readiness to fight to the bitter end, whereas a *martial* temperament

---

*Ana* analogous words     *Ant* antonyms     *Con* contrasted words     See also explanatory notes facing page 1

suggests qualities (as dauntlessness, spiritedness, and eagerness) that bespeak one likely to behave well and valiantly in war ⟨a *warlike* race⟩ ⟨tales of *warlike* feats —*Wordsworth*⟩ ⟨everything that might be of value to a *warlike* power—the muskets, the cutlasses—was thrown overboard—*Forester*⟩ ⟨the Huns, whose *warlike* fury had swept the earth like a living flame—*Stoker*⟩ **Military** is the broadest of these terms since it may imply reference to war, to arms, or to armed forces or might ⟨a *military* expedition⟩ ⟨the *military* needs of the nation⟩ ⟨a distinguished *military* career⟩ ⟨of *military* bearing, six feet in height, erect and compact, with black hair and commanding appearance—*Colegrove*⟩ Sometimes *military* in reference to armed forces is specifically opposed to *civil* or *civilian* ⟨a *military* governor⟩ ⟨it is beyond the scope of any *military* representative to effect a solution by political means—*Cilley*⟩ ⟨Spencer also could see only two main types of states, the *military*, fashioned primarily for war and extremely authoritarian, and the industrial state, set up chiefly for productive industry and implying democratic politics, extensive civil liberties and extreme limitation of state activities—*H. E. Barnes*⟩ or it may be restricted to land, or land and air, forces and is then opposed to *naval* ⟨among *military* and naval attachés, military rank takes precedence of "courtesy to the stranger"—*Squire*⟩
*Ana* *belligerent, bellicose, pugnacious, combative: *aggressive, militant: *spirited, high-spirited, mettlesome

**marvel** *n* *wonder, prodigy, miracle, phenomenon
*Ana* astonishment, amazement, surprise (see corresponding verbs at SURPRISE): perplexity, mystification, puzzle (see corresponding verbs at PUZZLE)

**masculine** *male, virile, manful, manly, manlike, mannish
*Ana* *vigorous, energetic, lusty, strenuous: robust, *healthy, sound
*Ant* feminine —*Con* womanly, ladylike, womanlike, womanish, *female

**mash** *vb* *crush, smash, bruise, squash, macerate
*Ana* pound, *beat

**mask** *n* portrait, photograph, *image, effigy, statue, icon

**mask** *vb* *disguise, cloak, dissemble, camouflage
*Ana* conceal, *hide, secrete, screen: protect, shield, *defend, guard, safeguard
*Con* discover, divulge, disclose, *reveal: expose, exhibit, display, flaunt, *show

**mass** *n* 1 *bulk, volume
*Ana* *aggregate, aggregation, conglomerate, conglomeration: *sum, amount, total, aggregate, whole
2 heap, pile, stack, shock, cock, bank (see under HEAP *vb*)
*Ana* accumulation, hoarding *or* hoard, amassment (see corresponding verbs at ACCUMULATE)

**mass** *vb* *heap, pile, stack, shock, cock, bank
*Ana* *gather, collect, assemble, congregate: *accumulate, amass, hoard: merge, blend, fuse, coalesce (see MIX): consolidate, *compact, unify, concentrate

**massacre** *n* Massacre, slaughter, butchery, carnage, pogrom are comparable when they mean a great and often wanton killing of human beings. **Massacre** implies promiscuous and wholesale slaying, especially of those who are not prepared to defend themselves and can make little or no resistance ⟨the tyrannous and bloody deed is done, the most arch act of piteous *massacre* that ever yet this land was guilty of—*Shak.*⟩ ⟨the vengeful murder of the mutiny's bloodthirsty ringleader, and the *massacre* of most of the surviving crew by natives—*Dulles*⟩ **Slaughter**, basically a butcher's term for the killing of animals used as food, suggests extensive and ruthless killing, whether the scene of that killing be a battle or a massacre ⟨the chief . . . cut his way through the enemy with great *slaugh-*

*ter*—*Irving*⟩ ⟨determined not to repeat the *slaughter* of the First World War, during which hundreds of thousands of soldiers were sacrificed in fruitless frontal attacks—*Bethe*⟩ ⟨it was no longer a battle but a *slaughter* . . . . From nine o'clock in the morning until seven o'clock in the evening, when it began to get dark, the killing went on—*Graves*⟩ **Butchery** adds to *slaughter* the implication of exceeding cruelty or of cold-blooded indifference to the sufferings of the victims ⟨boasting of his fights, his cruelties and his *butcheries*—*Kingsley*⟩ ⟨thus was the *butchery* waged while the sun clomb Heaven's eastern steep—*Shelley*⟩ **Carnage** is often not easily distinguishable from *slaughter*, except that it sometimes carries additional connotations similar to those of *massacre* ⟨a slight resistance was followed by a dreadful *carnage*—*Gibbon*⟩ ⟨war and all its deeds of *carnage*—*Whitman*⟩ **Pogrom** applies especially to an organized massacre of helpless people carried on usually with the connivance of officials. It is often applied specifically to such a massacre of Jews, especially in one of the European countries ⟨the *pogroms* at Gomel and Kishinev in Russia in 1903⟩ ⟨he carried on a full-scale *pogrom* against the Jews, slaughtering hundreds of thousands—*New Republic*⟩ ⟨the Hindus interpret every manifestation of individual violence . . . as the launching of a *pogrom* against them —*Edmond Taylor*⟩
*Ana* assassination, murdering *or* murder, slaying, killing (see corresponding verbs at KILL)

**massive**, massy, bulky, monumental, substantial are comparable when they mean impressively large or heavy. **Massive** distinctively stresses solidity and strength of construction and may imply an imposing appearance ⟨its ceilings . . . heavy with *massive* beams—*Dickens*⟩ ⟨the mainland of Asia, and especially that part of it occupied by the *massive* bulk of China—*Owen Lattimore*⟩ ⟨a man whose *massive* shoulders and determined cast of features ought to have convinced him that such an enterprise was nothing short of desperate—*Shaw*⟩ **Massy**, chiefly a literary word, carries a stronger implication of ponderousness than *massive*, but an equal implication of solidity and strength ⟨your swords are now too *massy* for your strengths and will not be uplifted—*Shak.*⟩ ⟨hast thou a goblet for dark sparkling wine? That goblet right heavy, and, *massy*, and gold?—*Keats*⟩ ⟨it was a castle, steadfast among storms, its side a *massy* wall —*Sinclair Lewis*⟩ **Bulky** stresses size rather than weight, and the excessive amount of space occupied rather than solidity or strength of construction ⟨a *bulky* parcel⟩ ⟨a *bulky* report⟩ ⟨its front door and steps were wide, presumably in order to permit the passage of *bulky* objects—*Chidsey*⟩ ⟨the museum finds it impossible to accept for display a great number of interesting but *bulky* items such as aircraft, guns or tanks—*Report on Nat'l Development (Ottawa)*⟩ **Monumental** implies greatness of size, but it distinctively suggests an imposing massiveness ⟨me, Goddess, bring to archèd walks of twilight groves, and shadows brown . . . of pine, or *monumental* oak— *Milton*⟩ ⟨the *monumental* fourpost bed has been taken down—*Daily Telegraph*⟩ ⟨a tall red-haired woman of *monumental* build—*Wharton*⟩ **Substantial** stresses solidity and strength of construction but it carries a weak implication of size or outwardly imposing appearance and a strong implication of established quality, worth, and stability ⟨the most *substantial* buildings in England today are the old Norman cathedrals⟩ ⟨the Philadelphia crowd in their drab, *substantial*, gray and brown clothes— *Dorothy Canfield*⟩ ⟨*substantial* homes, and *substantial* relatives of some sort or other, on whom we could fall back—*Galsworthy*⟩

---

A colon (:) separates groups of words discriminated. An asterisk (*) indicates place of treatment of each group.

*Ana* *heavy, weighty, ponderous: solid, hard, *firm: immense, enormous, *huge, gigantic, colossal

**massy** *massive, bulky, monumental, substantial
*Ana* ponderous, hefty, cumbrous, cumbersome, weighty, *heavy: *large, big, great: solid, *firm, hard

**master** *n* *chief, chieftain, head, leader

**masterful, domineering, imperious, peremptory, imperative** are comparable when they apply to persons or their acts, utterances, and demands and mean governed by, or manifesting, a strong tendency to impose one's will on another. One is **masterful** who by the strength and virility of his personality is able to enforce his will on others or who deals with affairs commandingly and compellingly ⟨the major was a *masterful* man; and I knew that he would not give orders for nothing—*Kipling*⟩ ⟨the man had such a *masterful* and magnetic personality . . . that it was impossible not to take fire at his ardor —*Huxley*⟩ One is **domineering** who tries to enforce his will or to make a show of his power by an overbearing or insolently tyrannical manner ⟨they are . . . not courageous, only quarrelsome; not determined, only obstinate; not masterful, only *domineering*—*Shaw*⟩ ⟨the European nations, arrogant, *domineering,* and rapacious, have done little to recommend the name of Christianity in Asia and Africa—*Inge*⟩ One is **imperious** who by temperament or by position is fitted to command or who assumes the air or manner of such a person; the term implies more arrogance than *masterful* and less insolence than *domineering* ⟨this ancient despot—this *imperious* old Louis XIV in a black front and a cap and ribbon—*Thackeray*⟩ ⟨one could not have passed him on the street without feeling his great physical force and his *imperious* will— *Cather*⟩ One is **peremptory** who insists, often with curtness, on an immediate response to his commands; the term usually implies authoritativeness and a refusal to brook disobedience or delay or to entertain objections however valid ⟨the general issued a *peremptory* summons⟩ ⟨two *peremptory* raps at the door—*Shaw*⟩ ⟨when we say of . . . a man that he has a great deal of character, we generally mean that he has disciplined his temperament, his disposition, into strict obedience to the behests of duty; that he has clear and *peremptory* ideas about right and wrong—*Brownell*⟩ One is **imperative** who, or whose behavior, is peremptory because of the urgency of the situation rather than because of a domineering temperament ⟨"Go back!" cried the old man, with an *imperative* jerk of the head—*M. E. Freeman*⟩ ⟨he heard her *imperative* voice at the telephone; he heard her summon the doctor—*Glasgow*⟩
*Ana* magisterial, *dictatorial, authoritarian, oracular, dogmatic, doctrinaire: arbitrary, *absolute, despotic, tyrannical

**masterly** *proficient, adept, skilled, skillful, expert
*Ana* *dexterous, deft, adroit: preeminent, superlative, transcendent, *supreme

**match** *vb* **Match, rival, equal, approach, touch** are comparable, especially in negative constructions, when they mean to come up to or nearly up to the level or standard of something else. One thing **matches** another when it proves to be its mate, rather than its duplicate, in power, strength, performance, beauty, or interest ⟨it has been said that no language can *match* French in expressing ideas with clarity and exactness⟩ ⟨the beauty of his person was *matched* by the grace and dignity of his spirit—*Buchan*⟩ ⟨no mortal builder's most rare device could *match* this winter palace of ice—*J. R. Lowell*⟩ ⟨we are prone to imitate the vices of those whose virtues we cannot *match*—*McCartney*⟩ One thing **rivals** another when it closely competes with it for superiority or in excellence ⟨but would

you sing, and *rival* Orpheus' strain, the wond'ring forests soon should dance again—*Pope*⟩ ⟨work of a beauty certainly not *rivaled* until we come to the Norman builders —*Quiller-Couch*⟩ ⟨some of them are furnished with colors that *rival* or excel the brilliance of the famous Morpho butterflies—*Curran*⟩ ⟨while my father could never have *rivaled* the sartorial magnificence of some of his friends, he dressed in the ceremonial manner of the time—*Brooks*⟩ One thing **equals** another when it rises to the same level or plane (as in quantity, value, or degree) and there is no question concerning a difference, especially a deficiency ⟨such a striking civility . . . ought to be imitated, though it could not be *equaled,* by some exertion of politeness on their side—*Austen*⟩ ⟨no other measure of our work *equals* the sight of the product put to its full uses— *Suzzallo*⟩ ⟨its society was formed by religion to an extent never *equaled* in any other epoch of its history—*M. W. Baldwin*⟩ One thing **approaches** another when it so nearly equals or matches the other that the difference, though detectable, is seldom important ⟨an adult reader with trained habits of . . . concentration will absorb the contents of a book with a speed and retentiveness which no child can *approach*—*Eliot*⟩ ⟨an unlettered speaker may startle you with his power of giving to the spoken word an urgent aptness that *approaches* the vivid instancy of an involuntary cry—*Montague*⟩ One thing **touches** another thing when it closely approaches the other (as in excellence or beauty) ⟨not another woman there to *touch* her—*W. J. Locke*⟩ ⟨Yeats, the last in the aristocratic tradition of poets . . . none of us can *touch* his later work—*Day Lewis*⟩
*Ana* correspond, harmonize, *agree, conform, square, accord
*Con* *differ: vary, *change, alter, modify

**material** *adj* **1 Material, physical, corporeal, phenomenal, sensible, objective** are comparable when they mean belonging to or having a relation to things that belong to the world of actuality or of things apparent to the senses. **Material** applies to whatever is formed of matter or relates to things formed of matter; it often implies an opposition to *spiritual,* but it may imply an antithesis to *ideal, formal, intangible,* or *impalpable* ⟨*material* objects⟩ ⟨transporting his *material* possessions⟩ ⟨believes in no other world than the *material* world⟩ ⟨busy with *material* affairs—*Conrad*⟩ ⟨bathrooms . . ., motorcars, and other *material* comforts of which that age was ignorant— *Russell*⟩ ⟨these poor Christians are not thrifty like our country people at home; they have no veneration for property, no sense of *material* values—*Cather*⟩ **Physical** (see also BODILY) differs from *material* chiefly in suggesting an opposition to *psychical, mental, metaphysical, imaginary,* and, less often, *spiritual;* it applies especially to things perceived by the senses or capable of being dealt with in the same manner as objects of sense, and it usually implies a contrast to things knowable only through thought or intuition or built up by the mind or imagination; thus, the *material* objects and the *physical* objects within one's reach may be exactly the same objects, but *material* suggests their substantial nature and *physical* suggests their susceptibility of perception and identification, or, what is more important in science, of being weighed and measured. In scientific use *physical* is also applicable to things that are not objects, but forces, actions, motions, or states which are operative in nature or in mechanics and which can be measured or calculated, or put to use, even though, strictly speaking, they cannot be handled ⟨*physical* properties of light⟩ ⟨*physical* effect of radiation⟩ ⟨everything *physical* is measurable by weight, motion, and resistance—*De Quincey*⟩ **Corporeal** (see also BODILY)

applies to what not only has physical existence but also is tangible or can be described as a body; thus, energy in itself has no *corporeal* existence though it is a *physical* power found usually in *corporeal* things ⟨in a monistic . . . sense "the mind" may be regarded as a living, growing "structure" even though it lacks *corporeal* tangibility —*Science*⟩ ⟨the spiritual life commences where the *corporeal* existence terminates—*Frazer*⟩ **Phenomenal** implies a relation to what is known or knowable through the senses and experience, as distinguished from what is knowable only through thought or intuition because beyond perception by the senses; the term is chiefly used in philosophy and science when there is an intent to mark the line between what is actually perceived and what has been ascertained by the reason, has been accepted by faith, or is theoretical or hypothetical ⟨*phenomenal* reality is often specifically called *actuality*⟩ ⟨*phenomenal* nature is reduced to an array of events in the four-dimensional continuum—*Jeans*⟩ ⟨her introspective bent has yielded more and more, in her recent writing, to a determination to capture the *phenomenal* world—*Redman*⟩ **Sensible** which basically applies to what is known or knowable through sense experience and thereby comprehends the specific terms *visible, audible, tangible, palpable* is sometimes opposed to *intelligible, conceptual,* or *notional* ⟨there is no *sensible* movement of the earth⟩ ⟨is this a dagger which I see before me, the handle toward my hand? Come, let me clutch thee . . . are thou not . . . *sensible* to feeling as to sight? or art thou but a dagger of the mind, a false creation—*Shak.*⟩ ⟨the man of science may carry us off into a world of symbols, but his symbols stand for features of the external world and he is bent on verifying them by *sensible* experience—*Alexander*⟩ **Objective** (see also FAIR) implies the same kind of existence as *phenomenal* and *sensible,* but it stresses the apartness of the thing known through the senses from the person who perceives it through his senses; the term, therefore, implies not only material existence but an existence which is or is felt as uncolored by the prejudices and preconceptions of the perceiver ⟨the ancient Hebrew . . . saw the rainbow as an *objective* structure set in the heavens for all men to behold—*Jeans*⟩ ⟨acosmism, the theory which denies the *objective* existence of the world or universe—*Inge*⟩
*Ana* *carnal, fleshly, sensual, animal: actual, true, *real: tangible, *perceptible, appreciable, palpable
*Ant* immaterial
2 *relevant, germane, pertinent, apposite, applicable, apropos
*Ana* important, significant, consequential, momentous (see corresponding nouns at IMPORTANCE): vital, cardinal, *essential, fundamental
*Ant* immaterial

**material** *n* *matter, substance, stuff
*Ana* *element, constituent, ingredient, component

**materialize** externalize, objectify, incarnate, embody, actualize, *realize, hypostatize, reify

**matériel** 1 *equipment, apparatus, machinery, paraphernalia, outfit, tackle, gear
2 *armament, munitions, arms, ordnance, artillery, ammunition

**matrimonial,** **marital, conjugal, connubial, nuptial, hymeneal** mean of, relating to, or characteristic of marriage. **Matrimonial** is the most general term applicable to whatever has to do both with matrimony and with marriage in most of its senses (see MARRIAGE) ⟨*matrimonial* vows⟩ ⟨the *matrimonial* state⟩ ⟨with close fidelity and love unfeigned, to keep the *matrimonial* bond unstained—*Cowper*⟩ ⟨*matrimonial* bliss⟩ **Marital** which sometimes implies specific reference to the husband and his part in

marriage ⟨*marital* rights⟩ ⟨*marital* authority⟩ is often used interchangeably with *matrimonial* ⟨*marital* vows⟩ ⟨the *marital* relationship⟩ *Conjugal* and *connubial* are frequently used interchangeably. More discriminatively, **conjugal** refers to persons who are married ⟨they flaunt their *conjugal* felicity in one's face—*Wilde*⟩ ⟨I count it my good fortune that never once in . . . my childhood was I the witness of any *conjugal* jar—*Ellis*⟩ and **connubial** to the marriage state ⟨of my friends who have been least successful in *connubial* contracts—*Johnson*⟩ ⟨enter the *connubial* state⟩ **Nuptial** has primary reference to the marriage rites or ceremony ⟨the *nuptial* torch—*Milton*⟩ ⟨the *nuptial* ceremony was then performed by the Superintendent—*Motley*⟩ **Hymeneal** is a poetic or literary word, suggestive of the splendors of marriage rites and festivities ⟨*hymeneal* songs⟩ ⟨chorus *hymeneal,* or triumphal chaunt matched with thine would be all but an empty vaunt—*Shelley*⟩ ⟨one fully expects that . . . the characters will join hands at the conclusion and dance off the stage to *hymeneal* music—*Booth*⟩

**matrimony** *marriage, wedlock, wedding, nuptial, espousal

**matter** *n* 1 Matter, substance, material, stuff are comparable when they mean what goes into the makeup or forms the being of a thing whether physical or not. In the relevant sense **matter** basically denotes that of which all physical objects are made, but to the physical scientist this may imply the component of the observable universe that includes among its properties extension, inertia, and gravitation and is held to consist ultimately of relatively few kinds of elementary particles, to be convertible into energy, and together with energy to form the basis of objective phenomena ⟨but what is more common than *matter*? We and the universe about us are *matter.* We know nothing of force or energy, nor of any physical phenomenon, except through the agency of *matter*—*Foley*⟩ ⟨*matter* is a form of energy and . . . presumably in nature processes go on in which *matter* is destroyed and transformed into more familiar forms of energy such as heat, radiation, and mechanical motion—*E. O. Lawrence*⟩ while to the philosopher it tends to imply an unordered material substratum distinguishable on the one hand from immaterial qualities (as spirit or energy) and on the other from form or formed bodies ⟨Aristotle defined the word *matter* figuratively and successfully when he said that *matter* is to substance what the bronze is to the statue—*Richard Robinson*⟩ ⟨it may be worth noting here the fundamentally opposed characters of Aristotle's *matter* and that of the new science. Aristotle's *matter* is the source of being, but not of intelligibility. To analyze an entity into its material components is to lose its essence. Modern science's *matter,* on the other hand, is the most intelligible of natural principles—*W. D. Oliver*⟩ In more general use *matter* often specifically applies to a particular portion or kind of physical matter ⟨strain the solid *matter* from the broth⟩ ⟨living *matter*⟩ **Substance** usually implies a particular kind of matter ⟨hard *substances*⟩ and often one of known chemical or physical nature ⟨gaseous *substances*⟩ ⟨an object may be either a homogeneous mass of a single *substance,* such as water, or a combination or mixture of different *substances,* as for instance a cup of tea—*Jeans*⟩ or it may distinctively suggest the particular matter or kind of matter that enters into the composition of something or gives it its characteristic properties ⟨the *substance* of this vase is porcelain⟩ ⟨are we not all of the same *substance*—men, planets and earth, born from the heart of darkness, returning to darkness, the consoling mother—*Sitwell*⟩ **Material** applies basically to matter or substance as a constituent of physical and especially of made things ⟨a cake made from the best *materials*⟩ ⟨the *material* of this dress is silk⟩ ⟨the sculptor, who is limited to a few *materials* like stone, wood and metal—*Read*⟩ But often it subordinates physical nature to the fact of being made and then may imply the idea of actuality or a basis in actuality rather than physical substance; thus, *raw materials* are usually physical substances capable of refinement or manufacture but they also may be events, ideas, or facts capable of further use (as in literary creation) ⟨adventures which would make good raw *materials* for several novels—*J. H. Burton*⟩ ⟨a region rich in coal, iron, and other raw *materials*⟩ ⟨is the whole creative effort of the artist an endeavor to form *material* so that it will be in actuality the authentic substance of a work of art?—*Dewey*⟩ **Stuff** may replace *material* or *substance* in reference to constituent materials or substances ⟨the house was built carelessly and of poor *stuff*⟩ ⟨creating out of raw material a skilled working class . . . they are the *stuff* of which The New Congo is made—*Marvel*⟩ but more often it refers to all the parts, parcels, objects, or items that make up an aggregate or a whole; in both cases it is likely to imply indeterminateness and suggest vaguely if at all the nature of the constituent materials or parts ⟨pick up the *stuff* you left on the table⟩ ⟨ambition should be made of sterner *stuff*—*Shak.*⟩ Sometimes, distinctively, *stuff* carries an inherent implication of inferiority ⟨not a line of the volume was ever included by Bryant in his later writings, and he spoke of the pamphlet with testy disgust as *stuff*—*Nevins*⟩ ⟨what was the psychological impulse behind the pedantic and elaborate *stuff* he called in the end *Finnegans Wake*? —*Desmond MacCarthy*⟩

**2** *affair, business, concern, thing

**3** *subject, subject matter, argument, topic, text, theme, motive, motif, leitmotiv

**matter-of-fact** *prosaic, prosy
*Ana* stolid, phlegmatic, *impassive: arid, *dry: downright, *forthright
*Con* fanciful, *imaginary, fantastic, chimerical, quixotic, visionary: ideal, transcendent, transcendental (see ABSTRACT *adj*): romantic, *sentimental

**mature** *adj* Mature, matured, ripe, mellow, adult, grown-up are comparable if not often interchangeable because they all bear the same underlying meaning "fully developed." **Mature**, in its basic use as applied to living things, stresses the completion of development; as applied specifically to persons, it usually implies attainment of the prime of life, when a person is at the height of his powers, physically and mentally ⟨a great writer of the past is known by the delight and stimulus which he gives to *mature* spirits in the present—*Brooks*⟩ ⟨the life has a *mature* tone, an intellectual alertness, a sense of proportion—*Laski*⟩ As applied to things, *mature* usually equals **matured**, which implies the completion of a course, process, or period; thus, a *matured* plan is a fully thought-out plan; a *matured* wine is one that has been allowed to age properly; a *matured* note is one that has reached the date when payment is due ⟨must be replaced by the *maturer* concept that virtue is its own reward—*Davies*⟩ ⟨a *matured* poetic intelligence is often happily fused with the creative beat of poetic imagination—*Horace Gregory*⟩ **Ripe**, though it implies maturity, stresses readiness for use or enjoyment; in its basic sense it is applied chiefly to such things as fruits ready for eating, grains or vegetables ready for harvesting, or seeds ready to germinate. In extended use it often connotes merely readiness or full preparedness for action, activity, or use ⟨*ripe* for exploits and mighty enterprises—*Shak.*⟩ ⟨to be careful, in teaching history, not to obtrude aspects which are in-

teresting to us until the child is *ripe* for them—*Russell*⟩ Sometimes, however, *ripe* connotes one or more of the characteristics of ripe things, especially ripe fruits, such as ruddiness, plumpness,. or richness ⟨Greek sculpture, in its *ripe* perfection—*Binyon*⟩ **Mellow** stresses either such agreeable qualities associated with ripe or slightly overripe fruits as softness, tenderness, sweetness, or the loss of their opposites, the signs of immaturity, such as hardness, harshness, or bitterness ⟨*mellow* cheese⟩ ⟨*mellow* wine⟩ ⟨the more *mellow* and cheerful outlook of his second book —*Buchan*⟩ **Adult** is the equivalent of *mature* in its application to the physical characteristics of living things ⟨a rhesus monkey . . . is infantile 1.5 years, juvenile 6.5 years, and *adult* some 20 years—*La Barre*⟩ It presupposes, however, a clearer line of demarcation, especially when used of human beings. An *adult* person physiologically is one that has passed beyond adolescence; in law, he is one that has attained his majority ⟨people born in this country who have not been within its borders in all the years of their *adult* lives—*Discovery No. 3*⟩ In extended use *adult* implies the attainment of that point in development where the weaknesses of immaturity or of imperfection are surmounted ⟨the difference [between Romanticism and Classicism] seems to me rather the difference between the complete and the fragmentary, the *adult* and the immature, the orderly and the chaotic —*T. S. Eliot*⟩ ⟨people supremely *adult* and specially schooled to comprehend ideas and employ logic—*Flanner*⟩ **Grown-up** is sometimes used in preference to *adult* when an antithesis to *childish* is needed ⟨adults incapable of *grown-up* behavior⟩
*Ant* immature: childish  —*Con* *childlike: *youthful, juvenile, boyish, puerile, maiden

**mature** *vb* Mature, develop, ripen, age are used in reference to living, growing things or to things with latent capacity for betterment and mean to come or cause to come to the state of being fit for use or enjoyment. When employed with reference to living things or their specific characters, **mature** stresses fullness of growth and readiness for normal functioning ⟨in warm climates human beings *mature* more rapidly than in cold climates⟩ ⟨in his *maturing* days, young Warren was a cheerful and attractive personality—*S. H. Adams*⟩ ⟨he was *matured* by six years' practical experience in a New York militia regiment— *Robert Lowell*⟩ while **develop** stresses the unfolding of all that is latent and the attainment of the perfection that is appropriate to the species or is possible to the individual ⟨the kitten's hunting instinct was not yet *developed*— *Russell*⟩ and **ripen** emphasizes the approach to or the attainment of the peak of perfection ⟨the fruits are now sufficiently *ripened*⟩ ⟨there is nothing here of slow budding, of fruits *ripening* in stillness—*Carlos Baker*⟩ ⟨at twenty-three she was still young enough to *ripen* to a maturer beauty—*Glasgow*⟩ **Age** may equal *mature* when it is applied to the young ⟨hard work *ages* a boy⟩ but more often and in other contexts, routinely, it implies approach to the period of decline or decay ⟨the leaders of the movement are *aging* rapidly⟩ ⟨as the individual matures and then *ages*, he constantly has to unlearn patterns of response which have ceased to be effective—*Linton*⟩
In their extended applications to things with latent capacity for improvement all these terms imply a perfecting with time. **Mature** suggests that something not fully formed undergoes completing changes ⟨*mature* a plan⟩ ⟨an art that toiling ages have but just *matured*— *Cowper*⟩ ⟨his ideas about the novel continued to develop and *mature*—*Cousins*⟩ while **develop** especially applies to the unfolding into full being or effectiveness of something that is potential, latent, or nebulous ⟨the environ-

ment fitted to *develop* . . . a genius at once so subtle and so humane as that of Socrates—*Dickinson*⟩ ⟨the sense of fact is something very slow to *develop*—*T. S. Eliot*⟩ Both *ripen* and *age* imply a becoming fit for some use, action, or purpose over a period of time. Distinctively, *ripen* tends to suggest the addition of desirable qualities ⟨time had *ripened* his life and mellowed its fruits—*Brooks*⟩ ⟨the civil law, which was in force in most of the countries of continental Europe and their colonies, was the accepted product of the *ripened* experience of many centuries of Roman jurisprudence—*Encyc. Americana*⟩ while *age* may suggest the elimination of unwanted qualities ⟨water for tropical fish should be *aged* by standing long enough for toxic substances to escape⟩ ⟨*aging* tends toward the restoration of real equilibrium in the metal, and away from any unstable condition induced by a prior operation—*Rusinoff*⟩ but often the two are used without distinction ⟨beef, mutton, venison, and game birds become more tender and palatable by the process of *ripening,* hanging, *aging,* or maturing—*Ashbrook*⟩
*Ana* *harden, season, acclimatize, acclimate: *habituate, accustom, inure, addict
**matured** *mature, ripe, mellow, adult, grown-up
*Ana* completed, finished (see CLOSE *vb*): *deliberate, considered, advised, designed, studied, premeditated
*Ant* unmatured: premature  —*Con* crude, green, callow, uncouth, *rude, rough, raw: *youthful, juvenile, puerile, boyish: childish, *childlike
**maudlin** mawkish, *sentimental, romantic, soppy, mushy, slushy
*Ana* confused, muddled, fuddled, addled, befuddled (see CONFUSE): embarrassed, rattled, fazed, discomfited, disconcerted (see EMBARRASS)
**mawkish** maudlin, *sentimental, romantic, soppy, mushy, slushy
*Ana* flat, vapid, jejune, *insipid, banal, inane
**maxim** *saying, saw, adage, proverb, motto, epigram, aphorism, apothegm
**may** *can
**meager,** scanty, scant, skimpy, scrimpy, exiguous, spare, sparse are comparable when they mean so small (as in amount, number, or size) as to fall short of what is normal, necessary, or desirable. **Meager** stresses thinness: as applied to persons or animals, it suggests emaciation ⟨*meager* were his looks, sharp misery had worn him to the bones—*Shak.*⟩ but as applied to things in general, it implies the absence of elements, qualities, or numbers necessary to a thing's richness, substance, or potency ⟨a *meager* diet⟩ ⟨an outline in itself is *meager,* truly, but it does not necessarily suggest a *meager* thing—*James*⟩ ⟨his austere and *meager* life bred too little sensuousness of nature and too few intellectual passions—*Parrington*⟩ ⟨*meager* appropriations which necessitated the most rigorous economies—*Pahlow*⟩ **Scanty** emphasizes insufficiency in amount, quantity, or extent ⟨a *scanty* supply of food for the winter⟩ ⟨the book . . . is not, like some biographical essays with *scanty* material, stuffed out with appreciation and conjecture—*T. S. Eliot*⟩ ⟨such a *scanty* portion of light was admitted . . . that it was difficult, on first coming in, to see anything—*Dickens*⟩ **Scant** may differ from *scanty* in suggesting a falling or a cutting short (as in amount or quantity) of what is desired or desirable rather than in what is necessary or essential ⟨the work of those hours was miserably *scant*—*Hardy*⟩ ⟨they were held in *scant* esteem—*Grandgent*⟩ **Skimpy** and the less common **scrimpy** as applied to things may be quite interchangeable with *meager* ⟨sufficiently recovered from her cold to climb out of bed and into a *skimpy,* strapless blue gown—*Capote*⟩ ⟨a reasonably thoughtful

appraisal of the new Russian leader, based on such *skimpy* evidence as is now available—*Uhl*⟩ ⟨four acres is *scrimpy* measure for a royal garden, even for a king of the heroic ages, whose daughter did the family washing —*Notes & Queries*⟩ but often they are more strongly colored by the related verbs, *skimp* and *scrimp,* and then usually suggest niggardliness or penury as the cause of the deficiency ⟨prevents *skimpy* construction that often leads to airfield shutdowns and aircraft accidents—*Livingston*⟩ ⟨European art books commonly come out with hundreds of huge, magnificent color plates. American art books, especially those produced by commercial publishers, are often *skimpy,* starved and inadequate by comparison—*Frankenstein*⟩ ⟨more proud of their breeding than they were of the *scrimpy,* almost stingy respectability of the ménage—*White*⟩ **Exiguous** stresses a smallness in size, amount, extent, or capacity that is more or less inherent in the thing under consideration and makes it compare unfavorably with other things of its kind ⟨brains too *exiguous* to hold more than half an idea at a time—*Amer. Speech*⟩ ⟨building ships to supplement his *exiguous* navy—*Buchan*⟩ ⟨a much larger dominion than the *exiguous* Dalriada—*Times Lit. Sup.*⟩ **Spare** (see also LEAN, SUPERFLUOUS) implies merely a falling short of what is easily or fully sufficient; unlike *scanty* and *meager,* it seldom suggests resulting loss or hardship ⟨a *spare* diet⟩ ⟨*spare,* alert, and jaunty figure—*Wolfe*⟩ ⟨the journals . . . are by no means always *spare* and laconic—*Dulles*⟩ **Sparse** stresses a lack of normal or desirable thickness or density; the term need not suggest insufficiency or inadequacy in numbers or in quantity, but it always connotes a thin scattering of the units ⟨the *sparse* population of the mountainous district⟩ ⟨facing the facts of her defeat and her poverty and by encouraging *sparse,* stringent living—*Anthony West*⟩ ⟨a *sparse* congregation of old women scattered over the church—*Bruce Marshall*⟩
*Ana* *thin, slender, slim, slight, tenuous, rare: thinned, attenuated, extenuated, diluted (see THIN *vb*): jejune, flat, *insipid, inane: penurious, *stingy, parsimonious
*Ant* ample: copious
**mean** *adj* **Mean, ignoble, abject, sordid** can all be applied to persons, their behavior, or the conditions in which they live with the meaning so low as to be out of keeping with human dignity or generally acceptable standards of human life or character. **Mean** usually suggests such repellent antisocial characteristics as malevolence or cupidity. It almost invariably connotes small-mindedness ⟨those who are tempted by the flesh have usually nothing to fear from avarice or the *meaner* vices—*Mackenzie*⟩ ⟨her father is a decidedly vulgar person, *mean* in his ideals and obtuse in his manners—*Erskine*⟩ Often *mean* implies conduct or an attitude that is detestable and unworthy of a human being ⟨Delane . . . flung him off like a thing too *mean* for human handling—*Wharton*⟩ ⟨now and then in his pages war flashes out in romantic or heroic episodes, but for the most part it is *mean* and degrading, a thing to be hated—*Parrington*⟩ **Ignoble,** like its opposite *noble,* usually implies qualities of mind or soul. It frequently comes close to *mean* except that it seldom connotes small-mindedness. Its distinguishing implication is loss or lack of some essential high quality (as spiritual elevation, moral dignity, or intellectual excellence) ⟨to see how those he has converted distort and debase and make *ignoble* parodies of his teaching—*Huxley*⟩ ⟨these are . . . as low and *ignoble,* as gutter-fallen and dispiriting, as can only be found in the gloomier literature of imperial Russia —*J. M. Brown*⟩ **Abject,** in its most inclusive sense, means little more than extremely low in station or in degree ⟨had not that fear of beautiful and rich things which renders

*abject* people incapable of associating costliness with comfort—*Shaw*⟩ Sometimes it is merely an intensive applied to something that is itself low in the scale ⟨the wars and their changing fortunes, which made *abject* ruin and undreamt-of power occurrences of every day— *L. G. Deruisseau*⟩ In discriminative use, however, *abject* carries the implication of being cast down and so variously implies abasement, debasement, or contemptible servility ⟨disgrace not so your king, that he should be so *abject*, base, and poor, to choose for wealth and not for perfect love—*Shak.*⟩ ⟨resolved to be a man who . . . would live no longer in subjection to the past with *abject* mind—*Wordsworth*⟩ ⟨the stagnation and the squalor that are the *abject* human realities left by the ebb of power and splendor—*Edmund Wilson*⟩ **Sordid** emphasizes the degrading baseness associated with physical or mental corruption ⟨the counterrevolution . . . ranks among the most *sordid* periods in Chinese history. Compromise, blackmail and treachery mark the pages devoted to this episode—*Lasker*⟩ ⟨books filled with *sordid*, filthy statements based on sexual deviations—*U.S. House of Representatives Report*⟩
*Ana* *base, low, vile: *contemptible, despicable, sorry, scurvy, cheap, beggarly, shabby, pitiable

**mean** *vb* **1** *intend, design, propose, purpose
*Ana* wish, want, *desire: *aim, aspire, pant

**2** Mean, denote, signify, import are comparable when they mean to convey to the mind a definite idea or interpretation. Not only words or phrases can be said to *mean, denote, signify,* or *import* something, but also whatever admits of interpretation or of being intellectually appraised (as a poem or an essay or an act of Congress, or the behavior of one person to another, or a set of circumstances). These words are commonly employed without distinction, but precision in their use is often possible and desirable. In their general application **mean** is the most common; it is often more expressive or poignant than the others when used to connote not only interpretation but also evaluation or appraisal ⟨he can have no idea of what it *means* to be the daughter of Mr. de Barral—*Conrad*⟩ ⟨national prosperity . . . has two surfaces: ability to sell *means* ability to buy; employment *means* production—*Benedict*⟩ **Denote**, in its widest application, is distinguished from the others by its taking for its subject things that serve as outward marks or visible indications; **signify**, by its taking for its subject things of a symbolic or representative character ⟨his somber expression *denoted* a worried mind⟩ ⟨slumped into a chair near the doorway, his posture *denoting* complete exhaustion—*Douglas*⟩ ⟨the scales in the hands of the figure of Justice *signify* impartiality⟩ ⟨the Eucharistic rite *signifies* one thing to Protestants and another to Catholics⟩ ⟨the "&c." *signified* that portion of King Henry's title . . . which, for the sake of brevity, was not written in full—*Maitland*⟩ *Signify* often suggests distinctiveness or importance ⟨events which *signify* little at the time of occurrence often attain significance when the history of that period is written⟩ ⟨I did not understand that I was living in a debtor land, nor what that *signified*—*White*⟩ **Import** frequently conveys an implication of carrying into the mind ⟨new ideas *import* little to those not intellectually fitted to receive them⟩ but it frequently comes close to *signify* ⟨what this *imported* I could ill divine—*Wordsworth*⟩ ⟨it *imports* little whether the sensible citizen is a Democrat or a Republican, an Episcopalian or a Presbyterian; it *imports* a good deal whether he is nationalist or internationalist— *Gerould*⟩
In their special use in reference to the interpretation of the content of a term, these words are not always dis-

tinguishable. **Mean**, however, is capable of implying reference to the term's full content, that is, to the idea or relation between ideas which it conveys to the mind and the suggestions which it evokes ⟨only a philosophically minded person can grasp what *beauty* and *truth mean* in Keats's lines "Beauty is truth, truth beauty,—that is all ye know on earth, and all ye need to know."⟩ **Signify** can, as *mean* usually does not, suggest symbolic relationship between the term and the idea it conveys ⟨the phrase "bread and butter" *signifies* the material needs of life⟩ **Denote** (see also DENOTE 2) can imply a logical definition in which the idea named or expressed by a term is clearly marked out and its application or range of application accurately determined ⟨"decoration" *denotes* one of three ideas, the act of adorning, or a thing used in adorning, or the results achieved by one who adorns⟩ **Import**, used with less frequency in relation to terms, is precise in its implications. A term *imports* not what it *denotes*, or bears as a definition, but any or all of the implications involved in its interpretation ⟨does it [the word "necessary"] always *import* an absolute physical necessity . . .?—*John Marshall*⟩
*Ana* *carry, convey, bear, transmit: *denote, connote: define, assign, *prescribe: *suggest, imply, intimate, hint

**mean** *n* **1** *average, median, norm, par

**2** Mean, instrument, instrumentality, agent, agency, medium, organ, vehicle, channel denote a person or thing through or by which work is performed or an end is effected. **Mean**, usually in the form **means** which may be either singular or plural in construction, is the most general of these words; it may be applied not only to persons and to such concrete things as implements, tools, and machines, but also to their actions or operations; it may also be applied to methods, policies, devices, and strategies ⟨the habit of regarding the laboring class as a mere *means* to the maintenance of the rest—*Dickinson*⟩ ⟨the manufacturer who doesn't look into every possible way and *mean* to show . . . where he may practically and economically find new business—*Harry Martin*⟩ ⟨the justification of barbarous *means* by holy ends—*Muller*⟩ ⟨the principal *means* of transportation was . . . Afghan camels—*Hoover*⟩ **Instrument** is applied especially to persons who merely carry out another's will or intention, often as tools, sometimes as dupes ⟨he . . . turned on me . . . suspecting perhaps that I only wished to make an *instrument* of him—*Hudson*⟩ ⟨if they [judges] were to be used as the *instruments*, and the knowing *instruments*, for violating what they swear to support—*John Marshall*⟩ When applied to concrete things, *instrument* often derives connotations from its musical sense (as susceptibility to manipulation and responsiveness to touch or use) ⟨he knew his brain was now a very uncertain *instrument*, sometimes quite good, sometimes a weary fount of half-formed ideas—*H. G. Wells*⟩ **Instrumentality** is interchangeable with *means* but not with *instrument* because its chief implication is effective action by, or effective use of, the instrument ⟨through the *instrumentality* of the police he was able to locate his relatives⟩ ⟨without the *instrumentality* of a free press liberty could not be preserved⟩ **Agent** is applied chiefly to persons and only by extension to things; the term usually names the one who does the work as distinguished from the one who wills, plans, or orders ⟨I often think, Jean, how you were an unconscious *agent* in the hands of Providence when you recalled me from Tucson—*Cather*⟩ ⟨ultimately these tattooed devils . . . were turned into effective *agents* for the maintenance of law and order—*Heiser*⟩ When applied to a thing, *agent* names what effects a desired result or serves as a cause producing a definite effect

⟨the cooling *agent* in making ice cream is a mixture of ice and rock salt⟩ **Agency,** like *instrumentality,* is not usually interchangeable with its related noun (*agent*) for it names the activity or operation of the agent or of something used to produce an effect. It is distinguished from *instrumentality* by its implication of causative, as opposed to effective, activity ⟨some communicable diseases are transmitted only through the *agency* of vermin or insects⟩ ⟨presumptuous thoughts that would assign mechanic laws to *agency* divine—*Wordsworth*⟩ **Medium** is more often applied to things than to persons; it designates especially a substance or material through which something, usually something intangible, is conveyed from one person or thing to another or given objective form ⟨air is the *medium* through which sound and light waves are transmitted⟩ ⟨language is the *medium* through which a person communicates his thoughts and feelings⟩ ⟨the sculptor's *medium* may be bronze, marble, or wood⟩ An **organ** is a part or representative that performs a particular function ⟨the political cartoon is one of the greatest *organs* of propaganda—*Harmsworth*⟩ or accomplishes a particular end ⟨the cabinet's function as a general *organ* of government without special regard to the king's wishes—*Times Lit. Sup.*⟩ or presents a particular point of view (see under JOURNAL). A **vehicle** is a medium that serves to carry and especially to carry effectively something which is to be revealed through it ⟨the play was an excellent *vehicle* for the genius of Booth⟩ ⟨we must find a new form of verse which shall be as satisfactory a *vehicle* for us as blank verse was for the Elizabethans—*T. S. Eliot*⟩ A **channel** is a medium that provides either an outlet or a fixed course through which something may flow from one to another ⟨the accident which directed my curiosity originally into this *channel* —*Lamb*⟩ ⟨submitting material to the Defense Department without going through the prescribed Army *channels*— *N. Y. Times*⟩
**Ana** *method, mode, manner, way, fashion, system: machinery, apparatus, *equipment, paraphernalia
**3** in plural form **means** resources, assets, effects, *possessions, belongings
**Ana** *money, cash, currency: riches, wealthiness, affluence, opulence (see corresponding adjectives at RICH)
**mean** *adj* average, median, par (see under AVERAGE *n*)
**Ant** extreme
**meander** stray, roam, ramble, *wander, rove, range, prowl, gad, gallivant, traipse
**meaning,** sense, acceptation, signification, significance, import are comparable when they denote the idea which something (as a word, a passage, a facial expression, an action, or a situation) conveys to the mind or is intended to convey to the mind. **Meaning,** the general term, may be used interchangeably with any of the remaining terms; it may be used of whatever can convey information when properly interpreted and therefore is not only applicable to language and expressions or gestures but to such more cryptic things as symbols and works of art ⟨a dictionary gives the *meanings* of words⟩ ⟨if *human* and the words formed from it can have an exact *meaning* . . . that *meaning* must refer to those qualities, characteristics, and powers which distinguish the human being—*Krutch*⟩ ⟨understand a plain man in his plain *meaning*—*Shak.*⟩ ⟨the sentence has *meaning* to Sam even if it will not have *meaning* to you. A great many ruminations, discoveries, and memories contribute their connotation—*Mailer*⟩ **Sense** (see also SENSE 2) denotes either the meaning or, more often, one of the specific or particular meanings, of a word or phrase, or sometimes of an allegory ⟨some words have many *senses*⟩ ⟨the literal and figurative *senses* of

*Pilgrim's Progress*⟩ ⟨in the *sense* usually implied by the word, Minneapolis has no slums, even though it admits to neighborhoods where substandard housing conditions prevail—*Amer. Guide Series: Minn.*⟩ More abstractly, it refers to intelligibility in general ⟨speaks things . . . that carry but half *sense*—*Shak.*⟩ ⟨in the first authentic edition . . . the words, I believe, ran "and a table of green fields," which has no *sense*—*Newman*⟩ ⟨if his work rarely has startling originality . . . it always has *sense* and penetration of judgment—*Schlesinger* b. 1917⟩ **Acceptation** (see also ACCEPTANCE) differs from *sense* as denoting a meaning of a term chiefly in its stress upon the actual use of that sense or upon its acceptance by a large number of writers and speakers ⟨it is necessary first to consider the different *acceptations* of the word knowledge—*Locke*⟩ ⟨[philosophy] in its common . . . *acceptation* . . . signifies the search after wisdom—*Fielding*⟩ ⟨where German has separate words for each subsidiary meaning, French is content with a general term, leaving it to the context to specify which particular *acceptation* is relevant—*Ullmann*⟩ **Signification** and *significance* (see *signify* under MEAN *vb* 2; *significance* under IMPORTANCE) are often used interchangeably in spite of the fact that they can be carefully differentiated in their meanings. **Signification** applies specifically to the established meaning of a term, a symbol, or a character, or to an established sense of a word; it usually implies that when a particular term or symbol or character is used only such an established idea is evoked in the mind of informed persons ⟨the *significations* of the characters which serve as Roman numerals⟩ ⟨I find it very . . . interesting to know the *signification* of names, and had written to ask him whether Jerusalem meant "the vision of peace" or "the foundation of peace" —*Arnold*⟩ ⟨the counsel for the appellee would . . . restrict a general term, applicable to many objects, to one of its *significations*. Commerce, undoubtedly, is traffic, but it is something more: it is intercourse—*John Marshall*⟩ **Significance,** on the other hand, applies specifically to the covert as distinguished from the established or the ostensible meaning of something; it may from its other sense (see IMPORTANCE) carry a connotation of weight or moment ⟨his language is so grandiose that one wonders if his speeches have any *significance*⟩ ⟨no one knows for a certainty the *significance* of some early Christian symbols⟩ ⟨for the mathematically illiterate, like myself, these things are . . . mere scribblings, without *significance* —*Huxley*⟩ ⟨explaining all the minute happenings of the ranch . . . as though each of them had a special joyous *significance*—*Mary Austin*⟩ **Import** (see also IMPORTANCE), like *significance,* may imply momentousness, but in contrast with that term, and like *signification,* it denotes the idea or the impression conveyed or to be conveyed to the mind by the medium of words ⟨spoke words in her ear that had an awful *import* to her—*Meredith*⟩ ⟨Kim gathered the *import* of the next few sentences—*Kipling*⟩
**Ana** suggestion, implication, intimation, hinting *or* hint (see corresponding verbs at SUGGEST): denotation, connotation (see under DENOTE)
**meaningful** significant, pregnant, sententious, *expressive, eloquent
**Ana** important, consequential, momentous, weighty (see corresponding nouns at IMPORTANCE)
**Ant** meaningless
**measly** paltry, trifling, trivial, puny, *petty, picayunish, picayune
**Ana** *contemptible, despicable, sorry, scurvy, cheap, beggarly, shabby: *stingy, parsimonious, penurious, miserly
**mechanic** workman, workingman, artisan, *worker, opera-

A colon (:) separates groups of words discriminated. An asterisk (*) indicates place of treatment of each group.

tive, hand, laborer, craftsman, handicraftsman, roustabout

**mechanical** automatic, instinctive, impulsive, *spontaneous

*Ana* stereotyped, hackneyed, *trite: dull, slow, *stupid, dense, crass, dumb

*Con* vital, cardinal, *essential, fundamental: *spirited, high-spirited, mettlesome, fiery, spunky, gingery

**mechanism** *machine, machinery, apparatus, engine, motor

**meddle,** interfere, intermeddle, tamper are comparable when they mean to busy or concern oneself with someone or something officiously, impertinently, or indiscreetly. One **meddles** *with* or *in* something that is not one's concern or is strictly the affair or the responsibility of another or of others; the term usually suggests the interposition of oneself without right or without permission or authorization ⟨it would be better if government *meddled* no farther with trade than to protect it—*Franklin*⟩ ⟨his enemies accused him . . . of . . . *meddling* in matters which did not belong to him—*Newman*⟩ ⟨it is inexpedient to *meddle* with questions of state in a land where men are highly paid to work them out for you—*Kipling*⟩ One **interferes** (see also INTERPOSE 2) *with* someone or something or *in* something when one meddles, whether intentionally or not, in such a way as to hinder, frustrate, molest, check, or defeat ⟨a physicist is not *interfering* with nature, any more than an architect is *interfering* with nature when he directs the building of a house—*Darrow*⟩ ⟨the Puritans made life in many ways a great deal less pleasant for the poor by *interfering* with their leisure —*Lewis & Maude*⟩ One **intermeddles** *with* or *in* something when one meddles impertinently and officiously and in such a way as to interfere ⟨the board of control had no right whatsoever to *intermeddle* in the business—*Burke*⟩ ⟨a petition to parliament sets forth how all kinds of unlearned men *intermeddle* with the practice of physic —*Coulton*⟩ One **tampers** *with* someone or something when one seeks to make unwarranted alterations, to perform meddlesome experiments, or to exert an improper influence; the term need not suggest corruption or clandestine operation ⟨provided, the farmer said, nobody had been *tampering* with any of his witnesses—*Meredith*⟩ ⟨money and sex are forces too unruly for our reason; they can only be controlled by taboos with which we *tamper* at our peril—*L. P. Smith*⟩ ⟨the goal of the search was fixed; it was sacrilegious and dangerous to *tamper* with the dogmas—*Thilly*⟩

*Ana* *intrude, obtrude, interlope, butt in: *interpose, interfere, intervene: discommode, incommode, trouble, *inconvenience

**meddlesome** *impertinent, intrusive, obtrusive, officious

*Ana* interfering, meddling, intermeddling, tampering (see MEDDLE): prying, snoopy, nosy, inquisitive, *curious

**median** *n* *average, mean, norm, par

**median** *adj* average, mean, par (see under AVERAGE *n*)

**mediate** intercede, intervene, *interpose, interfere

*Ana* arbitrate, *judge, ‘adjudge, adjudicate: conciliate, propitiate (see PACIFY): reconcile, accommodate, *adapt

**medicament, medication** medicine, *remedy, cure, specific, physic

**medicinal** *n* *drug, pharmaceutical, biologic, simple

**medicine** *remedy, cure, medicament, medication, specific, physic

**mediocre** *medium, middling, second-rate, moderate, average, fair, indifferent

*Ana* poor, wrong, *bad: *common, ordinary, vulgar

**meditate** *ponder, muse, ruminate

*Ana* contemplate, *consider, study, weigh: reflect, reason, speculate, deliberate, *think, cogitate: examine,

inspect, *scrutinize

**meditative** contemplative, speculative, *thoughtful, reflective, pensive

*Ana* pondering, musing, ruminating (see PONDER)

**medium** *n* *mean, instrument, instrumentality, agent, agency, organ, vehicle, channel

**medium** *adj* Medium, middling, mediocre, second-rate, moderate, average, fair, indifferent mean midway, or about midway, between the extremes of a scale or measurement or evaluation. Medium usually presupposes reference to some scale of measurement or comparison, whether by literal use of an instrument, or through mental power of measuring or gauging attained by experience ⟨a boy of *medium* height⟩ ⟨a book of *medium* size⟩ ⟨a *medium* grade of motor oil⟩ ⟨a *medium* gray⟩ ⟨the reports . . . received from about 70 publishers, large, *medium* and small, of hard-cover books—*Publishers' Weekly*⟩ ⟨cheddar . . . is mild, *medium,* or sharp, depending on the amount of acidity in the milk—*Standen*⟩ Middling is seldom used when accurate measurement or gradation is implied; it is employed chiefly in estimations (as of quality, rank, or value) to describe what is as far removed from the worst or lowest as it is from the best or highest. It may appropriately describe something that fails to measure up to the best or the first rate yet does not merit disapproval or rejection ⟨I discovered that I had been poised for an enormous sale or a failure—a *middling* success was cruel to take—*Mailer*⟩ ⟨both of the writers lauded highly . . . contemporaries who were certainly no better than *middling* performers in their several arts—*Montague*⟩ ⟨not all merchants were merchant princes. The great majority were *middling* people, mildly prosperous—*Plumb*⟩ In commercial use *middling* sometimes specifically designates the second of three grades ⟨carded yarn spun from 1-in. *middling* cotton—*Sheldon & Blake*⟩ Mediocre tends to be more depreciative than *middling*; thus, one who describes a moving picture as *middling* implies that it was good, but far from excellent, but one who describes it as *mediocre* gives ground for the inference that it was distinctly less than what one might call good. Often the word is modified by an adverb of degree ⟨it is a very *mediocre* poem⟩ ⟨he has only *mediocre* ability⟩ ⟨my performance is *mediocre* to the last degree—*Austen*⟩ ⟨a best seller is the gilded tomb of a *mediocre* talent—*L. P. Smith*⟩ Second-rate implies a ranking midway between extremes regarded as first-rate and as third-rate ⟨he is possessed of a good heart, and a *second-* or third-*rate* brain— *Erskine*⟩ ⟨fears that a strong continental coalition would soon surpass Britain . . . and the United Kingdom would gradually sink from the status of a *second-rate* to a third-rate power—*Patrick McMahon*⟩ Frequently *second-rate* loses all suggestion of a position on a scale of rating and then connotes inferiority and is used interchangeably with *mediocre* ⟨a *second-rate* singer⟩ ⟨a *second-rate* performance⟩ ⟨even an occasional notable critic like Edmund Wilson has dismissed him as *second-rate*—*Cordell*⟩ ⟨a gang of *second-rate* imitators who enjoyed moving in the reflected glory of the man who could outrun, outdrink, outfight, outlove, and outcuss any other man in the County —*Lockridge*⟩ Moderate (see also MODERATE 1) stresses limitations in quality, intensity, or degree; it implies distance from the extreme or from either of the extremes possible to a thing of its kind ⟨*moderate* wealth⟩ ⟨a man of *moderate* ability⟩ ⟨a *moderate* wind⟩ ⟨attain *moderate* success⟩ ⟨an infusion of *moderate* strength⟩ ⟨I was a *moderate* scholar and a competent athlete—*Benson*⟩ Average (see also under AVERAGE *n*) implies a theoretical level at which all things of a given kind, class, or category would find themselves or would seek, if their inequalities

were resolved ⟨published an article called "The Eclipse of the Highbrow," in which the *average* man was exalted —*Forster*⟩ ⟨an *average* June day⟩ However the term is applied more often to what seems of the common run or is undistinguished either by its superiority or its inferiority, or is not exceptional or outstanding in any way; thus, a man of *average* ability seems to have neither greater nor less ability than that of the ordinary man ⟨the only one . . . with whom he cared to probe into things a little deeper than the *average* level of club and chophouse banter— *Wharton*⟩ ⟨Mr. Shaw has understood everything but the *average* values of *average* living. His virtues, like his values, have all been exceptional—*J. M. Brown*⟩ **Fair** is applied to what is neither notably good nor bad, excellent nor poor, large nor small; often, only the context can reveal whether the implication is one of adequacy or of deficiency ⟨scraped together a *fair* breakfast⟩ ⟨the enrollment of 475 was composed largely of freshmen, with a *fair* representation from other classes—*Kinne*⟩ ⟨his health was only *fair*⟩ ⟨this region has had a *fair* amount of rain⟩ ⟨a *fair* knowledge of English and a smattering of Latin— *W. E. Smith*⟩ **Indifferent** is applied to what is difficult to rate because it is completely unimpressive, warranting neither praise nor censure ⟨play an *indifferent* game of bridge⟩ ⟨it is not cluttered up with *indifferent* and unimportant records, and aims at . . . the best—*Edward Sackville-West*⟩ ⟨the surprising obscurity and even *indifferent* Latinity of Locke the perfectionist—*Times Lit. Sup.*⟩
*Ana* mean, median, average, par (see under AVERAGE *n*): *common, ordinary, vulgar, popular

**meed** *n* guerdon, prize, award, reward, *premium, bounty, bonus
*Ana* recompensing *or* recompense, remuneration, satisfaction (see corresponding verbs at PAY)

**meek** modest, *humble, lowly
*Ana* gentle, mild (see SOFT): subdued, submissive, *tame: *compliant, acquiescent, resigned: *forbearing, tolerant, lenient: patient, long-suffering (see corresponding nouns at PATIENCE)
*Ant* arrogant —*Con* *proud, lordly, overbearing, haughty: *spirited, high-spirited, mettlesome, spunky: rebellious, contumacious, *insubordinate

**meet** *vb* **1** Meet, face, encounter, confront can all mean to come across or to run into someone or something face-to-face or as if face-to-face. **Meet** fundamentally implies the action of two or more persons or things which from different directions come across each other by design or by accident; often it implies nothing more ⟨the narrow strip of Syrian seaboard which they occupied when we first *meet* them in history—*Clodd*⟩ ⟨where the Mohawk *meets* the Hudson river⟩ ⟨the little girl ran to *meet* her father as he came up the hill⟩ Beyond this, the word may suggest such actions or intentions as finding, experiencing, or dealing with successfully ⟨I never *met* with such kindness before⟩ ⟨it is perhaps only in England that such ideas can be expressed without *meeting* anger or ridicule— *Sykes*⟩ ⟨Hobart . . . could talk; he could assert; produce opinions and information, but he couldn't *meet* or answer arguments—*Rose Macaulay*⟩ **Face** may imply nothing more than a standing or a meeting face-to-face (as of persons or things that merely present their faces or their fronts to each other) ⟨they *faced* each other across the table⟩ ⟨a very capacious couch *faced* a generous fireplace—*Sidney Lovett*⟩ but it more often emphasizes the act or intention of one who with courage or resolution or confidence, or with effrontery, or with desperation, looks upon or meets another person or thing ⟨the government *faces* a strong storm of protest over its decision—*Current History*⟩ ⟨the artist must *face* life and defy it—*Bambrick*⟩

⟨she couldn't *face* a lifetime of misery⟩ **Encounter** in its earliest and still not uncommon sense implies mutual hostility or active conflict ⟨the armies are now ready to *encounter* each other⟩ There has, however, been a progressive weakening of this implication, so that the word more frequently implies a running up against something that presents a difficulty, hardship, or obstacle ⟨after half an hour's free indulgence of grief . . . Catherine felt equal to *encountering* her friends—*Austen*⟩ ⟨the difficulties that had been *encountered* in attempting to perfect the machine—*Anderson*⟩ ⟨the innumerable hardships and discomforts to be *encountered* in the provinces—*Heiser*⟩ Often, even this notion of difficulty or hardship in turn is lost and the term means nothing more than *meet*, especially by chance or unexpectedly ⟨groping about, his hand *encountered* something warm that started at his touch— *Meredith*⟩ ⟨walked the whole of the six or seven miles . . . without *encountering* a soul—*Mackenzie*⟩ **Confront** more clearly than the other terms stresses the unavoidable face-to-face nature of the meeting and often also carries a strong implication of a resolute intent or firm determination to clarify an issue or settle a difficulty through such meeting ⟨he was *confronted* by several witnesses of the accident⟩ ⟨the predicament with which our civilization now finds itself *confronted*—*L. P. Smith*⟩ ⟨when he was *confronted* by accidental extinction, he had felt no will to resist—*Cather*⟩
*Ana* accost, greet, salute (see ADDRESS): collide, *bump, clash: *experience, undergo, sustain, suffer: *wrestle, grapple, tussle: forestall, anticipate (see PREVENT)
*Ant* avoid —*Con* evade, elude, shun, *escape
**2** *satisfy, fulfill, answer
*Ana* equal, approach, *match, touch: gratify, *please: content, *satisfy
*Ant* disappoint

**meet** *adj* suitable, proper, *fit, appropriate, fitting, apt, happy, felicitous
*Ana* adapted, adjusted, accommodated, conformed, reconciled (see ADAPT): right, *good: just, equitable, *fair
*Ant* unmeet

**melancholia** melancholy, *sadness, depression, dejection, gloom, blues, dumps

**melancholic** *adj* Melancholic, melancholy, atrabilious, hypochondriac are comparable when they mean gloomy or depressed, especially as a manifestation of one's temperament or state of health. *Melancholic* and *melancholy* are often used interchangeably without additional implications or suggestions ⟨the drawings Thurber has produced . . . calling into being an ineradicable population of fierce-looking women, furtive men, and gently *melancholic* dogs—*Newsweek*⟩ ⟨the Cape Colored, a gentle and *melancholy* people—*N. Y. Times*⟩ although each can be used discriminatingly to suggest the differences inherent in their related nouns (see *melancholia* and *melancholy* under SADNESS). In such use **melancholic** describes a person who is afflicted with or inclined to melancholia ⟨those recurring moods of *melancholic* suspicion which had so tortured me . . . remained absent and she seemed on the road to recovery—*Ellis*⟩ **Melancholy**, on the other hand, describes a person, or the mood, disposition, acts, or utterances of a person, who is excessively sad or detached in spirit and, usually, averse to what is cheerful or gay ⟨"They say you are a *melancholy* fellow." "I am so; I do love it better than laughing"—*Shak.*⟩ ⟨a changed smile flickered like sunlight over the *melancholy* countenance—*Wylie*⟩ ⟨there is no merriment . . . comparable to that of *melancholy* people escaping from the dark region in which it is their custom to keep themselves imprisoned —*Hawthorne*⟩ **Atrabilious** preserves the implication of an

---

A colon (:) separates groups of words discriminated. An asterisk (*) indicates place of treatment of each group.

unhealthy physical condition more strongly than the preceding words; often in modern use it suggests the morose or choleric disposition of the dyspeptic or the predilection for gloom of those who have been subjected to severe strain ⟨neither were those plump rosy-gilled Englishmen that came hither, but a hard-faced, *atrabilious,* earnest-eyed race—*J. R. Lowell*⟩ ⟨that the American genius was foredoomed to fail was the *atrabilious* Ames's firm conviction—*Brooks*⟩ **Hypochondriac** comes close to *atrabilious* in its suggestion of constitutional gloominess but it implies also an unwholesome anxiety about one's state of health ⟨she was rather *hypochondriac* and was gloating over the tale of her symptoms—*Edmund Wilson*⟩ ⟨the culture just had gone *hypochondriac,* and all members of the society, whatever their congenital individual dispositions, had fear and pessimism pounded into them from childhood on—*Kroeber*⟩
*Ana* *despondent, despairing, hopeless, forlorn, desperate: pessimistic, misanthropic, *cynical, misogynic

**melancholy** *n* *sadness, melancholia, dejection, gloom, depression, blues, dumps
*Ana* miserableness *or* misery, wretchedness (see corresponding adjectives at MISERABLE): despondency, despair, hopelessness, forlornness, desperation (see under DESPONDENT): *tedium, boredom, ennui, doldrums
*Ant* exhilaration —*Con* joy, delight, *pleasure, enjoyment, delectation, fruition: hopefulness, optimism (see corresponding adjectives at HOPEFUL)

**melancholy** *adj* **1** *melancholic, atrabilious, hypochondriac
*Ana* morose, gloomy, glum, *sullen, dour, saturnine: depressed, oppressed, weighed down (see DEPRESS): *despondent, despairing, hopeless, forlorn, desperate
**2** Melancholy, dolorous, doleful, lugubrious, rueful, plaintive are comparable when they mean expressing or suggesting sorrow or mourning. All of these words have, to a greater or less extent, weakened from their original meaning and are often used with a half-humorous connotation. **Melancholy** may stress a quality that inspires pensiveness or sad reflection or awakens mournful thoughts or recollections which are not only not necessarily painful or disagreeable, but often agreeable, especially to the poetic or thoughtful mind ⟨sweet bird, that shunn'st the noise of folly, most musical, most *melancholy!*—*Milton*⟩ ⟨the tender images we love to trace steal from each year a *melancholy* grace—*Rogers*⟩ ⟨I have in the present moment only the *melancholy* pleasure of an easy conscience—*Warren*⟩ The term more frequently applies to something which expresses or excites dejection or depression ⟨his *melancholy* old house on the hill—*Deland*⟩ ⟨that *melancholy* problem of a money-earning occupation which lay so heavily on my thoughts—*Ellis*⟩ **Dolorous** describes what is lamentable in its gloom or dismalness or is exaggeratedly dismal ⟨that *dolorous* aspect of human nature which in comedy is best portrayed by Molière—*T. S. Eliot*⟩ ⟨a rapid succession of warnings, as *dolorous* and pessimistic as the little booklets of possible mishaps that accompany the sale of English cars—*Gallant*⟩ **Doleful** and *lugubrious* are also frequently applied to what is exaggeratedly dismal or dreary, but **doleful** connotes a weight of woe ⟨a *doleful* and lackadaisical air⟩ ⟨the mourners, who are singing a very *doleful* dirge—*Goodenough*⟩ and **lugubrious,** an undue, and often an affected, heaviness or solemnity ⟨dark funereal barges like my own had flitted by, and the gondoliers had warned each other at every turning with hoarse, *lugubrious* cries—*Howells*⟩ ⟨a *lugubrious* obituary quality in the treatment given by the American press to Sir Winston's resignation—*Reporter*⟩ ⟨a *lugubrious* place which filled me with dread—*Henry Miller*⟩ **Rueful**

implies sorrow and regret but it often suggests a quizzical attitude ⟨the woebegone heroes . . . eyed each other with *rueful* countenances—*Irving*⟩ ⟨the fleeting glory of Napoleon, the *rueful* memory of Josephine and her somehow less enviable successor—*Cassidy*⟩ **Plaintive** applies chiefly to tones, sounds, utterances, or rhythms that suggest complaint or mourning or that excite pity or compassion ⟨the *plaintive* cries of a child⟩ ⟨he sighed, his voice became *plaintive*—*Huxley*⟩ ⟨the clarinet sings, in its eerie *plaintive* tone—*S. R. Watson*⟩
*Ana* pathetic, poignant, *moving, touching: hopeless, forlorn, despairing (see DESPONDENT): pensive, reflective, *thoughtful: discomposing, disquieting, perturbing, disturbing (see DISCOMPOSE)
*Con* happy, *glad, cheerful, joyous, joyful, lighthearted: *lively, vivacious, gay

**melee** fracas, row, *brawl, broil, rumpus, scrap
*Ana* altercation, *quarrel, wrangle, squabble: *confusion, disorder

**mellow** ripe, matured, *mature, adult, grown-up
*Ana* *tender, warm, sympathetic, responsive, warm-hearted
*Ant* unmellow: green —*Con* raw, crude, callow, uncouth, *rude, rough

**melodramatic** histrionic, theatrical, dramaturgic, *dramatic
*Ana* *showy, pretentious, ostentatious: *sentimental, romantic, maudlin, mawkish

**melody, air, tune** all denote a clearly distinguishable succession of rhythmically ordered tones. **Melody** stresses the sweetness or beauty of sound produced by such an arrangement of tones ⟨sweetest *melodies* are those that are by distance made more sweet—*Wordsworth*⟩ It also commonly suggests expressiveness or moving power and a carefully wrought pattern ⟨nerve-dissolving *melody* —*Tennyson*⟩ ⟨'tis a rich sobbing *melody,* with reliefs full and majestic—*Keats*⟩ Technically, as applied to complex musical structure, *melody* implies a contrast to *harmony;* it designates that kind of musical beauty produced by a continuous series of tones in one or more of the voice parts, in distinction from that produced by simultaneously sounded tones in all the voice parts. **Air** is applied technically to the dominating melody, usually carried by the upper voices (as in a chorale or part-song) ⟨and whistle all the *airs* from . . . *Pinafore*—*Gilbert*⟩ In more general use *air* is often applied to an easily remembered succession of tones which identifies a simple musical composition (as a song, a ballad, or a waltz) and which is more commonly and more precisely called **tune;** thus, one may refer to the *air,* or the *tune,* of a song ⟨hum the *air* of the *Marseillaise*⟩ ⟨left her fancywork and played for them some old Scotch *airs*—*Black*⟩ ⟨he . . . can invent a good *tune* which immediately captivates one—*Dyneley Hussey*⟩ **Tune** is also applied to the musical setting of a text (as a ballad, psalm, or lyric) ⟨a hymn *tune*⟩ and to a simple composition whether unison or harmonized ⟨a dance *tune*⟩ ⟨many hundred texts and *tunes* of English-Canadian folk songs—*Report on Nat'l Development (Ottawa)*⟩

**melt** *liquefy, deliquesce, fuse, thaw

**member** *part, portion, piece, detail, division, section, segment, sector, fraction, fragment, parcel
*Ana* *element, component, constituent: branch, limb, *shoot, bough

**memento** *remembrance, remembrancer, reminder, memorial, token, keepsake, souvenir
*Ana* token, earnest, *pledge: *gift, present, favor

**memoir** *biography, life, autobiography, confessions

**memorable** *noteworthy, notable

*Ana* remembered, recollected, recalled (see REMEMBER): salient, remarkable, *noticeable, outstanding, striking, arresting: *exceptional

**memorandum** *letter, epistle, missive, note, message, dispatch, report

**memorial** *n* *remembrance, remembrancer, reminder, memento, token, keepsake, souvenir

*Ana* monument, record (see DOCUMENT): *sign, mark, token

**memory, remembrance, recollection, reminiscence, mind, souvenir** are comparable though not wholly synonymous terms since all involve the ideas of remembering and of being remembered. **Memory** applies chiefly to the power or function of remembering what has been experienced or learned; in this sense it suggests the power to reproduce images of what is no longer before one, to retain something (as words, ideas, or skills) that has been learned, and to recognize and identify something previously known ⟨he has a remarkably good *memory* for names⟩ ⟨her *memory* . . . went slipping back upon the golden days— *Tennyson*⟩ *Memory* often occurs in the sense of something remembered either as an aggregate or as a single item. More than the other words *memory* as used in this sense suggests a keeping in mind rather than a bringing back and often, therefore, a treasuring as something intimate or personal ⟨a present moment of comfortable reality was worth a decade of *memories—Hardy*⟩ ⟨it was the merest *memory* now, vague and a little sweet—*Galsworthy*⟩ ⟨you must have had a charming evening . . . if I may judge from the way you have kept the *memory* green—*Conrad*⟩ **Remembrance** applies primarily to the act or the process, as distinguished from the faculty, power, or function, of remembering ⟨the *remembrance* of all that made life dear pierced me to the core—*Hudson*⟩ ⟨Roman soldiers . . . keep the restless Jews in *remembrance* of their provincial status—*Douglas*⟩ ⟨as April's green endures; or will endure like her *remembrance* of awakened birds—*Stevens*⟩ *Remembrance* also denotes the state or fact of being kept in the memory ⟨moments . . . that live again in *remembrance—Gibson*⟩ ⟨our literature is going to be our most perdurable claim on man's *remembrance—Quiller-Couch*⟩ **Recollection** often takes the place of *remembrance* but it may carry a strong suggestion of more voluntary and sometimes even more effortful recalling to mind often of something forgotten or for long unconsidered ⟨he looked . . . alarmed; but with a moment's *recollection* and a returning smile, replied— *Austen*⟩ ⟨half a word fixed upon or near the spot, is worth a cartload of *recollection—Gray*⟩ ⟨there came to him a slight uneasiness, a movement of the memory, a distant *recollection* of something, somewhere, he had seen before—*Dahl*⟩ But *recollection* is quite as often used of something remembered, especially as the result of conscious effort ⟨vivid indeed is my *recollection* of our halts before shaded homesteads, our protracted and usually successful parleys with lean housewives, hungry for conversation—*Grandgent*⟩ ⟨carried away from Casablanca an unpleasant *recollection* of indignities to which he believed he had been subjected—*Funk*⟩ **Reminiscence** carries a stronger implication of recovery through retrospection than any of the other terms. Like *remembrance* and *recollection* it denotes either the act or the process of remembering but it further suggests the recollection of what has been long unremembered, especially because it belongs to one's remote past ⟨the old man spent hour after hour indulging in *reminiscence*⟩ ⟨after another quarter of an hour of *reminiscence* they had got around to the things that had happened to each of them since they had last met—*Mary Austin*⟩ ⟨spurred into *reminiscence*

. . . revealed a strange tale told to him years earlier— *Rippin*⟩ The term is often used in place of *recollection* in the concrete sense where what is remembered serves as a contribution to biography, an autobiography, or a history ⟨the author's own *reminiscences* of childhood and youth—*Times Lit. Sup.*⟩ or is recalled from the past in conversation or in writing by an aging or aged person ⟨enjoy the *reminiscences* of the old veterans⟩ or is a phrase, a passage, a thought, or a custom that is so like one found in an earlier writer or people as to be regarded as an unconscious imitation or repetition or a survival ⟨the young poet's best phrases are *reminiscences* of Keats⟩ ⟨*reminiscences* of medieval pageants in modern carnivals⟩ ⟨here and there are to be found the *reminiscences* of Rimski-Korsakov's mannerisms—*Sargeant*⟩ **Mind** (see also MIND 2) is found in the sense here considered chiefly in certain idiomatic phrases where it means either the entity (as distinct from the function) which stores up what is remembered ⟨I shall keep your need in *mind*⟩ ⟨out of sight, out of *mind*⟩ or the power to remember ⟨like . . . assorted autocrats since time out of *mind*, always referred to himself in the third person—*Pynchon*⟩ **Souvenir,** which more commonly denotes a material memento, may sometimes replace *memory* ⟨then she carefully restored them, her mind full of *souvenirs* newly awakened— *Bennett*⟩

*Ana* *mind, intellect, soul, intelligence, brain, wit: remembering, minding, recalling, reminding (see REMEMBER): awareness, consciousness, cognizance (see corresponding adjectives at AWARE)

*Ant* oblivion

**menace** *vb* *threaten

*Ana* alarm, terrify, scare, *frighten: *intimidate, cow: presage, portend, forebode, forecast (see FORETELL)

**mend** *vb* **Mend, repair, patch, rebuild** are comparable when they mean to put into good or fitting order something that is injured, damaged, or defective. **Mend** basically implies a freeing from faults or defects ⟨*mend* your manners⟩ ⟨the wound *mended* slowly⟩ but in its most common use it specifically suggests a process of making whole or sound something that has been broken, torn, or injured (as by wear or use). In such use the term is especially applicable when the task calls for no extraordinary skill or unusual equipment; thus, one *mends* a dress by sewing up tears, darning holes, or reinforcing worn spots ⟨*mend* a broken dish with glue⟩ ⟨*mending* the stone wall with cobbles from the field⟩ ⟨over here the roads were never *mended* unless a few of the farmers agreed to give so much labor—*Glasgow*⟩ Often, and especially in extended use, *mend* stresses the resulting putting in order without much regard to the nature of the means of its attainment ⟨he *mended* the fire while he was speaking and the glow fell over the darkened room—*Roberts*⟩ ⟨whenever civilization palled upon him, he learned to *mend* his soul by going to sea—*Erskine*⟩ **Repair** is often interchangeable with *mend* in the sense of to make whole or sound, but typically it implies greater or more professional skill by the performer and usually correspondingly greater complexity both in the task involved and in the equipment used; thus, an old-time cobbler *mended* shoes so that they were good for further use but a modern specialist may *repair* them so well that his work cannot be detected; a boy may know how to *repair* a car but be unable to do so for lack of essential tools ⟨*mending* refers to minor restoration, not involving the replacement of any material or the separation of book from cover . . . . *Repairing* is the partial rehabilitation of a worn book, the amount of work done being less than the minimum involved in rebinding and more than the maximum involved in

A colon (:) separates groups of words discriminated. An asterisk (*) indicates place of treatment of each group.

*mending—Library Jour.⟩* In extended use, too, *repair* may be quite like *mend* ⟨the plain fact is that peace— or what passed for peace before it was broken—cannot be *mended*, cannot be *repaired*, cannot be restored— *MacLeish⟩* but often it more specifically implies a making good or making up for something ⟨reminds himself that he had not wept for the death of his mother a year or so earlier, and proceeds to *repair* the omission—*Times Lit. Sup.⟩* ⟨although his range of reading was wide, he could not in some respects *repair* the lack of early education— *Collis⟩* **Patch** basically implies a mending by covering, filling in, or reinforcing such a defect as a hole, rent, or weak spot, typically with the same or a similar material ⟨*patch* overalls worn thin at the knee⟩ ⟨*patch* holes in the road with asphalt⟩ ⟨*patch* an inner tube⟩ Sometimes, often with *up*, it implies careless, hurried, clumsy, or temporary mending ⟨$4,800,000 appropriated to start a new prison in New Jersey has been since diverted to *patch* up the 118-year-old penal slum at Trenton—*O'Leary⟩* and in much of its extended use this is the aspect stressed ⟨he hastily tries to *patch* up his marriage and purify his politics —*Bentley⟩* ⟨relations between the two men had to be *patched* up repeatedly—*Ishbel Ross⟩* Sometimes, often with *together*, *patch* implies a making from bits and pieces or odds and ends ⟨*patch* a quilt⟩ ⟨*patch* a car together from pieces out of the junkyard⟩ ⟨his life must be *patched* together from scattered references in the contemporary colonial records—*J. T. Adams⟩* **Rebuild**, which normally means to build again something which has been razed or ruined, is often preferred in industry and business to *repair* because it implies a thoroughgoing repairing with addition of new parts when necessary that makes a thing like new ⟨a *rebuilt* typewriter⟩ ⟨*rebuild* a carburetor⟩
*Ana* *improve, better, ameliorate, help: emend, remedy, redress, *correct, rectify, reform: *renew, restore, renovate, rejuvenate, refurbish: fix, *adjust, regulate

**mendacious** *dishonest, lying, untruthful, deceitful
*Ana* *false, wrong: prevaricating, equivocating, paltering, fibbing (see LIE *vb*)
*Ant* veracious　*—Con* *reliable, dependable, trustworthy: honest, *upright, just, scrupulous, conscientious, honorable

**menial** servile, slavish, *subservient, obsequious
*Ana* abject, *mean, sordid, ignoble: *base, low, vile: groveling, wallowing (see WALLOW)

**mental,** **intellectual, psychic, intelligent, cerebral** can mean of, relating to, or characteristic of that sum total of powers or functions called variously *mind, intellect, soul, psyche,* or *brain* (compare MIND 2). In general **mental** applies directly to what has to do with the mind as a real or as a purely theoretical entity ⟨his *mental* life⟩ ⟨a *mental* state⟩ ⟨*mental* diseases⟩ ⟨*mental* processes⟩ ⟨because every experience is constituted by interaction . . . between a self and its world, it is not itself either merely physical nor merely *mental*—*Dewey⟩* ⟨even if he dreads no physical betrayal, he suffers . . . at every hint of *mental* estrangement—*Santayana⟩* **Intellectual** differs from *mental* not only in its reference to the intellect, and therefore to such higher powers of the mind as the comprehension of the abstract or difficult and the ability to reason, but also because it is directly applicable to persons, their utterances, acts, and qualities ⟨an *intellectual* person⟩ It often carries an implied contrast to *emotional* and suggests an attachment to study and reflection ⟨all the *intellectual* qualities of the liberal mind—detachment, subtlety, complexity, understatement, irony—*Lerner⟩* ⟨the detective story, as created by Poe, is something as specialized and as *intellectual* as a chess problem—*T. S. Eliot⟩* ⟨it was only on her *intellectual* side that Elizabeth

touched the England of her day. All its moral aspects were simply dead to her—*J. R. Green⟩* **Psychic** implies a relation to the inner self or psyche and guides the attention away from notions of the physical, physiological, or organic ⟨you keep talking about maladies of the mind and soul. I don't accept the idea of *psychic* diseases analogous to mental diseases—*Mackenzie⟩* ⟨the humorist was a type that pioneer society required in order to maintain its *psychic* equilibrium—*Brooks⟩* **Intelligent** (see also INTELLIGENT 2) implies such a degree of mental power in a person or animal as to make possible appraisal of a situation and formulation of sound or reasonable decisions; it is often contrasted with *stupid* or *silly* ⟨men are *intelligent* beings⟩ ⟨some dogs are more *intelligent* than others⟩ ⟨*intelligent* self-interest⟩ ⟨friends, who were a little more *intelligent* and would understand— *Hersey⟩* **Cerebral** basically calls to mind the higher centers of the brain and may suggest intellectual activity or inclination especially as being coolly analytical and withdrawn from the sensuous and emotional aspects of the mental life ⟨the musical expression is sufficiently *cerebral* not to inflame anyone's libido—*Kolodin⟩* ⟨too *cerebral* a style, too baldly intellectual, to be wholly satisfactory—*Brand Blanshard⟩* ⟨doubtful if he ever can become a popular hero. He is too detached, too *cerebral*, and too rigid—*Gunther⟩*

**mention** *vb* **Mention, name, instance, specify** are comparable when they mean to make clear or specific by referring to something explicitly. **Mention** indicates a calling attention to, usually by name where possible, sometimes by a brief, cursory, or incidental reference ⟨I shall *mention* the accident which directed my curiosity originally into this channel—*Lamb⟩* ⟨intellectuals are such puritanical devils, that they usually recoil with horror when prayer is *mentioned*—*Forster⟩* ⟨usually the class is not directly *mentioned* in our statement; but there must be an implicit understanding, since otherwise the probability would be indeterminate—*Eddington⟩* ⟨*mentioning* several minor figures in his lecture on Shakespeare⟩ **Name** implies clear mention of a name and therefore may suggest greater explicitness ⟨*naming* Doe and Roe in the report and implicating their associates⟩ ⟨he *names* golf, tennis, and music as his chief means of recreation— *Current Biog.⟩* **Instance** may indicate clear explicit reference or definite emphasis as a typical example or special case ⟨examples can be *instanced* from the first to the twentieth century—*Latourette⟩* ⟨is it unfair to *instance* Marlowe, who died young?—*Quiller-Couch⟩* ⟨I have *instanced* his book because it was flagrant, not unique—*Leech⟩* **Specify** implies statement so explicit, detailed, and specific that misunderstanding is impossible ⟨the standards *specify* the names under which these five varieties must be sold—*Americana Annual⟩* ⟨as changes emerge from the storm of civil commotion, it is often just as hard to *specify* the exact day on which a government is born or dies—*Jessup⟩* ⟨to *specify* the structure of a skeleton is to *specify* the bones of which it consists and their interrelations—*Clement⟩*
*Ana* *refer, allude, advert: cite, *quote

**mephitic** toxic, *poisonous, venomous, virulent, pestilent, pestilential, miasmic, miasmatic, miasmal
*Ana* *offensive, loathsome, revolting, repulsive, repugnant: fetid, noisome, putrid, *malodorous: noxious, *pernicious, baneful

**mercantile** *commercial

**mercenary** *adj* **Mercenary, hireling, venal, hack** are comparable though not closely synonymous terms when they are applied to persons, or their acts, services, or products with the meaning actuated or motivated chiefly

---

by a desire for profit. **Mercenary** stresses self-interest and often self-seeking as the guiding motive; it usually, except when applied to soldiers who serve a foreign power for a wage, applies to persons or services that should be prompted by altruism or by noble aims or should be characterized by unselfishness or selflessness ⟨the faithful service of the heart; so rendered and so free from any *mercenary* taint—*Dickens*⟩ ⟨if a writer's attitude toward his characters and his scene is as vulgar as a showman's, as *mercenary* as an auctioneer's, vulgar and meretricious will his product for ever remain—*Cather*⟩ **Hireling** suggests the attitude of one who serves for the wage involved or is guided by servile motives; the term usually, especially in its more common opprobrious use, implies a motive no higher than that of the reward promised or foreseen ⟨prostituted muse and *hireling* bard—*Byron*⟩ ⟨the Quaker was a mystic . . . who denied the Scriptural validity of a Hebraized Calvinism and a *hireling* priesthood—*Parrington*⟩ **Venal** implies purchasability ⟨his initiation to *venal* love is sordid and mournful—*Peyre*⟩ The term often connotes the use of bribery and nearly always carries a strong implication of corruption or of corruptibility ⟨*venal* politicians⟩ ⟨*venal* members of the ill-paid police force discovered in opium a perquisite much greater than the customary squeeze—*Berrigan*⟩ ⟨women can take many forms . . . this gift for metamorphosis could be used to further all kinds of *venal* and petty schemes—*Cheever*⟩ **Hack** is used of a person, or of the work of such a person, willing to forfeit freedom of action and initiative or personal and professional integrity in return for an assured reward (as regular wages or political spoils). The term (and especially its corresponding noun **hack**) commonly combines some of the implications of *mercenary* and *venal*; like the former it implies self-interest and like the latter corruptibility. Distinctively, *hack* regularly stresses the mediocre and uninspired quality of the person or his work and may imply a background of previous professional failure or inherent low order of ability ⟨his voice had all the mechanical solicitude for unimportant facts common to a *hack* policeman anywhere in the world—*MacLennan*⟩ ⟨like a *hack* politician fighting the winged aggressor with yesterday's magic coat of ragged words—*MacNeice*⟩ ⟨some of the novels . . . were very good, some were so-so, some mere *hack* work—*Hass*⟩ ⟨the official Soviet histories and monographs, justly denounced . . . as crude travesties executed by official *hacks* and sycophants—*Times Lit. Sup.*⟩
*Ana* abject, \*mean, sordid, ignoble: \*covetous, greedy, acquisitive, grasping, avaricious: debased, corrupt, corrupted, depraved (see under DEBASE)

**merciful** clement, \*forbearing, tolerant, lenient, indulgent
*Ana* compassionate, \*tender: benignant, benign, \*kind, kindly: forgiving, pardoning, condoning (see EXCUSE *vb*)
*Ant* merciless —*Con* \*grim, implacable, relentless, unrelenting: cruel, fell, inhuman, \*fierce
**mercifully** forbearingly, tolerantly, clemently, leniently, indulgently (see under FORBEARING)
**mercifulness** clemency, forbearance, tolerance, leniency, indulgence (see under FORBEARING)
*Ana* \*mercy, clemency, lenity, charity, grace: compassion, commiseration, pity, ruth (see SYMPATHY)
*Con* severeness *or* severity, sternness (see corresponding adjectives at SEVERE): rigorousness *or* rigor, rigidity, strictness, stringency (see corresponding adjectives at RIGID)
**merciless** implacable, relentless, unrelenting, \*grim
*Ana* pitiless, ruthless, compassionless (see corresponding nouns at SYMPATHY): wanton, uncalled-for, gratuitous (see SUPEREROGATORY): cruel, fell, \*fierce: inexorable, obdurate, \*inflexible, adamant, adamantine

*Ant* merciful —*Con* clement, \*forbearing, tolerant, lenient, indulgent
**mercurial** \*inconstant, fickle, capricious, unstable
*Ana* volatile, effervescent, buoyant, expansive, \*elastic, resilient: \*changeable, changeful, variable, protean, mutable: mobile, \*movable: \*clever, adroit, cunning, ingenious
*Ant* saturnine
**mercy, charity, grace, clemency, lenity** are comparable when meaning the disposition to show compassion or kindness in one's treatment of others, especially of those who offend one and who are in one's power to punish or rebuke. **Mercy** implies compassion so great as to enable one to forbear, even when justice demands punishment, or to give help or comfort even to the lowliest or most undeserving ⟨earthly power doth then show likest God's when *mercy* seasons justice—*Shak.*⟩ ⟨souls who God's forbearance try, and those that seek his help, and for his *mercy* sigh—*Wordsworth*⟩ **Charity** stresses benevolence and goodwill, especially as it reveals itself not only in giving generously (for this sense see CHARITY 2) but in broad understanding of others and in kindly tolerance ⟨with malice toward none, with *charity* for all—*Lincoln*⟩ ⟨lack of another faculty: the faculty which theologians still call *charity*. Nowhere, in the whole of the volume, does any character act out of genuine kindness—*Time*⟩ ⟨it is far commoner at the University to meet men of great attainments combined with sincere humility and *charity*—*Benson*⟩ **Grace** implies a benignant attitude toward those who are dependent on one and a disposition to grant favors or to make concessions to them ⟨each in his place, by right, not *grace*, shall rule his heritage—*Kipling*⟩ ⟨that quiet but unabashed hospitality which is a common *grace* in Mexican households—*Cather*⟩ ⟨though the wages of sin are exacted with biblical sternness, a tender *grace* is present in a hundred minute particulars—*Gaither*⟩ **Clemency** (see also *clement* under FORBEARING) implies a mild or merciful disposition in one whose duty or function it is to administer justice or to punish offenses ⟨*clemency* . . . is the standing policy of constitutional governments, as severity is of despotism—*Hallam*⟩ ⟨off went poor Tom . . . . to rejoice in the *clemency* that spared his appearance at Sessions—*Meredith*⟩ **Lenity** differs from *clemency* only in its greater emphasis on lack of severity. It often suggests undue gentleness or softness or even at times undue leniency ⟨what makes robbers bold but too much *lenity*?—*Shak.*⟩ ⟨if it produces a proper *lenity* to our citizens in captivity, it will have the effect we meant—*Jefferson*⟩ ⟨errors which, had he been regarded with a less affectionate *lenity*, would have stood against his official account—*S. H. Adams*⟩
*Ana* compassion, ruth, pity, commiseration (see SYMPATHY): mercifulness, clemency, forbearance, tolerance, leniency, indulgence (see under FORBEARING)
*Con* vengeance, revenge, retribution, reprisal, \*retaliation: punishment, chastening, chastisement, disciplining *or* discipline, correction, castigation (see corresponding verbs at PUNISH)

**mere, bare** are often employed with little or no distinction in the sense of being such as the term qualified states but nothing more. But **mere** is commonly used to emphasize the limitations of a thing, as if it were declared to be "simply what it is and nothing more" ⟨it began to rain—not a *mere* hill-shower, but a good, tepid, monsoonish downpour—*Kipling*⟩ ⟨is *mere* living . . . without reference to any intrinsic values, a thing of any worth?—*Inge*⟩ ⟨the saying that we are members of one another is not a *mere* pious formula . . . without any meaning: it is a literal truth—*Shaw*⟩ **Bare** is stronger and frequently

---

A colon (:) separates groups of words discriminated. An asterisk (\*) indicates place of treatment of each group.

suggests that the thing just escapes falling short of what it actually is ⟨elected by a *bare* majority⟩ ⟨the short-lived Ukrainian Republic which lasted a *bare* four years before succumbing—*Current History*⟩ ⟨some must know higher mathematics, but the *bare* elements suffice for those to whom mathematics is distasteful—*Russell*⟩

**meretricious** *gaudy, tawdry, garish, flashy
*Ana* *showy, pretentious, ostentatious: vulgar, *coarse, gross: deceptive, delusive, delusory, *misleading

**merge** blend, fuse, coalesce, amalgamate, commingle, mingle, *mix
*Ana* consolidate, concentrate, *compact, unify: *unite, combine, conjoin: *integrate, concatenate, articulate

**merger** *consolidation, amalgamation

**meridian** culmination, zenith, apogee, *summit, peak, pinnacle, climax, apex, acme

**merit** *n* 1 *due, desert
*Ana* meed, reward, guerdon (see PREMIUM): *worth, value: gaining *or* gainings, winning *or* winnings (see GET)
2 *excellence, virtue, perfection
*Ant* fault: defect

**merit** *vb* *deserve, earn, rate
*Ana* reward, award (see corresponding nouns at PREMIUM): requite, recompense, repay (see PAY)

**merry,** blithe, jocund, jovial, jolly mean indicating or showing high spirits or lightheartedness often in play and laughter. **Merry** implies a gay, cheerful temper or mood and uninhibited enjoyment of frolic, festivity, or fun of any sort ⟨a *merrier* man, within the limit of becoming mirth, I never spent an hour's talk withal—*Shak.*⟩ ⟨let us drink and be *merry*, dance, joke, and rejoice—*Jordan*⟩ ⟨for the good are always the *merry*, save by an evil chance, and the *merry* love the fiddle, and the *merry* love to dance—*Yeats*⟩ **Blithe** carries a stronger implication of freshness, buoyancy, and lightheartedness than *merry*; it usually suggests carefree, innocent, or even heedless gaiety ⟨see this lovely child, *blithe*, innocent, and free. She spends a happy time with little care—*Shelley*⟩ ⟨he wrote *blithe* gay idiocies to me—*White*⟩ ⟨entertained by the author's *blithe* companionship and his engaging chatter—*Percy Atkinson*⟩ **Jocund** heightens the implication of gladness and usually also connotes liveliness, exhilaration of spirits, or elation ⟨a poet could not but be gay, in such a *jocund* company—*Wordsworth*⟩ ⟨he was . . . in that *jocund*, new-married mood—*Mary Austin*⟩ ⟨invested the matter with a clownish significance that perfectly fitted the spirit of the circus—*jocund*, yet charming—*E. B. White*⟩ **Jovial** connotes especially good-fellowship or conviviality ⟨a *jovial*, full-stomached, portly government servant with a marvelous capacity for making bad puns—*Kipling*⟩ ⟨his manner became more jaunty, *jovial*, half-jesting—*Wolfe*⟩ **Jolly** often suggests higher spirits than *jovial* and an even more manifest attempt by one to set others laughing (as by jesting, bantering, and playing tricks) ⟨I don't care; I'm not refined. I like the *jolly* old pantomime where a man sits on his top hat—*Chesterton*⟩ ⟨ran down the street . . . with so *jolly* an air that he set everyone he passed into a good humor—*Stevenson*⟩
*Ana* gay, vivacious, *lively, sprightly, animated: joyful, joyous, cheerful, *glad, happy, lighthearted: mirthful, gleeful, hilarious (see corresponding nouns at MIRTH)

**mesa** *mountain, mount, peak, alp, volcano

**message** missive, note, *letter, epistle, dispatch, report, memorandum

**metamorphose** *transform, transmute, convert, transmogrify, transfigure
*Ana* *change, vary, alter, modify: develop, *mature, age, ripen

**metamorphosis** transformation, transmutation, conversion, transmogrification, transfiguration (see under TRANSFORM)
*Ana* *change, mutation, alternation, permutation, vicissitude: change, variation, alteration, modification (see under CHANGE *vb*)

**metaphor** *simile, analogy

**metaphrase** *translation, version, paraphrase

**meter** *rhythm, cadence

**method,** mode, manner, way, fashion, system are comparable when they denote the means taken or the plan or procedure followed in doing a kind of work or in achieving an end. **Method** may denote either an abstraction or a concrete procedure, but in both cases it implies orderly, logical, and effective arrangements (as of one's ideas for an exposition or an argument, or of the steps to be followed in teaching, in investigation, in the treatment of a disease, or in any kind or piece of work); often, also, the term connotes regularity or formality in procedure ⟨his teaching is too informal to be said to have *method*⟩ ⟨the inductive *method* of reasoning⟩ ⟨the crude *methods* of trial and error—*Suzzallo*⟩ ⟨the *method* of unfolding the course of a plot must in some ways be different in a play meant for acting and in a book meant for reading—*Montague*⟩ ⟨always omitted the vowels in accordance with the Arabian *method* of orthography—*Krutch*⟩ ⟨surely not to leave to fitful chance the things that *method* and system and science should order and adjust—*Cardozo*⟩ **Mode** (see also FASHION 2; STATE) is sometimes used interchangeably with *method*, but it seldom stresses orderly or logical arrangement; rather, it denotes an order or course pursued as the result of custom, tradition, or personal preference ⟨the reasons given . . . do not seem very plausible to our *modes* of thought—*Binyon*⟩ ⟨a man to whom music was a necessary *mode* of expression—*Read*⟩ ⟨a study of fictional villains and the *mode* their villainy assumes—*Austin Warren*⟩ **Manner** is often used in place of *mode* where the reference is to a personal or peculiar course or procedure, or to a method, whether pursued by a number of persons or not, that seems to be individual or distinctive ⟨mark the *manner* of his teaching—*Shak.*⟩ ⟨the mathematician . . . is not capable of giving a reason in the same *manner* as the dialectician—*Jowett*⟩ ⟨it is not consistent with his *manner* of writing Latin—*Sellery*⟩ **Way** (see also WAY 1), the most general of these terms, may be used in place of any of the rest and is found in many familiar idiomatic expressions where theoretically *method*, *mode*, or *manner* might be more explicit ⟨religion implies not only a *way* of worship but a *way* of life⟩ ⟨it was the white man's *way* to assert himself in any landscape, to change it, make it over a little . . . it was the Indian's *way* to pass through a country . . . and leave no trace—*Cather*⟩ ⟨the century has brought us not only new things to see but new *ways* of seeing—*Day Lewis*⟩ ⟨Sally used to answer Robert's letters, sadly and patiently, and with no reproaches;—that was Sally's *way*—*Deland*⟩ **Fashion** differs from *way* not so much in denotation as in connotation derived in part from its commoner sense of *style* or *vogue* (see FASHION 2). The term often suggests an origin or source that is not so deep or a motivation that is not so abiding as those usually connoted by *way;* often also it is the idiomatic term in prepositional phrases introduced by *after* or *in* ⟨he will, after his sour *fashion*, tell you—*Shak.*⟩ ⟨subjects serious in themselves, but treated after my *fashion*, nonseriously—*Lamb*⟩ ⟨I have been faithful to thee, Cynara! in my *fashion*—*Dowson*⟩ ⟨we hear them talking . . . in different *fashions* under different moods—even as you and I—*Lowes*⟩ But *fashion* sometimes comes very close to *mode* when it means the way that is characteristic of

or peculiar to a group or type ⟨swim dog *fashion*⟩ ⟨a group of boys sprawl, teen-age *fashion*, on couches and chairs—*The Lamp*⟩ **System** suggests a fully developed and often carefully formulated method ⟨the mind can scarcely conceive a *system* for regulating commerce between nations which shall exclude all laws concerning navigation—*John Marshall*⟩ ⟨the *system* of classification used by botanists⟩ ⟨his manners, his speech and habits of thought all seemed so prescribed, so intricately connected to one another that they suggested a *system* of conduct —*Cheever*⟩ As an abstraction, however, meaning orderliness or plan in arrangement or procedure, *system* is often preferred to *method* ⟨housekeeping without *system*⟩ ⟨he follows no *system* in his reading⟩
*Ana* *process, procedure, proceeding: classification (see corresponding verb at ASSORT): disposition, *disposal
**methodical** *orderly, systematic, regular
*Ana* methodized, systematized, organized (see ORDER *vb*): *careful, meticulous, scrupulous: *logical, analytical
*Ant* unmethodical: desultory —*Con* *random, haphazard, casual, hit-or-miss: *irregular, unnatural: confused, disordered, chaotic, jumbled (see corresponding nouns at CONFUSION)
**methodize** systematize, organize, *order, arrange, marshal
*Ana* regulate, *adjust: *set, settle, fix, establish
**meticulous** *careful, scrupulous, punctilious, punctual
*Ana* fastidious, finicky, particular, fussy, pernickety, *nice: accurate, exact, precise, *correct
**mettle** *courage, spirit, resolution, tenacity
*Ana* *fortitude, backbone, sand, grit, pluck, guts: nerve, hardihood, *temerity, audacity: gallantry, valor, *heroism
**mettlesome** *spirited, high-spirited, spunky, fiery, peppery, gingery
*Ana* courageous, bold, audacious, intrepid, *brave: *impassioned, passionate, ardent, fervent: restive, *impatient, restless
**miasmic, miasmatic, miasmal** *poisonous, toxic, venomous, virulent, pestilent, pestilential, mephitic
*Ana* contagious, *infectious, catching: noxious, *pernicious, baneful, deleterious
**microbe** *germ, bacterium, bacillus, virus
**microscopic** minute, *small, little, diminutive, miniature, petite, wee, tiny, teeny, weeny
**middle** *n* *center, midst, core, hub, focus, nucleus, heart
**middling** *medium, mediocre, second-rate, moderate, average, fair, indifferent
**midget** *n* manikin, pygmy, *dwarf, homunculus, runt
**midst** middle, *center, core, hub, focus, nucleus, heart
**mien** demeanor, deportment, *bearing, port, presence
*Ana* air, *pose, affectation, mannerism: aspect, *appearance, semblance, look
**might** *n* strength, energy, *power, force, puissance
*Ana* vigorousness *or* vigor, strenuousness, energeticness, lustiness (see corresponding adjectives at VIGOROUS): potency, powerfulness, forcibleness, forcefulness (see corresponding adjectives at POWERFUL)
**mild** gentle, smooth, lenient, bland, *soft, balmy
*Ana* *forbearing, tolerant, clement, merciful, lenient, indulgent: delicate, dainty, exquisite, *choice: temperate, *moderate: *calm, serene, tranquil, placid
*Ant* harsh: fierce
**milieu** environment, setting, *background, mise-en-scène, backdrop
**militant** *aggressive, assertive, self-assertive, pushing, pushy
*Ana* bellicose, pugnacious, combative, contentious, *belligerent: combating, opposing, antagonizing *or* antagonistic (see corresponding verbs at RESIST): fighting, warring, contending, battling (see CONTEND)

*Con* *pacific, pacifist, pacifistic, peaceful, peaceable: acquiescent, resigned, *compliant
**military** *martial, warlike
**mime** *actor, player, performer, mummer, mimic, thespian, impersonator, trouper
**mimic** *n* *actor, player, performer, mummer, mime, thespian, impersonator, trouper
**mimic** *vb* *copy, imitate, ape, mock
*Ana* play, impersonate, *act: counterfeit, feign, simulate, sham, pretend, *assume
**mind** *n* 1 *memory, remembrance, recollection, reminiscence, souvenir
2 Mind, intellect, soul, psyche, brain, intelligence, wit are comparable when they mean the sum total of powers, often felt as a distinct entity, by means of which each individual knows and understands both his inner life and the external world and establishes effective relations between them and which are commonly felt as the distinctive possession of human beings. **Mind** indicates the complex of man's faculties involved in perceiving, remembering, considering, evaluating, and deciding; it contrasts variously with *body, heart, soul,* and *spirit* ⟨the *mind* must have its share in deciding these important matters, not merely the emotions and desires—*Rose Macaulay*⟩ *Mind* may indicate the peculiar complex of a particular individual as differing from all others ⟨the *mind* of a dreamer joined to the temperament of a soldier—*Buchan*⟩ **Intellect,** sometimes interchangeable with *mind,* may focus attention on the powers of knowing and thinking by which one may comprehend, consider, and conclude and especially the more coldly analytic powers, independent of and discrete from willing and feeling ⟨the emotionalist steeps himself or herself in luxurious feeling and pathetic imagination, which makes no severe call upon either the will or the *intellect*—*Inge*⟩ ⟨now the significance of Sir Thomas Browne lies in the fact that he was at once by *intellect* a force in the forward movement and by temperament a reactionary—*More*⟩ **Soul** (see also SOUL 2), used with considerable variation in meaning and suggestion, may indicate that principle which vitalizes, directs, selects, or inspires in matters emotional and volitional as well as mental ⟨my inner existence, that consciousness which is called the *soul*—*Jefferies*⟩ ⟨the *soul* is an intelligent, sensitive, and vital principle, a trinity which forms and moves the body predisposed to such action, as well as feels, thinks, and wills—*Thilly*⟩ **Psyche** may refer to the totality of self composed of all attributes, powers, and activities not purely bodily or somatic but definitely including the unconscious or subconscious ⟨by the *psyche* I understand the totality of all the psychic processes, both conscious as well as unconscious; whereas by soul, I understand a definitely demarcated function-complex that is best characterized as a "personality"—*Baynes*⟩ **Brain,** often as the plural **brains,** may more forcefully than *intellect* focus attention on powers of individual comprehension or independent thought ⟨it requires *brains* and education to follow the argument—*Inge*⟩ ⟨have I ever even felt inclined to write anything, until my emotions had been unduly excited, my *brain* immoderately stirred, my senses unusually quickened, or my spirit extravagantly roused?—*Galsworthy*⟩ **Intelligence** is likely to imply specific ability to cope with problems and situations and may apply to exhibition of the play of powers of the intellect or comparable ones ⟨had turned capable men into mere machines doing their work without *intelligence*—*Shaw*⟩ ⟨wild animals are not automata—they have *intelligence* if they lack intellect—*Clarke*⟩ **Wit,** often as the plural **wits,** may refer to a mind marked by inborn capacity, strong common sense, bright perception, or ready intelligence ⟨the un-

---

A colon (:) separates groups of words discriminated. An asterisk (*) indicates place of treatment of each group.

tutored natural *wit* of savages—*Shaw*⟩ ⟨everyone had to be a jack-of-all-trades, everyone had to live by his *wits*—*Brooks*⟩
*Ana* *power, function, faculty: *reason, understanding, intuition: wisdom, judgment, *sense, gumption
**mind** *vb* 1 *remember, recollect, recall, remind, reminisce, bethink
2 *obey, comply
*Ana* defer, *yield, submit, bow: accede, *assent, consent, agree, acquiesce
3 *tend, attend, watch
*Con* *neglect, ignore, disregard, forget, slight
**mingle** *mix, commingle, blend, merge, coalesce, amalgamate, fuse
*Ana* *join, combine, unite, conjoin, connect: consolidate, *compact, unify, concentrate
**miniature** *adj* minute, diminutive, *small, little, wee, tiny, teeny, weeny
**minimize** depreciate, *decry, belittle, disparage, derogate, detract
*Ant* magnify —*Con* aggrandize, *exalt: extol, eulogize, acclaim, laud, *praise
**minister** envoy, *ambassador, legate, nuncio, internuncio, chargé d'affaires
**minority** *infancy, nonage
*Ant* majority
**minstrel** bard, troubadour, *poet, versifier, rhymer, rhymester, poetaster
**minute** *n* *instant, moment, second, flash, jiffy, twinkling, split second
**minute** *adj* 1 *small, little, diminutive, miniature, wee, tiny, teeny, weeny
2 *circumstantial, particular, particularized, detailed, itemized
*Ana* meticulous, scrupulous, *careful, punctilious: precise, accurate, exact, right, nice, *correct
*Con* general, *universal: *abstract, ideal: comprehending *or* comprehensive, including *or* inclusive, embracing *or* embracive (see corresponding verbs at INCLUDE)
**miracle** *wonder, marvel, prodigy, phenomenon
**miraculous** *supernatural, supranatural, preternatural, superhuman
**mirage** hallucination, *delusion, illusion
**mirror** *n* *model, example, pattern, exemplar, ideal, standard, beau ideal
**mirth,** glee, jollity, hilarity are comparable when they mean the mood or temper of a person or a group of persons manifesting joy or high spirits especially in laughter, play, or merrymaking. **Mirth** often implies lightness of heart and a love of gaiety; it may, however, imply great amusement or cause for laughter ⟨Darcy was not of a disposition in which happiness overflows in *mirth*—*Austen*⟩ ⟨some of them literally throwing themselves down on the ground in convulsions of unholy *mirth*—*Kipling*⟩ ⟨they seem to quiver on the edge of *mirth,* as if some deep continual laughter was repressed—*Hallam Tennyson*⟩ **Glee** is often employed in reference to an individual who by reason of special circumstances is filled with joy, delight, or happiness, and shows his exultancy by laughter, smiles, and cries of joy ⟨full well they laughed, with counterfeited *glee,* at all his jokes, for many a joke had he—*Goldsmith*⟩ ⟨the best of constitutions will not prevent ambitious politicians from succumbing with *glee* and gusto to the temptations of power—*Huxley*⟩ But *glee* may express the exultation of one who takes more or less malicious delight in another's misfortunes or predicaments ⟨in great *glee* over his friend's embarrassment⟩ ⟨with malicious *glee* they quoted a previous boast of the President's—*F. L. Allen*⟩ ⟨it betrayed the *glee* felt by the mean-spirited when

they see people who do not deserve humiliation forced to suffer it—*West*⟩ **Jollity,** on the other hand, usually implies mirth in a group, especially a merrymaking group. Distinctively, however, it connotes exuberance and lack of constraint and may imply revelry of any kind ⟨midnight shout and revelry, tipsy dance and *jollity*—*Milton*⟩ ⟨contributed more than his share of the *jollity* by turning out puns by the hamperful—*Balliett*⟩ **Hilarity** fundamentally implies the exhilaration of spirits (as by wine, pleasurable excitement, or great amusement) ⟨wine gives not light, gay, ideal *hilarity,* but tumultuous, noisy, clamorous merriment—*Johnson*⟩ ⟨through all the works of Chaucer, there reigns a cheerfulness, a manly *hilarity*—*Coleridge*⟩ but it often carries implications of boisterousness or exuberance ⟨he entered wholeheartedly into the *hilarity* of the boys, till he too was talking only nonsense—*Rölvaag*⟩ ⟨the *hilarity* of a New Year's Eve celebration⟩
*Ana* cheerfulness *or* cheer, lightheartedness, joyfulness, gladness, happiness (see corresponding adjectives at GLAD): joy, *pleasure, delight: merriment, blitheness, jocundity, joviality (see corresponding adjectives at MERRY)
*Con* *sadness, depression, dejection, melancholy, blues, dumps: *tedium, boredom, ennui
**misanthropic** pessimistic, misogynic, *cynical
*Ant* philanthropic —*Con* benevolent, humane, humanitarian, *charitable, altruistic
**miscarriage** 1 *failure, neglect, default, dereliction
*Ana* abuse, maltreatment, misuse (see corresponding verbs at ABUSE)
2 *abortion
**miscellaneous,** assorted, heterogeneous, motley, promiscuous are comparable when they mean marked by diversity or variety and are applied to the things that make up a group, a collection, or a mass, or to a group, collection, or mass. **Miscellaneous** usually implies a mixture of many kinds, showing few signs of selection, and often suggesting dependence on chance ⟨there is always a *miscellaneous* assemblage at the meetings of the association⟩ ⟨Joyce's wide and *miscellaneous* acquaintanceship—*Colum*⟩ ⟨the contents of the chests were of the most *miscellaneous* description:—sewing utensils, marling spikes, strips of calico, bits of rope—*Melville*⟩ ⟨what appears at first to be a *miscellaneous* lot of books often reveals, on closer inspection, an interesting pattern of interrelationships—*Redman*⟩ **Assorted** (see also ASSORT) and the related noun **assortment** also imply a mixture but not a haphazard one; they carry the implications of a selection including various kinds *or* involving consideration of various tastes or needs ⟨a box of *assorted* candies⟩ ⟨there were passable performances of potpourri from *assorted* operas—*Copland*⟩ ⟨none of these authors has published books of *assorted* essays—*R. B. West*⟩ ⟨a case containing an *assortment* of tools⟩ **Heterogeneous** is applicable chiefly to masses or groups in which the individuals or the elements are in proximity or close relationship to each other by chance; it suggests not only variety or diversity in the individuals or the elements but also absence of uniformity or unity and little evidence of fusion ⟨the task of transforming a *heterogeneous* selection of mankind into a homogeneous nation—*Russell*⟩ ⟨the family is *heterogeneous* enough to make quite a good party in itself—*Rose Macaulay*⟩ ⟨the *heterogeneous* structure of granite⟩ ⟨a photograph lacks organization and unity . . . . It is haphazard, *heterogeneous,* aimless, and amorphous—just as is nature—*S. S. Van Dine*⟩ **Motley** adds to *heterogeneous* the suggestion of discordance in the individuals or elements or their striking contrast to each other; perhaps from the notion of discordance it is more depreciative than the foregoing terms and is more likely

---

*Ana* analogous words    *Ant* antonyms    *Con* contrasted words    See also explanatory notes facing page 1

to qualify groups made up of elements felt as inferior or undesirable ⟨one would enquire from whence this *motley* style did first our Roman purity defile—*Dryden*⟩ ⟨*motley* support drawn from Tammany Hall Irish, Wall Street bankers, and odds and ends of all factions—*Parrington*⟩ ⟨that *motley* aggregation of impudent and flattering camp followers—*Walker*⟩ **Promiscuous** may suggest haphazardness or the appearance of it, but it usually implies selection that is completely devoid of discrimination and that results in disorderly confusion; thus, a *miscellaneous* acquaintanceship may imply a catholicity of taste, but a *promiscuous* acquaintanceship implies an absence of taste and good judgment; from a description of a club's membership as *heterogeneous* one might infer its interesting diversity but from a description of it as *promiscuous* one can infer only a diversity that is distasteful and senseless from the point of view of the speaker or writer ⟨a classless, *promiscuous* world where *True Story* and London's *New Statesman and Nation* share the same rickety table—*Time*⟩ For this reason, *promiscuous* as applied specifically to people or their acts, emotions, and relations stresses not only lack of discrimination, but lack of restriction within bounds set (as by prudence, good sense, or sound morals); thus, *promiscuous* charity is imprudently lavish charity extended without reference to the needs of those helped; *promiscuous* blame suggests stupid indifference as to the persons or things one's censure may affect; *promiscuous* sexual intercourse implies licentious disregard of normal standards of conduct ⟨sanity involves some order and discrimination, rather than a *promiscuous* acceptance of all our impulses as good—*Cohen*⟩ ⟨the dangers to civil freedom of a *promiscuous* and unprincipled attack on radicalism—*Schlesinger* b. 1917⟩
*Ana* various, diverse, divergent, disparate, *different: multifarious, divers, sundry, *many
*Con* similar, alike, *like, identical, uniform
**mischance** *misfortune, adversity, mishap
*Ana* *accident, casualty, mishap: *disaster, calamity, catastrophe, cataclysm
**mischief** *injury, hurt, damage, harm
*Ana* perniciousness, detrimentalness *or* detriment, deleteriousness, noxiousness, banefulness *or* bane (see corresponding adjectives at PERNICIOUS): *evil, ill: impairment, marring, spoiling (see corresponding verbs at INJURE)
**mischievous** roguish, waggish, impish, *playful, frolicsome, sportive
*Ana* annoying, bothering *or* bothersome, vexing *or* vexatious, irking *or* irksome (see corresponding verbs at ANNOY): naughty, *bad, evil, ill, wicked: tricky, foxy, insidious, artful, *sly
**miscreant** *villain, scoundrel, blackguard, knave, rascal, rogue, scamp, rapscallion
*Ana* *criminal, malefactor, culprit, delinquent
**mise-en-scène** *background, setting, environment, milieu, backdrop
**miserable,** wretched both describe something (as a person's state of health or of mind, a state of affairs, a human being with reference to his condition or character, or a thing compared with others of its kind) that is deplorably or contemptibly bad or mean. A person is **miserable** if in misery or in a state either of extreme or acute distress of body or mind ⟨[Plato] would forbid any novelist to represent a good man as ever *miserable*—*Ellis*⟩ ⟨Gideon has been absolutely *miserable,* and gone about like a man half stunned, ever since it happened—*Rose Macaulay*⟩ or of pitiable poverty or degradation ⟨a *miserable* creature of a crazed aspect . . . shattered and made drunk by horror—*Dickens*⟩ A thing is *miserable* when it is exceedingly mean

or paltry, and provocative only of misery in the person affected or of strong distress or dislike in the observer ⟨a *miserable* cold⟩ ⟨a *miserable* dinner⟩ ⟨the squalor of mean and *miserable* streets—*Binyon*⟩ A person is **wretched** who is extremely unhappy or abjectly despondent (as from want, grief, oppression, affliction, or anxiety); a thing that relates closely to the happiness of a person is *wretched* if it produces such dejection or mental suffering ⟨O cruel death! To those you are more kind than to the *wretched* mortals left behind—*Waller*⟩ ⟨it was her unhappy lot to be made more *wretched* by the only affection which she could not suspect—*Conrad*⟩ ⟨she's "poor Ellen" certainly, because she had the bad luck to make a *wretched* marriage—*Wharton*⟩ A thing, in general, is *wretched* if it is extremely or deplorably bad ⟨a *wretched* French cabaret, smelling vilely—*Meredith*⟩ ⟨*wretched* crops⟩ ⟨it was the *wretched* truth, and not something I had conjured out of imagination—*Deasy*⟩
*Ana* forlorn, hopeless, despairing, *despondent: pitiable, piteous, *pitiful: doleful, dolorous, *melancholy
*Ant* comfortable
**miserly** penurious, parsimonious, niggardly, tight, tightfisted, *stingy, close, closefisted, cheeseparing, pennypinching
*Ana* avaricious, greedy, *covetous, grasping: *mean, sordid, abject, ignoble
*Con* bountiful, bounteous, openhanded, munificent, *liberal, generous: benevolent, *charitable, altruistic
**misery** *distress, suffering, agony, dolor, passion
*Ana* adversity, *misfortune: affliction, visitation, *trial, tribulation: melancholy, dejection, *sadness, depression
*Ant* felicity, blessedness —*Con* *happiness, beatitude, bliss: comfort, ease, repose (see REST)
**misfortune,** mischance, adversity, mishap are comparable when they denote bad luck or adverse fortune or an instance of this. **Misfortune** is both the most common and the most general term; it is applicable equally to the incident or conjunction of events that is the cause of an unhappy change of fortune ⟨by *misfortune* he lost his job⟩ or the ensuing state of distress ⟨a crass and stupid person who had fallen through luck into flowing prosperity. His every good fortune spattered others with *misfortune*—*Malamud*⟩ and it may denote a particular unfortunate incident ⟨they could by cooperation brave *misfortunes* and supplement each other's efforts in bettering the lot of the common man—*Middle East Jour.*⟩ **Mischance** rarely applies to a state of distress but is otherwise very close to *misfortune* from which it differs chiefly in greater objectivity. While sometimes used to imply grave affliction or even death it is especially appropriate when the situation involves no more than slight inconvenience or minor annoyance ⟨I threw a stone and hit a duck in the yard by *mischance*—*Yeats*⟩ ⟨they proceeded on their journey without any *mischance*—*Austen*⟩ **Adversity,** on the other hand, denotes the state or the instance but not the cause; it is distinctly the strongest of these words and in its typical use implies a state of grave and persistent misfortune ⟨a wretched soul, bruised with *adversity*—*Shak.*⟩ ⟨what fairy palaces we may build of beautiful thought—proof against all *adversity*—*Ruskin*⟩ In application to the instance *adversity* is normally used in the plural ⟨the many misfortunes and *adversities* Bolivia has suffered have brought this national spirit to a high pitch—*Americas*⟩ **Mishap,** (see also ACCIDENT) like *mischance,* commonly implies triviality ⟨directed the concert without any of the *mishaps* expected of a twenty-year-old's performance—*Current Biog.*⟩
*Ana* *disaster, calamity, catastrophe, cataclysm: *accident, casualty: *trial, tribulation, cross, affliction, visi-

---

A colon (:) separates groups of words discriminated. An asterisk (*) indicates place of treatment of each group.

tation
*Ant* happiness: prosperity  —*Con* felicity, bliss, blessedness, beatitude (see HAPPINESS): comfort, ease (see REST):
*victory, triumph
**misgiving** foreboding, presentiment, *apprehension
*Ana* mistrust, distrust (see under DISTRUST *vb*): suspicion,
doubt, skepticism, *uncertainty: *fear, alarm, dread,
fright
**mishap 1** *misfortune, mischance, adversity
**2** *accident, casualty
*Ana* *misfortune, mischance: *disaster, calamity:
*chance, fortune, hap, hazard
**mislay** *misplace
**mislead** delude, beguile, *deceive, betray, double-cross
*Ana* entice, inveigle, *lure, tempt, seduce: *dupe, gull,
hoodwink, hoax, bamboozle
**misleading, deceptive, delusive, delusory** all mean having
an appearance or character that leads one astray or into
error. **Misleading** is the general term applicable to something which, intentionally or otherwise, leads one away
from the right course or direction in thought or action
and, therefore, into confusion or error ⟨the bare statement
that "art is useless" is so vague as to be really meaningless,
if not inaccurate and *misleading*—*Ellis*⟩ ⟨it is not necessary to prove an injury to a competitor to stop *misleading*
advertising; it may be stopped merely because it is unfair and deceptive—*Fisk & Snapp*⟩ **Deceptive** applies
chiefly to things that by their aspect or appearance
give a false impression; the term need not imply the intention to deceive ⟨*deceptive* solemnity⟩ ⟨a *deceptive* air
of innocence⟩ ⟨while the communication was *deceptive*
and so intended, it was not technically mendacious—
*S.H. Adams*⟩ **Delusive** and **delusory**, though otherwise
similar to *deceptive*, carry a strong implication of befooling or cheating as well as misleading ⟨*delusive* hopes⟩
⟨*delusory* promises⟩ ⟨it is important for this Court to
avoid extracting from the very general language of the
Fourteenth Amendment a system of *delusive* exactness—
*Justice Holmes*⟩ ⟨arguments for universal selfishness
seemed to fall short of complete proof and some of them
appeared quite *delusive* and logically fallacious—*Garvin*⟩
⟨dangerously *delusory* habits of relying on industrial
potential *per se* as a bulwark in war—*C. B. Marshall*⟩
*Ana* fallacious, casuistical, sophistical (see under FAL-
LACY): *false, wrong: confounding, bewildering, distracting, perplexing, puzzling (see PUZZLE *vb*)
**misogynic** misanthropic, pessimistic, *cynical
*Con* benevolent, *charitable, altruistic
**misplace, mislay** both mean to put in the wrong place and
both in their basic use imply that the thing in question is
as unavailable as if lost though firmly believed to be still
in one's possession. **Misplace** basically implies a putting
of a thing in another than its proper or customary location
⟨*misplace* a book⟩ ⟨invoices continually being forgot or
*misplaced*—*Terry Southern*⟩ but it more often suggests
a setting or fixing of something where it should not be
⟨my confidence in him was *misplaced*⟩ ⟨she is suffering
from *misplaced* affections⟩ ⟨the globe and scepter in
such hands *misplaced*—*Cowper*⟩ **Mislay** usually implies
a misplacing in the basic sense but stresses a forgetfulness
of the place in which the thing has been put; it therefore
often means to lose through misplacing ⟨*mislaid* her
glasses in the excitement over the fire⟩ ⟨*mislay* an um-
brella⟩ In its extended use it differs little from *lose* ⟨almost
inevitably some of the literary qualities of *Darkness at
Noon* have been *mislaid* in the process of bringing it to the
stage—*J.M. Brown*⟩
*Ana* displace (see REPLACE): derange, disarrange, *disorder

**misrepresent, falsify, belie, garble** mean to present or
represent something in a manner that is contrary to the
truth. **Misrepresent** usually implies an intent to represent
or portray falsely, and therefore may take as its subject
not only a person or his utterance but also such things as
an organization, a political platform, or a cartoon; it often
carries a suggestion of deliberate lying, but it may suggest
bias or prejudice or a desire to do injustice ⟨*misrepresent*
a candidate's statement⟩ ⟨*misrepresent* the value of an
article⟩ ⟨the account *misrepresents* not only his actions
but his motives⟩ **Falsify** implies a perversion of the truth,
either by deliberately altering the facts in whole or in
part ⟨*falsify* bookkeeping records⟩ ⟨*falsified* her account
of the accident⟩ or by giving something an appearance
that does not accord with the truth or reality ⟨*falsify* the
meaning of a document by an incorrect translation⟩
⟨good breeding has made the tongue *falsify* the heart—
*Steele*⟩ ⟨a low-priced sunglass lens said to be completely
effective without *falsifying* the colors seen through it—
*Newsweek*⟩ **Belie** implies an impression given that contradicts or is at variance with the truth or the facts; it
usually takes as its subject an appearance, a manner, or
a form of speech, and lacks the implication of intent that
is usually present in the preceding words ⟨his confident
words were *belied* by his anxious look⟩ ⟨a brusque manner
that *belies* a real kindness of heart⟩ ⟨you are an Englishman . . . unless your physiognomy *belies* you—*Kingsley*⟩
**Garble** implies a mutilation or distortion of statements,
testimony, evidence, or messages that need not be deliberate but that creates a wrong impression of the original
and frequently gravely alters its tone or implications ⟨the
newspapers have sadly *garbled* the account of his speech⟩
⟨by the time the story had passed from mouth to mouth
until it reached him again, it was so *garbled* that its original form was barely recognizable⟩ ⟨the manufacture and
dissemination of propaganda literature, for the purpose
of rousing the passions of the people by *garbled* statements—*Inge*⟩
*Ana* *disguise, dissemble, cloak, mask, camouflage:
simulate, counterfeit, feign (see ASSUME): *lie, prevaricate,
equivocate, palter
**misrepresentation** *lie, falsehood, untruth, fib, story
*Ana* dishonesty, deceitfulness, mendaciousness *or* mendacity (see corresponding adjectives at DISHONEST): sophistication, doctoring, loading, weighting, adulteration
(see corresponding verbs at ADULTERATE): sophistry,
casuistry (see FALLACY)
**missive** *letter, epistle, note, message, dispatch, report,
memorandum
**mist** *n* *haze, fog, smog
**mistake** *vb* **Mistake, confuse, confound** are comparable
when they mean to mix up things, typically by taking one
thing for another. One **mistakes** one thing *for* another
when by an error of perception or of thought or as a result of a predisposition or a bias one fails to recognize
the thing or to comprehend its real nature and identifies
it with something not itself or with something of another
nature ⟨pointed out that Johnson's *a*'s and *o*'s have been
*mistaken* one for the other—*Sherbo*⟩ ⟨the tendency of
the rest of us to *mistake* gush for vigor and substitute
rhetoric for imagination—*Day Lewis*⟩ One **confuses** one
thing *with* another when one fails to distinguish two things
that have similarities or common characteristics or to
observe their lines of demarcation ⟨very possibly some of
the cases *confuse* the principles that govern jurisdiction
with those that govern merits—*Justice Holmes*⟩ ⟨far
too intellectually keen to *confuse* moral problems with
purely aesthetic problems—*Ellis*⟩ One **confounds** things,
or one thing *with* another, when one mixes them up so

hopelessly that one cannot detect their differences or distinctions. *Confound* usually carries a stronger connotation of mental bewilderment or of a muddled mind than the preceding words and accordingly is often preferred when the differences are more or less obvious to a clearheaded or intelligent person ⟨courage must not be *confounded* with brutality. Brutality is pleasure in forcing one's will upon other people; courage is indifference to personal misfortunes—*Russell*⟩ ⟨the temptation to *confound* accumulated knowledge and experience with intrinsic progress is almost irresistible—*Inge*⟩
*Ana* addle, muddle, *confuse
*Ant* recognize
**mistake** *n* *error, slip, lapse, blunder, faux pas, bull, howler, boner
*Ana* confusion, confounding, mistaking (see corresponding verbs at MISTAKE): inadvertence (see corresponding adjective at CARELESS): neglecting *or* neglect, omitting *or* omission, disregarding, slighting *or* slight (see corresponding verbs at NEGLECT)
**mistreat** maltreat, ill-treat, misuse, *abuse, outrage
*Ana* see those at ILL-TREAT
**mistrust** *n* **1** suspicion, skepticism, doubt, *uncertainty, dubiety, dubiosity
*Ana* misgiving, presentiment, foreboding, *apprehension
*Ant* trust: assurance  —*Con* confidence, faith, reliance, dependence (see TRUST): *certainty, certitude, conviction
**2** distrust (see under DISTRUST *vb*)
**mistrust** *vb* *distrust
*Ana* apprehend, anticipate, *foresee: alarm, *frighten, scare: appall, *dismay
*Con* *rely, trust, depend: confide, entrust, relegate, *commit
**misuse** *vb* *abuse, mistreat, maltreat, ill-treat, outrage
*Ana* hurt, *injure, harm, damage, impair, mar, spoil: pervert, *debase, corrupt
*Ant* respect  —*Con* esteem, regard (see under REGARD *n*): cherish, treasure, prize, *appreciate
**mite** bit, *particle, smidgen, whit, atom, iota, jot, tittle
**mitigate** allay, *relieve, alleviate, lighten, assuage
*Ana* temper, *moderate: abate, reduce, lessen, diminish, *decrease: *palliate, extenuate
*Ant* intensify  —*Con* aggravate, heighten, enhance (see INTENSIFY): *increase, augment
**mix,** mingle, commingle, blend, merge, coalesce, amalgamate, fuse denote to combine or become combined with resulting diffusion or interpenetration of particles, parts, or elements. **Mix,** the most comprehensive of these terms, need not imply loss of identities, but even when the elements are distinguishable it suggests a homogeneous character in the product ⟨*mix* salt and pepper⟩ ⟨*mix* colors for painting⟩ ⟨oil and water do not *mix*⟩ ⟨told in a style that *mixes* erudition and bawdiness—*Sat. Review*⟩ ⟨manual and intellectual labor seldom *mix* well—*Canby*⟩ So far as they differ, **mingle,** rather than *mix,* implies that the constituent elements are distinguished in the product ⟨the evil . . . strangely *mingled* with the good—*Babbitt*⟩ ⟨*mingling,* as no other school of dramatists has done, the oratorical, the conversational, the elaborate and the simple—*T. S. Eliot*⟩ ⟨he recognized in her look of *mingled* anxiety and pleasure the suspense of someone who introduces one part of life into another—*Cheever*⟩ **Commingle** may suggest a more intimate and often a harmonious union ⟨*commingled* with the gloom of imminent war, the shadow of his loss drew like eclipse, darkening the world—*Tennyson*⟩ ⟨the *commingling* in him of earthiness and sophistication—*Pick*⟩ **Blend** may be the equivalent of *mix* or *mingle* ⟨a tale that *blends* their glory with their shame—*Pope*⟩ but usually it implies a mixing of harmonious or

compatible things, a union so intimate as to obscure the individuality of the component parts and a sharing of their qualities by the resultant product ⟨*blended* teas⟩ ⟨offshore where sea and skyline *blend* in rain—*Kipling*⟩ ⟨the faltering accents of the supplicant, *blending* the cadences of the liturgy with those of perplexed brooding thought—*Edmund Wilson*⟩ **Merge** still more distinctly implies the loss in the whole of the constituent elements or the complete absorption of one element in another ⟨*merge* the private in the general good⟩ ⟨Archer often wondered how, after forty years of the closest conjugality, two such *merged* identities ever separated themselves enough for anything as controversial as a talking-over—*Wharton*⟩ ⟨all these people did not, however, *merge* anonymously into some homogeneous mass—*Handlin*⟩ **Coalesce** suggests a natural affinity for each other in the things merging and a resulting organic unity ⟨all these descriptive details do not *coalesce* for us into the distinct image of a living woman—*Babbitt*⟩ ⟨the vernaculars of the various groups began to *coalesce* into one recognized form of language somewhat distinct from the English of the mother country—*Mathews*⟩ **Amalgamate** implies a tendency to merge or draw together largely as a result of contact or association and sometimes suggests effective or harmonious union more than loss of identity ⟨the Indian race . . . formed no part of the colonial communities, and never *amalgamated* with them—*Taney*⟩ ⟨the "by-pass" engine tries to *amalgamate* the speed and the height characteristics of the pure jet with the fuel economy of the jet-prop—*Charles Gardner*⟩ **Fuse** stresses even more than *blend* and *merge* the loss of identity of each of the component elements, and, more than *coalesce,* the indissolubility of their union. It often implies a powerful cause which operates like heat melting and bringing into one mass disparate substances ⟨the Scotch nation, nobles and commons, ministers and people, wonderfully *fused* together by fiery enthusiasm—*Goldwin Smith*⟩ ⟨truth at white heat—the truth of terror and mystery and baleful beauty, *fused* into one flaming impression—*Lowes*⟩
*Ana* *join, combine, unite, conjoin
*Con* *separate, part, divide, sever, sunder
**mixture,** admixture, blend, compound, composite, amalgam denote a product formed by the combination of two or more things. **Mixture** is the most inclusive and most widely applicable term; it has, however, many specific applications; thus, a fabric made by interweaving yarns of different colors is a *mixture;* a pipe tobacco in which several varieties are combined to give a particular flavor or quality is a smoking *mixture.* The word often implies miscellaneousness ⟨"society" in a small town is very much of a *mixture*⟩ **Admixture** adds to *mixture* the suggestion of the alien character of one or more of the constituent elements ⟨the *admixture* of coffee with roasted and ground cereals or other inert adulterants—*Encyc. Americana*⟩ **Blend,** on the contrary, adds to *mixture* the implication of thorough mingling of usually similar or congruous elements or ingredients. Like *admixture,* it implies that the product is not pure or simple but, unlike it, it usually suggests harmony or complete integration ⟨a curious *blend* of humility and irony—*T. S. Eliot*⟩ ⟨unorthodox was the *blend* of executive responsibility, legislative power and financial control—*Buchan*⟩ **Blend** is applied in commerce to mixed whiskeys, teas, coffees, or tobaccos to indicate that a new product has been formed that combines the flavors of several varieties of the basic thing and that the products contain no other substance than such varieties. **Compound** usually implies the union of two or more distinguishable or analyzable parts, elements, or ingredients ⟨it was not fear, it was not ardor,—it was a *com-*

*pound* of both—*Scott*⟩ ⟨rare *compound* of oddity, frolic, and fun—*Goldsmith*⟩ In its technical senses *compound* is definitely restricted in application. In chemistry a compound is a distinct substance formed by a union of two or more elements or radicals in definite proportions by weight ⟨water is a *compound* of oxygen and hydrogen⟩ As applied to words, a compound is a word or group of word elements which is formed of recognizable parts but has a distinct sense often not inferable from the meanings of its component parts. A compound may be written solid (as *blackboard*), hyphenated (as *long-distance*), or open (as *all right*). **Composite** is often interchangeable with *compound* in its general sense, but there is a tendency to prefer *composite* when the constituent parts are artificially or fortuitously combined ⟨the American people is a *composite* of many races⟩ ⟨the opinions of America are formed from the *composite* of the voices of America, official and unofficial, true and false—*A. E. Stevenson*⟩ An **amalgam** is basically an alloy made by adding mercury to a metal; the term is particularly applicable to such alloys that are intended for use in dental restoration, usually contain several metals in addition to mercury, and set into a firm mass after a relatively brief period of time. In its extended use *amalgam* may draw on the notion of complexity of mixture ⟨one's judgment is inevitably an *amalgam* of impressions of the work and impressions of the man—*T. S. Eliot*⟩ or it may stress the hardening into final form ⟨a mixture of affection and contempt, which later days hardened into an *amalgam* of generosity and sadism—*Wecter*⟩
*Ana* joining, combining, uniting (see JOIN)

**moan** *n* groan, sigh, sob (see under SIGH *vb*)
*Ana* crying *or* cry, wailing *or* wail (see CRY): lamenting *or* lament, bemoaning, bewailing (see DEPLORE)

**moan** *vb* groan, *sigh, sob
*Ana* mourn, *grieve, sorrow: bemoan, bewail, lament, *deplore

**mob** *n* *crowd, throng, press, crush, rout, horde
*Ana* *multitude, army, host, legion

**mobile** *movable, motive
*Ana* fluid, *liquid: *changeable, changeful, protean, variable: *inconstant, unstable, mercurial, fickle, capricious
*Ant* immobile

**mock** *vb* 1 taunt, deride, *ridicule, twit, rally
*Ana* flout, *scoff, jeer, gird, gibe: caricature, parody, travesty, burlesque (see under CARICATURE *n*)
2 *copy, imitate, mimic, ape
*Ana* counterfeit, feign, affect, simulate, *assume

**mode** *n* 1 *state, condition, situation, posture, status
2 *method, manner, way, fashion, system
*Ana* trend, drift, *tendency, tenor: procedure, *process

**mode** *n* *fashion, style, vogue, fad, rage, craze, dernier cri, cry

**model** *n* Model, example, pattern, exemplar, ideal, standard, beau ideal, mirror are comparable when they denote something set or held before one for guidance or imitation in conduct or endeavor. **Model** applies to a person or thing set before one for imitation by oneself or another; the term may suggest nothing more ⟨art students painting the human figure from a *model*⟩ ⟨a child of three years old is a better *model* for a child one year old . . . because the things it does are more what the younger child would wish to do—*Russell*⟩ ⟨served as *model* for most of the State capitols built in the ensuing twenty-five years—*Amer. Guide Series: Minn.*⟩ Often the term applies to a person or thing that is eminently or even preeminently worthy of imitation ⟨there is no poet in any tongue . . . who stands so firmly as a *model* for all poets—*T. S. Eliot*⟩

⟨the Saint whose name is given to a child serves as . . . an ideal *model* to be imitated—*Nurnberg & Rosenblum*⟩ **Example** applies chiefly to a person (or his acts or conduct) that is or may be imitated by others; the term usually implies that the person, or the act, or the conduct, for some good reason is one that is likely to be imitated, whether good or bad, right or wrong ⟨a father should set a good *example* to his children⟩ ⟨she always followed the *example* of her mother in her social behavior⟩ ⟨one of the immortal *examples* of a true man in a world of bounders, cowards, and squeaking specters—*Sullivan*⟩ Sometimes, however, *example* applies to what is not intended to be imitated, but rather to serve as a warning ⟨let it profit thee to have heard, by terrible *example*, the reward of disobedience—*Milton*⟩ *Example* is also used in a highly abstract sense in antithesis to *precept*, then implying the setting of an example, usually but not necessarily a good example ⟨the mistake of thinking that all can be done by precept, when . . . *example* is no less potent a force—*Benson*⟩ **Pattern** applies either to the divine archetype of a thing or to a carefully worked out design or plan (as an architect's drawing) to be followed in fashioning a thing ⟨according to an heavenly *pattern* . . . which He had fashioned in his wise foresight, He man did make—*Spenser*⟩ ⟨almost all the common things we use now . . . are made by machinery, and are copies of an original *pattern*—*Jevons*⟩ In a more general sense (see also FIGURE 3) *pattern* applies to what merits or seems to merit imitation; it often differs from *model* in suggesting a more clearly worked out design, or a fuller presentation of details, or in connoting fixity or compelling power ⟨a housewife in bed, at table a slattern; for all an example, for no one a *pattern*—*Swift*⟩ ⟨the ancient *pattern* of life had been woven continuously for so many centuries that even illiterate farmers knew how to be courtly and dignified—*Blofeld*⟩ **Exemplar** often comes closer to *pattern* than to *example* because it usually applies to something set before one as worthy of imitation and, therefore, inherently good ⟨Christ is the . . . *exemplar* that all preachers ought to follow—*Latimer*⟩ ⟨dear . . . as an *exemplar* of goodness, probity, and pure life—*Thackeray*⟩ Sometimes, however, *exemplar* is specifically applied to a person or thing that exhibits a quality, or sums up all the characteristics that distinguish a type, whether that quality or type be in itself good or bad ⟨Sisyphus, the legendary *exemplar* of cunning—*Thirlwall*⟩ ⟨Stendhal's Julian Sorel . . . this *exemplar* of ruthless individualism—*Huxley*⟩ **Ideal** may specifically imply existence not in the actual world but in the mind and therefore may suggest a remoteness from reality and especially perfection exceeding what is possible in reality ⟨traditions grew up around his name, to be interpreted according to the hearers' own *ideals* of personality and education—*D. E. Smith*⟩ But *ideal* also may apply to a real person or thing that is held before one as embodying or representing the perfection one hopes to realize or attain ⟨the boy found his *ideal* in his father⟩ ⟨[Livia] embodied in her life the *ideal* of the Roman matron—*Buchan*⟩ Frequently *ideal* is almost indistinguishable from **standard** when it applies not to a person or object that serves as a pattern or exemplar, but to something (as a rule, a practice, an aim, or an established level of excellence) by which one seeks to maintain a high quality in a product or of performance ⟨the *ideal* of general cultivation has been one of the *standards* in education—*Eliot*⟩ ⟨[accuracy] is still a noble and inspiring *ideal*. It is the morality of the intellect: it prescribes what it ought to strive for—*Ballard*⟩ ⟨each generation . . . has its own *ideals* and its own *standards* of judgment—*Crothers*⟩ But *standard* (see also STANDARD 2) is inter-

*Ana* analogous words   *Ant* antonyms   *Con* contrasted words   See also explanatory notes facing page 1

changeable with *ideal* only when it applies to what is the test of perfection or of human perfection ⟨the very art . . . incommensurable with any *standard* except that of pure beauty—I refer of course to the art of music—*Dickinson*⟩ ⟨with the spread of impressionism literature has lost *standards* and discipline, and at the same time virility and seriousness—*Babbitt*⟩ **Beau ideal** applies to one and especially a person felt to be a fit model or ideal because of high excellence ⟨the *beau ideal* of all that was romantic, exquisite, and passionate—*Harrison Smith*⟩ **Mirror** applies to something so exemplary of its kind that it may serve as a model ⟨no modern building could act as a better *mirror* of functional needs . . . than this seventeenth-century Spanish mission—*Liturgical Arts*⟩
*Ana* criterion, touchstone, gauge, *standard

**moderate** *adj* **1 Moderate, temperate** are often used interchangeably to denote not excessive in degree, amount, or intensity ⟨a *moderate* allowance⟩ ⟨*temperate* heat⟩ When contrasted **moderate** often connotes absence or avoidance of excess and is opposed to *excessive* and *immoderate*, while **temperate** connotes deliberate restraint or restriction and is opposed to *intemperate* and *inordinate*; thus, "a *moderate* drinker" suggests free but far from excessive indulgence in intoxicants, and "a *temperate* drinker" suggests restrained and cautious indulgence; "*moderate* enthusiasm" suggests lukewarmness, "*temperate* enthusiasm" suggests keeping a hold over one's exhibition of feeling; one's anger may be far from *moderate*, yet one's reply may be *temperate*. Especially in technical language *moderate* and *temperate* often denote falling or staying within a range midway between extremes or designate a point (as in a scale) characterized neither by excess nor by deficiency of something understood. When so used they are not usually interchangeable, for custom or terminology has determined the selection ⟨*moderate* temperature⟩ ⟨a *moderate* breeze⟩ ⟨a *temperate* climate⟩ ⟨a *temperate* zone⟩ In this sense both *moderate* and *temperate* have two antonyms, one on the side of deficiency and the other on the side of excess. These antonyms are usually specific and vary according to the application, for example: *light* and *strong* (of breezes); *arctic* and *torrid* (of climate); *abstemious* and *gluttonous* (of eating); *mild* and *violent* (of something having force and intensity).
*Ana* ordinary, *common, familiar: gentle, mild, bland, *soft: *sparing, economical
*Ant* immoderate —*Con* *excessive, extreme, inordinate
**2** *medium, middling, mediocre, second-rate, average, fair, indifferent
*Ana* decent, *decorous, proper: *steady, even, equable, constant

**moderate** *vb* **Moderate, qualify, temper** are comparable when they mean to modify something so as to avoid an extreme or to keep within due bounds. **Moderate** stresses reduction of what is excessive, but it does not necessarily imply finding the happy mean ⟨the sun at midday *moderates* the cold⟩ ⟨you must *moderate* your demands if you wish to be listened to⟩ ⟨"*Moderate* your language, old man," I said; "remember that you are addressing a superior"—*Hudson*⟩ ⟨*moderating* his big voice to the dimensions of the room—*Clifton Daniel*⟩ **Qualify** emphasizes restriction or more precise definition that brings a thing closer to the truth or facts or that makes it less general, inclusive, or sweeping or that gives it a clearly defined quality or character of its own ⟨it is time to *qualify* the over simple account I have given of the artist's process of creation—*Alexander*⟩ ⟨almost every important point must be *qualified* with adverbs

and adjectives expressing uncertainty, approximation, tentativeness—*Urey*⟩ **Temper** strongly implies accommodation to the needs or requirements of someone or something; it need not suggest moderation or qualification, but it usually implies the addition of a counterbalancing or mitigating thing ⟨God *tempers* the wind to the shorn lamb—*Old Proverb*⟩ ⟨denunciation must be firm, *tempered* with sadness over the falling from grace—*MacInnes*⟩ ⟨*temper* justice with mercy⟩
*Ana* abate, reduce, lessen, diminish, *decrease: mitigate, alleviate, lighten, *relieve: slow, slacken (see DELAY)
*Con* *intensify, aggravate, heighten, enhance: augment, *increase

**modern** *adj* **1 Modern, recent, late,** though not close synonyms, are subject to confusion when they are used to date things or events which have taken place, come into existence, or developed in times close to the present. **Modern** (see also NEW) is the term of widest range of meaning; it may date anything that is not medieval or ancient ⟨the ancient languages have now been superseded by the *modern* languages in popular favor in high schools and colleges⟩ ⟨the date of the discovery of America, 1492, is often used arbitrarily as the beginning of *modern* history⟩ ⟨the weed-caught wrecks of ancient galleys, medieval ships and *modern* dreadnaughts—*Beebe*⟩ or anything that bears the marks of a period nearer in time than another ⟨*modern* surgical techniques⟩ ⟨the *modern* novel⟩ ⟨the ornate mansions of a bygone era mingle with more *modern* concepts of architecture—*N. Y. Times*⟩ or less clearly to anything that is new, fresh, or up-to-date ⟨she is very *modern* in her clothes and in her manners⟩ ⟨we all have to remember that what is *modern* today and up-to-date, what is efficient and practical, becomes obsolete and outworn tomorrow—*Roosevelt*⟩ In all these uses a change or contrast in character or quality is to some extent implied by the term *modern*. **Recent** is usually without such implication and may simply indicate a date that approximates that of the immediate past, though the time to which this term, too, refers depends upon the thing that is qualified; thus, "*recent* geological ages" designates those ages immediately preceding the present geological age, although, since each age may represent millions of years, *recent* is obviously used relatively; "Shakespeare is a more *recent* author than Chaucer" implies only a comparative status, for Shakespeare was born in the sixteenth century and Chaucer in the fourteenth; "we have all the *recent* books" implies an absolute relation to a time that may be described as the immediate past ⟨*recent* news⟩ ⟨*recent* rains⟩ ⟨a *recent* purchase⟩ ⟨a *recent* issue of a magazine⟩ **Late** (see also TARDY, DEAD) implies a series or succession of which the person or thing so described is the most recent in time ⟨the *late* war⟩ ⟨the servant's *late* master testified as to his honesty⟩ ⟨moose which of *late* years have been showing up around Stewartstown—*Holbrook*⟩ Sometimes the word carries an implication that is less definite and equivalent to "not long ago holding the position of or serving as" ⟨the firm's new director of research was the *late* professor of applied chemistry at the University⟩
**2** modernistic, *new, novel, new-fashioned, newfangled, original, fresh
*Ana* *contemporary, contemporaneous, coincident, concomitant, concurrent: *prevailing, current, prevalent
*Ant* antique: ancient

**modernistic** *new, new-fashioned, newfangled, novel, modern, original, fresh
*Ant* antiquated

**modest 1** *humble, meek, lowly
*Ana* retiring, withdrawing (see GO): *moderate, temperate

---

A colon (:) separates groups of words discriminated. An asterisk (*) indicates place of treatment of each group.

*Ant* ambitious —*Con* *showy, pretentious, ostentatious: arrogant, haughty, *proud, overbearing: *shameless, brazen, barefaced, impudent
2 *shy, bashful, diffident, coy
*Ana* reserved, reticent, *silent: shrinking, recoiling (see RECOIL): nice, seemly, proper (see DECOROUS)
3 decent, *chaste, pure
*Ana* *moral, virtuous: *decorous, proper, seemly, decent
*Ant* immodest —*Con* indecent, indelicate, *indecorous, unseemly, improper
**modification** change, alteration, variation (see under CHANGE *vb*)
*Ana* transformation, metamorphosis, conversion, transmogrification (see under TRANSFORM): qualification, tempering (see corresponding verbs at MODERATE)
**modify** *change, alter, vary
*Ana* temper, *moderate, qualify: *transform, convert, metamorphose, transmogrify
**modish** *stylish, fashionable, smart, chic, dashing
*Ant* antiquated
**moist** *wet, damp, humid, dank
*Con* *dry, arid
**molecule** atom, *particle, corpuscle
**mollify** appease, placate, *pacify, propitiate, conciliate
*Ana* *relieve, allay, mitigate, lighten: *moderate, temper, qualify: abate, lessen, reduce, *decrease
*Ant* exasperate
**mollycoddle** *vb* humor, pamper, *indulge, spoil, baby
**molt** *discard, cast, shed, slough, scrap, junk
**moment** 1 *instant, minute, second, flash, jiffy, twinkling, split second
2 *importance, consequence, significance, import, weight
*Ana* value, *worth: advantage, profit, avail, *use
**momentary** *transient, transitory, passing, ephemeral, fugitive, fleeting, evanescent, short-lived
*Ant* agelong
**momentum** impetus, *speed, velocity, pace, headway
**monastery** *cloister, convent, nunnery, abbey, priory
**monetary** *financial, pecuniary, fiscal
**money** *n* Money, cash, currency, legal tender, specie, coin, coinage are comparable when they mean pieces of stamped metal or their equivalents issued by a government, or by an authority recognized by the government, to serve as a medium of exchange in the country or section under the control of that government. **Money** applies to both coined gold, silver, copper, or other metal issued as a medium of exchange and to certificates or notes, often called specifically *paper money*, that sometimes promise payment in metal money, are issued by a government or governmentally recognized authority (as a bank), and pass like coined metal as a medium of exchange. **Cash** applies to money, sometimes specifically called *ready money*, actually in hand or immediate possession of an individual or a business or institution ⟨the firm's supply of *cash* was very low because the larger part of the day's accumulation had just been deposited in the bank⟩ **Currency** may apply to all of the money in circulation, as distinguished from that which is not in circulation for one reason or another ⟨the first panacea for a mismanaged nation is inflation of the *currency—Hemingway*⟩ but it may also apply to paper money as distinguished from coined metal. **Legal tender** applies specifically to the type of money which the law authorizes a debtor to offer and requires a creditor to receive as payment of money obligations and may or may not at any given time include all lawful money of a particular jurisdiction. **Specie, coin** (only in a collective sense), and **coinage** apply only to minted or coined money; they therefore imply an opposition to all forms of paper money (as treasury notes and bank notes) ⟨payments were demanded in *specie*, or in the *coin* of the realm⟩ ⟨we are far more concerned today with his debasement of the *coinage —Shaw*⟩
**monk** *religious, friar, nun
*Ana* *recluse, hermit, eremite, anchorite, cenobite
**monkeyshine** *n* *prank, caper, antic, dido
**monograph** treatise, disquisition, dissertation, thesis, *discourse
*Ana* article, paper, *essay
**monopolize, engross, absorb, consume** mean to take up completely. **Monopolize**, the general term, means to possess or control exclusively ⟨*monopolize* the year's crop of cotton⟩ ⟨a child should not be allowed to *monopolize* the attention of his family⟩ ⟨every railroad *monopolizes*, in a popular sense, the trade of some area—*Justice Holmes*⟩ ⟨the party in power at Washington can organize the two houses of the Congress . . . but it cannot *monopolize* the business of lawmaking—*Holcombe*⟩ ⟨never attempted to *monopolize* or even dominate the discussion—*J. G. Gray*⟩ Occasionally **engross** implies getting a physical control of (as by purchase of the available supply) ⟨the process of *engrossing* the land which attended the ascent to power of the aristocracy—*Becker*⟩ and this notion may persist in extended use ⟨the sun *engrossed* the east, the day controlled the world—*Emily Dickinson*⟩ but more often the verb takes an immaterial object and implies a preoccupying ⟨political theory has long *engrossed* the Indian mind—*Poleman*⟩ ⟨the works manager who . . . is *engrossed* chiefly with the engineering problem of securing maximum output with minimum input—*Hurff*⟩ **Absorb** is frequently interchangeable with *engross*, but it is less often predicated of persons as conscious agents and more often of things that have an inherent capacity for monopolization ⟨manual occupations do not engage the mind sufficiently . . . . But composition, especially of verse, *absorbs* it wholly—*Cowper*⟩ ⟨it is arithmetically impossible for every child to *absorb* the whole time of an adult tutor—*Russell*⟩ **Consume** comes into comparison with *engross* and *absorb* chiefly in an extended sense of each, implying monopolization of one's time, attention, or interest ⟨ Flané is determined that men and their convictions shall be given a true and proper evaluation. He is *consumed* with the idea of justice —*Boyle*⟩ ⟨the *consuming* anxiety of the ride still held him though the reason for it was gone—*Wheelwright*⟩
*Ana* possess, own, *have, hold: utilize, *use, employ: control, manage (see CONDUCT *vb*)
**monopoly, corner, pool, syndicate, trust, cartel** are comparable rather than synonymous terms when they apply to a means of controlling prices. **Monopoly** denotes the exclusive control of a service (as telephone or telegraph service) or traffic (as transportation of goods and passengers by railroad) or of a commodity (as wheat or petroleum) in a given market. *Monopoly* may imply exclusive control created by the state (as by franchise or patent or copyright). More frequently, however, the term is used to imply exclusive power to buy or sell a commodity or service in a given market, especially as a result of ownership or control of the sources of supply (as mines) or of the available stock of a commodity ⟨in the reign of Edward III [German traders] had a practical *monopoly* of the carrying trade—*Pattison*⟩ In extended use *monopoly* also denotes the group or organization having such control ⟨it might be that when a combination reached a certain size it might have attributed to it more of the character of a *monopoly* merely by virtue of its size than would be attributed to a smaller one—*Justice Holmes*⟩ A temporary or local monopoly (as of a particular security on a stock exchange or of a particular commodity on a produce exchange)

constitutes a **corner**, so called because it puts all those who are determined to buy into a corner, or position where they must pay the price asked ⟨maintained his *corner* on wheat for three days⟩ **Pool** in this relation applies primarily to a combination of property, or of interests of different persons or companies, by means of which a more or less permanent control or monopoly is acquired. Distinctively, however, *pool* implies a joint undertaking or end which cannot be attained unless the market is managed either by manipulating prices (as of a commodity or security) or by destroying the effects of competition (as through agreements concerning prices or rates, regulation of outputs, or division of earnings of each organization concerned). **Syndicate** is applied chiefly to a group of individuals, firms, or corporations (as banking houses) which organize for a limited time to accomplish a given purpose or more specifically such a group that is organized to market an issue of a security, makes its profit from the difference between the agreed-upon sum advanced to the issuing corporation for the securities and the fixed sale price at which they are marketed, assumes responsibility for absorbing any surplus securities not marketed, and dissolves when the marketing period is completed. Outside of the field of finance, the use of the term is extended in its application to any combination (as of newspapers, business concerns, or criminals) interested in a common project or enterprise, and often implies relation to a monopoly. **Trust** specifically applies to a merger in which stockholders in the merged corporations exchange their stock for trust certificates in the new corporation and surrender their rights to trustees who operate the combined corporations, but *trust* is often extended to any combination of business entities, especially when felt to represent a threat to healthy competition. **Cartel** implies an international combination for controlling production and sale of a product or group of products.

**monotonous** dreary, pedestrian, humdrum, *dull, stodgy
*Ana* wearisome, boring, *irksome, tedious, tiresome
*Con* varying, changing (see CHANGE *vb*): fresh, novel, *new: *interesting, absorbing, engrossing

**monstrous** 1 Monstrous, prodigious, tremendous, stupendous, monumental are comparable especially in their extended more or less hyperbolical senses in which they mean astonishingly impressive. **Monstrous** commonly applies to something abnormal, usually in actual or relative size, but often also in shape or character; the term frequently carries suggestions of deformity, extreme ugliness, or fabulousness ⟨the imagination turbid with *monstrous* fancies and misshapen dreams—*Wilde*⟩ ⟨he seemed of *monstrous* bulk and significance—*G. D. Brown*⟩ ⟨the *monstrous* way of living that mankind had made for itself out of the industrial revolution—*Connolly*⟩ **Prodigious** usually implies a marvelousness that exceeds belief; it sometimes applies to something entirely out of proportion to what is the previous or usual best, greatest, or largest ⟨the *prodigious* demand for steel in the First World War⟩ ⟨men have always reverenced *prodigious* inborn gifts, and always will—*Eliot*⟩ ⟨a mind with such *prodigious* capacity of development as Shakespeare's—*T. S. Eliot*⟩ **Tremendous** may come closer to awe-inspiring or terrifying in its immensity than to gigantic or enormous, its common denotations in more literal use ⟨must have made the animal in life look very much like a crocodile and the bite must have been *tremendous*—*Swinton*⟩ ⟨how shall we compare the cramped and limited vision of the universe which spread itself to the imagination of mankind in old time with the *tremendous* vistas opened out to us by modern science—*Inge*⟩ ⟨the spell and *tremendous* incantation of the thought of death—*L. P. Smith*⟩

⟨[he] too, had his appointed or acquired limits. He could never be *tremendous*—*Montague*⟩ **Stupendous** implies the power to stun or astound; it describes something that because of its size, its numbers, its complexity, or its greatness exceeds one's power to describe or explain ⟨all are but parts of one *stupendous* whole, whose body Nature is, and God the soul—*Pope*⟩ ⟨a *stupendous* catastrophe that occurred in the constellation Hercules 1300 years ago—*Kaempffert*⟩ **Monumental** in its extended sense (see also MASSIVE) applies to something as conspicuously impressive or as massively framed or constructed as such a monument as a great cathedral or an impressive memorial ⟨his magnum opus ... the five *monumental* volumes of his history of the writer in America—*Trilling*⟩ ⟨the Mexican peon has a *monumental* reserve beside which the Englishman becomes an idle chatterer—*Woodcock*⟩
*Ana* enormous, immense, *huge, vast, colossal, mammoth, gigantic
2 *outrageous, heinous, atrocious
*Ana* *flagrant, glaring, gross, rank: *ominous, portentous, fateful: flagitious, nefarious, infamous (see VICIOUS)

**monument** *document, record, archive

**monumental** 1 *monstrous, prodigious, tremendous, stupendous
*Ana* colossal, gigantic, enormous, mammoth (see HUGE): impressive, *moving
2 *massive, massy, bulky, substantial
*Ana* imposing, stately, majestic, august, magnificent, *grand

**mood,** humor, temper, vein mean a temporary state or frame of mind in which one emotion or desire or one set of emotions gains the ascendancy. **Mood** is the comprehensive term for any such frame of mind, regardless of its particular cause, its particular character, its effect on others, or its length of existence ⟨he indulged his *moods*. If he were surly, he did not bother to hide it—*Mailer*⟩ *Mood* carries a stronger implication of pervasiveness and of compelling power than the other terms; also, it may refer not only to the frame of mind ⟨feel in a *mood* to work⟩ ⟨a sullen *mood*⟩ but to its expression in a literary or artistic work ⟨the language, the stresses, the very structure of the sentences are imposed upon the writer by the special *mood* of the piece—*Cather*⟩ or to what is seen or heard in such a way as to evoke a mood or to harmonize with one's mood ⟨the *mood* of the landscape, achieved by the beauty of the evening light —*Kenneth Clark*⟩ ⟨watching land and water, rocks and trees, and their ever-changing hues and *moods*—*Semon*⟩ **Humor** (see also WIT 2) applies chiefly to a mood which is the result of one's peculiar temperament or of one's physical or mental condition at the moment; it may be preferable to *mood* when the idea of capriciousness or of whimsicality is to be suggested ⟨I am not in a *humor* to hear you further. Leave me, please—*Hardy*⟩ ⟨the women were horrified or admiring, as their *humor* moved them —*Wharton*⟩ ⟨victims of nature's cataclysmic humors—*Julian Dana*⟩ **Temper** (see also DISPOSITION 2) applies to a mood dominated by a single strong emotion, often specifically that of great anger ⟨"He is in a *temper*!" "I never knew him so out of patience with them"—*Millay*⟩ When qualified by an adjective indicating the controlling emotion, *temper* may apply to any humor that manifests itself in a display of feeling ⟨that meekness has done me more harm than the bitterest *temper*—*Hardy*⟩ ⟨she was evidently now in a gay, frolicsome *temper*—*Hudson*⟩ **Vein** (see also TOUCH) is often used in the sense of *mood* but with a stronger implication of transitoriness and seldom with any suggestion of a temperamental or physical

---

A colon (:) separates groups of words discriminated. An asterisk (*) indicates place of treatment of each group.

basis ⟨the merry *vein* you knew me in, is sunk into a turn of reflection—*Pope*⟩ ⟨the whole is written in a *vein* of ironic seriousness—*Laski*⟩
*Ana* *disposition, temper, temperament, character, personality, individuality: *soul, spirit: emotion, *feeling, affection

**moor** *vb* *secure, anchor, rivet
*Ana* *tie, bind: attach, *fasten, affix, fix: balance, steady, *stabilize, trim

**moral** *adj* **Moral, ethical, virtuous, righteous, noble** are comparable when they mean conforming to a standard of what is right and good. **Moral** is the most comprehensive term of the group; in all of its pertinent senses it implies a relationship to character or conduct viewed as good or bad or as right or wrong. Sometimes *moral* implies relationship to or concern with character or conduct as distinguished especially from intellectual or physical nature ⟨*moral* goodness may be distinguished from intellectual goodness or spiritual goodness⟩ ⟨the whole tendency of modern thought . . . is to extenuate the responsibility of human nature, not merely on the *moral* side, but equally on the spiritual side—*Mackenzie*⟩ ⟨we find ourselves confronted with a most disturbing *moral* problem . . . those situations, now of such frequent occurrence, in which good means have end results which turn out to be bad—*Huxley*⟩ **Moral** also applies to such things as literary works, works of art, and philosophies, or to writers, artists, and philosophers concerned with the determination or teaching of principles of right conduct or good living ⟨a *moral* tale⟩ ⟨*moral* essays⟩ ⟨paintings that convey a *moral* lesson⟩ ⟨tragedy . . . hath been ever held the gravest, *moralest*, and most profitable of all other poems—*Milton*⟩ The term also applies to men or communities, to acts, or to conduct in the sense of conforming to the accepted standard of what is right and good, often specifically in sexual conduct, or of conforming to the customs or conventions of a people regarded as binding laws ⟨lead a *moral* life⟩ ⟨a man of high *moral* character⟩ ⟨the *moral* ideals of the community⟩ ⟨I had a character who was ambitious, yet in his own way, *moral*, and with such a character one could travel deep into the paradoxes of the time—*Mailer*⟩ ⟨his nature was purely sensuous, and she strove to make him *moral*, religious—*D. H. Lawrence*⟩ **Ethical** primarily implies a relationship to ethics, the branch of philosophy which deals with moral principles, or more specifically with the principles governing ideal human character and with the ideal ends of human action ⟨an *ethical* system⟩ ⟨an *ethical* code⟩ Although *ethical* is often used interchangeably with *moral*, it characteristically gives a slightly different impression owing to certain subtle connotations; thus, *ethical* principles may, according to the context, convey a strong suggestion of principles derived from a certain school of ethics, or of a formulated code behind them, or of an idealistic quality; an action is often described as *ethical* rather than *moral* when it accords with what the writer or speaker believes to be a higher or finer standard of morality than the one generally accepted, or when it is in keeping with the code of ethics governing a profession (especially law and medicine); the phrase "an *ethical* person" often differs from the phrase "a *moral* person," in suggesting an assent to ethical principles or an attention to the niceties of ethics or to the ideal ends suggested by a system or code of ethics ⟨meanwhile we hear . . . the *ethical* instinct of mankind asserting itself with splendid courage and patience—*van Dyke*⟩ **Virtuous** implies the possession or manifestation of moral excellence in character; in its most general sense it implies rectitude, justice, integrity, and all other virtues, but in more restrictive use and especially as applied to women, it often means little more than chasteness or perfect fidelity in marriage ⟨poor people . . . whether they be lazy or busy, drunken or sober, *virtuous* or vicious—*Shaw*⟩ ⟨her life had been *virtuous*, her dedication to innocence had been unswerving—*Cheever*⟩ ⟨a man might grind the faces of the poor; but so long as he refrained from caressing his neighbors' wives and daughters, he was regarded as *virtuous*—*Huxley*⟩ **Righteous** differs from *virtuous* chiefly in its stronger implication of freedom from guilt or blame; as applied to persons, it often implies justification, especially worthiness of salvation in the theological sense ⟨I came not to call the *righteous*, but sinners to repentance—*Mk* 2:17⟩ ⟨what but thy malice moved thee to misdeem of *righteous* Job—*Milton*⟩ As applied to acts, conduct, and even displays of passion, it usually implies justifiability and often consciousness of rectitude ⟨*righteous* indignation⟩ But *righteous* is the one of these words that is freely used in a worsened sense to imply an invalid and sanctimonious assumption of the appearance of rectitude ⟨left most of the work to his assistants . . . and when he found that they were doing as they pleased, he was not *righteous* nor rebuking—*Sinclair Lewis*⟩ ⟨meets the resultant gossip, and the ruin of Lily's reputation, with a *righteous* indifference to either its unfairness or his share in it—*Harper's Bazaar*⟩ **Noble** (see also GRAND) applies to persons, their acts, utterances, careers, or lives, and implies the possession and exhibition of a conspicuously high character. Often the word carries no other clear implications and seems little more than a term of high praise implying moral or ethical eminence ⟨that *noble* passion for human rights and civil liberties possessed by . . . judicial libertarians—*Gressman*⟩ ⟨a *noble* aim, faithfully kept, is as a *noble* deed—*Wordsworth*⟩ At other times the term suggests not only moral eminence but the absence of all taint of any such petty or dubious thing as self-seeking, self-interest, or concern for the world's standards; it then often suggests independence, or magnanimity, or high courage, or some other outstanding moral excellence ⟨this was the *noblest* Roman of them all. All the conspirators, save only he, did that they did in envy of great Caesar; he only, in a general honest thought and common good to all—*Shak.*⟩ ⟨the disinterested search for truth is certainly one of the highest and *noblest* careers that a man can choose—*Inge*⟩
*Ana* right, *good: *upright, honest, just, honorable, scrupulous, conscientious: *chaste, pure, modest, decent: ideal, *abstract
*Con* *immoral, unmoral, amoral, nonmoral

**morale, discipline, esprit de corps** although not always close synonyms, are comparable when they mean a condition or spirit which holds together a body of persons. **Morale** usually applies to the qualities of an entire body of men (as an army or a regiment, a people, or a community) with respect especially to their courage and endurance under stress, but it sometimes may refer to an individual in his capacity of a member of a body held together by such qualities ⟨*morale* . . . describes the communal condition of mind and emotion, and it is incorrect to refer to the low or high *morale* of an individual, except in his or her relationship to the group—*Times Lit. Sup.*⟩ ⟨by military leadership we . . . mean . . . the capacity to weld 50 to 250 men into a unit of high *morale* and lead them into battle—*Psychiatry*⟩ **Discipline** applies to the order maintained and observed by a body or an individual that is or has been subjected to training (as in uniform behavior, in control over the passions or other individualistic traits, or in military exercises) so that the whole moves under command as one and the individual thinks of him-

---

*Ana* analogous words     *Ant* antonyms     *Con* contrasted words     See also explanatory notes facing page 1

self only in relation to others ⟨troops noted for their *discipline*⟩ ⟨true *discipline* is intelligent obedience of each for the consequent effectiveness of all—*Ageton*⟩ ⟨books . . . written by men who have subjected themselves in a superior degree to intellectual *discipline* and culture—*Dewey*⟩ **Esprit de corps** especially applies to the spirit of loyalty that is manifest in a body (as a profession or a society) by jealous regard for the honor or the interests of the body as a whole or for fellow members as belonging to it; often *esprit de corps* implies a spirit that distinguishes one body and brings it into opposition to others ⟨among the professions noted for their *esprit de corps*, that of physician ranks high⟩ ⟨*esprit de corps* . . . in each specialized part of the body politic, prompts measures to preserve the integrity of that part in opposition to other parts—*Spencer*⟩ ⟨though the development of a strong *esprit de corps* is most desirable, within a small and exclusive group it becomes dangerous . . . assumes the form of a closed club, the members of which can, in each other's eyes, do no wrong—*Political Science Quarterly*⟩ ⟨the inspired and faultless *esprit de corps* of her flesh and her bones and her blood; never were the features and the colors of a face in such serene and unassailable agreement, never had a skeleton been more singularly honored by the integument it wore—*Stafford*⟩
*Ana* *vigor, spirit, drive: self-confidence, self-possession, assurance, *confidence: nerving, steeling (see ENCOURAGE)
*Con* enervation (see corresponding verb at UNNERVE)
**morality** *goodness, virtue, rectitude
*Ana* integrity, probity, honor, *honesty: *excellence, perfection, virtue, merit
**morally** *virtually, practically
**morbid** *unwholesome, sickly, diseased, pathological
*Ana* hypochondriac, atrabilious, *melancholic: gloomy, morose, saturnine (see SULLEN)
*Ant* sound  —*Con* *healthy, wholesome, well, hale, robust: *healthful, healthy, hygienic
**mordant** *caustic, acrid, scathing
*Ana* *incisive, trenchant, cutting, biting, clear-cut, crisp: *pungent, poignant, piquant, racy, spicy, snappy: *sharp, keen, acute
**moreover** besides, furthermore, likewise, *also, too
**moron** imbecile, idiot, *fool, simpleton, natural
**morose** glum, gloomy, saturnine, dour, *sullen, surly, sulky, crabbed
*Ana* splenetic, choleric, *irascible, testy, cranky, cross: peevish, snappish, waspish, petulant, *irritable: brusque, gruff (see BLUFF)
**mortal** *adj* *deadly, fatal, lethal
*Ana* destructive (see corresponding verb DESTROY): virulent, venomous, *poisonous: implacable, unrelenting, relentless (see GRIM)
*Ant* venial (*especially of a sin*)
**mortified** *ashamed, chagrined
*Ana* harassed, harried, worried, annoyed (see WORRY *vb*): humiliated, humbled, abased (see ABASE): abashed, embarrassed, discomfited (see EMBARRASS)
**mostly** *largely, greatly, chiefly, mainly, principally, generally
**motif** *n* 1 device, design, pattern, *figure
2 *subject, matter, subject matter, argument, topic, text, theme, motive, leitmotiv
**motion** *n* Motion, movement, move, locomotion, stir mean the act or an instance of moving. **Motion** is the appropriate term in abstract use for the act or process of moving, without regard to what moves or is moved; in philosophical and aesthetic use it is an especially comprehensive term, for it may apply to manifestation of change or of changing not only from place to place, but from condition

to condition, or from step to step in a progression ⟨the laws of *motion*⟩ ⟨this vicissitude of *motion* and rest, which we call life—*Steele*⟩ ⟨in all the arts the principle of *motion* prevails increasingly over the principle of repose—*Babbitt*⟩ ⟨movement is always to be preferred to inaction. In *motion* a man has a chance, his body is warm, his instincts are quick—*Mailer*⟩ Ordinarily, however, the term implies discernible physical moving ⟨the *motion* of the planets⟩ ⟨I was lying . . . injured, and incapable of *motion*—*Hudson*⟩ ⟨the restless *motion* of the sea⟩ ⟨every step and every *motion* in the old dances had meaning—*Reginald & Gladys Laubin*⟩ **Movement** usually implies definite regulated motion; the term is used less often than *motion* to denote an abstraction, although it may be extended to denote a quality of representation in a work of art that suggests motion ⟨*movement* is one of the most striking characteristics of the Elgin marbles and of the Winged Victory⟩ ⟨the new freedom and variety in the *movements* of the Apostles in the boat . . . are proofs of Giotto's rare power of invention—*Fry*⟩ or a quality in literary work (as poetry) that suggests a definite rate of speed or progression (as in the meter, the rhythm, or the action) ⟨no one will so well render Homer's swift-flowing *movement* as he who has himself something of the swift-moving spirit of Homer—*Arnold*⟩ In concrete use *movement* implies a passage, whether self-initiated or under guidance or compulsion, from place to place, from situation to situation, or from condition to condition; it may, in this sense, be used interchangeably with *motion* in the collective singular or in the plural ⟨the *movements* of the planets⟩ ⟨the restless *movement* of the sea⟩ ⟨the *movement* of troops to the front was then in progress⟩ ⟨severe storms hindered the *movement* of trucks carrying supplies⟩ ⟨large regions in which, though earth *movement* has occurred rather recently, this has scarcely anywhere dislocated the land surface—*C. A. Cotton*⟩ ⟨there may be a complex double rhythm of annual *movement*; sowing in the north, extensive migration south in later winter, return for the harvest—*W. B. Fisher*⟩ **Movement** also is frequently used for an instance of moving ⟨a *movement* among the ferns attracted Adrian—*Meredith*⟩ ⟨every *movement* of the bird was watched by the cat⟩ **Move** is particularly likely to denote a beginning of a movement ⟨so shocked that no one made a *move* to leave⟩ or to apply to a definite instance of moving or moving something from one place to another ⟨make a *move* in a chess game⟩ The word may stress the notion of change and then is particularly applicable to a changing of one's abode ⟨planning a *move* to a new farm⟩ or to a physical or figurative moving to attain an end or objective ⟨viewed as a *move* to encourage . . . organized labor's full participation—*Current Biog.*⟩ ⟨the Turks would not be frightened into submission by any Russian *move*—*Collier's Yr. Bk.*⟩ **Locomotion** usually suggests travel especially by artificial means (as by boat, train, airplane, or automobile) ⟨every improvement of the means of *locomotion* benefits mankind morally and intellectually—*Macaulay*⟩ but it may apply to natural means (as wings or legs) ⟨pseudopodia and cilia are primitive organs of *locomotion*⟩ **Stir** applies to a motion or movement, often without an implication of changes of place or condition or of progress, that involves a not necessarily displeasing disturbance especially of what has been quiet or at rest or free from excitement, bustle, or agitation ⟨not a *stir* of child or mouse—*Stevenson*⟩ ⟨many persons find *stir*, and movement, and the presence of a crowd an agreeable stimulus—*Benson*⟩ ⟨it is an age of *stir* and change—*Galsworthy*⟩
*Ana* impetus, momentum, *speed, velocity, pace, headway

A colon (:) separates groups of words discriminated. An asterisk (*) indicates place of treatment of each group.

**motivate** actuate, *activate

*Ana* stimulate, quicken, *provoke, excite: arouse, rouse, *stir: inspire, animate, fire, *inform

**motive** *n* 1 Motive, spring, impulse, incentive, inducement, spur, goad all denote a stimulus inciting or prompting a person to act or behave in a definite way. **Motive** applies chiefly to such an emotion as fear, anger, hatred, or love or to a desire (as for fame, wealth, knowledge, supremacy, or revenge) or to such a physical appetite as hunger or sexual desire which operates on the will and definitely moves it to activity ⟨always seeking the *motive* of everyone's speech or behavior—*Brownell*⟩ ⟨whenever a man does a thoroughly stupid thing, it is always from the noblest *motives*—*Wilde*⟩ ⟨I could slay no living thing except from *motives* of hunger—*Hudson*⟩ ⟨even where some piece of knowledge is uninteresting in itself, a man can force himself to acquire it if he has an adequate *motive* for doing so—*Russell*⟩ **Spring**, often as the plural **springs**, is used in place of *motive* without much difference in meaning; however, it may refer to the underlying or basic motive which is often not fully recognized even by the person affected and is especially hidden from all but the most penetrating observers ⟨it is difficult . . . to come at the true *springs* of action—*Forrest*⟩ ⟨the love of gold was the sordid *spring* of the most brilliant enterprises of the republic—*Merivale*⟩ ⟨laying open to his view the *springs* of action in both parties—*Peacock*⟩ **Impulse** need not imply, as *motive* and *spring* regularly imply, actual performance of an act or engagement in an activity; the term stresses impetus, or driving power, rather than its effect; thus, one may check, or restrain, or forgo, or dismiss an *impulse*. In its more general sense *impulse* is applicable to a powerful incitement or instigation to activity, especially one arising within oneself as the result of a native propensity, one's peculiarity of temperament, or one's intellectual or emotional constitution ⟨he was not a man . . . to yield timidly to the *impulses* of others—*Prescott*⟩ ⟨in Brave New World . . . all are permitted to indulge their sexual *impulses* without let or hindrance—*Huxley*⟩ ⟨men like the elder Cato, Varro, and the elder Pliny liked to record the curiosities of nature, but they had not the systematizing *impulse*, the restless passion for order, of the Greeks —*Buchan*⟩ Specifically, *impulse* is applicable to a spontaneous and often unconsidered and nearly irresistible urge to do something ⟨Dr. Lavendar . . . said to himself, chuckling, "If I'd followed my *impulse*, I'd have married them then and there, and made no bones of it"—*Deland*⟩ ⟨the first *impulse* of a child in a garden is to pick every attractive flower—*Russell*⟩ ⟨Gard suffered an odd *impulse* to get up and kick his chair over; but people don't do those things. He kicked the back log instead—*Mary Austin*⟩ **Incentive** applies chiefly to a cause which incites and encourages action or activity and especially to one for which the person affected is not himself responsible or which does not originate within himself ⟨offer a bonus as an *incentive* to greater speed and efficiency in production⟩ ⟨with some pupils praise is not an *incentive* to study⟩ ⟨money is not the only *incentive* to work, nor the strongest—*Shaw*⟩ ⟨the great *incentive* to effort, all through life, is experience of success after initial difficulties—*Russell*⟩ ⟨people . . . cut off here without the influence of example or emulation, with no *incentive* but some natural yearning for order and security—*Cather*⟩ **Inducement** is narrower than *incentive*, for it consistently suggests an external influence and often an attempt to entice or allure to action or activity ⟨the chief *inducements* to serve were the pension and the right of citizenship which awaited a soldier on his discharge—*Buchan*⟩ ⟨his method of holding his followers together by culinary

and bibulous *inducements* has often been described— *L. M. Sears*⟩ **Spur** applies to an impetus to action which not only incites but stimulates the mind and increases its energy and ardor ⟨fame is the *spur* that the clear spirit doth raise . . . to scorn delights and live laborious days— *Milton*⟩ ⟨fear or despair may be a temporary *spur* to action—*Sat. Review*⟩ **Goad** applies to a stimulus to action or activity that keeps one going in spite of one's will or desire ⟨the daily *goad* urging him to the daily toil— *Macaulay*⟩ ⟨insecurity, considered by some management people as the indispensable *goad* for workers' efficiency— *Dun's Review*⟩

*Ana* *cause, determinant, antecedent, reason: *desire, appetite, urge, passion, lust: *feeling, emotion, passion: purpose, intent, *intention, aim, end

2 *subject, matter, subject matter, argument, topic, text, theme, motif, leitmotiv

**motive** *adj* *movable, mobile

*Ana* *active, operative, dynamic: moving, driving, impelling *or* impulsive (see corresponding verbs at MOVE)

**motley** *adj* 1 *variegated, parti-colored, checkered, checked, pied, piebald, skewbald, dappled, freaked

2 heterogeneous, *miscellaneous, assorted, promiscuous

*Ana* *different, diverse, divergent, disparate, various: discrepant, incompatible, uncongenial, incongruous (see INCONSONANT)

*Con* uniform, parallel, akin, alike, identical (see LIKE)

**motor** *machine, mechanism, machinery, apparatus, engine

**motorcade** *procession, parade, cortege, cavalcade

**mottle** *vb* *spot, spatter, sprinkle, fleck, stipple, marble, speckle, spangle, bespangle

**mottled** spotted, spattered, sprinkled, flecked, stippled, marbled, speckled, spangled, bespangled (see under SPOT *vb*)

**motto** proverb, adage, *saying, saw, maxim, epigram, aphorism, apothegm

**mount** *n* *mountain, peak, alp, volcano, mesa

**mount** *vb* 1 ascend, soar, *rise, arise, tower, rocket, levitate, surge

*Ant* drop

2 *ascend, climb, scale

*Ant* dismount

**mountain, mount, peak, alp, volcano, mesa** denote a relatively steep and high elevation of land. **Mountain**, the ordinary and inclusive term, varies somewhat in meaning according to locality. In general it designates an elevation higher and steeper than a hill, rising more or less abruptly from its surrounding country, and standing out conspicuously when viewed from a distance. **Mount** is often used in proper names of mountains. **Peak**, when applied to a mountain, designates one that rises to a sharp point; it may be isolated or one of a range. **Alp** suggests a towering, dizzy, or unscalable height ⟨yet do I sometimes feel a languishment . . . to sit upon an *alp* as on a throne, and half forget what world or worldling meant—*Keats*⟩ **Volcano** designates a cone-shaped mountain formed chiefly of ejected molten rock or ash and topped, usually, by a crater. **Mesa** is used especially in the southwestern part of the United States to designate a flat-topped elevation, usually comparable to a hill in height, but more suggestive of a mountain because of its steep clifflike sides.

*Ana* *height, altitude, elevation

**mountebank** *n* *impostor, faker, charlatan, quack

**mourn** sorrow, *grieve

*Ana* lament, bewail, bemoan (see DEPLORE): weep, keen, wail, *cry

*Con* rejoice, gladden, delight, *please

**movable, mobile, motive** mean capable of moving or of

being moved. **Movable** applies not to what has independent power of motion but to what can be moved by men or machines (as by lifting, drawing, pushing, or driving) ⟨a *movable* steam engine⟩ ⟨one's *movable* possessions⟩ ⟨some of these cabins were *movable*, and were carried on sledges from one part of the common to another —*Macaulay*⟩ or to what is not fixed in position or date ⟨printing from *movable* type⟩ ⟨a *movable* attachment for a machine⟩ ⟨*movable* feasts such as Easter and Whitsunday⟩ **Mobile** stresses facility or ease in moving or, less often, in being moved. It often describes the quality of flowing which distinguishes a fluid from a solid ⟨the *mobile* liquid passes into a compact rigid solid—*T. H. Huxley*⟩ or which characterizes an electric current or charge ⟨long-lasting circulation of the *mobile* charge, around and around the circuit—*Darrow*⟩ or the character which distinguishes something or someone that moves or is equipped or able to move quickly and readily, or to go (as from place to place or from one condition to another), from what is slow-moving or unlikely to engage in major moves ⟨a *mobile* army⟩ ⟨a *mobile* radio unit⟩ ⟨they attract the more ambitious, the more *mobile* young people—*Amer. Jour. of Sociology*⟩ ⟨American society, though highly *mobile* by European standards, is not classless—*Times Lit. Sup.*⟩ But equally often *mobile* describes features, faces, expressions of face, or thoughts which respond quickly and obviously to changing emotions, mental states, or external stimuli, often at the same time connoting either fickleness or instability or flexibility and versatility ⟨the gray restless eye, the thin *mobile* lips—*J. R. Green*⟩ ⟨you are as *mobile* as the veering air, and all your charms more changeful than the tide—*Millay*⟩ ⟨delicately sniffing the air to the left of him with his *mobile* nose end—*Dahl*⟩ **Motive** implies a moving only in the transitive sense of driving, or causing movement, or impelling to action; the term is used chiefly with reference to power or energy or their sources (as fuel, steam, or electricity) viewed as agent in a process of moving ⟨diesel engines supply the *motive* power for the new ship⟩ ⟨when horsepower and man power were alone employed, the *motive* agent was not bound up with the tool moved—*Spencer*⟩ Even when the reference is to something which constitutes a motive for action, "*motive* power," "*motive* force," or "*motive* energy" is likely to be used ⟨there was no *motive* power in experience. It was as little of an active cause as conscience itself—*Wilde*⟩ ⟨this new wave of *motive* energy began to penetrate the deep absorption in their own affairs of her husband and children—*Dorothy Canfield*⟩ ⟨his *motive* force is a blissful and naïve faith—*Rosten*⟩
**Ana** *changeable, changeful, variable, mutable
**Ant** immovable: stationary —**Con** fixed, set, settled, established (see SET *vb*)

**move** *vb* **1 Move, actuate, drive, impel** are comparable when they mean to set or keep going or in motion. **Move** is so general that the direction or nature of the motion can be gathered only from the context; it may imply an agent or an agency as the mover ⟨what power or force *moves* the rotating earth?⟩ ⟨the mechanism that *moves* the locomotive⟩ ⟨vessels *moved* by wind, steam, or electricity⟩ **Actuate** is more restricted in its reference than *move*, being used chiefly in connection with machinery and mechanisms; it stresses the communication of power to work or to set in action ⟨a turbine is *actuated* by the force of a current of fluid under pressure⟩ ⟨most of the hydraulically operated items of equipment are *actuated* by pistons and cylinders—*W. R. Sears*⟩ **Drive** implies forward and, usually, continuous rather than recurrent motion; it often emphasizes the effect produced,

as of speed, violence, or show of power, rather more than the impetus given ⟨a ship *driven* by wind and tide⟩ ⟨the washing machine is *driven* by electricity⟩ ⟨the heart *drives* the blood through the arteries⟩ ⟨air and petrol vapor . . . produce explosions powerful enough to *drive* the engine of a motorcar—*Toynbee*⟩ **Impel,** when used of physical motion, adds to *drive* the implication of great force in the impetus ⟨imitated the action of a man's being *impelled* forward by the butt ends of muskets—*Dickens*⟩

These words also are synonymous when they mean to excite or provoke a person to a given act or action or to given conduct or behavior. **Move** may imply an agent, an external influence, or an inner spring or motive as the mover ⟨if kingdom *move* thee not, let *move* thee zeal and duty—*Milton*⟩ ⟨he was, through the years, a hard man to *move*—*Malamud*⟩ **Actuate** presupposes such an inner stimulus as a desire, a feeling, or a motive ⟨it used to be the thing for parents to represent themselves as Olympians, immune from human passions and always *actuated* by pure reason—*Russell*⟩ ⟨would deny with indignation that they are *actuated* in their esteem for science by its material serviceability—*Dewey*⟩ **Drive** presupposes a compelling force, sometimes outer, sometimes inner, which affects the freedom of the will ⟨it was the crass materialism of America . . . that *drove* him to exasperation—*Parrington*⟩ ⟨what had I ever done to you that would *drive* you to such a step?—*Mary Austin*⟩ **Impel,** like *actuate*, implies an inner prompting, but it suggests greater urgency in the desire or motive and more headlong action ⟨a life of adventure . . . was that to which his nature irresistibly *impelled* him—*Arnold*⟩ ⟨she was a prey to shoddy, facile emotions . . . none of which had power to *impel* her to any action—*Rose Macaulay*⟩
**Ana** *activate, actuate, motivate: *provoke, excite, quicken, stimulate: *induce, persuade, prevail, get

**2 Move, remove, shift, transfer** are comparable when they mean to change or to cause to change from one place to another. All of these terms are general in that they do not in themselves and apart from the context imply a definite kind of agent or agency or a definite means of conveyance or transportation or give an indication of the extent of distance covered. **Move** is by far the most comprehensive term and is chiefly used when nothing more than the motion or activity involved in a change of place is to be indicated ⟨*move* a table from a corner to the center of the room⟩ ⟨*moved* his family from New York City to Chicago⟩ ⟨*move* a house across the street to a larger lot⟩ ⟨he will not *move* from that chair until he is called to dinner⟩ **Remove** adds to *move* the implication that the person or thing that changes or is changed from one place to another is moved from or quits a place which is his or its normal or original location, station, position, or occupation for one which is new or temporary ⟨*remove* the cover from a platter⟩ ⟨*remove* the dishes from the table⟩ When the idea of getting rid or eradicating is stressed, *remove* is appropriate ⟨*remove* a person from office⟩ ⟨they *removed* the cause of the epidemic of typhoid fever when they put the typhoid carrier under close surveillance⟩ **Shift** throws so much emphasis on change of location or direction that the implications of voluntary or guided motion or activity are seldom apparent; therefore the term is often preferred when unrest or uncertainty or instability is to be suggested ⟨the cargo *shifted* in the storm⟩ ⟨the wind will *shift* during the night to due east⟩ ⟨*shifting* his weight from one foot to another⟩ However, *shift* also is used when a mere change in position is implied ⟨*shifted* his quid of tobacco to the other side of his mouth before answering⟩ ⟨decided to *shift* his desk

A colon (:) separates groups of words discriminated. An asterisk (*) indicates place of treatment of each group.

into a better light⟩ **Transfer** (see also TRANSFER 2) commonly implies a change from hand to hand, or from one mode of conveyance to another, or from one depository to another; it is often used in a specific sense especially in the business of transportation ⟨you will need to *transfer* to another train at Albany⟩ ⟨there was no way in which he could *transfer* his own memories of European civilization into the Indian mind—*Cather*⟩
*Ana* displace, *replace, supplant, supersede: convey, *carry, bear, transport, transmit

**move** *n* movement, *motion, locomotion, stir
*Ana* change, alteration, variation, modification (see under CHANGE *vb*): transformation, metamorphosis, conversion, transmogrification (see under TRANSFORM)

**movement** *motion, move, locomotion, stir
*Ana* *action, act, deed: change, alteration, variation, modification (see under CHANGE *vb*): activity, operativeness *or* operation, dynamism, liveness (see corresponding adjectives at ACTIVE)

**moving, impressive, poignant, affecting, touching, pathetic** are comparable when they mean having the power to excite or the effect of exciting deep and usually saddening and solemn emotion. *Moving,* the most general of these words, can be used in place of any of the others; the rest, though not mutually exclusive in their implications, can be used very specifically. Something **moving** stirs one deeply or evokes a strong emotional response (as by thrilling, entrancing, agitating, or saddening) ⟨a *moving* scene in a play⟩ ⟨a *moving* appeal for help⟩ ⟨a modern version of the hero who for the good of mankind exposed himself to the agonies of the damned. It is always a *moving* subject—*Maugham*⟩ ⟨a *moving* revelation of child life in an orphanage—*MacColl*⟩ Something **impressive** imposes itself forcibly on the mind and compels a response (as of admiration, awe, wonder, or conviction) ⟨scenery . . . majestic without severity, *impressive* without showiness —*Hardy*⟩ ⟨ordinary men cannot produce really *impressive* artworks—*Shaw*⟩ ⟨I regret that I cannot put into more *impressive* words my belief that . . . the defendants were deprived of their rights—*Justice Holmes*⟩ Something **poignant** produces so painfully sharp an impression that it pierces one's heart or keenly affects one's sensitivities ⟨it was warm and yet fresh; blindfold, one could have mistaken it for a morning in early May: but this kind of day . . . had a more *poignant* loveliness in autumn than in spring, because it was a receding footfall, a waning moon —*Jan Struther*⟩ ⟨she left him with relief and a *poignant* sense of all she had wasted of the night—*Malamud*⟩ Something **affecting** moves one to tears or to some similar manifestation of feeling ⟨even the most callous found the play *affecting*⟩ ⟨an *affecting* reunion of a mother and her child⟩ ⟨it would spoil this *affecting* story to explain what happened; but the reader's sickening anxiety may be relieved to hear that Rosa escaped with her purity still white as driven snow—*Cunnington*⟩ ⟨the scenes of disappointment are quite *affecting*—*Whitman*⟩ Something **touching** arouses tenderness or compassion or melts the heart ⟨a clean sober little maid, with a very *touching* upward look of trust—*Galsworthy*⟩ ⟨*touching* not in the sense of pathos . . . but in the sense of sweetness, warmth, and gaiety—*Mannes*⟩ ⟨most men's *touching* illusion as to the frailness of women and their spiritual fragility—*Conrad*⟩ Something **pathetic** moves one to pity. Sometimes the word suggests pity induced by compassion for one in sorrow or distress ⟨a lonely old man . . . . Rather *pathetic!*—*Archibald Marshall*⟩ ⟨*pathetic* gropings after the fragments of a shattered faith—*Day Lewis*⟩ Sometimes it suggests pity mixed with contempt for what is weak, inadequate, or futile ⟨a *pathetic* confusion of aims—

*Binyon*⟩ ⟨a *pathetic* attempt to make a virtue of necessity —*Huxley*⟩
*Ana* exciting, stimulating, quickening, provoking (see PROVOKE): thrilling, electrifying (see THRILL): stirring, arousing, rousing, awakening, rallying (see STIR)

**muddle** *vb* *confuse, addle, fuddle, befuddle
*Ana* *puzzle, perplex, mystify, bewilder, distract, nonplus, confound, dumbfound: faze, rattle, discomfit, *embarrass: fluster, flurry, upset, agitate, *discompose
*Ant* enlighten

**muddle** *n* *confusion, disorder, chaos, disarray, jumble, clutter, snarl

**muddy** *turbid, roily
*Ana* murky, gloomy, obscure, *dark: confused, muddled, addle (see CONFUSE): *dirty, filthy, foul, nasty, squalid
*Con* *clear, transparent, translucent, lucid, limpid

**muff** *vb* *botch, bungle, fumble, cobble

**mug** *n* *face, countenance, visage, physiognomy, puss

**mulct** *penalize, fine, amerce
*Ana* exact, require, *demand, claim

**mulish** *obstinate, dogged, stubborn, pertinacious, stiff-necked, pigheaded, bullheaded
*Ana* headstrong, intractable, recalcitrant, refractory, ungovernable, *unruly: fixed, set (see SET)

**multifarious** divers, numerous, various, *many, several, sundry
*Ana* disparate, diverse, divergent, *different: incongruous, incompatible, uncongenial, discrepant, discordant, *inconsonant, inconsistent

**multiply** *increase, augment, enlarge
*Ana* propagate, reproduce, breed, *generate: expand, spread, stretch (see corresponding nouns at EXPANSE)
*Con* *decrease, diminish, lessen, reduce, abate

**multitude, army, host, legion** mean, both in the singular and plural, a very large number of persons or things. They do not (as do the words compared at CROWD) necessarily imply assemblage, but all of them can be used with that implication. **Multitude** stresses numerousness with respect to what is the standard for or the test of numerousness in the thing referred to; thus, in "that child always asks a *multitude* of questions" and "I never saw such a *multitude* of books before in one house" *multitude* obviously refers to a much smaller number in the first than in the second illustration ⟨we must not . . . expect systematic education to produce *multitudes* of highly cultivated and symmetrically developed persons—*Eliot*⟩ When applied to a group of persons taken as a whole, *multitude* suggests an assemblage of a large number of persons ⟨moved his arms with large pawing gestures, as though he were distributing lay blessings to a kneeling *multitude*—*Wharton*⟩ but *multitude* with a definite article suggests the masses of ordinary people or the populace ⟨speeches that sway the *multitude*⟩ ⟨a book that appeals to the *multitude*⟩ ⟨both scorns and seeks the understanding and approbation of the *multitude*—*Knight*⟩ **Army** usually adds to *multitude* the implications of orderly arrangement without a suggestion of crowding and often, especially in clearly figurative use, a progressive advance without any suggestion of halting or gathering ⟨they were served by a vast *army* of waiters⟩ ⟨an *army* of locusts⟩ ⟨we have considered science as a steadily advancing *army* of ascertained facts—*Inge*⟩ ⟨he discovered around him . . . a world whose existence he had neither known nor suspected, the *army* of persons who know no routine labor—*Purdy*⟩ **Host** has for its primary implication numerousness. It may mean nothing more ⟨she has a *host* of admirers⟩ ⟨he knows *hosts* of people⟩ ⟨the burning of *hosts* of unfortunate old women—and sometimes young ones—as witches—*Cobban*⟩ but it may suggest more

strongly than any of the other words a concentration in great numbers of the thing referred to; in such cases it often connotes an impressive or striking array ⟨a clear, cold night and a *host* of stars in the sky⟩ ⟨I saw a crowd, a *host*, of golden daffodils—*Wordsworth*⟩ ⟨a *host* of exquisite creations, the expression of a great artist's subtle vision and faultless technique—*Read*⟩ ⟨a very uneasy division, giving rise to a *host* of perplexities whose consideration has occupied the intervening centuries—*Whitehead*⟩ **Legion** in general use retains little suggestion of its basic application to the chief unit of the Roman army and but little more of its scriptural uses; typically it applies to an indefinitely or incalculably large number ⟨the windy arguments of this *legion* of aberrants—*McComas*⟩ ⟨the *legion* of animal owners is also rising fast—*Investor's Reader*⟩ ⟨a *legion* of friends hastened to his support—*W. B. Parker*⟩ ⟨armies of angels that soar, *legions* of demons that lurk—*Browning*⟩
*Ana* horde, throng, press, mob, crush, *crowd

**mummer** performer, mime, mimic, player, *actor, thespian, impersonator, trouper

**mummery** *gibberish, hocus-pocus, abracadabra

**mundane** worldly, *earthly, earthy, terrestrial, sublunary
*Ana* fleshly, sensual, *carnal, animal: secular, temporal, *profane
*Ant* eternal —*Con* *infinite, sempiternal, boundless: heavenly, *celestial, empyrean, empyreal

**munificent** bountiful, bounteous, openhanded, *liberal, generous, handsome
*Ana* benevolent, *charitable, philanthropic, eleemosynary, altruistic: *profuse, lavish, prodigal

**munitions** *armament, matériel, arms, ordnance, artillery, ammunition

**murder** *vb* *kill, slay, assassinate, dispatch, execute

**murky** obscure, gloomy, *dark, dim, dusky
*Ana* *turbid, muddy, roily: lowering, glowering, glooming *or* gloomy (see corresponding verbs at FROWN): lurid, grim, *ghastly
*Con* *bright, brilliant, radiant, effulgent: illuminated, illumined, lightened, enlightened (see ILLUMINATE): *clear, transparent, translucent, lucid

**muscular, brawny, sinewy, athletic, burly, husky** are applied to persons in the sense of strong and powerful in build or physique. **Muscular** implies well-developed, but not overdeveloped, muscles and, usually, a stalwart build ⟨hard exercise . . . built into a strong, *muscular* body what had been a frail and sickly frame—*White*⟩ **Brawny** implies the full development of the muscles; it carries no connotation of fatness but rather suggests the might that is associated with hard flesh and great size ⟨blond, healthy-looking fellows, with *brawny*, bare arms, who were approached with dread by all—*Zangwill*⟩ ⟨tough, weather-ruddied, *brawny* hunters of whales—*R. L. Cook*⟩ **Sinewy** attributes no less power to the muscles than *brawny,* but it suggests greater energy and quickness and seldom connotes hugeness. Rather it often implies a leanness, toughness, and litheness that are the result of training or of persistent exercise; thus, such people as blacksmiths, steelworkers, stevedores, and prizefighters are often described as *brawny,* but fencers, runners, and acrobats, more often as *sinewy* ⟨worthy fellows; and like to prove most *sinewy* swordmen—*Shak.*⟩ **Athletic** as used in anthropometry denotes a particular body build marked by heavy frame, large chest, and powerful well-developed muscles. In more general use *athletic* may suggest much the same type, but more often it stresses fitness for athletic activity and emphasizes muscularity, sinewiness, quick reflexes, and vigor of health ⟨a tall, *athletic* young man⟩ and it is with this latter aspect that the term is usually

extended to the mental life or its products ⟨imaginative skepticism and dramatic irony . . . keep the mind *athletic* and the spirit on the stretch—*Blackmur*⟩ ⟨she had tried . . . to shock and startle: and yet . . . had feared to begin with Shaw's *athletic* wit—*Yeats*⟩ **Burly** stresses massiveness of build to such an extent that it often carries connotations of corpulence, of coarseness, or of grossness and suggests the possession of brute force ⟨tall . . . *burly*, quite fearless, built with such a jaw that no man's rule could be his law—*Masefield*⟩ ⟨a great, *burly*, red-faced individual, huge in frame, with a stentorian voice—*Jesse*⟩ **Husky** implies a powerful athletic build and brawniness ⟨the *huskiest* members of a football team are placed on the line⟩ ⟨good food and leisure and heredity gave me a *husky* build—*S. E. White*⟩
*Ana* robust, *healthy, hale, sound: *strong, sturdy, stalwart, stout: *vigorous, lusty

**muse** *vb* *ponder, meditate, ruminate
*Ana* *consider, study, contemplate, weigh, excogitate: reflect, reason, *think

**museum, library, gallery, archives, treasury** are comparable but not synonymous terms when they mean a place serving as a repository for monuments (see DOCUMENT 1 for this sense) of the past. **Museum** is the most general of these terms; it usually implies the intention both to preserve and to exhibit for the education of the public. A *museum* may be an institution concerned with the preservation and exhibition of objects of historical or scientific interest, especially such as illustrate the development of human civilization or the evolution of species, or it may be one providing for the preservation and exhibition of works of fine art (as paintings and sculptures), or it may combine both purposes. Consequently, the term is usually qualified in proper names or in general designation ⟨the *Museum* of Fine Arts⟩ ⟨the *Museum* of Natural History⟩ ⟨an art *museum*⟩ **Library** is applicable to a place (as a room, building, or institution) which houses a collection of books not for sale but available for use by specified persons or sometimes the general public. But *library* is applicable also to a collection of literary material and as such may vary in scope from a handful of books making up a personal collection to a usually public collection consisting of a vast store of books of all kinds and of all ages, manuscripts, records, documents, files of journals, and often, in addition, works of art and serving primarily to preserve works of literature and of reference and documents in all fields of research and to make them available to scholars. **Gallery** (often *art gallery*) is used for a room, a suite, or a building housing and exhibiting works of art and especially paintings and pieces of sculpture. The term is used of a place housing a private as well as a public collection and (especially in the plural, *galleries*) of a place where works of art are exhibited for sale. **Archives**, when the term designates the place where a collection of old records, old documents, old files, and similar papers are kept rather than the collection itself (see DOCUMENT 1), may refer to a building or, as is more common, to a part of a building (as of a library or museum) where such a collection is housed ⟨the *archives* of the city hall⟩ ⟨the *archives* of the department of state⟩ ⟨place a manuscript in the *archives* of the Royal Society⟩ **Treasury** is used to designate a place, often a room, where possessions of intrinsic value and often historical significance are stored and in some instances displayed to visitors ⟨in the *treasury* of the cathedral . . . there is a fine, whole, uncut chasuble—*Rock*⟩ The term is often extended to things or places that are or are felt to be storehouses of precious things ⟨forests whose *treasury* of bird and beast and insect secrets had been only skimmed by collectors—*Beebe*⟩

---

A colon (:) separates groups of words discriminated. An asterisk (*) indicates place of treatment of each group.

⟨for quotable good things, for pregnant aphorisms, for touchstones of ready application, the opinions of the English judges are a mine of instruction and a *treasury* of joy—*Cardozo*⟩

**mushy** *sentimental, romantic, mawkish, maudlin, soppy, slushy

**muster** *summon, summons, call, cite, convoke, convene
*Ana* collect, congregate, assemble, *gather: marshal, organize, arrange, *order: align, *line, line up, range, array

**musty** fusty, *malodorous, stinking, fetid, noisome, putrid, rank, rancid
*Ana* dirty, filthy, foul, nasty, squalid: sloppy, *slipshod, unkempt, slovenly

**mutable** *changeable, changeful, variable, protean
*Ana* unstable, *inconstant, fickle: fluctuating, wavering, swinging, swaying (see SWING)
*Ant* immutable  —*Con* *steady, even, constant, uniform, equable: *lasting, permanent, durable, stable

**mutation** *change, permutation, vicissitude, alternation
*Ana* shifting *or* shift, moving *or* move, removing *or* remove (see MOVE): variation, modification, alteration (see under CHANGE *vb*)
*Con* stabilizing *or* stability, steadying *or* steadiness, poising *or* poise (see corresponding verbs at STABILIZE): fluctuation, wavering, swinging *or* swing (see corresponding verbs at SWING)

**mute** *adj* *dumb, speechless, inarticulate

**mutilate** 1 *maim, cripple, batter, mangle
*Ana* *injure, damage, hurt, spoil, mar: disfigure, *deface
2 *sterilize, castrate, spay, emasculate, alter, geld, caponize

**mutinous** rebellious, seditious, *insubordinate, factious, contumacious
*Ana* recalcitrant, refractory, intractable, *unruly, ungovernable: disaffected, alienated (see ESTRANGE)

**mutiny** *rebellion, revolution, uprising, revolt, insurrection, putsch, coup
*Ana* *sedition, treason: traitorousness, treacherousness, perfidiousness *or* perfidy, faithlessness (see corresponding adjectives at FAITHLESS)

**mutual** *reciprocal, common
*Ana* shared, participated, partaken (see SHARE): joined *or* joint, united, connected, related, associated (see corresponding verbs at JOIN)

**mysterious, inscrutable, arcane** mean beyond one's power to discover, understand, or explain. Something **mysterious** excites wonder, curiosity, or surmise yet baffles all attempts to explain it ⟨extremes in Nature equal ends produce, in Man they join to some *mysterious* use—*Pope*⟩ ⟨God moves in a *mysterious* way his wonders to perform —*Cowper*⟩ ⟨brought back a vivid report on remote and *mysterious* Tibet—*W. O. Douglas*⟩ Something **inscrutable** defies all one's efforts to examine or investigate it and leaves one with a sense of hopelessness or defeat ⟨great God, thy judgments are *inscrutable*!—*Browning*⟩ ⟨the plaything of an *inscrutable* power, called Fortune—*Bradley*⟩ The word is often applied to a person whose intentions, motives, or mental processes are so well concealed that they defy interpretation ⟨many fathers feel that, if they are to maintain their authority, they must be a little distant and *inscrutable*—*Benson*⟩ ⟨people who prefer to stand at the bar have, universally, an *inscrutable* look—*Pynchon*⟩ Something **arcane** is beyond comprehension because known or knowable only to the possessor of the secret (sometimes by implication God, Nature, the Fates, or the authorities). The word may come close to *occult* in meaning, but it stresses the reservation of what is necessary for comprehension rather than the supranatural or magical character of what is not understood ⟨by behaving as if he were a trickster, Shaw man-

aged to hide the *arcane* processes of his imaginative life —*Anthony West*⟩ ⟨not surprised to find his ways crossed and contested by his wife, who had her own *arcane* rites such as arranging flowers and cleaning closets—*Cheever*⟩
*Ana* occult, esoteric, *recondite, abstruse: cryptic, enigmatic, ambiguous, equivocal, *obscure: *mystical, mystic, anagogical, cabalistic

**mystery, problem, enigma, riddle, puzzle, conundrum** are comparable when they denote something which baffles or perplexes and challenges one's power to solve it. **Mystery** may, especially in theological use, imply the thing's incapacity for comprehension by the human reason, but it is also applicable to any of the facts of the world about us which defy all attempts to explain their cause or nature ⟨this *mystery* of growth and life—*Jefferies*⟩ ⟨we must be humble, for we are compassed by *mysteries*, and our spiritual faculties are poor and dull—*Inge*⟩ The term is also used to denote something which is guarded by secrecy or is in itself or by design mystifying while at the same time so intriguing as to compel speculation ⟨he always makes a *mystery* of his intentions⟩ ⟨it's a *mystery* to me how he can keep going⟩ ⟨Freud was a genius, an incredible mighty discoverer of secrets, *mysteries,* and new questions. But the answers he gave were doctrinaire, deathlike—*Mailer*⟩ ⟨lovers of *mystery* who like to think of some Wild Man of the Snows treading the heights, eating yaks and men, need not despair. Other monsters have successfully withstood the attempts of scientists to label them—*Country Life*⟩ **Problem** applies not only to a perplexing question that demands a solution ⟨a geometrical *problem*⟩ but also to a person or situation that causes perplexity or puts one in a predicament ⟨that child is a *problem* to his parents and teachers⟩ ⟨the *problem* . . . how to find healthy, happy leisure for all the working millions who are now being liberated by machines—*L. P. Smith*⟩ ⟨if a great hate and a great determination could solve the *problem*, Kelley would solve it—*Theodore Sturgeon*⟩ **Enigma** applies to whatever hides its meaning under obscure or ambiguous allusions so that one can only guess at its significance ⟨a metaphor should not be farfetched, for then it becomes an *enigma*⟩ ⟨the ancient oracles usually spoke in *enigmas*⟩ The term can be extended to whatever is inscrutable or beyond the range of unaided understanding ⟨Leonardo . . . worked so slowly, he left so much unfinished, he seemed to them so volatile and unstable. He was an *enigma* to which they never secured the key—*Ellis*⟩ ⟨the *enigmas* of history, of man's freedom and responsibility and of his guilt, cannot be solved as easily as modern culture assumed—*Niebuhr*⟩ **Riddle** applies to an *enigma* involving paradoxical or contradictory statements and definitely proposed to be guessed ⟨made up *riddles* for the amusement of her guests⟩ ⟨"What did one wall say to the other wall?" he asked shrilly. "It's a *riddle*!"—*Salinger*⟩ The term can be extended to any problem which is difficult because of its inner contradictions ⟨he tried to read the *riddle* of this girl's future—*Galsworthy*⟩ ⟨the *riddle* of Actium is not in the details of the fighting but in the minds of the combatants—*Buchan*⟩ **Puzzle** applies to a problem or enigma which tests one's ingenuity or skill in solution or which is peculiarly baffling ⟨hoary old *puzzles* of Ethics and Philosophy—*L. P. Smith*⟩ ⟨there are few things in the world so difficult to explain as real change; it appears to me that most scientists are far from realizing the complexity of this metaphysical *puzzle*—*Inge*⟩ **Conundrum** specifically applies to a riddle phrased as a question the answer to which involves a paradox or a pun or an equivocal use of words ⟨they roused him with jam and judicious advice: they set him *conundrums* to guess—*Lewis Car-*

---

*Ana* analogous words      *Ant* antonyms      *Con* contrasted words      See also explanatory notes facing page 1

_roll_⟩ The term can be extended to unsolved or unsolvable problems which provoke speculation rather than serious attempts at solution ⟨do you think life is long enough to let me speculate on _conundrums_ like that?—_Black_⟩ ⟨fail to touch on the political _conundrums_ involved, particularly the problem of how the richer areas of the South can be made to subsidize the poorer—_Cater_⟩

**mystic** _adj_ *mystical, anagogic, cabalistic
**Ana** occult, esoteric, *recondite, abstruse: *mysterious, inscrutable: visionary, quixotic, *imaginary

**mystic** _n_ *ascetic

**mystical, mystic, anagogic, cabalistic** are comparable when they denote having a meaning or character hidden from all except those who enjoy profound spiritual insight or are spiritually initiated. _Mystical_ and _mystic,_ though often interchangeable, can be distinguished in use. In general, **mystical** suggests comprehension of something beyond the range of the perceptive or ratiocinative powers; its use therefore often implies belief in the possibility of such comprehension and the word variously connotes penetration into sacred mysteries, holiness of life, idealism, detachment from material concerns, ecstatic contemplation, or spiritual rapture ⟨the _mystical_ philosophy of Plotinus⟩ ⟨_mystical_ religions such as Buddhism⟩ ⟨the _mystical_ poetry of William Blake⟩ ⟨there is something _mystical_ in this doctrine, this faith, as of Keats, that "what the Imagination seizes as Beauty must be Truth" —_L. P. Smith_⟩ **Mystic** is appropriately used when one wishes to avoid these special implications of _mystical_ or to suggest others more in keeping with a rationalistic or skeptical point of view. Therefore _mystic_ often imputes to the thing it describes: (1) an occult, esoteric, or visionary character ⟨_mystic_ ceremonies⟩ ⟨the _mystic_ symbolism of Blake's poetry⟩ (2) a mysterious, enigmatic, or sometimes nebulous quality ⟨words of _mystic_ import—_Shelley_⟩ ⟨[Guérin's] expression has . . ., more than Keats's, something _mystic,_ inward, and profound—_Arnold_⟩ (3) a connection with magic or the arts of magic ⟨_mystic_ numbers⟩ ⟨each silver vase in _mystic_ order laid—_Pope_⟩ Often its basic denotation is completely obscured and it means merely unintelligible, unfathomable, or incomprehensible ⟨the _mystic_ gulf from God to man—_Emerson_⟩ **Anagogic** refers basically to an ultimate underlying meaning, especially in the Bible, perceptible only to those of profound spiritual insight ⟨when Dante . . . describes his poetry as _polysemous,_ with literal, allegorical, moral, and _anagogic_ meaning levels, he at the same time insists that the literal meaning comes first in comprehension—_Burnham_⟩ ⟨looming in the distance, there was the final or _anagogic_ meaning that transformed the symbolic object into a spiritual truth—_Malcolm Cowley_⟩ **Cabalistic** in its primary meaning applies to a secret interpretation of Scriptures (_Cabala_) held to have been revealed to Moses and handed down orally through a line of chosen Jewish rabbis. The system came to be used by medieval magicians and sorcerers. Both aspects color the extended use of _cabalistic_ so that it sometimes comes close to _mystic_ in its connotations ⟨the power of the theurgic rite or _cabalistic_ word, understood only by the gods—_H. O. Taylor_⟩ ⟨self-conscious artists, working for the admiration of small followings and often requiring _cabalistic_ analysis before they could be fully understood—_Time_⟩ but commonly it is closer to _occult_ or _magic_ ⟨by describing with the

hands certain _cabalistic_ patterns on the air and uttering at the same time the proper Sanskrit formulas it was believed that goblins and demons . . . could be exorcised —_Noss_⟩
**Ana** profound, *deep, abysmal: *ultimate, absolute, categorical: spiritual, divine, sacred, *holy: *supernatural, supranatural, miraculous

**mysticism** asceticism (see under ASCETIC _n_)

**mystify** bewilder, perplex, *puzzle, distract, nonplus, confound, dumbfound
**Ana** discomfit, faze, rattle, *embarrass: *discompose, disquiet, perturb, disturb, agitate, upset
**Ant** enlighten

**myth** 1 **Myth, legend, saga** all mean a story which has come down from the past, which ostensibly relates a historical event or events, and of which the origin has been lost or forgotten. **Myth** varies considerably in its denotation and connotation depending on the persuasion of the user. Often the word is used to designate a usually fanciful and imaginative story that explains a natural phenomenon or a social practice, institution, or belief ⟨the old _myth,_ imported hazily from the East, which represented the cat-moon devouring the gray mice of twilight—_Repplier_⟩ It is also used to designate a story, belief, or notion commonly held to be true but utterly without factual basis ⟨the doubts that women have about themselves are manmade, and most women are so enslaved to the _myths_ of their own inferiority they are unable to see the truth for the _myths_—_Ashley Montagu_⟩ The word may be used with wide comprehensiveness in general writing or with narrow exclusiveness and specificity in more limited use ⟨_myths_ may be subdivided into such classifications as origin _myths,_ ritual _myths,_ incidents involving the lives of the gods, stories of culture heroes, trickster tales, journeys to the other world, human and animal marriages, adaptations of old world _myths,_ and retellings of biblical stories— _L. J. Davidson_⟩ ⟨_myths_ are said to be expressions or objectifications of "collective wishes" which are personified in the "leader" who is endowed by a given society with powers of social magic to fulfill the collective wish —_Kroeber_⟩ **Legend** is likewise used with latitude, but in its most typical use it is likely to apply to a story, incident, or notion attached to a particular person or place that purports to be historical and often has or seems to have a basis in historical reality although as a whole it is either incredible or unverifiable ⟨the medieval _legends_ of the saints⟩ ⟨the wrecking of the Palatine which, according to _legend,_ did not sink but rose flaming into the sky —_Zimmer_⟩ ⟨the violent deaths of several slaves quartered in them gave rise to a _legend_ that this part of the house is haunted—_Amer. Guide Series: Md._⟩ **Saga** may refer to a long, continued, heroic story that is action-packed but not especially romantic, that deals with a person or group, and that is historical or legendary or both ⟨the _Saga_ of Burnt Njal⟩ ⟨the building of the railroad in the Northwest was one of the great _sagas_ of man's enterprise— _Le Sueur_⟩
**Ana** *fiction, fable, fabrication, figment: invention, creation (see corresponding verbs at INVENT)
**2** *allegory, parable, fable

**mythical** *fictitious, fabulous, legendary, apocryphal
**Ana** *imaginary, visionary, fanciful, fantastic: invented, created (see INVENT)

A colon (:) separates groups of words discriminated. An asterisk (*) indicates place of treatment of each group.

# N

**naïve** unsophisticated, artless, ingenuous, *natural, simple
*Ana* *sincere, unfeigned: *spontaneous, impulsive, instinctive: fresh, original (see NEW)
**naked** *bare, nude, bald, barren
*Ana* revealed, disclosed, discovered (see REVEAL): *evident, manifest, palpable, obvious: uncolored, *colorless: *pure, simple, sheer
**name** *n* Name, designation, denomination, appellation, title, style mean the word or combination of words by which something is called and by means of which it can be distinguished or identified. **Name** is so general that it can be used of any such word or combination whether it distinguishes a person or an object, an individual or a class, a particular or a universal, a thing having distinct existence in fact or a thing having distinct existence only in thought ⟨all nouns are *names*⟩ ⟨love is the *name* of an emotion⟩ ⟨the child's *name* is John Joseph Brown⟩ Sometimes *name* is thought of as something apart from the real character of the thing to which it is attached ⟨what's in a *name*? that which we call a rose by any other *name* would smell as sweet—*Shak.*⟩ ⟨for sixty years he had been a *name*, not a figure—*Bennett*⟩ More often, however, the term connotes identification of the word with the thing or, especially, the person it names, so that what affects one affects the other ⟨[Oxford] home of lost causes, and forsaken beliefs, and unpopular *names*, and impossible loyalties!—*Arnold*⟩ ⟨if I discovered the worst, and it had to be exposed, I must see that Jane's *name* was kept entirely out of it—*Rose Macaulay*⟩ This common feeling of a mutual and almost inevitable relation between the name and the thing named is what distinguishes *name* from *designation, denomination, appellation,* all of which are thought of as given and therefore as having an artificial association with the thing and a utilitarian purpose such as description or identification. A **designation** is a name given primarily for the sake of distinguishing one thing, whether an individual or a class, from other things of the same general description ⟨the French revolutionists changed the traditional *designations* of days and months⟩ ⟨recognizing that this parasite was new, [he] . . . gave it the *designation Aphytis A*—*Jour. of Economic Entomology*⟩ ⟨Madame Curie chose *polonium* as the *designation* of the newly discovered radio element in honor of her native Poland⟩ **Denomination** (see also RELIGION) is the name given especially to a class, to a category, or to a closely knit group (as of persons); the idea of a class name is so deeply rooted in the word that in extended use it often means the kind or group distinguished by a particular name ⟨most of George Eliot's works come under the *denomination* of novel⟩ ⟨a roll of bills containing notes of every *denomination*⟩ ⟨in the classic world of antiquity they called outsiders, indiscriminately, *barbarians*—a *denomination* which took on an increasingly depreciative sense—*Ellis*⟩ **Appellation** is the name by which a thing or person is known or called; the term implies actual use and differs from *designation* and *denomination* in precluding the idea, but not necessarily the fact, of self-choice ⟨James Tubbington Brown, a boy better known to his fellows by the *appellation* Stinky⟩ ⟨the government of the United States has been emphatically termed a government of laws, and not of men. It will certainly cease to deserve this high *appellation*, if the laws furnish no remedy for the violation of a vested right—*John Marshall*⟩ A **title** is either a dis-

tinctive name given to a work (as a book, a picture, a play, or a musical composition) or an honorary appellation coming to a person by virtue of his rank, office, dignity, or descent or given to him as a mark of respect ⟨the head of the state must have a *title*—*Buchan*⟩ When used without reference to a particular work of art or person *title* is sometimes preferred to *denomination* because it connotes distinction and dignity ⟨any admixture of logical, of "prose" meaning detracts from the value of a poem, if it does not disqualify it for the *title* of poetry altogether—*Day Lewis*⟩ When used abstractly in preference to *name* or *designation* it often connotes the lack of an essential relation between the name and the thing it names ⟨things change their *titles*, as our manners turn—*Pope*⟩ **Style** is used to emphasize the exact form of a name and is applicable chiefly to such legal and formal titles as the legal name of a firm or corporation or the complete, formal designation of a royal or other exalted personage as used in documents or in ceremonial address ⟨a business incorporated under the *style* of the Globe Manufacturing Co.⟩ ⟨Thrones and Imperial Powers, offspring of Heaven, ethereal virtues! or these titles now must we renounce, and, changing *style*, be called Princes of Hell?—*Milton*⟩
**name** *vb* 1 *designate, nominate, elect, appoint
*Ana* *choose, select, prefer, elect, opt: *declare, announce, publish, advertise
2 *mention, instance, specify
*Ana* *refer, allude, advert: *designate: identify, recognize (see corresponding nouns at RECOGNITION): cite, *quote
**nap** *vb* catnap, doze, drowse, snooze, *sleep, slumber
**narcotic** *anodyne, opiate, nepenthe
**narrate** *relate, rehearse, recite, recount, describe, state, report
*Ana* tell, *reveal, disclose, discover: *discourse, expatiate, dilate, descant
**narrative** *story, tale, anecdote, yarn
*Ana* chronicle, *account, report, story, version: *fiction, fabrication, figment, fable
**narrow, narrow-minded** *illiberal, intolerant, bigoted, hidebound
*Ana* rigorous, *rigid, strict, stringent: obdurate, *inflexible, inexorable: provincial, parochial, local, small-town, *insular
*Ant* broad, broad-minded —*Con* *liberal, progressive, advanced, radical: tolerant, *forbearing, indulgent, lenient
**narrows** *strait, sound, channel, passage
**nasty** *dirty, filthy, squalid, foul
*Ana* *coarse, gross, vulgar, obscene, ribald: tainted, contaminated, polluted, defiled (see CONTAMINATE): indelicate, indecent, unseemly, improper, *indecorous
**nation** *race, people
**national** *n* *citizen, subject
**native** *adj* Native, indigenous, endemic, aboriginal, autochthonous all mean belonging to or associated with a particular place by birth or origin. A person or thing is **native** (opposed to *foreign, alien*) that has had his or its birth or origin in the place in question ⟨a *native* American⟩ ⟨a *native* New Yorker⟩ ⟨*native* tradition⟩ ⟨*native* artists left the state and studied . . . abroad—*Amer. Guide Series: Mich.*⟩ ⟨a one-story structure of *native* stone—*S. S. King*⟩ A person or thing is **indigenous** (opposed to *naturalized, exotic*) that is not only native but also has not been introduced from elsewhere into the place indicated ⟨maize is *indigenous* to America⟩ ⟨Southern Rhodesia at present

employs about half a million Africans, of whom half are *indigenous* and half are migrants from neighboring territories—*Peter Scott*⟩ ⟨no written flora anywhere in the world admits as *indigenous* that lusty weed . . . called Good-King-Henry—*Peattie*⟩ *Indigenous* is applied usually to kinds (as species or races) rather than to individuals and often implies reference to a larger area than *native* (as to a country, or to a region characterized by a particular type of climate). A thing is **endemic** (opposed to *exotic* and in medicine to *pandemic*) which not only is indigenous but is also peculiar to, or in the case of a disease, prevalent in, a restricted region because of special conditions favoring its growth or existence ⟨edelweiss is *endemic* in the Alps⟩ ⟨that complacency which is an *endemic* disease of academic groups—*Conant*⟩ A person or thing is **aboriginal** that belongs to the earliest known race inhabiting a country or to the people found there (as by explorers, colonists, and invaders); the term usually implies the lack of a known predecessor and often connotes a primitive culture ⟨Indians are the *aboriginal* Americans⟩ ⟨America must turn again to catch the spirit of her own dark, *aboriginal* continent—*D. H. Lawrence*⟩ ⟨the Kooboos, a primitive *aboriginal* race in the southeast of Sumatra—*Frazer*⟩ *Aboriginal* is more rarely applied to the earliest ascertainable native plants and animals. Something is **autochthonous** which has its origin in the place in which it is found ⟨*autochthonous* rocks⟩ ⟨an *autochthonous* flora⟩ When applied to races of men or their achievements, it implies purity of stock or freedom from all external influences ⟨as long as the States continue to . . . be dominated by the poetry of the Old World, and remain unsupplied with *autochthonous* song . . . so long will they stop short of first-class nationality —*Whitman*⟩

*Ant* alien, foreign

**natural** *adj* **1** *regular, normal, typical

*Ana* ordinary, *common, familiar: *usual, customary, habitual, accustomed, wonted

*Ant* unnatural: artificial: adventitious

**2 Natural, simple, ingenuous, naïve, unsophisticated, artless, unaffected** are applied to persons, their acts, and their utterances, in the sense of wholly free from pretension or calculation. **Natural** implies, on the one hand, freedom from every sign of artificiality, effort, constraint, or affectation and, on the other hand, an ease, a spontaneousness, or a flexibility that suggests nature rather than art; the term often implies opposition to whatever is labored, stiff, formal, or artificial ⟨set him to write poetry, he is limited, artificial, and impotent; set him to write prose, he is free, *natural*, and effective—*Arnold*⟩ ⟨it is of the essence of such talk that it should be *natural* and attractive, not professional or didactic—*Benson*⟩ ⟨she was so friendly and so *natural* that it was nice to talk to her about what was interesting him—*Archibald Marshall*⟩ ⟨the fact is that a poetic language which appears *natural* to one age will appear unnatural or artificial to another—*Day Lewis*⟩ **Simple** stresses complete freedom from everything that might suggest unconscious or conscious duplicity. It usually implies lack of confusion of aims, desires, interests, or values and therefore may carry one or the other of connotations as divergent as mental immaturity and intellectual ripeness, as the lack of experience characteristic of the child and the fullness of wisdom characteristic of the sage, or as the transparency of those who do not know how to conceal their nature or motives and that of those who have nothing to conceal ⟨nothing is more *simple* than greatness; indeed, to be *simple* is to be great—*Emerson*⟩ ⟨a man of mild and *simple* character who up to then had shown no interest in any-

thing at all except his collection of modern paintings —*Dahl*⟩ ⟨she was so *simple* and trustful that I always thought it would be as wicked to hurt her as to hurt a babe in swaddling clothes—*Webb*⟩ **Ingenuous** stresses inability to disguise or to conceal one's thoughts or feelings; it usually implies frankness or candor, lack of reserve, or freedom from dissimulation, often with a hint of childlike simplicity ⟨Father had set a dog on him. A less *ingenuous* character would be silent about such passages . . . but that is not his quality—*H. G. Wells*⟩ ⟨to post-Freudian ears this kind of language seems touchingly quaint and *ingenuous*—*Huxley*⟩ **Naïve** implies freedom from all that is artificial, conventional, or acquired; in early use and still often, especially in its derivative noun *naïveté*, it suggests freshness, spontaneity, and genuine expression of a nature untouched by worldly influences and without affectation or artifices ⟨by contrast with the poetry of Vergil, that of Homer seems strikingly *naïve*⟩ ⟨a delightfully *naïve* personality⟩ ⟨he claimed to himself to be innocent or *naïve*, but his pretense was the thinnest—*Cheever*⟩ But it may sometimes become a term of derogation and then often implies lack of worldly wisdom ⟨Sophia, the *naïve* ninny, had actually supposed that her walking along a hundred yards of pavement with a god by her side was not going to excite remark!— *Bennett*⟩ ⟨one does not ask favors, if it can be avoided, of persons one genuinely respects; one puts such burdens upon the *naïve* and colorless, upon what are called the good-natured—*Mencken*⟩ Equally often, especially in learned use, it suggests the point of view of the untutored or unenlightened person or of one whose judgments are not corrected by advanced scientific or philosophical knowledge and who therefore supposes that things are what they seem to be ⟨the *naïve* science of an earlier day merely took it for granted that space and time existed in their own right—*Jeans*⟩ ⟨that *naïve* patriotism which leads every race to regard itself as evidently superior to every other—*Krutch*⟩ **Unsophisticated** also stresses lack of wisdom, especially worldly wisdom. It does not, however, emphasize native simplicity as strongly as *naïve;* rather, it suggests lack of the experience or training necessary for worldly success or, more specifically, for graceful and adroit social relations ⟨she's not the type of the moment, not elegant or artificial, too much the *unsophisticated* child of nature—*Rose Macaulay*⟩ ⟨Italian civilization had, in short, everything to dazzle the imagination of *unsophisticated* northerners emerging into a period of prosperity—*T. S. Eliot*⟩ **Artless** lays the stress on the absence of design; it suggests naturalness that is the result of indifference to, or unawareness of, the effect or impression one is producing ⟨overflowing with . . . *artless* maternal gratitude—*Austen*⟩ ⟨almost every turn in the *artless* little maid's prattle touched a new mood in him —*Meredith*⟩ ⟨he hated to seem heavy or profound or anything but *artless* and spontaneous to Cecily—*H. G. Wells*⟩ **Unaffected** centers the attention on the absence of affectation, but it usually implies both naturalness and simplicity without any hint of childishness, unworldliness, guilelessness, or indifference ⟨a well-bred, *unaffected* girl⟩ ⟨he was extremely simple and *unaffected* in his attitude, and readily approachable—*MacCallum*⟩ ⟨gratified by his young guest's *unaffected* admiration for this treasure—*Wylie*⟩

*Ana* *spontaneous, impulsive, instinctive: ingrained, constitutional, *inherent

*Con* formal, conventional, ceremonious, *ceremonial: pretentious, ostentatious, *showy: affected, assumed, counterfeited, feigned (see ASSUME)

**natural** *n* *fool, idiot, imbecile, moron, simpleton

A colon (:) separates groups of words discriminated. An asterisk (*) indicates place of treatment of each group.

**nature** *type, kind, sort, stripe, kidney, ilk, description, character
*Ana* *structure, anatomy, framework: *disposition, temperament, character, personality: *form, figure, shape, conformation
**naughty** *bad, evil, ill, wicked
*Ana* mischievous, roguish, impish, waggish (see PLAYFUL): froward, balky, restive, wayward, *contrary, perverse
**nauseate** *vb* *disgust, sicken
*Ana* vomit, disgorge, *belch: *offend, outrage
**nautical** *marine, maritime, naval
**naval** nautical, *marine, maritime
**near** *adj & adv* *close, nigh, nearby
*Ant* far
**near** *vb* *approach, approximate
*Ana* rival, *match, touch, equal
*Con* vary, *change, alter, modify: *differ
**nearby** *adj & adv* *close, near, nigh
*Ant* far off
**nearest, next** are both superlative forms of *near*, but they are not always interchangeable. **Nearest** may be used wherever the intent is merely to indicate the highest degree of propinquity (as in space, time, or kinship) ⟨the *nearest* house is five miles distant⟩ ⟨their *nearest* neighbor lives two miles away⟩ ⟨her *nearest* relatives are her father and mother⟩ **Next** has lost this sense and usually implies immediate succession, or sometimes precedence, in an order, a series, or a sequence; thus, the *next* house is the house just beyond the one in mind in a row or series of houses; their *next* child is the one who comes after the child under consideration in order of birth; the *next* best is the second best in a rating or choice ⟨the *next* chapter of the story⟩ ⟨the *next* day⟩ ⟨the *next* time they met⟩ ⟨ask the *next* person we meet⟩ But in law one's *nearest* relative is one's "*next* of kin"; one's "*next* friend" is a person (as a near relative or natural guardian) who has the right or is appointed by a court to act for a person (as an infant) who by the law of the state has not full legal capacity to sue or make other legal moves. In ordinary language "*nearest* of kin" is found as often as "*next* of kin," but "*nearest* friend" applies distinctively to one's most intimate friend.

**nearly, almost, approximately, well-nigh** are comparable when they mean within a little of being, becoming, reaching, or sufficing. Their differences in meaning are often imperceptible. However, **nearly** is suitable when mere proximity is implied ⟨they are *nearly* at the end of their journey⟩ ⟨it is *nearly* six o'clock⟩ ⟨she was *nearly* hysterical with fright⟩ **Almost** is more explicit when the emphasis is on a falling short or a deficiency ⟨they had *almost* finished when they were interrupted⟩ ⟨she is *almost* out of her mind with grief⟩ ⟨the news is *almost* too good to be true⟩ **Approximately** is an appropriate choice when the difference is of no practical importance and a reasonable approach to accuracy is implied ⟨there were *approximately* 10,000 present⟩ ⟨government meteorologists make *approximately* correct forecasts⟩ **Wellnigh** often equals *virtually* ⟨he is *well-nigh* mad⟩ ⟨the difficulty of selecting the best of his short essays for a strictly limited space is *well-nigh* insuperable—*Desmond MacCarthy*⟩

**neat, tidy, trim, trig, snug, shipshape, spick-and-span** mean manifesting care and orderliness. **Neat** through all its variations in sense keeps as its basic implication clearness, such as the clearness from dirt or soil that is manifest chiefly in perfect cleanliness ⟨her house is as *neat* as a pin⟩ ⟨the cat is the *neatest* of domestic animals⟩ ⟨he was remarkably *neat* in his dress—*Johnson*⟩ ⟨it was

a *neat* place, with its piles of magazines and newspapers stacked in orderly fashion—*MacInnes*⟩ or the clearness that is indicated in simplicity and freedom from what clutters, complicates, or confuses or that indicates orderliness, deftness, or adroitness ⟨*neat* workmanship⟩ ⟨a *neat* style⟩ ⟨*neat* minds, who prefer things in their proper places, ticketed and pigeonholed—*Dixon*⟩ ⟨a *neat* retort⟩ **Tidy** commonly suggests a pleasing neatness and order diligently maintained ⟨he's always *tidy* without being smart; his coat is old and his trousers are uncreased, but they're both clean, and nothing's loose or torn—*Richard Harrison*⟩ As distinguished from *neat*, *tidy* throws the stress on orderliness, careful arrangement, or a place for everything, rather than on cleanliness or simplicity ⟨a *tidy* desk⟩ ⟨a *tidy* sewing basket⟩ ⟨once upon a time the universe was all *tidy*, with everything in its proper place, and . . . ever since then it has been growing more and more disorderly—*Russell*⟩ ⟨they have an unfailing instinct for doing things in a *tidy* way—their busy airports handle passengers with remarkable smoothness—*Rolo*⟩ **Trim** implies both neatness and tidiness; it stresses, however, such smartness or spruceness in appearance as is given by clean lines and excellent proportions ⟨a *trim* clipper ship⟩ ⟨a *trim* figure⟩ ⟨his shoes and buckles, too, though plain, were *trim*—*Dickens*⟩ ⟨a crisscross of *trim* . . . paths—*Lowes*⟩ **Trig**, though close to *trim*, tends to carry a stronger implication of compactness, of neatness, and of jauntiness of appearance and is especially applicable to persons or their clothes ⟨she has a *trig* new tailored suit⟩ ⟨his hair was hardly even gray, and he stood as straight and *trig* as a fence post—*Hersey*⟩ ⟨a wonderfully *trig* beret, wide and flat—*New Yorker*⟩ **Snug** (see also COMFORTABLE) in the present relation applies basically to ships and suggests a fine trimness of line and construction ⟨a *snug* little ship⟩ or adequate and orderly preparation for a voyage and especially for riding out a storm ⟨soon all was *snug* aloft, and we were allowed to go below—*Dana*⟩ In other applications the term may imply a neat, compact, ordered state that affords security or sheltered ease ⟨everything on this *snug* property was bright, thriving, and well kept—*Hardy*⟩ ⟨*snug* little shops that once offered Cornhill the best soups and jellies—*West*⟩ **Shipshape** is often used in place of *snug* to describe not only ships where tidiness and trimness prevail but whatever depends for its success or well-being upon habits of tidiness and orderliness ⟨his affairs are in *shipshape* condition⟩ ⟨look to the babes, and till I come again keep everything *shipshape*—*Tennyson*⟩ ⟨everything from rifles to shoelaces got a complete going over. It was my job to see that all was perfect. Finally, I felt confident everything was *shipshape*—*H. V. Kaltenborn*⟩ **Spickand-span**, which stresses the brightness and freshness of something new, is applicable also to what by care and cleanliness has been kept new in appearance or made to look like new ⟨*spick-and-span* white shoes⟩ ⟨the kitchen was *spick-and-span*⟩ ⟨*spick-and-span* machinery⟩ ⟨no spots came on his clothes. No slovenly habits crept upon him. He was always *spick-and-span*—*White*⟩
*Ana* *clean, cleanly: fastidious, *nice, dainty, finicky: exact, precise, *correct, accurate
*Ant* filthy —*Con* unkempt, disheveled, slovenly, *slipshod, sloppy: slack, lax, remiss, *negligent: confused, muddled, addled (see CONFUSE)
**neb** *bill, beak, nib
**necessary 1** *needful, requisite, indispensable, essential
*Ana* compelling *or* compulsory, obliging *or* obligatory, constraining (see corresponding verbs at FORCE): important, significant, momentous (see corresponding nouns at IMPORTANCE): cardinal, vital, *essential, fundamental

2 *certain, inevitable
*Ana* unavoidable, unescapable, inescapable, ineluctable, *inevitable: *infallible, inerrable, inerrant, unerring
**necessitous** *poor, indigent, needy, destitute, penniless, impecunious, poverty-stricken
*Ana* impoverished, drained, depleted, exhausted, bankrupt (see DEPLETE)
*Con* *rich, wealthy, affluent, opulent
**necessity** *need, exigency
*Ana* compelling *or* compulsion, constraining *or* constraint, obliging *or* obligation, coercing *or* coercion (see corresponding verbs at FORCE): indispensableness, requisiteness *or* requisition, needfulness (see corresponding adjectives at NEEDFUL)
**need** *n* Need, necessity, exigency may all denote either a state or condition requiring something as essential or indispensable or the thing required. **Need** implies pressure and urgency arising either from external or internal causes or forces; it may merely suggest the call of an appetite or demand for emotional or intellectual satisfaction ⟨he is in *need* of food⟩ ⟨children have a *need* for affection⟩ ⟨he felt the *need* of an education⟩ or it may imply circumstances (as a breakdown or interruption of activity, poverty, a storm, or a threat of war) that expose a lack of or create a demand for something indispensable (as to the well-being, protection, security, success, or functioning of those or the one concerned) ⟨the *need* of a city for an adequate water supply⟩ ⟨provide food and lodging for those in *need*⟩ ⟨the European war has taught Americans the *need* for a two-ocean navy⟩ ⟨order and discipline were the crying *needs—Malone*⟩ **Necessity**, though often interchanged with *need*, usually carries a stronger suggestion of an imperative demand or of a compelling cause ⟨telephone me only in case of *necessity*⟩ ⟨as soon as war is declared, every nation or institution must subordinate all other considerations to the *necessity* of victory—*Inge*⟩ ⟨*necessity* rather than charity was responsible for Republican commitments to the United Nations—*Feuer*⟩ ⟨amid these malign forces, our haunting anxiety and our paramount *necessity* is the defense of our country—*Hoover*⟩ **Necessity** may also apply to a compelling principle or abstract force inherent in nature or in the constitution of a thing and inevitable in its operation or inescapable in its results ⟨there is no logical *necessity* apparent in the conclusions you have reached⟩ ⟨such families get the *necessities* of life regardless of prices. To them differences in price levels mean only a difference in luxuries—*T. W. Arnold*⟩ ⟨one of the unhappy *necessities* of human existence is that we have to "find things out for ourselves"—*T. S. Eliot*⟩ **Exigency** (see also JUNCTURE) implies the compulsion of necessity or occasionally of an inherent compelling principle, especially as a result of such special circumstances as a crisis, an emergency, or an accident, that imposes severe restrictions or great stress and strain; in either case, the term emphasizes, more than either of the preceding words, extreme urgency, demands of a peremptory and exacting character, and difficulties that cannot be easily overcome ⟨figures which are doing nothing in particular . . . striking an attitude which is dictated not by the inner necessities of balance or motion, but by the *exigencies* of the composition—*Binyon*⟩ ⟨such travel *exigencies* as having to scout around for a room when you're tired—*Joseph*⟩ ⟨it may be argued that the *exigencies* of their work—the tension, the deadline . . . the abrupt arrivals and departures—drove them to alcohol—*Hubbell*⟩
*Ana* *stress, strain, pressure: *lack, want, dearth, absence, defect, privation: *poverty, indigence, penury, destitution, privation, want

**need** *vb* *lack, want, require
*Ana* *demand, require, claim, exact: *long, hanker, pine, yearn, hunger, thirst: crave, covet, *desire, wish
**needful,** necessary, requisite, indispensable, essential are comparable when meaning urgently required. **Needful** carries the weakest suggestion of urgency, but it applies to something that is required to supply a want or to fulfill a need ⟨forts, magazines, arsenals, dockyards, and other *needful* buildings—*U. S. Constitution*⟩ ⟨tradesmen carrying what was *needful* to British ports—*Repplier*⟩ ⟨a sensitive, flexible, resourceful adaptation to objective facts is especially *needful—Muller*⟩ **Necessary** implies more pressing need or urgent constraint but, except where the compulsion of necessity in the sense of an inherent, logically compelling principle ⟨a *necessary* consequence⟩ ⟨a *necessary* conclusion⟩ ⟨patience . . . is a *necessary* mark of the liberal mind—*Dewey*⟩ is suggested, the word need not connote that the thing so qualified cannot be done without but more often indicates it to be infinitely desirable rather than absolutely required; thus, tires are *necessary* to proper management of an automobile, but in a sufficient emergency one might drive without them ⟨his personal return was most required and *necessary—Shak.*⟩ ⟨it was nineteen-thirty-five and honeymoons in Europe were not considered *necessary* by anyone—*Flood*⟩ ⟨made himself so *necessary* to the company that by 1849 he was general superintendent of the road—*Harlow*⟩ ⟨always finding a more *necessary* article for which a less *necessary* had to be discarded—*Cather*⟩ ⟨of all the bitter and heavy things in this sorry old world, the not being *necessary* is the bitterest and heaviest—*Deland*⟩ **Requisite** differs from *necessary* chiefly in being applied to something that is specifically required by the nature of a thing, the end that is in view, or the purpose to be fulfilled; usually the adjective suggests an imposed requirement rather than an inner need and so suggests constraint from without or, often, from official sources ⟨complete the subjects *requisite* for college entrance⟩ ⟨the vigor *requisite* to success—*Grandgent*⟩ ⟨the *requisite* quorum of forty members was not present—*Schuyler*⟩ **Indispensable** not only carries a stronger implication of urgency than the preceding terms, but it also distinctly implies that the thing so qualified cannot be done without, especially if the implied or expressed end is to be attained ⟨there is no such thing as an *indispensable* person, though many persons have made themselves virtually *indispensable*⟩ ⟨the jury is the *indispensable* element in the popular vindication of the criminal law—*Frankfurter*⟩ ⟨rigid truthfulness in adults towards children is . . . absolutely *indispensable* if children are not to learn lying—*Russell*⟩ **Essential** (see also ESSENTIAL 2, INHERENT) is often used in place of *indispensable* as implying no less urgency but as being less extravagant in its suggestion; it usually also implies inherent necessity from the point of view of what a thing is or must be by its very nature or end ⟨knowledge of one's subject is *essential* to successful teaching⟩ ⟨*essential* raw materials⟩ ⟨you are *essential* to her perfect happiness—*Dickens*⟩ ⟨the builders must have begun with the central piers and the choir, because the choir was the only *essential* part of the church—*Henry Adams*⟩ ⟨the construction of the pier was desirable for the more convenient repair of warships, but it was not *essential—Justice Holmes*⟩
*Ana* wanted, needed, required, lacked (see LACK *vb*): vital, cardinal, *essential, fundamental
**needy** *adj* *poor, indigent, destitute, penniless, impecunious, poverty-stricken, necessitous
*Ana & Con* see those at NECESSITOUS
**nefarious** iniquitous, flagitious, infamous, corrupt, de-

A colon (:) separates groups of words discriminated. An asterisk (*) indicates place of treatment of each group.

generate, *vicious, villainous

*Ana* heinous, *outrageous, atrocious, monstrous: *flagrant, glaring, gross, rank

**negate** *nullify, annul, abrogate, invalidate

*Ana* negative, *neutralize, counteract

**negative** *adj* *neutral, indifferent

*Ant* affirmative

**negative** *vb* **1** *deny, gainsay, traverse, contradict, impugn, contravene

**2** *neutralize, counteract

*Ana* *nullify, negate, annul, abrogate, invalidate

**neglect** *vb* **Neglect, omit, disregard, ignore, overlook, slight, forget** are comparable when they mean to pass over something without giving it due or sufficient attention. **Neglect** usually implies intentional or unintentional failure to give full or proper attention, especially to something one is doing (as a task) or should do (as a duty) or to someone who has a claim upon one's care or attention ⟨he was changing into his dress clothes . . . . He had *neglected* to hang them up the night before, and for once they were bedraggled—*Mailer*⟩ ⟨he asked Mr. Powell with some brusqueness if the chief mate had *neglected* to instruct him that the captain was to be found on the port side—*Conrad*⟩ ⟨*neglect* his family⟩ **Omit** implies a leaving out of something which forms a part of a whole ⟨*omit* two stanzas of a hymn⟩ ⟨got up late and *omitted* breakfast⟩ a neglecting entirely through oversight, inattention, or absorption of an important detail, opportunity, or aspect ⟨Constance remembered small possessions of her own which she had *omitted* to remove from the cutting-out room—*Bennett*⟩ **Disregard** usually implies voluntary, sometimes deliberate, inattention; the term may or may not imply justifiable neglect ⟨*disregard* petty annoyances⟩ ⟨*disregard* an unimportant piece of evidence⟩ ⟨she persists in *disregarding* the wishes of her mother⟩ ⟨nearly all the humane alleviations of brutal violence, introduced and practised in the days when professional armies fought for a dynasty or for a point of honor, were *disregarded*—*Inge*⟩ ⟨flouting convention and *disregarding* his own clerical position—*Handlin*⟩ **Ignore** usually implies either an intention to disregard or a failure to regard something more or less obvious; it may even suggest a deliberate closing of the eyes to what one does not wish to recognize ⟨to those who agree with me I am uttering commonplaces and to those who disagree I am *ignoring* the necessary foundations of thought—*Justice Holmes*⟩ ⟨its mathematics approaches mysticism and its theory contains certain impossibilities which are *ignored* in practice—*Theodore Sturgeon*⟩ ⟨by tacit agreement they *ignored* the remarks and insinuations of their acquaintances—*D. H. Lawrence*⟩ **Overlook** implies an omitting or disregarding, sometimes through intention but more often through haste, or lack of care ⟨*overlook* an item in an account⟩ ⟨it is the practice of good nature to *overlook* the faults which have already, by the consequences, punished the delinquent—*Johnson*⟩ ⟨winced when he heard so young a man call him by nickname, but he *overlooked* this also in light of what had happened—*Purdy*⟩ **Slight** may imply neglect, omission, or disregard, but it also usually implies a contemptuous or an arrogant attitude that makes one undervalue a thing's importance, treat a person disdainfully, or be neglectful in performance of a task or duty ⟨nothing in the service was *slighted*, every phrase and gesture had its full value—*Cather*⟩ ⟨I have been *slighted*, tricked, threatened, insulted, made ill . . . but I am justified—*H. G. Wells*⟩ **Forget** (compare FORGETFUL) often retains in this relation the implication of losing the memory of something or someone, so that when it implies neglect, it usually carries a suggestion of willful ignoring or of a

failure to impress the thing neglected upon one's mind ⟨I shall not be surprised to be neglected and *forgot*—*Nelson*⟩ ⟨still, he told Hannah to get the boy better clothes—though he *forgot* to give her any money for the purpose—*Deland*⟩ ⟨it was—well, until yesterday—all but *forgotten*—put out of mind, I mean—*de la Mare*⟩

*Ant* cherish —*Con* *appreciate, value, prize, treasure: *nurse, nurture, foster, cultivate

**neglect** *n* **1** *failure, default, miscarriage, dereliction

*Ana* omitting *or* omission, disregarding *or* disregard, ignoring, slighting, forgetting, overlooking (see corresponding verbs at NEGLECT): forgetfulness, obliviousness (see adjectives at FORGETFUL)

**2** *negligence

*Ana* neglecting, omitting *or* omission, disregarding *or* disregard, ignoring, slighting, forgetting, overlooking (see corresponding verbs at NEGLECT)

**neglectful** *negligent, lax, slack, remiss

*Ana* *careless, heedless, thoughtless

*Ant* attentive —*Con* *thoughtful, considerate

**negligence, neglect** are not always clearly distinguished in use, even though the lines between them may be drawn with some clearness. **Negligence** stresses the quality or fact of being negligent or careless either as shown in a lack of care in the performance of a task, a duty, or a piece of work or in the operation or handling of a dangerous machine or mechanism which requires effort or close attention ⟨the amazing *negligence* of some housekeepers⟩ ⟨an act of criminal *negligence*⟩ ⟨no one has done more through *negligence* to corrupt the language—*Byron*⟩ ⟨most of these are involved in accidents through their own *negligence*—*Theodore Sturgeon*⟩ or as shown in a temperamental or assumed indifference to small niceties (as in dress, manners, or style) that gives an impression of casualness, artlessness, or lack of artificiality ⟨spoke with conviction, yet with a gentlemanly lightness, almost a *negligence*, as though to cancel any tone of dogmatism . . . in his words—*Wouk*⟩ ⟨his companion wore well-cut tweeds with a sort of aggressive *negligence*, as though he hated them—*I. A. R. Wylie*⟩ **Neglect**, on the other hand, applies either to the act or fact of leaving undone or carelessly, inadequately, or imperfectly done something which it is one's business or duty to do ⟨convicted of *neglect* of duty⟩ ⟨we made a nice tidy cleanup . . . . If I hadn't done it I ought either to have been shot for *neglect* or dismissed for incapacity—*H. G. Wells*⟩ ⟨in dealing with the infant . . . there is need of a delicate balance between *neglect* and indulgence—*Russell*⟩ or to the state or fact of being neglected, slighted, ignored, or forgotten ⟨rescue my poor remains from vile *neglect*—*Prior*⟩ ⟨a . . . motive for reading it . . . [that] ensured poetry against *neglect*—*Day Lewis*⟩ ⟨destined either to constantly inadequate execution or to complete *neglect*—*Virgil Thomson*⟩ For these reasons the phrase "the *negligence* of a person" always refers to a quality of character of the person as an agent or to its outward manifestation (as in an act, a piece of work, or an accident) while "the *neglect* of a person" refers to the act of another who neglects, slights, ignores, or forgets the person, thereby making the latter his victim.

*Ana* laxness, slackness, remissness (see corresponding adjectives at NEGLIGENT): indifference, unconcernedness *or* unconcern, incuriousness (see corresponding adjectives at INDIFFERENT)

*Ant* attention: solicitude —*Con* *care, concern, anxiety, worry: diligence, assiduity, sedulousness (see corresponding adjectives at BUSY)

**negligent, neglectful, lax, slack, remiss** are comparable when applied to persons, their ways of working or acting,

and the results of their work or activities with the meaning culpably careless or manifesting such carelessness. **Negligent** implies such culpable inattentiveness as is likely to result in imperfection, incompleteness, slovenliness, or danger or damage to others ⟨his family knew him to be . . . a most *negligent* and dilatory correspondent—*Austen*⟩ ⟨so *negligent* in his poetical style . . . so slovenly, slipshod, and infelicitous—*Arnold*⟩ ⟨a careless workman, *negligent* of detail—*Edith Hamilton*⟩ **Neglectful** is usually more derogatory or censorious than *negligent*, for it carries a stronger connotation of laziness or deliberate and blameworthy inattention ⟨parents *neglectful* of their children's health⟩ ⟨a government at once insatiable and *neglectful*—*Mill*⟩ ⟨show no trace of shame, and . . . are utterly *neglectful* of what we consider the first requirements of decency—*Westermarck*⟩ **Lax** (see also LOOSE) implies a usually blameworthy lack of necessary strictness, severity, or precision; the term applies chiefly to persons who do not satisfy the rigorous demands made upon them by their work or duties or to work or an activity performed or carried on without the close attention, constant care, or strict adherence to law or custom that is necessary ⟨a *lax* parent⟩ ⟨*lax* discipline⟩ ⟨*lax* morals⟩ ⟨a *lax* interpretation of a law⟩ ⟨scandalously *lax* in restraining drunkards from annoying the sober—*Trevelyan*⟩ ⟨we do not intend to leave things so *lax* that loopholes will be left for cheaters—*Roosevelt*⟩ **Slack** (see also LOOSE) stresses the want of proper or necessary diligence and expedition as well as of care; the term usually also implies indolence or sluggishness or indifference ⟨a *slack* workman⟩ ⟨we keep our wits *slack*— *H. G. Wells*⟩ When applied to what is accomplished by a slack worker, the term usually suggests neglect of important details necessary to the completeness, finish, or perfection of the work ⟨a three-quarters figure of admirable design, though of rather *slack* execution— *Stobart*⟩ ⟨a fine nose for what was *slack* in the play or insufficiently developed—*Mailer*⟩ **Remiss** implies culpable carelessness that shows itself in slackness and forgetfulness or in negligence; it is applied chiefly to something lax in performance or maintenance, but it may be applied to a person who is unduly careless or lax in the performance of his duties ⟨*remiss* housekeeping⟩ ⟨a *remiss* police officer⟩ ⟨it certainly had been very *remiss* of him, as Mayor . . . to call no meeting ere this—*Hardy*⟩ ⟨so *remiss* did they become in their attentions that we could no longer rely upon their bringing us the daily supply of food—*Melville*⟩
*Ana* *careless, heedless, thoughtless, inadvertent: *indifferent, unconcerned, incurious: *slipshod, slovenly
*Con* *rigid, strict, rigorous: *thoughtful, considerate, attentive

**negotiate** 1 parley, treat, *confer, commune, consult, advise
**2 Negotiate, arrange, concert** are comparable when they mean to bring about or accomplish by mutual agreement especially after discussion or parley. *Negotiate* and *arrange* both imply prior exchange of views and wishes and, sometimes, settlement by bargaining or compromise. **Negotiate**, however, is somewhat more formal and is especially appropriate when the dealings are carried on by diplomatic, business, or legal agencies, while **arrange** (see also ORDER) may retain some notion of its basic idea of putting in order and is especially applicable to dealings tending to the establishment or restoration of order or to those carried on by private persons or their representatives ⟨*negotiate* a treaty⟩ ⟨*arrange* a marriage⟩ ⟨*negotiate* a monetary understanding with the British government— *Current Biog.*⟩ ⟨*arrange* the settlement of a case out of

court⟩ ⟨a peace with the native chiefs was *arranged* and the crisis passed—*McPherson*⟩ **Concert** implies a planning together and especially a settling upon a joint course of action through conference and negotiation ⟨a conference of Commonwealth finance ministers . . . to discuss the balance-of-payments crisis in the sterling area and to *concert* action to deal with it—*Americana Annual*⟩ ⟨within another generation there will be another world war if the nations of the world do not *concert* the method by which to prevent it—*Woodrow Wilson*⟩
**neighborhood** *locality, district, vicinity
**neighborly** friendly, *amicable
*Ana* peaceful, peaceable, *pacific: *social, hospitable, gregarious, cooperative: cordial, sociable, *gracious
*Ant* unneighborly: ill-disposed —*Con* antagonistic, *adverse
**neophyte** *novice, novitiate, probationer, postulant, apprentice
**neoplasm** *tumor, malignancy, cancer
**nepenthe** *anodyne, opiate, narcotic
**neritic** *aquatic, marine, oceanic, thalassic, pelagic, abyssal, lacustrine, fluvial, fluviatile
**nerve** *n* effrontery, *temerity, audacity, hardihood, cheek, gall
*Ana* boldness, intrepidity (see corresponding adjectives at BRAVE): *fortitude, grit, pluck, sand, guts: foolhardiness, recklessness (see corresponding adjectives at ADVENTUROUS)
**nerve** *vb* *encourage, inspirit, hearten, embolden, cheer, steel
*Ana* *strengthen, invigorate, fortify, energize: rally, *stir, rouse, arouse: *renew, restore, refresh
*Ant* unnerve —*Con* enervate, unman, emasculate (see UNNERVE): *discourage, dishearten, dispirit, deject
**nervous** 1 *vigorous, lusty, energetic, strenuous
*Ana* forceful, forcible, potent, *powerful: *spirited, mettlesome: virile, manly (see MALE)
2 *impatient, restless, restive, unquiet, uneasy, fidgety, jumpy, jittery
*Ana* excited *or* excitable, stimulated, provoked *or* provocative (see corresponding verbs at PROVOKE): *inconstant, unstable, mercurial
*Ant* steady —*Con* constant, even, equable, uniform (see STEADY)
**nettle** provoke, exasperate, *irritate, aggravate, rile, peeve
*Ana* *annoy, irk, bother, vex: disturb, perturb, agitate, upset, *discompose: fret, chafe, gall (see ABRADE)
**network** *system, scheme, complex, organism, economy
**neurologist, psychiatrist, alienist, psychopathologist, psychotherapist, psychoanalyst** are comparable though not synonymous terms that denote a specialist in mental disorders. A **neurologist** is a physician skilled in the diagnosis and treatment of diseases of the nervous system, that is, of diseases (as epilepsy or locomotor ataxia) that involve structural or functional disorder of nervous tissue. *Psychiatrist, alienist, psychopathologist* all designate a physician who devotes himself to the diagnosis and treatment of diseases affecting the mind or emotions and especially, as distinguished from *neurologist*, of disorders (as neurasthenia, hysteria, and paranoia) not demonstrably of physical origin. **Psychiatrist** is the general term, applicable to any such physician, while **alienist** is the preferred term in medical jurisprudence and may especially suggest skill in detection of mental derangements or of insanity, and **psychopathologist** may specifically apply to a physician specializing in emotional disorders and dealing largely with the dynamic factors (as defects of personality or unfavorable environment) underlying such disorders. A **psychotherapist** may be either a physician or a layman (as

A colon (:) separates groups of words discriminated. An asterisk (*) indicates place of treatment of each group.

a psychologist, social worker, or clergyman) who treats mental or emotional disorder or maladjustment by psychological means and especially those involving verbal communication. A **psychoanalyst** is a psychotherapist and usually a physician (nonmedical psychoanalysts being often distinguished as *lay analysts*) who employs a form of psychotherapy, especially in the treatment of psychoneuroses, that is designed to bring unconscious and preconscious material into consciousness and involves largely the analysis of resistance and the establishment and analysis of a transference neurosis.

**neutral** *adj* Neutral, negative, indifferent are comparable when they mean lacking decisiveness or distinctiveness in character, quality, action, or effect. **Neutral,** in one of its earliest and still common senses, applies to states, governments, parties, or persons who refuse to take sides with either of two or any of several contending parties. The term need not imply an attitude of impartiality, but it usually implies either indecision or a refraining from positive action ⟨his family connections kept him *neutral,* and the household was never drawn into the war—*Buchan*⟩ ⟨revolutionary verse . . . makes the *neutral* reader wonder whether it is aimed to win him for the communist or fascist state—*Day Lewis*⟩ ⟨the bucks bridled a little when I came in, and then ignored me. Once the atmosphere had become *neutral* again, Thompson was willing to talk— *Mailer*⟩ When otherwise applied (as to colors or terms, to a character or personality, to a substance in chemistry, or to an entity in philosophy) *neutral* implies a quality, an appearance, or a reaction that belongs to neither of two opposites or extremes; the term therefore often connotes vagueness, indefiniteness, indecisiveness, ineffectualness; thus, a *neutral* character is one that reveals neither positive virtues nor positive vices; a chemically *neutral* substance (as distilled water) is neither acid nor basic; a *neutral* color (as taupe) is not clearly or positively any definite color, often because it verges on gray ⟨the artists of the Far East . . . use positive tints quite sparingly, giving them for foil large spaces of *neutral* tone—*Binyon*⟩ ⟨the land itself cannot be described as rich or poor, good or bad, favorable or unfavorable. The land is entirely *neutral*—*P. E. James*⟩ ⟨*atomic* . . . was until 1945 as emotionally *neutral* a word as *pyroborate* or *hygrometric.* But since the explosion at Hiroshima it has assumed a new implication—*Savory*⟩ **Negative** carries a stronger implication than *neutral* of absence of positive or affirmative (compare AFFIRMATIVE) characteristics or qualities; the term therefore usually implies inaction, ineffectiveness, or a failure to assume a definite or concrete form ⟨there is certainly a vague and widespread discontent with our present results [in education]; but it is all a *negative* opinion—*Benson*⟩ ⟨so much of the dream was described in *negative* . . . terms: no hostility, no friendliness, not feared, not welcomed, not grateful, not anxious—*Kelman*⟩ ⟨the *negative* happiness that follows the release from anxiety and tension—*Huxley*⟩ **Indifferent** (see also IN- DIFFERENT 1, MEDIUM) implies a character or appearance that does not readily define itself or fall into any clearly marked class or category; the term is applicable to things or occasionally to persons that stir up no feeling or elicit no decision as to whether they are good or bad, in accordance with one's principles or not, necessary or unnecessary, or pleasant or unpleasant ⟨though they disliked each other, they could converse at length upon *indifferent* subjects⟩ ⟨either one attitude is better than the other, or else it is *indifferent*—*T. S. Eliot*⟩ ⟨the injustice . . . in making penal an act which when committed seemed innocent or at least *indifferent*—*Radin*⟩ ⟨nature is *indifferent* to the survival of the human species, including

Americans—*A. E. Stevenson*⟩
**Con** biased, disposed, predisposed (see INCLINE *vb*): positive, *affirmative: *decided, decisive

**neutralize,** counteract, negative are comparable when they mean to make something inoperative or ineffective usually by means of an opposite force, influence, or effect. **Neutralize** implies an equalizing, making ineffectual or inoperative, or nullifying by an opposing force, power, agency, or effect ⟨a quinine that can *neutralize* his venom; it is called courage—*Davis*⟩ ⟨*neutralize* the effects of propaganda with counterpropaganda so as to render the international environment favorable—*Latham*⟩ ⟨our esteem for facts has not *neutralized* in us all religiousness—*James*⟩ **Counteract** may imply merely neutralizing or counterbalancing; it is often used in situations in which the good and bad or the beneficial and deleterious are opposed ⟨these two principles have often sufficed, even when *counteracted* by great public calamities and by bad institutions, to carry civilization rapidly forward— *Macaulay*⟩ ⟨frequently visited the Choctaws, in an effort to *counteract* the influence of the French and to win them to an alliance with the English—*Ghent*⟩ **Negative** implies an annulling, a contradicting, a making futile, useless, or ineffective, or a vitiating by an opposing force, effect, or trend ⟨as if the wind might blow it over, thus *negativing* the idea of solidity—*Bennett*⟩ ⟨it is only in literature that the paradoxical and even mutually *negativing* anecdotes in the history of a human heart can be juxtaposed and annealed by art into verisimilitude and credibility— *Faulkner*⟩
**Ana** offset, countervail, counterbalance, counterpoise (see COMPENSATE): defeat, overcome, subdue, *conquer

**new** *adj* New, novel, new-fashioned, newfangled, modern, modernistic, original, fresh can all mean having very recently come into existence or use or into a connection, a position, or a state (as of being recognized). A thing is **new** that has never before the time of its advent been known, thought of, manufactured, or experienced, or that is just ready for use, sale, or circulation, or that has just been acquired ⟨*new* books⟩ ⟨*new* ideas⟩ ⟨a *new* washing machine⟩ ⟨no man putteth *new* wine into old bottles— Mk 2:22⟩ ⟨a *new* way of dressing her hair⟩ A person is *new* if he has just been taken into a military, business, social, or other group ⟨a *new* soldier⟩ ⟨a *new* stenographer⟩ ⟨three *new* members⟩ or if he has received his first experience ⟨he was . . . frightened, being *new* to the sight—*Dickens*⟩ or if he has been renewed in spirit or in mind or in body ⟨the quiet hills which I am now seeing again, with a *new* and contented eye—*O'Connor*⟩ ⟨the hot food made a *new* man of him⟩ A thing is **novel** which is not only new but so out of the ordinary course as to strike one as strange, unusual, or unfamiliar ⟨*novel* forms of government, like those of Russia and Italy— *Frankfurter*⟩ ⟨*novel* schemes of salvation—*L. P. Smith*⟩ ⟨sermons . . . bold in thought and *novel* in language —*Wharton*⟩ A thing is **new-fashioned** which is so different in form, shape, style, or character from what was previously known that it challenges curiosity or has only recently met general acceptance ⟨*new-fashioned* modes of painting⟩ ⟨*new-fashioned* hats for women are regarded as absurd by many men⟩ ⟨the type of old-fashioned scholarship . . . the type of *new-fashioned* criticism— *S. E. Hyman*⟩ A thing is **newfangled** which strikes one as unnecessarily or as ingeniously novel; often, however, the term differs little from *new* except in suggesting disparagement ⟨*newfangled* toys⟩ ⟨*newfangled* theories of art⟩ ⟨a *newfangled* nomenclature—*Hamilton*⟩ ⟨quite a modern hostelry for its time. It had such *newfangled* doodads as mechanical dishwashers and potato peelers

---

*Ana* analogous words     *Ant* antonyms     *Con* contrasted words     See also explanatory notes facing page 1

*—Green Peyton⟩* A person or thing is **modern** that belongs to the present time or is especially characteristic of it; the term often implies up-to-dateness and novelty or a contrast with what has been long accepted and still is the choice of the conservative: in this special sense **modernistic** may be preferred to *modern,* but more often *modernistic* carries a contemptuous suggestion of the ephemerally novel ⟨when I refer to *modern* music, I do not mean necessarily *modernistic* music, much of which is a pale afterglow of the great and original modernism of yesteryear—*Virgil Thomson⟩ Modern,* however, is always preferred to *modernistic* when contemporaneousness only is implied ⟨in *modern* art atmosphere counts for so much—*Wilde⟩* ⟨this strange disease of *modern* life, with its sick hurry, its divided aims, its heads o'ertaxed, its palsied hearts—*Arnold⟩* But *modern* is also applicable to things of more remote origin than any of the other terms; as opposed to *ancient* and *medieval* it usually implies reference to the centuries beginning with the full Renaissance up to the present ⟨*modern* languages⟩ ⟨*modern* civilizations⟩ Often, however, the dividing line between what is modern and what is too far distant in time to be called modern has to be supplied by the context ⟨the Victorian era gave way to the *modern* age of machinery⟩ ⟨most *modern* well-to-do Englishmen and Americans, if they were transported by magic into the age of Elizabeth, would wish themselves back in the *modern* world —*Russell⟩* A person or thing is **original** that is or produces something new or novel and, at the same time, the first of its kind ⟨that he would be successful in an *original* way, or that he would go to the dogs in an *original* way, seemed equally probable—*Hardy⟩* ⟨they contain no new ideas . . . [he] was anything but an *original* thinker— *R. A. Hall⟩* ⟨some areas were occupied by savages, in others there were brilliant and *original* civilizations— *Poole⟩* A thing is **fresh** that is or seems so new that it has not had time to lose the signs of newness, such as liveliness, energy, brightness, or virginal quality ⟨*fresh* footprints⟩ ⟨receive a *fresh* impetus⟩ ⟨make a *fresh* start⟩ ⟨this was a new voice falling upon the attentive ears of youth—a *fresh* challenge to its native and impetuous generosity—*Repplier⟩* ⟨a great shouting at the coal works because a *fresh* vein of coal had been discovered—*Woolf⟩*
*Ant* old

**newfangled** *\*new, novel, new-fashioned, modernistic, modern, original, fresh

**new-fashioned** *\*new, novel, newfangled, modernistic, modern, original, fresh

**news,** tidings, intelligence, advice are comparable when they designate a report or the reports of occurrences and conditions not previously known. **News** stresses novelty and freshness of information ⟨the gossip was not *news* to her⟩ ⟨the letter contained no *news*⟩ ⟨wanted to tell her as quickly as he could his evil *news*—*Buck⟩* Since *news* is specifically applied to the information disseminated through public media (as radio and journals) shortly after the incidents have occurred, it also often implies distribution, even in its general sense ⟨experts in handling *news*⟩ or when used in combination ⟨*news*paper⟩ ⟨*news*-mongers⟩ **Tidings,** which may be singular in construction, is somewhat bookish; it is often appropriate when it refers to news orally communicated or disseminated (as by a herald or messenger) ⟨must have a courier who will carry the *tidings* of distress to those who are there to save when signals reach their ears—*Cardozo⟩* ⟨no trace or *tidings* of Lynchehaun was ever found—*Rooney⟩* **Intelligence** stresses the desirability or the practical value of the information rather than its freshness ⟨their visits

to Mrs. Philips were now productive of the most interesting *intelligence*—*Austen⟩* In specific military use *intelligence* suggests clandestine methods of gathering information (as by secret agents). It is therefore applied not only to the information gathered but to the branch of the service commissioned to gather it ⟨an enemy superior in numbers, who possessed also the advantage in armament, position, and more accurate *intelligence*—*Buchan⟩* In comparison with *intelligence,* which often suggests the gathering of important information, **advice** stresses the transmission of information and implies the immediacy of its value. It, or its plural **advices,** is often applied to the means (as letters, telegrams, or messengers) by which this information is communicated ⟨no doubt he had *advices* that Casale was sufficiently provisioned to last for many months, perhaps a year—*Belloc⟩* ⟨beginning their *advices* with the revelation that a rich potential for future prosperity and happiness had been discovered in atomic energy—*Burlingame⟩*

**newspaper** *\*journal, periodical, magazine, review, organ

**next** *\*nearest

**nib** *\*bill, beak, neb

**nice** 1 Nice, dainty, fastidious, finicky, finicking, finical, particular, fussy, squeamish, persnickety, pernickety can all mean exacting or displaying exacting standards (as in selection, judgment, or workmanship). **Nice** (see also CORRECT, DECOROUS) implies fineness of discrimination and power to distinguish the very good from the merely good; the term may connote more of intellectual quality than the other words ⟨an appetite for knowledge too eager to be *nice*—*Johnson⟩* ⟨he had a *nice* taste in literature and had edited Crashaw and Vaughan with conspicuous taste and much perception—*Mackenzie⟩ Nice* is also applicable to questions or problems which require such powers of discrimination and subtlety or delicacy in handling if the solution is to be found ⟨a *nice* experiment⟩ ⟨the situation raises a *nice* question⟩ ⟨it is a *nice* point in ethics whether it is dishonest to rob one's own money-box—*Lynd⟩* **Dainty** (see also CHOICE) usually implies a tendency to select carefully what does, or to reject with more or less disdain what does not, satisfy one's extremely delicate taste or sensibility; it usually connotes chariness or a tendency to pick and choose, especially in eating ⟨I have been silent—the hungry cannot be *dainty*—but it is useless to tell a pampered man this—*M. W. Shelley⟩* ⟨no shape but his can please your *dainty* eye—*Shak.⟩* ⟨it's all right to be *dainty* about money when you've lots of it as you have—*Behrman⟩* **Fastidious** implies a strong aversion to something that does not satisfy one's sense of what is right, proper, or in good taste; it may suggest the possession of ethical, artistic, social, or other standards that are so high that they impose a strain upon those who would meet them ⟨it is . . . an advantage for an author to have two or three *fastidious* readers whom he can imagine sniffing at his pages—*L. P. Smith⟩* ⟨he isn't always easy to work for, being *fastidious* in his standards and uncompromising in his demands—*Wechsberg⟩* or that cause suffering to the possessor when they are not satisfied ⟨the disorder was almost more than his *fastidious* taste could bear—*Cather⟩* or that foster extreme care in selection from what is offered or available ⟨why such a desperate orgy of literature? I thought you were of a more *fastidious* habit—not like Stanley, who insists on reading everything—*Rose Macaulay⟩* ⟨he liked people, was . . . not too *fastidious* to get along with barkeepers and party toughs and sufficiently cultivated to get along with gentlemen—*Commager⟩* **Finicky** and **finicking** as well as the less common **finical** imply an affected or overnice fastidiousness ⟨his reserve,

---

A colon (:) separates groups of words discriminated. An asterisk (*) indicates place of treatment of each group.

his delicacy, his distaste for many of the persons and things surrounding him . . . have produced an impression of Gray as being a man falsely fastidious, *finical*, effeminate—*Arnold*⟩ ⟨his voice is too soft, his manners too precise. He is genial, yet he is *finicky—Mailer*⟩ ⟨*finicking* fishermen demand almost as many rods as there are varieties of fish—*Monsanto Mag.*⟩ **Particular** implies an insistence that all details or circumstances must be exactly as one wishes them or that one's special or peculiar standards must be met. In contrast with *fastidious, particular* need not imply what others would call a high standard; the term usually suggests standards which the individual regards as high or exacting ⟨she is *particular* about the way steak should be broiled⟩ ⟨every year it used to get a nice coat of paint—Papa was very *particular* about the paint—*Hellman*⟩ ⟨when it came to sharing his walks, Henry was rather *particular*. Alcott served for a stroll, but the real art of walking was beyond him—*Brooks*⟩ ⟨as she approached, George Adams, who had a *particular* mother, rose, and Niel followed his example—*Cather*⟩ **Fussy** is applicable not only to fastidious or particular persons and to acts that manifest a disposition to be querulous or fidgety ⟨she was not one of the trivially *fussy* domesticated women—*Ellis*⟩ ⟨men who are finicky and a bundle of nerves. *Fussy* about their food, too—*Christie*⟩ ⟨in this matter Augustus moved slowly and tactfully. He was no lawyer, and he had not the *fussy* interest of Claudius in the work of the courts—*Buchan*⟩ ⟨indenting each paragraph half the width of a page, in a *fussy*, old-maidish sort of way—*Robert Lewis*⟩ but also to things that are especially difficult or complicated ⟨he looked like a natural for the *fussy* bookkeeping routine of an orderly room—*Birney*⟩ ⟨a *fussy* piece of work⟩ **Squeamish** implies a tendency to be easily nauseated by the sight, taste, smell, or hearing of something disagreeable ⟨the starved stomach is not *squeamish—Hudson*⟩ In its extended use it implies a disgust for or an aversion to anything that does not satisfy one's standards of what is decent, delicate, or nice; it therefore sometimes connotes extreme sensitiveness or prudishness or scrupulousness ⟨as to the nudities . . . they might well have startled a not very *squeamish* eye—*Hawthorne*⟩ ⟨our nerves . . . are unduly delicate, and our tastes too *squeamish—Stephen*⟩ ⟨he came of vigorous stock, prone to consult its own will and speak its opinions with no *squeamish* concern for a neighbor's views—*Parrington*⟩ ⟨since the daughter may fascinate the duke, and he would feel *squeamish* about incest, the relationship must be kept secret—*Times Lit. Sup.*⟩ **Persnickety** and **pernickety** convey the user's reaction of annoyance, exasperation, or disgust toward persons who are unduly fussy or finical, or tasks or problems that are so delicate or complicated as to impose severe strain on one's patience and good temper ⟨approached native food and drink pretty much like a *persnickety* peacetime tourist—*Pyle*⟩ ⟨the grammarian, the purist, the *pernickety* stickler for trifles —*Matthews*⟩ ⟨new mechanical devices . . . may be all right for those *pernickety* fellows, the exact scientists or the social scientists, but the humanities get along well enough without them—*H. M. Jones*⟩
*Ana* *wise, judicious, sage, sapient: punctilious, meticulous, scrupulous, *careful: discriminating, discerning, penetrating (see corresponding nouns at DISCERNMENT)
*Con* *coarse, gross, vulgar: crude, callow, green, uncouth, raw (see RUDE): *negligent, lax, remiss, neglectful, slack
**2** precise, exact, accurate, *correct, right
*Ana* strict, *rigid, rigorous, stringent: exquisite, delicate, rare (see CHOICE *adj*)
*Con* *random, haphazard, hit-or-miss, happy-go-lucky:

*careless, heedless, inadvertent
**3** proper, seemly, *decorous, decent
*Ana* fitting, *fit, appropriate, suitable, meet
**niggardly** parsimonious, penurious, miserly, *stingy, close, closefisted, tight, tightfisted, cheeseparing, penny-pinching
*Ana* *covetous, avaricious, grasping, greedy: *sparing, economical, frugal, thrifty: *mean, ignoble
*Ant* bountiful —*Con* *liberal, generous, bounteous, openhanded, munificent, handsome: *profuse, lavish, prodigal
**nigh** *adj & adv* *close, near, nearby
*Ant* far
**night** *adj* *nightly, nocturnal
**nightly, nocturnal, night** all mean of, relating to, or associated with the night. **Nightly,** opposed to *daily*, may mean no more than this ⟨all is quiet, no alarms; nothing fear of *nightly* harms—*Housman*⟩ ⟨the increase in body size may have been an important factor in releasing the early primates from their *nightly* or twilight feeding habits, by allowing them better to hold their own against aggressors —*LaBarre*⟩ But *nightly* is the one of these terms that usually carries a strong implication of recurrence and is especially appropriate to convey the idea of happening night after night ⟨there is only one novel this writer can recall which delves beneath the surface of the daily and *nightly* life and death of a great and influential newspaper—*Harrison Smith*⟩ **Nocturnal,** opposed to *diurnal*, is often interchangeable with *nightly*, especially in its more general sense ⟨the squares of light along the fifteenth story testified until midnight of their *nocturnal* industry—*Auchincloss*⟩ ⟨the changing beauty of *nocturnal* landscapes—*Bennett*⟩ but distinctively it may mean active at night ⟨shopping, working, theatergoing, and arguing hours in Barcelona never cease to amaze visitors from less *nocturnal* countries. Some shops stay open until well after midnight, and then are closed until the next noon—*Wechsberg*⟩ ⟨the eyes of most fish are adapted to the conditions of dim illumination associated with *nocturnal* feeding—*Dowdeswell*⟩ **Night** in much of its use is interchangeable with *nocturnal* and may be preferred to the latter when a less formal term is required ⟨*night* noises⟩ ⟨the *night* train⟩ ⟨a *night* ape⟩ Distinctively, the term is used to describe persons who work at night ⟨a *night* nurse⟩ ⟨ask the *night* clerk⟩ and things that occur or are intended for use at night ⟨*night* baseball⟩ ⟨a bank with a *night* depository⟩
*Ant* daily
**nightmare** dream, vision, *fancy, fantasy, phantasy, phantasm, daydream
*Ana* *delusion, hallucination, illusion: threatening *or* threat, menacing *or* menace (see corresponding verbs at THREATEN)
**nimble** *agile, brisk, spry
*Ana* sprightly, *lively, animated: alert, wide-awake, vigilant, *watchful: *supple, limber, lithe
**nip** *vb* *blast, blight
*Ana* check, *arrest: squeeze, *press: *frustrate, thwart, balk
**nip** *n* blast, blight (see under BLAST *vb*)
*Ana* arresting, checking (see ARREST *vb*): frigidity, freezing (see corresponding adjectives at COLD)
**nobility** *aristocracy, gentry, county, elite, society
**noble** **1** stately, majestic, imposing, august, magnificent, *grand, grandiose
*Ana* glorious, *splendid, resplendent, superb, sublime: illustrious, eminent (see FAMOUS)
*Ant* ignoble: cheap —*Con* despicable, *contemptible, sorry, scurvy, beggarly
**2** virtuous, righteous, *moral, ethical

---

*Ana* analogous words     *Ant* antonyms     *Con* contrasted words     See also explanatory notes facing page 1

*Ana* honorable, *upright, just, honest

*Ant* base (*of actions*): atrocious (*of acts, deeds*)

**nocturnal** *nightly

*Ant* diurnal

**noise** *n* *sound

*Ana* *din, uproar, babel, hubbub, clamor, racket, pandemonium

**noiseless** silent, quiet, *still, stilly

*Ana* *calm, tranquil, serene, placid

*Con* clamorous, *vociferous, strident, boisterous

**noisome** fetid, stinking, *malodorous, putrid, rank, rancid, fusty, musty

*Ana* foul, nasty, squalid, filthy, *dirty: noxious, baneful, *pernicious, deleterious: loathsome, *offensive, revolting

*Ant* balmy  —*Con* *odorous, fragrant, aromatic, redolent

**nomadic** *itinerant, peripatetic, ambulatory, ambulant, vagrant

**nom de guerre** *pseudonym, alias, pen name, nom de plume, incognito

**nom de plume** pen name, nom de guerre, *pseudonym, alias, incognito

**nominate** *designate, name, elect, appoint

*Ana* propose, *intend, mean, purpose: present, tender, *offer, proffer

**nominee** *candidate, aspirant, applicant

**nonage** *infancy, minority

*Ant* age

**nonchalant** unruffled, imperturbable, unflappable, *cool, composed, collected

*Ana* unconcerned, *indifferent, aloof, detached: lighthearted, cheerful, *glad: *easy, effortless, light, smooth

*Con* concerned, solicitous, anxious, worried, careful (see under CARE *n*)

**non compos mentis** *insane, mad, crazy, crazed, demented, deranged, lunatic, maniac

**nonconformist** *n* dissenter, sectary, sectarian, *heretic, schismatic

**nonesuch** *paragon, apotheosis, nonpareil

**nonmoral** unmoral, amoral, *immoral

**nonpareil** *paragon, apotheosis, nonesuch

**nonplus** bewilder, distract, confound, dumbfound, mystify, perplex, *puzzle

*Ana* faze, rattle, *embarrass, discomfit, disconcert: *confuse, muddle: baffle, balk, *frustrate

**nonreligious** unreligious, *irreligious, ungodly, godless

*Ana* secular, *profane, lay, temporal

**nonsense, twaddle, drivel, bunk, balderdash, poppycock, gobbledygook, trash, rot, bull** are comparable when they mean something said or proposed which is senseless or absurd. **Nonsense** is the most general of these terms; it may be referred to action or behavior as well as to utterances or to proposals, and it may imply foolery or humbuggery as well as absurdity or senselessness ⟨no throaty oratorical *nonsense* was there—*White*⟩ ⟨she told them she would stand no more of their *nonsense*⟩ ⟨then let Esther give up this *nonsense* of hers!—*Deland*⟩ **Twaddle** applies to silly empty utterance and suggests the speech of persons who know nothing about a subject yet talk or write about it foolishly, verbosely, or artlessly ⟨weary of the *twaddle* of theorists⟩ ⟨that reasoning was unadulterated *twaddle*—*Roosevelt*⟩ **Drivel** implies a flow of such idle, inane, or commonplace talk as might befit an imbecile or an idiot; it is a highly contemptuous term for nonsensical spoken or written utterances ⟨phrases which on the face of them may be platitudinous to a degree approaching *drivel*—*Montague*⟩ ⟨writes endless narcissistic *drivel* in a stream-of-consciousness and disorganized manner—*Deutsch*⟩ **Bunk** is an equivalent of

*nonsense* and applies especially to an utterance (as a speech, an opinion, or a doctrine) which, though lacking in real worth or substance, either by intent or by the gullibility of those who listen or accept, hits the popular fancy because it is pretentious, plausible, or high-sounding ⟨they denounced the scheme as *bunk*⟩ **Balderdash** and **poppycock** may apply to confused, turgid, complex utterances that lack or seem to lack sense ⟨a vexing combination of high-flown *balderdash* . . . and threadbare clichés —*Gibbs*⟩ ⟨the *Dissertations* are a fascinating farrago of the soundest linguistic common sense and the most egregious *poppycock*—*Pyles*⟩ but both words may imply an attempt to mislead or deceive by such utterances ⟨repeats more than once the old and obvious *balderdash* that the court . . . eschews the deciding of "political questions"—*Rodell*⟩ ⟨psychology is the youngest of the sciences, and hence chiefly guesswork, empiricism, hocus-pocus, *poppycock*—*Mencken*⟩ and both may suggest an unwillingness to see sense on the part of the one that uses them ⟨Uncle William, who thinks your views are all *poppycock*—*Glasgow*⟩ ⟨nothing looks stronger or less in need of scrutiny than a commonplace, up to the moment when, having outlived its usefulness, it begins to be called *poppycock*—*Gill*⟩ **Gobbledygook** is used of wordy unintelligible jargon especially when featuring the obscure or technical verbiage of some special field ⟨the current law is a masterpiece of complexity and *gobbledygook,* and few will contend that the law is successful at all in distinguishing excess profits from ordinary profits —*Magill*⟩ ⟨the all-too-common passion for pseudo-scientific *gobbledygook*—one of the ill-begotten offspring of excessive specialization—*Odegard*⟩ **Trash, rot,** and **bull** are applicable to utterances regarded as worthless or confusingly inaccurate or misleading. **Trash** may stress the empty worthlessness especially of written material ⟨this book is utter *trash* . . . pure quackery and without scientific standing—*Zirkle*⟩ and **rot,** the user's disbelief or disgust ⟨you are just the sort of woman to believe in that kind of *rot*—*Braddon*⟩ **Bull** in its more general use may apply to a grotesque or ludicrous blunder in language ⟨in their most telling appearance they are, to make a *bull* of it, invisible—*Liebling*⟩ but often it is a slang term denoting trivial, verbose, and commonly boastful or inaccurate utterance ⟨have no fear of "essay exams," even prefer them, and the instructor must watch out for the fine old custom of writing *bull*—*La Farge*⟩ ⟨sat around shooting the *bull*⟩ or facile speech intended to deceive ⟨he said bluntly, "You think I'm givin' you a line o' *bull*— *Harold Sinclair*⟩

*Ana* absurdity, preposterousness, silliness, foolishness (see adjectives at FOOLISH): asininity, fatuousness (see corresponding adjectives at SIMPLE)

**nonsocial** *unsocial, asocial, antisocial

**norm** *average, mean, median, par

**normal** *regular, typical, natural

*Ana* ordinary, *common, familiar: *usual, customary, habitual, wonted, accustomed

*Ant* abnormal

**nosy** *curious, inquisitive, prying, snoopy

*Ana* meddlesome, *impertinent, intrusive, obtrusive

**notable** *noteworthy, memorable

*Ana* *noticeable, remarkable, prominent, outstanding, extraordinary: eminent, celebrated (see FAMOUS)

**note** *vb* remark, notice, perceive, discern, observe, contemplate, survey, view, *see, behold, descry, espy

**note** *n* **1** *sign, mark, token, badge, symptom

*Ana* indication, betokening, bespeaking, attesting (see corresponding verbs at INDICATE): character, *quality, property, attribute, accident

---

A colon (:) separates groups of words discriminated. An asterisk (*) indicates place of treatment of each group.

**2** *remark, observation, comment, commentary, obiter dictum
*Ana* annotation, gloss (see under ANNOTATE): remembering, reminding *or* reminder, recalling (see corresponding verbs at REMEMBER)
**3** *letter, epistle, missive, message, dispatch, report, memorandum
**noteworthy, notable, memorable** mean having some quality that attracts one's attention. **Noteworthy** implies a quality and often a degree of excellence in a person or thing that justifies observation or remark ⟨enough to make a philosopher *noteworthy* . . . not enough to make him great—*Arnold*⟩ ⟨the appearance of a book which formulates a distinct philosophy of life is a rare and *noteworthy* event—*Cohen*⟩ **Notable** too stresses the power of a person or thing to attract attention, but often it distinctively connotes such a special feature as an excellence, a virtue, a value, or a significance that gives rise to its being noted or remembered ⟨the clock kept time with *notable* accuracy and pertinacity—*New Yorker*⟩ ⟨it is a symbol of the abnormality of our days that it should be *notable* when anyone dares stand up and criticize what is happening in America—*Bliven b.* 1889⟩ ⟨Elizabethan and Jacobean poetry . . . had this and that *notable* quality, but, when we wish to admit that it had defects, it is rhetorical—*T. S. Eliot*⟩ **Memorable** stresses the capacity in a person or thing not only of attracting attention but of being worthy to be remembered; it sometimes implies a personal reason for remembrance ⟨a girl with long black hair and a *memorable* figure—*Gibbs*⟩ ⟨for the irrepressible Lyovochka this first venture into the great world beyond the towered gates was a *memorable* event—*Simmons*⟩ ⟨this extravagant temperament endeared him and his work to the public, and it let him write and draw with *memorable* vividness—*Devoe*⟩ ⟨his very occasional compliments, steeped in vinegar though they always were, seem more *memorable* than those of others—*Osbert Sitwell*⟩
*Ana* *noticeable, remarkable, prominent, conspicuous: patent, manifest, *evident
**notice** *vb* remark, observe, note, perceive, discern, *see, behold, descry, espy, view, survey, contemplate
*Ana* recognize, *acknowledge: *refer, advert, allude
*Con* ignore, slight, overlook, disregard, *neglect
**noticeable, remarkable, prominent, outstanding, conspicuous, salient, signal, striking, arresting** can all mean attracting or compelling notice or attention. **Noticeable** implies that the thing so described is unlikely to escape observation ⟨a *noticeable* aversion to his company⟩ ⟨so slight a movement it was barely *noticeable*—a tiny pushing forward of the hand—*Dahl*⟩ **Remarkable** adds to *noticeable* the further implication of inviting comment or of demanding a call to others' attention; it commonly imputes to the thing so described an extraordinary or exceptional character ⟨he has a *remarkable* gift for making friends⟩ ⟨far too much has been written and said about ghosties and ghoulies . . . . They're *remarkable* enough, but have you ever realized that things that are *remarkable* are by definition rare?—*Theodore Sturgeon*⟩ **Prominent** seldom loses its basic implication of protuberance or projection above a level or beyond a surface; it is applied appropriately to things that noticeably protrude from their background ⟨a *prominent* nose⟩ ⟨feeble gleams . . . served to render sufficiently distinct the more *prominent* objects around—*Poe*⟩ In extended use it is applied to persons or things that stand out so clearly from their surroundings that they are often in evidence, are generally known or recognized, or are frequently pointed out; in such use it typically attributes superiority or importance to what it describes ⟨the church occupies a *prominent* position in

the community⟩ ⟨the second *prominent* fault in our reading and thinking is that we have not learned to fix our attention discriminatingly—*Mott*⟩ ⟨with regard to ill fortune . . . fate is given the most *prominent* part—*Linton*⟩ **Outstanding,** although it implies prominence, is applicable only to what rises above or beyond others of the same kind and is remarkable by comparison with them ⟨stories of *outstanding* legislators who had to resign simply because they couldn't afford to serve any longer—*Armbrister*⟩ **Conspicuous** is applicable chiefly to what is so obvious or patent that the eye or the mind cannot miss it ⟨*conspicuous* merit⟩ ⟨*conspicuous* bravery⟩ ⟨there was also some Yankee shrewdness here, for to be *conspicuous*—to be a hero—might entail some untoward financial responsibilities—*Cheever*⟩ It is also used to describe what strikes the eye or the mind, often unpleasantly, through its singularity ⟨wear *conspicuous* clothes⟩ ⟨made himself *conspicuous* by his affectations⟩ ⟨his supporters are *conspicuous* by their absence⟩ ⟨against spending money for cement sidewalks, which he considered *conspicuous* waste—*E. W. Smith*⟩ **Salient** stresses emphatic quality and is applied to what demands the attention or impresses itself insistently upon the mind; it imputes significance more often than obtrusiveness to the thing so described ⟨there are days rich in *salient* news and days far from rich in it—*Montague*⟩ ⟨pick the *salient* details out of dull verbiage—*Marquand*⟩ **Signal** suggests such distinction from what is ordinary or usual that the thing so described is in itself remarkable or memorable ⟨a *signal* mark of esteem⟩ ⟨such an appointment is a *signal* distinction though its value is mainly honorific—*Manoukian*⟩ ⟨Emily Dickinson is a *signal* illustration of this assertion. The imagination of this spinster . . . was constantly aware that the universe surrounded every detail of life—*Thornton Wilder*⟩ **Striking** is applicable to what impresses itself powerfully and deeply upon the observer's mind or vision ⟨one easily remembers the *striking* scenes in a play⟩ ⟨give a *striking* example of loyalty⟩ ⟨a woman of *striking* beauty⟩ ⟨one of the most *striking* and fearful figures in our early fiction—*Parrington*⟩ **Arresting** adds to *striking* the suggestion of capturing attention or of being of more than passing interest ⟨an *arresting* personality⟩ ⟨an *arresting* story⟩ ⟨the slight, steel-colored figure with steel-colored hair, was more *arresting* in its immobility than all the vociferations and gestures of the mob—*Galsworthy*⟩
*Ana* *evident, manifest, obvious, palpable, patent
**notify** apprise, advise, acquaint, *inform
*Ana* announce, *declare, proclaim, publish, promulgate, broadcast: *reveal, disclose, discover, divulge, tell
**notion** *idea, concept, conception, thought, impression
*Ana* *opinion, view, belief, conviction, persuasion, sentiment
**notoriety** reputation, repute, éclat, *fame, celebrity, renown, honor, glory
*Ana* *publicity, ballyhoo, promotion, propaganda
**notwithstanding, in spite of, despite** are often interchangeable prepositions. **Notwithstanding,** the least emphatic, merely implies the presence of an obstacle; **in spite of,** the most emphatic, suggests active opposition or strongly adverse considerations to be encountered; **despite** is somewhat lighter in its emphasis than *in spite of* and otherwise is closer to *notwithstanding* than to *in spite of* ⟨*notwithstanding* the rain, I shall go⟩ ⟨I shall go *in spite of* all your efforts to prevent me⟩ ⟨*despite* his assurances, I doubted him⟩
**nourish** *feed, pasture, graze
*Ana* *nurse, nurture, foster, cultivate
**nourishment** nutriment, sustenance, *food, aliment, pabu-

lum, pap

*Ana* support, keep, maintenance, sustenance, *\*living*

**novel** *adj* *\*new*, new-fashioned, newfangled, modern, modernistic, original, fresh

*Ana* *\*strange*, singular, unique, peculiar

*Con* *\*usual*, customary, habitual: ordinary, *\*common*, familiar

**novice,** **novitiate, apprentice, probationer, postulant, neophyte** are comparable when applied to one who is a beginner, especially in a trade, a profession, a career, or a sphere of life. **Novice** and the less common **novitiate** may be applied to anyone who comes under this description, since inexperience is their chief distinguishing implication ⟨a *novice* in writing⟩ ⟨a *novice* in mountain climbing had better not start with Mount Everest—*Guérard*⟩ ⟨acquaint the *novice* with the manuscripts about which the experts talk—*Monaghan*⟩ ⟨show the Communist *novitiate* as a human being with idealistic impulses— *Daniel Bell*⟩ ⟨*novitiates* to the druidic priesthood required twenty years' training in the mysteries—*C. W. Ferguson*⟩ **Novice** is specifically applied to a new member of a religious order who is undergoing training before taking first and usually not the final vows. **Apprentice** is applicable to a beginner who is serving under another as his master or teacher ⟨a graduate assistant would begin as an *apprentice* to a full-time staff member—*H. R. Bowen*⟩ ⟨the breathless, the fructifying adoration of a young *apprentice* in the atelier of some great master of the Renaissance— *Brooks*⟩ In such applications it emphasizes subjection to supervision and discipline rather than inexperience. It often denotes a young person who is starting his working career as a beginner at a skilled trade under an arrangement involving both work and on-the-job tuition and often a planned schedule of supplementary study or applies to an enlisted man in the United States Navy (usually called in full *apprentice seaman*) who is receiving instruction in seamanship, gunnery, and the rudiments of a general education. **Probationer** designates a beginner who is on trial for a period of time and must prove his aptitude for the work or life ⟨the young ones who are seeking recognition and establishment—the graduate students and the instructors—in general, the *probationers* in the field— *R. M. Weaver*⟩ ⟨the brevity and vanity of this life, in which we are but *probationers*—*Richardson*⟩ **Postulant** implies candidacy for admission (as into a religious order); it may also imply acceptance for a period of probation ⟨the Essenes had books of their own which the *postulant* for admission to their sect had to swear to preserve—*Jeffery*⟩ ⟨words . . . often answering to calls too subtle for analysis, are constantly presenting themselves as *postulants* for recognition—*Fitzedward Hall*⟩ **Neophyte** usually suggests initiation, and is applicable to one who is learning the ways, methods, or principles of something (as an art, a science, a society, a club, or a religious faith) with which he is newly connected ⟨such an encounter usually perplexes the *neophyte* at first—*M. C. Cooke*⟩ It often carries connotations of innocence and youthful eagerness derived from its association with a newly baptized person or convert to Christianity ⟨the old philosopher of Monticello was more than pleased with this ardent *neophyte* . . . . Not since his own years abroad had Jefferson seen such an eager student—*Brooks*⟩

*Ana* beginner, starter, commencer (see corresponding verbs at BEGIN): *\*amateur*, dilettante, dabbler, tyro

**novitiate** *\*novice*, apprentice, probationer, postulant, neophyte

**noxious** baneful, *\*pernicious*, deleterious, detrimental

*Ana* injurious, hurtful, harmful (see corresponding nouns at INJURY): *\*poisonous*, virulent, venomous, toxic, pes-

tilent, miasmatic: noisome, stinking, fetid, putrid (see MALODOROUS)

*Ant* wholesome, sanitary

**nuance** *\*gradation*, shade

*Ana* distinction, difference (see DISSIMILARITY): *\*touch*, suggestion, suspicion, soupçon, dash, tinge: *\*trace*, vestige

**nucleus** *\*center*, middle, midst, core, hub, focus, heart

**nude** *adj* *\*bare*, naked, bald, barren

*Ant* clothed

**nudge** *vb* *\*poke*, prod, jog

*Ana* *\*push*, thrust, shove

**nudge** *n* poke, prod, jog (see under POKE *vb*)

**nugatory** *\*vain*, otiose, idle, empty, hollow

*Ana* worthless, valueless (see affirmative nouns at WORTH): trifling, trivial, *\*petty*, paltry: ineffectual, *\*ineffective*, inefficacious: fruitless, bootless, *\*futile*, vain, abortive

**nullify,** **negate, annul, abrogate, invalidate** in general use are often interchangeable without marked loss. All then mean to deprive of effective or continued existence. One thing **nullifies** another when it reduces the latter to nothingness or deprives it of effectiveness, validity, or value ⟨[his] historical breadth in posing the problem of human life and destiny has been *nullified* . . . by his philosophic narrowness in seeking the answer—*Mumford*⟩ ⟨each of his virtues . . . was *nullified* by some rampant vice— *Buchan*⟩ ⟨when intelligent people murder themselves, or are *nullified* by inertia, or stereotyped by publicity, it's serious—*Morley*⟩ One thing **negates** another when one cannot coexist with the other or both are mutually destructive ⟨our actions often *negate* our principles⟩ ⟨in the water, however, buoyancy largely *negates* gravity, and a mass that would mean crushing death on land is supported under water without trouble—*Asimov*⟩ One thing **annuls** another (see also ANNUL) when it neutralizes the effect of the other or deprives it of power to act or work ⟨mystery does not *annul* meaning but enriches it—*Niebuhr*⟩ ⟨steady, appeasing; mitigating the need, *annulling* even the reason for action—*Boyle*⟩ One thing **abrogates** another (see also ANNUL) when it effectively dispenses with or abolishes the latter ⟨this law *abrogates* the rights of the minority⟩ ⟨*abrogated* their right to the atomic bomb when they drove a few leading scientists from their shores—*Berkner*⟩ One thing **invalidates** another when it deprives the latter of its force or legality. *Invalidate* usually implies failure to meet tests of soundness or to conform to imposed conditions ⟨a beneficiary under a will cannot witness the will without *invalidating* it⟩ ⟨let us try to discover how far the facts confirm or *invalidate* this proud claim—*Huxley*⟩ ⟨he . . . had the misuse of an extensive vocabulary and so was able to *invalidate* a great number of words and expressions—*Connolly*⟩

*Ana* *\*neutralize*, negative, counteract: offset, countervail, counterbalance, *\*compensate*: *\*limit*, restrict, confine

**number** *n* **1** quantity, whole, total, aggregate, *\*sum*, amount

**2 Number, numeral, figure, digit, integer** are comparable when they mean the character or characters by which an arithmetical value is designated. **Number** is the general term and is interchangeable with the others; it may refer to the word as well as to the character or characters ⟨the *number* forty-five⟩ and it may designate an abstraction or may have reference to concrete things ⟨6 is a perfect *number*, that is, it represents the sum of its divisors 1, 2, and 3⟩ ⟨the *number* of books was 1200⟩ A number may be classified as a *cardinal number*, according as it answers the question, how many? ⟨ten or 10 and thirty-three or

A colon (:) separates groups of words discriminated. An asterisk (\*) indicates place of treatment of each group.

33 are *cardinal numbers*⟩ or as an *ordinal number*, according as it indicates order or succession ⟨the *ordinal numbers* first or 1st and second or 2d⟩ **Numeral** is much narrower for it refers only to a cardinal number that is expressed by a character or characters; it therefore stresses the characters more than the values ⟨the Roman *numerals* I, V, X, L, C, D, M⟩ ⟨the Arabic *numerals* 1,2,3 . . .⟩ ⟨a license plate bearing both letters and *numerals*⟩ ⟨the *numerals* on the boys' sweaters indicate their class by telling the year when they will graduate⟩ **Figure** applies to the character representing a numerical value, and usually suggests use of Arabic notation. The term is frequently employed in the plural implying the use of these characters in expressing a number ⟨write all your *numbers* in *figures*⟩ ⟨the cost went into four *figures*⟩ ⟨legally, when there is a discrepancy in a document between *numbers* written out and expressed in *figures*, those written out are accepted⟩ **Digit** may refer to any of the whole numbers from one through nine or the numerals that denote these, or it may expressly refer to any one of the ten Arabic numerals (0, 1, 2, 3, 4, 5, 6, 7, 8, 9) by which all numbers can be expressed ⟨the nine *digits* in arithmetic —*Priestley*⟩ ⟨the numbers in arithmetic are expressed by the . . . ten *digits*—*Charles Hutton*⟩ **Integer** is a mathematical term for a number (*whole number*) that is not or does not contain a fraction ⟨11 2/3 is not an *integer*⟩ ⟨express your answers in *integers*, omitting all fractional parts⟩

**number** *vb* \*count, tell, enumerate
*Ana* \*calculate, compute, estimate, reckon
**numeral** *n* \*number, figure, digit, integer
**numerous** \*many, several, sundry, various, divers, multifarious
*Ana* \*large, great, big: abundant, \*plentiful, plenteous
**nun** \*religious, monk, friar
**nuncio** legate, internuncio, chargé d'affaires, \*ambassador, minister, envoy
**nunnery** \*cloister, monastery, convent, abbey, priory
**nuptial** *adj* \*matrimonial, conjugal, connubial, hymeneal, marital
**nuptial** *n* \*marriage, matrimony, wedlock, wedding, espousal
**nurse** *vb* Nurse, nurture, foster, cherish, cultivate are comparable especially when they mean to give the care necessary to the growth, development, or continued welfare or existence of someone or something. **Nurse** basically implies close care of and attention to someone (as an infant or a sick person) unable to care for himself with the idea of helping that one to grow strong and self-sufficient ⟨he was slowly *nursed* back to health⟩ In extended use the term implies similar sedulous attentions that feed or nourish and thereby strengthen what was at first weak, indefinite, or tentative ⟨when I would muse in boyhood . . . and *nurse* resolves and fancies—*Housman*⟩ ⟨we sat very quiet, not speaking at all, each *nursing* his own

fears and excitements—*Dahl*⟩ ⟨they sulkily avoid his eye, and *nurse* their wrath in silence—*Shaw*⟩ **Nurture** stresses the rearing and training, and so the determination of the course the person, or by extension the thing, will follow ⟨by solemn vision, and bright silver dream, his infancy was *nurtured*—*Shelley*⟩ ⟨reverence for age and authority, even for law, has disappeared; and in the train of these have gone the virtues they engendered and *nurtured*—*Dickinson*⟩ **Foster** implies encouragement or promotion of the growth or increase of something ⟨age, I find, *fosters* the finer feelings—*L. P. Smith*⟩ ⟨everything . . . had *fostered* in the princess a like conviction—*Henry James*⟩ ⟨the teaching that *fosters* these ends succeeds; the teaching which neglects them fails—*Suzzallo*⟩ ⟨governments have deliberately *fostered* nationalistic fervor to serve their own political purposes—*Huxley*⟩ **Cherish** stresses loving, protective care (as of a nurse or a parent for a child, or of a husband for a wife) ⟨to love and to *cherish*, till death do us part—*Anglican Marriage Service: Book of Common Prayer*⟩ In its extended use it is not always distinguishable from *nurse*, but it may retain its implications of holding dear or as a thing of value, and stress prizing and preserving rather than brooding over or causing to increase in strength ⟨tablecloths and napkins . . . washed and ironed again and again, mended and *cherished*—*Shirley Jackson*⟩ ⟨from the first, separately and together, she and I had *cherished* ideals of freedom and independence . . . and cast contempt on the narrow self-absorption of domestic love—*Ellis*⟩ ⟨Julius was a bold iconoclast about republican forms which had survived their usefulness; Augustus sought to *cherish* whatever of these forms could be made to work—*Buchan*⟩ **Cultivate** basically implies the care and attention given to land in order to increase its fertility or to plants in order to improve their condition. In its extended use it implies comparable and equally sedulous attentions to the improvement or growth of some usually desirable thing ⟨his sense of personal initiative is *cultivated* instead of being diminished—*Russell*⟩ ⟨we shall do well to foster the studies most conducive to the habits we wish to *cultivate*—*Grandgent*⟩ ⟨bred to patience—a barmaid since age thirteen—she had *cultivated* and perfected a vast cowlike calm which served her now in good stead—*Pynchon*⟩
*Ana* \*feed, nourish: promote, \*advance, further, forward: \*indulge, pamper, humor
**nurture** *vb* foster, \*nurse, cherish, cultivate
*Ana* raise, rear (see LIFT): train, educate, school, discipline (see TEACH): \*support, uphold, back
*Con* \*neglect, overlook, disregard, ignore
**nutriment** nourishment, sustenance, \*food, aliment, pabulum, pap
*Ana* maintenance, support, keep, bread and butter, \*living

---

*Ana* analogous words    *Ant* antonyms    *Con* contrasted words    See also explanatory notes facing page 1

# O

**obdurate** inexorable, *inflexible, adamant, adamantine
*Ana* *hardened, indurated, callous: *obstinate, stubborn, mulish, stiff-necked: *immovable, immobile
*Con* *tender, compassionate: yielding, submitting, succumbing, relenting (see YIELD)
**obedient,** docile, tractable, amenable, biddable mean submissive to the will, guidance, or control of another. Though applied chiefly to persons, they are sometimes extended to things. **Obedient** implies due compliance with the commands or requests of a person or power whose authority one recognizes or accepts ⟨*obedient* to the law⟩ ⟨he seemed to have lost all power of will; he was like an *obedient* child—*Maugham*⟩ When applied to things it implies compulsion by a superior force or movement in accordance with natural law ⟨tides *obedient* to the moon⟩ ⟨and floating straight, *obedient* to the stream, was carried towards Corinth—*Shak.*⟩ ⟨faces of others seem like stars *obedient* to symmetrical laws—*Spender*⟩ **Docile** implies a responsiveness to teaching, but it stresses either a predisposition to submit to guidance or control or an indisposition to resist impositions or to rebel against authority ⟨that is a question which you must excuse my child from answering. Not, sir, from want of will, for she is *docile* and obedient—*Hudson*⟩ ⟨whatever doctrine is best calculated to make the common people *docile* wage slaves—*Shaw*⟩ ⟨she is a gentle, *docile* person . . . . I think she can be molded into exactly what you would wish her to be —*Gibbons*⟩ **Tractable,** which is nearly as often applied to things as to persons and animals, suggests success or ease in handling or managing ⟨one of the most *tractable* liquid propellants is gasoline—*Space Handbook*⟩ Unlike *docile,* which in many ways it closely resembles, it seldom when applied to persons or animals implies a submissive temperament; thus, a *docile* child is always *tractable,* but a strong-willed child may prove *tractable* when he is wisely guided ⟨kept warning him that it really was pneumonia, and that if he wouldn't be *tractable* he might not get over it—*Day*⟩ ⟨a wave of rebelliousness ran through the countryside. Bulls which had always been *tractable* suddenly turned savage—*George Orwell*⟩ **Amenable** stresses a temperamental willingness or readiness to submit, not so much in the spirit of obedience as because of a desire to be agreeable or because of a natural openness of mind ⟨well, Joan had a broad brow; she thought things over; she was *amenable* to ideas—*H. G. Wells*⟩ ⟨one cannot say that Sean was *amenable,* but he was pliable, and more than that a wife does not need—*Maurice Walsh*⟩ ⟨the question they ask is, would he be *amenable*—would he play ball with the Regulars—*New Republic*⟩ **Biddable,** a more homely word than *docile,* is used chiefly of children ⟨well-behaved children, *biddable,* meek, neat about their clothes, and always mindful of the proprieties—*Cather*⟩ ⟨so used to being *biddable* that words and wishes said and shown by older folks were still like orders to her—*Guthrie*⟩
*Ana* *compliant, acquiescent, resigned: submissive, subdued, *tame: deferential, obeisant (see corresponding nouns at HONOR)
*Ant* disobedient: contumacious —*Con* *insubordinate, rebellious: *contrary, perverse, froward, wayward: recalcitrant, refractory, intractable, *unruly, ungovernable
**obeisance** deference, homage, *honor, reverence
*Ana* allegiance, fealty, loyalty, *fidelity: respect, esteem, *regard: veneration, reverence (see under REVERE)

**obese** corpulent, rotund, chubby, *fleshy, fat, stout, portly, plump
*Ant* scrawny —*Con* *lean, spare, angular, rawboned, lank, lanky, gaunt, skinny: *thin, slender, slim, slight
**obey,** comply, mind are comparable when they mean to follow the wish, direction, or command of another. **Obey** is the general term and implies ready or submissive yielding to the authority of another (as by the performance of his command or bidding) or subjection to a higher principle or to the agency, force, or impulse by which it is actuated ⟨honor and *obey* your father and mother⟩ ⟨the fiercest rebel against society . . . *obeys* most of its conventions—*Muller*⟩ ⟨in the feudal regime, disobedience to an order was treason—or even hesitation to *obey* —*Henry Adams*⟩ ⟨he marks how well the ship her helm *obeys*—*Byron*⟩ ⟨a wholesome and strenuous effort to *obey* at all costs the call of what was felt as "truth"—*Ellis*⟩ **Comply,** often with *with,* usually carries a stronger suggestion than *obey* of giving in to or yielding to a person's desires or expressed requests, the rules of an organization, the requirements of a law, or the conditions of one's environment ⟨she *complied* with them in order to get the instruction, but her own inner fancies broke through—*Dodd*⟩ It therefore often comes close to *conform* and *accommodate* and tends to imply complaisance, dependence, or lack of a strong opinion ⟨if he offered her any more sherry she would not be able to refuse, since all her instinct at this moment was to *comply*—*West*⟩ ⟨the rich woman can terrorize the poor woman by threatening to go to law with her if her demands are not *complied* with—*Shaw*⟩ ⟨on being invited by the brute to go outside, what could Gerald do but *comply?*—*Bennett*⟩ **Mind,** though often used in the sense of *obey,* especially in reference to children ⟨*mind* your mother, Bobby⟩ in a weaker sense carries the implication of heeding or attending to an expressed wish, demand, or command in order that one may comply with it ⟨now *mind,* mother, not a word about Uncle Richard yet—*Lytton*⟩ ⟨but if your reverence *minds* what my wife says, you won't go wrong—*Macdonald*⟩
*Ana* submit, *yield, defer, bow, succumb: accede, acquiesce, subscribe, agree, *assent
*Ant* command, order
**obfuscate** *obscure, dim, bedim, darken, eclipse, cloud, becloud, fog, befog
*Ana* *confuse, muddle, befuddle, fuddle, addle: stupefy, bemuse, *daze: perplex, mystify, bewilder, *puzzle
**obiter dictum** *remark, observation, comment, commentary, note
**object** *n* 1 *thing, article
*Ana* *affair, concern, matter, thing: *form, figure, shape, configuration
2 objective, goal, end, aim, design, purpose, *intention, intent
*Ana* *motive, incentive, inducement
*Con* result, *effect, consequence
**object** *vb* Object, protest, remonstrate, expostulate, kick mean to oppose something (as a course, a procedure, a policy, or a project) especially by making known one's arguments against it. **Object** carries so strong an implication of dislike or aversion that it often is lacking in a clear or definite implication of vocal or other outward opposition, though frequently such a reaction is suggested ⟨why do you always *object* to everything he wishes to do for you⟩ ⟨there's nothing wrong with being painted in the

A colon (:) separates groups of words discriminated. An asterisk (*) indicates place of treatment of each group.

nude; artists do it all the time. But our silly husbands have a way of *objecting* to that sort of thing—*Dahl*⟩ **Protest** (see also ASSERT 1) implies strong opposition and usually the presentation of objections in speech or in writing against the thing to which one objects ⟨the residents of the district unanimously *protested* against the granting of the license⟩ ⟨swearing and *protesting* against every delay in the work—*Anderson*⟩ ⟨she marched with the pickets, *protesting* atmospheric testing—*Kleiner*⟩ **Remonstrate** implies protestation but it carries so much stronger an implication of an attempt to convince or persuade than *protest* carries that it is especially appropriate when the objection is to something being done by a child, a friend, or a relative, rather than by an official or an impersonal agent, or when reproof is also implied ⟨now and then a well-meaning friend of Sir Austin's ventured to *remonstrate* on the dangerous trial he was making in modelling any new plan of education for a youth—*Meredith*⟩ ⟨"Father Joseph," he *remonstrated*, "you will never be able to take all these things back to Denver"—*Cather*⟩ **Expostulate** differs little from *remonstrate*, but it usually carries a heightened implication of firm, earnest, but friendly reasoning or insistence on the merits of one's arguments ⟨the priestly brotherhood . . . prompt to persuade, *expostulate*, and warn—*Cowper*⟩ ⟨lost his temper when reporters at his press conference *expostulated* against playing favorites—*New Republic*⟩ **Kick** implies strenuous protestation and, usually, an exhibition of recalcitrancy or defiance ⟨wherefore *kick* ye at my sacrifice and at mine offering—*1 Sam* 2:29⟩ ⟨when the tax rate was raised for the fourth successive year, everybody *kicked*⟩ ⟨I *kicked* at that and said that Asquith might be limited but he was honest—*Laski*⟩
*Ana* \*demur, balk, scruple, jib, boggle, shy, stick, stickle: \*criticize, denounce, reprobate
*Ant* acquiesce —*Con* \*assent, consent, agree, accede
**objectify** externalize, materialize, incarnate, embody, \*realize, actualize, hypostatize, reify
**objective** *adj* 1 \*material, physical, corporeal, phenomenal, sensible
*Ana* external, outside, \*outer, outward: tangible, palpable, \*perceptible
*Ant* subjective
2 impartial, unbiased, dispassionate, uncolored, \*fair, just, equitable
*Ana & Ant* see those at OBJECTIVE 1
**objective** *n* object, end, goal, aim, design, purpose, \*intention, intent
**objurgate** \*execrate, curse, damn, anathematize
*Ana* revile, vituperate (see SCOLD): condemn, denounce, reprobate, \*criticize
*Con* applaud, \*commend, compliment
**obligation** 1 Obligation, duty are comparable when they denote what a person is bound to do or refrain from doing or for the performance or nonperformance of which he is held responsible. In ordinary usage **obligation** typically implies immediate constraint and a specific reference ⟨he is under the *obligation* of supporting his aged mother⟩ ⟨the place in which folk assembled not only for worship but for the fulfillment of many other social *obligations*, civic, educational, and recreative—*Raven*⟩ ⟨it was plain that Greene was carrying out what he regarded as a fixed *obligation*—*Basso*⟩ ⟨the Ralstons fulfilled their *obligations* as rich and respected citizens—*Wharton*⟩ **Duty**, on the other hand, often suggests less compulsion from immediate circumstances but a greater impulsion on moral or ethical grounds; thus, a person weighed down by a sense of *duty* is keenly aware of what in general he ought to do; one has a sense of *obligation* only in a particular

case and for a particular reason ⟨Stern Daughter of the Voice of God! O *Duty*! if that name thou love who art a light to guide, a rod to check the erring—*Wordsworth*⟩ ⟨the old statesman was now in a sad frame of mind, torn between *duty* and self-interest—*Buchan*⟩ ⟨Russell tries hard to find a place for *duty* in his system; he suggests that we "ought" to do the act that would through its consequences satisfy the widest range of human desires—*Brand Blanshard*⟩
*Ana* compulsion, constraint, restraint (see FORCE *n*): responsibility, accountability, answerability (see corresponding adjectives at RESPONSIBLE)
2 \*debt, indebtedness, liability, debit, arrear
*Ana* burden, \*load: promising *or* promise, engagement, pledging *or* pledge (see corresponding verbs at PROMISE)
**oblige** 1 constrain, coerce, compel, \*force
*Ana* \*tie, bind
2 Oblige, accommodate, favor mean to do a service or courtesy. To **oblige** a person is to make him indebted by doing something that is pleasing to him ⟨Punch was always anxious to *oblige* everybody—*Kipling*⟩ ⟨most hotels . . . will *oblige* if on a particular occasion you wish your meal served at a special time—*Roetter*⟩ It is commonly used as a conventional acknowledgment of small courtesies or offices ⟨there is an oversight . . . which I shall be much *obliged* to you to correct—*Macaulay*⟩ **Accommodate**, when it is used of services, is often interchangeable with *oblige*. Sometimes, especially in the participial adjective, it implies gracious compliance ⟨an *accommodating* host⟩ or it may connote the intent to be of assistance ⟨I was willing to *accommodate* you by undertaking to sell the horse—*George Eliot*⟩ But *accommodate* often suggests a business transaction rather than an act of kindness, and an obligation to pay or repay. In such use it usually implies a loan of money or acceptance as a paying guest (see also CONTAIN) ⟨the bank *accommodated* him with a short-term loan⟩ ⟨the hotel could not *accommodate* the crowd⟩ To **favor**, by contrast, is to render an attention or a service out of goodwill and commonly without imposing an obligation on, or expecting a return from, the person favored ⟨luck *favored* him in all his enterprises⟩ ⟨it was possible for one *favored* by the accidents of pigmentation to pass surreptitiously outside the narrow confines set by the prevailing race conceptions—*Handlin*⟩ Sometimes there is a suggestion of gratuitousness or a patronizing character in the action ⟨*favor* a friend with advice⟩ ⟨the stupidity with which he was *favored* by nature—*Austen*⟩
*Ana* gratify, \*please: \*benefit, profit, avail: \*help, aid, assist: \*support, uphold, back
*Ant* disoblige —*Con* \*inconvenience, incommode, discommode, trouble
**obliging** good-natured, complaisant, \*amiable
*Ana* helping *or* helpful, aiding, assisting (see corresponding verbs at HELP): accommodating, favoring (see OBLIGE): \*compliant, acquiescent: \*thoughtful, considerate
*Ant* disobliging: inconsiderate
**oblique** \*crooked, devious
*Ana* \*awry, askance, askew: \*indirect, circuitous, roundabout
*Con* \*direct, immediate: \*straightforward, forthright: downright, \*forthright
**obliterate** efface, cancel, expunge, \*erase, blot out, delete
*Ana* \*abolish, annihilate, extinguish: \*destroy, raze: annul, abrogate, negate, invalidate, \*nullify
**oblivious** \*forgetful, unmindful
*Ana* disregarding, ignoring, forgetting, neglecting, overlooking (see NEGLECT *vb*)
*Con* \*aware, conscious, cognizant: \*thoughtful, attentive,

considerate: alert, vigilant, *watchful

**obloquy** 1 *abuse, vituperation, invective, scurrility, billingsgate
*Ana* censuring *or* censure, condemning *or* condemnation, denouncing *or* denunciation, criticizing *or* criticism (see corresponding verbs at CRITICIZE): calumny, *detraction, backbiting, slander, scandal
2 *disgrace, dishonor, disrepute, shame, infamy, ignominy, opprobrium, odium
*Ana* *stigma, brand, blot, stain: humiliation, humbling, degradation (see corresponding verbs at ABASE)

**obnoxious** distasteful, invidious, abhorrent, *repugnant, repellent
*Ana* *hateful, odious, detestable, abominable: *offensive, loathsome, repulsive, revolting
*Ant* grateful

**obscene** gross, vulgar, ribald, *coarse
*Ana* indecent, indelicate, *indecorous: lewd, lascivious, wanton, *licentious: foul, nasty, *dirty
*Ant* decent

**obscurantist** *n* Obscurantist, philistine, barbarian denote one inaccessible or opposed to enlightenment. An **obscurantist** is one who is precluded (as by prejudice, traditionalism, or bigotry) from intellectual candor and open-minded inquiry and who is opposed to the introduction of new and enlightened ideas and methods ⟨from this class of *obscurantists* who had hitherto resisted all Western innovations there now came young leaders eager to emulate Japan—*Peace Handbooks*⟩ ⟨if liberals have not always recognized this, their opponents—*obscurantists*, authoritarians, and enemies of enlightenment and scientific method—have amply done so—*Cohen*⟩ ⟨as soon as one begins to hint that the strain of wickedness in the human race . . . is still with us, he is called an *obscurantist* and is disqualified from further public hearing—*R. M. Weaver*⟩ A **philistine** is one whose attention is centered on material or worldly things, and is indifferent or blind to whatever makes an appeal only to the mind or soul. The term usually implies obtuseness and insensitiveness ⟨it is only the *Philistine* who seeks to estimate a personality by the vulgar test of production—*Wilde*⟩ ⟨the *Philistine* wants to talk about morals, not to understand what is morally wrong—*Farrell*⟩ **Barbarian** seldom wholly loses the notion of incompletely civilized that so strongly characterizes the adjective *barbarian*. As a result the term may be applied aptly to one whose cultural deficiency suggests that befitting a lower or more remote stage of civilization ⟨teachers of freshman composition and mathematics search in vain for even an awareness of the recurring problem of each year's new invasion by lovable but illiterate *barbarians* who have to be taught the elements of grammar and arithmetic —*Gideonse*⟩ ⟨have him take his meals in the dining room . . . . Let him sit with me, or he'll grow up a *barbarian*, with no manners—*Deland*⟩

**obscure** *adj* 1 murky, gloomy, *dark, dim, dusky
*Ana* shady, shadowy, umbrageous (see corresponding nouns at SHADE)
*Con* *clear, lucid: *bright, brilliant, luminous
2 Obscure, dark, vague, enigmatic, cryptic, ambiguous, equivocal are applied to language or expression (or less often to causes, motives, or thoughts) with the meaning not sufficiently intelligible or clearly understood. Something is **obscure** the true meaning of which is hidden or veiled, because of some fault or defect either in the thing itself or in the person trying to understand it ⟨that decorum and orderliness without which all written speech must be ineffective and *obscure*—*Ellis*⟩ ⟨this sordid, often *obscure* book, without visible motive or meaning—*Purdy*⟩ ⟨the mere text of the play will often look scrappy and disjointed

and *obscure* to a reader who does not bring to it the special theatrical imagination—*Montague*⟩ Something is **dark** which is imperfectly revealed and therefore mysterious ⟨I will utter *dark* sayings—*Ps* 78:2⟩ ⟨*dark* hints of revenge⟩ ⟨"Poison!" he whispered. But he pronounced it *pye-zn*, making it into a soft, *dark*, dangerous word—*Dahl*⟩ Something is **vague** which is lacking in distinct outlines or in clear definition, either because it is too general or because it is so imperfectly conceived or thought out that it is incapable of clear formulation ⟨managed to gain from Judith a *vague* half-promise that she would be ready as suggested—*Gibbons*⟩ ⟨we shall never gain power from *vague* discourse about unknown or unassimilated facts—*Grandgent*⟩ Something is **enigmatic** which puzzles, mystifies, and, often, baffles one seeking its true meaning or significance ⟨the *enigmatic* announcement was an appropriate addition to the tangled story of this country's oddest piece of real estate—*Thruelsen*⟩ ⟨here Shaw's stage direction . . . has the additional advantage of being so *enigmatic* that even the reader cannot understand it without aid from other Shavian sources—*Nethercot*⟩ ⟨puzzling out the threats, or the *enigmatic* promises, of a starry sky—*Pater*⟩ Something is **cryptic** which is stated or expressed darkly or enigmatically; the word often implies a definite intention to perplex or to challenge ⟨you had to intercede, with your *cryptic* innuendoes and mysterious head-waggings—*S. S. Van Dine*⟩ ⟨gave *cryptic* indications of his doubts but prudently refrained from open statements of them—*Davies*⟩ Something is **ambiguous** which admits of more than one interpretation, largely because of the use of words having a dual or multiple meaning without giving an indication of which sense is intended ⟨the title of this chapter is *ambiguous*. It promises a discussion of the end of the world, but it does not say which end—*Eddington*⟩ ⟨we are here not far from the *ambiguous* doctrine that art is "expression," for "expression" may be too easily confused with "communication"—*Ellis*⟩ Something is **equivocal** which permits a wrong or false impression, thereby admitting uncertainty and confusion or fostering error. As applied to use of words, *equivocal* is distinguishable from *ambiguous* in that it may suggest intent to deceive or evade ⟨nor could he find much pleasure in the subtle, devious, and *equivocal* utterances of Solomon—*Omnibook*⟩ ⟨veil the matter with utterances capable of more *equivocal* meaning—*H. O. Taylor*⟩ In extended use *equivocal* is applied to something such as an act or a mode of life that admits of two possible or plausible interpretations, one of which may be harmful or discreditable ⟨*equivocal* conduct⟩ ⟨an *equivocal* gesture⟩
*Ana* abstruse, *recondite, occult, esoteric: difficult, *hard: complicated, intricate, involved (see COMPLEX): *mysterious, inscrutable
*Ant* distinct, obvious: celebrated (*as a person*) —*Con* *clear, perspicuous, lucid: *evident, manifest, obvious: express, *explicit, definite

**obscure** *vb* Obscure, dim, bedim, darken, eclipse, cloud, becloud, fog, befog, obfuscate all mean to make dark, indistinct, or confused. Of these terms *obscure, dim, bedim,* and *darken* all suggest the effect obtained by the lessening or the removal of illumination—the making of an object difficult to see clearly or the weakening or impairing of the ability to see with the eye or the mind. **Obscure** stresses the indistinctness, often concealment, of the object or idea or the unclearness of the vision or the comprehension ⟨there are readers of papers who . . . like the ordinary, average day, with its good human humdrum; they do not want to have its nature denied or *obscured* —*Montague*⟩ ⟨the faded yellow building, its original

---

A colon (:) separates groups of words discriminated. An asterisk (*) indicates place of treatment of each group.

austerity of line somewhat *obscured* by a comfortable porch—*Amer. Guide Series: Vt.*⟩ **Dim** and **bedim** stress the diminishing of light or of clarity, intensity, or luster or the consequent diminishing of capacity to see, distinguish, or comprehend ⟨celestial tears *bedimmed* her large blue eyes—*Byron*⟩ ⟨the old patriotic glow began to *dim* its ineffectual fires—*H. M. Jones*⟩ **Darken**, although like *dim* and *bedim* suggesting a diminishing of illumination, is much richer metaphorically in suggesting strongly the alteration of an object or the impairment of clear or normal vision or mental comprehension by reason of confusion, ignorance, or evil ⟨the yearly migrations of passenger pigeons . . . literally *darkening* the sky—*Amer. Guide Series: Mich.*⟩ ⟨his intellect was indeed *darkened* by many superstitions and prejudices—*Macaulay*⟩ ⟨evils enough to *darken* all his goodness—*Shak.*⟩ **Eclipse** may stand alone in suggesting the effect of an actual astronomical eclipse, the partial or total darkening or concealment of one object by another and, hence, the overshadowing or supplanting of one object by another ⟨in the English field, Anglo-Saxon never *eclipsed* the study of Shakespeare or Milton—*Guérard*⟩ **Cloud, becloud, fog, befog,** and **obfuscate** all suggest the obstruction or impairment of vision by clouds, fog, or vapor or, in extended use, the making of the mental perception or object of that perception murky or confused. *Cloud* and *becloud* stress the obscuring of the object, or the murky view of the object, **becloud** being somewhat more literary than **cloud** ⟨the beginnings of our physical universe are necessarily *beclouded* in the swirling mists of countless ages past—*F. L. Whipple*⟩ ⟨smoke *clouding* the prospect before us⟩ ⟨the actual issues *clouded* by prejudice and politics⟩ ⟨reasoning *clouded* by hysteria⟩ *Fog* and *befog* are applied possibly more frequently than *cloud* and *becloud* to matters of the understanding or mental comprehension and usually suggest a greater obstruction or impairment of clear vision of eye and mind and, so, a greater and more unnecessary indistinctness, illogicality, or confusion; **fog**, however, occurs freely in both the basic sense and extended or metaphorical use while **befog** is uncommon in literal application ⟨their breaths *fogged* the windshield—*Hunter*⟩ ⟨a time of . . . pressure for him and, if his memory *fogged* slightly, he was not alone—*S. L. A. Marshall*⟩ ⟨questions of . . . shaking hands or not *befog* many people—*Miall*⟩ ⟨the willfully created misunderstandings that so often *befog* the American political scene—*Sandburg*⟩ **Obfuscate**, a somewhat pompous word, suggests strongly an avoidable, often willful, obscuring of an object or confusing of the mind by darkening or illogicality ⟨the process, not of enlightening, but of *obfuscating* the mind—*Thoreau*⟩
*Ana* *hide, conceal, screen: *disguise, cloak, mask, camouflage: *misrepresent, belie, falsify
*Ant* illuminate, illumine

**obsequious** *subservient, servile, slavish, menial
*Ana* deferential, obeisant (see corresponding nouns at HONOR): *compliant, acquiescent: sycophantic, parasitic, toadyish (see corresponding nouns at PARASITE): cringing, fawning, truckling, cowering (see FAWN *vb*)
*Ant* contumelious

**observation** *remark, comment, commentary, note, obiter dictum
*Ana* *opinion, view, belief: annotation, gloss (see under ANNOTATE): *criticism, critique

**observe** 1 *keep, celebrate, solemnize, commemorate
*Ana* respect, esteem, regard (see under REGARD *n*): *revere, reverence, venerate
*Ant* violate —*Con* *neglect, ignore, overlook, disregard, slight

2 survey, view, contemplate, notice, remark, note, perceive, discern, *see, behold, descry, espy
*Ana* *scrutinize, examine, scan, inspect

**observer** *spectator, beholder, looker-on, onlooker, witness, eyewitness, bystander, kibitzer

**obsolete** *old, antiquated, archaic, antique, ancient, venerable, antediluvian
*Ant* current

**obstacle, obstruction, impediment, bar, snag** denote something which seriously hampers action or progress. **Obstacle**, which is used of both material and immaterial things, applies to an object, condition, or situation which stands in one's way and must be removed or surmounted if one is to progress or attain one's ends ⟨love seats especially constructed for ardent couples who find such devices as armrests an *obstacle* to affectionate hips and hands—*Green Peyton*⟩ ⟨they smash themselves against the *obstacles* of circumstance—*Cloete*⟩ ⟨as to other social advancement, his record was an *obstacle*—*S. H. Adams*⟩ **Obstruction** may be used of immaterial things, but such use is often obviously figurative, for the word suggests a blocking of a way or passage ⟨an intestinal *obstruction*⟩ ⟨any phrase repeated too often becomes an *obstruction* to the flow of thought and feeling. It forms a clot—*Crothers*⟩ ⟨a very much denser *obstruction* is in the process of being erected now by literary critics—*Day Lewis*⟩ **Impediment** is applied to something material or immaterial which serves to hinder or delay action or progress until one is freed from it ⟨the refugee's limited knowledge of English was for a long time an *impediment* to his progress in his profession⟩ ⟨I have made my way through more *impediments* than twenty times your stop —*Shak.*⟩ ⟨legal restriction is a less effective *impediment* than the general sentiment that respectable people do not discuss birth control—*Petersen*⟩ **Bar** applies to something interposed, whether by nature or by man, which serves to prevent admission or escape as effectually as the bars of a cage or prison ⟨long sentences are a *bar* to easy reading—*Mott*⟩ Sometimes the word carries a strong suggestion of prohibition, especially when it applies to a law or condition that restrains ⟨under the immigration laws, a criminal record, an infectious disease, and illiteracy are *bars* to admission to the United States⟩ ⟨he found his infirmity no *bar* to his success in his profession⟩ ⟨must I new *bars* to my own joy create?—*Dryden*⟩ **Snag**, from its application to a stump of a tree with jagged points which lies hidden under water and proves a hazard to boats, is extended to an obstacle or impediment which is hidden from view and which one encounters suddenly and unexpectedly ⟨might run into a *snag* on the question of whether federal aid should be extended—*W. H. Lawrence*⟩ Sometimes *snag* suggests a mere temporary impediment ⟨after an early *snag* . . . he was able to proceed with his work—*The Irish Digest*⟩
*Ana* barrier, *bar: hindering *or* hindrance, blocking *or* block (see corresponding verbs at HINDER)

**obstinate, dogged, stubborn, pertinacious, mulish, stiffnecked, pigheaded, bullheaded** are comparable when they mean fixed or unyielding by temperament or nature. **Obstinate** implies persistent adherence, especially against persuasion or attack, to an opinion, purpose, or course; when applied to persons or to their ideas or behavior the term often suggests unreasonableness or perversity rather than steadfastness ⟨they will not be resolute and firm, but perverse and *obstinate*—*Burke*⟩ ⟨so yielding doubtful points that he can be firm without seeming *obstinate* in essential ones—*J. R. Lowell*⟩ ⟨she was—is—a damned *obstinate* old girl, and the more he swore it was Elsie, the more she swore it was Deacon—*Sayers*⟩ ⟨unfortunately

grammar is the subject that of all others arouses the most *obstinate* propensities in the human mind—*Richards*⟩ **Dogged** adds the implication of downright and tenacious, sometimes sullen, persistence; usually, also, it connotes great determination or an unwavering purpose ⟨*dogged* veracity⟩ ⟨*dogged* perseverance⟩ ⟨men whose hearts insist upon a *dogged* fidelity to some image or cause— *Hardy*⟩ ⟨his mother's influence was to make him quietly determined, patient, *dogged*, unwearied—*D. H. Lawrence*⟩ ⟨had a hard personality in those days . . . *dogged*, not altogether fair—*Mailer*⟩ **Stubborn** is often used interchangeably with *obstinate* and *dogged*, for it implies the unyielding adherence of the one and the tenacious determination of the other; more strongly than either of them, however, it carries an implication of a native fixedness of character or of a deeply rooted quality that makes a person sturdily resistant to attempts to change his purpose, course, or opinion, or that makes a thing highly intractable to those who would work it, treat it, or manipulate it ⟨there is something *stubborn* in him that makes him follow his own path even though he isn't certain where it goes— *Malcolm Cowley*⟩ ⟨Paddy and his old mare are teamed up . . . man and beast joined against *stubborn* nature— *A. F. Wolfe*⟩ ⟨it was all but impossible for the carpenter ever to admit himself in the wrong; but upon this occasion he swallowed his *stubborn* pride—*Nordhoff & Hall*⟩ ⟨poetry whose democracy is tempered by a *stubborn* conviction that democracy thwarts the development of the individual at its peril—*Lowes*⟩ **Pertinacious** lacks, as compared with *obstinate*, the implication of resistance, and as compared with *stubborn*, the suggestion of inherent quality; it usually implies a chosen course and stresses its pursuit with stick-to-itiveness and, often. with a persistence that is annoying or irksome ⟨a *pertinacious* beggar⟩ ⟨his originality lay not in any purely speculative views, but in the *pertinacious* curiosity, practical in its origin and aim, with which he attacked and sifted the ethical conceptions of his time—*Dickinson*⟩ ⟨arrive and look with becoming modesty at the photographers. These cynical and *pertinacious* gentlemen do not disappoint them— *Munro*⟩ **Mulish** suggests an obstinacy as characteristic or as unreasonable as that of a mule ⟨a *mulish* determination to make the worst of everything—*T. S. Eliot*⟩ ⟨a fierce, hot, hard, old, stupid squire . . . small brain, great courage, *mulish* will—*Masefield*⟩ **Stiff-necked,** more even than *obstinate* or *stubborn*, stresses inflexibility; it often also suggests a haughtiness or arrogance that makes one incapable of respecting the commands, wishes, or suggestions of others ⟨be ye not *stiff-necked*, as your fathers were, but yield yourselves unto the Lord —*2 Chron* 30:8⟩ ⟨she would have felt *stiff-necked* and ridiculous if she had resisted, like a republican who refuses to stand up in a London theater when "God Save the King" is played—*West*⟩ ⟨he was formidably upright . . . too *stiff-necked* to kneel—*Dorothy Thompson*⟩ **Pigheaded** and *bullheaded* suggest a particularly perverse or stupid kind of obstinacy; therefore they are chiefly terms of severe reproach; **pigheaded**, however, often suggests impenetrability to argument and **bullheaded**, headstrong determination ⟨many of the managing posts will be filled up by *pigheaded* people only because they happen to have the habit of ordering poor people about—*Shaw*⟩ ⟨there was to be no relieving intermission. Using my prerogative as author, I had been *bullheaded* on this point —*Paul Green*⟩ ⟨she's so *bullheaded*. She always has to have her way—*Ginder*⟩
*Ana* headstrong, willful, recalcitrant, *unruly: obdurate, inexorable, *inflexible: resolute, steadfast, staunch (see FAITHFUL)

*Ant* pliant, pliable  —*Con* *plastic, malleable, ductile: submitting *or* submissive, yielding, succumbing (see corresponding verbs at YIELD): *compliant, acquiescent
**obstreperous** *vociferous, clamorous, blatant, strident, boisterous
*Ana* *unruly, ungovernable, intractable, headstrong, refractory: uproarious, rackety (see corresponding nouns at DIN)
*Con* restrained, curbed, checked (see RESTRAIN): quiet, *still, silent, noiseless
**obstruct** impede, block, *hinder, bar, dam
*Ana* *prevent, preclude, obviate, avert: *restrain, check, curb, inhibit
**obstruction** *obstacle, impediment, bar, snag
*Ana* hindering *or* hindrance, blocking *or* block (see corresponding verbs at HINDER): arresting *or* arrest, checking *or* check, interruption (see corresponding verbs at ARREST)
*Ant* assistance  —*Con* forwarding, furthering, promoting *or* promotion, advancing *or* advancement (see corresponding verbs at ADVANCE)
**obtain** *get, procure, secure, acquire, gain, win
*Ana* gain, *reach, achieve, attain: effect, fulfill, accomplish, *perform
**obtrude** *intrude, interlope, butt in
*Ana* *interpose, interfere, intervene, mediate
**obtrusive** intrusive, meddlesome, *impertinent, officious
*Ana* inquisitive, *curious, prying, snoopy, nosy: blatant, strident (see VOCIFEROUS)
*Ant* unobtrusive: shy
**obtuse** *dull, blunt
*Ana* insensitive, *insensible, anesthetic, impassible: stolid, phlegmatic, *impassive
*Ant* acute  —*Con* *sharp, keen: sensitive, susceptible, open, exposed (see LIABLE)
**obverse** *n* *converse, reverse
**obviate** preclude, *prevent, avert, ward
*Ana* evade, elude, avoid, *escape: forestall, anticipate, *prevent: *interpose, interfere, intervene
**obvious** *evident, manifest, patent, distinct, apparent, palpable, plain, clear
*Ana* prominent, conspicuous, salient, signal, striking (see NOTICEABLE)
*Ant* obscure: abstruse
**occasion** *n* 1 *opportunity, chance, break, time
*Ana* *juncture, pass: situation, posture, condition, *state: moment, *instant
2 *cause, determinant, antecedent, reason
*Ana* incident, *occurrence, event: *origin, source, inception
**occasional** *infrequent, uncommon, scarce, rare, sporadic
*Ana* casual, desultory, *random: incidental, *accidental
*Ant* customary  —*Con* *usual, habitual, accustomed, wonted: constant, *continual, continuous
**occult** esoteric, *recondite, abstruse
*Ana* *mysterious, inscrutable, arcane: mystic, cabalistic, *mystical, anagogic
**occupation** employment, *work, calling, pursuit, business
**occur** *happen, chance, befall, betide, transpire
*Ana* rise, arise, *spring, emanate, issue, proceed: *follow, succeed, ensue, supervene
**occurrence,** **event, incident, episode, circumstance** are comparable when they denote something that happens or takes place. **Occurrence** is the general term for something which takes place ⟨such a happy and convenient *occurrence*, the princess's conversion—*H. G. Wells*⟩ ⟨chanced to witness Pussy's death—happily no common *occurrence*, as a cat, like an Englishman, considers dying a strictly private affair—*Repplier*⟩ ⟨I have not . . . quoted conversation or described *occurrence* from the private

---

A colon (:) separates groups of words discriminated. An asterisk (*) indicates place of treatment of each group.

life of named or recognizable living persons—*Yeats*⟩ **Event** is frequently regarded as arising from an antecedent state of things and is usually applied to a more or less important or noteworthy occurrence ⟨the *events* of the year⟩ ⟨the sequence of *events* that followed the declaration of war⟩ ⟨the course of human *events*—*U.S. Declaration of Independence*⟩ ⟨*events* acting upon us in unexpected, abrupt, and violent ways—*Dewey*⟩ ⟨the flat, monotonous plains stretch away . . . a single tree . . . becomes an *event*—*Moorehead*⟩ An **incident** (compare *incidental* under ACCIDENTAL) is commonly an occurrence of subordinate character or secondary importance, either a mere casual happening having little relation to major events or an occurrence that merely follows because of them ⟨her tone implied that bedroom fires were a quite ordinary *incident* of daily life in a place like Bursley—*Bennett*⟩ ⟨very few individuals can be considered as more than *incidents* in the life histories of the societies to which they belong—*Linton*⟩ The term may, however, be used of a single event that stands out or is marked off clearly from the other events (as in a story, a play, or a history) in its nature or significance ⟨the book narrates a series of thrilling *incidents*⟩ ⟨he was delighted and looked upon the *incident* as an adventure—*Anderson*⟩ ⟨and beat him she did—in just over 72 days—with only one dangerous *incident*. A "titled cad" tried to flirt with her—*Sat. Review*⟩ or applied to a critical event that provokes a break in diplomatic relations between countries or suggests the possibility of war ⟨border *incidents*⟩ **Episode** (see also DIGRESSION) is often used in place of *incident* in the sense of a single or outstanding event, but the term usually carries a stronger implication of distinctiveness or apartness from the main course than does *incident* ⟨a pretty little domestic *episode* occurred this morning—*Meredith*⟩ ⟨Clare would inevitably . . . come to regard her passion for Oliver Hobart and its tragic sequel as a romantic *episode* of girlhood—*Rose Macaulay*⟩ **Circumstance** is used as a synonym of *incident* only when the latter is thought of as a specific or significant detail ⟨before closing his door for the night, [he] stood reflecting on the *circumstances* of the preceding hours —*Hardy*⟩ The word is also occasionally used as a synonym for *event* in its more general sense ⟨a life every *circumstance* of which is regulated after an unchangeable pattern—*Wilde*⟩
*Ana* appearance, emergence (see corresponding verbs at APPEAR): *juncture, pass, exigency, emergency, contingency: posture, situation, condition, *state

**oceanic** *aquatic, marine, thalassic, neritic, pelagic, abyssal, lacustrine, fluvial, fluviatile

**odd** queer, quaint, *strange, singular, unique, peculiar, eccentric, erratic, outlandish, curious
*Ana* bizarre, grotesque, *fantastic: anomalous, *irregular, unnatural
*Con* *usual, customary, habitual: ordinary, *common, familiar: normal, *regular, typical, natural

**odds** *advantage, handicap, allowance, edge

**odious** *hateful, abhorrent, abominable, detestable
*Ana* *repugnant, repellent, distasteful, obnoxious: *offensive, loathsome, repulsive, revolting

**odium** obloquy, opprobrium, ignominy, infamy, *disgrace, dishonor, disrepute, shame
*Ana* *hate, hatred: *antipathy, aversion: abhorrence, abomination, detestation, loathing (see under HATE *vb*)

**odor** *smell, scent, aroma
*Ana* *fragrance, perfume, redolence, incense, bouquet

**odorous, fragrant, redolent, aromatic, balmy** mean emitting and diffusing scent. **Odorous** applies to whatever has a strong, distinctive smell, whether it is pleasant or not

⟨*odorous* flowers such as lilies, tuberoses, and narcissuses⟩ ⟨*odorous* chemicals are often malodorous⟩ ⟨*odorous* gums from the East—*Wilde*⟩ ⟨ability to detect and to identify infinitesimally small traces of *odorous* and savory materials—*Morrison*⟩ **Fragrant** applies to something with a sweet and agreeable odor, especially to flowers, fruits, spices, and beverages that through their lingering sweetness or richness of scent give sensuous delight ⟨*fragrant* roses⟩ ⟨where the *fragrant* limes their boughs unite, we met—and we parted forever!—*Crawford*⟩ ⟨perhaps far back . . . certain Chinese preferred *fragrant* tea to insipid water—*Heiser*⟩ ⟨the recollection that these unfortunates had once been *fragrant* children—*Cheever*⟩ **Redolent** occasionally means pleasantly odorous; in such use it applies not only to things that diffuse a scent but to the scent itself ⟨the *redolent* scent of pine⟩ ⟨every flower and every fruit the *redolent* breath of the warm seawind ripeneth—*Tennyson*⟩ More often it applies to a place or thing impregnated with odors, especially with those that are penetrating ⟨dim, shady wood roads, *redolent* of fern and bayberry—*Millay*⟩ ⟨ordinary salt air but stronger, *redolent* of seaweed, damp, and dead fish—*Nancy Hale*⟩ ⟨the air for half a block was *redolent* with the fumes of beer and whiskey—*Asbury*⟩ **Aromatic** is more restricted in its implications than *aroma*, for it distinctively suggests a pungent, often fresh, odor of the kind associated with the foliage of balsams, pine, and spruce, the wood of cedar, the dried leaves of lavender, such spices as cloves, and such gums as myrrh. It is therefore often applied to preparations scented with substances that are aromatic ⟨*aromatic* blends of tobacco⟩ ⟨as *aromatic* plants bestow no spicy fragrance while they grow; but crushed, or trodden to the ground, diffuse their balmy sweets around—*Goldsmith*⟩ ⟨*aromatic* spirit of ammonia⟩ **Balmy** applies chiefly to things which have a delicate and soothing aromatic odor ⟨the *balmy* winds breathed the animating odors of the groves around me—*Bartram*⟩ ⟨their tender beauty of *balmy*, flowery vegetation—*Muir*⟩
*Ant* malodorous: odorless —*Con* stinking, fetid, noisome, putrid, rank, rancid, fusty, musty (see MALODOROUS)

**offal** *refuse, waste, rubbish, trash, debris, garbage

**offend, outrage, affront, insult** mean to cause vexation or resentment or damage to self-respect. One **offends** by displeasing another, by hurting his feelings, or by violating his sense of what is proper or fitting ⟨if the First Amendment means anything, it means that a man cannot be sent to prison merely for distributing publications which *offend* a judge's esthetic sensibilities—*Potter Stewart*⟩ ⟨fangless perceptions which will please the conservative power and delight the liberal power, *offend* no one—*Mailer*⟩ ⟨knew that he had *offended* his father but guilt would have been too exact a word for the pain and uneasiness he felt—*Cheever*⟩ One **outrages** by offending another past endurance, or by offending his pride or his sense of justice or honor ⟨her power to make him do things which *outraged* all his upbringing—*Sackville-West*⟩ ⟨listened to the beginning of the uproar, the shrill cries of the ladies and the *outraged* unbelieving exclamations of the men— *Dahl*⟩ ⟨"Grief of two years' standing is only a bad habit." Alice started, *outraged*. Her mother's grief was sacred to her—*Shaw*⟩ One **affronts** who, either with an intent to offend or with deliberate indifference to civility or courtesy, humiliates or dishonors a person and arouses his deep resentment ⟨a moral, sensible, and well-bred man will not *affront* me, and no other can—*Cowper*⟩ One **insults** who wantonly and insolently offends another so as to cause him humiliation or shame ⟨you can annoy, you can *insult*, you cannot move me—*Meredith*⟩ ⟨he would *insult* them flagrantly; he would fling his hands in the air

and thunder at their ignorance—*Auchincloss*⟩
*Ana* *annoy, vex, irk, bother: exasperate, nettle, *irritate: pique, *provoke, excite: chafe, fret, gall (see ABRADE)
**offense** 1 offensive, aggression, *attack
*Ana* assault, *attack, onslaught, onset
2 **Offense, resentment, umbrage, pique, dudgeon, huff** are comparable when they mean a person's emotional reaction to what he regards as a slight, an affront, an insult, or an indignity. **Offense** implies an often extreme state of displeasure or of wounded feelings ⟨he is so sensitive that he takes *offense* at any unintentional or seeming slight⟩ ⟨this tiny breath of genuine criticism had given deep *offense*—*Forster*⟩ **Resentment** implies more indignation than *offense*, more prolonged dwelling upon what one regards as a personal injury or grievance, and, often, more ill will to the person who has offended ⟨as long as I am free from all *resentment* . . . I would be able to face the life with much more calm—*Wilde*⟩ ⟨have no right to trifle with their lives merely to gratify an old man's *resentment* of skepticism—*Anthony Boucher*⟩ **Umbrage**, used chiefly in the phrase "to take umbrage," differs from *offense* in carrying a clearer implication of being slighted or unfairly ignored; the term therefore generally suggests ruffled pride, resentful suspicion of others' motives, or jealousy of those favored ⟨he took such *umbrage* at Eliot —who had been delayed at his bank—arriving a few minutes late on the platform, that I doubt he ever forgave him—*Osbert Sitwell*⟩ Very often *umbrage* is not clearly distinguishable from *offense* ⟨the instance of a Southern defender who took *umbrage* at our saying that the leader of the Confederacy was outstandingly dumb—*N. Y. Herald Tribune Book Rev.*⟩ **Pique** applies to the reaction of one who has taken offense or umbrage, but it distinctively suggests a petty cause and a transient mood and often connotes wounded vanity ⟨when the wanton heroine chooses to . . . flirt with Sir Harry or the Captain, the hero, in a *pique*, goes off and makes love to somebody else—*Thackeray*⟩ ⟨had not for . . . years allowed his young green jealousy to show itself in words or *pique*—*Buck*⟩ **Dudgeon** applies chiefly to a fit of angry resentment or indignation provoked by opposition to one's views or a refusal of one's request ⟨left the recent meeting in high *dudgeon* when compulsory purchase powers were eventually granted—*Ian MacLennan*⟩ ⟨sometimes the employer . . . will in a *dudgeon* refuse to sit in the same room with the union representatives—*Bromley*⟩ **Huff**, like *dudgeon*, applies to a fit of anger, but it comes closer to *pique* in suggesting pettiness of cause and transitoriness; distinctively it implies petulance and a sulky refusal to have more to do with those who have offended ⟨at the first hint that we were tired of waiting and that we should like the show to begin, he was off in a *huff*—*Henry James*⟩ ⟨half of 'em will be disgusted, and go away in a *huff*— *De Morgan*⟩
*Ana* *affront, insult, indignity: indignation, wrath, *anger
*Con* *pleasure, delight, joy: gratifying *or* gratification, rejoicing (see corresponding verbs at PLEASE)
3 **Offense, sin, vice, crime, scandal** are comparable as general terms denoting a more or less serious or conspicuous infraction or transgression of law or custom. **Offense** is the term of widest application, being referable to a violation of any law, including the law of the state, the law of the church, natural law, moral law, or standards of propriety and taste set up (as by society or the arts). It is also applicable to any transgression regardless of its triviality or gravity or its voluntary or involuntary character, provided it injures or tends to injure the welfare or well-being or happiness of others ⟨O, my *offense* is rank, it smells to heaven; it hath the primal eldest curse upon't, a broth-

er's murder—*Shak.*⟩ ⟨had been a strike leader, which, though not a crime, was certainly an *offense* in New England in 1920—*Stong*⟩ ⟨the greater the number of laws, the greater the number of *offenses* against them—*Ellis*⟩ **Sin** primarily applies to an offense against the moral law especially as laid down in the Ten Commandments and in laws derived from them. Theologically its essential character is disobedience of the divine will and willful opposition to the law of God; in somewhat wider use it implies a failure to live up to the moral ideals of one's time or environment or to the moral ideal one has set as the standard of one's own conduct ⟨regarded stealing and lying as *sins*⟩ ⟨the *sin* of sacrilege⟩ ⟨nonobservance of the Sabbath was the *sin* most abhorred by the settlers of that region⟩ ⟨*sin*, remember, is a twofold enormity. It is a base consent to the promptings of our corrupt nature . . . and it is also a turning away from the counsel of our higher nature— *Joyce*⟩ ⟨it may not have been much of a culture, crude, bloodthirsty, harsh, and worst *sin* of all, different—*Agnew*⟩ **Vice** (see also FAULT 2), though frequently applied to any of the offenses that from the theological and religious points of view are called sins, often carries little direct suggestion of a violation of divine law; rather, it more uniformly imputes to such offenses a character suggestive of moral depravity, corruption, or degradation; also, the term less often applies to single acts or single transgressions than to habits and practices that debase the character of a person or group of persons ⟨spare then the person, and expose the *vice*—*Pope*⟩ ⟨treachery and cruelty, the most pernicious and most odious of all *vices* —*Hume*⟩ ⟨opium smoking was, and still is, considered a gentleman's *vice*—*Maurer & Vogel*⟩ ⟨our *vices* as well as our virtues have been imputed to bodily derangements till character has become identified with a chemical reaction—*Cardozo*⟩ **Crime** in its basic sense applies to an infraction of law, especially of common law or statute law, that is punishable by the state or by any power that constitutes itself as the guardian of such law; it is not a technical legal term, but it is often used in the courts and is sometimes defined in penal codes, usually as a general term applicable to any act or omission forbidden by law and punishable upon conviction. In such use the term comprehends many clearly distinguished types of offenses (as a misdemeanor, a felony, or an act of treason) ⟨the reason for excluding evidence obtained by violating the Constitution seems to me logically to lead to excluding evidence obtained by a *crime* of the officers of the law —*Justice Holmes*⟩ ⟨offenses against marriage such as adultery, which is a *crime* punishable by death in Papua and only a sin in civilized society—*Social Science Abstracts*⟩ ⟨human society may punish us for *crimes;* human monitors reprove us for vices; but God alone can charge upon us the sin, which He alone is able to forgive—*James Martineau*⟩ **Crime** and, less often, *sin* may be applied to offenses that are of exceedingly grave nature; in fact, this implication is often found in *crime*, even in its quasi-legal sense ⟨the betrayal by a people of itself is the ultimate historical *crime:* the final and the most degrading suicide —*MacLeish*⟩ ⟨I've not been guilty of anything more than an indiscretion . . . . I behaved foolishly, but that's not a *crime*—*Mackenzie*⟩ **Scandal** (see also DISGRACE) applies to an offense against a law that is also an offense in another sense of that word—that of an act, a condition, or a practice which offends the public conscience or which puts a stumbling block in the way of those who should obey the law or should be trained to obey it; unlike the words *sin*, *vice*, and *crime*, *scandal* carries no implication of probable or certain punishment or retribution but emphasizes the distressing effect it has on others or the discredit

A colon (:) separates groups of words discriminated. An asterisk (*) indicates place of treatment of each group.

it attaches to religion, morals, or respectability ⟨Catholics . . . could not appear in Protestant assemblies without causing *scandal* to the weaker brethren—*Froude*⟩ ⟨*scandal* is an act or omission that is sinful . . . and that is for another an occasion of sin—*Ferrell*⟩

*Ana* *injustice, injury, wrong, grievance: *breach, infraction, violation, transgression, trespass, infringement, contravention

**offensive** *adj* 1 attacking, aggressive (see under ATTACK *n*)
*Ana* invasive, incursive (see corresponding nouns at INVASION): assaulting, assailing, attacking, bombarding, storming (see ATTACK *vb*)

2 Offensive, loathsome, repulsive, repugnant, revolting are comparable when they mean utterly distasteful or repellent. Something *offensive* subjects one to painful or highly disagreeable sensations. Sometimes the term implies injured feelings as a result of an affront or insult ⟨Olly, though without the tact to perceive when remarks were untimely, was saved by her very simplicity from rendering them *offensive—Hardy*⟩ ⟨your attitude is *offensive.* Is any given truth any the less true for having been uttered more than once?—*Theodore Sturgeon*⟩ and frequently it suggests the evocation of such aversion that endurance involves mental strain or moral distaste ⟨a most untypical story for Alan to tell, a little out of place, not *offensive* exactly, but irritating and inconsequential—*Mailer*⟩ or it may imply a vileness (as of appearance or odor) that excites nausea or extreme disgust ⟨her head thrown back, her face discolored, her eyes bulging, her mouth wet and yawning: a sight horribly *offensive—Bennett*⟩ Something **loathsome** is so foul or obscene that one cannot look upon it, hear it, feel it, or have to do with it without a sense of deep disgust and abhorrence ⟨a most *loathsome* literary world, necrophilic to the core—they murder their writers, and then decorate their graves—*Mailer*⟩ Often the term is not clearly distinguishable from *offensive* in the sense of disgustingly nauseating but is applied more often to things which are generally or universally distasteful; thus, some people find the heavy fragrance of tuberoses *offensive*, but nearly everyone finds the sight and odor of meat rotting and crawling with maggots *loathsome* ⟨*loathsome* diseases⟩ ⟨*loathsome* prison conditions⟩ ⟨takes some dirty horrible incident or sight of the battlefront and describes it in *loathsome* detail—*Rose Macaulay*⟩ Something **repulsive** is so ugly in its appearance or so completely lacking in all that attracts or allures or charms or even challenges interest that it either drives one away or makes one unwilling to dwell on it ⟨Mary was not so *repulsive* and unsisterly as Elizabeth—*Austen*⟩ ⟨work which is now *repulsive* can be made no irksomer than the general run of necessary labor—*Shaw*⟩ ⟨in those days all school books were as *repulsive* as publishers could make them. Their appearance went a long way in discouraging any intimacy with their contents—*Repplier*⟩ ⟨he smiled at me, showing two rows of pale-pink, toothless gums, but it was a pleasant smile and there was nothing *repulsive* about the way the gums showed—*Dahl*⟩ Something **repugnant** (see also REPUGNANT 1 ) is highly offensive or loathsome because in direct conflict with one's nature, one's principles, and one's tastes and irreconcilable with them ⟨this frightful condition of internal strain and instability was . . . intensely *repugnant* to human nature, being a condition of chronic terror that at last became unbearable—*Shaw*⟩ ⟨the door is not barred and bolted for a solution less *repugnant* to our deepest intuitions—*Eddington*⟩ Something **revolting** is so extremely offensive, loathsome, repulsive, or repugnant to a person of delicate sensibilities that the sight or thought of it arouses in him a desire or determination to resist or rebel ⟨his whole

body shivered and started into awe-inspiring movement monstrous and inhuman, *revolting* as a spectacle of degrading vice—*O'Flaherty*⟩ ⟨to developed sensibilities the facts of war are *revolting* and horrifying—*Huxley*⟩ ⟨*revolting* cant about the duty of obedience and the wickedness of resistance to law—*Henry Adams*⟩
*Ana* repellent, *repugnant, abhorrent, distasteful, obnoxious, invidious: *hateful, odious, abominable, detestable

**offensive** *n* *attack, aggression, offense
*Ana* assault, *attack, onslaught, onset

**offer** *vb* Offer, proffer, tender, present, prefer can all mean to lay, set, or put something before another for acceptance. **Offer**, the most common of these words, frequently implies a putting before one something which may be accepted or rejected ⟨there was a crown *offered* him: and being *offered* him, he put it by—*Shak.*⟩ ⟨had he succeeded, he told me, he would have *offered* me the post of subeditor—*Ellis*⟩ ⟨*offer* a suggestion⟩ ⟨the dress department *offers* several new models this week⟩ ⟨he *offered* $10,000 for the house⟩ ⟨we must ask in the end what they have to *offer* in place of what they denounce—*T. S. Eliot*⟩ **Proffer** differs from *offer* chiefly in more consistently implying a putting or setting before one something that one is at liberty to accept or reject and in usually stressing voluntariness, spontaneity, or courtesy on the part of the agent ⟨*proffered* his arm to a lady having difficulty in crossing a street⟩ ⟨felt that it would be indelicate just then to ask for any information which Casaubon did not *proffer—George Eliot*⟩ ⟨rejecting the *proffered* assistance of a couple of officious friends—*Shaw*⟩ ⟨the flavor of social success is delicious, though it is scorned by those to whose lips the cup has not been *proffered—L. P. Smith*⟩ **Tender** was originally and still is a term in legal use meaning to offer something to the court or to a person concerned, according to the terms of the law, for formal acceptance or approval ⟨*tender* a thousand dollars in full satisfaction of a debt⟩ ⟨the defense will *tender* evidence to prove its contention that the defendant has a sound alibi⟩ ⟨will purchase all shares of preferred *tendered* to it before the redemption date—*Wall Street Jour.*⟩ ⟨*tender* the oath to a justice being sworn into office⟩ In general use *tender* differs from *offer* and *proffer* in carrying a stronger connotation of modesty, humility, or gentleness on the part of the one who makes the offer ⟨my gracious lord, I *tender* you my service—*Shak.*⟩ ⟨they are not judgments in name or form, but are expressed only as advice humbly *tendered* to Her Majesty —*Hogg*⟩ *Tender*, however, is the idiomatic or polite term in certain collocations ⟨three of us have already *tendered* our resignations—*Bretnor*⟩ ⟨this symposium is *tendered* to John Dewey as he enters the tenth decade of his life—*Sidney Hook*⟩ ⟨*tender* one's congratulations⟩ **Present** (see also GIVE) carries a stronger implication of ceremonious exhibition or of outward show than any of the preceding terms; otherwise it often suggests little more than *offer* in the sense of to lay or put before one for consideration, selection, or approval or for one's use or pleasure ⟨the butler *presented* the letter on a salver⟩ ⟨the producer will *present* a new play this week⟩ ⟨my last, least offering, I *present* thee now—*Cowper*⟩ ⟨whether Proust has not intended . . . for all his apparent deliquescent Romanticism, to *present* us with a realistic case history—*Edmund Wilson*⟩ ⟨the legislation was *presented* in July. The debate did little to clarify the specific issues —*Comstock*⟩ **Prefer** (see also CHOOSE) is disused in the sense of *proffer* or *present* except in some legal use ⟨*prefer* an indictment⟩ ⟨*prefer* a claim⟩ although common in writing up to late in the nineteenth century ⟨he spake, and to

---

*Ana* analogous words    *Ant* antonyms    *Con* contrasted words    See also explanatory notes facing page 1

her hand *preferred* the bowl—*Pope*⟩ ⟨I don't *prefer* any claim to being the soul of romance—*Dickens*⟩
*Ana* *give, present, bestow, confer: *adduce, advance: propose, design, purpose, *intend
*Con* accept, take, *receive: reject, refuse, *decline

**offhand** *extemporaneous, extempore, extemporary, improvised, impromptu, unpremeditated
*Ana* casual, desultory, *random: abrupt, hasty, sudden, *precipitate, impetuous: brusque, curt, blunt (see BLUFF)
*Con* studied, advised, considered, *deliberate

**office** *function, duty, province
*Ana* *work, business, calling: *task, job, chore, stint

**officious** meddlesome, intrusive, obtrusive, *impertinent
*Ana* meddling, interfering, intermeddling, tampering (see MEDDLE): annoying, vexing, irking, bothering (see ANNOY): pushing, assertive, *aggressive

**offset** countervail, balance, *compensate, counterbalance, counterpoise
*Ana* *neutralize, negative, counteract: *nullify, negate: redeem, reclaim, save, *rescue

**offspring, young, progeny, issue, descendant, posterity** are comparable when they mean those who follow in direct parental line. **Offspring** applies to those who are by birth immediately related to a parent; the term does not necessarily apply to human beings, for it may refer to animals or sometimes to plants ⟨at each farrow the sow produces many *offspring*⟩ ⟨the son endeavoring to appear the worthy *offspring* of such a father—*Steele*⟩ **Young** is used most often of the offspring of animals ⟨a bear surrounded by its *young*⟩ ⟨turtles bury their eggs in beaches and sandbanks and the *young* dig their way out when they hatch⟩ **Progeny** usually applies to the offspring of a father or a mother or of both; the term more often refers to those of human parentage, but it is used occasionally of the offspring of animals and plants ⟨from this union sprang a vigorous *progeny*—*Hawthorne*⟩ In comparison with *offspring*, however, it has somewhat extended use, being sometimes applied to those who trace their ancestry more remotely or to those who are the spiritual or intellectual successors of a great man ⟨all the *progeny* of David⟩ ⟨the intellectual *progeny* of Plato⟩ **Issue**, chiefly a legal term, is more abstract than the preceding terms and is used merely to call attention to the fact that a union has or has not reproduced its kind ⟨die without *issue*⟩ ⟨in the event of *issue*, the estate will pass to the children who are born of this union⟩ **Descendant**, on the other hand, applies to anyone who has or, in the plural, to all who have a right to claim relationship with a person as an ancestor in direct line; the degree of nearness does not matter, but the relationship of each as child, grandchild, great-grandchild, and so on must exist ⟨they are *descendants* of the first settlers of the town⟩ ⟨the claims of certain people to be *descendants* of George Washington are absurd, since he died without *issue*⟩ **Posterity** differs from *descendants* only in connoting all the descendants of a common ancestor ⟨the unnumbered *posterity* of William Bradford⟩ The term is also often used of the generations that come after a person, a race, or a people ⟨his fame will live to all *posterity*⟩ ⟨we are leaving many problems for *posterity* to solve⟩

**oft** *often, frequently, oftentimes

**often, frequently, oft, oftentimes** may be used with little or no distinction to mean again and again in more or less close succession. But **often** stresses the number of times a thing occurs, without regard to the interval of recurrence; **frequently** usually stresses repetition, especially at short intervals ⟨he came *often*⟩ ⟨he called *frequently*⟩ ⟨the disease is *often* fatal⟩ ⟨I *frequently* examined the color of the snow—*Tyndall*⟩ ⟨you will *often* find this to be true⟩

⟨unless you write me more *frequently* I shall feel out of touch with you⟩ *Oft* and *oftentimes* differ little from *often*; **oft**, however, is used chiefly in compound adjectives ⟨the *oft*-told tale of her hairbreadth escape—*Cerf*⟩ ⟨*oft* quoted statement⟩ or occasionally in formal discourse ⟨seemingly trifling events *oft* carry in their train great consequences—*Coolidge*⟩ and **oftentimes** is occasionally preferred for intonational reasons ⟨a sense of humor which was sometimes loud, *oftentimes* lewd, but never deliberately unkind—*Metalious*⟩

**oftentimes** *often, frequently, oft

**oil** *vb* **Oil, grease, lubricate, anoint, cream** all mean to smear or treat with an oily, fatty, or greasy substance, but they vary greatly in their implications of the substance used and the purpose for which it is employed and in their idiomatic applications. One **oils** the parts of a machine or mechanism subject to friction, typically by drops or squirts of a liquid substance, usually a mineral oil. Also, one *oils* a fabric (as cloth, silk, or paper) when one impregnates it with oil so as to make it waterproof. One **greases** a thing when one rubs on or in a thick fatty substance, often an animal fat or oil, for some purpose such as to increase speed by reducing friction ⟨*grease* axles⟩ or as a medicinal application ⟨*grease* the chest with lard and turpentine⟩ or as a preventive of cohesion ⟨*grease* a baking dish⟩ One **lubricates** when one oils, or greases, or provides for the feeding of a lubricant (as oil or grease or graphite or a silicone) to contiguous surfaces in a machine or mechanism to make them slippery, thereby reducing friction, eliminating roughness, and preventing cohesion. *Lubricate* stresses the effect intended or produced; *oil* and *grease*, the substance used or the method of its application. One **anoints** the body or a part of the body when one smears it with, or rubs into it an oily or fatty substance for some purpose (as a protection from the sun or an aid in massage). *Anoint*, however, is especially employed in reference to ceremonial uses of oil. In the application of oily or fatty cosmetics, especially those which are called creams, **cream** is the customary term.

**oily** unctuous, oleaginous, *fulsome, slick, soapy
*Ana* hypocritical, pharisaical, sanctimonious (see under HYPOCRISY): bland, politic, diplomatic, smooth (see SUAVE)

**old** 1 *aged, elderly, superannuated
*Ana* *weak, feeble, infirm, decrepit
*Ant* young

2 **Old, ancient, venerable, antique, antiquated, antediluvian, archaic, obsolete** all denote having come into existence or use in the more or less distant past. **Old**, opposed to *young* or *new* (see also AGED), applies to what has lived or existed long or has been long in use or has stood for a long time in a particular relation to something; **ancient**, opposed especially to *modern*, to what lived, existed, or happened long ago or has existed or come down from remote antiquity ⟨*old* wine⟩ ⟨*old* friends⟩ ⟨*old* as the hills⟩ ⟨O heavens, if you do love *old* men . . . if yourselves are *old*—*Shak.*⟩ ⟨this new exception condemns an advertising technique as *old* as history—*W. O. Douglas*⟩ ⟨from the *ancient* world those giants came—*Milton*⟩ ⟨some illustrious line so *ancient* that it has no beginning—*Gibbon*⟩ **Venerable** suggests the hoariness and dignity of age ⟨*venerable* as Anglo-Saxon is, and worthy to be studied as the mother of our vernacular speech—*Quiller-Couch*⟩ ⟨green ropes and leafy ladders hung down from the high limbs of a *venerable* bread tree—*Bemelmans*⟩ **Antique** applies to what has come down from former, ancient, or classical times or is in some way related to them; with regard to articles (as furnishings, implements, or bric-a-brac) the term suggests an old-fashioned type characteristic of an earlier period ⟨an *antique* highboy that had

A colon (:) separates groups of words discriminated. An asterisk (*) indicates place of treatment of each group.

belonged to his great-grandmother⟩ ⟨even a Leonardo regretted his failure to recover the *antique* symmetry, but he at least imitated the ancients vitally—*Babbitt*⟩ ⟨refreshing our minds with a savor of the *antique*, primeval world and the earliest hopes and victories of mankind—*Binyon*⟩ Something **antiquated** has gone out of vogue or fashion or has been for some time discredited; the word often implies some degree of contempt ⟨is it true that *antiquated* legal ideas prevent government from responding effectively to the demands which modern society makes upon it?—*Frankfurter*⟩ ⟨this very lack of manner keeps him from becoming *antiquated*. His style does not "date," like that of many of his contemporaries—*Tinker*⟩ ⟨cherished still their old rage against the northern invaders, a stout and defiant loyalty to their *antiquated* limitations—*Edmund Wilson*⟩ Something **antediluvian** is so antiquated and outmoded that it might have come from Noah's ark ⟨the whole system of traveling accommodations was barbarous and *antediluvian*—*De Quincey*⟩ ⟨those were *antediluvian* times. Unions were weak or nonexistent; employers were backed by the courts, the police, and the federal government—*Dwight Macdonald*⟩ Something **archaic** has the characteristics of an earlier, sometimes of a primitive, period; with regard to words, specifically, *archaic* applies to what is not in use in ordinary modern language but retained in special context or for special uses (as in biblical, ecclesiastical, and legal expressions and in poetry) ⟨we visited Medinin, a town so *archaic* and unreal in its architecture that it was difficult to believe that it was actually inhabited by the human race—*Hoffman*⟩ ⟨much of the remote past is conserved in the husk of convention, and *archaic* usages govern his conduct toward all the crucial issues of life—*Norman Lewis*⟩ ⟨to those who do not learn to read Shakespeare as a school text his *archaic* language presents formidable difficulties—*Bottrall*⟩ Something **obsolete** has gone out of use or has been or needs to be replaced by something newer, better, or more efficient that has subsequently come into being ⟨*obsolete* as the feudal baron—*Snaith*⟩ ⟨a scientific textbook is *obsolete* in a decade or less—*Lowes*⟩ ⟨it was she who had raised a fund for the granite horse trough . . . and who, when the horse trough became *obsolete*, had had it planted with geraniums —*Cheever*⟩ ⟨charged that United States Navy ships were equipped with *obsolete* torpedoes—*Current Biog.*⟩ *Ana* primitive, primeval, pristine, primal (see PRIMARY) *Ant* new

**oleaginous** oily, unctuous, *fulsome, slick, soapy *Ana* see those at OILY

**oligarchy, aristocracy, plutocracy** are comparable when they mean government by, or a state governed by, the few. The terms are often applied to governments or states that are ostensibly monarchies or republics but are, in the opinion of the user, actually governed by a clique. **Oligarchy** is the most inclusive term referable to a government or state where the power is openly or virtually in the hands of a few men ⟨democracy and *oligarchy* shade into each other and are chiefly distinguished by the degree of the citizens' participation in government—*McKean*⟩ **Aristocracy** basically and historically suggests the rule of the best citizens ⟨true *aristocracy* is just this, the government of the best, of a ruling class dedicated to the common well-being—*F. G. Wilson*⟩ but it retains this implication chiefly when it is used in distinction from *oligarchy* and the latter connotes power seized or held for selfish or corrupt reasons ⟨it ceased to be, in the Greek sense, an *aristocracy;* it became a faction, an *oligarchy*—*Thirlwall*⟩ Its more common implication is power vested in a privileged class, especially in a nobility

that is regarded as superior by birth and breeding and that by owning or controlling much of the land exercises direct control over a large portion of the population; in this sense Great Britain was until recent generations an *aristocracy* ⟨Clay was right . . . revolution was abroad among the people, shifting the basis of our government from *aristocracy* to democracy without destroying its essential republicanism—*Rossiter*⟩ **Plutocracy**, unlike the other terms, is usually derogatory; as a rule it implies concentration of power in the hands of the wealthy and, in consequence, a withholding of power from those to whom it properly belongs, either the people or their representatives ⟨Ward held that we must differentiate three types of democracy . . . the second *plutocracy*, or the control of the state by organized and predatory wealth—*H. E. Barnes*⟩ ⟨Carthage was a *plutocracy* and the real power of the state lay in the hands of a dozen big shipowners and mineowners and merchants—*van Loon*⟩

**omen** *n* augury, portent, *foretoken, presage, prognostic *Ana* *sign, mark, token, badge, note, symptom: foreboding, *apprehension, presentiment, misgiving

**ominous, portentous, fateful, inauspicious, unpropitious** basically mean having a menacing or threatening character or quality. What is **ominous** has or seems to have the character of an omen, especially of an omen forecasting evil; the term commonly suggests a frightening or alarming quality that bodes no good, and it may imply impending disaster ⟨there was something *ominous* about it, and in intangible ways one was made to feel that the worst was about to come—*London*⟩ ⟨my ears were startled by the . . . uproar of yelling and shouting. It sounded *ominous*, but . . . I had to go on—*Heiser*⟩ What is **portentous** has or seems to have the character of a portent; *portentous*, however, less often than *ominous* suggests a threatening character; it usually means little more than prodigious, monstrous, or almost frighteningly marvelous, solemn, or impressive ⟨his gravity was unusual, *portentous*, and immeasurable—*Dickens*⟩ ⟨the assertion that children of six are "mighty prophets, seers blessed," . . . seemed to him *portentous* nonsense—*Babbitt*⟩ ⟨it is *portentous* . . . that here at midnight, in our little town a mourning figure walks, and will not rest—*Lindsay*⟩ What is **fateful** has or seems to have the quality, character, or importance decreed for it by fate or suggests inevitability ⟨the *fateful* conference that brought on war⟩ ⟨to meet a Persian, any Persian, in New York seemed a *fateful* coincidence—*Mehdevi*⟩ but the term often means little more than momentous or appallingly decisive ⟨the great cases that make the work of the United States Supreme Court of *fateful* significance—*Cohen*⟩ What is **inauspicious** (compare *auspicious* under FAVORABLE) is or seems to be attended by signs that are distinctly unfavorable ⟨an *inauspicious* horoscope⟩ But *inauspicious* usually means nothing more than unlucky, unfortunate, or unlikely to succeed ⟨an *inauspicious* beginning of a great project⟩ ⟨you come at a singularly *inauspicious* moment, when I need all my strength to forget the world—*Sabatini*⟩ What is **unpropitious** (compare *propitious* under FAVORABLE) carries or seems to carry no sign of favoring one's ends or intentions ⟨*unpropitious* omens⟩ In its more common extended sense the term means merely unfavorable, discouraging, or harmful ⟨made a by-election necessary at a time highly *unpropitious* for the Government—*Cockburn*⟩ ⟨sleep and exercise are *unpropitious* to learning—*Jowett*⟩ *Ana* *sinister, baleful, malign, malefic, maleficent: threatening, menacing (see THREATEN)

**omit** *neglect, disregard, ignore, overlook, slight, forget *Ana* cancel, delete, efface, *erase: *exclude, eliminate

---

*Ana* analogous words  *Ant* antonyms  *Con* contrasted words  See also explanatory notes facing page 1

*Con* *remember, recollect, recall: *tend, attend, mind, watch

**omnipresent, ubiquitous** mean present or existent everywhere. Though they carry this as a basic meaning, they are often used hyperbolically. Something **omnipresent** is present everywhere at the same time. Though basically applicable to the Supreme Being ⟨*omnipresent* Deity⟩ the term is often, especially in a weakened sense, applied to something that is or is felt to be always present or existent (as in a class or a type wherever it may be found or in an area to which it belongs) ⟨an *omnipresent* sense of social obligation—*Eliot*⟩ ⟨the creeping, silent atmosphere of *omnipresent* fear that I have sensed in the capitals of the satellite countries—*Wechsberg*⟩ ⟨the mechanization of entertainment through . . . the *omnipresent* radio—*Millett*⟩ Something **ubiquitous** is found everywhere and, often, at the time or in the situation specified or implied ⟨electrons being so numerous and so *ubiquitous*—*Darrow*⟩ ⟨the big public services will have to be made practically *ubiquitous*—*Shaw*⟩ **Ubiquitous** is applicable to a type or an individual, often with the specific implication that one cannot escape him or it wherever one goes ⟨the *ubiquitous* American tourist⟩ ⟨the sad, *ubiquitous* spinster, left behind . . . by the stampede of the young men westward—*Brooks*⟩

**on 1** *at, in
**2** *at, in

**onerous, burdensome, oppressive, exacting** are comparable when they mean imposing severe trouble, labor, or hardships. All of these terms are applicable to a state of life, its duties or obligations, or to conditions imposed upon a person by that life or by another person; *oppressive* and *exacting* are applicable also to persons or agents responsible for these difficulties. **Onerous** stresses laboriousness and heaviness but often also implies irksomeness or distastefulness ⟨the tyranny of a majority might be more *onerous* than that of a despot—*Whitehead*⟩ ⟨"What were the conditions?" "Oh, they were not *onerous:* just to sit at the head of his table now and then"—*Wharton*⟩ **Burdensome** usually implies mental as well as physical strain and often emphasizes the former ⟨a *burdensome* tax⟩ ⟨*burdensome* Government regulations which are a nuisance to everyone—*Roosevelt*⟩ ⟨the *burdensome* and invidious job of a formal application to the Board of Trade—*Economist*⟩ **Oppressive** adds to *burdensome* the implication of extreme harshness or severity; it therefore usually connotes the unendurableness of what is imposed or inflicted, whether by nature or circumstances or by man, or cruelty or tyranny in the one responsible for the impositions or inflictions ⟨*oppressive* heat⟩ ⟨*oppressive* rulers⟩ ⟨there are more ways of coercing a man than by pointing a gun at his head. A pacifist society may be unjust and *oppressive*—*Inge*⟩ ⟨the women are . . . kind and they mean very well, but sometimes they get very *oppressive* —*Cheever*⟩ **Exacting**, like *oppressive,* implies severity of demands, but otherwise it differs because it commonly suggests rigor, sternness, or extreme fastidiousness rather than tyranny in the one who demands, or the tremendous care or pains required of the one who satisfies these demands ⟨an *exacting* technique⟩ ⟨an *exacting* employer⟩ ⟨the *exacting* life of the sea has this advantage over the life of the earth, that its claims are simple and cannot be evaded—*Conrad*⟩ ⟨the pity of it was that even the least *exacting* husband should so often desire something more piquant than goodness—*Glasgow*⟩
*Ana* *heavy, weighty, ponderous, cumbrous, cumbersome, hefty: arduous, *hard, difficult

**onlooker** looker-on, *spectator, observer, beholder, witness, eyewitness, bystander, kibitzer

**only** *adj* & *adv* **Only, alone** are often used interchangeably (though *alone* is not found in the attributive position), but seldom without a slight change in meaning or emphasis. **Only** is especially appropriate when restriction to what is specified or asserted is implied and the term is equivalent to *sole* or *solely;* thus, "I want *only* this book" implies a wish for one and no more; "of all the family *only* John and Helen came," that is, the specified persons and no more ⟨to distinguish . . . that which is established because it is right, from that which is right *only* because it is established—*Johnson*⟩ **Alone** may be chosen when the idea of the elimination of all other possibilities is expressed and the term is the equivalent of *exclusive* or, more often, *exclusively;* thus, "I want this book *alone*" implies a wish for a particular one and no other; "of all the family John *alone* came," that is, John and none of the others ⟨man shall not live by bread *alone*—*Mt* 4:4⟩

**onset** *attack, assault, onslaught
*Ana* aggression, offensive, offense, *attack: storming, bombarding, assailing (see ATTACK *vb*): *invasion, raid, incursion

**onslaught** *attack, assault, onset
*Ana* see those at ONSET

**onward, forward, forth** are comparable when they mean in the act of advancing or getting ahead (as in a movement, progression, series, or sequence). They are frequently used with little or no distinction, but **onward** often suggests progress or advance toward a definite goal, end, or place ⟨half a league *onward* . . . rode the six hundred—*Tennyson*⟩ ⟨*onward* into future lives—*Hawkridge*⟩ **Forward,** opposed to *backward,* has more specific reference to movement or advance with reference to what lies before rather than back in place (see *forward* under BEFORE) or in time ⟨his skill in reconciling conflicting points of view and his *forward*-looking spirit—*Dean*⟩ ⟨from this time *forward* Webster's bête noire was party spirit—*Warfel*⟩ or in a succession (as of incidents in a narrative or of steps in a process) ⟨the center has not yet been rebuilt, though they are . . . getting *forward* with it—*Rowse*⟩ **Forth** is often interchangeable with *forward* without loss ⟨expeditions went *forth* into the interior—*P. E. James*⟩ ⟨from that day *forth*⟩ but in certain idioms it may be quite distinctive and imply a making known, present, available, or real something previously unknown, lacking, unavailable, or hidden; thus, one brings *forth* from or as if from a place of concealment ⟨bring *forth* a precious jewel⟩ and one sets *forth* by providing ⟨set *forth* an ample supper⟩ or by making simple and clear ⟨in his charge to the grand jury . . . he set *forth* the democratic basis of the new state government—*Meriwether*⟩

**opalescent, opaline** iridescent, *prismatic

**open** *adj* **1** exposed, subject, prone, susceptible, sensitive, *liable
*Ant* closed
**2** plain, candid, *frank
*Ana* *straightforward, aboveboard, forthright: *natural, simple, ingenuous, naïve, unsophisticated: *fair, equitable, impartial
*Ant* close, closemouthed, close-lipped: clandestine

**openhanded** bountiful, bounteous, *liberal, generous, munificent, handsome
*Ant* closefisted, tightfisted —*Con* *stingy, niggardly, close, penurious

**operate** *act, behave, work, function, react

**operative** *adj* *active, dynamic, live
*Ana* *effective, effectual, efficacious, efficient: *fertile, fecund, fruitful
*Ant* abeyant

**operative** *n* mechanic, artisan, hand, workman, workingman, *worker, laborer, craftsman, handicraftsman, roust-about

**opiate** *anodyne, narcotic, nepenthe

**opinion,** view, belief, conviction, persuasion, sentiment are comparable when they mean a more or less clearly formulated idea or judgment which one holds as true or valid. An **opinion** is a more or less carefully thought-out conclusion concerning something that is or may be questioned. The word not only does not exclude the suggestion of consideration of all the evidence and of arguments on both sides, but it sometimes implies such consideration ⟨seek an expert *opinion* on the authenticity of a painting⟩ ⟨the word *opinion* . . . should be restricted to views entertained on subjects that admit of doubt and are open to controversy. . . . Matters that are not debatable are not open to *opinion—Corry*⟩ ⟨the attending physician said he would like the *opinion* of a consulting physician⟩ However, the term more consistently suggests even in the preceding instances a personal element in the judgment, the possibility of its being in error, and the strong probability that it will be disputed ⟨books . . . are a public expression of a man's *opinions*, and consequently they are submitted to the world for criticism—*Benson*⟩ ⟨the tolerant but untrained . . . will rarely know the difference between their tastes and their *opinions—Virgil Thomson*⟩ A **view** is an opinion more or less colored by the feeling, sentiment, or bias of the individual ⟨fond of airing his *views* in public⟩ ⟨each member was asked to state his *views* on the proposed change in the constitution⟩ ⟨must take the manly *view*, which is that the failure of the western democracies . . . is due to the failings of the democratic peoples—*Lippmann*⟩ ⟨in the fourth century . . . adopted the *view* that deceit and lying were virtues if in the interests of the Church—*Cohen*⟩ A **belief** differs from an opinion or view in that it is not necessarily formulated by the individual who holds it, but may have been proposed to him for acceptance (as in the form of a doctrine, a dogma, a proposition, or an authoritative opinion). The emphasis in *belief* is placed on intellectual assent or assurance of truth ⟨the *belief* that the whole system of nature is calculable in terms of mathematics and mechanics—*Inge*⟩ ⟨just one single example of real unreason is enough to shake our *belief* in everything—*Theodore Sturgeon*⟩ A **conviction** is a belief which one holds firmly and unshakably because one is undisturbed by doubt of its truth ⟨if any one had asked him the reason of this *conviction* he could not have told them; but *convictions* do not imply reasons—*Deland*⟩ ⟨the teacher should learn not to take sides, even if he or she has strong *convictions—Russell*⟩ ⟨he had overlooked this fact, borne along on his *conviction* of the abundance of life—*Cheever*⟩ A **persuasion** is usually at once an opinion and a belief. The term often implies that one's assurance of its truth is induced by one's feelings or wishes, rather than by argument or evidence ⟨it was the avowed opinion and *persuasion* of Callimachus . . . that Homer was very imperfectly understood even in his day—*Cowper*⟩ ⟨his strong interest in good government and the proper solution of social problems threw him more and more toward the Democratic *persuasion—Michener*⟩ **Sentiment** (see also FEELING 2) is becoming uncommon in this sense except in a few idiomatic phrases ⟨those are my *sentiments*⟩ The term applies to a more or less settled opinion, often with reference to something which involves one's feelings or which is formulated so as to suggest the stimulus of emotion ⟨there is no expression in the constitution, no *sentiment* delivered by its contemporaneous expounders, which would justify us—*John Marshall*⟩ ⟨it is the actions of men and not their *sentiments* which

make history—*Mailer*⟩ ⟨he would inform Miss Graves of his *sentiments* and she would translate them into a polite and brief answer—*Bemelmans*⟩
*Ana* thought, notion, impression, *idea, concept, conception: inference, deduction, conclusion, judgment (see under INFER): deciding *or* decision, determining *or* determination, settling *or* settlement (see corresponding verbs at DECIDE)

**opponent,** antagonist, adversary all denote one who expresses or manifests opposition. Unlike *enemy* they do not necessarily imply personal animosity or hostility. An **opponent** is one who is on the opposite side in a contest (as an argument, disputation, or election) or in a conflict (as of opinion) ⟨since [in France] opposition is never considered to be legitimate, the Government has no *opponents*—only enemies—*Revel*⟩ ⟨*opponents* of the desegregation decision have . . . largely founded their dissent on the principle that law cannot move faster than public opinion—*Roche & Gordon*⟩ **Antagonist** implies sharper opposition, especially in a struggle or combat for supremacy or control ⟨where you find your *antagonist* beginning to grow warm, put an end to the dispute by some genteel badinage—*Chesterfield*⟩ ⟨a swift voracious fish, a formidable *antagonist* for the angler—*J. L. B. Smith*⟩ **Adversary** ranges in connotation from the idea of mere opposition to that of active hostility ⟨do as *adversaries* do in law, strive mightily, but eat and drink as friends—*Shak.*⟩ ⟨your *adversary* the devil, as a roaring lion, walketh about, seeking whom he may devour—*I Pet* 5:8⟩
*Ana* *enemy, foe: rival, competitor, emulator (see corresponding verbs at RIVAL)

**opportune** *seasonable, timely, well-timed, pat
*Ana* happy, felicitous, appropriate, fitting (see FIT *adj*): propitious, auspicious, *favorable: ready, prompt, *quick, apt
*Ant* inopportune

**opportunity,** occasion, chance, break, time are comparable when they mean a state of affairs or a combination of circumstances favorable to some end. **Opportunity** is perhaps the most common of these terms; it applies to a situation which provides an opening for doing something, especially in line with one's inclinations, ambitions, purposes, or desires ⟨the suspect had both motive and *opportunity* for the murder⟩ ⟨to keep in the rear of *opportunity* in matters of indulgence is as valuable a habit as to keep abreast of *opportunity* in matters of enterprise—*Hardy*⟩ ⟨on the whole an infant's desire to learn is so strong that parents need only provide *opportunity* —*Russell*⟩ ⟨to strike out in search of new *opportunities* in new surroundings—*Truman*⟩ **Occasion** (see also CAUSE 1) carries the basic denotation characteristic of its leading senses—a definite moment or juncture, but it applies only to a moment that provides an opportunity or that calls for or prompts action of a definite kind or nature ⟨had *occasion* to prove the seaworthiness of this type of lifeboat in a gale—*N. B. Marshall*⟩ ⟨he took the *occasion* to satisfy his desire for revenge⟩ **Occasion** may suggest more strongly than *opportunity* a juncture that provokes or evokes action ⟨with great things charged he shall not hold aloof till great *occasion* rise—*Kipling*⟩ ⟨so long as a child is with adults, it has no *occasion* for the exercise of a number of . . . virtues . . . required by the strong in dealing with the weak—*Russell*⟩ ⟨it has also produced and spread *occasions* for diseases and weaknesses—*Dewey*⟩ **Chance** applies chiefly to an opportunity that comes seemingly by luck or accident ⟨they had no *chance* to escape⟩ ⟨it was war that gave Lenin his *chance*. He might have died in angry exile in Switzerland—*Brogan*⟩

---

*Ana* analogous words     *Ant* antonyms     *Con* contrasted words     See also explanatory notes facing page 1

Sometimes the word means little more than a fair or a normal opportunity, especially in negative expressions ⟨the feeling that the system under which we live deprives the majority of the *chance* of a decent life—*Day Lewis*⟩ **Break** applies to the occasion of a stroke of fortune that is usually good unless the term is qualified (as by an adjective indicating the kind of chance or suggesting its outcome) ⟨had been haunting . . . the tryouts, for two years: and this was her first *break*—*Wouk*⟩ ⟨ascribe his fortunes to luck, to getting the *breaks*—*Cozzens*⟩ ⟨she always did have a bad *break* if it was possible to get one—*Nevil Shute*⟩ ⟨shady folk . . . are generally given a fine *break*—*Lancaster*⟩ **Time** denotes a juncture that is well-timed or opportune (as for the execution of one's end or purpose) ⟨*time* and tide wait for no man⟩ ⟨the Mozartian scheme, in which the soloist bides his *time* in full confidence that he will be handsomely rewarded in the end—*Kolodin*⟩ ⟨the *time* has come to sift and synthesize the findings—*Towster*⟩ ⟨this is the *time* to buy stocks⟩
*Ana* *juncture, pass, contingency, emergency: posture, situation, condition, *state
**oppose** contest, fight, combat, conflict, antagonize, *resist, withstand
*Ana* *contend, fight, battle, war: *attack, assail, assault, storm, bombard: *defend, protect, shield, guard, safeguard
**opposite** *n* contradictory, contrary, antithesis, antipode, antonym (see under OPPOSITE *adj*)
**opposite** *adj* **Opposite, contradictory, contrary, antithetical, antipodal, antipodean, antonymous** are comparable chiefly as applied to abstractions and as meaning so far apart as to be or to seem irreconcilable with each other. The same differences in applications and implications are found in their corresponding nouns, **opposite, contradictory, contrary, antithesis, antipode, antonym,** when they mean one of two things which are opposite or contradictory. *Opposite* is the inclusive term; it may be used interchangeably with any of the others, though few of the others are interchangeable in precise use. **Opposite** may be used to describe the relation of either of two abstract elements (as ideas, terms, statements, qualities, or forces) to the other when they are set against each other so as to bring out sharply the contrast, conflict, or antagonism between them ⟨*opposite* views⟩ ⟨attraction and repulsion are *opposite* forces⟩ ⟨the plant does two *opposite* things at once. It is making sugar from carbon dioxide . . . and at the same time burning a little sugar—*Michael Graham*⟩ ⟨his private thesis that correction . . . entails retreat to a diametric *opposite* rather than any reasonable search for a golden mean—*Pynchon*⟩ **Contradictory,** though often used as an equivalent of *opposite*, may retain its fundamental implication of denial, and therefore, especially when it is applied to terms, propositions, and principles, may further imply that if one of the two opposites be true, the other must be false, or if one be false, the other must be true ⟨*contradictory* predictions are being made, some gloomy, some optimistic—*Farrell*⟩ Words, propositions, or principles that are *contradictory* in this strict sense are mutually exclusive and, therefore, admit no possibilities between; thus, "John is English" and "John is not English" are *contradictory* statements, one of which must be false if the other is true; *alive* and *dead* are *contradictory* terms because they cannot both be truly applied to the same thing ⟨stamped with the mint of our *contradictory* popular culture (where sex is sin and yet sex is paradise)—*Mailer*⟩ **Contrary** (see also CONTRARY 2) as applied to intentions, motives, and opinions usually implies extreme divergence with no basis for agreement ⟨take a *contrary* view of the situation⟩ ⟨from the center of capitalist and imperialistic America he seemed to diffuse

a *contrary* purely humanitarian influence—*Santayana*⟩ ⟨he maintained that the *contrary* was true⟩ But especially as applied to terms and propositions *contrary* may imply diametrical opposition or the greatest conceivable or possible difference between the things opposed. Contraries are poles apart; unlike contradictories both may be false, for they represent extremes and do not mutually exclude every other possibility; thus, *destitute* and *opulent* are *contrary* terms as applicable to a person's circumstances, but they may be inapplicable in a vast number of particular cases for they describe only the extremes; "John is parsimonious" and "John is prodigal" are *contrary* statements, but John in truth may be neither parsimonious nor prodigal, but merely close, or thrifty, or free, or liberal, in the expenditure of money ⟨a theory for which neither physics nor common sense can offer confirmatory or *contrary* evidence—*Clement*⟩ **Antithetical** and especially **antithesis** (see also COMPARISON) imply an intent to set the thing under consideration against its opposite, usually its diametrical opposite, in order to emphasize its significance or to reveal or define sharply its true nature. Both words are applicable to persons and things regarded objectively as well as to ideas, qualities, and terms ⟨*antithetical* symbolism of ice and flame—*Rees*⟩ ⟨that mystic faith in unseen powers which is the *antithesis* of materialism—*Rose Macaulay*⟩ ⟨the essential interests of men and women are eternally *antithetical*—*Mencken*⟩ Although **antipodal** or **antipodean** and the corresponding noun, **antipode,** which often occurs as the plural **antipodes** with singular or plural construction, also imply diametrical opposition, they do not suggest a logical relation but rather emphasize the unlikeness and the remoteness from each other of the things contrasted. So strong are these implications that often the things contrasted are only figuratively, not generically, opposites, and the contrast constitutes in a sense an inverse simile ⟨the unspannable gulf between the two brothers is widened by their *antipodal* attitudes toward money—*Behrman*⟩ ⟨flashy, crude, essentially shallow, but nevertheless at the *antipodes* from villainy. He is good-hearted and generous—*Walcutt*⟩ ⟨the very *antipode* of Gropius. Where the American is romantic, the German is rationalistic—*Werner*⟩ **Antonymous** and **antonym** are applicable only to a word or term which is so opposed to another in meaning that it, in effect, negates or nullifies every implication of it. Antonyms or antonymous words may be contradictory or contrary terms, as defined, or they may be terms which negate other terms by implying the undoing or reversing of what is denoted by them; thus, *retain* is the contradictory *antonym* of *lose*, but *recover* is the reverse *antonym* of *lose*.
*Ana* reverse, converse (see corresponding nouns at CONVERSE): antagonistic, *adverse, counter, counteractive
*Con* reconciling, conforming, adapting, adjusting (see ADAPT): consistent, compatible, congruous, congenial, *consonant
**oppress** 1 *depress, weigh
*Ana* *abuse, mistreat, maltreat, ill-treat, outrage: *worry, annoy, harass, harry
2 *wrong, persecute, aggrieve
*Ana* *afflict, torment, torture: overcome, subdue, subjugate, reduce, overthrow (see CONQUER)
**oppressive** *onerous, burdensome, exacting
*Ana* extorting *or* extortionate, extracting (see corresponding verbs at EDUCE): compelling *or* compulsory, coercing *or* coercion, constraining, obliging *or* obligatory (see corresponding verbs at FORCE): despotic, tyrannical, *absolute, arbitrary

---

A colon (:) separates groups of words discriminated. An asterisk (*) indicates place of treatment of each group.

*Con* humane, humanitarian (see CHARITABLE): compassionate, *tender

**opprobrious** *abusive, vituperative, contumelious, scurrilous
  *Ana* reviling, vituperating, railing, berating (see SCOLD): *malicious, malevolent, malign, malignant: *execrable, damnable, accursed

**opprobrium** obloquy, odium, ignominy, infamy, shame, *disgrace, dishonor, disrepute
  *Ana* *abuse, invective, vituperation, obloquy, scurrility: censure, denunciation, condemnation, reprehension (see corresponding verbs at CRITICIZE)
  *Con* prestige, authority, credit, *influence

**opt** *vb* *choose, select, elect, pick, cull, prefer, single
  *Ana* take, accept, *receive: *adopt, embrace, espouse

**optimistic** *hopeful, roseate, rose-colored
  *Ana* *confident, sanguine, assured: cheerful, lighthearted, joyous, *glad
  *Ant* pessimistic  —*Con* *cynical, misanthropic

**option** *choice, alternative, preference, selection, election
  *Ana* *right, prerogative, privilege

**opulent** 1 affluent, wealthy, *rich
  *Ana* lavish, *profuse, prodigal: *showy, pretentious, ostentatious
  *Ant* destitute: indigent
  2 sumptuous, *luxurious
  *Ana* luxuriant, lush, exuberant (see PROFUSE): *splendid, resplendent, gorgeous, superb

**opus** *work, product, production, artifact

**oracular** doctrinaire, dogmatic, *dictatorial, authoritarian, magisterial
  *Ana* positive, certain, *sure, cocksure

**oral** 1 *vocal, articulate
  *Ant* written
  2 **Oral, verbal** are often confused in use. **Oral** (see also VOCAL 1) implies utterance and speech; it is distinctively applicable to whatever is delivered, communicated, transacted, or carried on directly from one to another by word of mouth ⟨an *oral* as opposed to a written confession⟩ ⟨receive *oral* instructions⟩ ⟨*oral* teaching of the deaf as distinguished from teaching by signs⟩ **Verbal** stresses the use of words and may apply indifferently to what is written or spoken, for it carries no implication of the method of communication ⟨*verbal* difficulties caused by ambiguous or equivocal language⟩ ⟨he often loses himself in little trifling distinctions and *verbal* niceties—*Gray*⟩ The use of *verbal* as a substitute for *oral* fails to convey the intended distinction or suggests unintended or irrelevant distinctions or contrasts; thus, one would speak of an *oral* invitation or *oral* testimony when *spoken* is to be implied, because *verbal* would be ambiguous.

**oration** *speech, address, harangue, lecture, talk, sermon, homily

**orbit** *range, gamut, reach, radius, compass, sweep, scope, horizon, ken, purview

**ordain** *dictate, prescribe, decree, impose
  *Ana* order, *command, enjoin, direct

**order** *n* 1 *association, society, club
  2 *command, injunction, bidding, behest, mandate, dictate
  *Ana* instruction, direction, charging *or* charge (see corresponding verbs at COMMAND)

**order** *vb* 1 **Order, arrange, marshal, organize, systematize, methodize** are comparable when they mean to put (a number of persons or things) in proper place especially relatively or to bring about an orderly disposition of individuals, units, or elements that comprise (a thing). **Order** is somewhat outmoded when the idea of putting in a definite order is to be expressed; it more usually implies a straightening out and may connote either the elimination

of friction or confusion, often with resulting peace or harmony, or the imposition of a fixed and rigid discipline ⟨*ordered* his affairs in expectation of death⟩ ⟨it was a home strictly *ordered*, and he would have to conform to its *ordering*—*Archibald Marshall*⟩ ⟨the Greek states . . . were not well *ordered*; on the contrary, they were always on the verge, or in the act, of civil war—*Dickinson*⟩ ⟨a period of yearly relaxation in London, *ordered* and increasingly stately—*Sackville-West*⟩ **Arrange** is more often used than *order* where the idea of setting in proper sequence, relationship, or adjustment is uppermost. The word often implies a notion of what is orderly, fit, suitable, or right and a placing of things in accordance with this notion ⟨they are the great organizers . . . the Germans classify, but the French *arrange*—*Cather*⟩ ⟨*arrange* the furniture in a room⟩ ⟨*arrange* fruit in a dish⟩ ⟨each of us *arranges* the world according to his own notion of the fitness of things—*Conrad*⟩ Often the term implies a determination of the way in which the things are disposed by an end in view and then suggests careful management or manipulation ⟨we shall *arrange* matters so that you will not be inconvenienced⟩ ⟨*arrange* the details of a conference⟩ ⟨she *arranged* leave for a counselor whose mother was ill—*Auchincloss*⟩ ⟨political and economic life had been *arranged* in Utopian fashion—*Henry Miller*⟩ **Marshal** usually connotes generalship and implies assemblage and arrangement either for ease or advantage in management (as under stress) or for effectiveness in display or exhibition ⟨*marshal* troops for battle⟩ ⟨paused to *marshal* his thoughts before beginning his address⟩ ⟨*marshaled* like soldiers in gay company, the tulips stand arrayed—*Lowell*⟩ ⟨thanks to Mr. Dawson's erudition and his gift of *marshaling* facts, we begin to have a notion of what it is all about—*Huxley*⟩ **Organize** implies an arrangement in which all persons or things are so related to each other that they work as a unit, each individual having his or its proper function or duty ⟨*organize* the supporters of a candidate for the presidency⟩ ⟨part of this service is *organizing*—cataloging, classifying, and arranging on shelves—the collected literature—*Bercaw*⟩ ⟨the traditional logic was a logic for clarifying and *organizing* that which was already known—*Dewey*⟩ **Systematize** implies arrangement according to a definite and planned scheme; thus, one *systematizes* one's daily work when one reduces it to routine order ⟨if grammar was to become a rational science, it had to *systematize* itself through principles of logic—*H. O. Taylor*⟩ ⟨how Philosophy . . . blindly spinneth her geometric webs, testing and *systematizing* even her own disorders—*Bridges*⟩ **Methodize** differs from *systematize* in suggesting the imposition of orderly procedure rather than that of a fixed scheme; thus, one can *methodize* one's work without giving it the character of routine ⟨that art of reasoning . . . which *methodizes* and facilitates our discourse—*Shorthouse*⟩ ⟨philosophical decisions are nothing but the reflections of common life, *methodized* and corrected—*Thilly*⟩
  *Ana* *adjust, regulate: *line, line up, align, range, array
  2 *command, bid, enjoin, direct, instruct, charge
  *Ana* prohibit, *forbid, interdict, inhibit, ban
  *Con* permit, allow, *let: license, *authorize, commission

**orderly** *adj* **Orderly, methodical, systematic, regular** are comparable when they mean following closely a set arrangement, design, or pattern. **Orderly** implies observance of due sequence or proper arrangement especially in the harmonious or careful disposition of persons or things ⟨the guests passed in *orderly* groups into the ballroom⟩ ⟨an *orderly* placing of furniture⟩ or in obedience to the rules of conduct or behavior that guide disciplined persons ⟨an *orderly* group of children⟩ ⟨an *orderly* assem-

bly of citizens⟩ ⟨an *orderly* election⟩ or in keeping a place free from litter or confusion ⟨his study is always *orderly*⟩ ⟨an *orderly* housekeeper⟩ or in a scheme or system when all details stand in their proper relations, each playing its due part without interfering with that of any of the others ⟨a process calculated to reduce the *orderly* life of our complicated societies to chaos—*Huxley*⟩ ⟨the difference seems to me rather the difference between the complete and the fragmentary, the adult and the immature, the *orderly* and the chaotic—*T. S. Eliot*⟩ **Methodical** implies the observance of an order that has been carefully worked out so that the steps to be followed are exactly known or the pattern that is accepted seems logical or inevitable under the circumstances ⟨make a *methodical* search for evidence⟩ ⟨give *methodical* instructions to a new employee⟩ ⟨begin a *methodical* study of the Bible⟩ ⟨a *methodical* performance of daily duties⟩ **Systematic** comes close to *methodical* in ordinary use ⟨needed a *systematic* brain, and a sympathetic nature—*Andrew Buchanan*⟩ ⟨composing is self-expression and that is hard and *systematic* work—*Toch*⟩ but *systematic*, which always retains some notion of the ordered complex unity implied by the related noun (compare SYSTEM), may be preferred when the stress is not upon the order followed but upon the integrated and ordered whole involved; thus, *methodical* study implies study pursued in regular increments according to a predetermined schedule while *systematic* study implies study pursued according to a scheme in which each increment leads logically to the next and the end result is exposure to an integrated block of information ⟨the realization that all languages are *systematic* structures—*A. A. Hill*⟩ ⟨at the highest level, there stands . . . *systematic* theory, the conceptual framework within which a whole discipline is cast—*Easton*⟩ *Systematic* also may be used to suggest order in occurrence, in progression, and especially in repetition, still with some notion of an underlying system; thus, a *systematic* error is one that is inherent in a system of measurement or calculation and recurs whenever that system is used ⟨a *systematic* plan for world conquest⟩ ⟨they were not your gabbling, laughing eaters . . . they were quiet, *systematic*, devastating; they advanced steadily in good order from the first slice of ham to the last slice of chocolate cake—*Priestley*⟩ ⟨nowhere else in our literature can such a *systematic* and chill-blooded series of renderings, gorings, murders, suicides, and executions be found—*Aldridge*⟩ **Regular,** with its basic implication of conformance to a rule (see also REGULAR 1), may come very close to *orderly* ⟨even the most "realistic" work, if it is one of art, is not an imitative reproduction of the things that are so familiar, so *regular*, and so importunate that we call them real—*Dewey*⟩ ⟨the umbrageous trees, which rose in a *regular* line from either side—*De Quincey*⟩ The term may imply steadiness or uniformity (as in following a schedule) ⟨*regular* meals⟩ ⟨the gentleness of their morality, their *regular* and industrious habits—*de Tocqueville*⟩ or it may suggest occurrence and recurrence (as at fixed or stated intervals or in uniform amount) ⟨the *regular* ebb and flow of the tides⟩ ⟨the revenue of government from the taxes was not *regular* but capricious and exceptional—*Belloc*⟩
*Ana* tidy, *neat, trim, spick-and-span: formal, conventional, ceremonious (see CEREMONIAL): peaceable, *pacific, peaceful
*Ant* disorderly: chaotic

**ordinance** canon, precept, *law, rule, regulation, statute

**ordinary** *adj* *common, familiar, popular, vulgar
*Ana* *usual, customary, habitual, wonted, accustomed
*Ant* extraordinary —*Con* *abnormal, atypical, aber-

rant: *exceptional: *irregular, unnatural, anomalous

**ordnance** *armament, matériel, munitions, arms, artillery, ammunition

**organ** 1 medium, vehicle, channel, *mean, instrument, instrumentality, agent, agency
2 *journal, periodical, newspaper, magazine, review

**organism** *system, scheme, network, complex, economy

**organize** 1 systematize, methodize, *order, arrange, marshal
*Ana* design, project, plan, scheme (see under PLAN *n*): form, fashion, shape, *make
*Ant* disorganize
2 institute, *found, establish
*Ana* *begin, commence, start, initiate, inaugurate: *adjust, regulate

**oriel** *window, casement, dormer

**orifice** *aperture, interstice

**origin,** source, inception, root, provenance, provenience, prime mover denote the point at which something (as a process, a growth, a development, a custom, a habit, or an institution) begins its course or its existence. **Origin** applies chiefly to the point at which the thing under consideration has its rise or to the person or thing from which it is ultimately derived; it often applies specifically to the causes in operation before the thing itself is finally brought into being ⟨the *origin* of the custom of giving presents at Christmas⟩ ⟨is probable that the *origin* of language is not a problem that can be solved out of the resources of linguistics alone—*Sapir*⟩ Often, when used in reference to persons, it means little more than ancestry or parentage; it is then used either in the singular or the plural ⟨his father was of no great *origin*—*Belloc*⟩ ⟨quickly realized how far he had traveled from his *origins*—*Commins*⟩ **Source** basically applies to the point at which waters from a spring or fountain emerge to form the beginning point of a stream or river ⟨the *source* of the Hudson river⟩ In extended use *source* more often than *origin* applies to what serves as the ultimate beginning of a thing, especially an immaterial or intangible thing; however, since the term is sometimes qualified by such words as *immediate* or *secondary* which weaken or destroy this implication, it is often in this sense modified by *ultimate, fundamental,* or *primary* ⟨an ever-present energy, which is the *source* of all cosmical movement—*Inge*⟩ ⟨the power of concentrated attention as the fundamental *source* of the prodigious productiveness of great workers—*Eliot*⟩ ⟨theoretically the mob is the repository of all political wisdom and virtue; actually it is the ultimate *source* of all political power—*Mencken*⟩ *Source* is also applied to the one (as the person, book, manuscript, or document) from which a person derives information; in this sense a primary *source* is a person who has firsthand knowledge of a work that was written at the time under discussion, especially by one who had firsthand knowledge; a secondary *source* is a person who has learned the facts from others or a work which is based upon information gathered from others ⟨graduate students in history are discouraged from using secondary *sources*⟩ **Inception** is often preferred to *origin* when the reference is to the actual beginning (as of an undertaking, a project, an institution, or a practice); the term carries a weaker connotation of underlying causes than *origin*, yet does not, as *source* often does, carry a suggestion that the thing so called is the ultimate origin ⟨they joined the League of Nations Union. . . . Stanley did so, at its *inception*, and became, in fact, a speaker on platforms in the cause—*Rose Macaulay*⟩ ⟨the subject may and does change between the *inception* of the work and its completion—*Alexander*⟩ **Root** often suggests that the actual origin of a thing goes back to something very

---

A colon (:) separates groups of words discriminated. An asterisk (*) indicates place of treatment of each group.

deep and fundamental and that the thing itself is only an outward manifestation of its influence. *Root* therefore more often even than *source* applies to what is regarded as the first or final cause of a thing ⟨the love of money is the *root* of all evil—*1 Tim* 6:10⟩ ⟨John Brown has loosened the *roots* of the slave system; it only breathes—it does not live—*Phillips*⟩ **Provenance** and **provenience** are chiefly used to designate the place or, sometimes, the race or people from which a thing is derived or where or by whom or among whom it originated or was invented or constructed ⟨antiquities of doubtful *provenance*⟩ ⟨he would have some difficulty in guessing its *provenance*, and naming the race from which it was brought—*Lang*⟩ ⟨a fragment of a cast copper dagger had been discovered earlier, but its *provenience* is not certain—*Daifuku*⟩ ⟨in the *provenance*, or history of previous ownership, of many of the Duveen works appeared the names of kings and the mistresses of kings—*Behrman*⟩ **Prime mover** is chiefly used as a designation of an ultimate and original source of motion or motive power; when applied to a personal agent, it usually refers to an inciter or instigator of an action or course ⟨convinced that the great man is best understood as an effect or manifestation rather than as a *prime mover*—*L. A. White*⟩ ⟨the *prime mover* in the whole matter was Hugh the Great—*Freeman*⟩ In mechanics the term specifically applies to the natural or mechanical power which sets a thing moving or in motion; it has been used in reference to wind (as in driving a sailing ship), steam (as in driving a steamship), a waterwheel, a windmill, or a steam or diesel engine.
*Ana* beginning, commencement, initiation, starting (see corresponding verbs at BEGIN): derivation, origination, rising *or* rise (see corresponding verbs at SPRING): *ancestry, lineage

**original** *adj* **1** *initial, primordial
*Ana* beginning, commencing, starting (see BEGIN): *primary, primal, pristine, primeval: basic, *fundamental
*Con* deriving *or* derived, stemming *or* stemmed, proceeding *or* proceeded (see SPRING): imitated *or* imitating, copied *or* copying (see COPY): simulated *or* simulating (see ASSUME)
**2** *new, fresh, novel, new-fashioned, newfangled, modern, modernistic
*Ant* dependent: banal: trite

**originate** rise, derive, arise, *spring, flow, issue, emanate, proceed, stem
*Ana* *begin, commence, start

**ornament** *adorn, decorate, embellish, beautify, deck, bedeck, garnish
*Ana* enhance, heighten, *intensify

**ornate, rococo, baroque, flamboyant, florid** can all mean elaborately and often pretentiously decorated or designed. *Ornate* is applicable to anything heavily adorned or ornamented or conspicuously embellished ⟨an *ornate* style of architecture⟩ ⟨the room's communicating door, heavily *ornate* with late Renaissance panels and tarnished silver handles—*MacInnes*⟩ ⟨in the fiacre were Gerald and a woman. Gerald . . . was talking eagerly to his *ornate* companion—*Bennett*⟩ ⟨introduced the direct and colloquial manner upon the American public platform, as distinguished from the highly elaborated and often *ornate* style which had been established—*Higginson*⟩ **Rococo** basically applies to a French architectural style originating in the eighteenth century and characterized chiefly by the extravagant and often fantastic use of curves, shellwork, and fanciful excrescence. The term therefore implies the ornateness of design characteristic of this decorative style especially as evident in architectural details, in furniture, and in mirror and picture frames.

It is often extended to describe a style (as in painting or writing) that seems tastelessly or meaninglessly ornate or overadorned ⟨decided instead to have the wedding, *rococo* excess and all—*Wouk*⟩ ⟨doesn't mind getting caught out with a *rococo* phrase or an overstuffed image —*Los Angeles Times*⟩ **Baroque,** which is sometimes interchanged with *rococo,* basically applies to a style of art and architecture which prevailed from the latter part of the sixteenth century to nearly the end of the eighteenth century and which emphasized energy in conception, amplitude in design, the use of dynamic contrasts, extremely high relief, and the employment of curved and often contorted forms ⟨I entered this *baroque* interior, with its twisted columns and volutes and high-piled, hideous tombs, adorned with skeletons and allegorical figures and angels blowing trumpets—*L. P. Smith*⟩ In its extended sense *baroque* may suggest more grotesqueness and extravagance and less fancifulness than *rococo,* although it too may imply tasteless ornamentation ⟨*baroque* poetry with its frigid vehemence, its exhibitionistic forcefulness and false dynamism, its arbitrary twisting and distortions—*H. L. Davis*⟩ ⟨their literature, their modern painting and architecture, their music—it's all *baroque.* It gesticulates rhetorically, it struts across stages, it sobs and bawls in its efforts to show you how passionate it is—*Huxley*⟩ **Flamboyant** basically applies to a late French Gothic architectural style characterized by curves that suggest ascending flames (as in the tracery of windows). In its more general application *flamboyant* can suggest ornateness but more often stresses such elements as excess of color, conspicuous vigor and dash, or bold and daring display that suggest the freedom and brilliancy of flames ⟨a *flamboyant* display of courage⟩ ⟨*flamboyant* penmanship—*Dowden*⟩ ⟨the *flamboyant* period of prose—*Saintsbury*⟩ ⟨these . . . *flamboyant* tricks of virtuosity have gone quite out of fashion—*Quiller-Couch*⟩ ⟨some [people] are simply present at accidents, without being involved at all—catalysts of death, if you'll pardon a *flamboyant* phrase—*Theodore Sturgeon*⟩ **Florid** implies richness, usually overrichness, in details, shown particularly in the use of color, figures of speech, or flourishes, for their own sake; it implies, therefore, showy and ostentatious embellishment ⟨a *florid* style of poetry⟩ ⟨a *florid* musical composition⟩ ⟨the screen was an old one, of gilt Spanish leather, stamped and wrought with a rather *florid* Louis-Quatorze pattern—*Wilde*⟩ ⟨inexplicable how a book . . . can . . . be banned because of the manner in which it is advertised and sold. However *florid* its cover, whatever the pitch of its advertisements, the contents remain the same—*W. O. Douglas*⟩
*Ana* adorned, decorated, ornamented, embellished (see ADORN): flowery, aureate (see RHETORICAL): *luxurious, sumptuous, opulent: *showy, ostentatious
*Ant* chaste: austere

**orotund** *resonant, sonorous, ringing, resounding, vibrant
*Ana* *loud, stentorian, strident

**oscillate** *swing, sway, vibrate, fluctuate, pendulate, waver, undulate
*Ana* vacillate, waver, *hesitate, falter: shake, tremble, quiver, quaver

**ostensible** *apparent, seeming, illusory
*Ana* specious, *plausible, colorable: pretended, assumed, affected, simulated, feigned (see ASSUME)

**ostentatious** *showy, pretentious
*Ana* vainglorious, vain, proud (see under PRIDE): flaunting, parading, displaying (see SHOW *vb*): boasting, bragging, gasconading (see BOAST)

**ostracize** *banish, exile, expatriate, deport, transport, extradite

---

*Ana* analogous words      *Ant* antonyms      *Con* contrasted words      See also explanatory notes facing page 1

**otiose** *vain, nugatory, idle, empty, hollow
*Ana* *superfluous, supernumerary, surplus: *futile, vain, fruitless, bootless
**oust** *eject, expel, evict, dismiss
*Ana* *exclude, eliminate, shut out, rule out, debar, disbar: *dismiss, discharge, fire, cashier, sack
**out-and-out** *outright, unmitigated, arrant
**outcast** *n* Outcast, castaway, derelict, reprobate, pariah, untouchable are comparable when they mean one who has lost contact with or has been excluded from association with men in general or with a particular group. **Outcast** is usually applied to a person who has been rejected by society and is forced to live without its help, its companionship, or its approval; the term need not imply a degraded or abject condition, but it does suggest a loss of the comforts that accrue from one's association with other men ⟨the casual offender expiates his offense . . . and after devastating years is given back an *outcast* to the society that made him—*Cardozo*⟩ ⟨Arnold the heartbroken *outcast* from the snug household of faith—*Montague*⟩ **Castaway** usually implies abandonment as the result of shipwreck and suggests the wretched and pitiable condition of one isolated from both human society and normal human comforts ⟨took part . . . in that passage through the Straits of Gibraltar which landed him as a *castaway* on the Portuguese coast—*Sellery*⟩ ⟨a pitiful wreck of an old man he had picked up . . . a *castaway* Englishman, Henry Atkins by name—*Cather*⟩ **Derelict** basically applies to property and especially to a ship abandoned and left to the mercy of the elements. In application to human beings the term emphasizes a cutting off from normal social association particularly because of irresponsible or dissolute habits and more often than *outcast* or *castaway* suggests a debased state more or less voluntarily assumed ⟨chronic ne'er-do-wells, useless *derelicts* of society, seldom hired and then not for long —*F. L. Allen*⟩ ⟨strange things happen on a racetrack where human *derelicts* and equine aristocrats fashion bonds . . . beyond the comprehension of the outside world —*Gerald Beaumont*⟩ **Reprobate** basically applies to one who, because of his sins, is rejected by God. In extended use *reprobate* is more likely to imply the disapprobation of society than actual rejection by society, and, while it may impute grave wrongdoing, it is very likely to suggest a degree of social tolerance ⟨may paint his hero as a gay, devil-may-care *reprobate*, striding to the gallows with a twinkle in his eye—*Pawley*⟩ ⟨an old *reprobate* who acted as medicine man, astrologer, doctor, wizard, rainmaker—*Birtles*⟩ **Pariah** and *untouchable* are words basically used to denote specific socially inferior or unacceptable groups in India but in their more general applications often used without reference to the original meaning. **Pariah** in such general application typically denotes a person who especially as a member of a group is, justifiably or unjustifiably, rejected or despised by society ⟨with us, prison makes a man a *pariah*. I, and such as I am, have hardly any right to air and sun—*Wilde*⟩ ⟨many virile minds dare not speak out for fear of . . . becoming political *pariahs*—*L. L. Rice*⟩ ⟨a man who had disgraced himself in battle was a *pariah* in his native land—*Dickinson*⟩ ⟨hundreds of thousands of lepers still exist throughout the world as social *pariahs*—*Heiser*⟩ **Untouchable** is applicable not only to an individual but to a group (as a people, nation, or class) which another and supposedly superior group regards as beneath its notice or outside the sphere of its consideration ⟨those in Whitehall may go on thinking there is something extremely meritorious in treating Russia as a diplomatic *untouchable*—*Daily Express*⟩ ⟨that former *untouchable*

of the Atlantic, the Tourist-Class passenger—*Sutton*⟩
*Ana* *vagabond, vagrant, tramp, hobo
**outcome** *effect, result, consequence, upshot, aftereffect, aftermath, sequel, issue, event
*Ana* *fate, lot, portion, destiny: termination, *end
**outdo** excel, outstrip, transcend, surpass, *exceed
**outer,** **outward, outside, external, exterior** mean being or placed without something. Although in many cases interchangeable, they are more or less restricted in their applications and are therefore clearly distinguished in their implications. **Outer** usually retains its comparative force, then applying to what is farther out from something described as *inner* ⟨the *outer* as distinguished from the inner court⟩ ⟨the *outer* layer of skin is called the epidermis⟩ or is farther than another thing from the center ⟨shed one's *outer* garments⟩ ⟨the *outer* covering of a butternut is removed before the nut is cracked⟩ *Outer* is also applicable to what is definitely without as opposed to what is definitely within something, but in this sense the term rarely suggests spatial relations; thus, the *outer* man is the man as known in the flesh and as distinguished from the inner man, that is, the man as he really is in mind and soul; one's *outer* life is the part which is observable to one's fellows; the *outer* world is the world as known directly through the senses. **Outward** may be used of spatial relations; when it is so used it commonly implies motion or direction away from, or the reverse of, what is *inward* ⟨given to *outward* display⟩ ⟨*outward* travel from New York City is very heavy over the weekends⟩ ⟨the *outward* curve of a convex lens⟩ Like *outer*, the term is sometimes used of what is manifest to others in contrast with what is within and especially with what is spiritual or mental ⟨all *outward* actions, every overt thing we do —*Powys*⟩ ⟨obstinate questionings of sense and *outward* things—*Wordsworth*⟩ ⟨give *outward* and objective form to ideas that bubble inwardly and have a fascinating lure in them—*Mencken*⟩ **Outside** usually implies a position on or a reference to the outer parts or surface of a thing ⟨an *outside* stateroom on a ship⟩ ⟨*outside* shutters⟩ ⟨the *outside* paint is looking shabby⟩ But *outside*, in extended use, applies especially to a person or thing that is beyond implied borders, bounds, or limits; thus, an *outside* influence is one not emanating from the particular society, group, or community in mind; the *outside* world is the world beyond the scope or interest (as of a family group, community, or set) or the confines of a place (as an institution, a town, city, or a state); an *outside* broker is one who is not a member of an exchange; *outside* work is work in the open air in contrast with *inside* work under cover (as in an office, factory, or store) ⟨if it had condemned, Old Chester would not have cared in the very least. It looked down upon the *outside* world—*Deland*⟩ **External** and *exterior* are often used interchangeably without loss, for both come close in meaning to *outside* ⟨*external* appearance of an object⟩ ⟨the *exterior* form of a body⟩ But **external** may be preferred when location or situation beyond or away from the thing under consideration is implied ⟨our desires and wills are directed to some object *external* to us—*Alexander*⟩ ⟨the slavery which would be imposed upon her by her *external* enemies and her internal traitors—*Roosevelt*⟩ and **exterior** is often preferred when location or situation on the surface or on the outer limits of a thing is implied ⟨the *exterior* slope of a fortification⟩ ⟨the *exterior* parts of the human body⟩ ⟨thou, whose *exterior* semblance doth belie thy Soul's immensity—*Wordsworth*⟩ In addition, *external* sometimes comes close to *superficial* in implying mere appearance or semblance that has no relation or little relation to what the thing really is ⟨but under this *external*

A colon (:) separates groups of words discriminated. An asterisk (*) indicates place of treatment of each group.

appearance of ease she was covered with cold beads of sweat—*Wharton*⟩ ⟨beauty that is purely *external*⟩ and *exterior* may, like *outer* and *outward*, apply to what shows or is made apparent ⟨the *exterior* cold had stolen into the cars, forming lenses of ice on the inside surface of the windowpanes—*Capote*⟩ ⟨the absence of *exterior* demonstration of affection for my mother—*Wecter*⟩ *Ana* *extrinsic, extraneous, foreign, alien *Ant* inner —*Con* inward, inside, internal, interior, intestine (see INNER)

**outfit** *n* *equipment, apparatus, paraphernalia, tackle, machinery, gear, matériel

**outfit** *vb* *furnish, equip, appoint, accouter, arm

**outlander** *stranger, foreigner, alien, outsider, immigrant, émigré

**outlandish** *strange, singular, unique, peculiar, eccentric, erratic, odd, queer, quaint, curious *Ana* bizarre, grotesque, *fantastic, antic: alien, foreign, extraneous, *extrinsic

**outlast** *outlive, survive *Ana* endure, persist, abide, *continue: withstand, *resist

**outline** *n* **1** Outline, contour, profile, skyline, silhouette mean the boundary lines which give form or shape to a body, a mass, or a figure. **Outline** refers to a line which marks or seems to mark the outer edge or limits of a thing ⟨at night, the *outline* of the shore is traced in transparent silver by the moonlight and the flying foam—*Stevenson*⟩ ⟨looked at the big house. The dark *outline* against the dark sky made him hesitate—*Caldwell*⟩ ⟨in good years the *outline* of the cultivated area expands—*P. E. James*⟩ **Contour** does not fix the attention on an edge or limit but on the outer lines, particularly the curving lines, of a thing's shape as indicative of its grace or lack of grace, its fullness or slenderness, its softness or harshness ⟨the full and flowing *contour* of the neck—*Shelley*⟩ ⟨a child, of timid, soft *contours*—*Hewlett*⟩ ⟨the blurred *contour* of Rainbarrow obstructed the sky—*Hardy*⟩ Specifically, *contour* applies to lines (*contour lines*) in a map (*contour map*) that indicate the details of elevation of a country or tract of land. **Profile** applies primarily to the representation or the appearance of something in outline, especially of a face in side view showing the contour of the head and emphasizing the line from forehead to under the chin ⟨lips lovely in *profile*—a little too wide and hard . . . seen in front—*Ruskin*⟩ Consequently, *profile* is often preferred when a varied and sharply defined outline as seen against a background is implied ⟨out on the horizon you could see a tanker, small and neat in *profile* against the blue sea —*Hemingway*⟩ although **skyline** may be chosen as more specific when the background is the sky ⟨the *skyline* of New York City⟩ ⟨gracious towers and spires make up the loveliest man-made *skyline* in the world—*Pollock*⟩ **Silhouette** in its primary sense applies to a likeness of someone or something made by or as if by tracing the outline of his or its shadow on dark material (as black paper), cutting this out, and mounting it against a contrasting background. In extended use *silhouette*, even more than *outline* or *profile*, eliminates all consideration of such details as color, quality, and expression and implies an outline seen in or as if in a shadow ⟨from the distance at which we stood and because of the brightness of the sun behind them, we saw the two figures only in *silhouette*⟩ ⟨the *silhouette* made a blue-black stain on the opposite wall—*Lowell*⟩ ⟨with a little imagination, he could find . . . the face of a dead man in the *silhouette* of the mountains—*Bemelmans*⟩ *Ana* figure, *form, shape, conformation, configuration **2** sketch, diagram, delineation, draft, tracing, plot, blueprint (see under SKETCH *vb*)

**outline** *vb* *sketch, diagram, delineate, draft, trace, plot, blueprint

**outlive, outlast, survive** are comparable when they mean to remain in existence longer than another person or thing or after a given experience. **Outlive** carries a strong implication of a capacity for endurance and is especially appropriate when competition, struggle, or the surmounting of a difficulty is also connoted ⟨not marble, nor the gilded monuments of princes, shall *outlive* this powerful rhyme—*Shak.*⟩ ⟨the world has *outlived* much, and will *outlive* a great deal more—*J. R. Lowell*⟩ **Outlast** differs little from *outlive* but usually stresses greater length of duration rather than greater capacity for endurance and therefore may be employed when comparison is more important than a suggestion of superiority or when the fact of existing longer is more important than the length of time involved ⟨customs that have long *outlasted* their usefulness—*Inge*⟩ ⟨the sweet sensations of returning health made me happy for a time; but such sensations seldom *outlast* convalescence—*Hudson*⟩ **Survive** may be used as an intransitive as well as a transitive verb; in general it suggests merely a living or existing longer than another person or thing, or after some event (sometimes implied rather than expressed) which might bring about his or its end ⟨the elder sister *survived* the younger⟩ ⟨he is unlikely to *survive* the operation⟩ ⟨one in a million of these childish talents *survives* puberty—*Huxley*⟩ ⟨they had at least *survived* the old year and were alive for the next—*Irwin Shaw*⟩ ⟨all called their host "Mr. President." That much sense of the proprieties *survived* the reek of whiskey—*S. H. Adams*⟩ *Ana* endure, persist, abide, *continue: surpass, *exceed

**outlook** *n* *prospect, anticipation, foretaste *Ana* forecasting *or* forecast, predicting *or* prediction, prophesying *or* prophecy, presaging *or* presage (see corresponding verbs at FORETELL): possibility, probability, likelihood (see corresponding adjectives at PROBABLE)

**outrage** *vb* **1** *abuse, misuse, mistreat, maltreat, ill-treat *Ana* *wrong, persecute, oppress, aggrieve: corrupt, pervert, vitiate, deprave, *debase **2** *offend, affront, insult *Ana* vex, *annoy, irk, bother: mortify, chagrin (see corresponding adjectives at ASHAMED)

**outrageous, monstrous, heinous, atrocious** mean enormously or flagrantly bad or horrible. Something **outrageous** violates even the lowest standard of what is right or decent or exceeds one's power to suffer or tolerate ⟨an *outrageous* practical joke⟩ ⟨an *outrageous* cartoon⟩ ⟨the thought had already occurred to him, and it seemed *outrageous* to hear it repeated in what was, after all, the mouth of a prostitute—*Mailer*⟩ ⟨had induced her to come to Camp Tamarack with lies, bald *outrageous* lies—*Wouk*⟩ Something **monstrous** (see also MONSTROUS 1) is shockingly wrong, absurd, or horrible or is inconceivably fantastic, abnormal, or aberrant ⟨a *monstrous* falsehood⟩ ⟨a *monstrous* conception of morality⟩ ⟨the very horror with which men spoke, centuries after . . . plainly indicates that such a wholesale massacre was exceptional, *monstrous*—*Quiller-Couch*⟩ ⟨what is disturbing me most is . . . the knowledge that I have made a *monstrous* fool of myself—*Dahl*⟩ Something **heinous** is so flagrantly bad or so conspicuous for its enormity that it excites hatred or horror ⟨treason has always been regarded as a *heinous* crime⟩ ⟨these animal passions are felt most vividly when the community is animated with anger against some *heinous* offense—*Alexander*⟩ ⟨a murder, and a particularly *heinous* murder, for it involves the violation of hospitality and of gratitude—*Warren*⟩ Something **atrocious** excites condemnation for its savagery or barbarity

⟨*atrocious* cruelty⟩ ⟨*atrocious* acts which can only take place in a slave country—*Darwin*⟩ These words are frequently interchangeable, and all lend themselves to hyperbolic description of what is for the moment deprecated ⟨*outrageous* service in a restaurant⟩ ⟨awakened . . . by a *monstrous* hammering on his door—*G. D. Brown*⟩ ⟨time divorced from mechanical operations was treated as a *heinous* waste—*Mumford*⟩ ⟨*atrocious* weather⟩
*Ana* *flagrant, glaring, gross, rank: *excessive, inordinate, immoderate, extreme: flagitious, nefarious, iniquitous, *vicious

**outright** *adj* **Outright, out-and-out, unmitigated, arrant** are comparable when they are used hyperbolically as meaning not limited or qualified. They are often used interchangeably as intensives, but there are clear differences in meaning. What is **outright** has gone to the extreme and can be made neither better nor worse or is past recall ⟨he is an *outright* fool⟩ ⟨you speak *outright* nonsense⟩ ⟨torture more unmerciful than *outright* killing⟩ What is **out-and-out** is completely as described at all times or in every part or from every point of view ⟨an *out-and-out* fraud⟩ ⟨an *out-and-out* villain⟩ ⟨an *out-and-out* blessing⟩ What is **unmitigated** is or seems to be so utterly what it is as to be beyond the possibility of being lessened, softened, or relieved ⟨an *unmitigated* evil⟩ ⟨unrequited affections are in youth *unmitigated* woes—*L. P. Smith*⟩ What is **arrant** is all that is implied by the term that follows (usually a term of abuse) ⟨an *arrant* coward⟩ ⟨an *arrant* hypocrite⟩ ⟨an *arrant* liar⟩

**outside** *adj* *outer, outward, external, exterior
*Ana* *extrinsic, extraneous, alien, foreign
*Ant* inside —*Con* *inner, inward, internal, interior, intestine

**outsider** *stranger, foreigner, alien, outlander, immigrant, émigré

**outstanding** prominent, conspicuous, salient, signal, striking, arresting, remarkable, *noticeable
*Ana* *exceptional
*Ant* commonplace —*Con* *common, ordinary, familiar

**outstrip** outdo, *exceed, surpass, transcend, excel

**outward** *outer, outside, external, exterior
*Ana* extraneous, *extrinsic, alien, foreign
*Ant* inward —*Con* *inner, inside, internal, interior, intestine

**outwit** *frustrate, thwart, foil, baffle, balk, circumvent
*Ana* defeat, overcome, surmount (see CONQUER): *prevent, preclude, obviate, avert: overreach, *cheat, defraud

**over** *above
*Ant* beneath

**overbearing** supercilious, disdainful, lordly, arrogant, haughty, *proud, insolent
*Ana* domineering, *masterful, imperious: scorning *or* scornful, despising *or* despiteful, contemning (see corresponding verbs at DESPISE): autocratic, despotic, tyrannical, *absolute
*Ant* subservient

**overcome** surmount, overthrow, subjugate, rout, *conquer, vanquish, defeat, beat, lick, subdue
*Ana* capture, *catch: outstrip, outdo, *exceed: *suppress, repress

**overdue** *tardy, behindhand, late
*Ana* delayed, retarded, detained, slowed, slackened (see DELAY *vb*): deferred, postponed (see DEFER)

**overflow** *teem, swarm, abound

**overhang** *bulge, jut, stick out, protuberate, protrude, project, beetle
*Ana* *threaten, menace: suspend, *hang, dangle

**overlay, superpose, superimpose, appliqué** can all mean to add one thing to another by placing the former upon or over the latter. **Overlay** usually implies covering with another material or substance, sometimes thinly (as with a wash, glaze, or coat) ⟨plated silver is often a white metal *overlaid* with silver⟩ or sometimes thickly (as by encrusting, veneering, or plastering) ⟨a brick wall *overlaid* with stucco⟩ In extended use *overlay* usually implies accretions or additions that conceal or encumber the original thing or smother and stifle whatever there is of life in it ⟨the ancient world had its own complexities, but it was not, like ours, heavily *overlaid* with the debris of speculative systems—*Buchan*⟩ ⟨ages of fierceness have *overlaid* what is naturally kindly in the dispositions of ordinary men and women—*Russell*⟩ **Superpose** and *superimpose* are not always clearly distinguished, especially when they imply a putting of one thing on top of another, thereby extending the height of the original mass; thus, strata are layers of rock successively built up by sedimentary deposits, each layer being *superimposed* or *superposed* on the one previously formed. **Superpose**, however, is more often chosen when relative position only is indicated, and **superimpose** when the thing added rests upon or is supported by the original thing; thus, *superposed* columns do not necessarily have the columns of the lower row for their respective bases, but *superimposed* columns do; an overtone is strictly a *superposed* tone. *Superpose* is also the technical term when dealing with light rays or other energy waves that occupy the same position without destroying each other or losing their identities ⟨upon the large and general motion of the glacier, smaller motions are *superposed*—*Tyndall*⟩ ⟨originally they [two bright spots] were *superposed* on each other—*Darrow*⟩ *Superimpose* often, especially in extended use, carries the implications of imposition or the addition of something extraneous and unintegrated ⟨his symbolism is too often something *superimposed*—*Bentley*⟩ **Appliqué** basically implies an ornamenting with pieces, usually of contrasting material, that are cut or shaped and applied (as by sewing or pasting); the term is used primarily in reference to textile ornamentation ⟨*appliqué* a satin blouse with wool of the same color⟩ In extended use *appliqué* suggests overlaying with something obviously added and forming a pattern ⟨never taking his eyes off the pine trees, *appliquéd* against the blue water—*Cather*⟩ ⟨footnotes have been *appliquéd* to books that would have been better off without this factitious decoration—*D. C. Smith*⟩

**overlook** slight, forget, ignore, disregard, *neglect, omit

**overplus** *excess, superfluity, surplus, surplusage

**overreach** *cheat, cozen, defraud, swindle

**overrun** *infest, beset

**oversight, supervision, surveillance** all denote the function or duty of watching or guarding for the sake of proper control or direction. **Oversight** applies to the function or duty not only of one who is called an overseer or an inspector but of anyone whose duty it is to watch the progress of a piece of work so that no defects or imperfections may occur or to superintend the labors or efforts of a body of workers ⟨each foreman is charged with the *oversight* of the work done in his department⟩ ⟨his widow was to have the *oversight* of the portions left to the younger children —*Scudder*⟩ ⟨legislative *oversight* of administration is a familiar and well-grounded assumption of responsible government—*Macmahon*⟩ **Supervision** carries the strongest implication of authoritative powers, of responsibility, and of superintendence; it usually suggests more rigorous direction or closer management than *oversight* ⟨the architect had *supervision* of the construction of the building⟩ ⟨the majority plan advocated *supervision* of the processing of ores . . . that is, complete control of uranium and

A colon (:) separates groups of words discriminated. An asterisk (*) indicates place of treatment of each group.

thorium—*Current Biog.*⟩ **Surveillance** implies a close watch on persons suspected of being likely to commit misdeeds or offenses against the law or against morals or suffer untoward accidents ⟨the police are maintaining a strict *surveillance* of the suspect⟩ ⟨keep the inmates of a lunatic asylum under *surveillance*⟩ ⟨I cannot drink a milk shake or put on a pair of shoes without their friendly but implacable *surveillance*—A. E. *Stevenson*⟩ ⟨they subjected her to a pride-breaking foreign *surveillance*, and refused her even the lip service of recognition as an equal —*The Personalist*⟩

*Ana* management, direction, controlling *or* control (see corresponding verbs at CONDUCT): inspection, scrutiny, examination (see under SCRUTINIZE)

**overspread** *vb* *cover, envelop, wrap, shroud, veil

*Ana* *hide, conceal, screen: cloak, mask, *disguise, camouflage

**overstatement** *exaggeration, hyperbole

*Ant* understatement

**overthrow** *vb* 1 *overturn, subvert, upset, capsize

*Ana* *throw, cast, fling, hurl, toss

2 rout, surmount, overcome, vanquish, *conquer, defeat, beat, lick, subdue, subjugate, reduce

**overture** *n* Overture, approach, advance, tender, bid are words of somewhat indefinite application covering a variety of acts or actions by which one person or party tries to gain the goodwill of another person or party. **Overture** implies an attempt to begin a relationship. It may designate a formal proposal intended to open negotiations (as for peace, for a marriage between persons of royal blood, or for a merger of corporations). It is, however, often applied to an act or speech that may be construed as a search for an opening (as for friendship, for reconciliation, or for cooperation) ⟨she was not one of those backward and delicate ladies, who can die rather than make the first *overture*—*Fielding*⟩ ⟨"You are the new second officer, I believe." Mr. Powell answered in the affirmative, wondering if this was a friendly *overture*—*Conrad*⟩ **Approach**, often in the plural, may be used in place of *overture* when the latter is felt to be too formal ⟨the two girls made timid *approaches* to each other⟩ ⟨the minister is always tempted to break through . . . with intimate *approaches* to a congregation which are off the record—*Sperry*⟩ ⟨females who are most often involved in tavern pickups and in street *approaches* —*Kinsey et al*⟩ **Advance**, usually in the plural, may be applied to an attempt to gain love, friendship, or goodwill, whether it serve as an overture or as an effort to establish a closer relationship ⟨she tried to make talk, but Hugh answered all her *advances* . . . briefly—*Anderson*⟩ and it is the one of these terms that is freely used without qualification to suggest irregularity or impropriety in the overtures made ⟨Frances withstood the *advances* of the King, but she accepted his gift—*Sylvia Gray*⟩ ⟨if an officer with a higher rank than my husband's makes *advances* to me, do I have to submit if I want my husband to get promoted?—*Kaderli*⟩ **Tender** retains its primary meaning of offer, but it does not necessarily imply specific acts or a formal proposal. Sometimes it suggests little more than a sign or token ⟨"He hath, my lord, of late made many *tenders* of his affection to me." "Affection! pooh! you speak like a green girl. . . . Do you believe his *tenders*, as you call them?"—*Shak.*⟩ ⟨honored him by the *tender* of some important appointment—*J. D. Hicks*⟩ **Bid** adds to *advance* the implication of appeal or, sometimes, of invitation; it always requires qualification ⟨a *bid* for sympathy⟩ ⟨a *bid* for patronage⟩ Like the other words of this group, the specific nature of the act or action can be inferred only from the context ⟨de Gaulle's speech was generally considered a *bid* for the presidency—*Ehr-*

mann⟩ ⟨the establishing of a whaling colony as their first *bid* to fortune on the South river—*Amer. Guide Series: Del.*⟩

*Ana* *proposal, proposition: offering *or* offer, proffering (see corresponding verbs at OFFER)

**overturn, upset, capsize, overthrow, subvert** are comparable because they carry a common basic meaning—to cause to fall, or, intransitively, to fall, from the normal or proper position. Otherwise they vary widely in their applications and implications. **Overturn** is usually the least explicit in its additional implications; sometimes it implies a turning upside down ⟨the boat *overturned* and floated with its keel upwards⟩ but more often it implies a turning on the side so that the thing affected lies flat on the ground ⟨*overturn* a chair by hitting against it⟩ ⟨they *overturned* me in the dust, rubbed thistles into my hair, and left me—*Masters*⟩ Sometimes, especially when the thing affected is a state, an institution, or something which has been built up or become established, the term also implies a breaking down and consequently a ruining or destroying ⟨long-reverenced titles cast away as weeds; laws *overturned*—*Wordsworth*⟩ ⟨handed down a decision which *overturned* a century-old judicial rule—*Walter Goodman*⟩ ⟨a lever for prying apart and *overturning* the coalition —*Straight*⟩ **Upset** is the familiar term and implies especially a loss of balance, sometimes physical, sometimes mental, often emotional (for this sense of *upset* see DISCOMPOSE) as the result of some external or internal cause or agency ⟨no birds in last year's nests—the winds have torn and *upset* the mossy structures in the bushes—*Jefferies*⟩ ⟨a European war lays its blight on whole peoples, deranges their life, *upsets* their standards of judgement—*Montague*⟩ But *upset* more often than *overturn* is used to imply the abolition of something established or the demolishing of something built up ⟨the general's calculations were *upset* by the swift advance of the enemy⟩ ⟨we are bound to be very cautious in coming to the conclusion that the Fourteenth Amendment has *upset* what thus far has been established and accepted for a long time —*Justice Holmes*⟩ **Capsize** is specifically applicable to the upsetting or overturning of a boat; in more general use it usually suggests a complete overturning and is sometimes employed in an extended sense to imply a turning, especially a sudden turning, upside down or topsy-turvy, not only physically, but mentally or morally ⟨it may well have been the comedians who restored the theatre's balance when the tragedians threatened to *capsize* it into absurdity—*Bridges-Adams*⟩ **Overthrow** (see also CONQUER) carries a stronger implication of the exercise of force, violence, or strategy than any of the preceding terms; it often also implies consequent defeat, destruction, or ruin ⟨trees *overthrown* by a storm⟩ ⟨seek to *overthrow* religion⟩ ⟨my plans were *overthrown*—*Darwin*⟩ ⟨traditional beliefs which science may *overthrow*—*Cohen*⟩ **Subvert** implies an overturning or overthrowing of something held to be of intrinsic value (as a form of government, or morality, or religion) by undermining its supports or weakening its foundations; often it suggests the operation of insidious or corrupting influences ⟨this doctrine would *subvert* the very foundation of all written constitutions —*John Marshall*⟩ ⟨a . . . question . . . whether more harm will be done to morality by weakening or *subverting* established usage than good—*Alexander*⟩ ⟨representative government . . . easily may be, and in England has been, used to *subvert* equality and fraternity—*Brownell*⟩

*Ana* invert, *reverse, transpose

**own** *vb* 1 possess, hold, *have, enjoy

*Ana* control, manage, direct, *conduct: *keep, retain

2 *acknowledge, avow, admit, confess

---

*Ana* analogous words    *Ant* antonyms    *Con* contrasted words    See also explanatory notes facing page 1

*Ana* concede, \*grant, allow: \*reveal, disclose, divulge
*Ant* disown: repudiate

**oxygenate** \*aerate, ventilate, carbonate
**ozone** \*air, atmosphere, ether

# P

**pabulum** \*food, aliment, nutriment, nourishment, sustenance, pap

**pace** *n* \*speed, velocity, momentum, impetus, headway

**pacific, peaceable, peaceful, irenic, pacifist, pacifistic** are sometimes confused because they all involve the idea of affording or promoting peace. But **pacific** applies chiefly to persons or to utterances, acts, influences, or ideas that tend to make peace or to conciliate strife ⟨they flung out a challenge which even the most *pacific* Quaker in Philadelphia had to heed—*Charles & Mary Beard*⟩ ⟨seek the settlement of disputes only by *pacific* means—*R. H. Jackson*⟩ ⟨the *pacific* policy of Walpole was regarded by them as a national humiliation—*Plumb*⟩ **Peaceable** also applies to persons or to their actions or words, but it describes their character or quality as peace-loving, as disposed to avoid strife, or as inclined to keep peace, rather than their aims or tendencies ⟨the villagers were a quiet, *peaceable* folk⟩ ⟨our king the good Simonides . . . deserves so to be called for his *peaceable* reign and good government—*Shak.*⟩ ⟨the Mayans were a traditionally gentle and *peaceable* people—*Bracker*⟩ **Peaceful** applies especially to a life, a condition or state, a period or age, or a country or people in which peace prevails or there is no strife, but it may apply to whatever is indicative of peace, especially of mind, or provides an opportunity for such peace ⟨and may at last my weary age find out the *peaceful* hermitage—*Milton*⟩ ⟨the *peaceful* countenance of the old clergyman⟩ ⟨thou shouldst have seemed a treasure-house divine of *peaceful* years—*Wordsworth*⟩ ⟨man has laid down his weapons and resumed a *peaceful* way of life—*Bailey*⟩ ⟨the *peaceful* comportment of the seals had quieted my alarm—*London*⟩ **Irenic**, which applies primarily to peace in connection with religious controversy, may describe attitudes and measures likely to allay dispute ⟨the political equivalent of the dogfight on the human level is not made more *irenic* by the capacity of the participants to verbalize their animosities—*Murphy*⟩ ⟨Pieper lived to see his synod adopt a very *irenic* attitude towards its former antagonists —*Rohne*⟩ **Pacifist** and **pacifistic** apply chiefly to the views, arguments, writings, or attitudes of opponents of war or the use of military force for any purpose but they may also apply to the spirit or utterances of someone who conscientiously objects to wars or who would substitute arbitration for conflict in the settlement of any disputes ⟨*pacifistic* antagonism to conscription⟩ ⟨Grotius' *pacifistic* attitude is founded on his understanding of the humanitarian and cosmopolitan aspects of natural law— *Albert Salomon*⟩ ⟨as many *pacifist* writers argue, international warfare has consequences for the lives of people, in terms of spiritual sickness and the brutalizing of attitudes—*Garvin*⟩
*Ana* \*calm, placid, serene, tranquil: conciliating *or* conciliatory, propitiating *or* propitiatory, appeasing, pacifying *or* pacificatory (see corresponding verbs at PACIFY)
*Ant* bellicose —*Con* \*belligerent, pugnacious, combative, quarrelsome, contentious

**pacifist, pacifistic** \*pacific, peaceable, peaceful, irenic

**pacify, appease, placate, mollify, propitiate, conciliate** are comparable when they mean to quiet excited, aroused, or disturbed persons. **Pacify** implies a soothing or calming of anger, grievance, or agitation, or the quelling of insurrection especially by force ⟨seeing his mounting rage, friends did all they could to *pacify* and restrain him⟩ ⟨second-grade troops, useful mainly to occupy parts of the country that have already been *pacified*—*Crozier*⟩ **Appease** may indicate the quieting of agitation or insistent demand by the making of concessions ⟨open in manner, easy of access, a little quick of temper but readily *appeased* —*Buchan*⟩ ⟨he is utterly and absolutely implacable; no prayers, no human sacrifices can ever for one moment *appease* his cold, malignant rage—*L. P. Smith*⟩ and it may be used in reference to appetites, desires, and passions as well as persons and to imply a giving of quietening satisfaction ⟨there is always the drive to excel. Work, literacy, food and shelter . . . are minimum requirements of civilization, but they will not *appease* this ambition—*Edmund Wilson*⟩ ⟨a frantic effort to *appease* mounting discontent at home—*Willen*⟩ **Placate** is sometimes interchangeable with *appease* but may imply a more complete or lasting assuagement of bitter feeling ⟨each and every new route projected was liable to drastic alteration to *placate* local opposition—*O. S. Nock*⟩ ⟨federal officials who try to *placate* witch-hunting Congressmen—*New Republic*⟩ **Mollify** stresses softening of anger or abatement of hurt feelings by positive action (as flattery or concession) ⟨the propagandist . . . must be able to *mollify* and perhaps even convert the hostile—*Huxley*⟩ ⟨*mollified* when they heard that the patio, with its famous cottonwood tree will be left intact—*Green Peyton*⟩ **Propitiate** may refer to averting the anger or malevolence or winning the favor of a superior or of one possessing the power to injure greatly ⟨*propitiate* this far-shooting Apollo—*Grote*⟩ ⟨Aunty Rosa, he argued, had the power to beat him with many stripes . . . it would be discreet in the future to *propitiate* Aunty Rosa—*Kipling*⟩ ⟨the unlimited power of trustees to abuse their trust unless they are abjectly *propitiated*— *H. G. Wells*⟩ **Conciliate** may be used of situations in which an estrangement or dispute is settled by arbitration or compromise ⟨policy of *conciliating* and amalgamating conquered nations—*Repplier*⟩ ⟨instinctively friendly and wholly free from inflammatory rhetoric, he did much to *conciliate* more stubborn Northern sentiment concerning the South—*Gaines*⟩
*Ana* assuage, alleviate, allay, mitigate, \*relieve: \*moderate, qualify, temper
*Ant* anger

**pack** *n* \*bundle, bunch, package, packet, bale, parcel

**pack** *vb* **Pack, crowd, cram, stuff, ram, tamp** are comparable when they mean to fill tightly or cause to fill tightly something which holds a limited amount or presents a limited space. **Pack**, in its basic sense, implies a forming into packs or bundles for convenience in storing or transporting ⟨oranges are *packed* in crates for shipment⟩ ⟨*pack* books in cartons before moving them⟩ ⟨in this factory huge quantities of meat are processed, *packed*, and shipped to all parts of the country⟩ Additionally it may imply close, orderly arrangement in receptacles of determined size, and, as a corollary, compact and complete

A colon (:) separates groups of words discriminated. An asterisk (\*) indicates place of treatment of each group.

filling. In extended use it may suggest completeness of filling or, frequently, an excessive or uncomfortable filling, without any relation to the ideas of storing or transporting ⟨the play *packed* the theater⟩ ⟨the crowd in the bus was *packed* in like sardines⟩ ⟨*packs* an extraordinary amount of information into a few pages—*Times Lit. Sup.*⟩ **Crowd** (see also PRESS) implies the presence of great numbers of persons or things in proportion to the space, area, or time; the term often suggests numbers so great as to press upon or otherwise seriously inconvenience ⟨the harbor was *crowded* with ships⟩ ⟨*crowd* more persons into a hall than it can safely hold⟩ ⟨in revolutions men live fast: the experience of years is *crowded* into hours—*Macaulay*⟩ ⟨the road . . . was now *crowded* with people who had come up the hill for their Sunday afternoon walk—*Archibald Marshall*⟩ ⟨his mind was *crowded* with the detail he observed—*Nevil Shute*⟩ **Cram** carries a similar implication of pressing so as to bruise or squeeze, but the word usually also suggests a forcible and, sometimes, disorderly insertion into a receptacle or space of more than it can easily or comfortably or safely take ⟨*cram* a trunk full of clothes⟩ ⟨their storehouses *crammed* with grain—*Shak.*⟩ ⟨*crammed* his head full of knowledge⟩ ⟨*cram* for an examination⟩ ⟨most of the newcomers arrive with only such means as can be *crammed* into a bundle or two—*Hersey*⟩ **Stuff** implies the use of such a material as padding, wadding, or straw in expanding or distending ⟨*stuff* a pillow with feathers⟩ ⟨*stuff* a mattress with straw⟩ From this specific meaning comes the more general meaning of to fill so that a thing bulges or so that the filling protrudes ⟨*stuffed* his purse with bills⟩ ⟨*stuff* a turkey with dressing⟩ ⟨I have *stuffed* too many of the facts of history and science into my intellectuals—*L. P. Smith*⟩ ⟨as many hot hors d'oeuvres as the greediest guest could *stuff* into himself—*Wouk*⟩ **Ram** nearly always retains some notion of its basic implication of pounding and tamping ⟨*ram* home the charge in a muzzle-loading firearm by means of a ramrod⟩ but this implication is sometimes obscured or subordinated and that of stuffing or cramming as if by pounding in is stressed ⟨*ram* tobacco into his pipe⟩ ⟨I always *ram* my clothes into a box—*Bury*⟩ ⟨pronging great slices of meat onto his fork and *ramming* them into his mouth—*Bruce Marshall*⟩ **Tamp**, which often comes close to *ram* in meaning, originally meant and still means to plug up a drill hole above a blasting charge with clay, earth, or similar material. In its extended use it implies a series of blows which press something into a confined space or under, over, or about another thing that needs to be supported ⟨*tamping* the gravel back around the ties—*Laird*⟩ ⟨*tamp* tobacco into his pipe⟩
*Ana* \*compact, consolidate: \*press, squeeze, jam: compress, constrict, \*contract

**package** *n* packet, \*bundle, bunch, bale, parcel, pack

**packet** *n* package, pack, \*bundle, bunch, bale, parcel

**pact** compact, \*contract, bargain, treaty, entente, convention, cartel, concordat

**pain** *n* **1** Pain, ache, pang, throe, twinge, stitch are comparable when they mean a bodily sensation that causes acute discomfort or suffering. **Pain** may range in its application from a sensation that makes one uneasily aware of some bodily disturbance or injury to a sensation resulting from severe injuries or disease and of agonizing intensity; from a sensation that is purely local to one that affects the entire body ⟨a *pain* in the finger⟩ ⟨his *chest pains*⟩ ⟨his body was wracked with *pain*⟩ More technically, *pain* denotes a usually unpleasant sensation that results from a noxious stimulus to skin or tissues and leads to avoiding reactions. An **ache** is a steady, dull, and often generalized pain that is frequently associated with some underlying disorder ⟨the *ache* of an abscessed tooth⟩ ⟨back*ache* that accompanies kidney disease⟩ A **pang** is a sharp, sudden, and usually transitory pain of great intensity, especially one that recurs in spasms ⟨*pangs* have taken hold upon me, as the *pangs* of a woman that travaileth—*Isa* 21:3⟩ ⟨attacking them [fleas] was a waste of time, and unless a particularly savage *pang* forced you into action, you just sat and let yourself be devoured—*Stewart*⟩ A **throe** is a pang characteristic of a process (as of labor in childbirth). Because of its association with labor the term usually designates a violent and convulsive, as well as a recurrent pain ⟨in the *throes* of violent retching⟩ ⟨the *throes* of a mortal and painful disorder—*Scott*⟩ A **twinge** is a momentary shooting or darting pain, especially one causing muscular contraction or twitching; it is sometimes regarded as a premonitory symptom ⟨shrugged off *twinges* and creakings like mine as something quite to be expected in their early fifties—*E. M. Stern*⟩ ⟨feel a *twinge* in the region of the heart⟩ **Stitch** differs from *twinge* in suggesting something that runs through a part of a body (usually a muscle) like a piercing needle ⟨ran until he got a *stitch* in the side⟩

All of these words except the last designate also mental suffering. **Pain** commonly suggests sorrow (as for something lost or unattainable) ⟨my craving to hear from her was at times a gnawing *pain*—*Kenneth Roberts*⟩ **Ache** usually implies suffering that must be endured or longing not likely to be appeased ⟨there was an *ache* in his heart like the farewell to a dear woman—*Steinbeck*⟩ ⟨know the *ache* of loneliness⟩ **Pang** suggests a sudden sharp access of a painful emotion ⟨sharp *pangs* of envy⟩ ⟨*pangs* of remorse⟩ ⟨the next time I ran away just the same, and suffered the most ghastly *pangs* of fear—*John Reed*⟩ ⟨statements . . . made unhesitatingly, with no visible *pangs* of conscience—*Sanders*⟩ **Throe** presupposes the existence of mental agony and designates one of the recurrent spasms that characterize the state of mind ⟨fierce maternal passion . . . was now bowing her still lower, in the *throes* of a bitter renunciation—*Wharton*⟩ **Twinge** suggests less poignancy than *pang* but often connotes compunction ⟨*twinges* of conscience⟩ ⟨too painfully preoccupied to feel a *twinge* of self-reproach at this undeserved praise—*George Eliot*⟩ ⟨shot down his victims without shadow of provocation and who probably never felt a *twinge* of remorse—*Ghent*⟩
*Ana* agony, \*distress, suffering, passion: anguish, \*sorrow, grief, heartbreak
**2** in plural form **pains** \*effort, exertion, trouble
*Ana* labor, toil, travail, \*work: industriousness *or* industry, diligence, sedulousness, assiduousness (see corresponding adjectives at BUSY)

**pair** *n* \*couple, brace, yoke

**palatable,** appetizing, savory, sapid, tasty, toothsome, flavorsome, relishing mean agreeable or pleasant to the taste. **Palatable** is not emphatic in its implication of pleasantness; therefore it seldom suggests deliciousness and often, on the other hand, implies little more than acceptability ⟨provide *palatable* meals for her family⟩ ⟨the root, when properly cooked, was converted into a *palatable* and nutritious food—*Prescott*⟩ The term is used frequently of things which are mentally digested ⟨the rebuke was not *palatable*⟩ ⟨I'm afraid that my remarks have not been very *palatable*, but I can assure you that they were sincerely meant—*Mackenzie*⟩ **Appetizing** implies a whetting of the appetite; it is applicable to the smell and appearance as well as to the taste of food ⟨the *appetizing* odor of a roasting turkey⟩ ⟨a convalescent requires *appetizing* meals⟩ In its extended use the word is applicable to things that stimulate a desire for more or an

eagerness to go further ⟨an *appetizing* introduction to a subject⟩ ⟨the journalist with a nose for *appetizing* front-page tidbits—*Zirato*⟩ **Savory**, also, is applied to foods that have an agreeable odor as well as taste, but it conveys definite implications of piquancy; it is therefore applied to highly seasoned dishes as contrasted with sweet or bland dishes ⟨a bland meat sometimes needs a *savory* sauce⟩ ⟨a *savory* stuffing for the turkey⟩ In extended use *savory* may suggest a pleasantly stimulating and agreeable quality ⟨engaging books . . . neither autobiography, nor fiction, nor essays, but a *savory* mixture of all three—*N. Y. Times*⟩ but more often than not it is used in negative construction or with ironic implications ⟨the conquest of the West . . . is not among the more *savory* chapters in American history —*Agnew*⟩ **Sapid** is an uncommon and chiefly technical term that primarily applies to a substance able to stimulate taste receptors ⟨assuming that the *sapid* substance . . . initiates the electrical depolarization of the taste cell— *Beidler*⟩ In general use it may imply a marked taste or flavor ⟨a *sapid* dish⟩ or in extended use one that is distinctly keen or exhilarating ⟨a *sapid* and antiseptic quality of bright intelligence—*Ellis*⟩ **Tasty** implies a marked taste, but it suggests in addition an appetizing quality ⟨a *tasty* morsel⟩ ⟨a *tasty* cheese, like the cajú, which produce *tasty* fruits—*P. E. James*⟩ ⟨*tasty* ingredients for a good, breezy book—*Barrett*⟩ **Toothsome** heightens the implication of agreeableness in *palatable* and may add the suggestion of tenderness or of daintiness ⟨a *toothsome* dessert⟩ ⟨one of the most *toothsome* chicken dinners you'll ever munch—*Gelston Hardy*⟩ **Flavorsome** usually suggests richness rather than sharpness of taste, and often implies fragrance as well as savor ⟨*flavorsome* apricots⟩ ⟨incredibly *flavorsome* wild mushrooms from the forests— *Davenport*⟩ **Relishing** stresses gusto in enjoyment ⟨he found all this praise extremely *relishing*⟩ ⟨find ways in which the soldier's food could be made more *relishing*— *Current Biog.*⟩
*Ana* *delightful, delicious, delectable, luscious: piquant, *pungent, spicy
*Ant* unpalatable: distasteful

**palate** *taste, relish, gusto, zest

**pale** *adj* **1 Pale, pallid, ashen, ashy, wan, livid** mean devoid of natural or healthy color as applied to a complexion or deficient in vividness or intensity of hue as applied to a specific color. **Pale** is the least rich of these words in implications and connotations; it merely implies relative nearness to white and deficiency in depth and brilliance of coloring ⟨his face grew *pale*⟩ ⟨the sea is a *pale* green in this light⟩ **Pallid** adds to *pale* the suggestions of deprivation, rather than absence, of color and of an abnormal condition (as weakness or faintness, or intense weariness); thus, one may be naturally *pale* but a person made *pale* by illness would usually be called *pallid* ⟨his *pallid* face reveals the strain he has been under⟩ ⟨trembling limbs and *pallid* lips—*Shelley*⟩ ⟨its little smoke, in *pallid* moonshine, died—*Keats*⟩ **Ashen** and **ashy** definitely suggest not only the pale gray color of ashes but often, also, extreme pallor (as of the skin in death). A thing described as *ashen* or *ashy* may therefore be said to be deadly or ghastly pale ⟨the skies they were *ashen* and sober—*Poe*⟩ ⟨the *ashen* hue of age—*Scott*⟩ ⟨oft have I seen a timely-parted ghost, of *ashy* semblance—*Shak.*⟩ ⟨Mr. Cruncher, who was all in a tremble . . . with an *ashy* and solemn visage—*Dickens*⟩ **Wan** suggests the blanching associated with an unhealthy condition or waning vitality; it usually therefore denotes a sickly paleness ⟨the blasted stars looked *wan*—*Milton*⟩ ⟨her poor *wan* face with its wistful, pitiful little smile— *Hewlett*⟩ **Livid** basically means leaden-hued; it is chiefly used of things, especially of human faces that under the

influence of something that distorts them have lost their normal coloring and have assumed a dull grayish tinge ⟨he grew *livid* with rage⟩ ⟨in the greenish glass her own face looked far off like the *livid* face of a drowned corpse at the bottom of a pool—*Conrad*⟩ The word is also applied to various dull or dun colors when the hue is barely apparent ⟨the *livid* red of the sun seen through a heavy fog⟩ ⟨the *livid* yellow of a stormy sky⟩ ⟨his trembling lips are *livid* blue—*Scott*⟩
*Ana* *ghastly, macabre: cadaverous, *haggard, worn
**2 Pale, anemic, bloodless** are comparable in their extended senses when they are applied to things and mean weak and thin in substance or in vital qualities, as though drained of blood. **Pale** stresses deficiency in qualities necessary to give a thing its true color or character. Sometimes it connotes lack of vigor, force, or energy ⟨the French . . . shake in their fear and with *pale* policy seek to divert the English purposes—*Shak.*⟩ ⟨does *pale* little studies that are as innocuous as his earlier work was adventurous— *Coates*⟩ but more often it implies inadequacy or failure to measure up to the requirements of a type or standard ⟨her whole existence was too *pale*, too inadequate in some way—too unvital—*Farrell*⟩ **Anemic** in its extended applications to things implies deficiency in the elements that make for vigor or richness, especially intellectual or spiritual vigor or richness ⟨the African Negro has . . . joy of life, love of color, keen senses, beautiful voice, and ear for music—contributions that . . . might one day prove a tonic to an *anemic* and artless America—*Zangwill*⟩ ⟨not even a respectable vocabulary of indecency to draw upon in support of our *anemic* cussing—*Whicher*⟩ **Bloodless** stresses the absence of qualities necessary to life or lifelikeness (as vitality, warmth, color, and human emotion) ⟨now if I make this sound *bloodless*, I am exaggerating a bit—even an old habit is livened once in a while with color—*Mailer*⟩ ⟨books are good enough in their own way, but they are a mighty *bloodless* substitute for life—*Stevenson*⟩
*Ana* *insipid, wishy-washy, inane, jejune: *ineffective, ineffectual

**pall** cloy, surfeit, *satiate, sate, glut, gorge

**palliate,** extenuate, gloze, gloss, whitewash, whiten are comparable when they mean to give a speciously fine appearance to what is base, evil, or erroneous. **Palliate** may stress the concealing or cloaking or the condoning of the enormity of a crime or offense ⟨retracing thus his frolics ('tis a name that *palliates* deeds of folly and of shame)—*Cowper*⟩ ⟨we have not endeavored to conceal or even *palliate* his errors—*Lockhart*⟩ ⟨we cannot . . . explain away this deliberate act as due to the garrulity of age, or accept the other excuses with which his admirers have sought to *palliate* it—*L. P. Smith*⟩ The word also is used especially in reference to other than moral evils in the sense of to disguise the true nature or extent of so as to soften the bad effects ⟨minds which are keener and wills which are stronger than the average do not rest in "quiet desperation" *palliated* by illusion—*Krutch*⟩ ⟨resort to coercive force and suppression of civil liberties are readily *palliated* . . . when the cry is raised that "law and order" are threatened—*Dewey*⟩ **Extenuate** (see also THIN) implies the aim to lessen (as by excuses or explanations) the seriousness or magnitude of some crime, offense, or guilt ⟨when you shall these unlucky deeds relate, speak of me as I am; nothing *extenuate*, nor set down aught in malice—*Shak.*⟩ ⟨he did not *extenuate*, he rather emphasized, the criminality of Catiline and his confederates— *Froude*⟩ But the term is often used in the sense of to make excuses for ⟨had never forgiven Cromwell the execution of the martyr Charles; and to *extenuate* the conduct of the

great Roundhead captain, was to make Mrs. Doria despise and detest you—*Meredith*⟩ ⟨he permits himself . . . costly Havana cigars and an electric typewriter. There are circumstances that *extenuate* both indulgences—*Kahn*⟩ *Gloze* and *gloss* often followed by *over*, imply an aim to veil by more or less light dissembling (as by specious comments or by flattering talk) the true harshness, unpleasantness, or disagreeableness of something; often, the words suggest a representation of what is actually disagreeable as more or less agreeable or as not distinctly unpleasant; **gloze**, however, is usually more derogatory than **gloss** which is a relatively neutral word ⟨the explorer has succeeded in *glossing* over the hardships he endured⟩ ⟨not wish to *gloss* over the'fragmentary state of our present knowledge—*Eddington*⟩ ⟨with the tongue of flattery *glozing* deeds which God and Truth condemn—*Whittier*⟩ ⟨we *glozed* our fraud by conducting their necessary war purely and cheaply—*T. E. Lawrence*⟩ ⟨believed in youth and did not *gloze* the unpleasant consequences of age—*MacNeice*⟩ **Whitewash**, and less often **whiten**, imply an attempt to cover up (as a crime, a defect or fault, or a person's guilt) by some such means as a superficial investigation, or a perfunctory trial, or a special report that leads to a seeming acquittal or exoneration or that gives the person or persons accused an appearance of innocence or blamelessness ⟨a poet and an author will go as far in *whitewashing* a munificent tyrant—*Walpole*⟩ ⟨by selecting the evidence any society may be relatively blackened, and any other society relatively *whitened*—*Spencer*⟩ ⟨his object in attempting to *whitewash* the evildoers was not so clear—*Crofts*⟩
*Ana* mitigate, alleviate, lighten (see RELIEVE): condone, *excuse: *moderate, qualify, temper: cloak, mask, *disguise, dissemble, camouflage

**pallid** *pale, ashen, ashy, wan, livid

**palpable** 1 *perceptible, sensible, tangible, appreciable, ponderable
*Ana* *apparent, ostensible, seeming: believable, credible, colorable, *plausible
*Ant* insensible
2 plain, clear, *evident, apparent, manifest, patent, obvious, distinct
*Ana* *sure, certain, positive: *noticeable, remarkable, striking, arresting
*Ant* impalpable —*Con* *doubtful, dubious, questionable, problematic

**palpate** *vb* *touch, feel, handle, paw

**palpation** see under *palpate* at TOUCH *vb*

**palpitate** beat, throb, *pulsate, pulse
*Ana* vibrate, oscillate, fluctuate, *swing, sway

**palpitation** beat, throb, pulsation, pulse (see under PULSATE *vb*)
*Ana* vibration, oscillation, fluctuation, swinging, swaying (see corresponding verbs at SWING)

**palter** *lie, prevaricate, equivocate, fib
*Ana* evade, elude, *escape: *trifle, dally

**paltry** trifling, trivial, *petty, puny, measly, picayunish, picayune
*Ana* *contemptible, despicable, sorry, scurvy, cheap, beggarly, shabby: abject, ignoble, *mean: *base, low, vile

**pamper** *indulge, humor, spoil, baby, mollycoddle
*Ana* gratify, tickle, regale, *please: fondle, pet, cosset, *caress, dandle
*Ant* chasten

**pandect** *compendium, syllabus, digest, survey, sketch, précis, aperçu

**pandemonium** uproar, *din, hullabaloo, babel, hubbub, clamor, racket

**pander** *cater, purvey

*Ana* truckle, toady, *fawn, cringe: gratify, tickle, regale, *please

**panegyric** tribute, eulogy, *encomium, citation
*Ana* commendation, applauding *or* applause, complimenting *or* compliment (see corresponding verbs at COMMEND): acclaiming *or* acclaim, laudation, praising *or* praise, extolling *or* extollation (see corresponding verbs at PRAISE)

**pang** *pain, ache, throe, twinge, stitch
*Ana* agony, *distress, suffering: anguish, *sorrow, grief, heartache, heartbreak: torturing *or* torture, tormenting *or* torment (see AFFLICT)

**panic** terror, horror, trepidation, consternation, dismay, alarm, fright, dread, *fear
*Ana* agitation, upsetting *or* upset, perturbation, disquieting *or* disquiet, discomposing *or* discomposure (see corresponding verbs at DISCOMPOSE)
*Con* *confidence, assurance, self-possession, aplomb: equanimity, composure, sangfroid

**pant** aspire, *aim
*Ana* thirst, hunger, *long, yearn, pine: crave, covet, *desire, wish, want

**pap** *food, aliment, pabulum, nutriment, nourishment, sustenance

**paper** *n* 1 Paper, instrument, document all mean a writing (often typed, sometimes printed) that is of value to its owner or to others who come after him as a source of information or proof of a right, contention, or claim. **Paper** is the most general term, applicable to such writing (as a letter, deed, certificate, or writ) filed away for future use or reference ⟨state *papers*⟩ ⟨a peculiar difficulty I have experienced in dealing with Lord Macaulay's private *papers*—*G. O. Trevelyan*⟩ ⟨it was not until I was forty that my father put into my hands a few old family *papers* which furnished clues to an investigation of my more remote ancestry—*Ellis*⟩ **Instrument** is a legal term applicable to a paper (as a deed, a writ, a will, or a contract) that is made and executed according to the terms of the law, as concrete evidence of some legally defined action (as a transfer of property, the enforcement of a judgment, one's decisions as to who shall inherit one's property, or the terms of an agreement) ⟨set up a confederacy based upon a written *instrument*—*Nevins*⟩ **Document** (see also DOCUMENT 1) applies to a legal instrument or to an original or authentic copy of a letter, a record, or other paper that may be used as a source of information, evidence, or proof ⟨her letters I sent back except those of the quarreling correspondence, and those, being *documents*, are placed in the hands of a third person—*Byron*⟩ ⟨the Declaration of Independence stands out as one of the vital *documents* of history—*Canfield & Wilder*⟩
2 article, *essay, theme, composition

**par** *n* norm, *average, mean, median

**par** *adj* mean, median, average (see under AVERAGE *n*)

**parable** *allegory, myth, fable

**parade** *n* 1 *display, array, pomp
*Ana* showiness, ostentatiousness *or* ostentation, pretentiousness (see corresponding adjectives at SHOWY)
2 *procession, cavalcade, cortege, motorcade

**parade** *vb* flaunt, expose, display, exhibit, *show
*Ana* *reveal, disclose, divulge: *declare, proclaim, publish, advertise: vaunt, *boast, brag, gasconade
*Con* cloak, mask, *disguise, dissemble, camouflage

**paradox**, **antinomy**, **anomaly** are comparable terms that involve the idea of expressing or revealing an inner or inherent contradiction and are therefore not always clearly distinguished. A **paradox** is primarily a statement or proposition which contains a contradiction yet which, absurd as it seems to be, may still be true and in accordance with the facts and common sense ⟨the perfectly bred man is

---

*Ana* analogous words　　　*Ant* antonyms　　　*Con* contrasted words　　　See also explanatory notes facing page 1

born, not bred, if the *paradox* may be permitted—*Brownell*⟩ By extension *paradox* may apply to something which is known to exist, yet which when described or put in words seems incredible because it involves a logical contradiction ⟨the old will perennially become new at the hand of genius. That is the *paradox* of art—*Lowes*⟩ ⟨the colonel . . . is a *paradox*—a well-known secret agent—*Kobler*⟩ An **antinomy**, in philosophical use, is a contradiction between two laws, principles, or conclusions, both of which are held on good grounds or are correctly inferred from the same facts or premises; thus, the conclusions that every material thing can be explained by mechanical causes and that some material things cannot be explained unless a final cause is postulated, present an *antinomy*, but in the opinion of Kant both can be accepted as rules regulative of experience. In more general use the term is often applied to one thing that contradicts another thing and is irreconcilable with it ⟨form and expression . . . should stand toward one another not as clashing *antinomies* but as reconciled opposites—*Babbitt*⟩ or it may apply to a conflict (as of principles, beliefs, forces, tendencies, or aspirations) that is irresolvable in the light of present knowledge ⟨a mind that is not naturally analytical, and conscious of the *antinomies* of existence—*Amer. Speech*⟩ ⟨every dogma is but one side of an inevitable *antinomy*—*Cushing*⟩ ⟨the *antinomy* between contented security and adventure for gain, between equalitarian justice and the justice of rewards—an *antinomy* whose resolution calls for a reasonable compromise and not a clear-cut choice —*Aron*⟩ An **anomaly** is something that is contrary to what it should be. For example, it may be an exception or a contradiction to a rule; it may be a freak, a monster, a sport, or a contradiction to a type; it may be an anachronism or solecism, irreconcilable with its surroundings or conditions; it may be an action, a practice, or a mood, that is in effect a denial of what one believes or teaches ⟨there is no greater *anomaly* in nature than a bird that cannot fly—*Darwin*⟩ ⟨the *anomaly* of a war fought to preserve freedom by a people enslaved by prejudice—*Quentin Anderson*⟩ ⟨the political world must keep pace with the scientific world. A security league, in an age of flight, is an *anomaly*—*E. B. White*⟩

**paragon** *n* Paragon, apotheosis, nonpareil, nonesuch are comparable when they mean a person or thing of consummate quality or transcendent excellence in its kind. **Paragon** distinctively implies supremacy and incomparability ⟨an angel! or, if not, an earthly *paragon*—*Shak.*⟩ ⟨Mill's book is a *paragon* of expository writing—*Macy*⟩ ⟨neither the violent demagogue his enemies thought, nor the *paragon* his friends esteemed him—*Bonham*⟩ **Apotheosis** basically applies to a raising from an earthly to a divine or ideal status ⟨Wagner believed that Beethoven's Seventh Symphony . . . was an *apotheosis* of the dance—*Ellis*⟩ but it may be indistinguishable from *paragon* in denoting one that is the extreme and usually the highest of its kind ⟨here all is spotless grace, ethereal delicacy . . . the very *apotheosis* of womanhood—*Jameson*⟩ ⟨in the Third Reich the nation-state found both its zenith and its nadir, its *apotheosis* and its Black Mass—*Deutscher*⟩ **Nonpareil** and **nonesuch**, like *paragon* imply the absence of a rival or equal, but they sometimes impute uniqueness more strongly than excellence ⟨thou art the best o' the cutthroats: yet he's good that did the like for Fleance: if thou didst it, thou art the *nonpareil*—*Shak.*⟩ ⟨it was the strapping leader, the *nonpareil* of newspaperdom—*Swanberg*⟩ ⟨a *nonpareil* at her dimly lit specialties, but . . . certainly no Fitzgerald—*Hentoff*⟩ ⟨the Eiffel Tower, the mighty *nonesuch* of the Paris exposition—*Kobler*⟩ ⟨for more than fifty years a political boss, a

political *nonesuch*, and a general nuisance to the forces of political progress—*New Yorker*⟩

**paragraph,** verse, article, clause, plank, count are comparable when they denote one of the several and individually distinct statements of a discourse or instrument, each of which deals with a particular point or item. **Paragraph** primarily refers to a typographical division, usually indicated by beginning on a new line, and usually by indenting the first word, or by the use of ¶, but it also is applicable to a similar division in writing or typing. In rhetorical use the term usually implies a number of sentences which comprise a unit that coherently develops a topic or point, especially one of the subordinate topics or points of an essay or an argument. In more general use, brief, clear, or pointed statement of a single idea rather than its expansion and adequate exposition is stressed; the term is often used where statements follow in serial or numbered order and are neither developed individually nor logically related to each other ⟨see *paragraph* 4 of the accompanying instructions⟩ ⟨the witty *paragraphs* of a popular columnist⟩ **Verse** (see also VERSE 1) is applied specifically to one of the numbered paragraphs of the Bible, especially as printed in the Authorized and Douay versions ⟨Isaiah, chapter v, *verses* 23-25⟩ **Article** need not imply paragraph arrangement of each point or item, but it does imply that each is a distinct yet essential member of a whole. In its more common use it is applied to a statement that stands out distinctly, as, for example, one of the stipulations in a contract, or one of the doctrines in a creed, or one of the provisos of a statute; thus, the Thirty-nine *Articles* are the doctrines to which a clergyman of the Anglican Communion subscribes before being admitted to holy orders; the *articles* of the Apostles' Creed are not paragraphs or sentences, but brief phrases naming each of the dogmas professed by those Christians who hold this creed; the *articles* of an indenture, an agreement by which an apprentice is bound to a master, are the specific terms or conditions of that agreement. However, in some instruments, such as the Constitution of the United States of America, *article* designates one of the larger and more inclusive divisions, comprising many *articles* in the narrower sense. Therefore one usually speaks of a specific rule, regulation, specification, stipulation of that document, or of other constitutions, as a **clause.** *Clause* is also used more often than *article* in reference to a will, a deed, and a legislative bill, and with little difference in frequency in reference to such instruments as contracts and statutes ⟨he added two *clauses* to his will before signing it⟩ ⟨strike out *clause* 5 of the agreement⟩ **Plank** is applied to an article in a program as being something that those who accept that program implicitly agree to carry out if possible. It is chiefly used in designating one of the specific proposals or pledges in the platform of a political party ⟨the speaker argued for a platform with *planks* that were both specific and feasible⟩ **Count** is the legal designation for a particular allegation or charge in a declaration or indictment ⟨try the indicted man on two *counts*⟩

**parallel** *adj* *like, alike, similar, analogous, comparable, akin, uniform, identical
*Ana* *same, identical, equal, equivalent: corresponding, correlative (see RECIPROCAL)

**parallel** *n* **1** *comparison, contrast, antithesis, collation
*Ana* *likeness, similarity, resemblance, similitude
*Con* *dissimilarity, unlikeness, difference, divergence, divergency

**2** Parallel, counterpart, analogue, correlate are comparable when they denote a person or thing that corresponds in essentials to another person or thing, or closely resembles

A colon (:) separates groups of words discriminated. An asterisk (*) indicates place of treatment of each group.

the latter in the points under consideration. **Parallel** is especially appropriate when the two things compared are so like each other that their lack of divergence suggests two parallel lines; the term is often used in negative expressions ⟨we shall seek in vain a *parallel* for this situation⟩ ⟨it is hard to find a *parallel* for this mode of procedure⟩ ⟨none but thyself can be thy *parallel—Pope*⟩ Sometimes, especially when actual comparison is implied, the word suggests that the two things follow a similar course, order, or line of development ⟨cultural *parallels* found in the two hemispheres—*R. W. Murray*⟩ ⟨many interesting *parallels* are drawn with the historical plays of Shakespeare—*Times Lit. Sup.*⟩ **Counterpart** often suggests a complementary and sometimes an obverse relationship ⟨the two halves of a globe are *counterparts* of each other⟩ ⟨not an elaboration of Romanticism, but rather a *counterpart* to it, a second flood of the same tide—*Edmund Wilson*⟩ More commonly, however, the word implies a duplication, especially in another sphere, or age, or language ⟨synthetic chemistry has produced many a drug or perfume that has no *counterpart* in nature⟩ ⟨he saw that there was no mood of the mind that had not its *counterpart* in the sensuous life—*Wilde*⟩ ⟨French big businessmen and reactionary politicians have the support of their *counterparts* in the U.S.—*Gorrell*⟩ **Analogue** usually implies a more remote likeness than the preceding words and suggests comparison with something familiar and tangible for the sake of clarifying an explanation or enforcing an argument. Like *counterpart*, it often involves reference to something in another sphere, or order, or genus ⟨the gill in fishes is an *analogue* of the lung in quadrupeds⟩ ⟨the deepest and simplest reports of man's trouble have always been told in animal *analogues—Morley*⟩ ⟨civilization is . . . the process by which primitive packs are transformed into an *analogue*, crude and mechanical, of the social insects' organic communities—*Huxley*⟩ **Correlate** retains its primary implication of correspondence, but does not retain that of a complementary relationship. A thing which is a correlate of another is what corresponds to it from another point of view or in a different order of viewing ⟨the scientist asks what is the physical *correlate* of the rainbow⟩ ⟨words are the mental *correlates* of direct experience—*Weaver*⟩ ⟨fear persisted, and with it persisted an animosity toward the sister. Undoubtedly this is the psychological *correlate* of the incest taboo—*Dollard*⟩

**paralyze** *daze, stun, bemuse, stupefy, benumb, petrify
*Ana* *dismay, daunt, appall, horrify: disable, cripple, *weaken, enfeeble: astound, flabbergast (see SURPRISE): dumbfound, confound, nonplus (see PUZZLE)

**paramount** preponderant, preponderating, predominant, *dominant, sovereign
*Ana* *supreme, surpassing, preeminent, superlative: capital, foremost, principal, main, leading, *chief

**parapet** rampart, breastwork, *bulwark, bastion

**paraphernalia** apparatus, *equipment, machinery, outfit, tackle, gear, matériel

**paraphrase** *n* metaphrase, version, *translation

**parasite,** sycophant, favorite, toady, lickspittle, bootlicker, hanger-on, leech, sponge, sponger all signify a person who is supported or sustained or seeks support or sustenance, usually physical but sometimes social or intellectual, from another without right or justification. **Parasite** applies primarily to a person who as a matter of policy is supported more or less by another and gives nothing in return, but it is often extended to anyone who clings to a person of wealth, power, or influence in order to derive personal advantage or who is useless and unnecessary to society ⟨the ones who evade the earth and live upon the others

in some way they have devised. They are the *parasites*, and they are the despised—*Buck*⟩ ⟨a court society ridden with *parasites*⟩ ⟨as our present society disintegrates, this démodé figure will become clearer; the Bohemian, the outsider, the *parasite*, the rat—one of those figures which have at present no function either in a warring or peaceful world—*Forster*⟩ ⟨the poorer citizens were little more than *parasites*, fed with free state bread, amused by free state shows—*Buchan*⟩ **Sycophant** applies to one who clings to a person of wealth, power, or influence and wins or tries to win his favor by fawning, flattery, or adulation ⟨a man who rose in this world because he curried favor, a sycophant—*Kenneth Roberts*⟩ ⟨*sycophants* who kept him from wholesome contact with reality, who played upon his overweening conceit and confirmed him in his persecutional manias—*Overstreet*⟩ **Favorite** applies to a close associate or intimate of a king or noble who is unduly favored by him, especially with power; it may suggest parasitism or sycophancy on the part of the one favored and often connotes the exerting of undue or improper influence ⟨huge grants of land to court *favorites*—*W. C. Ford*⟩ ⟨reduced to the ranks every officer who had a good record and appointed scoundrelly *favorites* of his own in their places—*Graves*⟩ ⟨Pharaoh, his family and his *favorites*—*J. E. M. White*⟩ **Toady**, often interchangeable with *sycophant*, stresses more the servility and snobbery of the social climber ⟨he preens himself in the velvet coat, he spies out the land and sees that the Dowager is "the one"; he becomes the perfect *toady*—*Stevie Smith*⟩ ⟨this induced a sharp distaste for the flagrant political plunder, the obscene scramble for the loaves and fishes by the spoilsmen and their *toadies*—*Sidney Warren*⟩ **Lickspittle** and **bootlicker** are interchangeable in common speech with *sycophant* and *toady*, implying, however, even stronger contemptibleness ⟨characterized those who disagreed as *lickspittles* and toadies of official whiggery—*Asahel Bush*⟩ ⟨a *lickspittle* humility that went beyond flattery—*Moorehead*⟩ ⟨its principal characters were stupid and bemused commanders, or vicious *bootlickers* tainted with homosexuality—*Sutton*⟩ **Hanger-on** applies to someone who is regarded, usually contemptuously, as adhering to or depending unduly on another especially for favors ⟨there were the *hangers-on* who might be called domestics by inheritance—*Ybarra*⟩ ⟨a *hanger-on* at Court, waiting for the preferment that somehow eluded him—*Times Lit. Sup.*⟩ ⟨those rather *hangers-on* than friends, whom he treated with the cynical contempt that they deserved—*Graves*⟩ **Leech** stresses the persistence of clinging to or bleeding another for one's own advantage ⟨hatred for the freeloader or deadbeat. Yet, as a student of humanity, he tolerated these *leeches*—*Maule & Cane*⟩ ⟨*leeches* . . . hateful parasites feeding upon the blood of artists!—*Robertson Davies*⟩ **Sponge** and **sponger** stress a parasitic laziness, dependence, and indifference to the discomforts caused and usually a certain pettiness and constant regard for opportunities to cadge ⟨all social *sponges;* all satellites of the court; all beggars of the marketplace—*Drummond*⟩ ⟨a girl whose disappointment with the world has made her the prey of an unsuccessful crook and *sponger—Times Lit. Sup.*⟩
*Ana* fawner, cringer, truckler (see corresponding verbs at FAWN)

**parboil** *boil, seethe, simmer, stew

**parcel** *n* 1 *part, portion, piece, detail, member, division, section, segment, sector, fraction, fragment
2 *bundle, bunch, pack, package, packet, bale
3 *group, cluster, bunch, lot
*Ana* collection, assemblage (see under GATHER): *aggregate, aggregation, conglomerate, conglomeration

**parcel** *vb* *apportion, portion, ration, prorate
*Ana* *allot, assign, allocate, apportion: *grant, accord, award
**parch** *dry, desiccate, dehydrate, bake
*Ana* sear, scorch, char, *burn: shrivel, wizen, *wither
**pardon** *n* **Pardon, amnesty, absolution** in their legal and ecclesiastical senses mean a remission of penalty or punishment. **Pardon,** which is the comprehensive term, is often ambiguous; it denotes a release not from guilt but from the penalty imposed for a transgression of secular or spiritual law. Thus in civil and military affairs a *pardon* usually implies a release from prison, or from the payment of a fine, or from a sentence of death, and permission to go scot free, but not acquitted, though the term may suggest as a cause either executive clemency or the undoing of a judicial wrong. When a pardon is extended to an entire class (as an insurgent group) or to an entire community, it is called an **amnesty** ⟨a general *amnesty* and liberty of conscience were promised to parliament by Charles II in the Declaration of Breda (1660)⟩ *Amnesty* often suggests not only that past offenses will go unpunished, but that they will be forgotten. When, in ecclesiastical use and especially in the use of the Roman Catholic Church, a pardon is extended for sins confessed and atoned for according to the laws of the Church, it is specifically called **absolution** when it implies that the eternal punishment for sin has been remitted in the sacrament of penance.
**pardon** *vb* forgive, remit, *excuse, condone
*Ana* *free, release, liberate: acquit, absolve, *exculpate
*Ant* punish   —*Con* *penalize, fine, amerce: discipline, correct, chasten, castigate, chastise (see PUNISH)
**pardonable** *venial
**pare** peel, *skin, decorticate, flay
**pariah** *outcast, castaway, derelict, reprobate, untouchable
**parley** treat, negotiate, *confer, commune, consult, advise
*Ana* *discuss, debate, dispute, argue, agitate: converse, talk, *speak
**parochial** *insular, provincial, local, small-town
*Ana* circumscribed, restricted, limited, confined (see LIMIT *vb*): narrow, narrow-minded, *illiberal, intolerant, hidebound, bigoted
*Ant* catholic   —*Con* *universal, cosmopolitan, cosmic
**parody** *n* travesty, *caricature, burlesque
*Ana* skit, squib, lampoon, *libel
**parody** *vb* travesty, caricature, burlesque (see under CARICATURE *n*)
**paroxysm** spasm, convulsion, *fit, attack, access, -accession
**parry** *dodge, shirk, sidestep, duck, fence, malinger
*Ana* ward, avert, *prevent, preclude: forestall, anticipate (see PREVENT): elude, evade, avoid, shun (see ESCAPE)
**parsimonious** niggardly, penurious, *stingy, close, close-fisted, tight, tightfisted, miserly, cheeseparing, penny-pinching
*Ana* avaricious, *covetous, grasping, greedy: *sparing, frugal: *mean, ignoble, sordid, abject
*Ant* prodigal   —*Con* *profuse, lavish: *liberal, munificent, bountiful, bounteous, openhanded, generous
**part** *n* **Part, portion, piece, detail, member, division, section, segment, sector, fraction, fragment, parcel** are comparable when they mean something which is less than the whole but which actually is or is considered as if apart from the rest of the whole. **Part** is the most comprehensive of these terms; it may be used in place of any of the succeeding words in this group or even in place of such words as *element, component,* or *constituent* (see ELEMENT) ⟨all are but *parts* of one stupendous whole—*Pope*⟩ ⟨he spent

*part* of his life in China⟩ ⟨a large *part* of the estate went to the elder son⟩ ⟨the cup was broken into three *parts*⟩ ⟨the better *part* of valor is discretion—*Shak.*⟩ ⟨its basic assumption is that the social whole has greater worth and significance than its individual *parts—Huxley*⟩ **Portion,** although it denotes a part of a whole, does not always presuppose a compact or integral whole; it may suggest a whole that comprises all of an existing or a possible stock or store without any connotation of its assemblage ⟨he is a *portion* of the loveliness which once he made more lovely—*Shelley*⟩ ⟨she dreaded . . . taking from the small sum of peace they had in the world, adding to the *portion* of their unhappiness—*Malamud*⟩ But *portion* (see also FATE) is preferred to *part* when there is the intent to imply determination of amount or quantity or assignment or allotment, especially of a share ⟨divide a pie into six equal *portions*⟩ ⟨a *portion* of each day was given to this artistic labor—*Hudson*⟩ ⟨when the plant was set, a *portion* of water, nicely calculated as to quantity, ran down a pipe and was deposited at the plant roots—*Anderson*⟩ **Piece** applies to a separate or detached part or portion of a whole; thus, a *piece* of bread is a part of a larger whole such as a loaf; a *piece* of cloth may be a length cut from a bolt, a smaller length left after the larger part of that piece has been used, or a bit that serves as a swatch or sample ⟨break a stick of candy into *pieces*⟩ ⟨ask for a small *piece* of the cake⟩ But *piece* so stresses the implication of independence that the term may come close to *item* and then is often applied to a thing that is relatively complete in itself, and has reference to a whole only as it presupposes a mass from which it was taken, a collection of similar or related things, especially as produced by one person, one machine, or one factory ⟨the red-hot *piece* of iron upon the blacksmith's anvil⟩ ⟨each *piece* of furniture has been freshly polished⟩ ⟨a *piece* of poetry⟩ ⟨she had learned . . . that there really was more than one man in the world—the *piece* of knowledge that more than anything else divides women from girls—*Wouk*⟩ **Detail** (see also ITEM) applies to a part chiefly when the presupposed whole is a plan or design, or represents the working out of a plan or design; in this sense the term is used largely in the arts of painting, sculpture, and architecture, and often denotes a small but important part or feature ⟨reproduce a *detail* of a painting⟩ ⟨the sculptor's students were set to work, each modeling a *detail* of the Venus de Milo⟩ ⟨this blueprint shows the *details* of the façade⟩ ⟨she had her plan clearly in her head, with every *detail* as distinct as though the scheme had already been carried through—*Gibbons*⟩ **Member** applies to a part that constitutes one of the units of which a body (as a human or animal body, a social or legislative body, or a constructed or manufactured body) is comprised; the term, though it usually implies close association with the body under consideration, also usually implies separability of the unit in thought or in fact ⟨the legs, arms, and head are often specifically regarded as *members* of the human body⟩ ⟨the saddle seat is a distinctive *member* of a Windsor chair⟩ ⟨the flying buttress is an important architectural *member* of most of the great medieval Gothic cathedrals⟩ ⟨*members* of Congress⟩ ⟨the club has 500 *members*⟩ ⟨a lolling, impudent tongue—a truly unruly *member—Banfield*⟩ ⟨society is a joint-stock company, in which the *members* agree, for the better securing of his bread to each shareholder, to surrender the liberty and culture of the eater—*Emerson*⟩ **Division** and **section** apply to a distinct, often a detached, part formed by or as if by cutting or dividing. The terms are often used interchangeably, but *division* is usually applied to larger parts than is *section*; thus, one would refer to the *divisions*

A colon (:) separates groups of words discriminated. An asterisk (*) indicates place of treatment of each group.

of modern languages and of political sciences of a college but to the several *sections* into which a large class of students taking a course is divided ⟨there are twenty *sections* of freshman English⟩ Except in technical use, the terms carry no explicit suggestions as to size or extent; *division*, however, is more often used abstractly than *section*, which tends to be applied to a conspicuously distinct part (as of a writing, a people, a country, a territory, or a city) ⟨it is improper to speak of these different parts of the chemical industry as *divisions*, for the solidarity of the whole does not permit splitting it—*Morrison*⟩ ⟨the only important grape-growing *section* of Pennsylvania—*Amer. Guide Series: Pa.*⟩ ⟨the sports *section* of the newspaper⟩ ⟨entertained by all *sections* of the local community—*Moir*⟩ **Segment** is often preferred to *section* for a part cut off by natural lines of cleavage or necessitated by the nature of the thing's construction or design ⟨a *segment* of an orange⟩ ⟨a *segment* of a compound leaf⟩ ⟨invited to address a *segment* of the war college—*Michener*⟩ ⟨essential raw materials for a broad *segment* of American industry—*Crops in Peace and War*⟩ In mathematical use *segment* is distinguished from *sector* in that *segment* refers to any part of a plane or solid figure cut off from the whole by a line or plane ⟨a *segment* of a cylinder⟩ ⟨a *segment* of a circle is bounded by an arc and a chord⟩ while **sector** refers to any part of a circle bounded by an arc and two radii ⟨divide a circle into six *sectors*⟩ In more general use *sector* applies to a section that roughly corresponds to a mathematical sector; thus, a *sector* assigned to a commander of a division in war has arbitrary bounds on sides and rear but a front that is as extensive as the range of its guns ⟨consider the . . . problem as a whole and not in *sectors*—*Vandenberg*⟩ *Fraction* and *fragment* both apply to a part that is disconnected from a whole, especially by breaking; but **fraction**, probably by its confusion with the arithmetical sense of that word, often suggests a negligible part ⟨only a small *fraction* of mankind is capable of enthusiasm for language, for its own sake—*Inge*⟩ ⟨some little *fraction* . . . of your enjoyment of tragedy—*Montague*⟩ and **fragment** applies to a random bit and especially to one of the pieces left after most of the whole has been eaten, used, worn away, or lost ⟨they took up of the *fragments* . . . twelve baskets full—*Mt 14:20*⟩ ⟨only a *fragment* of the dramatic literature that once existed—*Altick*⟩ ⟨if the novel proves to be a novel and not a collage of extraordinary *fragments* —*Mailer*⟩ **Parcel** (see also BUNDLE) is used chiefly in law with reference to land and in such idiomatic phrases as *part and parcel;* in all its uses it carries an underlying notion of a part having a firm and unbreakable connection with the whole to which it belongs ⟨and I will die a hundred thousand deaths ere break the smallest *parcel* of this vow —*Shak.*⟩ ⟨a land *parcel*, insofar as it is a described area on the face of the earth, cannot be destroyed—*Babcock*⟩ *Ant* whole

**part** *vb* divide, *separate, sever, sunder, divorce
*Ana* *detach, disengage: apportion, *allot, allocate, assign: *tear, rend, cleave
*Ant* cleave (see STICK) —*Con* cling, *stick, adhere: *unite, combine, conjoin

**partake** *share, participate
*Ana* *separate, part, divide: take, *receive, accept: *have, hold, own, possess, enjoy: *get, obtain, procure, acquire

**partiality** prepossession, prejudice, bias, *predilection
*Ana* approving *or* approval, endorsing *or* endorsement (see corresponding verbs at APPROVE)
*Ant* impartiality

**participate** *share, partake

*Ana* *separate, divide, part: take, *receive, accept: *have, hold, own, possess, enjoy

**particle** 1 Particle, bit, mite, smidgen, whit, atom, iota, jot, tittle all mean a very small or insignificant piece or part. **Particle** is used in reference not only to substances which are actually divisible but to such things as a quality, a state, or a condition which are only theoretically so because they are intangible or ideal; usually it implies an amount within the range of visual or mental perception ⟨a *particle* of matter⟩ ⟨he hasn't a *particle* of sense⟩ ⟨her face was . . . beaded with small *particles* of rain— *Wolfe*⟩ ⟨there is not a *particle* of truth in any of these statements—*Ashley Montagu*⟩ **Bit** usually suggests a relatively minor or the least feasible amount, extent, or degree ⟨own a *bit* of land⟩ ⟨he doesn't like it a *bit*⟩ ⟨he is a *bit* of a coward⟩ ⟨distinction on the basis of sex is the only *bit* of gender we have left—*Laird*⟩ ⟨little trifling useless *bits* of deceit—*Black*⟩ ⟨if one wished to indulge in a *bit* of sentimentality, one could say that the truths of science become obsolete . . . but that the truth of the arts is everlasting—*Boas*⟩ **Mite** may stress either diminutiveness in size or minuteness in amount ⟨a *mite* of a boy⟩ ⟨a *mite* of a diamond⟩ ⟨he hasn't a *mite* of suspicion⟩ ⟨only a *mite* of what it could have taught was seen and learned—*Fitzsimmons*⟩ **Smidgen** may replace *bit* or *mite* ⟨yearning . . . for a *smidgen* of Broadway glamour—*New Yorker*⟩ but sometimes and especially in negative constructions it may go even farther in stressing minuteness or scarcity ⟨ate squirrel and rabbit, broiled over hot coals, for there was not a *smidgen* of grease left—*Atlantic*⟩ **Whit** is used chiefly in negative phrases in the sense of the least conceivable amount ⟨it matters not a *whit*⟩ ⟨he hasn't a *whit* of knowledge of the subject⟩ ⟨the civilized man is not a *whit* different from the savage in this respect—*Henry Miller*⟩ **Atom** (see also PARTICLE 2) implies an amount or a size beyond the possibility of further diminution ⟨not an *atom* of dust escaped her scrutiny⟩ ⟨it hasn't an *atom* of seriousness about it—a mere footnote to history—*Laski*⟩ **Iota** and **jot** both imply a minuteness suggestive of the character *iota* [ι], the smallest letter of the Greek alphabet, while **tittle**, used chiefly in the phrase *jot or tittle*, implies a minuteness suggestive of a small diacritical mark such as the dot over an *i;* the three are used interchangeably to mean the smallest or most minute detail or amount ⟨he hasn't added a *jot*, an *iota*, or a *tittle* to our knowledge of the subject⟩ *Iota*, however, sometimes denotes an insignificant amount, extent, or degree ⟨of statesmanship he had not an *iota*— *S. H. Adams*⟩ ⟨he who adds a *jot* to such knowledge creates new mind—*Shaw*⟩ ⟨he meant not to lose one *tittle* of enjoyment—*Churchill*⟩

2 Particle, corpuscle, atom, molecule in technical physical or chemical use can mean a submicroscopic division of matter. **Particle**, the oldest and most general of these terms, is applied especially to any of certain minute entities which have more specific designations such as *ion, molecule, atom, electron, proton,* and *alpha particle*. *Particle* is often used to emphasize the idea of indivisibility, commonly suggesting the entities (as protons, neutrons, and electrons) of which all matter is believed to be composed. **Corpuscle** may be interchangeable with *particle* ⟨they [alpha particles] are *corpuscles* endowed with charge, with mass, and with velocity—*Darrow*⟩ but more often it is specifically equivalent to *elementary particle* and may be applied to energy quanta (as photons or phonons) when these are considered as particulate entities ⟨let us assume that all lighted bodies emit *particles* of light, or *corpuscles*, which, falling on our eyes, create the sensation of light—*Einstein & Infeld*⟩ According to the common

modern concept, an **atom** is the smallest particle of an element that can exist either alone or in combination with smaller particles of the same or of a different element ⟨an *atom* of hydrogen⟩ **Molecule** denotes the smallest particle of an element or of a chemical combination (as a compound) that retains chemical identity with the substance in mass. Molecules are usually composed of two or more atoms, either of the same or of different elements ⟨a *molecule* of water is composed of two *atoms* of hydrogen and one *atom* of oxygen⟩

**parti-colored** *variegated, motley, checkered, checked, pied, piebald, skewbald, dappled, freaked

**particular** *adj* 1 *single, sole, separate, unique, lone, solitary
*Ant* general
2 individual, *special, specific, especial
*Ant* general, universal
3 particularized, detailed, itemized, *circumstantial, minute
*Ana* scrupulous, meticulous, *careful, punctilious
4 fussy, squeamish, *nice, dainty, fastidious, finicky, finicking, finical, persnickety, pernickety
*Ana* exacting, demanding, requiring (see DEMAND): strict, *rigid, rigorous

**particular** *n* *item, detail
*Ant* universal: whole: aggregate

**particularized** particular, detailed, itemized, *circumstantial, minute
*Ana* accurate, precise, exact, *correct
*Ant* generalized

**partisan** *follower, adherent, disciple, sectary, henchman, satellite
*Ana* supporter, upholder, backer, champion (see corresponding verbs at SUPPORT): helper, aider *or* aid, assistant (see corresponding verbs at HELP)
*Con* antagonist, *opponent, adversary

**partner**, copartner, colleague, ally, confederate all denote an associate but they differ markedly in connotation and are not freely interchangeable. **Partner** is especially an associate in a business (*partnership*) or one of two associates (as in some games, in a dance, or in marriage) ⟨in mind and character Mrs. Adams was a worthy *partner* throughout his career—*W. C. Ford*⟩ Since *partner* alone implies association, the addition of *co-*, with its implication of association, in **copartner** sometimes adds little or nothing to *partner;* thus, one may refer equally to *partners* or *copartners* in crime. **Copartner**, however, can distinctively imply fellow partner ⟨the authority of a *partner* to bind his *copartners*—*Encyc. Brit.*⟩ or equality of share ⟨a *copartner* in that sovereignty of the people—*Spence*⟩ **Colleague** applies typically to an associate in office or in professional or academic relations ⟨like their *colleagues* elsewhere, Illinois' lawmakers lack adequate facilities and staffs—*Armbrister*⟩ **Ally** and **confederate**, though referable to persons, more frequently denote an associated state or government. **Ally** suggests an often temporary association in a common cause (as the prosecution of a war) or in affairs of policy or statecraft ⟨it is not really the treaty that makes an *ally* of another nation—*Hayes*⟩ **Confederate** (see also CONFEDERATE 2) implies an entering into a confederacy or confederation and usually suggests a closer or more permanent union for strength and solidarity.
*Ant* rival

**party** 1 *company, band, troop, troupe
*Ana* clique, *set, coterie, circle: gathering, collection, assembly, assemblage, congregation (see under GATHER)
2 *combination, combine, bloc, faction, ring

**pasquinade** lampoon, squib, skit, *libel

**pass** *vb* Pass, pass away, elapse, expire mean to move or come to a termination or end. **Pass** and **pass away** imply gradual or gentle movement to another state or condition; they often imply a transition from life to death but they may suggest a transition from any one state or time or season to another ⟨all that lives must die, *passing* through nature to eternity—*Shak.*⟩ ⟨when those conditions have *passed away* and history returns to normal—*W. P. Webb*⟩ ⟨but yet I know, where'er I go, that there has *passed away* a glory from the earth—*Wordsworth*⟩ ⟨the strangeness of his life *passed*, and he began to feel what this city was—*Buck*⟩ **Elapse** suggests a movement that seems like the slipping and gliding away of something that moves silently or without notice; the word applies particularly to a period of time, either in reference only to itself or in reference to something that should have been accomplished within that time ⟨became burdensome to him as time *elapsed* and political conditions changed—*Malone*⟩ ⟨all prophecies make sad reading when their term has *elapsed*—*Krutch*⟩ ⟨the period for the payment of the debt had now *elapsed*⟩ **Expire** basically means to breathe one's last breath and hence to die; but it comprehends the extended senses as well as the ordinary sense of *die*, and is used in reference to many things that come to an end as if by death ⟨the flame of the candle suddenly *expired*⟩ ⟨the society *expired* after a single meeting⟩ ⟨in the *expiring*, diffused twilight—*Conrad*⟩ ⟨suddenly their whispers *expired*—*Bennett*⟩ It is often used with this underlying notion in reference to a period of time (as stated in a bond, a note, a promise, an agreement, a patent, or a lease) which has come to an end ⟨your note, which was due on June 24, has now *expired*⟩ ⟨the two years of grace which the bank gave the city will soon *expire*⟩ ⟨when this copyright *expires*, it cannot be renewed, unless there is a new edition of the book⟩ ⟨Antony regarded the triumvirate as having *expired* on the last day of 33 B.C. and did not wish it renewed—*Buchan*⟩
*Ana* depart, leave, quit, *go, withdraw: end, terminate (see CLOSE)

**pass** *n* passage, *way, route, course, artery

**pass** *n* *juncture, exigency, emergency, contingency, pinch, strait, crisis
*Ana* situation, condition, *state, posture: plight, *predicament, quandary

**passage** 1 pass, *way, route, course, artery
2 Passage, passageway, corridor, hall, hallway, gallery, arcade, cloister, aisle, ambulatory designate a typically long narrow way connecting parts of a building or affording access to a particular room or section in it. **Passage** (see also WAY 1) and **passageway** are the comprehensive terms, usually interchangeable with any of the others. A **corridor** is a passageway flanked on one or both sides by rooms, apartments, compartments, or offices or leading from one part of a building to another. **Hall** can be applied to a corridor or to a room that serves as an entrance to a house, but **hallway** is used only of the former. A **gallery** is a corridor having a continuous row of windows; it may be a part of the building or form an enclosed veranda. An **arcade** is an arched and covered passageway, usually between rows of shops but, sometimes, between the front of a row of shops and the street or an open court. A **cloister** is a similar structure in a monastery or in a building imitating monastic architecture, but it runs along one or more sides of an open court or patio, and is arcaded or colonnaded on the outer side. An **aisle** is, basically, not a passageway but a part of a church or other building divided from the central part, or *nave*, by a row of columns or piers. The term is also applied to a passage flanked by rows of seats (as in an auditorium, a theater, a railway car,

---

A colon (:) separates groups of words discriminated. An asterisk (*) indicates place of treatment of each group.

or a bus). An *ambulatory* is a passageway through which one may walk; it is specifically applied to the cloister of a monastery, and to the curved passageway between the choir of a church and the chapels of an apse.
**3** *strait, sound, channel, narrows
**passageway** *passage, corridor, hall, hallway, gallery, arcade, cloister, aisle, ambulatory
**pass away** *pass, elapse, expire
**passing** *n* *death, decease, demise
**passing** *adj* *transient, transitory, ephemeral, momentary, fugitive, fleeting, evanescent, short-lived
**passion** *n* **1** suffering, agony, dolor, *distress, misery
*Ana* *trial, tribulation, cross, visitation, affliction
**2** *feeling, emotion, affection, sentiment
*Ana* *inspiration, frenzy: *ecstasy, rapture, transport
**3** lust, appetite, *desire, urge
*Ana* craving, coveting (see DESIRE *vb*): longing, yearning, hungering *or* hunger, thirsting *or* thirst (see LONG *vb*): panting, aspiring, aiming (see AIM *vb*)
**4** Passion, fervor, ardor, enthusiasm, zeal denote intense, high-wrought emotion. **Passion** implies an overwhelming or driving emotion; it may be either the most abstract or the most concrete of these terms. It may be used without implication of a specific emotion; thus, a poet without *passion* is a poet incapable of feeling or of displaying vehement, agitating, or soul-stirring emotion; to be in the grip of *passion* is to be swayed by violent emotion, but without a hint from the context the nature of the emotion remains unknown ⟨Knipe also knew that *passion* was powerful, heady stuff, and must be prudently dispensed—*Dahl*⟩ *Passion* (see also FEELING, DESIRE) may specifically designate intense erotic love, or often lust, or it may designate violent rage ⟨she flew into a *passion*⟩ ⟨I am very sorry, good Horatio, that to Laertes I forgot myself . . . but, sure, the bravery of his grief did put me into a towering *passion*—*Shak.*⟩ *Fervor* and *ardor* both imply the kindling of emotion to a high degree of heat, but **fervor** more often suggests a steady glow or burning and **ardor** a restless or leaping flame. *Fervor* is associated especially with matters (as emotions that express themselves in prayer, contemplation, or devotion) involving persistent warmth; *ardor*, with those (as emotions that express themselves in eager longings, or zealous efforts) that suggest the violence and sometimes the transitoriness or wavering of flames ⟨the *fervor* of a nun⟩ ⟨the *ardor* of a missionary⟩ ⟨exhort with *fervor*⟩ ⟨dampened his *ardor*⟩ ⟨all prayed and hunted quail with equal *fervor* and died . . . at an advanced age—*Styron*⟩ ⟨in the prints of Harunobu there is an intense sympathy with youth, with its shyness, its tremulous *ardors*—*Binyon*⟩ **Enthusiasm** often comes very close to *ardor*, but it may differ in its emphasis on the rational grounds for the emotion, such as thoroughgoing admiration for a person or thing or conviction of the worthiness of a cause or end. *Ardor* may suggest aspiration without a clearly envisioned goal, but *enthusiasm* nearly always implies an objective, a cause, or an object of devotion; thus, a teacher may stimulate *ardor* in a pupil without necessarily directing the latter's emotion into a definite channel, but he stimulates *enthusiasm* only when he provides the pupil with something concrete to admire, to follow, or to fight for ⟨he showed in this cause not only the *enthusiasm* of an idealist, but the sagacity of a practical leader—*Inge*⟩ ⟨they are both weary of politics today, still radicals out of habit, but without *enthusiasm* and without a cause—*Mailer*⟩ **Zeal** retains from earlier senses a suggestion of a goading or driving passion expressed as great ardor or enthusiasm for a cause or end and coupled with energetic and unflagging activity in the service of the cause or in the pursuit of the end ⟨with all the *zeal* which

young and fiery converts feel—*Byron*⟩ ⟨it took the Franciscan movement about twenty years to lose the passion of its early *zeal*—*Huxley*⟩ ⟨worked in almost silent *zeal* and entire absorption—*Buck*⟩
*Ana* *ecstasy, rapture, transport: *anger, rage, fury, wrath: eroticism, amorousness (see corresponding adjectives at EROTIC)
**passionate** *impassioned, ardent, fervent, fervid, perfervid
*Ana* *intense, vehement, fierce, violent: impetuous, headlong, *precipitate, abrupt: excited, quickened, stimulated (see PROVOKE)
**passive** *inactive, inert, idle, supine
*Ana* *impassive, phlegmatic, stolid, apathetic
*Ant* active —*Con* live, operative, dynamic (see ACTIVE)
**paste** *n* *dough, batter
**pastoral** *rural, rustic, bucolic
**pasture** *vb* graze, *feed, nourish
**pat** *adj* *seasonable, timely, well-timed, opportune
*Ana* apt, happy, felicitous, appropriate, fitting (see FIT *adj*): pertinent, apposite, apropos, applicable (see RELEVANT)
**patch** *vb* *mend, repair, rebuild
*Ana* emend, remedy, redress, amend, *correct: fix, *adjust, regulate
**patent** *evident, manifest, distinct, obvious, apparent, palpable, plain, clear
*Ana* *noticeable, conspicuous, salient, prominent: *flagrant, glaring, gross, rank
*Ant* latent —*Con* *imperceptible, insensible, impalpable: hidden, concealed, secreted (see HIDE *vb*)
**pathetic** poignant, affecting, *moving, touching, impressive
*Ana* *pitiful, piteous, pitiable: plaintive, *melancholy, doleful
*Ant* comical
**pathological** *unwholesome, morbid, sickly, diseased
**pathos**, poignancy, bathos are comparable when they denote the quality found in human situations, or especially in works of art or literature, which moves one to pity or sorrow. **Pathos** is the common term in critical and literary use; because of its early and long-continued association with aesthetics it often implies the arousing of emotions which give pleasure rather than pain and it suggests the detachment of an observer rather than personal involvement in the perturbing events or situations ⟨*pathos* is the luxury of grief; and when it ceases to be other than a keen-edged pleasure it ceases to be *pathos*—*Patmore*⟩ Often, also, *pathos* implies not so much an effect produced on the person who sees, hears, or reads, as the art, device, or trick employed (as by a writer, speaker, or artist) in seeking to produce such an effect ⟨he passed without an effort from the most solemn appeal to the gayest raillery, from the keenest sarcasm to the tenderest *pathos*—*J. R. Green*⟩ ⟨"My poor children, what had I ever done to you that would drive you to such a step?" The touch of *pathos* was all that Jane needed to stiffen her—*Mary Austin*⟩ **Poignancy** is sometimes preferred by literary and art critics to *pathos* because it carries no suggestion of artificiality and centers the attention on the genuineness of the thing's emotional quality and of the emotions it arouses; it also specifically implies a power to pierce the mind or heart so that the reader, hearer, or observer feels acutely as well as with aesthetic pleasure the emotion aroused whether it be pity or sorrow or another overwhelming emotion ⟨the most famous of the women-poets of Japan, whose verse expresses with peculiar *poignancy* a sense of the glory of beauty and the *pathos* of it—*Binyon*⟩ ⟨felt the *poignancy* of the kakapo's plight and had somehow managed to slip in this intimation of pity for a fellow creature—*Tilford*⟩ **Bathos** is often applied to a false or pretentious

pathos and typically implies a maudlin sentimentality so detached from reality as to arouse disgusted contempt rather than the softer emotions that it is intended to elicit ⟨the poet seeks to render soulfully the blubbering of a happy idiot, and falls into *bathos—Ciardi*⟩ But *bathos* may also apply to a silly and artificially lugubrious reaction to something emotionally appealing that is akin to self-pity ⟨the voice of God, even at second-hand, should do more than make us sniff moistly in self-indulgent *bathos—Hatch*⟩

**patience,** long-suffering, longanimity, forbearance, resignation can all mean the power to endure or a capacity for enduring without complaint something which is disagreeable or requires effort. **Patience** stresses calmness or composure, not only under suffering or under provocation, but in awaiting an outcome that seems unduly or inordinately delayed, or in performing a task that makes severe demands upon one's attention ⟨upon the heat and flame of thy distemper sprinkle cool *patience—Shak.*⟩ ⟨he gathered . . . that he had been either a man of saintly *patience*, a masochist or a deaf-mute—*Theodore Sturgeon*⟩ ⟨bred to *patience* . . . she had cultivated and perfected a vast cowlike calm—*Pynchon*⟩ **Long-suffering** and **longanimity** imply extraordinary patience under provocation or trial. The former sometimes also suggests undue meekness or submissiveness ⟨it shows much *long-suffering* in you to put up with him, and keep him in your employ—*Hardy*⟩ ⟨the *long-suffering* type on whose bosom repentant tears always eventually fall—*Warren*⟩ The latter term more often than the former names a virtue, and so is chiefly found in abstract use ⟨in Isaac such simplicity, such *longanimity* in Jacob—*Hooker*⟩ ⟨the second window was to be devoted to *longanimity*, symbolized . . . by the passion-flower and the heavenly crown for long-suffering—*Killackey*⟩ **Forbearance** (see also under FORBEARING) adds to *long-suffering* the implication of restraint in the expression of one's feelings or in exacting punishment or one's due; it therefore often suggests toleration, for the sake of peace, of something that merits censure or castigation ⟨my lord Kew has acted with great *forbearance* and under the most brutal provocation—*Thackeray*⟩ **Resignation** implies a submission to suffering or evil or an acceptance of it because it must be endured or cannot be escaped; it sometimes connotes patience arising from submission to what is believed to be the Divine Will, but often it implies a stoical or fatalistic rather than a religious attitude ⟨*resignation* superadds to patience a submissive disposition . . . ; it acknowledges both the power and the right of a superior to afflict—*Cogan*⟩ ⟨a last-ditch fighter by nature . . . her philosophic *resignation* struck the girl as extremely suspicious—*Wouk*⟩ ⟨for a modern American or Englishman, waiting is a psychological torture. An Indian accepts the blank hours with *resignation—Huxley*⟩
*Ana* perseverance, persistence (see corresponding verbs at PERSEVERE): *fortitude, backbone, pluck, grit, sand, guts: *equanimity, composure
*Ant* impatience

**patois** *dialect, vernacular, lingo, jargon, cant, argot, slang

**patrician** *gentleman, aristocrat

**patrimony** *heritage, inheritance, birthright

**patron** *sponsor, surety, guarantor, backer, angel
*Ana* supporter, upholder, champion (see corresponding verbs at SUPPORT): benefactor, contributor (compare *benefaction, contribution,* at DONATION): protector, defender (see corresponding verbs at DEFEND)
*Ant* client: protégé

**patter** *vb* chatter, prate, *chat, gab, prattle, babble, gabble, jabber, gibber

**pattern** *n* 1 exemplar, example, *model, ideal, standard, beau ideal, mirror
*Ana* *paragon, apotheosis
2 *figure, design, motif, device
*Ana* *form, figure, shape, conformation, configuration

**paunch** *abdomen, belly, stomach, gut

**pause** *n* Pause, recess, respite, lull, intermission are comparable when they mean a temporary cessation especially in action, in activity, or in movement. **Pause,** though it carries an implication of expected resumption, stresses the fact of stopping without indicating, in itself, the duration or the cause of the stop. The term is often applied to such a letup in utterance as that marked in printing by a period or a caesura or as that caused by an interruption, by hesitation, or by awaiting an answer, but it may quite as readily be applied to a temporary cessation of activity (as for play, for sleep, or for relaxation) ⟨there was a short *pause* before he resumed speaking⟩ ⟨between the dark and the daylight . . . comes a *pause* in the day's occupations, that is known as the Children's Hour—*Longfellow*⟩ ⟨there is no *pause* in the invention of new and appalling weapons—*Grenville Clark*⟩ **Recess** implies a temporary cessation of work; usually it applies to an interval granted (as to legislators or students) for the sake of relaxation or diversion ⟨the smaller boys and girls are granted a *recess* of ten minutes each morning⟩ ⟨Parliament is now in *recess*⟩ ⟨the justices adjourned for their summer *recess—N. Y. Times*⟩ **Respite** implies a time of relief (as from labor, suffering, or war) or of delay (as before sentencing or executing) ⟨there will be no *respite* for such workers for the duration of the war⟩ ⟨a battle that seemed to be without *respite* and without end—*Rölvaag*⟩ ⟨a body of people . . . thrown together for a week or so without the possibility of *respite* or escape—*Lowes*⟩ **Lull** implies a temporary cessation or marked decline of activity (as in the course of a storm, in business, or in military activity between two offensives) ⟨after a *lull* the storm turned inland with increased fury⟩ ⟨running full tilt in most of its departments following a summer *lull—Ericson*⟩ ⟨there was a *lull* in the noises of insects as if they . . . were making a devotional pause—*Crane*⟩ **Intermission** basically implies a break in continuity but comes close to *lull* in stressing one caused by a temporary cessation (as of an action, a process, or a proceeding). However, its application is usually quite different since it usually suggests a pause available for some new or special activity (as for rest or recuperation) ⟨the habit of stern thrift, begun in 1870 and practiced without any *intermission* till . . . 1897—*Bennett*⟩ ⟨the attack recurred after a few days' *intermission*⟩ ⟨he often gives himself some *intermission* from such melancholy reflections—*Burke*⟩ ⟨several persons gathered around to talk during the *intermission* between the acts of a play⟩
*Ana* interruption, gap, interval, *break, interim: stopping *or* stop, ceasing *or* cessation (see corresponding verbs at STOP)

**paw** *vb* *touch, feel, palpate, handle

**pawn** *n* hostage, *pledge, earnest, token

**pay** *vb* Pay, compensate, remunerate, satisfy, reimburse, indemnify, repay, recompense are comparable when they mean to give money or an equivalent in return for something. **Pay** is the ordinary term when the giving or furnishing of money to discharge an obligation (as for services rendered or goods delivered) is implied ⟨*pays* good wages to his gardener⟩ ⟨*pay* ten dollars for a hat⟩ ⟨taxes are what we *pay* for civilized society—*Justice Holmes*⟩ ⟨could once more meet his running expenses, and with pinching and scrimping, even *pay* off some outstanding bills —*Malamud*⟩ When, in extended use, *pay* does not imply the actual giving of money, the term is often employed purely as a figure of speech ⟨nothing can *pay* him for his pains⟩ ⟨the hard knowledge of the hipster that you *pay* for what you get is usually too bitter for the beatnik— *Mailer*⟩ or it means merely to give as due or deserved ⟨*pay* a compliment⟩ or to give in the hope of a return in kind ⟨*pay* attention to a young woman⟩ **Compensate** is often preferred to *pay* when no legal obligation is implied or no payment for services is expected, because the term stresses a return, usually in money, that is regarded as an equivalent for a service given or for trouble taken or time spent ⟨*compensate* a waiter for his cheerful willing service⟩ ⟨*compensate* a neighbor for taking care of one's pets during the summer⟩ ⟨an epoch in which the immense costs of a war could never be *compensated* by any economic gains that came from it—*Lerner*⟩ In this sense (see also COMPENSATE 1) *compensate* often does not imply an obligation to another or the passing of money; it often suggests a counterbalancing (as of something unpleasant by something pleasant or of something lost by something gained) ⟨the beauty of the view *compensated* for the labor of the climb⟩ ⟨*compensate* for his feelings of loneliness by assertions of superiority—*Auden*⟩ **Remunerate**, like *pay*, usually implies the discharge of an obligation in money and, like *compensate*, usually suggests the giving of an equivalent for services rendered rather than for goods delivered ⟨goods with which the Cayuá is *remunerated* for his work for Brazilians—*J. B. Watson*⟩ but unlike both of these terms it often carries a suggestion, sometimes a mere hint, sometimes a distinct implication, of a reward ⟨he promised to *remunerate* the searchers handsomely⟩ ⟨the king *remunerated* them both, the former with an addition of honor, the latter with an accession of estate—*Fuller* d. 1661⟩ Both *compensate* and *remunerate* can replace *pay* when *pay* might seem offensive or indelicate ⟨the party always *remunerates* its faithful workers⟩ **Satisfy** (see also SATISFY 1 & 3) implies the payment of something that is asked, demanded, or required especially by the terms of the law or the decree of a court ⟨*satisfy* a claim⟩ ⟨*satisfy* a judgment⟩ ⟨death duties had been paid and the demands of creditors *satisfied*—*Gibbons*⟩ **Reimburse** implies a return for money that has been expended by oneself in hope of making a profit or by another (as one's agent or attorney) in doing one's business ⟨the profits of his business did not *reimburse* him for the money he had invested in it⟩ ⟨*reimbursed* his lawyer for earlier expenditures⟩ ⟨a promise of *reimbursing* . . . what the people should give to the king—*Bolingbroke*⟩ ⟨only Pennsylvania, of all the states, *reimbursed* loyalists for confiscated property—*Smelser & Kirwin*⟩ **Indemnify** implies promised or actual reimbursement for loss (as by fire), for injury (as by accident), or for damage (as by war or disaster) ⟨the basic purpose for which insurance exists is to *indemnify* persons subject to loss when such loss occurs—*Hedges*⟩ ⟨the governments of Louis XVIII and Louis Philippe so far as practicable *indemnified* the citizens of foreign states for losses caused by . . . Napoleon— *J. B. Moore*⟩ But *indemnify* may approach *compensate* and implies less a reimbursing than a counterbalancing ⟨he flogged them with merciless severity: but he *indemnified* them by permitting them to sleep on watch, to reel drunk about the streets, to rob, beat, and insult the merchants and the laborers—*Macaulay*⟩ *Repay* and *recompense* carry a weaker implication of giving or furnishing money than any of the preceding terms and a stronger implication of returning like for like; both therefore stress the demands of justice and usually the compulsion of an obligation. When the passing of money or of an equivalent is implied, **repay** may be preferred when

there is a suggestion of giving something back that has been paid out to one ⟨*repay* a loan⟩ and **recompense** when compensation for voluntary services or for losses or injuries sustained is suggested and a due or adequate return is implied ⟨*recompense* these people, and especially the priest, for their great kindness—*Kipling*⟩ But *repay* and *recompense* sometimes imply reciprocation of something given, advanced, or inflicted. *Repay* usually implies little more than paying back in kind or amount ⟨*repay* her scorn for scorn—*Keats*⟩ ⟨we never can *repay* your kindness⟩ ⟨Peacock's fidelity as a correspondent . . . was *repaid* by the magnificent series of letters from Shelley— *Garnett*⟩ but it is sometimes used when the return is not what might be expected but is its diametrical opposite ⟨*repay* love with hate⟩ ⟨*repaying* incredulity with faith— *Browning*⟩ ⟨these Indians enabled the Pilgrims to replenish their dwindling stores, a friendly act that was later *repaid* with treachery—*Amer. Guide Series: Me.*⟩ *Recompense* often in this extended sense specifically implies a desire to make amends or to atone for a wrong that has been inflicted ⟨in some part to *recompense* my rash but more unfortunate misdeed—*Milton*⟩

**pay** *n* *wage *or* wages, salary, stipend, fee, hire, emolument **Ana** *reparation, restitution, indemnity, redress, amends

**paying** *adj* **Paying, gainful, remunerative, lucrative, profitable** share the meaning of bringing in a return in money. **Paying** often implies only such a return, but it may imply a satisfactory return for the labor or effort or expenditure involved (as in a venture, a business, or a trade) ⟨a position as office boy was his first *paying* job⟩ ⟨oats proved a *paying* crop⟩ ⟨toolmaking is one of the better *paying* trades⟩ ⟨a *paying* investment⟩ ⟨important minerals found in *paying* quantities in Alabama include asbestos—*Willingham*⟩ **Gainful** applies chiefly to an endeavor (as a business or a trade) that leads to a money return whether large or small, but it may apply to persons or their acts that are motivated by a desire for gain ⟨*gainful* occupations⟩ ⟨the lawyer's profession is often preferred to government service as the more *gainful* career⟩ ⟨most girls choose to be *gainful* workers for at least a few years before marriage—*Landis*⟩ ⟨the hypocrisy that covers *gainful* exploitation by the pretext of a civilizing mission— *Hobson*⟩ **Remunerative** suggests a rewarding of labor, effort, or expenditure and often implies a profit or recompense that exceeds what is usual or customary ⟨it was a *remunerative* venture for all concerned⟩ ⟨some British farmers with land beside main lines of railways . . . find big boldly silhouetted advertisements to be the most *remunerative* of their crops—*Montague*⟩ ⟨the State has come nearer than usual to a useful and *remunerative* working partnership with the industry—*Macmillan*⟩ **Lucrative** carries a stronger implication of large returns and applies to a business, trade, or profession or to an enterprise or undertaking that succeeds beyond one's hopes ⟨he made a *lucrative* deal when he sold his house⟩ ⟨a *lucrative* speculation in cotton futures⟩ ⟨contributing to the town's prosperity and wealth was a *lucrative* smuggling trade—*Amer. Guide Series: La.*⟩ ⟨our rulers will best promote the improvement of the nation . . . by leaving capital to find its most *lucrative* course—*P. M. Fraser*⟩ **Profitable** also is applied to what is rewarding, but it need not imply a money return (see BENEFICIAL); however it usually suggests such returns, not necessarily in a lucrative manner but in any degree that is consonant with one's wishes or hopes ⟨he owns a *profitable* hardware business⟩ ⟨they hoped to make a *profitable* investment⟩ ⟨follow a *profitable* trade⟩ ⟨scientific research is the development of new, more *profitable* products and processes—*K. S. Davis*⟩ ⟨putting to *profitable* use his conviction that

---

*Ana* analogous words  *Ant* antonyms  *Con* contrasted words  See also explanatory notes facing page 1

the atmosphere of the music should determine its . . . presentation—*Kolodin*⟩ ⟨he spoke unreservedly and plainly . . . at a time when it would have been *profitable* to have been, at least, noncommittal—*Charles Graves*⟩
**peace** *truce, cease-fire, armistice
**peaceable** *pacific, peaceful, pacifist, pacifistic, irenic
*Ana* *amicable, friendly, neighborly: *amiable, complaisant: *calm, placid, serene, tranquil
*Ant* contentious: acrimonious —*Con* quarrelsome, bellicose, *belligerent: *martial, warlike
**peaceful 1** *calm, tranquil, serene, placid, halcyon
*Ana* *soft, gentle, mild: *still, stilly, quiet, silent, noiseless
*Ant* turbulent
**2** *pacific, peaceable, pacifist, pacifistic, irenic
*Ana* composed, collected, unruffled, *cool: equable, constant, *steady
*Con* disturbed, perturbed, disquieted, agitated, upset, discomposed (see DISCOMPOSE)
**peak 1** *mountain, mount, alp, volcano, mesa
**2** *summit, pinnacle, climax, apex, acme, culmination, meridian, zenith, apogee
**peculiar 1** individual, *characteristic, distinctive
*Ana* *special, especial, particular, specific: idiosyncratic, eccentric (see corresponding nouns at ECCENTRICITY)
**2** eccentric, odd, queer, *strange, singular, unique, quaint, outlandish, curious
*Ana* bizarre, grotesque, *fantastic: *abnormal, atypical, aberrant: unusual, uncustomary (see affirmative adjectives at USUAL)
**pecuniary** *financial, monetary, fiscal
**pedantic,** academic, scholastic, bookish are comparable as terms of derogation applied to thinkers, scholars, and learned men and their utterances. **Pedantic** often implies ostentatious display of knowledge, didacticism, and stodginess ⟨his opinions were as *pedantic* as his life was abstemious—*Froude*⟩ It may also connote undue attention to scholarly minutiae and small interest in significant issues ⟨much *pedantic* mistaking of notions for realities, of symbols and abstractions for the data of immediate experience —*Huxley*⟩ **Academic** rarely carries implications of disagreeable personal characteristics but it does stress abstractness, lack of practical experience and interests, and often the inability to consider a situation realistically ⟨there is so much bad writing . . . because writing has been dominated by . . . the *academic* teachers and critics— *Ellis*⟩ **Scholastic** is less fixed in its implications than the others, for sometimes the allusion is to philosophic Scholasticism and sometimes to modern education. As a rule it implies dryness, formalism, adherence to the letter, and sometimes subtlety ⟨it is very able, but harsh and crabbed and intolerably *scholastic*—*Laski*⟩ **Bookish** often suggests learning derived from books rather than from actualities ⟨the Greeks had a name for such mixture of learning and folly, which might be applied to the *bookish* but poorly read of all ages—*Adler*⟩ ⟨the gestures of Mr. Lutyens's heroes are a trifle *bookish*, too seldom of the dusty streets—*Times Lit. Sup.*⟩ and sometimes it implies a decided literary or rhetorical quality ⟨*bookish* words⟩ ⟨*bookish* interests⟩
*Ana* *learned, erudite: *recondite, abstruse
**pedestrian** *adj* *dull, humdrum, dreary, monotonous, stodgy
*Ana* commonplace, platitudinous, truistic (see corresponding nouns at COMMONPLACE): banal, jejune, inane, wishy-washy (see INSIPID): *irksome, wearisome, tiresome, boring
**pedigree** *ancestry, lineage
**peek** *n* peep, glimpse, glance, *look, sight, view
**peel** *vb* *skin, decorticate, pare, flay

**peel** *n* *skin, bark, rind, hide, pelt
**peep** *vb* *chirp, chirrup, cheep, tweet, twitter, chitter
**peep** *n* chirp, chirrup, cheep, tweet, twitter, chitter (see under CHIRP *vb*)
**peep** *n* glance, glimpse, peek, *look, sight, view
*Ana* peering *or* peer, gazing *or* gaze, staring *or* stare (see GAZE)
**peer** *vb* *gaze, gape, stare, glare, gloat
*Ana* peep, glance, glimpse, look (see corresponding nouns at LOOK)
**peerless** surpassing, preeminent, *supreme, superlative, transcendent, incomparable
*Ana* paramount, sovereign, *dominant, predominant: unmatched, unrivaled, unequaled (see affirmative verbs at MATCH)
**peeve** *vb* *irritate, exasperate, nettle, provoke, aggravate, rile
*Ana* vex, *annoy, irk, bother: chafe, fret, gall (see ABRADE)
**peevish** *irritable, fractious, snappish, waspish, petulant, pettish, huffy, fretful, querulous
*Ana* captious, carping, caviling, faultfinding, *critical
**pejorative** *derogatory, depreciatory, depreciative, disparaging, slighting
*Ana* contemptuous, despiteful, scornful, disdainful (see corresponding nouns under DESPISE *vb*): decrying, belittling, minimizing (see DECRY)
*Con* praising, acclaiming, lauding, extolling (see PRAISE): exalting, magnifying, aggrandizing (see EXALT)
**pelagic** *aquatic, marine, oceanic, thalassic, neritic, abyssal, lacustrine, fluvial, fluviatile
**pellucid** *clear, transparent, translucent, lucid, diaphanous, limpid
*Ana* *pure, sheer: *bright, brilliant, luminous, radiant
*Con* *turbid, muddy, roily
**pelt** *n* *skin, hide, rind, bark, peel
**pen** *vb* *enclose, envelop, fence, coop, corral, cage, wall
*Ana* confine, circumscribe, restrict, *limit
**penalize,** fine, amerce, mulct mean to punish by depriving of something. **Penalize** usually presupposes a violation of laws or rules intended to maintain discipline or fair treatment for all; it implies exaction by an authority of a pecuniary penalty or a forfeiture of an advantage or, especially in games, the imposition of a handicap ⟨*penalize* late taxpayers by adding interest to their unpaid taxes⟩ ⟨*penalize* a football team fifteen yards for holding⟩ **Fine** and *amerce* are chiefly found in technical legal use in reference to court cases, but their implications in extended use are not materially different. They and their corresponding nouns *fine* and *amercement* are distinguishable in that **fine** implies that the amount exacted is, within certain limits, prescribed by the law, while **amerce** and **amercement** indicate that it has been left to the discretion of the judge ⟨violators of the municipal parking ordinances may be *fined* from one to ten dollars⟩ ⟨the judge *amerced* the offender in the sum of fifty dollars⟩ ⟨millions of spirits for his fault *amerced* of heaven—*Milton*⟩ **Mulct** implies subjection to a superior power which can legally or illegally exact a penalty (usually in money) for a breach of discipline or for failure to comply with its edicts. Sometimes it merely implies a fine or amercement or a withholding of money due ⟨nonconformists were *mulcted* for attendance at services of their own communion⟩ Often the word suggests forcible imposition or exaction of a heavy or oppressive penalty ⟨the colonizers *mulcted* the natives of their gold whenever the latter showed signs of resistance⟩
*Ana* *punish, discipline, correct, chasten
**penchant** *leaning, propensity, proclivity, flair

A colon (:) separates groups of words discriminated. An asterisk (*) indicates place of treatment of each group.

*Ana* bent, turn, talent, knack, *gift: bias, prepossession, *predilection, prejudice

**pendant** *flag, ensign, standard, banner, color, streamer, pennant, pennon, jack

**pendent** *suspended, pendulous

**pendulate** *swing, sway, oscillate, vibrate, fluctuate, waver, undulate

**pendulous** *suspended, pendent

**penetrate 1** *enter, pierce, probe
*Ana* invade, entrench, encroach, *trespass: *perforate, puncture, bore, prick
**2** pervade, impenetrate, interpenetrate, *permeate, impregnate, saturate
*Ana* insert, insinuate, interpolate, *introduce: *soak, saturate, drench, steep

**penetration** insight, acumen, *discernment, discrimination, perception
*Ana* sharpness, keenness, acuteness (see corresponding adjectives at SHARP): shrewdness, astuteness, perspicaciousness *or* perspicacity, sagaciousness *or* sagacity (see corresponding adjectives at SHREWD)

**penitence, repentance, contrition, attrition, compunction, remorse** denote sorrow or regret for sin or wrongdoing. **Penitence** implies little more than such sorrow or regret ⟨the outward signs of *penitence*⟩ ⟨all calls to *penitence* fall on deaf ears. *Penitence* implies admission of guilt and no one wishes to stand accused—*Political Science Quarterly*⟩ ⟨he showed his *penitence* in many ways⟩ ⟨the majority . . . took the attitude that no sin is beyond forgiveness if it is followed by true *penitence*—*Latourette*⟩ **Repentance** is richer in its implications, for it also implies a change of heart, an awareness of one's shortcomings morally or spiritually, or of the evil of one's actions or life as a whole ⟨I came not to call the righteous, but sinners to *repentance*—*Lk* 5:32⟩ ⟨God of his mercy give you patience to endure, and true *repentance*—*Shak.*⟩ ⟨there's no *repentance* in the grave—*Watts*⟩ **Contrition** and *attrition* are both theological terms, and as such contrasted; only *contrition* is found in general use. Both imply deep sorrow for sin and the purpose of amendment, but in theological use **contrition** implies that one's sorrow arises out of love of God and a realization of one's failure to respond to his graces, and **attrition** that it arises from a lower motive, such as fear of hell or fear of the loss of heaven ⟨O may Thy love and pity supply whatsoever has been wanting in the sufficiency of my *contrition*—*Manual of Prayers*⟩ ⟨sacramental grace to raise our sorrow from *attrition* to *contrition*—*Manning*⟩ In general use *contrition* implies penitence that is manifest in signs of pain or grief ⟨you must—whether you feel it or no—present an appearance of *contrition*—*Meredith*⟩ ⟨Sophia thought that, after such a sin, the least Amy could do was to show *contrition*—*Bennett*⟩ **Compunction** and *remorse* both imply a painful sting of conscience, but **compunction** usually suggests a momentary reaction not only for something already done, but also for something being done or to be done, and **remorse** usually suggests prolonged and insistent self-reproach and often intense suffering for past wrongs and especially for those whose consequences cannot be escaped ⟨a heartless scoundrel who had . . . abandoned her in her poverty forevermore, with no touch of *compunction*—*Dickens*⟩ ⟨would not have hurt a gnat unless his party . . . told him to do so, and then only with *compunction*—*Sir Winston Churchill*⟩ ⟨not one of them . . . was showing any trifling *compunction* at deserting the rebel cause when it was most in need—*Kenneth Roberts*⟩ ⟨*remorse* that makes one walk on thorns—*Wilde*⟩ ⟨spent in Paris a year marked by futile indiscretions and equally futile *remorse*—*E. S. Bates*⟩ ⟨O, that the vain *remorse*

which must chastise crimes done, had but as loud a voice to warn, as its keen sting is mortal to avenge!—*Shelley*⟩
*Ana* regret, *sorrow, anguish: humiliation, humbling, degradation, debasement (see corresponding verbs at ABASE): *qualm, scruple
*Con* obdurateness *or* obduracy, inexorableness, adamant (see corresponding adjectives at INFLEXIBLE)

**pen name** *pseudonym, nom de plume, alias, nom de guerre, incognito

**pennant** *flag, ensign, standard, banner, color, streamer, pendant, pennon, jack

**penniless** *poor, indigent, needy, destitute, impecunious, poverty-stricken, necessitous
*Ana* impoverished, bankrupt, drained (see DEPLETE): penurious (see corresponding noun at POVERTY)
*Con* opulent, affluent, wealthy, *rich

**pennon** *flag, ensign, standard, banner, color, streamer, pennant, pendant, jack

**penny-pinching** *stingy, close, closefisted, tight, tightfisted, niggardly, parsimonious, penurious, miserly, cheeseparing

**pensive** *thoughtful, reflective, speculative, contemplative, meditative
*Ana* solemn, somber, *serious, earnest, sober, grave: musing, pondering, ruminating (see PONDER)

**penumbra** umbra, adumbration, umbrage, *shade, shadow

**penurious** parsimonious, niggardly, *stingy, close, closefisted, tight, tightfisted, miserly, cheeseparing, pennypinching
*Ana* avaricious, grasping, greedy, *covetous: *mercenary, venal: *mean, abject, sordid, ignoble

**penury** *poverty, indigence, want, destitution, privation
*Ana* *need, necessity, exigency: pinch, strait, pass, *juncture
*Ant* luxury

**people** *n* *race, nation

**peppery** fiery, gingery, *spirited, high-spirited, mettlesome, spunky
*Ana* impetuous, headlong, *precipitate, abrupt: *pungent, piquant, spicy, snappy

**perceive** discern, note, remark, notice, observe, contemplate, *see, behold, descry, espy, view, survey
*Ana* grasp, seize, *take: *apprehend, comprehend: *enter, penetrate, pierce, probe

**percept** sense-datum, sensum, *sensation, image
*Ana* *idea, concept, notion: recognition, acknowledgment (see corresponding verbs at ACKNOWLEDGE)

**perceptible, sensible, palpable, tangible, appreciable, ponderable** all mean capable of being apprehended through the senses or intellect as real and existent. **Perceptible** may be used inclusively to describe whatever comes within the range of one's senses and can be recognized in itself or by certain signs ⟨*perceptible* sounds⟩ ⟨the ship is barely *perceptible* on the horizon⟩ ⟨without argument, without any *perceptible* stages, the estrangement of almost a year was gone—*Wouk*⟩ ⟨something strange was in the air, *perceptible* to a little boy but utterly beyond his understanding—*H. G. Wells*⟩ It may also be used with or without qualification (as by *just, scarcely,* or *barely*) to describe something that just passes a borderline (as that between invisibility and visibility or inaudibility and audibility) ⟨a *perceptible* change in her tone⟩ ⟨there are *perceptible* differences between *surprise* and *astonish*⟩ ⟨a *perceptible* flavor of onion⟩ ⟨her remark had no *perceptible* relevance to the topic of conversation⟩ **Sensible** (see also MATERIAL, AWARE) may be used to describe whatever is clearly apprehended through the bodily senses or which impresses itself strongly on the mind through the medium of sensations ⟨a rich and thronging world of *sen-*

*sible* things—*Lowes*⟩ ⟨our true ideas of *sensible* things do indeed copy them—*James*⟩ In contrast with *perceptible*, however, *sensible* applies to what is more obvious, even sometimes to what is patent through its effects or signs; thus, a *sensible* change in tone is one which is immediately recognized; a *sensible* difference in a person's expression is one which is quickly detected ⟨the direct, *sensible* influence of Protestantism has been to isolate and to individualize—*Brownell*⟩ ⟨every owner is entitled to have the water come on to him without *sensible* diminution as regards quantity and *sensible* alteration as regards quality —*F. D. Smith & Barbara Wilcox*⟩ Both *palpable* and *tangible* in their primary senses may be used to describe anything which is perceptible through the sense of touch. **Palpable,** however, although it is used of what is felt by touching with the tips of the fingers ⟨a *palpable* powder is one that feels gritty⟩ ⟨touch beauty as though it were a *palpable* thing—*Maugham*⟩ ⟨before the clouded night dropped its mysterious veil, it was the immensity of space made visible—almost *palpable*—*Conrad*⟩ as often implies a sensation produced as a sensation sought and therefore may be applied to whatever evokes a response from tactile receptors in any part of the body ⟨there is a *palpable* chill in the air⟩ **Tangible,** on the other hand, is applied primarily to things which may be or are handled or grasped ⟨if an infant is not provided with light *tangible* objects, he will play with a sunbeam or shadow⟩ ⟨idols are gods or divinities in *tangible* form⟩ ⟨a cloud, a pillar of fire, a *tangible* physical something—*London*⟩ In their secondary senses these two words diverge widely. *Palpable,* in one of its most common meanings, implies a high degree of perceptibility (see under EVIDENT); in poetic use, especially when applied to an immaterial thing, it suggests an almost physical awareness of its existence or reality ⟨what happiness to live when every hour brings *palpable* access of knowledge—*Wordsworth*⟩ *Tangible* in its extended senses is applied to things that can be thought of as having real, independent, or objective existence whether they are apparent to the senses or not or whether they can be handled or not; thus, *tangible* ideas are those that can be grasped by the mind and made objects of thought; *tangible* advantages are those having a substantial character; *tangible* assets are those (as equipment and inventory) that can be appraised with reasonable accuracy as distinguished from those (as goodwill) that are *intangible* ⟨the conquest of a territory meant a *tangible* advantage to the conqueror—*Angell*⟩ **Appreciable** is applicable to whatever is large enough to be measured, weighed, valued, or otherwise estimated; thus, a *perceptible* change in the temperature may be so slight a change that it almost but not quite escapes notice; a *palpable* change in temperature may still be slight, but it is great enough to make it definitely felt; an *appreciable* change in temperature may also be slight, but its extent is determinable by reference to a thermometer ⟨the current . . . generated is small but *appreciable*—*Engel*⟩ ⟨a satellite must be launched above the *appreciable* atmosphere—*Newell*⟩ But *appreciable* may lose any clear notion of measurability and then often approaches *considerable* or *significant* in meaning ⟨there had been an *appreciable* feeling of strain, and a corresponding rise in your sense of the obligation of meeting it —*Mary Austin*⟩ ⟨there was no *appreciable* craft tradition in astronomy before modern times—*S. F. Mason*⟩ **Ponderable** is applicable to whatever can be weighed either physically or mentally ⟨something *ponderable* from the outer world—something of which we can say that its weight is so-and-so—*Jeans*⟩ The word tends, however, to be applied to what is appreciable in terms of weight or significance as distinguished from what is so intangible as

to elude such determination ⟨exert a *ponderable* influence upon the events of his time⟩
*Ana* *clear, lucid, perspicuous: *noticeable, conspicuous, signal: discerned *or* discernible, noted *or* notable, observed *or* observable (see corresponding verbs at SEE)
*Ant* imperceptible

**perception** penetration, insight, acumen, *discernment, discrimination
*Ana* appreciation, comprehension, understanding (see corresponding verbs at UNDERSTAND): sharpness, keenness, acuteness (see corresponding adjectives at SHARP)

**perch** *vb* *alight, light, land, roost

**percussion** concussion, clash, shock, *impact, impingement, collision, jar, jolt
*Ana* striking, hitting, smiting (see STRIKE): vibration, oscillation, fluctuation (see corresponding verbs at SWING)

**perdurable** durable, permanent, stable, *lasting, perpetual
*Ana* enduring, abiding, persisting, continuing (see CONTINUE): *everlasting, endless, interminable
*Ant* fleeting

**peremptory** imperative, imperious, *masterful, domineering
*Ana* decisive, *decided: positive, certain (see SURE): *dictatorial, dogmatic, oracular

**perennial** perpetual, incessant, unremitting, constant, *continual, continuous
*Ana* *lasting, perpetual, perdurable, stable: *everlasting, unceasing

**perfect** *adj* Perfect, whole, entire, intact are comparable when they mean not deficient, defective, or faulty in any particular. **Perfect** is the usual term to describe such a condition, for it may imply not only the presence of every part, every element, and every quality necessary to a thing in its finished or fully developed state, but the soundness, the proportionateness, and the excellence of each part, element, or quality ⟨a *perfect* set of teeth⟩ ⟨a *perfect* diamond⟩ ⟨a physically *perfect* infant⟩ ⟨the memory of that night remained intact and *perfect*—*Wylie*⟩ The term is also applicable where there is no more definite measure or test than correspondence to a very high standard of excellence ⟨a *perfect* gentleman⟩ ⟨*perfect* coloring⟩ ⟨a *perfect* poem like Lycidas, a *perfect* fiction like Esmond, a *perfect* handling of a theory like Newman's Idea of a University—*Pater*⟩ ⟨he is the most *perfect* writer of my generation, he writes the best sentences word for word, rhythm upon rhythm—*Mailer*⟩ or to an archetype, definition, or pattern ⟨a *perfect* hexagon⟩ ⟨a *perfect* Greek temple⟩ or to a conception that represents an ideal or personal vision of the highest possible of its kind ⟨*perfect* virtue⟩ The term is also used in the sense of *utter* or *complete* ⟨he is a *perfect* fool⟩ ⟨that is *perfect* nonsense⟩ *Whole* and *entire* (see also WHOLE 2) are somewhat elevated and often reminiscent of scriptural use. **Whole** usually implies a perfection, typically a moral or physical perfection, that can be sought and attained or that can be lost and regained; it usually suggests the attainment of or restoration to health, soundness, completeness ⟨here, with one balm for many fevers found, *whole* of an ancient evil, I sleep sound—*Housman*⟩ ⟨one silver spider of machine, so intricate and *whole* as to appear rightly sufficient in itself—*Terry Southern*⟩ ⟨daughter, be of good comfort; thy faith hath made thee *whole*—*Mt* 9:22⟩ **Entire** usually implies a physical, intellectual, moral, or spiritual perfection that derives from the completeness, integrity, soundness, and often the freedom from admixture of the thing so described; more than *whole*, it suggests a perfection that is unimpaired or without sign of previous imperfection; thus, a collection is *entire* when no constituent item is missing; an *entire* horse is an adult uncastrated male ⟨oh

---

A colon (:) separates groups of words discriminated. An asterisk (*) indicates place of treatment of each group.

grant me, Phoebus, calm content, strength unimpaired, a mind *entire—Conington*⟩ **Intact** usually implies the retention of the perfection of a thing in its finished or its natural or its original state; often it suggests its passage through some experience that might have destroyed its soundness, integrity, or wholeness ⟨that high courage which enabled Fielding . . . to keep his manly benevolence and love of truth *intact—Thackeray*⟩ ⟨had seen many storms, and had reached middle age with some illusions *intact—Michener*⟩ ⟨I am . . . thankful that I was among the last persons to see the original Rheims *intact*. The cathedral . . . remains enshrined . . . in my memory forever *—Ellis*⟩

*Ana* *pure, absolute, simple, sheer: *consummate, finished, accomplished: *impeccable, flawless, faultless, errorless

*Ant* imperfect  —*Con* *deficient, defective

**perfect** *vb* *unfold, evolve, develop, elaborate
*Ana* complete, finish (see CLOSE)

**perfection** virtue, merit, *excellence
*Ant* failing

**perfervid** fervid, *impassioned, passionate, ardent, fervent
*Ana* *intense, vehement, fierce, violent: heightened, enhanced, intensified (see INTENSIFY)

**perfidious** *faithless, false, disloyal, traitorous, treacherous
*Ana* *mercenary, venal: disaffected, alienated, estranged (see ESTRANGE): deceitful, *dishonest: perjured, forsworn (see PERJURE)

**perforate,** puncture, punch, prick, bore, drill mean to pierce through so as to leave a hole. **Perforate,** although it can mean to pierce, is used mainly with reference to the action of a machine or instrument which makes usually small round holes in a line or pattern (as for ready tearing, for ornamentation, or for marking with a symbol, device, or name) ⟨*perforate* a sheet of postage stamps⟩ ⟨*perforate* leather for the tips of shoes⟩ ⟨*perforate* laundry tabs⟩ ⟨a set of pins that *perforates* an entire sheet at one operation—*Al Burns*⟩ **Puncture** suggests the intentional or accidental entrance of a sharp pointed instrument or thing into a tissue, substance, or material ⟨*puncture* the arm with a hypodermic needle⟩ ⟨the tire was *punctured* by a sharp tack⟩ ⟨as the rush began, there flashed through my mind a picture of the ignominious fate which awaited me—*punctured* to death by umbrellas—*Heiser*⟩ Since *puncture* is often associated with the sudden release of air from an inflated object (as a balloon or a pneumatic tire) the word frequently connotes the sudden deflation of something inflated, unduly pretentious, or pompous ⟨*puncture* a scheme⟩ ⟨the effect of Mark Twain's humorous assault on the dignity of General Grant was to reduce him not to the human but to the common level, to *puncture* the reluctant reverence of the groundlings—*Brooks*⟩ **Punch** is often interchangeable with *perforate* especially when the use of a mechanical device called a *punch* is implied ⟨*punch* holes in a piece of brass⟩ ⟨railway conductors are instructed to *punch* the tickets presented them⟩ ⟨invented a system of dot-and-dash symbols which could be *punched* out on thick paper and read by touch at night—*Time*⟩ **Prick** implies a piercing with something that has a sharp fine point and therefore suggests a very small hole or a superficial wound ⟨*prick* oneself with a needle⟩ ⟨*prick* out a design on a piece of canvas⟩ In extended use *prick* usually stresses either the sharp sting that accompanies the pricking of the skin ⟨at the older man's laughter he felt his ready pride ruffle and *prick—Buck*⟩ or the delicacy and clearness of a pattern or design ⟨the design is *pricked* out, so to speak, by the rhymes—*Lowes*⟩ Both *bore* and *drill* imply the use of a mechanical

means in making a hole. But **bore** stresses the removal of materials and therefore is employed when there is a suggestion of excavation by hand or machinery ⟨*bore* a hole in the ground for a fence post⟩ ⟨*bore* a tunnel through a mountain⟩ or of the use of a rotary tool (as an auger or gimlet) ⟨*bore* holes in a plank⟩ or of the use of a boring tool designed for the finishing of roughly made holes by enlarging them and by making them exact in size and true with relation to a specified center line ⟨*bore* the barrel of a gun⟩ **Drill** commonly implies the use of an instrument or machine equipped with a pointed or sharp rotating tool for boring holes in such hard substances as metal and stone ⟨*drill* holes in a steel plate⟩ ⟨a dentist *drills* a tooth to remove decayed material and form a base for a filling⟩ In their extended senses *bore* and *drill* (see also PRACTICE) carry differing connotations, *bore* suggesting the slow or continuous forcing of a passage through ⟨*bore* one's way through a crowd⟩ ⟨the sound of an airplane *bored* ominously into the ears of the crowd—*Woolf*⟩ and *drill,* the forced entrance of something through a succession of efforts or through persistence ⟨is heavily and harshly written, and that is too bad, for the ideas are exciting if the reader can *drill* through to them—*Mailer*⟩

*Ana* *enter, penetrate, pierce, probe

**perform** *vb* Perform, execute, discharge, accomplish, achieve, effect, fulfill are comparable when they mean to carry out or into effect. **Perform,** sometimes merely a formal synonym for *do,* is more often used with reference to processes than to acts. One *performs* processes that are lengthy or exacting or ceremonial in character ⟨*perform* a play⟩ ⟨*perform* a surgical operation⟩ ⟨*perform* the marriage service⟩ ⟨a solemn sacrifice, *performed* in state —*Pope*⟩ One *performs* acts that are distinguished or striking ⟨*perform* feats of skill⟩ When the end rather than the means to the end is stressed, what is *performed* is, usually something undertaken or pledged ⟨lobbyists *perform* a legitimate, even necessary, function—*Armbrister*⟩ One **executes** what exists in design or intent by bringing it into being or by putting it into effect ⟨the heads of departments are . . . political or confidential agents . . . merely to *execute* the will of the president—*John Marshall*⟩ ⟨the escape was planned meticulously and *executed* boldly—*Edmond Taylor*⟩ Sometimes *execute* is used in place of *perform* of a process involving great skill or a highly exacting technique ⟨few dancers can *execute* an adagio beautifully⟩ One **discharges** duties or obligations when one goes through a required round of tasks ⟨I had *discharged* my confidential duties as secretary . . . to the general satisfaction—*De Quincey*⟩ **Accomplish** usually stresses the completion of a process rather than the means by which it is carried out. One *accomplishes* something begun or something which there is reason to expect ⟨it took us twenty-three days to *accomplish* the return journey—*Hudson*⟩ ⟨this project was so vast and so quickly *accomplished* that it has no parallel—*Stoumen*⟩ Sometimes *accomplish* implies the fruitfulness of effort or the value of the results obtained ⟨because of his efforts things are *accomplished—Anderson*⟩ ⟨there's very little to be *accomplished* by telling men anything. You have to show them—*Mary Austin*⟩ **Achieve** adds to *accomplish* the implication of conquered difficulties. One *achieves* a work, a task, or an enterprise that is of great importance and that makes unusual demands (as on one's energy, willpower, or resources) ⟨the American public schools *achieve* . . . the task of transforming a heterogeneous selection of mankind into a homogeneous nation—*Russell*⟩ **Effect** implies obstacles to be removed but, unlike *achieve,* it emphasizes inherent force in the agent rather than such personal qualities as daring and perseverance. Also, it is often predicated of things as well as of persons 〈only two prisoners *effected* their escape〉 〈taxation as an instrument for *effecting* a more equal distribution of income—*Shaw*〉 〈a neurotic general overcome with work may believe he has the power to *effect* nothing—*Mailer*〉 **Fulfill** implies a full realization of what exists potentially, or hitherto in conception, or is implicit in the nature or the sense of responsibility of the agent 〈a law that fails to *fulfill* its intended end〉 〈*fulfill* a promise〉 〈a sense of the failure of life to *fulfill* its ultimate expectations—*Rees*〉 **Ana** *reach, gain, compass, achieve, attain: finish, complete, conclude (see CLOSE *vb*)

**performer** *actor, player, mummer, mime, mimic, thespian, impersonator, trouper

**perfume** *fragrance, bouquet, redolence, incense **Ana** odor, scent, aroma, *smell

**peril** *danger, jeopardy, hazard, risk **Ana** menacing *or* menace, threatening *or* threat (see THREATEN): exposure, subjection, openness, liability (see corresponding adjectives at LIABLE)

**perilous** *dangerous, hazardous, risky, precarious **Ana** desperate, forlorn, hopeless (see DESPONDENT): chancy, chance, haphazard, *random

**perimeter** *circumference, periphery, circuit, compass

**period, epoch, era, age, aeon** all denote a portion or division of time; *epoch* and *era* can also denote an event regarded as the beginning of a portion or division of time. **Period** is the generic term, designating an extent of time of any length for whatever purpose delimited 〈request a one-minute *period* of silence as a tribute to a dead person〉 〈it began in 1915 in one of the darkest *periods* of the first world war—*Pollock*〉 〈was returned for eight successive Congresses—a *period* of seventeen years—*W. C. Ford*〉 **Epoch** can denote the starting point of a new period, especially as marked by striking or remarkable changes or events 〈this is an *epoch* . . . the end and the beginning of an age—*H. G. Wells*〉 or it may apply to such a new period 〈a phenomenon of our own special *epoch,* a man who couldn't . . . be a writer in the only meaning of the term, but who can and probably will write a book—*Purdy*〉 〈Dante's work . . . initiated a new *epoch* in literature—*R. A. Hall*〉 **Era** applies to a period characterized especially by some new order of things 〈a better intellectual *era* is dawning for the working men—*Kingsley*〉 〈the Victorian *era*〉 〈an *era* of singular crisis and upheaval—*Aldridge*〉 **Age,** usually interchangeable with but possibly more specific than *era,* is frequently used of a period dominated by some central figure or clearly marked feature 〈the *age* of Pericles〉 〈the Bronze *Age*〉 〈the French Revolution and its *age*—*Arnold*〉 **Aeon** applies to an immeasurably or indefinitely long period of time 〈*aeons* of primeval power have shaped that pillared bulk—*Gibson*〉 〈during the three terrible hours . . . he had lived centuries of pain, *aeon* upon *aeon* of torture—*Wilde*〉

**periodic** *intermittent, recurrent, alternate **Ana** *fitful, spasmodic, convulsive: sporadic, occasional (see INFREQUENT)

**periodical** *n* *journal, magazine, newspaper, review, organ

**peripatetic** *itinerant, ambulatory, ambulant, nomadic, vagrant

**periphery** *circumference, perimeter, circuit, compass **Ana** *limit, confine, bound, end

**periphrasis** *verbiage, redundancy, tautology, pleonasm, circumlocution

**peristyle** *colonnade, arcade, arcature, portico

**perjure, forswear** are comparable when they mean to violate one's oath or, when used reflexively, to make a false swearer of oneself. In general use **perjure** is often employed less precisely than in law, where it is a technical term meaning to make a willfully false statement of fact or sometimes of an intention to do something, while under oath or under a solemn affirmation to tell the truth 〈the judge was convinced that the witness had *perjured* himself〉 In general use *perjure* often implies making a liar of oneself whether one is under oath or not 〈when a native begins perjury he *perjures* himself thoroughly. He does not boggle over details—*Kipling*〉 〈he thanked her, with as much enthusiasm as he could muster without actually *perjuring* himself—*Archibald Marshall*〉 **Forswear** (see also ABJURE) often implies a violation of an oath, promise, or vow 〈he swore a thing to me on Monday night, which he *forswore* on Tuesday morning—*Shak.*〉 〈thou shalt not *forswear* thyself, but shalt perform unto the Lord thine oaths—*Mt* 5:33〉 but it may also suggest untruth or ill faith to something (as one's principles, one's beliefs, or the laws of one's country) as sacred as an oath 〈Shelley indignantly refused to *"forswear* his principles"* by accepting "a proposal so insultingly hateful"—*Arnold*〉 **Ana** *deceive, delude, mislead, beguile: *lie, prevaricate

**permanent** *lasting, perdurable, durable, stable, perpetual **Ana** perennial, constant, continuous, *continual **Ant** temporary: ad interim (*of persons*)

**permeate, pervade, penetrate, impenetrate, interpenetrate, impregnate, saturate** can all mean to pass or cause to pass through every part of a thing. **Permeate** may be used in reference to either a material or an immaterial thing and implies diffusion through all the pores or interstices of some substance or entity 〈the rain has *permeated* the soil〉 〈the air is *permeated* by the pungent scent of tobacco— *Amer. Guide Series: N. C.*〉 〈in . . . the Elizabethan age, English society at large was accessible to ideas, was *permeated* by them—*Arnold*〉 〈the sense of beauty had *permeated* the whole nation—*Binyon*〉 〈the religious issue *permeated* every meeting I conducted—*Michener*〉 **Pervade** is a very close synonym of *permeate,* but it distinctively carries a heightened suggestion of diffusion throughout every part or parcel of the whole and it is more often used in reference to such matters as places, writings, and works of art than to purely material things 〈a deep and solemn harmony *pervades* the hollow vale from steep to steep—*Wordsworth*〉 〈a principle which so entirely *pervades* the constitution . . . as to be incapable of being separated from it—*John Marshall*〉 〈a kind of easy morality seems to *pervade* all levels of the state government— *Armbrister*〉 **Penetrate** (see also ENTER 1) may be preferred to *permeate* or *pervade* when there is the intent also to suggest the entrance of something that goes deeply or profoundly into the essence or nature of a thing, thereby giving it its characteristic quality or efficient force 〈a whole nation . . . *penetrated* with an enthusiasm for pure reason, and with an ardent zeal for making its prescriptions triumph—*Arnold*〉 〈a letter *penetrated* with affection for the old plain edifice and its memories—*Quiller-Couch*〉 〈a commanding significance, which *penetrates* the whole, informing and ordering everything—*Leavis*〉 **Impenetrate** is an intensive of *penetrate* implying a more thorough and often a diffusive penetration 〈power to isolate and *impenetrate* Poland—*Gunther*〉 〈the church structure is backed up and *impenetrated* by the kinship structure—*Vogt & O'Dea*〉 **Interpenetrate,** too, may imply no more than thorough penetration or penetration into, within, or throughout 〈Westerners who *interpenetrated* the East in the nineteenth century—*Davis*〉 but distinctively it may imply a mutual penetration 〈the state and the economy *interpenetrate;* during slump, war, and boom, the tie-ins tend to become ever closer—*Labor and Nation*〉 〈had both imagination and a stubborn will, curiously balancing and *interpenetrating* each other—*Cather*〉 **Im-**

A colon (:) separates groups of words discriminated. An asterisk (*) indicates place of treatment of each group.

**pregnate** often carries a stronger implication of the operation of a causative power (as a human agent) than any of the preceding terms; it also suggests a filling of every available part or portion of a whole so that the thing which enters or is entered is diffused throughout the entire substance, structure, work, or group ⟨the water is *impregnated* with magnesia—*Huxley*⟩ ⟨any judge who has sat with juries knows that . . . they are extremely likely to be *impregnated* by the environing atmosphere—*Justice Holmes*⟩ ⟨a very notable poem *impregnated* with the pessimism of a time—*Lovett*⟩ **Saturate** (see also SOAK) implies impregnation to the point where no more of the thing which enters can be taken up or absorbed; the term is often used in preference to *permeate* or *pervade* when what permeates or pervades is highly obvious, deeply ingrained, or overabundant ⟨the smell, sweet and poignant beyond imagining, *saturated* the air—*Wouk*⟩ ⟨verse that is *saturated* with emotion—*Lowes*⟩ ⟨the air is *saturated* with golden light—*Diamant*⟩
*Ana* *infuse, imbue, ingrain: drench, steep, *soak, saturate: *inform, animate, inspire, fire
**permission,** **leave, sufferance** denote the sanction which enables one to do something that requires the consent of those in authority. **Permission** is the ordinary term except in some conventional phrases; it commonly implies the power or authority to grant or to refuse what is asked ⟨have the owner's *permission* to hunt on his estate⟩ ⟨"The horses can go in our barn. I'm sure Mr. Forrester would have no objection." She spoke as if he had asked her *permission*—*Cather*⟩ **Leave** differs very little from *permission*. It occurs chiefly in conventionally courteous phrases such as "by your *leave*," "to ask *leave*," and "give me *leave*," but it may be used elsewhere in place of *permission* ⟨ask for *leave* to remove papers from a file⟩ In military, naval, and some official use the term implies official permission to absent oneself from one's duties or from one's station for a fixed period of time, or the furlough or absence so permitted ⟨granted a *leave* of thirty days⟩ ⟨after being absent without *leave* for a month, the soldier was arrested as a deserter⟩ ⟨at home on sick *leave*⟩ **Sufferance** usually implies a neglect or refusal to forbid and therefore suggests either a tacit permission withdrawable on cause or, more often, merely allowing a person to be present or to do something ⟨you are here only on *sufferance* and if you want to stay, you must listen without interrupting⟩ ⟨he comes among us on *sufferance*, like those concert singers whom mamma treats with so much politeness—*Thackeray*⟩
*Ana* authorization, commissioning *or* commission, licensing *or* license (see corresponding verbs at AUTHORIZE): letting, allowing (see LET): sanctioning, approval, endorsement (see corresponding verbs at APPROVE)
*Ant* prohibition
**permit** *vb* *let, allow, suffer, leave
*Ana* *authorize, license, commission: sanction, endorse, *approve
*Ant* prohibit, forbid
**permutation** mutation, *change, vicissitude, alternation
*Ana* moving *or* move, shifting *or* shift, removing *or* remove (see MOVE): transformation, conversion, metamorphosis (see under TRANSFORM)
**pernicious,** **baneful, noxious, deleterious, detrimental** are comparable when they mean exceedingly harmful but they differ as to the kind and extent of the potential for harm. Something is either *pernicious* or *baneful* which is irreparably harmful but **pernicious** is more often applied to things that harm exceedingly or irreparably by evil or by insidious corrupting or enervating and **baneful** to those that poison or destroy ⟨*pernicious* anemia⟩ ⟨a *pernicious*

influence⟩ ⟨the effects of false and *pernicious* propaganda cannot be neutralized—*Huxley*⟩ ⟨*pernicious* social institutions which stifle the nobler impulses—*Parrington*⟩ ⟨the *baneful* notion that there is no such thing as a high, correct standard in intellectual matters—*Arnold*⟩ ⟨they were under as little personal restraint as was compatible with their protection from the *baneful* habit of swallowing one another—*Bierce*⟩ ⟨the full extent and degree of their *baneful* psychological influence is quite inadequately realized—*Moberly*⟩ Something is **noxious** which is harmful especially to health of body or mind ⟨a cold *noxious* wind—*Haughton*⟩ ⟨only when the educator shall have been educated, the air cleared of *noxious* fallacies . . . will the reign of Humbug come to an end—*Grandgent*⟩ **Deleterious** is used chiefly of something which causes harm when taken into the body (as into the digestive or respiratory tract) and may suggest obscure or ill-understood effects ⟨many drugs that seem so good in the first trials prove to have *deleterious* aftereffects—*Heiser*⟩ ⟨this gas was well known to be *deleterious*—*John Phillips*⟩ **Detrimental,** like *deleterious,* generally suggests a much lower degree of harmfulness than the remaining terms; typically it imputes an impairing or hampering quality to the agent or an impaired or hampered condition to the one acted upon ⟨a federal-scholarship program is a project worthy of our united support, provided it can be administered at the state level, free from political or other *detrimental* influences—*L. M. Chamberlain*⟩ ⟨they both ran down the theory as highly *detrimental* to the best interests of man—*Peacock*⟩ ⟨bismuth is considered to be a *detrimental* impurity in refined lead—*Pasternack*⟩ ⟨although too rich a diet is harmful to calves of both sexes, the *detrimental* effects are less marked in a bull calf than in a heifer—*Farmer's Weekly*⟩
*Ana* baleful, malign, *sinister, malefic, maleficent: *poisonous, venomous, toxic, pestilent, miasmatic: injurious, hurtful, harmful, mischievous (see corresponding nouns at INJURY)
*Ant* innocuous
**pernickety** persnickety, fastidious, finicky, finicking, finical, *nice, dainty, particular, fussy, squeamish
*Ana* exacting, demanding, requiring (see DEMAND): annoyed, vexed, irked (see ANNOY)
**perpendicular** *vertical, plumb
*Ana* *steep, abrupt, precipitous, sheer
*Ant* horizontal
**perpetrate** *commit
*Ana* accomplish, achieve, effect (see PERFORM)
**perpetual** 1 *lasting, permanent, perdurable, durable, stable
*Ana* *everlasting, endless, unceasing, interminable: eternal, sempiternal, *infinite
2 *continual, continuous, constant, incessant, unremitting, perennial
*Ana* enduring, persisting, abiding, continuing (see CONTINUE): set, settled, fixed, established (see SET *vb*)
*Ant* transitory, transient
**perplex** *puzzle, mystify, bewilder, distract, nonplus, confound, dumbfound
*Ana* disturb, perturb, upset, *discompose: baffle, balk, thwart (see FRUSTRATE): astound, amaze, astonish, *surprise
**perquisite** *right, prerogative, privilege, appanage, birthright
**persecute** oppress, *wrong, aggrieve
*Ana* *worry, annoy, harass, harry: torture, torment, rack (see AFFLICT): *bait, badger, hound, ride
*Con* *indulge, pamper, humor: favor, *oblige, accommodate: *support, uphold, champion, back

---

*Ana* analogous words     *Ant* antonyms     *Con* contrasted words     See also explanatory notes facing page 1

**persevere, persist** are both used in reference to persons in the sense of to continue in a given course in the face of difficulty or opposition. **Persevere** nearly always implies an admirable quality; it suggests both refusal to be discouraged by failure, doubts, or difficulties, and a steadfast or dogged pursuit of an end or an undertaking ⟨I will *persevere* in my course of loyalty, though the conflict be sore between that and my blood—*Shak.*⟩ ⟨for, strength to *persevere* and to support, and energy to conquer and repel — these elements of virtue, that declare the native grandeur of the human soul—*Wordsworth*⟩ ⟨I do not intend to take that cowardly course, but, on the contrary, to stand to my post and *persevere* in accordance with my duty—*Sir Winston Churchill*⟩ **Persist** (see also CONTINUE) may imply a virtue ⟨this is the poetry within history, this is what causes mankind to *persist* beyond every defeat—*J. S. Untermeyer*⟩ but it more often suggests a disagreeable or annoying quality, for it stresses stubbornness or obstinacy more than courage or patience and frequently implies opposition to advice, remonstrance, disapproval, or one's own conscience ⟨*persist* in working when ill⟩ ⟨it is hard to see how they can have *persisted* so long in inflicting useless misery—*Russell*⟩
*Ana* *continue, abide, endure, last
*Con* vary, *change, alter: waver, vacillate, falter, *hesitate

**persiflage** *badinage, raillery
*Ana* bantering *or* banter, chaffing *or* chaff (see BANTER): ridiculing *or* ridicule, twitting, deriding *or* derision (see corresponding verbs at RIDICULE)

**persist 1** *persevere
*Ant* desist —*Con* discontinue, cease, *stop, quit
**2** *continue, last, endure, abide
*Ant* desist —*Con* *stop, cease, discontinue

**persnickety** pernickety, fastidious, finicky, finicking, finical, *nice, dainty, particular, fussy, squeamish
*Ana* exacting, demanding, requiring (see DEMAND): annoyed, vexed, irked (see ANNOY)

**person** *entity, being, creature, individual

**personality** character, individuality, temperament, *disposition, temper, complexion

**perspicacious** *shrewd, sagacious, astute
*Ana* *sharp, keen, acute: penetrating, piercing, probing (see ENTER)
*Ant* dull

**perspicuous** *clear, lucid
*Ana* manifest, *evident, plain, distinct: *explicit, express, specific, definite
*Con* *turbid, muddy: inflated, flatulent, tumid, turgid

**persuade** *induce, prevail, get
*Ana* influence, *affect, touch, sway, impress: *move, drive, impel, actuate
*Ant* dissuade —*Con* *restrain, curb, check, inhibit: *hinder, impede, obstruct

**persuasion 1** conviction, belief, *opinion, view, sentiment
*Ana* *predilection, prepossession, bias, partiality, prejudice: tenet, dogma, *doctrine
**2** *religion, denomination, sect, cult, communion, faith, creed, church

**pert** *saucy, arch
*Ana* flippant, frivolous, volatile, light-minded (see corresponding nouns at LIGHTNESS): *impertinent, intrusive: brash, impudent (see SHAMELESS)
*Ant* coy

**pertain** *bear, relate, appertain, belong, apply
*Ana* connect, *join, combine, associate

**pertinacious** *obstinate, stubborn, dogged, mulish, stiff-necked, pigheaded, bullheaded
*Ana* tenacious, tough, stout, sturdy, *strong: persistent, persevering (see corresponding verbs at PERSEVERE):

resolute, steadfast, staunch (see FAITHFUL): headstrong, willful (see UNRULY)

**pertinent** *relevant, germane, material, apposite, applicable, apropos
*Ana* fitting, apt, happy, felicitous (see FIT): pat, *seasonable, opportune, timely, well-timed
*Ant* impertinent: foreign

**perturb** disturb, agitate, upset, *discompose, disquiet, fluster, flurry
*Ana* *annoy, vex, irk, bother: *confuse, muddle, addle: confound, nonplus, distract, bewilder, dumbfound (see PUZZLE *vb*)

**pervade** *permeate, penetrate, impenetrate, interpenetrate, impregnate, saturate
*Ana* *infuse, imbue, ingrain, leaven: *inform, animate, inspire, fire

**perverse** *contrary, restive, balky, froward, wayward
*Ana* *unruly, ungovernable, recalcitrant, refractory: *obstinate, stubborn, mulish, pigheaded, stiff-necked: fractious, *irritable, peevish

**pervert** *vb* deprave, corrupt, *debase, vitiate, debauch
*Ana* abuse, misuse, ill-treat, maltreat, mistreat, outrage: contort, distort, warp (see DEFORM)

**perverted** corrupted, depraved, debased, vitiated, debauched (see under DEBASE)
*Ana* distorted, contorted, warped (see DEFORM): abused, misused, outraged (see ABUSE)

**pessimistic** *cynical, misanthropic, misogynic
*Ana* gloomy, morose (see SULLEN): depressed, oppressed, weighed down (see DEPRESS)
*Ant* optimistic —*Con* sanguine, *confident, assured

**pester** plague, tease, tantalize, *worry, annoy, harass, harry
*Ana* *bait, badger, hector, heckle, chivy: fret, gall, chafe (see ABRADE): perturb, disturb, agitate, upset, *discompose

**pestilent, pestilential** *poisonous, venomous, virulent, toxic, mephitic, miasmic, miasmatic, miasmal
*Ana* *infectious, contagious, catching: noxious, *pernicious, baneful, deleterious

**pet** *vb* *caress, fondle, cosset, cuddle, dandle
*Ana* *indulge, humor, pamper, mollycoddle, baby

**petite** *small, little, diminutive, wee, tiny, teeny, weeny, minute, microscopic, miniature

**petition** *n* *prayer, suit, plea, appeal

**petition** *vb* pray, sue, plead, appeal (see under PRAYER)

**petrify 1** *harden, solidify, indurate, cake
*Ana* deposit, precipitate (see corresponding nouns at DEPOSIT): *compact, consolidate
**2** *daze, stun, bemuse, stupefy, benumb, paralyze
*Ana* terrify, alarm, *frighten, startle: appall, horrify, *dismay

**pettish** *irritable, fractious, peevish, petulant, snappish, waspish, huffy, fretful, querulous

**petty, puny, trivial, trifling, paltry, measly, picayunish, picayune** mean little and insignificant, often contemptibly so. Something is **petty** which by comparison with other things the same in kind but different in size, importance, gravity, or moment is among the smallest or least important ⟨a *petty* interest⟩ ⟨a *petty* prince⟩ ⟨giants beside whom we seem *petty*—*Sinclair Lewis*⟩ ⟨Hunt does one harm by making fine things *petty* and beautiful things hateful—*Keats*⟩ The word often connotes small-mindedness ⟨*petty* gossip⟩ ⟨explaining that only the *petty* vengeance of men who hated Roosevelt had produced the law that prohibited . . . a third term—*Michener*⟩ ⟨divine inhabitants of a world apart, for whom nothing sordid, nothing *petty*, and nothing painful had any existence—*Sackville-West*⟩ Something is **puny** which is so small or slight as to seem

A colon (:) separates groups of words discriminated. An asterisk (*) indicates place of treatment of each group.

impotent, feeble, or completely without vitality ⟨none of your thin, *puny,* yellow, hectic figures, exhausted with abstinence and hard study—*Smollett*⟩ ⟨one no sooner grasps the bigness of the world's work than one's own effort seems *puny* and contemptible—*J. R. Green*⟩ Something is **trivial** which seems petty and commonplace and scarcely worthy of special consideration or notice ⟨that strange interest in *trivial* things that we try to develop when things of high import make us afraid—*Wilde*⟩ ⟨he regarded no task as too humble for him to undertake, nor so *trivial* that it was not worth his while to do it well—*Huxley*⟩ The term is often applied to persons, minds, or activities which reveal engrossment in trivial affairs or a lack of serious or profound interests ⟨she knew him for a philanderer, a *trivial* taster in love and life—*Rose Macaulay*⟩ ⟨the incessant hurry and *trivial* activity of daily life—*Eliot*⟩ Something is **trifling** which is so small as to have little if any value or significance ⟨our ordinary distinctions become so *trifling,* so impalpable—*Hawthorne*⟩ ⟨a considerable sum was paid to Egmont and a *trifling* one to the Prince—*Motley*⟩ Something is **paltry** which is ridiculously or contemptibly small in comparison especially to what it should be ⟨a *paltry* allowance⟩ ⟨our little ambitions, our *paltry* joys—*Benson*⟩ ⟨the *paltry* prize is hardly worth the cost—*Byron*⟩ Something is **measly** which is contemptibly small (as in size or quantity) or petty ⟨a *measly* portion of pie⟩ ⟨snatch at a little *measly* advantage and miss the big one—*Anderson*⟩ Something is **picayunish** or **picayune** which is insignificant in its possibilities or accomplishments or hopelessly narrow in outlook or interests ⟨a *picayunish* policy⟩ ⟨a lifetime of *picayunish* drudgery in the company of louts—*H. L. Davis*⟩ ⟨the obvious futility, the *picayune,* question-begging character, of such ethical analyses—*Asher Moore*⟩ ⟨a *picayune* congressman⟩
*Ana* \*small, little, diminutive, minute
*Ant* important, momentous: gross
**petulant** \*irritable, fractious, peevish, pettish, snappish, waspish, huffy, fretful, querulous
*Ana* cross, cranky, touchy, testy (see IRASCIBLE): \*impatient, restive, fidgety
**phantasm** 1 \*apparition, phantom, wraith, ghost, spirit, specter, shade, revenant
*Ana* \*delusion, illusion, hallucination
2 \*fancy, fantasy, phantasy, vision, dream, daydream, nightmare
**phantasy** \*fancy, fantasy, phantasm, vision, dream, daydream, nightmare
**phantom** \*apparition, phantasm, wraith, ghost, spirit, specter, shade, revenant
*Ana* counterfeit, deception, \*imposture: \*delusion, illusion, hallucination
**pharisaical** hypocritical, sanctimonious, canting (see under HYPOCRISY)
**pharisaism** \*hypocrisy, sanctimony, cant
**pharmaceutical** *n* \*drug, medicinal, biologic, simple
**pharmacist** \*druggist, apothecary, chemist
**phase, aspect, side, facet, angle** are comparable when they denote one of the possible ways in which an object of contemplation may be seen or may be presented. **Phase** may distinctly imply a change in the appearance of a thing without a change in the observer's point of view. From its original denotation as one of the four different shapes which the moon apparently assumes during its waxing and waning it often suggests a cyclical change in appearance ⟨the wheel of the world swings through the same *phases.* . . . Summer passed and winter thereafter, and came and passed again—*Kipling*⟩ In extended use it is often applied to an outward and passing manifestation of a stage in growth, development, or unfolding ⟨the way children de-velop and the different *phases* they go through—*Barclay*⟩ but it also may apply to one of two or more distinctive appearances or values of something with little or no suggestion of cyclical or temporal succession ⟨the red fox occurs in several color *phases,* of which the silver *phase* has been found to breed true⟩ ⟨he was a shrewd, smooth political-financier, shady in both *phases*—*S. H. Adams*⟩ ⟨the two alternating forces or *phases* in the rhythm of the universe which Empedocles calls Love and Hate—*Toynbee*⟩ **Aspect** sometimes implies a change in appearance without a shifting in point of view, but unlike *phase* it usually suggests a superficial change, especially one brought about by unpredictable circumstances ⟨every time I look out of the window, the hills present a new *aspect*⟩ More distinctively it implies a change in appearance that is traceable to a change in the observer's point of view ⟨the one and only *aspect* of a rich and complex subject which I mean to treat—*Lowes*⟩ ⟨an entirely new *aspect* of the Everest massif filled our northwestern horizon—*Shipton*⟩ ⟨the two men lay whispering for hours, canvassing every *aspect* of Monck's situation—*Upton Sinclair*⟩ Thus, one who proposes to treat the *phases* of the depression of the nineteen-thirties implies that he intends to consider its stages as they manifested themselves outwardly; one who proposes to treat all *aspects* of that depression implies that he intends to consider it from every possible point of view (as the political, the economic, and the sociological). **Side,** though often used interchangeably with *phase* and *aspect,* may retain implications derived from other of its senses and is used chiefly in reference to something that may be thought of as having two or more faces and therefore not fully apprehensible unless it or its observer shifts position ⟨see life only on its pleasant *side*⟩ ⟨if you get on the wrong *side* of authority, you are executed or exiled—*Edmund Wilson*⟩ ⟨the history as a whole is deficient on the economic *side*—*Allen Johnson*⟩ But *side* differs from *phase* and *aspect* in less regularly connoting appearance or referring to physical or intellectual vision ⟨hear both *sides* of a dispute⟩ ⟨read all *sides* in a controversy⟩ ⟨on its theoretic and perceptive *side,* Morality touches Science; on its emotional *side,* poetic Art—*George Eliot*⟩ ⟨this kind of discussion went on all the time between the parents. They could take either *side* with ease—*Wouk*⟩ **Facet** differs from *side* in implying a multiplicity of other faces similar to or like the one singled out for attention ⟨noticed the different shades of green on the planes and *facets* of each clipped tree—*Dahl*⟩ ⟨the strength of the lyric lies in the complete statement of a single selected *facet* of experience—*Day Lewis*⟩ **Angle** denotes an aspect which is observable from a point of view restricted in its scope ⟨he knows only one *angle* of his subject⟩ ⟨it is necessary to consider all *angles* of the situation⟩ ⟨views these developments from a fresh *angle*—*Dumas Malone*⟩
*Ana* \*state, condition, situation, posture: \*appearance, look, semblance
**phenomenal** \*material, physical, corporeal, sensible, objective
*Ana* actual, \*real
*Ant* noumenal
**phenomenon** \*wonder, marvel, prodigy, miracle
*Ana* abnormality (see corresponding adjective at ABNORMAL): anomaly, \*paradox: singularity, peculiarity, uniqueness (see corresponding adjectives at STRANGE)
**philanthropic** \*charitable, benevolent, humane, humanitarian, eleemosynary, altruistic
*Ana* \*liberal, munificent, bountiful, bounteous, openhanded, generous: lavish, \*profuse, prodigal
*Ant* misanthropic

*Ana* analogous words　　*Ant* antonyms　　*Con* contrasted words　　See also explanatory notes facing page 1

**philanthropy** *charity
*Ant* misanthropy
**philippic** *n* *tirade, diatribe, jeremiad
*Ana* harangue, *speech, address, oration: condemnation, denunciation (see corresponding verbs at CRITICIZE)
**philistine** *n* *obscurantist, barbarian
**phlegm** 1 impassivity, stolidity, apathy, stoicism (see under IMPASSIVE)
*Ana* insensibility, insensitiveness, impassibility, anesthesia (see corresponding adjectives at INSENSIBLE)
2 *equanimity, composure, sangfroid
*Ana* imperturbability, nonchalance, coolness, collectedness (see corresponding adjectives at COOL): calmness *or* calm, tranquillity, serenity (see corresponding adjectives at CALM)

**phlegmatic** *impassive, stolid, apathetic, stoic
*Ana* *indifferent, unconcerned, incurious, aloof: cool, chilly, *cold, frigid: sluggish, *lethargic
**phony** *adj* *counterfeit, spurious, bogus, fake, sham, pseudo, pinchbeck
**photograph** *n* portrait, *image, effigy, statue, icon, mask
**phrase, idiom, expression, locution** mean a group of words which, taken together, express a notion and may be used as a part of a sentence. **Phrase** may apply to a group of words which for one reason or another recurs frequently (as in the language of a people, the writings of an author or school of authors, or the speech of a person or a clique of persons). Sometimes the word means little more than this ⟨this *phrase, a priori*, is in common most grossly misunderstood—*Southey*⟩ but more often it suggests a distinctive character, such as triteness ⟨to use the *phrase* of all who ever wrote upon the state of Europe, the political horizon is dark indeed—*Cowper*⟩ or pithiness or pointedness ⟨I summed up all systems in a *phrase*—*Wilde*⟩ ⟨"You don't understand a young philosopher," said the Baronet. "A young philosopher's an old fool!" returned Hippias, not thinking that his growl had begotten a *phrase*—*Meredith*⟩ In the combinations "noun *phrase*" and "verb *phrase*" it suggests one of the principal parts of a sentence. **Idiom** (see also LANGUAGE 1) applies to a combination of word elements which is peculiar to the language in which it occurs either in its grammatical structure or in the meaning which is associated with it but which cannot be derived from it when the elements are interpreted literally; thus, "to keep house," "to catch cold," "to strike a bargain" are examples of *idioms*. **Expression** and **locution** are sometimes used in place of *phrase* when the idea of a way of expressing oneself is uppermost. Although both terms may be applied to phrases that are generally current, they are perhaps more typically applied to those that are idiosyncratic. *Expression* is particularly used when accompanied by a characterizing adjective or clause or phrase ⟨he is in the habit of using telling *expressions*⟩ ⟨that is a very odd *expression*⟩ ⟨an *expression* that has gone out of use⟩ *Locution* is somewhat more bookish than *expression* and is therefore often preferred when the reference is to phrases that are peculiar to a language or a group as an idiom ⟨a pet *locution* of the author⟩ ⟨Carlyle and Carlylese were to leave their traces. Even the style of Thoreau was to be tinged faintly here and there with the rhythms and *locutions* of a writer whom lesser minds could not resist—*Brooks*⟩
**phraseology, phrasing** *language, vocabulary, diction, style
**physic** *n* *remedy, cure, medicine, medicament, medication, specific
**physical** 1 *bodily, corporeal, corporal, somatic
*Ana* fleshly, *carnal, sensual, animal
2 *material, corporeal, phenomenal, sensible, objective

*Ana* actual, *real, true: elemental, *elementary
**physiognomy** *face, countenance, visage, mug, puss
**physique, build, habit, constitution** all mean bodily makeup or structure or organization peculiar to an individual or to a group or kind of individuals. **Physique** applies to the structure, appearance, or strength of the body of an individual or of a race and may connote such qualities as capacity for endurance, stamina, or predisposition to disease ⟨a people of robust *physique*⟩ ⟨a man of slight *physique*⟩ **Build**, though often interchangeable with *physique*, may distinctively suggest not so much the makeup of a body as its conformation; it tends to call attention to such qualities as size, structure, and weight and rarely when used of man or an animal to health or the lack of it ⟨a horse of heavy *build*⟩ ⟨a person of fleshy *build* but of feeble physique⟩ **Habit** implies reference to the body as the outward evidence of natural or acquired characteristics that suggest the nature of one's physical condition and capabilities; thus, a full *habit* suggests an appearance marked by stoutness, redness, and congestion of the visible blood vessels ⟨a youth of consumptive *habit*⟩ ⟨old Mrs. Mingott's . . . being, like many persons of active mind and dominating will, sedentary and corpulent in her *habit*—*Wharton*⟩ **Constitution** applies to the makeup of the body, especially of an individual, as affected by the complex of mental or physical conditions which collectively determine its state (as of healthiness) and its powers (as of endurance and resistance) ⟨persons of sickly *constitutions* are given to worry⟩ ⟨buy them horses to ride, if you want them to enjoy good health and sound *constitutions*—*Jefferies*⟩ ⟨the key to her nature lay, I think, largely in her fragile *constitution*—*Ellis*⟩
*Ana* *body: *structure, framework, anatomy: *system, organism
**picayunish, picayune** *petty, trivial, trifling, puny, paltry, measly
**pick** *vb* *choose, select, elect, opt, cull, prefer, single
*Ana* *take, seize, grasp: determine, *decide, settle
*Con* reject, spurn, refuse, *decline
**picked** *select, elect, exclusive
**pickle** *n* *predicament, plight, dilemma, quandary, scrape, fix, jam
**pictorial** *graphic, vivid, picturesque
**picture** *vb* *represent, depict, portray, delineate, limn
*Ana* describe, *relate, narrate, recount: *sketch, outline
**picturesque** vivid, *graphic, pictorial
*Ana* charming, attractive, alluring (see under ATTRACT): conspicuous, salient, striking, arresting (see NOTICEABLE)
**piece** *n* *part, portion, detail, member, division, section, segment, sector, fraction, fragment, parcel
**pied, piebald** *adj* *variegated, parti-colored, motley, checkered, checked, skewbald, dappled, freaked
**pier** 1 *buttress, abutment
2 *wharf, dock, quay, slip, berth, jetty, levee
**pierce** penetrate, probe, *enter
*Ana* *perforate, bore, drill, puncture: rend, *tear, cleave, split, rive
**pietistic** sanctimonious, pious, *devout, religious
*Ana* reverencing *or* reverential, venerating, adoring, worshiping (see corresponding verbs at REVERE): fervid, perfervid, ardent, fervent (see IMPASSIONED): *sentimental, maudlin, romantic
**piety** devotion, *fidelity, allegiance, fealty, loyalty
*Ana* obedience, docility (see corresponding adjectives at OBEDIENT): fervor, ardor, zeal, enthusiasm, *passion: *holiness, sanctity
*Ant* impiety
**pigeonhole** *assort, sort, classify
*Ana* systematize, methodize, organize, arrange, *order

---

A colon (:) separates groups of words discriminated. An asterisk (*) indicates place of treatment of each group.

**pigheaded** *obstinate, stubborn, mulish, stiff-necked, bullheaded, dogged, pertinacious
*Ana* headstrong, willful, recalcitrant, refractory (see UNRULY): *contrary, perverse, froward

**pilaster** *pillar, column

**pile** *n* 1 heap, stack, mass, bank, shock, cock (see under HEAP *vb*)
2 *building, edifice, structure

**pile** *vb* *heap, stack, mass, bank, shock, cock
*Ana* *gather, collect, assemble, congregate: *accumulate, amass, hoard

**pilfer** *steal, filch, purloin, lift, pinch, snitch, swipe, cop
*Ana* seize, *take, grasp, grab, snatch: *catch, capture: *rob, rifle, loot, plunder

**pilgrimage** *journey, voyage, tour, trip, jaunt, excursion, cruise, expedition

**pillage** *vb* *ravage, devastate, waste, sack, despoil, spoliate
*Ana* plunder, loot, *rob, rifle: invade, encroach, *trespass: confiscate, *arrogate, appropriate, usurp

**pillar, column, pilaster** denote a structure that rises high from a base or foundation, is slender in comparison with its width, and usually has a monolithic and decorative appearance. **Pillar** is the general term and applies to any such structure whether it stands alone ⟨an obelisk is a kind of *pillar*⟩ or is a supporting architectural member of a building or similar structure ⟨the building was a spacious theater, half round on two main *pillars* vaulted high—*Milton*⟩ In extended use *pillar* usually applies to something which stays or supports ⟨the four *pillars* of government . . . religion, justice, counsel, treasure—*Bacon*⟩ ⟨the Classics have . . . lost their place as a *pillar* of the social and political system—*T. S. Eliot*⟩ but when the application is to persons the term usually suggests the character of one who supports, though it may also imply leadership or prominence ⟨he is a *pillar* of the church⟩ ⟨the middlemen . . . the *pillars* of society, the cornerstone of convention—*Lewis & Maude*⟩ **Column** in architectural use primarily applies to a supporting pillar that is often cylindrical and free at every point except its bottom and top. The term commonly also implies three more or less elaborate parts, the base, by which it is attached to the floor, the shaft, often a fluted or channeled cylinder which rises high from the base, and the capital, the uppermost member which crowns the shaft and takes the weight or its share of the weight of what rests on it ⟨a portico supported by a line of *columns*⟩ But *column* is also applicable to a monument or memorial fashioned in the manner of an architectural column ⟨the most conspicuous object in the whole churchyard, a broken *column* of white marble, on a pedestal—*Mary Fitt*⟩ By extension the term is also applicable to something that suggests a column especially in shape ⟨the wind sent *columns* of smoke into the tenement—*N. Y. Times*⟩ or in use or structure ⟨the spinal *column*⟩ Sometimes the suggestion is remote and the term is applied to anything that is long and relatively narrow ⟨the *columns* of a newspaper page⟩ ⟨a *column* of figures⟩ ⟨a *column* of infantry⟩ **Pilaster,** though used with reference to a supporting member of a piece of furniture, is chiefly employed with reference to an architectural member which in function is a pier (see *pier* under BUTTRESS) but which in design and treatment resembles a column. In this latter sense *pilaster* implies engagement or attachment to a wall and suggests a rectangular rather than cylindrical form.

**pilot** *vb* steer, *guide, lead, engineer
*Ana* direct, manage, *conduct, control: *handle, manipulate

**pimple** *abscess, boil, furuncle, carbuncle, pustule

**pinch** *vb* *steal, pilfer, filch, purloin, lift, snitch, swipe, cop

**pinch** *n* *juncture, pass, exigency, emergency, contingency, strait, crisis
*Ana* *difficulty, hardship, rigor, vicissitude

**pinchbeck** *adj* *counterfeit, spurious, bogus, fake, sham, pseudo, phony

**pinched** *haggard, cadaverous, worn, careworn, wasted
*Ana* gaunt, scrawny, skinny, angular, rawboned (see LEAN *adj*)
*Con* *strong, sturdy, stout, stalwart: robust, *healthy

**pinch hitter** *substitute, supply, locum tenens, alternate, understudy, double, stand-in

**pine** *vb* *long, yearn, hanker, hunger, thirst
*Ana* crave, covet, *desire: languish, enervate (see corresponding adjectives at LANGUID)

**pinnacle** *summit, peak, apex, acme, climax, culmination, meridian, zenith, apogee

**pious** *devout, religious, pietistic, sanctimonious
*Ana* *holy, sacred, divine, religious: worshiping, adoring, reverencing, venerating, revering (see REVERE): fervent, ardent, fervid (see IMPASSIONED)
*Ant* impious

**piquant** *pungent, poignant, racy, spicy, snappy
*Ana* *incisive, trenchant, cutting, biting, clear-cut
*Ant* bland —*Con* *insipid, flat, banal, jejune, inane

**pique** *n* *offense, resentment, umbrage, dudgeon, huff
*Ana* annoyance, vexation, irking *or* irk (see corresponding verbs at ANNOY): irritation, exasperation, provocation (see corresponding verbs at IRRITATE)

**pique** *vb* 1 *provoke, excite, stimulate, quicken, galvanize
*Ana* *stir, rouse, arouse: prick, punch (see PERFORATE): kindle, ignite (see LIGHT *vb*)
2 *pride, plume, preen

**pirate, freebooter, buccaneer, privateer, corsair** basically mean one who sails in search of plunder. **Pirate** suggests a person or a ship or its crew that without a commission from an established civilized state cruises about in quest of ships to plunder. Since *pirate* in this sense is seldom used of contemporary life, the word has been extended to name one who wanders over a wide territory in search of plunder ⟨a band of 400 desert *pirates* . . . raided the bazaar section and fled back across the river with their loot—*Time*⟩ or one who infringes upon a right legally restricted to another ⟨English books published by American *pirates*⟩ ⟨*pirates* of wavelengths in radio⟩ or one known for predatory business practices ⟨now my grandfather there who made the money . . . was a hard-boiled man of business. From your point of view he was a *pirate*—*Edmund Wilson*⟩ **Freebooter** often suggests a maritime plunderer who pursues his occupation without the excuse that his country is at war and then differs from *pirate* only in its connotations of membership in a less closely organized band and of use of less violent methods ⟨English *freebooters* who made life merry hell on the high seas for Spanish galleons waddling home from the Americas heavy-laden with gold—*Dodge*⟩ In extended use *freebooter* is often applied to one who seizes rights, privileges, and property on a large scale without regard to the restraints of law or of order ⟨many empire builders have been mere *freebooters*⟩ ⟨an era of comparably good feeling and incomparably good pickings. He took things easy, and his fellow *freebooters* took almost everything easily—*Hodding Carter*⟩ **Buccaneer,** primarily applied to early French residents of Haiti, is more generally used of these people and others who preyed, sometimes with the tacit consent of their own governments, on Spanish ships and settlements in the New World ⟨in the reign of Charles II, the *buccaneers* of the West Indian Islands were in the heyday of their romantic glory, as the unofficial maintainers of England's quarrels along the Spanish Main—*Trevelyan*⟩

---

*Ana* analogous words    *Ant* antonyms    *Con* contrasted words    See also explanatory notes facing page 1

The term is often extended to an unscrupulous adventurer (as in business or politics); in such use it need not be wholly disparaging but does regularly imply disregard of the rules observed by ordinary men ⟨one of the great building enterprises of the famous *buccaneer* out of which he is reputed to have made many millions—*Strunsky*⟩ ⟨there still exist outright *buccaneers*, men who will steal anything that isn't tied down—*Sat. Review*⟩ **Privateer** and **corsair** primarily apply to a ship privately owned but commissioned by its government (as in the 17th and 18th centuries) to prey upon other ships, usually those of an enemy, but in practice either term may designate a ship, its commander, or one of its crew. *Corsair* is applied chiefly to a ship, a commander, or a sailor of North African origin. Neither term has extensive extended use, but when so used they are quite distinct: *privateer* then applies to one doing in a private capacity what would normally be undertaken by a public official ⟨illegal [wire] taps by law enforcers and *privateers* continued unprosecuted—*Westin*⟩ but *corsair* attributes fury and rapacious cruelty to the one so-called ⟨*corsairs* among the reptiles—*Swinton*⟩ ⟨had lately attacked, in *corsair* fashion, the Greek philosophers and had disembowelled Plato, Aristotle, and the rest of them, to his complete satisfaction—*Norman Douglas*⟩

**pirouette** *vb* *turn, revolve, rotate, gyrate, circle, spin, twirl, whirl, wheel, eddy, swirl

**pitch** *vb* **1** hurl, fling, cast, *throw, toss, sling
*Ana* heave, *lift, raise, hoist: *move, drive, impel
**2** *plunge, dive
*Ana* *fall, drop, sink: *descend: *jump, leap, spring

**piteous** *pitiful, pitiable
*Ana* imploring, supplicating, entreating, beseeching (see BEG): *melancholy, doleful, dolorous, plaintive

**pith** *substance, purport, gist, burden, core
*Ana* *center, nucleus, heart, focus: spirit, *soul

**pithy** summary, compendious, *concise, terse, succinct, laconic
*Ana* sententious, pregnant, meaningful, *expressive: *brief, short
*Con* flatulent, *inflated, tumid, turgid: prolix, diffuse, *wordy, verbose

**pitiable 1** piteous, *pitiful
*Ana* sad, depressed, dejected, melancholy (see corresponding nouns at SADNESS): forlorn, hopeless, despairing, desperate, *despondent
**2** despicable, *contemptible, sorry, scurvy, cheap, beggarly, shabby
*Ana* *miserable, wretched: deplorable, lamentable (see corresponding verbs at DEPLORE)

**pitiful,** piteous, pitiable are comparable but not always interchangeable when they mean arousing or deserving pity or compassion. **Pitiful** applies especially to what actually excites pity or, sometimes, commiseration because it is felt to be deeply pathetic ⟨their distress was *pitiful*⟩ ⟨a long line of *pitiful* refugees⟩ ⟨her face looked pale and extinguished. . . . She struck Archer, of a sudden, as a pathetic and even *pitiful* figure—*Wharton*⟩ But *pitiful* may apply to something meriting pity or commiseration less as pathetic than as contemptible, especially in its inadequacy ⟨a *pitiful* attempt at housekeeping⟩ ⟨a *pitiful* wage scale⟩ **Piteous** implies not so much an effect on the observer as a quality in the thing that excites pity; thus, a cry is *piteous* if it implores or demands attention or pity; it is *pitiful* only if it actually excites pity; one may scorn a *piteous* appeal, but it would be a contradiction in terms to scorn a *pitiful* appeal ⟨Cashel cast a glance round, half *piteous*, half desperate, like a hunted animal—*Shaw*⟩ **Pitiable** (see also CONTEMPTIBLE) may be preferred to

*pitiful* when a contemptuous commiseration is implied, but contempt may be weakly or strongly connoted ⟨that *pitiable* husk of a man who a hundred years ago was a familiar figure in its streets, a shadow of his former insolence and splendor—*Lucas*⟩ ⟨felt a tender pity . . . mixed with shame for having made her *pitiable*—*Malamud*⟩
*Ana* touching, *moving, pathetic, affecting: *tender, compassionate, responsive, sympathetic
*Ant* cruel

**pittance** *ration, allowance, dole

**pity** *sympathy, compassion, commiseration, condolence, ruth, empathy
*Ana* *sadness, melancholy, dejection, depression: *pathos, poignancy: *charity, mercy, clemency, lenity

**pivotal** *central, focal
*Ana* *essential, cardinal, vital: important, significant, momentous (see corresponding nouns at IMPORTANCE): capital, principal, *chief

**placate** *vb* *pacify, appease, mollify, propitiate, conciliate
*Ant* enrage —*Con* *anger, infuriate, incense, madden: *stir, arouse, rouse: *provoke, excite, stimulate, pique

**place** *n* Place, position, location, situation, site, spot, station are comparable when they mean the point or portion of space occupied by or chosen for a thing. **Place,** the most general of these terms, carries as its basic implication the idea of extension in space, though often with no clear connotation of how great or how small that extent is; in some use it comes very close to *space* in meaning ⟨he passed the flaming bounds of *Place* and Time—*Gray*⟩ but it more usually implies a limited, though not always clearly defined, extent of space ⟨the *place* where we shall meet⟩ ⟨the *place* where they were born⟩ ⟨the cardplayers changed their *places* several times during the evening⟩ **Position** is capable of abstract as well as concrete use and therefore may be employed whether the thing referred to is immaterial or material, ideal or actual, or invisible or visible; it usually also implies place in relation to something in particular ⟨a point has definite *position* but no extent in space⟩ ⟨an instrument to find the *position* of an invisible target⟩ ⟨the 7th regiment took up its *position* on the left flank⟩ ⟨the blots of shade and flakes of light upon the countenances of the group changed shape and *position* endlessly—*Hardy*⟩ ⟨she dropped forks into their appointed *positions* with disdain—*Bennett*⟩ **Location** is used in a concrete sense implying a fixed but not necessarily a clearly definite place for something or sometimes a person; it may refer to the place as found or as usable as well as to the place actually occupied by a thing ⟨this is a most desirable *location* for your factory⟩ ⟨he knows the *location* of every house in the town built before 1800⟩ ⟨they visited Windsor. Mr. Beck said that if he had such a *location* he should always live there—*Besant & Rice*⟩ **Situation** may differ from *location* in being more specific about the character of the surroundings ⟨this is the best *situation* for the house, for the land is high and dry⟩ ⟨the *situation* of this camp was chosen with respect to its healthfulness and its nearness to the city⟩ ⟨not a place upon earth might be so happy as America. Her *situation* is remote from all the wrangling world—*Paine*⟩ **Site,** though close to *situation* in many ways, carries a clearer reference to the land on which something specific (as a building, a group of buildings, or a town) is built ⟨every ruined village on the road stands on the *site* of an ancient city—*J. L. Stephens*⟩ ⟨you may derive amusement from the historians when they . . . explain how Oxford and Cambridge . . . came to be chosen for *sites*—*Quiller-Couch*⟩ ⟨the *site* for the factory has been well selected⟩ ⟨the hill, with its view of the lake, affords excellent *sites* for summer cottages⟩ **Spot,** only in an extended sense, implies

A colon (:) separates groups of words discriminated. An asterisk (*) indicates place of treatment of each group.

a particular place, clearly defined in extent, which may be occupied or occupiable by a person or thing or may be the scene of an occurrence or activity; the word carries a stronger implication of restricted space than of its particular use ⟨it is one of the pleasantest *spots* in the Adirondacks⟩ ⟨we have found just the *spot* for the picnic⟩ ⟨he said he wouldn't move from the *spot*⟩ ⟨the *spot* where the corpse was found⟩ ⟨there was one *spot* in Rome which was calm amid all tumults—*Farrar*⟩ **Station** implies the place where a person or sometimes a thing stands or is set to stand; it usually carries an implication of accepted responsibility (as in performance of duty or participation in a game) ⟨waiters at their *stations* in the dining room⟩ ⟨every vessel in the squadron has its *station*⟩ ⟨the crew went to their battle *stations*⟩
*Ana* *locality, vicinity, district: region, tract, *area, zone: *field, territory, province
**placid** *calm, tranquil, serene, peaceful, halcyon
*Ana* imperturbable, nonchalant, *cool, collected, composed: gentle, mild, lenient, smooth (see SOFT): *steady, equable, even, constant
*Ant* choleric (*of persons*): ruffled (*of things*)
**plague** *vb* pester, tease, tantalize, harry, harass, *worry, annoy
*Ana* gall, fret, chafe (see ABRADE): *bait, badger, hector, hound, ride: torment, *afflict, try
*Con* *relieve, mitigate, lighten, assuage, alleviate
**plain** *adj* 1 plane, flat, *level, even, smooth, flush
*Ant* solid
2 clear, distinct, obvious, *evident, manifest, patent, apparent, palpable
*Ana* *clear, lucid, perspicuous: *explicit, express, definite, specific, categorical
*Ant* abstruse
3 **Plain, homely, simple, unpretentious** are comparable when they mean devoid of whatever embellishes or makes for superficial beauty. **Plain** stresses lack of anything (as ornamentation, complexity, extraneous matter, or strongly marked characteristics) likely to attract attention ⟨had no eccentricity even to take him out of the common run; he was just a good, dull, honest, *plain* man—*Maugham*⟩ ⟨a *plain* two-story frame house⟩ Additionally it may suggest elegance ⟨his brown stockings . . . were of a fine texture; his shoes and buckles, too, though *plain*, were trim—*Dickens*⟩ or frugality ⟨a *plain* skirt of serviceable gray flannel⟩ or, with reference to personal appearance, lack of positive characteristics, and then contrasts with *beautiful* but without implying positive ugliness ⟨was not a *plain* woman, and she might have been very pretty still—*Glasgow*⟩ In reference to houses, furniture, food, and other elements of domesticity, **homely** sometimes suggests *homey* and may indicate comfortable informality without ostentation ⟨his secluded wife ever smiling and cheerful, his little comfortable lodgings, snug meals, and *homely* evenings, had all the charms of novelty and secrecy—*Thackeray*⟩ It may connote warmth and simplicity ⟨a book-learned language, wholly remote from anything personal, native, or *homely*—*Cather*⟩ With reference to appearance *homely* in American but not usually in British usage often falls between *plain* and *ugly* ⟨she was certainly not bad-looking now and she could never have been so *homely* as she imagined—*Edmund Wilson*⟩ **Simple** may occasionally differ slightly from *plain* in implying choice rather than compulsive circumstance ⟨what was then called the *simple* life . . . is recognizable as the austere luxury of a very cultivated poet—*Repplier*⟩ ⟨a monk of Lindisfarne, so *simple* and lowly in temper that he traveled on foot on his long mission journeys—*J. R. Green*⟩ **Unpretentious,** stressing lack of vanity or affectation, may

praise a person but depreciate a possession ⟨an *unpretentious* family doctor without the specialist's curt loftiness⟩ ⟨an *unpretentious* and battered old car⟩
*Ana* *ugly, ill-favored, unsightly, hideous: barren, *bare, bald: unembellished, unadorned, undecorated, unornamented, ungarnished (see corresponding affirmative verbs at ADORN)
*Ant* lovely
4 *frank, candid, open
*Ana* forthright, *straightforward, aboveboard: blunt, *bluff: *sincere, unfeigned
**plaintive** dolorous, doleful, *melancholy, lugubrious, rueful
*Ana* pensive, reflective, meditative, *thoughtful: lamenting, deploring (see DEPLORE): *pitiful, piteous
**plait** *weave, knit, crochet, braid, tat
**plan** *n* **Plan, design, plot, scheme, project,** as nouns, denote a proposed method of doing or making something or of achieving a given end, and as verbs, to devise such a method. **Plan,** in its widest sense, regularly implies mental formulation of the method ⟨*plan* a trip to Europe⟩ ⟨make *plans* for the future of their children⟩ ⟨*plans* for an expansion of one's business⟩ ⟨she had her *plan* clearly in her head, with every detail . . . distinct—*Gibbons*⟩ ⟨it is a basic part of industrial technology that *planned* obsolescence should be built into every unit—*Pohl*⟩ In a narrower sense, the terms may imply a graphic representation of such a method (as by a mechanical drawing, a chart, a sketch, or a layout) ⟨an architect's set of *plans*⟩ ⟨*plan* a garden⟩ ⟨the basement of St. Katherine's Dock House is vast in extent and confusing in its *plan*—*Conrad*⟩ **Design** (see also INTENTION) adds to *plan* an emphasis on intention (as artistic or divine intention) in the disposition of individual members or details, often thereby suggesting a definite pattern; since it is used frequently in reference to a completed work, it often implies reference to the degree in which order, harmony, or integrity have been achieved in spite of diversity in the parts, or in which there is the beauty that results from unity in variety ⟨it . . . like most architecture erected since the Gothic age, was a compilation rather than a *design*—*Hardy*⟩ ⟨the most wonderful and delicate *design* composed entirely of flowers—*Dahl*⟩ ⟨knows how to *design* a part so that it develops and acquires momentum in performance—*Atkinson*⟩ ⟨a curious woman, whose dresses always looked as if they had been *designed* in a rage—*Wilde*⟩ **Plot** (see also PLOT *n* 2; SKETCH *vb*) usually connotes a laying out in clearly distinguished and carefully proportioned sections or divisions, and attention to proper placing and due relation of the parts, and to scale. It is found chiefly in technical use, such as that of surveying, where it suggests a ground plan ⟨*plot* a tract of land⟩ or in literature, where it refers to a fundamental design which the action of a drama or narrative follows ⟨there is plenty of action in this play, but no *plot*⟩ ⟨I cannot understand the sharp distinction some clever theorists make between story and *plot*. A *plot* is merely the pattern on which the story is arranged—*Maugham*⟩ ⟨in neatly *plotted* and tightly hedged domains of the corporate imperium, the freedom to adventure is gone—*W. H. Hamilton*⟩ **Scheme** has nearly lost its early implication of a diagram except in some technical senses where it suggests tabulation more often than outline drawing ⟨the rhyme *scheme* of a Shakespearean sonnet⟩ Nevertheless, the word often suggests, more than *plan* does, system and careful choice or ordering of details ⟨work out a *scheme* for the distribution of war refugees⟩ ⟨she seldom *schemed*, but when she did *scheme*, her plans showed . . . the comprehensive strategy of a general—*Hardy*⟩ The terms often connote, singly or

in combination, self-delusion, craftiness, or self-seeking on the part of the agent ⟨he doesn't *scheme* and twist things about trying to get the best of someone else— *Anderson*⟩ ⟨a lurking suspicion that our work was . . . a *scheme* to superimpose American economic control upon ingenuous foreign countries—*Heiser*⟩ **Project** comes close to *scheme* except in its connotations. Sometimes it suggests enterprise; sometimes, imaginative scope or vision; sometimes, mere extensiveness ⟨sanguine schemes, ambitious *projects*, pleased me less—*Wordsworth*⟩ ⟨such were my *projects* for the city's good—*Browning*⟩ ⟨I *projected*, and drew up a plan for the union—*Franklin*⟩ ⟨although his health was rapidly failing, he *projected* a new book—*Dinsmore*⟩
*Ana* *intention, intent, purpose: *idea, conception, notion: *chart, map, graph: diagram, outline, sketch (see under SKETCH *vb*)
**plan** *vb* design, plot, scheme, project (see under PLAN *n*)
*Ana* propose, purpose, *intend: *sketch, outline, diagram, delineate
**plane** *adj* plain, flat, *level, even, smooth, flush
*Ant* solid
**plank** *paragraph, verse, article, clause, count
**plastic, pliable, pliant, ductile, malleable, adaptable** are applied to things and to persons regarded as material susceptible of being modified in form or nature. Something **plastic** has the quality (as of wax, clay, or plaster) of being soft enough to be molded or to receive an impression yet capable of hardening into a final form ⟨a pill mass should be *plastic;* that is, it should be capable of being worked —*C. O. Lee*⟩ ⟨the language at the period during which the Bible was being translated into English was in its most *plastic* stage—*Lowes*⟩ ⟨life is *plastic:* it will assume any shape you choose to put on it—*Gogarty*⟩ Something **pliable** or **pliant** has the quality (as of willow twigs) of being supple enough to be easily bent or manipulated and therefore yielding without resistance. *Pliable,* in extended use, usually suggests the imposition of or submission to another's will ⟨I flatter myself that I have some influence over her. She is *pliable*—*Hardy*⟩ ⟨I've always been a *pliable* sort of person, and I let the ladies guide me—*Upton Sinclair*⟩ ⟨he was criticized as being too *pliable*, too eager to please—*Beverly Smith*⟩ *Pliant,* on the other hand, suggests flexibility rather than obedience ⟨art which is alive and *pliant* in the hands of men—*Quiller-Couch*⟩ ⟨ready to be used or not used, picked up or cast aside . . . , *pliant* to fate like a reed to the wind—*Goudge*⟩ Something **ductile** has the quality of a tensile metal (as copper) of being tenacious enough to be permanently drawn out or extended, or of water, of being made to flow through channels. In extended use *ductile* often approaches *plastic* and *pliant* but it may have distinctive connotations directly derived from its literal senses, such as quick responsiveness (as distinguished from submissiveness) to influences that would form, guide, or fashion ⟨verse . . . is easier to write than prose . . . . Mr. Shaw would have found his story still more *ductile* in the meter of *Hiawatha* —*Quiller-Couch*⟩ ⟨a vast portion of the public feels rather than thinks, a *ductile* multitude drawn easily by the arts of the demagogue—*Loveman*⟩ Sometimes fluidity within bounds is connoted ⟨smooth, *ductile*, and even, his fancy must flow—*Cowper*⟩ Something **malleable** is literally or figuratively capable of being beaten or pressed into shape, especially after being conditioned (as by heating) ⟨tempers . . . rendered pliant and *malleable* in the fiery furnace of domestic tribulation—*Irving*⟩ ⟨finds a sort of *malleable* mind in front of him that he can play with as he will—*Masefield*⟩ Something **adaptable** is capable of being modified or of modifying itself to suit other con-

ditions, other needs, or other uses. As applied to persons the term implies sometimes a pliant, but more often an accommodating, disposition and a readiness to make one's habits, one's opinions, and one's wishes correspond to those of one's present society or environment ⟨he was an *adaptable* person. He had yielded to Joyce's training in being quietly instead of noisily disagreeable—*Sinclair Lewis*⟩ ⟨anarchism has always been an elastic and *adaptable* faith, and looking round for a suitable machinery to replace state centralization—*Connolly*⟩
*Ana* flexible, supple, *elastic, resilient: tractable, amenable (see OBEDIENT)
*Con* rigid, *stiff, inflexible
**platitude** *commonplace, truism, bromide, cliché
*Ana* banality, inanity, vapidity, insipidity (see corresponding adjectives at INSIPID): mawkishness, sentimentality (see corresponding adjectives at SENTIMENTAL)
**plaudits** *applause, acclamation, acclaim
*Ana* cheering (see APPLAUD)
**plausible, credible, believable, colorable, specious** are comparable when they mean capable of impressing the observer, auditor, or reader as truly or genuinely possessing the quality or character that is set forth or claimed. A thing or sometimes a person is **plausible** that is capable of winning acceptance, approval, or belief by its or his apparent possession of qualities which make it or him seem pleasing, genuine, or reasonable at first sight or hearing; the word need not definitely imply a false outside, or an intention to deceive, or a lack of soundness, but it usually connotes such a possibility, even though it also clearly suggests an ingratiating or mentally satisfying character ⟨a *plausible* argument⟩ ⟨the most *plausible* and persuasive confidence man of his day—*S. H. Adams*⟩ ⟨that is a perfectly intelligible position, and it is *plausible* to the last degree—*Lowes*⟩ ⟨he learns that what is wanted is not an interesting or *plausible* story, but exact facts— *Notes and Queries on Anthropology*⟩ A thing or less often a person is **credible** that seems to be worthy of belief or of being credited, sometimes because of plausibility, but more often because of its or his support by known facts or by sound reasoning ⟨a *credible* explanation⟩ ⟨a *credible* witness⟩ ⟨right reason makes that which they say appear *credible*—*Hobbes*⟩ ⟨a theory which denies the truth of one of our fundamental convictions about our own minds must have very strong evidence from other quarters to make it *credible*—*Inge*⟩ A thing that is credible because it comes within the range of possibility or probability, or because it is in accordance with other facts that are known, is **believable** ⟨his undergraduate characters . . . are all alive and *believable*. With his older characters he is less convincing—*Havighurst*⟩ ⟨a down-to-earth, rat-chasing, thoroughly *believable* wharf cat—*Camper*⟩ ⟨demand for . . . *believable* explanations—*Fearing*⟩ A thing is **colorable** which at least on its face or outwardly seems true, just, or valid or which is capable to some extent of being sustained or justified ⟨no *colorable* evidence has as yet been presented in support of this theory⟩ ⟨the Chinese were given . . . a *colorable* excuse for joining in the fight. The excuse, of course, was much more than *colorable;* it was morally and practically ideal— *Purcell*⟩ A thing or, less often, a person is **specious** that is outwardly or apparently attractive, beautiful, valid, or sincere but that is inwardly or actually the reverse in character. *Specious* is the only one of these terms that clearly implies dissimulation or fraud or deceit or hypocrisy ⟨*specious* picturesqueness⟩ ⟨*specious* piety⟩ ⟨a *specious* rogue⟩ ⟨they sanctified the worse cause with the *specious* pretext of zeal for the furtherance of the best— *Cowper*⟩ ⟨effusions of fine sentiments about brotherly

A colon (:) separates groups of words discriminated. An asterisk (*) indicates place of treatment of each group.

love that are only a *specious* mask for envy and hatred of riches and success—*Babbitt*⟩
*Ana* smooth, bland, politic, diplomatic, *suave: likely, *probable, possible: unctuous, *fulsome, slick, oily

**play** *n* 1 sport, disport, frolic, rollick, romp, gambol (see under PLAY *vb* 1)
*Ana* enjoyment, delectation, *pleasure, delight: amusement, diversion, recreation, entertainment (see under AMUSE): *athletics, sports, games
*Ant* work
2 *fun, jest, sport, game
*Ant* earnest
3 *room, berth, elbowroom, leeway, margin, clearance

**play** *vb* 1 Play, sport, disport, frolic, rollick, romp, gambol can all as verbs mean to engage in exercise or other activity as a pleasure or amusement, and as nouns mean exercise or activities engaged in for the sake of pleasure or amusement. **Play**, the most general of these terms, suggests an opposition to *work*; like its antithesis it usually implies activity and often vigorous activity of body or mind, but it emphasizes the absence of any end except that of amusement, diversion, recreation, or pure enjoyment ⟨children *play* for hours at keeping house⟩ ⟨*play* chess⟩ ⟨*play* tennis⟩ ⟨no *play* is interesting to me unless it effects work, and no work is possible to me unless it possesses the amusement of *play*—*Ellis*⟩ ⟨they had been . . . transformed from a dejected, downcast, docile, uninterested people, who could not even *play*, into one which was healthy, alert—*Heiser*⟩ ⟨*playing* at one job and then another, too charged with impatience to plug at chores—*Mailer*⟩ **Sport** and **disport** suggest a complete release not only from work but from seriousness; the terms imply indulgence in something which cheers, makes merry, or serves as a pastime ⟨if all the year were playing holidays, to *sport* would be as tedious as as to work—*Shak.*⟩ ⟨*sport* that wrinkled Care derides—*Milton*⟩ ⟨see the children *sport* upon the shore—*Wordsworth*⟩ ⟨all the freedom and grace of healthy young animals, *sporting* in the shallows or playing in the warm sands—*Beaglehole*⟩ ⟨we make ourselves fools, to *disport* ourselves—*Shak.*⟩ ⟨a tiny fish *disporting* himself with me in the tub—*Beebe*⟩ **Frolic** suggests more gaiety, more levity, and more spontaneousness than any of the preceding terms; it often is used in reference to the lighthearted, joyous movements of children or young animals at play, but it also suggests the pastimes, antics, or pranks of those who have thrown off all care ⟨I come to *frolic* with you, and to cheer your drooping souls—*Ford & Dekker*⟩ ⟨children were allowed to *frolic* around on these piles of material to their heart's content—*Talbot*⟩ ⟨their sedateness is as comical as their *frolic*—*Meredith*⟩ **Rollick**, infrequent as a noun and used chiefly in the form *rollicking*, adds to *frolic* implications of exuberance in gaiety and of reveling and therefore is used especially in reference to youths or young adults ⟨*rollicking* blades⟩ ⟨"Q." appears as a *rollicking* humorist. . . . He *rollicks*, perhaps, a little too laboriously—*Pall Mall Gazette*⟩ **Romp** suggests the boisterous carefree frolicking of children, of rough boys, and of tomboys; it usually connotes running or racing in play ⟨first-to-sixth-graders . . . *romp* on the playground—*Cabell Phillips*⟩ ⟨I have been having a *romp* with my godson—*Braddon*⟩ **Gambol** suggests the leaping and skipping characteristic of lambs and young children; it comes close to *frolic*, but carries a stronger suggestion of joy in movement ⟨Gilda rose as limber as a 16-year-old, and *gambolled* the full length of the room—*Purdy*⟩ ⟨where be your gibes now? your *gambols*? your songs? your flashes of merriment . . .?—*Shak.*⟩ ⟨their pygmy king, and little fairy queen, in circling dances *gambolled* on the green—*Pope*⟩

*Ana* divert, entertain, recreate, *amuse: *trifle, toy, dally
2 *act, impersonate
*Ana* feign, simulate, counterfeit, *assume

**player** *actor, performer, mummer, mime, mimic, thespian, impersonator, trouper

**playful, frolicsome, sportive, roguish, waggish, impish, mischievous** mean given to play, jests, or tricks or indicative of such a disposition or mood. **Playful** stresses either lighthearted gaiety or merriment ⟨*playful* children⟩ ⟨in a *playful* mood⟩ ⟨a confiding, *playful* little animal, whom one . . . trained to do tricks—*Sackville-West*⟩ or a lack of seriousness or earnestness ⟨his words were serious, but in his eyes there was a *playful* gleam⟩ ⟨his pen was more *playful* than caustic—*Williams & Pollard*⟩ **Frolicsome** heightens the implications of *playful;* it carries a stronger suggestion of friskiness or prankishness or irresponsible merriment ⟨as *frolicsome* as a bird upon a tree, or a breeze that makes merry with the leaves—*Hawthorne*⟩ ⟨*frolicsome* sailors returning from their cruises . . . paraded through the streets—*Nevins & Commager*⟩ **Sportive** carries a stronger implication of jesting or of levity than either of the preceding words; the term sometimes implies merely excess of animal spirits, but it usually connotes a desire to evoke or provoke laughter ⟨three generations of serious and of *sportive* writers wept and laughed over the venality of the senate—*Macaulay*⟩ **Roguish** not only heightens the implications of *sportive,* but it suggests an engaging naughtiness or slyness ⟨"I don't think I shall want anything else when we've got a little garden; and I knew Aaron would dig it for us," she went on with *roguish* triumph—*George Eliot*⟩ ⟨not a pretty girl or a *roguish* buck in the lot—*Cooke*⟩ **Waggish** suggests a less engaging sportiveness than *roguish* and one less delicate in its character; usually also the term carries a stronger suggestion of jocoseness or of jocularity ⟨with all his overbearing roughness there was a strong dash of *waggish* good humor at bottom—*Irving*⟩ **Impish** adds to *roguish* a hint of elfish, malicious mockery ⟨teasing . . . with *impish* laughter half suppressed—*Hardy*⟩ ⟨he also displays *impish* ingenuity in picking his examples of error from the most dignified sources—*Brit. Book News*⟩ **Mischievous** combines the implications of *frolicsome* and *impish* ⟨took a secret and *mischievous* pleasure in the bewilderment of her attendants—*Stafford*⟩ Although it may imply the doing of mischief (see *mischief* under INJURY 1) or the causing of an injury to others it commonly retains some suggestion of mingled playfulness and malice ⟨the three *mischievous*, dark-eyed witches, who lounged in the stern of that comfortable old island gondola, . . . were a parcel of wicked hoydens, bent on mischief, who laughed in your face—*Melville*⟩ ⟨the little buried eyes still watching . . . in that *mischievous*, canny way, and . . . hatching out some further unpleasantness or scandal—*Dahl*⟩ Often it suggests little more than thoughtless indifference to the possible effects of one's sports, tricks, or practical jokes ⟨a garden ruined by *mischievous* boys⟩ ⟨she . . . was . . . waked by Meta, standing over her with a sponge, looking very *mischievous*—*Yonge*⟩
*Ana* gay, sprightly, *lively: *merry, blithe, jocund, jolly, jovial: mirthful, gleeful, hilarious (see corresponding nouns at MIRTH)

**plea** 1 *apology, apologia, excuse, pretext, alibi
*Ana* explanation, justification, rationalization (see corresponding verbs at EXPLAIN): defense, vindication (see corresponding verbs at MAINTAIN)
2 *prayer, suit, petition, appeal
*Ana* entreaty, supplication, imploring, beseeching, begging (see corresponding verbs at BEG)

---

*Ana* analogous words     *Ant* antonyms     *Con* contrasted words     See also explanatory notes facing page 1

**plead** *vb* pray, sue, petition, appeal (see under PRAYER) **Ana** entreat, implore, supplicate, beseech, *beg: intercede, mediate, intervene, *interpose

**Con** bestow, confer, present, *give: *grant, vouchsafe, accord

**pleasant, pleasing, agreeable, grateful, gratifying, welcome** are comparable when they mean highly acceptable to or delighting the mind or the senses. *Pleasant* and *pleasing* are often indistinguishable; however, **pleasant** usually imputes a quality to the object to which it is applied, and **pleasing** suggests merely the effect of the object upon one ⟨a *pleasant* garden⟩ ⟨she liked everything to be tidy and *pleasant* and comfortable about her—*Gibbons*⟩ ⟨a *pleasing* arrangement of colors⟩ ⟨the thought of gazing on life's Evening Star makes of ugly old age a *pleasing* prospect—*L. P. Smith*⟩ **Agreeable** implies harmony with one's tastes or likings ⟨an *agreeable* taste⟩ ⟨if I was obliged to define politeness, I should call it the art of making oneself *agreeable*—*Smollett*⟩ ⟨replied with an *agreeable*, cultured throaty intonation—*F. M. Ford*⟩ **Grateful** carries the implications of both *pleasing* and *agreeable;* in addition it stresses the satisfaction or relief afforded the senses or, somewhat less often, the mind ⟨they . . . lay down on the clean grass under the *grateful* shade of the tall cottonwoods—*Cather*⟩ ⟨only occasional voices from the road outside came to disturb the *grateful* sense of quiet and seclusion—*Archibald Marshall*⟩ **Gratifying** is applied chiefly to what affords mental pleasure to the individual by satisfying his desires, hopes, conscience, or vanity ⟨the reviews of his book were very *gratifying*⟩ ⟨the *gratifying* feeling that our duty has been done—*Gilbert*⟩ ⟨can satisfy their lust for power in a most *gratifying* way—*Huxley*⟩ **Welcome** even more than *pleasing* stresses the pleasure or satisfaction given by the thing to which it is applied; it often suggests prior need or an answer to one's longings ⟨the explorers found fresh fruit and vegetables a *welcome* addition to their diet⟩ ⟨the news was most *welcome*⟩ ⟨revivals offered *welcome* interludes in pioneer life—*Amer. Guide Series: Minn.*⟩

**Ana** charming, attractive, alluring (see under ATTRACT *vb*): *soft, gentle, mild, balmy, smooth

**Ant** unpleasant: distasteful: harsh

**please** *vb* **Please, gratify, delight, rejoice, gladden, tickle, regale** mean to make happy or to be a cause of happiness. **Please** usually implies an agreement with one's wishes, tastes, or aspirations and a happiness which ranges from mere content and the absence of grounds for displeasure to actual elation ⟨the family was *pleased* with the daughter's marriage⟩ ⟨the aim of poetry is to *please*⟩ ⟨the suggestion did not *please* him⟩ ⟨he may apply himself . . . to feeding and protecting his family, but he no longer need strain to *please*—*Edmund Wilson*⟩ ⟨fangless perceptions which will *please* the conservative power—*Mailer*⟩ **Gratify** (compare *gratifying* under PLEASANT) suggests an even stronger measure of satisfaction than *please* and is normally positive in its implication of pleasure ⟨it *gratifies* us to imagine that . . . we have reached a point on the road of progress beyond that vouchsafed to our benighted predecessors—*Ellis*⟩ ⟨it *gratified* him to have his wife wear jewels; it meant something to him—*Cather*⟩ ⟨he had a sense of humor in his peculiar quiet way, but he never *gratified* it by proofs of the obvious—*Theodore Sturgeon*⟩ **Delight** stresses the emotional rather than the intellectual quality of the reaction, though the latter is often also implied; it suggests intense, lively pleasure that is not only keenly felt but usually vividly expressed in outward signs ⟨O, flatter me; for love *delights* in praises—*Shak.*⟩ ⟨the girl was embarrassed and *delighted* by the effusive attention that

followed—*Hervey*⟩ ⟨she was as *delighted* as if he had given her a Christmas present all wrapped in shining paper—*MacInnes*⟩ **Rejoice** implies a happiness that exceeds bounds and reveals itself openly (as in smiles, in song, in festivities, or in enthusiastic effort) ⟨*rejoice*, you men of Angiers, ring your bells—*Shak.*⟩ ⟨Hendrik worked, *rejoicing* in the strength that God had given him —*Cloete*⟩ **Gladden** sometimes is indistinguishable from *rejoice* except in rarely suggesting excess of emotion and in being usually transitive ⟨a small pleasantry frankly uttered by a patron, *gladdens* the heart of the dependent— *Irving*⟩ It often, however, connotes a raising of the spirits, or a cheering or consoling in depression or grief ⟨the comrades of the dead girl assemble in the temple on certain days to *gladden* her spirit with songs and dances —*Hearn*⟩ **Tickle** and *regale* involve the idea of delight, but they are often less dignified in their connotations. **Tickle** implies such pleasurable sensations as tingles and thrills or suggests an almost physical gratification ⟨food that *tickles* the palate⟩ Sometimes, with reference to physical tickling, it suggests provocation of laughter ⟨the mimic court of justice in the orchard *tickled* him immensely —*Deland*⟩ ⟨the idea of himself as a parson *tickles* him: he looks down at the black sleeve on his arm, and then smiles slyly—*Shaw*⟩ **Regale** connotes huge enjoyment or a feasting upon what gives pleasure ⟨Mr. Sycamore was *regaling* himself with the discomfiture of Lady Charlotte —*H. G. Wells*⟩ ⟨would always *regale* them generously with madeira, sherry or whiskey, rich cake, and richer stories—*Chapman-Huston*⟩

**Ana** *satisfy, content: beguile, *while, wile

**Ant** displease: anger: vex

**pleasing** *pleasant, pleasing, agreeable, grateful, gratifying, welcome **Ana** winning (see GET): charming, attractive, alluring, enchanting (see under ATTRACT)

**Ant** displeasing: repellent

**pleasure, delight, joy, delectation, enjoyment, fruition** denote the agreeable emotion which accompanies the possession, acquisition, or expectation of something good or greatly desired. **Pleasure** so strongly implies a feeling of satisfaction or gratification that it sometimes carries no implication of visible happiness or actual gladness ⟨faintly unpleasant *pleasures* being atoned for by the dull unalleviated pain of guilt—*Styron*⟩ ⟨he owned over forty pairs of boots, and he had the same *pleasure* in handling them that jewels give—*Bemelmans*⟩ Often, however, the term suggests an excitement or exaltation of the senses or of the mind that implies positive happiness or gladness ⟨when these wild ecstasies shall be matured into a sober *pleasure—Wordsworth*⟩ ⟨a great work of art always gives *pleasure*⟩ ⟨she didn't want to ride on the roller coaster . . . her ideas of *pleasure* were more sophisticated—*Cheever*⟩ **Delight** carries a stronger implication of liveliness, intensity, or obviousness in the satisfaction or gratification induced than *pleasure* and often suggests a less stable or enduring emotion ⟨what pleasure the possession of my money could have afforded him I am unable to say; but . . . as it did give him evident *delight* I was not sorry that I had parted with it so readily— *Kipling*⟩ ⟨the errors he made in pitch and in language would be so amusing that the geishas would giggle with *delight—Mailer*⟩ ⟨next to their wondrous *delight* in each other came their delighted wonder at earth itself—*Theodore Sturgeon*⟩ **Joy** is often used in place of *pleasure* and still more often in place of *delight*. It is, however, especially appropriate when a deep-rooted, rapturous emotion is implied or when the happiness is so great as to be almost painful in its intensity ⟨and all its aching *joys* are now no more, and all its dizzy raptures—*Wordsworth*⟩

A colon (:) separates groups of words discriminated. An asterisk (*) indicates place of treatment of each group.

⟨it expressed her happiness, relieved the pressure of her *joy* at being alive—*Rose Macaulay*⟩ ⟨glad to be free, proud too . . . of stepping this famous pavement, *joy* of a kind, cheap, tinselly, if you like, but all the same rapture, flushed their faces—*Woolf*⟩ **Delectation** and *enjoyment* differ in the main from the other words of this group in denoting the state of mind or the sensuous or emotional reactions of one who takes pleasure, delight, or joy in something. But **delectation** often carries a strong connotation of amusement, diversion, or entertainment that gives occasion for delight ⟨her oddities afforded him the utmost *delectation*⟩ ⟨a superb eclipse of the sun, providentially arranged for the *delectation* of the Eastern seaboard cities —*F. L. Allen*⟩ ⟨revived ancient, joyful customs for the *delectation* of islanders and visitors—*Gruening*⟩ **Enjoyment**, on the other hand, usually implies an attitude or a circumstance or a favorable response to a stimulus that tends to make one gratified or happy ⟨he gave himself up to the vigorous *enjoyment* of his pipe for a silent minute or two—*Conrad*⟩ ⟨that ruling, however, has not entirely dimmed lawmakers' *enjoyment* of a ripping good time— *Armbrister*⟩ ⟨just as backbiting and gossip could be a source of *enjoyment*, so could friendliness and the exchange of . . . compliments—*Farrell*⟩ **Fruition** has become increasingly rare in its earlier sense of pleasure in possession or of enjoyment in attainment ⟨the sweet *fruition* of an earthly crown—*Marlowe*⟩ ⟨in love we must deserve nothing, or the fine bloom of *fruition* is gone—*Meredith*⟩ In extended use realization or fulfillment is stressed, though there is still some suggestion of accompanying pleasure ⟨how mature one has to be before learning . . . that growth is more desirable than *fruition*—*Lucas*⟩ *Ana* \*happiness, felicity, bliss: amusement, diversion, recreation, entertainment (see under AMUSE) *Ant* displeasure: anger: vexation

**plebiscite** \*mandate, initiative, referendum

**pledge** *n* **Pledge, earnest, token, pawn, hostage** are comparable when they denote something that is given or held as a sign of another's faith or intention to do what has been promised. **Pledge**, originally and still in some applications a technical legal term, applies in general to something handed over to another as a token ⟨bear her this jewel, *pledge* of my affection—*Shak.*⟩ or as security for the performance of an obligation or payment of a debt ⟨property of the debtor in the creditor's possession was held as a valid *pledge*—*Harvard Law Review*⟩ ⟨the pawnshop, where one waits nervously while the swarthy shrewd-eyed attendant squints contemptuously at the *pledges* one offers—*Donn Byrne*⟩ **Earnest**, basically the money or other thing of value given by a buyer to a seller to bind a bargain, in its extended sense applies to something which serves as a promise or assurance of more to come or which establishes a strong probability of it ⟨cutting off the heads of Empson and Dudley as an *earnest* of the great love he bare his people—*Trevelyan*⟩ ⟨it seemed to him a sort of *earnest* that Providence intended his rescue from worse consequences—*George Eliot*⟩ ⟨India must be granted her independence, as *earnest* to the subject peoples of the earth—*Griswold*⟩ **Token** (see also SIGN 1) applies to something given as a guaranty or proof of a person or thing's authority, authenticity, or good faith ⟨I do set my bow in the cloud, and it shall be for a *token* of a covenant between me and the earth— Gen 9:13⟩ ⟨from time to time said something . . . as a *token* of friendship—*Stewart*⟩ In specific concrete use *token* is applied to something which serves as a proof of an obligation, a right, a debt, or a payment; thus, a coin-like piece of metal sold by a transportation company for use as a ticket is usually called a *token;* coins or notes

issued by some countries, states, or cities as currency at a nominal or face value above their real value but redeemable at their face value are collectively called *tokens.* **Pawn** retains in anthropological use an earlier broad equivalence to a security pledge and then applies to a person held in servitude pending settlement of a debt ⟨*pawns* are debtors whose work serves as interest until the loan is repaid—*Amer. Anthropologist*⟩ In more general use *pawn* specifically refers to a personal chattel deposited as security for the money loaned on it by another, usually by a person called a *pawnbroker* whose business is the loaning of money on such security ⟨pledge and *pawn* were synonymous terms in the early common law. Modern usage tends to restrict the term *pawn* to the pledge of jewels and other personal chattels to pawnbrokers as security for small loans—*Restatement of the Law of Security*⟩ In extended use *pawn* often carries a suggestion of something held for a time and liable to redemption or withdrawal by the actual owner ⟨my life I never held but as a *pawn* to wage against thy enemies— *Shak.*⟩ ⟨I held what I inherited in thee, as *pawn* for that inheritance of freedom which thou hast sold—*Shelley*⟩ **Hostage** basically applies to a person handed over to another or kept by another as a guarantee of one's good or peaceable or submissive intentions or as a pledge until one's agreement or promise has been fulfilled ⟨*hostages* were taken in very large numbers from the civilian populations—*Nazi Conspiracy and Aggression*⟩ But sometimes the term is extended to other guarantees and pledges ⟨you know now your *hostages:* your uncle's word and my firm faith—*Shak.*⟩ *Ana* \*guarantee, guaranty, security, surety, bond, bail

**pledge** *vb* \*promise, engage, plight, covenant, contract *Ana* bind, \*tie: \*commit, consign, confide, entrust *Ant* abjure

**plenary** \*full, complete, replete *Ant* limited

**plenteous** \*plentiful, ample, abundant, copious *Ana & Ant* see those at PLENTIFUL

**plentiful, plenteous, ample, abundant, copious** denote in common more than adequate or sufficient yet not in excess. Something is **plentiful** or **plenteous** of which there is great or rich supply; *plenteous* is the more bookish term ⟨it is also a zone of *plentiful* food and therefore able to support an extensive fauna—*Dowdeswell*⟩ ⟨*plenteous* grace with Thee is found, grace to cleanse from ev'ry sin —*Wesley*⟩ Something is **ample** which is generously sufficient to satisfy a definite requirement ⟨*ample* apologies indeed for fifteen years of persecution—*Macaulay*⟩ ⟨their mother's fortune, though *ample* for her situation in life, could but ill supply the deficiency of his—*Austen*⟩ ⟨there would be an *ample* buffet available until the last guest left the premises—*Lucius Beebe*⟩ Something is **abundant** which is very plentiful or of which there is an unusually large supply ⟨his *abundant* vitality—*Bennett*⟩ ⟨the many small denominational colleges so *abundant* throughout the Middle West—*G. P. Merrill*⟩ **Abundant** sometimes implies profusion ⟨*abundant* beautiful bright tresses— *Meredith*⟩ ⟨we have lived in a broad and *abundant* land, and . . . we have made it flourish—*Roosevelt*⟩ Something is **copious** which is marked by great abundance; the term is especially applicable when emphasis is to be put on largeness of supply rather than fullness or richness. It is therefore not always interchangeable with the other words ⟨a *copious* supply of food⟩ ⟨there was a *copious* crop of potatoes this year⟩ ⟨*copious* eating and still more *copious* drinking—*Huxley*⟩ ⟨washed down with *copious* drafts of beer—*Green Peyton*⟩ In respect to language *copious* often implies profusion of words, richness of vocabulary,

or fullness of information ⟨declaimers of a *copious* vein —*Berkeley*⟩ ⟨French, English, or any other *copious* language—*Hobbes*⟩ ⟨be *copious* and distinct, and tell me a great deal of your mind—*Johnson*⟩
*Ana* fruitful, prolific (see FERTILE): sumptuous, opulent, *luxurious: *profuse, lavish, prodigal
*Ant* scanty, scant

**pleonasm** *verbiage, redundancy, tautology, circumlocution, periphrasis

**pliable** *plastic, pliant, ductile, malleable, adaptable
*Ana* lithe, limber, *supple: *elastic, resilient, springy, flexible: *compliant, acquiescent
*Ant* obstinate

**pliant** *plastic, pliable, ductile, malleable, adaptable
*Ana* see those at PLIABLE

**plight** *vb* *promise, engage, pledge, covenant, contract

**plight** *n* *predicament, dilemma, quandary, scrape, fix, jam, pickle
*Ana* situation, condition, *state, posture: *difficulty, rigor, hardship, vicissitude

**plot** *n* 1 *plan, design, scheme, project
*Ana* *chart, map, graph
2 Plot, intrigue, machination, conspiracy, cabal are comparable when they mean a secret plan devised to entrap or ensnare others. **Plot** implies careful planning of details and usually an intent to accomplish an evil, mischievous, or treacherous end; the action may involve one or more devisers and a person, a group, a class, or a people as the victim ⟨there is a *plot* against my life, my crown—*Shak.*⟩ ⟨the great Jesuit *plot* for the destruction of Protestant England—*Crothers*⟩ ⟨the conspirators roped into their scheme a whole network of the magnates. Nevers joined in the *plot*—*Belloc*⟩ **Intrigue** implies more complicated scheming or maneuvering than *plot* and often the use of petty underhand methods in an atmosphere of duplicity; it more often implies an attempt to gain one's own ends through clandestine means (as in politics, in business, or in love) than (as *plot* frequently implies) an attempt to destroy, to betray, or to usurp power ⟨Mr. Swift hath finely described that passion for *intrigue*, that love of secrecy, slander, and lying, which belongs to weak people, hangers-on of weak courts—*Thackeray*⟩ ⟨the party politicians forgot their good resolutions, and reverted to their familiar *intrigues*—*H. G. Wells*⟩ ⟨they had all stooped to folly and . . . here they were, alive, tanned, laughing, and like as not in some new *intrigue* with a waiter or a musician—*Wouk*⟩ **Machination**, usually in the plural, imputes hostility or treachery to the makers; often, also, it suggests craftiness in devising or contriving annoyances, injuries, or evils. If these ideas are to be connoted, it may be applied to a plot, an intrigue, or any of the secret plans named by the words in this group ⟨tortured by some black trouble of the soul, and given over to the *machinations* of his deadliest enemy—*Hawthorne*⟩ ⟨the devilish *machinations* of an enchanter masquerading as a pious hermit —*Lowes*⟩ **Conspiracy** differs from *plot* chiefly in implying a combination of persons or groups as the devisers and agents and in being applied chiefly to a plot that involves treason or great treachery ⟨these people he has been taking for granted are all part of an insidious *conspiracy* to undermine the world as he knows it—*Edmund Wilson*⟩ ⟨the conviction that World War I had been a crooked *conspiracy* of armament-manufacturers—*A. J. P. Taylor*⟩ In technical legal use the word implies the doing of an unlawful act or the use of unlawful means in accomplishing a lawful end ⟨monopoly . . . is *conspiracy* in restraint of trade, including under the term *conspiracy* all contracts and combinations entered into for the purpose of restraining trade—*The Amer. Individual Enterprise System*⟩ ⟨the

company brought suit against the strike leaders, charging them with *conspiracy* to ruin the business—*Amer. Guide Series: Conn.*⟩ **Cabal** applies usually to an intrigue in which a group combines to accomplish some end favorable to it but injurious or disastrous to the person or group, often, specifically, the government, affected ⟨the *cabal* against Washington found supporters exclusively in the north—*Bancroft*⟩ ⟨the innate character of the *cabal* and its purposes roused resentments and antagonisms in Congress which compelled its adherents to abandon the move . . . and . . . the scheme collapsed—*Fitzpatrick*⟩
*Ana* contrivance, *device, contraption: maneuver, stratagem, *trick, ruse, artifice
3 sketch, outline, diagram, delineation, draft, tracing, blueprint (see under SKETCH *vb*)

**plot** *vb* 1 plan, design, scheme, project (see under PLAN *n*)
*Ana* fashion, fabricate, forge, form, shape, *make
2 *sketch, outline, diagram, delineate, draft, trace, blueprint
*Ana* create, *invent: chart, map, graph (see under CHART *n*)

**ploy** *trick, ruse, stratagem, maneuver, gambit, artifice, wile, feint

**pluck** *n* *fortitude, grit, backbone, guts, sand
*Ana* *courage, spirit, mettle, resolution, tenacity: hardihood, audacity, *temerity

**plumb** *vb* *fathom, sound

**plumb** *adj* *vertical, perpendicular

**plume** *vb* *pride, pique, preen
*Ana* *appreciate, value, prize

**plump** *fleshy, stout, portly, rotund, chubby, fat, corpulent, obese
*Ant* cadaverous —*Con* *lean, spare, scrawny, skinny, lank, lanky: *haggard, pinched, wasted

**plunder** *vb* *rob, rifle, loot, burglarize
*Ana* despoil, spoliate, sack, pillage, *ravage: *strip, denude, bare

**plunder** *n* *spoil, booty, prize, loot, swag
*Ana* robbery, larceny, *theft

**plunge** *vb* Plunge, dive, pitch are comparable when they mean to throw or cast oneself or to be thrown or cast forward or downward with force or impetuosity into or as if into deep water. **Plunge** carries a more obvious implication than the others of the force with which one throws oneself or is thrown, but it does not always suggest a penetration of deep water; it may imply entrance into any penetrable medium, especially one that suggests a being lost to view, or into a state or condition in which one is overwhelmed or immersed, or into a course which marks a deep descent, a complete change, or a distinct involvement ⟨*plunge* bodily into the water after a forty-foot drop—*Forester*⟩ ⟨we are *plunged* once more into the war of nerves—*Times Lit. Sup.*⟩ ⟨he *plunged* into the crowd and was soon lost to view⟩ ⟨the singer drew breath and *plunged* into a new stanza—*Henri*⟩ **Dive**, though it implies an action very similar to that indicated by *plunge*, usually suggests deliberation or, at least, consciousness of an aim, more skill in execution, and less heaviness and more grace; thus, "he *dived* into the sea" usually implies intent where "he *plunged* headlong into the sea" may suggest either intent, accident, or impulsion by some force ⟨the gulls *dive* into the water for pieces of food⟩ ⟨an enormous water rat *dived* down from the bank—*Powys*⟩ ⟨"Clear out!" He raised his stick as he spoke. Katy shrieked, *dived* past him, and ran—*Deland*⟩ ⟨why not let a countable number of particles *dive* into it, and then weigh the tube?—*Darrow*⟩ ⟨she dove into the red pocketbook and, burrowing among the debris, came up at last with what she was after—*Helen Howe*⟩ **Pitch** (see also

THROW) is often used instead of *plunge* to imply a falling forward and downward usually without intent or design ⟨he *pitched* headlong over the cliff⟩ ⟨he tripped on a root and *pitched* forward on his face⟩ ⟨my anxiety to own the ducks caused me to *pitch* into the water with all my clothes on—*Wister*⟩ The term also is often used in reference to the alternate forward and backward plunging of a ship in a storm as distinguished from rolling or tossing from side to side ⟨the passengers found the *pitching* of the ship more disquieting than the rolling⟩ ⟨the sea was rough and my heart *pitched* with the small motorboat—*J. W. Brown*⟩
*Ana* submerge, immerse, *dip: *throw, cast, fling, hurl: *push, thrust, shove, propel

**plurality** *majority

**plutocracy** *oligarchy, aristocracy

**ply** *vb* *handle, manipulate, wield, swing
*Ana* exercise, *practice, drill: operate, work, function (see ACT *vb*): manage, direct, control, *conduct

**pocket** *n* *hole, hollow, cavity, void, vacuum

**poet, versifier, rhymer, rhymester, poetaster, bard, minstrel, troubadour** denote a composer who uses metrical or rhythmical language as his medium. **Poet** is used in a generic sense and in several highly specific senses. In its generic sense it applies to any writer or maker of verse; in its specific senses it applies only to a composer of verse who in his composition exhibits qualities regarded as essential by the age or time or by the writer or speaker who uses the term. With all its variations in implications in these specific senses, *poet* usually stresses creative and expressive power as the prime essential, sometimes without clear reference to skill in constructing verses ⟨every man, that writes in verse is not a *Poet*—*Ben Jonson*⟩ ⟨the *Poet* is chiefly distinguished from other men by a greater promptness to think and feel without immediate external excitement, and a greater power in expressing such thoughts and feelings—*Wordsworth*⟩ **Versifier** may designate a composer who uses verse as his medium without reference to qualities thought of as essential to poetry. In contrast to *poet*, it implies the lack of such a quality or qualities ⟨a clever *versifier* might have written Cowley's lines; only a *poet* could have made what Dryden made óf them—*T. S. Eliot*⟩ **Rhymer** and **rhymester**, once descriptive rather than depreciative, now tend to be even more definitely and consistently depreciatory than *versifier* in their implication of mediocrity or inferiority. **Poetaster** is a term of contempt applied to versifiers whose work is regarded as unimportant, trashy, or inane ⟨there are always *poetasters* enough; but of great poets . . . there are never so many as not to leave room for . . . more—*Julian Hawthorne*⟩ ⟨indicative of the mistakes of *poetasters* and would-be poets rather than of real poets—*Kilby*⟩ **Bard** basically applies to a tribal poet-singer (as among the ancient Celts) who composed verses praising heroes, chiefs, or warriors or recounting historical facts or traditions and who sang or recited them to the accompaniment of the harp or similar musical instrument. In extended use *bard* is a more or less romantic or florid synonym of *poet* used especially of one who writes impassioned, lyrical, or epic verse ⟨compile in all the lyrical poetry of the last 150 years a list of half a dozen first-class or even second-class *bards* who wrote primarily to be sung—*Quiller-Couch*⟩ **Minstrel** basically applies to a medieval public entertainer, often a strolling musician and mountebank, who sang songs (sometimes his own) to the accompaniment of a harp or other instrument and performed tricks; among its current extended applications is one in which it is close to *bard* in its implications, though it may place less emphasis on professional character and more on

natural lyrical power ⟨O black and unknown bards of long ago, how came your lips to touch the sacred fire? How, in your darkness, did you come to know the power and beauty of the *minstrel's* lyre?—*J. W. Johnson*⟩ **Troubadour** applies historically to a type of poet-musician found chiefly in southern France and northern Italy, frequently a knightly amateur, who composed lyrics (often also the music) in the Provençal tongue, usually of an amatory character and characteristically in a complicated metrical pattern; in extended use, the word loses its suggestion of artifice and technical skill in versifying and is often employed in place of *minstrel* in its extended sense ⟨known as a modern *troubadour*, for he wrote scores of verses for Irish folk tunes—*Bridgman & Curtis*⟩ or it may specifically denote one who uses his skill in expression for the promotion of some cause ⟨Mr. Bryan is one of the great *troubadours* . . . troubadouring is the thing he does best—*E. G. Lowry*⟩ ⟨I speak after my fancies, for I am a *Troubadour*, you know, and won the violet at Toulouse—*Tennyson*⟩
*Ana* *maker, creator, author: *writer, author, composer

**poetaster** *poet, versifier, rhymer, rhymester, bard, minstrel, troubadour

**pogrom** *massacre, slaughter, butchery, carnage

**poignancy** *pathos, bathos

**poignant** 1 *pungent, piquant, racy, spicy, snappy
*Ana* penetrating, piercing, probing (see ENTER): *sharp, keen, acute: *incisive, trenchant, cutting, biting, crisp
*Ant* dull (*reaction, sensation*)
2 *moving, touching, pathetic, impressive, affecting
*Ana* exciting, stimulating, provoking (see PROVOKE): disturbing, agitating, perturbing (see DISCOMPOSE)

**point** *vb* *direct, aim, level, train, lay
*Ana* bend (see CURVE *vb*): *direct, address, devote: steer, pilot, engineer, *guide

**point of view, viewpoint, standpoint, angle, slant** denote the position or attitude that determines which aspect of an object of contemplation is seen or presented. *Point of view, viewpoint,* and *standpoint* are often interchangeable, but **point of view** and **viewpoint** can suggest either a mental or a physical position and may permit the inference that there are other ways of looking at what is considered and therefore usually suggest lack of completeness in the vision, or one-sidedness in the views expressed or presented ⟨great literature enables us to see with another man's eyes . . . but only when we abandon ourselves for the time to his *point of view*—*Kilby*⟩ ⟨the general shape of the galaxy and the *point of view* from which we are looking at it—*B. J. Bok*⟩ ⟨all will benefit from exposure to the fresh *viewpoint* which he presents—*Harrison Brown*⟩ ⟨describes his own method of photographing motor races, and gives hints on the choice of subjects and *viewpoints*—*Kodak Abstract*⟩ **Standpoint** may have connotations which tend to distinguish it from *point of view* and *viewpoint*; it is more often restricted to the mental point of view ⟨consider totalitarianism from the German *standpoint*⟩ and it more often connotes than definitely implies a fixed way of looking justified by one's fundamental principles or one's stock of information and not necessarily resulting in a limited understanding ⟨from the poet-writer's *standpoint* all this prevalent talk about a New Order is sheer waste of time—*Forster*⟩ ⟨my criticism of what seem to me one-sided views will be better understood if my general *standpoint* is known—*Inge*⟩ **Angle** (see also PHASE) definitely implies one-sidedness or limitations in the scope of one's vision ⟨every man of genius sees the world at a different *angle* from his fellows, and there is his tragedy. But it is usually a measurable *angle*—*Ellis*⟩ ⟨in the rhetorical speeches from Shakespeare which have been cited, we have . . . a new clue to the character, in noting the *angle* from which he views himself—*T. S. Eliot*⟩ **Slant** stresses bias, but it may be bias derived from temperament, mental habits, or experience rather than from prejudice ⟨periodicals, not normally pro-Democratic in editorial *slant*—*Cater*⟩ ⟨no one sees anything without some personal *slant*—*S.R.L.*⟩ *Ana* *position, stand, attitude

**poise** *vb* *stabilize, steady, balance, ballast, trim *Ana* *support, uphold, back *Con* disturb, agitate, upset (see DISCOMPOSE): *overturn, overthrow, subvert

**poise** *n* 1 *balance, equilibrium, equipoise, tension *Ana* suspending *or* suspension, hanging (see corresponding verbs at HANG): *equanimity, composure
2 *tact, address, savoir faire *Ana* self-possession, aplomb, assurance, *confidence: calmness, tranquillity, serenity (see corresponding adjectives at CALM): grace, dignity, *elegance

**poison** *n* Poison, venom, virus, toxin, bane mean matter or a substance that when present in an organism or introduced into it produces an injurious or deadly effect. **Poison** is the most inclusive of these words and is applicable to any deadly or noxious substance whether introduced into or produced within the body of an organism ⟨killed by a *poison*-barbed arrow⟩ ⟨carbon monoxide gas, when inhaled, is a deadly *poison*⟩ ⟨keeping *poisons* out of the reach of children⟩ ⟨many alkaloids are dangerous *poisons*⟩ In extended use *poison* applies to whatever is felt to have the destructive effect of a physical poison ⟨fear uncontrolled is a *poison* that destroys all self-confidence⟩ **Venom** basically means a fluid containing a poison secreted by an animal (as a snake, scorpion, or bee) and injected into another animal during offensive or defensive action, usually by a bite or sting ⟨man spurns the worm, but pauses ere he wake the slumbering *venom* of the folded snake— *Byron*⟩ The term is occasionally extended to a poisonous secretion of a plant and in more general extended use applies especially to states of mind or utterances that are felt to have the malign quality of an animal venom ⟨their belief in *venom* and jealousy behind the war—*Paxson*⟩ ⟨spouting angry *venom* about his neighbors⟩ **Virus** (see also GERM), once equivalent to *venom*, retains this value only in extended use and then applies to something felt to have a corrupting quality that can poison the mind or spirit ⟨the force of this *virus* of prejudice—*V. S. Waters*⟩ **Toxin** applies to a complex organic poison that is a product of the metabolic activities of a living organism, is extremely poisonous when introduced into the tissues but usually destroyed by the digestive juices, and is usually able to induce antibody formation ⟨bacterial *toxins*, such as those of botulism and tetanus⟩ **Bane** may apply to any cause of ruin, destruction, or tribulation ⟨his wife is the *bane* of his life⟩ and in compounds denotes poison or something (as a plant) containing poison ⟨rats*bane*⟩ ⟨hen*bane* contains a poison resembling belladonna⟩

**poisonous,** venomous, virulent, toxic, mephitic, pestilent, pestilential, miasmic, miasmatic, miasmal are comparable when they mean having the properties or the effects of poison (see POISON). Basically **poisonous** implies that the thing so described will be fatal or exceedingly harmful if introduced into a living organism in sufficient quantities (as by eating, drinking, or inhaling) ⟨the most *poisonous* of mushrooms⟩ ⟨*poisonous* gases⟩ ⟨[aniline] is also *poisonous* but by proper chemical manipulation it becomes the parent of many beneficent medicines—*Morrison*⟩ In its extended use the term implies extreme noxiousness or perniciousness or power to corrode, rankle, or corrupt ⟨you might condemn us as *poisonous* of your honor—

*Shak.*⟩ ⟨the sentence was pronounced . . . in a stifling *poisonous* atmosphere—*Conrad*⟩ ⟨secret spreading of *poisonous* propaganda—*Roosevelt*⟩ **Venomous** applies equally to an animal (as a snake, scorpion, or bee) whose bite or sting introduces a venom (see *venom* under POISON) into an organism and to the bites, stings, or wounds inflicted by venomous creatures ⟨*venomous* insects⟩ ⟨a *venomous* snake bite⟩ The term has much extended usage; in this it implies extreme malevolence or destructive malignancy ⟨the most innocent intimacies would not have escaped misrepresentation from the *venomous* tongues of Roman society—*Froude*⟩ ⟨that many of you are frustrated in your ambitions, and undernourished in your pleasures, only makes you more *venomous*—*Mailer*⟩ **Virulent** implies the destructive or extremely deleterious properties of or as if of a strong poison; it is applied especially to infectious diseases of a particularly malignant or violent form or, somewhat less often, to notably venomous animals ⟨poverty produces outbreaks of *virulent* infectious disease . . . sooner or later—*Shaw*⟩ ⟨one of the most *virulent* types of the pneumococcus⟩ ⟨those mosquitoes must have been particularly *virulent*—*Farmer's Weekly*⟩ In extended use the term applies to something particularly violent in its display of an offensive or noxious nature or quality ⟨proceedings . . . dictated by *virulent* hatred— *George Eliot*⟩ ⟨the later stages of the campaign when the rumors became *virulent*—*Michener*⟩ **Toxic** sometimes implies the presence of properties or effects of a toxin (see *toxin* under POISON) ⟨a *toxic* goiter⟩ but more often implies only the character or the properties of a poison and therefore means little more than *poisonous* ⟨the *toxic* principle of a drug⟩ ⟨*toxic* gases⟩ ⟨over 200,000 fish were killed by the *toxic* wastes of one industrial plant—*Science*⟩ ⟨a *toxic* drug⟩ In its extended use *toxic* may imply insidious and destructive activity comparable to that of some toxins in the human organism ⟨there are emotionally *toxic* situations at work in the environment as manifestly injurious . . . as physical toxins—*McLean*⟩ **Mephitic** is applicable to something so offensive to the sense of smell that it is or is believed to be actually poisonous ⟨*mephitic* vapors rising from a swamp⟩ ⟨the *mephitic* air of a disused mine⟩ ⟨the *mephitic* verdure of the Malay peninsula— *Stafford*⟩ **Pestilent** and **pestilential** occasionally come close to *poisonous* in meaning, but they are chiefly used in the extended sense of exceedingly infectious or dangerous to the health, morals, or mental integrity, especially of the group as distinguished from the individual ⟨still fervently espouse the *pestilential* proposition that the world needs to be saved in a hurry by their own brand of righteousness —*Rolo*⟩ ⟨a *pestilent* land where people died like flies— *Maurice Carr*⟩ ⟨grew impatient with such *pestilent* heresies—*Parrington*⟩ ⟨blow up the blind rage of the populace, with a continued blast of *pestilential* libels—*Burke*⟩ **Miasmic, miasmatic,** and **miasmal** all imply a reference to *miasma,* or supposedly infectious or deadly emanations from swamps or jungles or from putrescent substances that float in the air ⟨the steaming, rain-drenched, *miasmic*, leech-filled Sumatran jungle—*Rex Lardner*⟩ ⟨the *miasmatic* northern and northeastern coast—*Encyc. Americana*⟩ ⟨the *miasmal* air of the closed, unventilated room— *C. M. Smith*⟩ Of these words only *miasmic* is common in extended use, where it often comes close to *pestilential* in implying a power to spread contamination or to poison the minds or souls of the multitude ⟨a *miasmic* little tale of degeneracy—*W. T. Scott*⟩ ⟨*miasmic* fear of Communism . . . has permeated Houston—*Houston Post*⟩ *Ana* mortal, fatal, lethal, *deadly: *pernicious, baneful, noxious, deleterious, detrimental

**poke** *vb* Poke, prod, nudge, jog are comparable when they

mean, as verbs, to thrust something into so as to stir up, urge on, or attract attention and, as nouns, the act or an instance of such thrusting. **Poke** implies primarily the use of a body part (as a finger or foot) or of some instrument or implement (as a stick, a rod, or a poker), but sometimes, especially in verbal use and in idiomatic phrases, it may imply the operation of something equally effective in stirring up or in rooting out ⟨walked up and down and *poked* among the rocks—*Masefield*⟩ ⟨he *poked* the man in front of him to attract his attention⟩ ⟨*poke* up the fire in a stove⟩ ⟨he handed one to Lonnie, *poking* it at him until Lonnie's attention was drawn from the hogs—*Caldwell*⟩ ⟨*poked* his head round the corner—*Sayers*⟩ ⟨liked to *poke* his nose into another person's affairs⟩ ⟨give the fire a *poke* or two⟩ **Prod** suggests the use of something sharp which can stab or prick or goad into action; it may be a physical thing (as a sharp pointed stick) ⟨probed and *prodded* and palpated that tortured and self-tortured flesh—*Styron*⟩ ⟨the cattle needed to be *prodded* along⟩ or it may be something less tangible but equally effective (as sharp words, a threat, or a taunt) ⟨the excitement of trying . . . to *prod* them into action—*J. R. Green*⟩ ⟨*prod* lazy schoolboys⟩ ⟨give Willis a *prod* on the subject of church attendance— *Mackenzie*⟩ **Nudge** suggests gentler action than the preceding terms; it may imply the use of an elbow in attracting attention especially under conditions when speech is impossible ⟨he *nudged* the person sitting next to him to allow him to pass⟩ ⟨Squeers then *nudged* Mrs. Squeers to bring away the brandy bottle—*Dickens*⟩ ⟨give him a *nudge* or he will not see her⟩ or it may imply a mere suggestion or hint ⟨what was not trimmed from our pages by an editor's *nudge* was given away in the hagglings of publisher and author—*Mailer*⟩ or it may imply repeated gentle action (as in moving or shifting) ⟨impudent little tugboats . . . *nudged* our ship out of its slip—*J. W. Brown*⟩ **Jog** implies a thrust or, often, a touch on or as if on the elbow or arm that to some extent shakes one up ⟨a bored-looking man, with a fashionably-dressed woman *jogging* his elbow —*Jerome*⟩ ⟨a *jog* to one's memory⟩ ⟨almost any idea which *jogs* you out of your current abstractions may be better than nothing—*Whitehead*⟩
*Ana* *push, shove, thrust: *stir, arouse, rouse, awaken: *provoke, excite, stimulate, galvanize, quicken
**poke** *n* prod, nudge, jog (see under POKE *vb*)
**polite** *civil, courteous, courtly, gallant, chivalrous
*Ana* *suave, urbane, diplomatic, politic: *thoughtful, considerate, attentive
*Ant* impolite
**politic** 1 *expedient, advisable
*Ana* practical, *practicable: *possible, feasible, practicable: *shrewd, astute, perspicacious, sagacious
2 diplomatic, bland, smooth, *suave, urbane
*Ana* unctuous, slick, oily, *fulsome: *wise, prudent, judicious
**politician,** statesman, politico are comparable when they denote a person who is versed in or engaged in politics or in the science or art of government, though they are often regarded as contrasting rather than as interchangeable terms. **Politician** regularly implies a personal and professional interest and a party affiliation and stresses to varying degrees the resulting bias; it is likely to suggest ability to deal with masses of people so as to accomplish such desired ends as election to a political office whether of oneself, or of one's chosen candidate, or the passage of bills or the acceptance of measures one upholds, or the settlement of especially difficult problems to the satisfaction of one's constituency or of the country as a whole ⟨a president . . . must be a good *politician,* adept at working with men, managing them, and inspiring their confidence—

*Ogg & Ray*⟩ Sometimes *politician* is used with a strong suggestion of derogation or contempt to imply scheming, self-interest, artifice, or intrigue in accomplishing one's ends ⟨made the better publicized pilfering of Washington *politicians* seem petty by comparison—*Woodward*⟩ ⟨known as a *politician* in the deprecatory sense of the word, with all its undertones of corruption and dirty deals and smoke-filled rooms—*Rodell*⟩ **Statesman** implies elevation above party conflict and a mind able to view objectively the needs and problems of the state and its citizens and to concern itself with the long-term greatest good of the greatest number. The term, often in contrast to *politician,* is likely to stress both eminence and ableness ⟨they were *statesmen* not *politicians;* they guided public opinion, but were little guided by it—*Henry Adams*⟩ ⟨the scornful may say that "a *statesman* is a dead *politician,*" but it is more truly said that a *statesman* lives by his principles and a *politician* is ruled by his interest—*H. D. Scott*⟩ ⟨the statesman differs from the ordinary *politician* in that he is able to envisage and inspire support for policies that are in the long-run, best interests of the most people—*Hallowell*⟩ **Politico** is virtually interchangeable with *politician* but perhaps more likely to stress concern with partisan political activity than with the actual business of government ⟨his strength rests on the support of veteran *politicos* throughout the state—*Shannon*⟩ ⟨some sharp *politicos* still think the President won't run again—*Wall Street Jour.*⟩ Like *politician,* it can be highly derogatory ⟨Machiavelli's *The Prince* in which the individual *politico* is shown how to succeed by ignoring all moral, social, and religious restraints on his own action—*Highet*⟩
**politico** *politician, statesman
**poll** *vb* *shear, clip, trim, prune, lop, snip, crop
*Ana* *cut, slash: sever, *separate
**pollute** *contaminate, defile, taint, attaint
*Ana* *debase, vitiate, corrupt, deprave, pervert: *abuse, outrage, mistreat: profane, desecrate, blaspheme (see corresponding nouns at PROFANATION)
**pomp** *n* *display, parade, array
*Ana* ceremony, ceremonial, liturgy, ritual, formality, *form: ostentatiousness *or* ostentation, showiness *or* show (see corresponding adjectives at SHOWY)
**ponder,** meditate, muse, ruminate can mean to consider or examine something attentively, seriously, and with more or less deliberation. **Ponder** characteristically retains its original implication of weighing and usually suggests consideration of a problem from all angles or of a thing in all its relations in order that nothing important will escape one; unlike *weigh* in a related sense (see CONSIDER 1) it does not usually suggest a balancing that leads to a conclusion ⟨the great Sung master was wont . . . to . . . spend the day *pondering* the subjects of his brush by the side of running streams—*Binyon*⟩ ⟨was *pondering* over the best style in which to address the unknown and distant relatives—*Gibbons*⟩ **Meditate** adds to *ponder* an implication of a definite directing or focusing of one's thought; in intransitive use, especially, it more often suggests an effort to understand the thing so considered in all its aspects, relations, or values than an effort to work out a definite problem ⟨*meditate* upon these things; give thyself wholly to them—*1 Tim 4:15*⟩ ⟨I sat down . . . to give way to the melancholy reflections called up by the sight before me. I know not how long I *meditated*—*Wilkie Collins*⟩ In transitive use *meditate* implies such deep consideration of a plan or project that it approaches *intend* or *purpose* in meaning ⟨meanwhile, he was *meditating* a book on Shakespearian questions—*H. J. Oliver*⟩ **Muse** comes close to *meditate* in implying focused attention but it suggests a less intellectual aim; often it implies absorption

and a languid turning over of a topic as if in a dream, a fancy, or a remembrance ⟨let him . . . read a certain passage of full poesy or distilled prose, and let him wander with it, and *muse* upon it . . . and dream upon it—*Keats*⟩ ⟨Cabot *mused* over the fact that the old bastard considered himself . . . one of the eminences of the great metropolis—*Purdy*⟩ ⟨still a pleasant mystery; enough to *muse* over on a dull afternoon—*Davis*⟩ **Ruminate** implies a going over the same problem, the same subject, or the same object of meditation again and again; it may be used in place of any of these words, but it does not carry as strong a suggestion of weighing as *ponder*, of concentrated attention as *meditate*, or of absorption as *muse*, and it more often implies such processes as reasoning or speculation ⟨I sit at home and *ruminate* on the qualities of certain little books like this one—little elixirs of perfection, full of subtlety and sadness—which I can read and read again—*L. P. Smith*⟩ ⟨forty years of *ruminating* on life, of glimpsing it in its simplest forms through microscopes—*Kaempffert*⟩
*Ana* weigh, *consider, contemplate: reflect, deliberate, speculate, *think, cogitate

**ponderable** appreciable, *perceptible, sensible, palpable, tangible
*Ana* important, significant, momentous, weighty, consequential (see corresponding nouns at IMPORTANCE)
*Con* trivial, trifling, *petty, paltry

**ponderous** cumbrous, cumbersome, *heavy, weighty, hefty
*Ana* *massive, massy, bulky, substantial: clumsy, *awkward, maladroit: *onerous, burdensome, oppressive, exacting

**pool** *n* *monopoly, corner, syndicate, trust, cartel

**poor** *adj* **1** Poor, indigent, needy, destitute, penniless, impecunious, poverty-stricken, necessitous are comparable when they mean having less money or fewer possessions than are required to support a full life. **Poor** describes a person, a people, or an institution that comes under this description; it is the most general term of the group, applying not only to those who are in actual want or to those in straitened circumstances, but also to those who, as compared to other groups, live below the level of what is regarded as comfortable ⟨despite the death of the breadwinner, his family was not left *poor*—*Wecter*⟩ ⟨it wasn't only that they were not rich . . . but that they were so *poor* that they couldn't afford things—*Mary Austin*⟩ Between **indigent** and **needy** there is very little difference in meaning, both implying urgent and pressing want; both, but especially *indigent*, may be used to express the state of want to which those who are poor are reduced ⟨the depression had left a number of them *indigent*, without state or federal relief—*Green Peyton*⟩ ⟨will make contributions to *needy* groups of all races and creeds—*Current Biog.*⟩ ⟨there are many *needy* persons in this town⟩ ⟨*needy* children are provided with hot luncheons, free of cost⟩ **Destitute** goes further than any of these words in its implication of acute and dire need. It implies a lack of fundamental resources or a deprivation of basic necessities of life ⟨the fire rendered several poor families absolutely *destitute*⟩ ⟨the death of a *destitute* widow from starvation—*Maclaren-Ross*⟩ **Penniless** may imply a state of destitution or of indigence but it also may suggest an often temporary state of being without money; consequently, the term is susceptible of wider use than any of the others, sometimes connoting poverty or an approach to it and sometimes a mere transitory inconvenience ⟨the bright but *penniless* youth whose climb to fame rivaled the most incredible of the Alger stories—*Amer. Guide Series: Minn.*⟩ ⟨returned from her shopping trip *penniless* but triumphant⟩ **Impecunious**, though it carries practically

the same basic suggestion as *penniless*, is not quite its equivalent; it may imply the deprivation of money but it more often suggests a habitual being without money and, sometimes, connotes also the habit of borrowing or of living upon one's friends ⟨I was, as many young barristers are, an *impecunious* party—*Gilbert*⟩ ⟨this eager *impecunious* young man who had fared so richly in his poverty—*Wharton*⟩ **Poverty-stricken** may be chosen as an especially vivid word suggesting the state of one who is extremely indigent or actually destitute; it often connotes the suffering caused by this condition ⟨a wretched, *poverty-stricken* old couple⟩ ⟨the bulk of the pioneers was formed by *poverty-stricken* people who migrated from densely populated areas—*J. F. Embree & W. L. Thomas*⟩ **Necessitous** comes close to *needy* in meaning but often carries a clearer connotation of insistent or persistent demands for relief ⟨it holds out a shadow of present gain to a greedy and *necessitous* public—*Burke*⟩ ⟨according to sample surveys . . . six percent are only "moderately in need." The rest are immoderately *necessitous*—*Liebling*⟩
*Ant* rich —*Con* wealthy, affluent, opulent (see RICH)
**2** *bad, wrong
*Ana* *deficient, defective: *petty, puny, trivial, trifling, paltry: *base, low, vile
*Con* *good, right: satisfying, fulfilling, meeting, answering (see SATISFY)

**poppycock** *nonsense, twaddle, drivel, bunk, balderdash, gobbledygook, trash, rot, bull

**popular** *common, ordinary, familiar, vulgar
*Ana* general, *universal, generic, common: accepted, received, admitted (see RECEIVE): prevalent, *prevailing, current
*Ant* unpopular: esoteric

**port** *n* *harbor, haven

**port** *n* presence, *bearing, deportment, demeanor, mien

**portal** *door, gate, doorway, gateway, postern

**portend** presage, augur, prognosticate, *foretell, predict, forecast, prophesy, forebode
*Ana* betoken, *indicate, bespeak, attest: signify, import, *mean, denote

**portent** *foretoken, presage, prognostic, omen, augury
*Ana* presentiment, foreboding, misgiving, *apprehension: forewarning, warning, cautioning *or* caution (see WARN)

**portentous** *ominous, unpropitious, inauspicious, fateful
*Ana* threatening, menacing (see THREATEN): prodigious, *monstrous: prophesying *or* prophetic, presaging, foreboding, predicting, foretelling (see corresponding verbs at FORETELL)

**portico** *colonnade, arcade, arcature, peristyle

**portion** *n* **1** *part, piece, detail, member, division, section, segment, sector, fraction, fragment, parcel
*Ana* quantity, amount (see SUM *n*): apportionment, rationing *or* ration (see corresponding verbs at APPORTION): allotment, assignment, allocation (see corresponding verbs at ALLOT)
**2** *fate, destiny, lot, doom
*Ana* distribution, dispensation, division, dealing (see corresponding verbs at DISTRIBUTE): fortune, hap, *chance, luck

**portion** *vb* *apportion, parcel, ration, prorate
*Ana* *allot, assign, allocate: *distribute, dispense, divide, deal

**portly** *fleshy, stout, plump, rotund, chubby, fat, corpulent, obese
*Ana* burly, husky, brawny, *muscular

**portrait** photograph, *image, effigy, statue, icon, mask

**portray** *represent, depict, delineate, picture, limn
*Ana* image, photograph (see corresponding nouns at

A colon (:) separates groups of words discriminated. An asterisk (*) indicates place of treatment of each group.

IMAGE): describe, *relate, narrate: reproduce, copy, duplicate (see corresponding nouns at REPRODUCTION)

**pose** *vb* *propose, propound
*Ana* *ask, question, query: *puzzle, confound: baffle (see FRUSTRATE)

**pose** *n* **1** Pose, air, affectation, mannerism are comparable when they mean an adopted rather than a natural way of speaking and behaving. **Pose** implies an attitude deliberately assumed in order to impress others or to call attention to oneself; it may be applied to opinions, policies, declared beliefs, and preferences as well as to manners ⟨his reticence is just a *pose*⟩ ⟨identified himself with the Great Commoner, and this seemed to me purely a *pose*, which verged upon demagoguery—*Edmund Wilson*⟩ **Air** in its more general related use may come close to *demeanor* (compare *demeanor* under BEARING), but as compared with *pose* it, especially in the plural **airs**, definitely implies artificiality and the intent to give a false appearance, and usually also implies a vulgar pretense of breeding, of grandeur, or of superiority ⟨the red-headed singer . . . dropped her patronizing *air*, offered her scotch from the bottle—*Wouk*⟩ ⟨there was no doubt at all that she had acquired insufferable *airs*—*Stafford*⟩ **Affectation** usually designates a specific trick of speech or behavior of one who obviously puts on airs or whose trick impresses others as deliberately assumed and insincere ⟨regarded carrying cigarettes in a case as an *affectation*—*Richard Burke*⟩ ⟨agitation for opera in English seems a particular *affectation* to those who have come to know the works in the original—*Dale Warren*⟩ **Mannerism** designates an acquired peculiarity or eccentricity in speech or behavior; it seldom implies insincerity, but it nearly always connotes habit or potential habit. A *mannerism* consciously assumed becomes thereby also an *affectation;* what begins as an *affectation* may become an unconscious and habitual trick of behavior, and so a *mannerism* ⟨he giggled, and she was surprised she had not noticed this *mannerism* in him before—*Purdy*⟩ ⟨those little *mannerisms* of hers . . . especially the way she has of pointing a finger at me to emphasize a phrase—*Dahl*⟩
**2** *posture, attitude

**posit** *vb* *presuppose, presume, assume, postulate, premise

**posit** *n* presupposition, presumption, assumption, postulate, premise (see under PRESUPPOSE)

**position** **1** Position, stand, attitude denote a more or less fixed mental point of view or way of regarding something. *Position* and *stand* both imply reference to a question at issue or to a matter about which there is difference of opinion. **Position,** however, is often the milder term, since it, unlike **stand,** seldom connotes aggressiveness or defiance of a widely held or popular opinion ⟨he was asked to make known his *position* on disarmament⟩ ⟨he took the *stand* that disarmament would not accomplish the ends its proponents had in view⟩ ⟨bases his *position* on a wide and shrewd scrutiny of man and his history—*Alain Locke*⟩ ⟨he . . . agreed thoroughly with my *stand* that no government or private organization could give health; people had to achieve it by their own efforts—*Heiser*⟩ **Attitude** suggests a personal or, sometimes, a group or communal point of view, especially one that is colored by personal or party feeling, is influenced by one's environment or the fashion of the moment, and is, on the whole, more the product of temperament or of emotion than of thought or conviction ⟨a humorous *attitude* to life⟩ ⟨the Greek *attitude* toward nature⟩ ⟨it was their *attitude* of acceptance . . . their complaisance about themselves and about their life—*Wolfe*⟩ ⟨their beliefs, *attitudes*, and prejudices were a crowd of inconsistencies—*Farrell*⟩
*Ana* *point of view, viewpoint, standpoint, angle, slant

**2** *place, location, situation, site, spot, station

**positive** **1** certain, *sure, cocksure
*Ana* *confident, assured, sanguine, sure: dogmatic, doctrinaire, oracular, *dictatorial
*Ant* doubtful
**2** *affirmative
*Ant* negative —*Con* *neutral, indifferent: nugatory, *vain, idle, hollow: nullifying, annulling (see NULLIFY)

**possess** own, enjoy, hold, *have
*Ana* control, manage, direct, *conduct: retain, *keep, reserve, withhold

**possessions,** belongings, effects, means, resources, assets can mean all the items that taken together constitute a person's or group's property or wealth. *Possessions, belongings, effects* stress ownership; *means, resources, assets* emphasize value and especially pecuniary value of what is owned. **Possessions** may be applied to the aggregate of things owned, regardless of the individual worth or significance of each thing; thus, one may speak of the *possessions* of an indigent old woman or of the *possessions* of a Rothschild, the former referring to a few articles of furniture and clothing, the latter to extensive properties and enormous invested capital. **Belongings** is applied commonly to an individual's more intimate personal possessions (as clothes, household goods, and valuables) ⟨left the house and took all his *belongings* with him⟩ ⟨my *belongings* were put away in the room—*Frank Perry*⟩ **Effects** may be more inclusive than *belongings,* but usually less so than *possessions.* It is often applied to personal as distinguished from real property, especially when the reference is to the estate of a deceased person ⟨he died leaving no *effects* of value⟩ ⟨all his *effects* were divided among his relatives before an administrator could be appointed⟩ Sometimes it is applied to movable articles as distinguished from those that are stationary ⟨a sale of household *effects*⟩ ⟨all his personal *effects* are in his one trunk⟩ **Means** usually applies to all the money that is available, in the form of revenue from capital, income, or ready money, for expenditure ⟨lived beyond his *means*⟩ ⟨a man of large *means*⟩ When unqualified *means* frequently implies some degree of affluence ⟨decked out with furs, gloves and a hat sewn with pearls—one of those middle-aged women of *means*—*Cheever*⟩ **Resources,** on the other hand, is applied to all possessions that have actual or potential, but not necessarily money, value and that may be depended upon in case of need or of deficiency ⟨a society which gives an increasing share of its *resources* to military purposes—*Science*⟩ Sometimes the term comprehends all tangibles and intangibles possessed whether they are actually used or are merely available for use; thus, a statement of a company's *resources* is a statement that covers every item that may be regarded as a part of the company's wealth ⟨the turn of the 20th century, when the financial *resources* of the well-to-do were matched by the national affluence—*Lucius Beebe*⟩ Often the term refers specifically to possessions held in reserve for emergencies or to sources of supply as yet untapped; thus, the natural *resources* of a country include its unmined minerals, unfelled timber, water sources, and wild life. **Assets** both in law and in accounting implies an opposition to *liabilities* and therefore suggests the possibility of an inequality between the two and a difference between one's ostensible and one's actual wealth. When the term is used in reference to the settlement of the estate of a deceased person or to the legal administration of the property of an insolvent or bankrupt person or concern, the assets include all the possessions of marketable value which may be turned into money to provide for the payment of the liabilities ⟨the *assets* of the estate were sufficient to cover all liabilities, including the decedent's debts and his legacies⟩ When used in reference to general balance sheets of a company or corporation, the term comprehends all items which from one point of view can be called resources having book value. But *assets* is never exactly the same as *resources,* because the latter word does not, as *assets* does, imply a comparison with *liabilities.*

**possible** 1 Possible, practicable, feasible can mean capable of being realized. **Possible** is used to dispel doubt that something may or does occur or exist or may come to exist ⟨the regime of religious toleration has become *possible* only because we have lost the primal intensity of religious conviction—*Cohen*⟩ ⟨although he still asserts that community of goods would be the ideal institution, he reluctantly abandons it as a basis for a *possible* state—*Dickinson*⟩ **Practicable** refers to what may be readily effected, executed, practiced, used, or put into operation ⟨trial by jury—an institution in which . . . we have the very abstract and essence of all *practicable* democratic government—*Mallock*⟩ ⟨the only *practicable* tactics to be pursued were those of the routine police procedure—*S. S. Van Dine*⟩ **Feasible** may designate what is likely to work out or be put into effect successfully or what in a difficult situation seems the expedient least liable to fail ⟨cheap iron and steel made it *feasible* to equip larger armies and navies than ever before—*Mumford*⟩ ⟨only the most simple types of utilization are *feasible*—*Van Valkenburg & Huntington*⟩
*Ana* practical, *practicable: *expedient, advisable
2 *probable, likely
*Ana* credible, believable, colorable, *plausible: potential, dormant, *latent

**posterior** *adj* Posterior, rear, hind, hinder, after, back are comparable when they mean behind in order of arrangement in space. **Posterior** is the usual technical term for whatever is situated behind and is opposed to *anterior* ⟨to an anatomical eye the *posterior* part of the skull is even more striking than the anterior—*T. H. Huxley*⟩ **Rear** belongs especially to military usage, but has general application with reference to such things as structures and vehicles ⟨the *rear* ranks of a column⟩ ⟨the *rear* wall of a house⟩ **Hind,** opposed to *front* or *fore,* is used most commonly with reference to related parts and designates the member or pair which is in the rear ⟨the *hind* wheels of a wagon⟩ ⟨the *hind* legs of a horse⟩ It has sometimes more general application ⟨had a boy-size pair of empty overhalls blowing out of his *hind* pocket—*Faulkner*⟩ **Hinder** is equivalent to *hind* or, in nontechnical use, to *posterior* ⟨a long oval forward part and a taillike *hinder* portion—*Coker*⟩ **After** is largely confined to nautical usage and applies to whatever is abaft the midship section, or in the rear part of a vessel, or relatively near to this part ⟨the *after* cabin⟩ ⟨the *after* hatchway⟩ **Back** applies to what is thought of as behind, remote from, or inferior or subsidiary to, the main or more important part ⟨*back* stairs⟩ ⟨*back* door⟩ ⟨the near woodlands and *back* pastures afford good hunting—*Amer. Guide Series: Tenn.*⟩
*Ant* anterior

**posterity** *offspring, young, progeny, issue, descendant
*Ant* ancestry  —*Con* lineage, pedigree (see ANCESTRY)

**postern** gate, *door, gateway, doorway, portal

**postpone** *defer, suspend, stay, intermit
*Ana* *delay, retard, slow, slacken

**postulant** *novice, novitiate, probationer, neophyte, apprentice

**postulate** *vb* *presuppose, presume, assume, premise, posit
*Ana* affirm, aver, predicate, *assert

**postulate** *n* presupposition, presumption, assumption,

premise, posit (see under PRESUPPOSE)
*Ana* *principle, axiom, theorem, fundamental, law: theory, *hypothesis

**posture** *n* 1 Posture, attitude, pose denote a position assumed by the body, or the disposition of the parts of the body with relation to one another. **Posture** applies to the relative arrangement of the different parts of the body. It may apply to a habitual or characteristic arrangement and then specifically means the way in which one holds oneself and refers to one's physical carriage or bearing ⟨her *posture* is excellent⟩ ⟨pictures illustrating defects of *posture*⟩ ⟨examples of correct *posture*⟩ ⟨an urbane alertness about the face, the *posture*—*Wouk*⟩ or it may apply to an arrangement determined with reference to the needs of the mood or the moment and then requires qualification ⟨a sitting *posture*⟩ ⟨a kneeling *posture*⟩ ⟨the *posture* of supplication⟩ ⟨his whole figure had a prowling and half-crouching *posture*—*Wolfe*⟩ or the assistance of the context to evoke a picture of how the parts of the body are disposed or to reveal the intention or end ⟨there's a *posture* for a man to fight in! His weight isn't resting on his legs—*Shaw*⟩ **Attitude** applies chiefly to a posture that is unconsciously expressive or is intentionally assumed, often as a result of a particular mood or state of mind ⟨they slipped into the embassy . . . so wary, so frightened and in such *attitudes* of wrongdoing—*Cheever*⟩ ⟨uttering platitudes in stained-glass *attitudes*—*Gilbert*⟩ **Pose** applies to an attitude or to a position of some part or parts of the body which is assumed for the sake of effect, or which, if unconscious, strikes the observer as effective or as affected ⟨the *pose* of a model⟩ ⟨the lofty *pose* of her head expressed an habitual sense of her own consequence —*Shaw*⟩ ⟨his *pose* was easy and graceful. A superb self-confidence radiated from him—*Gibbons*⟩
*Ana* *bearing, deportment, mien
2 situation, *state, condition, mode, status
*Ana* *position, stand, attitude: readiness, quickness, promptness (see corresponding adjectives at QUICK)

**pot** *bet, wager, stake, ante

**potent** *powerful, puissant, forceful, forcible
*Ana* *vigorous, energetic, strenuous, lusty: *effective, efficacious, effectual: *strong, sturdy, tenacious
*Ant* impotent

**potential** dormant, *latent, quiescent, abeyant
*Ant* active, actual

**pother** *n* flurry, fuss, ado, *stir, bustle
*Ana* *haste, hurry, speed, dispatch: agitation, upset, perturbation, disturbance (see corresponding verbs at DISCOMPOSE)
*Con* coolness, collectedness, composure (see corresponding adjectives at COOL)

**pouch** *bag, sack

**pound** *vb* *beat, pummel, buffet, baste, belabor, thrash
*Ana* *strike, hit, smite, slug: batter, mutilate (see MAIM)

**pour** *vb* Pour, stream, gush, sluice are comparable when they mean to send forth or cause to send forth copiously. **Pour** usually suggests an abundant emission of what is sent forth ⟨it never rains but it *pours*⟩ ⟨*pour* men and money into the Netherlands—*Barr*⟩ ⟨*pour* forth tributes⟩ ⟨letters *poured* in in answer to his inquiry⟩ but it sometimes implies a coming in a course or stream, usually a continuous stream (as from a mouth, a spout, an orifice, or a wound) ⟨crowds *poured* from every exit⟩ ⟨*pour* coffee from a pot⟩ ⟨ranges . . . *pour* rivers down to the coast—*M. Barnard Eldershaw*⟩ **Stream** suggests a flow that is circumscribed (as by issuance through a course or from an opening) ⟨tears *streamed* from her eyes⟩ ⟨light *streamed* through the open door⟩ ⟨hundreds of happy workers *streaming* in through the wide wrought iron gates—*Dahl*⟩

---

A colon (:) separates groups of words discriminated. An asterisk (*) indicates place of treatment of each group.

though it also may connote abundance or continuousness in that flow ⟨the guests *streamed* past, shaking hands, exchanging greetings—*Styron*⟩ **Gush** implies a sudden and copious emission of or as if of something released from confinement; it often connotes a coming in a jet or in spurts ⟨blood *gushed* from the wound⟩ ⟨he . . . suddenly *gushed* forth in streams of wondrous eloquence—*Stephen*⟩ ⟨beer began to *gush* . . . in a white cascade—*Pynchon*⟩ **Sluice** implies the operation of something like a sluice for the regulation or control of the flow of water; therefore the verb *sluice* suggests a sending of water or liquid over a surface in an abundant stream ⟨water so fresh . . . never *sluiced* parched throats before—*Thackeray*⟩ ⟨Mowgli, with the rain *sluicing* over his bare shoulders—*Kipling*⟩ *Ana* emerge, *appear: flow, issue, proceed, *spring

**poverty,** indigence, penury, want, destitution, privation all denote the state of one who is poor or without enough to live upon. **Poverty,** the most comprehensive of these terms, typically implies such deficiency of resources that one is deprived of many of the necessities and of all of the comforts of life ⟨in Syria he feathered his nest so successfully that in two years he raised himself from *poverty* to opulence—*Buchan*⟩ ⟨complaining of his *poverty* as if it were a new invention and he its first victim—*Malamud*⟩ **Indigence,** often opposed to *affluence,* does not suggest dire or absolute poverty, but it does imply reduced or straitened circumstances and therefore usually connotes the endurance of many hardships and the lack of comforts ⟨reduced to *indigence* in his old age⟩ ⟨our newfound European *indigence* now makes us more materialistic than we used to pride ourselves on being—*Times Lit. Sup.*⟩ **Penury** may or may not imply abject poverty, but it does suggest such a degree of need, especially of money, that one is cramped or oppressed by it ⟨chill *Penury* repressed their noble rage—*Gray*⟩ ⟨she has to take anything she can get in the way of a husband rather than face *penury*— *Shaw*⟩ But *penury* may imply the semblance of poverty that comes from miserliness or penuriousness (compare *penurious* under STINGY) ⟨her relatives considered that the *penury* of her table discredited the Mingott name, which had always been associated with good living— *Wharton*⟩ **Want** (see also LACK) and **destitution** both imply an extreme of poverty that leaves one without the basic necessities of life; both terms, but especially the latter, often imply starvation and homelessness or the urgent need of help ⟨he is in great *want*⟩ ⟨here to the homeless child of *want* my door is open still—*Goldsmith*⟩ ⟨sinking stage by stage from indigence to squalor, from squalor to grimy *destitution*—*Mumford*⟩ **Privation,** though implying a state that is comparable to the one suggested by *indigence,* does not, as the latter term does, necessarily suggest poverty; although it implies a condition of being without many of the comforts and sometimes of the necessities of existence or having only an insufficient supply of them, it may connote another cause of such a condition than a lack of money or of possessions of value ⟨an explorer must undergo prolonged *privations*⟩ ⟨months of *privation* after the crop failure had left them ill-nourished⟩
*Ana* necessity, *need, exigency: strait, pass, pinch (see JUNCTURE)
*Ant* riches

**poverty-stricken** *poor, indigent, needy, destitute, penniless, impecunious, necessitous

**power** *n* **1** Power, force, energy, strength, might, puissance mean the ability to exert effort for a purpose. **Power** is the most general of these terms and denotes an ability to act or be acted upon, to effect something, or to affect or be affected by something ⟨the finest machine in the world is

useless without a motor to give it *power*⟩ ⟨the mechanical *power* of the internal-combustion engine⟩ ⟨raise the productive *power* of the nation⟩ ⟨the sound of a great flood moving with majesty and *power*—*Cather*⟩ ⟨give an attorney the *power* to act for one⟩ ⟨in any link between past and present there was potent magic, some *power* to evoke allegiance—*Hervey*⟩ ⟨hateful to feel their *power* over me when I knew that they were nothing but fancies—*Hudson*⟩ **Force** (see also FORCE 2) implies the exhibition or the exercise of power; the term usually carries with it a suggestion of actually overcoming resistance (as by setting a thing in motion or accelerating its motion or driving a person or thing in the desired direction); thus, one having the *power* to do something exerts *force* only when he actually does it ⟨a wind gathers *force*⟩ ⟨accumulated *force* which drove them as if discharged from a crossbow —*Jefferies*⟩ ⟨a hard and rebellious element not to be conquered mainly by skill . . . but mainly by *force*—*Ellis*⟩ ⟨the perverse wish to flee . . . not from the laws and customs of the world but from its *force* and vitality— *Cheever*⟩ Therefore *force* is often applied to a person or thing that exerts its power with marked efficacy or efficiency ⟨they believed that the Church was the only *force* which could consolidate the nation—*Inge*⟩ ⟨art is but the expression of a harmony of life, a fine balance of all the *forces* of the human spirit—*Binyon*⟩ **Energy** in general use and especially as applied to persons implies stored-up power releasing itself in work or craving such release ⟨the prodigious *energy* put forth by industry in time of war—*Morrison*⟩ ⟨in spite of his small size and fragile build, the man was a dynamo of *energy* and could perform the labors of a Titan—*Wolfe*⟩ ⟨it was marvelous . . . that the *energy* of her spirit could carry through so triumphantly her frail nervous system—*Ellis*⟩ **Strength** applies to the power that resides in a person or thing as a result of qualities or properties that enable him or it to exert force or to manifest energy or to resist pressure, strain, stress, or attack. Physically *strength* implies soundness (as of health or of construction or design) ⟨the tensile *strength* of a rope⟩ ⟨I was not delicate, not physically; when it was a matter of *strength* I had as much as the next man— *Mailer*⟩ while mentally and morally it may imply capacity for endurance or resolution or intrepidity ⟨show *strength* in temptation⟩ ⟨*strength* to surmount the horrors and humiliations of . . . defeat—*O'Donovan*⟩ When applied to military forces it usually implies power manifest in such things as numbers, equipment, and resources ⟨estimate the *strength* of the enemy⟩ ⟨a fleet incomparable in *strength*⟩ **Might** and **puissance** are rather rhetorical or poetic words meaning operative or effective power or force. **Might** often suggests great or superhuman power; it is therefore appropriate when the reference is to supernatural beings or supranatural forces or to human power that is so strong that it cannot be gainsaid ⟨protect us by thy *might*, Great God, our King—*S. F. Smith*⟩ ⟨let us have faith that right makes *might*—*Lincoln*⟩ ⟨the pride and *might* and vivid strength of things—*Galsworthy*⟩ **Puissance** is often indistinguishable from *might*, but it can also connote an impressive display of power ⟨we should advance ourselves to look with forehead bold and big enough upon the power and *puissance* of the King— *Shak.*⟩ ⟨the sapience and *puissance* of the American businessman in general—*G. W. Johnson*⟩
*Ana* *ability, capacity, capability: *gift, genius, talent, faculty: qualification, competence (see corresponding adjectives at ABLE)
*Ant* impotence

**2** Power, faculty, function can all mean an ability of a living being to act or perform in a given way or a capacity for a particular kind of action or performance. **Power**, the comprehensive term of this group, may apply to a capacity for action or performance that does not or apparently does not call the mind into play ⟨the *power* to digest food⟩ ⟨the *power* of reflex movement⟩ but it more frequently applies to an ability or capacity that involves either mental activity or mental receptiveness ⟨the *power* to think clearly⟩ ⟨the human mind is a fearful instrument . . . in its mysterious *powers* of resilience, self-protection, and self-healing—*Wolfe*⟩ **Faculty** in general, as distinct from technical psychological or metaphysical use, is applicable to those powers which are the possession of every normal human being, though not always manifested in the first months of infancy or the earliest years of childhood ⟨the *faculty* of hearing⟩ ⟨the *faculty* of speech⟩ or it may apply to any one of the several specific powers of the mind (as will, memory, and reason) that are often felt as discrete and discoverable ⟨the truth is that memory and imagination, the two most important human *faculties*, are scarcely cultivated at all—*Grandgent*⟩ Sometimes *faculty* means no more than a distinguishable capacity of the functioning mind or soul ⟨once a thing did become pertinent, he had an amazing *faculty* for absorbing it wholly—*Terry Southern*⟩ ⟨her *faculty* for moral perception had withdrawn into that dim neutrality—*Hervey*⟩ ⟨it is the one occasion when violent grief, disturbing his *faculties*, appears in his correspondence—*Belloc*⟩ **Function** may denote an activity which can be more or less definitely associated with the brain or the central nervous system or a part of either ⟨all mental activities, such as seeing, hearing, perceiving, conceiving, imagining, recalling, etc., are termed *functions*—*Murchison*⟩ or it may apply to one (as digestion or respiration) in which the mental component is slight or obscure.

**3 Power, authority, jurisdiction, control, command, sway, dominion** are comparable when they mean the right or prerogative of determining, ruling, or governing or the exercise of that right or prerogative. **Power** even in this specific sense never loses its fundamental implication of ability, but in this case it is a capacity for rule that may derive from rank, office, or even character or personality ⟨in an absolute monarchy the king has sole *power*⟩ ⟨it is a strange desire, to seek *power*, and to lose liberty; or to seek *power* over others, and to lose *power* over a man's self—*Bacon*⟩ ⟨for thine is the kingdom, and the *power*, and the glory, for ever—*Mt* 6:13⟩ *Power* when used with reference to a definite person or body or office commonly connotes divisibility or strict limitation ⟨the trustees have *power* of appointment⟩ ⟨the charter gives the city *power* to tax sales⟩ ⟨he was given *power* of attorney to act for his brother⟩ ⟨it is not enough that a statute goes to the verge of constitutional *power*. We must be able to see clearly that it goes beyond that *power* —*Justice Holmes*⟩ **Authority** is often used interchangeably with *power;* nevertheless, there can be an essential difference in meaning, since *authority* usually refers to power resident in or exercised by another than oneself; thus, one may have *power*, rather than *authority*, to determine one's own actions, but a parent or a master or a ruler has the *authority*, rather than the *power*, to determine the actions of those under him; children are obedient to *authority* rather than to *power* ⟨they were both getting childish and needed care and yet they resented any loss of *authority*—*Buck*⟩ ⟨the object is to induce the child to lend of his own free will; so long as *authority* is required, the end aimed at has not been achieved—*Russell*⟩ ⟨*authority* in the religious sphere generally means absolute or infallible *authority*, such as Catholics ascribe to the Church—*Inge*⟩ *Power* and *authority*, especially

in the plural, often refer to the persons who have or hold power or authority as defined. *Powers*, however, usually occurs in the phrase "the *powers* that be" and is either somewhat more comprehensive or less explicit in its reference than "the *authorities*," which often means the persons who have authority in the special instance to direct, to decide, or to punish ⟨he is always in instinctive opposition to the *powers* that be⟩ ⟨he threatened to report the offense to the *authorities*⟩ **Jurisdiction** implies possession of legal or actual power to determine, to rule, or to govern within definitely assigned limits, and of the authority to so act in all matters coming within the sphere of that power ⟨the principle of law is too well settled to be disputed, that a court can give no judgment for either party, where it has no *jurisdiction*—*Taney*⟩ ⟨this new and populous community must, for the present, the Kansas Bishop wrote, be accounted under Father Latour's *jurisdiction*—*Cather*⟩ **Control** stresses possession of the authority to restrain or curb and its effective exercise, or of actual power to regulate or keep responsive to one's will not only persons but things; thus, a teacher who has lost *control* of his class has reached a point where the pupils no longer recognize his authority; a fire has gone beyond *control* when those who are fighting it have lost all power to check it ⟨completely out of *control*, the woman had shrugged off her husband's embarrassed efforts to stop her— *Wouk*⟩ ⟨he was at last in triumphant *control* of his destiny—*Wolfe*⟩ **Command** implies such control as makes one the master of men, and such authority that obedience to one's order or one's will either inevitably follows or is inexorably enforced; thus, one speaks of the officer in *command*, rather than in *control*, of a regiment; a person has *command* of a situation when he completely dominates it or has all persons or things involved in it under control ⟨how, in one house, should many people, under two *commands*, hold amity?—*Shak.*⟩ *Command* is also used in reference to things which one has mastered so thoroughly that one encounters no resistance or interference in using, recalling, or controlling them ⟨his brush did its work with a steady and sure stroke that indicated *command* of his materials—*Jefferies*⟩ ⟨something beyond disorderly or careless thinking, something close to a complete loss of emotional *command*—*Anthony West*⟩ **Sway** tends to be slightly rhetorical because its use in this sense was originally figurative and the word still carries a hint of its original implications of swinging or sweeping through an arc or circle; hence, when a word is desired that means power but also connotes extent or scope and such added matters as preponderant influence, compelling authority, or potency, *sway* is the appropriate choice ⟨the British Empire extended its *sway* to every quarter of the earth⟩ ⟨primal spirits beneath his *sway*— *Shelley*⟩ ⟨the law of compensation rules supreme in art, as it holds *sway* in life—*Lowes*⟩ **Dominion** imputes sovereignty to the power in question or supremacy to the authority in question ⟨God of our fathers, known of old, Lord of our far-flung battle line, beneath whose awful Hand we hold *dominion* over palm and pine—*Kipling*⟩ ⟨foreign *dominion* in any shape would soon become hateful—*Freeman*⟩

*Ana* \*right, privilege, prerogative, birthright: management, direction (see corresponding verbs at CONDUCT): ascendancy, \*supremacy

**powerful,** potent, puissant, forceful, forcible are comparable when they mean having or manifesting power to effect great or striking results. **Powerful** is applicable to something which stands out from the rest of its kind as exceeding the others in its display of strength or force or in its manifestation of energy; the word also usually implies

A colon (:) separates groups of words discriminated. An asterisk (\*) indicates place of treatment of each group.

an effectiveness that has been proved rather than attributed ⟨the most *powerful* ruler of his age⟩ ⟨a *powerful* fleet⟩ ⟨a *powerful* influence for good—*Walcutt*⟩ ⟨a *powerful* cathartic⟩ **Potent,** though it implies powerfulness, is applicable chiefly to something which derives or seems to derive that character from some hidden or latent virtue or quality rather than from an observable or measurable power or force ⟨he exercised a *potent* spell over her imagination⟩ ⟨how *potent* is this Oriental blood in Napoleon, in Goethe, in Heine, Victor Hugo—*J. R. Lowell*⟩ ⟨illusions . . . no longer *potent* because they are no longer really believed—*Krutch*⟩ **Puissant,** a bookish word, refers typically to persons, to military or naval forces, or to bodies politic and connotes more the outward attributes of power; it commonly suggests a great and abiding strength ⟨most . . . mighty, and most *puissant* Caesar—*Shak.*⟩ ⟨one of the nation's most *puissant* labor leaders—*Time*⟩ ⟨methinks I see in my mind a noble and *puissant* nation rousing herself like a strong man after sleep—*Milton*⟩ The last two words of the group, though somewhat more restrained in their suggestion of power, nevertheless imply an ability to effect impressive results. **Forceful** stresses the possession or manifestation of force as a quality; it therefore suggests marked vigor or energy or strength regardless of whether it is being exercised or not. The word is applicable even to something which makes no display of effort or violence, provided it impresses its undoubted force on the observer ⟨a *forceful* personality⟩ ⟨he relied more on a *forceful* clarity to convince his readers than on the brilliant and exciting ambiguities of propagandist eloquence—*Huxley*⟩ ⟨physically, he suggests at once a *forceful* spit-and-polish officer—*Knight*⟩ **Forcible,** on the other hand, suggests the actual exertion of power or force; it often implies the use of physical violence in attaining one's ends ⟨*forcible* disarmament and military occupation can only be temporary—*Times Lit. Sup.*⟩ ⟨take *forcible* possession of goods not paid for⟩ ⟨favor *forcible* measures in treating unruly prisoners⟩ Sometimes it is used in place of *forceful* to add to that term implications of aggressiveness, militancy, or decided potency ⟨win a chess game with a series of *forcible* moves⟩ ⟨more than thirty years have passed and I have seen no *forcible* young man of letters brave the metropolis—*Yeats*⟩
*Ana* \*able, capable, competent: efficacious, effectual, \*effective, efficient: \*vigorous, energetic, strenuous
*Ant* powerless: inefficacious

**powerless, impotent** both mean unable to effect one's purpose, intention, or end. **Powerless** denotes merely lack of power or efficacy which is often temporary or relative to a specific purpose or situation ⟨he suddenly found himself *powerless* to move⟩ ⟨*powerless* as an infant—*De Quincey*⟩ ⟨I hope that the luxuries of this palatial mansion are *powerless* to corrupt your heart—*Shaw*⟩ ⟨that mood of hopeless apathy that comes over men *powerless* to help themselves—*Nordhoff & Hall*⟩ **Impotent** (see also STERILE) implies not only powerlessness but positive weakness or, especially, complete ineffectiveness ⟨an angry little spitfire sea continually . . . thrashes with *impotent* irascibility—*Stevenson*⟩ ⟨*impotent* aristocrats talking about the code of chivalry but unable to bring it to life—*Time*⟩ ⟨terrible and *impotent* rage—*Wilde*⟩
*Ana* inert, \*inactive, passive, supine: feeble, \*weak, infirm, decrepit
*Ant* powerful: efficacious  *—Con* \*effective, efficient
**practicable** 1 feasible, \*possible
*Ana* operating *or* operable, working *or* workable, functioning (see corresponding verbs at ACT)
*Ant* impracticable

2 **Practicable, practical** are not close synonyms and not interchangeable, but they are sometimes confused when they imply a capacity for being used or turned to account. **Practicable** (see also POSSIBLE 1) applies chiefly to something immaterial (as a plan, project, scheme, or design) which has not been tested in practice or to something material (as a new machine, a new form of entertainment, or a new implement) which has not been proved successful in operation or use ⟨aviation was his predominant interest. He was one of the first to consider aerial locomotion *practicable*—*W. C. Langdon*⟩ ⟨the lovely combes running down to the sea are infested with cars in the summer season wherever there is a *practicable* road—*Brit. Book News*⟩ ⟨a serviceable concept on which to base a *practicable* policy—*Hobson*⟩ **Practical** applies not only to things both concrete and immaterial but also as *practicable* does not, to persons. The term in all of its senses stresses an opposition to what is *theoretical, speculative, ideal, unrealistic,* or *imaginative* and implies a relation to the actual life of man, his daily needs, or the conditions which must be met. When the term also implies a capacity for use, it emphasizes actual usefulness rather than highly probable or merely discovered usableness; thus, a plan might be *practicable* in that it could be put into practice though not *practical* because inefficient, too costly, or superfluous; the modern low-slung high-speed automobile was *practicable* long before improved roads and fuels made it *practical* ⟨those most *practical* machines of our modern life, the dynamo and the telephone—*Ellis*⟩ Hence, *practical* may apply to whatever is such in kind, character, amount, or effect that it is definitely useful or serviceable in actual life ⟨to make the gas turbine *practical* for the ordinary driver, controls would have to be simple and . . . fuel consumption . . . lowered—*Modern Industry*⟩ ⟨*practical* sciences, in which knowledge is pursued as a means to conduct rather than as an end in itself—*Thilly*⟩ ⟨he was eminently *practical,* seeking a sound, workable system adapted to the conditions of the people—*Schafer*⟩ ⟨in everything he undertook he demanded a utilitarian purpose and a *practical* result—*Buchan*⟩
**practical** \*practicable
**practically** \*virtually, morally
**practice** *vb* **Practice, exercise, drill** are comparable when they mean, as verbs, to perform or cause one to perform an act or series of acts repeatedly and, as nouns, such repeated activity or exertion. **Practice** fundamentally implies doing, especially doing habitually or regularly, often in contrast to thinking, believing, and professing or to theory and precept ⟨*practice* what you preach⟩ ⟨the *practice* of one's religion⟩ ⟨*practice* a profession⟩ ⟨in theory every citizen votes, but in *practice* rarely more than half avail themselves of the privilege⟩ ⟨thinking piously of saints and others who *practiced* mortification—*Cheever*⟩ **Practice** also implies a doing over and over again of certain acts for the sake of acquiring proficiency, dexterity, or skill or in the hope of attaining perfection ⟨*practice* makes perfect⟩ ⟨*practice* on the piano each day⟩ ⟨rifle *practice*⟩ ⟨I am not normally a scheming person; I . . . have had no *practice* in it whatsoever—*Dahl*⟩ **Exercise** fundamentally implies a keeping busy or a setting to work; it usually presupposes the possession of a power or of powers which can be developed or strengthened by activity, especially repeated activity, or can be manifested only in practice ⟨give him plenty of opportunities to *exercise* his intelligence⟩ ⟨a wise father avoids the *exercise* of authority except when other means fail⟩ ⟨he had liberality, and he had the means of *exercising* it—*Austen*⟩ ⟨so long as a child is with adults, it has no

---

*Ana* analogous words     *Ant* antonyms     *Con* contrasted words     See also explanatory notes facing page 1

occasion for the *exercise* of a number of important virtues, namely, those required by the strong in dealing with the weak—*Russell*⟩ ⟨will can only be *exercised* in the presence of something which retards or resists it—*Inge*⟩ Like *practice, exercise* may be used also to imply acts performed repeatedly for the sake of an ulterior end, but *exercise* refers especially to those directed to the attainment of health or vigor (as of body or mind) ⟨Tom was being *exercised* like a raw recruit⟩ ⟨grow mentally dull through lack of physical *exercise*⟩ ⟨*exercise* is good for the muscles of mind and to keep it well in hand for work—*J. R. Lowell*⟩ ⟨poetry is in France an *exercise*, not an expression. It is to real French expression, to prose, what gymnastics and hygiene are to health—*Brownell*⟩ **Drill** fundamentally connotes an intention to fix physical or mental habits as deeply as though they were bored in by the use of a drill; the term stresses repetition (as of military evolutions, of word pronunciations, or of grammatical rules) as a means of training and disciplining the body or mind or of forming correct habits ⟨*drill* troops in marching and handling arms⟩ ⟨a *drill* in arithmetic⟩ ⟨this is a real danger in modern education, owing to the reaction against the old severe *drill*. The mental work involved in the *drill* was good; what was bad was the killing of intellectual interests—*Russell*⟩
*Ana* *perform, execute, fulfill: *follow, pursue: *repeat, iterate

**practice** *n* **1** *habit, habitude, usage, custom, use, wont
*Ana* procedure, *process, proceeding: *method, system, way, fashion, mode, manner
**2** exercise, drill (see under PRACTICE *vb*)
*Ana* *use, utility, usefulness: usage, *form, convention, convenance: pursuit, calling, *work
*Ant* theory: precept

**praise,** laud, acclaim, extol, eulogize mean to express approbation or esteem. **Praise** often implies no more than warmly expressed commendation ⟨what we admire we *praise*, and when we *praise*, advance it into notice—*Cowper*⟩ When specifically referred to persons, it frequently suggests the judgment of a superior ⟨*praise* a pupil for his diligence⟩ ⟨he's given you every encouragement. He's *praised* you to the skies—*Wouk*⟩ However, it is also used in reference to God or a god or to a saint; then it implies glorification by such acts of homage as song or prayer ⟨*praise* God from whom all blessings flow—*Ken*⟩ **Laud** implies high, sometimes excessive, praise ⟨history written by the conqueror, *lauding* to the skies the victories of its sublime troops—*Americas*⟩ ⟨both of the writers *lauded* highly . . . contemporaries who were certainly no better than middling performers in their several arts—*Montague*⟩ **Acclaim** usually suggests enthusiastic and public expression of approval ⟨he was *acclaimed* not only in his own country but throughout the civilized world—*Heiser*⟩ ⟨a new British film that has been widely *acclaimed* by the critics and public as a classic of its kind—*Gillett*⟩ **Extol** retains its original implication of lifting up or raising and suggests praise that exalts or magnifies ⟨*extol* the Lamb with loftiest song, ascend for him our cheerful strain—*R. A. West*⟩ It is often used when a contrast between approbation or esteem and their opposites is enforced ⟨an age must always decry itself and *extol* its forbears—*Galsworthy*⟩ **Eulogize,** sometimes interchangeable with *extol*, may differ from it in implying formality both in the method and in the occasion; very frequently it suggests a set composition or oration (*eulogy*) suitable for a funeral or testimonial ⟨he *eulogized* constitutional government as immeasurably superior to despotism—*Lecky*⟩ ⟨one of those rare days in June *eulogized* by poets—*Barkins*⟩

*Ana* *commend, applaud, compliment: *exalt, magnify, aggrandize
*Ant* blame —*Con* asperse, *malign, traduce, vilify, calumniate, defame, libel: disparage, *decry, detract, belittle: reprehend, reprobate, censure, denounce, *criticize

**prank** *n* Prank, caper, antic, monkeyshine, dido mean a playful, often a mischievous, act or trick. **Prank** carries the strongest implication of devilry of all these words, though there is little suggestion of malice and primary emphasis upon the practical joke ⟨the sons are wild and wanton sons, and perform all the *pranks* to be expected of them—*T. S. Eliot*⟩ ⟨when, with elfin delight, he perpetrates a successful practical joke—or when somebody makes him the butt of such a *prank*—*J. A. Morris*⟩ **Caper** can suggest carefree frisking and bounding like a kid and is especially applicable to capricious or reckless escapades ⟨relaxed acceptance of the most outlandish *capers*—*Spectorsky*⟩ ⟨it will be sad if his journalistic facility, his quirks and *capers*, obscure his excellence as a writer—*A. C. Ward*⟩ **Antic** stresses the ludicrousness and grotesqueness of the movements, gestures, and postures rather than the spirit in which the acts or tricks are performed ⟨the deliberately childish *antics* of comedians: the affected high voices, the giggles, the silly faces —*Wouk*⟩ ⟨the *antics* of a clown⟩ Sometimes, however, it suggests showing off ⟨watch the *antics* of boys climbing poles⟩ ⟨a small boy whose *antics* were somewhat amusing, but not understandable—*Terry Southern*⟩ **Monkeyshine** may be applied to a caper or antic, but, especially in the plural, the term typically applies to behavior or a trick that attracts attention by its inappropriateness and often impropriety ⟨scientists on the alert for any atomic *monkeyshines*—*McCarten*⟩ ⟨have been at this *monkeyshine* for a generation. Today a loaf of "bread" looks deceptively real—*Philip Wylie*⟩ ⟨students of political *monkeyshines*—*Newsweek*⟩ **Dido,** also frequently used in the plural, applies to an absurd, foolish, or mischievous act and may come close to *monkeyshine* in suggesting obtrusive inappropriateness ⟨this and ancillary *didoes* culminate in a whopper of an orgy—*Perelman*⟩ ⟨onetime mayor . . . whose unstatesmanlike *didoes* made a circus of municipal affairs—*Time*⟩
*Ana* frolic, gambol, rollick, sport, play (see under PLAY *vb*): levity, *lightness, frivolity: vagary, *caprice, freak, fancy, whim, whimsy, conceit

**prate** chatter, *chat, gab, patter, prattle, babble, gabble, jabber, gibber

**prattle** chatter, patter, prate, gab, *chat, babble, gabble, jabber, gibber

**pray** plead, petition, appeal, sue (see under PRAYER)
*Ana* supplicate, entreat, beseech, implore, *beg

**prayer,** suit, plea, petition, appeal mean an earnest and usually a formal request for something and their corresponding intransitive verbs **pray, sue, plead, petition, appeal** mean to make such a request. **Prayer** and **pray** imply that the request is made to a person or body invested with authority or power or especially to God or a god; the words usually therefore connote humility in approach and often fervor in entreating ⟨we do *pray* for mercy; and that same *prayer* doth teach us all to render the deeds of mercy —*Shak.*⟩ In religious use, where *prayer* and *pray* always imply an act of worship, they may or may not connote a request or petition. The implication of making a request is retained, however, in the specific legal use of these terms in a court of equity, where formally one *prays* for relief; the *prayer* in a bill in equity is the part that specifies the kind of relief sought. The words are also used in formal petitions or remonstrances to a legislative body. **Suit** and **sue** imply

a deferential and formal solicitation sometimes for help or relief but often for a favor, a grace, or a kindness. Except in legal use (see SUIT *n* 2), in reference to the addresses of a man to the lady he hopes to marry, and in some idiomatic phrases such as "*sue* for peace," the words are somewhat old-fashioned in flavor ⟨his *suit* to the Muse . . . relies too much on exertions and capacities—*The Nation*⟩ ⟨she *sued* year after year . . . for acceptance by a society of dreary dowagers—*E. K. Brown*⟩ **Plea** (see also APOLOGY) and **plead** often suggest a court of law, the status of a defendant or of an accused person, and formal statements in answer to a plaintiff's allegations or the state's charge. In general use both terms imply argument or urgent entreaty, of which self-justification, a desire for vindication or support, or strong partisanship is usually the motive ⟨make a *plea* for forgiveness⟩ ⟨*plead* for a more tolerant attitude⟩ ⟨she dreaded the arguments, their tear-stained *pleas*—*Malamud*⟩ ⟨I *plead* frankly for the theistic hypothesis as involving fewer difficulties than any other—*Inge*⟩ **Petition** and its verb **petition** imply a formal and specific request, often in writing, presented to the person or body that has power to grant it. The words carry little or no connotation of abject humility or of entreaty; rather, they suggest a right to make a request, as one of the sovereign people or as one who is confident that it will be judged on its merits ⟨the flood of *petitions* from business interests begging relief from the political crisis—*Woodward*⟩ ⟨she neither *petitioned* for her right, nor claimed it—*Meredith*⟩ **Appeal**, as noun and verb, basically implies a call for attention to and favorable consideration of one's plea ⟨*appeal* for mercy⟩ ⟨*appeal* to one's family for help⟩ Often it additionally connotes an insistence on being heard and hence a change of plea from an inferior to a superior power (as a higher court or a higher authority) or to an emotion in an attempt to evoke a favorable response or judgment ⟨*appeal* to the supreme court for a new trial⟩ ⟨to what sources of information do I *appeal* for guidance?—*Cardozo*⟩ ⟨Mantalinis and Dobbins who pursue women with *appeals* to their pity or jealousy or vanity—*Shaw*⟩ Sometimes, used alone, either noun or verb implies a sympathetic or favorable response or a compelling quality ⟨an *appealing* child⟩ ⟨the song has a human *appeal*⟩
**Ana** supplication, entreaty, beseeching, imploring, begging (see corresponding verbs at BEG): worship, adoration (see under REVERE)

**preamble** *introduction, prologue, prelude, preface, foreword, exordium

**precarious** *dangerous, hazardous, perilous, risky
**Ana** *doubtful, dubious, questionable: distrustful, mistrustful (see corresponding verbs at DISTRUST): chance, chancy, haphazard, *random
**Con** *safe, secure: *steady, even, equable, constant

**precedence** *priority
**Ana** leading *or* lead, guiding *or* guide (see GUIDE): antecedence, foregoing (see corresponding adjectives at PRECEDING)

**precedent** *adj* *preceding, antecedent, foregoing, previous, prior, former, anterior

**preceding, antecedent, precedent, foregoing, previous, prior, former, anterior** are comparable when they mean being before, especially in time or in order of arrangement. **Preceding,** opposed to *succeeding* and *following,* is restricted to time and place; it usually means immediately before ⟨the *preceding* day⟩ ⟨the *preceding* clause⟩ ⟨events *preceding* the opening of the story⟩ **Antecedent,** opposed to *subsequent* and *consequent,* usually implies order in time, but unlike *preceding,* it often suggests an indefinite intervening interval ⟨events *antecedent* to the opening of the story⟩ ⟨Chaucer's poems were written in a period *antecedent* to the Elizabethan Age⟩ Very often, also, the word implies a causal or a logical, as well as a temporal, relation ⟨to understand the success of modern dictators we must have a knowledge of *antecedent* conditions⟩ ⟨a conclusion is based on a chain of *antecedent* inferences⟩ **Precedent** often applies to one thing which must precede another thing if the latter is to be valid or become effective; thus, a condition *precedent* in law is a condition that must be fulfilled before an estate can be vested in one or before a right accrues to one. **Foregoing,** opposed to *following,* applies almost exclusively to statements ⟨the *foregoing* citations⟩ ⟨the *foregoing* argument⟩ *Previous* and *prior,* opposed to *subsequent,* are often used almost interchangeably ⟨his life *previous* to his marriage⟩ ⟨this will cancels all *prior* wills⟩ But **prior** sometimes implies greater importance than **previous**; thus, a *previous* obligation suggests merely an obligation entered into earlier in point of time, whereas a *prior* obligation is one which surpasses the other in importance and must be fulfilled in advance of any other; a *prior* preferred stock is one whose claim to dividends or to a specified sum in liquidation comes before other preferred stocks of a company. **Former,** opposed to *latter,* even more definitely than *prior,* implies comparison; thus, there can be a *former* engagement only when there is also a later one; a *previous* or *prior* engagement may prevent one's making a second. **Anterior,** opposed to *posterior,* also comparative in force, applies to position, usually in space, sometimes in order or time ⟨the *anterior* lobe of the brain⟩ ⟨organization must presuppose life as *anterior* to it—*Coleridge*⟩
**Ant** following

**precept** rule, *law, canon, regulation, statute, ordinance
**Ana** *principle, fundamental, axiom: *doctrine, tenet, dogma: injunction, behest, bidding (see COMMAND *n*)
**Ant** practice: counsel

**precious** *costly, expensive, dear, valuable, invaluable, priceless
**Ana** *choice, exquisite, recherché, rare: valued, prized, appreciated, cherished (see APPRECIATE)

**precipitate** *vb* *speed, accelerate, quicken, hasten, hurry
**Ana** drive, impel (see MOVE *vb*): *force, compel, coerce, constrain

**precipitate** *n* *deposit, sediment, dregs, lees, grounds

**precipitate** *adj* **Precipitate, headlong, abrupt, impetuous, hasty, sudden** as applied to persons or their acts or behavior denote characterized by excessive haste and unexpectedness. **Precipitate** especially stresses lack of due deliberation; sometimes it suggests prematureness and is therefore especially applicable to decisions or to actions based on decisions ⟨she was resolved to lose nothing by neglect or delay, but also she meant to do nothing *precipitate*—*H. G. Wells*⟩ **Headlong** throws the emphasis on rashness and lack of forethought; it is used to describe not only persons and their acts but the qualities exhibited by such persons or in such acts ⟨*headlong* folly⟩ ⟨*headlong* haste⟩ ⟨the *headlong* torrent of her feelings scared her—*Wouk*⟩ **Abrupt** when applied to actions suggests complete lack of warning or, sometimes, unceremoniousness ⟨an *abrupt* departure⟩ ⟨the story came to an *abrupt* end⟩ and when applied to manners or words, it usually implies curtness ⟨an *abrupt* refusal⟩ **Impetuous** implies violence or vehemence; as applied to persons, it often also suggests impulsiveness or, at times, extreme impatience ⟨no necessity exists for any hurry, except in the brain of that *impetuous* boy—*Meredith*⟩ ⟨they had been *impetuous* and daring, making up their minds in a couple of flashes—*Farrell*⟩ **Hasty** stresses quickness of response and often suggests thoughtlessness and hot temper rather than impul-

siveness ⟨often *hasty* in her judgment of strangers—*Dahl*⟩ ⟨too passionate and *hasty* to keep pace with the deliberate steps of his leader—*Philip Marsh*⟩ **Sudden** is distinguishable from *sudden* meaning unexpected only by its added implications of extreme hastiness or impetuosity ⟨given to *sudden* rages⟩ ⟨now and then an access of . . . *sudden* fury . . . would lay hold on a man or woman—*Kipling*⟩
*Ana* headstrong, willful, refractory (see UNRULY)
*Ant* deliberate  *—Con* leisurely, *slow
**precipitous** *steep, abrupt, sheer
*Ana* soaring, towering, rocketing, ascending, rising (see RISE)
**précis** sketch, aperçu, survey, *compendium, syllabus, digest, pandect
**precise** exact, accurate, *correct, nice, right
*Ana* definite, express, *explicit: strict, *rigid, rigorous, stringent
*Ant* loose  *—Con* lax, slack (see LOOSE): *careless, heedless
**preciseness** *precision
**precision, preciseness** both denote the quality or character of what is precise. **Precision** denotes a quality that is sought for or is attained usually as a highly desirable thing. When used in reference to language it implies expression with such exactitude that neither more nor less than what applies to the thing under consideration is said ⟨defining words with utmost care, they fashioned their statements of doctrine with meticulous *precision*—*Dinsmore*⟩ ⟨a vague term of abuse for any style that is . . . so evidently bad or second-rate that we do not recognize the necessity for greater *precision* in the phrases we apply to it—*T. S. Eliot*⟩ When used in reference to the arts and sciences, the term usually implies such clearness of definition or such sharpness in distinction or in distinguishing that there is no confusion about outlines, boundaries, dividing lines, or movements ⟨however we may disguise it by veiling words we do not and cannot carry out the distinction between legislative and executive action with mathematical *precision*—*Justice Holmes*⟩ ⟨acting, singing, and dancing seem to me the best methods of teaching aesthetic *precision*—*Russell*⟩ **Precision** is also used in reference to an instrument, a machine, or a part of a machine that must be made with such exactness of measurements that an infinitesimal fraction of an inch would debar it from fulfilling its function ⟨*precision* instruments⟩ ⟨tiny, Swiss-made replicas, they were *precision* machined and finely detailed, all scaled to perfection—*Terry Southern*⟩ **Preciseness** is rarely interchangeable with *precision*, since it carries so strong an implication of severity or of strictness, or sometimes of overnicety in the observance of religious laws, the code of one's profession, or the proprieties as dictated by one's class or social equals that it is depreciative as often as it is laudatory ⟨savoring of Puritanism and overstrict *preciseness*—*Prynne*⟩ ⟨the letter . . . had the *preciseness* of an imperial mandate—*Meredith*⟩ ⟨there was a certain amount of *preciseness* about the young man, and his approach to Texas was in the best striped-trousers tradition—*T. D. Clark*⟩
**preclude** *prevent, obviate, avert, ward
*Ana* *hinder, obstruct, impede, block, bar: *stop, discontinue, quit, cease: *exclude, eliminate, shut out, debar
**precocious** untimely, forward, *premature, advanced
*Ana* *immature, unmatured, unripe
*Ant* backward
**precursor** *forerunner, harbinger, herald
*Ana* *sign, mark, token, symptom: antecedent, determinant, *cause, reason
**predicament, dilemma, quandary, plight, scrape, fix, jam,**

**pickle** can all denote a situation from which one does or can extricate himself only with difficulty. **Predicament** carries the implication that the situation constitutes a problem for those who are involved in it and may additionally imply lack of freedom to do what one wishes or finds essential for some reason, or it may imply deep perplexity as to ways out of the situation ⟨advice . . . may be of such nature that it will be painful to reject and yet impossible to follow it; and in this *predicament* I conceive myself to be placed—*Crabbe*⟩ ⟨the *predicament* with which our civilization now finds itself confronted—the problem, namely, how to find healthy, happy leisure for all the working millions who are now being liberated by machines—*L. P. Smith*⟩ **Dilemma** applies to a situation which constitutes a predicament from which one can escape only by a choice of equally unpleasant or unsatisfactory alternatives ⟨faced with a *dilemma:* if they discard obsolete headings, the librarians may suffer; and if they do not discard them, the user may be penalized—*Lawler*⟩ **Quandary** differs from *dilemma* chiefly in its stress on puzzlement or perplexity; in fact, this implication is often so emphasized that the suggestion of a dilemma or an unavoidable choice between alternatives is lost or obscured ⟨he was in a *quandary* as to how he could keep his appointment⟩ ⟨all his *quandaries* terminated in the same catastrophe; a compromise—*Disraeli*⟩ The remaining words all definitely imply a difficulty, often a very disagreeable situation. **Plight** suggests an unfortunate, trying, or unhappy situation ⟨the *plight* in which the world finds itself today—*Hobson*⟩ ⟨the *plight* of the ten million forgotten men and women living at or below the destitution level—*Crossman*⟩ **Scrape** applies to a specific difficulty in which one is involved through one's own fault; often it suggests a being in disgrace or disfavor ⟨he escapes from trouble only to become idiotically conceited; and . . . plunges dementedly into a more ghastly *scrape*—*Swinnerton*⟩ **Fix** and **jam** are somewhat casual terms that stress involvement and entanglement from which extrication is difficult ⟨he will be in a *fix* if he doesn't settle his debts⟩ ⟨they get sick and it puts them in a *jam* and they end up under a pile of bills—*Basso*⟩ **Pickle** applies to a particularly distressing or sorry plight ⟨but when I was left ashore in Melbourne I was in a pretty *pickle.* I knew nobody, and I had no money—*Shaw*⟩
*Ana* *state, situation, condition, posture: pass, pinch, strait, emergency, exigency, *juncture
**predicate** *vb* affirm, declare, profess, *assert, aver, protest, avouch, avow, warrant
**predict** *foretell, forecast, prophesy, prognosticate, augur, presage, portend, forebode
*Ana* *foresee, foreknow, divine: *warn, forewarn, caution: surmise, *conjecture, guess
**predilection, partiality, prepossession, prejudice, bias** are comparable when they mean an attitude of mind which predisposes one to make a certain choice or judgment or to take a certain view without full consideration or reflection. **Predilection** implies a strong liking that results from one's temperament, one's principles, or one's previous experience and that predisposes one to prefer certain kinds of things (as friends, books, foods, or methods) or to accept a thing without reference to any other test ⟨a *predilection* for the strange and whimsical—*Coleridge*⟩ ⟨one or two authors of fiction for whom I have a *predilection*—*Benson*⟩ **Partiality** implies a disposition to favor a particular person or thing because of some predilection or, more often, because of undue fondness or partisanship; it may connote unfairness ⟨show *partiality* in appointments to office⟩ ⟨fond *partiality* for their own daughters' performance, and total indifference to any other person's—

---

A colon (:) separates groups of words discriminated. An asterisk (*) indicates place of treatment of each group.

*Austen*⟩ ⟨I have a *partiality* for a man who isolates an issue and pleads to it, not all around the bush—*Cozzens*⟩ **Prepossession** implies a fixed idea or conception in the light of which a new person, new idea, or new experience is judged ⟨no approach opens on anything except from its own point of view and in terms of its own *prepossessions*— *Blackmur*⟩ ⟨the *prepossessions* of childhood and youth— *Dugald Stewart*⟩ **Prejudice** applies to a judgment made before evidence is available and typically to an unfavorable preconception marked by suspicion and antipathy ⟨those who use their reason do not reach the same conclusions as those who obey their *prejudices*—*Lippmann*⟩ ⟨I do not think I speak only from my *prejudices,* although in justice I must admit that I approached Riesman's work with animus—*Mailer*⟩ **Bias** implies a lack of balance or distortion in one's judgment owing to the pull in a predictable or consistent direction of a predilection or a prepossession or of partiality or prejudice and a resulting inclination in favor of or against a person or thing ⟨it is as well that you be able to allow for my personal *bias*—*Shaw*⟩ ⟨the most pernicious kind of *bias* consists in falsely supposing yourself to have none—*Moberly*⟩
*Ana* \*leaning, propensity, proclivity, flair: bent, turn, knack, aptitude, \*gift
*Ant* aversion

**predispose** dispose, \*incline, bias
*Ana* influence, sway, \*affect, touch, impress, strike

**predominant** \*dominant, paramount, preponderant, preponderating, sovereign
*Ana* controlling, directing, conducting, managing (see CONDUCT *vb*): \*prevailing, prevalent: \*chief, principal, leading, main, foremost
*Con* \*subordinate, secondary, dependent, subject

**preeminent** surpassing, transcendent, superlative, \*supreme, peerless, incomparable
*Ana* \*dominant, predominant, paramount: excelling *or* excellent, outdoing, outstripping (see corresponding verbs at EXCEED): \*consummate, finished

**preempt** \*arrogate, usurp, appropriate, confiscate
*Ana* \*take, seize, grasp, grab: \*exclude, eliminate, shut out, debar

**preen** plume, \*pride, pique
*Ana* congratulate, \*felicitate

**preface** *n* \*introduction, prologue, prelude, foreword, exordium, preamble

**prefatory** \*preliminary, introductory, preparatory
*Ana* preparing, fitting, readying (see PREPARE)

**prefer** 1 \*choose, select, elect, opt, pick, cull, single
*Ana* accept, \*receive, admit, take: \*approve, endorse, sanction: favor, \*oblige, accommodate
2 \*offer, proffer, tender, present

**preferable** \*better, superior

**preference** selection, election, \*choice, option, alternative
*Ana* \*predilection, prepossession, partiality

**preferment** \*advancement, promotion, elevation
*Ana* advance, progress (see under ADVANCE *vb* 2): rising *or* rise, ascending *or* ascent (see corresponding verbs at RISE)

**pregnant** meaningful, significant, \*expressive, eloquent, sententious
*Ana* weighty, momentous, consequential, significant, important (see corresponding nouns at IMPORTANCE)

**prejudice** *n* bias, partiality, prepossession, \*predilection
*Ana* predisposition, disposition, inclination (see corresponding verbs at INCLINE): \*leaning, penchant

**preliminary** *adj* Preliminary, introductory, preparatory, prefatory describe something that serves to make ready the way for something else. **Preliminary** suggests reference to what must be done or made ready or acquired before

entrance into some definitive state or activity becomes possible ⟨the small amount of trouble involved in this *preliminary* measure will prove to be well worthwhile in avoiding muddle—*Dowdeswell*⟩ ⟨a *preliminary* education obtained at home and in the local schools—*Phalen*⟩ ⟨the ideal of cultivation cannot be appealed to as a standard without *preliminary* explanations and interpretations— *Eliot*⟩ ⟨the scientific spirit demands . . . a wish to find out the truth. . . . There must be *preliminary* uncertainty, and subsequent decision according to the evidence—*Russell*⟩ **Introductory** usually implies reference to the first steps in a process and therefore seldom applies to what is a prerequisite, as does *preliminary,* but rather to what sets an action, a work, or a process going ⟨the *introductory* scene should present the situation to be developed⟩ ⟨an *introductory* sketch of equity courts and their jurisdiction— *Wilkinson*⟩ **Preparatory** comes close to *preliminary* in meaning, but it throws the emphasis upon matters that should be attended to in order to make a person or thing ready for what ensues or may ensue ⟨take *preparatory* measures against a possible air raid⟩ ⟨a note on sources and a bibliography . . . indicate the wide range of the author's *preparatory* reading—*Bruun*⟩ **Prefatory** usually suggests not absolute need of *preparation* but a desire on the part of someone to prepare others (as for reading, for hearing, for action, or for understanding) ⟨remarks *prefatory* to the customary toasts⟩ ⟨he introduces each of them with a really distinguished little group of *prefatory* passages—*Bierstedt*⟩
*Ana* \*primary, primal: \*elementary, elemental: basic, \*fundamental

**prelude** \*introduction, prologue, preface, foreword, exordium, preamble

**premature, untimely, forward, advanced, precocious** are comparable though rarely interchangeable when they mean unduly early in coming, happening, or developing. **Premature** applies usually to something which takes place before its due or proper time ⟨a *premature* birth⟩ ⟨a *premature* announcement⟩ or comes into existence before it is fully grown or developed or ready for presentation ⟨a *premature* baby⟩ ⟨a *premature* conclusion⟩ or to actions or persons that manifest overhaste or impatience ⟨I have been a little *premature,* I perceive; I beg your pardon—*Austen*⟩ **Untimely** usually means little more than unseasonable but when it is applied to something which comes or occurs in advance of its due or proper time, it approaches very close to *premature* in meaning; the term, however, applies not so often to what begins a life or outward existence before its proper time as to what ends or destroys a life, a season, or a growing or developing thing before it has run its normal, natural, or allotted course ⟨*untimely* falling of fruit from a tree⟩ ⟨the *untimely* death of the son and heir⟩ ⟨the *untimely* frosts that brought summer's beauty to an end⟩ ⟨whose harvest . . . perished by *untimely* blight—*Brontë*⟩ **Forward** applies chiefly to young living things or to growing crops, but also sometimes to seasons, that show signs of progress beyond those that are normal or usual for things of its kind at the time in question ⟨an unusually *forward* spring⟩ ⟨a child very *forward* in mental development for his age⟩ **Advanced** tends to supplant *forward* when by comparison with other persons, other growing things, or other seasons of the same kind or class the one so described is notably ahead of the others ⟨the most *advanced* children in the school⟩ ⟨conflict between the economic interests of the *advanced* and backward peoples—*Hobson*⟩ **Precocious** basically implies an exceptional earliness in development (as in the germinating of seeds, the flowering of plants, the occurring of a process, or especially in the maturing

of the mind) ⟨inhibition of *precocious* germination of seeds—*Chronica Botanica*⟩ ⟨a *precocious* youth bursting with ideas—*Henry Miller*⟩ The term is also applied to qualities, conditions, or circumstances which properly belong to maturity but come or belong to one who is otherwise immature ⟨his *precocious* dignities were hard for youth to support without arrogance—*Buchan*⟩ ⟨Shaw is dramatically *precocious*, and poetically less than immature—*T. S. Eliot*⟩
*Ana* *immature, unmatured, unripe, unmellow: abortive, fruitless (see FUTILE): *precipitate, hasty, sudden, abrupt
*Ant* matured
**premeditated** *deliberate, considered, advised, designed, studied
*Ana* intended, purposed, meant (see INTEND): *voluntary, intentional, willful
*Ant* unpremeditated: casual, accidental —*Con* *precipitate, abrupt, headlong, hasty, sudden
**premise** *n* postulate, posit, presupposition, presumption, assumption (see under PRESUPPOSE)
*Ana* ground, *reason: proposition, *proposal
**premise** *vb* postulate, posit, *presuppose, presume, assume
**premium, prize, award, reward, meed, guerdon, bounty, bonus** are comparable when they mean something which is bestowed upon a person as a recompense for cooperation, greater effort, superior merit, or supremacy in competition. **Premium** is applied usually to something extra or additional that serves as an incentive to buy, sell, loan, compete, or strive ⟨the worker who does more . . . is rewarded by a *premium*, which is usually a percentage of the amount the additional work would cost—*G. D. Halsey*⟩ ⟨racking their brains last fall for a new *premium* that would intrigue . . . the breakfast-food public—*Cerf*⟩ ⟨ask a *premium* as well as interest for a loan⟩ **Prize** is applied to something which is striven for or, sometimes, which may be won by chance; it is bestowed upon the winner in a contest or competition or in a lottery ⟨bridge *prizes*⟩ ⟨a *prize* for the best composition⟩ ⟨at last the Dodo said, "Everybody has won, and all must have *prizes*" —*Lewis Carroll*⟩ In extended use *prize* commonly implies effort, struggle, and uncertainty in the seeking and often imputes value or worth to what is sought or competed for ⟨let a man contend to the uttermost for his life's set *prize*, be it what it will!—*Browning*⟩ ⟨he had embarked early upon that desperate game of which the *prize* was a throne, and the forfeit, life—*Repplier*⟩ ⟨the leading chairmanships are regarded as great *prizes*—*Nevins*⟩ **Award** implies both a decision of judges and a bestowal of a prize or an honor; it is therefore often preferred to *prize* when the recipients have not been competitors in the strict sense but have in their work or performances fulfilled the conditions required by those who offer prizes ⟨receive an *award* for civic service⟩ ⟨the urge to make the most of ourselves and to get *awards* varying with our success—*J. T. Adams*⟩ *Award* is also applicable to the act of awarding a prize or to the decision in a particular competition ⟨the judges may conceivably find themselves . . . unable to make an *award* —*Barkham*⟩ **Reward** strongly involves the idea of recompense for something good or meritorious or ironically for something evil; it may be used in reference to a prize or premium only when that has been earned (as by effort or sacrifice); thus, a winner of a *prize* for the best novel of the year may feel that he has been given a *reward* for intense effort; a *reward* is offered for the return of a lost article ⟨he scorned to take a *reward* for doing what in justice he ought to do—*Steele*⟩ ⟨it may come as a shock to the cynical that the mere embrace of wickedness is no guarantee of financial *reward*—*Sat. Review*⟩ **Meed** and **guerdon** are close synonyms of *reward*, often employed

without distinction, but the former tends to suggest a reward recognizing merit and proportioned to it, and the latter a prize or honor conferred as a reward ⟨he must not float upon his watery bier unwept, and welter to the parching wind, without the *meed* of some melodious tear— *Milton*⟩ ⟨finds his *guerdon* in the consciousness of work done perfectly—*Beerbohm*⟩ ⟨verse, like the laurel, its immortal *meed*, should be the *guerdon* of a noble deed— *Cowper*⟩ **Bounty** and *bonus* are applicable chiefly to a sum of money or its equivalent given as a premium or reward. **Bounty** is usually applied to a premium promised by a government or governmental agency as an inducement to some act ,(as enlistment in the army or navy, emigration to a distant colony, or destruction of noxious animals or pests) or as a subsidy to industry ⟨the State pays a *bounty* for every wildcat killed⟩ ⟨generous *bounties* for enlistment were offered by federal, state, and local authorities—*T. A. Bailey*⟩ **Bonus**, in contrast, is usually applied to something given over and above what is regularly received or due, either as a reward or encouragement or as a distribution of surplus ⟨a soldier's *bonus*⟩ ⟨the subsidies became only a *bonus* for inefficiency—*T. W. Arnold*⟩ ⟨*bonus* . . . includes extra payments for night work, hazardous work, regular attendance, and overtime, as well as any annual or regular allotment such as a Christmas *bonus*—*Glossary of Currently-Used Wage Terms*⟩ ⟨the reader is given a *bonus* of material not ordinarily found in meteorology texts—*Science*⟩
*Ana* *gift, present, gratuity, favor: enhancement, intensification, heightening (see corresponding verbs at INTENSIFY)
**preoccupied** *abstracted, absent, absentminded, distraught
*Ana* *intent, engrossed, absorbed: *forgetful, oblivious, unmindful
**preparatory** *preliminary, introductory, prefatory
*Ana* fitting, preparing, qualifying, readying, conditioning (see PREPARE)
**prepare, fit, qualify, condition, ready** are comparable when they mean to make someone or something ready. **Prepare** is the most inclusive of these terms; it implies a process, often a complicated process, involving a making ready, a getting ready, or a putting in readiness one or more persons or things ⟨*prepare* ground for a crop⟩ ⟨*prepare* a corpse for burial⟩ ⟨*prepare* a person for bad news⟩ ⟨made a few notes for a paper I was *preparing*—*Dahl*⟩ **Fit** is more limited in its scope than *prepare*: it suggests a making a person or thing fit for or suitable to a particular end or objective ⟨accomplishments, *fitting* him to shine both in active and elegant life—*Irving*⟩ ⟨I had *fitted* myself to do everything, from sweeping out to writing the editorials— *White*⟩ ⟨the soldier's efforts to *fit* himself into the new world made possible by his sweat and blood—*Wecter*⟩ **Qualify** (see also MODERATE) stresses the implication that a person's fitness for a duty, office, function, or status requires the fulfillment of some necessary conditions, such as taking certain courses of study or training, an examination, or an oath ⟨do not let druggists prescribe for you; they are not *qualified* to treat syphilis—*Fishbein*⟩ ⟨his extensive knowledge of foreign languages specially *qualified* him for such service—*A. P. Wills*⟩ **Condition** implies a getting into or a bringing to the condition that is proper or necessary for a person or, more often, a thing to satisfy a particular purpose or use ⟨*condition* air by purification, humidification, and adjustment of temperature⟩ ⟨*condition* an athletic team by exercise and practice⟩ ⟨*condition* cattle for show or market⟩ **Ready** emphasizes a putting a thing into order, especially for use, or a making ready a person for action ⟨*ready* a bedroom for the use of a guest⟩ ⟨the whole town took part in helping to *ready* the outdoor

A colon (:) separates groups of words discriminated. An asterisk (*) indicates place of treatment of each group.

theater—*Marguerite Johnson*⟩ ⟨the expedition *readied* itself during the summer—*Handlin*⟩
*Ana* *provide, supply, furnish: endow, endue, *dower: equip, outfit (see FURNISH): predispose, dispose, *incline

**preponderant, preponderating** *dominant, predominant, paramount, sovereign
*Ana* *supreme, preeminent, transcendent, surpassing: outstanding, salient, signal (see NOTICEABLE)

**prepossession** partiality, prejudice, bias, *predilection
*Ana* bent, turn, knack, aptitude, *gift: *leaning, penchant: predisposition, inclination (see corresponding verbs at INCLINE)

**preposterous** absurd, *foolish, silly
*Ana* *irrational, unreasonable: bizarre, grotesque, *fantastic

**prerequisite** requisite, *requirement
*Ana* necessity, *need, exigency

**prerogative** *right, privilege, perquisite, appanage, birthright
*Ana* immunity, *exemption: *claim, title: *freedom, license, liberty

**presage** *n* *foretoken, prognostic, omen, augury, portent
*Ana* *sign, symptom, mark, token: forewarning, warning (see WARN)

**presage** *vb* augur, portend, forebode, prognosticate, *foretell, predict, forecast, prophesy
*Ana* *indicate, betoken, bespeak: signify, import, denote, *mean

**prescribe** 1 *dictate, ordain, decree, impose
*Ana* order, *command, enjoin, bid: exact, *demand, require
2 **Prescribe, assign, define** mean to fix arbitrarily or authoritatively for the sake of order or of a clear understanding. **Prescribe** stresses dictation, especially by one in command, and usually implies that the aim is to give explicit directions or clear guidance to those who accept one's authority or are bound to obey one's injunctions ⟨the Constitution *prescribes* the conditions under which it may be amended⟩ ⟨the attending physician *prescribes* the medicines for his patient⟩ ⟨the fixed routine of *prescribed* duties—*Wilde*⟩ ⟨the code of behavior which the culture *prescribes* for child training—*Franz Alexander*⟩ **Assign** (see also ALLOT, ASCRIBE) usually has some suggestion of allotment or ascription; it implies arbitrary but not despotic determination for the sake of some practical end such as harmony in operation or functioning, the proper distribution of a number of things, or the settlement of a dispute by agreement ⟨the city charter *assigns* the duties of each elected official and the limits of his authority⟩ ⟨the clause, *assigning* original jurisdiction to the supreme court—*John Marshall*⟩ ⟨impersonal words, such as those *assigning* latitude, longitude, and date—*Russell*⟩ **Define** implies an intent to mark boundaries between things so as to prevent confusion, conflict, or overlapping ⟨the issues here are not too well *defined,* but deliberation at this point may be fruitful in that respect—*Terry Southern*⟩ ⟨obscure symbolisms which *define* the relation of various age groups to each other—*Sapir*⟩ ⟨the Constitution of the United States prescribes the powers of the government, assigns the limits to each, and *defines* the functions of each branch⟩
*Ana* *set, settle, fix, establish: direct, enjoin, instruct, order, *command

**prescription** *receipt, recipe

**presence** *bearing, deportment, demeanor, mien, port
*Ana* personality, individuality (see DISPOSITION): aspect, *appearance, look

**present** *n* *gift, gratuity, favor, boon, largess
*Ana* contribution, *donation, benefaction: grant, subven-

tion (see APPROPRIATION)

**present** *vb* 1 *give, bestow, confer, donate, afford
*Ana* *grant, award, accord
2 *offer, tender, proffer, prefer
*Ana* exhibit, display, parade, *show: advance, *adduce, allege, cite

**presentiment** misgiving, foreboding, *apprehension
*Ana* *fear, dread, alarm, terror: foretaste, anticipation, *prospect: disquieting *or* disquietude, discomposing *or* discomposure, disturbance, perturbation (see corresponding verbs at DISCOMPOSE)

**presently, shortly, soon, directly** are comparable when they mean after a little while or before long. **Presently** carries this as its chief meaning; it is a term of rather vague implication as to the time indicated ⟨the doctor will be here *presently*⟩ ⟨he said he would tell them the full story *presently*⟩ ⟨I shall forget you *presently,* my dear, so make the most of this, your little day—*Millay*⟩ ⟨I cannot attend to this at once but will do so *presently*⟩ **Shortly** is often less vague as to the exact time indicated; it frequently retains one of its earlier implications of following quickly or with little delay ⟨your father will be home *shortly,* for it is after five o'clock⟩ ⟨the ship will leave the wharf *shortly,* but perhaps you can catch it⟩ ⟨the two concluding volumes which will appear *shortly*—*P. H. Douglas*⟩ ⟨questions of vital importance came up for solution *shortly* after his appointment—*Knott*⟩ **Soon** (see also EARLY) implies that the thing narrated or predicted happened or will happen without much loss of time; otherwise the term is indefinite and may suggest any length of time that seems short, depending on the nature of the matter involved ⟨they will *soon* repent their anger⟩ ⟨the rout *soon* became general⟩ ⟨the doctor will see you very *soon*⟩ ⟨the plants *soon* took root⟩ **Directly** often replaces its more basic sense of without delay by a value in which it is interchangeable with *shortly* and implies with little, or a minimum of, delay ⟨I shall be back *directly* after sundown—*Hichens*⟩ ⟨I expect Rachel in *directly,* as she said she should not stay a moment—*Henning*⟩

**preserve** *vb* *save, conserve
*Ana* *rescue, deliver, redeem, ransom: protect, guard, safeguard (see DEFEND)

**press** *n* throng, crush, *crowd, mob, rout, horde
*Ana* *multitude, army, host, legion

**press** *vb* **Press, bear, bear down, squeeze, crowd, jam** mean to exert pressure upon something or someone continuously or for a length of time. They are not close synonyms because of added implications and connotations which often give them distinct or specific senses. **Press** fundamentally implies an effect involving a weighing upon or a steady pushing or thrusting and may suggest little more than this ⟨*press* down the soil with his feet⟩ ⟨the crowd *pressed* against them⟩ ⟨*press* clothes with a hot iron⟩ More often, however, the word is used in any of several extended senses in which it additionally implies such ideas as constraint or compulsion ⟨he *pressed* the agitated girl into a seat—*Hardy*⟩ or urgency in driving or in prosecuting ⟨the work was *pressed* forward with the same feverish haste—*Henry Adams*⟩ ⟨you see, my people believe Gideon killed Hobart, and are determined to *press* the matter—*Rose Macaulay*⟩ or importunity in urging ⟨next morning, though they were *pressed* to stay, the lama insisted on departure—*Kipling*⟩ ⟨she *pressed* me to take some cream crackers also—*Joyce*⟩ or, especially in the intransitive, a pushing or shoving to an objective (as in great numbers or with speedy movement) ⟨he *pressed* on rapidly . . . towards what was evidently a signal light—*Hardy*⟩ **Bear** (see also CARRY, BEAR 3) implies the exertion of weight or of pressure upon another person or thing

⟨the ceiling *bears* down upon the columns⟩ ⟨misfortune *bore* heavily upon him⟩ Like *press,* the term has extended use; it and **bear down** may imply the achievement of any end consistent with the action of pressing down or heavily upon ⟨Clan Alpine's best are backward *borne—Scott*⟩ ⟨his activity and zeal *bore down* all opposition—*Macaulay*⟩ **Squeeze** usually implies the exertion of pressure on both sides or on all sides strongly enough and for a long enough time to accomplish a flattening, a crushing, a shaping, an emptying, or a compression ⟨in washing silk stockings be sure to *squeeze* them, not wring them⟩ ⟨the child had *squeezed* the wax doll out of shape⟩ Usually, however, the term carries an added implication that gives it an extended or specific meaning while often retaining its basic implication; sometimes it implies nothing more than an expression of affection ⟨he *squeezed* his friend's hand⟩ but at other times it implies such a different idea as extraction ⟨*squeeze* the juice from a lemon⟩ ⟨approximates a laugh formed by . . . *squeezing* guttural sounds out of the throat—*Pynchon*⟩ or eliciting with difficulty ⟨we *squeezed* out of him an admission that he was leaving⟩ or extortion ⟨*squeezing* the people . . . of all the wealth that could be drained out of them—*Froude*⟩ Squeeze is also susceptible to use even when there is no suggestion of exerting force on another but a clear suggestion of forcing someone, often oneself, or something into a space that is extremely small or is very circumscribed ⟨*squeeze* through a half-opened window⟩ ⟨*squeezes* his hand into the hole and grasps the prize—*Stevenson-Hamilton*⟩ **Crowd** (see also PACK) implies the exertion of pressure upon and usually suggests such a force as a number of persons or of things closely packed together ⟨great numbers of the birds were *crowded* to death⟩ ⟨I hope not too many try to *crowd* in here at once. It isn't a very big room—*Steinbeck*⟩ ⟨never have more startling twists been *crowded* into the concluding scene of a melodrama—*J. M. Brown*⟩ ⟨the multitude of weeds *crowded* out the flowers⟩ Sometimes *crowd* implies pressure exerted by one or more persons in pushing or shoving through a crowd ⟨the speakers *crowded* their way through the throng to the platform⟩ **Jam** in its most frequent meaning carries an implication of being wedged in so that pressure on all sides ensues and movement or escape is made impossible ⟨the courts need not be *jammed* with negligence cases—*S. H. Hofstadter*⟩ ⟨just above McCauslin's, there is a rocky rapid, where logs *jam* in the spring—*Thoreau*⟩ ⟨traffic was completely *jammed* by the crowd—*Current Biog.*⟩ Sometimes, however, the term implies not pressure upon all sides but (as in reference to a gun, an engine, or a machine) the presence of an obstacle or an obstruction or the displacement of a part which prevents operation ⟨her propeller got foul of a rope, so that the shaft was *jammed,* and the engines could not be worked—*Herschell*⟩

*Ana* *push, thrust, propel, shove: drive, impel, *move: *pack, cram, stuff, ram

**pressing** *adj* **Pressing, urgent, imperative, crying, importunate, insistent, exigent, instant** are comparable when they mean demanding or claiming attention and especially immediate attention. **Pressing** often implies directly or indirectly the use of pressure by persons in calling for immediate attention to their wishes ⟨managed to pay his most *pressing* debts⟩ ⟨without ever subordinating his high ideals to the *pressing* demands of popular opinion—*Cohen*⟩ but it may also imply, without reference to personal agents, a claim to quick attention which cannot be denied ⟨it was business of the most *pressing* importance which had brought them—*Doyle*⟩ ⟨it would be a great mistake for a government to concern themselves only with short-term problems, *pressing* as these are—*Attlee*⟩

**Urgent** is stronger than *pressing* and places greater stress upon the constraint or compulsion of attention (as by a vehement urging), and it also usually connotes the need of promptness (as in replying, considering, or relieving) ⟨an *urgent* telegram⟩ ⟨the *urgent* needs of the war—*Costain*⟩ ⟨the more power the people are given the more *urgent* becomes the need for some rational and well-informed superpower to dominate them—*Shaw*⟩ ⟨if human ingenuity fails in an *urgent* task, fate may take a hand—*Buchan*⟩ **Imperative** (see also MASTERFUL) stresses the obligatory nature of a task, need, or duty, but it also usually implies that immediate attention is essential ⟨I feel it my *imperative* duty to warn you⟩ ⟨a remonstrance had become *imperative—Butler* d. 1902⟩ ⟨military necessity makes it *imperative* that the bridge should be blown up—*Peter Forster*⟩ **Crying** stresses the demand for attention but adds the implication of the extreme or shocking conspicuousness of the need ⟨an organizer of genius in a day when order and discipline were the *crying* needs—*Malone*⟩ ⟨our *crying* need is for more blood donors⟩ **Importunate** carries a strong implication of pertinacity in demanding or claiming attention; often therefore it is applied to persons or to their acts ⟨an *importunate* beggar⟩ ⟨an *importunate* knocking at a door⟩ ⟨when people are *importunate,* and will not go away when asked, they had better come in—*Shaw*⟩ but it is also much used in reference to impersonal matters (as problems or difficulties) which persistently and naggingly make claims upon one's full and immediate attention ⟨the demands of the dance becoming . . . too *importunate* for a divided attention—*Austen*⟩ ⟨it is a work which ought to be studied by anyone to whom the relation of Church and State is an actual and *importunate* problem—*T. S. Eliot*⟩ Like *importunate,* **insistent** basically implies a quality of persons, that of insisting or maintaining or asserting persistently ⟨how continual and *insistent* is the cry for characters that can be worshiped—*Galsworthy*⟩ ⟨de Vaca was *insistent,* and Charles approached the table—*Hergesheimer*⟩ and it too is often used in reference to a quality which enforces attention by its perseverance or compels it by obtruding itself upon one's consciousness ⟨an *insistent* noise⟩ ⟨an *insistent* voice⟩ ⟨the *insistent* odor of fertilizer—*Amer. Guide Series: Md.*⟩ ⟨we who read poetry are ridden and haunted by no such *insistent* problem—*Lowes*⟩ **Exigent** implies less a demand for immediate attention than one for action (as by way of giving assistance or settling problems); nevertheless the term comes very close to *urgent* or *pressing* in its emphasis on the exacting or the imperative nature of that demand ⟨that *exigent* cry for help—*Clarendon*⟩ ⟨demands upon him had never been *exigent* before. He had selected a course of life which required only easy and congenial effort—*S. H. Adams*⟩ **Instant** may come very close to *urgent* and like it often implies a temporal pressure; distinctively it may suggest perseverance or the need of perseverance ⟨rejoicing in hope; patient in tribulation; continuing *instant* in prayer—*Rom* 12:12⟩ ⟨I thought there was not such *instant* haste —*Scott*⟩ ⟨the single-hearted force of him who sees the *instant* need—*Buchan*⟩ ⟨the need to study precision in writing has grown far more *instant* since men of science have abandoned the "universal language"—*Quiller-Couch*⟩

*Ana* immediate, *direct: demanding, claiming, requiring, exacting (see DEMAND): compelling, constraining, forcing, obliging (see FORCE)

**pressure** *stress, strain, tension

**prestige** *influence, authority, weight, credit

*Ana* ascendancy, *supremacy: *power, sway, dominion: reputation, repute, honor, glory, *fame

---

A colon (:) separates groups of words discriminated. An asterisk (*) indicates place of treatment of each group.

**presume** *presuppose, postulate, premise, posit, assume
*Ana* surmise, *conjecture: deduce, *infer, judge, gather, conclude

**presumption** presupposition, assumption, postulate, premise, posit (see under PRESUPPOSE)
*Ana* view, *opinion, conviction, belief: conjecture, surmise (see under CONJECTURE *vb*)

**presumptuous** *confident, assured, sanguine, sure
*Ana* self-confident, self-assured, self-possessed (see corresponding nouns at CONFIDENCE): presuming, assuming (see PRESUPPOSE): positive, cocksure, certain, *sure: arrogant, insolent, overbearing (see PROUD)

**presuppose,** presume, assume, postulate, premise, posit are comparable when they mean to take something for granted or as true or existent especially as a basis for action or reasoning. Their corresponding nouns **presupposition, presumption, assumption, postulate, premise, posit** when they denote something that is taken for granted or is accepted as true or existent are distinguishable in general by the same implications and connotations as the verbs. **Presuppose** and **presupposition,** the most inclusive of these words, need not imply dubiousness about what is taken for granted. At the one extreme they may suggest nothing more than a hazy or imperfectly realized belief that something exists or is true or an uncritical acceptance of some hypothesis, in either case casting doubt on what is taken for granted ⟨a lecturer who talks above the heads of his listeners *presupposes* too extensive a knowledge on their part⟩ ⟨a school of theology that *presupposed* the total depravity of human nature⟩ ⟨it *presupposes* an opposition between the end of the individual and that of the State, such as was entirely foreign to the Greek conception—*Dickinson*⟩ At the other extreme the terms may be used in reference to something that is taken for granted because it is the logically necessary antecedent of a thing known to be true or the truth of which is not presently in question ⟨an effect *presupposes* a cause⟩ ⟨so deliberate a murder *presupposes* a motive⟩ ⟨belief in the supernatural *presupposes* a belief in natural law—*Inge*⟩ **Presume** and **presumption** may imply conjecture ⟨I *presume* they are now in London⟩ but ordinarily they carry the implication that whatever is taken for granted is entitled to belief until it is disproved. Therefore one *presumes* only something for which there is justification in experience, or which has been shown to be sound in practice or in theory or which is the logical inference from such facts as are known ⟨until a man or an organization has been condemned by due process of law he or it must be *presumed* innocent—*Hutchins*⟩ ⟨the fact that a custom is ancient and is still revered creates a *presumption* in its favor⟩ ⟨it cannot be *presumed* that any clause in the constitution is intended to be without effect—*John Marshall*⟩ **Assume** and **assumption** stress the arbitrary acceptance as true of something which has not yet been proved or demonstrated or about which there is ground for a difference of opinion ⟨some debaters weaken their case by *assuming* too much⟩ ⟨for the sake of argument let us *assume* that the accident occurred as is contended⟩ ⟨I know of nothing more false in science or more actively poisonous in politics . . . than the *assumption* that we belong as a race to the Teutonic family—*Quiller-Couch*⟩ ⟨I . . . *assume* that one purpose of the purchase was to suppress competition—*Justice Holmes*⟩ ⟨she was amazed and at a loss. She had *assumed* that Elfine's family would be overjoyed at their offspring's luck—*Gibbons*⟩ **Postulate,** either as verb or noun, differs from *assume* or *assumption* in being more restricted in its application and more exact in its implications. One can *assume* or make an *assumption* at any point in a course of reasoning, but one *postulates* something or lays down a proposition as a *postulate* only as the groundwork for a single argument or for a chain of reasoning or for a system of thought. *Postulate,* therefore, has reference to one of the underlying assumptions, which are accepted as true but acknowledged as indemonstrable and without which thought or action or artistic representation is impossible because of the limitations of human knowledge or of human reason or of art ⟨the ordinary man always *postulates* the reality of time and of space⟩ ⟨the dramatist *postulates* certain conventions which it is necessary for the audience to accept⟩ ⟨belief in the uniformity of nature, which is said to be a *postulate* of science—*Russell*⟩ ⟨the prevailing theological system is one which *postulates* the reality of guidance by a personal God—*Huxley*⟩ ⟨what I'm *postulating* in all this . . . is that the unconscious, you see, has an enormous teleological sense—*Mailer*⟩ **Premise** is often used as though it were identical in meaning with *postulate. Premise,* the noun, in logic denotes a proposition, or one of the two propositions in a syllogism, from which an inference is drawn. In more general use it may refer to a proposition which is the starting point in an argument. But a premise is not a proposition that is frankly an assumption, as a postulate often is; it may have been previously demonstrated or it may be admitted as true or axiomatic, but it is always advanced as true and not as assumed ⟨his listeners could not assent to his conclusion because they doubted the truth of his *premises*⟩ ⟨begin with a simple statement which is the *premise* for all that I have to say—*F. C. James*⟩ *Premise,* the verb, means to lay down as a premise or to base on or introduce by a premise or other pertinent matter and usually refers to the broader rather than to the technical meaning of the noun ⟨he *premised* his argument on a proposition which all but a few of his readers accept as true⟩ ⟨it was quickly evident that the decision was not *premised* upon any abhorrence of the test oath technique—*New Republic*⟩ ⟨these observations are *premised* solely for the purpose of rendering more intelligible those which apply more directly to the particular case under consideration—*John Marshall*⟩ **Posit,** as noun and verb, comes close to *postulate* in implying the laying down of a proposition as a base for an argument, a line of reasoning, or a system of thought, but it may differ in suggesting subjective and arbitrary grounds rather than, as *postulate* regularly does, objective and rational grounds for selection of the proposition ⟨if she needs salvation, she will *posit* a savior—*Santayana*⟩ ⟨he did not *posit* a world of wormless apples to set off the fruit he reported in such wonderful detail—*Grattan*⟩ ⟨materialism at that time *posited* the premise that character was the product of environment, and this was the basis for Zola's naturalism—*Farrell*⟩ but even when it connotes actual falsity it remains very close to *postulate* ⟨such *posits* or postulated entities are myths from the standpoint of the level below them, the phenomenalistic level—*Hofstadter*⟩ ⟨kill or be killed, the sergeants cried, discriminating Die from Live, and spoke the truth. And also lied, *posited* false alternative—*Gibson*⟩
*Ana* surmise, *conjecture, guess: *infer, deduce, gather, judge

**presupposition** presumption, assumption, postulate, premise, posit (see under PRESUPPOSE)
*Ana* surmise, conjecture, guess (see under CONJECTURE *vb*): inference, deduction, judgment (see under INFER): belief, conviction, *opinion, view

**pretend** *assume, affect, simulate, feign, counterfeit, sham
*Ana* *disguise, dissemble, cloak, mask, camouflage: *deceive, delude, mislead, beguile

**pretense** 1 pretension, *claim, title
*Ana* plea, pretext, excuse, *apology, apologia: *right,

birthright, privilege

**2 Pretense, pretension, make-believe** are comparable though seldom interchangeable when they involve the idea of offering something false or deceptive as real or true. **Pretense** may denote false show in general, or the evidence of it ⟨she is utterly devoid of *pretense*⟩ ⟨there is too much *pretense* in his piety⟩ ⟨the *pretense* that eludes the detection of others and that which deceives the pretender himself—*Brownell*⟩ ⟨confuse dignity with pomposity and *pretense—Cerf*⟩ The term may apply also to an act that is performed, an appearance that is assumed, or a statement that is made in the hope that it will convince others of the truth or reality of something that is false or unreal ⟨rushing away from the discussion on the transparent *pretense* of quieting the dog—*Conrad*⟩ ⟨my mother's affectionate *pretense* of his being the head of the family—*Mary Austin*⟩ **Pretension** (see also CLAIM, AMBITION) is rarely used in place of *pretense* as a concrete act, appearance, or statement, but it is often used in the sense of false show or the evidence of it, with, however, somewhat differing implications. Where *pretense* in this general sense often implies hypocrisy or intentional deceit, *pretension* suggests rather an unwarranted assumption that one possesses certain desirable qualities or powers, and therefore more often implies overweening conceit or self-deception ⟨his disdain of affectation and prudery was magnificent. He hated all *pretension* save his own *pretension—Mencken*⟩ ⟨this mannerism which has become so offensive . . . is Roslyn's social *pretension*. Perhaps I should say intellectual *pretension*. She entertains people as if she were conducting a salon—*Mailer*⟩ ⟨annoyed with . . . the *pretensions* of simplicity and homeliness in her parlor—*Cheever*⟩ **Make-believe** applies usually to pretense or pretenses that arise not so much out of a desire to give others a false impression as out of a strong or vivid imagination (as that of children or poets who like to take what their fancies create as real or as true) ⟨in children, the love of *make-believe* usually expresses itself in games⟩ The term is occasionally used to denote the acceptance against one's better judgment of something manifestly unreal or untrue because of some power in the thing itself or in its accompaniments ⟨tells us that the *make-believe* of the stage is a higher reality than life outside—*Bentley*⟩

*Ana* humbug, fake, sham, fraud, deceit, deception, *imposture: affectation, *pose, air, mannerism

**pretension 1** *claim, title, pretense

*Ana* *right, privilege, prerogative: assertion, affirmation, declaration, protestation (see corresponding verbs at ASSERT)

**2** *pretense, make-believe

*Ana* *hypocrisy, sanctimony, cant: dissimulation, duplicity, guile, *deceit

**3** *ambition, aspiration

*Ana* hoping *or* hope, expectation (see corresponding verbs at EXPECT): dream, vision, *fancy

**pretentious 1** *showy, ostentatious

*Ana* *gaudy, garish, flashy: *ornate, flamboyant, florid, baroque, rococo

*Ant* unpretentious

**2** *ambitious, utopian

*Ana* aiming, aspiring, panting (see AIM *vb*): conspicuous, striking, arresting (see NOTICEABLE)

**preternatural** *supernatural, supranatural, miraculous, superhuman

*Ana* unnatural, anomalous (see IRREGULAR): *abnormal, atypical: outstanding, remarkable, salient (see NOTICEABLE): *exceptional

**pretext** excuse, plea, alibi, *apology, apologia

*Ana* ruse, *trick, maneuver, stratagem: *deception: justification, vindication, defending *or* defense (see corresponding verbs at MAINTAIN)

**pretty** bonny, comely, fair, *beautiful, lovely, handsome, good-looking, beauteous, pulchritudinous

*Ana* charming, attractive, alluring (see under ATTRACT): dainty, delicate, exquisite (see CHOICE *adj*)

**prevail** *induce, persuade, get

*Ana* *move, actuate, drive, impel: influence, *affect, impress, sway

**prevailing, prevalent, rife, current** are comparable when they mean general (as in circulation, acceptance, or use) especially in a given place or at a given time. **Prevailing** applies especially to something which is predominant or which generally or commonly obtains at the time or in the place indicated or implied ⟨the *prevailing* winds are westerly⟩ ⟨the *prevailing* opinion among booksellers⟩ ⟨their frankly barbarous outlook and *prevailing* grossness of expression—*Bridges-Adams*⟩ **Prevalent** applies especially to something which is general or very common over a given area or at a given time. The term, however, does not suggest, as *prevailing* usually suggests, a predominance in frequency or in favor; rather, it connotes a frequency without necessarily implying that it is the most frequent; thus, the *prevailing* or usual wind in a region is from the southeast, but southwest winds may, nevertheless, be *prevalent* there; colds and grippe are *prevalent* in northern states during the winter; a widely *prevalent* pronunciation of a word may not necessarily be the *prevailing* pronunciation ⟨so *prevalent* is urban blight that the nickname "Garden State" seems a macabre joke—*Armbrister*⟩ **Rife** adds to *prevalent* an implication such as the rapid spread of the thing so qualified, or a great increase in the number of its instances, or merely its commonness or abundance ⟨rumor is already *rife* here as to Dr. Trefoil's successor—*Trollope*⟩ ⟨in a national political campaign, when issues are hotly contested and prejudices are *rife—Mott*⟩ ⟨was a considerable poet himself in days when poets were *rife—Gogarty*⟩ **Current** applies especially to things (as language, philosophy, or fashion) that are constantly in process of change or development, or to things (as coins or diseases) that circulate constantly from one person or thing to another; hence, *current* so often describes what is widespread in its use, adoption, or acceptance at the time in question that it has come to imply the present if no other time is indicated; thus, *current* English is the English language of the present time; a *current* notion is one that is widely accepted at the moment; banknotes, postage stamps, or coins of the *current* series are those still being printed or minted for circulation or sale ⟨*current* styles in hats⟩ ⟨*current* tendencies in fiction⟩ ⟨a *current* practice⟩ However, when the term applies to things (as periodicals) that come out in a series or in installments, *current* describes the one appearing during the present period (as the week or month) or the latest to appear ⟨the *current* issue of a magazine⟩ ⟨the *current* installment of a new novel appearing serially in a periodical⟩ But *current* is often used in the place of the other words of this group when the time or place is definitely indicated and merely the passing from one person to another is stressed ⟨Shakespeare used the *current* language of his day—*J. R. Lowell*⟩ ⟨as *current* in her time, the Evangelical creed was simple—*Ellis*⟩ ⟨she had been given, at fourteen, the *current* version of her origin—*Wharton*⟩

*Ana* *dominant, predominant, preponderant: *common, ordinary, familiar: general, *universal

**prevalent** *prevailing, rife, current

*Ana* *common, ordinary, familiar: pervading, impreg-

---

A colon (:) separates groups of words discriminated. An asterisk (*) indicates place of treatment of each group.

nating, saturating (see PERMEATE): *usual, wonted, accustomed, customary

**prevaricate** *lie, equivocate, palter, fib

*Ana* evade, elude, *escape: *misrepresent, falsify, belie, garble

**prevent 1 Prevent, anticipate, forestall** can mean to be or get ahead of or to deal with beforehand, with reference especially to a thing's due time or to its actual occurrence or to the action of another. *Prevent* implies frustration (as of an intention or plan) or an averting (as of a threatened evil) or a rendering impossible (as by setting up an obstacle or obstacles) ⟨the surest way to *prevent* aggression is to remain strong enough to overpower and defeat any who might attack—*Lawrence*⟩ Sometimes the emphasis upon hindrance (see PREVENT 2) is so strong that other implications are nearly lost, but in the sense here considered advance provision or preparation against something possible or probable is clearly implied ⟨medical science knows how to limit these evils and can do much to *prevent* their destructiveness—*Eliot*⟩ ⟨steps had therefore to be taken to *prevent* or impede these unseemly displays—*Thornton*⟩ ⟨who stands safest? tell me, is it he? . . . whose *preventing* care in peace provides fit arms against a war?—*Pope*⟩ **Anticipate** (see also FORESEE) takes the place of *prevent* when merely getting ahead of another especially as a precursor or forerunner is implied ⟨most of the great European thinkers of the eighteenth and early nineteenth centuries were in some measure inspired, influenced, or *anticipated* by Shaftesbury—*Ellis*⟩ ⟨a "Teacher of Righteousness" who seemed in some ways to *anticipate* Jesus—*Edmund Wilson*⟩ Like *prevent*, *anticipate* sometimes suggests frustrating another in carrying out an intention or plan, but implies its prior performance or execution rather than interposition of obstacles to its performance ⟨he would probably have died by the hand of the executioner had not been *anticipated* by the populace—*Macaulay*⟩ ⟨in October came Commodore T. A. C. Jones, palpitating lest Great Britain *anticipate* him in seizing California—*H. I. Priestley*⟩ Distinctively, the word implies dealing with (as by using, paying, or acting) in advance of the due time or proper order but it often involves another implication which can be gathered only from the context; thus, one *anticipates* a payment on a loan by making a payment before it is due; one *anticipates* his salary by spending its equivalent before it is earned ⟨*anticipate* some details in telling a story⟩ **Forestall**, in what has become perhaps the less common meaning, carries over from its earliest sense so strong an implication of intercepting that it means merely to stop in its course ⟨something you were not in the least prepared to face, something you hurried to *forestall*—*Mary Austin*⟩ ⟨*forestalled* by the watchful Jelks who fetched it for him—*Dahl*⟩ But often the word loses most of its suggestion of intercepting and then implies beforehand action that serves to render a thing, and especially something inevitable, powerless to harm or merely useless ⟨to *forestall* public opinion and guide its judgment—*L. P. Smith*⟩ ⟨posterity will still be explaining me, long after I am dead. Why, then, should I *forestall* their labors? —*Rose Macaulay*⟩

*Ana* *frustrate, thwart, foil, baffle, balk: *arrest, check, interrupt: avoid, shun, eschew, evade, *escape

**2 Prevent, preclude, obviate, avert, ward** are comparable when they mean to hinder or stop something that may occur or, in the case of *prevent* and *preclude*, to hinder or stop someone from doing something. *Prevent* usually implies the existence of something which serves as an insurmountable obstacle or an impediment ⟨there is no law to *prevent* you from erecting a building on this spot⟩

⟨the authority of his presence and the purposefulness of his manner at least *prevent* the role becoming a minor one—*Bentley*⟩ ⟨he *prevents* an innocent man going to the gallows—*New Books*⟩ **Preclude** differs from *prevent* in stressing the existence of some situation or condition or the taking of anticipatory measures that effectually shuts out every possibility of a thing's occurring or of a person's doing something ⟨he makes everything so clear that all misunderstanding is *precluded*⟩ ⟨death *precluded* him from completing his investigation⟩ ⟨the doctrine . . . was adopted, not to promote efficiency but to *preclude* the exercise of arbitrary power—*Brandeis*⟩ ⟨the roar of the motor *precluded* further conversation—*Gerald Beaumont*⟩ **Obviate** usually implies the use of intelligence or forethought; *preclude* also often implies these but sometimes it suggests the operation of chance. The chief distinction between these words when anticipatory measures are implied is that *obviate* usually connotes an attempt to forestall disagreeable eventualities by clearing away obstacles or by disposing of difficulties ⟨the use of bills of exchange *obviates* the risk in transporting money from one country to another⟩ ⟨no care, no art, no organization of society, could *obviate* the inherent incompatibility of individual perfection with the course of nature—*Dickinson*⟩ **Avert** and **ward,** the latter usually with *off,* differ from the other words of this group in implying prevention of an approaching or oncoming evil. They suggest therefore immediate and effective measures in the face of what threatens. **Avert,** however, suggests the use of active measures to force back the evil before it is actually encountered ⟨*avert* a catastrophe by prompt action⟩ ⟨the satisfaction of *averting* war—*J. R. Green*⟩ ⟨it was very doubtful whether the consequences could be *averted* by sealing my lips—*Shaw*⟩ **Ward,** on the other hand, implies a close encounter and the use of defensive measures ⟨*ward* off an opponent's blow⟩ in order to avoid the evil or to diminish its disastrous effects ⟨*ward* off a chill with hot drinks⟩ ⟨a magic charm to *ward* off evil—*Herskovits*⟩ ⟨our nation has *warded* off all enemies—*Eisenhower*⟩

*Ana* *hinder, impede, obstruct, block, bar, dam: debar, shut out (see EXCLUDE): prohibit, *forbid, interdict, inhibit

*Ant* permit

**previous** foregoing, prior, *preceding, antecedent, precedent, former, anterior

*Ant* subsequent: consequent

**prey** *n* *victim, quarry

*Ana* *spoil, booty, prize

**price** *n* **Price, charge, cost, expense** can mean what is given or asked in payment for a thing or for its use, or for services. *Price* and *charge* in their ordinary nontechnical use commonly designate what is asked or demanded— in the case of **price,** especially for goods or commodities; in the case of **charge,** especially for services ⟨what is the *price* of this book?⟩ ⟨the *price* of meat has risen greatly⟩ ⟨the market *price* of wheat⟩ ⟨the *charge* for haulage⟩ ⟨goods delivered free of *charge* within a radius of one hundred miles⟩ ⟨there is a small *charge* for registering a deed⟩ In economics, however, *price* does not necessarily refer to a fixed sum of money asked by a seller, but to the quantity or number of units of one thing exchangeable in barter or sale for another thing ⟨labor was the first *price,* the original purchase money that was paid for all things— *Smith*⟩ *Charge,* especially in accounting, also applies to what is imposed on one as a financial burden ⟨the fixed *charges* of a business include rentals, taxes, interest, and liens⟩ *Cost* and *expense* in their ordinary nontechnical use apply to what is given or surrendered for something —*cost* often implying somewhat specifically the payment of the price asked and **expense** often designating the aggregate amount actually disbursed for something ⟨they found the *cost* of the piano made too severe a drain on their resources⟩ ⟨the *cost* of provisions⟩ ⟨traveling *expenses*⟩ ⟨the heavy *expense* of a long illness⟩ But *cost* sometimes replaces *price* with, however, a difference in connotation. Since *cost* applies to whatever must be given or sacrificed to obtain something, to produce something, or to attain some end whether it be money, labor, or lives or whether it is actually given or sacrificed, it, when replacing *price*, tends to suggest what will be taken or accepted from one in exchange rather than what the item is worth ⟨the *price* of this article is below the *cost* of its manufacture⟩ ⟨victory will be won only at great *cost* of life⟩ ⟨he felt that the *cost* in effort was greater than he could afford⟩ *Expense* also may denote expenditure especially but not only of money ⟨fresh news is got only by enterprise and *expense—Justice Holmes*⟩ ⟨a convenient way of producing the maximum amount of "copy" with the minimum *expense* of intellect—*Babbitt*⟩

**priceless** invaluable, precious, *costly, expensive, dear, valuable
*Ana* cherished, treasured, prized, valued (see APPRECIATE)

**prick** *vb* 1 punch, puncture, *perforate, bore, drill
*Ana* *enter, pierce, probe, penetrate: *cut, slit, slash
2 *urge, egg, exhort, goad, spur, prod, sic
*Ana* stimulate, excite, pique, *provoke: *activate, actuate, motivate: compel, constrain, *force

**pride** *n* Pride, vanity, vainglory are comparable when they mean the quality or the feeling of a person who is keenly or excessively aware of his own excellence or superiority. The same distinctions in implications and connotations are found in their corresponding adjectives **proud, vain, vainglorious. Pride** and **proud** may imply either justified or unjustified self-esteem, insofar as what one regards as a merit or a superiority is real or imagined, and insofar as the feeling manifests itself either in proper self-respect and distaste for what is beneath one's standards or in inordinate and arrogant conceit. In the "unjustified" interpretation, pride is a sin or vice and the antithesis of humility ⟨those that walk in *pride* he is able to abase—*Dan* 4:37⟩ ⟨*pride* in the sense of contemning others less gifted than herself deserves the two lowest circles of a vulgar woman's Inferno—*Holmes*⟩ ⟨he had gone on for years deceiving himself—too *proud*, too self-conscious, maybe just too stupid to realize it—*Styron*⟩ but in the "justified" interpretation, pride is a virtue or at least a highly pardonable, even commendable, feeling or quality that is the antithesis of shame and that spurs one to equal or better one's best or gives one rightful gratification ⟨take *pride* in our work⟩ ⟨*proud* of his skill in fencing⟩ ⟨the solemn *pride* that must be yours to have laid so costly a sacrifice upon the altar of freedom—*Lincoln*⟩ ⟨she might grieve . . . but she was gallant, she was *proud;* she would not whine—*Sackville-West*⟩ **Vanity** and **vain** imply an excessive desire to win the notice, approval, or praise of others; both connote an interest centered on oneself and often suggest a concentration on things of little or no importance relatively ⟨had . . . not the gay, tail-spreading peacock *vanity* of his son—*Carlyle*⟩ ⟨he was conceited and *vain*, and he was endlessly trying to enjoy what he thought he appeared to be in the eyes of others—*Farrell*⟩ ⟨looked only at himself; he had nothing but a small and worthless mortification, which was only wounded *vanity—Deland*⟩ **Vainglory** and **vainglorious** imply excessive pride which manifests itself in boastfulness and arrogant display of one's power, skill, or influence ⟨*vainglorious* boastings—*Irving*⟩ ⟨American historians . . . with much of the *vainglorious* pedantry that Irving

burlesqued—*Brooks*⟩ ⟨have blockaded their minds behind . . . walls of nationalistic egoism and *vainglory*, symptoms of collective paranoia—*Yale Review*⟩
*Ana* arrogance, haughtiness, superciliousness, disdainfulness *or* disdain, insolence (see corresponding adjectives at PROUD): complacency, smugness, priggishness (see corresponding adjectives at COMPLACENT): self-esteem, self-love, egotism, egoism, *conceit
*Ant* humility: shame

**pride** *vb* Pride, plume, pique, preen are all reflexive verbs meaning to congratulate oneself because of something one is, has, or has done or achieved. **Pride** usually implies a taking credit to oneself on or upon something that redounds to one's honor or gives just cause for pride in oneself ⟨he *prides* himself on his ancestry⟩ ⟨Mark *prided* himself upon maintaining outwardly a demeanor that showed not the least trace of overstrung nerves—*Mackenzie*⟩ ⟨he *prided* himself on his part in the new century, but he resisted the installation of a telephone—*Frank*⟩ **Plume** adds to *pride* the implication of a display of vanity or of a more obvious exhibition of one's gratification; the term usually suggests less justification than does *pride* ⟨the Viceroy *plumed* himself on the way in which he had instilled notions of reticence into his staff—*Kipling*⟩ ⟨Cicero *plumed* himself on flirting with disreputable actresses—*Buchan*⟩ ⟨authors who *plume* themselves on writing history with "popular appeal"—*L. B. Wright*⟩ **Pique** (see also PROVOKE 1) differs from *plume* chiefly in carrying a hint of stirred-up pride or satisfaction; usually the cause of the pride is a special accomplishment ⟨every Italian or Frenchman of any rank *piques* himself on speaking his own tongue correctly—*Walpole*⟩ ⟨"Pride," observed Mary, who *piqued* herself upon the solidity of her reflections, "is a very common failing, I believe" —*Austen*⟩ **Preen** is occasionally used in place of *plume*, sometimes with a slight suggestion of adorning oneself with one's virtues ⟨he *preened* himself upon his sapience—*Lowell*⟩ ⟨men have admired, in theory, feminine virtue and *preened* themselves on the fear they aroused in the timid sex—*Cunnington*⟩
*Ana* *boast, brag, vaunt, crow, gasconade: congratulate, *felicitate

**priggish** 1 smug, self-complacent, self-satisfied, *complacent
*Ana* righteous, ethical, *moral: conceited, egotistic, self-esteeming, self-loving (see corresponding nouns at CONCEIT)
2 *prim, prissy, prudish, puritanical, straitlaced, stuffy
*Ana* see those at PRIGGISH 1

**prim** *adj* Prim, priggish, prissy, prudish, puritanical, straitlaced, stuffy mean excessively concerned with what one regards as proper or right. *Prim* and *priggish* (see also COMPLACENT) both imply an excessive and conscious fastidiousness in manners and morals that often more or less displeases an observer. **Prim**, however, often suggests stiffness and preciseness of manner as well as extreme decorousness, and **priggish** connotes a more or less offensive, but not necessarily conscious, assumption of moral superiority, so that they are rarely interchangeable. Further, *prim* is often applied to the dress, words, or actions of persons but *priggish* is seldom referred to anything but the person or to something that directly reveals his personality ⟨in the reign of James I the conduct of ladies and gentlemen was not marked by the same *prim* propriety as in the reign of the highly respectable Victoria—*Ellis*⟩ ⟨Charlotte Lovell was meant to be an old maid . . . . There was something *prim* about her in spite of her fiery hair—*Wharton*⟩ ⟨a widower, a man with a *prim* sour mouth and an expression of eternal disapproval

all over his face—*Dahl*⟩ ⟨there is . . . no moralizing of that offensively *priggish* kind which the instinct of boys teaches them to despise and mistrust—*Pall Mall Gazette*⟩ ⟨it was, as you warned me, very expensive. But I have no *priggish* objections to a little luxury—*Ambler*⟩ **Prissy,** though sometimes very close to *prim* in meaning, is applied to a person who shows, or to a thing that manifests, an exaggerated sense of what is proper or precise; the term connotes sissiness but usually as a feminine concern for niceties of expression, of conduct, or of design and may imply a lack of forcefulness or virility ⟨an outspoken candidate who offended the *prissiest* members of his party⟩ ⟨shock words may wear out their welcome just as readily as *prissy* ones—*New Republic*⟩ ⟨a shockable, narrow, *prissy* people obeying the rules . . . and protecting their treasured, specialized pruderies—*Theodore Sturgeon*⟩ **Prudish** implies a modesty and decorousness so marked as to seem affected or overasserted; the term, however, seldom suggests pretense but rather an undue consciousness of propriety or fear of impropriety or an excessive sense of the importance of modesty and decorum ⟨a verse, not fettered in its movements, or *prudish* in its expressions—*Edinburgh Review*⟩ ⟨tried to condemn her own attitude as old-fashioned, *prudish*. There was no such thing as an adulteress anymore, she told herself—*Wouk*⟩ ⟨had become so serious, so *prudish* almost, since she had given up balls and taken to visiting the poor—*Wharton*⟩ **Puritanical,** often capitalized, may refer specifically to the religion of the Puritans especially as it showed itself in strict regulation of behavior, but in ordinary uncapitalized use it more often suggests only an excessive narrowness or illiberality in judgment (as of books, plays, or pictures), in regulation (as of manners and morals), or in narrowly determining the boundary between what is good and what is bad ⟨the *puritanical* suspicion of beauty⟩ ⟨that Fielding in his hatred for humbug should have condemned purity as *puritanical*, is clearly lamentable—*Stephen*⟩ ⟨he held old-fashioned and rather *puritanical* views as to the vice of luxury and the sin of idleness—*Woolf*⟩ ⟨afraid that if it became known he might jeopardize his position in the rather *puritanical* community, he avoided consulting any of the Coltertown doctors—*Elmer Rice*⟩ **Straitlaced** and **stuffy** are derogatory terms applicable to persons or things that are markedly puritanical or prudish; **straitlaced** refers more often to a person or his principles from a less subjective point of view than does **stuffy,** which is usually a term of contempt expressive of their effect upon the observer ⟨"*Stuffy,* my lord; it's an expression a good deal used in modern Society." "What does it mean?" "*Straitlaced,* my lord"—*Galsworthy*⟩ ⟨a *stuffy* book⟩ ⟨abiding by the rather involved, *stuffy* code of ethics—*Riggs*⟩ ⟨set himself incautiously to the business of assailing the *straitlaced* authorities of Boston—*Parrington*⟩
*Ana* precise, *correct, nice: *decorous, proper: *stiff, rigid, wooden

**primal** primordial, primitive, pristine, primeval, *primary, prime
*Ana* *ultimate, absolute, categorical: original, fresh, *new

**primary,** primal, primordial, primitive, pristine, primeval, prime mean first in some respect (as order, character, or importance). Something **primary** comes first in the order of development or of progression. Sometimes the term means little more than *initial* ⟨the *primary* lesion of a disease⟩ but sometimes it acquires the implications of *fundamental, elemental,* or *elementary,* and describes the part or element that is first (as in time or in importance) or one of such parts or elements in a complicated structure,

substance, or system ⟨the *primary* xylem tissue of a tree⟩ ⟨*primary* schools⟩ ⟨the raw material of music is sound. Sound is a *primary,* a "pure" medium . . . . It has no meaning except in a context—*Day Lewis*⟩ and at other times it means *original* in the sense of not being derived ⟨the *primary* colors⟩ ⟨the *primary* qualities of matter⟩ ⟨the *primary* cause⟩ ⟨basic research in the *primary* sciences such as physics and chemistry—*Univ. of Fla. Bulletin*⟩ But *primary* may convey little or no suggestion of a time order and imply superiority in importance, thereby coming close to *principal* ⟨the *primary* object of education⟩ ⟨the *primary* end of poetry⟩ ⟨all of us in the news business ought to remember that our *primary* responsibility is to the man who buys his newspaper, or turns on his radio, expecting . . . the whole truth—*Davis*⟩ **Primal** applies to what is primary in the sense of *initial, fundamental,* or *elemental* ⟨some who maintain that the regime of religious toleration has become possible only because we have lost the *primal* intensity of religious conviction—*Cohen*⟩ ⟨not philosophy, after all, not humanity, just sheer joyous power of song, is the *primal* thing in poetry—*Beerbohm*⟩ or to what goes back to the origin or to the beginnings, especially of the human race ⟨it hath the *primal* eldest curse upon't, a brother's murder—*Shak.*⟩ ⟨the Biblical vocabulary is compact of the *primal* stuff of our common humanity—*Lowes*⟩ ⟨ultimate issues, *primal* springs—*Kipling*⟩ **Primordial** applies to what serves as the starting point in a course of development or growth or is the earliest in order or in formation. The term often suggests a rudimentary quality or state; thus, the *primordial* ooze is thought of as the substance out of which the earth was formed; a *primordial* cell is in biology the first and least specialized of a line of cells ⟨*primordial* germ cells⟩ ⟨*primordial* man⟩ ⟨assuming that the sun, planets, and their satellites had all originated from a *primordial* mass of gas—*S. F. Mason*⟩ Something **primitive** belongs to or is associated with an early stage, often but not necessarily a remote stage, in the development of something (as the human race). Often, when used in reference to art or manufacture, the term suggests lack of knowledge of such modern techniques or conventions as perspective in painting or modes in mensurable music or automation in industry ⟨*primitive* potteries⟩ ⟨the symmetry of the body provides the archetype of *primitive* design in most religious art—*Binyon*⟩ When used in reference to persons, their ways of living, or their instincts, emotions, or laws, it usually suggests either a connection with a very rudimentary civilization or a retention of a character or quality associated with such a civilization ⟨a *primitive* but effective police inquiry—*T. S. Eliot*⟩ ⟨*primitive* laws to protect inheritance, to safeguard property—*Rose Macaulay*⟩ ⟨genuinely *primitive* traits that reveal themselves in the childhood of either the individual or the race—*Babbitt*⟩ ⟨he worked in the seed gardens, learned the *primitive* pharmacy of roots, barks, and herbs—*Genzmer*⟩ Often, however, the term merely stresses an opposition to what is highly civilized or sophisticated and therefore unduly complicated, and may suggest naturalness or simplicity ⟨life is very *primitive* here—which doesn't mean that one is getting down to anything fundamental, but only going back to something immediate and simple—*H. G. Wells*⟩ ⟨the town band, a very *primitive* affair, brings up the rear, playing "Yankee Doodle"—*Shaw*⟩ **Pristine** applies to something in its earliest and freshest and newest state ⟨an image of the *pristine* earth—*Wordsworth*⟩ ⟨the qualities of *pristine* Christianity⟩ ⟨restored to its *pristine* freshness⟩ ⟨a *pristine* form of air conditioning—*Mumford*⟩ **Primeval** in its basic sense applies to something which belongs to or is characteristic of the first ages of the earth ⟨for food you must still go to the earth and to the sea, as in *primeval* days—*Jefferies*⟩ ⟨drawings have a harsh, *primeval* definiteness, as though the world were in the throes of creation—*Eric Newton*⟩ Often, however, the term merely suggests extreme antiquity or the absence of all signs of human trespass or influence ⟨*primeval* ages⟩ ⟨behind the *primeval* curtain of trees and swamps the old tribal and pagan life went on—*Cutforth*⟩ **Prime** in its basic sense comes very close to *primordial* and *primitive* in designating what is first in order of time ⟨high heaven and earth ail from the *prime* foundation—*Housman*⟩ but in its more common use it applies specifically to what is first in rank, degree, or dignity ⟨makes his moral being his *prime* care—*Wordsworth*⟩ ⟨a matter of *prime* importance⟩ or sometimes to what is merely choice or excellent of its kind ⟨*prime* beef⟩ ⟨a *prime* claret⟩

**Ana** initiating *or* initial, beginning, commencing, starting (see corresponding verbs at BEGIN): elemental, *elementary: basic, *fundamental, radical: *chief, leading, principal

**Con** following, succeeding, ensuing (see FOLLOW): secondary, *subordinate

**prime** *adj* *primary, primal, primordial, primitive, pristine, primeval

**Ana** *chief, leading, principal, main: *choice, exquisite, recherché

**prime mover** *origin, source, provenance, provenience, inception, root

**primeval** pristine, primitive, primordial, primal, *primary, prime

**Ana** aboriginal, *native, indigenous, autochthonous: original, *new

**primitive** *primary, primal, primordial, pristine, primeval, prime

**Ana** *fundamental, basic, radical: elemental, *elementary: aboriginal, *native

**primordial** 1 primeval, pristine, primitive, primal, *primary, prime
2 *initial, original

**princely** *kingly, regal, royal, queenly, imperial

**Ana** *luxurious, sumptuous, opulent: munificent, bountiful, bounteous, openhanded, *liberal

**principal** *adj* *chief, main, leading, foremost, capital

**Ana** *dominant, predominant, paramount: vital, cardinal, fundamental, *essential: preeminent, *supreme, superlative

**principally** mainly, chiefly, mostly, *largely, greatly, generally

**principle,** axiom, fundamental, law, theorem are comparable when they denote a proposition or other formulation stating a fact or a generalization accepted as true and basic. **Principle** applies to a generalization that provides a basis for reasoning or a guide for conduct or procedure ⟨the *principle* of free speech⟩ ⟨his remarkable grasp of *principle* in the remaining field, that of historical geography—*Farrington*⟩ ⟨the same hankering as their pious ancestors for a cozy universe, a closed system of certainties erected upon a single *principle*—*Muller*⟩ ⟨the *principle* was established that no officer or employee . . . was entitled to any classified information whatever unless it was necessary for the performance of his duties —*Baxter*⟩ ⟨I do not mean to assert this pedantically as an absolute rule, but as a *principle* guiding school authorities—*Russell*⟩ **Axiom** can apply to a principle that is not open to dispute because self-evident and is usually one upon which a structure of reasoning is or may be erected ⟨the *axioms* of Euclidean geometry⟩ Perhaps more frequently the term implies a principle universally

accepted or regarded as worthy of acceptance rather than one necessarily true ⟨the journalistic *axiom* that there is nothing as dead as yesterday's newspaper—*G. W. Johnson*⟩ ⟨the superficial commonplaces which pass as *axioms* in our popular intellectual milieu—*Cohen*⟩ **Fundamental** usually applies to a principle, but sometimes a fact, so essential to a philosophy, religion, science, or art that its rejection would destroy the intellectual structure resting upon it ⟨the *fundamentals* of scientific research⟩ ⟨developed the arch and other *fundamentals* of architecture—*R. W. Murray*⟩ ⟨what they deemed the *fundamentals* of the Christian faith—*Latourette*⟩ **Law** applies to a formulation stating an order or relation of phenomena which is regarded as always holding good ⟨the conquest of nature's procreative forces, through the discovery of the *laws* of agriculture and animal husbandry—*R. W. Murray*⟩ ⟨the *laws* of the rain and of the seasons here are tropic laws—*M. S. Douglas*⟩ ⟨it is a *law* that no two electrons may occupy the same orbit—*Eddington*⟩ **Theorem** applies to a proposition that admits of rational proof and, usually, is logically necessary to succeeding logical steps in a structure of reasoning ⟨theoretical economics puts the patterns of uniformity in a coherent system [of which] the basic propositions are called assumptions or postulates, the derived propositions are called *theorems*—*Lange*⟩ ⟨the error that was to prove most durable of all, the *theorem* that only a very short land traverse would be found necessary from Missouri to Pacific waters—*De Voto*⟩

**Ana** basis, foundation, ground (see BASE): *law, rule, canon, precept: *form, usage, convention

**print** *n* *impression, impress, imprint, stamp

**Ana** mark, token, *sign: *trace, vestige

**printing** *edition, impression, reprinting, reissue

**prior** previous, foregoing, precedent, anterior, former, antecedent, *preceding

**Ana** ahead, *before, forward

**Con** behind, *after

**priority,** precedence can both mean the act, the fact, or, especially, the right of preceding another. When the reference is to the right, both terms usually imply an established or accepted code that determines which shall precede the other. **Priority** is the usual term in law and the sciences and chiefly concerns an order of time. When there is merely a question concerning the time relations of events, the term implies antecedence in occurrence ⟨the courts established the *priority* of the wife's death in an accident⟩ ⟨the right to inherit a title is dependent mainly on *priority* of birth⟩ ⟨they disputed *priority* of invention of the regenerative electron-tube circuit—*C. B. Fisher*⟩ When, however, the question concerns a number of things (as debts or cases) which cannot be taken care of or dealt with all at once and must be arranged in order of time, *priority* suggests a rule of arrangement that determines the order in which one goes before another ⟨in payment of debts he must observe the rules of *priority*—*Blackstone*⟩ ⟨liens on a property take *priority* in bankruptcy settlements⟩ ⟨the "law of *priority*" in biological classification is the principle that the first published name of a genus or species has preference over any one subsequently published⟩ ⟨where roads cross one another without a sign on either, there is no absolute *priority*, but it is usual to give way to the vehicle on one's right—*Joseph*⟩ **Precedence,** though frequent in general use, is, in the sense under consideration, primarily a term of formal etiquette; it then implies an established order (as in receiving, greeting or seating) which gives preference to those who are superior in rank, dignity, or position ⟨among ambassadors of equal rank, *precedence* is usually determined by order

A colon (:) separates groups of words discriminated. An asterisk (*) indicates place of treatment of each group

of seniority or length of service⟩ ⟨the order of *precedence* was very rigidly observed, for the visiting maids and valets enjoyed the same hierarchy as their mistresses and masters—*Sackville-West*⟩ In more general use the term often suggests a prior place, chance, or seat accorded to one, often because of age, sex, social position, or as a mere courtesy ⟨no one lost anything by granting *precedence* to a man so flawlessly urbane—*Repplier*⟩ ⟨to give organizations *precedence* over persons is to subordinate ends to means—*Huxley*⟩

*Ana* ordering *or* order, arrangement (see corresponding verbs at ORDER): ascendancy, *supremacy: preeminence, transcendence (see corresponding adjectives at SUPREME)

**priory** *cloister, monastery, nunnery, convent, abbey

**prismatic,** **iridescent, opalescent, opaline** are comparable when they mean marked by or displaying a variety of colors. **Prismatic** implies an exhibition of the colors of the spectrum (as when a ray of light is refracted by a prism) or of a rainbow. In its nontechnical and extended use it merely suggests a brilliant or striking variety of colors ⟨Jeremy Taylor's style is *prismatic*. It unfolds the colors of the rainbow—*Hazlitt*⟩ ⟨have you ever observed a hummingbird moving about in an aerial dance among the flowers—a living *prismatic* gem that changes its color with every change of position?—*Hudson*⟩ **Iridescent** implies a rainbowlike play of shifting, merging colors such as is exhibited by a soap bubble, by mother of pearl, and by the plumage of some birds ⟨the whole texture of his mind, though its substance seem plain and grave, shows itself at every turn *iridescent* with poetic feeling like shot silk—*J. R. Lowell*⟩ ⟨something *iridescent,* like the shining of wet sand—*Repplier*⟩ **Opalescent** and the less frequent **opaline** imply both the soft milky quality and the iridescence of an opal ⟨Titian hardly ever paints sunshine, but a certain *opalescent* twilight which has as much of human emotion as of imitative truth in it—*Ruskin*⟩ ⟨the *opaline* light which comes through these lateral bays, and makes a sort of veil . . . under the lofty vaulting—*Henry Adams*⟩

**prisoner,** **captive** both denote one who is deprived of his liberty. **Prisoner** is the general term, applicable to anyone so deprived, but it is frequently used in a more specific sense, and applied to one who is confined to a prison or held under guard ⟨*prisoners* of war⟩ ⟨take one *prisoner*⟩ ⟨the *prisoners* in the penitentiary⟩ **Captive** implies seizure by force (as in war, conquest, or brigandage); it also often implies bondage or slavery rather than imprisonment, and sometimes suggests capture for ransom ⟨he hath brought many *captives* home to Rome, whose ransoms did the general coffers fill—*Shak.*⟩

**prissy** *prim, priggish, prudish, puritanical, straitlaced, stuffy

*Ana* womanish, effeminate, ladylike, *female: finicky, fastidious, *nice, squeamish: scrupulous, punctilious, meticulous, *careful

**pristine** primeval, primordial, primitive, primal, *primary, prime

*Ana* original, fresh, *new

**privateer** *pirate, freebooter, buccaneer, corsair

**privation** 1 *lack, want, dearth, absence, defect

*Ana* negation, nullification, annulling, abrogation (see corresponding verbs at NULLIFY)

2 *poverty, want, destitution, indigence, penury

*Ana* depletion, draining, exhaustion, impoverishment (see corresponding verbs at DEPLETE): *need, necessity, exigency: pinch, strait (see JUNCTURE)

**privilege** *right, prerogative, birthright, perquisite, appanage

*Ana* concession, *allowance: favor, boon (see GIFT):

*claim, title

**prize** *n* *premium, award, reward, meed, guerdon, bounty, bonus

*Ana* recompensing *or* recompense, compensation (see corresponding verbs at PAY): winning *or* winnings (see GET)

*Ant* forfeit

**prize** *vb* value, treasure, cherish, *appreciate

*Ana* esteem, respect, admire, regard (see under REGARD *n*): *estimate, evaluate, assess, assay, rate

**prize** *n* *spoil, booty, plunder, loot, swag

**probable,** **possible, likely** are comparable when they mean not now certain but such as may be, or may become, true, real, or actual. Something **probable** has so much evidence in its support or seems so reasonable that it commends itself to the mind as worthy of belief, though not to be accepted as a certainty; thus, the most *probable* conclusion from evidence at hand is the one which the weight of evidence supports even though it does not provide proof; the *probable* thief is the one at whom so much of the evidence points as to give grounds for a presumption that he is guilty; the "*probable* life" of a person, in the language of actuaries, is the period during which one half the persons of a given age at a given time will remain alive according to mortality tables ⟨the *probable* cause of a fire⟩ ⟨the *probable* expenses of a trip⟩ ⟨far from being a madman's dream . . . Burr's chance of success was uncomfortably *probable*—*Hervey Allen*⟩ ⟨it is not *probable* that any enemy would . . . attack us by landing troops in the United States—*Roosevelt*⟩ Something **possible** is within the powers of performance, attainment, or conception of an agent or agency, especially a human agent ⟨it is *possible* to cross the Atlantic in an airplane⟩ ⟨knowledge *possible* only to God⟩ or which is within the widest limits of a person's ability or a thing's capacity as determined by nature, necessity, or circumstances ⟨it is not *possible* to carry more than a thousand gallons of gasoline in this airplane⟩ ⟨communication with the stars may never be *possible*⟩ ⟨the number of *possible* amusements is small until the child has learned to grasp objects that it sees—*Russell*⟩ or which, though not probable, may happen by chance or is dependent on a contingency ⟨his election is *possible*, but not probable⟩ ⟨it is *possible* that she will come this way⟩ ⟨I think that "so near as to obstruct" means so near as actually to obstruct—and not merely near enough to threaten a *possible* obstruction—*Justice Holmes*⟩ Something **likely** (see also APT 2) is to all appearances as alleged, suggested, or required; in contrast with *probable, likely* does not as often or as definitely suggest grounds sufficient to warrant a presumption of truth, but in contrast with *possible*, it usually implies many more chances in favor of its being true or coming about; thus, the *probable* murderer is the suspect whose guilt is nearly but not completely established by the evidence; a *possible* murderer is merely one against whom suspicion is directed for some reason, or one known to have had opportunity; the *likely* murderer is the one among the *possible* murderers who, especially from a more or less superficial point of view, has had the strongest motive and the best opportunity, or toward whom the circumstantial evidence most distinctly points as the murderer ⟨no *likely* heir to the bachelor millionaire's estate has been mentioned⟩ ⟨the *likely* outcome of the war changes from month to month⟩ ⟨if there is failure in one quarter, no matter which, it is a *likely* sign of failure in the other—*Blackmur*⟩ *Likely* is also often used in the sense of *promising* because of appearances or ability to win favor ⟨a *likely* young man⟩ ⟨a *likely* candidate⟩ and sometimes in that of *suitable* because of apparent fitness or adapta-

---

*Ana* analogous words  *Ant* antonyms  *Con* contrasted words  See also explanatory notes facing page 1

tion to some end ⟨watching for a *likely* place to picnic⟩ ⟨chose the eastern part of the island as the more *likely* district for discovery of prehistoric remains—*Clodd*⟩
*Ana* credible, believable, colorable, *plausible: reasonable, *rational
*Ant* certain: improbable
**probationer** *novice, novitiate, apprentice, postulant, neophyte
**probe** *n* investigation, *inquiry, inquisition, inquest, research
**probe** *vb* pierce, penetrate, *enter
*Ana* examine, inspect, *scrutinize: *prove, try, test
**probity** *honesty, honor, integrity
*Ana* uprightness, justness, conscientiousness, scrupulousness (see corresponding adjectives at UPRIGHT): *truth, veracity: rectitude, *goodness, virtue
**problem** *mystery, enigma, riddle, puzzle, conundrum
*Ana* perplexity, mystification, bewilderment, distraction (see corresponding verbs at PUZZLE): *predicament, dilemma, plight, quandary
*Ant* solution
**problematic** *doubtful, dubious, questionable
*Ana* ambiguous, equivocal, *obscure, vague, cryptic, enigmatic: uncertain, suspicious, mistrustful (see corresponding nouns at UNCERTAINTY)
**procedure** *process, proceeding
*Ana* ordering *or* order, arrangement (see corresponding verbs at ORDER): *method, system, manner, way: conducting *or* conduct, management (see corresponding verbs at CONDUCT)
**proceed** issue, emanate, stem, flow, derive, *spring, arise, rise, originate
*Ana* *follow, succeed, ensue: *come, arrive
**proceeding** *n* *process, procedure
*Ana* *action, act, deed: *affair, business, concern: operation, functioning, working (see corresponding verbs at ACT)
**process, procedure, proceeding** denote the series of actions, operations, or motions involved in the accomplishment of an end. **Process** is particularly appropriate when progress from a definite beginning to a definite end is implied and something is thereby made, produced, or changed from one thing into another; the term usually suggests a division of the entire sequence of events into steps or stages ⟨describe the *process* of making sugar from sugarcane⟩ ⟨the *process* of digestion⟩ ⟨perfect knowledge is no mere intellectual *process*—*Inge*⟩ ⟨I have always liked the *process* of commuting; every phase of the little journey is a pleasure to me—*Dahl*⟩ The idiomatic phrase "in *process*" means in the course of being made, produced, built, constructed, evolved, or attained ⟨for men in practical life perfection is something far off and still in *process* of achievement—*James*⟩ **Procedure** stresses the method followed or the routine to be followed, whether in carrying through an industrial, a chemical, a mental, or other process, or in doing some specific thing (as conducting a meeting, a trial, a conference, or a business, or performing an experiment or an operation, or prosecuting an investigation or a search) ⟨study the rudiments of parliamentary *procedure*⟩ ⟨knows laboratory *procedure* thoroughly⟩ ⟨correct legal *procedure*⟩ ⟨you know what a stickler she is for *procedure*—"red tape" I called it to her—*Terry Southern*⟩ ⟨this Byzantine court, which is trying to adapt its *procedure* to the ideals of its Western education—*Edmund Wilson*⟩ **Proceeding**, a much less definite term than the others of this group, applies not only to the sequence of events, actions, or operations directed toward the attainment of an end, but also to any one of such events, acts, or operations. The term throws more stress on the individ-

ual or collective items than on their closely knit relation to each other or on the final end which they have in view, and often the term means little more than an instance, sometimes a course, of conduct or behavior ⟨the law . . . stepped in to prevent a *proceeding* which it regarded as petty treason to the commonwealth—*Froude*⟩ ⟨record the *proceedings* of a meeting of a society⟩ ⟨the precise habits, the incredible *proceedings* of human insects—*L. P. Smith*⟩ ⟨legislative *proceedings* frequently veer off into areas of somewhat less than momentous significance—*Armbrister*⟩
*Ana* progress, advance (see under ADVANCE *vb*): conducting *or* conduct, management, controlling *or* control, direction (see corresponding verbs at CONDUCT): performance, execution, accomplishment, fulfillment (see corresponding verbs at PERFORM)
**procession, parade, cortege, cavalcade, motorcade** mean a body (as of persons and vehicles) moving along in order. **Procession** stresses the orderly arrangement and smooth procedure; often it suggests formality, solemnity, and pomp ⟨a funeral *procession*⟩ ⟨and all the priests and friars in my realm shall in *procession* sing her endless praise—*Shak.*⟩ ⟨and delegate Dead from each past age and race, viewless to man, in large *procession* pace—*Lanier*⟩ **Parade** is used of a usually large and formal procession. The term also implies marching in a more or less military fashion to the accompaniment of a band and often suggests other evidences of pomp and display (see also DISPLAY) ⟨the Fourth of July program includes a *parade* and fireworks⟩ ⟨the annual *parades* of both organizations . . . open-air festivals, with colorful banners, drum and fife bands—*Mogey*⟩ ⟨there was a *parade* in honor of the successful candidate for governor⟩ **Cortege**, sometimes used in the meaning of a retinue or train, usually means a procession of mourners at a funeral; it can refer either to those who follow the casket on foot or to those who follow in vehicles ⟨declared that the *cortege* of the dead emperor must set forth on the journey homeward—*Buck*⟩ **Cavalcade** throws the emphasis upon the moving of men on horseback or in vehicles; often it applies specifically to a dignitary and his retinue ⟨the king's *cavalcade* through the gates of the city the day before his coronation—*Walpole*⟩ and only indirectly does it suggest the appeal of a spectacle or spectacular procession. **Motorcade** may replace *cavalcade* when the intent is to stress mechanized as distinguished from equine power; otherwise the two terms are similar in values ⟨with a *motorcade* of more than 2,000 vehicles, New York yesterday celebrated its traffic safety record for the first quarter—*N. Y. American*⟩ ⟨more than 300 floats will form a brilliant *motorcade* to the fairgrounds—*Brooklyn Daily Eagle*⟩ ⟨the three heads of state motored to Arlington Cemetery. It was raw and windy as the *motorcade* entered the cemetery—*Time*⟩
*Ana* *succession, sequence, train: pomp, array (see DISPLAY)
**proclaim** *declare, announce, publish, advertise, promulgate, broadcast
*Ana* *reveal, disclose, discover, divulge, tell: voice, utter, vent, ventilate (see EXPRESS *vb*): *inform, apprise
**proclamation** declaration, announcement, publication, advertisement, promulgation, broadcasting (see under DECLARE)
**proclivity** propensity, *leaning, penchant, flair
*Ana* knack, aptitude, *gift, bent, turn: inclination, disposition, predisposition (see corresponding verbs at INCLINE): *predilection, prepossession, prejudice, bias
**procrastinate** *delay, lag, dawdle, loiter
*Ana* *defer, suspend, stay, postpone: protract, prolong (see EXTEND)

A colon (:) separates groups of words discriminated: An asterisk (*) indicates place of treatment of each group.

*Ant* hasten, hurry

**procreate** *generate, engender, beget, get, sire, breed, propagate, reproduce

**procure** *get, obtain, secure, acquire, gain, win
*Ana* *negotiate, arrange, concert: *reach, compass, gain, achieve, attain

**prod** *vb* 1 *poke, nudge, jog
*Ana* prick, punch, bore (see PERFORATE): goad, spur (see corresponding nouns at MOTIVE): pierce, penetrate (see ENTER)
2 *urge, egg, exhort, goad, spur, prick, sic
*Ana* *incite, instigate: stimulate, excite, pique, *provoke

**prod** *n* poke, nudge, jog (see under POKE *vb*)
*Ana* *stimulus, stimulant, incitement, impetus

**prodigal** *adj* *profuse, lavish, exuberant, luxuriant, lush
*Ana* extravagant, exorbitant, immoderate, *excessive: abundant, *plentiful, plenteous, ample, copious: *supererogatory, uncalled-for, gratuitous
*Ant* parsimonious: frugal —*Con* niggardly, penurious, *stingy: economical, *sparing, thrifty

**prodigal** *n* *spendthrift, profligate, waster, wastrel
*Ana* spender, expender, disburser (see corresponding verbs at SPEND)

**prodigious** *monstrous, tremendous, stupendous, monumental
*Ana* enormous, immense, *huge, vast, gigantic, mammoth, colossal: amazing, astounding, flabbergasting (see SURPRISE)

**prodigy** *wonder, marvel, miracle, phenomenon
*Ana* abnormality (see corresponding adjective at ABNORMAL): monstrosity (see corresponding adjective at MONSTROUS): anomaly, *paradox

**produce** *vb* *bear, yield, turn out
*Ana* *generate, breed, propagate: *make, form, shape, fabricate, manufacture: create, *invent

**produce** *n* *product, production

**product** 1 *work, production, opus, artifact
*Ana* forming *or* form, fabrication, manufacturing *or* manufacture (see corresponding verbs at MAKE): article, object, *thing
2 **Product, production, produce** are comparable when they denote something produced or brought into being by a process or operation, especially one involving labor or effort. **Product** is the most general of these terms, applicable to anything produced by generation, growth, labor, or thought or by any industrial, chemical, mental, or other process or by the operation of causes in no way controllable by man ⟨the literary *products* of the Age of Reason⟩ ⟨soot is usually the *product* of the imperfect combustion of fuel⟩ ⟨even the simplest poem is the *product* of much . . . work—*Highet*⟩ ⟨he is a *product* of his party machine, in which he has had his whole existence—*Edmund Wilson*⟩ **Production,** in the sense of the thing produced, is generally restricted in its application to human products involving intellectual or artistic labor, and it is the usual term in theatrical and motion-picture use. A work of sculpture, a philosophical or historical treatise, or a theatrical representation of a play may be described as a *production* ⟨the greatest *production* of Hamlet that this country has been privileged to see and hear⟩ ⟨the finest *productions* of Praxiteles or Zeuxis—*Froude*⟩ ⟨Wagner believed Parsifal the climactic *production* of his career⟩ But *production* is also used in a collective sense to denote all the things, often of a specified or implied kind, manufactured or grown to satisfy human wants ⟨an increase of steel *production* is anticipated⟩ ⟨this chart shows the relationship between pork *production* and pork prices—*Sat. Review*⟩ **Produce** is ordinarily a collective

noun applied to natural and especially agricultural as distinguished from industrial products ⟨the meager *produce* of the land—*Cowper*⟩ ⟨able to exist for a fortnight in the western Mediterranean where less sea *produce* was forthcoming—*N. B. Marshall*⟩ ⟨the *produce* that is likely to result from the mating of one individual with another—*Wynmalen*⟩ Sometimes the term is applied specifically to vegetables and fruits ⟨stripping the country of hogs and cattle, *produce* and flour—*Mason*⟩ and sometimes it is applied to products of human and especially human intellectual effort ⟨nine-tenths of modern science is . . . the *produce* of men whom their contemporaries thought dreamers—*Bagehot*⟩

**production** 1 *work, product, opus, artifact
·*Ana* execution, fulfillment, performance (see corresponding verbs at PERFORM): *effort, exertion
2 *product, produce

**profanation, desecration, sacrilege, blasphemy** can all mean a violation or a misuse of something regarded as sacred. **Profanation** applies to an irreverent outrage shocking to those who cherish and hold sacred the thing mistreated; although it may suggest base callousness, it often applies to vulgar intrusion or insensitive irreverence (as of vandals) ⟨these sages attribute the calamity to a *profanation* of the sacred grove—*Frazer*⟩ **Desecration** applies especially to any action whereby sacred character is impaired or lost; often it indicates loss of that character through defilement, often malicious or malign and culpable ⟨*desecration* of the cathedrals by the invading barbarians⟩ ⟨the last priest, feeling there was no work to be done in such a dreary outpost, burned the chapel in 1706 to prevent its *desecration*—*Amer. Guide Series: Mich.*⟩ **Sacrilege** may refer technically to reception or administration of a religious sacrament by one unworthy; it refers commonly to any outrageous profanation ⟨the execution was not followed by any *sacrilege* to the church or defiling of holy vessels—*Cather*⟩ ⟨above all things they dread any contact with the spirits of the dead. Only a sorcerer would dare to commit such a *sacrilege*, an offense punishable with death—*Frazer*⟩ **Blasphemy** (see also BLASPHEMY 1; compare *blasphemous* under IMPIOUS) may refer to any strong irreverence, often one involving or suggesting reviling, defying, mocking, or otherwise treating with indignity something sacred ⟨he cooperated with me in sending the pious elders to unspeakable corners of hell; we arranged a wordless language of *blasphemy* and signaled to each other across the laps of the godly—*Brace*⟩
*Ana* defilement, pollution, contamination (see corresponding verbs at CONTAMINATE): debasement, vitiation, corruption, perversion (see corresponding verbs at DEBASE): violation, transgression, trespass (see BREACH)

**profane** *adj* 1 **Profane, secular, lay, temporal** mean not dedicated or set apart for religious ends or uses. **Profane** specifically implies an opposition to *sacred* (see HOLY); in this sense it is purely descriptive and not derogatory; thus, *profane* history is history dealing with nations or peoples rather than with biblical events or characters; *profane* literature comprises all literature except the Scriptures, other sacred writings, and sometimes writings having a definite religious end or use; *profane* love applies to human love as between man and woman, as distinguished from the love of man for God and of God for man ⟨the *profane* poet is by instinct a naturalist. He loves landscape, he loves love, he loves the humor and pathos of earthly existence—*Santayana*⟩ The term also is used to imply an opposition to *holy, religious, spiritual* ⟨I have observed that *profane* men living in ships, like the holy men gathered together in monasteries, develop traits of profound resemblance—*Conrad*⟩ **Secular** usually

implies a relation to the world as distinguished from the church or religion or the religious life; it may come close to *profane* ⟨*secular* music⟩ ⟨the *secular* drama⟩ or it may be opposed to *regular* in the sense of governed by a monastic rule; thus, a *secular* priest is a priest who does not belong to a religious order; a *regular* priest is one who does. The term is most often opposed to *religious* in the sense of belonging to or serving the ends of a religion or church, then coming close to *civil* or *public* ⟨*secular* schools⟩ ⟨*secular* journals⟩ ⟨the *secular* authority⟩ ⟨there are peoples in the world who have no *secular* dances, only religious dances—*Ellis*⟩ ⟨believing that no creed, religious or *secular,* can be justified except on the basis of reason and evidence—*Times Lit. Sup.*⟩ **Lay** is applied to persons, or sometimes to their activities, interests, or duties, that do not belong to the clergy and particularly the regularly ordained clergy; it therefore usually implies an opposition to *clerical* or *ecclesiastical* ⟨*lay*men and *lay*women of the parish⟩ ⟨a *lay* preacher⟩ ⟨*lay* sermon⟩ ⟨*lay* delegates to a diocesan convention⟩ In religious orders the term is applied to a class of religious who are occupied chiefly with domestic and manual work as distinguished from those who are occupied with liturgical observances, teaching, and study ⟨the *lay* brothers in a monastery⟩ *Lay* is often extended to other than the clerical profession (compare *lay analyst* under NEUROLOGIST) in the sense of nonprofessional or of not having a professional source or character; thus, a *lay* opinion on a question of law is merely an opinion delivered by one who is neither a lawyer nor a judge ⟨the doctrine of scienter . . . in the *lay* mind has been converted into the popular half truth that a dog is entitled to his first bite—*Field-Fisher*⟩ **Temporal** implies an opposition to *spiritual* (in the sense of being concerned not with material or mundane but with immaterial and eternal ends) and is applied chiefly to sovereigns, rulers, or dignitaries having political authority or civil power; thus, lords *temporal* are those members of the British House of Lords who are not bishops or archbishops (these latter being called lords *spiritual*) ⟨the Papacy had no *temporal* power between 1870, the year of the fall of the Papal State, and 1929, the year of the establishment of Vatican City⟩ ⟨persuading the Church to forego its claim to *temporal* authority and confine its attention to spiritual benefactions—*Littlefield*⟩
*Ana* worldly, mundane, *earthly, terrestrial
*Ant* sacred —*Con* *holy, divine, religious, spiritual
2 *impious, blasphemous, sacrilegious
*Ana* foul, filthy, *dirty, nasty: ungodly, godless, *irreligious: iniquitous, nefarious, villainous, *vicious
**profanity** *blasphemy, cursing, swearing
*Ana* imprecation, *curse, malediction: execration, objurgation, damning (see corresponding verbs at EXECRATE)
**profess** *assert, declare, affirm, aver, protest, avouch, avow, predicate, warrant
*Ana* allege, *adduce, advance
**profession** art, handicraft, craft, *trade
**proffer** *offer, tender, present, prefer
*Ana* propose, design, *intend: confer, bestow, present, *give
*Con* reject, spurn, refuse, *decline
**proficient,** adept, skilled, skillful, expert, masterly are comparable when they mean having the knowledge and experience necessary to success in a given line especially of work or endeavor. When applied to things rather than persons, all these terms carry the implication that the quality of the person has been attributed to the thing. **Proficient** implies training and practice as the source of competency beyond the average ⟨*proficient* in the art of self-defense—*Shaw*⟩ ⟨Jane began to type. It bored her,

but she was fairly *proficient* at it—*Rose Macaulay*⟩ **Adept** implies proficiency but stresses aptitude and often cleverness ⟨*adept* at legerdemain⟩ ⟨so *adept* at the lovely polishing of every grave and lucent phrase—*Gibbons*⟩ **Skilled,** often interchangeable with *proficient,* may distinctively suggest mastery of the details of a trade or handicraft or of the technique of an art or profession. In modern industrial use *skilled* simply connotes that one has met a standard set up by employers for a special type of work or job ⟨*skilled* labor⟩ ⟨the *skilled* trades⟩ ⟨by long practice, he was *skilled* in the arts of teaching—*Gibbon*⟩ ⟨professors, students, and *skilled* employees make a varied assault upon the mysteries of marine biology—*Parshley*⟩ **Skillful** implies adeptness coupled with dexterity in execution or performance ⟨a *skillful* operator of an automobile⟩ ⟨a *skillful* teacher⟩ ⟨in little danger with a *skillful* hand at the helm—*Nordhoff & Hall*⟩ ⟨the solution achieved by a *skillful* minority in face of a hostile majority —*Parrington*⟩ **Expert** applies to one who has attained extraordinary proficiency or is exceptionally adept ⟨an *expert* accountant⟩ ⟨an *expert* bridge player⟩ ⟨*expert* knowledge of engines⟩ ⟨neither of them was *expert* in the roping of cattle—*Mary Austin*⟩ ⟨explaining at length, but with an *expert* lucidity, some basic point of law —*Edmund Wilson*⟩ **Masterly,** applied more often to the thing executed or the quality displayed than to the person who executes or displays, is close to *expert* in its implication of proficiency and adeptness, but it commonly adds a suggestion of confident control ⟨he compressed into the *masterly* introductory essays . . . his entire theory of the progress of the United States—*Bidwell*⟩ ⟨his *masterly* dissimulation—*Motley*⟩ ⟨how *masterly* is he in all the points of his profession—*Trollope*⟩
*Ana* efficient, effectual, *effective: capable, *able, competent, qualified: finished, accomplished, *consummate: practiced, drilled, exercised (see PRACTICE *vb*)
*Con* *awkward, clumsy, maladroit, inept, gauche: *ignorant, untaught
**profile** *outline, contour, silhouette, skyline
**profit** *n* *use, service, advantage, account, avail
*Ana* reward, award, meed, guerdon (see PREMIUM): gaining *or* gain, winning (see GET)
**profit** *vb* *benefit, avail
*Ana* *get, gain, win: *advance, progress
**profitable** 1 *beneficial, advantageous
*Ana* *favorable, auspicious, propitious: *expedient, advisable, politic
*Ant* unprofitable —*Con* detrimental, deleterious (see PERNICIOUS): harming *or* harmful, injurious, hurting *or* hurtful (see corresponding verbs at INJURE)
2 *paying, gainful, remunerative, lucrative
*Ana* fruitful (see FERTILE): compensating, recompensing, repaying (see PAY): valuable, precious (see COSTLY)
**profligate** *adj* dissolute, reprobate, *abandoned
*Ana* debauched, corrupted, depraved, debased, perverted (see under DEBASE): degenerate, corrupt, *vicious: *loose, relaxed, slack, lax
**profligate** *n* *spendthrift, prodigal, wastrel, waster
*Ana* debauchee, pervert, corrupter (see corresponding verbs at DEBASE): libertine, lecher (see corresponding adjectives at LICENTIOUS)
**profound** *deep, abysmal
*Ana* penetrating, probing, piercing (see ENTER): scrutinizing, inspecting, examining (see SCRUTINIZE)
*Ant* shallow
**profuse,** lavish, prodigal, luxuriant, lush, exuberant carry as their basic meaning giving out or given out in great abundance. What is *profuse* seems to pour or be poured forth in abundance, without restraint, or in a stream ⟨*pro-*

*fuse* apologies⟩ ⟨*profuse* sweating⟩ ⟨pourest thy full heart in *profuse* strains of unpremeditated art—*Shelley*⟩ ⟨a land where life was great . . . and beauty lay *profuse*—*Browning*⟩ What is **lavish** is so exceedingly profuse as to suggest, positively, munificence or extravagance or, negatively, the absence of all stint or moderation ⟨*lavish* gifts⟩ ⟨a *lavish* feast⟩ ⟨*lavish* expenditures⟩ ⟨the *lavish* attentions of his mother—*Meredith*⟩ ⟨our *lavish* use of a bountiful supply of crude oil—*Morrison*⟩ What is **prodigal** gives or is given so lavishly and so recklessly as to suggest waste or the ultimate exhaustion of resources ⟨chary of praise and *prodigal* of counsel—*Stevenson*⟩ ⟨the *prodigal* expenditures of the recent war—*M. W. Childs*⟩ ⟨he had been *prodigal* with his money and she probably imagined that he was still in funds—*Cliff Farrell*⟩ What is **luxuriant** produces or is produced in great and rich abundance; the term usually connotes not only profusion but gorgeousness or splendor in what is produced ⟨her *luxuriant* hair⟩ ⟨the *luxuriant* imagination of Milton⟩ ⟨this damp and mild climate makes possible the most *luxuriant* forest growth—*Forde*⟩ ⟨rich and *luxuriant* beauty; a beauty that shone with deep and vivid tints—*Hawthorne*⟩ What is **lush** is not only luxuriant but has reached the peak of its perfection; the term distinctively connotes richness, fullness of development, or luxuriousness ⟨how *lush* and lusty the grass looks! how green!—*Shak.*⟩ ⟨the *lush* . . . full-blown landscape of the south through which they had set out that morning—*Jan Struther*⟩ ⟨the fabulous period of the Nineties, that *lush*, plush, glittering era with all its sentimentality and opulence and ostentation—*S. H. Hay*⟩ What is **exuberant** produces or is produced so abundantly or luxuriantly as to suggest exceedingly great vigor, vitality, or creative power; the term applies chiefly to persons or their words, emotions, or qualities that display a vigor or vitality that is almost rampant ⟨an *exuberant* fancy⟩ ⟨the *exuberant* genius of Shakespeare⟩ ⟨to restrain my too *exuberant* gesture—*Mary Austin*⟩ ⟨*exuberant* energy⟩ ⟨actually, in the present context, all our *exuberant* post-Sputnik talk is irrelevant and even nonsensical—*Huxley*⟩
*Ana* copious, abundant (see PLENTIFUL): *excessive, immoderate, extravagant: *liberal, bountiful, bounteous, openhanded, munificent, generous
*Ant* spare, scanty, scant —*Con* *meager, skimpy, scrimpy, exiguous, sparse

**progenitor** *ancestor, forefather, forebear
*Ant* progeny

**progeny** *offspring, young, issue, descendant, posterity
*Ant* progenitor

**prognosis** *diagnosis

**prognostic** *foretoken, presage, omen, augury, portent
*Ana* indication, betokening, bespeaking (see corresponding verbs at INDICATE): symptom, *sign, mark, token

**prognosticate** *foretell, predict, forecast, prophesy, augur, presage, portend, forebode
*Ana* *indicate, betoken, bespeak: *foresee, foreknow, apprehend, divine, anticipate

**program, schedule, timetable, agenda** denote a formulated plan listing things to be done or to take place, especially in their time order. **Program** is the term of widest application. It may refer to a mental plan or to one that is written or printed; it may be applied not only to a plan for a meeting, an entertainment, or a service but to one made by an individual in ordering his own day or his own future or to one made by a group that has certain ends in view and proposes their orderly achievement ⟨what is your *program* for today?⟩ ⟨the *program* of a concert⟩ ⟨theater *programs*⟩ ⟨the Five-Year Plan was the name given the industrialization *program* of the Soviet Union⟩ **Schedule**

and **timetable** stress the importance of the time element and imply a plan of procedure which establishes not only the chronological order of events or steps but also their time limits ⟨the *schedule* for a college year⟩ ⟨a *schedule* of production in a factory⟩ ⟨the *timetable* life of a New York University student—*N. Y. Times*⟩ ⟨the *timetable* for expansion of Soviet power and influence in Asia has been seriously upset—*Mosely*⟩ **Schedule** is sometimes used, but *timetable* distinctly more often, for a tabulated list of regularly recurring events (as arrivals and departures of trains or buses) ⟨a *schedule* of classes⟩ ⟨it was in October 1839 that George Bradshaw issued the first *timetable* to show all trains then running in this country—*O. S. Nock*⟩ **Agenda** is applied chiefly to a schedule of the order of business for a meeting.

**progress** *n* 1 advance (see under ADVANCE *vb* 2)
*Ana* improvement, betterment (see corresponding verbs at IMPROVE): headway, impetus (see SPEED *n*)
2 **Progress, progression** are not always clearly distinguished, although they can be more or less sharply differentiated. Both denote movement forward. **Progress** (see also *progress n* under ADVANCE *vb* 2) usually applies to a movement considered as a whole, stressing such aspects as the distance covered, the change or changes taking place, and the amount of improvement made ⟨we made little *progress* that day⟩ ⟨note the extent of his *progress* during the past year⟩ ⟨delightful never-ending *progress* to perfection—*Hazlitt*⟩ ⟨the history of educational *progress*⟩ ⟨the rapid *progress* of a disease⟩ **Progression** (see also SUCCESSION) commonly applies to a movement in itself or in its detail, often implying a continuous series of steps, degrees, or stages toward an objective but sometimes implying little more than a moving on more or less continuously ⟨mode of *progression*⟩ ⟨that slow *progression* of things, which naturally makes elegance and refinement the last effect of opulence and power—*Reynolds*⟩ ⟨every generation . . . adds . . . its own discoveries in a *progression* to which there seems no limit—*Peacock*⟩

**progress** *vb* *advance
*Ana* *move, drive, impel: further, forward, promote, *advance: develop, *mature
*Ant* retrogress

**progression** 1 *succession, series, sequence, chain, train, string
2 *progress

**progressive** *liberal, advanced, radical
*Ant* reactionary

**prohibit** *forbid, inhibit, enjoin, interdict, ban
*Ana* *prevent, preclude, obviate: debar, shut out, *exclude: *hinder, impede, obstruct: *restrain, curb, check
*Ant* permit —*Con* *let, allow, suffer: tolerate, endure, *bear

**project** *n* scheme, design, plot, *plan
*Ana* sketch, delineation, draft, outline, diagram (see under SKETCH *vb*): *device, contrivance

**project** *vb* 1 scheme, design, plot, plan (see under PLAN *n*)
*Ana* propose, purpose, *intend: *sketch, outline, diagram, delineate
2 *bulge, jut, stick out, protuberate, protrude, overhang, beetle
*Ana* *extend, prolong, lengthen: swell, distend, *expand

**projection, protrusion, protuberance, bulge** all denote something which extends beyond a level or a normal outer surface. **Projection** is applicable to anything that juts out, especially at a sharp angle ⟨buttresses are *projections* which serve to support a wall or a building at a point of great strain or pressure⟩ ⟨machinery set in motion to keep a level smooth . . . feels the least *projection*, and

---

*Ana* analogous words      *Ant* antonyms      *Con* contrasted words      See also explanatory notes facing page 1

tries to flatten it out—*Hearn*⟩ ⟨the appendix is a small fingerlike *projection* from the large bowel—*Fishbein*⟩ **Protrusion** applies to something which is thrust out or which pushes out so that it seems an excrescence or deformity ⟨a *protrusion* of lava in the form of a thousand-foot pinnacle⟩ ⟨the fantastic gables, pinnacles, and *protrusions* which intercepted the light—*Samuel Lucas*⟩ A **protuberance** swells or pushes out, often in rounded rather than angular form ⟨warty *protuberances* on a potato⟩ ⟨balconies, bay windows and *protuberances* which make their fronts look like bemedaled chests—*Hauser*⟩ A **bulge** is a protuberance or expansion of a surface caused usually by pressure from within or below ⟨a *bulge* in a wall⟩ ⟨there is a slight *bulge* in the soil before the first stalk of a plant appears⟩

**prolific** fruitful, *fertile, fecund
*Ana* teeming, swarming, abounding (see TEEM): generating, breeding, propagating, reproducing *or* reproductive (see corresponding verbs at GENERATE)
*Ant* barren, unfruitful

**prolificacy** fruitfulness, fertility, fecundity (see under FERTILE)
*Ant* barrenness, unfruitfulness

**prolix** *wordy, verbose, diffuse, redundant
*Ana* tedious, *irksome, tiresome, wearisome: prolonged, protracted (see EXTEND): pleonastic, circumlocutory, redundant, tautological (see corresponding nouns at VERBIAGE)

**prologue** *introduction, prelude, preface, foreword, exordium, preamble

**prolong** protract, *extend, lengthen, elongate
*Ana* *continue, last, persist, endure: *increase, augment, enlarge: *expand, amplify
*Ant* curtail —*Con* *shorten, abridge, abbreviate, retrench

**prominent** remarkable, conspicuous, salient, outstanding, signal, *noticeable, striking, arresting
*Ana* *chief, leading, main, principal: important, significant (see corresponding nouns at IMPORTANCE)

**promiscuous** heterogeneous, motley, *miscellaneous
*Ana* mixed, mingled, blended, merged (see MIX): *random, haphazard, desultory, casual: *indiscriminate, wholesale, sweeping: *licentious, lewd, wanton, lascivious
*Con* discriminating, perceiving, discerning (see corresponding nouns at DISCERNMENT): discreet, prudent, forethoughtful (see under PRUDENCE)

**promise** *vb* Promise, engage, pledge, plight, covenant, contract are comparable when they mean to give one's word that one will act in a specified way (as by doing, making, giving, or accepting) in respect to something stipulated. **Promise** implies a giving assurance either orally or in writing but it suggests no further grounds for expectation of the fulfillment of what is promised ⟨he is a man of his word, what he *promises* he performs⟩ ⟨he *promised* that he would pay his bill⟩ ⟨*promised* to do painting, trimming and repairing with all possible expertness—*Riker*⟩ ⟨*promised* to reexamine all loyalty cases cleared by the Democrats—*Ginzburg*⟩ ⟨she has *promised* herself a trip to Bermuda⟩ **Engage** implies a more binding agreement or more definite commitment than *promise*. Typically it is used in formal or consequential situations, sometimes specifically implying an agreement to marry and sometimes an agreement to accept as an employee. It ordinarily implies a promise regarded as binding and to be relied on and especially one concerning conduct over a period of time ⟨to Him whose truth and faithfulness *engage* the waiting soul to bless—*Walford*⟩ ⟨study material about Gen. Grant, whose biography he had *engaged* to prepare—*Caffey*⟩ ⟨the United

States . . . *engaged* to exclude peddlers from their country —*Foreman*⟩ ⟨an *engaged* couple⟩ **Pledge** (compare PLEDGE *n*), aside from uses in connection with drives and charities ⟨*pledged* a dollar a week to the church building fund⟩, may imply the giving of a promise by some act or words that suggest the giving of a solemn assurance or the provision of a formal guarantee ⟨*pledged* their loyalty to their sovereign⟩ ⟨*pledge* themselves to maintain and uphold the right of the master—*Taney*⟩ ⟨Austria swarmed with excited and angry men *pledged* to destroy the Church—*Belloc*⟩ **Plight** implies a solemn promising ⟨if for America it is too violent a wrench to *plight* its fate with Europe's, even . . . to prevent war—*Peffer*⟩ and persists chiefly in a few stereotyped phrases such as "plight one's troth." **Covenant** implies at least two parties to the promise, each making a solemn agreement with the other ⟨a man cannot grant anything to his wife, or enter into convenant with her: for . . . to *covenant* with her, would be only to *covenant* with himself—*Blackstone*⟩ ⟨*covenanted* to defeat the present conspiracy to set up a Home Rule Parliament in Ireland—*Rose Macaulay*⟩ **Contract** (see also CONTRACT *vb* 3, INCUR) implies the entry into a solemn and usually legally binding agreement (see CONTRACT *n*) ⟨*contract* for a large loan⟩ ⟨the company has *contracted* to supply the schools of the state with textbooks⟩ ⟨the good wife realizes that in becoming a wife she *contracts* to forget self and put her husband's happiness above her own—*D. F. Miller*⟩
*Ana* agree, consent, *assent, accede: assure, *ensure, insure

**promote** forward, further, *advance
*Ana* *help, aid, assist: *speed, quicken, hasten, hurry
*Ant* impede —*Con* *hinder, obstruct, block, bar

**promotion** 1 *advancement, preferment, elevation
*Ana* *progress, progression: exaltation, magnifying, aggrandizement (see corresponding verbs at EXALT)
*Ant* demotion —*Con* degradation, humiliation, debasement (see corresponding verbs at ABASE)
2 *publicity, ballyhoo, propaganda
*Ana* advertisement, promulgation, broadcasting (see corresponding verbs at DECLARE)

**prompt** *adj* *quick, ready, apt
*Ana* alert, wide-awake, vigilant, *watchful: expeditious, speedy, swift (see FAST): trained, disciplined (see TEACH): *eager, keen, avid
*Con* remiss, lax, slack (see NEGLIGENT): dilatory, *slow

**promulgate** proclaim, announce, *declare, publish, advertise, broadcast
*Ana* *reveal, disclose, divulge, discover: profess, affirm, aver, avow, avouch (see ASSERT): *communicate, impart

**promulgation** proclamation, declaration, announcement, publication, advertisement, broadcasting (see under DECLARE)

**prone** 1 subject, exposed, open, *liable, susceptible, sensitive
*Ana* inclined, predisposed, disposed (see INCLINE *vb*): addicted, habituated, accustomed (see HABITUATE)
2 Prone, supine, prostrate, recumbent, couchant, dormant are comparable when they mean lying upon a surface (as the ground or a floor). **Prone** implies a position with the face, chest, or abdomen lying on or turned toward the supporting surface ⟨if we ourselves lie *prone* upon the floor we can exemplify the characteristic relationship, for our internal cavity is nearest to the floor, above it is our backbone—*Swinton*⟩ ⟨Her Majesty, *prone* but queenly, stretched out on the deck . . . to try her hand at target shooting—*Time*⟩ **Supine** applies to a position with the back against a supporting surface, the face upward, and may suggest lethargy, abjectness, or inertness

A colon (:) separates groups of words discriminated. An asterisk (*) indicates place of treatment of each group.

⟨lying *supine* in the bottom of the canoe and staring upward at the immaculate azure of the sky—*Wylie*⟩ ⟨jaded people lolling *supine* in carriages—*Shaw*⟩ **Prostrate** basically applies to full-length proneness as in submission, fear, or helplessness; the term also may apply to a horizontal position either prone or supine that is typically brought about by a fall or weakness or shock ⟨*prostrate* in homage, on her face, silent—*Bottomley*⟩ ⟨lying *prostrate* on my chest, I took a long draft of clear cold water—*Hudson*⟩ ⟨stood over the bloody and *prostrate* form—*Nordhoff & Hall*⟩ **Recumbent** may apply to lying down in any position of comfortable repose ⟨if the patient is greatly weakened or prostrated, he must be kept reasonably warm, *recumbent*—*Fishbein*⟩ ⟨*recumbent* upon the brown pine-droppings—*Meredith*⟩ **Couchant** and **dormant**, mainly technical heraldic terms in the senses here involved, apply to a prone body position, the former suggesting that the head is raised as if in watchfulness, the latter that it is lowered in sleep.
*Ana* flat, *level: groveling, wallowing, weltering (see WALLOW): crawl, *creep
*Ant* erect
**pronounce** *articulate, enunciate
**proof** 1 ground, *reason, argument
*Ana* demonstration, trial, test (see under PROVE): corroboration, confirmation, substantiation, verification (see corresponding verbs at CONFIRM)
2 demonstration, test, trial (see under PROVE)
*Ant* disproof
**prop** *vb* *support, sustain, bolster, buttress, brace
*Ana* uphold, back (see SUPPORT): hoist, heave, boost, *lift
**propaganda** *publicity, ballyhoo, promotion
*Ana* propagation, engendering, generating (see corresponding verbs at GENERATE): spread, stretch (see EXPANSE): inculcation, instillment, implanting (see corresponding verbs at IMPLANT)
**propagate** 1 *generate, engender, breed, beget, procreate, sire, reproduce
*Ana* *increase, multiply, augment: *continue, persist: *extend, lengthen, prolong
2 *spread, circulate, disseminate, diffuse, radiate
*Ana* *scatter, disperse, dissipate: *distribute, dispense: *teach, instruct, educate: *communicate, impart: inculcate, instill, *implant
**propel** *push, shove, thrust
*Ana* *move, drive, impel: *force, compel, constrain, oblige
**propensity** *leaning, proclivity, penchant, flair
*Ana* *predilection, prejudice, bias, prepossession: *gift, aptitude, bent, turn, knack: predisposition, disposition, inclination (see corresponding verbs at INCLINE)
*Ant* antipathy
**proper** 1 meet, appropriate, fitting, apt, happy, felicitous, *fit, suitable
*Ana* congruous, congenial, compatible, *consonant: *correct, nice, right: *due, rightful, condign
*Ant* improper —*Con* wrong, *false
2 seemly, *decorous, decent, nice
*Ana* formal, conventional, ceremonious, *ceremonial
**property** *quality, character, attribute, accident
*Ana* peculiarity, individuality, characteristic (see corresponding adjectives at CHARACTERISTIC)
**prophecy** *revelation, vision, apocalypse
*Ana* communication, impartation (see corresponding verbs at COMMUNICATE): *inspiration
**prophesy** predict, forecast, *foretell, prognosticate, augur, presage, portend, forebode
*Ana* *foresee, foreknow, divine, apprehend, anticipate

**propinquity** *proximity
*Ana* closeness, nearness (see corresponding adjectives at CLOSE): relatedness *or* relationship, kindredness *or* kindred (see corresponding adjectives at RELATED)
**propitiate** *pacify, appease, placate, mollify, conciliate
*Ana* reconcile, conform, adjust, *adapt: *satisfy, content: intercede, mediate (see INTERPOSE)
**propitious** auspicious, *favorable, benign
*Ana* benignant, *kind, kindly: fortunate, *lucky, providential, happy
*Ant* unpropitious: adverse —*Con* *sinister, malefic, maleficent, malign, baleful: *ominous, inauspicious, portentous, fateful
**proportion** *symmetry, balance, harmony
**proportional, proportionate, commensurate, commensurable** are often used without marked distinction because all mean being duly proportioned to something else. *Proportional* and *proportionate* both imply due proportions either to a related thing or things, or of things that are related (as by belonging to the same set, series, design, or construction, or by being the effect of a cause or the response to a stimulus). **Proportional** is the more usual term when a constant and often mathematically precise ratio between corresponding aspects (as size, amount, number, or length) of related things is under consideration; thus, a *proportional* tax is one assessed as a constant percentage of the value (as of income or realty) being taxed; a *proportional* wage is a fixed percentage (as of gross sales or profits) ⟨the circumferences of all circles are *proportional* to the lengths of their radii⟩ ⟨a detailed plan for *proportional* . . . disarmament to be achieved by stages—*Grenville Clark*⟩ *Proportional* may be used, but **proportionate** is more often used, when the term is intended to imply the adjustment and sometimes the deliberate adjustment of one thing that bears a reciprocal relationship to another thing, so that both are in keeping with each other or not out of keeping with what is just, fair, due, or reasonable ⟨the punishment should be *proportionate* to the crime⟩ ⟨ponderous bodies forced into velocity move with violence *proportionate* to their weight—*Johnson*⟩ ⟨most state taxes produce a yield *proportionate* only to general economic growth—*Armbrister*⟩ ⟨they rushed into freedom and enjoyment . . . with an energy *proportional* to their previous restraint—*Dickinson*⟩ **Commensurate** and **commensurable** differ from the preceding words chiefly in carrying a stronger implication of equality between related things each of which has a value (as of measure, degree, or intensity) that is intimately related to that of the other ⟨the meagerness of the result was *commensurate* with the crudity of the methods—*Buchan*⟩ ⟨the two punishments must be perfectly *commensurable*—*Bentham*⟩ Sometimes both terms, but especially *commensurable,* differ from the other words in implying a common scale of values by which outwardly different things can be shown to be equal or proportionate in some significant way ⟨if two magnitudes can both be expressed in whole numbers in terms of a common unit, they are *commensurable*—*W. G. Shute et al*⟩ ⟨all civilization[s] . . . are *commensurable,* and . . . are but ramifications (if not historically, at least phenomenologically) of the one idea of civilization—*Schrecker*⟩ ⟨the measure of a rancher's ability to take care of livestock while not on public land . . . is referred to as his commensurability and the property so used is his *commensurate* property—*Appraisal Terminology & Handbook*⟩
*Ana* corresponding, correlative, *reciprocal: relative, contingent, *dependent
**proportionate** *proportional, commensurate, commensurable
*Ana* corresponding, correlative, *reciprocal

---

*Ana* analogous words    *Ant* antonyms    *Con* contrasted words    See also explanatory notes facing page 1

*Ant* disproportionate

**proposal, proposition** denote something which is proposed to another for consideration. **Proposal** usually carries a clear suggestion of the act of proposing; thus, one receives a *proposal*, or entertains a *proposal*, or listens to a *proposal*. It also commonly implies an offer (as of oneself as a husband, or of a sum of money in return for the transferring of a piece of property) ⟨a *proposal* of marriage⟩ ⟨he offered to sweep the floor of the gymnasium then and there. This *proposal* convinced the Skenes—*Shaw*⟩ ⟨the steel industry refused to make any wage *proposals* until it obtained federal clearance for higher steel prices—*Current History*⟩ But it may imply the suggestion of a scheme, a plan, or a project which may be accepted or rejected at the will of the one to whom it is proposed ⟨every *proposal* for a grant, a subsidy, a loan, is being examined more carefully and less enthusiastically than at any previous time—*Harsch*⟩ ⟨this *proposal* was distinctly treasonable, but Burr probably never seriously intended to carry it out—*Cox*⟩ **Proposition** applies primarily to a usually affirmative statement that is propounded for discussion, argument, proof, or disproof ⟨demonstrate the truth of a *proposition*⟩ ⟨at first sight the *proposition* seemed absurd⟩ ⟨the fanatical and ordered mobs . . . proved, if the *proposition* needed proof, that in a time of crisis men will act from passion—*MacLeish*⟩ ⟨it is a *proposition* too plain to be contested, that the constitution controls any legislative act repugnant to it—*John Marshall*⟩ The term is also applicable to an implied or expressed principle that is or may be questioned or is regarded from the point of view of its truth or its falsity ⟨who still fervently espouse the pestilential *proposition* that the world needs to be saved in a hurry by their own brand of righteousness—*Rolo*⟩ **Proposition** has been and to a restricted extent still is used instead of *proposal* in the sense of a proposal made formally that some course of action be followed, some policy be adopted, or some honor granted ⟨we hold it essential to our success . . . that the *proposition* of Sir George Clerk should be adopted—*Wilberforce*⟩ ⟨parking meters for Bakersfield again will be a *proposition* on the June 3 ballot—*Los Angeles Examiner*⟩ **Proposition** may replace *proposal* in implying an act of proposing ⟨if you wish to buy this land, make me a *proposition*⟩ but in such use it and especially the corresponding verb **proposition** may carry a hint of irregularity or impropriety that *proposal* lacks; thus, one offers a *proposal* of marriage but a *proposition* of less formal sexual relation ⟨propositioned him to work for the Soviets after his return to the United States—*Expose of Soviet Espionage*⟩

**propose** 1 purpose, *intend, mean, design
*Ana* *aim, aspire: plan, plot, scheme, project (see under
PLAN *n*)
2 **Propose, propound, pose** can all mean to set before the mind for consideration. **Propose** (see also INTEND) fundamentally implies an invitation to consider, discuss, settle, or agree on some question or some proposition clearly stated ⟨in the last chapter I *proposed* the hypothesis that a pure poetry exists—*Day Lewis*⟩ ⟨someone *proposed* that he had really done it the night before by moonlight—*Stafford*⟩ or an offering for consideration or acceptance of someone as a candidate or aspirant or of something by way of a suggestion ⟨he *proposed* Mr. Smith for secretary of the club⟩ ⟨*propose* marriage⟩ ⟨with a swarm of fantastic reforms being every day suggested . . . perhaps we may *propose* one as fantastic as any other—*Sullivan*⟩ **Propound** implies the stating of a question or proposition for discussion; it usually suggests neither personal bias nor an attempt to prove or disprove on the part of the one setting it forth or in the manner of setting it forth. The term is there-

fore often used when the writer or speaker wishes to convey no implications of how the one propounding would answer the question or deal with the proposition ⟨the query is *propounded* whether the privilege should be accorded to a physician of putting a patient painlessly out of the world when there is incurable disease—*Cardozo*⟩ ⟨*propound* the thesis that the great artist is an unconscious artist—*T. S. Eliot*⟩ ⟨if we may judge from his . . . facility in the *propounding* of theories—*Huxley*⟩ **Pose** often equals *propound*, except that it frequently implies that no attempt will be or can be made to seek an immediate answer ⟨the problems *posed* by this situation in the control of cancer and diseases of the heart are receiving the most serious study—*Morrison*⟩ ⟨I shall try at least to *pose* basic issues that underlie all our political problems—*Frankfurter*⟩
*Ana* state (see RELATE): *offer, tender, present

**proposition** *proposal
**propound** *propose, pose
*Ana* *ask, question, query: state (see RELATE)
**propriety** *decorum, decency, etiquette, dignity
*Ana* grace, *elegance, dignity: *form, usage, convention, convenance
**prorate** *apportion, portion, parcel, ration
**prosaic, prosy, matter-of-fact** all denote having a plain, practical, unimaginative, unemotional character or quality. **Prosaic** implies an opposition to *poetic* in the extended sense of that word. Although the term suggests the quality of prose, it seldom refers to literary prose as such but rather to the ordinary language of men in communicating their wants, their ideas, or their experiences, or in rendering intelligible what is difficult to understand or make clear; hence, *prosaic* usually implies a commonplace, unexciting quality, and the absence of everything that would stimulate feeling or awaken great interest ⟨to make verse speak the language of prose, without being *prosaic* . . . is one of the most arduous tasks a poet can undertake—*Cowper*⟩ ⟨a certain irreverent exuberance which prompts him never to choose a *prosaic* example for his concrete illustrations—*Times Lit. Sup.*⟩ ⟨the eighteenth century, from the religious point of view, is a period of rather cold and *prosaic* common sense—*Inge*⟩ ⟨a record of mediocrities, of the airless *prosaic* world of a small college town—*E. K. Brown*⟩ **Prosy**, on the other hand, suggests a relation to *prose,* the verb, rather than to *prose,* the noun, and heightens the implication in the verb of turning what is poetry or interesting prose into dull plain prose (as by paraphrasing or by translating). Consequently, *prosy* stresses extreme dullness or tediousness and usually implies a tendency to talk or write at length in a boring or uninviting manner ⟨made me wish that he would be long-winded and *prosy* instead of twitching me from one thing to another—*Sassoon*⟩ ⟨all *prosy* dull society sinners, who chatter and bleat and bore—*Gilbert*⟩ **Matter-of-fact** stresses a lack of interest in the imaginative, speculative, visionary, romantic or ideal; sometimes it connotes accuracy in detail, but often it suggests concern only for the obvious and a neglect of the deeper or spiritual reality or an absence of emotional quality ⟨a *matter-of-fact* account of his experience⟩ ⟨a *matter-of-fact* historian⟩ ⟨faced with this *matter-of-fact* skepticism you are driven into pure metaphysics—*Shaw*⟩ ⟨Lilly, who was *matter-of-fact* and in whom introspection, poetry or contemplation had no place—*Ethel Wilson*⟩
*Ana* practical, *practicable: boring, tedious, *irksome
**proscribe** *sentence, condemn, damn, doom
**proselyte** *convert
**prospect, outlook, anticipation, foretaste** are comparable when they mean an advance realization of something to

come, especially of something foreseen or expected. *Prospect* and *outlook* both imply a conjuring up of a picture or mental vision of what the future, usually the near future, holds in store. **Prospect** is chiefly applied to particular events or situations, especially to those of interest to one as an individual and evocative of an emotional response ⟨the *prospect* of a quick, easy conquest of Greece . . . proved too big a temptation for the strutting Fascist Caesar to resist—*Shirer*⟩ ⟨Coverly felt a dim rumble of homosexual lust . . . . Then the lash of his conscience crashed down . . . at the *prospect* of joining this pale-eyed company—*Cheever*⟩ ⟨he had just received a box of new books . . . and had preferred the *prospect* of a quiet Sunday at home —*Wharton*⟩ **Outlook** suggests an attempt to forecast the future from the point of view of an intellectual (as an economist or a philosopher) or from that of a practical man (as a politician or businessman) who is concerned not only with immediate but remote possibilities, and who demands accuracy in detail and soundness in conclusions ⟨the *outlook* for business has been declared favorable⟩ ⟨the *outlook,* domestic and international, was still what those who think in terms of color call black—*Rose Macaulay*⟩ ⟨in Pennsylvania the *outlook* is equally gloomy. Today the state has a surplus. But . . . that surplus will evaporate soon—*Armbrister*⟩ **Anticipation** usually implies a prospect or outlook, but in addition it involves the implication of advance suffering or enjoyment of what is envisioned ⟨Lord Beaconsfield once said that the worst evil one has to endure is the *anticipation* of the calamities that do not happen—*Benson*⟩ ⟨the young Bishop lay down in Benito's deep feather bed, thinking how different was this night from his *anticipation* of it—*Cather*⟩ **Foretaste** also implies advance experience or prior enjoyment or suffering, but it does not necessarily connote, as does *anticipation,* a mental as distinguished from an actual experience. It implies sufficient experience to give one a hint of what is to come, but the experience, or taste, may be actual enjoyment or suffering or a fleeting but poignant anticipation of it ⟨for whatever wrong she had done, she would pay through a thousand tortured days. Already the *foretaste* of them was upon her—*Hervey*⟩ ⟨giving me amid the fretful dwellings of mankind a *foretaste* . . . of the calm that Nature breathes among the hills and groves—*Wordsworth*⟩
*Ana* hope, expectation (see corresponding verbs at EXPECT): foreseeing *or* foresight, foreknowing *or* foreknowledge, divining *or* divination (see corresponding verbs at FORESEE)

**prosper** *succeed, thrive, flourish
*Ana* *increase, augment, multiply: *bear, yield, produce, turn out

**prostrate** *prone, supine, recumbent, couchant, dormant
*Ana* flat, *level: abject (see MEAN)

**prosy** *prosaic, matter-of-fact
*Ana* *insipid, jejune, banal, inane: *irksome, boring, tedious

**protean** *changeable, changeful, variable, mutable

**protect** shield, guard, safeguard, *defend
*Ana* *save, preserve, conserve: *ensure, insure, assure: shelter, *harbor

**protest** *vb* 1 avouch, avow, profess, affirm, aver, *assert, declare, predicate, warrant
2 *object, remonstrate, expostulate, kick
*Ana* oppose, *resist, combat, fight: *demur, scruple, balk
*Ant* agree (sense 1)

**protract** prolong, *extend, lengthen, elongate
*Ana* *delay, retard, slow, slacken: *defer, suspend, stay, postpone
*Ant* curtail —*Con* *shorten, abridge, abbreviate

**protrude** *bulge, jut, stick out, protuberate, project, overhang, beetle
*Ana* obtrude (see INTRUDE): *extend, prolong: swell, distend, *expand

**protrusion** *projection, protuberance, bulge

**protuberance** *projection, protrusion, bulge

**protuberate** *bulge, jut, stick out, protrude, project, overhang, beetle
*Ana* swell, distend, *expand

**proud** 1 Proud, arrogant, haughty, lordly, insolent, overbearing, supercilious, disdainful can mean in common filled with or showing a sense of one's superiority and scorn for what one regards as in some way inferior. **Proud** (see also *proud* under PRIDE *n*) usually connotes a lofty or imposing manner, attitude, or appearance that may be interpreted as dignified, elevated, spirited, imperious, satisfied, contemptuous, or inordinately conceited according to the circumstances ⟨oh, why should the spirit of mortal be *proud*? Like a swift-flitting meteor, a fast-flying cloud . . . he passeth from life to his rest in the grave—*William Knox*⟩ ⟨she's a stuck-up *proud* girl, and she hasn't a proper decency—*Buck*⟩ ⟨a dictator convinced that destiny lies in his own hands is bound to be *proud,* ruthless and ultimately destructive—*Billy Graham*⟩ **Arrogant** implies a disposition to claim for oneself, often domineeringly or aggressively, more consideration or importance than is warranted or justly due ⟨the Junker developed into a rude, domineering, *arrogant* type of man, without cultivation or culture—*Shirer*⟩ ⟨in holidays the atmosphere of home is apt to be dominated by the young people. Consequently they tend to become *arrogant* and hard—*Russell*⟩ **Haughty** implies a strong consciousness of exalted birth, station, or character, and a more or less obvious scorn of those who are regarded as beneath one ⟨pride goeth before destruction, and an *haughty* spirit before a fall—*Prov* 16:18⟩ ⟨his walk, his *haughty,* indifferent manner spoke his scorn for the two . . . men who accompanied him—*Hervey*⟩ The last four words of this group are more specific than the preceding terms and refer more to the ways in which arrogance or haughtiness is exhibited than to the temperament or attitude. **Lordly** usually suggests pomposity, strutting, or an arrogant display of power or magnificence ⟨a *lordly* indifference to making money by his writings—*Stephen*⟩ ⟨a *lordly* foreman in a shoe factory —a man who, in distributing the envelopes, had the manner of a prince doling out favors to a servile group of petitioners—*Dreiser*⟩ **Insolent** implies both haughtiness and extreme contemptuousness; it carries a stronger implication than the preceding words of a will to insult or affront the person so treated ⟨she could not determine whether the silent contempt of the gentlemen, or the *insolent* smiles of the ladies, were more intolerable—*Austen*⟩ ⟨vile food, vile beyond belief, slapped down before their sunken faces by *insolent* waiters—*K. A. Porter*⟩ **Overbearing** suggests a bullying or tyrannical disposition, or intolerable insolence ⟨an *overbearing* employer⟩ ⟨back country militiamen whose rough *overbearing* manners sorely tried the Indians' patience—*Amer. Guide Series: Tenn.*⟩ **Supercilious** stresses such superficial aspects of haughtiness as a lofty patronizing manner intended to repel advances. It refers to one's behavior to others rather than to one's conceit of oneself, though the latter is always implied; often it suggests not only scorn but also incivility ⟨they have no blood these people. Their voices, their *supercilious* eyes that look you up and down—*Galsworthy*⟩ ⟨*supercilious* and haughty they [camels] turn this way and that, like the dowagers of very aristocratic families at a plebeian evening party—*Huxley*⟩ **Disdainful** implies a more passionate scorn for what is beneath one than does *supercilious;* it as often as not suggests justifiable pride or justifiable scorn ⟨very elegant in velvet and broadcloth, with delicately cut, *disdainful* features,—one had only to see him cross the room . . . to feel the electric quality under his cold reserve—*Cather*⟩ ⟨a democracy smugly *disdainful* of new ideas would be a sick democracy —*Eisenhower*⟩

*Ana* contemptuous, scornful, disdainful (see corresponding nouns under DESPISE): pretentious, ostentatious (see SHOWY): imperious, domineering, *masterful

*Ant* humble: ashamed

**2** vain, vainglorious (see under PRIDE *n*)

*Ana* exalted, magnified, aggrandized (see EXALT): self-satisfied, *complacent, smug: contented, satisfied (see under SATISFY)

*Ant* ashamed: humble

**prove 1** Prove, try, test, demonstrate are comparable when they mean to establish a given or an implied contention or reach a convincing conclusion by such appropriate means as evidence, argument, or experiment. The same distinctions in implications and connotations are evident in their corresponding nouns **proof, trial, test, demonstration** when they denote the process or the means by which a contention is established or a convincing conclusion is reached. **Prove** and **proof** (see also INDICATE, REASON *n* 1) are the most widely useful of these terms, employable not only in reference to contentions and conclusions, but also in reference to persons or things whose quality (as of strength, genuineness, or fitness) is in question. When used in reference to contentions or to conclusions reached by study, they imply that evidence sufficient in amount and sufficiently reliable in its character has been adduced to bring conviction of the truth of the contentions or conclusions and to make other contentions or other conclusions untenable ⟨this proposition may or may not be true; at present there is certainly no evidence sufficient to *prove* it true—*Russell*⟩ ⟨the legislation of the different colonies furnishes positive and indisputable *proof* of this fact—*Taney*⟩ But *prove* and *proof* when used in reference to persons or things about which there is doubt in some particular imply the settlement of this doubt or the establishing of certainty of his or its quality by subjecting the thing to an experiment or by giving the person a chance to manifest his quality in experience, or by such means as assaying, verifying, or checking ⟨we want to realize our spontaneity and *prove* our powers, for the joy of it—*Justice Holmes*⟩ ⟨*prove* a cannon⟩ ⟨*proved* his courage in action⟩ ⟨put a man's loyalty to the *proof*⟩ ⟨the *proof* of the pudding is in the eating⟩ **Try** and **trial** (see also ATTEMPT *vb*, TRIAL 2) carry implications from their earliest senses of to separate, or the separation of, the good from the bad in a person or thing, and therefore stress not the conclusion reached but the process by which the guilt or innocence of a person is definitely proved, or a thing's genuineness or falsity, its worth or worthlessness, or its degree of strength or validity is definitely established ⟨*try* a person for theft⟩ ⟨a boy does not like to be called a fool, and is usually ready to *try* the question with his fists—*Meredith*⟩ ⟨some other apparently inaccessible peak on which to *try* their ardor and endurance—*Mais*⟩ ⟨the new employee is on *trial*⟩ ⟨a brief *trial* of the plan would convince the people of its futility—*Ogg & Ray*⟩ **Test**, both as a verb and as a noun, implies a putting to decisive proof by means of experiment, use, experience, or comparison with a high standard, or through subjection to a thorough examination or trial for the sake of such proof or a determination of the facts ⟨experience is the surest standard by which to *test* the real tendency of the existing constitution—*Wash-*

*ington*⟩ ⟨the first time he made a helmet, he *tested* its capacity for resisting blows, and battered it out of shape; next time he did not *test* it but "deemed" it to be a very good helmet—*Russell*⟩ ⟨one *test* of a writer's value lies in the series of illusions and superstitions which surround his work—*Geismar*⟩ **Demonstrate** and **demonstration** (see also SHOW *vb* 1) imply the conclusive proof of a contention or the reaching of a conclusion about which there can be no doubt. In such use, *prove* and *demonstrate* and their corresponding nouns are not distinguishable except that in *demonstrate* the emphasis is upon the resulting certainty or formality of method ⟨[Lyell] first imagined, and then *demonstrated*, that the geologic agencies are not explosive and cataclysmal, but steady and patient— *Eliot*⟩

*Ana* corroborate, verify, substantiate, *confirm: *justify, warrant

*Ant* disprove

**2** *indicate, betoken, attest, bespeak, argue

*Ana* evidence, manifest, evince, *show, demonstrate

**provenance, provenience** *origin, source, inception, root, prime mover

*Ana* beginning, commencement, starting (see corresponding verbs at BEGIN)

**provender** *food, fodder, forage, feed, victuals, viands, provisions, comestibles

**proverb** maxim, adage, motto, *saying, saw, epigram, aphorism, apothegm

**provide, supply, furnish** mean to give or to get what is desired by or needed for someone or something. The words are often used interchangeably without seeming loss ⟨*provide* what is needed for an army⟩ ⟨*supply* daily rations of food⟩ ⟨*furnish* enough men for the expedition⟩ but sometimes one of them rather than either of the others may be selected because of the implications or connotations that it stresses. **Provide** may suggest foresight and stress the idea of making adequate preparation for something by stocking or equipping; the agent of the action in such cases is usually personal ⟨*provide* for the common defense— *U. S. Constitution*⟩ ⟨through the long painful days of inaction his wife sought by every possible means to *provide* him with occupation—*Current Biog.*⟩ ⟨federal old-age and survivors insurance *provides* retirements benefits to workers—*Collier's Yr. Bk.*⟩ **Supply** may stress the idea of replacing, of making up what is needed, or of satisfying a deficiency ⟨cards . . . and the polished die, the yawning chasm of indolence *supply*—*Cowper*⟩ ⟨unable to *supply* the public demand⟩ ⟨an age which *supplied* the lack of moral habits by a system of moral attitudes and poses—*T. S. Eliot*⟩ ⟨the book would be incomplete without some such discussion as I have tried to *supply*— *Inge*⟩ **Furnish** (see also FURNISH) may emphasize the idea of fitting something or someone with whatever is necessary or, sometimes, normal or desirable (as for use, occupancy, service, or emergencies) ⟨a small salary out of which she had to *furnish* her own wardrobe—*Current Biog.*⟩ ⟨the . . . tail of this bird . . . is *furnished* with proper quills— *Winchell*⟩ ⟨the southeast trade winds and the tropical foliage *furnish* alleviating coolness—*Chippendale*⟩

*Ana* *prepare, fit, ready: equip, outfit, arm (see FURNISH): purvey, *cater

**provided** *if

**providence** *prudence, foresight, forethought, discretion

*Ana* *care, solicitude, concern: thoughtfulness, consideration (see corresponding adjectives at THOUGHTFUL): frugality, thriftiness, economy (see corresponding adjectives at SPARING)

*Ant* improvidence

**provident** prudent, foresighted, forethoughtful, discreet

(see under PRUDENCE)
*Ana* careful, solicitous, concerned (see under CARE *n*): *thoughtful, considerate: *sparing, economical, frugal, thrifty
*Ant* improvident

**providential** *lucky, fortunate, happy
*Ana* benign, auspicious, propitious, *favorable: benignant, kindly, *kind

**providing** see under *provided* at IF

**province** 1 *field, domain, sphere, territory, bailiwick
*Ana* *limit, confine, bound, end
2 *function, office, duty
*Ana* *work, calling, pursuit, business: *task, duty, job

**provincial** *insular, parochial, local, small-town
*Ana* circumscribed, confined, limited, restricted (see LIMIT *vb*): narrow, narrow-minded, *illiberal, intolerant, hidebound, bigoted
*Ant* catholic —*Con* cosmic, cosmopolitan, *universal: *liberal, progressive

**provision** 1 *condition, stipulation, terms, proviso, reservation, strings
*Ana* clause, article, *paragraph: prerequisite, requisite, *requirement
2 in plural form **provisions** *food, feed, victuals, viands, comestibles, provender, fodder, forage

**provisional** 1 Provisional, tentative are comparable when they mean not final or definitive. Something **provisional** is adopted only for the time being and will be discarded when the final or definitive form is established or when the need which called it into being no longer exists. *Provisional*, therefore, is used to describe something made or devised while its permanent successor is in process of formation or construction ⟨a *provisional* government⟩ ⟨these *provisional* assemblies would decide the conditions under which elections should be held—*Cronyn*⟩ or when circumstances prevent introduction of a corresponding definitive or permanent thing; thus, a *provisional* order of a government agency is one subject to review and revision by the legislative branch; a *provisional* license or certificate (as of a driver or a teacher) is one destined to be replaced by a permanent license or certificate if the holder maintains certain standards or meets certain additional qualifications. Something **tentative** is of the nature of a trial or experiment or serves as a test of a thing's practicability or feasibility ⟨the awakening of the modern world to consciousness, and its first *tentative*, then fuller, then rapturous expression of it— J. R. *Lowell*⟩ ⟨it would be folly to treat the first *tentative* results as final—*Jeans*⟩ ⟨Maria was entranced with this reverent gesture, and her *tentative* approval of her cousin settled into awed respect—*Hervey*⟩
*Ana* *temporary: conditional, *dependent, contingent
*Ant* definitive
2 *temporary, ad interim, acting, supply

**proviso** *condition, stipulation, terms, provision, reservation, strings
*Ana* clause, article, *paragraph: limitation, restriction (see corresponding verbs at LIMIT): contingency, exigency (see JUNCTURE)

**provoke** 1 Provoke, excite, stimulate, pique, quicken, galvanize can all mean to rouse one into doing or feeling something or to call something into existence by so rousing a person. **Provoke** stresses a power in the agent or agency sufficient to produce such an effect, but it is often the least explicit of these terms as to the nature or character of that power and may imply nothing more than the effecting of the stated result ⟨it is not in . . . the emotions *provoked* by particular events in his life, that the poet is in any way remarkable or interesting—*T. S. Eliot*⟩ ⟨inoculate you

with that disease . . . in order to *provoke* you to resist it as the mud *provokes* the cat to wash itself—*Shaw*⟩ ⟨his candor *provoked* a storm of controversy—*Times Lit. Sup.*⟩ **Excite** carries so strong an implication of a rousing that stirs up, moves profoundly, or serves as a challenge to one's powers that the term is often used merely in the sense of to rouse in any of these ways ⟨the ideas which *excited* my own generation— *Æ*⟩ ⟨a city beautiful enough to delight the romantic, picturesque enough to *excite* the jaded—*Cassidy*⟩ Often, however, *excite* adds to these implications those found in *provoke*, and thereby becomes a more explicit or richer word than the latter by suggesting the powerful or stirring nature of the agent or agency and the degree or intensity of the activity stirred up ⟨the curiosity *excited* by his long absence burst forth in . . . very direct questions—*Austen*⟩ ⟨the ruler's rivals, driven to outrage or *excited* to great envy, can topple governments built on stilts—*Flora Lewis*⟩ **Stimulate** suggests a provoking or exciting by or more often as if by a prick, a spur, or a goad; sometimes therefore it connotes a rousing out of lethargy, indifference, inaction, or inactivity, or a bringing forth into play something that is latent, dormant, or quiescent ⟨the stupidity of the opposition *stimulated* him, and made him resolute— *Mencken*⟩ ⟨I have always believed that it is better to *stimulate* than to correct, to fortify rather than to punish —*Benson*⟩ Often *stimulate* specifically implies excitement or reexcitement of interest, especially of an intellectual interest ⟨some subjects, which are remarkably *stimulating* to the mind of the pupil, are neglected, because they are not well adapted for examinations—*Inge*⟩ ⟨it's *stimulating* to be outside the law. It makes you look sharp, it simplifies the day's job—*Wouk*⟩ **Pique,** a term of more restricted application, suggests provocation or stimulation by or as if by something that pricks or irritates ⟨a show of secrecy always *piques* her curiosity⟩ ⟨*piqued* . . . by what he considered to be a premature disclosure of the plan—*Armbrister*⟩ **Quicken** implies a stimulation of life, vigor, energy, or activity with consequent beneficial results ⟨the mistress which I serve *quickens* what's dead —*Shak.*⟩ ⟨with his feeling for history *quickened* and sharpened, he was to find another stimulus to follow up this interest of his boyhood—*Brooks*⟩ **Galvanize** suggests a highly artificial stimulating or quickening, especially of something old, or stiff, or dying ⟨he seemed a mere automaton, *galvanized* into moving and speaking—*Hardy*⟩ ⟨*galvanize* the government into vehement and extraordinary preparation—*Sir Winston Churchill*⟩
*Ana* arouse, rouse, *stir: *thrill, electrify, enthuse: *incite, instigate, foment
2 *irritate, exasperate, nettle, aggravate, rile, peeve
*Ana* affront, *offend, insult, outrage: *anger, incense, madden: agitate, upset, perturb (see DISCOMPOSE)
*Ant* gratify

**prowess** *heroism, valor, gallantry
*Ana* bravery, boldness, audacity, intrepidity (see corresponding adjectives at BRAVE): *courage, mettle, spirit: strength, might, puissance, *power

**prowl** *vb* *wander, stray, roam, ramble, rove, range, gad, gallivant, traipse, meander

**proximity,** propinquity are often used almost interchangeably to denote nearness. **Proximity,** however, commonly implies simple and often temporary nearness in space; it may be used with reference to either persons or things found in the same vicinity or neighborhood ⟨for centuries and centuries their nests have been placed in the closest *proximity* to man—*Jefferies*⟩ ⟨his office geographically was just down the corridor from George's, a *proximity* which Harry had insisted on—*Auchincloss*⟩ ⟨affected

---

*Ana* analogous words     *Ant* antonyms     *Con* contrasted words     See also explanatory notes facing page 1

much as he might have been by the *proximity* of a large dog of doubtful temper—*Shaw*⟩ **Propinquity** may imply proximity, but it then usually distinctively suggests closeness, sometimes even contact ⟨we read a book because it happens to be near us and it looks inviting. It is a case where *propinquity* is everything—*Crothers*⟩ ⟨they are jammed into such *propinquity* with one another in their new suburbia—*Whyte*⟩ But it is more often used as *proximity* is not, to imply nearness in relationship ⟨here I disclaim all my paternal care, *propinquity*, and property of blood—*Shak.*⟩ or closeness in association, in age, or in tastes ⟨environment and *propinquity* make for a desire to graduate from marihuana to opiates—*Maurer & Vogel*⟩ or even closeness in time ⟨events occurring in close *propinquity* to each other⟩ ⟨thereby was declared the *propinquity* of their desolations, and that their tranquility was of no longer duration than those soon decaying fruits of summer—*Browne*⟩ *Ana* nearness, closeness (see corresponding adjectives at CLOSE): adjacency, contiguousness, juxtaposition (see corresponding adjectives at ADJACENT) *Ant* distance

**proxy** deputy, attorney, *agent, factor

**prudence, providence, foresight, forethought, discretion** are comparable when they denote a quality that enables a person to choose the wise and sensible course, especially in managing his practical affairs. The same differences in implications and connotations are apparent in the corresponding adjectives **prudent, provident, foresighted, forethoughtful, discreet. Prudence** and **prudent** (see also WISE), the most comprehensive of these words, imply both that one does not act rashly or unadvisedly and that one has foreseen the probable consequences of one's act. Consequently the terms usually imply habitual caution and circumspection ⟨that type of person who is conservative from *prudence* but revolutionary in his dreams—*T. S. Eliot*⟩ ⟨*prudence* is a virtue that reviews all of the values at stake and then assigns to each its proper weight— *JAMA*⟩ ⟨had judged it more *prudent* to hide than to fight —*Heiser*⟩ **Providence** and **provident** imply thought for the future, especially with reference to its difficulties and its needs and, usually, the provision in advance of what will then be required ⟨the intellectual *providence* to acquire . . . vast stores of dry information—*Bagehot*⟩ ⟨a *provident*, rather thoughtful people, who made their livelihood secure by raising crops and fowl—*Cather*⟩ **Foresight** and **foresighted** stress a power, usually the result of a highly developed intelligence, of seeing what is likely to happen and of being prepared for it ⟨the more we study the making of the principate, the more we shall be impressed with the grasp and *foresight* of its founder— *Buchan*⟩ ⟨incapable of the *foresighted* control and adjustment of action which are the essence of all the higher forms of behavior—*McDougall*⟩ **Forethought** and the less frequent **forethoughtful** suggest due consideration of contingencies ⟨in choosing the Yankee dialect, I did not act without *forethought*—*J. R. Lowell*⟩ ⟨every newcomer, be he never so *forethoughtful,* finds himself lacking tools —*Bell*⟩ **Discretion** and **discreet** stress qualities (as good judgment, caution, and self-control) which make for prudence or compel prudent action; they often imply the power to restrain oneself when one is tempted to be temerarious, passionate, incensed, or loquacious ⟨encountered an eagerness to talk and a candor of expression among officials that . . . has heavily taxed my *discretion*— *A. E. Stevenson*⟩ ⟨I dare say he will be a *discreeter* man all his life, for the foolishness of his first choice—*Austen*⟩ *Ana* caution, circumspection, calculation (see under CAUTIOUS): expediency, advisableness (see corresponding

adjectives at EXPEDIENT): frugality, thriftiness *or* thrift (see corresponding adjectives at SPARING)

**prudent** 1 judicious, sensible, sane, *wise, sage, sapient *Ana* *intelligent, brilliant, bright, smart, alert: *shrewd, perspicacious, sagacious, astute: disciplined, schooled (see TEACH)
2 provident, foresighted, forethoughtful, discreet (see under PRUDENCE) *Ana* *cautious, circumspect, calculating, wary: politic, *expedient, advisable: economical, frugal, thrifty, *sparing
3 **Prudent, prudential** are sometimes confused in use. **Prudent** applies to persons or their acts or utterances and implies such qualities of mind or character as caution, circumspection, and thrift (see *prudent* under PRUDENCE), or as wisdom in practical affairs (see WISE) ⟨a *prudent* man⟩ ⟨a *prudent* course⟩ ⟨a *prudent* way of life⟩ ⟨people who are both dissolute and *prudent*. They want to have their fun, and they want to keep their position—*Sackville-West*⟩ **Prudential**, on the other hand, applies not to individuals but either to habits, motives, policies, or considerations which are dictated or prescribed by prudence, forethought, business sense, or practical wisdom ⟨in a *prudential* light it is certainly a very good match for her—*Austen*⟩ ⟨from obvious *prudential* considerations the Pacific has been principally sailed over in known tracts—*Melville*⟩ or to committees, groups, or associations having charge of practical affairs such as expenditures or exercising discretionary or advisory powers in regard to these ⟨a *prudential* investment society⟩ ⟨the *prudential* committee of a Congregational church⟩ *Ana* politic, *expedient, advisable: advising, counseling (see corresponding verbs under ADVICE)

**prudential** *prudent

**prudish** *prim, priggish, prissy, puritanical, straitlaced, stuffy *Ana* *rigid, strict: stern, *severe, austere: formal, conventional, solemn (see CEREMONIAL)

**prune** *vb* trim, lop, *shear, poll, clip, snip, crop *Ana* enhance, heighten (see INTENSIFY): eliminate, *exclude

**prying** *curious, inquisitive, snoopy, nosy *Ana* meddlesome, officious, *impertinent, intrusive, obtrusive

**pseudo** *counterfeit, spurious, bogus, fake, sham, pinchbeck, phony *Ana* *false, wrong: *misleading, deceptive, delusive, delusory

**pseudonym, alias, nom de guerre, pen name, nom de plume, incognito** all denote a name other than one's true or legal name. **Pseudonym** usually implies assumption of a fictitious name as an accepted practice of writers, prizefighters, actors, and entertainers; it does not suggest a discreditable motive for one's attempt to conceal one's identity. **Alias,** in legal use, covers not only assumed names, but those ascribed by others; thus, a boy's true name may be John Potter but is better known by the *alias* John Rhoads (Rhoads being his stepfather's name). In more general use *alias* is associated regularly with offenders against the law and usually connotes an attempt to free oneself by a change of name from the onus of a criminal record. **Nom de guerre** is a pseudonym assumed by one who seeks anonymity or freedom of scope typically as an adventurer, a critic, or a controversialist; **pen name** or **nom de plume** is the pseudonym of a writer. **Incognito** can denote a name or character adopted especially by a person of rank or eminence from a desire to remain unrecognized or as a polite fiction by which the honors due his rank or eminence may be avoided ⟨the Prince

A colon (:) separates groups of words discriminated. An asterisk (*) indicates place of treatment of each group.

of Wales often traveled under the *incognito* of Baron Chester⟩

**psyche** *mind, intellect, soul, brain, intelligence, wit

**psychiatrist** *neurologist, alienist, psychopathologist, psychotherapist, psychoanalyst

**psychic** *mental, intellectual, intelligent, cerebral

**psychoanalyst** *neurologist, psychiatrist, alienist, psychopathologist, psychotherapist

**psychopathologist** *neurologist, psychiatrist, alienist, psychotherapist, psychoanalyst

**psychosis** *insanity, lunacy, mania, dementia

**psychotherapist** *neurologist, psychiatrist, alienist, psychopathologist, psychoanalyst

**puberty, pubescence** *youth, adolescence

**public** *n* *following, clientele, audience

**publication** declaration, announcement, advertisement, proclamation, promulgation, broadcasting (see under DECLARE)

**publicity, ballyhoo, promotion, propaganda** are comparable when they mean either a systematic effort to mold public opinion in respect to something or the means or the matter used in such an effort. Each implies a specialized form of advertising. **Publicity** is used especially in reference to the activities of and the information disseminated by a person or persons in the employ of individuals, corporations, organizations, associations, or institutions that seek advertising through more or less indirect means in order to attract attention to themselves, their products, or their objectives or that wish to provide a source of authoritative information on matters concerning themselves that are of interest to the public; thus, the work of a theatrical press agent and of a public relations counsel is *publicity*; in the first case, for an actor or producer seeking favorable notices in the press; in the second, for a corporation or institution that seeks to control the kind of information regarding itself that is published ⟨some of his carefully planned speeches, always made in the presence of the right listener, are perfect of their kind—their kind being advertisement, or, as we say now, *publicity*—*Lucas*⟩ ⟨the object of all commercial *publicity* is to persuade someone to exchange his money for what the advertiser has for sale—*H. H. Smith*⟩ **Ballyhoo** is indiscriminately applied to any kind of advertising, publicity, or promotion which the speaker or writer regards as noisy, sensational, insincere, misleading, or unduly obtrusive ⟨the candidate's preconvention campaign was attended with too much *ballyhoo*⟩ ⟨every face powder must claim a "scientific" uniqueness, and by this *ballyhoo* millions are impressed—*Benedict*⟩ **Promotion** is specifically applied to the systematic efforts of a business organization to gain advance publicity for something new (as a venture, a product, a motion picture, or an issue of bonds) in order to ensure its favorable reception by the public when it is launched ⟨$50,000 was appropriated for the *promotion* of the company's new line of soups⟩ ⟨attractive *promotions* of spring clothing helped to allay the usual post-Easter drop in retail volume—*Dun's Review*⟩ **Propaganda** is applied to the concerted or systematic effort of a group that tries to convert others or to hold others to its way of thinking, and to the means employed and the matter circulated. The term has chiefly derogatory, but occasionally underogatory use. In derogatory use it frequently implies publicity sought through objectionable, usually underhand, methods or for a cause that cannot work in the open, and with the intent to win over the gullible or the unwary ⟨attempt to undermine the people's faith in democracy by communist *propaganda*⟩ ⟨he must acquire an armed following of his own, by lavish expenditure and adroit *propaganda*—*Buchan*⟩ In nonde-

rogatory use *propaganda* often implies the ends of convincing a prejudiced or ignorant public and of inducing it to accept something it is disposed to reject. Even in this use the word usually suggests indirect methods ⟨gradually the terror it [a leper colony] caused was lost through our educational *propaganda*—*Heiser*⟩
*Ana* advertisement, publication, announcement, promulgation, broadcasting (see under DECLARE)

**publish** *declare, announce, advertise, proclaim, promulgate, broadcast
*Ana* divulge, disclose, *reveal, discover: *communicate, impart: vent, ventilate, utter, broach, *express

**puerile** *youthful, juvenile, boyish, virgin, virginal, maiden
*Ana* *immature, unmatured, unripe: raw, callow, green, *rude
*Ant* adult —*Con* virile (see MALE)

**puff** *n* *criticism, critique, review, blurb

**pugnacious** combative, *belligerent, bellicose, quarrelsome, contentious
*Ana* *aggressive, militant, assertive, self-assertive, pushing, pushy
*Ant* pacific

**puissance** might, strength, *power, force, energy

**puissant** *powerful, potent, forceful, forcible
*Ant* impuissant

**pulchritudinous** beauteous, good-looking, comely, bonny, pretty, handsome, fair, lovely, *beautiful

**pull** *vb* **Pull, draw, drag, haul, hale, tug, tow** mean to cause to move in the direction determined by the person or thing that exerts force. **Pull**, the general term, is often accompanied by an adverb or adverbial phrase to indicate the direction ⟨two locomotives *pull* the heavy train up the grade⟩ ⟨*pull* a person toward one⟩ ⟨*pull* down goods from a shelf⟩ ⟨*pull* out a drawer⟩ ⟨he felt *pulled* this way and that way by duty and by ambition⟩ **Draw** usually implies a pulling forward or toward the person or thing that exerts the force; commonly it implies a steadier and smoother and often gentler motion than *pull* ⟨*draw* a chair to the fireside⟩ ⟨the coach was *drawn* by six horses⟩ ⟨*draw* a sled over the snow⟩ ⟨*draw* the curtains⟩ ⟨*draw* lots from an urn⟩ In extended use *draw* often specifically implies a result dependent on a drawing by lot ⟨*draw* a prize⟩ ⟨*draw* a jury⟩ or by extracting ⟨*draw* a tooth⟩ or by an inferring ⟨*draw* a conclusion⟩ or by attracting ⟨the parasol *drew* him like a magnet—*Wharton*⟩ ⟨the *drawing* power of a play⟩ or a bringing forth or eliciting from a source of supply ⟨*draw* money from the bank⟩ ⟨a . . . being from whom we *draw* power and refreshment —*Day Lewis*⟩ **Drag** implies a pulling slowly and heavily after the agent or thing exerting force over the ground or a surface; it usually suggests active or passive resistance ⟨the horses *dragged* the overturned carriage half a mile⟩ ⟨the ship *dragged* her moorings in the storm⟩ ⟨*drag* the laden net to the shore⟩ ⟨*drag* logs to the river⟩ ⟨the attempt which is now being made to *drag* Anglicanism away from its history and traditions—*Inge*⟩ **Haul** implies a forcible pulling, sometimes a dragging ⟨when the hawser fell into the water, there was no means of *hauling* the boat to shore⟩ ⟨*haul* down the sails⟩ ⟨that dangling figure was *hauled* up forty feet above the fountain—*Dickens*⟩ ⟨began to kiss all the girls, young and old, until his wife . . . *hauled* him aside and calmed him down—*Styron*⟩ *Haul* may imply transportation of heavy materials in a vehicle or conveyance ⟨wagons *hauling* loads of wood⟩ ⟨trucks *hauling* gravel⟩ ⟨trains that *haul* coal from the mines⟩ **Hale** may occasionally replace *haul* in the sense of pulling forcibly ⟨the rope that *haled* the buckets from the well—*Tennyson*⟩ but more often it is used of the constraining, compelling, or dragging of a reluctant person ⟨natives,

*Ana* analogous words    *Ant* antonyms    *Con* contrasted words    See also explanatory notes facing page 1

*haled* long distances to court as liquor witnesses—*Colby*⟩ **Tug** implies a strenuous, usually spasmodic pulling, but it may or may not suggest actual movement ⟨the child *tugged* at his father's hand⟩ ⟨*tugged* at the chains with the aid of two husky comrades—*Costain*⟩ ⟨the Old Inhabitant chuckled and *tugged* at his little goatee—*Brandt*⟩ **Tow** implies pulling or drawing (as by a rope or chain) something which is not using or is unable to use its own power ⟨*tow* a ship into its berth⟩ ⟨*tow* a wrecked automobile to a garage⟩ ⟨a truck comes out from headquarters, and *tows* the wagon—*G. R. Stewart*⟩

**pulsate, pulse, beat, throb, palpitate** can mean to manifest a rhythmical movement such as or similar to the one which occurs in the circulatory system when blood is forced along by alternate contractions and relaxations of the ventricles of the heart. The same distinctions in implications and connotations are to be found in the nouns **pulsation, pulse, beat, throb, palpitation** when they are used of this rhythmical movement or of one distinct step in it. **Pulsate** and **pulsation** carry few specific or distinguishing connotations, but they usually imply regularity, continuity, and vigor in the rhythm whether it is apparent in movements or in sounds ⟨when the heart no longer *pulsates,* death occurs⟩ ⟨great effort *pulsating* from the heart of this small island—*Sir Winston Churchill*⟩ ⟨the *pulsations* of its engine had died away—*Bennett*⟩ ⟨long heavy *pulsation* of airplanes passing over—*Thirkell*⟩ **Pulse,** the verb, carries a strong implication of impelled movement; in distinction from *pulsate* it may also connote a lively succession of spurts, waves, or gushes; thus, the arteries *pulsate* as the blood *pulses* through them. The term is more common in general and literary than in technical use. It sometimes takes as its subject what flows or moves in this fashion (as the blood) and at other times what evidences the rhythmical movement (as the heart or blood vessels) ⟨the *pulsing* waters of the sea⟩ ⟨through the tensed veins on his forehead the blood could be seen to *pulse* in nervous, staccato bounds—*Donn Byrne*⟩ ⟨Eustacia . . . set inwardly *pulsing* by his words—*Hardy*⟩ ⟨they move and breathe in an environment that *pulses* and glows—*Mencken*⟩ **Pulse,** the noun, is chiefly a technical term; even its extended use is affected by or dependent on the term's meaning in physiology. In this sense, *pulse* usually denotes the number of pulsations of the arteries in a minute as observed commonly by feeling the radial artery of the wrist ⟨a normal *pulse*⟩ ⟨feel a patient's *pulse*⟩ ⟨an intermittent *pulse*⟩ ⟨in his eardrums hammers his heavy *pulse*—*Lowell*⟩ In extended use *pulse,* when it does not take the place of *pulsation* is usually a metaphoric extension of the technical use ⟨Rome was the heart and *pulse* of the empire . . . and on its well-being hung the future of the civilized world—*Buchan*⟩ ⟨one felt the *pulse* of the village in the pub—*Mais*⟩ **Beat,** both verb and noun, is the ordinary nontechnical word often used in place of *pulsate* and *pulsation* and sometimes in place of *pulse.* It stresses rhythmical recurrence of sounds more often than rhythmical and continuous alternation in movement ⟨he could hear the *beat* of his heart⟩ ⟨his breathing was hard and . . . the blood *beat* in his ears and eyes—*Robertson Davies*⟩ ⟨a question was *beating* unanswered at the back of his brain—*Glasgow*⟩ It is the more usual designation for something (as the tick of a clock, a stroke on a drum, and the accented syllable in verse or note in music) that strikes the ear at regular intervals ⟨the *beat* of a bird's wing against a windowpane⟩ ⟨the *beating* of tom-toms⟩ Both the noun and verb **throb** imply vigorous and often violent or painful pulsation ⟨*throb* of drum and timbal's rattle—*Housman*⟩ ⟨the *throbbing* of an abscessed tooth⟩ Either is especially appropriate when there is the intent to imply excitement,

strain, or emotional stress ⟨the love which fills the letter, which *throbs* and burns in it—*H. O. Taylor*⟩ ⟨here is a captain, let him tell the tale; your hearts will *throb* and weep to hear him speak—*Shak.*⟩ ⟨the *throb* of their activity is felt throughout the whole body politic—*R. M. Dawson*⟩ **Palpitate** and **palpitation** imply rapid, often abnormally rapid and fluttering, pulsation. In medical use the terms commonly imply overexertion, violent emotion, or a diseased condition; in extended use, however, the words more often imply a rapid vibration, quivering, or shaking, without any connotation of something amiss ⟨then, delicate and *palpitating* as a silver reed, she stood up in the soft light of the morning—*Hewlett*⟩ ⟨though the book *palpitates* with l'amour, nothing like simple ordinary human love is to be seen anywhere—*Barrett*⟩
*Ana* vibrate, fluctuate, waver, oscillate (see SWING): quiver, shudder, quaver, tremble (see SHAKE)

**pulsation** pulse, beat, throb, palpitation (see under PULSATE)

**pulse** *n* pulsation, beat, throb, palpitation (see under PULSATE)
*Ana* *rhythm, cadence, meter: vibration, fluctuation (see corresponding verbs at SWING)

**pulse** *vb* *pulsate, beat, throb, palpitate
*Ana* *move, drive, impel: vibrate, fluctuate, oscillate (see SWING)

**pummel** *vb* *beat, pound, buffet, baste, belabor, thrash
*Ana* *strike, hit, smite, slug, punch

**punch** *vb* **1** *strike, hit, smite, slug, slog, swat, clout, slap, box, cuff
*Ana* *beat, pound, pummel, baste, belabor
**2** *perforate, puncture, prick, bore, drill
*Ana* pierce, penetrate, probe, *enter

**punch** *n* *vigor, vim, spirit, dash, esprit, verve, élan, drive

**punctilious** punctual, meticulous, scrupulous, *careful
*Ana* particular, fussy, squeamish, fastidious, *nice: formal, conventional, ceremonious, *ceremonial

**punctual** punctilious, meticulous, scrupulous, *careful
*Ana* *quick, prompt, ready: precise, *correct, nice, right

**puncture** *vb* *perforate, punch, prick, bore, drill
*Ana* pierce, penetrate (see ENTER): deflate, shrink (see CONTRACT *vb*)

**pungent, piquant, poignant, racy, spicy, snappy** are comparable when they mean characterized by sharpness, zest, and a piercing or gripping quality. **Pungent** applies especially to a sharp, piercing, stinging, biting, or penetrating quality, primarily of odors; it may suggest power to excite or stimulate keen interest or telling force and cogency ⟨her perfume, a sweet *pungent* odor . . . evocative and compelling—*Styron*⟩ ⟨the *pungent* reek of a strong cigar—*Doyle*⟩ ⟨his *pungent* pen played its part in rousing the nation to its later struggle with the Crown—*J. R. Green*⟩ ⟨the mob needs concrete goals and the *pungent* thrill of hate in order to give vent to its destructive impulses—*Cohen*⟩ **Piquant** may indicate an interesting or appetizing tartness, sharpness, or pungency that stimulates or a zestful, arch, provocative, challenging, or exciting quality that is individual or peculiar ⟨a *piquant* sauce⟩ ⟨*piquant* with the tart-sweet taste of green apples and sugar—*Spitzer*⟩ ⟨*piquant* touch of innocent malice in his narration—*Coulton*⟩ ⟨those *piquant* incongruities, which are the chief material of wit—*Montague*⟩ **Poignant** (see also MOVING) may describe what is sharply or piercingly effective upon the senses or stirring to one's inmost consciousness or deepest emotions ⟨the air of romantic poverty which Rosalie found so tragically *poignant*—*Wylie*⟩ ⟨with *poignant* finality, as a lover might put away a rose from a lost romance—*Turnbull*⟩ ⟨a vague but *poignant* sense of discouragement that the sacrifices of the

A colon (:) separates groups of words discriminated. An asterisk (*) indicates place of treatment of each group.

war had not been justified by its results spread over the country—*Handlin*⟩ **Racy** may suggest verve, dash, tang, or vitality manifested with lively free heartiness ⟨writes a *racy,* sometimes almost lusty prose, entirely suited to describing a group of down-to-earth hard-living people—*Sherberg*⟩ ⟨a rare and *racy* sense of humor—*Maugham*⟩ Sometimes the term may carry the additional hint of passing beyond the bounds of propriety or good taste ⟨considered too *racy* for the ladies and was read aloud only at a stag meeting—*Newsweek*⟩ ⟨if men yawn . . . the singers will sweep into an especially *racy* and obscene offering—*Julian Dana*⟩ **Spicy** describes what is seasoned or made redolent of spice; in extended uses it may suggest the piquant, smart, spirited, sensational, or scandalous ⟨flair for a *spicy* zestful vernacular in dialogue—*Rees*⟩ ⟨*spicy* tales of the type which usually appear in paper-bound copies, in which bishops are forced to visit nudist camps in their underwear—*Robertson Davies*⟩ **Snappy** suggests briskness, animation, dash, wit, or risqué quality ⟨spoken in a *snappy,* matter-of-fact way—*Lindsay*⟩ ⟨the renditions, if not especially lovely, were at all times spirited, neat, and *snappy*—*Virgil Thomson*⟩ ⟨taken one look at . . . a campus publication, decided that the contents are too *snappy,* and expelled the editor—*N. Y. Times*⟩

*Ana* *incisive, trenchant, biting, cutting: penetrating, piercing, probing (see ENTER): exciting, stimulating, provoking *or* provocative (see corresponding verbs at PROVOKE)

*Ant* bland

**punish,** chastise, castigate, chasten, discipline, correct mean to inflict pain, loss, or suffering upon a person for his sin, crime, or fault. **Punish** implies imposing a penalty for violation of law, disobedience of authority, or intentional wrongdoing ⟨if ye will not . . . hearken unto me, then I will *punish* you—*Lev* 26:18⟩ ⟨American society *punishes* the ex-Communist who voluntarily repents about as severely as it does the one caught Red-handed—*Bliven b.* 1889⟩ **Chastise** may suggest the infliction of corporal punishment and sometimes implies an acting in anger, but more often with a view to reformation or amendment ⟨my father hath *chastised* you with whips, but I will *chastise* you with scorpions—*1 Kings* 12:11⟩ Sometimes *chastise* implies verbal censure or denunciation ⟨moral and intellectual weaklings that she felt herself appointed to *chastise*—*Tennessee Williams*⟩ and then comes close to **castigate** which usually implies severe and often public lashing by tongue or pen rather than by whip or rod, and so suggests painful censure or bitter rebuke ⟨not even the ablest critic can *castigate* an artless generation into repentance and creative vigor—*Barnouw*⟩ **Chasten** usually implies subjection to affliction or trial with the aim not so much of punishment as of a testing whereby one may emerge humbled and purified or strengthened ⟨for whom the Lord loveth he *chasteneth* . . . . If ye endure *chastening,* God dealeth with you as with sons—*Heb* 12:6-7⟩ ⟨such bliss, he tells himself, cannot last forever; fortune must balance it now and then with a *chastening* blow—*Durant*⟩ **Discipline** (see also TEACH) implies punishment, chastisement, or sometimes chastening, with the intent to subjugate, subdue, or bring under one's control ⟨the duty of parents to *discipline* their children⟩ ⟨a thorn in the side of those in authority, his position . . . made it impossible to ignore or effectively to *discipline* him—*Fish*⟩ **Correct** implies punishment having for its aim the amendment or reformation of the offender ⟨his faults lie open to the laws; let them, not you, *correct* him —*Shak.*⟩ ⟨must moreover know how to *correct* without wounding—*Barzun*⟩

*Ana* *penalize, fine, amerce, mulct: *imprison, incarcer-

ate, immure: *avenge, revenge

*Ant* excuse: pardon  —*Con* *exculpate, acquit, exonerate, absolve, vindicate

**puny** *petty, trivial, trifling, paltry, measly, picayunish, picayune

*Ana* feeble, *weak, frail, infirm: *small, little, diminutive: slight, tenuous (see THIN *adj*)

**purblind** *blind, sightless

**purchase** *vb* *buy

*Ana* gain, win, *get, obtain, procure, secure

**pure 1** Pure, absolute, simple, sheer denote free from everything that is foreign to the true nature or the essential character of the thing specified. **Pure** distinctively suggests freedom from intermixture. When applied to concrete things, it usually implies lack of contamination, adulteration, or pollution ⟨*pure* water⟩ ⟨a *pure* breed⟩ When applied to an abstraction or to a concrete example of an abstraction, it implies the absence of everything that would obscure the thing in its essence or in its ideal character ⟨*pure* poetry⟩ ⟨an institute devoted to *pure* physics, as distinct from applied physics—*Endeavour*⟩ ⟨as there is a constant mingling of Hebrew and Aramaic passages, the Aramaic is not *pure*—*Barton*⟩ **Absolute** implies freedom from relation to or dependence on anything else; it is applied chiefly to abstractions (as space, time, and magnitude) viewed independently of experience and considered in their ultimate ideal character; thus, *absolute* space, as used in physics, is space conceived of as apart from the things which occupy it, and which limit or determine the ordinary person's notion of it. Because of such use, *absolute* often comes close to *real,* as opposed to *apparent. Absolute* music, in theory, is music that depends solely on such distinctive properties of that art as tone, harmony, and rhythm to produce its effects, and avoids, in contrast to program music, all suggestion or characterization of external things. *Absolute* is applied to substances less often than is *pure,* but both are applied to alcohol: *pure* alcohol is free from other matter except for a modicum of water; *absolute* alcohol is both pure and completely dehydrated. **Simple** stresses singleness of character and is distinguished from what is *compound* or *complex.* It can connote homogeneity and incapacity for analysis or further reduction ⟨an element is a *simple* substance⟩ ⟨quality and relation are *simple* notions⟩ ⟨was now confronted by *simple* beauty, pure and undeniable—*Gibbons*⟩ ⟨too-elaborate deference paid them by the neighbors embarrassed them and caused them to clothe their wealth in muted, *simple* gray—*Styron*⟩ *Simple,* as applied to abstractions or conceptions, often suggests artificial freedom from complexity, and sometimes also unreality or untruth, when the simplicity is attained by eliminating essential factors ⟨the world to which your philosophy professor introduces you is *simple* . . . . The contradictions of real life are absent from it—*James*⟩ **Sheer,** more than any of these words, tends to lose its significance and to become a mere intensive ⟨*sheer* nonsense⟩ However, it can distinctively imply such a dissociation from everything else that the pure and essential character of the quality (as a trait, virtue, or power) to which it is applied is clearly displayed ⟨the "Ancient Mariner" . . . is a work of *sheer* imagination —*Lowes*⟩ ⟨he was part *sheer* technician, part delighted child when he could demonstrate his sound system—*Theodore Sturgeon*⟩

*Ana* elemental, *elementary: *clear, transparent, lucid, limpid: genuine, *authentic

*Ant* contaminated, polluted: adulterated (*of foods, metals*): applied (*of science*)

**2** *chaste, modest, decent

*Ana* *clean, cleanly: virtuous, *moral, ethical

---

*Ant* impure: immoral

**purge** *vb* *rid, clear, unburden, disabuse
*Ana* cleanse, *clean: eliminate, *exclude, debar, shut out, rule out: *eject, oust, dismiss, expel: expunge, *erase, efface, delete

**puritanical** *prim, priggish, prissy, prudish, straitlaced, stuffy
*Ana* *rigid, rigorous, strict: *plain, simple, homely, unpretentious: *illiberal, narrow, narrow-minded, hidebound, intolerant, bigoted

**purloin** *steal, pilfer, filch, lift, pinch, snitch, swipe, cop
*Ana* abstract, *detach: *rob, plunder, rifle, loot, burglarize

**purport** *n* *substance, gist, burden, core, pith
*Ana* significance, import, *meaning, signification: tenor, *tendency, drift, trend

**purported** *supposed, supposititious, suppositious, reputed, putative, conjectural, hypothetical

**purpose** *n* *intention, intent, design, aim, end, object, objective, goal
*Ana* *ambition, aspiration: proposition, *proposal: *plan, project, scheme

**purpose** *vb* propose, design, *intend, mean
*Ana* meditate, *ponder: weigh, *consider, contemplate: plan, plot, scheme, project (see under PLAN *n*): determine, *decide

**pursue** *follow, chase, trail, tag, tail
*Ana* *persevere, persist: *practice, exercise: persecute, oppress (see WRONG *vb*): hound, ride, *bait, badger
*Con* flee, fly, *escape: avoid, evade, elude, shun (see ESCAPE)

**pursuit** calling, occupation, employment, *work, business

**purvey** *cater, pander
*Ana* *furnish, equip, outfit

**purview** *range, gamut, reach, radius, compass, sweep, scope, orbit, horizon, ken

**push** *vb* **Push, shove, thrust, propel** mean to use force upon a thing so as to make it move ahead or aside. **Push** implies the application of force by a body (as a person) already in contact with the body to be moved onward, aside, or out of the way ⟨*push* a wheelbarrow along the road⟩ ⟨*push* a door open⟩ ⟨*push* a man over a cliff⟩ ⟨an extra locomotive was needed at the rear to *push* the long train up the grade⟩ ⟨*push* the excited children into another room⟩ **Shove** often differs from *push* in carrying a stronger implication of the exercise of muscular strength and of forcing something along a surface ⟨the boys *shoved* the furniture up against the walls⟩ ⟨I picked him up trying to *shove* in the front door. There wouldn't been any door in a minute—*Hellman*⟩ Often, when muscular exertion is not strongly implied, haste or roughness or rudeness in pushing is suggested ⟨*shoved* the paper into his pocket⟩ ⟨*shove* the articles on the desk into a box⟩ ⟨*shove* a person out of one's way⟩ ⟨I can't say that I took the drink. It got *shoved* into my hand—*Warren*⟩ **Thrust** differs from *push* in carrying a weaker implication of steadiness or continuousness in the application of force and a stronger suggestion of rapidity in the movement effected or of violence in the force that is used; often the use of actual physical force is not clearly implied ⟨Abraham . . . *thrust* the old man out of his tent—*Taylor*⟩ ⟨*thrust* her hands in her coat pockets in a coquettish pose—*Wouk*⟩ Often, also, it implies the sudden and forcible pushing (as of a weapon, implement, or instrument) so that it enters into the thing aimed at ⟨*thrust* a spear into an opponent's breast⟩ ⟨*thrusting* their money into a stranger's hand—*Wolfe*⟩ **Propel** implies a driving forward or onward by a force or power that imparts motion. In some use it implies pressure exerted from outside or behind, usually by some power that is not human ⟨the flow of air which *propels* the slow-sailing clouds—*Lowes*⟩ ⟨she walked—as if she were being *propelled* from the outside, by a force that she neither knew nor could control—*Tate*⟩ Additionally, it is the usual term when the use of a mechanical aid or of an actuating power (as steam or electrical power) is implied ⟨ships *propelled* by steam⟩ ⟨a galley *propelled* by fifty oars⟩ ⟨automobiles are usually *propelled* by internal-combustion engines⟩

In extended uses **push** implies a pressing or urging forward (as with insistence, with vigor, or with impetuousness) so that one's end may be gained, one's work may be completed, or one's goal be reached ⟨*push* the nation into war⟩ ⟨*push* a theory to an extreme⟩ ⟨he directed a year-long probe . . . then *pushed* through sweeping reforms—*Armbrister*⟩ **Shove** often suggests obtrusiveness or intrusiveness or lack of finesse in attaining an end or making a way for oneself or another ⟨*shove* oneself into society⟩ ⟨*shoving* the boring tiring jobs off onto other people—*Ann Bridge*⟩ **Thrust** implies a forcing upon others of something that is not wanted, desired, or sought for ⟨some have greatness *thrust* upon 'em—*Shak.*⟩ ⟨Amy had a grievance . . . because Sophia had recently *thrust* upon her a fresh method of cooking green vegetables—*Bennett*⟩ **Propel** is sometimes used in place of *impel* when a strong inner urge or appetite is implied as pushing one on, especially toward what one desires ⟨anxiety is not the only force that *propels* us, but it is surely one of the most potent—*Binger*⟩
*Ana* *move, drive, impel: *force, compel, constrain, oblige

**pushing, pushy** *aggressive, militant, assertive, self-assertive
*Ana* *vigorous, energetic, strenuous: officious, intrusive, obtrusive (see IMPERTINENT): self-confident, confident, self-assured, assured (see corresponding nouns at CONFIDENCE)

**puss** *n* *face, countenance, visage, physiognomy, mug

**pustule** *abscess, boil, furuncle, carbuncle, pimple

**putative** *supposed, supposititious, suppositious, reputed, purported, conjectural, hypothetical
*Ana* alleged, advanced (see ADDUCE): assumed, pretended, simulated (see ASSUME)

**putrefy** rot, decompose, *decay, spoil, disintegrate, crumble
*Ana* corrupt, vitiate, deprave, *debase: deliquesce (see LIQUEFY)

**putrid** fetid, noisome, stinking, *malodorous, rank, rancid, fusty, musty
*Ana* decomposed, decayed, rotten, putrefied (see DECAY): corrupted, vitiated (see under DEBASE)

**putsch** *rebellion, revolution, uprising, revolt, insurrection, mutiny, coup

**put up** *reside, live, dwell, sojourn, lodge, stay, stop

**puzzle** *vb* **Puzzle, perplex, mystify, bewilder, distract, nonplus, confound, dumbfound** are comparable when they mean to disturb and baffle mentally or throw into mental confusion. The first three words express various mental reactions to what is intricate, complicated, or involved. **Puzzle** implies such complication or intricacy that the mind finds it exceedingly, often distressingly, difficult to understand or to solve ⟨a great poet may tax our brains, but he ought not to *puzzle* our wits—*Birrell*⟩ ⟨there was much that impressed, *puzzled* and troubled a foreign observer about the new Germany—*Shirer*⟩ **Perplex** adds to *puzzle* the implications of worry and uncertainty, especially about reaching a decision on a course of action or the right solution of a personal problem ⟨Southerners . . . were terribly *perplexed* and torn when the conceptions on which

A colon (:) separates groups of words discriminated. An asterisk (*) indicates place of treatment of each group.

they had been living began to be broken down—*Edmund Wilson*⟩ To **mystify** is to perplex, sometimes by playing upon one's credulity, but more often by concealing important facts or factors or by obscuring issues ⟨when she was weary of *mystifying* foreign statesmen, she turned to find fresh sport in *mystifying* her own ministers—*J. R. Green*⟩ ⟨once prescriptions were written almost altogether in Latin. This was not done to *mystify* the patient—*Fishbein*⟩ **Bewilder** often implies perplexity, but it stresses a confused state of mind that makes clear thinking and complete comprehension practically impossible ⟨*bewildered* by contradictory statements and orders⟩ ⟨do not run to the Socialists or the Capitalists, or to your favorite newspaper, to make up your mind for you: they will only unsettle and *bewilder* you—*Shaw*⟩ **Distract** implies strong agitation arising from divergent or conflicting considerations or interests ⟨she seemed nervous and *distracted*, kept glancing over her shoulder, and crushing her handkerchief up in her hands—*Cather*⟩ ⟨conscious of . . . a current of unsaid speeches, which would *distract* her feelings and perhaps confuse a little her thoughts—*Gibbons*⟩ The last three words imply less mental disturbance and distress than some of the preceding terms, but they heighten the implication of bafflement and mental confusion. **Nonplus** implies blankness of mind or utter inability to find anything

worth saying or doing ⟨the problem which *nonplusses* the wisest heads on this planet, has become quite a familiar companion of mine. What is reality?—*L. P. Smith*⟩ ⟨she was utterly *nonplussed* by the pair of them . . . . What on earth were they?—*Goudge*⟩ **Confound** (see also MISTAKE) implies mental confusion, but it stresses the implication either of mental paralysis or of profound astonishment ⟨so spake the son of God; and Satan stood a while as mute, *confounded*—*Milton*⟩ ⟨language to him is a means of communication . . . . He does not wish to dazzle or *confound* his friends, but only to make himself understood—*Crothers*⟩ ⟨this sorrow . . . seemed to have *confounded* him beyond all hope—*Styron*⟩ **Dumbfound** tends to replace *confound* in casual and oral use ⟨I cannot wriggle out of it; I am *dumbfounded*—*Darwin*⟩ ⟨he captured the public and *dumbfounded* the critics—*Macy*⟩ Sometimes *dumbfound* so strongly implies astonishment that it is used in place of *astound* ⟨I was *dumbfounded* to hear him say that I was on a quixotic enterprise—*William Lawrence*⟩
*Ana* amaze, astound, flabbergast (see SURPRISE): *confuse, muddle, addle: *embarrass, disconcert, discomfit
**puzzle** *n* *mystery, problem, enigma, riddle, conundrum
**pygmy** *dwarf, midget, manikin, homunculus, runt

# Q

**quack** *n* *impostor, faker, mountebank, charlatan
*Ana* pretender, simulator, counterfeiter, shammer (see corresponding verbs at ASSUME): *deceit, duplicity, dissimulation, cunning, guile
**quail** *vb* *recoil, shrink, flinch, wince, blench
*Ana* cower, cringe (see FAWN): falter, waver, vacillate, *hesitate: quake, quaver, tremble, shudder (see SHAKE)
**quaint** *strange, odd, queer, outlandish, curious, peculiar, eccentric, erratic, singular, unique
*Ana* *fantastic, bizarre, grotesque: droll, funny, *laughable: archaic, antiquated, antique (see OLD)
**quake** *vb* *shake, tremble, totter, quiver, shiver, shudder, quaver, wobble, teeter, shimmy, dither
*Ana* quail, shrink, *recoil: vibrate, fluctuate, waver (see SWING): falter, vacillate, *hesitate
**qualified** competent, capable, *able
*Ana* trained, instructed, disciplined (see TEACH): examined, quizzed, catechized (see ASK): tested, tried, proved (see PROVE)
*Ant* unqualified
**qualify** 1 *moderate, temper
*Ana* modify, vary, alter, *change: *adapt, adjust, conform, accommodate, reconcile
2 *characterize, distinguish, mark
*Ana* *ascribe, impute, attribute, assign: predicate (see ASSERT)
3 *prepare, fit, condition, ready
*Ana* empower, *enable: endow, endue (see DOWER): train, instruct, *teach
**quality** 1 Quality, property, character, attribute, accident all denote one of the intelligible marks or indications by means of which a thing may be identified or its constitution be understood. **Quality** is the term of widest application and may designate any such mark, material or immaterial, individual or generic ⟨distinguishing *qualities* of iron are tensile strength and corrosiveness⟩ ⟨there was only

one *quality* in a woman that appealed to him—charm—*Galsworthy*⟩ ⟨the persistent contemporariness that is a *quality* of all good art—*Huxley*⟩ ⟨her self-conscious . . . awkwardness lent her a dangerous amateur *quality*—*Salinger*⟩ A **property** is a quality that is proper to a species or type; it therefore belongs to a thing by virtue of that thing's true or essential nature ⟨the eye has this strange *property*: it rests only in beauty—*Woolf*⟩ ⟨rhythm is a *property* of words—*Rickword*⟩ ⟨Sir Joseph Thomson . . . pointed out that weight is only an "apparently" invariable *property* of matter—*Ellis*⟩ A **character** is a peculiar or distinctive quality more often of a class than of an individual. The term is used especially in scientific and philosophical writing with reference to the properties which distinguish an isolable subgroup (as a species) within a larger group (as a genus) ⟨wheat and oats share the properties of cereal grasses but have specific *characters* that clearly differentiate them⟩ ⟨hauynite and noselite show *characters* like sodalite, but they differ from it in containing the radical $SO_4$ in the place of chlorine—*Pirsson*⟩ An **attribute** is a quality that is ascribed to a thing. The term may imply a lack of definite knowledge of the thing in question; thus, one can speak of the *attributes* of God, meaning the qualities men ascribe to him ⟨to endow her with all the *attributes* of a mythological paragon upon Olympus—*Wylie*⟩ ⟨historical personages become invested with romantic *attributes*—*Wright*⟩ More often *attribute* denotes a quality that, though ascribed, is felt as an essential concomitant which must belong to a thing by reason of its nature ⟨mercy is . . . an *attribute* to God himself—*Shak.*⟩ ⟨this Confederation had none of the *attributes* of sovereignty in legislative, executive, or judicial power—*Taney*⟩ An **accident** basically is a nonessential trait; in philosophical use, however, the term often means one of the qualities by which a thing manifests itself and implies, therefore, a contrast with the substance—or the real, but unapparent, nature—of the thing ⟨waves [on a Japanese artist's screen] such as these, divested of all *accident* of appearance, in their naked impetus of movement and recoil —*Binyon*⟩ In more general use *accident* usually implies fortuitousness or lack of intrinsic value ⟨rhyme is . . . an *accident* rather than an essential of verse—*Lowes*⟩ ⟨certainly many mystics have been ascetic. But that has been the *accident* of their philosophy, and not the essence of their religion—*Ellis*⟩

*Ana* predication, affirmation (see corresponding verbs at ASSERT): peculiarity, individuality, characteristic (see corresponding adjectives at CHARACTERISTIC)

**2 Quality, stature, caliber** are often interchangeable as indicating, when used without modifiers, distinctive merit or superiority. **Quality** implies a complex of qualities (see QUALITY 1) and is therefore always singular in use. The term usually implies a high order of excellence, virtue, strength of character, or worth ⟨splendid writing, of course, but to no purpose . . . . It's not *quality* we look for in a novel, but mileage—*Purdy*⟩ ⟨they're all made by machinery now. The *quality* may be inferior, but that doesn't matter. It's the cost of production that counts —*Dahl*⟩ ⟨this little Tania had *quality;* she carried her scars without a whimper—*Bambrick*⟩ **Stature** implies that the one considered has reached or is in process of reaching the height or greatness possible to one of his kind ⟨probings in the realms of life and matter have seemed to diminish man's *stature* and to belittle his dignity—*Marquand*⟩ ⟨every piece of work you do adds something to your *stature,* increases the power and maturity of your experience—*Wolfe*⟩ **Caliber** suggests extent or range especially of one's mind or powers; it may connote unusual but measurable range, scope, or breadth of ability or intellect but often depends on qualification to supply a standard of reference or comparison or to indicate the direction of deviation from the norm ⟨a man of high moral *caliber*⟩ ⟨the milieu of her youth where the size of the engagement ring determines the *caliber* of the bridegroom—*Geismar*⟩ ⟨is at his relaxed best because he is accompanied by musicians of the first *caliber*—*John Hammond*⟩ ⟨pundits of big and little *caliber*—*Craig Thompson*⟩

*Ana* *excellence, virtue: value, *worth

**qualm, scruple, compunction, demur** can all denote a feeling of doubt or hesitation as to the rightness or wisdom of something one is doing or is about to do. **Qualm** implies an uneasy, often a sickening, sensation that one is not following the dictates of his conscience or of his better judgment ⟨have no *qualms* at all in committing adultery —*Book-of-the-Month Club News*⟩ ⟨how few little girls can squash insects and kill rabbits without a *qualm*— *Rose Macaulay*⟩ ⟨we go on spreading culture as if it were peanut butter . . . but we feel *qualms* about the result —*Barzun*⟩ **Scruple** denotes mental disturbance occasioned by doubt of the rightness, the propriety, the fairness, or, sometimes, the outcome of an act; it often implies a principle as the source of the disturbance, and it may imply an overnice conscience or an extremely delicate sense of honor ⟨she has no *scruples* about carrying away any of my books⟩ ⟨began to have *scruples,* to feel obligations, to find that veracity and honor were . . . compelling principles—*Shaw*⟩ ⟨he has not pretended an apprehension which he does not feel, but has candidly disclosed his conscientious *scruples*—*Meltzer*⟩ **Compunction** (see also PENITENCE) implies a usually transitory prick or sting of conscience that warns a person that what he is about to do or is doing is wrong, unfair, unjust, or improper; it may additionally suggest a degree of concern for a potential

victim ⟨showed no *compunction* in planning devilish engines of military destruction—*Ellis*⟩ ⟨he has to be taught . . . to feel *compunction* when he has wantonly caused tears—*Russell*⟩ **Demur** stresses hesitation to such an extent that it carries a stronger implication of delay than any of the other terms; it usually suggests, however, a delay caused by objections or irresolution rather than by an awakened conscience or by a scruple or compunction ⟨he doubts with a persistence of *demur* and question that might well have surprised Descartes himself—*Times Lit. Sup.*⟩ ⟨with some misgivings but without *demur* his committee accepted the decision—*Time*⟩

*Ana* misgiving, *apprehension, foreboding, presentiment: doubt, mistrust, suspicion, *uncertainty

**quandary** *predicament, dilemma, plight, scrape, fix, jam, pickle

*Ana* *juncture, pass, exigency, emergency, contingency, crisis: *difficulty, hardship, vicissitude: puzzling *or* puzzle, mystification, perplexity, bewilderment (see corresponding verbs at PUZZLE)

**quantity** amount, *sum, aggregate, total, whole, number

**quarrel** *n* **Quarrel, wrangle, altercation, squabble, bickering, spat, tiff** are comparable when they mean a dispute marked by anger or discord on both sides. The same distinctions in implications and connotations are found in their corresponding verbs, **quarrel, wrangle, altercate, squabble, bicker, spat, tiff. Quarrel** usually implies heated verbal contention, but it stresses strained or severed relations which may persist even after verbal strife has ceased ⟨patch up a *quarrel*⟩ ⟨she hated any kind of *quarrel* . . . she shuddered at raised voices and quailed before looks of hate—*Stafford*⟩ ⟨the middle class had taken over the reins. It *quarreled* with James I, beheaded Charles I —*Barr*⟩ **Wrangle** implies undignified and often futile disputation with noisy insistence on each person's opinion ⟨a vulgar *wrangle* was unknown, and indeed it was only among the upper servants that . . . jealous friction existed —*Sackville-West*⟩ ⟨makes them *wrangle* interminably about petty details—*Laski*⟩ **Altercation** and the rare verb **altercate** imply fighting with words as the chief weapons, though blows may also be connoted ⟨I have an extreme aversion to public *altercation* on philosophic points— *Franklin*⟩ ⟨Lydia, foreseeing an *altercation,* and alarmed by the threatening aspect of the man, attempted to hurry away—*Shaw*⟩ ⟨it becomes us not . . . to *altercate* on the localities of the battle—*Lytton*⟩ **Squabble** stresses childish and unseemly wrangling over a petty matter; it does not necessarily imply anger or bitter feeling ⟨they had always *squabbled* . . . but their scenes, with the shouting, the insults, the threats, and the flare-ups of mutual revulsion had gradually increased—*Farrell*⟩ ⟨a mere *squabble* in the children's schoolroom—*Moorehead*⟩ **Bickering** and **bicker** imply constant and petulant verbal sparring or interchanges of cutting remarks; they suggest an irritable mood or mutual antagonism ⟨the tearing worries of political snarls, of strife between capital and labor, of factional *bickering*—*Sulzberger*⟩ ⟨though men may *bicker* with the things they love, they would not make them laughable in all eyes, not while they loved them —*Tennyson*⟩ **Spat** also implies an insignificant cause but, unlike *squabble* and *bicker,* it suggests an angry outburst and a quick ending without hard feelings ⟨it wasn't a fight, really—more of a *spat* than anything else— *Heggen*⟩ ⟨a teen-ager who . . . is *spatting* with her mother over unchaperoned dates—*Time*⟩ **Tiff** differs from *spat* chiefly in implying a disagreement that manifests itself in ill humor or temporarily hurt feelings ⟨at the trial circumstantial evidence piled up against him, including his earlier *tiff* . . . which was offered as a motive—*Hilton*⟩

---

A colon (:) separates groups of words discriminated. An asterisk (*) indicates place of treatment of each group.

⟨he retired after *tiffing* with Hitler—*Hal Boyle*⟩
*Ana* *brawl, broil, fracas, melee, row, rumpus, scrap: contention, dissension, conflict, difference, variance, strife, *discord
**quarrel** *vb* wrangle, altercate, squabble, bicker, spat, tiff (see under QUARREL *n*)
*Ana* *contend, fight, battle, war: dispute, agitate, argue, *discuss
*Con* *agree, concur, coincide
**quarrelsome** pugnacious, combative, bellicose, *belligerent, contentious
*Ana* antagonistic, *adverse, counter: hostile, inimical, antipathetic, rancorous (see corresponding nouns at ENMITY)
**quarry** *victim, prey
**quash** 1 *annul, abrogate, void, vacate
2 *crush, quell, extinguish, suppress, quench
*Ana* *destroy: *ruin, wreck: *suppress, repress
**quaver** *vb* *shake, tremble, shudder, quake, totter, quiver, shiver, wobble, teeter, shimmy, dither
*Ana* falter, waver, vacillate, *hesitate: vibrate, fluctuate, sway (see SWING)
**quay** *wharf, dock, pier, slip, berth, jetty, levee
**queenly** regal, royal, *kingly, imperial, princely
**queer** *adj* *strange, odd, erratic, eccentric, peculiar, quaint, outlandish, curious
*Ana* dubious, *doubtful, questionable: droll, funny, *laughable: bizarre, grotesque, *fantastic
**quell** *crush, extinguish, suppress, quench, quash
*Ana* *destroy: wreck, *ruin: subdue, subjugate, overcome, vanquish, *conquer
*Ant* foment
**quench** *crush, quell, extinguish, suppress, quash
*Ana* repress, *suppress: end, terminate (see CLOSE)
**querulous** fretful, petulant, pettish, huffy, *irritable, peevish, fractious, snappish, waspish
*Ana* crying, weeping, wailing, whimpering, blubbering (see CRY *vb*): touchy, cranky, cross (see IRASCIBLE): lamenting, deploring, bemoaning (see DEPLORE)
**query** *vb* *ask, question, interrogate, inquire, examine, quiz, catechize
**quest** *adventure, enterprise
*Ana* exploit, *feat, achievement
**question** *vb* *ask, interrogate, query, inquire, examine, quiz, catechize
*Ant* answer —*Con* reply, respond (see ANSWER *vb*)
**questionable** *doubtful, dubious, problematic
*Ana* uncertain, suspicious (see corresponding nouns at UNCERTAINTY): *obscure, vague, equivocal
*Ant* authoritative: unquestioned
**quick** 1 fleet, swift, rapid, *fast, speedy, expeditious, hasty
*Ana* brisk, nimble, *agile: abrupt, impetuous, *precipitate, headlong
2 **Quick, prompt, ready, apt** are comparable when they apply to persons, their mental operations, their acts, and their words and mean having or manifesting the ability to respond without delay or hesitation. **Quick** stresses instancy of response to such an extent that it usually connotes native rather than acquired power ⟨*quick* eyes⟩ ⟨*quick* in perception⟩ ⟨examined the hall and the men who passed, with the same *quick*, sharp cunning—*O'Flaherty*⟩ Very often the word suggests marked capacity for learning or for absorbing what is taught ⟨even as a child she had had a *quick* mind, a gift of mimicry, an excellent memory —*Wouk*⟩ **Prompt** also implies instancy of response, but it may or may not imply native quickness. Often it carries a suggestion of preparation (as by training or discipline) that fits one for quick response when the occasion demands

it ⟨*prompt* service⟩ ⟨*prompt* eloquence⟩ ⟨*prompt* insight into the workings of complex apparatus—*F. H. Garrison*⟩ Sometimes the word carries so strong an implication of willingness or eagerness that a lack of normal inhibitions is also suggested ⟨they press so eagerly to savor the purity, the heroism, that matches their *prompt* imaginings —*Hackett*⟩ **Ready**, like *prompt*, implies previous training or a strong predisposition as well as instancy of response, but it more often characterizes the person or his powers than his performance or his expression of thought or feeling. It therefore often implies, as *prompt* does not, skill, facility, fluency, or ease in attainment ⟨reading maketh a full man, conference a *ready* man—*Bacon*⟩ ⟨he was not a *ready* speaker, and so . . . had written out what he had to say—*Scudder*⟩ The word is often applied to the bodily organ or to the instrument one uses in manifesting skill or fluency ⟨he has a *ready* tongue⟩ ⟨a pair of *ready* hands⟩ **Apt** (see also FIT; APT 2) does not throw the emphasis on the quickness of the response, though that is involved in its meaning, but on the possession of qualities (as a high degree of intelligence, a particular talent or gift, or a strong bent) which make for such quickness. It is therefore especially appropriate when the person in mind responds quickly only to particular stimuli or shows a capacity for a definite kind of work ⟨she is *apt* at drawing but not at arithmetic⟩ ⟨supple, sinew-corded, *apt* at arms—*Tennyson*⟩ ⟨*apt* as he was in attack or report . . . [he] was readier still to give mercy—*Maxwell Anderson*⟩
*Ana* *intelligent, clever, smart, quick-witted: deft, adroit, *dexterous: *sharp, acute, keen
*Ant* sluggish

**quicken** *vb* 1 **Quicken, animate, enliven, vivify** can mean to make alive or lively, but the words diverge more or less widely in their implications. **Quicken** stresses either the renewal of life, especially of suspended life or growth, or the rousing of what is inert into fullness of activity. Sometimes the rekindled life is physical but more often it is spiritual, intellectual, or imaginative ⟨it is the Spirit that *quickeneth* . . . the words that I speak unto you, they are spirit, and they are life—*Jn* 6:63⟩ ⟨its characters never *quicken* with the life one feels lurks somewhere within them—*Jerome Stone*⟩ **Animate** (compare *animated* under LIVING and LIVELY) emphasizes the imparting of vitality or of motion and activity or the giving of liveliness or of the appearance of life to something previously deficient in or lacking such a quality ⟨that which *animates* all great art—spiritual ferment—*Clive Bell*⟩ ⟨vendors and shoppers . . . *animate* its lanes—*W. R. Moore*⟩ **Enliven** suggests a stimulating influence that kindles, exalts, or brightens; it therefore presupposes dullness, depression, or torpidity, in the thing affected ⟨the sun . . . was wonderfully warm and *enlivening*—*D. H. Lawrence*⟩ ⟨but soon the feel of the paint on the canvas begins to *enliven* his mind; and the mind thus quickened conceives a livelier curiosity about the creature before him—*Montague*⟩ **Vivify** sometimes, like *quicken,* implies the renewal of life and at other times, like *animate*, implies the giving of the appearance of life. In each case it usually also suggests a freshening or energizing effect and implies vitality more often than activity or motion ⟨in . . . the Elizabethan age, English society at large was accessible to ideas, was permeated by them, was *vivified* by them —*Arnold*⟩ ⟨the room was dead. The essence that had *vivified* it was gone—*O. Henry*⟩ ⟨that Promethean fire, which animates the canvas and *vivifies* the marble— *Reynolds*⟩
*Ana* activate, *vitalize, energize: rouse, arouse, *stir
*Ant* deaden

2 excite, stimulate, *provoke, pique, galvanize
*Ana* *activate, actuate, motivate: spur, goad, induce (see corresponding nouns at MOTIVE): *incite, foment
*Ant* arrest
3 hasten, hurry, *speed, accelerate, precipitate
*Ant* slacken
**quick-witted** clever, bright, smart, *intelligent, alert, knowing, brilliant
*Ana* ready, prompt, *quick, apt: *sharp, keen, acute: *witty, humorous, facetious
**quiescent** *latent, dormant, potential, abeyant
*Ana* quiet, *still, silent: inert, *inactive, passive, supine
**quiet** *adj* silent, noiseless, *still, stilly
*Ana* *calm, serene, placid, tranquil, peaceful
*Ant* unquiet —*Con* *rough, harsh: disturbed, agitated, upset, disquieted, perturbed (see DISCOMPOSE): *vociferous, clamorous, boisterous, blatant, strident
**quiet, quieten** *vb* *calm, compose, still, lull, soothe, settle, tranquilize
*Ana* allay, alleviate, assuage, *relieve: abate, lessen, *decrease
*Ant* disquiet: arouse, rouse —*Con* *stir, awaken, rally: excite, stimulate, *provoke, quicken
**quip** *joke, jest, jape, witticism, wisecrack, crack, gag
**quit** 1 acquit, comport, deport, demean, conduct, *behave
*Ana & Con* see those at ACQUIT
2 *go, leave, depart, withdraw, retire
*Ana* forsake, desert, *abandon: *relinquish, surrender, resign: *escape, flee, fly, abscond
3 *stop, cease, discontinue, desist
**quiver** *vb* *shake, shiver, shudder, quaver, totter, tremble, quake, wobble, teeter, shimmy, dither
*Ana* *pulsate, pulse, beat, throb, palpitate: flutter, flicker, flitter (see FLIT)
**quixotic** chimerical, fantastic, visionary, fanciful, *imaginary

*Ana* *sentimental, romantic: utopian, *ambitious: ideal, transcendental, *abstract
**quiz** *vb* *ask, question, interrogate, examine, catechize, query, inquire
**quote, cite, repeat** are not close synonyms, though all mean to speak or write again something already said or written by another. Quote usually implies a use of another's words, commonly with faithful exactness or an attempt at it, for some special effect like adornment, illustration, close examination ⟨I will *quote* a passage which is unfamiliar enough to be regarded with fresh attention —*T. S. Eliot*⟩ But sometimes *quote* is applied to a more general referral to someone as the author or source of information without implication of precise reproduction of an original statement ⟨don't *quote* me as your authority⟩ ⟨in one sense we are *quoting* all the time. To whistle Tin Pan Alley's latest inanity is to *quote.* . . . To transmit the tired gag of a television comic is to *quote*—*Fadiman*⟩ **Cite** is likely to stress the idea of adducing, bringing forward, or mentioning for a particular reason, like substantiation or proof, with or without the idea of uttering another's words ⟨the critic *cited* in the opening of this chapter—*Leavis*⟩ ⟨asked a senator if he could *cite* a single piece of legislation enacted solely for the benefit of the public—*Armbrister*⟩ **Repeat** stresses the fact of a saying or writing over again of someone else's words often with no reference to the source ⟨*repeat* a rumor⟩ Typically it carries none of the implication of formal or dignified reasons for the procedure that attaches to *quote* and *cite* ⟨unrealistic to go on *repeating* phrases about the connection of industry with personal independence—*Dewey*⟩
*Ana* *adduce, allege, advance
**quotidian** *daily, diurnal, circadian

# R

**rabid** *furious, frantic, frenzied, wild, frenetic, delirious
*Ana* maddened, enraged, infuriated, incensed, angered (see ANGER *vb*): violent, compulsive (see corresponding nouns at FORCE): *insane, crazed, crazy, demented, deranged
**race** 1 Race, nation, people, even though in technical use they are commonly differentiated, are often used popularly and interchangeably to designate one of a number of great divisions of mankind, each made up of an aggregate of persons who are thought of, or think of themselves, as comprising a distinct unit. In technical discriminations, all more or less controversial and often lending themselves to great popular misunderstanding or misuse, **race** is anthropological and ethnological in force, usually implying a distinct physical type with certain unchanging characteristics (as a particular color of skin or shape of skull) ⟨the Caucasian *race*⟩ ⟨the Mongolian *race*⟩ Sometimes, and more controversially, other presumed common factors are chosen, as place of origin ⟨the Nordic *race*⟩ or common root language ⟨the Aryan *race*⟩ In popular use *race* can apply to any more or less clearly defined group thought of as a unit usually because of a common or presumed common past ⟨the Anglo-Saxon *race*⟩ ⟨the Celtic *race*⟩ ⟨the Hebrew *race*⟩ **Nation,** primarily political in force, usually designates the citizenry as a whole of a sovereign state and implies a certain homogeneity because of com-

mon laws, institutions, customs, or loyalty ⟨the British *nation*⟩ ⟨the French *nation*⟩ ⟨the house must have been built before this country was a *nation*—*Tate*⟩ ⟨what is a *nation*? A group of human beings recognizing a common history and a common culture, yearning for a common destiny, assuming common habits, and generally attached to a specific piece of the earth's surface—*David Bernstein*⟩ Sometimes it is opposed to *state* ⟨a state is accidental; it can be made or unmade; but a *nation* is something real which can be neither made nor destroyed—*J. R. Green*⟩ and often not clearly distinguishable from *race* in comprising any large group crossing national boundaries and with something significantly in common ⟨the children of the world are one *nation;* the very old, another—*Jan Struther*⟩ ⟨for the two *nations* that inhabit the earth, the rich and the poor—*Sitwell*⟩ ⟨the Gypsy *nation*⟩ **People,** sometimes interchangeable with *nation* though stressing a cultural or social rather than a national unity, can apply to a body of persons, as a whole or as individuals, who show a consciousness of solidarity or common characteristics suggesting a common culture or common interests or ideals and a sense of kinship ⟨the Mexican *people*—*Prewett*⟩ ⟨the British and American *peoples*—*Sir Winston Churchill*⟩ ⟨we, the *people* of the United States—*U. S. Constitution*⟩ ⟨we, the *peoples* of the United Nations—*U. N. Charter*⟩ ⟨a new government, which, for certain purposes,

A colon (:) separates groups of words discriminated. An asterisk (*) indicates place of treatment of each group.

would make the people of the several states one *people* —*Taney*⟩
2 *variety, subspecies, breed, cultivar, strain, clone, stock
**rack** *vb* torment, torture, try, *afflict
*Ana* persecute, oppress (see WRONG *vb*): harry, harass, *worry, annoy
**racket** *din, uproar, pandemonium, hullabaloo, babel, hubbub, clamor
**racking** *excruciating, agonizing
*Ana* torturing, tormenting (see AFFLICT): *intense, vehement, fierce, exquisite, violent: *fierce, ferocious, barbarous, savage, cruel, inhuman
**racy** *pungent, piquant, poignant, spicy, snappy
*Ana* exciting, stimulating, quickening, provoking *or* provocative (see corresponding verbs at PROVOKE): *spirited, mettlesome, fiery, gingery, peppery
*Con* *insipid, flat, jejune, banal, inane
**radiant** brilliant, *bright, luminous, lustrous, effulgent, refulgent, beaming, lambent, lucent, incandescent
*Ana* *splendid, resplendent, glorious, sublime: sparkling, glittering, gleaming, flashing, scintillating (see FLASH *vb*)
**radiate** *spread, circulate, disseminate, diffuse, propagate
*Ana* *distribute, dispense: disperse, *scatter, dissipate: diverge (see SWERVE)
**radical** *adj* 1 *fundamental, basic, basal, underlying
*Ana* cardinal, *essential, vital: *inherent, intrinsic, constitutional
*Ant* superficial
2 advanced, progressive, *liberal
**radius** *range, gamut, reach, compass, sweep, scope, orbit, horizon, ken, purview
**rag** *vb* *banter, chaff, kid, rib, josh, jolly
**rage** *n* 1 *anger, ire, fury, indignation, wrath
*Ana* *acrimony, asperity, acerbity: frenzy, *mania, hysteria: agitation, upset, perturbation (see corresponding verbs at DISCOMPOSE)
2 *fashion, style, mode, vogue, craze, cry, dernier cri, fad
*Ana* *caprice, freak, conceit, vagary, crotchet, whim, fancy
**raid** *n* *invasion, incursion, inroad
*Ana* *attack, assault, onslaught, onset
**rail** *vb* revile, vituperate, rate, berate, upbraid, *scold, tongue-lash, jaw, bawl, chew out, wig
*Ana* censure, denounce, condemn, reprobate, reprehend, *criticize: reprimand, rebuke, *reprove, reproach
**raillery** *badinage, persiflage
*Ana* bantering *or* banter, chaffing *or* chaff (see BANTER): sport, *fun, game, jest, play: satire, sarcasm, irony (see WIT)
**raiment** apparel, attire, *clothes, clothing, dress
**raise** *vb* 1 *lift, elevate, hoist, heave, rear, boost
*Ana* *rise, ascend, mount, soar: *exalt, magnify, aggrandize: *advance, promote, forward, further
2 *build, construct, erect, frame, rear
*Ant* raze
**rally** *vb* *stir, rouse, arouse, awaken, waken
*Ana* excite, stimulate, quicken, *provoke: fire (see LIGHT *vb*): *renew, restore, refresh
**rally** *vb* *ridicule, deride, mock, taunt, twit
*Ana* *scoff, jeer, gibe, flout: tease, tantalize, *worry, harass, harry
**ram** *vb* *pack, crowd, cram, stuff, tamp
*Ana* *press, squeeze, jam: *compact, concentrate, consolidate: compress (see CONTRACT)
**ramble** *vb* *wander, stray, roam, rove, range, prowl, gad, gallivant, traipse, meander
**rampant** *rank

*Ana* luxuriant, lush, exuberant, *profuse, lavish: immoderate, *excessive, inordinate
*Con* *moderate, temperate: restrained, curbed, checked (see RESTRAIN)
**rampart** *bulwark, breastwork, parapet, bastion
**rancid** *malodorous, stinking, fetid, rank, noisome, putrid, fusty, musty
*Ana* decomposed, decayed, spoiled (see DECAY): *offensive, loathsome, repulsive
**rancor** antagonism, animosity, animus, antipathy, *enmity, hostility
*Ana* hate, hatred, detestation, abhorrence, abomination (see under HATE *vb*): spite, *malice, malevolence, malignity, malignancy, spleen, grudge
**random,** haphazard, chance, chancy, casual, desultory, hit-or-miss, happy-go-lucky are comparable when they mean having a cause or a character that is determined by accident rather than by design or by method. What is **random** comes, goes, occurs, or is done or made without a fixed or clearly defined aim, purpose, or evidence of method or system or direction; the term implies an absence of guidance by a governing mind, eye, or objective ⟨a *random* shot⟩ ⟨a *random* answer to a question⟩ ⟨my choice was as *random* as blindman's buff—*Burns*⟩ ⟨the tail end of the conference was becoming frayed and *random*—*Rand*⟩ ⟨the clerks become tired and bored and start making *random* mistakes—*Martin Gardner*⟩ What is **haphazard** is done, made, arranged, used, or said without concern or without sufficient concern for its fitness, its effectiveness, or its possible ill effects, and is more or less at the mercy of chance or whim or of natural or logical necessity ⟨a *haphazard* policy⟩ ⟨the disorder . . . the *haphazard* scattering of stray socks, shirts and collars, old shoes, and unpressed trousers—*Wolfe*⟩ ⟨not . . . a collection of *haphazard* schemes, but rather the orderly component parts of a connected and logical whole—*Roosevelt*⟩ What is described as **chance** comes or happens to one or is done or made by one without prearrangement or preawareness or without preparation; the term is applicable not only to things but to persons with whom one comes into contact more or less by accident ⟨a *chance* acquaintance⟩ ⟨a *chance* meeting with an old friend⟩ ⟨found it increasingly difficult to welcome *chance* visitors with his usual affability—*Graves*⟩ What is **chancy** involves uncertainty and risk because its results, actions, responses, or condition cannot be predicted; the term applies more often to situations and things than to persons ⟨a *chancy* road to take at night⟩ ⟨a *chancy* appeal, at best, to the shifting and unguessable 'sympathies of their readers—*Morse*⟩ ⟨despite recent advances in geophysics, oil drilling is still a *chancy* business—*Kane*⟩ What is **casual** (see also ACCIDENTAL) leaves or seems to leave things to chance, and works, acts, comes, or goes haphazardly or by chance, or without method or deliberation or indication of intent or purpose; the term often also suggests offhandedness ⟨a *casual* remark⟩ ⟨his treatment of his friends is *casual*⟩ or lightness or spontaneity ⟨she was constantly referring to dear friends . . . in a *casual* and familiar way—*Ellis*⟩ or lack of definiteness in terms or intention ⟨their policy was opportunist at home and *casual* abroad—*Spectator*⟩ ⟨the *casual* allusion, the chance reference to her—*Henry Adams*⟩ What is **desultory** is not governed by method or system but jumps or skips erratically from one thing to another; the term may imply additionally such consequences as irregular or inconsistent performance or lack of continuity or plan or persistence ⟨make reading have a purpose instead of being *desultory* —*Russell*⟩ ⟨its growth from 1900 to 1950 had been *desultory*—*Michener*⟩ ⟨a dragged-out ordeal of worry,

*Ana* analogous words   *Ant* antonyms   *Con* contrasted words   See also explanatory notes facing page 1

aimless wandering, and *desultory* shopping—*Wouk*⟩ What is **hit-or-miss** is so haphazard in its character or operation as to be or appear so wholly lacking in plan, aim, system, or care that one is indifferent as to how it turns out or as to what pattern or arrangement it makes ⟨*hit-or-miss* patchwork⟩ ⟨a *hit-or-miss* policy was pursued by the Department of Justice—*Ripley*⟩ ⟨his . . . training had given him a profound prejudice against inexact work, experimental work, *hit-or-miss* work—*Forester*⟩ A person is **happy-go-lucky** who leaves everything to chance or who accepts with happiness or easy indifference whatever comes; a thing is *happy-go-lucky* that is governed by such a disposition ⟨a radical pragmatist on the other hand is a *happy-go-lucky* . . . sort of creature—*James*⟩ ⟨a funny little *happy-go-lucky* native-managed railway—*Kipling*⟩ *Ana* fortuitous, \*accidental, casual: vagrant, vagabond, truant (see corresponding nouns at VAGABOND)

**range** *n* 1 \*habitat, biotype, station

2 **Range, gamut, reach, radius, compass, sweep, scope, orbit, horizon, ken, purview** can denote the extent that lies within the powers of something to cover, grasp, control, or traverse. **Range** is the general term indicating the extent of one's perception or the extent of powers, capacities, or possibilities ⟨safe, well out of the *range* of the pursuers⟩ ⟨a beautiful voice with a wide *range* between the high and the low tones—*Ellis*⟩ ⟨a creative writer can do his best only with what lies within the *range* and character of his deepest sympathies—*Cather*⟩ ⟨the whole *range* of Greek political life—*Dickinson*⟩ **Gamut** suggests a graduated series running from one possible extreme to another ⟨types of light each occupying its particular place in that far-reaching roster or *gamut* which is called the spectrum—*Darrow*⟩ **Reach** suggests an extent of perception, knowledge, ability, or activity attained to or experienced by or as if by stretching out ⟨moving step by step toward the widest generalizations within his *reach*—*L. J. Henderson*⟩ ⟨out of *reach* of the first invading forces⟩ ⟨anything like sustained reasoning was beyond his *reach*—*Stephen*⟩ **Radius** suggests a usually circular area (as of activity) implied by a known or determined center ⟨the town's history has been the history of coal; within a *radius* of five miles are 12 large mines—*Amer. Guide Series: Pa.*⟩ **Compass** implies an extent, sometimes more limited than that suggested by *range,* of perception, knowledge, or activity; it is likely to connote a bounding circumference ⟨the powers expressly granted to the government . . . are to be contracted . . . into the narrowest possible *compass*—*John Marshall*⟩ ⟨here we get in very small *compass* . . . as many different reminders of the continuity of the country . . . as you will find anywhere—*Mais*⟩ **Sweep** suggests extent, often circular or arc-shaped, of motion or activity, which latter notion it more strongly suggests than the preceding terms ⟨the boldness and *sweep* of Webster's original scheme appear plainly—*Malone*⟩ ⟨in the *sweep* of their universal robbery, they showed at least no discrimination between native and foreign victims—*Osbert Sitwell*⟩ **Scope** is applicable to an area of activity, an area predetermined and limited, but an area of free choice within the set limits ⟨its *scope* was widened by the legislature to include other departments—*Amer. Guide Series: Texas*⟩ ⟨the infinite *scope* for personal initiative in business—*Shaw*⟩ **Orbit** suggests a range of activity or influence, often circumscribed and bounded, within which forces work toward accustoming, integrating, or absorbing ⟨communities . . . outside the *orbit* of modernity—*Lippmann*⟩ ⟨the war as a gigantic cosmic drama, embracing every quarter of the globe and the whole *orbit* of man's life—*Buchan*⟩ **Horizon** suggests an area, per-

haps arc-shaped or semicircular, of knowledge, interest, perception; it may suggest the new or the potential or envisioned ⟨science has provided a new frontier with unlimited *horizons*—*Compton*⟩ ⟨possibilities he hadn't known were upon its *horizon*—*Mary Austin*⟩ **Ken** tends to apply to personal or individual range of perception or cognizance ⟨they seemed trivial at the time they came into his *ken*—*White*⟩ ⟨the bulk of his known reading, until the great Italians swam into his *ken*, was French—*Lowes*⟩ **Purview** may indicate either range of perception or knowledge or range of authority or competence ⟨the inclusion of dependent areas within the *purview* of Point Four—*Rupert Emerson*⟩ ⟨the problem of ethnic variation falls very definitely within the *purview* of the student of the social life of man—*Ashley Montagu*⟩ *Ana* extent, area (see SIZE): \*field, domain, province, sphere, territory: spread, stretch, \*expanse, amplitude

**range** *vb* 1 \*line, line up, align, array *Ana* arrange, \*order, marshal: \*assort, sort, classify: \*incline, dispose, predispose, bias

2 \*wander, rove, ramble, roam, stray, prowl, gad, gallivant, traipse, meander

**rank** *adj* 1 **Rank, rampant** mean growing or increasing at an immoderate rate. **Rank** applies primarily to vegetation and implies vigorous, luxuriant, and often unchecked or excessive growth ⟨behold, seven ears of corn came up upon one stalk, *rank* and good—*Gen* 41:5⟩ ⟨its garden was . . . *rank*, too thickly crowded with trees and bushes and plants—*West*⟩ The term is common in metaphoric extension ⟨weed your better judgments of all opinion that grows *rank* in them—*Shak.*⟩ **Rampant** is more widely applicable than *rank;* it implies rapid, often unrestrained or wild, spreading and is frequently applicable not only to what literally grows but to what extends or increases by contagion or diffusion ⟨it grieved him to see ignorance and impiety so *rampant*—*Fuller* d. 1661⟩ ⟨that curiosity which is so *rampant*, as a rule, in an Indian village—*Kipling*⟩ ⟨rumor ran *rampant* . . . the other day—*Breit*⟩ *Ana* \*coarse, gross, vulgar: exuberant, \*profuse, lavish, luxuriant

2 fusty, musty, rancid, \*malodorous, stinking, fetid, noisome, putrid *Ana* dank, humid (see WET): \*offensive, loathsome, repulsive: decomposed, decayed, spoiled (see DECAY) *Ant* balmy

3 \*flagrant, glaring, gross *Ana* conspicuous, outstanding, \*noticeable: foul, filthy, squalid, nasty (see DIRTY): \*outrageous, heinous, atrocious, monstrous

**rank** *n* \*line, row, file, echelon, tier

**rank** *vb* \*class, grade, rate, graduate, gradate *Ana* \*order, arrange: classify, \*assort, sort: divide, \*separate

**ransack** search, hunt, rummage, \*seek, scour, comb, ferret out *Ana* investigate (see corresponding noun at INQUIRY): penetrate, pierce, probe (see ENTER): examine, inspect, \*scrutinize

**ransom** *vb* \*rescue, deliver, redeem, reclaim, save *Ana* \*free, release, liberate, emancipate, manumit: \*expiate, atone

**rant** *n* \*bombast, fustian, rodomontade, rhapsody *Ana* inflatedness *or* inflation, turgidity, tumidity, flatulence (see corresponding adjectives at INFLATED)

**rap** *n* tap, knock, thump, thud (see under TAP *vb*) *Ana* beating, pummeling, pounding (see BEAT *vb*)

**rap** *vb* \*tap, knock, thump, thud *Ana* smite, \*strike: pummel, \*beat

**rapacious** ravening, ravenous, gluttonous, \*voracious

---

A colon (:) separates groups of words discriminated. An asterisk (\*) indicates place of treatment of each group.

*Ana* ferocious, *fierce: greedy, grasping, *covetous

**rapacity** greed, *cupidity, avarice

*Ana* covetousness, avariciousness, greediness, grasping-ness (see corresponding adjectives at COVETOUS): exaction, demanding *or* demand, claiming *or* claim (see corresponding verbs at DEMAND)

**rapid** *adj* *fast, swift, fleet, quick, speedy, hasty, expeditious

*Ana* brisk, nimble, *agile: hurried, quickened (see SPEED *vb*)

*Ant* deliberate: leisurely

**rapscallion** *villain, scoundrel, blackguard, knave, rascal, rogue, scamp, miscreant

*Ana* *vagabond, vagrant, tramp, hobo, bum

**rapt** absorbed, engrossed, *intent

*Ana* ecstatic, transported, rapturous (see corresponding nouns at ECSTASY): enchanted, captivated, fascinated (see ATTRACT)

*Con* *indifferent, unconcerned, incurious, uninterested, disinterested

**rapture** *ecstasy, transport

*Ana* bliss, beatitude, blessedness, felicity, *happiness

**rare** 1 tenuous, slight, *thin, slender, slim

2 delicate, dainty, exquisite, *choice, elegant, recherché

*Ana* excelling *or* excellent, transcending *or* transcendent, surpassing (see corresponding verbs at EXCEED): superlative, *supreme, incomparable

3 scarce, *infrequent, uncommon, occasional, sporadic

*Ana* *exceptional: singular, unique, curious, *strange

*Con* *usual, customary, wonted, accustomed, habitual: *common, ordinary, familiar

**rarefy** *thin, attenuate, extenuate, dilute

*Ana* diminish, reduce, lessen, *decrease: *expand, distend, inflate

**rascal** *villain, scoundrel, blackguard, knave, rogue, scamp, rapscallion, miscreant

**rash** daring, daredevil, reckless, foolhardy, *adventurous, venturesome

*Ana* *precipitate, abrupt, impetuous, sudden, hasty: desperate, forlorn (see DESPONDENT)

*Ant* calculating —*Con* *cautious, circumspect, wary, chary

**rasp** *vb* *scrape, scratch, grate, grind

*Ana* *abrade, excoriate, chafe, fret: *irritate, exasperate, aggravate: *annoy, vex, irk, bother

**rate** *vb* berate, upbraid, *scold, tongue-lash, jaw, bawl, chew out, wig, rail, revile, vituperate

*Ana* *reprove, reproach, rebuke, reprimand, admonish, chide: censure, condemn, denounce, reprehend, reprobate, *criticize

**rate** *vb* 1 value, evaluate, appraise, *estimate, assess, assay

*Ana* *calculate, compute, reckon, estimate: *decide, determine, settle

2 *class, grade, rank, graduate, gradate

*Ana* *order, arrange, systematize, methodize: *assort, sort, classify

**ratify, confirm** are comparable when they mean to make something legally valid or operative. Both terms presuppose previous action by a person or body with power of appointing, of legislating, or of framing such a document as a constitution, a treaty, or a contract, and imply reference therefore only to the act of the person or body endowed with the power to accept or to veto the appointment, bill, or document. The terms are occasionally interchanged without loss, but **ratify** usually carries a stronger implication of approval than *confirm* and is therefore used by preference when the acceptance of something (as a constitution, a treaty, or a course of action) that has

been framed or proposed by a committee or a small body is put up to a larger body (as a society, legislature, or nation) for a vote that testifies to its approval ⟨the men who had written and signed the Constitution became the leaders of the fight to *ratify* it—*Smelser & Kirwin*⟩ **Confirm,** on the other hand, stresses the giving of formal or decisive assent as necessary to a thing's validity; it applies specifically to appointments made by an executive (as a president or governor) that according to the constitution of a nation or state require the consent of a body (as a senate, a legislature, or a council) before they are definitely settled and made legally valid ⟨the other executive function of the Senate, that of *confirming* nominations submitted by the president—*Bryce*⟩ ⟨the Senate's powers to *ratify* treaties and *confirm* appointments of ambassadors —*Dimond &Pflieger*⟩

*Ana* *authorize, accredit, license, commission: sanction, *approve, endorse: validate, authenticate (see CONFIRM)

**ratiocination** *inference

*Ant* intuition

**ratiocinative** inferential (see under INFERENCE)

*Ant* intuitive

**ration** *n* Ration, allowance, dole, pittance denote the amount of food, supplies, or money allotted to an individual. **Ration** implies apportionment and, often, equal sharing. Specifically it is applied in military and naval use to the daily supply of provisions given each man, and in stock-breeding to the daily or periodical supply of food for each animal. In these uses it generally implies dietary variety and restricted amounts of each food. When used of a particular food or commodity (as meat or gasoline) it implies a shortage in the supply and a limitation on the amount allowed each person. **Allowance,** though often interchangeable with *ration,* is wider in its range of application. Both imply restriction in amount, but *allowance* stresses granting rather than sharing and is applicable to money and many other things besides food or commodities ⟨a daily *allowance* of tobacco for the old pensioners⟩ ⟨a schoolboy's weekly *allowance*⟩ ⟨the court determines an heir's *allowance* during his minority⟩ **Dole** tends to imply a grudging division and needy or sometimes grasping recipients ⟨cold charity's unwelcome *dole*—*Shelley*⟩ ⟨no rich man's largess may suffice his soul, nor are the plundered succored by a *dole*—*E. V. Cooke*⟩ In current, chiefly British, use *dole* is applied to a payment to unemployed workers, whether in the form of relief or insurance, by the national government. **Pittance** is likely to suggest, or even stress, scantiness or meagerness. It is applicable to a ration, an allowance, a dole, or a wage, the context usually making the reference clear ⟨and gained, by spinning hemp, a *pittance* for herself—*Wordsworth*⟩ ⟨in England, such a dowry would be a *pittance,* while elsewhere it is a fortune—*Byron*⟩

*Ana* apportionment, portioning *or* portion (see corresponding verbs at APPORTION): sharing *or* share, participation, partaking (see corresponding verbs at SHARE)

**ration** *vb* *apportion, portion, prorate, parcel

*Ana* divide, *distribute, dispense, deal, dole: *share, partake, participate

**rational, reasonable** may be applied to men, their acts, utterances, or policies in the senses of having or manifesting the power to reason, or of being in accordance with what reason dictates as right, wise, or sensible. **Rational** usually implies a latent or active power to make inferences from the facts and to draw from such inferences conclusions that enable one to understand the world about him and to relate such knowledge to the attainment of personal and common ends; often, in this use, *rational* is opposed to *emotional* or *animal* ⟨we are *rational;* but we are animal too—*Cowper*⟩ ⟨the *rational,* the intelligent, the orderly processes of behavior—*Mumford*⟩ ⟨to cure this habit of mind, it is necessary . . . to replace fear by *rational* prevision of misfortune—*Russell*⟩ When the term is applied to policies, projects, systems, or to something conceived or formulated, *rational* is preferred when justification on grounds that are satisfactory to the reason is specifically implied ⟨the advantages of a *rational* orthography—*Grandgent*⟩ ⟨let's just entertain the notion as a *rational* hypothesis which may or may not be true—*Mailer*⟩ **Reasonable** usually carries a much weaker implication than *rational* of the power to reason in general, or of guidance by conclusions drawn by the reasoning powers; typically it applies to actions, decisions, choices, or proposals that avoid obvious mistakes and that are practical, sensible, just, or fair ⟨if that belief, whether right or wrong, may be held by a *reasonable* man, it seems to me that it may be enforced by law—*Justice Holmes*⟩ ⟨asking me some *reasonable* if openly ignorant questions about the nature of the bullfight—*Mailer*⟩ ⟨the formation of *reasonable* habits, of method, of punctuality . . . makes enormously for the happiness and convenience of every one about us—*Benson*⟩

*Ant* irrational: animal (*of nature*): demented (*of state of mind*): absurd (*of actions, behavior*)

**rationalize** *explain, account, justify

**rattle** faze, *embarrass, discomfit, disconcert, abash
*Ana* *confuse, muddle, addle: agitate, upset, perturb, disturb, fluster, flurry (see DISCOMPOSE): bewilder, distract, perplex (see PUZZLE *vb*)

**raucous** *loud, stentorian, earsplitting, hoarse, strident, stertorous
*Ana* *rough, harsh: gruff, brusque (see BLUFF)

**ravage, devastate, waste, sack, pillage, despoil, spoliate** are comparable when they mean to lay waste or bare by acts of violence (as plundering or destroying). **Ravage** implies violent, severe, and often cumulative destruction accomplished typically by depredations, invasions, raids, storms, or floods ⟨four major disasters had *ravaged* the country—*Leakey*⟩ ⟨the psychic disease which *ravaged* Europe as mercilessly as the Spanish influenza—*Day Lewis*⟩ ⟨an Indian hunt was never a slaughter. They *ravaged* neither the rivers nor the forest—*Cather*⟩ **Devastate** stresses the ruin and desolation which follow upon ravaging; it suggests eradication of buildings, of forests, and of crops by or as if by demolition or burning ⟨behind him were the ruins of a city, shattered, *devastated,* crumbled piles of concrete and stone that glowed—*Styron*⟩ ⟨a succession of cruel wars had *devastated* Europe—*Macaulay*⟩ ⟨had *devastated* the neighboring county to get timber—*Ellis*⟩ **Waste** may be a close synonym for *devastate* but it tends to suggest a less complete destruction or desolation, produced more gradually or less violently ⟨he fell suddenly on the Nervii with four legions, seized their cattle, *wasted* their country—*Froude*⟩ ⟨the broad gray summit is barren and desolate-looking . . . *wasted* by ages of gnawing storms—*Muir*⟩ **Sack** basically suggests the acts of a victorious army when it takes a town that has been captured and stripping it of all its possessions of value by looting or destruction ⟨we *sacked* the city after nine months' siege—*Heywood*⟩ ⟨the retreating Federals *sacked* and burned as they went—*Amer. Guide Series: La.*⟩ The term may be extended to other than military activity but consistently retains the notion of stripping of valuables and usually of destruction ⟨a crowd sympathetic with the employees *sacked* the newspaper's offices—*Dilliard*⟩ ⟨men . . . who'll *sack* a railroad or lay siege to a corporation with the idea they're ordained to grab the other fellow's property—*Everybody's Mag.*⟩

**Pillage** stresses ruthless plundering such as is characteristic of an invading or victorious army, but it carries a weaker implication of devastation than *sack* ⟨he *pillaged* many Spanish towns, and took rich prizes—*Fuller* d.1661⟩ ⟨the houses, first *pillaged,* were then fired—*Prescott*⟩ In nonmilitary use *pillage* still implies ruthlessness but it carries a stronger implication of appropriation to oneself of something that belongs to another (as by fleecing, plagiarizing, or robbing) ⟨humbugged by their doctors, *pillaged* by their tradesmen—*Shaw*⟩ ⟨libraries *pillaged* to supply grocers with paper—*Schultz*⟩ **Despoil,** like *sack,* implies a stripping of valuables ⟨the English buccaneers . . . fell upon their cities and *despoiled* them—*Haskin*⟩ but it does not so often refer to a violent ransacking for booty; it more often suggests a pillaging, sometimes under a guise of legality, or a heedless or inadvertent destruction ⟨magnificent stands of pine . . . *despoiled* by naval-stores operators and loggers—*Amer. Guide Series: Fla.*⟩ ⟨a law which restored . . . an immense domain of which they had been *despoiled*—*Macaulay*⟩ ⟨the *despoiling* of the English monasteries in the 16th century⟩ ⟨*despoiled* of innocence, of faith, of bliss—*Milton*⟩ **Spoliate** is chiefly a legal term; in its meaning it comes close to *despoil* and is particularly applicable to destruction inflicted on a neutral, a noncombatant, or a victim of piracy ⟨from the ages, from the barbarians, the land has been burnt and *spoliated*—*Richard Llewellyn*⟩ or, in more general use, when the gaining of spoils by means of exactions, graft, or various venal practices is suggested ⟨the Tweed Ring was charged with *spoliating* the people of New York City⟩
*Ana* *destroy, demolish, raze: plunder, loot, *rob: *ruin, wreck: invade, *trespass, encroach

**ravening** rapacious, ravenous, gluttonous, *voracious
*Ana* greedy, acquisitive, grasping, *covetous

**ravenous** ravening, rapacious, *voracious, gluttonous
*Ana* grasping, greedy, acquisitive, *covetous: *fierce, ferocious

**ravish** *transport, enrapture, entrance
*Ana* rejoice, delight, regale (see PLEASE)

**raw** crude, callow, green, *rude, rough, uncouth
*Ana* *elementary, elemental: *ignorant, untaught, untutored: *immature, unmatured, unripe
*Con* practiced, exercised, drilled (see PRACTICE *vb*): seasoned, hardened (see HARDEN): *mature, matured, ripe, adult, grown-up

**rawboned** gaunt, angular, *lean, lank, lanky, spare, scrawny, skinny

**ray, beam** are comparable when they denote a shaft of light. This conception of light as a shaft is fixed in our language but is not always in keeping with modern scientific views of the nature of light. **Ray** suggests emanation from a center or point in the manner of the spokes of a wheel; its typical application is to one of the apparently thin lines of light that seem to extend from a radiant body (as the sun or a candle) or that are flashed from a reflective surface (as of steel or a mirror glittering in the sun) ⟨the more numerous the facets of a diamond the more numerous the *rays* of light it reflects⟩ **Beam** implies not a line but a long bar; it suggests therefore a bar made up of a bundle of rays of light; thus, a *beam* of white light is split by a prism into *rays* of light of the various colors of the spectrum ⟨the *beam of* an automobile headlight⟩ ⟨a searchlight throws a narrow *beam*⟩ ⟨where a sun*beam* enters, every particle of dust becomes visible—*Ruskin*⟩ ⟨how far that little candle throws his *beams*!—*Shak.*⟩ A small beam is sometimes called a *ray* ⟨a tiny hole in the window shade admitted a *ray* of sunlight into the room⟩

**raze** demolish, *destroy

---

A colon (:) separates groups of words discriminated. An asterisk (*) indicates place of treatment of each group.

*Ana* efface, obliterate (see ERASE): eradicate, extirpate (see EXTERMINATE): *ruin, wreck: *abolish, extinguish, annihilate

**reach** *vb* **Reach, gain, compass, achieve, attain** can mean to arrive at a point by effort or work. **Reach** is the most general term, being capable of reference to whatever can be arrived at by exertion of any degree and applicable to such diverse matters as a point in space, in time, or in a development, or as a destination, a goal, or a position of eminence ⟨they *reached* the city that night⟩ ⟨after a long discussion they *reached* an understanding⟩ In extended use *reach* may be predicated even of inanimate things ⟨the hour hand has *reached* two⟩ ⟨the depression has *reached* bottom⟩ **Gain** usually implies a struggle to reach a contemplated or desired destination or goal ⟨*gained* the confidence of the mountain people by his . . . sympathetic approach—*Persons*⟩ ⟨I had *gained* the frontier and slept safe that night—*Browning*⟩ **Compass** implies efforts to get around difficulties or to transcend limitations; it often connotes skill or craft in management ⟨a writer who is attempting a higher strain of elevation or pathos than his powers can *compass*—*Montague*⟩ ⟨if you can *compass* it, do cure the younger girls of running after the officers—*Austen*⟩ **Achieve** can stress the skill or the endurance as well as the efforts involved in reaching an end ⟨some are born great, some *achieve* greatness—*Shak.*⟩ ⟨no government or private organization could give health; people had to *achieve* it—*Heiser*⟩ Often it implies accomplishment of something that is in itself a feat or triumph ⟨a complete moral unity such as England *achieved*—*Belloc*⟩ **Attain** connotes more strongly than any of the others the spur of aspiration or ambition ⟨his constant efforts to *attain* his ends⟩ It is therefore especially referable to ends beyond the vision, the scope, or the powers of most men ⟨this indispensable condition of the safety and civilization of the world is, indeed, very difficult to *attain*—*Hobson*⟩ ⟨a fine balance of all the forces of the human spirit such as but once or twice has been *attained* in the world's history—*Binyon*⟩
*Ana* effect, fulfill, execute, accomplish, *perform: *get, obtain, procure, secure

**reach** *n* *range, gamut, radius, compass, sweep, scope, orbit, horizon, ken, purview
*Ana* extent, area, magnitude (see SIZE): spread, stretch, *expanse: capacity, capability, *ability

**react** operate, work, function, *act, behave

**readiness,** ease, facility, dexterity are comparable when they mean the power of doing something without evidence of effort, or the quality of work that manifests such effortlessness. **Readiness** lays stress on the quickness or promptitude with which something is done ⟨his *readiness* in repartee⟩ ⟨a happy *readiness* of conversation—*Austen*⟩ **Ease,** which is probably more often used of the quality than of the power, suggests not only a lack of all signs of strain or care but an absence of signs of hesitation or uncertainty, with resulting evenness in performance and, especially in spoken or written discourse, fluency, directness, grace, and simplicity in expression ⟨true *ease* in writing comes from art, not chance—*Pope*⟩ ⟨*ease* and strength, effort and weakness, go together—*Shaw*⟩ ⟨Constance was surprised at the *ease* which he displayed in the conduct of practical affairs—*Bennett*⟩ **Facility** is sometimes used in a derogatory sense nearly equivalent to shallowness ⟨his *facility* in language has been fatal only too often to his logic and philosophy—*J. C. Van Dyke*⟩ More frequently this feeling is lost and *facility* may be interchangeable with *ease*, though it tends more often than *ease* to express the power, proceeding from practice and use, of performing an act or dispatching a task with

lightness and address ⟨by the use of a few English words and the dramatic *facility* to express complex thoughts in pantomime, she was quite capable of carrying on extended conversations—*Mailer*⟩ ⟨I loathed algebra at first, although afterwards I had some *facility* in it—*Russell*⟩ **Dexterity** implies both readiness and facility, but it carries a stronger implication than any of the preceding words of previous training or practice and of proficiency or skill ⟨his amazing *dexterity* in argument⟩ ⟨absorbed in his own *dexterity* and in the proposition of trying to deceive a fish with a bird's feather and a bit of hair—*Cheever*⟩
*Ana* quickness, promptness, aptness (see corresponding adjectives at QUICK): alacrity, *celerity, legerity: fluency, eloquence, volubility (see corresponding adjectives at VOCAL)
*Con* *effort, exertion, pains, trouble

**ready** *adj* *quick, prompt, apt
*Ana* expert, adept, skilled, skillful, *proficient, masterly: *active, live, dynamic

**ready** *vb* *prepare, fit, qualify, condition

**real,** actual, true, and their derivative nouns reality, actuality, truth are often interchangeable in general, as distinct from technical philosophical or critical, language without marked loss when they mean correspondent to or what is correspondent to all the facts known and knowable; thus, one may say the *real*, or the *actual*, or the *true* state of affairs in the foregoing sense without evident and inherent difference in meaning. The terms are also often used interchangeably, but with distinct loss in clearness and precision, when their common implication is merely that of having or constituting substantial objective existence. **Real,** in this more inclusive sense, implies genuineness, or correspondence between what the thing appears or pretends to be and what it is ⟨this is a *real* diamond⟩ ⟨the British sovereign has little *real* power⟩ ⟨he has a *real* interest in art⟩ ⟨to know the difference between *real* and sham enjoyment—*Shaw*⟩ **Actual** emphasizes occurrence or manifest existence often in contrast with possible or theoretical or expected occurrence or existence; it is applied to what has emerged into the sphere of action or fact and is inapplicable to abstractions ⟨*actual* events⟩ ⟨give me an *actual* instance of the workings of this law⟩ ⟨the *actual* tests of the new airplane are yet to be made⟩ ⟨sculpture and painting are not . . . capable of *actual* movement, but they suggest movement—*Binyon*⟩ ⟨I'm no judge of the feelings of *actual* or prospective parents—*Rose Macaulay*⟩ ⟨the possible way—I am far from asserting it was the *actual* way—in which our legendary Socrates arose—*Ellis*⟩ **True** implies conformity either to what is real or to what is actual. If the former is intended, the term presupposes a standard, a pattern, a model, a technical definition, or a type by which what is true is determined ⟨a *true* Christian⟩ ⟨the ladybug is not a *true* bug, but a beetle⟩ ⟨the whale is not a *true* fish, but a mammal⟩ ⟨in the seventh and eighth centuries there were no *true* kings of England—*Malone*⟩ ⟨the *true* refinement . . . that in art . . . comes only from strength—*Wilde*⟩ When *true* stresses conformity to what is actual, it presupposes the test of correspondence to what exists in nature or to all the facts known and knowable ⟨*true* sidereal time⟩ ⟨run *true* to type⟩ ⟨a *true* story⟩ ⟨the *true* version of a story⟩ ⟨fiction is *truer* than history, because it goes beyond the evidence—*Forster*⟩
*Ana* being, existing *or* existent, subsisting *or* subsistent (see corresponding verbs at BE): *certain, necessary, inevitable
*Ant* unreal: apparent (sense 2): imaginary

**realize** 1 Realize, actualize, embody, incarnate, material-

ize, externalize, objectify, hypostatize, reify are the chief words in English meaning to give concrete or objective existence to something that has existed as an abstraction or a conception or a possibility. They are seldom freely interchangeable, because their implications vary widely and their applications are largely determined by idiom. **Realize** commonly implies emergence into the sphere of actual things (as of something that has been a dream, an ideal, a hope, or a plan) ⟨the project was never *realized* owing to a lack of funds⟩ ⟨he did not *realize* his ambition until he was past middle life⟩ The implication of attainment, of achievement, or of fulfillment is at times so strong in *realize* as to obscure or subordinate this fundamental idea of coming into existence ⟨to achieve a beautiful relation to another human being is to *realize* a part of perfection—*Binyon*⟩ ⟨however evolution . . . is effected, a divine purpose is being *realized* in it—*Inge*⟩ **Actualize,** though sometimes used interchangeably with *realize,* is found chiefly in philosophical or technical writings with the implication of emergence (as of something that has existed only in potentiality) either into fullness or perfection of existence ⟨powers of the mind never *actualized*⟩ or into act or action ⟨potential energy becomes kinetic energy when it is *actualized* by motion⟩ **Embody** and **incarnate** sometimes imply investment with an outward or visible form of something abstract (as a principle, an idea, a trait, or a quality) ⟨the poet cannot *embody* his conceptions so vividly and completely as the painter—*Binyon*⟩ ⟨Dickens *incarnated* hypocrisy in his Uriah Heep⟩ **Materialize** stresses emergence into the sphere of what is perceptible or tangible and usually presupposes prior vagueness, haziness, or elusiveness ⟨I had the glimmering of an idea, and endeavored to *materialize* it in words—*Hawthorne*⟩ *Externalize* and *objectify* emphasize the projection of what is subjective (as a thought, an emotion, or a desire) so that it takes form apart from the mind. **Externalize** often suggests a conscious or unconscious urge for expression or relief ⟨madness has produced . . . valuable art . . .; the artist attempts to rid himself of his abnormality . . . by *externalizing* it into the work of art—*Day Lewis*⟩ **Objectify** is more likely to suggest a conscious attempt to overcome the limitations of subjectivity and sometimes to contemplate one's own mental processes ⟨art has always attempted to express, to *objectify* the dynamic processes of our inner life—*Robert Humphrey*⟩ **Hypostatize** and **reify** occur chiefly in philosophical and technical writing. They imply conversion by the mind of something that is a concept or abstraction into a thing that has real and objective even if not tangible existence ⟨our ingrained habit of *hypostatizing* impressions, of seeing things and not sense-data—*Langer*⟩ ⟨it is people, real flesh and blood human beings—not a *reified* entity called "culture"—who do things—*L. A. White*⟩
Ana effect, fulfill, execute, accomplish, achieve, *perform

2 *think, conceive, imagine, fancy, envisage, envision
Ana *understand, comprehend, appreciate

**reap, glean, gather, garner, harvest** are comparable when they mean to do the work or a given part of the work of collecting ripened crops. **Reap** applies to the cutting down and usually collecting of ripened grain; in extension, it may suggest a return or requital ⟨*reap* early wheat for market⟩ ⟨the lucky artisan producing something they could use would *reap* a fortune—*Billington*⟩ **Glean** basically applies to the stripping of a field or vine that has already been gone over once but may be extended to any picking up of valuable bits from here and there and especially to a gathering of what has been left or missed ⟨*glean* in the fields after the reapers have gone⟩ ⟨assembled a multitude of facts *gleaned* from many and varied sources—*Amer. Guide Series: Wash.*⟩ ⟨she had *gleaned* all the information the library contained—*Robertson Davies*⟩ ⟨data *gleaned* from the questionnaire—*Terry*⟩ **Gather,** the most general of these terms, applies to the collecting or bringing together of the produce of the farm, plantation, or garden; in extension, it can apply to any similar amassing or accumulating ⟨the fruit is *gathered* in late July and August—*Amer. Guide Series: Tenn.*⟩ ⟨workers who *gathered* rubber—*P. E. James*⟩ ⟨she had traveled by safari to *gather* her material—*Current Biog.*⟩ ⟨the multitude of pitfalls in the *gathering,* writing, and processing of the news—*Mott*⟩ ⟨mail is *gathered* and distributed by electrically operated conveyors—*Amer. Guide Series: Minn.*⟩ **Garner** implies the storing of produce (as grain); in extension, it can apply to a laying away of a store ⟨more harvest than one man can *garner*—*Buck*⟩ ⟨a skilled picker may *garner* 100 quarts—*Amer. Guide Series: Ark.*⟩ ⟨wisdom *garnered* through the years—*Hambly*⟩ ⟨these short pieces *garnered* from a magazine catering to the masculine taste—*Lisle Bell*⟩ **Harvest,** the general term, may imply any or all of these processes or be extended in meaning to apply to any gathering together or husbanding ⟨the *harvesting* of cranberries—*Garside*⟩ ⟨the *harvesting* of shellfish—*Amer. Guide Series: Conn.*⟩ ⟨busy *harvesting* your crop of furs—*Nat'l Fur News*⟩ ⟨he had sown pain and *harvested* regret—*Samuel*⟩
Ana collect, assemble (see GATHER)

**rear** vb 1 *build, construct, erect, frame, raise
2 raise, *lift, elevate, hoist, heave, boost
Ana *rise, ascend, mount, soar: *nurse, nurture, foster: breed, propagate (see GENERATE)

**rear** adj *posterior, after, back, hind, hinder
Ant front

**reason** n 1 Reason, ground, argument, proof are comparable when they mean a point or series of points offered or capable of being offered in support of something questioned or disputed. **Reason** usually implies the need of justification, either to oneself or another, of some practice, action, opinion, or belief; it is usually personal in its reference; thus, a father asks the *reason* for his son's disobedience; a person gives the *reasons* for his preference. *Reason* is often applied to a motive, consideration, or inducement which one offers in explanation or defense ⟨so convenient it is to be a "reasonable creature," since it enables one to find or make a *reason* for everything one has in mind to do—*Franklin*⟩ **Ground** is often used in place of *reason* because it too implies the intent to justify or defend. When, however, the emphasis is on evidence, data, facts, or logical reasoning rather than on motives or considerations, *ground* is the acceptable word; thus, the *reasons* for a belief may explain why it is held, but the *grounds* for it give evidence of the validity of that belief; a scientist presents the *grounds* for his conclusion. *Ground* also suggests more solid support in fact and therefore greater cogency and objectivity than *reason;* thus, one may speak of frivolous or of trumped-up *reasons* but not *grounds* ⟨the future as we see it offers no *grounds* for easy optimism—*Current Biog.*⟩ ⟨*grounds* for divorce⟩ **Argument** stresses the intent to convince or to bring him into agreement with one's view or position. It can imply the use of evidence and reasoning in the making and stating of a point in support of one's contention ⟨the debaters came well provided with *arguments*⟩ ⟨a party organ, providing usable facts and *arguments,* in terse paragraphs—*Boatfield*⟩ but often it suggests reasoning without reference to fact ⟨one of the commonest of all evasions;

A colon (:) separates groups of words discriminated. An asterisk (*) indicates place of treatment of each group.

the *argument* which is not an *argument* but an appeal to the emotions—*Woolf*⟩ **Proof** in much of its use (see *proof* under PROVE) emphasizes not an intent but an effect: that of conclusive demonstration; therefore, a *proof* is a piece of evidence (as a fact or a document) or of testimony (as of a witness or expert) or an argument that evokes a feeling of certainty in those who are to be convinced ⟨these arguments [for the existence of God] are sometimes called *proofs*, though they are not demonstrations; they are, however, closely inwoven with the texture of rational experience—*Inge*⟩ ⟨Euclid, the author of the Elements, who gave irrefutable *proofs* of the looser demonstrations of his predecessors—*Farrington*⟩ *Ana* explanation, justification, rationalization (see corresponding verbs at EXPLAIN)
**2** *cause, determinant, antecedent, occasion
*Ana* *motive, incentive, inducement, impulse: basis, foundation, ground (see BASE *n*)
**3 Reason, understanding, intuition** can all denote that power of the intellect by which man arrives at truth or knowledge. **Reason** centers attention on the faculty for order, sense, and rationality in thought, inference, and conclusion about perceptions ⟨the maintenance of *reason*—the establishment of criteria, by which ideas are tested empirically and in logic—*Dorothy Thompson*⟩ ⟨*reason* is logic; its principle is consistency; it requires that conclusions shall contain nothing not already given in their premises—*Kallen*⟩ **Understanding** may sometimes widen the scope of *reason* to include both most thought processes leading to comprehension and also the resultant state of knowledge ⟨*understanding* is the entire power of perceiving and conceiving, exclusive of the sensibility; the power of dealing with the impressions of sense, and composing them into wholes—*Coleridge*⟩ ⟨philosophy is said to begin in wonder and end in *understanding*—*Dewey*⟩ **Intuition** (see under *intuitive* at INSTINCTIVE) stresses quick knowledge or comprehension without orderly reason, thought, or cogitation ⟨all this . . . I saw, not discursively, or by effort, or by succession, but by one flash of horrid simultaneous *intuition*—*De Quincey*⟩ ⟨do we not really trust these faint lights of *intuition,* because they are lights, more than reason, which is often too slow a councillor—*Æ*⟩ Used in connection with 19th century literary and philosophic notions, *understanding* often suggests the cold analytical order usually associated with *reason* and *reason* in turn suggests the spontaneity of *intuition* ⟨the *understanding* was the faculty that observed, inferred, argued, drew conclusions . . . the cold, external, practical notion of life. . . . The *reason* was the faculty of *intuition*, warm, perceptive, immediate, that represented the mind of young New England—*Brooks*⟩
*Ana* *mind, intellect, intelligence, brain: ratiocination, *inference

**reason** *vb* reflect, *think, deliberate, speculate, cogitate
*Ana* *infer, deduce, conclude, judge, gather

**reasonable** *rational
*Ana* sensible, sane, prudent, judicious, *wise: *fair, equitable, just
*Ant* unreasonable

**rebate** *deduction, abatement, discount

**rebel** *n* **Rebel, insurgent, iconoclast** are comparable when they denote one who rises up against constituted authority or the established order. **Rebel** carries the strongest implication of a refusal to obey or to accept dictation and of actual, often armed, resistance to what one opposes; the term does not necessarily imply antagonism to a government but is comprehensive enough to cover one who defies a generally accepted authority (as of a law, a tradition, or a custom) ⟨all their friends were protesters

and *rebels* and seceders—*H. G. Wells*⟩ ⟨one is a *rebel* or one conforms, one is a frontiersman in the Wild West of American night life, or else a Square cell, trapped in the totalitarian tissues of American society—*Mailer*⟩ **Insurgent** applies chiefly to a rebel who rises in revolt but who is not regarded by the authorities as having the status of an enemy or belligerent; thus, *rebels* in a colony or dependency of an empire may, from the imperial point of view, be designated as *insurgents*, even though they call themselves *rebels* ⟨at the beginning of the war Lincoln held the idea that the Southerners were *insurgents* and that those captured in arms should be punished as traitors —*Muzzey*⟩ In a more extended use *insurgent* applies to a rebel (as in a political party, a church, or a group of artists or writers) who rises in revolt not so much in an attempt to destroy the organization or institution or its laws or conventions as in the hope of effecting changes or reforms believed to be necessary ⟨the progressives, who favored giving the voters more control over the nation's political and economic life, were called *insurgents*—*Canfield & Wilder*⟩ ⟨the free verse movement was led by a group of *insurgents*⟩ **Iconoclast**, historically applicable to one of a party of insurgents in the Eastern Church in the 8th and 9th centuries who opposed the use of images, is applied in an extended sense to a person who, especially in the capacity of a reformer, violently attacks an established belief, custom, tradition, or institution ⟨I have become a reformer, and, like all reformers, an *iconoclast*. . . . I shatter creeds and demolish idols—*Shaw*⟩ ⟨the blundering crudity of the tough-minded *iconoclast*—*Garvin*⟩
*Ana* *opponent, antagonist, adversary: assailant, attacker (see corresponding verbs at ATTACK)

**rebellion, revolution, uprising, revolt, insurrection, mutiny, putsch, coup** can all denote a war or an armed outbreak against a government or against powers in authority. **Rebellion** implies open, organized, and formidable armed resistance to constituted authority or to the government in power; the term is usually applied after the event to an instance of such resistance as has failed to overthrow the powers that be ⟨Jack Straw's *Rebellion*⟩ ⟨the Jacobite *rebellions* of 1715 and 1745⟩ **Revolution** applies to a rebellion that has been successful to the extent that the old government is overthrown and a new one substituted ⟨the French *Revolution*⟩ ⟨the American *Revolution*⟩ The term, however, does not invariably imply a war or a warlike outbreak ⟨effected a bloodless *revolution* by a coup d'etat⟩ The words are often applied to the same event according to the point of view of the user or sometimes according to the time in which it is used; thus, the American Civil War of 1861-1865 was called the "War of the *Rebellion*" by Northerners, not only during its progress but for a long time after; a *revolution* is often called a *rebellion* by the overthrown government or its supporters until bitterness has faded ⟨the English Civil War (1642-1652) was, after the Restoration (1660), and still sometimes is, called the Great *Rebellion*⟩ **Uprising** is a somewhat general term applicable to an act of violence that indicates a popular desire to defy or overthrow the government; it is often used in reference to a small and ineffective movement that flares up suddenly and violently among an insurgent class or section of the people but it is applicable also to the first signs of a general or widespread rebellion ⟨there was fear of *uprisings* in different parts of the country⟩ ⟨whenever the whole nation should join together in one sudden and vigorous *uprising*—*Freeman*⟩ **Revolt** and **insurrection** apply to an armed uprising which does not attain the extent of a rebellion, either because it is quickly put down or is

immediately effective. **Revolt**, however, carries a stronger suggestion of a refusal to accept conditions or continue in allegiance than does **insurrection**, which often suggests such a seditious act as an attempt to seize the governing power or to gain control for one's party ⟨the Reformation . . . was no sudden *revolt*, but the culmination of a long agitation for national independence in religious matters —*Inge*⟩ ⟨Baltazar's tyranny grew little by little, and the Acoma people were sometimes at the point of *revolt* —*Cather*⟩ ⟨*insurrections* of base people are more furious in their beginnings—*Bacon*⟩ ⟨excess of obedience is . . . as bad as *insurrection*—*Meredith*⟩ **Mutiny** applies chiefly to an insurrection against military or especially maritime or naval authority ⟨the ship's master feared *mutiny* long before it occurred⟩ ⟨the *mutiny* of a regiment made the situation desperate for the invaders⟩ **Putsch** may apply to a small popular uprising or demonstration, or a planned attempt to seize power ⟨the Munich beer hall *Putsch* of Hitler's supporters in 1923⟩ **Coup**, in full **coup d'etat**, applies to a sudden overthrowing of a government by other than normal constitutional means; typically it implies careful planning on the part of a comparatively small opposition that usually has such backing from the military forces as insures the success of its effort, often without the need for bloodshed ⟨General Naguib's *coup*, peaceful only because of the lack of resistance on the part of the faltering king . . . well illustrates the old definition of a dictator—one who receives a bankrupt country—*Atyeo*⟩ ⟨it's not in our usual tradition of *coups d'etat* at all. Normally, nobody is killed in a *coup d'etat*. A certain amount of firing, yes, but over the heads of the crowds, just to show people they are serious—*Rama Rau*⟩ ⟨Czechoslovakia was absorbed by a *coup* under the direct threat of nearby Russian military force—*Isaacs*⟩
*Ana* \*sedition, treason: resistance, opposition, combating, withstanding (see corresponding verbs at RESIST)

**rebellious** \*insubordinate, mutinous, seditious, factious, contumacious
*Ana* recalcitrant, refractory, intractable, \*unruly, ungovernable: estranged, alienated, disaffected (see ESTRANGE)
*Ant* acquiescent, resigned: submissive

**rebound,** reverberate, recoil, resile, repercuss are comparable when they mean to spring back to an original position or shape. **Rebound** basically implies a springing back after a collision or impact ⟨the ball readily *rebounds* when thrown against a wall⟩ In extended use the term implies a springing back from one extreme to another or from an abnormal condition to one that is normal ⟨literature is *rebounding* again from the scientific-classical pole to the poetic-romantic one—*Edmund Wilson*⟩ **Reverberate** is used chiefly of rays or waves, most typically of sound waves, which are forced back in the manner of an echo or series of echoes or are repelled or reflected from side to side or from one surface to another ⟨the evening gun thundered from the fortress, and was *reverberated* from the heights—*Hawthorne*⟩ but it may be extended to other matters giving a similar effect ⟨presents even simple subjects with a perceptiveness that makes them *reverberate* in the mind—*Babette Deutsch*⟩ **Recoil** (see also RECOIL 1) often implies a springing back after being stretched, strained, or depressed ⟨a spring *recoiling* after pressure has been removed⟩ or a sudden or violent backward movement ⟨a gun *recoils* when it is fired⟩ Sometimes it carries the suggestion of a return to the source or point of origin in the manner of a boomerang ⟨that evidence missed the mark at which it was aimed, and *recoiled* on him from whom it proceeded—*Macaulay*⟩ But *recoil* often implies a springing back in the sense of

being forced back by or as if by a blow; it then may connote a retreat, a receding, or a reeling ⟨ten paces huge he back *recoiled*—*Milton*⟩ ⟨as deep *recoiling* surges foam below —*Burns*⟩ ⟨commentators *recoiled* from the spectacle as if it were too loathsome for remark—*S. L. A. Marshall*⟩ **Resile**, much less common than its corresponding adjective *resilient*, like *recoil* may imply a springing back (as of an elastic body) into the original state or position, but in practice it is largely restricted to an essentially legal use in which it implies a withdrawing from something to which one has previously committed oneself ⟨the suggestion which he had brought . . . meant that India was seeking to *resile* from its solemn international commitments—*Pakistan Affairs*⟩ **Repercuss**, also much less common than its corresponding noun *repercussion* and adjective *repercussive*, is a close synonym of *reverberate* and *rebound*, for it implies the return of something moving ahead with great force or, in extended use, set in motion or operation, back to or toward the starting point. However it distinctively suggests repulsion upon impact and a return with undiminished force, or sometimes even greater force, and often, when persons are involved, with a marked effect upon the ones who initiated the action ⟨the waves dashed against the rocks and *repercussed* with a great roar⟩ ⟨sickness produces an abnormally sensitive emotional state . . . and in many cases the emotional state *repercusses* . . . on the organic disease —*Peabody*⟩
*Ana* bound, \*skip, ricochet

**rebuild** \*mend, repair, patch
*Ana* \*renew, restore, renovate, refresh

**rebuke** \*reprove, reprimand, admonish, reproach, chide
*Ana* rate, upbraid, \*scold, berate: \*criticize, reprehend, reprobate

**rebut** \*disprove, refute, confute, controvert

**recalcitrant** refractory, intractable, headstrong, willful, \*unruly, ungovernable
*Ana* rebellious, \*insubordinate, factious, contumacious: \*obstinate, stubborn: resisting, opposing, withstanding (see RESIST)
*Ant* amenable (sense 2)

**recall** *vb* 1 recollect, \*remember, remind, reminisce, bethink, mind
*Ana* evoke, elicit, extract, \*educe: \*stir, rouse, arouse, waken, awaken
2 \*revoke, reverse, repeal, rescind
*Ana* \*annul, abrogate, void: retract, \*abjure, recant

**recant** retract, \*abjure, renounce, forswear
*Ana* withdraw, remove

**recede,** retreat, retrograde, retract, back can all mean to move or seem to move in a direction that is exactly the opposite of ahead or forward. **Recede** stresses marked and usually gradually increasing distance from a given point, line, or position, but it implies movement on the part of what recedes only when a fixed point of view is indicated or understood ⟨the tide is *receding*⟩ ⟨until the flood waters *recede*⟩ ⟨while I stood gazing, both the children gradually grew fainter to my view, *receding*, and still *receding*—*Lamb*⟩ When the point of view is that of a traveler or the distance is in time rather than in space, the receding thing is stationary and the point of view changes. In such a case either a gradual disappearance (as from view or consciousness) or a change in perspective is implied ⟨he stood at the ship's stern watching the shore *recede* from view⟩ ⟨past events as they *recede* appear in truer proportions—*L. P. Smith*⟩ ⟨the possibility of certain ultimate solutions has rather *receded* than approached as the years went by—*Krutch*⟩ When used of persons and their ideas or attitudes, *recede* suggests departure from a

A colon (:) separates groups of words discriminated. An asterisk (\*) indicates place of treatment of each group.

fixed idea, or determined attitude, or a definite stand ⟨he was far too self-willed to *recede* from a position, especially as it would involve humiliation—*Hardy*⟩ **Retreat** implies withdrawal from a point or position reached, usually because of uncertainty, or of imminent defeat or danger, or in obedience to orders ⟨after the failure of the first attack, the army *retreated*⟩ ⟨he had *retreated* inside himself, as into a dense thicket—*Hervey*⟩ ⟨they frequently approached this theme, and always *retreated* from it—*Meredith*⟩ **Retrograde** implies movement contrary to what is expected, normal, or natural; thus, a planet *retrogrades* when it moves or seems to move from east to west, or in a direction opposite to that of the usual planetary course. The verb is also used to imply the reverse of progress in the course of development (as of an institution, a species, or an individual) ⟨some races have been stationary, or even have *retrograded*—*Lubbock*⟩ ⟨in his Latin and Greek he was *retrograding*—*Meredith*⟩ ⟨we have no control over the process by which the arts or sciences advance or *retrograde*—*Whitehead*⟩ Occasionally it is used to imply a going backward in time or an inversion of the chronological order ⟨our narrative *retrogrades* to a period shortly previous to the incidents last mentioned —*Scott*⟩ **Retract** suggests a drawing backward or inward from a forward or exposed position, often in reference to those parts of an organism which can be thrust forward or drawn backward ⟨a cat *retracting* its claws⟩ ⟨throwing out and *retracting* their left fists like pawing horses—*Shaw*⟩ **Back** applies to any retrograde motion and is often qualified by an adverb (as *up, out,* or *down*) ⟨*back* an automobile⟩ ⟨the water in a drain *backs* up when a pipe cannot carry it off⟩ ⟨*back* out of a room⟩ ⟨a wind *backs* when it shifts to a counterclockwise direction⟩ Often when followed by *out* or *down* it implies a receding from a stand or attitude, or a retreating from a promise or an engagement ⟨he will never *back* down once his word is given⟩ ⟨he is trying to *back* out now that he sees how much work the project entails⟩ ⟨the opposition forced the governor to *back* down and to recall his recommendations⟩

*Ana* withdraw, retire, depart (see GO): *rebound, recoil

*Ant* proceed: advance (sense 2)

**receipt** *n* **1** *reception

**2** Receipt, recipe, prescription are comparable when they mean a formula or set of directions for the compounding of ingredients especially in cookery and medicine. **Receipt** is often employed as a designation of a formula for making a homemade medicine ⟨she has an excellent *receipt* for a cough syrup⟩ Though also often used in reference to cookery formulas, the term in this sense is commonly felt as old-fashioned or dialectal and is being gradually displaced by *recipe*. **Recipe** is perhaps the most general of these terms since it can apply not only to a formula or set of instructions for making or doing something but to a method or procedure for attaining some end ⟨*recipes* are used in making steel, and each ingredient is measured to a fraction of one percent—*Hot-Metal Magic*⟩ ⟨reading good books . . . is the *recipe* for those who would learn to read—*Adler*⟩ In application to medicinal formulas *recipe* may come close to *receipt* or it may suggest an old-fashioned empirical remedy as distinct from a modern pharmaceutical product ⟨some of his *recipes* are printed in pharmacopoeias of today—*Norman Douglas*⟩ In cookery *recipe* is the usual and standard English term for a set of directions for preparing a made dish ⟨a family *recipe* for plum pudding⟩ The usual term for a physician's direction to a pharmacist for the compounding or dispensing of a medicine is **prescription**. That term is also applied to a medicine which is compounded or dispensed according to such a direction ⟨his doctor gave him three

*prescriptions*⟩ ⟨he is still taking the *prescription* for bronchitis⟩

**receive, accept, admit, take** can all mean to permit to come into one's possession, presence, group, mind, or substance. They are seldom interchangeable except within a narrow range and, even then, rarely without modification of the thought expressed. **Receive** very often implies nothing more than what has been stated in the common definition; it may be predicated of persons or of things ⟨he did not *receive* the news gladly⟩ ⟨the barrel *receives* excess rain water⟩ In general *receive* implies passiveness in the receiver even when the subject is a person and his response is indicated in the context ⟨an infant merely *receives* impressions, for he does not understand them⟩ ⟨soft wax *receives* the impression of anything that touches it⟩ Only when it implies welcoming or recognition does *receive* connote activity in the receiver ⟨after some delay, the king *received* the ambassador⟩ ⟨the social leaders refused to *receive* the newcomers⟩ ⟨the indifference and hostility with which his earlier work was *received*—*Day Lewis*⟩ **Accept** adds to *receive* an implication of some measure of mental consent, even of approval; thus, a person may be *received* but not necessarily *accepted* in society; an idea may be *received* but not *accepted* by the mind; one may *receive* without necessarily *accepting* an apology. Frequently *accept* suggests tacit acquiescence rather than active assent or approval. Sometimes it connotes an uncritical attitude ⟨the man who . . . *accepted* simply, as a matter of course, the tradition—*Dickinson*⟩ Sometimes it implies a surrender to the inevitable ⟨it is the business of the sensitive artist in life to *accept* his own nature as it is, not to try to force it into another shape—*Huxley*⟩ **Admit** is synonymous with *receive* only when the agent (the one that lets in) is the one that receives rather than introduces ⟨the king *admitted* the ambassador to his presence⟩ ⟨the heart *admits* fluid through these apertures⟩ *Admit*, in this restricted sense, is distinguishable from *receive* by slight syntactical differences but chiefly by its strong implications of permission, allowance, or sufferance; thus, a judge *admits* evidence only after its admissibility has been questioned and he has allowed its entrance. The situation remains the same when the subject is impersonal ⟨the archway was wide enough to *admit* ten men abreast⟩ *Admit*, in contrast with *accept*, often adds the implication of concession; thus, one who *admits* the truth of a contention *accepts* it more or less unwillingly; one can *accept* a proposition without question, but one *admits* it only after he has questioned it. **Take** is a synonym of *receive* only when it suggests no reaching out on one's own part or of one's own initiative to get hold of something (see also TAKE 1) or when it suggests an offering, presenting, conferring, or inflicting by another; it then implies merely a letting something be put into one's hands, mind, possession, or control ⟨this gift was meant for you: *take* it or leave it as you please⟩ ⟨he *takes* whatever fortune sends him⟩ ⟨the British showed that they can *take* the German bombing⟩ ⟨what was it that made men follow Oliver Cromwell and *take* at his hands that which they would not receive from any of his contemporaries?—*Crothers*⟩ ⟨you don't have to *take* anything from him, or to stand his bad manners—*Cather*⟩

*Ana* *enter, penetrate: seize, *take, grasp

**recent** *modern, late

*Ana* fresh, *new, new-fashioned

**reception, receipt** both mean a receiving, but they are not often interchangeable, their use being dependent upon accepted idiom. **Reception** is the more appropriate term when what is received is a person, especially a caller, a visitor, or a guest; the term may then apply to the act, fashion, or manner of receiving ⟨she gave all her friends a warm *reception*⟩ or the manner of being received ⟨much pleased with the *reception* she had—*Pepys*⟩ or a ceremonious receiving or entertaining ⟨invite one's circle of friends to a *reception*⟩ ⟨hold a *reception* for the out-of-town delegates and their wives⟩ or an admission or entrance (as into a place, a society, or a company) ⟨the house is ready for the *reception* of its new tenants⟩ ⟨call attention to the *reception* of several new members into the society⟩ When what is received is a thing, *reception* is employed when to the idea of receiving is added the idea of admitting into or as if into a space or enclosure ⟨the tower is large enough for the *reception* of several bells⟩ or of apprehension (as by a sense, the senses, or the mind) ⟨their minds are not ready for the *reception* of such ideas⟩ ⟨the proposal met a favorable *reception*⟩ ⟨television *reception* was poor during the storm⟩ **Receipt** (see also RECEIPT 2) stresses the simple fact of receiving and is the customary term when what is received is a thing (as money, goods, or a letter) given or sent by another and delivered into one's custody or possession ⟨acknowledge the *receipt* of goods ordered⟩ ⟨I am awaiting the *receipt* of a letter before making my decision⟩ *Receipt* is also applied to a signed paper or document testifying to the receiving of money due or of goods delivered.

**recess** *n* \*pause, respite, lull, intermission
*Ana* withdrawal, retirement (see corresponding verbs at GO): \*break, interruption, interval, gap: relaxation, leisure, \*rest

**recherché** elegant, \*choice, exquisite, delicate, dainty, rare
*Ana* fresh, original, \*new, novel: \*select, exclusive, picked
*Ant* banal

**recipe** \*receipt, prescription

**reciprocal** **1** Reciprocal, mutual, common mean shared, experienced, or shown by each of the persons or things concerned. **Reciprocal** has for its distinctive implication the return in due measure by each of two sides of whatever is offered, given, or manifested by the other. Usually therefore it implies not only a quid pro quo but an equivalence in value, though not necessarily in kind, on each side (as of love, hate, understanding, courtesies, concessions, or duties) ⟨the connection between law and political theory has not been one-sided; it has been completely *reciprocal*—*Cairns*⟩ ⟨the *reciprocal* feelings of man and woman towards each other—*T. S. Eliot*⟩ **Mutual** is often used in place of *reciprocal* when the idea of return or interchange is suggested and that of sharing equally or jointly is stressed ⟨*mutual* affection⟩ ⟨*mutual* enthusiasm⟩ But *mutual* is applicable, as *reciprocal* is not, to two persons who entertain reciprocal feelings toward each other ⟨*mutual* friends⟩ ⟨*mutual* foes⟩ When there is little or no suggestion of a reciprocal relation (as between thoughts or feelings) and the emphasis is upon the fact that the two persons or things involved entertain the same feelings towards each other, perform the same actions, or suffer the same results, *mutual* is more appropriate than *reciprocal* ⟨their eyes held and the air was eloquent of *mutual* suspicion—*Hervey*⟩ ⟨even Shelley sometimes mingles poetry and propaganda to their *mutual* disaster—*Lowes*⟩ Both *reciprocal* and *mutual* are sometimes used when more than two persons, classes, or things are involved ⟨*mutual* recriminations, long suppressed, broke out between the Fuehrer's captains—*Shirer*⟩ but when there is no implication of reciprocity, **common** is the more usual term; thus, one says "we (two, three, or more persons) are *mutual* friends," meaning that all are friends each of the other but "they have *common* friends," meaning that each has friends who

also are friends of the others; the members of a group may have a *common* purpose. *Common* (see also COMMON 3; UNIVERSAL 2) implies joint participation or possession by two or more persons, and differs from *mutual* in not being restricted as to the number involved and in not carrying a suggestion of a reciprocal relation or of an equivalence of feeling, performance, or effort ⟨make *common* cause against an enemy⟩ ⟨their *common* fund of intellectual interests and curiosities made their talks exhilarating—*Wharton*⟩ ⟨death and other incidents of our *common* fate—*Cohen*⟩
*Ana* shared, participated, partaken (see SHARE): interchanged, exchanged (see EXCHANGE): balancing, compensating, counterpoising (see COMPENSATE)

**2** Reciprocal, corresponding, correlative, complementary, complemental, convertible are not close synonyms, although in some instances they are interchangeable, and all are comparable in meaning like, equivalent, or similarly related to each other (as in kind, quality, or value). **Reciprocal** (see also RECIPROCAL 1) implies that the likeness or equivalence of two things or of one thing to another rests on the fact of their being returns or its being a return in kind, value, or quality for what one side has given to the other ⟨*reciprocal* courtesies⟩ ⟨a treaty providing for *reciprocal* trade privileges⟩ ⟨each flexor muscle which contracts has its *reciprocal* extensor muscle which operates in the reverse direction—*Wier*⟩ ⟨public and private systems engage in *reciprocal* services—*Lepawsky*⟩ **Corresponding** implies a likeness or equivalence proceeding from the fact that one answers to the other or conforms to it so that they are fitted to each other, or proportionate to or commensurate with each other, or in perfect accord with each other ⟨*corresponding* sides of similar triangles are in proportion—*G. F. Wilder*⟩ ⟨the light, with its *corresponding* shadow—*Kitson*⟩ ⟨all rights carry with them *corresponding* responsibilities —*Paepke*⟩ **Correlative** implies a close relationship rather than a likeness and is applicable chiefly to two things, or one of two things, which cannot exist independently of each other either because one logically implies the other ⟨*husband* and *wife, father* and *child*, are *correlative* terms⟩ or one cannot exist without the other ⟨the "right" of the worker to demand work on reasonable terms, and the *correlative* obligation of the organized community to provide it—*Hobson*⟩ In more casual use *correlative* may imply nothing more than so close a correspondence or relation between two or sometimes more things that they come naturally, necessarily, or logically together ⟨two *correlative* rules: first, that no one shall be allowed to undertake important work without having acquired the necessary skill; secondly, that this skill shall be taught to the ablest of those who desire it—*Russell*⟩ ⟨disorder in any one of nature's *correlative* hierarchies—physical, political, psychological—automatically produces disorder in the others—*Bingham*⟩ **Complementary** also implies a close relationship rather than a likeness; the term carries a strong suggestion that one thing is so necessary to another or to others that without it an entire or perfect whole is not possible ⟨it is important to recognize that these two uses of the surplus are *complementary* and not competitive—*Hobson*⟩ ⟨the corpuscular and undulatory concepts of light must be regarded as *complementary* rather than *antithetical*—*Jeans*⟩ **Complemental** has essentially the same meaning, differing only in applying usually to a quantitative completing ⟨revelation is regarded by many theologians as *complemental* to reason⟩ **Convertible** implies so strong a likeness that the things, though not identical, are virtually interchangeable ⟨the law, and the opinion of the judge, are not always *con-*

_vertible_ terms, or one and the same thing—_Blackstone_⟩ ⟨truth and beauty have never been recognized as identical, and . . . to employ their names as _convertible_ terms would lead to no end of confusion—_Quiller-Couch_⟩
**Ana** equivalent, identical, *same: related, associated, linked, united (see JOIN)

**reciprocate,** **retaliate, requite, return** can mean to give back usually in kind or in quantity. **Reciprocate** may imply a mutual, equivalent, or roughly equivalent, exchange or a paying back of what one has received. The connotations of alternating movements and of correspondence between what is interchanged are usually stressed ⟨he touched his friend's glass lightly and _reciprocated_ the former toast —_Joyce_⟩ ⟨he . . . is peevish and sensitive when his advances are not _reciprocated_—_Shaw_⟩ ⟨I hope in a few days to _reciprocate_ for your verses by sending you a few remarks suggested by reading . . . Gény—_Justice Holmes_⟩ **Retaliate** denotes chiefly a paying back of an injury and usually implies return in exact kind, often vengefully ⟨terrorist violence erupts . . . troops _retaliate_ quickly —_N. Y. Times_⟩ ⟨schoolmates quick to recognize a victim who would never _retaliate_—_Gorer_⟩ ⟨though at first he considers the possibility . . . of _retaliating_ on those who have injured him—_Krutch_⟩ **Requite** can imply simply a paying back, usually reciprocally, but additionally it can imply a paying back according to what one construes as the merits of the case and then need not imply satisfaction to both parties concerned ⟨his servility was _requited_ with cold contempt—_Macaulay_⟩ ⟨Drake . . . had _requited_ the wrongs inflicted by the Inquisition on English seamen— _J. R. Green_⟩ ⟨_requited_ their hospitality by robbing them of much of their supplies—_Amer. Guide Series: Me._⟩ **Return** (see also RETURN _vb_) does not emphasize the idea of interchanging as strong in _reciprocate_ but rather that of paying back whatever has been given, usually in kind but sometimes by way of contrast ⟨_return_ a visit⟩ ⟨_return_ a blow⟩ ⟨_return_ good for evil⟩ ⟨he _returns_ my envy with pity—_Steele_⟩ ⟨devotion that it was not in her nature to _return_—_Naomi Lewis_⟩
**Ana** interchange, *exchange: repay, compensate, recompense (see PAY)

**recite** rehearse, recount, *relate, narrate, describe, state, report
**Ana** enumerate, tell, *count, number: detail, itemize, particularize (see corresponding adjectives at CIRCUMSTANTIAL)

**reckless** daring, daredevil, rash, foolhardy, venturesome, *adventurous
**Ana** *precipitate, sudden, hasty, headlong, impetuous, abrupt: desperate, hopeless (see DESPONDENT)
**Ant** calculating —**Con** *cautious, circumspect, wary, chary

**reckon** _vb_ 1 *calculate, compute, estimate
**Ana** enumerate, *count, number: figure, total, *add, sum, cast, foot
2 *consider, regard, account, deem
**Ana** *think, conceive, imagine, envision: *conjecture, surmise, guess
3 count, bank, *rely, trust, depend

**reclaim** save, ransom, redeem, deliver, *rescue
**Ana** *renew, restore, renovate: reform, rectify, remedy, *correct, amend
**Ant** abandon —**Con** desert, forsake (see ABANDON)

**recluse,** **hermit, eremite, anchorite, cenobite** all designate a person who lives apart from the world usually in order to devote himself to prayer, contemplation, and penance. _Recluse_ and _hermit_ are also applied to persons who avoid intercourse with men for other than religious motives, but even in such extended use they retain their original

distinguishing implications, for **recluse** stresses retirement from the world and the life of the world into seclusion but not necessarily into physical isolation and **hermit,** a solitary life lived apart from men and usually in a place or under conditions where there is little likelihood of intrusion. _Recluse_ is the broader term; it may be applied to a hermit or to a religious who lives in a cloistered community. _Hermit_ is often applied to a member of one of the very few religious orders (as the Carthusians) whose members dwell alone and meet other members of the community only in church and in the refectory on Sundays. **Eremite,** archaic as a variant of _hermit_, is sometimes chosen to unequivocally designate a solitary who is under a religious vow. _Anchorite_ and _cenobite_ are contrasted terms for the two leading types of recluses in the Eastern and in the Western Church. **Anchorite** designates the type known as _hermit_ or _eremite;_ **cenobite,** the type that dwells in a community, especially a strictly cloistered community of monks or nuns.

**recognition,** **identification, assimilation, apperception** are comparable when they designate a form of cognition which relates a perception of something new to knowledge already acquired. **Recognition** implies that the thing now perceived (as by seeing, hearing, or smelling) has been previously perceived, if not in itself then in another instance of the same kind, and that the mind is aware that the two things are identical or of the same kind. **Identification** implies not only recognition, but such previous knowledge as permits one to recognize the thing as an individual member of a class of things. **Assimilation** implies that the mind responds to new facts, new ideas, or new experiences by interpreting them in the light of what is already known, thereby making them also an integral part of one's body of knowledge. **Apperception** differs from _assimilation_ in implying that the mind responds to new facts, ideas, or situations when and only when it can relate them to what is already known.

**recognize** *acknowledge
**Ana** accept, admit, *receive: notice, note, observe, remark (see SEE)

**recoil** _vb_ 1 **Recoil, shrink, flinch, wince, blench, quail** can all mean to draw back from something, usually through fear, faintheartedness, or disgust. **Recoil** more than any of the succeeding terms suggests the physical signs of such drawing back or the sensations that accompany it. The term may imply a start or a sudden movement away ⟨had so great a dread of snakes that he instinctively _recoiled_ at the sight of one—_Costain_⟩ ⟨she makes a gesture as if to touch him. He _recoils_ impatiently—_Shaw_⟩ but often the term suggests an inner or not outwardly apparent shaking or stirring that affects one mentally more than physically ⟨she was principally aware of the sentiment of fear. She _recoiled_ from the future—_Bennett_⟩ ⟨the tendency to _recoil_ from the expression of repressed feelings, such as hate—_Garvin_⟩ **Shrink** implies an instinctive recoil (as from something painful or unpleasant or horrible); it often implies cowardice, but it may imply extreme sensitiveness or scrupulousness ⟨guilt and misery _shrink,_ by a natural instinct, from public notice—_De Quincey_⟩ ⟨she _shrank_ from the words which would have expressed their mutual consciousness, as she would have _shrunk_ from flakes of fire—_George Eliot_⟩ ⟨he might have _shrunk_ from defending himself at the expense of a frightened, unhappy girl—_Rose Macaulay_⟩ **Flinch** implies a failure in resolution or an inability to overcome one's desire to avoid or evade something that is painful, difficult, or abhorrent ⟨he looked his fate in the face without _flinching_—_Burroughs_⟩ ⟨she read and took notes incessantly, mastering facts with painful laboriousness, but never _flinching_ from

---

**Ana** analogous words    **Ant** antonyms    **Con** contrasted words    See also explanatory notes facing page 1

her self-imposed task—*Hardy*⟩ ⟨the process of purgation is alway perilous, though it is . . . still more perilous to *flinch* from making the attempt—*Toynbee*⟩ *Flinch* is sometimes used but **wince** more often when by some involuntary, often slight, physical movement (as starting or recoiling) one manifests pain, fear, disgust, or acute sensitiveness ⟨cannot bear the slightest touch without *flinching*—*Smollett*⟩ ⟨his horse stands *wincing* at the flies, giving sharp shivers of his skin—*Hunt*⟩ ⟨old Lady Kew's tongue was a dreadful thong which made numbers of people *wince*—*Thackeray*⟩ ⟨Mr. Warburton *winced* when he heard so young a man call him by nickname—*Purdy*⟩ **Blench** may be indistinguishable from *flinch;* it often, however, carries a stronger suggestion of faintheartedness or of signs of fear ⟨this painful, heroic task he undertook, and never *blenched* from its fulfillment—*Jeffrey*⟩ ⟨though his death seemed near he did not *blench*—*Masefield*⟩ To **quail** is to shrink coweringly, as from something which strikes terror ⟨the most formidable woman I have ever known . . . eminent men invariably *quailed* before her—*Russell*⟩ ⟨I am never known to *quail* at the fury of a gale—*Gilbert*⟩
*Ana* waver, falter, *hesitate: shy, balk, stick, stickle (see DEMUR)
*Ant* confront: defy
2 *rebound, reverberate, resile, repercuss
*Ana* retreat, *recede, back, retract: *return, revert
**recollect** *remember, recall, remind, reminisce, bethink, mind
*Ana* *stir, rouse, arouse, rally, waken, awaken
**recollection** *memory, remembrance, reminiscence, mind, souvenir
**recommend** *commend, compliment, applaud
*Ana* *approve, endorse, sanction: *praise, extol, acclaim
**recommendation** testimonial, *credential, character, reference
*Ana* approval, endorsement (see corresponding verbs at APPROVE): commendation (see corresponding verb at COMMEND)
**recompense** *vb* reimburse, indemnify, repay, satisfy, remunerate, compensate, *pay
*Ana* award, accord, vouchsafe, *grant: balance, offset, *compensate
**reconcile** conform, accommodate, adjust, *adapt
*Ana* harmonize, accord, square, *agree: *correct, rectify, amend, revise
**recondite,** abstruse, occult, esoteric can all mean being beyond the power of the average intelligence to grasp or understand. **Recondite** stresses difficulty resulting from the profundity of the subject matter or its remoteness from ordinary human interest. It often, especially as applied to persons, implies scholarly research carried beyond the bounds of apparent usefulness ⟨the *recondite* and occult in human nature alike attract the insurgent temper—*Lowes*⟩ ⟨profound and scholarly, but often *recondite* to the point of obscurity—*Woodring*⟩ **Abstruse** suggests extreme complexity or abstractness in the material as well as its remoteness from the ordinary range of human experience or interest ⟨the vast army of illiterate or semiliterate people who distrust the learned world, especially the *abstruse* world of science—*Meyer*⟩ ⟨the last quartets and piano sonatas of Beethoven, which are some of the most *abstruse* music ever written—*Whitehead*⟩ **Occult** basically implies secret, mysterious knowledge purporting to be attainable only through special and often supernatural or magical agencies and not through ordinary channels of human reason ⟨the *occult* sciences⟩ ⟨whether it be from natural predisposition or from some *occult* influence of the time—*J. R. Lowell*⟩ But often the word

is used with much weakened force to mean little more than mysterious ⟨the sense of *occult* rivalry in suitorship was so much superadded to the palpable rivalry of their business lives—*Hardy*⟩ ⟨juries selected by some *occult* procedure satisfactory to the judges—*Amer. Guide Series: Nev.*⟩ **Esoteric** basically implies knowledge guarded by, and imparted only to, members of a cult or inner circle of initiates ⟨the *esoteric* sects, which guard a mystery known only to the initiated—*Sperry*⟩ but it is extended in general use to describe knowledge in the possession only of adepts, students, and specialists ⟨as far as the general public was concerned the museum was an *esoteric*, occult place in which a mystic language was spoken —*Saarinen*⟩
*Ana* scholarly, erudite, *learned: *pedantic, scholastic, academic
**record** *vb* Record, register, list, enroll, catalog can mean to commit to writing for the sake of immediate or future use. **Record** usually implies as its purpose the making of an exact or official entry or statement which gives evidence of the facts involved; the act serves as an aid or a check to memory or as a means of supplying details unlikely to be remembered indefinitely ⟨*record* the proceedings of a meeting⟩ ⟨*record* the events of each day in a diary⟩ ⟨*record* a deed in the county clerk's office⟩ ⟨in all *recorded* history, nothing like this has happened before⟩ **Register** usually implies accurate entry into a formal record of facts or particulars of a certain kind which require or deserve recording ⟨required by law to *register* all births⟩ ⟨all purchases are *registered* in our books⟩ Sometimes *register* carries a further or a slightly different implication; thus, one *registers* a letter by payment of a special fee and obtaining a receipt to ensure its safe delivery by requiring a record of each person who handles it; a thermometer *registers* the temperature when the mercury expands or contracts to a certain mark in degrees. **List** implies an entering in a list (as of names, figures, needs, or events) ⟨*list* the achievements of an athlete⟩ ⟨*list* alphabetically the books you have read⟩ ⟨*list* the survivors of an accident⟩ ⟨*list* the food needed for the party⟩ ⟨*list* your expenses carefully⟩ **Enroll** may add to *list* the notion of setting apart those entered in a distinctive category (as members of a body or adherents of a person or cause) and therefore may connote a winning over, an enlisting, or an admission to membership ⟨interested persons are invited to *enroll* themselves as members of the society⟩ ⟨those who are . . . tempted to *enroll* themselves as soldiers—*Malthus*⟩ ⟨as he goes on, he . . . *enrolls* a following—*Montague*⟩ **Enroll** is sometimes also used of things in the sense of *record*, but in its more usual extended sense, it also includes the connotation of honoring ⟨*enroll* your triumphs o'er the seas and land—*Pope*⟩ **Catalog** commonly implies an enumeration of all items making up a class or group, usually with descriptive or defining details ⟨*catalog* the books in a library⟩ ⟨the porcelains in the collection needed to be *cataloged*⟩ ⟨allowing time to *catalog* the items to be sold at auction⟩ **Catalog** may also imply assignment of an item to its proper place in a list or sometimes in a category ⟨the book has not yet been *cataloged*⟩ ⟨a specimen impossible to *catalog* in the existent classification often turns out to be a new species⟩
*Ana* *enter, admit, introduce
**record** *n* *document, monument, archive
**recount** recite, *relate, rehearse, narrate, describe, state, report
*Ana* enumerate, *count, number, tell: detail, itemize, particularize (see corresponding adjectives at CIRCUMSTANTIAL)

A colon (:) separates groups of words discriminated. An asterisk (*) indicates place of treatment of each group.

**recoup** *vb* recruit, retrieve, regain, *recover
*Ana* *compensate, balance, offset, counterpoise
**recover** 1 Recover, regain, retrieve, recoup, recruit can mean to get back something that has been let go or lost. Recover, the most comprehensive of these terms, may imply a finding or obtaining something material or immaterial that has been lost ⟨*recover* a lost watch⟩ ⟨*recovered* his health⟩ ⟨*recover* peace of mind⟩ ⟨*recovered* his balance⟩ or a getting of something in reparation or compensation ⟨*recover* damages in a lawsuit⟩ **Regain,** though often used interchangeably with *recover,* carries a stronger implication of winning back or getting once more into one's possession something of which one has been deprived ⟨*regain* a fortress⟩ ⟨*regain* a person's good will⟩ ⟨*regained* his sight⟩ ⟨*regained* freedom⟩ *Regain* also may imply, as *recover* seldom implies, success in reaching again a place or point at which one has been before ⟨in his efforts to *regain* his hotel—*Meredith*⟩ ⟨the trench allowed the performers, after being thrust down into perdition, to *regain* the greenroom unobserved—*Quiller-Couch*⟩ **Retrieve** implies a recovering or regaining after assiduous effort or search ⟨desperate efforts to *retrieve* lost territory⟩ ⟨it now seemed impossible to *retrieve* the foreign trade lost by war⟩ ⟨his desire to *retrieve* his military reputation—*Belloc*⟩ ⟨marveling at the silent untiring activity with which her popularity had been *retrieved—Wharton*⟩ But *retrieve* sometimes takes for its object such words as *loss, error, failure,* or *disaster,* then implying not recovery but a setting right or a making what is bad good, or a reparation by making up for what was wrong or unsuccessful ⟨life is not long enough to *retrieve* so many mistakes⟩ ⟨one false step is ne'er *retrieved—Gray*⟩ ⟨he is to *retrieve* his father's failure, to recover the lost gentility of a family that had once been proud—*Brooks*⟩ **Recoup,** basically a legal term implying a rightful deduction by a defendant of part of a claim awarded to a successful plaintiff in a lawsuit, can in its general and extended use imply recovery or retrieval, usually in equivalent rather than identical form, of something lost ⟨able to *recoup* his gambling losses by more careful play⟩ ⟨Elizabeth had lost her venture; but if she was bold, she might *recoup* herself at Philip's cost—*Froude*⟩ **Recruit** fundamentally implies growth through fresh additions; in military use it can imply an increase in numbers through drafting and enlisting or a filling of vacancies in a force resulting from casualties ⟨it was his custom to *recruit* his army with conquered people—*Newton*⟩ In more general use it may imply a regaining of what has been lost (as vigor through illness, or money through extravagance or heavy expenditures) by fresh additions or replenishment of the supply ⟨*recruiting* his strength with a good plain dinner—*Dickens*⟩ ⟨[the middle class] is continually *recruited* from the capitalist families—*Shaw*⟩
*Ana* redeem, reclaim (see RESCUE): *compensate, offset, balance
2 *improve, recuperate, convalesce, gain
*Ana* restore, refresh, rejuvenate, *renew: revive, resuscitate, revivify (see RESTORE)
**recreant** *n* *renegade, apostate, turncoat, backslider
*Ana* treacherousness *or* treachery, perfidiousness *or* perfidy, traitorousness (see corresponding adjectives at FAITHLESS)
**recreate** *amuse, divert, entertain
*Ana* *renew, restore, refresh, rejuvenate: enliven, *quicken, animate
**recreation** amusement, diversion, entertainment (see under AMUSE)
*Ana* relaxation, repose, ease (see REST): play, sport, frolic, rollick (see under PLAY *vb*): *mirth, jollity, hilarity
**recrudesce** *return, revert, recur

*Ana* *renew, renovate, refurbish
*Con* *suppress, repress: *stop, cease, discontinue
**recrudescence** return, reversion, recurrence (see under RETURN *vb*)
*Ana* renewal, restoration, refreshment, renovation (see corresponding verbs at RENEW)
*Con* suppression, repression (see corresponding verbs at SUPPRESS)
**recruit** *vb* *recover, regain, retrieve, recoup
*Ana* *renew, restore, renovate, refresh: repair, *mend, rebuild
**rectify** *correct, emend, amend, reform, revise, remedy, redress
*Ana* *improve, better, help, ameliorate: *mend, repair, rebuild: *adjust, regulate, fix
**rectitude** virtue, *goodness, morality
*Ana* integrity, probity, *honesty, honor: righteousness, nobility (see corresponding adjectives at MORAL): uprightness, justness, conscientiousness, scrupulousness (see corresponding adjectives at UPRIGHT)
**recumbent** *prone, supine, prostrate, couchant, dormant
*Ant* upright, erect
**recuperate** *improve, recover, convalesce, gain
*Ana* invigorate, *strengthen, fortify, energize
**recur** *return, revert, recrudesce
*Ana* *repeat, iterate, reiterate
**recurrence** return, reversion, recrudescence (see under RETURN *vb*)
*Ana* relapse (see under LAPSE *vb*): repeating *or* repetition, iteration (see corresponding verbs at REPEAT)
**recurrent** *intermittent, periodic, alternate
*Ana* rhythmic, metrical (see corresponding nouns at RHYTHM): returning, reverting, recrudescing (see RETURN): *fitful, spasmodic
**redact** *edit, compile, revise, rewrite, adapt
**redeem** deliver, *rescue, ransom, save, reclaim
*Ana* *free, liberate, release, emancipate, manumit: restore, *renew, renovate: *recover, regain
**redolence** *fragrance, perfume, incense, bouquet
*Ana* odor, aroma, *smell: balminess, aromaticness *or* aromaticity (see corresponding adjectives at ODOROUS)
**redolent** aromatic, balmy, fragrant, *odorous
*Ana* *pungent, poignant, piquant, racy, spicy: penetrating, piercing (see ENTER)
**redress** *vb* emend, remedy, amend, *correct, rectify, reform, revise
*Ana* *relieve, lighten, alleviate, assuage, mitigate, allay: repair, *mend
**redress** *n* *reparation, amends, restitution, indemnity
*Ana* compensation, offsetting, balancing (see corresponding verbs at COMPENSATE): *retaliation, reprisal, vengeance, retribution
**reduce** 1 *decrease, lessen, diminish, abate, dwindle
*Ana* *shorten, abridge, abbreviate, curtail, retrench: *contract, shrink, condense
*Con* *increase, augment, enlarge, multiply: *extend, lengthen, elongate, prolong, protract: *expand, swell, amplify
2 *conquer, vanquish, defeat, subjugate, beat, overcome, lick, subdue, surmount, overthrow, rout
*Ana* *weaken, cripple, disable, undermine, enfeeble: humble, humiliate, degrade, debase (see ABASE)
3 *degrade, demote, declass, disrate
*Ana* humble, humiliate, debase (see ABASE)
**redundancy** *verbiage, tautology, pleonasm, circumlocution, periphrasis
*Ana* wordiness, verbosity, prolixity, diffuseness (see corresponding adjectives at WORDY): inflatedness *or* inflation, turgidity, tumidity, flatulence (see corresponding

adjectives at INFLATED): *bombast, rant, fustian

**redundant** *wordy, verbose, prolix, diffuse
*Ana* *superfluous, surplus, supernumerary, extra, spare: repeating *or* repetitious, iterating, reiterating (see corresponding verbs at REPEAT)
*Ant* concise —*Con* terse, succinct, laconic, pithy, summary (see CONCISE): compact, *close

**reef** *n* *shoal, bank, bar

**reel** *vb* **Reel, whirl, stagger, totter** are comparable when they mean to move or seem to move uncertainly or uncontrollably (as in weakness, in giddiness, or in intoxication). **Reel** usually implies a turning round and round, or a sensation of so turning or being turned ⟨for, while the dagger gleamed on high, *reeled* soul and sense, *reeled* brain and eye—*Scott*⟩ ⟨in these lengthened vigils his brain often *reeled*—*Hawthorne*⟩ But it may also imply a being thrown off balance (as an army that recoils before a mighty attack, a ship that has lost its equilibrium, or a person affected by exhaustion, a wound, faintness, or intoxication) ⟨giddy and restless, let them *reel* like stubble from the wind—*Milton*⟩ ⟨when Church and State were *reeling* to their foundations—*Stanley*⟩ ⟨he . . . placed his open palm gently against the breast of Lucian, who instantly *reeled* back as if the piston rod of a steam engine had touched him —*Shaw*⟩ **Whirl** (see also TURN) is often used like *reel*, especially when referred to the head or to the brain ⟨the dim brain *whirls* dizzy with delight—*Shelley*⟩ but it more frequently implies swiftness or impetuousness of movement often by someone or something being carried along blindly or furiously ⟨in popular commotions, each man is *whirled* along with the herd—*Lytton*⟩ **Stagger** stresses uncertainty or uncontrollability of movement, typically of a person walking while weak, giddy, intoxicated, or heavily burdened, but sometimes of whatever meets with difficulty or with adverse conditions; thus, a boat that labors, a mind that is perplexed, confused, or bewildered, and a faith, opinion, or purpose that meets heavy opposition can all be said to *stagger* ⟨a porter half my size who . . . *staggered* through the shallow water under what must have been an almost overwhelming weight—*Heiser*⟩ ⟨at whose immensity even soaring fancy *staggers*—*Shelley*⟩ **Totter** (see also SHAKE) implies not only weakness or unsteadiness as a cause of uncertain movement but often also suggests an approaching complete collapse ⟨from the day of Cressy feudalism *tottered* slowly but surely to its grave —*J. R. Green*⟩ ⟨[the waning moon] like a dying lady, lean and pale, who *totters* forth, wrapt in a gauzy veil—*Shelley*⟩
*Ana* *turn, spin, revolve, rotate: sway, waver, *swing: wobble, teeter, quiver (see SHAKE)

**refer** 1 assign, credit, accredit, *ascribe, attribute, impute, charge
*Ana* associate, relate, connect (see JOIN): *direct, aim, point, lay
2 *resort, apply, go, turn
*Ana* consult, *confer, commune, advise: address, *direct
3 **Refer, allude, advert** are comparable when they mean to mention something so as to call or direct attention to it. **Refer,** when unqualified, usually suggests intentional introduction and distinct mention ⟨a day or two later she *referred* to the matter again—*Mary Austin*⟩ ⟨we may here again *refer*, in support of this proposition, to the plain and unequivocal language of the laws—*Taney*⟩ but often it is so qualified as to add the idea of judging to that of mentioning ⟨inclined at times to give a subjective interpretation to mathematical-physical theories and to *refer* to them as fictions—*Cohen*⟩ **Allude,** though often close to *refer* in the latter's more general sense, distinctively implies indirect reference (as by a hint, a suggestive phrase, a

roundabout or covert method of expression, or a figure of speech); it may suggest mere casual interest, modesty, timidity, or reticence in the one who alludes ⟨fruit . . . gives him that intestinal condition I *alluded* to—*Stafford*⟩ ⟨the traveling facilities *alluded* to . . . would date the story as between 1842 and 1844—*O. S. Nock*⟩ Sometimes, however, it connotes bias or ill will ⟨proposals, which were never called proposals, but always *alluded* to slightingly as innovations—*Mackenzie*⟩ **Advert,** which basically means to turn the mind or attention to something (see ADVERT 1), is sometimes interchangeable with *refer* but in such use it may distinctively imply a slight or glancing reference interpolated in a text or utterance ⟨regards as truly religious certain elevated ethical attitudes and cosmologies that Freud, when he *adverted* to them at all, regarded as too highbrow to be given the name of religion—*Riesman*⟩ ⟨letters from Franklin to his wife's grandmother . . . in which he *adverted* to having had to do with her education—*Justice Holmes*⟩
*Ana* *introduce, insert, interpolate: *quote, cite

**referee** *n* umpire, arbiter, *judge, arbitrator

**reference** testimonial, recommendation, character, *credential

**referendum** initiative, *mandate, plebiscite

**refinement** *culture, cultivation, breeding
*Ana* suavity, urbanity (see corresponding adjectives at SUAVE): courtesy, politeness, civility (see corresponding adjectives at CIVIL): *elegance, grace, dignity
*Ant* vulgarity

**reflect** *think, cogitate, reason, speculate, deliberate
*Ana* *consider, contemplate, study, weigh: *ponder, muse, meditate, ruminate

**reflection** *animadversion, stricture, aspersion
*Ana* imputing *or* imputation, ascribing *or* ascription (see corresponding verbs at ASCRIBE): criticizing *or* criticism, reprehending *or* reprehension, blaming *or* blame (see corresponding verbs at CRITICIZE): *attack, assault, onslaught, onset: disparagement, derogation, depreciation (see corresponding verbs at DECRY)

**reflective** *thoughtful, contemplative, meditative, pensive, speculative
*Ana* thinking, reasoning, deliberating, cogitating (see THINK): analytical, *logical, subtle

**reform** *vb* *correct, rectify, emend, amend, remedy, redress, revise
*Ana* *mend, repair, rebuild: better, *improve, help, ameliorate

**reform** *n* *reformation

**reformation, reform** can both denote a making better or a giving of a new and improved form or character and are sometimes interchangeable without loss ⟨the *reformation* of a criminal⟩ ⟨the *reform* of society⟩ **Reformation** is the more usual term as a designation of a movement that has brought about many revolutionary amendments or improvements, especially in morals or religious practices ⟨the Protestant *Reformation*⟩ It is also appropriate when the idea of making over so as to eradicate defects is stressed ⟨not directed to the *reformation* of what was ill —*Belloc*⟩ ⟨never came *reformation* in a flood, with such a heady currance, scouring faults—*Shak.*⟩ ⟨it is the moral basis of this *reformation* that I wish to lay—*Hobson*⟩ **Reform,** on the other hand, is more usual as a designation of an attempt to remove abuses, correct corrupt practices, or to make changes for the better ⟨hostile to all persons advocating *reform*⟩ ⟨Boeotia, choose *reform* or civil war! —*Shelley*⟩ ⟨a wave of municipal *reform* had passed over it—*Ellis*⟩ *Reform* also applies, as *reformation* does not, to a particular or specific amendment, whether achieved or proposed, as a measure of reform ⟨initiate sweeping

---

A colon (:) separates groups of words discriminated. An asterisk (*) indicates place of treatment of each group.

*reforms* in the government⟩ ⟨a *reform* worthy of a good prince and of a good parliament—*Macaulay*⟩

**refractory** recalcitrant, intractable, ungovernable, *unruly, headstrong, willful
*Ana* *contrary, perverse, froward, wayward: *insubordinate, rebellious, contumacious
*Ant* malleable: amenable (sense 2)

**refrain, abstain, forbear** are comparable when they mean to keep or withhold oneself voluntarily from something to which one is moved by desire or impulse. **Refrain** is especially suitable when the checking of a momentary inclination is implied ⟨*refrain* from laughter⟩ At times, to *refrain* from an action implies merely its nonperformance ⟨no tolerable parent could *refrain* from praising a child when it first walks—*Russell*⟩ **Abstain** is more emphatic than *refrain*, because it usually stresses deliberate renunciation or self-denial on principle and often implies permanency of intent ⟨early Christians . . . *abstained* from the responsibilities of office—*Acton*⟩ ⟨I have . . . *abstained* from the use of many expressions, in themselves proper and beautiful, but which have been foolishly repeated by bad poets—*Wordsworth*⟩ It is used especially in reference to those natural appetites and passions whose control or renunciation are a part of self-discipline ⟨from this personal blow stemmed, I believe, an act of renunciation, his decision to *abstain* from meat—*Shirer*⟩ **Forbear** usually implies self-restraint rather than self-denial, be it from patience, charity, or clemency, or from discretion, or from stoicism ⟨he was so poison-mean that the marsh mosquitoes *forbore* to bite him—*S. H. Adams*⟩ ⟨wherever he has not the power to do or *forbear* any act according to the determination or thought of the mind, he is not free—*Thilly*⟩ But often *forbear* is but vaguely distinguishable from *refrain* ⟨I cannot *forbear* quoting what seems to me applicable here—*Justice Holmes*⟩
*Ana* check, *arrest, interrupt: *restrain, curb, inhibit

**refresh** *renew, restore, rejuvenate, renovate, refurbish
*Ana* enliven, *quicken, animate, vivify: recruit, *recover, regain: recreate, *amuse, divert
*Ant* jade, addle

**refuge** asylum, sanctuary, *shelter, cover, retreat
*Ana* safety, security (see corresponding adjectives at SAFE): stronghold, citadel, *fort, fortress: *harbor, haven, port

**refulgent** effulgent, luminous, radiant, lustrous, *bright, brilliant, beaming, lambent, lucent, incandescent

**refurbish** renovate, *renew, refresh, restore, rejuvenate

**refuse** *vb* *decline, reject, repudiate, spurn
*Ana* *deny, gainsay: balk, baffle, *frustrate, thwart, foil: debar, *exclude, shut out

**refuse** *n* Refuse, waste, rubbish, trash, debris, garbage, offal can all mean matter that is regarded as worthless and fit only for throwing away. **Refuse**, ordinarily the most comprehensive term of the group, stresses the rejection of the matter, or its uselessness from the point of view of the owner (as a manufacturer, processor, builder, or housekeeper) and usually implies its being cast aside or thrown away. The term includes anything covered by this description without regard to whether another will find use for it ⟨a stream polluted by *refuse* from a manufacturing plant⟩ ⟨heaps of *refuse* left by the former tenant⟩ ⟨arrangements made by the city to collect *refuse*⟩ ⟨a road surfaced with the hardened *refuse* from a neighboring tannery⟩ **Waste** may also be a comprehensive term approaching *refuse* in meaning, but it typically applies to material that is unused by its producer but can or could be useful in other ways or in other circumstances or to other people ⟨wiped his hands on a wad of cotton *waste*⟩ **Rubbish** is likely to mean

an accumulation of useless material and worn-out, broken-down, used up, worthless things ⟨throw it in the *rubbish* barrel⟩ ⟨her closets heaped with *rubbish*⟩ **Trash** stresses material of no account (as something worn-out or exhausted of what was good in it or parts discarded in shaping, trimming, or clipping). In general use *trash* is often employed in place of *rubbish* as a name for waste materials requiring disposition, but both terms in this sense usually exclude refuse that is animal or vegetable matter. **Debris** usually applies to what remains from the breaking up, the disintegration, or the destruction of something (as a building, a wall, or a tree); the term usually suggests a loose accumulation of detritus or broken fragments ⟨a pile of *debris* was the only sign that a house was once there⟩ ⟨the sandstone cliffs . . . are battered down and their *debris* carried out to sea—*Geikie*⟩ ⟨after the air raid nothing was left of the building but a pile of rubble and *debris*⟩ **Garbage** chiefly applies to organic refuse (as from a kitchen, a store, or a market) including waste of animal or vegetable origin or animal or vegetable matter that is or is regarded as unfit for human food. **Offal** may refer to something (as chips of wood or pieces of leather) cut off in dressing or fitting for use, but the term is usually applied specifically to the parts of a butchered animal that are removed in dressing the carcass, that consist chiefly of viscera (as liver, kidneys, and heart) and of trimmings (as tail, hooves, blood, and head meat), and that include edible meats and raw materials for processing as well as refuse. But *offal* may also be applied to carrion and other worthless or distasteful refuse and tends then and in extended use to stress offensiveness or disagreeableness.

All these terms except *waste* also have extended use; **refuse** refers usually to something left after the available supply has been thoroughly picked over and therefore implies the worst, the meanest, or the least desirable of the lot ⟨the *refuse* of society⟩ **Rubbish** may be applied to something (as inferior merchandise or a ridiculous or nonsensical idea, argument, or discussion) that in its worthlessness suggests a heap of trash ⟨much of the goods in bargain sales is mere *rubbish*⟩ ⟨most of the stuff talked about Nordics and Aryans is simply *rubbish*—*Huxley*⟩ **Trash** retains its implication of relative worthlessness ⟨who steals my purse steals *trash*—*Shak.*⟩ ⟨most of these paintings are *trash*, but there are two or three good things⟩ **Debris** may be applied to something immaterial or intangible that remains as evidence of what the original thing once was ⟨those eastern lands which were the *debris* of Alexander's empire—*Buchan*⟩ **Garbage** also may be applied to something that in comparison with other things of the same sort may be described as filthy or foul ⟨she flew with voracious appetite to sate herself on the *garbage* of any circulating library—*Porter*⟩ **Offal** ordinarily applies to persons considered as the lowest or meanest of refuse or as offscourings ⟨wretches . . . whom everybody now believes to have been . . . the *offal* of gaols and brothels—*Macaulay*⟩

**refute** confute, rebut, *disprove, controvert
*Ana* contradict, impugn, traverse, negative, contravene (see DENY)

**regain** *recover, recruit, recoup, retrieve
*Ana* gain, *reach, compass, attain, achieve: redeem, reclaim, save (see RESCUE): restore, *renew

**regal** royal, *kingly, queenly, imperial, princely
*Ana* majestic, imposing, stately, magnificent, august (see GRAND): *splendid, resplendent, glorious, sublime

**regale** tickle, gratify, delight, *please, rejoice, gladden
*Ant* vex

**regard** *n* Regard, respect, esteem, admiration, and their

corresponding verbs (**regard, respect, esteem, admire**) are comparable when they mean a feeling, or to have a feeling, for someone or something which involves recognition of that person's or thing's worth and some degree of liking. **Regard** is the most colorless as well as the most formal of these words ⟨please give him my *regards*⟩ It usually requires qualification to reinforce and orient its meaning ⟨held in slight *regard* by his neighbors⟩ ⟨she learned to hope that it [the past] . . . might not cost her Henry's entire *regard*—*Austen*⟩ ⟨Steve had not been highly *regarded* in his hometown—*Anderson*⟩ **Respect** usually implies careful evaluation or estimation of the worth of a person or thing and of the measure of recognition which is due him or it ⟨he *respected* their views even though he could not agree with them⟩ ⟨he held their opinions in slight *respect*⟩ ⟨one wants to produce in the child the same *respect* for the garden that restrains the grown-ups from picking wantonly—*Russell*⟩ Often *respect* implies such a show of deference or veneration as is proper from a junior or an inferior ⟨the *respect*, amounting almost to worship, he sometimes saw in the eyes of the people—*Anderson*⟩ Sometimes it suggests observance of what is proper or fitting ⟨show *respect* for the dead⟩ ⟨*respected* the wishes of his parents⟩ and sometimes it suggests recognition of something as sacred or inviolable ⟨*respect* a person's privacy⟩ ⟨have *respect* for the rights of others⟩ **Esteem** adds to *respect* the implications of a high valuation with a consequent prizing and of warmth of feeling or attachment ⟨what things there are most abject in regard and dear in use! What things again most dear in the *esteem* and poor in worth!—*Shak.*⟩ ⟨in the Renaissance, no Latin author was more highly *esteemed* than Seneca—*T. S. Eliot*⟩ **Admiration** and **admire**, like *esteem*, imply a recognition of superiority, but they usually connote more enthusiastic appreciation, and sometimes suggest genuine affection ⟨Miss Welwood, I have long felt the deepest *esteem* for you, and your present courageous attitude in this distressing financial crisis has added *admiration* to *esteem*—*Deland*⟩ Sometimes the words stress the personal attractiveness of the object of admiration, and weaken the implication of *esteem* ⟨what sight . . . is sadder than the sight of a lady we *admire admiring* a nauseating picture?—*L. P. Smith*⟩
*Ana* deference, \*honor, homage, reverence: appreciation, cherishing, prizing, valuing (see corresponding verbs at APPRECIATE)
*Ant* despite —*Con* contempt, scorn, disdain (see under DESPISE)
**regard** *vb* 1 respect, esteem, admire (see under REGARD *n*)
*Ana* \*appreciate, cherish, value, prize, treasure
*Ant* despise —*Con* contemn, scorn, disdain (see DESPISE): reject, repudiate, spurn (see DECLINE *vb*)
2 \*consider, account, reckon, deem
*Ana* rate, \*estimate, value, assess, assay
**regarding** \*about, concerning, respecting
**region** \*area, tract, zone, belt
*Ana* \*locality, vicinity, district, neighborhood: section, sector, division, \*part: \*field, territory, province
**register** *n* \*list, table, catalog, schedule, roll, roster, inventory
**register** *vb* \*record, list, enroll, catalog
*Ana* \*enter, admit: insert, \*introduce: fix, establish, \*set: preserve, conserve, \*save
**regressive** retrogressive, retrograde, \*backward
*Ant* progressive
**regret** *n* \*sorrow, grief, heartache, heartbreak, anguish, woe
*Ana* compunction, remorse, \*penitence, repentance, contrition: \*qualm, scruple, demur

**regular** *adj* 1 Regular, normal, typical, natural can all mean being of the sort or kind that is expected as usual, ordinary, or average. A person or, more often, a thing is **regular**, as opposed to *irregular*, that conforms to what is the prescribed rule or standard or the established pattern for its kind ⟨a *regular* verb⟩ ⟨a *regular* meeting of a society⟩ A person or a thing is **normal**, as opposed to *abnormal* or *exceptional*, that does not deviate in any marked way from what has been discovered or established as the norm (see *norm* under AVERAGE *n*) for one of its kind. In contrast with *regular*, *normal* carries a stronger implication of conformity within prescribed limits or under given conditions and therefore sometimes admits a wide range of difference among the things that may be described as normal for a class or kind ⟨*normal* winter weather⟩ ⟨a perfectly *normal* child physically as well as mentally⟩ ⟨his pulse is *normal* for a person of his age⟩ ⟨her intensity . . . would leave no emotion on a *normal* plane—*D. H. Lawrence*⟩ When applied to persons, *normal* often specifically connotes mental balance or sanity ⟨his actions are not those of a *normal* person⟩ but it may connote merely an approach to the average in mentality, implying the exclusion of those below or above this average ⟨the twins, since they had gone to Oxford, never admitted that they cared for any books that *normal* people cared for—*Rose Macaulay*⟩ A person or thing is **typical**, as opposed to *individual*, that markedly exhibits the characters or characteristics identifying the type, class, species, or group to which he or it belongs, often to the exclusion or the obscuring of any that differentiate him or it individually ⟨a *typical* example of Browning's style⟩ ⟨I would suggest that the most *typical*, as it is probably the oldest of the arts, is the Dance—*Binyon*⟩ ⟨peculiar to himself, not *typical* of Greek ideas—*Dickinson*⟩ ⟨a *typical* English country town with wide High Street, narrow Market Street, picturesque Market Square—*Mackenzie*⟩ A person or thing is **natural** (see also NATURAL 2) that acts, behaves, or operates in accordance with the nature or essence of his or its kind or constitution; the term also applies to what is normal in or suitable to one because of such nature or constitution ⟨the father is the *natural* protector of his children⟩ ⟨the *natural* love of a mother⟩ ⟨flesh is the *natural* food of a dog⟩ ⟨he died from *natural* causes⟩
*Ana* \*usual, habitual, customary: \*common, ordinary, familiar
*Ant* irregular
2 \*orderly, methodical, systematic, regular
*Ana* fixed, set, settled (see SET): constant, even, equable, \*steady, uniform
*Ant* irregular
**regulate** \*adjust, fix
*Ana* \*order, arrange, organize, systematize, methodize: temper, \*moderate: \*correct, rectify
**regulation** rule, \*law, precept, statute, ordinance, canon
*Ana* instruction, direction, bidding (see corresponding verbs at COMMAND): deciding *or* decision, determination, ruling (see corresponding verbs at DECIDE)
**regurgitate** \*belch, burp, vomit, disgorge, spew, throw up
**rehearse** \*relate, narrate, describe, recite, recount, state, report
*Ana* \*repeat, iterate, reiterate: detail, itemize, particularize (see corresponding adjectives at CIRCUMSTANTIAL)
**reify** \*realize, actualize, embody, incarnate, materialize, externalize, objectify, hypostatize
**reimburse** indemnify, repay, recompense, compensate, remunerate, satisfy, \*pay
*Ana* recoup, \*recover: \*compensate, balance, offset
**reinforce** \*strengthen, invigorate, fortify, energize

---

A colon (:) separates groups of words discriminated. An asterisk (\*) indicates place of treatment of each group.

*Ana* *increase, augment, multiply, enlarge: *support, sustain, prop, bolster, buttress

**reissue** *n* *edition, impression, reprinting, printing

**reiterate** *repeat, iterate, ingeminate

**reject** *vb* repudiate, spurn, refuse, *decline
*Ana* *discard, cast, shed: oust, expel, dismiss, *eject: *exclude, debar, shut out, eliminate
*Ant* accept: choose, select

**rejoice** delight, gladden, *please, gratify, tickle, regale
*Ant* grieve: aggrieve: bewail

**rejoin** *answer, respond, reply, retort
*Con* question, interrogate, *ask, inquire, query, catechize, examine

**rejoinder** answer, response, reply, retort (see under ANSWER *vb* 1)
*Ana* returning *or* return, reverting *or* reversion (see under RETURN *vb*): *retaliation, reprisal

**rejuvenate** *renew, restore, refresh, renovate, refurbish

**relapse** *n* lapse, backsliding (see under LAPSE *vb*)
*Ana* *reversion, atavism, throwback: degeneration, decline, declension, decadence, *deterioration

**relapse** *vb* *lapse, backslide
*Ana* revert, *return: degenerate, decline, deteriorate (see corresponding nouns at DETERIORATION)

**relate** *vb* 1 Relate, rehearse, recite, recount, narrate, describe, state, report are comparable when they mean to tell orally or in writing the details or circumstances necessary to others' understanding or knowledge of a real or imagined situation or combination of events. **Relate** implies the giving of a usually detailed or orderly account of something one has witnessed or experienced ⟨*related* the story of his life⟩ ⟨then Father Junípero and his companion *related* fully their adventure—*Cather*⟩ **Rehearse** usually suggests a repetition; it may imply a summary of what is known ⟨let us *rehearse* the few facts known of the inconspicuous life of Thomas Traherne —*Quiller-Couch*⟩ or a second or third or oft-repeated telling ⟨designed to fool the easily fooled . . . it *rehearsed* all the lies with which we are now familiar—*Shirer*⟩ or a going over and over something in one's mind, or with another person, or in privacy before relating or sometimes performing or presenting it to others or to an audience ⟨Mr. Hynes hesitated a little longer . . . . He seemed to be *rehearsing* the piece in his mind—*Joyce*⟩ ⟨felt certain . . . that his smile was as he had *rehearsed* it, polished and genially satanic—*Hervey*⟩ **Recite** and the more common **recount** imply greater particularity of detail than the preceding terms; in fact, the implication of enumeration or of mention of each particular is so strong that both verbs usually take a plural object; thus, one *relates* an experience, but he *recites* or *recounts* his experiences ⟨*recite* the events of the day⟩ ⟨as with all mysteries, it cannot be rationally explained, merely *recounted*— *Shirer*⟩ **Narrate** suggests the employment of devices characteristic of the literary narrative such as plot, creation of suspense, and movement toward a climax ⟨what verse can sing, what prose *narrate* the butcher deeds of bloody Fate—*Burns*⟩ ⟨the discovery of Madeira is *narrated* with all the exaggerations of romance—*Southey*⟩ **Describe** usually implies emphasis upon details that give the hearers or readers a clear picture or that give not only a visual representation but one that appeals to the other senses ⟨bitter sea and glowing light, bright clear air, dry as dry,—that *describes* the place—*Jefferies*⟩ ⟨*described* her . . . as "a dear little thing. Rather brainy, but quite a nice little thing"—*Gibbons*⟩ **State** stresses particularity, clearness, and definiteness of detail, and suggests the aim of presenting material (as facts, ideas, or feelings) in their naked truth so that they will be distinctly understood or

fixed in others' minds ⟨Dryden's words . . . are precise, they *state* immensely, but their suggestiveness is often nothing—*T. S. Eliot*⟩ ⟨one should know what one thinks and what one means, and be able to *state* it in clear terms —*Rose Macaulay*⟩ **Report** implies a recounting and narrating, often after investigation, for the information of others ⟨*report* the progress on defense projects to the cabinet⟩ ⟨he was assigned to *report* the murder trial for the local newspaper⟩ ⟨in his letters Thaddeus *reported* approaching an island in an outrigger one evening —*Cheever*⟩
*Ana* tell, *reveal, disclose, divulge: detail, itemize, particularize (see corresponding adjectives at CIRCUMSTANTIAL)

2 associate, link, connect, *join, conjoin, combine, unite
*Ana* attach, *fasten, fix: refer, assign, credit, impute, *ascribe
*Con* disengage, *detach, abstract: divorce, sever, sunder, *separate

3 *bear, pertain, appertain, belong, apply

**related, cognate, kindred, allied, affiliated** can all mean connected by or as if by close family ties. **Related,** when referred to persons, usually implies consanguinity, but sometimes implies connection by marriage ⟨the royal families in Europe are nearly all *related* to each other⟩ When applied to things, *related* suggests an often close connection, the particular nature of which is to be gathered from the context ⟨*related* species⟩ ⟨*related* events⟩ ⟨*related* activities⟩ ⟨every part of an organism is *related* to the other parts⟩ ⟨body and soul are contrasted, but *related*, concepts⟩ **Cognate** differs from *related* chiefly in being referable only to things that are generically alike or that can be shown to have a common ancestor or source or to be derived from the same root or stock ⟨*cognate* races⟩ ⟨*cognate* languages⟩ ⟨*cognate* words in various languages, such as *pater, Vater, father*⟩ ⟨physics and chemistry are *cognate* sciences⟩ **Kindred,** in its primary sense, stresses blood relationship ⟨*kindred* members of a community⟩ In its more common extended sense, it implies such likenesses as common interests, tastes, aims, or qualities that might be characteristic of a family. When the reference is to persons, congeniality is usually connoted ⟨he would never be popular . . . but he might appeal to a little circle of *kindred* minds—*Joyce*⟩ When applied to things, a more obvious connection or a closer likeness is implied than in *related* ⟨*kindred* qualities in two otherwise alien tongues [Hebrew and English]—*Lowes*⟩ **Allied** more often implies connection by union than by origin, and especially by marriage or by voluntary association. It often connotes a more remote family connection than *related* ⟨the Raycie blood was . . . still to be traced in various *allied* families: Kents, Huzzards, Cosbys—*Wharton*⟩ In its extended use it usually stresses relation based on the possession of common characters, qualities, aims, or effects which lead either to union or to inclusion in the same class or category ⟨*allied* physical types⟩ ⟨*allied* societies⟩ ⟨*allied* diseases⟩ **Affiliated** also stresses connection by union, but it may imply a dependent relation such as that of a child to a parent. Sometimes it implies the adoption of the weaker by the stronger ⟨a small college *affiliated* to a university⟩ Sometimes it connotes a loose union in which the affiliating units retain their independence, but derive support or strength from the main, central, or parent body, or cooperate in its work ⟨Monte Cassino and *affiliated* monasteries⟩ ⟨the CIO and its *affiliated* unions⟩
*Ana* associated, connected (see JOIN): *reciprocal, corresponding, correlative, convertible, complementary: akin, identical, alike, analogous (see LIKE): *relevant,

---

*Ana* analogous words     *Ant* antonyms     *Con* contrasted words     See also explanatory notes facing page 1

germane, pertinent

**relative** *dependent, contingent, conditional
*Ant* absolute

**relaxation** *rest, repose, leisure, ease, comfort
*Ana* amusement, diversion, recreation (see under AMUSE *vb*): relieving *or* relief, assuagement, alleviation, mitigation (see corresponding verbs at RELIEVE)

**relaxed** *loose, slack, lax
*Ana* mitigated, lightened, alleviated, assuaged, relieved (see RELIEVE): flexuous, sinuous (see WINDING): *soft, mild, gentle, lenient
*Ant* stiff —*Con* strict, *rigid, rigorous, stringent: *severe, stern, austere, ascetic

**release** *vb* *free, liberate, emancipate, manumit, deliver, discharge, enfranchise
*Ana* *detach, disengage: *exculpate, exonerate, acquit: surrender, resign, yield, *relinquish
*Ant* detain (*as a prisoner*): check (*as thoughts, feelings*): oblige

**relegate** *vb* *commit, entrust, confide, consign
*Ana* refer, assign, credit, accredit, charge (see ASCRIBE)

**relent** *yield, submit, capitulate, succumb, defer, bow, cave
*Ana* comply, acquiesce (see corresponding adjectives at COMPLIANT): forbear, *refrain, abstain: *abate, subside, wane, ebb

**relentless** unrelenting, merciless, implacable, *grim
*Ana* inexorable, obdurate, adamant, *inflexible: strict, stringent, *rigid, rigorous: *fierce, ferocious, cruel, inhuman
*Con* *soft, lenient, mild, gentle: *tender, compassionate: yielding, submitting *or* submissive (see corresponding verbs at YIELD)

**relevant,** germane, material, pertinent, apposite, applicable, apropos are comparable when they mean having a relation to or a bearing upon the matter in hand or the present circumstances. Something **relevant** has a traceable connection, especially logical connection, with the thing under consideration and has significance in some degree for those who are engaged in such consideration ⟨the judge decided that the evidence was *relevant* and therefore admissible⟩ ⟨great books are universally *relevant* and always contemporary; that is, they deal with the common problems of thought and action that confront men in every age and every clime—*Adler*⟩ Something **germane** is so closely related (as in spirit, tone, or quality) to the subject, the matter, the occasion, or the issue that the fitness or appropriateness of their association is beyond question ⟨enliven his lecture by introducing amusing anecdotes *germane* to his subject⟩ ⟨an interesting point but not *germane* to the issue⟩ ⟨the passionate cravings which are *germane* to the hermit life—*H. O. Taylor*⟩ Something **material** is so closely related to the matter in hand that it cannot be dispensed with without having an evident and especially a harmful effect ⟨the motion is supported by an affidavit showing that the evidence is *material*—*B. F. Tucker*⟩ ⟨certain passages *material* to his understanding the rest of this important narrative—*Scott*⟩ Something **pertinent** is so decisively or significantly relevant that it touches the real point at issue or contributes materially to the understanding of what is under discussion or to the solution of what is in question ⟨once a thing did become *pertinent*, he had an amazing faculty for absorbing it wholly—*Terry Southern*⟩ ⟨it is more *pertinent* to observe that it seems to me that logically and rationally a man cannot be said to be more than once in jeopardy in the same cause, however often he may be tried—*Justice Holmes*⟩ Something **apposite** is relevant and germane to such a degree that it strikes one both by its pertinency and by its felicitousness ⟨an *apposite* illustration⟩ ⟨*apposite* quotations. . . came easily to his pen to grace the pellucid flow of his English—*Parrington*⟩ ⟨whatever she did, she made her circumstances appear singularly *apposite* and becoming—*Sackville-West*⟩ Something **applicable** may be brought to bear upon or be used fittingly in reference to a particular case, instance, or problem ⟨the word *tool* is *applicable* to a plow only when used in a general sense⟩ ⟨the principle is not *applicable* to the case in question⟩ ⟨although . . . I do not get much help from general propositions in a case of this sort, I cannot forbear quoting what seems to me *applicable* here—*Justice Holmes*⟩ Something **apropos** is both appropriate and opportune ⟨a person who is not aware of an undercurrent of feeling may make remarks that are far from *apropos*⟩ ⟨we . . . find a new pleasure in the hackneyed words. They are really not quite *apropos*—*Julian Huxley*⟩ Sometimes it can suggest relevancy rather than appropriateness or opportuneness ⟨he is not witty but Frenchly *apropos*—*Flanner*⟩
*Ana* *related, cognate, allied: fitting, appropriate, proper (see FIT): important, significant, weighty (see corresponding nouns at IMPORTANCE)
*Ant* extraneous —*Con* alien, foreign, *extrinsic

**reliable,** dependable, trustworthy, trusty, tried can be applied to persons, their utterances, views, methods, or instruments to mean having or manifesting qualities which merit confidence or trust. **Reliable** describes what one can count upon not to fail in doing what is expected ⟨she is a very *reliable* servant⟩ ⟨one of the most *reliable* of our employees⟩ ⟨a *reliable* washing machine⟩ or to give or tell the exact truth ⟨a *reliable* work of reference⟩ ⟨*reliable* testimony⟩ **Dependable** is very close to *reliable;* it may suggest steadiness or trustworthiness in time of need or in an emergency ⟨ask a friend to recommend a *dependable* physician⟩ ⟨he is the most *dependable* of our friends⟩ ⟨a *dependable* source of information⟩ **Dependable** is also used merely as a descriptive term implying a character that is predictable or that is the antithesis of what is fickle or capricious ⟨Laura wasn't pretty, but . . . healthy-looking and *dependable*—*Mary Austin*⟩ A person or occasionally a thing is **trustworthy** that merits or has earned one's complete confidence in his or its soundness, integrity, veracity, discretion, or reliability ⟨a *trustworthy* confidant⟩ ⟨a *trustworthy* witness⟩ ⟨a *trustworthy* wife⟩ ⟨the most *trustworthy* comment on the text of the Gospels and the Epistles is to be found in the practice of the primitive Christians—*Macaulay*⟩ **Trusty** applies to a person or thing that has been found by experience to be reliable and trustworthy ⟨a *trusty* guide⟩ ⟨a *trusty* servant⟩ or that has been found never to have failed one in need or in an emergency or that has been found dependable whenever needed ⟨his *trusty* sword—*Spenser*⟩ ⟨he wrapped the *trusty* garment about him—*Cather*⟩ **Tried** also stresses proved reliability, dependability, trustworthiness, or trustiness ⟨a *tried* and true friend⟩ ⟨a *tried* remedy⟩ ⟨a *tried* soldier⟩ ⟨his *tried* expedients—*Bagehot*⟩
*Ana* *safe, secure: *infallible, inerrable, inerrant, unerring: cogent, *valid, sound, convincing, compelling, telling
*Ant* dubious —*Con* *doubtful, problematic, questionable

**reliance** *trust, confidence, dependence, faith
*Ana* credence, credit, *belief, faith: assurance, conviction, certitude, *certainty

**relieve,** alleviate, lighten, assuage, mitigate, allay are comparable when they mean to make something tolerable or less grievous. Though they are often used interchangeably, they are clearly distinguishable. **Relieve** implies a lifting of enough of a burden to make it definitely endurable or temporarily forgotten ⟨drugs that *relieve* pain⟩ ⟨taking steps to control the fire and *relieve* the suffering it entailed—*Milner*⟩ Occasionally *relieve*, when used in the passive, implies a release from anxiety or fear ⟨they were greatly *relieved* when her letter came⟩ Sometimes it suggests a break in monotony or in routine ⟨I've had some trouble to get them together to *relieve* the dullness of your incarceration—*Meredith*⟩ **Alleviate** stresses the temporary or partial nature of the relief and usually implies a contrast with *cure* and *remedy* ⟨oil of cloves will *alleviate* a toothache⟩ ⟨to help *alleviate* New York's chronic traffic problem—*Current Biog.*⟩ **Lighten** implies reduction in the weight of what oppresses or depresses; it often connotes a cheering or refreshing influence ⟨his interest in his work *lightened* his labors⟩ ⟨that blessed mood . . . in which the heavy and the weary weight of all this unintelligible world is *lightened*—*Wordsworth*⟩ **Assuage** suggests the moderation of violent emotion by influences that soften or mollify or sometimes sweeten ⟨the good gods *assuage* thy wrath—*Shak.*⟩ ⟨the life-giving zephyrs that *assuage* the torment of the summer heat—*Cloete*⟩ **Mitigate** also suggests moderation in the force, violence, or intensity of something painful; it does not, as *assuage* does, imply something endured but something inflicting or likely to inflict pain ⟨*mitigate* the barbarity of the criminal law—*Inge*⟩ ⟨group friction and conflict are generally *mitigated* when people realize their common interests—*Cohen*⟩ **Allay**, though it seldom implies complete release from what distresses or disquiets, does suggest an effective calming or quieting ⟨the report *allayed* their fears⟩ ⟨his suspicions were *allayed*⟩ ⟨these . . . words . . . *allayed* agitation; they composed, and consequently must make her happier—*Austen*⟩

*Ana* *comfort, console, solace: *moderate, qualify, temper: diminish, reduce, lessen, *decrease

*Ant* intensify: embarrass: alarm

**religion, denomination, sect, cult, communion, faith, creed, persuasion, church** can all denote a system of religious belief and worship or the body of persons who accept such a system. **Religion,** the usual uncolored term, may apply to a system (as Christianity or Buddhism) which represents the beliefs and worship of all those who accept a given revelation or to one (as Anglicanism) which represents the beliefs and practiced worship of a specific body of those who accept the same revelation ⟨the *religion* of the Arabs⟩ ⟨the *religion* of the Scribes and Pharisees⟩ **Denomination** basically applies to a body of people holding common and distinctive religious beliefs and called by a particular name so as to distinguish them from a more inclusive body ⟨Methodists form one *denomination* of Protestants⟩ ⟨the leading Christian *denominations*⟩ **Sect** is applied to a group cut off from a larger body or, more specifically, from an established or a parent church through discontent with some matter of doctrine or observance; thus, one speaks of the Christian *religion* as comprising all who accept the New Testament as divine revelation, but of the various *sects* into which the seventeenth-century and eighteenth-century Protestant *denominations* were divided. **Cult** though widely varied in usage is typically applied either to a system of beliefs and ritual associated with a particular and sometimes nontheistic worship that is devoutly observed by a usually small group and often viewed as unorthodox or spurious by nonadherents or to the group which practices such a form of worship ⟨ever since the close of the Punic War foreigners had been thronging to Rome, bringing with them their foreign *cults*—*Buchan*⟩ ⟨the romantic error has been . . . in short, to turn the nature *cult* into a *religion*

—*Babbitt*⟩ **Communion** stresses not difference from others but union in essentials (as of religious belief and discipline); the term can apply not only to a large body ⟨the Roman Catholic *communion*⟩ but to one comprising several smaller bodies or organizations (as national churches) which exhibit such union ⟨the Anglican *communion* includes all who are united with the Church of England in matters of faith and order⟩ or to small sects and cults isolated by their special beliefs or practices. **Faith** and **creed** apply to a system of belief and worship that is clearly formulated and definitely accepted ⟨men of all *faiths* were present⟩ ⟨*creeds* are often a cause of division⟩ **Persuasion** may suggest the conviction produced by evangelism and exhortation; it is frequently equivalent to *faith* or *denomination*. **Church** usually has implications that closely relate it to *denomination*. Distinctively it suggests a clearly defined character, both as a system of beliefs or as a body of persons, and often carries a stronger connotation of organization than *denomination* carries; it may imply specifically Christian as contrasted with non-Christian worship ⟨to what *church* does he belong?⟩ ⟨some *churches* that forbade dancing now countenance it⟩

**religious** *adj* 1 *devout, pious, pietistic, sanctimonious
*Ana* *faithful, staunch, steadfast, true: virtuous, righteous, noble, *moral, ethical: *upright, just, honorable, honest
*Ant* irreligious —*Con* ungodly, godless (see IRRELIGIOUS)
2 spiritual, *holy, sacred, divine, blessed
*Ant* secular (*of schools, journals, authorities*): profane (*of music, drama*)

**religious** *n* **Religious, monk, friar, nun** all mean a member of a religious order whose members are bound by the monastic vows of poverty, chastity, and obedience and who lead to a greater or lesser extent a cloistered life. **Religious** is the comprehensive term applicable either to a man or to a woman; it implies a living apart from the world either in a cloistered community formed of members of the same order or as a hermit (see RECLUSE) under the governance of the superior of an order. **Monk** in general use may designate a male religious; in precise technical use the term applies to a member of a religious order for men (as the Benedictine or Cistercian order) whose members live an ascetic life in a cloistered community, and devote themselves mainly to contemplation and prayer and liturgical observances, and to some assigned and usually scholarly, artistic, or scientific employment. **Friar** applies to a member of a mendicant order under whose original regulations neither personal nor community tenure of property was allowed and whose members lived by alms and wandered from place to place preaching the Gospel and administering the sacraments or to a member of an order patterned after them, whether he lives as a mendicant or in a cloistered community and whether he serves as a pastor, a curate, a missionary, a preacher, or a teacher. **Nun** applies only to a female religious; since there are no terms to distinguish nuns according to the severity of their discipline, the rigor of their cloistered life, and the nature of their duties, the word is generally applied to any member of a religious order of women who wear a habit and devote themselves to prayer, contemplation, and work.

**relinquish, yield, leave, resign, surrender, cede, abandon, waive** are comparable when they mean to let go from one's control or possession or to give up completely. **Relinquish** in itself seldom carries any added implication, but it often acquires color from the words with which it is associated or from the character of the thing given up ⟨disinclined to *relinquish* his command⟩ ⟨*relinquished* his

grasp only after a struggle⟩ ⟨he had let something go . . . : something very precious, that he could not consciously have *relinquished*—*Cather*⟩ **Yield** adds to *relinquish* the implication of concession or compliance; in some collocations it does not even suggest finality—a prevailing but not always necessary implication in the words of this group—but rather, a giving way as a favor, or as a sign of weakness, or as an indulgence ⟨*yield* not thy neck to fortune's yoke, but let thy dauntless mind still ride in triumph over all mischance—*Shak.*⟩ **Leave** is often used in place of *relinquish* but distinctively it can imply a forsaking ⟨we have *left* all, and have followed thee—*Mk* 10:28⟩ ⟨he has *left* me . . . quitted me! abandoned me!—*Bennett*⟩ Like *relinquish* it can be strongly colored by context and may convey such dissimilar notions as a giving up or letting go that constitutes sacrifice ⟨the opium eater who cannot *leave* his drug—*Wolfe*⟩ or neglect ⟨by all ye *leave* or do, the silent, sullen peoples shall weight your Gods and you—*Kipling*⟩ or concession ⟨the constitution *leaves* them [the States] this right in the confidence that they will not abuse it—*John Marshall*⟩ or even imposition upon others ⟨she *leaves* most of the work to her sister⟩ **Resign** emphasizes voluntary or deliberate sacrifice without struggle; it usually connotes either renunciation or acceptance of the inevitable ⟨the ambition which incites a man to seize power seldom allows him to *resign* it—*Times Lit. Sup.*⟩ ⟨in her face . . . was that same strange mingling of *resigned* despair and almost eager appeal—*Galsworthy*⟩ **Surrender** distinctively implies the existence of external compulsion or demand; it commonly suggests submission after a struggle or after resistance or show of resistance ⟨when they saw all that was sacred to them laid waste, the Navaho . . . did not *surrender;* they simply ceased to fight—*Cather*⟩ At times the implication of resistance is blurred and that of conscious sacrifice, as for a greater advantage, is heightened ⟨*surrender* rights to a portion of an estate⟩ **Cede** is narrower in its application than *surrender;* as a rule it suggests juridical pressure as expressed in a court decision, the findings of arbitrators, or the terms of a treaty, though it may suggest previous negotiation, and is used in reference to the transfer of lands, territory, or rights ⟨the territory *ceded* by France, under the name of Louisiana—*Taney*⟩ **Abandon** (see also ABANDON 1) stresses finality and completeness in relinquishment, especially of intangible things (as hopes, opinions, methods, or schemes) ⟨no, no; you stick to your prejudices, or at any rate don't *abandon* them on my account—*Mackenzie*⟩ **Waive**, like *yield*, need not imply finality and often suggests a concession, but unlike *yield* and the other terms of this group, it seldom implies the compulsion of force or necessity. Its main implication is a refusal to insist on something (as a right, a claim, one's preference, one's immunity, or obedience to a rule, law, or convention) usually for the sake of courtesy, simplicity, or concentration on what is relatively more important ⟨*waive* extradition proceedings⟩ ⟨*waive* a jury trial⟩ ⟨he *waived* his right to be heard in his own defense⟩ ⟨he *waived* the ceremony of introduction—*Burney*⟩ ⟨if art can enthrall him, he is willing to *waive* all question of logic or rationality—*Babbitt*⟩
*Ana* *abdicate, renounce, resign: *abandon, desert, forsake: *forgo, forbear, abnegate, sacrifice: *discard, shed, cast
*Ant* keep

**relish** *n* **1** savor, tang, flavor, *taste, smack
**2** *taste, palate, gusto, zest
*Ana* liking, loving, enjoying, relishing (see LIKE): *predilection, partiality, prepossession, prejudice, bias: propensity, *leaning, flair, penchant

**relish** *vb* fancy, dote, enjoy, *like, love
*Ana* appreciate, *understand, comprehend: *approve, endorse, sanction

**relishing** *palatable, appetizing, savory, sapid, tasty, toothsome, flavorsome
*Ana* pleasing, gratifying, delighting, rejoicing, tickling, regaling (see PLEASE)
*Con* flat, *insipid, jejune, banal, inane

**reluctant** *disinclined, indisposed, hesitant, loath, averse
*Ana* *cautious, circumspect, chary, wary, calculating: *antipathetic, unsympathetic
*Con* inclined, disposed, predisposed (see INCLINE *vb*): *eager, avid, keen

**rely, trust, depend, count, reckon, bank** can all mean to have or place full confidence. One *relies on* or *upon* someone or something that one believes will never fail in giving or doing what one wishes or expects. *Rely* usually connotes a judgment based on previous experience and, in the case of persons, actual association ⟨he *relies* on his father to help him out of trouble⟩ ⟨he never *relies* on the opinions of others⟩ ⟨a physician upon whom all his patients *rely*⟩ ⟨bitter experience soon taught him that lordly patrons are fickle and their favor not to be *relied* on—*Huxley*⟩ ⟨he is entitled to one or two men whose personal loyalty he can *rely* upon—*Michener*⟩ One **trusts,** or *trusts in* or *to,* when one is completely assured or wholly confident that another will not fail one in need. *Trust* stresses unquestioning faith which need not be based on actual experience ⟨take short views, hope for the best, and *trust* in God—*Sydney Smith*⟩ ⟨because he *trusted* his own individual strength, he was hostile to planning—*Commager*⟩ One **depends** *on* or *upon* someone or something when one, with or without previous experience, rests confidently on him or it for support or assistance. *Depend* may connote a lack of self-sufficiency or even weakness; it often implies so strong a belief or so confident an assumption that the hoped-for support or assistance is forthcoming that no provision for the contrary is made ⟨his diffidence had prevented his *depending* on his own judgment . . . but his reliance on mine made everything easy—*Austen*⟩ ⟨the captain of the ship at sea is a remote, inaccessible creature . . . *depending* on nobody—*Conrad*⟩ ⟨the man never cared; he was always getting himself into crusades, or feuds, or love, or debt, and *depended* on the woman to get him out—*Henry Adams*⟩ One **counts** or **reckons** *on* something when one takes it into one's calculations as certain or assured; the words often imply even more confidence in expectation than *depend* and may carry even more than the latter's frequent suggestion of possible distress or disaster if one's expectations are not fulfilled ⟨they told me I was going to get a pension. I *counted* on it. And now they take it away —*Upson*⟩ ⟨Christian souls who *counted* on the slaves for their bread and butter—*Brooks*⟩ ⟨the Oriental writer *reckons* largely on the intellectual cooperation of his reader—*Cheyne*⟩ But these terms are often weakened in use to the point that they mean little more than *expect* ⟨the Soviet economic administration . . . *reckons* on good rather than poor crops—*Van Valkenburg & Huntington*⟩ ⟨he had not *counted* on having to pay for a room —*Irwin Shaw*⟩ One **banks** *on* something or someone in which one's confidence is as strong as it would be in a bank to which one would entrust one's money; hence, the term is appropriate when one wishes to express near absolute certainty without any of the other implications inherent in *depend, count,* and *reckon* ⟨the kind of people you could *bank* on in a tight place—*J. D. Adams*⟩ ⟨you can *bank* on his honesty⟩ ⟨had reliable sources of information, and you could *bank* on what he said⟩

---

A colon (:) separates groups of words discriminated. An asterisk (*) indicates place of treatment of each group.

*Ana* confide, entrust, *\*commit:* hope, *\*expect,* look, await

**remain** *\*stay,* wait, abide, tarry, linger

*Ant* depart

**remainder,** residue, residuum, remains, leavings, rest, balance, remnant can all mean what is left after the subtraction or removal of a part. **Remainder** is the technical term for the result in the arithmetical process of subtraction ⟨subtract 8 from 10 and the *remainder* is 2⟩ It is otherwise a comprehensive term for things that remain after the others of a collection, assemblage, or stock have been taken away, used up, or accounted for, or for any persons that remain after the others of the group have departed ⟨he spent the *remainder* of his life in seclusion⟩ ⟨it took a week to eat up the *remainder* of their Thanksgiving feast⟩ ⟨the *remainder* of the exploring party turned homeward⟩ *Residue* and *residuum* are often interchanged with *remainder,* but they usually imply whatever may be left of a former whole, often a previously intact whole, after it has been subjected to some process which depletes or diminishes it but does not annihilate it. Both terms, but especially **residue,** have acquired specific meanings; thus, a testator, after making certain bequests and providing for the payment of all his debts and charges, usually leaves the *residue* of his estate to a legatee, or to legatees, of his choice; water after evaporation often leaves a *residue* of mineral material; the *residue* of something destroyed by burning is called ash or ashes. **Residuum** is frequently used in place of *residue,* especially when evaporation or combustion is implied, and it may be preferred to *residue* when what is left after a process, whether physical or chemical or mental, is such that it cannot be ignored or left out of account or may have value as a product or significance as a result ⟨the *residuum* of the process by which sugar is extracted from cane is called molasses⟩ ⟨there is always a *residuum* of air in the lungs after the most forcible expiration possible⟩ ⟨one might say that every fine story must leave in the mind of the sensitive reader an intangible *residuum* of pleasure—*Cather*⟩ **Remains** is chiefly used of what is left after death, decay, decline, disintegration, or consumption; the term is specifically applied to a corpse, to the unpublished works of a dead author, and to the ruins of an ancient civilization ⟨they buried Keats's *remains* in the Protestant cemetery in Rome⟩ ⟨appointed executor of a friend's literary *remains*⟩ ⟨the *remains* of Pompeii⟩ ⟨the *remains* of a meal⟩ **Leavings** usually implies that the valuable or useful parts or things have been culled out and used up or taken away or that what is left has been rejected or discarded ⟨how like the *leavings* of some vast overturned scrap basket—*Brooks*⟩ **Rest** is seldom distinguishable from *remainder* (except in the latter's technical arithmetical sense), and the two are commonly used interchangeably without loss. However it may be preferred to *remainder* when it means simply the persons or things not previously referred to or mentioned (as in an enumeration or list) and carries no implication of subtraction, deduction, or depletion ⟨England, as well as the *rest* of Europe, awaited the effect of the ultimatum with anxiety⟩ ⟨only two stories in this book are interesting and the *rest* are uniformly dull⟩ **Balance** is sometimes used in the simple sense of *remainder* or *rest* ⟨answers will be given in the *balance* of this chapter—*R. W. Murray*⟩ But *balance* is more often found in technical and especially commercial use; thus, in reference to a banking account, *balance* usually is applied only to the amount left after withdrawals and other charges have been deducted from the deposits and accumulated interest; in a mercantile

charge account, *balance* is usually applied to the amount owed after credits have been deducted from the debits ⟨a *balance* in the bank is a sum of money to the depositor's credit⟩ ⟨a *balance* of a bill is an amount still owed by the debtor⟩ ⟨a *balance* in hand is an amount left when all assets are reckoned after all liabilities have been discharged⟩ **Remnant** and its plural *remnants* are applied to a remainder that is small in size or numbers or that represents only an insignificant part or piece left from a former whole ⟨the *remnant* of a once powerful army⟩ ⟨a sale of *remnants* of cloth⟩ ⟨living in Santa Fe on the *remnants* of the family fortune—*Mary Austin*⟩ ⟨sleeping bits of woodlands—*remnants* of the great forests in which Tom had worked as a boy—*Anderson*⟩

**remains** leavings, residue, *\*remainder,* residuum, rest, balance, remnant

**remark** *vb* 1 notice, note, observe, perceive, discern, *\*see,* behold, descry, espy, view, survey, contemplate 2 Remark, comment, commentate, animadvert are comparable when they mean to make observations or to pass judgment but they diverge in their implications regarding the motive and the nature of these observations and judgments. **Remark** usually implies little more than a desire to call attention to something ⟨a bore *remarks* upon everything he sees⟩ ⟨a metropolitan newspaper *remarked* that no one today hopes for progress—*Bierstedt*⟩ **Comment** stresses interpretation (as by bringing out what is not apparent or by adding details that help to clarify) ⟨the dramatic reader frequently interrupted his performance to *comment* upon a scene⟩ ⟨neither could be induced to make an oral report on his country or to *comment* during general discussions—*Boesen*⟩ Occasionally the word carries some hint of the unfavorable interpretation that is often a feature of the related noun ⟨we cannot help *commenting* on a certain meanness of culture—*T. S. Eliot*⟩ **Commentate** is sometimes used as a substitute for *comment* to suggest a purely expository or interpretative intent ⟨*commentating* upon and collating of the works of former times—*H. E. Cushman*⟩ ⟨emerged from routine *commentating* to dramatic . . . reporting and interpreting—*Life*⟩ but the verb is less frequently used than its agent noun, **commentator** ⟨radio *commentators* on the news of the day⟩ **Animadvert** (compare ANIMADVERSION) implies a remarking or commentating on something that may be based on careful judgment ⟨I went to an old-fashioned school. All those who wish to *animadvert* on education ought to be able to begin that way—*Calisher*⟩ but this basic implication is often obscured by an emphasis on passing an adverse judgment ⟨we talked of gaming, and *animadverted* on it with severity—*Boswell*⟩

**remark** *n* Remark, observation, comment, commentary, note, obiter dictum can all denote a brief expression intended to enlighten, clarify, or express an opinion. A **remark** is a more or less casual expression in speech or writing of an opinion or judgment (as of something seen in passing, something read for the first time, or something to which one's attention has been called); the term usually carries no implication of a final or considered judgment ⟨comments I have to make . . . on the man . . . . Brief *remarks,* absolutely not exhaustive—*Mailer*⟩ ⟨had a genius for remembering the most telltale gestures as well as the most self-revelatory *remarks* . . . of his master—*Krutch*⟩ **Observation** may suggest a reasoned judgment based on more or less careful scrutiny of the evidence ⟨he apparently was impressed by my *observation* that disease had made it largely impossible for Indians to smile—*Heiser*⟩ ⟨intimate letters . . . even when containing valuable critical *observations,* should not be published in the same volume as achieved works—*Wyndham Lewis*⟩

---

*Ana* analogous words   *Ant* antonyms   *Con* contrasted words       See also explanatory notes facing page 1

**Comment** applies to a remark or an observation made in criticism, in interpretation, or in elucidation of something ⟨felt . . . that her own conduct must be carefully regulated so as not to give rise to a breath of adverse *comment—Gibbons*⟩ ⟨puts in from time to time some critical *comment* that often extraordinarily clears up any subject one is talking round—*Rose Macaulay*⟩ **Commentary** may be used in place of *comment* for an annotation or gloss of a passage or text. More often, however, it is employed as a collective noun, designating a series of annotations or glosses provided for the elucidation of a text or literary work ⟨the translation is good, but . . . its usefulness could have been . . . enhanced by a *commentary—Brit. Book News*⟩ Even more often the word is used of a running sequence of oral comments (as on a sports event or the news) made on radio or television or sometimes accompanying a film projection ⟨we have the *commentary*, which takes its shape from the day's news, giving us a chronicle with pauses for explanation, interpretation, or speculation—*Milton Crane*⟩ **Note** applies chiefly to a written or printed comment or gloss on a particular point (as the historical origin of an idea, the exact meaning of a term, or the source of the writer's information) made either by the reader of an article or book on the margin of a page or by the author or editor to be printed at the bottom of the page (then called a *footnote*) or, with other comments or glosses, in an appendix ⟨the author . . . was advised . . . to subjoin some few explanatory *notes—Gray*⟩ **Note** is also applicable to a brief statement jotted down (as one of the minutes of a meeting, a memorandum of a point developed or to be developed in a speech, or of a point made by a speaker or lecturer) ⟨I've . . . jotted down a few revealing *notes* on the bride as I knew her—*Salinger*⟩ **Obiter dictum** is applied in law to an incidental opinion delivered by a judge on a matter bearing upon but not material to the case being tried, and therefore having no binding force. In general use it is usually applied to a remark or observation made more or less on the spur of the moment and not intended to be taken as a final opinion or definitive statement ⟨their tendency to wander off into *obiter dicta* on the iniquities of music publishers—*New Yorker*⟩ ⟨his *obiter dicta* were echoed from pulpits—*S. H. Adams*⟩

**remarkable** *noticeable, prominent, outstanding, conspicuous, salient, signal, striking, arresting
*Ana* *exceptional: important, significant, weighty, momentous (see corresponding nouns at IMPORTANCE): singular, unique, peculiar, *strange

**remedial** restorative, *curative, sanative, corrective
*Ana* healing, curing (see CURE *vb*)

**remedy** *n* Remedy, cure, medicine, medicament, medication, specific, physic are comparable when they mean something prescribed or used for the treatment of disease. **Remedy** applies to a substance or treatment that is known or regarded as effective in bringing about recovery or restoration of health or the normal functioning of the body ⟨patent medicines and cold *remedies*⟩ ⟨a toothache *remedy*⟩ ⟨much has been written on the subject of fear and many inspirational and emotional *remedies* have been suggested—*Reilly*⟩ ⟨psychoanalysis as a *remedy* for mental ills⟩ **Cure,** more positive than *remedy* in implying complete recovery or restoration of health, is a common term to designate anything advocated as being or thought to be conducive to complete recovery ⟨the climate was advertised during the eighties as a *cure* for tuberculosis—*Amer. Guide Series: Minn.*⟩ ⟨reaching into the medicine cabinet for a *cure* for the baby—*Reilly*⟩ ⟨all current surgical intervention in mental disease is not proposed as a *cure—Collier's Yr. Bk.*⟩ **Medicine** is the ordinary term for a substance or preparation taken in-

ternally in treating a disturbance of the normal functions of the body ⟨most *medicines* are alleviative in their action and not definitely curative—*Morrison*⟩ ⟨the witch doctor is there to give them some magic *medicine* to drink —*Frazer*⟩ **Medicament** and *medication* are general terms used especially by doctors and pharmacists for all medicinal substances and preparations whether taken internally or applied externally ⟨doctors admit that they can do more for their patients now that they do not have to worry about the size of their bills and the cost of *medicaments—New Statesman*⟩ ⟨made the rounds of her five patients with a *medicament* of her own—a quart of Grandfather's best bonded bourbon—*Maxwell*⟩ Sometimes, however, **medicament** is applied specifically to a medicinal substance or compound that is the active ingredient of a remedy ⟨different *medicaments* may be added for specific types of ulcers: sulfanilamide for streptococci, ethyl aminobenzoate for painful ulcers —*Science News Letter*⟩ and **medication,** to a compounded remedy containing one or more medicaments together with adjuvants (as flavoring agents and vehicles) ⟨ordinary cold cream or any similar *medication—Fishbein*⟩ **Specific** is applied to something, usually a drug, known to be effective in curing a specific disease ⟨various rheumatism *specifics* containing cinchophen, found to have notably injurious effects on the liver—*Encyc. Americana*⟩ **Physic** is an old-fashioned equivalent of *medicine* ⟨his first revolt against authority took the form of refusing *physic* when he was ill—*Repplier*⟩ but in modern use it has specialized to become synonymous with *purgative* or *cathartic*.

**remedy** *vb* 1 *cure, heal
2 *correct, rectify, emend, amend, redress, reform, revise
*Ana* *relieve, assuage, alleviate, lighten, mitigate: restore, *renew, refresh
*Con* *intensify, aggravate, heighten

**remember,** recollect, recall, remind, reminisce, bethink, mind all carry as their basic meaning to put an image or idea from the past into the mind. **Remember** usually implies a putting oneself in mind of something. The term carries so strong an implication of keeping in one's memory that it often implies no conscious effort or willing ⟨he *remembers* every detail of that occurrence as though it happened yesterday⟩ ⟨the average reader of the newspaper or short story reads to forget, not to *remember—Eliot*⟩ ⟨years—so many of them that no one *remembered* the exact number—*Roark Bradford*⟩ **Recollect** implies a gathering of what has been scattered; it is distinguished from *remember* in presupposing a letting go from rather than a retaining in one's memory and therefore implies a bringing back, sometimes with effort, to one's own mind what has not been in it for an appreciable period of time ⟨she tried to *recollect* some instance of goodness, some distinguished trait of integrity or benevolence, that might rescue him from the attacks of Mr. Darcy—*Austen*⟩ ⟨beasts and babies remember, that is, recognize: man alone *recollects—Coleridge*⟩ ⟨certain phrases . . . which I have often found myself *recollecting* from a distant past —*Lucas*⟩ When used reflexively, *recollect* usually implies a remembrance of something (as one's manners or intention) one has forgotten (as from eagerness, excitement, anger, or haste) ⟨Catherine, *recollecting* herself, grew ashamed of her eagerness—*Austen*⟩ ⟨he pointed a foot; *recollected* himself; took it back—*Sackville-West*⟩ **Recall** often comes close to *recollect* in implying volition or an effort to bring back what has been forgotten, but it differs from *recollect* in suggesting a summons rather than a process of thought; often, also, it connotes a telling of what is brought back ⟨let me *recall* a case within my

A colon (:) separates groups of words discriminated. An asterisk (*) indicates place of treatment of each group.

own recent experience—*Mencken*⟩ ⟨I will permit my memory to *recall* the vision of you, by all my dreams attended—*Millay*⟩ But *recall* may imply, as *recollect* does not, an agent or an agency other than oneself, and in such use suggests the awakening or evocation of a memory ⟨forty years later Mr. Wilson *recalled* this circumstance to my memory—*Repplier*⟩ ⟨that tree always awakened pleasant memories, *recalling* a garden in the south of France where he used to visit young cousins—*Cather*⟩ **Remind** implies the evocation of something forgotten, or not at the time in one's mind, by some compelling power or agent. Often also it strongly implies a jogging of one's memory. Usually the agent or agency is someone or something external that causes one to remember ⟨he *reminded* me of my promise⟩ ⟨this incident *reminded* him of another and similar one⟩ ⟨he *reminded* himself that he had made an appointment for eight o'clock⟩ ⟨he found it necessary to keep on *reminding* himself that the time was short and the work must be finished according to schedule⟩ **Reminisce** can imply the process of recollecting or of recalling something ⟨how do people remember anything? How do they *reminisce?*—*Lang*⟩ but often it suggests a nostalgic dredging up and retelling of events and circumstances of one's past life ⟨well, anyhow, we old fellows can *reminisce*—*Garland*⟩ ⟨he cut me short to *reminisce* of his schoolmates—*Hervey Allen*⟩ **Bethink,** a commonly reflexive verb little used today, can distinctively imply recollection or recalling after reflection or a reminding oneself by thinking back ⟨I have *bethought* me of another fault—*Shak.*⟩ ⟨to *bethink* themselves how little they may owe to their own merit—*Helps*⟩ **Mind** (see also TEND) in the sense of *remember* is sometimes chosen to convey a dialectal feeling of simplicity or quaintness ⟨I *mind* him coming down the street—*Tennyson*⟩ ⟨the lads you leave will *mind* you till Ludlow tower shall fall—*Housman*⟩ ⟨I can *mind* her well as a nursing mother—a comely woman in her day—*Quiller-Couch*⟩

*Ant* forget —*Con* ignore, disregard, *neglect, overlook

**remembrance** 1 *memory, recollection, reminiscence, mind, souvenir

*Ant* forgetfulness

2 **Remembrance, remembrancer, reminder, memorial, memento, token, keepsake, souvenir** denote something that serves to keep a person or thing in mind. **Remembrance** and the less common **remembrancer** are applied to an object which causes one to call back to mind someone or something, especially someone dead or far away or an event or occurrence of the past, often the distant past ⟨I desire your acceptance of a ring, a small *remembrance* of my father—*Swift*⟩ ⟨every article she possessed . . . is separately bequeathed as an affectionate *remembrance*—*Ellis*⟩ ⟨the apricot scent of the gorse, which was ever afterwards to be the *remembrancer* of their love —*Kaye-Smith*⟩ **Reminder** suggests something (as a memorandum) that keeps one from forgetting; the term need not suggest a wish to remember ⟨occasional sawmills, *reminders* of the once-active lumber industry—*Amer. Guide Series: Me.*⟩ **Memorial** suggests a wish or desire to preserve the memory of something (as a person or event) and therefore applies to a reminder (as a building, a monument, an endowment, or an observance) that is of a kind fitted to endure ⟨the Lincoln *Memorial* in Washington⟩ ⟨the *memorials* of the rule of the Pharaohs are still engraved on the rocks of Libya—*Newman*⟩ ⟨it was the white man's way to assert himself in any landscape . . . to leave some mark or *memorial* of his sojourn— *Cather*⟩ The remaining words more consistently suggest a personal association between the thing intended as a

remembrance or reminder and the person, experience, or place to be remembered. **Memento** typically applies to something small or trivial kept to satisfy a desire to renew the remembrance of some past interest; often the word suggests that the thing itself has no longer any value ⟨the drawer was filled with *mementos* of her girlhood —dance programs, love letters, a glove⟩ **Token** often refers to something treasured as a memento, but it usually denotes a gift presented to one as a sign of affection, esteem, or regret at parting ⟨a handkerchief, an antique *token* my father gave my mother—*Shak.*⟩ ⟨I leave in every house some little *token*, a rosary or a religious picture—*Cather*⟩ **Keepsake** represents the attitude of the receiver rather than of the giver; otherwise it differs little in general use from *token* and *memento* ⟨perhaps the strongest *keepsake* is a slice of her . . . wedding cake— *Green Peyton*⟩ But *keepsake* may apply specifically to a giftbook, often one made up for a particular group or occasion or as a specimen of fine printing. **Souvenir** (see also MEMORY) usually implies a material reminder not necessarily given nor received that remains or is kept as a memento (as of a place visited or of an experience worthy of remembrance) ⟨pockmarks in the masonry . . . are *souvenirs* of the bomb that exploded there—*John Brooks*⟩

*Ana* *gift, present, favor

**remembrancer** *remembrance, reminder, memorial, memento, token, keepsake, souvenir

**remind** *remember, recollect, recall, reminisce, bethink, mind

*Ana* *suggest, intimate, hint, imply

**reminder** *remembrance, remembrancer, memorial, memento, token, keepsake, souvenir

*Ana* memorandum (see LETTER): intimation, hint, suggestion (see corresponding verbs at SUGGEST)

**reminisce** *remember, recollect, recall, remind, bethink, mind

**reminiscence** *memory, remembrance, recollection, mind, souvenir

**remiss** lax, slack, neglectful, *negligent

*Ana* *careless, heedless, thoughtless: *forgetful, oblivious, unmindful: indolent, slothful, faineant, *lazy

*Ant* scrupulous

**remit** 1 pardon, forgive, *excuse, condone

*Ana* *exculpate, exonerate, acquit, vindicate, absolve

2 forward, transmit, route, ship, *send, dispatch

**remnant** *remainder, residue, residuum, remains, leavings, rest, balance

*Ana* *part, piece, fragment, segment, section: vestige, *trace

**remonstrate** expostulate, *object, protest, kick

*Ana* oppose, combat, *resist, withstand, fight: *criticize, denounce, reprobate

**remorse** *penitence, repentance, contrition, attrition, compunction

*Ana* regret, *sorrow, grief: *qualm, scruple, compunction, demur

**remote** *distant, far, faraway, far-off, removed

*Ant* close

**remove** *vb* *move, shift, transfer

*Ana* convey, *carry, bear, transport, transmit: eradicate, extirpate, uproot (see EXTERMINATE)

**removed** remote, far-off, faraway, far, *distant

**remunerate** *pay, compensate, satisfy, reimburse, indemnify, repay, recompense

*Ana* award, accord, vouchsafe, *grant

**remunerative** *paying, gainful, lucrative, profitable

*Ana* handsome, bountiful, munificent, *liberal: lavish, prodigal, *profuse

---

*Ana* analogous words    *Ant* antonyms    *Con* contrasted words    See also explanatory notes facing page 1

**rend** *vb* split, cleave, rive, rip, *tear
*Ana* *separate, divide, sever, sunder
**rendezvous** tryst, *engagement, appointment, assignation, date
**renegade,** **apostate, turncoat, recreant, backslider** are strongly derogatory terms denoting a person who forsakes his faith or party, a cause, or an allegiance, and aligns himself with another. **Renegade,** originally applied to a Christian who became a Mohammedan, came to mean one who completely denies all he has been brought up to believe by going over to the enemy or the opposition ⟨venom the *renegade* can summon up against his former beliefs and associates—*New Yorker*⟩ **Apostate** stresses the giving up, either voluntarily or under compulsion, of something (as one's religious beliefs or political or intellectual principles) one has formerly professed and the acceptance of others which are usually, by implication, of a less exalted character. *Apostate* therefore usually connotes surrender, but it need not, as *renegade* often does, imply treachery or hostility to what is forsaken ⟨that incomparable *apostate* from intelligence—*Laski*⟩ ⟨prepared to welcome back even the *apostate*, if he shows repentance and remorse—*Bienenstok*⟩ **Turncoat,** a contemptuous designation, differs from *renegade* and *apostate* chiefly in its implications that profession of faith or allegiance is regarded lightly and that convenience or profit rather than conviction motivates the change ⟨an American who went abroad and stayed, without an official excuse . . . was regarded as a *turncoat*—*Brooks*⟩ **Recreant,** like *apostate,* implies a retreat from a stand one has taken, but it stresses cowardice and meanspiritedness, and usually connotes treachery to the party or cause once supported ⟨all such *recreants* as either refused to sail with the colonists or having sailed with them should afterwards desert—*Frazer*⟩ **Backslider,** in contrast to the other terms, usually implies a previous conversion and a reversion to the old indifference or the old beliefs; thus, a convert who goes back to his earlier state morally or to his earlier religious affiliation is regarded as a *backslider* by one adherent to the position he held as a convert.
*Ana* *rebel, insurgent, iconoclast: deserter, forsaker, abandoner (see corresponding verbs at ABANDON): *heretic, schismatic
*Ant* adherent
**renew,** **restore, refresh, renovate, refurbish, rejuvenate** are comparable when they mean to give a person or thing that has become old, worn, or exhausted the qualities or appearance of what is fresh or new or young. **Renew** is so inclusive a term that it may imply a making something new to replace the old that has died, decayed, or disintegrated ⟨each spring the trees *renew* their foliage⟩ ⟨I think I will be extravagant enough to *renew* my entire wardrobe—*Shaw*⟩ or a remaking so that it seems like new of a thing which has depleted its vitality or force or has lost its freshness ⟨they that wait upon the Lord shall *renew* their strength—*Isa* 40:31⟩ ⟨to *renew* and rebuild civilization, and save the world from suicide—*T.S. Eliot*⟩ or a making a fresh start ⟨*renewed* his efforts⟩ ⟨*renewed* his offer of assistance⟩ **Restore** (see also RESTORE 2) definitely implies a return to an original state or to a prime condition typically after depletion, exhaustion, or illness ⟨*restored* his vigor⟩ ⟨*restored* his good humor⟩ ⟨a long rest *restored* him to health⟩ or after being marred, injured, or wrecked (as by passage of time, use, accident, or assault in war) ⟨Rheims Cathedral was *restored* after World War I⟩ ⟨an attempt to *restore* a picture⟩ or after the loss of a vital or essential quality or character ⟨if I quench thee, thou flaming minister, I can again thy former light *restore*, should I repent me—*Shak.*⟩ **Refresh** often

implies the supplying of something necessary to restore lost strength, animation, or power ⟨sleep *refreshes* both body and mind⟩ ⟨a cool, *refreshing* drink⟩ or to make up for what has been lost through forgetfulness or disuse ⟨he made it his business to see Dr. Lavendar, and be *refreshed* as to facts—*Deland*⟩ Equally often the term implies the imparting of freshness to something by or as if by cooling, wetting, or allaying thirst; it then usually connotes an enlivening, invigorating, or exhilarating effect ⟨the springs . . . under the earth . . . break forth to *refresh* and gladden the life of flowers and the life of man —*Binyon*⟩ ⟨it *refreshes* me to find a woman so charmingly direct—*Bromfield*⟩ **Renovate** and **refurbish** differ from the preceding terms chiefly in being referred almost exclusively to material things and as a consequence in not having the poetic connotations so often found in *renew, restore,* and *refresh.* **Renovate** is often used in place of *renew* when cleansing, repairing, or rebuilding is implied ⟨*renovate* an old colonial house⟩ ⟨drawn into a sequence of violent episodes that cause him to *renovate* his attitudes toward life and death—*Martin Levin*⟩ while **refurbish** implies the restoration of newness or freshness by or as if by scouring or polishing and suggests here little more than a freshening up of the appearance or the external aspects of a thing ⟨*refurbish* an old table by sandpapering and waxing it⟩ and therefore occasionally is used in depreciation ⟨hoped to reform national conduct . . . by reforming our vocabulary . . . . But it does seem a good bit to achieve with nothing more tangible than a *refurbished* vocabulary—*Laird*⟩ ⟨the *refurbishing* of trite thoughts is the sole accomplishment of many would-be poets⟩ **Rejuvenate** implies a restoration of youthful vigor, powers, appearance, or activities; sometimes it merely suggests a giving a youthful aspect to something old ⟨he . . . had the air of an old bachelor trying to *rejuvenate* himself—*Irving*⟩ ⟨outworn themes may be *rejuvenated* by taking on contemporary garb—*Lowes*⟩
*Ana* *mend, repair, rebuild: reform, revise, rectify, *correct
*Con* exhaust, *deplete, drain, impoverish, bankrupt
**renounce 1** *abdicate, resign
*Ana* sacrifice, abnegate, *forgo, forbear, eschew
*Ant* arrogate: covet (sense 2) —*Con* usurp, preempt, appropriate (see ARROGATE)
**2** *abjure, forswear, recant, retract
*Ana* reject, repudiate, spurn (see DECLINE *vb*): *forgo, forbear, eschew
*Ant* confess: claim
**renovate** refurbish, rejuvenate, *renew, restore, refresh
*Ana* *mend, repair, patch: *clean, cleanse
**renown** *fame, honor, glory, celebrity, reputation, repute, notoriety, éclat
*Ana* prestige, authority, *influence, weight, credit
*Con* contempt, despite, disdain, scorn (see under DESPISE): disrepute, *disgrace, dishonor, obloquy
**renowned** *famous, famed, celebrated, eminent, illustrious
*Ana* praised, acclaimed, lauded, extolled (see PRAISE): outstanding, signal, prominent (see NOTICEABLE)
**rent** *vb* *hire, let, lease, charter
**rent** *n* *breach, break, split, schism, rupture, rift
*Ana* separation, severance, division (see corresponding verbs at SEPARATE): tearing *or* tear, cleaving *or* cleavage (see corresponding verbs at TEAR): interruption, gap, hiatus (see BREAK)
**renunciation,** **abnegation, self-abnegation, self-denial** can all mean voluntary surrender or putting aside of something desired or desirable. **Renunciation** (see also under *renounce* at ABDICATE) commonly connotes personal sacrifice for a higher end (as the good of others, or moral

A colon (:) separates groups of words discriminated. An asterisk (*) indicates place of treatment of each group.

discipline, or the attainment of the highest good) ⟨she had learnt the lesson of *renunciation*, and was as familiar with the wreck of each day's wishes as with the diurnal setting of the sun—*Hardy*⟩ Historically **abnegation** is scarcely distinguishable from **self-abnegation**, although the trend is toward preference for the latter or its equivalent *abnegation of self*. Both words more often denote a quality of character than an act, and both imply a high degree of unselfishness or a capacity for putting aside all personal interests or desires ⟨individuals who are willing to abandon the pleasures of the world for lepers are rare, but, when found, usually exhibit complete *abnegation* of self—*Heiser*⟩ ⟨his *self-abnegation* prevented him from taking credit for the victory—*Fitzpatrick*⟩ **Self-denial**, unlike *abnegation*, is usually applied to an act or a practice. Though it means denial of oneself or forbearance from gratifying one's own desires, it does not necessarily connote nobility in the act, its motive, or its end and is therefore applicable to a larger range of instances than either *abnegation* or *renunciation* ⟨her still face, with the mouth closed tight from suffering and disillusion and *self-denial*—*D. H. Lawrence*⟩
*Ana* sacrificing *or* sacrifice, forgoing, forbearing, eschewing (see FORGO)

**repair** *vb* *mend, patch, rebuild
*Ana* remedy, redress, amend, emend, rectify, *correct: *renew, renovate, refurbish, restore

**reparation,** **redress, amends, restitution, indemnity** are comparable when they mean a return for something lost or suffered, usually through the fault of another. **Reparation** implies an attempt to restore things to their normal or sound condition. It is chiefly applied to recompense for material losses or damages or reimbursement for repairs ⟨war *reparations*⟩ ⟨seek *reparation* from the state for flood damages⟩, but it is applied also to atonement for an offense, especially one incurring injury to others ⟨educated . . . at royal expense as *reparation* for the death of his father—*Nixon*⟩ ⟨I am sensible of the scandal I have given by my loose writings, and make what *reparation* I am able—*Dryden*⟩ **Redress** heightens the implications of a grievance and therefore connotes compensation or satisfaction, or even, at times, retaliation or vengeance ⟨victims of the swindle sought *redress* in the courts⟩ ⟨*redress* is always to be had against oppression, by punishing the immediate agents—*Johnson*⟩ ⟨the civil law by which contracts are enforced, and *redress* given for slanders and injuries—*Shaw*⟩ ⟨particular grievances call not only for *redress,* but also for the formulation of universally valid reasons why they should be redressed—*Huxley*⟩ **Amends** is as strong as *redress* in its suggestion of due satisfaction but weaker in its implication of a grievance. It often implies a correction or restoration of a just balance ⟨if I did take the kingdom from your sons, to make *amends*, I'll give it to your daughter—*Shak.*⟩ ⟨love, freedom, comrades, surely make *amends* for all these thorns through which we walk to death—*Masefield*⟩ **Restitution** implies the restoration in kind or in value of what has been unlawfully taken ⟨a *restitution* of civil rights⟩ ⟨expressing willingness to offer *restitution* to those Jews who had been robbed . . . by the Third Reich—*Hirsch*⟩ **Indemnity** is the specific term for money given (as by an insurance company) in reparation for losses (as from fire, accident, illness, or disaster) or for payments made by a defeated country for losses caused by war ⟨an attempt to make palatable to the country what . . . amounts to imposing a war *indemnity* upon it—*Schumpeter*⟩
*Ana* expiation, atonement (see under EXPIATE): compensation, remuneration, recompensing *or* recompense (see corresponding verbs at PAY)

**repartee** *wit, humor, irony, sarcasm, satire
*Ana* retort, rejoinder, response (see under ANSWER *vb*): *badinage, persiflage, raillery

**repay** *pay, compensate, remunerate, recompense, satisfy, reimburse, indemnify
*Ana* balance, offset, *compensate: accord, award (see GRANT *vb*)

**repeal** *vb* *revoke, reverse, rescind, recall
*Ana* abrogate, *annul, void: cancel, expunge (see ERASE)

**repeat** *vb* **1** Repeat, iterate, reiterate, ingeminate can all mean to say again. **Repeat,** the word in ordinary use, may apply to what is said or uttered or done again, whether once or many or an indefinite number of times ⟨*repeat* a command⟩ ⟨the teacher *repeated* her question not once but three times⟩ ⟨wondered what would have happened if he had *repeated* his earlier tantrum—*Purdy*⟩ ⟨*repeat* an attempt to swim the river⟩ ⟨*repeat* a step in a process⟩ ⟨wish to *repeat* a pleasant experience⟩ *Repeat* sometimes implies a change in the speaker or doer ⟨please do not *repeat* what I have told you⟩ ⟨the teacher asked the children to *repeat* the verses after her⟩ ⟨falsehoods and half-truths . . . uncritically *repeated* from writer to writer—*Altick*⟩ **Iterate** usually implies one repetition after another, especially of something that is said ⟨the bird in the dusk *iterating, iterating,* his one phrase—*Aiken*⟩ There is very little difference between *iterate* and **reiterate,** except that *iterate* occasionally refers to a second saying or uttering or sometimes doing and *reiterate* carries an even more emphatic implication of manifold repetitions; consequently the two words are often used together when insistency is implied ⟨scientific research *iterates* and *reiterates* one moral . . . the greatness of little things—*Sat. Review (London)*⟩ When only one term is desired to make this point, *reiterate* is especially appropriate ⟨over and over again, in a somber, bullfrog voice, he *reiterates* his favorite theme—*Armbrister*⟩ **Ingeminate,** a somewhat uncommon term, implies reiteration for special emphasis or impressiveness. It therefore seldom implies indefinite repetition but rather duplication or triplication for the sake of the effect produced ⟨that peace-loving habit of mind . . . which made so many nations, in the years before 1939, *ingeminate* "Peace" when there was no peace—*Ernest Barker*⟩ ⟨"He was the tramp," he *ingeminated*. "He was the tramp."—*Buchan*⟩
*Ana* *return, recur, revert, recrudesce: rehearse, recite, recount, *relate
**2** *quote, cite

**repellent** *repugnant, abhorrent, distasteful, obnoxious, invidious
*Ana* *offensive, loathsome, repulsive, revolting
*Ant* attractive: pleasing —*Con* alluring, charming, captivating, bewitching (see under ATTRACT): enticing, seductive, tempting, luring (see corresponding verbs at LURE)

**repentance** *penitence, contrition, attrition, remorse, compunction
*Ana* regret, *sorrow, grief
*Con* complacency, self-complacency, self-satisfaction (see corresponding adjectives at COMPLACENT)

**repercuss** reverberate, recoil, *rebound, resile

**replace,** **displace, supplant, supersede** are rarely interchangeable terms, but they can carry the same basic meaning—to put a person or thing out of his or its place or into the place of another. **Replace** implies supplying a substitute for what has been lost, destroyed, used up, worn out, or dismissed ⟨a broken toy should not be immediately *replaced* if it has been broken by the child's carelessness—*Russell*⟩ ⟨*replace* a servant⟩ ⟨constant flow of conversation from dawn till dark . . . only to be *re-*

*placed* by a night shift of resounding snores—*Theodore Sturgeon*⟩ or it may imply a preferring of one of two or more things that could satisfy a need ⟨nor would I admit that the human actor can be *replaced* by a marionette —*T. S. Eliot*⟩ and sometimes it implies a putting back into a proper or assigned place ⟨*replace* a book on a shelf⟩ ⟨the guard soon *replaced* his blunderbuss in his arm-chest —*Dickens*⟩ **Displace** implies a dislodging, ousting, or putting or crowding out followed by a replacing. This dual implication of putting out of place and of replacing is the chief distinction of *displace* in contrast with *replace* ⟨the weight of water *displaced* by a floating body is equal to that of the *displacing* body⟩ However one of these ideas is sometimes stressed more than the other so that the emphasis is either on ousting ⟨American democracy was the response to challenge of Europeans *displaced* to a continental wilderness and cut loose from many ancient ties—*Dorothy Thompson*⟩ or on replacing ⟨as he became more conscious of the bar accounts, of the kitchen expenses, the benevolence was *displaced* by calculation—*Gorer*⟩ **Supplant** basically implies a dispossessing or ousting by craft, fraud, or treachery and a taking or usurping of the place, possessions, or privileges of the one dispossessed or ousted ⟨you three from Milan did *supplant* good Prospero—*Shak.*⟩ ⟨the pretty young wife finds herself in the humiliating position of having been *supplanted* by a brisk, unlovely woman—*Bullett*⟩ ⟨eager to succeed Louis and even to *supplant* him—*Belloc*⟩ But *supplant* sometimes implies an uprooting and replacing rather than a dispossessing and usurping; in such cases trickery or treachery is no longer implied ⟨his tutor tried to *supplant* his fears by arousing his sense of curiosity⟩ ⟨don't claim that the Divine revelation has been *supplanted* . . . but that it has been amplified—*Mackenzie*⟩ ⟨the architect, to serve the vogue, uptilts greenhouses thirty stories high on stilts, *supplanting* walls of stone with sheets of glass—*Hillyer*⟩ **Supersede** implies a causing of another to be set aside, abandoned, or rejected as inferior, no longer of use or value, or obsolete ⟨the old-fashioned fishing luggers with their varicolored sails have been *superseded* by motorboats—*Amer. Guide Series: La.*⟩ ⟨that is the worst of erudition —that the next scholar sucks the few drops of honey that you have accumulated, sets right your blunders, and you are *superseded*—*Benson*⟩
*Ana* restore, *renew: *change, alter: *recover, regain, recoup, retrieve

**replete** *full, complete, plenary
*Ana* abundant, *plentiful: sated, satiated, surfeited (see SATIATE)

**replica** facsimile, *reproduction, duplicate, copy, carbon copy, transcript

**reply** *vb* *answer, respond, rejoin, retort
*Con* *ask, question, interrogate, query, inquire, catechize, examine: *accuse, charge, impeach, indict: salute, greet, *address

**reply** *n* answer, response, rejoinder, retort (see under ANSWER *vb* 1)
*Ana* acknowledgment, recognition (see corresponding verbs at ACKNOWLEDGE)
*Con* asking, requesting *or* request, solicitation (see corresponding verbs at ASK): accusation, charging *or* charge (see corresponding verbs at ACCUSE): *argument, dispute: *greeting, salute

**report** *n* 1 Report, rumor, gossip, hearsay are comparable when they mean common talk or an instance of it that spreads rapidly. **Report** is the most general and least explicit of these terms; it need not imply an authentic basis for the common talk, but it often suggests some

ground for the belief unless specifically qualified (as by *false*, *untrue*, or *wild*) ⟨my brother Jaques he keeps at school and *report* speaks goldenly of his profit—*Shak.*⟩ ⟨denies the common *report* that he ghosted the whole document—*Bliven* b.1889⟩ ⟨spread a false *report*⟩ **Rumor** applies to a report that flies about, often gains in detail as it spreads, but lacks both an evident source and clear-cut evidence of its truth ⟨almost every newspaper issue brought *rumors* of reduction in their salaries—*Heiser*⟩ ⟨we make our blunders . . . as *rumor* has it that you make your own—*Cardozo*⟩ **Gossip** applies to idle talk, chiefly about personal affairs and behavior, that is the source of or means of propagating rumors or reports, and is sometimes used in the sense of a rumor or report ⟨neighborhood *gossip*⟩ ⟨my presence killed the *gossip* on her tongue—*Barrie*⟩ ⟨*gossip* about the party leader and his beautiful blond niece was inevitable—*Shirer*⟩ ⟨this girl's . . . intimate *gossip* about well-known people—*Wouk*⟩ **Hearsay** carries a strong implication of the means by which a report or rumor comes to one, that is, by hearing rather than by seeing or knowing directly ⟨the qualifications and doubts that distinguish critical science from *hearsay* knowledge—*Cohen*⟩ It is sometimes extended to a report or rumor based upon such hearsay ⟨the *hearsays* bandied about by the medievalists—*Behrman*⟩
*Ana* talking *or* talk, conversing *or* conversation, speaking *or* speech (see corresponding verbs at SPEAK): chatting, chattering *or* chatter, prating (see CHAT): *news, tidings, intelligence, advice
2 *account, story, chronicle, version
3 dispatch, message, note, *letter, epistle, missive, memorandum

**report** *vb* *relate, narrate, describe, state, recite, recount, rehearse
*Ana* *communicate, impart: *reveal, disclose, discover, tell, divulge

**repose** *n* *rest, relaxation, leisure, ease, comfort
*Ana* calmness, tranquillity, serenity, placidity, peacefulness (see corresponding adjectives at CALM): refreshment, restoration, renewal (see corresponding verbs at RENEW)
*Con* *work, labor, toil, grind, drudgery: *stress, strain: agitation, perturbation, discomposure (see corresponding verbs at DISCOMPOSE)

**reprehend** *criticize, censure, reprobate, condemn, denounce, blame
*Ana* *reprove, rebuke, reprimand, admonish, reproach, chide: *scold, upbraid, berate, rate

**represent,** depict, portray, delineate, picture, limn can mean to present an image or lifelike imitation of (as in art). **Represent** implies a placing before the mind as if real or as if living through the medium of one of the arts (as painting, sculpture, or literature); the term may imply either a presentation of reality or of imagined reality or a treatment of an abstraction or a spiritual being in terms of real things ⟨the painting *represents* a spring scene⟩ ⟨the Holy Ghost is *represented* as a dove in the Pentecostal window⟩ ⟨there are several classic procedures for *representing* visual images by means of music—*Virgil Thomson*⟩ ⟨paintings . . . to produce a specific aesthetic sensation rather than merely to *represent* nature—*Current Biog.*⟩ **Depict,** primarily meaning to represent in terms of painting, may stress the implication of graphic, vivid representation more than the form of art employed; it is applied to such arts as literature or drawing which suggest color and detail in some other way than by pigments ⟨painters are sometimes accused of calling upon their imagination when they are really *depicting* fact —*Jefferies*⟩ ⟨a novelist noted especially for his skill in *depicting* character⟩ ⟨drama may be achieved by action

---

A colon (:) separates groups of words discriminated. An asterisk (*) indicates place of treatment of each group.

as well as by speech. Action can tell a story . . . and *depict* every kind of human emotion, without the aid of a word—*Justice Holmes*⟩ **Portray** suggests the making of a detailed representation of individual persons, or of specific characters, emotions, or qualities (as by drawing, engraving, painting, acting, or describing) ⟨in literature are *portrayed* all human passions, desires, and aspirations —*Eliot*⟩ ⟨a star who unquestionably conveyed to audiences the very essence of the character he was *portraying* —*J. F. Wharton*⟩ **Delineate** (see also SKETCH) basically implies representation by an art (as engraving or drawing) that uses lines to gain its effects, but, like *portray*, it is often used to stress care for accuracy of detail and fullness of outline ⟨his brush did its work with a steady and sure stroke that indicated command of his materials. He could *delineate* whatever he elected with technical skill— *Jefferies*⟩ **Picture** less than any of these terms implies the employment of a particular art; it emphasizes the ability to realize a thing in a pictorial or vivid way and may either imply graphic description ⟨those villages Mark Twain . . . has *pictured* for us—*Brooks*⟩ or sensible representation in any form ⟨her emotions are all *pictured* in her face⟩ or, sometimes with "to oneself," mere imaginative power ⟨the girl was in his mind a lot . . . he had always had a good imagination. He *pictured* her as she came down the stairs in the morning—*Malamud*⟩ ⟨they tried, in their sympathetic grief, to *picture* to themselves all that she had been through in her life—*Bennett*⟩ **Limn** is used chiefly as an equivalent of *depict* or *delineate*, often implying the art of painting vividly and with color ⟨since not every ancestral likeness had been *limned* by the brush of a maestro, dignity . . . sometimes seemed merely bovine —*Warren*⟩ ⟨had too much taste to bare all these grubby secret details, but she *limned* a general picture for him —*Stafford*⟩
**Ana** exhibit, display, *show: *suggest, hint: *sketch, outline, draft, delineate: describe, narrate, *relate
**representative** *n* *delegate, deputy
**repress** *suppress
**Ana** *restrain, curb, check, inhibit: subdue, overcome (see CONQUER)
**reprimand** *vb* *reprove, rebuke, reproach, admonish, chide
**Ana** upbraid, rate, berate, *scold: censure, denounce, blame, reprehend, reprobate, *criticize
**reprinting** *edition, impression, printing, reissue
**reprisal** *retaliation, retribution, revenge, vengeance
**reproach** *vb* chide, admonish, *reprove, rebuke, reprimand
**Ana** *criticize, reprehend, censure, reprobate: *warn, forewarn, caution: counsel, advise (see under ADVICE)
**reprobate** *vb* censure, reprehend, *criticize, blame, condemn, denounce
**Ana** *decry, derogate, detract, depreciate, disparage: reject, repudiate, spurn (see DECLINE *vb*): reprimand, rebuke, *reprove
**reprobate** *adj* *abandoned, profligate, dissolute
**Ana** *vicious, iniquitous, corrupt, degenerate: *blameworthy, guilty, culpable
**Ant** elect (*in theology*) —**Con** righteous, virtuous, *moral, ethical
**reprobate** *n* *outcast, castaway, derelict, pariah, untouchable
**Ana** sinner, offender (see corresponding nouns at OFFENSE): transgressor, trespasser (see corresponding nouns at BREACH): *villain, scoundrel, blackguard
**reproduce** propagate, *generate, engender, breed, beget, get, sire, procreate
**Ana** produce, *bear, yield: multiply (see INCREASE)

**reproduction,** duplicate, copy, carbon copy, facsimile, replica, transcript are comparable when they mean one thing which closely or essentially resembles something that has already been made, produced, or written. **Reproduction** may imply identity in material or substance, in size, and in quality, or it may imply differences, provided that the imitation gives a fairly true likeness of the original; thus, a *reproduction* of an Elizabethan theater may be on a very small scale; a *reproduction* of a Sheraton chair may be in cherry rather than in the mahogany of the original ⟨the present director, on tour in Western Canada, discovered the need for *reproductions* of Canadian pictures—*Report on Nat'l Development (Ottawa)*⟩ ⟨the late works look finer in *reproduction* than they do in the original—*Kitson*⟩ A **duplicate** is a double of something else; the word may be used of something that exactly corresponds to or is the counterpart of any object whatsoever ⟨a *duplicate* of a bill of sale⟩ ⟨this postage stamp is a *duplicate* of one in my collection⟩ ⟨make out a receipt in *duplicate*⟩ ⟨plans a movie of the salvage operations, and will sail a *duplicate* vessel on the course taken— *Current Biog.*⟩ A **copy** is a reproduction of something else, often without the exact correspondence which belongs to a duplicate; however *copy*, rather than *duplicate* (which logically implies that there is but a single reproduction), is applicable to any one of a number of things printed from the same type format, struck off from the same die, or made in the same mold ⟨a thousand *copies* of a magazine⟩ ⟨production costs of popular records vary, of course, but a sales figure of sixty thousand *copies* is the . . . break-even point—*Robert Rice*⟩ ⟨modern *copies* of sixteenth-century chess sets—*New Yorker*⟩ ⟨mimeographed *copies* of a letter⟩ **Carbon copy** stresses the idea of exactness found in *duplicate* ⟨the full moon rising like an immense red *carbon copy* of the earth seen from a distance—*Peggy Bennett*⟩ ⟨the civilians . . . seem well-content to let our foreign policy be a *carbon copy* of the strategy worked out by the military—*Atlantic*⟩ A **facsimile** is a close but usually not exact reproduction; the term may imply differences (as in scale) but it implies as close an imitating in details and material as possible or feasible ⟨the heavy chandeliers were loaded with flattened brass balls, magnified *facsimiles* of which crowned the uprights of the . . . massively-framed chairs —*Shaw*⟩ ⟨a screen cast . . . presses hard for emotional impact. What results is less a *facsimile* than a parody of the original—*Hatch*⟩ ⟨looking for an intellectual equal, or at least the *facsimile* of an intellectual equal—*Mailer*⟩ **Replica** applies specifically to an exact reproduction of a statue, a painting, or a building made by or under the direction of the same artist, architect, or artisan; thus, one does not speak accurately of a modern *replica* of the Winged Victory, but of a modern *reproduction;* one may speak of the confusing tendency of some Renaissance artists to make *replicas* of their paintings. However the word is often used merely to emphasize very close likeness ⟨collection of miniature sports cars. Tiny, Swiss-made *replicas*, they were precision machined and finely detailed, all scaled to perfection—*Terry Southern*⟩ **Transcript** applies only to a written, typed, or printed copy made directly from an original or from shorthand notes ⟨a stenographer's *transcript* of a letter⟩ ⟨ask for a *transcript* of a will⟩
**reprove,** rebuke, reprimand, admonish, reproach, chide can all mean to criticize adversely, especially in order to warn of or to correct a fault. To **reprove** is to blame or censure, often kindly or without harshness and usually in the hope of correcting the fault ⟨his voice sounded so bright and cheerful . . . that she could not find it in her

heart to *reprove* him—*Rölvaag*⟩ **Rebuke** implies sharp or stern reproof ⟨he could not evade the persistent conviction that she was the Church speaking, *rebuking* him —*Hervey*⟩ **Reprimand** suggests reproof that is formal, and often public or official ⟨a word . . . which the Duke of Wellington, or Admiral Stopford, would use in *reprimanding* an officer—*Macaulay*⟩ **Admonish** stresses the implication of warning or counsel ⟨count him not as an enemy, but *admonish* him as a brother—*2 Thess* 3:15⟩ ⟨a highly sensitive dog, and cannot bear reproof. Perhaps this is because he is not *admonished* sufficiently at home —*Littell*⟩ **Reproach** and *chide* imply dissatisfaction or displeasure; **reproach** usually connotes criticism or faultfinding; **chide** implies mild reproof or a slight scolding ⟨if he came home late, and she *reproached* him, he frowned and turned on her in an overbearing way—*D. H. Lawrence*⟩ ⟨it is not fitting for men of dignity to threaten and *reproach* because women have had a falling out—*Shirley Jackson*⟩ ⟨the gentle irony with which he *chides* the overzealousness of modern critics—*Joseph Frank*⟩ *Ana* *criticize, reprehend, censure, reprobate: chasten, correct, discipline, *punish

**repudiate** 1 spurn, reject, refuse, *decline
*Ana* renounce, *abjure: *forgo, forbear, eschew, sacrifice
*Ant* adopt —*Con* *acknowledge, own, admit, avow, confess: embrace, espouse (see ADOPT)
2 *disclaim, disavow, disown, disallow
*Ana* *abandon, desert, forsake: *discard, cast
*Ant* own —*Con* *acknowledge, admit, avow, confess: *grant, concede, allow

**repugnant** 1 Repugnant, repellent, abhorrent, distasteful, obnoxious, invidious are comparable when they mean so alien or unlikable as to arouse antagonism and aversion. **Repugnant** is applied to something so incompatible with one's ideas, principles, or tastes as to stir up resistance and loathing ⟨soon the pressures of male eyes, eyes expressing sex . . . became *repugnant* to her—*Peggy Bennett*⟩ ⟨the nonlegal methods of the magistrates in dispensing judgment, so *repugnant* to the spirit of the common law—*Parrington*⟩ **Repellent** usually implies a forbidding or unlovely character in something that causes one to back away from it ⟨the mediocre was *repellent* to them; cant and sentiment made them sick—*Rose Macaulay*⟩ ⟨what he does say is that hanging is barbarous and sickening, that electrocution and the gas chamber are no less brutal and *repellent*—*Rovere*⟩ **Abhorrent** (see also HATEFUL) is applied to something that is incapable of association or existence with something else, and it often implies profound antagonism ⟨dictatorial methods *abhorrent* to American ways of thinking—*Forum*⟩ **Distasteful** is applied to something that one instinctively shrinks from not because it in itself is necessarily unlikable but because it is contrary to one's particular taste or inclination ⟨even the partition of the world into the animate and the inanimate is *distasteful* to science, which dislikes any lines that cannot be crossed—*Inge*⟩ ⟨she finds it *distasteful* to think of using the personal belongings of . . . previous occupants—*Kenneth Roberts*⟩ **Obnoxious** is applied to what is so highly objectionable, usually on personal grounds, that one cannot endure the sight or presence of it or him with equanimity ⟨the nation had sulked itself into a state of tacit rebellion against the *obnoxious* Volstead Law—*S. H. Adams*⟩ ⟨an opportunity to . . . make himself generally *obnoxious*—*Simeon Ford*⟩ **Invidious** is applied to something that cannot be used (as a word) or made (as a distinction) or undertaken (as a task or project) without arousing or creating ill will, envy, or resentment ⟨the *invidious* word usury—*Hume*⟩ ⟨what I would urge, therefore, is that no *invidious* distinction

should be made between the Old Learning and the New —*J. R. Lowell*⟩ ⟨undertake the *invidious* task of deciding what is to be approved and what is to be condemned— *Daniel Jones*⟩
*Ana* foreign, alien, extraneous, *extrinsic: uncongenial, incompatible, incongruous, *inconsonant: *antipathetic, averse, unsympathetic
*Ant* congenial
2 repulsive, revolting, *offensive, loathsome
*Ana* odious, *hateful, abominable, detestable: foul, nasty (see DIRTY): vile, *base, low

**repulsive** repugnant, revolting, *offensive, loathsome
*Ana* repellent, *repugnant, abhorrent, obnoxious
*Ant* alluring, captivating

**reputation** repute, *fame, renown, honor, glory, celebrity, éclat, notoriety
*Ana* credit, weight, *influence, authority, prestige

**repute** *n* reputation, *fame, renown, celebrity, notoriety, éclat, honor, glory
*Ant* disrepute

**reputed** *supposed, supposititious, suppositious, putative, purported, conjectural, hypothetical
*Ana* assumed, presumed (see PRESUPPOSE)

**request** *vb* *ask, solicit
*Ana* *beg, entreat, beseech, implore, supplicate, importune: appeal, petition, sue, pray (see under PRAYER)

**require** 1 exact, claim, *demand
*Ana* *prescribe, assign, define: warrant, *justify
2 *lack, want, need

**requirement, requisite, prerequisite** can all mean something that is regarded as necessary to the success or perfection of a thing. Although **requirement**, the more general term, may be employed in place of *requisite*, it is the customary term when the idea to be conveyed is of something more or less arbitrarily demanded or expected, especially by those who lay down conditions (as for admission to college, for enlistment in the army or navy, for membership in a church, or for entrance into a course) ⟨college entrance *requirements*⟩ ⟨a list of *requirements* for all campers⟩ ⟨action was instituted . . . to compel the school board to revoke the oath *requirement* —*Clinton*⟩ **Requisite** is the customary term when the stress is on the idea of something that is indispensable to the end in view, or is necessitated by a thing's nature or essence or is otherwise essential and not arbitrarily demanded ⟨the first *requisite* of literary or artistic activity, is that it shall be interesting—*T. S. Eliot*⟩ ⟨the *requisites* of our present social economy are capital and labor⟩ ⟨intellectual freedom . . . is the prime *requisite* for a free people—*Science*⟩ **Prerequisite** differs from *requisite* only in a stress on the time when something becomes indispensable; it applies specifically to things which must be known, or accomplished, or acquired as preliminaries (as to the study of a subject, the doing of a kind of work, or the attainment of an end) ⟨answered the questions put to him by the Senators as a *prerequisite* to his confirmation—*Current Biog.*⟩ ⟨he possesses the *prerequisite* of an original poet—a percipience unifying, exact and exhilarating—*Day Lewis*⟩

**requisite** *adj* *needful, necessary, indispensable, essential
*Ana* compelled *or* compulsory, constrained, obliged *or* obligatory (see corresponding verbs at FORCE): fundamental, *essential, cardinal, vital

**requisite** *n* *requirement, prerequisite

**requite** *reciprocate, retaliate, return
*Ana* repay, recompense, compensate (see PAY): *satisfy, content: revenge (see AVENGE)

**rescind** *revoke, reverse, repeal, recall
*Ana* cancel, expunge, *erase: abrogate, *annul, void

A colon (:) separates groups of words discriminated. An asterisk (*) indicates place of treatment of each group.

**rescue** *vb* **Rescue, deliver, redeem, ransom, reclaim, save** are comparable when they mean to free a person or thing from confinement, danger of death or destruction, or a serious evil. One **rescues** a person who is in imminent danger (as of death, of capture, or of assault) by prompt or vigorous action ⟨we are beset with thieves; *rescue* thy mistress—*Shak.*⟩ ⟨*rescue* the crew of a sinking ship⟩ ⟨*rescue* the perishing, care for the dying, snatch them in pity from sin and the grave—*Crosby*⟩ Less often one *rescues* a thing that is in danger of destruction, or that has been forcibly seized, by freeing it from danger or from its captors ⟨diamonds that I *rescued* from the tarn—*Tennyson*⟩ ⟨a main object of his teaching to *rescue* the idea of justice from identification with the special interest of the strong—*Dickinson*⟩ One **delivers** a person by setting him free from something (as prison, confinement, suffering, temptation, or embarrassment) ⟨lead us not into temptation, but *deliver* us from evil—*Mt* 6:13⟩ ⟨to *deliver* mankind from the paralyzing grip of determinism—*Inge*⟩ ⟨the population of Russia had only just been *delivered*, nominally at least, from serfdom—*Ellis*⟩ One **redeems** a person from bondage, from captivity, or from suffering the consequences of his sin or crime, or a thing from pawn or from neglect, deterioration, or decay by making some commensurate expenditure (as of money, of effort, or of time) ⟨let me *redeem* my brothers both from death—*Shak.*⟩ ⟨a plot of land *redeemed* from the heath, and after long and laborious years brought into cultivation—*Hardy*⟩ ⟨labored for eighty years, *redeeming* them to Christianity—*Norman Douglas*⟩ One **ransoms** a person who has been captured, enslaved, or kidnapped by paying the amount that is demanded by his captor or owner ⟨he was back in Quebec with a number of Iroquois captives whom he had *ransomed*—*Wynne*⟩ *Ransom* is often employed in place of *redeem* in religious use, especially in reference to Christ as the Redeemer, when the emphasis is on the price he paid in accepting crucifixion ⟨his brethren, *ransomed* with his own dear life—*Milton*⟩ One **reclaims** what has become debased, wild, savage, waste, or desert by bringing it back to its former state of usefulness. Specifically one *reclaims* a person who has wandered from rectitude or has become a sinner, a reprobate, or a degenerate when one reforms him or restores him to moral, decent ways of life ⟨I fear he is not to be *reclaimed;* there is scarcely a hope that anything in his character or fortunes is reparable now—*Dickens*⟩ or one *reclaims* a thing that has been abandoned or neglected when one works with it so that it becomes productive or finds a new use or is made to give up what is still usable in it ⟨*reclaim* long-abandoned farms⟩ ⟨filled in valleys, diverted creeks and *reclaimed* swamps—*G. R. Gilbert*⟩ ⟨*reclaim* discarded wool⟩ One **saves** (see also SAVE 2) a person when one rescues, delivers, redeems, ransoms, or reclaims him and enables him not only to be free from the evil that involves or threatens but to continue in existence, to enjoy security or happiness, or to be of future use or service ⟨his life was *saved* by an operation⟩ ⟨the lifeguard *saved* him from drowning⟩ ⟨the book he had written himself, the *Navigator,* had *saved* countless lives—*Brooks*⟩
*Ana* *free, release, liberate, emancipate, manumit: preserve, conserve (see SAVE): *extricate, disentangle, disembarrass

**research** investigation, *inquiry, inquisition, inquest, probe

**resemblance** *likeness, similarity, similitude, analogy, affinity
*Ana* correspondence, agreement, harmonizing *or* harmony, conformity (see corresponding verbs at AGREE): *comparison, parallel

*Ant* difference: distinction

**resentment** *offense, umbrage, pique, dudgeon, huff
*Ana* rancor, animus, animosity, antipathy, antagonism (see ENMITY): ill will, spite, *malice, malignity, malignancy

**reservation** *condition, stipulation, terms, provision, proviso, strings
*Ana* limitation, restriction, circumscription (see corresponding verbs at LIMIT): exception (see corresponding adjective at EXCEPTIONAL)

**reserve** *vb* *keep, keep back, keep out, hold, hold back, retain, withhold, detain
*Ana* *save, preserve, conserve: appropriate, preempt, confiscate, *arrogate

**reserved** *silent, reticent, uncommunicative, taciturn, secretive, close, close-lipped, closemouthed, tight-lipped
*Ana* aloof, detached, uninterested, disinterested (see INDIFFERENT): *shy, diffident, modest, bashful: formal, ceremonious, conventional (see CEREMONIAL)
*Ant* affable: expansive: blatant

**reside, live, dwell, sojourn, lodge, stay, put up, stop** can all mean to abide in a particular place as one's habitation or domicile. *Reside* and *live* express this idea, often without further implications. Usually, however, when the term is intended to suggest the fixed, settled, or legal abode of a person or group such as a family, **reside** is the more appropriate word; when the idea to be emphasized is the spending of one's time in a given place and the carrying on of the normal activities of one's way of life, **live** is more explicit ⟨the senator *resides* in San Francisco but he *lives* for the better part of the year in Washington⟩ When the reference is not to persons but to things, *reside* is the term to be used when the thing referred to is a quality, an element, or a condition ⟨the power of decision *resides* in the electorate⟩ ⟨his peculiar merit as a critic ... *resided* in the combination of this personal gusto and curiosity—*T. S. Eliot*⟩ ⟨when we have in our minds the idea of art as imitation, we are prone to think of beauty as *residing* in particular objects, particular colors—*Binyon*⟩ When the thing is something concrete and the idea of making one's abode or home is suggested, *live* may be used ⟨they say that sherry ought to *live* for a while in an old brandy-cask, so as to contract a certain convincing quality from the cask's genial timbers—*Montague*⟩ **Dwell** is a close synonym of these words ⟨more people than he could count (and yet, he thought, less than had *dwelled* in his own town)—*Forester*⟩ but it is more frequently found in elevated language ⟨she *dwelt* among the untrodden ways beside the springs of Dove—*Wordsworth*⟩ In extended use *dwell* carries a stronger implication of abiding (as in thought or in spirit) ⟨the bad poet *dwells* partly in a world of objects and partly in a world of words, and he never can get them to fit—*T. S. Eliot*⟩ ⟨these men had *dwelt* so long in that weariness they called success—*R. H. Newman*⟩ **Sojourn** differs from the preceding terms in usually implying a temporary habitation or abode or a more or less uncertain place or way of living ⟨for what purpose, it may be asked, was the world created, and immortal spirits sent to *sojourn* in it—*Inge*⟩ **Lodge** (see also HARBOR) also implies an abode for a time or for the time being; it typically also implies having restricted accommodations (as in a hotel or rooming house) often without meals ⟨he *lodges* at the Y.M.C.A. when he is in town⟩ ⟨a convenience to me as well as to him if he would *lodge* on the cot in the spare room—*Davis*⟩ **Stay** is the term commonly used in language in place of *sojourn* and often of *lodge* ⟨he is *staying* at Miami Beach for the winter⟩ ⟨whenever he was in Paris he *stayed* at that hotel⟩ **Put up** is also a common equivalent for *lodge*

and usually suggests the status of a guest either in a hotel or in a private home ⟨two seasons ago I *put up* at a farmhouse—*T. H. White*⟩ ⟨where does he *put up* when he is in Chicago?⟩ **Stop**, which is often used in the sense of *stay* ⟨he is *stopping* at the largest hotel in the city⟩ often specifically implies the breaking of a trip or journey by a short stay ⟨where shall we *stop* for the night?⟩
*Ana* remain, abide (see STAY): *continue, endure

**residence** *habitation, dwelling, abode, domicile, home, house

**resident** *n* *inhabitant, denizen, citizen

**residue** residuum, remains, leavings, *remainder, rest, balance, remnant

**residuum** residue, *remainder, remains, leavings, rest, balance, remnant

**resign** 1 yield, surrender, leave, abandon, *relinquish, cede, waive
*Ana* *forgo, eschew, sacrifice, forbear, abnegate: *abjure, renounce, forswear
2 *abdicate, renounce

**resignation** 1 compliance, acquiescence (see under COM-PLIANT)
*Ana* submitting *or* submission, yielding, deferring *or* deference (see corresponding verbs at YIELD): meekness, modesty, humbleness *or* humility, lowliness (see corresponding adjectives at HUMBLE)
2 *patience, long-suffering, longanimity, forbearance
*Ana* endurance, toleration, suffering *or* sufferance (see corresponding verbs at BEAR): *fortitude, backbone, pluck

**resigned** *compliant, acquiescent
*Ana* submissive, subdued (see TAME): reconciled, adjusted, adapted, accommodated, conformed (see ADAPT)
*Ant* rebellious

**resile** recoil, *rebound, reverberate, repercuss

**resilient** 1 *elastic, springy, flexible, supple
*Ana* recoiling, resiling, rebounding (see REBOUND): recovering, regaining, retrieving (see RECOVER)
*Con* rigid, *stiff, inflexible, tense
2 *elastic, expansive, buoyant, volatile, effervescent
*Ana* responsive, sympathetic (see TENDER): *spirited, high-spirited, mettlesome
*Ant* flaccid

**resist, withstand, contest, oppose, fight, combat, conflict, antagonize** are comparable when they mean to set one person or thing against another in a hostile or competing way, and they may be roughly distinguished according to the degree to which one of the things or forces takes the initiative against the other. *Resist* and *withstand* suggest generally that the initiative lies wholly with the person or force competed against. **Resist** implies an overt recognition of a hostile or threatening force and a positive effort to counteract it, repel it, or ward it off ⟨the very region which had *resisted* and finally destroyed the Roman Empire—*Malone*⟩ ⟨it is hard to *resist* the thought that metaphor is one of the most important heuristic devices —*R. M. Weaver*⟩ ⟨*resist* the pressure of political orthodoxy⟩ **Withstand** may suggest a more passive yet often successful resistance in which if nothing is gained, at least nothing is lost ⟨most plants cannot *withstand* frost⟩ ⟨built to *withstand* work and worry—*Yoder*⟩ ⟨having *withstood* the pressure of her parents—*Rose Macaulay*⟩ *Contest* and *oppose* suggest a more positive action against a threatening or objectionable force. **Contest** often stresses the raising of the issue or the bringing into open question of the matter over which there is conflict ⟨the board's power to inspect private welfare agencies was later *contested* and restricted—*Amer. Guide Series: N. Y.*⟩ ⟨it is impossible to *contest* your principle—*Meredith*⟩

⟨attempt to reconcile *contesting* parties⟩ **Oppose**, perhaps the most general of the terms, can indicate almost any degree of protesting attitude from mild objection to positive belligerence, and can suggest any action from a mere contrastive setting of one thing against another to open violence against an opposing force, although in all instances positive action is implied ⟨the chronic objector, who *opposes* every popular measure—*Crothers*⟩ ⟨he had been much *opposed* by women, crossed, balked, wronged, misled—*Hackett*⟩ ⟨the only man in public life who dared *oppose* wholesale executions of the Sioux captives—*Amer. Guide Series: Minn.*⟩ ⟨human art, as *opposed* to mere tools and mechanical contrivances—*Clodd*⟩ *Fight* and *combat* suggest strong action. **Fight** puts the initiative clearly in the hands of the subject of the verb and stresses the forthrightness or belligerence of the action ⟨my father was a servant of the people who *fought* Boston's biggest and crookedest politician fiercely—*Cummings*⟩ ⟨the steel companies . . . *fought* the strike with every weapon at their disposal—*Amer. Guide Series: Ind.*⟩ ⟨had to open his mouth wide and *fight* for breath—*Caldwell*⟩ **Combat** more often suggests a resisting than an initiating and stresses the force or impact or urgency of the resulting action, though it says nothing about the success of the resistance ⟨*combat* aggression⟩ ⟨Jefferson believed . . . that error of opinion may be tolerated so long as truth is free to *combat* it—*Davis*⟩ ⟨attempts to *combat* discriminatory practices were . . . evident—*Collier's Yr. Bk.*⟩ ⟨Russell *combats* the philosophers who denied the possibility of a three-dimensional non-Euclidean space— *Kline*⟩ *Conflict* and *antagonize* do not fit easily into the scale. **Conflict** indicates merely the fact of competition, friction, or hostility between two forces ⟨two logical principles often *conflict*⟩ ⟨there was the smell of tar and ropes and sawdust to *conflict* with that of unsalt water faintly tinged with decaying vegetation—*Archibald Marshall*⟩ ⟨where his feeling *conflicted* with the facts, his vision flickered—*Lippmann*⟩ ⟨if the *conflicting*, indigenous elements in Korea and in Viet Nam were left to fight it out among themselves, which would prevail . . .?— *Toynbee*⟩ **Antagonize** has lost in general use the idea of placing oneself in opposition or in the position of an antagonist, a sense which persists in technical usage ⟨a new synthetic steroid . . . that *antagonized* the renal excretory effects of aldosterone—*Science*⟩ In current general use the term carries only the idea of arousing antagonism or making antagonistic ⟨it was inexpedient to *antagonize* these people—*Cather*⟩ ⟨they resented his extreme militancy . . . he even *antagonized* a few of his fellow workers—*Warner*⟩
*Ana* assail, *attack, assault: impugn, gainsay, contravene (see DENY): thwart, baffle, balk, foil, *frustrate
*Ant* submit: abide

**resolute** steadfast, staunch, *faithful, true, loyal
*Ana* determined, decided, resolved (see DECIDE): intrepid, valiant, *brave, courageous: stubborn, *obstinate, pertinacious

**resolution** 1 analysis, dissection, breakdown (see under ANALYZE)
*Ana* separation, division (see corresponding verbs at SEPARATE): elucidation, interpretation, expounding *or* exposition, explaining *or* explanation (see corresponding verbs at EXPLAIN)
2 mettle, spirit, tenacity, *courage
*Ana* pluck, grit, *fortitude, backbone, guts

**resolve** 1 *analyze, dissect, break down
*Ana* *separate, part, divide: reduce, diminish (see DECREASE): melt, fuse (see LIQUEFY)
*Ant* blend

A colon (:) separates groups of words discriminated. An asterisk (*) indicates place of treatment of each group.

2 determine, *decide, settle, rule

*Ana* purpose, propose, design, *intend, mean: plan, scheme, project (see under PLAN *n*)

3 *solve, unfold, unravel, decipher

*Ana* dispel, dissipate, disperse (see SCATTER): clear, *rid, purge, disabuse

**resonant,** sonorous, ringing, resounding, vibrant, orotund are applied to the sounds or tones of speech and music and mean conspicuously full and rich. **Resonant** implies intensification or enrichment of tone by sympathetic vibration (as by the soundboard and body of a violin or by columns of air above and below the vocal cords in the larynx). It applies especially to musical tones ⟨the tones produced by this piano are very *resonant*⟩ ⟨heard the beating of the small drums—a hollow, *resonant* sound—*Nordhoff & Hall*⟩ but in more general use it is applicable to a sound (as of speech or a bird note) that seems more than naturally full and rich ⟨his deep *resonant* voice that makes even a line from a financial statement have the ringing, rhythmic tones of a Yeats quotation—*Saarinen*⟩ **Sonorous** implies a quality of tone or speech suggesting the reverberant sound elicited by striking some metals (as copper or brass) or some kinds of glass; it may apply to a voice that is high and clear or, more often, to one that is deep and rich, but loudness and fullness are usually clearly implied ⟨a herald chosen for his *sonorous* voice—*Frazer*⟩ ⟨the deep, *sonorous* voice of the red-bearded Duke, which boomed out like a dinner gong—*Doyle*⟩ As applied to language or utterance as distinct from voice *sonorous* may suggest depth and richness ⟨its earnestness and patience, and its utter lack of synthetic drama, give many of its pages the *sonorous* sureness of pure philosophy—*Marquand*⟩ but is more likely to suggest an obscuring or the absence of real meaning by lush verbiage or florid presentation ⟨detains thought within pompous and *sonorous* generalities wherein controversy is as inevitable as it is incapable of solution—*Dewey*⟩ ⟨adept at distilling from the *sonorous* official speeches the three or four words that contain the meaning the speechmakers sought to conceal—*New Yorker*⟩ **Ringing** usually implies a sound made by or as if by a bell; the word suggests a vigorous, stirring quality ⟨her beautiful, *ringing,* honest voice, the expression of her whole personality—*Ellis*⟩ ⟨a perfect ecstasy of song—clear, *ringing,* copious—*Burroughs*⟩ **Resounding** applies not only to vocal or instrumental sounds but to any sound that seems to reecho or to awaken echoes. It usually implies the increase of sound by something that throws it back ⟨the sound of a great underground river, flowing through a *resounding* cavern—*Cather*⟩ but it may imply a loudness and fullness of sound that seem to call forth echoes ⟨put into circulation many *resounding* phrases which rang from the hustings—*Krock*⟩ ⟨closed the door behind him with a *resounding* bang—*Brennan*⟩ **Vibrant,** when used of sounds or tones, suggests vibration but not necessarily resonance; rather it implies qualities of life, vigor, or strong feeling ⟨the speaker paused a moment, his low *vibrant* tones faltering into silence—*Zangwill*⟩ ⟨it concentrates in one *vibrant* poem the despairs and the hopes of millennia—*Edmund Wilson*⟩ **Orotund** usually describes an acquired or an affected quality of speech. It implies fullness, roundness, and dignity of utterance which may be regarded either objectively or contemptuously ⟨it is rather the exquisite craftsmanship of France than the surging and *orotund* utterances of *Leaves of Grass* that has given to free verse . . . its most distinctive qualities—*Lowes*⟩ ⟨the voice was like no voice ever heard before—*orotund,* massive, absolute, like the sound of thunder—*Styron*⟩

*Ana* *full, replete: *rich, opulent: intensified, enhanced, heightened (see INTENSIFY)

**resort** *n* *resource, expedient, shift, makeshift, stopgap, substitute, surrogate

*Ana* see those at RESOURCE 2

**resort** *vb* **Resort,** refer, apply, go, turn are comparable when they mean to betake oneself or to have recourse when in need of help or relief. **Resort** often implies that one has encountered difficulties or has tried ineffectually to surmount them; when it carries the latter implication, it often also connotes an approach to desperation ⟨he found he could not get relief, unless he *resorted* to the courts⟩ ⟨most powers conceivably may be exercised beyond the limits allowed by the law . . . . But we do not on that account *resort* to the blunt expedient of taking away the power—*Justice Holmes*⟩ **Refer** usually suggests a need of authentic information and recourse to someone or something that will supply such information ⟨every time he comes across a new word he *refers* to the dictionary⟩ ⟨most men *refer* to their own watches when someone reports the time⟩ **Apply** suggests having direct recourse (as in person or by letter) to one having the power to grant a request or petition ⟨*apply* to a hospital for aid⟩ ⟨*apply* to the court for relief⟩ ⟨determined, that if he persisted in considering her repeated refusals as flattering encouragement, to *apply* to her father, whose negative might be uttered in such a manner as must be decisive—*Austen*⟩ **Go** and **turn** are more general but often more picturesque or dramatic terms than the words previously considered, for they directly suggest action or movement ⟨the president decided to *go* to the people with his plan for reorganization⟩ ⟨there was no one to whom she could *go* for sympathy⟩ ⟨she had taken fright at our behavior and *turned* to the captain pitifully—*Conrad*⟩

*Ana* *direct, address, devote: *use, employ, utilize

**resounding** *resonant, sonorous, ringing, vibrant, orotund

*Ana* *loud, stentorian, earsplitting: intensified, heightened (see INTENSIFY)

**resource** 1 in plural form **resources** assets, belongings, effects, *possessions, means

2 **Resource,** resort, expedient, shift, makeshift, stopgap, substitute, surrogate can all denote something to which one turns for help or assistance in difficulty or need when the usual means, instrument, or source of supply fails one, is not at hand, or is unknown to one. **Resource** applies to an action, activity, person, method, device, or contrivance upon which one falls back when in need of support, assistance, or diversion ⟨he has exhausted every *resource* he can think of⟩ ⟨I must e'en hasten to matters of fact, which is the comfortable *resource* of dull people—*Shenstone*⟩ ⟨I am doomed to be the victim of eternal disappointments; and I have no *resource* but a pistol—*Peacock*⟩ ⟨with all the *resources* of her slovenliness, she was cunningly protecting herself against him by inducing him to believe she was a slut—*Callaghan*⟩ **Resort** is less often used than *resource* except when qualified by *last* or in the phrase "to have *resort* to" ⟨have *resort* to a fortune-teller⟩ ⟨thus the income tax became a . . . last *resort*—*Shaw*⟩ ⟨for many plankters transparency of body is a chief *resort* for concealment—*Coker*⟩ ⟨courts are the ultimate *resorts* for vindicating the Bill of Rights—*Frankfurter*⟩ **Expedient** applies to a means, device, or contrivance which serves in place of what is usual or ordinary, or sometimes as a means, a device, or a contrivance to accomplish a difficult end easily or without waste of time ⟨everything is brought about . . . through the medium of the author's reflections, which is the clumsiest of all *expedients*—*Scott*⟩ ⟨is not this a desperate *expedient,* a last refuge likely to appeal only to the leaders of a lost cause?—*Krutch*⟩ A **shift** is commonly a ten-

tative or temporary and often imperfect expedient; the term when applied to plans or stratagems typically implies evasiveness or trickery ⟨the dear delicious *shifts* I used to be put to, to gain half a minute's conversation with this fellow!—*Sheridan*⟩ ⟨not amused by her *shifts* and her shameful deceit—*Tinker*⟩ **Makeshift** is even more derogatory than *shift* for it implies substitution of the inferior for the superior and often it imputes carelessness, indifference, or laziness to the one who chooses or makes use of it ⟨his ingenuity had been sharpened by all the recent necessity to employ *makeshifts*—*Forester*⟩ ⟨three or four rooms . . . have been kept nearly habitable by *makeshifts* of patchings—*Pierce*⟩ **Stopgap** applies to a person or thing that momentarily or temporarily supplies an urgent need or fills a gap, hole, or vacancy ⟨both vigilantes and mass meeting were looked upon as temporary *stopgaps*, to be disbanded as soon as governmental machinery was provided—*Billington*⟩ **Substitute** (see also SUBSTITUTE 2) does not carry as strong a suggestion of an emergency or exigency as the preceding terms do; the word is applicable to something one chooses, accepts, or prefers, whether rightly or wrongly, rationally or irrationally , in place of the usual or original thing, or which has been invented or devised to take its place or to do its work ⟨a *substitute* for milk . . . could be manufactured from the soya bean—*Heiser*⟩ ⟨daydreams, in adult life, are recognized as more or less pathological, and as a *substitute* for efforts in the sphere of reality—*Russell*⟩ ⟨this mock king who held office for eight days every year was a *substitute* for the king himself—*Frazer*⟩ **Surrogate** is a somewhat learned word for a substitute ⟨slang is . . . a facile *surrogate* for thought—*Lowes*⟩ It is frequently applied to people whether as literal replacements or as replacement figures in psychological or sociological analyses ⟨college presidents or their *surrogates* appealed for a revival of idealism—*Adler*⟩ ⟨to primitive men the cranes were . . . the *surrogates* of the resurgent sun-god —*E. A. Armstrong*⟩ ⟨the relationship to the mother *surrogate* retains the qualities . . . of the little boy's attachment to his mother—*Scientific American*⟩
*Ana* \*device, contrivance, contraption: invention, creation (see corresponding verbs at INVENT): \*method, manner, way, fashion, mode, system

**respect** *n* \*regard, esteem, admiration
*Ana* \*reverence, awe, fear: \*honor, homage, deference: veneration, reverence, worship, adoration (see under REVERE)
*Ant* contempt

**respect** *vb* regard, esteem, admire (see under REGARD *n*)
*Ana* reverence, \*revere, venerate: value, prize, cherish, \*appreciate
*Ant* abuse: misuse

**respecting** concerning, regarding, \*about

**respectively** \*each, apiece, severally, individually

**respite** \*pause, recess, lull, intermission
*Ana* leisure, ease, \*rest: interruption, interval, \*break

**resplendent** \*splendid, gorgeous, glorious, sublime, superb
*Ana* effulgent, refulgent, radiant, brilliant, \*bright: blazing, glowing, flaming (see BLAZE *vb*)

**respond** \*answer, reply, rejoin, retort
*Ana* react, behave, \*act
*Con* stimulate, excite, quicken (see PROVOKE)

**response** answer, reply, rejoinder, retort (see under ANSWER *vb* 1)

**responsible, answerable, accountable, amenable, liable** can all mean subject to an authority which may exact redress in case of default. *Responsible, answerable,* and *accountable* are very close, all meaning capable of being called upon to answer or to make amends to someone for

something. Although often used interchangeably they are capable of distinction based on their typical applications. One is **responsible** for the performance of a task or duty, or the fulfillment of an obligation, or the execution of a trust, or the administration of an office to the person or body that imposes the task, duty, or trust or delegates the power ⟨the governor is *responsible* to the electorate for the administration of the laws⟩ Sometimes the *to* phrase or the *for* phrase is suppressed but still implied ⟨the salesmen are *responsible* to the manager and the manager is *responsible* to the owner⟩ ⟨a teacher is *responsible* for the conduct of pupils in the classroom⟩ ⟨the ideally free individual is *responsible* only to himself—*Henry Adams*⟩ ⟨while held *responsible* for the bank's operations, the president has powers considered largely nominal—*Current Biog.*⟩ Sometimes when both phrases are suppressed, *responsible* implies manifest ability to fulfill one's obligations especially by reason of developed powers of judgment and sense of moral obligation ⟨his record shows that he is a *responsible* person⟩ One is **answerable** to someone for something who, because of a moral or legal obligation or because of the acceptance of such an obligation for another, may be called upon to pay the penalty for a violation of the law or a neglect of duty; the term usually indicates or implies the existence of a judge or tribunal ⟨men in business, who are *answerable* with their fortunes for the consequences of their opinions—*Hazlitt*⟩ ⟨there was something ineradicably corrupt inside her for which her father was not *answerable*—*E. K. Brown*⟩ ⟨the minister who is *answerable* to Parliament for the affairs of the BBC—*Beachcroft*⟩ One is **accountable** to someone for something who because of something entrusted to him is bound to be called upon to render an account of how that trust has been executed. *Accountable* is much more positive than *responsible* or *answerable* in its suggestion of retributive justice in case of default ⟨if the physicist discovers new sources of energy that may be readily released for destructive purposes, he should not be held *accountable* for their use—*Gauss*⟩ ⟨the Russian leaders . . . are not *accountable* to their people—*The Reporter*⟩ *Amenable* and *liable* especially stress subjection and suggest the contingency rather than the probability or certainty of being called to account. One is **amenable**, usually to something, whose acts are subject to the control or the censure of a higher authority and who, therefore, is not self-governing or absolute in power ⟨is it to be contended that the heads of departments are not *amenable* to the laws of their country?—*John Marshall*⟩ ⟨scholar and teacher alike ranked as clerks . . . *amenable* only to the rule of the bishop—*J. R. Green*⟩ One is **liable** that by the terms of the law may be made answerable in case of default ⟨a surety is *liable* for the debts of his principal⟩ ⟨the present United States . . . took nothing by succession from the Confederation . . . was not *liable* for any of its obligations—*Taney*⟩ *Liable* does not, however, always imply answerability. It may imply mere contingent obligation ⟨every citizen is *liable* for jury duty⟩ ⟨he is only 39, and *liable* for military service under the new act—*Shaw*⟩
*Ana* subject, open, exposed (see LIABLE): \*reliable, dependable, trustworthy

**responsive** 1 \*sentient, sensitive, impressible, impressionable, susceptible
*Ana* answering, responding, replying (see ANSWER *vb*): reacting, acting, behaving (see ACT *vb*)
*Ant* impassive
2 sympathetic, warm, warmhearted, compassionate, \*tender
*Ana* gentle, mild, lenient (see SOFT): sensible, conscious,

---

A colon (:) separates groups of words discriminated. An asterisk (*) indicates place of treatment of each group.

alive, awake, *aware: sensitive, susceptible, prone (see LIABLE)

**rest** *n* Rest, repose, relaxation, leisure, ease, comfort are comparable when they mean freedom from toil or strain. Rest, the most general term, implies withdrawal from all labor or exertion and suggests an opposition to the term *work;* it does not in itself explicitly imply a particular way of spending one's time, but it does suggest as an aim or as a result the overcoming of physical or mental weariness 〈there the wicked cease from troubling; and there the weary be at *rest—Job* 3:17〉 〈night came, and with it but little *rest—Hardy*〉 〈there was *rest* now, not disquietude, in the knowledge—*Glasgow*〉 Repose implies freedom from motion or movement and suggests not only physical quiet (as in sleeping or slumbering) but also mental quiet and freedom from anything that disturbs, annoys, agitates, or confuses. Typically the term suggests tranquillity or peace or the refreshment that comes from complete quiet or rest 〈heavily passed the night. Sleep, or *repose* that deserved the name of sleep, was out of the question—*Austen*〉 〈eighteen years of commotion had made the majority of the people ready to buy *repose* at any price—*Macaulay*〉 〈walls . . . that shut out the world and gave *repose* to the spirit—*Cather*〉 Relaxation may imply rest that comes from diversion or recreation but it usually stresses either a releasing of the tension that keeps muscles taut and fit for work or the mind keyed up to the processes of clear and prolonged thinking, or a physical and mental slackening that finally induces repose 〈those who wish *relaxation* from analysis . . . the tired scientist, and the fagged philologist and the weary man of business—*Babbitt*〉 〈now and then came *relaxation* and lassitude, but never release. The war towered over him like a vigilant teacher—*H. G. Wells*〉 〈found *relaxation* in her unobtrusive company—*Shirer*〉 Leisure implies exemption from the labor imposed upon one by a trade or profession or by duties; it may apply to the hours in which one is not engaged in one's daily work, or to the period in which one is on vacation, or to the entire time of a person who is not compelled to earn his living 〈have little *leisure* for reading〉 〈he looked forward to the prospect of a full month of *leisure*〉 〈those who lead lives of *leisure*〉 Leisure, therefore, stresses freedom from compulsion, or routine, or continuous work; it usually suggests not freedom from activity but the freedom to determine one's activities 〈labor is doing what we must; *leisure* is doing what we like; rest is doing nothing whilst our bodies and minds are recovering from their fatigue—*Shaw*〉 Ease (see also READINESS) stresses exemption from toil, but it also implies a freedom from whatever worries or disturbs and from what demands physical or mental activity. In contrast to *leisure* it implies rest and repose; in addition it suggests either complete relaxation of mind and body or a state of mind that finds no attraction in work or activity 〈all day I sit in idleness, while to and fro about me thy serene, grave servants go; and I am weary of my lonely *ease—Millay*〉 But *ease* may also imply absence of strain, especially mental or nervous strain, rather than freedom from toil 〈not only devoted, but resourceful and intelligent, one who would be at his *ease* with all sorts of men—*Cather*〉 Comfort differs from the other words of this group in carrying little if any suggestion of freedom from toil; it applies rather to a state of mind induced by relief from all that strains or inconveniences or causes pain, disquiet, or discontent. Positively it suggests perfect wellbeing and a feeling of quiet enjoyment or content 〈he had bought for himself out of all the wealth streaming through his fingers neither adulation nor love, neither splendor nor *comfort—Conrad*〉 〈this sudden calm and

the sense of *comfort* that it brought created a more genial atmosphere over the whole ship—*Dahl*〉 〈spent every dollar he earned on the *comfort* of his family—*Wouk*〉 *Ana* intermitting *or* intermission, suspending *or* suspension, deferring (see corresponding verbs at DEFER): stillness, quietness *or* quiet, silentness *or* silence (see corresponding adjectives at STILL): calmness *or* calm, tranquillity, serenity (see corresponding adjectives at CALM)

**rest** *vb* *base, found, ground, bottom, stay
*Ana* *depend, hang, hinge: *rely, depend, count

**rest** *n* *remainder, residue, residuum, remains, leavings, balance, remnant
*Ana* *excess, superfluity, surplus, surplusage, overplus

**restful** *comfortable, cozy, snug, easy
*Ana* *soft, gentle, mild, lenient: *still, quiet, silent: placid, peaceful, *calm, serene, tranquil

**restitution** amends, redress, *reparation, indemnity
*Ana* repayment, recompense, reimbursement (see corresponding verbs at PAY)

**restive** 1 *contrary, perverse, balky, froward, wayward
*Ana* intractable, *unruly, ungovernable, refractory: *obstinate, stubborn, mulish, stiff-necked, pigheaded
2 restless, *impatient, nervous, unquiet, uneasy, fidgety, jumpy, jittery
*Ana* see those at RESTLESS

**restless** restive, *impatient, nervous, unquiet, uneasy, fidgety, jumpy, jittery
*Ana* *fitful, spasmodic: *inconstant, capricious, unstable, fickle: agitated, disquieted, perturbed, discomposed (see DISCOMPOSE)

**restorative** *adj* *curative, remedial, corrective, sanative
*Ana* stimulating, quickening (see PROVOKE)

**restore** 1 *renew, refresh, rejuvenate, renovate, refurbish
*Ana* save, reclaim, redeem, *rescue: reform, revise, amend (see CORRECT *vb*): *recover, regain, retrieve, recoup, recruit
2 Restore, revive, revivify, resuscitate can all mean to regain or cause to regain signs of life and vigor. Restore (see also RENEW) implies a return to consciousness, to health, or to vigor often through the use of remedies or of treatments 〈it took many months to *restore* him to health〉 〈gave her aromatic spirits of ammonia to *restore* her to consciousness〉 Revive, when used in reference to a person, implies recovery from a deathlike state (as stupor or a faint or shock); it carries a stronger suggestion of apparent death in the victim and a less positive suggestion of restored health and vigor than does *restore* 〈slowly *revived* from the effects of shock〉 〈revived her by throwing water on her face〉 But the term is often applied to spirits or to feelings that are depressed, to plants that seem withering, to states, arts, industries, or fashions that are not flourishing and implies a return to a prior state (as of animation, freshness, or activity) 〈the flowers have been *revived* by the shower〉 〈ambitious hopes which had seemed to be extinguished, had *revived* in his bosom—*Macaulay*〉 Revivify differs from *revive* in suggesting an adding of new life and in not carrying so strong a suggestion of prior loss or depletion of vital power; hence, it is applicable to normal persons or to their powers 〈a good night's sleep *revivifies* every healthy person〉 〈cessation in his lovemaking had *revivified* her love—*Hardy*〉 The term is also applicable to something that tends to become exhausted of interest through long usage or familiarity and then suggests a freshening or a vitalizing from a new source 〈being a true poet, he was able . . . to *revivify* them [old, much-used words] as poetic agents—*Day Lewis*〉 〈tradition is dead; our task is to *revivify* life that has passed away—*Buchan*〉 Resuscitate implies commonly a restora-

---

*Ana* analogous words　　　*Ant* antonyms　　　*Con* contrasted words　　　See also explanatory notes facing page 1

tion to consciousness, but in comparison with *revive* it usually also implies a condition that is serious and that requires arduous efforts to correct or relieve ⟨uncertain of success in *resuscitating* the boy they had taken from the water⟩ Especially in extended use it can suggest a bringing again to a quick or vital state of someone or something in which life appears to be extinct ⟨*resuscitate* an old interest⟩ ⟨it was Delia's turn to be silent. The past was too overwhelmingly *resuscitated* in Charlotte's words —*Wharton*⟩

*Ana* *cure, heal, remedy: arouse, rouse, rally, *stir

**restrain, curb, check, bridle, inhibit** are comparable when they mean to hold a person or thing back from doing something or from going too far in doing something. **Restrain,** the most comprehensive of these terms, may imply the intent either to prevent entirely or to keep under control or within bounds, but it usually suggests the operation of some force, authority, or motive that is sufficiently strong or compelling as to achieve the desired end ⟨to produce in the child the same respect for the garden that *restrains* the grown-ups from picking wantonly—*Russell*⟩ ⟨her voice is not usually one of her assets . . . the whines, the snarls and the sneers of a poor childhood are *restrained* with difficulty—*Mailer*⟩ **Curb** can imply either a sharp, drastic method of bringing under control ⟨attempts to *curb* lynching by legislation—*F. W. Coker*⟩ or a guiding or controlling influence that tends to restrain or moderate something or to restrict a person's freedom of action ⟨the sober scientific method does not stimulate the imagination; it *curbs* it—*Crothers*⟩ ⟨it was necessary to set up devices for *curbing* the swindles of the speculators—*Edmund Wilson*⟩ ⟨the feudal nobility was *curbed* here—*Coulton*⟩ **Check** (see also ARREST 1) often implies the use of a method suggestive of a checkrein which holds up a horse's head and prevents him from getting the bit between his teeth ⟨Father Latour *checked* his impetuous vicar—*Cather*⟩ but it may carry implications derived from other senses of the noun such as those of delaying or impeding motion or progress ⟨the ship, hauled up so close as to *check* her way—*Conrad*⟩ ⟨a spot where her footsteps were no longer *checked* by a hedgerow—*George Eliot*⟩ or of attacking or defeating some force or influence ⟨the ambition of churchmen . . . disciplined and *checked* by the broader interests of the Church—*Henry Adams*⟩ ⟨*check* for a time the inward sweeping waves of melancholy—*Bromfield*⟩ **Bridle** (see also STRUT) carries a strong implication of bringing or keeping under one's control (as by subduing, moderating, or holding in); it is used chiefly in respect to strong or vehement emotions or desires ⟨*bridle* his wrath⟩ ⟨potential violence of feeling is *bridled* by good form— *N. Y. Herald Tribune Book Rev.*⟩ ⟨strong in censuring and *bridling* the wicked—*H. O. Taylor*⟩ ⟨*bridled* his curiosity⟩ ⟨he could no longer *bridle* his passion⟩ **Inhibit** (see also FORBID) is a synonym of these terms in a predominantly psychological sense in which it implies the repression or suppression of certain emotions, desires, or thoughts by a curbing influence (as one's conscience or religious principles or the social conventions of one's class) ⟨a people long *inhibited* by the prevailing taboos— *Ellery*⟩

*Ana* *arrest, check, interrupt: abstain, *refrain, forbear: *hinder, impede, obstruct, block

*Ant* impel: incite: activate: abandon (*oneself*)

**restraint** constraint, compulsion, *force, coercion, duress, violence

*Ana* curbing, checking, inhibiting (see RESTRAIN): hindering, impeding, obstructing, blocking (see HINDER)

*Ant* incitement: liberty

**restrict** *limit, circumscribe, confine

*Ana* bind, *tie: *contract, shrink: *restrain, curb, check

*Con* *extend, lengthen: *expand, amplify, swell: enlarge, *increase

**result** consequence, *effect, upshot, aftereffect, aftermath, sequel, issue, outcome, event

*Ana* concluding *or* conclusion, ending *or* end, closing *or* close, termination (see corresponding verbs at CLOSE): *product, production

*Con* *origin, source, root: *cause, determinant, antecedent

**resuscitate** *vb* *restore, revive, revivify

*Ana* reanimate (see base word at QUICKEN): rekindle (see base word at LIGHT *vb*)

**retain** *keep, keep back, keep out, detain, withhold, reserve, hold, hold back

*Ana* *have, hold, own, possess, enjoy: *save, preserve, conserve

*Con* *discard, shed, cast: *relinquish, surrender, abandon, yield: *abdicate, resign: *abjure, renounce, forswear, recant, retract

**retaliate** *reciprocate, requite, return

*Ana* revenge, *avenge: repay, recompense, compensate (see PAY)

**retaliation, reprisal, revenge, vengeance, retribution** can all mean both the act of inflicting or the intent to inflict injury in return for injury, and the injury so inflicted. **Retaliation** implies a return of like for like, commonly a return of evil for evil ⟨so astonished by a blow as to lose the opportunity for *retaliation*⟩ ⟨he is never satisfied until he inflicts a *retaliation* for every injury, real or fancied⟩ ⟨sanguinary *retaliation* on the part of a rejected office-seeker—*Swanberg*⟩ ⟨could catch us flat-footed, could destroy our air fleet and its bases, and . . . there would then be no *retaliation* at all—*Vannevar Bush*⟩ **Reprisal** applies specifically to an act of retaliation indulged in for the sake of gaining redress of a grievance or of compelling an enemy or antagonist to cease unlawful acts. The term in legal use usually implies the seizure of property by force either as a means of getting compensation for one's own injuries or of inflicting punishment; when used in reference to nations, it need not imply an act of war ⟨declared an embargo in *reprisal* for the seizing of ships⟩ ⟨*reprisals* are illegal if they are not preceded by a request to remedy the alleged wrong—*Cases & Materials on International Law*⟩ ⟨American correspondents, too, sometimes work in danger of personal *reprisals* other than expulsion—*Mott*⟩ **Revenge** usually carries a strong implication of vindictiveness or sometimes of justifiable anger that is lacking in *retaliation;* the term more often applies to the desire or intent to inflict injury or to the gratification of that desire than to the actual infliction of injury ⟨he had his *revenge*⟩ ⟨'tis sweet to love; but when with scorn we meet, *revenge* supplies the loss with joys as great— *Granville*⟩ ⟨she went through agonies of jealousy and remorse, and fantasies of *revenge,* which amazed her with their violence—*Wouk*⟩ **Vengeance** may imply the avenging of a wrong done to oneself or another by measures that punish the offender so that he suffers in the same degree as his victim, but the term is also applicable to an act committed in gratification of one's revenge ⟨*vengeance* is mine; I will repay, saith the Lord. Therefore if thine enemy hunger, feed him; if he thirst, give him drink— *Rom* 12:19-20⟩ ⟨there was a time in my imprisonment, when my desire for *vengeance* was unbearable—*Dickens*⟩ ⟨the burning of a rick is an act of *vengeance,* and a plowman out of employ is a vengeful animal—*Meredith*⟩ **Retribution** also applies chiefly to a punishment inflicted in return for a wrong done. Distinctively it stresses the operation of strict justice, and is especially appropriate

---

A colon (:) separates groups of words discriminated. An asterisk (*) indicates place of treatment of each group.

when merited punishment is administered, not by the victim, but by a higher power or impersonal chance ⟨his coat pockets . . . a mess of broken eggs, studded with coins and miscellaneous objects. This mishap was *retribution* for robbing nests—*C. L. Barrett*⟩ ⟨to be left alone and face to face with my own crime, had been just *retribution*—*Longfellow*⟩
*Ana* punishment, disciplining *or* discipline, correcting *or* correction (see corresponding verbs at PUNISH): recompensing *or* recompense, indemnification, repayment (see corresponding verbs at PAY)

**retard** *delay, slow, slacken, detain
*Ana* reduce, lessen, *decrease: *arrest, check, interrupt: clog, fetter, *hamper: balk, baffle (see FRUSTRATE)
*Ant* accelerate: advance, further

**reticent** *silent, reserved, uncommunicative, taciturn, secretive, close, close-lipped, closemouthed, tight-lipped
*Ana* restrained, inhibited, curbed, checked (see RESTRAIN): discreet, prudent (see under PRUDENCE)
*Ant* frank —*Con* candid, open, plain (see FRANK)

**retire** withdraw, *go, leave, depart, quit
*Ana* *recede, retreat: recoil, *rebound, resile: *relinquish, yield, surrender, abandon

**retort** *vb* rejoin, reply, *answer, respond

**retort** *n* rejoinder, answer, reply, response (see under ANSWER *vb* 1)
*Ana* *retaliation, reprisal, revenge: repartee (see WIT)

**retract** 1 retrograde, back, *recede, retreat
*Ant* protract
2 recant, *abjure, renounce, forswear
*Ana* eliminate, *exclude, suspend, rule out

**retreat** *n* *shelter, cover, refuge, asylum, sanctuary
*Ana* *harbor, haven, port: safety, security (see corresponding adjectives at SAFE): seclusion, *solitude

**retreat** *vb* *recede, retrograde, back, retract
*Ana* withdraw, retire, depart, *go: *recoil, shrink, quail

**retrench** curtail, abridge, *shorten, abbreviate
*Ana* *decrease, lessen, reduce, diminish

**retribution** reprisal, vengeance, revenge, *retaliation
*Ana* *reparation, redress, amends, restitution: visitation, tribulation, *trial, affliction
*Con* *mercy, clemency, lenity, grace: forgiveness, pardoning *or* pardon, remitting *or* remission (see corresponding verbs at EXCUSE)

**retrieve** *recover, regain, recoup, recruit
*Ana* amend, remedy, redress, reform (see CORRECT *vb*): repair, *mend, rebuild
*Ant* lose

**retrograde** *adj* *backward, retrogressive, regressive
*Ana* reversed, inverted (see REVERSE *vb*): relapsing, lapsing, backsliding (see LAPSE *vb*)

**retrograde** *vb* *recede, retreat, back, retract
*Ana* *return, revert: *reverse, invert: relapse, *lapse, backslide

**retrogressive** regressive, retrograde, *backward
*Ana* reversing, inverting (see REVERSE *vb*): receding, retreating, retrograding (see RECEDE)
*Ant* progressive —*Con* advancing, furthering, forwarding (see ADVANCE *vb*): improving, bettering (see IMPROVE)

**return** *vb* 1 Return, revert, recur, recrudesce are comparable when they mean to go or come back (as to a person or to a place or condition). The same distinctions in implications and connotations are evident in their corresponding nouns return, reversion, recurrence, recrudescence. Return is the ordinary term of this group; it usually implies either a going back to a starting place or a source ⟨they *returned* as wolves *return* to cover, satisfied with the slaughter that they had done—*Kipling*⟩ ⟨the sickness of a child caused their sudden *return*⟩ or it may imply, especially

in the case of the noun, a coming back to a former or proper place or condition ⟨now shall the kingdom *return* to the house of David—*1 Kings* 12:26⟩ ⟨look forward to the *return* of spring⟩ ⟨he was greeted with enthusiasm on his *return* home⟩ ⟨he *returns* here tomorrow⟩ ⟨sorry to hear you had a *return* of your rheumatism—*Whitman*⟩ Revert and reversion (see also REVERSION 2) most frequently imply a going back to a previous, often a lower, state or condition ⟨the conception of a lordly splendid destiny for the human race, to which we are false when we *revert* to wars and other atavistic follies—*Russell*⟩ ⟨in the last hours of his life he *reverted* to the young man he had been in the gutter days in Vienna—*Shirer*⟩ ⟨the *reversion* to barbarism in political trials and punishments —*Cobban*⟩ Both terms, however, are often used when a return after an interruption is implied (as to a previous owner, to a previous topic, or to a previous decision) ⟨when the lease expires, the property *reverts* to the lessor⟩ ⟨thought that he would not pass between these two, then he decided that he would hurry up and do so, then he *reverted* to his former decision—*H. G. Wells*⟩ ⟨on *reversion* to private trading in aluminium in this country —*Financial Times*⟩ Recur and recurrence imply a return, or sometimes repeated returns at more or less regular intervals, of something that has previously happened, that has previously affected a person or thing, that has previously been in one's mind, or that has been previously known or experienced ⟨the idea kept *recurring*, and growing stronger each time it came back—*Cloete*⟩ ⟨they came back to her as a dream *recurs*—*Bennett*⟩ ⟨a melancholy tempered by *recurrences* of faith and resignation and simple joy—*Joyce*⟩ ⟨incessant *recurrence* without variety breeds tedium; the overiterated becomes the monotonous—*Lowes*⟩ Recrudesce and the more frequent recrudescence imply a return to life or activity; usually the terms imply a breaking out again of something that has been repressed, suppressed, or kept under control ⟨the general influence . . . which is liable every now and then to *recrudesce* in his absence—*Gurney*⟩ ⟨the *recrudescence* of an epidemic of influenza⟩
*Ana* *advert, revert: *turn, rotate, revolve: restore, *renew: *recover, regain: reverberate, repercuss, *rebound
2 *reciprocate, retaliate, requite
*Ana* repay, recompense, compensate (see PAY): *give, bestow

**return** *n* reversion, recurrence, recrudescence (see under RETURN *vb*)

**reveal,** discover, disclose, divulge, tell, betray can all mean to make known what has been or should be concealed or is intended to be kept concealed. Reveal implies a setting forth or exhibition by or as if by lifting a curtain that veils or obscures. It can apply to supernatural or inspired revelation of truths beyond or above the range of ordinary human sight or reason ⟨sacred laws . . . unto him *revealed* in vision—*Spenser*⟩ ⟨in laws divine, deduced by reason, or to faith *revealed*—*Wordsworth*⟩ ⟨the artist, the man of genius, raises this veil and *reveals* Nature to us—*Ellis*⟩ ⟨he must feel as a man what he *reveals* as a poet—*Day Lewis*⟩ or to simple disclosure (as of information or a secret) ⟨a foreboding crept into him that if he said nothing now, he would someday soon have a dirtier past to *reveal*—*Malamud*⟩ or it may carry no suggestions of an intentional communication but imply rather an affording of signs or other evidence from which the truth may be inferred ⟨the paradox of both distrusting and burdening government *reveals* the lack of a conscious philosophy of politics—*Frankfurter*⟩ ⟨England, where the speech of a self-made man and of a . . . university

---

*Ana* analogous words     *Ant* antonyms     *Con* contrasted words     See also explanatory notes facing page 1

graduate will almost always *reveal* the differences in their formal education—*Joseph*⟩ **Discover** (see also DIS-COVER 2, INVENT) implies an exposing to view by or as if by uncovering; the term usually suggests that the thing discovered has been hidden from sight or perception but is not, as often in the case of *reveal*, in itself beyond the range of human vision or comprehension ⟨go draw aside the curtains and *discover* the several caskets to this noble prince—*Shak.*⟩ ⟨it is a test which we may apply to all figure-painters—a test which will often *discover* the secret of unsatisfactory design—*Binyon*⟩ **Disclose** is more often used in this sense than *discover* ⟨a black dress which *disclosed* all she decently could of her shoulders and bosom—*Wouk*⟩ ⟨the stress of passion often *discloses* an aspect of the personality completely ignored till then by its closest intimates—*Conrad*⟩ More often *disclose* implies the making known of something that has not been announced or has previously been kept secret ⟨the court refused to *disclose* its decision before the proper time⟩ ⟨the confessions of St. Austin and Rousseau *disclose* the secrets of the human heart—*Gibbon*⟩ ⟨the Bishop did not *disclose* his objective, and the Vicar asked no questions—*Cather*⟩ **Divulge** differs little from *disclose* in this latter sense except in often carrying a suggestion of impropriety or of a breach of confidence ⟨his voice became secretive and confidential, the voice of a man *divulging* fabulous professional secrets—*Dahl*⟩ ⟨he knew of the conspiracy and did not *divulge* it—*Belloc*⟩ or in implying a more public disclosure ⟨it seemed to me an occasion to *divulge* my real ideas and hopes for the Commonwealth—*L. P. Smith*⟩ **Tell** (see also COUNT 1) may come very close to *divulge* in the sense of making known something which should be kept a secret ⟨gentlemen never *tell*⟩ but more often it implies the giving of necessary or helpful information, especially on request or demand ⟨*tell* me the news⟩ ⟨why didst thou not *tell* me that she was thy wife?—*Gen* 12:18⟩ ⟨she never *told* her love—*Shak.*⟩ **Betray** (see also DECEIVE) often implies a divulging of a secret, but it carries either a stronger and more obvious suggestion of a breach of faith ⟨had . . . written no letters that would *betray* the conspiracy he had entered into—*Anderson*⟩ or of a disclosure (as through signs or appearances) against one's will ⟨life moves on, through whatever deserts, and one must compose oneself to meet it, never *betraying* one's soul—*Rose Macaulay*⟩ ⟨the stamp of desire on his face had *betrayed* him once and he did not want to be *betrayed* by disappointment or anger—*Cheever*⟩
*Ana* impart, *communicate: *suggest, adumbrate, shadow: *declare, announce, publish
*Ant* conceal

**revelation,** vision, apocalypse, prophecy are comparable when they mean disclosure or something disclosed by or as if by divine or preternatural means. **Revelation** is often specifically applied to the religious ideas transmitted by writers of books regarded as sacred or divinely inspired, especially the Bible; by extension it has come to mean a body of knowledge distinguishable from that attained by the ordinary human processes of observation, experiment, and reason ⟨'tis *revelation* satisfies all doubts, explains all mysteries, except her own—*Cowper*⟩ ⟨*revelation* differs from natural knowledge, he says, not by being more divine or more certain than natural knowledge, but by being conveyed in a different way—*Arnold*⟩ **Vision** implies, as *revelation* does not, a seeing of something not corporeally present; often, especially in mystical and poetic language, it suggests a profound intuition of something not comprehensible to the ordinary or unaided reason and often implies the operation of some agent

(as the Holy Spirit) or the gift or accession of some inexplicable power (as genius or poetic rapture) not attributable to all men. *Vision,* however, unlike *revelation,* does not necessarily imply that what is seen or realized is true or of value to oneself or others ⟨and some had *visions,* as they stood on chairs, and sang of Jacob, and the golden stairs—*Lindsay*⟩ ⟨the ecstasy of imaginative *vision,* the sudden insight into the nature of things, are also experiences not confined to the religious—*Edmund Wilson*⟩ ⟨an age in which men still saw *visions* . . . seeing *visions* . . . was once a more significant, interesting, and disciplined kind of dreaming—*T. S. Eliot*⟩ **Apocalypse** in religious use denotes a type of sacred book (of which the Book of Revelation is an example) which presents a vision of the future in which the enemies of Israel or of Christianity are defeated and God's justice and righteousness prevail. In its general application *apocalypse* usually denotes a vision of the future, when all the mysteries of life shall be explained and good shall magnificently triumph over evil. The noun and still more its adjective **apocalyptic** often carry one or more connotations as various as those of a spectacular splendor or magnitude suggestive of the Book of Revelation or of wild and extravagant dreams of the visionary or passionate reformer ⟨the *apocalyptic* imagination of Michelangelo—*N. Y. Times*⟩ ⟨this allegedly universal religion is challenged today by another secular religion with an alternative *apocalypse* of history—*Niebuhr*⟩ ⟨the writers of political *apocalypse* and other forms of science fiction . . . have dealt in absolutes—*Davis*⟩ **Prophecy** has become rare in its original meaning except in learned use and in some religious use. Its occasional connotation of the prediction of future events has been emphasized to such an extent that its historical implications have almost been lost, with the result that the word in older writings is often misinterpreted. *Prophecy* in this narrow sense implies a commission to speak for another, especially and commonly for God or a god. It therefore further implies that the prophet has been the recipient of divine communications or revelations or that he has been granted a vision or visions ⟨though I have the gift of *prophecy,* and understand all mysteries, and all knowledge . . . and have not charity, I am nothing—*1 Cor* 13:2⟩ ⟨*prophecy* is not prediction, it is not a forecasting of events. Rather, it is the vision which apprehends things present in the light of their eternal issues—*Seaver*⟩
*Ant* adumbration

**revenant** *apparition, phantasm, phantom, wraith, ghost, spirit, specter, shade

**revenge** vb *avenge
*Ana* recompense, repay (see PAY): vindicate, defend, justify (see MAINTAIN)

**revenge** n vengeance, *retaliation, retribution, reprisal
*Ana* *reparation, redress, amends: recompensing *or* recompense, repayment (see corresponding verbs at PAY)

**revengeful** *vindictive, vengeful
*Ana* implacable, relentless, unrelenting, merciless, *grim: inexorable, obdurate, adamant, *inflexible

**reverberate** repercuss, *rebound, recoil, resile
*Ana* *return, revert, recur

**revere,** reverence, venerate, worship, adore can all mean to regard with profound respect and honor. All imply a recognition of the exalted character of what is so respected and honored, but they can differ in regard to their objects and to the feelings and acts which they connote. Their differences in implication extend to their corresponding nouns, **reverence** (for both verbs *revere* and *reverence*), **veneration, worship,** and **adoration.** One **reveres** with tenderness and deference not only persons or institutions entitled to respect and honor but also their accomplish-

ments or attributes or things associated with or symbolic of such persons or institutions ⟨that makes her loved at home, *revered* abroad—*Burns*⟩ ⟨*revered* for the wisdom of his counsels and the nobility of his character—*Collier*⟩ ⟨islands and cities which he *revered* as the cradle of civilization—*Buchan*⟩ ⟨towards Johnson . . . his [Boswell's] feeling was not sycophancy, which is the lowest, but *reverence*, which is the highest of human feelings—*Carlyle*⟩ One **reverences** things more often than persons, especially things (as laws and customs) which have an intrinsic claim to respect or are commonly regarded as inviolable ⟨we *reverence* tradition, but we will not be fettered by it—*Inge*⟩ ⟨sincerity and simplicity! if I could only say how I *reverence* them—*Benson*⟩ ⟨pledged to *reverence* the name of God—*Steck*⟩ One **venerates** persons as well as things that are regarded as holy, sacred, or sacrosanct because of character, associations, or age ⟨*venerate* saints and heroes⟩ ⟨for Socrates he had an almost religious *veneration*—*Nicholls*⟩ In a narrow sense one **worships** only a divine being, God, a god, or a thing deified, when one pays homage by word or ceremonial ⟨churches are buildings in which God is *worshiped*⟩ ⟨pagans *worship* idols, the sun, and the stars⟩ In wider use *worship* implies a kind of veneration that involves the offering of homage or the attribution of an especially exalted character, whether the object is a divine being or not ⟨there is a difference between admiring a poet and *worshiping* at a shrine—*Repplier*⟩ ⟨in his calm, unexcited way, he *worships* success—*Rose Macaulay*⟩ **Adore** (see also ADORE 2) is often used for *worship* in application to divinity; *worship*, however, usually suggests the group approach, and *adore* the personal approach, to deity. *Adore* therefore commonly implies love and the performance of individual acts of worship that express unquestioning love and honor (as by obeisance, prostration, and prayer) ⟨[the devil] said to him: all these will I give thee, if falling down thou wilt *adore* me—*Mt* 4:9⟩ ⟨quiet as a nun breathless with *adoration*—*Wordsworth*⟩ In more general application *adore* implies an extremely great and usually unquestioning love ⟨his staff *adored* him, his men worshiped him—*White*⟩
*Ana* esteem, respect, regard, admire (see under REGARD *n*): cherish, prize, value, treasure, *appreciate
*Ant* flout

**reverence** *n* 1 *honor, homage, deference, obeisance
*Ana* piety, devotion, fealty, loyalty, *fidelity: esteem, respect, *regard, admiration
2 veneration, worship, adoration (see under REVERE)
*Ana* fervor, ardor, zeal, *passion: devoutness, piousness, religiousness (see corresponding adjectives at DEVOUT)
3 **Reverence, awe, fear** are comparable when they denote the emotion inspired by something which arouses one's deep respect or veneration. **Reverence** distinctively implies a recognition of the sacredness or inviolability of the person or thing which stimulates the emotion ⟨a profound *reverence* for and fidelity to the truth—*Mencken*⟩ ⟨Richelieu's *reverence* for the throne was constant—*Belloc*⟩ ⟨I feel a *reverence* for this place. Wherever humanity has made that hardest of all starts and lifted itself out of mere brutality, is a sacred spot—*Cather*⟩ **Awe**, in all of its shades of meaning, fundamentally implies a sense of being overwhelmed or overcome by great superiority or impressiveness, typically manifested by an inability to speak in its presence or to come near to it. Otherwise, it may suggest any of such widely different reactions as adoration, profound reverence, wonder, terror, submissiveness, or abashment ⟨stood in *awe* of his teachers⟩ ⟨my heart standeth in *awe* of thy word—*Ps* 119:161⟩ ⟨make me as the poorest vassal is that doth with *awe* and

terror kneel—*Shak.*⟩ ⟨he is a great man of the city, without fear, but with the most abject *awe* of the aristocracy—*T. S. Eliot*⟩ **Fear** (see also FEAR 1) occurs, in the sense here considered, chiefly in religious use ⟨the *fear* of the Lord is the beginning of wisdom—*Ps* 111:10⟩ In this sense and as referred chiefly to the Supreme Being as its cause, it implies awed recognition of his power and majesty and, usually, reverence for his law ⟨and calm with *fear* of God's divinity—*Wordsworth*⟩

**reverence** *vb* venerate, worship, adore, *revere
*Ana* love, enjoy (see LIKE): esteem, respect, regard, admire (see under REGARD *n*)

**reverse** *vb* 1 **Reverse, transpose, invert** can all mean to change to the contrary or opposite side or position. **Reverse** is the most general of these terms, implying a change to the opposite not only in side or position but also in direction, order, sequence, relation, or bearing; thus, to *reverse* a coin is to turn it upside down; to *reverse* a process is to follow the opposite order of sequence; to *reverse* a judgment is to change a previous judgment to another that is contrary to it; to *reverse* a garment or part of a garment is to turn it inside out; to *reverse* the direction of a locomotive is to make it go backward instead of forward ⟨having his shield *reversed*—*Scott*⟩ ⟨half were put on a diet of unpolished rice; half on polished. The latter group came down with beriberi. Then the diets were *reversed*—*Heiser*⟩ **Transpose** implies a change in position, usually by reversing the order of two or more units (as letters or words) or by an exchange of position ⟨the printer was instructed to *transpose* the letters *sr* in the word set as *vesre*⟩ ⟨if the term b in the equation $a + b = c$ is *transposed*, the result obtained is $a = c - b$⟩ But *transpose* often, especially in grammar or anatomy, implies merely a change in the natural order or position ⟨he frequently *transposes* words for the sake of effect⟩ ⟨a *transposed* heart⟩ **Invert** implies a change from one side to another chiefly by turning upside down but occasionally, especially in surgery, by turning inside out or outside in ⟨*invert* a tumbler⟩ ⟨*invert* a comma⟩ ⟨*invert* the uterus⟩ ⟨the photograph of the pond showed the *inverted* images of the trees on its bank⟩ In its secondary senses it approaches *reverse* but applies within narrower limits ⟨*invert* the order of words in a sentence⟩ ⟨*invert* the relation of cause and effect⟩ ⟨the custom . . . to *invert* now and then the order of the class so as to make the highest and lowest boys change places—*Thomas Moore*⟩
*Ana* *overturn, upset, capsize
2 *revoke, repeal, rescind, recall
*Ana* upset, *overturn: retract, recant, *abjure, forswear: abrogate, *annul

**reverse** *n* *converse, obverse
*Ana* back, rear, posterior (see corresponding adjectives at POSTERIOR): opposite, contrary (see under OPPOSITE *adj*)

**reversion** 1 return, recurrence, recrudescence (see under RETURN *vb*)
2 **Reversion, atavism, throwback** are comparable when they mean return to an ancestral type or an instance of such return. The same distinctions in implications and connotations are evident in the adjectival forms **reversionary** and **atavistic**. **Reversion** and **reversionary** are the technical terms in the biological sciences for the reappearance of an ancestral character or characters in an individual, or for an organism or individual that manifests such a character ⟨we could not have told, whether these characters in our domestic breeds were *reversions* or only analogous variations—*Darwin*⟩ ⟨similar mutations are paired together; divergent or *reversionary* individuals are eliminated —*J. A. Thomson*⟩ **Atavism** and **atavistic** are widely used

both in general and in technical English. Their implication is of an apparent reversion to a remote rather than to an immediate ancestral type through the reappearance of remote, even primitive, characters after a long period of latency. Often, in general use, this connotation of primitiveness carries with it a suggestion of barbarism or even degeneration ⟨a magnificent *atavism*, a man so purely primitive—*London*⟩ ⟨those who had made England what it was had done so by sticking where they were, regardless of their own *atavistic* instincts, which might have led them back to France or Denmark—*Brooks*⟩ **Throwback** is preferred to *reversion* or *atavism* by those who seek a picturesque or less technical word. It is chiefly applied to the concrete instance and is often extended to other than living things ⟨the racial laws which excluded the Jews from the German community seemed . . . a shocking *throwback* to primitive times—*Shirer*⟩ ⟨an aristocrat of the old line, a *throwback* to another century—*White*⟩ *Ana* relapse, lapse, backsliding (see under LAPSE *vb*)
**reversionary** atavistic (see under REVERSION)
**revert** 1 *return, recur, recrudesce
*Ana* *recede, retreat, retrograde, back: *lapse, relapse, backslide
2 *advert
*Ana* *return, recur
**review** *n* 1 *criticism, critique, blurb, puff
2 *journal, periodical, magazine, organ, newspaper
**revile** vituperate, rail, berate, rate, upbraid, *scold, tongue-lash, jaw, bawl, chew out, wig
*Ana* vilify, calumniate, *malign, traduce, defame, asperse, slander, libel: *execrate, objurgate, curse
*Ant* laud —*Con* *praise, extol, eulogize, acclaim
**revise** 1 *correct, rectify, emend, remedy, redress, amend, reform
*Ana* *improve, better, ameliorate: *change, alter, modify
2 *edit, compile, redact, rewrite, adapt
*Ana* amend, emend, *correct, rectify: *improve, better
**revive** *restore, revivify, resuscitate
*Ana* *recover, recruit, regain: recuperate, *improve, gain: refresh, rejuvenate, *renew
**revivify** *restore, revive, resuscitate
*Ana* reanimate (see base word at QUICKEN): *vitalize, activate, energize: galvanize, quicken, stimulate (see PROVOKE)
**revoke, reverse, repeal, rescind, recall** are close synonyms when they mean to abrogate by undoing something previously done, especially in legal context. **Revoke** implies a calling back, annulling, abrogating; thus, a testator may *revoke* his will and make a new one; a benefactor may *revoke* a gift to an institution; a license board may *revoke* a license ⟨the court *revoked* its sentence of death⟩ ⟨the Edict of Nantes was *revoked* by King Louis XIV⟩ **Reverse** (see also REVERSE) usually implies the action of a higher court in overthrowing a law, a decree, or a decision previously made; it commonly suggests that the earlier law, decree, or decision has been disputed and that the case is now settled by this annulment, unless there is still a higher court to which an appeal may be carried. *Reverse* is, however, still occasionally used in the broader sense of *revoke*, with an implication of upsetting, when it applies to actions, decisions, or judgments of a personal or official but not judicial nature ⟨the teacher *reversed* his judgment of the boy when he heard the full story⟩ ⟨the umpire *reversed* his decision after conferring with his colleague⟩ **Repeal** applies to a law or statute which is revoked by authority, usually by the authority of the body that made it, but sometimes by the executive power or by the vote of the suffrage ⟨the Eighteenth Amendment to the Constitution of the United States was *repealed* when the

Twenty-first Amendment was passed⟩ ⟨Parliament has *repealed* several of the statutes made against nonconformists⟩ **Rescind** implies the exercise of the proper authority in abolishing or making void. It may suggest exercise of legal, judicial, or legislative authority, or it may suggest the exercise of the summary authority of a sovereign, dictator, master, or parent ⟨the council of ten had . . . power over the senate and other magistrates, *rescinding* their decisions—*Hallam*⟩ ⟨the monks petitioned, and the vote was *rescinded*—*Freeman*⟩ In legal use *rescind* as applied to a contract means that it is voided and is as though it never had been. **Recall** (see also REMEMBER) is not a technical term though used sometimes of legal or judicial acts. It is capable of wider use than any of the other of these terms and can on occasion replace any of the others ⟨*recall* a bid in bridge⟩ ⟨one cannot *recall* a sentence to death, if it has been carried out⟩ ⟨they *recalled* the hasty decree—*Gibbon*⟩ *Ana* *annul, abrogate, void: cancel, expunge, *erase: invalidate, *nullify
**revolt** *n* revolution, uprising, insurrection, *rebellion, mutiny, putsch, coup
*Ana* insubordination, seditiousness *or* sedition, factiousness, contumaciousness *or* contumacy (see corresponding adjectives at INSUBORDINATE)
**revolting** *offensive, loathsome, repulsive, repugnant
*Ana* *horrible, horrid, horrific: repellent, distasteful, obnoxious, abhorrent (see REPUGNANT): odious, *hateful, abominable
**revolution** *rebellion, uprising, revolt, insurrection, mutiny, putsch, coup
*Ana* overthrowing *or* overthrow, subverting *or* subversion, upsetting *or* upset, overturning *or* overturn (see corresponding verbs at OVERTURN): change, modification, alteration (see under CHANGE *vb*)
**revolve** *turn, rotate, gyrate, circle, spin, twirl, whirl, wheel, eddy, swirl, pirouette
*Ana* *swing, sway, oscillate, vibrate
**reward** *n* *premium, prize, award, meed, guerdon, bounty, bonus
**rewrite** *vb* *edit, compile, revise, redact, adapt
**rhapsody** *bombast, rant, fustian, rodomontade
**rhetorical, grandiloquent, magniloquent, aureate, flowery, euphuistic, bombastic** are comparable when they mean emphasizing style often at the expense of thought. **Rhetorical** describes a style, discourse, passage, phrase, or word which, however skillfully constructed or chosen and however effective, impresses the reader or hearer as not natural or effortless, but the result of conscious endeavor to produce an effect ⟨Burke catches your eye by *rhetorical* inversions—*Quiller-Couch*⟩ ⟨an essay on friendship, high-flown, *rhetorical*—*Canby*⟩ **Grandiloquent** implies excess (as of elevation or color) and applies to an exaggerated, high-flown, and often pompous manner or style especially in language ⟨the *grandiloquent* advertisement speaks at multitudes of people, and leaves them unmoved—*Kleppner*⟩ ⟨a great stone building like the *grandiloquent* boast of weak men—*Greene*⟩ **Magniloquent** is not always distinguishable from *grandiloquent*, but it more often suggests boastfulness or extravagance than a high-flown eloquence ⟨the *magniloquent* utterances of the drunken Falstaff⟩ ⟨continues his comic oration . . . bent on the choice of *magniloquent* phrase—*E. K. Brown*⟩ **Aureate** implies excessive embellishment of style by strained figures of speech and rhetorical flourishes, strange or high-sounding words, and foreign phrases; in ordinary language and in reference to writings which have no pretensions to literature the same quality is described by **flowery** ⟨the *aureate* prose of the Eliza-

A colon (:) separates groups of words discriminated. An asterisk (*) indicates place of treatment of each group.

bethans⟩ ⟨the *flowery* style of her letters⟩ **Euphuistic** describes specifically a highly rhetorical and aureate style of the reign of Elizabeth I; in extended use it more often suggests extreme artificiality and a straining after effects that distract attention from the thought, rather than the affectation of elegance and the excessive use of alliteration, antithesis, and similes that characterized the original euphuism and are implied in *euphuistic* when used in its strict historical sense ⟨in *Love's Labour's Lost* Shakespeare burlesqued many *euphuistic* affectations of language of his own time⟩ ⟨the bizarre quips and turns in which the . . . *euphuistic* writers delighted—*Miles*⟩ **Bombastic** implies inflation or grandiosity of style. It suggests verbosity and grandiloquence rather than a straining for rhetorical effects ⟨a style that combines realism and old-fashioned emotionalism without becoming *bombastic* —*Abbott*⟩ ⟨Rubens' love for big canvases and mighty subjects led him over the boundary from the eloquent into the *bombastic*—*Coates*⟩

**Ana** eloquent, articulate, *vocal, fluent, voluble, glib: florid, *ornate, flamboyant: *inflated, turgid, tumid, flatulent

**rhymer, rhymester** *poet, versifier, poetaster, bard, minstrel, troubadour

**rhythm, meter, cadence** can all mean the more or less regular rise and fall in intensity of sounds that one associates chiefly with poetry and music. **Rhythm**, which of these three terms is the most inclusive and the widest in its range of application, implies movement and flow as well as an agreeable succession of rising and falling sounds; it need not suggest regular alternation of these sounds, but it fundamentally implies the recurrence at fairly regular intervals of the accented or prolonged syllable in poetry or of the heavy beat or the accented note in music, so that no matter how many unaccented or unstressed syllables or notes lie between these, the continuing up and down movement is strongly apparent to the senses. Consequently *rhythm* is used not only in reference to speech sounds and musical tones ordered with relation to stress and time, but also to dancing, games, and various natural phenomena where a comparable pulsing movement is apparent, and even to the arts of design, where fluctuations in line or pattern suggest a pulsing movement ⟨the wavering, lovely *rhythms* of the sea—*Rose Macaulay*⟩ ⟨every one learned music, dancing, and song. Therefore it is natural for them to regard *rhythm* and grace in all the actions of life—*Ellis*⟩ ⟨lost their talent in the deadening *rhythms* of war, its boredom, its concussion, and . . . its injustice—*Mailer*⟩ **Meter** implies the reduction of rhythm to system and measure. Poetry that has meter has a definite rhythmical pattern which determines the typical foot or sometimes the arrangement of feet in each line and either the number of feet in every line or, if a stanzaic pattern is implied, in each verse of a stanza ⟨the revolt against *meter* in poetry in the late nineteenth and early twentieth centuries⟩ ⟨the only strict antithesis to prose is *meter*— *Wordsworth*⟩ In music *meter* implies the division of the rhythm into measures, all of which are uniform in number of beats or time units, and each of which begins with the accented tone. **Cadence** is the least clearly fixed in meaning of these words. The term has often been used as though it were equal to *rhythm*, or sometimes to *meter*, especially when the reference is to poetry ⟨golden *cadence* of poesy —*Shak.*⟩ ⟨wit will shine through the harsh *cadence* of a rugged line—*Dryden*⟩ ⟨poetry can never again become a popular art until the poet gives himself wholly to "the *cadence* of consenting feet"—*Read*⟩ **Cadence** often stresses the rise and fall of sound or the rhythm as heard, whether in prose or in poetry, and as influenced by tone or

modulation, choice of words, and association of sound and feeling ⟨great music like that of Prospero's speech in *The Tempest* or the *cadence* of Cleopatra's "Give me my robe"—*Alexander*⟩ ⟨I could hear the *cadence* of his voice and that was all, nothing but the measured rise and fall of syllables—*Marquand*⟩ ⟨the singsong *cadence* which jarred on her the more because she was still trying to free her own speech of it—*Wouk*⟩

**rib** *vb* *banter, chaff, kid, rag, josh, jolly

**ribald** obscene, gross, *coarse, vulgar

**Ana** *offensive, loathsome: indecent, indelicate (see INDECOROUS): lewd, lascivious, wanton (see LICENTIOUS): scurrilous, opprobrious (see ABUSIVE)

**ribbon** fillet, band, *strip, stripe

**rich, wealthy, affluent, opulent** are applied both to persons and to things. The last three are close synonyms of *rich*, the general term, but they are more explicit in their implications and more limited in their range of application. One is **rich** that possesses more than enough to gratify normal desires and needs. *Rich*, therefore, may describe anyone or anything above what is felt as average or normal in possessions. When used of persons, without qualification, it implies the possession of money or of property, especially income-producing property ⟨a *rich* citizen⟩ ⟨a *rich* state⟩ In its extended use one may be *rich* in friends, in talents, or in interests; a soil may be *rich* in nitrogen; a poem may be *rich* in meaning, a career in promise, a flower in fragrance. Also, something is *rich* which is above the line dividing the cheap from the costly or precious or dividing the stinted in elements or ingredients from the bountifully supplied ⟨a *rich* fabric⟩ ⟨a *rich* tone⟩ ⟨a *rich* red⟩ ⟨a *rich* cake⟩ One is **wealthy** that possesses money, income-producing property, or intrinsically valuable things in great abundance. *Wealthy* is rarer than *rich* in extended use and usually connotes material possessions. It also more often than *rich* implies a way of living in keeping with one's income and a commanding position in the community, state, or world ⟨power is in the hands of the *wealthy*⟩ ⟨the *wealthy* nations of Europe⟩ ⟨she was indeed rich, according to the standards of the Square; nay, *wealthy*!—*Bennett*⟩ One is **affluent** that is prosperous and therefore continually increasing one's material possessions ⟨men . . . obviously *affluent* by their excellent clothes and careful grooming—*MacInnes*⟩ *Affluent*, though often used to describe persons, groups, or nations, is more often applied to their circumstances or to their state; thus, a rich man is in *affluent* circumstances if his income is increasing or, at least, not decreasing; one is reduced from an *affluent* position but not from riches or wealth, for only *affluent* implies increase and therefore suggests decrease as its opposite. One is **opulent** that is ostensibly and ostentatiously rich; thus, a person in *affluent* circumstances may or may not maintain an *opulent* establishment, for *affluent* suggests the inflow of money and *opulent* lavish expenditure. Hence *opulent* usually qualifies things that are luxurious, prodigal, expensively splendid, or sumptuous ⟨*opulent* decorations⟩ ⟨*opulent* entertainment⟩ When applied to persons *opulent* usually qualifies a specific term which harmonizes with it in implications ⟨an *opulent* aristocracy⟩ Occasionally *opulent* does not connote display but inexhaustible richness ⟨the *opulent* genius of Shakespeare⟩

**Ant** poor —**Con** destitute, indigent, penurious (see corresponding nouns at POVERTY)

**ricochet** *vb* *skip, bound, hop, curvet, lope, lollop

**rid, clear, unburden, disabuse, purge** are comparable when they mean to set a person or thing free of something that encumbers. **Rid** is a rather general term but is likely to refer to concrete or specific matters which are burdensome or pestiferous ⟨England had in the meantime *ridded* herself of the Stuarts, worried along under the Hanoverians—*Repplier*⟩ ⟨a lazy man's expedient for *ridding* himself of the trouble of thinking and deciding—*Cardozo*⟩ **Clear** is likely to be used to refer to tangible matters which obstruct progress, clutter an area, or block vision ⟨wars which . . . enabled the United States first to *clear* its own territory of foreign troops—*Bemis*⟩ ⟨rose from the food she had barely tasted and began to *clear* the table—*Glasgow*⟩ and may be used also in relation to ideas that hinder progress ⟨of service to his fellow Methodists in *clearing* away obstructions to modern thinking—*H. K. Rowe*⟩ **Unburden** typically implies a freeing of oneself from something taxing or something distressing the mind or spirit, in the latter situation often by confessing, revealing, or frankly discussing ⟨insisted that he *unburden* himself of most of the weighty chores that go with the job of majority leader—*Time*⟩ ⟨conquers his own submissiveness and *unburdens* himself, before his domineering wife, of all the accumulated resentment and dislike of years—*S. M. Fitzgerald*⟩ **Disabuse** is appropriately chosen to refer to freeing the mind from an erroneous notion or an attitude or feeling making clear straightforward thought difficult ⟨if men are now sufficiently enlightened to *disabuse* themselves of artifice, hypocrisy, and superstition—*Adams*⟩ ⟨neither familiarity with the history and institutions of Old World nations nor contact with them during two wars *disabused* the average American of his feeling of superiority—*Commager*⟩ **Purge** may refer to cleansing out of or purification from whatever is impure or alien or extrinsic ⟨*purged* of all its unorthodox views—*Shaw*⟩ ⟨the room had never quite been *purged* of the bad taste of preceding generations—*Edmund Wilson*⟩ In political matters it may suggest ruthless elimination ⟨the dictator has *purged* academic faculties of every savant suspected of being opposed to his regime—*H. M. Jones*⟩

*Ana* *free, release, liberate: *exterminate, extirpate, eradicate, uproot: *abolish, extinguish

**riddle** *n* puzzle, conundrum, enigma, problem, *mystery

**ride** *vb* 1 **Ride, drive** as verbs (transitive and intransitive) and as nouns may both involve the idea of moving in or being carried along in a vehicle or conveyance or upon the back of something. The basic meaning of **ride** is a being borne along in or upon something; when this idea is uppermost, it makes little difference who or what controls the animal, the vehicle, or mechanism by which one is borne along; thus, one *rides* or *rides* on a horse, a bicycle, or a motorcycle when, mounted upon it, one controls its operation or movements, but a woman seated on a pillion behind the saddle may also be said to *ride* the horse, and a person in the rear seat of a tandem bicycle may be said to *ride* the bicycle, but a person in a sidecar of a motorcycle *rides* in the sidecar (not *rides* the motorcycle). Sometimes *ride*, the transitive verb, is preferred when the management of the horse and vehicle is also implied, and *ride*, the intransitive verb, when merely the being mounted upon a moving horse or vehicle is suggested ⟨when he *rides* his horse his small daughter usually *rides* on it with him⟩ The basic meaning of **drive** (see MOVE 1) is a causing to move along; the term therefore primarily refers to the action of an agent that controls the movement of a vehicle whether it is drawn by an animal or self-propelled ⟨*drove* a four-horse brewery wagon⟩ ⟨it is usually wise to have your child taught to *drive* by a professional⟩ There is usually a further distinction between *ride* and *drive* when movement in a vehicle or conveyance is implied. *Ride* usually suggests movement in a vehicle (as a train, a bus, or a stranger's automobile) which is not in any sense under one's control ⟨it is a long train *ride* from New York to

Chicago⟩ ⟨he said he preferred *riding* in a bus to *riding* in a train⟩ ⟨will you give me a *ride* to the next town?⟩ *Drive* often suggests movement in a horse-drawn or motor vehicle the course of which is in some way or in some degree under one's control, whether one is the actual driver or one (as an employer, patron, or guest) whose wishes the actual driver observes ⟨take a *drive* along the shore of the lake⟩ ⟨we are going for a short *drive*⟩

2 *bait, badger, heckle, hector, chivy, hound

*Ana* *worry, annoy, harass, harry: persecute, oppress (see WRONG *vb*): torment, torture (see AFFLICT)

**ride** *n* drive (see under RIDE *vb*)

*Ana* *journey, tour, trip, excursion, expedition

**ridicule** *vb* **Ridicule, deride, mock, taunt, twit, rally** are comparable when they mean to make a person or thing the object of laughter. **Ridicule** implies deliberate and often malicious belittling of the person or thing ridiculed ⟨the old State religion which Augustine attacks, *ridiculing* the innumerable Roman godlings whose names he perhaps found in Varro—*Inge*⟩ ⟨the man who wants to preserve his personal identity is *ridiculed* as an eccentric—*Harris*⟩ **Deride** implies a bitter or contemptuous spirit ⟨he took his revenge on the fate that had made him sad by fiercely *deriding* everything—*Huxley*⟩ ⟨sardonic wisecracks in which supposedly lofty ideals are mercilessly *derided*—*Times Lit. Sup.*⟩ **Mock** stresses scornful derision and usually implies words or gestures or sometimes acts expressive of one's defiance or contempt ⟨nowhere can men be entirely happy while human nature is still being *mocked* and tortured on other parts of the globe—*Kennan*⟩ When used in reference to things, *mock* often implies a setting at naught that suggests scorn or derision ⟨a perishing that *mocks* the gladness of the spring!—*Wordsworth*⟩ ⟨a joke was a good way to *mock* reality, to dodge an issue, to escape involvement—*MacInnes*⟩ **Taunt** implies both mockery and reproach; it often connotes jeering insults ⟨*taunted* in fun or in earnest with the foibles and shortcomings of their fathers—*de Laguna*⟩ ⟨he . . . took no part in the revivals and usually teased and *taunted* those who did—*J. M. Hunt*⟩ **Twit** may come close to *taunt* and imply a mocking or cruel casting something up to someone ⟨the absence of ideas with which Matthew Arnold *twits* them—*Inge*⟩ ⟨a British author snooting American food is like the blind *twitting* the one-eyed—*Liebling*⟩ but *twit*, like *rally*, may imply no more than good-natured raillery or friendly ridicule ⟨the paper delights in *twitting* new laws—*Newsweek*⟩ ⟨a useful place for getting away from the cheery *rallying* of . . . the English governess—*Nancy Hale*⟩

*Ana* *scoff, flout, jeer, gibe: caricature, burlesque, travesty (see under CARICATURE *n*)

**ridiculous** *laughable, risible, ludicrous, droll, funny, comic, comical, farcical

*Ana* absurd, preposterous, *foolish, silly: amusing, diverting, entertaining (see AMUSE): *fantastic, grotesque, bizarre, antic

**rife** *prevailing, prevalent, current

*Ana* abundant, *plentiful, copious, ample: *common, ordinary, familiar

**rifle** *vb* plunder, *rob, loot, burglarize

*Ana* despoil, spoilate, *ravage, pillage, sack, devastate: *steal, pilfer, purloin, filch

**rift** *n* *breach, break, split, schism, rent, rupture

*Ana* *crack, cleft, fissure: gap, interval, hiatus, interruption (see BREAK): separation, division (see corresponding verbs at SEPARATE)

**right** *adj* 1 *good

*Ant* wrong

2 *correct, accurate, exact, precise, nice

---

A colon (:) separates groups of words discriminated. An asterisk (*) indicates place of treatment of each group.

*Ana* fitting, proper, meet (see FIT): *decorous, decent, seemly
*Ant* wrong

**right** *n* **Right, prerogative, privilege, perquisite, appanage, birthright** can all mean something to which a person has a just or legal claim. They differ in their implications both of the nature of the thing claimed and of the grounds of the claim. **Right,** the most inclusive term, may designate something (as a power, a condition of existence, or a possession) to which one is entitled by nature, by the principles of morality, by grant, by the laws of the land, or by purchase ⟨the *right* to life, liberty, and the pursuit of happiness⟩ ⟨*rights* in a patent⟩ ⟨we do not lose our *right* to condemn either measures or men because the country is at war—*Justice Holmes*⟩ ⟨every person has a *right* to a certain amount of room in the world, and should not be made to feel wicked in standing up for what is due to him—*Russell*⟩ **Prerogative** denotes a right which belongs to an actual or a legal person by virtue of status (as in sex, rank, office, or character) and which thereby gives precedence, superiority, or an advantage over others ⟨the fundamental fact is that eminent domain is a *prerogative* of the State—*Justice Holmes*⟩ ⟨endurance and stamina in the last analysis are *prerogatives* of the male—*Gerald Beaumont*⟩ **Privilege** applies to a special right either granted as a favor or concession or belonging to one as a prerogative; *privilege* often implies an advantage over others ⟨equal rights for all, special *privileges* for none—*Jefferson*⟩ ⟨a propertied class struggling for its *privileges* which it honestly deems to be its rights—*White*⟩ ⟨what men prize most is a *privilege*, even if it be that of chief mourner at a funeral—*J. R. Lowell*⟩ **Perquisite** signifies something, usually money or a thing of monetary value, to which one is entitled, especially by custom, as an addition to one's regular revenue, salary, or wages ⟨fees that constitute the *perquisites* of an office⟩ ⟨a domestic servant often regards her mistress's cast-off clothing as her *perquisite*⟩ ⟨the petty graft and favoritism which are normal *perquisites* of machine rule—*Green Peyton*⟩ **Appanage** is often used as if it meant merely an adjunct or appurtenance ⟨whose literary work had become a mere *appanage* of his domestic life—*Brooks*⟩ but more precisely it can denote something to which one has a claim through custom, through tradition, or through natural necessity ⟨the religious supremacy became a kind of *appanage* to the civil sovereignty—*Milman*⟩ ⟨beauty, which is the natural *appanage* of happiness—*Patmore*⟩ ⟨their acquired prestige as a token of power and dignity made gloves an *appanage* of the ruling classes—*Anny Latour*⟩ **Birthright,** which basically applies to the property or possessions belonging to one by right of inheritance (see HERITAGE), has acquired extended use in which it differs from *right* only in being restricted to a right to which one is entitled by some reason connected with one's nativity (as by being a man, a native-born citizen, or a descendant of a particular family line) ⟨we sell our *birthright* whenever we sell our liberty for any price of gold or honor—*Whipple*⟩ ⟨the poetic imagination that was his Elizabethan *birthright—Parrington*⟩
*Ana* *claim, title: *freedom, license, liberty

**righteous** virtuous, noble, *moral, ethical
*Ana* *upright, honest, just, honorable
*Ant* iniquitous —*Con* *vicious, nefarious, flagitious, corrupt: profligate, dissolute, reprobate, *abandoned

**rightful** *due, condign
*Ana* *fair, equitable, just, impartial: *lawful, legal, legitimate

**rigid** 1 *stiff, inflexible, tense, stark, wooden
*Ana* *firm, hard, solid: compact, *close: tough, tenacious, *strong

*Ant* elastic —*Con* resilient, flexible, supple, springy (see ELASTIC)

2 **Rigid, rigorous, strict, stringent** are often used interchangeably in the sense of extremely severe and stern, especially when applied to laws or imposed conditions or to the persons who enforce them. There are, however, differences in implications and in range of application. Basically *rigid* and *rigorous* imply extreme stiffness or utter lack of elasticity or flexibility, while *strict* and *stringent* imply tightness so extreme as to permit no looseness, laxity, or latitude. These implications are preserved in their extended uses. **Rigid** (see also STIFF) in extended use is applied less often to persons than to their acts or to the conditions the persons make for themselves or others; it usually suggests uncompromising inflexibility ⟨*rigid* laws⟩ ⟨*rigid* discipline⟩ ⟨a *rigid* system, faithfully administered, would be better than a slatternly compromise—*Benson*⟩ **Rigorous** is applied to persons, to their acts, to their way of life, and to the natural or artificial conditions under which they live. It commonly implies imposed severities or hardships; thus, a *rigid* rule admits of no change or compromise, but a *rigorous* rule imposes exacting or harsh conditions; a *rigorous* enforcement of a law makes the people feel its rigors; a *rigid* enforcement of a law admits of no relaxations in anyone's favor; one can speak of a *rigorous* winter, a *rigorous* disciplinarian, the *rigorous* life of an explorer or a monk. **Strict** is applied chiefly to persons or their acts and denotes showing or demanding undeviating conformity to rules, standards, conditions, or requirements; thus, a *strict* rule demands obedience; a *strict* teacher may impose *rigorous* discipline and adhere to a *rigid* system of grading; a *strict* watch admits no relaxing of vigilance, and *strict* silence no freedom to speak; a *strict* construction of a law is one confined to the letter of that law ⟨the *strictest* obligations of intellectual honesty—*Inge*⟩ ⟨*strict* justice, either on earth or in heaven, was the last thing that society cared to face—*Henry Adams*⟩ **Stringent** is to *strict* as *rigorous* is to *rigid*, in that it usually emphasizes the effect or effects rather than the presence of a quality in an agent or his act. Both *stringent* and *rigorous* connote imposition, but *stringent* suggests impositions that limit, curb, or sometimes coerce; thus, a *stringent* rule narrows one's freedom or range of activities; a *stringent* interpretation of the constitution may either be narrower or more restrictive in its effects than the letter of the constitution warrants; poverty may be described as *stringent* when it narrows one's opportunities to satisfy one's aspirations; necessity may be called *stringent* when it forces one to live within bounds or forces one into distasteful acts ⟨he endeavors by the most *stringent* regulations to prevent the growth of inequalities of wealth—*Dickinson*⟩ ⟨colleges with the most *stringent* admissions requirements—*Frederiksen*⟩ ⟨with energy sufficiently great to burst the bounds of the most *stringent* confinement—*Rogow*⟩
*Ana* *inflexible, inexorable, obdurate, adamant, adamantine: stern, *severe, austere
*Ant* lax

**rigor** *difficulty, hardship, vicissitude
*Ana* austerity, severity, sternness (see corresponding adjectives at SEVERE): harshness, roughness (see corresponding adjectives at ROUGH): *trial, tribulation, visitation, affliction
*Ant* amenity

**rigorous** *rigid, strict, stringent
*Ana* *stiff, rigid, inflexible: stern, austere, ascetic, *severe: exacting, *onerous, burdensome, oppressive
*Con* *easy, facile, light, smooth, effortless

**rim** brim, brink, *border, margin, verge, edge

---

*Ana* analogous words  *Ant* antonyms  *Con* contrasted words  See also explanatory notes facing page 1

**rind** *skin, bark, peel, hide, pelt

**ring** n *combination, combine, party, bloc, faction

**ring** vb *surround, environ, encircle, circle, encompass, compass, hem, gird, girdle
*Ana* confine, circumscribe, *limit, restrict: *enclose, corral, wall

**ringing** adj *resonant, sonorous, resounding, vibrant, orotund

**rip** vb *tear, rend, split, cleave, rive

**ripe** *mature, matured, mellow, adult, grown-up
*Ana* *seasonable, timely, well-timed: *consummate, finished, accomplished
*Ant* green: unripe —*Con* raw, *rude, crude, callow: *immature, unmatured, unmellow

**ripen** *mature, develop, age
*Ana* *improve, better: enhance, heighten, *intensify: season (see HARDEN)

**rise** vb 1 *spring, arise, originate, derive, flow, issue, emanate, proceed, stem
*Ana* *appear, emerge, loom
*Ant* abate (sense 3) —*Con* ebb, subside, wane (see ABATE)
2 Rise, arise, ascend, mount, soar, tower, rocket, levitate, surge are comparable when they mean to move or come up from a lower to a higher level. **Rise** is the comprehensive term interchangeable with all the others, but often at a sacrifice of explicitness or picturesqueness. *Rise* is idiomatic, and therefore the preferred word, when used: (1) in reference to persons or sometimes animals that get up from a recumbent position (as in bed or after a fall) or from a sitting or kneeling position ⟨*rise* every morning at six⟩ ⟨the injured horse was unable to *rise*⟩ ⟨the audience *rose* when the national anthem was sung⟩ or (2) in reference to things that give the impression of coming up into view ⟨the sun *rises* at 5:30⟩ or to an object that seems to lift itself up ⟨the hills *rise* in the distance⟩ or (3) in reference to fluid (as water) under the influence of some natural force that sends it upward ⟨the river *rises* regularly each spring⟩ ⟨the mercury is *rising*⟩ or to any natural phenomenon indicated by such rising of water or other fluid ⟨the tide *rises* early tonight⟩ ⟨the temperature is *rising*⟩ The word may be used more widely than these instances indicate, but in these and in closely related extensions and metaphoric applications *rise* is specifically necessary ⟨for the first two weeks, or three . . . the work *rose* about him like a tide—*Mary Austin*⟩ ⟨now he felt his mother counting the week's money, and her wrath *rising*—*D. H. Lawrence*⟩ ⟨felt the color *rising* in her face—*Sedgwick*⟩ **Arise** (see also SPRING) is narrower in its range of application than *rise* and in most uses is felt to be rhetorical or poetic excepting perhaps the senses of to get up in the morning after a night's sleep or to rise from the grave ⟨*arise, arise;* awake the snorting citizens with the bell —*Shak.*⟩ ⟨the temple rends, the rocks burst, the dead *arise*—*Steele*⟩ **Ascend** and **mount** (see also ASCEND 2) carry a stronger suggestion of continuous or progressive upward movement and of climbing than *rise* and may therefore be used in distinction from the latter word; thus, the sun *rises* at dawn, but it *ascends* from dawn to noon; smoke *rises* from a fire and *ascends* to the treetops; a lark *rises* from the ground and *mounts* to the skies; a scientist's hopes *rise* at the first indication of his success and *mount* as one experiment after another turns out as expected ⟨the third day he *rose* again from the dead, he *ascended* into heaven—*Apostles' Creed: Book of Common Prayer*⟩ **Soar** even in metaphoric use suggests the straight upward flight of a bird that mounts on rising currents without flapping of wings; it therefore usually connotes continuous, often swift, ascent into high altitudes especially intellectually, spiritually, or aesthetically ⟨[the skylark] singing still dost *soar,* and *soaring* ever singest— *Shelley*⟩ ⟨up from the eastern sea *soars* the delightful day—*Housman*⟩ ⟨young *soaring* imaginations—*John Reed*⟩ ⟨the *soaring* melody of the rondo in the Waldstein sonata is Beethoven's . . . transfiguration of the air of a ribald folk song—*Lowes*⟩ **Tower** is used more often in reference to things that attain conspicuous height through growth or thrusting upward, or building than in reference to things that actually move upward; it also frequently connotes extension to a height beyond that of such comparable neighboring objects as buildings, trees, mountains, or, when eminence is suggested, persons ⟨the Empire State Building *towers* above New York City⟩ ⟨full thirty foot she *towered* from waterline to rail—*Kipling*⟩ ⟨this *towering* but erratic genius . . . combined in his tempestuous character so many of the best and the worst qualities—*Shirer*⟩ When the word does imply movement upward, it usually evokes a picture of something shooting up so as to suggest a tower or steeple ⟨the nimble flames *towered,* nodded, and swooped through the surrounding air—*Hardy*⟩ **Rocket** suggests the inordinately swift ascent of a projectile; it is used chiefly with reference to things that rise with extraordinary rapidity or wildly and uncontrollably (as under the impetus of events) ⟨prices have *rocketed* sky-high—*Kent*⟩ ⟨cock pheasants *rocket* from the misty spinneys—*Glover*⟩ ⟨Indian pride was reawakened; Indian hopes *rocketed*—*J. M. Brown*⟩ **Levitate** implies a rising or floating in or as if in air that suggests the intervention of antigravity; the term connotes actual or induced lightness or buoyancy and ease of movement ⟨a 1/2-in. niobium sphere *levitated* in a liquid helium bath—*J. L. Taylor*⟩ ⟨we are *levitated* between acceptance and disbelief—*O'Faolain*⟩ ⟨dwellings . . . *levitated* by his imagination into new structural creations—*Flanner*⟩ The word is sometimes specifically associated with supranormal and especially spiritualistic practices ⟨the *levitation* of a table at a séance⟩ and with illusory risings ⟨it is asserted that a man or a woman *levitated* to the ceiling, floated about there, and finally sailed out by the window— *T. H. Huxley*⟩ **Surge** suggests the upward heaving or spurting of waves. It is used often with *up*, in reference to emotions and thoughts that rise powerfully from the depths of subconsciousness ⟨strong emotions *surged* through him as he strode on—*Rölvaag*⟩ ⟨things half-guessed, obscurely felt, *surged* up from unsuspected depths in her—*Wharton*⟩ Quite as often, usually with an adverb of direction, it suggests a rolling movement comparable to that of oncoming waves ⟨the troops *surged* forward⟩ ⟨traffic *surging* past⟩
*Ana* climb, *ascend, mount, scale: *increase, enlarge, augment: *lift, raise, elevate
*Ant* decline: set (*as the sun*)

**rise** n *beginning, genesis, initiation
*Ana* *origin, source, inception, root, provenance, provenience: derivation, origination (see corresponding verbs at SPRING)
*Ant* fall

**risible** droll, funny, *laughable, ludicrous, ridiculous, comic, comical, farcical
*Ana* amusing, diverting, entertaining (see AMUSE)

**risk** n hazard, *danger, peril, jeopardy
*Ana* *chance, fortune, luck, accident: exposedness *or* exposure, liableness *or* liability, openness (see corresponding adjectives at LIABLE)
*Con* safety, security (see corresponding adjectives at SAFE): *exemption, immunity

**risk** vb *venture, hazard, chance, jeopardize, endanger, imperil

---

*Ana* dare, brave, beard, *face, defy: confront, encounter, *meet

**risky** precarious, hazardous, *dangerous, perilous
*Ana* *adventurous, venturesome: chancy, *random, haphazard, hit-or-miss, happy-go-lucky

**rite** ritual, liturgy, ceremonial, ceremony, *form, formality

**ritual** rite, liturgy, ceremonial, ceremony, *form, formality

**rival** *vb* **1 Rival, compete, vie, emulate** can all mean to strive to equal or surpass another or his achievements. **Rival** (see also MATCH) usually suggests an attempt to outdo each other ⟨a work . . . which contending sects have *rivaled* each other in approving—*Heber*⟩ **Compete** and **vie,** usually with the opponent explicitly stated after *with* and the objective after *for,* may sometimes omit direct reference to one or both of these ⟨a modified apple syrup to *compete* in the . . . market of syrups for infant feeding —*Crops in Peace and War*⟩ **Compete** stresses a struggle for an objective (as position, favor, profit, or a prize); unlike *rival,* it need not suggest a conscious attempt to outdo another but may imply a quite impersonal striving ⟨athletes *competing* in track sports⟩ ⟨colleges *compete* with each other, promotionally, for public favor—*Hoff*⟩ ⟨the buyer does not *compete* with the seller. He bargains with him; he *competes* with other buyers—*C. E. Griffin*⟩ **Vie** carries less suggestion of arduous struggle to hold one's own or to excel than *compete,* but it may suggest more conscious awareness of the opponent ⟨the calypso singers who . . . *vie* with one another in duels of lyrical improvisation—*The Lamp*⟩ It sometimes suggests the excitement of contest that is a game rather than a combat ⟨the boys *vied* with each other in showing off⟩ ⟨they *vied* with each other in enlivening their cups by lamenting the depravity of this degenerate age—*Peacock*⟩ **Emulate** implies a conscious effort to equal or surpass someone or something by imitation or by using him or it as a model ⟨a simplicity *emulated* without success by numerous modern poets—*T. S. Eliot*⟩ ⟨these young . . . heroes, reared on the immense empty western plains, seek to *emulate* an eastern sophistication—*Geismar*⟩ ⟨*emulated* the proverbial and sagacious rat; he got off in time— *S. H. Adams*⟩
*Ana* strive, struggle, try, *attempt: *contend, fight
**2** *match, equal, approach, touch

**rive** *vb* cleave, split, rend, *tear, rip
*Ana* sever, sunder, divide, *separate: *cut, hew, chop

**rivet** *vb* *secure, anchor, moor
*Ana* *fasten, attach, affix, fix: *join, unite, connect, link

**roam** *wander, stray, ramble, rove, range, prowl, gad, gallivant, traipse, meander

**roar** *vb* **Roar, bellow, bluster, bawl, vociferate, clamor, howl, ululate** are comparable when they mean to make a very loud and often a continuous or protracted noise. The same distinctions in implications and connotations are to be found in their nouns, all of which are identical in spelling with the corresponding verbs except **vociferation** and **ululation. Roar** implies such a heavy, hoarse, and prolonged sound as is made by the booming sea, by thunder that reverberates, by a lion, or by persons when they lose control (as in rage or in boisterous merriment) ⟨far away guns *roar*—*Woolf*⟩ ⟨the harsh north wind . . . *roared* in the piazzas—*Osbert Sitwell*⟩ ⟨it's the same to her, whether we coo like turtledoves or *roar* like twenty lions—*Meredith*⟩ ⟨his anecdotes sent the audience into *roars* of laughter⟩ **Bellow** suggests the loud, hollow crying of a bull; by extension, it applies to sound that seems to reverberate loudly from a cavity or to come insistently from a distance ⟨*bellowing* with hoarse merriment—*Kenneth Roberts*⟩ ⟨the *bellow* of crocodiles—*Forester*⟩ **Bluster** suggests not only the violence or turbulence of a windstorm but the

lashing quality of its blasts ⟨when autumn *blusters* and the orchard rocks—*Browning*⟩ It is applicable not only to violent weather but also to something (as loud boastful swaggering or empty but noisy threats or protests) that suggests such weather. The term in extended use often carries a connotation of useless or futile effort ⟨do their work without *bluster* or ostentation—*Walker*⟩ ⟨she expressed her opinion gently but firmly, while he *blustered* for a time and then gave in—*Anderson*⟩ **Bawl** is sometimes interchangeable with *bellow,* but typically it suggests less depth and resonance and more persistence ⟨cattle *bawling* for water⟩ As applied to human utterance, *bawl* is more or less derogatory ⟨despite all political *bawls* and bellows about . . . prices—*Time*⟩ Even when applied specifically to unrestrained weeping and wailing it tends to call up an unsympathetic image of dishevelment and disorder ⟨collapsed in an armchair in the lobby and *bawled* . . . uncontrollably—*Kahn*⟩ **Vociferate** and **vociferation,** like *bawl,* imply loud and urgent human utterance, but they are far less derogatory, if derogatory at all, more adapted to writing than to speech, and more likely to suggest a reason (as rage or excitement), a call for help, or a protest, than mere temperament ⟨an atmosphere of shrieks and moans; prayers *vociferated* like blasphemies— *Conrad*⟩ ⟨the perpetual *vociferation* of inflammatory opinion—*Sampson*⟩ **Clamor** implies, usually, loud noises in confusion; it may suggest a mingling of voices or sounds. The term can apply to loud sounds, whatever their source. As applied to human utterances, it commonly gains the suggestion of vehemence (as in insisting, urging, or protesting) ⟨half-starved men and women *clamoring* for food —*Kenneth Roberts*⟩ ⟨Europe has begun to *clamor* for political disciplinarians to save her—*Shaw*⟩ ⟨*clamored* their piteous prayer incessantly—*Longfellow*⟩ **Howl** often stresses such loudness and mournfulness as is characteristic of the protracted cry of dogs and wolves; it may be used not only of animals but also of persons or things that make doleful or agonized and often prolonged sounds ⟨a legion of foul fiends . . . *howled* in my ears— *Milton*⟩ ⟨*howls* of mingled rage and pain⟩ ⟨the *howling* of the wind on a stormy night⟩ Especially when used of human utterance, *howl* may suggest not only the quality of the sound but the unrestrained character of the utterance or of its underlying emotion ⟨he . . . chortled at their errors, *howled* at their inconsistencies—*Martin Gardner*⟩ ⟨*howled* at a brother for his low-down ways, his prowling, guzzling, sneak-thief days—*Lindsay*⟩ ⟨from faint doubt to uneasy suspicion, from the stirring of resentment to the *howl* of outraged protest—*Lewis & Maude*⟩ **Ululate** and **ululation** are less common and more literary than *howl,* from which they differ chiefly in carrying less suggestion of unrestrained emotion and a stronger implication of wailing, often giving a hint of the peculiar rhythm of the sounds ⟨*ululating* coyotes⟩ ⟨an *ululating* baritone mushy with pumped-up pity—*E. B. White*⟩ ⟨who uttered in public or in private such high-pitched notes of *ululation*— *Swinburne*⟩
*Ana* reverberate, repercuss, *rebound: yell, *shout: bay, *bark, growl, yelp

**rob** *vb* **Rob, plunder, rifle, loot, burglarize** are comparable when they mean to take unlawfully possessions of a person or from a place. All in this basic use imply both an owner of and value inherent in the thing taken. In its basic and legal use **rob** implies the taking of personal property or valuables from another or from a place in a felonious manner (as by the exercise of violence, by intimidation, or by trickery or fraud) ⟨*rob* a bank⟩ ⟨*rob* a man of his savings by selling him worthless securities⟩ In extended use *rob* implies deprivation by unjust means or by powers

beyond one's control ⟨*rob* a person of his good name⟩ ⟨the high winds *robbed* the trees of their fruit⟩ ⟨a tree *robs* the adjacent soil of moisture and fertility⟩ **Plunder** implies a despoliation by force (as by armies in war or organized gangs and bandits); it often suggests robbery on an extensive scale or a ravaging or pillaging of a territory ⟨travelers through the remote sections of the country were in constant danger of being *plundered*⟩ ⟨*plunder* a warehouse⟩ ⟨*plundering* wrecked ships . . . was a well-established business in many places on our shores—*Shaw*⟩ Sometimes it is extended to wasting or destroying that suggests a pillaging ⟨the reduction of soil erosion and *plundering* of the soil—*Farmer's Weekly*⟩ ⟨big business which serves the great metropolis, or *plunders* it—*Upton Sinclair*⟩ **Rifle**, like *plunder*, usually implies a despoliation of possessions or valuables, but it distinctively stresses a breaking into and ransacking and therefore usually takes as its object a place, building, treasury, or receptacle ⟨*rifle* a strongbox⟩ ⟨*rifle* a palace⟩ ⟨*rifle* a man's pockets⟩ But the word may also be used when ransacking for the sake of finding something is the chief implication ⟨awakened . . . to find him *rifling* through her desk in a desperate search for writing materials—*Brand Blanshard*⟩ **Loot** differs from *plunder* chiefly in its suggestion of circumstances which explain the despoliation or make it exceedingly reprehensible; it sometimes implies defiance of all laws governing civilized conduct ⟨*loot* the bodies of those killed in a wreck⟩ or desperation ⟨if we left them to starve they would begin by breaking our windows and end by *looting* our shops and burning our houses—*Shaw*⟩ or utter venality ⟨pressing indelicate questions about . . . the *looting* of the forest and mineral reserves—*G. W. Johnson*⟩ but it quite commonly refers to pillaging by undisciplined soldiers or by mobs ⟨soldiers *looted* the town after it was captured⟩ **Burglarize** implies an act of breaking and entering by night in order to steal; usually, however, it carries, as *burglary* in law does not necessarily carry, an implication that one's purpose has been accomplished ⟨the house was *burglarized* while its occupants were asleep⟩
*Ana* *steal, pilfer, purloin, filch, lift: defraud, swindle, *cheat: despoil, pillage, sack, *ravage
**robber** thief, burglar (see under THEFT)
**robbery** larceny, *theft, burglary
**robe** *vb* *clothe, attire, dress, apparel, array
**robust** *healthy, sound, wholesome, hale, well
*Ana* *strong, sturdy, stout, stalwart: athletic, husky, *muscular, sinewy: *vigorous, energetic, lusty
*Ant* frail, feeble
**rock** *vb* *shake, agitate, convulse
*Ana* *swing, sway, undulate, oscillate: totter, quake, tremble (see SHAKE)
**rocket** *vb* *rise, arise, ascend, mount, soar, tower, levitate, surge
**rococo** *adj* *ornate, baroque, flamboyant, florid
**rodomontade** *bombast, rhapsody, rant, fustian
*Ana* boasting, bragging, vaunting (see BOAST *vb*): vainglory, vanity, *pride: magniloquence, grandiloquence (see corresponding adjectives at RHETORICAL)
**rogue** *villain, scoundrel, blackguard, knave, rascal, scamp, rapscallion, miscreant
*Ana* *vagabond, vagrant, tramp, hobo, bum: malefactor, culprit, delinquent (see CRIMINAL)
**roguish** *playful, frolicsome, sportive, waggish, impish, mischievous
**roily** *turbid, muddy
**roll** *n* *list, table, catalog, schedule, register, roster, inventory
**rollick** *vb* frolic, disport, sport, *play, romp, gambol

**rollick** *n* frolic, disport, sport, play, romp, gambol (see under PLAY *vb*)
**romantic** *adj* *sentimental, mawkish, maudlin, soppy, mushy, slushy
*Ana* fanciful, *imaginary, quixotic, fantastic, visionary: invented, created (see INVENT): picturesque, pictorial, vivid, *graphic
**romp** *n* frolic, rollick, gambol, disport, sport, play (see under PLAY *vb*)
**romp** *vb* frolic, rollick, gambol, disport, sport, *play
**room** *n* **1** Room, chamber, apartment all denote space in a building enclosed or set apart by a partition. **Room** is the word in ordinary use. **Chamber** is somewhat elevated; it is used chiefly of a private room, especially of a bedroom on an upper floor ⟨high in her *chamber* up a tower to the east—*Tennyson*⟩ ⟨he . . . hardly ever slept two nights successively in one *chamber*—*Southey*⟩ **Apartment** is decreasingly frequent in the sense of a single room ⟨her morning room was an airy *apartment* on the first floor—*Braddon*⟩
**2** Room, berth, play, elbowroom, leeway, margin, clearance can all mean enough space or scope for free movement. **Room**, the general term, often means sufficient or ample space for doing something (as working, growing or developing, sitting, passing, or entering or leaving) ⟨space is *room* . . . and *room* is roominess, a chance to be, live and move—*Dewey*⟩ But the word may also mean an occasion, an opportunity, or an opening that admits or permits something ⟨there is *room* for hope⟩ ⟨believing Mexico's behavior left no *room* for peaceful settlement—*Billington*⟩ ⟨in search of a wider naturalism which will find *room* for life, mind, and spirit within the scheme of nature—*Inge*⟩ **Berth**, basically a nautical term meaning maneuvering space for a ship, in more general use denotes a space kept between one and some source of potential danger ⟨an orderly place to which outlaws and criminals gave wide *berth*—*Holbrook*⟩ **Play** (see also PLAY, FUN) can specifically imply freedom of movement and action especially with reference to two or more things which must work together in close relation or without interference or conflict ⟨some *play* must be allowed to the joints if the machine is to work—*Justice Holmes*⟩ ⟨the free *play* of passion and thought . . . were crushed out of existence under this stern and rigid rule—*Dickinson*⟩ **Elbowroom** does not greatly differ from *room* except that it is somewhat more forceful and definitely implies freedom from interference or constraint as well as space for movement or for action ⟨which would give him more *elbowroom* to act against France—*Chesterfield*⟩ **Leeway**, basically a nautical term meaning the drift to leeward especially of a sailing vessel, in its closest extended sense means a falling off from the line of progress and therefore may connote something (as a shortage) to be made up ⟨Africa has been late in its emergence into modern civilization and it has still considerable *leeway* to make up—*Simnett*⟩ More frequently, however, *leeway* tends to mean room or margin for freedom of action ⟨educational programs . . . must allow *leeway* for interests which can develop into avocations—*Sat. Review*⟩ ⟨the president was given wide *leeway* in deciding what constituted a threat to public safety—*C. E. Black & K. D. White*⟩ ⟨he asked his creditors to allow him a little *leeway*⟩ **Margin** (see also BORDER) implies an amount (as of time, money, or material) additionally allowed or made available so as to provide for contingencies or emergencies which cannot be foreseen ⟨the King, in his instructions, left a wide *margin* of discretion to the generals—*Froude*⟩ ⟨an enormous *margin* of luxury . . . against which we can draw for our vital needs—*Lippmann*⟩ **Clearance** stresses lack of obstruction.

A colon (:) separates groups of words discriminated. An asterisk (*) indicates place of treatment of each group.

Typically it implies a carefully calculated amount of space between two physical objects such as the water level and the underside of a bridge, or a roadway and the underside of a viaduct above it, or a shaft and the hole into which it is fitted easily but not loosely ⟨the railway tunnel has just sufficient *clearance* to permit passage of the new freight cars⟩ Sometimes it may apply to intangible obstructions and then stress removal (as by the satisfying of legal or official requirements) rather than planned avoidance ⟨security *clearance* of those with access to secret atomic information—*Palfrey*⟩

**roost** *vb* perch, *alight, light, land

**root** *n* *origin, source, inception, provenance, provenience, prime mover
*Ana* beginning, commencing *or* commencement, starting *or* start (see corresponding verbs at BEGIN): foundation, basis, ground (see BASE)

**root** *vb* *applaud, cheer

**roseate** *hopeful, optimistic, rose-colored

**rose-colored** *hopeful, optimistic, roseate

**roster** *list, table, catalog, schedule, register, roll, inventory

**rot** *vb* *decay, decompose, putrefy, spoil, disintegrate, crumble

**rot** *n* *nonsense, twaddle, drivel, bunk, balderdash, poppycock, gobbledygook, trash, bull
*Ana* corrupt, vitiate, *debase: taint, *contaminate, pollute, defile

**rotate** 1 *turn, revolve, gyrate, circle, spin, twirl, whirl, wheel, eddy, swirl, pirouette
2 Rotate, alternate can both mean to succeed or cause to succeed each other in turn. **Rotate** may be used in reference to two or more persons or things; it implies indefinite repetition of the order of succession. Thus, persons *rotate* in jobs or offices when they periodically interchange their jobs or offices according, usually, to a predetermined scheme; one *rotates* crops who grows different things on the same land in successive seasons in an order calculated to maintain soil fertility or to enrich exhausted soil. **Alternate** differs from *rotate* in being referable only to two persons or things; though it also implies repetition of the order, it does not convey so strong a suggestion of continuity ⟨*alternate* workers on an exhausting job⟩ ⟨*alternate* hot and cold applications in the treatment of a bruise⟩ ⟨the weather *alternated* between blinding sandstorms and brilliant sunlight—*Cather*⟩
*Ana* interchange, *exchange, bandy: succeed, *follow, ensue

**rotter** *cad, bounder

**rotund** plump, chubby, portly, stout, *fleshy, fat, corpulent, obese
*Ant* angular —*Con* *lean, spare, lank, lanky, gaunt, rawboned, skinny, scrawny

**rough** *adj* 1 Rough, harsh, uneven, rugged, scabrous are comparable when they mean not having a smooth or even surface, exterior, or texture. **Rough,** the usual and comprehensive word, basically applies to whatever may be said to have a surface or an exterior which to the sense of touch or to the sight is not smooth but is covered with perceptible inequalities (as points, bristles, projections, or ridges) ⟨*rough* ground⟩ ⟨a *rough* block of stone⟩ ⟨the *rough* skin of chapped hands⟩ ⟨a *rough* tweed⟩ ⟨a *rough,* unshaved face⟩ Often when applied to materials and substances employed in the arts and in manufacturing, *rough* means lacking a final finish (as of polishing, smoothing, or dressing) ⟨a *rough* diamond⟩ ⟨*rough* steel⟩ ⟨*rough* lumber⟩ By extension the term applies also to things which impress another than the tactile sense or one's nerves or feelings as lacking in smoothness and evenness ⟨*rough*

words⟩ ⟨*rough* winds⟩ ⟨*rough* sounds⟩ ⟨he has had a *rough* time⟩ (see also RUDE). **Harsh** suggests a more definitely disagreeable sensation or impression than *rough;* when applied to what is felt with the hand, it implies a surface or texture that is distinctly unpleasant to the tactile sense ⟨a *harsh* fabric⟩ ⟨*harsh* sand⟩ or when applied to something heard, it suggests a rasping, grating quality ⟨*harsh* voices⟩ ⟨*harsh* din broke the fair music —*Milton*⟩ and when applied to something seen, tasted, or smelled, it suggests a character or quality that is offensive or repellent to a sensitive person ⟨a *harsh* liquor⟩ ⟨*harsh* features⟩ ⟨a *harsh* combination of colors⟩ Unlike *rough, harsh* in its extended senses seldom implies lack of polish or refinement, but rather it suggests a nature that is unfeeling, cruel, and indifferent to the pain it inflicts ⟨a *harsh* critic⟩ ⟨a *harsh* parent⟩ or when applied to things, effectiveness in promoting discomforts or in imposing rigors ⟨a *harsh* rebuke⟩ ⟨a *harsh* climate⟩ ⟨a *harsh* sentence⟩ **Uneven** applies either to surfaces or to lines and suggests a lack of uniformity in height through all the points of the surface ⟨an *uneven* road⟩ ⟨an *uneven* floor⟩ or a lack of straightness and the presence of curves or angles ⟨an *uneven* edge⟩ ⟨an *uneven* hem⟩ In extended use it implies a lack of uniformity especially in excellence or agreeableness in all the parts (as of a life, a performance, or a work of art) ⟨the artist's brushwork in this painting is *uneven*⟩ ⟨the trio's playing of the sonata was *uneven*⟩ **Rugged,** more often applied to persons so strong and healthy or machines so strongly made that they can survive great stress and strain, is not uncommonly employed in the sense of *rough;* in such use it applies chiefly to surfaces broken by ridges, prominences, gorges, and gullies that can offer serious difficulty to the traveler or worker ⟨a *rugged* road up a mountain⟩ or which (as in the case of faces or countenances) are gaunt, seamed, or heavy-featured and suggest strength or maturity ⟨any resemblance between you, with your *rugged* strong face and your coal-black hair, and this young Adonis—*Wilde*⟩ ⟨his face had already lost its youthful chubbiness, and was becoming somewhat like William's—rough-featured, almost *rugged*—*D. H. Lawrence*⟩ **Rugged** is also applicable to writing which has not been made smooth, flowing, and agreeable to the ear, sometimes, but not necessarily, through lack of care or skill ⟨the most *rugged*-seeming of prose dialogue, the kind . . . that people sometimes praise as "simply a page torn from the book of life"—*Montague*⟩ **Scabrous** applies basically to a surface that is rough to the touch though not necessarily uneven; in this sense it is a generic term including such species as *scaly, scurfy, scabby, thorny, prickly, knobby,* and *knotty* when applied to surfaces ⟨a *scabrous* leaf⟩ ⟨a *scabrous* hide⟩ In extended use *scabrous* applies chiefly to subject matter or to writings and works of art having subject matter that is prickly or thorny, or difficult to treat, often because it is offensive to the tastes or morals of the community ⟨what writer . . . has spoken more acutely on the somewhat *scabrous,* but none the less important subject of feminine "temperament"?—*Huxley*⟩
*Ana* hard, solid, *firm: *coarse, gross: *rank, rampant
*Ant* smooth
2 *rude, crude, uncouth, raw, callow, green
*Ana* brusque, crusty, gruff, curt, blunt, *bluff: ungracious, uncivil, discourteous, impolite (see RUDE): *indecorous, unseemly, indecent, indelicate
*Ant* gentle

**roundabout** *indirect, circuitous
*Ana* sinuous, *winding, tortuous, flexuous

**rouse** arouse, *stir, awaken, rally, waken

---

*Ana* analogous words      *Ant* antonyms      *Con* contrasted words      See also explanatory notes facing page 1

*Ana* enliven, *quicken, animate, vivify: stimulate, excite, *provoke: *incite, foment, instigate

**roustabout** *worker, workman, workingman, laborer, mechanic, artisan, operative, ˌhand, craftsman, handicraftsman

**rout** *n* *crowd, throng, press, crush, mob, horde

**rout** *vb* *conquer, vanquish, defeat, subdue, subjugate, reduce, overcome, surmount, overthrow, beat, lick

**route** *n* *way, course, passage, pass, artery

**route** *vb* forward, transmit, remit, ship, *send, dispatch

**rove** *wander, stray, roam, ramble, range, prowl, gad, gallivant, traipse, meander

**row** *n* *line, rank, file, echelon, tier

*Ana* series, sequence, *succession, train

**row** *n* *brawl, broil, fracas, melee, rumpus, scrap

*Ana* fight, affray, fray, combat, conflict, *contest: altercation, wrangle, *quarrel, squabble

**royal** regal, *kingly, queenly, imperial, princely

*Ana* *splendid, resplendent, glorious, superb: august, majestic, stately, imposing (see GRAND)

**rubbish** *n* *refuse, waste, trash, debris, garbage, offal

**rube** bumpkin, hick, yokel, clodhopper, clown, lout, *boor, churl

**rude** 1 Rude, rough, crude, raw, callow, green, uncouth mean deficient in the qualities that make for finish or for perfection in development or in use. **Rude,** as applied to men and their minds, suggests a comparatively low state of culture or a dearth of learning more often than savagery or barbarism, although it may suggest the latter ⟨like a *rude* and savage man of Ind—*Shak.*⟩ ⟨a *rude*, domineering, arrogant type of man, without cultivation or culture —*Shirer*⟩ As applied to the things which men make or do, *rude* suggests the makers' ignorance of technique or of proper materials, their inexpertness or inexperience or a deficiency of materials ⟨*rude* attempts at verse⟩ ⟨*rude* implements⟩ ⟨*rude* workmanship⟩ ⟨a *rude* hut⟩ ⟨our father Adam sat under the Tree and scratched with a stick in the mold; and the first *rude* sketch that the world had seen was joy to his mighty heart—*Kipling*⟩ **Rough** (see also ROUGH 1) usually suggests more harshness or violence than *rude* and a more culpable ignorance or inexperience. As applied to men and their manners, the term usually implies the absence of signs not only of polish and refinement but of gentleness, politeness, and often even civility. It does not, however, necessarily imply boldness, insolence, boorishness, or other unpleasant qualities ⟨a plain, *rough*, honest man, and wise, tho' not learned—*Addison*⟩ ⟨Phil was *rough* and frank . . . she had brought herself up in a hard school—*Sackville-West*⟩ ⟨use *rough* language⟩ As applied to men's works and products, *rough* suggests less lack of expertness or deficiency of materials than offhandedness, haste, or indifference to technique; it is typically applied to things which are not carefully made because they suffice for the purpose or are not yet finished, being in an early stage of a process or development ⟨make a first *rough* draft of a speech⟩ ⟨a *rough* guess⟩ ⟨the style of the work lost its polish, became *rough* —*Mailer*⟩ **Crude** may be applied to men and their acts, words, or products, but it gets its fundamental implications from its historically earlier application to things which have not been touched by man (as in processing, refining, or treating) and are as yet in their natural state or in an undeveloped state ⟨*crude* petroleum⟩ ⟨*crude* rubber⟩ Consequently when applied to men or their acts, words, or products, *crude* implies the far remove of what is so described from what is perfected, highly developed, or fully civilized ⟨*crude* colors⟩ ⟨*crude* methods⟩ ⟨a *crude* philosophy⟩ ⟨the guests . . . made a decorous beeline for the champagne. There was whisky and gin, too,

. . . for *cruder* palates—*Styron*⟩ **Raw,** which in the earliest of its present senses describes the condition of uncooked food, is often further applied to natural products which are gathered, mined, or otherwise removed from their native places but are not yet processed or are in the earliest stage of manufacture or processing; thus, *raw* silk names the fiber from the cocoons of the silkworm as it is drawn from them and reeled; *raw* hides are stripped from the carcasses of animals but are not yet tanned or dressed; *raw* milk is as yet unpasteurized; the *raw* materials from which the miller produces flour are various cereal grains ⟨the *raw* material of music is sound—*Day Lewis*⟩ As applied to men, their minds, or their product, *raw*, more than *crude*, suggests the elementariness of the untried and the inexperienced ⟨*raw* recruits⟩ ⟨compared with her, he felt vague and *raw*, incapable of coming to terms with life— *Sackville-West*⟩ ⟨over and over again he had seen her take some *raw* youth, twist him, turn him, wake him up; set him going—*Woolf*⟩ **Callow** is nearly always applied to youths or to those who retain the signs of immaturity in manhood; it usually suggests naïveté, simplicity, lack of sophistication, but not so strikingly as does *crude*, and its suggestions of inexperience or present unfitness are not so strong as those of *raw* ⟨souls and wits which have never got beyond the *callow* and boarding-school stage—*Arnold*⟩ ⟨an embarrassingly *callow* master of ceremonies—*New Yorker*⟩ ⟨in its *callow* days, modern science used to amuse itself by frightening the rest of us with its bogies—*Gauss*⟩ **Green** derives most of its connotations from *green* as applied to fruit and implying unripeness and unfitness for use. The term often comes close to *raw* when applied to persons and their abilities because it suggests inexperience and lack of necessary training ⟨employ *green* hands in a factory⟩ Often, however, it additionally connotes simplicity or gullibility ⟨he had not . . . allowed his young *green* jealousy to show itself in words or pique—*Buck*⟩ ⟨wasn't so *green* as to expect suspicious characters to look suspicious—*Chesterton*⟩ But *green* is also used of products or sometimes of the raw materials of manufacture or processing which are not yet fully seasoned or cured ⟨*green* liquors⟩ ⟨*green* pelts⟩ **Uncouth** retains from other senses a strong implication of strangeness ⟨*outlandish* meant in the beginning only what doesn't belong to our own land, and *uncouth* was simply "unknown"—*Lowes*⟩ and is appropriately applied to what seems strange in comparison to what is felt as normal or finished or excellent, whether because crude and clumsy especially in appearance ⟨though living in as refined a home as could be found in that part of the world, Breckinridge found conditions rough and *uncouth*—*Coulter*⟩ ⟨armored catfish . . . — *uncouth* creatures, with outrageously long feelers and tentacles, misplaced fins, and mostly ensconced in bony armor—*Beebe*⟩ or because lacking in polish and grace ⟨the inherent courtesy and tenderness of the untutored and *uncouth* human being—*Harrison Smith*⟩ ⟨artists who were rude and *uncouth*, yet possessed a high degree of technical skill and strong powers of imagination—*Eliot*⟩ or because deficient in cultivation and refinement ⟨people who are, though kind, still *uncouth* or inconsiderate; . . . uncouthness and inconsiderateness, are, however tolerable, nowhere agreeable qualities in a positive sense—*Brownell*⟩ ⟨they were unaccustomed, painfully *uncouth* in the simplest social intercourse, suffering, and yet insolent in their superiority—*D. H. Lawrence*⟩

*Ana* boorish, churlish, clownish, loutish (see under BOOR): rustic, *rural, bucolic: barbarous, savage, *barbarian: primitive, *primary, primeval

**2 Rude, ill-mannered, impolite, discourteous, uncivil, ungracious** can all mean not observant of the manners or forms required by good breeding. **Rude** suggests lack of delicacy or consideration for the feelings of others; it does not necessarily suggest lack of breeding, for it is applicable to persons of all stations or conditions. It usually stresses impudence, insolence, or a generally insulting manner ⟨a *rude* answer⟩ ⟨demanding an explanation of the *rude* familiarity with which Jim had treated him—*Anderson*⟩ **Ill-mannered** is a more general and less explicit term, and it seldom carries a suggestion of an intent to offend or insult such as *rude* usually carries; it is therefore applicable to a person, act, or utterance that shows ignorance of, indifference to, or a disregard of the proprieties ⟨the tone . . . seems to me as gratuitously *ill-mannered* as the sentence itself is foolish—*Corke*⟩ **Impolite, discourteous,** and **uncivil,** as the negatives of *polite, courteous, civil* (for all three, see CIVIL), imply merely the reverse of the care in observing the proprieties of good or formal society that is suggested by *polite* ⟨scientists may form schools of thought, but these can never become cults because there is always some *impolite* maverick pointing to some new unassimilated fact—*La Barre*⟩ or of the considerate, dignified politeness that is suggested by *courteous,* thereby implying something like rudeness ⟨the clergyman was much humiliated by the *discourteous* reply to his appeal⟩ or of the modicum of good manners that is suggested by *civil,* thereby implying an utter disregard of the decent consideration expected in social intercourse among civilized persons ⟨no profanity, Señor. We want nothing from you but to get away from your *uncivil* tongue—*Cather*⟩ **Ungracious** (compare GRACIOUS) stresses the lack of kindliness or courtesy resulting from awkwardness, callowness, surliness, or irritation ⟨an *ungracious* refusal⟩ ⟨an *ungracious* answer⟩ ⟨these criticisms of a book that is a labor of love and piety may seem *ungracious*—*Cohen*⟩
*Ana* brusque, curt, gruff, crusty (see BLUFF): *impertinent, intrusive, meddlesome: surly, crabbed (see SULLEN)
*Ant* civil: urbane

**rueful** dolorous, doleful, lugubrious, plaintive, *melancholy
*Ana* depressed, weighed down, oppressed (see DEPRESS): piteous, *pitiful: despairing, *despondent, hopeless

**rugged** *rough, scabrous, harsh, uneven
*Ana* robust, *healthy: burly, brawny, husky, *muscular: *rank, rampant: arduous, *hard, difficult
*Ant* fragile

**ruin** *n* **Ruin, havoc, devastation, destruction** are comparable when they mean the bringing about of disaster or what is left by a disaster. They are general terms which do not definitely indicate the cause or the effect yet suggest the kind of force operating to produce the kind of disaster involved. **Ruin** implies generally a falling or tumbling down and is applicable to anything that through decay, corruption, neglect, or loss is unable to maintain its wholeness or soundness and so gives way or falls apart; this idea underlies all of the many uses of the word ⟨the old castle has fallen to *ruin*⟩ ⟨this carelessness . . . was to be his *ruin*—*M. A. Hamilton*⟩ ⟨cases of hopeless *ruin* . . . in which the body has first been ruined through neglect or vice—*Eliot*⟩ ⟨the possessive instinct . . . when pushed too far becomes the cause of the *ruin* of . . . society—*Ellis*⟩ **Havoc** suggests an agent that pillages, despoils, or ravages and brings confusion and disorder with it ⟨appalled by the *havoc* and loss of life caused by the earthquake—*Crowley*⟩ ⟨he was now blockaded . . . for Agrippa had worked *havoc* with his sea communications—*Buchan*⟩ ⟨hookworms live a long, long time in the small intestine,

creating *havoc* all the while—*Heiser*⟩ **Devastation** basically implies a laying waste, usually of a widespread territory (as by war or a natural catastrophe) ⟨the terrible *devastation* wrought by the great tidal wave which followed the earthquake at Lima—*T. H. Huxley*⟩ but it also is applicable to something (as disease) that overwhelms the individual or his property or resources like a natural catastrophe ⟨those [letters] . . . make clear the *devastation* in her health that was soon to be revealed —*Ellis*⟩ **Destruction** implies an unbuilding or pulling down or apart, but, since it is used alike of material and of immaterial things, it may suggest not only demolition but a killing, an undoing, or an annihilation; also, although it often connotes a conscious attempt to pull down, it as often suggests rather an inevitableness or an irony in the effect produced ⟨an unjust society wreaks cruel if subtle imprisonments and *destructions* of personal energy—*Mailer*⟩ ⟨the *destruction* of a man's edifice [lifework] by his own instruments of construction—*Belloc*⟩
*Ana* disintegration, crumbling (see corresponding verbs at DECAY)

**ruin** *vb* **Ruin, wreck, dilapidate** can all mean to subject a person or more often a thing to forces that are destructive of soundness, worth, or usefulness. **Ruin** usually suggests a bringing to an end the structural or mental integrity, the value, beauty, or the well-being of something or of someone through such destructive agencies as weather, age, or neglect, through partial destruction by fire, flood, or collision, or through loss of something vital to happiness or success (as one's fortune, one's good name, or one's chastity) ⟨the storm has *ruined* the garden⟩ ⟨the firm's reputation was *ruined* by rumors⟩ ⟨there was in all of them [persons] something *ruined,* lost or broken—some precious and irretrievable quality which had gone out of them and which they never could get back again—*Wolfe*⟩ **Wreck** implies a ruining by or as if by crashing or being shattered. Basically it is used in reference to a ship, a train, a vehicle, or an airplane ⟨the ship was *wrecked* on the rocky coast⟩ In its extended sense *wreck* is often used in place of *ruin* when there is an intent to imply injury, often to something intangible such as one's career, one's credit, or one's prospects, past all hope of repair or of reconstruction ⟨his health was *wrecked* by dissipation⟩ ⟨their plans were *wrecked* by the unexpected change in weather⟩ When the pulling down of a building is implied, *wreck* is often preferred to *demolish* or *destroy* because it does not necessarily carry the suggestion implicit in those words of the uselessness of that which is left. **Dilapidate** historically implies ruin especially of a building, or of developed property, or of one's fortune or financial resources through neglect or through wastefulness; the term in such use carries, as the other terms do not, a strong implication of culpability ⟨men bent . . . upon intriguing for places at court, for salaries, and for fragment after fragment of the Royal fortune which they were *dilapidating*—*Belloc*⟩ ⟨the church . . . was . . . shamefully suffered to *dilapidate* by deliberate robbery and frigid indifference—*Johnson*⟩ In more general use *dilapidate* implies a shabby, run-down, and often tumbledown condition and is used chiefly in the past-participial form as an adjective ⟨negotiating the *dilapidated* and purblind vehicle over the curving roads—*Cheever*⟩ ⟨an aged man, traveling alone, and wearing the *dilapidated* look of a retired missionary—*Glasgow*⟩
*Ana* *destroy, demolish, raze: *deface, disfigure: *maim, mutilate, mangle

**rule** *n* *law, regulation, precept, statute, ordinance, canon
*Ana* order, mandate, dictate, *command: *principle, axiom, fundamental: etiquette, *decorum, propriety

---

*Ana* analogous words     *Ant* antonyms     *Con* contrasted words     See also explanatory notes facing page 1

**rule** *vb* **1** *govern
*Ana* *guide, lead: manage, direct, control, *conduct
**2** *decide, determine, settle, resolve
*Ana* conclude, judge, gather, deduce, *infer
**rule out** eliminate, debar, *exclude, shut out, suspend, disbar, blackball
*Ana* bar, block (see HINDER): *prevent, preclude, obviate
**ruminate** muse, meditate, *ponder
*Ana* *consider, weigh, excogitate: reflect, deliberate, speculate, cogitate, *think
**rummage** comb, ransack, search, hunt, *seek, scour, ferret out
*Ana* examine, inspect, *scrutinize
**rumor** *n* *report, gossip, hearsay
**rumpus** *brawl, broil, fracas, melee, row, scrap
**runt** *dwarf, pygmy, midget, manikin, homunculus
**rupture** *n* *breach, break, split, schism, rent, rift
*Ana* separation, division, parting, severance, divorce (see corresponding verbs at SEPARATE): estrangement, alienation (see corresponding verbs at ESTRANGE)
**rural, rustic, pastoral, bucolic** are comparable when they mean of or characteristic of the country as distinguished from city life. **Rural** is the most comprehensive term; in its widest meaning it implies open country whether uninhabited or sparsely settled; more narrowly it suggests agricultural pursuits or simple community life. In distinction from *rustic*, however, *rural* suggests the pleasant aspects of country life; *rustic* commonly implies a contrast with the refinements of the city or the town and often connotes rudeness or lack of polish ⟨he had no taste for *rural* loveliness, green fields and vineyards . . . but he would often have his tongue in his cheek at the simplicity of *rustic* dupes—*Stevenson*⟩ **Pastoral** and *bucolic* derive some or most of their connotations from the literary treatment of rural life. **Pastoral,** when it does not refer directly to the life of shepherds, suggests either green pastures and grazing sheep or a life primitive in its simplicity or idyllic in its peace and apartness from the world ⟨to *pastoral* dales, thin-set with modest farms—*Wordsworth*⟩ ⟨no more shall . . . Peace pipe on her *pastoral* hillock a languid note—*Tennyson*⟩ **Bucolic,** a curiously dichotomous word, may be a close synonym of *pastoral* in stressing the charm of rural environment and life ⟨there is here

a *bucolic* atmosphere of peculiar beauty and inspiration—*Sacheverell Sitwell*⟩ or may come close to *rustic* in emphasizing the crudity and lack of refinement of rural life or people ⟨to give up all the city's life . . . for the *bucolic* tedium of a Pennsylvania farm—he couldn't do it—*Wolfe*⟩
**ruse** *n* *trick, stratagem, maneuver, gambit, ploy, artifice, wile, feint
*Ana* chicane, trickery, *deception: expedient, shift, makeshift, *resource, resort
**rush, dash, tear, shoot, charge** can all mean to move or cause to move forward with speed. **Rush** suggests either impetuosity or intense hurry on account of some exigency, and often carelessness about the concomitant effects of the precipitate action ⟨*rush* for a train⟩ ⟨*rush* a research paper into print⟩ ⟨a flying rout of suns and galaxies, *rushing* away from the solar system—*Forster*⟩ ⟨business *rushed* forward into the glittering years—*Amer. Guide Series: Ind.*⟩ **Dash** is likely to suggest running or moving at a wild unrestrained top speed ⟨gyroscopically controlled trains that can make 150 miles an hour . . . and *dash* across an abyss on a steel cable—*Kaempffert*⟩ ⟨*dashed* on like a spurred blood horse in a race—*Byron*⟩ **Tear** in this sense may suggest extreme swiftness with impetus, violence, and abandon ⟨then he *tóre* out of the study—*Turnbull*⟩ ⟨disheveled atoms *tear* along at 100 miles a second—*Kaempffert*⟩ **Shoot** may imply the precipitate headlong rushing or darting of something impelled, as though discharged from a gun ⟨leaped to one side and out of reach of those wicked horns. The bull *shot* past—*Gipson*⟩ ⟨the Bridal Veil *shoots* free from the upper edge of the cliff by the velocity the stream has acquired—*Muir*⟩ ⟨*shooting* out in their motorcars on errands of mystery—*Woolf*⟩ **Charge** is likely to suggest a rapid, violent onslaught gathering forceful momentum calculated to overpower ⟨down we swept and *charged* and overthrew—*Tennyson*⟩ ⟨one morning he *charged*—he was a very burly man—into Rossetti's studio—*Osbert Sitwell*⟩
*Ana* *speed, hurry, hasten: dart, *fly, scud
**rustic** *rural, pastoral, bucolic
**ruth** *n* commiseration, compassion, pity, condolence, *sympathy, empathy
*Ana* *mercy, grace, charity, clemency, lenity: forbearance, tolerance, indulgence (see under FORBEARING)

# S

**sack** *n* *bag, pouch
**sack** *vb* *dismiss, discharge, cashier, drop, fire, bounce
**sack** *vb* pillage, despoil, spoliate, *ravage, devastate, waste
*Ana* plunder, *rob, loot, rifle: *destroy, demolish, raze: *strip, bare, denude
**sacred 1** *holy, divine, blessed, spiritual, religious
*Ana* dedicated, consecrated, hallowed (see DEVOTE): cherished, treasured, valued (see APPRECIATE)
*Ant* profane —*Con* secular, lay, temporal (see PROFANE)
**2 Sacred, sacrosanct, inviolate, inviolable** can all mean having such a character as to be protected by law, custom, tradition, or human respect against breach, intrusion, defilement, or profanation. **Sacred** (see also HOLY) implies either a setting apart for a special and often exclusive use or end ⟨among civilized peoples, property is regarded as *sacred* to its owner⟩ ⟨a fund *sacred* to charity⟩ ⟨the den was *sacred* to the father of the family⟩ or a special char-

acter or quality which makes the person or thing held sacred an object of almost religious veneration or reverence ⟨[Louis XIII] saw that the things which happened increasingly strengthened the Royal Office which was *sacred* to him—*Belloc*⟩ ⟨"Grief of two years' standing is only a bad habit." Alice started, outraged. Her mother's grief was *sacred* to her—*Shaw*⟩ **Sacrosanct,** which in technical religious use implies the utmost of holiness or sacredness, in its more general use may retain this implication ⟨the strikers . . . respected the *sacrosanct* character of the mails, and were willing to undertake their delivery to the pier—*Heiser*⟩ but often tends to suggest an imputed rather than a genuinely possessed character justifying freedom from attack or violation; its emphasis in such use is usually somewhat ironical and occasionally slightly derisive ⟨etymology is after all not *sacrosanct*—*Darrow*⟩ ⟨she rebuffed explanations . . . they intruded on her privacy, that closely guarded preserve—as *sacrosanct* as her bureau drawers—*Mary McCarthy*⟩ Inviolate and *inviolable* apply to things (as laws, principles, treaties, agreements, institutions, persons, places, or objects) that for one reason or another are secure from breach, infringement, attack, intrusion, or injury; the terms differ from each other chiefly in that **inviolate** suggests the fact of not having been violated while **inviolable** implies a character which does not permit or which distinctly forbids violation; thus, one holds a vow *inviolable* but keeps his vow *inviolate* ⟨what seemed *inviolable* barriers are burst asunder in a trice—*Meredith*⟩ ⟨the Navahos . . . believed that their old gods dwelt in the fastnesses of that canyon . . . an *inviolate* place—*Cather*⟩

*Ana* protected, shielded, defended, guarded (see DEFEND): revered, reverenced, venerated (see REVERE)

**sacrifice** *vb* abnegate, forbear, *forgo, eschew

*Ana* renounce, *abdicate: surrender, yield, resign, *relinquish

**sacrilege** desecration, *profanation, blasphemy

*Ana* defilement, pollution (see corresponding verbs at CONTAMINATE): violation, transgression, trespass, *breach: sin, crime, scandal, *offense

**sacrilegious** blasphemous, *impious, profane

*Ana* polluting, defiling (see CONTAMINATE): profaning, desecrating (see corresponding nouns at PROFANATION)

**sacrosanct** inviolate, inviolable, *sacred

*Ana* respected, regarded, esteemed (see corresponding verbs under REGARD *n*): revered, venerated, reverenced (see REVERE)

**saddle** *vb* *burden, encumber, cumber, weigh, weight, load, lade, tax, charge

**sadness, depression, melancholy, melancholia, dejection, gloom, blues, dumps** are comparable when they mean a state of mind in which one is unhappy or low-spirited or an attack of low spirits. Sadness is the general term; apart from the context it carries no explicit suggestions of the cause of the low spirits or of the extent to which one is deprived of cheerfulness ⟨a feeling of *sadness* and longing that is not akin to pain—*Longfellow*⟩ ⟨we feel his underlying *sadness* . . . but Rome may have felt more strongly than we do his hopefulness and pride—*Buchan*⟩ ⟨the leafless trees left her with unearned *sadness*. She mourned the long age before spring and feared loneliness in winter —*Malamud*⟩ **Depression** applies chiefly to a mood in which one feels let down, discouraged, and devoid of vigor or to a state of mind, usually outwardly manifested by brooding, in which one is listless, despondent, or sullen; the term usually implies a precipitating or predisposing cause which may be external but is as often inherent in the nature of the affected individual ⟨as for his look, it was a natural cheerfulness, striving against *depression* from without, and not quite succeeding—*Hardy*⟩ ⟨Tina's love was a stormy affair, with continual ups and downs of rapture and *depression*—*Wharton*⟩ ⟨a defeat would bring me closer to a general *depression*, a fog bank of dissatisfaction with myself—*Mailer*⟩ **Melancholy** often applies to a not unpleasant or displeasing mood or a mental state characterized by sadness, pensiveness, and deep but not depressing or heavy seriousness ⟨lend our hearts and spirits wholly to the influence of mild-minded *melancholy*—*Tennyson*⟩ ⟨the lively, curious mind, the wit, the gaiety of spirit tinged with a tender *melancholy*—*Hudson*⟩ ⟨fate did not bring her dreamed-of-love. Instead, it gave her cause for *melancholy*, disappointment, and disillusionment—*Farrell*⟩ ⟨in spite of her civic zeal, she had a taste for *melancholy*—for the smell of orange rinds and wood smoke—*Cheever*⟩ **Melancholia** may denote a disordered mental state characterized by a settled deep depression ⟨the excited phase is called mania and

its counterpart is known as *melancholia* . . . . The latter phase is marked by mournful and self-accusatory ideas and a countenance disfigured by despair—*Ellery*⟩ **Dejection** suggests especially the mood of one who is downcast, discouraged, or dispirited; the term differs from *depression* chiefly in its suggestion of an external cause and in its more frequent application to a mood than to a prolonged state of mind ⟨it was the last of the regiment's stay in Meryton, and all the young ladies in the neighborhood were drooping apace. The *dejection* was almost universal—*Austen*⟩ ⟨full of the *dejection* of a nice child whose toy has been snatched from its hand—*Tracy*⟩ **Gloom** applies either to the effect produced by melancholy, depression, dejection, or extreme sadness on the person afflicted or to the atmosphere which a person of low spirits or a depressing event creates; the term carries a suggestion of darkness and dullness and it further connotes lack of all that enlivens or cheers ⟨the leaden *gloom* of one who has lost all that can make life interesting, or even tolerable—*Hardy*⟩ ⟨the idea that I am being studied fills me, after the first outburst of laughter, with a deepening *gloom*—*Huxley*⟩ Blues and *dumps* are familiar, expressive terms for an attack of low spirits. **Blues** may suggest an acute attack of depression or melancholy which afflicts one almost as if an illness ⟨a fit of the *blues*⟩ ⟨I believe that the attack of intense *blues* which caught me in that moment would have taken weeks to shake off—*Ingamells*⟩ while **dumps**, usually in the phrase *in the dumps*, is more likely to suggest a deep sullen persistent dejection of spirits ⟨doleful *dumps* the mind oppress—*Shak.*⟩ ⟨where someone else would have been in the dolefullest *dumps* . . . this young fellow took it out in joking—*Overstreet*⟩

*Ana* *sorrow, grief, anguish, woe: despondency, despair, hopelessness, forlornness (see under DESPONDENT)

*Ant* gladness

**safe, secure** can both mean free from danger or apprehension of danger. Safe may imply that one has passed through dangers or has run some risk (as of injury or of being lost) without incurring harm or damage ⟨arrived home *safe* and sound after their long journey⟩ or it can apply to persons or possessions whose situation or position involves neither risk nor exposure to destruction or loss ⟨let the great world rage! We will stay here *safe* in the quiet dwellings—*Shelley*⟩ ⟨build shelters where the people might go to be *safe* from falling bombs⟩ ⟨he felt that his money was *safe* when it was in a bank⟩ ⟨sat in a niche of the tower where her somewhat faded beauty was *safe* from the sun —*Bemelmans*⟩ or to things (as highways, bridges, or vehicles, or as policies, actions, or courses) which are so constructed or designed that they expose one to few or no risks ⟨a *safe* harbor⟩ ⟨a *safe* fire escape⟩ ⟨a *safe* investment⟩ ⟨'tis never *safe* to despise an enemy—*Defoe*⟩ or to a cautious procedure which keeps one out of danger or free from the risk of making an error or blunder ⟨it is *safer* to generalize about institutions than individuals —*Levin*⟩ **Secure** in a few idiomatic phrases implies freedom from anxiety or apprehension of danger ⟨most people like to feel *secure*⟩ In more general use *secure* tends to stress freedom from anxiety not as merely a subjective state but as a frame of mind induced by grounds that are or appear to be good and sufficient. Sometimes the grounds are intellectual and imply sufficient evidence to establish the certainty of something that has been doubted ⟨send the author off to other publishers, *secure* in his belief that only an ugly moneyed attitude separates his work from the public—*Frugé*⟩ Sometimes the grounds are material, such as the existence of sufficient money, the possession or definite expectation of property, or a definite means of livelihood which enables one to live or

---

*Ana* analogous words    *Ant* antonyms    *Con* contrasted words    See also explanatory notes facing page 1

make a venture without fear, or the provision of safeguards or protective devices which make a thing safe to use or follow ⟨the offer of a partnership by making his future *secure* also made his marriage possible⟩ ⟨now that the foundations were in good repair they regarded the bridge as *secure*⟩ ⟨a provident, rather thoughtful people, who made their livelihood *secure* by raising crops and fowl—*Cather*⟩ ⟨an independent, stubborn man who knew what he wanted, a man who was firmly rooted, established, *secure* against calamity and want—*Wolfe*⟩ Often the term suggests not only a freedom from fear of danger but a position, condition, or situation free from all hazards ⟨has made a *secure* place for himself in the history of English poetry⟩ ⟨university graduates who had been unable to find suitable jobs or any *secure* place in normal society—*Shirer*⟩
*Ana* protected, guarded, shielded (see DEFEND): *reliable, dependable, tried
*Ant* dangerous —*Con* precarious, hazardous, risky, perilous (see DANGEROUS)
**safeguard** *vb* guard, shield, protect, *defend
*Ana* conserve, preserve, *save: secure, insure, *ensure, assure
**sag** *vb* *droop, wilt, flag
*Ana* sink, slump, subside, *fall, drop: *hang, dangle, suspend
**saga** *myth, legend
**sagacious** perspicacious, astute, *shrewd
*Ana* *sharp, keen, acute: penetrating, piercing, probing (see ENTER): *wise, judicious, sage, sapient
**sage** *adj* *wise, sapient, judicious, prudent, sensible, sane
*Ana* *intelligent, knowing, brilliant: *learned, erudite: sagacious, perspicacious (see SHREWD)
**sail** *vb* float, skim, scud, shoot, dart, *fly
**sailor** *mariner, seaman, tar, gob, bluejacket
**salary** *wage *or* wages, stipend, pay, hire, emolument, fee
**salient** conspicuous, outstanding, signal, striking, arresting, prominent, remarkable, *noticeable
*Ana* significant, important, weighty (see corresponding nouns at IMPORTANCE): impressive, *moving: obtrusive, intrusive (see IMPERTINENT)
**salubrious** *healthful, healthy, wholesome, salutary, hygienic, sanitary
*Ana* *beneficial, advantageous: benign, *favorable
**salutary** wholesome, *healthful, healthy, salubrious, hygienic, sanitary
*Ana* *beneficial, advantageous, profitable
*Ant* deleterious: evil
**salutation** *greeting, salute
**salute** *vb* *address, greet, hail, accost
**salute** *n* *greeting, salutation
**same**, selfsame, very, identical, identic, equivalent, equal, tantamount can mean either not different from the other or others or not differing from each other. Same may imply, and selfsame invariably implies, that the things under consideration are in reality one and not two or three different things ⟨this is the *selfsame* book that John once owned⟩ ⟨they go to the *same* summer resort year after year⟩ ⟨voted out of power . . . by the *selfsame* people who had put them into office in the first place—*Fairless*⟩ ⟨perhaps the *selfsame* owl that used to fly overhead—*Eve Langley*⟩ But *same* may also be applied to things actually distinct but with no appreciable difference in quality, kind, appearance, amount, or significance ⟨saw Wheeler riding in state in the great Dewey parade . . . in 1898, wearing the *same* uniform that Miles and Merritt wore—*Long*⟩ ⟨would be looked upon as one of the afterguard, and would eat the *same* rations as the captain—*Chippendale*⟩ Very, like *selfsame*, implies

complete absence of difference and therefore oneness in the things under consideration ⟨you are the *very* man I have been anxious to see⟩ ⟨that is the *very* thing that I was saying—*Shelley*⟩ ⟨here in this *very* town there was once a café—*McCullers*⟩ Identical (see also LIKE) implies either selfsameness ⟨I found it at the *identical* spot where I left it⟩ ⟨the authors of the anonymous *Waverley* and of the popular *Lady of the Lake* were found to be *identical*⟩ or absolute agreement in all details (as of quality, shape, and appearance) ⟨since the sculptures are *identical* one must be a replica of the other⟩ ⟨no two leaves from the same tree are *identical*⟩ ⟨twins that are *identical* develop from a single fertilized egg⟩ ⟨a thousand *identical* gaunt gray houses—*Rouéché*⟩ ⟨the same measures . . . may flow from distinct powers; but this does not prove that the powers themselves are *identical*—*John Marshall*⟩ Identic occurs chiefly in diplomatic or governmental use and like *identical* implies absolute agreement in all details ⟨the Allies sent *identic* answers to the ultimatum⟩ ⟨*identic* notes utilized by the powers in making joint representation to a government —*Stuart*⟩ Equivalent is used of things that amount to the same thing or are freely interchangeable in some respect (as worth, force, significance, or import) ⟨some heirs received their legacies in cash, some in real estate of *equivalent* value⟩ ⟨in economics, the *equivalent* of a beautifully composed work of art is the smoothly running factory in which the workers are perfectly adjusted to the machines—*Huxley*⟩ Equal implies complete correspondence (as in number, amount, magnitude, or value) and therefore equivalence but not selfsameness ⟨*equal* salaries⟩ ⟨*equal* quantities⟩ ⟨*equal* merit⟩ ⟨divide in *equal* shares⟩ ⟨the General . . . greeted Mrs. Churchill in English, and spoke it throughout the meal. To make things *equal*, I spoke French—*Sir Winston Churchill*⟩ Tantamount, otherwise identical with *equivalent*, is restricted in application to one of a pair of usually immaterial things that are in effect equivalent the one to the other (as in value, significance, or effect) ⟨such a movement . . . would be *tantamount* to a confession of failure —*Trollope*⟩ ⟨refusal to prolong the truce . . . would be *tantamount* to a threat—*Current Biog.*⟩
*Ana* alike, *like, akin, parallel, uniform
*Ant* different
**sample** *n* specimen, example, *instance, case, illustration
*Ana* piece, *part, portion, segment, fragment
**sanative** remedial, *curative, restorative, corrective
*Ana* salutary, hygienic, sanitary, *healthful: healing, curing, remedying (see CURE *vb*)
**sanctimonious** 1 pietistic, religious, *devout, pious
*Ana* see those at SANCTIMONIOUS 2
2 hypocritical, pharisaical, canting (see under HYPOCRISY)
*Ana* affected, feigned, simulated, counterfeited, assumed, pretended (see ASSUME): perfervid, fervid, ardent, fervent (see IMPASSIONED)
**sanctimony** *hypocrisy, pharisaism, cant
*Ana* pretending *or* pretense, simulation, feigning, counterfeiting, affecting *or* affectation (see corresponding verbs at ASSUME): enthusiasm, zealotry, fanaticism (see nouns at ENTHUSIAST)
**sanction** *vb* *approve, endorse, accredit, certify
*Ana* *authorize, license, commission: confirm, *ratify: *enforce, implement
*Ant* interdict
**sanctity** *holiness
**sanctuary** refuge, asylum, *shelter, cover, retreat
*Ana* safety, security (see corresponding adjectives at SAFE): protection, shielding *or* shield, guarding *or* guard

---

A colon (:) separates groups of words discriminated. An asterisk (*) indicates place of treatment of each group.

(see corresponding verbs at DEFEND)

**sand** *n* *fortitude, grit, backbone, pluck, guts
  *Ana* *courage, mettle, spirit, resolution, tenacity

**sane** *wise, judicious, prudent, sensible, sage, sapient
  *Ana* *rational, reasonable: right, *good: sound, cogent, convincing, compelling (see VALID)
  *Ant* insane

**sangfroid** phlegm, composure, *equanimity
  *Ana* indifference, unconcernedness *or* unconcern, aloofness, detachment (see corresponding adjectives at INDIFFERENT): self-possession, aplomb, self-assurance, assurance, self-confidence, *confidence

**sanguinary** *bloody, sanguine, sanguineous, gory

**sanguine** 1 also **sanguineous** *bloody, sanguinary, gory
  *Ant* bloodless
  2 assured, *confident, sure, presumptuous
  *Ana* *hopeful, optimistic: positive, certain, *sure
  *Ant* afraid

**sanitary** *healthful, hygienic, salutary, salubrious, healthy, wholesome
  *Ana* curing *or* curative, healing, remedying (see corresponding verbs at CURE): *effective, efficacious, effectual
  *Ant* noxious

**sanitize** disinfect, *sterilize, fumigate

**sap** *vb* undermine, enfeeble, *weaken, debilitate, cripple, disable
  *Ana* drain, *deplete, exhaust, impoverish: *ruin, wreck: *destroy

**sapid** *palatable, appetizing, savory, tasty, toothsome, flavorsome, relishing
  *Ant* insipid —*Con* vapid, flat, inane, jejune (see INSIPID): bland, *soft, mild

**sapient** sage, *wise, judicious, prudent, sensible, sane
  *Ana* *learned, erudite, scholarly: sagacious, perspicacious (see SHREWD)

**sarcasm** satire, irony, *wit, humor, repartee
  *Ana* incisiveness, trenchancy, bitingness, cuttingness (see corresponding adjectives at INCISIVE): mockery, taunting, derision (see corresponding verbs at RIDICULE)

**sarcastic,** **satiric, ironic, sardonic** can mean having or manifesting bitterness and power to cut or sting. A person, a mood, a remark, or an expression is **sarcastic** when he or it manifests an intent to inflict pain by deriding, taunting, or making ridiculous ⟨*sarcastic* comments on an actor's performance⟩ ⟨the atmosphere is less chilly and *sarcastic,* more warm and compassionate—*Orville Prescott*⟩ ⟨she was accepted . . . as one of them. The *sarcastic* nickname she had been tagged with, "Sweetness and Light," fell into disuse—*Wouk*⟩ A person or his utterance, expression, or spirit is **satiric** when he or it manifests the intent to censure someone or something by holding him or it up for ridicule and reprobation ⟨hers was the rarest of *satiric* gifts. She . . . could ridicule without wounding —*S.R.L.*⟩ ⟨all this comedy was filled with bitter *satiric* strokes against a certain young lady—*Thackeray*⟩ Not only a person or an utterance, mood, or expression but also a situation or an event may be described as **ironic** when he or it manifests the power to evoke amused but often startled or unpleasant reflection on the difference between what is said and what is intended or between what happens and what was aimed at or what was expected ⟨how his [Fielding's] *ironic* lightning plays around a rogue and all his ways!—*Dobson*⟩ ⟨how exquisitely *ironic* is the entertainment we can derive from our disillusions— *L. P. Smith*⟩ ⟨it is an *ironic* likelihood that had he written less he would be held in higher esteem—*D. S. Davis*⟩ A person or more often a person's smile, expression, or words may be described as **sardonic** when he or it manifests scorn, mockery, and derision ⟨an eccentric, gangling

man, whose *sardonic* wit somewhat compensated for his shallow mind—*Shirer*⟩ ⟨got a *sardonic* twist to his mouth, the way of a man who feels that the breaks are against him—*Mary Austin*⟩ ⟨came to the funeral, full of calm, *sardonic* glee, and without being asked—*Bennett*⟩ *Ana* biting, cutting, trenchant, *incisive: *caustic, scathing, mordant

**sardonic** ironic, satiric, *sarcastic
  *Ana* *bitter, acrid: deriding *or* derisive, mocking, taunting, ridiculing (see corresponding verbs at RIDICULE): *sinister, malign

**sate** *vb* *satiate, surfeit, cloy, pall, glut, gorge
  *Ana* *satisfy, content: *indulge, pamper, humor: gratify, regale (see PLEASE)

**satellite** *follower, adherent, henchman, partisan, disciple, sectary
  *Ana* sycophant, *parasite, favorite, toady, lickspittle, bootlicker, hanger-on: devotee, votary, *addict

**satiate,** **sate, surfeit, cloy, pall, glut, gorge** are comparable when they mean to fill or become filled to the point of repletion. Although both **satiate** and **sate** can imply no more than a complete satisfying, both terms more often imply an overfilling or an overfeeding so that there is no longer a pleasure in what once pleased or seemed desirable ⟨the ordinary Roman . . . *satiated* alike with the fervors of the democrats and the rigidity of the conservatives— *Buchan*⟩ ⟨I wondered even then if a few common words of explanation, a few sober words of promise, would not have satisfied the crowd, already *sated* with eloquence—*Repplier*⟩ ⟨so overwhelmed by information . . . that curiosity becomes *sated,* discrimination dulled— *W. R. Parker*⟩ **Surfeit** distinctly implies a feeding or supplying to excess with consequent nausea or disgust ⟨*surfeited* herself with candy⟩ ⟨*surfeit* a person with flattery⟩ ⟨readers *surfeited* with the . . . wild overstatements and wild understatements of public dispute— *Montague*⟩ ⟨if music be the food of love, play on; give me excess of it, that, *surfeiting,* the appetite may sicken, and so die—*Shak.*⟩ **Cloy** stresses the resulting disgust or boredom more than the surfeit which induces them ⟨and thus, with sinning *cloyed,* has died each Murgatroyd —*Gilbert*⟩ ⟨poetic wit itself is a rarity . . . . Large indiscriminate doses of it tend to *cloy—Horace Gregory*⟩ **Pall** differs from *cloy* only in its greater emphasis upon the loss of all power in something with which one is surfeited to challenge one's interest or attention or to whet one's appetite; the term therefore refers rather to things that tend to satiate than to the persons whose appetites or desires have been sated by such things ⟨there anguish does not sting; nor pleasure *pall—Keats*⟩ ⟨common sense does *pall* on a husband sometimes—*Deland*⟩ ⟨at that point the scene begins to *pall* and the senses dull. Defeat . . . can be as monotonous as tropical rain—*S. L. A. Marshall*⟩ **Glut,** like *surfeit,* implies excess in feeding or supplying but it stresses the consequent overloading rather than the extinction of appetite or desire; often it also suggests the stimulation of a greed that knows no limits except those imposed upon it by physical necessity ⟨its hunger was already all but *glutted,* and its purpose seemed to be, mainly, to kill—*C. G. D. Roberts*⟩ *Glut* may be used also in reference to impersonal things, implying merely an overloading, and carrying no suggestion of greed or satiation ⟨banks *glutted* with unpaid commercial paper—*Lehrman*⟩ **Gorge** usually implies the stimulation of greed but it distinctively suggests a glutting to the point almost of choking or bursting; the term therefore often implies the frustration rather than the satisfying of that greed ⟨*gorge* oneself with chocolate⟩ ⟨Dick fell upon eggs and bacon and *gorged* till he could *gorge* no

---

*Ana* analogous words      *Ant* antonyms      *Con* contrasted words      See also explanatory notes facing page 1

more—*Kipling*⟩ ⟨heaven can *gorge* us with our own desires—*Defoe*⟩
*Ana* \*satisfy, content: pamper, humor, \*indulge: gratify, regale (see PLEASE)

**satiny** silky, silken, velvety, glossy, \*sleek, slick

**satire** irony, \*wit, humor, sarcasm, repartee
*Ana* raillery, persiflage, \*badinage: lampoon, pasquinade, \*libel, skit: ridiculing *or* ridicule, deriding *or* derision, taunting (see corresponding verbs at RIDICULE)

**satiric** ironic, sardonic, \*sarcastic
*Ana* \*pungent, piquant, poignant: ridiculing, deriding *or* derisive, taunting, mocking (see corresponding verbs at RIDICULE): mordant, \*caustic, scathing

**satisfied** content (see under SATISFY)
*Ana* gratified, gladdened, pleased (see PLEASE): appeased, pacified (see PACIFY)

**satisfy** 1 **Satisfy, content** can both mean to appease desires or longings. The same distinctions in implications are also found in their corresponding adjectives **satisfied** and **content** or **contented**. **Satisfy** implies full appeasement not only of a person's desires or longings but also of his needs or requirements ⟨walks that *satisfy* a wish for exercise⟩ ⟨he was always ready to *satisfy* every one of her desires⟩ ⟨the bosses are able to maintain the required tension in their followers and at the same time can *satisfy* their lust for power in a most gratifying way—*Huxley*⟩ ⟨Flora was *satisfied*. She had done what she had hoped to do—*Gibbons*⟩ **Content** implies appeasement to the point where one is not disquieted or disturbed by a desire for what he does not have, even though every wish is not fully gratified ⟨he was *content* with the world, not because he thought reality good . . . but because he possessed immense imaginative resources with which to evade it—*Paulding*⟩ ⟨when I was at home, I was in a better place: but travelers must be *content*—*Shak.*⟩ ⟨my own garden must *content* me this year—*Quiller-Couch*⟩
*Ana* gratify, gladden, \*please: appease, \*pacify: \*satiate, sate
*Ant* tantalize
2 recompense, compensate, remunerate, repay, \*pay, reimburse, indemnify
*Ana* balance, \*compensate, offset
3 **Satisfy, fulfill, meet, answer** all can mean to measure up to a condition, a need, a claim, a hope, or a requirement. They are seldom interchangeable, however, without loss of precision or expressiveness or without violation of idiom. **Satisfy**, with this meaning (compare SATISFY 1), is used chiefly in reference to things or to persons considered impersonally which are submitted to a test (as a condition, a requirement, or a hypothesis) and found to be such in constitution or makeup as not to fall short ⟨there is one condition that a lyric ought to *satisfy;* it ought to pass the test of being read aloud—*Binyon*⟩ ⟨he will *satisfy* Newman's famous definition of a gentleman as one who never inflicts pain—*Montague*⟩ **Fulfill** usually connotes more than adequacy or richness and fullness of measure; also what is *fulfilled* is not determined by something calculable but usually by something indefinite or immeasurable (as expectations, hopes, desires, or needs) ⟨a son seldom *fulfills* his father's hopes⟩ ⟨the trip *fulfilled* all the claims made for it⟩ ⟨the objective of our country . . . is to achieve human decency to meet human needs and to *fulfill* human hopes—*A. E. Stevenson*⟩ **Meet** implies exact agreement with the test or measure and therefore usually connotes mathematical equivalence; thus, "the new machine *meets* expectations" is slightly more tempered praise than "the new machine *fulfills* expectations" ⟨we must expand the concept of conservation to *meet* the imperious problems of the new age—*Kennedy*⟩

⟨the grocer could once more *meet* his running expenses —*Malamud*⟩ **Answer** usually implies even more moderation in praise than *meet;* while it does not quite imply dissatisfaction it seldom connotes complete content ⟨this knife will *answer* the purpose⟩ ⟨his school grades *answered* his parents' expectations⟩ ⟨she could ask herself now . . . if any other reasonably attractive man would have *answered* as well in his place—*Glasgow*⟩
*Ana* \*prove, test, try, demonstrate: verify, substantiate, corroborate, \*confirm: \*match, equal, rival, approach, touch

**saturate** 1 \*soak, steep, impregnate, drench, sop, waterlog
*Ana* \*dip, immerse, submerge: \*absorb, imbibe, assimilate
2 impregnate, impenetrate, interpenetrate, penetrate, \*permeate, pervade
*Ana* \*infuse, imbue, ingrain, inoculate: penetrate, pierce, probe (see ENTER)

**saturnine** dour, gloomy, \*sullen, glum, morose, surly, sulky, crabbed
*Ana* grave, \*serious, solemn, somber, staid: taciturn, reserved, uncommunicative, \*silent
*Ant* genial: mercurial

**saucy, pert, arch** are comparable when they mean flippant and bold rather than serious and respectful in one's manner or attitude. **Saucy** is rarely strongly derogatory though it implies some degree of lack of proper respect ⟨a *saucy* pupil⟩ ⟨a *saucy* retort⟩ Usually it also implies piquancy and levity with a hint of smartness or of amusing effrontery ⟨a little *saucy* rosebud minx can strike death-damp into the breast of doughty king—*Browning*⟩ Sometimes it is applied also to birds and small animals on similar grounds ⟨some *saucy* puppies on their hind legs—*Ruskin*⟩ ⟨the mistle thrush is very bold and *saucy*, and has been known to fly in the face of persons who have disturbed the sitting bird—*Burroughs*⟩ **Pert** implies a saucy freedom that may suggest presumption or affectation rather than insolence ⟨a *pert* jackanapes, full of college petulance and self-conceit—*Smollett*⟩ ⟨a little upstart, vulgar being . . . with all her airs of *pert* pretension—*Austen*⟩ In some contexts the word carries additional implications (as of cleverness or sprightliness) found in its other senses ⟨a little, upright, *pert*, tart, tripping wight—*Burns*⟩ **Arch** usually implies roguish or coquettish audacity or mischievous mockery sometimes carried to the point that it seems forced or awkward ⟨simpering expressions and *arch* posturing—*Osbert Lancaster*⟩ ⟨Elizabeth . . . turned to him with an *arch* smile, and said—"You mean to frighten me, Mr. Darcy, by coming in all this state to hear me?"—*Austen*⟩
*Ana* flippant, frivolous, volatile, light-minded (see corresponding nouns at LIGHTNESS): intrusive, obtrusive, meddlesome, \*impertinent: brash, impudent (see SHAMELESS): piquant, snappy (see PUNGENT)

**saunter, stroll, amble** can all mean to walk slowly and more or less aimlessly, especially in the open air. **Saunter** suggests a leisurely pace and an idle and carefree mind ⟨*sauntering* about the streets, loitering in a coffeehouse —*Fielding*⟩ ⟨he had stepped out into the street well ahead of the man *sauntering* toward the doorway— *MacInnes*⟩ **Stroll** differs from *saunter* chiefly in its implications of an objective (as sight-seeing or exercise) pursued without haste and sometimes with wandering from one place to another ⟨then we *strolled* for half the day through stately theaters—*Tennyson*⟩ ⟨the notables of the town . . . *stroll* past with the dignity of Roman senators —*Huxley*⟩ **Amble** occasionally conveys the same implications as *saunter* or sometimes *stroll*, but it more often suggests merely an easy, effortless gait comparable to that

---

A colon (:) separates groups of words discriminated. An asterisk (\*) indicates place of treatment of each group.

of an ambling horse ⟨you were just *ambling* around that party, eating, drinking, carefree as a bird—*Wouk*⟩

**savage** *adj* **1** *fierce, ferocious, barbarous, inhuman, cruel, fell, truculent
*Ana* implacable, relentless, unrelenting, merciless, *grim: rapacious, *voracious, ravenous
*Con* gentle, mild, lenient (see SOFT): humane, benevolent, *charitable
**2** barbaric, *barbarian, barbarous
*Ana* primitive, primeval (see PRIMARY): *rough, harsh: untaught, untutored, *ignorant
*Con* *tame, submissive, subdued: ˙civilized, cultured (see corresponding nouns at CIVILIZATION)

**save** *vb* **1** deliver, redeem, *rescue, ransom, reclaim
*Ana* *free, release, liberate, emancipate: *defend, protect, shield, guard, safeguard: *recover, retrieve, recoup, recruit
*Ant* lose: waste: damn (*in theology*)
**2** Save, preserve, conserve can mean to keep free or secure from injury, decay, destruction, or loss. Save may imply measures taken to protect something from danger of loss, injury, or destruction ⟨they had her in a Sunday-go-to-meeting dress . . . never washed or worn, just *saved*—*Welty*⟩ ⟨*saved* his papers in a vault⟩ ⟨he wavered around an atomistic explanation of the world, yet held fast to the Biblical Creation, to *save* his orthodoxy—*H. O. Taylor*⟩ but, more often, it suggests rescue or delivery from a dangerous situation (see under RESCUE). Preserve stresses the idea of resistance to destructive agencies and hence implies the use of means to keep something in existence or intact ⟨old records are *preserved* by protecting them from light and moisture⟩ ⟨*preserve* food for winter use⟩ ⟨constitutions are intended to *preserve* practical and substantial rights, not to maintain theories—*Justice Holmes*⟩ ⟨there's nothing like routine and regularity for *preserving* one's peace of mind—*Dahl*⟩ Conserve, on the other hand, suggests keeping sound and unimpaired and implies the use of means to prevent unnecessary or excessive change, loss, or depletion ⟨a convalescent must *conserve* his energy if he is to make rapid progress⟩ ⟨our constitutional rights can be *conserved* only by an intelligent electorate⟩ ⟨the air is recirculated within the cabin in order to *conserve* heat—*Armstrong*⟩ ⟨sipped his coffee, made from his carefully *conserved* supply brought with him from England—*Bambrick*⟩
*Ana* *have, hold, own, possess, enjoy: *keep, retain, reserve
*Ant* spend: consume

**savoir faire** poise, *tact, address
*Ana* grace, dignity, *elegance: ease, *readiness, dexterity, facility: self-possession, self-assurance, aplomb, *confidence
*Con* awkwardness, clumsiness, ineptness, maladroitness, gaucherie (see corresponding adjectives at AWKWARD)

**savor** *n* *taste, flavor, tang, relish, smack
*Ana* *quality, property, character, attribute: peculiarity, individuality, characteristic, distinctiveness (see corresponding adjectives at CHARACTERISTIC): *impression, impress, print, stamp

**savory** *palatable, appetizing, sapid, tasty, toothsome, flavorsome, relishing
*Ant* bland (*to taste*): acrid (*in taste and smell*)

**saw** *n* *saying, adage, proverb, maxim, motto, epigram, aphorism, apothegm

**say** *vb* Say, utter, tell, state are comparable when they mean to put into words. Say often means merely to articulate or pronounce ⟨*say* the words after me⟩ ⟨the baby has not yet learned to *say* "mama" or "daddy"⟩ or is used in reporting something voiced ⟨he *said* over the telephone that he would be late in coming home⟩ ⟨"I am going now," he *said*⟩ Say may also imply the fact of putting in speech or in writing without necessarily suggesting the actual wording ⟨you must learn to *say* what you mean⟩ ⟨he meant what he *said*⟩ ⟨do as I *say* and everything will be all right⟩ Utter (see also EXPRESS) stresses the act of putting into speech or spoken words, often with reference only to the use of the voice and with no indication of motive or impulse in speaking ⟨she sat still, not *uttering* a single word⟩ ⟨just as the actor *uttered* his first speech⟩ ⟨he formed this speech with his lips many times before he could *utter* it—*Dickens*⟩ Tell (see also COUNT, REVEAL) carries no clear implication of whether what is said is put into speech or writing, for the stress is upon imparting an idea or thought and not upon the method used. Consequently *tell* may suggest a putting into spoken or written words, or it may connote an equally clear or forcible means of impressing an idea upon the mind of a person or of revealing a condition or a sequence of events ⟨I am *telling* you the truth⟩ ⟨the rocks *tell* the story of past ages⟩ State (see also RELATE) is often used in place of *say* when the added implication of clearness and definiteness is necessary ⟨perhaps I had better take this opportunity of *stating* he need have no expectations from me; all my money will go in public bequests—*Deland*⟩ ⟨one should know what one thinks and what one means, and be able to *state* it in clear terms—*Rose Macaulay*⟩
*Ana* pronounce, *articulate, enunciate: *express, voice,ˎ broach: *speak, talk: *declare, announce, proclaim: note, observe (see SEE): comment, animadvert, *remark: *explain, expound: cite, *quote, repeat: *assert, affirm, aver, avow, protest

**saying,**   saw, adage, proverb, maxim, motto, epigram, aphorism, apothegm can all denote a sententious expression of a general truth. A saying is a brief current or habitual expression that may be anonymous, traditional, or attributable to a specific source ⟨the *saying* is true, "The empty vessel makes the greatest sound"—*Shak.*⟩ A saw is an oft-repeated and usually traditional or old saying ⟨full of wise *saws* and modern instances—*Shak.*⟩ ⟨the old *saw* that ignorance is bliss—*M. W. Childs*⟩ An adage is a saying given credit by long use and general acceptance ⟨if there is verity in wine, according to the old *adage*—*Thackeray*⟩ ⟨there's an *adage* to the effect that a good horse eventually comes back to his best form—*Audax Minor*⟩ A proverb is an adage couched, usually, in homely and vividly concrete or figurative phrase ⟨accused (in the phrase of a homely *proverb*) of being "penny-wise and pound-foolish"—*Spectator*⟩ ⟨we hear, that we may speak. The Arabian *proverb* says, "A fig tree, looking on a fig tree, becometh fruitful"—*Emerson*⟩ A maxim offers a general truth, fundamental principle, or rule of conduct often in the form of a proverb ⟨the difference between principles as universal laws, and *maxims* of conduct as prudential rules—*Robinson*⟩ ⟨we have reversed the wise *maxim* of Theodore Roosevelt: "Speak softly and carry a big stick"—*Warburg*⟩ A motto is usually a maxim or moral aphorism adopted by a person, a society, or an institution as a guiding principle or as a statement of an aim or ideal ⟨William of Wykeham's old *motto* that "Manners makyth Man"—*Quiller-Couch*⟩ ⟨he adopted the maxim, "Napoleon is always right," in addition to his private *motto* of "I will work harder" —*George Orwell*⟩ The last three terms, *epigram, aphorism,* and *apothegm,* commonly imply known authorship and a conscious literary quality. An epigram gets its effectiveness from its terseness and a witty turn of phrase; it characteristically presents a paradox or a cleverly pointed antithesis ⟨what is an *epigram*? A dwarfish whole,

---

*Ana* analogous words     *Ant* antonyms     *Con* contrasted words     See also explanatory notes facing page 1

its body brevity, and wit its soul—*Coleridge*⟩ An **aphorism** is a pithy epigram that requires some thought ⟨when Mark Twain utters such characteristic *aphorisms* as "Heaven for climate, hell for society"—*Brooks*⟩ An **apothegm** is a sharply pointed and often startling aphorism such as Johnson's remark, "Patriotism is the last refuge of a scoundrel."

**scabrous** *rough, harsh, uneven, rugged
*Ant* glabrous: smooth

**scale** *vb* climb, mount, *ascend

**scamp** *villain, scoundrel, blackguard, knave, rascal, rogue, rapscallion, miscreant
*Ana* malefactor, culprit, delinquent, *criminal

**scamper** *vb* *scuttle, scurry, skedaddle, sprint
*Ana* *speed, hurry, hasten: *rush, dash, shoot

**scan** *scrutinize, examine, inspect, audit
*Ana* *consider, study, contemplate: observe, survey, remark, notice (see SEE)

**scandal** *n* 1 *offense, sin, vice, crime
*Ana* indignity, insult, *affront: offending *or* offense, outraging *or* outrage (see corresponding verbs at OFFEND): wrong, grievance, injury, *injustice
2 *detraction, calumny, slander, backbiting
*Ana* gossiping *or* gossip, tattling (see corresponding verbs at GOSSIP): maligning, defaming *or* defamation, traducing (see corresponding verbs at MALIGN)

**scanning** scrutiny, examination, inspection, audit (see under SCRUTINIZE)
*Ana* study, application, *attention, concentration: *oversight, supervision, surveillance: analysis, dissection (see under ANALYZE)

**scant** scanty, skimpy, scrimpy, *meager, exiguous, spare, sparse
*Ana* *deficient, defective: scarce, rare, *infrequent
*Ant* plentiful: profuse

**scanty** scant, skimpy, scrimpy, *meager, exiguous, spare, sparse
*Ana* *deficient
*Ant* ample, plentiful: profuse

**scarce** rare, uncommon, *infrequent, occasional, sporadic
*Ana* *deficient: curtailed, abridged, shortened (see SHORTEN)
*Ant* abundant

**scare** *vb* alarm, *frighten, fright, terrify, terrorize, startle, affray, affright
*Ana* daunt, appall, *dismay: *intimidate, cow, browbeat: astound, amaze, flabbergast, astonish, *surprise
*Ant* entice

**scathing** *caustic, mordant, acrid
*Ant* scorching, searing, burning (see BURN): *fierce, ferocious, truculent, savage: *incisive, biting, cutting, trenchant

**scatter** 1 Scatter, disperse, dissipate, dispel can mean to cause a group, mass, or assemblage to separate or break up. **Scatter** may imply the use or operation of force which drives the persons or things in different directions ⟨the hurricane *scattered* the ships of the fleet⟩ ⟨the heavy assault *scattered* the troops⟩ ⟨the wind *scattered* the leaves⟩ ⟨but the whip—in fancy he cracked it aloft and sent his adversaries *scattering*—*Hervey*⟩ On the other hand, *scatter* may imply little more than throwing or casting so that the things thrown will fall by or as if by chance ⟨*scatter* pennies⟩ ⟨*scatter* seeds⟩ **Disperse** usually implies a wider separation of the units than *scatter* and a complete breaking up of the mass or assemblage ⟨the rain quickly *dispersed* the crowd⟩ ⟨in a few years, the Bureau was dismembered, its staff *dispersed*—*Heiser*⟩ ⟨a sea where all the ships in the world might be so *dispersed* as that none should see another—*Cowper*⟩

**Dissipate** suggests definitely the idea of complete disintegration or dissolution (as by evaporation, crumbling, squandering, or blowing away) and consequent vanishing ⟨the sun *dissipates* the mist⟩ ⟨*dissipated* her energy in futile efforts⟩ ⟨from the far-off wooded hills the haze . . . had not yet *dissipated*—*D. H. Lawrence*⟩ ⟨had a small patrimony . . . that he *dissipated* before he left college —*Meredith*⟩ **Dispel** carries less suggestion of separation of units or particles than any of these words but it stresses a driving away as if by scattering of something that clouds, confuses, or bothers ⟨the rising sun *dispelled* the darkness⟩ ⟨a blind man whose darkness no street lamp can dispel—*Shaw*⟩ ⟨truth and frankness *dispel* difficulties —*Russell*⟩ ⟨if there were any lingering doubts in his mind they were *dispelled* by an incident which occurred . . . on February 17—*Shirer*⟩
*Ana* *throw, cast, fling, toss: *distribute, dispense, divide: *discard, shed, cast
*Con* *accumulate, amass, hoard: collect, *gather, assemble: *compact, concentrate
2 *strew, straw, broadcast, sow
*Ana* *spread, disseminate: *sprinkle, besprinkle

**scent** *n* *smell, odor, aroma
*Ana* emanation, issuing *or* issue (see corresponding verbs at SPRING)

**schedule** *n* 1 *list; table, catalog, register, roll, roster, inventory
2 *program, timetable, agenda

**scheme** *n* 1 *plan, design, plot, project
*Ana* *proposal, proposition: arrangement, ordering (see corresponding verbs at ORDER): *device, contrivance: expedient, shift, makeshift (see RESOURCE)
2 *system, network, complex, organism, economy
*Ana* organization, arrangement, ordering (see corresponding verbs at ORDER): whole, total, *sum

**scheme** *vb* plan, design, plot, project (see under PLAN *n*)
*Ana* propose, purpose, *intend: *aim, aspire: manipulate, *handle, swing, wield

**schism** split, rupture, *breach, break, rent, rift
*Ana* division, separation, severance (see corresponding verbs at SEPARATE): estrangement, alienation (see corresponding verbs at ESTRANGE): *discord, dissension

**schismatic** *n* *heretic, sectarian, dissenter, nonconformist

**scholarly** *learned, erudite
*Ana* academic, scholastic, *pedantic: abstruse, *recondite: accurate, exact, precise (see CORRECT)

**scholarship** learning, erudition, *knowledge, science, information, lore

**scholastic** academic, *pedantic, bookish
*Ana* *conversant, versed: *dry, arid: formal, conventional (see CEREMONIAL)

**school** *vb* discipline, train, *teach, instruct, educate
*Ana* *practice, exercise, drill: *guide, lead: *conduct, control, direct, manage

**science** 1 *knowledge, learning, erudition, scholarship, information, lore
2 *art

**scintillate** *flash, gleam, glance, glint, sparkle, glitter, glisten, coruscate, twinkle

**scoff**, jeer, gibe, fleer, gird, sneer, flout can all mean to show one's scorn or contempt in derision or mockery. **Scoff** stresses insolence, irreverence, lack of respect, or incredulity as the motives for one's derision or mockery ⟨it is an easy thing to *scoff* at any art or recreation; a little wit mixed with ill nature, confidence, and malice, will do it—*Walton*⟩ ⟨fools, who came to *scoff*, remained to pray—*Goldsmith*⟩ ⟨in jesting mood his comrades heard his tale, and *scoffed* at it—*Lowell*⟩ **Jeer** carries a stronger implication of loud derisive laughter than *scoff*; it usually

A colon (:) separates groups of words discriminated. An asterisk (*) indicates place of treatment of each group.

connotes a coarser and more vulgar or, at least, a less keenly critical attitude than *scoff* ⟨how does it come that men . . . walk in its streets and *jeer* and speak their hate —*Keesing*⟩ ⟨unsuccessful experiments had been *jeered* down with an I-told-you-so that rang from coast to coast —*Dos Passos*⟩ ⟨inclined to *jeer* at those slightly older than himself who show any tendency to abandon the —to him—rational preoccupations of childhood—*Krutch*⟩ **Gibe** stresses taunting, often in derisive sarcasm, sometimes in good-natured raillery ⟨you . . . with taunts did *gibe* my missive out of audience—*Shak.*⟩ ⟨after one of her visitations you *gibed* each other good-naturedly over the extent to which you found yourself shifted from the firm ground of reasoned conclusion—*Mary Austin*⟩ ⟨generosity of spirit which had prevented him from *gibing* at individuals for characteristics beyond their control—*Gwethalyn Graham*⟩ **Fleer** throws the emphasis upon derisive grins, grimaces, and laughs rather than on utterances ⟨look like two old maids of honor got into a circle of *fleering* girls and boys—*Gray*⟩ ⟨he listened with a *fleering* mouth to his father's long dogmatic grace before meat—*Hergesheimer*⟩ **Gird** implies an attack marked by scoffing, gibing, or jeering ⟨the subprior was bidden to sing . . . the "Elegy of the Rose"; the author *girding* cheerily at the clerkly man's assumed ignorance of such compositions—*Pater*⟩ ⟨it worked off steam and got its comedy largely by *girding* at the great ones of the past— *Times Lit. Sup.*⟩ **Sneer** carries the strongest implication of cynicism and ill-natured contempt of any of these terms; it often suggests the use of irony or satire the real purport of which is indicated by an insultingly contemptuous facial expression, tone of voice, or manner of phrasing ⟨it has become . . . fashionable to *sneer* at economics and emphasize "the human dilemma"—*Mailer*⟩ ⟨people are nowadays so cynical—they *sneer* at everything that makes life worth living—*L. P. Smith*⟩ **Flout** may imply any of the actions suggested by the preceding terms, but it carries a heightened implication not only of disdain and contempt but of refusal to heed or of a denial of a thing's truth or power ⟨that bids him *flout* the law he makes, that bids him make the law he *flouts*—*Kipling*⟩ ⟨no form of Christianity which *flouts* science is in the true line of progress—*Inge*⟩ ⟨for the past eight years they had watched an administration purposely *flout* the intellectual life—*Michener*⟩
*Ana* *ridicule, deride, mock, taunt: scorn, disdain, scout, contemn, *despise

**scold** *n* shrew, vixen, termagant, *virago, amazon

**scold** *vb* Scold, upbraid, rate, berate, tongue-lash, jaw, bawl, chew out, wig, rail, revile, vituperate can all mean to reprove, reproach, or censure angrily, harshly, and more or less abusively. **Scold,** the term most common in ordinary use, usually implies a rebuking in a mood of irritation or ill temper, with or without sufficient justification ⟨his father *scolded* him for staying out late⟩ ⟨our great authors have *scolded* the nation more than they praised it. Often their *scolding* has been . . . wholly justified, but often too it has been eccentric or ill-informed—*Malcolm Cowley*⟩ **Upbraid** stresses reproaching or censuring on more definite grounds than *scold* does and usually suggests justification or justifiable anger ⟨the judge *upbraided* the parents for the delinquency of their children⟩ ⟨I think he'd meant to *upbraid* me for sneaking off, but he didn't—*Cather*⟩ ⟨he had so often *upbraided* her for her superficiality— *Sackville-West*⟩ **Rate** and the more common **berate** usually imply more or less prolonged, angry, and sometimes abusive scolding either in censuring or in reprimanding ⟨the voice continued violently *rating* me —*Hudson*⟩ ⟨hearing Ed Hall *berate* a farmer who doubted

the practicability of the machine—*Anderson*⟩ Fairly close synonyms of *rate* and *berate* are the expressive **tongue-lash** which stresses the punitive effect on the person berated ⟨*tongue-lashed* them in a way that could be heard blocks off—*Fast*⟩ ⟨suffer from a fifteen-minute *tongue-lashing*⟩ and the crude terms **jaw, bawl,** usually with *out,* **chew out,** and **wig** (chiefly British), which emphasize the noisy prolonged ranting which usually attends a berating ⟨I have been *jawed* for letting you go —*Marryat*⟩ ⟨you'll get *bawled* out when you pull a boner —*Mathewson*⟩ ⟨some niggling Quartermaster lieutenant *chewed* them *out* because they were a few hundred cases short—*Liebling*⟩ ⟨a subordinate . . . who presumably had been severely *wigged* by his chief—*The Times*⟩ **Rail** carries a more definite implication of either abusive or scoffing language than *rate* or *berate* ⟨enemies . . . *rail* at him for crimes he is not guilty of—*Junius*⟩ ⟨the couples *railed* at the chant and the frown of the witchmen lean, and laughed them down—*Lindsay*⟩ **Revile** carries a much stronger implication of abusive, scurrilous language than *rail* does but little, if any, suggestion of scoffing; it often also implies deliberate vilification ⟨the words humiliated her, the tone *reviled* her . . . they were the clashes of naked hate—*Farrell*⟩ ⟨her tenants, who have to earn the money she spends abroad . . . *revile* her as a fugitive and an absentee—*Shaw*⟩ **Vituperate** implies more violence in the censure and in the method of attack than does *revile,* but otherwise they are close synonyms ⟨he *vituperated* from the pulpit the vices of the court— *Froude*⟩ ⟨the last image that crossed his mind was Sir James with his angry face and his trembling hands *vituperating* him—*Archibald Marshall*⟩
*Ana* reprehend, reprobate, censure, blame, *criticize: reproach, reprimand, *reprove, rebuke, admonish, chide: *execrate, objurgate

**scoop** *vb* *dip, bail, ladle, spoon, dish

**scope** *range, gamut, reach, radius, compass, sweep, orbit, horizon, ken, purview
*Ana* *expanse, amplitude, spread, stretch: *field, domain, sphere, territory, province: extent, area, *size

**scorch** *vb* *burn, char, sear, singe
*Ana* *wither, shrivel

**scorn** *n* disdain, contempt, despite (see under DESPISE)
*Ana* superciliousness, insolence, disdainfulness (see corresponding adjectives at PROUD): scoffing, flouting, jeering, gibing (see SCOFF): deriding *or* derision, ridiculing *or* ridicule, taunting, mocking *or* mockery (see corresponding verbs at RIDICULE)

**scorn** *vb* disdain, scout, *despise, contemn
*Ana* repudiate, spurn, reject (see DECLINE *vb*): flout, *scoff, jeer, gibe: deride, mock, taunt, *ridicule

**Scotch, Scottish, Scots** can all apply to what constitutes, belongs to, or derives from Scotland or its people. **Scotch** is most widely used outside Scotland, especially in the spoken language ⟨the entire *Scotch* people⟩ ⟨the inconvenience of having nothing in England like the *Scotch* one-pound note—*Todd*⟩ ⟨a schism in the *Scotch* Church —*Justice Holmes*⟩ ⟨the overwhelming proportion being English, *Scotch,* or Irish in descent—*Carnegie Mag.*⟩ ⟨a *Scotch* painter⟩ ⟨not all the Scottish names that survive today are truly *Scotch* in origin—*Mencken*⟩ **Scottish** has a more literary, less casual flavor and use ⟨the zest, courage, and good humor of the nineteenth-century *Scottish* author are infectious—*Bloom*⟩ ⟨she left for Edinburgh the following year to assume the *Scottish* crown —*Bruun & Commager*⟩ ⟨the *Scottish* Universities— *Winant*⟩ ⟨*Scottish* literature⟩ **Scots** is used in the same way as *Scottish* ⟨the names of *Scots* and English shipowners—*Conrad*⟩ ⟨a *Scots* writer—*H. M. Jones*⟩ except

---

*Ana* analogous words   *Ant* antonyms   *Con* contrasted words   See also explanatory notes facing page 1

that *Scots* is sometimes preferred in reference to law and in historical references to money ⟨a pound *Scots*⟩ In Scotland itself *Scottish* and *Scots* are often preferred to *Scotch* ⟨a delegation of *Scottish* editors—*The Scotsman*⟩ ⟨*Scottish* cricket—*The Scotsman*⟩ ⟨the *Scots* community in New York—*The Scotsman*⟩ ⟨new *Scots* air link—*The Scotsman*⟩ but *Scotch* also is used ⟨the signs confirmed my recollection that the *Scotch* Scotch are not ashamed of the word *Scotch* and do not go about protesting that *Scottish* and *Scots* are preferable forms —*Liebling*⟩ especially with regard to the products of Scotland ⟨wool jersey . . . and *Scotch* tweeds are favorite fabrics—*Women's Wear Daily*⟩

**Scottish, Scots** *adj* *Scotch

**scoundrel** *villain, blackguard, knave, rascal, rogue, scamp, rapscallion, miscreant
*Ana* *criminal, felon, malefactor, culprit

**scour** *vb* *seek, search, hunt, ransack, rummage, comb, ferret out
*Ana* investigate (see corresponding noun at INQUIRY): *scrutinize, inspect, examine: range, roam, rove, *wander

**scout** *vb* scorn, *despise, contemn, disdain
*Ana* flout, *scoff, sneer, jeer: deride, taunt, mock, *ridicule

**scowl** *vb* *frown, glower, lower, gloom
*Ana* glare, stare, *gaze

**scrap** *vb* *discard, junk, cast, shed, molt, slough

**scrap** *n* *brawl, broil, fracas, melee, row, rumpus
*Ana* *quarrel, altercation, squabble, wrangle: fight, affray, fray, combat (see CONTEST)

**scrape** *vb* **Scrape, scratch, grate, rasp, grind** are comparable when they mean to apply friction to something by rubbing it with or against a thing that is harsh, rough, or sharp. **Scrape** usually implies the removal of something from a surface with an edged instrument; the term then commonly suggests a purpose (as erasing, smoothing, or freeing from dirt, paint, skin, or peel). Additionally the term commonly implies the making of a distinctive and often unpleasant sound ⟨*scrape* the dishes before washing⟩ ⟨*scrape* potatoes⟩ ⟨*scrape* off paint⟩ ⟨a twinge that *scraped* upon the very parchment of his soul as a lead pencil upon a slate—*Powys*⟩ ⟨chairs were *scraped* along the floor—*Anderson*⟩ **Scratch** differs from *scrape* in its common implication of less purposiveness in the agent and of definite damage to the thing that is scratched; it usually also suggests the use of a pointed rather than an edged instrument which gouges a line or furrow in a surface and seldom stresses the noise produced ⟨a substance hard enough to *scratch* glass⟩ ⟨*scratched* by the thorns of a rose⟩ ⟨*scratch* a mosquito bite⟩ ⟨this pen *scratches*⟩ ⟨his wooden plow scarcely more than *scratched* the surface of the earth—*A. R. Williams*⟩ **Grate** usually stresses the harsh sound or the sensation of harshness made by rubbing something with or against a rough indented or cutting surface (as of a file); the term implies removal of material from a body in particles, and in itself as distinct from context suggests nothing about the aims or effects (as abrasion, wearing or rubbing away, or pulverization) ⟨*grate* nutmeg⟩ ⟨*grate* cheese⟩ Often *grate* implies little more than a harsh or creaking sound made by friction ⟨a key *grated* in the lock⟩ ⟨till *grates* her keel upon the shallow sand—*Byron*⟩ In extended use the term tends to be used in reference to things that irritate, exasperate, or harass with the implication that their effect is like the harsh sound or the sensation of harshness characteristic of a physical grating ⟨an unctuous heartiness . . . which *grated* upon David's ear—*Turnbull*⟩ **Rasp** usually implies a harsher or rougher and more disagreeable effect than either *scrape* or *grate*. It may suggest

the use of or as if of a rough instrument (as a coarse file called a *rasp*) or of something equally effective or as trying to the nerves ⟨thin a stick by *rasping*⟩ ⟨these rocks are known to have their angles *rasped* off, and to be fluted and scarred by the ice—*Tyndall*⟩ ⟨her hard, metallic voice had *rasped* the invalid's nerves—*Carey*⟩ ⟨when you laid a tight hold on your fiddlestick . . . you could do nothing but *rasp*—*Shaw*⟩ **Grind** implies a sharpening of the edge or point of a tool or weapon or the smoothing of a surface (as of glass) by friction; in both uses the sound made in the act of grinding is often stressed ⟨I have *ground* the axe myself; do you but strike the blow —*Shak.*⟩ ⟨*grind* lenses for eyeglasses⟩ In extended use the word often implies a wearing down by friction and also often suggests a particularly harsh or rough method of gaining one's ends or of making one's way ⟨laws *grind* the poor, and rich men rule the law—*Goldsmith*⟩ ⟨we went aground—*grinding, grinding*, till the ship trembled in every timber—*Martineau*⟩
*Ana* *erase, efface, delete: remove (see MOVE): *rid, clear: *abrade, chafe, excoriate

**scrape** *n* *predicament, dilemma, quandary, plight, fix, jam, pickle
*Ana* *difficulty, vicissitude: perplexity, bewilderment, distraction (see corresponding verbs at PUZZLE): embarrassment, discomfiture (see corresponding verbs at EMBARRASS)

**scratch** *vb* *scrape, grate, rasp, grind
*Ana* *tear, rend: *injure, damage, mar, impair, hurt: *deface, disfigure

**scrawny** skinny, lank, lanky, *lean, spare, gaunt, rawboned, angular
*Ana* *thin, slim, slender: *meager, exiguous
*Ant* brawny: fleshy: obese

**scream** *vb* shriek, screech, yell, *shout, squeal, holler, whoop
*Ana* pierce, penetrate (see ENTER): vent, utter, voice, *express, air

**scream** *n* shriek, screech, yell, shout, squeal, holler, whoop (see under SHOUT *vb*)

**screech** *vb* scream, shriek, yell, *shout, squeal, holler, whoop

**screech** *n* scream, shriek, yell, shout, squeal, holler, whoop (see under SHOUT *vb*)

**screen** *vb* *hide, conceal, secrete, cache, bury, ensconce
*Ana* *defend, protect, shield, guard, safeguard: *disguise, dissemble, cloak, mask, camouflage

**scrimpy** *meager, scanty, scant, skimpy, exiguous, spare, sparse
*Ana* *thin, slight, slender, slim: niggardly, *stingy, penurious, parsimonious

**scruple** *n* demur, *qualm, compunction
*Ana* *hesitation, hesitancy: doubt, *uncertainty, suspicion, mistrust: misgiving, *apprehension

**scruple** *vb* *demur, balk, jib, shy, boggle, stickle, stick, strain
*Ana* *hesitate, waver, falter, vacillate: *object, protest

**scrupulous** 1 meticulous, punctilious, punctual, *careful
*Ana* fastidious, particular, finicky, fussy (see NICE): exact, accurate, precise (see CORRECT)
*Ant* remiss
2 conscientious, *upright, honest, just, honorable
*Ana* *moral, ethical, righteous, virtuous, noble: *rigid, rigorous, strict
*Ant* unscrupulous

**scrutinize,** scan, inspect, examine, audit can all mean to look at or over critically and searchingly. The same distinctions in implications and connotations are observable in their corresponding nouns **scrutiny, scanning,**

---

A colon (:) separates groups of words discriminated. An asterisk (*) indicates place of treatment of each group.

inspection, examination, and audit. Scrutinize and scrutiny imply close observation and attention to minute detail ⟨scores of plain-dress detectives closely *scrutinized* the bidden guests as they arrived—*Lucius Beebe*⟩ ⟨living among the absurd magpie *scrutinies* of wife, children, colleagues, patients . . . most analysts are obliged to be more proper than proper—*Mailer*⟩ Scan and scanning are usually employed in reference to something that is surveyed from point to point; the terms may imply careful observation or study but sometimes imply the opposite and suggest a cursory glancing from one point to another; thus, to *scan* the newspaper each morning may admit of either interpretation. Only a context can make the implication clear ⟨the more one *scans* the later pages of Mark Twain's history the more one is forced to the conclusion that there was something gravely amiss with his inner life—*Brooks*⟩ ⟨*scanned*, with raised brows, yesterday's Jewish paper that he had already thoroughly read—*Malamud*⟩ ⟨a quick *scanning* of the items will help you—*S. L. Payne*⟩ Inspect and inspection in general use often imply little more than a careful observation ⟨he had perched himself upon the edge of the desk . . . and was absorbed in an unabashed *inspection* of her—*Hervey*⟩ but in legal, military, governmental, and industrial use they imply a searching scrutiny for possible errors, defects, flaws, or shortcomings ⟨every length of cloth is *inspected* before it leaves the factory⟩ ⟨the troops prepared for the daily *inspection*⟩ ⟨this report will not pass *inspection*⟩ ⟨freshly picked grapes are *inspected* and cleansed before delivery—*Amer. Guide Series: Pa.*⟩ Examine (see also ASK 1) and examination imply a close scrutiny or investigation to determine the facts about a thing or the real nature, character, or condition of a thing or to test a thing's quality, validity, truth, or functioning ⟨the critic refused to give an opinion before he had *examined* the painting closely⟩ ⟨the doctor sent him to the hospital for a thorough *examination*⟩ ⟨they *examined* the house from cellar to attic before deciding to purchase it⟩ ⟨could it be the intention of those who gave this power, to say that . . . a case arising under the constitution should be decided without *examining* the instrument under which it arises?—*John Marshall*⟩ ⟨he began to . . . *examine* the speeches of its leaders, study its organization, reflect on its psychology and political techniques—*Shirer*⟩ ⟨*examination* of the bedroom has convinced me that it was possible for them to have escaped . . . as they said they did—*Prewett*⟩ Audit, as verb or noun, implies a searching examination of accounts in order to determine their correctness ⟨an annual *audit* of the tax books⟩ ⟨each bank is *audited* annually by a certified public accountant—*Safety for Your Savings*⟩ In its extended sense *audit* often carries a suggestion of a final accounting ⟨the general day of account and *audit* to be made at the throne of God—*Udall*⟩ ⟨when it comes to the *audit* before high heaven—*Lowes*⟩
*Ana* *consider, study, contemplate, weigh: *analyze, resolve, dissect: penetrate, pierce, probe (see ENTER)
**scrutiny** examination, scanning, inspection, audit (see under SCRUTINIZE)
*Ana* investigation, research, probe, *inquiry, inquisition: surveying *or* survey, observing *or* observation, viewing *or* view (see corresponding verbs at SEE)
**scud** skim, shoot, sail, *fly, dart, float
**scuffle** *vb* *wrestle, tussle, grapple
*Ana* fight, *contend: clash, conflict, collide, *bump
**sculpture, sculpt, sculp** *carve, chisel, engrave, incise, etch
*Ana* shape, fashion, form (see MAKE): depict, portray, *represent
**scum** *foam, froth, spume, lather, suds, yeast

**scurrility** *abuse, billingsgate, invective, vituperation, obloquy
*Ana* vilifying *or* vilification, maligning, traducing, calumniation (see corresponding verbs at MALIGN): reviling, berating, upbraiding, rating, scolding (see SCOLD)
**scurrilous** *abusive, opprobrious, vituperative, contumelious
*Ana* ribald, obscene, gross, *coarse, vulgar: insulting, outraging, offending *or* offensive (see corresponding verbs at OFFEND): foul, filthy, *dirty
**scurry** *vb* *scuttle, scamper, skedaddle, sprint
*Ana* *rush, dash, shoot, tear, charge: dart, *fly, scud: hurry, *speed, hasten
**scurvy** *adj* *contemptible, despicable, pitiable, sorry, cheap, beggarly, shabby
*Ana* *base, low, vile: *mean, abject
**scuttle** *vb* Scuttle, scurry, scamper, skedaddle, sprint are comparable when they mean to move briskly by or as if by running. *Scuttle, scurry,* and *scamper* all imply a rapid erratic progress of or as if of a small active animal but each may carry quite distinctive suggestions. Scuttle tends to suggest an irregular, precipitous, and seemingly awkward gait (as of a spider or crab) in which speed often appears to be attained with effort ⟨landladies *scuttling* sideways like crabs in their crustacean silk gowns—*Sitwell*⟩ ⟨a flock of sparrows *scuttled* like brown leaves over the pavement—*Glasgow*⟩ ⟨a little motorcar so small that it *scuttled* up the road, shot around, and stopped . . . with the abruptness of a wound-up toy—*Wolfe*⟩ Scurry more often conveys the impression of a neat briskness (as of a mouse or squirrel) and often of abrupt changes in direction or speed ⟨sent him *scurrying* down a zigzag, crisscross, confused trail—*Hervey*⟩ ⟨[the squirrel] changed his mind. For no apparent reason he whisked about, *scurried* across the ground to the big elm, ran straight up the tall trunk, and disappeared—*C. G. D. Roberts*⟩ ⟨his still restless and curious intelligence went *scurrying* back through the past, savoring the quality of his experience, sniffing at souvenirs of his fights and his triumphs—*James Gray*⟩ Scamper suggests nimbleness in movement and typically applies to playful gamboling (as of children or young animals) ⟨tiny chipmunks no bigger than half-grown rats *scampered* fearlessly about—*S. E. White*⟩ ⟨lambs *scampering* after their mothers⟩ but it may stress urgency and then imply such motives as fear or need of shelter ⟨he could let his harried mind and spirit *scamper* in thought to this quiet male refuge and there find solace—*Ferber*⟩ ⟨the resulting roar . . . sent several persons under the marquee *scampering* into the store for safety—*N. Y. Times*⟩ Skedaddle typically applies to human movement and distinctively implies a hasty departing for cause, sometimes even a panic flight ⟨the children around our place all own hideouts where they *skedaddle* whenever that old ogre, Work, rears his ugly head—*Perkins*⟩ ⟨the claim's played out, the partnership's played out, and the sooner we *skedaddle* out of this the better—*Harte*⟩ Sprint implies movement at top speed and typically suggests an output of energy that can only briefly be maintained; it is particularly appropriate when the notion to be conveyed is one of an urgent effort of speed to attain an immediate end ⟨the commuter has no time to read the editorials as he *sprints* alternately from train to ferry and from ferry to train—*Amer. Guide Series: N. J.*⟩ ⟨hoping to get a shot at a rabbit *sprinting* back to cover from far out in the field—*T. H. White*⟩ ⟨the . . . Brens at once began to blaze away and under their cover the rest of the patrol *sprinted* back about fifty yards—*Majdalany*⟩
*Ana* shoot, tear, dash, *rush, charge: *fly, scud: hurry,

*speed, hasten

**seaman** *mariner, sailor, tar, gob, bluejacket

**sear** *vb* *burn, scorch, char, singe

**search** *vb* *seek, scour, hunt, comb, ransack, rummage, ferret out
*Ana* investigate (see corresponding noun at INQUIRY): inspect, examine, *scrutinize: penetrate, pierce, probe (see ENTER)

**season** *vb* *harden, acclimatize, acclimate
*Ana* *habituate, accustom, inure: train, school, discipline (see TEACH): *practice, exercise, drill

**seasonable, timely, well-timed, opportune, pat** can mean occurring or coming with peculiar appropriateness as to moment or present situation. What is **seasonable** is perfectly suited to the season or time of year ⟨*seasonable* menus for hot August days⟩ ⟨*seasonable* weather⟩ or, by extension, fits in perfectly with the needs of the moment or the character of the occasion ⟨his caution was . . . *seasonable*, and his advice . . . good—*Defoe*⟩ ⟨weaves a *seasonable* garland of legend and fact from the flora of Christmas—*London Calling*⟩ What is **timely** is not only seasonable but comes or occurs at such a moment as to be of genuine value or service ⟨a *timely* book⟩ ⟨to me alone there came a thought of grief: a *timely* utterance gave that thought relief—*Wordsworth*⟩ ⟨valuable objects may be saved from the flames by *timely* aid—*Dickens*⟩ What is **well-timed** is so timely as to suggest the appearance or the actual exercise of care, forethought, or design ⟨their *well-timed* and rapid charge decided the conflict —*Gibbon*⟩ ⟨the instruments needed to make their movements precise and *well-timed* were necessarily reduced to uniformity too—*Mumford*⟩ What is **opportune** fits directly into a given concurrence of circumstances or comes as if by accident in the nick of time and works to the advantage of those concerned ⟨the moment was not *opportune* for an uprising⟩ ⟨as if this was an encounter which was something more than convenient, something really *opportune*—*West*⟩ ⟨the literary scene was too full of chaotic and short-lived movements to make the launching of a large work *opportune*—*Barzun*⟩ What is **pat** is perfectly adapted to the situation or the moment ⟨a *pat* quotation⟩ or comes or occurs at the very moment it is needed ⟨a story so *pat*, you may think it is coined—*Cowper*⟩ ⟨had assuredly the air of a miracle, of something dreamed in a dream, of something pathetically and impossibly appropriate—*pat*, as they say—*Bennett*⟩
*Ana* apropos, apposite, pertinent, *relevant: appropriate, happy, felicitous, apt (see FIT): welcome, grateful, gratifying (see PLEASANT)
*Ant* unseasonable

**seclude** *isolate, segregate, insulate, sequester
*Ana* *enclose, envelop, fence, pen, cage, wall: confine, circumscribe, *limit, restrict

**seclusion** *solitude, isolation, alienation
*Ana* retirement, withdrawal (see corresponding verbs at GO): separation, parting, severing *or* severance (see corresponding verbs at SEPARATE)
*Con* *intercourse, communication, commerce, dealings, communion

**second** *n* *instant, moment, minute, flash, jiffy, twinkling, split second

**secondary** *adj* *subordinate, dependent, subject, tributary, collateral
*Ana* *auxiliary, accessory, subservient, subsidiary, contributory: incidental, *accidental, adventitious
*Ant* primary

**second-rate** mediocre, middling, *medium, moderate, average, fair, indifferent

**secret** *adj* Secret, covert, stealthy, furtive, clandestine, sur-

reptitious, underhand, underhanded are comparable when they mean done, carried on, operated, or accomplished so as not to attract attention or observation. **Secret,** the most general of these terms and the widest in its range of application, implies a hiding or concealing or a being hidden or concealed ⟨virtues are the hidden beauties of a soul, the *secret* graces which cannot be discovered by a mortal eye—*Spectator*⟩ ⟨she seized a lamp . . . and hurried towards the *secret* passage—*Walpole*⟩ ⟨for eighteen years a *secret* and an unaccused prisoner in the Bastille—*Dickens*⟩ ⟨a beautiful woman exquisitely finished . . . shrewd, mature, *secret*, betraying her real self to none—*Sackville-West*⟩ **Covert** applies to something that is done as it were under cover, and is not open or avowed ⟨he would find out the facts, the good and the bad, and set them down without any *covert* attack or special pleading—*MacInnes*⟩ ⟨his *covert* alliance against the House of Austria—*Belloc*⟩ **Stealthy** usually suggests an intent to elude, to spy upon, or to gain one's ends without attracting attention; it is frequently a term either of derogation or of censure, connoting deliberateness and quietness in decoying, entrapping, or deceiving ⟨murder . . . with his *stealthy* pace . . . towards his design moves like a ghost—*Shak.*⟩ ⟨a series of gradual and *stealthy* encroachments on the rights of the people—*Freeman*⟩ ⟨he came sidling up the driveway with a *stealthy*, soft-treading gait, making no noise at all —*Dahl*⟩ **Furtive** agrees with *stealthy* in suggesting an intent to escape observation but it carries clearer suggestions of cautiousness, watchfulness, or slyness, and is used to describe not only movements and acts but also faces, features, or expressions which reveal these or similar characteristics ⟨the man in black, after a *furtive* glance, did not look me in the face—*Borrow*⟩ ⟨small *furtive* eyes—*George Eliot*⟩ ⟨it would be possible for them, by breaking the law discreetly, to get all they want without discomfort; but . . . they . . . refuse to be the *furtive* evaders of a rule—*Huxley*⟩ ⟨the *furtive* sex fumbling that all boys her own age considered natural and in fact obligatory—*Wouk*⟩ **Clandestine** implies concealment (as in working out a plan) and usually an evil or illicit end; it commonly suggests stealthy or furtive methods or a fear that others may know what is occurring ⟨*clandestine* meetings of the lovers⟩ ⟨a *clandestine* marriage⟩ ⟨the past when even the girls in the Library of Congress—even the archivists—could be booked for a *clandestine* weekend at Virginia Beach—*Cheever*⟩ ⟨Germany's *clandestine* rearmament under the auspices of the Reichswehr—*Shirer*⟩ **Surreptitious** applies not only to stealthy and furtive actions but also to emotions or desires and to concrete things which are concealed for fear of their discovery usually because they involve violation of a right, a law, a custom, or a standard (as of conduct or propriety) ⟨there he kept his *surreptitious* quids of tobacco, his pipe, and his small hoards—*M. E. Freeman*⟩ ⟨over the paling of the garden we might obtain an oblique and *surreptitious* view—*Henry James*⟩ ⟨cherish a *surreptitious* liking for romantic love stories⟩ ⟨the *surreptitious* removal of his stock by a merchant about to be forced into bankruptcy⟩ **Underhand** and **underhanded** consistently carry an implication of fraud, deceit, or unfairness, in addition to that of secrecy in dealings or surreptitiousness in methods ⟨he had suspected his agent of some *underhand* dealings—*Austen*⟩ ⟨it seemed deceitful and *underhand* to try such a thing—*Pritchett*⟩ ⟨he did not look quite like a professional gambler, but something smooth and twinkling in his countenance suggested an *underhanded* mode of life—*Cather*⟩
*Ana* *mysterious, inscrutable, arcane: puzzling, per-

A colon (:) separates groups of words discriminated. An asterisk (*) indicates place of treatment of each group.

plexing, mystifying (see PUZZLE *vb*): hidden, concealed, secreted, screened (see HIDE)

**secrete** *hide, conceal, screen, cache, bury, ensconce
*Ana* dissemble, cloak, mask, *disguise, camouflage
**secretive** close, close-lipped, closemouthed, tight-lipped, *silent, uncommunicative, taciturn, reticent, reserved
*Ana* *cautious, circumspect, wary: restrained, inhibited (see RESTRAIN)
*Con* *talkative, loquacious, garrulous, voluble, glib: candid, open, plain, *frank
**sect** *religion, denomination, cult, communion, faith, creed, persuasion, church
**sectary** 1 adherent, *follower, disciple, partisan, henchman, satellite
*Ana* devotee, votary, *addict
2 also **sectarian** *heretic, schismatic, dissenter, nonconformist
*Ana* *enthusiast, zealot, fanatic, bigot
**section** *n* sector, segment, division, *part, portion, piece, detail, member, fraction, fragment, parcel
*Ana* district, *locality, vicinity: region, tract, *area, zone, belt: *field, sphere, territory
**sector** segment, section, division, *part, portion, piece, detail, member, fraction, fragment, parcel
**secular** temporal, lay, *profane
*Ana* worldly, mundane, *earthly, earthy, terrestrial
*Ant* religious (*as schools, journals, authorities*): profane (*as music, drama*): regular (*as priests*)
**secure** *adj* *safe
*Ana* *firm, solid: protected, shielded, guarded, safeguarded, defended (see DEFEND): certain, positive, *sure: impregnable, unassailable, invulnerable, *invincible
*Ant* precarious, dangerous
**secure** *vb* 1 Secure, anchor, moor, rivet can all in extended use mean to fasten or fix firmly or immovably. They are, however, not often interchangeable because of implications derived from their primary senses. One **secures** something that may get lost, may escape, or may permit invasion or intrusion if allowed to remain loose or to work loose; the word usually implies care or protection as the end of the action ⟨*secure* doors and windows before retiring to keep out intruders⟩ ⟨replace the nut, and tighten it down to *secure* the capacitor to the panel—*J. A. Stanley*⟩ ⟨getting intelligence which . . . will *secure* your own countrymen against brutality and outrages—*Kenneth Roberts*⟩ One **anchors** or **moors** something unstable or subject to tugging or pulling by external forces or influences to another thing strong enough to hold it down or in place or powerful enough to counterbalance or counteract the opposing forces ⟨most classrooms had benches and desks lined up in rows and *anchored* to the floor—*Mumford*⟩ ⟨*anchor* the cables of a suspension bridge to towers at either end⟩ ⟨*moored* to the rock on two sides, the cabin stood firm—*Tyndall*⟩ But *moor*, which in its primary sense implies a making fast between two anchors or two or more lines or cables, may in extended use suggest greater steadiness or an even balancing of forces that make for stability ⟨her reticent childhood sweetheart —whose idea of the good life is *anchored* to his dream of a French version of an American drugstore—*N. Y. Times Book Rev.*⟩ ⟨some of the tiny cone-shaped hats are attached to chenille snoods . . . which *moor* them on firmly —*P. J. Reynolds*⟩ ⟨said a network executive proudly: "While they're with us they [actors on contract] 'll be *moored* to television—they can't do any Broadway plays or movies."—*Time*⟩ One **rivets** one thing to another when one joins things normally or actually separate from each other as closely together as though a rivet had been driven through them ⟨fear *riveted* him to his chair⟩ ⟨why should

I write this down, that's *riveted*, screwed to my memory —*Shak.*⟩ ⟨the head of the state, in whose name he insisted that all his victories were won, to *rivet* the loyalty of the army to the civil administration—*Buchan*⟩ ⟨stood *riveted* to the earth . . . in the fascination of that dreaded gaze—*Le Fanu*⟩
*Ana* establish, *set, settle, fix: *fasten, attach, affix
2 *ensure, insure, assure
*Ana* protect, *defend, safeguard, guard, shield: preserve, conserve, *save: guarantee, guaranty (see corresponding nouns at GUARANTEE): warrant, *justify
3 procure, obtain, *get, acquire, gain, win
*Ana* seize, *take, grasp: *reach, attain, achieve, gain: *have, hold, own, possess
**security** surety, guaranty, *guarantee, bond, bail
*Ana* *pledge, earnest, token
**sedate** grave, staid, earnest, sober, *serious, solemn, somber
*Ana* placid, *calm, serene, tranquil: collected, composed, imperturbable (see COOL): *decorous, seemly, proper
*Ant* flighty
**sediment** *n* *deposit, precipitate, dregs, lees, grounds
**sedition,** treason are comparable when they mean an offense against a state to which or a sovereign to whom one owes allegiance. Sedition applies to conduct that is not manifested in an overt act but that incites commotion and resistance to lawful authority without in itself amounting to insurrection ⟨*sedition* is . . . a matter of expressing opinions, not of committing acts—*The Reporter*⟩ Treason applies to conduct that is manifested by an overt act or acts, is variously defined by various governments and at various times but typically has for its aim the violent overthrow of the government, the death of the sovereign, or betrayal to or aid and comfort of the enemy ⟨one cannot commit *treason* simply by talking or conspiring against the government; he must actually *do* something, and there must be witnesses—*Ogg & Ray*⟩ ⟨*sedition* has come to be applied to practices which tend to disturb internal public tranquility by deed, word, or writing but which do not amount to *treason* and are not accompanied by or conducive to open violence—*Chafee*⟩ ⟨*sedition* . . . is traitorous behavior that falls short of *treason* because it does not actively levy war against the United States or give aid to an enemy of the United States. It stirs up resistance to law or encourages conduct that may become *treason*—*Smelser & Kirwin*⟩
*Ana* *rebellion, revolt, revolution, uprising, insurrection, mutiny, putsch, coup: disaffection, alienation, estrangement (see corresponding verbs at ESTRANGE)
*Con* *fidelity, allegiance, loyalty, fealty
**seditious** mutinous, rebellious, factious, *insubordinate, contumacious
*Ana* traitorous, treacherous, perfidious, disloyal, *faithless: disaffected, alienated (see ESTRANGE)
**seduce** tempt, entice, inveigle, *lure, decoy
*Ana* mislead, beguile, delude, *deceive: corrupt, debauch, deprave, pervert, *debase: bewitch, captivate, allure (see ATTRACT)
**sedulous** assiduous, diligent, industrious, *busy
*Ana* persevering, persistent (see corresponding verbs at PERSEVERE): untiring, unwearied, *indefatigable, tireless
**see** *vb* 1 See, behold, descry, espy, view, survey, contemplate, observe, notice, remark, note, perceive, discern can all mean to take cognizance of something by physical or sometimes mental vision. See, the most general of these terms, may be used to imply little more than the use of the organs of vision ⟨he cannot *see* the crowd for he is blind⟩ but more commonly it implies a recognition or

appreciation of what is before one's eyes ⟨they can *see* a great deal in Paris, but nothing in an English meadow —*Jefferies*⟩ ⟨if the policeman *saw* him at all, he probably observed him with misgiving—*Wolfe*⟩ ⟨the . . . look of one who has *seen* all, borne all, known all—*Styron*⟩ The term may imply the exercise of other powers than the sense of sight, including a vivid imagination ⟨I can *see* her plainly now, as she looked forty years ago⟩ ⟨"Methinks I *see* my father." "Where, my lord?" "In my mind's eye, Horatio"—*Shak.*⟩ or mental insight ⟨he was the only one who *saw* the truth⟩ or powers of inference ⟨though he appeared calm, I could *see* he was inwardly agitated⟩ **Behold** carries a stronger implication of a definite ocular impression and of distinct recognition than *see;* it also suggests looking at what is seen ⟨we have sailed many weeks, we have sailed many days, (seven days to the week I allow), but a Snark, on the which we might lovingly gaze, we have never *beheld* till now—*Lewis Carroll*⟩ ⟨a whole tribe living in a craterlike valley, every member of which believes it would be death for him or her to *behold* the sea—*Frazer*⟩ **Descry** and *espy* imply a seeing in spite of difficulties (as distance, darkness, or partial concealment). **Descry** often suggests an effort to discover or a looking out for someone or something ⟨the grass was high in the meadow, and there was no *descrying* her —*George Eliot*⟩ ⟨Sir Austin ascended to the roof . . . and *descried* him hastening to the boathouse by the river-side—*Meredith*⟩ but **espy** usually implies skill in detection (as of what is small, or not clearly within the range of vision, or is trying to escape detection) ⟨the seamen *espied* a rock within half a cable's length of the ship— *Swift*⟩ ⟨flowers we *espy* beside the torrent growing; flowers that peep forth from many a cleft and chink— *Wordsworth*⟩ **View** and *survey*, on the contrary, imply the seeing of what is spread before one or what one can examine steadily or in detail. Both terms as often imply mental consideration as a physical seeing or looking over. **View** usually implies or requires a statement of a particular way of looking at a thing or a particular purpose in considering it ⟨*view* the panorama with delight⟩ ⟨*viewed* a piece of property that he thought of buying⟩ ⟨*view* a painting from various angles⟩ ⟨*view* the industry of the country, and see how it is affected by inequality of income—*Shaw*⟩ ⟨the effort is an interesting one if you *view* it in terms of the techniques of political symbolism—*Lerner*⟩ **Survey** more often implies a detailed scrutiny or inspection by the eyes or the mind so that one has a picture or idea of something as a whole ⟨the captain *surveyed* him from cap to waistcoat and from waistcoat to leggings for a few moments— *Hardy*⟩ ⟨he *surveyed* the room from the weathered blue jalousies to the frayed rush mats, from the inevitable spiders on the ceiling to the ants . . . over the floor—*Hervey*⟩ ⟨a man *surveying* Europe today discovers this strange anomaly: it is one great culture, yet it is at deadly issue with itself—*Belloc*⟩ **Contemplate** (see also CONSIDER 1) implies little more than a fixing of the eyes upon something, sometimes in abstraction, but more often in enjoyment or in reference to some end in view ⟨he had a way of looking her over from beneath lowered lids, while he affected to be examining a glove-button or *contemplating* the tip of his shining boot—*Wharton*⟩ **Observe** and *notice* both imply a heeding and not passing over; they commonly imply seeing but may suggest the use of another sense ⟨he *observed* every detail in the arrangement⟩ ⟨did you *notice* the man who just passed us?⟩ ⟨he *noticed* a peculiar odor⟩ Especially in scientific use **observe** may carry a stronger implication of directed attention ⟨in order to get fresh light on this subject, I have *observed*

my own children carefully—*Russell*⟩ ⟨keeping an ear pricked to *observe* the movements of the Viceroy and his group—*Woolf*⟩ ⟨things which are always about us . . . are the easiest to *observe* with accuracy—*Grandgent*⟩ **Notice** often implies some definite reaction to what is seen or sometimes heard, felt, or sensed such as making a mental note of it or a remark about it or, if what is noticed is a person, recognizing him by a salute or a greeting ⟨by Mrs. Hurst and Miss Bingley they were *noticed* only by a curtsey—*Austen*⟩ ⟨she didn't *notice*. She drove single-minded and unaware there was anyone next to her— *Pynchon*⟩ **Remark** (see also REMARK) and *note* carry an even stronger implication than *notice* of registering mentally one's impression. But **remark** is more likely to suggest a judging or criticizing of what is noticed ⟨a young lady was talking and laughing with two young gentlemen. I *remarked* their English accents and listened vaguely— *Joyce*⟩ ⟨I could not help *remarking* the position of her left arm—*Quiller-Couch*⟩ and **note** to suggest a recording, sometimes by a mental note, but sometimes in writing or in speech ⟨a certain ungraciousness, *noted* in later years by his nearest colleagues—*Ellis*⟩ ⟨he carried a map and *noted* every stream and every hill that we passed⟩ **Perceive** carries a stronger implication of the use of the mind in observation than any of the preceding terms. The word basically implies apprehension or obtaining knowledge of a thing, not only through the sense of sight but through any of the senses. It is often used in place of *see* in the simple sense of that word, but since it always implies distinct recognition of what is seen, the words are sometimes used in contrast, especially by psychologists ⟨an infant *sees* objects long before it is able to *perceive* them as definite persons or things⟩ ⟨when he drew nearer he *perceived* it to be a spring van, ordinary in shape, but singular in color—*Hardy*⟩ In its richer meaning *perceive* suggests not only dependence on other senses than that of sight but also usually keen mental vision or special insight and penetration ⟨disgusted with every person who could not *perceive* . . . these obvious truths— *Bennett*⟩ ⟨his lightning dashes from image to image, so quick that we are unable at first to *perceive* the points of contact—*Day Lewis*⟩ **Discern**, like *descry*, often implies little more than a making out of something by means of the eyes ⟨at length he *discerned*, a long distance in front of him, a moving spot, which appeared to be a vehicle— *Hardy*⟩ ⟨sometimes we *discern* the city afar off—*Benson*⟩ In its more distinctive use the term usually implies the powers of deeply perceiving and of distinguishing or discriminating what the senses perceive ⟨ye can *discern* the face of the sky; but can ye not *discern* the signs of the times?—*Mt* 16:3⟩ ⟨his grave eyes steadily *discerned* the good in men—*Masefield*⟩ ⟨he tried quickly to think of somthing else, lest with her uncanny intuition she *discern* the cloud of death in his mind—*Buck*⟩
**Ana** *scrutinize, scan, examine, inspect: pierce, penetrate, probe (see ENTER): *consider, study, contemplate

**2 See, look, watch** can all mean to perceive something by means of the eyes. **See** (see also SEE 1) stresses the reception of visual impressions ⟨he is now able to *see* clearly⟩ ⟨have the power of *seeing*⟩ **Look** stresses the directing of the eyes to something or the fixing of the eyes on something in order to see it ⟨if you will only *look*, you will be able to see what I am doing⟩ ⟨he refused to *look* in the mirror the nurse gave him⟩ **Watch** (see also TEND) implies a following of something with one's eyes, so as to observe every movement, every change, a sign of danger, or a favorable opportunity ⟨*watch* for a while and tell us what you see⟩ ⟨spend the night *watching* a sick friend⟩ ⟨*watching* the clock as closely as a cat *watches* a mouse⟩

---

A colon (:) separates groups of words discriminated. An asterisk (*) indicates place of treatment of each group.

*Ana* \*gaze, gape, stare, glare

**seedy** \*shabby, dilapidated, dingy, faded, threadbare

*Ana* drooping, flagging, sagging, wilting (see DROOP): sickly, \*unwholesome, morbid: worn (see HAGGARD)

**seek, search, scour, hunt, comb, ferret out, ransack, rummage** are comparable when they mean to look for or go in quest of in the hope of finding. **Seek** has become widely extended in application and may take as its object either a person or a concrete thing or something intangible or abstract and may imply either a quest that involves great effort or one that makes slight demands; the term is more often used in the written than the spoken language ⟨they *sought* him among their kinsfolk and acquaintance. And when they found him not, they turned back again to Jerusalem, *seeking* him—*Lk* 2:44-45⟩ ⟨*seek* the truth⟩ ⟨a small sadistic streak that caused me to *seek* a more subtle and painful punishment for my victim—*Dahl*⟩ ⟨wisdom must be *sought* for its own sake or we shall not find it—*Inge*⟩ **Search** implies both effort and thoroughness. It differs from *seek* especially in taking as its object the place in which or the person on whom something is sought; it therefore connotes an investigating, an exploring, a penetrating scrutinizing, or a careful examining ⟨*search* every section of the country for spies⟩ ⟨*search* the house from top to bottom for a lost ring⟩ ⟨I have *searched* every nook and cranny⟩ ⟨*search* all the persons present when the money disappeared⟩ ⟨*searched* his memory for a name⟩ ⟨the book was edited in a way no editor could ever have time or love to find; it was *searched* sentence by sentence, word for word—*Mailer*⟩ **Scour,** which means in general to run over or to traverse swiftly especially in pursuit or in search, can be used more narrowly to mean to make an exhaustive search of a territory or of something comparable to a territory for a thing that must be found ⟨*scour* the coast for lurking submarines⟩ ⟨*scour* the neighborhood for the missing child⟩ ⟨the next morning Archer *scoured* the town in vain for more yellow roses—*Wharton*⟩ ⟨*scoured* the coppices and woods and old quarries, so long as a blackberry was to be found—*D. H. Lawrence*⟩ **Hunt** basically comes close to *scour* in its general sense for it implies a pursuit of and often a search for something, but especially game. In the extended sense in which the term is here considered it implies specifically a vigorous and, often, unavailing search for something as elusive as game ⟨they *hunted* till darkness came on, but they found not a button, or feather, or mark—*Lewis Carroll*⟩ ⟨*hunt* evidence far and wide⟩ ⟨I've *hunted* for the lost papers everywhere but I can't find them⟩ ⟨in . . . *hunting* up earlier quotations for recent words—*Murray*⟩ **Comb** implies methods of searching as painstaking or thoroughgoing as those involved in going through the hair with a fine comb ⟨*comb* the countryside for the escaped convicts⟩ ⟨*comb* the factories for more men for the army⟩ ⟨the Pacific Ocean between San Francisco and Hawaii is being *combed* today by aircraft and shipping for signs of the two planes —*Morning Post*⟩ **Ferret out** stresses the finding of something that is difficult to get at and usually suggests a vigorous, arduous, persistent and, often, tricky method of search ⟨*ferret out* a secret⟩ ⟨one of the professor's specialties being to *ferret out* captured . . . political commissars for execution—*Shirer*⟩ ⟨I have *ferreted out* evidence— *Dickens*⟩ **Ransack** and *rummage* imply a search usually of a limited area; both tend to stress the manner of going through what is examined and suggest a haphazard and often disorderly or heedless pulling about and turning over of miscellaneous items. Though the two are often interchangeable, **ransack** is especially appropriate when one wishes to stress careless haste, lack of regard for the rights of others, or improper motives on the part of the searcher, while **rummage** may be chosen when a more neutral word is needed or when lack of a definite object of search is to be implied; thus, a thoughtless child might *ransack* the refrigerator to make himself a snack and then go *rummage* through his toys after a lost ball; a thief *ransacks* a house in search of loot, but *rummages* through a drawer with no clear and specific notion of what he may find ⟨pass a rainy day *rummaging* about in the attic⟩ ⟨the men *ransacked* the thatched huts, *rummaged* among the pots, the fishing gear, the shell ornaments—*M. S. Douglas*⟩ ⟨apparently unlimited search, such as *ransacking* parts of an office can never be justified—*Paul Wilson*⟩ ⟨*ransacked* his father's shelves, dipped into a multitude of books—*Macaulay*⟩ ⟨stooped and deliberately *rummaged* in the dust at his feet, as if searching for the squirming threads of death it might contain—*Wylie*⟩ ⟨the impatience with which a community without tradition *rummages* through ways of life which other peoples, other cities have worked out for themselves slowly and painfully —*Gordimer*⟩

*Ana* inquire, question, \*ask, interrogate: pursue, chase, \*follow, trail

**seem, look, appear** can mean to be as stated in one's view or judgment, but not necessarily in fact. Often they are used interchangeably with apparently no difference in meaning ⟨he *seems* tired⟩ ⟨the students *look* eager⟩ ⟨the orchestra *appeared* ready to begin⟩ But even in such phrases **seem** suggests an opinion based on subjective impressions and personal reaction rather than on objective signs ⟨a tiny pebble in the middle of your back *seems* to grow all night, and by the crack of dawn has grown to boulder size—*Boy Scout Handbook*⟩ ⟨my other visits to Greece were over twenty years ago. How would it *seem* after such a long time, and seen in such a different way— *Chubb*⟩ while **look** implies that the opinion is based on a general visual impression ⟨her . . . lips *looked* parched and unnatural—*Glasgow*⟩ **Appear** may convey the same implication as *look* but it sometimes suggests a distorted impression such as can be produced by an optical illusion, a restricted point of view, or another's dissembling ⟨his tongue . . . could make the worse *appear* the better reason—*Milton*⟩ ⟨the attempt has been made to make it *appear* that this conflict is not between religion and science, but between the latter and theology. This seems to me a cheap and worthless evasion—*Cohen*⟩

*Ana* \*infer, gather, judge, deduce, conclude

**seeming** \*apparent, illusory, ostensible

*Ana* \*plausible, specious, credible: dissembling, disguising, masking, cloaking, camouflaging (see DISGUISE)

**seemly** proper, nice, \*decorous, decent

*Ana* fitting, suitable, appropriate, meet (see FIT): congruous, compatible, congenial, consistent, \*consonant

*Ant* unseemly

**seethe** \*boil, simmer, parboil, stew

**segment** section, sector, division, \*part, portion, piece, detail, member, fraction, fragment, parcel

**segregate** *vb* \*isolate, seclude, insulate, sequester

*Ana* \*separate, divide, part, sever: \*detach, disengage: \*choose, select, single

**seize** \*take, grasp, clutch, snatch, grab

*Ana* \*catch, capture, snare, ensnare, trap, entrap: appropriate, confiscate, usurp, \*arrogate

**select** *adj* **Select, elect, picked, exclusive** can mean marked by a superior character or quality which distinguishes the person, the thing, or the group so qualified from others (as in value, excellence, or favor). **Select** implies that the person or thing has been chosen with discrimination in preference to others of the same class or kind ⟨the hotel caters to a *select* clientele⟩ ⟨the Milton of poetry is, in his own

words again, the man of "industrious and *select* reading" —*Arnold*⟩ *Select* is also often used, with little or no implication of choice or selection, in the sense of *superior* or *exceptional* ⟨a *select* audience⟩ ⟨persecution of that sort which bows down and crushes all but a very few *select* spirits—*Macaulay*⟩ **Elect** commonly implies careful or discriminating selection and it carries a stronger implication than *select* of admission to some carefully restricted or inner circle; sometimes it also suggests the award of special privileges ⟨that delicious phantom of being an *elect* spirit . . . unlike the crowd—*Kingsley*⟩ ⟨Darwin was one of those *elect* persons in whose subconscious, if not in their conscious, nature is implanted the realization that "science is poetry"—*Ellis*⟩ **Picked,** like *select,* may or may not imply actual choice; the term commonly applies to what is conspicuously superior or above the average though it may suggest little more than the best available ⟨a *picked* team⟩ ⟨the candidates are all *picked* men⟩ ⟨the *picked* moments of exaltation and vision which great tragedy brings—*Montague*⟩ **Exclusive** in its most general sense implies a character in a thing that forces or inclines it to rule out whatever is not congruous or compatible with it or is its opposite or antithesis in constitution or character ⟨mutually *exclusive* colors when mixed in the right proportions form a neutral gray⟩ ⟨*exclusive* concepts—animal and vegetable, for instance—*Bowen*⟩ ⟨didacticism and a sense of humor are mutually *exclusive* qualities—*Lowes*⟩ As applied especially to persons, groups, or institutions *exclusive* implies tendencies or rules which prevent free acceptance or admission of those not conforming to imposed standards or not satisfying the requirements of those who are fastidious, snobbish, or highly critical ⟨a weak, critical, fastidious creature, vain of a little *exclusive* information or of an uncommon knack in Latin verse—*Eliot*⟩ ⟨the *exclusive* caste system of a rigid feudalism—*Binyon*⟩
*Ana* *choice, exquisite, rare, delicate, dainty, recherché: superlative, surpassing, peerless, *supreme
*Ant* indiscriminate
**select** *vb* *choose, elect, prefer, opt, pick, cull, single
*Ana* *assort, sort, classify: discriminate, discern (see corresponding nouns at DISCERNMENT)
*Ant* reject —*Con* refuse, repudiate, spurn (see DECLINE *vb*)
**selection** *choice, preference, election, option, alternative
*Ana* choosing, culling, picking (see CHOOSE): discrimination, *discernment, insight, acumen
*Ant* rejection
**self-abnegation** *renunciation, abnegation, self-denial
*Ana* sacrificing *or* sacrifice, forbearance, forgoing, eschewal (see corresponding verbs at FORGO): surrendering *or* surrender, resignation, abandonment, relinquishment (see corresponding verbs at RELINQUISH)
**self-assertive** assertive, *aggressive, pushing, pushy, militant
*Ana* obtrusive, intrusive, officious, meddlesome, *impertinent: bold, audacious (see BRAVE): positive, certain, *sure, cocksure
**self-assurance** assurance, *confidence, self-confidence, aplomb, self-possession
*Ana* coolness, collectedness, imperturbability (see corresponding adjectives at COOL): composure, sangfroid, *equanimity
*Con* diffidence, shyness, bashfulness, modesty (see corresponding adjectives at SHY)
**self-complacent** *complacent, self-satisfied, smug, priggish
*Ana & Con* see those at COMPLACENT
**self-confidence** *confidence, assurance, self-assurance,

self-possession, aplomb
*Ana* composure, *equanimity: sureness, sanguineness (see corresponding adjectives at CONFIDENT)
**self-denial** self-abnegation, abnegation, *renunciation
*Ana* sacrificing *or* sacrifice, forbearance (see corresponding verbs at FORGO): abstaining, refraining (see REFRAIN): restraining *or* restraint, curbing *or* curb, checking *or* check (see corresponding verbs at RESTRAIN)
**self-esteem** self-love, *conceit, egotism, egoism, amour propre
*Ana* *pride, vanity: self-respect, self-regard, self-admiration (see base words at REGARD *n*)
*Ant* self-distrust
**self-love** self-esteem, *conceit, egotism, egoism, amour propre
*Ana* *pride, vanity, vainglory: complacency, self-complacency, smugness, priggishness (see corresponding adjectives at COMPLACENT)
*Ant* self-forgetfulness
**self-possession** *confidence, self-confidence, assurance, self-assurance, aplomb
*Ana* *equanimity, composure: coolness, collectedness, imperturbability, nonchalance (see corresponding adjectives at COOL): poise, savoir faire, *tact
**selfsame** *same, very, identical, identic, equivalent, equal, tantamount
*Ana* alike, *like, identical, uniform
*Ant* diverse
**self-satisfied** *complacent, self-complacent, smug, priggish
*Ana* satisfied, content (see under SATISFY): conceited, egoistic, egotistic (see corresponding nouns at CONCEIT)
**semblance** *appearance, look, aspect
*Ana* *likeness, similitude, resemblance, analogy, affinity: *pose, affectation, air: *form, figure, shape
**semiannual** *biannual, biennial
**sempiternal** eternal, *infinite, boundless, illimitable, uncircumscribed
*Ana* *everlasting, endless, interminable, unceasing: *immortal, deathless, undying: *lasting, perdurable
**send,** dispatch, forward, transmit, remit, route, ship are comparable when they mean to cause to go or to be taken from one place or person or condition to another. **Send,** the most general term, carries a wide range of implications and connotations and is capable of replacing any of the remaining terms especially when joined with a suitable modifying adverb. Basically it implies the action of an agent or sometimes an agency or instrumentality that initiates passage of one to another typically by ordering or directing ⟨*sent* a messenger to the bank⟩ ⟨if the body is rotated in any dimension of space, certain definite and fixed messages will be *sent* to the brain by the vestibular sense —*Armstrong*⟩ or by using force ⟨*send* an arrow into a target⟩ ⟨there can come a cloudburst, an inch or two or three falling within an hour to wash out fields, *send* rivers flooding, wreck houses—*La Farge*⟩ or by employing some available facility or inherent capacity or power ⟨*send* a letter by airmail⟩ ⟨the burning forest *sent* smoke over the city⟩ ⟨diseases that rack the human frame and *send* epidemics of sickness over great tracts of the earth's surface—*Swinton*⟩ Often the term carries special connotations characteristic of particular idioms; thus, when one *sends* a child to college, one makes it possible for him to go by providing funds; when a teacher *sends* her pupils back to their books after recess she leads them to shift their focus from one activity (play) to another (study); when a story *sends* its hearers into gales of laughter it impels attention and alters mood; when something (as music or a personality) *sends* one, it induces an intense

A colon (:) separates groups of words discriminated. An asterisk (*) indicates place of treatment of each group.

emotional response. **Dispatch** tends to suggest speed in sending and to heighten notions of specific destination or cause, though the use of a speedy means is as likely to be stated as implied ⟨the police chief *dispatched* several detectives to the scene of the murder⟩ ⟨two destroyers were *dispatched* to the aid of the sinking vessel⟩ ⟨*dispatch* word to them by radio⟩ ⟨a messenger was *dispatched* with a reprieve but failed to arrive before the soldier had been shot—*Amer. Guide Series: Conn.*⟩ **Forward** (see also ADVANCE) implies a sending on or forward especially of something that has been delayed or stopped before reaching the person to whom it is to be delivered ⟨the letter had been *forwarded* from his old address—*J. D. Beresford*⟩ or, in commercial use, of something that has been asked for or ordered ⟨the goods ordered will be *forwarded* by parcel post⟩ **Transmit** (see also CARRY) fundamentally implies a sending or passing from one place, person, or point to another; it often emphasizes the means rather than the fact of sending ⟨the information can be most rapidly *transmitted* by radio⟩ ⟨the virus of yellow fever is *transmitted* by a mosquito⟩ ⟨prophets, who are . . . a vehicle through which to *transmit* a revelation—*W. W. Howells*⟩ **Remit** (see also EXCUSE) especially in reference to money can mean merely to send ⟨profits, dividends, interest, rents and royalties may be *remitted* to any country—*Mikesell*⟩ but often implies a sending in response to a demand ⟨please *remit* the balance due on your account⟩ In more general and in legal use the term is likely to imply a sending or referring back (as for further action or consideration) ⟨where an appellate court . . . reverses an original sentence . . . and *remits* the record for appropriate action, the lower court may proceed to sentence the defendant anew in proper form and according to law—*U. S. v. Keenan*⟩ ⟨there may be disputes whether an issue belongs to the side of civil or to that of administrative law. Such conflicts and disputes are *remitted* . . . to the arbitrating authority—*Ernest Barker*⟩ **Route** implies a sending along of something according to a predetermined route, and often suggests the reaching in proper succession of one person or place after another ⟨*route* a memorandum to the various staff members⟩ ⟨*route* the films to a chain of motion-picture theaters⟩ **Ship** applies to the sending especially of heavy goods or articles specifically by ship or more generally by any normal commercial transportation channel ⟨*ship* coal to distant lands⟩ ⟨*ship* freight by rail⟩ ⟨kept busy . . . *shipping* mackerel and cod—*C. R. Sumner*⟩
*Ana* *speed, quicken: direct, order (see COMMAND): *go, leave, depart

**senescence** *age, senility, dotage
*Ant* adolescence
**senility** dotage, *age, senescence
*Ana* infirmity, feebleness, weakness, decrepitude (see corresponding adjectives at WEAK): childishness, childlikeness (see corresponding adjectives at CHILDLIKE): decay, disintegration (see DECAY *vb*)
**sensation** 1 Sensation, percept, sense-datum, sensum, image can denote the experience or process which is the result of the activity of a sense organ and its associated neural structures. **Sensation** (see also SENSATION 2), the most general of these terms, is applicable to a specific awareness (as of heat, pain, or odor) resulting from adequate stimulation of a sensory receptor by a stimulus from without or within the body, whether this awareness enters fully into consciousness or not; specifically it means an impression received by a sensory end organ (as the retina of the eye, the taste buds of the tongue, or the tactile corpuscles of the skin) or by a combination of such end organs ⟨the four basic taste *sensations*, sweet, sour, bitter, and salty⟩ ⟨gave himself up to the enjoyment of the sen-

sations provided by a perfect spring day⟩ ⟨a reptile that appears . . . to squander more than two-thirds of its existence in a joyless stupor, and be lost to all *sensation* for months together—*Gilbert White*⟩ **Percept, sense-datum,** and **sensum** are technical terms especially of epistemology that are subject to widely varied interpretation, but that typically denote a strictly individual and personal neural event occurring centrally in response to sensory stimulation and constituting an immediate unanalyzable private object of sensation ⟨it makes for a neat little burlesque of the central debate between concept—the large, institutionalized idea, and *percept*—the irreducibly personal vision which must be coped with in its own terms—*Rago*⟩ ⟨instead of an irregular mass of pink sensation mixed with blue and red and topped with brown, he recognizes his mother's face. These emerging organized groups of sensations which cluster together (and soon seem to belong together) and serve to indicate things in the physical environment are called *percepts;* these may be defined briefly as "sensations plus meaning"—that is, groups of sensations that have become organized into meaningful wholes or patterns. Thus every physical object represents a *percept*, or at least a potential one—*Hunter Mead*⟩ ⟨observation of physical objects is primarily the noticing of *sense-data;* and each person has and observes his own color and sound *sensa*, just as he has and observes his own twinges, nausea and touch *sense-data*—*A. C. Garnett*⟩ ⟨a *sense-datum* is by definition whatever appears to the senses and in so far as we confine ourselves to a description of our *sense-data* we cannot possibly be in error—*Pap*⟩ ⟨our sense organs must select certain predominant forms, if they are to make report of *things* and not of mere dissolving *sensa*—*Langer*⟩ **Image** (see also IMAGE 1) applies to a sensation that results in a mental representation of the thing seen, the sound heard, and the odor smelled and in the retention of that mental representation in the memory ⟨after I had looked long at it, and passed on, the *image* of that perfect flower remained . . . persistently in my mind—*Hudson*⟩ ⟨I had never spoken to her, except for a few casual words, and yet her . . . *image* accompanied me even in places the most hostile to romance—*Joyce*⟩ *Image* also refers to a mental representation that can be evoked in the mind in the absence of the thing represented; in this case, the term may apply to a mental representation that is in the memory as a result of previous sense experience or that is a construction of the imagination or fancy out of various bits of sense experience or as a result of a verbal description ⟨when I recall London, Paris, Rome . . . the *image* that first presents itself is the earliest one—*Grandgent*⟩ ⟨a succession of efforts to call up before us veracious *images* of a bedroom, a bed, pillows, a lighted candle, a woman asleep, a man speaking to himself—*Montague*⟩
*Ana* *impression, impress, print, stamp: feeling, feel (see ATMOSPHERE): consciousness, awareness (see corresponding adjectives at AWARE)
2 Sensation, sense, feeling, sensibility are comparable when they mean the power to respond or the capacity for or the act of responding to stimuli, especially external physical stimuli. **Sensation** in technical use often denotes nothing more than the mere seeing, hearing, smelling, tasting, or feeling and does not imply recognition or comprehension ⟨the first step, which most children take at the age of about five months, is to pass beyond mere pleasures of *sensation*, such as food and warmth, to the pleasure of social approbation—*Russell*⟩ In more general use the term usually suggests somewhat more than mere receiving of impressions and may imply not only recognition but more or less clearly defined intellectual and emotional

reactions (as pleasure or pain or curiosity). It therefore may apply to responses to other than purely physical stimuli ⟨the *sensation* of finding a command of no avail is to the mind what sitting down upon a suddenly withdrawn chair is to the body—*Deland*⟩ ⟨there are *sensations* you cannot describe. You may know what causes them but you cannot tell what portions of your mind they affect nor yet, possibly, what parts of your physical entity —*F. M. Ford*⟩ **Sense** is applied specifically to any one of the perceptive powers associated with the sensory end organs ⟨the *sense* of taste⟩ ⟨the *sense* of smell⟩ or in the plural (occasionally in the singular) to the combined powers which enable a sentient being to establish relations between itself and what is external to itself ⟨the sudden, violent shock almost took away my *senses*—*Hudson*⟩ ⟨my brain immoderately stirred, my *senses* unusually quickened—*Galsworthy*⟩ but it differs from *sensation*, when applied to the power or act of responding to stimuli, in suggesting a less corporeal and a more intellectual reaction and often a less objective stimulus. In fact its most emphatic implication in this sense is often that of intense awareness or of full consciousness ⟨she had no *sense* at all of any word I said—*W. H. Davies*⟩ ⟨filled with a *sense* of pleasure so great that it constantly gave me pins and needles all along the lower parts of my legs—*Dahl*⟩ ⟨with a haze suspended all around them so that . . . their *sense* of direction and their *sense* of time were obscured—*Cheever*⟩ ⟨a deep *sense* of loss . . . a *sense* of loss and unbelief such as one might feel to discover suddenly that some great force in nature had ceased to operate—*Wolfe*⟩ **Feeling** (see also FEELING 2; ATMOSPHERE 2) in its most specific meaning denotes the sense that has its end organs in the skin; usually it signifies the sense of touch ⟨had no *feeling* in his fingertips⟩ but often it is more inclusive and suggests other sensations (as heat, cold, or pressure) that are typically perceived through stimulation of the skin ⟨a *feeling* of chill in the air⟩ But *feeling* is also used to denote a response to a stimulus or a set of stimuli that is a combination of sensation, emotion, and a degree of thought ⟨judged a situation by his *feelings* rather than by the facts⟩ ⟨you know her *feelings* about the vulgarity of these people⟩ Often also, the term denotes not the response, but the power to respond in general or as a characteristic ⟨he complains that she has no *feeling*⟩ ⟨the delicacy of his *feeling* makes him sensibly touched—*Hume*⟩ In this latter sense *feeling* is often replaced by **sensibility**, especially when a keenly impressionable nature and unusually delicate powers of appreciation or its opposite are implied ⟨the extreme *sensibility* to physical suffering which characterizes modern civilization—*Inge*⟩ ⟨she was a creature of palpitating *sensibility*, with feelings so delicate that they responded to every breath—*Crothers*⟩ Sometimes sentimental or affected responsiveness is suggested ⟨the nerveless sentimentalist and dreamer, who spends his life in a weltering sea of *sensibility*—*James*⟩
*Ana* perceptibleness *or* perceptibility, tangibleness *or* tangibility, palpableness *or* palpability, ponderableness *or* ponderability (see corresponding adjectives at PERCEPTIBLE): reaction, action, behavior (see corresponding verbs at ACT): response, answer (see under ANSWER *vb*)
**sense** *n* 1 *sensation, feeling, sensibility
*Ana* awareness, consciousness, cognizance (see corresponding adjectives at AWARE): perception, *discernment, discrimination, penetration
2 **Sense, common sense, good sense, horse sense, gumption, judgment, wisdom** can all mean the quality of mind or character which enables one to make intelligent choices or decisions or to reach intelligent conclusions. **Sense,**

because of its numerous significations, is often, when this meaning is intended, called **common sense, good sense,** or **horse sense** . All four terms imply a capacity—usually a native capacity—for seeing things as they are and without illusion or emotional bias, for making practical choices or decisions that are sane, prudent, fair, and reasonable and that commend themselves to the normal or average good mind ⟨when it came to taking care of myself, I had little to offer next to the practical *sense* of an illiterate sharecropper—*Mailer*⟩ ⟨"Jane is a goose," said the doctor, irritably. "Maggy is the only one that has any *sense* in that family"—*Deland*⟩ ⟨the *common sense* of common men . . . has not been seriously affected by these still academic aberrations of our alleged wise men—*Niebuhr*⟩ ⟨women have often more of what is called *good sense* than men. They have fewer pretensions; are less implicated in theories; and judge of objects . . . more truly and naturally—*Hazlitt*⟩ **Gumption** implies native wit or sound common sense often combined with initiative and drive ⟨there isn't a grain of intelligence in it. Nobody with more *gumption* than a grasshopper could go and sit and listen—*D. H. Lawrence*⟩ ⟨in practical talk, a man's common sense means his good judgment, his freedom from eccentricity, his *gumption*—*James*⟩ **Judgment** seldom applies to a native quality though it usually suggests a foundation in native good sense. But it also suggests intellectual qualities (as discernment of facts or conditions that are not obvious as well as knowledge of those that are ascertainable and an ability to comprehend the significance of those facts and conditions and to draw correct unbiased conclusions from them) which are the result of training, discipline, and experience ⟨'tis true that strength and bustle build up a firm. But *judgment* and knowledge are what keep it established—*Hardy*⟩ ⟨the ultimate test of true worth in pleasure, as in everything else, is the trained *judgment* of the good and sensible man—*Dickinson*⟩ **Wisdom** is of all these terms the one of highest praise. It often suggests great soundness of judgment in practical affairs and unusual sagacity ⟨common sense in an uncommon degree is what the world calls *wisdom*—*Coleridge*⟩ but it is also capable of suggesting an ideal quality of mind or character that is the result of a trained judgment exercised not only in practical affairs but in philosophical speculation, of wide experience in life and thought, of great learning, and of deep understanding ⟨for *wisdom* is better than rubies; and all the things that may be desired are not to be compared to it—*Prov* 8:11⟩ ⟨*wisdom* is said to be the funded experience which man has gathered by living; but for so many harvests the crop is still a light one. Knowledge he has gained and power, but not goodness and understanding—*Repplier*⟩
*Ana* *prudence, foresight, discretion: understanding, comprehension, appreciation (see corresponding verbs at UNDERSTAND): intelligence, brain, wit (see MIND)
3 *meaning, acceptation, signification, significance, import
*Ana* denotation, connotation (see under DENOTE)
**sense-datum** sensum, percept, *sensation, image
**sensibility** feeling, sense, *sensation
*Ana* perception, *discernment, penetration, discrimination, insight: sensitiveness, susceptibility (see corresponding adjectives at LIABLE): emotion, *feeling, affection
**sensible** 1 *material, physical, corporeal, phenomenal, objective
*Ant* intelligible
2 *perceptible, palpable, tangible, appreciable, ponderable
*Ana* sensational, perceptual, imaginal (see corresponding nouns at SENSATION): obvious, patent, manifest, *evident: *carnal, fleshly, sensual
*Ant* insensible

A colon (:) separates groups of words discriminated. An asterisk (*) indicates place of treatment of each group.

3 *aware, conscious, cognizant, alive, awake
*Ana* perceiving, noting, remarking, observing, seeing (see SEE): knowing, *intelligent: understanding, comprehending, appreciating (see UNDERSTAND): sensitive, susceptible (see LIABLE)
*Ant* insensible (of *or* to) —*Con* impassible, insensitive, anesthetic (see INSENSIBLE)
4 prudent, sane, judicious, *wise, sage, sapient
*Ana* sagacious, perspicacious, astute, *shrewd: foresighted, discreet, provident (see under PRUDENCE): reasonable, *rational
*Ant* absurd, foolish: fatuous, asinine

**sensitive** 1 susceptible, subject, exposed, open, *liable, prone
*Ana* impressed, influenced, affected (see AFFECT): predisposed, disposed, inclined (see INCLINE *vb*)
*Ant* insensitive
2 *sentient, impressible, impressionable, responsive, susceptible
*Ana* alert, *watchful, vigilant, wide-awake: *sharp, keen, acute: *aware, conscious, cognizant, sensible, alive

**sensual** 1 *carnal, fleshly, animal
*Ana* *bodily, physical, corporeal, somatic: *coarse, gross, vulgar: lewd, lascivious, lustful, wanton (see LICENTIOUS)
2 *sensuous, luxurious, voluptuous, sybaritic, epicurean
*Ana* see those at SENSUAL 1

**sensum** sense-datum, percept, *sensation, image

**sensuous, sensual, luxurious, voluptuous, sybaritic, epicurean** are comparable when they mean having to do with the gratification of the senses or providing pleasure by gratifying the senses. Both *sensuous* and *sensual* can imply reference to the sense organs and to perceptions based on the reactions of these organs and then come very close to *sensory* in meaning, but more typically both apply to things of the senses as opposed to things of the spirit or intellect. In this use **sensuous** is more likely to imply gratification of the senses for the sake of the aesthetic pleasure or the delight in beauty of color, sound, or form that is induced while **sensual** (for fuller treatment see CARNAL) tends to imply the gratification of the senses or the indulgence of the appetites (as of gluttony and lust) as an end in itself ⟨nobody can resist the Bay of Naples, or if he can, then all the simple and *sensuous* delights of this world must turn to bitterness and ashes in his mouth— *Mackenzie*⟩ ⟨arise and fly the reeling faun, the *sensual* feast—*Tennyson*⟩ ⟨he liked the morning plunge in his great sunken tub, the *sensual* warmth of sudsy water— *Wolfe*⟩ ⟨Chinese painters are not, like the Persians, absorbed in expressing their *sensuous* delight in the wonder and glory of the world—*Binyon*⟩ As applied to persons or their natures, *sensuous* often carries an implication of indifference to things of the spirit but it practically never suggests the carnality so often connoted by *sensual* ⟨the *sensuous*, self-indulgent nature she [Elizabeth] derived from Anne Boleyn—*J. R. Green*⟩ ⟨his nature was purely *sensuous*, and she strove to make him moral, religious— *D. H. Lawrence*⟩ ⟨the young boy's love is a spiritual passion . . . without any sensory, still less any *sensual*, elements—*Ellis*⟩ **Luxurious** (see also LUXURIOUS 2) implies indulgence, often self-indulgence, in sensual or, more often, sensuous pleasures, especially pleasures that induce a pleasant languor, delightful ease, or particularly a grateful peace of mind ⟨the emotionalist steeps himself or herself in *luxurious* feeling and pathetic imagination, which make no severe call upon either the will or the intellect—*Inge*⟩ ⟨the fatuous air of *luxurious* abandon . . . as she danced with the prince—*Connolly*⟩ **Voluptuous** also implies giving oneself up to the pleasures of sense

but it carries a stronger implication of abandonment to such pleasure for its own sake than does *luxurious;* also it more frequently carries a suggestion of sensual rather than of sensuous enjoyment ⟨fair fallacious looks . . . softened with pleasure and *voluptuous* life—*Milton*⟩ ⟨a temper too indolent to inquire, too bigoted to doubt, a *voluptuous* devotionality allied perhaps to refined aestheticism, but totally alien to the austerity and penetrating sincerity of the Gospel—*Inge*⟩ ⟨he had worked himself up in lecherous and *voluptuous* anticipation of this date—*Farrell*⟩ **Sybaritic** implies voluptuousness of an overrefined and effeminate sort; usually it suggests indulgence in the rarest and choicest foods and drinks amid surroundings calculated to charm and soothe the senses ⟨it was a *sybaritic* repast, in a magnificent apartment—*Thackeray*⟩ ⟨*sybaritic* grandeur which eclipses the splendor of a sultan's harem—*Green Peyton*⟩ **Epicurean** may imply sensuality and voluptuousness but more often suggests sensuous rather than sensual delight in the pleasures of eating and drinking and a delicate and fastidious rather than a gross taste ⟨warming their palace kitchens, and from thence their unctuous and *epicurean* paunches— *Milton*⟩ ⟨nothing to mar the sober majesties of settled, sweet, *epicurean* life—*Tennyson*⟩ ⟨drinking his tea with *epicurean* satisfaction—*Powys*⟩
*Ana* sensational, imaginal (see corresponding nouns at SENSATION): delicious, delectable, luscious, *delightful: aesthetic, *artistic

**sentence** *vb* **Sentence, condemn, damn, doom, proscribe** can all mean to decree the fate or punishment of a person or sometimes a thing that has been adjudged guilty, unworthy, or unfit. **Sentence** is used in reference to the determination and pronouncement of punishment or penalty following an act of judging and an adverse verdict ⟨was tried on the charge of inciting to riot and *sentenced* to thirty days in jail—*E. S. Bates*⟩ ⟨he tries and *sentences* them on their merits, in the swift summary way of boys, as good, bad, interesting, silly—*Emerson*⟩ **Condemn** (see also CRITICIZE) implies both an adverse judgment and a sentence which carries with it a penalty (as forfeiture of one's freedom, one's rights, or one's life) ⟨Napoleon was *condemned* to exile⟩ ⟨cells for *condemned* prisoners⟩ ⟨was not inexorably *condemned*, as so many had feared at first, to be a vassal state in Hitler's unspeakable New Order—*Shirer*⟩ or, in the case of a thing, a forfeiture of its existence or of some status which has legally protected it from invasion; thus, to *condemn* an old building is legally to decree its destruction; to *condemn* a piece of property is to take it over for the uses of the state, on payment of its appraised value. **Damn**, akin to *condemn*, is not employed in modern law. In theological use it implies the condemnation of the soul to hell or to eternal punishment ⟨he that believeth and is baptized shall be saved; but he that believeth not shall be *damned*—Mk 16:16⟩ In general use, when it carries this implication, it is often employed in curses, imprecations, or expressions of strong disapproval ⟨I give thee sixpence! I will see thee *damned* first—*Canning*⟩ Otherwise it usually implies a verdict that is destructive or annihilating in its effects ⟨if we fail, then we have *damned* every man to be the slave of fear—*Baruch*⟩ **Doom** adds to *condemn* the implication of a punishment or penalty that cannot be evaded or escaped because imposed by an inexorable power ⟨I am thy father's spirit, *doomed* for a certain term to walk the night—*Shak.*⟩ ⟨he does certain things that are very brave . . . he gambles that he can be terribly, tragically wrong, and therefore be *doomed*, you see, *doomed* to Hell—*Mailer*⟩ This idea of fate or destiny is so strongly stressed in *doom* that in some cases the impli-

---

*Ana* analogous words     *Ant* antonyms     *Con* contrasted words     See also explanatory notes facing page 1

cation of an adverse judgment is lost or obscured ⟨the city was *doomed* to destruction⟩ ⟨the substance of a scientific paper is incorporated into the general stock of knowledge; but the paper itself is *doomed* to oblivion— *Huxley*⟩ **Proscribe** implies the publication or posting of a decree condemning a person to banishment or death or announcing his status as an outlaw and the forfeiture of his property or of his civil rights ⟨a declaration . . . *proscribed* Napoleon as a public enemy, with whom neither peace nor truce could be concluded—*Alison*⟩ ⟨still a *proscribed* fugitive, but with the knowledge that he could at any time cause a formidable revolt—*Stenton*⟩ The word in more general uses suggests ostracism or interdiction as the result of a judgment by some authoritative or influential body or group ⟨dancing was once *proscribed* by many churches⟩ ⟨you . . . your rites, your garb *proscribed*, must yet receive one degradation more —*Browning*⟩ ⟨the individual is often blacklisted not because he is guilty of anything, but because he is . . . regarded as controversial and therefore *proscribed*— *Elmer Rice*⟩

*Ana* \*judge, adjudge, adjudicate: condemn, denounce, blame (see CRITICIZE): determine, settle, rule, \*decide

*Con* acquit, absolve, vindicate, exonerate, \*exculpate

**sententious** pregnant, meaningful, significant, \*expressive, eloquent

*Ana* formal, conventional, ceremonious (see CEREMONIAL): \*showy, ostentatious: terse, pithy, compendious (see CONCISE)

**sentient,** sensitive, impressible, impressionable, responsive, susceptible can all mean readily affected by stimuli, usually external stimuli. **Sentient** implies a capacity to be affected through the senses; it may describe inclusively the lowest thing in animal life that feels, or the infant aware only of rudimentary sensation, or the man with the most highly developed powers of sensation or perception. The term *sentient creature* or *sentient being* may apply to a creature or being within these classes or between them ⟨the flowers in remote forests that no eye has ever seen, the shells of delicate form and rare color hidden forever in the deep waters of the sea—these fulfil the ends of their existence, though they have delighted no *sentient* being—*Binyon*⟩ ⟨whatever fate may have in store for the most *sentient* . . . the most civilized, the most socially developed people of the modern world—*Brownell*⟩ or it may apply to something animate or inanimate to which similar powers are ascribed ⟨it seemed the *sentient* earth must feel the summer—*Mary Austin*⟩ **Sensitive** (see also LIABLE) applies usually to human beings who are quick or sharp in sensing anything. It may imply senses that respond to the most delicate of stimuli ⟨to enjoy her [style] the reader must have . . . a *sensitive* ear; especially must he have a sense of "pitch" in writing—*Cather*⟩ or it may imply quick emotional reactions that are the outward signs of one's being easily moved or stirred ⟨of age indeed and of death they had a horror proportional to their acute and *sensitive* enjoyment of life—*Dickinson*⟩ or an acuteness of mind that is linked with acuteness of sense and of emotion ⟨France, the most intellectually *sensitive* of modern nations—*Babbitt*⟩ Sometimes *sensitive* is applied not only to a part of the body (as a section of skin or an organ) which is abnormally or excessively reactive to stimuli but to inanimate things (as a photographic film, a thermometer, or an explosive) which responds quickly to some specific influencing factor (as light, heat, or shock) ⟨the high vacuum tubes which constitute the *sensitive* brain of modern radio—*Morrison*⟩ **Impressible** implies occasionally and **impressionable** regularly a readiness to be influenced, not only by a stronger power, but by a

power that succeeds in producing an impression. They do not imply, as *sensitive* usually does, a power to judge accurately and delicately; rather they suggest crudeness or immaturity or indifference to the quality of the thing that impresses ⟨the mind *impressible* and soft with ease imbibes and copies what she hears and sees—*Cowper*⟩ ⟨what he couldn't think of was David submitting, during his most *impressionable* years, to the worst superstitions of Capitalism—*Mary Austin*⟩ **Responsive,** which implies sensitiveness to stimuli in particular or in general, suggests in addition a readiness to respond or react in the way that is wanted. Since it usually occurs only in a good sense, it is likely to connote alertness, cooperativeness, and enthusiasm ⟨we shall presumably find them most *responsive* to the language, literature, and history of their own country—*Inge*⟩ ⟨she took up life, and became alert to the world again, *responsive*, like a ship in full sail, to every wind that blew—*Rose Macaulay*⟩ **Susceptible** (see also LIABLE) suggests a fitness in disposition or in temperament to be affected by certain stimuli. Though it comes close to *impressionable* or *responsive* it more often implies weakness than does either of them, the weakness sometimes being stated but more frequently implied or suggested (as by the person considered or the circumstances attending) ⟨in France it is . . . bad manners to be too *susceptible*—*Brownell*⟩ ⟨she is *susceptible* to flattery⟩ ⟨he is very young and very *susceptible* to the charms of women⟩ ⟨his temper was not very *susceptible* of . . . enthusiasm—*Gibbon*⟩

**sentiment** 1 emotion, affection, \*feeling, passion

*Ana* thought, impression, notion, \*idea: ideal, standard, exemplar (see MODEL)

2 \*opinion, view, belief, conviction, persuasion

*Ana* \*truth, verity: conclusion, judgment (see under INFER)

**sentimental,** romantic, mawkish, maudlin, soppy, mushy, slushy are comparable when they mean unduly or affectedly emotional. **Sentimental** usually suggests emotion that does not arise from genuine or natural feeling but is evoked by an external cause, by a particular mood, by an excess of sensibility, or for the sake of the thrill, or is merely an affectation that is temperamental, the moment's fashion, or designed to achieve an end ⟨*sentimental* songs⟩ ⟨his sense of character is nil, and he is as pretentious as a rich whore, as *sentimental* as a lollipop— *Mailer*⟩ ⟨a *sentimental* person, interested in pathetic novels and all unhappy attachments—*Thackeray*⟩ ⟨we are all for tooting on the *sentimental* flute in literature —*Stevenson*⟩ ⟨he had an alert and a *sentimental* mind and worried about the health of Mr. Hiram's cart horse and . . . the inmates of the Sailor's Home—*Cheever*⟩ **Romantic** implies emotion that has little relation to things as they actually are, but is derived more from one's imagination of what they should be ideally or from one's conceptions of them as formed by literature, art, or daydreams ⟨the process of growing from *romantic* boyhood into cynical maturity—*Shaw*⟩ ⟨its premise is *romantic*, if only because it assumes that every sparrow . . . is a warbler, if not a nightingale—*J. M. Brown*⟩ ⟨it has become the fashion to smile a little at *romantic* hopes for the world . . . . But it could be that it is precisely such dreams and visions that are needed—*Edman*⟩ **Mawkish,** when it implies sentimentality, suggests a kind that creates loathing or disgust because of its insincerity, emotional excess, or other signs of weakness or futility ⟨stale epithets, which, when I only seem to smell their *mawkish* proximity, produce in me a slight feeling of nausea—*L. P. Smith*⟩ ⟨stories simpering with delight and *mawkish* with pathos—*J. D. Hart*⟩ **Maudlin** stresses a lack of balance or self-restraint

A colon (:) separates groups of words discriminated. An asterisk (\*) indicates place of treatment of each group.

that shows itself in emotional excess (as unrestrained tears and laments); usually also it suggests extreme or contemptible silliness ⟨the mob became not only enthusiastic but *maudlin—Disraeli*⟩ ⟨saying things that were inept, *maudlin*, unhinged, and knowing then that these very words must drive him on and on toward . . . more helpless depths of drunkenness—*Styron*⟩ **Soppy,** *mushy,* and *slushy* come close to *mawkish* in their suggestion of distasteful and disgusting sentimentality. **Soppy** (chiefly in British use) often carries a strong suggestion of silliness in showing affection ⟨they do not permit themselves to show much family affection, so who are we to object if they go *soppy* over a few four-footed friends?—*Hahn*⟩ ⟨a naturally sad but never *soppy* poet—*Fraser*⟩ **Mushy** may suggest softness or wishy-washiness ⟨Stuffy rolled over on her back and paddled the air hysterically, a hypocrite, trading shamelessly on her sex and the *mushy* hearts of humans—*Panter-Downes*⟩ ⟨you may . . . be a sharp, cynical sort of person; or you may be a nice, *mushy,* amiable, good-natured one—*Shaw*⟩ **Slushy** applies chiefly to utterances or personalities that are so sentimental or emotionally confused as to seem senseless ⟨*slushy* stories⟩ ⟨pander to everything that's shoddy and *slushy* and third-rate in human nature—*Buchan*⟩
*Ana* emotional, affectionate, feeling, passionate (see corresponding nouns at FEELING): affecting, *moving, pathetic, touching: affected, pretended, counterfeited, feigned, simulated (see AFFECT)

**separate** *vb* **Separate, part, divide, sever, sunder, divorce** can all mean to become or cause to become disunited or disjoined. **Separate** implies a putting or keeping apart; it may suggest a scattering or dispersion of units ⟨forces that *separate* families⟩ ⟨*separate* the parts of a watch⟩ or a removal of one from the other ⟨*separate* a husband from his wife⟩ ⟨the business of government cannot and should not be *separated* from the day-to-day lives of the human beings who conduct it—*T. E. Dewey*⟩ ⟨*separate* the wheat from the chaff⟩ ⟨*separated* his feelings from his work⟩ or the presence of an intervening thing or things ⟨the Atlantic *separates* Europe from America⟩ ⟨a thousand miles *separate* the two branches of the family⟩ ⟨"What *separates* the men and the girls? A fence or something?" "Just foliage, dear, and upbringing"—*Wouk*⟩ **Part** usually suggests the separation of two persons or things in close union or association; often also it suggests a complete or final separation (as by death or violence) ⟨if aught but death *part* thee and me—*Ruth* 1:17⟩ ⟨*part* two combatants⟩ **Divide** commonly stresses the idea of parts, groups, or sections resulting from literal or figurative cutting, breaking, or branching ⟨*divide* a pie into six pieces⟩ ⟨*divide* the government into the executive, legislative, and judicial branches⟩ ⟨he that will *divide* a minute into a thousand parts—*Shak.*⟩ *Divide* often, in addition, carries an implication of apportioning, distributing, or sharing ⟨*divide* the candy among the children⟩ ⟨*divide* profits⟩ ⟨the grocer got along well with his assistant. They *divided* tasks and waited on alternate customers —*Malamud*⟩ ⟨*divided* his estate equitably among his heirs⟩ Often *divide* is used in place of *separate,* especially when mutual antagonism or wide separation is connoted ⟨united we stand, *divided* we fall⟩ ⟨the broad and deep gulf which . . . *divides* the living from the dead, the organic from the inorganic—*Inge*⟩ ⟨the suspicion which the Citizens' Committee predicted would *divide* neighbor from neighbor—*Clinton*⟩ **Sever** adds the implication of violence by or as if by cutting and frequently applies to the separation of a part from the whole or of persons or things that are joined in affection, close affinity, or natural association ⟨*sever* a branch from the trunk by one blow of the

ax⟩ ⟨*sever* the head from the body⟩ ⟨*severed* from thee, can I survive?—*Burns*⟩ ⟨the hour is ill which *severs* those it should unite—*Shelley*⟩ ⟨finding herself *severed* from formal and religious education, she struggled with a sense of guilt—*Hervey*⟩ **Sunder** often implies a violent rending or wrenching apart ⟨even as a splitted bark, so *sunder* we—*Shak.*⟩ ⟨the Romans *sundered* copper-bearing rock by alternately playing fire and water on it—*New Yorker*⟩ ⟨man's most significant personal relationship is *sundered* in an atmosphere of chicanery and buffoonery—*Cohn*⟩ **Divorce** implies the separation of two or more things so closely associated that they interact upon each other or work well only in union with each other ⟨its academic tendency to *divorce* form from matter—*Day Lewis*⟩ ⟨you cannot *divorce* accurate thought from accurate speech—*Quiller-Couch*⟩ *Divorce* can specifically refer to the legal dissolution of a marriage, a use in which it contrasts with *separate* which implies a mutually agreed ending of cohabitation without actual legal termination of the marital state.
*Ana* cleave, rend, split, rive (see TEAR): *estrange, alienate: disperse, dispel, *scatter: *detach, disengage
*Ant* combine

**separate** *adj* **1** *distinct, several, discrete
*Ana* diverse, disparate, *different, divergent, various: *free, independent
**2** *single, solitary, particular, unique, sole, lone
*Ana* *special, especial, specific, individual: peculiar, distinctive (see CHARACTERISTIC): detached, disengaged (see DETACH)

**sequel** outcome, issue, *effect, result, consequence, upshot, aftereffect, aftermath, event
*Ana* termination, *end, ending: conclusion, closing, finishing *or* finish (see corresponding verbs at CLOSE)

**sequence** series, *succession, progression, chain, train, string
*Ana* ordering *or* order, arrangement (see corresponding verbs at ORDER)

**sequent, sequential** *consecutive, successive, serial

**sequester** *vb* *isolate, segregate, seclude, insulate
*Ana* *separate, sever, sunder

**serene** tranquil, *calm, peaceful, placid, halcyon
*Ana* *still, stilly, silent, noiseless, quiet: *cool, collected, composed: smooth, effortless, *easy
*Con* disturbed, disquieted, agitated, upset (see DISCOMPOSE)

**serial** *adj* *consecutive, successive, sequent, sequential
*Ana* following, ensuing, succeeding (see FOLLOW): continuous, *continual

**series** *succession, progression, sequence, chain, train, string

**serious, grave, solemn, somber, sedate, staid, sober, earnest** may be applied to persons, their looks, or their acts with the meaning not light or frivolous but actually or seemingly weighed down by deep thought, heavy cares, or purposive or important work. **Serious** implies absorption in work rather than in play, or concern for what matters rather than for what merely amuses ⟨the features . . . were *serious* and almost sad under the austere responsibilities of infinite pity and power—*Henry Adams*⟩ ⟨there was no great warmth or fervor in those daily exercises, but rather a *serious* and decorous propriety—*Stowe*⟩ **Grave** implies both seriousness and dignity but it usually implies also an expression or attitude that reflects the pressure of weighty interests or responsibilities ⟨a *grave* voice which, falling word by word upon his consciousness, made him stir inside with . . . fear—*Styron*⟩ ⟨his air was *grave* and stately, and his manners were very formal—*Austen*⟩ *Grave* is more likely than *serious* to be used when a mere

*Ana* analogous words     *Ant* antonyms     *Con* contrasted words     See also explanatory notes facing page 1

appearance is to be implied ⟨loved to exaggerate, to astonish people by making extravagant statements with the *gravest* air—*Hall*⟩ and it may be used of things with qualities suggestive of human gravity ⟨the richness and *grave* dignity of its carved staircase and interior wood-work—*Amer. Guide Series: Pa.*⟩ ⟨my father's many-volumed edition of the Talmud . . . the look of those pages—*grave*, wide, solid columns of text—*Behrman*⟩ **Solemn** usually heightens the suggestion of impressiveness or awesomeness often implicit in *grave* ⟨perhaps it was natural . . . to mistake *solemn* dignity for sullenness—*Shirer*⟩ ⟨the *solemn* splendor of that most wonderful poem, the story of Job—*Quiller-Couch*⟩ ⟨it was a *solemn* moment, for these were the last words of Augustus to his people—*Buchan*⟩ **Somber** applies to a melancholy or depressing gravity, completely lacking in color, light, or cheer ⟨the Scots, famed for *somber* Calvinism and its intellectual theologizing, did not expect to warm to the enthusiastic kind of religion—*P. D. Whitney*⟩ **Sedate** implies composure and decorous seriousness in character or speech and often a conscious avoidance of lightness or frivolity ⟨good sense alone is a *sedate* and quiescent quality—*Johnson*⟩ ⟨her habitual expression was *sedate* and serious, a permanent reproof, as it were, to those who were first attracted by the voluptuous quality of her admirable figure—*Linklater*⟩ **Staid** implies a settled sedate-ness, often a prim self-restraint, and an even stronger negation of volatility or frivolity than *sedate* ⟨the side streets here are excessively maiden-lady-like . . . the knockers have a very *staid*, serious, nay almost awful, quietness about them—*Keats*⟩ ⟨the *staid* Roman citizen was repelled by the wild dances and the frenzied paeans—*Buchan*⟩ **Sober** sometimes stresses seriousness of purpose ⟨if our pupils are to devote *sober* attention to our in-struction—*Grandgent*⟩ but it more often suggests gravity that proceeds from control over or subdual of one's emotions or passions ⟨come, pensive Nun, devout and pure, *sober*, steadfast, and demure—*Milton*⟩ ⟨this work is certainly of more *sober* mien than most of its author's others. It is very long and very serious, and both these qualities are certainly deliberate observances—*Virgil Thomson*⟩ **Earnest** implies seriousness of purpose as well as sincerity and, often, zealousness and enthusiasm ⟨an *earnest* student⟩ ⟨and men are merry at their chores, and children *earnest* at their play—*Millay*⟩ ⟨she set out on an *earnest* and grim quest for the dollar—*Wouk*⟩
*Ana* austere, stern, *severe, ascetic: *thoughtful, re-flective, contemplative, meditative: *deep, profound
*Ant* light, flippant　—*Con* frivolous, flighty, volatile (see corresponding nouns at LIGHTNESS)

**sermon** homily, *speech, address, oration, harangue, talk, lecture

**serpentine** *winding, sinuous, tortuous, flexuous
*Ana* circuitous, roundabout, *indirect: *crooked, devious

**service** *n* *use, advantage, profit, account, avail
*Ana* usefulness, utility (see USE *n*): *worth, value: helping *or* help, aiding *or* aid, assistance (see corresponding verbs at HELP)

**servile** *subservient, menial, slavish, obsequious
*Ana* *mean, abject, ignoble: fawning, cringing, truckling, cowering (see FAWN)
*Ant* authoritative

**servitude, slavery, bondage** agree in meaning the state of subjection to a master. **Servitude** may refer to the state of a person, or of a class of persons, or of a race that is bound to obey the will of a master, a lord, or a sovereign, and lacks the freedom to determine his or their own acts, laws, and conditions of living. The term is often vague or rhetorical, sometimes implying lack of political freedom, sometimes lack of liberty to do as one pleases ⟨I am as free as Nature first made man, ere the base laws of *servitude* began, when wild in woods the noble savage ran—*Dryden*⟩ More specifically *servitude* denotes the condition of one who must give service to a master and perform labor for him, whether he has bound himself (see BOUND *adj*) voluntarily or is a convict sentenced to penal *servitude* or a slave. **Slavery** implies subjection to a master who is the owner of one's person or who may treat one as his property ⟨taken by the insolent foe and sold to *slavery*—*Shak.*⟩ or entire loss of personal freedom and subjugation to another ⟨is life so dear, or peace so sweet, as to be purchased at the price of chains and *slavery*?—*Henry*⟩ **Bondage** applies to the state of one bound as a serf to the soil and sold with the land when conveyed to a new owner; it can apply also to a state of subjection from which there is no hope of escape except by breaking one's chains ⟨what more oft, in nations grown corrupt, and by their vices brought to servitude, than to love *bondage* more than liberty—*Milton*⟩

**set** *vb* **1 Set, settle, fix, establish** mean to cause someone or something to be put securely in position. **Set** is the most inclusive of these terms, sometimes implying placing in a definite location, especially to serve some definite purpose ⟨*set* a light at each window⟩ ⟨*set* out trees⟩ ⟨*set* food on the table⟩ or to permanently fill some void ⟨*set* a diamond in a ring⟩ or establish some limit ⟨*set* a limit to discussion⟩ ⟨the law of God determines the laws of this world and *sets* the bounds and the character of the institutions and activi-ties of men—*Donald Harrington*⟩ ⟨the question of whether human nature is *set* by heredity or can be changed by environmental factors—*Bauer*⟩ and sometimes im-plying a placing under orders (as in an occupation, a situation, an office, or a sphere of life) or under conditions where something or someone must perform an allotted or prescribed function ⟨*set* a boy to work⟩ ⟨*set* the maids to cleaning house⟩ ⟨*set* proctors to watch the students⟩ or occasionally suggesting a prescribing or ordaining of an object or objects on which one or one's efforts, mind, heart, or eyes concentrates ⟨*set* the subject for a debate⟩ ⟨*set* a goal for his efforts⟩ ⟨*set* his heart on winning a prize⟩ ⟨*set* duty before pleasure⟩ **Settle** comes close to *set* but carries a much stronger implication of putting a person or thing in a place or condition of stability, rest, or repose and often a weaker implication of regulative or dictatorial power ⟨*settle* an invalid in an easy chair⟩ ⟨*settle* themselves in their new home⟩ ⟨offered to escort her to Paris and see her *settled* in a reasonably cheap hotel—*Wouk*⟩ ⟨the tendency to *settle* standards on the level of the "common man"—*Edmund Wilson*⟩ Often the word carries an implication of decisive quieting, calming, or ordering of something that is disturbed, upset, unstable, or fluctuating ⟨*settle* a person's stomach⟩ ⟨*settle* his doubts⟩ ⟨the white of an egg will *settle* the coffee⟩ ⟨everything's *settled* now. You need not worry, Reuben; there will be no fuss—*Gibbons*⟩ ⟨there's nothing will *settle* me but a bullet—*Swift*⟩ **Fix** (see also ADJUST 1; FASTEN) usually implies more stability and permanence in position, condition, or character than *set* or even *settle* ⟨his resolution was already *fixed*—*Buchan*⟩ ⟨truth which the scientist strives to catch and *fix*—*Lowes*⟩ ⟨his place in the McCoy household had become *fixed*—*Anderson*⟩ ⟨what I have most at heart is, that some method should be thought of for ascertaining and *fixing* our language forever —*Swift*⟩ ⟨the undifferentiated, inchoate religious sense is thus intensified and *fixed*, to the great and lasting injury of the spiritual life—*Inge*⟩ **Establish** (see also FOUND) stresses not so much the putting in place or the bringing into existence as the becoming fixed, stable, or immovable,

---

A colon (:) separates groups of words discriminated. An asterisk (*) indicates place of treatment of each group.

although in some use both ideas are connoted ⟨do not transplant a tree once it is *established*⟩ ⟨American sculptors . . . whose reputation was already *established* —*Wharton*⟩ ⟨the child initiates new processes of thought and *establishes* new mental habits much more easily than the adult—*Eliot*⟩ ⟨the novel as I have described it has never really *established* itself in America—*Trilling*⟩ ⟨at the end of the first growing season, the grass was firmly *established*—*Farmer's Weekly*⟩
*Ana* *implant: *fasten, attach, fix, affix: *prescribe, assign, define
*Con* eradicate, deracinate, uproot (see EXTERMINATE): *abolish, annihilate, extinguish: displace, supplant, *replace
2 *coagulate, congeal, curdle, clot, jelly, jell
*Ana* *harden, solidify: *compact, consolidate, concentrate
**set** *n* Set, circle, coterie, clique can all denote a more or less carefully selected or exclusive group of persons having a common interest. Set applies to a comparatively large group, especially of society men and women bound together by common tastes ⟨a solid citizen of the fast and frantic international *set*—*Kenneth Fearing*⟩ ⟨I was myself living in several *sets* that had no connection with one another—*Maugham*⟩ ⟨her college *set* had stayed rigidly in a zigzag path . . . which they considered smart —*Wouk*⟩ Circle implies a common center of the group (as a person or a cause that draws persons to him or it) or a common interest, activity, or occupation ⟨the work of the younger writers . . . has even penetrated into academic *circles*—*Day Lewis*⟩ ⟨like *sex*, the word *segregation* was not mentioned in the best *circles*—*Lillian Smith*⟩ ⟨she felt violently the gaps that death made in her *circle*—*Pritchett*⟩ ⟨an active figure in Madrid's literary and theatrical *circles*—*Current Biog.*⟩ Coterie stresses the notion of selectness or of congeniality within the small circle; **clique** heightens the implication of an often selfish or arrogant exclusiveness ⟨we three formed a little *coterie* within the household—*Symonds*⟩ ⟨the poetry of revolt is apt to become the poetry of a *coterie*—*Lowes*⟩ ⟨the best English society—mind, I don't call the London exclusive *clique* the best English society—*Coleridge*⟩ ⟨the corruption and debauchery of the homosexual *clique*—*Shirer*⟩ ⟨every hoodlum in every crack gang and *clique* who fancied himself with the blade—*Mailer*⟩
**setting** *background, environment, milieu, mise-en-scène, backdrop
**settle** 1 *set, fix, establish
*Ana* *secure, anchor, moor, rivet: *order, arrange
*Ant* unsettle
2 *calm, compose, quiet, quieten, still, lull, soothe, tranquilize
*Ana* placate, appease, *pacify, mollify, conciliate
*Ant* unsettle —*Con* *discompose, disquiet, disturb, perturb, agitate, upset
3 determine, *decide, rule, resolve
*Ana* *judge, adjudge, adjudicate: *close, end, conclude, terminate
**sever** *separate, sunder, part, divide, divorce
*Ana* rive, cleave, rend, split (see TEAR): *cut, hew, chop: *detach, disengage
**several** 1 *distinct, separate, discrete
*Ana* individual, particular, *special, especial
2 *many, sundry, various, divers, numerous, multifarious
*Ana* *single, separate, particular: detached, disengaged (see DETACH)
**severally** individually, respectively, *each, apiece
**severe, stern, austere, ascetic** can all mean given to or characterized by strict discipline and firm restraint.

Severe is applicable to persons and their looks, acts, thoughts, and utterances or to things (as laws, penalties, judgments, and styles) for which persons are responsible. In all these applications it implies rigorous standards of what is just, right, ethical, beautiful, or acceptable and unsparing or exacting adherence to them; it not only excludes every hint of laxity or indulgence but often suggests a preference for what is hard, plain, or meager ⟨a *severe* teacher⟩ ⟨*severe* impartiality⟩ ⟨*severe* in dress⟩ ⟨these bleak and *severe* Sunday mornings, though they left me with a respect for the Bible, had the effect of antagonizing me against it—*Edmund Wilson*⟩ Very often the word suggests harshness or even cruelty ⟨a *severe* penalty⟩ ⟨*severe* discipline⟩ ⟨*severe* criticism⟩ ⟨a *severe* test of his endurance⟩ It is then by extension referable also to things for which persons are not responsible but which similarly impose pain or acute discomfort ⟨a *severe* attack of lumbago⟩ ⟨I do not think that she anticipated anything so *severe* as arsenic on her blackberries—*Shirley Jackson*⟩ ⟨a *severe* winter⟩ **Stern,** though it often implies severity when applied to persons or their acts or words, stresses inflexibility or inexorability of temper; thus, a *severe* judge may appear kindly though dispassionately just, but a *stern* judge reveals no disposition to be mild or lenient; to be made of *stern* stuff is to have an unyielding will or an extraordinarily resolute character ⟨he wanted to bang on his desk, arise magisterially, like a good confessor, being purposeful and *stern*—*Styron*⟩ In extended use *stern* is applied to what cannot be escaped or evaded ⟨*stern* necessity⟩ ⟨the *stern* compulsion of facts—*Buchan*⟩ or to what is harsh and forbidding in its appearance or in its external aspects ⟨the *stern* and rockbound land . . . on which his lot was cast—*Faulkner*⟩ ⟨a marble bath that made cleanliness a luxury instead of one of the *sternest* of the virtues, as it seemed at home—*Shaw*⟩ **Austere** is chiefly applied to persons, their habits, their modes of life, the environments they create, or the works of art they produce; in these applications *austere* implies the absence of appealing qualities (as feeling, warmth, color, animation, and ornament) and therefore positively implies dispassionateness, coldness, reserve, or barrenness ⟨my common conversation I do acknowledge *austere*, my behavior full of rigor—*Browne*⟩ ⟨secretly, these *austere* tyrants seized with delight upon so estimable an excuse for censuring a member of the set they deprecated—*Sackville-West*⟩ Sometimes the word tends to add such connotations as restraint, self-denial, economy of means, and stark simplicity and becomes a term of praise rather than of depreciation ⟨the *austere* dignity and simplicity of their existence—*Pater*⟩ ⟨mathematics, rightly viewed, possesses not only truth, but supreme beauty—a beauty cold and *austere*, like that of sculpture—*Russell*⟩ ⟨a landscape lightly strewn with snow, and rendered graciously *austere* by long, converging lines of leafless poplars—*Wylie*⟩ **Ascetic** implies laborious and exacting spiritual training or discipline, self-denial, abstention from what is pleasurable, and even the seeking of what is painful or disagreeable ⟨strong-willed and *ascetic*, he discovered in discipline the chief end for which the children of Adam were created —*Parrington*⟩ ⟨a people possessed of the epicurean rather than the *ascetic* ideal in morals—*Brownell*⟩ The idea of discipline, especially by abstention from what is pleasurable or easy or self-indulgent for the sake of spiritual or intellectual ends may be emphasized ⟨for science is *ascetic*. It is a discipline and a control of personal impulse that could arise only in a relatively mature civilization—*Baker Brownell*⟩ ⟨there was in him a real nobility, an even *ascetic* firmness and purity of

---

*Ana* analogous words      *Ant* antonyms      *Con* contrasted words      See also explanatory notes facing page 1

character—*Ellis*⟩

*Ana* exacting, oppressive, *onerous, burdensome: *rigid, rigorous, strict, stringent: *hard, difficult, arduous: harsh, rugged, uneven, *rough

*Ant* tolerant: tender　—*Con* lenient, clement, *forbearing, merciful, indulgent: gentle, mild, *soft

**shabby** 1 Shabby, dilapidated, dingy, faded, seedy, threadbare refer to the appearance of persons and of things and mean showing signs of wear and tear. Shabby applies to persons and places and suggests a lack of freshness or newness in those items that contribute to appearance; sometimes the term applies directly to the things, especially clothes, which so contribute. Poverty is often suggested as the cause of this run-down condition but various other causes (as neglect or indifference) may also be suggested ⟨old Bart, *shabby* and inconspicuous, dunking pound cake with his dirty fingers—*W. S. Burroughs*⟩ ⟨villages . . . with their *shabby*, unpainted shacks, dropping with decay—*Brooks*⟩ ⟨everything had been done to make the accused look as *shabby* as possible. They were outfitted in nondescript clothes—*Shirer*⟩ ⟨the old house . . . is too elegant for poor people, and too large; too *shabby*, in too *shabby* a neighborhood, for the rich—*Tate*⟩ **Dilapidated** (compare *dilapidate* under RUIN) implies a worse appearance than *shabby*, usually suggesting a broken-down or tumbledown condition resulting from neglectful lack of repairs or from careless abuse ⟨a *dilapidated* fence with its gate hanging from one hinge⟩ ⟨sat down in a *dilapidated* easy chair minus a cushion—*Purdy*⟩ ⟨an old toy is so much better . . . . The very fact that it was worn and *dilapidated* caused it to create a feeling of warmth—*Henry Miller*⟩ **Dingy** applies to what is no longer fresh or new in appearance and shows the effects of gradual soiling that dulls the colors or dims the brightness ⟨out of his *dingy* retreat, dirty and uncomfortable, he would appear resplendent—*Osbert Sitwell*⟩ ⟨*shabby* in attire, *dingy* of linen—*Thackeray*⟩ ⟨counting another man's money . . . in a *dingy* office—*Shaw*⟩ ⟨he flashed from *dingy* obscurity into splendor—*H. G. Wells*⟩ **Faded** also implies lack of freshness but it connotes the loss of vigor or brightness that shows that a person or thing has passed its prime and is revealing signs of drooping and withering ⟨her slightly stale and *faded* gush about Chopin and her memories of Paris in the spring—*Edmund Wilson*⟩ ⟨she lives with her mother, a *faded* tired woman who played Lady Capulet—*Wilde*⟩ ⟨her clothes were always the same and it is hard to remember what she wore. She seemed to sink into the *faded* anonymity of the old street—*Tate*⟩ ⟨so many of the old friends are dead, and those who live are older and changed, and everything seems a bit *faded* and drab—*H. L. Matthews*⟩ **Seedy** does not go so far as *shabby* in implying deterioration and lack of freshness but it does suggest some loss of those signs that marked a person or thing as strong or at the peak of value and usefulness ⟨sordid squabbling with his landlady about the rent he owes on a *seedy* room —*McCarten*⟩ ⟨an English setter, a bitch, and rather *seedy* now and smelly—*Henry Miller*⟩ ⟨a table on which was a clutter of *seedy* Western souvenirs—a rusted, beat-up placer pan . . . and the shellacked tail of a beaver—*Stafford*⟩ **Seedy** is also used in reference to a person who feels himself not really sick but not up to the mark ⟨we were all feeling *seedy*, and we were getting nervous about it —*Jerome*⟩ **Threadbare** (see also TRITE) in its basic use implies such wear of fabric that all nap is worn away and the threads are visible ⟨the curves of hips and breasts already discernible under the too short and often *threadbare* clothes—*Metalious*⟩ but often this basic notion is lost and the emphasis is on the shabby state typical of

or the fact of extreme grinding poverty ⟨the only opportunity . . . to find escape from the grim, drab, *threadbare* unpicturesque poverty of her inharmonious home —*Dorothy Canfield*⟩ ⟨England, which has a *threadbare* Treasury—*Sulzberger*⟩ ⟨finally got *threadbare* enough and hungry enough to overlook my scruples—*O'Leary*⟩

*Ana* worn (see HAGGARD): dowdy, frowzy, *slatternly: shopworn, *trite: decrepit (see WEAK)

*Con* trim, trig, spick-and-span, *neat, tidy: *new, fresh, new-fashioned

2 *contemptible, despicable, pitiable, sorry, scurvy, cheap, beggarly

*Ana* *mean, sordid, ignoble: *base, low, vile

**shackle** *vb* fetter, clog, trammel, *hamper, manacle, hog-tie

*Ana* *restrain, curb, check, inhibit: *hinder, impede, obstruct, block, bar: restrict, circumscribe, confine, *limit

*Con* disencumber, disembarrass, *extricate: release, liberate, *free

**shade** *n* 1 Shade, shadow, umbrage, umbra, penumbra, adumbration can mean the comparative darkness caused by something which intercepts rays of light. Shade carries no implication of a darkness that has a particular form or definite limit but the term often stresses protection from the glare, heat, or other effect of the light that is cut off ⟨the forest, one vast mass of mingling *shade*— *Shelley*⟩ ⟨chiaroscuro, by which light reveals [in paintings] the richness of *shade* and *shade* heightens the brightness of light—*Ellis*⟩ ⟨the trees afforded *shade* and shelter— *Cather*⟩ **Shadow** usually applies to shade which preserves something of the form of the object which intercepts the light ⟨it [the garden] . . . has neither arbor, nor alcove, nor other shade, except the *shadow* of the house —*Cowper*⟩ ⟨saw . . . the *shadow* of some piece of pointed lace, in the Queen's *shadow*, vibrate on the walls—*Tennyson*⟩ ⟨the shadowless winter, when it is all shade and therefore no *shadow*—*Jefferies*⟩ In extended use *shade* implies darkness or obscurity; *shadow*, insubstantiality or unreality ⟨there no *shade* can last in that deep dawn behind the tomb—*Tennyson*⟩ ⟨'tis but the *shadow* of a wife you see, the name and not the thing—*Shak.*⟩ **Umbrage** (see also OFFENSE) applies chiefly to the shade cast by heavy foliage or trees, though sometimes it refers to the mass of trees or foliage which make for heavy shade ⟨branches . . . spreading their *umbrage* to the circumference of two hundred and seven feet—*Strutt*⟩ ⟨the thrush sings in that *umbrage*—*L. P. Smith*⟩ Its occasional extended use can draw meaning from either of these aspects and suggest, on the one hand, an indistinct indication, as if of something seen in deep shadow ⟨the least *umbrage* of a reflection upon this accident—*North*⟩ or, on the other, an overshadowing influence ⟨to compete in the *umbrage* of big city . . . wages and other costs he had to simplify his . . . process—*J. R. Malone*⟩ Umbra and *penumbra* are largely astronomical and optical terms. Umbra applies to the perfect or complete shadow cast on the moon or the earth in an eclipse, and **penumbra** to the imperfect or partly illuminated shadow which often surrounds the umbra. *Umbra* rarely and *penumbra* often are used in extended senses, the former implying a complete overshadowing or eclipse, the latter denoting the marginal region or border between areas which are themselves clearly one thing or the other, or in which the exact differences between one thing or another are so obscure as not to be clearly discernible ⟨his memory was eclipsed in the *umbra* of a more compelling personality—*Cobb*⟩ ⟨physiology having rudely investigated its phenomena upon the same level as other biological processes, it [love] has been stripped of the mystical *penumbra* in whose shadow its transcendental value seemed real, though hid—*Krutch*⟩ ⟨the great ordinances of the Constitution do not establish and divide fields of black and white. Even the more specific of them are found to terminate in a *penumbra* shading gradually from one extreme to the other—*Justice Holmes*⟩ **Adumbration** applies to something that is so faint or obscure a figure, sketch, or outline of something which actually exists or is to come that it serves as a foreshadowing of it or a hinting at it ⟨the lugubrious harmony of the spot with his domestic situation was too perfect for him, impatient of effects, scenes, and *adumbrations*—*Hardy*⟩ ⟨if the Parthenon has value, it is only as an *adumbration* of something higher than itself—*Babbitt*⟩

*Ana* darkness, dimness, obscurity (see corresponding adjectives at DARK): *shelter, cover, retreat
*Con* brightness, brilliancy, radiance, effulgence (see corresponding adjectives at BRIGHT): glare, glow, blaze (see under BLAZE *vb*)
2 ghost, spirit, specter, *apparition, phantasm, phantom, wraith, revenant
3 *blind, shutter
4 tint, *color, hue, tinge, tone
5 *gradation, nuance
*Ana* distinction, difference (see DISSIMILARITY): *touch, suggestion, suspicion, soupçon, dash, tinge
6 *touch, suggestion, suspicion, soupçon, tinge, smack, spice, dash, vein, strain, tincture, streak
*Ana* *trace, vestige: tint, tinge (see COLOR)

**shadow** *n* *shade, umbrage, umbra, penumbra, adumbration
*Ana* *form, figure, shape, conformation, configuration: darkness, obscurity, dimness (see corresponding adjectives at DARK): silhouette, contour, *outline

**shadow** *vb* *suggest, adumbrate
*Ana* *foretell, forecast, predict, prognosticate: *foresee, foreknow, divine
*Con* *reveal, disclose, discover, divulge, tell

**shake** *vb* 1 Shake, tremble, quake, totter, quiver, shiver, shudder, quaver, wobble, teeter, shimmy, dither are comparable when they mean to exhibit vibratory, wavering, or oscillating movement often as an evidence of instability. Shake, the ordinary and the comprehensive term, can apply to any such movement, often with a suggestion of roughness and irregularity ⟨the earth itself seemed to *shake* beneath my feet—*Hudson*⟩ ⟨he *shook* with fear⟩ ⟨his body *shook* with laughter⟩ **Tremble** applies specifically to a slight, rapid shaking of the human body, especially when one is agitated or unmanned (as by fear, passion, cold, or fatigue) ⟨she stood with her hand on the doorknob, her whole body *trembling*—*Anderson*⟩ ⟨she is so radiant in her pure beauty that the limbs of the young man *tremble*—*Meredith*⟩ The term may apply also to things that shake in a manner suggestive of human trembling ⟨not a breath of breeze even yet ruffled the water: but momentarily it *trembled* of its own accord, shattering the reflections—*Richard Hughes*⟩ **Quake** may be used in place of *tremble* but it commonly carries a stronger implication of violent shaking or of extreme agitation ⟨his name was a terror that made the dead *quake* in their graves—*Ouida*⟩ ⟨his accusing hand . . . stiffly extended, *quaking* in mute condemnation—*Terry Southern*⟩ Often the term suggests either an internal convulsion (as an earthquake or something suggestive of one) or an external event which rocks a person or thing to its foundations ⟨the sounding of the clock in *Venice Preserved* makes the hearts of the whole audience *quake*—*Addison*⟩ ⟨I thought of the sounds that must be coming from those men, and at that thought my insides *quaked;* I thanked God we couldn't hear them—*Kenneth Roberts*⟩ **Totter**

usually suggests great physical weakness (as that associated with infancy, extreme old age, or disease); it therefore often connotes a shaking that makes movement extremely difficult and uncertain or that forebodes a fall or collapse ⟨the mast *tottered* before it fell⟩ ⟨the little calf that's standing by the mother . . . *totters* when she licks it with her tongue—*Frost*⟩ **Quiver** suggests a slight, very rapid shaking comparable to the vibration of the strings of a musical instrument; it differs from *tremble* chiefly in being more often applied to things ⟨aspen leaves *quiver* in the slightest breeze⟩ ⟨it is not a dead mass of stone and metal, but a living thing, *quivering* and humming like a great ship at sea. A splendid piece of architecture—*Highet*⟩ or in carrying a less necessary suggestion of fear or passion and a stronger implication of emotional tension ⟨the little boy's lips *quivered* as he tried not to cry⟩ ⟨I was *quivering* and tingling from head to foot—*Kipling*⟩ ⟨eagerness that made their flanks *quiver*—*Roberts*⟩ ⟨Seymour sat whimpering and *quivering* with panic and temper and discomfort—*Davenport*⟩ **Shiver** and **shudder** usually imply a momentary or short-lived quivering, especially of the flesh. **Shiver** typically suggests the effect of cold ⟨came into the house snow-covered and *shivering*⟩ but it may apply to a similar quivering that results from an emotional or mental cause (as an anticipation, a premonition, a foreboding, or a vague fear) ⟨such thoughts . . . may make you *shiver* at first—*Montague*⟩ ⟨he *shivered* with pleasure as he conceived robberies, assaults—murders if it had to be—*Malamud*⟩ or to a sudden, often seeming, quivering of a thing ⟨his heart *shivered,* as a ship *shivers* at the mountainous crash of the waters—*Bennett*⟩ ⟨when the first star *shivers* and the last wave pales—*Flecker*⟩ **Shudder** usually suggests the effect of something horrible or revolting; physically it implies a sudden sharp quivering that for the moment affects the entire body or mass ⟨the splotched shadow of the heaven tree *shuddered* and pulsed monstrously in scarce any wind—*Faulkner*⟩ ⟨"I am afraid of it," she answered, *shuddering*—*Dickens*⟩ ⟨it was one of those illnesses from which we turn away our eyes, *shuddering*—*Deland*⟩ ⟨the chill of an age-old recognition *shuddered* my spine; a voice was sounding in the dimly lit air—*Miller*⟩ **Quaver** sometimes implies irregular vibration or fluctuation, especially as an effect of something that disturbs ⟨the breeze . . . set the flames of the streetlamps *quavering*—*Stevenson*⟩ but often it stresses tremulousness especially in reference to voices and utterances affected by weakness or emotion ⟨a reedy, *quavering* voice—*Doyle*⟩ ⟨dread returned, and the words *quavered* as she spoke them—*Meredith*⟩ ⟨the *quavering,* envenomed voice of . . . Scrooge—*Styron*⟩ **Wobble** implies an unsteadiness that shows itself in tottering, or in a quivering characteristic of a mass of soft flesh or of a soft jelly, or in a shakiness characteristic of rickety furniture ⟨this table *wobbles*⟩ ⟨bumping when she trots, and *wobbling* when she canters—*Whyte-Melville*⟩ ⟨antique French automobiles *wobbling* giddily along the roads—*Panter-Downes*⟩ ⟨picked up his glass and half emptied it. His hand *wobbled* so that some of it ran down his chin—*Charteris*⟩ **Teeter** implies an unsteadiness that reveals itself in seesawing motions ⟨an inebriated man *teetering* as he stands⟩ ⟨stood on chairs and *teetered* on stepladders—*Dos Passos*⟩ **Shimmy** suggests the fairly violent shaking of the body from the shoulders down which is characteristic of the dance of that name and, therefore, may suggest vibratory motions of an abnormal nature ⟨all kinds of starlets get an opportunity to *shimmy* around for the edification of Pharaoh and his court—*McCarten*⟩ ⟨a lizard *shimmied* across her path—*Millar*⟩ ⟨I often see the

walls of my house *shimmying* a bit—*Lucas*⟩ ⟨the *shimmying* of unbalanced front wheels of an automobile⟩ **Dither** implies a shaking or a hesitant vacillating movement often as a result of nervousness, confusion, or lack of purpose ⟨*dithering* to his feet, he crept downstairs—*Cronin*⟩ *Ana* oscillate, fluctuate, vibrate, waver, *swing, sway
**2 Shake, agitate, rock, convulse** can mean to cause to move to and fro or up and down with more or less violence. **Shake**, the most general of these words, in its specific senses usually retains this basic meaning ⟨as there is a high wind blowing nearly all the time, the nests are continually *shaken*—*Seago*⟩ but it seldom conveys merely this idea. Very often its meaning is narrowed but enriched by an implication of the particular intent or purpose of the movement; thus, to *shake* a rug implies an intent to dislodge dust; to *shake* a tree, to bring down its fruit; to *shake* a cocktail, to mix ingredients; to *shake* hands, to greet or to acknowledge an introduction; to *shake* one's fist, to threaten. Even in its extended use *shake* commonly implies movement, usually physical movement ⟨he was visibly *shaken* by the news⟩ ⟨the exposure of unsuspected depravity in the highest circles *shook* the social fabric to its foundations—*Lucius Beebe*⟩ ⟨just one single example of real unreason is enough to *shake* our belief in everything—*Theodore Sturgeon*⟩ **Agitate** usually carries a much stronger implication of tossing or of violent stirring than *shake;* it often also suggests a prolongation of the movement ⟨a churn has a dasher for *agitating* cream⟩ ⟨the leaves on the trees were *agitated* as if by a high wind—*Hudson*⟩ ⟨brown water in the basin . . . slightly *agitated* by concentric ripples, as though someone had recently thrown a stone into it—*James Helvick*⟩ When the recipient of the action is a person *agitate* connotes emotional disturbance or excitement ⟨he started a discussion which has *agitated* thinkers ever since —*Whitehead*⟩ ⟨the physician interposes, frightens the family, *agitates* the patient to the utmost—*Overstreet*⟩ **Rock** suggests a swinging or swaying motion; it tends to lose the implication of lulling derived from its earliest associations with the movement of a cradle and to emphasize those of upheaving, derived from the violent swaying (as of a ship in a storm or of the earth in an earthquake) ⟨the wind *rocked* the house⟩ ⟨the entire city was *rocked* by the explosion⟩ ⟨Tokyo *rocks* under the weight of our bombs—*Truman*⟩ Often, especially in extended use, *rock* suggests, as *shake* does not, tottering and peril of falling ⟨the stock market was *rocked* by the rumor of war⟩ ⟨constant insinuations finally *rocked* his faith in his friend⟩ ⟨the explosions that *rock* the world today are nothing less than the stirring of the common man the world over—*Hansen*⟩ **Convulse** often implies more violence in the motion than any of the others; it also commonly suggests a pulling to and fro or a wrenching or twisting (as of the body in a paroxysm or of the earth in seismic disturbances) ⟨Lucetta . . . *convulsed* on the carpet in the paroxysms of an epileptic seizure—*Hardy*⟩ ⟨they were *convulsed* with laughter⟩ ⟨the ferment of change that has *convulsed*, distorted, and reshaped our twentieth-century world—*A. E. Stevenson*⟩
*Ana* *move, drive, impel: flourish, brandish, *swing, wave: disturb, derange, unsettle, *disorder
**3** *swing, wave, flourish, brandish, thrash
**shallow** *adj* *superficial, cursory, uncritical
*Ana* slim, slight, slender, *thin: trivial, trifling, *petty, paltry: empty, hollow, idle, *vain
**sham** *n* *imposture, cheat, fake, humbug, fraud, deceit, deception, counterfeit
*Ana* *pretense, pretension, make-believe: *trick, ruse, feint, wile, gambit, ploy

**sham** *vb* feign, simulate, counterfeit, pretend, *assume, affect
*Ana* *invent, create: ape, mock, mimic, imitate, *copy
**sham** *adj* *counterfeit, spurious, bogus, fake, pseudo, pinchbeck, phony
*Ana* feigned, assumed, affected (see ASSUME): hoaxing, bamboozling, hoodwinking, duping (see DUPE): deceptive, delusive, delusory, *misleading
**shame** *n* *disgrace, dishonor, disrepute, infamy, ignominy, opprobrium, obloquy, odium
*Ana* humiliation, degradation, abasement (see corresponding verbs at ABASE): mortification, chagrin (see corresponding adjectives at ASHAMED)
*Ant* glory: pride
**shameless, brazen, barefaced, brash, impudent** can apply to persons and their acts that defy the moral code or social decorum when they mean characterized by boldness and a lack of a sense of shame. **Shameless** implies a lack of effective restraints (as modesty, a sense of decency, an active conscience, or concern for the respect of others) ⟨a *shameless* neglect of her children⟩ ⟨*shameless* gossips⟩ ⟨*shameless* graft⟩ ⟨regards every compromise his comrades have made to get the machine going as a *shameless* betrayal of principle—*West*⟩ ⟨no composer . . . makes such *shameless* use of patriotic feelings to advertise his product—*Virgil Thomson*⟩ **Brazen** implies not only complete shamelessness but defiant insolence ⟨at first a furtive, now a *brazen*, thief⟩ ⟨a *brazen* minister of state, who bore for twice ten years the public hate—*Swift*⟩ ⟨solicited praise and power with the *brazen*, businesslike air of a streetwalker on the prowl—*Rovere*⟩ **Barefaced** implies absence of all effort to disguise or to mask one's transgressions; it connotes extreme effrontery ⟨a *barefaced* lie⟩ ⟨*barefaced* tyranny⟩ ⟨however *barefaced* their deceptions, they manage to convince themselves at the time that they are speaking the truth—*Muggeridge*⟩ **Brash** so strongly implies impetuousness that it does not stress shamelessness as clearly as the preceding words; however, it is often used in place of *shameless* when heedlessness and temerity make one indifferent to the claims of conscience or one's sense of decency ⟨a *brash* intrusion on another's privacy⟩ ⟨*brash* reporters⟩ ⟨deeply I repented of *brash* and boyish crime—*Lindsay*⟩ ⟨felt secure enough in his wealth to make several *brash*, futile attempts at joining the country club—*Styron*⟩ **Impudent** adds to *shameless* implications of bold or pert defiance of considerations of modesty or decency ⟨conduct so sordidly unladylike that even the most *impudent* woman would not dare do it openly—*Shaw*⟩ ⟨women are getting *impudent* all over again and corsetieres, dreaming of the old, elegant, secure, confining days, may well despair— *Lois Long*⟩ ⟨she has a passion for *impudent* adventure, and . . . has quite properly explored a number of improper relationships—*Payne*⟩
*Ana* *abandoned, profligate, dissolute: *hardened, indurated, callous: *vicious, villainous, iniquitous
*Con* modest, pure, *chaste, decent: *shy, diffident, bashful
**shape** *vb* *make, form, fashion, fabricate, manufacture, forge
**shape** *n* *form , figure, conformation, configuration
*Ana* *outline, contour, profile, silhouette: *appearance, look, aspect, semblance
**shapeless** *formless, unformed
*Ana* *rude, rough, crude
*Ant* shapely —*Con* proportionate, *proportional, commensurate
**share, participate, partake** can mean to have, get, use, exercise, experience, or engage in something in common

A colon (:) separates groups of words discriminated. An asterisk (*) indicates place of treatment of each group.

with another or others. **Share** implies that one as the original owner or holder grants the part use, enjoyment, or possession to another ⟨willing to *share* her room at the convention⟩ ⟨*sharing* lunch with a squirrel⟩ or that one as the receiver accepts the part use, enjoyment, or possession of something that belongs to or comes from another ⟨she asked all to *share* in the salad⟩ ⟨I *shared* my sister's room last night when we had a guest⟩ ⟨the employees *shared* in the profits⟩ ⟨she *shared* unwillingly the grocer's fate though . . . her dissatisfaction went no farther than nagging—*Malamud*⟩ But *share* may also take for its subject a group and imply a community of possession or use ⟨you do not *share* the great earth among you fairly —*Jefferies*⟩ ⟨flowers have always been sinister to me when they are lovely—they seem to *share* the elusive promise of a woman who is beautiful—*Mailer*⟩ **Participate** implies that one has or takes a part or a share in a thing (as a work, an experience, or an enterprise) ⟨*participate* in a discussion⟩ ⟨may I ask you whether your wife *participates* in this undertaking?—*Meredith*⟩ ⟨the commerce of the United States with foreign nations, is that of the whole United States. Every district has a right to *participate* in it—*John Marshall*⟩ ⟨they *participated*, with a curious, restrained passion, in the speech made by the red-haired man. He spoke for them—*Isherwood*⟩ **Partake** implies that one accepts, takes, or acquires a portion of a thing (as food, drink, a pleasure, or a burden) ⟨both *partook* of salted bread that a slave proffered —*Hervey*⟩ ⟨we do not only meet to share each other's burdens, but to *partake* in each other's joys—*Spurgeon*⟩ ⟨adventurers who were willing to *partake* his fortunes —*Kinglake*⟩ or comes to have some of the essential or distinguishing characters of a thing ⟨the story itself ceases to be merely melodramatic, and *partakes* of true drama—*T. S. Eliot*⟩

*Ana* \*communicate, impart: divide, dispense, \*distribute

**sharp, keen, acute** can all mean having a fine point or edge, but it is in several of their extended senses that they are most likely to come into comparison. As applied to persons or their qualities, especially of intellect, all three can indicate possession of alert competence and clear understanding. In such use *sharp* is likely to suggest an incisive self-centered quality, sometimes manifest in alert rationality, sometimes in devious cunning ⟨she could never hear enough of this girl's worldly wisdom, vulgar *sharp* wit, and intimate gossip about well-known people—*Wouk*⟩ ⟨a man whose *sharp* face and sharp voice seemed wholeheartedly dedicated to chicanery and lewdness—*Cheever*⟩ ⟨the mumbo jumbo . . . interested him. He was *sharp* enough to guess that these formalities were in the honor of some god—*Forester*⟩ ⟨Russell's critique of these works and their philosophical bases is *sharp*, limpid, and yet profound. With sovereign ease he handles subtleties and ambiguities, disposes of mathematical paradoxes and philosophical paralogisms, refutes errors, and dissipates confusion—*Kline*⟩ **Keen** (see also EAGER) usually stresses eager enthusiasm, clear-sightedness, and quick penetrating character of mind ⟨now hath the child grown greater, and is *keen* and eager of wit and full of understanding—*Morris*⟩ ⟨candidates shall be selected on the basis of future promise of leadership, strength of character, *keen* mind, a balanced judgment—*Official Register of Harvard Univ.*⟩ but it may imply no more than shrewd astuteness ⟨able businessmen . . . as *keen* in their bargains as they were faithful to their engagements —*Scudder*⟩ **Acute** (see also ACUTE) may come close to *keen* in implying a penetrating quality of mind but it is more likely to stress sensitivity and depth and effectiveness of perception especially in the making of subtle

distinctions ⟨his creative tendencies were restrained, however, by an *acute* critical sense, a liking for research, and his genius for teaching—*Starr*⟩ ⟨my very *acute* grandmother, who at eighty-eight is clear and definite in her political convictions—*Current Biog.*⟩ ⟨the *acutest* philosophers have succeeded in liberating themselves completely from the narrow prison of their age and country —*Huxley*⟩ As applied to something perceptible through the senses *sharp* often suggests a disagreeably cutting or biting quality ⟨*sharp* as vinegar⟩ ⟨a *sharp* voice⟩ ⟨a *sharp* flash⟩ ⟨a *sharp* wind⟩ or it may emphasize distinctness or clearness of definition ⟨a *sharp* outline⟩ ⟨*sharp* contrasts⟩ ⟨had happened close on twenty years ago. Yet how short a time it seemed, so *sharp* was still the impression of that night—*Mackenzie*⟩ **Keen**, in contrast, may suggest a bracing, zestful, or piquant quality ⟨the wind came *keen* with a tang of frost—*Masefield*⟩ ⟨very *keen* is the savor of the roast beef that floats up—*Benson*⟩ **Acute**, less common in this sense, may impute an intensely perceptible and often distasteful quality to what it qualifies ⟨the stench was *acute*— *Mailer*⟩ ⟨the sound rose to an almost painfully acute note⟩ As applied to the senses themselves, all imply exceptional functional efficiency and choice is predicated on idiom; thus, *sharp* is used especially of sight and hearing, *keen*, of sight and smell, and *acute*, of hearing. As characterizing pleasures and pains, *sharp* suggests most definitely something that seems to cut or pierce, *keen* implies intensity, and *acute* implies poignancy ⟨a *sharp* pain⟩ ⟨*keen* zest⟩ ⟨*acute* anguish⟩

*Ana* \*incisive, trenchant, cutting, biting: mordant, \*caustic, scathing: piercing, penetrating, probing (see ENTER): tricky, cunning, artful, wily, guileful, \*sly

*Ant* dull: blunt

**shatter** *vb* shiver, \*break, crack, burst, bust, snap

*Ana* demolish, \*destroy: \*ruin, wreck: rend, split, rive (see TEAR)

**shave** *vb* \*brush, graze, glance, skim

*Ana* touch, contact (see corresponding nouns at CONTACT): \*escape, avoid

**shear** *vb* Shear, poll, clip, trim, prune, lop, snip, crop are comparable when they mean to cut off something (as a piece, an excrescence, or a limb). **Shear** is the most general word of this group; it usually implies the use of a sharp cutting instrument (as shears, a razor, or a sharp knife) and, as its result, a close and even or a clean cut through, or off, or away, or from something. The term may or may not imply injury and suggests improvement more often than destruction ⟨a machine with blades strong enough to *shear* a steel bar at one stroke⟩ ⟨*shear* the fleece from sheep⟩ ⟨each year he *sheared* his sheep⟩ ⟨a shark's curved razor-like teeth *shear* cleanly through the bone—*Heiser*⟩ **Poll** implies the cutting of the hair as closely as if shaved; in this sense the verb seldom takes the person as its object, but the part affected ⟨David . . . was in such grief that he had not *polled* his head—*Whiston*⟩ ⟨monks with *polled* crowns⟩ It sometimes refers to the cutting off of the top or head of trees (as willows), often in order to provide new growth suitable for basketry, but sometimes in order to encourage the throwing out of branches from below ⟨there were some beautiful willows, and now the idiot Parson has *polled* them into wretched stumps—*Morris*⟩ **Clip** suggests a cutting evenly or closely without any indication of how much or how little is cut off ⟨*clipped* her little son's curls⟩ ⟨*clipped* the shrubs into elaborate forms⟩ ⟨*clip* an article from a newspaper⟩ **Trim** (see also STABILIZE) always implies the removal of something unwanted or overlong by or as if by cutting or clipping in order to improve the appearance of a thing, or to adjust it to something, or to prepare it for a definite use ⟨*trim* a straggly hedge⟩ ⟨*trimmed* his hair and beard⟩ ⟨*trim* the rough edges from a piece of cloth⟩ ⟨what was not *trimmed* from our pages by an editor's nudge was given away in the hagglings of publisher and author—*Mailer*⟩ **Prune** implies a trimming of a plant (as a tree or shrub) by cutting out superfluous parts (as dead branches) not only to improve its shape but to promote its growth or bearing ⟨*prune* the rosebushes in the garden⟩ Consequently *prune* in broader use implies a cutting down or out or excision so as to remove useless or needless material (as in written matter) ⟨*prune* a manuscript before sending it to the printer⟩ ⟨a good personal library, like a tree, must be *pruned* occasionally to stay healthy—*L. L. Day*⟩ **Lop** implies a cutting off or away by or as if by an axe, especially of what is superfluous; typically it suggests pruning and the removal of dead or unnecessary branches or boughs, but it may suggest the similar removal of something that may be regarded as improperly associated or as an excrescence, a nuisance, or an interference ⟨superfluous branches we *lop* away, that bearing boughs may live—*Shak.*⟩ ⟨Virginia, even after Maryland had been *lopped* off, remained a dominion of imperial extent—*Morison*⟩ **Snip**, like *clip*, may imply the employment of scissors, but it may also suggest the use of sharp fingernails or of any other instrument by which a part may be pinched or cut off; it differs from *clip* in emphasizing suddenness and quickness in movement. It, therefore, often suggests a cutting off of a small piece at a time or a cutting into bits ⟨*snip* off a loose thread⟩ ⟨*snip* the dead flowers from a plant⟩ ⟨the child, with its newfound toy, a pair of scissors, was *snipping* the newspaper into pieces⟩ **Crop**, in most of its meanings, implies the cutting off of the top (as of a tree or grass), but when it emphasizes that implication, it usually suggests cutting off of a piece at the top (as for identification or punishment) or a cutting extremely close (as of the hair) ⟨the stiff-necked sectaries . . . who had been glad to stand in pillories and suffer their ears to be *cropped* rather than put bread in the mouths of priests—*Brooks*⟩ ⟨his hair . . . had been *cropped* by the prison barber—*Yeats*⟩

*Ana* \*cut, slit, slash, hew: split, rive, cleave (see TEAR)

**shed** *vb* \*discard, cast, molt, slough, scrap, junk

*Ana* remove, shift, transfer (see MOVE): reject, repudiate, spurn (see DECLINE *vb*)

**sheen** \*luster, gloss, glaze

*Ana* gleaming *or* gleam, glittering *or* glitter, flashing *or* flash (see FLASH)

**sheer** *adj* **1** \*pure, simple, absolute

*Ana* \*outright, out-and-out, arrant, unmitigated

**2** precipitous, abrupt, \*steep

*Ana* perpendicular, \*vertical

**sheer** *vb* \*turn, divert, deflect, avert

**shelter** *n* **Shelter, cover, retreat, refuge, asylum, sanctuary** can mean the state or a place in which one is safe or secure from whatever threatens or disturbs. **Shelter** usually implies the protection of something that temporarily covers (as a shield or a roof) or that prevents the entrance or approach of something that would harm or annoy ⟨seek *shelter* in a cave from an approaching storm⟩ ⟨*shelters* must be provided for sheep in winter⟩ ⟨the trees afforded shade and *shelter*—*Cather*⟩ ⟨the little boy would run yelping to the *shelter* of Mrs. Dixon's petticoats—*Kenneth Roberts*⟩ ⟨religious discipline is nothing but a permanent psychic *shelter*. You stay inside it, and you're less vulnerable—*Wouk*⟩ **Cover** usually stresses concealment; it is often applied to a place of natural shelter (as a copse, thicket, or dense growth of brush) or, by extension, to something similarly thick or protective ⟨they returned as wolves return to cover—*Kipling*⟩ ⟨the blackout, whose *cover* enabled a number of persons . . . to get about on various subversive missions—*Shirer*⟩ **Retreat** stresses usually voluntary retirement from danger or annoyance and escape to a condition or place promising safety or security or peace. It often suggests remoteness, solitude, quiet, or, in religious use, conditions affording opportunities for prayer and meditation ⟨a hermit's *retreat*⟩ ⟨ah, for some *retreat* deep in yonder shining Orient—*Tennyson*⟩ ⟨regard the hut as a *retreat* and a camp rather than a home—*Canby*⟩ **Refuge** also suggests an attempt to escape whatever threatens one's peace, safety, or happiness, but it usually implies fleeing from an attack or from pursuers, or something (as a thought or emotion) that harasses like a pursuer ⟨refuse *refuge* to political exiles⟩ ⟨the escaped convict found *refuge* in a deserted house⟩ ⟨our clubs are . . . not *refuges* for bored husbands and homeless bachelors—*Brownell*⟩ ⟨millions of people . . . feel . . . the secrecy of the voting booth is their last *refuge*—*Seldes*⟩ **Asylum** adds to *refuge* the implications of exemption from seizure or plundering and the finding of safety (as in the care of a protector or in a place outside the jurisdiction of the law) ⟨the embezzler sought *asylum* in a country that had no extradition treaty⟩ ⟨during the war that followed, Britain gave *asylum* to many exiles from different lands—*Victor Ross*⟩ **Sanctuary** stresses the sacredness of the place and its claim to reverence or inviolability; thus, a *sanctuary* for wildlife is an area which is exempt from intrusion by hunters and trappers and in which predators commonly are controlled so that the forms of life which are their prey may flourish ⟨if thou breathest aught that can attaint the honor of my house, by Saint George! not the altar itself shall be a *sanctuary*—*Scott*⟩ ⟨the most important single event . . . in our history is that it is our turn to be freedom's shield and *sanctuary*—*A. E. Stevenson*⟩

*Ana* protection, safeguarding *or* safeguard (see corresponding verbs at DEFEND): \*harbor, haven, port

**shelter** *vb* \*harbor, lodge, house, entertain, board

*Ana* \*defend, protect, shield, guard, safeguard: \*receive, accept, admit

**shibboleth** \*catchword, byword, slogan

**shield** *vb* protect, guard, safeguard, \*defend

*Ana* preserve, conserve, \*save: \*harbor, shelter, lodge, house

**shift** *vb* \*move, remove, transfer

*Ana* displace, \*replace: \*change, alter, vary: veer, \*swerve, deviate

**shift** *n* **1** makeshift, expedient, \*resource, resort, stopgap, substitute, surrogate

*Ana* \*device, contrivance, contraption: ruse, \*trick, stratagem, maneuver, gambit, ploy, wile, feint, artifice

**2** tour, trick, turn, \*spell, stint, bout, go

*Ana* \*change, alternation: allotment, assignment (see corresponding verbs at ALLOT)

**shimmy** *vb* \*shake, tremble, quake, totter, quiver, shiver, shudder, quaver, wobble, teeter, dither

**ship** *n* \*boat, vessel, craft

**ship** *vb* forward, transmit, remit, route, \*send, dispatch

**shipshape** \*neat, tidy, trim, trig, snug, spick-and-span

**shirk** *vb* \*dodge, parry, sidestep, duck, fence, malinger

*Ana* evade, elude, avoid, \*escape: \*recoil, shrink, quail, flinch

**shiver** *vb* shatter, \*break, crack, burst, bust, snap

**shiver** *vb* quiver, shudder, quaver, \*shake, tremble, quake, totter, wobble, teeter, shimmy, dither

**shoal** *n* **Shoal, bank, reef, bar** can all mean a shallow place in a body of water. In ordinary use **shoal** is applied

---

A colon (:) separates groups of words discriminated. An asterisk (\*) indicates place of treatment of each group.

to a shallow place, especially one that is difficult to navigate ⟨dangerous *shoals* in uncharted waters⟩ **Bank,** often as the plural *banks,* is applied to one that is formed by a muddy, sandy, or gravelly elevation but is deep enough to make navigation safe for lighter craft (as fishing boats) ⟨the Grand *Bank,* also called the *Banks* of Newfoundland, is a noted fishing ground⟩ and **reef,** to one where rock lies dangerously close to the surface ⟨the *reef*-bound shores of Bermuda⟩ Technically *shoal* is applied to elevations which are not rocky and on which the water is not more than 6 fathoms deep, *bank* to a similar elevation rising from the continental shelf and usually having a broad flat top under deeper water, and *reef* to a rocky elevation on which the water at low tide is 6 fathoms or less in depth. **Bar** carries implications found in many senses (as of length, narrowness, and hindrance). It is applied to a ridge of sand or gravel piled up at and often across or nearly across a river's mouth or an entrance to a harbor and obstructing navigation.

**shock** *n* cock, stack, heap, pile, mass, bank (see under HEAP *vb*)

**shock** *vb* cock, stack, *heap, pile, mass, bank

**shock** *n* collision, clash, concussion, *impact, impingement, percussion, jar, jolt   •
*Ana* *encounter, skirmish: *attack, assault, onslaught, onset: shaking, rocking, agitation, convulsion (see corresponding verbs at SHAKE)

**shocking** appalling, *fearful, awful, dreadful, frightful, terrible, terrific, horrible, horrific
*Ana* *ghastly, gruesome, lurid, macabre, grisly, grim: odious, abhorrent, abominable, *hateful: *repugnant, repellent, distasteful, obnoxious

**shoot** *vb* 1 *fly, dart, float, skim, scud, sail
*Ana* *speed, hasten, hurry, quicken
2 *rush, dash, tear, charge
*Ana* dart, *fly, scud: *speed, hasten, hurry

**shoot** *n* Shoot, branch, bough, limb can mean one of the members of a plant and especially a shrub or a tree that are outgrowths from a main stem or from one of its divisions. *Shoot* and *branch* are referable to most plants as well as to shrubs and trees and both imply development from a bud. *Shoot,* however, stresses actual growing and therefore applies chiefly to a young undeveloped member. *Branch* suggests a spreading out by dividing and subdividing and applies typically to a more or less fully developed member, whether it arises directly from the trunk or stem or from an outgrowth or a subdivision of an outgrowth. *Bough* is not interchangeable with *shoot,* for it usually suggests foliage and fruit or flowers. Although it is often used interchangeably with *branch* and is sometimes thought of as a large or main branch, it carries a comparatively weak implication of ramification and a strong connotation of full seasonal development; thus, *bough* may be preferred when the shrub or tree is in leaf or bloom and *branch* when the shrub or tree is stripped of foliage or its members are thought of as barren or dead ⟨*boughs* loaded with fruit⟩ ⟨pine *boughs* for Christmas decorations⟩ ⟨bare *branches*⟩ ⟨superfluous *branches* we lop away, that bearing *boughs* may live—*Shak.*⟩ ⟨in a drearnighted December, too happy, happy tree, thy *branches* ne'er remember their green felicity—*Keats*⟩ **Limb** applies usually to a large branch that grows directly out of the trunk of a tree or to a member produced by the forking of the trunk ⟨the knotty *limbs* of an enormous oak—*Shelley*⟩

**shopworn** *trite, hackneyed, stereotyped, threadbare
*Ana* wasted (see HAGGARD): attenuated, diluted, thinned (see THIN *vb*): antiquated, obsolete, archaic (see OLD)

**shore** *n* Shore, coast, beach, strand, bank, littoral, fore-

**shore** are comparable when they mean land bordering a body or stream of water. **Shore** is the general word for the land immediately bordering on the sea, a lake, or a large stream. **Coast** denotes the land along the sea regarded especially as a boundary. **Beach** applies to the pebbly or sandy shore washed by the sea or a lake ⟨a rocky shore with here and there a cove with a *beach*⟩ Both *shore* and *beach* may denote a resort frequented for pleasure or vacation. In this use *shore* more specifically indicates proximity to the sea ⟨spend the summer at the *shore*⟩ and *beach* a place adapted (as by the presence of a sandy beach) to the use of swimmers or sunbathers ⟨spend a part of each day at the *beach*⟩ **Strand** is elevated for *shore* or *beach* ⟨to this lakeside, as to the holiest *strand* in Europe, pilgrims full of soul were drawn in thousands—*L. P. Smith*⟩ **Bank** denotes the steep or sloping margin of a stream. **Littoral** is a technical or somewhat pretentious term occurring especially in geographic, political, and scientific writings for the whole coast or an extended, clearly specified portion of the coast of a particular sea or country; it may imply extension farther inland than *coast* usually implies ⟨the whole Mediterranean *littoral* is . . . subject to earthquakes—*Scribner's Mag.*⟩ **Foreshore** is applied sometimes to the part of the shore between high and low watermarks but at other times is extended to include the beach.

**short** 1 *brief
*Ana* decreased, lessened, reduced, diminished (see DECREASE): shortened, abridged, abbreviated, curtailed (see SHORTEN): *concise, terse, laconic
*Ant* long
2 crisp, brittle, friable, *fragile, frangible

**shortcoming** *imperfection, deficiency, fault
*Ana* defect, flaw, *blemish: failing, frailty, foible, *fault
*Con* *excellence, merit, virtue, perfection

**shorten,** curtail, abbreviate, abridge, retrench can all mean to reduce in extent, especially by cutting. **Shorten** commonly implies reduction in length or duration ⟨*shorten* a road by eliminating curves⟩ ⟨to *shorten* a visit⟩ It is also often used of apparent rather than actual length ⟨they *shortened* the journey by telling stories⟩ ⟨if we really have a murderer in our midst, your easiest method of *shortening* your own young life would be to let him know how clever you are—*Mary Fitt*⟩ ⟨the vaccines will not even *shorten* the course of a cold—*Fishbein*⟩ **Curtail** adds to *shorten* the implication of making cuts that impair completeness or cause deprivation ⟨the interruption *curtailed* his speech⟩ ⟨the outdoor ceremony was *curtailed* because of the storm⟩ ⟨*curtailed* rights⟩ ⟨emergency order drastically *curtailing* the use of fuel—*Current Biog.*⟩ **Abbreviate** implies reducing by omitting some normally present or following part; thus one *abbreviates* a word by cutting out or cutting off letters; one *abbreviates* a discussion by bringing it to a close sooner than planned or anticipated ⟨their outing was *abbreviated* by a sudden drenching downpour⟩ ⟨a stocky square-jawed man of great physical strength and energy, though of *abbreviated* intelligence—*Shirer*⟩ **Abridge** expresses reduction in compass or scope rather more than in length ⟨I feel you do not fully comprehend the danger of *abridging* the liberties of the people—*Lincoln*⟩ but it may imply the retention of all that is essential and the relative completeness of the result ⟨*abridge* a dictionary⟩ **Retrench** stresses reduction in extent or costs of something felt to be in excess ⟨*retrench* expenses⟩ ⟨the lords are *retrenching* visibly, and are especially careful to avoid any form of ostentation—*Nancy Mitford*⟩
*Ana* reduce, *decrease, lessen, diminish: *contract, shrink, condense

---

*Ana* analogous words     *Ant* antonyms     *Con* contrasted words     See also explanatory notes facing page 1

*Ant* lengthen, elongate: extend

**short-lived** *transient, transitory, passing, ephemeral, momentary, fugitive, fleeting, evanescent
*Ant* agelong

**shortly** *presently, soon, directly

**shout** *vb* Shout, yell, shriek, scream, screech, squeal, holler, whoop are comparable when they mean as verbs to make or utter a loud and penetrating sound that tends or is intended to attract attention and, as nouns, a sound or utterance of this character. All, when used in reference to human utterance, can apply to either meaningful speech or inarticulate cries. **Shout** ordinarily implies vocal utterance in an energetically raised voice intended to carry a considerable distance or to rise above conflicting sound; in itself and apart from context the term carries no information about the emotional or meaning content or the tonal quality of the sound ⟨the peddlers . . . *shout* their wares with a cry which is like the howl of a wolf—*Gardner*⟩ ⟨the geishas followed us, *shouting* insults in English, Japanese and pantomime—*Mailer*⟩ ⟨the lusty yells of the brown-shirted masses or the *shouts* of the Fuehrer blaring from the loudspeakers—*Shirer*⟩ ⟨the cuckoo *shouts* all day at nothing in leafy dells alone—*Housman*⟩ In its extended use *shout* stresses attention-gaining quality ⟨the brassy, peremptory *shout* of the ship's siren sounded . . . urgent and startling—*R. B. Robertson*⟩ ⟨his conservatory in winter is a *shout* of warring geraniums, which fills his heart with joy—*G. W. Johnson*⟩ **Yell** is used chiefly with reference to human utterance and implies not only loudness but sharpness and stridency of sound and usually either the uncontrolled expression of an emotion (as horror, fear, rage, or triumph) or an urgent attempt to attract attention ⟨the two boys *yelled* with fear—*Buck*⟩ ⟨faced a waiting crowd that let out a tumultuous *yell* of greeting—*Sandburg*⟩ ⟨heard the boy *yell* for help⟩ In its extended use *yell* may apply to a sound suggesting a human yell ⟨heard the lacerating *yell* of a scared bird shrill in his ears—*Gibson*⟩ ⟨the long, sunless winters, with their wild snows, their *yelling* gales—*C. G. D. Roberts*⟩ or to an urgent appeal ⟨they have exposed the flimsiness of satellite power, which—when the chips are down—must *yell* for Red Army help—*Goldstein*⟩ **Shriek** implies a piercingly shrill sound or tone and, as applied to human utterance, suggests a strong emotional background (as of fear, horror, or anguish or less often of some pleasant or neutral emotion) ⟨a case of goods from Paris to examine with little *shrieks* of excitement—*Jesse*⟩ ⟨the heavy booming of surf . . . could not drown the *shriek* of tortured metal in her damaged forepart—*Porteous*⟩ ⟨this instant's hesitation seemed to fill him with a tremendous, fantastic contempt, and he damned them in *shrieked* sentences—*Crane*⟩ ⟨I threatened the three men with my revolver, but they *shrieked* for mercy and I did not fire—*R. H. Davis*⟩ In extended use *shriek*, like *shout*, stresses attention-gaining quality ⟨the slogans and hyperboles of boundless confidence. The advertising columns *shrieked* with them—*F. L. Allen*⟩ ⟨the *shriek* of red furnaces against the sky—*Brand*⟩ **Scream** in its basic use differs little from *shriek* ⟨how quick the crows come flapping with their *screams*—*Vance*⟩ ⟨she *screamed* and fainted and came to and *screamed* and fainted all over again—*Bromfield*⟩ ⟨*screaming* to God for death by drowning—*Millay*⟩ and it may be similar in extended use ⟨the growing industries of Utah are *screaming* for water— —*Time*⟩ ⟨the papers carried *screaming* headlines— *Lovett*⟩ but more often its extension refers to something of which the action or occurrence is accompanied by or suggestive of physical screaming ⟨every one of you will *scream* your lives out at the block within a year—*George*

*Orwell*⟩ ⟨while smoke-black freights . . . *screaming* to the west coast, *screaming* to the east, carry off a harvest, bring back a feast—*Lindsay*⟩ ⟨smells of concentration camps and the basements of secret police. There are *screaming* nerves in it—*Priestley*⟩ **Screech** implies a prolonged, typically inarticulate shriek that is conspicuously harsh or discordant or trying to the nerves ⟨the groan . . . had changed to a *screech* like an electric butcher saw on bone—*Wouk*⟩ ⟨three overfed fish house cats were *screeching* at each other—*Joseph Mitchell*⟩ ⟨their ungreased wooden wheels *screeching* a cacophony that could be heard for miles—*Amer. Guide Series: Minn.*⟩ In extended uses it is closely comparable to such uses of *scream* ⟨many photographers . . . congratulate themselves when they have almost blown you down with *screeching* hues alone—a bebop of electric blues, furious reds, and poison greens—*Fortune*⟩ ⟨the driver applied his brakes with a jerk, and the car *screeched* to a standstill—*Bruce Marshall*⟩ **Squeal** implies a sharp shrill sound that is not necessarily especially loud and that, if of human origin, is ordinarily less emotion-charged than a shriek, scream, or screech ⟨the hulk of this man belied the *squeal* of his piping voice like a run-down wheel —*Salomon*⟩ ⟨on the stage the talk of Mr. Steinbeck's characters occasionally hits the ear with the effect of chalk *squealing* on a slate—*Lardner*⟩ Often the term is used with specific reference to the natural cries of certain animals ⟨the urgent *squeals* of a hungry pig⟩ ⟨rats *squealing* between the walls⟩ **Holler** ordinarily refers to human utterance that in tone and volume is equivalent to *shout* ⟨his *holler* and shout made the bobcat shiver—*Warren*⟩ Often it implies a purpose (as of warning or attracting attention) ⟨*hollered* again and again until the boy turned⟩ or an expression (as of surprise or distress or anger) ⟨let out a *holler* as the stone whizzed by his head⟩ In extended use the term stresses vehemence (as in expostulating or criticizing or demanding) ⟨the correspondents *holler* so . . . because the legend of the profession demands that one must be objective in all things—*Belden*⟩ ⟨I didn't see he'd taken my line at first and when I did I put up a *holler*—*Brace*⟩ ⟨in spite of six rate increases in the last seven years, casualty companies are already getting ready to *holler* for more—*Time*⟩ **Whoop**, like *holler*, usually refers to human utterance equivalent in quality to *shout*, but ordinarily it implies eagerness, enthusiasm, or enjoyment as a cause ⟨made a man want to cry and *whoop* all at the same time—*Krey*⟩ In its varied extended uses it is likely to suggest exuberant, often noisy vigor or vitality ⟨*whoops* up a selling boom—*Stegner*⟩ ⟨*whooped* through on a voice vote a stopgap foreign aid appropriation bill—*Current Biog.*⟩
*Ana* *roar, bellow, bawl, howl

**shout** *n* yell, shriek, scream, screech, squeal, holler, whoop (see under SHOUT *vb*)
*Ana* bellow, vociferation, clamor, bawl, roar (see under ROAR *vb*)

**shove** *vb* *push, thrust, propel
*Ana* *force, constrain, oblige, compel, coerce: impel, drive, *move

**show** *vb* **1** Show, manifest, evidence, evince, demonstrate are comparable when they mean to reveal something outwardly by or as if by a sign or to serve to make something outwardly apparent or visible. **Show** implies enabling others to see, but in this case what is revealed can only be inferred (as from acts, words, or looks) ⟨he never *shows* what he thinks⟩ ⟨Tony . . . asked a question or two designed to *show* his intelligence—*Archibald Marshall*⟩ ⟨in this decision he *showed* his capacity for extreme boldness—*Buchan*⟩ ⟨slackness among civilians

---

A colon (:) separates groups of words discriminated. An asterisk (*) indicates place of treatment of each group.

. . . *showed* plainly in public life—*Wecter*⟩ **Manifest** implies a fuller, plainer, and more indubitable revelation than *show* ⟨in handwriting the Chinese believe that the inner personality of the writer is directly *manifested*— *Binyon*⟩ ⟨it is said that . . . a race *manifests* in all its history the same innate mental and emotional character- istics—*Benedict*⟩ ⟨the devotion *manifested* for these cherished beasts sometimes produced uncomfortable results—*Repplier*⟩ **Evidence** is often used in place of *show* ⟨*evidenced* his appreciation⟩ but it specifically implies that the outward act or utterance serves as proof of the existence or the actuality of something not fully proved or in question ⟨argued that their hostility was *evidenced* by their acts⟩ ⟨initiative is *evidenced* by willingness to accept responsibility—*McCain*⟩ ⟨chaste, elegant, entirely in the contemporary mode, *evidencing* stylistic affiliations only with other contemporary buildings —*Mumford*⟩ **Evince** implies some outward marks or tokens (as of an interest, an emotion, or a power) ⟨he has *evinced* no interest in the project⟩ ⟨Cashel, bitterly humiliated by his own tears, and exasperated by a certain cold triumph which his captor *evinced* on witnessing them—*Shaw*⟩ ⟨the first paragraph *evinces* an ignorance of religious poetry, or an indifference to it—*Tate*⟩ ⟨he had never *evinced* any special interest in countries be- yond our immediate borders—*S. H. Adams*⟩ **Demonstrate** (see also PROVE 1) is used chiefly in reference to feelings; it ordinarily implies obvious or even deliberately dis- played external signs (as effusiveness, enthusiasm, emo- tional excitement, or significant actions) ⟨*demonstrate* his approval by loud applause⟩ ⟨Paul was a person who *demonstrated* all his sentiments—*Thackeray*⟩ ⟨*demon- strated* his own brand of intransigence—*Funk*⟩

*Ana* *reveal, disclose, discover: present, *offer, proffer, tender

*Con* *hide, conceal, secrete

**2 Show, exhibit, display, expose, parade, flaunt** can all mean to present in such a way as to invite notice or atten- tion. One **shows** something which he enables others to see or look at (as by putting it forward into view inten- tionally or inadvertently or by taking another where he may see it) ⟨*showed* his tongue to the doctor⟩ ⟨*show* our new home to friends⟩ ⟨*show* the city to an out-of- town guest⟩ ⟨the picture purported to *show* the earth's convexity—*Martin Gardner*⟩ ⟨I don't think he ever *showed* his full powers—*Laski*⟩ One **exhibits** something which he puts forward prominently or openly, either with the express intention or with the result of attracting others' attention or inspection ⟨*exhibit* the museum's collection of Whistler engravings⟩ ⟨*exhibit* articles made by children in school⟩ ⟨in many fashionable gown shops, garments are not *exhibited* but are shown only to prospective purchasers⟩ ⟨*exhibit* unreasonable fear⟩ ⟨if any crave redress of injustice, they should *exhibit* their petitions in the street—*Shak.*⟩ ⟨he *exhibited* with peculiar pride two cream-colored mules—*Cather*⟩ ⟨a group of rectangular buildings, *exhibiting* the stark functionalism of a toy village—*Marquand*⟩ One **displays** something when he spreads it out before the view of others or puts it in a position where it can be seen to advantage or with great clearness ⟨the exhibition was criticized because many paintings were not properly *displayed*⟩ ⟨the male makes a play for the female . . . by strutting before her, *dis- playing* his accomplishments, his prowess, his charms— *Edmund Wilson*⟩ One **exposes** something when he brings it out of hiding or concealment or from under cover and shows, exhibits, or displays it consciously or unconscious- ly. The term sometimes means little more than to exhibit or display ⟨he . . . looked me over as if I had been *ex-*

*posed* for sale—*Conrad*⟩ ⟨the tide was low and the mud- banks were *exposed* and reeking—*Cheever*⟩ Often it means to reveal publicly something and especially some- thing disagreeable that has been or should be concealed ⟨afraid to *expose* his ignorance by asking questions⟩ ⟨it was my duty to leave no stone unturned to discover and *expose* the awful truth—*Rose Macaulay*⟩ Frequently it carries the additional implication of unmasking ⟨it was . . . his friends . . . that he attacks in this terrible story of the passing stranger who took such a vitriolic joy in *exposing* their pretensions and their hypocrisy—*Brooks*⟩ One **parades** something by displaying it ostentatiously or arrogantly ⟨smugly *parading* his honesty⟩ ⟨I can't believe that God wants the strong to *parade* their strength —*Hellman*⟩ ⟨he is a writer who does not raise his voice. He avoids emphasis. His finest phrases . . . are tucked away, not *paraded*—*J. M. Brown*⟩ Sometimes the term implies not merely ostentation or arrogance but an intent to deceive or mislead ⟨*parades* her love for her husband only because she actually did not love him—*Parshley*⟩ ⟨speaking with open contempt of mature persons who *paraded* their deference to the wishes of a father—*Krutch*⟩ One **flaunts** something when one parades it shamelessly, often boastfully, and offensively ⟨they *flaunt* their con- jugal felicity in one's face—*Wilde*⟩ ⟨ye vaunted your fathomless power, and ye *flaunted* your iron pride— *Kipling*⟩ ⟨over this was an unbelievable *flaunting* of opulence—*Hervey*⟩

*Ana* *indicate, betoken, attest, bespeak, argue, prove: intimate, hint, *suggest

*Ant* disguise

**show** *n* *exhibition, exhibit, exposition, fair

**showy, pretentious, ostentatious** can mean making or presenting an outward display that is by implication greater than what is necessary or justifiable. **Showy,** the ordinary term, carries less definite implications than the other words. It implies an imposing, striking, or impressive appearance, but it often suggests cheapness, inferiority, or poor taste ⟨*showy* brass ware—*Shaw*⟩ ⟨*showy* fur- niture⟩ ⟨*showy* decorations⟩ or undue conspicuousness or gaudiness ⟨a *showy* wallpaper design⟩ ⟨*showy* peonies⟩ or overattention to superficial qualities ⟨the *showy* talents, in which the present age prides itself—*Newman*⟩ **Pre- tentious** (see also AMBITIOUS 2) suggests even less warrant for display, for it usually implies an appearance that is not justified by the thing's actual value or actual cost or by the person's actual worth, rank, performance, or capability; the term therefore implies a criticism of what- ever is so described ⟨I'd rather you didn't call me "sir" . . . it might give rise to the idea that I had asked you to . . . . It might appear rather *pretentious*—*Mackenzie*⟩ ⟨his sense of character is nil, and he is as *pretentious* as a rich whore, as sentimental as a lollipop—*Mailer*⟩ ⟨a brilliant sham, which, like a badly built and *pretentious* house, looks poor and shabby after a few years—*Cather*⟩ **Ostentatious** stresses vainglorious display or parade but it does not necessarily imply either showiness or preten- tiousness ⟨*ostentatious* public charities—*Wilde*⟩ ⟨the *ostentatious* simplicity of their dress—*Macaulay*⟩ ⟨thought their cortege *ostentatious* . . . slaves marching ahead with drums, porters bearing food and . . . gifts, and an armed escort—*Hervey*⟩

*Ana* *gaudy, tawdry, garish, flashy, meretricious: re- splendent, gorgeous (see SPLENDID): opulent, sumptuous, *luxurious

**shrew** scold, vixen, termagant, *virago, amazon

**shrewd, sagacious, perspicacious, astute** can all mean acute in perception and sound in judgment, especially in reference to practical affairs. **Shrewd** implies native

cleverness, acumen, and an exceptional ability to see below the surface; it often also connotes hardheadedness ⟨a *shrewd* bargain⟩ ⟨a *shrewd* observer⟩ ⟨a *shrewd* remark⟩ ⟨the *shrewd* wisdom of an unlettered old woman —*Pater*⟩ ⟨the hard mind of a *shrewd* small-town boy, the kind of boy who knows you have a real cigar only when you are the biggest man in town—*Mailer*⟩ ⟨she had had a mania for buying and selling land, and was a *shrewd* judge of values—*Wolfe*⟩ **Sagacious** is usually applied to persons or their decisions; their judgments, and their methods of pursuing their ends; it stresses penetration, discernment, judiciousness, and often, farsightedness ⟨the auctioneer, a small *sagacious* individual . . . , was directing his two blue-jowled assistants in the business of displaying to their best advantage the remaining pieces —*Wylie*⟩ ⟨he left an estate of approximately $172,000, accumulated through *sagacious* investments—*Dilliard*⟩ **Perspicacious** is applied chiefly to mental sight or insight and suggests unusual power to see through and to understand what is dark, hidden, mysterious, or puzzling ⟨a *perspicacious* reader of character⟩ ⟨a *perspicacious* critic⟩ ⟨we must make allowance also for those blind spots which are found in the most *perspicacious* mortals —*L. P. Smith*⟩ ⟨some *perspicacious* manufacturer of another product . . . beat the rap the same way—*Ace*⟩ ⟨it occurred to the *perspicacious* reddleman that he would have acted more wisely by appearing less unimpressionable—*Hardy*⟩ **Astute** implies a combination of shrewdness and perspicacity and often, in addition, connotes an ability to keep one's counsel or an incapacity for being fooled, especially where one's own interests are concerned ⟨savages . . . are often as . . . *astute* socially as trained diplomatists—*James*⟩ ⟨the man who can make millions by an *astute* business deal—*Hobson*⟩ **Astute**, opprobriously used, heightens the suggestion, sometimes present in *perspicacious*, of artfulness, diplomacy, or craft. It may connote merely shrewd discernment and sagacity ⟨I have described above our low-caliber presidents—they, too, are more or less *astute* party hacks— *Edmund Wilson*⟩
*Ana* knowing, *intelligent, smart, clever, quick-witted: politic, diplomatic, smooth (see SUAVE): *wise, prudent, sensible, judicious: penetrating, piercing, probing (see ENTER): *sharp, keen, acute

**shriek** *vb* *shout, yell, scream, screech, squeal, holler, whoop
*Ana* vociferate, clamor, bellow, *roar: vent, ventilate, air, voice, *express

**shriek** *n* shout, yell, scream, screech, squeal, holler, whoop (see under SHOUT *vb*)
*Ana* vociferation, clamor, bellow, roar (see under ROAR *vb*)

**shrink** 1 *contract, constrict, compress, condense, deflate
*Ana* *decrease, reduce, diminish, lessen: *shorten, abridge, retrench, curtail
*Ant* swell —*Con* *expand, amplify, distend, dilate, inflate
2 *recoil, flinch, quail, blench, wince
*Ana* cringe, cower (see FAWN): retreat, *recede: balk, shy, boggle, scruple, *demur

**shrivel** *wither, wizen
*Ana* parch, desiccate, *dry: sear, scorch, *burn

**shroud** *vb* *cover, overspread, envelop, wrap, veil
*Ana* *hide, conceal, screen, bury: cloak, mask, camouflage, *disguise

**shudder** *vb* shiver, quiver, quaver, *shake, tremble, quake, totter, wobble, teeter, shimmy, dither

**shun** avoid, evade, elude, *escape, eschew
*Ana* *decline, refuse, reject: balk, shy, scruple, *demur,

stick, stickle: scorn, disdain, *despise
*Ant* habituate

**shut** *vb* *close

**shut out** eliminate, *exclude, debar, rule out, blackball, disbar
*Ana* *prevent, preclude, obviate: *hinder, obstruct, block, bar

**shutter** *n* *blind, shade

**shy** *adj* **Shy, bashful, diffident, modest, coy** can mean showing disinclination to obtrude oneself in the presence or company of others. **Shy** implies a shrinking, sometimes constitutional, sometimes the result of inexperience, from familiarity or contact with others; shyness usually manifests itself in a certain reserve of manner or in timidity in approaching others ⟨the savage . . . is a *shy* person, imbued with the notion that certain things are not to be talked of to strangers—*Inge*⟩ ⟨*shy* in the presence of strangers and bold with people she knew well—*Anderson*⟩ **Bashful** implies an instinctive or constitutional shrinking from public notice that usually expresses itself in awkwardness of demeanor and is especially characteristic of childhood and adolescence; as applied to mature persons it connotes abnormal or excessive shyness and lack of savoir faire ⟨he hesitated, awkward and *bashful*, shifted his weight from one leg to the other—*London*⟩ ⟨as he grew up, he became increasingly *bashful*, and he never had a close friend of either sex—*Donovan*⟩ **Diffident** implies a distrust, which may or may not be warranted, of one's own ability, opinions, or powers that gives rise to hesitation in their exercise ⟨he was conservative and *diffident* by nature, and even after all these years he felt tongue-tied in the presence of those stricken by grief— *Styron*⟩ **Modest,** without implying self-distrust, may denote an absence of all undue confidence in oneself or one's powers ⟨the most *modest*, silent, sheepfaced and meek of little men—*Thackeray*⟩ but often it stresses not an inner lack of confidence but a manner free from brashness, boldness, and self-assertiveness ⟨stood at ease . . . with the *modest* air of a man who has given his all and is reasonably assured it is enough—*Wolfe*⟩ ⟨entirely natural, *modest*, and unaffected in manner—*Eliot Clark*⟩ **Coy** suggests assumed or affected shyness, often with the further implication of coquetry ⟨I was vexed, and resolved to be even with her by not visiting the wood for some time. A display of indifference on my part would, I hoped, result in making her less *coy* in the future— *Hudson*⟩ ⟨without being in the least *coy*, Mrs. Gross displayed a certain half smiling modesty—*Terry Southern*⟩
*Ana* *timid, timorous: wary, chary, *cautious, circumspect
*Ant* obtrusive

**shy** *vb* balk, boggle, scruple, *demur, jib, stickle, stick, strain
*Ana* *recoil, shrink, quail, blench: *hesitate, waver, falter, vacillate

**sic** *vb* *urge, egg, exhort, goad, spur, prod, prick
*Ana* *incite, instigate, abet: encourage, countenance, *favor

**sicken** *disgust, nauseate
*Ana* revolt, offend, repulse (see corresponding adjectives at OFFENSIVE)

**sickly** *unwholesome, morbid, diseased, pathological
*Ana* ailing (see corresponding noun at DISEASE): *weak, feeble, frail, infirm: mawkish, mushy, maudlin (see SENTIMENTAL)
*Ant* robust —*Con* *healthy, sound, wholesome, hale, well

**side** *phase, aspect, facet, angle

**sidereal** *starry, stellar, astral

---

A colon (:) separates groups of words discriminated. An asterisk (*) indicates place of treatment of each group.

**sidestep** *vb* *dodge, parry, shirk, duck, fence, malinger
*Ana* avoid, evade, elude, shun (see ESCAPE)

**siege** *n* *blockade

**sigh** *vb* **Sigh, sob, moan, groan** are comparable as verbs when they mean to emit a sound, commonly an inarticulate sound, indicative of mental or physical pain or distress and as nouns, such a sound. **Sigh** implies a deep audible respiration that is a usually involuntary expression of grief, intense longing, regret, discouragement, weariness, or boredom ⟨*sigh* no more, ladies, *sigh* no more, men were deceivers ever—*Shak.*⟩ ⟨a *sigh* uttered from the fullness of the heart—*Hazlitt*⟩ ⟨the stranger sometimes seemed to be under stress, *sighed* much and muttered inaudibly to himself—*Malamud*⟩ **Sob** implies a sound made by a convulsive catching of the breath when weeping or when both speaking and crying or when trying to restrain tears; the noun, however, more often refers solely to this sound than does the verb, which often implies accompanying tears and speech ⟨"Ah!" It was a long, grieving sound, like a sigh—almost like a *sob*—*Dickens*⟩ ⟨the mother . . . knelt by his side, and they prayed, and their joint *sobs* shook their bodies, but neither of them shed many tears—*Meredith*⟩ ⟨she *sobbed* out her story⟩ ⟨like a child *sobbing* itself to sleep⟩ **Moan** implies a low, prolonged, usually inarticulate sound, especially one that is indicative of intense suffering of mind or body ⟨they are quick to hear the *moans* of immemorial grief—*Blunden*⟩ ⟨Polly *moaned*, overwhelmed with retrospective shame and embarrassment—*Huxley*⟩ ⟨to hear the piteous *moan* that Rutland made—*Shak.*⟩ The term, however, is often extended to sounds suggestive of pain, complaint, or murmuring ⟨the *moan* of the wind⟩ ⟨the *moan* of doves in immemorial elms—*Tennyson*⟩ ⟨the rain and the wind splashed and gurgled and *moaned* round the house—*Kipling*⟩ **Groan** implies a heavier sound than *moan* and more often suggests an unbearable weight of suffering or a strong spirit of rebelliousness to pain or discomfort ⟨thy *groans* did make wolves howl—*Shak.*⟩ ⟨the whole creation *groaneth* and travaileth in pain together until now—*Rom 8:22*⟩ Often however, in extended use the term carries no hint of suffering but implies noises made in strong disapproval or in pretended suffering ⟨greet a speaker with *groans*⟩ or by something that moves or swings heavily ⟨trees *groaning* in the wind⟩ ⟨the door upon its hinges *groans*—*Keats*⟩ ⟨the *groan* under the floorboard had changed to a screech—*Wouk*⟩
*Ana* lament, *deplore, bemoan, bewail: *long, yearn, pine, hunger, thirst

**sigh** *n* groan, moan, sob (see under SIGH *vb*)
*Ana* regret, *sorrow, grief

**sight** *n* *look, view, glance, glimpse, peep, peek
*Ana* *prospect, outlook: vision, *revelation

**sightless** *blind, purblind

**sign** *n* **1** **Sign, mark, token, badge, note, symptom** can denote a sensible and usually visible indication by means of which something not outwardly apparent or obvious is made known or revealed. **Sign** is the most comprehensive of these terms, being referable to a symbol (see also CHARACTER 1) or a symbolic device or act ⟨the mace is the *sign* of authority⟩ ⟨make the *sign* of the cross⟩ or to a visible or sensible manifestation of a mood, a mental or physical state, or a quality of character ⟨good manners are *signs* of good breeding⟩ ⟨they are gestures of exclusion—not snobbery, merely *signs* of a private life with all its unique standards—*Fadiman*⟩ ⟨suicide is the *sign* of failure, misery, and despair—*Ellis*⟩ or to a trace or vestige of someone or something ⟨the *signs* of her fate in a footprint here, a broken twig there, a trinket

dropped by the way—*Conrad*⟩ or to objective evidence that serves as a presage or foretoken ⟨*signs* of an early spring⟩ ⟨there are *signs* that poetry is beginning to occupy itself again with the possibilities of sound—*Day Lewis*⟩ ⟨two men that night watched for a *sign*, listened for a wonder—*Gwyn Jones*⟩ and concretely to a placard, board, tablet, or card that serves to identify, announce, or direct ⟨watch for a road *sign*⟩ ⟨a brilliantly lighted bar *sign*⟩ ⟨did you see the *sign* announcing the new play?⟩ ⟨"for rent" *signs* in the dingy windows⟩ **Mark** (see also CHARACTER 1) may be preferred to *sign* when the distinguishing or revealing indication is thought of as something impressed upon a thing or inherently characteristic of it, often in contrast to something outwardly apparent or displayed ⟨the bitter experience left its *mark* on him⟩ ⟨courtesy is the *mark* of a gentleman⟩ ⟨the distinguishing *marks* of Victorian poetry⟩ ⟨what, then, are the *marks* of culture and efficiency?—*Suzzallo*⟩ ⟨the unrealized schemes of [the] past . . . have usually left their *mark* in the shape of some unfinished pier, half completed parade—*Angus Wilson*⟩ Concretely also *mark* is applied either (1) to some visible trace (as a scar or a stain or a track) left upon a thing ⟨birth*mark*⟩ ⟨the *marks* of smallpox⟩ ⟨the high-water *mark* is observable on the pier's supports⟩ ⟨the *marks* of an army's passage⟩ ⟨they found not a button, or feather, or *mark*, by which they could tell that they stood on the ground where the Baker had met with the Snark—*Lewis Carroll*⟩ or (2) to something that is affixed in order to distinguish, identify, or label a particular thing or to indicate its ownership ⟨a trade*mark*⟩ ⟨a laundry *mark*⟩ **Token** (see also PLEDGE) can replace *sign* and also *mark* except in their specific concrete applications when the sensible indication serves as a proof of or is given as evidence of the actual existence of something that has no physical existence ⟨how could he doubt her love when he had had so many *tokens* of her affection?⟩ ⟨the savages bore gifts as *tokens* of their desire for peace and friendship⟩ ⟨*tokens* tossed his way—an occasional salute, a "well done" for the preflights . . . a tense smile—were hoarded fervently—*Pynchon*⟩ **Badge** designates a piece of metal or a ribbon carrying an inscription or emblem and worn upon the person as a token of one's membership in a society or as a sign of one's office, employment, or function ⟨a policeman's *badge*⟩ ⟨each delegate wore a *badge*⟩ ⟨a gold key is the *badge* of membership in Phi Beta Kappa⟩ In extended use *badge* often is employed in place of *sign*, *mark*, or *token* when it is thought of in reference to a class, a group, a category of persons, or as a distinctive feature of their dress, their appearance, or their character ⟨for sufferance is the *badge* of all our tribe—*Shak.*⟩ ⟨essentially we were taught to regard culture as a veneer, a *badge* of class distinction—*Malcolm Cowley*⟩ ⟨the diplomat wearing his *badge* of office, the Homburg—*Siler*⟩ **Note** usually means a distinguishing or dominant mark or characteristic; it differs from *mark*, its closest synonym, in suggesting something emitted or given out by a thing, rather than something impressed upon that thing ⟨a fertile oasis possesses a characteristic color scheme of its own . . . . The fundamental *note* is struck by the palms—*Huxley*⟩ ⟨you walk on stage . . . and somehow you're alive, and inside the part, and yet you're projecting a peculiar *note*, your own —*Wouk*⟩ ⟨the *note* of sadness . . . which . . . poets were to find so much more to their taste than the *note* of gladness —*Henry Adams*⟩ *Note* may be used in place of *mark* for a characteristic that seems to emanate from a thing that strikes one as true or authentic and therefore is the test of a similar thing's truth, genuineness, or authoritativeness ⟨the grand manner that is the *note* of great poetry⟩

*Ana* analogous words     *Ant* antonyms     *Con* contrasted words     See also explanatory notes facing page 1

⟨tolerance, moderation, and pity are the abiding *notes* which help to keep Chaucer's poetry level with life— *H. S. Bennett*⟩ **Symptom** can apply to any of the physical or mental changes from the normal which can be interpreted as evidence of disease, but in medical use it is commonly restricted to the subjective evidences of disease primarily apparent to the sufferer and is then opposed to *sign*, which is applied to the objective evidences of abnormality that are primarily determined by tests and instruments ⟨*symptoms* and *signs* taken together constitute the evidence on which a diagnosis can be based⟩ In extended use the term tends to follow popular rather than professional medical use and is applicable to an outward indication of an inner change (as in an institution, a state, or the body politic) or to an external phenomenon that may be interpreted as the result of some internal condition (as a weakness, defect, or disturbance) ⟨even that . . . is treated lightly as a foible of the age, and not as a *symptom* of social decay and change—*T. S. Eliot*⟩ ⟨the belief that a young man's athletic record is a test of his worth is a *symptom* of our general failure to grasp the need of knowledge and thought in mastering the complex modern world—*Russell*⟩ ⟨she wanted . . . to be alone so that she could study and afterwards remember each *symptom* of this excitement that had caught her—*Auchincloss*⟩
*Ana* indication, betokening, attesting *or* attestation (see corresponding verbs at INDICATE): manifestation, evidencing *or* evidence, demonstration, showing *or* show (see corresponding verbs at SHOW): intimation, suggestion (see corresponding verbs at SUGGEST)
**2 Sign, signal** can both mean a motion, an action, a gesture, or a word by which a command or wish is expressed or a thought is made known. **Sign** (see also SIGN 1; CHARACTER 1) is the general term that in itself carries no explicit connotations; it is used in reference to a bodily motion (as a shrug) or a gesture (as a beckoning) or an action (as a pantomime) by which one conveys a thought, a command, a direction, or a need to another with whom one either cannot communicate orally (as by reason of deaf-mutism, or lack of a common language, or distance) or does not wish to communicate orally (as from consideration of others or desire for secrecy) ⟨put a finger to her lips as a *sign* for quiet⟩ ⟨the explorer made *signs* to the natives to show his friendly intentions⟩ **Signal** usually applies to a conventional and recognizable sign that typically conveys a command, a direction, or a warning ⟨she was startled by a ring at the door, the certain *signal* of a visitor—*Austen*⟩ ⟨the flying of the first champagne cork gave the *signal*, and a hum began to spread— *Meredith*⟩ ⟨at a *signal* given by the train conductor, the engineer climbed into his engine—*Anderson*⟩ **Signal** is also applied to mechanical devices which by operating lights, moving barriers, or sounding an alarm, take the place of a guard, a watchman, or a policeman ⟨traffic *signals*⟩ ⟨railroad *signals*⟩
*Ana* *gesture, gesticulation: *symbol, emblem
**3** symbol, *character, mark
*Ana* *device, contrivance
**signal** *n* *sign
*Ana* *alarm, tocsin, alert: *gesture, gesticulation: *motion, movement: *device, contrivance, contraption
**signal** *adj* salient, striking, arresting, outstanding, prominent, remarkable, *noticeable, conspicuous
*Ana* distinctive, individual, peculiar, *characteristic: eminent, illustrious, *famous, renowned
**significance** **1** signification, import, *meaning, sense, acceptation
*Ana* denotation, connotation (see under DENOTE):

suggestion, implication, intimation (see corresponding verbs at SUGGEST)
**2** *importance, import, consequence, moment, weight
*Ana* *worth, value: *influence, authority, credit, prestige: merit, *excellence, virtue, perfection
**significant** *expressive, meaningful, pregnant, eloquent, sententious
*Ana* cogent, telling, convincing, compelling, *valid, sound: forcible, forceful, *powerful: important, momentous, weighty (see corresponding nouns at IMPORTANCE)
**signification** significance, import, *meaning, sense, acceptation
*Ana* signifying, meaning, denoting (see MEAN *vb*): denotation, connotation (see under DENOTE 2)
**signify** import, *mean, denote
*Ana* convey, *carry, bear: *denote, connote: imply, *suggest
**silent 1 Silent, uncommunicative, taciturn, reticent, reserved, secretive, close, close-lipped, closemouthed, tight-lipped** are comparable when they mean showing restraint in speaking to or with others. **Silent** and **uncommunicative** often imply a tendency to say no more than is absolutely necessary as a matter of habit ⟨he had had a rather unhappy boyhood; and it made him a *silent* man—*Conrad*⟩ ⟨a stern, *silent* man, long a widower—*Cather*⟩ ⟨whose *uncommunicative* heart will scarce one precious word impart—*Swift*⟩ or an abstinence from speech on some particular occasion typically because of caution or the stress of emotion ⟨a *silent*, shaky embrace, each afraid to entrust words to her trembling lips—*Styron*⟩ ⟨she found the presidential nominee *uncommunicative* regarding plans to put women in high office—*Current Biog.*⟩ **Taciturn** implies a temperamental disinclination to speech; it usually also connotes unsociableness or the nature of one who grudgingly converses when necessary ⟨Benson was . . . a *taciturn* hater of woman—*Meredith*⟩ ⟨always *taciturn*, he now hardly spoke at all— *Cloete*⟩ ⟨the farmer was *taciturn* and drove them speechlessly to the house—*Buck*⟩ **Reticent** implies the disposition to keep one's own counsel or the habit or fact of withholding much that might be said, especially under particular circumstances; the term does not usually connote silence but, rather, sparing speech or an indisposition to discuss one's private affairs ⟨all subsequent autobiographies and confessions seem in comparison *reticent*, wanting in detail—*L. P. Smith*⟩ ⟨he had been characteristically *reticent* regarding the details of his own financial affairs—*Marquand*⟩ ⟨it was a matter upon which he was *reticent*, and with persons of his kidney a direct question is never very discreet—*Maugham*⟩ **Reserved** implies reticence but it also suggests formality, standoffishness, or a temperamental indisposition to the give and take of friendly conversation or familiar intercourse ⟨a *reserved* and distant demeanor⟩ ⟨grave, though with no formal solemnity, *reserved* if not exactly repressed . . . she was yet a woman of unmistakable force of character —*Ellis*⟩ ⟨habitually was *reserved* in speech, withholding her opinion—*Sackville-West*⟩ **Secretive** also implies reticence, but it adds an implication of disparagement that *reticent* usually lacks, for it suggests an opposition to *frank* or *open* and often connotes an attempt to hide or conceal something that might properly be told ⟨a *secretive* public official is the despair of reporters⟩ ⟨the rapport between this man and his parents was so intense and tacit that it seemed *secretive*—*Cheever*⟩ ⟨his voice became *secretive* and confidential, the voice of a man divulging fabulous professional secrets—*Dahl*⟩ **Close** (see also CLOSE 1 & 2) comes near to *reticent* and *secretive* in its meaning but it usually denotes a dis-

A colon (:) separates groups of words discriminated. An asterisk (*) indicates place of treatment of each group.

position rather than an attitude or manner and, therefore, often suggests taciturnity 〈he was too *close* to name his circumstances to me—*Dickens*〉 **Close-lipped** and **close-mouthed** are often used in place of *close* not only as more picturesque terms but also as more clearly implying a determined refusal to disclose something that another desires to know 〈he is always *closemouthed* about his plans〉 〈she proved a good secretary because she was *close-lipped* about all matters of a confidential nature〉 〈those few who knew actual combat destination kept *close-lipped*—*Dodson*〉 〈the family has been . . . extraordinarily *closemouthed* about even the broad outline of its commercial affairs—*Freeman Lincoln*〉 **Tight-lipped** carries a stronger implication of resolute but not necessarily temperamental reticence 〈infinite caution, *tight-lipped*, unshakable patience, these must be his rule —*Buchan*〉
*Ana* restrained, curbed, checked, inhibited (see RE-STRAIN): discreet, prudent (see under PRUDENCE)
*Ant* talkative —*Con* *vocal, articulate, fluent, voluble, glib: loquacious, garrulous (see TALKATIVE)
**2** *still, stilly, quiet, noiseless
*Ana* *calm, serene, tranquil, placid, peaceful
**silhouette** *outline, contour, profile, skyline
*Ana* shadow, *shade, adumbration
**silken, silky** *sleek, slick, glossy, velvety, satiny
*Ana* lustrous, luminous, lambent (see BRIGHT)
**silly 1** *simple, foolish, fatuous, asinine
*Ana* *irrational, unreasonable: *stupid, slow, dull, dense, crass, dumb: vacuous, *empty
**2** *foolish, absurd, preposterous
*Ana* inane, wishy-washy, *insipid: puerile, juvenile (see YOUTHFUL): ridiculous, ludicrous, *laughable
**similar** *like, alike, analogous, comparable, akin, parallel, uniform, identical
*Ana* *same, equivalent, equal, identical: corresponding, correlative, complementary, *reciprocal
*Ant* dissimilar —*Con* *different, disparate, diverse: *opposite, contradictory, contrary, antithetical, antonymous
**similarity** *likeness, resemblance, similitude, analogy, affinity
*Ana* *comparison, contrast, collation, parallel: agreement, accordance, harmonizing *or* harmony, correspondence (see corresponding verbs at AGREE)
*Ant* dissimilarity
**simile** *analogy, metaphor
**similitude** *likeness, similarity, resemblance, analogy, affinity
*Ant* dissimilitude, dissimilarity
**simmer** *vb* *boil, seethe, parboil, stew
**simper** *vb* *smile, smirk, grin
**simper** *n* smile, smirk, grin (see under SMILE *vb*)
**simple** *adj* **1** *pure, absolute, sheer
*Ana* elemental, *elementary: *single, sole
*Ant* compound: complex
**2** *easy, facile, light, effortless, smooth
*Ana* clear, plain, distinct, obvious, *evident, manifest: *clear, lucid, perspicuous
*Ant* complicated: difficult
**3** *plain, homely, unpretentious
*Ana* ordinary, *common, familiar: lowly, *humble: insignificant, unimportant (see affirmative nouns at IMPORTANCE)
**4** *natural, ingenuous, naïve, unsophisticated, artless
*Ana* *sincere, unfeigned: *childlike, childish: open, plain, *frank, candid
*Con* affected, pretended, assumed (see ASSUME): pretentious, ostentatious, *showy

**5 Simple, foolish, silly, fatuous, asinine** can all mean actually or apparently deficient in intelligence. **Simple,** when it implies actual deficiency in intelligence, is applied chiefly to persons whose intelligence is that of a child and who are incapable of dealing with ideas or situations that involve much mental effort. It may imply either illiteracy coupled with a lack of native shrewdness, or feeblemindedness that does not amount to imbecility 〈this poor, *simple* boy. Half-witted, they call him; and surely fit for nothing but to be happy—*Hawthorne*〉 When used as a term of criticism of normal persons or their acts it suggests little more than failure to use one's intelligence 〈Marcia was a *simple* woman and easily deceived—*Graves*〉 〈he knew they thought him *simple* . . . . Not *simple*, perhaps, but strange and imperceptive —*Cloete*〉 **Foolish** (see also FOOLISH 2) as a term of criticism of normal persons and their acts is stronger than *simple* because it imputes either the appearance of idiocy or imbecility or a want of intelligence or of good judgment that makes one blind to dangers or consequences 〈he looks and acts *foolish* when he drinks too much〉 〈oh, *foolish* youth! Thou seek'st the greatness that will overwhelm thee—*Shak.*〉 〈in his younger days he had been very *foolish*. He had flirted and giggled—*Woolf*〉 〈feeling herself a rather *foolish* figure, with her stockings rolled around her ankles and her brassiere loose—*Mary McCarthy*〉 **Silly** is applied to persons who, though not mentally deficient in a technical sense, fail to act as rationally guided beings either by showing a lack of common sense or ordinary good judgment or by behaving in a manner that makes them ridiculous in the eyes of others 〈she wasn't a weak and *silly* creature, with running faucets in her eyes. She didn't swoon and give way to feelings and emotions—*Farrell*〉 〈although we maintained a blackout at night, we felt *silly* about it—*Liebling*〉 **Fatuous** does not often imply a pathological lack of intelligence, but it does imply an appearance of this and regularly suggests a combination of foolishness, stupidity, and inanity. It is a term of contempt rather than of impersonal description, and is capable of additional connotations (as fatheadedness, vacuousness, obtuseness, or loss of a sense of proportion) 〈do you doubt that the most *fatuous* of the Georges, whichever it was, thought himself Newton's superior?—*Landor*〉 〈Prescott . . . was no *fatuous* optimist—*Brooks*〉 〈a *fatuous* and at the same time arrogant epistle, abounding in nonsense and lies and subterfuge—*Shirer*〉 〈she still indulged in those *fatuous* remarks that had no point. Remarks like: Marriage is an institution made chiefly for men and women—*Abse*〉 **Asinine** is also a term of contempt; it suggests an intelligence comparable to that of a donkey, considered the stubbornest and most stupid of the beasts of burden. As applied to persons or their acts, choices, or opinions it connotes an utter failure to exercise intelligence or thinking unworthy of a rational being 〈an *asinine* choice of profession〉 〈an *asinine* use of his leisure time〉 〈what is one to think of a man so *asinine* that he looks for gratitude in this world?—*Mencken*〉 〈the most *asinine* and inept movie that has come out of Hollywood in years —*McCarten*〉
*Ana* childish, *childlike: dull, dense, dumb, slow, *stupid, crass: *ignorant, illiterate, untaught
*Ant* wise
**simple** *n* *drug, medicinal, pharmaceutical, biologic
**simpleton** *fool, moron, imbecile, idiot, natural
**simulate** feign, counterfeit, sham, pretend, *assume, affect
*Ana* dissemble, *disguise, cloak, mask, camouflage: ape, mock, mimic, imitate, *copy

---

*Ana* analogous words     *Ant* antonyms     *Con* contrasted words     See also explanatory notes facing page 1

**simultaneous** synchronous, coincident, *contemporary, contemporaneous, coeval, coetaneous, concomitant, concurrent

*Ana* concurring, coinciding, agreeing (see AGREE)

*Con* *preceding, foregoing, antecedent, previous: following, succeeding, ensuing (see FOLLOW)

**sin** *n* *offense, vice, crime, scandal

*Ana* transgression, trespass, *breach, violation: *error, lapse, slip: *fault, failing, frailty

**since** *conj* *because, for, as, inasmuch as

**sincere,** **wholehearted, whole-souled, heartfelt, hearty, unfeigned** can mean genuine in feeling or expression or showing such genuineness. Sincere stresses the absence of hypocrisy, dissimulation, or falsification in any degree; it therefore usually connotes a strict adherence to truth, a revelation of just what one feels, thinks, or sees and no more, and an unwillingness to embellish, exaggerate, or make pretenses of any sort ⟨the loathing with which he describes the sodden Vienna working classes is . . . so *sincere* that one thinks for a moment that out of it must come a people's rebel—*Dorothy Thompson*⟩ ⟨in spite of her confusion, something strong and *sincere* and questing emanated from her—*Styron*⟩ **Wholehearted** and **whole-souled** imply the absence of all reservations and therefore stress not only sincerity, but also qualities (as earnestness or devotion or zealousness) which suggest that one's whole being is stirred or moved ⟨the service they one and all gave . . . was *wholehearted* and even passionate—*Sackville-West*⟩ ⟨*whole-souled* dislike of totalitarianism⟩ ⟨who could help liking her? her generous nature, her gift for appreciation, her *wholehearted*, fervid enthusiasm?—*L. P. Smith*⟩ ⟨demonstrated a *whole-souled* allegiance to the democratic world—*Limb*⟩ **Heartfelt** places the emphasis upon the depth and genuineness of the feeling which finds expression in words, in signs of emotion (as tears), or in acts; the term suggests that one is deeply stirred or moved, and it is applied usually to what might, by contrast, be formally or conventionally expressed or outwardly indicated ⟨*heartfelt* interest in the poor and suffering⟩ ⟨our sympathy for you therefore is *heartfelt*, for we are sharing the same sufferings—*Sir Winston Churchill*⟩ **Hearty** comes closer to *wholehearted* than to *heartfelt*, but it carries a stronger implication than *wholehearted* of vigor or energy in expression or manifestation, and may connote simple honesty, great warmth, or exuberance in the display of feeling ⟨receive a *hearty* welcome⟩ ⟨a *hearty* laugh⟩ ⟨in the *hearty* tones natural when the words demanded by politeness coincide with those of deepest feeling—*Hardy*⟩ ⟨the overwhelming mass of American citizens are in *hearty* accord with these basic policies—*Roosevelt*⟩ **Unfeigned** is often used in place of *sincere*, especially when the absence of simulation is to be stressed; the term usually emphasizes spontaneousness as well as genuineness ⟨I confess to *unfeigned* delight in the insurgent propaganda—*Lowes*⟩ ⟨an *unfeigned* interest in people and scenes—*Bruun*⟩

*Ana* candid, open, *frank, plain: honest, honorable, conscientious, scrupulous, *upright: *straightforward, aboveboard, forthright

*Ant* insincere

**sinewy** *muscular, athletic, husky, brawny, burly

*Ana* robust, *healthy, sound: *strong, tough, tenacious, sturdy: nervous, *vigorous, energetic

**sing** *vb* Sing, **troll, carol, descant, warble, trill, hymn, chant, intone** all mean to produce musical tones by or as if by means of the voice. **Sing** is the general term used of human beings and of animals and things that produce musical or sustained tones. In its primary application to human beings it usually implies utterance in words with musical inflections or modulations and often suggests such modulated utterance as an art to be practiced, studied, or learned ⟨*sing* an aria⟩ ⟨*sing* the part of Faust⟩ ⟨*sing* a plaintive song⟩ ⟨she studied *singing* diligently but lacked the voice to profit from instruction⟩ ⟨grasshoppers chirping, and birds *singing*—*Shaw*⟩ ⟨the rigging *sang* in the wind⟩ **Troll** usually suggests the use of full round tones in singing ⟨while mountains were unloosing their hair to the music waterfalls *trolled* like bells for the wedding—*Babette Deutsch*⟩ and is especially applicable to the hearty voices of jovial men raised in singing or the resonant celebration in song of great events or deeds ⟨let us be jocund. Will you *troll* the catch you taught me but whilere?—*Shak.*⟩ ⟨strange adventure that we're *trolling*: modest maid and gallant groom—*Gilbert*⟩ **Carol** suggests the voices of youthful, lively, or joyous singers, usually of persons, sometimes of birds; it may or may not suggest the singing of carols, but it often implies merriment or effortlessness and spontaneity ⟨used to *carol* cheerfully in the morning, locked in the single bathroom—*Canby*⟩ ⟨a wren on a tree stump *caroled* clear—*Masefield*⟩ **Descant** (see also DISCOURSE) implies part singing or, especially, the singing of a higher part in harmony with the plainsong of the tenor in a contrapuntal treatment. *Descant* often merely implies harmonious singing or singing in harmony with ⟨they will . . . sing so sweetly, and withall *descant* it so finely and tunably—*Topsell*⟩ ⟨a device by which several singers appear to be *descanting*, when in fact only one is doing so—*Grove's Dict. of Music*⟩ **Warble** frequently implies singing in a soft and gentle voice but with various modulations (as turns and trills and quavers); often it means no more than to sing melodiously or with sweetness ⟨*warble* his native woodnotes wild—*Milton*⟩ ⟨the skylark *warbles* high his trembling thrilling ecstasy—*Gray*⟩ **Trill** basically means to sing with trills or vibrations (as by rapidly alternating two notes a degree apart) ⟨*trill* like a canary⟩ but it is often extended to refer to the making of sounds involving vibration without much thought of musical quality ⟨with a shrill *trilling* from the countless leaves in between gusts of wind—*Idriess*⟩ ⟨*trilled* his soup into his mouth with a swift sucking vibration—*The Use of English*⟩ ⟨could hear the noise of a telephone *trilling*—*James Helvick*⟩ **Hymn** implies a lifting of the voice in songs of worship or praise, especially of God ⟨evening by evening, as they came to the setting sun, they *hymned* Father, Son, and Holy Ghost—*Pusey*⟩ ⟨the thrush concerting with the lark that *hymned* on high—*Pollok*⟩ **Chant** may mean little more than *sing*, but often it is used specifically to imply the method of singing adopted by priests or choristers singing unmetrical verse where the emphasis is upon musical recitation of phrases, measured even tones, and a reverential spirit. **Intone** also comes very close to the specific sense of *chant* in meaning but sometimes carries a stronger connotation of reciting in sustained monotone ⟨the Psalms were *chanted*⟩ ⟨the priest *intoned* the Gospel of the Mass⟩ ⟨I joined with choirs of monks, *intoning* their deep sonorous dirges—*L. P. Smith*⟩ ⟨they would take hands and ring-a-rosy about him, *chanting* at the tops of their voices, until good humor was restored—*Mary Austin*⟩

**singe** sear, *burn, scorch, char

**single** *adj* 1 *unmarried, celibate, virgin, maiden

2 **Single, sole, unique, lone, solitary, separate, particular** can all mean one as distinguished from two or more or all others. Something **single** is not accompanied or supported by, or combined or united with, another ⟨a *single* instance may be cited⟩ ⟨the strength of the lyric lies in

the complete statement of a *single* selected facet of experience—*Day Lewis*⟩ ⟨that was the greatest *single* thing that had ever happened to her. No one had ever looked at her and made a respectful gesture before—*Theodore Sturgeon*⟩ Something **sole** is the only one that exists, that acts, that has power or relevance, or that is to be or should be considered ⟨he is the *sole* heir⟩ ⟨this is his *sole* invention⟩ ⟨your conscience must be the *sole* judge in this case⟩ ⟨acquire the *sole* rights of publication⟩ ⟨his *sole* object was to study the form of his sitter's head in every detail—*Alexander*⟩ ⟨California is not the *sole* repository of political virtue in the United States—*Armbrister*⟩ Something **unique** (see also STRANGE) may be the only one of its kind in existence ⟨the medal is *unique*, for no duplicates were made⟩ ⟨of the world's geniuses he strikes me as being *unique*—*Mailer*⟩ or it may stand alone because of its unusual character ⟨the *unique* character of the English conquest of Britain—*Malone*⟩ ⟨they stand alone, *unique*, objects of supreme interest—*Osborne*⟩ Something **lone** (see also ALONE) is not only single but also separated or isolated from others of its kind; the word often replaces *single* in technical or poetic context ⟨to sit beneath a fair *lone* beechen tree—*Keats*⟩ ⟨ the ambitious Aaron Burr, who played a *lone* hand against the field—*Parrington*⟩ ⟨constitutes the *lone* industry of the community—*Amer. Guide Series: Vt.*⟩ Something **solitary** (see also ALONE) stands by itself, either as the sole instance or as a unique thing ⟨her world was the Church, in which she hoped that her *solitary* child would some day be a polished pillar—*Buchan*⟩ ⟨began to eat again fiercely, like a great strong animal, tackling the *solitary* meal of its day—*O'Flaherty*⟩ Something **separate** (see also DISTINCT 1) is not only single, but disconnected from or unconnected with any of the others in question ⟨turning over in his thoughts every *separate* second of their hours together—*Wharton*⟩ ⟨group consciousness . . . makes the individual think lightly of his own *separate* interests—*Cohen*⟩ Something **particular** (see also SPECIAL; CIRCUMSTANTIAL; NICE 1) is the single or numerically distinct instance, member, or example of the whole or the class considered or under consideration ⟨a special provision for a known and *particular* territory—*Taney*⟩ ⟨Richard . . . replied that he had an engagement at a *particular* hour, up to which he was her servant—*Meredith*⟩ ⟨reality is a succession of concrete and *particular* situations—*Huxley*⟩
*Ana* individual, particular, *special, especial, specific
*Ant* accompanied: supported: conjugal
**single** *vb* prefer, *choose, select, elect, opt, pick, cull
*Ana* *take, seize, grasp, grab: accept, *receive, admit: *decide, determine, settle
**singular** *strange, unique, peculiar, eccentric, erratic, odd, queer, quaint, outlandish, curious
*Ana* *different, diverse, divergent, disparate: *exceptional: *abnormal, atypical, aberrant
*Con* ordinary, *common, familiar: *usual, customary, habitual
**sinister,** baleful, malign, malefic, maleficent all mean seriously threatening, portending, or promising evil or disaster, usually imminent or already initiated evil or disaster. **Sinister** is the most commonly employed of these words and the widest in its range of reference. It may be applied not only to something perceptible ⟨a *sinister* cloud⟩ ⟨a *sinister* look⟩ but to something imperceptible ⟨a *sinister* influence⟩ ⟨a *sinister* intention⟩ In either case *sinister* often expresses a judgment based on experience or on an interpretation of outward signs and implies on the part of the observer a resulting

fear or apprehension of approaching evil or of lurking dangers; thus, a cloud is describable as *sinister* when it has the color, shape, or general character of one that the observer believes to precede a tornado; a person's influence may be interpreted as *sinister* when it is judged in the light of some of its visible effects ⟨she was about half a mile from her residence when she beheld a *sinister* redness arising from a ravine a little way in advance—*Hardy*⟩ ⟨some of the customers did look *sinister* enough—scar-faced toughs in ragged caps—*Wouk*⟩ ⟨I did not wish him to know that I had suspected him of harboring any *sinister* designs—*Hudson*⟩ **Sinister** is also applied to something that works or operates so covertly, insidiously, or obliquitously that it is likely to find those whose well-being it threatens off guard ⟨a *sinister* disease⟩ ⟨a *sinister* policy⟩ ⟨the *sinister* power exercised . . . by the combination in keeping rivals out of the business and ruining those who already were in—*Justice Holmes*⟩ **Baleful** carries an even stronger suggestion of menace than *sinister* for it implies inevitable suffering, misery, or destruction; often it imputes perniciousness, noxiousness, or hellishness to the thing so described. It is applicable to something that works openly and without indirection ⟨this dread power . . . can be made a giant help to humanity, but science does not show us how to prevent its *baleful* use—*Baruch*⟩ as well as to something that works occultly or obliquely ⟨deceit contrived by art and *baleful* sorcery—*Shak.*⟩ ⟨culling their potent herbs and *baleful* drugs—*Milton*⟩ ⟨the *baleful* power of fanaticisms and superstitions—*Edmund Wilson*⟩ ⟨the *baleful* horoscope of Abdallah had predicted the downfall of Granada—*Prescott*⟩ **Malign** (see also MALICIOUS) carries over from its earliest sense a suggestion of an inherently evil or harmful tendency or disposition, even though the term in this sense is characteristically applied to immaterial things (as appearances, aspects, forces, or influences) rather than to persons ⟨the eyes were no longer merely luminous points; they looked into his own with a meaning, a *malign* significance—*Bierce*⟩ ⟨believe that lions will only kill humans under a *malign* human influence—*Wyatt*⟩ It also carries connotations (as of boding evil or disaster) derived from its reference in astrology to the aspects or the influences of the stars ⟨a struggle between two forces, the one beneficent, the other *malign*—*Bryce*⟩ ⟨the spirit of competition, which, according to Rousseau, was one of the earliest of the *malign* fruits of awakening intelligence—*Grandgent*⟩ ⟨dense masses of smoke hung amid the darting snakes of fire, and a red *malign* light was on the neighboring leafage—*Meredith*⟩ and occasionally suggests a force or power contributory to boded disaster ⟨the prickly topic of symbolism, with its *malign* power to set the wise by the ears—*Montague*⟩ **Malefic** and **maleficent** carry a stronger suggestion of balefulness than does *malign*, for both regularly imply not only a tendency toward but an active force productive of evil or disaster; thus, a *malign* influence bodes disaster; a *malefic* or *maleficent* influence is putting the threat of disaster into effect ⟨the *malefic* arts of sorcery, witchcraft, and diabolism⟩ ⟨conjurations for the expulsion of *malefic* demons—*Norman Douglas*⟩ ⟨Saturn . . . represents *malefic* force. Cold, hostile, merciless . . . he blights all that he gazes on—*Evangeline Adams*⟩ ⟨like everything that has outlived its usefulness nationalism has changed from a beneficent into a *maleficent* force—*C. K. Streit*⟩ ⟨at times his *maleficent* power burst open the peak, sent fire through the jagged holes, and destroyed villages—*Diez de Medina*⟩
*Ana* *ominous, portentous, fateful, unpropitious, inauspicious: *secret, covert, furtive, underhand, under-

handed: *malicious, malignant, malevolent, spiteful

**sink** *vb* *fall, drop, slump, subside
*Ana* *droop, sag, flag, wilt: submerge, immerse, *dip: ebb, *abate, wane: disappear, *vanish

**sinuous** *winding, flexuous, serpentine, tortuous
*Ana* circuitous, roundabout, *indirect: *crooked, devious

**sire** *vb* beget, get, procreate, *generate, engender, breed, propagate, reproduce

**site** *n* *place, position, location, situation, spot, station
*Ana* *area, tract, region, zone: *field, territory, province: section, sector (see PART): *locality, district

**situation** 1 *place, position, location, site, spot, station
*Ana* *area, region, tract, zone: section, sector (see PART): *locality, district, vicinity, neighborhood
2 *state, condition, mode, posture, status
*Ana* *juncture, pass, crisis, exigency, emergency: *predicament, plight, quandary, dilemma: case, *instance

**size** *n* Size, dimensions, area, extent, magnitude, volume are here compared primarily as terms meaning the amount of space occupied or sometimes of time or energy used by a thing and determinable by measuring. Size usually refers to things having length, width, and depth or height; it need not imply accurate mathematical measurements but may suggest a mere estimate of these ⟨the *size* of this box is 10 inches long, 8 inches wide, and 5 inches deep⟩ ⟨these trees are not the right *size*⟩ ⟨what is the *size* of the room?⟩ ⟨that exceptional mushroom, skull-like in its proportions and bold in *size—Mailer*⟩ Size is also referable to things which cannot be measured in themselves, but can be computed in terms of the number of individuals which comprise them or the amount of space occupied by those individuals ⟨the mere complexity and *size* of a modern state is against the identification of the man with the citizen—*Dickinson*⟩ Since *dimension* means measurement in a single direction (as the line of length, or breadth, or depth) the plural **dimensions**, used collectively, is a close synonym of *size;* in contrast, however, it usually implies accurate measurements that are known or specified ⟨the window frames must be exactly alike in *dimensions*⟩ ⟨the *dimensions* of the universe are not calculable⟩ ⟨the *dimensions* of the lot are 75 by 100 feet⟩ ⟨no reliable calipers exist long enough to stretch into the next century and measure the *dimensions* of greatness—*Fadiman*⟩ **Area** is referable only to things measurable in the two dimensions length and breadth. It is used of plane figures or of plane surfaces (as the ground, a floor, or an arena) and is computed in square measure ⟨the estate is 200 acres in *area*⟩ ⟨the forest fire covered an *area* of ten square miles⟩ ⟨the *area* of a rectangle is computed by multiplying its length by its breadth⟩ ⟨the major *areas* of the world are in the throes of revolutionary social change—*Geismar*⟩ **Extent** is referable chiefly to things that are measured in one dimension; it may be the length or the breadth, but it is usually thought of as the length ⟨the driveway's *extent* is 100 feet⟩ ⟨the wings of the airplane are 75 feet in *extent*⟩ However it is often used as though it were the equivalent of *area* ⟨the basement of St. Katherine's Dock House is vast in *extent* and confusing in its plan—*Conrad*⟩ ⟨the reports . . . constantly express amazement at the *extent* and severity of Russian attacks and counterattacks—*Shirer*⟩ The word is also referable to measured time or to space measured in terms of time; thus, the duration of a thing is the *extent* of its existence ⟨few lives reach the *extent* of one hundred years⟩ ⟨Germany was . . . a nine days' march from north to south, and of incalculable *extent* from west to east—*Buchan*⟩ **Magnitude,** largely a mathematical and technical term, may be used in reference to

size or two-dimensional extent ⟨a queer little isolated point in time, with no *magnitude*, but only position— *Rose Macaulay*⟩ It may be used also in reference to something measurable whose exact quantity, extent, or degree may be expressed in mathematical figures; thus, the *magnitude* of a star is indicated by a number that expresses its relative brightness ⟨an alpha particle bearing a positive charge equal in *magnitude* to twice the electron charge—*Darrow*⟩ ⟨the *magnitude* of the structure as a whole and the massive nature of its details are never obtrusive—*O. S. Nock*⟩ **Volume** (see also BULK) is also a technical term; it is used in reference to something that can be measured or considered in terms of cubic measurements; thus, the *volume* of a solid cylinder is equal to the cubic measure of air it displaces, and that of a hollow one, to the cubic measure of its capacity; two objects that are equal in *volume* may differ greatly in weight; when a thing expands, it increases in *volume* ⟨we could readily store a million times as many stars in the present *volume* of the system—*B. J. Bok*⟩ ⟨you may say that the waves . . . are not like real waves; but they move, they have force and *volume—Binyon*⟩
*Ana* amplitude, *expanse, spread, stretch: *bulk, mass, volume

**skedaddle** *scuttle, scurry, scamper, sprint
*Ana* flee, fly, *escape, decamp: retreat, *recede: withdraw, retire (see GO)

**skeleton** *structure, anatomy, framework

**skepticism** *uncertainty, doubt, dubiety, mistrust

**sketch** *n* 1 outline, diagram, delineation, draft, tracing, plot, blueprint (see under SKETCH *vb*)
*Ana* design, plot, *plan, scheme, project: *chart, map
2 précis, aperçu, *compendium, syllabus, digest, pandect, survey

**sketch** *vb* Sketch, outline, diagram, delineate, draft, trace, plot, blueprint are comparable when they mean to present or to represent something by or as if by drawing its lines or its features. The same distinctions in implications and connotations are observable in the corresponding nouns sketch, outline, diagram, delineation, draft, tracing, plot, blueprint. Sketch may imply a drawing, a painting, a model, or a verbal presentation (as in a description or exposition) of the main lines, features, or points with the result that a clear, often a vivid, but not a detailed impression or conception of the whole is given ⟨then, in a calm historian's tone, he proceeded to *sketch* . . . some pictures of the corruption which was rife abroad— *Joyce*⟩ ⟨this lecture is a humble attempt to *sketch* out a metaphysics of natural science—*Inge*⟩ ⟨a sculptor's *sketch* of his design for a memorial⟩ ⟨in some of Miss Jewett's earlier books . . . one can find first *sketches*, first impressions, which later crystallized into almost flawless examples of literary art—*Cather*⟩ **Outline** (compare OUTLINE *n* 1) differs from *sketch* in suggesting emphasis upon the contours of a thing that is represented or the main points of a thing expounded and in implying more or less inattention to the details which fill up, amplify, or particularize; the term therefore usually implies a more rigid selection and greater economy in treatment and less consideration for qualities which give pleasure than *sketch* implies and, often, suggests a presentation of a thing as a simplified whole ⟨*outlining* a plan for a future investigation—*Conant*⟩ ⟨the detailed study of history should be supplemented by brilliant *outlines*, even if they contained questionable generalizations—*Russell*⟩ ⟨the gist of these books was preserved in a series of small *outlines—Southern*⟩ **Diagram** implies presentation by means of a graphic design (as a mechanical drawing, a pattern showing arrangement and distribution of parts,

---

A colon (:) separates groups of words discriminated. An asterisk (*) indicates place of treatment of each group.

or a chart, map, or graph) of something which requires explanation rather than representation or portrayal ⟨*diagram* the nervous system⟩ ⟨he *diagrammed* his route on the tablecloth—*Cather*⟩ ⟨spread out on the table a number of maps and aerial photographs that *diagrammed* what the Authority is up to—*Robert Rice*⟩ ⟨there was little or no desire to amend the comprehensive *diagram* of . . . constitutional theory—*Times Lit. Sup.*⟩ **Delineate** and **delineation** come close to *describe* and *description* and *depict* and *depiction*. Though they carry a strong implication of drawing a thing so as to show its lines or features with great distinctness, they tend to stress amplifying details and therefore often imply greater fullness or richness in treatment than the preceding words ⟨his brush did its work with a steady and sure stroke that indicated command of his materials. He could *delineate* whatever he elected with technical skill—*Jefferies*⟩ ⟨the cult of beauty and the *delineation* of ugliness are not in natural opposition —*Pound*⟩ ⟨he had a capacity for *delineating* emotions he had never felt—*Edman*⟩ **Draft**, especially as a verb, implies accurate drawing to scale, especially of an architect's plan for a building to be constructed or of a design (as for a ship, a machine, or an engine) ⟨young architects usually spend their first years in *drafting* plans rather than in designing buildings⟩ The term may apply to the drawing up of a preliminary statement which when corrected, polished, and copied will serve as a final statement ⟨*draft* me a proper letter to send him—*Shaw*⟩ ⟨I have three or four *drafts* of each essay or chapter that I have written, and . . . all of them run to about twice the length of the finished piece—*Geismar*⟩ ⟨the legislature did pass a measure . . . yet the controls were suggested—some insist *drafted*—by the industry itself—*Armbrister*⟩ **Trace** and **tracing** in their perhaps most common use refer to redrawing an existent design by following its lines as seen through a superimposed transparent sheet, but they can also apply when a precise and detailed pattern is to be formed by or as if by drawing. The terms are more likely to suggest accuracy in or as if in following or sometimes shakiness resulting from or as if from following a continuous line than they are to imply anything about the qualities of what is to be traced ⟨*trace* an outline to be colored with crayons⟩ ⟨make a *tracing* of a diagram⟩ ⟨continuous blood pressure *tracings* have been recorded—*Armstrong*⟩ ⟨time was *tracing* purple reminders on his nose and cheeks —*Costain*⟩ ⟨Kurler swore, a palsied, tottering sound, and traced his name, a shaking, wandering line—*Lowell*⟩ ⟨with my eyes I *traced* the line of the horizon, thin and fine, straight around till I was come back to where I'd started from—*Millay*⟩ ⟨his fumbling brain had *traced* the braille of an enduring and bitter truth—*Hervey*⟩ **Plot** is often used in place of *diagram* or *draft* or, less often, *sketch* when a map, chart, or graph rather than a design is implied; distinctively it throws emphasis upon the indicating of specific locations (as points, areas, sections, or objectives) so that their relation to each other or the whole is clear; thus, one who diagrammatically represents the condition of business during a given year by means of a graph is said to *plot* a graph or to make a *plot* of the curve of business activity ⟨*plot* the course of a hurricane⟩ ⟨*plot* . . . the exact position of the ship—*Heaton*⟩ **Blueprint**, from its common application to a photograph in white lines on blue paper of a draftsman's mechanical drawing or of an architect's plan, in extended use implies precise and detailed sketching or delineation; it suggests not the act of drawing or drawing up but the effect produced by what is drawn or drawn up ⟨people engaged in the amusing and innocuous pastime of *blueprinting* a new social order— *The Commonweal*⟩ ⟨the political leaders of the two coun-

tries are guided by the same political *blueprints*—*Bevan*⟩ *Ana* design, plot, plan, scheme, project (see under PLAN *n*): chart, map, graph (see under CHART *n*)

**skewbald** *variegated, parti-colored, motley, checkered, checked, pied, piebald, dappled, freaked

**skid** *vb* *slide, slip, glide, glissade, slither, coast, toboggan

**skill** *art, cunning, craft, artifice
*Ana* proficiency, adeptness, expertness (see corresponding adjectives at PROFICIENT): efficiency, effectiveness (see corresponding adjectives at EFFECTIVE): *readiness, facility, dexterity, ease

**skilled** skillful, *proficient, adept, expert, masterly
*Ana* apt, ready, *quick, prompt: practiced, exercised, drilled (see PRACTICE *vb*): competent, qualified, *able, capable
*Ant* unskilled

**skillful** *proficient, adept, expert, skilled, masterly
*Ana* *dexterous, adroit, deft: efficient, *effective: *conversant, versed
*Ant* unskillful —*Con* *awkward, clumsy, inept, maladroit, gauche

**skim** 1 float, *fly, dart, scud, shoot, sail
2 *brush, graze, glance, shave
*Ana* *slide, glide, slip, slither: float, scud, shoot, sail, dart, *fly: *flit, hover

**skimpy** scrimpy, exiguous, *meager, scanty, scant, spare, sparse

**skin** *n* Skin, hide, pelt, rind, bark, peel can all denote an outer removable coat which adheres to and protects the inner tissues of a body or organism. **Skin**, the most general term, applies especially to the outer covering of animals, whether it is as delicate as the one which covers the human body or as tough as the one which covers a rhinoceros; it is used also of the outer coverings of various fruits, plants, and seeds especially when they are thin and tight ⟨the *skin* of an apple⟩ ⟨the *skin* of an almond⟩ *Skin* applies to this integument whether it covers the living organism or has been stripped from it. **Hide** applies to the tough skin of large animals (as the rhinoceros or the horse); in commercial use it is applied specifically to the raw or undressed skins of cattle, horses, and other large animals, sometimes in distinction from those of calves, sheep, and goats, which are commonly described merely as *skins*. **Pelt** is applied chiefly to the skin of an animal that is covered with hair, fur, or wool; in commerce it usually denotes an undressed skin of any of these animals and especially of a furred animal. It is applied also to the skin of a sheep or goat stripped of wool or hair and ready for tanning. **Rind** applies chiefly to the thick, tough, and often inelastic outer layer which covers certain fruits (as oranges and melons) or the stems and roots of some woody perennial plants (then usually called **bark**). The hardened skin on smoked meats (as bacon) and the hardened crust of molded cheeses are also called *rinds*. A skin or rind of a fruit or a portion of it that is or may be stripped free is called **peel** ⟨slip on a banana *peel*⟩ ⟨candied orange *peel*⟩

**skin** *vb* Skin, decorticate, peel, pare, flay can mean to divest something of its skin or thin outer covering. **Skin** is the most general of these terms, being applicable to any animal as well as to any plant or plant part that is covered by or as if by a skin ⟨*skin* calves slaughtered for the market⟩ ⟨do not *skin*, but wash the eggplants in iced water—*Dione Lucas*⟩ ⟨*skin* the bark off a birch tree⟩ **Decorticate** is applicable when an outer layer (as of bark, fiber, or husk) is to be removed by stripping ⟨obviated the necessity of fully *decorticating* the canna stalks—*Edward Samuel*⟩ ⟨the *decorticated* seeds are crushed and pressed—*Riegel*⟩ **Peel** and **pare** are frequently interchanged but distinctively **peel** may imply that the skin or outer covering can be removed by stripping or by pulling off while **pare** tends to be used when it requires to be cut off, usually with some of the adjoining substance; thus, freshly boiled potatoes can be easily *peeled*, but uncooked ones must be either scraped or *pared;* one speaks usually of *peeling* an orange because its rind may be stripped by the hand; one speaks usually of *paring* an apple since the skin is not easily detached from the flesh; one *peels* a hard-boiled egg. But *pare* may also be used of anything that is cut close and so is applicable to many things which do not have a skin or rind ⟨*pared* his toenails⟩ ⟨*pare* expenses to a minimum⟩ **Flay** tends to be applied largely to persons often in threats or in descriptions of torture or of cruel punishment (as scourging) ⟨he said he would *flay* the man alive if he again caught him prowling around⟩ ⟨they killed and *flayed* a number of slaves and captives—*Coon*⟩ ⟨campaign pledge to ban the medieval practice of *flaying* unruly convicts—*Time*⟩ ⟨the son and his mother *flay* one another with their words—*Fowlie*⟩

**skinny** scrawny, rawboned, angular, gaunt, lank, lanky, *lean, spare

*Ant* fleshy

**skip** *vb* **Skip, bound, hop, curvet, lope, lollop, ricochet** can all mean to move or advance with successive springs or leaps. The first three words are commonly referable to persons or animals but they may be used in reference to inanimate things. **Skip** suggests quick, light, graceful movement and a continuous alternation of touching a surface and springing clear of it; often also when referred to living creatures it connotes sportiveness or excess of animal spirits ⟨wanton as a child, *skipping*—*Shak.*⟩ ⟨small yachts *skipped* here and there—*Villiers*⟩ **Bound** (see also JUMP) implies longer and more vigorous springs than *skip* and carries a stronger suggestion of elasticity and buoyancy of spirit ⟨like a roe I *bounded* o'er the mountains—*Wordsworth*⟩ ⟨I saw her *bounding* down the rocky slope like some wild, agile creature—*Hudson*⟩ ⟨the ball struck the earth and *bounded* across the field⟩ **Hop** suggests a less flowing or springy movement than the two preceding words; at times it connotes jerkiness and lack of dignity in movement. It implies a succession of small quick leaps (as of birds, toads, or grasshoppers) ⟨he does not waltz, he *hops*⟩ and in reference to children it suggests a jumping on one foot only ⟨chalked out a hop-scotch game and began to *hop* around its squares—*Dorothy Canfield*⟩ **Curvet** may suggest a leap of a horse in which he raises both forelegs at once and as they are falling lifts both hind legs so that for an instant all his legs clear the surface, or in more general application it may imply frisking and gamboling or flightiness ⟨would you sell or slay your horse for bounding and *curvetting* in his course . . . ?—*Cowper*⟩ ⟨a gang of merry roistering devils, frisking and *curvetting* on a flat rock—*Irving*⟩ **Lope** evokes a picture of the long easy bounds of a lithe and agile animal (as a wolf or fox) on the run ⟨the long, *loping* stride of a mountaineer⟩ ⟨he progressed at an uneven pace, *loping* forward almost recklessly for many yards . . . then pausing fearfully for seconds—*Mailer*⟩ ⟨when it came time to feed them, he would . . . bang on the bottom of a tin pan; the fat cats would come *loping* up, like leopards, from all corners of the saloon—*Joseph Mitchell*⟩ **Lollop,** on the other hand, implies a clumsy, irregular bounding that suggests awkwardness or heaviness of movement ⟨its doors opened; out poured, *lolloped*, flopped a villainous crew, mostly foxhounds too old or too young—*Punch*⟩ ⟨the other buffalo also extricated itself from the slime and *lolloped* away—*George Orwell*⟩

**Ricochet** is referable almost exclusively to things which are thrown, shot, or cast. It suggests a skipping caused by a series of glancing rebounds after the object first strikes a surface ⟨the smaller the angle, under which a shot is made to *ricochet*, the longer it will preserve its force and have effect—*Spearman*⟩ ⟨fretting as her husband *ricocheted* from job to job—*E. W. Pike*⟩ ⟨our minds *ricochet* from the race problem to the housing problem, from the problem of foreign trade to the problem of displaced persons—*C. W. Ferguson*⟩

**skirmish** *n* *encounter, brush

*Ana* *contest, conflict, combat, fight, affray, fray: engagement, action, *battle

**skit** *libel, squib, lampoon, pasquinade

**skulk** *lurk, couch, slink, sneak

*Ana* secrete, *hide, conceal

*Con* emerge, *appear, loom

**skyline** profile, contour, *outline, silhouette

**slack** *adj* 1 lax, remiss, *negligent, neglectful

*Ana* *lazy, indolent, slothful, faineant: *indifferent, unconcerned, detached, aloof: sluggish, *lethargic

*Con* diligent, sedulous, industrious, *busy, assiduous: expeditious, quick, *fast

2 relaxed, *loose, lax

*Ana* *weak, feeble, infirm: inert, supine, passive, *inactive: *slow, leisurely, laggard

*Con* *tight, taut, tense: *steady, constant, uniform, even, equable: *firm, hard

**slacken** *delay, retard, slow, detain

*Ana* abate, reduce, lessen, *decrease: *restrain, curb, check, inhibit: *moderate, temper, qualify

*Ant* quicken

**slander** *n* calumny, *detraction, backbiting, scandal

*Ana* defamation, vilification, aspersion, traducing (see corresponding verbs at MALIGN): *abuse, vituperation, invective, obloquy, scurrility

**slander** *vb* defame, libel, calumniate, *malign, traduce, asperse, vilify

*Ana* *decry, depreciate, detract, derogate, disparage, belittle: *injure, damage, hurt: *attack, assail

**slang** *dialect, vernacular, patois, lingo, jargon, cant, argot

**slant** *vb* **Slant, slope, incline, lean** are comparable when they mean to diverge or cause to diverge from a vertical or horizontal line. **Slant** carries the sharpest and clearest implication of such divergence of any of these terms but it carries no explicit implication of how great or how little the divergence is; consequently it is accepted generally as the comprehensive term implying a noticeable physical divergence ⟨the Tibetans are of Mongol race, but their eyes *slant* less than those of the Japanese or Chinese—*Harrer*⟩ ⟨lines of gray, plunging tropic rain *slanted* across the whole world—*Beebe*⟩ ⟨one side of his body seemed to *slant* towards the other, he settled so much more heavily upon one foot—*M. E. Freeman*⟩ **Slope** is often used interchangeably with *slant*, but it is especially likely to be chosen when the reference is to a surface or a side of an elevation (as a hill or a roof) and there is an intent to suggest a gradual divergence from a vertical or horizontal line; thus, "the ground *slopes* to the left" usually suggests a lack of steepness; "a *sloping* roof," unless qualified by such adverbs as *sharply* or *steeply*, usually implies a gradual slant ⟨the road *slopes* downward from this point⟩ ⟨enjoyed their wide *sloping* lawns with the sprinklers idly turning —*Auchincloss*⟩ ⟨wooded valleys and rolling hills *slope* away to the horizon—*Amer. Guide Series: Pa.*⟩ **Incline** (see also INCLINE 2) carries a stronger implication of bending or tipping or of being bent or tipped; it is therefore

*A colon (:) separates groups of words discriminated. An asterisk (\*) indicates place of treatment of each group.*

especially appropriate not only when human or similar agency is implied but when what is bent or tipped is an immaterial thing (as one's will, one's thoughts, or one's intentions) ⟨just as the twig is bent, the tree's *inclined* —*Pope*⟩ ⟨*inclined* his head to the right ⟩ ⟨the garden terraces *incline* to the south⟩ ⟨there is another theory to which the late Professor Freeman *inclined* (if so sturdy a figure could be said to *incline*)—*Quiller-Couch*⟩ **Lean** differs from *incline* in carrying either a stronger implication of a definite directing of the inclination by a human agent or by some shaping or molding force ⟨the old man *leaned* the mast . . . against the wall—*Hemingway*⟩ ⟨olive trees *leaning* from the hillsides, twisted by the sun—*Davenport*⟩ ⟨without looking up at him she *leaned* towards him—*Marsh*⟩ or of a resting or an intent to rest either literally or figuratively against a support ⟨both items *lean* heavily on nostalgia, both bring happy memories of an era unfortunately ended—*Cerf*⟩ ⟨the others treated me gingerly, fearing to be classed as Bolsheviks by association. Naturally, I *leaned* toward those who *leaned* towards me—*Dent*⟩

*Ana* veer, *swerve, deviate, diverge

**slant** *n* *point of view, viewpoint, standpoint, angle
*Ana* attitude, *position, stand: bias, prejudice, *predilection

**slap** *vb* *strike, hit, smite, punch, slug, slog, swat, clout, cuff, box

**slash** *vb* slit, *cut, hew, chop, carve
*Ana* rive, rend, cleave, split (see TEAR): penetrate, pierce, *enter

**slatternly,** dowdy, frowzy, blowsy can all mean deficient in neatness, freshness, or smartness, especially in dress or appearance. **Slatternly** stresses notions of slovenliness, unkemptness, and sordidness ⟨a small, *slatternly* looking craft, her hull and spars a dingy black, rigging all slack and bleached nearly white, and everything denoting an ill state of affairs aboard—*Melville*⟩ ⟨lived with them, in the *slatternly* apartment among the unwashed dishes in the sink and on the table, the odor of stale tobacco smoke, the dirty shirts and underwear piled in corners—*Warren*⟩ **Dowdy** is likely to imply a complete lack of taste typically marked by a blend of something untidy, drab, or tawdry ⟨her shoes were bought a long time ago and have no relation to the dress, and the belt of her dress has become untied and is hanging down. She looks clean and *dowdy*—*Hellman*⟩ ⟨surely . . . it was old-fashioned, *dowdy*, savored of moth-eaten furs, bugles, cameos and black-edged notepaper, to go ferreting into people's pasts? —*Woolf*⟩ ⟨so dreadfully *dowdy* that she reminded one of a badly bound hymnbook—*Wilde*⟩ **Frowzy** suggests a lazy lack of neatness, order, and cleanliness ⟨a dumpy, *frowzy* woman, clad in old dress and apron—*Coutts*⟩ ⟨theater packed, and just as dirty and *frowzy* as when I first entered it in the year 1903—*Bennett*⟩ but *frowzy* also may apply to a natural and not unwholesome disorder ⟨white spruce, and the *frowzy*, slender jack pine thrive on the high land—*Rowlands*⟩ ⟨a live oak, *frowzy* with dry Resurrection ferns that the first rain startles to green life —*M. S. Douglas*⟩ or it may suggest drab misery and squalor as an inevitable result of circumstances ⟨a *frowzy* feeling, a mean, sleepy, stupid, fed-up, incomplete feeling—*Jonas*⟩ ⟨one may see women like this in poor districts . . . not quite anxious, not quite starved, but by circumstances reduced to a daily diet of *frowzy* economy —*Swinnerton*⟩ ⟨if a fully fed, presentably clothed, decently housed, fairly literate and cultivated and gently mannered family is not better than a half-starved, ragged, *frowzy*, overcrowded one, there is no meaning in words —*Shaw*⟩ **Blowsy** implies dishevelment or disorder ⟨her

hair, so untidy, so *blowsy*—*Austen*⟩ to which is often added a notion of crudity or coarseness or grossness ⟨that *blowsy* hoyden of an America that existed when Grant was accounted a statesman and Longfellow an epic poet— *Sinclair Lewis*⟩ ⟨the pleasant but plebeian scent of Bouncing Bet, that somewhat *blowsy* pink of old English gardens—*Peattie*⟩
*Ana* slovenly, unkempt, disheveled, sloppy, *slipshod
*Con* *neat, tidy, trim, spick-and-span

**slaughter** *n* *massacre, butchery, carnage, pogrom

**slavery** *servitude, bondage

**slavish** servile, menial, *subservient, obsequious
*Ana* *mean, abject, ignoble, sordid: *tame, subdued, submissive: *miserable, wretched

**slay** *kill, murder, assassinate, dispatch, execute

**sleazy** *limp, flimsy, floppy, flaccid, flabby
*Ana* *thin, tenuous, slight: *loose, slack

**sleek,** slick, glossy, velvety, silken, silky, satiny are comparable when they mean having a smooth bright surface or appearance. *Sleek* and *slick* are sometimes interchangeable with this meaning ⟨dark *slick* leaves—*Langley*⟩ ⟨the *sleek* blue plums—*Wylie*⟩ but more often **sleek** connotes a smoothness or brightness that is the result of close attention or is an indication, especially when the reference is to a person or animal, of being in excellent physical condition ⟨let me have men about me that are fat: *sleek*-headed men and such as sleep o' nights—*Shak.*⟩ ⟨a beautiful panther . . . so bright of eye, so *sleek* of coat— *Thackeray*⟩ ⟨the metal felt *sleek* and warm to his touch —*Cloete*⟩ ⟨a child's mind thrills at the touch of fur because it is *sleek*—*Montague*⟩ and it may also suggest a smoothness of finish resulting from overattention to or overrefinement in dress and appearance ⟨curse me the *sleek* lords with their plumes and spurs—*Lindsay*⟩ ⟨something *sleek* about him, something that suggested a well-bred dog—*Anderson*⟩ ⟨the poise, assurance, and sophistication of all these *sleek* faces—*Wolfe*⟩ **Slick,** by contrast, is more likely to apply when the intent is to suggest such an extreme of smoothness as to provide an unsafe or slippery surface ⟨the grass was *slick* from the night's dew, and the men slipped frequently—*Mailer*⟩ In extended use *slick* is less likely than *sleek* to suggest desirable qualities and often carries more than a hint of contempt ⟨as much a *slick*-surfaced commercial product as a serious piece of literary art—*Gurko*⟩ ⟨new hotels . . . so *slick* and shiny—*Basso*⟩ ⟨everything was to be *slick*, which was Marvin's term of approbation; but not too *slick*, which was his abomination—*Mary Austin*⟩ **Glossy** implies a surface that is exceedingly smooth and shining, whether by nature or by art ⟨the *glossy* leaves of the beech tree⟩ ⟨downy peaches and the *glossy* plum— *Dryden*⟩ ⟨*glossy* as black rocks on a sunny day cased in ice—*Dorothy Wordsworth*⟩ **Velvety** implies the extreme softness associated with the surface or appearance of velvet. The word is often used of things as they appeal to the sense of touch or of sight or of both ⟨a *velvety* skin⟩ ⟨a *velvety* flower⟩ ⟨a land of *velvety* meadows and lush gardens—*Mumford*⟩ ⟨the *velvety* flanks of the cattle—*Glasgow*⟩ but it is also applicable to sounds that caress the ear or to tastes or odors that are delightfully bland ⟨even her high notes are *velvety*⟩ ⟨the boy reading in his queer, *velvety* bass voice—*Galsworthy*⟩ **Silken** implies the smoothness and luster as well as the softness of silk ⟨*silken* hair⟩ ⟨to what green altar . . . lead'st thou that heifer lowing at the skies, and all her *silken* flanks with garlands dressed—*Keats*⟩ ⟨the lazy movement of their bodies beneath their *silken* doeskins—*O'Meara*⟩ The term is used in reference both to things that appeal to other senses than those of touch or sight and to imma-

---

*Ana* analogous words     *Ant* antonyms     *Con* contrasted words     See also explanatory notes facing page 1

terial things that are softly soothing and pleasant to the spirit or mind ⟨a *silken* voice⟩ ⟨the *silken* sonority of the strings—*Virgil Thomson*⟩ ⟨*silken* words⟩ **Silky** is sometimes used in place of *silken* ⟨fingers, *silky* and soft—*Watts-Dunton*⟩ ⟨blue, *silky* October days—*Glover*⟩ ⟨his eyes between his *silky* lashes gone soft—*Boyle*⟩ but when the reference is to persons or their voices, manners, or productions it, more often than *silken*, suggests an ingratiating or a specious quality ⟨put his talent for writing *silky* satire to most profitable unliterary uses—*Derwent May*⟩ ⟨Tchaikovsky's *Meditation* was no *silky* simper of tone, but something that glowed inside—*Cassidy*⟩ ⟨there have been many able varmints since, but none quite as *silky* or loathsome—*Perelman*⟩ **Satiny** applies to what is not only soft but smooth and shining ⟨the *satiny* petals of a flower⟩ ⟨beautiful women with *satiny* backs were moving through the crowd—*Wolfe*⟩

*Ana* *bright, lustrous, brilliant: smooth, even (see LEVEL)

**sleep** *vb* **Sleep, slumber, drowse, doze, nap, catnap, snooze** mean to take rest by a suspension of consciousness. **Sleep,** the usual term, implies ordinarily the periodical repose of this sort in which men and animals recuperate their powers after activity, but it may imply such repose indulged in temporarily or at odd times ⟨the young baby *sleeps* most of the time⟩ ⟨he *sleeps* fitfully⟩ ⟨they *slept* soundly all night⟩ ⟨*slept* away his fatigue⟩ ⟨*sleep* off the effects of an opiate⟩ ⟨doped to make him *sleep* away the hours of travel—*Ervine*⟩ *Sleep* can also refer to a condition (as dormancy, indolence, or death) felt to resemble true sleep ⟨the restless enmity of the Angevin never *slept*—*Freeman*⟩ ⟨beneath those rugged elms . . . the rude forefathers of the hamlet *sleep*—*Gray*⟩ **Slumber** implies sleeping but it has acquired connotations that usually distinguish it from *sleep.* When applied to persons it usually suggests a sleeping quietly and easily ⟨covered the sleeper with a blanket and the girl *slumbered* peacefully to Buffalo—*LaCossitt*⟩ ⟨hush, my dear, lie still and *slumber*! holy angels guard thy bed!—*Watts*⟩ In extended use it is likely to connote the repose of death and inactivity and suggest prolonged heavy sleep ⟨that I may *slumber* in eternal sleep—*Shak.*⟩ ⟨this New England of ours *slumbered* from the dawn of creation until the beginning of the seventeenth century—*Coolidge*⟩ **Drowse** suggests a dull heavy condition of body and mind when one is falling asleep or is half asleep ⟨sit *drowsing* by the fire⟩ ⟨it is idle to pretend that a man lectures as well if half his audience are *drowsing*—*Whitehead*⟩ In extension it implies a sluggishness that makes something move or act slowly ⟨the villages that once *drowsed* in the sun about the placid center squares—*Theodore White*⟩ **Doze** carries somewhat the same implications as *drowse* but the term often suggests a falling asleep, unintentionally or naturally, and does not emphasize a previous drowsy condition; often it suggests a falling asleep for a brief period or a drifting in and out of sleep, and it may imply a state of bewilderment when suddenly awakened ⟨he had just *dozed* off when the explosion occurred⟩ ⟨the sun drowsing on crooked streets, old men *dozing* in the parks—*Green Peyton*⟩ ⟨I have been *dozing* over a stupid book—*Sheridan*⟩ ⟨she *dozed* off for a moment or two, and then she got up and began . . . washing her hands—*Goudge*⟩ **Nap** basically implies a taking of a short light sleep, especially in the daytime; in extended use it commonly implies an opposition to *watch* or *be on the alert* and does not necessarily suggest the taking of a nap but merely a relaxation of care or activity (as in preventing, protecting, or detecting) ⟨while I nodded, nearly *napping*—*Poe*⟩ ⟨the Tory party is organized now; they will not catch us *napping* again—*Dis-*

*raeli*⟩ **Catnap** implies a frequent taking of brief refreshing naps, usually at odd intervals fitted between one's periods of activity ⟨stays in top form by *catnapping* whenever he has a spare moment—*Time*⟩ **Snooze,** a somewhat casual or slangy term, may be used in place of *nap* and others of the preceding terms but without any emphasis on their distinctive or figurative connotations ⟨*snooze* by the fire⟩ ⟨the smaller, quieter resorts, where *snoozing* in a deck chair on the beach, salon orchestras and ornamental gardens are emphasized—*Kenneth Young*⟩

*Ana* rest, repose, relax (see corresponding nouns at REST)

**sleepy, drowsy, somnolent, slumberous** mean affected by a desire to sleep or inducing such a desire. **Sleepy,** the ordinary term of this group, applies not only to persons but to things that suggest a resemblance to persons who show a readiness to fall asleep ⟨away, you rogue, away! I am *sleepy*—*Shak.*⟩ ⟨a *sleepy* town⟩ ⟨the quiet, *sleepy* railroad station—*Anderson*⟩ The term also applies to conditions or to things which incline one to sleep or to dozing or dreaming ⟨the yellowhammer trills his *sleepy* song in the noonday heat—*L. P. Smith*⟩ **Drowsy** differs from *sleepy* in carrying a stronger implication of the heaviness or loginess associated with sleepiness than of the actual need of rest ⟨become *drowsy* after a heavy dinner⟩ ⟨when the sun should burn through the leaves . . . Mrs. Barkley would grow *drowsy* . . . and go off to take a nap—*Deland*⟩ When applied to things rather than to persons, *drowsy* connotes more obviously than *sleepy* a soporific power ⟨not poppy, nor mandragora, nor all the *drowsy* syrups of the world, shall ever medicine thee to that sweet sleep which thou owedst yesterday—*Shak.*⟩ ⟨*drowsy* tinklings lull the distant folds—*Gray*⟩ ⟨the leisurely swishing of the water to leeward was like a *drowsy* comment on her progress—*Conrad*⟩ **Somnolent** may be used in place of *drowsy;* usually, however, it connotes the sluggishness or inertness characteristic of one who is sleepy or drowsy or the capacity for inducing this rather than the actual impulse to sleep or doze ⟨a *somnolent* want of interest—*De Quincey*⟩ ⟨Eustacia waited, her *somnolent* manner covering her inner heat and agitation—*Hardy*⟩ ⟨the *somnolent* pages of a three-volume novel⟩ **Slumberous** is often used in the sense of *sleepy* or *drowsy* or *somnolent;* occasionally it carries a distinctive connotation in which it usually suggests quiescence or the repose of latent powers ⟨I . . . heard the mountain's *slumberous* voice—*Shelley*⟩ ⟨Eustacia's manner was as a rule of a *slumberous* sort, her passions being of the massive rather than the vivacious kind—*Hardy*⟩

*Ana* *lethargic, sluggish, comatose

**slender** *thin, slim, slight, tenuous, rare

*Ana* *lean, spare, lanky, skinny: flimsy, flaccid, flabby, *limp: trivial, trifling, *petty, paltry, puny

**slick** *adj* **1** *sleek, glossy, velvety, silken, satiny, silky

*Ana* finished, *consummate: flawless, *impeccable, faultless: shallow, *superficial

**2** *fulsome, oily, unctuous, oleaginous, soapy

*Ana* bland, smooth, diplomatic, politic, *suave, urbane: specious, *plausible

**slide** *vb* **Slide, slip, glide, skid, glissade, slither, coast, toboggan** can mean to move along easily and smoothly over or as if over a surface. **Slide** usually implies accelerating motion and continuous contact with a smooth and slippery surface; it is used not only in reference to persons and to moving things (as vehicles) ⟨boys like to *slide* down banisters⟩ ⟨the fool *slides* o'er the ice that you should break—*Shak.*⟩ ⟨when it's quiet you can *slide* in there in a skiff—*Gardner*⟩ but also, especially in extended use, with reference to things which pass rapidly

---

A colon (:) separates groups of words discriminated. An asterisk (*) indicates place of treatment of each group.

before one because of one's own swift and easy motion ⟨house after house *slid* by as we neared the city⟩ or which move easily, unobtrusively, or gradually from one place or condition to another ⟨prose that *slides* into poetry⟩ ⟨shadows *slid* along the huge wooden tables— *Sinclair Lewis*⟩ ⟨*slide* one's hand into another's pocket⟩ ⟨it was inevitable that existentialism should *slide* out of men's minds—*Cousins*⟩ **Slip** carries a stronger implication than *slide* of a frictionless and unobstructed surface but a weaker suggestion of continued contact; it typically suggests involuntary rather than voluntary sliding, often definitely implying a loss of footing and a fall ⟨*slip* on the ice⟩ ⟨he had hurt his elbow through dropping his stick and *slipping* downstairs—*Bennett*⟩ ⟨half-*slipped*, half-slid down toward the wide level ribbon that marked the frozen Schuylkill—*Mason*⟩ When only swift, easy motion is implied, *slip* heightens the emphasis upon quietness, stealth, or skillfulness ⟨while we were talking, he *slipped* from the house⟩ Things are said to *slip* that pass quickly or without notice (as from one's grasp, one's control, one's memory, or one's observation) ⟨the book *slipped* from her feeble hands⟩ ⟨the details have *slipped* from his mind⟩ ⟨it leaves us without our being aware that it is *slipping* away—*J. M. Brown*⟩ ⟨a father can't make offhand remarks to a 4-year-old and have them gently *slip* into oblivion—*McNulty*⟩ or as a result of one's negligence or inattention ⟨the bus *slipped* by while they were engrossed in conversation⟩ ⟨the tool *slipped* and cut his hand⟩ ⟨he *slips* into occasional inaccuracies— *Anthony Boucher*⟩ **Glide** comes closer to *slide* than to *slip* in its stress upon such continued smooth, easy, usually silent motion as is characteristic of some dances, but it may or may not imply unintermittent contact with a surface and, apart from its context, it seldom carries any suggestion of danger ⟨they *glide*, like phantoms, into the wide hall—*Keats*⟩ ⟨even the swallows, the restless swallows, *glided* in an effortless way through the busy air—*Jefferies*⟩ ⟨two monsterlike cameras on trucks that *glided* backwards and forwards—*Edmund Wilson*⟩ ⟨I *glide* over these interesting items to dwell at some length on two men, now dead—*Henry Miller*⟩ Often, like *slide* and, to a lesser extent, *slip, glide* is used in reference to things that apparently move because the observer is moving ⟨the landward marks have failed, the fogbank *glides* unguessed—*Kipling*⟩ ⟨soft fell the splash of the oars . . . softly the banks *glided* by—*Meredith*⟩ **Skid** is employed especially in regard to wheeled vehicles the tires of which on an icy, wet, or dusty road fail to grip the roadway, thereby causing the wheels to slide without rotating and the vehicle to go out of control ⟨the car *skidded* on the icy patch and ran into a telegraph pole⟩ In extended use *skid*, like *slip*, usually implies an element of danger or recklessness or a lack of complete control or grasp ⟨he ran fast, occasionally *skidding* on an icy patch, but always quickly recovering his balance⟩ ⟨a jet plane . . . crashed into a house in northwest Kansas City, *skidded* across a street and plowed into another home—*Wall Street Jour.*⟩ ⟨his timid, tired voice *skidding* into a hoarse whisper—*Capote*⟩ **Glissade**, basically a mountaineering term implying a long slide down a snow-covered slope, carries the major implications of both *slide* and *glide* but stresses skillful technique and control ⟨the danger of *glissading*, for inexperienced persons, is that they may *glissade* in the wrong place—*Conway*⟩ ⟨Wilkins and I *glissaded* down the long snow slopes, and our porters . . . came sliding and tumbling after—*Hillary*⟩ In extended reference to things *glissade* tends to lose its implication of skill and differs little from *slide, slip,* or *glide* ⟨rock fragments are streaming or *glissading* down from

above—*C. A. Cotton*⟩ ⟨you will really feel the buoyancy of the craft as it *glissades* over the Atlantic swell—*The Motor*⟩ **Slither** typically implies a sliding down or along a rocky, pebbly, or other rough surface with noise and clatter ⟨the rest [of the tile] bounced on the roof and then *slithered* down it and off it—*Masefield*⟩ ⟨the *African Queen* was *slithering* and grating over the mud and the tree roots—*Forester*⟩ or it may suggest a gliding, sliding, sometimes undulating motion suggestive of a snake's movement ⟨crawling through walls and *slithering* along the ground—*de Kruif*⟩ ⟨a crocodile *slithering* down a sandbank into a stream—*Moorehead*⟩ ⟨a muffled *slithering* sound which he knew could be made only by men moving through a thin patch of jungle—*Mailer*⟩ Both *coast* and *toboggan* basically imply a downward movement (as of a sled or toboggan) on a smooth or slippery course under the influence of gravity and thereby come close to *slide* and *glide* ⟨*coasted* his car down the long hill to the village⟩ ⟨as Boylston Place ran downhill, it afforded in winter an irresistible chance for *coasting*, that is, for *tobogganing* with single or even with double or longer sleds—*Santayana*⟩ But they differ in their extended use, for **coast** usually stresses movement in the absence of continuously applied force (as of momentum or gravity) ⟨to *coast* from Earth to the moon . . . we must achieve a velocity of 25,000 mph—*A. C. Clarke*⟩ ⟨swallows were *coasting* in and out the smashed mill roof— *Bartlett*⟩ and often suggests an easy drifting ⟨the country . . . seems in a mood to *coast* along—*U.S. News and World Report*⟩ while **toboggan** is likely to stress a building up of momentum and a resulting wild speed in a usually uncontrollable downward movement ⟨three depth charges, each weighing 400 pounds, broke loose and *tobogganed* wildly on the main deck—*Bigart*⟩ ⟨could it be possible that man, who fondly called himself *Homo sapiens,* was *tobogganing* into another self-destructive war while the wounds of the last were still throbbing?—*Pinckney*⟩ ⟨the Chinese dollar, which, amid all the speculating, had been *tobogganing* steadily—*Vanya Oakes*⟩

**slight** *adj* tenuous, rare, \*thin, slender, slim
*Ana* \*imperceptible, imponderable, impalpable, intangible, insensible, inappreciable: trifling, trivial, puny, \*petty, paltry: minute, diminutive, wee, little, \*small
**slight** *vb* \*neglect, ignore, overlook, disregard, omit, forget
*Ana* scorn, disdain, contemn, \*despise: flout, \*scoff
**slighting** \*derogatory, depreciatory, depreciative, disparaging, pejorative
*Ana* contemptuous, disdainful, scornful, despiteful (see corresponding nouns under DESPISE *vb*)
**slim** \*thin, slender, slight, tenuous, rare
*Ana* \*lean, spare, skinny, scrawny: \*meager, exiguous, scant, scanty: lithe, lithesome, lissome (see SUPPLE)
*Ant* chubby *(of persons)*
**sling** *vb* furl, fling, pitch, toss, \*throw, cast
*Ana* heave, hoist, \*lift, raise: impel, drive (see MOVE): propel, shove, thrust, \*push
**sling** *vb* \*hang, suspend, dangle
**slink** \*lurk, skulk, sneak
**slip** *vb* \*slide, glide, skid, glissade, slither, coast, toboggan
**slip** *n* 1 \*wharf, dock, pier, quay, berth, jetty, levee
2 lapse, \*error, mistake, blunder, faux pas, bull, howler, boner
*Ana* accident, \*chance: inadvertence, carelessness, heedlessness (see corresponding adjectives at CARELESS): \*fault, failing, foible, frailty, vice
**slipshod** *adj* Slipshod, slovenly, unkempt, disheveled, sloppy are comparable when applied to persons and their appearance or to their mental and manual processes, performances, or products, and mean manifesting conspicuous

negligence or carelessness. **Slipshod** implies an easygoing tolerance of details that are inaccurate, incongruous, or lacking in precision, or careless indifference to the niceties of technique or to qualities that make for perfection (as thoroughness, soundness, and fastidiousness) ⟨a *slipshod* style⟩ ⟨a *slipshod* piece of carpentry⟩ ⟨a *slipshod* performance of a symphony⟩ ⟨was at first a *slipshod* observer . . . he had a positive distaste for exactitude—*Peattie*⟩ ⟨had the conscientious craftsman's contempt for *slipshod* work—*Spaeth*⟩ **Slovenly,** a stronger term than *slipshod*, implies laziness and disorderliness which is evident throughout and is not merely a matter of detail. The term may be used of a person or his appearance and imply diametrical opposition to *neat* or *tidy* ⟨a *slovenly* housekeeper⟩ ⟨his person showed marks of habitual neglect; his dress was *slovenly*—*George Eliot*⟩ ⟨the beatnik is *slovenly*—to strike a pose against the middle class you must roil their compulsion to be neat—*Mailer*⟩ or it may be applied to processes, technique, or workmanship without significant change in value ⟨*slovenly* thinking⟩ ⟨the *slovenly* manner in which the dinner was served—*Conrad*⟩ ⟨a tendency to think that a fine idea excuses *slovenly* workmanship—*Lowell*⟩ **Unkempt** is applied usually to something that requires to be kept in order if a favorable impression is to be produced. It implies extreme negligence amounting to neglect ⟨*unkempt* hair⟩ ⟨an *unkempt* garden⟩ ⟨add to this *unkempt*, untended, this grammatically anarchical Russian tongue the jargon of German Marxism: no simile can cope with the situation—*Edmund Wilson*⟩ ⟨most of the shops . . . had become pettifogging little holes, *unkempt*, shabby, poor—*Bennett*⟩ **Disheveled** is more likely to describe a temporary state of ruffled disorder or disarray following intense effort (as in doing something or coping with some emergency) ⟨she hoped she appeared calm. She was conscious of a *disheveled* appearance—*Hervey*⟩ or in extended application a lack of normal planned orderliness (as of concept or development) ⟨a *disheveled* movie that charges futilely about—*McCarten*⟩ **Sloppy** implies a general effect of looseness and of spilling over. When applied to a person or his appearance it usually suggests loose, ill-fitting, unpressed garments, but it often also carries connotations of slovenliness ⟨his *sloppy* appearance at breakfast offended her⟩ ⟨her hair was thin and tied in a *sloppy* knot at the back of her not too clean neck—*Metalious*⟩ When applied to ideas or their expression, style, or manners or to a work or its workmanship, the word usually suggests a lack of control and precision or of confinement within proper limits, manifested in incoherency, emotional excess, or formlessness ⟨it is a *sloppy* bit of reporting, poorly organized, loaded with pointless personal details—*Sugrue*⟩
*Ana* \*negligent, neglectful, slack, lax, remiss: \*careless, heedless, inadvertent: \*indifferent, unconcerned: \*slatternly, dowdy, frowzy, blowsy
*Con* precise, accurate, exact, \*correct: fastidious, finicky, \*nice

**slit** *vb* slash, \*cut, hew, chop, carve

**slither** \*slide, slip, glide, skid, glissade, coast, toboggan

**slog** \*strike, hit, smite, punch, slug, swat, clout, slap, cuff, box

**slogan** \*catchword, byword, shibboleth
*Ana* \*phrase, expression, locution, idiom

**slope** *vb* \*slant, incline, lean
*Ana* deviate, diverge, veer, \*swerve

**sloppy** slovenly, unkempt, disheveled, \*slipshod
*Ana* \*negligent, neglectful, slack, remiss, lax: mawkish, maudlin, soppy, slushy (see SENTIMENTAL): \*slatternly, dowdy, frowzy, blowsy
*Con* \*careful, meticulous, scrupulous, punctilious: fas-

tidious, finicky, \*nice

**slothful** indolent, faineant, \*lazy
*Ana* \*inactive, inert, supine, passive, idle: slack, remiss, lax, \*negligent, neglectful: \*slow, leisurely, deliberate, dilatory, laggard
*Ant* industrious —*Con* \*busy, diligent, sedulous, assiduous

**slough** *vb* \*discard, cast, shed, molt, scrap, junk

**slovenly** \*slipshod, unkempt, disheveled, sloppy
*Ana* \*slatternly, dowdy, frowzy, blowsy: \*indifferent, unconcerned: \*negligent, neglectful, slack, lax, remiss
*Con* \*orderly, methodical: \*neat, tidy, trim, spick-and-span

**slow** *adj* **1** \*stupid, dull, dense, crass, dumb
**2 Slow, dilatory, laggard, deliberate, leisurely** can apply to persons, their movements, or their actions, and mean taking a longer time than is necessary, usual, or sometimes, desirable. **Slow** (see also STUPID), the term that is the widest in its range of application, may also be used in reference to a thing (as a mechanism, a process, or a drug) that is the opposite of quick or fast in its motion, its performance, or its operation. In its varying applications *slow* often suggests a reprehensible or discreditable cause (as stupidity, lethargy, indolence, or inaction) ⟨a *slow* student⟩ ⟨*slow* wits⟩ ⟨*slow* movements⟩ ⟨he is as *slow* as a snail⟩ ⟨*slow* in getting results⟩ ⟨an unimaginative man, *slow* of comprehension—*Times Lit. Sup.*⟩ but it may suggest either extreme care or caution ⟨a *slow* but capable worker⟩ ⟨*slow* to take offense⟩ ⟨he is *slow* in making changes⟩ ⟨he spoke with a *slow*, slightly thick precision, making elegant gestures—*Wouk*⟩ or a tempo that is required by nature, art, or a plan or schedule ⟨a *slow* convalescence⟩ ⟨a *slow* stream⟩ ⟨a *slow* movement in music⟩ ⟨a *slow* train⟩ or a falling behind because of structural or mechanical defects or untoward difficulties ⟨a *slow* watch⟩ ⟨the train is *slow* tonight because of the snowstorm⟩ **Dilatory** is relatively a term of restricted application referable to persons or to things for which persons are responsible as their actors, performers, or creators and implying slowness that is the result of inertness, procrastination, or indifference ⟨a *dilatory* correspondent⟩ ⟨though *dilatory* in undertaking business, he was quick in its execution—*Austen*⟩ ⟨he was temporizing, making, with unconscious prudence, a *dilatory* opposition to an impending catastrophe—*Bierce*⟩ **Laggard** is even more censorious a term than *dilatory*, for it implies a failure to observe a schedule (as for arriving or performing) or to obey a call or demand promptly; it frequently suggests loitering or waste of time ⟨*laggard* pupils keep a whole class back⟩ ⟨for Love was *laggard*, O, Love was slow to come—*Millay*⟩ ⟨in its coverage of spot news events, radio has been especially *laggard*—*Rovere*⟩ ⟨directed him and another general to . . . prod *laggard* manufacturers into speeding up production—*Kahn*⟩ **Deliberate** (see also DELIBERATE 2) applies to persons, usually directly but sometimes indirectly, and then is applied to things for which a person is responsible; the term suggests absence of hurry or agitation and a slowness that is the result of care, forethought, calculation, or self-restraint ⟨*deliberate* enunciation⟩ ⟨*deliberate* movements⟩ ⟨he returned with the same easy, *deliberate* tread—*Cather*⟩ ⟨she ate her food in the *deliberate*, constrained way, almost as if she recoiled a little from doing anything so publicly—*D. H. Lawrence*⟩ **Leisurely** also implies a lack of hurry or a slowness that suggests that there is no pressure for time; the term applies not only to persons and their acts but to things that have no relation to persons ⟨breakfast was a *leisurely* meal—*Archibald Marshall*⟩ ⟨his departure, like all his movements, was *leisurely*. He did not take the first

---

A colon (:) separates groups of words discriminated. An asterisk (\*) indicates place of treatment of each group.

available boat or the second—*Waugh*⟩ ⟨took *leisurely* leave, with kisses all around, of a half dozen young men— *K. A. Porter*⟩

*Ant* fast

**slow** *vb* slacken, *delay, retard, detain

*Ana* *moderate, temper, qualify: reduce, abate, *decrease, lessen

*Ant* speed  —*Con* accelerate, quicken, hasten, hurry (see SPEED *vb*)

**slug** *vb* *strike, hit, smite, punch, slog, swat, clout, slap, cuff, box

**sluggish** *lethargic, torpid, comatose

*Ana* inert, *inactive: indolent, slothful, *lazy: listless, languishing, *languid

*Ant* brisk: expeditious: quick (*of mind*)

**sluice** *vb* *pour, stream, gush

*Ana* flood, inundate, deluge (see corresponding nouns at FLOOD): drench, *soak

**slumber** *vb* *sleep, drowse, doze, nap, catnap, snooze

*Ana* relax, rest, repose (see corresponding nouns at REST)

**slumberous** *sleepy, drowsy, somnolent

**slump** *vb* *fall, drop, sink, subside

*Ana* *plunge, dive, pitch: sag, flag, *droop

**slushy** *sentimental, mushy, romantic, mawkish, maudlin, soppy

**sly, cunning, crafty, tricky, foxy, insidious, wily, guileful, artful** are comparable when they mean having or showing a disposition to attain one's ends by devious or indirect means. *Sly* implies a lack of candor which shows itself in secretiveness, in suggestiveness rather than in frankness, in underhandedness, or in furtiveness or duplicity in one's dealings with others ⟨with knowing leer and words of *sly* import—*Irving*⟩ ⟨because the state is hostile, writers have become *sly*, circumspect and disingenuous—*Philip Toynbee*⟩ More often than the remaining words, *sly* is used with weakened force to imply a lightly arch or roguish quality ⟨he was unpretentious, earnest, full of *sly* humor —*Rollo Brown*⟩ **Cunning** (see also CLEVER 2) stresses the use of intelligence in overreaching or circumventing; nevertheless, it often suggests sly inventiveness rather than a high-grade mentality, and a perverted sense of morality ⟨every man wishes to be wise, and they who cannot be wise are almost always *cunning*—*Johnson*⟩ ⟨all gods are cruel, bitter, and to be bribed, but women-gods are mean and *cunning* as well—*Bottomley*⟩ ⟨the fellow's eyes were now sly and *cunning* as a cat's, now hard and black as basalt—*Wolfe*⟩ **Crafty** also implies a use of intelligence but it usually suggests a higher order of mentality than *cunning*: that of one capable of devising stratagems and adroit in deception ⟨he disappointeth the devices of the *crafty*, so that their hands cannot perform their enterprise—*Job* 5:12⟩ ⟨as a *crafty* envoy does his country's business by dint of flirting and conviviality— *Montague*⟩ ⟨*crafty* senior tactician for the Republicans and a man with an astonishing record of maintaining political control of his county—*Michener*⟩ **Tricky** usually suggests unscrupulousness and chicanery in dealings with others; in general it connotes shiftiness and unreliability rather than skill in deception or in maneuvering ⟨here was Woman, with a capital W, *tricky* and awful, inconstant as the weather—*Styron*⟩ ⟨he avoided the mean and *tricky*: he was always an honorable foe—*W. C. Ford*⟩ **Foxy** implies shrewdness in dodging discovery or in practicing deceptions so that one may follow one's own devices or achieve one's own ends; it usually connotes experience and is rarely applied to the young or to novices ⟨where one was legitimate—and a *foxy* play—the other was a snide trick—*Lieb*⟩ ⟨this time the lecherous Alsatian uses a *foxier* gambit to achieve his ends—*Perelman*⟩ ⟨a *foxy*

old man⟩ **Insidious** suggests a lying in wait or a gradualness of effect or approach and applies especially to devious and carefully masked underhandedness ⟨an *insidious* tempter⟩ ⟨persuaded that these people . . . are all part of an *insidious* conspiracy to undermine the world as he knows it—*Edmund Wilson*⟩ ⟨that form of bias which is most *insidious*, precisely because it pretends to be unbiased—*Moberly*⟩ **Wily** and **guileful** stress an attempt to ensnare or entrap; they usually imply treacherous astuteness or sagacity and a lack of scruples regarding the means to one's end ⟨nor trust in the *guileful* heart and the murder-loving hand—*Morris*⟩ ⟨shun the insidious arts that Rome provides, less dreading from her frown than from her *wily* praise—*Wordsworth*⟩ ⟨the headmaster, *wily*, had not confiscated these articles; he had merely informed the parents concerned—*Bennett*⟩ **Artful** implies insinuating or alluring indirectness of dealing; it usually also connotes sophistication or coquetry or clever designs ⟨being *artful*, she cajoled him with honeymouthed flattery until his suspicion was quieted—*John Bennett*⟩ ⟨oddly enough, they stayed sober. The *artful* Henry had told them that all the wine in Panama was poisoned—*Chidsey*⟩

*Ana* furtive, clandestine, stealthy, covert (see SECRET): devious, oblique, *crooked: astute, *shrewd

**smack** *n* 1 *taste, flavor, savor, tang, relish
2 *touch, suggestion, suspicion, soupçon, tincture, tinge, shade, spice, dash, vein, strain, streak

**small, little, diminutive, petite, wee, tiny, teeny, weeny, minute, microscopic, miniature** can all mean conspicuously below the average in magnitude, especially physical magnitude. *Small* (opposed to *large*) and *little* (opposed to *big, great*) are often used without distinction. But **small**, more frequently than *little*, applies to things whose magnitude is determined by number, size, capacity, value, or significance ⟨a *small* attendance⟩ ⟨a *small* boy⟩ ⟨a *small* box⟩ ⟨a *small* house⟩ ⟨*small* change⟩ ⟨a *small* income⟩ ⟨a *small* matter⟩ ⟨fear of life, memory of hard times, dread of *small* slights in the community . . . combined to keep the household temperature low—*Buck*⟩ *Small* is also preferred when words like *quantity, amount, size*, and *capacity* are qualified ⟨give me a *small* quantity of flour⟩ ⟨they have only a *small* amount of money⟩ ⟨the *small* size of the rooms was disappointing⟩ *Small* also applies to intangible and immeasurable things which, however, may be said to be limited in some pertinent or significant way ⟨he has a *small* mind⟩ ⟨her sadness at the *small* prospect of seeing him again—*Archibald Marshall*⟩ ⟨"I never . . . thought you could be so *small* about anything," said Selena, who was just angry enough to use the word *small*—*Salinger*⟩ **Little** is usually more absolute in its implications than *small*, which often connotes less magnitude than is ordinary or is to be expected or is desirable; it may be preferred to *small*, therefore, when there is the intent to convey a hint of pettiness, of pettiness, or of insignificance in size, amount, quantity, or extent ⟨take *little* interest in politics⟩ ⟨a foolish consistency is the hobgoblin of *little* minds—*Emerson*⟩ ⟨the bull Bill . . . had picked out was a fierce, waspy *little* animal—*Gipson*⟩ ⟨he enjoyed the *little* vices and luxuries —coffee, fresh water, women—*T. E. Lawrence*⟩ ⟨this *little* man, whose intellectual resources were hardly more than a combination of prejudice and syntax—*Sheean*⟩ ⟨how unsubstantial then appear our hopes and dreams, our *little* ambitions, our paltry joys!—*Benson*⟩ *Little* is also appropriate in the sense of a small amount, a small quantity, or a small extent; thus, one asks for a *little* sugar or a *small* quantity of sugar; one sees that the garden is *little* or of *small* extent ⟨spading up a *little* culture along with the history—*Schulberg*⟩ *Little* is also appropriate

when the context carries a note of tenderness, pathos, or affection ⟨our *little* house⟩ ⟨the air turned cold . . . so that the *littlest* kids cried from cold as much as fright— *Grau*⟩ ⟨her pathetic *little* smile⟩ ⟨sleep, my *little* one —*Tennyson*⟩ **Diminutive** not only carries a stronger implication of divergence from a normal or usual size or scale than *small* or *little*, but it often carries the meaning of extremely or even abnormally small or little ⟨the bedrooms are small but the parlor is *diminutive*⟩ ⟨in so hot a climate peach trees will produce only *diminutive* fruits in very small quantities⟩ ⟨the horses are so *diminutive* that they might be, with propriety, said to be Lilliputian —*Cowper*⟩ ⟨a *diminutive* financial wizard, who looked like a Kewpie doll—*J. D. Hart*⟩ **Petite** is the usual term to describe a trim, well-shaped woman or girl of diminutive size ⟨a bit incongruous that such a *petite* woman should write such huge tomes—*Fisher*⟩ **Wee** is found especially in dialectal use in place of *small* or *little* ⟨a *wee* lad⟩ ⟨a *wee* drop of whisky⟩ or in more general use as an equivalent of *diminutive* ⟨a little *wee* face, with a little yellow beard—*Shak.*⟩ ⟨the one to the bachelor uncle . . . was sweetly girlish, and just a *wee* bit arch—*Gibbons*⟩ **Tiny** goes further than *diminutive* or *wee* in suggesting extreme littleness or a smallness out of proportion to most things of its kind or in comparison with all other things ⟨they were prominent eyes yellowed with *tiny* red veins —*Avram Davidson*⟩ ⟨the behavior of the invisible, intangible, inconceivably *tiny* electrons and atoms— *Darrow*⟩ ⟨*tiny*, Swiss-made replicas . . . each . . . about the size of a small, oblong wristwatch—*Terry Southern*⟩ **Teeny** and **weeny**, found chiefly in childish or playful use, occur also in paired or reduplicated forms (as *teeny-weeny* and *teeny-tiny*) ⟨one day this *teeny-tiny* woman put on her *teeny-tiny* bonnet and went out of her *teeny-tiny* house to take a *teeny-tiny* walk—*Fairy Tale*⟩ ⟨he gave a *weeny, weeny* yawn—*Wiggin*⟩ **Minute** means extremely small on an absolute scale, usually a microscopic or near-microscopic scale ⟨a *minute* animalcule⟩ ⟨*minute* grains of sand⟩ ⟨ants that marched their *minute* columns over the floor—*Hervey*⟩ ⟨the tremendous forces imprisoned in *minute* particles of matter—*Inge*⟩ **Microscopic** applies to what is so minute that it is literally observable only under a microscope ⟨*microscopic* organisms⟩ or is of a comparable minuteness in its class ⟨no matter how *microscopic* his wage, he forced himself to save a dollar or two a year—*Irving Stone*⟩ ⟨the lady of the dreadnaught class with a leash on the *microscopic* Chihuahua—*Cross*⟩ **Miniature** applies to what is complete in itself but is built, drawn, or made on a very small scale ⟨in circus parades, Tom Thumb and his ménage rode together in a *miniature* red coach, drawn by two small ponies—*Green Peyton*⟩ ⟨it was one of the *miniature* Italian cities . . . all compact and complete, on the top of a mountain—*L. P. Smith*⟩ ⟨we may thus picture an atom as a *miniature* solar system—*Eddington*⟩
*Ana* \*petty, puny, paltry, trifling, trivial
*Ant* large  —*Con* big, great (see LARGE): vast, \*huge, immense, enormous

**smaller** \*less, lesser, fewer

**small-town** \*insular, provincial, parochial, local
*Ana* narrow, narrow-minded, \*illiberal, intolerant, hidebound, bigoted: circumscribed, limited, confined, restricted (see LIMIT *vb*)
*Ant* cosmopolitan

**smart 1** bright, knowing, quick-witted, \*intelligent, clever, alert
*Ana* \*sharp, keen, acute: \*quick, ready, prompt, apt: \*shrewd, astute, perspicacious
*Ant* dull (*of mind*)

**2** modish, fashionable, \*stylish, chic, dashing
*Ana* elegant, exquisite (see CHOICE *adj*): finished, \*consummate
*Ant* dowdy, frowzy, blowsy

**smash** *vb* \*crush, mash, bruise, squash, macerate
*Ana* shatter, burst, crack, \*break: \*press, squeeze, crowd, jam

**smell, scent, odor, aroma** all denote a property of a thing that makes it perceptible to the olfactory sense. **Smell** not only is the most general of these terms but tends to be the most colorless. It is the appropriate word when merely the sensation is indicated and no hint of its source, quality, or character is necessary ⟨our horses . . . often reared up and snorted violently at *smells* which we could not perceive—*Landor*⟩ ⟨the *smells* of these offices—the *smell* of dental preparations, floor oil, spittoons and coal gas —*Cheever*⟩ It is also the preferred term when accompanied by explicitly qualifying words or phrases ⟨the rank *smell* of weeds—*Shak.*⟩ ⟨the rented coarse black gown . . . gave out a musty *smell*, as though it had been lying long disused—*Wouk*⟩ ⟨a *smell* of marigold and jasmine stronger even than the reek of the dust—*Kipling*⟩ and occasionally, even when unqualified, it implies offensiveness ⟨traced the *smell* to a stopped-up drain⟩ ⟨Cobden was much upset when he saw the middle classes leaving the *smells* of the . . . towns for the scents of the countryside—*Lewis & Maude*⟩ **Scent** tends to call attention to the physical basis of the sense of smell and is particularly appropriate when the emphasis is on the emanations or exhalations from an external object which reach the olfactory receptors rather than on the impression produced in the olfactory centers of the brain ⟨the *scent* of the first wood fire upon the keen October air—*Pater*⟩ ⟨if the air was void of sound, it was full of *scent*—*Galsworthy*⟩ ⟨the heavy *scent* of damp, funereal flowers—*Millay*⟩ ⟨presently a *scent* came with it, dank and pervasive. It was the must of the forest—*Hervey*⟩ but *scent* can apply specifically to emanations evidencing the passing of a body (as an animal) and may suggest a high level of sensory efficiency in a perceiver ⟨the dog caught the *scent* of a rabbit⟩ or from its use as a synonym of *perfume* the term may suggest a pleasant quality ⟨the rich, vital *scents* of the plowed ground—*Glasgow*⟩ **Odor** is oftentimes indistinguishable from *scent*, for it too can be thought of as something diffused and as something by means of which external objects are identified by the sense of smell. But the words are not always interchangeable, for *odor* usually implies abundance of effluvia and therefore does not suggest, as *scent* often does, the need of a delicate or highly sensitive sense of smell ⟨the *odors* of the kitchen clung to her clothes⟩ ⟨he smelled her perfume, a sweet pungent *odor*, intimately coquettish—*Styron*⟩ ⟨gave off a kind of sweetish rich animal-vegetable *odor*, such as one associates with the tropics—*Purdy*⟩ For these reasons *odor* usually implies general perceptibility and is the normal word in scientific use especially when the classification or description of types is attempted ⟨science, while recognizing the potency of our sense of smell, has not yet satisfactorily classified and catalogued the many varieties of *odors* that we recognize—*Morrison*⟩ **Aroma** usually adds to *odor* the implication of a penetrating, pervasive, or, sometimes, a pungent quality; it need not imply delicacy or fragrance, but it seldom connotes unpleasantness, and it often suggests something to be savored, with the result that it is used of things that appeal both to the sense of smell and taste or by extension to one's aesthetic sense ⟨the fresh river smell, rank and a little rotten, and spiced among these odors was the sultry *aroma* of strong boiling coffee—*Wolfe*⟩ ⟨an atmosphere, impalpable as a

---

A colon (:) separates groups of words discriminated. An asterisk (*) indicates place of treatment of each group.

perfume yet as real, rose above the heads of the laughing guests. It was the *aroma* of enjoyment and gaiety— *Gibbons*⟩ ⟨the *aroma* of a wood fire is the significant part of a camper's delight—*Morrison*⟩
*Ana* *fragrance, redolence, perfume, bouquet, incense: savor, flavor (see TASTE)

**smidgen** *particle, bit, mite, whit, atom, iota, jot, tittle

**smile** *vb* Smile, grin, simper, smirk are comparable as verbs meaning to express amusement or pleasure or satisfaction or, sometimes, contempt or indulgence, by a brightening of the eyes and an upward curving of the corners of the mouth and as nouns denoting such an expression. **Smile** is the general term, capable of being qualified so as to suggest malign as well as benign pleasure or amusement ⟨*smile* tenderly⟩ ⟨*smile* derisively⟩ ⟨a bright *smile*⟩ ⟨she wears a fixed *smile* . . . and it never varies, no matter to whom she speaks. I never heard her laugh spontaneously—*Mills*⟩ ⟨she *smiled* slowly then, the same slow *smile* that ended before it reached her eyes —*Buck*⟩ **Grin** implies a broad smile that shows the teeth. It often carries some suggestion of grimacing in anger or pain in its not infrequent implication of unnaturalness, of bewilderment, or senselessness ⟨they could not see the bitter smile behind the painted *grin* he wore—*Sill*⟩ More often, however, *grin* tends to imply naïve cheerfulness, mirth, or impishness ⟨she saw too clearly now that what had been his weary, decadent smile, was, after all, simply a boyish *grin*—*Terry Southern*⟩ ⟨did a little prancing jig on his toes to show how fit he was, then he looked up at me and *grinned*—*Dahl*⟩ ⟨how cheerfully he seems to *grin,* how neatly spreads his claws, and welcomes little fishes in with gently smiling jaws!—*Lewis Carroll*⟩ **Simper** implies a silly, affected, or languishing smile ⟨so much vanity and outmoded affectation. The thin lips are curved into a *simper* that is the worst of all possible substitutes for a smile—*Horace Gregory*⟩ ⟨it was Ellen who came off best, bearing all the laurels, with all the *simpering* critics trotting attendance—*Bromfield*⟩ **Smirk,** too, suggests affectation together with self-conscious complacency or embarrassment ⟨had grown so conceited that he wouldn't deign to talk to his brother; he kept fussing and *smirking* around his father all the time— *Rölvaag*⟩ ⟨the solemnity of the ceremony was broken by *smirks,* whispered jokes and repressed titters—*Graves*⟩ ⟨a few *smirked* . . . as if they had been caught coming out of a bawdy house—*Gruber*⟩
*Ant* frown

**smile** *n* simper, smirk, grin (see under SMILE *vb*)
*Ant* frown

**smirch** *soil, dirty, sully, tarnish, foul, befoul, besmirch, grime, begrime

**smirk** *vb* simper, grin, *smile

**smirk** *n* simper, grin, smile (see under SMILE *vb*)

**smite** *strike, hit, punch, slug, slog, swat, clout, slap, cuff, box
*Ana* *beat, pummel, buffet: *punish, discipline, correct

**smog** fog, mist, *haze

**smooth** *adj* 1 even, plane, plain, flat, *level, flush
*Ana* *sleek, slick, glossy
*Ant* rough  —*Con* harsh, uneven, rugged, scabrous (see ROUGH)
2 effortless, *easy, light, simple, facile
*Ana* agreeable, *pleasant, pleasing, gratifying, grateful: serene, tranquil, *calm, placid, peaceful
*Ant* labored  —*Con* *hard, difficult, arduous
3 bland, diplomatic, politic, *suave, urbane
*Ana* polite, courteous, courtly (see CIVIL): oily, unctuous, slick, *fulsome
*Ant* bluff  —*Con* blunt, brusque, curt, gruff, crusty

(see BLUFF)
4 *soft, bland, mild, gentle, lenient, balmy

**smother** *vb* *suffocate, asphyxiate, stifle, choke, strangle, throttle

**smug** self-complacent, self-satisfied, priggish, *complacent
*Ana* self-respecting, self-esteeming, self-admiring (see base words under REGARD *n*): pharisaical, sanctimonious, hypocritical (see under HYPOCRISY)

**smuggled, bootleg, contraband** are comparable in meaning transported in defiance of the law but each has implications and applications not shared with the others. **Smuggled** applies to what is taken out of or brought into an area (as a nation or district) clandestinely, especially to avoid payment of taxes or dues or to contravene the law ⟨*smuggled* diamonds⟩ ⟨the same route that the pirates used in taking their *smuggled* goods to market—*Amer. Guide Series: La.*⟩ In extended use it may stress deftly evasive action or surreptitious procedure ⟨make use of local knowledge and *smuggled* information to sow alarm among Communist officials—*Economist*⟩ ⟨to the ordinary beholder there seem to be so many *smuggled* assumptions in the literature of social science—*R. M. Weaver*⟩ **Bootleg** denotes a material thing (as liquor) made in or imported into a country or district and offered for sale or distribution in defiance of its prohibition in that country or of legal restrictions (as by rationing or licensing) on its use ⟨*bootleg* whiskey⟩ The term can imply fraud, deceit, and often secretiveness or concealment; thus, *bootleg* wiring is done by one who is not a legally qualified electrician and who may disregard safety requirements; *bootleg* prizefights are conducted without legal sanction and often with disregard of the welfare of fighters or patrons ⟨Congress arbitrarily said, "We know better than unions what is good for employees." . . . Today several thousand employers and several million employees are operating under *bootleg* agreements in flagrant violation of the statute—*A. E. Stevenson*⟩ **Contraband** applies to something of which the importation or exportation is declared illegal by law, proclamation, or treaty. Often the term is perfectly interchangeable with *smuggled* ⟨waterfront resorts were notorious as smuggling centers . . . *contraband* cargoes were carried aboard motorboats and dories—*Amer. Guide Series: Mich.*⟩ or it may nearly replace *bootleg* ⟨Benzedrine . . . has been extremely common as a *contraband* item for introduction into prisons and correctional institutions—*Maurer & Vogel*⟩ but it alone is specifically applied to something of which the exportation to belligerents is expressly prohibited and which, therefore, is liable to seizure ⟨eventually Great Britain was seizing as *contraband* almost everything sent to Germany and to the neutral states on Germany's borders—*Roehm et al*⟩

**snag** *n* *obstacle, obstruction, impediment, bar
*Ana* *projection, protuberance: *difficulty, hardship, vicissitude: barring *or* bar, blocking *or* block, hindering *or* hindrance (see corresponding verbs at HINDER)

**snap** *vb* 1 *jerk, twitch, yank
*Ana* seize, snatch, clutch, grasp (see TAKE)
2 *break, crack, burst, bust, shatter, shiver
*Ana* part, *separate, sever, sunder

**snappish** *irritable, fractious, peevish, waspish, petulant, pettish, huffy, fretful, querulous
*Ana* testy, touchy, cranky, *irascible: surly, crabbed, morose (see SULLEN)

**snappy** *pungent, piquant, poignant, racy, spicy
*Ana* *sharp, keen, acute: vivacious, *lively, animated: *quick, prompt, ready: smart, dashing, chic, modish (see STYLISH)

**snare** *n* trap, *lure, bait, decoy
*Ana* trickery, *deception, chicanery, chicane

---

*Ana* analogous words     *Ant* antonyms     *Con* contrasted words     See also explanatory notes facing page 1

**snare** *vb* ensnare, trap, entrap, bag, *catch, capture
*Ana* *lure, entice, inveigle, tempt, seduce, decoy
**snarl** *n* *confusion, disorder, chaos, disarray, jumble, clutter, muddle
*Ana* complexity, complication, intricateness *or* intricacy (see corresponding adjectives at COMPLEX): *difficulty, hardship
**snarl** *vb* *bark, bay, howl, growl, yelp, yap
**snatch** *vb* grasp, grab, clutch, seize, *take
*Ana* *catch, capture: *pull, drag, draw
**sneak** *vb* slink, skulk, *lurk
**sneer** *vb* *scoff, jeer, gird, flout, gibe, fleer
*Ana* deride, taunt, mock, *ridicule: scout, *despise, scorn, disdain
**snip** *vb* *shear, poll, clip, trim, prune, lop, crop
*Ana* *cut, slit, slash, chop: *bite
**snitch** *steal, pilfer, filch, purloin, lift, pinch, swipe, cop
**snoopy** *curious, inquisitive, prying, nosy
*Ana* meddlesome, officious, intrusive, *impertinent, obtrusive: interfering, interposing (see INTERPOSE)
**snooze** *vb* *sleep, slumber, drowse, doze, nap, catnap
**snug** 1 trim, trig, shipshape, *neat, tidy, spick-and-span
*Ana* compact, *close: *orderly, methodical, systematic
2 *comfortable, cozy, easy, restful
*Ana* *safe, secure: *familiar, intimate, close: sheltered, harbored (see HARBOR *vb*)
**so** *therefore, hence, consequently, then, accordingly
**soak** *vb* **Soak, saturate, drench, steep, impregnate, sop, waterlog** can mean to permeate or be permeated with or as if with water. **Soak** suggests immersion in a liquid so that the substance absorbs the moisture and usually becomes thoroughly wetted, softened, or dissolved ⟨*soak* a sponge in water⟩ ⟨the blotter *soaked* up the spilled ink⟩ ⟨*soak* out the dirt from soiled clothes⟩ ⟨*soak* tapioca before cooking it⟩ In its extended use the term implies a comparable immersion of one thing in another so that the latter is taken up by or enters into the very being of the former and becomes a part of it ⟨he *soaked* himself in the poetry of the great romanticists⟩ ⟨the shadowy copse was *soaked* in piny sweetness, golden and dim—*Rose Macaulay*⟩ ⟨*soaked* in the best prejudices and manners of his class—*Galsworthy*⟩ **Saturate** (see also PERMEATE) may or may not imply a soaking; distinctively it stresses absorption (as of a liquid) up to a point where no more can be absorbed; thus, the air is said to be *saturated* when it can retain no more moisture in the form of vapor; one's clothes may be described as *saturated* when they are so damp that the addition of further moisture would make them dripping wet; a solution (as of salt in water) is said to be *saturated* when the liquid has dissolved as much of the substance as it can retain under the circumstances (as of heat and atmospheric pressure). Consequently in its extended use *saturate* usually implies a becoming imbued or infused with something in exactly the right measure or to the most useful degree ⟨to a mind not thoroughly *saturated* with the tolerating maxims of the Gospel—*Burke*⟩ ⟨the entire poem is *saturated* with imagination⟩ ⟨*saturated* with experience of a particular class of materials, an expert intuitively feels whether a newly reported fact is probable or not—*James*⟩ **Drench** basically implies a thorough wetting by liquid and especially rainwater ⟨they were in an open buggy and were *drenched* to the skin—*Cather*⟩ In its extended use the term carries an implication of being soaked or saturated by something that pours or is poured down upon one ⟨the solid mountains shone . . . *drenched* in empyrean light—*Wordsworth*⟩ ⟨the new life with which it *drenches* the spirits—*Shelley*⟩ **Steep** implies a complete immersion and soaking in a liquid; it usually suggests the extraction

of the essence of one thing so that it becomes part and parcel of the other; thus, one *steeps* tea leaves in boiling water in order to make the beverage tea. In extended use the acquirement of the qualities of one thing by a process suggestive of such steeping is often implied ⟨epistles . . . *steeped* in the phraseology of the Greek mysteries —*Inge*⟩ ⟨language simple and sensuous and *steeped* in the picturesque imagery of what they saw and felt —*Lowes*⟩ but often the term means little more than to envelop with or as if with the quality (as color or light) shed from or emanated by something else ⟨her tall spars and rigging *steeped* in a bath of red-gold—*Conrad*⟩ ⟨the world was all *steeped* in sunshine—*D. H. Lawrence*⟩ **Impregnate** (see also PERMEATE) commonly carries a suggestion of soaking in something other than water; it implies the interpenetration of one thing by another until the former is everywhere imbued with the latter ⟨*impregnate* rubber with sulphur⟩ ⟨when my mind was, as it were, strongly *impregnated* with the Johnsonian ether—*Boswell*⟩ ⟨this poem, everywhere *impregnated* with original excellence—*Wordsworth*⟩ **Sop** usually applies to food soaked in meat juices or wine ⟨*sop* bread in gravy⟩ ⟨serve cake *sopped* in sherry and covered with a soft custard⟩ but it may apply also to something (as soil) that is heavily soaked with liquid ⟨*sopping* wet clothes⟩ ⟨*sop* plants with too much water⟩ **Waterlog** suggests a thorough soaking or drenching that makes a thing either useless or too heavy and sodden (as for floating or cultivating) ⟨a *waterlogged* rowboat⟩ ⟨soil *waterlogged* by lack of proper drainage⟩
*Ana* *dip, immerse, submerge: *permeate, pervade, penetrate
**soak** *n* *drunkard, inebriate, alcoholic, dipsomaniac, sot, toper, tosspot, tippler
**soapy** slick, *fulsome, oily, unctuous, oleaginous
**soar** *rise, arise, ascend, mount, tower, rocket, levitate, surge
*Ana* *fly, dart, shoot: aspire, *aim
**sob** *vb* moan, groan, *sigh
*Ana* weep, wail, *cry, blubber
**sob** *n* moan, groan, sigh (see under SIGH *vb*)
*Ana* weeping, wailing, crying, blubbering (see CRY *vb*)
**sober** 1 **Sober, temperate, continent, unimpassioned** can mean having or manifesting self-control or the mastery of one's emotions, passions, or appetites. **Sober** basically describes moderation in the use of food and drink and often specifically implies freedom from intoxication; this implication is often found with another (as of habitual abstinence from intoxicating liquors or merely of not being drunk at the time in question) ⟨he is, by reputation, a *sober* man⟩ ⟨Gilda, in a drink coma, squealed on Cabot Wright. Later, *sober*, she denied her own story —*Purdy*⟩ In more general application *sober* implies a cool head, composure especially under strain or excitement, and freedom from passion, prejudice, fear, or any unreasonable excess ⟨sound, *sober* advice⟩ ⟨a man of *sober* judgment⟩ ⟨his bearing was *sober*, his comments courteous—*Wouk*⟩ ⟨a *sober* book, written without hysteria or excitement—*A. T. Steele*⟩ **Temperate** (see also MODERATE 1) implies control over the expression of one's feelings, passions, appetites, or desires or the restrained exercise of one's rights, powers, or privileges, with the result that one never exceeds the bounds of what is right or proper ⟨in what *temperate* language Horace clothes his maxims . . . not a flourish! Not a gesture!— *Repplier*⟩ ⟨he was a scholar and a stoic; what *temperate* virtues he owned had been hard won—*Styron*⟩ **Continent** (compare *continence* under TEMPERANCE) carries a stronger implication of deliberate restraint placed upon

A colon (:) separates groups of words discriminated. An asterisk (*) indicates place of treatment of each group.

oneself, upon one's feelings seeking expression, or upon one's desires, especially sexual desires, seeking satisfaction ⟨my past life hath been as *continent,* as chaste, as true, as I am now unhappy—*Shak.*⟩ ⟨their strength was the strength of men geographically beyond temptation: the poverty of Arabia made them simple, *continent,* enduring—*T. E. Lawrence*⟩ ⟨not . . . a subject of irregular and interrupted impulses of virtue, but a *continent,* persisting, immovable person —*Emerson*⟩ **Unimpassioned** so stresses the absence of heat, ardor, or fervor that it often connotes lack of feeling and, therefore, coldness, stiffness, or hardness of heart ⟨when love is not involved in a union, any differences are likely to settle into . . . *unimpassioned* enmity—*Hervey*⟩ ⟨he was tired, excited, on fire, and Deborah seemed so *unimpassioned*—*Webb*⟩ but it often implies a subduing of feeling or passion by rationality ⟨the *unimpassioned* administration of disciplinary measures⟩ ⟨his manner resembled their manner, reserved, logical, *unimpassioned,* and intelligent—*W. C. Ford*⟩
*Ana* abstaining, refraining, forbearing (see REFRAIN): forgoing, eschewing, abnegating (see FORGO): *cool, collected, composed: reasonable, *rational
*Ant* drunk: excited
**2** grave, *serious, sedate, staid, solemn, somber, earnest
*Ana* *decorous, decent, proper: *calm, placid, tranquil, serene: dispassionate, impartial, *fair, equitable
*Ant* gay —*Con* light, frivolous, flippant, light-minded (see corresponding nouns at LIGHTNESS)

**sobriety** *temperance, abstinence, abstemiousness, continence
*Ana* moderateness, temperateness (see corresponding adjectives at MODERATE): quietness, stillness (see corresponding adjectives at STILL): seriousness, gravity, somberness, sedateness (see corresponding adjectives at SERIOUS)
*Ant* drunkenness: excitement

**sociable** *gracious, cordial, affable, genial
*Ana* *social, companionable, convivial, gregarious: intimate, *familiar, close: *amiable, obliging, complaisant, good-natured
*Ant* unsociable

**social** *adj* Social, gregarious, cooperative, convivial, companionable, hospitable are comparable rather than synonymous terms that all involve and often stress the idea of having or manifesting a liking for or attraction to the company of others. Social, a broadly inclusive word, is distinctly dichotomous. On the one hand it stresses sociability and the pleasant relation between individuals, singly or in groups ⟨a *social* club⟩ ⟨spent a *social* evening with her friends⟩ ⟨Adams was known as a man of *social* talent, a good talker, admired for his richness of recollection and apt illustration—*W. C. Ford*⟩ ⟨of a jovial, *social* disposition, with a host of friends—*Westcott*⟩ and may come close to *sociable* (which see under GRACIOUS) in meaning ⟨having to drive home, and not feeling very *social,* I drank very little—*Balchin*⟩ ⟨Miss Pinckney is one of the most *social* of beings . . . Her hospitality is famous—*Stoney*⟩ On the other hand it can stress relation to society and the community and approach *societal* in meaning; when applied with this notion to the individual or kind of individual it implies membership in or adherence to a more or less definitely organized society; thus, the common reference to man as a *social* animal implies that human beings as a result of qualities inherent in their fundamental animal nature tend to live in societies rather than in solitude ⟨there is every reason to believe that the origin of culture derives from the fact that man is a *social* animal. *Social* species are those whose very

existence depends on interaction among their members. It is important to repeat that these *social* essentials are not peculiarly human but are a basic fact in the existence of all mammalian species—*Kimball Young*⟩ In relation to immaterial things *social* may imply no more than relation to society ⟨established *social* custom⟩ ⟨the *social* aspects of cultures are the material traces of ideas and ideals in the habits and associations of men—*McKeon*⟩ but more often it stresses the consideration and responsibility of society for its members and especially its weaker members ⟨legislation which is enacted to protect and aid those who cannot help themselves is often called *social* legislation —*W. H. Wilson & E. S. Eyster*⟩ ⟨*social* rights—the right to work, to rest and leisure, to education, to material security in old age and in case of illness or disability —*Mendel*⟩ As applied to lower animals, *social* heightens the notion of *societal* and implies not mere physical association but association in a community with specialization of function and often of form ⟨the honeybee is a common *social* insect with the colony members specialized for reproduction or for work⟩ **Gregarious** sometimes approaches the first aspect of *social* ⟨a cheery, relaxed, fun-loving young man who enjoyed his own humor but enjoyed it all the more if it were shared by an appreciative audience. He was therefore *gregarious,* friendly, outgoing and extroverted—*C. W. M. Hart*⟩ ⟨always *gregarious* and eager for companionship, Tony tried twice to draw abreast of the men plodding along the unmarked trail—*Herron*⟩ but in its commoner societal applications it tends, in distinction to *social,* to imply a need or desire for contiguity ⟨he renounced . . . a life of solitude, and became a *gregarious* creature—*Cowper*⟩ ⟨impelled by *gregarious* instincts, Peter followed the crowd—*H. G. Wells*⟩ ⟨the *gregarious* bustle goes on as a matter of routine. Streets intersect, shops advertise, homes have party walls, and fellow citizens depend upon the same water supply; but there is no cooperation between human beings— *Joyce*⟩ or a living contiguously rather than an active participation in the life of an integrated society ⟨the ordinary *gregarious* human life, led by us in contact with others and in the stress of our normal pursuits—*Powys*⟩ ⟨many solitary insects are *gregarious,* that is, they share certain common needs or react in the same way to certain external stimuli so that dense populations assemble locally —*O. W. Richards*⟩ ⟨it is at least plausible that the domestication of animals—which are almost exclusively *gregarious* animals—is based on the relation of the hunter to the wild herd—*Franz Boas*⟩ The remaining terms describe particular aspects of being social. **Cooperative** implies the existence of common ends which serve as the objectives of a group, a community, or society at large and of the need of mutual assistance in the attainment of those ends; the term therefore usually suggests shared effort, helpfulness, and a willingness to work for the welfare or well-being of the entire group ⟨leadership of a *cooperative* rather than of a competitive type—*Sellars*⟩ ⟨capacity for *cooperative* industrial effort—*Mumford*⟩ ⟨with regard to a young English statesman, we want to know two things mainly—his intrinsic value, and his *cooperative* capacity—*Pall Mall Gazette*⟩ ⟨if we are to develop a *cooperative* foreign policy, we shall have to learn to consult continuously with other nations—*Dean*⟩ **Convivial** is applied chiefly to persons, groups, or activities that manifest enjoyment of the company of others especially in festive joviality and eating and drinking ⟨at the insistence of a *convivial* uncle . . . she permits herself to drink three glasses of champagne—*Edmund Wilson*⟩ ⟨has a *convivial* temperament . . . gets on a first-name basis quickly—*Dwight Macdonald*⟩ ⟨dinners *convivial*

---

*Ana* analogous words   *Ant* antonyms   *Con* contrasted words   See also explanatory notes facing page 1

and political—*Shelley*⟩ ⟨she was a somewhat somber figure in that *convivial* household—*Cather*⟩ **Companionable** implies a special fitness by nature or disposition for friendly and intimate association with others ⟨thus we lived on unsocially together. More *companionable* . . . were the large crawling, running insects—crickets, beetles, and others—*Hudson*⟩ and it is often applied to things (as situations or writings) that are felt to convey such a quality ⟨they [swans] paddle in the cold *companionable* streams or climb the air—*Yeats*⟩ ⟨the book is above all *companionable*, and has an insinuation of appeal that no other work quite possesses—*More*⟩ **Hospitable** usually implies a disposition to receive and to entertain not only one's friends but especially strangers; it therefore stresses receptiveness and generosity more than any of the preceding terms ⟨it was no small joy to these west-movers . . . to find this *hospitable*, talkative man who was everywhere bustling about, trying to be of service to them—*Rölvaag*⟩ ⟨your criticism, so *hospitable* to ideas, so inflexible in judging right from wrong—*Quiller-Couch*⟩

**Ana** *gracious, cordial, sociable, genial, affable: *amicable, neighborly, friendly

**Ant** unsocial, antisocial, asocial

**society** 1 elite, *aristocracy, nobility, gentry, county
2 *association, order, club

**soft** *adj* **Soft, bland, mild, gentle, smooth, lenient, balmy** are applied to things with respect to the sensations they evoke or the impressions they produce and mean pleasantly agreeable because devoid of all harshness or roughness. **Soft** is applied chiefly to what soothes, calms, or induces a sensation of delicious quiet ⟨as sweet as balm, as *soft* as air, as *gentle*—*Shak.*⟩ ⟨a *soft* answer turneth away wrath—*Prov* 15:1⟩ ⟨ever, against eating cares, lap me in *soft* Lydian airs—*Milton*⟩ ⟨to feel forever its *soft* fall and swell—*Keats*⟩ This positive connotation is often apparent in the use of *soft* even when its major implication is the absence or the subduing of some quality (as pungency, vividness, intensity, or force); thus, a *soft* fragrance is lacking in richness but is quietly agreeable and not overpowering; a *soft* color is lacking in vividness, but it is mellow rather than dull; a *soft* voice though lacking in resonance is not faint or feeble but is pleasantly low and without harshness or stridency ⟨the far shore of the river's mouth was just *soft* dusk—*Galsworthy*⟩ ⟨the *soft* shock of wizened apples falling from an old tree—*Millay*⟩ ⟨listen to Yuriko's voice as it floated, breathlike and *soft*, through the frail partitions—*Mailer*⟩ **Bland** (see also SUAVE) may be interchangeable with *soft*, but it generally suggests smoothness and suavity and stresses the absence of whatever might disturb, excite, stimulate, or irritate; thus, foods and beverages which are not unpleasant to the taste yet tend toward the insipid or are lacking in pungency, tang, or richness of flavor or ingredients may be described as *bland;* a *bland* climate not only is free from extremes but is neither stimulating nor depressing ⟨*bland* fruits such as bananas⟩ ⟨the doctor prescribed a *bland* diet⟩ ⟨there was an unusual softness to the dark air and the *bland* starlight and an unusual density to the darkness—*Cheever*⟩ ⟨the whole shabby performance . . . the *bland* reassurances instead of the hard dichotomies—*Michener*⟩ ⟨full, clear, with something *bland* and suave, each note floated through the air like a globe of silver—*Cather*⟩ Both *mild* and *gentle* stress moderation; they are applied chiefly to things that are not, as they might be or often are, harsh, rough, strong, violent, unduly stimulating, or irritating and are therefore pleasant or agreeable by contrast ⟨a *mild* cigar⟩ ⟨*mild* weather⟩ ⟨a man of *mild* and simple character who

. . . had shown no interest in anything at all except his collection of modern paintings—*Dahl*⟩ ⟨a *gentle* breeze⟩ ⟨a *gentle* heat⟩ However, both words are capable of connoting positively pleasurable sensations, **mild** often being applied to what induces a feeling of quiet measured beauty or of serenity and **gentle** to what evokes a mood of placidity or tranquillity, or a sense of restrained power or force ⟨a *mild*, rosy spring evening in which blackbirds sang on the budding boughs of the elms—*Gibbons*⟩ ⟨some did shed a clear *mild* beam like Hesperus, while the sea yet glows with fading sunlight—*Shelley*⟩ ⟨O *gentle* sleep, nature's soft nurse—*Shak.*⟩ ⟨he was *gentle*, waiting for whatever he awaited with a grace she respected—*Malamud*⟩ ⟨she had a *gentle* face, and her eyes were filled with compassion—*Theodore Sturgeon*⟩ **Smooth** (see also EASY, LEVEL) in most of its senses suggests the absence or removal of all unevennesses or obstacles (as to use or enjoyment); often it comes close to *mild* in stressing the pleasant quality of what might be harsh or irritating, but unlike *mild* and *bland* it rarely if ever hints at weakness or insipidness. Distinctively it may approach *mellow* (which see under MATURE) and suggest qualities of excellence that come with time (as through ripening or aging) or are the result of careful and skilled handling that eliminates all harshness ⟨a *smooth* whiskey⟩ ⟨dancing every night to the island's *smoothest* orchestra —*N. Y. Times*⟩ In reference to persons or their works and accomplishments (as in the arts) *smooth* may carry further the notion of care and skill in handling and suggest a polished finish stemming from experienced knowledgeability or craftsmanship ⟨Gottfried's style is urbane and *smooth* and full of understatement, but the story he tells is one of wild passion—*Artz*⟩ ⟨behind the *smooth* performance of choir, organ and minister were hours of preparation and careful timing—*Dawson & Wilson*⟩ ⟨they themselves were *smooth* in manner, and they saw to it that in their presence life had no rough edges—*Webb*⟩ or, in a less complimentary sense, a slick sophistication or meretricious attractiveness ⟨he may be an authentic wonder-worker, but he's also a *smooth* customer—*Gilman*⟩ ⟨a *smooth* little blonde glides out of the bedroom —*Time*⟩ ⟨a *smooth* wolf who has a highly polished technique in sidestepping marriage—*Tilden*⟩ **Lenient** (see also FORBEARING) is applicable chiefly to things that are grateful to the senses or to the mind because they exert an emollient, relaxing, softening, or assuasive influence ⟨earthly sounds, though sweet and well combined, and *lenient* as soft opiates to the mind—*Cowper*⟩ ⟨in the *lenient* hush, strong torpid rhythms somehow flowed— *E. P. O'Donnell*⟩ ⟨I poured her a *lenient* rum and water —*Morley*⟩ **Balmy** also implies a soothing influence on the senses or mind, but beyond this it suggests refreshment and sometimes exhilaration. Coupled with one or another of these implications there is also frequently a suggestion of fragrance, especially the aromatic fragrance of balm-producing trees ⟨all *balmy* from the groves of Tahiti, came an indolent air—*Melville*⟩ ⟨a lovely soft spring morning at the end of March, and unusually *balmy* for the time of year—*Butler* d. 1902⟩ ⟨in the *balmy* atmosphere of that second victory she basks today—*Fishwick*⟩

**Ana** moderated, tempered (see MODERATE *vb*): smooth, effortless, *easy: velvety, silken, *sleek, slick: serene, tranquil, *calm, placid, peaceful

**Ant** hard: stern —**Con** *rough, harsh, uneven, rugged: *intense, vehement, fierce, violent

**soil,** **dirty, sully, tarnish, foul, befoul, smirch, besmirch, grime, begrime** can all mean to make or become unclean. **Soil** basically implies fundamental defilement or pollution (as of the mind or spirit) ⟨why war *soils* and disarranges whatever it touches, I cannot say—*Kenneth Roberts*⟩ ⟨making that room our Chapter, our one mind where all that this world *soiled* should be refined—*Masefield*⟩ but in much of its use it applies to a making or becoming superficially and literally unclean (as by spotting or staining or smudging) ⟨dressed in gray shirt and trousers appropriately *soiled* and wrinkled from a day's work—*MacInnes*⟩ In this sense the word is very close to the corresponding sense of **dirty**, which is slightly stronger in its implication of uncleanliness and especially of disagreeable uncleanliness; thus, "to *soil* one's clothes" may merely imply that the freshness of a clean or new thing is lost, but "to *dirty* one's clothes" usually implies some activity which has plainly left its unclean traces upon the garments. In its extended use, too, *dirty* tends to stress the unpleasant effect and typically suggests a making squalid or nasty of something that in itself is normal, wholesome, or clean ⟨their religion took most of the rural whites' pleasures away from them, *dirtying* sex and the human body until it was a nasty thing—*Lillian Smith*⟩ ⟨a burlesque which *dirties* the idea of chivalry—*Canby*⟩ **Sully** implies the staining or soiling of something that is pure, fresh, limpid, or innocent ⟨they would not *sully* their fingers when eating human flesh—*Elisofon*⟩ It is used more often in reference to immaterial or spiritual than to physical soiling ⟨if it is bounderish to traduce one's host, it is an even worse breach of etiquette to *sully* one's own nest—*Guérard*⟩ ⟨those sins of the body which smear and *sully* , debase and degrade, destroy and ruin, condemn to the deepest pits of Hell—*Farrell*⟩ ⟨a merciless massacre *sullied* the fame of his earlier exploits—*J. R. Green*⟩ **Tarnish** basically implies the dulling or dimming of the luster of a thing by chemical action (as of air, dust, or dirt) ⟨silver *tarnished* by the sulfur in egg yolk⟩ In extended use it suggests a dimming rather than a total sullying of something of value ⟨with similar scandals . . . it is not surprising that the image of state government is woefully *tarnished*—*Armbrister*⟩ ⟨her tawdry, shoddy, garish components are exposed as never before; yet her overall beauty is scarcely *tarnished*—*Temple Fielding*⟩ **Foul** and the intensive form **befoul** stress a making filthy or nasty and apply either to a material or an immaterial thing. They often suggest pollution or defiling by something highly offensive or disagreeable ⟨earth was scarred by mining pits and railway tracks; air was *fouled* and darkened by factory soot—*J. D. Hart*⟩ ⟨it is senseless to *foul* our municipal personnel with unproved charges of general corruption—*Moses*⟩ ⟨having *befouled* their own minds for hire, they made their living by *befouling* the minds of others—*Anderson*⟩ ⟨Milton was . . . virtuous after *befouling* himself; once smeared with the sluttish filth of an evil woman, he had finally been won over—*Styron*⟩ **Smirch** and the intensive form **besmirch** may emphasize a discoloring by or as if by soot, smoke, or mud; usually they come close to *sully* in implying a destruction of immaculateness ⟨now, with the singular ratiocination of the politician *besmirched*, he sought to go before the electorate and be washed whiter than snow by their votes—*S. H. Adams*⟩ ⟨the parson's well-practiced and spellbinding condemnation of the *besmirching*, degrading, befouling, hideous, and bestial sins of the flesh —*Farrell*⟩ but they seldom carry as clear an implication of an effect on real virtue or purity as they do of a darkening or blackening of appearance, reputation, honor, or good name ⟨their infamy spreads abroad, *smirching* the whole class to which they belong—*Jefferies*⟩ ⟨as blackhearted a brigand as ever *smirched* a page of Highland history—*Joseph*⟩ ⟨her reputation . . . was not *smirched* by gossip, for she was known to love her husband and to be

virtuous—*Bowers*⟩ **Grime** and the more usual **begrime** intensify the meaning of *dirty* and typically suggest deeply imbedded dirt often accumulated over a prolonged period ⟨a rudely cut inscription *grimed* with dust of many a year—*Henry Phillips*⟩ ⟨she was always filthy, her legs *grimed*, her hair bedraggled, her face anything but clean —*W. C. Williams*⟩ ⟨wearing a dress that virtually swept the street; that would in fact actually sweep it from time to time, battering and *begriming* the hem—*F. L. Allen*⟩ ⟨they had stood, *begrimed* with train smoke—*Stafford*⟩

**sojourn** *vb* *reside, lodge, stay, put up, stop, live, dwell

**solace** *vb* *comfort, console
*Ana* *relieve, assuage, mitigate, allay, alleviate, lighten: gladden, rejoice, delight, *please, gratify

**sole** *adj* *single, unique, solitary, lone, separate, particular
*Ana* alone, *only: exclusive, picked, *select

**solecism** *anachronism

**solemn** 1 *ceremonial, ceremonious, formal, conventional
*Ana* liturgical, ritualistic (see corresponding nouns at FORM): *full, complete, plenary: imposing, august, majestic, magnificent (see GRAND)
2 *serious, grave, somber, sedate, earnest, staid, sober
*Ana* impressive, *moving: sublime, superb (see SPLENDID): ostentatious (see SHOWY)

**solemnize** celebrate, observe, *keep, commemorate

**solicit** 1 *ask, request
*Ana* *resort, refer, apply, go, turn: *beg, entreat, beseech, implore, supplicate
2 *invite, bid, court, woo
*Ana* importune, adjure (see BEG): *demand, claim, exact: evoke, elicit, extract, extort, *educe

**solicitor** *lawyer, attorney, counselor, barrister, counsel, advocate

**solicitous** careful, concerned, anxious, worried (see under CARE *n*)
*Ana* apprehensive, *fearful, afraid: agitated, disturbed, disquieted, upset (see DISCOMPOSE): uneasy, fidgety, jittery (see IMPATIENT)
*Ant* unmindful: negligent

**solicitude** *care, concern, anxiety, worry
*Ana* misgiving, *apprehension, foreboding, presentiment: compunction, *qualm, scruple: *fear, alarm, consternation, dismay
*Ant* negligence: unmindfulness

**solid** *firm, hard
*Ana* compact, *close, dense: consolidated, concentrated, compacted (see COMPACT *vb*)
*Ant* fluid, liquid

**solidarity** *unity, union, integrity
*Ana* consolidation, concentration, unification (see corresponding verbs at COMPACT): cooperation, concurrence, combination (see corresponding verbs at UNITE)

**solidify** *harden, indurate, petrify, cake
*Ana* *compact, consolidate, concentrate: condense, *contract, compress: *congeal, coagulate, set, clot, jelly, jell

**solitary** 1 *alone, lonely, lonesome, lone, forlorn, lorn, desolate
*Ana* isolated, secluded (see corresponding nouns at SOLITUDE): retired, withdrawn (see GO): forsaken, deserted, abandoned (see ABANDON)
2 *single, sole, unique, lone, separate, particular
*Ana* alone, *only

**solitude,** isolation, alienation, seclusion mean the state of one that is alone. **Solitude** applies not only to a physical condition where there are no others of one's kind with whom one can associate ⟨this man [the lighthouse keeper]

in his wild *solitude*, forced to live only with himself, almost forgets the common language of men—*Ellis*⟩ but often to the state, physical or mental, of one who by wish or by compulsion is cut off from normal contacts (as with colleagues, neighbors, friends, or family) ⟨my spirits will not bear *solitude*, I must have employment and society—*Austen*⟩ ⟨these are the voices which we hear in *solitude*, but they grow faint and inaudible as we enter into the world—*Emerson*⟩ Sometimes the term refers entirely to a mental state and comes very close in meaning to *loneliness*, implying a lack of intimate association with, rather than a separation from, others ⟨had not been able to escape from the *solitude* imposed by existence in hotels. Since her marriage she had never spoken to a woman in . . . intimacy—*Bennett*⟩ ⟨aye, *solitude*, black *solitude* indeed, to meet a million souls and know not one—*W. H. Davies*⟩ **Isolation** stresses detachment from others either because of causes beyond one's control or because of one's own wish. Since the term may refer to communities and to things as well as to individuals, it often suggests a cutting off physically rather than such a frame of mind as loneliness or depression ⟨the solemn *isolation* of a man against the sea and sky—*Stevenson*⟩ ⟨axiomatic that the artist and man of letters ought not to work in cloistral *isolation*, removed from public affairs—*Quiller-Couch*⟩ ⟨we are exposed to *isolation* imposed on us from the outside by unfriendly powers—*Ascoli*⟩ ⟨many words and phrases have no significance in *isolation* but contribute to the significance only of whole sentences—*Russell*⟩ **Alienation** stresses estrangement and lack or loss of adjustment either between the individual and his environment and especially his social or intellectual environment so that he is in fact isolated even when physically surrounded by multitudes of his kind ⟨*alienation* . . . can mean estrangement *from* society or estrangement *from self through* society. The delinquent is estranged but so, too, is the organization man—*Harold Rosenberg*⟩ or sometimes between the creator and his creation ⟨his *alienation* seems more fully acknowledged and extreme than ever before—*Times Lit. Sup.*⟩ **Seclusion** implies a shutting away or a keeping apart of oneself or another so that one is either inaccessible to others or accessible only under difficult conditions. The term may connote a condition (as confinement in an asylum or prison or withdrawal from the world or from human companionship) that makes contact difficult or repels the efforts of others to establish contact ⟨the *seclusion* of their life was such that she would hardly be likely to learn the news except through a special messenger—*Hardy*⟩ ⟨the time would come when she could no longer live in *seclusion*, she must go into the world again—*Stafford*⟩ ⟨even in the *seclusion* of the convent, Sister had heard the rumors —*Ruth Park*⟩ ⟨it had a deep New England tendency to *seclusion* and secrecy—*Time*⟩
*Ana* retreat, refuge, asylum (see SHELTER *n*): retirement, withdrawal (see corresponding verbs at GO)

**solve, resolve, unfold, unravel, decipher** can all mean to make clear or apparent or intelligible what is obscure or mysterious or incomprehensible. **Solve** is the most general in meaning and suggestion in this group; it implies the finding of a satisfactory answer or solution, usually to something of at least moderate difficulty ⟨the mystery and disquieting meaninglessness of existence . . . were *solved* for me now—*L. P. Smith*⟩ ⟨create a difficulty rather than *solve* one—*A. M. Young*⟩ **Resolve** (see also ANALYZE), as contrasted with *solve*, is likely to indicate analytic arrangement and consideration of the various phases or items of a problem or situation rather than finding a final

solution or answer and is likely to suggest dispelling of confusion or perplexity by a clear formulation of questions or issues ⟨you may find it of some interest to be told that the law has had to struggle with these problems and to know how it has *resolved* them—*Cardozo*⟩ In some situations this process may achieve an answer, especially a ready or summary one ⟨he was at the same time *resolving* successive tangles of intrigue against himself and his policy—*Belloc*⟩ ⟨it was realized that the method of *resolving* apparent contradictions by liquidating one of the contradictories is not the way to arrive at true solutions —*Times Lit. Sup.*⟩ **Unfold** implies continuous opening up, clarifying, and making more and more clear and patent until a full solution or resolution is apparent ⟨went around and through and behind a situation, *unfolding* it . . . to include possibilities he hadn't known were upon its horizon—*Mary Austin*⟩ ⟨saw the great truth of evolution *unfolded*—*Kaempffert*⟩ ⟨the method of *unfolding* the course of a plot must in some ways be different in a play meant for acting and in a book meant for reading—*Montague*⟩ **Unravel** stresses the notion of making a clear and orderly rearrangement of something entangled or a simple ordering of something complicated, especially by patient endeavor ⟨the details are difficult to *unravel* at this distance of time—*H. O. Taylor*⟩ ⟨a whole elaborate plot may be *unraveled* by discovering the one relevant detail—*Aydelotte*⟩ **Decipher** stresses the notion of finding the meaning or significance of something very obscure, clouded, cryptic, or enigmatic ⟨placing of a writer or other artist in his proper rank or in *deciphering* the less obvious intentions of his work—*Montague*⟩ ⟨the results, so far as they could be *deciphered* from the puzzling procedure and twisted combinations, confirmed what had gone before —*Atlantic*⟩
*Ana* *decide, determine, settle: *illuminate, enlighten: interpret, elucidate, *explain

**somatic** *bodily, physical, corporeal, corporal
**somber** *serious, grave, solemn, sedate, staid, sober, earnest
*Ana* gloomy, *dark, murky: *dismal, bleak, cheerless: melancholy (see MELANCHOLIC)
*Ant* garish
**somnolent** *sleepy, drowsy, slumberous
*Ana* sluggish, comatose, *lethargic: inert, *inactive, passive, supine
**sonorous** *resonant, ringing, resounding, vibrant, orotund
*Ana* *deep, profound: *rich, opulent: *loud, stentorian
**soon** *adv* 1 *presently, shortly, direct
2 *early, beforehand, betimes
**soothe** *calm, compose, quiet, quieten, still, lull, settle, tranquilize
*Ana* mollify, appease, placate, *pacify, propitiate, conciliate: allay, alleviate, assuage, mitigate, *relieve
*Ant* annoy: excite
**sop** *soak, saturate, drench, steep, impregnate, waterlog
**sophism** sophistry, casuistry, *fallacy
**sophistical** fallacious, casuistical (see under FALLACY)
*Ant* valid —*Con* cogent, sound, convincing, compelling, telling (see VALID)
**sophisticate** *adulterate, load, weight, doctor
**sophisticated,** worldly-wise, worldly, blasé, disillusioned are synonymous when they apply to persons, to their attitudes and actions, or to products of human skill and effort and mean experienced or revealing experience in the ways of the world. **Sophisticated** may be a term of reproach or of commendation according to the point of view of the speaker or writer, but it regularly implies a loss of naturalness, simplicity, or spontaneity through experience. From one point of view the term connotes

artificiality of manner, overrefinement, and absence of enthusiasm as the price paid for experience that brings knowledge of men and their ways ⟨the Negro . . . could rarely afford the *sophisticated* inhibitions of civilization, and so he kept for his survival the art of the primitive, he lived in the enormous present—*Mailer*⟩ From another point of view it implies a type of mentality marked by distinction, urbanity, cleverness, together with an indifference to all that is simple or banal in life ⟨she didn't want to ride on the roller coaster and he guessed that her ideas of pleasure were more *sophisticated*—*Cheever*⟩ From still another it may imply a cultivation that enables a man to rise above the ordinary or usual ⟨the lack of a body of *sophisticated* and civilized public opinion, independent of plutocratic control and superior to the infantile philosophies of the mob—*Mencken*⟩ ⟨photographs realistic enough to catch the quality of the milieu which produced Pope John, surely the world's simplest and most *sophisticated* of men—*Casey*⟩ **Worldly-wise** and **worldly** imply a wisdom gained by attention to the things and ways of the world. Often they stress alienation from true spiritual interests and, as a result, devotion to aims that will make one happy in this world, typically suggesting a concentration upon material ends or aims or upon a wealth of worldly experience ⟨we apply the term "*worldly-wise*" to a man who skillfully chooses the best means to the end of ambition; but we should not call such a man "wise" without qualification—*Sidgwick*⟩ ⟨religion has been leading man toward a nobler vision, a better day, a higher hope, and a fuller life. The church, on the other hand, has been *worldly*, obscurantist, arrogant and predatory—*Pfeffer*⟩ **Blasé** implies a lack of responsiveness to things which have once been a joy or delight. It usually suggests satiety, but also it tends to suggest such real or affected overexperience and overcultivation as leads to disdain for all that arouses the average person's interest ⟨the *blasé* indifference of both the authorities and the people to the war was like cold water . . . on my spirits—*Belden*⟩ ⟨I was going through a period of adolescent awfulness in which I was trying to appear pale, interesting, and world-weary (the popular term . . . was "*blasé*"), and incapable of any reaction to sentiment—*Skinner*⟩ **Disillusioned** implies having had experiences that have completely destroyed a person's illusions, with resulting hopelessness; it applies to a person who from experience is no longer capable of enthusiasm or of idealistic motives and who has grown not only realistic but scornful of the sentimental, the visionary, the emotional ⟨in a few years the young [newspaper] man will become a cynic, appraising the world and his fellows with *disillusioned* eyes, even with bitterness—*Walker*⟩ ⟨the world, grown *disillusioned* and afraid, has neglected the one source that answers every problem, fills every need—*Oursler*⟩
*Ana* cultivated, cultured (see corresponding nouns at CULTURE): intellectualized (see corresponding adjective at MENTAL): knowing, brilliant, *intelligent, clever, alert
*Ant* unsophisticated　—*Con* *natural, simple, ingenuous, naïve, artless: crude, uncouth, callow, raw (see RUDE)
**sophistry** *fallacy, sophism, casuistry
*Ana* plausibility, speciousness (see corresponding adjectives at PLAUSIBLE): equivocation, *ambiguity, tergiversation: evading *or* evasion, avoiding *or* avoidance (see corresponding verbs at ESCAPE)
**soppy** *sentimental, romantic, mawkish, maudlin, mushy, slushy
**sorcery** *magic, witchcraft, witchery, wizardry, alchemy, thaumaturgy
**sordid** *mean, ignoble, abject

*Ana* *mercenary, venal: squalid, foul, filthy, nasty, *dirty: *contemptible, despicable, sorry, scurvy, cheap, beggarly, shabby
**sorrow** *n* Sorrow, grief, heartache, heartbreak, anguish, woe, regret, though not close synonyms, share the idea of distress of mind. **Sorrow** is the most general term, implying a sense of loss or of guilt ⟨when you depart from me, *sorrow* abides and happiness takes his leave—*Shak.*⟩ ⟨virginity she thought she had parted with without *sorrow*, yet was surprised by torments of conscience—*Malamud*⟩ **Grief** denotes intense emotional suffering or poignant sorrow especially for some real and definite cause (compare GRIEVE) ⟨a stifled, drowsy, unimpassioned *grief*, which finds no natural outlet—*Coleridge*⟩ ⟨I have lain in prison . . . . Out of my nature has come wild despair; an abandonment to *grief* that was piteous even to look at; terrible and impotent rage; bitterness and scorn—*Wilde*⟩ but *grief* may also denote a more mundane distress of mind that is representative of the distress and trials of day-to-day life or often of a particular situation in life ⟨he had a thankless job which gave him all of the *grief* of running a war and none of the glory—*Time*⟩ **Heartache** is used especially of persistent and deep sorrow that is slow to heal but that often gives little or no outward indication ⟨the *heartaches* of a would-be author⟩ ⟨the *heartache* of a hunted race—*Zangwill*⟩ ⟨the dumb *heartaches* of those days—*Churchill*⟩ **Heartbreak** can imply a yet deeper and more crushing grief ⟨the sorrow and the *heartbreak* which . . . abide in the homes of so many of our neighbors—*Truman*⟩ **Anguish** implies a distress of mind that is excruciating or torturing almost beyond bearing ⟨*anguish* so great that human nature is driven by it from cover to cover, seeking refuge and finding none—*Rose Macaulay*⟩ ⟨a mild perturbation . . . about as like real *anguish* as three little eruptions on your arm are like confluent smallpox—*Montague*⟩ ⟨then came another sob, more violent than the first—a strangled gasp of *anguish*—*Rölvaag*⟩ **Woe** implies a deep or inconsolable misery or distress usually induced by grief ⟨the suffering people whose *woes* he has not alleviated—*W. P. Webb*⟩ ⟨outcast from God . . . condemned to waste eternal days in *woe*—*Milton*⟩ **Regret** seldom implies a sorrow that shows itself in tears or sobs or moans; usually it connotes such pain of mind as deep disappointment, fruitless longing, heartache, or spiritual anguish; consequently the term is applicable within a wide range that begins with the disappointment one feels, sometimes sincerely but sometimes merely as suggested by the language required by convention, in declining an invitation and ends with the pangs of remorse for something done or left undone or of hopeless repining for what can never be restored ⟨with a sigh that might have been either of *regret* or relief—*Wharton*⟩ ⟨in moments of *regret* we recognize that some of our judgments have been mistaken—*Cohen*⟩ ⟨that expression of mildly cynical *regret* and acceptance that one often notices in people who have seen much of life, and experienced its hard and seamy side—*Wolfe*⟩
*Ana* mourning, grieving (see GRIEVE): *distress, suffering, misery, agony: melancholy, dejection, *sadness, depression
*Ant* joy
**sorrow** *vb* mourn, *grieve
*Ana* *cry, weep, wail, keen: sob, moan, groan (see SIGH *vb*)
**sorry** pitiable, *contemptible, despicable, scurvy, cheap, beggarly, shabby
*Ana* *mean, ignoble, sordid, abject: *miserable, wretched: paltry, *petty, trifling, trivial

---

*Ana* analogous words　　*Ant* antonyms　　*Con* contrasted words　　See also explanatory notes facing page 1

**sort** *n* \*type, kind, stripe, kidney, ilk, description, nature, character

**sort** *vb* \*assort, classify, pigeonhole
*Ana* arrange, methodize, systematize, \*order: cull, pick, \*choose, select

**sot** \*drunkard, inebriate, alcoholic, dipsomaniac, soak, toper, tosspot, tippler

**soul** 1 \*mind, intellect, psyche, brain, intelligence, wit
*Ana* powers, faculties, functions (see singular nouns at POWER)
2 Soul, spirit can both denote an immaterial entity that is held to be distinguishable from and felt as superior to the body with which it is associated during the life of the individual and that in most religious beliefs is regarded as immortal, surviving the death of the body. Soul (see also MIND 2) may be preferred when the emphasis is upon the thing considered as an entity having specific functions, responsibilities, aspects, or destiny, while spirit (see also COURAGE, APPARITION) may be preferred when the stress is upon the quality, the constitution, the movement, or the activity of that entity ⟨hoped to save his *soul*⟩ ⟨willing to sell his *soul*⟩ ⟨pray for the *souls* of the dead⟩ ⟨do the right thing for your *soul's* sake⟩ ⟨come close to God in *spirit*⟩ ⟨a man fervent in *spirit*⟩ ⟨the *spirit* indeed is willing, but the flesh is weak—*Mt* 26:41⟩ Soul, both in the sense here emphasized and in the extended meanings derived from that sense, usually suggests a relation to or a connection with a body or with a physical or material entity to which it gives life or power; *spirit* in both its restricted and extended senses suggests an opposition or even an antithesis to what is physical, corporeal, or material and often a repugnance to the latter ⟨it often takes a war to lay bare the *soul* of a people⟩ ⟨obey the *spirit* rather than the letter of a law⟩ ⟨Gibbon's magnificent saying, that the Greek language gave a *soul* to the objects of sense and a body to the abstractions of metaphysics—*Quiller-Couch*⟩ ⟨those who believe in the reality of a world of the *spirit*—the poet, the artist, the mystic—are at one in believing that there are other domains than that of physics—*Jeans*⟩ Spirit only, and not *soul*, is used of incorporeal beings (as angels or devils) ⟨I can call *spirits* from the vasty deep—*Shak.*⟩
*Ant* body

**sound** *adj* 1 \*healthy, wholesome, robust, hale, well
*Ana* \*vigorous, lusty, nervous, energetic, strenuous: \*strong, sturdy, stalwart, stout: intact, whole, entire, \*perfect
2 \*valid, cogent, convincing, compelling, telling
*Ana* \*impeccable, flawless, faultless, errorless: \*correct, exact, precise, accurate: \*rational, reasonable
*Ant* fallacious

**sound** *n* Sound, noise both mean a sensation or effect produced by the stimulation of the auditory receptors of the ear and the auditory centers of the brain. Sound is the general term applicable to anything that is heard regardless of its loudness or softness, its pleasantness or unpleasantness, or its meaningfulness or meaninglessness ⟨he waited a good half hour after the last *sounds* of the departing enemy came down the wind—*Mason*⟩ ⟨it is impossible, words being what they are, to read the *sound* without reading the sense at the same time—*MacLeish*⟩ ⟨heard a *sound*, rather shrill and tentative, swell into hoarse, high clamor, and suddenly die out—*Galsworthy*⟩ ⟨approximates a laugh formed by . . . squeezing guttural *sounds* out of the throat—*Pynchon*⟩ Noise basically applies to confused sounds emanating from many persons and usually suggests a clamor made by mingled outcries or shouts; in more general use, it may apply to a disagreeably loud or harsh sound, whatever its source

⟨the terrific *noise* of an explosion⟩ ⟨a *noise* like that from just one stringy throat must be an impossibility, and yet, there it was—*Theodore Sturgeon*⟩ ⟨dense jungle, restless with the shrill *noise* of wild life—*Shipton*⟩ ⟨he could not endure the *noise* of the machine shop⟩ ⟨the hell of distracting *noises* made by the carts, the cabs, the carriages—*Mallock*⟩ Although the connotations of unpleasantness and discordance typically distinguish *noise* from *sound, noise* may sometimes be applied to a sound that merely engages the attention ⟨still the sails made on a pleasant *noise* till noon, a *noise* like of a hidden brook—*Coleridge*⟩ ⟨the wetted earth gave out a cool delicious fragrance; there was a *noise* of birds—*Huxley*⟩
*Ant* silence

**sound** *n* \*strait, channel, passage, narrows

**sound** *vb* \*fathom, plumb

**soupçon** suspicion, suggestion, \*touch, tincture, tinge, shade, smack, spice, dash, vein, strain, streak

**sour, acid, acidulous, tart, dry** mean having a taste devoid of sweetness. All but *dry* suggest the taste of lemons, vinegar, or of most unripe fruits. Sour and acid are often interchangeable, but sour is more likely to be chosen to describe something that through fermentation has lost its natural sweet or neutral taste or, sometimes, smell ⟨*sour* milk⟩ ⟨*sour* wine⟩ and the term may additionally suggest a spoiled or rancid state ⟨*sour* garbage⟩ Acid, on the other hand, is appropriately used to describe something having a sharp sweetless taste in its natural state usually due to the presence of chemical acids ⟨*acid* fruits⟩ ⟨*acid* drinks⟩ Acidulous and tart are applied, as a rule, to things which may be described as *acid, acidulous* implying a modest degree of acidity and tart, a sharp but often agreeable acidulousness or, sometimes, acidity ⟨some mineral waters are pleasantly *acidulous*⟩ ⟨most cooks prefer *tart* apples for pies and puddings⟩ Dry is usually applied to wines which, although without any sweetness, are bland and therefore neither definitely acid nor definitely sour.
In their extended senses sour applies especially to what is crabbed or morose ⟨a man with a prim *sour* mouth and an expression of eternal disapproval—*Dahl*⟩ and acidulous and tart to what is characterized by asperity, pungency, or sharpness ⟨*tart* temper never mellows with age—*Irving*⟩ ⟨what has been dull and dead in your years is now *tart* to the taste—*Mailer*⟩ ⟨said in *acidulous* jest that in Congress the South takes a recurrent and unending revenge in behalf of the long-dead Lee—*W. S. White*⟩ Acid, partly by allusion to the corrosive powers of some acids, is likely to describe what is biting or caustic ⟨his wit became *acid;* his letters are filled with caustic comment to sharpen the temper of those on the fighting line—*Parrington*⟩ while dry may suggest matter-of-fact impersonal presentation of what is humorous, ironic, or sarcastic ⟨there seemed to be a faint tinge of appeal in his eyes, curiously contrasted with the *dry* tone and the mocking words—*Wouk*⟩ ⟨a story . . . *dry* and ironical in its beginning—*Pritchett*⟩
*Ana* \*bitter, acrid: \*sharp, keen: morose, \*sullen, glum, crabbed, saturnine, dour

**source** \*origin, root, inception, provenance, provenience, prime mover
*Ana* beginning, commencement, starting *or* start (see corresponding verbs at BEGIN): \*cause, determinant, antecedent
*Ant* termination: outcome

**souse** \*dip, immerse, submerge, duck, dunk
*Ana* \*soak, steep, saturate, impregnate

**souvenir** 1 \*remembrance, remembrancer, reminder, memorial, memento, token, keepsake

---

A colon (:) separates groups of words discriminated. An asterisk (\*) indicates place of treatment of each group.

2 remembrance, recollection, *memory, reminiscence, mind

**sovereign** *adj* 1 *dominant, predominant, paramount, preponderant, preponderating
*Ana* *supreme, transcendent, surpassing: absolute, *ultimate
2 independent, *free, autonomous, autarchic, autarkic
*Ana* highest, loftiest (see positive adjectives at HIGH): *chief, principal, foremost: governing, ruling (see GOVERN): commanding, directing (see COMMAND *vb*)

**sovereignty** independence, freedom, autonomy, autarky, autarchy (see under FREE *adj*)
*Ana* *supremacy, ascendancy: command, sway, control, dominion, *power, authority

**sow** *vb* *strew, straw, scatter, broadcast

**spacious, commodious, capacious, ample** are comparable when they mean larger in extent than the average. **Spacious** implies great length and breadth and, sometimes, height; primarily, it is applied to things that have bounds or walls ⟨*spacious* rooms⟩ ⟨*spacious* gardens⟩ ⟨the whole interior . . . a dim, *spacious*, fragrant place, afloat with golden lights—*Pater*⟩ ⟨none of them were mansions but they were *spacious* and faced on neat lawns—*Styron*⟩ In its extended use, though it usually implies limits, it suggests largeness, sweep, and freedom within those limits ⟨the *spacious* times of great Elizabeth—*Tennyson*⟩ ⟨one great *spacious* golden morning followed another—*Powys*⟩ **Commodious** stresses roominess and freedom from hampering constriction along with convenience and comfortableness ⟨my mother's room is very *commodious*, is it not? Large and cheerful looking—*Austen*⟩ ⟨the *commodious* first-class grandstand . . . is built not only for comfort but for pleasant living—*Dobie*⟩ **Capacious** stresses the ability to hold, contain, and, sometimes, receive or retain, more than the ordinary thing of its kind ⟨the dull girls, with their slow but *capacious* memories—*Gallant*⟩ ⟨provides a *capacious* rack in its clubrooms which is daily filled with press releases—*Mott*⟩ ⟨fumbled in a *capacious* pocket of the old-fashioned sort —*Sayers*⟩ ⟨the *capacious* soul of Shakespeare—*Hazlitt*⟩ **Ample** basically means more than adequate or sufficient (as in size, expanse, or amount) ⟨*ample* funds⟩ ⟨an *ample* garden⟩ It may suggest fullness and bulk ⟨she held the child beneath the folds of her *ample* cloak⟩ ⟨an imposing creature, tall and stout, with an *ample* bust and an obesity girthed in alarmingly—*Maugham*⟩ and in extended use it often suggests freedom to expand or absence of trammels or limitations ⟨a government, entrusted with such *ample* powers—*John Marshall*⟩ ⟨religious experience which opens to him an even *ampler* world, even greater issues—*R. W. Livingstone*⟩
*Ana* vast, immense, enormous (see HUGE): *broad, wide, deep: extended *or* extensive (see corresponding verb at EXTEND)

**spade** *vb* *dig, delve, grub, excavate

**spangle** *vb* *spot, spatter, sprinkle, mottle, fleck, stipple, marble, speckle, bespangle

**spangled** spotted, spattered, sprinkled, mottled, flecked, stippled, marbled, speckled, bespangled (see under SPOT *vb*)

**spare** *adj* 1 extra, *superfluous, surplus, supernumerary
*Ana* *excessive, immoderate, exorbitant, inordinate
2 *lean, lank, lanky, skinny, scrawny, gaunt, rawboned, angular
*Ana* *thin, slender, slim, slight: sinewy, athletic (see MUSCULAR)
*Ant* corpulent —*Con* fat, *fleshy, obese, portly, plump
3 *meager, exiguous, sparse, scanty, scant, skimpy, scrimpy

*Ana* economical, *sparing, frugal, thrifty
*Ant* profuse

**sparing** *adj* **Sparing, frugal, thrifty, economical** can all mean exercising or manifesting careful and unwasteful use of one's money, goods, and resources. **Sparing** connotes abstention or restraint ⟨*sparing* in the expenditure of money⟩ ⟨*sparing* in giving praise⟩ ⟨he was lavish of encouragement, *sparing* of negation—*S. H. Adams*⟩ ⟨he had always been a *sparing* eater of plain foods but now he ate heartily—*Buck*⟩ **Frugal** suggests the absence of all luxury and lavishness especially in food and ways of living and dress; positively it implies simplicity, temperance, and, often, content ⟨Roman life was a *frugal* thing, sparing in food, temperate in drink, modest in clothing, cleanly in habit—*Buchan*⟩ ⟨the cost of the war was appalling to his *frugal* mind—*Forester*⟩ ⟨he likes *frugal* fighters. Every kind of serious trouble a fighter can get into, he says, has its origin in the disbursement of currency —*Liebling*⟩ **Thrifty** implies industry, good management, and prosperity as well as frugality ⟨lived in affluence for half a century; but memories of her early straits had made her excessively *thrifty*—*Wharton*⟩ ⟨their sober, *thrifty*, industrious life, concentrated upon moneymaking —*Mumford*⟩ ⟨the difference between a miserly man who hoards money out of avarice and a *thrifty* man who saves money out of prudence—*Empson*⟩ **Economical** often is used interchangeably with *thrifty* when the sparing use of money and goods is emphasized ⟨an *economical* housekeeper⟩ However the word often implies more than saving, for its chief implication is prudent management or use to the best advantage, without waste, and it is therefore far more widely applicable than *thrifty*, which refers only to persons or their expenditures ⟨the verse, which nowhere bursts into a flame of poetry, is yet *economical* and tidy, and formed to extract all the dramatic value possible from the situation—*T. S. Eliot*⟩ ⟨historically, sea power is the most mobile and therefore the most *economical* form of military force—*Time*⟩ ⟨he applied his skill to the *economical* use of words, the brief but vivid description—*Fellows*⟩
*Ana* *meager, exiguous, spare: *stingy, niggardly, parsimonious, penurious: *moderate, temperate
*Ant* lavish —*Con* *profuse, prodigal, exuberant

**sparkle** *vb* *flash, gleam, glance, glint, glitter, glisten, scintillate, coruscate, twinkle

**sparse** *meager, spare, exiguous, scanty, scant, skimpy, scrimpy
*Ana* scattered, dispersed (see SCATTER): sporadic, occasional, *infrequent, uncommon: *thin, slim, slender
*Ant* dense —*Con* *close, thick, compact

**spasm** paroxysm, convulsion, *fit, attack, access, accession

**spasmodic** *fitful, convulsive
*Ana* *intermittent, alternate, recurrent, periodic: *irregular, unnatural: *abnormal, aberrant, atypical
*Con* *steady, even, constant, equable, uniform: regular, methodical, *orderly

**spat** *n* bickering, squabble, *quarrel, wrangle, altercation, tiff
*Ana* dispute, controversy, *argument: contention, difference, variance, *discord
*Con* agreement, concurrence, coincidence (see corresponding verbs at AGREE)

**spat** *vb* bicker, squabble, quarrel, wrangle, altercate, tiff (see under QUARREL *n*)
*Ana* dispute, argue, agitate, debate (see DISCUSS): *differ, disagree
*Con* *agree, concur, coincide

**spate** *n* *flood, deluge, inundation, torrent, cataract

---

*Ana* analogous words     *Ant* antonyms     *Con* contrasted words     See also explanatory notes facing page 1

**Ana** *flow, stream, current, tide: *succession, progression, series

**spatter** *spot, sprinkle, mottle, fleck, stipple, marble, speckle, spangle, bespangle
**Ana** bespatter, asperse, splash (see SPRINKLE)

**spattered** spotted, sprinkled, mottled, flecked, stippled, marbled, speckled, spangled, bespangled (see under SPOT *vb*)

**spay** castrate, *sterilize, emasculate, alter, mutilate, geld, caponize

**speak, talk, converse** can all mean to articulate words so as to express one's thoughts. **Speak** is, in general, the broad term and may refer to utterances of any kind, however coherent or however broken or disconnected, and with or without reference to a hearer or hearers ⟨not able to *speak* above a whisper⟩ ⟨I shall *speak* to him about it⟩ ⟨let him *speak* for the organization⟩ ⟨most of the material in this book was *spoken* before it was printed, as may perhaps be inferred from the style—*Davis*⟩ ⟨she repeated them, angered . . . but once the words were *spoken* she was sorry—*McCullers*⟩ ⟨the Bellman looked scared, and was almost too frightened to *speak*—*Lewis Carroll*⟩ **Talk**, on the other hand, usually implies an auditor or auditors and connected colloquy or discourse ⟨he left the room because he did not care to *talk*⟩ ⟨we *talk* in the bosom of our family in a way different from that in which we discourse on state occasions—*Lowes*⟩ ⟨she *talked* and *talked* and *talked*, yet it seemed to Marjorie that she could never hear enough of this girl's worldly wisdom—*Wouk*⟩ But *speak* is also used of relatively weighty or formal speech (often public speech), and *talk*, of what is more or less empty or frivolous ⟨a fool may *talk*, but a wise man *speaks*—*Ben Jonson*⟩ ⟨a good old man, sir; he will be *talking*—*Shak.*⟩ ⟨yet there happened in my time one noble speaker who was full of gravity in his *speaking* . . . . No man ever *spake* more neatly, more pressly, more weightily, or suffered less emptiness, less idleness, in what he uttered—*Ben Jonson*⟩ **Converse** implies an interchange in talk of thoughts and opinions ⟨in the press conference the President can *converse* with the public rather than preach to it—*Cater*⟩ ⟨don't ever remember hearing my parents *converse*, and they never even chatted. My father would expound on law and ritual, my mother would listen—*Behrman*⟩
**Ana** pronounce, *articulate, enunciate: *stammer, stutter: *discourse, expatiate, dilate, descant

**special** *adj* Special, especial, specific, particular, individual are closely related terms because all carry the meaning relating to or belonging to one thing or one class especially as distinguished from all the others. Both *special* and *especial* imply differences which distinguish the thing so described from others of its kind, and the two can often be interchanged without significant loss. However **special** may be preferred when the differences give the thing concerned a quality, character, identity, or use of its own ⟨the mistress of the boardinghouse refused to serve *special* food to any of her guests⟩ ⟨the baby requires a *special* soap because of his sensitive skin⟩ ⟨if the whole of nature is purposive, it is not likely that we can discern *special* purposes operating—*Inge*⟩ ⟨a *special* aspect of a more general malady—*Babbitt*⟩ Often, in addition, *special* implies being out of the ordinary or being conspicuously unusual and therefore comes close to *uncommon* or *exceptional* ⟨it's not like ordinary photographs. There's something *special* about it—*Bennett*⟩ ⟨Mom was drunk most of the time and sometimes used to tear up the whole neighborhood, but all the same she had very *special* ideas about being respectable—*Theodore Sturgeon*⟩ ⟨preventing the perpetuation of an hereditary upper class with *special*

privileges and better education—*Edmund Wilson*⟩ **Special** is also applicable to something added (as to a schedule, a series, or a sequence) for an exceptional or extraordinary purpose, reason, or occasion ⟨*special* trains will be run to Washington for the inauguration⟩ ⟨a *special* dividend⟩ **Especial** is more likely to be chosen when there is the intent to convey the idea of preeminence or of being such as is described over and above all the others ⟨his *especial* friend⟩ ⟨a matter of *especial* importance⟩ ⟨this has no *especial* reference to any one person⟩ ⟨Egypt, as the granary of the ancient world, had *especial* need for Pussy's services—*Repplier*⟩ ⟨an elegantly written piece in the author's own *especial* version of the neoclassic manner—*Virgil Thomson*⟩ **Specific** (see also EXPLICIT) basically implies unique and peculiar relationship to a kind or category or individual ⟨*specific* evidence of disease⟩ ⟨the *specific* virtue of a drug⟩ ⟨*specific* nutritional needs of the aged⟩ In some (as philosophical, biological, or critical) uses it can suggest opposition to *generic* and imply a relation to a particular species as distinguished from a more comprehensive category to which that species belongs ⟨*specific* characters by which members of the genus *Rosa* can be differentiated⟩ ⟨groups of *specific* rank⟩ but in more general use it tends to stress uniquity and to imply a relation to one thing or one individual as distinguished from all others that can be felt to fall into a category with that one ⟨whether the *specific* freedoms we know and cherish . . . can be maintained—*Sidney Hook*⟩ ⟨make it possible for the imaginative talent to develop along those lines that reward with *specific* fruition—*Hudson Review*⟩ ⟨the binding of some ions is highly *specific* with respect to the protein involved—*Cannan & Levy*⟩ However, *specific* also may mean no more than explicitly mentioned, or called into or brought forward for consideration ⟨if such injuries . . . result in any of the following *specific* losses—*insurance policy*⟩ ⟨would be glad to hear of *specific* cases of scholars having difficulty with either passports or visas—*ACLS Newsletter*⟩ ⟨interested in any *specific* field only for its contribution to a view of the world as a totality—*Cohen*⟩ In this last sense of *specific* **particular** is sometimes preferred on the ground that the term is clearly opposed to *general* and that it is a close synonym of *single* (for fuller treatment see SINGLE). The differences between the two words in this sense are not easily discoverable, but *specific* seems to be chosen more often when the ideas of specification or of illustration are involved, and *particular*, when the distinctness of the thing as an individual is to be suggested; thus, one gives a *specific* illustration to indicate a word's normal use but describes the *particular* uses of the word ⟨in this connection, one of Don Quixote's adventures deserves *particular* mention—*Muggeridge*⟩ ⟨we get a sense for *particular* beauties of nature, rather than a sense for Nature herself—*Binyon*⟩ **Particular** is often used also in the sense of *special* and *especial* ⟨some half-dozen *particular* friends—*Dickens*⟩ ⟨the Debussy selection was the *particular* gem of the evening—*Watt*⟩ In logic *particular* is opposed to *universal* and applies to matters (as propositions, judgments, and conceptions) which have reference to a single member or to some members of a class rather than to all; thus, "some men are highly intelligent" is a *particular* proposition, but "all men make mistakes" is a *universal* proposition. Often, in less technical use, *particular* implies an opposition to *general* as well as to *universal* ⟨one is apt to amplify a *particular* judgment into a general opinion—*Mackenzie*⟩ ⟨we shall venture beyond the *particular* book in search of qualities that group books together—*Woolf*⟩ **Individual** unequivocally im-

A colon (:) separates groups of words discriminated. An asterisk (*) indicates place of treatment of each group.

plies reference to one of the class or group as clearly distinguished from all the others ⟨the aspect of every *individual* stone or brick—*Conrad*⟩ ⟨one could hardly maintain the courage to be *individual*, to speak with one's own voice—*Mailer*⟩ ⟨it was not the magnitude or multiplicity of burdens that created martyrs and saints; it was the *individual* capacity to bear suffering—*Hervey*⟩ *Ana* distinctive, peculiar, individual, *characteristic: *exceptional: uncommon, occasional, rare (see INFREQUENT)
*Con* *common, ordinary, familiar: *usual, customary, habitual

**specie** cash, currency, *money, legal tender, coin, coinage
**species** *class, category, genus, denomination, genre
*Ana* *type, kind, sort, description, character, nature
**specific** *adj* 1 *special, especial, particular, individual
*Ant* generic
2 definite, *explicit, express, categorical
*Ana* designating, naming (see DESIGNATE): *clear, lucid, perspicuous: precise, exact (see CORRECT *adj*)
*Ant* vague
**specific** *n* *remedy, cure, medicine, medicament, medication, physic
**specify** *mention, name, instance
*Ana* cite, *quote: stipulate (see corresponding noun under CONDITION)
**specimen** example, sample, illustration, *instance, case
**specious** *plausible, believable, colorable, credible
*Ana* *vain, nugatory, empty, hollow, idle: delusory, delusive, *misleading, deceptive: deceitful, *dishonest, untruthful, mendacious, lying
**speckle** *vb* *spot, spatter, sprinkle, mottle, fleck, stipple, marble, spangle, bespangle
**speckled** spotted, spattered, sprinkled, mottled, flecked, stippled, marbled, spangled, bespangled (see under SPOT *vb*)
**spectator,** observer, beholder, looker-on, onlooker, witness, eyewitness, bystander, kibitzer are comparable when they mean one who sees or looks upon something. **Spectator** can be used precisely in place of *auditor* for one that attends an exhibition, performance, or entertainment which does not involve an appeal to the sense of hearing; thus, one tends to speak of the *spectators* at a football game, a prizefight, a pageant, a pantomime, or a circus but of the *auditors* or the *audience* at a concert, a lecture, or a play. Very often, however, the term is used more broadly to denote one who regards himself or is felt to be wholly apart from and in no manner identified with what is presented to his attention (as by his sight, hearing, or understanding) ⟨it is only the *spectator* of morals who can assume the calm aesthetic attitude—*Ellis*⟩ ⟨the narrator . . . is a sensitive young artist, nominally a Communist, actually a *spectator* of history, a camera not much involved in life—*Ludwig*⟩ **Observer** may or may not imply an intent to see, but it usually does suggest, whether one sees by intention or by accident, that one attends closely to details and often keeps a record of them; the term applies especially to those (as scientists) who gather evidence by carefully noting phenomena or the results of experiments or to military or diplomatic officials who are sent by countries not participating in a war or in a meeting of representatives from other nations to watch proceedings closely and to make a report of them; it is also applicable to whoever has formed similar habits and can be more or less relied upon for accuracy ⟨it is the man of science who speaks, the unprejudiced *observer*, the accepter of facts—*Huxley*⟩ ⟨an *observer* for the United States at assemblies of the United Nations⟩ ⟨you go about a lot amongst all sorts of people. You are a tolerably honest

*observer*—*Conrad*⟩ ⟨I had once been a cool *observer* because some part of me knew that I had more emotion than most and so must protect myself with a cold eye —*Mailer*⟩ **Beholder** sometimes carries a stronger implication of watching or regarding intently than either of the preceding terms, but it may mean little more than one who sees ⟨all the *beholders* take his part with weeping —*Shak.*⟩ The term is often applicable to one who has been privileged to look intently upon or, sometimes, consider deeply a person or thing with the result that he obtains a clear and accurate impression of that person or thing and is moved by the qualities (as beauty, power, tenderness, or pathos) of what is seen ⟨to what extent is beauty subjective, existing only in the mind of the *beholder* —*Hunter Mead*⟩ ⟨what the *beholder* must realize as he looks and ponders is that history is not something in books—*Duffus*⟩ **Looker-on** and **onlooker** differ from *beholder* chiefly in their suggestions of casualness or detachment and in their definite implication of lack of participation ⟨there was a great crowd of *lookers-on* at the fire⟩ ⟨the surgeon refused to operate in the presence of *onlookers*⟩ Either term is sometimes used in place of *spectator* when the distinction between the one who sees and what he sees is stressed ⟨the *onlookers*, not the participants, see most of the game⟩ ⟨*lookers-on* often see what familiarity obscures for the participants—*Moberly*⟩ ⟨they dropped, panting, while the *onlookers* repeated that it was a shame and somebody ought to stop them—*Davis*⟩ **Witness** specifically denotes one who has firsthand knowledge and therefore is competent to give testimony ⟨no person shall be convicted of treason, unless on the testimony of two *witnesses* to the same overt act—*U. S. Constitution*⟩ The term sometimes applies to a person who knows because he has seen ⟨standing there, I was *witness* of a little incident that seemed to escape the rest —*Quiller-Couch*⟩ but since *witness* does not necessarily imply seeing, **eyewitness** is often preferred as more explicitly implying actual sight ⟨there were no *eyewitnesses* of the collision⟩ ⟨incontrovertible evidence, with occasional corroboration from the *eyewitness* accounts of the few survivors—*Shirer*⟩ **Bystander** primarily denotes one who stands by when something is happening; sometimes it carries the implication of *onlooker* ⟨the policeman took the names of all the *bystanders*⟩ ⟨men have been haunted recurrently by the question "Am I my brother's keeper?". . . It is what makes being a *bystander* more and more impossible—*Rothman*⟩ but at other times it suggests little more than presence at a place ⟨difficult for each member of the society really to participate . . . . He begins to be an onlooker at most of it, then a *bystander*, and may end up with indifference to the welfare of his society—*Kroeber*⟩ ⟨a *bystander* was injured by the explosion⟩ **Kibitzer** specifically applies to one who watches a card game by looking over the shoulders of the players and who may annoy them by offering advice; in extended use the word denotes an onlooker who meddles or makes unwelcome suggestions.

**specter** spirit, ghost, *apparition, phantasm, phantom, wraith, shade, revenant
**speculate** reason, reflect, *think, cogitate, deliberate
*Ana* *ponder, meditate, muse, ruminate: *consider, weigh, study, contemplate, excogitate
**speculative** 1 contemplative, meditative, *thoughtful, reflective, pensive
*Ana* conjecturing *or* conjectural, surmising, guessing (see corresponding verbs at CONJECTURE): pondering, musing, ruminating (see PONDER)
2 *theoretical, academic
**speech** 1 *language, tongue, dialect, idiom

**2 Speech, address, oration, harangue, lecture, talk, sermon, homily** designate a discourse delivered to an audience. Speech can apply to a public discourse irrespective of its quality or its degree of preparation, of its aim (as to influence, instruct, or entertain), or of the caliber of its speaker or audience ⟨the senator was called upon to make a *speech*⟩ ⟨after-dinner *speeches*⟩ ⟨"The rest of my *speech*" (he exclaimed to his men) "you shall hear when I've leisure to speak it"—*Lewis Carroll*⟩ Address implies formality and usually careful preparation; it often connotes distinction in the speaker or gives emphasis to the importance of the speech ⟨commencement *address*⟩ ⟨the president is scheduled to deliver three *addresses* on his trip⟩ ⟨an article developed from his *address* to friends and admirers at a recent testimonial dinner—*Sat. Review*⟩ Oration suggests eloquence, rhetorical style, and usually a dignified but sometimes a high-flown or long-winded appeal to the emotions of a large audience or assembly ⟨a Fourth of July *oration*⟩ ⟨the *oration* of Mr. Webster was worthy of his fame, and what is much more, was worthy of the august occasion—*Emerson*⟩ Harangue, once nearly equivalent to *oration* except for its added implications of vehemence and passion, commonly retains only these distinctive implications and connotes either length and tediousness of speech or an impassioned appeal to the audience ⟨if you do not believe that emotion . . . is the basic social force, listen to the *harangue* of any successful politician—*Furnas*⟩ Lecture often implies reading; it commonly designates a carefully prepared speech on a special topic intended to give information and instruction to a group of students or studious persons ⟨they are still using *lectures* to pass out information which could be got by the student more rapidly and accurately from . . . books—*Lynn White*⟩ Talk stresses informality; it may be used to designate either a lecture or an address when the speaker wishes to emphasize his desire to speak directly and simply to his auditors as individuals ⟨this is a *talk* rather than an oration . . . . It is surely unnecessary to say how well, and with what an individual attitude and selectiveness Mr. Forster talks—*Times Lit. Sup.*⟩ Sermon and *homily* both commonly imply religious instruction by an ordained preacher and a church congregation as the listeners; in such use *sermon* usually connotes a theme drawn from a scriptural text, while *homily* suggests practical moral counsel rather than doctrinal discussion. But both terms have extended use in which they denote a usually didactic talk or discussion on a moral theme ⟨copious drafts of exhortation and *homily* administered . . . by reformers—*Cardozo*⟩ ⟨going around the country, preaching *sermons* on the need of defending the freedom of the mind—*Davis*⟩

**speechless** *dumb, mute, inarticulate

**speed** *n* **1** *haste, hurry, expedition, dispatch
*Ana* *celerity, legerity, alacrity: fleetness, rapidity, swiftness, quickness (see corresponding adjectives at FAST): velocity, pace, headway (see SPEED)

**2 Speed, velocity, momentum, impetus, pace, headway** are comparable but not all mutually synonymous terms that basically apply to motion through space. Speed (see also HASTE *n*) denotes rate of motion, a value computable by dividing the distance covered by the time taken ⟨a car that covers 300 miles in 6 hours has an average *speed* of 50 miles an hour⟩ Velocity denotes the speed of something that is directed along a given path. Ordinarily *velocity* suggests rate of motion in a straight line (*linear velocity*) or in an arc or circle (*angular velocity*) ⟨the *velocity* of a bullet⟩ ⟨the *velocity* of a skier⟩ ⟨*velocity* of a wind⟩ ⟨*velocity* of light⟩ ⟨a body rotating about a fixed axis with a constant angular *velocity*⟩ Momentum in

general or casual use may take the place of *speed* or *velocity*, but in technical use it denotes not rate of motion but quantity of motion, a value determinable by multiplying the mass of a moving body by its velocity ⟨a falling stone gathers *momentum*⟩ ⟨the *momentum* of an iron ball rolling down an inclined plane is greater than that of a cork ball of the same diameter rolling with the same velocity⟩ ⟨as photons are always in motion, we may also speak of the *momentum* of a photon, much as we speak of the *momentum* of a motorcar—*Jeans*⟩ Impetus (see also STIMULUS) is a popular rather than technical synonym of *momentum*. In practice it is a closer synonym of *impulse* in the sense of the effect of an impelling force, for it regularly carries an implication of a rushing upon or an onset, with the result that it usually suggests great momentum or implies a powerful driving force as the cause of such momentum ⟨whether the steam . . . retains sufficient *impetus* to carry it to our shores—*T. H. Huxley*⟩ ⟨the circulating blood receives a new *impetus* from the contraction of the ventricles of the heart⟩ Pace belongs here not as a technical term but as a term in general use to denote the speed of or as if of one (as a person or horse) going afoot ⟨he set the *pace* for his companions on the hike⟩ ⟨the *pace* was too slow for the rest of the party⟩ *Pace* often finds extended use in describing such things as activities, progress, or rate of production ⟨keep *pace* with the times⟩ ⟨the factories were asked to increase their *pace*⟩ ⟨in New York he had moved on from speed to speed and from height to height, keeping *pace* with all the most magnificent developments in the furious city—*Wolfe*⟩ Headway basically applies to motion forward and in this sense is used chiefly in reference to ships ⟨he started the screw turning until the *African Queen* was just making *headway* against the current—*Forester*⟩ However it frequently denotes rate of movement ahead and then is used in reference not only to ships but to whatever is capable of advancing or making progress ⟨our mutual security program had suffered a year of lost *headway*—*Barnett*⟩ ⟨the independent movements of nominalism and German mysticism made great *headway*—*Thilly*⟩

**speed** *vb* **Speed, accelerate, quicken, hasten, hurry, precipitate** can mean to go or make go fast or faster. Speed emphasizes rapidity of motion or progress; as a transitive verb it suggests an increase in tempo; as an intransitive verb, a high degree of swiftness ⟨*speed* up an engine⟩ ⟨*speed* up the work in a factory⟩ ⟨the bullet *sped* through the air⟩ ⟨arrested for *speeding*⟩ ⟨the stoutest of the boatmen seized the staff out of turn and *sped* our craft forward—*Waln*⟩ Accelerate stresses increase in rate of motion or progress; it does not necessarily imply speed ⟨*accelerated* his pace so as to overtake the leaders⟩ ⟨a rich soil *accelerates* the growth of most plants⟩ ⟨*accelerate* the speed of a car⟩ ⟨History of late has *accelerated* her pace. Where once she moved slowly . . . she has within the past decade raced forward jet-propelled—*J. M. Brown*⟩ ⟨excitement was *accelerating* moment by moment, like the wheels of the train—*Capote*⟩ Quicken stresses shortening of the time consumed, often with a suggestion of animation or stimulation ⟨exercise *quickens* the pulse⟩ ⟨a broad and continuous education that *quickens* understanding of the modern world—*Sidney Hook*⟩ Hasten implies urgent quickness or a quick or premature outcome ⟨*hastened* to apologize⟩ ⟨the annoyance and terror he lived in must have greatly *hastened* his early and unhappy death—*Stevenson*⟩ ⟨the science of archaeology is advancing into the past almost as rapidly as physics and electronics are *hastening* the future—*Time*⟩ Hurry implies haste that causes confusion or prevents concentrated attention ⟨his aim was *hurried* and his shot went wide of the mark⟩

A colon (:) separates groups of words discriminated. An asterisk (*) indicates place of treatment of each group.

⟨a second fear . . . which madly *hurries* her she knows not whither—*Shak.*⟩ ⟨these defects might pass more easily in a turbulent romanticist, *hurrying* pell-mell to get expressed some moving and dramatic scene, careless of details—*Fry*⟩ **Precipitate** implies impetuousness, suddenness, or abruptness ⟨men will not bide their time, but will insist on *precipitating* the march of affairs—*Buckle*⟩ ⟨its ruin was *precipitated* by religious persecution—*J. R. Green*⟩

*Ana* *advance, forward, further, promote: *adjust, regulate, fix

**speedy** expeditious, quick, swift, fleet, rapid, *fast, hasty

*Ana* brisk, nimble, *agile: prompt, *quick, ready

*Ant* dilatory

**spell** *n* Spell, shift, tour, trick, turn, stint, bout, go can mean a limited period or amount of some activity that often follows a schedule. **Spell** is ordinarily used in reference to very heavy or trying work which must be interrupted by a period of rest; the period may vary according to the laboriousness of the activity and the need of relief from it ⟨each *spell* of work was followed by a brief rest⟩ **Shift** suggests a change in time or hours of duty and therefore a change in the workers employed; it is used especially in reference to an industrial plant which is in continuous operation, and is applied variously to the period of work or to the body of workers engaged to work during that period ⟨the third *shift* begins work at midnight⟩ ⟨the factory works on a schedule of three *shifts* each day⟩ **Tour** occurs chiefly in the phrase *tour of duty;* it usually suggests a change in the character of the work and in its typical use (as of military or naval personnel) implies assignment for a definite term (as of weeks, months, or years) to a particular type of duty or to duty in a particular place ⟨his next *tour* of duty will be in Ceylon⟩ ⟨after a year at sea the commander was given a *tour* of shore duty⟩ **Trick**, like *spell*, usually implies the time allotted to one for working at or as if at the helm of a ship, and it may differ little from *shift* as applied to a period of work ⟨to take his *trick* at the wheel—*Marryat*⟩ ⟨the night *trick* in a newspaper office⟩ **Turn** in general use suggests an opportunity of a specified kind (as for work or play) or for a particular period that comes in alternation, rotation, or at more or less regular intervals ⟨I'll take a *turn* at that job now⟩ ⟨the boys lined up, each waiting for his *turn* at bat⟩ ⟨if we each took our *turn* and did our bit in peace as we had to do during the war—*Shaw*⟩ **Stint** (see also TASK) implies either an assigned amount of work or an assigned amount of time in which to accomplish it. The term is used widely in reference to one's own occupation, to the work of running a home, a farm, or a business, or to work in an industrial field especially where regular hours for a day's work are not or cannot be easily established ⟨the author assigned himself a daily *stint* of three pages⟩ ⟨Spinoza was forced to grind his *stint* of lenses before he could gratify his love for philosophy⟩ ⟨in some countries miners' wages are regulated not by days but by *stints*⟩ **Bout**, which has many specific applications and is perhaps more widely employed than any of the preceding terms, in general suggests an activity or condition that is marked by a definite beginning and end in time; specifically it may refer to a fight, an attack of illness and especially to a recurrent illness, or a spell (as of drinking, of work, or of exercise), but in every case it implies a beginning or end that marks it off from what precedes and follows ⟨a wrestling *bout*⟩ ⟨a *bout* of malaria⟩ ⟨he had been given to *bouts* only, and was not a habitual drunkard—*Hardy*⟩ ⟨copious eating and still more copious drinking, interrupted by *bouts* of . . . domes-

tic horseplay—*Huxley*⟩ ⟨showing the effect of his past in . . . *bouts* of neurotic excitement—*Buchan*⟩ **Go** is often not clearly defined in meaning, but it comes close to *bout, spell*, and *turn*, in suggesting a restricted period ⟨a *go* with the gloves⟩ ⟨have a *go* at farming⟩

*Ana* *period: allotment, assignment, apportionment (see corresponding verbs at ALLOT)

**spend, expend, disburse** can mean to pay out money or an equivalent of money for something or in expectation of some return. **Spend** is the ordinary term; it may be used regardless of the amount dealt out in the purchase of something ⟨*spend* a nickel for candy⟩ ⟨*spend* fifty dollars for a dress⟩ ⟨the government during the first year of the war *spent* billions of dollars⟩ In intransitive use it requires usually an adverb or adverbial phrase to indicate the extent to which money or, by extension, its equivalent, is paid out ⟨he has never known how it feels to *spend* freely⟩ ⟨the Pentagon *spends* so wastefully that we could cut our military budget by at least 25 percent—*Catton*⟩ ⟨this world in arms is not *spending* money alone. It is *spending* the sweat of its laborers, the genius of its scientists, the hopes of its children—*Eisenhower*⟩ However the word is often used with so little implication of an immediate or direct or commensurate return and with objects so remotely equivalent to money that it comes to imply a using in such a manner as to exhaust, drain, or deplete ⟨*spend* six months searching for the home they wished to buy⟩ ⟨*spent* her small store of energy with caution⟩ ⟨man after man *spends* himself in this cause—*Carlyle*⟩ ⟨decided on a whim to *spend* the day like a yo-yo shuttling on the subway back and forth underneath 42nd Street—*Pynchon*⟩ ⟨*spend* his life and his blood in the service of the king⟩ **Expend** comes very close to *spend* in meaning, but it tends to be used more in reference to business, industry, finance, or government than in reference to private persons and therefore to imply larger sums or more determinate ends ⟨the social services upon which public revenue is *expended*—*Hobson*⟩ In its extended use, too, *expend* tends to imply largeness of outgo and often, like *spend*, suggests a depleting or exhausting of what is being used ⟨we have *expended* our resources—both human and natural—without stint—*Truman*⟩ ⟨youth is always giving itself, *expending* itself—*Yeats*⟩ but it not infrequently carries an added suggestion of futility that is not apparent in *spend* ⟨much thought had been *expended*, but little accomplished—*Dawson & Wilson*⟩ ⟨the tons of printer's ink and newsprint *expended* during the course of the hearings—*Wall Street Jour.*⟩ ⟨all the social feeling and intellectual effort . . . seemed to have *expended* themselves—*John Morley*⟩ **Disburse** basically implies the paying out of money (as from public revenues, a huge fortune, an institutional income, or a society's funds), but it also may imply distribution (as to pensioners or among heirs) and often stresses an acting under authority in such paying or distributing ⟨the treasurer has *disbursed* nearly five thousand dollars of emergency funds for repair of the clubhouse⟩ ⟨our time and our money, even though *disbursed* by governmental authority—*Hambly*⟩ ⟨waiting for the teller to *disburse* those complex payroll accounts—*Morley*⟩ When extended to nonmonetary matters, *disburse* is likely to stress distribution ⟨the hundred kilograms of uranium . . . was designated for research only, and was to be *disbursed* under strictly bilateral agreements—*Lear*⟩

*Ana* *distribute, dispense, divide, deal, dole: *allot, assign, allocate, apportion: *scatter, disperse, dissipate: *pay, compensate, remunerate

*Ant* save

**spendthrift,** prodigal, profligate, waster, wastrel are

---

*Ana* analogous words　　*Ant* antonyms　　*Con* contrasted words　　See also explanatory notes facing page 1

comparable when they denote a person who dissipates his resources foolishly and wastefully. All are more or less pejorative terms but they may differ significantly in emphasis and application. *Spendthrift* and *prodigal* are the most nearly neutral terms and in themselves, as apart from context, carry little suggestion of moral obliquity; they are, however, the members of the group with specific legal applications and are generally applicable when the basic notion is one of unwise and wasteful expenditure usually of material resources (as wages, wealth, or property). **Spendthrift** stresses lack of prudence in spending and usually implies imbalance between income and outgo rather than lavishness ⟨to *spendthrifts* . . . there is only one limit to their fortune,—that of time; and a *spendthrift* with only a few crowns is the Emperor of Rome until they are spent—*Stevenson*⟩ ⟨a *spendthrift* is a man . . . who saves nothing, spends fifty-eight cents of every dollar on living expenses, forty cents on recreation and one cent each on education and alms—*Brooklyn Daily Eagle*⟩ In legal and quasi-legal use the term implies such expenditure in relation to income and resources as are likely to leave the spendthrift and his dependents public charges. **Prodigal** (compare *prodigal adj* under PROFUSE) is more likely to suggest such lavish expenditure as can deplete the most abundant resources ⟨this royal *prodigal*, lavishing the nation's wealth on palaces and parks while the people starved⟩ ⟨the Irish produce great writers because they're temperamentally *prodigals*—they're willing to squander their lives on the gratuitous work that great art demands —*Edmund Wilson*⟩ In legal and quasi-legal use the term applies specifically to one held legally incompetent to manage his property or to incur debts because of demonstrated incapacity to avoid foolish dissipation of property. While **profligate** may imply the habits of a spendthrift, it is more likely to stress such extravagant, even vicious expenditure of one's personal powers (as of mind and body) that mere economic waste becomes a secondary matter; characteristically it suggests the utmost of debauchery and dissoluteness ⟨they were not cautious schemers, husbanding their resources. Julius Caesar was a notorious *profligate*, who piled up enormous debts —*Inge*⟩ ⟨the wretched *profligate* found himself again plunged into excesses—*J. R. Green*⟩ **Waster** often comes very close to *spendthrift* in meaning, but it carries a stronger implication of worthlessness than does the former word. It often suggests the habits of a loafer or ne'er-do-well but it is sometimes applied to men of inherited wealth who spend their lives in idleness or in frivolities ⟨he who will not work, must . . . leave the town, as they will not sweat themselves for an healthy, idle *waster*—*Adair*⟩ ⟨the palaces and pleasure seats of the plutocrats are used for the recreation of workers instead of for the enervation of extravagant *wasters*—*Shaw*⟩ ⟨they're a bunch of *wasters*. All they do . . . is just dance and chatter and show off their clothes—*Sinclair Lewis*⟩ **Wastrel**, though it often implies the wasting of money and other resources, more often is applied to a good-for-nothing, whether young or old, especially to one who is a drain upon the community; the prevailing implication is that of disreputableness ⟨if we are to avoid the danger of so shaping them that they shall be mere mechanisms in working hours and mere *wastrels* in the rest—*Grandgent*⟩ ⟨even allowing for a large element of intentional exaggeration . . . there remains the basic fact that . . . we have the expression of the twisted psyche of an embittered, penniless *wastrel*— *R. A. Hall*⟩

**spew** *vb* *belch, burp, vomit, disgorge, regurgitate, throw up

**sphere** *field, domain, province, territory, bailiwick

*Ana* dominion, sway, jurisdiction, control, *power: *range, reach, scope, compass: *function, office, duty, province

**spice** *touch, suggestion, suspicion, soupçon, tincture, tinge, shade, smack, dash, vein, strain, streak

**spick-and-span** *neat, tidy, trim, trig, snug, shipshape
*Ana* *clean, cleanly: fresh, *new
*Ant* filthy

**spicy** *pungent, piquant, poignant, racy, snappy
*Ana* *spirited, high-spirited, gingery, fiery, peppery: aromatic, redolent, balmy, *odorous

**spin** *vb* *turn, revolve, rotate, gyrate, circle, twirl, whirl, wheel, eddy, swirl, pirouette
*Ana* *swing, sway, oscillate, vibrate

**spine, backbone, back, vertebrae, chine** designate the articulated column of bones which is the central and axial feature of the skeleton of human beings and other vertebrate animals. *Spine, backbone, back,* and *vertebrae* can be used without distinction, but one of the first three is more likely to be chosen when the structure is considered as a unit, and the last when its composite structure is pertinent. *Spine* and *backbone* are more often used in reference to human beings than to lower vertebrates; **spine** is often felt as more technical than **backbone** and is likely to be preferred when the intent is to appear informed or knowledgeable ⟨the doctor recommended an operation on my brother's *spine*⟩ ⟨don't sit like that, you'll kink your *backbone*⟩ but *spine* is also appropriate when *vertebrae* could be misleading ⟨fractured his *spine* and injured three vertebrae⟩ **Back**, more often than *spine* or *backbone*, applies to the bony column together with ligaments and muscles that support it and collectively make up a distinguishable part of the vertebrate body ⟨broke his *back* in a fall⟩ ⟨a badly wrenched *back*⟩ **Vertebrae** is likely to occur in technical anatomical use and in general use is often preferred when the reference is to other than human beings. **Chine** has lost this basic meaning except indirectly in application to meat animals, in which it is applied to a cut of meat including part of the backbone ⟨a *chine* of beef⟩

**spirit** *n* **1** *soul
*Ana* *mind, intellect, soul, psyche
**2** ghost, *apparition, phantasm, phantom, wraith, specter, shade, revenant
**3** *courage, mettle, resolution, tenacity
*Ana* *fortitude, pluck, grit, backbone, sand, guts: zeal, fervor, ardor, *passion, enthusiasm: energy, strength, might, *power, force
**4** *vigor, vim, dash, esprit, verve, punch, élan, drive
*Ana* vitality, animation, aliveness (see corresponding adjectives at LIVING): vivacity, liveliness, gaiety, sprightliness (see corresponding adjectives at LIVELY)

**spirited, high-spirited, mettlesome, spunky, fiery, peppery, gingery** mean having or manifesting a high degree of vitality, spirit, and daring. **Spirited** implies not only fullness of life but such signs of excellent physical, or sometimes mental, health as ardor, animation, energy, and enthusiasm; the term's implications vary widely, but it usually carries a suggestion of vigorous vitality, exaltation, or stimulation ⟨his words, *spirited* as they were in meaning, contrasted sadly with the weakness of the voice—*Stevenson*⟩ ⟨a *spirited* turn to a jaded commonplace has achieved an opening that is flawlessly organic—*Lowes*⟩ ⟨the defense is *spirited* and extreme and nothing is given to the enemy —*Sykes*⟩ ⟨shaking his head backward, somewhat after the manner of a *spirited* horse—*George Eliot*⟩ **High-spirited** can add to *spirited* a strong suggestion of dashing vigor and even of a temperamental unwillingness to accept guidance and control ⟨a sensibly unheroic man who is

A colon (:) separates groups of words discriminated. An asterisk (*) indicates place of treatment of each group.

led into wild shooting frays by a *high-spirited* girl— *Anthony Boucher*⟩ ⟨too *high-spirited* to be passive instruments in his hand—*William Robertson*⟩ ⟨they were *high-spirited*, perhaps a little insolent as well as reckless —*Ellis*⟩ **Mettlesome** differs little from *high-spirited* except in its tendency to stress fearlessness and vigor more than restiveness ⟨he found himself immediately at grips with one of the watch, a *mettlesome* fellow who fought like a wildcat—*Costain*⟩ ⟨his occasional sarcasms are no more than a high-spirited gaiety and his quarrels no more frequent or violent than might be normal in any *mettlesome* youngster—*Edgar Johnson*⟩ **Spunky** often implies qualities similar to those suggested by *high-spirited* and *mettlesome* but it carries a stronger implication of quickness in taking fire and of an incapacity for being downed or daunted; also, the term is often applied to unlooked-for courage in persons or animals ⟨she was under five feet and weighed less than ninety pounds, but he would have had an armful of *spunky* vitality— *Thurber*⟩ ⟨one of the great subjects for biography is that *spunky*, crotchety, illiterate, and wonderfully gifted maker of things, Henry Ford—*Gill*⟩ *Fiery, peppery,* and *gingery* are used as synonyms of the preceding terms when one prefers a more concrete term. **Fiery,** suggesting the heat of flame or fire, implies impetuousness, passionateness, or sometimes irascibility in addition to spiritedness ⟨a *fiery* soul, which, working out its way, fretted the pygmy body to decay—*Dryden*⟩ ⟨a *fiery*, tortured spirit, aiming at something greater than could be conceived by anything that was bound up with the flesh—*Maugham*⟩ ⟨the *fiery* thinker who flattened a generation with the hail of his words—*Tracy*⟩ **Peppery** adds to *spirited* suggestions of a hotness or pungency characteristic of pepper and often distinctively connotes asperity or excitability ⟨a *peppery* response⟩ ⟨Master Rickey is a *peppery* young man. Love and war come as natural to him as bread and butter—*Meredith*⟩ ⟨as he makes clear in *peppery* footnotes and caustic asides, he has aimed at an absolute precision of factual detail—*Kazin*⟩ **Gingery** carries a heightened suggestion of a zest, spiciness, or snap associated with ginger ⟨in *gingery* good health at 55—*Newsweek*⟩ ⟨he learned the high quick *gingery* ways of thoroughbreds—*Masefield*⟩
*Ana* courageous, intrepid, bold, audacious, valiant, *brave: impetuous, *precipitate: *eager, avid, keen: passionate, enthusiastic, zealous, fervent, ardent (see corresponding nouns at PASSION)
*Ant* spiritless
**spiritless** *languid, languishing, languorous, listless, enervated, lackadaisical
*Ana* *lethargic, sluggish, comatose: dull, slow, *stupid, dense, crass: *tame, subdued, submissive
*Ant* spirited
**spiritual** *adj* 1 *immaterial, incorporeal
*Ant* physical —*Con* *material, corporeal, phenomenal, sensible, objective: *bodily, corporal, somatic
2 *holy, sacred, divine, religious, blessed
*Ana* *supernatural, supranatural: *celestial, heavenly
*Ant* physical: carnal: material: temporal
**spite** *n* despite, malignity, malignancy, spleen, grudge, *malice, ill will, malevolence
*Ana* rancor, animus, antipathy (see ENMITY): vindictiveness, revengefulness *or* revenge, vengefulness *or* vengeance (see corresponding adjectives at VINDICTIVE)
**spiteful** malignant, *malicious, malevolent, malign
*Ana* rancorous, antipathetic, antagonistic, hostile (see corresponding nouns at ENMITY): *vindictive, revengeful, vengeful
**spleen** malignity, malignancy, grudge, spite, despite,

*malice, malevolence, ill will
*Ana* animosity, antipathy, animus, rancor, antagonism (see ENMITY): venom, *poison: vindictiveness, revengefulness (see corresponding adjectives at VINDICTIVE)
**splendid, resplendent, gorgeous, glorious, sublime, superb** can mean having or displaying outstanding or transcendingly impressive qualities. Although, like most adjectives implying transcendence, they are often used interchangeably in hyperbole or in general expressions of great admiration or satisfaction, they are capable of being used more precisely in ways that convey quite distinctive images and impressions. **Splendid** implies an outshining of the usual or customary (as in brilliancy, luster, grandeur, or magnificence) or an impressing of the observer (as by surpassing brilliancy, luster, or grandeur) ⟨a fine— yea even a *splendid* room, of great height, and carved grandeur—*Galsworthy*⟩ ⟨the *splendid* efflorescence of genius in Russia during . . . the last century—*Ellis*⟩ ⟨blocks set there like markers of a *splendid* city yet unbuilt which would rise grandly from the hills—*Wolfe*⟩ ⟨there was a majestic quality about this woman, something *splendid*, almost stately—*Dahl*⟩ **Resplendent** implies a glowing or blazing splendor ⟨girls, *resplendent* in fine red or green cloth coats with big fur collars framing the flashing vivacity of their faces—*Ferber*⟩ ⟨Juliet died, but not before she had shown how great and *resplendent* a thing love could be—*Krutch*⟩ **Gorgeous** is likely to apply to the sumptuously splendid in color or display of colors ⟨the July sun shone over Egdon and fired its crimson heather to scarlet. It was the one season of the year, and the one weather of the season, in which the heath was *gorgeous*—*Hardy*⟩ The term sometimes stresses showiness or elaborateness rather than splendor of coloring ⟨a *gorgeous* feast⟩ ⟨quite *gorgeous* archway with gates at the head of the staircase, covered and festooned with pink roses—*Wouk*⟩ **Glorious** implies a being radiant with light or beauty or a standing out as eminently worthy of admiration, renown, or distinction ⟨now is the winter of our discontent made *glorious* summer by this sun of York—*Shak.*⟩ ⟨he soon saw within ken a *glorious* Angel stand . . . his back was turned, but not his brightness hid— *Milton*⟩ ⟨as often happens after a gray daybreak the sun had risen in a warm and *glorious* splendor—*Conrad*⟩ ⟨this *glorious* vision of manly strength and beauty—*Shaw*⟩ **Sublime** applies distinctively to what is so elevated or exalted that the mind in contemplating or picturing it cannot reach full comprehension of it and must, in part at least, feel or imagine the vastness of its extent, power, beauty, or nobility ⟨the main force of *sublime* art was spent in the creation of *sublime* figures, the images of those enlightened ones who in the clear beam of their purified vision beheld and understood the sorrows, the struggles, the vain angers and hatreds of imperfect mortality—*Binyon*⟩ ⟨the thunderstorm when it is felt to be *sublime* has lost in part at least the terrors it possesses as a natural event—*Alexander*⟩ ⟨he ran the gamut of denunciation, rising to heights of wrath that were *sublime* and almost Godlike—*London*⟩ **Superb** describes what exceeds the merely grand, magnificent, sumptuous, or splendid and reaches the highest conceivable point of competence, brilliance, grandeur, magnificence, or splendor ⟨a *superb* wine⟩ ⟨a *superb* performance⟩ ⟨the author's style is brilliant, his command of words and images superb —*Harrison Smith*⟩ ⟨as a boat builder he was *superb* .... The boat was sculptured rather than built—*Steinbeck*⟩ ⟨*superb* figures, breathing health and strength—*Binyon*⟩ ⟨he had the *superb* vitality of early youth—*Cather*⟩
*Ana* radiant, effulgent, luminous, brilliant, *bright: illustrious, eminent (see FAMOUS): excelling *or* excellent,

*Ana* analogous words   *Ant* antonyms   *Con* contrasted words   See also explanatory notes facing page 1

surpassing, transcending *or* transcendent (see corresponding verbs at EXCEED)

**splenetic** *irascible, choleric, testy, touchy, cranky, cross
*Ana* morose, *sullen, glum, gloomy: *irritable, querulous, peevish, snappish: captious, carping, caviling (see CRITICAL)

**split** *vb* rend, cleave, rive, rip, *tear
*Ana* *separate, part, divide, sever: *cut, chop, hew

**split** *n* *breach, break, schism, rent, rupture, rift
*Ana* *crack, cleft, fissure: estrangement, alienation (see corresponding verbs at ESTRANGE): schism, heresy (see corresponding nouns at HERETIC)

**split second** *instant, moment, second, minute, flash, jiffy, twinkling

**spoil** *n* Spoil, plunder, booty, prize, loot, swag can mean something of value that is taken from another by force or craft. **Spoil** applies to the movable property of a defeated enemy, which by the custom of old-time warfare belongs to the victor and of which he strips a captured city or place ⟨fire the palace, the fort, and the keep—leave to the foeman no *spoil* at all—*Kipling*⟩ With changes in methods and customs of warfare *spoil*, and especially its plural **spoils**, tends to be applied not only to property or land taken over by conquering forces in actual warfare or demanded by them from the conquered as a condition of making peace but also to whatever by custom and often unethical custom belongs to a victor whether in warlike endeavor or more peaceful pursuits; thus, in political use *spoils* applies chiefly to appointive public offices and their emoluments which the successful party in an election regards as its peculiar property to be bestowed as its leaders wish. But *spoil* may also apply to something gained by skill or effort ⟨the *spoils* of a conservative industrial life—*Brooks*⟩ or sometimes acquired as casually as if by looting ⟨the car filled with country *spoils*⟩ ⟨brought back all sorts of frivolous *spoils* from her trip⟩ **Plunder** implies open violence (as of marauders) and is a more inclusive term than *spoil* because not restricted to warfare; it consistently implies robbery, whether as incidental to war or as dissociated from it and is applicable to what has been seized not only by spoilers, pillagers, and sackers but by such ruffians as bandits, brigands, and highwaymen ⟨often the pirates were glad to accept money instead of *plunder*, and ransom for the slaves—*Forester*⟩ ⟨a useless compiler, who fills letters and sermons with the *plunder* of the ancients and Holy Writ—*H. O. Taylor*⟩ **Booty**, like *plunder*, is applicable to martial spoils as well as to what is seized by or as if by robbery or theft ⟨birds like the berries. They gather them, fly to top branches where they can be on the lookout for danger, and eat their *booty*—*Dorrance*⟩ ⟨a cat springing on an oriole and marching proudly off with her golden *booty* projecting . . . from her mouth—*Brooks*⟩ In international law *booty* is technically used in distinction from **prize**, *booty* referring to spoils taken on land, and *prize*, to spoils captured on the high seas or in the territorial waters of the enemy ⟨finished, but never published, a Latin treatise on the right of seizing *prizes* at sea—*Barr*⟩ **Loot** may be used in place of *plunder, booty,* or *spoils* when a highly derogatory or condemnatory term is desired ⟨drawn into the conflict by a hope of sharing in the *loot* of the Church—*Belloc*⟩ ⟨they believed that the revolution which they had fought by brawling in the streets would bring them *loot* and good jobs—*Shirer*⟩ The term is also applied specifically to the plunder of those who rob the dead or helpless victims of a catastrophe or who steal anything left of value in the ruins of buildings wholly or partly destroyed (as by fire, flood, earthquake, or violent storm) ⟨prowlers among the ruins

in search of *loot*⟩ In more general use the term is applicable to gains felt as ill-gotten ⟨corrupt officials enriched by the *loot* of years⟩ **Swag** is also often used in place of *loot* or *plunder* especially to imply a collection or sackful of valuables gathered by or as if by thieves ⟨asserted that the *swag* from . . . graft was kept hidden . . . in a metal box buried in the backyard—*F. L. Allen*⟩ ⟨certain the great *swag* of doubloons was there—if he could only find it—*Dobie*⟩
*Ana* *theft, robbery, larceny, burglary: acquisitions, acquirements (see singular nouns at ACQUIREMENT)

**spoil** *vb* 1 *injure, harm, hurt, damage, impair, mar
*Ana* *ruin, wreck: *destroy, demolish
*Con* preserve, conserve, *save: amend, redress, remedy (see CORRECT *vb*)
2 *indulge, pamper, humor, baby, mollycoddle
*Ana* *injure, harm, hurt, damage: favor, accommodate, *oblige: *debase, deprave, vitiate, debauch
3 *decay, decompose, rot, putrefy, disintegrate, crumble
*Ana* corrupt, vitiate (see DEBASE): *ruin, wreck: impair, harm, *injure

**spoliate** despoil, *ravage, devastate, waste, sack, pillage
*Ana* *rob, plunder, rifle, loot: defraud, swindle, *cheat

**sponge, sponger** *parasite, sycophant, favorite, toady, lickspittle, bootlicker, hanger-on, leech

**sponsor** *n* Sponsor, patron, surety, guarantor, backer, angel are comparable when they denote a person who in a greater or less degree accepts responsibility for another person or for a particular venture or undertaking. **Sponsor** usually implies public acceptance of a responsibility and a definite engagement to perform what is promised; the word implies making a pledge in behalf of another and thereby accepting responsibility for its fulfillment; thus, the *sponsor* of an infant in baptism makes the promises in the child's name and pledges himself to be responsible for the child's religious training if the latter is deprived of his natural guardians. In a wider sense *sponsor* suggests assumption of the role of promoter or supporter and may imply acceptance of any degree of responsibility from one that is complete ⟨it is my way, when I have finished a book, to let it drop with a resigned shrug . . . . The charm it once possessed for me, its *sponsor*, has long since vanished—*Thomas Mann*⟩ to one that is indirect or remote and often purely economic ⟨the major *sponsors* of scientific research, governments and business corporations—*Flew*⟩ ⟨for every person whose passage was paid to Virginia, the *sponsor* received fifty acres of land—*Smelser & Kirwin*⟩ **Patron** stresses the acceptance of the relation as a protector or benefactor especially in return for service, honors, or devotion; it often implies the obligation to assist, support, or defend; thus, a *patron* of an artist or of a poet is a wealthy or influential person who makes him a protégé presumably in return for honors paid him; the *patron* of an institution, a cause, or a charity is one whose generous and regular contributions to its support are publicly recognized. **Surety** and **guarantor** imply answerability for another's debt or performance of duty in case of default because of prior acceptance of responsibility. **Backer**, less specific in denotation than the other terms, is used chiefly in relation to enterprises (as of sports, politics, and the theater); it often implies the giving of financial support, sometimes merely moral support or encouragement, but it carries no implication that responsibility for debts is assumed ⟨the success of a publication is the success of its editors, and not of its business managers and its *backers*—*Hendrick*⟩ **Angel** is a somewhat derogatory or contemptuous term for a financial backer, especially of a theatrical enterprise.
*Ana* supporter *or* support, upholder, champion, advoca-

tor *or* advocate (see corresponding verbs at SUPPORT): promoter, furtherer (see corresponding verbs at ADVANCE)

**spontaneity** abandon, *unconstraint
*Ana* spontaneousness, instinctiveness, impulsiveness (see corresponding adjectives at SPONTANEOUS): extemporaneousness, offhandedness, unpremeditatedness (see corresponding adjectives at EXTEMPORANEOUS): naturalness, simplicity, unsophistication, naïveté, ingenuousness (see corresponding adjectives at NATURAL)

**spontaneous** 1 Spontaneous, impulsive, instinctive, automatic, mechanical in application to persons or their movements, acts, and utterances mean acting or activated without apparent thought or deliberation. **Spontaneous** can describe whatever is not affected or effected by an external or internal compulsion of the will and comes about so naturally that it seems unpremeditated as well as unprompted ⟨a *spontaneous* burst of applause⟩ ⟨a *spontaneous* expression of feeling⟩ ⟨the *spontaneous* wish to learn, which every normal child possesses . . . should be the driving-force in education—*Russell*⟩ ⟨the witticisms are never planted: they are *spontaneous* and over in a flash, like the quick striking of a match—*Edmund Wilson*⟩ **Impulsive** applies to someone or something actuated suddenly and impetuously under the stress of the feeling or spirit of the moment and seeming to be involuntary and forced by emotion rather than voluntary and natural ⟨an *impulsive* act of generosity⟩ ⟨my heart, *impulsive* and wayward—*Longfellow*⟩ ⟨he made an *impulsive* gesture, and opened his lips; but he dared not speak—*Deland*⟩ ⟨to promote the carefree, *impulsive* purchasing of new items—*Packard*⟩ **Instinctive** implies the guiding influence of instinct and a native and unreasoned prompting to actions characteristic of the species and presumably contributing to its life and well-being; when referred to human beings, the term is applied to actions, movements, or feelings which are instantaneous, unwilled, and often unconscious (as reflex movements, habitual actions, or specific responses to stimuli) ⟨the most prolonged and difficult operations of our minds may yet become instantaneous, or, as we call it, *instinctive*—*Shaw*⟩ ⟨her attitude was not a matter of reason. It was as *instinctive* as the humping-up of a cat at a dog—*Wouk*⟩ **Automatic** and *mechanical* apply to what at least to outward appearances seems to engage neither the mind nor the emotions and to suggest the operation of a machine. But **automatic**, like *instinctive*, stresses promptness in the response. It differs from *instinctive*, however, in implying adaptability to changing circumstances and readiness to react or to respond immediately and unvaryingly each time a given situation or stimulus recurs ⟨the responses of a well-trained soldier to commands are *automatic*⟩ ⟨he pulled the hall door open, and he held it, in *automatic* and habitual caution, scarcely ajar—*Boyle*⟩ ⟨in fact, voting is so nearly *automatic* that a cynic might ask why we have election campaigns at all—*Bliven* b.1889⟩ **Mechanical**, on the other hand, stresses the lifeless and, often, the perfunctory character of the response. It does not, as *automatic* often does, suggest perfect discipline; rather, it suggests a mind dulled by repetition of the act, motion, or operation and capable only of routine performance ⟨he would deal you out facts in a dry *mechanical* way as if reading them in a book—*Hudson*⟩ ⟨engaged in futile and *mechanical* lovemaking, compulsive drinking, and considerations of suicide—*Aldridge*⟩
*Ana* *extemporaneous, extempore, impromptu, improvised, offhand, unpremeditated: *natural, simple, ingenuous, unsophisticated
2 *automatic

**spoon** *vb* ladle, dish, *dip, bail, scoop

**sporadic** occasional, rare, scarce, *infrequent, uncommon
*Ana* scattered, dispersed (see SCATTER): sparse, exiguous, *meager

**sport** *vb* *play, disport, frolic, rollick, romp, gambol
*Ana* divert, *amuse, recreate, entertain: *skip, bound, hop

**sport** *n* 1 play, disport, frolic, rollick, romp, gambol (see under PLAY *vb*)
*Ana* amusement, diversion, recreation, entertainment (see under AMUSE): merriment, jollity (see corresponding adjectives at MERRY)
2 *fun, jest, game, play
*Ana* *mirth, glee, hilarity, jollity
3 in plural form **sports** *athletics, games

**sportive** *playful, frolicsome, roguish, waggish, impish, mischievous
*Ana* blithe, *merry, jocund, jovial, jolly: mirthful, gleeful, hilarious (see corresponding nouns at MIRTH )

**spot** *n* *place, position, location, situation, site, station
*Ana* *locality, district, neighborhood, vicinity: region, *area, tract, belt, zone: section, sector (see PART)

**spot** *vb* Spot, spatter, sprinkle, mottle, fleck, stipple, marble, speckle, spangle, bespangle can mean to cover or to mark or to become covered or marked with spots or streaks. The same distinctions in implications or connotations are found in their participial adjectives (often used as simple adjectives) **spotted, spattered, sprinkled, mottled, flecked, stippled, marbled, speckled, spangled, bespangled.** Spot usually suggests either accident or a result of nature. When accident or carelessness is suggested, a staining or smirching is often connoted ⟨*spot* a dress with mud⟩ ⟨*spot* a cloth with iodine⟩ ⟨the book was *spotted* with grease⟩ ⟨*spotted* her stockings in the rain⟩ but, when the agency of art or nature is suggested, some design is usually implied that decorates, covers, or distinguishes; this use occurs mainly in the participial adjective ⟨*spotted* muslin⟩ ⟨no *spotted* pony is ever pure Shetland—*Riker*⟩ ⟨a *spotted* leopard⟩ ⟨a *spotted* orchid⟩ **Spatter** (see also SPRINKLE) essentially implies a dispersing or scattering in fragments; in general it presupposes an action (as of boiling grease, of dashing rain, or of a person washing) that causes something to fly out in drops or bits upon something or someone ⟨do not get the lard too hot, for it will *spatter* all over you⟩ ⟨spray from one of the hoses *spattered* over the longshoremen—*Pizer*⟩ ⟨his every good fortune *spattered* others with misfortune—*Malamud*⟩ ⟨do ´ye wait for the *spattered* shrapnel ere ye learn how a gun is laid?—*Kipling*⟩ **Sprinkle** (see also SPRINKLE) implies an effect of or as if of scattering a liquid in small drops; the term may emphasize the numbers or frequency of tiny spots or the thin strewing of larger ones ⟨his ill-fitting clothes were usually *sprinkled* with cigarette ashes—*Lubell*⟩ ⟨the massed rows of black skullcaps and white prayer shawls, ´sprinkled here and there with the frilly hats . . . of women—*Wouk*⟩ ⟨a heavily wooded section, *sprinkled* with small lakes—*Amer. Guide Series: Pa.*⟩ **Mottle** stresses an irregular spotting (as in streaks or blotches or patches) usually with another color; therefore what is mottled tends to present a clouded or a broken appearance or a surface covered with unevenly placed spots ⟨drifting clouds *mottled* the sea—*Michener*⟩ ⟨books bound in *mottled* calf⟩ ⟨his eyes were opaque as paving stones, and his cheeks a *mottled* gray—*Kenneth Roberts*⟩ **Fleck** may imply a spot or blemish (as of the skin); usually, however, it suggests a light spotting by specks (as of snow, of color, of light, or of clouds) ⟨overhead the still blue is scarcely *flecked* by a cloud—*Black*⟩ ⟨one hillside is *flecked* by a herd of black goats—*Edmund Wilson*⟩ ⟨immature birds . . . recognizable by their dark, *flecked* plumage—*E. A. Armstrong*⟩ **Stipple** . basically refers to a technique in engraving, painting, or drawing in which dots or short touches rather than lines are used, especially to depict masses or to indicate shadows. The term is often extended to other things that suggest this technique or its effect ⟨accidentally joggled his arm in such wise as to *stipple* ink over the coat—*Perelman*⟩ ⟨sunlight that fell through the trees and *stippled* the sidewalks—*Basso*⟩ ⟨the quail that spins out of the *stippled* corn to windy air—*Southerly*⟩ ⟨a play *stippled* alternately with tenderness and dynamite—*Nathan*⟩ **Marble** comes close to *mottle*, but it is specifically used when by intent or by nature the irregularly streaked effect of variegated marble is reproduced ⟨for the endpapers we use . . . handmade paper *marbled* by hand—*Notes on The Art of Bookbinding*⟩ ⟨well-*marbled* beef⟩ ⟨his uneven eyes, one blind, *marbled* and sunken in his skull—*Malcolm Cowley*⟩ **Speckle** suggests a covering with small and often crowded spots (as of color); the term is sometimes used with a suggestion of the cause or nature of the marks ⟨a few drops of unenthusiastic rain . . . *speckled* the shoulders of his coat —*Charteris*⟩ ⟨his arms were *speckled* from wrists to biceps with the punctures of a hypodermic needle—*Kobler*⟩ ⟨bright stars *speckled* the sky—*Mansfield*⟩ **Spangle** and **bespangle** suggest a thick strewing with tiny sparkling bits (as of shiny metal) or with something giving a similar effect ⟨an evening sheath . . . *spangled* with black sequins —*Lois Long*⟩ ⟨the *spangled* palaces of sin and fancy dancing in the false West of the movies—*Steinbeck*⟩ ⟨grass . . . all *bespangled* with dewdrops—*Cowper*⟩ ⟨a cold perspiration *bespangled* his brow—*Gilbert*⟩ **Ana** splash, bespatter, besprinkle, asperse (see SPRINKLE): *soil, sully, dirty, smirch, besmirch: variegate, checker, dapple, freak (see corresponding adjectives at VARIEGATED)

**spotted** spattered, sprinkled, mottled, flecked, stippled, marbled, speckled, spangled, bespangled (see under SPOT *vb*)

**sprain** *n* *strain

**sprain** *vb* strain (see under STRAIN *n*)

**spread** *vb* Spread, circulate, disseminate, diffuse, propagate, radiate can all mean to extend or cause to extend over an area or space. **Spread** basically implies a drawing or stretching out to the limit ⟨*spread* a net⟩ ⟨*spread* a cloth on the ground⟩ ⟨the bird *spreads* its wings⟩ ⟨*spread* a sail⟩ and in the sense here considered emphasizes distribution or dispersion (as by strewing or scattering or being strewed or scattered) over an extent of space that may be large or small or incalculable or calculable ⟨*spread* fertilizer over a field⟩ ⟨this troublesome weed has *spread* over a large section of the country⟩ Often it suggests an applying in or a taking the form of a thin layer ⟨*spread* butter on bread⟩ ⟨the paint *spreads* thinly and evenly⟩ ⟨the clouds shifted, *spread* against the sky . . . and enveloped everything below—*Styron*⟩ or a making or becoming more prevalent or more widely known or felt ⟨don't go on *spreading* that nonsense—*Rose Macaulay*⟩ ⟨the heretic should be crushed before his heresy can *spread*— *Fitzroy Maclean*⟩ ⟨news of us might *spread* far beyond that town—*Shipton*⟩ **Circulate** may imply in its primary and largely technical use a continuous or repeated movement over the same course from starting point to starting point ⟨the blood *circulates* from the heart through the arteries and veins back to the heart again⟩ ⟨steam *circulating* through a heating system⟩ In its more general applications the term tends to stress a moving about or a causing to move about freely and continuously, often to the more or less complete loss of the notion of going over the same course again and again ⟨the seats were being filled up rapidly and a pleasant noise *circulated* in the auditorium—*Joyce*⟩ ⟨the satire, *circulating* in manuscript copies, had a great local vogue—*Lucas*⟩ ⟨all of us *circulating* ominously, and incognito, throughout the city, sizing up elevator operators—*Salinger*⟩ **Disseminate** implies much the same as *spread* when that word suggests distribution here and there ⟨*disseminate* information⟩ ⟨the London ladies were indignant, and naturally they started *disseminating* a vast amount of fruity gossip about the new Lady Turton—*Dahl*⟩ ⟨in those days the Boy Scout movement was already in existence, but it had still to *disseminate* sound views about knot-tying among the rising generation—*H. G. Wells*⟩ **Diffuse** suggests a spreading throughout a space; it is applied primarily to things (as sound, light, odor, or vapor) that in moving permeate the medium through which they move and in its extended sense to things (as education, knowledge, fame, and spirit) that have or are felt to have a similar pervasive quality in their dissemination ⟨the colors of the sky are due to minute particles *diffused* through the atmosphere—*Tyndall*⟩ ⟨it would surely be hard to find any country . . . where instruction is more widely *diffused* —*Ellis*⟩ ⟨a State in which power is concentrated will . . . be more bellicose than one in which power is *diffused* —*Russell*⟩ ⟨the so-called "correct speech" is being *diffused* to the mass of the populace through migration, mass education, and . . . communication media—*Amer. Sociological Review*⟩ **Propagate** (see also GENERATE; compare *propaganda* under PUBLICITY) implies extension for the sake of increase (as of believers or members or of activity or operation) ⟨*propagate* the faith⟩ ⟨*propagate* a false rumor⟩ ⟨I am bound by my own definition of criticism: a disinterested endeavor to learn and *propagate* the best that is known and thought in the world—*Arnold*⟩ ⟨extraordinary plebeians who rise sharply . . . and so *propagate* the delusion that all other plebeians would do the same thing if they had the chance—*Mencken*⟩ **Radiate** implies a spreading from a center outward in or as if in rays; in general use it is often applied to the spreading of something material or immaterial from a fixed center ⟨soulsearching Freedom! here assume thy stand, and *radiate* hence to every distant land—*Barlow*⟩ ⟨her face . . . was still pretty, even with the web of little wrinkles that *radiated* from the corners of her eyes—*Basso*⟩ ⟨a superb self-confidence *radiated* from him, as it does from any healthy animal—*Gibbons*⟩ but in its common technical use the term is largely restricted in reference to diffusion in the form of rays (as of heat or light) ⟨the sun *radiates* both light and heat⟩

**Ana** *distribute, dispense, deal: *scatter, dissipate

**spread** *n* *expanse, amplitude, stretch

**Ana** extent, area, magnitude, *size: *range, reach, scope, compass

**sprightly** *lively, animated, vivacious, gay

**Ana** *active, live, dynamic: *agile, nimble, brisk, spry: *merry, blithe, jocund

**spring** *vb* 1 Spring, arise, rise, originate, derive, flow, issue, emanate, proceed, stem can mean to come up or out of something into existence. **Spring** stresses sudden or surprising emergence especially after a period of concealment or hidden existence or preparation ⟨plants *spring* from seed⟩ ⟨thoughts that *sprang* up in his mind⟩ ⟨he had not chosen his course. It had *sprung* from a necessity of his nature—*Brooks*⟩ ⟨freedom of the mind, the basic freedom from which all other freedoms *spring*—*Davis*⟩ **Arise** emphasizes the fact of coming into existence or into notice more than the conditions attending the event; often it conveys no clear suggestion of a prior state ⟨a rumor *arose* and was widely circulated⟩ ⟨after Alfred no rival native

A colon (:) separates groups of words discriminated. An asterisk (*) indicates place of treatment of each group.

house *arose* to dispute the throne with Alfred's heirs—*Malone*⟩ When used with *from*, however, it usually implies a causal connection between what is the object of the preposition and what is the subject of the verb; in such cases it is synonymous with *result*, though it neither loses nor obscures its primary implication of coming into existence ⟨mistakes often *arise* from ignorance⟩ ⟨the mischief *arose* from careless gossip⟩ ⟨the depression, the shock *arising* from what had happened abovestairs, left him almost at once—*Bromfield*⟩ Sometimes, when the context suggests a cause, the *from* phrase is omitted ⟨where there is continued discontent, trouble is certain to *arise*⟩ ⟨the right never existed, and the question whether it has been surrendered cannot *arise*—*John Marshall*⟩ Rise and *arise* (see also under RISE 2) are often used interchangeably, but usage usually favors *arise* except where, in addition to the implication of beginning, there is either in the word or the context a strong suggestion of ascent ⟨new nations *rise* only to fall⟩ ⟨mighty forces *rise* from small beginnings⟩ ⟨the Gothic cathedrals *rose* in England in the first half of the thirteenth century —*Saunders*⟩ ⟨great regimes *rose*, based upon the irrational and negative in man's nature—*Straight*⟩ Originate suggests a definite source or starting point which may be specified or located ⟨the theory of evolution did not *originate* with Darwin⟩ ⟨the fire *originated* in the basement⟩ ⟨the newsreel, *originated* . . . in France, was introduced in the United States in 1910—*Mott*⟩ ⟨its founding *originated* in the Puritans' conviction that learning was essential for godliness—*Murdock*⟩ Derive also suggests a source; usually it does not imply, as *originate* implies, actual inception but presupposes a prior existence in another form or in another person or thing and connotes descent (as by inheritance, endowment, transference, or deduction) ⟨the power of the executive *derives* from the people⟩ ⟨our thoughts often *derive* from our wishes⟩ ⟨the principle of symmetry *derives*, I suppose, from contemplation of the human form—*Binyon*⟩ ⟨much of our thinking about the rights and duties of the citizen *derives* directly from Greco-Roman thought—*Highet*⟩ Flow, issue, emanate in common imply a passing from one thing to another, the former being the source from which the latter is derived. All of these words are colored by their basic meanings. Flow suggests passage like water, easily as if from a spring or abundantly as if from a reservoir ⟨praise God, from whom all blessings *flow*—*Ken*⟩ ⟨the oleaginous sentences *flowed* easily from her pen—*Gibbons*⟩ Issue most frequently suggests emergence into existence, as if from a womb ⟨how far Arnold is responsible for the birth of Humanism would be difficult to say; we can at least say that it *issues* very naturally from his doctrine—*T. S. Eliot*⟩ ⟨if the naturalist's logic rests on wind, and *issues* in echoing phrases devoid of substance—*Sullivan*⟩ Emanate is used largely in reference to immaterial constructions (as a law, a principle, a power, or a system of thought); it connotes the passage of something impalpable or invisible and suggests a less obvious causal connection between the source and the thing derived than *flow* or *issue* ⟨but the house . . . was Carrie's and it was from her that *emanated* the atmosphere of a home—*Purdy*⟩ ⟨the government of the Union . . . is, emphatically, and truly, a government of the people. In form and in substance it *emanates* from them—*John Marshall*⟩ Proceed stresses place of origin or, sometimes, parentage, derivation, or cause ⟨no public benefit which you receive but it *proceeds* or comes from them to you and no way from yourselves—*Shak.*⟩ ⟨assuring her that his seeming inattention had only *proceeded* from his being involved in a profound meditation—*Peacock*⟩ Stem suggests a growing out (as of a

stem from a root or of a branch from a trunk) and is used chiefly in reference to things that come into existence through the influence of a predecessor either as a natural outgrowth or as a subordinate development ⟨the good portrait painters . . . *stem* from Rubens—*Mather*⟩ ⟨it spread to the lower officers and the troops in the field—or perhaps it *stemmed* from them—*Shirer*⟩
*Ana* emerge, loom, *appear: *come, arrive: *begin, commence, start
2 *jump, leap, bound, vault
*Ana* frolic, rollick, gambol, disport (see PLAY)
**spring** *n* 1 *motive, impulse, incentive, inducement, spur, goad
*Ana* *origin, source, root; inception: *cause, determinant, antecedent: *stimulus, stimulant, excitant, incitement, impetus
2 jump, leap, bound, vault (see under JUMP *vb*)
**springy** *elastic, resilient, flexible, supple
*Ana* yielding, submitting (see YIELD): recoiling, rebounding (see REBOUND)
**sprinkle** *vb* *spot, spatter, mottle, fleck, stipple, marble, speckle, spangle, bespangle
**sprinkled** spotted, spattered, mottled, flecked, stippled, marbled, speckled, spangled, bespangled (see under SPOT *vb*)
**sprint** *vb* *scuttle, scurry, scamper, skedaddle
*Ana* *rush, dash, charge, shoot, tear: *speed, hurry, hasten: dart, *fly, scud
**spry** *agile, brisk, nimble
*Ana* *quick, ready, prompt: *vigorous, energetic, strenuous: hale, *healthy, sound, robust
*Ant* doddering
**spume** *foam, froth, scum, lather, suds, yeast
**spunky** *spirited, high-spirited, mettlesome, fiery, peppery, gingery
*Ana* dauntless, undaunted, bold (see BRAVE): daring, venturesome (see ADVENTUROUS): restive, restless, *impatient
**spur** *n* goad, spring, *motive, impulse, incentive, inducement
*Ana* *stimulus, stimulant, excitant, incitement, impetus: activation, actuation, motivation (see corresponding verbs at ACTIVATE): *cause, determinant: provoking *or* provocation, exciting *or* excitement (see corresponding verbs at PROVOKE)
**spur** *vb* *urge, egg, exhort, goad, prod, prick, sic
*Ana* rouse, arouse, *stir, awaken, rally: *incite, instigate: excite, *provoke, stimulate: encourage, countenance, *favor
*Ant* curb —*Con* *restrain, inhibit, check
**spurious** *counterfeit, bogus, fake, sham, pseudo, pinchbeck, phony
*Ana* *false: simulated, feigned, shammed (see ASSUME): supposititious, reputed, putative (see SUPPOSED)
*Ant* genuine —*Con* *authentic, veritable, bona fide: true, *real, actual
**spurn** reject, repudiate, refuse, *decline
*Ana* disdain, scorn, scout, *despise, contemn: flout, *scoff, sneer
*Ant* crave: embrace
**squabble** *n* *quarrel, wrangle, altercation, bickering, spat, tiff
*Ana* dispute, controversy, *argument: row, rumpus, scrap, *brawl, broil
**squabble** *vb* quarrel, wrangle, altercate, bicker, spat, tiff (see under QUARREL *n*)
*Ana* *contend, fight, battle, war: struggle, strive (see ATTEMPT *vb*): dispute, agitate, argue (see DISCUSS)
**squalid** *dirty, nasty, filthy, foul

---

*Ana* analogous words    *Ant* antonyms    *Con* contrasted words    See also explanatory notes facing page 1

*Ana* slovenly, unkempt, disheveled, sloppy, *slipshod: sordid, abject (see MEAN *adj*): *slatternly, frowzy

**squander** *vb* *waste, dissipate, fritter, consume
*Ana* *scatter, disperse, dissipate, dispel: *spend, expend, disburse

**square** *vb* *agree, conform, accord, harmonize, correspond, tally, jibe
*Ana* equal, *match, approach, touch, rival: balance, offset (see COMPENSATE): concur, coincide (see AGREE)

**squash** *vb* *crush, mash, smash, bruise, macerate
*Ana* *press, squeeze, jam, crowd: *compact, concentrate, consolidate

**squat** *adj* *stocky, thickset, thick, chunky, stubby, dumpy
*Ant* lanky

**squeal** *vb* *shout, yell, shriek, scream, screech, holler, whoop
*Ana* *cry, wail

**squeal** *n* shout, yell, shriek, scream, screech, holler, whoop (see under SHOUT *vb*)

**squeamish** finicky, finicking, finical, particular, fussy, persnickety, pernickety, fastidious, *nice, dainty
*Ana* exacting, demanding, requiring (see DEMAND): hypercritical, *critical, faultfinding, caviling, captious, carping

**squeeze** *vb* *press, bear, bear down, crowd, jam
*Ana* compress, *contract: extract, elicit, *educe, extort: *force, compel, constrain, coerce

**squib** *libel, skit, lampoon, pasquinade

**squirm** *writhe, agonize
*Ana* twist, bend (see CURVE *vb*): wince, flinch, blench, shrink, *recoil

**stabilize, steady, poise, balance, ballast, trim** are comparable when they mean to maintain or cause to maintain position or equilibrium. Despite their agreement in basic meaning they vary widely in their implications and in their range of application and are seldom interchangeable. **Stabilize** is used chiefly in reference to something which is fluctuating or is subject to fluctuation and which requires either external aids or regulation ⟨Greece was an infant state, without *stabilizing* traditions or profound culture—*Durant*⟩ ⟨serve the whole nation by policies designed to *stabilize* the economy—*Eisenhower*⟩ ⟨the tendency of science is necessarily to *stabilize* terms, to freeze them into strict denotations—*Cleanth Brooks*⟩ ⟨a gyroscope for *stabilizing* an airplane⟩ **Steady** is used chiefly in reference to something which is losing its customary or necessary stability or equilibrium and is demonstrating instability (as by rocking, shaking, fluttering, or tipping) ⟨*steady* a table by putting a piece of wood under one of its legs⟩ ⟨medics *steadied* trays of instruments against bomb concussions—*Alcine*⟩ ⟨drew a deep breath and *steadied* himself with an effort of will—*Huxley*⟩ **Poise** is used chiefly in reference to something that maintains its equilibrium perfectly under adverse conditions or in opposition to external forces (as gravity); it implies a proper distribution of weight with reference to the supporting medium (as air or water) or to the part (as a base, a foot, the hand, or a column) that bears the weight ⟨the ballet dancer *poised* on tiptoe for an instant⟩ ⟨Mrs. Buffo, *poised* on her rampart . . . took the full impact of the onslaught—*Pynchon*⟩ In extended use, when employed in reference to the mind or spirit, *poise* implies either acquired control over the faculties or an inner serenity that enables one to remain steady or impervious to disquieting or disturbing influences ⟨he owed his reputation . . . to this particular trait, the ability to *poise* himself, invulnerable to surprise—*Theodore Sturgeon*⟩ ⟨self-collected, *poised*, and steady—*Wordsworth*⟩ **Balance** also implies an equilibrium that is the result of the proper distribution of weight, but it carries none of the suggestions of sustained position or equilibrium so strong in *poise;* thus, one *balances* a boat by adjusting its cargo so that there is no excess weight at any one point, and one *balances* a flywheel by removing portions where the weight is excessive or by adding weight in its lighter sections, but in either case the equilibrium may be lost if the cargo shifts or a section of the flywheel alters in weight. Though both *balance* and *poise* imply that the thing affected is steadied, *balance* often carries so strong an implication of uncertain equilibrium that it suggests wavering or rocking ⟨in a moment of inattention, the child crept to the edge, and was *balanced* on the very verge. To call to it, to touch it, would have insured its destruction—*Jefferies*⟩ ⟨the musicians struggled toward the raft in hip-deep water, *balancing* themselves with outthrust trombones and cornets—*Styron*⟩ ⟨caution warned her not . . . to disturb her equilibrium; her present peace of mind was too precious—and too precariously *balanced*—*Hervey*⟩ **Ballast** is used in reference to what needs to be held down because too light or too buoyant; it implies the addition of something heavy or solid enough to ensure stability ⟨*ballast* a ship with stone or metal⟩ ⟨*ballast* a free balloon with bags of sand⟩ *Ballast* is occasionally found in extended use with reference especially to the mind and the moral character that might otherwise suffer from volatility, frivolousness, or unwieldiness ⟨'tis charity must *ballast* the heart—*Hammond*⟩ ⟨like many other men of high intellectual gifts, Arnold was *ballasted* with a just proportion of . . . practical wisdom—*Montague*⟩ **Trim** is chiefly nautical; it implies proper balancing of a boat or ship so that it sits well on the water or fulfills any of the conditions that make for steadiness in sailing ⟨they could be *trimmed* on an even keel . . . like scales, in which the weight on one side must be counterpoised by a weight in the other—*Jefferies*⟩
*Ana* regulate, *adjust, fix: *set, settle, establish

**stable** *adj* *lasting, durable, perdurable, permanent, perpetual
*Ana* enduring, persisting, abiding (see CONTINUE): secure, *safe: *steady, constant: staunch, steadfast, resolute (see FAITHFUL)
*Ant* unstable: changeable

**stack** *n* heap, pile, mass, bank, shock, cock (see under HEAP *vb*)

**stack** *vb* *heap, pile, mass, bank, shock, cock
*Ana* collect, *gather, assemble: amass, *accumulate, hoard

**stagger** *vb* *reel, whirl, totter
*Ana* sway, waver, fluctuate (see SWING): *stumble, lurch, blunder, flounder

**staid** sedate, grave, *serious, somber, sober, earnest
*Ana* *decorous, decent, seemly: *cool, collected, composed: smug, priggish, self-complacent, *complacent
*Ant* jaunty

**stain** *n* *stigma, blot, brand
*Ana* *blemish, defect, flaw: mark, *sign, token: *disgrace, dishonor

**stake** *bet, wager, pot, ante

**stalemate** *n* *draw, tie, deadlock, standoff

**stalwart** *strong, stout, sturdy, tough, tenacious
*Ana* husky, brawny, *muscular, sinewy, athletic: lusty, nervous, *vigorous: robust, sound, *healthy

**stammer** *vb* **Stammer, stutter** both mean to speak in a faltering, hesitating, or stumbling manner. **Stammer** usually implies a proximate cause (as fear, embarrassment, or a sudden shock) which deprives one for the time being of control over his vocal organs and inhibits his power to speak straightforwardly; the word can suggest a blocking in which one either cannot form sounds or a slow confused articulation or an involuntary repetition of sounds or words ⟨the eloquent tongue forgot its office. Cicero *stammered*, blundered, and sat down—*Froude*⟩ ⟨"Why— why—" *stammered* the youth struggling with his balking tongue—*Crane*⟩ **Stutter** usually stresses the involuntary repetition of sounds, especially of consonantal or syllabic sounds. It is less likely than *stammer* to imply a proximate cause and typically, especially in medical use, implies a constitutional defect (as a nervous affliction or a speech defect) which results in a habitual and persistent speech problem ⟨no two persons *stutter* alike . . . a stutterer who stumbles over the initial of "Peter" may have no trouble with any other *p* in . . . "Peter Piper's peppers"—*Scripture*⟩ ⟨this gentleman has . . . a small natural infirmity; he *stutters* a little—*Foote*⟩ In nontechnical use the terms are often used interchangeably especially in their extended senses, in which both terms are freely employed either in reference to a fluctuating repetitive sound or to something that halts or progresses by fits and starts like the speech of a stammerer or stutterer ⟨climbed into his Ford and *stuttered* down the hill—*Steinbeck*⟩ ⟨her pen sometimes *stammers* with the intensity of the emotion that she controlled—*Woolf*⟩ ⟨a brilliant idea stands still and *stuttering*—*Pritchett*⟩

**stamp** *vb* *mark, brand, label, tag, ticket
*Ana* impress, imprint, print (see corresponding nouns at IMPRESSION): authenticate, validate (see CONFIRM): avouch, warrant (see ASSERT)

**stamp** *n* 1 *impression, impress, imprint, print
2 mark, brand, label, tag, ticket (see under MARK *vb*)
**stand** *vb* tolerate, brook, *bear, suffer, endure, abide
**stand** *n* *position, attitude
*Ana* *point of view, standpoint, viewpoint, slant, angle
**standard** *n* 1 *flag, ensign, banner, color, streamer, pennant, pendant, pennon, jack
2 Standard, criterion, gauge, yardstick, touchstone can all mean a measure by which one judges a thing as authentic, good, or adequate or the degree to which it is authentic, good, or adequate. **Standard** applies to an authoritative rule, principle, or measure used to determine the quantity, weight, or extent or especially the value, quality, level, or degree of a thing ⟨each generation . . . has its own ideals and its own *standards* of judgment—*Crothers*⟩ ⟨the ideal of general cultivation has been one of the *standards* in education—*Eliot*⟩ ⟨the building . . . by all the *standards* of St. Botolph's . . . would be condemned as expensive, pretentious, noisy and unsafe—*Cheever*⟩ **Criterion** denotes the thing, whether formulated into a rule or principle or not, by appeal to which one arrives at or confirms a given judgment (as of value, quality, fitness, or correctness) ⟨the sole *criterion* of the truth of illusion is its inner congruity—*Lowes*⟩ ⟨the size of sunspots is a meaningless *criterion* in predicting the havoc which may occur to radio transmission—*Dawes*⟩ ⟨no exact *criterion* for a just and fruitful apportionment of the surplus wealth—*Hobson*⟩ ⟨these laws . . . did establish useful *criteria* of conduct—*Handlin*⟩ **Gauge**, concretely a standard measure or scale or an instrument for measuring something that fluctuates (as in size or height), can in extension apply to a standard measure whether tangible or not ⟨a piece of 1/8 inch thickness fiber or wood makes a convenient *gauge* in setting brush holders—*Mill & Factory*⟩ ⟨the inarticulate, whose ferocity was a *gauge* of the injustices they had suffered—*Bruce Marshall*⟩ ⟨the degree of public acceptance of the opinions of leaders is the ultimate *gauge* of the importance and validity of those opinions—*Rafferty*⟩ **Yardstick**, basically a measuring stick a yard long and subdivided into inches and fractions of inches, is often extended to standards

or criteria especially for something intangible or immaterial ⟨no absolute or universal *yardstick* about what constitutes a frustration—*Kardiner*⟩ ⟨the consumption of petroleum products, an accurate *yardstick* of economic growth— *The Lamp*⟩ **Touchstone** can apply to a simple device by which authenticity or value may be determined and especially to an authentic or superior instance of a class of things by comparison with which another thing may be judged authentic or superior ⟨consistency is a *touchstone* by which the basic doctrine can often be distinguished from the propaganda line—*L. C. Stevens*⟩ ⟨a Marxist critic using economic determinants, social perspectives, and class consciousness as his *touchstones*—*Glicksberg*⟩ ⟨the chief *touchstone* to folklore is the manner in which it is transmitted: one man tells another, one man shows another—*Emrich*⟩
*Ana* norm, median, par, mean, *average: rule, *law: *principle, fundamental, axiom: *model, pattern, exemplar
3 ideal, beau ideal, *model, pattern, exemplar, example, mirror
*Ana* see those at STANDARD 2

**stand-in** *substitute, supply, understudy, double, locum tenens, alternate, pinch hitter

**standoff** *n* *draw, tie, stalemate, deadlock

**standpoint** *point of view, viewpoint, angle, slant
*Ana* stand, *position, attitude

**stanza** *verse

**stare** *vb* *gaze, gape, glare, peer, gloat
*Ana* look, watch, *see: glower, lower, scowl, *frown

**stark** *stiff, rigid, inflexible, tense, wooden
*Ana* settled, established, fixed, set (see SET *vb*)
*Con* *elastic, resilient, springy, flexible, supple: fluid, *liquid

**starry**, **stellar, astral, sidereal** can mean of, referring to, or suggestive of a star or group of stars. **Starry** is the ordinary nontechnical term, capable of being used in reference to stars of various kinds (as the celestial bodies known as stars or the geometrical figure with five, six, or more points that is the conventionalized star) ⟨a *starry* night⟩ ⟨a *starry* banner⟩ ⟨*starry* eyes⟩ ⟨here are the skies, the planets seven, and all the *starry* train— *Housman*⟩ ⟨*starry* towers of Babylon Noah's freshet never reached—*Yeats*⟩ **Stellar** has the same range of reference as *starry*, but, since the connotations of the words are not the same, they are rarely interchangeable; *starry* gathers its connotations (as of brilliancy, remoteness, and beauty) chiefly from the appearance of the celestial stars to the ordinary observer; *stellar* derives its suggestions chiefly from astrological lore of the stars as influencing all things and as shaping human destinies or from astronomical knowledge of the constitution, arrangement, and classification of stars; thus, one tends to speak of a *stellar*, rather than a *starry*, influence or aspect; of a *stellar*, rather than *starry*, eclipse or nebula ⟨these soft fires . . . shed down their *stellar* virtue on all kinds that grow on Earth—*Milton*⟩ ⟨Kapteyn worked nearly alone in the field of *stellar* astronomy—*G. W. Gray*⟩ *Stellar* is also used more often than *starry* of theatrical or cinematic stars ⟨*stellar* roles in operas and musical festivals—*Current Biog.*⟩ and it alone is freely used to imply outstanding quality or position in other relations ⟨a dependable working staff, and a *stellar* panel of consultants—*Hartwell*⟩ ⟨he just wasn't a *stellar* naval officer in the eyes of his subordinates—*Lois & Don Thorburn*⟩ **Astral** is in much of its use a technical term in theosophy and similar cults, and in more general use it is likely to bear connotations of spirituality, mysticism, and remoteness from the fleshly that derive largely from mythological

---

*Ana* analogous words    *Ant* antonyms    *Con* contrasted words    See also explanatory notes facing page 1

and other conceptions of the stars as the abode of celestial spirits or of supersensible beings whose nature and constitution are rarer and finer than those of earthly human beings ⟨enchantments that unlock a crystal cage; an alphabet with *astral* fire seasoned—*Wylie*⟩ ⟨an *astral* thinker with disturbing, visionary thoughts of helping the whole world—*Newsweek*⟩ ⟨an *astral* myth⟩ ⟨a state of mind which may resemble that of a soul in its *astral* body looking back upon its corporeal one—*Beebe*⟩ **Sidereal** is sometimes interchangeable with the other terms ⟨walls of interlocked magnolias, *sidereal* with white, fragrant blossoms—*Nat'l Geog. Mag.*⟩ ⟨I felt that he was an Intelligence which had borrowed form and substance in deference to the requirements of *sidereal* politeness— *Henry Miller*⟩ but distinctively it is used in opposition to *solar*, especially as applied to periods of time measured by the rotation of the earth with reference to a given star; thus, the *sidereal* day, determined by reference to Aries, is 3 minutes and 55.91 seconds shorter, as measured in solar time, than the mean solar day.

**start** *vb* *begin, commence, initiate, inaugurate
*Ana* institute, *found, establish, organize: *enter, penetrate: originate, proceed, *spring

**startle** scare, alarm, terrify, terrorize, *frighten, fright, affray, affright
*Ana* *surprise, astonish, astound: rouse, arouse, *stir: electrify, *thrill

**state** *n* State, condition, mode, situation, posture, status can all mean the way in which a person or thing manifests his or its existence or the circumstances under which he or it exists or by which he or it is given a definite character. **State** may be used so generally that it denotes merely a form of existence which has little or no relation to material being (as in space or time or as substance) but is purely immaterial and typically mental or spiritual ⟨[Dante's *Inferno*] reminds us that Hell is not a place but a *state*— *T. S. Eliot*⟩ The term may also be used specifically to name the combination of circumstances affecting a person or thing at a given time or the sum of the relations, qualities, or characteristics involved in his or its existence at the time under consideration ⟨live fifty years happily in the *state* of matrimony⟩ ⟨the present *state* of industry⟩ ⟨the historian . . . visited Alexandria during the reign of this king. He was disgusted with its *state*—*Farrington*⟩ ⟨parents have probably gone too far in one direction and nature's reacting, trying to get back to the *state* of equilibrium—*Huxley*⟩ **Condition** is interchangeable with *state* only when the effect or influence of present circumstances on actual or concrete existence is implied ⟨the present *condition* of the country⟩ ⟨it is a *condition* which confronts us, not a theory—*Cleveland*⟩ It regularly carries a stronger implication than *state* of a relation to the causes or circumstances which produced or are producing the effect and a weaker suggestion of the duration of that effect; also, *condition* may be used in the plural in the sense of combination of circumstances and of qualities or characteristics, as *state* may not ⟨his physical *condition* improved with rest and sufficient exercise⟩ ⟨under the best *conditions*, a voyage is one of the severest tests to try a man—*Emerson*⟩ ⟨I probably had been hoping . . . the book would not change my life too much. I wished at that time to protect a modest *condition*—*Mailer*⟩ ⟨there is no possible method of compelling a child to feel sympathy or affection; the only possible method is to observe the *conditions* under which these feelings arise spontaneously, and then endeavor to produce the *conditions*—*Russell*⟩ This suggestion of a relation to an external cause or causes is often so strong that the word frequently denotes a circumstance that serves as a causative influence or prerequisite rather than a combination of circumstances that form a state of being (see under CONDITION 1) **Mode** (see also METHOD; FASHION 2) is basically a philosophical term; typically it implies an opposition to the underlying reality which can be known only from its external manifestations (as color, form, and texture), and it usually applies to the combination of characters by which substance is manifested in a particular individual or instance ⟨no *mode* . . . can exist except as the *mode* or modification of a substance; the substance is the abiding principle, the *mode* is transitory. The particular *mode* . . . is but a temporal expression of the substance—*Thilly*⟩ ⟨nearly all [painters] use color as a *mode* of form. They design in color, that is in colored shapes—*Clive Bell*⟩ In somewhat less restricted use the term can apply to something that expresses or exemplifies a typical form or value of a larger class; thus, the mathematical *mode* is the most frequent value in a statistical array; the *mode* of a rock is its specific mineral composition as distinguished from the norm of its kind ⟨Rouse's *mode* unit is the smallest isolated item pertaining to a prehistoric manufacture . . . . This *mode*, or attribute, is a concept many archeologists work with in pottery classification—*Willey*⟩ **Situation** applies to a state or condition that represents a combination of definite concrete circumstances, often such a conjunction of particular circumstances that the whole has a peculiarly interesting character; more than *state* or *condition*, *situation* implies an arrangement of these circumstances not only with reference to each other but also with respect to the character or circumstances of the persons involved so as to make for a particular resulting condition (as of difficulty or advantage, embarrassment or elation, or uncertainty or security) ⟨such views of life were to some extent the natural begettings of her *situation* upon her nature—*Hardy*⟩ ⟨there was a dizzy succession of events and of constantly changing *situations* for a politician to watch—*Shirer*⟩ ⟨that slender, unrigid erectness, and the fine carriage of head, which always made him seem master of the *situation*—*Cather*⟩ The term is also applied to a comparably striking and interesting combination of events in a narrative, especially one whose outcome involves uncertainty or suspense ⟨one knows the *situation* in fiction—the desperate girl appealing out of her misery to the Christian priest for help. So many women have this touch of melodrama, this sense of a *situation*—*Rose Macaulay*⟩ ⟨a master of plot and *situation*, of those elements of drama which are most essential to melodrama —*T. S. Eliot*⟩ **Posture** (see also POSTURE 1) may be used in the sense of *condition* when that represents a state into which one is forced by need of preparation for something to come ⟨put a warship in a *posture* of defense⟩ ⟨[Christ] insisted upon a certain . . . *posture* of the soul as proper to man's reception of this revelation—*Liddon*⟩ ⟨Spanish chants have no solemnity: . . . which doesn't preclude a general devout *posture* of mind—*Santayana*⟩ The term is often a closer synonym of *situation* than of *condition* ⟨a virgin of thirty-two, already lapsing, though naturally attractive and sprightly, into the mental *posture* of old maidhood—*Follett*⟩ ⟨production which will permit us to maintain both a strong economy and a strong military *posture*—*Truman*⟩ **Status** may indicate an individual's state or condition as determined with some definiteness for legal administrative purposes or by social or economic considerations ⟨the change in the *status* of the Negro, under the Thirteenth Amendment, from three fifths of a person to a whole person in computing state apportionment —*C. L. Thompson*⟩ ⟨a married woman's *status* was determined entirely by that of her husband—*Ogg & Ray*⟩

---

A colon (:) separates groups of words discriminated. An asterisk (*) indicates place of treatment of each group.

⟨the job which a person is supposed to do . . . is what Linton and others call his role. The position which he occupies on the social ladder, as a result of his general practice of leading or following, supervising or being supervised, in the totality of his activities, is his *status—Coon*⟩ ⟨the social sciences have been, since their institution, jealous of their *status* as science—*R. M. Weaver*⟩ ⟨the city's *status* as a tourist attraction—*Sargeant*⟩ Sometimes the term specifically denotes a superior state or condition and then implies elevated rank in a hierarchy ⟨make him feel a man of *status* in the community—*Beaglehole*⟩ ⟨the *status* seekers . . . continually straining to surround themselves with visible evidence of the superior rank they are claiming—*Packard*⟩ ⟨because she could not accept less than twenty pounds a week without loss of *status* and got it but rarely, she was doomed to remain an amateur—*Yeats*⟩ Even in uses in which it comes close to the specific aspect of *state* or the corresponding aspect of *condition, status* tends to retain some suggestion of a hierarchical relation and correspondingly, of comparison; thus, one might comment "his mental *state*, or *condition*, is a cause for concern" as a simple declaration, but "his mental *status* is unsatisfactory" implies comparison ⟨established the bank's *status* as an independent international organization—*Collier's Yr. Bk.*⟩ ⟨Keynes regards the rate of interest and the marginal efficiency of capital as possessing something like the *status* of independent variables—*Feuer*⟩ ⟨a quiet German-American farming community, a *status* it managed to maintain for nearly two decades —*Amer. Guide Series: Mich.*⟩
*Ana* *phase, aspect: plight, *predicament, quandary, dilemma: pass, *juncture, exigency, emergency, crisis

**state** *vb* 1 *say, utter, tell
2 report, *relate, rehearse, recite, recount, narrate, describe
*Ana* expound, *explain, elucidate, interpret: *assert, affirm, declare, profess

**stately** magnificent, imposing, majestic, august, *grand, noble, grandiose
*Ana* princely, regal, royal, *kingly, imperial: *splendid, glorious, superb, sublime: sumptuous, opulent, *luxurious

**statesman** *politician, politico

**station** *n* 1 *place, position, location, situation, site, spot
*Ana* *locality, district, vicinity, neighborhood: region, *area, zone, belt, tract
2 *habitat, biotype, range

**statue** *image, effigy, icon, portrait, photograph, mask

**stature** *quality, caliber
*Ana* capacity, *ability: competence, qualification (see corresponding adjectives at ABLE)

**status** situation, posture, condition, *state, mode

**statute** 1 ordinance, regulation, *law, rule, precept, canon
2 *bill, act, law

**staunch** *faithful, loyal, true, constant, steadfast, resolute
*Ana* trusty, trustworthy, *reliable, dependable, tried: stout, *strong, tough, tenacious, sturdy, stalwart
*Con* *inconstant, fickle, mercurial, unstable, capricious

**stay** *vb* 1 Stay, remain, wait, abide, tarry, linger can mean to continue to be in one place for a noticeable time. Stay, the most general of these terms, stresses continuance in a place or sometimes in a specified condition; it often specifically connotes the status of visitor or guest ⟨they could not decide whether to *stay* or to go⟩ ⟨they went for tea and *stayed* for dinner⟩ ⟨*staying* a while at the Joneses, he could quietly insinuate . . . hilarious things about the Joneses when he weekended with the Browns—*Theodore*

*Sturgeon*⟩ Remain is often used interchangeably with *stay* but distinctively means to stay behind or to be left after others have gone ⟨few *remained* in the building after the alarm was given⟩ ⟨a little verse my all that shall *remain—Gray*⟩ ⟨she remembered her decision to send the young people of the village into the woods. There would have been many more casualties had they *remained* —*Linklater*⟩ Wait implies a staying in expectation or in readiness ⟨at his request no one *waited* for him at the pier⟩ ⟨the taxi *waited* while they were shopping⟩ ⟨the lights in the window had a leering, *waiting* look, like that on the faces of old pimps who sit in the cafés—*Gibbons*⟩ Abide implies prolonged staying or remaining after at length and usually connotes either stable residence or patient waiting for an outcome ⟨she hated the change; she felt like one banished; but here she was forced to *abide—Hardy*⟩ Tarry implies staying when it is time to depart or to proceed ⟨do not *tarry* if you wish to catch the noon train⟩ ⟨some children like to *tarry* on the way to school⟩ ⟨the celebrated trade winds . . . ceased to blow, and over the island a horrid stillness *tarried—Stafford*⟩ Linger, like *tarry*, usually implies outstaying one's appointed or allotted time; frequently, however, it also implies either deliberate delay or disinclination to depart ⟨strange, that now she was released she should *linger* by him—*Meredith*⟩ ⟨she shouldn't have come to the hotel suite. She shouldn't have *lingered*—this was fatal—after the others had left—*Wouk*⟩ ⟨after the guests had *tarried* long over their tea and had done with their jokes, the woman still *lingered—Buck*⟩
*Ana* *delay, procrastinate, lag, loiter: *arrest, check, interrupt: *continue, persist
2 sojourn, lodge, put up, stop, *reside, live, dwell
3 *defer, postpone, suspend, intermit
*Ana* *delay, retard, slow, slacken, detain: *restrain, check, curb: *hinder, obstruct, impede

**stay** *vb* *base, found, ground, bottom, rest

**steadfast** staunch, resolute, constant, true, *faithful, loyal
*Ana* settled, established, set, fixed (see SET *vb*): *steady, constant: stable, durable, perdurable, *lasting: enduring, persisting, abiding (see CONTINUE)
*Ant* capricious

**steady** *adj* Steady, uniform, even, equable, constant are comparable when they mean neither markedly varying nor variable but much the same throughout its course or extent. Steady is the most widely applicable of these terms; in general it suggests regularity and lack of deviation, especially in movement, but it may imply such fixity in position as to be immovable or unshakable ⟨*steady* as a rock⟩ ⟨a *steady* pole⟩ or such consistency in character or conduct as to be perfectly reliable ⟨a *steady* workman⟩ ⟨maybe she'd marry the first nice and good *steady* fellow with a steady job who'd be a *steady* provider—*Farrell*⟩ When movement, motion, or direction is implied, the term may connote lack of fluctuation ⟨a *steady* market⟩ ⟨*steady* prices⟩ ⟨a *steady* flame⟩ ⟨you can't make millions on books, but it's a *steady* respectable business—*Buck*⟩ or lack of nervousness ⟨with hinged knees and *steady* hand to dress wounds—*Whitman*⟩ ⟨a *steady* voice⟩ or a constant uninterrupted flow or pursuit ⟨a *steady* stream⟩ ⟨a *steady* rain⟩ ⟨*steady* work⟩ Uniform stresses the sameness or alikeness of the elements, parts, units, or instances that comprise a whole (as an aggregate, a series, a combination of instances, a course, or a texture) ⟨the cells of the human organism are not *uniform* in structure and function⟩ ⟨the progress of civilization is not wholly a *uniform* drift towards better things—*Whitehead*⟩ ⟨one of the most fundamental social interests is that law shall be *uniform* and impartial—*Cardozo*⟩ ⟨the

various tackle blocks and planks of the wooden ships were cut to *uniform* measure—*Mumford*⟩ **Even** stresses steadiness more than uniformity; it often connotes a dead level (as in quality or in character) which is unvaryingly maintained or which is incapable of alteration or disturbance ⟨her monotonous *even* voice⟩ ⟨the *even* flow of his verse⟩ ⟨I mean to . . . support with an *even* temper, and without any violent transports of mind, a sudden gust of prosperity—*Fielding*⟩ **Equable** usually implies some inherent quality which makes for invariability, such as uniformity ⟨an *equable* stride⟩ ⟨an *equable* pulse⟩ or freedom from extremes or sudden marked changes ⟨there is an *equable* climate in the most populated parts, warm and tempting to leisure—*Peffer*⟩ ⟨an *equable* temper⟩ or a temperamental calmness ⟨low *equable* tones, curiously in contrast to the strident babble—*Kipling*⟩ ⟨she won and lost, with the same *equable* sangfroid—*Rose Macaulay*⟩ **Constant** (see also FAITHFUL, CONTINUAL) implies fixity in character, quality, or condition or persistence in kind or type under the same conditions ⟨the sand is frequently yellow . . . but this color is by no means *constant*—*Lyell*⟩ ⟨science has to deal . . . with scores of chemical energies which it knows little about except that they always seem to be *constant* to the same conditions—*Henry Adams*⟩
*Ana* stable, durable, perdurable, perpetual, *lasting: enduring, persisting, continuing (see CONTINUE): staunch, steadfast, resolute, constant (see FAITHFUL): persevering, persisting (see PERSEVERE)
*Ant* unsteady: nervous, jumpy

**steady** *vb* *stabilize, poise, balance, ballast, trim
*Con* *shake, rock, agitate, convulse

**steal, pilfer, filch, purloin, lift, pinch, snitch, swipe, cop** are comparable when they mean to take another's possession without right and without his knowledge or permission. **Steal,** the commonest and most general of the group, can refer to any act of taking without right, although it suggests strongly a furtiveness or secrecy in the act ⟨*steal* a pocketbook⟩ ⟨*steal* jewels⟩ ⟨*steal* a kiss⟩ ⟨*steal* a glance at someone⟩ **Pilfer** suggests stealing in small amounts or with cautious stealth and often bit by bit ⟨the pantry mouse that *pilfers* our food—*Gustafson et al*⟩ ⟨the ladies of unexceptionable position who are caught *pilfering* furs in shops—*L. P. Smith*⟩ ⟨*pilfer* the secret files of the foreign office—*Morgenthau*⟩ **Filch** is close to *pilfer* but may suggest more strongly the use of active though surreptitious means, especially quick snatching ⟨in pursuit of a thief who had *filched* an overcoat—*McKenzie Porter*⟩ ⟨a lot of fellows were too hungry to wait, and so some of the rations were *filched*—*Autry*⟩ ⟨a bulky, dark youth in spectacles . . . *filching* biscuits from a large tin—*Sayers*⟩ **Purloin** usually shifts the stress onto the idea of removal or making away with for one's own use, often becoming generalized to include such acts as plundering or plagiarism ⟨had *purloined* $386,920 from the New York realty management firm for which he worked, then absconded—*Time*⟩ ⟨added theft to her other sin, and having found your watch in your bedroom had *purloined* it—*Butler* d. 1902⟩ ⟨to quote him is not to *purloin*—*Dryden*⟩ **Lift,** when it does not mean specifically to steal by surreptitiously taking from counters or displays in stores, is used frequently in spoken English in the sense of *purloin* ⟨women shoplifters often work in gangs of three. Two act as shields while the third does the *lifting*—*The Irish Digest*⟩ ⟨*lift* money from the cash register⟩ ⟨imitators who *lifted* everything except the shirt off his back—*F. S. Fitzgerald*⟩ **Pinch, swipe, snitch,** and *cop* are virtually interchangeable with *filch*. **Pinch** and **swipe** are often used in place of *steal* to suggest an act morally less reprehensible ⟨*loot* having been *pinched* by him from the British ship *Mary Dyer*—*Sydney Bulletin*⟩ or sometimes more dashing ⟨well-dressed crooks really did steal the Gold Cup at Ascot . . . drove up in a handsome car . . . and *pinched* the cup out of the Royal Enclosure—*J. D. Carr*⟩ ⟨the bloke who *pinched* my photographs—*Richard Llewellyn*⟩ and occasionally to suggest a petty meanness ⟨hovering outside the dying butler's bedroom waiting to . . . pop in and *swipe* the old man's private notebooks—*Time*⟩ **Snitch** possibly stresses more the removal by quick, furtive snatching ⟨while he was bathing, somebody *snitched* his uniform—*Wodehouse*⟩ ⟨*snitched* people's ideas without telling them—*Sayers*⟩ **Cop** usually lays stress upon quick, often spur-of-the-moment filching or purloining ⟨some woman put on a dinner gown, mingled with guests, *copped* fifty thousand bucks in jewelry—*Gardner*⟩ ⟨ran home and *copped* a piece of beefsteak from his old lady—*Farrell*⟩
*Ana* *rob, plunder, rifle, loot, burglarize

**stealthy** *secret, covert, furtive, clandestine, surreptitious, underhand, underhanded
*Ana* *sly, cunning, crafty, artful, tricky, wily: sneaking, slinking, skulking (see LURK)

**steel** *vb* *encourage, inspirit, hearten, embolden, cheer, nerve
*Ana* fortify, reinforce, invigorate, *strengthen: determine, resolve (see DECIDE)
*Con* *unnerve, enervate, emasculate, unman: sap, undermine, *weaken, enfeeble: *discourage, dishearten, dispirit, deject

**steep** *adj* Steep, abrupt, precipitous, sheer mean having an incline approaching the perpendicular. The words are here arranged in ascending order of degree of perpendicularity. **Steep** implies so sharp a slope or pitch that ascent or descent is difficult ⟨a military road, which rises . . . by an acclivity not dangerously *steep*, but sufficiently laborious—*Johnson*⟩ ⟨the trail . . . then struck up the side of the mountain, growing *steeper* every foot of the way—*Quillin*⟩ **Abrupt** adds to *steep* the suggestion of a sharper pitch or angle of ascent or descent and usually of a sudden break in a level ⟨high *abrupt* banks in places become hanging cliffs with a drop of 100 feet or more—*Amer. Guide Series: N. C.*⟩ **Precipitous** suggests extreme steepness and an abruptness like that of a precipice ⟨a *precipitous* height⟩ ⟨a deep gorge, with *precipitous*, volcanic walls which no man could scale—*London*⟩ **Sheer** implies precipitousness approaching the perpendicular and showing no break in its line ⟨*sheer* cliffs that fell from the summit to the plain, more than a thousand feet—*Cather*⟩
*Ana* elevated, lifted, raised (see LIFT): lofty, *high

**steep** *vb* *soak, saturate, impregnate, drench, sop, waterlog
*Ana* *infuse, imbue, ingrain: penetrate, pierce, probe (see ENTER)

**steer** *vb* *guide, lead, pilot, engineer
*Ana* *conduct, direct, manage, control: *govern, rule

**stellar** *starry, sidereal, astral

**stem** *vb* proceed, issue, emanate, derive, flow, originate, *spring, arise, rise

**stentorian** *loud, earsplitting, hoarse, raucous, strident, stertorous
*Ana* resounding, orotund, *resonant: *vociferous, clamorous, blatant: harsh, *rough

**stereotyped** *trite, hackneyed, threadbare, shopworn
*Ana* conventional, formal (see CEREMONIAL): obsolete, archaic, antiquated (see OLD): used, employed, utilized, applied (see USE)
*Ant* changeful

**sterile, barren, impotent, unfruitful, infertile** mean not

A colon (:) separates groups of words discriminated. An asterisk (*) indicates place of treatment of each group.

having or not manifesting the power to produce offspring or to bear literal or figurative fruit. **Sterile**, opposed to *fertile*, in its basic application to living things implies an inability to reproduce ⟨*sterile* hyphae that protect the fruiting body of a fungus⟩ ⟨a *sterile* marriage⟩ ⟨the workers among ants and bees are *sterile*⟩ ⟨the attempt will be made to distinguish between those who are childless from choice and those who are *sterile*—*Jour. of Heredity*⟩ But *sterile* is widely extendible to things that might reasonably be expected to be fruitful but that in fact are not so; thus, poor worthless land in which plants will not grow is described as *sterile;* minds deficient in ideas are *sterile;* funds left in a safe-deposit box and drawing no interest are *sterile;* whatever offers no return (as of pleasure, profit, value, or use) is *sterile* ⟨beneath his fun lurked the *sterile* bitterness of the still young man who has tried and given up—*Wharton*⟩ ⟨his unsatisfactory relations with women; and his impulses toward a *sterile* and infantile perversity—*Edmund Wilson*⟩ **Barren** (see also BARE 1) applies especially to a female who has borne no offspring or who is or is believed to be incapable of bearing any ⟨a *barren* heifer⟩ ⟨she hath also conceived a son in her old age: and this is the sixth month with her, who was called *barren*—*Lk* 1:36⟩ In extended use the term can imply a lack of return or profit ⟨a *barren* conquest which brought him no special repute—*Buchan*⟩ **Impotent** (see also POWERLESS) applies to the male and implies a lack of the ability to copulate and a corresponding inability to reproduce his kind ⟨a pink Sultan with his pale harem maidens and a yellow slob of eunuch lolling *impotent* in the background—*Murchie*⟩ Only rarely is the term in this sense used of other than the male animal, and in such use it approaches the aspect of *impotent* discriminated at *powerless* ⟨whole groups of animals and plants are rendered *impotent* by the same unnatural conditions—*Darwin*⟩ **Unfruitful** is sometimes used in place of *barren* not only as applied to the female but as applied to land, vegetation, or efforts which bear no fruit ⟨an *unfruitful* tree⟩ ⟨*unfruitful* soil⟩ ⟨this unsavory and *unfruitful* piece of research—*Cater*⟩ **Infertile** is often interchanged with *sterile* ⟨an *infertile* egg⟩ ⟨*infertile* matings⟩ but it is as likely to imply deficiency as absence of fertility and is appropriately used when a relative rather than an absolute sterility is to be implied ⟨the *infertile* grazings of those hills—*Allan Fraser*⟩ ⟨an *infertile* strain of beef cattle⟩ ⟨has our history shown that liberty is so *infertile* a principle that with it we are unable to compete in the world struggle . . . ?—*Chenery*⟩ ⟨animals and plants, when removed from their natural conditions, are often rendered in some degree *infertile*—*Darwin*⟩
*Ana* *bare, barren, bald, naked: arid, *dry: *meager, exiguous: empty, hollow, nugatory, *vain
*Ant* fertile: exuberant —*Con* bearing, yielding, producing, turning out (see BEAR): fecund, fruitful, prolific (see FERTILE)

**sterilize** 1 Sterilize, castrate, spay, emasculate, alter, mutilate, geld, caponize mean to make incapable of producing offspring. **Sterilize**, the most general of these terms, is applicable to both human beings and animals and is used whether the end is attained accidentally (as by undue exposure to X rays which kill germ cells) or deliberately (as by a surgical operation which prevents the germ cells from reaching the site where fertilization can occur or by removal of the gonads). *Sterilize* often suggests a legalized procedure undertaken to prevent the reproduction of undesirables (as imbeciles and habitual criminals); the term does not imply physical disfigurement and does not in itself necessarily imply interference with the capacity for copulation. **Castrate**, a narrower term than *sterilize*, means to deprive of the testes, the male reproductive glands. It is used of both human beings and animals and usually implies a surgical procedure and a loss of libido as well as of procreative power. By extension *castrate* may also mean to deprive of the ovaries, the female reproductive glands, and therefore is often used in place of **spay**, the specific term for this operation. **Emasculate** is often preferred to *castrate* when the reference is to human males and especially when there is the intent to stress the loss of virile or masculine qualities. **Alter** may replace *castrate* especially in reference to domestic pets and when an ambiguous or euphemistic term is appropriate. **Mutilate** (see also MAIM) is sometimes substituted for *castrate* especially when the intent is to convey strongly the idea of physical disfigurement or violence or when a euphemism is desired. **Geld**, meaning to castrate, is used chiefly in reference to domestic animals, especially the horse, and **caponize**, also meaning to castrate, most commonly has reference to the male domestic fowl, but both are sometimes used contemptuously of human beings.
*Ant* fertilize
2 Sterilize, disinfect, sanitize, fumigate can mean to subject to a process or treatment for the destruction of living organisms, especially microorganisms. **Sterilize** suggests drastic methods (as the application of intense heat, boiling, or the use of strong chemicals) with the intent of destroying all microorganisms whether they are disease-producing or not. The term usually suggests means taken to avoid infection. **Disinfect** also suggests vigorous methods (as exposure to strong sunlight and fresh air, thorough washing, and the use of special chemicals) with the intent of destroying all infective agents; the term usually suggests an intent to free from germs something that is known or feared to be infected. **Sanitize**, which basically means to make sanitary, is often preferred by public health officials when the reference is to preventive measures affecting the health of a community (as the treatment of drinking water or the cleansing of food processing facilities) and when neither *sterilize* (because it suggests complete destruction of microorganisms and often implies the taking of measures too drastic for general use) nor *disinfect* (because it suggests the actual presence of disease germs) exactly fits their needs or makes clear their intention. **Fumigate** is associated with these terms only because fumigation was once the usual method of disinfection; it implies the use of fumes (as smoke or gas) that are destructive not only of microorganisms but of such pests as cockroaches, beetles, and bedbugs.

**stern** *adj* *severe, austere, ascetic
*Ana* strict, *rigid, rigorous, stringent: *grim, implacable, unrelenting: *inflexible, inexorable: disciplined, trained, schooled (see TEACH)
*Ant* soft: lenient

**stertorous** *loud, stentorian, earsplitting, hoarse, raucous, strident
*Ana* harsh, *rough

**stew** *vb* *boil, seethe, simmer, parboil

**stick** 1 Stick, adhere, cohere, cling, cleave can mean to be or become closely, firmly, or indissolubly attached. **Stick** implies attachment by affixing; one thing or a person *sticks* to another, or things or persons *stick* together when they are literally or figuratively glued together and can be separated only by tearing or forcing apart ⟨the stamp *sticks* to the envelope⟩ ⟨by *sticking* together they gained their objective⟩ ⟨marriage . . . was nothing more than a token that a couple intended to *stick* to each other—*F. M. Ford*⟩ ⟨whether . . . there will be anyone so beyond suspicion that no slander can *stick* to him—

*Davis*⟩ ⟨I'm the celestial drudge . . . and I *stick* to my work till I drop at it—*Gilbert*⟩ When referred to things, **adhere** is interchangeable with *stick* ⟨the mud *adhered* to their shoes⟩ It is narrower in idiomatic range than *stick* but is the usual term when the attachment results from growth of parts normally distinct or separate ⟨abdominal tissues sometimes *adhere* after an operation⟩ When referred to persons, *adhere* usually implies deliberate or voluntary acceptance (as of the creed of a church, the platform of a political party, or the doctrines of a philosopher) ⟨he believes passionately that India will *adhere* to her traditional democracy if it can be made to work—*Jerome Ellison*⟩ ⟨he liked a certain order in his life; when he had made a plan he liked to *adhere* to it—*Sackville-West*⟩ ⟨the then current fashion, which royal ladies have *adhered* to ever since—*Rose Macaulay*⟩ **Cohere** takes for its subject a collective singular or a plural noun that names things that stick together to produce a mass, a body, or a unified whole ⟨the dry ingredients of a cake *cohere* only when liquid is added⟩ ⟨did not the whole composition *cohere*, were its unity broken, it would not be *one* picture or *one* quartet—*Edman*⟩ ⟨passing his hand over his cool forehead, he closed his eyes. The sounds *cohered* as in delirium—*Stafford*⟩ But occasionally when the notion of producing a unified whole is to be stressed *cohere* may replace *stick* or *adhere* ⟨the necessity that he shall conform, that he shall *cohere*—*T. S. Eliot*⟩ ⟨with weariness, anger, and disappointment I passed out and fell with my heavy musket . . . to the floor. Arms and the man did not *cohere*—*Lovett*⟩ **Cling** usually implies attachment by hanging on (as by the arms, by roots, or by tendrils) and may suggest, often strongly, a need of support in one that clings ⟨*cling* to a capsized boat⟩ ⟨the vine *clings* to the wall⟩ ⟨man whose breeches *clung* to his bony legs as if he'd been wading waist-high in a river—*Kenneth Roberts*⟩ In its extended use *cling* may add to the suggestion of need of support one of dependence ⟨she *clung* to her father and mother even after her marriage⟩ but at other times it suggests tenacity in holding on to something possessed, believed, or used ⟨*clung* to the superstitions of his childhood⟩ ⟨*clung* stubbornly to their hopes of being saved at the last minute by a miracle—*Shirer*⟩ **Cleave** implies closeness and strength of attachment; when applied to persons, it commonly suggests depth of devotion and fidelity in affection ⟨my tongue *cleave* to my roof within my mouth, unless a pardon ere I rise or speak—*Shak.*⟩ ⟨he remains . . . for more essential reasons than mere responsibility. Even if there were no children, he would probably *cleave* to her—*Mailer*⟩

*Ana* *tie, bind: attach, *fasten, affix, fix: *implant
*Con* sever, sunder, part, divide, *separate: *detach, disengage

**2 stickle, balk, shy, boggle, *demur, scruple, jib, strain**

**stickle** *vb* balk, shy, boggle, jib, *demur, scruple, stick, strain
*Ana* *hesitate, vacillate, falter, waver: *object, kick, protest

**stick out** *bulge, jut, protuberate, protrude, project, overhang, beetle
*Ana* *extend, prolong, elongate, lengthen: *expand, swell, distend: obtrude (see INTRUDE)

**stiff** *adj* **Stiff, rigid, inflexible, tense, stark, wooden** can mean so firm, hard, or tough in texture, consistency, or quality as to be impossible or highly difficult to bend or enliven. **Stiff**, the most common word of this group, is applicable where this condition exists in any noticeable degree; it may describe either a desirable or an undesirable quality, because, except in its extended senses, it merely implies a condition and carries neither depreciative nor commendatory connotations ⟨an edition of a book with *stiff* covers⟩ ⟨he wants a cane that is very *stiff*⟩ ⟨dislike a *stiff* custard⟩ ⟨every gust made a noise like the rattling of dry bones in the *stiff* toddy palms outside—*Kipling*⟩ ⟨sitting . . . on the edge of a *stiff* chair—*F. S. Fitzgerald*⟩ In its extended senses *stiff*, when applied to persons or their manners and their expression, usually suggests either extreme formality and coldness ⟨he replied with *stiff* condescension⟩ ⟨she preferred the easygoing parties of this day to the *stiff* entertainments she had known in her youth⟩ or a lack of ease, grace, or graciousness in dealing with others ⟨seemed to be struggling with her *stiff* reserve to give him comfort—*Archibald Marshall*⟩ ⟨Brutus had . . . a hard face, a pedantic style in speech and writing, and a *stiff* ungracious character—*Buchan*⟩ ⟨he seemed suddenly uneasy . . . I could tell by the drop of the head and by the *stiff* intent set of the body—*Dahl*⟩ When applied to something that must be overcome or must be accomplished, the term implies unusual difficulty or the need of great exertion ⟨a *stiff* ascent⟩ ⟨a *stiff* opposition⟩ ⟨a *stiff* examination⟩ ⟨a *stiff* task⟩ ⟨the casual reader will find certain parts of this book *stiff* going—*Linton*⟩ and when applied to something that under particular circumstances or in a particular case has lost its usual or typical pliancy or pliability, *stiff* implies difficulty (as in using, moving, or handling) ⟨branches *stiff* with ice⟩ ⟨limbs *stiff* with cold⟩ ⟨he grew *stiff* with fear⟩ In a variety of other senses, *stiff* implies harshness or extreme severity ⟨a *stiff* sentence⟩ ⟨a *stiff* penalty⟩ or great strength or violence ⟨a *stiff* breeze⟩ ⟨a *stiff* dose⟩ ⟨the two drinks he had drunk, both *stiff* ones, had clouded his mind—*Styron*⟩ **Rigid** (for extended senses see RIGID 2) implies so high a degree of stiffness that the thing so described cannot be bent or flexed without breaking it ⟨an airship with a *rigid* hull⟩ ⟨a bridge supported by a series of *rigid* masonry arches⟩ ⟨a *rigid* crosspiece⟩ **Inflexible** (for extended sense see INFLEXIBLE 2) differs from *rigid* only in suggesting a lack of limberness or an incapacity for being bent rather than a texture or consistency that resists bending or deforming. Consequently it is often used when a less precise term is needed and merely an approach to rigidity is suggested ⟨an *inflexible* metal⟩ ⟨snakes . . . with portions of their bodies still numb and *inflexible*, waiting for the sun to thaw them out—*Thoreau*⟩ **Tense** (see also TIGHT 1) occurs especially in reference to bodily structures (as muscles, fibers, or membranes) that are stretched so tight, or so strained by effort or excitement, that they have lost their elasticity or flexibility either for the time being or permanently ⟨*tense* arteries⟩ ⟨*tense* nerves⟩ ⟨with muscles as *tense* as those of a tiger about to spring⟩ ⟨only his *tense* movements, the rather rigid way he held himself, the habitual drumming of his fingers, were in any way abnormal—*Wouk*⟩ **Stark** usually suggests a stiffness that is associated with loss of life, warmth, power, vitality, or fluidity and therefore often also connotes desolation, barrenness, death, or present valuelessness; frequently it is accompanied by *stiff* or *rigid* ⟨many a nobleman lies *stark* and stiff—*Shak.*⟩ ⟨cut flowers before they actually die . . . stretch themselves out with a palpable jerk, *stark* and rigid—*Powys*⟩ ⟨here all the surfaces remained *stark* and unyielding, thin and sharp—*Santayana*⟩ ⟨rats . . . danced comically before they died, and lay in the scuppers *stark* and ruffled—*Sinclair Lewis*⟩ Often *stark* is merely an intensive (often an adverb) meaning little more than such as is stated or described without qualification ⟨rich men who were once *stark* poor—*Brinig*⟩ ⟨he stood in *stark* terror⟩ ⟨they . . . wrote *stark* nonsense—*Quiller-Couch*⟩ **Wooden**

A colon (:) separates groups of words discriminated. An asterisk (*) indicates place of treatment of each group.

suggests not only the hardness and inflexibility of wood but its dryness and its lack of suppleness and plasticity; consequently the term suggests not only stiffness and lack of life and grace but often clumsiness or deadness or heaviness of spirit ⟨Kim took a few paces in a stiff *wooden* style—*Kipling*⟩ ⟨the courtroom scene was . . . prosy, *wooden*, and lifeless—*Elmer Rice*⟩ ⟨he appears *wooden*, remote, often addicted to incredible posturings—*Rothman*⟩
*Ana* tough, tenacious, *strong, stout: *firm, hard, solid: formal, conventional, ceremonious (see CEREMONIAL): frigid, *cold, cool: difficult, *hard, arduous
*Ant* relaxed: supple
**stiff-necked** *obstinate, stubborn, mulish, dogged, pertinacious, pigheaded, bullheaded
**stifle** *suffocate, asphyxiate, smother, choke, strangle, throttle
**stigma, brand, blot, stain** can denote a mark of shame left on a name, reputation, or character. **Stigma**, though often implying dishonor or public shame, usually applies to a mark or a charge or judgment that is fastened upon a person or thing or is attached to it so as to discredit it and cause it to be generally disapproved or condemned ⟨curmudgeonly inability to praise others which has ever been the *stigma* by which we may recognize the ungenerous—*Partridge*⟩ ⟨they can attach a social *stigma* to the relief by taking away the pauper's vote—*Shaw*⟩ **Brand** carries stronger implications of disgrace and infamy than *stigma;* it often suggests impossibility of removal, permanent social ostracism, and public condemnation ⟨for the sorrow and the shame, the *brand* on me and mine, I'll pay you back in leaping flame—*Kipling*⟩ ⟨it may mean nothing very much to you, but . . . those words carry the ultimate, ignominious *brand* of incompetency and failure—*Sayers*⟩ ⟨segregation, however "equal" the physical facilities, does put the *brand* of inferiority on Negro pupils in the schools—*N. Y. Times*⟩ **Blot** and **stain** imply a blemish that diminishes the honor of a name or a reputation or that sullies one's reputation for purity or virtue but does not bring either name or reputation into utter disrepute ⟨thou noteless *blot* on a remembered name—*Shelley*⟩ ⟨there are *blots* on the chronicle, moments of the petulance . . . and the unhappy record of the meaningless and aimless slighting of General de Gaulle. But these are minor blemishes—*Anthony West*⟩ ⟨to have loved one peerless, without *stain*—*Tennyson*⟩ ⟨England will have a nasty *stain* on her flag if she sees this man go down without a hand lifted to save him—*Parker*⟩
*Ana* *disgrace, dishonor, opprobrium, odium, shame: contamination, tainting *or* taint, defilement, pollution (see corresponding verbs at CONTAMINATE)
**still** *adj* **Still, stilly, quiet, silent, noiseless** can all mean making no stir or noise. **Still** applies to what is motionless or at rest, often with the further implication of hush or absence of sound; sometimes one implication is stressed, sometimes the other, and sometimes both ⟨ha! no more moving? *still* as the grave—*Shak.*⟩ ⟨the crowd remained *still*, quietly stupefied, and with a shaky reverence—*Styron*⟩ ⟨that chair, when you arose and passed out of the room, rocked silently a while ere it again was *still*—*Millay*⟩ **Stilly** emphasizes the absence of sounds, but it usually implies also the absence of stir or motion ⟨oft, in the *stilly* night, ere Slumber's chain has bound me—*Thomas Moore*⟩ ⟨the rigidly haughty forms stretched out, with crossed arms upon their *stilly* hearts, in everlasting and undreaming rest—*Melville*⟩ ⟨a mad rush of heavy feet went past his door, to speed over the *stilly* house—*O'Casey*⟩ **Quiet**, like *still*, may imply absence of perceptible motion or sound or of both, but it carries

stronger suggestions of lack of excitement, agitation, or turbulence, and of tranquillity, serenity, restfulness, or repose ⟨through the green evening *quiet* in the sun —*Keats*⟩ ⟨the happy stillness of dawn . . . the *quiet* morning air—*Meredith*⟩ ⟨a *quiet* town filled with people who lived *quiet* lives and thought *quiet* thoughts—*Anderson*⟩ ⟨all the impetuous restlessness of her girlhood had left her and she had bloomed into a *quiet* half-indolent calm—*Buck*⟩ **Silent** and **noiseless** differ from the other words of this group in being frequently applied to motion, movement, or stir that is unaccompanied by sound. **Silent** usually carries more positive suggestions of stillness or quietness ⟨the Earth . . . from West her *silent* course advance[s]—*Milton*⟩ ⟨three mountaintops, three *silent* pinnacles of aged snow—*Tennyson*⟩ whereas **noiseless** usually connotes absence of commotion or of sounds of activity or movement ⟨along the cool sequestered vale of life they kept the *noiseless* tenor of their way—*Gray*⟩ ⟨this quiet sail is as a *noiseless* wing to waft me from distraction—*Byron*⟩ ⟨I looked out on a thoroughfare crowded with traffic, but yet a *noiseless* one—*Fairchild*⟩
*Ana* *calm, tranquil, serene, placid, peaceful: restful, *comfortable
*Ant* stirring: noisy
**still** *vb* *calm, compose, quiet, quieten, lull, soothe, settle, tranquilize
*Ana* allay, assuage, alleviate, *relieve: *pacify, placate, mollify, appease: silence (see corresponding adjective at STILL)
*Ant* agitate
**stilly** *still, quiet, silent, noiseless
*Ana* *soft, gentle, mild, bland: placid, peaceful, *calm, tranquil, serene
*Con* agitated, disturbed (see DISCOMPOSE)
**stimulant** *stimulus, excitant, incitement, impetus
*Ana* provocation, excitement, stimulation, quickening, galvanizing (see corresponding verbs at PROVOKE): incentive, spur, goad, *motive
*Ant* anesthetic: anodyne
**stimulate** excite, *provoke, quicken, pique, galvanize
*Ana* *quicken, animate, enliven, vivify: activate, energize, *vitalize: rouse, arouse, *stir, rally, waken, awaken
*Ant* unnerve: deaden
**stimulus, stimulant, excitant, incitement, impetus** can all mean an agent that arouses a person or a lower organism or a particualr organ or tissue to activity. Only the first three words have definite and common technical use. **Stimulus**, in this use chiefly a physiological or psychological term, applies basically to something (as a change in temperature, light, sound, or pressure) that occurs in the internal or external environment of an organism, is perceived by sense organs, and if sufficiently intense induces a neural or equivalent (as tropistic) response ⟨any physical energy that acts upon a receptor of a living organism. A *stimulus* causes a reaction in an organism, but not necessarily a response (a reaction of a muscle or gland)—*Charles Morris*⟩ ⟨so long as a system recognizes *stimuli*, and reacts to them with fitting responses, it exercises control. And it may then remain intact and functioning, despite stresses which would otherwise upset its internal coordination—*Weisz*⟩ **Stimulant**, typically a medical term, applies chiefly to a chemical substance and especially to a medicament that does or is intended to vitalize bodily activity, either generally or in respect to a particular system or organ or function ⟨tea, coffee, and cocoa are true *stimulants* to the heart, nervous system, and kidneys; coffee is more stimulating to the brain, cocoa to the kidneys, while tea occupies a happy position between the two, being mildly stimulating to most of our

---

*Ana* analogous words    *Ant* antonyms    *Con* contrasted words    See also explanatory notes facing page 1

bodily functions—*Ukers*⟩ ⟨drugs which speed up cell activity are called *stimulants—Clemensen et al*⟩ ⟨alcohol produces a false sense of well-being and efficiency, but actually it is a depressant rather than a *stimulant—T. L. Engle*⟩ **Excitant** can come very close to *stimulant* in some of its uses; thus, one may speak of a substance as a *stimulant* or an *excitant* of intestinal motility. But distinctively *excitant* can apply to either a sought or an unwanted reaction and it can imply, as *stimulus* often but *stimulant* rarely does, either the initiating or the vitalizing of a process or activity ⟨these amines, being *excitants* of the central nervous system, increase intellectual and motor activity, produce insomnia, nervousness, and tremors and have the property of antagonizing mild drug depression—*Thienes*⟩ ⟨a great many allergists believed that pine pollen contained little or no *excitant* of allergy. That is to say, the element within the pollen which stimulates antibody production was absent in pine pollen —*Swartz*⟩

In their more general use these three terms are seldom as clearly differentiable as in their basic use. **Stimulus** and **stimulant** are usually interchangeably applicable to whatever exerts an impelling or invigorating effect (as on a process, an activity, or a mind) ⟨whenever an idea loses its immediate felt quality, it ceases to be an idea and becomes, like an algebraic symbol, a mere *stimulus* to execute an operation without the need of thinking—*Dewey*⟩ ⟨to borrow from commercial banks increases the money supply and is a business *stimulant—F. M. Knight*⟩ ⟨the colonial-development money is the extra *stimulus* to generate development faster than would otherwise be possible—*Lewis*⟩ but **excitant**, here too, is more likely to suggest an initiating ⟨we hold that ethical statements are expressions and *excitants* of feeling which do not necessarily involve any assertions—*Ayer*⟩ and it is applicable when unwanted or undesirable ends result ⟨the desire to gain vast and lucrative readership and audiences is the major *excitant* to the excesses of which so many are aware—*Newsweek*⟩ **Incitement** applies to something that moves or impels usually a course of action; the term tends to emphasize an urging or pressing intended to drive one into moving or acting quickly rather than the result attained ⟨to issue a solemn public condemnation and warning that this attack against the Jewish people is an *incitement* to massacre—*The Nation*⟩ ⟨energies slumbering in him which the *incitements* of the day do not call forth—*James*⟩ ⟨nor could all the *incitements* of its master induce the beast again to move forward—*Galsworthy*⟩ **Impetus** (see also SPEED 2) usually stresses the stimulation of an increase in the momentum of activity already initiated ⟨what also gave an unusual *impetus* to the mind of men at this period was the discovery of the New World—*Hazlitt*⟩ ⟨in estimating the social importance of this movement, we must be careful to discount the temporary . . . *impetus* it received from the economic slump of this period—*Day Lewis*⟩ But the term sometimes applies also to a stimulus that initiates action ⟨it is the *impetus* that I ask of you: the will to try—*Quiller-Couch*⟩ *Ana* spur, goad, incentive, *motive, inducement: excitement, piquing, provocation (see corresponding verbs at PROVOKE): irritation, nettling (see corresponding verbs at IRRITATE)

**stingy, close, closefisted, tight, tightfisted, niggardly, parsimonious, penurious, miserly, cheeseparing, penny-pinching** can mean unwilling or manifesting unwillingness to share one's goods with others or to give to another a part of one's possessions. **Stingy** implies mainly a lack of generosity; the term is applicable whenever there is a suggestion of a mean or illiberal spirit ⟨if I want anything,

he says that it cannot be afforded. I never thought before that he was *stingy*, but I am sure now that he must be a miser at heart—*Trollope*⟩ ⟨*stingy* at heart, Cabot, refusing to plunk down what they were asking for movies and plays, began browsing in a . . . public library—*Purdy*⟩ **Close** and **closefisted** and **tight** and **tightfisted** usually imply stinginess of nature, but they also ordinarily suggest the power to keep a tight grip upon whatever one has acquired ⟨*closefisted* in all his expenditures⟩ ⟨men and women who are *closefisted* and make a gift do not want their next week's mail loaded with appeals—*William Lawrence*⟩ ⟨he wasn't as *tight* as you . . . but he was a little bit *close*. So the bargain hung fire—*Hammett*⟩ ⟨must be eagle-eyed and *tightfisted* about these expenditures—*A. E. Stevenson*⟩ **Niggardly** implies the character of one who is so stingy and so closefisted that he grudgingly gives the smallest portion or amount possible; the term may refer not only to the giving or spending of money or the giving of material goods but to the provision of what would add to the comfort, happiness, or well-being of oneself or of others ⟨as poor and *niggardly* as it would be to set down no more meat than your company will be sure to eat up—*Swift*⟩ ⟨his *niggardly* allowance for rent and food⟩ ⟨they were not *niggardly*, these tramps, and he who had money did not hesitate to share it among the rest—*Maugham*⟩ ⟨literature is so lavish with wealth and titles . . . the real world is so *niggardly* of these things—*Huxley*⟩ **Parsimonious** stresses frugality, but it suggests also niggardliness; because of this double connotation the term usually suggests not a virtue but a fault or, often, a vice ⟨a lonely bachelor life in caring for his property and in adding to it by *parsimonious* living—*Long*⟩ **Penurious** adds to *parsimonious* the suggestion of a niggardliness so great as to give the appearance of extreme poverty or of excessive closefistedness ⟨a grudging master . . . a *penurious* niggard of his wealth—*Milton*⟩ ⟨I had a rich uncle . . . a *penurious* accumulating curmudgeon—*Irving*⟩ **Miserly** implies penuriousness but it stresses obsessive avariciousness as the motive ⟨her expenditure was parsimonious and even *miserly—J. R. Green*⟩ ⟨a *miserly* man who hoards money out of avarice—*Empson*⟩ **Cheeseparing** and **penny-pinching** suggest frugality and parsimoniousness carried to the extreme ⟨the *cheeseparing* guardians of the city's finances⟩ ⟨a campaign of administrative *cheeseparing—Alan*⟩ ⟨a *penny-pinching* appropriation for relief⟩ *Ana* *mean, sordid, ignoble: scrimpy, skimpy, *meager: greedy, acquisitive, avaricious, *covetous, grasping: *sparing, economical, frugal, thrifty *Ant* generous —*Con* *liberal, bountiful, bounteous, openhanded, munificent: *profuse, lavish, prodigal

**stinking** *malodorous, fetid, noisome, putrid, rank, rancid, fusty, musty *Ana* foul, filthy, nasty, *dirty: *offensive, repulsive, revolting

**stint** *n* 1 *task, duty, assignment, job, chore *Ana* quantity, amount (see SUM): allotment, apportionment (see corresponding verbs at ALLOT): prescribing *or* prescription, assigning (see corresponding verbs at PRESCRIBE): sharing *or* share, participation (see corresponding verbs at SHARE) 2 *spell, bout, shift, tour, trick, turn, go

**stipend** *wage *or* wages, salary, fee, emolument, pay, hire *Ana* remuneration, compensation, recompensing *or* recompense (see corresponding verbs at PAY)

**stipple** *vb* *spot, spatter, sprinkle, mottle, fleck, marble, speckle, spangle, bespangle

**stippled** spotted, spattered, sprinkled, mottled, flecked, marbled, speckled, spangled, bespangled (see under

A colon (:) separates groups of words discriminated. An asterisk (*) indicates place of treatment of each group.

SPOT *vb*)

**stipulation** *condition, terms, provision, proviso, reservation, strings

*Ana* specification (see corresponding verb at MENTION): restriction, circumscription (see corresponding verbs at LIMIT)

**stir** *vb* **Stir, rouse, arouse, awaken, waken, rally** can all mean to cause to shift from quiescence or torpor into activity. **Stir,** often followed by *up,* usually presupposes excitement to activity by something which disturbs or agitates and so brings to the surface or into outward expression what is latent or dormant ⟨a dreamy, faraway look came into Mr. Bohlen's eyes, and he smiled. Then he *stirred* himself and began leafing through the plans —*Dahl*⟩ ⟨if the . . . teacher longs to *stir* the sluggish mind of one of her scholars, she must first find out what the sluggishness is due to—*Eliot*⟩ ⟨she wants *stirring* up. She's got into a rut—*Bennett*⟩ Sometimes the word suggests the evoking of rebellion or revolt ⟨movements that begin by *stirring* up hostility against a group of people—*Dewey*⟩ More often it implies the evocation of profound, agitating, but usually agreeable, emotion ⟨peace has no drums and trumpets to *stir* the pulse—*Loveman*⟩ ⟨men lacking an arm or leg *stirred* universal pity —*Wecter*⟩ **Rouse, arouse, awaken, waken** all presuppose a state of rest or repose, often that of sleep. **Rouse** derives its implications from its application to the starting of game from coverts or lairs by the cries of hunters or by beating of bushes and often suggests incitement to activity by startling, frightening, or upsetting. In addition it commonly implies intense or vigorous activity and often ensuing commotion or turbulence ⟨every tent *roused* by that clamor dread—*Shelley*⟩ ⟨*roused* out of sleep by a heavy pounding on the door—*Wechsberg*⟩ ⟨Antony . . . had spoken words which *roused* the mob to fury—*Buchan*⟩ **Arouse,** though frequently used interchangeably with *rouse,* tends to be weaker in its implications and often means little more than to start into activity and conveys no hint of what follows; thus, a noise in the night *arouses* a sleeping soldier if he merely wakes up into consciousness of it, but it *rouses* him when he also makes determined efforts to trace its source or hastily arms himself; a fear may be *aroused* and immediately dispelled; passions are *roused* when they are so stirred up that they exert a compelling influence ⟨now I had to guard against *arousing* the emotions of others—*Mailer*⟩ ⟨the new force stirred and *aroused* the people—*Anderson*⟩ **Awaken** and **waken,** like *arouse,* frequently imply an ending of sleep; in extended use they are employed chiefly in reference to mental or spiritual powers or faculties which need only the proper stimulation to be called forth into activity or to be elicited ⟨*waken* love⟩ ⟨the conscience of the nation was *awakened*⟩ ⟨her eyes brightened, her features appeared gradually to *awaken,* and life flowed back into her face—*Farrell*⟩ ⟨had *wakened* and heard the lion— *Hemingway*⟩ ⟨*waken* to the point about seven minutes after—*Laski*⟩ ⟨that tree always *awakened* pleasant memories, recalling a garden in the south of France —*Cather*⟩ **Rally** (see also RIDICULE) presupposes a diffusion of forces or a lack of concentration that promotes lethargy or inaction; it therefore implies a gathering together that stirs up or rouses ⟨he *rallied* his strength for a final blow—*Prescott*⟩ ⟨as if his memory were impaired . . . [he] made an effort to *rally* his attention— *Dickens*⟩ ⟨they stirred and *rallied* a divided, defeated people—*Shirer*⟩

*Ana* excite, *provoke, stimulate, quicken, galvanize: *incite, foment, instigate: activate, energize, *vitalize: *move, drive, impel, actuate

**stir** *n* **1** *motion, movement, move, locomotion

*Ana* acting *or* activity, working *or* work, behaving *or* behavior, reaction (see corresponding verbs at ACT): change, alteration, variation, modification (see under CHANGE *vb*)

**2** **Stir, bustle, flurry, pother, fuss, ado** all denote the signs of excitement or hurry that accompany an act, action, or an event. **Stir** suggests brisk or restless movement and ordinarily implies a crowd ⟨he liked to hear the paper talked about. He liked to have a *stir* and rumpus going on—*White*⟩ ⟨as some messenger arrived . . . a *stir* would pass through the throng so full of swagger and of youth—*Osbert Sitwell*⟩ **Bustle** adds the implication of a noisy, obtrusive, or self-important display of energy, especially when used in reference to an individual ⟨she needs the *bustle* of life in a good hotel—*Bennett*⟩ ⟨'tis true that strength and *bustle* build up a firm. But judgment and knowledge are what keep it established—*Hardy*⟩ ⟨the meaningless and vulgar *bustle* of newspaper offices —*Gibbons*⟩ **Flurry** stresses nervous agitation and undue haste ⟨so now began a great *flurry* . . . . There is no part of the world where there doesn't have to be excitement over a wedding—*Upton Sinclair*⟩ ⟨the resilience and strength of purpose that persist like deeply banked fires beneath a surface that is frequently all *flurry* and crepitation—*Times Lit. Sup.*⟩ **Pother** and **fuss** both imply flurry and fidgety activity; **pother** often distinctively stresses commotion or confusion and **fuss** needless worry or effort ⟨he is always in a *pother* about something or other⟩ ⟨she had invited her parents to come on the fiesta weekend, calculating that the excitement and *fuss* would distract their attention from herself— *Wouk*⟩ ⟨it had made a dreadful *pother* and was still remembered uneasily—*Mencken*⟩ ⟨even this *pother* about gods reminds one that something is worthwhile —*Pound*⟩ **Ado** usually suggests fussiness or waste of energy ⟨go to work without any more *ado*⟩ It also often implies trouble or difficulty ⟨there was much *ado* before their affairs were straightened out⟩

*Ana* agitation, disturbance, disquieting *or* disquiet (see corresponding verbs at DISCOMPOSE): excitement, stimulation (see corresponding verbs at PROVOKE): *din, uproar, hubbub, pandemonium

*Ant* tranquillity

**stitch** *n* *pain, twinge, ache, pang, throe

**stock** *n* *variety, subspecies, race, breed, cultivar, strain, clone

**stocky, thickset, thick, chunky, stubby, squat, dumpy** are comparable when they apply to build of the human body and mean being relatively compact in form. **Stocky** implies a short and wide or thick build and is likely to be complimentary in suggesting compact sturdiness ⟨*stocky* though not chubby—*White*⟩ ⟨a *stocky* hard-hitting catcher⟩ **Thickset** may describe a thick, solid, burly body ⟨too *thickset* for jockeying—*Masefield*⟩ **Thick** may be used for bodily parts ⟨*thick* lips⟩ ⟨*thick* legs⟩ more often than for body build. **Chunky** may indicate a body type ample but robust and solid ⟨short and *chunky,* not quite fat—*Harold Sinclair*⟩ ⟨a well-fed, *chunky,* healthy boy⟩ **Stubby,** less apt than others in this set to describe human body types, indicates noteworthy lack of height or length and corresponding shortness ⟨outfielders' gloves have longer fingers . . . infielders' gloves have relatively *stubby* fingers—*New Yorker*⟩ **Squat** and **dumpy** are usually uncomplimentary. **Squat** may indicate unshapely lack of height as though suggesting a person squatting ⟨the *squat* misshapen figure that flattened itself into the shadow—*Wilde*⟩ ⟨anchored vessels of every sort from *squat* Baltic timber carriers—*Wheel-*

---

*Ana* analogous words     *Ant* antonyms     *Con* contrasted words     See also explanatory notes facing page 1

*wright*⟩ **Dumpy** may suggest short, lumpish gracelessness of body ⟨stumpy, *dumpy* girls with their rather coarse features, big buttocks and heavy breasts—*Koestler*⟩

**stodgy** *dull, humdrum, dreary, monotonous, pedestrian
*Ana* *heavy, weighty, ponderous: *irksome, tedious, wearisome, tiresome, boring: stuffy, straitlaced, prudish (see PRIM)

**stoic** *impassive, phlegmatic, apathetic, stolid
*Ana* detached, aloof, *indifferent, unconcerned: imperturbable, composed, collected, *cool: unassailable, indomitable (see INVINCIBLE): patient, long-suffering, resigned (see corresponding nouns at PATIENCE)

**stoicism** impassivity, phlegm, apathy, stolidity (see under IMPASSIVE)
*Ana* *fortitude, grit, backbone, pluck, guts, sand: detachment, aloofness, indifference, unconcernedness *or* unconcern (see corresponding adjectives at INDIFFERENT)

**stolid** *impassive, phlegmatic, apathetic
*Ana* *dull, blunt, obtuse: *stupid, slow, dull, dense, crass, dumb: *heavy, ponderous: passive, supine, inert, *inactive
*Ant* adroit (sense 2)

**stolidity** impassivity, phlegm, apathy, stoicism (see under IMPASSIVE)
*Con* quickness, promptness, readiness, aptness (see corresponding adjectives at QUICK): animation, enlivening, quickening (see corresponding verbs at QUICKEN): *passion, fervor, ardor, zeal, enthusiasm

**stomach** *abdomen, belly, paunch, gut

**stoop** *vb* **Stoop, condescend, deign** can mean to descend below the level (as in rank or dignity) where one belongs or thinks he belongs to do something. **Stoop** implies a descent not only in rank or dignity but also, and more often, from a relatively high moral plane to a lower one; the term, therefore, can suggest disgraceful or shameful action ⟨*stoop* to fraud⟩ ⟨to think that you should *stoop* to lying⟩ Often the term implies a lowering of one's standards (as of conduct) or a debasement of one's principles for some unworthy end (as to satisfy greed or ambition) ⟨aspiring to be the leader of a nation of third-rate men, he had to *stoop* to the common level—*Mencken*⟩ ⟨his ambition was still to paint huge historical pictures; but meanwhile, to keep the pot boiling, he was prepared to *stoop* to a pettier kind of art—*Huxley*⟩ ⟨but on the material side, Mr. Archer, if one may *stoop* to consider such things—*Wharton*⟩ **Condescend** may imply the stooping of one who is actually exalted in power, rank, or dignity so as to accommodate himself to intercourse with those who are his inferiors; in this sense the term usually suggests graciousness and courtesy and a waiving of formalities ⟨Spain's mighty monarch, in gracious clemency, does *condescend*, on these conditions, to become your friend—*Dryden*⟩ Often, however, the term implies an assumption of superiority and a patronizing manner that tends to offend or affront the person who is regarded as an inferior ⟨no beggar ever felt him *condescend*, no prince presume—*J. R. Lowell*⟩ ⟨those who thought they were honoring me by·*condescending* to address a few words to me—*F. W. Robinson*⟩ ⟨he had, of course, every right to *condescend*. He was the success, the young man of twenty-three with a hit on Broadway—*Wouk*⟩ **Deign** implies a temperament or frame of mind that makes one haughty, arrogant, or contemptuous more often than it implies high rank or dignity or high standards of conduct; it usually means to stoop to what one believes is not fully in keeping with one's dignity or to something that one is reluctant to do or say or offer; therefore the term is most common with *scarcely, hardly*, or in negative constructions ⟨[the] very dog will hardly *deign* to bark at you—*Arnold*⟩

⟨my father she *deigned* to talk with because he was a simple and friendly man and vaguely a relation—*Bromfield*⟩ ⟨never *deigned* to make money in any considerable amount; but he has no doubt that he could do so if he tried —*Gorer*⟩
*Ana* *abase, demean, humble: vouchsafe, accord, *grant, concede: favor, accommodate, *oblige

**stop** *vb* **1 Stop, cease, quit, discontinue, desist** are comparable when they mean to suspend or cause to suspend activity. **Stop** applies primarily to action or progress or to what is thought of as moving or progressing; **cease** applies primarily to states and conditions or to what is thought of as being or as having existence; thus, a train *stops* but does not *cease;* the noise it makes both *stops* and *ceases;* one *stops* a car but may *cease* driving a car; one *stops* work on a book but *ceases* one's efforts to perfect its style ⟨when I have fears that I may *cease* to be—*Keats*⟩ *Stop* frequently connotes a sudden or definite, *cease* a gradual suspension of activity ⟨*stop* a quarrel⟩ ⟨*cease* quarreling⟩ ⟨I gave commands; then all smiles *stopped* together—*Browning*⟩ ⟨you hear the grating roar . . . begin, and *cease*, and then again begin—*Arnold*⟩ **Quit** (see also GO) may suggest finality in ceasing an activity, sometimes with an implication of accepting frustration or failure ⟨he *quit* coming⟩ ⟨*quit* smoking⟩ ⟨since he has *quit* Party work, he has studied a great deal—*Mailer*⟩ ⟨a few came, straggling and reluctant and not at all constant: most *quit* after the first day—*Pynchon*⟩ **Discontinue** implies the suspension of some activity, especially one that has become a form of occupation or employment or is a practice or habit ⟨*discontinue* a correspondence⟩ ⟨*discontinue* a subscription to a journal⟩ ⟨she found it necessary to *discontinue* her studies—*Current Biog.*⟩ ⟨the English abstracts that were formerly printed in Russian technical periodicals have been *discontinued*—*Martin Gardner*⟩ **Desist** usually stresses forbearance or restraint as the motive for stopping or ceasing but it may imply the futility of one's efforts ⟨*desist* from further questioning⟩ ⟨an order . . . requiring such person . . . to cease and *desist* from the violation of the law so charged—*U. S. Code*⟩ ⟨Paul *desisted*, because he had read in the newspaper satirical remarks about initial-carvers, who could find no other road to immortality—*D. H. Lawrence*⟩ ⟨he had made two attempts to shave but his hand had been so unsteady that he had been obliged to *desist*—*Joyce*⟩
*Ana* *arrest, check, interrupt: intermit, suspend, stay, *defer, postpone: *frustrate, thwart, foil, balk, circumvent
*Con* start, *begin, commence, initiate: *go, depart, leave

**2** stay, put up, lodge, sojourn, *reside, live, dwell

**stopgap** makeshift, shift,· expedient, *resource, resort, substitute, surrogate

**storm** *vb* bombard, assault, assail, *attack

**story** **1** *account, report, chronicle, version
*Ana* *history, chronicle, annals: relation, rehearsing, recital, recounting (see corresponding verbs at RELATE)
**2 Story, narrative, tale, anecdote, yarn** all denote a recital of happenings less elaborate than a novel. **Story** is the most general and the familiar word and may be interchanged with any of the others of the group, except in its generalized sense of legendary lore ⟨snowy summits old in *story*—*Tennyson*⟩ A story may be oral or written, factual or fictitious, in prose or in verse, and designed to inform or to entertain but characteristically treats of a connected series of events or incidents rather than a single incident ⟨his life *story*⟩ ⟨the *story* of an opera⟩ ⟨the *story* of the Crusades⟩ ⟨a *story* full of incident⟩ ⟨he had told the *story* simply, without any visible attempt to work on her sympathy. Probably it was a true memory—

---

A colon (:) separates groups of words discriminated. An asterisk (*) indicates place of treatment of each group.

*Malamud*〉 The short story and a newspaper story may treat of but one incident. **Narrative** in its common use is more often factual than imaginative 〈his part of the book is impeccable; the *narrative* is a pleasure to read and the material of great interest—*Geographical Jour.*〉 〈historical *narrative*〉 〈a *narrative* of discovery〉 As a literary composition *narrative* usually suggests a plot or causally connected series of motived incidents; thus, a chronicle or a diary is not ordinarily called a *narrative* 〈at this point he spun into the *narrative* a little yarn which he had fabricated last night in bed—*Rölvaag*〉 **Tale** suggests, in consequence of its historical connection with oral telling, a more leisurely and more loosely organized recital, characteristically treating legendary or imaginary happenings, often those of ancient times, and may be in verse 〈Oriental *tales*〉 〈folk *tales*〉 〈*tales* of the court of King Arthur〉 〈*tales* based on folklore, legends of great men and small—*Mahler*〉 **Anecdote**, retaining something of its original sense of an unpublished item, applies to a brief story of a single detachable incident of curious or humorous interest, often illustrative of a truth or principle or of the character or foibles of a notable person 〈an *anecdote* of Lincoln's boyhood〉 〈during the meal he entertained them with *anecdotes* of his travels—*Meredith*〉 〈an occasional *anecdote*, given as an example of the indignities she was made to suffer—*Sackville-West*〉 **Yarn** often suggests a rambling and rather dubious tale of exciting adventure, marvelous or incredible, ingenious or fanciful, and not always reaching a clear-cut outcome 〈without motive a story is not a novel, but only a *yarn*—*Caine*〉 〈the uncle . . . would arrive from Australia once every few years bringing no gifts but his wonderful *yarns*. As far as Victoria remembered, he'd never repeated himself—*Pynchon*〉
*Ana* narration, description (see corresponding verbs at RELATE): *fiction, fable, fabrication
**3** *lie, falsehood, untruth, fib, misrepresentation
**stout** *adj* **1** *strong, sturdy, stalwart, tough, tenacious
*Ana* *brave, bold, intrepid, valiant, valorous: indomitable, *invincible: resolute, staunch, steadfast (see FAITHFUL): *vigorous, energetic, lusty
**2** *fleshy, fat, portly, corpulent, obese, plump, rotund, chubby
*Ana* thick, thickset, *stocky: burly, brawny, husky, *muscular
*Ant* cadaverous　—*Con* *lean, lank, lanky, spare, angular, rawboned, skinny, scrawny
**straightforward, forthright, aboveboard** when applied to persons, their actions, or their methods mean honest and open. Something **straightforward** is consistently direct and free from deviations or evasiveness 〈a *straightforward* course of action〉 〈a *straightforward* answer〉 〈he is a man; with clear, *straightforward* ideas, a frank, noble presence—*Disraeli*〉 Something **forthright** has directness like that of a thrust, or goes straight to the point without swerving or hesitating 〈a *forthright* appeal for votes〉 〈thought that this must be the true air of success: no conceit or obvious triumph, but a *forthright* glance, a confident smile, a new erectness in the shoulders—*Wouk*〉 Something **aboveboard** is free from all traces of deception or duplicity. *Aboveboard* is chiefly used predicatively and applies more often to actions or methods than to persons 〈one whose life had been so well-ordered, balanced, and *aboveboard*—*Galsworthy*〉 〈the peace of mind that comes from being completely honest and *aboveboard*—*Haupt*〉 **Straightforward, forthright,** and *aboveboard* are also used adverbially with the same implications and connotations as their adjectival forms.
*Ana* honest, *upright, honorable, just: *fair, equitable,

impartial: candid, *frank, open, plain
*Ant* devious: indirect
**strain** *n* **1** *variety, subspecies, race, breed, cultivar, clone, stock
**2** streak, vein, *touch, suggestion, suspicion, soupçon, tincture, tinge, shade, smack, spice, dash
**strain** *vb* **1** sprain (see under STRAIN *n*)
**2** *demur, scruple, balk, jib, shy, boggle, stickle, stick
**strain** *n* **1** *stress, pressure, tension
**2 Strain, sprain** as nouns can mean an injury to a part of the body through overstretching and as verbs to cause or to suffer such an injury to a part of the body. **Strain,** the more general and less technical term, usually implies an injury to a body part or organ or to muscles as a result of overuse, overexercise, or overexertion or of over-effort (as in an attempt to regain one's balance or to lift too heavy an object); the injury may range from a slight soreness or stiffness to a disabling damage; thus, eye*strain* is a condition of the eye or of the muscles of the eye involving pain and fatigue such as occurs in those who do close work with their eyes or in those who suffer from uncorrected defects of vision; *charley horse* is a familiar term for a stiffness resulting from muscular *strain* in the arm or leg (as of an athlete) 〈*strained* his back while trying to avoid a fall on a slippery sidewalk〉 But *strain* may specifically apply to an injury resulting from a wrench or twist and involving overstretching of muscles and ligaments and is then nearly interchangeable with, though typically suggesting less severe injury than, **sprain** which definitely implies an injury to a joint, usually as a result of a wrenching, with stretching or tearing of its ligaments, damage to the synovial membrane, swelling and pain, and disablement of the joint; thus, one may *strain* or *sprain* an ankle by a sudden slip that wrenches it 〈crippled by a *sprain* of the hip〉
**strained** *forced, labored, farfetched
*Ana* tense, taut, *tight: *artificial, factitious: unnatural (see IRREGULAR): *stiff, rigid, inflexible, wooden
**strait** *n* **1 Strait, sound, channel, passage, narrows** can all denote a long and comparatively narrow stretch of water connecting two larger bodies. **Strait,** often as the plural *straits* with either singular or plural construction, denotes a relatively short and very narrow waterway 〈the *Strait* of Dover connecting the English Channel and the North Sea〉 〈the *Straits* of Gibraltar connecting the Atlantic Ocean and the Mediterranean Sea〉 **Sound** applies to a longer and more extensive waterway than a strait; the term is often applied to a long passage of water between the mainland and an island or group of islands and therefore at each end opening into the same ocean or sea or arms of the same ocean or sea 〈Long Island *Sound* lying between the Connecticut shore and the north shore of Long Island and connecting the East River and the Atlantic Ocean〉 〈the Chandeleur *Sound* lying between the southeast coast of Louisiana and the Chandeleur Islands and opening at both ends into the Gulf of Mexico〉 **Channel** is less frequent than *strait* or *sound* as a technical term in the sense here considered, but when it is so used it denotes a relatively large sound 〈the English *Channel* between southeastern England and the north coast of France〉 〈the Mozambique *Channel* between the coast of southeastern Africa and Mozambique Island〉 **Passage** is practically synonymous with *channel*, denoting a connecting body of water wider than a strait 〈Mona *Passage* between the islands of Hispaniola and Puerto Rico〉 **Narrows** designates a strait or a contracted part of a body of water; it is especially used of the necklike part of a bottle-shaped harbor 〈the *Narrows* of New York harbor〉

2 pass, exigency, pinch, emergency, *juncture, contingency, crisis
*Ana* *difficulty, hardship, vicissitude, rigor: perplexity, bewilderment, mystification (see corresponding verbs at PUZZLE): plight, *predicament, fix, quandary

**straitlaced** *prim, priggish, prissy, prudish, puritanical, stuffy
*Ana* narrow, narrow-minded, hidebound, intolerant (see ILLIBERAL): *rigid, rigorous, strict
*Ant* libertine

**strand** *shore, coast, beach, bank, littoral, foreshore

**strange,** singular, unique, peculiar, eccentric, erratic, odd, queer, quaint, outlandish, curious can mean varying from what is ordinary, usual, and to be expected. Strange, the most comprehensive of these terms, suggests unfamiliarity; it may apply to what is foreign, unnatural, inexplicable, or new ⟨some *strange* and potent élan was released in Cabot shortly after the second treatment . . . . He bloomed, as so few men do—*Purdy*⟩ ⟨to most of us the art of China and Japan, however much it may attract and impress, is *strange*—*Binyon*⟩ ⟨the people in the streets have their usual air, tranquil and indolent. No curiosity, no emotion in their faces. A *strange* people! —*Edmund Wilson*⟩ **Singular** distinctively implies difference from every other instance of its kind and therefore stresses individuality ⟨a distinguished and *singular* excellence—*Mencken*⟩ ⟨the taxi driver had lugged the parcel . . . for the woman, and then—proving himself a *singular* example of his species—had broken a ten-dollar bill for her—*Kahn*⟩ Often, however, the word suggests strangeness that puzzles one or piques one's curiosity ⟨I experienced a *singular* sensation on reading the first sentence . . . . There are sensations you cannot describe—*F. M. Ford*⟩ ⟨'tis *singular* that even within the sight of the high towers of Antioch you could lose your way—*Shelley*⟩ **Unique** implies not only singularity but the fact of being unparalleled without suggesting, as *singular* does, a strange or baffling character or quality ⟨personality always contains something *unique*—*Justice Holmes*⟩ ⟨he has the almost *unique* distinction of having made speeches which were both effective when delivered and also models of literary eloquence—*Inge*⟩ ⟨the majestic, the enduring novels treat of subjects which are rarely *unique*—*Elizabeth Bowen*⟩ **Peculiar** (see also CHARACTERISTIC) implies marked or conspicuous distinctiveness in character or quality ⟨this difference arises . . . from the *peculiar* character of the Government of the United States—*Taney*⟩ ⟨the *peculiar* etiquette attached to elevators was rigidly observed by members of both households—*Bemelmans*⟩ ⟨only subtle and delicate minds . . . catch the characteristic aroma, the *peculiar* perfume—*Brownell*⟩ Often *peculiar* is employed where one of the succeeding terms (as *eccentric* or *queer*) might well be used ⟨he is growing very *peculiar*⟩ ⟨made little effort to remember the day; with its *peculiar* quality of dementia it seemed not a commonplace and civilized social event but a nightmare—*Styron*⟩ **Eccentric** implies divergence from the beaten track; **erratic** adds to *eccentric* a stronger implication of caprice and unpredictability ⟨an *eccentric* preference for beginning his dinner . . . in the late afternoon—*Cather*⟩ ⟨the house had grown, reflecting the stubborn and *eccentric* turns of Justina's mind—*Cheever*⟩ ⟨the workings of his mind were *erratic*⟩ ⟨this towering but *erratic* genius . . . who combined in his tempestuous character so many of the best and the worst qualities of the German—*Shirer*⟩ **Odd** stresses a departure from the usual, the normal, or the regular; it sometimes suggests an element of the fantastic; **queer** even more strongly implies eccentricity and often suggests

that the thing so qualified is dubious or questionable ⟨great men whose *odd* habits it would have been glorious piety to endure—*George Eliot*⟩ ⟨the *oddest* sense of being herself invisible; unseen; unknown—*Woolf*⟩ ⟨Alice was not much surprised at this, she was getting so well used to *queer* things happening—*Lewis Carroll*⟩ ⟨completely out of control . . . her voice had become louder and her smile *queerer*—*Wouk*⟩ **Quaint** implies pleasant or especially old-fashioned oddness; **outlandish,** uncouth or bizarre oddness ⟨a *quaint* village, full of half-timbered houses⟩ ⟨to post-Freudian ears, this kind of language seems touchingly *quaint* and ingenuous—*Huxley*⟩ ⟨an *outlandish* custom⟩ ⟨he wore the prophet's robe with a difference. He never let it look *outlandish* —*Montague*⟩ ⟨he introduced *outlandish* or unbelievable people and situations into his work; that is, . . . fantasy was not a mode of escape but a device of satire—*Fitzell*⟩ **Curious** usually implies extraordinary oddness or a singularity that invites close attention, study, or inquiry. When the word is employed as an equivalent of one or another of the foregoing words it tends to retain to a greater or less degree the notion of extraordinariness and often suggests that the thing so described merits notice or investigation ⟨a *curious* sickening smell⟩ ⟨*curious* bits of folklore⟩ ⟨*curious* customs and habits of speech surviving from an earlier age⟩ ⟨my only guiding principle has been that the examples should be *curious,* striking and even, in certain cases, extravagant—*Huxley*⟩ ⟨a *curious* sensation, sitting only a yard away from this man who fifty years before had made me so miserable that I had once contemplated suicide—*Dahl*⟩ ⟨loneliness, far from being a rare and *curious* circumstance—*Wolfe*⟩
*Ana* *abnormal, atypical, aberrant: *fantastic, bizarre, grotesque: surprising, astonishing, amazing, flabbergasting (see SURPRISE)
*Ant* familiar

**stranger,** foreigner, alien, outlander, outsider, immigrant, émigré can all designate a person who comes into a community from the outside and is not recognized as a member of that community. This is the primary denotation of some of the words, but the secondary sense of the others, especially the last three. *Stranger* and *foreigner* may both apply to one who comes from another country or sometimes from another section as a resident or visitor. They have somewhat different implications, however, **stranger** stressing the person's unfamiliarity with the language and customs and **foreigner** the fact that he speaks a different language, follows different customs, or bears allegiance to another government ⟨the time came when I was the observant *foreigner,* examining education in France. To tell the truth, I was not a *stranger* to it, having lived in France as a child and again as a youth—*Grandgent*⟩ **Alien** emphasizes allegiance to another sovereign or government and is often opposed to *citizen;* thus, one may be called a *foreigner* after naturalization, but not with accuracy an *alien.* In extended use *alien* can imply either exclusion from full privileges of or inability to identify oneself with a group ⟨the older I grow, the more of an *alien* I find myself in the world; I cannot get used to it, cannot believe that it is real—*L. P. Smith*⟩ ⟨he is anesthetic to their theological and political enthusiasms. He finds himself an *alien* at their feasts of soul—*Mencken*⟩ **Outlander,** in its general sense, is preferred to *foreigner* only for a literary or rhetorical reason or because it carries the implications of *outlandish* ⟨to this vast matriarchal blackness he had returned, bringing a bride, an *outlander*— *Hervey*⟩ ⟨his neighbors were . . . *outlanders* of that particular type to which . . . his own fastidiousness found the greatest objection—*Tarkington*⟩ **Outsider** usually

A colon (:) separates groups of words discriminated. An asterisk (*) indicates place of treatment of each group.

implies nonmembership in a group, clique, or caste largely because of essential differences in origin, interests, backgrounds, customs, and manners ⟨was the only *outsider* in a company of which every member was privy to the origin, developments, and existing state of its complications—*Sackville-West*⟩ *Immigrant* and *émigré* are often used of foreigners who are residents and no longer aliens. **Immigrant** usually is applied to a foreigner who has come voluntarily, typically in search of a better means of earning a living or a more satisfying way of life; *émigré* implies that the foreigner is a fugitive or refugee from his native land or, in a weaker sense, that he has left his abiding place rather from dissatisfaction than from strong hope for a better future ⟨Hemingway, whom the young *émigrés* to Montparnasse . . . had hailed as a major prophet of the emptiness of everything—*F. L. Allen*⟩

**strangle** *vb* \*suffocate, asphyxiate, stifle, smother, choke, throttle

**stratagem** \*trick, ruse, maneuver, gambit, ploy, artifice, wile, feint

*Ana* \*device, contrivance, contraption: expedient, shift, \*resource, resort: machination, intrigue, conspiracy, \*plot

**strategic** tactical, logistic (see under STRATEGY)

**strategy, tactics, logistics** as used in relation to warfare are not always clearly distinguished. **Strategy** is the art or science involved in the direction of the forces at his disposal by the commander in chief of a belligerent nation or by those assisting him. The term usually implies the planning of major operations intended to gain the objectives of the war, and often, but not necessarily, connotes the effective presence of these officers at home or behind the lines. **Tactics** is the art or science of handling forces in the field or in action; the term implies not only the presence of the enemy as affecting the disposition or maneuvering of troops, ships, planes, and matériels but the direction of a commanding officer upon the scene ⟨the theater of war is the province of *strategy*, the field of battle is the province of *tactics—Hamley*⟩ **Logistics** is the art or science of military supply and transportation; the term usually implies both planning and implementation and covers such varied matters as design and development, acquisition, stockpiling, shipping and distribution, upkeep, and ultimate evacuation and disposition of matériel; acquisition, preparation, assignment, distribution, and physical care of personnel; preparation, operation, upkeep, and disposal of facilities; and provision of services. Broadly *logistics* constitutes the theory and practice of military housekeeping ⟨generals and admirals and their staffs plan campaigns. That is *strategy*. They fight battles and these combat operations are known as *tactics*. A third element determines the success or failure of *strategy* and *tactics*. This is called *logistics*. A large part of an army, a fleet, or an air force, and nearly the entire civilian population today play a role in *logistics*. What they accomplish in producing and distributing the resources needed to implement *strategy* and *tactics* controls the outcome of war—*Donald Armstrong*⟩

The same differences in meaning are also found in **strategic, tactical,** and **logistic** (or **logistical**) as referred to the conduct of a war ⟨*strategic* air war now being conducted so effectively upon German cities and factories by the Royal Air force and the United States 8th air force will in due time be supplemented or in part substituted by *tactical* air operations on which our ground forces will depend to cover advances of troops and to devastate the huge fortifications erected by the Nazis in northern France, Belgium and along the northern coast of the continent—*David Lawrence*⟩ ⟨the outstanding military lesson of this campaign was the continuous, calculated application of air power . . . in the most intimate *tactical* and *logistical* union with ground forces—*MacArthur*⟩

**straw** *vb* \*strew, scatter, sow, broadcast

**stray** *vb* \*wander, roam, ramble, rove, range, prowl, gad, gallivant, traipse, meander

**streak** *n* strain, vein, \*touch, suggestion, suspicion, soupçon, tincture, tinge, shade, smack, spice, dash

**stream** *n* \*flow, current, flood, tide, flux

**stream** *vb* \*pour, gush, sluice

*Ana* flow, issue, emanate, proceed (see SPRING): flood, deluge, inundate (see corresponding nouns at FLOOD)

**streamer** pennant, pendant, pennon, banner, \*flag, ensign, standard, color

**strength** \*power, force, might, energy, puissance

*Ana* stoutness, sturdiness, toughness, tenaciousness (see corresponding adjectives at STRONG): soundness, healthiness (see corresponding adjectives at HEALTHY): \*possessions, means, resources, assets

**strengthen, invigorate, fortify, energize, reinforce** can mean to make strong or stronger. **Strengthen** is the most general term, applicable not only to persons or their physical, mental, or moral powers but also to things material or immaterial (as a structure, a system, an aggregation, or an influence); the word can connote increase either in force, energy, vigor, and power of resistance, or in intensity, authority, or effectiveness ⟨their friendship *strengthened* as they grew older⟩ ⟨exercise is necessary to *strengthen* the body⟩ ⟨opposition will only *strengthen* their belief⟩ ⟨his case was greatly *strengthened* by the newly discovered evidence⟩ ⟨the handle of the tool had been bound by ordinary picture wire, apparently to *strengthen* a fracture in the wood—*Hynd*⟩ ⟨impulses to submission *strengthened* by habits of obedience bred in the past—*Dewey*⟩ ⟨after a period of hoarse whispering, her voice changes its tone and *strengthens—Hearn*⟩ **Invigorate** is commonly used in reference to living things or of some power or activity of a living thing and is sometimes extended to things that have powers suggestive of life; it implies an increase in vigor or vitality or active or effective strength or force ⟨their minds and bodies were *invigorated* by exercise—*Gibbon*⟩ ⟨the series of Midwestern novels that followed shocked and *invigorated* American thought—*S. R. L.*⟩ ⟨the general run of Canadians are *invigorated* when our athletes win recognition in the United States—*D. M. Fisher*⟩ ⟨a passing priest heard of Kaldi's discovery and thought that he would try these *invigorating* berries since he was inclined to fall asleep during his prayers—*Charles Cooper*⟩ ⟨*invigorating* sea breezes⟩ **Fortify**, which primarily means to strengthen a town or city by defensive structures, in a more general sense means to strengthen against attack or stress of any sort ⟨a certain uneasiness had come upon her, and even *fortified* by food she could not bring herself to go—*Boyle*⟩ ⟨*fortified* himself with a stiff drink⟩ ⟨I have been *fortified* in my belief by the utterances of this Court from the time of Chief Justice Taney to the present day—*Justice Holmes*⟩ ⟨set up on a pedestal, *fortified* by the strongest bulwark in executive acts, those principles which we would abandon at our peril—*Vannevar Bush*⟩ ⟨the old-fashioned polemical sermon followed, *fortified* with texts and garnished with quotations in Greek—*Brooks*⟩ **Energize** implies a strengthening in the form of supplying the active power for working or for being ready for work and, therefore, is used of whatever can be roused into strong activity or infused with a desire to act ⟨the office of Inspector General was greatly improved, and *energized*, during

*Ana* analogous words    *Ant* antonyms    *Con* contrasted words    See also explanatory notes facing page 1

the first administration of Mr. Pitt—*Chalmers*⟩ ⟨as between husband and wife, hers was definitely the stronger spirit. She was more highly *energized*, more industrious, more ambitious—*S. H. Adams*⟩ ⟨he *energized* the Garden-Suburb ethos with a certain original talent and the vigor of a prolonged adolescence—*Leavis*⟩ **Reinforce** implies the making of what is weak stronger or of what is strong still stronger by or as if by an addition that stiffens and supports, and thereby adds effectiveness, powers of resistance, cogency, or durability ⟨*reinforce* concrete by embedding steel bars or mesh in it⟩ ⟨*reinforce* an argument by additional evidence⟩ ⟨*reinforce* a stocking at heel and toe⟩ ⟨the stimulus given by his dialectics to their keen and eager minds was supplemented and *reinforced* by the appeal to their admiration and love of his sweet and virile personality—*Dickinson*⟩ ⟨Maria's distrust returned, *reinforced* by resentment. Yet she said nothing—*Hervey*⟩ ⟨experience in Brazil seems to show that in mixed marriages the black element, if not *reinforced*, is absorbed by the white within a few generations—*William Tate*⟩

*Ana* embolden, steel, nerve, *encourage, inspirit, hearten, cheer: *vitalize, activate: galvanize, quicken, stimulate (see PROVOKE): *intensify, heighten, aggravate

*Ant* weaken —*Con* enfeeble, debilitate, sap, undermine, cripple, disable (see WEAKEN): *discourage, dishearten, dispirit, deject: *unnerve, enervate, unman, emasculate

**strenuous** energetic, *vigorous, lusty, nervous

*Ana* virile, manful, manly (see MALE): dynamic, live, *active, operative: *spirited, high-spirited, mettlesome: vehement, *intense, fierce, violent

**stress** *n* **1** Stress, strain, pressure, tension are comparable terms when they apply to the action or effect of force exerted within or upon a thing. *Stress* and *strain* are the comprehensive terms of this group and are sometimes used interchangeably ⟨put *stresses* and *strains* on parts of the body that were not constructed to bear that burden—*Fishbein*⟩ ⟨if sufficiently large *stresses* are applied to any crystal, it remains at least partly deformed when the *stresses* are removed—*Seitz*⟩ ⟨the wrench is an instrument for exerting a twisting *strain*, as in turning bolts and nuts —*Burghardt & Axelrod*⟩ ⟨by a powerful *strain* upon the reins, raising his horse's forefeet from the ground—*De Quincey*⟩ ⟨the breakup due to tremendous *strains* experienced in bad weather have time and again proven the fatal power of squalls over dirigibles—*Furnas*⟩ Although **stress** is frequently used in technical contexts in the above sense of a force applied to deform a body, it is also used, especially in physics, of the equal and opposite forces with which the body resists being deformed ⟨a weight suspended from a rod tends to pull the rod apart. The *stress* developed in the rod to resist being pulled apart is called tensile *stress*—*Samuel Slade & Louis Margolis*⟩ **Strain** in technical contexts and especially in physics usually denotes the deformation of a body as a result of applied force ⟨a new device . . . conveniently measures *strain* in vulcanized rubber . . . after application of a predetermined *stress*—*Technical News Bulletin*⟩ ⟨it is generally held that most earthquakes are caused by the sudden release of elastic *strain* when this becomes greater than the strength of the rock—*Science*⟩ **Pressure** commonly applies to a stress which is characterized by a weighing down upon or a pushing against a surface and which, in fluids, is distributed uniformly in all directions; it is usually measurable per unit area of surface affected ⟨the normal atmospheric *pressure* is about 14.7 pounds per square inch—*Van Nostrand's*⟩ ⟨the *pressure* of the blood against the walls of blood vessels⟩ ⟨steam *pressure*⟩ **Tension** applies to either of two balancing forces causing or tending

to cause elongation of an elastic body or to the stress resulting from the elongation of such a body ⟨a steel bar can safely bear a pull or *tension* of 16,000 lb. for each square inch of its cross section—*Samuel Slade & Louis Margolis*⟩

**2** *emphasis, accent, accentuation

**stretch** *n* *expanse, amplitude, spread

*Ana* *area, tract, region: extent, magnitude, *size

**strew,** straw, scatter, sow, broadcast can mean to throw loosely or at intervals. **Strew** and the less common **straw** usually imply a spreading at intervals, but the intervals may be so fine as not to be obvious or so great that each thing may be separately identified ⟨ground *strewn* with leaves⟩ ⟨*strew* a path with gravel⟩ ⟨as he sits in the armchair, the Sunday papers are *strewn* around him—*Mailer*⟩ ⟨he looked . . . over the great mesa-*strewn* plain far below —*Cather*⟩ ⟨petty ordinances . . . of no more weight than dandelion fluff *strawed* by the wind—*Clement Wood*⟩ ⟨the tent of night in tatters *straws* the sky-pavilioned land —*Housman*⟩ **Scatter** (see also SCATTER) implies a separation of parts or pieces, but it distinctively implies a throwing that lets the things fall where they will ⟨*scatter* pennies⟩ ⟨*scatter* bread crumbs⟩ ⟨no railroad *scatters* its soot over the neat white frame houses—*Corey Ford*⟩ ⟨a story . . . attacking tuberculars for coming to San Antonio and *scattering* their deadly germs about this innocent city—*Green Peyton*⟩ **Sow** basically implies the strewing of seeds where they will sprout and develop ⟨surrounding fields have been *sown* . . . with squash, pumpkin, and maize—*Science*⟩ or in its extended use the strewing of something comparable to seed that can be disseminated (as throughout a group, a community, or an organization) ⟨*sow* discord among the club members⟩ ⟨*sow* seeds of reason and understanding throughout the world—*A. E. Stevenson*⟩ **Broadcast** (see also DECLARE) implies a scattering widely or in all directions ⟨it is best to *broadcast* very fine seed⟩ ⟨early in April, just before a rain begins, *broadcast* 3 pounds of white clover seed—*H. S. Pearson*⟩

*Ana* *spread, disseminate: disperse, dissipate (see SCATTER)

**strict** stringent, *rigid, rigorous

*Ana* stern, *severe, austere, ascetic: *inflexible, inexorable: exacting, oppressive, *onerous, burdensome

*Ant* lax: loose: lenient, indulgent

**stricture** *animadversion, aspersion, reflection

*Ana* criticism, censuring *or* censure, condemnation, denouncing *or* denunciation (see corresponding verbs at CRITICIZE)

*Ant* commendation

**strident** **1** *loud, stentorian, earsplitting, hoarse, raucous, stertorous

*Ana* harsh, *rough: resounding, *resonant

**2** blatant, clamorous, *vociferous, boisterous, obstreperous

*Ana* harsh, uneven, *rough

**strife** *discord, conflict, contention, dissension, difference, variance

*Ana* combat, conflict, fight, affray, fray (see CONTEST): dispute, controversy, *argument: *brawl, broil, fracas: altercation, wrangle, *quarrel, squabble

*Ant* peace: accord

**strike** *vb* **1** Strike, hit, smite, punch, slug, slog, swat, clout, slap, cuff, box are comparable when they mean to come or bring into contact with or as if with a sharp blow. *Strike, hit,* and *smite* are the more general terms. **Strike,** the most general of the words, may indicate the motion of aiming or dealing the blow, the motion prior to contact with the hand, fist, instrument, weapon, or missile ⟨*strike* at the enemy and miss⟩ ⟨*strike* out at random⟩ It may

---

A colon (:) separates groups of words discriminated. An asterisk (*) indicates place of treatment of each group.

indicate various types of contact from a light, often stroking contact ⟨the light breeze *struck* the ship on the north side⟩ to a forcible collision or blasting contact ⟨the car *struck* a post and overturned⟩ ⟨the lightning *struck* the house⟩ ⟨*strike* a man down with a heavy blow⟩ ⟨the enemy *struck* with full force⟩ It may suggest several types of physical or emotional effect or impression ⟨*strike* someone dead⟩ ⟨*strike* a line on paper⟩ ⟨*strike* out a name from a list⟩ ⟨to be *struck* by the beauty of the scenery⟩ ⟨grief-*stricken*⟩ ⟨conscience-*stricken*⟩ or it may be used to indicate any of the types of contact suggested by the other words in this group. **Hit**, although it is used in most of the situations in which *strike* occurs, emphasizes more than the latter the physical or figurative contact with or impact upon an object, usually one aimed at; it tends to stress forcefulness ⟨*hit* a child on the wrist⟩ ⟨the shell *hit* the tank and tore through the side⟩ ⟨the disaster . . . *hit* him hard—*H. G. Wells*⟩ ⟨*hit* the right road home⟩ ⟨*hit* the winning number in a lottery⟩ **Smite**, likely to appear in rhetorical or bookish contexts, commonly stresses the injuriousness or destructiveness of the contact and often suggests a motivation of anger or desire for vengeance ⟨with the hammer she *smote* Sisera, she *smote* off his head—*Judg 5:26*⟩ ⟨conscience-*smitten*⟩ ⟨*smitten* with grief⟩ *Punch, slug, slog, swat,* and *clout* are generally used to suggest the giving of various kinds of usually sharp or heavy blows. **Punch** suggests a quick blow with or as if with the fist ⟨would handcuff everybody rather than face the risk of having their noses *punched* by somebody—*Shaw*⟩ **Slug** emphasizes the heaviness of the impact and may suggest a certain viciousness in the delivery of the blow ⟨was attacked by an assault suspect, who *slugged* him with a 5-ft. iron pipe—*Time*⟩ **Slog** emphasizes the heavy and typically haphazard quality of the blows ⟨"*Slog* them on the head with your club . . . ," shouted Tammers. And as the twisted knot of men reeled conveniently towards me I did what execution I could—*Strand Mag.*⟩ and in sports (as cricket or golf) it may stress power as opposed to finesse ⟨hayfields fringed the very putting greens . . . and a man had to *slog* and *slog* again before he got out of them—*Bernard Darwin*⟩ **Swat** suggests a forceful, slapping blow, usually with an instrument (as a bat, weapon, or flyswatter) ⟨in off moments he would *swat* the regiments of cockroaches—*de Kruif*⟩ ⟨*swat* flies⟩ ⟨*swat* a baseball out of the ball park⟩ **Clout** suggests a heavy careless blow (as with the hand or fist) ⟨a shoe *clouted* his skull and inflicted a fracture—*McCrae*⟩ ⟨they *clout* our heads the moment our conclusions differ from theirs—*Shaw*⟩ *Slap, cuff,* and *box* all denote blows of varying force with the open hand. **Slap** is the most general and indicates a sharp, stinging blow with or as if with the palm of the hand ⟨*slap* a person in the face⟩ ⟨*slapped* the coverlet angrily—*Kenneth Roberts*⟩ **Cuff** suggests a blow often forcible enough to dizzy or throw off balance and often dealt with the back of the hand ⟨it was pointed out . . . that children could be hurried and delayed, *cuffed* or bribed, into becoming adults—*Mead*⟩ ⟨I swear I'll *cuff* you, if you strike again—*Shak.*⟩ **Box** suggests the delivery of an openhanded blow but is ordinarily limited to one against the ears ⟨the mother *boxed* her child's ears in a fit of temper⟩
*Ana* *beat, pummel, buffet, pound, baste, belabor, thrash
**2** impress, touch, influence, *affect, sway
**striking** arresting, signal, salient, conspicuous, outstanding, *noticeable, remarkable, prominent
*Ana* *effective, effectual, efficacious: telling, convincing, compelling, cogent (see VALID): forcible, forceful, *powerful: impressive, *moving

**string** *n* **1** *succession, progression, series, sequence, chain, train
**2** in plural form **strings** *condition, stipulation, terms, provision, proviso, reservation
**stringent** strict, *rigid, rigorous
*Ana* *severe, austere, stern: limiting, restricting, circumscribing, confining (see LIMIT *vb*): restraining, curbing (see RESTRAIN): exacting, oppressive, *onerous
**strip** *vb* Strip, divest, denude, bare, dismantle can mean to deprive a person or thing of what clothes, furnishes, or invests him or it. **Strip** stresses a pulling or tearing off rather than a laying bare, though the latter implication is frequent; it often connotes more or less violent action or complete deprivation ⟨*strip* the bark from a tree⟩ ⟨he was quickly *stripped* of his clothes⟩ ⟨where pasturing cattle *stripped* the ground⟩ ⟨once start *stripping* poetry of what you imagine are inessentials and you will find . . . the anatomy is made visible but the life will have gone —*Day Lewis*⟩ ⟨I had *stripped* a few of my habits, seconal and benzedrine at any rate, but I was . . . tense and brain-deadened—*Mailer*⟩ **Divest**, in contrast to *strip*, does not suggest violence; it usually implies a taking away of what a person or thing has been clothed or equipped with especially as a sign of power, rank, influence, or prestige ⟨*divesting* capitalists of further increments of power—*Cohen*⟩ Therefore it often connotes an undoing or a dispossession or a degrading ⟨*divest* an officer of all authority⟩ ⟨naturalism *divests* life, whether physical or spiritual, of all that separates it from the inanimate and inorganic—*Inge*⟩ ⟨the king is thus *divested* of his kingship and now becomes merely a corpse—*Frazer*⟩ **Denude** implies a stripping or divesting, but distinctively it implies a resulting bareness or nakedness ⟨*stripped* of its vines and *denuded* of its shrubbery, the house would probably have been ugly enough—*Cather*⟩ ⟨a ghostly lunar rainbow —the spectrum cleansed and *denuded* of all the garish colors of day—*Beebe*⟩ ⟨modern agriculture . . . *denudes* the land of the protective cover and food that wild creatures need—*G. S. Perry*⟩ **Bare**, although it suggests a removal of what covers or clothes, seldom carries implications of violent or complete stripping; it is chiefly used in idiomatic phrases which imply more than the mere act; thus, to *bare* one's head is to take off one's hat usually as a sign of respect or reverence; to *bare* one's sword is to unsheathe it and to have it ready for action; to *bare* one's heart to another is to reveal feelings one has concealed; to *bare* the secrets of the grave is to disclose, often as a result of a discovery of documents, something which had been known only to persons now dead ⟨no hidden secrets are *bared* in this biography—*Lubell*⟩ ⟨*bared* her teeth at the audience with comic ferocity—*Wouk*⟩ **Dismantle** is used chiefly with reference to the act of stripping a house, a building, a ship, or a complex installation (as of machinery) of its entire equipment and furnishings ⟨*dismantle* a factory⟩ ⟨the cottage itself was built of old stones from the long *dismantled* Priory—*Hardy*⟩ ⟨hurriedly *dismantled* a second bomb that he had brought along—*Shirer*⟩
*Ana* despoil, spoliate, devastate, waste, *ravage: rifle, loot, plunder, *rob
*Ant* furnish: invest
**strip** *n* Strip, stripe, band, ribbon, fillet are comparable when they mean a relatively long and narrow piece or section. *Strip* and *stripe* both imply length and comparative narrowness and approximate uniformity of width. However **strip** commonly suggests separation from a larger piece ⟨tear old linen into *strips* for bandages⟩ ⟨cut a sheet of paper into *strips*⟩ and **stripe** stresses a contrast (as in color, texture, or pattern) between the section of

a surface referred to and the sections bordering upon it ⟨each white petal had a *stripe* of red⟩ ⟨gray cloth with alternate *stripes* of blue and red⟩ ⟨when one or more *strips* of braid have been sewn on a soldier's sleeve to indicate his rank or his length of service, they are called *stripes*⟩ If actual separation is not implied *strip* may be employed when the difference between the portion of surface referred to and its neighboring portions is a matter of use, ownership, or physical character ⟨the *strip* between sidewalk and curb belongs to the city⟩ ⟨each man on relief was allotted a *strip* of land for raising vegetables⟩ However *stripe* may be used in such cases in preference to *strip* when the division is made evident by a contrast in appearance ⟨narrow *stripes* of ice separated from each other by parallel moraines—*Tyndall*⟩ ⟨*stripes* of cultivated land in various shades of green⟩ **Band** (see also BOND 1) may mean either a strip or stripe but often also connotes either an encircling with or without a suggestion of confining or uniting or a horizontal position rather than the vertical position so often connoted by *stripe* ⟨the lower parts of the sleeves and of the skirt were adorned with *bands* of blue silk⟩ ⟨*bands* of colored light in the sky at dawn⟩ ⟨at closer range, the mountain showed three *bands*, the lowest green, the middle gray, and the highest white⟩ **Ribbon** designates concretely a length of narrow woven material with selvage edges, usually one that is fine and firm in texture and is used for ornamental bands, ties, and bows. In extended use *ribbon* is often used in place of *strip* when the strips are very long, very narrow, and very thin and when the material is flexible enough to appear like ribbon or to be handled like ribbon ⟨steel *ribbon* for use in springs⟩ ⟨*ribbons* of red, green, and gold paper for tying Christmas packages⟩ ⟨the sails were torn by the hurricane into *ribbons*⟩ ⟨the road was a *ribbon* of moonlight over the purple moor—*Noyes*⟩ **Fillet**, which basically denotes a narrow strip of ornamental material (as a band of ribbon for restraining the hair or a narrow molding or beading that forms the inner part of a picture frame), is often extended to various things that have no inherent ornamental quality and are otherwise describable as strips, ribbons, or bands (as a metal strip or ribbon from which coins are punched, a very thin molding, one of certain bands of white matter in the brain, or a long narrow piece of meat or fish without bone).

**stripe** *n* **1** *strip, band, ribbon, fillet
**2** character, description, nature, *type, kind, sort, kidney, ilk

**strive** struggle, endeavor, *attempt, essay, try
*Ana* work, labor, toil, travail (see corresponding nouns at WORK): *contend, fight

**striving** *n* struggle, endeavor, essay, attempt, try (see under ATTEMPT *vb*)
*Ana* *work, labor, toil, travail: contending (see CONTEND): *contest, conflict, combat, fight

**stroll** *vb* *saunter, amble

**strong, stout, sturdy, stalwart, tough, tenacious** can all mean having or manifesting great power or force (as in acting or resisting). **Strong**, the most inclusive of these terms, fundamentally implies the possession of great physical power and may connote such varied causes as sound health or physical size and vigor or soundness of construction and substance ⟨a *strong* constitution⟩ ⟨the hammock is not *strong* enough to bear the weight of two persons⟩ ⟨a *strong* foundation⟩ ⟨his hands were large. They looked neither *strong* nor competent—*Salinger*⟩ but in extended use it may apply to groups whose force is dependent upon numbers, organization, or discipline ⟨a *strong* army⟩ ⟨a *strong* majority forced

a wavering minority along the road of rectitude—*Replier*⟩ or to a spiritual or mental power or faculty that acts with force and vigor ⟨a *strong* mind⟩ ⟨a *strong* will⟩ ⟨a *strong* critical instinct⟩ or to some very potent or powerful thing ⟨*strong* liquor⟩ ⟨a *strong* poison⟩ ⟨a *strong* current⟩ ⟨a *strong* battery⟩ ⟨the memorandum was couched in *strong* language and the Russians replied to it . . . with equally stern words—*Shirer*⟩ or to something (as color or light or emotion or sentiment) that is particularly intense or violent ⟨a *strong* purple⟩ ⟨the *strong* light of the setting sun⟩ ⟨*strong* love⟩ ⟨a *strong* attachment⟩ ⟨the impulse to fight is something so *strong*, so deep-seated, so uncontrollable by . . . reason—*Edmund Wilson*⟩ **Stout** (see also FLESHY) carries a stronger implication than does *strong* of an ability to resist aggression or destructive forces or of an ability to endure hard use, severe pain, or great temptation without giving way. When applied to persons, it often suggests resolution, doggedness, or fearlessness ⟨a *stouter* champion never handled sword—*Shak.*⟩ ⟨and let our hearts be *stout*, to wait out the long travail . . . to impart our courage unto our sons—*Roosevelt*⟩ When applied to things, *stout* usually also suggests solid, substantial construction ⟨a *stout* cane⟩ ⟨a *stout* ship⟩ or a texture that resists stress or strain ⟨*stout* canvas⟩ ⟨a *stout* paper⟩ ⟨their feet were protected by *stout* boots—*Mason*⟩ In fact the term is generally applicable when the suggestion of power to resist or endure is more emphatic than that of a power to do or to effect. **Sturdy** implies qualities in inanimate as well as in animate things that suggest the possession of rugged health; the term carries no suggestion of powers derived from such qualities as size, intensity, or vehemence but connotes rather an inner strength typically derived from healthy vigorous growth, close solid construction, or a determined spirit that gives it staying power and stoutness ⟨the little fellow has *sturdy* legs⟩ ⟨was a *sturdy*, handsome, high-colored woman—*Van Doren*⟩ ⟨it is the *sturdiest* of creepers, facing the ferocious winds of the hills, the tremendous rains that blow up from the sea, and bitter frost—*Jefferies*⟩ ⟨our people are . . . conspicuous for a *sturdy* independence—*Inge*⟩ **Stalwart** usually implies strength derived from what is so deeply established or firmly rooted that it is unassailable or impregnable or is completely dependable ⟨William Law . . . was a *stalwart* Churchman, and showed no sympathy with the sectaries—*Inge*⟩ ⟨Dryden brings his *stalwart* common sense to bear upon the problem, and clarifies the issue—*Lowes*⟩ ⟨what is best in our society will have to be saved by the advocates of some older and more *stalwart* system of thought—*Kirk*⟩ When applied to persons with reference to their physique or prowess, *stalwart* regularly suggests great strength, but it often throws the emphasis upon heroic build or largeness of frame ⟨a *stalwart* man, limbed like the old heroic breeds—*J. R. Lowell*⟩ **Tough** suggests the strength that comes from a texture or a spirit that is firm and unyielding and effectively resists attempts to pierce, destroy, or overcome; it stresses hardiness rather than vigor, resistant elasticity or wiriness rather than hardness or solidity, or a capacity for yielding that is just sufficient to increase rather than to destroy a person's or thing's strength or stoutness ⟨a *tough* membrane⟩ ⟨a *tough* opponent⟩ ⟨*tough* resistance⟩ ⟨any type who reached the age of six . . . was a pint of iron man, so *tough*, so ferocious, so sharp in the teeth that the wildest alley cat would have surrendered a freshly caught rat rather than contest the meal—*Mailer*⟩ ⟨physically fragile, she was spiritually *tough*—*Sackville-West*⟩ **Tenacious** comes very close to *tough* in its most general implications, but it places greater emphasis upon

A colon (:) separates groups of words discriminated. An asterisk (*) indicates place of treatment of each group.

retentiveness of what has been gained or of adherence to a support, position, or idea; it carries a strong suggestion of holding on, of adhesiveness, or of maintaining strength or position in spite of all opposing forces that would dislodge, dispossess, thwart, or weaken ⟨he had always held with *tenacious* devotion to one of the ancient traditions of his race—*Wolfe*⟩ ⟨he seemed to hold on to life by a single thread only, but that single thread was very *tenacious*—*Arnold*⟩ When applied to material things and especially to substances it may suggest a powerful clinging quality and extraordinary resistance to forces that tend to effect separation or pulling apart ⟨*tenacious* mud⟩ ⟨bold and *tenacious* as the bamboo shooting up through the hard ground of winter—*Binyon*⟩ When applied to persons it suggests a stubborn hold upon something (as a possession or an opinion) that defies the efforts of others to break ⟨Italians in possession are probably as *tenacious* of their rights as any one else—*Lucas*⟩
*Ana* *vigorous, energetic, lusty: *powerful, potent, forcible, forceful: robust, sound, *healthy: vehement, *intense, fierce, exquisite, violent
*Ant* weak

**stronghold** citadel, *fort, fortress, fastness

**structure 1** *building, edifice, pile
**2 Structure, anatomy, framework, skeleton** are often used interchangeably. **Structure** is by far the richest in implications and the widest in its range of application. In general it denotes the formation, arrangement, and articulation of parts in something built up by nature or made by man. Often the word implies reference to everything that enters into the makeup of a particular body, organism, edifice, fabric, or substance; thus, a study of the *structure* of a brain involves attention to the two kinds of matter (gray and white) of which it is composed, to the three parts (forebrain, midbrain, hindbrain) into which it is divided, to the subdivisions of each of these parts, to the connections and interrelations between all these divisions, and to any peculiarities in form or arrangement of parts. Sometimes, however, *structure* implies a reference to certain features only, as for example: the parts or elements which distinguish kinds rather than individuals ⟨crocodiles and alligators exhibit certain differences in *structure*⟩ or the parts or features which are essential or necessary to a thing's existence as distinguished from those that are removable, detachable, or dispensable ⟨in Gothic architecture the pointed arch · is part of the *structure* and is not a decorative addition⟩ or the parts or features that reveal the underlying design as opposed to those that complete the work or bring it into fullness of being ⟨study the *structure* of a poem⟩ **Anatomy** may be preferred when the typical structure of an organism or of an organ is to be denoted ⟨the *anatomy* of an ape⟩ ⟨the *anatomy* of the heart⟩ *Framework* and *skeleton* are applied to the underlying or supporting structure. **Framework** is used chiefly in reference to an artificial construction which serves as a prop and a guide in building but which is not visible in the completed thing ⟨the *framework* of a sofa⟩ ⟨the carpenters are now working on the *framework* for the house⟩ **Skeleton** is frequently used in the building trades for a rigid framework, especially one made of steel; it is often used in place of *structure, design, outline* in reference to literary constructions, sometimes to imply that the design is carefully developed and its parts definitely articulated ⟨the *skeleton* of his argument is now finished⟩ but more often, probably, to indicate a sketchy conception of the whole which serves as a starting point ⟨he has the *skeleton* of his plot in mind⟩ In either case it is usually further implied that the writing out in literary form and the elaboration of atmosphere,

details, characters remain to be accomplished.
*Ana* integration, articulation, concatenation (see under INTEGRATE): organization, arrangement (see corresponding verbs at ORDER): *system, organism, scheme, complex

**struggle** *vb* strive, endeavor, essay, *attempt, try
*Ana* *contend, fight: compete, vie, *rival, emulate: toil, labor, work, travail (see corresponding nouns at WORK)

**struggle** *n* striving, endeavor, essay, attempt, try (see under ATTEMPT *vb*)
*Ana* toil, labor, *work, travail: *contest, conflict, fight, affray, fray: contending (see CONTEND)

**strut** *vb* **Strut, swagger, bristle, bridle** can all mean to assume an air of dignity or importance. **Strut** implies a pompous or theatrical affectation of dignity, especially as shown in one's gait or by one's bearing in movement ⟨a poor player that *struts* and frets his hour upon the stage—*Shak.*⟩ ⟨Dr. Goldsmith . . . went . . . *strutting* away and calling to me with an air of superiority—*Boswell*⟩ **Swagger** implies ostentation, a conviction of one's superiority, and, often, an insolent or overbearing gait or manner ⟨scarcely deigned to set a foot to ground, but *swaggered* like a lord about his hall—*Dryden*⟩ ⟨what a *swaggering* puppy must he take me for—*Goldsmith*⟩ **Bristle** implies an aggressive manifestation sometimes of anger or of zeal but often of an emotion or desire that causes one to display conspicuously one's sense of dignity or importance ⟨all the time he stuck close to her, *bristling* with a small boy's pride of her—*D. H. Lawrence*⟩ ⟨the bourgeoisie, *bristling* with prejudices and social snobberies —*Rose Macaulay*⟩ **Bridle** usually suggests awareness of a threat to one's dignity or state and a reaction (as of hostility, protest, scorn, or resentment) typically expressed by a lofty manner with a tossing up of one's head and a drawing in of one's chin ⟨by her *bridling* up I perceived she expected to be treated hereafter not as Jenny Distaff, but Mrs. Tranquillus—*Tatler*⟩ ⟨everything that poses, prances, *bridles*, struts, bedizens, and plumes itself— *Ward*⟩ ⟨military commanders who had *bridled* against . . . interference—*Time*⟩
*Ana* expose, exhibit, flaunt, parade (see SHOW *vb*)
*Con* cringe, cower, *fawn, truckle: grovel (see WALLOW)

**stubborn** *obstinate, dogged, pertinacious, mulish, stiff-necked, pigheaded, bullheaded
*Ana* rebellious, contumacious, *insubordinate: intractable, recalcitrant, refractory (see UNRULY): obdurate, adamant, inexorable, *inflexible
*Con* pliable, pliant, adaptable (see PLASTIC): tractable, amenable (see OBEDIENT)

**stubby** *stocky, thickset, thick, chunky, squat, dumpy
**studied** *deliberate, considered, advised, premeditated, designed
*Ana* *thoughtful, considerate, attentive: intentional, *voluntary, willing, willful
*Con* *spontaneous, impulsive, instinctive

**study** *n* concentration, application, *attention
*Ana* consideration, contemplation, weighing (see corresponding verbs at CONSIDER): reflection, thought, speculation (see corresponding verbs at THINK): pondering, musing, meditation, rumination (see corresponding verbs at PONDER)

**study** *vb* *consider, contemplate, weigh, excogitate
*Ana* scrutinize, examine, inspect: *ponder, muse, meditate: *think, reflect, reason, speculate

**stuff** *n* *matter, substance, material
*Ana* constituent, ingredient, component, *element: *item, detail, particular
**stuff** *vb* *pack, crowd, cram, ram, tamp
*Ana* distend, *expand, swell: squeeze, jam, *press:

gorge, glut, surfeit, sate, *satiate

**stuffy** *prim, priggish, prissy, prudish, puritanical, strait-laced

**Ana** stodgy, *dull, humdrum: *irksome, tedious: narrow, narrow-minded, *illiberal, hidebound

**stumble, trip, blunder, lurch, flounder, lumber, galumph, lollop, bumble** can mean to move unsteadily, clumsily, or with defective equilibrium (as in walking, in doing, or in proceeding). *Stumble, trip, blunder, lurch,* and *flounder* as applied to physical movement or gait usually suggest a departure from the normal and imply some extraneous influence to be responsible for such departure. **Stumble** characteristically implies striking an obstacle or impediment which hinders free movement or direct progress and therefore usually suggests a fall or a check or a cause of embarrassment or perplexity ⟨the horse *stumbled* over a stone and threw its rider⟩ ⟨he found himself running from tree to tree . . . *stumbling* wildly towards the cleared ground—*Caldwell*⟩ ⟨his thought staggers, and reels, and *stumbles*—*Martin Gardner*⟩ ⟨the classic instance of the second-rate man who is offered a first-rate destiny, and who, in *stumbling* after it, loses his way in the world—*Buchan*⟩ Occasionally *stumble* implies nothing more than accidental discovery or a coming upon without design ⟨she tried to rationalize his death as we will, *stumbling* onto such conclusions as that it was time for him to go; he was meant to die young—*Cheever*⟩ **Trip** definitely implies a loss of footing or of something comparable to a loss of footing, often on account of the interposition of an unseen obstacle; therefore in extended use *trip* often connotes a falling into a trap, a lapsing in speech, or making a wrong move ⟨his plump hands wavering uncertainly away from his body as he *tripped,* and caught up and *tripped,* trying desperately not to fall behind the men running—*Mailer*⟩ ⟨how I rejoiced when I found an author *tripping*—*Tyndall*⟩ ⟨his tongue *tripped* over the word⟩ ⟨any military man familiar with firearms could *trip* you up, and if you were found out, you'd be hanged —*Kenneth Roberts*⟩ **Blunder** stresses awkward confusion in movement or in proceeding that may suggest blindness, aimlessness, clumsiness, ignorance, or a failure to perceive where one is going or what is to be accomplished ⟨unsteady on his feet and taken completely by surprise, he *blundered* headlong through the open doorway . . . and fell sprawling—*Isherwood*⟩ ⟨there was the constant danger of *blundering* into a house at a time when it was being ransacked by the Gestapo—*Valtin*⟩ ⟨the van . . . *blundered* away down the cart track like a drunken bee— *Jan Struther*⟩ ⟨various *blundering* attempts were made at alliance between various branches of thought—*T. S. Eliot*⟩ **Lurch** suggests the heavy, ungainly rolling or swaying movement of a ship in a storm or of a drunken man; when applied more generally to persons, it usually implies loss of muscular control or extreme clumsiness ⟨the distraught and frightened man . . . raised himself on his hands and *lurched* forward—*Anderson*⟩ ⟨sometimes, down the trough of darkness formed by the path under the hedges, men came *lurching* home—*D. H. Lawrence*⟩ ⟨the conductor . . . *lurches* through the car asking for tickets —*Styron*⟩ **Flounder** stresses stumbling, struggling, or sprawling rather than rolling and usually implies an effort to proceed when one is out of one's element (as a fish out of water or a horse in the mire) or when one does not know the road or the way ⟨went swiftly into the forest, leaping with sure feet over logs and brush. Pilon *floundered* behind him—*Steinbeck*⟩ ⟨they *floundered* on foot some eight miles to a squatter's cabin—*Cather*⟩ In its extended use *flounder* usually implies the confusion of mind and the uncertainty of one who is completely muddled or at a loss but nevertheless proceeds ⟨individuals who can't get a foothold in life, who *flounder* about in bewildered desperation—*Deutsch*⟩ ⟨nature has been *floundering* along for a great many millions of years to get things as they are—*Furnas*⟩ Lumber, galumph, lollop, and bumble by contrast with the foregoing terms tend to suggest clumsiness, irregularity, or heaviness as a natural or usual manner of movement or gait. **Lumber** implies a ponderousness or clumsiness in movement (as of one heavily burdened or of great weight) ⟨the jeep, opening its siren at a column of Quartermaster's trucks that *lumbered* along half a mile ahead, summoned them with stentorian wails to move over—*Cozzens*⟩ ⟨a veritable mountain of a man, [he] deeply resented the attention he invariably attracted when he *lumbered* down a Manhattan thoroughfare— *Cerf*⟩ In extended use it implies comparable ponderousness or clumsiness in proceeding or accomplishing ⟨widespread exasperation with the union leadership and at the *lumbering* slowness of the machinery of negotiation —*New Statesman*⟩ ⟨where so many other historical novels *lumber* along beneath their load of conscientious detail, Mr. Graves's imagination is invariably stimulated by what he finds—*Strong*⟩ **Galumph** adds to *lumber* the suggestion of a thumping, bumping, weighty gait ⟨Frankie lived by day beside the ceaseless, dumping shuffle of the three-legged elephant which was the laundry's sheet-rolling machine. When he piled onto his narrow pad in the long dim-lit dorm at night and turned his face to the white-washed wall, the three-legged elephant of the mangle roller followed, *galumphing,* through dreams—*Algren*⟩ ⟨doors banged, voices rose shrilly, several pairs of feet *galumphed* down the passage—*Monica Stirling*⟩ The notion of thumping or of heavy, lurching irregularity is often prominent in extended use ⟨I was sweating in the cool air, my heart *galumphing* as I stood up—*McHugh*⟩ ⟨the mornings are enlivened by the spectacle of high-ranking naval and Air Force officers, who will be horse-borne in the procession, uneasily *galumphing* along the bridle path on their mounts—*Panter-Downes*⟩ but sometimes it retains an earlier implication of gaily clumsy prancing ⟨to a country that liked to think of its leaders as . . . mad but never without their dignity, Low brought the manhandling democratic touch. He made rank and office commonplace, turned politics into a *galumphing* merry-go-round—*Pritchett*⟩ **Lollop** is more likely to suggest bounding irregularity than clumsiness or heaviness ⟨calves *lolloped* in long grass—*Patrick White*⟩ ⟨the lioness . . . started to charge and seemed to come on in great bounds. She appeared to be *lolloping* along with a lot of up-and-down motion—*F. G. Stewart*⟩ ⟨an interurban trolley line (which terrified me the way it went *lolloping* around curves)—*Palmer*⟩ ⟨the breeze blew *lolloping* along the corridors, blowing the blinds out—*Woolf*⟩ **Bumble** suggests a blundering, haphazard progress ⟨the hot auditorium where the June bugs *bumbled* foolishly against the window screens—*Stafford*⟩ ⟨plane . . . hit the ground, her tail wheel exploded, and she came leaping like a grasshopper up the runway on a flat tail wheel . . . . She bumped and *bumbled* up to the line—*Steinbeck*⟩ and, especially in its extended use, may carry more than a suggestion of floundering and blundering ⟨this novel describes a whole small town as it *bumbles* its way towards an acceptable life under conditions it never made—*Graham Bates*⟩ ⟨so long as we continue pursuing so shortsighted and blind a policy, so long, I believe, will we *bumble* and stumble into error—*Cherin*⟩

**Ana** stagger, totter, *reel: *plunge, pitch, dive: falter, *hesitate, waver, vacillate: chance, *venture: encounter, *meet, confront

---

A colon (:) separates groups of words discriminated. An asterisk (*) indicates place of treatment of each group.

**stun** *daze, bemuse, stupefy, benumb, paralyze, petrify
*Ana* astound, amaze, flabbergast (see SURPRISE): bewilder, dumbfound, nonplus, confound (see PUZZLE)

**stupefy** *daze, stun, bemuse, benumb, paralyze, petrify
*Ana* *confuse, muddle, addle, fuddle, befuddle: faze, rattle (see EMBARRASS): dumbfound, nonplus, bewilder, mystify (see PUZZLE)

**stupendous** tremendous, prodigious, monumental, *monstrous
*Ana* enormous, immense, *huge, vast, colossal, gigantic: astounding, amazing, astonishing (see SURPRISE)

**stupid** *adj* Stupid, slow, dull, dense, crass, dumb are comparable when they mean conspicuously lacking in intelligence or power to absorb ideas or impressions or exhibiting such a lack. **Stupid** can apply to a sluggish slow-witted lack of intelligence, typically congenital or habitual, or it can apply to a usually more or less transitory benumbed or dazed state of mind that is typically the result of drunkenness, shock, or illness; although the term seldom is applied to the insane or the imbecile, it often also suggests senselessness ⟨*stupid* with age—*Shak.*⟩ ⟨*stupid* with drink⟩ ⟨he could not stand *stupid* people, especially those who are made *stupid* by education—*Wilde*⟩ ⟨there emerged gradually a picture of *stupid* chicanery and petty corruption for *stupid* and petty ends —*Faulkner*⟩ ⟨he had gone on for years deceiving himself— too proud, too self-conscious, maybe just too *stupid* to realize it—*Styron*⟩ **Slow** implies stupidity manifested especially in lack of quickness in comprehension or reaction; often the term is little more than a euphemistic substitute for *stupid* ⟨the too great length of neck and limb, which made him loose and slow in body, as he was somewhat loose and *slow* in mind—*Kingsley*⟩ ⟨offers *slow* or retarded boys an adjusted program of education— *advt.*⟩ **Dull** (see also DULL 2) suggests a labored slowness or sluggishness of mind that may be constitutional, or the result of lack of mental exercise, or of overwork, or of a physical condition, and is unrelieved by any hint of quickness, brightness, or liveliness ⟨there were cows and they looked at him dully with their great *dull* eyes —*James Baldwin*⟩ ⟨had a warm spot in his heart for this *dull*, stupid, fumbling man—*Shirer*⟩ ⟨find the book long-winded, incredibly boring . . . and deadly *dull*— *John O' London's Weekly*⟩ **Dense** implies a quality of mind that makes it impervious to ideas. Additionally it may imply qualities (as obtuseness or stolidity) that reveal lack of perception, sensitiveness, or subtlety ⟨a woman may be a fool, a sleepy fool, an agitated fool, a too awfully noxious fool, and she may even be simply stupid. But she is never *dense*—*Conrad*⟩ ⟨never offered to take me over the house, though I gave her the broadest hints. She's very *dense*—*Clive Arden*⟩ **Crass** suggests a gross unfeeling quality that makes the mind incapable of delicate mental processes (as analysis, discrimination, and evaluation) or impervious to refined or spiritual ideas ⟨*crass* ignorance⟩ ⟨those dedicated guardians of man's aspiration who somehow redeem their *crass* society by being simultaneously its exiles, queer ducks and catalysts—*Viereck*⟩ ⟨the new business buildings in the City of London represent British philistinism in its most *crass* and shortsighted form—*Mumford*⟩ ⟨he resented him as a *crass* and stupid person who had fallen through luck into flowing prosperity—*Malamud*⟩ **Dumb** (see also DUMB 1) is a term of contempt that may be used in place of any of the preceding terms especially when obtuseness and inarticulateness are also implied ⟨how *dumb* do you think people are? Or how obtuse are you, actually?—*Wouk*⟩ ⟨too *dumb* to do things in the right way—*Reilly*⟩
*Ana* foolish, silly, *simple, fatuous, asinine: sluggish,

comatose, *lethargic: inert, idle, supine, *inactive: phlegmatic, stolid, *impassive
*Ant* intelligent

**stupor** torpor, torpidity, lassitude, *lethargy, languor
*Ana* phlegm, impassivity, stolidity (see under IMPASSIVE): inertness *or* inertia, passivity, supineness, inactivity, idleness (see corresponding adjectives at INACTIVE): insensibility, anesthesia (see corresponding adjectives at INSENSIBLE)

**sturdy** stout, *strong, stalwart, tough, tenacious
*Ana* sound, robust, *healthy: *vigorous, energetic, lusty: dogged, pertinacious (see OBSTINATE)
*Ant* decrepit

**stutter** *stammer

**stygian** *infernal, chthonian, Hadean, Tartarean, hellish

**style** *n* 1 diction, phraseology, phrasing, *language, vocabulary
*Ana* *taste, zest, gusto, relish: *form, convention, usage, convenance
2 *fashion, mode, vogue, fad, rage, craze, dernier cri, cry
*Ana* modishness, smartness, chicness, stylishness, fashionableness (see corresponding adjectives at STYLISH)
3 *name, designation, title, denomination, appellation

**stylish, fashionable, modish, smart, chic, dashing** can mean conforming to the choice and usage of those who set the vogue (as persons of wealth and taste or often the avant-garde). **Stylish** is likely to stress currency and, correspondingly, transitoriness ⟨a *stylish* address in the new part of the city⟩ ⟨recently it has been more *stylish* to assume that the author of a story is a complete victim and tool, either of his purse and social position or of his parents' neuroses and theories about child-raising— *Smart*⟩ ⟨a former college classmate of mine, . . . he had been a big wheel under the elms, a miracle of scholarship and coordination, and classified, in the jargon then *stylish*, as a snake, or suave operator—*Perelman*⟩ ⟨she has restored delight . . . to poetry, has written her poems with the completest possible clarity (here you will find no *stylish* obscurantism, so dear to the avant-garde)— *Charles Jackson*⟩ **Fashionable** is often interchangeable with *stylish* ⟨a *fashionable* neighborhood⟩ ⟨it has become . . . *fashionable* to sneer at economics and emphasize "the human dilemma"—*Mailer*⟩ but *fashionable* is distinctly more likely to imply conformance to what is established and generally accepted than to a transitory or restricted vogue ⟨the Episcopal church—that's kind of the *fashionable* church in Paterson, where the nicest people go, or at least the ones with the most money— *Chidsey*⟩ ⟨one of the rare French intellectuals who has the courage to be publicly and outspokenly pro-American in France, a country where it is nowadays *fashionable* to ridicule the United States—*Padover*⟩ **Modish** stresses conformity to the latest styles ⟨all the ornaments deemed essential to a *modish* Victorian drawing room—*New Yorker*⟩ but sometimes it suggests a step beyond what is describable as *stylish* or *fashionable* and may apply to what from another point of view might be called *daring*, *extreme*, or *startling* ⟨tend to regard the pursuit of the new as necessarily silly and *modish*—*Bentley*⟩ ⟨nothing is so transitory as the *modish*. It is on the way out at the very moment that it comes in—*J. M. Brown*⟩ ⟨he was English enough to feel a contempt for *modish* philosophers who went about preaching a profitable brand of nihilism, blandly informing their fellow creatures that they were already in hell and there was no point in struggling against it—*Wain*⟩ **Smart** comes close to *modish* in suggesting the height of what is stylish or fashionable, but it implies a position in the forefront of what is acceptably stylish

---

*Ana* analogous words     *Ant* antonyms     *Con* contrasted words     See also explanatory notes facing page 1

or fashionable rather than one beyond this point ⟨he was handsome, he was rich, he was a sportsman and he was good company. . . . he had been long established as one of the *smartest* men in London—*Maugham*⟩ ⟨her college set had stayed rigidly in a zigzag path through the town, traversing a few hotel bars, nightclubs, and eating places which they considered *smart—Wouk*⟩ ⟨black is often used in *smart*, sophisticated interiors—*Hazel & Julius Rockow*⟩ **Chic** is sometimes used simply as an equivalent to *modish* or *smart* ⟨the good corporation wife does not make her friends uncomfortable by clothes too blatantly *chic—Whyte*⟩ or even of *fashionable* ⟨whether or not he [the artist] liked it, he became *chic—Harper's*⟩ However it may not imply conformity to the latest style so much as an effectiveness in style which suggests the exercise of a knack or skill and the achievement of distinction ⟨the natural elegance which enables her to look *chic* in camouflaged parachutist's overalls—*Edmond Taylor*⟩ ⟨decided to put her culinary tricks into book form for other women who want to whip up a *chic* meal—*Butcher*⟩ ⟨achieved so great a virtuosity that now he not only can do anything but does everything, fluctuating between a wistful religiosity and a *chic* diablerie—*Untermeyer*⟩ **Dashing** applies to people or to things which they wear or use; it implies not only stylishness or, more often, modishness but a bold, shining quality that enables one to cut a figure in any group or assemblage ⟨you're willing to be a *dashing* knight, but you also want to be a careful knight—*Gardner*⟩ ⟨he was a tall, handsome, *dashing* chap . . . whose magnificent disregard for money cut a wide swathe in the social life of the town—*Amer. Guide Series: N. J.*⟩ ⟨a pair of *dashing* young brokers⟩

*Ana* \*new, novel, new-fashioned, newfangled, modernistic: \*showy, ostentatious, pretentious

**suave, urbane, diplomatic, bland, smooth, politic** as applied to persons, their demeanor, and their utterances can mean conspicuously and ingratiatingly tactful and well-mannered. These words at times can convey so strong a suggestion of insincerity or of a surface manner that their distinctive implications are obscured. It is chiefly in their nonderogatory use that essential differences in meaning are apparent. **Suave** suggests qualities that are or have the appearance of being acquired through discipline and training and that encourage or are intended to encourage easy and frictionless intercourse with others. Negatively, it suggests the absence of everything that may offend or repel; positively, it suggests such qualities as affability without fulsomeness, politeness without stiffness, and persuasiveness without evident desire to force one's opinion on others ⟨what gentle, *suave*, courteous tones!—*Jackson*⟩ ⟨a slight disturbance of his ordinary *suave* and well-bred equanimity—*Lytton*⟩ ⟨they could be as *suave* in advancing their bromides as we could be gauche in establishing our originalities—*J. M. Brown*⟩ **Urbane** implies a high degree of cultivation, poise, and wide social experience; it also commonly suggests an ingrained or inbred courtesy which makes for pleasant and agreeable intercourse among all kinds of men regardless of their social or intellectual standing ⟨writes with fluent charm, in the easy, *urbane*, richly allusive manner of an Oxford and Cambridge savant—*Wecter*⟩ ⟨men of delicate fancy, *urbane* instinct and aristocratic manner—in brief, superior men—in brief, gentry—*Mencken*⟩ Since urbanity and an ability to deal with difficult or ticklish situations with great tact are theoretically the qualities of the typical diplomat, the adjective **diplomatic**, when used in reference to nondiplomats, carries these implications, often adding in addition a hint of artfulness in gaining one's own ends ⟨Gabrielle's busy, active, *diplomatic* managing of the

party—*E. E. Hale*⟩ ⟨the *diplomatic* manner . . . of a government official whose career depended on politeness to his equals and deference to his superiors—*MacInnes*⟩ ⟨I have grown to believe that the one thing worth aiming at is simplicity of heart and life; that one's relations with others should be direct and not *diplomatic—Benson*⟩ **Bland** is negative as well as positive in its implications, for it usually implies the absence of irritating qualities as strongly as it suggests serenity, mildness, and gentility. Nevertheless, in spite of this vagueness, the term often carries a hint of benignity or the appearance of it and usually directly implies an ingratiating pleasantness ⟨his manners were gentle, complying, and *bland—Goldsmith*⟩ ⟨he's simply a distinguished-looking old cleric with a sweet smile and a white tie: he's just honorable and *bland* and as cold as ice—*Santayana*⟩ ⟨most of the time he sat behind a look of *bland* absorption, now and then permitting himself an inscrutable smile—*Hervey*⟩ **Smooth** differs from *bland* chiefly in being more positive in its implications and in being more consistently derogatory. Sometimes it stresses suavity, often an assumed suavity ⟨the words of his mouth were *smoother* than butter, but war was in his heart—*Ps* 55:21⟩ At other times it carries even a stronger implication of tactfulness and craft than *diplomatic* ⟨I was not even my parents' son in 1928 but a devilishly *smooth* imposter, awaiting their slightest blunder . . . to assert my true identity—*Salinger*⟩ ⟨the sales talk of our government for the second one was a *smooth* and professional job—*Edmund Wilson*⟩ **Politic** (see also EXPEDIENT) when applied to persons implies both shrewdness and tact; the term usually suggests the ability to gain one's ends or to avoid friction through ingratiating means or diplomatic methods. It varies considerably, however, in its implication of artfulness, sometimes connoting cunning or craft and sometimes little more than just the right degree of suavity ⟨I . . . am an attendant lord . . . deferential, glad to be of use, *politic*, cautious, and meticulous—*T. S. Eliot*⟩ ⟨the mayors and corporations as a rule guided their cities through difficult times with *politic* shrewdness—*Edwin Benson*⟩

*Ana* \*gracious, cordial, affable, genial, sociable: courteous, courtly, polite (see CIVIL): \*fulsome, unctuous, slick
*Ant* bluff

**subdue** subjugate, reduce, overcome, surmount, overthrow, rout, \*conquer, vanquish, defeat, beat, lick
*Ana* control, manage, direct (see CONDUCT *vb*): discipline, \*punish, correct: foil, thwart, circumvent, \*frustrate: \*suppress, repress
*Ant* awaken (sense 2), waken

**subdued** \*tame, submissive
*Ana* meek, \*humble, modest, lowly: \*timid, timorous: docile, tractable, amenable (see OBEDIENT)
*Ant* intense: barbaric (*of taste*): bizarre (*of effects*): effervescent (*of character and temperament*)

**subject** *n* 1 \*citizen, national
*Ant* sovereign
2 **Subject, matter, subject matter, argument, topic, text, theme, motive, motif, leitmotiv** can mean the basic idea or the principal object of thought or attention in a discourse or artistic composition. **Subject** is the most widely applicable as well as the least definite in denotation of these words; it implies merely some restriction in one's field of choice and a governing principle determining the selection of one's material and demanding some concentration in the treatment of it (as in a discourse or work of art) ⟨what is the *subject* of his painting?⟩ ⟨your *subject* is too comprehensive to be treated adequately in so short an article⟩ ⟨it was the first of the . . . major mistakes in World War II and became a *subject* of violent controversy

A colon (:) separates groups of words discriminated. An asterisk (\*) indicates place of treatment of each group.

*—Shirer*⟩ **Matter** and the more usual **subject matter** are often used as close synonyms of *subject* ⟨hail, Son of God, Saviour of men! Thy name shall be the copious *matter* of my song—*Milton*⟩ ⟨Mr. Lytton Strachey . . . chose, as *subject matter* of a book, four people of whom the world had heard little but good—*Repplier*⟩ As often, however, these terms refer not to the idea, object, or situation selected for treatment but to a restricted field or range of material from which one selects the specific subject he intends to treat ⟨*Alexander's Bridge* was my first novel, and does not deal with the kind of *subject matter* in which I now find myself most at home—*Cather*⟩ **Argument** (see also REASON, ARGUMENT 2) can denote the subject, especially the carefully delimited subject, for a particular discourse (as a poem or a part of a poem) that is planned in advance of execution ⟨the *argument* of the book is as simple as you could wish for—*Parris*⟩ The word sometimes implies explicit statement of the leading idea or a summarizing of its development ⟨Pope prefaced each epistle of his *Essay on Man* with an *argument* of it⟩ **Topic** applies to a subject, usually of general interest, chosen because of its possibilities for individual or original treatment or for discussion by different persons holding diverse views ⟨the students were asked to write an essay on one of the assigned *topics*⟩ ⟨I can't remember in a prolonged conversation what *topic*'s been covered and what hasn't—*Purdy*⟩ **Text** can mean a verse or passage, usually from Scripture, chosen as providing or suggesting a subject for a sermon or similar discourse ⟨the excellency of this *text* is that it will suit any sermon; and of this sermon, that it will suit any *text*—*Sterne*⟩ In extended use it is often applied to whatever suggests itself as a good starting point for a discourse the subject of which is yet to be defined or which lacks a definite subject ⟨my *text* for this chapter is . . . any good daily newspaper—*La Barre*⟩ **Theme** denotes a subject which one selects for literary or artistic treatment; it is applicable to something (as an idea, proposition, text, melodic phrase, or mood) which a writer, composer, or artist proposes to develop (as in a poem), to elaborate upon (as in a movement of a symphony), or to illustrate (as in a mural or series of murals) or which can be detected in a completed work as the dominant object of his concern ⟨fools are my *theme*, let satire be my song—*Byron*⟩ ⟨waterfalls are from very early times a favorite *theme* for the painter —*Binyon*⟩ **Theme** does not necessarily suggest a clearer definition than *subject* or *topic*, but, in distinction from them, it invites comparison with the treatment and calls attention to the quality, the form, the design, or the execution of the completed work; thus, an overworked *theme* implies a lack of freshness in the thought or design; a compelling *theme* suggests force and enthusiasm in its treatment ⟨to produce a mighty book you must choose a mighty *theme*—*Melville*⟩ **Motive** and **motif** are restricted in reference to works of art to those in which design or pattern is the important element. In music they are interchangeable in this sense with *theme*, the leading phrase which is repeated with variations during the course of a composition or movement; in the decorative arts they apply to the figure which stands out as the salient and dominant feature of the design and is repeated at appropriate intervals ⟨the chief *motif* of the design is the peacock one, much favored by decorative artists⟩ ⟨don't speak. Don't think. This is, of course, a familiar refrain . . . . It is the *motif* of the great dark stories of the 1930's—*Geismar*⟩ **Leitmotiv** designates a specific melodic phrase that is associated with a particular person, mood, or situation (as in an opera) and that is repeated each time this person, mood, or situation reappears. The word

has considerable extended use and is often applied to an insistent or recurrent idea that becomes the dominant theme of an author or of a work ⟨"Fate went its way uncompromisingly to the terrible end." This is the *leitmotiv* of this interesting, dignified apologia of one of Austria's Elder Statesmen—*S. R. L.*⟩

**subject** *adj* **1** dependent, *subordinate, secondary, tributary, collateral
*Ana* *subservient, servile, slavish: conditional, contingent, *dependent, relative
*Ant* sovereign, dominant
**2** *liable, open, exposed, prone, susceptible, sensitive
*Ana* *apt, likely, liable
*Ant* exempt
**subject matter** *subject, matter, argument, topic, text, theme, motive, motif, leitmotiv
**subjoin** *add, append, annex, superadd
*Ana* attach, affix, *fasten: *unite, conjoin, combine
*Con* *detach, disengage: *separate, part, sever
**subjugate** subdue, reduce, overcome, surmount, overthrow, rout, *conquer, vanquish, defeat, beat, lick
*Ana* circumvent, outwit, foil, thwart, *frustrate: compel, coerce, *force
**sublime** glorious, *splendid, superb, resplendent, gorgeous
*Ana* transcendent, transcendental, ideal, *abstract: divine, spiritual, sacred, *holy: majestic, august, noble, stately (see GRAND)
**sublunary** *earthly, terrestrial, earthy, mundane, worldly
**submerge** immerse, duck, *dip, souse, dunk
*Ana* *soak, saturate, drench, impregnate
**submission** *surrender, capitulation
*Ana* yielding, submitting, succumbing, bowing, caving in (see YIELD): compliance, acquiescence, resignation (see under COMPLIANT)
*Ant* resistance
**submissive** *tame, subdued
*Ana* docile, tractable, amenable, biddable, *obedient: meek, lowly, *humble: *subservient, servile, slavish, menial
*Ant* rebellious
**submit** *yield, capitulate, succumb, relent, defer, bow, cave
*Ana* surrender, abandon, resign, *relinquish: abide, endure, suffer, *bear
*Ant* resist, withstand
**subordinate** *adj* **Subordinate, secondary, dependent, subject, tributary, collateral** are comparable when they mean placed in or belonging to a class, rank, or status lower than the highest or the first in importance or power. **Subordinate** applies to a person or thing that is lower than another in some such essential respect as by being under his or its authority ⟨all officers of an independent army below the rank of general are *subordinate* officers⟩ ⟨Montholon, up to that moment *subordinate* to the Grand Marshal, was entrusted with the management of the Emperor's household—*Maurois*⟩ or by having a less important or less conspicuous place, position, or status in the scheme of a whole than some other member, part, or element ⟨the relation of dominating to *subordinate* features —*Binyon*⟩ ⟨ceremony is *subordinate* in the scheme of life, as color is in a painting—*Ellis*⟩ or by loss of independence and reduction to a lower or inferior position ⟨at that time considered as a *subordinate* and inferior class of beings . . . subjugated by the dominant race—*Taney*⟩ ⟨it does tell us . . . why a complex of beliefs is dominant at one time and *subordinate* at another—*Howe*⟩ **Secondary** differs from *subordinate* mainly in suggesting a much narrower range of difference, for it implies a position

or an importance that is just below what may be described as *primary, main, chief,* or *leading* ⟨what they actually believe is of *secondary* consequence; the main thing is what they say—*Mencken*⟩ ⟨the valuation of an object is thus *secondary* to the apprehension of it—*Alexander*⟩ ⟨each stage of the climb from valley to intermediate shoulders and crags, to a *secondary* and thence to the highest point—*W. O. Douglas*⟩ In reference to order of development or derivation *secondary* is opposed to *original* or *first* and carries no necessary implication of inferiority in importance ⟨the *secondary* meaning of a word⟩ ⟨his primary tools, the fundamental cutting tools with which he makes his *secondary* tools —*R. W. Murray*⟩ **Dependent** (see also DEPENDENT 1) implies subordination to someone or something, but it also connotes the position or the status of one that hangs on, leans on, or relies on the other for support or for the provision of what is lacking in itself; thus, a *dependent* clause in a sentence is not completely intelligible apart from the main clause; a *dependent* child is not old enough to support himself and therefore must rely upon his parents or guardians. In its commonest use *dependent* implies a loss, through subjugation or through weakness, of one's independence; it therefore frequently stresses powerlessness or debasement more than subordination ⟨England, long *dependent* and degraded, was again a power of the first rank—*Macaulay*⟩ ⟨Maggie is not *dependent* on Honora—she could get a better job tomorrow— *Cheever*⟩ **Subject** definitely implies subordination to a dominant power but never carries, as *subordinate* sometimes carries, an implication of relative importance within a scheme of the whole; it often tends to suggest loss of those powers which imply a degree of freedom, responsibility, self-discipline, and self-sufficiency ⟨a *subject* race⟩ ⟨aristocracy is out of date, and *subject* populations will no longer obey even the most wise and virtuous rulers—*Russell*⟩ **Tributary** basically applies to peoples, races, or nations that have been conquered and made subject to another people, race, or nation and that are forced to pay tribute to their conquerors, but in more general use it is often interchangeable with *subject* ⟨no conquering race ever lived or could live . . . among a *tributary* one without begetting children on it—*Quiller-Couch*⟩ In another sense it is also applicable to whatever has an outlet into another and larger thing of the same kind and thereby yields supplies (as a flow of water or material) which increase the size or importance of the latter ⟨the *tributary* streams of the Mississippi river⟩ ⟨the lane, receiving two *tributary* lanes from who should say what remote hamlets, widened out with this accession —*Mackenzie*⟩ **Collateral** implies a being side by side, but it suggests not equivalence in value but subordination of one through or as if through an indirect relation to or a loose connection with the other; thus, a *collateral* cause of a war, though by implication operative at the same time as the most important or primary cause, is subordinate to the latter; a *collateral* issue is not the main issue; a *collateral* descendant is not a direct or lineal descendant but one in a different line (as of a brother or sister) ⟨the union had engaged successfully in many *collateral* activities such as banking and cooperative housing—*Soule*⟩ ⟨the limiting of inquiry to the immediate, with total disregard of the *collateral* or circumstantial events—*Poe*⟩
*Ana* *auxiliary, subsidiary, subservient, contributory, adjuvant: *accidental, incidental, fortuitous
*Ant* chief, leading: dominant
**subordinate** *n* *inferior, underling
*Ant* chief  —*Con* head, master, leader (see CHIEF)

**subscribe** agree, acquiesce, *assent, consent, accede
*Ana* concur, coincide, *agree: *approve, endorse, sanction: *promise, pledge, covenant
*Ant* boggle
**subservient** 1 *auxiliary, subsidiary, contributory, ancillary, adjuvant, accessory
*Ana* *subordinate, secondary, dependent, subject
2 **Subservient, servile, slavish, menial, obsequious** can mean showing or characterized by extreme compliance or abject obedience. **Subservient** (see also AUXILIARY) applies directly or indirectly to those who occupy a subordinate or dependent condition or who manifest the state of mind of one in such a position; the term stresses subordination and may connote cringing or truckling ⟨editors and journalists who express opinions in print that are opposed to the interests of the rich are dismissed and replaced by *subservient* ones—*Shaw*⟩ ⟨a certainty that she would always worship him and be nice and *subservient* —*Farrell*⟩ **Servile** suggests a lowly status and a mean or cringing submissiveness ⟨*servile* labors⟩ ⟨mean, *servile* compliance—*Burns*⟩ ⟨in no country . . . did the clergy become by tradition so completely *servile* to the political authority—*Shirer*⟩ ⟨they are not loyal, they are only *servile*—Shaw⟩ **Slavish** suggests the status or attitude of a slave and typically implies an abject or debased servility unbecoming to a free man ⟨a *slavish* yes-man to the party bosses—*S. H. Adams*⟩ ⟨Oriental literature . . . is based on a *slavish* acceptance by the pupil of the authority of the master—*Cohen*⟩ ⟨fear took hold on me from head to foot—*slavish* superstitious fear—*Stevenson*⟩ ⟨she also became increasingly assiduous in her *slavish* attentions, until . . . one would almost have thought that her duty toward him was her very life—*Wolfe*⟩ Both *servile* and *slavish* are used of unduly close dependence upon an original or model ⟨it is the business of art to imitate nature, but not with a *servile* pencil—*Goldsmith*⟩ ⟨a *slavish* devotion to tradition⟩ **Menial** in its typical extended reference applies to occupations requiring no special skill or intellectual attainment or ranked low in economic or social status and stresses the humbleness and degradation of or like that of one bound to such an occupation ⟨niggers were ineducable and would therefore always be *menial*—*Mayer*⟩ ⟨competing against a mass of unemployed, they accepted the most *menial* and worst paid jobs—*Handlin*⟩ ⟨encouraged to rise from the *menial* and mechanical operations of his craft—*Mumford*⟩ ⟨most *menial* of stations in that aristocratic old Boston world— *Parrington*⟩ **Obsequious** may apply to persons who are actual inferiors or to the words, actions, or manners by which they reveal their sense of inferiority in the presence of their superiors ⟨a duteous and knee-crooking knave . . . doting on his own *obsequious* bondage— *Shak.*⟩ ⟨be civil, but not *obsequious*—*Meredith*⟩ The word may imply a servile, often a sycophantic, attitude ⟨brutal and arrogant when winning, they are bootlicking and servilely *obsequious* when losing—*Cohn*⟩ ⟨on the second Saturday evening after he got his new position, the tobacconist, a rather *obsequious* man, called him Mr. Hall—*Anderson*⟩ or extreme attentiveness in service or to the niceties of service ⟨following him out, with *obsequious* politeness—*Dickens*⟩
*Ana* fawning, cringing, truckling, cowering (see FAWN): *compliant, acquiescent, resigned: *mean, ignoble, abject
*Ant* domineering: overbearing
**subside** 1 *fall, drop, sink, slump
*Ana* sag, flag, *droop, wilt: shrink, *contract, constrict
2 *abate, wane, ebb
*Ana* dwindle, diminish, *decrease

A colon (:) separates groups of words discriminated. An asterisk (*) indicates place of treatment of each group.

**subsidiary** *auxiliary, contributory, subservient, ancillary, adjuvant, accessory

**subsidy** grant, subvention, *appropriation

**subsist** exist, live, *be

**subsistence** *living, livelihood, sustenance, maintenance, support, keep, bread, bread and butter

**subspecies** *variety, race, breed, cultivar, strain, clone, stock

**substance** 1 Substance, purport, gist, burden, core, pith can denote the inner significance or central meaning of something written or said. **Substance** implies the essence of what has been said or written devoid of details and elaborations; the term is used especially when such an essence is repeated for the sake of others, but it may be used also of what characterizes a discourse and gives it body as distinguished from the frills or rhetorical froth that give it finish ⟨give the *substance* of a speech⟩ ⟨the *substance* of a scientific paper is incorporated into the general stock of knowledge; but the paper itself is doomed to oblivion—*Huxley*⟩ ⟨to strip her lines of all ornament, of all effective appeal, in order to contemplate better the *substance* of her poem—*Fitts*⟩ **Purport** lays the stress upon purpose or intent but when used of written or spoken discourse it applies to what is intended to be conveyed or imparted and so actually refers to the central meaning. It is often interchangeable with *substance* but always with the implication of the speaker's or writer's purpose ⟨the . . . *purport* of his letter was to inform them that Mr. Wickham has resolved on quitting the militia—*Austen*⟩ ⟨he has received just sufficient education to make him understand half the *purport* of the orders he receives—*Kipling*⟩ **Gist** refers to the material part (as of a question, an argument, or a discourse); it is the substance thereof reduced to its lowest terms ⟨the *gist* of the thing grows, at each stage of the progress, terser, more pungent, more crystal clear—*Montague*⟩ ⟨within an hour the Voice of America had begun translating the *gist* of the decision into thirty-four languages—*Beverly Smith*⟩ **Burden** implies the part most insisted upon or most often repeated and usually means the main topic or theme ⟨the *burden* of his conversation was that there was no escape "of no kind whatever"—*Kipling*⟩ ⟨that desire to hear lost laughter which is the *burden* of every century's lament —*Repplier*⟩ **Core** can apply to various things that give the effect of being whatever remains after the outer or superficial part is stripped off; in application to what is written or said it emphasizes the centrality of the meaning and the relative unimportance of the other aspects ⟨the true center of the book is its *core* of irony, insight into the contrast between illusion and reality in the story of the West—*Kohler*⟩ ⟨when we have cut away all his errors, exaggerations, prejudices and nonsense, we shall find a hard *core* of truth—*Day Lewis*⟩ **Pith** often equals *substance* in the sense of *body;* actually, however, it implies substance which gives a discourse its concentrated force, vigor, or vitality and is, therefore, a narrower and more expressive term ⟨there is *pith* in this essay⟩ ⟨such counsels, rather than the systematic doctrine . . . contain the *pith* of what he has to say—*J. M. Cameron*⟩
*Ana* *center, nucleus, heart, core, focus: *principle, fundamental: foundation, *base, groundwork
2 *matter, material, stuff

**substantial** *massive, massy, bulky, monumental
*Ant* airy, ethereal

**substantiate** verify, corroborate, *confirm, authenticate, validate
*Ana* *prove, demonstrate, try, test

**substitute** *n* 1 surrogate, *resource, resort, expedient,

shift, makeshift, stopgap
*Ana* *device, contrivance, contraption: duplicate, copy, *reproduction
2 Substitute, supply, locum tenens, alternate, understudy, double, stand-in, pinch hitter designate a person who performs or is prepared to perform the duties of another during the latter's absence or incapacitation. **Substitute** is the general term interchangeable with any of the others; specifically it is often applied to a teacher not appointed to a full-time position but held in reserve for service when needed. A **supply** is a clergyman who substitutes for the regular preacher. A **locum tenens** is often a substitute for a professional man with a practice or clientele which needs to be cared for while he is away for a length of time; the term is used especially with respect to physicians and clergymen. An **alternate** is one appointed or elected to take the place of another (as a delegate to a convention, a holder of a fellowship, the winner of an award, or a juror) if the latter should be incapacitated or disqualified. An **understudy** is a reserve actor or actress prepared to take the part of a regular actor or actress on short notice. A **double** is a person sufficiently like another to be able to substitute for him in public and especially an anonymous actor or actress in motion pictures who substitutes in shots or scenes where the required action is considered too risky or onerous for the regular player. A **stand-in** in motion pictures is one whose chief duty is to substitute for a star during the preparation (as in arranging lighting) for actual shooting of scenes. A **pinch hitter** is a baseball player sent in to bat to replace a weak hitter when a hit is particularly needed or, by extension, a person who substitutes for another in an emergency; the term may connote competence or ability to rise to the demands of the situation but is frequently a more graphic equivalent of *substitute.*

**subsume** *include, comprehend, embrace, involve, imply

**subtle** *logical, analytical
*Ana* penetrating, piercing, probing (see ENTER): *deep, profound: abstruse, *recondite
*Ant* dense (*in mind*): blunt (*in speech*)

**subtract** *deduct
*Ant* add

**subvention** grant, *appropriation, subsidy

**subvert** *overturn, overthrow, capsize, upset
*Ana* *ruin, wreck: *destroy, demolish: corrupt, pervert, deprave, *debase
*Ant* uphold, sustain

**succeed** 1 *follow, ensue, supervene
*Ana* displace, supplant, *replace, supersede
*Ant* precede
2 Succeed, prosper, thrive, flourish can mean to attain or to be attaining a desired end. **Succeed** (see also FOLLOW) implies little more than this. Both persons and things *succeed* when they are effective in gaining their purposes or ends, in particular or in general; the term implies an antithesis to *fail* ⟨the teaching that fosters these ends *succeeds;* the teaching which neglects them fails—*Suzzallo*⟩ ⟨the little man had *succeeded* in disturbing the boy with his absurd proposal—*Dahl*⟩ ⟨the revolt against the tyranny of mathematics and physics is justified by the fact that these sciences have not *succeeded* in explaining the phenomena of life—*Inge*⟩ **Prosper** carries an implication of continued or long-continuing success; it usually also suggests increasing success. Only through the context is it clear whether the success is in the continuation or the increase of health, of wealth, or of well-being ⟨*prosper* in business⟩ ⟨Milenka was soon *prospering.* His coat came in soft and shining; his purr cleared and his eyes lost the milkiness that had clouded them—

*Stafford*⟩ ⟨did all the naughty things little . . . children were punished for, did them and *prospered* in body and mind—*Lillian Smith*⟩ **Thrive** adds the implication of vigorous growth; it often also implies succeeding noticeably because of or in spite of conditions or circumstances stipulated by the context ⟨plants that *thrive* in an acid soil⟩ ⟨he worked hard and his business *thrived*⟩ ⟨the children *throve* under good care and proper feeding⟩ ⟨like most great revolutionaries he could *thrive* only in evil times—*Shirer*⟩ ⟨states *thrive* or wither as moons wax and wane—*Cowper*⟩ **Flourish** implies a period of vigorous growth and expansion (as in an institution, a business, an art, or a science) at or towards the peak of development or productivity and without signs of decay or decadence; it carries no suggestion of how far this growth will be maintained and sometimes by implication hints at a future decline ⟨if physics and chemistry and biology have *flourished*, morals, religion, and aesthetics have withered—*Krutch*⟩ ⟨a pleasant white-haired widow surrounded by many potted plants that seemed to bloom and *flourish* in the fertile climate of her disposition—*Cheever*⟩ ⟨the sciences cannot fully *flourish*, and may be badly damaged, in a society which gives an increasing share of its resources to military purposes—*Science*⟩ It is also used of an individual to indicate the period of his prime or time of high success ⟨Spenser and Fairfax both *flourished* in the reign of Queen Elizabeth—*Dryden*⟩
*Ana* attain, achieve, gain, compass, *reach: effect, fulfill (see PERFORM)
*Ant* fail: attempt

**succession,** progression, series, sequence, chain, train, string are comparable when they mean a number of things that follow each other in some order. **Succession** implies that the units, whether things or persons, follow each other, typically in order of time or, less often, of place and usually without break or interruption ⟨a *succession* of disasters⟩ ⟨a *succession* of mild winters⟩ ⟨there was a dizzy *succession* of events and of constantly changing situations—*Shirer*⟩ ⟨a *succession* of rooms, one after the other, extending over a great length—*Amer. Guide Series: La.*⟩ ⟨reality is a *succession* of concrete and particular situations—*Huxley*⟩ **Progression** (see also PROGRESS 2) applies to a succession in which there is movement and flow, and often change, so that a pattern is formed or an advance is indicated. The word is most frequent in mathematics and in music; in the former it denotes a succession of quantities between every two of which there is a particular but an unvarying relation ⟨arithmetical *progression*⟩ ⟨all the following systems are based on a *progression* by which the amount of a bet is increased after a loss—*Morehead & Mott-Smith*⟩ In music it denotes a succession of chords which constitute a harmony ⟨a short melodic line without addition of simultaneous harmony, containing mostly stepwise *progressions*, moderately interspersed with leaps—*Hindemith*⟩ **Series** applies to a number of things of similar or uniform character that stand in the same relation to each other or achieve the same end; often the term is indistinguishable from *succession*, but the combined or total effect of the units is rather more stressed than the fact that they follow each other ⟨a *series* of notes⟩ ⟨a *series* of visits⟩ ⟨a *series* of payments⟩ ⟨it all came together in my understanding, as a *series* of experiments do when you begin to see where they are leading—*Cather*⟩ ⟨some so-called *series* are nothing more than miscellaneous collections of books published at the same price and in the same style—*McColvin*⟩ **Sequence** is more restricted in meaning than *series* and implies a closer causal or logical connection between the things involved

(as a numerical or chronological order or a settled recurrence in the same order) ⟨the *sequence* of the seasons⟩ ⟨his thoughts flow in logical *sequence*⟩ ⟨preferring rather to get the news in weekly retrospect, from the periodicals —for these organs treated events of a preceding week as an understandable *sequence* and gave them discernible pattern—*Terry Southern*⟩ ⟨our presidents have run in *sequences*, and . . . have tended to be classifiable under three main types—*Edmund Wilson*⟩ **Chain** applies to a succession or series which forms a logical or causal sequence ⟨a *chain* of arguments⟩ ⟨a *chain* of effects⟩ ⟨the long *chain* of development which makes the very language of the English Bible what it is—*Lowes*⟩ ⟨there is no climactic choice in the story; it moves evenly on a *chain* of circumstances—*Walcutt*⟩ **Train** applies to a number of persons, animals, or concrete things or of effects or ideas that follow as attendants or as consequences or sometimes (as in the case of causes) that precede ⟨she always has a *train* of admirers⟩ ⟨I invite your Highness and your *train* to my poor cell—*Shak.*⟩ ⟨a long *train* of causes⟩ ⟨the August afternoon that the little *train* of silent people carried her out of her own door up to the family burying ground—*Deland*⟩ ⟨somebody who wrote and wrote and wrote and never finished even one *train* of thought to the very end—*Purdy*⟩ **String** applies to a series or succession so uniform (as in character, size, or quality) that its units are or seem to be strung on a thread; usually there is little implication of chronological, logical, or causal connection ⟨a *string* of victories⟩ ⟨his long *string* of single-handed successes made rich fare for . . . crime reporters—*Spiers*⟩ ⟨launched at once into a *string* of stories—*Dawson & Wilson*⟩
*Ana* consecutiveness, successiveness (see corresponding adjectives at CONSECUTIVE): articulation, concatenation, integration (see under INTEGRATE)

**successive** *consecutive, sequent, sequential, serial
*Ana* continuous, *continual, constant, incessant: rotating, alternating (see ROTATE)

**succinct** terse, *concise, laconic, summary, pithy, compendious
*Ana* *brief, short: compressed, condensed, contracted (see CONTRACT *vb*): compact, *close: curt, brusque, blunt (see BLUFF)
*Ant* discursive

**succumb** *yield, submit, capitulate, relent, defer, bow, cave
*Ana* surrender, abandon, resign, *relinquish

**sudden** hasty, *precipitate, headlong, abrupt, impetuous
*Ana* quickened, hurried, speeded, accelerated (see SPEED *vb*): *fast, rapid, swift, fleet, expeditious

**suds** *foam, froth, spume, lather, scum, yeast

**sue** pray, plead, petition (see under PRAYER)
*Ana* entreat, beseech, *beg, importune, implore, supplicate: solicit, request, *ask: *demand, claim, exact, require

**suffer** 1 *bear, endure, abide, tolerate, stand, brook
*Ana* accept, *receive, admit: *yield, submit, bow
2 *experience, undergo, sustain
*Ana* submit, succumb, defer, *yield
3 permit, allow, *let, leave

**sufferance** *permission, leave
*Ana* toleration, endurance (see corresponding verbs at BEAR): acquiescence, resignation, compliance (see under COMPLIANT)

**suffering** *distress, misery, agony, dolor, passion
*Ana* affliction, tribulation, *trial, visitation: adversity, *misfortune: *sorrow, grief, anguish, woe, heartache, heartbreak

**suffocate,** asphyxiate, stifle, smother, choke, strangle,

A colon (:) separates groups of words discriminated. An asterisk (*) indicates place of treatment of each group.

throttle can all mean to interrupt the normal course of breathing. **Suffocate** commonly refers to conditions in which breathing is impossible through lack of available oxygen or through presence of noxious or poisonous gas ⟨prisoners *suffocated* in the underground dungeon⟩ *Suffocate* also refers to situations in which breathing is impossible because mouth and nose are covered ⟨*suffocating* under the mud and earth which had fallen over his head⟩ **Asphyxiate** is likely to refer to situations in which death comes through poisonous gases in the air or through lack of sufficient oxygen ⟨*asphyxiated* by the chlorine gas in the cellar⟩ **Stifle** is appropriately used to refer to situations in which breathing is difficult or impossible through lack of adequate fresh air and, often, presence of heat ⟨closing a hatch to stop a fire and the destruction of a cargo was justified even if it was known that doing so would *stifle* a man below—*Justice Holmes*⟩ **Smother** is likely to be used in situations in which the supply of oxygen is inadequate for life; it often suggests a deadening pall of smoke, dust, or impurity in the air ⟨*smothered* by the dust after the explosion⟩ ⟨a smell of soot which *smothered* the scent of wistaria and iris—*Bromfield*⟩ *Smother* also refers to situations in which the mouth and nose are covered so that one cannot breathe ⟨was *smothered* with a cushion⟩ **Choke** suggests difficulty in breathing through constriction, obstruction, or extreme irritation within the throat ⟨*choked* to death by a brutal marauder⟩ ⟨gasping and *choking* as the harsh liquor burned his throat⟩ ⟨*choking* as he breathed the acrid smoke⟩ **Strangle** also refers to constriction of the throat, obstruction of the windpipe, or irritation, but it is more likely to indicate fatality or quite serious condition ⟨fingers itched to *strangle* him—*R. W. Buchanan*⟩ ⟨*strangling* on a chicken bone⟩ **Throttle** usually suggests external compression of the throat done forcefully for the purpose of subduing or overcoming resistance ⟨heartbeats . . . so violent that they seemed . . . *throttling* hands to her throat—*Wharton*⟩

**suffrage** *n* Suffrage, franchise, vote, ballot mean the right, privilege, or power of expressing one's choice or wish (as in an election or in the determination of policy). **Suffrage** is the usual term when the emphasis is upon the extent to which this privilege or power is enjoyed in a state or community or upon the kinds of citizens in a representative government who legally exercise this power; the word is frequently modified by a term indicating such extent or restriction ⟨universal *suffrage*⟩ ⟨the long-fought battle that brought about woman *suffrage*⟩ ⟨household *suffrage*, or the restriction of the right to vote to male householders, existed in Great Britain from 1867 to 1918⟩ **Franchise** may be chosen when the privilege or power is thought of as conferred by the government or as a statutory or legal right ⟨the *franchise* was long withheld from British citizens who were not householders⟩ ⟨yet some people hesitate to give women the *franchise*! actually, a miserable privilege which any poor fool of a man may exercise—*Jefferies*⟩ **Vote** is appropriate when the stress is on the power of each of the individuals on whom the franchise has been conferred to express his choice or opinion in the approved way, thereby aiding in the task of determining the will of the people ⟨to have the *vote* and not to exercise it is to show oneself unworthy of one's citizenship⟩ ⟨a class that has not the *vote* lacks the power to assert its rights⟩ ⟨every American citizen has a like *vote* in choosing those who will make the laws⟩ **Ballot**, which specifically implies some method of secret voting, is likely to be used when the emphasis is on the power to vote freely, effectively, and without coercion, on the expressed will of the majority, or on the ethical use of the vote ⟨the *ballot* is the citizens' means of getting the kind of government they want⟩ ⟨among free men there can be no successful appeal from the *ballot* to the bullet, and . . . they who take such appeal are sure to lose their case and pay the cost—*Lincoln*⟩

**suffuse** *infuse, imbue, ingrain, inoculate, leaven
*Ana* *introduce, interpose, interject: impregnate, penetrate, pervade (SEE PERMEATE)

**suggest** **1** Suggest, imply, hint, intimate, insinuate can all mean to convey an idea or the thought of something by indirect means. **Suggest** emphasizes a putting into the mind as the result of an association of ideas, an awakening of a desire, or an initiating of a train of thought ⟨the militant severity of his judgments, and the caustic wit of his comments, *suggest* . . . how long and bitter would be the struggle—*Parrington*⟩ ⟨designing attractive books (with jackets that truly *suggest* their contents)—*Malcolm Cowley*⟩ ⟨he can *suggest* in his work the immobility of a plain or the extreme action of a bolt of lightning, without showing either—*Nichols*⟩ **Imply** (see also INCLUDE) is in general opposed to *express;* the term stresses a suggesting, or putting into the mind, of an idea, a thought, or a meaning that is involved in a statement, an action, a situation, or a word and forms a part, but not necessarily an obvious part, of its full signification or significance ⟨the philosophy of Nature which is *implied* in Chinese art—*Binyon*⟩ ⟨dislikes intensely to say this; in chapter after chapter he approaches it and *implies* it, only to draw back from saying it quite baldly—*Brand Blanshard*⟩ Very often the difference between *suggest* and *imply* is not clear, though *suggest* often connotes the necessity of delicate perception and *imply* connotes the need of inference ⟨a competent portraitist knows how to *imply* the profile in the full face—*Huxley*⟩ ⟨the "sayings" of a community, its proverbs, are its characteristic comment upon life; they *imply* its history, *suggest* its attitude toward the world and its way of accepting life—*Cather*⟩ **Hint** implies the use of a remote or covert suggestion and often also connotes lack of candor, frankness, or straightforwardness ⟨looking for a minute at the soft *hinted* green in the branches against the sky—*Shirley Jackson*⟩ ⟨he was not candid with her about his feelings; for once, when he had merely *hinted* at them to her, she had laughed—*Dell*⟩ ⟨the Star Route frauds, *hinted* at while Hayes was president, were uncovered before the death of Garfield—*Paxson*⟩ **Intimate** frequently implies a lighter or more elusive suggestion than *hint* but it connotes delicacy of approach rather than lack of candor or frankness ⟨he said that he had to be prudent or might not be able to say all that he thought, thus *intimating* to his hearers that they might infer that he meant more—*Justice Holmes*⟩ **Insinuate** (see INTRODUCE 2) implies an artful hinting or a conveying, especially of an unpleasant or depreciative suggestion, in an underhanded or devious manner ⟨by his tone and expression, rather than by his words, he *insinuated* that the boy was not to be trusted⟩ ⟨he could quietly *insinuate* the most scandalously hilarious things about the Joneses—*Theodore Sturgeon*⟩ ⟨the voice that *insinuates* that Jews and Negroes and Catholics are inferior excrescences on our body politic—*Lerner*⟩ *Ana* present, *offer: *infuse, imbue, inoculate, leaven: *advance, further: allude, *refer, advert: connote, *denote
*Ant* express

**2** Suggest, adumbrate, shadow are comparable when they are predicated of things that serve indirectly to represent another thing because they evoke a thought, an image, or a conception of it. One thing **suggests** another when it brings to mind something that is not objectively present, immediately apparent, or directly represented. The thing

---

*Ana* analogous words     *Ant* antonyms     *Con* contrasted words     See also explanatory notes facing page 1

that *suggests* may be an outward sign which prompts an inference ⟨a certain well-to-do air about the man *suggested* that he was not poor for his degree—*Hardy*⟩ It may be a symbol, which calls to mind whatever it conventionally represents ⟨the fleur-de-lis *suggests* the royal power of France⟩ It may be a fragment which evokes an image of a whole or a concrete detail that gives an inkling of something abstract or incapable of representation ⟨the curve of the greyhound is not only the line of beauty, but a line which *suggests* motion—*Jefferies*⟩ It may be a word or a phrase that calls up a train of associations and reveals more than it actually denotes ⟨phrases flat and precise on the surface yet *suggesting* mystery below—*Day Lewis*⟩ ⟨the business of words in prose is primarily to state; in poetry, not only to state, but also (and sometimes primarily) to *suggest*—*Lowes*⟩ One thing **adumbrates** another when the former faintly or darkly or sketchily suggests the latter. *Adumbrate* seldom takes a material object and is especially appropriate for use with one that is or is felt as beyond the present level or sometimes the reach of human comprehension or imagination ⟨the Soviet demands, flatly presented or delicately *adumbrated* at Potsdam—*Mosely*⟩ ⟨this concept is *adumbrated*, but not yet distinctly conceived —*Lowie*⟩ ⟨both in the vastness and the richness of the visible universe the invisible God is *adumbrated*—*Isaac Taylor*⟩ When one thing **shadows** (or *shadows forth*) another thing, it represents that thing obscurely (as by a symbol or other indirect means). Sometimes the word comes close to *prefigure* or *foreshadow*, but as a rule precedence is not implied ⟨to the Chinese painters this world of nature seemed a more effective way of *shadowing* forth the manifold moods of man than by representing human figures animated by these moods—*Binyon*⟩ *Ant* manifest

**suggestion** *touch, suspicion, soupçon, tincture, tinge, shade, smack, spice, dash, vein, strain, streak

**suit 1** *prayer, plea, petition, appeal
*Ana* entreaty, importuning *or* importunity, imploring, supplication (see corresponding verbs at BEG): asking, requesting *or* request, soliciting *or* solicitation (see corresponding verbs at ASK)
**2 Suit, lawsuit, action, cause, case** are all used to designate legal proceedings instituted for the sake of demanding justice or enforcing a right. Though often used interchangeably in the sense of *lawsuit*, they may have certain differences in their connotations and their applications. **Suit** stresses the attempt of a complainant through litigation to gain an end (as redress for a wrong, recognition of a claim, or the enforcement of law); it therefore may be used of the proceedings from the time of formal application through the prosecution ⟨win a *suit*⟩ ⟨withdraw a *suit*⟩ ⟨a *suit* in equity⟩ **Lawsuit** can add to *suit* the implication of actual trial in court and often that of judicial decision; it may therefore refer to the entire proceedings ⟨the *lawsuit* of Brown versus Jones ended in victory for the defendant⟩ **Action** comes very close to *suit*, but it is relatively colorless and throws the emphasis on actual proceedings rather than on petition ⟨bring an *action* in Circuit Court⟩ In technical legal use, however, it is a proceeding in a court of law which is distinguished from a suit in equity and which has for its end the ascertainment of facts. If the complainant's position is found correct in such an action, an appropriate legal remedy may then be applied. **Cause** emphasizes the grounds on which one institutes a suit; consequently, like *suit*, it implies the plaintiff's point of view, but it suggests even more strongly his sense of the justice of his demand ⟨the customary arts of the pleader, the appeal to the sympathies of the

public . . . he rejected as unworthy of himself and of his *cause*—*Dickinson*⟩ **Case**, like *cause*, may imply rather the grounds of action than the actual proceedings but, unlike *cause*, may view or present these grounds from either or both points of view ⟨the plaintiff has a good *case*⟩ ⟨the defendant's attorney stated his *case*⟩ However *case* often is applied to the entire proceedings in a lawsuit including the judicial decision ⟨one of the famous *cases* in legal history⟩ ⟨a study of historic capital *cases*⟩

**suitable** *fit, meet, proper, appropriate, fitting, apt, happy, felicitous
*Ana* *decorous, decent, seemly, proper, nice: advisable, *expedient, politic: *due, rightful, condign
*Ant* unsuitable: unbecoming

**sulky** surly, morose, glum, *sullen, crabbed, saturnine, dour, gloomy
*Ana* cranky, cross, testy, touchy (see IRASCIBLE): peevish, petulant, fretful, querulous, *irritable

**sullen, glum, morose, surly, sulky, crabbed, saturnine, dour, gloomy** can mean governed by or showing, especially in one's aspect, a forbidding or disagreeable mood or disposition. One is **sullen** who is, often by disposition, gloomy, silent, and ill-humored and who refuses to be sociable, cooperative, or responsive ⟨Sheridan was generally very dull in society, and sat *sullen* and silent—*Scott*⟩ ⟨he made them go back to the fields immediately after supper and work until midnight. They went in *sullen* silence—*Anderson*⟩ ⟨the furious quarrels, and always, always the bitter *sullen* face of the boy brooding over his work—*Dahl*⟩ One is **glum** who is dismally silent either because of low spirits or depressing circumstances ⟨we have of course good reason to look *glum* and little reason to laugh . . . now deprived of most of the things that make for gaiety and high spirits—*Mais*⟩ ⟨the two of you . . . sitting there as *glum* as a pair of saints in hell—*Deasy*⟩ One is **morose** who is austerely sour or bitter and inclined to glumness ⟨a *morose* ill-conditioned, ill-natured person—*South*⟩ ⟨should there be any cold-blooded and *morose* mortals who really dislike this book—*Boswell*⟩ One is **surly** who adds churlishness or gruffness of speech and manner to sullenness or moroseness ⟨he indulged his moods. If he were *surly*, he did not bother to hide it; if he were aggressive, he would swear at her—*Mailer*⟩ ⟨"Sam, put it out of your mind," I snapped in a rather *surly* rebuff—*Michener*⟩ ⟨the somewhat *surly* goodness, the hard and unattractive pieties into which she cannot really enter—*Pater*⟩ One is **sulky** who manifests displeasure, discontent, or resentment by giving way childishly to a fit of peevish sullenness ⟨though he had come in *sulky* unwillingness, he was impressed by the supper—*Sinclair Lewis*⟩ ⟨we were a precious pair: I *sulky* and obstinate, she changeable and hot-tempered—*Shaw*⟩ One is **crabbed** who is actually or seemingly ill-natured, harsh, and forbidding. The term often refers to one's aspect and manner of speaking and usually implies a sour or morose disposition or a settled crossness ⟨divine Philosophy! Not harsh and *crabbed*, as dull fools suppose—*Milton*⟩ ⟨the querulous, exacting father could not help . . . exasperating the children whom, in his own *crabbed* way, he yet genuinely loved—*Woolf*⟩ One is **saturnine** who presents a heavy, forbidding, taciturn gloom ⟨driven to *saturnine* and scornful silence by Gerald's godless conversation—*Wylie*⟩ ⟨Sheridan's humor, or rather wit, was always *saturnine*, and sometimes savage; he never laughed—*Byron*⟩ but *saturnine* may come close to *sardonic* (which see under SARCASTIC) and then suggests less a depressing heaviness and gloom than a wry mocking disdain and skepticism that is often at least superficially attractive ⟨novels . . . in which evil is personified by *saturnine* persons who

A colon (:) separates groups of words discriminated. An asterisk (*) indicates place of treatment of each group.

own yachts and look good in evening dress—*Anthony West*⟩ ⟨he felt worldly and *saturnine* like a character in a movie—*Cheever*⟩ One is **dour** who gives a sometimes superficial effect of severity, obstinacy, and grim bitterness of disposition ⟨though the Filipino seldom smiled, he was by no means *dour*. Kindliness was one of his most charming traits—*Heiser*⟩ ⟨he was silent, gloomy and *dour*, frequently irritable, unfriendly—*C. W. M. Hart*⟩ One is **gloomy** who is so depressed by events or conditions or so oppressed by melancholy that all signs of cheerfulness or optimism are obscured, so that he appears sullen, glum, or dour as well as low-spirited ⟨take a *gloomy* view of world conditions⟩ ⟨when she is *gloomy* she makes everyone unhappy⟩ ⟨he was constitutionally *gloomy*, a congenital pessimist who always saw the doleful side of any situation —*White*⟩
*Ana* lowering, glowering, frowning, scowling (see FROWN): spiteful, malevolent, *malicious, malign: *cynical, pessimistic
**sully** *soil, dirty, tarnish, foul, befoul, smirch, besmirch, grime, begrime
*Ana* *spot, spatter, sprinkle: defile, pollute, taint, *contaminate
**sum** *n* Sum, amount, number, aggregate, total, whole, quantity denote a result obtained by putting or taking together all in a given group or mass. **Sum** denotes the result of simple addition, usually of figures, sometimes of particulars ⟨four is the *sum* of two and two⟩ **Amount** denotes the result reached by combining all the sums or weights or measures that form a whole ⟨the *amount* of his purchases⟩ ⟨the *amount* of cotton raised in one year⟩ **Number**, with its strong suggestion of enumerating, is usually applied to a countable aggregate of persons or things and is clearly distinct from *amount*, which ordinarily applies to things in bulk or mass; thus, one may pick a large *number* of apples to make a large *amount* of applesauce. **Aggregate** denotes the result reached by counting and considering together all the distinct individuals or particulars in a group or collection ⟨though his errors are individually insignificant, their *aggregate* is so large as to destroy confidence in his accuracy⟩ ⟨it is not true that a social force or effort is the mere *aggregate* of individual forces and efforts—*Hobson*⟩ **Total** and *whole* suggest the completeness or inclusiveness of the result; **total** often further implies magnitude in the result, and **whole**, unity in what is summed up ⟨a grand *total* of ten millions⟩ ⟨the *whole* is the sum of its parts⟩ **Quantity** in general use is employed chiefly of things which are measured in bulk, even though they can be counted ⟨a *quantity* of apples⟩ In technical and scientific use *quantity* is not limited to an aggregate or bulk but may be used of anything that is measurable in extent, duration, volume, magnitude, intensity, or value ⟨spatial *quantity*⟩ ⟨the *quantity* of a vowel⟩ ⟨electrical *quantities*⟩ ⟨*quantity* of heat⟩ ⟨*quantity* of work performed by a machine⟩
**sum** *vb* *add, total, tot, cast, figure, foot
*Ana* compute, *calculate, estimate, reckon: *count, enumerate, number
**summary** *adj* pithy, compendious, *concise, terse, succinct, laconic
*Ana* *brief, short: *quick, prompt, ready, apt: compacted *or* compact, concentrated (see COMPACT *vb*)
*Ant* circumstantial
**summative** *cumulative, accumulative, additive
**summit**, peak, pinnacle, climax, apex, acme, culmination, meridian, zenith, apogee can mean the highest point attained or attainable. **Summit** is applied to what represents the topmost level attainable by effort or to what is the highest in its type or kind of attainable things ⟨this scaleless

monster, eight or nine feet long, sprawling in the shade by the side of the mud pools . . . was the *summit* of labyrinthodont evolution—*Swinton*⟩ ⟨the Bar's outstanding figure by acclaim . . . in the fullness of his powers and at the *summit* of his fame—*Lustgarten*⟩ **Peak** usually implies a point rather than a level ⟨the *peak* of enthusiasm⟩ It is frequently applied to something that is or can be represented in a graph; used absolutely it designates the highest point reached in a course or during a stated or implied length of time ⟨security prices reached new *peaks* this year⟩ ⟨his vocal control was at its *peak* when he did the recording—*Paul Hume*⟩ **Pinnacle** is applied chiefly to what has reached a dizzy and, often, insecure height ⟨the word *theater* means different things to different groups. To some its very *pinnacle* is *South Pacific*, which is despised by the aesthetes—*Miller*⟩ ⟨a *pinnacle* of happiness— *Brooks*⟩ ⟨never achieved the *pinnacle* of public life, the presidency, when lesser men did—*Sevareid*⟩ **Climax** implies a scale of ascending values; it is applied to the highest point in force, in intensity, in interest, or in impressiveness in an ascending movement or series. The word often suggests an end or close ⟨reserve your strongest argument for the *climax* of your speech⟩ ⟨the quarrel had been only the *climax* of a long period of increasing strain—*Davis*⟩ ⟨the Marxist version of history, according to which the seeming harmonies of our society would blow up in a catastrophic *climax*—*Niebuhr*⟩ **Apex** is applied to the highest or culminating point (as in time or of accomplishment) to which everything in a career, a system of thought, or a cultural development ascends and in which everything is concentrated ⟨if terrestrial culture were a pyramid, at the *apex* (where the power is) would sit a blind man, for . . . only by blinding ourselves, bit by bit, may we rise above our fellows—*Theodore Sturgeon*⟩ ⟨the British people, who look upon the king as the *apex* of their national and social aspirations—*Bolitho*⟩ ⟨the argument is that Wordsworth's economic, political, religious, and "sexual" unorthodoxies dawned gradually, reaching an *apex* about 1793—*Carlos Baker*⟩ **Acme** is applied to what embodies or represents the perfection or pure essence of a thing ⟨Sir Philip Sidney was the *acme* of courtesy⟩ ⟨to say "mither" instead of "mother" seems to many the *acme* of romance—*Wilde*⟩ ⟨seemed to consider this the very *acme* of humor, for he fairly hooted at us—*R. H. Davis*⟩ **Culmination** can denote an apex that is the outcome of a movement, a growth, a development, or a progress and that represents its natural end or attained objective ⟨this joint effort of church and crown . . . found its *culmination* under Louis XIV, when the nobles were definitely conquered by the crown and the Reformation by the church—*Brownell*⟩ ⟨the recent use of the atomic bomb . . . is the *culmination* of years of Herculean effort—*Stimson*⟩ but often *culmination* suggests a coming to a head or issue rather than to a high point ⟨war is a *culmination* of evils, a sudden attack on the very existence of the body politic—*Roosevelt*⟩ ⟨the Reformation . . . was . . . the *culmination* of a long agitation for national independence in religious matters—*Inge*⟩ **Meridian** is applied to the prime or period of fullest development or vigor in a life (as of a person, a race, or an institution); it connotes not only prior ascent but ensuing decline ⟨I have touched the highest point of all my greatness: and, from that full *meridian* of my glory, I haste now to my setting—*Shak.*⟩ ⟨the past eighteen years have constituted one of the great historical *meridians* of the presidency— *Rossiter*⟩ **Zenith** adds to *meridian* the implications of luster and distinction ⟨he had reached the *zenith* of his powers⟩ ⟨classical studies reached their *zenith* in the twelfth century—*H. O. Taylor*⟩ **Apogee**, like *meridian*, is applied to the highest point (as in a course, a career, or a movement), but it seldom connotes being at the prime or height of glory ⟨the French Revolution reached its *apogee* in the Reign of Terror⟩ ⟨a rangy man whose deeply burned, granular face reached an *apogee* of redness in his beard—*Hervey*⟩

**summon, summons,** call, cite, convoke, convene, muster mean to demand the presence of persons or, by extension, things. **Summon** implies the exercise of authority or of power; it usually suggests a mandate, an imperative order or bidding, or urgency ⟨the king *summoned* his privy councilors to the palace⟩ ⟨*summoned* his secretary⟩ ⟨*summon* a person to appear in court⟩ ⟨I *summon* your Grace to his Majesty's parliament—*Shak.*⟩ ⟨a confiding, playful little animal, whom one alternately trained to do tricks and then *summoned* to jump snuggling upon one's knee—*Sackville-West*⟩ ⟨she could *summon* tears and delights as one *summons* servants—*H. G. Wells*⟩ **Summons,** sometimes interchangeable with *summon*, usually implies the actual serving with a legal writ to appear in court. **Call** is often used in place of *summon*, especially when less formality is implied or the imperativeness of the bidding is not stressed, or when actual shouting is suggested ⟨*call* men to arms⟩ ⟨*call* witnesses to court⟩ ⟨*call* a servant⟩ ⟨the president *called* congress together for an extra session⟩ ⟨I can *call* spirits from the vasty deep—*Shak.*⟩ Often, however, there is a suggestion of an impulsion of God, of Nature, or of necessity ⟨the young man felt that he was *called* to the ministry⟩ ⟨America is *called* to greatness—*A. E. Stevenson*⟩ ⟨he felt *called* upon to speak⟩ **Cite** (see also ADDUCE) may occasionally replace *summon* or *summons*, especially in legal use ⟨Andrew was *cited* to appear and testify—*W. B. Parker*⟩ ⟨he hath *cited* me to Rome, for heresy—*Tennyson*⟩ **Convoke** implies a summons to assemble, especially for legislative or deliberative purposes ⟨the king *convoked* parliament⟩ ⟨the Italian government *convoked* great congresses of physicists and engineers—*Darrow*⟩ ⟨he *convoked* the chiefs of the three armed services . . . and laid down the law—*Shirer*⟩ **Convene** is related to *convoke* somewhat as *call* is to *summon;* it is weaker in its suggestions of the exercise of authority and of imperativeness, but otherwise it is often not distinguishable ⟨*convene* the students in the school auditorium⟩ ⟨the Senate was *convened* by the tribunes—*Froude*⟩ ⟨the court-martial, perhaps fortunately, was never *convened*—*Powell*⟩ **Muster** implies the summoning of an army or other body of troops or of a ship's company (as for military action, inspection, parade, or exercise). In extended use it implies the assembling of a number of things that form a collection or a group in order that they may be exhibited, displayed, or utilized as a whole ⟨a daw that had a mind to be sparkish, tricked himself up with all the gay feathers he could *muster* together—*L'Estrange*⟩ ⟨before the residents could *muster* a fighting force, the marauders had filled their boats with plunder and were gone—*Laird*⟩ **Muster** is used in place of *summon* with such objects as *courage* or *strength*, especially when the context implies the previous dissipation of the quality mentioned ⟨at length you have *mustered* heart to visit the old place—*Dickens*⟩
*Ana* *command, order, bid, enjoin: evoke, elicit, *educe

**sumptuous** *luxurious, opulent
*Ana* magnificent, stately, majestic, *grand: *splendid, resplendent, gorgeous, superb: *showy, ostentatious, pretentious: lavish, prodigal (see PROFUSE)

**sunder** *vb* sever, divide, part, *separate, divorce
*Ana* rend, rive, cleave, split (see TEAR)
*Ant* link

**sundry** *many, several, various, divers, numerous, multifarious

*Ana* *different, disparate, diverse, divergent: *distinct, separate: individual, distinctive, peculiar (see CHARACTERISTIC)

**superadd** annex, append, subjoin, *add
*Ana* *fasten, attach, affix

**superannuated** *aged, old, elderly

**superb** *splendid, resplendent, glorious, gorgeous, sublime
*Ana* superlative, transcendent, surpassing, *supreme: sumptuous, *luxurious, opulent: imposing, stately, majestic, magnificent, *grand

**supercilious** disdainful, overbearing, arrogant, haughty, *proud, lordly, insolent
*Ana* vain, vainglorious (see under PRIDE): contemptuous, scornful (see corresponding nouns under DESPISE *vb*)

**supererogatory,** gratuitous, uncalled-for, wanton are comparable when they mean given or done freely and without compulsion or provocation or without warrant or justification. **Supererogatory** basically implies a giving above or beyond what is required or is laid down in the laws or rules; the word then suggests a devotion or loyalty that is not satisfied merely with the doing of what is required and that finds expression in the performance of additional labors, works, or services beyond those expected or demanded ⟨the *supererogatory* services of representatives in Congress⟩ In other usage the term is definitely depreciative in that it implies not a giving freely over and above what is required but a giving or adding of what is not needed or wanted and is therefore an embarrassment or encumbrance ⟨for a mind like his, education seemed *supererogatory*. Training would only have destroyed his natural aptitudes—*Huxley*⟩ ⟨the virtual unity of language, laws, general race-ideals would seem to render protection of frontiers *supererogatory* —*Angell*⟩ **Gratuitous** may apply to a giving voluntarily without expectation of recompense, reward, or compensation ⟨the *gratuitous* education provided by the public schools of the United States⟩ but it often stresses a giving without provocation of something disagreeable, offensive, troublesome, or painful ⟨a *gratuitous* insult⟩ ⟨a *gratuitous* . . . imposition of labor—*Mann*⟩ **Gratuitous** often means little more than **uncalled-for,** which suggests not only a lack of provocation but a lack of need or justification and therefore implies impertinence or absurdity, often logical absurdity ⟨the *gratuitous* assumption that the new must surpass the old—*Grandgent*⟩ ⟨*uncalled-for* interference⟩ ⟨*uncalled-for* advice⟩ **Wanton** (see also LICENTIOUS) also implies want of provocation, but it stresses capriciousness and the absence of a motive except reckless sportiveness or arbitrariness or pure malice ⟨a *wanton* attack⟩ ⟨*wanton* destruction⟩ ⟨the *wanton* horrors of her bloody play—*Shelley*⟩ ⟨believing the deed [the burning of a haystack] to have been unprovoked and *wanton*—*Meredith*⟩ ⟨tyranny consists in the *wanton* and improper use of strength by the stronger—*Bryce*⟩
*Ana* *free, independent, autonomous: *excessive, extreme, exorbitant: *superfluous, supernumerary, extra, spare

**superficial,** shallow, cursory, uncritical can mean lacking in depth, solidity, and comprehensiveness. **Superficial** applies chiefly to persons, their minds, their emotions, their attainments, or their utterances or writings, but it is also applicable to things (as circumstances, factors, conditions, or qualities). The term usually implies a concern with surface aspects or obvious features or an avoidance of all but these aspects or features ⟨he had time for no more than a *superficial* examination of the report⟩ ⟨multiple *superficial* wounds of the left and right thigh . . . . Profound wounds of right knee—*Hemingway*⟩ ⟨the tendency . . . of prose drama

A colon (:) separates groups of words discriminated. An asterisk (*) indicates place of treatment of each group.

is to emphasize the ephemeral and *superficial;* if we want to get at the permanent and universal we tend to express ourselves in verse—*T. S. Eliot*⟩ Often the term is definitely depreciative and adds implications of unpleasing qualities (as pretense, ostentation, slightness, lack of thoroughness, insignificance, or insincerity) ⟨the lecture was very *superficial*⟩ ⟨our political theory is hopelessly sophomoric and *superficial—Mencken*⟩ ⟨its treatment of what is one of the important themes of our day seems generally too slick and *superficial* to be taken seriously— *Merle Miller*⟩ **Shallow** regularly implies a lack of depth ⟨a *shallow* stream⟩ ⟨*shallow* breathing⟩ and when applied to persons, their knowledge, their reasoning, or their emotions, is almost invariably derogatory and differs little from *superficial* used derogatorily except in its freedom from implication of outward show or of apparent but not genuine significance ⟨do you suppose this eternal *shallow* cynicism of yours has any real bearing on a nature like hers?—*Shaw*⟩ ⟨he continued to prop up this utterly muddled man, this confused and *shallow* "philosopher," as the intellectual mentor of the Nazi movement— *Shirer*⟩ ⟨people who are property-grabbers, *shallow* and callous egoists . . . are not capable of so noble and selfish a feeling as love—*Salisbury*⟩ **Cursory** stresses a lack of thoroughness or of care for details rather than a concentration on the obvious; it often also suggests haste and casualness ⟨even from a *cursory* reading of the book, I judge that it is a very fine piece of work⟩ ⟨knowing the nature of women, your *cursory* observations might prove to be more exacting . . . than my own—*Terry Southern*⟩ ⟨the coffeehouse must not be dismissed with a *cursory* mention—*Macaulay*⟩ ⟨as they worked, they cursed us— not with a common *cursory* curse, but with long, carefully thought-out, comprehensive curses—*Jerome*⟩ **Uncritical** implies a superficiality or shallowness unbefitting to a critic or sound judge, whether of literature or the arts or of more general matters (as data, statements, or events) which must be evaluated, related, estimated, or judged ⟨an *uncritical* judgment of a book⟩ ⟨she was absolutely *uncritical*, she believed everything—*Audrey Barker*⟩ ⟨I would not have you so *uncritical* as to blame the Church or its clergy for what happened—*Quiller-Couch*⟩
*Ant* radical (sense 1)

**superfluity** *excess, surplus, surplusage, overplus
*Ana* overflowing *or* overflow, teeming, swarming (see TEEM): exuberance, profusion, lavishness, prodigality (see corresponding adjectives at PROFUSE)

**superfluous,** **surplus, supernumerary, extra, spare** all describe what is above or beyond what is needed or indispensable. **Superfluous** implies a superabundance or excess that requires elimination or pruning ⟨many people . . . found themselves *superfluous* and, in their turn, were compelled to emigrate—*Handlin*⟩ ⟨artists . . . not tempted, as are those who work direct from nature, to transcribe *superfluous* detail because it happens to be before their eyes—*Binyon*⟩ Sometimes the term either loses its implication of richness of supply or places no emphasis on that idea and comes to mean little more than *nonessential* or *dispensable*, if circumstances require its sacrifice ⟨art, music, literature, and the like—in short . . . , *superfluous* things—*Sherman*⟩ ⟨gradually the heat, the exertion had consumed all *superfluous* energy—*Hervey*⟩ or *unnecessary, useless,* or *needless* ⟨authority, like a good educator, ought to aim at making itself *superfluous—Inge*⟩ **Surplus** applies to what remains over when what is needed or required for all present purposes has been used ⟨there will be no *surplus* wheat this year⟩ ⟨each year the *surplus* funds of the institution were invested⟩ ⟨the task of in-

ducing those with *surplus* land to part with it voluntarily to the landless—*Masani*⟩ ⟨transporting its troops to Manchuria, giving it *surplus* airplanes—*Richard Watts*⟩ **Supernumerary** implies something added to a number that is normal, adequate, or prescribed; it need not necessarily suggest that there is no need or no use for what is added, though in reference to a physical condition it often implies a departure from the normal ⟨extra ribs, as well as other *supernumerary* internal parts—*Science News Letter*⟩ ⟨a *supernumerary* member of a cast used for mob scenes⟩ ⟨offered the *supernumerary* position of inspector general—*Roucek*⟩ **Extra** is often used in place of *supernumerary* ⟨buy a few *extra* Christmas presents in case someone has been forgotten⟩ ⟨was looking at Kitty as if she had suddenly sprouted an *extra* head—*Rolfs*⟩ but it may also apply to an addition not in number but in amount ⟨he was subjected to *extra* work as acting chairman of the House Committee—*C. H. Lincoln*⟩ or in price ⟨there is an *extra* charge for coffee⟩ **Spare** is often used in place of *surplus* but it carries a stronger suggestion of being held for future use, often a special use ⟨a *spare* suit of clothes⟩ ⟨the *spare* room is the guest room⟩ ⟨a pouch for carrying tobacco, tinder, and *spare* arrow-poison —*Huntingford*⟩ ⟨carry a *spare* tire for an automobile⟩ or of not having any demands on it for a particular use ⟨he never has any *spare* cash⟩ ⟨bring along a little *spare* time, too, and some extra patience, to work these fast . . . streams of New England—*Corey Ford*⟩ or of being easily spared ⟨have you a *spare* cigarette on you?⟩
*Ana* *supererogatory, gratuitous, uncalled-for, wanton: *profuse, lavish, prodigal, exuberant: *excessive, inordinate, extravagant, extreme

**superhuman** preternatural, miraculous, supranatural, *supernatural
*Ana* potent, puissant, *powerful, forcible, forceful: Herculean, cyclopean, titanic, gigantic (see HUGE)

**superimpose** *overlay, superpose, appliqué

**superior** *adj* *better, preferable
*Ant* inferior

**superlative** *adj* *supreme, transcendent, surpassing, peerless, incomparable, preeminent
*Ana* *consummate, finished, accomplished: *splendid, glorious, sublime, superb

**supernatural,** **supranatural, preternatural, miraculous, superhuman** are overlapping rather than strictly synonymous terms whose meanings all involve a contrast with what is natural or, sometimes, normal or predictable. All, with the possible exception of the uncommon *supranatural*, are used hyperbolically to mean exceeding usual or likely human standards and then are generally equivalent to such terms as *extraordinary, exceptional, or wonderful;* thus, in an emergency a man may exhibit *supernatural* strength; one may show *preternatural* awareness of small sounds when alone at night; a scholar may decipher a manuscript with *miraculous* accuracy; a player may win against odds by a *superhuman* effort. **Supernatural** stresses deviation from the natural that is felt as above or beyond what is observable and capable of being experienced by ordinary means; in much of its use it suggests spirituality and implies a relation to God or to divine powers ⟨a *supernatural* religion⟩ ⟨the gods in Homer do exert *supernatural* effects; for when Zeus nods, all Olympus shakes—*Noss*⟩ ⟨medieval theologians who did so much to establish and define the terminology of Christianity spoke of man's *supernatural* life, the life of the soul above the natural life of the body—*M. W. Baldwin*⟩ ⟨the belief in a *supernatural* power, in God, was natural to him who felt that he could plow and plant, but that only God made his work produce grain and fruit—

---

*Ana* analogous words    *Ant* antonyms    *Con* contrasted words    See also explanatory notes facing page 1

*Wood*⟩ but sometimes the word loses these suggestions and implications and can then denote more or less neutrally a transcending of the natural and comprehensible or known ⟨not to him, as to us, a world . . . mapped, botanized, zoologized; a tiny planet about which everybody knows, or thinks they know everything: but a world infinite, magical, *supernatural*—because unknown—*Kingsley*⟩ ⟨richer, warmer, more vibrant with love and yearning and compassion, a wonderful, mysterious, *supernatural* Voice spoke from above their heads—*Huxley*⟩ or it can apply to things commonly felt as matters of superstition rather than of divine spirituality and then often carries a depreciatory note ⟨books that describe fraudulent production of *supernatural* phenomena—*G. R. Price*⟩ ⟨his Northmen kept away from Amneran Heath and Morven, on account of the *supernatural* beings you were always apt to encounter thereabouts—*Cabell*⟩ ⟨going without a companion, he had taken my revolver to preserve him from dangers—meaning those of a *supernatural* kind—*Hudson*⟩ **Supranatural** implies a transcending of what is natural and especially of what is comprehensible or capable of becoming comprehensible; it is likely to be chosen when the theistic connotations of *supernatural* are to be avoided ⟨the *supernatural* phenomena investigated by parapsychologists⟩ ⟨a mystic who resorts to *supranatural* explanations for two of history's greatest riddles—*Werner*⟩ **Preternatural** applies chiefly to what is not regarded as natural or being within the usual range or compass of nature. Usually the term means abnormal or strange and inexplicable to an extreme or startling degree ⟨a degree of acumen which appears to the ordinary apprehension *preternatural*—*Poe*⟩ ⟨the *preternatural* prowess of the hero—*Emerson*⟩ ⟨preserved the *preternatural* neatness of a man who is often tempted and deeply familiar with sloth—*Cheever*⟩ **Miraculous** applies particularly to events or effects in the physical world that are out of the ordinary course of things or that deviate from the known laws of nature either in kind or degree ⟨the plant, his hope, which he had deemed dead, blossomed with *miraculous* suddenness—*Bennett*⟩ ⟨for the last two years he was like a flame burning on in *miraculous* disregard of the fact that there was no more fuel to justify its existence—*Huxley*⟩ In its also common religious use *miraculous* applies to what is regarded or accepted as performed by divine power or happening as a result of divine intervention ⟨the medical man's way of saying that, short of *miraculous* intervention, you may as well order the coffin—*Sayers*⟩ ⟨the *miraculous* transformation of water into wine at the wedding in Cana⟩ ⟨*miraculous* cures attributed to a saint⟩ **Superhuman** is sometimes used in the sense of *supernatural* but in this use it tends to stress the notion of being higher than mankind or sometimes than average or ordinary mankind and it does not carry a clear implication of divinity as *supernatural* often does ⟨superstitious belief in *superhuman* agency—*Mozley*⟩ ⟨if a man believes that he is a *superhuman* servant of a living god it is not difficult to persuade him that he has a right to . . . make use of the toil of his merely human neighbor—*Floyd Taylor*⟩ ⟨you can't expect me to be *superhuman* like you. If you can forgive everything, that's your good luck—*Bellow*⟩ **Ana** divine, spiritual, sacred, *holy, blessed: *infinite, eternal, boundless, illimitable

**supernumerary** surplus, extra, spare, *superfluous

**superpose** superimpose, *overlay, appliqué

**supersede** *replace, displace, supplant

**Ana** repudiate, spurn, reject (see DECLINE *vb*): *abandon, desert, forsake: stay, suspend, intermit (see DEFER)

**supervene** *follow, succeed, ensue

**Ana** *add, append, annex, subjoin, superadd: combine, *unite, conjoin, cooperate

**supervision** *oversight, surveillance

**Ana** controlling *or* control, management, direction, conducting *or* conduct (see corresponding verbs at CONDUCT): leading, guiding (see GUIDE)

**supine 1** *prone, prostrate, recumbent, couchant, dormant

**2** *inactive, inert, passive, idle

**Ana** slothful, *lazy, indolent, faineant: *lethargic, sluggish, torpid: apathetic, *impassive, phlegmatic

**supplant** displace, *replace, supersede

**Ana** *eject, oust, dismiss, expel: uproot, eradicate, extirpate, *exterminate

**supple 1** flexible, resilient, *elastic, springy

**Ana** pliable, pliant, *plastic: *soft, gentle, mild

**Ant** stiff

**2 Supple, limber, lithe, lithesome, lissome** can all apply to bodily movements and mean showing freedom and ease in bending and twisting. **Supple** implies great flexibility of muscles and joints, perfect muscular coordination, and rapidity yet smoothness in change of posture or movement ⟨the light *supple* spring of a cat from its hiding place⟩ ⟨the Bishop stood watching the flowing, *supple* movements of their arms and shoulders, the sure rhythm of their tiny moccasined feet—*Cather*⟩ ⟨in good condition —not fat, like grass-fed cattle, but trim and *supple*, like deer—*Burroughs*⟩ **Limber** also implies great flexibility of muscles and joints and the power to move quickly or easily, but it carries no clear suggestion of grace or of muscular coordination ⟨*limber* country boys jumping from rock to rock⟩ ⟨Gilda rose as *limber* as a 16-year-old, and gamboled the full length of the room—*Purdy*⟩ **Lithe** is applied chiefly to persons or animals that are slender, supple, nimble, and usually graceful in movements ⟨a *lithe* dancer⟩ ⟨they climbed the wall—your lady must be *lithe*—*Browning*⟩ ⟨a *lithe* movement of her apparently boneless little figure—*Jesse*⟩ **Lithesome** may suggest an agility and vigor that makes for sure graceful movement ⟨the warlike carriage of the men, and their strong, *lithesome*, resolute step—*Kinglake*⟩ ⟨an altogether more *lithesome* and nonetheless useful wolfhound—*Nat'l Geog. Mag.*⟩ **Lissome** tends to suggest a light easy supple grace in bearing or in movement ⟨she only wanted wings to fly away, easy and light and *lissome*—*Ransom*⟩ ⟨she dismounted with *lissome* grace, beaming welcomingly —*Wodehouse*⟩ ⟨the *lissome* grace of the cat tribe—*Stevenson-Hamilton*⟩

**Ana** graceful, elegant (see corresponding nouns at ELEGANCE): *easy, smooth, effortless, facile

**supplement** *n* **1** *complement

**2** *appendix, addendum, addenda

**supplement** *vb* complement (see under COMPLEMENT *n*)

**Ana** *improve, better: heighten, enhance, aggravate, *intensify

**supplicate** implore, beseech, entreat, importune, *beg, adjure

**Ana** pray, sue, plead, appeal, petition (see under PRAYER): *ask, request, solicit

**supply** *vb* *provide, furnish

**Ana** *replace, supplant, supersede: compensate, satisfy, recompense (see PAY): fulfill, *satisfy, answer: sustain, *support, prop, bolster, buttress

**supply** *n* *substitute, locum tenens, alternate, understudy, pinch hitter, double, stand-in

**supply** *adj* *temporary, provisional, ad interim, acting

**support** *vb* **1 Support, sustain, prop, bolster, buttress, brace** are comparable when they mean to hold up either literally or figuratively, though they vary greatly in their specific

A colon (:) separates groups of words discriminated.. An asterisk (*) indicates place of treatment of each group.

senses and in the range of their applicability. **Support** suggests the presence of a foundation or base and is applicable in diverse uses with the general meaning or suggestion of carrying from or as if from below, of maintaining or holding up the weight or pressure of, and of forestalling sinking or falling back, or sometimes, merely, of enduring the difficulties or rigors of without yielding and without undue distress ⟨pillars *supporting* the balcony⟩ ⟨he *supports* the greater muscular tension involved with less evident fatigue—*Brownell*⟩ ⟨*support* the Constitution⟩ ⟨found the Roman winter . . . too poignant for his anatomy to *support* without pain—*Wylie*⟩ **Sustain** may center attention on the fact of constantly holding up or of maintaining undiminished ⟨*sustain* the weight of office⟩ ⟨found it difficult to *sustain* an interest in their talk—*Douglas*⟩ or it may more specifically imply an upholding by aiding or backing up ⟨for nine years, Napoleon has been *sustained* by the people of France with a unanimity such as the United States never knew—*Aguecheek*⟩ or by supplying the physical or mental nutriments needed for strength ⟨this intellectual interest is great enough to *sustain* the reader through the analytical labyrinths we must search together—*Hunter Mead*⟩ **Prop** may imply a weakness, a tendency to fall, sink, or recede, or a need for strengthening or reinforcing on the part of the thing being treated ⟨*propping* up the table with a packing case⟩ ⟨trying to *prop* up the decaying structures of last-century imperialism—*G. L. Kirk*⟩ ⟨the plot, a slim tale of vengeance, is psychologically shallow and *propped* up by unpardonable coincidences—*Anthony Boucher*⟩ **Bolster** blends the suggestions of *sustain* and *prop;* it may suggest a supporting comparable to that afforded an invalid by pillows ⟨*bolster* up the falling fortunes of the East India Company—*Parrington*⟩ ⟨*bolster* the diminishing lumber trade within the next 75 years—*Amer. Guide Series: N.J.*⟩ ⟨assign some extra instruments to *bolster* the choir's volume of sound—*P. H. Lang*⟩ **Buttress** tends to suggest strengthening, reinforcing, or stabilizing, sometimes massive, at a stress point in the manner of an architectural buttress ⟨combat business slumps and to *buttress* the economy so that danger of another depression will be reduced to a minimum—*Newsweek*⟩ ⟨a code of laws *buttressed* by divine sanctions which should be unshakable —*Farrington*⟩ ⟨the popular success formula is *buttressed* by evidence from the careers of an impressive minority— *R. B. Morris*⟩ **Brace** may suggest supporting or strengthening so that the thing treated is made firm, unyielding, or rigid against pressure ⟨*brace* the shelf with an angle iron⟩ ⟨then he *braced* himself against a giant oak on his front lawn and experienced a savage kind of exaltation as the elements raged around him—*Cerf*⟩ ⟨the shoring up of a tottering political system, which is precisely the problem that we face in trying to *brace* the western democracies— *G. W. Johnson*⟩
*Ana* \*carry, bear, convey: endure, \*bear, suffer, stand: evidence, evince, \*show: \*indicate, attest, argue, betoken: uphold, advocate, back, champion (see SUPPORT 2)
**2 Support, uphold, advocate, back, champion** are comparable when they mean to favor actively and in some concrete manner a person or thing that meets opposition. **Support** is general and comparatively colorless. One *supports* a candidate for election whether one merely votes for him or takes a leading part in his campaign; one *supports* a cause whether one merely announces one's stand in favor of it or contributes money and time to furthering its interests ⟨any politician who *supported* her husband was regarded with favor by Mrs. Lincoln—*R. P. Randall*⟩ ⟨it is not enough to *support* the capitalist system; to escape abuse as an iconoclast, you must publicly venerate

it as well—*Bliven* b. 1889⟩ **Uphold** carries an implication of keeping erect or from falling or breaking down; it is appropriately used in reference to something that already exists but is attacked or challenged ⟨those who *uphold* the ideal of pure poetry—*Day Lewis*⟩ ⟨tried to *uphold* the morale of the occupied capital—*Paxson*⟩ ⟨he is the Philistine who *upholds* and aids the heavy, cumbrous, blind, mechanical forces of society—*Wilde*⟩ **Advocate** implies vocal support either in speeches or in writings; often it connotes urging or pleading ⟨I believe that our political leaders should live by faith . . . but I doubt that they should *advocate* faith, if only because such advocacy renders a few people uncomfortable—*E. B. White*⟩ ⟨the few local believers in world government brought to town a play that *advocated* it—*Davis*⟩ **Back** often implies strong support from the rear to be used whenever assistance is needed to prevent the failure of a person or of his ventures or efforts. Sometimes it connotes reserve forces or the use of force; sometimes it implies money reserves or the promise of financial assistance ⟨his father said he would *back* him in business⟩ ⟨states, large and small, with . . . their very practical traders pushing for foreign markets, and their navies and armies to *back* the traders and annex these markets—*Shaw*⟩ ⟨there would be more talk, but talk *backed* by armed force—*Cloete*⟩ Often *back* derives its implications from its use in betting and suggests a willingness to hazard something and especially money on a person's or thing's chance for success ⟨I *back* you to hold your own against them all—*Wharton*⟩ ⟨the wife of a Dublin civil servant prohibited her husband from *backing* horses, but he continued to gamble secretly —*The Irish Digest*⟩ **Champion** implies public defense of a person or thing believed to be unjustly attacked or too weak to advocate its own cause and may therefore connote distinction or gallantry in the one who champions ⟨who . . . *championed* every cause I called my heart's cause, loving as I loved, hating my hates, spurned falsehood, *championed* truth—*Browning*⟩
*Ana* \*approve, endorse, sanction: espouse, embrace, \*adopt: \*defend, protect, shield
**support** *n* maintenance, sustenance, \*living, livelihood, subsistence, keep, bread
*Ant* adversary, antagonist
**supposed, supposititious, suppositious, reputed, putative, purported, conjectural, hypothetical** can mean accepted or advanced as true, real, or in accordance with the facts on the basis of less than conclusive evidence. All imply a measure of doubt of what is asserted and may serve as a disclaimer of responsibility for the assertion. **Supposed** is likely to imply rather general or common acceptance of what is asserted, though suggesting the presence of uncertainty or conflicting evidence or the likelihood of error ⟨the identity thus asserted with its *supposed* though sometimes debated poetic essence—*Kolodin*⟩ ⟨there has not been a reputable student of grammar for a long time who believed the grammar books which are in common use. But we, the people, are loyal to our *supposed* grammar —*Laird*⟩ ⟨have we not in the present censorship an ineffectual check on certain *supposed* evils which perhaps are not very real evils?—*Walkley*⟩ **Supposititious** occasionally comes close to *supposed* ⟨we have no reason to conclude that my idea of the absent thing has only such meaning as can be expressed in anticipatory terms —whether the anticipation be mine or that of a *supposititious* observer—*Victor Lowe*⟩ but usually it carries distinct and positive suggestions of fraudulence or spuriousness ⟨ready to lend his last cent to a man in distress or *supposititious* distress—*Herzberg*⟩ ⟨dispatched a lawyer . . . to enlarge upon the theme of his father's *supposi ti-*

*tious* affluence—*Kobler*⟩ **Suppositious** is used chiefly to imply that a belief or assertion is based on theory or on a postulate or hypothesis, and lacks factual support ⟨this was no *suppositious* contract between ruler and ruled in prehistoric times—*Parrington*⟩ ⟨it [magic] comes down to a *suppositious*, misguided philosophy, a pseudo science —*Howells*⟩ **Reputed**, *putative*, and *purported* imply a basis in tradition or in popular belief. **Reputed** in itself is usually a thoroughly neutral word ⟨Ferdinand Latizar, *reputed* to have been a Mexican—*Amer. Guide Series: La.*⟩ ⟨Ross's goose, which was *reputed* to be near extinction—*Times Lit. Sup.*⟩ but can be strongly colored by context ⟨naturally, no lady would willingly admit that she had been ignored; so that the *reputed* prowess of Danny may be somewhat overstated—*Steinbeck*⟩ **Putative** describes something that is commonly or generally accepted but about which the describer reserves certain doubts ⟨that much of the time so saved was frittered away . . . is a fact which diminished the *putative* efficiency of the new regime—*Mumford*⟩ ⟨the U. S. Fascists met . . . its slapstick Waterloo, when a small detachment of Philadelphia cops stormed headquarters and captured the entire *putative* army, all of them generals—*C. W. Ferguson*⟩ In its common legal use it applies to a thing or person that may be subject to proof that it is not what it is generally accepted to be; thus, a *putative* marriage is one duly formalized but to a greater or less degree invalid because of some impediment (as consanguinity) ⟨proceedings to establish paternity and provide for the support of a child born out of wedlock may be instituted . . . within one year after the *putative* father has ceased making contributions for the support of such child—*U. S. Code*⟩ **Purported** may differ little from *reputed* and *putative* ⟨payments of allowances based on a *purported* marriage and made prior to judicial annulment or termination of such marriage —*U. S. Code*⟩ ⟨the *purported* head of the family is an ancient and garrulous lush; his helpmate is a domineering crone—*McCarten*⟩ but especially in its common journalistic use the word tends to stress the writer's disclaimer of responsibility for the matter asserted (compare *alleged* under ADDUCE) and may approach *rumored* in meaning ⟨the weekly reproduced a *purported* letter from De Gasperi, apparently addressed to a British officer in 1944—*Time*⟩ ⟨a list containing the names of 380 *purported* Communists in the United States—*Current Biog.*⟩ **Conjectural** implies inference from incomplete or defective evidence, and what is so described is offered as a possibility or likelihood but not as a fact ⟨the *conjectural* etymology of a word⟩ ⟨*conjectural* emendations in a faulty text⟩ ⟨*conjectural* causes of a depression⟩ **Hypothetical** describes someone or something (as a principle, a situation, or a question) that is invented or put forward as possibly true or as likely to be true in the main if not in detail, or as the tentative basis for continuing an argument or investigation ⟨a *hypothetical* explanation of nebulae⟩ ⟨this land claimed by the Spaniards—a *hypothetical* claim, all the interiors being still in the hands of the Indians —*Amer. Guide Series: Texas*⟩ ⟨my French visitor—who was a real, flesh-and-blood visitor, and not, like most of his kind, a *hypothetical* foreigner invented to point a moral —*Grandgent*⟩ ⟨this study is *hypothetical*—i.e., tentative propositions derived from the existing body of social theory and empirical knowledge, but not yet refined into tested theoretical generalizations—*A. K. Davis*⟩
*Ana* assumed, presumed, presupposed, postulated (see PRESUPPOSE): tentative, *provisional: *doubtful, dubious, questionable: *theoretical, speculative, academic: alleged (see under ADDUCE)
*Ant* certain

**suppositious, suppositious** *supposed, reputed, putative, purported, conjectural, hypothetical
*Ana* pretended, simulated, feigned, shammed, counterfeited *or* counterfeit (see ASSUME): questionable, dubious, *doubtful: factitious, *artificial
**suppress** 1 *crush, quell, extinguish, quench, quash
*Ana* subdue, overcome, surmount, *conquer: *abolish, annihilate: *destroy: *ruin, wreck
2 **Suppress, repress** both mean to hold back by the use of more or less force someone or something that seeks an outlet (as by expression or activity). **Suppress** carries a strong implication of putting down or keeping back completely. It usually implies the exercise of great or oppressive power or even of violence. It often is a synonym of such words as *overpower, crush, abolish, destroy, eliminate,* or *stifle,* but in each case it tends strongly to suggest the prompt use of effective methods ⟨*suppress* an insurrection⟩ ⟨ungovernable passions . . . *suppressed* by the very same means which keep the rest of us in order —*Conrad*⟩ ⟨the bishop was purple with *suppressed* wrath—*Sherman*⟩ ⟨a regime of terror designed to brutally *suppress* . . . freedom, culture and national life—*Shirer*⟩ **Repress**, on the other hand, implies little more than a checking or restraining sometimes by an external force, sometimes by the power of the will or mind. It often suggests that the thing so held back may break out again or in a different way and so comes close to *inhibit, bridle,* or *curb* ⟨*repressed* his curiosity⟩ ⟨*repressed* her desire to weep⟩ ⟨his breathing was a little quickened; but he *repressed* all other signs of agitation—*Dickens*⟩ ⟨money and religion: yes, those are the two *repressed* subjects in the modern novel upon which furtively we open the door—*Pritchett*⟩ ⟨it is necessary to *repress* a natural scorn of the master of the glad hand and the soft soap —*H. A. Burton*⟩ ⟨as she passed the elm tree . . . a thrill of recollected fear would run through her; but she *repressed* the temptation to talk about it—*Mary Fitt*⟩ In psychology *suppress* is commonly used with reference to desires, instincts, and emotions which are consciously and forcibly inhibited by the mind from seeking expression or overt activity; *repress* usually suggests an unconscious or subconscious process by which a desire or an impulse that is regarded as unacceptable because of one's religious, moral, or social training is inhibited by a refusal to recognize it or to permit consideration of it and so is left to operate in the unconscious.
*Ana* *arrest, check, interrupt: extinguish, *abolish, annihilate: *forbid, prohibit, ban: subdue, overcome, surmount, *conquer
**supranatural** *supernatural, miraculous, preternatural, superhuman
**supremacy,** ascendancy denote the position of being first (as in rank, power, or influence). **Supremacy** implies superiority over all others (as in utility, in quality, in efficiency, in desirability, or in prestige) ⟨in the Sahara, the automobile has begun to challenge the *supremacy* of the camel—*Huxley*⟩ ⟨the British concept of the *supremacy* of the home . . . was so deep and so great that not even the Crown could enter the home—*Wayne Morse*⟩ ⟨last summer American atomic *supremacy* gave place to something like atomic equality between "the two great colossi"—*New Statesman*⟩ **Ascendancy** may or may not imply supremacy, but it always involves the idea of domination or of autocratic power ⟨an idea has *ascendancy* over his imagination when it has the latter completely under its sway⟩ ⟨the whole system of oppression and cruelty by which dominant castes seek to retain their *ascendancy*—*Russell*⟩ ⟨a speaker can get an *ascendancy* over the House, if he has a strong personality and the

A colon (:) separates groups of words discriminated. An asterisk (*) indicates place of treatment of each group.

ability to regain the thread of his speech—*Woodrow Wyatt*⟩ ⟨the rays of the gas lamps, feeble at first in their struggle with the dying day, had now at length gained *ascendancy—Poe*⟩

*Ana* preeminence, transcendence, superlativeness, peerlessness, incomparability (see corresponding adjectives at SUPREME): *power, authority, dominion, control, sway

**supreme** *adj* **Supreme, superlative, transcendent, surpassing, preeminent, peerless, incomparable** can all mean highest in a scale of values. All of these words may be interchangeable when used rhetorically or bombastically with the resulting loss in definiteness, but all are capable of discriminative use in which they carry distinctive implications and connotations. **Supreme** is applicable to what is not only the highest in rank, power, or quality but has no equals in that status, all others of the same class or kind being inferior in varying degrees ⟨the *Supreme* Court of the United States⟩ ⟨Shakespeare is generally regarded as the *supreme* dramatic poet⟩ ⟨I did not detect in his playing the fire and dash that I look for in the work of a *supreme* virtuoso—*Sargeant*⟩ ⟨he smiled again with an air of *supreme* contentment. "It's the first time I've ever done what I wanted to do"—*Bromfield*⟩ **Superlative** is applicable to whatever, by comparison with all other things of the same kind or with all other manifestations of the same quality, admits of no superior especially in commendatory qualities, for *superlative* may admit equals but it excludes superiors ⟨the *superlative* genius of Goethe⟩ ⟨his *superlative* rudeness⟩ ⟨what makes him a great artist is a high fervor of spirit, which produces a *superlative*, instead of a comparative, clarity of vision—*Galsworthy*⟩ ⟨there is a smaller proportion than usual of superior books and a minuscule number of *superlative* ones—*Kinkead*⟩ ⟨enhanced with a *superlative* commentary . . . it is commendable in all respects—*McCarten*⟩ **Transcendent** and **surpassing** are applicable to whatever goes beyond everything else of its kind or in its quality; both can connote an exceeding even of the superlative, but **transcendent** suggests realization of the ideal, and **surpassing** suggests almost inconceivable attainment ⟨the *transcendent* acting of Duse⟩ ⟨Cleopatra's reputation for *transcendent* beauty⟩ ⟨his *surpassing* skill in surgery⟩ ⟨the geometric pattern is of a *surpassing* intricacy—*Rovere*⟩ ⟨[his] native gifts are perhaps not of a *transcendent* kind; they have their roots in a quality of mind that ought to be as frequent as it is modest—*Trilling*⟩ **Preeminent** is applicable to what goes beyond all others in achieving distinction or eminence; it implies both superlativeness and uniqueness within the limits indicated, but it seldom carries a suggestion of direct supremacy or transcendency ⟨the *preeminent* general in that war⟩ ⟨the *preeminent* film of the year⟩ ⟨the *preeminent* example of magnanimity⟩ ⟨although his own case is *preeminent*, there are a sufficient number of others—*J. D. Adams*⟩ **Peerless** and **incomparable** both imply the absence of equals but, commonly, **peerless** connotes the absence of superiors and **incomparable** connotes the impossibility of being equaled; while both normally refer to commendatory qualities, *incomparable* is also freely referable to qualities that merit condemnation ⟨a *peerless* performance of *Hamlet*⟩ ⟨Philip Sidney, called the *peerless* one of his age—*Quiller-Couch*⟩ ⟨the *incomparable* refinement with which he has drawn this interior with its two youthful figures—*Binyon*⟩ ⟨nothing—simply nothing at all—transcends a cat's *incomparable* insincerity—*Theodore Sturgeon*⟩ ⟨*peerless* among women; perfect in beauty, perfect in courtliness—*H. O. Taylor*⟩

*Ana* *chief, foremost, leading, capital: predominant, *dominant, paramount, sovereign

**sure** 1 assured, *confident, sanguine, presumptuous

*Ana* relying, trusting, depending, counting, banking (see RELY): inerrant, unerring, *infallible: *safe, secure

2 **Sure, certain, positive, cocksure** mean having or showing no doubt. *Sure* and *certain* are often interchangeable. But **sure** frequently emphasizes the mere subjective state of assurance; **certain** often suggests more strongly a conviction that is based on definite grounds or on indubitable evidence ⟨"I know my hour is come." "Not so, my lord." "Nay, I am *sure* it is"—*Shak.*⟩ ⟨be out of hope, of question, of doubt; be *certain—Shak.*⟩ ⟨in the library he too seemed *surer* of himself—though once they were on their way home he became almost remote, strangely watchful—*Malamud*⟩ ⟨they were *sure* and *certain*, forever wrong, but always confident. They had no hesitation, they confessed no ignorance or error—*Wolfe*⟩ **Positive** often suggests overconfidence or dogmatism, but it implies conviction or full confidence in the rightness or correctness of one's statement or conclusion ⟨an assertive *positive* man . . . had his own notion of what a young man should be—*Anderson*⟩ ⟨so much more *positive* than most of his customers, and he impressed his own convictions on them so determinedly, that he had his own way—*Scudder*⟩ ⟨an easy and elegant skepticism was the attitude expected of an educated adult: anything might be discussed, but it was a trifle vulgar to reach very *positive* conclusions—*Russell*⟩ **Cocksure** tends to carry a strong implication of presumption or overconfidence in positiveness ⟨certitude is not the test of certainty. We have been *cocksure* of many things that were not so—*Justice Holmes*⟩ ⟨people . . . regarded as brash to the point of arrogance, *cocksure* to the verge of folly—*MacLeish*⟩

*Ana* decisive, *decided: self-assured, assured, self-confident (see corresponding nouns at CONFIDENCE): dogmatic, doctrinaire, oracular (see DICTATORIAL)

*Ant* unsure

**surety** 1 security, bond, *guarantee, guaranty, bail

*Ana* *pledge, earnest, token, hostage, pawn

2 guarantor, *sponsor, backer, patron, angel

**surfeit** *vb* *satiate, sate, cloy, pall, glut, gorge

*Ant* whet

**surge** *vb* *rise, arise, ascend, mount, soar, tower, rocket, levitate

**surly** morose, glum, *sullen, crabbed, sulky, saturnine, dour, gloomy

*Ana* *rude, ungracious, ill-mannered, discourteous: boorish, churlish (see under BOOR): snappish, waspish, fractious, *irritable

*Ant* amiable —*Con* *gracious, cordial, affable, genial

**surmise** *vb* *conjecture, guess

*Ana* *infer, gather, judge, deduce, conclude: *think, conceive, fancy, imagine: *consider, regard, deem

**surmise** *n* conjecture, guess (see under CONJECTURE *vb*)

*Ana* inference, deduction, conclusion (see under INFER): *hypothesis, theory

**surmount** overcome, overthrow, rout, *conquer, vanquish, defeat, subdue, subjugate, reduce, beat, lick

*Ana* surpass, transcend, outdo, outstrip, excel, *exceed

**surpass** transcend, excel, outdo, outstrip, *exceed

*Ana* surmount, overcome, beat (see CONQUER)

**surpassing** transcendent, *supreme, superlative, preeminent, peerless, incomparable

*Ana* excelling, outdoing, outstripping (see EXCEED): *consummate, finished, accomplished

**surplus** *n* *excess, superfluity, surplusage, overplus

*Ana* *remainder, residue, residuum

*Ant* deficiency

**surplus** *adj* *superfluous, supernumerary, extra, spare

---

*Ana* analogous words     *Ant* antonyms     *Con* contrasted words     See also explanatory notes facing page 1

*Con* *needful, necessary, requisite, indispensable, essential

**surplusage** surplus, superfluity, overplus, *excess

*Ana & Ant* see those at SURPLUS *n*

**surprise** *vb* **1** Surprise, waylay, ambush are comparable when they mean to attack unawares. Surprise is in military as well as in general use. As a technical term it implies strategy in the disposition and movement of troops and equipment and secrecy in the operations; it need not suggest that the attack has been successful ⟨an army suddenly attacked within the lines which it had reckoned upon to ward off its enemy is in a military sense *surprised*—*Maurice*⟩ ⟨R.A.F. bombers *surprised* a large invasion training exercise and inflicted heavy losses—*Shirer*⟩ In more general use one may *surprise* a person or something he is concealing by coming on him when he is off guard ⟨housemaids must vanish silently if *surprised* at their tasks—*Sackville-West*⟩ ⟨high instincts before which our mortal nature did tremble like a guilty thing *surprised*—*Wordsworth*⟩ **Waylay** commonly suggests a lying in wait on a road or highway. Sometimes it implies concealment by the roadside and an often evil intent to disturb or interfere with (as by robbery or assault) ⟨he was *waylaid* on his return from the bank⟩ ⟨I am *waylaid* by Beauty . . . . Oh, savage Beauty, suffer me to pass—*Millay*⟩ Sometimes it carries no suggestion of hostility or evil intent but implies intercepting a person in his progress and detaining him ⟨unable any longer to bear not seeing her, he *waylaid* her in the street. She would not speak to him, but he insisted on speaking to her—*Maugham*⟩ ⟨riding in the park . . . Carola beheld her intended galloping furiously down the Row, and left her sister Clementina's side to *waylay* him—*Meredith*⟩ **Ambush** tends to evoke the image of would-be attackers concealed in a thicket; it is often used in reference to guerrilla warfare ⟨his body was brought after he had been *ambushed* by Indians on nearby Wolf Run—*Amer. Guide Series: Pa.*⟩ but it can be extended to other situations in which one is caught as if by an ambush (see AMBUSH *n*) ⟨the same kind of feeling *ambushed* me a few weeks ago—*Jan Struther*⟩ ⟨the woman clasped her hands together; the butterfly sleeves fluttered as though *ambushed*—*Harriet La Barre*⟩

*Ana* *catch, capture: *take, seize, grasp, grab

**2** Surprise, astonish, astound, amaze, flabbergast can mean to impress one forcibly because unexpected or startling or unusual. **Surprise** can mean to come upon another suddenly and with startling effect, or, more broadly, it can apply to an unexpected or unanticipated development that tends to arouse some degree of surprise, amazement, or wonder; both senses imply a lack of preparation or a reversal of what is anticipated ⟨her friends planned to *surprise* her on her birthday with a gift⟩ ⟨apt not only to be interested but also to be *surprised* by the experience life was holding in store for him—*Conrad*⟩ ⟨the morning skies . . . *surprised* her daily as if they were uncommon things—*West*⟩ **Astonish** can imply a dazing or silencing ⟨it is the part of men to fear and tremble, when the most mighty gods by tokens send such dreadful heralds to *astonish* us—*Shak.*⟩ or it may mean to surprise so greatly as to seem incredible ⟨while still an undergraduate . . . [he] had *astonished* the scientific world by his acceleration of the metamorphosis of the tadpole—*Mackenzie*⟩ ⟨the former corporal showed an *astonishing* grasp of military strategy and tactics—*Shirer*⟩ or sometimes merely unusual ⟨he . . . *astonished* his fellows by buying and smoking ten-cent cigars—*Anderson*⟩ **Astound** stresses a stunning or overwhelming emotional effect and usually implies so great a difference between what one believes

possible and what one discovers to be true that one can find no precedent for it; thus, a piece of news *surprises* one when it is unexpected; it *astonishes* when one finds it hard to believe; it *astounds* when one cannot account for it by any previous knowledge or experience; the successful laying of the Atlantic cable *astounded* everybody, while its later breaks *astonished* no one, but after it was finally in operation, many said that no future human invention could *surprise* them ⟨*astounded* his congregation by putting up for sale a mulatto slave girl—*Amer. Guide Series: N.Y. City*⟩ **Amaze**, though it carries an implication of astonishment, stresses rather bewilderment, perplexity, or wonder ⟨that he should even speak to her was *amazing*!—but to speak with such civility—*Austen*⟩ ⟨went through agonies of jealousy and remorse, and fantasies of revenge, which *amazed* her with their violence—*Wouk*⟩ **Flabbergast** is a picturesque and often hyperbolical synonym of *astonish* or *amaze;* it suggests vividly the physical signs of a sudden dumbfounding ⟨a delightful letter . . . that *flabbergasted* me as usual with your critical knowledge—*Justice Holmes*⟩ ⟨some off-the-cuff retort that will excite the reporters but *flabbergast* the President's aides—*Cater*⟩

*Ana* startle, alarm, scare (see FRIGHTEN): bewilder, nonplus, confound, dumbfound (see PUZZLE *vb*): *embarrass, disconcert, discomfit, rattle, faze

**surrender** *vb* abandon, resign, *relinquish, yield, leave, cede, waive

*Ana* *abdicate, renounce: *forgo, forbear, sacrifice, eschew: submit, capitulate, succumb (see YIELD): *commit, consign, confide, entrust

**surrender** *n* Surrender, submission, capitulation denote the act of yielding up one's person, one's forces, or one's possessions to another person or power. **Surrender** usually implies a state of war and present domination by a victor or by an admittedly stronger power; in addition it often also implies the immediate cessation of fighting ⟨the commander replied that no terms except an unconditional and immediate *surrender* could be accepted⟩ **Submission** often implies surrender (as of an army, its supplies, and its fortifications), but it stresses the acknowledgment of the power or authority of another and often suggests loss of independence; it is used especially of those who rebel or of those whose weak condition leaves them at the mercy of a stronger power or subject to its threats. Unlike *surrender, submission* often implies not a previous state of war but a threat of disastrous warfare ⟨*submission*, Dauphin! 'tis a mere French word; we English warriors wot not what it means—*Shak.*⟩ ⟨declaring my *submission* to your arms—*Browning*⟩ **Capitulation** also implies surrender, but it suggests a conditional one on terms agreed upon between the parties or the commanders of the forces concerned ⟨in Greece to offer earth and water was the sign of *capitulation*—*Newman*⟩ ⟨after Lee's surrender at Appomattox Buckner . . . negotiated terms of *capitulation* . . . for the trans-Mississippi armies—*Coulter*⟩

**surreptitious** underhand, underhanded, *secret, covert, stealthy, furtive, clandestine

*Ana* sneaking, slinking, skulking, lurking (see LURK): hidden, concealed, screened (see HIDE)

**surrogate** substitute, shift, makeshift, expedient, *resource, resort, stopgap

**surround**, environ, encircle, circle, encompass, compass, hem, gird, girdle, ring can mean to close in or as if in a ring about something. **Surround** is a general term without specific connotations; it implies enclosure as if by a circle or a ring ⟨the town was once *surrounded* by a wall⟩ ⟨a crowd *surrounded* the victim of the accident⟩ ⟨the ships

---

A colon (:) separates groups of words discriminated. An asterisk (*) indicates place of treatment of each group.

are *surrounded* by a veil of smoke⟩ ⟨whole divisions were frequently overrun or *surrounded* and cut to pieces when a timely withdrawal would have saved them—*Shirer*⟩ Often the term denotes not a literal enclosure but something which forms the circumstances, the environment, or the border of something ⟨*surrounded* by luxury⟩ ⟨a pleasant white-haired widow *surrounded* by many potted plants—*Cheever*⟩ ⟨those mental and moral barriers with which the average Englishman *surrounds* himself—*Bagot*⟩ **Environ** also implies enclosure as if by a circle or a ring, but it often differs somewhat from *surround* in carrying a clearer implication of the permanent or continuing existence of what environs; thus, "a nation *environed* by foes" does not clearly imply as immediate danger as "an army *surrounded* by foes" does, but the former does suggest a persistent or ever-present danger in a way that the latter cannot. The difference is often slight but usually perceptible ⟨the passions and motives of the savage world which underlies as well as *environs* civilization—*Howells*⟩ ⟨persuading the doubter that our human spirits are *environed* by other and vaster spiritual powers—*Whiteley*⟩ ⟨there are old buildings still . . . but they are usually overshadowed by an *environing* swarm of new stucco— *H. L. Davis*⟩ **Encircle** is not quite the equal of *surround* though very like it in meaning and often interchangeable with it; it more definitely suggests an enclosing circle and therefore often is suited to a more concrete use; in this sense it is often equal to **circle** ⟨I found myself *encircled* in the arms of my . . . Father—*Richardson*⟩ ⟨a wreath *encircles* the brow of Apollo⟩ ⟨the close which *encircles* the venerable cathedral—*Macaulay*⟩ ⟨its frame residences —many of them aged—*circle* a small business district— *Amer. Guide Series: Texas*⟩ Also, *encircle* and *circle* may denote to proceed in a circle about something, a meaning unknown to *surround* ⟨*circled* the house in his search⟩ ⟨as a hungry wolf might have *encircled* . . . the firelit camp of a hunter—*Anderson*⟩ ⟨at this speed, 186,000 miles per second, it would take us only about one seventh of a second to *circle* the earth—*B. J. Bok*⟩ **Encompass** suggests something that closes in or shuts off a place or person; it often also suggests a motive (as protection or homage or hostility) ⟨the flaming Seraph, fearless, though alone, *encompassed* round with foes, thus answered bold —*Milton*⟩ ⟨the love of all thy sons *encompass* thee— *Tennyson*⟩ ⟨for an instant . . . he contained within himself illimitable space and power, enough to *encompass* and hold all the ships and men that at this moment lay between heaven and the Atlantic—*Hervey*⟩ **Compass** implies a being surrounded or encompassed usually by something that covers and protects or by something that weighs down upon and depresses ⟨those wild regions of obscurity which are vaguely felt to be *compassing* us about in midnight dreams of flight and disaster—*Hardy*⟩ ⟨we must be humble, for we are *compassed* by mysteries, and our spiritual faculties are poor and dull—*Inge*⟩ ⟨the Great Peace beyond all this turmoil and fret *compassed* me around—*L. P. Smith*⟩ **Hem,** usually followed by an adverb and especially *in*, carries the strongest implication of confinement or of perfect enclosure of any of these words and often suggests difficulty or impossibility of escape ⟨the constables were *hemmed* in so closely that they could make no use of their pikes—*Costain*⟩ ⟨a mule generally becomes most evil-eyed and active when you try to *hem* him up so you can slip the bridle on—*Amer. Guide Series: Ark.*⟩ ⟨low hills which *hem* the valley— *Ernestine Evans*⟩ ⟨lone flower, *hemmed* in with snows, and white as they—*Wordsworth*⟩ **Gird** and *girdle* both basically apply to an encircling of the waist with a belt or girdle. **Gird** is sometimes preferred when the meaning

of to surround or encircle is expressed and the idea of a strong or insuperable barrier is implied ⟨I *girded* thee, though thou hast not known me—*Isa 45:5*⟩ ⟨like to his island, *girt* in with the ocean—*Shak.*⟩ ⟨*girt* with a chain he cannot wish to break—*Cowper*⟩ ⟨shut up as in a crumbling tomb, *girt* round with blackness as a solid wall —*Tennyson*⟩ **Girdle,** on the other hand, tends to imply an encirclement suggestive of a belt or sash or constituting a zone ⟨great coastal plain which *girdles* the United States —*Morgan*⟩ and seldom connotes a tight or confining quality in what encircles ⟨the whole harbor looks like Coleridge's Xanadu, the walls and towers *girdled* round with radiance—*Atkinson*⟩ **Ring** carries a vivid picture of formation in a ring, but beyond this it has no particular implication. It is frequently chosen as a picturesque word in the senses of *surround, encircle,* and *hem in* ⟨a girdle of mist will *ring* the slopes, while the heights rise clear in the upper air—*W. C. Smith*⟩ ⟨a septuagenarian whose few sad last grey hairs, *ringing* an otherwise completely bald head—*The Irish Digest*⟩
*Ana* *enclose, envelop, wall, fence, cage, coop: circumscribe, confine, *limit

**surveillance** *oversight, supervision
*Ana* inspection, scrutiny, examination (see under SCRUTI-NIZE)

**survey** *vb* view, espy, descry, behold, *see, observe, notice, remark, note, perceive, discern
*Ana* *scrutinize, scan, inspect, examine: *see, look, watch

**survey** *n* *compendium, syllabus, digest, pandect, sketch, précis, aperçu

**survive** *outlive, outlast
*Ana* endure, *continue, persist, last: withstand, *resist, fight

**susceptible** 1 sensitive, subject, exposed, prone, *liable, open
*Ana* inclined, disposed, predisposed (see INCLINE *vb*): alive, awake, sensible, conscious (see AWARE)
*Ant* immune
2 *sentient, sensitive, impressible, impressionable, responsive
*Ana* affected, impressed, touched, influenced, swayed (see AFFECT): stirred, aroused, roused (see STIR)
*Con* resisting, withstanding (see RESIST): frustrating, thwarting, baffling (see FRUSTRATE)

**suspend** 1 disbar, shut out, *exclude, eliminate, debar, blackball, rule out
*Ana* *eject, dismiss, oust: *banish, exile, ostracize
2 stay, intermit, postpone, *defer
*Ana* *arrest, check, interrupt: *stop, cease, discontinue: *delay, detain, retard
3 *hang, sling, dangle
*Ana* poise, balance, steady, *stabilize

**suspended, pendent, pendulous** can mean hanging from or remaining in place as if hanging from a support. **Suspended** may imply attachment from a point or points above so that a thing swings freely or is held steady in its proper place or position ⟨*suspended* from his neck was a medallion—*R. H. Brown*⟩ ⟨chimes are a set of metal tubes *suspended* from a frame and struck by wooden mallets— *McConathy et al*⟩ ⟨a *suspended* ceiling⟩ or it may suggest a being poised or a being upheld (as by buoyancy) ⟨they neither float nor fly, they are *suspended*—*Jefferies*⟩ ⟨water free from *suspended* silt⟩ **Pendent** usually describes something which hangs downward from a support or from one point of attachment; it seldom carries any further implication and so is applicable both to what is motionless and to what swings or moves or is in danger of falling ⟨a trailing creeper with curving leaf and twining tendril, and *pendent* bud and blossom—*Hudson*⟩ ⟨the smokehouse, its sooty rafters jeweled with fat hams like eardrops and *pendent* strips of cured middling meat—*Cobb*⟩ **Pendulous** adds to *pendent* the specific implication of swaying or swinging, sometimes carrying a suggestion of actual floating in space ⟨a *pendulous* nest⟩ ⟨breasts . . . grown flabby and *pendulous* with many children—*Buck*⟩ ⟨steep cliffs . . . hung with *pendulous* vines, swinging blossoms in the air—*Melville*⟩ ⟨so blend the turrets and shadows there that all seems *pendulous* in air—*Poe*⟩

**suspicion** 1 mistrust, *uncertainty, doubt, dubiety, dubiosity, skepticism
*Ana* misgiving, foreboding, presentiment, *apprehension: distrust, mistrust (see under DISTRUST *vb*)
2 *touch, suggestion, soupçon, tincture, tinge, shade, smack, spice, dash, vein, strain, streak

**sustain** 1 *support, prop, bolster, buttress, brace
*Ana* *continue, persist, endure, abide: uphold, back (see SUPPORT): *prove, demonstrate
*Ant* subvert
2 *experience, undergo, suffer
*Ana* *receive, accept, take: endure, *bear, stand, brook: *meet, encounter, face, confront

**sustenance** 1 nourishment, nutriment, *food, aliment, pabulum, pap
2 maintenance, support, *living, livelihood, subsistence, keep, bread

**suture** *n* *joint, articulation

**swag** *n* *spoil, plunder, loot, booty, prize

**swagger** *vb* *strut, bristle, bridle
*Ana* flourish, brandish, shake, *swing, wave: brag, *boast, vaunt, crow, gasconade
*Con* cower, cringe, truckle (see FAWN): shrink, quail, blench, wince (see RECOIL)

**swallow** *vb* *eat, ingest, devour, consume
*Ana* *receive, accept, take: believe, credit (see corresponding nouns at BELIEF): *absorb, imbibe, assimilate

**swarm** *vb* *teem, abound, overflow

**swat** *vb* *strike, hit, smite, *punch, slug, slog, clout, slap, cuff, box
*Ana* *beat, pound, pummel, baste, belabor

**sway** *vb* 1 *swing, oscillate, fluctuate, pendulate, vibrate, waver, undulate
*Ana* *shake, rock, agitate, convulse
2 influence, impress, strike, touch, *affect
*Ana* control, direct, manage, *conduct: rule, *govern: bias, *incline, dispose, predispose

**sway** *n* dominion, control, command, *power, authority
*Ana* *supremacy, ascendancy: *range, reach, scope, sweep: spread, stretch, amplitude, *expanse

**swearing** *blasphemy, profanity, cursing

**sweep** *n* *range, gamut, reach, radius, compass, scope, orbit, horizon, ken, purview
*Ana* *expanse, amplitude, spread

**sweeping** *indiscriminate, wholesale
*Ana* promiscuous, heterogeneous, motley, *miscellaneous

**sweet, engaging, winning, winsome, dulcet** are comparable when they are applied to persons or things with respect to the sensations they evoke or the impressions they produce and mean distinctly pleasing or charming because devoid of all that irritates, annoys, or embitters. **Sweet** when extended beyond its primary application to one of the basic taste sensations, whether to things that produce other sensory impressions or to persons or things that induce emotional or intellectual response, is ordinarily a term of mild general approbation for what pleases, attracts, or charms without stirring deeply or arousing a profound response ⟨what a *sweet* little cottage⟩ ⟨twilight, *sweet* with the smell of lilac and freshly turned earth—*Corey Ford*⟩ ⟨flower motifs and emblems, all printed in *sweet* colors—*Rosner*⟩ ⟨has been very *sweet*. He wants to help, but of course there's nothing he can do—*Auchincloss*⟩ but in this as in its primary application *sweet* may also imply an excess of what in more moderate quantity is pleasing and then comes close to *surfeiting* or *cloying* (compare SATIATE) ⟨the flaw in her book is the *sweet* side, the Pollyanna note, that fatal emphasis on the happy ending—*Rosemary Benét*⟩ **Engaging** and *winning* come very close to one another, both implying a power to attract favorable attention and strongly suggesting a power to please or delight; **engaging**, however, more often stresses the power of a thing to attract such attention, whereas **winning** usually emphasizes the power of a person to please or delight ⟨an *engaging* story⟩ ⟨*engaging* manners⟩ ⟨she has *winning* ways⟩ ⟨a *winning* smile⟩ ⟨affectionate, cheerful, happy, his sweet and *engaging* personality drew all men's love—*H. O. Taylor*⟩ ⟨simple as a child, with his gentle, *winning* voice and grave smile—*Brooks*⟩ **Winsome** is chiefly applied to persons or to their attractions; the term is somewhat more inclusive in meaning than the others, for it usually implies an engaging quality, a cheerful disposition, pleasing though not striking looks, and often a childlike quality ⟨tears came to his eyes as he remembered her childlike look, and *winsome* fanciful ways—*Wilde*⟩ **Dulcet** suggests an appealing and gratifying or soothing quality whether to the senses (as of some, especially musical, sounds) or to the feelings or emotions ⟨the voice was . . . *dulcet* as the hum of heavy honeybees amid orange blossoms—*Wouk*⟩ ⟨could not . . . expect such *dulcet* weather to last—*Sackville-West*⟩ ⟨the classic, *dulcet*, but difficult art of architecture—*R. W. Kennedy*⟩
*Ana* *pleasant, pleasing, agreeable, gratifying, grateful, welcome: delicious, delectable, luscious, *delightful: lovely, fair, *beautiful: ineffable (see UNUTTERABLE)
*Ant* sour: bitter

**swell** *vb* *expand, amplify, distend, inflate, dilate
*Ana* *extend, elongate, lengthen: *intensify, heighten, enhance: *increase, augment, enlarge
*Ant* shrink —*Con* *contract, condense, compress, constrict

**swerve, veer, deviate, depart, digress, diverge** mean to turn aside from a straight line or a defined course. **Swerve** may refer to a turning aside, usually somewhat abruptly, by a person or material thing ⟨at that point the road *swerves* to the left⟩ ⟨the great roots of a tree *swerve* upward out of the design—*Binyon*⟩ or it may suggest a mental, moral, or spiritual turning aside ⟨had never *swerved* from what she conceived to be her duty—*A. J. Kennedy*⟩ ⟨if I be false, or *swerve* a hair from truth—*Shak.*⟩ ⟨our affections and passions put frequently a bias . . . so strong on our judgments as to make them *swerve* from the direction of right reason—*Bolingbroke*⟩ **Veer** is frequently used in reference to a change in the course of a wind or of a ship; often it suggests either a frequent turning this way or that or a series of turnings in the same direction, especially of the wind in a clockwise direction ⟨the wind *veered* to the east⟩ ⟨[the ship] plunged and tacked and *veered*—*Coleridge*⟩ ⟨the wind had *veered* round, and the Aurora was now able to lay up clear of the island of Maritimo—*Marryat*⟩ In extended use the term commonly implies a change or series of changes of direction or course under an external influence comparable to the wind ⟨his thought, *veering* and tacking as the winds blew—*Parrington*⟩ or a turning aside for a tactical reason ⟨as to avoid an undue influence⟩ ⟨the plan has worked. . . .

---

A colon (:) separates groups of words discriminated. An asterisk (*) indicates place of treatment of each group.

the state . . . has not only *veered* away from bankruptcy; it has also improved its services—*Armbrister*⟩ **Deviate** implies a turning aside from a customary, chosen, allotted, or prescribed course ⟨finding it no easy matter to make my way without constantly *deviating* to this side or that from the course I wished to keep—*Hudson*⟩ It is commonly used in reference to persons, or their minds, their morals, and their actions, with the suggestion of a swerving from a norm or standard or from a right or lawful procedure or course ⟨when the aesthetic sense *deviates* from its proper ends to burden itself with moral intentions . . . it ceases to realize morality—*Ellis*⟩ ⟨had told him the story many times and . . . never *deviated* in the telling—*Costain*⟩ ⟨from a fundamental sincerity he could not *deviate*— *T. S. Eliot*⟩ The next three words of this group usually imply a turning aside from a literal or figurative way (as a path, course, track, or standard) which still continues. **Depart** stresses the turning away from and leaving an old path, a customary course, or an accepted type or standard; it may further imply a forsaking of the antiquated, conventional, or traditional ⟨[books] which *depart* widely from the usual type—*Grandgent*⟩ or a deviation from what is right, true, or normal ⟨forced by circumstance to *depart* from the principles of his own logic—*W. P. Webb*⟩ **Digress** commonly implies a departure from the subject of one's discourse that may be voluntary and made with the intent to return ⟨let me *digress* for a few minutes to indicate the possible results of this condition⟩ or involuntary and the result of an inability to think coherently or to stick to the point to be developed ⟨I shall not pursue these points further for fear of *digressing* too far from my main theme—*Spilsbury*⟩ **Diverge** is sometimes used in the sense of *depart* ⟨let them [professors] *diverge* in the slightest from what is the current official doctrine, and they are turned out of their chairs—*Mencken*⟩ but more typically it suggests a separation of a main, old, or original course or path into two or more courses or paths that lead away from each other ⟨they proceeded along the road together till . . . their paths *diverged*—*Hardy*⟩ ⟨two roads *diverging* like the branches of a Y—*Belloc*⟩
*Ana* *turn, divert, deflect, sheer, avert: *curve, bend
**swift** *fast, rapid, fleet, quick, speedy, hasty, expeditious
*Ana* *easy, effortless, smooth, facile: headlong, *precipitate, sudden
**swimming** *adj* *giddy, dizzy, vertiginous, dazzled
*Ana* reeling, whirling, tottering (see REEL): swaying, wavering, fluctuating (see SWING)
**swindle** *vb* *cheat, overreach, cozen, defraud
*Ana* *dupe, gull, bamboozle, hoodwink, trick: *steal, pilfer, purloin, filch
**swing** *vb* 1 Swing, wave, flourish, brandish, shake, thrash are comparable when they mean to wield or to handle something so that it moves alternately backward and forward or upward and downward or around and around. **Swing** often implies regular oscillations ⟨impassable, *swinging* hands with their escorts . . . they dawdled up the hill toward the college—*Faulkner*⟩ ⟨he spun the typewriter around, and tested the action of the bell several times, *swinging* the carriage back and forth—*Bliven b. 1916*⟩ It may, however, imply continuous rotatory movements ⟨*swung* a pail over his head⟩ **Wave** distinctively implies undulating or fluttering motions without rhythmical regularity ⟨*wave* a flag⟩ ⟨*wave* a handkerchief⟩ and usually additionally implies, according to the nature of the thing waved and the way in which it is waved, a specific intent or purpose (as of signaling, ordering, displaying an emotion, or greeting) ⟨then grave Clarissa graceful *waved* her fan; silence ensued—*Pope*⟩ ⟨*waved* my arm to warn them off—*Tennyson*⟩ ⟨you cannot *wave* a wand over

the country and say "Let there be Socialism": at least nothing will happen if you do—*Shaw*⟩ **Flourish** implies ostentation, triumph, or bravado in swinging or waving something held in the hand (as a weapon, a stick, or a rod) ⟨with their swords *flourished* as if to fight—*Wordsworth*⟩ ⟨he walked with a gay spring . . . *flourishing* his cane —*Bennett*⟩ ⟨Painless *flourished* the forceps, planted himself square in front of his patient, heaved a moment, and triumphantly held up in full view an undoubted tooth—*S. E. White*⟩ **Brandish** stresses menace or threat as *flourish* seldom does; otherwise it suggests somewhat similar motions ⟨I shall *brandish* my sword before them—*Ezek 32:10*⟩ ⟨he *brandishes* his pliant length of whip, resounding oft—*Cowper*⟩ ⟨the . . . speech was a curious mélange of olive branches and *brandished* fists— *Frye*⟩ **Shake** (see also SHAKE 2) can come very close to *wave* or *flourish* ⟨with his mighty wind shall he *shake* his hand over the river—*Isa 11:15*⟩ ⟨*shaking* her fingers playfully in the direction of the vehicle—*Thackeray*⟩ but like *brandish* it commonly suggests a menacing or threatening or warning intent ⟨people passing by . . . *shake* their fists and curse—*Housman*⟩ ⟨"Take heed, Oliver! take heed!" said the old man, *shaking* his right hand before him in a warning manner—*Dickens*⟩ **Thrash** (see also BEAT 1) implies a noisy vigorous swinging suggestive of the motions of a flail in threshing grain ⟨*thrashing* his arms to keep warm⟩ ⟨*thrashed* his legs in swimming⟩ ⟨on a blanket on the nursery floor and watched him proudly while he *thrashed* his sturdy arms and legs— *Davenport*⟩
*Ana* parade, flaunt, display, exhibit (see SHOW *vb*)
2 Swing, sway, oscillate, vibrate, fluctuate, pendulate, waver, undulate mean to move to and fro, back and forth, or up and down. **Swing** (see also SWING 1) implies movement in an arc of something attached only at one side or at one end (as by being suspended, hinged, or pivoted); apart from the context the term conveys no definite implication of whether the movement is induced or is automatic, whether it is occasional or constant, or whether it is rhythmical and regular or intermittent and irregular ⟨the red amaryllises . . . *swung* in heavy clusters—*Stark Young*⟩ ⟨the door *swung* open⟩ ⟨suddenly Gil's head *swung* sharply to the right—*Mason*⟩ ⟨a pendulum *swings* with great regularity⟩ **Sway** implies a slow swinging motion, especially in a flexible or unsteady object that yields to lack of support or to pressure from one side or another ⟨to hear the *swaying* of the branches of the giant pine—*Binyon*⟩ ⟨she stood up; she seemed to *sway* a little as she stood—*Mary Austin*⟩ ⟨caravans of camels, *swaying* with their padded feet across the desert—*L. P. Smith*⟩ **Oscillate** implies a swinging motion of or as if of something suspended so that it moves through a regular arc; the term usually implies a movement from one side or place or from one condition, attitude, or position to another, with more or less regularity ⟨hurricanes frequently move along an irregular path that *oscillates* about the relatively straight or smooth curved path that the storms were depicted as following . . . before the 1940's—*R. C. Gentry & R. H. Simpson*⟩ ⟨Bohemianism has continuously *oscillated* between the poles of escape and revolt—*Levin*⟩ ⟨American attitudes *oscillate* between such poles as withdrawal and intervention, optimism and pessimism, idealism and cynicism—*Bundy*⟩ **Vibrate** is sometimes used in the sense of *oscillate* ⟨the double complex pendulum, when it *vibrates* in one plane—*Encyc. Brit.*⟩ but it more typically implies rapid periodic oscillations usually over an arc of small amplitude and may suggest the rapid pulsations of the string of a musical instrument (as the piano or violin) when touched by a hammer or bow or

---

*Ana* analogous words  *Ant* antonyms  *Con* contrasted words  See also explanatory notes facing page 1

the rapid beating of some wings (as of a hawkmoth or hummingbird) ⟨you know that if you strike a note of music, all the octave notes will *vibrate—Manning*⟩ ⟨ultrasonic . . . waves *vibrate* so fast they can't be heard by the human ear—*Boyd Wright*⟩ In a more extended sense *vibrate* may imply a trembling, a quavering, or a throbbing suggestive of the movements of musical strings when an instrument is being played ⟨on summer evenings when the air *vibrated* with the song of insects—*Anderson*⟩ ⟨nerve and bone of that poor man's body *vibrated* to those words—*Stowe*⟩ **Fluctuate** occasionally implies a tossing up and down restlessly like the waves of the sea or like something floating on such waves, but is chiefly used in an extended sense implying constant irregular alternations suggestive of the movement of waves ⟨stock prices that *fluctuate* from day to day⟩ ⟨the old unquiet breast, which neither deadens into rest, nor ever feels the fiery glow that whirls the spirit from itself away, but *fluctuates* to and fro—*Arnold*⟩ ⟨causes the respiration, pulse, and blood pressure of the test subject to *fluctuate* widely from the normal—*Armstrong*⟩ ⟨there are about seven hundred and fifty of them . . . but the number *fluctuates* rapidly with the demands of the situation—*Hahn*⟩ **Pendulate**, a somewhat uncommon word, is a near synonym of *oscillate* in implying a swinging between two extremes, but it often comes close to *fluctuate* in its strong suggestion of constant change ⟨the ill-starred scoundrel *pendulates* between Heaven and Earth—*Carlyle*⟩ ⟨he *pendulated* between extremes, between adding to his poetic masterpieces and to his notorious "Don Juan list"—*Cournos*⟩ ⟨saw the Colonel *pendulating* between Perkins' room and Pinchot's room. He would toddle out of one room . . . and enter another—*White*⟩ **Waver** (see also HESITATE) carries a stronger implication of unsteadiness or of uncertainty in swinging than does *sway* or *oscillate* ⟨banners and pennons *wavering* with the wind—*Berners*⟩ ⟨he needed assurance, his plump hands *wavering* uncertainly away from his body—*Mailer*⟩ ⟨a great misery spoke from the hold. It *wavered* eerily about the fringes of her consciousness—*Hervey*⟩ **Undulate** is more often used than *fluctuate* when a wavelike motion is implied; especially in its extended use it seldom suggests violent changes, but rather the continuous rolling or rippling that is associated with the steady flow of waves ⟨the ripe corn under the *undulating* air *undulates* like an ocean—*Shelley*⟩ ⟨the . . . flame . . . made the jades *undulate* like green pools—*Lowell*⟩ ⟨the great serpent drew back like a flash, and turning, *undulated* slowly away—*Beebe*⟩
*Ana* *turn, spin, whirl, wheel, revolve, rotate, gyrate: *shake, tremble, quiver, quaver, quake
**3** wield, manipulate, *handle, ply
*Ana* control, manage, direct, *conduct
**swipe** *vb* *steal, pilfer, filch, purloin, lift, pinch, snitch, cop
**swirl** *vb* circle, spin, twirl, whirl, wheel, eddy, *turn, revolve, rotate, gyrate, pirouette
**sybaritic** *sensuous, sensual, luxurious, voluptuous, epicurean
**sycophant** *parasite, favorite, toady, lickspittle, bootlicker, hanger-on, leech, sponge, sponger
*Ana* blandisher, cajoler, wheedler (see corresponding verbs at COAX): fawner, truckler (see corresponding verbs at FAWN)
**syllabus** *compendium, digest, pandect, survey, sketch, précis, aperçu
*Ana* conspectus, synopsis, epitome, *abridgment, brief, abstract
**symbol** **1** Symbol, emblem, attribute, type can all denote a perceptible thing that stands for or suggests something invisible or intangible. *Symbol* and *emblem* are often used interchangeably but they can be so used as to convey clearly distinguishable notions. **Symbol** is applicable to whatever serves as an outward sign of something spiritual or immaterial; thus, the cross is to Christians the *symbol* of salvation because of its connection with the Crucifixion; the circle, in medieval thought, was the *symbol* of eternity because it, like eternity, has neither beginning nor end. This close and natural connection between the symbol and what it makes visible or partly intelligible is not always so strongly implied; it may be a traditional, conventional, or even an arbitrary association of one thing with another that is suggested ⟨a king's crown is the *symbol* of his sovereignty and his scepter the *symbol* of his authority⟩ ⟨upstairs suites and private dining rooms whose *symbol* became a hot bird and a cold bottle served by a graying waiter in sideburns—*Lucius Beebe*⟩ ⟨a flock of sheep is not the *symbol* of a free people—*New Republic*⟩ **Emblem**, as distinguished from *symbol*, implies representation of an abstraction or use in representation; it is applicable chiefly to a pictorial device or a representation of an object or a combination of objects (as on a shield, a banner, or a flag) intended to serve as an arbitrary or chosen symbol of the character or history of one (as a family, a nation, a royal line, or an office) that has adopted it; thus, the spread eagle, the usual *emblem* of the United States, is found in its coat of arms and on some of its coins and postage stamps; the *emblem* of Turkey, a crescent and a star, appears on its flag ⟨the *emblem* of the school is a dolphin, token of the marine source of the founder's wealth—*Thorogood*⟩ ⟨remembering this flower . . . as the feminine *emblem* of the big college football games—*Edmund Wilson*⟩ *Emblem* is also applied to what is technically known in painting and sculpture as an **attribute**, some object that is conventionally associated with the representation either of a character (as a Greek divinity or a Christian saint) or of a personified abstraction, and is the means by which the character or abstraction is identified; thus, in fine art the balance is the *emblem,* or *attribute,* of Justice; the turning wheel, of Fortune; the club, of Hercules; and the spiked wheel, of St. Catherine of Alexandria ⟨Saint Helena is always painted with a cross beside her, or holding one, as a reminder that it was she who found the original cross. In this instance the cross is an *attribute,* not a symbol—*G. W. Benson*⟩ **Type**, especially in theological use, is applied to a person or thing that prefigures or foreshadows someone or something to come and that stands therefore as his or its symbol until the reality appears. In theology, biblical interpretation, and religious poetry, it usually also implies a divine dispensation whereby the spiritual or immaterial reality is prefigured by a living person, event, experience, or the like; thus, in medieval religious poetry Jerusalem is the *type* of heaven (the heavenly Jerusalem); in allegorical interpretation of Scriptures, the paschal lamb is the *type* of Christ, the victim on the Cross ⟨spiritual wisdom . . . is unchanging and eternal; it is communicated to us in *types* and shadows dim—in symbols—till we grow up into the power of understanding it—*Inge*⟩ ⟨concludes that the whole of the Old Testament is one great prophecy, one great *type* of what was to come—*Maas*⟩
*Ana* *sign, mark, token, badge: device, motif, design, *figure, pattern
**2** *character, sign, mark
*Ana* *device, contrivance: diagram, delineation, outline, sketch (see under SKETCH *vb*)
**symbolism** *allegory
**symmetry,** proportion, balance, harmony are comparable chiefly as used in the arts of design and decoration to

---

A colon (:) separates groups of words discriminated. An asterisk (*) indicates place of treatment of each group.

mean a quality which gives aesthetic pleasure and which depends upon the proper relating of details and parts to each other (as in magnitude, or arrangement) and to the consequent effect produced by the whole. **Symmetry** implies a median line or an axis on either side of which the details correspond (as in size, form, and placing). Often it implies such mathematical precision especially in arrangement of elements or parts as is observable in the corresponding halves of a perfect crystal, in a geometrically regular star, or in the conventionalized leaf or flower of decorative design ⟨*symmetry* is the keynote of most formal gardens⟩ ⟨the *symmetry* of a Greek temple⟩ ⟨abandoned the decent gown for a short coat or jacket and displayed the *symmetry* of their legs— *Trevelyan*⟩ but, in its stress of mechanical precision, *symmetry* may sometimes suggest an arid sterile quality, lacking in true artistic expression ⟨*symmetry* is a condition of perfect but inert balance; it will be entirely useless in a composition—*Taubes*⟩ **Proportion** implies a grace or beauty, independent of a thing's actual magnitude, duration, or intensity, that stems from the measured fitness of every one of its details and the consequent perfection of the whole ⟨we care for size, but inartistically; we care nothing for *proportion*, which is what makes size count—*Brownell*⟩ ⟨an impressive structure of Greek design, notable for its beauty of *proportion* and simplicity of detail—*Amer. Guide Series: Minn.*⟩ **Balance** is sometimes employed as an equivalent of *symmetry*, but it can be used distinctively to imply equality of values rather than repetition of details or parts and a massing of different things (as light and shade, sharply contrasted colors, or figures and background) so that each one tends to offset the other or to reduce the other's emphasis without loss of significance on either side. *Balance* implies as its aesthetic object an inducing of a pleasant satisfaction in the thing's quiet beauty or of a delight in the unified yet varied effect of the whole ⟨it is a similar principle of unsymmetrical *balance* which the Taoist artists sought in design. Space therefore, empty space, becomes a positive factor, no longer something not filled and left over, but something exerting an attractive power to the eye, and balancing the attractive power of forms and masses —*Binyon*⟩ ⟨every good statue is marked by a certain air of repose; every fine picture exists in a state of stable equilibrium brought about by the *balance* of its masses —*Krutch*⟩ ⟨*balance* is a subtler quality than *symmetry*. *Symmetry* means repetition . . . . *Balance*, which is a free, almost irregular extension of the concept of *symmetry*, implies, unlike *symmetry*, the element of risk—*Charles Johnson*⟩ **Harmony**, when used specifically in reference to the arts of design and decoration, retains as its leading implication the same idea as is involved in its general sense (see HARMONY 1), that of beauty resulting from a perfect interrelation of details and their fusion into an agreeable whole. However it often denotes specifically the aesthetic impression produced by something which manifests symmetry, proportion, or balance, or these qualities in combination ⟨a coloring *harmony* obtained by the aid of a long experience in the effects of light on translucent surfaces—*Henry Adams*⟩ ⟨we hear harmonious tones; but . . . the pleasure they give us . . . [is] the pleasure of their relational form which makes us attribute to them and their physical combination a quality which we call *harmony—Alexander*⟩ ⟨choosing with care and with a good eye for *harmony* the shoes, socks, shirt, and necktie he would wear—*Wolfe*⟩

**sympathetic** 1 *consonant, congenial, congruous, compatible, consistent
*Ana* agreeing, harmonizing *or* harmonious, accordant,

correspondent (see corresponding verbs at AGREE)
2 *tender, compassionate, warm, warmhearted, responsive
*Ana* kindly, *kind, benign, benignant: understanding, appreciating, comprehending (see UNDERSTAND)
*Ant* unsympathetic

**sympathy** 1 *attraction, affinity
*Ana* reciprocality, correspondence (see corresponding adjectives at RECIPROCAL): *harmony, consonance, accord, concord
*Ant* antipathy
2 **Sympathy, pity, compassion, commiseration, condolence, ruth, empathy** are comparable though often not interchangeable when they mean a feeling for the suffering or distress of another. **Sympathy** is the most general term, ranging in meaning from friendly interest or agreement in taste or opinion to emotional identification, often accompanied by deep tenderness ⟨*sympathy* with my desire to increase my . . . knowledge—*Fairchild*⟩ ⟨*sympathies* were . . . with the Roman Stoics—*Ellis*⟩ ⟨satire had its roots not in hatred but in *sympathy—Perry*⟩ **Pity** has the strongest emotional connotation; the emotion may be one of tenderness, love, or respect induced by the magnitude of another's suffering or of fellowship with the sufferer ⟨*pity* is the feeling which arrests the mind in the presence of whatsoever is grave and constant in human sufferings and unites it with the human sufferer—*Joyce*⟩ ⟨*pity* that made you cry . . . not for this person or that person who is suffering, but . . . for the very nature of things. . . . out of *pity* comes the balm which heals— *Saroyan*⟩ *Pity* sometimes may suggest a tinge of contempt for one who is inferior whether because of suffering or from inherent weakness; there is also a frequent suggestion that the effect if not the purpose of pity is to keep the object in a weak or inferior state ⟨*pity* for the man who could think of nothing better—*T. S. Eliot*⟩ ⟨the parents of a crippled child should give him understanding and challenge rather than *pity*⟩ **Compassion**, which originally meant fellowship in suffering between equals, has come to denote imaginative or emotional sharing of the distress or misfortune of another or others who are considered or treated as equals; it implies tenderness and understanding as well as an urgent desire to aid and spare ⟨one of his neighbor women cooked a chicken and brought it in to him out of pure *compassion—Cather*⟩ ⟨with understanding, with *compassion* (so different from pity) she shows the sordid impact . . . on the lives of the natives—*Campion*⟩ ⟨when Jesus came in his gentleness with his divine *compassion— Bridges*⟩ but while *compassion* suggests a greater dignity in the object than *pity* often does, it also implies a greater detachment in the subject ⟨as a priest he regards all history from that eminence of spiritual objectivity which is called *compassion—Albright*⟩ **Commiseration** and *condolence* agree in placing the emphasis on expression of a feeling for another's affliction, rather than on the feeling itself. **Commiseration** denotes a spontaneous and vocal expression, often one made in public or by a crowd ⟨there was a murmur of *commiseration* as Charles Darnay crossed the room . . . the soft and compassionate voices of women —*Dickens*⟩ **Condolence** denotes a formal expression of sympathy especially for the loss of a relative through death and refers strictly to an observance of etiquette without an implication as to the underlying feeling ⟨a *condolence* call⟩ ⟨they received many *condolences*⟩ **Ruth** denotes softening of a stern or indifferent disposition ⟨look homeward, Angel, now, and melt with *ruth—Milton*⟩ **Empathy**, of all the terms here discussed, has the least emotional content; it describes a gift, often a cultivated gift, for vicarious feeling, but the feeling need not be one of sorrow; thus *empathy* is often used as a synonym for

some senses of *sympathy* as well as in distinction from *sympathy* ⟨what he lacks is not *sympathy* but *empathy*, the ability to put himself in the other fellow's place —*G. W. Johnson*⟩ *Empathy* is frequently employed with reference to a nonhuman object (as a literary character or an idea, culture, or work of art) ⟨a fundamental component of the aesthetic attitude is *sympathy*, or—more accurately—*empathy*. In the presence of any work of art . . . the recipient . . . must surrender his independent and outstanding personality, to identify himself with the form or action presented by the artist—*Read*⟩
*Ana* tenderness, warmheartedness, warmth, responsiveness (see corresponding adjectives at TENDER): kindliness, kindness, benignness, benignancy (see corresponding adjectives at KIND)

**symptom** *sign, mark, token, badge

**synchronous** coeval, coetaneous, contemporaneous, *contemporary, simultaneous, coincident, concomitant, concurrent

**syndicate** *n* *monopoly, corner, pool, trust, cartel

**syndrome** *disease, disorder, condition, affection, ailment, malady, complaint, distemper

**synopsis** brief, conspectus, epitome, *abridgment, abstract

**synthetic** *artificial, ersatz, factitious

**system** 1 System, scheme, network, complex, organism, economy can mean an organized integrated whole made up of diverse but interrelated and interdependent parts. System usually implies that the component units of an aggregate exist and operate in unison or concord according to a coherent plan for smooth functioning ⟨the digestive *system*⟩ ⟨amid a *system* where the classic principles of capitalism still work successfully—*Laski*⟩ ⟨comprehend all experience in a closed *system*—*Inge*⟩ ⟨it does not form an independent *system*, like the universe: it exists as an element in human culture—*Mumford*⟩ Scheme may replace *system* but tends to stress an overall design for the interrelation of components, often a design carefully calculated or planned detail ⟨the cheerful, sanguine, courageous *scheme* of life, which was in part natural to her and in part slowly built up—*Ellis*⟩ ⟨our complex system, presenting the rare and difficult *scheme* of one general government, whose action extends over the whole —*John Marshall*⟩ ⟨the Newtonian *scheme* of the universe does not banish God from the universe—*Times Lit. Sup.*⟩ but sometimes *scheme* may carry a suggestion of irony or

depreciation that is absent from *system* (see also PLAN). Network suggests a system with interconnection or intercrossing at salient points sometimes involved but susceptible to analysis or control ⟨a *network* of abandoned narrow-gage logging roads penetrates the wooded areas—*Amer. Guide Series: Mich.*⟩ ⟨even the lowliest savages live in a social world characterized by a complex *network* of traditionally conserved habits, usages, and attitudes—*Sapir*⟩ Complex stresses an elaborate interweaving, interconnection and interrelationship of components difficult to trace ⟨for these ancestors of ours, in one half of their thoughts and acts, were still guided by a *complex* of intellectual, ethical and social assumptions of which only medieval scholars can today comprehend the true purport—*Trevelyan*⟩ ⟨this *complex* of conditions which taxes the terms upon which human beings associate and live together is summed up in the word *culture*—*Dewey*⟩ ⟨modern science, with infinite effort, has discovered and announced that man is a bewildering *complex* of energies —*Henry Adams*⟩ Organism basically applies to systems having life, but it is sometimes extended to systems felt as analogous to biological systems (as in capacity for growth and development) ⟨not because of an interest in the individual himself as a matured and single *organism* of ideas but in his assumed typicality for the community as a whole—*Sapir*⟩ ⟨the Church grew, like any other *organism*, by responding to its environment—*Inge*⟩ Economy implies a system concerned with needs and their regulation and fulfillment by individual, species, household, business, or government ⟨the plantation *economy*, with its base in slavery, was not conducive to the growth of industrial enterprise—*Amer. Guide Series: N. C.*⟩ ⟨the principle may operate successfully in the close *economy* of a good family, or even within a small religious community—*Hobson*⟩
*Ant* chaos
2 *method, mode, manner, way, fashion
*Ana* *plan, project, scheme, design: procedure, *process, proceeding

**systematic** *orderly, methodical, regular
*Ana* systematized, organized, ordered, arranged (see ORDER *vb*): *logical, analytical

**systematize** organize, methodize, *order, arrange, marshal
*Ana* *adjust, regulate, fix

# T

**table** *n* *list, catalog, schedule, register, roll, roster, inventory

**taciturn** *silent, uncommunicative, reserved, reticent, secretive, close, close-lipped, closemouthed, tight-lipped
*Ana* *dumb, mute, inarticulate: restrained, inhibited, curbed, checked (see RESTRAIN)
*Ant* garrulous: clamorous (*especially of crowds*): convivial (*of habits*)

**tackle** *n* *equipment, apparatus, machinery, paraphernalia, outfit, gear, matériel

**tact, address, poise, savoir faire** can all mean the skill and grace with which a well-bred person conducts himself in his relations with others. Tact stresses skill and considerateness in one's association with or handling of others, whether social equals or not. It implies delicate and sympathetic perception, especially of what is fit, graceful, or

considerate under given circumstances ⟨of political wisdom . . . Elizabeth had little or none; but her political *tact* was unerring—*J. R. Green*⟩ ⟨had been known to correct her mistress—with the utmost *tact* and respect —on a point of historical accuracy—*Sackville-West*⟩ ⟨without the *tact* to perceive when remarks were untimely —*Hardy*⟩ Address stresses dexterity and grace in approach (as in meeting strangers or in coping with new or with difficult situations). It often connotes adroitness and suavity and commonly implies success in winning favor or in attaining one's ends ⟨to bring the thing off as well as Mike has done requires *address*—*Wouk*⟩ ⟨his acute and flexible logic could support, with equal *address* . . . the adverse sides of every possible question—*Gibbon*⟩ Poise often implies both tact and address; it stresses, however, self-possession or equanimity in meeting em-

---

A colon (:) separates groups of words discriminated. An asterisk (*) indicates place of treatment of each group.

barrassing or upsetting situations ⟨mental *poise* . . . a balance of mind and temper that neither challenged nor avoided notice, nor admitted question of superiority or inferiority—*Henry Adams*⟩ ⟨would look into his eyes, the reserve, the statuesque *poise* all going to pieces—*Styron*⟩ **Savoir faire** may stress worldly or social experience and a knowledge of what is the proper thing to say or do or of how to act under all circumstances ⟨the inexperience and want of *savoir faire* in high matters of diplomacy of the Emperor and his ministers—*Greville*⟩ But it as often suggests a seemingly intuitive ability to act appropriately and with the utmost ease and tact rather than one based on breadth of experience ⟨the alcoholic usually has memories of occasions when liquor seemed to sharpen his wits, polish his manners and infuse him with *savoir faire—Seliger*⟩
*Ana* diplomaticness *or* diplomacy, politicness *or* policy, suavity, urbanity (see corresponding adjectives at SUAVE): *courtesy, amenity, gallantry
*Ant* awkwardness

**tactical** strategic, logistic (see under STRATEGY)
**tactics** *strategy, logistics
**tag** *n* mark, brand, stamp, label, ticket (see under MARK *vb*)
**tag** *vb* 1 *mark, brand, stamp, label, ticket
2 *follow, pursue, chase, trail, tail
**tail** *vb* *follow, pursue, chase, trail, tag
**taint** *vb* *contaminate, pollute, defile
*Ana* *debase, deprave, corrupt, vitiate: spoil, decompose, rot, putrefy, *decay: imbue, inoculate, *infuse
**take** 1 Take, seize, grasp, clutch, snatch, grab are comparable when they mean to get hold of by or as if by reaching out the arm or hand. **Take** is not only the most general but also the only colorless term in this group. In ordinary use, especially with reference to physical things, it may imply nothing more than a movement of the hand to get hold of something ⟨*take* the lamp from the table⟩ ⟨*take* meat from a platter⟩ or it may imply, with reference not only to physical but to immaterial or intangible things, numerous and often difficult operations by means of which one gets possession of or control over something ⟨*take* a city⟩ Between these two extremes *take* may imply, in innumerable idiomatic applications, a very wide range of methods of getting hold of something or possessing it in some way; thus, one *takes* a prize by winning it in a competition; one *takes* a cottage by renting it; one *takes* the temperature of a room by observing the thermometer ⟨*take* a bath⟩ ⟨*take* the air⟩ ⟨*take* a rest⟩ **Seize** usually suggests a sudden and forcible taking or getting hold of, and it therefore is interchangeable with *take* only when emphasis is placed upon these qualities ⟨the hungry children *seized* the food that was offered them⟩ ⟨the policeman *seized* the thief in the act of escaping⟩ ⟨the fort was *seized* before its defenders had time to repel the assault⟩ ⟨*seizing* between his teeth the cartilage of the trainer's ear—*Shaw*⟩ In extended use, especially when the thing seized or the thing seizing is something immaterial or intangible, the term usually suggests a catching of something fleeting or elusive ⟨*seize* an opportunity⟩ ⟨*seize* the attention of the crowd⟩ or the capture of something by force and, usually, surprise ⟨*seize* the throne⟩ ⟨the Breton *seized* more than he could hold; the Norman took less than he would have liked—*Henry Adams*⟩ or the ready understanding of something difficult to apprehend or analyze ⟨the character of Louis XIII is difficult to *seize*, for it comprised qualities hardly ever combined in one man—*Belloc*⟩ **Grasp** basically implies a laying hold of with the hands, teeth, or claws so as to hold firmly ⟨thy hand is made to *grasp* a palmer's staff —*Shak.*⟩ In extended use the term implies a comparable ability to comprehend fully or adequately something

difficult to comprehend either inherently or by reason of circumstances ⟨understood the words I heard, but couldn't seem to *grasp* their meaning—*Kenneth Roberts*⟩ ⟨the evil of the corruption and falsification of law, religion, education, and public opinion is so enormous that the minds of ordinary people are unable to *grasp* it—*Shaw*⟩ **Clutch** in its basic use implies more haste, more avidity, more urgency, and often less success in getting hold of the thing desired than *grasp* ⟨I . . . *clutched* desperately at the twigs as I fell—*Hudson*⟩ Only when success is clearly indicated is a tight hold or a clenching suggested ⟨I gave him all the money in my possession . . . . Gunga Dass *clutched* the coins, and hid them at once in his ragged loincloth—*Kipling*⟩ ⟨he *clutched* Father Joseph's hand with a grip surprisingly strong—*Cather*⟩ In extended use the term usually suggests a mental or emotional grasping at or seizing that is comparable to a physical clutching ⟨they *clutch* childishly at straws of optimism—*Wouk*⟩ ⟨can you never like things without *clutching* them as if you wanted to pull the heart out of them?—*D. H. Lawrence*⟩ **Snatch** carries the strongest implication of a sudden, hurried movement, but it seldom carries as strong a suggestion of the use of force as does its closest synonym, *seize;* rather, it often implies stealth ⟨*snatch* a purse⟩ ⟨*snatch* a kiss⟩ or promptness in rescuing ⟨*snatch* a child from the flames⟩ ⟨*snatched* from the jaws of death⟩ or rudeness or roughness ⟨*snatched* the book from her hand⟩ Consequently in extended use one *snatches* only what one can get by chance, surreptitiously, or by prompt action ⟨*snatch* a free moment for writing a letter⟩ ⟨youngsters *snatching* at fun while they chased the dream of a happy marriage—*Wouk*⟩ **Grab** commonly implies more rudeness or roughness than *snatch*, and it also usually implies as much force or violence as *seize;* distinctively it often suggests vulgarity and indifference to the rights of others or to the standards of the community, or a more or less open unscrupulousness in getting what one wants for oneself ⟨*grab* all the meat from the platter⟩ ⟨*grabbed* his hat and ran⟩ ⟨*grab* power⟩ ⟨Hitler had been helpless to prevent the Russians from *grabbing* the Baltic States—*Shirer*⟩
*Ana* *have, hold, own, possess: *catch, capture: confiscate, appropriate, preempt (SEE ARROGATE)
2 *receive, accept, admit
*Ana* acquiesce, accede, *assent, consent, subscribe
3 *bring, fetch
*Ana* *carry, convey, bear
**tale** *story, narrative, anecdote, yarn
*Ana* *fiction, fable: *myth, legend, saga
**talent** genius, *gift, faculty, aptitude, knack, bent, turn
*Ana* capacity, *ability, capability: *art, skill, craft, cunning: endowment (see corresponding verb at DOWER)
**talisman** *fetish, charm, amulet
**talk** *vb* *speak, converse
*Ana* *discuss, dispute, argue: *discourse, expatiate, dilate, descant: *chat, chatter, prate
**talk** *n* *speech, address, oration, harangue, lecture, sermon, homily
**talkative**, loquacious, garrulous, voluble, glib are comparable chiefly as applied to persons and their moods and as meaning given to talk or talking. The same distinctions in implications and connotations are also seen in their corresponding nouns **talkativeness, loquacity** *or* **loquaciousness, garrulity** *or* **garrulousness, volubility** *or* **volubleness,** and **glibness. Talkative** and **talkativeness,** the least explicit of these terms, may imply nothing more than a readiness to engage in talk, or they may suggest fluency and ease in talking or a disposition to enjoy conversation ⟨a *talkative* boy learns French sooner in France than a silent

boy—*Sydney Smith*⟩ ⟨he was *talkative*, he had a natural curiosity—*Styron*⟩ ⟨among them they noticed a beautiful, slim, *talkative* old man, with bright black eyes and snow-white hair—*L. P. Smith*⟩ **Loquacious** and **loquacity** more commonly imply fluency and ease in speech or, sometimes, an undue talkativeness ⟨had lost his usual *loquacity* and quaint humor—*Kingsley*⟩ ⟨talks in a rapid and persuasive fashion (he is described as *loquacious* and good-natured)—*Current Biog.*⟩ ⟨a *loquaciousness* at times rising to eloquence—*Walter Cerf*⟩ **Garrulous** and **garrulity** imply prosy, tedious, or rambling loquacity and usually suggest much idle talk about trivial things ⟨a fond *garrulous* old man, who loved to indulge his mind in reminiscences of the past—*Trollope*⟩ ⟨his petty vanities and anxieties, are set down with a naïve, irresistible *garrulity*—*Brit. Book News*⟩ **Voluble** and **volubility** suggest a free, flowing, and seemingly unending loquacity ⟨perhaps it was an overwhelming shock for the *voluble* French to discover that foreigners could enjoy conversation, too—*MacInnes*⟩ ⟨realizing that she had made a faux pas, was uneasy and *voluble*—*S. H. Adams*⟩ ⟨he sang of the lark, and it was the lark's *voluble* self—*Pater*⟩ ⟨for it was not a fault in him to dislike Aunt Charlotte, whose *volubility* must have assorted ill with his customary reserve—*Archibald Marshall*⟩ **Glib** and **glibness** are often interchangeable with *voluble* and *volubility*, but distinctively they may suggest a facility indicative of superficiality, trickery, or deceitfulness ⟨as usual when bemused, he flung out a smoke screen of his own variety of *glib* chatter—*Theodore Sturgeon*⟩ ⟨a *glib* excuse⟩ ⟨to train students as speakers, while neglecting them as listeners, is to foster *glibness* and deceitfulness—*Wendell Johnson*⟩
*Ana* *vocal, fluent, articulate, voluble, glib, eloquent: *vociferous, clamorous
*Ant* silent —*Con* reticent, reserved, uncommunicative, secretive (see SILENT)
**talkativeness** loquacity, garrulity, volubility, glibness (see under TALKATIVE)
*Ana* fluency, articulateness, eloquence, volubility, glibness (see corresponding adjectives at VOCAL)
*Ant* silence
**tall** *high, lofty
*Ant* short
**tally** *vb* *agree, square, accord, harmonize, correspond, conform, jibe
*Ana* *match, equal: coincide, concur (see AGREE)
*Con* *differ
**tame** *adj* Tame, subdued, submissive are comparable when they mean docile and tractable or incapable of asserting one's will either permanently or for the time being. **Tame** implies opposition to *wild* and in its basic sense applies chiefly to animals that have been domesticated and therefore accustomed to control by men ⟨*tame* horses⟩ In extended use it also applies to persons, or less directly to the acts and words of persons, whose wills have been broken or who have allowed themselves to be dominated by the will of another ⟨the tribunal lately so insolent, became on a sudden strangely *tame*—*Macaulay*⟩ Often the term implies little more than a temperamental lack of proper spirit or independence, or undue docility or timidity ⟨a *tame* reply⟩ ⟨*tame* acquiescence in tradition and routine—*Babbitt*⟩ **Subdued** stresses quietness and in its most general sense implies a toning down with a loss or veiling of all vehemence or intensity ⟨a *subdued*, passionate, desperate voice—*Styron*⟩ ⟨*subdued* colors⟩ In reference to persons, their acts, words, or characters, it implies a real or apparent domination by or subjection to another, or a similar response to circumstances, and a

resulting quietness or meekness that suggests a broken will, complete dependence, or excessive timorousness ⟨Zeke's natural manner with his mother was well-trained deception, a *subdued* mockery—*Farrell*⟩ ⟨she had a mild, *subdued*, expiring look—*Crabbe*⟩ ⟨in such a man, so gentle and *subdued* . . . a race illustrious for heroic deeds, humbled, but not degraded, may expire—*Wordsworth*⟩ **Submissive** implies the state of mind of one who has yielded his will to control by another and who unquestioningly or humbly obeys what is ordered or accepts what is given ⟨meek, humble, timid persons . . . who are cautious, prudent, and *submissive*, leave things very much as they find them—*Benson*⟩ ⟨the bigot is conventional, rigid . . . is *submissive* to authority, suppressive of the weak —*Ernst*⟩ ⟨the perverse, negative will . . . has to be made *submissive* before it can become positive and integrated with the heart and mind—*Henry Miller*⟩
*Ana* tractable, amenable, docile, biddable, *obedient: *timid, timorous: pliant, pliable (see PLASTIC)
*Ant* fierce
**tamp** *vb* *pack, crowd, cram, stuff, ram
*Ana* *press, squeeze, jam, crowd: *compact, consolidate, concentrate
**tamper** *meddle, interfere, intermeddle
*Ana* *interpose, interfere, intervene: trouble, discommode, *inconvenience
**tang** *taste, flavor, savor, relish, smack
*Ana* pungency, piquancy, raciness (see corresponding adjectives at PUNGENT)
**tangent** *adj* abutting, adjoining, *adjacent, contiguous, conterminous, juxtaposed
**tangible** sensible, *perceptible, palpable, appreciable, ponderable
*Ana* *material, physical, corporeal, objective: actual, *real, true: obvious, *evident, manifest
*Ant* intangible
**tantalize** tease, harass, harry, *worry, annoy, plague, pester
*Ana* vex, *annoy, irk, bother: torment, torture, try, *afflict: *bait, badger
*Ant* satisfy
**tantamount** *same, selfsame, very, identical, identic, equivalent, equal
*Ana* *like, alike, uniform, similar
**tap** *vb* Tap, knock, rap, thump, thud can mean, as verbs, to strike or hit audibly or, as nouns, the sound or effect produced by such striking or hitting. **Tap** implies a light blow usually repeated (as to attract attention to one's presence, needs, or wishes) ⟨*tap* at her door⟩ ⟨*tapping* on the window⟩ ⟨she *tapped* her pencil on the desk for order⟩ **Knock** implies a more forcible blow than *tap*, often a pounding or hammering (as on a door to call attention to one's need for admittance or on a person's body or head in an attack or a collision) ⟨there came a heavy *knock* on the door⟩ ⟨the messenger *knocked* loudly to awaken us⟩ In extended use *knock* may imply a sound or an effect that suggests a knocking ⟨an automobile engine may *knock* because of uneven combustion⟩ **Rap** suggests a smart, vigorous striking (as with the knuckles) on a hard surface so as to produce a sharp, quick sound or succession of sounds ⟨the chairman *rapped* sharply for order⟩ ⟨a *rap* at the door⟩ In extended use *rap* implies utterance that comes as quick and as sharp as rapping ⟨*rap* out a series of commands⟩ ⟨the tired businessman . . . wants his poems snapped at him, *rapped* at him—*Lowes*⟩ **Thump** implies the dull, heavy, yet resonant sound made by something that pounds or beats (as the fist upon a table or heavy feet upon the ground) or by something that pulsates forcibly and noisily ⟨hear the

---

A colon (:) separates groups of words discriminated. An asterisk (*) indicates place of treatment of each group.

*thump* of many feet⟩ ⟨the *thumping* of a big drum⟩ ⟨the *thump* of a boat against the pier⟩ ⟨everybody's heart was *thumping* as hard as possible—*Thackeray*⟩ **Thud** places more emphasis upon the sound made than upon the action which produces it and carries a less strong suggestion of repetition; also, it more often suggests the sound made by something falling and striking than by something being struck; otherwise it differs only by suggesting a flatter or hollower and less resonant sound than *thump* ⟨the dull *thud* of a heavy body striking the floor⟩ ⟨a bullet *thudded* into the wall above me—*Hubert Wales*⟩
*Ana* \*strike, smite: \*beat

**tap** *n* rap, knock, thump, thud (see under TAP *vb*)

**tar** *n* \*mariner, sailor, seaman, gob, bluejacket

**tardy** *adj* **Tardy, late, behindhand, overdue** can all designate persons or things that do not arrive or take place at the time set, the time due, or the expected and usual time. **Tardy** implies a lack of promptness or punctuality or a coming or happening or doing after the proper or appointed moment; it need not imply slowness in movement but may suggest rather a being delayed in starting or beginning ⟨ten years is a long time for a courtship, and she summons courage to spur her *tardy* swain—*Seamus Kelly*⟩ ⟨the *tardier* indicators of business activity have finally begun to turn down—*Fortune*⟩ **Late** implies an opposition to *early* and usually connotes a failure to come or take place at the time due because of procrastination, slowness of movement or growth, or the interference of obstacles; it is applied especially to persons or to things that are governed by a schedule ⟨be *late* for work⟩ ⟨you are too *late* to get your dinner⟩ ⟨the train is very *late* today⟩ ⟨spring is very *late* this year⟩ **Behindhand** usually applies either directly or indirectly to persons who are in arrears (as in the payment of debts or in the fulfillment of obligations) or who are slower than normal (as in mental progress, in the acceptance of fashions, or in taking action) ⟨*behindhand* in the payment of his rent⟩ ⟨a whole class who were *behindhand* with their lessons—*Hawthorne*⟩ ⟨Spain, usually so *behindhand* in matters of art, displayed expressionism . . . even nonobjectivists—*Gómez Sicre*⟩ **Overdue** is applied to things that are affected by a person's being, or less often to a person that is, markedly late or behindhand; thus, a person is *behindhand* in the payment of his rent, but the rent is *overdue* when such a situation occurs; a ship is *overdue* when it is seriously or conspicuously behind its scheduled time of arrival ⟨her gallant was now more than an hour *overdue*—*Barclay*⟩ ⟨a peremptory demand . . . for the settlement of an account long *overdue* —*Norris*⟩ Overdue also may refer to something that might logically or suitably have appeared or occurred a long time before ⟨colonies that are *overdue* for liberation—*Landman*⟩ ⟨the valuable work . . . received long *overdue* recognition—*Kuney*⟩
*Ana* dilatory, laggard, \*slow: delayed, detained, retarded (see DELAY)
*Ant* prompt

**tarnish** *vb* \*soil, dirty, sully, foul, befoul, smirch, besmirch, grime, begrime   •
*Ana* darken, dim, bedim, \*obscure: defile, pollute, taint, \*contaminate
*Ant* polish —*Con* cleanse, \*clean: \*illuminate, illumine, lighten

**tarry** \*stay, remain, wait, abide, linger
*Ana* \*delay, procrastinate, lag, loiter, dawdle

**tart** *adj* \*sour, acid, acidulous, dry
*Ana* piquant, \*pungent: \*sharp, keen: curt, brusque, blunt (see BLUFF): \*irritable, snappish, waspish

**Tartarean** \*infernal, chthonian, Hadean, stygian, hellish

**task, duty, assignment, job, stint, chore** are comparable

when they mean a piece of work which one is asked to do and is expected to accomplish. **Task** refers to a specific piece of work or service usually imposed by authority or circumstance but sometimes undertaken voluntarily ⟨some person or some organization whose *task* it is to realize the daydreams of the masses—*Huxley*⟩ ⟨the spirit in which judge or advocate is to look upon his *task*—*Cardozo*⟩ **Duty** is likely to indicate work, service, or conduct enjoined on a person because of his rank, status, occupation, or affiliation; it is more likely in most uses to suggest obligation, often moral, than specific imposition by a taskmaster ⟨it is emphatically the province and *duty* of the judicial department to say what the law is—*John Marshall*⟩ ⟨some of the military branches having a preferred status . . . had higher pay scales for less dangerous *duties*— *Kingsley Davis*⟩ **Assignment** suggests a specific amount of work or sort of service assigned authoritatively ⟨it is not our *assignment* to settle specific questions of territories —*Truman*⟩ **Job** is a general term wide in suggestion ranging from voluntary undertaking of some signal service down to an assigned bit of menial work ⟨a *job* that suffers from some relative poverty in charm, such as totting up endless small sums at a desk or feeding coal in at the door of a furnace—*Montague*⟩ **Stint** stresses carefully or equitably measured or timed apportionment of work ⟨took to doing "German Romance" as my daily work, ten pages daily my *stint*—*Carlyle*⟩ **Chore** is likely to suggest minor routine activity necessary for continuing satisfactory operating (as of farm or office) ⟨leisure after the *chores* and happy meeting places where the farmer and his family might play—*Burlingame*⟩
*Ana* \*function, office, duty, province: \*work, labor, toil: employment, occupation, business (see WORK)

**taste** *n* **1 Taste, flavor, savor, tang, relish, smack** can all mean the property of a substance which makes it perceptible to the gustatory sense. **Taste** not only is the most inclusive of these terms but it gives no suggestion of a specific character or quality ⟨dislike the *taste* of olives⟩ ⟨the fundamental *tastes* are acid, sweet, bitter, and salt⟩ **Flavor** applies to the property of a thing which is recognized by the cooperation of the olfactory and gustatory and to some extent tactile senses. The term therefore usually denotes the combination of tastes and smells perceived when eating or drinking a thing. Usually, also, it suggests the blend of tastes and odors and textures that give a substance a distinctive or peculiar character ⟨this peach has a particularly fine *flavor*⟩ ⟨the *flavor* of a fine tea has been described as "a bouquet which can be tasted"⟩ **Savor** stresses sensitiveness of palate or of nose and may refer to the odor of something cooking as well as to the flavor of something eaten ⟨caught the rich *savor* of roasting meat as they passed the window⟩ ⟨sipping slowly to enjoy the full *savor* of the wine⟩ **Tang** applies chiefly to a sharp penetrating savor, flavor, or odor; it usually implies a live, pungent quality ⟨prefer apples with a *tang*⟩ ⟨the *tang* of dry champagne⟩ ⟨the *tang* of a salt breeze⟩ *Relish* and *smack* are comparatively rare in this sense; **relish** (see also TASTE 2) comes close to *savor* and usually suggests enjoyment of the taste ⟨a Laplander . . . has no notion of the *relish* of wine— *Hume*⟩ ⟨my first endeavor must be to distinguish the true taste of fruits, refine my palate, and establish a just *relish* in the kind—*Shaftesbury*⟩ **Smack** comes close to *flavor* but applies usually to one that is added to or is different from the typical flavor of a substance ⟨ale with a burnt musty *smack*⟩ ⟨a good *smack* of pepper in this stew⟩

In extended use these words usually call up one or more suggestions from their basic senses. **Taste** usually denotes a strong impression or a heightened sense of the quality of

---

*Ana* analogous words     *Ant* antonyms     *Con* contrasted words     See also explanatory notes facing page 1

something ⟨the book leaves a bad *taste* in the mouth⟩ ⟨the first *taste* of sudden death and destruction from the skies —*Shirer*⟩ **Flavor** implies a predominant or distinctive and pervasive quality ⟨imparted an unwonted lachrymose *flavor* to his tone—*Purdy*⟩ ⟨the passing hour's supporting joys have lost the keen-edged *flavor*—*Meredith*⟩ ⟨*flavor*, in fine, is the spirit of the dramatist projected into his work—*Galsworthy*⟩ **Savor** differs from *flavor* largely in suggesting a stimulating or enlivening character or quality that, like salt, spice, or other seasoning, gives life or pungency to a thing ⟨an odd blend of bitter naturalism and quiet humor . . . gives it a *savor* quite its own —*Anthony Boucher*⟩ ⟨no one treats me like a child now, and the *savor* has gone out of my life—*Ellis*⟩ **Tang, relish,** and **smack** come still closer to their basic senses ⟨the language has a *tang* of Shakespeare—*Gray*⟩ ⟨Yankeeisms . . . whose salt-sea flavor has its own peculiar *tang* in it —*J. R. Lowell*⟩ ⟨the full flavor, the whole *relish* of delight —*Beecher*⟩ ⟨your lordship . . . hath yet some *smack* of age in you, some *relish* of the saltness of time—*Shak.*⟩ ⟨the Saxon names of places, with the pleasant, wholesome *smack* of the soil in them—*Arnold*⟩

**2 Taste, palate, relish, gusto, zest** are comparable when they mean a liking for or an enjoyment of something because of qualities that give the sense of taste a pleasurable sensation or that produce comparably pleasant mental or aesthetic impressions. **Taste** (see also TASTE 1) may imply a liking that is either natural or acquired; the term is often used to designate a deep-seated or ingrained longing for something that lies behind one's predilection for it, one's bent to it, one's aptitude for it, or a predisposition to enjoy one thing more than another ⟨cultivate a *taste* for olives⟩ ⟨he had no *taste* for the study of law⟩ ⟨she had a *taste* for melancholy—for the smell of orange rinds and woodsmoke—that was extraordinary—*Cheever*⟩ More often *taste* refers to a liking that is based upon an understanding of peculiar excellences, especially aesthetic excellences, and that gives one a more or less discerning appreciation of a thing's beauty or perfection (as of form, design, and color) or grace and dignity and consequently greater enjoyment of it ⟨a connoisseur, possessing above all things an exquisite *taste*—*Dahl*⟩ ⟨all *tastes* are legitimate, and it is not necessary to account for them—*Virgil Thomson*⟩ ⟨without any technical knowledge she had acquired a good *taste* in music—*Ellis*⟩ In this sense *taste* is often so close to another sense of *taste*, namely, the power of discriminating aesthetic judgment, that the two meanings tend to overlap. In the first case, however, *taste* is not an abstraction but a concrete thing referable to an individual or a group of individuals ⟨we have our *tastes* in painting as in confectionery. Some of us prefer Tintoretto to Rembrandt, as we do chocolate to coconut— *Brownell*⟩ In the latter sense *taste* is an abstraction used commonly without reference to individuals. In general it implies a capacity for discerning true excellence and the setting up of standards whereby all may be taught to appreciate the excellence they discern; sometimes it denotes the body of standards so set up ⟨you do have talent, but you're pitifully ignorant of the first principles of *taste*— *Wouk*⟩ **Palate** may imply either the literal physical sensation or sense of taste ⟨a wine taster must have a discriminating *palate*⟩ ⟨people who considered cider was just like champagne. It was a matter of *palate*—*Hilton*⟩ or a corresponding intellectual reaction and then suggest pleasure afforded the mind ⟨in the midst of such beauty . . . one's body is all one tingling *palate*—*Muir*⟩ ⟨had no philosophy, but things distressed his *palate*, and two of those things were International propaganda and the Organized State—*Yeats*⟩ **Relish** often suggests a more distinct or a more exciting flavor in the thing that evokes enjoyment or liking; but especially it tends to imply a keener or more personal gratification than *taste* ⟨a man of . . . a quick *relish* for pleasure—*Macaulay*⟩ ⟨seemed to speak all his words with an immense wet-lipped *relish*, as though they tasted good on the tongue—*Dahl*⟩ ⟨[the artist's brain] can go further and build up, always with a passionate *relish* for what it is producing—*Montague*⟩ **Gusto** can imply either the hearty relish with which one sometimes may attack a meal, execute a piece of work, or go about the performance of an act (as a task or duty), or a quality in the thing which is executed or in the act which is performed that indicates vital or enthusiastic interest, keen delight, and intense imaginative or emotional energy in the doing of it ⟨ambitious politicians . . . succumbing with glee and *gusto* to the temptations of power—*Huxley*⟩ ⟨this dramatic sense . . . gives Rostand's characters— Cyrano at least—a *gusto* which is uncommon on the modern stage—*T. S. Eliot*⟩ **Zest**, like *gusto*, applies either to the spirit in which one approaches something one likes to do, make, or encounter or the quality imparted to the thing done, made, or envisioned as a result of this spirit. In contrast with *gusto* it suggests eagerness, avidity, or a perception of a thing's piquancy or peculiar flavor rather than a hearty appetite indicative of abounding energy ⟨the Elizabethan theater had its cause in an ardent *zest* for life and living—*Arnold*⟩ ⟨his robustiousness, his *zest* for malicious humor—*Hervey*⟩

*Ana* \*predilection, prepossession, partiality: appreciation, understanding, comprehension (see corresponding verbs at UNDERSTAND): inclination, disposition, predisposition (see corresponding verbs at INCLINE): \*discernment, discrimination, penetration, insight, acumen

*Ant* antipathy

**tasty** savory, sapid, \*palatable, appetizing, toothsome, flavorsome, relishing

*Ant* bland

**tat** *vb* \*weave, knit, crochet, braid, plait

**tattle** \*gossip, blab

*Ana* divulge, disclose, betray, \*reveal

**taunt** *vb* mock, deride, \*ridicule, twit, rally

*Ana* \*scoff, jeer, gibe, flout: affront, insult, \*offend, outrage: scorn, disdain, scout (see DESPISE): chaff, \*banter

**taut** \*tight, tense

**tautology** \*verbiage, redundancy, pleonasm, circumlocution, periphrasis

**tawdry** \*gaudy, garish, flashy, meretricious

*Ana* \*showy, pretentious: vulgar, gross, \*coarse: flamboyant, \*ornate, florid

**tax** *vb* \*burden, encumber, cumber, weigh, weight, load, lade, charge, saddle

**teach, instruct, educate, train, discipline, school** are comparable when they mean to cause to acquire knowledge or skill. **Teach** implies a direct showing to another with the intent that he will learn; it usually suggests the imparting of information, but in addition it often also connotes the giving of help that will assist the learner in mastering such difficulties as are involved in putting the new knowledge to use or in making it a part of his mental or physical equipment ⟨*teaching* the young to read⟩ ⟨*teach* arithmetic⟩ ⟨*taught* the boys how to swim⟩ ⟨that same prayer does *teach* us all to render the deeds of mercy—*Shak.*⟩ **Instruct** stresses the furnishing, especially the methodical furnishing, of necessary knowledge or skill to someone else ⟨schoolmasters will I keep within my house, fit to *instruct* her youth—*Shak.*⟩ ⟨he is wise who can *instruct* us and assist us in the business of daily virtuous living —*Carlyle*⟩ **Educate**, although it implies or presupposes teaching or instruction as the means, stresses the intention or the result, the bringing out or development of qualities or capacities latent in the individual or regarded as essential to his position in life ⟨schools that *educate* boys for the ministry⟩ ⟨in my eyes the question is not what to teach, but how to *educate*—*Kingsley*⟩ ⟨*educate* the masses into becoming fit for self-government—*Huxley*⟩ **Train,** even when it is used as a close synonym of *educate,* almost invariably suggests a distinct end or aim which guides teachers and instructors; it implies, therefore, such subjection of the pupil as will form him or fit him for the state in view ⟨universities exist . . . on the one hand, to *train* men and women for certain professions—*Russell*⟩ *Train* is especially employed in reference to the instruction of persons or sometimes animals who must be physically in excellent condition, mentally proficient, or quickly responsive to orders for a given occupation or kind of work ⟨*train* a dog to point game⟩ ⟨troops . . . equipped and *trained* to fight in the bitter cold and the deep snow —*Shirer*⟩ **Discipline,** even more than *train,* implies subordination to a master or subjection to control, often self-control ⟨he consciously seeks to *discipline* himself in fine thinking and right living—*Ellis*⟩ ⟨feeling . . . the rush of old jealousy he had thought long since *disciplined* from him—*Buck*⟩ **School** is sometimes interchangeable with *educate* ⟨some of them have been *schooled* at Eton and Harrow—*Shaw*⟩ or with *teach* or *instruct* ⟨*schooled* by my guide, it was not difficult to realize the scene—*S. C. Hall*⟩ but it is more often used in the sense of *train* or *discipline,* frequently with the added implication of learning to endure what is hard to bear ⟨that I can bear. I can *school* myself to worse than that—*Wilde*⟩ ⟨groomed and faultless, *schooled* in power, he bowed greetings—*Wolfe*⟩ *Ana* impart, *communicate: *practice, drill, exercise: inculcate, instill, *implant

**tear** *vb* **Tear, rip, rend, split, cleave, rive** can all mean to separate forcibly one part of a continuous material or substance from another, or one object from another with which it is closely and firmly associated. **Tear** implies pulling apart or away by or as if by main force; it often suggests jagged rough edges or laceration ⟨*tore* his coat on a nail⟩ ⟨*tear* a piece of paper lengthwise⟩ ⟨he took hold of it with his powerful hands and *tore* it out by the roots—*Anderson*⟩ ⟨flood *tore* a . . . gorge through the township—*Amer. Guide Series: Vt.*⟩ ⟨grief *tears* her heart⟩ **Rip** usually implies a forcible pulling or breaking apart typically along a line or juncture (as a seam, a joint, or a connection) ⟨Macduff was from his mother's womb untimely *ripped*—*Shak.*⟩ ⟨*rip* the shingles from a roof⟩ **Rend** implies greater violence than *tear* and either heightens the implication of a lacerating effect or adds that of severing or sundering ⟨*rend* your heart, and not your garments—*Joel* 2:13⟩ ⟨the black volume of clouds . . . *rent* asunder by flashes of lightning—*Irving*⟩ ⟨his pride and vanity had been *rent* by her ultimate rejection—*H. G. Wells*⟩ **Split** implies a cutting or breaking apart in a continuous, straight, and usually lengthwise direction or in the direction of grain or layers ⟨*split* a log with a wedge⟩ ⟨great rocks *split* by an earthquake⟩ In extended use the term implies force or intensity sufficient to split something ⟨*split* their sides with laughter⟩ ⟨pain that seemed about to *split* his head⟩ ⟨let sorrow *split* my heart, if ever I did hate thee—*Shak.*⟩ ⟨ear-*splitting* outcries⟩ **Cleave,** a somewhat rhetorical word, may come close to *split,* but more often it conveys the notion of laying open by or as if by a stroke of an edged weapon ⟨struck the final blow, *cleaving* the Archbishop's skull—*Lucas*⟩ ⟨his acumen *clove* clean to the heart of a piece of writing —*Mandelbaum*⟩ **Rive** is elevated for *split* ⟨blunt wedges *rive* hard knots—*Shak.*⟩ ⟨all thoughts to *rive* the heart

are here, and all are vain—*Housman*⟩
*Ana* slit, slash, *cut: *pull, drag: damage, *injure, impair 2 *rush, dash, shoot, charge
*Ana* *speed, hasten, hurry: dart, *fly, scud
**tease** tantalize, pester, plague, harass, harry, *worry, annoy
*Ana* *bait, badger, hector, chivy: importune, adjure, *beg: fret, chafe, gall (see ABRADE)
**tedious** *irksome, tiresome, wearisome, boring
*Ana* burdensome, *onerous, oppressive: fatiguing, exhausting, fagging, jading (see TIRE *vb*): *slow, dilatory, deliberate
*Ant* exciting
**tedium, boredom, ennui, doldrums** are comparable when they denote a state of dissatisfaction and weariness. **Tedium** suggests a repression of energy for lack of a proper or adequate outlet, and dullness or lowness of spirits resulting from irksome inactivity or from the irksome monotony of one's pursuits or surroundings ⟨incessant recurrence without variety breeds *tedium*—*Lowes*⟩ ⟨able boys and girls will go through endless *tedium* . . . to acquire some coveted knowledge or skill—*Russell*⟩ **Boredom** adds to *tedium* suggestions of listlessness, dreariness, and unrest resulting either from a lack of interest in one's pursuits or surroundings or from the fact that they pall or fail to excite interest ⟨I suppose I shall go on "existing" till the *boredom* of it becomes too great—*J. R. Green*⟩ ⟨wealthy indolent women . . . who got up at noon and spent the rest of the day trying to relieve their *boredom*—*Dahl*⟩ **Ennui** stresses profound dissatisfaction, discontent, or weariness of spirit; usually it suggests physical depression, languor, or lassitude as well as boredom ⟨that *ennui,* that terrible taedium vitae, that comes on those to whom life denies nothing—*Wilde*⟩ ⟨the inexhaustible power and activity of his mind leave him no leisure for *ennui*—*Arnold*⟩ **Doldrums** applies to a phase or period of depression that in persons may be marked by listlessness, despondency, and flagging energy ⟨Lotharioism is simple monogamy's *doldrums* multiplied, and with thrice monogamy's duties—*Nathan*⟩ or in more general applications (as to economic activity) may be marked by inactivity and dullness.
*Ana* irksomeness, tediousness, tiresomeness, wearisomeness (see corresponding adjectives at IRKSOME): melancholy, dumps, blues, gloom (see SADNESS)
**teem, abound, swarm, overflow** can all mean to be plentifully supplied (*with*) or to be rich (*in*). Though they are often interchangeable, each of these words may carry distinctive implications. **Teem** implies productiveness or fecundity ⟨the rivers *teem* with fish⟩ ⟨his mind *teems* with plans⟩ It often suggests little more than crowding and activity ⟨Tozeur, which has a railway station and positively *teems* with French officials—*Huxley*⟩ **Abound** implies plenitude in numbers or amount; usually it stresses profusion ⟨distant forests aglow with tropical colors and *abounding* with strange forms of life—*Jefferies*⟩ It is as often used with reference to qualities as to things ⟨the young soldiers *abound* in vigor and courage⟩ **Swarm** in its relevant extended sense implies even more strongly than *teem* motion and thronging ⟨a marketplace *swarming* with buyers and sellers—*Macaulay*⟩ It is also more capable of suggesting infestation ⟨the house *swarmed* with flies⟩ **Overflow** in its extended sense adds to *abound* the implication of exceeding capacity ⟨he *overflows* with good nature⟩ Sometimes it suggests glutting ⟨the market *overflows* with goods⟩
*Ana* *bear, produce, yield, turn out: *generate, engender, breed, propagate: multiply, augment, *increase
**teeny** tiny, little, diminutive, *small, petite, wee, weeny,

---

*Ana* analogous words     *Ant* antonyms     *Con* contrasted words     See also explanatory notes facing page 1

minute, microscopic, miniature

**teeter** *vb* *shake, tremble, quake, totter, quiver, shiver, shudder, quaver, wobble, shimmy, dither

**tell** *vb* **1** *count, enumerate, number

**2** *say, utter, state

**3** divulge, discover, *reveal, disclose, betray
*Ana* impart, *communicate: *relate, rehearse, recite, recount: *inform, acquaint, apprise

**telling** compelling, convincing, cogent, sound, *valid
*Ana* forceful, forcible, *powerful, potent: *effective, effectual, efficacious: *conclusive, decisive, determinative, definitive

**temerity, audacity, hardihood, effrontery, nerve, cheek, gall** are comparable when they mean conspicuous or flagrant boldness (as in speech, behavior, or action). Temerity usually implies contempt of danger and consequent rashness; often it suggests, especially when a proposal or project is under discussion, a failure to estimate one's chances of success ⟨impetuously brushed aside the legalistic twaddle of the lawyers . . . and they frowned on such *temerity*—*Bowers*⟩ ⟨tenth-rate critics and compilers, for whom any violent shock to the public taste would be a *temerity* not to be risked—*Arnold*⟩ **Audacity** implies either a bold and open disregard of the restraints imposed by prudence, convention, decorum, or authority or undue presumption in making advances ⟨he had committed the supreme *audacity* of looking into her soul —*Sackville-West*⟩ ⟨the moral *audacity,* the sense of spiritual freedom, that one gets from certain scenes in the Gospels—*Edmund Wilson*⟩ **Hardihood** stresses firmness of purpose and often additionally implies considered defiance (as of conventions or decorum). It may be used without depreciative intent, but it is frequently employed as a term of contempt almost equivalent to *insolence* or *impudence* ⟨no historian or astronomer will have the *hardihood* to maintain that he commands this God's-eye view—*Toynbee*⟩ ⟨the reviewers . . . were staggered by my *hardihood* in offering a woman of forty as a subject of serious interest to the public—*Bennett*⟩ **Effrontery** is definitely derogatory; it is used in place of any of the three preceding words when one wishes to impute flagrant disregard of the laws of courtesy, propriety, or fair dealing or an arrogant assumption of a privilege ⟨had the damnable *effrontery* to tell me my father's delay was occasioned . . . by his addiction to immoral practices—*Cheever*⟩ ⟨she had won her way to success by strength of will and hardness of heart, and a kind of haughty *effrontery*—*Wharton*⟩ Nerve, cheek, and gall are close to *effrontery,* **nerve,** however, often carrying a strong suggestion of hardihood, **cheek** of impudent self-assurance, and **gall** of outrageous insolence ⟨had the ghastly *nerve* to tell you . . . that you were being vulgar—*Wouk*⟩ ⟨the *cheek* of him . . . imagine a miserable-looking leprechaun like Pat Dolan to be having notions of a fine girl like Maria—*Laverty*⟩ ⟨the small stockholder who . . . has the *gall* to ask questions about the management—*Cohn*⟩
*Ana* rashness, recklessness, foolhardiness, daring, venturesomeness (see corresponding adjectives at ADVENTUROUS): precipitateness, impetuosity, abruptness (see corresponding adjectives at PRECIPITATE): impertinence, intrusiveness, officiousness (see corresponding adjectives at IMPERTINENT)
*Ant* caution

**temper** *vb* *moderate, qualify
*Ana* *adjust, regulate, fix: mitigate, alleviate, lighten, assuage, allay, *relieve: mollify, *pacify, appease
*Ant* intensify

**temper** *n* **1** *mood, humor, vein
*Ana* mettle, spirit (see COURAGE): emotion, *feeling,

affection, passion: attitude, *position, stand

**2** *disposition, temperament, complexion, character, personality, individuality
*Ana* *state, condition, posture, situation: *quality, property, attribute

**temperament** *disposition, temper, complexion, character, personality, individuality
*Ana* *mind, soul: nature, kind, *type

**temperance, sobriety, abstinence, abstemiousness, continence** can all mean self-restraint in the gratification of appetites or passions. In its more general sense **temperance** implies simply habitual moderation and the exercise of judgment ⟨*temperance* in eating and drinking⟩ ⟨exaggeration, exaltation, the fanatic spirit, are extremely rare. *Temperance* is the almost universal rule in speech, demeanor, taste, and habits—*Brownell*⟩ But *temperance* may be used specifically in reference to the use of intoxicating beverages and then tends to imply not merely moderation but abstention; thus, a *temperance* hotel is one where no intoxicating liquors are sold or served. **Sobriety,** like *temperance,* suggests avoidance of excess not only in drinking ⟨what would be *sobriety* for a billiard marker would be ruinous drunkenness for a . . . billiard player—*Shaw*⟩ but also in thought or action. Often it connotes the idea of seriousness or of avoidance of ostentation ⟨*sobriety* in dress⟩ ⟨admired him for his cleanliness, *sobriety* and industry—*Cheever*⟩ **Abstinence** implies voluntary deprivation ⟨the Cynic preached *abstinence* from all common ambitions, rank, possessions, power, the things which clog man's feet—*Buchan*⟩ ⟨the man who has made a virtue of *abstinence* secretly regrets, when he grows old, the discretions of his youth—*Abel*⟩ **Abstemiousness** and its much commoner adjective **abstemious** suggest habitual self-restraint, moderation, or frugality especially in eating or drinking ⟨the most *abstemious* of men . . . he held old-fashioned and rather puritanical views—*Woolf*⟩ **Continence** emphasizes self-restraint in regard to one's impulses or desires ⟨he knew what to say, so he knows also when to leave off, a *continence* which is practiced by few writers—*Dryden*⟩ In its specific sense it stresses self-restraint in sexual indulgence. Sometimes it implies chastity or complete abstention; often, when referred to husband and wife, it implies avoidance of undue indulgence ⟨chastity is either abstinence or *continence.* Abstinence is that of virgins or widows; *continence,* of married persons—*Taylor*⟩
*Ana* forgoing, forbearing *or* forbearance, sacrificing *or* sacrifice, eschewal (see corresponding verbs at FORGO): frugality, sparingness, thriftiness (see corresponding adjectives at SPARING): restrained, curbed, checked (see RESTRAIN)

**temperate 1** *moderate
*Ana* mild, gentle, lenient, *soft: *steady, even, equable, constant: restrained, curbed, checked (see RESTRAIN)
*Ant* intemperate: inordinate

**2** *sober, continent, unimpassioned
*Ana* *sparing, frugal, economical: abstaining, refraining, forbearing (see REFRAIN): dispassionate, just, equitable, *fair

**temporal** *profane, secular, lay
*Ana* *material, objective, physical, corporeal
*Ant* spiritual

**temporary, provisional, ad interim, acting, supply** can all be applied to a person holding a post for a limited time, to the post held by that person, or to his appointment. **Temporary** merely implies that the post is not held on tenure but may be terminated at the will of those having the appointive power. It is interchangeable with many of the other words but is not so explicit ⟨a *temporary* position⟩

---

A colon (:) separates groups of words discriminated. An asterisk (*) indicates place of treatment of each group.

⟨*temporary* clerks⟩ ⟨a *temporary* appointment⟩ **Provisional** is applied chiefly to a government or to the head or leading officials of a government that is set up in a new state or after a revolution until a permanent government can be established. **Ad interim** definitely suggests appointment for an intervening period (as between the death or resignation of an incumbent and the appointment or election of his successor) ⟨an *ad interim* pastor⟩ The term is also applied to an appointment made by the president of the United States when the Senate is not in session and confirmation is not possible until after the recess ⟨an *ad interim* appointment as ambassador⟩ **Acting** is applied to the person who during a vacancy in an office or during the absence of the incumbent assumes temporarily, by appointment or by fixed procedure, the powers given the person regularly appointed or elected ⟨the president of the common council becomes *acting* mayor when the mayor is on vacation⟩ **Supply** implies the performance of duties of another or service as a locum tenens ⟨a *supply* pastor⟩ ⟨a *supply* teacher⟩
*Ant* permanent

**tempt** entice, inveigle, *lure, decoy, seduce
*Ana* allure, *attract: *invite, solicit, court, woo: *induce, persuade, prevail, get

**tenacious** tough, stout, *strong, sturdy, stalwart
*Ana* dogged, pertinacious, *obstinate, stubborn: resolute, staunch, steadfast, true (see FAITHFUL): persevering, persisting (see PERSEVERE)

**tenacity** resolution, spirit, mettle, *courage
*Ana* pluck, grit, guts, sand, *fortitude, backbone: hardihood, audacity, nerve (see TEMERITY)

**tend,** **attend, mind, watch** are comparable when they mean to take charge of or look after someone or something especially as a duty or in return for remuneration. **Tend** usually retains some notion of an earlier sense in which it means to pay attention; hence, it is appropriately used in situations to which this notion is relevant. Often it is used in reference to menial, unskilled, or routine employments and then typically takes for its object something that requires attention (as in anticipating wishes or needs, looking out for accidents, mishaps, or signs of danger, or maintaining effective mechanical operation); thus, one who *tends* a lock is employed to work the devices adjusting the level of the water in the canal when a boat approaches; a shepherd is one who *tends* a flock of sheep; a stoker *tends* a furnace and supplies it with fuel when needed ⟨standard roses *tended* by her hands—*Meredith*⟩ *Tend* is used in reference to the care of persons when a menial or a ministering rather than a professional relationship is implied ⟨employ a girl to *tend* to the children for a few hours each day⟩ ⟨sacrificing her leisure to *tend* the sick and helpless poor in their homes⟩ **Attend,** which is more likely to be colored by a sense meaning to take charge, is appropriate when the services given are of a professional character or are the prerogatives of a post that one holds as a mark of honor or merit ⟨the new doctor *attended* the governor in his last illness⟩ **Mind** is closer to *tend* than to *attend,* but it distinctively suggests a guarding or protecting (as from harm, injury, or failure) ⟨a neighbor *minds* the children when their mother is at work⟩ ⟨the men . . . were gone to dinner: I stayed to *mind* the furnace—*Edgeworth*⟩ **Watch** (see also SEE 2) may come close to *mind,* but it tends to imply a more constant or more professional relationship and to suggest a more definite need of vigilance and usually the intention of forestalling danger ⟨employed a man to *watch* the factory when the machines were idle⟩ ⟨wilt thou receive this weighty trust when I am o'er the sea? To *watch* and ward my castle strong, and to protect my land—*Scott*⟩

*Ana* *defend, protect, shield, guard, safeguard: *nurse, nurture, foster, cherish, cultivate

**tendency,** **trend, drift, tenor** can mean a movement or course having a particular direction and character or the direction and character which such a movement or course takes. **Tendency** usually implies an inherent or acquired inclination in a person or thing that causes him or it to move in a definite direction so long as no one or nothing interferes. Often, when used in reference to persons, the word means little more than *leaning, propensity,* or *disposition* ⟨a growing *tendency* to disastrously underestimate the potential strength of the United States—*Shirer*⟩ ⟨he worked to destroy the *tendency* to dreams in himself—*Anderson*⟩ More often, especially when used in reference to groups or communities or their activities or the course or direction they take with or without consciousness or intent, the term implies a driving force behind the direction or course taken and an insusceptibility to its being controlled or changed ⟨gave the King a policy at once plausible and insidious, temporizing and yet thick with *tendency*—*Hackett*⟩ ⟨the whole *tendency* of evolution is towards a diminishing birthrate—*Ellis*⟩ ⟨the *tendencies* which Lycurgus had endeavored to repress by external regulation reasserted themselves—*Dickinson*⟩ **Trend** is used primarily in reference to something that follows an irregular or winding course and denotes the general direction maintained in spite of these irregularities ⟨jagged ranges of mountains with a north and south *trend*⟩ In its extended use *trend* may differ from *tendency* in implying a direction subject to change through the interposition of a sufficiently strong force or agency, in implying a course taken at a given time by something subject to change and fluctuation, or in implying the general direction followed by a changing or fluctuating thing throughout its entire course or within given limits of space or of time ⟨the current *trends* toward intolerance and the garrison state—*Mowrer*⟩ ⟨Aristotle, the most balanced of all the Greek thinkers and the best exponent of the normal *trend* of their ideas—*Dickinson*⟩ **Drift** may apply to a tendency whose direction or course is determined by such external influences as a wind or the movement of flowing water or a fashion or a state of feeling ⟨the *drift* of public opinion went steadily against him—*Parrington*⟩ ⟨stoutly opposed the *drift* toward national prohibition and equal suffrage—*Sam Acheson*⟩ but it may apply also to the direction or course taken by something (as speech, writing, or teaching) that has a meaning, a purpose, or an objective which is not definitely stated or made clear but which is inferable; in this sense the word is scarcely distinguishable from *intention, purport,* or *import* ⟨for the *drift* of the Maker is dark, an Isis hid by a veil—*Tennyson*⟩ ⟨write it down . . . and then maybe I can get the *drift* of it—*Stafford*⟩ ⟨I see the whole *drift* of your argument—*Goldsmith*⟩ **Tenor** is a very close synonym of *drift* in this latter sense but it more often refers to utterances or documents and carries a much stronger implication of clearness of meaning or purport ⟨the general *tenor* . . . of the talks—*Bernard Smith*⟩ Both in this sense and in its more common sense of a course or movement having a particular clearly observable direction *tenor* carries a strong implication of continuity in that course and of absence of fluctuation in its direction; therefore it frequently suggests unaltered, often unalterable, procedure ⟨along the cool sequestered vale of life they kept the noiseless *tenor* of their way—*Gray*⟩ ⟨the village . . . was . . . away from the main road and the *tenor* of its simple agricultural economy had not been disturbed—*Iengar*⟩ ⟨even a foible is forgiven so long as it ruffles not the calm *tenor* of respectability—*Gogarty*⟩

*Ana* analogous words    *Ant* antonyms    *Con* contrasted words    See also explanatory notes facing page 1

*Ana* *leaning, propensity, penchant, proclivity: inclination, disposition, predisposition (see corresponding verbs at INCLINE): bent, turn, genius, aptitude (see GIFT)

**tender** *adj* Tender, compassionate, sympathetic, warm, warmhearted, responsive are comparable when they mean expressing or expressive of feeling that reveals affectionate interest in another especially in his joys, sorrows, or welfare. **Tender** implies a sensitiveness to influences that awaken gentle emotions (as love, affection, pity, or kindliness) and often a capacity for expressing such emotions with a delicacy and gentleness that are especially grateful to the person concerned ⟨his mother was very *tender* with him . . . . she saw the effort it was costing—*D. H. Lawrence*⟩ ⟨the inflections of their voices, when they were talking to each other very privately, were often *tender*, and these sudden surprising tendernesses secretly thrilled both of them—*Bennett*⟩ **Compassionate** implies a temperament or a disposition that is either easily moved by the sufferings or hardships of another or is quick to show pity with tenderness or mercy ⟨not cold and blaming . . . but an older and wiser brother, very *compassionate—Sinclair Lewis*⟩ ⟨to wax *compassionate* over a bird, and remain hard as flint to a beast, is possible only to humanity—*Repplier*⟩ **Sympathetic** is a more comprehensive term than *compassionate;* it implies a temperament or a disposition that enables one to enter into the life of another and share his sorrows, his joys, his interests, his antipathies, and his ways of thinking and feeling and to give that other the impression that he is not alone or that he is being fairly and justly understood ⟨thus a tête-à-tête with a man of similar tastes, who is just and yet *sympathetic*, critical yet appreciative . . . is a high intellectual pleasure—*Benson*⟩ ⟨though some considered her arrogant and forbidding, I found her personality *sympathetic—Edmund Wilson*⟩ *Sympathetic* is also applicable to attitudes or treatments that reveal a capacity for appraising or treating men and their experiences with great fairness and understanding ⟨a penetrating and profoundly *sympathetic* portrayal of the shifting, fluctuating impulses of a woman yielding both against and with her will—*Lowes*⟩ **Warm** implies a capacity for feeling and expressing love, affection, or interest with depth, ardor, or fervency; it suggests less softness of feeling or compassion than *tender*, but more heartiness, cordiality, or force ⟨a perfect gentleman, unaffected, *warm*, and obliging—*Austen*⟩ ⟨we common people are all one way or the other—*warm* or cold, passionate or frigid—*Hardy*⟩ ⟨a wave of genial friendliness flowed from the *warm* silly hearts of Britons towards the conquered foe—*Rose Macaulay*⟩ **Warmhearted** differs little from *warm* in meaning, but it usually carries a stronger implication of generosity, unselfishness, and, often, compassionateness ⟨she is *warmhearted*, impulsive, kind, and independent—*Kaplan*⟩ ⟨his portrait of the metropolis is *warmhearted* and accurate—*Bracker*⟩ **Responsive** differs from the preceding terms in usually suggesting sensitiveness to another's display of tenderness, compassion, sympathy, or warmth and a capacity for responding to that emotion; it stresses impressionableness and suggests a reaction, rather than a taking of the initiative ⟨rushed to Moscow as the new British ambassador in the hope of striking a more *responsive* chord among the Bolsheviks—*Shirer*⟩ ⟨she took up life, and became alert to the world again, *responsive*, like a ship in full sail, to every wind that blew—*Rose Macaulay*⟩

*Ana* gentle, lenient, mild, *soft: humane, benevolent, *charitable, altruistic: *pitiful, piteous

*Ant* callous: severe

**tender** *vb* *offer, proffer, present, prefer

*Ana* propose, purpose, design (see INTEND): *suggest,

intimate

**tender** *n* *overture, approach, advance, bid

**tenet** *doctrine, dogma

*Ana* belief, conviction, persuasion, view (see OPINION): *principle, fundamental, axiom

**tenor** drift, trend, *tendency

*Ana* movement, *motion, move: procedure, proceeding (see PROCESS): *meaning, significance, import

**tense** *adj* **1** *tight, taut

*Ana* strained (see corresponding noun at STRAIN): nervous, unquiet, uneasy, jittery (see IMPATIENT)

**2** *stiff, rigid, inflexible, stark, wooden

*Ana* tough, tenacious, stout (see STRONG): *firm, hard

*Ant* expansive —*Con* *loose, relaxed, lax, slack: *limp, flaccid, flabby

**tension** **1** *stress, strain, pressure

**2** equilibrium, equipoise, *balance, poise

**tentative** *provisional

*Ana* *temporary, ad interim, acting: testing, trying, demonstrating, proving (see PROVE)

*Ant* definitive

**tenuous** *thin, rare, slender, slim, slight

*Ana* ethereal, aerial, *airy

*Ant* dense

**tergiversation** *ambiguity, equivocation, double entendre

**term** *n* **1** end, confine, bound, *limit

**2** *word, vocable

**3** in plural form **terms** *condition, stipulation, provision, proviso, reservation, strings

*Ana* restriction, limit (see corresponding verbs at LIMIT): requisite, prerequisite, *requirement

**termagant** *virago, scold, shrew, vixen, amazon

**terminal** *adj* final, concluding, *last, latest, eventual, ultimate

*Ana* closing, ending, terminating, concluding (see CLOSE)

*Ant* initial

**terminate** end, *close, conclude, finish, complete

*Ana* *abolish, extinguish, abate: *stop, cease, discontinue

**termination** *end, ending, terminus

*Ana* result, issue, outcome (see EFFECT): concluding *or* conclusion, completion, closing *or* close (see corresponding verbs at CLOSE)

*Ant* inception: source

**terminus** *end, termination, ending

*Ant* starting point

**terrace** avenue, boulevard, drive, parkway, *road, roadway, highway, highroad, street, thoroughfare, byway, lane, alley, alleyway

**terrestrial** *earthly, earthy, mundane, worldly, sublunary

*Ant* celestial

**terrible** terrific, frightful, dreadful, *fearful, awful, horrible, horrific, shocking, appalling

*Ana* frightening, alarming, startling (see FRIGHTEN): agitating, upsetting, disturbing, perturbing (see DISCOMPOSE)

**terrific** terrible, frightful, dreadful, *fearful, horrible, horrific, awful, shocking, appalling

*Ana* frightening, alarming, terrorizing (see FRIGHTEN): agitating, upsetting, disquieting (see DISCOMPOSE)

**terrify** *frighten, fright, scare, alarm, terrorize, startle

*Ana* agitate, upset, perturb, disquiet (see DISCOMPOSE): *dismay, appall, horrify, daunt: cow, *intimidate, browbeat, bulldoze

**territory** domain, province, *field, sphere, bailiwick

*Ana* region, tract, *area, zone, belt: limits, confines, bounds (see singular nouns at LIMIT)

**terror** panic, consternation, *fear, dread, fright, alarm, dismay, horror, trepidation

*Ana* apprehensiveness, fearfulness (see corresponding

---

A colon (:) separates groups of words discriminated. An asterisk (*) indicates place of treatment of each group.

adjectives at FEARFUL): agitation, disquiet, perturbation, upsetting *or* upset (see corresponding verbs at DISCOMPOSE): appalling, daunting, dismaying (see DISMAY)

**terrorize** terrify, *frighten, fright, alarm, scare, startle, affray, affright
*Ana* *intimidate, cow, bulldoze, browbeat: coerce, compel, *force: drive, impel, *move: agitate, upset (see DISCOMPOSE)

**terse** *concise, succinct, laconic, summary, pithy, compendious
*Ana* *brief, short: compact, *close: *expressive, sententious, meaningful: *incisive, crisp, clear-cut

**test** *n* trial, proof, demonstration (see under PROVE)
*Ana* examination, inspection, scrutiny (see under SCRUTINIZE): verification, substantiation, corroboration, confirmation (see corresponding verbs at CONFIRM)

**test** *vb* try, *prove, demonstrate
*Ana* essay (see ATTEMPT *vb*): examine, inspect, *scrutinize: verify, substantiate, *confirm

**testimonial** *n* recommendation, *credential, character, reference
*Ana* commendation (see corresponding verb at COMMEND): approval, endorsement (see corresponding verbs at APPROVE)

**testimony** *evidence, deposition, affidavit
*Ana* trial, test, proof, demonstration (see under PROVE): witnessing *or* witness, attesting *or* attestation, certifying *or* certification, vouching for (see corresponding verbs at CERTIFY)

**testy** *irascible, choleric, splenetic, touchy, cranky, cross
*Ana* *irritable, peevish, snappish, waspish: hasty, sudden, impetuous (see PRECIPITATE): captious, carping, caviling, faultfinding (see CRITICAL)

**text** topic, argument, theme, *subject, matter, subject matter, motive, motif, leitmotiv

**thalassic** *aquatic, marine, oceanic, neritic, pelagic, abyssal

**thankful** *grateful
*Ana* appreciating *or* appreciative, valuing, prizing, cherishing, treasuring (see corresponding verbs at APPRECIATE): satisfied, content (see under SATISFY)
*Ant* thankless

**thaumaturgy** *magic, sorcery, witchcraft, witchery, wizardry, alchemy

**thaw** *vb* melt, *liquefy, deliquesce, fuse
*Ant* freeze

**theatrical** *adj* *dramatic, dramaturgic, melodramatic, histrionic
*Ana* *artificial, factitious: formal, conventional, *ceremonial, ceremonious: affecting, pretending, assuming, simulating, feigning (see ASSUME): *showy, pretentious, ostentatious

**theft, larceny, robbery, burglary** mean the act or crime of stealing, though they have differences in legal application. The same differences in implications and applications are observable in the agent nouns **thief, larcener** *or* **larcenist, robber, burglar**, denoting one who steals. **Theft** and **thief** are the most general and the least technical of these terms; they imply the taking and removing of another's property usually by stealth or without his knowledge and always without his consent. The terms are often so broad that they may include reference to any taking of another's property without his consent (as by pilfering, purloining, swindling, embezzling, or plagiarizing) ⟨the *theft* of a purse⟩ ⟨the *theft* of the city's money by grafters⟩ ⟨a *thief* removed his watch from his pocket⟩ **Larceny** and the less common agent nouns **larcener** and **larcenist** are legal terms implying direct theft but excluding such specialized forms as swindling, embezzlement, and plagiarizing. The terms connote an unlawful or felonious act, a removal of another's property from the place where it belongs, and complete possession, even for a moment, by the thief ⟨the shoplifter was not apprehended until she had left the store, so that there would be proof of *larceny*⟩ ⟨the maid was found guilty of *larceny*⟩ *Grand larceny* and *petty larceny* are common in ordinary use as indicating respectively a theft of an appreciable amount and a theft of a negligible amount. **Robbery** and **robber** in their precise legal use imply the taking of another's property from his person or in his presence by means of violence or intimidation ⟨highway *robbery*⟩ ⟨the paymaster was attacked and the payroll money was seized by armed *robbers*⟩ **Burglary** and **burglar** in legal use imply a breaking and entering with an intent to commit a felony, usually that of larceny or robbery. In the laws of different states and nations the detailed specifications of the crime, for example, the time of occurrence (nighttime often being stipulated) or the actual commission of the felony, may or may not be considered material to the charge ⟨the *burglary* of their home was committed during their absence for the evening⟩ ⟨she lived in constant fear of *burglars*⟩

**theme** 1 text, topic, argument, *subject, matter, subject matter, motive, motif, leitmotiv
2 composition, paper, *essay, article

**then** *therefore, hence, consequently, accordingly, so

**theorem** *principle, axiom, fundamental, law

**theoretical, speculative, academic** can be applied to minds, types of reasoning or philosophizing, or branches of learning as meaning concerned principally with abstractions and theories, sometimes at the expense of practical basis or application. **Theoretical** in its most usual and nonderogatory sense applies to branches of learning (as sciences) which deal with the inferences drawn from observed facts and from the results of experiments and with the laws or theories that explain them ⟨the distinguishing feature of *theoretical* science is the anticipation of facts from experience—*Georg von Wright*⟩ In this sense the term is often opposed to *applied*, which describes branches of learning which have to do with the putting of such laws and theories into use (as in mechanics, in industry, or in social reform) ⟨*theoretical* versus applied chemistry⟩ ⟨applied ethics is grounded upon *theoretical* ethics⟩ ⟨a purely *theoretical* definition would be that a person is emotionally sensitive when many stimuli produce emotions in him—*Russell*⟩ But *theoretical* often implies a divorce from actuality or reality that makes one unable to see things as they are and usually makes him see them only in the terms of preexistent ideas or theories. In this sense it is opposed to *practical* ⟨seems compelled to establish that . . . the book does have great practical importance in spite of its predominantly *theoretical* character—*M. G. White*⟩ ⟨things that had seemed drearily *theoretical*, dry, axiomatic, platitudinal, showed themselves to be great generalizations from a torrent of human effort and mortal endeavor—*Benson*⟩ **Speculative** (see also THOUGHTFUL 1) may go further than *theoretical* in suggesting a deep interest in theorizing or in forming theories or hypotheses and often additionally implies a daring use of the imagination ⟨the rights of man . . . were necessarily more abstract, more detached from usage and concrete applicability, more open to *speculative* interpretation—*Sabine*⟩ ⟨so vaguely *speculative* are they that their author found it necessary to explain them in lengthy prefaces—*W. J. Fisher*⟩ Often, however, there is very little difference evident in the use of these terms ⟨was a great inventor and builder, but in the *speculative* and theoretic side of science he had little interest—*Buchan*⟩

⟨this is about as far as *speculative* chemistry will take one in this field; and the rest of the subject is experimental—*Furnas*⟩ **Academic** (see also PEDANTIC) carries a much stronger implication of a habit of looking at a thing, or things in general, abstractly, without reference to real life or practical concerns, and often in terms of the theories and dicta of a particular school (as of literature or art) ⟨*academic* thinkers and schoolmen, men whom the free spaces of thought frightened and who felt safe only behind secure fences—*Parrington*⟩ ⟨apart from its *academic* tendency to divorce form from matter, I cannot believe that any such theory of poetry, built on a neurosis, is admirable or adequate—*Day Lewis*⟩
*Ana* conjectural, hypothetical (see SUPPOSED): postulated, premised, presupposed (see PRESUPPOSE)
**theory** *hypothesis, law
*Ana* judgment, conclusion, deduction, inference (see under INFER): postulate, presumption, assumption, presupposition (see under PRESUPPOSE)
*Ant* practice
**therefore, hence, consequently, then, accordingly, so** are adverbs used as connectives to indicate logical or causal sequence. They vary in the degree of closeness of connection suggested as well as in the kind of sequence implied. *Therefore* and *hence* are employed chiefly to indicate that what follows is a necessary deduction from what has preceded. **Therefore** commonly introduces a conclusion ⟨all men are rational beings, John Jones is a man, *therefore* John Jones is a rational being⟩ **Hence,** though often interchangeable with *therefore,* stresses the importance of what precedes ⟨both statements may be false, but both cannot be true since they are contradictory; *hence,* if A be true, B is false, or if B be true, A is false⟩ **Consequently,** though often used to introduce a deduction, does not always imply necessity in the inference. Rather it suggests good grounds for the conclusion or implies a strong antecedent probability ⟨he said he would come; *consequently* I expect him⟩ It also may indicate that what follows is a result of what precedes ⟨he said he would come; *consequently* I am waiting for him⟩ **Then,** when used to indicate logical sequence, is employed chiefly in the consequent clause or conclusion in a conditional sentence ⟨if A is true, *then* B is false⟩ **Accordingly** usually indicates logical or causal sequence but connotes naturalness or usualness in what follows as a consequence rather than necessity or inevitability ⟨he said he was hungry; *accordingly* they shared their meager lunch with him⟩ **So** is typically found in more casual expression and is often indefinite in its suggestion of which kind of sequence is indicated ⟨the day was fine and *so* we set out⟩
**thesis** dissertation, treatise, monograph, disquisition, *discourse
*Ana* *exposition: *argumentation, disputation: article, paper, *essay
**thespian** *actor, player, impersonator, trouper, performer, mummer, mime, mimic
**thick** 1 thick, thickset, *stocky, chunky, stubby, squat, dumpy
*Ana* *broad, wide, deep
*Ant* thin —*Con* slender, slim, slight, tenuous, rare (see THIN *adj*): *lean, spare
2 compact, *close, dense
*Ana* condensed, compressed, contracted (see CONTRACT *vb*): concentrated, compacted (see COMPACT *vb*)
3 close, confidential, chummy, *familiar, intimate
**thickset** *stocky, thick, chunky, stubby, squat, dumpy
*Ana* bulky, *massive, massy: *fleshy, stout, portly, plump
**thief** robber, burglar (see under THEFT)
**thin** *adj* Thin, slender, slim, slight, tenuous, rare are in

general referable not only to measure in width or amount but also to quantity or quality and agree in meaning not broad, not thick, not abundant, nor dense. **Thin** basically implies comparatively little extension between two surfaces of a thing ⟨a *thin* layer of cement⟩ ⟨a *thin* stratum of rock⟩ ⟨a *thin* coin⟩ or the comparatively small diameter of a cylindrical or nearly cylindrical thing in proportion to its height or length ⟨a *thin* body⟩ ⟨the *thin* trunk of a tree⟩ ⟨*thin* wire⟩ In its extended senses the term usually implies the lack of the flesh or substance that fills out a thing to its normal or usual extent and gives it fullness, richness, substantiality, compactness, or density ⟨a *thin* face⟩ ⟨*thin* wine⟩ ⟨a *thin* argument⟩ ⟨a *thin* forest⟩ ⟨*thin* hair⟩ ⟨*thin*, pebbly earth, which was merely the rock pulverized by weather—*Cather*⟩ ⟨like the air of a mountaintop—*thin*, but pure and bracing—*Inge*⟩ ⟨would make a sound as *thin* and sweet as trees in country lanes—*Millay*⟩ **Slender,** as applied to the bodies of men and of animals, implies leanness or spareness without any suggestion of gauntness or lankiness and usually carries a distinct connotation of gracefulness and of good proportions ⟨a *slender* girl⟩ ⟨a *slender* dog⟩ ⟨*slender* white hands—*Anderson*⟩ *Slender* is preferred to *thin* in describing things of narrow extension when the thinness is an element of beauty and gracefulness of line ⟨a *slender* vase⟩ ⟨the *slender* legs of a Sheraton chair⟩ ⟨the pure *slender* lines of water falling from the abrupt wooded crag—*Binyon*⟩ In its extended use *slender* is often employed with little distinction from *thin*, but it is often preferred when quantity or amount rather than quality is stressed ⟨a few attempts had been made . . . with *slender* success—*Macaulay*⟩ ⟨packed up her *slender* belongings—*Kipling*⟩ ⟨with *slender* forces he had to face the formidable Sextus—*Buchan*⟩ ⟨such a vision [of life] as might come as the result of few or *slender* experiences—*T. S. Eliot*⟩ **Slim** differs little from *slender* when applied to the figures of persons or animals; it may sometimes suggest fragility or gauntness rather than grace, and lack of flesh rather than excellent proportions. In its extended senses, however, *slim* usually carries a clearer implication of meagerness or scantiness than *slender*, which, though it suggests smallness in amount or quantity, implies less commonly than *slim* a falling short of adequacy or sufficiency; thus, *slim* resources are by suggestion more meager than *slender* resources ⟨he has a *slim* chance of recovery⟩ ⟨his hopes for success are *slim*⟩ ⟨there was a *slim* attendance at the meeting⟩ **Slight** through most of its variations in meaning carries a more obvious implication of smallness than of thinness; when applied to persons, it seldom suggests height or length, as *slender* usually does or *slim* sometimes does ⟨a *slight*, middle-aged man⟩ When applied to things, it is often derogatory and usually implies a failure to come up to a level of what is commensurate, adequate, or significant ⟨a *slight* and transient fancy—*Arnold*⟩ ⟨a *slight* difference⟩ ⟨his success was *slight*⟩ ⟨there is . . . ground to recognize a *slight* intellectual superiority in the upper social class—*Ellis*⟩ ⟨he liked the folksong, because it was a *slight* thing, born of immediate impulse—*Huxley*⟩ **Tenuous** basically implies extreme thinness or even absence of perceptible thickness; the term is literally applicable to things (as lines, cords, or wires) of great length or height and of minute diameter ⟨the most *tenuous* of threads⟩ ⟨as *tenuous* as the filament of a spider's web⟩ or to fabrics and textiles which are exceedingly sheer or gauzy ⟨*tenuous* fabrics such as tulle and chiffon⟩ In its extended senses *tenuous* often describes something which covers an expanse but lacks density, compactness, or solidity ⟨some [stars] are extremely dense and compact, others extremely

---

A colon (:) separates groups of words discriminated. An asterisk (*) indicates place of treatment of each group.

tenuous—*Eddington*⟩ ⟨*tenuous* evening mists—*Darrow*⟩ or something which is so finespun or so fine-drawn as to be exceedingly subtle, abstruse, or visionary ⟨a *tenuous* idealism—*Binyon*⟩ ⟨poetry . . . so *tenuous* in thought and feeling that only the most exquisite diction can justify its perpetuation in cold print—*Grandgent*⟩ ⟨I did not despise the golden, *tenuous* imaginings . . . starting in my own spirit—*Galsworthy*⟩ **Rare** in the sense of rarefied (see also INFREQUENT, CHOICE) is applied chiefly to gases and especially to air ⟨he was miles high . . . nearly slumping in the *rare* air—*Cozzens*⟩ In its uncommon extended use it suggests tenuity or sometimes extreme exaltation or elevation ⟨reared in the *rarest* air of German intellectualism—*Time*⟩ ⟨if we try to express almost any poems of his in prose, we find it impossible; its *rare* spirit evaporates in the process—*Day Lewis*⟩

*Ana* *lean, spare, lank, lanky, gaunt: *meager, exiguous, scanty: cadaverous, pinched, wasted, *haggard: attenuated, extenuated, diluted (see THIN *vb*)

*Ant* thick

**thin** *vb* **Thin, attenuate, extenuate, dilute, rarefy.** **Thin** is the most inclusive of these terms and is interchangeable with any of the others, though not without some loss of precision or of specific connotations. Basically it implies reduction in thickness or in density; in extended use it implies a comparable diminution (as of strength, depth, or intensity) ⟨*thin* a forest by removing surplus trees⟩ ⟨*thin* wine by adding water⟩ ⟨the voice *thins* when one raises its pitch⟩ ⟨*thin* paint with turpentine⟩ ⟨constant use *thins* silver⟩ **Attenuate** implies thinning as the result of some such process as drawing out, spinning fine, or culturing (as a strain of bacteria) repeatedly or as the effect of conditions (as disease or starvation) which emaciate ⟨*attenuate* wire by drawing it through successively smaller holes⟩ ⟨hammer brass in order to *attenuate* it⟩ ⟨a wave of current *attenuates* in magnitude and phase as it travels along a transmission line⟩ ⟨*attenuate* a virus by heating it⟩ ⟨the powerful frame *attenuated* by spare living—*Dickens*⟩ In its frequent extended use *attenuate* implies the loss of properties that are necessary to a thing's strength, richness, effectiveness, or vitality, and it often connotes overrefining, oversubtilizing, or overemphasis of an opposing quality ⟨we may reject and reject till we *attenuate* history into sapless meagerness —*Palgrave*⟩ ⟨if she had had a little more self-control she would have *attenuated* the emotion to nothing by sheer reasoning—*Hardy*⟩ ⟨illusions which science can *attenuate* or destroy, but which it is powerless to enrich—*Krutch*⟩ **Extenuate** in a somewhat learned use can suggest attrition either by literally emaciating and exhausting (see also PALLIATE) ⟨peasants . . . so *extenuated* by hunger that they could scarcely hold the spade—*Lecky*⟩ or by a gradual diminishing of a thing's importance or significance ⟨the . . . tendency . . . to *extenuate* the responsibility of human nature, not merely on the moral side, but equally on the spiritual side—*Mackenzie*⟩ **Dilute** implies a thinning of what is concentrated by the addition or, in extended use, sometimes by the influence of something that weakens it, neutralizes it, or destroys its vigor or intensity ⟨*dilute* peppermint oil with alcohol⟩ ⟨*dilute* hydrochloric acid with water⟩ ⟨the pioneer spirit has been *diluted* by new race mixtures, its confidence shaken by new social trends—*Amer. Guide Series: Minn.*⟩ ⟨the rough, spontaneous conversation of men they [clergymen] do not hear, but only a mincing and *diluted* speech—*Emerson*⟩ **Rarefy** implies a thinning in density and usually an expansion in volume or a decrease in weight or pressure ⟨the *rarefied* air of mountainous regions⟩ ⟨the expansive power of moisture *rarefied* by heat—*Macaulay*⟩

The word occurs in extended use chiefly with reference to ideas, emotions, and intellectual powers, sometimes suggesting their spiritualization or refinement and the elimination of all grossness and impurity and sometimes imputing to them a vaporous or tenuous quality ⟨plain truths lose much of their weight when they are *rarefied* into subleties—*Cudworth*⟩ ⟨love is a gentle flame that *rarefies* and expands her whole being—*Hazlitt*⟩

*Ana* reduce, lessen, diminish, *decrease: *liquefy, melt

*Ant* thicken

**thing** 1 matter, concern, business, *affair

2 **Thing, object, article** are comprehensive terms applicable to whatever is apprehended as having actual, distinct, and demonstrable existence. They vary, however, in their range of application. **Thing** is the term of widest reference. In its most inclusive sense it need not imply direct knowledge through the senses but is equally applicable to something so known and to something the existence of which is inferred from its signs or its effects; thus, one thinks of the state, the church, literature, and the law as *things* rather than as ideas or abstractions; a friend's affection is as real a *thing* as is his house or his hand; one distinguishes a word from the *thing* it names ⟨name the *things* that are on this table⟩ ⟨wanted to do the right *thing*⟩ ⟨a blind person recognizes *things* through such qualities as shape, texture, smell, taste, and sound⟩ In somewhat more restricted use *thing* can denote specifically an entity having existence in space or time as distinguished from one existing only in thought ⟨virtue is not a *thing* but an attribute of a *thing*⟩ or in still more restricted use an inanimate entity and especially a material possession as distinguished from living beings and especially persons ⟨more interested in *things* than in human beings⟩ Often the word is used idiomatically to mention without specifically identifying an item that cannot or need not be further identified or whose nature is implicit in the context; thus, in "be sure to wear warm *things*," clothing is implied; in "bring in the tea *things*," the necessary collection of dishes, implements, and foods is implied ⟨what's that *thing* in your hand?⟩ Occasionally *thing* may be used in reference to persons when contempt is expressed or derogation intended ⟨do you call that *thing* a man?⟩ **Object** has for its primary implications externality to the mind or existence outside the observer. In philosophic and scientific use it is applied to something that is put before one as an entity capable of being seen, observed, or contemplated ⟨a thinker may make an abstraction, such as love, art, or justice, an *object* of thought⟩ ⟨modern physicists are concentrating on the atom as an *object* of study⟩ This basic implication of *object* is its chief distinction from *thing* when either word is used to denote something that can be perceived by one or more of the senses. For *object* in this, its ordinary sense, is applied chiefly to what has body and usually substance and shape ⟨he groped his way in the darkness with hands outstretched to detect any *objects* in his path⟩ ⟨in the glare of the torch they saw moving *objects* in the distance⟩ **Article** is the most limited in its range of application, being used chiefly of objects that are thought of as members of a group, kind, or class ⟨meat is an important *article* of food⟩ ⟨*articles* of merchandise⟩ ⟨a chair is an *article* of furniture⟩ ⟨*articles* of apparel⟩

*Ana* *item, detail, particular

**think** 1 **Think, conceive, imagine, fancy, realize, envisage, envision** are comparable when they mean to form an idea or notion of something in the mind. **Think,** the most general and least explicit word of this group, may imply nothing more than the entrance of an idea or notion into one's mind ⟨please do not *think* of it⟩ but often it suggests some consideration or reflection typically resulting in a decision or judgment ⟨*think* one plot better than another⟩ ⟨*think* that a change in occupation is desirable⟩ or it implies a conscious mental act such as a recalling or recollection ⟨try to *think* how the accident happened⟩ or a bringing of a definite picture or a clear idea into one's mind ⟨one cannot *think* infinity⟩ ⟨*think* what a sacrifice he has made⟩ or the framing of a purpose or intention ⟨he . . . *thought* he would send for his mother; and then he *thought* he would not—*Hardy*⟩ **Conceive** implies a bringing forth in the mind of an organized product of thought (as an idea, a plan, a project, or a design); often the term suggests the growth and development of that idea as the mind dwells upon it and brings it into being ⟨it was among the ruins of the Capitol that I first *conceived* the idea of a work which has amused and exercised near twenty years of my life—*Gibbon*⟩ ⟨they're philosophers . . . . They can't help *conceiving* the highest good in terms of intelligence and morality—*Wouk*⟩ **Imagine** carries a stronger implication than *conceive* does of visualization or of definitely creating a mental image of a thing; thus, one can *conceive*, but scarcely *imagine*, a world of more than three dimensions ⟨the girl was in his mind . . . . He couldn't help it, *imagined* seeing her in the things that were hanging on the line—*Malamud*⟩ ⟨I could *imagine* easily original plots for stories or plays, but never received any impulse to write them—*Æ*⟩ **Fancy** (see also LIKE) may differ little from *imagine*, but it commonly suggests unreality or a degree of untruth in the idea conceived or the image developed; sometimes it even implies a tendency to cut oneself off from facts and to be governed by one's dreams or desires ⟨*fancied* himself as an infallible prophet . . . and master of such powers that they awed even him—*Ogdon*⟩ ⟨some *fancied* she might marry again, but others didn't think she ever would, being too independent—*Phillpotts*⟩ **Realize** (see also REALIZE 1) implies a very vivid conception or imagination through which a grasp of the significance of a thing is attained ⟨burning with the passion of infinitely *realized* and therefore eternally restless love—*Sullivan*⟩ ⟨people say that they cannot *realize* these big numbers. But that is the last thing anyone wants to do with big numbers—to *realize* them—*Eddington*⟩ **Envisage** and **envision** imply a conception or imagination actually or potentially so clear or so detailed that one does or can contemplate it as though it were before one ⟨education . . . as Hitler *envisaged* it, was not to be confined to stuffy classrooms but to be furthered by a Spartan, political and martial training—*Shirer*⟩ ⟨*envisaging* the future without fear—*Bennett*⟩ ⟨he had *envisioned* the starred face of the night with high exaltation and noble inspiration—*Wolfe*⟩

*Ana* *consider, weigh, study, contemplate: *understand, comprehend, appreciate: surmise, *conjecture, guess

**2 Think, cogitate, reflect, reason, speculate, deliberate** can all mean to use one's powers of conception, judgment, or inference in regard to any matter or subject which concerns one or interests one. **Think** is the general term implying mental activity for the sake of forming ideas or of reaching conclusions; the term need not suggest closeness of application, clearness in the ideas formed, or correctness in the conclusions reached, though when used without qualification it often does suggest the attainment or approximation of these ⟨when I was a child, I spoke as a child, I understood as a child, I *thought* as a child: but when I became a man, I put away childish things—*1 Cor* 13:11⟩ ⟨colleges are places where at least some men learn to *think*—*Lippmann*⟩ ⟨I am even prepared to be told that when you paid the price of this book you were paying me to *think* for you—*Shaw*⟩ **Cogitate** places more stress on the process than upon the results of thinking; it is often used to suggest the appearance or the atmosphere of profound but not necessarily productive thinking ⟨still *cogitating* and looking for an explanation in the fire—*Dickens*⟩ ⟨Mrs. Berry had not *cogitated* long ere she pronounced distinctly and without a shadow of dubiosity: "My opinion is . . . "—*Meredith*⟩ **Reflect** usually implies a turning of one's thoughts back upon or back to something that exists, has occurred, or needs reexamining; it implies quiet, unhurried, and serious consideration or study ⟨stood *reflecting* on the circumstances of the preceding hours—*Hardy*⟩ ⟨all the most important things in his life, [he] sometimes *reflected*, had been determined by chance—*Cather*⟩ ⟨began to . . . study its organization, *reflect* on its psychology and political techniques and ponder the results—*Shirer*⟩ **Reason** implies consecutive logical thought, beginning with a postulate, a premise, or definite data or evidence and proceeding through inferences drawn from these to a conclusion or judgment ⟨since, where all is uncertain, we must *reason* from what is probable of human nature—*Quiller-Couch*⟩ ⟨no man as near death as I was feeling, could, I *reasoned*, be absorbed by such trifles—*Lucas*⟩ **Speculate** implies the processes of reasoning but stresses either the uncertainty of the premises or the incompleteness of the data and therefore usually imputes a hypothetical or theoretical character to the conclusions reached ⟨the two women *speculated* with deep anxiety on whether or not little Pamela had died of exposure—*Cheever*⟩ ⟨it is interesting to *speculate* whether it is not a misfortune that two of the greatest masters of diction in our language, Milton and Dryden, triumph with a dazzling disregard of the soul—*T. S. Eliot*⟩ **Deliberate** suggests slow and careful thought or reasoning and fair consideration of various aspects in an attempt to reach a conclusion often on a matter of public interest ⟨lawmakers . . . can—and do—spend huge amounts of time *deliberating* matters of absolute insignificance—*Armbrister*⟩ ⟨please you, *deliberate* a day or two—*Shak.*⟩ ⟨the future relations of the two countries could now be *deliberated* on with a hope of settlement—*Froude*⟩

*Ana* *ponder, meditate, muse, ruminate: *infer, deduce, conclude, judge

**thirst** *vb* hunger, pine, yearn, *long, hanker
*Ana* covet, crave, *desire, wish, want

**though, although, albeit** introduce subordinate clauses stating something that is or may be true in spite of what is asserted in the main clause. **Though,** the most widely used of these words, can introduce a clause that states an established fact or one that offers only a supposition, either a hypothesis or an admission of possibility or probability ⟨*though* philology was Bede's chief interest and concern, he by no means stopped there—*Malone*⟩ ⟨remembered a great deal of classical literature, badly taught *though* it was—*Highet*⟩ ⟨let us not defer our trip, *though* it rain tomorrow⟩ **Although,** which is freely interchangeable with *though*, is often preferred when it introduces an assertion of fact and when the subordinate clause precedes the main clause ⟨*although* they worked hard . . . their movements seemed painfully slow—*Forester*⟩ ⟨*although* the war was still on, the diamond trade began to show signs of recovery—*Hahn*⟩ **Albeit** is especially appropriate when the idea of admitting something that seems a contradiction is stressed ⟨a worthy fellow, *albeit* he comes on angry purpose now—*Shak.*⟩ ⟨passages of moving, *albeit* restrained, eloquence—*N. Y. Herald Tribune Book Rev.*⟩

**thought** *idea, concept, conception, notion, impression
*Ana* *opinion, view, sentiment, belief, conviction, persuasion

---

A colon (:) separates groups of words discriminated. An asterisk (*) indicates place of treatment of each group.

**thoughtful** 1 Thoughtful, reflective, speculative, contemplative, meditative, pensive can be applied to persons or their moods, attitudes, expressions, and utterances as meaning characterized by or showing the power to engage in thought, especially in concentrated thinking. Thoughtful may imply either the act of thinking concentratedly or the disposition to apply oneself to the careful and serious consideration of problems or questions at issue ⟨he has a shrewd rather than a *thoughtful* face⟩ ⟨Marlowe—not excepting Shakespeare or Chapman, the most *thoughtful* and philosophical mind, though immature, among the Elizabethan dramatists—*T. S. Eliot*⟩ ⟨a *thoughtful* book on a serious subject—*Seltzer*⟩ Reflective differs from *thoughtful* in its stronger implication of orderly processes of thought, such as analysis and logical reasoning, and in its suggestion of a definite aim, such as the understanding of a thing's nature or of its relation to other things or the reaching of a definite conclusion ⟨men of *reflective* and analytical habit, eager to rationalize its [plutocracy's] instincts and to bring it into some sort of relationship to the main streams of human thought—*Mencken*⟩ Speculative implies a tendency or inclination to think about things of which direct knowledge is either impossible or so limited that any conclusions are bound to be uncertain ⟨economics is regarded by many persons as a *speculative* science⟩ ⟨*speculative* writing about the state—*Frankfurter*⟩ Hence the term often implies theorizing or conjecturing without consideration of the evidence or with little attention to the evidence ⟨about a thousand practical and positive topics the Frenchman, who speaks from experience and examination, takes our views *speculative* and immature—*Brownell*⟩ ⟨the philosophical background of Chinese culture has always tended to create reflective rather than *speculative* thinkers—*Hart*⟩ Contemplative carries a stronger implication than the other words of an attention fixed on the object of one's thoughts; it may imply as its object something perceivable by the senses or something abstract yet comprehensible by the mind, or it may suggest a habit of mind ⟨a *contemplative* thinker, withdrawn from active life—*Theodore Spencer*⟩ ⟨practical curiosity becomes *contemplative* and examines things for their own sake when . . . man . . . having arrived at the stage of ideas and thought, applies them to the data presented by sensible experience—*Alexander*⟩ ⟨the *contemplative* life which is concerned with human feeling and thought and beauty—*Ruskin*⟩ Meditative, except in religious use, where it comes very close to *contemplative,* usually implies a tendency to ponder or muse over something without necessarily implying any such intellectual purpose as understanding a thing or reaching a conclusion regarding it. The term therefore often comes close to *thoughtful,* though it usually implies some consecutive reasoning and sometimes suggests pleasure rather than seriousness in the exercise of thought ⟨indulge in many a *meditative* walk⟩ ⟨a *meditative* temperament⟩ ⟨sympathies . . . that steal upon the *meditative* mind, and grow with thought—*Wordsworth*⟩ Pensive is not always clearly distinguishable from *meditative,* though at times it carries a stronger suggestion of dreaminess, of wistfulness, or of melancholy ⟨for oft, when on my couch I lie in vacant or in *pensive* mood—*Wordsworth*⟩ ⟨silent and *pensive,* idle, restless, slow—*Byron*⟩
*Ana* *serious, earnest, grave, sober: engrossed, absorbed, *intent: *abstracted, preoccupied

2 Thoughtful, considerate, attentive are applied to persons and their acts in the sense of being mindful of the comfort or happiness of others. Thoughtful usually implies unselfish concern for others or the capacity for anticipating another's needs ⟨in his *thoughtful* wish of escorting them

through the streets of the rough, riotous town—*Gaskell*⟩ Considerate stresses concern for the feelings of others or thoughtfulness in preventing or in relieving pain, suffering, or distress ⟨the French poor people are very *considerate* where they see suffering—*Meredith*⟩ ⟨too courteous and *considerate* to make stubborn subordinates bend properly to his will—*Nevins & Commager*⟩ Attentive emphasizes continuous thoughtfulness or implies repeated acts of kindness or courtesy ⟨Emmy had always been good and *attentive* to him. It was she who ministered to his comforts—*Thackeray*⟩ ⟨I was never more surprised than by his behavior to us. It was more than civil; it was really *attentive*—*Austen*⟩
*Ana* solicitous, concerned, careful, anxious (see under CARE): courteous, polite, gallant, chivalrous (see CIVIL)
*Ant* thoughtless

**thoughtless** *careless, heedless, inadvertent
*Ana* rash, reckless, foolhardy (see ADVENTUROUS): *indifferent, unconcerned, incurious, aloof: lax, remiss, *negligent
*Ant* thoughtful

**thrash** *vb* 1 *beat, pound, pummel, buffet, baste, belabor
*Ana* *strike, smite, slug, slap
2 flourish, brandish, shake, *swing, wave
*Ana* wield, manipulate, swing, ply, *handle

**threadbare** 1 *shabby, dilapidated, dingy, faded, seedy
*Ana* damaged, injured, impaired (see INJURE): worn (see HAGGARD)
2 shopworn, *trite, hackneyed, stereotyped
*Ana* antiquated, obsolete, archaic (see OLD): exhausted, depleted, drained, impoverished (see DEPLETE)

**threaten,** menace both mean to announce or forecast (as by word or look) an impending or probable infliction (as an evil or an injury). Threaten basically implies an attempt to dissuade or influence by promising punishment or the infliction of reprisals upon those who disobey an injunction or perform acts objectionable to the speaker ⟨the magistrates . . . solicited, commanded, *threatened,* urged—*Milton*⟩ ⟨another form of lying, which is extremely bad for the young, is to *threaten* punishments you do not mean to inflict—*Russell*⟩ However the term has been so extended in its meaning that it is often used with reference to things (as events, conditions, or symptoms) which presage or otherwise indicate something, and typically something dire or disturbing, to be about to or likely to happen ⟨overcast skies that *threaten* rain⟩ ⟨lived on the margin of survival, constantly *threatened* by famine and disease—*Geddes*⟩ ⟨without invoking the rule of strict construction I think that "so near as to obstruct" means so near as actually to obstruct—and not merely near enough to *threaten* a possible obstruction—*Justice Holmes*⟩ Menace is a somewhat more literary term than *threaten,* and it carries a much weaker implication of an attempt to dissuade or influence and a much stronger suggestion of an alarming or a definitely hostile character or aspect ⟨conditions that *menace* our liberty⟩ ⟨is it not experience which renders a dog apprehensive of pain, when you *menace* him?—*Locke*⟩ ⟨the devastating weapons which are at present being developed may *menace* every part of the world—*Attlee*⟩
*Ana* *intimidate, bulldoze, cow, browbeat: forebode, portend, presage, augur (see FORETELL): *warn, forewarn, caution

**thrifty** economical, *sparing, frugal
*Ana* provident, prudent, foresighted (see under PRUDENCE): saving, preserving, conserving (see SAVE)
*Ant* wasteful

**thrill** *vb* Thrill, electrify, enthuse are comparable when they mean to fill with emotions that stir or excite physically

---

*Ana* analogous words    *Ant* antonyms    *Con* contrasted words    See also explanatory notes facing page 1

and mentally or to be stirred by such emotions. **Thrill** suggests pervasion by emotions that set one atingle or aquiver (as with pleasure, horror, or excitement); commonly it implies an agreeable sensation even when the exciting cause is potentially distressing or painful ⟨a *thrilling* detective story⟩ ⟨by carefully copying what other people did, she would manage to get through . . . this *thrilling*, agonizing, exquisite ordeal—*Sackville-West*⟩ ⟨why should not mind be able to pass on to mind its *thrilled* sense of a storm or a flower . . .?—*Montague*⟩ **Electrify** differs from *thrill* in suggesting effects comparable to those produced by an electric current that shocks rather than stuns; it implies a sudden, startling, and violent stimulation by a power that for the time being holds one obedient to its will or under its sway ⟨the blue-eyed girl whose silvery tones and immense vitality had *electrified* audiences—*Tomkins*⟩ ⟨she was not eating anything, she was using up all her vitality to *electrify* these heavy lads into speech—*Cather*⟩ **Enthuse** can be used effectively in respect to an arousing of enthusiasm in someone or an experiencing of enthusiasm about something ⟨Lubichov, *enthused* by the music of his native land, beat his baton with more and more zest—*Bambrick*⟩ ⟨as a dogmatic theologian, the Bishop did not *enthuse* himself and he did not understand other people's enthusiasms—*Frank O'Connor*⟩ ⟨the War Dance [among Indians] was a ceremony to arouse the community and *enthuse* the warriors—*Wissler*⟩
*Ana* excite, stimulate, galvanize, quicken (see PROVOKE): *stir, arouse, rouse, rally: penetrate, pierce, probe (see ENTER): quiver, tremble, shiver (see SHAKE)

**thrive** *succeed, prosper, flourish
*Ana* *increase, augment, multiply, enlarge
*Ant* languish

**throb** *vb* beat, *pulsate, pulse, palpitate
**throb** *n* beat, pulsation, pulse, palpitation (see under PULSATE)

**throe** *pain, ache, pang, twinge, stitch

**throng** *n* *crowd, press, crush, mob, rout, horde
*Ana* *multitude, army, host, legion: assembly, congregation, gathering, collection (see under GATHER)

**throttle** *vb* *suffocate, asphyxiate, stifle, smother, choke, strangle

**through** *by, with

**throw,** cast, fling, hurl, pitch, toss, sling can all mean to cause to move swiftly forward, sideways, upward, or downward by a propulsive movement (as of the arm) or by means of a propelling instrument or agency. **Throw,** the general word, is often interchangeable with the others; basically it implies a distinctive propelling motion of the bent arm and wrist, but in practice it is applicable in respect to almost any propulsive action ⟨people who live in glass houses should not *throw* stones⟩ ⟨the fire engine *throws* a long stream of water⟩ ⟨this gun *throws* a huge shell⟩ ⟨*threw* off his coat⟩ ⟨the skeptic cannot *throw* his opponent if his own feet are in the air—*Inge*⟩ **Cast** is sometimes interchangeable with *throw,* but it typically is used when what is thrown is light ⟨*cast* a net⟩ ⟨*cast* dice⟩ and is either directly aimed ⟨*cast* his line in angling⟩ or scattered more or less carefully ⟨*cast* seed⟩ or is thrown only in a figurative sense ⟨*cast* a black look⟩ **Fling** implies more violence and less control in propulsion than either of the preceding words; it often implies a force gained from strong emotion (as anger, contempt, or enthusiasm) ⟨then he loathed his own beauty, and, *flinging* the mirror on the floor, crushed it into silver splinters beneath his heel—*Wilde*⟩ ⟨the opening pages irritated him . . . in the end, in exasperation, he *flung* them aside—*Malamud*⟩ **Hurl** stresses driving and im-

petuous force that makes for speed and distance in throwing ⟨him the Almighty Power *hurled* headlong flaming from the ethereal sky—*Milton*⟩ **Pitch** sometimes means no more than to throw lightly or carelessly ⟨could take up a sack of grain and with ease *pitch* it over a packsaddle—*Zane Grey*⟩ ⟨when you get your new outfit, *pitch* out that dress—*Ethel Wilson*⟩ but distinctively it more than any of the preceding words stresses a sense of direction and a definite target in throwing ⟨*pitch* horseshoes⟩ ⟨*pitching* hay onto the high load⟩ ⟨*pitching* matchbooks at a crack . . . was the favorite sport—*James Jones*⟩ ⟨possible . . . to run up to their enemy's lines and roll, bowl, or *pitch* their grenades among the legs of their opponents—*Wintringham*⟩ **Toss** implies light, careless, or more or less aimless throwing ⟨he . . . *tossed* me some pieces of money—*Dickens*⟩ ⟨she rested on a log and *tossed* the fresh chips—*Frost*⟩ ⟨*toss* a coin to decide who should go⟩ The term often also suggests a throwing to and fro or up and down ⟨an hour's play in *tossing* a ball⟩ ⟨they . . . discussed a doubt and *tossed* it to and fro—*Tennyson*⟩ **Sling** suggests propelling with a sweeping or swinging motion, usually with force and suddenness ⟨grabbed the boy's collar and *slung* him against the wall⟩
*Ana* drive, impel (see MOVE *vb*): propel, thrust, shove, *push: heave, raise, *lift, boost

**throwback** *reversion, atavism

**throw up** *belch, burp, vomit, disgorge, regurgitate, spew

**thrust** *vb* *push, shove, propel
*Ana* *throw, cast, fling: drive, impel, *move: *enter, penetrate, pierce

**thud** *vb* thump, knock, rap, *tap
*Ana* hit, *strike, smite: pound, *beat
**thud** *n* thump, knock, rap, tap (see under TAP *vb*)
*Ana* slumping, falling (see FALL)

**thump** *vb* thud, knock, rap, *tap
*Ana* pound, *beat, belabor: punch, smite, *strike
**thump** *n* thud, knock, rap, tap (see under TAP *vb*)
*Ana* pounding, beating, pummeling (see BEAT *vb*)

**thwart** foil, *frustrate, baffle, balk, circumvent, outwit
*Ana* *hinder, impede, obstruct, block, bar: defeat, overcome, surmount (see CONQUER): check, curb, *restrain: *prevent, forestall, anticipate

**ticket** *n* mark, brand, stamp, label, tag (see under MARK *vb*)
**ticket** *vb* *mark, brand, stamp, label, tag
*Ana* affix, attach, *fasten: append, *add

**tickle** *please, regale, gratify, delight, rejoice, gladden
*Ana* divert, *amuse, entertain: *thrill, electrify

**tide** *n* flood, *flow, stream, current, flux

**tidings** *news, intelligence, advice

**tidy** *neat, trim, trig, snug, shipshape, spick-and-span
*Ana* *orderly, methodical, systematic
*Ant* untidy —*Con* *slipshod, slovenly, sloppy, unkempt, disheveled

**tie** *n* 1 *bond, band
2 *draw, stalemate, deadlock, standoff
*Ana* equality, equivalence (see corresponding adjectives at SAME)
**tie** *vb* **Tie, bind** both mean to make fast or secure. They are often used interchangeably without marked loss, but since in both their primary and extended senses they carry fundamentally distinct connotations, greater precision in their use is often possible. **Tie** basically implies the use of a cord or rope to attach one thing that may wander or move to another that is stable ⟨I'll *tie* them [our horses] in the wood—*Shak.*⟩ **Bind,** on the other hand, implies the use of a band or bond (see BOND *n*) to attach two or more things so that they are held firmly together or brought into union ⟨gather ye together first the tares, and *bind* them in bundles—*Mt 13:30*⟩ ⟨*bind* a sprained

ankle⟩ ⟨a fillet *binds* her hair—*Pope*⟩ ⟨*bind* a person hand and foot⟩ In extended use, especially when what is tied or bound is a person, both terms imply a deprivation of liberty and an imposed restraint. *Tie*, however, specifically suggests a being held down by something stronger than oneself and an inability to get away or free oneself ⟨*tied* to a job⟩ ⟨*tied* to an unsympathetic wife⟩ *Bind*, on the other hand, either suggests a being held together in a close union, for the sake of strength or mutual support ⟨the common danger *bound* all classes together⟩ ⟨and vows of faith each to the other *bind*—*Shelley*⟩ or a being held down by such a bond, as a pledge, a compact, a duty, or an obligation, or by a bond of blood, marriage, or friendship ⟨and vows, that *bind* the will, in silence made—*Wordsworth*⟩ ⟨"Are you engaged?" . . . "There's someone . . . . We don't want to spoil things by having anything definite and *binding*"—*Gibbons*⟩ *Ana* *fasten, attach: *secure, rivet, anchor, moor: *join, connect, link
*Ant* untie

**tier** *line, row, rank, file, echelon

**tiff** *n* *quarrel, bickering, spat, squabble, wrangle, altercation
*Ana* scrap, rumpus, row, *brawl, broil: difference, variance, dissension, contention, *discord

**tiff** *vb* spat, bicker, quarrel, squabble, wrangle, altercate (see under QUARREL *n*)
*Ana* dispute, argue (see DISCUSS): *differ, disagree: *contend, fight

**tight** **1** Tight, taut, tense are comparable chiefly in their basic senses in which they mean drawn or stretched to the point where there is no looseness or slackness. **Tight** implies a drawing around or about something in a way that constricts or binds it or a drawing of the edges of something firmly together ⟨a *tight* belt⟩ ⟨a *tight* coat⟩ ⟨Tom has eaten . . . till his little skin is as *tight* as a drum—*Hughes*⟩ When applied to a structure, *tight* more often suggests a drawing together of all parts so that nothing can enter or escape ⟨a *tightly* built house⟩ ⟨if the granary be not *tight*, the grain will leak out almost as fast as it is shoveled in—*Grandgent*⟩ When applied to a situation, it suggests that those involved in it are cornered or squeezed unmercifully ⟨those who take refuge in gaps find themselves in a *tight* place when the gaps begin to close—*Inge*⟩ ⟨a genius for fast talking in *tight* situations —and this was the *tightest* and most precarious of his stormy life—*Shirer*⟩ When the emphasis is upon pulling or stretching a cord, a rope, or a fabric to the point where it can be stretched no more without breaking or without putting undue strain upon its supports, *tight* is often used but **taut** is the more explicit word and therefore the more appropriate; thus, a *tight* cord may be one which ties up a bundle closely and firmly or is stretched to the limit between two points but a *taut* cord is one which is tight only in the second of these senses ⟨*taut* as a drumhead⟩ ⟨he is *taut* as one of the hawsers of his own boat—*Brooks*⟩ ⟨her sails are loose, her tackles hanging, waiting men to seize and haul thém *taut*—*Lowell*⟩ In other than nautical or mechanical use, *taut* often carries a suggestion of strain, especially of nervous strain ⟨in appearance and manner, she was formidable and astringent, with hands that seemed forever *taut*—*Hervey*⟩ ⟨so frightened by his driving that she couldn't enjoy the night . . . . tense, *taut*, and curdling up inside—*Farrell*⟩ When there is an implication of tightness or tautness that involves severe physical or, more often, nervous strain or that manifests itself in signs of such strain, **tense** may be preferred ⟨a cat crouched for a spring, with muscles *tense*⟩ ⟨help him to unbend his too *tense* thought—*Arnold*⟩ ⟨just as a bicycle chain may be

too tight, so may one's carefulness and conscientiousness be so *tense* as to hinder the running of one's mind—*James*⟩ ⟨the rat was crouching, very *tense,* sensing extreme danger, but not yet frightened—*Dahl*⟩
*Ana* strict, stringent (see RIGID): *close, compact: constricted, contracted, compressed, condensed, shrunken (see CONTRACT *vb*): snug, shipshape (see NEAT)
*Ant* loose
**2** also **tightfisted** *stingy, close, closefisted, niggardly, parsimonious, penurious, miserly, cheeseparing, penny-pinching
*Ana* *mean, ignoble, sordid, abject
**3** tipsy, intoxicated, *drunk, drunken, inebriated

**tight-lipped** *silent, uncommunicative, taciturn, close, close-lipped, closemouthed, reticent, reserved, secretive

**time** *n* *opportunity, occasion, chance, break
*Ana* *juncture, contingency, emergency, exigency

**timely** well-timed, opportune, *seasonable, pat
*Ana* appropriate, fitting, meet, proper, suitable (see FIT): fortunate, *lucky, happy, providential
*Ant* untimely

**timetable** *program, schedule, agenda

**timid,** **timorous** both mean so fearful and apprehensive as to hesitate or hold back. **Timid** stresses lack of courage and daring and usually implies extreme cautiousness and fearlessness of change or of venture into the unknown or uncertain ⟨a *timid* investor⟩ ⟨*timid* as a deer⟩ ⟨*timid* about making decisions⟩ ⟨a *timid* person would rather remain miserable than do anything unusual—*Russell*⟩ **Timorous** stresses domination by fears and apprehensions; it implies a temporary or habitual frame of mind which causes one to shrink from an action or activity which requires independence, decision, or self-assertiveness and suggests terror rather than extreme caution ⟨Murray, the most *timorous,* as Byron called him, of all God's booksellers—*Scott*⟩ ⟨in another moment she seemed to have descended from her womanly eminence to helpless and *timorous* girlhood—*Wharton*⟩ ⟨*timorous* and fearful of challenge—*Mencken*⟩
*Ana* *fearful, apprehensive, afraid: *cautious, circumspect, calculating, wary, chary
*Con* *brave, courageous, unafraid, fearless, intrepid, valiant, bold, audacious

**timorous** *timid
*Ana* *fearful, apprehensive, afraid: recoiling, shrinking, quailing, blenching (see RECOIL): trembling, quivering, shivering, shuddering (see SHAKE)
*Ant* assured

**tincture** *n* *touch, suggestion, tinge, suspicion, soupçon, shade, smack, spice, dash, vein, strain, streak

**tinge** *n* **1** tint, shade, hue, *color, tone
**2** tincture, *touch, suggestion, shade, suspicion, soupçon, smack, spice, dash, vein, strain, streak

**tint** *n* hue, shade, *color, tinge, tone

**tiny** minute, miniature, diminutive, wee, *small, little, teeny, weeny

**tippler** *drunkard, inebriate, alcoholic, dipsomaniac, sot, soak, toper, tosspot

**tipsy** intoxicated, inebriated, *drunk, drunken, tight

**tirade,** **diatribe, jeremiad, philippic** can all mean a violent, often long-winded, and usually denunciatory speech or writing. **Tirade** implies a swift emission of heated language, sometimes critical, sometimes abusive, but usually long-continued and directed against persons or things that the speaker or writer believes worthy of castigation ⟨screaming a *tirade* of protest and rage—*Davenport*⟩ ⟨the King . . . had . . . to impose silence on the *tirades* which were delivered from the University pulpit—*J. R. Green*⟩ **Diatribe** carries a stronger implica-

---

*Ana* analogous words      *Ant* antonyms      *Con* contrasted words      See also explanatory notes facing page 1

tion of bitterness and, often, of long-windedness than *tirade* ⟨a rambling, bitter *diatribe* on the wrongs and sufferings of the laborers—*Kingsley*⟩ ⟨a *diatribe* in some . . . paper which neglected to mention what I had said, it merely indicated that it had been awful—*Mailer*⟩ **Jeremiad** stresses the implication of dolefulness or lugubriousness, but it usually applies to a diatribe in that strain ⟨a *jeremiad* against a civilization that values knowledge above wisdom—*Durrell*⟩ **Philippic** applies to an oration or harangue that constitutes a denunciatory attack filled with acrimonious invective and often directed against a public person, a way of life, an aggressive power, or some dictatorial assumption ⟨gave full rein to his mingled exasperation and boredom in a *philippic* so withering that it roused a lethargic Senate—*S. H. Adams*⟩ ⟨delivered a violent *philippic* against democracy—*S. R. L.*⟩ *Ana* harangue, oration, *speech: invective, vituperation, *abuse: denunciation, censure, condemnation (see corresponding verbs at CRITICIZE)

*Ant* eulogy

**tire** *vb* Tire, weary, fatigue, exhaust, jade, fag, tucker can all mean to make or in some cases to become disinclined or unable to continue because of loss of strength or endurance. **Tire** is the general and ordinary word and usually implies the draining of one's strength or patience; it may suggest such causes as overexertion, long continuance at a task, boredom, or a sense of futility and usually it requires textual amplification to indicate the cause and the degree of the effect ⟨it *tires* me to death to read how many ways the warrior is like the moon, or the sun, or a rock, or a lion, or the ocean—*Walpole*⟩ ⟨music that gentlier on the spirit lies, than *tired* eyelids upon *tired* eyes—*Tennyson*⟩ ⟨spoke exclusively from the larynx, as if he were altogether too *tired* to put any diaphragm breath into his words—*Salinger*⟩ ⟨we shall not fail or falter; we shall not weaken or *tire*—*Sir Winston Churchill*⟩ **Weary** as often suggests an incapacity for enduring more of the same thing or an unwillingness to continue one's effort or one's interest as a depletion of that strength or that interest ⟨the others would never even raise their eyes when this happened, as men too well aware of the futility of their fellows' attempts and *wearied* with their useless repetition —*Kipling*⟩ ⟨ah, I am worn out—I am *wearied* out— it is too much—I am but flesh and blood, and I must sleep— *Millay*⟩ ⟨I have only one prayer—that I *weary* of you before you tire of me—*Mailer*⟩ ⟨*wearied* of her husband's infidelities, and could not bear them any more—*Rose Macaulay*⟩ **Fatigue** is stronger than *tire* and implies great lassitude brought on by overstrain or undue effort. It usually implies an incapacity for further strain or effort without damaging effects ⟨I rested . . . in a shrubbery, being, in my enfeebled condition, too *fatigued* to push on —*H. G. Wells*⟩ ⟨she flung herself upon a sofa, protesting . . . that she was *fatigued* to death—*Burney*⟩ **Exhaust** (see also DEPLETE) heightens *fatigue's* implications of drained strength or a worn-out condition of mind or of body ⟨she is too *exhausted* to sleep⟩ ⟨*exhausted* and addled by the frustration of their failures—*Mailer*⟩ **Jade** implies weariness or fatigue that makes one lose all freshness, spirit, animation, or interest and become dull and languid. The term seldom carries a suggestion of physical or mental overexertion as *fatigue* and often implies satiety even more clearly than *weary;* it is especially useful when the implication of overindulgence in something or the overworking of a particular sense or faculty is to be conveyed ⟨to minds *jaded* with debauches of overemphasis it does contrive to give a thrill—*Montague*⟩ ⟨to the *jaded* . . . eye it is all dead and common . . . flatness and disgust—*James*⟩ **Fag** implies work until

one droops with weariness or fatigue ⟨I worked . . . at correcting manuscript, which *fags* me excessively—*Scott*⟩ ⟨with a gasp for breath said, "Lord, what a run. I'm *fagged* to death"—*Masefield*⟩ **Tucker** closely approaches *fatigue* or *exhaust* in meaning but sometimes carries the additional suggestion of loss of breath ⟨too *tuckered* to finish a job—*Leavitt*⟩ ⟨seemed *tuckered* out from listening to long speeches—*Dorothy Canfield*⟩

*Ana* irk, vex, *annoy, bother: *deplete, drain, exhaust, impoverish, bankrupt

**tireless** *indefatigable, weariless, untiring, unwearying, unwearied, unflagging

*Ana* assiduous, sedulous, diligent, industrious, *busy: energetic, strenuous, *vigorous

**tiresome** *irksome, wearisome, tedious, boring

*Ana* oppressive, burdensome, *onerous, exacting: fatiguing, exhausting, jading, fagging (see TIRE *vb*): arduous, *hard, difficult

**titanic** *huge, vast, immense, enormous, elephantine, mammoth, giant, gigantic, gigantean, colossal, gargantuan, Herculean, cyclopean, Brobdingnagian

**title** n 1 *claim, pretension, pretense

*Ana* *right, privilege, prerogative, birthright: *reason, ground, argument, proof: *due, desert, merit

2 *name, designation, denomination, appellation, style

**tittle** *particle, bit, mite, smidgen, whit, atom, iota, jot

**toady** *n* *parasite, sycophant, favorite, lickspittle, bootlicker, hanger-on, leech, sponge, sponger

**toady** *vb* *fawn, truckle, cringe, cower

*Ana* *follow, tag, trail, tail: blandish, cajole, wheedle (see COAX)

**toboggan** *vb* coast, *slide, slip, glide, skid, glissade, slither

**tocsin** *alarm, alert

*Ana* signal, *sign

**toil** *n* labor, *work, travail, drudgery, grind

*Ana* *effort, exertion, pains, trouble: employment, occupation, calling, pursuit, business (see WORK)

*Ant* leisure

**token** 1 *sign, mark, symptom, badge, note

*Ana* *symbol, emblem, attribute: *evidence, testimony: indication, proving *or* proof, betokening (see corresponding verbs at INDICATE)

2 *pledge, earnest, pawn, hostage

*Ana* *guarantee, guaranty, security, surety

3 *remembrance, remembrancer, reminder, memorial, memento, keepsake, souvenir

*Ana* *gift, present, favor

**tolerance** forbearance, leniency, indulgence, clemency, mercifulness (see under FORBEARING)

*Ana* *mercy, charity, grace, lenity: *patience, longsuffering, longanimity

*Ant* intolerance: loathing

**tolerant** *forbearing, lenient, indulgent, clement, merciful

*Ana* *charitable, benevolent, humane: forgiving, excusing, condoning (see EXCUSE *vb*)

*Ant* intolerant: severe

**tolerantly** forbearingly, clemently, mercifully, leniently, indulgently (see under FORBEARING)

**tolerate** endure, abide, *bear, suffer, stand, brook

*Ana* accept, *receive: submit, *yield, bow, succumb

**tone** *color, hue, shade, tint, tinge

**tongue** *language, dialect, speech, idiom

**tongue-lash** *vb* upbraid, rate, berate, *scold, jaw, bawl, chew out, wig, rail, revile, vituperate

**too** *also, likewise, besides, moreover, furthermore

**tool** *implement, instrument, appliance, utensil

*Ana* *device, contrivance, contraption, gadget: *machine, mechanism, apparatus: *mean, instrument, instrumentality, agent, agency

---

A colon (:) separates groups of words discriminated. An asterisk (*) indicates place of treatment of each group.

**toothsome** *palatable, appetizing, savory, sapid, tasty, flavorsome, relishing

**toper** *drunkard, inebriate, alcoholic, dipsomaniac, sot, soak, tosspot, tippler

**topic** *subject, matter, subject matter, argument, text, theme, motive, motif, leitmotiv

**torment** *vb* torture, rack, *afflict, try
*Ana* *worry, annoy, harry, harass, plague, pester: distress, *trouble: *bait, badger, hector: agonize, *writhe

**tornado** *whirlwind, cyclone, typhoon, hurricane, waterspout, twister

**torpid** *lethargic, sluggish, comatose
*Ana* inert, *inactive, idle, passive: phlegmatic, *impassive, stolid
*Ant* agile

**torpidity** torpor, stupor, *lethargy, languor, lassitude
*Ana* inertness, inactivity, idleness, passiveness (see corresponding adjectives at INACTIVE)

**torpor** torpidity, stupor, *lethargy, languor, lassitude
*Ana* apathy, phlegm, impassivity, stolidity (see under IMPASSIVE): inertness *or* inertia, passiveness, inactivity (see corresponding adjectives at INACTIVE)
*Ant* animation

**torrent** *n* *flood, deluge, inundation, spate, cataract

**tortuous** *winding, sinuous, serpentine, flexuous
*Ana* *crooked, devious: roundabout, circuitous, *indirect

**torture** *vb* rack, torment, *afflict, try
*Ana* *writhe, agonize: persecute, oppress, *wrong: *distress, trouble: *worry, annoy, harry, harass: *maim, mutilate, mangle

**toss** *vb* pitch, sling, *throw, cast, fling, hurl
*Ana* impel, drive (see MOVE *vb*): thrust, propel (see PUSH *vb*)

**tosspot** *drunkard, inebriate, alcoholic, dipsomaniac, sot, soak, toper, tippler

**tot** *vb* total, *add, sum, cast, figure, foot

**total** *adj* *whole, entire, all, gross
*Ana* complete, *full, plenary: including *or* inclusive, comprehending *or* comprehensive (see corresponding verbs at INCLUDE)

**total** *n* *sum, aggregate, whole, amount, number, quantity

**total** *vb* tot, *add, sum, figure, cast, foot

**totalitarian** *adj* Totalitarian, authoritarian, as applied to a government or state, require discrimination, for, although applicable to the same states, they actually carry a different emphasis. Totalitarian implies as an objective an undivided state in which all power, whether political, economic, commercial, cultural, or religious, is vested in the government and in which the people as a unit sanction and support this government and obey its orders. Practically, it implies toleration of but one political party, the one which supports the government, and the concentration of authority in the hands of one person or group, theoretically the mouthpiece of the people. Authoritarian implies a type of governmental organization in which professedly as well as actually all political power is ultimately concentrated in the hands of an individual head (as a sovereign, a leader, or a dictator) and not (as in democratic countries) in the people or in a representative body. No matter how the various powers vested in the government may be distributed for practical purposes, an *authoritarian* state is so organized that the final and determining authority is its head. Practically an *authoritarian* government, though professing political power, often extends its control over the economic and cultural life of the people; thus, Italy, with the rise of Mussolini and the Fascists to power in 1922, became an *authoritarian* state; Germany, with the election of Hitler as Chancellor in 1933, became a *totalitarian* state.

**totter** 1 *shake, tremble, quake, quaver, quiver, shiver, shudder, wobble, teeter, shimmy, dither
*Ana* rock, agitate, *shake, convulse: sway, *swing, fluctuate, oscillate, waver
2 *reel, stagger, whirl
*Ana* *stumble, lurch, blunder, flounder, trip

**touch** *vb* 1 Touch, feel, palpate, handle, paw can all mean to lay the hand or fingers or an equally sensitive part of the body upon so as to get or produce a sensation often in examination or exploration. Touch usually stresses the act which leads to or produces the sensation or the resulting knowledge, but it does not invariably imply the act of placing a bodily part in contact with the object considered for it may suggest the use of an instrument which induces a specific sensation or produces another sensation (as that of sounds heard) ⟨*touch* an iron lightly with a wet finger to see if it is hot enough for ironing⟩ ⟨*touch* the strings of a violin lightly with the bow⟩ ⟨if you *touch* the baby he will awaken⟩ or it may suggest an immaterial contact ⟨it is essential that the College . . . be strengthened in its enduring task of *touching* creatively the lives of those many who will study here—*N. M. Pusey*⟩ Feel stresses the sensation induced or produced; usually it suggests a sensation on the part of the person touching but may connote a sensation on the part of the one touched ⟨come near . . . that I may *feel* thee, my son—*Gen* 27:21⟩ ⟨the natural philosopher concerned himself with almost anything that he could see or hear or *feel*—*Darrow*⟩ ⟨all that the saints and mystics say about the irradiation of the whole personality by the *felt* presence of the Holy Spirit—*Inge*⟩ Although *touch* and *feel* often connote examination or exploration, they do not throw the emphasis on that end; on the other hand, **palpate** (as well as the noun **palpation**), especially in medical use, stresses the feeling of the surface of a body, usually a human body, as a means of discovering the condition of organs that cannot be seen ⟨the doctor *palpated* the swollen mass and said no bone was broken⟩ ⟨examine the condition of the abdominal organs by *palpation*⟩ ⟨having probed and prodded and *palpated* that tortured . . . flesh until it was as familiar as his own—*Styron*⟩ Handle (see also HANDLE, TREAT) implies a laying of the hands or fingers upon so as to get the feel of a thing, or a taking up into the hands so as to determine its qualities (as of weight, condition, or finish) by the sense of touch ⟨she insists upon *handling* cloth before she buys it⟩ ⟨*handle* this fur and feel its softness yet strength⟩ ⟨*handle* me, and see; for a spirit hath not flesh—*Lk* 24:39⟩ Paw implies a touching or stroking with the hand, often but not always involving the connotation of getting or stimulating a sensation; the term is often used when the action is clumsy or offensive ⟨the inspectors . . . *pawing* through his papers, consulting dusty books of regulations—*W. S. Burroughs*⟩ ⟨kept trying to kiss and hug and *paw* her—*Wouk*⟩
*Ana* examine, inspect, *scrutinize: investigate (see corresponding noun at INQUIRY)
2 *affect, influence, impress, strike, sway
*Ana* arouse, *stir: excite, stimulate, quicken (see PROVOKE): *injure, harm, damage, hurt, impair
3 approach, rival, *match, equal

**touch** *n* 1 *contact
*Ana* feeling, sense, *sensation, sensibility: tangibleness, palpableness (see corresponding adjectives at PERCEPTIBLE): *impact, impingement, shock, clash
2 Touch, suggestion, suspicion, soupçon, tincture, tinge, shade, smack, spice, dash, vein, strain, streak are comparable when they mean a perceptible trace of something foreign, extraneous, or peculiar. Touch can suggest an impression left on someone or something by or as if by

contact with another, but in general it implies little more than an appreciable trace ⟨in the air was a *touch* of frost—*Galsworthy*⟩ ⟨he was a very active lad, fair-haired, with a *touch* of the Dane or Norwegian about him—*D. H. Lawrence*⟩ ⟨occasionally the wrinkled serenity of her face became a *touch* grim—*Styron*⟩ **Suggestion** implies an outward sign that is just enough to give one a hint or an inkling of the presence or existence of something ⟨his voice conveyed a *suggestion* of fear⟩ ⟨the taste of the fowl delicately dominant over the tart *suggestion* of Burgundy—*Wouk*⟩ **Suspicion** and **soupçon** differ little from *suggestion,* but they tend to imply a fainter trace requiring more delicate perception or evoking less certainty ⟨tea with a *suspicion* of brandy⟩ ⟨add a *soupçon* of red pepper⟩ ⟨just a *suspicion* . . . of saturnine or sarcastic humor—*A. W. Ward*⟩ ⟨a *soupçon* of army rank had slipped . . . insidiously into his voice—*Salinger*⟩ *Tincture, tinge,* and *shade* are terms used primarily in describing color. **Tincture** and **tinge** usually imply an admixture with something that gives the thing affected a faint cast or an appearance suggestive of a lightly suffused coloring ⟨what he said had plausibility and perhaps a *tincture* of sincerity—*Hackett*⟩ ⟨both young men were Whigs of a radical *tincture*—*Current History*⟩ ⟨a subjective *tinge* entered into the nineteenth-century description of nature—*Jeans*⟩ ⟨eyes that . . . had some *tinge* of the oriental—*Edmund Wilson*⟩ **Shade** implies enough of a trace to suggest the smallest possible degree of some quality; it usually derives its implications from the meaning of *shade* as a gradation in the darkening of a color ⟨he smiled; in that smile there was a *shade* of patronage—*Galsworthy*⟩ ⟨eyes that were too small and a *shade* too close together—*Dahl*⟩ ⟨the distinction between French plums and stewed prunes is . . . not to be overlooked by those sensitive to these nice *shades*—*Sackville-West*⟩ **Smack, spice,** and *dash* are used primarily in relation to the stimulation of the sense of taste. **Smack** suggests a trace which is pronounced enough or decided enough for one to savor it ⟨the Saxon names of places, with the pleasant, wholesome *smack* of the soil in them—*Arnold*⟩ **Spice** and **dash** suggest a slight admixture or infusion, especially such as gives zest, relish, or pungency ⟨there was a *spice* of obstinacy about Miss Dale—*Trollope*⟩ ⟨a king of England should have a *spice* of the devil in his composition—*Smollett*⟩ ⟨he is a man with a *dash* of genius in him—*Arnold*⟩ ⟨his ancestry was chiefly English, with some Scotch and a *dash* of both French and Dutch—*Kellogg*⟩ *Vein, strain,* and *streak* all suggest linearity and imply continuity though not necessarily evident continuity to the thing, usually a quality or condition, so designated. **Vein** applies to a trace that runs through a personality, a work, or a movement in the manner of a vein so that it lies below or within the substance or character of the thing as a whole and occasionally shows on the surface or crops out ⟨in Swift he discovered an inimitable *vein* of irony—*Johnson*⟩ ⟨he had always had a *vein* of childish obstinacy—*M. E. Freeman*⟩ **Strain** and **streak** can both denote a distinctive characteristic that runs through and modifies the whole of which it is a part ⟨throughout the speech . . . ran a curious *strain,* as though he himself were dazed at the fix he had got himself into—*Shirer*⟩ They are used especially of a personal characteristic that is clearly distinguishable from or even contrasts sharply with the rest of one's qualities ⟨a *strain* of eccentricity, amounting in some cases almost to insanity—*L. P. Smith*⟩ ⟨the *streak* of extreme stubbornness . . . was both his strength and his misfortune —*Galbraith*⟩ ⟨a *streak* of Indian blood in him—*Long*⟩ *Ana* \*trace, vestige: contamination, pollution, defile-

ment, tainting (see corresponding verbs at CONTAMINATE): \*impression, impress, imprint, stamp, print

**touching** affecting, \*moving, impressive, poignant, pathetic
*Ana* \*tender, responsive, sympathetic, compassionate: \*pitiful, piteous, pitiable

**touchstone** criterion, \*standard, gauge, yardstick
*Ana* test, proof, trial, demonstration (see under PROVE)

**touchy** \*irascible, choleric, splenetic, testy, cranky, cross
*Ana* \*irritable, fractious, snappish, waspish, peevish: captious, caviling, faultfinding, carping (see CRITICAL)
*Ant* imperturbable

**tough** tenacious, stout, sturdy, \*strong, stalwart
*Ana* resisting *or* resistant, withstanding, opposing (see corresponding verbs at RESIST): \*firm, hard: intractable, refractory, recalcitrant, headstrong (see UNRULY): dogged, pertinacious, \*obstinate, stubborn
*Ant* fragile

**tour** *n* **1** shift, trick, turn, \*spell, stint, bout, go
**2** \*journey, voyage, trip, cruise, expedition, jaunt, excursion, pilgrimage

**tow** *vb* tug, haul, hale, \*pull, draw, drag

**tower** *vb* mount, ascend, soar, rocket, \*rise, arise, levitate, surge

**toxic** \*poisonous, venomous, virulent, mephitic, pestilent, pestilential, miasmic, miasmatic, miasmal

**toxin** \*poison, venom, virus, bane

**toy** *vb* \*trifle, dally, flirt, coquet
*Ana* \*play, sport, disport, frolic: fondle, \*caress, pet, cosset, cuddle, dandle

**trace** *n* **Trace, vestige, track** can all mean a visible or otherwise sensible sign left by something that has passed or has taken place. **Trace** basically applies to a line (as of footprints) or a rut made by someone or something that has passed ⟨follow the *traces* of a deer through the snow⟩ ⟨the clear *trace* of a sleigh⟩ ⟨when the hounds of spring are on winter's *traces*—*Swinburne*⟩ The term is often extended to suggest a mark, whether material or immaterial, that is evidence of something that has happened or has influenced a person or thing ⟨the child carefully removed the *traces* of jam from his mouth⟩ ⟨would tell him they had detected in the book some slight *traces* of a talent which . . . could be schooled to produce, in time, a publishable book—*Wolfe*⟩ ⟨the stimulation of violent emotions may leave permanent *traces* on the mind—*Inge*⟩ **Vestige** may be preferred to *trace* when the reference is to something that remains or still exists to give evidence of or testimony to the existence of something in the past; it often applies to remains (as a fragment, a remnant, or a relic) that constitutes a tangible or sensible reminder of what has gone before ⟨of this ancient custom no *vestige* remained—*Gibbon*⟩ ⟨the *vestiges* of some knowledge of Latin still appear . . . in his sentences—*The Nation*⟩ ⟨some embryonic organs neither disappear nor take on permanent function, but rather persist throughout life as *vestiges*—*Arey*⟩ ⟨a remote outpost, with only a *vestige* of its former commerce in livestock—*P. E. James*⟩ **Track** has come to be used more often than *trace* in the sense of a line of perceptible marks, especially in hunting, where it also may mean the scent followed by the hounds, and in geology, where it usually means a line of fossilized footprints ⟨the hounds are on the *track* of the fox⟩ ⟨the *track* of a dinosaur⟩ ⟨he could just discern the marks made by the little feet on the virgin snow, and he followed their *track* to the furze bushes—*George Eliot*⟩
*Ana* \*sign, mark, token

**trace** *vb* \*sketch, outline, diagram, delineate, draft, plot, blueprint
*Ana* copy, duplicate, reproduce (see corresponding nouns at REPRODUCTION): map, chart, graph (see under CHART *n*)

A colon (:) separates groups of words discriminated. An asterisk (*) indicates place of treatment of each group.

**tracing** *n*   sketch, outline, diagram, delineation, draft, plot, blueprint (see under SKETCH *vb*)
*Ana* *reproduction, copy, duplicate: *plan, project, scheme, plot, design

**track** *n* *trace, vestige
*Ana* print, stamp, imprint (see IMPRESSION): *sign, mark, token

**tract** *area, region, zone, belt
*Ana* *expanse, stretch, spread, amplitude: *locality, district, vicinity: section, sector, *part, portion

**tractable** amenable, biddable, docile, *obedient
*Ana* pliant, pliable, *plastic: submissive, subdued (see TAME): *compliant, acquiescent
*Ant* intractable: unruly —*Con* ungovernable, refractory, headstrong, willful (see UNRULY): stubborn, *obstinate

**trade** *n* 1 Trade, craft, handicraft, art, profession are general terms which designate a pursuit followed as an occupation or means of livelihood and requiring technical knowledge and skill. Trade is applied chiefly to pursuits involving skilled manual or mechanical labor and the management of machinery or tools ⟨the *trade* of a carpenter⟩ ⟨a blacksmith's *trade*⟩ ⟨he is a plumber by *trade*⟩ Craft is not always clearly distinguished from *trade*, but it tends to be used of those pursuits that involve not only manual or mechanical labor but allow more or less freedom for the exercise of taste, skill, and ingenuity; many of the crafts were once or are still carried on independently in the small shop or home; thus, weaving, tailoring, and goldsmithing are often spoken of as *crafts;* the village shoemaker practised a *craft*, but the latter in a modern shoe factory follows a *trade*. Handicraft implies handwork and usually suggests dexterity in manipulation of instruments or of materials; in comparison with *craft* it tends to imply more definite independence from machinery and it more often applies to an activity carried on for other than purely economic reasons; thus, basketmaking, embroidery, lacemaking, and bookbinding are *handicrafts* when carried out with the use of simple hand tools whether the products are primarily a source of livelihood or not. Art as applied to an occupation (compare ART 1) implies the use of knowledge and skill by the practitioner and often comes very close to *craft* in such phrases as the manual *arts*, industrial *arts*, household *arts*, practical *arts*. But *art*, when unqualified, usually designates one of the creative pursuits (as painting or sculpture) that, whether practised as an occupation or an avocation, involve an elaborate technique, great skill, definite ends to be achieved, and the possession and exercise of highly personal creative judgment and taste. Further, *art* is so freely applicable to the general principles or underlying system of rules, methods, and procedures on which a trade or craft, or a creative pursuit, or a branch of learning or doing, or an aspect of human affairs is based, that it is often difficult, apart from the context, to determine whether the word denotes a pursuit or a technique ⟨the *art* of navigation⟩ ⟨the *art* of interior decorating⟩ ⟨dancing as an *art*, a profession, an amusement—*Ellis*⟩ ⟨proficient in the *art* of self-defense—*Shaw*⟩ ⟨literature is an *art* and therefore not to be pondered only, but practiced—*Quiller-Couch*⟩ Profession is, in general, applied only to a pursuit that requires prolonged study and training before one is ready to follow it as a means of livelihood; the term also often implies that one has undergone tests of one's fitness and has won a degree or has given proof of one's qualifications and has been licensed to practice; it often also implies devotion to an end other than that of personal profit or the earning of a livelihood ⟨law, medicine, architecture, and teaching are pro-

*fessions*⟩ ⟨a person may be a clergyman, a nurse, a civil engineer, or a dentist by *profession*⟩
*Ana* *work, employment, occupation, pursuit
2 commerce, *business, industry, traffic

**traduce** *malign, asperse, vilify, calumniate, defame, slander, libel
*Ana* *decry, detract, derogate, depreciate, disparage: revile, vituperate (see SCOLD *vb*)

**traffic** *n* 1 *business, commerce, trade, industry
*Ana* transportation, conveyance, carrying (see corresponding verbs at CARRY)
2 *intercourse, commerce, dealings, communication, communion, conversation, converse, correspondence
*Ana* familiarity, intimacy, closeness (see corresponding adjectives at FAMILIAR)

**trail** *vb* *follow, pursue, chase, tag, tail

**train** *n* *succession, progression, series, sequence, chain, string

**train** *vb* 1 *teach, discipline, school, instruct, educate
*Ana* *practice, exercise, drill: *habituate, accustom: *harden, season
2 aim, *direct, point, level, lay
*Ana* *turn, divert, deflect

**traipse** *wander, stray, roam, ramble, rove, range, prowl, gad, gallivant, meander

**trait** *characteristic, feature
*Ana* *quality, character, property, attribute

**traitorous** treacherous, perfidious, *faithless, false, disloyal
*Ana* recreant, renegade, apostate (see corresponding nouns at RENEGADE): seditious, mutinous, rebellious (see INSUBORDINATE): disaffected, estranged, alienated (see ESTRANGE)

**trammel** *hamper, fetter, shackle, clog, manacle, hog-tie
*Ana* *hinder, impede, obstruct, block, bar: *restrain, curb, check, inhibit: *limit, restrict, circumscribe, confine

**tramp** *n* *vagabond, vagrant, hobo, truant, bum

**tranquil** serene, placid, *calm, peaceful, halcyon
*Ana* quiet, *still, silent, noiseless: *soft, gentle, mild: restful, *comfortable: *cool, composed, collected
*Ant* troubled

**tranquilize** *calm, compose, quiet, quieten, still, lull, soothe, settle
*Ana* allay, assuage, alleviate, *relieve: mollify, appease, *pacify
*Ant* agitate

**transcend** surpass, *exceed, excel, outdo, outstrip
*Ana* surmount, overcome (see CONQUER)

**transcendent** 1 surpassing, superlative, *supreme, peerless, preeminent, incomparable
*Ana* *consummate, finished, accomplished: *perfect, entire, whole, intact
2 transcendental, ideal, *abstract
*Ana* absolute, *ultimate, categorical: *infinite, boundless, eternal

**transcendental** transcendent, ideal, *abstract
*Ana* *supernatural, supranatural: categorical, *ultimate

**transcript** copy, carbon copy, duplicate, *reproduction, facsimile, replica

**transfer** *vb* 1 *move, remove, shift
*Ana* *carry, convey, transport, transmit: *commit, consign
2 Transfer, convey, alienate, deed are comparable chiefly as legal terms meaning to make over property from one owner to another. Transfer is the general term; it is applicable when the property is real or personal and when it is passed from one owner to another by a lawful means (as sale, gift, or foreclosure). Convey stresses the legalistic aspects of the transfer; it is the precise term when a sealed

---

*Ana* analogous words     *Ant* antonyms     *Con* contrasted words     See also explanatory notes facing page 1

writing or deed plays an essential part in the transfer and is used chiefly of the transfer of real property and of ships. Alienate is not always clearly distinguished from *transfer* or *convey;* in precise legal use, however, it implies the passing of a title by the act of the owner as distinguished from its passing by the operation of the law (as in the case of inheritance by descent) ⟨entailed property cannot be *alienated*⟩ *Alienate,* however, may be used when the sale of property is not voluntary but is ordered or enforced by a court (as in foreclosure or in condemnation proceedings). In ordinary nonlegal use *alienate* often implies diversion (as by force or by a sovereign power or an imperative need) ⟨he pleaded for the resumption by clerics of Church revenues *alienated* into lay hands—*Belloc*⟩ **Deed,** a popular rather than a technical legal term, is equivalent to *convey.*

**transfiguration** transformation, metamorphosis, transmutation, conversion, transmogrification (see under TRANSFORM)
*Ana* exaltation, magnification (see corresponding verbs at EXALT): enhancing, heightening, intensifying (see INTENSIFY)

**transfigure** *transform, metamorphose, transmute, convert, transmogrify
*Ana* *exalt, magnify: heighten, enhance, *intensify

**transform, metamorphose, transmute, convert, transmogrify, transfigure** can all mean to turn or change one thing into another or a different thing or from one form into another and different form. In general, the same differences in implications and connotations are observable in the corresponding nouns **transformation, metamorphosis, transmutation, conversion, transmogrification, transfiguration. Transform** may imply a mere changing of outward form or appearance ⟨a Hunter senior *transformed* into a bride floating in a white brilliant mist, on the arm of an awkward trapped-looking young man—*Wouk*⟩ ⟨the placid sunshine . . . seems to have been *transformed* in a moment into imperious angry fire—*Pater*⟩ or it may imply a basic changing of character, nature, or function ⟨*transform* electrical energy into light⟩ ⟨to Samarcand . . . we owe the art of *transforming* linen into paper—*Newman*⟩ ⟨the task of *transforming* a heterogeneous selection of mankind into a homogeneous nation—*Russell*⟩ ⟨too much organization *transforms* men and women into automata—*Huxley*⟩ **Metamorphose** may add implications not often present in *transform* such as that of a supernaturally or magically induced change ⟨men were by the force of that herb *metamorphosed* into swine—*Steele*⟩ or of a fundamental change in structure and habits that characterizes the development of some forms of animal life ⟨the caterpillar is a larva which finally *metamorphoses* into a butterfly or moth⟩ or of a transformation specifically induced by chemical or physical agencies ⟨rocks *metamorphosed* by heat⟩ In more general use the term carries a much stronger implication than *transform* in a moment of an abrupt, startling, or violent change ⟨the little song . . . later *metamorphosed* into one of the noblest chorales—*P. L. Miller*⟩ ⟨a convention of maidenly modesty has *metamorphosed* many a fine woman into an embittered, disillusioned old maid —*Kyne*⟩ ⟨if you deny man his intelligence, you *metamorphose* him into a machine⟩ **Transmute** usually suggests a fundamental change, especially one involving a metamorphosis of a lower element or thing into a higher one ⟨a simple romantic narrative *transmuted* by sheer glow or beauty into a prose poem—*Galsworthy*⟩ ⟨Shakespeare, too, was occupied with the struggle—which alone constitutes life for a poet—to *transmute* his personal and private agonies into something rich and strange, something universal and impersonal—*T. S. Eliot*⟩ ⟨in order to *trans-*

*mute* energy to higher and more subtle levels one must first conserve it—*Henry Miller*⟩ **Convert** carries a slighter suggestion of change in kind, nature, or structure than the preceding terms but a stronger one of such changes in details or properties as fit something for a given use or function or for a new use or function ⟨*convert* iron into steel⟩ ⟨nature *converts* the fallen trunks of trees into coal⟩ ⟨having conducted their lame guest to a room in the Georgian corridor hastily *converted* to a bedroom—*Galsworthy*⟩ ⟨every possible industry was *converted* to produce war goods—*Morris Sayre*⟩ ⟨that a new seam of richest material has been opened up and that poets are learning how to *convert* that raw material to their own uses—*Day Lewis*⟩ **Transmogrify** implies a thoroughgoing metamorphosis that is often grotesque, bewildering, or even preposterous ⟨see Social life and Glee sit down, all joyous and unthinking, till, quite *transmogrified,* they're grown Debauchery and Drinking—*Burns*⟩ ⟨wondering how the caricatured capitalism of his forebears can be *transmogrified* into a harmonious . . . way of life—*Current Biog.*⟩ ⟨the classical heroes and heroines were *transmogrified* into medieval knights and ladies—*Lowes*⟩ **Transfigure** is often interchangeable with *transform* or *metamorphose* ⟨her face was *transfigured* by uncontrollable passion—*Bennett*⟩ but more typically it suggests an exaltation or glorification of the outward appearance ⟨Jesus . . . was *transfigured* before them: and his face did shine as the sun—*Mt* 17:1-2⟩ ⟨if she be guilty, 'twill transform her to manifest deformity . . . if innocent, she will become *transfigured* into an angel—*Shelley*⟩ ⟨the moment when good verse . . . is *transfigured* into a thing that takes the breath away—*Day Lewis*⟩
*Ana* *change, alter, modify, vary

**transformation** metamorphosis, transmutation, conversion, transmogrification, transfiguration (see under TRANSFORM)
*Ana* change, alteration, modification, variation (see under CHANGE *vb*): evolution, *development

**transgression** trespass, violation, infraction, *breach, infringement, contravention
*Ana* encroachment, invasion, entrenchment (see corresponding verbs at TRESPASS): slip, lapse, *error: *offense, sin, vice, crime

**transient** *adj* Transient, transitory, passing, ephemeral, momentary, fugitive, fleeting, evanescent, short-lived are comparable when they mean lasting or staying only for a short time. *Transient* and *transitory* are often used as if they were interchangeable; but **transient** more frequently applies to what is actually short in its duration or stay ⟨the summer hotel does not take *transient* guests⟩ ⟨*transient* sorrows—*Wordsworth*⟩ ⟨an ancient folk tradition whose *transient* resting-place was the Bronx—*Geismar*⟩ and **transitory,** like its close synonym **passing,** to what is by its nature or essence bound to change, pass, or come to an end sooner or later ⟨objects of sense . . . are *transitory* and ephemeral—*Thilly*⟩ ⟨wise men will apply their remedies to . . . the causes of evil which are permanent, not to . . . the *transitory* modes in which they appear—*Burke*⟩ ⟨a *passing* fancy⟩ ⟨the confounding of the *Passing* with the Permanent—*Austin*⟩ **Ephemeral** may imply existence for only a day ⟨*ephemeral* insects⟩ ⟨*ephemeral* flowers⟩ In extended use, it implies marked shortness of life or of duration (as of influence or appeal) ⟨jazz is perishable, *ephemeral,* elusive—*Balliett*⟩ **Momentary** implies duration for a moment or a similar very short time ⟨a *momentary* irritation—*Hardy*⟩ **Fugitive** and **fleeting** apply to what passes swiftly, and is gone; but **fugitive** carries a stronger implication of the difficulty of catching or fixing ⟨oh joy! . . . that nature yet remembers what was so *fu-*

A colon (:) separates groups of words discriminated. An asterisk (*) indicates place of treatment of each group.

*gitive!—Wordsworth*⟩ ⟨both crucifix and river ... offered contentment and poignant, *fugitive* hints of another world —*Styron*⟩ and **fleeting**, of the impossibility of holding back or restraining from flight ⟨a calm and studious expression, but touched with a curious, *fleeting* light of triumph—*Styron*⟩ ⟨a *fleeting* wisdom told her that ... one does not love another for his good character—*Hervey*⟩ **Evanescent** implies momentariness, but it stresses quick and complete vanishing, and it usually connotes a delicate, fragile, or airy quality ⟨*evanescent* visitations of thought and feeling ... arising unforeseen and departing unbidden—*Shelley*⟩ ⟨all was unstable; quivering as leaves, *evanescent* as lightning—*Hardy*⟩ ⟨it is poetry of the most *evanescent* type, so tenuous in thought and feeling that only the most exquisite diction can justify its perpetuation in cold print —*Grandgent*⟩ **Short-lived** implies extreme brevity of life or existence often of what might be expected to last or live longer ⟨*short-lived* fame⟩ ⟨their satisfaction was *short-lived*⟩ ⟨trade unions have pressed their demands regardless of the fact that sellers' market conditions would be *short-lived*—*The Scotsman*⟩
*Ant* perpetual —*Con* *lasting, permanent, perdurable, stable, durable

**transitory** *transient, passing, ephemeral, momentary, fugitive, fleeting, evanescent, short-lived
*Ant* everlasting: perpetual

**translation, version, paraphrase, metaphrase** can all denote a restating in intelligible language of the meaning or sense of a passage or work or the passage or work that is the product of such a restatement. **Translation** implies a turning from one language into another ⟨English *translations* of the Bible⟩ ⟨a literal *translation*⟩ ⟨*translation* is an art that involves the re-creation of a work in another language, for readers with a different background—*Malcolm Cowley*⟩ **Version** (see also ACCOUNT 2) may be used in place of *translation* especially to imply a rendering that adheres rather to the spirit than to a literal translating of the original ⟨the year 1632 saw a complete *version* of the Aeneid by Vicars—*Conington*⟩ but often it is used to denote one of the translations of a given work, and especially of the Bible ⟨the Authorized or King James *Version*⟩ ⟨the Douay *Version* is used by English-speaking Roman Catholics⟩ **Paraphrase** may apply to a very free translation the purpose of which is to present the meaning rather than the phrasing of a passage or work ⟨a *translation* must be a *paraphrase* to be readable—*FitzGerald*⟩ It may apply also to an imitation with enough changes to obscure its indebtedness to an original in another tongue ⟨[Latin] plays which were not *paraphrases* from the Greek —*Buchan*⟩ Commonly, however, the term denotes a free, amplified, and often, interpretative rendering of the sense of a difficult passage in the same language ⟨write a *paraphrase* of Milton's Lycidas⟩ ⟨*paraphrases* of the Psalms in the Authorized Version⟩ **Metaphrase** is occasionally used by learned writers to denote a translation that is almost slavishly faithful to the original (what is often called a *literal translation*) to distinguish it from a *paraphrase* or free translation ⟨the way I have taken [in a translation of the Aeneid] is not so straight as *metaphrase*, nor so loose as *paraphrase*—*Dryden*⟩

**translucent** lucid, pellucid, diaphanous, limpid, *clear, transparent
*Ana* luminous, radiant, brilliant, effulgent, *bright: iridescent, opalescent, *prismatic

**transmit 1** forward, remit, route, ship, *send, dispatch
**2** *carry, bear, convey, transport
*Ana* *move, remove, shift, transfer: *communicate, impart: propagate, breed, engender, *generate

**transmogrification** transformation, metamorphosis, trans-

mutation, conversion, transfiguration (see under TRANSFORM)

**transmogrify** *transform, metamorphose, transmute, convert, transfigure

**transmutation** transformation, metamorphosis, conversion, transmogrification, transfiguration (see under TRANSFORM)

**transmute** *transform, metamorphose, convert, transmogrify, transfigure

**transparent** *clear, lucid, pellucid, diaphanous, translucent, limpid
*Ant* opaque —*Con* *turbid, muddy, roily

**transpire** *happen, occur, chance, befall, betide

**transport** *vb* **1** *carry, bear, convey, transmit
*Ana* *move, remove, shift, transfer: *bring, fetch, take
**2 Transport, ravish, enrapture, entrance** can all mean to carry away by strong and usually pleasurable emotion. **Transport** need not suggest that the transporting emotion is joy or delight; it may be an emotion (as rage, amazement, fear, or wonder) strong enough to exceed ordinary limits; usually, the term implies excessive agitation or excitement ⟨the test of greatness in a work of art is ... that it *transports* us—*Read*⟩ ⟨*transported* with rage⟩ **Ravish** can imply a seizure by emotion and in this use is typically an emphatic term for a being filled with joy or delight ⟨his eye was *ravished* by a thin sunshine of daffodils spread over a meadow—*Clemence Dane*⟩ ⟨a sound of angelic chimes infinitely *ravishing* to my senses —*Sabatini*⟩ ⟨I was given my first taste of music in the high sense, and never, surely, could a youth from a small country town have been more *ravished* by such an experience—*Hall*⟩ **Enrapture** basically implies a putting into a state of rapture and typically suggests an intense, even ecstatic, delight, often in one of the arts ⟨he is *enrapturing* us with his extraordinary powers to make us see and feel beauty—*Welty*⟩ ⟨he may never achieve a full understanding of the medium of the art that *enraptures* him—*Tassovin*⟩ But sometimes *enrapture* stresses the bemusing aspect of rapture and then tends to suggest a bedazzling and often a suppressing of the powers of clear thinking ⟨gives him a weary skepticism before the *enraptured* claims—*Schlesinger b. 1917*⟩ ⟨[his] personality simply has not *enraptured* the voters—*Rowland Evans & Robert Novak*⟩ **Entrance** implies a throwing into a state of mind resembling a trance; it usually suggests a being held spellbound by something that awakens an overmastering emotion (as joy, fear, or wonder) ⟨*entranced* with this reverent gesture ... her tentative approval of her cousin settled into awed respect—*Hervey*⟩ ⟨he felt his head whirl. Her complete abandon was *entrancing*—*Buck*⟩ ⟨the beauty of the land *entranced* them—*Baily*⟩
*Ana* quicken, stimulate, excite, *provoke: agitate, upset, perturb (see DISCOMPOSE): *lift, elevate
**3** deport, *banish, exile, expatriate, ostracize, extradite
*Ana* expel, *eject, oust

**transport** *n* *ecstasy, rapture
*Ana* enthusiasm, *passion, fervor, ardor: *inspiration, fury, frenzy: bliss, beatitude, blessedness, felicity, *happiness

**transpose** *reverse, invert
*Ana* *exchange, interchange: transfer, shift (see MOVE)

**trap** *n* *lure, bait, decoy, snare
*Ana* stratagem, ruse, *trick, maneuver, gambit, ploy, artifice, wile, feint: *ambush, ambuscade: intrigue, machination, *plot, conspiracy

**trap** *vb* entrap, snare, ensnare, bag, *catch, capture
*Ana* seize, *take, clutch, grasp: betray, beguile, delude (see DECEIVE)

---

*Ana* analogous words     *Ant* antonyms     *Con* contrasted words     See also explanatory notes facing page 1

**trash** *n* 1 \*refuse, waste, rubbish, debris, garbage, offal
2 \*nonsense, twaddle, drivel, bunk, balderdash, poppy-cock, gobbledygook, rot, bull
**trauma, traumatism** \*wound, lesion, bruise, contusion
**travail** labor, \*work, toil, drudgery, grind
*Ana* \*effort, exertion, pains, trouble
**traverse** \*deny, gainsay, contradict, negative, impugn, contravene
*Ana* controvert, confute, refute, \*disprove, rebut
*Ant* allege
**travesty** *n* \*caricature, parody, burlesque
**travesty** *vb* caricature, parody, burlesque (see under CARICATURE *n*)
*Ana* \*copy, mimic, ape, mock, imitate
**treacherous** perfidious, traitorous, \*faithless, false, disloyal
*Ana* betraying, deceiving, misleading, double-crossing (see DECEIVE): seditious, mutinous, rebellious (see INSUBORDINATE): \*dangerous, perilous
**treason** \*sedition
*Ana* revolution, revolt, \*rebellion, uprising, insurrection: betrayal, deceiving *or* deception, double-crossing (see corresponding verbs at DECEIVE): overthrowing *or* overthrow, subverting *or* subversion (see corresponding verbs at OVERTURN)
*Ant* allegiance
**treasure** *vb* prize, value, \*appreciate, cherish
*Ana* esteem, respect, regard, admire (see under REGARD *n*): \*revere, reverence, venerate: \*save, preserve, conserve
**treasury** \*museum, library, gallery, archives
**treat** *vb* 1 parley, negotiate, \*confer, commune, consult, advise
*Ana* \*discuss, dispute, argue, debate: \*consider, weigh, study: \*think, reason, deliberate
2 **Treat, deal, handle** are comparable when they mean to have to do with a person or thing in a way specified in the context. **Treat** in the sense of doing about, serving, or coping with is usually accompanied by context indicating an attitude, temperament, or point of view determining behavior or a manner of approach or execution ⟨*treat* all controversial questions impartially⟩ ⟨*treat* a subject realistically⟩ ⟨*treat* with care⟩ ⟨*treating* her guests cavalierly by *treating* with scorn nearly all the ancient virtues—*Hummel*⟩ ⟨before Massasoit died he made his sons promise to *treat* the Brown family kindly—*Clift*⟩ **Deal**, followed by *with*, may suggest managing, controlling, or authoritative disposing ⟨she *dealt* with moral problems as a cleaver *deals* with meat—*Joyce*⟩ ⟨the dean *dealt* with the matter promptly⟩ ⟨the only previous meeting . . . had *dealt* essentially with the immediate problems of military cooperation—*Deakin*⟩ and sometimes it suggests a relationship between persons or parties on a more or less even basis ⟨we're *dealing* with a ruthless foe that knows exactly what he wants—*L. B. Salomon*⟩ **Handle** is often interchangeable with *treat* and *deal* (with); it may suggest a placing, directing, disposing, or manipulating with or as if with the hand ⟨*handle* an ax skillfully⟩ ⟨*handle* the distribution of tickets⟩ ⟨*handling* the arrangement of flowers⟩ ⟨the federal government picked up a group of unfilled functions that the states could not *handle—Berle*⟩ ⟨occasionally he wondered—if and when they were married—how on earth he would *handle* her —*Styron*⟩
*Ana* \*conduct, manage: regard, respect (see under REGARD *n*): \*consider, account: \*estimate, appraise, evaluate, value, rate
**treatise** disquisition, dissertation, thesis, monograph, \*discourse

*Ana* article, paper, \*essay: \*exposition
**treaty** \*contract, bargain, compact, pact, entente, convention, cartel, concordat
**tremble** \*shake, quake, quiver, shiver, shudder, quaver, totter, wobble, teeter, shimmy, dither
*Ana* \*thrill, electrify: falter, waver (see HESITATE): quail, shrink, wince (see RECOIL)
**tremendous** stupendous, monumental, prodigious, \*monstrous
*Ana* enormous, immense, \*huge, vast, gigantic, colossal: astounding, amazing, flabbergasting (see SURPRISE): terrifying, alarming, startling, frightening (see FRIGHTEN)
**trenchant** \*incisive, clear-cut, cutting, biting, crisp
*Ana* piercing, penetrating, probing (see ENTER): \*sharp, keen, acute: \*sarcastic, satiric, ironic, sardonic: \*caustic, mordant, acrid, scathing: poignant, \*pungent, piquant
**trend** \*tendency, drift, tenor
*Ana* movement, \*motion, move: inclination, disposition, predisposition (see corresponding verbs at INCLINE): progression, \*progress
**trepidation** horror, terror, panic, consternation, \*fear, dread, fright, alarm, dismay
*Ana* apprehensiveness, fearfulness (see corresponding adjectives at FEARFUL): anxiety, worry, concern, solicitude, \*care: awe, \*reverence, fear
**trespass** *n* transgression, violation, infraction, \*breach, infringement, contravention
*Ana* invading *or* invasion, entrenchment, encroachment (see corresponding verbs at TRESPASS): intrusion, obtrusion (see corresponding verbs at INTRUDE): \*offense, sin, vice, crime
**trespass** *vb* **Trespass, encroach, entrench, infringe, invade** all mean to make inroads upon the property, territory, or rights of another. **Trespass** implies an intrusion, often one that is either an unwarranted and unpardonable or an unlawful and offensive intrusion ⟨warn hunters against *trespassing* on his land⟩ ⟨shall probably *trespass* on your hospitality till the Saturday se'nnight following—*Austen*⟩ ⟨it is essential that . . . an artist should consciously or unconsciously draw a circle beyond which he does not *trespass—T. S. Eliot*⟩ **Encroach** usually implies gradual or stealthy entrance upon another's territory or assumption of another's rights or possessions; the term may imply either the act of a person or the agency of a thing ⟨impertinence . . . ever *encroaches* when it is tolerated—*Burney*⟩ ⟨houses *encroaching* . . . upon the desolation of the marshland—*Styron*⟩ ⟨the motive of simplicity is to prevent frivolities of fashion from *encroaching* upon our time—*Inge*⟩ ⟨today . . . the expert *encroaches* on the artist —*Mailer*⟩ **Entrench** may throw less emphasis than do the preceding words upon unlawful intrusion and more upon cutting or digging into what belongs to another, what should be used in another way, or what is outside one's sphere ⟨demands that *entrenched* too much upon his time⟩ ⟨it does not appear that he *entrenched* upon his own or his mother's private fortune—*Buchan*⟩ **Infringe** implies an encroachment that is a clear breach of the law or violation of the rights of another ⟨*infringe* a patent⟩ ⟨he was *infringing* upon the liberties of a man who had never done him any injury—*Edgeworth*⟩ ⟨the statute proposed would *infringe* fundamental principles as they have been understood by the traditions of our people and our law—*Justice Holmes*⟩ **Invade** implies a definite entrance into the territory or rights of another usually with hostile intent or injurious effect ⟨the gangrene has *invaded* healthy tissues⟩ ⟨where there is a legal right, there is also a legal remedy by suit, or action at law, whenever that right is *invaded—Blackstone*⟩ ⟨a crowd of tourists *invades* the town each weekend⟩ ⟨she'll probably insult you for *invading* what

---

A colon (:) separates groups of words discriminated. An asterisk (\*) indicates place of treatment of each group.

she calls their privacy—*Basso*⟩
*Ana* *intrude, obtrude, interlope, butt in: interfere, intervene, *interpose
**trial** **1** test, proof, demonstration (see under PROVE)
*Ana* inspection, examination, scanning, scrutiny (see under SCRUTINIZE): *process, proceeding, procedure
**2** **Trial, tribulation, affliction, visitation, cross** are comparable when they denote suffering, misery, or unhappiness regarded as an infliction which cannot be escaped or avoided. **Trial** implies a trying (as of one's endurance, patience, self-control, courage, or power to resist temptation). The word is applicable not only to distressing situations or conditions but to persons or things that cause distress or annoyance ⟨the *trials* and tribulations of traveling over desert—*T. D. Clark*⟩ ⟨he has always been a *trial* to his parents⟩ ⟨hotels are a *trial* of both spirit and flesh—*Peffer*⟩ **Tribulation,** when not completely interchangeable with *trial,* heightens the emphasis on the suffering or anguish involved in *trial* ⟨out of this time of trial and *tribulation* will be born a new freedom and glory for all mankind—*Sir Winston Churchill*⟩ and often connotes divinely permitted suffering as a test of virtue ⟨the just shall . . . after all their *tribulations* long, see golden days—*Milton*⟩ **Affliction** stresses the implication of imposed suffering that challenges one's powers of endurance; the term need not suggest a relation between suffering and deserts ⟨if severe *afflictions* borne with patience merit the reward of peace, peace ye deserve —*Wordsworth*⟩ ⟨the dark and senseless *afflictions* of a nightmare—*Kenneth Roberts*⟩ **Visitation** heightens the implications of *affliction* by stressing the severity of suffering and by suggesting an ordeal; distinctively it often connotes retribution or retributive justice ⟨many people regarded the disastrous flood as a *visitation*⟩ ⟨woe unto them! for their day is come, the time of their *visitation—Jer* 1:27⟩ **Cross** in its applications closely parallels *trial* and *tribulation* but it may differ from them in its implications of suffering accepted and borne for the sake of a larger, unselfish good rather than as a test of character ⟨leaving her . . . solemnly elate at the recognition of the *cross* on which she must agonize for the happiness of some other soul—*Deland*⟩ The word often directly alludes to the words of Jesus to the rich young man: "Come, take up the *cross,* and follow me" as recorded in the Gospel according to Mark, or to his own carrying of the cross to the place of his crucifixion.
*Ana* *distress, suffering, misery, agony: *sorrow, grief, anguish, woe, heartbreak: *misfortune, adversity: *difficulty, hardship, vicissitude, rigor
**tribulation** *trial, affliction, visitation, cross
*Ana* oppression, persecution, wronging *or* wrong (see corresponding verbs at WRONG): *sorrow, grief, anguish, woe: *distress, suffering, misery, agony
*Ant* consolation
**tributary** *adj* *subordinate, secondary, dependent, subject, collateral
*Ana* conquered, vanquished, subjugated, subdued (see CONQUER): *auxiliary, subsidiary, ancillary, adjuvant, contributory
**tribute** *n* *encomium, eulogy, panegyric, citation
**trick** *n* **1** **Trick, ruse, stratagem, maneuver, gambit, ploy, artifice, wile, feint** are comparable when they mean an act or an expedient whereby one seeks to gain one's ends by indirection and ingenuity and often by cunning. **Trick** implies cheating or deceiving and often evil intention ⟨*tricks* and devices to conceal evasions and violations of ethical principles—*Wagner*⟩ ⟨she could not be entirely sure that . . . he was not after all merely using a *trick* to get rid of her—*Bennett*⟩ The word may, however,

imply nothing more than roguishness or playfulness and be used to designate an antic, a prank, a practical joke, or a harmless hoax ⟨the brothers were fond of playing *tricks* on their sisters⟩ ⟨the *tricks* of the clowns in a circus⟩ It may also be applied to a dexterous device or contrivance that pleases, persuades, deludes, or evokes surprise or wonder ⟨an auctioneer who knows all the *tricks* of his trade⟩ ⟨illusion in the theater is often accomplished by *tricks* of lighting⟩ ⟨that idle *trick* of making words jingle which men of Nuflo's class in my country so greatly admire—*Hudson*⟩ **Ruse** implies an attempt to give a false impression (as by diverting others' attention from one's real purposes or by making what is untrue seem true) ⟨her "falling" through the glass skylight . . . must be construed by him as a form of reckless intrepidity, the hardened *ruse* of a dyed-in-the-wool newspaper woman —*Purdy*⟩ ⟨a favorite *ruse* of the opium smugglers was to insert a hypodermic needle into an egg, withdraw carefully all the albumen and then refill the cavity with opium— *Heiser*⟩ **Stratagem,** though commonly applied to a ruse by which an advantage is gained over an enemy (as by outwitting or surprising him), is not restricted to military operations; in extended use it usually implies a clear objective such as entrapping or circumventing and a more or less elaborate plan for achieving one's end ⟨on our guard against the *stratagems* of evil rhetoric—*R. M. Weaver*⟩ ⟨some women . . . are driven to every possible trick and *stratagem* to entrap some man into marriage—*Shaw*⟩ **Maneuver** usually suggests tactics or handling and moving of troops or ships for the accomplishment of definite ends. In extended use it commonly implies adroit or dexterous manipulation of persons or things ⟨the Longbourn party were the last of all the company to depart, and, by a *maneuver* of Mrs. Bennet, had to wait for their carriage a quarter of an hour after everybody else was gone— *Austen*⟩ It may, however, be applied to a single strategic move comparable to one in a game of chess ⟨unless indeed, all her talk of flight had been a blind, and her departure no more than a *maneuver—Wharton*⟩ **Gambit** in chess denotes an opening that risks a pawn or minor piece to gain an advantage in position; in extended use it can apply to a device that is intended or serves to launch a conversation ⟨opened, safely as I thought, with the *gambit* of inquiring whether present conditions were satisfactory—*Jeremy Potter*⟩ ⟨he could not, if he had pondered conversational *gambits* for an hour, have hit on a more successful one—*Day Lewis*⟩ ⟨always carried turtle eggs in his pockets and bounced them on bars as a conversational *gambit—Bergen Evans*⟩ Perhaps more often the advantage-gaining aspect of the basic meaning of *gambit* is stressed, and the term is applied to a trick or tactic designed to gain its user a competitive advantage often by harassing or embarrassing an opponent ⟨from the Russian point of view it is no mere diplomatic *gambit* to keep Germany weak and disunited: it is a doctrine of self-preservation—*Harold Nicolson*⟩ ⟨if a stranger just ahead drops a rosary, don't take any notice. That's the opening *gambit* of the oldest trick in the world—*Aldor*⟩ ⟨to avoid the multitude of taxes and assessments, the standard *gambit* of the peasant was to "dress poor" and "talk poor"—*Idzerda*⟩ ⟨nobody could be sure whether his anti-market talk was real, or simply a Gaullist *gambit* designed to enhance the French bargaining position— *Scheingold*⟩ **Ploy** carries a suggestion of finesse and often of roguishness and can come very close to the last-mentioned value of *gambit* ⟨this summer's *ploy* in the game of oneupmanship, is to holiday in Europe *without* doing the great museums. . . . little out-of-the-way museums and provincial churches are admissible. But to

score special points one must visit really distinguished collections in private houses—*Genauer*⟩ ⟨perhaps the most common *ploy* of stockholders at annual meetings is imparting ideas on how the business should be run—*Wall Street Jour.*⟩ or it can be used of an individual maneuver in the development of a gambit ⟨subplays or individual maneuvers of a gambit are usually referred to as *ploys*—*Stephen Potter*⟩ However in their common conjoined use *gambit* and *ploy* are seldom distinguishable ⟨demonstrates his Gamesmanship technique for inducing embarrassment and discomfort, and offers *ploys* and *gambits* for use against such rivals as fishing companions, wine experts, and fellow club members—*New Yorker*⟩ ⟨among the *ploys* and *gambits* the President may have used in the process were the White House breakfast . . . the fireside chat . . . the press conference . . . the dangled patronage—*Rossiter*⟩ **Artifice** suggests the employment of devices or contrivances; it usually connotes ingenuity, but it need not connote an intent to deceive or overreach ⟨the *artifices* by which friends endeavor to spare one another's feelings—*Shaw*⟩ ⟨he was witnessing a remarkable performance? Not a show of *artifice* . . . but a genuine creative effort—*Hervey*⟩ **Wile** usually suggests an attempt to entrap or ensnare by allurements or by false and deceptive appearances; it may connote slyness and imposture, but it often suggests coquetry or an attempt to charm ⟨the Devil was helping him and made him sly and foxier than the fox with all the *wiles*, and the cunning, and the craftiness—*Farrell*⟩ ⟨he was no longer a mild old man to be worked on by the *wiles* of engaging youth, but a stern-spoken person in high authority—*Archibald Marshall*⟩ **Feint** basically applies to a thrust (as of a rapier or a fist) seemingly directed at one part of an opponent's body but actually designed to divert his attention and his guards away from the part at which it is really aimed. In extended use the term commonly implies the employment of a stratagem or maneuver which distracts attention from one's actual intention until it is accomplished ⟨I love to think the leaving us was just a *feint*—*Browning*⟩ ⟨smiled a little embarrassedly at his colleague who, whether in *feint* or truth, was too occupied to take a part—*Terry Southern*⟩ ⟨believed the dropping of parachutists was merely an Allied *feint* to cover their main landings—*Shirer*⟩
*Ana* *imposture, deceit, deception, counterfeit, humbug, fake, cheat, fraud: *fun, jest, sport, game, play
**2** turn, tour, shift, *spell, stint, bout, go

**trick** *vb* gull, befool, hoax, *dupe, hoodwink, bamboozle
*Ana* *deceive, delude, beguile, mislead: outwit, circumvent (see FRUSTRATE): cajole, wheedle, blandish, *coax

**trickery** *deception, double-dealing, chicanery, chicane, fraud
*Ana* *deceit, dissimulation, guile, cunning, duplicity: *imposture, cheat, fraud, sham, fake, humbug, counterfeit

**tricky** crafty, foxy, insidious, cunning, *sly, wily, guileful, artful
*Ana* *crooked, devious, oblique: deceptive, delusive, *misleading, delusory: deceitful, *dishonest

**tried** *reliable, dependable, trustworthy, trusty
*Ana* staunch, steadfast, constant, *faithful: proved, demonstrated, tested (see PROVE)

**trifle, toy, dally, flirt, coquet** can all mean to deal with a person or thing without seriousness, earnestness, close attention, or purpose. **Trifle**, the most comprehensive term of the group, may be used interchangeably with any of the others, implying any of such varied attitudes as playfulness, unconcern, indulgent contempt, or light amorousness ⟨dabbled in poetry, delivered ironical orations, . . . *trifled* with some of the radical doctrines then

current—*Lerner*⟩ ⟨knows when to be serious and when to *trifle*, and he has a sure tact which enables him to *trifle* with gracefulness and to be serious with effect—*Newman*⟩ ⟨she began to *trifle* with plans of retirement, of playing in Paris, of taking a theatre in London, and other whims —*Shaw*⟩ **Toy** implies a dealing with a person or thing in a way that keeps one pleasantly occupied but does not engage one's full attention or evoke serious intention ⟨since Plutarch, innumerable hands have *toyed* with historical biography, but not until our time has it become perfected as an art form—*Mandel*⟩ ⟨he lapsed into becoming an observer of life, *toying* on the margin of women and politics—*Lowenthal*⟩ ⟨there is evidence that Augustus, like Julius, *toyed* with the idea of giving the Assemblies greater power and making them representative of the whole body of citizens in Italy—*Buchan*⟩ **Dally** stresses indulgence in something (as thoughts or plans) as a pastime or amusement rather than as leading to something definite or serious; it usually retains some hint of deliberate dawdling, the notion predominant in another of its senses ⟨*dallied* with him, and liked him well enough, but there was a more glittering catch on her horizon—*Kathleen Fitzpatrick*⟩ ⟨poetry . . . is not a mere exercise in fancy, not a *dallying* with pretty little nothings—*Kilby*⟩ ⟨for so, to interpose a little ease, let our frail thoughts *dally* with false surmise—*Milton*⟩ **Flirt**, which in several of its senses implies quick jerky movement, in this extended use stresses vagrancy and superficiality of interest, attention, or liking and often a tendency to pass heedlessly from one person or concern to another ⟨German leaders were *flirting* with the idea of a deal with Russia—*Time*⟩ ⟨the bright young people *flirting* with new isms—*O'Hearn*⟩ ⟨afraid to have either war or peace with the enemy, we *flirt* with both prospects—*Ascoli*⟩ **Coquet** primarily refers to a trifling in love, such as is characteristic of a flirtatious woman ⟨she *coquetted* with the solid husbands of her friends, and with the two or three bachelors of the town—*Dorothy Parker*⟩ but it is also used in reference to things which catch one's interest but with which one will not come fairly to terms ⟨there were none of those external indications of Christmas which are so frequent at "good" Jewish houses . . . . Mrs. Henry Goldsmith did not countenance these *coquettings* with Christianity—*Zangwill*⟩
*Ana* palter, fib, equivocate, prevaricate, *lie: waver, vacillate, falter, *hesitate: dawdle (see DELAY)

**trifling** trivial, *petty, puny, paltry, measly, picayunish, picayune
*Ana* inane, wishy-washy, banal, jejune, vapid, *insipid: *vain, idle, otiose, nugatory, empty, hollow: *venial, pardonable

**trig** trim, *neat, tidy, spick-and-span, snug, shipshape
*Ana* *orderly, methodical

**trill** *vb* *sing, troll, carol, descant, warble, hymn, chant, intone

**trim** *vb* **1** *shear, poll, clip, prune, lop, snip, crop
**2** *stabilize, steady, poise, balance, ballast
*Ana* *adjust, regulate, fix: counterbalance, counterpoise, offset, *compensate

**trim** *adj* *neat, tidy, trig, snug, shipshape, spick-and-span
*Ana* *clean, cleanly: compact, *close
*Ant* frowzy

**trip** *vb* *stumble, blunder, lurch, flounder, lumber, galumph, lollop, bumble
*Ana* totter, stagger, *reel: *fall, drop

**trip** *n* *journey, voyage, tour, excursion, cruise, expedition, jaunt, pilgrimage

**trite, hackneyed, stereotyped, threadbare, shopworn** are comparable when they describe something, especially a

once effective idea or expression in writing or art or a dramatic plot, lacking the power to evoke attention or interest because it lacks freshness. **Trite** applies to something spoiled by too long familiarity with it and suggests commonplaceness or total lack of power to impress ⟨the foregoing remarks doubtless sound *trite* and commonplace—*Cohen*⟩ ⟨it is as true as it is *trite* to liken the desert to a sea and the camel to a ship—*Coon*⟩ ⟨one could wish however that he had found a less *trite* and commonplace way of ending his chapters—*Geographical Jour.*⟩ **Hackneyed,** often interchangeable with *trite*, stresses the idea of such constant use that all significance or force is dulled or destroyed ⟨the *hackneyed* pictures we have seen again and again—*C. M. Smith*⟩ ⟨used the *hackneyed* old theme of the vanity of earthly power for one of his best poems —*Langer*⟩ ⟨a *hackneyed* and cheap melodrama⟩ **Stereotyped** stresses an imitative quality and a usually total lack of originality or creativity ⟨most advertising today is *stereotyped*—using the same words, the same ideas that we have had for more than 50 years—*Printers' Ink*⟩ ⟨a *stereotyped* novel about a young girl growing to womanhood⟩ **Threadbare** applies to what has been used or exploited so much that its possibilities of interest have been totally exhausted ⟨when one writer hit upon a good phrase the others took it up and used it until it became *threadbare* —*Walker*⟩ ⟨this charge is becoming *threadbare* with repetition—*Pollack*⟩ ⟨our self-deceptive pretence of jollity at a *threadbare* joke—*Hawthorne*⟩ **Shopworn** suggests a loss, from constant use, of some or most of the qualities that appeal or arouse interest ⟨there hardly exists a more *shopworn* plot than the one about the show that during its preparation has to battle against all sorts of obstacles to emerge in the end a sensational success— *Baum*⟩ ⟨when a book as unusual as this appears the old adjectives seem too *shopworn* to do it justice—*Graham Bates*⟩ ⟨he has devoted his very considerable talents to a *shopworn* theme: the building of the first space platform —*McComas*⟩
*Ana* *old, antiquated, archaic, obsolete: banal, flat, jejune, *insipid, vapid: depleted, exhausted, drained, impoverished (see DEPLETE)
*Ant* original: fresh

**triumph** *n* *victory, conquest
*Ana* vanquishing, subjugation, surmounting, overthrowing, routing (see corresponding verbs at CONQUER)

**trivial** trifling, *petty, puny, paltry, measly, picayunish, picayune
*Ana* *small, little, diminutive: *futile, vain, fruitless, bootless: slight, slim, slender, *thin, tenuous
*Ant* weighty: momentous

**troll** *vb* *sing, carol, descant, warble, trill, hymn, chant, intone

**troop** *n* band, troupe, *company, party
*Ana* *crowd, throng, press: assembly, gathering, collection (see under GATHER): legion, host, army, *multitude

**troubadour** *poet, versifier, rhymer, rhymester, poetaster, bard, minstrel

**trouble** *vb* 1 Trouble, distress, ail can all mean to cause to be uneasy or upset. **Trouble** suggests loss of tranquillity or serenity and implies disturbance of any sort that interferes with efficiency, convenience, comfort, health of body, or peace of mind ⟨'tis not my speeches that you do mislike, but 'tis my presence that doth *trouble* ye—*Shak.*⟩ ⟨let not your heart be *troubled:* ye believe in God, believe also in me—*Jn* 14:1⟩ ⟨it was his face which was so startling, so *troubling:* limber-jawed, twitching all over with emotion—*Styron*⟩ **Distress** implies subjection to strain or pressure that causes such reactions as tension, pain, worry, or grief; thus, a cough *distresses* when it is

tight and persistent; the formation of gas in the stomach *distresses* by its pressing bloating effect; a person is *distressed* in mind when anxiety distracts or crushes him; a person is financially *distressed* when he is in circumstances so straitened that he cannot pay his debts or satisfy his needs ⟨it was this unseeing quality . . . that *distressed* Maria, that left her with a mingling of compassion and apprehension—*Hervey*⟩ **Ail** implies that something has gone wrong or is the matter; in contrast to *trouble* and *distress* it is used only in respect to unspecified causes; thus, a cough may be said to *trouble* or to *distress* a person but not to *ail* him; one can be *troubled* or *distressed* but not *ailed* by something disturbing ⟨few American industries have gone to such lengths . . . to find out what was *ailing* it—*Nation's Business*⟩ ⟨that . . . was what *ailed* the Jews: they never knew when they were whipped—*Douglas*⟩
*Ana* *discompose, disquiet, disturb, perturb, upset, agitate: vex, irk, *annoy, bother
2 *inconvenience, incommode, discommode
*Ana* *embarrass, discomfit, disconcert, abash: *worry, annoy, plague, pester: perplex, *puzzle, distract

**trouble** *n* *effort, exertion, pains
*Ana* flurry, fuss, ado, *stir, bustle, pother: labor, toil, *work: *difficulty, rigor, vicissitude, hardship

**troupe** troop, band, *company, party

**trouper** *actor, player, performer, mummer, mime, mimic, thespian, impersonator

**truant** *n* *vagabond, vagrant, tramp, hobo, bum

**truce, cease-fire, armistice, peace** are comparable when they mean a state of suspension of hostilities or an agreement for suspending hostilities. The first three terms are commonly interchangeable and each of them can sometimes replace *peace*, yet all four terms can so differ in emphasis and in connotation as to permit them to be used distinctively and with a degree of precision. **Truce** is the most general term and can apply to an understanding or agreement for the suspension of hostilities or to a resulting suspension, not only on the part of military forces and nations but equally in the case of disputes (as between labor and management) and of individuals engaged in disputing ⟨a volume of essays . . . where the parts of his complex and tortured spirit come together in a *truce* of amity and concord—*Woolf*⟩ ⟨their present chilly marital *truce*—*F. H. Bullock*⟩ Historically *truce* denotes an interruption of hostilities for a predetermined and specified period, and it remains the most appropriate term when this notion is prominent ⟨on Christmas Eve the Communist high command called a *truce* for the holidays— *Collier's Yr. Bk.*⟩ ⟨wants a two or three year *truce* on tariffs—*Vernon*⟩ *Truce* also is appropriately used when the agreement is local rather than general ⟨agree to a *truce* to bury the dead⟩ or when there is a clear indication that no general or permanent termination of hostilities is proposed ⟨in international law, [*truce* is] an agreement between belligerent parties by which they mutually engage to forbear all acts of hostility against each other for some time, the war still continuing—*Collegiate Law Dict.*⟩ **Cease-fire** is the most recent of these terms and is rarely used except in relation to actual military engagement. Basically it applies to a literal order to desist from firing on an enemy ⟨efforts to secure full observance of a *cease-fire*— *Lie*⟩ As applied to a suspension of hostilities it may imply an intermitting of acts of active hostility for the duration of a period of negotiation ⟨the *cease-fire* was over; the peace talks had failed—*Newsweek*⟩ or as a preliminary step toward a more permanent or more substantial suspension ⟨the first stage is a *cease-fire*. This is already in effect. The second is the signing of a truce agreement to make the

---

*Ana* analogous words    *Ant* antonyms    *Con* contrasted words    See also explanatory notes facing page 1

*cease-fire* permanent—*U. N. Bulletin*⟩ but more often it implies a cessation of hostilities for an indefinite period of time with the warring parties, typically in a state of military readiness, remaining in the positions they held at the time hostilities ceased or withdrawing a short distance to create a demilitarized zone and without the implication of a permanent peaceful settlement ⟨the fighting should be stopped by an armistice agreement. A *cease-fire* leaving opposing forces where they now are would be unsatisfactory—*Tillman Durdin*⟩ ⟨press for a reduction in the military strength of the parties holding the *cease-fire* line—*U. N. Background Papers*⟩ *Cease-fire* may additionally suggest the intercession of a neutral party in securing the cessation of hostilities ⟨had two weeks in which to persuade Nationalists and Communists to quit shooting at each other before sitting down together; he arranged a *cease-fire* just 30 minutes before the conference began—*Time*⟩ ⟨*cease-fire* arrangements by the United Nations—*Landis*⟩ and in supervising its observance ⟨contribute contingents to the United Nations for . . . the supervision of agreed *cease-fires*—*Munro*⟩ **Armistice** (in full, **general armistice**) basically applies to a formal agreement at the highest level for the laying down of arms and a suspension of military operations; though it does not ordinarily suggest a permanent state, it does commonly imply one that persists either indefinitely or until termination of hostilities by a peace treaty ⟨an *armistice* is a written agreement, usually between the highest authorities of the warring powers, which suspends military operations for a definite or indefinite period of time . . . . A General Armistice is broader in scope, embodying both military and political principles and usually precedes peace negotiations—*Coast Artillery Jour.*⟩ ⟨no treaty followed the *armistice*, which was never more than an imperfect cease-fire—*Liebling*⟩ But sometimes *armistice* (in full, **local armistice**) applies to a merely local or temporary suspension and is then indistinguishable from *truce* in a similar sense ⟨[an *armistice* is] an agreement for the general cessation of active hostilities between two or more belligerents. Distinguished from general armistices are arrangements for a short-term or partial suspension of arms called local armistice or truce which may be made between commanders in the field, for a variety of purposes such as burying the dead. General armistices are made by commanders in chief, usually pursuant to political decision of the governments concerned. An *armistice* does not put an end to the state of war—*Gross*⟩ In its occasional extended use *armistice* usually stresses the temporariness and uncertainty of the state ⟨he had learned to live in the land and had established an uneasy *armistice* between himself and the hostility of rocks and elements —*Mowat*⟩ **Peace** (compare *peaceable* and *peaceful* under PACIFIC) can denote a state of mutual concord between governments or more specifically the state resulting from the termination of hostilities ⟨if ever there is to be a *peace* which is not an armistice, men must learn to live at least as well as they now know how to die—*J. M. Brown*⟩ ⟨today there is a truce in Korea. After 3 years of hostilities, we are now in the first year of an armed *peace*— *Eisenhower*⟩ or it can apply to an agreement by which such a state is attained ⟨the purpose of some overtures, it could be foreseen, would be to test out Allied solidarity by offering a tempting separate *peace* to one or the other —*Feis*⟩ ⟨the severely punitive *peace* . . . which the Allies attempted to impose upon Turkey—*Kennan*⟩ Unlike the other terms *peace* imputes permanence or an intention of permanence to the state of or the agreement for suspension of hostilities ⟨Adler says flatly that there can be no *peace* between sovereign states; at best there can be

nothing more than an uneasy "truce," a period of jockeying and diplomatic cheating preliminary to the next outbreak of armed conflict—*Time*⟩

**truckle** *fawn, toady, cringe, cower
**Ana** defer, succumb, bow, cave, *yield, submit: *follow, tag, trail, tail
**truculent** *fierce, ferocious, barbarous, savage, inhuman, cruel, fell
**Ana** intimidating, cowing, bulldozing, browbeating, bullying (see INTIMIDATE): terrorizing, terrifying, frightening (see FRIGHTEN): threatening, menacing (see THREATEN)
**true** 1 *faithful, loyal, constant, staunch, steadfast, resolute
**Ana** *reliable, dependable, trustworthy, tried: persevering, persisting (see PERSEVERE): *sincere, wholehearted, whole-souled, unfeigned
**Ant** false (sense 2): fickle
2 *real, actual
**Ana** genuine, *authentic, veritable, bona fide: exact, precise, *correct, right: typical, natural, *regular
**Ant** false
**truism** *commonplace, platitude, bromide, cliché
**Ana** triteness, threadbareness (see corresponding adjectives at TRITE): banality, jejuneness, inanity (see corresponding adjectives at INSIPID)
**trust** *n* **1 Trust, confidence, reliance, dependence, faith** can all mean the fact of feeling sure or the state of mind of one who feels sure that a person or thing will not fail him. **Trust** implies an absolute and assured resting on something or someone; it often suggests a basis upon other grounds than experience or sensible proofs. It is the most frequent term in religious use ⟨O God . . . in thee is my *trust*—*Ps* 141:8⟩ but it occurs also in secular use, especially when an intimate knowledge of or a deep affection for someone is implied ⟨he was a gentleman on whom I built an absolute *trust*—*Shak.*⟩ or when there has been no cause for changing an instinctive or intuitive judgment respecting a person's or thing's reliability ⟨the ways in which some of the most highly placed and powerful figures in the state have betrayed the public *trust*—*Armbrister*⟩ **Confidence** need not imply such definite grounds for one's assurances as the support of experience or of convincing evidence; when it does, it carries less suggestion of emotional factors than *trust* and a stronger implication of an assurance based upon the evidence of one's senses ⟨those in whom we had no *confidence*, and who reposed no *confidence* in us—*Burke*⟩ When it does not imply such grounds, it usually suggests less reliable grounds for that feeling than does *trust* ⟨he had . . . an unquenchable *confidence* in himself and a deep, burning sense of mission—*Shirer*⟩ **Reliance** implies not only an attitude or feeling but also an objective expression of it in act or action ⟨he had such *reliance* on the doctor's skill that he allowed himself to be operated upon at once⟩ ⟨his diffidence had prevented his depending on his own judgment in so anxious a case, but his *reliance* on mine made everything easy— *Austen*⟩ ⟨Mark had written out his Christmas sermon with a good deal of care and an excessive *reliance* on what other preachers had said before him—*Mackenzie*⟩ **Dependence** differs from *reliance* chiefly in suggesting greater subordination of self ⟨affectionate *dependence* on the Creator—*Thomas Erskine*⟩ ⟨he had a . . . mixture of conceit and terrible self-doubt, and . . . he shifted between extremes of emotional *dependence* and independence— *Wouk*⟩ **Faith** (see also BELIEF 1) implies confidence, but it often suggests a degree of credulity or an unquestioning acceptance of something capable of being objectively tested and proved or disproved; it is often used when the person or thing in which one has faith is open to question or suspicion ⟨he has great *faith* in a popular patent medi-

cine⟩ ⟨my *faith* in Germanism had not wavered—*H. S. Chamberlain*⟩
*Ana* assurance, conviction, certitude, *certainty: *belief, faith, credence, credit
*Ant* mistrust
2 *monopoly, corner, pool, syndicate, cartel
**trust** *vb* *rely, depend, count, reckon, bank
*Ana* confide, entrust, *commit, consign: hope, *expect, look
**trustworthy** *reliable, dependable, trusty, tried
*Ana* *safe, secure: veracious, truthful (see corresponding nouns at TRUTH): staunch, constant, steadfast, *faithful: honest, *upright, scrupulous
*Ant* deceitful: dubious
**trusty** trustworthy, tried, *reliable, dependable
*Ana* *faithful, staunch, steadfast, constant
**truth, veracity, verity, verisimilitude** are comparable when they mean the quality or property of keeping close to the facts or to things as they are and avoiding such distortions as lies, fictions, or misrepresentations. **Truth** is a general term ranging in meaning from a transcendent idea to an indication of conformity with fact and of avoidance of error, misrepresentation, or falsehood ⟨the *truths* of religion are more like the *truths* of poetry than like the *truths* of science; that is, they are vision and insight, apprehended by the whole man, and not merely by the analyzing mind—*Times Lit. Sup.*⟩ ⟨*truth* as the opposite of error and of falsehood—*Eliot*⟩ **Veracity** usually implies rigid and unfailing adherence to, observance of, or respect for truth ⟨question an opponent's *veracity*⟩ ⟨his passion for *veracity* always kept him from taking any unfair rhetorical advantages of an opponent—*Huxley*⟩ ⟨I cannot, indeed, guarantee the absolute *veracity* of any of my apparently authentic law reports—*Sutherland*⟩ **Verity** typically designates the quality of a state or thing in being true or entirely in accordance with factual reality or with what should be so regarded; sometimes the word designates what is marked by lasting, ultimate, or transcendent value ⟨most primitive and national religions have also started out, naturally enough, with the assumption of their own *verity* and importance—*Kroeber*⟩ ⟨the old *verities* and truths of the heart, the old universal truths lacking which any story is ephemeral and doomed—love and honor and pity and pride and compassion and sacrifice—*Faulkner*⟩ **Verisimilitude** describes the quality of a representation that causes one to accept it as true ⟨to convey human nature in fiction requires the highest degree of *verisimilitude;* events that seem just like those of life as the reader's experience has led him to conceive of life must happen to people who seem just like human beings in a succession which seems just like the course of human affairs——*E. K. Brown*⟩ ⟨the mathematical picture . . . so far as we know . . . depicts the phenomena of nature with complete *verisimilitude*—*Jeans*⟩
*Ana* exactness, precision, correctness, rightness (see corresponding adjectives at CORRECT): authenticity, genuineness, veritableness (see corresponding adjectives at AUTHENTIC)
*Ant* untruth: lie, falsehood
**try** *vb* 1 test, *prove, demonstrate
*Ana* *judge, adjudge, adjudicate: inspect, examine, *scrutinize
2 *afflict, torment, torture, rack
*Ana* *worry, harass, harry, plague, pester: *trouble, distress: irk, vex, bother, *annoy
3 *attempt, endeavor, essay, strive, struggle
*Ana* *aim, aspire: *intend, mean, propose, purpose, design
**try** *n* attempt, endeavor, essay, striving, struggle (see

under ATTEMPT *vb*)
*Ana* *effort, exertion, trouble, pains: test, trial, proof (see under PROVE)
**tryst** rendezvous, assignation, *engagement, appointment, date
**tucker** fatigue, exhaust, jade, fag, *tire, weary
*Ana* *deplete, drain, exhaust, impoverish, bankrupt
**tug** *vb* tow, hale, haul, drag, *pull, draw
**tumid** *inflated, flatulent, turgid
*Ana* expanded, distended, swollen, dilated (see EXPAND): pretentious, *showy, ostentatious: bombastic, grandiloquent, magniloquent, *rhetorical
**tumor, neoplasm, malignancy, cancer** can all denote an abnormal growth or mass of tissue. **Tumor,** the most general term, is applicable to any such growth or mass in or on the surface of the body of a human being, animal, or plant ⟨the term *tumor* literally means a swelling, and thus has been applied to the prominence caused by an overdistended bladder, to the enlargement of pregnancy, to the swelling produced by an abscess, to the overgrowth of tissue (hyperplasia) associated with injury and consequent inflammation, and to numerous other phases of tissue enlargement directly connected with recognized disease processes—*Mohler*⟩ **Neoplasm** often replaces *tumor* in technical use when the reference is specifically to a more or less unrestrained new growth of cells that serves no physiological purpose or to a mass formed by such growth ⟨a *neoplasm* is an uncontrolled new growth of tissue—*Shields Warren*⟩ **Malignancy** in application to a neoplasm denotes a growth that because of unrestrained proliferation and tendency to spread and invade other tissues constitutes a danger to life. This use, though deplored by some purists, is common in technical literature and often used euphemistically in discussion with a patient or his associates. **Cancer** is the usual popular and technical term for a malignant neoplasm, though sometimes it is applied specifically to such neoplasms arising in epithelial tissues (as skin or membrane) which are more often distinguished as *carcinomas* from the other great class of cancers, the *sarcomas,* that originate in nonepithelial tissues (as bone, muscle, or connective tissue).
**tumult** *commotion, agitation, turmoil, turbulence, confusion, convulsion, upheaval
*Ana* agitation, perturbation, disturbance (see corresponding verbs at DISCOMPOSE): uprising, insurrection, *rebellion, revolt, mutiny: disorder, unsettlement (see corresponding verbs at DISORDER): *din, uproar, pandemonium
**tune** *n* *melody, air
**tune** *vb* *harmonize, attune
*Ana* *adjust, regulate, fix: *adapt, accommodate, reconcile, conform
**turbid, muddy, roily** are comparable when they mean not clear or translucent but clouded with or as if with sediment. **Turbid** describes something (as a liquid or, in extended use, an idea, affair, or feeling) which is stirred up and disturbed so that it is made opaque or becomes obscured or confused ⟨the *turbid* water of a river in flood⟩ ⟨careless handling of a bottle makes wine *turbid*⟩ ⟨the *turbid* ebb and flow of human misery—*Arnold*⟩ ⟨the air without had the *turbid* yellow light of sandstorms —*Cather*⟩ ⟨*turbid* feelings, arising from ideas not fully mastered, had to clarify . . . themselves—*H. O. Taylor*⟩ **Muddy** describes something which is turbid or opaque as a result of being mixed with mud or with something suggestive of mud or which is merely mud-colored ⟨*muddy* coffee⟩ ⟨a *muddy* pond⟩ In extended use the term carries a stronger suggestion than *turbid* of a dull, heavy, or muddled character ⟨a *muddy* complexion⟩ ⟨a *muddy*

thinker, but a superb artist—*J. D. Adams*⟩ ⟨the *muddy* and slow-moving plot has something to do with spying and counterspying—*H. H. Holmes*⟩ **Roily** describes something which is turbid and agitated ⟨where the *roily* Monongahela meets the clear Allegheny—*Weed*⟩ ⟨the human rubble . . . washed up by the *roily* wake of the war—*Woodburn*⟩

*Ana* obscure, *dark, murky: *dirty, foul, nasty

*Ant* clear: limpid

**turbulence** *commotion, agitation, tumult, turmoil, confusion, convulsion, upheaval

*Ana* *din, uproar, babel, pandemonium: agitation, perturbation, disturbance (see corresponding verbs at DISCOMPOSE)

**turgid** tumid, *inflated, flatulent

*Ana* expanded, distended, amplified, swollen (see EXPAND): magniloquent, grandiloquent, *rhetorical, bombastic

**turmoil** *commotion, agitation, tumult, turbulence, confusion, convulsion, upheaval

*Ana* agitation, disquiet, disturbance, perturbation (see corresponding verbs at DISCOMPOSE): restlessness, nervousness, uneasiness, jitteriness (see corresponding adjectives at IMPATIENT)

**turn** *vb* **1** Turn, revolve, rotate, gyrate, circle, spin, twirl, whirl, wheel, eddy, swirl, pirouette can all mean to go or move or cause to go or move in a circle. **Turn** is a general rather colorless word implying movement in circle after circle or in a single full circle or through an arc of a circle. It is interchangeable with most of the other terms in their less specific uses ⟨a wheel *turning* on its axle⟩ ⟨*turned* to speak to his friend⟩ **Revolve** may suggest regular circular motion on an orbit around something exterior to the item in question ⟨the earth *revolves* around the sun⟩ It may refer to the dependence of the less important, the secondary, on something cardinal or pivotal which resolves or determines ⟨though local questions, such as the State Bank and state aid to railroads, gave rise to sharp contests, politics usually *revolved* around national questions—*A. B. Moore*⟩ ⟨everything in that house *revolved* upon Aunt Mary—*Deland*⟩ **Rotate** is likely to suggest a circular motion on an interior axis within the thing under consideration which may be not moving otherwise ⟨the earth *rotates* on its axis while it revolves in its orbit⟩ **Gyrate** may suggest the regularity of *revolve,* but it is more likely to be used to indicate a fluctuating or swinging back and forth which describes circular or spiral patterns ⟨stocks *gyrated* dizzily on uncertainty over the foreign situation—*Wall Street Jour.*⟩ ⟨a low cloud of dust raised by the dog *gyrating* madly about—*Conrad*⟩ **Circle** basically applies to a movement around in a more or less circular pattern, but it can also be used with reference to a lack of straight directness in a winding course ⟨a flock of black ibises *circled* high overhead wheeling endlessly on the ascending air currents—*Dillon Ripley*⟩ ⟨the essayist's license to *circle* and meander—*Woolf*⟩ or, specifically, to a curved or arched course followed in avoiding something ⟨the soldiers were *circling* homewards in high spirits at a safe distance from the war area—*Waln*⟩ **Spin** implies rapid sustained rotation on an inner axis or fast circling around an exterior point ⟨he who but ventures into the outer circle of the whirlpool is *spinning*, ere he has time for thought, in its dizzy vortex—*Bayard Taylor*⟩ **Twirl** can add to the ideas of *spin* those of dexterity, lightness, or easy grace ⟨this . . . book . . . I toss i' the air, and catch again, and *twirl* about—*Browning*⟩ **Whirl** stresses force, power, speed, and impetus of rotary or circular motion ⟨and collections of opaque particles *whirled* to shore by the eddies—*Bartram*⟩ ⟨the withered

leaves had gathered violence in pursuit, and were *whirling* after her like a bevy of witches—*Glasgow*⟩ **Wheel** may suggest either going in a circular or twisted course or turning on an arc or curve to a new course ⟨a familiar sight is the turkey vulture *wheeling* against the skies to the north—*Amer. Guide Series: Ariz.*⟩ ⟨she had crossed the threshold to the porch, when, *wheeling* abruptly, she went back into the hall—*Glasgow*⟩ **Eddy** suggests the circular movement, sometimes fast, sometimes slow, of an eddy; it may be used in situations involving indirection, futility, or isolation from main currents ⟨as the smoke slowly *eddied* away—*Crane*⟩ ⟨the dead leaves which *eddied* slowly down through the windless calm—*West*⟩ ⟨waves of friends and reporters *eddied* through the . . . apartment —*Time*⟩ **Swirl** suggests more rapidity, flow, or graceful attractiveness than *eddy* ⟨further than ever comet flared or vagrant star dust *swirled*—*Kipling*⟩ ⟨the black water was running like a millrace and raising a turbulent coil as it *swirled* and tossed over the ugly heads of jutting rocks —*Costain*⟩ ⟨her dark hair *swirled* about her face—*Helen Howe*⟩ **Pirouette** suggests the light graceful turning of a ballet dancer ⟨ashes *pirouetted* down, coquetting with young beeches—*Tennyson*⟩

*Ana* *swing, oscillate, vibrate, fluctuate, pendulate, undulate

**2** Turn, divert, deflect, avert, sheer are comparable when they mean to change or cause to change course or direction. **Turn** is the most comprehensive of these words and the widest in its range of application. It may be used in reference to any change in course or direction of something movable, no matter how small or how large an arc is traversed, but it usually requires qualification ⟨here the river *turns* slightly to the north⟩ ⟨he *turned* the car just in time to avoid a collision⟩ ⟨the force of the impact *turned* the boat completely around⟩ It may also be used in reference to something (as things that show a drift, a bent, or a tendency or persons or things that can respond to an influence) which follows a figurative course or proceeds in a definite direction ⟨*turn* the conversation to livelier topics⟩ ⟨*turn* public opinion against a person⟩ ⟨*turn* an enemy into a friend⟩ ⟨even the younger men had *turned* against me—*Yeats*⟩ ⟨in his need his thoughts *turned* to the sea which had given him so much . . . congenial solitude—*Conrad*⟩ **Divert** may be preferred to *turn* when there is an implication of an imposed change in an existent or a natural course or direction ⟨*divert* a river by providing a new channel⟩ ⟨the unfounded belief that a lightning rod is capable of *diverting* lightning from a building it is about to strike⟩ ⟨the machinery of our economic life has been *diverted* from peace to war—*Attlee*⟩ When used in reference to a person's concerns (as thoughts, interests, attention, or intentions) it often presupposes mental concentration, fixity of attention, or resoluteness of purpose; therefore, when an attempt to alter the situation (as by distracting, dissuading, or sidetracking) is to be suggested, *divert* is the appropriate word ⟨hard to *divert* his attention when he is engrossed in study⟩ ⟨had I spoke with her, I could have well *diverted* her intents—*Shak.*⟩ ⟨could France or Rome *divert* our brave designs, with all their brandies or with all their wines? —*Pope*⟩ **Deflect,** in contrast to *divert,* implies a turning (as by bouncing, refracting, or ricocheting) from a straight course or a fixed direction ⟨*deflect* a ray of light by passing it through a prism⟩ ⟨*deflect* a magnetic needle⟩ In its extended use it is chiefly referred to thoughts, purposes, or interests that pursue a rigid or clearly defined course or direction; consequently the word sometimes connotes deviation or aberration ⟨he underwent all those things— but none of them *deflected* his purpose—*Belloc*⟩ ⟨after

---

A colon (:) separates groups of words discriminated. An asterisk (*) indicates place of treatment of each group.

all, she had perhaps purposely *deflected* the conversation from her own affairs—*Wharton*⟩ **Avert** implies a turning away from what is before one physically or mentally; it is used chiefly in reference to something at which one has been looking or of which one has been thinking and carries commonly a strong implication of avoidance and, often, a further suggestion of repugnance ⟨tried to *avert* her eyes; but like a child irresistibly drawn to peek at the monster in a horror movie . . . kept glancing at Mr. Greech—*Wouk*⟩ ⟨the last drop of her magnanimity had been spent, and she tried to *avert* her shuddering mind from Charlotte—*Wharton*⟩ **Sheer** is used basically in reference to the turning of a boat or ship from its course especially in an emergency ⟨the yachts *sheered* to so that their captains could speak to each other⟩ ⟨*sheer* off the boat just in time to avoid collision with a rock⟩ In its extended use the word commonly implies a sudden or conspicuous turning aside from a path or course that has been followed ⟨an age when the interests of popular liberty and of intellectual freedom had *sheered* off from the church—*J. R. Green*⟩
*Ana* *swerve, veer, deviate, diverge, digress, depart: *move, shift
3 *resort, refer, apply, go
4 *depend, hinge, hang
**turn** *n* 1 trick, tour, shift, *spell, stint, bout, go
2 *gift, bent, faculty, aptitude, genius, talent, knack
*Ana* inclination, disposition, predisposition, bias (see corresponding verbs at INCLINE): propensity, proclivity, penchant, *leaning, flair
**turncoat** *renegade, apostate, recreant, backslider
*Ana* deserter, forsaker, abandoner (see corresponding verbs at ABANDON)
**turn out** *bear, produce, yield
*Ana* *make, form, fashion, shape, manufacture, fabricate: propagate, breed, *generate, engender
**tussle** *vb* *wrestle, grapple, scuffle
*Ana* *contend, fight: *resist, combat, withstand, oppose: compete, vie, *rival
**twaddle** *n* *nonsense, drivel, bunk, balderdash, poppycock, gobbledygook, trash, rot, bull
**tweet** *n* chirp, chirrup, cheep, peep, twitter, chitter (see under CHIRP *vb*)
**tweet** *vb* *chirp, chirrup, cheep, peep, twitter, chitter
**twine** *vb* *wind, coil, curl, twist, wreathe, entwine
*Ana* *curve, bend: interweave, interplait (see base words at WEAVE): *entangle, enmesh
**twinge** *n* *pain, ache, pang, throe, stitch
**twinkle** *vb* *flash, gleam, glance, glint, sparkle, glitter, glisten, scintillate, coruscate
**twinkling** *instant, moment, minute, second, flash, jiffy, split second
**twirl** *vb* *turn, revolve, rotate, gyrate, circle, spin, whirl, wheel, eddy, swirl, pirouette
**twist** *vb* 1 *wind, coil, curl, twine, wreathe, entwine
*Ana* combine, unite, associate (see JOIN): plait, braid, knit, *weave: encircle, *surround
2 bend, *curve
*Ana* spin, twirl, whirl (see TURN *vb*): contort, distort (see DEFORM)
**twister** *whirlwind, cyclone, typhoon, hurricane, tornado, waterspout
**twit** *vb* *ridicule, deride, mock, taunt, rally
*Ana* reproach, chide, *reprove: reprehend, blame, censure (see CRITICIZE): *scoff, jeer, gibe
**twitch** *vb* *jerk, snap, yank
*Ana* *pull, drag, tug: clutch, snatch, grasp (see TAKE)
**twitter** *vb* *chirp, chirrup, cheep, peep, tweet, chitter
**twitter** *n* chirp, chirrup, cheep, peep, tweet, chitter (see under CHIRP *vb*)

**type** *n* 1 *symbol, emblem, attribute
*Ana* *sign, mark, token: intimation, suggestion (see corresponding verbs at SUGGEST 1): adumbration, shadowing (see corresponding verbs at SUGGEST 2)
*Ant* antitype
2 **Type, kind, sort, stripe, kidney, ilk, description, nature, character** are comparable when they denote a number of individuals thought of as a group or class because of one or more shared and distinctive characteristics. **Type** may suggest strong, clearly marked, or obvious similarities throughout the items included so that the distinctiveness of the group that they form cannot be overlooked ⟨the landforms are related to these rock *types*—*Trueman*⟩ ⟨that most dangerous *type* of critic: the critic with a mind which is naturally of the creative order—*T. S. Eliot*⟩ **Kind** in most uses is likely to be very indefinite and involve any criterion of classification whatever ⟨each *kind* of mental or bodily activity—*Spencer*⟩ ⟨their soil yields treasures of every *kind*—*Buckle*⟩ ⟨the *kind* of fear here treated of is purely spiritual—*Lamb*⟩ but it may suggest criteria of grouping dependent natural, intrinsic characteristics ⟨Sinic philosophers conceived yin and yang as two different *kinds* of matter . . . yin symbolized water and yang fire—*Toynbee*⟩ **Sort** is often a close synonym of *kind* ⟨the *sort* of culture I am trying to define—*Powys*⟩ and may be used in situations having a suggestion of disparagement ⟨the *sort* of journals put out by the learned societies—*New Republic*⟩ ⟨Victorianism of a meaner and baser *sort*—*Millett*⟩ ⟨what *sort* of idiots have you got around here?—*Long*⟩ *Type, kind,* and *sort* are usually interchangeable and are used most of the time without attention to special connotations. **Stripe** and **kidney** are used mostly of people rather than things; the first may suggest political attitude or affiliation, the second persuasion, disposition, or social level ⟨all Fascists are not of one mind, one *stripe*—*Hellman*⟩ ⟨economic dogmatists of whatever *stripe*—*Atlantic*⟩ ⟨the crown representative and comptroller, were political appointees; and like many men of that *kidney* had never done a fair share of the work —*Morison*⟩ **Ilk** may suggest grouping on the basis of status, attitude, or temperament ⟨no matter if . . . your ancestors spoke only to Cabots and their *ilk*—*Walker*⟩ ⟨one great composer is worth twenty of your *ilk*—*Bella & Samuel Spewack*⟩ *Description, nature,* and *character* are close synonyms of *type* and *kind* mostly in phrases beginning with *of*. **Description** may suggest a grouping in which all salient details of description or definition are involved; **nature** may suggest inherent, essential characteristics rather than superficial, ostensible, or tentative ones; and **character** may stress distinctive or individualizing criteria ⟨all embargoes are not of this *description*. They are sometimes resorted to . . . with a single view to commerce—*John Marshall*⟩ ⟨the few hitherto known phenomena of a similar *nature*—*Amer. Jour. of Science*⟩ ⟨until the invention of printing advertising was necessarily of this primitive *character*—*Presbrey*⟩
*Ana* exemplar, example, *model, pattern
**typhoon** *whirlwind, cyclone, hurricane, tornado, waterspout, twister
**typical** *regular, natural, normal
*Ana* generic, general, *universal, common: specific (see SPECIAL)
*Ant* atypical: distinctive
**tyrannical, tyrannous** despotic, arbitrary, *absolute, autocratic
*Ana* *dictatorial, authoritarian, magisterial: *totalitarian, authoritarian: domineering, imperious, *masterful
**tyro** *amateur, dilettante, dabbler
*Ana* *novice, apprentice, probationer, neophyte

---

*Ana* analogous words　　*Ant* antonyms　　*Con* contrasted words　　See also explanatory notes facing page 1

# U

**ubiquitous** *omnipresent

**ugly, hideous, ill-favored, unsightly** are comparable when they mean contrary to what is beautiful or pleasing especially to the sight. **Ugly** is the comprehensive term which may apply not only to what is distasteful to the sight but also to the hearing or occasionally to another sense or to whatever gives rise to repulsion, repugnance, dread, or extreme moral distaste in the mind ⟨acres of *ugly* wooden tenement houses line the drab streets—*Amer. Guide Series: Mass.*⟩ ⟨these evenings . . . ended up in a welter of *ugly* words, tears, misunderstandings—*Styron*⟩ ⟨it is essential to sweep away in art all that is . . . fundamentally *ugly*, whether by being, at the one end, distastefully pretty, or, at the other, hopelessly crude—*Ellis*⟩ ⟨how eager we are to reveal all sorts of . . . *ugly* secrets about ourselves—*Mailer*⟩ ⟨life in the moment . . . seemed *ugly* and brutal—*Anderson*⟩ **Hideous** carries an even stronger implication of the personal impression produced by something *ugly* by stressing the suggestions of induced horror or loathing; it may on occasion be applied to something which, without regard to any surface ugliness, arouses intense personal distaste ⟨an altogether *hideous* room—expensive but cheesy—*Salinger*⟩ ⟨the papers of the students dismayed me as a *hideous* revelation of the abysses of noneducation that are possible in the United States—*Edmund Wilson*⟩ **Ill-favored** applies especially to the features or to the general aspect or appearance of a person or sometimes an animal that may be described as ugly; the word emphasizes the unpleasing or disagreeable character, so far as the eyes are concerned, but seldom suggests marked distaste, repugnance, or dread ⟨an *ill-favored* thing, sir, but mine own—*Shak.*⟩ ⟨a scrawny, *ill-favored* little girl, always untidily dressed—*Mead*⟩ **Unsightly** usually refers to things, especially material things, upon which the eye dwells with no pleasure; it often is used in place of *ugly* when a connotation of distaste is not strongly marked ⟨their *unsightly* hovels were not visible from his melancholy old house on the hill—*Deland*⟩ ⟨an *unsightly* swamp and dump grounds—*Amer. Guide Series: Minn.*⟩
*Ana* *plain, homely: grotesque, bizarre (see FANTASTIC) *Ant* beautiful —*Con* fair, lovely, handsome, pretty, comely, good-looking (see BEAUTIFUL)

**ultimate** 1 *last, latest, final, terminal, concluding, eventual 2 **Ultimate, absolute, categorical,** despite great differences in implications, mean in common so fundamental as to represent the extreme limit of actual or possible knowledge. Something **ultimate** represents the utmost limit attained or attainable either by analysis or by synthesis ⟨that lofty musing on the *ultimate* nature of things—*Huxley*⟩ ⟨the fugue was considered the *ultimate* vehicle for profound musical expression—*Wier*⟩ Something **absolute** (see also PURE 1; ABSOLUTE 2) has the character of being above all imperfection because it is not derived but original, not partial but complete, not subject to qualification because unlimited, and not dependent on anything else because self-sufficient. What is *absolute* has, as a rule, ideal existence and implies an opposite in actuality lacking the marks of absoluteness ⟨*absolute* reality as opposed to reality as known⟩ ⟨*absolute*, as opposed to human, justice⟩ ⟨truth . . . is no *absolute* thing, but always relative—*Galsworthy*⟩ ⟨Luther . . . was led to set up the text of the Bible as a sort of visible *absolute,* a true and perfect touchstone in matters religious—

*Babbitt*⟩ Something **categorical** (see also EXPLICIT) is so fundamental that human reason cannot go beyond it in a search for generality or universality and has therefore an affirmative, undeniable character; thus, the *categorical* concepts or *the categories* as they are often called, are the few concepts (as quantity, quality, and relation) to which all human knowledge can be reduced, inasmuch as no more general conceptions can be found to include them.

**ululate** *roar, bellow, bluster, bawl, vociferate, clamor, howl
*Ana* wail, keen, weep, *cry: bewail, lament (see DEPLORE)
**ululation** see under *ululate* at ROAR *vb*

**umbra** penumbra, *shade, shadow, umbrage, adumbration

**umbrage** 1 shadow, *shade, umbra, penumbra, adumbration
2 *offense, resentment, pique, dudgeon, huff
*Ana* annoyance, vexation, irking (see corresponding verbs at ANNOY): irritation, exasperation, provocation, nettling (see corresponding verbs at IRRITATE): indignation, rage, fury, wrath, *anger, ire

**umpire** *n* referee, *judge, arbiter, arbitrator

**unaffected** artless, *natural, simple, ingenuous, naïve, unsophisticated

**unafraid** fearless, dauntless, undaunted, bold, intrepid, audacious, *brave, courageous, valiant, valorous, doughty
*Ana* *cool, composed, imperturbable: *confident, assured, sure
*Ant* afraid —*Con* *fearful, apprehensive: *timid, timorous

**unassailable** impregnable, inexpugnable, invulnerable, *invincible, unconquerable, indomitable
*Ana* stout, sturdy, tenacious, tough, *strong, stalwart

**unavoidable** *inevitable, ineluctable, inescapable, unescapable
*Ana* certain, positive, *sure

**unbecoming** *indecorous, improper, unseemly, indecent, indelicate
*Ana* unfitting, inappropriate, unsuitable (see UNFIT): inept, *awkward, maladroit, gauche, clumsy

**unbelief, disbelief, incredulity** are comparable when they mean the attitude or state of mind of one who does not believe. **Unbelief** stresses the lack or absence of belief especially in respect to something (as religious revelation) above and beyond one's personal experience or capacity ⟨a sense of loss and *unbelief* such as one might feel to discover suddenly that some great force in nature had ceased to operate—*Wolfe*⟩ ⟨if thou canst believe, all things are possible to him that believeth. And straightway the father of the child cried out . . . Lord, I believe; help thou mine *unbelief—Mk* 9:23-24⟩ **Disbelief** implies a positive rejection of what is stated or asserted ⟨a *disbelief* in ghosts and witches was one of the most prominent characteristics of skepticism in the seventeenth century —*Lecky*⟩ ⟨a disbeliever in aristocracy, he never perceived the implications of his *disbelief* where education was concerned—*Russell*⟩ ⟨comprehension flooded Maria's mind, followed by a sort of stupefying *disbelief* —*Hervey*⟩ **Incredulity** implies indisposition to believe or, more often, a skeptical frame of mind ⟨there is a vulgar *incredulity*, which . . . finds it easier to doubt than to examine—*Scott*⟩ ⟨was looking interestedly around . . . when suddenly he started forward . . . and in an instant, his face seemed suddenly to go ashen with bitter *in-*

---

A colon (:) separates groups of words discriminated. An asterisk (*) indicates place of treatment of each group.

credulity—*Terry Southern*⟩
*Ana* *uncertainty, doubt, dubiety, dubiosity, skepticism
*Ant* belief

**unbeliever** freethinker, *atheist, agnostic, infidel, deist

**unbiased** impartial, dispassionate, *fair, just, equitable, uncolored, objective
*Ana* uninterested, disinterested, detached, aloof (see INDIFFERENT)
*Ant* biased

**unburden** *rid, clear, disabuse, purge
*Ana* disencumber, unload, discharge (see base words at BURDEN *vb*): *free, release, liberate
*Ant* burden —*Con* encumber, load, lade, weight, tax, saddle (see BURDEN)

**uncalled-for** gratuitous, wanton, *supererogatory
*Ana* *impertinent, intrusive, officious: *foolish, silly, absurd, preposterous

**uncanny** *weird, eerie
*Ana* *strange, singular, erratic, eccentric, odd, queer: *mysterious, inscrutable

**unceasing** *everlasting, endless, interminable

**uncertainty, doubt, dubiety, dubiosity, skepticism, suspicion, mistrust** can all mean a feeling of unsureness about someone or something. **Uncertainty** stresses the lack of certainty or certitude that may range from a mere falling short of these to an almost complete lack of knowledge or conviction especially about the result or outcome of something ⟨suffered an agonizing *uncertainty* concerning his son's fate⟩ ⟨she drove without any *uncertainty* or hesitation as to her route—*Deland*⟩ ⟨if you are really in love, there is no *uncertainty:* there must not be, or else your marriage would always be . . . a gamble—*MacInnes*⟩ ⟨waited in eagerness and impatience, and then in *uncertainty,* in anxiety, in hurt pride, in anger—*Farrell*⟩ **Doubt** implies both an uncertainty about the truth or reality or status of something and an inability to make a decision, often even after study or investigation; frequently the term implies such a feeling or state of mind in respect to religious beliefs or doctrines ⟨he never felt a *doubt* of God's existence⟩ ⟨there crept into the diary . . . signs of *doubt* and then of despair—*Shirer*⟩ ⟨longed for some reassurance in the midst of the dismay and *doubt* which possessed her—*Gibbons*⟩ ⟨no man likes to have his intelligence or good faith questioned, especially if he has *doubts* about it himself—*Henry Adams*⟩ **Dubiety** (compare *dubious* under DOUBTFUL) comes closer to *uncertainty* than to *doubt,* for it stresses a lack of sureness rather than an inability to reach a decision as to where the truth lies. But it regularly carries, as *uncertainty* does not, a strong implication of wavering or of fluctuations between one conclusion and another ⟨faith free from all *dubiety*⟩ ⟨the twilight of *dubiety* never falls upon him —*Lamb*⟩ ⟨cannot escape the *dubieties* and problems of his day and . . . finds himself swerved from his certainties and confronted with the tenuousness of his preconceptions—*Sat. Review*⟩ **Dubiosity** is not always distinguishable from *dubiety* ⟨men . . . swallow falsities for truths, *dubiosities* for certainties—*Browne*⟩ Sometimes, however, it suggests not uncertainty, but vagueness, indistinctness, or mental confusion ⟨had not cogitated long ere she pronounced distinctly and without a shadow of *dubiosity:* "My opinion is . . . ."—*Meredith*⟩ **Skepticism** suggests in this, its general sense, an unwillingness to believe without demonstration or an incredulity while any plausible evidence to the contrary exists; it usually refers to a habitual or temperamental state of mind or to a customary reaction to something proposed for belief ⟨an easy and elegant *skepticism* was the attitude expected of an educated adult; anything might be discussed, but it was a

trifle vulgar to reach very positive conclusions—*Russell*⟩ ⟨has found that *skepticism* rather than dogmatism is the key to human freedom—*New Republic*⟩ **Suspicion** stresses conjecture or apprehension that someone or something is not true, real, or right or that he or it has worked or is working evil or injury, but it also implies that the conjecture or apprehension is accompanied by uncertainty or doubt, often to the extent that the term comes close to *doubt* ⟨seized with unwonted *suspicion* of his own wisdom—*Meredith*⟩ ⟨a glance of defiant nonchalance which . . . became a look of *suspicion,* and, finally, of rude disdain—*Terry Southern*⟩ ⟨the most ordinary actions became . . . entangled in complicated webs of apprehension and *suspicion*—*Gibbons*⟩ ⟨a stranger . . . regarded with *suspicion,* if not actual hostility—*Hudson*⟩ **Mistrust** (see also DISTRUST) implies doubt that is based upon suspicion and that therefore precludes the possibility of one's having faith or confidence or trust in a person or thing ⟨intracommunity bickering, conflict, and *mistrust* obscure the steady vision of extracommunity danger— *A. E. Stevenson*⟩ ⟨man is only weak through his *mistrust* and want of hope—*Wordsworth*⟩
*Ant* certainty —*Con* certitude, conviction, assurance (see CERTAINTY)

**uncircumscribed** boundless, illimitable, *infinite, sempiternal, eternal
*Ant* circumscribed

**uncivil** *rude, ill-mannered, impolite, discourteous, ungracious
*Ana* boorish, loutish, churlish (see under BOOR): brusque, blunt, gruff, crusty (see BLUFF)
*Ant* civil

**uncolored** 1 *colorless, achromatic
2 dispassionate, impartial, objective, unbiased, *fair, just, equitable

**uncommon** *infrequent, scarce, rare, occasional, sporadic
*Ana* *strange, singular, unique: *exceptional: *choice, exquisite
*Ant* common

**uncommunicative** *silent, taciturn, reticent, reserved, secretive, close, close-lipped, closemouthed, tight-lipped
*Ant* communicative

**unconcerned** *indifferent, incurious, aloof, detached, uninterested, disinterested
*Ana* *cool, collected, composed, nonchalant: apathetic, *impassive, stolid, phlegmatic
*Ant* concerned —*Con* solicitous, anxious, worried, careful (see under CARE)

**uncongenial** unsympathetic, incompatible, *inconsonant, inconsistent, incongruous, discordant, discrepant
*Ana* *antipathetic, unsympathetic, averse: *repugnant, repellent, abhorrent, obnoxious
*Ant* congenial —*Con* companionable, cooperative, *social: pleasing, *pleasant, agreeable

**unconquerable** *invincible, indomitable, impregnable, inexpugnable, unassailable, invulnerable
*Ant* conquerable

**unconstraint, abandon, spontaneity** can all denote the free and uninhibited expression of one's thoughts or feelings or the quality of mood or style resulting from a free yielding to impulse. **Unconstraint** is the most general term and may be used in place of either of the others, though it is less positive in its implication ⟨the old red blood and stainless gentility of great poets will be proved by their *unconstraint*—*Whitman*⟩ **Abandon** adds to *unconstraint* the implication either of entire loss of self-control ⟨weep with *abandon*⟩ or of the absence or impotence of any influence hampering free, full, or natural expression of feeling ⟨had the fire and *abandon* that alone

---

*Ana* analogous words     *Ant* antonyms     *Con* contrasted words     See also explanatory notes facing page 1

can arouse audiences to fever pitch—*Copland*⟩ ⟨jazz is the passion of movement, excitement, *abandon*, sex —*Overstreet*⟩ **Spontaneity** suggests an unstudied naturalness and agreeable freshness of expression or manner; sometimes it connotes lack of deliberation and obedience to the impulse of the moment ⟨Keats' letters . . . have a deceptive *spontaneity* which invites the mind to pass over them . . . without pausing to penetrate below the surface—*Murry*⟩
*Ana* spontaneousness, impulsiveness, instinctiveness (see corresponding adjectives at SPONTANEOUS): naturalness, simplicity, unsophistication, ingenuousness, naïveté (see corresponding adjectives at NATURAL)

**uncouth** *rude, rough, crude, raw, callow, green
*Ana* *awkward, clumsy, gauche

**uncritical** *superficial, shallow, cursory
*Ant* critical —*Con* discerning, discriminating, penetrating (see corresponding nouns at DISCERNMENT): comprehending, understanding, appreciating (see UNDERSTAND)

**unctuous** *fulsome, oily, oleaginous, slick, soapy
*Ana* bland, politic, smooth, diplomatic (see SUAVE): obsequious (see SUBSERVIENT)
*Ant* brusque

**undaunted** *brave, courageous, unafraid, fearless, intrepid, valiant, valorous, dauntless, doughty, bold, audacious
*Ana* resolute, staunch, steadfast (see FAITHFUL): *confident, assured, sanguine, sure
*Ant* afraid —*Con* *fearful, apprehensive: cowed, browbeaten, bullied (see INTIMIDATE)

**under** *below, beneath, underneath

**undergo** *experience, sustain, suffer
*Ana* *bear, endure, abide, tolerate: accept, *receive: submit, bow, *yield, defer

**underhand, underhanded** *secret, covert, stealthy, furtive, clandestine, surreptitious
*Ana* deceitful, *dishonest: *crooked, devious, oblique: *sly, cunning, crafty, tricky, insidious, wily, guileful
*Ant* aboveboard —*Con* *straightforward, forthright: open, plain, *frank, candid

**underling** *n* *inferior, subordinate
*Ant* leader, master

**underlying** basic, *fundamental, basal, radical
*Ana* *essential, cardinal, vital, fundamental: requisite, indispensable, necessary, *needful

**undermine** *weaken, enfeeble, debilitate, sap, cripple, disable
*Ana* *ruin, wreck: *injure, damage, impair: thwart, foil, *frustrate
*Ant* reinforce

**underneath** *below, under, beneath

**understand, comprehend, appreciate** mean to have a clear idea or conception or full and exact knowledge of something. *Understand* and *comprehend* both imply an obtaining of a mental grasp of something and in much of their use are freely interchangeable ⟨"You begin to *comprehend* me, do you?" cried he . . . . "Oh! Yes—I *understand* you perfectly"—*Austen*⟩ ⟨the artist, it seemed . . . had thoughts so subtle that the average man could *comprehend* them no more than a mongrel could *understand* the moon he bayed at—*Wolfe*⟩ But **understand** may stress the fact of attained grasp, and **comprehend** may stress the process by which it is attained; thus, one *understands* a decision when he knows what it involves even though he fails to *comprehend* the reasoning process on which it was based; a person may *understand* a foreign language without *comprehending* exactly how he learned it ⟨for well on a thousand years there have been universities in the Western world; to *understand* the present institutions, we must therefore *comprehend* something of their history—*Conant*⟩ Sometimes the difference is more subtle, for *understand* can imply the power to receive and register a clear and exact impression, and *comprehend* can imply the mental act of grasping clearly and fully; thus, the concept of infinity can be *understood* theoretically though scarcely *comprehended* as a verity ⟨in order fully to *understand* America, it is helpful to have some grasp of the origins, culture and problems of the racial and religious groups which are gradually being fused into one people—*Current History*⟩ ⟨the average layman—or Congressman—is deemed unable to *comprehend* the mystic intricacies and intrigues of foreign affairs— *Kennedy*⟩ ⟨felt in Russia the presence of elements he could not *understand* and never would *understand*, and . . . some of our official representatives said they shared with him this feeling of bafflement—*Edmund Wilson*⟩ ⟨being untutored in local history . . . in no way detracted from my sense of enjoyment, nor lessened my ability to *comprehend* the real beauty of all that surrounded me— *Carruthers*⟩ **Appreciate** (see also APPRECIATE 2) implies a just judgment or the estimation of a thing's true or exact value; therefore the word is used in reference to persons or things which may be misjudged (as by underestimating or overestimating or by undervaluing or overvaluing) ⟨you are of an age now to *appreciate* his character— *Meredith*⟩ ⟨the public opinion which thus magnifies patriotism into a religion is a force of which it is difficult to *appreciate* . . . the strength—*Brownell*⟩ ⟨a new type of State Department man with a most aggressive determination to see, to know and to *appreciate* all of his command —*Michener*⟩
*Ana* conceive, realize, envision, envisage (see THINK): interpret, elucidate, construe (see EXPLAIN): penetrate, pierce, probe (see ENTER)

**understanding** 1 *reason, intuition
*Ana* comprehension, apprehension (see under APPREHEND): *discernment, discrimination, insight, penetration
2 *agreement, accord

**understudy** *n* *substitute, supply, locum tenens, alternate, pinch hitter, double, stand-in

**undulate** waver, *swing, sway, oscillate, vibrate, fluctuate, pendulate
*Ana* *pulsate, pulse, beat, throb, palpitate

**undying** *immortal, deathless, unfading
*Ana* *everlasting, endless, unceasing, interminable

**unearth** *discover, ascertain, determine, learn
*Ana* *dig, delve: expose, exhibit, *show: *reveal, disclose, discover

**uneasy** *impatient, nervous, unquiet, restless, restive, fidgety, jumpy, jittery
*Ana* anxious, worried, solicitous, concerned, careful (see under CARE): disturbed, perturbed, agitated, disquieted (see DISCOMPOSE)

**uneducated** *ignorant, illiterate, unlettered, untaught, untutored, unlearned
*Ana* *rude, crude, rough, raw, callow, green, uncouth
*Ant* educated

**unerring** *infallible, inerrable, inerrant
*Ana* *reliable, dependable, trustworthy: exact, accurate, precise, *correct

**unescapable** *inevitable, ineluctable, inescapable, unavoidable
*Ana & Ant* see those at INESCAPABLE

**uneven** *rough, harsh, rugged, scabrous
*Ant* even —*Con* *level, flat, plane, smooth: equable, even, uniform, *steady, constant

**unfading** *immortal, deathless, undying

---

A colon (:) separates groups of words discriminated. An asterisk (*) indicates place of treatment of each group.

*Ana* *everlasting, endless: *lasting, perdurable, perpetual

**unfeigned** *sincere, wholehearted, whole-souled, heartfelt, hearty

*Ana* genuine, veritable, bona fide, *authentic: *natural, simple, naïve: *spontaneous, impulsive

**unfit,** unsuitable, improper, inappropriate, unfitting, inapt, unhappy, infelicitous are comparable when they mean not right with respect to what is required or expected under the circumstances or demanded by the end, use, or function in view. Except for this denial of rightness, the terms otherwise correspond in applications and in implications to the affirmative adjectives as discriminated at FIT. *Ant* fit —*Con* adaptable, pliable, malleable (see PLASTIC): *able, capable, competent, qualified

**unfitting** inappropriate, improper, unsuitable, *unfit, inapt, unhappy, infelicitous

*Ana* unbecoming, unseemly, *indecorous

*Ant* fitting

**unflagging** unwearied, unwearying, tireless, untiring, *indefatigable, weariless

*Ana* persevering, persisting *or* persistent (see corresponding verbs at PERSEVERE): *steady, constant

*Con* indolent, faineant, slothful, *lazy

**unflappable** *cool, composed, collected, unruffled, imperturbable, nonchalant

**unfold** 1 Unfold, evolve, develop, elaborate, perfect can all mean to cause something to emerge from a state where its potentialities are not apparent or not realized into a state where they are apparent or fully realized. Unfold suggests usually a natural process by which is unveiled or disclosed the true character, the real beauty or ugliness, or the significance or insignificance of someone or something ⟨the bud *unfolds* itself into the flower⟩ ⟨I see thy beauty gradually *unfold*, daily and hourly, more and more— *Tennyson*⟩ ⟨they were theater people, and the *unfolding* of a new creative work was a solemnity—*Wouk*⟩ Evolve implies an unfolding or unrolling itself gradually and in orderly process; the term is particularly applicable when the slowness of the process and the complications involved in it are to be suggested ⟨the Protozoa . . . *evolved* the types that were transitional to higher animals—*Miner*⟩ ⟨societies are *evolved* in structure and function as in growth—*Spencer*⟩ ⟨life has *evolved* according to a Creator's plan—*Marquand*⟩ However *evolve* is often used with weakened emphasis on the implications of slowness and complexity to imply specifically the production of a result (as an idea, a theory, or an aesthetic effect) from within or as if from within ⟨twilight combined with the scenery of Egdon Heath to *evolve* a thing majestic without severity, impressive without showiness —*Hardy*⟩ ⟨this novel and intensely exacting technique, *evolved* . . . by the critical genius of a few . . . Frenchmen and of Henry James—*Montague*⟩ Develop (see also MATURE) implies a passing through several stages and stresses the coming out or unfolding of latent possibilities in a thing, whether by a natural process or through human means (compare DEVELOPMENT) ⟨there were different ideas of how the paper should *develop*. They wanted it to be successful; I wanted it to be outrageous—*Mailer*⟩ ⟨shorter than his wife—a jolly pink-faced man with a quietness that might have been *developed* to complement the noise she made—*Cheever*⟩ ⟨most of the great European thinkers of the eighteenth and early nineteenth centuries . . . helped to *develop* the conception Shaftesbury first formulated—*Ellis*⟩ Elaborate distinctively stresses attention to detail and increasing complication by means of which the latent possibilities of a thing are more fully or completely developed ⟨the sun, under whose influence one plant *elaborates* nutriment for man and

another poison—*Southey*⟩ ⟨the constitutional system which was in course of being gradually *elaborated*— *Gladstone*⟩ ⟨the Negro discovered and *elaborated* a morality . . . an ethical differentiation between the good and the bad in every human activity—*Mailer*⟩ Perfect stresses a freeing from faults, defects, or blemishes, and it can additionally imply an unfolding or development of something so that it stands as a complete or finished product ⟨she had cultivated and *perfected* a vast cowlike calm which served her now in good stead—*Pynchon*⟩ ⟨he first conceives, then *perfects* his design, as a mere instrument in hands divine—*Cowper*⟩ ⟨a new determination to complete and *perfect* his plant-setting machine had taken possession of him—*Anderson*⟩

*Ana* *show, manifest, evidence, evince, demonstrate: exhibit, display, expose (see SHOW)

2 *solve, resolve, unravel, decipher

**unformed** *formless, shapeless

*Ant* formed —*Con* *definite, definitive: developed, matured (see MATURE): fashioned, fabricated, manufactured, made (see MAKE)

**unfortunate** *unlucky, disastrous, ill-starred, ill-fated, calamitous, luckless, hapless

*Ana* baleful, malefic, *sinister: *miserable, wretched: unhappy, infelicitous (see UNFIT)

*Ant* fortunate —*Con* *lucky, providential, happy: auspicious, propitious, *favorable

**unfounded** *baseless, groundless, unwarranted

*Ana* *false, wrong: *misleading, deceptive: mendacious, *dishonest, untruthful

**unfruitful** barren, *sterile, infertile, impotent

*Ant* fruitful, prolific —*Con* *fertile, fecund

**ungodly** *irreligious, godless, unreligious, nonreligious

*Ana* wicked, evil, ill, *bad: reprobate, *abandoned, profligate: *impious, blasphemous, profane

**ungovernable** *unruly, intractable, refractory, recalcitrant, willful, headstrong

*Ana* *contrary, perverse, froward, wayward: contumacious, *insubordinate, rebellious, factious

*Ant* governable: docile —*Con* submissive, subdued, *tame: tractable, amenable, *obedient

**ungracious** *rude, ill-mannered, impolite, discourteous, uncivil

*Ana* churlish, boorish (see under BOOR): brusque, gruff, blunt, curt (see BLUFF)

*Ant* gracious

**unhappy** infelicitous, inapt, unsuitable, improper, inappropriate, unfitting, *unfit

*Ana* inept, maladroit, gauche, *awkward

*Ant* happy

**uniform** *adj* 1 *like, alike, similar, analogous, comparable, akin, parallel, identical

*Ana* *same, equivalent, equal

*Ant* various

2 *steady, constant, even, equable

*Ana* consistent, *consonant, compatible: regular, *orderly

*Ant* multiform

**unify** consolidate, concentrate, *compact

*Ana* *integrate, articulate, concatenate: organize, systematize (see ORDER *vb*): *unite, combine, conjoin

**unimpassioned** *sober, temperate, continent

*Ana* *cool, composed, collected, imperturbable: *calm, serene, placid, tranquil: *impassive, stolid, stoic, phlegmatic

*Ant* impassioned

**uninterested** *indifferent, unconcerned, incurious, aloof, detached, disinterested

**union** *unity, solidarity, integrity

---

*Ana* integration, articulation, concatenation (see under INTEGRATE): *harmony, consonance, accord, concord

**unique** 1 *single, sole, lone, solitary, separate, particular
*Ana* *only, alone
2 singular, *strange, peculiar, eccentric, erratic, odd, queer, quaint, outlandish, curious
*Ana* *exceptional: uncommon, rare, *infrequent

**unite** 1 conjoin, combine, *join, connect, link, associate, relate
*Ana* *mix, blend, merge, amalgamate: *weave, knit: *integrate, concatenate, articulate
*Ant* divide: alienate

2 **Unite, combine, conjoin, cooperate, concur** are comparable especially when they are applied to people or groups or categories of people or to human institutions and when they mean to join forces so as to act together or to form a larger unit. **Unite** may suggest either of these ends ⟨to *unite* their strength to maintain international peace and security—*Dean*⟩ ⟨states which would be politically independent but economically *united*—*Current Biog.*⟩ but it more commonly suggests the formation of a new or larger unit (as by merging) ⟨slowly *uniting* the Middle Eastern peoples in a strong emotional, religious nationalism—*Atyeo*⟩ **Combine** (see also JOIN) is often used interchangeably with *unite,* but it may be preferred when a somewhat looser or more temporary association is to be suggested ⟨several citizens *combined* to lead the campaign for the adoption of the city-manager form of government⟩ ⟨it is not so difficult to *combine* matrimony and a career in a small city—*Hobby*⟩ **Combine** also is the one of these words that is at all likely to carry derogatory connotations (compare *combine* under COMBINATION) ⟨no man is at liberty to *combine,* conspire and unlawfully agree to regulate the whole body of workingmen—*J. N. Welch & Richard Hofstadter*⟩ **Conjoin** (see also JOIN) stresses firmness of the combination ⟨the English army, that divided was into two parties, is now *conjoined* in one—*Shak.*⟩ ⟨despotism, priestcraft, and proletariat have ever been good friends; a kind of freemasonry . . . has *conjoined* them from time immemorial against the honest and educated classes—*Norman Douglas*⟩ **Cooperate** implies a combining for the sake of action or mutual support or assistance ⟨it is . . . difficult to induce a number of free beings to *cooperate* for their mutual benefit— *Goldsmith*⟩ ⟨because the states can so seldom *cooperate* on common problems, federal intervention is inevitable—*Armbrister*⟩ **Concur** in this relation retains the notion of agreement from another of its senses (which see under AGREE 2) and specifically implies a joining in agreement ⟨was also a member of the Senate Finance Committee, with which he *concurred* in a recommendation of lowered income taxes—*Current Biog.*⟩ ⟨the Scotch philosopher believed that there was a moral discipline in nature . . . . Bryant and Cole *concurred* in this opinion —*Ringe*⟩
*Ana* mingle, commingle, coalesce, fuse (see MIX): adhere, cohere, *stick, cling, cleave
*Ant* part

**unity,** solidarity, integrity, union can all denote a combining of all the parts, elements, or individuals into an effective whole, or the property or character of the whole achieved by such a combining. **Unity** is the comprehensive term applicable to wholes formed either of persons or of things; it may characterize such diverse things as a people, a nation, a church, an association, or a natural or artificial structure (as the human body or a cathedral) or a work of art (as a drama, an epic, a painting, or a bas-relief). In every case it implies oneness, especially of what is varied or diverse rather than uniform in its elements, that is

gained by the interdependence of parts or individuals and by the cooperation of all so that each within its proper limits helps in effecting the end of the whole ⟨the indispensable *unity* of a beautiful design—*Alexander*⟩ ⟨the wish to impose order upon confusion, to bring harmony out of dissonance and *unity* out of multiplicity is a kind of intellectual instinct, a primary and fundamental urge of the mind—*Huxley*⟩ **Unity** often implies a oneness of spirit that results in a group of persons when there is harmony and concord ⟨what he sought was *unity* of sentiment, not an unfeatured uniformity, and he attained it—*Buchan*⟩ **Solidarity** denotes a kind of unity in a group (as a class, a community, or an institution) which enables it to show its strength, express its opinion, or exert its influence both through individuals and through the whole with the force of an undivided mass; the term implies unwillingness in individuals or in subgroups to go counter to the interests, aspirations, or will of the group as a whole ⟨one secret of their power is their mutual good understanding . . . . They have *solidarity,* or responsibleness, and trust in each other—*Emerson*⟩ ⟨instead of national *solidarity* following the war, we have only a revival of Know-Nothingism; one faction of hyphenates tries to exterminate another faction—*Mencken*⟩ ⟨the Mingotts had not proclaimed their disapproval aloud: their sense of *solidarity* was too strong—*Wharton*⟩ **Integrity** is used chiefly in reference to wholes that have been built up so that each stands as a thing marked by completeness and a unity dependent on the perfection of its parts and their mutual interdependence; the term usually stresses soundness, undividedness, or freedom from impairment ⟨guarantee the *integrity* of the British Empire forever—*Upton Sinclair*⟩ ⟨the *integrity,* the clean drive and the unforced power that distinguishes the good "primitive" novel— —*Morton*⟩ **Union** is the general term for the act of uniting several things to form a whole or for the body or organization which results from such a uniting ⟨the *union* of thirteen states to form the United States⟩ However the term can carry the deeper implications of a thorough integration of parts and of their harmonious cooperation ⟨such harmony alone could hold all Heaven and Earth in happier *union*—*Milton*⟩ ⟨the *union,* peace and plenty of the kingdom—*Clarendon*⟩ ⟨thanks to . . . God, who has restored *union* to my family—*Scott*⟩
*Ana* identification, incorporation, embodiment, assimilation (see corresponding verbs at IDENTIFY): cooperation, concurrence, uniting, combining (see corresponding verbs at UNITE): integration, concatenation, articulation (see under INTEGRATE)

**universal** 1 **Universal, cosmic, ecumenical, catholic, cosmopolitan** can all mean worldwide or at least extremely widespread (as in extent, range, influence, appeal, or use). **Universal** is likely to suggest what is worldwide rather than pertinent to or characteristic of the whole universe; it is often further narrowed to refer to the world of men and human affairs or to important or significant parts of this world. It is likely to indicate a unanimity or conformity of practice or belief or a broad comprehensiveness ⟨no other theory which has won *universal* acceptance— *Binyon*⟩ ⟨the *universal* favor with which the New Testament is outwardly received—*Thoreau*⟩ ⟨replaced a philosophy which was crude and raw and provincial by one which was, in comparison, catholic, civilized, and *universal*—*T. S. Eliot*⟩ **Cosmic** is used to suggest matters pertinent to the whole universe as opposed to the earth, especially in suggestions of infinite vastness, distance, or force ⟨sardonic phantoms, whose vision is *cosmic,* not terrestrial—*Lowes*⟩ ⟨the great *cosmic* rhythm of the spirit which sets the currents of life in motion—*Binyon*⟩ **Ecu-**

**menical** applies to situations involving people throughout the whole world or all people in groups or divisions as indicated, often in religious contexts ⟨the incorporation of all the broken fragments of the former Iranic and Arabic societies into the wholly different structure of a Western World which has grown into an *ecumenical* "Great Society"—*Toynbee*⟩ **Catholic** may stress an attitude involved, as well as a fact, in the including, comprehending, or appreciating of all or many peoples, places, or periods ⟨he was a *catholic* nature lover. The tropics, the desert, the tundra, the glaciers and the prairies all found a place in his heart—*Peattie*⟩ **Cosmopolitan** may imply an understanding and appreciation of other lands, sections, nations, or cities coming about through personal experience in traveling or living elsewhere; it often contrasts with *provincial* ⟨one of the most entertaining and most *cosmopolitan* of novelists. Born in Tuscany, he was educated in New England, England, Germany, and Italy, became interested in Sanskrit, edited a newspaper in India—*Van Doren*⟩
*Ana* *earthly, terrestrial, worldly, mundane: *whole, entire, all, total

**2 Universal, general, generic, common** are comparable when they mean characteristic of, belonging or relating to, comprehending, or affecting all or the whole. **Universal** as used chiefly in logic and philosophy implies reference to each one of a whole (as a class, a category, or a genus) without exception; thus, "all men are animals" is a *universal* affirmative proposition, and "no man is omniscient" is a *universal* negative proposition; color is a *universal* attribute of visible objects, but chroma is not ⟨prolongation of the . . . war, with its increasing danger of *universal* catastrophe—*Science*⟩ ⟨habits both *universal* among mankind and peculiar to individuals—*Allport*⟩ ⟨if we want to get at the permanent and *universal* we tend to express ourselves in verse—*T. S. Eliot*⟩ **General** can imply reference to all, either of a precisely definable group (as a class, type, or species) ⟨ladies, a *general* welcome from his grace salutes ye all—*Shak.*⟩ ⟨these first assemblies were *general*, with all freemen bound to attend—*Amer. Guide Series: Md.*⟩ or of a more or less loosely or casually combined or associated number of items. In contrast to *universal, general* tends to be used with less precise boundaries and often implies no more than reference to nearly all or to most of the group ⟨ethylene has come into *general* but not yet *universal* favor with surgeons—*Morrison*⟩ ⟨the ideal of *general* cultivation has been one of the standards in education —*Eliot*⟩ But when used with respect to words, language, ideas, or notions, *general* tends to suggest lack of precision in use or signification ⟨some rather weak cases must fall within any law which is couched in *general* words—*Justice Holmes*⟩ **Generic** is often used in place of *general* when a term implying reference to every member of a genus or often of a clearly defined scientific or logical category and the exclusion of all other individuals is needed; thus, a *general* likeness between two insects may be a likeness that is merely observable, whereas a *generic* likeness is one that offers proof that they belong to the same genus or that enables a student to assign a hitherto unknown insect to its proper category; the use of words is a *general* characteristic of writing but the use of meter is a *generic* characteristic of poetry ⟨there is no such thing as a *generic* "Asian mind"—*R. A. Smith*⟩ ⟨the novel has always had a *generic* habit of reaching out to the extremes of literary expression—*Schorer*⟩ ⟨absolute *generic* unity would obtain if there were one summum genus under which all things without exception could be eventually subsumed—*James*⟩ **Common** (see

also COMMON 3; RECIPROCAL 1) differs from *general* in implying participation, use, or a sharing by all members of the class, group, or community of persons or, less often, of things under consideration ⟨a thing . . . practiced for two hundred years by *common* consent—*Justice Holmes*⟩ ⟨crowds . . . swept along by a *common* animating impulse —*Binyon*⟩ ⟨our *common* tongue—*Lowes*⟩
*Ant* particular

**universe** cosmos, macrocosm, *earth, world

**unkempt** slovenly, sloppy, *slipshod, disheveled
*Ana* frowzy, *slatternly, blowsy, dowdy: *negligent, neglectful, lax, slack, remiss

**unlawful, illegal, illegitimate, illicit** are comparable when they mean contrary to, prohibited by, or not in accordance with law or the law. Otherwise than this negation in character, the words in general carry the same differences in implications and connotations as the affirmative adjectives discriminated at LAWFUL. But there are a few recognizable differences. **Illegitimate** tends to be more narrowly used than *legitimate;* its most common application is to children born out of wedlock or to a relation which leads to such a result ⟨the *illegitimate* son of the Duke⟩ ⟨their union was *illegitimate*⟩ but it is occasionally referred to something that is not proper according to the rules (as of logic) or to the authorities or to precedent ⟨your inference is *illegitimate*⟩ ⟨it is *illegitimate* to suppose a chasm between the brute facts of physical nature . . . and the most abstract principles—*Alexander*⟩ ⟨I am far from thinking, with some modern theoretic purists, that it is *illegitimate* in painting to play on the power of association—*Binyon*⟩ **Illicit** is used much more widely than *illegitimate;* it may imply a lack of conformity to the provisions of a law intended to regulate the performance, the carrying on, or the execution of something that comes under the law of state or of church ⟨*illicit* liquor traffic⟩ ⟨an *illicit* marriage according to the Church may still be a legal marriage from the point of view of the State⟩ but it is also applied to something that is obtained, done, or maintained unlawfully, illegally, or illegitimately ⟨most persons . . . have long believed that happiness, being as they suspect somehow *illicit* at best, must have its locus beyond ourselves, beyond this world—*Edman*⟩ ⟨the tradition that *illicit* love affairs are at once vicious and delightful—*Shaw*⟩ ⟨the . . . monk who loved Virgil had to study him with an *illicit* candle—*Quiller-Couch*⟩
*Ant* lawful —*Con* iniquitous, nefarious, flagitious (see VICIOUS)

**unlearned** *ignorant, illiterate, unlettered, uneducated, untaught, untutored
*Ana* crude, *rude, rough, raw, callow, green, uncouth

**unlettered** illiterate, *ignorant, uneducated, untaught, untutored, unlearned

**unlikeness** *dissimilarity, difference, divergence, divergency, distinction
*Ana* diversity, *variety: disparity, variousness (see corresponding adjectives at DIFFERENT): discrepancy, discordance, incongruousness, incompatibility, inconsistency, inconsonance (see corresponding adjectives at INCONSONANT)
*Ant* likeness

**unlucky, disastrous, ill-starred, ill-fated, unfortunate, calamitous, luckless, hapless** can all mean having, meeting, or promising an outcome that is distinctly unfavorable (as to hopes, plans, or well-being). **Unlucky** implies that in spite of efforts or merits one meets with bad luck, often chronically, or that a specific occasion or action will be or has proved to be unfavorable especially in its outcome or consequences ⟨the child who is born on an *unlucky* day—*Kardiner*⟩ ⟨the loss of over $200,000 in an

---

*Ana* analogous words    *Ant* antonyms    *Con* contrasted words    See also explanatory notes facing page 1

*unlucky* coffee speculation—*H. G. Pearson*⟩ ⟨it was the *unluckiest* step we ever made to admit him into the bosom of our family—*Lytton*⟩ *Disastrous* and *ill-starred* both carry the astrological implication that the stars are adverse to the person or thing in question and both suggest a more or less dire fate for him or it ⟨the intrepid but *ill-starred* General . . . met with an airplane accident . . . and was burned to death—*Peers*⟩ Though *disastrous* and *ill-starred* often imply a calamitous result as inevitable ⟨in his fury made sudden decisions which would prove utterly *disastrous* to the fortunes of the Third Reich—*Shirer*⟩ ⟨the period and the region that produced Burr's *ill-starred* conspiracy—*H. E. Davis*⟩ *disastrous* is not infrequently used in a much weakened sense without a hint of inevitability or, often, an implication of consequences more serious than that of a turning of the tables upon one or the other of the participants or contenders ⟨a . . . denial of poetic possibilities . . . is liable to *disastrous* refutation by a triumphant instance of the "poetizing" . . . of that very word—*Lowes*⟩ **Ill-starred,** on the other hand, is close to **ill-fated** in meaning in that both imply an evil and unavoidable destiny awaiting a person or an action ⟨the holiday was *ill-starred* from the outset, and a series of minor catastrophes culminated in a blowout on a lonely road—*Cerf*⟩ ⟨the *ill-fated* attempt to collect the old war debts—*Soule*⟩ ⟨served as a wagoner with General Braddock's *ill-fated* army—*J. M. Brown*⟩ **Unfortunate,** though often interchangeable with *unlucky*, carries a much weaker implication of the intervention of chance ⟨had an *unfortunate* day at the races⟩ and a much stronger suggestion of misfortune, misery, unhappiness, or desolation, often to the extent of eliminating all suggestions of luck or of chance; occasionally it means nothing much more than *regrettable* or *disastrous* in its weakened sense ⟨a most *unfortunate* family⟩ ⟨an *unfortunate* choice of words⟩ ⟨expecting some *unfortunate* woman to instruct simultaneously a crowd of fifty urchins of all degrees of ignorance—*Grandgent*⟩ **Calamitous,** which is used of events rather than persons, resembles *unfortunate* in its frequent elimination of all suggestion of luck or chance and in sometimes meaning little more than *regrettable* or *upsetting* ⟨mother was afraid to leave the house in case something *calamitous* would happen, so we had a little extra time for dressing—*Molly Weir*⟩ but it, like the noun *calamity* (which see under DISASTER) often suggests dire misery or the utmost of woeful distress typically stemming from some grave and extraordinary event ⟨in that *calamitous* year of 1932 a total of 277,952 foreclosures forced people out of their homes—*O'Brien*⟩ ⟨men naturally admire Hannibal though the success of his cause might have been *calamitous* to the progress of civilization —*Cohen*⟩ ⟨there was more news than ever before, practically all of it *calamitous*—*Catton*⟩ **Luckless** and **hapless** are more or less rhetorical terms implying that the person or thing so described has or reveals less than average good luck or good fortune (as in his undertakings or in their outcome); usually these words mean nothing more than *unhappy, miserable,* or *wretched* ⟨she had disobeyed—and at the wrong time. Ah, the horrible, chancy, *luckless* wrong time—*Styron*⟩ ⟨*hapless* beings caught in the grip of forces we can do little about—*Whyte*⟩ ⟨the other victims . . . met an even more *hapless* fate—*E. S. Bates*⟩
*Ana* inept, *awkward: distressing, troubling (see TROUBLE): *sinister, malign, baleful
*Ant* lucky —*Con* auspicious, propitious, *favorable, benign: fortunate, happy, providential (see LUCKY)

**unman** *unnerve, emasculate, enervate
*Ana* sap, undermine, *weaken, enfeeble, debilitate: *abase, degrade: *deplete, drain, exhaust, impoverish,

bankrupt

**unmarried,** single, celibate, virgin, maiden are comparable as adjectives when they mean not united in bonds of marriage. **Unmarried** merely states the fact; it is usually applied to those who have not yet married, but in law, it is applicable to a person who has been divorced and has not remarried and, sometimes, to one who has been widowed ⟨an *unmarried* woman⟩ ⟨he said he would remain *unmarried*⟩ ⟨the question of being both unchaste and *unmarried* apparently never arises—*Marcuse*⟩ **Single** is applied to those who are not yet married but is commonly used of those who remain unmarried through life ⟨housing problems of *single* men and women⟩ ⟨has to take anything she can get in the way of a husband rather than face penury as a *single* woman—*Shaw*⟩ **Celibate** may be applied to the state of one having no expectation of marrying and it is especially applicable to that of one who is bound by a solemn vow to abstain from taking a mate. It is used chiefly of priests, monks, and nuns, of others who have dedicated their lives to religion, or of men or women who have accepted a way of life incompatible with having a spouse or children ⟨the masses of [Orthodox] believers preferred to confess to the *celibate* holy men . . . in the distant monastery—*Burks*⟩ ⟨the dandy must be *celibate,* cloistral; is, indeed, but a monk with a mirror for beads and breviary—an anchorite, mortifying his soul that his body may be perfect—*Beerbohm*⟩ **Virgin** tends to stress a pure unsullied state of chastity. It usually applies to the unmarried but it may also be referred to the married when the marital relation has not been consummated, usually on grounds of choice ⟨Saint Ursula and her *virgin* companions⟩ ⟨the young chief could not be told . . . for he was married, and the secret could be given only to a *virgin* youth—*Corlett*⟩ **Maiden** holds much the same implications as *virgin*, but it often differs in its heightened implication of not having married and in its subdued suggestion of purity and freedom from sexual intercourse ⟨he has two *maiden* sisters⟩ ⟨his mind partly on a slit-skirted *maiden* cyclist—*Birney*⟩

**unmatured** *immature, unripe, unmellow
*Ant* matured —*Con* *mature, adult, grown-up

**unmellow** *immature, unmatured, unripe
*Ana* mellow, mellowed —*Con* developed, ripened, matured (see MATURE *vb*)

**unmindful** *forgetful, oblivious
*Ana* heedless, thoughtless, *careless, inadvertent: *negligent, neglectful, remiss
*Ant* mindful: solicitous —*Con* careful, concerned, anxious, worried (see under CARE): *thoughtful, considerate, attentive

**unmitigated** *outright, out-and-out, arrant

**unmoral** *immoral, amoral, nonmoral

**unnatural** anomalous, *irregular
*Ana* *abnormal, aberrant, atypical: *monstrous, prodigious: *fantastic, grotesque, bizarre
*Ant* natural

**unnerve,** enervate, unman, emasculate can all mean to deprive of strength or vigor and of the capacity for endurance, overcoming difficulties, or making progress. **Unnerve** implies marked loss of courage, steadiness, and self-control or of power to act or fight usually as a result of some calamity or sudden shock ⟨government was *unnerved,* confounded, and in a manner suspended—*Burke*⟩ ⟨that beloved name *unnerved* my arm—*Arnold*⟩ ⟨entered . . . hesitantly, *unnerved* and bewildered—*Styron*⟩ ⟨the narcotic and *unnerving* property of these stimulants has been thoroughly established—*Day Lewis*⟩ **Enervate** implies a more gradual physical or moral weakening or dissipation of one's strength until one is too feeble

---

A colon (:) separates groups of words discriminated. An asterisk (*) indicates place of treatment of each group.

to make effort; usually the term implies a weakening of moral fiber under the influence of such debilitating factors as luxury, indolence, or effeminacy ⟨those unhappy people whose tender minds a long course of felicity has *enervated—Bolingbroke*⟩ ⟨Plato asserts that a life of drudgery disfigures the body and . . . *enervates* the soul —*Dickinson*⟩ **Unman** implies loss of manly fortitude or spirit; it often suggests a shameful reduction to tears, tremors, extreme timidity, or other state regarded as womanish ⟨what, quite *unmanned* in folly? . . . . Fie, for shame!—*Shak.*⟩ ⟨the strangeness of the night . . . the dead man they had left in the field had unsettled them all and had *unmanned* at least one of them—*Cheever*⟩ **Emasculate** (see also STERILIZE 1) implies a loss of essential or effective power especially by the removal of something (as a factor or a condition) which has made for strength (as of a person, a group, or a law) ⟨Hellenism . . . was not destroyed, though it was *emasculated*, by the loss of political freedom—*Inge*⟩ ⟨many states *emasculate* such civil rights statutes as exist—*Swindler*⟩
*Ana* upset, agitate, perturb (see DISCOMPOSE): bewilder, distract, confound (see PUZZLE *vb*): *weaken, enfeeble, sap, undermine
**unoffending** *harmless, innocuous, innocent, inoffensive
**unpremeditated** *extemporaneous, extempore, extemporary, improvised, impromptu, offhand
*Ant* premeditated —*Con* *deliberate, considered, designed, studied
**unpretentious** *plain, homely, simple
*Ana* *natural, unsophisticated, simple, ingenuous, unaffected: unassuming (see corresponding affirmative verb at ASSUME)
**unpropitious** *ominous, portentous, fateful, inauspicious
*Ana* *sinister, baleful, malign, malefic, maleficent: threatening, menacing (see THREATEN): *adverse, antagonistic, counter
*Ant* propitious
**unqualified** incompetent, *incapable
*Ana* disabled, crippled, weakened, debilitated (see WEAKEN): *unfit, unsuitable
*Ant* qualified —*Con* *able, capable, competent
**unquiet** *impatient, nervous, restless, restive, uneasy, fidgety, jumpy, jittery
*Ana* agitated, upset, perturbed, disquieted, disturbed (see DISCOMPOSE): worried, anxious, solicitous, concerned, careful (see under CARE)
*Ant* quiet
**unravel** *solve, resolve, unfold, decipher
*Ana* disentangle, untangle, *extricate: elucidate, explicate, interpret, *explain, expound
**unreasonable** *irrational
*Ana* absurd, preposterous, *foolish, silly: *simple, fatuous, asinine: *excessive, immoderate, inordinate
*Ant* reasonable
**unrelenting** *grim, implacable, relentless, merciless
*Ana* inexorable, obdurate, *inflexible, adamant: *stiff, rigid: *severe, stern
*Ant* forbearing
**unreligious** *irreligious, ungodly, godless, nonreligious
**unremitting** constant, incessant, *continual, continuous, perpetual, perennial
*Ana* unceasing, interminable, endless (see EVERLASTING): assiduous, sedulous, diligent (see BUSY): *indefatigable, untiring
*Con* remiss, lax, slack (see NEGLIGENT): *fitful, spasmodic: sporadic, *infrequent: desultory, haphazard, *random
**unripe** *immature, unmatured, unmellow
*Ana* crude, raw, green, callow, *rude: *premature, un-

timely, forward, precocious
*Ant* ripe —*Con* matured, ripened, developed (see MATURE *vb*)
**unruffled** imperturbable, unflappable, nonchalant, *cool, composed, collected
*Ana* *calm, placid, peaceful, serene, tranquil: poised, balanced (see STABILIZE)
*Ant* ruffled: excited
**unruly,** ungovernable, intractable, refractory, recalcitrant, willful, headstrong are comparable when they mean not submissive to government or control. **Unruly** stresses a lack of discipline or an incapacity for discipline; in addition it often connotes such qualities as turbulence, disorderliness, waywardness, or obstreperousness ⟨*unruly* children⟩ ⟨whatever my *unruly* tongue may say—*J. R. Green*⟩ ⟨the *unruly* passions—*T. S. Eliot*⟩ ⟨cleared the land, dug ditches and dammed *unruly* streams—*Amer. Guide Series: Ariz.*⟩ **Ungovernable** implies either an incapacity for or an escape from guidance or control. When applied directly or indirectly to persons, it usually suggests either no previous subjection to restrictions or a state of having thrown off previous restrictions ⟨the fiercest and most *ungovernable* part of the . . . population —*Macaulay*⟩ or the loss of all power to control oneself or to be controlled by others ⟨he fell into an *ungovernable* rage⟩ When used in reference to things, it usually suggests their incapacity for human direction or control ⟨that . . . *ungovernable* wonder the wind—*Hawthorne*⟩ ⟨genius was as valuable and as unpredictable, perhaps as *ungovernable*, as the waves of the sea—*Buck*⟩ **Intractable** and *refractory* both imply resistance to all attempts to bring under one's control, management, or direction. When applied to persons, **intractable** suggests a disposition to resist guidance or control ⟨an *intractable* child⟩ ⟨an *intractable* temper⟩ ⟨his rough, *intractable* spirit—*John Wesley*⟩ ⟨a young man who resisted his mistress' wishes was an *intractable* young man indeed—*Sackville-West*⟩ When applied to things, it suggests a more or less marked resistance to working, manipulation, treatment, or management ⟨*intractable* soil⟩ ⟨an *intractable* metal⟩ ⟨Shakespeare was unable to impose this motive successfully upon the *intractable* material of the old play—*T. S. Eliot*⟩ **Refractory**, on the other hand, often implies active resistance indicated by manifest disobedience, open protest, or rebelliousness ⟨it becomes my duty to struggle against my *refractory* feelings—*Burney*⟩ ⟨there is no use in making the *refractory* child feel guilty; it is much more to the purpose to make him feel that he is missing pleasures which the others are enjoying—*Russell*⟩ or, when the reference is to an inanimate thing, a degree of intractability that offers especially great resistance or presents unusual difficulties ⟨bricks and other *refractory* substances are used to line furnaces⟩ ⟨cheerfulness is in ethics what fluorspar is in metallurgy. It is a flux absolutely necessary in dealing with *refractory* moral elements —*Crothers*⟩ **Recalcitrant** carries an even stronger implication of active and violent resistance or of obstinate rebellion; it usually suggests defiance of another's will, order, or authority ⟨his father became *recalcitrant* and cut off the supplies—*Stevenson*⟩ ⟨in Russia a minority of devoted Marxists maintain by sheer force such government as is possible in the teeth of an intensely *recalcitrant* peasantry—*Shaw*⟩ The term is less often applied to things than *intractable* and *refractory*, but there is some use when seemingly insuperable difficulties are implied ⟨he discovers poetry in the most unlikely places and wrings it out of the most *recalcitrant* material—*Day Lewis*⟩ **Willful** usually implies intractability because of an overweening desire or an obstinate determination to

have one's own way and an unwillingness to be guided by those who are wise or experienced ⟨to *willful* men, the injuries that they themselves procure must be their schoolmasters—*Shak.*⟩ ⟨we know we haven't finality, and so we are open and receptive, rather than *willful*—H. G. *Wells*⟩ **Headstrong** implies violent self-will that makes for refractoriness or recalcitrance ⟨the *headstrong* young ruler, who had taken his country out of its alliance . . . into a foolish neutrality—*Shirer*⟩ ⟨they are testy and *headstrong* through an excess of will and bias—*Emerson*⟩ *Ana* *insubordinate, rebellious, contumacious: obstreperous, boisterous, strident (see VOCIFEROUS): *contrary, perverse, froward, wayward: fractious, *irritable, snappish, waspish
*Ant* tractable, docile
**unseemly** *indecorous, improper, unbecoming, indecent, indelicate
*Ana* unfitting, unsuitable, inappropriate (see UNFIT): incongruous, incompatible, inconsistent, *inconsonant
*Ant* seemly
**unsettle** *disorder, derange, disarrange, disorganize, disturb
*Ana* discommode, incommode, trouble (see INCONVENIENCE): upset, agitate, perturb, *discompose, disquiet
*Ant* settle
**unsightly** *ugly, hideous, ill-favored
*Ana* distasteful, obnoxious, repellent, *repugnant: *hateful, odious, detestable, abominable
**unsocial,** asocial, antisocial, nonsocial are comparable in meaning not social and therefore opposed in some way to what is social. However, they are not ordinarily interchangeable. **Unsocial** is applied chiefly to persons or to their temperaments, acts, and motives, and implies a distaste for the society of others or an aversion to companionship or fraternization ⟨he is a withdrawn, *unsocial* person⟩ ⟨an *unsocial* disposition⟩ **Asocial** is also applied to persons, but especially to their behavior, their thoughts, or their acts regarded objectively (as from the psychologist's point of view); it implies a lack of all the qualities which are suggested by the word *social* especially as opposed to *individual*. What is *asocial* lacks reference to, or orientation towards or in respect to, or significance for others and is by implication, individualistic, self-centered, egocentric, or egoistic ⟨*asocial* interests⟩ ⟨dreaming is an *asocial* act⟩ **Antisocial** is applied chiefly to things (as ideas, movements, acts, or writings) which are regarded as harmful to or destructive of society or the social order or institutions (as the state and church) ⟨anarchists are both *asocial* in their thinking and *antisocial* in their propaganda⟩ ⟨*antisocial* theories⟩ ⟨*antisocial* conduct⟩ **Nonsocial** is applied only to things which cannot be described as *social* in any sense of the word ⟨*nonsocial* questions⟩ ⟨*nonsocial* activities⟩
*Ant* social
**unsophisticated** *natural, simple, ingenuous, naïve, artless
*Ana* candid, *frank, open, plain: genuine, bona fide, *authentic: crude, callow, green, uncouth (see RUDE)
*Ant* sophisticated
**unspeakable** *unutterable, inexpressible, ineffable, indescribable, indefinable
*Ana* *offensive, loathsome, repulsive, revolting: *repugnant, repellent, obnoxious, distasteful: abominable, odious, *hateful, detestable
**unstable** *inconstant, fickle, capricious, mercurial
*Ana* *changeable, variable, mutable, protean: volatile, effervescent, buoyant, resilient, *elastic
*Ant* stable
**unsuitable** *unfit, improper, inappropriate, unfitting, inapt, unhappy, infelicitous

*Ana* unbecoming, unseemly, *indecorous, indecent: inept, maladroit, *awkward, clumsy, gauche
*Ant* suitable
**unsympathetic** 1 uncongenial, discordant, incongruous, incompatible, *inconsonant, inconsistent, discrepant
*Ant* sympathetic —*Con* harmonizing *or* harmonious, accordant, correspondent (see corresponding verbs at AGREE)
2 *antipathetic, averse
*Ana* *indifferent, unconcerned, incurious, aloof: *hardened, callous, indurated
*Ant* sympathetic
**untangle** disentangle, *extricate, disencumber, disembarrass
*Ana* *free, release, liberate
*Con* *hamper, fetter, manacle, shackle, trammel
**untaught** *ignorant, illiterate, unlettered, uneducated, untutored, unlearned
*Ant* taught
**untimely** *premature, forward, advanced, precocious
*Ana* *immature, unmatured, unripe, unmellow
*Ant* timely —*Con* *seasonable, opportune, well-timed, pat
**untiring** *indefatigable, tireless, weariless, unwearying, unwearied, unflagging
*Ana* unceasing, interminable, *everlasting: assiduous, sedulous, diligent (see BUSY): persevering, persisting (see PERSEVERE)
**untouchable** *n* *outcast, castaway, derelict, reprobate, pariah
**untruth** *lie, falsehood, fib, misrepresentation, story
*Ana* mendaciousness *or* mendacity, dishonesty, deceitfulness (see corresponding adjectives at DISHONEST): equivocation, tergiversation (see AMBIGUITY)
*Ant* truth —*Con* veracity, verity (see TRUTH): *honesty, integrity, probity, honor
**untruthful** lying, mendacious, *dishonest, deceitful
*Ana* *false, wrong: *misleading, deceptive, delusive, delusory
*Ant* truthful —*Con* honest, *upright, scrupulous: veracious (see corresponding noun at TRUTH)
**untutored** *ignorant, illiterate, unlettered, uneducated, untaught, unlearned
*Ant* tutored
**unutterable,** inexpressible, unspeakable, ineffable, indescribable, indefinable mean incapable of being told or described. All are often nothing more than intensives implying an extreme that goes beyond the power of words to express. In its more explicit denotations **unutterable** can imply such various reasons why the thing so qualified cannot be voiced or spoken, as the greatness of one's awe ⟨my tongue . . . attempts th' *unutterable* Name, but faints—*Watts*⟩ **Inexpressible** usually applies to what is so delicate, so immaterial, or so subtle, that there are no words to reveal its true or exact nature ⟨speech able to express subleties . . . that before seemed *inexpressible*—*Ellis*⟩ **Unspeakable** differs little from *unutterable* in its explicit meaning ⟨joy *unspeakable* and full of glory—*1 Pet* 1:8⟩ ⟨a thousand memories . . . *unspeakable* for sadness—*Tennyson*⟩ ⟨the bawdy thoughts that come into one's head—the *unspeakable* words—L. P. *Smith*⟩ More often, perhaps, *unspeakable* means too unpleasant, disgusting, or horrible to describe in detail ⟨twisted shapes of lust, *unspeakable,* abominable—*Tennyson*⟩ ⟨a pledge which enabled . . . officers to excuse themselves from any personal responsibility for the *unspeakable* crimes which they carried out—*Shirer*⟩ **Ineffable** is a near synonym of *inexpressible*, but carries a stronger suggestion of a character that transcends expression be-

A colon (:) separates groups of words discriminated. An asterisk (*) indicates place of treatment of each group.

cause of some elusive quality (as etherealness, spirituality, or ideality ⟨*ineffable* tenderness⟩ ⟨the eyes remained distant and serious, as if bent on some *ineffable* vision —*Wharton*⟩ ⟨to explore the delicate involutions of consciousness, the microscopically sensuous and all but *ineffable* frissons of mental becoming—*Mailer*⟩ ⟨who shall say that in this silence, in this hovering wan light, in this air bereft of wings, and of all scent save freshness, there is less of the *ineffable*, less of that before which words are dumb?—*Galsworthy*⟩ **Indescribable** and **indefinable** may imply to the thing a quality or sometimes the lack of any quality or to the would-be describer or definer a deficiency (as of perceptiveness, understanding, or language) that makes precise description, definition, narration, or explanation impossible ⟨I keep being conscious of some subtle smell . . . . It's not exactly a smell, either! It's more than that. It's a taste in the mouth and a strange *indescribable* feeling through every pore of the body—*Powys*⟩ ⟨an *indescribable* horror . . . . I myself could hardly put it into words. But the effect it has upon me I *could* describe; only that would make you as miserable as I am—*Powys*⟩ ⟨our men have fought with *indescribable* and unforgettable gallantry—*Roosevelt*⟩ ⟨she lacks the *indefinable* charm of weakness—*Wilde*⟩ ⟨if an idea cannot be analyzed into any function of a given set of primitive ideas, it is *indefinable* relative to that set —*Richard Robinson*⟩ ⟨men may attribute to women mysterious, *indefinable* traits which finally prove to be mere caprice—*Blankenagel*⟩

**unwarranted** *baseless, groundless, unfounded
*Ana* unauthorized, unaccredited (see corresponding affirmative verbs at AUTHORIZE): unapproved, unsanctioned (see corresponding affirmative verbs at APPROVE)
*Ant* warranted

**unwearied** *indefatigable, tireless, weariless, untiring, unwearying, unflagging
*Ana* persevering, persisting *or* persistent (see corresponding verbs at PERSEVERE): unceasing, interminable (see EVERLASTING): constant, *steady

**unwearying** *indefatigable, tireless, weariless, untiring, unwearied, unflagging
*Ana* see those at UNTIRING

**unwholesome**, morbid, sickly, diseased, pathological apply to what is unhealthy or unhealthful in any of various ways. Unwholesome is applicable not only to what is not healthy or healthful physically and mentally but also to what is morally corruptive ⟨sick at heart, and enfeebled by *unwholesome* diet—*Bancroft*⟩ ⟨*unwholesome* surroundings in which to bring up children⟩ ⟨an aura . . . of *unwholesome* cleverness—*J. V. Baker*⟩ ⟨an *unwholesome* influence⟩ **Morbid**, in the sense of showing the effects of disease, is somewhat old-fashioned ⟨a *morbid* condition of the liver⟩ ⟨*morbid* tissue⟩ The term is more often descriptive of a physical, emotional, mental, or social condition or of fancies, feelings, or behavior that are abnormal or are a sign of abnormality (as derangement, decadence, or deterioration) ⟨displayed a *morbid* interest in the gruesome details of the accident⟩ ⟨in this vision . . . there is something of *morbid* suspicion—*Edmund Wilson*⟩ ⟨her thoughts had been more and more preoccupied with death, and with her *morbid* shame lest someone see her in the state of nature after she was dead —*Wolfe*⟩ ⟨but one feels gradually creeping on . . . the *morbid* excitement of the high-tensioned life around her —*Ellis*⟩ **Sickly**, more than any of these words, implies the appearance of weakness or wanness characteristic of poor health, or an inherent lack of robustness or virility; it applies not only to persons but to animals and to plants, not only to bodies but to minds and souls, not

only to thoughts, feelings, and behavior, but to objective things (as colors, odors, or lights) that suggest the quality or character of a person weakened or wasted by disease ⟨*sickly* children⟩ ⟨a *sickly* plant⟩ ⟨a pallor that gave his dark skin a *sickly* look—*Hervey*⟩ ⟨the chronic habits of the *sickly* soul—*Crabbe*⟩ **Diseased** applies not only to something (as a part or an organism) that is attacked by disease, but, like *morbid*, is often extended to whatever is deranged, disordered, dying, or abnormal ⟨a *diseased* skin⟩ ⟨canst thou not minister to a mind *diseased*?— *Shak.*⟩ ⟨when love grows *diseased*, the best thing we can do is to put it to a violent death—*Etherege*⟩ **Pathological** is applied to physical, mental, and moral conditions which have their origin in disease or which constitute gross deviations from the usual, expected, or normal, and, by implication, the wholesome ⟨enormously sensitive and resilient, almost *pathological* in his appetite for activity. —*Mencken*⟩ ⟨the beguiling Alice-world of *pathological* curves, some of which bound a small finite area and yet are infinite in length, while others entirely fill squares, cubes, and hypercubes, and some cross themselves at all points—*Gridgeman*⟩ ⟨this irrational age, governed by absolute violence and *pathological* hate—*Mumford*⟩
*Ana* detrimental, deleterious, noxious, *pernicious, baneful: toxic, *poisonous: injurious, hurtful, harmful, mischievous (see corresponding nouns at INJURY)
*Ant* wholesome  —*Con* *healthful, salubrious, salutary, hygienic: *healthy, robust, sound

**upbraid** *scold, rate, berate, tongue-lash, revile, vituperate, jaw, bawl, chew out, wig, rail
*Ana* reprehend, reprobate, blame, censure, denounce (see CRITICIZE): reproach, reprimand, rebuke, *reprove

**upheaval** *commotion, agitation, tumult, turmoil, turbulence, confusion, convulsion
*Ana* heaving, raising, lifting (see LIFT *vb*): alteration, change (see under CHANGE *vb*): cataclysm, catastrophe, *disaster

**uphold** *support, advocate, back, champion
*Ana* *help, aid, assist: defend, vindicate, justify, *maintain: sanction, *approve, endorse
*Ant* contravene: subvert

**upright**, honest, just, conscientious, scrupulous, honorable are comparable when they are applied to men or their acts and words and mean having or exhibiting a strict regard for what is morally right. **Upright** implies manifest rectitude and an uncompromising adherence to high moral principles ⟨the old-fashioned word *upright*. It's a good word, comprises a good many things—all the straight qualities, like loyalty, truthfulness, the right sort of pride —*Goudge*⟩ ⟨we shall exult, if they who rule the land, be men . . . wise, *upright*, valiant; not a servile band— *Wordsworth*⟩ **Honest** implies a recognition of and strict adherence to solid virtues (as truthfulness, candor, respect for others' possessions, sincerity, and fairness) ⟨it was fiction, but it was made as all *honest* fiction must be, from the stuff of human life—*Wolfe*⟩ It is more widely applicable than *upright* which often implies independence of spirit and self-mastery and which is therefore referable chiefly to thoughtful and highly disciplined men. *Honest*, on the other hand, may be used in reference to the ignorant as well as the learned, and to the simple as well as the wise ⟨the *honest* heart that's free frae a' intended fraud or guile—*Burns*⟩ ⟨if we be *honest* with ourselves, we shall be *honest* with each other—*Macdonald*⟩ **Just** (see also FAIR) may stress conscious choice and regular practice of what is right or equitable ⟨a *just* man, and one that feareth God, and of good report among all the nation of the Jews—*Acts* 10:22⟩ ⟨human beings are a good deal less rational and innately *just* than the optimists of the

eighteenth century supposed—*Huxley*⟩ *Conscientious* and *scrupulous* both imply an active moral sense which governs all one's actions. **Conscientious** stresses painstaking efforts to follow that guide at all costs, especially in one's observance of the moral law or in the performance of one's duty ⟨his whole character ... was far too sturdily *conscientious* to allow of any suspicion being cast upon his rectitude—*A. W. Ward*⟩ ⟨*conscientious* and incorruptible and right-minded, a young man born to worry —*Styron*⟩ **Scrupulous** (see also CAREFUL 2), on the other hand, implies either anxiety in obeying strictly the dictates of conscience or meticulous attention to the morality of the details of conduct as well as to the morality of one's ends ⟨Sebastian was *scrupulous*, and certain accepted conventions had forced him to satisfy his conscience— *Sackville-West*⟩ **Honorable** (see also HONORABLE 1) implies the guidance of a high sense of honor or of a sense of what one should do in obedience not only to the dictates of conscience but to the demands made by social position or office, by the code of his profession, or by the esteem in which he is held ⟨Leopold's defenders ... believed that he had done the right and *honorable* thing in sharing the fate of his soldiers and of the Belgian people—*Shirer*⟩ ⟨did this vile world show many such as thee, thou perfect, just, and *honorable* man—*Shelley*⟩
*Ana* *moral, ethical, virtuous, righteous: *fair, equitable, impartial: *straightforward, aboveboard
**uprising** *rebellion, revolution, revolt, insurrection, mutiny, putsch, coup
*Ana* fight, combat, conflict, fray (see CONTEST): strife, contention, dissension (see DISCORD): aggression, *attack
**uproar** *din, pandemonium, hullabaloo, babel, hubbub, clamor, racket
*Ana* strife, contention, dissension, *discord, conflict, variance: *confusion, disorder, chaos: fracas, *brawl, broil, melee
**uproot** eradicate, deracinate, extirpate, *exterminate, wipe
*Ana* *abolish, extinguish, annihilate, abate: supplant, displace, *replace, supersede: subvert, overthrow, *overturn: *destroy, demolish
*Ant* establish: inseminate
**upset** *vb* 1 *overturn, capsize, overthrow, subvert
*Ana* invert, *reverse: bend (see CURVE *vb*)
2 agitate, perturb, disturb, disquiet, *discompose, fluster, flurry
*Ana* bewilder, distract, confound (see PUZZLE *vb*): discomfit, rattle, faze, *embarrass: *unnerve, unman
**upshot** outcome, issue, result, consequence, *effect, aftereffect, aftermath, event, sequel
*Ana* *end, termination, ending: climax, culmination (see SUMMIT): concluding *or* conclusion, finishing *or* finish, completion (see corresponding verbs at CLOSE)
**urbane** *suave, smooth, diplomatic, bland, politic
*Ana* courteous, polite, courtly, *civil: poised, balanced (see STABILIZE): cultured, cultivated, refined (see corresponding nouns at CULTURE)
*Ant* rude: clownish, bucolic
**urge** *vb* **Urge, egg, exhort, goad, spur, prod, prick, sic** mean to press or impel to action, effort, or speed. **Urge** implies the exertion of influence or pressure either from something or someone external or from something within (as the conscience or the heart); specifically it suggests an inciting or stimulating to or toward a definite end (as greater speed or a prescribed course or objective) often against the inclinations or habits of the one urged ⟨the crowd *urged* on their favorites with shouts of encouragement⟩ ⟨his conscience *urged* him to battle for the cause⟩ ⟨with remarkable speed the four guests ... saddled their

mules and *urged* them across the plain—*Cather*⟩ ⟨his new young life, so strong and imperious, was *urged* towards something else—*D. H. Lawrence*⟩ **Egg** usually presupposes a hesitant, inert, or lagging will and usually suggests an encouraging or even an abetting ⟨schemers and flatterers would *egg* him on—*Thackeray*⟩ ⟨she *egged* me to borrow the money—*Kipling*⟩ **Exhort** may suggest the arts of a preacher or orator inciting men to good or better lives or actions and usually implies a fervor or zeal characteristic of a preacher in stimulating through admonition, encouragement, or pleading ⟨William *exhorted* his friend to confess, and not to hide his sin any longer—*George Eliot*⟩ ⟨he may probably be *exhorted* to "do well in his examination"—*Inge*⟩ **Goad** basically denotes the use of a pointed rod in driving cattle and carries in its extended use a strong implication of something that irritates or inflames and drives one on in spite of inclinations or habit of yielding to other desires or motives ⟨many of them ... had been *goaded* by petty persecution into a temper fit for desperate enterprise—*Macaulay*⟩ ⟨man's inquisitive nature has *goaded* him on to look deeply into these matters —*Morrison*⟩ **Spur** basically applies to a spiked device attached to the heels of a rider and used to urge on a lagging horse; it is likely to suggest in its extended use a superior impulsion that makes up for the weakness or reluctance of one's nature or will ⟨love will not be *spurred* to what it loathes—*Shak.*⟩ ⟨he is ... *spurred* on by yearnings after an unsearchable delight—*Symonds*⟩ ⟨reproaches too, whose power may *spur* me on ... to honorable toil —*Wordsworth*⟩ **Prod** implies a being driven or forced into action as if by means of a stick or goad and may suggest a thrust or a push and an impelling against one's will ⟨the excitement of trying ... to *prod* them into action —*J. R. Green*⟩ ⟨Indians grew hungry and hatred of the white man *prodded* them into open hostilities—*Julian Dana*⟩ **Prick** comes close to *spur* in implying an impulsion from something sharp-pointed or irritating that serves to urge or drive ⟨rely on their animal instinct and developed reflexes to *prick* them into awareness when danger threatened—*Majdalany*⟩ ⟨*pricked* on by knightly spur of female eyes—*J. R. Lowell*⟩ **Sic** basically means to urge on a dog to chase or attack someone; with persons it often implies exhorting or goading to attack or worry ⟨a civilized nation *sicced* on the Barbary whelps to tear the peaceful passerby—*Spears*⟩
*Ana* impel, drive, actuate, *move: stimulate, excite, quicken, *provoke
**urge** *n* *desire, lust, passion, appetite
*Ana* *motive, spring, spur, goad, incentive: longing, yearning, pining (see LONG): craving, coveting, desiring (see DESIRE *vb*)
**urgent** *pressing, imperative, crying, importunate, insistent, exigent, instant
*Ana* impelling, driving (see MOVE): constraining, compelling, obliging (see FORCE *vb*)
**usage** 1 practice, custom, use, *habit, habitude, wont
*Ana* *method, mode, manner, way, fashion: procedure, proceeding, *process: guiding *or* guidance, leading *or* lead (see corresponding verbs at GUIDE): *choice, preference
2 *form, convention, convenance
*Ana* formality, ceremony, *form
**use** *n* 1 **Use, service, advantage, profit, account, avail** can all mean a useful or valuable end, result, or purpose. **Use** stresses either employment for some purpose or end of practical value ⟨turn every scrap of material to *use*⟩ or the practical value of the end promoted or attained ⟨the findings in the investigation were of little *use*⟩ ⟨sweet are the *uses* of adversity—*Shak.*⟩ **Service,** though often

---

A colon (:) separates groups of words discriminated. An asterisk (*) indicates place of treatment of each group.

interchangeable with *use*, is especially appropriate when the reference is to persons or animals or their work or actions ⟨the horse was unfit for *service—Scott*⟩ ⟨render a *service* to a friend⟩ *Service* often implies that the result of one's act or works is beneficial ⟨I have done the state some *service*, and they know't—*Shak.*⟩ **Advantage** adds to *use* the implication of improvement or enhancement (as in value or position) ⟨he uses every penny to *advantage*⟩ ⟨her beauty proved to be of great *advantage* to her in her stage career⟩ ⟨Constance had never before seen him to such heroic *advantage—Bennett*⟩ ⟨true Wit is Nature to *advantage* dressed—*Pope*⟩ **Profit** distinctively implies reward or the rewarding character of what is attained, and often implies pecuniary gain ⟨the student worked hard but to no *profit*⟩ ⟨he found moral *profit* also in this self-study; for how, he asked, can we correct our vices if we do not know them—*L. P. Smith*⟩ ⟨coal and steel interests were merging with mutual *profit—Amer. Guide Series: Pa.*⟩ **Account** is used chiefly in fixed phrases ⟨turn his musical talent to *account*⟩ ⟨of little *account*⟩ It is sometimes interchangeable with *use*, *advantage*, or *profit*, but distinctively it suggests calculable value ⟨a book that turns to *account* the conclusions of other recent German theorists—*Babbitt*⟩ Sometimes it is nearly equivalent to *importance* ⟨our family . . . whose honor is of so much *account* to both of us—*Dickens*⟩ **Avail** so strongly suggests effectualness or effectiveness in the end attained that the negative idiomatic phrases in which it is often found are equivalent to *ineffectual* or *ineffectually* ⟨the search was of no *avail*⟩ ⟨he labored unceasingly without *avail* to move the rock⟩ ⟨he studied hard but to no *avail*⟩

*Ana* benefit, profit (see corresponding verbs at BENEFIT): value, *worth: *function, office, duty: purpose, *intention, object

**2 Use, usefulness, utility** are comparable when they mean the character or the quality of serving or of being able to serve an end or purpose. **Use** (see also USE 1; HABIT) is the most general or least explicit of these terms; it usually implies little more than suitability for employment for some purpose stated or implied ⟨our gymnasium . . . is of excellent *use*, and all my girls exercise in it—*Meredith*⟩ ⟨she said she would have saved the pieces had they been of any *use*⟩ **Usefulness**, on the other hand, is employed chiefly with reference to definite concrete things that serve or are capable of serving a practical purpose ⟨demonstrated the *usefulness* of his device⟩ ⟨her [the cat's] sacred character was in no wise impaired by her *usefulness* —*Repplier*⟩ ⟨libraries have moved into that wider area of *usefulness* which today makes them one of the most effective instruments for ensuring a democratic way of life —*Collier's Yr. Bk.*⟩ **Utility**, which comes very close to *usefulness*, may be preferred in technical, economic, and philosophical speech or writing, where it is often regarded as a property that can be measured or altered (as in quantity or quality) or that can be viewed as an abstraction ⟨the extent to which the price of motorcars per unit of *utility* has fallen—*Schumpeter*⟩ ⟨in economics production is simply the creation of *utility* . . . adding some kind of *utility* to raw materials so that they will satisfy consumers' wants—*Goodman & Moore*⟩ ⟨universities exist for two purposes; on the one hand, to train men and women for certain professions; on the other hand, to pursue learning and research without regard to immediate *utility—Russell*⟩

*Ana* applicability, relevance, pertinence (see corresponding adjectives at RELEVANT): suitability, fitness, appropriateness (see corresponding adjectives at FIT)

**3** wont, practice, usage, custom, *habit, habitude

*Ana* *form, usage: rite, ceremony, formality (see FORM *n*)

**use** *vb* **Use, employ, utilize, apply, avail** can all mean to deal with something so as to give it a practical value or to make it serviceable to oneself or others. One **uses** a thing, or a person when regarded as a passive object, as a means or instrument to the accomplishment of a purpose or as an aid to the attainment of an end; the thing may be concrete ⟨*use* a hoe in cultivating⟩ ⟨*used* a dictionary to build up his vocabulary⟩ ⟨*use* a person as a tool⟩ or it may be abstract ⟨*use* patience in dealing with children⟩ ⟨*use* discretion in investing money⟩ ⟨the way to learn to *use* words is to read some good literature often and carefully—*Russell*⟩ ⟨his sense of being *used* rose suddenly above the treacherous sympathy he had begun to feel for her—*Tarkington*⟩ One **employs** a person or thing that is idle, inactive, or not in use, when he puts him or it to work or finds a profitable use for him or it ⟨she had . . . *employed* her leisure in reading every book that came in her way— *Shaw*⟩ ⟨the student crammed full of knowledge which he cannot *employ—Grandgent*⟩ ⟨craftsmen were finding in the new land raw materials on which they could *employ* all their artistry—*Amer. Guide Series: Pa.*⟩ Although *use* and *employ* are often interchanged, there can be a perceptible difference in meaning: wherever the idea of serving as the means or instrument is uppermost, *use* is likely to be preferred; wherever the idea of engaging or selecting, of keeping occupied or busy, or of turning to account is uppermost, *employ* is the desirable and often the necessary choice; thus, a writer *uses* words effectively who knows what ones he should *employ* in a given context; a teacher often *uses* his pupils as monitors when he should keep them *employed* in study. One **utilizes** something when he finds a profitable use for it or discovers how to employ it for a practical purpose ⟨he even tried to figure out a way to *utilize* the small limbs cut from the tops of the trees—*Anderson*⟩ ⟨charged against him that he *utilized* his military office for private gain—*R. G. Adams*⟩ One **applies** something when he brings it into contact or into relation with something else where it will prove its usefulness or acquire practical value. This suggestion of making a connection or bringing into contact is strong in all senses of *apply* (see also DIRECT, RESORT); in the present sense it can not only affect the construction but can even obscure the implication of usefulness; thus, one *uses* a mustard plaster to relieve a chest pain, but one *applies* a mustard plaster to the chest. The same implication distinguishes *apply* from the other words when the idea of usefulness is stressed; thus, one who knows how to *employ* words reveals his ability to select those words that express his exact meaning, no more and no less, but one who knows how to *apply* words reveals his ability to use them relevantly, that is, in reference to the things or ideas with which they are idiomatically associated ⟨foreigners learning English find difficulty in *applying* certain words and phrases (as *evening dress* and *nightdress*, *tool* and *instrument*, or *bad* and *naughty*)⟩ ⟨our own word *virtue* is *applied* only to moral qualities; but the Greek word which we so translate should properly be rendered "excellence," and includes a reference to the body as well as to the soul—*Dickinson*⟩ The implication of a useful or definite end is strongest in *apply* when the word carries the further suggestion of relating what is general or theoretical to what is particular or concrete, for some such practical purpose as identification ⟨we can discover if this fabric is woolen by *applying* specific tests⟩ or clarification of a problem ⟨before forming an opinion, the judges must know what laws *apply* to the particular case⟩ or invention ⟨most modern inventions and discoveries are the result of a fresh outlook in *applying* the laws of physics and chemistry⟩ ⟨the law does all that

---

*Ana* analogous words    *Ant* antonyms    *Con* contrasted words    See also explanatory notes facing page 1

is needed when it does all that it can, indicates a policy, *applies* it to all within the lines, and seeks to bring within the lines all similarly situated—*Justice Holmes*⟩ ⟨it is a test which we may *apply* to all figure painters—a test which will often discover the secret of unsatisfactory design—if we ask whether the figures are really occupied by what they are doing—*Binyon*⟩ One **avails** (*oneself of*) something or someone that is at hand or is offered by using it or him to one's own benefit or advantage ⟨far from resenting such tutelage I am only too glad to *avail* myself of it—*Shaw*⟩ ⟨takes us . . . into the consciousness of his characters, and in order to do so, he has *availed* himself of methods of which Flaubert never dreamed—*Edmund Wilson*⟩
*Ana* *handle, manipulate, ply, wield: *practice, exercise
**usefulness** *use, utility
*Ana* value, *worth: *excellence, merit
**usual, customary, habitual, wonted, accustomed** can mean familiar through frequent or regular repetition. **Usual** stresses the absence of strangeness and is applicable to whatever is normally expected or happens in the ordinary course of events ⟨they paid the *usual* fee⟩ ⟨open for business as *usual*⟩ ⟨it appeared to him to be the *usual* castle, and he saw nothing unusual in the manner of his reception by the *usual* old lord—*Henry Adams*⟩ ⟨the characters were better drawn than is *usual* in romantic drama—*Quinn*⟩ ⟨darkness caused them to speak much louder than *usual*—*Dahl*⟩ **Customary** often implies characteristic or distinguishing quality, and is applied to whatever is according to the usual or prevailing practices, conventions, or usages of a particular person or, especially, of a particular community ⟨having her *customary* cup of tea before walking down the road to the bus stop—*Salinger*⟩ ⟨we had no idea how men behave when their *customary* way of life is disrupted—*Lippmann*⟩ Sometimes invariable or fixed quality is implied ⟨the assumption that whatever has been *customary* must be bad, and that anything which is or seems novel must be good—*Grandgent*⟩ **Habitual** implies settled or established practice, and is commonly applied to what has settled by long

repetition into a habit ⟨his *habitual* energy⟩ ⟨a *habitual* smile⟩ ⟨I stop ashamed, for I am talking *habitual* thoughts, and not adapting them to her ear—*Yeats*⟩ ⟨shut away from all that was familiar and *habitual* to him—*Hervey*⟩ **Wonted**, a somewhat bookish word, stresses habituation, but tends to be applied to what is favored, sought, or purposefully cultivated ⟨in revolutionary times when all our *wonted* certainties are violently called in question—*Moberly*⟩ ⟨robbed him of his peace, destroying his pleasure in *wonted* things—*Parrington*⟩ **Accustomed** is often interchangeable with *wonted* and *customary*, but it is a more familiar word than the first and is weaker in its suggestions of custom and fixity than the second ⟨work with *accustomed* diligence⟩ ⟨even his evening clothes were as habitual as his breath and hung on him with a weary and *accustomed* grace as if he had been born in them—*Wolfe*⟩
*Ana* *regular, natural, normal, typical: *common, ordinary, familiar: prevalent, *prevailing, rife, current
**usurp** *arrogate, preempt, appropriate, confiscate
*Ana* seize, *take, grab, grasp
*Ant* abdicate
**utensil** *implement, tool, instrument, appliance
*Ana* *device, contrivance, contraption, gadget
**utility** *use, usefulness
*Ana* suitability, fitness, appropriateness (see corresponding adjectives at FIT): value, *worth
**utilize** *use, employ, apply, avail
*Ana* *benefit, profit: *handle, manipulate, ply, wield: forward, further, promote, *advance
**utopian** *ambitious, pretentious
*Ana* impracticable, unfeasible, impossible (see affirmative adjectives at POSSIBLE): visionary, quixotic, chimerical (see IMAGINARY): ideal, transcendental, *abstract
**utter** *vb* **1** *say, tell, state
*Ana* enunciate, *articulate, pronounce: *speak, talk
**2** *express, vent, voice, broach, air, ventilate
*Ana* enunciate, *articulate, pronounce: *reveal, disclose, discover, divulge: *declare, announce, publish, advertise

# V

**vacant** *empty, blank, void, vacuous
*Ana* *bare, barren: destitute, void, *devoid: idiotic, imbecilic, foolish (see corresponding nouns at FOOL)
*Con* *full, complete, replete
**vacate** *annul, abrogate, void, quash
**vacillate** *hesitate, waver, falter
*Ana* fluctuate, sway, oscillate (see SWING): *demur, scruple, boggle
**vacuous** *empty, vacant, blank, void
*Ana* barren, *bare: inane, wishy-washy, *insipid
*Con* *full, replete
**vacuum** *n* void, cavity, *hole, hollow, pocket
**vagabond, vagrant, truant, tramp, bum, hobo** mean a person who wanders at will or as a habit. **Vagabond** may apply to a homeless wanderer lacking visible means of support ⟨apprehend all nightwalkers . . . *vagabonds* and disorderly persons—*Philadelphia Ordinances*⟩ but more often it lacks derogatory implications and emphasizes the mere fact of wandering and implies a carefree fondness for a roaming life ⟨Rousseau . . . that young *vagabond* of genius—*L. P. Smith*⟩ ⟨an exquisite defense of the fine

art of irresponsible travel, and an encomium on the "cultured *vagabond*"—*Nock*⟩ **Vagrant** is more likely to imply disreputableness and in its common legal use it denotes a person without fixed or known residence whose habits or acts are such that he is likely to become a public menace or a public charge ⟨arrested as a *vagrant*⟩ ⟨the jail is the winter home of many *vagrants*⟩ Even in more general use the term tends to carry stronger implications of disreputableness and waywardness than *vagabond* ⟨every beggar, *vagrant*, exile-by-choice and peregrine-at-large . . . . This whole hard-up population—*Pynchon*⟩ ⟨a chronic *vagrant* from the spirit's home—*Sapir*⟩ **Truant** carries as its strongest implication the habit of wandering away from where one ought to be or of loitering when one ought to be elsewhere and especially at school ⟨I have a *truant* been to chivalry—*Shak.*⟩ ⟨by *truant* we mean a boy of school age who intentionally stays away from school for no other reason than that he does not wish to go—*Powers & Witmer*⟩ **Tramp** is the ordinary and generally derogatory word for one who leads a wandering life; it can apply to any such person whether

A colon (:) separates groups of words discriminated. An asterisk (*) indicates place of treatment of each group.

he moves about in search of work, especially seasonal work, or whether he lives by beggary and thievery ⟨whoever, not being under seventeen, a blind person or a person asking charity within his own town, roves about from place to place begging, or living without labor or visible means of support, shall be deemed a *tramp*— *General Laws of the Commonwealth of Mass.*⟩ ⟨a distinct class of these gentlemen *tramps,* young men no longer young, who wouldn't settle down, who disliked polite society and the genteel conventions—*Santayana*⟩ **Bum** basically applies to a lazy, idle, and often drunken, good-for-nothing, who will not work but habitually sponges on others ⟨dwells in a black-and-white world where a guy is either your pal or probably a *bum*—*Hal Boyle*⟩ ⟨the local ne'er-do-well, the traditional village *bum*⟩ But *bum,* especially when qualified, may denote one who wanders in pursuit of a particular occupation or activity ⟨fruit *bums* who follow the harvests north⟩ ⟨a ski *bum*⟩ **Hobo** is often distinguished from *tramp,* sometimes in terms of willingness to work, sometimes in terms of methods of travel, the *tramp* being then taken as one who typically tramps the roads, the *hobo* as one who typically rides surreptitiously on freight trains. A common application of *hobo* is to the migratory worker who roves about following such seasonal occupations as harvesting and crop picking ⟨*hoboes* are traveling workers, *tramps* are traveling shirkers and *bums* are stationary shirkers— *Cleveland Plain Dealer*⟩ ⟨in Western parlance a *hobo* is not a tramp. A *hobo* is a migratory laborer, who carries his blankets on his back, looking for work—*World's Work*⟩ *Ana* wanderer, roamer, rover (see corresponding verbs at WANDER)

**vagary** *caprice, freak, fancy, whim, whimsy, conceit, crotchet
*Ana* *mood, humor, temper, vein: *fancy, fantasy, dream, daydream: notion, *idea

**vagrant** *n* *vagabond, truant, tramp, hobo, bum
*Ana* wanderer, roamer, rover (see corresponding verbs at WANDER)

**vagrant** *adj* *itinerant, peripatetic, ambulatory, ambulant, nomadic
*Ana* moving, shifting (see MOVE *vb*): wandering, roaming, roving, rambling, straying, ranging (see WANDER): strolling, sauntering (see SAUNTER)

**vague** *obscure, dark, enigmatic, cryptic, ambiguous, equivocal
*Ana* *formless, unformed: *doubtful, dubious: abstruse, *recondite
*Ant* definite: specific: lucid —*Con* *clear, perspicuous: express, *explicit

**vain** 1 Vain, nugatory, otiose, idle, empty, hollow are comparable when they mean devoid of worth or significance. Something **vain** (see also FUTILE) is devoid of all value, either absolutely because worthless, superfluous, or unprofitable or relatively because there are other things which are of infinitely greater value, greater necessity, or greater profitableness ⟨*vain* pleasures of luxurious life, forever with yourselves at strife—*Wordsworth*⟩ ⟨unless the forces of destruction . . . are brought under control, it is *vain* to plan for the future—*Attlee*⟩ ⟨*vain* pomp and glory of this world—*Shak.*⟩ Something **nugatory** is trifling or insignificant or, especially in legal use, inoperative ⟨in the decorative arts, the freedom given to the individual is rendered *nugatory* by the absence of cultural recognition of the innovator—*Mead*⟩ ⟨a literary work . . . likely to be despised as ephemeral and *nugatory*—*J. W. Clark*⟩ ⟨limiting the right to pass laws for the execution of the granted powers, to such as are indispensable, and without which the power would be *nugatory*—*John Marshall*⟩

⟨the book is so one-sided that as a constructive contribution it is *nugatory*—*Times Lit. Sup.*⟩ Something **otiose** has no excuse for being or serves no purpose and is usually an encumbrance or a superfluity ⟨mummified customs that have long outlasted their usefulness, and *otiose* dogmas that have long lost their vitality—*Inge*⟩ ⟨it ought to be comparatively easy to decide . . . what kinds of criticism are useful and what are *otiose*—*T. S. Eliot*⟩ ⟨you were drastic . . . . A firm hand pruned your lines; a sharp ear tested their music. Nothing soft, *otiose,* irrelevant cumbered your pages—*Woolf*⟩ Something **idle** has no solidity, either being baseless or groundless or being incapable of having any worthwhile effects or result ⟨*idle* theorizing⟩ ⟨*idle* dreams⟩ ⟨there is nothing that can control speculation, and preserve legitimate theory from *idle* fancy, but a strict adherence to the essential principles of science—*Dingle*⟩ ⟨it is *idle* to illustrate further, because to those who agree with me I am uttering commonplaces and to those who disagree I am ignoring the necessary foundations of thought—*Justice Holmes*⟩ Something **empty** or **hollow** is destitute of substance or reality and is only apparently or deceivingly sound, real, worthwhile, genuine, or sincere ⟨*empty* threats⟩ ⟨a *hollow* victory⟩ ⟨in itself unreal, *empty,* of no importance, and discardable overnight—*Wouk*⟩ ⟨*empty* profundities to which no operational meaning can possibly be attached—*Huxley*⟩ ⟨they were married with the bright *hollow* panoply attending such military affairs—*Styron*⟩
*Ana* worthless, valueless (see affirmative nouns at WORTH): ineffectual, *ineffective, inefficacious: fruitless, bootless, *futile, abortive
*Con* effectual, *effective, efficacious
2 *futile, fruitless, bootless, abortive
*Ana* *ineffective, ineffectual, inefficacious: trivial, trifling, puny, *petty, paltry: delusive, delusory, *misleading
3 proud, vainglorious (see under PRIDE *n*)
*Ana* self-satisfied, self-complacent, *complacent, priggish, smug: conceited, egoistic, egotistic (see corresponding nouns at CONCEIT)
*Con* *humble, meek, modest: diffident, *shy, bashful

**vainglorious** proud, vain (see under PRIDE *n*)
*Ana* arrogant, haughty, supercilious, disdainful, insolent, *proud: boasting *or* boastful, bragging, vaunting, gasconading (see corresponding verbs at BOAST)

**vainglory** *pride, vanity
*Ana* pomp, *display, parade: flaunting, parading, exhibition (see corresponding verbs at SHOW): rhapsody, rodomontade, rant, *bombast

**valiant** *brave, courageous, unafraid, fearless, intrepid, valorous, dauntless, undaunted, doughty, bold, audacious
*Ana* stout, sturdy, tenacious, stalwart (see STRONG): indomitable, unconquerable, *invincible
*Ant* timid: dastardly

**valid,** **sound, cogent, convincing, compelling, telling** can all be applied directly or indirectly to arguments, reasons, principles, or processes of thought or to their presentation and mean having or manifesting the power to impress themselves on others as right and well-grounded. *Valid* and *sound* both imply that the power is inherent in the rationality or logicality of the thought apart from its presentation. Something is **valid** against which no objections can be maintained, because it conforms strictly to the law or regulations (as of the state or the church) ⟨hold a *valid* title to a piece of property⟩ ⟨a *valid* ordination⟩ ⟨a *valid* marriage⟩ or because it is supported by facts and correct reasoning ⟨a *valid* argument⟩ ⟨*valid* evidence⟩ ⟨universally *valid* principles—*Inge*⟩ or, less often, because it is fully in accordance with claims

---

*Ana* analogous words    *Ant* antonyms    *Con* contrasted words    See also explanatory notes facing page 1

or promises made for it and is entirely effectual or efficacious ⟨a *valid* method of testing intelligence⟩ ⟨these folkways remain *valid* for anybody who gets solace from them—*Wouk*⟩ A person or a thing is **sound** that is free from error or fault in his or its processes of thought and that avoids fallacies, insufficient evidence, hasty conclusions, or superficiality. The term not only suggests flawlessness in reasoning but solidity in the grounds upon which this reasoning is based ⟨a *sound* thinker⟩ ⟨his assurance that he had never used an argument which he did not believe to be *sound*—*Inge*⟩ ⟨to admit . . . that reason cannot extend into the religious sphere is absolutely *sound* so long as we realize that reason has a coordinate right to lay down the rules in its own sphere of intelligence—*Ellis*⟩ Something *cogent* or *convincing* or *compelling* commands mental assent. But **cogent** tends to stress a power or force resident in the argument or reasoning that makes it conclusive, **convincing** suggests a power to overcome doubt, opposition, or reluctance to accept, and **compelling** calls particular attention to the substantial nature of the objective evidence ⟨the remarks of Gibbon [on universities and their degrees] are still . . . *cogent*— *Aldington*⟩ ⟨there are other ways of making a thing . . . *convincing* . . . besides merely appealing to one's logic and sense of fact—*Babbitt*⟩ ⟨so expressed, the argument does not sound strongly *convincing;* but it is really *cogent,* and the conclusion is sound—*Darrow*⟩ ⟨though his logic is often unconvincing, his documentation is always *compelling*—*Muller*⟩ Something **telling** produces at once the desired effect; frequently the term implies the compelling of assent but it seldom directly suggests soundness or cogency though, in general, it does not deny the existence of these qualities ⟨the first speaker for the affirmative used far more *telling* arguments than the second speaker⟩ ⟨every point made by the prosecuting attorney was *telling*⟩ The term is often applied to words, phrases, tones of expression, or rhetorical methods which convince, persuade, or win admiration and support because of their pertinency, their suitability, or their forcibleness ⟨a *telling* illustration of what Darwin unintentionally did to the minds of his disciples—*Shaw*⟩ ⟨such *telling* effects of contrast as the Japanese [artists] produced by an empty space—*Binyon*⟩
*Ana* *conclusive, determinative, definitive, decisive: *effective, effectual: legal, *lawful, licit: *logical, analytical, subtle
*Ant* fallacious, sophistical

**validate** *confirm, authenticate, substantiate, verify, corroborate
*Ana* *certify, attest, witness, vouch
*Ant* invalidate

**valor** *heroism, prowess, gallantry
*Ana* *courage, mettle, tenacity, spirit, resolution: indomitableness, unconquerableness, invincibility (see corresponding adjectives at INVINCIBLE): *fortitude, guts, sand, backbone

**valorous** *brave, courageous, unafraid, fearless, intrepid, valiant, dauntless, undaunted, doughty, bold, audacious
*Ana* venturesome, daring (see ADVENTUROUS): stout, sturdy, tenacious, stalwart, tough, *strong

**valuable** *adj* precious, invaluable, priceless, *costly, expensive, dear
*Ana* estimated, appraised, evaluated (see ESTIMATE): valued, appreciated, prized, treasured (see APPRECIATE): esteemed, admired, respected (see corresponding verbs under REGARD *n*)

**value** *n* *worth
*Ana* *price, charge, cost, expense: *importance, consequence, significance, weight: *use, usefulness, utility

**value** *vb* **1** *estimate, appraise, evaluate, rate, assess, assay
*Ana* *calculate, compute, reckon: *judge, adjudge, adjudicate
**2** prize, treasure, *appreciate, cherish
*Ana* esteem, respect, admire (see under REGARD *n*): love, enjoy (see LIKE): *revere, reverence, venerate

**vanish, evanesce, evaporate, disappear, fade** can all mean to pass from view or out of existence. **Vanish** implies a complete, often mysterious, and usually sudden passing; it commonly suggests absence of all trace or of any clue that would permit following until found ⟨no facts on the mother's disappearance. Died in childbirth, ran off with someone, committed suicide: some way of *vanishing* painful enough to keep Sidney from ever referring to it —*Pynchon*⟩ ⟨all those emotions of fear and abhorrence . . . *vanished* instantly from my mind—*Hudson*⟩ ⟨Addison complained that in his time the very appearances of Christianity had *vanished*—*Huxley*⟩ **Evanesce** differs from *vanish* in its greater stress on the process (as effacement or dissipation) by which a thing passes from visibility or thought; sometimes the term distinctly suggests a gradual process ⟨I touch a scarf and it falls into air and light and seems to *evanesce*—*Goyen*⟩ ⟨the sun-streaming clarity of checkered beach parasols, of friendly boys digging castles in the sand, faded in outline, *evanesced* from the bright precision of reality to vagueness of storm and fog—*Joseph Bennett*⟩ **Evaporate** suggests a vanishing as silently and inconspicuously as water does into vapor ⟨because of future expenses already mandated by the legislature, that surplus will *evaporate* soon—*Armbrister*⟩ The term is often used in respect to tenuous qualities, but it may be employed to describe stealthy or prudent or sudden departures or withdrawings of persons ⟨people whose faith, so tenuous anyway, had *evaporated* upon the threatening winds of a "cosmic cataclysm"— *Styron*⟩ ⟨looking at the high gray-green grass. A man could *evaporate* in that stuff in a second—*R. O. Bowen*⟩ ⟨if we try to express almost any poem of his in prose, we find it impossible; its rare spirit *evaporates* in the process —*Day Lewis*⟩ **Disappear** stresses only the passing from sight or thought; the passing implied may be sudden or gradual, permanent or temporary, but such suggestions are mostly contextual and not in the word ⟨the traditional view, that the world was made up of a vertical scale of creatures, gradually *disappeared*—*S. F. Mason*⟩ ⟨some say, let us go back to Palestine, else Judaism will *disappear* —*Cohen*⟩ ⟨seldom have other writers been able to *disappear* from their narrative as completely as Faulkner does—*Robert Humphrey*⟩ **Fade,** often with *out* or *away,* implies a gradual diminution in clearness and distinctness until the thing becomes invisible ⟨the ship gradually *faded* from sight⟩ ⟨all other certainties had *faded* or eroded away in growing up—*Wouk*⟩ ⟨this story seems to have *faded* out of the popular mind—*Norman Douglas*⟩
*Ana* *escape, flee, fly: dispel, disperse, dissipate, *scatter
*Ant* appear: loom

**vanity** *pride, vainglory
*Ana* self-esteem, self-love, *conceit, egotism, egoism, amour propre: complacency, self-complacency, self-satisfaction, smugness, priggishness (see corresponding adjectives at COMPLACENT): show, ostentation, pretense (see corresponding adjectives at SHOWY)

**vanquish** *conquer, defeat, beat, lick, subdue, subjugate, reduce, overcome, surmount, overthrow, rout
*Ana* *frustrate, foil, outwit, circumvent: *overturn, subvert
*Con* surrender, submit, capitulate (see corresponding nouns at SURRENDER): *yield, succumb

**vanquisher** *victor, conqueror, winner, champion

A colon (:) separates groups of words discriminated. An asterisk (*) indicates place of treatment of each group.

**vapid** *insipid, flat, jejune, banal, wishy-washy, inane
*Ana* *soft, bland, gentle, mild: *tame, subdued, submissive: mawkish, maudlin, soppy, slushy, mushy,
*sentimental
*Con* racy, spicy, *pungent, piquant: trenchant, crisp,
*incisive: *expressive, significant, pregnant, meaningful
**variable** *adj* *changeable, protean, changeful, mutable
*Ana* *fitful, spasmodic: fickle, mercurial, unstable, *inconstant, capricious: mobile, *movable
*Ant* constant: equable
**variance** *discord, contention, dissension, difference,
strife, conflict
*Ana* difference, diversity, divergency, disparateness (see
corresponding adjectives at DIFFERENT): separation,
division, severing, sundering (see corresponding verbs at
SEPARATE): incongruousness, uncongeniality, incompatibility, discordance, discrepancy (see corresponding
adjectives at INCONSONANT)
**variation** change, alteration, modification (see under
CHANGE *vb*)
*Ana* *variety, diversity: difference, divergence, divergency, *dissimilarity: *deviation, deflection, aberration
**variegated,** parti-colored, motley, checkered, checked,
**pied, piebald, skewbald, dappled, freaked** can all mean
having a pattern involving different colors or shades of
color. **Variegated** implies variation in the color (as of a
single piece, object, or specimen) without indication of
what colors or what forms—spots, streaks, blotches—are
involved ⟨disliked the *variegated* hues of the buildings
—they reminded him of the garish brilliance in the lower
town—*Norman Douglas*⟩ ⟨*variegated* tulips⟩ **Parti-
colored** implies the presence of two or more colors but
stresses not so much the presence of different colors as
their clear demarcation and distinct presentation. **Motley**
in most uses is likely to suggest presence of colors of very
noticeable diversity in a chance, haphazard, or very
capricious arrangement ⟨birds of *motley* colors and varied
cries—*Chesterton*⟩ ⟨the *motley* dress of a court jester⟩
**Checkered** indicates a regular alternation of rectangular
shapes different in color or shade like a checkerboard,
especially an alternation between black and white or dark
and light ⟨the *checkered* fabric of Constable's pictures,
their deep undertones overlaid with variegated passages
of crumbling impasto and strewn with particles of white
light—*Ironside*⟩ **Checked** indicates much the same thing
but is admissible in situations where figures are less
certainly rectangular; it is common in reference to fabrics
⟨a gambler's *checked* vest⟩ **Pied** suggests patches,
blotches, or spots of colors on a contrasting background
and especially the white on black of a magpie's plumage.
**Piebald** suggests similar coloration, especially in reference
to the markings of a horse or dog, and **skewbald** implies
an arrangement of spots and background involving white
and some color other than black ⟨*piebald* strictly means
spotted white and black and *skewbald* white and any color
but black—*Simpson*⟩ **Dappled** describes a marking with
small spots, patches, or specks of color or shade differing
from that of the background ⟨it lay *dappled* with sun and
shade, still, clear, and irresistible—*Ertz*⟩ **Freaked** may
suggest bold streaks of contrasting color ⟨tall bare fells,
capped and *freaked* with snow—*Brophy*⟩ ⟨the woods were
*freaked* and pied with fresh transparent leaves and
flowers—*Wylie*⟩
*Ana* flecked, stippled, marbled, mottled, spattered,
spotted (see under SPOT *vb*)
**variety** 1 Variety, diversity are comparable when they are
used in reference to a group, class, or complex whole and
denote the state or quality of being composed of different
parts, elements, or individuals. **Variety** may imply that

the things which differ, whether they are fundamentally
similar or completely dissimilar, are related because they
contribute to the same end or play a part in the formation
of the same whole ⟨his *variety* is to be praised . . . what is
distressing . . . is his style—*Mailer*⟩ ⟨most workers would
prefer some *variety* in their work, but they cannot get it—
*Hobson*⟩ **Diversity,** though often used interchangeably
with *variety,* distinctively stresses the marked difference
or divergence of the individuals, parts, or elements, and
seldom suggests even a class or categorical likeness ⟨the
practical reduction of human *diversity* to subhuman uniformity, of freedom to servitude—*Huxley*⟩ ⟨the moral and
intellectual explosion needed . . . to reestablish tolerance
of qualitative *diversity* and intellectual freedom as the
true basis of democracy—*Julian Huxley*⟩ ⟨the great
*diversity* among human beings⟩
*Ana* *dissimilarity, unlikeness, difference, divergence,
divergency: multifariousness, variousness (see corresponding adjectives at MANY): miscellaneousness *or*
miscellany, heterogeneousness *or* heterogeneity, assort-
edness *or* assortment (see corresponding adjectives at
MISCELLANEOUS)
2 Variety, subspecies, race, breed, cultivar, strain, clone,
**stock** are comparable when they mean a group of related
plants or animals narrower in scope than a species. These
terms tend to be variable in application and subject to
confusing overlap in use, but all can carry distinctive
implications. **Variety** stresses deviation from a type;
historically, it denotes an infraspecific category differing
from the typical form of the species in characters that are
too trivial or too inconstant to justify its separation as a
distinct species. In modern use it is appropriately selected
when it is desirable to call attention to such deviation
without making any specific taxonomic suggestion or it
may be used specifically of any such divergent group
developed under human control (as by selective breeding,
hybridization, and cultivation) ⟨an early *variety* of peach⟩
⟨developing new *varieties* to meet special conditions⟩
**Subspecies,** which stresses subordinate status, is primarily
a taxonomic term applicable to a morphologically distinguishable subdivision of a species that is geographically
isolated but physiologically capable of interbreeding with
other comparable subdivisions of the same species. **Race**
stresses common ancestry and differentiation based on
readily discernible hereditary characters ⟨a *race* of albino
mice⟩ As applied to the human species (*Homo sapiens*),
*race* is a highly controversial term that basically denotes
any of the primary subdivisions of recent man historically
native to distinct parts of the world and distinguished by
relatively fixed characters in physical type (as skin color,
hair form, and skull shape) ⟨the Caucasoid *race*⟩ ⟨the
Mongoloid *race*⟩ In more general use *race* may apply
to either large or small groups within a species. Though
often used as if interchangeable *race* and *variety* are not
exactly correspondent; while they sometimes agree, they
more often overlap in their reference. For *race* emphasizes a common descent, while *variety* stresses divergence
from a type. **Breed** can refer to a group within a species
of animals or occasionally of plants the members of which
presumably share a common ancestry and are visibly
similar in most characters. More specifically *breed* refers
to such a group (as Jersey cattle or beagle dogs) that has
been developed under human control chiefly through selective breeding and the fixing of desired qualities. **Cultivar** applies specifically to a race or breed of plants originated (as
by selection or hybridization) under cultivation. **Strain,** like
*variety,* stresses difference, but it is more likely to be used
of subdivisions of subdivisions (as subspecies, or especially breeds or varieties) than, as *variety* typically is, of

primary subdivisions of the species. It is especially applicable when the distinguishing character is a physiological quality (as vigor, or yield, or virulence); the term may imply human control as a means of gaining this result (as through crossing or inbreeding) or it may imply chance variation ⟨the appearance of virulent and antibiotic-resistant bacterial *strains*⟩ or controlled conditions ⟨an improved *strain* of Golden Bantam corn⟩ ⟨superior milking *strains* have been developed in most dual-purpose breeds of cattle⟩ **Clone** is the most precisely delimited term of this set; it denotes all the individuals that constitute the asexually produced progeny of a single parent and are therefore genetically identical. Though applicable to organisms (as bacteria and protozoans) that reproduce asexually in nature, it is used typically of economic plants that are propagated by such means as dividing, budding, or grafting and in such use may come close to *variety, race,* or *strain;* thus, one can speak of the Baldwin *variety* of apple or the Baldwin *clone.* **Stock** places emphasis upon community of origin and genetically close relationship in the group but its range of reference is not clearly defined. Often also it carries over from other senses of the word the notion of being a source or original ⟨culled out a vigorous *stock* from which he selected several clones⟩ ⟨the several *stocks* developed by inbreeding were crossed to gain hybrid vigor⟩

**various** 1 *different, diverse, divergent, disparate
*Ana* *distinct, separate: distinctive, peculiar, individual (see CHARACTERISTIC): varying, changing (see CHANGE *vb*)
*Ant* uniform: cognate
2 *many, several, sundry, divers, numerous, multifarious
*Ana* *miscellaneous, heterogeneous, assorted
*Con* *same, identical, equivalent, equal: similar, alike, *like

**vary** 1 *change, alter, modify
*Ana* deviate, diverge, digress, depart (see SWERVE): *transform, metamorphose, convert
2 *differ, disagree, dissent
*Ana* deviate, diverge, digress, depart (see SWERVE): *separate, divide, part

**vast** *huge, immense, enormous, elephantine, mammoth, giant, gigantic, gigantean, colossal, gargantuan, Herculean, cyclopean, titanic, Brobdingnagian
*Ana* stupendous, tremendous, prodigious, *monstrous: *large, big, great: *spacious, capacious

**vault** *vb* *jump, leap, spring, bound
*Ana* surmount (see CONQUER): mount, ascend, *rise, soar

**vault** *n* jump, leap, spring, bound (see under JUMP *vb*)
*Ana* surmounting (see CONQUER): rising, mounting, ascending, soaring (see RISE)

**vaunt** *vb* *boast, brag, crow, gasconade
*Ana* parade, flaunt, exhibit, display, *show: magnify, aggrandize, *exalt

**veer** *swerve, deviate, depart, digress, diverge
*Ana* shift, transfer, *move: *turn, divert, deflect, sheer

**vehement** *intense, fierce, exquisite, violent
*Ana* forcible, forceful, *powerful, potent: fervid, perfervid, *impassioned, passionate, ardent: *furious, frantic, wild, rabid, delirious

**vehicle** *mean, instrument, instrumentality, agent, agency, medium, organ, channel

**veil** *vb* *cover, overspread, envelop, wrap, shroud
*Ana* mask, cloak, camouflage, *disguise: conceal, *hide, secrete, screen

**vein** 1 *mood, humor, temper
*Ana* *disposition, temper, complexion, temperament
2 strain, streak, *touch, suggestion, suspicion, soupçon, tincture, tinge, shade, smack, spice, dash

**velocity** *speed, momentum, impetus, pace, headway

*Ana* *celerity, legerity, alacrity: *haste, hurry, expedition, dispatch

**velvety** silken, silky, satiny, glossy, slick, *sleek

**venal** *mercenary, hireling, hack
*Ana* corrupt, nefarious, iniquitous, *vicious, infamous, flagitious: sordid, ignoble (see MEAN *adj*)

**venerable** *old, ancient, antique, antiquated, archaic, obsolete, antediluvian
*Ana* venerated, revered, reverenced (see REVERE): *aged, old

**venerate** *revere, reverence, worship, adore
*Ana* esteem, respect, admire, regard (see under REGARD *n*): cherish, prize, treasure, value, *appreciate

**veneration** reverence, worship, adoration (see under REVERE)
*Ana* deference, homage, obeisance, *honor

**vengeance** revenge, retribution, *retaliation, reprisal
*Ana* punishment, disciplining *or* discipline, castigation (see corresponding verbs at PUNISH): avenging, revenging (see AVENGE): recompensing *or* recompense, repayment (see corresponding verbs at PAY)

**vengeful** *vindictive, revengeful
*Ana* rancorous, inimical, hostile, antagonistic (see corresponding nouns at ENMITY): malevolent, spiteful, *malicious, malignant

**venial, pardonable** are applied to faults, sins, or errors and mean of such a character as not to warrant punishment or the imposition of a penalty. **Venial** in most use implies an opposition to *grave, serious,* or *grievous* ⟨he had learned to see what was really criminal in what he had done, and what was *venial—Trollope*⟩ and in theological use to *mortal* (see *mortal* under DEADLY); consequently it often means *trifling, not willful,* or *harmless* ⟨the fastidious could carp at many minor slips or infelicities; but they seem fairly *venial—R. H. Bowers*⟩ ⟨the *venial* indiscretions of youth—*Southey*⟩ ⟨[Esperanto's] flaws, which are obvious, are *venial* compared with those of the best natural languages—*Guérard*⟩ **Pardonable** implies that such excuse or justification may be offered for the fault or error that it is not worthy of consideration ⟨her heart innocent of the most *pardonable* guile—*Conrad*⟩ ⟨able to add, with *pardonable* pride, "it was a costly and a noble act"—*Coulton*⟩
*Ant* heinous: mortal (*in Roman Catholic theology*)

**venom** *poison, toxin, virus, bane

**venomous** *poisonous, virulent, toxic, mephitic, pestilent, pestilential, miasmic, miasmatic, miasmal
*Ana* malignant, malign, malevolent (see MALICIOUS): baleful, malefic, maleficent (see SINISTER): *pernicious, baneful, noxious, deleterious, detrimental

**vent** *vb* *express, utter, voice, broach, air, ventilate
*Ana* *reveal, disclose, discover, divulge: *assert, declare, aver, avow
*Ant* bridle (sense 1) —*Con* *restrain, inhibit, check, curb: *suppress, repress

**ventilate** 1 *aerate, oxygenate, carbonate
2 *express, vent, air, utter, voice, broach
*Ana* expose, exhibit, display, *show: disclose, divulge, discover, *reveal: publish, advertise, broadcast (see DECLARE)

**venture** *vb* **Venture, hazard, risk, chance, jeopardize, endanger, imperil** can all mean to expose to the chance of being unsuccessful, lost, or injured. **Venture** implies a daring to stake something (as the success of an action or undertaking, one's life, or one's property) on the chance of getting an advantage or gain whether great or small; the term implies only the chances taken and the contingencies foreseen and does not, apart from the context, indicate its outcome ⟨he determined to *venture* his life and his fortunes

---

for the cause of freedom⟩ ⟨you have deeply *ventured;* but all must do so who would greatly win—*Byron*⟩ But *venture* is often used in a weakened sense to mean little more than *dare* or, sometimes, *attempt* ⟨imagine the fate of a university don of 1860, or 1870, or 1880, or even 1890 who had *ventured* to commend *Leaves of Grass* to the young gentlemen—*Mencken*⟩ ⟨his class fellows were all rather gloomily polite to him, and one or two *ventured* awkward words of condolence—*Archibald Marshall*⟩ **Hazard** usually implies the putting of something to the chance of losing it; the term suggests more uncertainty or precariousness than *venture* and less hope of a favorable outcome and is often used in place of *venture* because of this implication ⟨men that *hazard* all do it in hope of fair advantages—*Shak.*⟩ ⟨his own possessions, safety, life, he would have *hazarded* for Lucie and her child, without a moment's demur—*Dickens*⟩ Like *venture, hazard* is also often used in a much weaker sense but it comes closer to *dare* than to *attempt* ⟨sometimes as he hunted he got a glimpse of the giraffe moving through the bush, but was never near enough to *hazard* a shot—*Cloete*⟩ ⟨no Elizabethan dramatist offers greater temptation: to the scholar, to *hazard* conjecture of fact; and to the critic, to *hazard* conjecture of significance—*T. S. Eliot*⟩ **Risk** carries a still stronger implication of exposure to real dangers and of taking actual chances ⟨Captain Cook had sailed straight through the middle of the group, not *risking* a landing because of the fierce aspect of the natives—*Heiser*⟩ **Chance** may suggest a trusting to luck and a sometimes irresponsible disregarding of the risks involved in an action or procedure ⟨decided to withdraw from Kentucky rather than *chance* defeat in enemy territory—*Hay*⟩ ⟨I'll *chance* it, if it kills me⟩ **Jeopardize** carries further the implication of exposure to dangers; it implies not only that they are a constant threat but that the odds in one's favor are equally or even unfavorably balanced with those against one ⟨found it difficult to steer a course that should not *jeopardize* either his loyalty or his honesty—*Sidney Lee*⟩ ⟨no traveler from abroad, however fair-minded, could tell the truth about us without *jeopardizing* his life, liberty, and reputation—*Brooks*⟩ **Endanger** and **imperil** both stress exposure to dangers or perils, and do not in themselves throw emphasis upon a taking of chances. *Imperil* may imply more certainty or more imminence to the predicted risk than *endanger* but the two words are often used interchangeably without significant loss ⟨not so great a wind as to *endanger* us—*Defoe*⟩ ⟨condemned the abolitionists as agitators who actually *endangered* the cause of freedom—*Cole*⟩ ⟨a jungle of aggressive power politics which *imperils* internal reconversion, the healing of the wounds of war, and the creation of the political apparatus necessary for one world—*Mark Starr*⟩ ⟨new technical processes and devices litter the countryside with waste and refuse, contaminate water and air, *imperil* wildlife and man and *endanger* the balance of nature itself—*Kennedy*⟩

**venturesome** *adventurous, daring, daredevil, rash, reckless, foolhardy

*Ana* bold, audacious, intrepid, *brave: stout, sturdy, stalwart (see STRONG)

*Con* *timid, timorous: *fearful, apprehensive, afraid

**veracity** *truth, verity, verisimilitude

*Ana* integrity, probity, *honesty, honor

**verbal** *oral

**verbiage, redundancy, tautology, pleonasm, circumlocution, periphrasis** are comparable when they denote a fault of style or a form or mode of expression involving the use of too many words. **Verbiage** may imply delight in words for their own sake (as for their sound, their color, or their suggestions) and overindulgence in their use for these

reasons; the term, however, often suggests a pointless or habitual wordiness that tends to make what is written dull, meaningless, obscure, or unduly heavy reading ⟨his concise and well-informed speeches were welcomed amid the common *verbiage* of debate—*Buchan*⟩ ⟨the almost luscious richness of Aunt Phoebe's imagination, her florid *verbiage*, her note of sensuous defiance—*H. G. Wells*⟩ **Redundancy** does not in general carry the implications of expansiveness, floridity, or heaviness so often apparent in *verbiage;* but the term sometimes implies the use of more words than are required by idiom or syntax and so suggests a fault of style ⟨*redundancies* result . . . when the writer fails to perceive the scope of a word—*Westley*⟩ ⟨the . . . florid *redundancy* of Italian prose—*Ellis*⟩ **Tautology** is needless or useless repetition of the same idea in different words ⟨he cautioned his students to beware of such *tautologies* as "visible to the eye" and "audible to the ear"⟩ **Pleonasm** implies the use of syntactically unnecessary words as in "the man he said." Sometimes pleonastic expressions are acceptable means of emphasis and are thought of as figures of speech ⟨it is a *pleonasm*, a figure usual in Scripture, by a multiplicity of expressions to signify one notable thing—*South*⟩ **Circumlocution** and **periphrasis** denote a roundabout or indirect way of saying a thing ⟨the gift of the pamphleteer, who cuts through academic *circumlocution*—*Dean*⟩ ⟨this was not however a question to be asked point-blank, and I could not think of any effective *circumlocution*—*Conrad*⟩ ⟨one of those anomalous practitioners in lower departments of the law who . . . deny themselves all indulgence in the luxury of too delicate a conscience (a *periphrasis* which might be abridged considerably)—*De Quincey*⟩ ⟨"The answer is in the negative" is a *periphrasis* for "no"—*Time*⟩

*Ana* wordiness, verboseness, prolixity, diffuseness (see corresponding adjectives at WORDY)

**verbose** *wordy, prolix, diffuse, redundant

*Ana* grandiloquent, magniloquent, flowery, bombastic (see RHETORICAL): loquacious, voluble, glib, garrulous, *talkative

*Ant* laconic —*Con* *concise, terse, succinct: compact, *close

**verge** *n* edge, rim, brim, brink, *border, margin

*Ana* bound, *limit, end, confine: *circumference, perimeter, compass

**verify** corroborate, substantiate, *confirm, authenticate, validate

*Ana* *prove, test, try, demonstrate: *certify, attest, witness, vouch: establish, settle (see SET *vb*)

**verisimilitude** *truth, veracity, verity

*Ana* agreement, accordance, harmonizing *or* harmony, correspondence (see corresponding verbs at AGREE): *likeness, similitude, resemblance

**veritable** *authentic, genuine, bona fide

*Ana* actual, *real, true

*Ant* factitious

**verity** *truth, veracity, verisimilitude

**vernacular** *dialect, patois, lingo, jargon, cant, argot, slang

**versatile, many-sided, all-around** can all mean marked by or showing skill or ability or capacity or usefulness of many different kinds. When applied to persons, **versatile** stresses aptitude and facility in many different activities requiring skill or ability, especially the ability to turn with no diminution in skill from one activity to another without a hitch; applied to things, it stresses their multiple and diverse qualities, uses, or possibilities ⟨a *versatile* student⟩ ⟨the most *versatile* soprano now active—*Kolodin*⟩ ⟨*versatile* interests⟩ ⟨a *versatile* combat weapon⟩ ⟨a *versatile* building material⟩ **Many-sided** applied to persons stresses

breadth or diversity of interests or accomplishments; applied to things, their diversity of aspects, attributes, or uses ⟨a *many-sided* scholar and citizen⟩ ⟨a *many-sided* and truly civilized life—*Trevelyan*⟩ ⟨a *many-sided* personality⟩ ⟨a *many-sided* agreement—*Manchester Guardian*⟩ **All-around** implies completeness or symmetry in development, either general or within a single activity with many phases; the term need not imply special or great attainments but rather a general ability to do oneself credit; when applied to things, it implies an analogous general usefulness ⟨many observers have called him the best *all-around* reporter in the country—*Walker*⟩ ⟨the *all-around* adaptability and quality of our men—*Vosseller*⟩
*Ana* gifted, talented (see corresponding nouns at GIFT): accomplished, finished, *consummate: ready, apt, *quick, prompt

**verse 1 Verse, stanza** both mean a unit of metrical writing. **Verse** is both wider and more varied in its popular usage since it can denote a single line of such writing, such writing as a class, or, along with **stanza**, a group of lines forming a division of a poem and typically following a fixed metrical and sometimes rhythmical pattern. *Verse* may also specifically denote the part of a song preceding the refrain or chorus or a comparable part of an anthem or hymn. But in technical use and in discussion of prosody *verse* is restricted to the single line of metrical writing and *stanza* is regularly employed for the group of lines that forms a division of a poem.
**2** *paragraph, article, clause, plank, count

**versed** *conversant
*Ana* *learned, erudite: informed, acquainted (see INFORM): intimate, *familiar

**versifier** *poet, rhymer, rhymester, poetaster, bard, minstrel, troubadour

**version 1** *translation, paraphrase, metaphrase
**2** *account, report, story, chronicle

**vertebrae** *spine, backbone, back, chine

**vertex** *apex

**vertical, perpendicular, plumb** can mean situated at right angles to the plane of the horizon or extending from that plane at such an angle. **Vertical** suggests a relation to the vertex or topmost point (see APEX 1); it is used most often when the thing so described actually extends upward from the plane of the horizon or from its base or support in such a direction that if its direction line were produced, it would reach the zenith ⟨*vertical* threads in a tapestry⟩ ⟨a *vertical* piston⟩ ⟨walls not quite *vertical*⟩ **Vertical** is, of these terms, the most frequently applied to abstractions and the most common in extended use ⟨the *vertical* organization of society⟩ **Perpendicular** differs from *vertical* in being normally applied to things that extend upward or downward from the horizontal or both upward and downward; thus, one looks up or down the *perpendicular* face of a cliff ⟨a *perpendicular* fall of water⟩ Consequently, *perpendicular* is used more often than *vertical* to suggest little more than precipitousness or extreme steepness or stiffness and straightness of line ⟨a *perpendicular* descent⟩ ⟨a stiff *perpendicular* old maid—*Mitford*⟩ **Plumb** is largely a builder's term used particularly in judging the exact verticality or perpendicularity of something by its conformity to the direction of a plumb line ⟨the wall was *plumb*⟩
*Ant* horizontal

**vertiginous** *giddy, dizzy, swimming, dazzled
*Ana* reeling, whirling, staggering, tottering (see REEL)

**verve** *vigor, vim, spirit, dash, esprit, punch, élan, drive
*Ana* vivacity, animation, liveliness (see corresponding adjectives at LIVELY): buoyancy, resiliency, elasticity (see corresponding adjectives at ELASTIC)

**very** selfsame, *same, identical, identic, equivalent, equal, tantamount

**vessel** ship, *boat, craft

**vestige** *trace, track
*Ana* print, imprint, *impression, stamp

**vex** irk, *annoy, bother
*Ana* chafe, fret, gall (see ABRADE): *irritate, exasperate, nettle, provoke
*Ant* please, regale  —*Con* *pacify, appease, mollify, propitiate

**viands** provisions, comestibles, *food, feed, victuals, provender, fodder, forage

**vibrant** *resonant, sonorous, ringing, resounding, orotund
*Ana* pulsating, pulsing, throbbing, beating (see PULSATE): thrilling, electrifying (see THRILL)

**vibrate** *swing, sway, oscillate, fluctuate, pendulate, waver, undulate
*Ana* *pulsate, pulse, beat, throb, palpitate: quiver, quaver, tremble, *shake

**vice 1** *fault, failing, frailty, foible
*Ana* defect, flaw, *blemish: infirmity, weakness (see corresponding adjectives at WEAK)
**2** *offense, sin, crime, scandal
*Ana* transgression, trespass, violation, *breach, infraction: immorality (see corresponding adjective at IMMORAL): *evil, ill
*Ant* virtue

**vicinity** neighborhood, district, *locality
*Ana* region, *area: section, sector (see PART *n*)

**vicious, villainous, iniquitous, nefarious, flagitious, infamous, corrupt, degenerate** are comparable when they mean highly reprehensible or offensive in character, nature, or conduct. **Vicious** may imply an addiction to or connection with vice or immorality; usually it suggests moral depravity and is the diametrical opposite of *virtuous* ⟨form *vicious* habits⟩ ⟨we cannot afford to have poor people anyhow, whether they be lazy or busy, drunken or sober, virtuous or *vicious*—*Shaw*⟩ Often the word implies a particular highly reprehensible quality (as ugliness or violence of temper or deliberate cruelty) ⟨the horseman delivered one last *vicious* cut with his whip—*Kipling*⟩ ⟨he looked at the piece of meat and crust, and suddenly, in a *vicious* spurt of temper, flung it into the fire—*D. H. Lawrence*⟩ or it may imply a debasing ⟨the multiplication of critical books and essays may create . . . a *vicious* taste for reading about works of art instead of reading the works themselves—*T. S. Eliot*⟩ or complete vitiation by faults, defects, or irremediable conditions ⟨a *vicious* system of financing⟩ ⟨discriminate between thoroughly *vicious* ideas and those which should have a chance to be heard—*Chafee*⟩ **Villainous** is a more condemnatory term than *vicious*; it may suggest specifically qualities which can be associated with a villain, a rascal, or a scoundrel or it may be little more than an intensifying equivalent of *vicious* ⟨a *villainous* assault⟩ ⟨a *villainous* practice⟩ ⟨a *villainous* temper⟩ ⟨dreams bizarre and frantic, *villainous* beyond men's wildest imaginings—*Styron*⟩ **Iniquitous** is more fixed in its meaning than the preceding terms; it commonly implies the absence of all signs of justice or fairness or a complete indifference to the standards or principles which govern the conduct of civilized or law-abiding men ⟨*iniquitous* disregard of the rights of small nations⟩ ⟨that quenchless hunger for raw, quick, dirty money in American politics, which hardly sugarcoats its bribes, which glazes over its most *iniquitous* corruption—*White*⟩ **Nefarious** is often used in place of *iniquitous* when one wishes an even more censorious form of expression. The word implies impiety in its deepest sense or a breach of laws and traditions which have immemorially been honored, but it commonly

A colon (:) separates groups of words discriminated. An asterisk (*) indicates place of treatment of each group.

means extremely or flagrantly wicked ⟨the *nefarious* neglect of their aged parents⟩ ⟨race prejudice is most *nefarious* on its politer levels—*Clurman*⟩ **Flagitious** and **infamous** both imply shameful and scandalous badness or wickedness, but the former is somewhat less rhetorical and more closely descriptive than the latter ⟨in the beginning, the common law applied only to acts that all men, everywhere, admitted were *flagitious*—*G. W. Johnson*⟩ ⟨forced and *flagitious* bombast—*T. S. Eliot*⟩ ⟨else, perhaps, I might have been entangled among deeds, which, now, as *infamous,* I should abhor—*Wordsworth*⟩ ⟨Alice ... would have scouted as *infamous* any suggestion that her parent was more selfish than saintly—*Shaw*⟩ **Corrupt** (see also DEBASE 1) may be applied to persons in an official capacity or to their acts, then implying a loss or lack of moral integrity or probity that makes one accessible to bribes or other inducements to go contrary to sworn duties or obligations ⟨control of municipal government in . . . many . . . American cities had fallen into the clutches of *corrupt* political machines—*Armbrister*⟩ ⟨bent only on turning each to his own personal advantage the now *corrupt* machinery of administration and law—*Dickinson*⟩ or the term may be more generally applied, and then suggests degradation or depravity ⟨those moral wildernesses of civilized life which the Square automatically condemns as delinquent or evil or immature or morbid or self-destructive or *corrupt*—*Mailer*⟩ ⟨humanity they knew to be *corrupt* and incompetent—*Henry Adams*⟩ **Degenerate** stresses a descent and deterioration from a presumed original or earlier high type or condition to one that is very low in the scale morally, intellectually, physically, or artistically. However it additionally carries so strong an implication of corruption, and so often suggests extreme viciousness that it is generally used to describe what is especially reprehensible and offensive from the historical point of view or in comparison to other members of its class or other instances of the type ⟨preferred to prop up an effete and *degenerate* dynasty rather than face a vigorous reformed China—*G. F. Hudson*⟩ ⟨what he has to say is inspired by revolt against the *degenerate* practice of his times—*Binyon*⟩ ⟨we are solemnly warned that in the hands of modern writers language has fallen into a morbid state. It has become *degenerate*—*Ellis*⟩
*Ana* debased, depraved, debauched, perverted (see under DEBASE): dissolute, profligate, *abandoned, reprobate: lewd, lascivious, wanton, lecherous, libidinous (see LICENTIOUS)
*Ant* virtuous

**vicissitude 1** *change, alternation, mutation, permutation
*Ana* turning, rotation, revolving *or* revolution (see corresponding verbs at TURN): reversal, transposition (see corresponding verbs at REVERSE): *succession, progression, sequence, series: *variety, diversity
**2** *difficulty, hardship, rigor
*Ana* *misfortune, mischance, adversity: *trial, tribulation, affliction

**victim, prey, quarry** denote a person or animal killed or injured for the ends of the one who kills or injures. **Victim** primarily applies to a living creature, usually an animal, sometimes a person, that is killed and offered as a sacrifice to a divinity; in more general use it applies to one who has been destroyed, ruined, seriously injured, or badly treated by some ruthless person or impersonal power before which he has been helpless ⟨the *victims* of a pestilence⟩ ⟨spent much time in the back of the grocery, complaining of his poverty as if it were a new invention and he its first *victim*—*Malamud*⟩ ⟨was the girl born to be a *victim*; to be always disliked and crushed as if she were too fine for this world?—*Conrad*⟩ ⟨all are *victims* of circumstances;

all have had characters warped in infancy and intelligence stunted at school—*Russell*⟩ **Prey** applies to animals hunted and killed for food by more powerful carnivorous animals ⟨the hungry family flew like vultures on their *prey*—*Johnson*⟩ In extended sense *prey* applies to a victim of something that seizes or captures or fells in a manner suggestive of the action of a predatory animal ⟨Hitler, having taken his plunge, and with such reckless bravado, now suddenly was *prey* to doubts—*Shirer*⟩ ⟨people who make solemn talk about art and are the natural *prey* of the artists of *Punch*—*Montague*⟩ **Quarry** is predominantly a hunting term referable to a victim of the chase, especially one taken with hounds or hawks; it may be applied to the animal as pursued as well as the animal as taken after pursuit ⟨the startled *quarry* bounds amain, as fast the gallant greyhounds strain—*Scott*⟩ In extended use *quarry* usually applies to a person or thing determined upon as a victim and vigorously and relentlessly pursued ⟨you think . . . you are the pursuer and she the pursued. . . . Fool: it is you who are the pursued, the marked-down *quarry,* the destined prey—*Shaw*⟩ ⟨sometimes a man has to stalk his *quarry* with great caution, waiting patiently for the right moment to reveal himself—*Dahl*⟩

**victor, winner, conqueror, champion, vanquisher** can all denote one who gains the mastery in a contest, conflict, or competition. **Victor,** the more literary term, and **winner,** the ordinary term, usually stress the fact of defeating one's opponents; additionally *victor* can connote a triumph or a glorious proof of one's powers. The terms are applicable when the test is one of strength, strategy, skill, or endurance ⟨the *winner* in the oratorical contest⟩ ⟨he who battles on her [Justice's] side, God, though he were ten times slain, crowns him *victor* glorified, *victor* over death and pain—*Emerson*⟩ ⟨life is a contest between people in which the *victor* generally recuperates quickly and the loser takes long to mend—*Mailer*⟩ ⟨he undoubtedly was going to be a very rich man. So her boss said. And her boss picked *winners*—*Donn Byrne*⟩ **Conqueror** stresses the defeat and subjugation of an enemy or opposing force; the term is seldom used appropriately in respect to friendly games or competitions where *winner* is the regular term, for it usually presupposes a warlike struggle or an attempt to crush by getting the upper hand ⟨England never did, nor never shall, lie at the proud foot of a *conqueror*—*Shak.*⟩ ⟨there was also in it . . . a note of the triumphant *conqueror,* the defier of the world—*Shirer*⟩ **Champion** applies to the one who gains acknowledged supremacy through a contest or in a field of competition (as in an athletic contest or in a given sport). The term does not apply to a winner of any test, but only of a test in which one meets all of those of highest rank in the field or meets the one who holds the title of champion or one who challenges one's own right to hold that title ⟨the heavyweight *champion* of the world⟩ ⟨he could end up being *champion* for a while. But I doubt if he could hold the title in a strong field—*Mailer*⟩ **Vanquisher** is often used in place of *conqueror* and, often ironically or somewhat hyperbolically, in place of *victor* or *winner,* when there is an intent to imply an overpowering or an overwhelming or crushing defeat ⟨but I shall rise victorious, and subdue my *vanquisher*—*Milton*⟩ ⟨realized that gold is not always the *vanquisher* of every obstacle—*Cable*⟩

**victory, conquest, triumph** can mean the result achieved by one who gains the mastery in a contest or struggle. *Victory* and *conquest* in their basic use carry the same implications and suggestions as the corresponding agent nouns (see VICTOR) ⟨"*Victory*," said Nelson, "is not a name strong enough for such a scene"; he called it a *conquest*—*Southey*⟩ In their common extended use, **victory**

---

*Ana* analogous words    *Ant* antonyms    *Con* contrasted words    See also explanatory notes facing page 1

is likely to suggest a gaining of superiority or success, often in intellectual or spiritual fields ⟨a first instance of the *victory* of technical knowledge . . . over the traditional crafts—*Michael Barbour*⟩ ⟨his mental *victory* over this cruel illness is . . . inspiring—*Patterson*⟩ ⟨music . . . starts off at the point where the *victory* of the spirit over musical instruments is complete—*Spender*⟩ while **conquest** is more likely to imply a bringing of something under one's control, especially so that it may be put to use ⟨man's *conquest* of the soil—*Shaplen*⟩ ⟨art is essentially a *conquest* of matter by the spirit—*Binyon*⟩ **Triumph** may apply either to a brilliant or decisive victory or an overwhelming conquest and suggest the acclaim and personal satisfaction accruing to the winner ⟨his [Wellington's] *triumph* will be sung . . . far on in summers that we shall not see—*Tennyson*⟩ ⟨it is surely questionable whether we . . . should desire their *triumph*, a degree of success that clearly implies the full accomplishment of all their ends, good and bad—*The Commonweal*⟩ In its extended use *triumph* tends to stress decisiveness and brilliance of the result ⟨the *triumph* of industrialism and the spread of urbanism—*Glicksberg*⟩ or to express the pleasure of the successful person ⟨she was clearly conscious of her success . . . . There was a little prance of *triumph* in her walk—*Dahl*⟩

*Ana* winning, gaining (see GET): ascendancy, *supremacy: control, sway, dominion, command, *power, authority

*Ant* defeat

**victuals** *food, feed, viands, provisions, comestibles, provender, fodder, forage

**vie** *rival, compete, emulate

*Ana* *contend, fight: strive, struggle, essay, endeavor (see ATTEMPT *vb*)

**view** *n* 1 *look, sight, glance, glimpse, peep, peek

*Ana* scrutiny, scanning, inspection, examination (see under SCRUTINIZE)

2 *opinion, belief, conviction, persuasion, sentiment

*Ana* *idea, thought, concept, conception: inference, deduction, conclusion, judgment (see under INFER)

**view** *vb* survey, contemplate, observe, note, remark, notice, perceive, discern, *see, behold, descry, espy

*Ana* scan, *scrutinize, inspect, examine: *consider, regard, account

**viewpoint** *point of view, standpoint, angle, slant

*Ana* *position, stand, attitude: ground, *reason

**vigilant** alert, wide-awake, *watchful

*Ana* anxious, agog, keen, avid, *eager: circumspect, wary, chary, *cautious: *quick, ready, prompt: *sharp, keen, acute

*Con* *negligent, neglectful, lax, slack, remiss: *forgetful, unmindful, oblivious

**vigor, vim, spirit, dash, esprit, verve, punch, élan, drive** can all denote a quality of force, forcefulness, or energy. **Vigor** implies a strength that proceeds from a fundamental soundness or robustiousness or a display of energy or forcefulness deriving from this or befitting it ⟨the physical and intellectual *vigor* and toughness which the trial lawyer needs—*Robert Hale*⟩ ⟨the tendency . . . to mistake gush for *vigor* and substitute rhetoric for imagination—*Day Lewis*⟩ **Vim** stresses the display of usually enthusiastic energy put into the work of doing or making something ⟨fights with *vim*⟩ ⟨the workmen . . . are always busy; there is a hearty *vim* to their work that proves interest—*Century*⟩ **Spirit** (see also COURAGE, SOUL, APPARITION) stresses vivacity, animation, and liveliness which usually derive from mood, disposition, or temperament ⟨all in arms . . . as full of *spirit* as the month of May—*Shak.*⟩ ⟨the pieces . . . were written in deadest winter of the dead years . . . and few of the contributions had *spirit*—*Mailer*⟩

⟨sing it with a *spirit* that will start the world along—*Work*⟩ **Dash** may imply the presence of any of these qualities, vigor, vim, and spirit, often in the form of a bold devil-may-care force; it tends to stress the impact of the thing upon the mind of the observer or reader or listener ⟨drawn with Dureresque vigor and *dash*—*Hardy*⟩ ⟨the two sisters were not beautiful . . . but they had the *dash* . . . that a later generation came to call sex appeal—*Shaplen*⟩ **Esprit** is not quite equivalent to *spirit;* like spirit it implies a quality which has its basis in nature and is manifested in mood or temperament; unlike it, it suggests the force displayed by an exceedingly active and subtle mind and so comes close to meaning cleverness, brains, or wit usually with an added suggestion of vivacity (as in conversation) ⟨one man who is a little too literal can spoil the talk of a whole tableful of men of *esprit*—*Holmes*⟩ ⟨the industrial *esprit* that could spark general economic advance—*Riesman*⟩ **Verve** also comes close to *spirit*, but it often carries a clearer implication of a characteristic or peculiar force or energy, the exact description of which only the context can supply or suggest ⟨writing with the *verve* and gusto dear to the mid-nineteenth century—*Mary Ross*⟩ ⟨the spirit of their times is in them. There is the same tremendous energy and *verve* and vitality—*Edith Hamilton*⟩ ⟨his manly *verve* for the enlivening of that gray court—*Belloc*⟩ **Punch** suggests a quality that carries with it the power to gain its aim; it may imply a convincing or commanding quality, but it stresses forcefulness and immediate effectiveness ⟨the searing *punch* of cloud to ground lightning—*Dillon*⟩ ⟨verbs that have *punch*—*Westley*⟩ **Élan** approaches *dash* in meaning, but it carries a stronger connotation of impetuosity and assurance or of ardor in the display of force and energy ⟨his stories . . . are told in a formal style and exhibit the attempt to recapture a certain note of urbanity, wit, and *élan*—*Mailer*⟩ ⟨performed with great *élan* in a sophisticated style—*Dance Observer*⟩ **Drive** also, like *dash* and *élan*, suggests a quality that affects others, but it carries a richer implication than either of the display of power to force through to the ends in view and to carry the observers, especially the readers, along with it ⟨the city had lost . . . the surging *drive* that supposedly was so characteristically American—*Harold Sinclair*⟩ ⟨the dynamic core of a society, its central impulse and *drive*—*Maughan*⟩ ⟨this titan's spirit which gave such *drive* and strength to the mightiest of his plays—*J. M. Brown*⟩

*Ana* strength, force, *power, might, energy: soundness, healthiness (see corresponding adjectives at HEALTHY): virility (see corresponding adjectives at MALE)

**vigorous, energetic, strenuous, lusty, nervous** can all mean having or manifesting great vitality and force. A person or thing is **vigorous** that has or manifests active strength or force and exhibits no signs of a depletion of the powers associated with freshness or robustness of body or mind ⟨seemed as *vigorous* as a youth half his age⟩ ⟨a *vigorous*, fast-growing tree⟩ ⟨the *vigorous* mother of a large family⟩ ⟨a *vigorous* argument—*Edmund Wilson*⟩ ⟨Kate was a bold, *vigorous* thinker—*Anderson*⟩ A person or thing is **energetic** that displays abundant force or a capacity for great activity; the term does not necessarily connote the reserve vitality and force that *vigorous* implies and it sometimes even suggests an exertion of effort or a bustling activity that has little to do with inherent physical or mental strength; therefore the term may be used to suggest compliment or, less often, slight depreciation ⟨to be counted among the strong, and not the merely *energetic* —*J. R. Lowell*⟩ ⟨capable and *energetic* women, as fit to intimidate local government boards as to control the domestic economy of their own homes—*Sackville-*

A colon (:) separates groups of words discriminated. An asterisk (*) indicates place of treatment of each group.

*West*⟩ ⟨received by bustling male assistants very *energetic* and rapid—*Bennett*⟩ ⟨a less *energetic* expulsion of air from the lungs—*Grandgent*⟩ A person that is **strenuous** is continuously and zealously energetic, while a thing that is *strenuous* makes constant demands on one's vigor, energy, and zeal; in both cases the term implies no flagging of ardor or no avoidance of the arduous ⟨to hustle and to be *strenuous* . . . seem to be prominent American virtues—*Cohen*⟩ ⟨*strenuous* liberty—*Milton*⟩ ⟨the spirit of our religion calls for *strenuous* opposition to the current principles and practice of the world—*Inge*⟩ A person or thing is **lusty** that exhibits exuberant vigor or energy ⟨therefore my age is as a *lusty* winter, frosty, but kindly—*Shak.*⟩ ⟨Pete Gurney was a *lusty* cock turned sixty-three, but bright and hale—*Masefield*⟩ ⟨a *lusty* appetite⟩ A thing (as a quality, a style, or an utterance) is **nervous** that conveys a feeling of continuing often forceful activity such as results from mental vigor and energy ⟨the *nervous* alertness of youthful brains, and the stamina of youthful bodies—*Amer. Guide Series: Mich.*⟩ ⟨Tyndale's own diction was singularly simple, energetic, *nervous*, and yet restrained—*Lowes*⟩ ⟨his rhythm has a pulsating and *nervous* vitality—*Collet*⟩

*Ana* virile, manly, manful (see MALE): *muscular, athletic, sinewy, husky: stout, sturdy, stalwart, *strong, tough
*Ant* languorous: lethargic

**vile** *base, low
*Ana* depraved, corrupted, perverted, debased, debauched (see under DEBASE): *coarse, vulgar, obscene, gross: foul, filthy, nasty, *dirty: *mean, abject, sordid: *offensive, repulsive, revolting, loathsome

**vilify** *malign, traduce, asperse, calumniate, defame, slander, libel
*Ana* *abuse, outrage, mistreat, misuse: assail, *attack: revile, vituperate, berate (see SCOLD)
*Ant* eulogize

**villain,** scoundrel, blackguard, knave, rascal, rogue, scamp, rapscallion, miscreant can all denote a low, mean, and reprehensible person utterly lacking in principles. **Villain** describes one utterly given to crime, evil, and baseness ⟨are not made *villains* by the commission of a crime, but were *villains* before they committed it—*Ruskin*⟩ **Scoundrel** may suggest blended worthlessness, meanness, and unscrupulousness ⟨a crew of pirates . . . will elect a boatswain to order them about and a captain to lead them and navigate the ship, though the one may be the most insufferable bully and the other the most tyrannical *scoundrel* on board—*Shaw*⟩ **Blackguard** may imply inveterate depravity; sometimes it is used with a suggestion of angry contempt as the antithesis of *gentleman* ⟨you must employ either *blackguards* or gentlemen, or, best of all, *blackguards* commanded by gentlemen, to do butcher's work with efficiency and dispatch—*Kipling*⟩ **Knave** may suggest sly trickery and deceit ⟨cheating *knaves* gathered at the taverns⟩ ⟨more fool than *knave*⟩ **Rascal** may suggest base dishonesty ⟨your true *rascal* is today your only true citizen of the world. He plunders all nations without pride in one or prejudice against another—*Linklater*⟩ **Rogue** often suggests the blended roughness and wiliness of a vagabond ⟨sturdy *rogues* taking to the roads as highwaymen⟩ but both *rascal* and *rogue* are freely used with greatly weakened force and then imply no more than a more or less pleasing mischievousness ⟨tell me about . . . the dear little *rogues*—*Whitman*⟩ ⟨the Yankee . . . was already established as a comic *rascal*—*Bergen Evans*⟩ **Scamp** may describe one given to artful cheating, clever robbery, or interesting escapades ⟨a *scamp* who had pinched pennies out of the teacups of the poor by various shenanigans, who was distributing his largess to divert

attention from his rascality—*White*⟩ and it, too, is often used with weakened force, then suggesting impish and often childish trickery ⟨the most audacious *scamp* in all the animal kingdom is Bugs Bunny—*My Baby Magazine*⟩ **Rapscallion** may refer to an ill-dressed rogue or rascal rarely successful ⟨the *rapscallions* of the river, the Black Gangs—*Le Sueur*⟩ **Miscreant** typically refers to a singularly conscienceless villain ⟨a sordid glamour about imprisonment which makes the young *miscreant* feel important; he has the inverted satisfaction of being treated like a grown-up gangster—*Times Lit. Sup.*⟩
*Ana* offender, sinner (see corresponding nouns at OFFENSE): *criminal, malefactor

**villainous** *vicious, iniquitous, nefarious, flagitious, infamous, corrupt, degenerate
*Ana* debased, depraved, perverted (see under DEBASE): atrocious, *outrageous, heinous: dissolute, profligate, *abandoned

**vim** *vigor, spirit, dash, esprit, verve, punch, élan, drive
*Ana* force, strength, *power, energy

**vindicate** 1 justify, defend, *maintain, assert
*Ana* *support, uphold, advocate
2 exonerate, *exculpate, absolve, acquit
*Ana* *disprove, refute, confute: *defend, protect, shield, guard
*Ant* calumniate

**vindictive,** revengeful, vengeful are close synonyms often used interchangeably to mean showing or motivated by a desire for vengeance. Distinctively **vindictive** tends to stress this reaction as inherent in the nature of the individual and, therefore, is especially applicable when no specific motivating grievance exists ⟨there was nothing *vindictive* in his nature; but, if revenge came his way, it might as well be good—*Stevenson*⟩ The term can imply a persistent emotion or a tendency to seek revenge for real or fancied wrongs or slights, sometimes with implacable malevolence, sometimes with spiteful malice ⟨a *vindictive* man will look for occasions of resentment—*James Martineau*⟩ ⟨his zeal . . . was mingled with a *vindictive* hatred of the Puritans, which did him little honor either as a statesman or as a Christian—*Macaulay*⟩ ⟨it is not true that suffering ennobles the character; happiness does that sometimes, but suffering, for the most part, makes men petty and *vindictive*—*Maugham*⟩ but occasionally it implies no more than a punitive or retributive intent ⟨a *vindictive* purpose,—a purpose to punish you for your suspicion—*Cowper*⟩ ⟨the prison sentence handed down by a court that was more puzzled than *vindictive* was mild—*Purdy*⟩ ⟨the punishments in Dante's *Inferno*, though seldom devoid of a certain horrible appropriateness, are essentially *vindictive* in their nature. Retributive punishment is the essential of medieval justice—*Cohen*⟩ **Revengeful** and **vengeful** are more likely to suggest the state of one specifically provoked to action and truculently ready to seek revenge ⟨no creature is so *revengeful* as a proud man who has humbled himself in vain—*Macaulay*⟩ ⟨such a close farmer, as to grudge almost the seed to the ground, whereupon *revengeful* Nature grudged him the crops which she granted to more liberal husbandmen—*Thackeray*⟩ ⟨knowing that by one word—Yes or Forgive or Love—she might have . . . released all of the false and *vengeful* and troubling demons right up into the encompassing air of night, and everything would be right again —*Styron*⟩ ⟨to some *vengeful* people the treaty seemed too easy upon Germany; to many liberals it seemed too harsh—*Nevins & Commager*⟩ Additionally *revengeful* and especially *vengeful* can apply to an agent or weapon by which vengeance is won ⟨may my hands . . . never brandish more *revengeful* steel—*Shak.*⟩ ⟨provide thee

---

*Ana* analogous words      *Ant* antonyms      *Con* contrasted words      See also explanatory notes facing page 1

proper palfries, black as jet, to hale thy *vengeful* wagon swift away—*Shak.*⟩ ⟨they unnerve us with *vengeful* roar of wheel—*Lewisohn*⟩
*Ana* implacable, unrelenting, relentless, merciless, *grim: spiteful, *malicious, malignant, malign
**violation** *breach, infraction, transgression, trespass, infringement, contravention
*Ana* *offense, sin, vice, crime, scandal: desecration, *profanation, sacrilege, blasphemy: invading *or* invasion, encroachment, entrenchment (see corresponding verbs at TRESPASS)
**violence** *force, compulsion, coercion, duress, constraint, restraint
*Ana* vehemence, intensity, fierceness (see corresponding adjectives at INTENSE): *effort, exertion, pains, trouble: *attack, assault, onslaught, onset
**violent** *intense, vehement, fierce, exquisite
*Ana* *powerful, potent, forceful, forcible: *excessive, immoderate, inordinate, extreme, extravagant
**virago,** amazon, termagant, scold, shrew, vixen can all mean a woman of pugnacious temperament. *Virago* and *amazon* are often interchangeable; both tend to suggest physical vigor and size and often a masculine quality of mind or interests ⟨viragoes with red faces, thick necks, and tousled lint-colored hair screamed at all present to come and have a shy at the wooden figures—*Lynd*⟩ ⟨an *amazon* of a woman appeared suddenly in the doorway. She was well over six feet and well over two hundred pounds—*Nancy Rutledge*⟩ ⟨a few daring *amazons* of the horsey set—*Dos Passos*⟩ and both may apply to a woman engaged in typically masculine pursuits and especially fighting ⟨their leader was a fiery little Mexican *virago* scarcely out of her teens—*Green Peyton*⟩ ⟨Charles XII of Sweden had a bearded female grenadier in his army, a reputedly beautiful *amazon*—*Joseph Mitchell*⟩ ⟨the warrior maiden Marfisa, a true *virago* and amazon— *R. A. Hall*⟩ Distinctively **virago** can imply fierceness of temper and a domineering nature ⟨sometimes she abjures her femininity, she hesitates between chastity, homosexuality, and an aggressive *virago* attitude—*Parshley*⟩ ⟨certain *viragoes*, who made life a burden to the brothers —*G. W. Johnson*⟩ while **amazon** is more likely to suggest heroic qualities (as of dedication and competence) ⟨a magnificent, tousled, ragged *amazon* of a woman, on fire with the spirit of revolt against oppression—*Linguaphone Mag.*⟩ ⟨you can . . . while some intellectual *amazon* at your right tells you all about Péguy and Beethoven and Karl Marx, smile at your wife and be glad she has just the mind she has—*Le Beau*⟩ **Termagant** carries a strong implication of habitual disorderly turbulence, boisterousness, and uncontrollable temper ⟨a foulmouthed *termagant*, who screamed abuse and vile scurrility at her husband from morning till night—*The Scotsman*⟩ ⟨what she was trying to accomplish was to get rid of all his relatives . . . . She became a *termagant*—a confirmed scold—*Howard*⟩ **Scold, shrew,** and *vixen* designate women who habitually inflict bad temper on others. A **scold** indulges herself in vulgar, abusive, and often castigating speech ⟨really was a *scold* . . . had fought life single-handed . . . with all the ferocity of outraged sensibilities, and had come out of the fight scratched and disheveled, with few womanly graces—*Stowe*⟩ ⟨she laid on external things the blame of her mind's internal disorder, and thus became by degrees an accomplished *scold*— *Peacock*⟩ while a **shrew** possesses a bitter tongue and a nagging disposition ⟨a *shrew*, a woman with the temper of a fiend—*Forester*⟩ and a **vixen,** a fiery temperament and often a tendency to snappish asperity ⟨a woman tropical, intense . . . she blended in a like degree the *vixen*

and the devotee—*Whittier*⟩
**virgin** *adj* 1 *unmarried, single, celibate, maiden
2 also **virginal** maiden, boyish, *youthful, juvenile, puerile
*Ana* *chaste, pure, modest, decent: fresh, *new
**virile** manful, manly, *male, masculine, manlike, mannish
*Ant* effeminate: impotent '(sense 2)
**virtual** *implicit, constructive
*Ant* actual
**virtually, practically, morally** can all mean not absolutely or actually, yet so nearly so that the difference is negligible. So close are these words in meaning that they (especially the first two) are often interchanged although each can carry specific implications that make discriminative use possible. **Virtually** may imply that the difference is merely that between what a thing is in name or outward seeming and what it is in fact, in essence, in effect, or, sometimes, in potentiality ⟨the prime minister is *virtually* the ruler of his country⟩ ⟨their father's request is *virtually* a command⟩ ⟨the British contended that the American colonies were *virtually* represented⟩ **Practically** implies a difference between what is enough for practical purposes or from the point of view of use, value, or effectiveness and what satisfies the requirements formally or absolutely ⟨badly spotted fruit is *practically* worthless⟩ ⟨a road is *practically* finished when traffic can pass over it freely and without interruptions⟩ **Morally** implies a difference between what satisfies one's judgment and what is required for proof by law or by logic ⟨the jurors were *morally* certain of the defendant's guilt, but owing to a lack of evidence, they were compelled to render a verdict of "not guilty"⟩ When *morally* qualifies words such as "impossible," it occurs in a statement of a conviction and is slightly less positive than "absolutely" ⟨it is *morally* impossible to accomplish more under the circumstances⟩
**virtue** 1 *goodness, morality, rectitude
*Ana* honor, *honesty, integrity, probity: *fidelity, piety, fealty, loyalty: righteousness, nobility, virtuousness (see corresponding adjectives at MORAL)
*Ant* vice
2 *excellence, merit, perfection
*Ana* *worth, value: effectiveness, efficacy, effectualness (see corresponding adjectives at EFFECTIVE): strength, might, *power, force
**virtuoso** *expert, adept, artist, artiste, wizard
**virtuous** *moral, ethical, righteous, noble
*Ana* pure, *chaste, modest, decent: *upright, just, honorable
*Ant* vicious
**virulent** *poisonous, venomous, toxic, mephitic, pestilent, pestilential, miasmic, miasmatic, miasmal
*Ana* *deadly, mortal, fatal, lethal: *pernicious, noxious, baneful, deleterious: malignant, malign (see MALICIOUS)
**virus** 1 *poison, venom, toxin, bane
2 *germ, microbe, bacterium, bacillus
**visage** *face, countenance, physiognomy, mug, puss
**vision** 1 *revelation, prophecy, apocalypse
2 *fancy, fantasy, phantasy, phastasm, dream, daydream, nightmare
*Ana* illusion, *delusion, hallucination, mirage: *imagination, fancy, fantasy
**visionary** *adj* *imaginary, fanciful, fantastic, chimerical, quixotic
*Ana* romantic, *sentimental, maudlin: utopian, *ambitious, pretentious: ideal, transcendent, transcendental (see ABSTRACT): illusory, seeming, *apparent
**visit** *n* **Visit, visitation, call** are comparable when they mean a coming to stay with another, usually for a brief time, as a courtesy, an act of friendship, or a business or professional duty. **Visit** applies not only to such a stay with

*A colon (:) separates groups of words discriminated. An asterisk (*) indicates place of treatment of each group.*

another ⟨pay a *visit* to a friend⟩ ⟨a physician's bill for *visits*⟩ ⟨a welfare worker's *visit*⟩ but also, to a more prolonged stay as a house guest or in a place where one goes for rest, entertainment, or sightseeing ⟨a week's *visit* in a friend's summer home⟩ ⟨off for a *visit* to Washington⟩ ⟨plan a *visit* to Europe⟩ **Visitation** (see also TRIAL 2) is chiefly employed in reference to a formal or official visit (as to a church, a college, or a ship) made by one in authority (as an ecclesiastical superior, a school superintendent, or a medical inspector) ⟨parochial *visitations* of a bishop⟩ ⟨a *visitation* and search of a merchant ship can be made only by an authorized official⟩ The term may also be used of something that visits one, often by or as if by the will of a superior power ⟨ye gentle *visitations* of calm thought—*Shelley*⟩ or that is visited upon one and that is usually regarded as an affliction ⟨an illness, a maiming accident or some other *visitation* of blind fate—*Conrad*⟩ **Call** applies only to a brief visit, such as one makes upon a person who is not a friend, but with whom one has social or official relations ⟨a society woman must give a portion of her time to formal *calls*⟩ or by a person in quest of business or of a business order ⟨the morning *call* of the grocer's boy⟩ The term, however, may be used in place of *visit* for a short social visit.

**visitant** *visitor, guest, caller

**visitation 1** *visit, call
**2** *trial, tribulation, affliction, cross
*Ana* *misfortune, mischance, adversity: calamity, catastrophe, *disaster: hardship, vicissitude (see DIFFICULTY)

**visitor, visitant, guest, caller** mean one who visits another or comes to pay a visit. **Visitor** is the general word applicable to anyone who comes under this description ⟨there are *visitors* in the drawing room⟩ ⟨summer *visitors*⟩ but it is especially applicable to one who makes a friendly visit or one who comes in the cause of charity, social service, or investigation ⟨a frequent *visitor* at his friend's house⟩ ⟨the *visitor* from the Red Cross found no one at home⟩ **Visitant** is applied especially to a visitor who is or seems to be from ánother sphere (as heaven or hell) ⟨supernatural *visitant*⟩ ⟨at the sound of this the *visitant* returned . . . . Markheim . . . thought he bore a likeness to himself: and always, like a lump of living terror, there lay in his bosom the conviction that this thing was not of the earth—*Stevenson*⟩ As compared with *visitor*, **guest** emphasizes the idea of hospitable entertainment; it applies therefore chiefly to one who comes as a result of an invitation ⟨they had ten *guests* at dinner⟩ ⟨we shall have no *guests* until the children are perfectly well⟩ It also is often used, sometimes in the expanded form *paying guest*, of a lodger or boarder, and is used regularly for patrons of a restaurant or hotel. **Caller** is applicable not only to one who comes for a social or business call (see under VISIT) but to anyone regardless of his intentions who seeks entrance to one's home or office ⟨told her maid that she would not be at home to *callers* that day⟩

**vital 1** *living, alive, animate, animated
*Ana* *vigorous, energetic, lusty: *active, live, dynamic
**2** fundamental, *essential, cardinal
*Ana* important, significant, consequential, weighty, momentous (see corresponding nouns at IMPORTANCE): indispensable, requisite, necessary, *needful

**vitalize, energize, activate** can all mean to arouse to activity, animation, or life something inactive, inert, latent, or arrested (as in development). **Vitalize** may stress the arousal of something more or less inert or lifeless to vital activity, often by communicating an impetus or force, or an imparting of significance or interest to (something) or a making one aware of its inherent significance or interest; the term usually suggests a vigor, freshness, or health in the effect ⟨a force which can *vitalize* or destroy men—*Cunnington*⟩ ⟨a power of description that *vitalizes* his words—*Christian Science Monitor*⟩ ⟨a resurgent democracy *vitalized* . . . through a mobilization of the total resources of the community—*Melby*⟩ **Energize** implies an arousing to activity by an imparting of strength or a source of power that increases capacity for activity or an acting with a vitality presumably induced by such power ⟨oats are, without doubt, the best *energizing* food for horses—*Wynmalen*⟩ ⟨storage batteries *energize* railroad block signal circuits— *Orsino & Lynes*⟩ ⟨it is Christianity which *energized* the special genius that made the West what it is—*Cogley*⟩ ⟨when a man and woman are successfully in love, their whole activity is *energized* and victorious. They walk better . . . they think more clearly —*Lippmann*⟩ **Activate** implies a passing from an inactive to an active state; though the process involved can be equivalent to that implied by *energize* the stress is quite different and is consistently upon an arousing to activity by the influence of an external agent ⟨breaks contact with the photoelectric cell and *activates* an alarm—*Hynd*⟩ ⟨the report has done much to crystallize and *activate* official and private opinion—*Walter White*⟩ ⟨vitamin D *activated* by sunlight⟩ ⟨political and legal hacks whose function it was to supply the docile social machinery for cleverer men to *activate* and guide— *Mattingly*⟩
*Ana* animate, *quicken, enliven, vivify: stimulate, galvanize, excite, *provoke
*Ant* atrophy

**vitiate** *debase, deprave, corrupt, pervert, debauch
*Ana* pollute, defile, taint, *contaminate: degrade, demean, *abase: impair, spoil, *injure, damage: annul, invalidate, *nullify

**vitiated** debased, depraved, corrupted, debauched, perverted (see under DEBASE)
*Ana* defiled, polluted, contaminated, tainted (see CONTAMINATE): impaired, spoiled, injured (see INJURE): invalidated, annulled (see NULLIFY)

**vituperate** revile, berate, rate, upbraid, *scold, tongue-lash, jaw, bawl, chew out, wig, rail
*Ana* condemn, denounce, censure, blame, reprehend, reprobate (see CRITICIZE): vilify, asperse, traduce, *malign, calumniate: *execrate, objurgate
*Con* *commend, applaud, compliment: *praise, extol, eulogize

**vituperation** *abuse, invective, obloquy, scurrility, billingsgate
*Ana* *animadversion, aspersion, stricture, reflection: *attack, assault, onslaught, onset: condemnation, denunciation, censuring *or* censure (see corresponding verbs at CRITICIZE): vilifying *or* vilification, maligning, calumniation (see corresponding verbs at MALIGN)
*Ant* acclaim, praise

**vituperative** *abusive, opprobrious, contumelious, scurrilous
*Ana* *coarse, vulgar, gross, obscene: insulting, offending, outraging (see OFFEND): condemning *or* condemnatory, denouncing *or* denunciatory (see corresponding verbs at CRITICIZE)

**vivacious** *lively, animated, gay, sprightly
*Ana* buoyant, effervescent, volatile (see ELASTIC): *merry, blithe, jocund: frolicsome, sportive, *playful
*Ant* languid

**vivid** *graphic, picturesque, pictorial
*Ana* *sharp, keen, acute: *dramatic, dramaturgic, theatrical: *expressive, eloquent, meaningful: nervous, lusty, *vigorous: *clear, lucid, perspicuous
*Con* *obscure, vague, enigmatic

**vivify** *quicken, animate, enliven
*Ana* *vitalize, energize, activate: *renew, restore, refresh: *stir, rouse, arouse: stimulate, galvanize, excite (see PROVOKE)

**vixen** shrew, scold, termagant, *virago, amazon

**vocable** *n* *word, term

**vocabulary** *language, phraseology, diction, phrasing, style

**vocal** 1 Vocal, articulate, oral can all mean uttered by the voice or having to do with utterance. **Vocal** implies the use of voice, but not necessarily of speech or language; thus, *vocal* sounds are sounds produced by a creature that has *vocal* organs; *vocal* music is contrasted with instrumental music because the musical tones are produced by the voice rather than by a musical instrument. **Articulate** implies the use of distinct intelligible language; thus, speech is the uttering of *articulate* sounds; *articulate* cries are those that are expressed in meaningful words rather than in meaningless sounds ⟨Constance nodded her head in thorough agreement. She did not trouble to go into *articulate* apologies—*Bennett*⟩ **Oral** implies the use of the voice rather than the hand (as in writing or typing) in communicating (as thoughts, wishes, orders, questions, or answers) ⟨an *oral* examination⟩ ⟨an *oral* command⟩ ⟨the *oral* transmission of tradition⟩
2 Vocal, articulate, fluent, eloquent, voluble, glib can mean being able to express oneself clearly or easily, or showing such ability. **Vocal** usually implies ready responsiveness to an occasion for expression or free and usually forceful, insistent, or emphatic voicing of one's ideas or feelings ⟨earth's millions daily fed, a world employed in gathering plenty yet to be enjoyed, till gratitude grew *vocal* in the praise of God—*Cowper*⟩ ⟨this instantaneous indignation of the most impulsive and *vocal* of men was diligently concealed for at least six weeks, with reporters camped upon his doorstep day and night—*Mencken*⟩ **Articulate** is as often applied to thoughts and emotions with reference to their capacity for expression as to persons or their utterances. It implies the use of language which exactly and distinctly reveals or conveys what seeks expression ⟨the deepest intuitions of a race are deposited in its art; no criticism can make these wholly *articulate*—*Binyon*⟩ ⟨the primitive poet . . . was used by the community to make its spiritual needs *articulate*—*Day Lewis*⟩ ⟨how can you write about a literary subject . . . when you yourself are hardly *articulate*, can scarcely express the most commonplace thoughts—*Edmund Wilson*⟩ **Fluent** stresses facility in speaking or writing and copiousness in the flow of words; unlike *vocal* and *articulate*, it refers chiefly to the manner of the expression rather than to the matter seeking expression ⟨it was his gift to be *fluent* on anything or nothing—*Stevenson*⟩ The word can carry a definite suggestion of depreciation or contempt ⟨politically at the mercy of every bumptious adventurer and *fluent* charlatan—*Shaw*⟩ but it also is the only one of these words capable of implying facility and ease in the use of a foreign language ⟨had a *fluent* command of idiomatic French⟩ **Eloquent** usually implies fluency but it suggests also the stimulus of powerful emotion and its expression in fervent and moving language; it is applicable not only to speakers but to writers and can be extended to things that convey similar suggestions (see also EXPRESSIVE) ⟨pressed his arm reassuringly, and the gesture was more *eloquent* than any words could be—*Wolfe*⟩ ⟨Tully was not so *eloquent* as thou, thou nameless column with the buried base—*Byron*⟩ ⟨the wording of the Weimar Constitution was sweet and *eloquent* to the ear of any democratically minded man—*Shirer*⟩ **Voluble** and *glib* both imply loquacity and are usually derogatory. **Voluble** sug-

gests a flow of language that is not easily stemmed ⟨indulge in *voluble* explanations⟩ ⟨a *voluble* person, but at last the flow of words stopped—*Glasgow*⟩ **Glib** implies such facility in utterance as to suggest superficiality or emptiness in what is said or slipperiness or untrustworthiness in the speaker ⟨a *glib* reply⟩ ⟨he has a *glib* tongue⟩ ⟨their only virtue, a *glib* conversance with such topics as came up for discussion—*Sackville-West*⟩
*Ana* expressing, voicing, venting (see EXPRESS *vb*): *expressive, sententious, eloquent

**vociferate** *roar, bellow, bluster, bawl, clamor, howl, ululate
*Ana* *shout, yell, shriek, scream, screech, holler

**vociferation** see under *vociferate* at ROAR *vb*

**vociferous, clamorous, blatant, strident, boisterous, obstreperous** are comparable when they mean so loud and noisy, especially vocally, as to compel attention, often unwilling attention. **Vociferous** implies both loud and vehement cries or shouts; it often suggests also a deafening quality ⟨watermen, fishwomen, oysterwomen, and . . . all the *vociferous* inhabitants of both shores—*Fielding*⟩ ⟨*vociferous* vindications of their innocence—*Irving*⟩ ⟨*vociferous* protests⟩ **Clamorous** can imply insistency as well as vociferousness in demanding or protesting ⟨it was impossible to yield to her *clamorous* demands—*Repplier*⟩ but as often it stresses the notion of sustained din or confused turbulence ⟨the district had been *clamorous* with trucks arriving, backing in and out . . . the drivers bawling and cursing—*Peggy Bacon*⟩ **Blatant** implies a tendency to bellow or be conspicuously, offensively, or vulgarly noisy or clamorous ⟨they were heretics of the *blatant* sort, loudmouthed and shallow-minded—*Expositor*⟩ ⟨building against our *blatant*, restless time an unseen, skillful, medieval wall—*Lindsay*⟩ **Strident** basically implies a harsh and discordant quality characteristic of some noises that are peculiarly distressing to the ear; it is applied not only to loud, harsh sounds but also to things which, like these, irresistibly and against one's will force themselves upon the attention ⟨the colors are too *strident*⟩ ⟨the *strident* yellow note of the cockerel shot up into the sunshine—*Gibbons*⟩ ⟨there was no *strident* old voice to bid him do this or that; no orders to obey, no fierce and insane faultfinding—*Deland*⟩ **Boisterous** has usually an implication of rowdy high spirits and flouting of customary order and is applied to persons or things that are extremely noisy and turbulent, as though let loose from all restraint ⟨from the distant halls the *boisterous* revelry floated in broken bursts of faint-heard din and tumult—*Jerome*⟩ ⟨*boisterous* spring winds—*Cather*⟩ **Obstreperous** suggests unruly and aggressive noisiness, typically occurring in resistance to or defiance of authority or restraining influences ⟨the most careless and *obstreperous* merriment —*Johnson*⟩ ⟨disrespectful of Parliamentary decorum, they are so *obstreperous* that sittings sometimes have to be suspended to stop their hubbub—*Flanner*⟩
*Ana* noisy, sounding (see corresponding nouns at SOUND): bewildering, distracting (see PUZZLE *vb*)

**vogue** mode, *fashion, style, fad, rage, craze, dernier cri, cry

**voice** *vb* *express, utter, vent, broach, air, ventilate
*Ana* *reveal, disclose, tell, discover, divulge: *communicate, impart: *speak, talk

**void** *adj* 1 *empty, vacant, blank, vacuous
*Ana* exhausted, depleted, drained (see DEPLETE): *bare, barren: hollow, empty, nugatory, *vain
2 *devoid, destitute

**void** *n* vacuum, *hole, hollow, cavity, pocket
*Ana* emptiness, vacancy, vacuity (see corresponding adjectives at EMPTY): abyss, *gulf, abysm

---

A colon (:) separates groups of words discriminated. An asterisk (*) indicates place of treatment of each group.

**void** *vb* vacate, *annul, abrogate, quash

**volatile** effervescent, buoyant, expansive, resilient, *elastic

*Ana* unstable, mercurial, *inconstant, fickle, capricious: light-minded, frivolous, flippant, flighty (see corresponding nouns at LIGHTNESS): variable, *changeable, protean

**volatility** *lightness, light-mindedness, levity, frivolity, flippancy, flightiness

*Ana* vivaciousness *or* vivacity, gaiety, liveliness, animation, sprightliness (see corresponding adjectives at LIVELY): unstableness *or* instability, mercurialness, inconstancy (see corresponding adjectives at INCONSTANT): variability, changeableness (see corresponding adjectives at CHANGEABLE)

**volcano** *mountain, mount, peak, alp, mesa

**volition** *will, conation

*Ana* *choice, election, option

*Con* *force, coercion, compulsion, duress

**volubility** glibness, garrulity, loquacity, talkativeness (see under TALKATIVE)

*Ana* fluency, glibness, eloquence, articulateness (see corresponding adjectives at VOCAL)

**voluble** 1 fluent, glib, eloquent, *vocal, articulate

*Ana* copious, abundant, *plentiful: *easy, facile, effortless, smooth

*Ant* stuttering, stammering

2 glib, garrulous, loquacious, *talkative

*Ant* curt

**volume** 1 magnitude, *size, extent, dimensions, area

2 *bulk, mass

**voluntary, intentional, deliberate, willful, willing** can mean constituting or proceeding from an exercise of free will. **Voluntary,** the most widely applicable of these terms, often implies not only freedom from constraint but freedom from the control of an influence that might suggest, prompt, or incite action; it does not necessarily imply that these influences have not been operative, but it usually suggests that the decision is the result of one's free choice ⟨a *voluntary* renunciation of his inheritance⟩ ⟨a *voluntary* confession⟩ ⟨a *voluntary* system . . . which possessed a certain pleasant dignity denied to the systems of a more compulsory sort—*Sackville-West*⟩ Often the term carries another, sometimes a different, implication, such as that of spontaneity ⟨*voluntary* contributions⟩ ⟨our *voluntary* service he requires not—*Milton*⟩ or, especially when the opposition is to *involuntary,* that of subjection to or regulation by the will ⟨*voluntary* movements of the eyes⟩ ⟨*voluntary* muscles⟩ or that of prior consideration and clear choice ⟨*voluntary* manslaughter⟩ or that of absence of any legal obligation or compulsion (as to do or make) ⟨*voluntary* bankruptcy⟩ or of any valuable consideration in return for doing or making ⟨*voluntary* conveyance of property⟩ **Intentional** applies chiefly to acts or processes entered into in order to achieve a desired end or purpose or to the end or purpose so willed or effected; the use of the word eliminates all suggestion of the possibility of accident or inadvertence ⟨an *intentional* insult⟩ ⟨not one in a thousand . . . perpetrates any *intentional* damage to fish, fowl, or flowers—*Jefferies*⟩ **Deliberate** (see also DELIBERATE 2, SLOW) adds the implication of full knowledge or full consciousness of the nature of one's intended act and a decision to go ahead in spite of such knowledge or consciousness ⟨a *deliberate* falsehood⟩ ⟨*deliberate* murder⟩ ⟨an organized and *deliberate* attack—carefully planned and calculated—*N.Y. Times*⟩ **Willful** (see also UNRULY) adds to *deliberate* the implications of a refusal to be taught, counseled, or commanded, and of an obstinate determination to follow one's own will or choice in full consciousness of the influences or arguments opposed to the attitude adopted or the action or deed contemplated ⟨*willful* murder⟩ ⟨*willful* ignorance⟩ ⟨his *willful* abuse of his children⟩ ⟨*willful* blindness to ascertained truth—*Inge*⟩ **Willing** carries, in contrast, an implication of characteristics (as agreeableness, openness of mind, or absence of reluctance) that makes one ready or eager, without suggestion or without coercion, to accede to the wishes or instructions of others or to do something or effect some end pleasing to them ⟨how curious is that instinct which makes each sex, in different ways, the *willing* slave of the other!—*Jefferies*⟩ ⟨*willing* service⟩ ⟨where ears are *willing,* talk tends to be loud and long—*Huxley*⟩

*Ana* chosen, elected, opted (see CHOOSE): *free, independent, autonomous

*Ant* involuntary: instinctive (sense 2) —*Con* compelled, coerced, forced (see FORCE *vb*)

**voluptuous** luxurious, sybaritic, epicurean, *sensuous, sensual

*Ana* indulging *or* indulgent, pampering (see corresponding verbs at INDULGE): *luxurious, opulent, sumptuous

*Ant* ascetic

**vomit** *belch, burp, disgorge, regurgitate, spew, throw up

*Ana* *eject, expel, oust

**voracious, gluttonous, ravenous, ravening, rapacious** can all mean excessively greedy and can all apply to persons, their appetites and reactions, or their behavior. **Voracious** implies habitual gorging with food or drink, or with whatever satisfies an excessive appetite ⟨a *voracious* eater⟩ ⟨a *voracious* reader⟩ ⟨*voracious* birds, that hotly bill and breed, and largely drink—*Dryden*⟩ **Gluttonous** differs from *voracious* chiefly in its common suggestions of covetous delight (as in food) and of acquiring or eating past need or to the point of satiety ⟨he was *gluttonous* for jewels—*Gunther*⟩ ⟨though a Norman was not *gluttonous,* he was epicurean—*Lytton*⟩ ⟨his *gluttonous* appetite for food, praise, pleasure—*Guérard*⟩ **Ravenous** implies excessive hunger and suggests violent or grasping methods of dealing with food or with whatever satisfies an appetite ⟨he contracted a habit of eating with *ravenous* greediness. . . . The sight of food affected him as it affects wild beasts and birds of prey—*Macaulay*⟩ ⟨he had mad hungers that grew more *ravenous* as he fed them—*Wilde*⟩ **Ravening** is sometimes employed in place of *ravenous* ⟨the hordes of *ravening* ants—*Beebe*⟩ but more often it comes close to **rapacious** in suggesting a violent tendency to seize or appropriate to oneself in the manner of a bird of prey or a predatory animal ⟨beware of false prophets, which come to you in sheep's clothing, but inwardly they are *ravening* wolves—*Mt 7:15*⟩ **Rapacious** may imply the seizure of food ⟨*rapacious* animals we hate: kites, hawks, and wolves, deserve their fate—*Gay*⟩ but more often it suggests excessive and utterly selfish acquisitiveness or cupidity ⟨the Indians, who, though often *rapacious,* are devoid of avarice—*Parkman*⟩ ⟨the European nations, arrogant, domineering, and *rapacious,* have done little to recommend the name of Christianity in Asia and Africa —*Inge*⟩

*Ana* greedy, grasping, acquisitive, *covetous: satiating, sating, surfeiting, gorging (see SATIATE)

**vortex** *eddy, whirlpool, maelstrom

**votary** *addict, devotee, habitué

*Ana* *enthusiast, fanatic, zealot, bigot

**vote** *n* *suffrage, franchise, ballot

**vouch** *certify, attest, witness

*Ana* *support, uphold: *confirm, substantiate, verify, corroborate

**vouchsafe** *grant, accord, concede, award

*Ana* *give, bestow, confer, present: condescend, deign, *stoop: *oblige, accommodate, favor

---

*Ana* analogous words      *Ant* antonyms      *Con* contrasted words      See also explanatory notes facing page 1

**voyage** n *journey, tour, trip, excursion, cruise, expedition, jaunt, pilgrimage

**vulgar 1** *common, ordinary, familiar, popular
*Ana* *universal, general: *prevailing, prevalent, current, rife: *usual, customary: crude, *rude, rough, uncouth:

sordid, ignoble, *mean
**2** *coarse, gross, obscene, ribald
*Ana* low, *base, vile: *offensive, loathsome, repulsive, revolting: indelicate, indecent, *indecorous

# W

**wage** or **wages, salary, stipend, fee, pay, hire, emolument** can all mean the price paid a person for his labor or services. **Wage** or **wages** applies chiefly to an amount paid on a daily, hourly, or piecework basis and typically at weekly intervals for labor, especially labor that involves more physical than mental effort ⟨a gardener's *wages*⟩ ⟨a steelworker's daily *wage*⟩ **Salary** and **stipend** both usually apply to compensation at a fixed, often annual, rate that is paid in regular (as weekly or monthly) installments but *stipend* is more likely to apply to the compensation of a teacher, a clergyman, or a magistrate, or it may denote money received from a scholarship or a pension ⟨many a parson has brought up a family on a *stipend* of seventy pounds a year—*Shaw*⟩ **Fee** applies to the price usually in the form of a fixed charge, asked or paid for the service of a professional (as a physician, lawyer, musician, or artist) when such service is requested or required ⟨pay the surgeon's *fee* for a major operation⟩ ⟨a lawyer's retaining *fee*⟩ ⟨a pianist's *fee* for a concert⟩ **Pay** can replace *wages, salary*, or *stipend* ⟨fired and told to draw his *pay*⟩ ⟨a teacher's *pay*⟩ ⟨even a preacher needs adequate *pay*⟩ and is the one of these four terms freely used in combination and attributively ⟨waiting for *pay*day⟩ ⟨*pay*check⟩ ⟨crumpled his empty *pay* envelope⟩ **Hire**, which basically denotes payment made for the temporary use of something (as the property or money of another), is occasionally and especially in legal use applied to compensation for labor or services and is then equivalent to *wages* or *salary* ⟨the laborer is worthy of his *hire*—*Lk* 10:7⟩ ⟨lends his pen for small *hires*—*Meredith*⟩ **Emolument**, usually in the plural, often means the financial reward of one's work or office ⟨the *emoluments* of a profession—*Gibbon*⟩ ⟨a worthier successor wears his dignity and pockets his *emoluments*—*Hawthorne*⟩ or more specifically rewards and perquisites other than wages or salary ⟨*emoluments* of value, like pension and insurance benefits, which may accrue to employees—*Boyce*⟩ ⟨salary £550 with no *emoluments*—*Farmer and Stock-Breeder*⟩
*Ana* remuneration, recompensing or recompense (see corresponding verbs at PAY)

**wager** *bet, stake, pot, ante

**waggish** sportive, frolicsome, *playful, impish, mischievous, roguish
*Ana* facetious, jocose, jocular, humorous, *witty: jovial, jolly (see MERRY): comic, comical, *laughable, droll, ludicrous, funny
*Con* *serious, earnest, sober, grave, sedate, staid

**wail** vb weep, *cry, whimper, blubber, keen
*Ana* mourn, *grieve: lament, bewail, bemoan, *deplore: moan, sob, *sigh, groan

**wait** *stay, remain, abide, tarry, linger
*Ana* *delay, loiter
*Con* depart, leave, *go, withdraw, retire

**waive** cede, yield, resign, abandon, surrender, *relinquish, leave
*Ana* *forgo, forbear, sacrifice: concede, *grant, allow

*Con* *demand, claim, require, exact: assert, *maintain, defend

**waken** awaken, arouse, rouse, *stir, rally
*Ana* excite, stimulate, quicken, galvanize, *provoke: fire, kindle (see LIGHT): impel, *move, actuate, drive
*Ant* subdue —*Con* *pacify, mollify, placate

**wall** vb *enclose, envelop, fence, pen, coop, corral, cage
*Ana* *surround, environ, encircle, hem: confine, circumscribe, *limit, restrict

**wallow, welter, grovel** can imply heavy clumsy movement and, when the reference is to man, a debased, pitiable, or ignoble condition. **Wallow** basically implies a lurching or rolling to and fro (as of a pig in the mire or a ship in the trough of a wave) ⟨whenever the animals grew hot and tired, they would lie down and *wallow*—*Heiser*⟩ ⟨a jeep came *wallowing* through the mud—*Mailer*⟩ In extended use the term may suggest the state of an animal wallowing in mud and then variously imply complete self-abandonment ⟨*wallowing* in self-pity⟩ or absorption ⟨enjoyed sitting . . . and *wallowing* in the sensual melodies—*Osbert Sitwell*⟩ or helpless involvement ⟨the economic catastrophe in which they were . . . *wallowing*—*J. P. O'Donnell*⟩ or especially sensual enjoyment and indifference to the defilement or degradation that the condition suggests ⟨publicly *wallowed* in his infamies—*Merle Miller*⟩ ⟨in port Rootes would roar off to the fleshpots, in which he would *wallow* noisily until an hour before takeoff—*Theodore Sturgeon*⟩ **Welter** is often employed in place of *wallow*, but it frequently carries a stronger implication of rolling or tossing helplessly or confusedly or at the mercy of the elements or other external forces ⟨he must not float upon his watery bier unwept, and *welter* to the parching wind—*Milton*⟩ ⟨beneath the *weltering* of the restless tide —*Shelley*⟩ ⟨the mass of the people were *weltering* in shocking poverty whilst a handful of owners *wallowed* in millions—*Shaw*⟩ *Welter*, however, may not always imply movement, as when it suggests the position of one who has been killed and lies soaked in blood ⟨they lie—the fifty corpses—*weltering* in their blood—*Mitchell*⟩ ⟨score technical successes, even if their backers *welter* in red ink— *Gabriel*⟩ **Grovel** implies a crawling or wriggling with face close to the ground (as in abject fear, awe, self-abasement, or complete humiliation or degradation) ⟨upon thy belly *groveling* thou shalt go, and dust shalt eat all the days of thy life—*Milton*⟩ ⟨one moment he towered in imagination, the next he *groveled* in fear—*G. D. Brown*⟩
*Ana* crawl, *creep: defile, pollute, *contaminate, taint: *debase, debauch, corrupt, deprave, pervert
*Con* soar, mount, ascend, *rise

**wan** pallid, *pale, ashen, ashy, livid
*Ana* blanched, whitened, decolorized (see WHITEN): *languid, languishing, languorous: *haggard, cadaverous, worn

**wander, stray, roam, ramble, rove, range, prowl, gad, gallivant, traipse, meander** can mean to move about more or less aimlessly or without a plan from place to place or

A colon (:) separates groups of words discriminated. An asterisk (*) indicates place of treatment of each group.

from point to point. Most of these verbs may imply walking, but most are not restricted in their reference to human beings or to any particular means of locomotion. **Wander** implies the absence of a fixed course or more or less indifference to a course that has been fixed or otherwise indicated; the term may imply the movement of a walker whether human or animal or of any traveler, but it may be used of anything capable of direction or control that is permitted to move aimlessly ⟨*wand'ring* thoughtful in the silent wood—*Pope*⟩ ⟨his eyes *wandered* over the landscape⟩ ⟨his mind *wandered* and he was unsure of himself—*Shirer*⟩ ⟨she *wandered* frequently from her subject⟩ **Stray** carries a stronger suggestion of deviation from a fixed, true, or proper course, and often connotes a being lost or a danger of being lost ⟨fallows grey, where the nibbling flocks do *stray*—*Milton*⟩ ⟨we have erred, and *strayed* from thy ways like lost sheep—*Book of Common Prayer*⟩ ⟨though we stumbled and we *strayed*, we were led by evil counsellors—*Kipling*⟩ **Roam** carries a stronger suggestion of freedom and of scope than *wander;* it usually carries no implication of a definite object or goal, but it seldom suggests futility or fruitlessness and often connotes delight or enjoyment ⟨like us, the Libyan wind delights to *roam* at large—*Arnold*⟩ ⟨let the winged Fancy *roam*—*Keats*⟩ ⟨type of the wise who soar, but never *roam*—*Wordsworth*⟩ ⟨the charm of a quiet watch on deck when one may let one's thoughts *roam* in space and time—*Conrad*⟩ **Ramble**, in contrast, suggests carelessness in wandering and more or less indifference to one's path or goal ⟨to *ramble* through the country and to talk about books—*Marquand*⟩ It often, especially in its extended uses, implies a straying beyond bounds, an inattention to details that ought to serve as guides, or an inability to proceed directly or under proper restrictions ⟨a vine, remarkable for its tendency, not to spread and *ramble*, but to mass and mount—*Cather*⟩ ⟨great temptation . . . to *ramble* on interminably in praise of the delights of sailing—*Schoettle*⟩ **Rove** comes close to *roam* in its implication of wandering over extensive territory, but it usually carries a suggestion of zest in the activity, and does not preclude the possibility of a definite end or purpose ⟨invaders *roved* through the country burning and pillaging homes in their pathway⟩ ⟨ravenous beasts freely *roving* up and down the country—*Fuller* d. 1661⟩ ⟨to seek thee did I often *rove* through woods and on the green—*Wordsworth*⟩ **Range** is often used in place of *rove* without loss; it may be preferred when literal wandering is not implied or when the stress is on the sweep of territory covered rather than on the form of locomotion involved ⟨earth ships had *ranged* the cosmos far and wide—*Theodore Sturgeon*⟩ ⟨her imperious and hoarse voice *ranged* over a complete octave of requited social ambitions—*Cheever*⟩ ⟨his thoughts always *ranged* far afield—*Mencken*⟩ **Prowl** implies a stealthy or furtive roving, especially in search of prey or booty. It is used not only of animals ⟨even a tomcat who cannot get the tabby he wants will *prowl* around her prison for days—*Edmund Wilson*⟩ but often also of human beings intent on marauding ⟨now goes the nightly thief *prowling* abroad—*Cowper*⟩ but it is also applied with little or no connotation of an evil intention to persons, especially those of a restless or vagabond temperament, who rove, often singly, through the streets or the fields in a quiet and leisurely manner ⟨if I should *prowl* about the streets a long time, don't be uneasy—*Dickens*⟩ **Gad** and **gallivant** imply a wandering or roving especially by those who ought to be under restrictions (as servants, children, husbands or wives, and persons who have not much strength or enough money). **Gad**, usually with *about*, may suggest a bustling from place

to place idly or for the most trivial ends and often to the detriment of one's actual duties ⟨her upper housemaid and laundry maid, instead of being in their business, are *gadding* about the village all day long—*Austen*⟩ ⟨he disapproved of her *gadding* about by herself—*Galsworthy*⟩ **Gallivant** adds to *gad* the implication of a search for pleasure or amusement or the use of an opportunity to display one's finery ⟨her father refused to allow her to go *gallivanting* around with any of her suitors⟩ ⟨young girls dressed in their Sunday best *gallivanting* along the highways⟩ **Traipse**, which commonly suggests more vigor in movement and less aimlessness in intent than the remaining terms, may come close to *come, go,* or *travel* in meaning ⟨in her late sixties she *traipsed* over Europe with a crony of equal years—*Leavitt*⟩ ⟨how old . . . does he think a man should be before he is barred from *traipsing* around making political speeches—*N.Y. Times*⟩ ⟨here *traipsed* into town a little thing from away off down in the country—*Welty*⟩ Even when used with reference to an erratic course *traipse* ordinarily implies a positive purpose ⟨they lacked the time and energy to *traipse* around looking for the sort of thing they had in mind—*Kahn*⟩ or stresses a bustling activity ⟨other crowds like this: the yellow-faced swarm that pours out of shipyards, say, at five o'clock, the swarm that *traipses* Oxford Street, the mad swarms at the greyhound tracks—*Pritchett*⟩ or a wearying expenditure of energy ⟨she *traipsed* around the provinces playing small parts in second-rate companies at a miserable salary—*Maugham*⟩ ⟨kings . . . *traipsed* here and there with frenetic energy—*J. E. M. White*⟩ Sometimes the term loses most of its reference to a course and then stresses a dashing or flaunting manner of going ⟨people . . . who *traipsed* about in trite monotonous flippery—*Peggy Bennett*⟩ ⟨I got a job . . . as a model. I'd *traipse* around stepping through lace hems and gabbing to the customers—*New Yorker*⟩ **Meander** may be used in reference to persons and animals but more characteristically in reference to things (as streams, paths, or roads) that follow a winding or intricate course in such a way as to suggest aimless or listless wandering ⟨rivers that . . . *meandered* across the vast plains—*Haggard*⟩ ⟨across the ceiling *meandered* a long crack—*Galsworthy*⟩ ⟨the gray gelding *meandered* along through the hills—*Anderson*⟩

**wane** \*abate, subside, ebb
*Ana* \*decrease, dwindle, lessen, diminish
*Ant* wax —*Con* \*increase, augment: mount, soar, tower, surge, \*rise

**want** *vb* 1 \*lack, need, require
*Ana* \*demand, claim, exact
*Con* \*have, hold, own, possess, enjoy
2 \*desire, wish, crave, covet
*Ana* \*long, yearn, hanker, pine, hunger, thirst: aspire, pant, \*aim
*Con* refuse, \*decline, reject, repudiate, spurn

**want** *n* 1 \*lack, dearth, absence, defect, privation
*Ana* \*need, necessity, exigency: deficiency (see corresponding adjective at DEFICIENT)
*Con* plentifulness *or* plenty, abundance, copiousness (see corresponding adjectives at PLENTIFUL)
2 destitution, \*poverty, indigence, privation, penury
*Ana* pinch, strait, pass, exigency (see JUNCTURE): meagerness, scantiness, exiguousness (see corresponding adjectives at MEAGER)
*Con* affluence, opulence, riches, wealth (see corresponding adjectives at RICH)

**wanton** 1 \*licentious, libertine, lewd, lustful, lascivious, libidinous, lecherous
*Ana* \*immoral, unmoral, amoral: \*abandoned, profligate,

dissolute, reprobate

*Ant* chaste —*Con* pure, modest, decent (see CHASTE): virtuous, *moral

2 *supererogatory, uncalled-for, gratuitous

*Ana* *malicious, malevolent, spiteful: wayward, *contrary, perverse

**war** *vb* battle, *contend, fight

*Ana* *resist, withstand, combat, oppose, fight: strive, struggle, endeavor, essay, *attempt

**warble** *vb* *sing, troll, carol, descant, trill, hymn, chant, intone

**ward** avert, *prevent, preclude, obviate

*Ana* block, bar, obstruct, impede, *hinder: forestall, anticipate (see PREVENT): *frustrate, balk, thwart, foil

*Ant* conduce to

**wariness** chariness, caution, circumspection, calculation (see under CAUTIOUS)

*Ana* alertness, watchfulness (see corresponding adjectives at WATCHFUL): *prudence, discretion, foresight, forethought, providence

*Ant* foolhardiness: brashness (of *persons*) —*Con* carelessness, heedlessness, thoughtlessness, inadvertence (see corresponding adjectives at CARELESS): recklessness, rashness (see corresponding adjectives at ADVENTUROUS)

**warlike** *martial, military

*Ana* bellicose, *belligerent, pugnacious, combative, contentious: fighting, warring, contending, battling (see CONTEND)

*Con* *pacific, peaceable, peaceful

**warm** *adj* warmhearted, sympathetic, *tender, compassionate, responsive

*Ana* *loving, affectionate: cordial, *gracious, affable: ardent, fervent, passionate (see IMPASSIONED): *sincere, heartfelt, hearty, wholehearted

*Ant* cool: austere

**warmhearted** warm, sympathetic, *tender, compassionate, responsive

*Ana* *loving, affectionate: *kind, kindly, benign, benignant: heartfelt, hearty, wholehearted, *sincere

*Ant* coldhearted —*Con* austere, *severe, stern: *cold, cool, frosty, frigid

**warn, forewarn, caution** can mean to let one know of approaching or possible danger or risk. **Warn** is the most comprehensive of these terms; in most of its senses it stresses a timely notification that makes possible the avoidance of a dangerous or inconvenient situation ⟨*warn* ships of an approaching hurricane⟩ ⟨five minutes before the end of the class period, a bell rings to *warn* teachers and pupils⟩ ⟨the steamship company *warned* those who had taken tickets of the advanced sailing⟩ Additionally, the word may carry an implication of admonition ⟨*warned* him of the consequences of his folly⟩ or of exhortation ⟨the priestly brotherhood . . . prompt to persuade, expostulate, and *warn*—*Cowper*⟩ or of threats of punishment, reprisal, or personal violence ⟨I shall not take him at his word about fishing, as he might change his mind another day, and *warn* me off his grounds—*Austen*⟩ **Forewarn** carries a stronger implication of advance notification than *warn* and may also suggest impending though not imminent danger or peril ⟨I will arm me, being thus *forewarned*—*Shak.*⟩ ⟨he knew not one *forewarning* pain—*Wordsworth*⟩ **Caution** commonly emphasizes advice that puts one on one's guard or that suggests precautions ⟨*cautioned* him against unwarranted expectations⟩ ⟨the doctor *cautioned* him against overindulgence in strenuous exercise⟩

*Ana* apprise, *inform, advise, notify: admonish (see REPROVE): advise, counsel (see under ADVICE)

**warp** *vb* distort, contort, *deform

*Ana* twist, bend (see CURVE *vb*): *injure, damage, impair, mar

**warrant** *vb* 1 *assert, declare, profess, affirm, aver, protest, avouch, avow, predicate

*Ana* state (see RELATE): *maintain, assert: assure, *ensure, insure

2 *justify

*Ana* vindicate, justify (see MAINTAIN): sanction, *approve, endorse: *authorize

**wary** chary, *cautious, circumspect, calculating

*Ana* alert, *watchful: prudent, discreet, foresighted, forethoughtful, provident (see under PRUDENCE)

*Ant* foolhardy: brash (*of persons*) —*Con* *careless, . heedless, thoughtless, inadvertent: reckless, rash, venturesome (see ADVENTUROUS)

**waspish** snappish, *irritable, fractious, peevish, petulant, pettish, huffy, fretful, querulous

*Ana* testy, touchy, cranky, cross, *irascible: *impatient: *contrary, perverse: spiteful, *malicious

**waste** *n* 1 **Waste, desert, badlands, wilderness** can mean a tract or region of land not usable for cultivation or general habitation. **Waste** is the general term applicable to a tract or region which because of natural features (as poor stony soil, excessive wetness or dryness, or abrupt elevations) or because of barrenness induced by human agency is unfit or unsuitable for cultivation or human habitation ⟨at this . . . point of its nightly roll into darkness the great and particular glory of the Egdon *waste* began —*Hardy*⟩ ⟨*wastes* of sand and thorns—*Montague*⟩ **Desert** tends to stress aridity; it calls to mind arid regions where areas of shifting sand prevail and there is little or no vegetation ⟨the Sahara *desert*⟩ but technical use generally applies it to regions that have less than ten inches of annual rainfall or are incapable of supporting a significant population without an artificial water supply. **Badlands** applies to a barren waste where soft rocks that suffer from continual erosion prevail and hills are steep, furrowed, and often fantastic in form, drainage is labyrinthine, and watercourses are normally dry ⟨there are extensive *badlands* in southwest South Dakota and northwest Nebraska⟩ **Wilderness** may apply to a waste which human beings find not only incapable of cultivation or habitation but difficult to make their way through for lack of actual or even possible paths or trails, but perhaps more often the term denotes an area or region that has not been extensively occupied or cultivated by man without implying anything about its potential uses ⟨oh for a lodge in some vast, *wilderness*, some boundless contiguity of shade—*Cowper*⟩ ⟨O my poor kingdom . . . thou wilt be a *wilderness* again, peopled with wolves—*Shak.*⟩

2 *refuse, rubbish, trash, debris, garbage, offal

**waste** *vb* 1 devastate, *ravage, sack, pillage, despoil, spoliate

*Ana* plunder, loot, *rob, rifle: *destroy, demolish: *ruin, wreck

*Ant* conserve, save

2 **Waste, squander, dissipate, fritter, consume** are comparable when they mean to spend or expend freely or futilely. **Waste** often implies careless or prodigal expenditure (as of money or of things which cost money) but it may also imply useless or fruitless expenditure (as of time, talent, or energy) ⟨allowing no money to be *wasted* on whims and luxuries—*Shaw*⟩ ⟨the windows were thickly frosted over, so that Mr. Povey's art in dressing them was quite *wasted*—*Bennett*⟩ **Squander** heightens the implications of *waste* by emphasizing reckless or lavish expenditures that tend to deplete or exhaust; often it suggests impoverishment or complete exhaustion ⟨the money, after all, was theirs; seeing it all *squandered* on a house and

---

A colon (:) separates groups of words discriminated. An asterisk (*) indicates place of treatment of each group.

a garden, why didn't they rise up . . . ?—*Huxley*⟩ ⟨willing to *squander* their lives on the gratuitous work that great art demands—*Edmund Wilson*⟩ ⟨the most brilliant journalist of my generation . . . often *squanders* his genius for invective—*T. S. Eliot*⟩ **Dissipate**, in the specific sense here considered (see also SCATTER), implies loss by extravagance, as if what is expended had been scattered to the four winds; it goes further than *waste* or *squander*, which do not, as does *dissipate*, in themselves imply exhaustion or near exhaustion of the store or stock ⟨its endowment *dissipated* in worthless securities, the institution was closed—*Amer. Guide Series: N.C.*⟩ ⟨the face of one whose essential innocence could not be *dissipated* by maturity, even tragedy—*Hervey*⟩ **Fritter**, usually with *away*, implies expenditure on trifles or by bits; it usually suggests a gradual disappearance (as of money, of property, or of something of value) ⟨the friend had lost $300,000, and Lasker had *frittered* away almost as much—*Cerf*⟩ ⟨if we *fritter* and fumble away our opportunity in needless, senseless quarrels—*L. B. Johnson*⟩ **Consume** basically stresses a devouring or destroying ⟨the house was *consumed* by fire⟩ (see also EAT, MONOPOLIZE), but it can mean to waste or squander entirely as if by devouring. In this use it is decreasingly frequent with regard to money or property ⟨having then *consumed* all his estate he grew very melancholy—*Anthony Wood*⟩ but in reference to time or energy spent unprofitably, it is not uncommon ⟨the day was *consumed* attending to a multitude of little things⟩ ⟨the heat, the exertion had *consumed* all superfluous energy—*Hervey*⟩
*Ana* *spend, expend, disburse: *distribute, dispense: *scatter, disperse, dispel: *deplete, drain, exhaust, impoverish
*Ant* save: conserve

**wasted** pinched, cadaverous, *haggard, worn, careworn
*Ana* gaunt, scrawny, skinny, angular, rawboned (see LEAN *adj*)
*Con* sturdy, *strong, stout, stalwart: robust, *healthy

**waster** *spendthrift, profligate, prodigal, wastrel
*Ana* idler, loafer, lounger (see corresponding verbs at IDLE): squanderer, dissipater, fritterer (see corresponding verbs at WASTE)

**wastrel** *spendthrift, profligate, prodigal, waster
*Ana* reprobate, *outcast: loafer, idler, lounger (see corresponding verbs at IDLE): scoundrel, rascal, rogue, scamp (see VILLAIN)

**watch** *vb* 1 *tend, mind, attend
*Ana* guard, protect, shield, safeguard (see DEFEND)
2 look, *see
*Ana* *gaze, gape, stare, glare: *scrutinize, scan, inspect, examine

**watchful**, vigilant, wide-awake, alert are comparable when they mean on the lookout especially for danger or for opportunities. **Watchful** is the general word ⟨the five *watchful* senses—*Milton*⟩ ⟨became almost remote, strangely *watchful*, looking back from time to time as though they were being followed—*Malamud*⟩ **Vigilant** implies keen, courageous, often wary, watchfulness ⟨be sober, be *vigilant*; because your adversary the devil, as a roaring lion, walketh about, seeking whom he may devour—*1 Pet 5:8*⟩ ⟨we should be eternally *vigilant* against attempts to check the expression of opinions that we loathe—*Justice Holmes*⟩ **Wide-awake** stresses keen awareness, more often of opportunities and relevant developments than of dangers ⟨merchants who . . . were . . . *wide-awake* and full of energy—*van Loon*⟩ **Alert** stresses readiness or promptness in apprehending and meeting a danger, an opportunity, or an emergency ⟨not only watchful in the night, but *alert* in the drowsy after-

noon—*Pater*⟩ ⟨our wits are much more *alert* when engaged in wrongdoing . . . than in a righteous occupation —*Conrad*⟩
*Ana* *cautious, wary, chary, circumspect: *quick, ready, prompt
*Con* *careless, heedless, thoughtless, inadvertent

**waterlog** *soak, drench, saturate, steep, impregnate, sop

**waterspout** *whirlwind, cyclone, typhoon, hurricane, tornado, twister .

**wave** *vb* *swing, flourish, brandish, shake, thrash
*Ana* wield, swing, manipulate, *handle, ply: undulate, sway, *swing, fluctuate: *shake, quiver, quaver

**waver** *vb* 1 fluctuate, oscillate, pendulate, vibrate, *swing, sway, undulate
*Ana* flicker, flutter, hover, *flit, flitter: quiver, quaver, tremble, *shake
2 falter, *hesitate, vacillate
*Ana* balk, boggle, stickle, scruple, *demur, shy: fluctuate, oscillate (see SWING)

**way** *n* 1 Way, route, course, passage, pass, artery mean, in common, a track or path traversed in going from one place to another. **Way** is general and inclusive of any track or path; it can specifically signify a thoroughfare especially in combinations and in fixed phrases ⟨high*way*⟩ ⟨live across the *way*⟩ ⟨the city accepted the new street as a public *way*⟩ ⟨long inclined *ways*, paved with cobblestones, leading down between great warehouses to the water's edge—*Santayana*⟩ or a direction or track that is, or can or should be, followed ⟨lost his *way*⟩ ⟨the short *way* to town⟩ ⟨the only other village was one day's mule trip farther into the interior, but the *way* was so steep and slippery in places that we walked almost as much as we rode—*Hitchcock*⟩ ⟨the water continues its *way* down the valley for 5 kilometers—*Heiden*⟩ The term also can be extended to what leads in a specified or implied nonspatial direction or toward a specified or implied end ⟨cleared the *way* for a more purely rational interpretation of the world—*Ashley Montagu*⟩ ⟨the *way* was now open for the final act—*W. C. Ford*⟩ **Route** signifies a way, often circuitous, followed with regularity by a person or animal or laid out to be followed (as by a tourist or army) ⟨a paper *route*⟩ ⟨a milk truck following a morning delivery *route*⟩ ⟨the dog team trails and canoe *routes* of trader, trapper and missionary in the bush country—*Granberg*⟩ ⟨a much traveled main *route* from Boston to Albany⟩ **Course** may be interchangeable with *route* but more often implies a path followed by or as if by a stream, star, or other moving natural object impelled by or in a path determined by natural forces ⟨the *course* of a river⟩ ⟨a meteor's *course*⟩ ⟨a ship's *course*⟩ ⟨the *course* of the seasons⟩ or a predetermined or more or less compulsory way or route followed in human activities or enterprises ⟨a *course* of study for an academic degree⟩ ⟨a golf *course*⟩ ⟨a race*course*⟩ **Passage** stresses a crossing over or a passing through, often designating the thing passed through, usually something narrow where transit might be restricted ⟨a rough *passage* to America by boat⟩ ⟨a narrow *passage* from kitchen to basement⟩ ⟨restrict the *passage* into the stomach⟩ **Pass** usually designates a passage through or over something that presents an obstacle (as a mountain or river) ⟨a narrow *pass* over the Alps⟩ ⟨a shallow ford constituted the only *pass* across the river⟩ **Artery** is applied to one of the great continuous traffic channels (as a central rail route, river, or highway) from which branch off smaller or shorter channels ⟨the Congo river would remain the main traffic *artery*—*Weigend*⟩ ⟨the main *artery* between Buffalo and Niagara Falls—*Retailing Daily*⟩ ⟨the need for improvement of main *arteries* interconnecting cities and for express highways in cities—

---

*Ana* analogous words    *Ant* antonyms    *Con* contrasted words    See also explanatory notes facing page 1

Britannica Bk. of the Yr.⟩

2 *method, mode, manner, fashion, system

*Ana* procedure, *process, proceeding: *plan, design, scheme: practice, *habit, habitude, custom, use, usage, wont

**waylay** *surprise, ambush

*Ana* *attack, assault, assail: *prevent, forestall

**wayward** perverse, froward, restive, *contrary, balky

*Ana* *insubordinate, contumacious, rebellious: refractory, recalcitrant, intractable, headstrong, *unruly: capricious, *inconstant, fickle, unstable

*Con* amenable, tractable, *obedient: *compliant, acquiescent

**weak, feeble, frail, fragile, infirm, decrepit** can mean not strong enough to bear, resist, or endure strain or pressure or to withstand difficulty, effort, or use. **Weak** is by far the widest in its range of application, being not only interchangeable with all of the succeeding words but also capable of being applied where they are not. Fundamentally it implies deficiency or inferiority in strength; it may apply to the body, the will, the mind, or the spirit ⟨a character too *weak* to resist temptation⟩ ⟨she wasn't a *weak* and silly creature . . . . She didn't swoon and give way to feelings and emotions—*Farrell*⟩ ⟨thou, though strong in love, art all too *weak* in reason—*Wordsworth*⟩ Often it implies a lack of power, skill, efficiency or ability to control ⟨a *weak* government⟩ ⟨a *weak* team⟩ ⟨a *weak* influence⟩ It may also suggest a sign of impairment of a thing's strength (as a defect, a fault, or a dilution) ⟨a *weak* tread in a stairway⟩ ⟨*weak* tea⟩ ⟨a *weak* argument⟩ ⟨*weak* facetious echoes of a style . . . ten years outmoded —*Wouk*⟩ **Feeble** not only is more restricted than *weak* in its range of application but also carries a stronger implication of lamentableness or pitiableness in that weakness. It is chiefly applied to human beings and their acts and utterances, then usually implying a manifest lack or impairment of physical, mental, or moral strength ⟨a *feeble*, tottering old man⟩ ⟨a *feeble* attempt to resist the enemy's advance⟩ ⟨rigid principles often do for *feeble* minds what stays do for *feeble* bodies—*Macaulay*⟩ As applied to things, *feeble* implies faintness, indistinctness, impotency, or inadequacy ⟨a *feeble* light⟩ ⟨a *feeble* sound⟩ ⟨a sense of *feeble* lust, of desire that mumbled incoherently as in a restless dream—*Hervey*⟩ **Frail**, when it implies physical weakness, suggests not so much the impairment of strength as natural delicacy of constitution or slightness of build ⟨a small, *frail* man, all heart and will—*Masefield*⟩ ⟨it was marvelous that . . . the energy of her spirit could carry through so triumphantly her *frail* nervous system and her delicate constitution—*Ellis*⟩ As applied to things the term usually implies liability to failure or destruction if the thing has physical existence ⟨shoot the rapids in a *frail* canoe⟩ ⟨I would lie . . . and listen to Yuriko's voice as it floated . . . through the *frail* partitions—*Mailer*⟩ or, if immaterial, an incapacity for dealing with forces or powers opposed to it, or tending to destroy it ⟨beauty, *frail* flow'r that ev'ry season fears—*Pope*⟩ When *frail* is applied to the will, the conscience, the moral nature of man, it carries an even stronger implication of lack of power to resist than *weak* ⟨if he prove unkind, (as who can say but being man, and therefore *frail*, he may)—*Cowper*⟩ **Fragile** (see also FRAGILE 1) is frequently used in place of *frail*, but it usually carries even a stronger suggestion of delicacy and of likelihood of destruction ⟨physically *fragile*, she was spiritually tough—*Sackville-West*⟩ ⟨passionately realizing the moment, its fleeting exquisiteness, its still, *fragile* beauty—*Rose Macaulay*⟩ **Infirm** usually implies a loss of strength, especially of physical strength, °with consequent instability, unsoundness, or insecurity ⟨elevators

in loft buildings . . . that, *infirm* and dolorous to hear, seem to touch on our concepts of damnation—*Cheever*⟩ As referred to human beings, it implies illness or more often old age ⟨a poor, *infirm*, weak, and despised old man— *Shak.*⟩ As referred, however, to the tempers, the designs, or the intentions of men, it often implies wavering or serious vacillation ⟨*infirm* of purpose! Give me the daggers—*Shak.*⟩ **Decrepit** is as applicable to things as to persons that are worn out or broken down by use or age ⟨such is its misery and wretchedness, that it resembles a man in the last *decrepit* stages of life—*Fielding*⟩ ⟨the bus is *decrepit* and the seats and several of the windows are held together with friction tape—*Cheever*⟩

*Ana* debilitated, weakened, enfeebled (see WEAKEN): *powerless, impotent

*Ant* strong —*Con* stout, sturdy, tough, stalwart, tenacious (see STRONG)

**weaken, enfeeble, debilitate, undermine, sap, cripple, disable** can mean to lose or cause to lose, strength, vigor, or energy. **Weaken**, the most general term of this group, most frequently implies loss of the physical strength or functional efficiency characteristic of a healthy living thing or of any of its parts or loss of the soundness or stability characteristic of a strong material structure ⟨overexercise has *weakened* his heart⟩ ⟨unfertilized plants *weaken* and die⟩ ⟨the illness has *weakened* him considerably⟩ ⟨decay has *weakened* the wooden supports of the bridge⟩ but it may imply a loss in quality, intensity, or effective power in something material or immaterial (as by a natural or forced reduction in resources, numbers, means of support, or strengthening principle) ⟨wearing down the *weakening* defenders in battles of attrition—*Shirer*⟩ ⟨the growing power of Parliament *weakened* the authority of the sovereign⟩ ⟨*weaken* tea with water⟩ ⟨the spirit of adventure is not stimulated but *weakened* by poverty—*Cohen*⟩ **Enfeeble** implies a more obvious and a more pitiable condition than *weaken;* it suggests the state of a person greatly weakened by old age, by severe or prolonged illness, or by a state comparable to it and usually implies helplessness or powerlessness more strongly than *weaken* does ⟨so *enfeebled* by illness that he will probably never walk again⟩ ⟨a country crushed and *enfeebled* by war⟩ **Debilitate** may be used in place of *enfeeble* but it tends to suggest a somewhat less marked and often more gradually developed impairment of strength or vitality ⟨her frail nervous system and her delicate constitution, still further *debilitated* by the slow progress of disease—*Ellis*⟩ ⟨a *debilitating* climate⟩ **Undermine** and **sap** imply a weakening by something or someone working surreptitiously or insidiously and may further suggest a draining of strength or a caving in or breaking down ⟨her health has been *undermined* by lack of rest and proper food⟩ ⟨some of the new philosophies *undermine* the authority of science, as some of the older systems *undermined* the authority of religion—*Inge*⟩ ⟨but sloth had *sapped* the prophet's strength—*Newman*⟩ ⟨his moral energy is *sapped* by a kind of skepticism—*Dowden*⟩ **Cripple** basically means to deprive of the use of a limb; in extended use it suggests a deprivation of something causing a loss of strength or effectiveness comparable to that resulting from the loss of a limb ⟨*crippling* diseases⟩ ⟨*crippled* by arthritis⟩ ⟨the obstacles which stunt and *cripple* the mind—*Inge*⟩ ⟨the war economy which marries full production to a necessarily *crippled* market—*Mailer*⟩ ⟨a writer possessing . . . a sense of style only partially *crippled* by his reckless fecundity—*A. C. Ward*⟩ **Disable** implies an intervention (as an event, an injury, or an influence) that deprives of strength or competence ⟨these consoling yet nonetheless *disabling* illusions—*Straight*⟩ ⟨*disabled* soldiers⟩ ⟨do

A colon (:) separates groups of words discriminated. An asterisk (*) indicates place of treatment of each group.

not let your mind be *disabled* by excessive sympathy —*Shaw*⟩
*Ana* enervate, emasculate, *unnerve, unman: impair, *injure, damage: dilute, *thin, attenuate, extenuate
*Ant* strengthen —*Con* energize, *vitalize, activate: *improve, better

**wealthy** *rich, affluent, opulent
*Ant* indigent

**wean** *estrange, alienate, disaffect
*Ana* *separate, part, divide, sunder, sever, divorce
*Ant* addict

**weariless** unwearying, unwearied, tireless, *indefatigable, untiring, unflagging
*Ana* dogged, pertinacious (see OBSTINATE): assiduous, sedulous, diligent (see BUSY)
*Con* lagging, dawdling, procrastinating (see DELAY): indolent, faineant, slothful, *lazy

**wearisome** tiresome, tedious, boring, *irksome
*Ana* fatiguing, exhausting, fagging, tiring (see TIRE *vb*): dull, slow, *stupid
*Con* exciting, stimulating, quickening (see PROVOKE)

**weary** *vb* *tire, fatigue, exhaust, jade, fag, tucker
*Ana* debilitate, enfeeble, *weaken: *depress, oppress, weigh
*Con* energize, *vitalize: animate, *quicken, enliven, vivify

**weave, knit, crochet, braid, plait, tat** mean to make a fabric or textile or to form an article by interlacing threads or strands of material. **Weave** usually implies crossing rows of threads or strands interlaced into a web, irrespective of method, material, or pattern ⟨*weave* baskets⟩ Specifically the term means to interlace warp and weft yarns, by means of a loom, into a textile fabric, the yarns being passed over and under each other according to a predetermined pattern. **Knit** implies the use of a single strand, commonly of yarn, to produce an elastic fabric and, in its specific sense, the use of two smooth-pointed needles alternately holding the material and forming a new row of interlacing loops ⟨*knit* a sweater⟩ ⟨*knit* stockings⟩ ⟨*knitted* fabrics⟩ **Crochet** specifically differs from *knit* by implying the use of a single hooked needle and in not necessarily suggesting a building up by successive rows ⟨*crochet* an afghan⟩ ⟨*crochet* lace⟩ **Braid** implies the entwining of three or more strands (as of hair, cord, or cloth strips) by passing one strand over another in such a manner that each strand winds a sinuous course through the ribbonlike or ropelike contexture that is thus produced ⟨*braid* rag strips to make a rug⟩ ⟨a whip of *braided* rawhide⟩ **Plait** is sometimes identical in meaning with *braid*, but it tends to be used especially of the braiding of strands of hair or of the interlacing of straw or reeds (as in hatmaking or basketmaking) whether the method approaches that of braiding or weaving. **Tat** implies the making of lace by the use of a single thread and of one or more shuttles by means of which a series of sliding knots and, usually, loops is formed in that thread.

**wedding** *marriage, matrimony, nuptial, espousal, wedlock

**wedlock** *marriage, matrimony, nuptial, espousal, wedding

**wee** diminutive, tiny, teeny, weeny, *small, little, minute, microscopic, miniature, petite

**weeny** tiny, teeny, wee, diminutive, minute, microscopic, miniature, little, *small

**weep** *cry, wail, keen, whimper, blubber
*Ana* bewail, bemoan, lament, *deplore: sob, moan, *sigh, groan

**weigh 1** *consider, study, contemplate, excogitate
*Ana* *ponder, meditate, ruminate, muse: *think, reflect, cogitate, reason, speculate
**2** *burden, encumber, cumber, weight, load, lade, tax, charge, saddle
*Ana* balance, ballast, trim, poise (see STABILIZE): *set, settle
**3** *depress, oppress
*Ana* *worry, annoy, harass, harry: torment, torture, *afflict, try, rack
*Con* lighten, *relieve, alleviate, assuage, mitigate, allay

**weight** *n* **1** significance, *importance, moment, consequence, import
*Ana* *worth, value: magnitude, *size, extent: seriousness, gravity (see corresponding adjectives at SERIOUS)
**2** *influence, authority, prestige, credit
*Ana* effectiveness, efficacy (see corresponding adjectives at EFFECTIVE): *emphasis, stress: powerfulness, potency, forcefulness, forcibleness (see corresponding adjectives at POWERFUL)

**weight** *vb* **1** load, *adulterate, sophisticate, doctor
**2** *burden, encumber, cumber, weigh, load, lade, tax, charge, saddle
*Ana* see those at WEIGH 2

**weighty** *heavy, ponderous, cumbrous, cumbersome, hefty
*Ana* *onerous, burdensome, oppressive, exacting

**weird, eerie, uncanny** can all mean fearfully and mysteriously strange or fantastic. **Weird** may be used in the sense of unearthly or preternaturally mysterious ⟨when night makes a *weird* sound of its own stillness—*Shelley*⟩ ⟨*weird* whispers, bells that rang without a hand—*Tennyson*⟩ or it may mean little more than strangely or absurdly queer ⟨had somehow absorbed . . . a *weird* mixture of the irresponsible, megalomaniacal ideas which erupted from German thinkers during the nineteenth century—*Shirer*⟩ **Eerie** does not connote ordinary justifiable or explainable fear but rather a vague consciousness that unearthly or mysterious and often malign powers or influences are at work; the term is used chiefly to create atmosphere rather than to define the character of the thing so described ⟨found awe creeping over her as her brother's voice filled the vault of the temple, chanting words thousands of years old, in an *eerie* melody from a dim lost time—*Wouk*⟩ **Uncanny** has in general use an implication of uncomfortable strangeness or of unpleasant mysteriousness that makes it applicable not only to persons or concrete things but to abstractions (as sensations, feelings, or thoughts) ⟨the alien elements of the Soviet Union affect him as disquieting, *uncanny*, because they turn up in fusion with pretenses at Western discipline, Western logic—*Edmund Wilson*⟩
*Ana* *mysterious, inscrutable: *fearful, awful, dreadful, horrific: *strange, odd, queer, curious, peculiar

**welcome** *adj* *pleasant, pleasing, agreeable, grateful, gratifying
*Ana* satisfying, contenting (see SATISFY): congenial, sympathetic (see CONSONANT)
*Ant* unwelcome —*Con* distasteful, *repugnant, repellent, obnoxious

**well** *adj* *healthy, sound, wholesome, robust, hale
*Ant* unwell, ill —*Con* infirm, frail, feeble, *weak

**well-nigh** *nearly, almost, approximately

**well-timed** timely, *seasonable, opportune, pat
*Ana* apt, happy, felicitous, appropriate, fitting (see FIT *adj*)
*Con* *premature, untimely: late, *tardy, behindhand

**welter** *wallow, grovel
*Ana* struggle, strive (see ATTEMPT *vb*)

**wet, damp, dank, moist, humid** are comparable when they mean covered or more or less soaked with liquid. **Wet** may be used with no further implications or it may specifically imply saturation ⟨*wet* clothes⟩ ⟨the rain lies in puddles on the *wet* ground⟩ Often, however, the term refers to a surface covered with liquid ⟨*wet* pavements⟩ ⟨*wet* hands⟩ ⟨cheeks *wet* with tears⟩ But *wet* often means merely not dry, or not yet dry, especially when used in reference to something (as paint, ink, or glue) which has been applied to or used on a surface. **Damp** differs from *wet* chiefly in implying a slight or moderate absorption or covering and often in connoting the presence of unpleasant or disagreeable wetness ⟨*damp* shoes⟩ ⟨the sheets on the bed are *damp*⟩ ⟨a *damp* house⟩ However *damp* usually implies less wetness than is commonly suggested by the adjective *wet* ⟨sheets should be *damp* when they are ironed⟩ **Dank** unequivocally applies to what is disagreeably, penetratingly or, from the point of view of health or comfort, dangerously, wet ⟨a cold *dank* mist⟩ ⟨*dank* forests⟩ ⟨a *dank* cellar⟩ **Moist** often suggests little more than the absence of dryness or a not unpleasant dampness ⟨*moist* eyes⟩ ⟨*moist* air⟩ ⟨*moist* heat⟩ **Humid** is chiefly used to imply an oppressive degree of moisture in warm air ⟨the *humid* atmosphere of early August⟩ ⟨the *humid* prairie heat, so nourishing to wheat and corn, so exhausting to human beings—*Cather*⟩ ⟨a firefly . . . on a *humid* summer's night—*Furnas*⟩

*Ana* soaked, saturated, drenched, waterlogged (see SOAK *vb*)

*Ant* dry

**wharf,** dock, pier, quay, slip, berth, jetty, levee signify a structure used by boats and ships for taking on or landing cargo or passengers. **Wharf** applies to a structure projecting from the shore that permits boats or ships to lie alongside for loading or unloading ⟨a ship maneuvering slowly up to the *wharf*⟩ ⟨the townsfolk rush to the *wharves* to welcome with cheers and banners the precious cargo of food—*Life*⟩ ⟨at the foot of this street . . . a rude *wharf* of logs was chained together and moored—*Amer. Guide Series: Vt.*⟩ ⟨a boy sitting on the edge of the *wharf*, his feet dangling in the water⟩ **Dock** is usually interchangeable with *wharf* but can be restricted to signify an enclosed basin which permits the entrance of a vessel for loading or unloading or which, with floodgates and a method of exhausting water, can be used for building or repairing ships ⟨a summer lake cottage with a short *dock* for canoes and rowboats⟩ ⟨a *dock* on Occoquan Creek—*Amer. Guide Series: Va.*⟩ ⟨the New York *docks*⟩ ⟨bring a ship into *dock* for repairs⟩ **Pier** is interchangeable with *dock* or *wharf* especially as applied to a large or long structure shooting out quite a distance into a body of water ⟨a sloping earthen *pier* for the launching of boats—*G. S. Perry*⟩ ⟨a fishing dragger unloading its catch at a *pier*— *Don Smith*⟩ ⟨pulled the canoe up on the *pier* to empty it⟩ ⟨the New York harbor *piers*⟩ **Quay** usually refers to an artificial enbankment lying along or projecting from a shore and mainly used for loading or unloading; the term normally applies to wharves or piers characteristic of small places ⟨so she, also, got into the small boat; and together they went in to the *quay*, and got ashore—*Black*⟩ ⟨a *quay* is a docking facility at which vessels lie parallel to the shoreline—*N.Y. Times*⟩ **Slip** can apply to a sloping ramp usually constructed or used where the shore is high and shore water shallow ⟨on the *slip* a thick water hose was connected from a hydrant to the ship—*Pizer*⟩ ⟨rolling barrels down a *slip* into the ship's hold⟩ but it, like **berth**, can denote the space between two piers or wharves which gives room for a ship when anchored or not in use, and is more common for such a space intended or used for ferryboat landings or boardings ⟨about to sail from her *berth* at the foot of Fifth Street—*Ships and the Sea*⟩ ⟨a deep-chested liner rears through the thin haze, easing her way to a Hudson river *berth*—*Amer. Guide Series: N.Y. City*⟩ ⟨transatlantic liners in adjoining *slips* down at the docks⟩ ⟨a series of steamship piers and ferry *slips*⟩ **Jetty** although commonly applied to a structure serving as a

breakwater for a harbor applies also to a small and usually not very substantial pier of timbers ⟨the harbor, from 30 to 60 feet deep, is protected by white marble *jetties*— *Amer. Guide Series: Fla.*⟩ ⟨fishermen . . . take their accustomed places on the wharves and *jetties* for the summer sport of gawking—*Anable*⟩ ⟨a *jetty* is usually built so that it lies parallel with the direction of the tidal stream, and at such *jetties* ships should always berth against the stream—*Manual of Seamanship*⟩ **Levee** primarily applies to an embankment for confining or restricting floodwaters but in the South and West, where a levee is often used for landing, the term is often the equivalent of *quay* ⟨build emergency *levees* to control a dangerously rising river⟩ ⟨down by the river's borders the new *levees* proclaim the grandsons' plans for a resurrected river traffic—*Amer. Guide Series: Minn.*⟩

**wheedle** blandish, cajole, *coax

*Ana* entice, inveigle, *lure, seduce, decoy

*Con* bully, browbeat, bulldoze, cow, *intimidate

**wheel** *vb* *turn, revolve, rotate, gyrate, circle, spin, twirl, whirl, swirl, pirouette, eddy

**while, wile, beguile, fleet** mean to pass time, especially leisure time, without being bored. One **whiles** or **wiles** *away* a space of time by causing it to be filled by something pleasant, diverting, or amusing ⟨they can *while* away an hour very agreeably at a card table—*Lamb*⟩ ⟨attempt to *wile* away the long days . . . telling a story to his sister— *Woolf*⟩ One **beguiles** a space of leisure time or its tedium or irksomeness by occupying that time with some agreeable and not necessarily time-wasting employment ⟨and, skilled in legendary lore, the lingering hours *beguiled* —*Goldsmith*⟩ ⟨others . . . *beguiled* the little tedium of the way with penny papers—*Hawthorne*⟩ ⟨to *beguile* his enforced leisure, I tried to teach him sundry little tricks —*Grandgent*⟩ One **fleets** the time by causing it to pass quickly or imperceptibly; the term may or may not imply an effort to while time away ⟨many young gentlemen . . . *fleet* the time carelessly—*Shak.*⟩ ⟨*fleeting* the quiet hour in observation of his pets—*Lewes*⟩

*Ana* divert, *amuse, entertain

**whim** freak, fancy, *caprice, whimsy, conceit, vagary, crotchet

*Ana* inclination, disposition (see corresponding verbs at INCLINE): *fancy, fantasy, vision, dream: notion, *idea

**whimper** *vb* weep, *cry, blubber, wail, keen

**whimsy** *caprice, freak, fancy, whim, conceit, vagary, crotchet

*Ana* see those at WHIM

**whirl** *vb* **1** twirl, spin, wheel, swirl, *turn, revolve, rotate, gyrate, circle, pirouette, eddy

**2** *reel, stagger, totter

**whirlpool** *eddy, maelstrom, vortex

**whirlwind,** cyclone, typhoon, hurricane, tornado, waterspout, twister share the basic notion of a rotary motion of the wind. **Whirlwind** is applied to a small windstorm which begins with an inward and upward spiral motion of the lower air and is followed by an outward and upward spiral motion until, usually, there is a progressive motion at all levels. **Cyclone,** in technical use, is applicable to a system of winds that rotate, counterclockwise in the northern hemisphere, about a center of low atmospheric pressure; such a system of winds originating in the tropics (a *tropical cyclone*) may rotate at the rate of 75 miles per hour or more, sometimes exceeding 200 miles per hour. **Typhoon** is used of a severe tropical cyclone in the region of the western Pacific ocean. A tropical cyclone in the tropical north Atlantic and tropical western Pacific, with winds rarely exceeding 150 miles an hour, occasionally moving into temperate latitudes, is called a **hurricane**. In popular use, especially in the midwestern U.S., *cyclone* may take the place of **tornado**, the usual technical term, for an extremely violent whirling wind which is accompanied by a funnel-shaped cloud and which moves with great speed in a narrow path over a stretch of territory, often causing great destruction. A **waterspout** is a tornado that occurs over water. **Twister** is a familiar term often applied to a whirlwind, tornado, or waterspout.

**whit** mite, jot, iota, bit, *particle, smidgen, tittle, atom

**whiten** *vb* 1 **Whiten, blanch, bleach, decolorize, etiolate** can all mean to change from an original color to white or almost to white. To **whiten** is to make white usually by the application or addition of something from without ⟨*whiten* shoes with pipe clay⟩ To **blanch** is to whiten by the removal or withdrawal of color ⟨*blanch* almonds by scalding which removes the brown skin⟩ or by preventing it from developing ⟨*blanch* celery by covering the stalks with earth, so as to exclude the sunlight⟩ To **bleach** is to whiten or lighten in color, especially by exposure to sun and air or by chemical processes ⟨*bleach* linen by spreading it on the grass in the sun⟩ ⟨*bleach* hair by use of peroxide⟩ **Decolorize** implies the deprivation of color (as by processes of bleaching or blanching) but does not carry as strong an implication of whitening as do *bleach* and *blanch* ⟨*decolorize* a colored fabric by the use of chloride of lime⟩ **Etiolate** is a scientific term used in reference chiefly to plants from which sunlight has been excluded with the result that the natural coloring of chlorophyll is not formed ⟨*etiolated* plants look sickly⟩
*Ant* blacken
2 whitewash, gloze, gloss, *palliate, extenuate
*Ana* see those at WHITEWASH

**whitewash** *vb* whiten, gloze, gloss, *palliate, extenuate
*Ana* *disguise, cloak, mask, dissemble, camouflage: condone, *excuse

**whole** *adj* 1 entire, *perfect, intact
*Ana* sound, well, *healthy, robust, wholesome: complete, plenary, *full
*Con* *deficient, defective: impaired, damaged, injured, marred (see INJURE)
2 **Whole, entire, total, all, gross** are comparable when they mean including each and every part, particle, individual, or instance of without exception. **Whole** implies that nothing has been omitted, ignored, abated, or removed ⟨he devoted his *whole* energy to the task⟩ ⟨the *whole* congregation approved the pastor's policy⟩ ⟨the *whole* army will be mobilized⟩ ⟨the *whole* country was affected⟩ **Entire** may be used in place of *whole* in any of these illustrations; it also can, as *whole* cannot, imply actual completeness or perfection from which not only nothing has been taken but to which nothing can be added ⟨an *entire* stallion⟩ ⟨whom to obey is happiness *entire*—*Milton*⟩ ⟨granting *entire* liberty of conscience—*Macaulay*⟩ **Total** implies that everything without exception has been counted, measured, weighed, or somehow included ⟨the *total* amount expended for welfare payments⟩ ⟨the *total* output of the factory last year⟩ Sometimes especially when applied to something that is often incomplete, *total* is used as an indication that no reservation is made ⟨*total* eclipse⟩ ⟨*total* blindness⟩ ⟨a *total* silence⟩ **All** sometimes equals *whole* ⟨all the city was in an uproar⟩, sometimes it comes closer to *entire* ⟨all their affection was centered on their children⟩, and sometimes it equals *total* ⟨all their earnings were insufficient for their needs⟩ **Gross** is used especially in financial statements in place of *total* to indicate that deductions (as for costs or expenses) have not yet been made ⟨*gross* earnings⟩ ⟨*gross* receipts⟩
*Ant* partial
**whole** *n* total, aggregate, *sum, amount, number, quantity

*Ant* part: constituent: particular —*Con* portion, piece, detail (see PART *n*): *item, detail: component, *element
**wholehearted** whole-souled, heartfelt, hearty, unfeigned, *sincere
*Ana* ardent, fervent, *impassioned, passionate: genuine, bona fide, *authentic: earnest, *serious
**wholesale** *indiscriminate, sweeping
**wholesome** 1 *healthful, healthy, salubrious, salutary, hygienic, sanitary
*Ant* noxious —*Con* deleterious, detrimental, *pernicious
2 sound, *healthy, robust, hale, well
*Ana* *strong, sturdy, stalwart, stout
**whole-souled** wholehearted, heartfelt, hearty, unfeigned, *sincere
*Ana* see those at WHOLEHEARTED
**whoop** *vb* *shout, yell, shriek, scream, screech, squeal, holler
**whoop** *n* shout, yell, shriek, scream, screech, squeal, holler (see under SHOUT *vb*)
**wicked** evil, *bad, ill, naughty
*Ana* *immoral, unmoral, amoral: iniquitous, *vicious, villainous: *abandoned, reprobate, profligate, dissolute
*Con* *moral, virtuous, righteous, ethical, noble
**wide** *broad, deep
*Ana* *spacious, capacious, ample: extended *or* extensive (see corresponding verb at EXTEND)
*Ant* strait —*Con* limited, restricted, confined (see LIMIT *vb*)
**wide-awake** *watchful, vigilant, alert
*Ana* *aware, alive, awake, conscious, sensible
**wield** swing, *handle, manipulate, ply
*Ana* *swing, flourish, brandish, shake, wave: control, direct, manage, *conduct: exercise, drill, *practice
**wig** *vb* tongue-lash, jaw, bawl, chew out, berate, *scold, upbraid, rate, rail, revile, vituperate
*Ana* reprimand, reproach, rebuke, *reprove, chide
**wild** *adj* *furious, frantic, frenzied, frenetic, delirious, rabid
*Ana* distracted, bewildered, perplexed (see PUZZLE): confused, muddled, addled (see CONFUSE): agitated, upset, perturbed (see DISCOMPOSE): mad, crazy, demented, deranged (see INSANE)
**wilderness** *waste, desert, badlands
**wile** *n* artifice, feint, ruse, maneuver, *trick, stratagem, gambit, ploy
*Ana* *deception, fraud, trickery, chicanery, chicane: cunning, *deceit, duplicity, dissimulation, guile
**wile** *vb* *while, beguile, fleet
*Ana* see those at WHILE *vb*
**will** *n* **Will, volition, conation** can all refer to the power or act of making or effecting a choice or decision. **Will** applies not only to this power or act but also to the complex of rational and irrational, conscious and unconscious forces within a person that is the agent of this power and to the process by which one makes his choice, resolves it into an intention, and puts that intention into effect. In all of these senses *will* may vary greatly in its specific meaning; it may denote a dominant desire or inclination which determines one's choice ⟨when he was confronted by accidental extinction, he had felt no *will* to resist—*Cather*⟩ or it may denote a power that derives from one's conception of what is good or right and that tests and accepts or rejects one's desires or inclinations ⟨appetite is the *will's* solicitor, and the *will* is appetite's controller; what we covet according to the one, by the other, we often reject—*Hooker*⟩ **Will** often denotes mainly the determination that is inseparable from action or the effecting of one's decisions ⟨in the government of self, Bismarck's

*Ana* analogous words    *Ant* antonyms    *Con* contrasted words    See also explanatory notes facing page 1

*will* broke down from time to time, as Richelieu's never did; and, after all, the government of self is the supreme test of *will*—*Belloc*⟩ but it may be used when frustration or impossibility of action is suggested ⟨spirits disillusioned, who still pathetically preserve the *will* to conquer, even when life no longer presents them with anything worth winning—*Binyon*⟩ Further *will* may designate a subjective power, act, or process ⟨luxurious feeling and pathetic imagination, which make no severe call upon . . . the *will* —*Inge*⟩ or an objective force which must be encountered, challenged, or obeyed ⟨submit oneself to the *will* of God⟩ ⟨this method of consulting the popular *will*—*Bryce*⟩ **Volition**, in contrast to *will*, is a comparatively simple term. In its ordinary and most sharply distinguished sense, it designates merely the act of making a choice or decision; it usually carries an implication of deliberation, but it rarely suggests struggle or determination to put one's decision or choice into effect. Therefore it may be preferred when no other implications are desirable or important ⟨surrendered his authority of his own *volition*⟩ ⟨our children do not seek school of their own *volition*— *Grandgent*⟩ ⟨the primal necessity for the faithful is that by an act of the will,—not necessarily an emotional act, but an act of pure and definite *volition*,—they should associate themselves with the true and perfect sacrifice —*Benson*⟩ **Conation** usually implies a striving to get or achieve what is desired or willed. The term need not imply a conscious goal; it may suggest clearly directed striving or it may connote the restless aimless strivings which the mind cannot interpret or explain, but it stresses effort rather than choice ⟨Religion or the desire for the salvation of our souls, Art or the desire for beautification, Science or the search for the reasons of things—these *conations* of the mind . . . are really three aspects of the same profound impulse—*Ellis*⟩
*Ana* *intention, intent, purpose, design: *choice, election, preference: character, *disposition, temper, temperament
**will** *vb* **Will, bequeath, devise, leave, legate** all mean to give a part or the whole of one's possessions to another by one's last will and testament. **Will** implies the provision or the existence of a legal instrument (a *will*) disposing of one's property after one's death ⟨he has *willed* that his property be divided among his wife and children⟩ ⟨he *willed* his money to various charities⟩ **Bequeath** is much used in wills by the testator ⟨I *bequeath* all my property to my wife⟩ and is frequent in legal, historical, and literary use; it may imply nothing more than a proved intention (as by a will or a definite oral or written statement) ⟨William had *bequeathed* Normandy to his eldest son, Robert —*J. R. Green*⟩ In legal use *bequeath* is commonly distinguished from **devise**, the one implying a gift of personalty, the other a gift of realty ⟨every article she possessed . . . , every pot and pan, every garment, is separately *bequeathed* as an affectionate remembrance—*Ellis*⟩ ⟨I had never imagined rings as things one bought for oneself . . . . They were things given, or *bequeathed* by grandaunts —*Repplier*⟩ ⟨was the son of a white man by one of his slaves, and his father executed certain instruments to manumit him, and *devised* to him some landed property— *Taney*⟩ **Leave** is the common and ordinary unspecific term for any of the preceding terms ⟨he *left* a legacy to his nephew⟩ ⟨he *left* his land, money, books, pictures to Harvard University⟩ **Legate** is not manifestly different from *bequeath* except that it invariably implies a formal will ⟨the oval inlaid table I *legate* to _____—*Law Reports, House of Lords*⟩

**willful** 1 deliberate, intentional, *voluntary, willing
*Ana* determined, decided, resolved (see DECIDE): intended, purposed (see INTEND): *obstinate, stubborn,

dogged, pertinacious
*Con* acquiescent, *compliant: submissive, *tame
2 headstrong, intractable, refractory, recalcitrant, *unruly, ungovernable
*Ana* rebellious, contumacious, factious, *insubordinate: *obstinate, mulish, bullheaded, pigheaded
*Ant* biddable —*Con* tractable, docile, amenable, *obedient
**willing** *voluntary, intentional, deliberate, willful
*Ana* prone, open (see LIABLE): inclined, predisposed, disposed (see INCLINE *vb*)
*Ant* unwilling —*Con* reluctant, loath, *disinclined, indisposed, averse
**wilt** *droop, flag, sag
*Ana* slump, sink, drop, *fall: languish (see corresponding adjective at LANGUID)
**wily** *sly, cunning, crafty, tricky, foxy, insidious, guileful, artful
*Ana* astute, sagacious, *shrewd: deceitful, cunning (see corresponding nouns at DECEIT)
**win** gain, acquire, *get, obtain, procure, secure
*Ana* achieve, accomplish, effect (see PERFORM): attain, *reach, compass: *induce, persuade, prevail, get
*Ant* lose
**wince** *recoil, flinch, shrink, blench, quail
*Ana* cringe, cower (see FAWN): balk, shy, stick, stickle (see DEMUR): squirm, *writhe
**wind, breeze, gale, hurricane, zephyr** are comparable rather than synonymous terms that can all basically mean air in motion. **Wind** is the general term referable to any sort of natural motion whatever its degree of velocity or of force ⟨a strong *wind*⟩ ⟨there is no *wind* tonight⟩ **Breeze** in general use is applied to relatively light but fresh wind, usually a pleasant or welcome one ⟨the fair *breeze* blew, the white foam flew, the furrow followed free—*Coleridge*⟩ In technical meteorological use the term specifically denotes a wind with a velocity of from 4 to 31 miles an hour. *Breezes* are sometimes further described as *light* (4–7 miles an hour), *gentle* (8–12), *moderate* (13–18), *fresh* (19–24), *strong* (25–31). **Gale** in ordinary use is applied to a high, destructive wind of considerable velocity and force; technically the term is applied specifically to a wind between 32 and 63 miles an hour; a *whole gale* is one having a velocity between 55 and 63 miles an hour. **Hurricane** is sometimes applied popularly to an exceedingly violent or devastating windstorm but technically the term denotes a rotating windstorm with winds of particular velocities (see also WHIRLWIND). **Zephyr** is a poetical term for a very light gentle breeze that delicately touches objects ⟨fair laughs the morn, and soft the *zephyr* blows—*Gray*⟩
*Ana* *whirlwind, cyclone, typhoon, tornado, twister
**wind** *vb* **Wind, coil, curl, twist, twine, wreathe, entwine** mean to follow a circular, spiral, or writhing course or to make or form a corresponding figure. **Wind** fundamentally implies an axis or something suggestive of an axis around which another thing is turned so as to encircle, enclose, or enfold ⟨*wind* thread on a spool⟩ ⟨*wind* a bandage around his arm⟩ Often the word is extended in meaning to imply a result accomplished (as tightening, tensing, or lifting) by or as if by winding ⟨*wind* a watch⟩ ⟨*wind* the strings of a mandolin⟩ ⟨her nerves are all *wound* up⟩ ⟨*wound* up his affairs⟩ At other times the word implies movement or direction in a curving, sinuous, or devious manner (compare WINDING) ⟨the road . . . *wound* on between low, quickset hedges or wooden palings—*Mackenzie*⟩ ⟨a wagon . . . light enough and narrow enough to *wind* the mountain gorges beyond Pueblo—*Cather*⟩ **Coil** implies a curving so as to take the form of a spiral, often a flat

spiral; it is used chiefly in reference to something (as a rope, a wire, a hose, or a snake) which is wound or winds itself in such a manner ⟨ropes *coiled* on the deck and everything shipshape⟩ ⟨*coil* the hose before putting it away⟩ ⟨the snake *coiled* itself to strike⟩ **Curl** basically implies the formation of the hair into large or small ringlets either by nature or by art; in extended use it is applied to something that forms itself or is formed into a curl or coil ⟨*curled* his lip in disgust⟩ ⟨tree leaves *curled* by drought⟩ ⟨the smoke *curled* up from the chimney⟩ ⟨the dog *curled* itself up on the sofa⟩ ⟨shavings *curled* by the plane⟩ ⟨huge waves with crests *curling* over as they broke on the beach⟩ **Twist** and *twine* can both refer to a step in the process of spinning or throwing in which two or more filaments are turned about each other to form yarn or thread. **Twist** retains this or a similar sense in more general use ⟨form a cable by *twisting* several folds of wire together⟩ Often in its extended senses *twist* implies a turning this way and that, a sudden turning around, a contorting, or a distorting ⟨*twisted* his ankle when he fell⟩ ⟨caught the ball, *twisted* to avoid a tackler, then ran ten yards to a touchdown⟩ ⟨a sluggish stream *twisting* and turning through the meadowland⟩ ⟨*twist* the testimony of the witness so as to give it a new significance⟩ **Twine** has nearly lost its implication of a mechanical process and usually emphasizes a winding around something by another thing which is flexible ⟨let me *twine* mine arms about that body—*Shak.*⟩ ⟨let wreaths of triumph now my temples *twine*—*Pope*⟩ ⟨the bucket and rope had been encircled by *twining* tendrils of convolvulus—*Binyon*⟩ **Wreathe** may come close to *coil, twist,* or *wind* ⟨about his neck a green and gilded snake had *wreathed* itself—*Shak.*⟩ ⟨therefore . . . are we *wreathing* a flowery band to bind us to the earth—*Keats*⟩ ⟨the smoke from his pipe *wreathing* about his head⟩ **Entwine** usually implies a twisting together (as two or more similar things) and it often suggests the idea of interweaving, interlacing, or entangling ⟨the lamp base looks like two snakes *entwined*⟩ ⟨the branches of the bushes were so thoroughly *entwined* that passage was impossible⟩ But the word may imply nothing more than a winding about ⟨*entwine* the lampposts with Christmas greens⟩
*Ana* twist, bend, *curve: *surround, encircle, circle, gird, girdle: *enclose, envelop

**winding,** sinuous, serpentine, tortuous, flexuous can all mean curving first one way and then another. **Winding,** the general and the ordinary term, often implies spiral ascent ⟨*winding* stairs⟩ ⟨a *winding* mountain road⟩ When applied to things in a horizontal plane it implies little more than weaving from side to side or in and out through some length, often without apparent plan ⟨a *winding* path through a forest⟩ ⟨a *winding* cave⟩ ⟨following the serpent lightning's *winding* track—*Shelley*⟩ **Sinuous** fundamentally suggests frequent departures from a straight or direct line by curving ⟨streams . . . *sinuous* or straight, now rapid and now slow—*Cowper*⟩ In its extended use where it may imply moral deviation this implication remains strong, but in respect to material things the word tends to stress the presence of curves in every line, bend, and movement and the absence of angularity, awkwardness, or stiffness ⟨the stealthy terror of the *sinuous* pard—*Thompson*⟩ ⟨the *sinuous* movements of the leading lady⟩ ⟨gardens bright with *sinuous* rills—*Coleridge*⟩ **Serpentine** implies curving in a pattern suggested by the smooth and flowing curves of a moving snake; it need not imply regularity in the size and shape of the inward and outward curves ⟨up the heathy waste, [the road] mounts, as you see, in mazes *serpentine*—*Wordsworth*⟩ As applied to a type of compound curve or to the front of a bureau or

sideboard having such a curve the word implies that the bulging or convex curve is in the center. **Tortuous,** like *sinuous,* suggests lack of straightness and directness, but in contrast it stresses the number and intricacy of bendings, twistings, and turnings rather than the constant flow of curves ⟨the course of the river became more *tortuous* as we neared its source⟩ ⟨there remained but a *tortuous* defile for carriages down the center of the street—*Hardy*⟩ **Flexuous,** commoner in technical than general use, basically suggests alternation of gentle opposite curves or an easy zigzag course ⟨a *flexuous* leaf margin⟩ ⟨*flexuous* stems⟩ In extended use it implies a lack of rigidity in action, and so comes very close to *flexible* ⟨[a bacterium that] appears to move by changing the shape of its body which is not rigid but very *flexuous* and elastic—*Biological Abstracts*⟩ ⟨René's comings and goings, and each of his *flexuous* moods—*E. P. O'Donnell*⟩
*Ana* curving, bending, twisting (see CURVE *vb*): circuitous, *indirect, roundabout: *crooked, devious: meandering (see WANDER)
*Ant* straight

**window,** casement, dormer, oriel can mean an opening in the wall of a building that is usually covered with glass and serves to admit light and air. **Window** is the ordinary general term for the entire structure, including both its framework and the glass or the movable sashes which that framework encloses ⟨come to the *window,* sweet is the night air—*Arnold*⟩ **Casement** basically denotes a window sash attached to one of the upright sides of the frame by hinges; in ordinary use, however, the term is applied to a window or a series of windows (sometimes called *casement* window) with sashes of this character ⟨magic *casements,* opening on the foam of perilous seas, in faery lands forlorn—*Keats*⟩ **Dormer** denotes a window which stands out from a sloping roof and is typically enclosed by a gable-topped structure. An **oriel** differs from a dormer in projecting from a wall of a building rather than from a roof, in being at least three-sided and usually either semihexagonal or semisquare in shape, and in being supported by a corbel or bracket rather than by a rafter.

**wing** ell, extension, *annex

**wink** *vb* Wink, blink both mean to move one's eyelids. **Wink** usually means to close and open the eyelids rapidly and usually involuntarily ⟨houses so white that it makes one *wink* to look at them—*Dickens*⟩ or to close one eye part way mischievously or teasingly or as a hint or a command ⟨Asiatics do not *wink* when they have outmaneuvered the enemy, but . . . Mahbub Ali . . . came very near it—*Kipling*⟩ To **blink** is to wink involuntarily and with eyes nearly shut as if dazzled, partly blind, half asleep, or suddenly startled ⟨*blink* when roused from a sound sleep⟩ ⟨*blink* at the report of a gun⟩ ⟨he was . . . hauled up . . . *blinking* and tottering . . . into the blessed sun—*Stevenson*⟩ In extended use *wink* implies connivance, and *blink* suggests evasion or shirking ⟨*wink* at neglect of duty⟩ ⟨*blink* the issue⟩

**winner** *victor, conqueror, champion, vanquisher
*Ant* loser

**winning** *adj* *sweet, engaging, winsome, dulcet
*Ana* charming, alluring, captivating, enchanting, bewitching, attractive (see under ATTRACT *vb*)

**winsome** *sweet, engaging, winning, dulcet
*Ana* see those at WINNING

**wipe** *exterminate, extirpate, eradicate, uproot, deracinate
*Ana* obliterate, *erase, efface, expunge, blot out: *abolish, extinguish, annihilate: *destroy, demolish

**wisdom** judgment, *sense, gumption
*Ana* discretion, *prudence, foresight: judiciousness, sageness, saneness, sapience (see corresponding adjectives at

WISE): sagacity, perspicacity, shrewdness (see corresponding adjectives at SHREWD)

*Ant* folly: injudiciousness

**wise, sage, sapient, judicious, prudent, sensible, sane** are comparable when they mean having or manifesting the power to recognize the best ends and the best means to attain those ends. **Wise** applies to one or the acts or views of one who is so discerning in his understanding of persons, conditions, or situations that he knows how to deal with them, how to correct what is wrong in them, how to get the best out of them considering their limitations or difficulties, or how to estimate them fairly and accurately; often also the term implies a wide range of experience or of knowledge or learning ⟨prudent and conservative, Edward was *wise* enough to know that these two qualities . . . were not enough—*Buck*⟩ ⟨knowing himself *wise* in a mad world—*Meredith*⟩ ⟨it is *wise* to be cautious in condemning views and systems which are now out of fashion—*Inge*⟩ **Sage** characterizes one who is eminently wise and typically philosophical by temperament and experience. The term can suggest a habit of profound reflection upon men and events and an ability to reach conclusions of universal as well as immediate value, and has been applied chiefly to persons and utterances that are venerated for their wisdom and good counsel ⟨what the *sage* poets, taught by the heavenly Muse, storied of old in high immortal verse—*Milton*⟩ ⟨for I, who hold *sage* Homer's rule the best—*Pope*⟩ ⟨the natural crown that *sage* Experience wears—*Wordsworth*⟩ In somewhat lighter use *sage* often suggests the affectation or the appearance of great wisdom or knowledge, whether the matters concerned be of significance or not ⟨the older women seemed to have a kind of secret among themselves, a reason for *sage* smiles and glances—*Sackville-West*⟩ **Sapient** describes one exhibiting the utmost sagacity ⟨contain valuable insights and *sapient* advice to educators—*Larrabee*⟩ ⟨the *sapient* leader who shall bring order out of the wild misrule—*Parrington*⟩ but often the term is used ironically to imply a mere hollow sham of such sagacity ⟨the generals . . . turned attractive profiles in their [photographers'] direction and put on expressions of *sapient* authority—*Linklater*⟩ ⟨a *sapient*, instructed, shrewdly ascertaining ignorance—*Pater*⟩ **Judicious** applies to one who is capable of arriving at wise decisions or just conclusions; the term usually suggests the ability to distinguish fact from falsehood and to eliminate all bias so that one's judgments are fair, well-balanced, and level-headed as well as sound ⟨I am perfectly indifferent to the judgment of all, except the few who are indeed *judicious*—*Cowper*⟩ ⟨I really think that, for wise men, this is not *judicious*—*Burke*⟩ ⟨the love of knowledge is not perhaps as insatiable as with us, but it is infinitely more *judicious*—*Brownell*⟩ **Prudent** (see also under PRUDENCE; PRUDENT 3) applies to one who is so rich in practical wisdom that he is able to keep himself, his passions, and his actions under control and obedient to what he knows as right and necessary. In this sense *prudent* implies the use of one's reason in the attainment of the moral virtue that leads to right living, as distinguished from its use in the attainment of knowledge of things which transcend experience ⟨the *prudent* man looketh well to his going—*Prov* 14:15⟩ **Sensible** (see also AWARE, PERCEPTIBLE, MATERIAL) describes one who in speech or action does not exceed the bounds of common sense or of good sense; the term suggests a display of intelligence rather than of wisdom and of natural reasonableness rather than the exercise of the reason ⟨to discuss the ultimate career of a child nine years old would not be the act of a *sensible* parent—*Bennett*⟩ ⟨whatever he took up he did in the same matter-of-fact *sensible* way; without

a touch of imagination, without a spark of brilliancy—*Woolf*⟩ **Sane** characterizes one who shows healthy-mindedness and level-headedness in prudent, judicious, or sensible acts and words ⟨*sane* . . . persons who are so well balanced that they can adjust themselves to the conditions of every civilization—*Ellis*⟩ ⟨thankful in his heart and soul that he had his mother, so *sane* and wholesome—*D. H. Lawrence*⟩

*Ana* discreet, prudent, foresighted (see under PRUDENCE): *cautious, circumspect, calculating: sagacious, perspicacious, *shrewd, astute: knowing, *intelligent, alert, bright, smart

*Ant* simple

**wisecrack** *n* crack, gag, *joke, jest, jape, quip, witticism

**wish** *vb* *desire, want, crave, covet

*Ana* *long, yearn, hanker, pine, hunger, thirst: aspire, pant, *aim: hope, *expect

*Con* spurn, refuse, *decline, reject, repudiate: scorn, *despise, disdain

**wishy-washy** *insipid, vapid, flat, jejune, banal, inane

*Ana* spiritless, enervated, *languid, listless: *weak, feeble: diluted, attenuated, thinned (see THIN *vb*)

*Con* *spirited, high-spirited, mettlesome, spunky, fiery, peppery, gingery: stimulating, exciting, piquing, provoking (see PROVOKE)

**wit** *n* **1** intelligence, brain, *mind, intellect, soul, psyche

*Ana* *reason, understanding, intuition: comprehension, apprehension (see under APPREHEND): sagaciousness *or* sagacity, perspicaciousness *or* perspicacity (see corresponding adjectives at SHREWD)

**2** Wit, humor, irony, sarcasm, satire, repartee are comparable when they denote a mode of expression which has for its aim the arousing of sudden sharp interest that is accompanied by amusement or laughter or a quality of mind which leads or predisposes to such expression. **Wit** which can denote reasoning power or mental capacity more typically implies intellectual brilliance and quickness in perception combined with the talent for expressing one's ideas in a sparkling effective manner; in this sense *wit* need not imply the evocation of laughter, but it suggests a delighting and entertaining ⟨they never meet but there's a skirmish of *wit* between them—*Shak.*⟩ ⟨true *wit* is nature to advantage dressed, what oft was thought, but ne'er so well expressed—*Pope*⟩ Sometimes the implication of a power to evoke laughter or smiles becomes prominent and the term without any loss of its earlier suggestions of mental acuteness and swift perception, especially of the incongruous, adds notions of verbal felicity, especially as shown in the expression's unexpectedness of turn and aptness of application ⟨if thou hast *wit*, and fun, and fire, and ne'er good wine did fear—*Burns*⟩ **Humor** is often contrasted with *wit*, especially as one of two similar yet strikingly different modes of expression in literature. *Humor* may designate the peculiar disposition that leads one to perceive the ludicrous, the comical, or the ridiculous, and to express one's perceptions so as to make others see or feel the same thing ⟨she was always saved by her crisp sense of *humor*, her shrewd and mischievous wit—*Ellis*⟩ or it may imply more human sympathy, more tolerance, more kindliness than *wit*, a deeper sense of the inherent incongruities in human nature and human life, and a feeling for the not readily perceived pathos as well as for the not readily perceived absurdness of characters, of situations, or of consequences ⟨writers distinguish the *humor* of Chaucer and Shakespeare from the *wit* of Dryden and Pope; the *wit* of Molière's comedies from the *humor* of Don Quixote; ⟨you expect *wit* from every man of any eminence in the eighteenth century. But of that sympathetic enjoyment of all the manifold contrasts

A colon (:) separates groups of words discriminated. An asterisk (*) indicates place of treatment of each group.

and incongruities of life which we call *humor*, I think Wesley had very little—*Winchester*⟩ **Irony** applies chiefly to a way of speaking or writing in which the meaning intended is contrary to that seemingly expressed ⟨"Of course Constance is always right," observed Sophia, with . . . *irony*—*Bennett*⟩ ⟨she was assisted by an impetuous girl called Caroline . . . who by the *irony* of language "waited" at table—*Mackenzie*⟩ In a deeper sense *irony* applies both to the quality of mind of a person (as a poet, dramatist, or philosopher) who perceives discrepancies in life and in character (as between the appearance and the reality, or between what is promised and what is fulfilled, or between what is attempted and what is accomplished) and to the form of humor or wit which has for its aim the revelation of the mockery implicit in these contradictions ⟨there must be some meaning beneath all this terrible *irony*—*Shaw*⟩ ⟨a kind of understatement which recalls to us at once the grim and conscious *irony* of those who knew that "their feet had come to the end of the world"—*Day Lewis*⟩ **Sarcasm** applies chiefly to a savage, bitter form of humor intended to cut or wound. *Sarcasm* need not imply the use of verbal irony, sometimes suggesting no more than plain speaking, but it regularly implies as its aim the intent to make the victim an object of ridicule ⟨in the intercourse of familiar life, he indulged his disposition to petulance and *sarcasm*—*Johnson*⟩ ⟨the arrows of *sarcasm* are barbed with contempt—*Gladden*⟩ **Satire** primarily designates writing intended to hold up vices or follies (as of a people or an age) for ridicule and reprobation ⟨Jonson's drama is only incidentally *satire*, because it is only incidentally a criticism upon the actual world . . . that is, it does not find its source in any precise emotional attitude or precise intellectual criticism of the actual world—*T. S. Eliot*⟩ **Repartee** applies chiefly to the power or art of answering quickly, pointedly, skillfully, and with wit or humor or, less often, irony or sarcasm ⟨as for *repartee* in particular, as it is the very soul of conversation, so it is the greatest grace of comedy—*Dryden*⟩ ⟨I hadn't known Jane spoke so well. She has a clever, coherent way of making her points, and is concise in reply if questioned, quick at *repartee* if heckled—*Rose Macaulay*⟩
*Ana* quick-wittedness, alertness, brightness, brilliancy, cleverness, smartness, intelligence (see corresponding adjectives at INTELLIGENT): raillery, *badinage, persiflage: pungency, piquancy, poignancy (see corresponding adjectives at PUNGENT)

**witchcraft** wizardry, witchery, sorcery, *magic, alchemy, thaumaturgy

**witchery** *magic, sorcery, witchcraft, wizardry, alchemy, thaumaturgy

**with** *by, through

**withdraw** *go, leave, depart, quit, retire
*Ana* abscond, decamp, *escape, flee, fly: retreat, *recede
*Con* arrive, *come

**wither, shrivel, wizen** mean to lose or cause to lose freshness and smoothness of appearance. **Wither** implies a loss of vital moisture (as sap or body fluids) with consequent fading or drying up and ultimate decay or death ⟨*withered* leaves⟩ ⟨[blossoms] which fall before they *wither*—*Binyon*⟩ The term is often used in an extended sense implying a similar loss of vitality, vigor, or animation ⟨age cannot *wither* her, nor custom stale her infinite variety—*Shak.*⟩ ⟨art, he thought, should flower from an immediate impulse towards self-expression or communication, and should *wither* with the passing of the impulse—*Huxley*⟩ **Shrivel** carries a stronger implication of becoming wrinkled or crinkled or shrunken in size than *wither;* usually also it implies a cause (as a blasting or blighting by or as if by intense heat) or a lack of invigorating

influences (as rain or, in extended use, encouragement, stimulation, or variety of employments) ⟨the leaves *shrivel* in the hot sun⟩ ⟨age has *shriveled* her skin⟩ ⟨the man whose . . . practical life [is] *shriveled* to an insignificant routine—*Ellis*⟩ **Wizen**, especially in the past participle, is often preferred to *wither* or *shrivel* when the ideas of shrinking in size, and the wrinkling of the face or other surface especially through age, lack of nourishment, or failing vitality are especially stressed ⟨a *wizened* old man⟩ ⟨the *wizened* face of a poorly nourished boy⟩ ⟨a *wizened* shrub, a starveling bough—*Browning*⟩
*Ana* *dry, parch, desiccate: shrink, *contract, constrict

**withhold** detain, keep back, keep out, retain, hold, hold back, reserve, *keep
*Ana* *restrain, curb, check, bridle, inhibit: refuse, *decline
*Con* accord, *grant, concede, award, vouchsafe

**withstand** *resist, contest, oppose, fight, combat, conflict, antagonize
*Ana* *bear, endure, stand, tolerate, suffer: thwart, baffle, balk, foil, *frustrate: assail, *attack, assault
*Con* submit, *yield, capitulate

**witness** *n* *spectator, observer, beholder, looker-on, onlooker, eyewitness, bystander, kibitzer

**witness** *vb* *certify, attest, vouch
*Ana* subscribe (see ASSENT)

**witticism** *joke, jest, jape, quip, wisecrack, crack, gag
*Ana* *wit, humor, sarcasm, satire, irony, repartee

**witty, humorous, facetious, jocular, jocose** are comparable when they apply to persons and their utterances and mean provoking or intended to provoke laughter or smiles. **Witty** (compare WIT) suggests a high degree of cleverness and quickness in discerning amusing congruities or incongruities; it may connote sparkling pleasantry, especially in repartee, but it often suggests sarcasm or causticity ⟨her tongue was as sharp and *witty* as ever—*Sackville-West*⟩ ⟨there's no possibility of being *witty* without a little ill-nature; the malice of a good thing is the barb that makes it stick—*Sheridan*⟩ **Humorous** is a generic term applied to whoever or whatever provokes laughter ⟨a *humorous* account of a picnic⟩ ⟨a *humorous* lecture⟩ ⟨the *humorous* characters of Shakespeare's plays⟩ As opposed to *witty*, *humorous* often suggests sensibility rather than intellect, sympathy rather than aloofness in criticism, and sometimes, whimsicality rather than direct insight; thus, Pope is often described as a *witty*, Burns as a *humorous*, poet ⟨whose *humorous* vein, strong sense, and simple style may teach the gayest, make the gravest smile—*Cowper*⟩ ⟨the genius of the Italians is acute . . . but not subtle; hence, what they think to be *humorous* is merely *witty*—*Coleridge*⟩ **Facetious** usually applies to clumsy or inappropriate jesting or, somewhat derogatorily, to attempts at wittiness or humorousness that please their maker more than others ⟨probably the most tedious bore on earth is the man who feels it incumbent upon him always to be *facetious* and to turn everything into a joke—*Fiske*⟩ ⟨her lines were weak *facetious* echoes of a style of college slang ten years outmoded—*Wouk*⟩ **Jocular** also implies a fondness for jesting and joking but suggests as its motive the desire to make others laugh or to keep them amused. It need not imply loquaciousness but it tends to suggest a sustained jolly mood or habit of temperament ⟨his more solemn and stately brother, at whom he laughed in his *jocular* way—*Thackeray*⟩ ⟨the watercolor lesson enlivened by the *jocular* conversation of the kindly, humorous old man was always great fun—*Conrad*⟩ **Jocose** suggests waggishness or sportiveness in jesting and joking; it often comes close to *facetious* in suggesting clumsy inappropriate jesting ⟨sundry *jocose* proposals that the ladies should sit in the gentlemen's laps—*Dickens*⟩

---

*Ana* analogous words     *Ant* antonyms     *Con* contrasted words     See also explanatory notes facing page 1

*Ana* amusing, diverting, entertaining (see AMUSE): sparkling, scintillating (see FLASH *vb*): *caustic, mordant, acrid, scathing: penetrating, piercing, probing (see ENTER)

**wizard** *expert, adept, artist, artiste, virtuoso

**wizardry** witchcraft, witchery, sorcery, *magic, alchemy, thaumaturgy

**wizen** *wither, shrivel

*Ana* shrink, *contract: dwindle, diminish, reduce, *decrease

**wobble** teeter, totter, shimmy, quiver, shiver, shudder, quaver, quake, *shake, tremble, dither

**woe** grief, anguish, heartache, heartbreak, *sorrow, regret

*Ana* *distress, suffering, misery, agony, dolor: lamenting, bewailing, bemoaning, deploring (see DEPLORE)

*Con* *happiness, bliss, felicity

**woebegone** disconsolate, dispirited, dejected, depressed, *downcast

*Ana* *melancholy, lugubrious, doleful: forlorn, *despondent: spiritless, listless (see LANGUID)

**woman** *female, lady

**womanish** womanlike, womanly, ladylike, feminine, *female, effeminate

*Ant* mannish —*Con* manlike, virile, masculine, manly, *male

**womanlike** womanly, womanish, ladylike, feminine, *female, effeminate

*Con* feminine, womanly, womanlike, womanish, ladylike (see FEMALE)

**womanly** womanlike, ladylike, womanish, feminine, *female, effeminate

*Ana* *mature, matured, grown-up, adult

*Ant* unwomanly, manly —*Con* mannish (see MALE): *youthful, juvenile, virgin, virginal, maiden

**wonder** *n* 1 Wonder, marvel, prodigy, miracle, phenomenon can all mean something that causes astonishment or admiration. **Wonder** applies specifically to whatever excites surprise, astonishment, or amazement (as by its perfection, its greatness, or its inexplicableness) ⟨the hotels were *wonders* of comfort—*White*⟩ ⟨the real *wonder* of jujitsu is . . . in the uniquely Oriental idea which the whole art expresses—*Hearn*⟩ ⟨Chinese painters are not . . . absorbed in expressing their sensuous delight in the *wonder* and glory of the world—*Binyon*⟩ **Marvel** applies to something that excites surprise or astonishment especially by its extraordinariness, its strangeness, or its curiousness ⟨"All I ask from them is discreetness." "Ay," said Adrian, whose discreetness was a *marvel*—*Meredith* ⟩ ⟨had never believed that such *marvels* of the cooking art really existed —*Wouk*⟩ ⟨for the Roman army was still strong, and was to remain for centuries one of the *marvels* of the world—*Buchan*⟩ **Prodigy** may name some extraordinary or abnormal fact or circumstance in nature seen as an omen or portent ⟨were not comets formerly dreaded, as awful *prodigies* intended to alarm the world?—*Jeremiah Joyce*⟩ or apply to something that makes one marvel because of its oddness or unusualness especially in degree of some quality (as skill, endurance, size, or achievement) ⟨wondering whether her husband, a despotic and pitiless pedant, would have tried to turn their boy into a *prodigy*—*Edmund Wilson*⟩ ⟨women performing *prodigies* of endurance, bravery, and hope—*Newsweek*⟩ **Miracle** applies to something that is accomplished or occurs which seems to those who are witnesses or have undergone the experience to exceed human powers and to require a supernatural or superhuman explanation ⟨wonders ye have done; *miracles* ye cannot—*Tennyson*⟩ In its nonreligious sense *miracle* retains its implication of wonder in its insistence on the fact that the person or thing so designated is beyond ordinary human comprehension or capacity to do or produce;

only occasionally does it suggest a supernatural or superhuman agent or agency ⟨clung to their candles with an instinctive feeling that these primitive instruments were . . . more to be trusted than the *miracles* of science—*Wolfe*⟩ ⟨the *miracle* which we call genius—*Lowes*⟩ ⟨it was a *miracle* that the two men survived so many days' exposure in an open boat⟩ ⟨it was a *miracle* of rare device, a sunny pleasure dome with caves of ice!—*Coleridge*⟩ **Phenomenon** in its more popular sense, which is somewhat contrary in meaning to *phenomenon* as used by scientists and philosophers (compare *phenomenal* under MATERIAL), implies something exceptional or extraordinary; it applies to a person, animal, or thing that is regarded as a prodigy or marvel or occasionally merely as an oddity ⟨the captain—a *phenomenon* during prohibition because he was honest—*Dinneen*⟩ ⟨Beat . . . the first *phenomenon* in years to come out of the Great Unwashed which Madison Avenue hadn't rigged, manipulated or foreseen—*Mailer*⟩

2 Wonder, wonderment, amazement, admiration can denote the complex emotion aroused by something that is inexplicable or incomprehensible and, often, awe-inspiring. **Wonder** and **wonderment** commonly suggest novelty or strangeness in what excites the emotion and astonishment or perplexity in the person affected ⟨still the *wonder* grew that one small head could carry all he knew—*Goldsmith*⟩ ⟨showed no great zest . . . a quiet *wonderment* rather, faintly tinged with pleasure—*Cather*⟩ In its richest use *wonder* often implies rapturous awe ⟨nor any power above or under ever made us mute with *wonder*—*Shelley*⟩ **Amazement** stresses bewilderment or loss of power to collect one's thoughts; it rarely gives an indication of like or dislike for the object exciting the emotion ⟨reports . . . which constantly express *amazement* at the extent and severity of Russian attacks . . . and despair at the German setbacks—*Shirer*⟩ **Admiration**, which in its most general sense implies an often enthusiastic recognition of superiority (see REGARD *n*), can add an implication of absorbed or ecstatic attention (as to the rare, the beautiful, or the sublime) that approaches awe in its elevation and intensity ⟨respect which in the lay mind may well mount to *admiration* and even to awe—*More*⟩ ⟨considered the emotion of reverence to be very complex. Into it enters awe which itself is a blend of fear and *admiration*. *Admiration*, in turn, represents a fusion of negative self-feeling and wonder—*G. W. Allport*⟩ ⟨a Kioto painter . . . who burnt a hole in his roof to admire a moonlight effect, and in his rapt *admiration* omitted to notice that he had set a whole quarter of the city on fire—*Binyon*⟩

*Ana* awe, *reverence, fear: astonishment, amazement (see corresponding verbs at SURPRISE): perplexity, puzzlement, bewilderment (see corresponding verbs at PUZZLE)

**wonderment** *wonder, amazement, admiration

**wont** *n* *habit, habitude, practice, usage, custom, use

*Ana* way, manner, fashion (see METHOD)

**wonted** accustomed, customary, habitual, *usual

*Ana* familiar, *common, ordinary: natural, *regular, normal, typical

**woo** *vb* court, solicit, *invite, bid

*Ana* allure, *attract: *lure, entice, seduce: blandish, *coax, cajole, wheedle: pursue, chase, *follow, trail

**wooden** *stiff, rigid, inflexible, tense, stark

*Ana* *firm, hard, solid: *heavy, weighty, ponderous: clumsy, *awkward

*Con* pliant, pliable, *plastic: *supple, limber

**word, vocable, term** can mean a letter or combination of letters or a sound or combination of sounds capable of being pronounced and expressing an idea that is by tradition or common consent associated with the letters or the sounds. **Word** applies to a letter or combination of

A colon (:) separates groups of words discriminated. An asterisk (*) indicates place of treatment of each group.

letters or a sound or a combination of sounds that forms an indivisible whole constituting one of the ultimate units of a language. **Vocable** throws emphasis upon a word as pronounced or spelled rather than as a unit of meaning ⟨a flat denial of poetic possibilities, in the case of any *vocable*, is liable to disastrous refutation—*Lowes*⟩ ⟨accustomed to songs in which the words are often merely convenient *vocables* with the melody usually more important than the text—*Scholl*⟩ **Term** applies both to words and to phrases that express a whole idea and form one of the units of expression in a language, applying especially to units with a more or less precise technical use or meaning ⟨the *term* communism is used today to describe both a political philosophy and its translation into reality—*Gatzke*⟩ ⟨"The most important woman in Finland" is a *term* which has been applied—*Current Biog.*⟩ ⟨all professions are likely to develop innumerable *terms* that constitute an almost private jargon⟩

*Ana* expression, idiom, \*phrase, locution

**wordy, verbose, prolix, diffuse, redundant** can all mean using or marked by the use of more words than are necessary to express the thought. **Wordy** often carries no further implications, though it may suggest garrulousness or loquacity when the reference is to speech ⟨went into considerable detail about the Fuehrer's thoughts and policies on almost every conceivable subject, being more *wordy* than any previous letter . . . to his Italian partner—*Shirer*⟩ ⟨a *wordy*, prolegomenous babbler—*Stevenson*⟩ **Verbose** suggests overabundance of words as a literary fault characteristic especially of a writer or public speaker or of a work or speech; it often implies resulting dullness or obscurity of expression or a lack of incisiveness, confusion of ideas, or grandiloquence ⟨a *verbose* style⟩ ⟨a dull *verbose* narrative⟩ ⟨his letters are full of interesting details but they are never *verbose*⟩ **Prolix** implies such attention to minute details as to extend what is written or told beyond due bounds; the term carries a stronger implication of tediousness or wearisomeness than *verbose* ⟨the belief, so prevalent abroad, that it is typical of Russian literature to be formless, *prolix* and hysterical—*Edmund Wilson*⟩ ⟨this, then, was Nuflo's story, told not in Nuflo's manner, which was infinitely *prolix*—*Hudson*⟩ **Diffuse** usually implies verbosity, but it throws the emphasis upon the lack of organization and of the compactness and condensation needed for pointedness and for strength of style; it often attributes flabbiness, looseness, or desultoriness to what is written ⟨the one can be profuse on occasion; the other is *diffuse* whether he will or no—*J. R. Lowell*⟩ ⟨though Seneca is long-winded, he is not *diffuse;* he is capable of great concision—*T. S. Eliot*⟩ **Redundant** can apply to whatever is superfluous ⟨older . . . occupations are becoming *redundant* and obsolete—*Barkin*⟩ but in its specific application to words and phrases the term implies a superfluity that results from being repetitious or unneeded for clarity and accuracy of expression ⟨revision of technical prose requires word by word review and elimination of whatever is *redundant*⟩ In its corresponding application to writers, speakers, or utterances *redundant* implies the use of redundancies (see *redundancy* under VERBIAGE) ⟨the naturally copious and flowing style of the author is generally *redundant*—*Mackintosh*⟩ ⟨she had been, like nearly all very young writers, superfluous of phrase, *redundant*—*Rose Macaulay*⟩ ⟨in sharp comment . . . quite demolished the emptiness and the pretentiousness of this *redundant* plan—*Michener*⟩

*Ana* \*inflated, turgid, tumid, flatulent: bombastic, \*rhetorical: loquacious, garrulous, voluble, glib, \*talkative

*Con* laconic, \*concise, terse, succinct, summary, pithy, compendious

**work** *n* **1** **Work, labor, travail, toil, drudgery, grind** are comparable when they mean effort or exertion directed to the accomplishment of an end, or an employment or activity which involves such expenditure of effort or exertion. **Work** is the most comprehensive of these terms, for it may imply activity of body, mind, or machine or, in its largest sense, of a natural force. It is applicable not only to the exertion and to the employment which involves such exertion ⟨six days shalt thou labor, and do all thy *work*—*Exod* 20:9⟩ but also to what is accomplished or produced by such exertion ⟨this statue is the *work* of a gifted but unknown sculptor⟩ ⟨you have done a day's *work* in three hours⟩ and to the material upon which one is employed ⟨put your *work* away⟩ **Labor** differs from *work* not so much in its specific denotations as in its implications; as a rule it implies human work and therefore suggests physical or intellectual exertion only, but it may suggest work of strenuous, onerous, or fatiguing kind ⟨*labor* is doing what we must; leisure is doing what we like—*Shaw*⟩ ⟨the larger part of the *labor* of an author in composing his work is critical *labor;* the *labor* of sifting, combining, constructing, expunging, correcting, testing—*T. S. Eliot*⟩ ⟨Sir William Meredith, anticipating the *labors* of Romilly, protested against the barbarity and the inefficacy of a criminal code—*G. O. Trevelyan*⟩ **Travail** carries a stronger implication of painful effort or exertion than does *labor;* that connotation is often so strong that the term tends to denote suffering rather than labor ⟨the sentimentalist escapes the stern *travail* of thought—*Lowes*⟩ ⟨it breaks his heart . . . that all his hours of *travail* here for men seem yet in vain—*Lindsay*⟩ **Toil** suggests labor that is prolonged and highly fatiguing but not necessarily physical ⟨for years he led a life of unremitting physical *toil*—*Buchan*⟩ **Drudgery** implies dull, irksome, and distasteful labor ⟨thereafter, through . . . all the days she served in the store, the job was nothing but exasperating *drudgery*—*Wouk*⟩ ⟨labor of the hands . . . pursued to the verge of *drudgery*—*Thoreau*⟩ **Grind** applies to labor that one finds toilsome and trying or exhausting to mind or body ⟨the long *grind* of teaching the promiscuous and preoccupied young—*Henry James*⟩

*Ana* exertion, \*effort, pains, trouble: \*task, duty, job, chore

*Ant* play

**2** **Work, employment, occupation, calling, pursuit, business** can all denote the specific kind of labor or activity in which a person engages seriously especially as a means of earning a livelihood. **Work** is the most general of these terms; it applies to any kind of labor, whether physical or intellectual, whether carried on by the hour, day, week, month, or longer period, and whether done for pay or not and, if the former, whether compensated for by an employer or out of fees for services or the profits of a business ⟨be out of *work*⟩ ⟨his *work* is that of a railroad engineer⟩ ⟨he is at *work* on his book⟩ **Employment** implies work for which one has been engaged and is being paid by an employer ⟨he is unable to find *employment*⟩ ⟨his *employment* is that of a bookbinder⟩ ⟨I . . . went from town to town, working when I could get *employment*—*Goldsmith*⟩ **Occupation**, though often used interchangeably with *employment*, can be more inclusive, for it does not necessarily connote service under an employer and may be referred to the work of a kind in which one engages habitually or for which one has been trained; thus, one seeks *employment* but follows a particular *occupation* ⟨unable to find *employment* in his old *occupation*, he turned to common labor⟩ ⟨he is by *occupation* a teacher⟩ ⟨these are the chief questions which a man would ask . . . whom circumstances allowed to choose his *occupation*—*Inge*⟩ **Calling** is sometimes used in place of *occupation* but is typically used of occupations which can be described as vocations or professions and to which one is likely to have been called by one's nature or special tastes ⟨his *calling* is that of a preacher⟩ ⟨the learned *callings*⟩ ⟨Miss Jekyll had received that luckiest of fairy gifts, a *calling* . . . something that she loved to do—*L. P. Smith*⟩ **Pursuit**, too, may be used in place of *occupation* but more specifically in the sense of a trade, craft, profession, business, or art that is followed often as a means of earning one's living ⟨they never have to learn to adjust themselves to people whose tastes and *pursuits* are different from their own—*Russell*⟩ ⟨though it was supposed to be proper for them to have an occupation, the crude fact of moneymaking was still regarded as derogatory, and the law, being a profession, was accounted a more gentlemanly *pursuit* than business— *Wharton*⟩ **Business** is often used in the sense of *work* or sometimes of *occupation* ⟨the *business* of keeping a lunatic asylum—*Denman*⟩ ⟨I hated, and still hate, the awful *business* of research—*Bennett*⟩

*Ana* *trade, craft, handicraft, art, profession

**3 Work, product, production, opus, artifact** can all denote a concrete thing that is made or brought into being by the exertion of effort and the exercise of skill. **Work** is applied to what comes under this general definition (as something that is manufactured or that is constructed or built) only when used without reference to a particular thing ⟨the *work* reveals the workman⟩ or when used with a possessive ⟨the cabinetmaker is proud of his *work*⟩ ⟨every church that is known as Christopher Wren's *work*⟩ or in certain combinations ⟨fire*works*⟩ ⟨wax*works*⟩ Otherwise it is applied to a thing that results from mental labor, especially one involving composition and artistry in execution and specifically called a *work of art* ⟨the *works* of Keats include his poems and usually his prefaces⟩ ⟨the *works* of Beethoven are all his musical compositions⟩ ⟨*The Thinker* is one of Rodin's *works*⟩ ⟨the new history of literature promises to be a monumental *work*⟩ **Product** (see also PRODUCT 2) is applied chiefly to articles of manufacture whether they are made by hand or with the aid of machinery ⟨the factory seeks a market for its *products*⟩ ⟨she was unwilling to part with the embroideries and laces that were the *products* of her handiwork⟩ ⟨synthetic materials impart their special properties to perfumes and flavors and when properly used, increase rather than diminish the value of the *product*—*Morrison*⟩ When *product* rather than *work* is used of a poem, novel, statue, or painting, it is often either depreciative in its connotations or definitely noncommittal ⟨this dull *product* of a scoffer's pen—*Wordsworth*⟩ ⟨shall a literary *product* reveal the spirit of its age and be silent as to the spirit of its author—*Matheson*⟩ **Production** is sometimes used where *work* would be the commoner and more idiomatic term, but it has a formal or slightly bombastic effect except when qualified by a superlative ⟨the noblest *productions* of literary genius⟩ ⟨the finest *productions* of Michelangelo⟩ ⟨so one [Pygmalion] whose story serves at least to show men loved their own *productions* long ago, wooed an unfeeling statue [Galatea] for his wife—*Cowper*⟩ The term also is specifically applied to a theatrical or similar performance viewed as the work of a producer or director who is responsible for all the details ⟨the recent Shakespearian *productions*⟩ **Opus** is applied chiefly to a musical composition or group of compositions and in this use it is commonly followed by a number designating the order of publication or, sometimes, execution ⟨Beethoven's *opus* 27⟩ The term also has some specific application (as to work in mosaic or embroidery) and is used in light criticism of a work of art or literature often with a suggestion

of facetious pomposity ⟨British books on statistics are ever so much sprightlier and clearer than American *opera* on the subject—*Forbes*⟩ ⟨an instance of misplaced creativity, perhaps the first but not the last in Wright's prodigious *opus*—*Mumford*⟩ **Artifact** basically denotes an artificial as distinguished from a natural product; it usually implies human workmanship, largely as a general designation for primitive weapons and implements as well as works of art ⟨flints, arrowheads, and other *artifacts* of stone⟩

*Ana* article, object, *thing: accomplishment, achievement, performance (see corresponding verbs at PERFORM)

**work** *vb* operate, function, *act, behave, react

**worker,** workman, workingman, laborer, craftsman, handicraftsman, mechanic, artisan, hand, operative, roustabout can all mean one who earns his living by labor, especially by manual labor. **Worker,** the most comprehensive and least specific of these terms, applies to someone who earns his living by work of hand or brain ⟨office *workers*⟩ ⟨factory *workers*⟩ **Workman** does not imply a specific kind of work, but in all but its extended senses it commonly implies manual labor. It may be applied to one engaged to do a specified piece of work or to help in the construction of something requiring many workers; it may also be applied to a skilled or to an unskilled worker. Usually it implies opposition to *employer*, or *manager*, or *foreman* ⟨there were 50 *workmen* on the job⟩ In extended use the term is applicable to a worker whether he works with his hands or with his mind provided he makes, constructs, invents, or creates something ⟨high-minded and untiring *workmen*, they have spared no pains to produce a poetry finer than that of any other country in our time— *Lowell*⟩ **Workingman** is more restricted in its range of application than *workman*, and is, in spite of varying legal definitions, applied commonly to a wage earner who at an hourly, daily, or weekly rate pursues a trade (as carpentry, masonry, or plumbing) or is similarly employed in a mercantile, manufacturing, or industrial establishment as distinguished especially from an industrialist, a merchant, and a professional man. **Laborer** commonly designates one whose work demands more strength and physical exertion than skill (as on a construction or excavation job) ⟨day *laborers*⟩ ⟨farm *laborers*⟩ **Craftsman** and handicraftsman basically apply to one who is a skilled workman in a craft or handicraft (see *craft, handicraft* under TRADE 1). Unlike the foregoing terms these two are common in general use and may apply as freely with reference to an avocation as to an employment. But the former may apply distinctively to a worker who is a competent technician or who is versed in the technique of his art, profession, or trade. It is especially used of artists, writers, playwrights, or skilled artificers ⟨Pope . . . one of the most consummate *craftsmen* who ever dealt in words—*Lowes*⟩ ⟨the good *craftsman* constructs his product as perfectly as he can . . . . He becomes an artist in so far as he treats his materials also for themselves—*Alexander*⟩ **Mechanic** applies specifically to a workman skilled in the repair or adjustment of machines ⟨an automobile *mechanic*⟩ ⟨an aviation *mechanic*⟩ **Artisan** is more often opposed to *artist* (for this sense see under ARTIST 1) than employed as a designation of a particular type of workman. When applied to workingmen as such and without thought of opposition to *artist*, the term comes very close to *craftsman* and is commonly applied to one who is skilled in a trade (as carpentry, weaving, or shoemaking) that involves learned skills and their appropriate application as well as physical labor ⟨we pass from the weavers of cloth to a different class of *artisans*—*Macaulay*⟩ **Hand** is applied to one of a crew, a force, or a gang of workmen or some-

---

A colon (:) separates groups of words discriminated. An asterisk (*) indicates place of treatment of each group.

times to an owner's or proprietor's helper or assistant ⟨a deck*hand*⟩ ⟨a farm*hand*⟩ ⟨mill *hands*⟩ ⟨my son has lately lost his principal *hand* by death—*Franklin*⟩ **Operative,** a general term suggestive of modern industrial conditions, applies to a workman employed in a mill, a manufactory, or an industry utilizing machines ⟨the steelworks employ as many as 2000 *operatives*⟩ **Roustabout** usually adds to *laborer* distinguishing implications of muscular fitness for exceedingly heavy work, roughness, and, often, migratory habits ⟨longshoremen and other *roustabouts*⟩
*Ant* idler

**workingman** workman, laborer, *worker, craftsman, handicraftsman, mechanic, artisan, operative, hand, roustabout

**workman** *worker, workingman, laborer, craftsman, handicraftsman, mechanic, artisan, operative, hand, roustabout

**world** universe, *earth, cosmos, macrocosm

**worldly** 1 mundane, *earthly, terrestrial, earthy, sublunary
*Ana* temporal, *profane, secular: *material, physical, corporeal: *carnal, fleshly, sensual
*Con* *celestial, heavenly, empyrean, empyreal: sacred, *holy, spiritual, divine, religious
2 *sophisticated, worldly-wise, blasé, disillusioned

**worldly-wise** worldly, *sophisticated, blasé, disillusioned

**worn** *haggard, careworn, pinched, wasted, cadaverous
*Ana* exhausted, tired, wearied, fatigued, fagged, jaded (see TIRE *vb*): gaunt, scrawny, skinny, *lean
*Con* refreshed, restored, rejuvenated (see RENEW): *vigorous, lusty, energetic, strenuous

**worried** anxious, concerned, careful, solicitous (see under CARE *n*)
*Ana* apprehensive, afraid, *fearful: troubled, distressed (see TROUBLE *vb*): harassed, harried (see WORRY *vb*)
*Con* comforted, solaced, consoled (see COMFORT *vb*)

**worry** *vb* **Worry, annoy, harass, harry, plague, pester, tease, tantalize** can all mean to torment so as to destroy one's peace of mind or to disturb one acutely. **Worry** stresses incessant attacking or goading and an intention or sometimes an effect of driving the victim to desperation or defeat ⟨pursue a policy of *worrying* the enemy⟩ ⟨*worry* him out till he gives his consent—*Swift*⟩ ⟨brother should not war with brother, and *worry* and devour each other—*Cowper*⟩ **Annoy** (see also ANNOY 1) implies continued molesting, interfering with, intruding on, or bedeviling until the victim is angry or upset ⟨wilt thou then serve the Philistines with that gift which was expressly given thee to *annoy* them?—*Milton*⟩ ⟨clouds of flies . . . *annoyed* our horses—*Borrow*⟩ ⟨my movements are all along a regular beat, which enables me to avoid things that bore or *annoy* me—*Edmund Wilson*⟩ **Harass** usually implies persecution, especially continued petty persecutions, or burdensome demands or exactions that drive one to distraction or exhaust one's nervous or mental power ⟨it is good for boys and girls to know that their father can be *harassed* by worries and their mother worn out by a multiplicity of details—*Russell*⟩ ⟨securing air and naval bases from which he could *harass* and blockade the British Isles—*Shirer*⟩ **Harry,** though often used interchangeably with *harass,* more vividly suggests maltreatment and oppression ⟨Button and Miss Wace had been *harried* and chivied . . . the latter getting visibly flustered, for tears came into her eyes—*Sackville-West*⟩ ⟨how on earth can you rack and *harry* and post a man for his losings, when you . . . live in the same station with him?—*Kipling*⟩ **Plague** basically implies an affliction or infliction comparable to that of a devastating epidemic disease and even with greatly weakened implications tends to suggest a tormentor and

an agonized or suffering victim ⟨the gods are just, and of our pleasant vices make instruments to *plague* us—*Shak.*⟩ ⟨the kind of unhappy phrase that could *plague* a candidate right down to the wire—*Michener*⟩ ⟨misfortune *plagued* the plotters at every turn—*Shirer*⟩ **Pester** implies the power to annoy past endurance (as by numbers or by repetition of attacks suggestive of the discomforts of an infestation of vermin) ⟨*pester* the authorities with complaints⟩ ⟨Adrian . . . would accept him entirely as he seemed, and not *pester* him . . . by trying to unlock his heart—*Meredith*⟩ **Tease** may imply repeated attempts to break down resistance by successive appeals or importunities ⟨the children were *teasing* to be taken to the circus⟩ ⟨I have not been to the Rooms this age . . . except . . . last night with the Hodges's . . . they *teased* me into it—*Austen*⟩ or it may imply an attempt to provoke or upset by raillery or tormenting ⟨gets me mad when my analyst friends ask me some *teasing* question . . . . Implying they know a hell of a lot more about me than I do—*Wouk*⟩ ⟨not soon provoked, however stung and *teased,* and, if perhaps made angry, soon appeased—*Cowper*⟩ **Tantalize** stresses the repeated awakening of expectation and then its frustration ⟨because they are so fabulous and beautiful, they create an atmosphere of suspense . . . something *tantalizing,* breathtaking—*Dahl*⟩ ⟨merciful love that *tantalizes* not, one-thoughted, never-wandering, guileless love—*Keats*⟩
*Ana* disquiet, disturb, *discompose, perturb, agitate, upset: torment, try, torture (see AFFLICT): oppress, persecute, *wrong, aggrieve
*Con* *comfort, solace, console

**worry** *n* anxiety, concern, *care, solicitude
*Ana* *apprehension, foreboding, misgiving, presentiment: anguish, woe, heartache (see SORROW): *uncertainty, doubt, mistrust
*Con* *equanimity, composure, sangfroid: *certainty, assurance, certitude

**worship** *n* adoration, veneration, reverence (see under REVERE *vb*)
*Ana* *honor, homage, obeisance: respect, *regard, esteem, admiration
*Con* *profanation, desecration, sacrilege: execration, cursing (see corresponding verbs at EXECRATE)

**worship** *vb* 1 adore, venerate, *revere, reverence
*Ana* *exalt, magnify: respect, esteem (see under REGARD *n*)
*Con* *execrate, curse: *despise, scorn, disdain, contemn
2 *adore, idolize
*Ana* love, dote (see LIKE): admire, regard (see under REGARD *n*)
*Con* *hate, abhor, detest

**worth** *n* **Worth, value** are close synonyms in more than one of their senses, often differentiated by demands of idiom rather than by differences of meaning or connotation. Both *worth* and *value* denote the equivalent in money or sometimes in goods or services given or asked in exchange for another thing; thus, the *value* or *worth* of these coins to collectors is much greater than their monetary *worth* or *value* ⟨the current exchange *value* of the dollar⟩ ⟨he always gets his money's *worth*⟩ ⟨gets full *value* for his money⟩ When, however, *worth* and *value* mean the quality of being useful, important, excellent in its kind, or highly desirable or meritorious, they do not always come so closely together. In such use **worth** more often than *value* applies to what is excellent intrinsically (as by being superior morally, spiritually, intellectually, or aesthetically) ⟨of ancient race by birth, but nobler yet in his own *worth*—*Dryden*⟩ ⟨Archer's . . . coherent thinking, his sense of the *worth* of order and workmanship—*Montague*⟩

⟨assumption . . . that the social whole has greater *worth* and significance than its individual parts—*Huxley*⟩ **Value**, on the other hand, applies more frequently than *worth* to the qualities (as excellence, usefulness, or importance) imputed to a person or thing or to the degree in which that person or thing is regarded as excellent, useful, or important especially in its relation to other things ⟨a special association may give an inflated *value* to a certain poem⟩ ⟨there is always a gap between their appreciation of a man's *value* at any moment and his real weight—*Belloc*⟩ ⟨nothing in the [church] service was slighted, every phrase and gesture had its full *value*—*Cather*⟩ Further, *value* may be applied, as *worth* is not, to something (as a principle, a quality, a condition, or a substance) which is regarded as important, useful, desirable, or of value, sometimes in its relation to other things, sometimes in the degree which seems proper or fitting to it, and sometimes absolutely ⟨we may call food a *value* for the animal . . . because it is nutritious and fills his need of life—*Alexander*⟩ ⟨the opinion . . . that while science . . . contemplates a world of facts without *values*, religion contemplates *values* apart from facts—*Inge*⟩ ⟨prolongation of the . . . war . . . threatens not only the lives of millions, but the humanitarian *values* and goals which we are striving to maintain—*Science*⟩

*Ana* \*excellence, merit, virtue, perfection: \*use, usefulness, utility

**wound** *n* Wound, trauma, traumatism, lesion, bruise, contusion are comparable when they mean an injury to one of the organs or parts of the body. **Wound** generally denotes an injury that is inflicted by a hard or sharp instrument (as a knife, a bullet, or a club) forcibly driven or applied, and is characterized by breaking of the skin or mucous membrane and usually by damage to the tissues beneath ⟨deep *wounds* made by a bayonet⟩ ⟨a bite *wound* is likely to become infected⟩ In extended use *wound* can apply to a figurative hurt or blow (as to the mind or to society) ⟨inflicts *wounds* upon the human spirit which no surgery can heal—*Woolf*⟩ ⟨the perfect way to heal many of the world's worst *wounds*—*Mazur*⟩ **Trauma** basically applies to a wound or other injury (as a strain, fracture, or concussion) resulting from external force or violence (as from a fall, a blow, a shot, a stab, or a burn) or from a cause incidental to birth or surgery. Often the term is extended to a mental or emotional blow or stress that results in disordered feelings or behavior or leaves a lasting abnormal impression on the mind ⟨hysteria is a condition that often results from a psychic *trauma*⟩ ⟨great social *traumas* like the French Revolution and the American Civil War—*Heard*⟩ ⟨what psychologists call a *trauma*, a shock whose increasing aftereffects . . . testified to the susceptibility of the saint to sin—*Thomas Mann*⟩ In this connection *trauma* tends to pass in meaning from the injury received to the effect it produces ⟨the disillusion of the older generation had become the spiritual *trauma* of the younger—*Aldridge*⟩ ⟨a postwar boom that got us over the physical *trauma* of the 1930's—*Galantière*⟩ **Traumatism** in general use is seldom clearly distinguished from *trauma* ⟨the *traumatisms* of history with time . . . become embedded in the culture of a people—*Edmond Taylor*⟩ but in technical use it tends to be applied specifically to the local or general disordered state that results from injury or wounding ⟨fractures, sprains . . . burns and similar *traumatisms*—*JAMA*⟩ **Lesion** basically implies an injury or impairment ⟨the severe control . . . is no *lesion* to inward harmony and happiness—*Muirhead*⟩ but in medical use it applies specifically to a usually clearly circumscribed pathological change in tissue that may be caused by a wound or injury or be symptomatic of a disease or degenerative process

⟨tuberculous *lesions* in the lung⟩ ⟨syphilitic *lesions*⟩ ⟨a traumatic *lesion*⟩ In much of its general use *lesion* is an extension of the medical sense and implies a damaged or defective point or a weak spot ⟨a comic example of the *lesions* in Shakespeare studies—*Margery Bailey*⟩ ⟨crime has . . . become the symptom of a radical *lesion* in the stamina of humanity—*Zabel*⟩ **Bruise** is the general and **contusion** the more technical term for an injury, ordinarily due to impact, that results in more or less disorganization of tissues beneath the skin without breaking it but with black and blue discoloration due to oozing of blood into the tissues ⟨his letter talks of a disjointed thumb, a *contusion* on the hip, and a sightless eye—*Lucas*⟩ Only *bruise* has appreciable extended use and in this it tends to be strictly metaphoric ⟨the social and economic *bruises* that have come from our violence to nature—*Sears*⟩ ⟨all sensitiveness, at bottom is an intimation of pain and of fear . . . a shrinking from the *bruise*, and an awareness of transitoriness—*Behrman*⟩

*Ana* \*injury, hurt: burning *or* burn (see BURN)

**wraith** \*apparition, phantasm, phantom, ghost, spirit, specter, shade, revenant

**wrangle** *vb* quarrel, altercate, squabble, bicker, spat, tiff (see under QUARREL *n*)

*Ana* argue, dispute, debate (see DISCUSS): fight, \*contend

*Con* \*agree, concur, coincide

**wrangle** *n* \*quarrel, altercation, squabble, bickering, spat, tiff

*Ana* \*argument, dispute, controversy: \*discord, contention, dissension, conflict

**wrap** *vb* \*cover, overspread, envelop, shroud, veil

*Ana* \*enclose, envelop: \*surround, encompass, environ, gird, girdle: cloak, mask, camouflage (see DISGUISE)

**wrath** rage, indignation, ire, fury, \*anger

*Ana* resentment, dudgeon, \*offense: \*acrimony, acerbity, asperity

**wrathful** irate, indignant, \*angry, mad, wroth, acrimonious

*Ana* infuriated, incensed, enraged (see ANGER *vb*)

*Con* \*forbearing, tolerant, clement, lenient, indulgent, merciful

**wreathe** \*wind, coil, curl, twist, twine, entwine

**wreck** *vb* \*ruin, dilapidate

*Ana* \*destroy, demolish, raze: \*injure, damage, impair

*Con* \*save, preserve, conserve

**wrench** *vb* Wrench, wrest, wring can all basically mean to turn or twist forcibly, but they tend to vary widely in the implied purpose or result of the action. **Wrench** denotes a twisting or turning with considerable force, often with an abrupt tug or yank, so that the thing affected is twisted, distorted, or forced out of position; it may stress the violence of exertion in pulling or yanking ⟨carelessly *wrenching* the pipe until it bent⟩ ⟨a *wrenching* effect on the basic structural line—*Sidney Hyman*⟩ ⟨jerked and *wrenched* savagely at his bridle, stopping the hard-breathing animal with a furious pull near the colonel—*Crane*⟩ **Wrest** commonly implies a twisting or wrenching, sometimes with crude violence, sometimes with continuing deftness and dexterity, from another's possession into one's own ⟨*wrested* the knife from his attacker⟩ The term is common in extended use in which it implies a seizing, usurping, capturing, or extorting by such means ⟨through the efforts of bold and ambitious men who *wrest* the power from the lords—*Thilly*⟩ ⟨while one group of Mississippi valley pioneers advanced into the Southwest to *wrest* Texas from its Mexican owners—*Billington*⟩ ⟨when we could *wrest* the initiative from our enemies—*Roosevelt*⟩ **Wring** applies basically to a compressive twisting together, often to express or extract ⟨*wring* out wet clothes⟩ but in its extended use often implies a forcing or extorting (as by

A colon (:) separates groups of words discriminated. An asterisk (\*) indicates place of treatment of each group.

urgent demands or threats) that suggests a physical wringing ⟨*wring* a confession from a suspect⟩ ⟨more farm output, both of foodstuffs and raw materials, must be *wrung* from the hard-pressed peasants—*Lieberman*⟩ ⟨*wringing* more blackmail from this unwarlike nation—*Forester*⟩ **Ana** twist, bend (see CURVE): *force, compel, coerce, constrain: strain, sprain (see under STRAIN *n*)

**wrest** *vb* *wrench, wring
**Ana** twist, bend (see CURVE): usurp, *arrogate, confiscate: extort, extract, elicit (see EDUCE): distort, contort (see DEFORM)

**wrestle, tussle, grapple, scuffle** mean to struggle with an opponent at close quarters. **Wrestle** basically implies a struggle for mastery by gripping with hands, arms, and legs, often in ways governed by fixed rules; the term connotes the exercise of skill and ingenuity as well as strength. In its extended use *wrestle* also implies a struggle for mastery, but it may suggest either a striving for superiority or for a particular advantage or a laborious effort (as in understanding, in seeking, or in overcoming) ⟨compelled to *wrestle* with the increasing difficulties of his office⟩ ⟨the perfectionist's instinct for *wrestling* with a problem until he had shaped it to his mental image—*Kolodin*⟩ ⟨the man who has never *wrestled* with his early faith . . . has missed not only a moral but an intellectual discipline—*Ellis*⟩ **Tussle** also suggests a struggle for mastery, but it implies determination rather than skill or ingenuity and willingness to accept the rough-and-tumble conditions of such a struggle ⟨the boys *tussled* long and hard⟩ ⟨*tussle* with a problem in mathematics⟩ ⟨a strong man who could *tussle* with evil and conquer—*Caspary*⟩ **Grapple** stresses the action of taking hold of or coming to grips with; the term carries a stronger implication of being in a position to gain the mastery and, usually, of a successful struggle ⟨*grappled* with his assailant, pinning one of his arms behind him⟩ ⟨the architect has *grappled* with more problems than one need hope to see solved in any single church—*Henry Adams*⟩ ⟨it has been mainly the academicians who have attempted to *grapple* with the . . . intricacies of Joyce's mysticism of the flesh—*Mailer*⟩ **Scuffle** may imply brief, confused, usually not very serious fighting involving much scrambling and noise ⟨boys *scuffled* with each other in the schoolyard⟩ It may suggest hurry or superficiality in overcoming difficulties ⟨you go to school and *scuffle* on the best way you can—*Runciman*⟩
**Ana** *contend, fight, battle, war: *resist, withstand, combat, oppose: strive, endeavor, essay (see ATTEMPT): labor, toil, travail (see corresponding nouns at WORK)

**wretched** *miserable
**Ana** *despondent, forlorn, hopeless, despairing: doleful, dolorous, *melancholy: abject, sordid, *mean: pitiable, piteous, *pitiful

**wring** *vb* *wrench, wrest
**Ana** *press, squeeze: *crush, mash, smash, bruise: extract, extort, elicit (see EDUCE): distort, contort (see DEFORM): twist, bend (see CURVE)

**writer, author, composer** can all denote a person who gives expression to his ideas or feelings, but they are not as a rule synonyms. **Writer** is a comprehensive term applied to someone whose occupation or chief employment is that of expressing something in words, especially for others to read. As an occupational designation, it implies that one's profession is writing for publication, and it covers such persons as novelists, essayists, dramatists, editors, and journalists ⟨a free-lance *writer*⟩ ⟨news *writers*⟩ ⟨a *writers'* club⟩ **Author** in its comprehensive sense (see under MAKER) is applicable to a producer or source (as of a work of art) ⟨the *author* of my being⟩ but it can be applied specifically to a person who has written for publi-

cation. It differs from *writer* in placing less stress upon the profession and more upon the fact of having written and published something (as a book or an article under one's own name or a pen name) ⟨decide to become a *writer*⟩ ⟨the *authors* of some well-known books were not *writers* by profession⟩ *Author* in this sense, too, implies an originator or source and is distinguished from *reviser, adapter, editor,* or *dramatizer*. **Composer**, like *author,* may be used generally and specifically. But because it emphasizes the bringing together of a number of things so as to form a whole (a composition), it is applied most frequently to those expressions of ideas or feelings achieved by bringing together musical tones, words, colors, or shapes so as to form an artistic pattern. It is the specific term for the author of a musical composition ⟨the *composer* of the Peer Gynt suite⟩ but, although this is its commonest application, it is also applicable to poets, painters, designers, and others when composition rather than creation or representation is the end ⟨Shakespeare was not only a dramatist but a *composer* of lyrics and sonnets⟩

**writhe, agonize, squirm** are comparable when they mean to twist or turn in physical or mental distress. **Writhe** regularly carries vivid suggestions of convulsive contortions (as of one in the throes of death, in a paroxysm, in an instrument of torture, or in a trap) and of fruitless struggling to escape. When used in reference to physical distress, it commonly implies also great pain ⟨childhood and youth and age *writhing* in savage pains—*Shelley*⟩ When extended to refer to mental distress, it usually implies a torturing sense of shame, of bafflement, or of frustration ⟨thus, at every march, the hidden enemy became bolder and the regiment *writhed* . . . under attacks it could not avenge—*Kipling*⟩ ⟨corrupt men in the machines *writhe* in the presence of his obvious integrity—*Helen Fuller*⟩ **Agonize** sometimes evokes the image of one in the pangs of death, struggling and in anguish; sometimes it evokes the picture of one wrestling or straining arduously to achieve a difficult victory ⟨bled, groaned, and *agonized,* and died in vain—*Cowper*⟩ ⟨pages which cost a week of unremitting and *agonizing* labor—*Huxley*⟩ **Squirm** evokes images of a less dignified or a more familiar character; it usually does not imply profound distress, but great unease (as in aversion to restraint or discipline) or a shrinking or wincing (as under sarcasm or criticism) ⟨sleek-haired subalterns who *squirmed* painfully in their chairs when they came to call—*Kipling*⟩ ⟨a grueling cross-examination . . . in which he is going to make me *squirm* in front of the grand jury—*Gardner*⟩
**Ana** twist, bend (see CURVE *vb*): distort, contort (see DEFORM): wince, blench, flinch, *recoil

**wrong** *n* *injustice, injury, grievance
**Ana** damage, *injury, harm, mischief: violation, infraction, *breach, trespass, transgression: hardship, *difficulty

**wrong** *adj* **1** *false
**Ana** fallacious, sophistical (see under FALLACY): *misleading, deceptive, delusive, delusory
**Ant** right —**Con** *correct, exact, accurate, precise
**2** *bad, poor
**Ana** improper, *unfit, inappropriate, unfitting, unsuitable, inapt, unhappy, infelicitous
**Con** proper, *fit, appropriate, suitable, fitting: *awry, askew: *amiss, astray

**wrong** *vb* **Wrong, oppress, persecute, aggrieve** can mean to inflict injury upon a person without just cause or in an outrageous manner. One **wrongs** another who injures him by unjustifiably depriving him of his property or his good name or by violating something he holds sacred ⟨receive

---

*Ana* analogous words    *Ant* antonyms    *Con* contrasted words    See also explanatory notes facing page 1

us; we have *wronged* no man, we have corrupted no man, we have defrauded no man—*2 Cor* 7:2⟩ ⟨such an air of *wronged* nobility—*Cheever*⟩ One **oppresses** another who inhumanely lays upon him burdens too heavy to be endured or exacts of him more than he can possibly perform ⟨how reviving to the spirits of just men long *oppressed*, when God into the hands of their deliverer puts invincible might—*Milton*⟩ ⟨may have missed the tender love of her parents . . . or been *oppressed* by her elderly uncle—*Cheever*⟩ One **persecutes** another who relentlessly or unremittingly subjects him to annoyance or suffering ⟨if a boy has abnormal mental powers in some direction, com-

bined with poor physique and great nervousness, he . . . may be so *persecuted* [by normal boys] as to be driven mad—*Russell*⟩ One **aggrieves** another or, more often, causes him to be or to feel *aggrieved* who by wronging, oppressing, or persecuting him gives him ground for protest ⟨several nations were *aggrieved* by the terms of the Treaty of Versailles⟩ ⟨so the bargain stood: they broke it, and he felt himself *aggrieved*—*Browning*⟩
*Ana* \*abuse, mistreat, maltreat, ill-treat, outrage: \*injure, harm, hurt
**wroth** \*angry, irate, indignant, wrathful, acrimonious, mad

# Y

**yank** *vb* \*jerk, snap, twitch
*Ana* \*pull, drag, tug: snatch, clutch (see TAKE): \*wrench, wrest
**yap** *vb* \*bark, bay, howl, growl, snarl, yelp
**yardstick** \*standard, criterion, gauge, touchstone
**yarn** tale, \*story, narrative, anecdote
**yearn** \*long, pine, hanker, hunger, thirst
*Ana* crave, \*desire, wish, want, covet: aspire, pant, \*aim
**yeast** \*foam, froth, spume, scum, lather, suds
**yell** *vb* \*shout, shriek, scream, screech, squeal, holler, whoop
*Ana* vociferate, \*roar, clamor, bellow, bawl
**yell** *n* shout, shriek, scream, screech, squeal, holler, whoop (see under SHOUT *vb*)
**yelp** *vb* \*bark, bay, howl, growl, snarl, yap
**yield** *vb* **1** produce, turn out, \*bear
*Ana* \*generate, engender, breed, propagate: create, \*invent: form, shape, \*make, fabricate, fashion
**2** \*relinquish, surrender, cede, abandon, leave, resign, waive
*Ana* \*forgo, forbear, abnegate, eschew, sacrifice: \*abdicate, renounce, resign
*Con* \*keep, keep back, retain, withhold: appropriate, \*arrogate, confiscate
**3** Yield, submit, capitulate, succumb, relent, defer, bow, cave can all mean to give way to someone or something that one cannot further resist. **Yield** (see also RELINQUISH; BEAR 2), when the reference is to a person implies being overcome (as by force, argument, or entreaty) ⟨*yield* to persuasion⟩ ⟨*yield* to temptation⟩ ⟨he never *yields* except when the matter under discussion is of no significance to him⟩ ⟨the great principle in a contest with a child is: do not *yield* but do not punish—*Russell*⟩ but when the reference is to a thing, the word implies elasticity, or lack of firmness, strength, or endurance in the thing that gives way ⟨the door suddenly *yielded* to her hand—*Austen*⟩ ⟨the house they went to was . . . a human burrow or habitation that had *yielded* at every point to the crotchets and meanderings of a growing family—*Cheever*⟩ **Submit** carries a more definite implication of contention or conflict than *yield* and, therefore, suggests more strongly a surrender after resistance to another's will, or because of a thing's strength or inevitableness ⟨all is not lost—the unconquerable will . . . and courage never to *submit*—*Milton*⟩ ⟨the Indian summer of her heart, which was slow to *submit* to age—*Stevenson*⟩ ⟨a long diatribe against Pitt for having tamely *submitted* to the rebuffs of the French Directory—*Quiller-Couch*⟩ ⟨*submitted* to their joking with the best grace she could—*Wouk*⟩ **Capitulate**

can mean to surrender on terms definitely agreed upon, but in its common extended use, it more often centers attention on a definite submission to a force or power that one has not the strength, the skill, or the will to overcome ⟨I always tip for special services rendered but I will not *capitulate* before sheer impertinence—*Wechsberg*⟩ ⟨the universities would *capitulate* to a young, vigorous and revolutionary creed—*Moberly*⟩ **Succumb** carries a stronger implication than any of the preceding terms of weakness or helplessness in the person or thing that gives way or of strength or irresistibility in the person or more often the thing that causes the giving way. The suggestion of sinking under that force or power is usually so strong in *succumb* that the word frequently implies a disastrous outcome (as death, destruction, or subjugation) ⟨*succumb* to pneumonia⟩ ⟨the best of constitutions will not prevent ambitious politicians from *succumbing* . . . to the temptations of power—*Huxley*⟩ ⟨true passion . . . must be crushed before it will *succumb*—*Meredith*⟩ All of the preceding terms usually imply a giving way on the part of a person or sometimes a thing that has not or cannot maintain the upper hand; they therefore often imply a weakening of the one that gives way. **Relent**, by contrast, implies a yielding on the part of the one who has the upper hand and who has been severe or harsh in his attitude to another person or fixed in his determination (as to punish, to interfere, or to frustrate). The term therefore implies a softening or mollifying that turns him from his previous course ⟨can you hear a good man groan, and not *relent*?—*Shak.*⟩ ⟨when a second appeal, couched in more urgent terms, was dispatched to him, he *relented*—*Cerf*⟩ **Defer** implies a yielding or submitting to because of respect or reverence for another or in recognition of another's authority or superior knowledge ⟨everybody must *defer* . . . a nation must wait upon her decision, a dean and chapter truckle to her wishes—*Sackville-West*⟩ ⟨clearly conscious of her success and of the way these Londoners were *deferring* to her—*Dahl*⟩ **Bow** is a picturesque equivalent of *defer* or *submit;* it may suggest a yielding through courtesy or through subjugation ⟨*bow* to the inevitable⟩ ⟨*bow* to established authority⟩ ⟨he admired the tribal discipline which made May *bow* to this decision—*Wharton*⟩ **Cave**, usually with *in*, can be a close synonym of *succumb*, but it often suggests resistance to pressure to the point of exhaustion and sudden collapse ⟨in the end government *caved* in, and unconditionally agreed to inquiry—*Punch*⟩
*Ana* surrender, cede, waive (see RELINQUISH): concede, accord, award, \*grant

---

A colon (:) separates groups of words discriminated. An asterisk (\*) indicates place of treatment of each group.

**yoke** *couple, pair, brace

**yokel** bumpkin, hick, rube, clodhopper, clown, lout, *boor, churl

**young** *n* *offspring, progeny, issue, descendant, posterity

**youth, adolescence, puberty, pubescence** are sometimes used interchangeably to denote the period in life when one passes from childhood to maturity. **Youth** is the most general of these terms, being applied sometimes to the whole early part of life from childhood or infancy to maturity ⟨*youth*, maturity, senility⟩ More often, however, *youth* is applied to the period between the maturing of the sexual organs and the attaining of full maturity. *Youth* often connotes the freshness, vigor, inexperience, or impetuosity characteristic of the young. **Adolescence** designates the same period as *youth* in the restricted sense, but it carries a stronger connotation of immaturity. *Adolescence* suggests the awkwardness resulting from the rapid growth during this period and also the mental and emotional instability resulting from the physiological changes. In legal use *adolescence* designates the period extending from puberty to the attainment of full legal age or majority. Basically **puberty** designates the age at which the signs of the maturing of the sexual organs appear (as the beard and changed voice in boys and the development of the breasts in girls); in law this age is commonly fixed at fourteen for boys and twelve for girls. In broader use *puberty* often designates the period covering the earlier years of adolescence during which the secondary sex characteristics are unfolding. **Pubescence** is sometimes used as equivalent to *puberty*, but often it applies distinctively to the condition of attaining the characteristics (as genital hair) of developing sexuality.
*Ant* age (sense 1)

**youthful, juvenile, puerile, boyish, virgin, virginal, maiden** are comparable when they mean relating to or characteristic of one who is between childhood and adulthood; although their basic meaning is the same, they are seldom interchangeable because of widely differing implications and applications. **Youthful** suggests the possession or the appearance of youth, or of qualities appropriate to youth; it can be employed laudatorily or in extenuation ⟨*youthful* aspirations⟩ ⟨*youthful* indiscretions⟩ **Juvenile** often suggests immaturity of mind or body or lack of experience; it is applied especially to what is suited to or designed for boys and girls in their early teens ⟨*juvenile* dances⟩ ⟨*juvenile* fiction⟩ **Puerile** is applied especially to acts and utterances which, though excusable in a boy or girl or characteristic of immaturity, would be unpardonable or out of character in an adult; the word finds its commonest use in depreciatory reference to acts or utterances of the mature ⟨what seemed sapient discourse in 1940 is rather *puerile* chatter now—*G. W. Johnson*⟩ ⟨time and again the suspicion wounds us that we are *puerile* people, fetal minds, illegible tapestries—*Peggy Bennett*⟩ **Boyish** (compare *mannish* under MALE), though referred commonly to boys, is sometimes used in reference to girls or their clothes, appearance, or qualities. The term often suggests some of the engaging qualities or the physical attractiveness of normal, vigorous boys ⟨a *boyish* smile⟩ ⟨*boyish* charm⟩ ⟨*boyish* enthusiasm⟩ **Virgin** and **virginal**, though referable usually to girls, in the extended use in which they suggest the freshness, innocence, purity, and inexperience that are associated with youthful virginity are applicable also to boys ⟨that beautiful mixture of manly courage and *virginal* modesty—*Farrar*⟩ ⟨he smiled like a girl, or like clear winter skies, a *virginal* light making stars of his eyes—*Lindsay*⟩ **Maiden** in its extended sense carries an even stronger suggestion than *virgin* or *virginal* of youthful lack of experience; it also implies that one's qualities (as virtue, worth, competence, or strength) have not been tried or tested ⟨a *maiden* speech⟩ ⟨his *maiden* effort at authorship⟩
*Ana* *immature, unmatured
*Ant* aged  —*Con* *mature, matured, grown-up

# Z

**zeal** enthusiasm, fervor, ardor, *passion
*Ana* energy, force (see POWER): zest, gusto (see TASTE): earnestness, seriousness (see corresponding adjectives at SERIOUS): intensity, vehemence, fierceness (see corresponding adjectives at INTENSE)
*Ant* apathy  —*Con* impassivity, phlegm, stolidity (see under IMPASSIVE)

**zealot** *enthusiast, fanatic, bigot
*Ana* partisan, sectary, adherent, disciple, *follower: devotee, votary (see ADDICT)

**zenith** apogee, culmination, meridian, *summit, peak, pinnacle, climax, apex, acme
*Ant* nadir

**zephyr** *wind, breeze, gale, hurricane

**zest** relish, gusto, *taste, palate
*Ana* enthusiasm, fervor, ardor, zeal, *passion: spiritedness *or* spirit, high-spiritedness (see corresponding adjectives at SPIRITED): enjoyment, delight, delectation, *pleasure

**zone** belt, *area, tract, region
*Ana* *locality, district: section, sector, segment (see PART *n*)

---

*Ana* analogous words     *Ant* antonyms     *Con* contrasted words     See also explanatory notes facing page 1

# LIST OF AUTHORS QUOTED

The entries in italic type in the left-hand column are the actual forms used in citations in the *Vocabulary* of this Dictionary. These entries are arranged in the alphabetical order of surnames or titles. The right-hand column supplies an identification for each author or source cited. Only readily understood abbreviations (such as Amer. for American and Eng. for English) are used in this column.

As the names of books of the Bible are given wherever cited in the *Vocabulary*, these names are omitted from the list below. Unless otherwise stated at the citation itself in the *Vocabulary*, all biblical quotations are from the Authorized Version (or King James Bible). Quotations from other versions are indicated by the addition of the abbreviations *R. V.* for Revised Version (of 1885), *D. V.* for Douay Version (or Douay Bible).

*Abbott* . . . George Francis Abbott (1889– ) Amer. playwright

*J. S. C. Abbott* John Stevens Cabot Abbott (1805–1877) Amer. historian

*Abel* . . . . Darrel Abel (1911– ) Amer. educator

*Abend* . . . Hallett Edward Abend (1884–1955) Amer. editor

*Abernethy* Cecil Emory Abernethy (1908– ) Amer. educator

*Abse* . . . . Dannie Abse (1923– ) Brit. poet

*Ace* . . . . Goodman Ace (1899– ) Amer. writer

*Acheson* . . Dean Gooderham Acheson (1893–1971) Amer. diplomat

*Sam Acheson* Sam Hanna Acheson (1900– ) Amer. editor

*Ackerman* Saul Benton Ackerman (1887– ) Amer. educator

*ACLS Newsletter* Amer. Council of Learned Societies

*Acton ●* . . . Jon Emerich Edward Dalberg-Acton (1834–1902) 1st baron Acton. Eng. historian

*Adair* . . . James Adair (1709?–?1783) Amer. (Irish-born) pioneer

*Adams* . . John Adams (1735–1826) 2d president of the U.S.

*Evangeline Adams* Evangeline Smith Adams (1872 1932) Amer. astrologist

*F. A. Adams* Francis A. Adams (fl. 1952) Amer. businessman

*Henry Adams* Henry Brooks Adams (1838–1918) Amer. historian

*J. D. Adams* James Donald Adams (1891–1968) Amer. critic

*J. Q. Adams* John Quincy Adams (1767–1848) 6th president of the U.S.

*J. T. Adams* James Truslow Adams (1878–1949) Amer. historian

*R. G. Adams* Randolph Greenfield Adams (1892–1951) Amer. librarian

*S. H. Adams* Samuel Hopkins Adams (1871–1958) Amer. author

*William Adams* William Adams (1706–1789) Eng. clergyman

*Addison* . . Joseph Addison (1672–1719) Eng. essayist

*Adler* . . . Mortimer Jerome Adler (1902– ) Amer. philosopher

*Æ* . . . . . *pseud.* of George William Russell (1867–1935) Irish author

*African Abstracts* Brit. quarterly

*African Wild Life* So. African quarterly

*Agar* . . . . Herbert Sebastian Agar (1897– ) Amer. writer

*Ageton* . . . Arthur Ainsley Ageton (1900–1971) Amer. naval officer

*Agnew* . . Seth Agnew (1921–1967) Amer. publisher

*Aguecheek* *pseud.* of Charles Bullard Fairbanks (1827–1859) Amer. writer

*Aiken* . . . Conrad Potter Aiken (1889– ) Amer. poet

*Ainsworth* William Harrison Ainsworth (1805–1882) Eng. nov.

*Alan* . . . . Ray Alan (fl. 1953) Brit. journalist

*Albright* . . William Foxwell Albright (1891–1971) Amer. orientalist

*Alcine* . . . Bill Alcine (fl. 1945) Amer. soldier

*Alcott* . . . Louisa May Alcott (1832–1888) Amer. author

*Aldington* . . Richard Aldington (1892–1962) Eng. writer

*Aldor* . . ✓. . Francis Aldor, *The Good Time Guide to London* (1951)

*Aldrich* . Thomas Bailey Aldrich (1836–1907) Amer. author

*Aldridge* . . John Watson Aldridge (1922– ) Amer. critic

*Alexander* . . Samuel Alexander (1859–1938) Austral. philosopher

*Franz Alexander* Franz Gabriel Alexander (1891–1964) Amer. (Hung.-born) psychiatrist

*H. B. Alexander* Hartley Burr Alexander (1873–1939) Amer. philosopher

*Algren* . . . Nelson Algren (1909– ) Amer. author

*Alison* . . . Sir Archibald Alison (1792–1867) Scot. historian

*Allen* . . . Alexander Viets Griswold Allen (1841–1908) Amer. clergyman

*F. L. Allen* Frederick Lewis Allen (1890–1954) Amer. editor

*Grant Allen* Grant Allen (1848–1899) Canad. author

*Hervey Allen* (William) Hervey Allen (1889–1949) Amer. author

*Allport* . . . Floyd Henry Allport (1890– ) Amer. psychologist

*G. W. Allport* Gordon Willard Allport (1897–1967) Amer. psychologist

*Alpert* . . . Hollis Alpert (1916– ) Amer. writer

*Alsop* . . . Stewart Johonnot Oliver Alsop (1914– ) Amer. journalist

*Altamira y Crevea* Rafael Altamira y Crevea (1866–1951) Span. jurist

*Altick* . . . Richard Daniel Altick (1915– ) Amer. educator

*Altschul* . . Frank Altschul (1887– ) Amer. businessman

*Ambler* . . Eric Ambler (1909– ) Brit. writer

*Amer. Anthropologist* Amer. bimonthly

*Amer. Fabrics* Amer. quarterly

*Amer. Guide Series* Federal Writers' Project of the Works Progress Administration

*Americana Annual* Amer. yearbook

*Americas* . . Pan American Union monthly

*The Amer. Individual Enterprise System* Economic Principles Commission, Nat'l Assoc. of Manufacturers of the U. S.

*Amer. Jour. of Science* Amer. monthly

*Amer. Jour. of Sociology* Amer. bimonthly

*Amer. Mercury* Amer. monthly

*Amer. Naturalist* Amer. bimonthly

*Amer. Sociological Review* Amer. bimonthly

*Amer. Speech* Amer. quarterly

*Anable* . . . Anthony Anable, Jr. (fl. 1953) Amer. editor

*Anderson* . . Sherwood Anderson (1876–1941) Amer. writer

*Ethel Anderson* Ethel Mason Anderson (1904–1958) Austral. writer

*Maxwell Anderson* Maxwell Anderson (1888–1959) Amer. playwright

*M. L. Anderson* Marcia Lee Anderson (1916– ) Amer. educator

*Quentin Anderson* Quentin Anderson (1912– ) Amer. educator

*W. H. Anderson* William Harry Anderson (1905– ) Amer. educator

*Andrewes* . . Sir Christopher Andrewes (1896– ) Eng. physician

*Andrews* . . Wayne Andrews (1913– ) Amer. curator

*Angell* . . . Sir Norman Angell (1872–1967) Eng. author

*Angoff* . . . Charles Angoff (1902– ) Amer. (Russ.-born) author

*Anspacher* Louis Kaufman Anspacher (1878–1947) Amer. dramatist

*Appraisal Terminology & Handbook* Amer. Institute of Real Estate Appraisers

*Archer* . . . William Archer (1856–1924) Scot. critic

*Arden* . . . Ringgold Arden, *Textile Industries* (1954)

*Clive Arden* *pseud. of* Lily Clive Nutt (1888– ) Eng. author

*Arendt* . . . Hannah Arendt (1906– ) Amer. (Ger.-born) political philosopher

*Arey* . . . . Leslie Brainerd Arey (1891– ) Amer. anatomist

*Argus* . . . Seattle weekly newspaper

*Arke* . . . C. H. Arke, *English Digest* (1953)

*Armbrister* Trevor Armbrister (1933– ) Amer. writer

*Armstrong* Harry George Armstrong (1899– ) Amer. surgeon

*Donald Armstrong* Donald Armstrong (1889– ) Amer. army officer

*E. A. Armstrong* Edward Allworthy Armstrong (1900– ) Brit. clergyman

*Arnold* . . . Matthew Arnold (1822–1888) Eng. poet

*Edwin Arnold* Sir Edwin Arnold (1832–1904) Eng. poet

*T. W. Arnold* Thurman Wesley Arnold (1891–1969) Amer. lawyer

*W. R. Arnold* W. R. Arnold, *The Postmark* (1955)

*Aron* . . . Raymond Aron (1905– ) French sociologist

*Artz* . . . . Frederick Binkerd Artz (1894– ) Amer. historian

*Asbury* . . . Herbert Asbury (1891–1963) Amer. author

*Ascham* . . Roger Ascham (1515–1568) Eng. scholar

*Ascoli* . . . Max Ascoli (1898– ) Amer. (Ital.-born) author

*Ashbrook* . . Frank Getz Ashbrook (1892– ) Amer. biologist

*Ashley* . . . Frederick William Ashley (1863–1943) Amer. librarian

*Asimov* . . Isaac Asimov (1920– ) Amer. (Russ.-born) educator

*Aswell* . . . James R. Aswell (1906–1955) Amer. author

*Athenaeum* Eng. weekly incorporated in *The Nation and Athenaeum* 1921

*Atkinson* . . (Justin) Brooks Atkinson (1894– ) Amer. critic

*Percy Atkinson* Percy L. Atkinson (1886–1950) Amer. advertising executive

*Atlantic* . . Amer. monthly

*Attlee* . . . Clement Richard Attlee (1883–1967) 1st earl Attlee. Brit. statesman

Atyeo . . . Henry Clay Atyeo (1905– ) Amer. educator

Auchincloss Louis Stanton Auchincloss (1917– ) Amer. writer

Auden . . . Wystan Hugh Auden (1907– ) Amer. (Eng.-born) poet

Austen . . . Jane Austen (1775–1817) Eng. nov.

Austin . . . Alfred Austin (1835–1913) Eng. poet

Mary Austin Mary Hunter Austin (1868–1934) Amer. nov.

Sarah Austin Sarah Austin (1793–1867) Eng. translator

Autry . . . Asa Autry (fl. 1945) Amer. soldier

Axelrod . . Aaron Axelrod (fl. 1919) Amer. educator

Aydelotte . . William Osgood Aydelotte (1910– ) Amer. historian

Ayer . . . . Alfred Jules Ayer (1910– ) Eng. writer

Baab . . . Otto J. Baab (1896–1958) Amer. educator

Babbitt . . Irving Babbitt (1865–1933) Amer. scholar

Babcock . . Frederick Morrison Babcock, *Valuation of Real Estate* (1932)

Bacon . . . Francis Bacon (1561–1626) 1st baron Verulam. Eng. author

A. M. Bacon Alice Mabel Bacon (1858–1918) Amer. educator

Peggy Bacon Peggy Bacon (1895– ) Amer. artist

T. D. Bacon Theodore Davenport Bacon (1863–1930) Amer. author

Baerlein . . Henry Baerlein (1875–1960) Eng. author

Bagby . . . English Bagby (1891–1955) Amer. psychologist

Bagehot . . Walter Bagehot (1826–1877) Eng. economist

Bagot . . . Richard Bagot (1860–1921) Eng. nov.

Bailey . . . Alfred Marshall Bailey (1894– ) Amer. curator

Margery Bailey Margery Bailey (1891– ) Amer. educator

T. A. Bailey Thomas Andrew Bailey (1902– ) Amer. historian

Baily. . . . Joe Baily, Jr. (fl. 1954) Amer. newspaperman

Bainton . . Roland Herbert Bainton (1894– ) Amer. (Eng.-born) theologian

Baker . . . Christina Hopkinson Baker (1873–1959) Amer. author

Carlos Baker Carlos Heard Baker (1909– ) Amer. educator

Dorothy Baker Dorothy Dodds Baker (1907–1968) Amer. nov.

J. H. Baker John Hopkinson Baker (1894– ) Amer. conservationist

J. V. Baker James Volant Baker (1903– ) Amer. educator

R. H. Baker Robert Horace Baker (1883– ) Amer. astronomer

Balchin . . Nigel Marlin Balchin (1908–1970) Eng. author

Baldwin . . Faith Baldwin (1893– ) Amer. nov.

James Baldwin James Baldwin (1924– ) Amer. author

M. W. Baldwin Marshall Whithed Baldwin (1903– ) Amer. historian

Ballard . . Philip Boswood Ballard (1865–1950) Brit. educator

Balliett . . Whitney Balliett (1926– ) Amer. writer

Bambrick . . Winifred Bambrick (fl. 1946) Canad. author

Banay . . . Ralph Steven Banay (1896–1970) Amer. (Hung.-born) psychiatrist

Bancroft . . George Bancroft (1800–1891) Amer. historian

Banfield . . Edmund James Banfield (1852–1923) Austral. naturalist

Bangs . . . John Kendrick Bangs (1862–1922) Amer. humorist

Barbour . . Thomas Barbour (1884–1946) Amer. naturalist

Michael Barbour Michael Barbour, *Geographical Jour.* (1954)

Barclay . . Dorothy Edith Barclay (1918– ) Amer. journalist

Barham . . Richard Harris Barham (1788–1845) Eng. author

Baring . . . Maurice Baring (1874–1945) Eng. writer

Baring-Gould Sabine Baring-Gould (1834–1924) Eng. clergyman

Barker . . . Squire Omar Barker (1894– ) Amer. writer

Audrey Barker Audrey Lilian Barker (1918– ) Eng. writer

Ernest Barker Sir Ernest Barker (1874–1960) Eng. political scientist

Barkham . . John Barkham (1908– ) Amer. editor

Barkin . . . Solomon Barkin (1907– ) Amer. economist

Barkins . . Evelyn Werner Barkins (1918– ) Amer. author

Barkley . . Alben William Barkley (1877–1956) U.S. vice-president (1949–1953)

Barlow . . . Joel Barlow (1754–1812) Amer. poet

Barnes . . . Margaret Ayer Barnes (1886–1967) Amer. author

H. E. Barnes Harry Elmer Barnes (1889–1968) Amer. sociologist

Barnett . . Vincent MacDowell Barnett (1913– ) Amer. educator

Barnouw . . Adriaan Jacob Barnouw (1877–1968) Amer. (Du.-born) philologist

Barr . . . . Stringfellow Barr (1897– ) Amer. educator

Barrett . . William Barrett (1913– ) Amer. educator

C. L. Barrett Charles Leslie Barrett (1879– ) Austral. naturalist

Barrie . . . Sir James Matthew Barrie (1860–1937) Scot. author

Barrow . . . Isaac Barrow (1630–1677) Eng. theologian

Barth . . . Alan Barth (1906– ) Amer. editor

Bartlett . . Paul Bartlett (1881– ) Amer. author

Barton . . . George Aaron Barton (1859–1942) Amer. (Canad.-born) educator

Bartram . . William Bartram (1739–1823) Amer. naturalist

Baruch . . . Bernard Mannes Baruch (1870–1965) Amer. businessman

Barzun . . . Jacques Barzun (1907– ) Amer. (Fr.-born) educator

Basso . . . (Joseph) Hamilton Basso (1904–1964) Amer. nov.

Bateman . . John Henry Bateman (1892–1953) Amer. educator

A. M. Bateman Alan Mara Bateman (1889–1971) Amer. geologist

Bates. . . . Katharine Lee Bates (1859–1929) Amer. poet

E. S. Bates Ernest Sutherland Bates (1879–1939) Amer. editor

Graham Bates Gladys Graham Bates (1890–1962) Amer. editor

Battenhouse Roy Wesley Battenhouse (1912– ) Amer. educator

Bauer . . . Raymond Augustine Bauer (1916– ) Amer. educator

Baum . . . Vicki Baum (1896–1960) Amer. (Austrian-born) nov.

Baxter . . . James Phinney Baxter (1893– ) Amer. educator

Baynes . . . Helton Godwin Baynes (1882–1943) Eng. physician

Beach . . . Joseph Warren Beach (1880–1957) Amer. educator

Stewart Beach Stewart Taft Beach (1899– ) Amer. editor

Beachcroft Thomas Owen Beachcroft (1902– ) Brit. author

Beaglehole Ernest Beaglehole (1906–1965) N. Z. psychologist

Beale . . . Howard Kennedy Beale (1899–1959) Amer. historian

Charles Beard Charles Austin Beard (1874–1948) Amer. historian

Mary Beard Mary Ritter Beard (1876–1958) Amer. historian; wife of Charles

Beaumont Francis Beaumont (1584–1616) Eng. dramatist

Gerald Beaumont Gerald Beaumont (d. 1926) Amer. nov.

Beck . . . Warren Beck (fl. 1948) Amer. educator

Becker . . . Howard Paul Becker (1899–1960) Amer. sociologist

Beckford . . William Beckford (1760–1844) Eng. author

Beebe . . . (Charles) William Beebe (1877–1962) Amer. naturalist

Lucius Beebe Lucius Morris Beebe (1902–1966) Amer. author

Beecher . . Henry Ward Beecher (1813–1887) Amer. clergyman

Barbara Beecher Barbara Beecher, *Britain Today* (1953)

Beerbohm Max Beerbohm (1872–1956) Eng. critic

Behrman . . Samuel Nathaniel Behrman (1893– ) Amer. playwright

Beidler . . . Lloyd Mumbauer Beidler (1922– ) Amer. educator

Bejarano . . Jorge Bejarano (1888– ) Colombian physician

Belden . . . Jack Belden (1910– ) Amer. author

Bell . . . . Adrian Hanbury Bell (1901– ) Eng. author

Clive Bell . . Arthur Clive Howard Bell (1881–1964) Eng. critic

Daniel Bell Daniel Bell (1919– ) Amer. educator

E. T. Bell . . Eric Temple Bell (1883–1960) Amer. (Scot.-born) mathematician

Lisle Bell . . Lisle Bell (1893–1952) Amer. literary critic

Belloc . . . Hilaire Belloc, *pen name of* (Joseph) Hilary (Pierre) Belloc (1870–1953) Brit. author

Bellow . . . Saul Bellow (1915– ) Amer. (Canad.-born) nov

Belluschi . . Pietro Belluschi (1899– ) Amer. (Ital.-born) architect

Bemelmans Ludwig Bemelmans (1898–1962) Amer. (Austrian-born) author and artist

Bemis . . . Samuel Flagg Bemis (1891– ) Amer. historian

Bendiner . . Robert Marvin Bendiner (1909– ) Amer. writer

Benedict . . Ruth Fulton Benedict (1887–1948) Amer. anthropologist

Benét . . . William Rose Benét (1886–1950) Amer. writer

Rosemary Benét Rosemary Carr Benét (1900– ) Amer. writer

S. V. Benét Stephen Vincent Benét (1898–1943) Amer. poet

Benfield . . Adalbert Edwin Benfield (1911– ) Amer. educator

Benjamin . . Judah Philip Benjamin (1811–1884) Amer. (Brit.-born) lawyer

Bennett . . (Enoch) Arnold Bennett (1867–1931) Eng. nov.

H. S. Bennett Henry Stanley Bennett (1889– ) Eng. educator

John Bennett John Bennett (1865–1956) Amer. writer

Joseph Bennett Joseph Bennett (1922–1972) Amer. editor

Lowell Bennett Lowell Bennett (1920– ) Amer. journalist

Peggy Bennett Peggy Bennett (1925– ) Amer. writer

Benson . . . Arthur Christopher Benson (1862–1925) Eng. educator

Edwin Benson Edwin Benson, *Life in a Mediaeval City* (1920)

G. W. Benson George Willard Benson, *The Cross: Its History & Symbolism* (1934)

Bentham . . Jeremy Bentham (1748–1832) Eng. philosopher

Bentley . . Eric Russell Bentley (1916– ) Amer. (Eng.-born) educator

Bercaw . . . Louise Oldham Bercaw (1894– ) Amer. librarian

Beresford . . James Beresford (1764–1840) Eng. writer

J. D. Beresford John Davys Beresford (1873–1947) Eng. nov.

Berger . . . John Peter Berger (1926– ) Eng. art critic

Bergin . . . Thomas Goddard Bergin (1904– ) Amer. educator

Berkeley . . George Berkeley (1685–1753) Irish bishop

Berkner . . Lloyd Viel Berkner (1905–1967) Amer. physicist

Berle . . . Adolf Augustus Berle (1895–1971) Amer. diplomat

Berners . . John Bourchier (1467–1533) 2d baron Berners. Eng. politician

Bernstein . . Walter Saul Bernstein (1919– ) Amer. author

David Bernstein David Bernstein (1915– ) Amer. writer

Berrigan . . Darrell Berrigan (fl. 1954) Amer. journalist

Besant . . . Sir Walter Besant (1836–1901) Eng. author

Bester . . . Alfred Bester (1913– ) Amer. writer

Bethe . . . Hans Albrecht Bethe (1906– ) Amer. (Ger.-born) physicist

Beuf . . . . Carlo Maria Luigi Beuf (1893– ) Amer. (Ital.-born) writer

Bevan . . . Aneurin Bevan (1897–1960) Brit. socialist leader

Biddle . . . Francis Biddle (1886–1968) Amer. lawyer

Bidwell . . . Percy Wells Bidwell (1888–1970) Amer. educator

Bienenstok Theodore Rozeney Bienenstok (1907– ) Amer. (Pol.-born) anthropologist

Bierce . . . Ambrose Gwinnett Bierce (1842–?1914) Amer. author

Bierstedt . . Robert Bierstedt (1913– ) Amer. sociologist

Bigart . . . Homer Bigart (1907– ) Amer. journalist

Billington . . Ray Allen Billington (1903– ) Amer. educator

L. E. Billington Lillian Emily Billington (fl. 1950) Amer. educator

Binger . . . Carl Alfred Lanning Binger (1889– ) Amer. psychiatrist

Bingham . . Robert Worth Bingham (1871–1937) Amer. journalist

Binyon . . . Laurence Binyon (1869–1943) Eng. author

Biological Abstracts Amer. periodical

Birney . . . Alfred Earle Birney (1904– ) Canad. educator

Birrell . . . Augustine Birrell (1850–1933) Eng. author

Birtles . . . Francis Birtles (fl. 1935) Austral. explorer

Black . . . William Black (1841–1898) Scot. nov.

C. E. Black Cyril Edwin Black (1915– ) Amer. educator

Blackie . . John Stuart Blackie (1809–1895) Scot. classical scholar

Blackmore Richard Doddridge Blackmore (1825–1900) Eng. nov.

Blackmur Richard Palmer Blackmur (1904–1965) Amer. writer

Blackstone Sir William Blackstone (1723–1780) Eng. jurist

Blair . . . Hugh Blair (1718–1800) Scot. clergyman

Blake . . . J. J. Blake (1893–1964) Amer. engineer

Blankenagel John Charles Blankenagel (1886– ) Amer. educator

Blanshard . . Paul Blanshard (1892– ) Amer. author

Brand Blanshard Brand Blanshard (1892– ) Amer. philosopher; twin brother of preceding

Bliven b. 1889 Bruce Bliven (1889– ) Amer. journalist

Bliven b. 1916 Bruce Bliven (1916– ) Amer. writer; son of preceding

Blofeld . . . John Eaton Calthorpe Blofeld (1913– ) Brit. author

Bloom . . . Edward Alan Bloom (1914– ) Amer. educator

Blue Book Amer. monthly

Blum . . . Gerald Saul Blum (1922– ) Amer. educator

Blumer . . . George Blumer (1872–1962) Amer. (Eng.-born) pathologist

Blunden . . Edmund Charles Blunden (1896– ) Eng. author

Blunt . . . John Henry Blunt (1823–1884) Eng. historian

Boas . . . George Boas (1891– ) Amer. educator

Franz Boas Franz Boas (1858–1942) Amer. (Ger.-born) anthropologist

Boatfield . . Helen C. Boatfield (1899– ) Amer. historian

Boesen . . . Victor Boesen (1908– ) Amer. writer

Bogue . . . Donald Joseph Bogue (1918– ) Amer. sociologist

Bok . . . . Edward William Bok (1863–1930) Amer. (Du.-born) editor

B. J. Bok . . Bart Jan Bok (1906– ) Amer. (Du.-born) astronomer

Bolander . . Louis H. Bolander (1890–1957) Amer. librarian

Bolingbroke Henry St. John (1678–1751) 1st viscount Bolingbroke. Eng. statesman

Bolitho . . (Henry) Hector Bolitho (1898– ) Brit. writer

Bonham . . Milledge Louis Bonham (1880–1941) Amer. educator

Bonney . . Walter T. Bonney (1909– ) Amer. government official

Book of Common Prayer The service book of the Anglican Communion (Church of England ed.)

Book-of-the-Month Club News Amer. periodical

Booth . . . Bradford Allen Booth (1909– ) Amer. educator

Borrow . . George (Henry) Borrow (1803–1881) Eng. author

Boschen . . Henry C. Boschen (1906– ) Amer. business executive

Boston Journal Boston daily newspaper consolidated (1917) with the Boston Herald

Boswell . . James Boswell (1740–1795) Scot. author

Alexander Boswell Sir Alexander Boswell (1775–1822) Scot. poet

Botteghe Oscure Italian multilingual periodical

Bottomley . . Gordon Bottomley (1874–1948) Eng. poet

Bottrall . . (Francis James) Ronald Bottrall (1906– ) Eng. poet

Anthony Boucher pen name of William Anthony Parker White (1911–1968) Amer. writer

Bowen . . . Francis Bowen (1811–1890) Amer. philosopher

C. D. Bowen Catherine Drinker Bowen (1897– ) Amer. author

Elizabeth Bowen Elizabeth Dorothea Cole Bowen (1899– ) Brit. author

H. R. Bowen Howard Rothmann Bowen (1908– ) Amer. educator

R. O. Bowen Robert Owen Bowen (1920– ) Amer. author

Bowers . . . Claude Gernade Bowers (1878–1958) Amer. historian

Faubion Bowers Faubion Bowers (1917– ) Amer. writer

R. H. Bowers Robert Hood Bowers (1906– ) Amer. educator

Boyce . . . Carroll W. Boyce (fl. 1950) Amer. editor

Boyd . . . Julian Parks Boyd (1903– ) Amer. educator

Boyle . . . Kay Boyle (1903– ) Amer. author

Hal Boyle Harold Vincent Boyle (1911– ) Amer. journalist

Boy Scout Handbook Boy Scouts of America

Boys' Life Amer. monthly

Brace . . . Gerald Warner Brace (1901– ) Amer. educator

Bracker . . Milton Bracker (1909–1964) Amer. journalist

Bradbury . . Ray Douglas Bradbury (1920– ) Amer. writer

Braddon . . Mary Elizabeth Braddon (1837–1915) Eng. nov.

Braddy . . Haldeen Braddy (1908– ) Amer. educator

Braden . . . Thomas Wardell Braden (1918– ) Amer. editor

Bradford . . Gamaliel Bradford (1863–1932) Amer. biographer

Roark Bradford Roark Bradford (1896–1948) Amer. writer

Bradley . . Andrew Cecil Bradley (1851–1935) Eng. literary critic

Braithwaite Warwick Braithwaite (1896–1971) Brit. conductor

Brand . . . Millen Brand (1906– ) Amer. author

Brandeis . . Louis Dembitz Brandeis (1856–1941) Amer. jurist

Brandt . . . Carl Brandt, New England Journeys (1954)

Brecht . . . Charles A. Brecht, Bulletin (1949)

Breck . . . Edward Breck (1861–1929) Amer. author

Breit . . . Harvey Breit (1913–1968) Amer. writer

Brennan . . Robert Brennan, The Irish Digest (1953)

Bretnor . . Reginald Bretnor (fl. 1953) Amer. editor

Ann Bridge pen name of Mary Dolling (Sanders). Lady O'Malley (1889– ) Eng. author

Bridges . . Robert Seymour Bridges (1844–1930) Eng. poet

Bridges-Adams William Bridges-Adams (1889–1965) Brit. theatrical producer

Bridgman William Charles Bridgman (1887– ) Amer. educator

Brief . . . Amer. periodical

Brinig . . . Myron Brinig (1900– ) Amer. nov.

Britain Today Brit. monthly

Britannia & Eve Brit. monthly

Britannica Bk. of the Yr. Amer. yearbook

Brit. Book News Brit. monthly

Brittain . . Robert Edward Brittain (1908– ) Amer. writer

Brodkey . . Harold Brodkey (fl. 1955) Amer. writer

Brogan . . . Sir Denis William Brogan (1900– ) Brit. political scientist

Bromfield Louis Bromfield (1896–1956) Amer. writer

Bromley . . Dorothy Dunbar Bromley (1896– ) Amer. editor

Brontë . . . Charlotte Brontë (1816–1855) Eng. nov.

Brooke . . Henry Brooke (1703?–1783) Irish author

Rupert Brooke Rupert Brooke (1887–1915) Eng. poet

Brooklyn Daily Eagle New York daily

Brooks . . . Van Wyck Brooks (1886–1963) Amer. author

Cleanth Brooks Cleanth Brooks (1906– ) Amer. educator

John Brooks John Nixon Brooks (1920– ) Amer. journalist

Phillips Brooks Phillips Brooks (1835–1893) Amer. bishop

Brophy . . . John Brophy (1899–1965) Eng. author

Brougham Henry Peter Brougham (1778–1868) Baron Brougham and Vaux. Scot. jurist

Brown . . . Kenneth Irving Brown (1896– ) Amer. educator

Douglas Brown Douglas Brown (1921–1964) Eng. writer

E. K. Brown Edward Killoran Brown (1905–1951) Amer. (Canad.-born) educator

F. M. Brown Frederick Martin Brown (1903– ) Amer. physiologist

G. D. Brown George Douglas Brown (1869–1902) Scot. nov.

Harrison Brown Harrison Scott Brown (1917– ) Amer. educator

J. M. Brown John Mason Brown (1900–1969) Amer. drama critic

J. W. Brown June Wilcoxson Brown (fl. 1953) Amer. writer

Lawrason Brown Lawrason Brown (1871–1937) Amer. physician

R. H. Brown Ralph Hall Brown (1898–1948) Amer. educator

Rollo Brown Rollo Walter Brown (1880–1956) Amer. author

R. W. Brown Roger William Brown (1925– ) Amer. psychologist

T. E. Brown Thomas Edward Brown (1830–1897) Brit. poet

Browne . . Sir Thomas Browne (1605–1682) Eng. author

Brownell . . William Crary Brownell (1851–1928) Amer. critic

Baker Brownell Baker Brownell (1887–1965) Amer. educator

Browning . . Robert Browning (1812–1889) Eng. poet

E. B. Browning Elizabeth Barrett Browning (1806–1861) Eng. poet; wife of Robert

Bruun . . . (Arthur) Geoffrey Bruun (1898– ) Amer. (Canad.-born) historian

Bryant . . . William Cullen Bryant (1794–1878) Amer. poet

Bryce . . . James Bryce (1838–1922) Viscount Bryce. Brit. jurist

Bryson . . . Lyman Lloyd Bryson (1888–1959) Amer. educator

Buchan . . Sir John Buchan (1875–1940) 1st baron Tweedsmuir. Scot. author

*Buchanan*    Daniel Crump Buchanan (1892– ) Amer. (Jap.-born) orientalist

*Alfred Buchanan*    Alfred Buchanan (1874–1941) Austral. writer

*Andrew Buchanan*    Andrew Buchanan (1897– ) Brit. film producer

*R. W. Buchanan*    Robert Williams Buchanan (1841–1901) Brit. writer

*Buck* . . .    Pearl Buck (1892– ) Amer. nov.

*Buckle* . .    Henry Thomas Buckle (1821–1862) Eng. historian

*Bulletin* . .    *Bulletin of the Nat'l Catholic Educational Assoc.*

*Bullett* . . .    Gerald William Bullett (1893–1958) Eng. author

*Bullock* . .    Alan Louis Bullock (1914– ) Eng. educator

*F. H. Bullock*    Florence Haxton Bullock (1891– ) Amer. writer

*Bunche* . .    Ralph Johnson Bunche (1904–1971) Amer. diplomat

*Bundy* . .    McGeorge Bundy (1919– ) Amer. educator

*Bunyan* . .    John Bunyan (1628–1688) Eng. preacher

*Burghardt*    Henry D. Burghardt (fl. 1919) Amer. educator

*Burk* . . .    John Naglee Burk (1891– ) Amer. writer

*Burke* . . .    Edmund Burke (1729–1797) Brit. statesman

*K. D. Burke*    Kenneth Duva Burke (1897– ) Amer. critic

*Richard Burke*    Richard Burke (1886– ) Amer. author

*Burkholder*    Edwin V. Burkholder (fl. 1954) Amer. writer

*Burks* . . .    Richard Voyles Burks (1913– ) Amer. educator

*Burlingame*    (William) Roger Burlingame (1889–1967) Amer. author

*Burnet* . .    Gilbert Burnet (1643–1715) Brit. bishop

*Burney* . .    Frances Burney (1752–1840) *Madame d'Arblay*. Eng. nov.

*Burnham* . .    James Burnham (1905– ) Amer. author

*Burns* . . .    Robert Burns (1759–1796) Scot. poet

*Al Burns* . .    Al Burns (fl. 1934) Amer. stamp editor

*Burroughs*    John Burroughs (1837–1921) Amer. naturalist

*W. S. Burroughs*    William Seward Burroughs (1914– ) Amer. writer

*Burton* . .    Robert Burton (1577–1640) Eng. author

*H. A. Burton*    Howard A. Burton (1916– ) Amer. educator

*J. H. Burton*    John Hill Burton (1809–1881) Scot. historian

*R. F. Burton*    Sir Richard Francis Burton (1821–1890) Brit. explorer

*Bury* . . . .    Lady Charlotte Susan Maria Bury (1775–1861) Eng. nov.

*Bush* . . . .    (John Nash) Douglas Bush (1896– ) Amer. (Canad.-born) educator

*Asahel Bush*    Asahel Bush (1824–1913) Amer. banker

*Vannevar Bush*    Vannevar Bush (1890– ) Amer. engineer

*Butcher* . .    Fanny Butcher (1888– ) Amer. journalist

*Butler d. 1680*    Samuel Butler (1612–1680) Eng. satirist

*Butler d. 1902*    Samuel Butler (1835–1902) Eng. nov.

*Bp. Butler*    Bishop Joseph Butler (1692–1752) Eng. theologian

*J. R. Butler*    Judson Rea Butler (1895– ) Amer. educator

*Butterfield*    Lyman Henry Butterfield (1909– ) Amer. educator

*Donn Byrne*    Brian Oswald Donn-Byrne (1889–1928) Amer. nov.

*Byron* . . .    George Gordon Byron (1788–1824) Eng. poet

*Cabell* . . .    James Branch Cabell (1879–1958) Amer. author

*Cable* . . .    George Washington Cable (1844–1925) Amer. author

*Caffey* . . .    Francis Gordon Caffey (1868–1951) Amer. jurist

*Cain* . . .    Robert E. Cain (1938– ) Amer. librarian

*Caine* . . .    Sir (Thomas Henry) Hall Caine (1853–1931) Eng. nov.

*Cairns* . . .    Huntington Cairns (1904– ) Amer. lawyer

*Caldwell* . .    Erskine Caldwell (1903– ) Amer. nov.

*Calisher* . .    Hortense Calisher (1911– ) Amer. author

*Callaghan*    Morley Edward Callaghan (1903– ) Canad. nov.

*Callender*    Guy Stevens Callender (1865–1915) Amer. educator

*Cameron* . .    Norman Alexander Cameron (1896– ) Amer. (Canad.-born) psychopathologist

*James Cameron*    James Cameron (1911– ) Brit. journalist

*J. M. Cameron*    James Munro Cameron (1910– ) Eng. educator

*Campbell* . .    Thomas Campbell (1777–1844) Brit. poet

*Joseph Campbell*    Joseph Campbell (1904– ) Amer. educator

*Camper* . .    Shirley Camper (1922– ) Amer. writer

*Campion* . .    Sarah Campion (fl. 1949) Eng. author

*Canad. Forum*    Canadian monthly

*Canad. Jour. of Economics & Political Science*    Canadian quarterly

*Canby* . . .    Henry Seidel Canby (1878–1961) Amer. editor

*Cane* . . .    Melville Henry Cane (1879– ) Amer. lawyer

*Canfield*    Leon Hardy Canfield (1886– ) Amer. educator

*Dorothy Canfield*    Dorothy Canfield Fisher (1879–1958) Amer. nov.

*Cannan* . .    Robert Keith Cannan (1894–1971) Amer. educator

*Canning* . .    George Canning (1770–1827) Brit. statesman

*Victor Canning*    Victor Canning (1911– ) Eng. author

*Capern* . .    Edward Capern (1819–1894) Eng. poet

*Capote* . . .    Truman Capote (1924– ) Amer. author

*Cardozo* . .    Benjamin Nathan Cardozo (1870–1938) Amer. jurist

*Carey* . . .    Rosa Nouchetté Carey (1840–1909) Eng. writer

*Cargill* . . .    Oscar Cargill (1898–1972) Amer. educator

*Car Life* . .    Amer. publication

*Carlyle* . .    Thomas Carlyle (1795–1881) Scot. essayist

*J. W. Carlyle*    Jane Baillie Welsh Carlyle (1801–1866) Scot. writer; wife of Thomas

*Carnegie Mag.*    Carnegie Institute of Technology

*Carr* . . .    Lowell Juillard Carr (1885– ) Amer. educator

*J. D. Carr*    John Dickson Carr (1906– ) Amer. author

*Maurice Carr*    Maurice Carr (1913– ) Brit. journalist

*R. K. Carr*    Robert Kenneth Carr (1908– ) Amer. educator

*Carrel* . . .    Alexis Carrel (1873–1944) French surgeon

*Lewis Carroll*    *pseud.* of Charles Lutwidge Dodgson (1832–1898) Eng. storywriter

*Carruth* . .    Hayden Carruth (1921– ) Amer. poet

*Carruthers*    (Alexander) Douglas (Mitchell) Carruthers (1881–1962) Eng. naturalist

*Carson* . .    Saul Carson (1895?–1971) Amer. writer

*Carter* . . .    George Goldsmith Carter (1911– ) Brit. author

*Hodding Carter*    Hodding Carter (1907–1972) Amer. editor

*H. W. Carter*    Henry William Carter (fl. 1954) Brit. businessman

*John Carter*    John Carter (1905– ) Eng. bibliographer

*Cary* . . .    (Arthur) Joyce (Lunel) Cary (1888–1957) Brit. nov.

*Cases & Materials on International Law*    New York (1950)

*Casey* . . .    Genevieve Mary Casey (1916– ) Amer. librarian

*Caspary* . .    Vera Caspary (1904– ) Amer. writer

*Cassidy* . .    Claudia Cassidy (fl. 1954) Amer. music and drama critic

*Cater* . . .    Douglass Cater (1923– ) Amer. editor

*Cather* . . .    Willa Sibert Cather (1873–1947) Amer. nov.

*Catton* . . .    Bruce Catton (1899– ) Amer. writer

*Cecil* . . .    Lord (Edward Christian) David Cecil (1902– ) Eng. biographer

*Century* . .    *The Century Illustrated Monthly Magazine* Amer. periodical

*Cerf* . . . .    Bennett Alfred Cerf (1898–1971) Amer. publisher

*Walter Cerf*    Walter Cerf (1907– ) Ger.-born educator

*Chafee* . .    Zechariah Chafee (1885–1957) Amer. lawyer

*Chalmers* .    George Chalmers (1742–1825) Scot. historian

*Chamberlain*    John Rensselaer Chamberlain (1903– ) Amer. critic

*H. S. Chamberlain*    Houston Stewart Chamberlain (1855–1927) Ger. (Eng.-born) writer

*L. M. Chamberlain*    Leo Martin Chamberlain (1896– ) Amer. educator

*Chambers*    Ephraim Chambers (d. 1740) Eng. encyclopedist

*Chandler* .    Raymond Thornton Chandler (1888–1959) Amer. author

*Channing d. 1842*    William Ellery Channing (1780–1842) Amer. clergyman

*Channing d. 1901*    William Ellery Channing (1818–1901) Amer. poet

*Chapman* .    Stuart Webster Chapman (1907– ) Amer. educator

*Arnold Chapman*    (George) Arnold Chapman (1917– ) Amer. educator

*Chapman-Huston*    Desmond Chapman-Huston (1884–1952) Brit. author

*Charles I* .    Charles I of England (1600–1649); king (1625–49)

*Charteris* .    Leslie Charteris (1907– ) Amer. (Brit.-born) author

*Chase* . . .    Stuart Chase (1888– ) Amer. economist

*F. H. Chase*    Frank Herbert Chase (1870–1930) Amer. librarian

*Chatham* .    William Pitt (1708–1778) 1st earl of Chatham. Eng. statesman

*Chaucer* . .    Geoffrey Chaucer (1340?–1400) Eng. poet

*Cheek* . . .    Leslie Cheek (1908– ) Amer. museum director

*Cheever* . .    John Cheever (1912– ) Amer. writer

*Chenery* . .    William Ludlow Chenery (1884– ) Amer. publisher

*Cheney* . .    Sheldon Warren Cheney (1886– ) Amer. critic

*Cherin* . .    David Cherin, *N. Y. Times Mag.* (1955)

*Chesterfield*    Philip Dormer Stanhope (1694–1773) 4th earl of Chesterfield. Eng. statesman

*Chesterton*    Gilbert Keith Chesterton (1874–1936) Eng. writer

*Cheyne* . .    Thomas Kelley Cheyne (1841–1915) Eng. theologian

*Cheyney* .    Edward Potts Cheyney (1861–1947) Amer. historian

*Chidsey* . .    Donald Barr Chidsey (1902– ) Amer. author

*Child* . . .    Francis James Child (1825–1896) Amer. scholar

*Childe* . . .    Vere Gordon Childe (1892–1957) Eng. anthropologist

*Childs* . . .    George William Childs (1829–1894) Amer. publisher

*M. W. Childs*    Marquis William Childs (1903– ) Amer. journalist

*Chilton* . .    Alexander Wheeler Chilton (1886– ) Amer. army officer

*Chippendale*    Harry Allen Chippendale (1879–1953) Amer. sea captain

*Chisholm* .    Sir Roderick Milton Chisholm (1916–1967) Amer. educator

*I-Kua Chou*    I-Kua Chou (fl. 1955) Chinese-born educator

*Christian Century*    Amer. weekly

*Christian Science Monitor*    Boston daily

*Christie* . .    Agatha (Mary Clarissa) Christie (1891– ) Brit. writer

*Chronica Botanica*    Amer. bimonthly

*Chubb* . . .    Mary Alford Chubb (1903– ) Eng. writer

Churchill .. Winston Churchill (1871–1947) Amer. nov.

Charles Churchill Charles Churchill (1731–1764) Eng. satirist

Sir Winston Churchill Sir Winston Leonard Spencer Churchill (1874–1965) Brit. statesman

Ciardi ... John Anthony Ciardi (1916– ) Amer. poet

Cibber ... Colley Cibber (1671–1757) Eng. dramatist

Cilley .... George E. Cilley (fl. 1953) Amer. army officer

Clare ... John Clare (1793–1864) Eng. poet

Clarendon Edward Hyde (1609–1674) 1st earl of Clarendon. Eng. historian

Clark ... Joseph Thomas Clark (1911– ) Amer. educator

Eliot Clark Eliot Candee Clark (1883– ) Amer. artist

Grenville Clark Grenville Clark (1882–1967) Amer. lawyer

J. W. Clark John Williams Clark (1907– ) Amer. educator

Kenneth Clark Sir Kenneth McKenzie Clark (1903– ) Eng. art connoisseur

Michael Clark Michael K. Clark (1919– ) Amer. journalist

T. D. Clark Thomas Dionysius Clark (1903 ) Amer. historian

W. G. Clark William George Clark (1821–1878) Eng. scholar

W. V. T. Clark Walter Van Tilburg Clark (1909–1971) Amer. author

Clarke .. John Smith Clarke (1885–1959) Scot. author

A. C. Clarke Arthur Charles Clarke (1917– ) Eng. author

Cowden Clarke Charles Cowden Clarke (1787–1877) Eng. scholar

Clemensen Jessie Williams Clemensen (1901– ) Amer. educator

Clement .. William C. Clement, Philosophical Review (1953)

Cleveland (Stephen) Grover Cleveland (1837–1908) 22d and 24th president of the U. S.

Cleveland Plain Dealer Cleveland daily

Clift .... John Russell Clift (fl. 1955) Amer. writer

Clinton . David Clinton, The Nation (1953)

Clodd ... Edward Clodd (1840–1930) Eng. banker

Cloete ... (Edward Fairly) Stuart (Graham) Cloete (1897– ) So. African nov.

Cloud ... Wilbur Frank Cloud (1895– ) Amer. engineer

Clough ... Arthur Hugh Clough (1819–1861) Eng. poet

Clurman . Harold Edgar Clurman (1901– ) Amer. stage director

Coast Artillery Jour. Amer. bimonthly

Coates ... Robert Myron Coates (1897– ) Amer. author

Cobb.... Irvin Shrewsbury Cobb (1876–1944) Amer. humorist

Cobban .. Alfred Cobban (1901– ) Eng. educator

Cobbett . William Cobbett (1763–1835) Eng. political writer

Cockburn Stewart Cockburn (fl. 1954) Austral. writer

Cogan ... Thomas Cogan (1736–1818) Eng. philosopher

Cogley .. John Cogley (1916– ) Amer. journalist

Cohen ... Morris Raphael Cohen (1880–1947) Amer. (Russ.-born) philosopher

A. A. Cohen Arthur Allen Cohen (1928– ) Amer. writer

Cohn ... David Lewis Cohn (1896– ) Amer. writer

Coke ... Sir Edward Coke (1552–1634) Eng. jurist

Coker ... Robert Ervin Coker (1876–1967) Amer. zoologist

F. W. Coker Francis William Coker (1878–1963) Amer. educator

Colby ... Elbridge Colby (1891– ) Amer. author

Cole .... Arthur Charles Cole (1886– ) Amer. historian

Taylor Cole Robert Taylor Cole (1905– ) Amer. educator

Colegrove Kenneth Wallace Colegrove (1886– ) Amer. educator

Coleman .. Emily Coleman (fl. 1949) Amer. music and dance editor

Coleridge .. Samuel Taylor Coleridge (1772–1834) Eng. poet

Collegiate Law Dict. compiled by J. J. Lewis (1925)

Collet ... Robert Collet, The Score and I.M.A. Mag. (1954)

Collie ... Robert Collie (fl. 1964) Amer. clergyman

Collier ... Theodore Collier (1874–1963) Amer. historian

Collier's Yr. Bk. Amer. yearbook

Collins ... Frederic William Collins (1906– ) Amer. newspaperman

Tom Collins pseud. of Joseph Furphy (1843–1912) Austral. author

Wilkie Collins (William) Wilkie Collins (1824–1889) Eng. nov.

Collis ... Ernest Harry Collis (fl. 1948) Austral. writer

Colum ... Padraic Colum (1881–1972) Amer. (Irish-born) author

Colvin ... Sir Sidney Colvin (1845–1927) Eng. critic

Combat Forces Jour. Amer. monthly

Comfort . Alexander Comfort (1920– ) Brit. author

Commager Henry Steele Commager (1902– ) Amer. historian

Commentary Amer. monthly

Commins . Saxe Commins (1892–1958) Amer. editor

The Commonweal Amer. weekly

Compendium of Meteorology Amer. Meteorological Society

Compton . Arthur Holly Compton (1892–1962) Amer. physicist

Comstock . Alzada Peckham Comstock (1888–1960) Amer. educator

Conant ... James Bryant Conant (1893– ) Amer. educator

Congressional Record U. S. periodical

Congreve . William Congreve (1670–1729) Eng. dramatist

Conington John Conington (1825–1869) Eng. translator

Conklin . Edwin Grant Conklin (1863–1952) Amer. biologist

Connally . F. G. Connally, The New Scholasticism (1953)

Connolly . Cyril Vernon Connolly (1903– ) Brit. journalist

Conrad ... Joseph Conrad (1857–1924) Brit. nov.

Barnaby Conrad Barnaby Conrad (1922– ) Amer. author

Contemporary Review Brit. monthly

Conway .. William Martin Conway (1856–1937) 1st baron. Eng. explorer

Cook .... Captain James Cook (1728–1779) Eng. explorer

R. L. Cook Reginald Lansing Cook (1903– ) Amer. educator

T. I. Cook Thomas Ira Cook (1907– ) Amer. (Eng.-born) educator

Cooke ... (Alfred) Alistair Cooke (1908– ) Amer. (Brit.-born) writer

E. V. Cooke Edmund Vance Cooke (1866–1932) Amer. author

M. C. Cooke Mordecai Cubitt Cooke (1825–1913) Brit. mycologist

R. P. Cooke Richard Platt Cooke (1904– ) Amer. writer

Coolidge . Calvin Coolidge (1872–1933) 30th president of the U.S.

Coon .... Carleton Stevens Coon (1904– ) Amer. anthropologist

Coons ... Hannibal Coons (fl. 1954) Amer. writer

Cooper . James Fenimore Cooper (1789–1851) Amer. nov.

Charles Cooper Charles Cooper, London Calling (1954)

Copland . Aaron Copland (1900– ) Amer. composer

Cordell .. Richard Albert Cordell (1896– ) Amer. educator

Corke ... Hilary Corke (fl. 1955) Eng. educator

Corlett ... William Thomas Corlett (1854–1948) Amer. physician

Corry ... James Alexander Corry (1899– ) Canad. educator

Corsini .. Ray Pierre Corsini (fl. 1954) Amer. author

Cort .... David Cort (1904– ) Amer. editor

Corwin .. Edward Samuel Corwin (1878–1963) Amer. educator

Costain .. Thomas Bertram Costain (1895–1965) Amer. (Canad.-born) writer

Cotgrave . John Cotgrave (fl. 1655) Eng. compiler

Cotton .. Nathaniel Cotton (1705–1788) Eng. physician

C. A. Cotton Charles Andrew Cotton (1885– ) N. Z. geologist

Cottrell .. Leonard Slater Cottrell (1899– ) Amer. psychologist

Coulter . Ellis Merton Coulter (1890– ) Amer. historian

Coulton .. George Gordon Coulton (1858–1947) Eng. historian

Country Life Brit. weekly

The Countryman Brit. quarterly

Cournos . John Cournos (1881–1966) Amer. (Russ.-born) writer

Cousins .. Norman Cousins (1912– ) Amer. editor

Coutts ... Alan John Coutts (fl. 1950) Austral. dramatist

Cowen ... Robert Churchill Cowen (1927– ) Amer. writer

Cowie ... Alexander Cowie (1896– ) Amer. educator

Cowley .. Abraham Cowley (1618–1667) Eng. poet

Malcolm Cowley Malcolm Cowley (1898– ) Amer. literary critic

Cowper .. William Cowper (1731–1800) Eng. poet

Cox .... Isaac Joslin Cox (1873– ) Amer. educator

Coxe .... Louis Osborne Coxe (1918– ) Amer. educator

Cozzens . James Gould Cozzens (1903– ) Amer. author

Crabbe .. George Crabbe (1754–1832) Eng. poet

Craig .... Gerald Spellman Craig (1893– ) Amer. educator

H. A. L. Craig H. A. L. Craig (fl. 1955) Irish writer

Cram ... Ralph Adams Cram (1863–1942) Amer. architect

Crane ... Stephen Crane (1871–1900) Amer. writer

Hart Crane Hart Crane (1899–1932) Amer. poet

Milton Crane Milton Crane (1917– ) Amer. educator

Cranston . Maurice William Cranston (1920– ) Eng. author

Crashaw . Richard Crashaw (1613?–1649) Eng. poet

Crawford . Julia Crawford (1800–1885) Irish writer

W. R. Crawford William Rex Crawford (1898– ) Amer. educator

Crawley . Aidan Merivale Crawley (1908– ) Eng. journalist

The Critic Amer. periodical merged 1906 with Putnam's Monthly

Crofts ... Freeman Wills Crofts (1879–1957) Irish writer

Croly ... Herbert Croly (1869–1930) Amer. editor

Cronin .. Archibald Joseph Cronin (1896– ) Eng. nov.

Cronk ... Paul B. Cronk (1896– ) Amer. Coast Guard officer

Cronyn... George William Cronyn (1888– ) Amer. writer

Crops in Peace and War U.S. Dept. of Agriculture Yearbook

Crosby .. Frances Jane Crosby known as Fanny (1820–1915) Amer. hymn writer

Cross ... John W. Cross (1909– ) Amer. dog fancier

Crossman Richard Howard Stafford Crossman (1907– ) Brit. politician

Crothers . Samuel McChord Crothers (1857–1927) Amer. clergyman

Crowley . Francis Joseph Crowley (1902– ) Amer. educator

Crowther . Bosley Crowther (1905– ) Amer. journalist

Crozier . . Brian Crozier (1918– ) Brit. (Austral.-born) writer

Cruickshanks Evelyn G. Cruickshanks (1930– ) Eng. historian

Cruise . . . William Cruise (d. 1824) Brit. legal writer

Cudworth Ralph Cudworth (1617–1688) Eng. philosopher

Cummings Edward Estlin Cummings (1894–1962) Amer. poet

Ridgely Cummings Ridgely Cummings (fl. 1953) Amer. writer

Cunnington Cecil Willett Cunnington (1878–1961) Eng. physician

Curran . . . Charles Howard Curran (1894– 1972) Canad. entomologist

Current Biog. Amer. periodical

Current History Amer. monthly

Currier . . . Charles Warren Currier (1857– 1918) Amer. bishop

Curtis . . . Louis Woodson Curtis (1885– ) Amer. educator

Cushing . . Harvey Cushing (1869–1939) Amer. surgeon

Cushman . . Robert Eugene Cushman (1889–1969) Amer. political scientist

C. F. Cushman Clarissa Fairchild Cushman (fl. 1942) Amer. writer

H. E. Cushman Herbert Ernest Cushman (1865– 1944) Amer. educator

Cutforth . . René Cutforth (1912– ) Brit. reporter

Cutsforth . . Thomas Darl Cutsforth (1893– ) Amer. psychologist

Dahl . . . Roald Dahl (1916– ) Brit. author

Daifuku . . Hiroshi Daifuku (1920– ) Amer. anthropologist

Daily Express London newspaper

Daily Mail London newspaper

Daily Telegraph London newspaper

Damon . . Samuel Foster Damon (1893– 1971) Amer. educator

Dana . . . Richard Henry Dana (1815– 1882) Amer. author

Julian Dana Julian Dana (1907– ) Amer. writer

Dance Observer Amer. monthly

Clemence Dane pseud. of Winifred Ashton (1888–1965) Eng. nov.

Daniel . . . Samuel Daniel (1562–1619) Eng. poet

Clifton Daniel (Elbert) Clifton Daniel (1912– ) Amer. newspaperman

Darrow . . Karl Kelchner Darrow (1891– ) Amer. physicist

Darwin . . Charles Robert Darwin (1809– 1882) Eng. naturalist

Bernard Darwin Bernard Darwin (1876–1961) Eng. golf correspondent

Davenant . . Sir William Davenant (1606– 1668) Eng. poet

Davenport Marcia Davenport (1903– ) Amer. author

Basil Davenport Basil Davenport (1905–1966) Amer. anthologist

Davidson . . Donald Grady Davidson (1893– 1963) Amer. educator

Avram Davidson Avram Davidson (1923– ) Amer. writer

L. J. Davidson Levette Jay Davidson (1894– 1957) Amer. educator

Davies . . . Arthur Powell Davies (1902– 1957) Amer. (Eng.-born) clergyman

C. M. Davies Charles Maurice Davies (1828– 1910) Brit. author

Robertson Davies Robertson Davies (1913– ) Canad. editor

W. H. Davies William Henry Davies (1871– 1940) Brit. poet

Davis . . . Elmer Holmes Davis (1890– 1958) Amer. newscaster

A. K. Davis Arthur Kyle Davis (1897– ) Amer. educator

A. V. Davis A. V. Davis (fl. 1953) Eng. schoolteacher

C. B. Davis Clyde Brion Davis (1894–1962) Amer. nov.

D. S. Davis Dorothy Salisbury Davis (1916– ) Amer. author

H. E. Davis Harold Eugene Davis (1902– ) Amer. educator

H. L. Davis Harold Lenoir Davis (1896– 1960) Amer. writer

H. M. Davis Harry Meyer Davis (1911– 1949) Amer. scientist

J. L. Davis Joe Lee Davis (1906– ) Amer. educator

Kingsley Davis Kingsley Davis (1908– ) Amer. sociologist

K. S. Davis Kenneth Sydney Davis (1912– ) Amer. author

R. G. Davis Robert Gorham Davis (1908– ) Amer. educator

R. H. Davis Richard Harding Davis (1864– 1916) Amer. writer

Davy . . . Sir Humphry Davy (1778–1829) Eng. scientist

Dawes . . . Chester Laurens Dawes (1886– ) Amer. electrical engineer

Dawson . . Virginia Douglas Dawson (1909– ) Amer. author

R. M. Dawson Robert MacGregor Dawson (1895–1958) Canad. educator

Day . . . Clarence Shepard Day (1874– 1935) Amer. author

L. L. Day L. L. Day, Sat. Rev. (1955)

Deakin . . . Frederick William Dampier Deakin (1913– ) Eng. educator

Dean . . . Vera Micheles Dean (1903– 1972) Amer. (Russ.-born) scholar

Deasy . . . Mary Margaret Deasy (1914– ) Amer. author

Defoe . . . Daniel Defoe (1659?–1731) Eng. nov.

de Kiewiet Cornelis Willem de Kiewiet (1902– ) Amer. (Du.-born) educator

Dekker . . . Thomas Dekker (1572?–1632) Eng. playwright

de Kruif . . Paul Henry de Kruif (1890– 1971) Amer. bacteriologist

de Laguna Frederica Annis de Laguna (1906– ) Amer. anthropologist

de la Mare Walter de la Mare (1873–1956) Eng. author

Deland . . . Margaret Wade Deland (1857– 1945) Amer. nov.

Dell . . . . Floyd Dell (1887–1969) Amer. nov.

De Morgan William Frend De Morgan (1839–1917) Eng. nov. and artist

Denman . . Thomas Denman (1779–1854) 1st baron Denman. Eng. judge

J. V. Denney Joseph Villiers Denney (1862– 1935) Amer. educator

Dent . . . Lewis Dent (fl. 1953) Amer. writer

De Quincey Thomas De Quincey (1785– 1859) Eng. author

L. G. Deruisseau pseud. of Anny Latour q.v.

de Tocqueville Alexis de Tocqueville (1805– 1859) French political writer

Deutsch . . Albert Deutsch (1905–1961) Amer. author

Babette Deutsch Babette Deutsch (1895– ) Amer. writer

Deutscher . Isaac Deutscher (1907–1967) Brit. (Pol.-born) writer

Deutschman Paul E. Deutschman (fl. 1955) Amer. foreign correspondent

Devlin . . . Christopher Devlin (1907– 1961) Eng. clergyman

Devoe . . . Alan Taylor Devoe (1909– 1955) Amer. naturalist

De Voto . . Bernard Augustine De Voto (1897–1955) Amer. author

Dewey . . . John Dewey (1859–1952) Amer. philosopher

T. E. Dewey Thomas Edmund Dewey (1902– 1971) Amer. politician

The Dial . . Amer. monthly, 1880–1929

Diamant . . Gertrude Diamant (1901–1969) Amer. author

Dibdin . . . Charles Dibdin (1745–1814) Eng. songwriter

Dick . . . Sir Alexander Dick (1703– 1785) Scot. physician

Everett Dick Everett Dick (1898– ) Amer. educator

Dickens . . Charles (John Huffam) Dickens (1812–1870) Eng. nov.

Dickinson Goldsworthy Lowes Dickinson (1862–1932) Eng. essayist

Emily Dickinson Emily Elizabeth Dickinson (1830–1886) Amer. poet

Dict. of Occupational Titles U.S. Employment Service

Diehl . . . Edith Diehl (1876–1953) Amer. hand bookbinder

Diez de Medina Fernando Diez de Medina (1908– ) Bolivian industrialist

Dilliard . . Irving Dilliard (1904– ) Amer. writer

Dillon . . . J. C. Dillon (fl. 1953) Canad. forest ranger

Dimnet . . Ernest Dimnet (1869–1954) French abbé

Dimond . . Stanley Ellwood Dimond (1905– ) Amer. educator

Dingle . . . Herbert Dingle (1890– ) Eng. educator

Dinkler . . Erich Dinkler (1909– ) Ger. theologian

Dinneen . . Joseph Francis Dinneen (1897– ) Amer. newspaperman

Dinsmore Charles Allen Dinsmore (1860– 1941) Amer. clergyman

DiSalle . . . Michael Vincent DiSalle (1908– ) Amer. politician

Discovery No. 3 Collection of new writings

Diseases of Cattle U.S. Bureau of Animal Industry

Disraeli . . Benjamin Disraeli (1804–1881) 1st earl of Beaconsfield. Brit. statesman

D'Israeli . . Isaac D'Israeli (1766–1848) Eng. writer; father of Benjamin Disraeli

Ditmars . . Raymond Lee Ditmars (1876– 1942) Amer. naturalist

Dixon . . . William Macneile Dixon (1866– 1946) Eng. educator

Dobie . . . James Frank Dobie (1888– 1964) Amer. folklorist

Dobson . . (Henry) Austin Dobson (1840– 1921) Eng. poet

Dobzhansky Theodosius Dobzhansky (1900– ) Amer. (Russ.-born) zoologist

Dock Leaves Brit. review incorporated 1950 in The Anglo-Welsh Review (Pembroke Dock, Wales)

Dodd . . . Marion C. Dodd (fl. 1947) Amer. editor

Dodge . . . David Dodge (1910– ) Amer. author

Dodson . . Kenneth MacKenzie Dodson (1907– ) Amer. sea captain

Doherty . . Edward Joseph Doherty (1890– ) Amer. editor

Dole . . . Charles Fletcher Dole (1845– 1927) Amer. clergyman

Dollard . . John Dollard (1900– ) Amer. psychologist

Donne . . . John Donne (1573–1631) Eng. poet

Donovan . . Robert John Donovan (1912– ) Amer. journalist

Dorrance . . Anne Dorrance (1873– ) Amer. author

Dos Passos John Roderigo Dos Passos (1896–1970) Amer. writer

Doty . . . Robert Clark Doty (1915– ) Amer. journalist

Douglas . . Lloyd Cassel Douglas (1877– 1951) Amer. nov.

Lewis Douglas Lewis Williams Douglas (1894– ) Amer. businessman

M. S. Douglas Marjory Stoneman Douglas (1890– ) Amer. author

Norman Douglas Norman Douglas (1868–1952) Eng. author

P. H. Douglas Paul Howard Douglas (1892– ) Amer. senator

W. O. Douglas William Orville Douglas (1898– ) Amer. jurist

Dowden . . Edward Dowden (1843–1913) Irish literary critic

Dowdeswell Wilfred Hogarth Dowdeswell (1914– ) Brit. ecologist

Dowson . . Ernest Christopher Dowson (1867–1900) Eng. poet

Doyle . . . Sir Arthur Conan Doyle (1859–1930) Brit. author

Drake . . . Francis Vivian Drake (1894– 1971) Amer. (Eng.-born) editor

Draper . . . William Henry Draper (1894– ) Amer. economist

Dreiser . . . Theodore Dreiser (1871–1945) Amer. nov.

Drew . . . Elizabeth A. Drew (1887–1965) Amer. literary critic

Drinker . . Henry Sandwith Drinker (1890– ) Amer. lawyer

Driscoll . . David Driscoll (fl. 1953) Amer. writer

Drummond Henry Drummond (1851–1897) Scot. writer

| | |
|---|---|
| *William Drummond* | William Drummond (1585–1649) Scot. poet |
| Dryden | John Dryden (1631–1700) Eng. poet |
| *Duffus* | Robert Luther Duffus (1888– ) Amer. author |
| *C. E. Dull* | Charles Elwood Dull (1878–1947) Amer. educator |
| Dulles | Foster Rhea Dulles (1900–1970) Amer. author |
| *du Maurier* | George Louis Palmella Busson du Maurier (1834–1896) Brit. artist and nov. |
| *Duncan-Kemp* | Alice Monkton Duncan-Kemp (fl. 1935) Austral. author |
| Dunglison | Robley Dunglison (1798–1869) Eng. physician |
| *Dunham* | William Huse Dunham (1901– ) Amer. educator |
| *C. C. Dunsmoor* | Clarence Clifford Dunsmoor (1899– ) Amer. educator |
| *Dun's Review* | Amer. monthly |
| *Durant* | William James Durant (1885– ) Amer. educator |
| *Durdin* | Peggy Durdin, *N. Y. Times Mag.* (1955) |
| *Tillman Durdin* | Tillman Durdin, *N. Y. Times* (1954) |
| Durrell | Lawrence George Durrell (1912– ) Brit. writer |
| *Dworkin* | Martin S. Dworkin (fl. 1954) Amer. writer |
| *Eastman* | Max Forrester Eastman (1883–1969) Amer. editor |
| *Easton* | David Easton (1917– ) Amer. educator |
| *Eaton* | Walter Prichard Eaton (1878–1957) Amer. educator |
| *Eccles* | Marriner Stoddard Eccles (1890– ) Amer. economist |
| *Economist* | Brit. weekly |
| *Eddington* | Sir Arthur Stanley Eddington (1882–1944) Eng. astronomer |
| *Edgeworth* | Maria Edgeworth (1767–1849) Brit. nov. |
| *Edinburgh Review* | Scot. journal |
| *Edman* | Irwin Edman (1896–1954) Amer. educator |
| *Edmunds* | Henry M. Edmunds, *Land Reborn* (1953) |
| *Educational Review* | Canad. periodical |
| *Education Digest* | Amer. monthly |
| *Edwards* | John Edwards (1637–1716) Eng. Calvinist |
| *Ehrmann* | Henry Walter Ehrmann (1908– ) Amer. (Ger.-born) educator |
| *Einstein* | Albert Einstein (1879–1955) Amer. (Ger.-born) physicist |
| *Eisenhower* | Dwight David Eisenhower (1890–1969) 34th president of the U.S. |
| *M. Barnard Eldershaw* | *pseud. of* Marjorie Faith Barnard (1897– ) and Flora Sydney Patricia Eldershaw (1897– ) Austral. writers |
| *Eliot* | Charles William Eliot (1834–1926) Amer. educator |
| *George Eliot* | *pseud. of* Mary Ann Evans (1819–1880) Eng. nov. |
| *T. S. Eliot* | Thomas Stearns Eliot (1888–1965) Brit. (Amer.-born) poet and critic |
| *Elisofon* | Eliot Elisofon (1911– ) Amer. photographer |
| *Ellery* | Reginald Spencer Ellery (fl. 1945) Austral. psychiatrist |
| *Ellis* | (Henry) Havelock Ellis (1859–1939) Eng. psychologist |
| *F. H. Ellis* | Frank Hale Ellis (1916– * ) Amer. educator |
| *Ellison* | Ralph Waldo Ellison (1914– ) Amer. author |
| *Jerome Ellison* | Jerome Ellison (1907– ) Amer. editor |
| *Elton* | Sir Charles Abraham Elton (1778–1853) Eng. author |
| *J. F. Embree* | John Fee Embree (1908– ) Amer. social anthropologist |
| *Emerson* | Ralph Waldo Emerson (1803–1882) Amer. essayist |
| *Rupert Emerson* | Rupert Emerson (1899– ) Amer. educator |
| *Emporia Gazette* | 'Emporia (Kansas) daily |
| *Empson* | William Empson (1906– ) Eng. critic |

| | |
|---|---|
| *Emrich* | Duncan Emrich (1908– ) Amer. writer |
| *Encore* | Amer. monthly |
| *Encounter* | Amer. monthly |
| *Encyc. Americana* | *Encyclopedia Americana* |
| *Encyc. Brit.* | *Encyclopaedia Britannica* |
| *Endeavour* | Brit. quarterly |
| *Engel* | Leonard Engel (1916–1964) Amer. journalist |
| *Engle* | Paul Hamilton Engle (1908– ) Amer. poet |
| *T. L. Engle* | Thelburn LaRoy Engle (1901– ) Amer. educator |
| *English Digest* | Brit. monthly |
| *Enright* | Elizabeth Enright (1909–1968) Amer. author and illustrator |
| *Enters* | Angna Enters (1907– ) Amer. dancer |
| *Epoch* | Amer. quarterly |
| *Ericson* | George Ericson (1883– ) Amer. editor |
| *Ernst* | Morris Leopold Ernst (1888– ) Amer. lawyer |
| *Erskine* | John Erskine (1879–1951) Amer. educator |
| *Thomas Erskine* | Thomas Erskine (1788–1870) Scot. biblical scholar |
| *Ertz* | Susan Ertz (fl. 1938) Brit. writer |
| *Ervine* | St. John Greer Ervine (1883–1971) Brit. author |
| *Etherege* | Sir. George Etherege (1635?–1691) Eng. dramatist |
| *Eurich* | Alvin Christian Eurich (1902– ) Amer. educator |
| *Evans* | Sir (B.) Ifor Evans (1899– ) Eng. educator |
| *Bergen Evans* | Bergen Baldwin Evans (1904– ) Amer. educator |
| *Ernestine Evans* | Ernestine Evans (1889–1967) Amer. author |
| *L. B. Evans* | Lawrence Boyd Evans (1870–1928) Amer. lawyer |
| *Rowland Evans* | Rowland Evans (1921– ) Amer. columnist |
| *Evelyn* | John Evelyn (1620–1706) Eng. diarist |
| *Everett* | Edward Everett (1794–1865) Amer. clergyman |
| *Everybody's Mag.* | Amer. periodical |
| *Evett* | Robert Evett (fl. 1953) Amer. editor |
| *Ewer* | William Norman Ewer (1885– ) Brit. writer |
| *Expose of Soviet Espionage* | U.S. Bureau of Investigation |
| *Expositor* | Brit. monthly |
| *E. S. Eyster* | Elvin S. Eyster (1902– ) Amer. educator |
| *Fadiman* | Clifton Fadiman (1904– ) Amer. writer |
| *Fairchild* | David Grandison Fairchild (1869–1954) Amer. botanist |
| *Fairless* | Benjamin Franklin Fairless (1890–1962) Amer. industrialist |
| *Falk* | Werner David Falk (fl. 1953) German-born educator |
| *Farmer and Stock-Breeder* | Brit. weekly |
| *Farmer's Weekly* | Bloemfontein (So. Africa) newspaper |
| *Farrar* | Frederic William Farrar (1831–1903) Eng. clergyman |
| *Farrell* | James Thomas Farrell (1904– ) Amer. nov. |
| *Cliff Farrell* | Cliff Farrell (fl. 1957) Amer. author |
| *Farrelly* | John Farrelly (fl. 1949) Amer. writer |
| *Farrington* | Benjamin Farrington (1891– ) Eng. educator |
| *Fast* | Howard Melvin Fast (1914– ) Amer. author |
| *Fathauer* | George Harry Fathauer (1918– ) Amer. anthropologist |
| *Faulkner* | William Falkner *or* Faulkner (1897–1962) Amer. nov. |
| *H. U. Faulkner* | Harold Underwood Faulkner (1890–1968) Amer. educator |
| *Fay* | Sidney Bradshaw Fay (1876–1967) Amer. historian |
| *Fearing* | Franklin Smith Fearing (1892–1962) Amer. educator |
| *Kenneth Fearing* | Kenneth Fearing (1902–1961) Amer. author |
| *Federal Probation* | U.S. Govt. quarterly journal |

| | |
|---|---|
| *Feis* | Herbert Feis (1893–1972) Amer. historian |
| *Feld* | Rose Caroline Feld (1895– ) Amer. (Romanian-born) author |
| *Fellows* | Otis Edward Fellows (1908– ) Amer. educator |
| *Ferber* | Edna Ferber (1887–1968) Amer. writer |
| *Ferguson* | John DeLancey Ferguson (1888–1966) Amer. educator |
| *C. W. Ferguson* | Charles Wright Ferguson (1901– ) Amer. editor |
| *Fergusson* | Harvey Fergusson (1890–1971) Amer. writer |
| *Ferrell* | William F. Ferrell (fl. 1947) Amer. clergyman |
| *Ferril* | Thomas Hornsby Ferril (1896– ) Amer. poet |
| *Feuer* | Lewis Samuel Feuer (1912– ) Amer. educator |
| *Fforde* | Sir Arthur (Frederic Brownlow) Fforde (1900– ) Brit. educator |
| *Fiedler* | Leslie Aaron Fiedler (1917– ) Amer. educator |
| *Field* | Eugene Field (1850–1895) Amer. poet |
| *Field-Fisher* | Thomas Gilbert Field-Fisher, *Animals and the Law* (1950) |
| *Fielding* | Henry Fielding (1707–1754) Eng. nov. |
| *Temple Fielding* | Temple Hornaday Fielding (1913– ) Amer. author |
| *Fienburgh* | Wilfred Fienburgh (1919–1958) Eng. statesman |
| *Financial Times* | London daily |
| *Richard Findlater* | *pseud. of* Kenneth Bruce Findlater Bain (1921– ) Eng. writer |
| *Fine* | Benjamin Fine (1905– ) Amer. educator |
| *Finlay* | Sir Campbell Kirkman Finlay (1875–1937) Eng. jurist |
| *Firth* | Raymond William Firth (1901– ) Eng. anthropologist |
| *Fischer* | Louis Fischer (1896–1970) Amer. journalist |
| *Fish* | Carl Russell Fish (1876–1932) Amer. historian |
| *Fishbein* | Morris Fishbein (1889– ) Amer. physician |
| *Fisher* | Vardis Fisher (1895–1968) Amer. author |
| *C. B. Fisher* | Charles Boddy Fisher (1908– ) Canad. engineer |
| *D. M. Fisher* | Douglas Mason Fisher (1919– ) Canad. librarian |
| *W. B. Fisher* | William Bayne Fisher (1916– ) Eng. geographer |
| *W. J. Fisher* | William J. Fisher (1919– ) Amer. educator |
| *Fishwick* | Marshall William Fishwick (1923– ) Amer. historian |
| *Fisk* | McKee Fisk (1900– ) Amer. educator |
| *Fiske* | John Fiske (1842–1901) Amer. historian |
| *Mary Fitt* | *pseud. of* Kathleen Freeman (1897–1959) Brit. educator |
| *Fitts* | Dudley Fitts (1903–1968) Amer. educator |
| *Barbara Fitts* | Barbara Fitts (fl. 1955) Amer. research assistant; wife of W.T. |
| *W. T. Fitts* | William Thomas Fitts (1915– ) Amer. surgeon |
| *Fitzell* | Lincoln Fitzell (1903–1958) Amer. author |
| *FitzGerald* | Edward FitzGerald (1809–1883) Eng. poet |
| *C. P. Fitzgerald* | Charles Patrick Fitzgerald (1902– ) Austral. educator |
| *F. S. Fitzgerald* | Francis Scott Fitzgerald (1896–1940) Amer. writer |
| *S. M. Fitzgerald* | S. M. Fitzgerald (fl. 1953) Amer. writer |
| *Fitzpatrick* | John Clement Fitzpatrick (1876–1940) Amer. historian |
| *Kathleen Fitzpatrick* | Kathleen Elizabeth Fitzpatrick (1905– ) Austral. educator |
| *Fitzsimmons* | Tom Fitzsimmons (fl. 1953) Amer. journalist |
| *Fixx* | James F. Fixx (1932– ) Amer. editor |
| *Flanner* | Janet Flanner (1892– ) Amer. writer; pen name Genêt |
| *Flecker* | (Herman) James Elroy Flecker (1884–1915) Eng. poet |

*Fleming* . . Denna Frank Fleming (1893– ) Amer. educator

*Fletcher* . . John Fletcher (1579–1625) Eng. dramatist

*Joseph Fletcher* Joseph Fletcher (1905– ) Amer. educator

*S. E. Fletcher* Sydney E. Fletcher (d. 1953) Amer. author

*Flew* . . . Anthony Garrard Newton Flew (1923– ) Eng. philosopher

*Flint* . . . . Austin Flint (1812–1886) Amer. physician

*Flood* . . . Charles Bracelen Flood (1929– ) Amer. author

*Fogg.* . . . Rushworth Fogg, *The Irish Digest* (1953)

*Foley.* . . . Arthur Lee Foley (1867–1945) Amer. physicist

*Follett* . . . Wilson Follett (1887–1963) Amer. editor

*Foote* . . . Samuel Foote (1720–1777) Eng. dramatist

*Forbes* . . . Amer. periodical

*Alexander Forbes* Alexander Forbes (1882–1965) Amer. physiologist

*Forcey* . . . Charles Budd Forcey (1925– ) Amer. educator

*Ford.* . . . John Ford (1586–1639) Eng. dramatist

*Corey Ford* Corey Ford (1902–1969) Amer. humorist

*F. M. Ford* Ford Madox Ford (1873–1939) Eng. author

*James Ford* James Ford (1884–1944) Amer. sociologist

*Simeon Ford* Simeon Ford (1855–1933) Amer. hotelkeeper

*W. C. Ford* Worthington Chauncey Ford (1858–1941) Amer. statistician

*Forde* . . . Cyril Daryll Forde (1902– ) Eng. educator

*Ford Times* Ford Motor Co.

*Fordyce* . . James Fordyce (1720–1796) Scot. clergyman

*Foreign Affairs* Amer. quarterly

*Foreman* . . Grant Foreman (1869–1953) Amer. author

*Forester* . . Cecil Scott Forester (1899–1966) Eng. nov.

*Forrest.* . . Thomas Forrest (1729?–?1802) Eng. navigator

*Forster* . . . Edward Morgan Forster (1879–1970) Eng. nov.

*Peter Forster* Peter Forster (1926– ) Eng. writer

*Fortnight* . . Los Angeles periodical

*Fortune* . . . Amer. monthly

*Forum* . . . Amer. periodical merged into *Forum and Century* 1930, into *Current History and Forum* 1940

*Fosbroke* . . Hughell Edgar Woodall Fosbroke (1875–1957) Amer. (Eng.-born) theologian

*Foulkes.* . . Siegmund Heinz Foulkes, *Horizon* (1946)

*Fowler* . . . Harold S. Fowler, *Wall Street Journal* (1954)

*Guy Fowler* Guy Fowler (1893–1966) Amer. author

*W. M. Fowler* Willis Marion Fowler (1900– ) Amer. physician

*Fowlie* . . . Wallace Fowlie (1908– ) Amer. educator

*Fox* . . . . Sir Lionel Wray Fox (1895–1961) Eng. penologist

*Fox-Davies* Arthur Charles Fox-Davies (1871–1928) Eng. barrister and heraldist

*Frank* . . . Waldo David Frank (1889– ) Amer. author

*Joseph Frank* Joseph Frank (1916– ) Amer. educator

*Frankel* . . . Charles Frankel (1917– ) Amer. educator

*Frankenstein* Alfred Victor Frankenstein (1906– ) Amer. editor

*Frankfurter* Felix Frankfurter (1882–1965) Amer. jurist

*Franklin* . . Benjamin Franklin (1706–1790) Amer. philosopher and statesman

*Miles Franklin* Stella Maria Sarah Miles Franklin (1879–1954) Austral. writer

*Fraser* . . . George Sutherland Fraser (1915– ) Eng. author

*Allan Fraser* Allan Fraser (1900– ) Scot. animal husbandman

*P. M. Fraser* Peter MacGregor Fraser (1891– ) Amer. life insurance executive

*Fraser's Mag.* Brit. periodical

*Frazee* . . . Steve Frazee (1909– ) Amer. writer

*Frazer* . . . Sir James George Frazer (1854–1941) Scot. anthropologist

*Frederiksen* Norman Oliver Frederiksen (1909– ) Amer. psychologist

*Freeman* . . Edward Augustus Freeman (1823–1892) Eng. historian

*D. S. Freeman* Douglas Southall Freeman (1886–1953) Amer. historian

*M. E. Freeman* Mary Eleanor Freeman née Wilkins (1852–1930) Amer. writer

*French* . . . Thomas Ewing French (1871–1944) Amer. educator

*R. M. French* Reginald Michael French (1883–1961) Eng. clergyman

*Friedlander* Paul J. C. Friedlander (fl. 1953) Amer. writer

*Friendly* . . Alfred Friendly (1911– ) Amer. editor

*Frohman* . . Charles Frohman (1860–1915) Amer. theater manager

*Frost.* . . . Robert Frost (1874–1963) Amer. poet

*Froude* . . . James Anthony Froude (1818–1894) Eng. historian

*Frugé* . . . August Frugé (1909– ) Amer. publisher

*Fry* . . . . Roger Eliot Fry (1866–1934) Eng. painter

*Christopher Fry* Christopher Fry (1907– ) Eng. dramatist

*Frye* . . . . William R. Frye (1918– ) Amer. journalist

*Fuess* . . . Claude Moore Fuess (1885–1963) Amer. educator

*Fuller d. 1661* Thomas Fuller (1608–1661) Eng. clergyman

*Fuller d. 1734* Thomas Fuller (1654–1734) Eng. physician

*Edmund Fuller* Edmund Fuller (1914– ) Amer. author

*Helen Fuller* Helen Fuller (1914?–1972) Amer. editor

*Fulton* . . . John Farquhar Fulton (1899–1960) Amer. physiologist

*Funk.* . . . Arthur Layton Funk (1914– ) Amer. educator

*Furnas* . . . Clifford Cook Furnas (1900–1969) Amer. chemist

*J. C. Furnas* Joseph Chamberlain Furnas (1905– ) Amer. writer

*Furphy* . . . Joseph Furphy (1843–1912) Austral. author

*Fussell* . . . George Edwin Fussell (1889– ) Eng. historian

*Gabriel.* . . Gilbert Wolf Gabriel (1890–1952) Amer. author

*Gaines* . . . Francis Pendleton Gaines (1892–1963) Amer. educator

*Gaither.* . . Frances Ormond Jones Gaither (1889–1955) Amer. author

*Gaitskell* . . Hugh Todd Naylor Gaitskell (1906–1963) Brit. socialist leader

*Galantière* Lewis Galantière (1893– ) Amer. writer

*Galbraith* . . John Kenneth Galbraith (1908– ) Amer. (Canad.-born) economist

*Gallagher.* . Buell Gordon Gallagher (1904– ) Amer. educator

*Gallant.* . . Mavis Gallant (1922– ) Canad. author

*Galsworthy* John Galsworthy (1867–1933) Eng. author

*Galt* . . . . John Galt (1779–1839) Scot. nov.

*Gardner* . . Erle Stanley Gardner (1889–1970) Amer. writer

*Charles Gardner* Charles Gardner (1912– ) Brit. pilot and journalist

*G. E. Gardner* George Edward Gardner (1904– ) Amer. psychiatrist

*Martin Gardner* Martin Gardner (1914– ) Amer. author

*Garland* . . Hamlin Garland (1860–1940) Amer. nov.

*Garnett.* . . Richard Garnett (1835–1906) Eng. editor

*A. C. Garnett* Arthur Campbell Garnett (1894– ) Austral.-born educator

*David Garnett* David Garnett (1892– ) Eng. author

*Garrigue* . . Jean Garrigue (1914–1972) Amer. poet

*Garrison* . . William Lloyd Garrison (1805–1879) Amer. abolitionist

*F. H. Garrison* Fielding Hudson Garrison (1870–1935) Amer. librarian

*Garside.* . . Edward Ballard Garside (1907– ) Amer. author

*Garvin* . . . Lucius Garvin (1908– ) Amer. educator

*Gaskell.* . . Elizabeth Cleghorn Gaskell (1810–1865) Eng. nov.

*Gatzke* . . . Hans Wilhelm Gatzke (1915– ) Amer. (Ger.-born) educator

*Gauss* . . . Christian Gauss (1878–1951) Amer. educator

*Gay* . . . . John Gay (1685–1732) Eng. author

*Geddes* . . . Arthur Geddes (1895– Brit. geographer

*Gee* . . . . Harold F. Gee (1899– ) Amer. writer

*Gehman* . . Richard Boyd Gehman (1921–1972) Amer. writer

*Geikie* . . . Sir Archibald Geikie (1835–1924) Scot. geologist

*Geismar* . . Maxwell David Geismar (1909– ) Amer. literary critic

*Gelatt* . . . Roland Gelatt (1920– ) Amer. music critic

*Geldard* . . Frank Arthur Geldard (1904– ) Amer. educator

*Genauer* . . Emily Genauer (1911– ) Amer. art critic

*R. C. Gentry* Robert Cecil Gentry (1916– ) Amer. meteorologist

*Genzmer* . . George Harvey Genzmer (1896– ) Amer. educator

*Geographical Jour.* Brit. quarterly

*George.* . . Edwin Black George (1896–1963) Amer. economist

*Gerber* . . . Henry Gerber, *Amer. Mercury* (1947)

*Gerould* . . Katharine Fullerton Gerould (1879–1944) Amer. author

*E. M. Geyer* Ellen Mary Geyer (1879–1953) Amer. educator

*Ghent* . . . William James Ghent (1886–1942) Amer. author

*Gibb.* . . . Hamilton Alexander Rosskeen Gibb (1895–1971) Eng. orientalist

*Gibbon* . . . Edward Gibbon (1737–1794) Eng. historian

*Charles Gibbon* Charles Gibbon (1843–1890) Brit. (Scot.-born) author

*Gibbons* . . Stella Dorothea Gibbons (1902– ) Eng. writer

*Gibbs* . . . Wolcott Gibbs (1902–1958) Amer. writer

*Gibson* . . . Wilfrid Wilson Gibson (1878–1962) Eng. poet

*Gideonse* . . Harry David Gideonse (1901– ) Amer. educator

*Giese.* . . . Arthur Charles Giese (1904– ) Amer. educator

*Gifford* . . . Humphrey Gifford (fl. 1580) Eng. poet

*Gilbert* . . . Sir William Schwenk Gilbert (1836–1911) Eng. librettist and poet

*G. R. Gilbert* Gavin Robert Gilbert (1917– ) N. Z. writer

*Joseph Gilbert* Joseph Gilbert (1779–1852) Eng. clergyman

*Gill* . . . . Brendan Gill (1914– ) Amer. writer

*Susan Gillespie* pseud. of Edith Constance (Bradshaw) Turton-Jones (1906– ) Brit. author

*Gillett* . . . Eric Walkey Gillett (1893– ) Amer. educator

*Gillis.* . . . James Martin Gillis (1876–1957) Amer. clergyman

*D. H. Gillis* Donald Hugh Gillis (fl. 1953) Canad. educator

*Gilman.* . . LaSelle Gilman (1909– ) Amer. writer

*Gilpin* . . . William Gilpin (1724–1804) Eng. clergyman

*Gilroy* . . . Norman Cardinal Gilroy (1896– ) Austral. cardinal

*Ginder* . . . Richard Ginder (1914– ) Amer. clergyman

*Giniger* . . . Henry Giniger (1922– ) Amer. journalist

*Ginnetti* . . P. Adhelidi Ginnetti, *Jour. of Philosophy* (1954)

*Ginzburg* . . Benjamin Ginzburg (1898– ) Amer. government official )

Gipson . . . Frederick Benjamin Gipson (1908– ) Amer. author

Girard . . . Rene Noel Girard (1923– ) Amer. (Fr.-born) educator

Gladden . . Washington Gladden (1836–1918) Amer. clergyman

Gladstone . William Ewart Gladstone (1809–1898) Brit. statesman

Glanvill . . Joseph Glanvill (1636–1680) Eng. philosopher

Glasgow . . Ellen Anderson Gholson Glasgow (1874–1945) Amer. nov.

Glicksberg Charles Irving Glicksberg (1901– ) Amer. (Polish-born) educator

Gloag . . . John Edwards Gloag (1896– ) Eng. architect

Glossary of Currently-Used Wage Terms U.S. Dept. of Labor

Glover . . . C. Gordon Glover (1908– ) Brit. writer

Godwin . . William Godwin (1756–1836) Eng. philosopher

Gogarty . . Oliver St. John Gogarty (1878–1957) Irish author

Gohdes . . . Clarence Louis Frank Gohdes (1901– ) Amer. educator

Gold . . . Herbert Gold (1924– ) Amer. author

Goldsmith . . Oliver Goldsmith (1728–1774) Brit. author

Goldstein . . Thomas Eugen Goldstein (1913– ) Amer. (Ger.-born) educator

Gómez Sicre José Gómez Sicre (fl. 1954) Cuban sociologist

Goodenough Ward Hunt Goodenough (1919– ) Amer. anthropologist

Goodman . . Kennard Everett Goodman (1899– ) Amer. educator

E. J. Goodman Edward John Goodman (fl. 1887) Eng. author

Walter Goodman Walter Goodman (1927– ) Amer. writer

Gordimer . . Nadine Gordimer (1923– ) So. African author

Gordon . . Milton Myron Gordon (1918– ) Amer. sociologist

A. C. Gordon Armistead Churchill Gordon (1897–1953) Amer. educator

Gore . . . John Francis Gore (1885– ) Eng. journalist

Gorer . . . Geoffrey Edgar Gorer (1905– ) Brit. anthropologist

Gorrell . . . Frank Gorrell (fl. 1954) Amer. writer

Gosse . . . Sir Edmund William Gosse (1849–1928) Eng. poet and critic

Goudge . . . Elizabeth de Beauchamp Goudge (1900– ) Brit. writer

Goudy . . . Frederic William Goudy (1865–1947) Amer. typographer

Gould . . . Jay Gould (1836–1892) Amer. financier

Gowers . . . Sir Ernest Arthur Gowers (1880–1966) Brit. government official

Goyen . . . (Charles) William Goyen (1915– ) Amer. author

Graham . . Frank Porter Graham (1886–1972) Amer. government official

Billy Graham William Franklin Graham (1918– ) Amer. evangelist

Gwethalyn Graham Gwethalyn Graham (1913–1965) Canad. author

Michael Graham (Godfrey) Michael Graham (1898– ) Eng. naturalist

Grahame . . Georgina S. Grahame (fl. 1902) Brit. writer

Grainger . . Thomas Hutcheson Grainger (1913– ) Amer. bacteriologist

Granberg . . Wilbur John Granberg (1906– ) Amer. writer

Grandgent Charles Hall Grandgent (1862–1939) Amer. educator

Granite . . . Harvey Granite (fl. 1947) Amer. writer

Grant . . . Ulysses Simpson Grant (1822–1885) 18th president of the U.S.

Granville . . George Granville or Grenville (1667–1735) Baron Lansdowne. Eng. writer

Grattan . . . Clinton Hartley Grattan (1902– ) Amer. author

Grau . . . Shirley Ann Grau (1929– ) Amer. author

Graves . . . Robert von Ranke Graves (1895– ) Brit. author

Charles Graves Charles Graves (1868–1948) Amer. (Eng.-born) clergyman

Mortimer Graves (Frederick) Mortimer Graves (1893– ) Amer. educator

Gray . . . . Thomas Gray (1716–1771) Eng. poet

G. W. Gray George William Gray (1886–1960) Amer. scientific writer

Henry Gray Henry Gray (1825–1861) Eng. anatomist

James Gray James Gray (1899– ) Amer. writer

J. G. Gray Jesse Glenn Gray (1913– ) Amer. philosopher

Sylvia Gray Sylvia Gray, London Calling (1954)

Green . . . Matthew Green (1696–1737) Eng. poet

J. R. Green John Richard Green (1837–1883) Eng. historian

Paul Green Paul Eliot Green (1894– ) Amer. author

Greene . . . Graham Greene (1904– ) Eng. nov.

J. D. Greene Jerome Davis Greene (1874–1959) Amer. banker

Greenhall . . Arthur M. Greenhall (1911– ) Amer. zoologist

Gregory . . Lady Augusta Gregory (1859?–1932) Irish playwright

Horace Gregory Horace Victor Gregory (1898– ) Amer. poet

Grenfell . . Russell Grenfell (1892–1954) Eng. naval officer

Gressman . . Eugene Gressman (1917– ) Amer. lawyer

Greville . . . Charles Cavendish Fulke Greville (1794–1865) Eng. diarist

Grey . . . Sir Edward Grey (1862–1933) Eng. statesman

Zane Grey Zane Grey (1875–1939) Amer. nov.

Gridgeman Norman Theodore Gridgeman (1912– ) Eng. statistician

Griffin . . . Harold John Griffin (1912– ) Canad. newspaperman

C. E. Griffin Clare Elmer Griffin (1892– ) Amer. educator

Grigson . . Geoffrey Grigson (1905– ) Brit. author

Griswold . . Alfred Whitney Griswold (1906–1963) Amer. educator

Grosart . . . Alexander Balloch Grosart (1827–1899) Scot. scholar

Gross . . . Leo Gross (1903– ) Amer. (Austrian-born) educator

Grote . . . George Grote (1794–1871) Eng. historian

Groves . . . Harold Martin Groves (1897–1969) Amer. educator

Grove's Dict. of Music Grove's Dictionary of Music and Musicians

Gruber . . . Ruth Gruber (1911– ) Amer. journalist

Gruening . . Ernest Gruening (1887– ) Amer. politician

Guérard . . Albert Léon Guérard (1880–1959) Amer. (Fr.-born) educator

Guest . . . Edgar Albert Guest (1881–1959) Amer. poet

Guild . . . Leo Guild (1911– ) Amer. writer

Gunn . . . Harold Dale Gunn (1918– ) Amer. anthropologist

Gunther . . John Gunther (1901–1970) Amer. writer

Gurko . . . Leo Gurko (1914– ) Amer. (Pol.-born) educator

Gurney . . . Edmund Gurney (1847–1888) Eng. philosopher

Gustafson . Axel Ferdinand Gustafson (1880–1949) Amer. agronomist

Gutheim . . Frederick Albert Gutheim (1908– ) Amer. editor

Guthrie . . . Alfred Bertram Guthrie (1901– ) Amer. nov.

Gwyn . . . Rhys Gwyn, Dock Leaves (1958)

Hacker . . . Andrew Hacker (1929– ) Amer. political scientist

Hackett . . Francis Hackett (1883–1962) Amer. (Irish-born) writer

Hadley . . . Frederick Brown Hadley (1880– ) Amer. veterinarian

Haggard . . Sir Henry Rider Haggard (1856–1925) Eng. nov.

Hahn . . . Emily Hahn (1905– ) Amer author

Hale . . . Sir Matthew Hale (1609–1676) Eng. jurist

E. E. Hale Edward Everett Hale (1822–1909) Amer. clergyman

Nancy Hale Nancy Hale (1908– ) Amer. nov.

Robert Hale Robert Hale (1889– ) Amer. lawyer

Hall . . . James Norman Hall (1887–1951) Amer. nov.

Fitzedward Hall Fitzedward Hall (1825–1901) Amer. philologist

R. A. Hall Robert Anderson Hall (1911– ) Amer. educator

S. C. Hall Samuel Carter Hall (1800–1889) Eng. editor

Hallam . . . Henry Hallam (1777–1859) Eng. historian

Hallowell . . John Hamilton Hallowell (1913– ) Amer. educator

Halsey . . . Ashley Halsey (1908– ) Amer. editor

G. D. Halsey George Dawson Halsey (1889– ) Amer. business administrator

Margaret Halsey Margaret Frances Halsey (1910– ) Amer. author

Hambly . . William Frank Hambly (1908– ) Austral. educator

Hamburger Michael Hamburger (1924– ) Eng. poet

Philip Hamburger Philip Paul Hamburger (1914– ) Amer. writer

Hamerton . . Philip Gilbert Hamerton (1834–1894) Brit. artist

Hamilton . . Sir William Hamilton (1788–1856) Scot. philosopher

Edith Hamilton Edith Hamilton (1867–1963) Amer. classicist

M. A. Hamilton Mary Agnes Hamilton (1883–1966) Brit. writer

W. H. Hamilton Walton Hale Hamilton (1881–1958) Amer. educator

Hamley . . Sir Edward Bruce Hamley (1824–1893) Eng. general

Hammett . . Samuel Dashiell Hammett (1894–1961) Amer. writer

Hammond Henry Hammond (1605–1660) Eng. clergyman

John Hammond John Hammond (1910– ) Amer. executive

Hamrah . . Louise A. Hamrah, Bulletin (1949)

Handler . . M. S. Handler (fl. 1954) Amer. foreign correspondent

Handlin . . Oscar Handlin (1915– ) Amer. educator

Hanscom . . Elizabeth Deering Hanscom (1865–1960) Amer. educator

Hansen . . . Alvin Harvey Hansen (1887– ) Amer. educator

Hanson . . Howard Hanson (1896– ) Amer. composer

Han Suyin pseud. of Elizabeth Chow Comber (1917– ) Chin. author

Hardwick . . Elizabeth Hardwick (1916– ) Amer. nov.

Hardy . . . Thomas Hardy (1840–1928) Eng. author

Gelston Hardy Gelston Hardy, New England Journeys (1955)

Harlow . . . Alvin Fay Harlow (1875–1963) Amer. author

Harmsworth Albert Charles William Harmsworth (1865–1922) Viscount Northcliffe. Eng. (Irish-born) publisher

Harper's Amer. monthly

Harper's Bazaar Amer. monthly

Harradon . . Harry Durward Harradon (1883– ) Amer. librarian

Harrer . . . Heinrich Harrer (1912– ) Austrian geographer

Harrington Richard Harrington (fl. 1952) Canad. photographer

Donal Harrington Donald Harrington (fl. 1954) Amer. clergyman

Harris . . . Sydney Justin Harris (1917– ) Amer. (Eng.-born) journalist

Harrison . . Frederic Harrison (1831–1923) Eng. author

Gordon Harrison Gordon Andrews Harrison (1914– ) Amer. writer

G. R. Harrison George Russell Harrison (1898– ) Amer. physicist

Richard Harrison Richard Harrison (1901– ) Eng. writer

Harsch . . Joseph Close Harsch (1905– ) Amer. journalist

Hart . . . . Henry Hersch Hart (1886– ) Amer. sinologue

C. W. M. Hart     Charles William Merton Hart (1905– ) Austral. anthropologist

J. D. Hart   James David Hart (1911– ) Amer. educator

Harte . . . (Francis) Brett Harte (1836–1902) Amer. short-story writer

Hartford . . (George) Huntington Hartford (1911– ) Amer. financier

Hartford Times    Hartford (Conn.) daily

Hartmann   Frederick Howard Hartmann (1922– ) Amer. educator

Hartwell . . Wayne Hartwell, Sat. Review (1954)

Harvard Law Review   Harvard Univ. periodical

Harvey . . . Sir Henry Paul Harvey (1869–1948) Brit. editor

Haskin . . . Frederic J. Haskin (1872–1944) Amer. journalist

Hass . . . . Victor P. Hass (fl. 1949) Amer. editor

Hastings' . . Dict. of the Bible, ed. James Hastings

Hatch . . . Robert Hatch (fl. 1950) Amer. movie critic

Haughton . . Samuel Haughton (1821–1897) Irish scientist

Haupt . . . Richard J. Haupt, The Spectator (1953)

Hauser . . . Ernest Otto Hauser (1910– ) Amer. (Ger.-born) author

Havighurst   Walter Edwin Havighurst (1901– ) Amer. educator

Christopher Hawkes   (Charles Francis) Christopher Hawkes (1905– ) Brit. archaeologist

Jacquetta Hawkes   Jacquetta Hawkes (1910– ) Brit. archaeologist

Hawkridge   Emma Lois Hawkridge (1889– ) Amer. author

Hawthorne   Nathaniel Hawthorne (1804–1864) Amer. author

Julian Hawthorne   Julian Hawthorne (1846–1934) Amer. author; son of Nathaniel

Hay . . . . Thomas Robson Hay (1888– ) Amer. historian

S. H. Hay   Sara Henderson Hay (1906– ) Amer. poet

Hayes . . . Samuel Perkins Hayes (1910– ) Amer. educator

Hays . . . . Will Harrison Hays (1879–1954) Amer. lawyer

Hayward . . Sir John Hayward (1564?–1627) Eng. historian

Hazlitt . . . William Hazlitt (1778–1830) Eng. essayist

Healey . . . Denis Winston Healey (1917– ) Brit. politician

Heard . . . (George) Alexander Heard (1917– ) Amer. educator

Hearn . . . Lafcadio Hearn (1850–1904) Greek-born writer of Irish-Greek descent

Heaton . . . Peter Heaton (1919– ) Eng. writer

Heber . . . Reginald Heber (1783–1826) Eng. prelate

Hecht . . . Ben Hecht (1894–1964) Amer. writer

Hedges . . . Joseph Edward Hedges (1904–1966) Amer. economist

Hedley . . . George Percy Hedley (1899– ) Amer. (Chin.-born) educator

Heggen . . . Thomas Orle Heggen (1919–1949) Amer. author

Heiden . . . Noland Rall Heiden (1919– ) Amer. geographer

Heinold . . . George Heinold (1913– ) Amer. writer

Heiser . . . Victor George Heiser (1873–1972) Amer. physician

Heitner . . . Joseph Heitner, Automotive Mechanics (1953)

Heller . . . Judith Bernays Heller (1893– ) Amer. writer

Hellman . . Lillian Hellman (1905– ) Amer. playwright

E. C. Helmreich   Ernst Christian Helmreich (1902– ) Amer. educator

Helps . . . Sir Arthur Helps (1813–1875) Eng. historian

Helsel . . . Paul R. Helsel (1888–1961) Amer. educator

James Helvick   pseud. of Claud Cockburn (1904– ) Brit. writer

Hemingway   Ernest Hemingway (1899–1961) Amer. writer

Hendel . . . Charles William Hendel (1890– ) Amer. educator

Henderson   Thomas Greenshields Henderson (1906–1969) Canad. educator

L. J. Henderson   Lawrence Joseph Henderson (1878–1942) Amer. biochemist

Hendrick . . Burton Jesse Hendrick (1871–1949) Amer. biographer

Kimmis Hendrick   Kimmis Hendrick (1910– ) Amer. editor

Henley . . . William Ernest Henley (1849–1903) Eng. author

Henning . . Rachel Biddulph Henning (1826–1914) Austral. writer

Henri . . . Florette Henri (fl. 1950) Amer. nov.

Henry . . . Patrick Henry (1736–1799) Amer. statesman

O. Henry . . pseud. of William Sydney Porter (1862–1910) Amer. short-story writer

Hentoff . . . Nathan Irving Hentoff (1925– ) Amer. editor

Herbert . . . George Herbert (1593–1633) Eng. poet

Hergesheimer   Joseph Hergesheimer (1880–1954) Amer. nov.

Herrick . . . Robert Herrick (1591–1674) Eng. poet

Herron . . . Edward Albert Herron (1912– ) Amer. writer

Herschell . . Farrar Herschell (1837–1899) 1st baron. Eng. jurist

Hersey . . . John Hersey (1914– ) Amer. nov.

Herskovits . Melville Jean Herskovits (1895–1963) Amer. anthropologist

Hervey . . . Harry Clay Hervey (1900–1951) Amer. explorer

Herzberg . . Max John Herzberg (1886–1958) Amer. educator

Hewes . . . Henry Hewes (1917– ) Amer. drama critic

Hewitt . . . James Hewitt (1928– ) Irish author

Hewlett . . . Maurice Henry Hewlett (1861–1923) Eng. nov.

Heywood . . Thomas Heywood (1574?–1641) Eng. dramatist

Hichens . . Robert Smythe Hichens (1864–1950) Eng. nov.

Hicks . . . Granville Hicks (1901– ) Amer. author

J. D. Hicks   John Donald Hicks (1890– ) Amer. educator

Higginson . Thomas Wentworth Storrow Higginson (1823–1911) Amer. clergyman

Highet . . . Gilbert Arthur Highet (1906– ) Amer. (Scot.-born) educator

High School Biology   Amer. Institute of Biological Sciences

Hildreth . . Gertrude Howell Hildreth (1898– ) Amer. educator

Hill . . . . Aaron Hill (1635–1750) Eng. dramatist

A. A. Hill . . Archibald Anderson Hill (1902– ) Amer. educator

Hillary . . . Sir Edmund Percival Hillary (1919– ) N.Z. alpinist

Hillyer . . . Robert Silliman Hillyer (1895–1961) Amer. poet

Hilton . . . James Hilton (1900–1954) Eng. nov.

Himstead . . Ralph Ebner Himstead (1893–1955) Amer. educator

Hindemith   Paul Hindemith (1895–1963) Amer. (Ger.-born) composer

Hirsch . . . Felix Edward Hirsch (1902– ) Amer. (Ger.-born) librarian

Hitchcock . . Charles Baker Hitchcock (1906–1969) Amer. geographer

Hobbes . . . Thomas Hobbes (1588–1679) Eng. philosopher

Hobby . . . Oveta Culp Hobby (1905– ) Amer. newspaper publisher

Hobson . . . John Atkinson Hobson (1858–1940) Eng. economist

Hocking . . Richard Boyle O'Reilly Hocking (1906– ) Amer. philosopher

R. E. Hodgson   Ralph Edward Hodgson (1906– ) Amer. dairy husbandman

Hoff . . . . Charles Worthington Hoff (1898–1965) Amer. banker

Hoffman . . Malvina Hoffman (1887–1966) Amer. sculptor

Hofstadter . Albert Hofstadter (1910– ) Amer. educator

Richard Hofstadter   Richard Hofstadter (1916–1970) Amer. educator

S. H. Hofstadter   Samuel H. Hofstadter (1894–1970) Amer. (Austrian-born) jurist

Hogarth . . William Hogarth (1697–1764) Eng. painter

Hogben . . . Lancelot Hogben (1895– ) Eng. scientist

Hogg . . . . Quintin McGarel Hogg formerly Lord Hailsham (1907– ) Eng. statesman

Holbrook . . Stewart Hall Holbrook (1893–1964) Amer. author

Holcombe . . Arthur Norman Holcombe (1884– ) Amer. political scientist

Holland . . Josiah Gilbert Holland (1819–1881) Amer. author

Holley . . . Donald L. Holley (fl. 1947) Amer. educator

Hollywood Reporter   Los Angeles daily

Holman . . Emile Frederic Holman (1890– ) Amer. surgeon

Holmer . . Paul LeRoy Holmer (1916– ) Amer. educator

Holmes . . Oliver Wendell Holmes (1809–1894) Amer. author

H. H. Holmes   pseud. of William Anthony Parker White (1911– ) Amer. writer

Justice Holmes   Oliver Wendell Holmes (1841–1935) associate justice, U.S. Supreme Court

Holt . . . . Lucius Hudson Holt (1881–1953) Amer. author

Emily Holt   Emily Holt, The Complete Housekeeper (1903)

Hood . . . . Thomas Hood (1799–1845) Eng. poet

Hook . . . . Theodore Edward Hook (1788–1841) Eng. nov.

Sidney Hook   Sidney Hook (1902– ) Amer. philosopher

Hooker . . . Richard Hooker (1554?–1600) Eng. theologian

Edward Hooker   Edward Hooker (fl. 1683) Eng. editor

Hooper . . . John Hooper (d. 1555) Eng. prelate

Hoover . . . Herbert Clark Hoover (1874–1964) 31st president of the U.S.

Hope . . . . Clifford Ragsdale Hope (1893– ) Amer. businessman

Horizon . . Brit. quarterly

Horner . . . Durbin Lee Horner (1910– ) Amer. editor

Horney . . . Karen (Danielsen) Horney (1885–1952) Amer. (Ger.-born) psychoanalyst

Hot-Metal Magic   Union Carbide and Carbon Corp.

Household   Geoffrey Edward West Household (1900– ) Eng. nov.

Housman . . Alfred Edward Housman (1859–1936) Eng. poet

Houston . . Clifford Granville Houston (1903– ) Amer. psychologist

Houston Post   Houston (Texas) daily

Howard . . Walter Lafayette Howard (1872–1949) Amer. horticulturist

Howe . . . . Irving Howe (1920– ) Amer. educator

Helen Howe   Helen Huntington Howe (1905– ) Amer. author

Howells . . William Dean Howells (1837–1920) Amer. author

W. W. Howells   William White Howells (1908– ) Amer. anthropologist

Hubbell . . . Albert Hubbell (1908– ) Amer. writer

Hubbs . . . Carl Leavitt Hubbs (1894– ) Amer. zoologist

Hudson . . . William Henry Hudson (1841–1922) Brit. naturalist

G. F. Hudson   Geoffrey Francis Hudson (1903– ) Eng. author

Hudson Review   Amer. quarterly

Hughes . . . Thomas Hughes (1822–1896) Eng. author

D. P. Hughes   Dorothea Price Hughes (1904– ) Brit. author

| | | | | | |
|---|---|---|---|---|---|
| *Richard Hughes* | Richard Arthur Warren Hughes (1900– ) Eng. writer | *Jack* | Theodore Henley Jack (1881–1964) Amer. educator | *Daniel Jones* | Daniel Jones (1881–1967) Eng. phonetician |
| *Richard Hull* | *pseud. of* Richard Henry Sampson (1896– ) Eng. author | *Jackson* | Helen Maria Hunt Jackson (1830–1885) Amer. nov. | *Gwyn Jones* | Gwyn Jones (1907– ) Eng. educator |
| *Hume* | David Hume (1711–1776) Scot. philosopher | *Charles Jackson* | Charles Reginald Jackson (1903–1968) Amer. author | *H. M. Jones* | Howard Mumford Jones (1892– ) Amer. educator |
| *Paul Hume* | Paul Chandler Hume (1915– ) Amer. music critic | *Holbrook Jackson* | Holbrook Jackson (1874–1948) Eng. editor | *James Jones* | James Jones (1921– ) Amer. author |
| *Hummel* | Arthur William Hummel (1884– ) Amer. educator | *R. E. Jackson* | Reid Ethelbert Jackson (1908– ) Amer. educator | *R. M. Jones* | Rufus Matthew Jones (1863–1948) Amer. educator |
| *Humphrey* | Hubert Horatio Humphrey (1911– ) U.S. vice-president (1965–1969) | *R. H. Jackson* | Robert Houghwout Jackson (1892–1954) Amer. jurist | *William Jones* | Sir William Jones (1746–1794) Eng. orientalist |
| *Hugh Humphrey* | Hugh Humphrey, *Car Life* (1954) | *Shirley Jackson* | Shirley Jackson (1919–1965) Amer. writer | *Ben Jonson* | Benjamin Jonson (1573?–1637) Eng. author |
| *Robert Humphrey* | Robert Clay Humphrey (1919– ) Amer. educator | *Jacobs* | Robert Durene Jacobs (1918– ) Amer. educator | *Jordan* | Thomas Jordan (1612?–1685) Eng. poet |
| *Humphreys* | (Travers) Christmas Humphreys (1901– ) Brit. lawyer | *JAMA* | *The Journal of the American Medical Association* | *H. D. Jordan* | Henry Donaldson Jordan (1897– ) Amer. educator |
| *Hunt* | (James Henry) Leigh Hunt (1784–1859) Eng. writer | *James* | William James (1842–1910) Amer. philosopher | *Joseph* | Richard Joseph (1910– ) Amer. writer |
| *J. M. Hunt* | Joseph McVicker Hunt (1906– ) Amer. psychologist | *C. L. R. James* | Cyril Lionel Robert James (1901– ) West Indian author | *Josephson* | Matthew Josephson (1899– ) Amer. author |
| *William Hunt* | William Hunt (1842–1931) Eng. historian | *F. C. James* | Frank Cyril James (1903– ) Brit. educator | *Jour. of Economic Entomology* | Amer. bimonthly |
| *Hunter* | Evan Hunter (1926– ) Amer. author | *G. P. R. James* | George Payne Rainsford James (1799–1860) Eng. nov. | *Jour. of Geology* | Amer. bimonthly |
| *Huntingford* | George Wynn Brereton Huntingford (1901– ) Eng. anthropologist | *Henry James* | Henry James (1843–1916) Brit. (Amer.-born) writer | *Jour. of Heredity* | Amer. bimonthly |
| *Huntington* | Ellsworth Huntington (1876–1947) Amer. explorer | *P. E. James* | Preston Everett James (1899– ) Amer. geographer | *Jour. of Philosophy* | Amer. periodical |
| *Hurd* | Richard Hurd (1720–1808) Eng. bishop | *Jameson* | Anna Brownell Jameson (1794–1860) Irish author | *Jour. of Religion* | Amer. quarterly |
| *Hurff* | George Brian Hurff (1900– ) Amer. economist | *C. G. Jameson* | Colin G. Jameson (fl. 1954) Amer. writer | *Jowett* | Benjamin Jowett (1817–1893) Eng. scholar |
| *Hurlbut* | Cornelius Searle Hurlbut (1906– ) Amer. mineralogist | *Jarratt* | Vernon Jarratt (fl. 1951) Brit. film editor | *Joyce* | James Joyce (1882–1941) Irish writer |
| *Hussey* | Christopher Edward Clive Hussey (1899–1970) Eng. architectural historian | *Jarrell* | Randall Jarrell (1914–1965) Amer. writer | *Jeremiah Joyce* | Jeremiah Joyce (1764–1816) Eng. clergyman |
| *Dyneley Hussey* | Dyneley Hussey (1893– ) Brit. music critic | *Jeans* | Sir James Hopwood Jeans (1877–1946) Eng. physicist | *Jung* | Carl Gustav Jung (1875–1961) Swiss psychologist |
| *Hutchins* | Robert Maynard Hutchins (1899– ) Amer. educator | *Jefferies* | Richard Jefferies (1848–1887) Eng. naturalist | *Junius* | *Letters of Junius* (176?–1772), reputedly by Philip Francis (1708?–1773) Eng. writer |
| *Hutchinson* | George Evelyn Hutchinson (1903– ) Amer. (Eng.-born) biologist | *Jeffers* | (John) Robinson Jeffers (1887–1962) Amer. poet | *Kaderli* | Elizabeth Land Kaderli (fl. 1954) Amer. writer |
| *Hutton* | (David) Graham Hutton (1904– ) Eng. economist | *Jefferson* | Thomas Jefferson (1743–1826) 3d president of the U.S. | *Kaempffert* | Waldemar Bernhard Kaempffert (1877–1957) Amer. writer |
| *Charles Hutton* | Charles Hutton (1737–1823) Eng. mathematician | *Jeffery* | Arthur Jeffery (1892–1959) Austral.-born educator | *Kahn* | Ely Jacques Kahn (1916– ) Amer. author |
| *Huxley* | Aldous (Leonard) Huxley (1894–1963) Eng. author | *Jeffrey* | Francis Jeffrey (1773–1850) *Lord Jeffrey* Scot. literary critic | *Kalischer* | Peter Kalischer (fl. 1951) Amer. journalist |
| *Julian Huxley* | Sir Julian Sorell Huxley (1887– ) Eng. biologist; brother of Aldous | *Jekyll* | Joseph Jekyll (1752–1837) Eng. politician | *Kallen* | Horace Meyer Kallen (1882– ) Amer. educator |
| *T. H. Huxley* | Thomas Henry Huxley (1825–1895) Eng. biologist; grandfather of preceding | *Jenkins* | Edward Hopkins Jenkins (1850–1931) Amer. chemist | *H. V. Kaltenborn* | Hans von Kaltenborn (1878–1965) Amer. newscaster |
| *Hyman* | Harold Melvin Hyman (1924– ) Amer. educator | *Jennett* | Seán Jennett (1912– ) Brit. author | *Kandel* | Isaac Leon Kandel (1881–1965) Romanian educator |
| *S. E. Hyman* | Stanley Edgar Hyman (1919–1970) Amer. educator | *Jennings* | James Jennings (fl. 1825) Eng. philologist | *Kane* | Harnett Thomas Kane (1910– ) Amer. author |
| *Sidney Hyman* | Sidney Hyman (fl. 1954) Amer. writer | *Jernigan* | Muriel Molland Jernigan (fl. 1954) Eng. author | *Kaplan* | Charles Kaplan (1919– ) Amer. educator |
| *Hynd* | Alan Hynd (1908– ) Amer. writer | *Jerome* | Jerome Klapka Jerome (1859–1927) Eng. author | *Kardiner* | Abram Kardiner (1891– ) Amer. psychiatrist |
| *Idriess* | Ion Llewellyn Idriess (1890– ) Austral. writer | *Jesse* | Fryniwyd Tennyson Jesse (d. 1958) Eng. author | *Karsten* | Rafael Karsten (1879–1956) Finnish anthropologist |
| *Idzerda* | Stanley John Idzerda (1920– ) Amer. educator | *Jessup* | Philip Caryl Jessup (1897– ) Amer. jurist | *Kaufmann* | Felix Kaufmann (1895–1949) Austrian philosopher |
| *Iengar* | H. V. R. Iengar (1902– ) Indian banker | *Jevons* | William Stanley Jevons (1835–1882) Eng. economist | *Kaye-Smith* | Sheila Kaye-Smith (1887–1956) Eng. nov. |
| *Iglesias* | Antonio Iglesias (1903–1953) Amer. (Mex.-born) journalist | *ohn O'London's Weekly* | Brit. publication | *Kazin* | Alfred Kazin (1915– ) Amer. writer |
| *Infantry Jour.* | Amer. monthly | *Johnson* | Samuel Johnson (1709–1784) Eng. lexicographer | *Keats* | John Keats (1795–1821) Eng. poet |
| *Infeld* | Leopold Infeld (1898–1968) Polish physicist | *Allen Johnson* | Allen Johnson (1870–1931) Amer. editor | *Keble* | John Keble (1792–1866) Eng. clergyman |
| *Ingamells* | Rex Ingamells (1913–1955) Austral. poet | *Alvin Johnson* | Alvin Saunders Johnson (1874–1971) Amer. economist | *Keene* | Frances White Keene (1908– ) Amer. writer |
| *Inge* | William Ralph Inge (1860–1954) Eng. clergyman | *Charles Johnson* | Charles William Heaton Johnson (1896– ) Eng. art lecturer | *Keesing* | Nancy Florence Keesing (1923– ) Austral. writer |
| *Ingelow* | Jean Ingelow (1820–1897) Eng. poet | *Edgar Johnson* | Edgar Johnson (1901– ) Amer. educator | *Kefauver* | Estes Kefauver (1903–1963) Amer. politician |
| *Inside Detective* | Amer. monthly | *G. W. Johnson* | Gerald White Johnson (1890– ) Amer. author | *Keightley* | Thomas Keightley (1789–1872) Irish author |
| *Investor's Reader* | Amer. monthly | *J. W. Johnson* | Josephine Winslow Johnson (1910– ) Amer. nov. | *Keith* | Agnes Newton Keith (1901– ) Amer. author |
| *The Irish Digest* | Irish monthly | *L. B. Johnson* | Lyndon Baines Johnson (1908– ) 36th president of the U.S. | *Kelleher* | John Vincent Kelleher (1916– ) Amer. educator |
| *Ironside* | Robin Ironside (1912– ) Eng. painter | *Marguerite Johnson* | Marguerite Marie Johnson (1916– ) Amer. educator | *Kellogg* | Vernon Lyman Kellogg (1867–1937) Amer. zoologist |
| *Irving* | Washington Irving (1783–1859) Amer. essayist | *Pyke Johnson* | Pyke Johnson, Jr. (fl. 1954) Amer. editor | *Kelly* | James Kelly (1912– ) Amer. author |
| *Isaacs* | Harold Robert Isaacs (1910– ) Amer. author | *Wendell Johnson* | Wendell A. L. Johnson (1906–1965) Amer. speech pathologist | *Seamus Kelly* | Seamus Brian Kelly (1912– ) Irish drama critic |
| *Isherwood* | Christopher William Bradshaw Isherwood (1904– ) Amer. (Eng.-born) author | *Jonas* | Carl Stebbins Jonas (1913– ) Amer. nov. | *Kelman* | Norman Joseph Kelman (1914– ) Amer. psychiatrist |
| | | *Jones* | Chester Lloyd Jones (1881–1941) Amer. educator | *Ken* | Thomas Ken *or* Kenn (1637–1711) Eng. prelate |
| | | | | *Kennan* | George Frost Kennan (1904– ) Amer. historian |
| | | | | *Kennedy* | John Fitzgerald Kennedy (1917–1963) 35th president of the U.S. |

*A. J. Kennedy* Albert Joseph Kennedy (1879– ) Amer. settlement worker

*R. W. Kennedy* Robert Woods Kennedy (1911– ) Amer. architect

*Kent* . . . . Patrick Kent, *The Irish Digest* (1952)

*Kenyon Review* Amer. quarterly

*Kerouac* . . Jack Kerouac (1922–1969) Amer. author

*Kersh* . . . Cyril Kersh, *The Irish Digest* (1953)

*Gerald Kersh* Gerald Kersh (1911–1968) Amer. (Eng.-born) journalist

*Kerwin* . . Jerome G. Kerwin (1896– ) Amer. political scientist

*Kettering* . Charles Franklin Kettering (1876–1958) Amer. engineer

*Key* . . . . Francis Scott Key (1779–1843) Amer. lawyer

*Kiene* . . Hugh Edward Kiene (1902– ) Amer. psychiatrist

*Kilby* . . . Clyde Samuel Kilby (1902– ) Amer. educator

*Killackey* . Edward R. Killackey (1931– ) Amer. missionary priest

*Kimble* . . . David Kimble (1921– ) Brit. educator

*King* . . . . Clarence King (1842–1901) Amer. geologist

*S. S. King* . Seth S. King, *N.Y. Times* (1954)

*W. T. C. King* Wilfred Thomas Cousins King (1906– ) Eng. economist

*Kingdon-Ward* Frank Kingdon-Ward (1885–1958) Eng. botanist

*Kinglake* . Alexander William Kinglake (1809–1891) Eng. historian

*Kingsley* . Charles Kingsley (1819–1875) Eng. nov.

*Kingston* . William Henry Giles Kingston (1814–1880) Eng. writer

*Kinkead* . Katharine T. Kinkead, *New Yorker* (1951)

*Kinne* . . Ernest Webber Kinne (1904– ) Amer. educator

*Kinross* . . John Patrick Balfour (1904– ) Lord Kinross Eng. author

*Kinsey* . . . Alfred Charles Kinsey (1894–1956) Amer. zoologist

*Kipling* . . . Rudyard Kipling (1865–1936) Eng. author

*Kirby* . . . Ellwood Kirby, *New England Journeys* (1955)

*Kirk* . . . . Russell Amos Kirk (1918– ) Amer. author

*G. L. Kirk* Grayson Louis Kirk (1903– ) Amer. educator

*Kirwin* . . Harry Wynne Kirwin (1911–1963) Amer. historian

*Kitchell* . . Iva Kitchell (1912– ) Amer. dancer

*Kitson* . . Michael Kitson (fl. 1955) Eng. writer on art

*Kleiner* . . Dick Kleiner (fl. 1966) Amer. newspaperman

*Kleppner* . Otto Kleppner, *Advertising Procedure* (1925)

*Kline* . . . . Morris Kline (1908– ) Amer. educator

*G. L. Kline* George Louis Kline (1921– ) Amer. educator

*Knight* . . . Arthur Knight (fl. 1953) Amer. movie critic

*F. M. Knight* Francis McMaster Knight (1890–1958) Amer. banker

*Knott* . . . H. W. Howard Knott (d. 1930) Amer. educator

*Knox* . . . . Israel Knox (1906– ) Amer. (Russ.-born) educator

*John Knox* John Knox (1505–1572) Scot. reformer

*William Knox* William Knox (1789–1825) Scot. poet

*Kobler* . . John Kobler (1910– ) Amer. writer

*Kodak Abstract* Eastman Kodak monthly

*Kodak Reference Handbook* The Eastman Kodak Co.

*Koestler* . . Arthur Koestler (1905– ) Brit. (Hung.-born) author

*Kogan* . . . Herman Kogan (1914– ) Amer. editor

*Kohler* . . . Dayton Kohler (1907– ) Amer. educator

*Kolodin*. . . Irving Kolodin (1908– ) Amer. music critic

*Koontz* . . . Harold Dayton Koontz (1908– ) Amer. educator

*Krey*. . . . Laura Lettie Krey (1890– ) Amer. nov.

*Krim*. . . . Seymour Krim (1922– ) Amer. writer

*Kristol* . . . Irving Kristol (fl. 1954) Eng. editor

*Krock* . . . Arthur Krock (1886– ) Amer. journalist

*Kroeber* . . Alfred Lewis Kroeber (1876–1960) Amer. anthropologist

*Kronenberger* Louis Kronenberger (1904– ) Amer. drama critic

*Krout* . . . John Allen Krout (1896– ) Amer. educator

*Krutch* . . . Joseph Wood Krutch (1893–1970) Amer. critic

*Kuney* . . . Joseph H. Kuney (fl. 1949) Amer. editor

*Kupferberg* Herbert Kupferberg (1918– ) Amer. journalist

*Kurtz* . . . Paul Winter Kurtz (1925– ) Amer. educator

*Kyne*. . . . Peter Bernard Kyne (1880–1957) Amer. author

*La Barre* . . Weston La Barre (1911– ) Amer. anthropologist

*Harriet La Barre* Harriet La Barre (fl. 1954) Amer. author

*Labor and Nation* Amer. bimonthly

*Lack*. . . . Arthur Lack (1931– ) Amer. journalist

*LaCossitt* . . Henry LaCossitt (1901–1962) Amer. editor

*La Farge* . . Oliver Hazard Perry La Farge (1901–1963) Amer. author

*Christopher La Farge* Christopher La Farge (1897–1956) Amer. poet

*Laird* . . . Charlton Grant Laird (1901– ) Amer. educator

*Lamb* . . . Charles Lamb (1775–1834) Eng. essayist

*The Lamp*. . Standard Oil Company (N.J.)

*Lancaster*. . Bruce Lancaster (1896–1963) Amer. nov.

*Osbert Lancaster* Osbert Lancaster (1908– ) Eng. writer

*Lancet* . . . Brit. weekly

*Landis* . . . Paul H. Landis (1901– ) Amer. sociologist

*Landman* . . David Landman (1917– ) Amer. writer

*Landor* . . . Walter Savage Landor (1775–1864) Eng. author

*Land Reborn* Amer. periodical

*Lang*. . . . Andrew Lang (1844–1912) Scot. author

*Daniel Lang* Daniel Lang (1915– ) Amer. journalist

*John Lang*. . John Lang (fl. 1852–1878) Brit. nov.

*P. H. Lang* Paul Henry Lang (1901– ) Amer. (Hung.-born) musicologist

*Langdon* . . William Russell Langdon (1891– ) Amer. foreign service officer

*W. C. Langdon* William Chauncey Langdon (1871–1947) Amer. author

*Lange* . . . Oscar Richard Lange (1904–1965) Pol. diplomat

*Langer* . . . Susanne (Katherina Knauth) Langer (1895– ) Amer. educator

*W. L. Langer* William Leonard Langer (1896– ) Amer. educator

*Langfeld* . . Herbert Sidney Langfeld (1879–1958) Amer. psychologist

*Langley* . . Adria Locke Langley (fl. 1945) Amer. author

*Eve Langley* Eve Langley (1908– ) N. Z. nov.

*Lanier* . . . Sidney Lanier (1842–1881) Amer. poet

*Lans* . . . . Asher B. Lans (1918– ) Amer. attorney

*Lardner* . . John Abbott Lardner (1912–1960) Amer. writer

*Rex Lardner* Rex Lardner (1881–1941) Amer. journalist

*Ring Lardner* Ringgold Wilmer Lardner (1885–1933) Amer. writer

*Larrabee* . . Harold Atkins Larrabee (1894– ) Amer. educator

*Lasker* . . . Bruno Lasker (1880–1965) Amer. (Ger.-born) sociologist

*Laski* . . . Harold Joseph Laski (1893–1950) Eng. political scientist

*Lasswell* . . Mary Clyde Grayson Lubbock Lasswell (1905– ) Amer. author

*Latham*. . . Earl Ganson Latham (1907– ) Amer. political scientist

*Lathrop* . . George Parsons Lathrop (1851–1898) Amer. author

*Latimer* . . Hugh Latimer (1485?–1555) Eng. Protestant martyr

*Anny Latour* Anny Latour (fl. 1956) French art historian

*Latourette* . Kenneth Scott Latourette (1884–1968) Amer. religious historian

*Eleanor Lattimore* Eleanor Holgate Lattimore (1895–1970) Amer. author; wife of Owen

*Owen Lattimore* Owen Lattimore (1900– ) Amer. orientalist

*Lauber* . . . Patricia Grace Lauber (1924– ) Amer. author

*Gladys Laubin* Gladys Laubin (fl. 1949) Amer. dancer; wife of Reginald

*Reginald Laubin* Reginald Laubin (fl. 1949) Amer. dancer

*Laver* . . . James Laver (1899– ) Eng. writer

*Laverty*. . . Maura Laverty (1907–1966) Irish nov.

*Lawler* . . . John Lawrence Lawler (1916– ) Amer. newspaperman

*Lawrence* . . David Leo Lawrence (1889–1966) Amer. politician

*David Lawrence* David Lawrence (1888– ) Amer. journalist

*D. H. Lawrence* David Herbert Lawrence (1885–1930) Eng. nov.

*E. O. Lawrence* Ernest Orlando Lawrence (1901–1958) Amer. physicist

*Robert Lawrence* Robert Lawrence (1912– ) Amer. conductor

*T. E. Lawrence* Thomas Edward Lawrence (1888–1935) *Lawrence of Arabia* Brit. soldier

*W. H. Lawrence* William Howard Lawrence (1916–1972) Amer. broadcaster

*William Lawrence* William Lawrence (1850–1941) Amer. bishop

*Lawson*. . . Ted W. Lawson (1917– ) Amer. Army Air Force officer

*Law Times* Eng. weekly journal

*Leakey* . . . Louis Seymour Bazett Leakey (1903–1972) Brit. paleontologist

*Lear* . . . . John Lear (1909– ) Amer. writer

*Leary* . . . Lewis Gaston Leary (1906– ) Amer. educator

*Leavis* . . . Frank Raymond Leavis (1895– ) Eng. educator

*Leavitt* . . . Robert Keith Leavitt (1895– ) Amer. author

*Le Beau* . . Walter L. Le Beau (fl. 1954) Amer. priest

*Lebon* . . . John Harold George Lebon (1909– ) Brit. educator

*Lecky* . . . William Edward Hartpole Lecky (1838–1903) Irish historian

*Ledig-Rowohlt* Heinrich Maria Ledig-Rowohlt (fl. 1955) Ger. publisher

*Lee* . . . . Charles Lee (1913– ) Amer. educator

*C. O. Lee*. . Charles Oren Lee (1883– ) Amer. educator

*Sidney Lee* Sir Sidney Lee (1859–1926) Eng. editor

*Leech* . . . Margaret Leech (1893– ) Amer. author

*Leedy* . . . Haldon A. Leedy (1910– ) Amer. research executive

*Le Fanu* . . Joseph Sheridan Le Fanu (1814–1873) Irish nov.

*Lehrer* . . . Thomas Andrew Lehrer (1928– ) Amer. songwriter

*Lehrman* . . Harold Arthur Lehrman (1911– ) Amer. writer

*Leland* . . . Charles Godfrey Leland (1824–1903) Amer. humorist

*Lengyel* . . . Emil Lengyel (1895– ) Amer. (Hung.-born) educator

*Leonard* . . Jonathan Norton Leonard (1903– ) Amer. journalist

*Lepawsky*. . Albert Lepawsky (1908– ) Amer. educator

*Lerner* . . . Max Lerner (1902– ) Amer. (Russ.-born) author

*L'Estrange* — Sir Roger L'Estrange (1616–1704) Eng. journalist

*Le Sueur* . . — Meridel Le Sueur (1900– ) Amer. writer

*Levin*. . . . — Harry (Tuchman) Levin (1912– ) Amer. educator

*Martin Levin* — Martin Levin (fl. 1963) Amer. editor

*Levy* . . . . — Milton Levy (1903– ) Amer. scientist

*Lewes* . . . — George Henry Lewes (1817–1878) Eng. writer

*Lewis* . . . — Roy Lewis (1913– ) Eng. economist

*C. I. Lewis* — Clarence Irving Lewis (1883–1964) Amer. philosopher

*C. S. Lewis* — Clive Staples Lewis (1898–1963) *Clive Hamilton* Eng. writer

*Day Lewis* — Cecil Day Lewis (1904–1972) Eng. author; pen name *Nicholas Blake*

*D. B. Lewis* — Diana Bonner Lewis, *N.Y. Herald Tribune Book Rev.* (1953)

*Flora Lewis* — Flora (Gruson) Lewis (1922– ) Amer. writer

*G. M. Lewis* — George Morris Lewis (1899–1966) Amer. (Canad.-born) physician

*Naomi Lewis* — Naomi Lewis (fl. 1953) Eng. writer

*Norman Lewis* — Norman Lewis (fl. 1955) Brit. author

*Oscar Lewis* — Oscar Lewis (1893– ) Amer. author

*Robert Lewis* — Robert Lewis (1909– ) Amer. theatrical director

*Sinclair Lewis* — Sinclair Lewis (1885–1951) Amer. nov.

*W. A. Lewis* — Sir (William) Arthur Lewis (1915– ) Eng. political economist

*Wyndham Lewis* — Wyndham Lewis (1884–1957) Brit. painter

*Lewisohn* — Ludwig Lewisohn (1883–1955) Amer. (Ger.-born) author

*Library Jour.* — Amer. monthly

*Liddon* . . . — Henry Parry Liddon (1829–1890) Eng. clergyman

*Lie* . . . . — Trygve Halvdan Lie (1896–1968) Norw. statesman; secy.-gen. of U.N.

*Lieb* . . . . — Frederick George Lieb (1888– ) Amer. sportswriter

*Lieberman* — Henry R. Lieberman (1916– ) Amer. newspaperman

*Liebling* . . — Abbott Joseph Liebling (1904–1964) Amer. journalist

*Life* . . . . — Amer. weekly

*Limb*. . . . — Ben Chik Limb (1893– ) Korean diplomat

*Lincoln*. . . — Abraham Lincoln (1809–1865) 16th president of the U.S.

*C. H. Lincoln* — Charles Henry Lincoln (1869– ) Amer. editor

*F. C. Lincoln* — Frederick Charles Lincoln (1892–1960) Amer. biologist

*Freeman Lincoln* — (Joseph) Freeman Lincoln (1900–1962) Amer. journalist

*Lindeman*. . — Eduard Christian Lindeman (1885–1953) Amer. educator

*Lindner*. . . — Robert Mitchell Lindner (1914–1956) Amer. psychologist

*Lindsay*. . . — (Nicholas) Vachel Lindsay (1879–1931) Amer. poet

*Linebarger* — Paul Myron Anthony Linebarger (1913–1966) Amer. educator

*Lingard*. . . — John Lingard (1771–1851) Eng. historian

*Linguaphone Mag.* — The Linguaphone Institute, London

*Link*. . . . — Arthur Stanley Link (1920– ) Amer. educator

*Linklater*. . — Eric Linklater (1899– ) Brit. author

*Linton* . . . — Ralph Linton (1893–1953) Amer. anthropologist

*Lippincott*. . — Isaac Lippincott (1881–1959) Amer. educator

*Lippmann*. . — Walter Lippmann (1889– ) Amer. writer

*Littell* . . . — Robert Littell (1896–1963) Amer. writer

*Littlefield*. . — Henry Wilson Littlefield (1905– ) Amer. educator

*Littleton* . . — Ananias Charles Littleton (1886– ) Amer. accountant

*Liturgical Arts* — Amer. quarterly

*Livingston* — John Joseph Livingston (1906– ) Amer. military engineer

*Livingstone* — David Livingstone (1813–1873) Scot. explorer

*R. W. Livingstone* — Sir Richard Winn Livingstone (1880–1960) Brit. classical scholar

*Richard Llewellyn* — pen name of Richard Dafydd Vivian Llewellyn Lloyd (1907– ) Brit. author

*Locke* . . . — John Locke (1632–1704) Eng. philosopher

*Alain Locke* — Alain Leroy Locke (1886–1954) Amer. educator

*W. J. Locke* — William John Locke (1863–1930) Brit. nov.

*Lockhart* . . — John Gibson Lockhart (1794–1854) Scot. biographer

*Lockridge*. . — Ross Franklin Lockridge (1914–1948) Amer. educator

*Lockyer* . . — Sir Joseph Norman Lockyer (1836–1920) Eng. astronomer

*Lodge* . . . — John Davis Lodge (1903– ) Amer. diplomat

*Loewy* . . . — Raymond Fernand Loewy (1893– ) Amer. (Fr.-born) industrial designer

*London*. . . — Jack London (1876–1916) Amer. writer

*London Calling* — Brit. weekly (BBC)

*Long*. . . . — Augustus White Long (fl. 1939) Amer. author

*Lois Long*. . — Lois Long (1901– ) Amer. writer

*Longfellow* — Henry Wadsworth Longfellow (1807–1882) Amer. poet

*Lord* . . . . — Russell Lord (1895– ) Amer. writer

*Los Angeles Examiner* — Los Angeles daily

*Los Angeles Times* — Los Angeles daily

*Lovelace* . . — Richard Lovelace (1618–1658) Eng. poet

*Loveman* . . — Amy Loveman (1881–1955) Amer. editor

*Lover* . . . — Samuel Lover (1797–1868) Irish nov.

*Lovett* . . . — Robert Morss Lovett (1870–1956) Amer. educator

*Sidney Lovett* — Sidney Augustus Lovett (1890– ) Amer. theologian

*Lowe*. . . . — Robert Lowe (1811–1892) Viscount Sherbrooke. Brit. political leader

*Victor Lowe* — Victor Augustus Lowe (1907– ) Amer. educator

*Lowell* . . . — Amy Lowell (1874–1925) Amer. poet

*J. R. Lowell* — James Russell Lowell (1819–1891) Amer. author

*Robert Lowell* — Robert (Traill Spence) Lowell (1917– ) Amer. poet

*Lowenthal*. . — Marvin Lowenthal (1890–1969) Amer. author

*Lowes* . . . — John Livingston Lowes (1867–1945) Amer. educator

*Lowie* . . . — Robert Harry Lowie (1883–1957) Amer. (Austrian-born) anthropologist

*Lowrie* . . . — Walter Lowrie (1868–1959) Amer. clergyman

*Lowry* . . . — Robert James Lowry (1910– ) Amer. nov.

*E. G. Lowry* — Edward George Lowry (1876–1943) Amer. journalist

*Lubbock* . . — Sir John Lubbock (1834–1913) 1st baron Avebury. Eng. author

*Lubell* . . . — Samuel Lubell (1911– ) Amer. (Pol.-born) writer

*Lucas* . . . — Edward Verrall Lucas (1868–1938) Eng. writer

*Dione Lucas* — Dione Narona Margaris (Wilson) Lucas (1909–1971) Eng. restaurateur

*Samuel Lucas* — Samuel Lucas (1818–1865) Eng. writer

*Ludwig* . . . — Jack Barry Ludwig (1922– ) Canad.-born educator

*Lueders* . . — Edward George Lueders (1923– ) Amer. editor

*Lukens* . . . — Raymond James Lukens (1930– ) Amer. plant pathologist

*Lustgarten* — Edgar Marcus Lustgarten (1907– ) Brit. nov.

*Lydgate* . . — William Anthony Lydgate (1909– ) Amer. editor

*Lyell*. . . . — Sir Charles Lyell (1797–1875) Brit. geologist

*Lynch* . . . — Thomas Toke Lynch (1818–1871) Eng. hymn writer

*Lynd*. . . . — Robert Lynd (1879–1949) Irish journalist

*Lynes* . . . — Thomas C. Lynes (fl. 1948) Amer. research chemist

*Lytton* . . . — Edward George Earle Lytton Bulwer-Lytton (1803–1873) 1st baron Lytton. Eng. author

*Maas* . . . — Anthony J. Maas (1858–1927) Amer. (Ger.-born) priest

*McAllister* — (Samuel) Ward McAllister (1827–1895) Amer. society leader

*MacArthur* — Douglas MacArthur (1880–1964) Amer. general

*Macaulay*. . — Thomas Babington Macaulay (1800–1859) 1st baron Macaulay. Eng. historian

*Rose Macaulay* — Dame Rose Macaulay (1881–1958) Eng. nov.

*McAuliffe*. . — Mike McAuliffe, *The Irish Digest* (1952)

*McCain* . . — Arthur Williamson McCain (1894– ) Amer. banker

*MacCallum* — William George MacCallum (1874–1944) Amer. (Canad.-born) pathologist

*McCarten* . — John McCarten (1916– ) Amer. writer

*M'Carthy* . . — Justin M'Carthy (1830–1912) Irish writer

*Desmond MacCarthy* — Desmond MacCarthy (1878–1952) Eng. journalist

*J. McCarthy* — Rev. J. McCarthy, *The Irish Digest* (1954)

*Mary McCarthy* — Mary Therese McCarthy (1912– ) Amer. author

*McCartney* — Eugene Stock McCartney (1883– ) Amer. educator

*McCloskey* — John Clement McCloskey (1895– ) Amer. educator

*McClung* . . — Paul McClung, *Inside Detective* (1958)

*McClure's Mag.* — Amer. monthly

*MacColl* . . — Mary MacColl (fl. 1936) Amer. educator

*McColvin*. . — Lionel Roy McColvin (1896– ) Eng. librarian

*McComas* . — J. Francis McComas (fl. 1954) Amer. editor

*McConathy et al* — Osbourne William McConathy (1875–1947) Amer. music editor

*McCourt* . . — Edward Alexander McCourt (1907– ) Canad. (Irish-born) educator

*McCrae* . . — Hugh Raymond McCrae (1876– ) Austral. poet

*McCrone* . . — Guy McCrone (1896– ) Scot. nov.

*McCullers* — Carson Smith McCullers (1917–1967) Amer. author

*Macdonald* — George Macdonald (1824–1905) Scot. writer

*Alexander MacDonald* — Alexander MacDonald (1889– ) Amer. writer

*Dwight Macdonald* — Dwight Macdonald (1906– ) Amer. journalist

*McDougall* — William McDougall (1871–1938) Brit. psychologist

*MacFall* . . — Haldane MacFall (1860–1928) Brit. nov.

*McFee* . . . — William McFee (1881–1966) Eng. writer

*McGiffert* . — Arthur Cushman McGiffert (1861–1933) Amer. theologian

*McGranery* — James Patrick McGranery (1895–1962) Amer. jurist

*McHugh* . . — Vincent McHugh (1904– ) Amer. writer

*MacInnes* . — Helen MacInnes (1907– ) Amer. (Scot.-born) author

*MacIver* . . — Robert Morrison MacIver (1882–1970) Scot. sociologist

*Mackay* . . — Charles Mackay (1814–1889) Scot. poet

*McKean* . . — Dayton David McKean (1904– ) Amer. educator

*Mackenzie* — Sir Compton Mackenzie (1883–1972) Eng. nov.

*Henry Mackenzie* — Henry Mackenzie (1745–1831) Scot. nov.

*McKeon* . . — Richard Peter McKeon (1900– ) Amer. educator

*McKinley*. . — William McKinley (1843–1901) 25th president of the U.S.

*Mackintosh*   Sir James Mackintosh (1765–1832) Scot. philosopher

*Maclaren-Ross*   Julian Maclaren-Ross (fl. 1954) Eng. author

*McLean* .   Alan Angus McLean (1925– ) Amer. psychiatrist

*Fitzroy Maclean*   Sir Fitzroy Hew Maclean (1911– ) Brit. politician

*H. N. Maclean*   Hugh Norman Maclean (1919– ) Canad. educator

*Maclean's*   Canad. periodical

*MacLeish* .   Archibald MacLeish (1892– ) Amer. poet

*MacLennan*   Hugh MacLennan (1907– ) Canad. nov.

*Ian Mac-Lennan*   Ian MacLennan (fl. 1958) Scot. journalist

*Macmahon*   Arthur Whittier Macmahon (1890– ) Amer. educator

*Patrick McMahon*   Patrick McMahon (fl. 1953) Amer. editor

*Macmillan*   William Miller Macmillan (1885– ) So. African (Scot.-born) historian

*MacNeice*   Louis MacNeice (1907–1963) Brit. (Irish-born) poet

*McNulty* .   John McNulty (1895–1956) Amer. journalist

*Faith McNulty*   Faith McNulty (1918– ) Amer. writer

*McPherson*   John Hanson Thomas McPherson (1865–1953) Amer. historian

*Macy* . . .   John Albert Macy (1877–1932) Amer. author

*Magill* . . .   Roswell Foster Magill (1895–1963) Amer. lawyer

*Mahan* . . .   Alfred Thayer Mahan (1840–1914) Amer. historian

*Maher* . . .   Nellie Maher (fl. 1953) Irish writer

*Mahler* . . .   Jane Gaston Mahler (1906– ) Amer. educator

*Mailer* . . .   Norman Mailer (1923– ) Amer. author

*Mais* . . . .   Stuart Petre Brodie Mais (1885– ) Eng. writer

*Maitland* . .   Frederic William Maitland (1850–1906) Eng. legal historian

*Majdalany*   Fred Majdalany (1913– ) Eng. author

*Malahoff* .   Alexander Malahoff, *Science* (1966)

*Malamud* .   Bernard Malamud (1914– ) Amer. writer

*Malcolm* .   Donald F. Malcolm (fl. 1955) Amer. writer

*Malik* . . .   Charles Habib Malik (1906– ) Lebanese diplomat

*Malinowski*   Bronislaw Kasper Malinowski (1884–1942) Pol. anthropologist

*Mallock* . .   William Hurrell Mallock (1849–1923) Eng. writer

*Mallon* . . .   James Joseph Mallon (1875–1961) Eng. sociologist

*Malone* . . .   Kemp Malone (1889–1971) Amer. educator

*Dumas Malone*   Dumas Malone (1892– ) Amer. historian

*J. R. Malone*   John R. Malone, *New Printing Methods* (1949)

*Malthus* . .   Thomas Robert Malthus (1766–1834) Eng. economist

*Manchester Examiner*   Brit. daily

*Manchester Guardian*   Brit. newspaper

*Mandel* . . .   Siegfried Mandel (1922– ) Ger.-born educator

*Mandelbaum*   David Goodman Mandelbaum (1911– ) Amer. anthropologist

*Mandeville*   Bernard Mandeville (1670?–1733) Eng. (Du.-born) satirist

*Mann* . . .   Horace Mann (1796–1859) Amer. educator

*Thomas Mann*   Thomas Mann (1875–1955) Amer. (Ger.-born) author

*Mannes* . .   Marya Mannes (1904– ) Amer. writer

*Manning* . .   Henry Edward Manning (1808–1892) Eng. cardinal

*Mannix* . .   Jule Mannix, *Omnibook* (1954)

*Manoukian*   Madeline Manoukian (1921– ) Brit. social worker

*Mansfield* . .   Katherine Mansfield (1888–1923) Brit. writer

*Manship* . .   Paul Manship (1885–1966) Amer. sculptor

*Manual for Courts-Martial*   U.S. Dept. of Defense 1949

*Manual of Prayers*   a manual of prayers for the use of the Catholic laity

*Manual of Seamanship*   Admiralty, London

*Manual of Style*   Univ. of Chicago Press

*Marcuse* . .   Jacques Marcuse (fl. 1964) Belgian-born foreign correspondent

*Margolis* . .   Joseph Zalman Margolis (1924– ) Amer. educator

*Louis Margolis*   Louis Margolis (fl. 1922) Amer. engineer

*Markham* . .   (Charles) Edwin Markham (1852–1940) Amer. poet

*Mark Twain*   *pseud. of* Samuel Langhorne Clemens (1835–1910) Amer. author

*Marlowe* . .   Christopher Marlowe (1564–1593) Eng. dramatist

*Marquand*   John Phillips Marquand (1893–1960) Amer. writer

*Marryat* . .   Frederick Marryat (1792–1848) Eng. naval officer & nov.

*Marsh* . . .   Dame Ngaio Marsh (1899– ) N. Z. writer

*Philip Marsh*   Philip Merrill Marsh (1893– ) Amer. educator

*Marshak* . .   Robert Eugene Marshak (1916– ) Amer. physicist

*Marshall* . .   George Catlett Marshall (1880–1959) Amer. army officer

*Archibald Marshall*   Archibald Marshall (1866–1934) Eng. nov.

*Bruce Marshall*   Bruce Marshall (1899– ) Scot. nov.

*C. B. Marshall*   Charles Burton Marshall (1908– ) Amer. author

*Edison Marshall*   Edison Marshall (1894–1967) Amer. author

*John Marshall*   John Marshall (1755–1835) chief justice, U.S. Supreme Court

*N. B. Marshall*   Norman Bertram Marshall (1915– ) Eng. naturalist

*S. L. A. Marshall*   Samuel Lyman Atwood Marshall (1900– ) Amer. military critic

*Martin* . . .   Sir Theodore Martin (1816–1909) Brit. writer

*Harry Martin*   Harry Martin, *Retailing Daily* (1954)

*J. B. Martin*   John Bartlow Martin (1915– ) Amer. journalist

*John Martin*   John Martin (1893– ) Amer. dance critic

*J. S. Martin*   James Stewart Martin (1911– ) Amer. author

*Pete Martin*   Pete Martin (1901– ) Amer. editor

*Martineau*   Harriet Martineau (1802–1876) Eng. nov.

*ames Martineau*   James Martineau (1805–1900) Eng. theologian; brother of Harriet

*Marvel* . . .   Tom Marvel (1901–1970) Amer. author

*Masani* . . .   Minocheher Rustom Masani (1905– ) Indian diplomat

*Masefield* . .   John Masefield (1878–1967) Eng. poet

*Mason* . . .   Francis Van Wyck Mason (1897– ) Amer. nov.

*S. F. Mason*   Stephen Finney Mason (1923– ) Eng. scientist

*Masson* . . .   David Masson (1822–1907) Scot. author

*Masters* . . .   John Masters (1915– ) Eng. author

*Mather* . . .   Frank Jewett Mather (1868–1953) Amer. educator

*K. F. Mather*   Kirtley Fletcher Mather (1888– ) Amer. geologist

*Matheson* . .   George Matheson (1842–1906) Scot. clergyman

*Mathews* . .   Mitford McLeod Mathews (1891– ) Amer. editor

*Mathewson*   Christopher (Christy) Mathewson (1880–1925) Amer. baseball player

*Matthews* . .   (James) Brander Matthews (1852–1929) Amer. educator

*H. L. Matthews*   Herbert Lionel Matthews (1900– ) Amer. journalist

*Matthiessen*   Francis Otto Matthiessen (1902–1950) Amer. educator

*Mattingly* . .   Garrett Mattingly (1900–1962) Amer. historian

*Maude* . . .   Angus Edmund Upton Maude (1912– ) Eng. economist

*Mauer* . . .   Edgar Frank Mauer (1908– ) Amer. physician

*Maugham* . .   (William) Somerset Maugham (1874–1965) Eng. author

*Maughan* . .   Charles Maughan, *Britain Today* (1953)

*Maule* . . .   Harry Edward Maule (1886–1971) Amer. editor

*Maurer* . . .   David W. Maurer (1906– ) Amer. educator

*Maurice* . .   Sir John Frederick Maurice (1841–1912) Eng. writer

*Maurois* . .   André Maurois (1885–1967) French author

*Maury* . . .   Matthew Fontaine Maury (1806–1873) Amer. scientist

*Maxwell* . .   James A. Maxwell (1912– ) Amer. writer

*May* . . . .   Sir Thomas Erskine May (1815–1886) 1st baron Farnborough. Eng. jurist

*Derwent May*   Derwent May (1930– ) Brit. writer

*Mayer* . . .   Milton Sanford Mayer (1908– ) Amer. educator

*Mazur* . . .   Paul Myer Mazur (1892– ) Amer. investment banker

*Mead* . . .   Margaret Mead (1901– ) Amer. anthropologist

*Hunter Mead*   Hunter Mead (1907–1961) Amer. educator

*Meeker* . .   Oden Meeker (fl. 1954) Amer. author

*Mehdevi* . .   Anne Sinclair Mehdevi (fl. 1954) Amer. author

*Melby* . . .   Ernest Oscar Melby (1891– ) Amer. educator

*Melden* . . .   Abraham Irving Melden (1910– ) Canad. philosopher

*Meltzer* . .   Bernard Nathan Meltzer (1916– ) Amer. sociologist

*Melville* . .   Herman Melville (1819–1891) Amer. nov.

*Mencken* . .   Henry Louis Mencken (1880–1956) Amer. editor

*Mendel* . . .   Arthur Paul Mendel (1927– ) Amer. educator

*Menen* . . .   Aubrey Menen (1912– ) Brit. author

*Menninger*   Karl Augustus Menninger (1893– ) Amer. psychiatrist

*Mercantile Marine Mag.*   Brit. magazine

*Mercer* . . .   Samuel Alfred Brown Mercer (1880– ) Amer. (Eng.-born) Egyptologist

*Meredith* . .   George Meredith (1828–1909) Eng. author

*Mereness* . .   Newton Dennison Mereness (1868– ) Amer. editor

*Merivale* . .   Charles Merivale (1808–1893) Eng. historian

*Meriwether*   Robert Lee Meriwether (1890– ) Amer. educator

*Merrill* . . .   Paul Willard Merrill (1887–1961) Amer. astronomer

*G. P. Merrill*   George Perkins Merrill (1854–1929) Amer. geologist

*Merriman* . .   Roger Bigelow Merriman (1876–1945) Amer. historian

*Messenger*   Donald Messenger (1898– ) Brit. journalist

*Metalious* . .   Grace de Repentigny Metalious (1925–1964) Amer. author

*H. C. Metcalfe*   Harold Clark Metcalfe (1919– ) Amer. educator

*Meyer* . . .   Agnes Elizabeth Meyer (1887–1970) Amer. publisher

*A. G. Meyer*   Alfred George Meyer (1920– ) Amer. (Ger.-born) political scientist

*Mezger* . . .   Fritz Mezger (1893– ) Amer. (Ger.-born) educator

*Miall* . . .   Agnes MacKenzie Miall (1892– ) Eng. author

*Michelson*   Edward J. Michelson (fl. 1954) Amer. reporter

*Michener* . .   James Albert Michener (1907– ) Amer. author

*Middle East Jour.*   Amer. quarterly

*Middleton*   Thomas Middleton (1570?–1627) Eng. dramatist

*Drew Middleton*   Drew Middleton (1913– ) Amer. journalist

*Miers* . . .   Earl Schenck Miers (1910–1972) Amer. editor

**Mikesell** . . Raymond Frech Mikesell (1913– ) Amer. economist

**Miles** . . . Josephine Miles (1911– ) Amer. educator

**Mill** . . . . James Mill (1773–1836) Scot. philosopher

**J. S. Mill** . . John Stuart Mill (1806–1873) Brit. philosopher; son of James

**Millan** . . . Verna Carleton Millan (fl. 1939) Amer. author

**Mill & Factory** Amer. monthly

**Millar** . . . Margaret Ellis Millar (1915– ) Amer. (Canad.-born) author

**Millard** . . . Joseph John Millard (1908– ) Amer. writer

**Millay** . . . Edna St. Vincent Millay (1892–1950) Amer. poet

**Miller** . . . Arthur Miller (1915– ) Amer. playwright

**D. F. Miller** Rev. D. F. Miller, *The Irish Digest* (1953)

**G. A. Miller** George Armitage Miller (1920– ) Amer. educator

**Henry Miller** Henry Miller (1891– ) Amer. writer

**L. M. Miller** Leonard M. Miller (fl. 1942) Amer. educator

**Merle Miller** Merle Miller (1919– ) Amer. author

**P. L. Miller** Philip Lieson Miller (1906– ) Amer. librarian

**Millett** . . . Fred Benjamin Millett (1890– ) Amer. educator

**Mills** . . . Charles Wright Mills (1916–1962) Amer. sociologist

**Millstein** . . Gilbert Millstein (fl. 1955) Amer. writer

**Milman** . . . Henry Hart Milman (1791–1868) Eng. historian

**Milner** . . . Donald Rigby Milner (1923– ) Brit. reporter

**Milton** . . . John Milton (1608–1674) Eng. poet

**Mims** . . . Edwin Mims (1872–1959) Amer. educator

**Miner** . . . Roy Waldo Miner (1875–1955) Amer. curator

**Audax Minor** *pseud.* of George F. T. Ryall (fl. 1955) Amer. sportswriter

**Mitchell** . . Donald Grant Mitchell (1822–1908) Amer. author

**Joseph Mitchell** Joseph Mitchell (1908– ) Amer. author

**Mitford** . . Mary Russell Mitford (1787–1855) Eng. author

**Nancy Mitford** Nancy Mitford (1904– ) Eng. author

**Mizener** . . Arthur Moore Mizener (1907– ) Amer. educator

**Moberly** . . Sir Walter (Hamilton) Moberly (1881– ) Eng. educator

**Modern Industry** Amer. magazine

**Modern Language Notes** Amer. periodical

**Modern Textiles Mag.** Amer. monthly

**Mogey** . . . John McFarland Mogey (1915– ) Irish-born sociologist

**Mohler** . . . John Robbins Mohler (1875–1952) Amer. pathologist

**Moir** . . . Guthrie Moir, *London Calling* (1954)

**Moley** . . . Raymond Moley (1886– ) Amer. journalist

**Monaghan** James (Jay) Monaghan (1891– ) Amer. author

**Monroe** . . Elizabeth Monroe (1905– ) Brit. educator

**Monsanto Mag.** Monsanto Chemical Co.

**Montagu** . . Lady Mary Wortley Montagu (1689–1762) Eng. writer

**Ashley Montagu** (Montague Francis) Ashley Montagu (1905– ) Amer. (Eng.-born) anthropologist

**Montague** . . Charles Edward Montague (1867–1928) Eng. writer

**Montrose** . . James Graham (1612–1650) 1st marquis of Montrose. Scot. soldier

**Moody** . . . William Vaughn Moody (1869–1910) Amer. author

**M. H. Moody** Minnie Hite Moody (1901– ) Amer. author

**Mooney** . . Hughson F. Mooney (fl. 1954) Amer. educator

**Moore** . . . William Levi Moore (1889– ) Amer. educator

**A. B. Moore** Albert Burton Moore (1887–1967) Amer. educator

**Asher Moore** Asher Moore (1919– ) Amer. educator

**George Moore** George Moore (1852–1933) Irish author

**J. B. Moore** John Bassett Moore (1860–1947) Amer. jurist

**John Moore** John Moore (1729–1802) Scot. physician

**Thomas Moore** Thomas Moore (1779–1852) Irish poet

**W. R. Moore** William Robert Moore (1899– ) Amer. writer

**Moorehead** Alan McCrae Moorehead (1910– ) Austral. writer

**Morby** . . . Edwin Seth Morby (1909– ) Amer. educator

**More** . . . Paul Elmer More (1864–1937) Amer. author

**Morehead** . . Albert Morehead (1910–1966) Amer. editor

**Morgan** . . . Forrest Morgan (1852–1924) Amer. librarian

**Morgenthau** Hans Joachim Morgenthau (1904– ) Amer. (Ger.-born) educator

**Morison** . . Samuel Eliot Morison (1887– ) Amer. historian

**Morley** . . . Christopher Darlington Morley (1890–1957) Amer. writer

**Felix Morley** Felix Muskett Morley (1894– ) Amer. educator; brother of Christopher

**John Morley** John Morley (1838–1923) Viscount Morley of Blackburn. Eng. author

**Morning Post** London daily

**Morris** . . . William Morris (1834–1896) Eng. poet and artist

**Charles Morris** Charles William Morris (1901– ) Amer. educator

**Clara Morris** Clara Morris (1848–1925) Amer. (Canad.-born) actress

**Edita Morris** Edita Morris (1902– ) Amer. (Swed.-born) author

**I. V. Morris** Ira Victor Morris (1903– ) Amer. author

**J. A. Morris** Joe Alex Morris (1904– ) Amer. journalist

**R. B. Morris** Richard Brandon Morris (1904– ) Amer. educator

**Morrison** . . Abraham Cressy Morrison (1864–1951) Amer. chemist

**Arthur Morrison** Arthur Morrison (1863–1945) Eng. author

**Morse** . . . Robert Morse (1906– ) Amer. writer

**Wayne Morse** Wayne Lyman Morse (1900– ) Amer. politician

**Morton** . . . Frederic Morton (1924– ) Amer. (Austrian-born) nov.

**Mosely** . . . Philip Edward Mosely (1905–1972) Amer. educator

**Moses** . . . Robert Moses (1888– ) Amer. public official

**Moss** . . . . Claude Beaufort Moss (1888–1964) Eng. prelate

**Howard Moss** Howard Moss (1922– ) Amer. writer

**Motley** . . . John Lothrop Motley (1814–1877) Amer. historian

**The Motor** Brit. weekly

**Mott** . . . . Frank Luther Mott (1886–1964) Amer. journalist

**Mott-Smith** Geoffrey Mott-Smith (1902–1960) Amer. mathematician

**Mowat** . . . Farley McGill Mowat (1921– ) Canad. author

**Mowrer** . . . Edgar Ansel Mowrer (1892– ) Amer. columnist

**Mozley** . . . James Bowling Mozley (1813–1878) Eng. theologian

**Muggeridge** Malcolm Muggeridge (1903– ) Eng. editor

**Muir** . . . . John Muir (1838–1914) Amer. (Scot.-born) naturalist

**Muirhead** . . John Henry Muirhead (1855–1940) Brit. philosopher

**Mullahy** . . . Patrick Mullahy, *New Republic* (1952)

**Muller** . . . Herbert Joseph Muller (1905– ) Amer. educator

**F. M. Müller** Friedrich Max Müller (1823–1900) Brit. philologist

**Mumford** . . Lewis Mumford (1895– ) Amer. writer

**Munro** . . . Sir Leslie (Knox) Munro (1901– ) N. Z. diplomat

**Murchie** . . Guy Murchie (1907– ) Amer. author

**Murchison** Carl Murchison (1887–1961) Amer. psychologist

**Murdock** . . Kenneth Ballard Murdock (1895– ) Amer. educator

**Murphy** . . Arthur Edward Murphy (1901–1962) Amer. educator

**Murray** . . . Sir James Augustus Henry Murray (1837–1915) Brit. lexicographer

**G. W. Murray** George William Murray (1885– ) Eng. geographer

**R. W. Murray** Raymond William Murray (1893– ) Amer. clergyman

**William Murray** William Murray (1926– ) Amer. journalist

**Murry** . . . John Middleton Murry (1889–1957) Eng. author

**Musical America** Amer. monthly

**Muzzey** . . . David Saville Muzzey (1870–1965) Amer. historian

**My Baby Mag.** Amer. monthly

**Myers** . . . Frederic William Henry Myers (1843–1901) Eng. writer

**W. S. Myers** William Starr Myers (1877–1956) Amer. political scientist

**Nagel** . . . Ernest Nagel (1901– ) Amer. (Czech-born) educator

**Namier** . . . Sir Lewis Bernstein Namier (1888–1960) Brit. historian

**Nash** . . . . Thomas Nash (1567–1601) Eng. author

**Nathan** . . . George Jean Nathan (1882–1958) Amer. editor

**The Nation** Amer. weekly

**Nation's Business** Amer. monthly

**Nat'l Fur News** Amer. monthly

**Nat'l Geog. Mag.** Amer. monthly

**Nat'l Jewish Monthly** Amer. periodical

**The Naval Reservist** U.S. Government

**Nazi Conspiracy and Aggression** U.S. Government Printing Office

**Nebel** . . . Frederick Nebel (fl. 1954) Amer. writer

**Neff** . . . . Frederick Clifton Neff (1913– ) Amer. educator

**Neill** . . . Thomas Patrick Neill (1915– ) Amer. educator

**Nelson** . . . Horatio Nelson (1758–1805) Viscount Nelson. Eng. admiral

**J. C. Nelson** James Cecil Nelson (1908– ) Amer. educator

**N. E. Nelson** Norman Edward Nelson (1899– ) Amer. educator

**Nemerov** . . Howard Nemerov (1920– ) Amer. educator

**Nemetz** . . . Anthony Nemetz (1923– ) Amer. educator

**Nethercot** . . Arthur Hobart Nethercot (1895– ) Amer. educator

**Neuberger** Richard Lewis Neuberger (1912–1960) Amer. politician

**Neumann** . . Robert Gerhard Neumann (1916– ) Amer. (Austrian-born) educator

**Nevins** . . . Allan Nevins (1890–1971) Amer. historian

**New Books** Hodder & Stoughton (London)

**Newcomb** . . Theodore Mead Newcomb (1903– ) Amer. educator

**Newell** . . . Homer Edward Newell (1915– ) Amer. physicist

**New England Journeys** Ford Motor Co.

**Newhall** . . . Richard Ager Newhall (1888– ) Amer. educator

**Newman** . . John Henry Newman (1801–1890) Eng. cardinal

**Al Newman** Albert Henry Newman (fl. 1954) Amer. writer

**J. P. Newman** John Philip Newman (1826–1899) Amer. clergyman

**R. H. Newman** Robert H. Newman (1917– ) Amer. author

**New Republic** Amer. weekly

**The New Scholasticism** Amer. quarterly

**New School Bulletin** New School for Social Research, N.Y.

*News Front* Amer. monthly
*New* Brit. weekly
*Statesman*
*Newsweek* Amer. weekly
*Newton*. . . Sir Isaac Newton (1642–1727) Eng. mathematician
*Eric* Eric Newton (1893–1965) Eng.
*Newton* art critic
*New Yorker* Amer. weekly
*Nicholls* . . Norton Nicholls (1742?–1809) Eng. clergyman
*Nichols*. . . Dale Nichols (1904– ) Amer. artist
*Nicholson*. . Meredith Nicholson (1866–1947) Amer. author
*Nicolaeva-* Nadine Nicolaeva-Legat (fl.
*Legat* 1947) Russ. dancer
*Nicolson* . . Lionel Benedict Nicolson (1914– ) Eng. journalist
*Harold* Sir Harold George Nicolson
*Nicolson* (1886–1963) Eng. author
*Nida* . . . . Eugene Albert Nida (1914– ) Amer. linguist
*Niebuhr* . . Reinhold Niebuhr (1892–1971) Amer. theologian
*Nixon* . . . Herman Clarence Nixon (1886– ) Amer. educator
*Nock*. . . . Albert Jay Nock (1872–1945) Amer. historian
*O. S. Nock* Oswald Stevens Nock (1905– ) Eng. engineer
*Nordhoff* . . Charles Bernard Nordhoff (1887–1947) Amer. author
*Norris* . . . Charles Gilman Norris (1881–1945) Amer. nov.
*North* . . . Roger North (1653–1734) Eng. lawyer
*North Amer-* Amer. quarterly
*ican Review*
*Norton* . . . Charles Eliot Norton (1827–1908) Amer. educator
*Noss* . . . . John Boyer Noss (1896– ) Amer. educator
*Notes &* Brit. monthly
*Queries*
*Notes and* Royal Anthropological Insti-
*Queries on* tute of Great Britain and
*Anthro-* Ireland
*pology*
*Notes on The* London (1952)
*Art of*
*Bookbind-*
*ing*
*Robert* Robert David Sanders Novak
*Novak* (1931– ) Amer. journal-ist
*Noyes* . . . Alfred Noyes (1880–1958) Eng. poet
*W. A. Noyes* William Albert Noyes (1898– ) Amer. chemist
*Nurnberg* . . Maxwell W. Nurnberg (fl. 1951) Amer. educator
*Nursing* Amer. monthly
*World*
*N.Y. Ameri-* New York daily
*can*
*N.Y. Evening* New York daily
*Post*
*N.Y. Herald* New York daily
*Tribune*
*N.Y. Times* New York daily
*Vanya Oakes* pseud. of Virginia Armstrong Oakes (1909– ) Amer. author
*O'Brien* . . Patrick Joseph O'Brien (1892–1938) Amer. writer
*O'Casey* . . Sean O'Casey (1880–1964) Irish playwright
*O'Connor* . . Michael Patrick O'Connor, *The Irish Digest* (1955)
*Frank* pseud. of Michael Joseph
*O'Connor* O'Donovan (1903–1966) Irish author
*Johnson* Johnson O'Connor (1891– )
*O'Connor* Amer. psychometrician
*O'Dea* . . . Thomas Francis O'Dea (1915– ) Amer. educator
*Odegard* . . Peter H. Odegard (1901–1966) Amer. educator
*O'Donnell* Cyril James O'Donnell (1900– ) Amer. educator
*E. P. O'Don-* Edwin P. O'Donnell (1895–
*nell* 1943) Amer. writer
*J. P. O'Don-* James Preston O'Donnell
*nell* (1917– ) Amer. journal-ist
*O'Donovan* Patrick Antony O'Donovan (1918– ) Brit. journalist
*O.E.D.* . . *A New English Dictionary on Historical Principles*, Oxford Univ. Press
*O'Faolain* . Sean O'Faolain (1900– ) Irish writer

*O'Flaherty* Liam O'Flaherty (1896– ) Irish nov.
*Ogdon* . . . William D. Ogdon (fl. 1955) Amer. editor
*Ogg* . . . . Frederic Austin Ogg (1878–1951) Amer. educator
*O'Hearn* . . Walter O'Hearn (1910?–1969) Canad. army officer
*O'Leary* . . Frank O'Leary (1902– ) Amer. journalist
*Oliphant* . . Margaret Oliphant (1828–1897) Scot. nov.
*Oliver* . . . Frederick Scott Oliver (1864–1934) Brit. jurist
*H. J. Oliver* Harold James Oliver (1916– ) Austral. educator
*W. D. Oliver* William Donald Oliver (1907– ) Amer. educator
*Olivier* . . . Warner Olivier, *Sat. Evening Post* (1954)
*O'Meara* . . Walter Andrew O'Meara (1897– ) Amer. author
*Omnibook* Amer. monthly
*O'Nolan* . . Brian O'Nolan (1912–1966) Irish nov.
*Oppenheimer* Julius Robert Oppenheimer (1904–1967) Amer. physicist
*Orsino* . . . Joseph Anthony Orsino (1908– ) Amer. (Ital.-born) chemist
*Orth* . . . . Allen Orth (1902– ) Amer. writer
*George* pseud. of Eric Blair (1903–1950)
*Orwell* Eng. author
*Osborne* . . Albert B. Osborne (1866–1913) Amer. writer
*Osler* . . . . Sir William Osler (1849–1919) Canad. physician
*Ouida* . . . pen name of Marie Louise de la Ramée (1839–1908) Eng. nov.
*Oursler* . . . (Charles) Fulton Oursler (1893–1952) Amer. writer
*Overstreet* Harry Allen Overstreet (1875–1970) Amer. educator
*Packard* . . Vance Oakley Packard (1914– ) Amer. writer
*Padover* . . Saul Kussiel Padover (1905– ) Amer. historian
*Paepke* . . . Walter Paul Paepke (1896–1960) Amer. businessman
*Page* . . . . Walter Hines Page (1855–1918) Amer. diplomat
*William Page* William Page (1861–1934) Eng. editor
*Paget* . . . Henry William Paget (1768–1854) 1st marquis of Angle-sey. Eng. soldier
*Pahlow* . . . Edwin William Pahlow (1878–1942) Amer. historian
*Paine* . . . Thomas Paine (1737–1809) Amer. (Eng.-born) political philosopher
*Pakistan* Embassy of Pakistan, Washing-
*Affairs* ton, D.C.
*Paley* . . . . William Paley (1743–1805) Eng. theologian
*Palfrey* . . . John Gorham Palfrey (1919– ) Amer. government official
*Palgrave* . . Sir Francis Palgrave (1788–1861) Eng. historian
*Pall Mall* London daily
*Gazette*
*Palmer*. . . Charles B. Palmer (1908–1968) Amer. writer
*Panter-* Mollie Panter-Downes (1906–
*Downes* ) Eng. journalist
*Pap* . . . . Arthur Pap (1921–1959) Amer. (Swiss-born) philosopher
*Pares* . . . Sir Bernard Pares (1867–1949) Eng. historian
*Pargellis* . . Stanley Pargellis (1898–1968) Amer. librarian
*Park* . . . . Orlando Park (1901– ) Amer. educator
*Ruth Park* Ruth Park (fl. 1947) N. Z. au-thor
*Parker* . . . Sir Gilbert Parker (1862–1932) Canad. author
*Dorothy* Dorothy Rothschild Parker
*Parker* (1893–1967) Amer. writer
*George* George Parker (fl. 1953) Amer.
*Parker* banker
*W. B. Parker* William Belmont Parker (1871–1934) Eng.-born editor
*W. R. Parker* William Riley Parker (1906–1968) Amer. educator
*Parkman* . . Francis Parkman (1823–1893) Amer. historian
*Parrington* Vernon Louis Parrington (1871–1929) Amer. literary historian

*Parris* . . . Robert Parris (fl. 1955) Amer. writer
*Parshley* . . Howard Madison Parshley (1884–1953) Amer. zoologist
*Partridge* . . Eric Honeywood Partridge (1894– ) Brit. lexicog-rapher
*Pasternack* Richard Pasternack (fl. 1948) Amer. chemist
*Pater*. . . . Walter Horatio Pater (1839–1894) Eng. writer
*Patmore* . . Coventry Kersey Dighton Pat-more (1823–1896) Eng. poet
*Derek Pat-* Derek Coventry Patmore
*more* (1908– ) Eng. author
*Paton* . . . William Andrew Paton (1889– ) Amer. educator
*A. S. Paton* Alan Stewart Paton (1903– ) So. African writer
*Pattee* . . . Fred Lewis Pattee (1863–1950) Amer. educator
*Patterson* . . Ellen Day Patterson (fl. 1954) Amer. writer
*Pattishall* . . Beverly W. Pattishall (1916– ) Amer. lawyer
*Pattison* . . Mark Pattison (1813–1884) Eng. scholar
*Patton* . . . Frances Gray Patton (1906– ) Amer. author
*G. S. Patton* George Smith Patton (1885–1945) Amer. general
*Paul* . . . . Elliot Harold Paul (1891–1958) Amer. editor
*Paulding* . . C. Gouverneur Paulding (fl. 1956) Amer. editor
*Pawley* . . . Kenneth Pawley (1916– ) Brit. barrister-at-law
*Paxson* . . . Frederic Logan Paxson (1877–1948) Amer. historian
*Payne* . . . (Pierre Stephen) Robert Payne (1911– ) Amer. (Eng.-born) author
*S. L. Payne* Stanley LeBaron Payne (1911– ) Amer. writer
*Payton* . . . J. Russell T. Payton (1910– ) Canad. lawyer
*Peabody* . . Francis Weld Peabody (1881–1927) Amer. physician
*Peace Hand-* 25 vols., Historical Section of
*books* (British) Foreign Office (1920)
*Peacock* . . Thomas Love Peacock (1785–1866) Eng. nov.
*Max Peacock* pseud. of Dennis Max Cornelius Woodruffe-Peacock (1899– ) Brit. author
*Pearson* . . Charles Chilton Pearson (1879–1956) Amer. historian
*H. G.* Henry Greenleaf Pearson
*Pearson* (1870–1939) Amer. educator
*H. S. Pearson* Haydn Sanborn Pearson (1901–1967) Amer. writer
*Peattie* . . . Donald Culross Peattie (1898–1964) Amer. botanist
*Peden* . . . William Harwood Peden (1913– )Amer. educator
*Peerman* . . Dean Gordon Peerman (1931– ) Amer. editor
*Peers*. . . . Edgar Allison Peers (d. 1952) Eng. educator
*Peffer* . . . Nathaniel Peffer (1890–1964) Amer. educator
*Pegler* . . . Westbrook Pegler (1894–1969) Amer. columnist
*Penn* . . . . William Penn (1644–1718) Eng. founder of Pennsylvania
*Pepper* . . . Stephen Coburn Pepper (1891–1972) Amer. educator
*Pepys* . . . Samuel Pepys (1633–1703) Eng. diarist
*Perelman* . . Sidney Joseph Perelman (1904– ) Amer. writer
*Perkins*. . . Gwen Kirtley Perkins (1918– ) Amer. writer
*Perry* . . . Bliss Perry (1860–1954) Amer. educator
*Frank Perry* Frank Anthony Perry (1921– ) Amer. physician
*G. S. Perry* George Sessions Perry (1910–1956) Amer. author
*O. H. Perry* Oliver Hazard Perry (1785–1819) Amer. naval officer
*The Personal-* Amer. quarterly
*ist*
*Personnel* Amer. monthly
*Jour.*
*Persons*. . . Frederick Torrel Persons (1869–1948) Amer. librarian
*Petersen* . . William Petersen (1912– ) Amer. sociologist
*Peyre* . . . Henri Maurice Peyre (1901– ) Amer. (Fr.-born) edu-cator

*Green Peyton* Green Peyton Wertenbaker (1907– ) Amer. author

*Pfeffer* . . . Leo Pfeffer (1910– ) Amer. (Hung.-born) lawyer

*Pflieger* . . Elmer F. Pflieger (fl. 1957) Amer. educator

*Phalen* . . . James Matthew Phalen (1822–1954) Amer. physician

*Pharr* . . . Clyde Pharr (1885– ) Amer. educator

*Phelan* . . . Patrick J. Phelan, *The Irish Digest* (1952)

*Phelps* . . . Clyde William Phelps (1897– ) Amer. economist

*Phillips* . . Wendell Phillips (1811–1884) Amer. orator

*Cabell Phillips* Cabell Phillips (1904– ) Amer. journalist

*Henry Phillips* Henry Phillips (1838–1895) Amer. writer

*J. D. Phillips* James Duncan Phillips (1876–1954) Amer. publisher

*John Phillips* John Phillips (1800–1874) Eng. geologist

*U. B. Phillips* Ulrich Bonnell Phillips (1877–1934) Amer. educator

*Phillpotts* . Eden Phillpotts (1862–1960) Eng. nov.

*Philosophical Review* Amer. quarterly

*Pick* . . . . Robert Pick (1898– ) Amer. (Austrian-born) author

*Pierce* . . . Ovid Williams Pierce (1910– ) Amer. nov.

*Pike* . . . . James Albert Pike (1913–1969) Amer. bishop

*E. W. Pike* Elizabeth Wecter Pike, *Sat. Review* (1953)

*Pimlott* . . . John Alfred Ralph Pimlott (1909–1969) Eng. government official

*Pinckney* . . Josephine Pinckney (1895–1957) Amer. nov.

*Pirsson* . Louis Valentine Pirsson (1860–1919) Amer. geologist

*Pizer* . . . . Vernon Pizer (1918– ) Amer. writer

*Plamenatz* John Petrov Plamenatz (1912– ) Eng. lecturer

*Ploscowe* Morris Ploscowe (1904– ) Amer. (Pol.-born) lawyer

*Plucknett* . . Theodore Frank Thomas Plucknett (1897–1965) Brit. historian

*Plumb* . . . John Harold Plumb (1911– ) Eng. historian

*Plummer* . Alfred Plummer (1896– ) Eng. educator

*PMLA* . . . *Publications of The Modern Language Association of America*

*Poe* . . . . Edgar Allan Poe (1809–1849) Amer. author

*Pohl* . . . . Frederik Pohl (1919?– ) Amer. author

*Poleman* . . Horace Irvin Poleman (1905–1965) Amer. orientalist

*Political Science Quarterly* Amer. periodical

*Pollack* . . . Jack Harrison Pollack (1914– ) Amer. author

*Pollard* . . . John Albert Pollard (1901–1968) Amer. educator

*Pollet* . . . Elizabeth Pollet, *Botteghe Oscure* (1953)

*Pollitzer* . . Anita Pollitzer (fl. 1950) Amer. suffragist

*Pollock* . . . Sam Pollock (1903– ) Brit. broadcaster

*Pollok* . . . Robert Pollok (1798–1827) Scot. poet

*Poole* . . . Derek Michael Poole (d. 1953) Brit. geographer

*Poore* . . . Charles Graydon Poore (1902–1971) Amer. writer

*Pope* . . . . Alexander Pope (1688–1744) Eng. poet

*Porteous* . . Richard Sydney Porteous (fl. 1954) Austral. writer

*Porter* . . . Jane Porter (1776–1850) Eng. nov.

*K. A. Porter* Katherine Anne Porter (1890– ) Amer. writer

*McKenzie Porter* McKenzie Porter, *Maclean's* (1953)

*Portz* . . . . John Portz (fl. 1955) Amer. literary critic

*The Postmark* Canad. Postal Service (Ottawa)

*Potter* . . . George Edwin Potter (1898– ) Amer. zoologist

*Jeremy Potter* Jeremy Potter (1922– ) Brit. publisher

*Stephen Potter* Stephen Potter (1900–1969) Eng. author

*Pound* . . . Ezra Loomis Pound (1885–1972) Amer. poet

*Roscoe Pound* Roscoe Pound (1870–1964) Amer. jurist

*Powell* . . . Anthony Dymoke Powell (1905– ) Eng. nov.

*Power* . . . William Longford Power (1909– ) Amer. (Austral.-born) educator

*Powers* . . . Edwin Powers (1896– ) Amer. psychologist

*Powys* . . . John Cowper Powys (1872–1963) Eng. author

*Praed* . . . Winthrop Mackworth Praed (1802–1839) Eng. poet

*Pratt* . . . . Fletcher Pratt (1897–1956) Amer. author

*Presbrey* . . Charles Presbrey (1882– ) Amer. businessman

*Prescott* . . William Hickling Prescott (1796–1859) Amer. historian

*Orville Prescott* Orville Prescott (1906– ) Amer. journalist

*Pressey* . . . Sidney Leavitt Pressey (1888– ) Amer. psychologist

*Prewett* . . . Virginia Prewett (1911– ) Amer. author

*Price* . . . . Lucien Price (1883–1964) Amer. writer

*E. T. Price* Edward Thomas Price (1915– ) Amer. educator

*G. R. Price* George Rennie Price (1909– ) Amer. educator

*Priest* . . . Ivy Baker Priest (1905– ) Amer. politician

*Priestley* . . John Boynton Priestley (1894– ) Eng. author

*H. I. Priestley* Herbert Ingram Priestley (1875–1944) Amer. historian

*Printers' Ink* Amer. weekly

*Prior* . . . . Matthew Prior (1664–1721) Eng. poet

*Pritchett* . . Victor Sawdon Pritchett (1900– ) Eng. journalist

*Progressive* Amer. monthly

*Prynne* . . . William Prynne (1600–1669) Eng. Puritan pamphleteer

*Psychiatry* Amer. quarterly

*Publishers' Weekly* Amer. periodical

*Puckle* . . . Sir Frederick Puckle (1889– ) Eng. government official

*Punch* . . . London weekly

*Purcell* . . . Victor William Williams Saunders Purcell (1896–1965) Eng. historian

*Purdy* . . . James Purdy (1923– ) Amer. author

*Purtell* . . . William Arthur Purtell (1897– ) U.S. politician

*Pusey* . . . Edward Bouverie Pusey (1800–1882) Eng. theologian

*N. M. Pusey* Nathan Marsh Pusey (1907– ) Amer. educator

*Putnam* . . . Samuel Putnam (1892–1950) Amer. writer

*Pyle* . . . . Ernie Pyle (1900–1945) Amer. journalist

*Pyles* . . . Thomas Pyles (1905– ) Amer. educator

*Pynchon* . . Thomas Pynchon (1936– ) Amer. nov.

*Quarles* . . . Francis Quarles (1592–1644) Eng. poet

*Quiller-Couch* Sir Arthur Thomas Quiller-Couch (1863–1944) Eng. author

*Quillin* . . . H. D. Quillin, *True* (1954)

*Quinn* . . . Arthur Hobson Quinn (1875–1960) Amer. educator

*Rabi* . . . . Isidor Isaac Rabi (1898– ) Amer. (Austrian-born) physicist

*Radcliffe* . . Ann Radcliffe (1764–1823) Eng. nov.

*Radin* . . . Max Radin (1880–1950) Amer. (Pol.-born) educator

*E. D. Radin* Edward David Radin (1909–1966) Amer. author

*Rafferty* . . . Keen (Alexander) Rafferty (1902– ) Amer. educator

*Rago* . . . . Henry Anthony Rago (1915–1969) Amer. educator

*Raleigh* . . . Sir Walter Alexander Raleigh (1861–1922) Eng. writer

*Rama Rau* Santha Rama Rau (1923– ) Indian-born author

*Ramsay* . . . David Ramsay (1749–1815) Amer. historian

*Ramsdell* . . Charles William Ramsdell (1877–1942) Amer. educator

*Rand* . . . . Christopher Rand (1912–1968) Amer. journalist

*Randall* . . . John Herman Randall (1899– ) Amer. educator

*R. P. Randall* Ruth Painter Randall (1892–1971) Amer. author

*Ransom* . . John Crowe Ransom (1888– ) Amer. poet

*Raven* . . . Charles Earle Raven (1885– ) Eng. educator

*Rawlings* . Marjorie Kinnan Rawlings (1896–1953) Amer. author

*Ray* . . . . Perley Orman Ray (1875– ) Amer. educator

*Read* . . . . Sir Herbert Read (1893–1968) Eng. writer

*Reade* . . . Charles Reade (1814–1884) Eng. nov.

*Reckless* . . Walter C. Reckless (1899– ) Amer. criminologist

*Redman* . . Ben Ray Redman (1896–1961) Amer. author

*Alvin Redman* Alvin Redman (fl. 1954) Brit. publisher

*Reed* . . . . Henry Hope Reed (1808–1854) Amer. educator

*John Reed* . John Reed (1887–1920) Amer. writer

*Rees* . . . . Leslie Clarke Rees (1905– ) Austral. writer

*Reese* . . . Lizette Woodworth Reese (1856–1935) Amer. poet

*Reeves* . . . Jesse Siddall Reeves (1872–1942) Amer. political scientist

*Reid* . . . . Robert Reid (1895– ) Brit. broadcaster

*Reilly* . . . William John Reilly (1899– ) Amer. educator

*Reinhardt* . . Kurt Frank Reinhardt (1896– ) Amer. (Ger.-born) educator

*Renwick* . . William Lindsay Renwick (1889–1970) Scot. educator

*The Reporter* Amer. biweekly

*Report on Nat'l Development (Ottawa)* Royal Commission on National Development in the Arts, Letters, and Sciences, 1949–1951

*Repplier* . . Agnes Repplier (1855–1950) Amer. essayist

*Restatement of the Law of Security* American Law Institute

*Retailing Daily* New York newspaper

*Revel* . . . Jean-Francois Revel (fl. 1965) Fr. writer

*Révész* . . . Géza Révész (1878–1955) Hungarian-born psychologist

*Reynolds* . . Sir Joshua Reynolds (1723–1792) Eng. portrait painter

*L. G. Reynolds* Lloyd G. Reynolds (1910– ) Amer. (Canad.-born) economist

*P. J. Reynolds* P. Joyce Reynolds, *Country Life* (1951)

*Rice* . . . . James Rice (1843–1882) Eng. writer

*Elmer Rice* Elmer L. Rice (1892–1967) Amer. playwright

*L. L. Rice* . Laban Lacy Rice (1870– ) Amer. educator

*P. B. Rice* . Phillip Blair Rice (1904–1956) Amer. philosopher

*Robert Rice* Robert Rice (1916– ) Amer. writer

*Richards* . . Ivor Armstrong Richards (1893– ) Eng. educator

*O. W. Richards* Owain Westmacott Richards (1901– ) Eng. entomologist

*Richardson* Samuel Richardson (1689–1761) Eng. nov.

*Ricketts* . . Charles Ricketts (1866–1931) Brit. artist

*Rickword* . . C. H. Rickword (fl. 1948) Brit. writer

*Riegel* . . . Emil Raymond Riegel (1882– ) French-born educator

*Riesman* . . David Riesman (1909– ) Amer. social scientist

*Riggs* . . . Robert Langmuir Riggs (1901– ) Amer. newspaperman

*Riker* . . . Ben H. Riker (1889?–1962) Amer. bookseller

*Riley* . . . . James Whitcomb Riley (1849–1916) Amer. poet

*Ringe* . . . Donald Arthur Ringe (1923– ) Amer. educator

Ripley . . . William Zebina Ripley (1867–1941) Amer. economist

Dillon Ripley (Sidney) Dillon Ripley (1913– ) Amer. zoologist

Rippin . . . Richard C. Rippin, *Ships and the Sea* (1953)

Ritchie . . . Leitch Ritchie (1800?–1865) Scot. nov.

Road and Track Amer. monthly

Roberts . . . Elizabeth Madox Roberts (1886–1941) Amer. nov.

C. G. D. Roberts Sir Charles George Douglas Roberts (1860–1943) Canad. poet

Kenneth Roberts Kenneth Lewis Roberts (1885–1957) Amer. nov.

Robertson Alexander Robertson (d. 1970) Brit. author

F. W. Robertson Frederick William Robertson (1816–1853) Eng. clergyman

R. B. Robertson Robert Blackwood Robertson (1913– ) Scot. writer

William Robertson William Robertson (1721–1793) Scot. historian

Robinson . . Henry Crabb Robinson (1775–1867) Eng. diarist

Cyril Robinson Cyril Edward Robinson (1884– ) Brit. historian

E. A. Robinson Edwin Arlington Robinson (1869–1935) Amer. poet

F. N. Robinson Fred Norris Robinson (1871–1966) Amer. educator

F. W. Robinson Frederick William Robinson (1830–1901) Eng. nov.

Richard Robinson Richard Robinson (fl. 1950) Brit. writer

Robson . . . William Alexander Robson (1895– ) Eng. educator

Roche . . . John Pierre Roche (1889–1960) Amer. advertising executive

Rock. . . . Daniel Rock (1799–1871) Eng. ecclesiologist

Hazel Rockow Hazel Marcia (Kory) Rockow (1909– ) Amer. interior decorator

Julius Rockow Julius Rockow (1912– ) Amer. interior decorator

Rodell . . . Fred Rodell (1907– ) Amer. educator

Roehm . . . A. Wesley Roehm (1908– ) Amer. educator

Roetter . . . Charles Roetter (fl. 1953) Brit. editor

Rogers . . . Samuel Rogers (1763–1855) Eng. poet

Rogow . . . Lee Rogow (fl. 1954) Amer. writer

Rohne . . . John Magnus Rohne, *Dict. o Amer. Biog.*

Rolfs . . . Mary Jane Rolfs (1916– Amer. writer

Rolo . . . . Charles James Rolo (1916– ) Amer. editor

Rölvaag . . Ole Edvart Rölvaag (1876–1931) Amer. (Norw.-born) educator

Romulo . . . Carlos Pena Romulo (1901– ) Filipino editor

Roney . . . James Givens Roney (1918– ) Amer. physician

Rooney . . . Philip Rooney (1909– ) Irish author

Roosevelt . . Franklin Delano Roosevelt (1882–1945) 32d president of the U.S.

Eleanor Roosevelt (Anna) Eleanor Roosevelt (1884–1962) Amer. writer; wife of preceding

Rorick . . . Isabel Scott Rorick (1900– ) Amer. author

Rose. . . . George Rose III (fl. 1908) Amer. writer

Rosebery . . Archibald Philip Primrose (1847–1929) 5th earl of Rosebery. Eng. statesman

Rosen . . . Harold Rosen (1908– ) Amer. physician

Rosenberg Bernard Rosenberg (1923– ) Amer. educator

Harold Rosenberg Harold Rosenberg (fl. 1964) Amer. writer

Rosenblum Morris Rosenblum (fl. 1951) Amer. educator

Rosenfeld . . Isaac Rosenfeld (1918–1956) Amer. educator

Rosenthal . . Abraham Michael Rosenthal (1922– ) Amer. (Canad.-born) journalist

Harold Rosenthal Harold David Rosenthal (1917– ) Eng. music critic

Rosenzweig Saul Rosenzweig (1907– ) Amer. psychologist

Rosner . . . Charles Rosner (1902– ) Amer. (Hung.-born) artist

Ross. . . . Emory Ross (1887– ) Amer. missionary

Ishbel Ross Ishbel Ross (1897– ) Amer. (Scot.-born) author

Mary Ross Mary Margaret Ross (1918– ) Amer. author

Victor Ross Victor Ross (1919– ) Brit. army officer

Rossetti . . Christina Georgina Rossetti (1830–1894) Eng. poet

Rossiter . . Clinton Lawrence Rossiter (1917–1970) Amer. educator

Rosten . . . Leo Calvin Rosten (1908– ) Amer. (Pol.-born) author

Rothman . . Nathan L. Rothman (1904– ) Amer. writer

Roucek. . . Joseph Slabey Roucek (1902– ) Amer. (Czech.-born) social scientist

Roueché . . Berton Roueché (1911– ) Amer. writer

Rourke. . . Constance Mayfield Rourke (1885–1941) Amer. author

Rovere . . . Richard Halworth Rovere (1915– ) Amer. author

Rowe . . . Nicholas Rowe (1674–1718) Eng. dramatist

D. N. Rowe David Nelson Rowe (1905– ) Amer. educator

H. K. Rowe Henry Kallock Rowe (1869–1941) Amer. educator

Rowlands . . John James Rowlands (1892– ) Canad. writer

Rowse . . . Alfred Leslie Rowse (1903– ) Eng. historian

Roy . . . . Ralph Lord Roy (1928– ) Amer. theologian

Rubinstein Ronald Rubinstein (1896–1947) Brit. writer

Rufus . . . Will Carl Rufus (1876–1946) Amer. astronomer

Rukeyser . . Muriel Rukeyser (1913– ) Amer. poet

Runciman. . James Runciman (1852–1891) Eng. writer

Rusinoff . . Samuel Eugene Rusinoff (1894– ) Amer. (Russ.-born) engineer

Ruskin . . . John Ruskin (1819–1900) Eng. author

Russell . . . Bertrand Arthur William Russell (1872–1970) 3d earl Russell. Eng. philosopher

Nancy Rutledge pseud. of Leigh Bryson (fl. 1956) Amer. author

Ryan . . . Abram Joseph Ryan (1838–1886) Amer. priest

W. L. Ryan William L. Ryan (1911– ) Amer. journalist

Ryle . . . . Gilbert Ryle (1900– ) Eng. educator

Saarinen . . Aline Bernstein Saarinen (1914–1972) Amer. art critic

Sabatini . . Rafael Sabatini (1875–1950) Eng. (Ital.-born) author

Sabine . . . George Holland Sabine (1880–1961) Amer. political philosopher

Sackville-West Victoria Mary Sackville-West (1892–1962) Eng. writer

Edward Sackville-West Edward Charles Sackville-West (1901–1965) 5th baron. Eng. author

Sacramento Bee Sacramento (Calif.) daily

Safety for Your Savings Mutual Savings Central Fund

Saintsbury George Edward Bateman Saintsbury (1845–1933) Eng. critic

Salinger . . Jerome David Salinger (1919– ) **Amer. nov.**

Salisbury . . Harrison Evans Salisbury (1908– ) Amer. journalist

Salomon . . Isidore Lawrence Salomon (1899– ) Amer. poet

Albert Salomon Albert Salomon (1891–1966) German-born sociologist

L. B. Salomon Louis Bernard Salomon (1908– ) Amer. educator

Sampley . . Arthur McCullough Sampley (1903– ) Amer. college administrator

Sampson . . George Sampson (1873–1950) Eng. educator

Samuel. . . Maurice Samuel (1895– ) Amer. (Romanian-born) author and translator of Sholem Asch

Edward Samuel Edward Samuel, *Farmer's Weekly* (1953)

Sandburg . . Carl Sandburg (1878–1967) **Amer. author**

Sanders . . Jacquin Sanders (1922– ) Amer. editor

Sandwell . . Bernard Keble Sandwell (1876–1954) Canad. journalist

Santayana George Santayana (1863–1952) Span.-Amer. philosopher

Sapir. . . . Edward Sapir (1884–1939) Amer. linguist

Sargeant . . Winthrop Sargeant (1903– ) Amer. music critic

Saroyan . . William Saroyan (1908– ) Amer. writer

Sassoon . . Siegfried Lorraine Sassoon (1886–1967) Eng. writer

Sat. Evening Post Amer. periodical

Sat. Review (London) Brit. weekly

Sat. Review (of Literature) Amer. weekly

Saunders . . O. Elfrida Saunders (fl. 1932) Eng. art historian

Savory . . . Theodore Horace Savory (1896– ) Eng. biologist

Sawyer. . . Walter Warwick Sawyer (1911– ) Eng. mathematician

Saxon . . . Lyle Saxon (1891–1946) Amer. author

Sayers . . . Dorothy Leigh Sayers (1893–1957) Eng. writer

Sayre . . . Wallace Stanley Sayre (1905–1972) Amer. political scientist

Morris Sayre Morris Sayre (1885–1953) Amer. businessman

Scalia . . . Samuel Eugene Scalia (1903– ) Amer. educator

Schafer. . . Joseph Schafer (1867–1941) Amer. historian

Schapiro . . Jacob Salwyn Schapiro (1879– ) Amer. historian

Scheingold Stuart A. Scheingold (fl. 1966) Amer. educator

Scherman. . Harry Scherman (1887–1969) Amer. economist

Schlesinger d. 1965 Arthur Meier Schlesinger (1888–1965) Amer. historian

Schlesinger b. 1917 Arthur Meier Schlesinger (1917– ) Amer. historian; son of preceding

Schoettle . Edwin J. Schoettle (fl. 1949) Amer. yachtsman

Scholl . . . Evelyn Harwood Scholl (1899– ) Amer. educator

School and Society Amer. weekly

Schorer. . . Mark Schorer (1908– ) Amer. educator

Schrecker. . Paul Schrecker (1889–1963) Amer. (Austrian-born) educator

Schreiner . . Olive Schreiner (1855–1920) So. African nov.

Schulberg. . Budd Schulberg (1914– ) Amer. author

Schultz. . . Howard Schultz (1907– ) Amer. educator

Schumpeter Joseph Alois Schumpeter (1883–1950) Amer. (Ger.-born) economist

Schuyler . . Robert Livingston Schuyler (1883–1966) Amer. educator

Schwartz . . Delmore Schwartz (1913-1966) Amer. poet

Schytt . . . Valter Schytt (1919– ) Swedish geologist

Science. . . Amer. weekly

Science News Letter Amer. weekly

Scientific American Amer. monthly

Scientific Monthly **Amer. monthly**

The Score and I.M.A. Mag. Brit. quarterly

The Scotsman Edinburgh daily

Scott. . . . Sir Walter Scott (1771–1832) **Scot. nov. & poet**

F. N. Scott Fred Newton Scott (1860–1930) Amer. educator

G. G. Scott Sir George Gilbert Scott (1811–1878) Brit. architect

H. D. Scott Hugh Doggett Scott (1900– ) U.S. senator

**H. S. Scott** — Hugh Stowell Scott (1862–1903); *pseud.* of Henry Seton Merriman. Eng. nov.

**Peter Scott** — Peter Scott (1922– ) Brit. educator

**W. T. Scott** — Winfield Townley Scott (1910–1968) Amer. writer

**Scribner's Mag.** — Amer. monthly

**Scripture** — Edward Wheeler Scripture (1864–1943) Amer. phonetician

**Scudder** — Horace Elisha Scudder (1838–1902) Amer. author

**Seago** — John Seago, *London Calling* (1954)

**Sears** — Paul Bigelow Sears (1891– ) Amer. botanist

**L. M. Sears** — Louis Martin Sears (1885– ) Amer. educator

**W. R. Sears** — William Rees Sears (1913– ) Amer. engineer

**Seaver** — George Seaver (1890– ) Brit. clergyman

**Seccombe** — Thomas Seccombe (1866–1923) Eng. biographer

**Sedgwick** — Anne Douglas Sedgwick (1873–1935) Amer. nov.

**Sédillot** — René Sédillot (1906– ) French historian

**Seitz** — Frederick Seitz (1911– ) Amer. physicist

**Seldes** — Gilbert Vivian Seldes (1893–1970) Amer. journalist

**Seliger** — Robert Victor Seliger (1900–1953) Amer. psychiatrist

**Sellars** — Roy Wood Sellars (1880– ) Amer. (Canad.-born) educator

**Sellery** — George Clarke Sellery (1872–1962) Amer. educator

**Seltzer** — Leon Eugene Seltzer (1918– ) Amer. writer

**Semon** — Richard Wolfgang Semon (1859–1918) Ger. naturalist

**Service to Youth** — Division of Youth Service of the Commonwealth of Massachusetts

**Sevareid** — (Arnold) Eric Sevareid (1912– ) Amer. broadcaster

**F. E. Seymour** — Francis Eugene Seymour (1883– ) Amer. educator

**Shaftesbury** — Anthony Ashley Cooper (1671–1713) 3d earl of Shaftesbury. Eng. philosopher

**Shak.** — William Shakespeare (1564–1616) Eng. dramatist

**Shalowitz** — Aaron Louis Shalowitz (1892– ) Amer. engineer

**Shannon** — William Vincent Shannon (1927– ) Amer. author

**Shaplen** — Robert Modell Shaplen (1917– ) Amer. author

**Sharp** — Margery Sharp (1905– ) Eng. nov.

**Shaw** — George Bernard Shaw (1856–1950) Brit. author

**Irwin Shaw** — Irwin Shaw (1913– ) Amer. author

**Desmond Shawe-Taylor** — Desmond Shawe-Taylor (1907– ) Eng. music critic

**Joseph Shearing** — *pseud.* of (Margaret) Gabrielle Long (1888–1952) Eng. author

**Sheean** — Vincent Sheean (1899– ) Amer. writer

**Sheffield** — John Sheffield (1648–1721) 1st duke of Buckingham. Eng. writer

**Shehan** — Lawrence Joseph Shehan (1898– ) Amer. cardinal

**Sheldon** — Arthur N. Sheldon (1877– ) Amer. engineer

**Shelley** — Percy Bysshe Shelley (1792–1822) Eng. poet

**M. W. Shelley** — Mary Wollstonecraft Shelley (1797–1851) Eng. nov.

**Shenstone** — William Shenstone (1714–1763) Eng. poet

**Shepard** — Francis Parker Shepard (1897– ) Amer. geologist

**Shepherd** — Massey Hamilton Shepherd (1913– ) Amer. clergyman

**Sherberg** — M. Sherberg, *Nat'l Jewish Monthly* (1953)

**Sherbo** — Arthur Sherbo (1918– ) Amer. educator

**Sheridan** — Richard Brinsley Sheridan (1751–1816) Irish dramatist

**Clare Sheridian** — Clare Consuelo Sheridan (1885–1970) Eng. sculptor

**Sherman** — Stuart Pratt Sherman (1881–1926) Amer. critic

**Shields** — Dan B. Shields, *The Caduceus of Kappa Sigma* (1952)

**Shils** — Edward Albert Shils (1911– ) Amer. educator

**Ships and the Sea** — Amer. quarterly

**Shipton** — Eric Earle Shipton (1907– ) Eng. mountaineer

**Shirer** — William Lawrence Shirer (1904– ) Amer. journalist

**Shirley** — James Shirley (1596–1666) Eng. dramatist

**Luke Short** — *pseud.* of Frederick Dilley Glidden (1908– ) Amer. writer

**Shorthouse** — Joseph Henry Shorthouse (1834–1903) Eng. nov.

**Shreve** — Randolph Norris Shreve (1885– ) Amer. chemical engineer

**Nevil Shute** — *full name* Nevil Shute Norway (1899–1960) Eng. nov.

**W. G. Shute** — William George Shute (1887– ) Amer. mathematician

**Siberts** — Bruce Siberts (1868–1952) Amer. writer

**Sidgwick** — Henry Sidgwick (1838–1900) Eng. philosopher

**Sidney** — Sir Philip Sidney (1554–1586) Eng. poet

**Siler** — Thomas Terrill Siler (1909– ) Amer. writer

**Sill** — Edward Rowland Sill (1841–1887) Amer. poet

**Silveus** — Marian Silveus (1904– ) Amer. educator

**Simmons** — Ernest Joseph Simmons (1903–1972) Amer. educator

**Simnett** — William Edward Simnett (1880–1958) Eng. writer

**Simpson** — George Gaylord Simpson (1902– ) Amer. paleontologist

**R. H. Simpson** — Robert H. Simpson (fl. 1956) Amer. writer

**Sinclair** — May Sinclair (1865?–1946) Eng. nov.

**Harold Sinclair** — Harold Augustus Sinclair (1907–1966) Amer. nov.

**Upton Sinclair** — Upton Beall Sinclair (1878–1968) Amer. author

**Sisk** — John Paul Sisk (1914– ) Amer. educator

**Sitwell** — Dame Edith Sitwell (1887–1964) Eng. author

**Osbert Sitwell** — Sir Osbert Sitwell (1892–1969) Eng. author; brother of preceding

**Sacheverell Sitwell** — Sacheverell Sitwell (1897– ) Eng. author; brother of preceding

**Skidmore** — Hobert Douglas Skidmore (1909– ) Amer. nov.

**Skinner** — Cornelia Otis Skinner (1901– ) Amer. actress

**Samuel Slade** — Samuel Slade (fl. 1922) Amer. engineer

**Smart** — Charles Allen Smart (1904–1967) Amer. author

**Smelser** — Marshall Taylor Smelser (1912– ) Amer. historian

**Smith** — Adam Smith (1723–1790) Scot. economist

**A. D. H. Smith** — Arthur Douglas Howden Smith (1887– ) Amer. author

**Bernard Smith** — Bernard Smith (1916– ) Austral. educator

**Beverly Smith** — Beverly Waugh Smith (1898–1972) Amer. editor

**C. M. Smith** — Cecil Michener Smith (1906–1956) Amer. music critic

**D. C. Smith** — Datus Clifford Smith (1907– ) Amer. publisher

**D. E. Smith** — David Eugene Smith (1860–1944) Amer. educator

**Don Smith** — Don Smith (1909– ) Amer. writer

**E. W. Smith** — Edmund Ware Smith (1900– ) Amer. writer

**F. D. Smith** — Frederick Daniel Smith (fl. 1950) Eng. author

**Goldwin Smith** — Goldwin Smith (1823–1910) Eng. historian

**Harrison Smith** — Harrison Smith (1888–1971) Amer. editor

**H. G. Smith** — Hugh G. Smith, *N. Y. Times* (1954)

**H. H. Smith** — Herbert Heebner Smith (fl. 1941) Amer. writer

**H. L. Smith** — Henry Ladd Smith (1906– ) Amer. educator

**Horace Smith** — Horace Smith (1779–1849) Eng. poet

**J. L. B. Smith** — James Leonard Brierly Smith (1897–1968) So. African ichthyologist

**Lillian Smith** — Lillian Eugenia Smith (1897–1966) Amer. author

**L. P. Smith** — Logan Pearsall Smith (1865–1946) Amer. essayist

**M. O. Smith** — Martha Otis Smith (fl. 1947) Amer. educator

**Mortimer Smith** — Mortimer Brewster Smith (1906– ) Amer. writer

**P. J. Smith** — Paul James Smith (fl. 1945) Amer. educator

**Preserved Smith** — Preserved Smith (1880–1941) Amer. historian

**R. A. Smith** — Robert Aura Smith (1899–1959) Amer. journalist

**R. B. Smith** — Reginald Bosworth Smith (1839–1908) Eng. historian

**R. R. Smith** — Rolland Ryther Smith (1894– ) Amer. educator

**S. F. Smith** — Samuel Francis Smith (1808–1895) Amer. hymn writer

**Stevie Smith** — *pen name* of Florence Margaret Smith (1902–1971) Eng. poet

**Sydney Smith** — Sydney Smith (1771–1845) Eng. essayist

**W. C. Smith** — Walter Chalmers Smith (1824–1908) Scot. poet

**W. E. Smith** — William Ernest Smith (1892– ) Amer. educator

**W. P. Smith** — Wendell P. Smith (1892– ) Amer. ornithologist

**Smollett** — Tobias George Smollett (1721–1771) Brit. author

**Smythe** — George Franklin Smythe (1852–1934) Amer. clergyman

**Snaith** — John Collis Snaith (1876–1936) Eng. nov.

**Snapp** — James Cecil Snapp (1907– ) Amer. educator

**Soby** — James Thrall Soby (1906– ) Amer. art critic

**Social Science Abstracts** — Amer. monthly

**Sokolsky** — George (Ephraim) Sokolsky (1893–1962) Amer. columnist

**Sorokin** — Pitirim Alexandrovitch Sorokin (1889–1968) Amer.(Russ.-born) educator

**Soule** — George Henry Soule (1887–1970) Amer. editor

**South** — Robert South (1634–1716) Eng. clergyman

**Southerly** — Austral. periodical

**Southern** — Richard William Southern (1912– ) Eng. educator

**Terry Southern** — Terry Southern (1924– ) Amer. author

**Southey** — Robert Southey (1774–1843) Eng. writer

**Space Handbook** — U. S. Government Printing Office

**Spaeth** — John Duncan Spaeth (1868–1954) Amer. educator

**Spaulding** — Oliver Lyman Spaulding (1875–1947) Amer. army officer

**Spearman** — James Morton Spearman (fl. 1828) Brit. artillerist

**Spears** — John Randolph Spears (1850–1936) Amer. writer

**Spectator** — Eng. daily newspaper

**The Spectator** — Eng. weekly

**Spectorsky** — Auguste Comte Spectorsky (1910–1972) Amer. (Fr.-born) editor

**Spence** — James Spence (fl. 1861) Brit. writer

**Spencer** — Herbert Spencer (1820–1903) Eng. philosopher

**Theodore Spencer** — Theodore Spencer (1902–1949) Amer. educator

**Spender** — Stephen Spender (1909– ) Eng. poet

**Spenser** — Edmund Spenser (1552?–1599) Eng. poet

**Sperry** — Willard Learoyd Sperry (1882–1954) Amer. theologian

**Bella Spewack** — Bella Spewack (1899– ) Amer. (Romanian-born) playwright; wife of Samuel

**Samuel Spewack** — Samuel Spewack (1899–1971) Amer. (Russ.-born) playwright

**Spicer** — Edward Holland Spicer (1906– ) Amer. anthropologist

Spiers . . . Al Spiers, *Sat. Evening Post* (1954)
Spilsbury . . R. J. Spilsbury (fl. 1953) Brit. educator
Spina . . . Michele Spina, *Kenyon Review* (1949)
Spitzer . . . Silas Spitzer (fl. 1954) Amer. writer
Spock . . . Benjamin McLane Spock (1903– ) Amer. physician
Sprigge . . Cecil Jackson Squire Sprigge (1896–1959) Eng. journalist
Springfield Republican Springfield (Mass.) daily
Springfield Union Springfield (Mass.) daily
Spurgeon . . Charles Haddon Spurgeon (1834–1892) Eng. preacher
Squire . . . Anne Squire (fl. 1929) Amer. writer
S. R. L. . . *Saturday Review of Literature*
Stafford . . Jean Stafford (1915– ) Amer. author
Stahl . . . Ernest Ludwig Stahl (1902– ) Eng. (So. African-born) linguist
Stamp . . . Sir (Laurence) Dudley Stamp (1898–1966) Brit. geographer
Standen . . Nika Standen (1912– ) Amer. (Ital.-born) writer
Robert Standish pseud. of Digby George Gerahty (1898– ) Eng. author
Stanley . . Arthur Penrhyn Stanley (1815–1881) Eng. clergyman
J. A. Stanley Jay A. Stanley, *Electronics for the Beginner* (1960)
Starr . . . Harris Elwood Starr (1875– ) Amer. biographer
Mark Starr Mark Starr (1894– ) Amer. (Brit.-born) author
Statesman's Year-Book Brit. annual
Stead . . . William Henry Stead (1899–1959) Amer. economist
Steck . . . Francis Borgia Steck (1884–1962) Amer. clergyman
Steegmuller Francis Steegmuller (1906– ) Amer. author
Steele . . . Sir Richard Steele (1672–1729) Brit. essayist
A. T. Steele Archibald Trojan Steele (1903– ) Amer. (Canad.-born) correspondent
Steen . . . Marguerite Steen (1894– ) Eng. writer
Stefansson Vilhjalmur Stefansson (1879–1962) Canad. arctic explorer
Stegner . . Wallace Earle Stegner (1909– ) Amer. author
Stein . . . Sol Stein (1926– ) Amer. publisher
Steinbeck John Ernst Steinbeck (1902–1968) Amer. nov.
Steiner . . Walter Ralph Steiner (1870–1940) Amer. physician
Stenton . . Sir Frank Merry Stenton (1880–1967) Eng. educator
Stephen . . Sir Leslie Stephen (1832–1904) Eng. philosopher
Stephens . . James Stephens (1882–1950) Irish writer
J. L. Stephens John Lloyd Stephens (1805–1852) Amer. author
Sterling . . Claire Sterling (fl. 1956) Amer. writer
Stern . . . James (Andrew) Stern (1904– ) Brit. author
E. M. Stern Edith Mendel Stern (1901– ) Amer. author
Sterne . . . Laurence Sterne (1713–1768) Brit. nov.
Stevens . . Wallace Stevens (1879–1955) Amer. poet
L. C. Stevens Leslie Clark Stevens (1895–1956) Amer. naval officer
W. E. Stevens Wayne Edson Stevens (1892–1959) Amer. historian
Stevenson Robert Louis Stevenson (1850–1894) Scot. author
A. E. Stevenson Adlai Ewing Stevenson (1900–1965) Amer. diplomat
Stevenson-Hamilton James Stevenson-Hamilton (1867–1957) Brit. author
Stewart . . Douglas Alexander Stewart (1913– ) Austral. writer
Dugald Stewart Dugald Stewart (1753–1828) Scot. philosopher
F. G. Stewart Dr. F. Gordon Stewart, *African Wild Life* (1948)
G. R. Stewart George Rippey Stewart (1895– ) Amer. educator
Potter Stewart Potter Stewart (1915– ) Amer. jurist

Stimson . . Henry Lewis Stimson (1867–1950) Amer. statesman
Stirling . . Sir William Alexander (1567?–1640) Earl of Stirling. Scot. poet
Monica Stirling Monica Stirling (1916– ) Brit. author
Stobart . . John Clarke Stobart (1878–1933) Brit. archaeologist
Stoddard . . Ernest M. Stoddard (1889–1965) Amer. plant pathologist
Stoker . . . Bram Stoker (1847–1912) Brit. writer
Stokes . . . George Stewart Stokes (fl. 1950) Amer. educator
Stone Irving Randall Stone, *Brief* (1952) Irving Stone (1903– ) Amer. writer
Jerome Stone Jerome Stone, *Sat. Review* (1954)
Stoney . . . Samuel Gaillard Stoney (1891– ) Amer. architect
Stong . . . Philip Duffield Stong (1899–1957) Amer. writer
Storrs . . . Sir Ronald Storrs (1881–1955) Brit. government official
Stoumen . . Louis C. Stoumen (fl. 1945) Amer. soldier
Stowe . . . Harriet Beecher Stowe (1811–1896) Amer. author
Strachey . . Evelyn John St. Loe Strachey (1901–1963) Eng. socialist
Straight . . Michael Whitney Straight (1916– ) Amer. editor
Strand Mag. Brit. monthly
Strange . . W. E. Strange, *Science* (1966)
Strauss . . Harold Strauss (1907– ) Amer. editor
Street . . . Julian Leonard Street (1902– ) Amer. writer
Streeten . . Paul Patrick Streeten (1917– ) Eng. economist
Streit . . . Peggy Streit (fl. 1964) Amer. writer
C. K. Streit Clarence Kirshman Streit (1896– ) Amer. writer
Stringer . . Arthur John Arbuthnott Stringer (1874–1950) Canad. author
Strong . . . Leonard Alfred George Strong (1896–1958) Eng. writer
Strunsky . . Simeon Strunsky (1879–1948) Amer. (Russ.-born) writer
Jan Struther pseud. of Joyce Maxtone Graham (1901–1953) Eng. author
Strutt . . . Jacob George Strutt (fl. 1850) Brit. painter
Stuart . . . Graham Henry Stuart (1887– ) Amer. educator
Stubbs . . . William Stubbs (1825–1901) Eng. historian
Theodore Sturgeon pseud. of Edward Hamilton Waldo (1918– ) Amer. author
Styron . . . William Styron (1925– ) Amer. author
Suckow . . Ruth Suckow (1892–1960) Amer. author
Sugrue . . . Thomas Sugrue (1907–1953) Amer. author
Sullivan . . William Lawrence Sullivan (1903–1967) Amer. educator
Walter Sullivan Walter Seagar Sullivan (1918– ) Amer. writer
Sulzberger Cyrus Leo Sulzberger (1912– ) Amer. journalist
Sumner . . William Graham Sumner (1840–1910) Amer. sociologist
C. R. Sumner Cid Ricketts Sumner (1890–1971) Amer. author
Sutherland James Runcieman Sutherland (1900– ) Brit. educator
Sutton . . . Horace Ashley Sutton (1919– ) Amer. editor
Suzzallo . . Henry Suzzallo (1875–1933) Amer. educator
Swaim . . . Joseph Carter Swaim (1904– ) Amer. theologian
Swanberg . . William Andrew Swanberg (1907– ) Amer. author
Swartz . . . Harry Felix Swartz (1911– ) Amer. physician
Sweeney . . James Johnson Sweeney (1900– ) Amer. art museum director
Sweet . . . William Warren Sweet (1881–1959) Amer. educator
W. J. Sweetman W. J. Sweetman (fl. 1947) Amer. dairy husbandman

Swift . . . Jonathan Swift (1667–1745) Eng. (Irish-born) satirist
E. H. Swift Emerson Howland Swift (1889– ) Amer. educator
Swinburne Algernon Charles Swinburne (1837–1909) Eng. poet
Swindler . . William Finley Swindler (1913– ) Amer. educator
Swinnerton Frank Arthur Swinnerton (1884– ) Eng. nov.
Swinton . . William Elgin Swinton (1900– ) Brit. paleontologist
Sydney Bulletin Sydney (Australia) weekly
Sykes . . . Christopher Hugh Sykes (1907– ) Eng. author
Sylvester . . Harry Sylvester (1908– ) Amer. author
Symonds . . John Addington Symonds (1840–1893) Eng. author
Symons . . Arthur Symons (1865–1945) Brit. writer
Taffel . . . Alexander Taffel (1911– ) Amer. educator
Talbot . . . Godfrey Walker Talbot (1908– ) Eng. news reporter
Taney . . . Roger Brooke Taney (1777–1864) chief justice, U.S. Supreme Court
Tarkington (Newton) Booth Tarkington (1869–1946) Amer. nov.
Tasaki . . . Hanama Tasaki (1913– ) Jap. journalist
Tassovin . . Paul Tassovin (fl. 1953) Brit. writer
Tate . . . . (John Orley) Allen Tate (1899– ) Amer. author
William Tate William Arnold Tate (1911– ) Brit. broadcaster
Tatler . . . Brit. weekly; merged 1940 in *Tatler and Bystander*
Taubes . . . Frederic Taubes (1900– ) Amer. (Austrian-born) artist
Taylor . . . Jeremy Taylor (1613–1667) Eng. author
A. J. P. Taylor Alan John Percivale Taylor (1906– ) Eng. historian
Ann Taylor Ann Taylor (1782–1866) Eng. nursery-rhyme writer
Bayard Taylor (James) Bayard Taylor (1825–1878) Amer. writer
Edmond Taylor Edmond Lapierre Taylor (1908– ) Amer. writer
Elizabeth Taylor Elizabeth Taylor (1912– ) Eng. author
Floyd Taylor Floyd Taylor (1902–1951) Amer. journalist
Henry Taylor Sir Henry Taylor (1800–1886) Eng. poet
H. O. Taylor Henry Osborn Taylor (1856–1941) Amer. historian
Isaac Taylor Isaac Taylor (1787–1865) Eng. author
ane Taylor Jane Taylor (1783–1824) Eng. nursery-rhyme writer; sister of Ann
J. L. Taylor Jack L. Taylor, *Laboratory Techniques in Space Environment Research NASA* (1962)
Richard Taylor Richard Taylor (1919– ) Amer. philosopher
R. L. Taylor Robert Lewis Taylor (1912– ) Amer. journalist
W. W. Taylor Walter Willard Taylor (1913– ) Amer. anthropologist
Technical News Bulletin U.S. National Bureau of Standards monthly publication
Temple . . . Sir William Temple (1628–1699) Brit. statesman
Tennyson . . Alfred Tennyson (1809–1892) 1st baron Tennyson. Eng. poet
Hallam Tennyson Hallam Tennyson (1921– ) Eng. writer
Terrien . . . Samuel Lucien Terrien (1911– ) Amer. (Fr.-born) clergyman
Terry . . . Estelle Clarke Terry (1908– ) Amer. educator
Textile Industries Amer. monthly
Thackeray William Makepeace Thackeray (1811–1863) Eng. author
Thesiger . . Wilfred Patrick Thesiger (1910– ) Brit. explorer
Thienes . . Clinton Hobart Thienes (1896– ) Amer. pharmacologist
Thilly . . . Frank Thilly (1865–1934) Amer. educator
Third Degree Mystery Writers of America, Inc.

*Thirkell* . . Angela Margaret Thirkell (1890–1961) Eng. nov.

*Thirlwall* . . Connop Thirlwall (1797–1875) Eng. historian

*Thomas* . . Norman Mattoon Thomas (1884–1968) Amer. socialist

*W. L. Thomas* William Leroy Thomas (1920– ) Amer. anthropologist

*Thompson* Francis Thompson (1859–1907) Eng. poet

*C. L. Thompson* Carol Lewis Thompson (1918– ) Amer. editor

*Craig Thompson* Craig Thompson (1907– ) Amer. journalist

*Dorothy Thompson* Dorothy Thompson (1894–1961) Amer. journalist

*P. W. Thompson* Paul Williams Thompson (1906– ) Amer. army engineer

*W. S. Thompson* Warren Simpson Thompson (1887– ) Amer. sociologist

*Thomson* . James Thomson (1700–1748) Scot. poet

*Archbishop Thomson* William Thomson (1819–1890) Brit. clergyman

*J. A. Thomson* Sir John Arthur Thomson (1861–1933) Scot. biologist

*Virgil Thomson* Virgil Thomson (1896– ) Amer. composer

*Don Thorburn* Donaldson Bride Thorburn (1907– ) Amer. writer

*Lois Thorburn* Lois Long, *q.v., formerly* Lois Long Thorburn

*Thoreau* Henry David Thoreau (1817–1862) Amer. author

*Guy Thorne* *pseud. of* Cyril Arthur Edward Ranger Gull (1876–1923) Eng. author

*Thornton* . . William Thornton (fl. 1953) Brit. writer

*Thorogood* Horace Thorogood, *Country Life* (1951)

*Thorp* . . . Raymond W. Thorp (1896– ) Amer. writer

*Thruelsen* . Richard Delmar Thruelsen (1908– ) Amer. editor

*Thurber* . . James Grover Thurber (1894–1961) Amer. author

*Tilden* . . . David Tilden, *N.Y. Herald Tribune Book Rev.* (1953)

*Tilford* . . John Emil Tilford (1912– ) Amer. educator

*Timasheff* . Nicholas S. Timasheff (1886–1970) Amer. (Russ.-born) educator

*Time* . . . Amer. weekly

*The Times* London daily

*Times Lit. Sup.* *Times Literary Supplement,* Brit. weekly

*Tinker* . . . Chauncey Brewster Tinker (1876–1963) Amer. educator

*Toch* . . . Ernst Toch (1887–1964) Amer. (Austrian-born) composer

*Todd* . . . John Aiton Todd (1875–1954) Brit. economist

*Tomkins* . . Alan Tomkins, *The Irish Digest* (1953)

*Tomkinson* . Joan Tomkinson, *Wesfarmers News* (1955)

*Topsell* . . Edward Topsell (1572–1625) Eng. naturalist

*Toulmin* . . Harry Aubrey Toulmin (1890–1965) Amer. author

*Towster* . . Julian Towster (1905– ) Amer. (Pol.-born) educator

*Toynbee* . . Arnold Joseph Toynbee (1889– ) Eng. historian

*Philip Toynbee* (Theodore) Philip Toynbee (1916– ) Eng. nov.

*Tracy* . . . Honor Tracy (1915– ) Eng. author

*Travis* . . . Martin Bice Travis (1917– ) Amer. educator

*Trench* . . . Richard Chenevix Trench (1807–1886) Eng. archbishop

*Trevelyan* George Macaulay Trevelyan (1876–1962) Eng. historian

*G. O. Trevelyan* Sir George Otto Trevelyan (1838–1928) Eng. historian; father of George Macaulay

*Trewartha* Glenn Thomas Trewartha (1896– ) Amer. geographer

*Triebel* . . Louis Augustus Triebel (1890– ) Austral. writer

*Trilling* . . Lionel Trilling (1905– ) Amer. educator

*Trollope* . . Anthony Trollope (1815–1882) Eng. nov.

*Troy* . . . William E. Troy (1904–1961) Amer. educator

*True* . . . . Amer. monthly

*Trueman* . . Sir Arthur Elijah Trueman (1894–1956) Eng. educator

*Truman* . . Harry S Truman (1884–1972) 33d president of the U.S.

*Tucker* . . Abraham Tucker (1705–1774) Eng. philosopher

*B. F. Tucker* B. Fain Tucker (1899– ) Amer. jurist

*Tunley* . . . Roul Tunley (1912– ) Amer. writer

*Turnbull* . . Agnes Sligh Turnbull (1888– ) Amer. author

*Tyndall* . . John Tyndall (1820–1893) Brit. physicist

*Udall* . . . Stewart Lee Udall (1920– ) Amer. secretary of the interior

*Uhl* . . . . Alexander Herbert Uhl (1899– ) Amer. journalist

*Uhlan* . . . Edward Uhlan (1912– ) Amer. publisher

*Ukers* . . . William Harrison Ukers (1873–1954) Amer. author

*Ulich* . . . Robert Ulich (1890– ) Amer. (Ger.-born) educator

*Ullmann* . . Stephen Ullmann (1914– ) Brit. educator

*Ullyett* . . Kenneth Ullyett (1908– ) Eng. author

*U.N. Background Papers* United Nations publication

*Uniform Code of Military Justice* U.S. Government Printing Office (1951)

*Univ. of Fla. Bulletin* University of Florida (1953)

*Untermeyer* Louis Untermeyer (1885– ) Amer. poet

*J. S. Untermeyer* Jean Starr Untermeyer (1886–1970) Amer. poet

*Upjohn* . . Everard Miller Upjohn (1903– ) Amer. educator

*Upson* . . . William Hazlett Upson (1891– ) Amer. writer

*Urban* . . John Urban (fl. 1947) Amer. educator

*Urey* . . . Harold Clayton Urey (1893– ) Amer. chemist

*U. S. Code* Code of the Laws of the U.S. (1934 ed.)

*The Use of English* Brit. quarterly

*Usher* . . . Roland Greene Usher (1880–1957) Amer. historian

*U. S. News and World Report* Amer. weekly

*Ustinov* . . Peter (Alexander) Ustinov (1921– ) Eng. actor

*Utley* . . . Francis Lee Utley (1907– ) Amer. educator

*Valentine* . . Alan Valentine (1901– ) Amer. educator

*Valtin* . . . Jan Valtin (1904–1951) Ger. author

*Van Alstyne* Richard Warner Van Alstyne (1900– ) Amer. historian

*Vance* . . . Thomas Hume Vance (1908– ) Amer. educator

*Vandenberg* Arthur Hendrick Vandenberg (1884–1951) Amer. politician

*Van der Spuy* Una van der Spuy (fl. 1953) So. African writer

*S. S. Van Dine* *pseud. of* Willard Huntington Wright (1888–1939) Amer. writer

*Van Doren* Carl Clinton Van Doren (1885–1950) Amer. editor

*Mark Van Doren* Mark Van Doren (1894–1972) Amer. author

*van Dyke* Henry van Dyke (1852–1933) Amer. author

*J. C. Van Dyke* John Charles Van Dyke (1856–1932) Amer. educator

*Van Loan* Herbert Carroll Van Loan (1924– ) Amer. stock adviser

*van Loon* . Hendrik Willem van Loon (1882–1944) Amer. (Du.-born) historian

*Van Nostrand's* Van Nostrand's Scientific Encyclopedia

*Van Valkenburg* Samuel Van Valkenburg (1891– ) Dutch geographer

*Van Vechten* Carl Van Vechten (1880–1964) Amer. writer

*Vanzetti* . . Bartolomeo Vanzetti (1888–1927) Ital.-Amer. anarchist

*Vaughan* . . Robert Alfred Vaughan (1823–1857) Eng. clergyman

*Vaughan-Thomas* Wynford Vaughan-Thomas (1908– ) Brit. commentator

*Veblen* . . . Thorstein Bunde Veblen (1857–1929) Amer. social scientist

*Vernon* . . Raymond Vernon (1913– ) Amer. educator

*Vierck* . . . Charles John Vierck (1906– ) Amer. educator

*Viereck* . . Peter Viereck (1916– ) Amer. educator

*L. A. Viereck* Leslie A. Viereck (1930– ) Amer. research botanist

*Viets* . . . Henry Rouse Viets (1890– ) Amer. neurologist

*Villiers* . . Alan John Villiers (1903– ) Austral. author

*Visalberghi* Aldo Visalberghi, *Jour. of Philosophy* (1953)

*Vogel* . . . Victor Hugh Vogel (1905– ) Amer. physician

*Vogt* . . . . Evon Zartman Vogt (1918– ) Amer. anthropologist

*von Engeln* Oskar Diedrich von Engeln (1880–1965) Amer. geologist

*Von Mises* Ludwig Edler Von Mises (1881– ) Amer. (Austrian-born) economist

*Vorse* . . . Mary Heaton Vorse (1881–1966) Amer. writer

*Vosseller* . Aurelius B. Vosseller (1903– ) Amer. naval officer

*Vucinich* . Wayne S. Vucinich (1913– ) Amer. historian

*Waage* . . . Thomas Olaf Waage (1912– ) Amer. banker

*Waggoner* Hyatt Howe Waggoner (1913– ) Amer. educator

*Wagley* . . Charles Walter Wagley (1913– ) Amer. anthropologist

*Wagner* . . Herman Alexander Wagner (1864–1960) Amer. (N. Z.-born) engineer

*Wain* . . . John Barrington Wain (1925– ) Brit. writer

*Walcutt* . . Charles Child Walcutt (1908– ) Amer. educator

*Walden* . . David Walden, *The Season* (1942)

*Hubert Wales* *pseud. of* William Pigott (1870–1943) Eng. nov.

*Walford* . . William W. Walford (fl. 1849) Eng. clergyman

*Walinsky* . Louis Joseph Walinsky (1908– ) Amer. (Eng.-born) economist

*Walker* . . . Stanley Walker (1898–1962) Amer. journalist

*Walkley* . . Arthur Bingham Walkley (1855–1926) Eng. drama critic

*Wallace* . . Pat Wallace, *Punch* (1953)

*Waller* . . . Edmund Waller (1606–1687) Eng. poet

*Wall Street Jour.* New York daily

*Waln* . . . Nora Waln (1895–1964) Amer. writer

*Walpole* . . Horace Walpole (1717–1797) 4th earl of Orford. Eng. author

*Hugh Walpole* Sir Hugh Seymour Walpole (1884–1941) Eng. nov.

*Walsh* . . . Thomas Walsh (1875–1928) Amer. writer

*Maurice Walsh* Maurice Walsh (1879–1964) Irish nov.

*Walton* . . Izaak Walton (1593–1683) Eng. author

*Warburg* . . James Paul Warburg (1896–1969) Amer. (Ger.-born) banker

*Warburton* William Warburton (1698–1779) Eng. bishop

*Ward* . . . Mrs. Humphry Ward, née Mary Augusta Arnold (1851–1920) Eng. nov.

*A. C. Ward* Alfred Charles Ward (1891– ) Brit. literary critic

*A. W. Ward* Sir Adolphus William Ward (1837–1924) Eng. historian

*Barbara Ward* Barbara Ward (1914– ) *Lady Jackson.* Brit. economist

*Warfel* . . Harry Redcay Warfel (1899–1971) Amer. educator

*Warner* . . John Warner (fl. 1954) Amer. labor expert

*S. T. Warner* Sylvia Townsend Warner (1893– ) Eng. writer

*Warren* . . Robert Penn Warren (1905– ) Amer. writer

| | |
|---|---|
| *Austin Warren* | Austin Warren (1899– ) Amer. educator |
| *Dale Warren* | (Frank) Dale Warren (1897– ) Amer. publisher |
| *Earl Warren* | Earl Warren (1891– ) Amer. jurist |
| *Shields Warren* | Shields Warren (1898– ) Amer. pathologist |
| *Sidney Warren* | Sidney Warren (1916– ) Amer. historian |
| *Warton* .. | Thomas Warton (1728–1790) Eng. poet |
| *Washington* | George Washington (1732–1799) 1st president of the U.S. |
| *Waters* .... | Frank Waters (1902– ) Amer. author |
| *V. S. Waters* | Vincent Stanislaus Waters (1904– ) Amer. bishop |
| *Waterton* .. | Charles Waterton (1782–1865) Eng. naturalist |
| *Watkins* .. | Gordon S. Watkins (1889– ) Amer. (Welsh-born) economist |
| *Watnick* .. | Morris Watnick (fl. 1948) Amer. educator |
| *Watson* .. | Sir William Watson (1858–1935) Eng. poet |
| *J. B. Watson* | James Bennett Watson (1918– ) Amer. educator |
| *Ralph Watson* | Ralph Watson, *New Yorker* (1956) |
| *S. R. Watson* | Sara Ruth Watson (1909– ) Amer. educator |
| *Watt* .... | Douglas Benjamin Watt (1914– ) Amer. music critic |
| *Watts* .... | Isaac Watts (1674–1748) Eng. hymn writer |
| *Richard Watts* | Richard Watts (1898– ) Amer. journalist |
| *Watts-Dunton* | Walter Theodore Watts-Dunton (1832–1914) Eng. writer |
| *Waugh* .. | Evelyn Arthur St. John Waugh (1903–1966) Eng. author |
| *Coulton Waugh* | Coulton Waugh (1896– ) Amer. cartoonist |
| *Weaver* . | Andrew Thomas Weaver (1890–1965) Amer. educator |
| *R. M. Weaver* | Richard Malcolm Weaver (1910–1963) Amer. educator |
| *Warren Weaver* | Warren Weaver (1894– ) Amer. mathematician |
| *Webb* ... | Mary Gladys Meredith Webb (1881–1927) Eng. nov. |
| *W. P. Webb* | Walter Prescott Webb (1888–1963) Amer. educator |
| *Webber* .. | Howard Webber, *New Yorker* (1963) |
| *Webster* .. | Daniel Webster (1782–1852) Amer. statesman |
| *John Webster* | John Webster (1580?–?1625) Eng. dramatist |
| *Wechsberg* | Joseph Wechsberg (1907– ) Amer. (Czech-born) writer |
| *Wecter* .. | Dixon Wecter (1906–1950) Amer. educator |
| *Weed* ... | John Merrill Weed (1897– ) Amer. engineer |
| *Weeks* ... | Edward Augustus Weeks (1898– ) Amer. editor |
| *Raymond Weeks* | Raymond Weeks (1863–1954) Amer. educator |
| *Weidman* . | Jerome Weidman (1913– ) Amer. author |
| *Weigend* .. | Guido Gustav Weigend (1920– ) Amer. (Austrian-born) educator |
| *Weir* .... | Charles Weir, Jr., *Univ. of Toronto Quarterly* (1944) |
| *Molly Weir* | Molly Weir (fl. 1956) Scot. actress |
| *Weiss* ... | Emilio Weiss (1918– ) Amer. bacteriologist |
| *T. R. Weiss* | Theodore Russell Weiss (1916– ) Amer. poet |
| *Weisz* ... | Paul B. Weisz (1921– ) Amer. (Austrian-born) biologist |
| *J. N. Welch* | Joseph Nye Welch (1890–1960) Amer. lawyer |
| *Weldon* .. | Thomas Dewar Weldon (1896–1958) Eng. educator |
| *René Wellek* | René Wellek (1903– ) Amer. (Austrian-born) educator |
| *Welles* .. | Sumner Welles (1892–1961) Amer. diplomat |
| *Wellington* | Arthur Wellesley (1769–1852) 1st duke of Wellington. Brit. general |
| *Wellman* . | Paul Iselin Wellman (1898–1966) Amer. author |
| *Wells* ... | Carolyn Wells (1869–1942) Amer. writer |

| | |
|---|---|
| *H. G. Wells* | Herbert George Wells (1866–1946) Eng. author |
| *Welty* ... | Eudora Welty (1909– ) Amer. author |
| *Wendell* .. | Barrett Wendell (1855–1921) Amer. educator |
| *Werner* .. | Alfred Werner (1911– ) Amer. (Austrian-born) author |
| *Wescott* .. | Glenway Wescott (1901– ) Amer. nov. |
| *Wesfarmers News* | Austral. periodical |
| *Wesley* ... | Charles Wesley (1707–1788) Eng. clergyman; brother of John |
| *John Wesley* | John Wesley (1703–1791) Eng. founder of Methodism |
| *West* ... | Dame Rebecca West, *pseud.* of Mrs. Henry Maxwell Andrews (1892– ) Eng. nov. |
| *Anthony West* | Anthony Panther West (1914– ) Amer. (Eng.-born) author |
| *R. A. West* | Robert Athow West (fl. 1844) Amer. (Eng.-born) writer |
| *R. B. West* | Ray Benedict West (1908– ) Amer. educator |
| *Westcott* .. | Allan Ferguson Westcott (1882–1953) Amer. educator |
| *Westerby* .. | Robert Westerby (1909– ) Eng. nov. |
| *Westermarck* | Edward Alexander Westermarck (1862–1939) Finnish anthropologist |
| *Westin* .. | Alan Furman Westin (1929– ) Amer. educator |
| *Westley* .. | Bruce Hutchinson Westley (1915– ) Amer. educator |
| *Weston* .. | Christine Weston (1904– ) Amer. (Indian-born) nov. |
| *Weygandt* | Cornelius Weygandt (1871–1957) Amer. educator |
| *Wharton* .. | Edith Newbold Wharton (1862–1937) Amer. nov. |
| *J. F. Wharton* | John Franklin Wharton (1894– ) Amer. lawyer |
| *Whately* .. | Richard Whately (1787–1863) Eng. theologian |
| *Wheatley* .. | Henry Benjamin Wheatley (1838–1917) Eng. bibliographer |
| *Wheelwright* | Jere Hungerford Wheelwright (1905–1961) Amer. author |
| *Philip Wheelwright* | Philip Ellis Wheelwright (1901– ) Amer. educator |
| *Whicher* .. | George Frisbie Whicher (1889–1954) Amer. educator |
| *Whipple* .. | Edwin Percy Whipple (1819–1886) Amer. writer |
| *F. L. Whipple* | Fred Lawrence Whipple (1906– ) Amer. astronomer |
| *Whiston* .. | William Whiston (1667–1752) Eng. theologian |
| *White* ... | William Allen White (1868–1944) Amer. journalist |
| *A. D. White* | Andrew Dickson White (1832–1918) Amer. educator |
| *E. B. White* | Elwyn Brooks White (1899– ) Amer. writer |
| *G. H. White* | George H. White, *Addresses on Current Issues in Higher Education* (1951) |
| *Gilbert White* | Gilbert White (1720–1793) Eng. naturalist |
| *J. E. M. White* | Jon Ewbank Manchip White (1924– ) Welsh author |
| *K. D. White* | Kenneth Douglas White (fl. 1953) So. African writer |
| *L. A. White* | Leslie Alvin White (1900– ) Amer. anthropologist |
| *Lynn White* | Lynn Townsend White (1907– ) Amer. educator |
| *M. G. White* | Morton Gabriel White (1917– ) Amer. philosopher |
| *Patrick White* | Patrick Victor Martindale White (1912– ) Austral. author |
| *S. E. White* | Stewart Edward White (1873–1946) Amer. nov. |
| *T. H. White* | Terence Hanbury White (1906–1964) Eng. writer |
| *Theodore White* | Theodore Harold White (1915– ) Amer. author |
| *Walter White* | Walter Francis White (1893–1955) Amer. author |
| *W. H. White* | Sir William Henry White (1845–1913) Eng. naval architect |
| *W. S. White* | William Smith White (1907– )Amer. journalist |

| | |
|---|---|
| *Whitehead* | Alfred North Whitehead (1861–1947) Eng. mathematician |
| *A. C. Whitehead* | Albert Carlton Whitehead (1875– ) Amer. author |
| *William Whitehead* | William Whitehead (1715–1785) Eng. poet |
| *Whiteley* .. | Charles Henry Whiteley (fl. 1950) Eng. educator |
| *Whitman* .. | Walt Whitman (1819–1892) Amer. poet |
| *Whitney* .. | William Dwight Whitney (1827–1894) Amer. philologist |
| *P. D. Whitney* | Peter Dwight Whitney (1915– ) Amer. writer |
| *Whittier* .. | John Greenleaf Whittier (1807–1892) Amer. poet |
| *Whyte* ... | William Hollingsworth Whyte (1917– ) Amer. writer |
| *Whyte-Melville* | George John Whyte-Melville (1821–1878) Brit. nov. |
| *Wicker* .. | Tom Wicker (1926– ) Amer. journalist |
| *Wiener* ... | Norbert Wiener (1894–1964) Amer. mathematician |
| *Wier* .... | Albert Ernest Wier (1879–1945) Amer. music editor |
| *Wiggam* .. | Albert Edward Wiggam (1871–1957) Amer. author |
| *Wiggin* .. | Kate Douglas Wiggin (1856–1923) Amer. author |
| *Wilberforce* | Samuel Wilberforce (1805–1873) Eng. bishop |
| *Barbara Wilcox* | Barbara Wilcox (fl. 1950) Eng. author |
| *Wilde* ... | Oscar Fingal O'Flahertie Wills Wilde (1854–1900) English (Irish-born) writer |
| *Wilder* ... | Howard Baker Wilder (1901– ) Amer. educator |
| *G. F. Wilder* | George F. Wilder (fl. 1927) Amer. educator |
| *Thornton Wilder* | Thornton (Niven) Wilder (1897– ) Amer. author |
| *Wiles* ... | Peter William Wiles (1930– ) Eng. writer |
| *Wilkinson* | Vernon Lee Wilkinson (1909– ) Amer. lawyer |
| *Willen* ... | Paul Willen (fl. 1953) Amer. writer |
| *Willets* ... | Harry Willets, *Russia Under Khrushchev* (1962) |
| *Willey* ... | Gordon Randolph Willey (1913– ) Amer. anthropologist |
| *Williams* . | Stanley Thomas Williams (1888–1956) Amer. educator |
| *A. R. Williams* | Albert Rhys Williams (1883–1962) Amer. author |
| *Greer Williams* | Greer Williams (1909– ) Amer. writer |
| *G. V. Williams* | George Valentine Williams (1883–1946) Eng. writer |
| *H. A. Williams* | Harrison Arlington Williams (1919– ) U.S. senator |
| *Howel Williams* | Howel Williams (1898– ) Amer. (Eng.-born) geologist |
| *J. E. Williams* | John E. Williams (fl. 1960) Amer. educator |
| *Philip Williams* | Philip Williams (1918–1955) Amer. educator |
| *Tennessee Williams* | Tennessee Williams (1911– ) Amer. playwright |
| *W. C. Williams* | William Carlos Williams (1883–1963) Amer. writer |
| *Wirt Williams* | Wirt Alfred Williams (1921– ) Amer. educator |
| *Willingham* | Henry J. Willingham (1868–1948) Amer. educator |
| *Willis* ... | Nathaniel Parker Willis (1806–1867) Amer. editor |
| *H. P. Willis* | Harry Parker Willis (1874–1937) Amer. economist |
| *Willkie* .. | Wendell Lewis Willkie (1892–1944) Amer. politician |
| *Wills* ... | Colin Wills (1906– ) Austral. author |
| *A. P. Wills* | Albert Potter Wills (1873–1937) Amer. educator |
| *Wilson* ... | Betty Douglas Wilson (1906– ) Amer. writer |
| *Angus Wilson* | Angus Frank Johnstone Wilson (1913– ) Eng. writer |
| *Edmund Wilson* | Edmund Wilson (1895–1972) Amer. writer |
| *Ethel Wilson* | Ethel Davis Wilson (1890– ) Canad. nov. |
| *F. G. Wilson* | Francis Graham Wilson (1901– ) Amer. educator |
| *Henry Wilson* | Henry Wilson (1812–1875) U.S. vice-president (1873–1875) |